THE POCKET Oxford American Dictionary of Current English

THE POCKET Oxford American Dictionary of Current English

New York Oxford
Oxford University Press

OXFORD
UNIVERSITY PRESS

Oxford New York
Athens Auckland Bangkok Buenos Aires
Cape Town Chennai Dar es Salaam Delhi Hong Kong Istanbul
Karachi Kolkata Kuala Lumpur Madrid Melbourne Mexico City Mumbai
Nairobi São Paulo Shanghai Singapore Taipei Tokyo Toronto

and an associated company in Berlin

First published in 1999 as *The Oxford American Dictionary of Current English*
First issued as a Pocket Oxford University Press paperback, 2002
Oxford University Press
198 Madison Avenue, New York, NY 10016

Library of Congress Cataloging-in-Publication Data
is available:
0-19-515082-1

3 5 7 10 9 8 6 4
Printed in the United States of America

Contents

Preface

The Pocket Oxford American Dictionary of Current English covers an extensive range of contemporary American English vocabulary. The text was specially compiled for this edition by Oxford's U.S. Dictionaries Program, in keeping with the renowned lexicographic tradition of Oxford University Press. Oxford's unrivaled language research, including the North American Reading Program (NARP), constantly monitors growth and change in American English. Using computerized search-and-analysis tools developed originally for the 20-volume *Oxford English Dictionary,* our American lexicographers can quickly explore more than 45 million words of citation text collected by NARP, and consult many other massive English language databases. The result is a more sharply refined picture of the language of today, elucidating many complex aspects of meaning, grammar, and usage.

This dictionary reflects the scholarly guidance of Oxford's academic advisors, as well as the experience of specialist consultants in many fields of endeavor. And with the Internet and the World Wide Web, Oxford lexicographers are now able to stay in daily contact with expert sources worldwide, receiving answers to their queries almost instantly.

The text is accompanied by hundreds of examples, illustrations, usage notes, and word histories that clarify definitions and provide guidance on the subtleties of appropriate usage. Biographical and geographical sections in the back of the book offer essential information on the key people and places of the world. Finally, special reference appendices provide quick-reference information for a variety of subjects that are of frequent interest.

The Oxford American Dictionary of Current English is an excellent choice for business people, students, and all those who wish to use English with clarity and style. With its attention to accuracy, currency, and thoroughness, this new American dictionary builds on the tradition of Oxford—the world's most trusted name in dictionaries.

Frank R. Abate
Editor in Chief, U.S. Dictionaries
Oxford University Press, Inc.

How to Use This Dictionary

1 MAIN ENTRIES

Each main entry is printed in bold roman type:

> **ad•um•brate** /ádumbrayt/ *v.tr.* **1** indicate faintly. **2** represent in outline. **3** foreshadow; typify. **4** overshadow. □□ **ad•um•bra•tion** /–bráyshən/ *n.*

Main entries are arranged in letter-by-letter alphabetical order. Different words that are spelled the same way (homographs) are distinguished by raised numerals:

> **font**[1] /font/ *n.* **1** a receptacle in a church for baptismal water. **2** the reservoir for oil in a lamp.
> **font**[2] /font/ *n. Printing* a set of type of one face or size.

2 PRONUNCIATION

Guidance on the pronunciation of a main entry will be found in most cases immediately after the main entry, enclosed in oblique strokes / /. In some cases, more than one pronunciation is given: that given first is the more frequent or preferred pronunciation. Guidance on the pronunciation of derivatives of the main entry is limited to cases in which the main entry pronunciation would be of no help in establishing the correct pronunciation of the derivative. The dictionary uses a simple respelling system to represent pronunciation. This is meant to be self-explanatory and easily readable by the lay person without constant recourse to a table of special characters.

For details on the pronunciation symbols, see the "Key to Pronunciation" below.

3 PART OF SPEECH

The grammatical identity of words as noun, verb, adjective, and so on, is given for all main entries and derivatives, and for compounds and phrases when necessary to aid clarity. The same part-of-speech labeling is used for groups of more than one word when the group has the function of a particular part of speech, e.g., *ad hoc*; *vacuum cleaner*. When a main entry has more than one part of speech, a list is given at the beginning of the entry, and the treatment of the successive parts of speech is introduced by a bullet in each case:

> **ac•ci•den•tal** /áksidént'l/ *adj. & n.* • *adj.* **1** happening by chance or unexpectedly. **2** not essential to a conception. • *n.* **1** *Mus.* a sign indicating a momentary departure from the key signature. **2** something not essential to a conception. □□ **ac•ci•den•tal•ly** *adv.*

The standard part-of-speech names are used, and the following additional explanations should be noted:

- Nouns used attributively are designated *attrib.* when their function does not include predicative use (e.g., *model* in a *model student;* but *the student is very model* is not acceptable usage; see also at "Adjectives", next).
- Adjectives are labeled *attrib.* (= attributive) when they are normally placed before the word they modify (e.g., *acting* in *acting manager*), and *predic.* (= predicative) when they normally occur (usually after a verb) in the predicate of a sentence (e.g., *afraid* in *he was afraid*). When an adjective can occur either attributively or predicatively, the simple designation *adj.* is used.
- The designation *absol.* (= absolute) refers to uses of transitive verbs with an object implied but not stated (as in *smoking kills* and *let me explain*).
- The designation "in *comb.*" (= in combination), or "also in *comb.*," refers to uses of words (especially adjectives and nouns) as an element joined by a hyphen to another word, as with *crested* (which often appears in forms such as *red-crested, large-crested*) or *footer* (as in *six-footer*).

4 VARIANTS

Variant spellings are given before the definition; in all such cases the form given as the main entry is the preferred form. Variant forms are also given at their own places in the dictionary when these are three or more entries away from the main form.

Variant spellings given at the beginning of an entry normally apply to the whole entry, including any phrases and undefined derivatives. When variants apply only to certain functions or senses of a word, these are given in parentheses at the relevant point in the entry.

Variant British spellings are indicated by the designation *Brit.* These variants are often found in British use in addition to or instead of the main forms given.

Pronunciation of variants is given when it differs significantly from the pronunciation of the main entry.

5 INFLECTED FORMS

Inflected forms of words (i.e., plural, past tenses, etc.) are given after the part of speech concerned:

> **broad·cast** /bráwdkast/ *v., n., adj., & adv.* •*v.* (*past* **broadcast** or **broadcasted**; *past part.* **broadcast**) **1** *tr.* **a** transmit by radio or television. **b** disseminate (information) widely. **2** *intr.* undertake or take part in a radio or television transmission. **3** *tr.* scatter (seed, etc.) over a large area. •*n.* a radio or television program or transmission. •*adj.* **1** transmitted by radio or television. **2** widely disseminated. •*adv.* over a large area. □□ **broad·cast·er** *n.* **broad·cast·ing** *n.*

The forms given are normally those in use in American English. Pronunciation of inflected forms is given when it differs significantly from the pronunciation of the main entry. The designation "*pronunc.* same" denotes that the pronunciation, despite a change of form, is the same as that of the main entry. In general, the inflection of nouns, verbs, adjectives, and adverbs is given when it is irregular (as described further below) or when, though regular, it causes difficulty (as with forms such as *budgeted*, *coos*, and *taxis*).

Plurals of nouns

Nouns that form their plural regularly by adding *-s* (or *-es* when they end in *-s*, *-x*, *-z*, *-sh*, or soft *-ch*) receive no comment. Other plural forms are given, notably in cases where the singular is a noun that:

- ends in *-i* or *-o*.
- ends in *-y*.
- is a Latinate form ending in *-a* or *-um*, etc.
- has more than one plural form, e.g., *fish* and *aquarium*.
- has a plural involving a change in the stem, e.g., *foot*, *feet*.
- has a plural form identical to the singular form, e.g., *sheep*.
- ends in *-ful*, e.g., *handful*.

Forms of verbs

The following verb forms are regarded as regular:

- third person singular present tense forms adding *-s* to the stem, or *-es* to stems ending in *-s*, *-x*, *-z*, *-sh*, or soft *-ch* (e.g., *bite/bites; pass/passes*)
- past tenses and past participles adding *-ed* to the stem, dropping a final silent *-e* (e.g., *changed*; *danced*).
- present participles adding *-ing* to the stem, dropping a final silent *-e* (e.g., *changing*; *dancing*).

Other forms are given, notably those that involve:

- doubling of a final consonant, e.g., *bat*, *batted*, *batting*.
- strong and irregular forms involving a change in the stem, e.g., *come*, *came*, *come*, and *go*, *went*, *gone*.
- irregular inflections of borrowed words, e.g., *polka'd*.

Comparative and superlative of adjectives and adverbs

Words of one syllable adding *-er* or *-est* and those ending in silent *-e* dropping the *-e* (e.g., *braver*, *bravest*) are regarded as regular. Most one-syllable words have these forms, but participial adjectives (e.g., *pleased*) do not. Those that double a final consonant (e.g., *hot*, *hotter*, *hottest*) are given, as are two-syllable words that have comparative and superlative forms in *-er* and *-est* (of which very many are forms ending in *-y*, e.g., *lucky*, *luckier*, *luckiest*), and their negative forms (e.g., *unluckier*, *unluckiest*). It should be noted that specification of these forms indicates only that they are available; it is usually also possible to form comparatives with *more* and superlatives with *most* (as in *more lucky*, *most unlucky*), which is the standard way of proceeding with adjectives and adverbs that are not regularly inflected.

Adjectives in *-able* formed from transitive verbs

These are given as derivatives when there is sufficient evidence of their currency; in general they are formed as follows:

- verbs drop silent final *-e* except after *c* and *g* (e.g., *movable* but *changeable*).
- verbs of more than one syllable ending in *-y* (preceded by a consonant or *qu*) change *y* to *i* (e.g., *enviable*, *undeniable*).
- a final consonant is often doubled as in normal inflection (e.g., *conferrable*, *regrettable*).

6 DEFINITION

Definitions are listed in a numbered sequence in order of relative familiarity and importance, with the most current and important senses given first. They are subdivided into lettered senses (**a**, **b**, etc.) when these are closely related or call for collective treatment.

7 GRAMMAR NOTES

Definitions are often accompanied by explanations in parentheses of how the word or phrase in question is used in context. Often, the comment refers to words that usually follow ("foll. by") or precede ("prec. by") the word being explained:

> **ac·cred·it** /əkrédit/ *v.tr.* (**accredited, accrediting**) **1** (foll. by *to*) attribute (a saying, etc.) to (a person). **2** (foll. by *with*) credit (a person) with (a saying, etc.). **3** (usu. foll. by *to* or *at*) send (an ambassador, etc.) with credentials. □□ **ac·cred·i·ta·tion** /–táyshən/ *n.*

The formula "foll. by *to* + infin." means that the word is followed by a normal infinitive with *to*, as after *want* in *wanted to leave* and after *ready* in *ready to burst*. The formula "foll. by *that* + clause" indicates the routine addition of a clause with *that*, as after *say* in *said that it was late* or after *warn* in *warned him that he was late too often*. The formulas "*pres. part.*" and "*verbal noun*" denote verbal forms in *-ing* that function as adjectives and nouns respectively, as in *set him laughing* and *tired of asking*.

8 ILLUSTRATIVE EXAMPLES

Examples of words in use are given to support or clarify the definitions. These appear in italics following the definition, enclosed in parentheses. They are meant to amplify meaning and (especially when following a grammatical point) illustrate how the word is used in context.

9 USAGE AND LABELS

If the use of a word is restricted in any way, this is indicated by one of several labels printed in italics, as explained in the following.

Geographical labels

US indicates that the use is found chiefly in American English (often including Canada), but not in British English except as a conscious Americanism.

Brit. indicates that the use is found chiefly in British English (and often also in Australian and New Zealand English, and in other parts of the British Commonwealth), but not typically in American English.

Other geographical labels (e.g., *Austral., NZ, S. Afr.*) indicate that usage is largely restricted to the areas designated.

These usage labels should be distinguished from comments of the type "(in the UK)" preceding definitions, which denote that the thing defined is associated with the country named. For example, *Parliament* is a British institution, but the term is not restricted to British English.

Register labels

Levels of usage, or registers, are indicated as follows:

- *formal* indicates uses that are normally restricted to formal (esp. written) English, e.g., *commence*.
- *colloq.* (= colloquial) indicates a use that is normally restricted to informal (esp. spoken) English.
- *sl.* (= slang) indicates an informal use (typically a word that is equivalent in meaning to a "standard" word), unsuited to written English and often restricted to a particular social group, while *coarse sl.* is used to show that an expression is regarded as vulgar or unacceptable even in spoken use in most social contexts.
- *archaic* indicates a word that is obsolete in general use and is restricted to special contexts such as legal or religious use, or is used for special effect.
- *literary* indicates a word or use that is found chiefly in literature.
- *poet.* (= poetic) indicates uses confined to poetry or other similar contexts.
- *joc.* (= jocular) indicates uses that are intended to be humorous or playful.
- *derog.* (= derogatory) denotes uses that are intentionally disparaging.
- *offens.* (= offensive) denotes uses that cause offense, whether intentionally or not.
- *disp.* (= disputed) indicates a use that is disputed or controversial. When further explanation is needed a usage note (see below) is given as well or instead.
- *hist.* (= historical) denotes a word or use that is confined to historical reference, normally because the thing referred to no longer exists.
- *propr.* (= proprietary) denotes a term that is asserted to have the status of a trademark (see the Note on Proprietary Status, below).

Subject labels

Subject labels, e.g., *Law, Math., Naut.*, show that a word or sense is used in a particular field of activity, and is not in widespread general use.

Usage notes

These give extra information not central to the definition, and to explain points of grammar and style. They are introduced by the symbol ▶. The purpose of these notes is not to prescribe usage but to alert the user to a difficulty or controversy attached to particular uses.

10 PHRASES AND IDIOMS

These are listed (together with compounds) in alphabetical order after the treatment of the main senses and introduced by the symbol □. The words *a*, *the*, *one*, and *person* do not count for purposes of alphabetical order. They are normally defined under the first key word in the phrase, except when a later word is more clearly the key word or is the common word in a phrase with variants.

11 DERIVATIVES

Words formed by adding a standard suffix to another word are in many cases listed at the end of the entry for the main word, introduced by the symbol □□. These are not defined since they can be understood from the sense of the main entry plus that of the suffix concerned. When further definition is called for they are given main entries in their own right (e.g., *changeable*).

12 PREFIXES, SUFFIXES, AND COMBINING FORMS

A large selection of these is given in the main body of the text; prefixes are given in the form **ex-**, **re-**, etc., and suffixes in the form **-ion**, **-ness**, etc. These entries should be consulted to explain the many routinely formed derivatives given at the end of entries (see 11 above). Combining forms (e.g., *bio-*, *-graphy*) are semantically significant elements that can be attached to words or elements as explained in the usage note at the entry for *combining form*.

13 WORD HISTORIES

Brief paragraphs explaining the origin of a word are given as boxed features accompanying certain entries in the dictionary. Generally speaking, these word histories tell a particularly interesting story about how a word originated or developed, and are often helpful in understanding and remembering the meaning.

14 CROSS REFERENCES

Cross references appear in small capitals if the reference is to a main entry and in italics if the reference is to a compound, idiom, or phrase within an entry. References in italics to compounds and defined phrases and idioms are to the entry for the first word, unless another word is specified.

Abbreviations

Listed below are abbreviations that occur within the text of entries, except for those in general use (such as etc. and i.e.), which have their own entries in the dictionary itself.

abbr.	abbreviation
acc.	according
adj.	adjective
adv.	adverb
Aeron.	Aeronautics
Amer.	America, American
Anat.	Anatomy
anc.	ancient
Anthropol.	Anthropology
Antiq.	Antiquities, Antiquity
Archaeol.	Archaeology
Archit.	Architecture
Arith.	Arithmetic
assoc.	associated, association
Astrol.	Astrology
Astron.	Astronomy
Astronaut.	Astronautics
attrib.	attributive
Austral.	Australia, Australian
aux.	auxiliary
back-form.	back-formation
Bibl.	Biblical
Bibliog.	Bibliography
Biochem.	Biochemistry
Biol.	Biology
Bot.	Botany
Brit.	British
c.	century
c.	*circa*
Can.	Canada, Canadian
cf.	compare
Ch.	Church
Chem.	Chemistry
Cinematog.	Cinematography
coarse sl.	coarse slang
collect.	collective(ly)
colloq.	colloquial(ly)
comb.	combination, combining
compar.	comparative
compl.	complement
Conchol.	Conchology
conj.	conjunction
contr.	contraction
corresp.	corresponding
Criminol.	Criminology
Crystallog.	Crystallography
def.	definite
Demog.	Demography
demons.	demonstrative
deriv.	derivative
derog.	derogatory
dial.	dialect(al)
disp.	disputed (use or pronunciation)
Eccl.	Ecclesiastical
Ecol.	Ecology
Econ.	Economics
Electr.	Electricity
ellipt.	elliptical(ly)
emphat.	emphatic(ally)
Engin.	Engineering
Engl.	England, English
Entomol.	Entomology
erron.	erroneous(ly)
esp.	especial(ly)
euphem.	euphemism
Eur.	Europe, European
exclam.	exclamation
fam.	familiar
fem.	feminine
fig.	figurative(ly)
fl.	flourished
foll.	followed, following
gen.	general
Geog.	Geography
Geol.	Geology
Geom.	Geometry
Gk	Greek
Gk Hist.	Greek History
Gram.	Grammar
Hist.	History
hist.	with historical reference
Horol.	Horology
Hort.	Horticulture
imper.	imperative
impers.	impersonal
incl.	including, inclusive
ind.	indirect
indef.	indefinite
infin.	infinitive
int.	interjection
interrog.	interrogative(ly)
intr.	intransitive
iron.	ironical(ly)
irreg.	irregular(ly)
joc.	jocular(ly)
lang.	language
lit.	literal(ly)
masc.	masculine
Math.	Mathematics
Mech.	Mechanics
Med.	Medicine
med.	medieval
metaph.	metaphorical
Meteorol.	Meteorology
Mil.	Military
Mineral.	Mineralogy
mod.	modern
Mus.	Music
Mythol.	Mythology
n.	noun
N.Amer.	North America, North American
Nat.	National
Naut.	Nautical
neg.	negative(ly)
neut.	neuter
N.Engl.	New England
No. of Engl.	North of England
north.	northern
n.pl.	noun plural
num.	numeral
NZ	New Zealand
obj.	object, objective
obs.	obsolete
Obstet.	Obstetrics
occas.	occasional(ly)
offens.	offensive
opp.	(as) opposed (to), opposite (of)
orig.	origin, original(ly)
Ornithol.	Ornithology
Paleog.	Paleography
Parl.	Parliament, Parliamentary
part.	participle
past part.	past participle
Pathol.	Pathology
pejor.	pejorative
pers.	person(al)
Pharm.	Pharmacy, Pharmacology
Philol.	Philology
Philos.	Philosophy
Phonet.	Phonetics
Photog.	Photography
phr.	phrase
Phrenol.	Phrenology
Physiol.	Physiology
pl.	plural
poet.	poetical
Polit.	Politics
pop.	popular, not technical
poss.	possessive
prec.	preceded, preceding
predic.	predicate, predicative(ly)
prep.	preposition
pres.part.	present participle
pron.	pronoun
pronunc.	pronunciation
propr.	proprietary term
Psychol.	Psychology
RC Ch.	Roman Catholic Church
ref.	reference
refl.	reflexive(ly)
rel.	related, relative
Relig.	Religion
rhet.	rhetorical(ly)
Rom.	Roman
Rom.Hist.	Roman History
S.Afr.	South Africa, South African
S.Amer.	South America, South American
Sci.	Science
sing.	singular
sl.	slang
Sociol.	Sociology
spec.	special(ly)
Stock Exch.	Stock Exchange
subj.	subject, subjunctive
superl.	superlative
syll.	syllable
symb.	symbol
syn.	synonym
techn.	technical(ly)
Telev.	Television
Theatr.	Theater, Theatrical
Theol.	Theology
tr.	transitive
transf.	in transferred sense
Typog.	Typography
univ.	university
US	United States; in use in the United States
usu.	usual(ly)
v.	verb
var.	variant(s)
v.aux.	auxiliary verb
Vet.	Veterinary
v.intr.	intransitive verb
v.refl.	reflexive verb
v.tr.	transitive verb
Zool.	Zoology

Key to Pronunciation

This dictionary uses a simple respelling system to show how entries are pronounced, using the following symbols:

a, á	*as in*	**pat** /pat/, **fasten** /fásən/
aa, áa	*as in*	**father** /fáathər/, **barnyard** /báarnyaard/
air, áir	*as in*	**fair** /fair/, **share** /shair/, **heir** /air/
aw, áw	*as in*	**law** /law/, **caught** /kawt/, **thought** /thawt/
ay, áy	*as in*	**day** /day/, **raid** /rayd/, **made** /mayd/, **prey** /pray/
ch	*as in*	**church** /chərch/, **picture** /píkchər/
e, é	*as in*	**men** /men/, **said** /sed/
ee, ée	*as in*	**feet** /feet/, **receive** /riséev/
ə	*as in*	**along** /əlóng/, **soda** /sṓdə/, **civil** /sívəl/
ər, ə́r	*as in*	**parade** /pəráyd/, **bitter** /bítər/, **person** /pə́rsən/
g	*as in*	**get** /get/, **exhaust** /igzáwst/, **egg** /eg/
i, í	*as in*	**pin** /pin/, **guild** /gild/, **women** /wímin/
ī, ī́	*as in*	**time** /tīm/, **fight** /fīt/, **guide** /gīd/
īr, ī́r	*as in*	**fire** /fīr/, **desire** /dizī́r/
j	*as in*	**judge** /juj/, **carriage** /kárij/
kh	*as in*	**loch** /lokh/, **Bach** /baakh/
N	*as in*	**en route** /oN root/ (preceding vowel is nasalized)
ng	*as in*	**sing** /sing/, **anger** /ánggər/
o, ó	*as in*	**rob** /rob/, **pocket** /pókit/
ō, ṓ	*as in*	**go** /gō/, **promote** /prəmṓt/
ö, ö́	*as in*	**jeu** /zhö/, **schön** /shön/
ŏŏ, ŏŏ́	*as in*	**wood** /wŏŏd/, **football** /fŏŏ́tbawl/
ōō, ōṓ	*as in*	**food** /fōōd/, **music** /myōṓsik/
ow, ów	*as in*	**mouse** /mows/, **coward** /kówərd/
oy, óy	*as in*	**boy** /boy/, **noisy** /nóyzee/
r	*as in*	**run** /run/, **fur** /fər/, **spirit** /spírit/
sh	*as in*	**shut** /shut/, **social** /sṓshəl/, **action** /ákshən/
th	*as in*	**thin** /thin/, **truth** /trōōth/
th	*as in*	**then** /then/, **mother** /múthər/
u, ú	*as in*	**cut** /kut/, **blood** /blud/, **enough** /inúf/
y	*as in*	**yet** /yet/, **accuse** /əkyōṓz/
Y	*as in*	**aperçu** /aapersY/
zh	*as in*	**measure** /mézhər/, **vision** /vízhən/

More than one acceptable pronunciation may be given, with commas between the variants; for example:

news /nōōz, nyōōz/

If the pronunciations of a word differ only in part, then the syllable or syllables affected are shown as follows:

bedroom /bédrōōm, –rōōm/, **forest** /fáwrist, fór–/

The same principle applies to derivative forms that are given within the main entry; for example:

complete /kəmpléet/, **completion** /–pléeshən/

STRESS

The mark that appears over the vowel symbol in words of more than one syllable indicates the part of the word that carries the stress. Where a word has two or more stress markers then the main stress may vary according to the context in which a word is used; for example:

afternoon /áftərnōṓn/

In the phrase "afternoon tea" the main stress falls on the first syllable /áftər–/, but in the phrase "all afternoon" the main stress falls on the last syllable /–nōṓn/.

A

A[1] /ay/ *n.* (also **a**) (*pl.* **As** or **A's**) **1** the first letter of the alphabet. **2** *Mus.* the sixth note of the diatonic scale of C major. **3** the first hypothetical person or example. **4** the highest class or category (of academic grades, etc.). **5** (usu. **a**) *Algebra* the first known quantity. **6** a human blood type of the ABO system.

A[2] /ay/ *abbr.* (also **A.**) **1** ampere(s). **2** answer. **3** Associate of. **4** atomic (energy, etc.).

a[1] /ə, ay/ *adj.* (also **an** before a vowel) **1** (as an unemphatic substitute) one; some; any. **2** one like (*a Judas*). **3** one single (*not a thing in sight*). **4** the same (*all of a size*). **5** in, to, or for each (*twice a year*).

a[2] /ə/ *prep.* (usu. as *prefix*) **1** to; toward (*ashore*). **2** (with verb in pres. part. or infin.) in the process of; in a specified state (*a-hunting*). **3** on (*afire*). **4** in (*nowadays*).

Å *abbr.* ångström(s).

a- /ay, a/ *prefix* not; without (*amoral*; *apetalous*).

-a /ə/ *suffix colloq.* **1** of (*kinda*; *coupla*). **2** have (*mighta*; *coulda*). **3** to (*oughta*).

AA *abbr.* **1** Alcoholics Anonymous. **2** Associate of Arts. **3** *Mil.* antiaircraft.

AAA *abbr.* **1** American Automobile Association. **2** Amateur Athletic Association. **3** antiaircraft artillery.

aard·vark /aárdvaark/ *n.* a nocturnal mammal of southern Africa, *Orycteropus afer*, with a tubular snout and a long tongue, that feeds on termites.

aard·wolf /aárdwoolf/ *n.* (*pl.* **aardwolves** /–woolvz/) an African mammal, *Proteles cristatus*, of the hyena family, with gray fur and black stripes, that feeds on insects.

AAU *abbr.* Amateur Athletic Union.

AB[1] /áybeé/ *n.* a human blood type of the ABO system.

AB[2] *abbr.* Bachelor of Arts.

a·back /əbák/ *adv. archaic* backward; behind. □ **take aback** surprise; disconcert (*I was greatly taken aback by the news*).

ab·a·cus /ábəkəs, əbákəs/ *n.* (*pl.* **abacuses**) an oblong frame with rows of wires or grooves along which beads are slid, used for calculating.

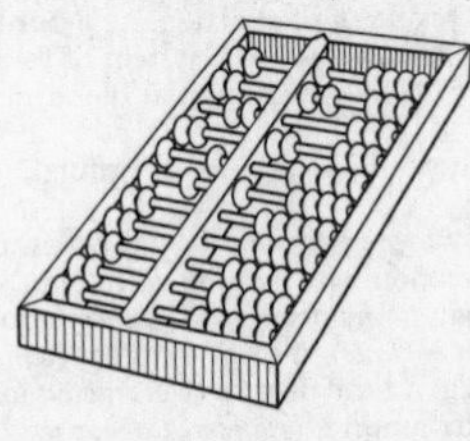

abacus

a·baft /əbáft/ *adv. & prep. Naut.* • *adv.* in the stern half of a ship.• *prep.* nearer the stern than; aft of.

ab·a·lo·ne /ábəlṓnee/ *n.* any mollusk of the genus *Haliotis*, with a shallow ear-shaped shell having respiratory holes, and lined with mother-of-pearl.

a·ban·don /əbándən/ *v. & n.* • *v.tr.* **1** give up completely or before completion (*abandoned hope*; *abandoned the game*). **2 a** forsake or desert (a person or a post of responsibility). **b** leave or desert (a motor vehicle, ship, etc.). **3 a** give up to another's control or mercy. **b** *refl.* yield oneself completely to a passion or impulse. • *n.* lack of inhibition or restraint. □□ **a·ban·don·ment** *n.*

a·ban·doned /əbándənd/ *adj.* **1 a** (of a person or animal) deserted; forsaken (*an abandoned child*). **b** (of a building, vehicle, etc.) left empty or unused (*an abandoned car*). **2** (of a person or behavior) unrestrained; profligate.

a·base /əbáys/ *v.tr. & refl.* humiliate or degrade. □□ **a·base·ment** *n.*

a·bash /əbásh/ *v.tr.* (usu. as **abashed** *adj.*) embarrass; disconcert. □□ **a·bash·ment** *n.*

a·bate /əbáyt/ *v.* **1** *tr. & intr.* make or become less strong, severe, etc. **2** *tr. Law* **a** quash (a writ or action). **b** put an end to (a nuisance). □□ **a·bate·ment** *n.*

ab·at·toir /ábətwaar/ *n.* a slaughterhouse.

ab·ax·i·al /abákseeəl/ *adj. Bot.* facing away from the stem of a plant, esp. of the lower surface of a leaf (cf. ADAXIAL).

ab·bess /ábis/ *n.* a woman who is the head of certain communities of nuns.

ab·bey /ábee/ *n.* (*pl.* **·beys**) **1** the building(s) occupied by a community of monks or nuns. **2** the community itself.

ab·bot /ábət/ *n.* a man who is the head of an abbey of monks. □□ **ab·bot·ship** *n.*

ab·bre·vi·ate /əbreévee-ayt/ *v.tr.* shorten (a word, etc.).

ab·bre·vi·a·tion /əbreévee–áyshən/ *n.* **1** an abbreviated form, esp. a shortened form of a word or phrase. **2** the process or result of abbreviating.

ABC /áybeeseé/ *n.* **1** the alphabet. **2** (also **ABC's**) the rudiments of any subject. **3** an alphabetical guide.

ab·di·cate /ábdikayt/ *v.tr.* give up or renounce (a throne, duty, etc.). □□ **ab·di·ca·tion** /–káyshən/ *n.*

ab·do·men /ábdəmən, abdṓ–/ *n.* **1** the part of the body containing the stomach, bowels, reproductive organs, etc. **2** *Zool.* the hind part of an insect, crustacean, spider, etc. □□ **ab·dom·i·nal** /abdóminəl/ *adj.*

ab·duct /əbdúkt/ *v.tr.* carry off or kidnap (a person) illegally by force or deception. □□ **ab·duc·tion** /–dúkshən/ *n.* **ab·duc·tor** *n.*

a·beam /əbeém/ *adv.* on a line at right angles to a ship's or an aircraft's length.

a·bed /əbéd/ *adv. archaic* in bed.

a·bele /əbeél, áybəl/ *n.* the white poplar, *Populus alba.*

A·be·na·ki /abənaákee/ *n.* (also **Ab·na·ki** /abnaákee/) **1 a** a N. American people native to northern New England and adjoining parts of Quebec. **b** a member of this people. **2** either of the two languages of this people.

ab·er·rant /əbérənt, ábə–/ *adj.* **1** esp. *Biol.* diverging from the normal type. **2** departing from an accepted standard. □□ □□ **ab·er·rance** /–rəns/ *n.* **ab·er·ran·cy** *n.*

ab·er·ra·tion /ábəráyshən/ *n.* **1** a departure from what is normal or accepted or regarded as right. **2** a moral or mental lapse. **3** *Biol.* deviation from a normal type. **4** *Optics* the failure of rays to converge at one focus because of a defect in a lens or mirror.

a·bet /əbét/ *v.tr.* (**abetted, abetting**) (usu. in **aid and abet**) encourage or assist (an offender or offense).

a·bet·tor /əbétər/ *n.* (also **a·bet·ter**) one who abets.

a·bey·ance /əbáyəns/ *n.* (usu. prec. by *in*) temporary disuse or suspension.

ab·hor /əbháwr/ *v.tr.* (**abhorred, abhorring**) detest; regard with disgust and hatred. ▫▫ **ab·hor·rer** *n.*

ab·hor·rence /əbháwrəns, –hór–/ *n.* **1** disgust; detestation. **2** a detested thing.

ab·hor·rent /əbháwrənt, –hór–/ *adj.* (often foll. by *to*) (of conduct, etc.) inspiring disgust; repugnant; hateful; detestable.

a·bide /əbíd/ *v.* (*past* **abode** /əbṓd/or **abided**) **1** *tr.* (usu. in *neg.* or *interrog.*) tolerate; endure (*can't abide him*). **2** *intr.* (foll. by *by*) **a** act in accordance with (*abide by the rules*). **b** remain faithful to (a promise). **3** *intr. archaic* dwell. ▫▫ **a·bid·ance** *n.*

a·bid·ing /əbíding/ *adj.* enduring; permanent (*an abiding sense of loss*). ▫▫ **a·bid·ing·ly** *adv.*

a·bil·i·ty /əbílitee/ *n.* (*pl.* **·ties**) **1** (often foll. by *to* + infin.) capacity or power. **2** cleverness; talent; mental power (*a person of great ability; has many abilities*).

-ability /əbílitee/ *suffix* forming nouns of quality from, or corresponding to, adjectives in *-able* (*capability; vulnerability*).

a·bi·o·gen·e·sis /áybīōjénisis/ *n.* **1** the formation of living organisms from inanimate substances. **2** the supposed spontaneous generation of living organisms. ▫▫ **a·bi·o·gen·ic** /–jénik/ *adj.*

ab·ject /ábjekt, abjékt/ *adj.* **1** miserable; wretched. **2** degraded; self-abasing; humble. **3** despicable. ▫▫ **ab·jec·tion** /əbjékshən/ *n.* **ab·ject·ly** *adv.* **ab·ject·ness** *n.*

ab·jure /əbjŏŏr/ *v.tr.* renounce under oath (an opinion, cause, claim, etc.). ▫▫ **ab·ju·ra·tion** /–ráyshən/ *n.*

ab·la·tion /ablάyshən/ *n.* **1** the surgical removal of body tissue. **2** *Geol.* the wasting or erosion of a glacier, iceberg, or rock by melting, evaporation, or the action of water. **3** *Astronaut.* the evaporation or melting of part of the outer surface of a spacecraft through heating by friction with the atmosphere. ▫▫ **ab·late** *v.tr.*

ab·la·tive /áblətiv/ *n. & adj. Gram.* • *n.* the case (esp. in Latin) of nouns and pronouns (and words in grammatical agreement with them) indicating an agent, instrument, or location. • *adj.* of or in the ablative.

ab·laut /áblowt/ *n.* a change of vowel in related words or forms, e.g., in *sing, sang, sung.*

a·blaze /əbláyz/ *predic.adj. & adv.* **1** on fire. **2** (often foll. by *with*) glittering; glowing; radiant.

a·ble /áybəl/ *adj.* (**abler, ablest**) **1** (often foll. by *to* + infin.) having the capacity or power (*was not able to come*). **2** having great ability; clever; skillful.

-able /əbəl/ *suffix* forming adjectives meaning: **1** that may or must be (*forgivable; payable*). **2** that can be made the subject of (*dutiable*). **3** that is relevant to or in accordance with (*fashionable; seasonable*). **4** (with active sense, in earlier word formations) that may (*comfortable; suitable*).

a·ble-bod·ied *adj.* fit; healthy.

a·bloom /əblŏŏm/ *predic. adj.* blooming; in flower.

ab·lu·tion /əblŏŏshən/ *n.* (usu. in *pl.*) **1** the ceremonial washing of parts of the body or sacred vessels, etc. **2** *colloq.* the ordinary washing of the body. ▫▫ **ab·lu·tion·ar·y** *adj.*

a·bly /áyblee/ *adv.* capably; cleverly; competently.

-ably /əblee/ *suffix* forming adverbs corresponding to adjectives in *-able.*

ABM *abbr.* antiballistic missile.

ab·ne·gate /ábnigayt/ *v.tr.* **1** give up or deny oneself (a pleasure, etc.). **2** renounce or reject (a right or belief). ▫▫ **ab·ne·ga·tor** *n.*

ab·ne·ga·tion /ábnigáyshən/ *n.* **1** the rejection of a doctrine. **2** = SELF-ABNEGATION.

ab·nor·mal /abnáwrməl/ *adj.* deviating from what is normal or usual; exceptional. ▫▫ **ab·nor·mal·ly** *adv.*

ab·nor·mal·i·ty /ábnawrmálitee/ *n.* (*pl.* **·ties**) **1** an abnormal quality, occurrence, etc. **2** the state of being abnormal.

a·board /əbáwrd/ *adv. & prep.* on or into (a ship, aircraft, train, etc.).

a·bode[1] /əbṓd/ *n.* a dwelling; one's home.

a·bode[2] *past* of ABIDE.

a·bol·ish /əbólish/ *v.tr.* put an end to (esp. a custom or institution). ▫▫ **a·bol·ish·ment** *n.*

ab·o·li·tion /ábəlíshən/ *n.* the act or process of abolishing or being abolished.

ab·o·li·tion·ist /ábəlíshənist/ *n.* one who favors the abolition of a practice or institution, esp. of capital punishment or slavery. ▫▫ **ab·o·li·tion·ism** *n.*

A-bomb /áybom/ *n.* = ATOM BOMB.

a·bom·i·na·ble /əbóminəbəl/ *adj.* **1** detestable; loathsome. **2** *colloq.* very bad or unpleasant (*abominable weather*). ▫▫ **a·bom·i·na·bly** *adv.*

a·bom·i·na·ble snow·man *n.* a humanoid or bearlike animal said to exist in the Himalayas; a yeti.

a·bom·i·nate /əbóminayt/ *v.tr.* detest; loathe.

a·bom·i·na·tion /əbóminάyshən/ *n.* **1** loathing. **2** an odious habit or act. **3** an object of disgust.

ab·o·rig·i·nal /ábəríjinəl/ *adj. & n.* • *adj.* **1** inhabiting or existing in a land from the earliest times or before the arrival of colonists. **2** (**Aboriginal**) of the Australian Aborigines. • *n.* **1** an aboriginal inhabitant. **2** (**Aboriginal**) an aboriginal inhabitant of Australia.

ab·o·rig·i·ne /ábəríjinee/ *n.* (usu. in *pl.*) **1** an aboriginal inhabitant. **2** (**Aborigine**) an aboriginal inhabitant of Australia. **3** an aboriginal plant or animal.

a·bort /əbáwrt/ *v.* **1** *intr.* **a** (of a woman) undergo abortion; miscarry. **b** (of a fetus) undergo abortion. **2** *tr.* **a** effect the abortion of (a fetus). **b** effect abortion in (a mother). **3 a** *tr.* cause to end fruitlessly or prematurely. **b** *intr.* end unsuccessfully or prematurely. **4 a** *tr.* abandon or terminate (a space flight or other technical project) before its completion. **b** *intr.* terminate such an undertaking.

a·bor·ti·fa·cient /əbáwrtifáyshənt/ *adj. & n.* • *adj.* effecting abortion. • *n.* a drug or other agent that effects abortion.

a·bor·tion /əbáwrshən/ *n.* **1** the expulsion of a fetus (naturally or esp. by medical induction) from the womb before it is able to survive independently, esp. in the first 28 weeks of a human pregnancy. **2** a stunted or deformed creature or thing.

a·bor·tion·ist /əbáwrshənist/ *n.* a person who carries out abortions, esp. illegally.

a·bor·tive /əbáwrtiv/ *adj.* **1** fruitless; unsuccessful; unfinished. **2** resulting in abortion. ▫▫ **a·bor·tive·ly** *adv.*

ABO sys·tem /áybee–ṓ/ *n.* a system of four types (A, AB, B, and O) by which human blood may be classified.

a·bound /əbównd/ *v.intr.* **1** be plentiful. **2** (foll. by *in*) be rich.

a·bout /əbówt/ *prep. & adv.* • *prep.* **1 a** on the subject of; in connection with (*a book about birds*). **b** relating to (*something funny about this*). **c** in relation to (*symmetry about a plane*). **d** so as to affect (*can do nothing about it*). **2** at a time near to (*come about four*). **3 a** in; around; surrounding (*wandered about the town*). **b** all around from a center (*look about you*). **4** at points throughout (*toys lying about the house*). **5** at a point or points near to (*fighting going on about us*). • *adv.* **1 a** approximately. **b** *colloq.* used to indicate understatement (*just about had enough*). **2** here and there; at points nearby (*a lot of flu about*). **3** all around; in every direction (*look about*). **4** on the move; in action (*out and about*). **5** in partial rotation or alteration from a given position (*the wrong way about*). **6** in rotation or succession (*turn and turn about*). **7** *Naut.* on or to the opposite tack (*put about*). ▫ **be about to** be on the point of (doing something).

a·bout-face /əbówtfáys/ *n., v., & int.* •*n.* **1** a turn made so as to face the opposite direction. **2** a change of opinion or policy, etc. •*v.intr.* make an about-face. •*int. Mil.* a command to make an about-face.

a·bove /əbúv/ *prep., adv., adj., & n.* •*prep.* **1** over; on the top of; higher than. **2** more than (*above average*). **3** higher in rank, position, importance, etc., than. **4 a** too great or good for (*is not above cheating*). **b** beyond the reach of; not affected by (*above my understanding*). •*adv.* **1** at or to a higher point; overhead (*the floor above; the clouds above*). **2** upstairs (*lives above*). **3** (of a text reference) further back on a page or in a book (*as noted above*). **4** in addition (*over and above*). **5** *rhet.* in heaven (*Lord above!*). •*adj.* mentioned earlier; preceding (*the above argument*). •*n.* (prec. by *the*) what is mentioned above (*the above shows*). □ **above all** most of all; more than anything else.

a·bove·board /əbúvbawrd/ *adj. & adv.* fair or fairly; open or openly.

ab·ra·ca·dab·ra /ábrəkədábrə/ *n.* **1** a word used by magicians in performing a trick. **2** jargon or gibberish.

a·brade /əbráyd/ *v.tr.* scrape or wear away by rubbing. □□ **a·brad·er** *n.*

a·bra·sion /əbráyzhən/ *n.* **1** scraping or wearing away. **2** a damaged area resulting from this.

a·bra·sive /əbráysiv/ *adj. & n.* •*adj.* **1 a** tending to rub or abrade. **b** capable of polishing by rubbing. **2** harsh in manner •*n.* an abrasive substance.

ab·re·ac·tion /ábreeákshən/ *n. Psychol.* the free expression and consequent release of a previously repressed emotion. □□ **ab·re·ac·tive** *adj.*

a·breast /əbrést/ *adv.* **1** side by side and facing the same way. **2 a** (often foll. by *with*) up to date. **b** (foll. by *of*) well-informed (*abreast of all the changes*).

a·bridge /əbríj/ *v.tr.* shorten (a book, movie, etc.). □□ **a·bridg·a·ble** or **a·bridge·a·ble** *adj.* **a·bridg·er** *n.*

a·bridg·ment /əbríjmənt/ *n.* (also **a·bridge·ment**) **1** shortened version, esp. of a book. **2** the process of producing this.

a·broad /əbráwd/ *adv.* **1** in or to a foreign country or countries. **2** over a wide area; in different directions (*scatter abroad*). **3** in circulation (*there is a rumor abroad*).

ab·ro·gate /ábrəgayt/ *v.tr.* repeal or abolish (a law or custom). □□ **ab·ro·ga·tion** /–gáyshən/ *n.*

ab·rupt /əbrúpt/ *adj.* **1** sudden and unexpected; hasty (*his abrupt departure*). **2** (of speech, manner, etc.) lacking continuity; curt. **3** steep; precipitous. □□ **ab·rupt·ly** *adv.* **ab·rupt·ness** *n.*

ABS *abbr.* antilock brake (or braking) system.

ab·scess /ábses/ *n.* a swollen area accumulating pus within a body tissue. □□ **ab·scessed** *adj.*

ab·scis·sa /əbsísə/ *n.* (*pl.* **abscissae** /–ee/ or **abscissas**) *Math.* (in a system of coordinates) the shortest distance from a point to the vertical or *y*-axis (cf. ORDINATE).

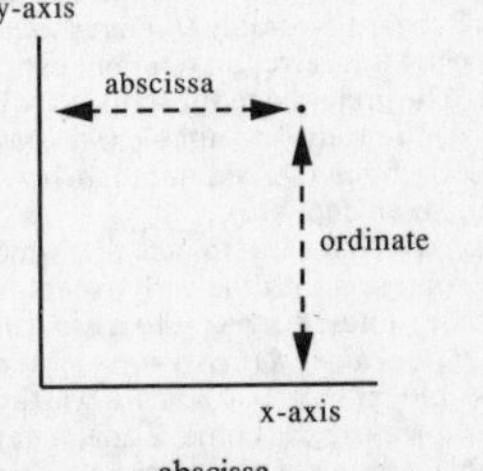

abscissa

ab·scis·sion /əbsízhən/ *n.* the act or an instance of cutting off.

ab·scond /əbskónd/ *v.intr.* depart hurriedly, esp. unlawfully. □□ **ab·scond·er** *n.*

ab·sence /ábsəns/ *n.* **1** the state of being away from a place or person. **2** the time or duration of being away. **3** (foll. by *of*) the nonexistence or lack of. □ **absence of mind** inattentiveness.

ab·sent *adj. & v.* •*adj.* /ábsənt/ **1** not present. **2** not existing. **3** inattentive. •*v.refl.* /absént/ **1** stay away. **2** withdraw. □□ **ab·sent·ly** *adv.* (in sense 3 of *adj.*).

ab·sen·tee /ábsəntée/ *n.* a person not present, esp. one who is absent from work or school.

ab·sen·tee bal·lot *n.* a ballot, usu. returned by mail, for a voter who cannot be present at the polls.

ab·sen·tee·ism /ábsənteéizəm/ *n.* the practice of absenting oneself from work or school, etc., esp. frequently or illicitly.

ab·sen·tee land·lord *n.* a landlord who rents out a property while living elsewhere.

ab·sent·mind·ed /ábsəntmíndid/ *adj.* habitually forgetful or inattentive. □□ **ab·sent·mind·ed·ly** *adv.* **ab·sent·mind·ed·ness** *n.*

ab·sinthe /ábsinth/ *n.* (also **ab·sinth**) a green anise-flavored liqueur based on wormwood.

ab·so·lute /ábsəlóot/ *adj. & n.* •*adj.* **1** complete; utter (*an absolute fool*). **2** unconditional; unlimited (*absolute authority*). **3** ruling arbitrarily or with unrestricted power (*an absolute monarch*). **4** (of a standard or other concept) universally valid; not relative or comparative. **5** *Gram.* **a** (of a construction) syntactically independent of the rest of the sentence, as in *dinner being over, we left the table.* **b** (of an adjective or transitive verb) used or usable without an expressed noun or object (e.g., *the deaf; guns kill*). **6** (of a legal decree, etc.) final. •*n. Philos.* a value, standard, etc., which is objective and universally valid. □□ **ab·so·lute·ness** *n.*

ab·so·lute·ly /ábsəlóotlee/ *adv.* **1** completely; utterly (*absolutely marvelous*). **2** (foll. by *neg.*) (no or none) at all (*absolutely no chance*). **3** *Gram.* in an absolute way, esp. (of a verb) without a stated object. **4** *colloq.* (used in reply) quite so; yes.

ab·so·lute ze·ro *n.* a theoretical lowest possible temperature, calculated as zero on the Kelvin scale, equivalent to –273.15°C.

ab·so·lu·tion /ábsəlóoshən/ *n.* **1** a formal release from guilt, obligation, or punishment. **2** an ecclesiastical declaration of forgiveness of sins.

ab·so·lut·ism /ábsəlóotizəm/ *n.* the acceptance of or belief in absolute principles in political, philosophical, ethical, or theological matters. □□ **ab·so·lut·ist** *n. & adj.*

ab·solve /əbzólv, –sólv/ *v.tr.* **1** (often foll. by *from, of*) set or pronounce free from blame or obligation, etc. **2** pardon or give absolution for (a sin, etc.).

ab·sorb /əbsáwrb, –záwrb/ *v.tr.* **1** include or incorporate as part of itself or oneself. **2** take in; suck up (liquid, heat, knowledge, etc.). **3** reduce the effect or intensity of; deal easily with (an impact, sound, difficulty, etc.). **4** consume (income, time, resources, etc.). **5** engross the attention of. □□ **ab·sorb·a·ble** *adj.* **ab·sorb·er** *n.*

ab·sorbed /əbsáwrbd, –záwrbd/ *adj.* intensely engaged or interested. □□ **ab·sorb·ed·ly** /–bidlee/ *adv.*

ab·sorb·ent /əbsáwrbənt, –záwr–/ *adj. & n.* •*adj.* having a tendency to absorb (esp. liquids) •*n.* an absorbent substance. □□ **ab·sorb·en·cy** /–bənsee/ *n.*

ab·sorp·tion /əbsáwrpshən, –záwrp–/ *n.* **1** the process or action of absorbing or being absorbed. **2** mental engrossment. □□ **ab·sorp·tive** *adj.*

ab·stain /əbstáyn/ *v.intr.* **1 a** (usu. foll. by *from*) refrain from indulging in (*abstained from candy*). **b** refrain from drinking alcohol. **2** formally decline to use one's vote. □□ **ab·stain·er** *n.*

ab·ste·mi·ous /abstéemeeəs/ *adj.* moderate, esp. in eating and drinking. □□ **ab·ste·mi·ous·ly** *adv.* **ab·ste·mi·ous·ness** *n.*

ab·sten·tion /əbsténshən/ *n.* the act of abstaining from voting.

ab·sti·nence /ábstinəns/ *n.* the act of abstaining, esp. from food, alcohol, or sexual relations.

ab·sti·nent /ábstinənt/ *adj.* practicing abstinence.

ab·stract *adj., v., & n.* • *adj.* /ábstrakt/ **1 a** to do with or existing in thought rather than matter, or in theory rather than practice. **b** (of a word, esp. a noun) denoting a quality or condition or intangible thing rather than a concrete object. **2** (of art) achieving its effect by shapes and colors rather than by the recognizable representation of physical reality. • *v.* /əbstrákt/ **1** *tr.* (often foll. by *from*) take out of; extract; remove. **2** *tr.* summarize (an article, book, etc.). • *n.* /ábstrakt/ **1** a summary or statement of the contents of a book, etc. **2** an abstract work of art. □□ **ab·stract·ly** *adv.* **ab·stract·or** *n.* (in sense 2 of *v.*).

ab·stract·ed /əbstráktid/ *adj.* inattentive; preoccupied. □□ **ab·stract·ed·ly** *adv.*

ab·strac·tion /əbstrákshən/ *n.* **1** the act or an instance of abstracting or taking away. **2** an abstract or visionary idea. **3** abstract qualities (esp. in art). **4** absentmindedness.

ab·struse /abstróos/ *adj.* hard to understand. □□ **ab·struse·ly** *adv.* **ab·struse·ness** *n.*

ab·surd /əbsə́rd/ *adj.* wildly unreasonable, illogical, or ludicrous. □□ **ab·surd·ly** *adv.* **ab·surd·ness** *n.*

ab·surd·i·ty /əbsə́rditee/ *n.* (*pl.* **·ties**) **1** wild inappropriateness or incongruity. **2** an absurd statement or act.

a·bun·dance /əbúndəns/ *n.* **1** a great quantity; more than enough. **2** wealth; affluence.

a·bun·dant /əbúndənt/ *adj.* **1** existing or available in large quantities; plentiful. **2** (foll. by *in*) having an abundance of. □□ **a·bun·dant·ly** *adv.*

a·buse *v. & n.* • *v.tr.* /əbyóoz/ **1** use to bad effect or for a bad purpose. **2** insult verbally. **3** maltreat; assault (esp. sexually) • *n.* /əbyóos/ **1** incorrect or improper use (*the abuse of power*). **2** insulting language (*a torrent of abuse*). **3** unjust or corrupt practice. **4** maltreatment (*child abuse*). □□ **a·bus·er** /əbyóozər/ *n.*

a·bu·sive /əbyóosiv/ *adj.* **1** using insulting language. **2** (of language) insulting. **3** given to physical abuse. □□ **a·bu·sive·ly** *adv.* **a·bu·sive·ness** *n.*

a·but /əbút/ *v.* (**abutted, abutting**) **1** *intr.* (foll. by *on*) (of countries, etc.) adjoin (another). **2** *intr.* (foll. by *on*) (of part of a building) touch or lean on (another) with a projecting end or point. **3** *tr.* abut on.

a·but·ment /əbútmənt/ *n.* the lateral supporting structure of a bridge, arch, etc.

a·buzz /əbúz/ *adv. & adj.* in a state of excitement or activity.

a·bys·mal /əbízməl/ *adj.* **1** *colloq.* extremely bad (*abysmal weather*). **2** profound; utter (*abysmal ignorance*). □□ **a·bys·mal·ly** *adv.*

a·byss /əbís/ *n.* **1** a deep or seemingly bottomless chasm. **2 a** an immeasurable depth (*abyss of despair*). **b** a catastrophic situation as contemplated.

a·byss·al /əbísəl/ *adj.* at or of the ocean depths or floor.

AC *abbr.* **1** (also **ac**) alternating current. **2** air conditioning.

Ac *symb. Chem.* the element actinium.

a/c *abbr.* account.

a·ca·cia /əkáyshə/ *n.* **1** any tree of the genus *Acacia*, with yellow or white flowers. **2** (also **false acacia**) the locust tree, *Robinia pseudoacacia.*

ac·a·deme /ákədeem/ *n.* **1** the world of learning. **2** universities collectively.

ac·a·de·mi·a /ákədéemeeə/ *n.* the academic world.

ac·a·dem·ic /ákədémik/ *adj. & n.* • *adj.* **1 a** scholarly; to do with learning. **b** of or relating to a scholarly institution (*academic dress*). **2** abstract; not of practical relevance. **3** *Art* conventional; overly formal • *n.* a teacher or scholar in a university or college. □□ **ac·a·dem·i·cal·ly** *adv.*

a·cad·e·my /əkádəmee/ *n.* (*pl.* **·mies**) **1** a place of study or training in a special field (*military academy*). **2** (usu. **Academy**) a society or institution of distinguished scholars, artists, scientists, etc. (*Royal Academy*). **3** a secondary school, esp. one that is private.

A·ca·di·an /əkáydeeən/ *n. & adj.* • *n.* **1** a native or inhabitant of Acadia in Nova Scotia. **2** a descendant of French-speaking Nova Scotian immigrants in Louisiana • *adj.* of or relating to Acadians.

a·can·thus /əkánthəs/ *n.* **1** any herbaceous plant of the genus *Acanthus*, with spiny leaves. **2** *Archit.* a conventionalized representation of an acanthus leaf.

a cap·pel·la /aá kəpélə/ *adj. & adv.* (also **al·la cap·pel·la** /álə/) *Mus.* (of choral music) unaccompanied.

a·car·pous /əkaárpəs/ *adj. Bot.* (of a plant, etc.) without fruit or that does not produce fruit.

ac·cede /akséed/ *v.intr.* (often foll. by *to*) **1** assent or agree. **2** take office, esp. become monarch. **3** formally subscribe to a treaty or other agreement.

ac·cel·er·an·do /əksélərándō, aachéləraán–/ *adv. & adj. Mus.* with a gradual increase of speed.

ac·cel·er·ate /əksélərayt/ *v.* **1** *intr.* **a** (of a moving body) increase speed. **b** (of a process) happen more quickly. **2** *tr.* **a** cause to increase speed. **b** cause to happen more quickly.

ac·cel·er·a·tion /əkséləráyshən/ *n.* **1** the process or act of accelerating. **2** (of a vehicle, etc.) the capacity to gain speed (*the car has good acceleration*).

ac·cel·er·a·tor /əksélәraytər/ *n.* **1** a device for increasing speed, esp. the pedal that controls the speed of a vehicle's engine. **2** *Physics* an apparatus for imparting high speeds to charged particles. **3** *Chem.* a substance that speeds up a chemical reaction.

ac·cel·er·om·e·ter /əksélərómitər/ *n.* an instrument for measuring acceleration.

ac·cent *n. & v.* • *n.* /áksent/ **1** a mode of pronunciation, esp. one associated with a particular region or group. **2** prominence given to a syllable by stress or pitch. **3** a mark on a letter or word to indicate pitch, stress, or the quality of a vowel. **4** emphasis (*an accent on comfort*). **5** *Mus.* emphasis on a particular note or chord • *v.tr.* also /aksént/ **1** pronounce with an accent; emphasize. **2** write or print accents on (words, etc.). **3** *Mus.* play with an accent.

ac·cen·tu·ate /aksénchooayt/ *v.tr.* emphasize; make prominent. □□ **ac·cen·tu·a·tion** /–áyshən/ *n.*

ac·cept /aksépt/ *v.tr.* **1** (also *absol.*) consent to receive (a thing offered). **2** (also *absol.*) give an affirmative answer to. **3** regard favorably (*her mother-in-law never accepted her*). **4 a** receive (an opinion, explanation, etc.) as valid. **b** be prepared to subscribe to (a belief, philosophy, etc.). **5** receive as suitable (*the hotel accepts traveler's checks*). **6** tolerate; submit to (*accepted the umpire's decision*). □□ **ac·cept·er** *n.*

▶**Accept**, which means 'to take that which is offered,' may be confused with the verb **except**, which means 'to exclude.' Thus: *I accept your terms, but I wish to except the clause calling for repayment of the deposit.*

ac·cept·a·ble /akséptəbəl/ *adj.* **1 a** worthy of being accepted. **b** pleasing; welcome. **2** adequate; satisfactory. **3** tolerable (*an acceptable risk*). □□ **ac·cept·a·bil·i·ty** /–bílitee/ *n.* **ac·cept·a·ble·ness** *n.* **ac·cept·a·bly** *adv.*

ac·cept·ance /əkséptəns/ *n.* **1** willingness to receive or accept. **2** an affirmative answer to an invitation or proposal. **3 a** approval; belief (*found wide acceptance*). **b** willingness or ability to tolerate.

ac•cep•tor /akséptər/ *n.* **1** *Commerce* a person who accepts a bill. **2** *Physics* an atom or molecule able to receive an extra electron, esp. an impurity in a semiconductor. **3** *Chem.* a molecule or ion, etc., to which electrons are donated in the formation of a bond. **4** *Electr.* a circuit able to accept a given frequency.

ac•cess /ákses/ *n. & v.* •*n.* **1** a way of approaching or reaching or entering (*a building with rear access*). **2 a** (often foll. by *to*) the right or opportunity to reach or use or visit; admittance (*has access to secret files*). **b** accessibility. •*v.tr. Computing* gain access to (data, a file, etc.).

ac•ces•si•ble /aksésibəl/ *adj.* (often foll. by *to*) **1** that can readily be reached, entered, or used. **2** (of a person) readily available (esp. to subordinates). **3** (in a form) easy to understand. ▫▫ **ac•ces•si•bil•i•ty** /–bílitee/ *n.* **ac•ces•si•bly** *adv.*

ac•ces•sion /akséshən/ *n. & v.* •*n.* **1** entering upon an office (esp. the throne) or a condition (as adulthood). **2** (often foll. by *to*) a thing added (e.g., a book to a library). **3** assent; the formal acceptance of a treaty, etc. •*v.tr.* record the addition of (a new item) to a library or museum.

ac•ces•so•rize /aksésərīz/ *v.tr.* provide (clothing, etc.) with accessories.

ac•ces•so•ry /aksésəree/ *n. & adj.* •*n.* (*pl.* **•ries**) **1** an additional or extra thing. **2** (usu. in *pl.*) **a** a small attachment or fitting. **b** a small item of (esp. a woman's) dress (e.g., shoes, gloves, etc.). **3** (often foll. by *to*) a person who helps in or knows the details of an (esp. illegal) act, without taking part in it. •*adj.* additional; aiding in a minor way; dispensable. ▫▫ **ac•ces•so•ri•al** /áksesáwreeəl/ *adj.*

ac•cess time *n. Computing* the time taken to retrieve data from storage.

ac•ciac•ca•tu•ra /əchaákətóorə/ *n. Mus.* a grace note performed as quickly as possible before an essential note of a melody.

ac•ci•dent /áksidənt/ *n.* **1** an event that is without apparent cause, or is unexpected. **2** an unfortunate event, esp. one causing physical harm or damage, brought about unintentionally. **3** occurrence of things by chance; the working of fortune (*accident accounts for much in life*). ▫ **by accident** unintentionally.

ac•ci•den•tal /áksidént'l/ *adj. & n.* •*adj.* **1** happening by chance or unexpectedly. **2** not essential to a conception. •*n.* **1** *Mus.* a sign indicating a momentary departure from the key signature. **2** something not essential to a conception. ▫▫ **ac•ci•den•tal•ly** *adv.*

ac•ci•dent-prone *adj.* (of a person) subject to frequent accidents.

ac•claim /əkláym/ *v. & n.* •*v.tr.* **1** praise publicly. **2** (foll. by compl.) hail as (*was acclaimed the winner*). •*n.* **1** applause; public praise. **2** a shout of acclaim.

ac•cla•ma•tion /ákləmáyshən/ *n.* **1** loud and eager assent. **2** (usu. in *pl.*) shouting in a person's honor. **3** the act or process of acclaiming.

ac•cli•mate /áklimayt, əklímit/ *v.tr.* acclimatize.

ac•cli•ma•tion /ákləmáyshən/ *n.* acclimatization.

ac•cli•ma•tize /əklímətīz/ *v.* **1** *tr.* accustom to a new climate or to new conditions. **2** *intr.* become acclimatized. ▫▫ **ac•cli•ma•ti•za•tion** /–tizáyshən/ *n.*

ac•cliv•i•ty /əklívitee/ *n.* (*pl.* **•ties**) an upward slope. ▫▫ **ac•cliv•i•tous** *adj.*

ac•co•lade /ákəláyd/ *n.* an acknowledgment of merit.

ac•com•mo•date /əkómədayt/ *v.tr.* **1** provide lodging or room for. **2** adapt; harmonize; reconcile. **3** do a service or favor to.

ac•com•mo•dat•ing /əkómədayting/ *adj.* obliging; compliant. ▫▫ **ac•com•mo•dat•ing•ly** *adv.*

ac•com•mo•da•tion /əkómədáyshən/ *n.* **1** (in *pl.*) lodgings; a place to live. **2 a** an adjustment or adaptation to suit a special or different purpose. **b** a convenient arrangement; a settlement or compromise.

ac•com•pa•ni•ment /əkúmpənimənt/ *n.* **1** *Mus.* an instrumental part supporting a solo instrument, voice, or group. **2** an accompanying thing.

ac•com•pa•nist /əkúmpənist/ *n.* a person who provides a musical accompaniment.

ac•com•pa•ny /əkúmpənee/ *v.tr.* (**•nies, •nied**) **1** go with; escort. **2** (usu. in *passive*; foll. by *with, by*) be done or found with; supplement. **3** *Mus.* support with accompaniment.

ac•com•plice /əkómplis, əkúm–/ *n.* a partner or helper, esp. in a crime.

accomplice mid-16th cent.: alteration (probably by association with ACCOMPANY) of Middle English *complice* 'an associate,' via Old French from late Latin *complex, complic-* 'allied,' from *com-* 'together' + the root of *plicare* 'to fold.'

ac•com•plish /əkómplish/ *v.tr.* perform; complete; succeed in doing.

ac•com•plished /əkómplisht/ *adj.* clever; skilled; well trained or educated.

ac•com•plish•ment /əkómplishmənt/ *n.* **1** the fulfillment or completion (of a task, etc.). **2** an acquired skill, esp. a social one. **3** a thing done or achieved.

ac•cord /əkáwrd/ *v. & n.* •*v.* **1** *intr.* (often foll. by *with*) (esp. of a thing) be in harmony; be consistent. **2** *tr.* **a** grant (permission, a request, etc.). **b** give (a welcome, etc.). •*n.* **1** agreement; consent. **2** harmonious correspondence in pitch, tone, color, etc. ▫ **of one's own accord** on one's own initiative; voluntarily.

ac•cord•ance /əkáwrd'ns/ *n.* harmony; agreement.

ac•cord•ing /əkáwrding/ *adv.* (foll. by *to*) **1** as stated by or in (*according to my sister*). **2** in a manner corresponding to; in proportion to (*he lives according to his principles*).

ac•cord•ing•ly /əkáwrdinglee/ *adv.* **1** as suggested or required by the (stated) circumstances. **2** consequently; therefore.

ac•cor•di•on /əkáwrdeeən/ *n.* a portable musical instrument with reeds blown by bellows and played by means of keys and buttons. ▫▫ **ac•cor•di•on•ist** *n.*

accordion

ac•cost /əkáwst, əkóst/ *v.tr.* approach and address (a person), esp. boldly.

ac•couche•ment /ákooshmóɴ/ *n.* **1** childbirth. **2** the period of childbirth.

ac•count /əkównt/ *n. & v.* •*n.* **1** a narration or description. **2 a** an arrangement or facility at a bank, etc., for commercial or financial transactions, esp. for depositing and withdrawing money. **b** an arrangement at a store for buying goods on credit. **3** (often in *pl.*) a record or statement of money, goods, or services received or expended, with the balance. •*v.tr.* (foll. by *to be* or compl.) consider; regard as (*account him wise*; *account*

him to be guilty). □ **account for 1** serve as or provide an explanation or reason for (*that accounts for their misbehavior*). **2 a** give a reckoning of or answer for (money, etc., entrusted). **b** answer for (one's conduct). **3** succeed in killing, destroying, or defeating. **4** make up a specified amount or proportion of (*rent accounts for 50 percent of expenditures*). **call to account** require an explanation from (a person). **keep account of** keep a record of; follow closely. **of no account** unimportant. **on account 1** (of goods or services) to be paid for later. **2** (of money) in part payment. **on account of** because of. **on no account** under no circumstances. **on one's own account** for one's own purposes. **take account of** (or **take into account**) consider along with other factors (*took their age into account*).
▶Use with *as* (*we accounted him as wise*) is considered incorrect.

ac·count·a·ble /əkówntəbəl/ *adj.* responsible; required to account for one's conduct (*accountable for one's actions*). □□ **ac·count·a·bil·i·ty** /–bílitee/ *n.* **ac·count·a·bly** *adv.*

ac·count·an·cy /əkównt'nsee/ *n.* the profession or duties of an accountant.

ac·count·ant /əkównt'nt/ *n.* a professional keeper or inspector of accounts.

ac·count·ing /əkównting/ *n.* the process of or skill in keeping accounts.

ac·cou·tre·ment /əkóotrəmənt, –tərmənt/ *n.* (also **ac·cou·ter·ment** /–tərmənt) (usu. in *pl.*) **1** equipment; trappings. **2** *Mil.* a soldier's outfit other than weapons and garments.

ac·cred·it /əkrédit/ *v.tr.* (**accredited, accrediting**) **1** (foll. by *to*) attribute (a saying, etc.) to (a person). **2** (foll. by *with*) credit (a person) with (a saying, etc.). **3** (usu. foll. by *to* or *at*) send (an ambassador, etc.) with credentials. □□ **ac·cred·i·ta·tion** /–táyshən/ *n.*

ac·cred·it·ed /əkréditid/ *adj.* (of a person or organization) officially recognized.

ac·crete /əkréet/ *v.* **1** *intr.* grow together or into one. **2** *intr.* (often foll. by *to*) form around or on, as around a nucleus. **3** *tr.* attract (such additions).

ac·cre·tion /əkréeshən/ *n.* **1** growth by organic enlargement. **2 a** the growing of separate things into one. **b** the product of such growing. **3** extraneous matter added to anything. □□ **ac·cre·tive** *adj.*

ac·crue /əkróo/ *v.intr.* (**accrues, accrued, accruing**) (often foll. by *to*) come as a natural increase or advantage, esp. financial. □□ **ac·cru·al** *n.* **ac·crued** *adj.*

ac·cul·tur·ate /əkúlchərayt/ *v.* **1** *intr.* adapt to or adopt a different culture. **2** *tr.* cause to do this. □□ **ac·cul·tur·a·tion** /–ráyshən/ *n.* **ac·cul·tur·a·tive** /–rətiv/ *adj.*

ac·cu·mu·late /əkyóomyəlayt/ *v.* **1** *tr.* **a** acquire an increasing number or quantity of. **b** produce or acquire (a resulting whole) in this way. **2** *intr.* form an increasing mass or quantity.

ac·cu·mu·la·tion /əkyóomyəláyshən/ *n.* **1** the act or process of accumulating or being accumulated. **2** an accumulated mass.

ac·cu·mu·la·tive /əkyóomyəlaytiv, –lətiv/ *adj.* **1** arising from accumulation; cumulative (*accumulative evidence*). **2** arranged so as to accumulate.

ac·cu·mu·la·tor /əkyóomyəlaytər/ *n.* a person who accumulates things.

ac·cu·ra·cy /ákyərəsee/ *n.* exactness or precision.

ac·cu·rate /ákyərət/ *adj.* **1** careful; precise; lacking errors. **2** conforming exactly with a qualitative standard. □□ **ac·cu·rate·ly** *adv.*

ac·curs·ed /əkɔ́rsid, əkɔ́rst/ *adj.* **1** under a curse; ill-fated. **2** *colloq.* detestable; annoying.

ac·cu·sa·tion /ákyəzáyshən/ *n.* **1** the act or process of accusing or being accused. **2** a statement charging a person with an offense or crime.

ac·cu·sa·tive /əkyóozətiv/ *n.* & *adj. Gram.* • *n.* the case of nouns, pronouns, and adjectives expressing the object of an action or the goal of motion • *adj.* of or in this case.

ac·cu·sa·to·ri·al /əkyóozətáwreeəl/ *adj. Law* (of proceedings) involving accusation by a prosecutor and a verdict reached by an impartial judge or jury.

ac·cu·sa·to·ry /əkyóozətawree/ *adj.* of or implying accusation.

ac·cuse /əkyóoz/ *v.tr.* **1** (foll. by *of*) charge (a person, etc.) with a fault or crime (*accused them of murder*). **2** lay the blame on. □□ **ac·cus·er** *n.* **ac·cus·ing·ly** *adv.*

ac·cus·tom /əkústəm/ *v.tr.* & *refl.* (foll. by *to*) make (a person or thing or oneself) used to (*the army accustomed him to discipline*).

ac·cus·tomed /əkústəmd/ *adj.* **1** (foll. by *to*) used to. **2** customary.

ace /ays/ *n.* & *adj.* • *n.* **1** a playing card, domino, etc., with a single spot. **2 a** a person who excels in some activity. **b** *Mil.* a pilot who has shot down many enemy aircraft. **3** (in tennis) a service too good for the opponent to touch. **4** *Golf* a hole in one. • *adj. sl.* excellent.

a·ce·di·a /əséediə/ *n.* laziness; sloth; apathy.

a·cel·lu·lar /aysélyoolər/ *adj. Biol.* **1** having no cells; not consisting of cells. **2** (esp. of protozoa) consisting of one cell only; unicellular.

a·ceph·a·lous /əséfələs, əkéf–/ *adj.* **1** headless. **2** having no chief. **3** *Zool.* having no part of the body specially organized as a head.

a·cer·bic /əsérbik/ *adj.* **1** astringently sour. **2** bitter in speech, manner, or temper. □□ **a·cer·bi·cal·ly** *adv.* **a·cer·bi·ty** *n.* (*pl.* **·ties**).

ac·e·tab·u·lum /ásitábyooləm/ *n.* (*pl.* **acetabulums** or **acetabula** /–lə/) *Zool.* **1** the socket for the head of the thighbone, or of the leg in insects. **2** a cup-shaped sucker of various organisms.

a·ce·ta·min·o·phen /əseetəmínəfən/ *n.* a crystalline substance, $C_8H_9NO_2$, that is used medically to reduce fever and relieve pain.

ac·e·tate /ásitayt/ *n.* **1** a salt or ester of acetic acid. **2** a fabric made from cellulose acetate.

a·ce·tic /əséetik/ *adj.* of or like vinegar.

a·ce·tic ac·id *n.* the clear liquid acid that gives vinegar its characteristic taste.

ac·e·tone /ásitōn/ *n.* a colorless, volatile liquid valuable as a solvent of organic compounds, esp. paints.

a·ce·tous /ásitəs, əsée–/ *adj.* **1** having the qualities of vinegar. **2** producing vinegar. **3** sour.

a·ce·tyl·cho·line /ásitilkóleen, ásitīl–/ *n.* a compound serving to transmit impulses from nerve fibers.

a·cet·y·lene /əsétileen/ *n.* a colorless hydrocarbon gas, burning with a bright flame, used esp. in welding.

a·ce·tyl·sal·i·cyl·ic ac·id /ásitīlsálisílik/ *n.* = ASPIRIN.

A·chae·an /əkéeən/ *adj.* & *n.* • *adj.* **1** of or relating to Achaea in ancient Greece. **2** *literary* Greek. • *n.* **1** an inhabitant of Achaea. **2** *literary* a Greek.

ache /ayk/ *n.* & *v.* • *n.* **1** a continuous or prolonged dull pain. **2** mental distress • *v.intr.* **1** suffer from or be the source of an ache. **2** (foll. by *to* + infin.) desire greatly. □□ **ach·ing·ly** *adv.*

---

ache Old English *æce* (noun), *acan* (verb). In Middle and early modern English the noun was spelled *atche* and pronounced so as to rhyme with 'batch,' the verb was spelled and pronounced as it is today. The noun began to be pronounced like the verb around 1700. The modern spelling is largely due to Dr. Johnson, who mistakenly assumed its derivation to be from Greek *akhos* 'pain.'

---

a·chene /əkéen/ *n. Bot.* a small, dry, one-seeded fruit that does not open to liberate the seed (e.g., a strawberry pip).

A·cheu·li·an /əshóōliən/ *adj.* *&n.* (also **Acheulean**) • *adj.* of the Paleolithic period in Europe, etc., following the Abbevillian and preceding the Mousterian. • *n.* the culture of this period.

a·chieve /əchéev/ *v.tr.* **1 a** reach or attain by effort (*achieved victory*). **b** acquire; gain (*achieved notoriety*). **2** accomplish or carry out (a feat or task). **3** *absol.* attain a desired level of performance. □□ **a·chiev·a·ble** *adj.* **a·chiev·er** *n.*

a·chieve·ment /əchéevmənt/ *n.* **1** something achieved. **2** the act of achieving.

A·chil·les heel /əkíleez/ *n.* a person's weak or vulnerable point.

A·chil·les ten·don /əkíleez/ *n.* the tendon connecting the heel with the calf muscles.

a·chro·mat·ic /ákrōmátik/ *adj.* *Optics* **1** that transmits light without separating it into constituent colors (*achromatic lens*). **2** without color. □□ **a·chro·mat·i·cal·ly** *adv.* **a·chro·ma·tism** /əkrṓmətizəm/ *n.*

ach·y /áykee/ *adj.* (**achier, achiest**) full of or suffering from aches.

ac·id /ásid/ *n. & adj.* • *n.* **1** *Chem.* any of a class of substances that liberate hydrogen ions in water, are usu. sour and corrosive, turn litmus red, and have a pH of less than 7. **2** (in general use) any sour substance. **3** *sl.* the drug LSD. • *adj.* **1** sharp-tasting; sour. **2** biting; sharp (*an acid wit*). **3** *Chem.* having the essential properties of an acid. **4** (of a color) intense; bright. □□ **a·cid·ic** /əsídik/ *adj.* **ac·i·dim·e·try** /ásidímitree/ *n.* **ac·id·ly** *adv.*

ac·id·head /ásidhed/ *n. sl.* a user of the drug LSD.

a·cid·i·fy /əsídifī/ *v.tr. & intr.* (**·fies, ·fied**) make or become acid. □□ **a·cid·i·fi·ca·tion** /–fikáyshən/ *n.*

a·cid·i·ty /əsíditee/ *n.* (*pl.* **·ties**) an acid quality or state, esp. an excessively acid condition of the stomach.

ac·id rain *n.* acid formed in the atmosphere, esp. from industrial waste gases, and falling with rain.

ac·id test *n.* **1** a severe or conclusive test. **2** a test in which acid is used to test for gold, etc.

a·cid·u·late /əsídyoolayt/ *v.tr.* make somewhat acid. □□ **a·cid·u·la·tion** /–láyshən/ *n.*

a·cid·u·lous /əsídyooləs/ *adj.* somewhat acid.

ac·i·nus /ásinəs/ *n.* (*pl.* **acini** /–nī/) **1** any of the small elements that make up a compound fruit of the blackberry, raspberry, etc. **2** the seed of a grape or berry. **3** *Anat.* **a** any multicellular gland with saclike secreting ducts. **b** the terminus of a duct in such a gland.

ack-ack /ákák/ *adj. colloq.* antiaircraft.

ac·knowl·edge /əknólij/ *v.tr.* **1 a** recognize; accept. **b** (often foll. by *to be* + compl.) recognize as. **c** (often foll. by *that* + clause or *to* + infin.) admit that something is so. **2** confirm the receipt of. **3 a** show that one has noticed. **b** express appreciation of (a service, etc.). □□ **ac·knowl·edge·a·ble** *adj.*

ac·knowl·edg·ment /əknólijmənt/ *n.* (also **ac·knowl·edge·ment**) **1** the act or an instance of acknowledging. **2 a** a thing given or done in return for a service, etc. **b** a letter confirming receipt of something. **3** (usu. in *pl.*) an author's statement of indebtedness to others.

ACLU *abbr.* American Civil Liberties Union.

ac·me /ákmee/ *n.* the highest point or period; the peak of perfection.

ac·ne /áknee/ *n.* a skin condition characterized by red pimples. □□ **ac·ned** *adj.*

ac·o·lyte /ákəlīt/ *n.* **1** a person assisting a priest. **2** an assistant; a beginner.

ac·o·nite /ákənīt/ *n.* **1 a** any poisonous plant of the genus *Aconitum*. **b** the drug obtained from this. Also called ACONITINE. **2** (in full **winter aconite**) any ranunculaceous plant of the genus *Eranthis*, with yellow flowers.

a·con·i·tine /əkóniteen/ *n. Pharm.* a poisonous alkaloid obtained from the aconite plant.

a·corn /áykorn/ *n.* the fruit of the oak, a smooth nut in a rough cuplike base.

a·cot·y·le·don /əkótiléed'n/ *n.* a plant with no distinct seed leaves. □□ **acotyledonous** *adj.*

a·cous·tic /əkóōstik/ *adj. & n.* • *adj.* **1** relating to sound or hearing. **2** (of a musical instrument or recording) not having electrical amplification. **3** (of building materials) used for soundproofing. • *n.* **1** (usu. in *pl.*) the properties or qualities (esp. of a room or hall) in transmitting sound. **2** (in *pl.*; usu. treated as *sing.*) the science of sound. □□ **a·cous·ti·cal** *adj.* **a·cous·ti·cal·ly** *adv.*

a·cous·tic cou·pler *n. Computing* a modem that converts digital signals into audible signals and vice versa.

ac·ous·ti·cian /ákoostíshən/ *n.* an expert in acoustics.

ac·quaint /əkwáynt/ *v.tr. & refl.* (usu. foll. by *with*) make (a person or oneself) familiar with.

ac·quaint·ance /əkwáyntəns/ *n.* **1** (usu. foll. by *with*) slight knowledge. **2** the fact of being acquainted. **3** a person one knows slightly. □□ **ac·quaint·ance·ship** *n.*

ac·qui·esce /ákwee–és/ *v.intr.* **1** agree, esp. tacitly. **2** (foll. by *in*) accept (an arrangement, etc.). □□ **ac·qui·es·cence** *n.* **ac·qui·es·cent** *adj.*

ac·quire /əkwír/ *v.tr.* **1** gain by and for oneself; obtain. **2** come into possession of. □□ **ac·quir·a·ble** *adj.* **ac·quire·ment** *n.*

ac·quired char·ac·ter·is·tic *n. Biol.* a characteristic caused by the environment, not inherited.

ac·quired im·mune de·fi·cien·cy syn·drome *n. Med.* see AIDS.

ac·qui·si·tion /ákwizíshən/ *n.* **1** something acquired, esp. if regarded as useful. **2** the act or an instance of acquiring.

ac·quis·i·tive /əkwízitiv/ *adj.* eager to acquire things. □□ **ac·quis·i·tive·ly** *adv.* **ac·quis·i·tive·ness** *n.*

ac·quit /əkwít/ *v.* (**acquitted, acquitting**) **1** *tr.* (often foll. by *of*) declare (a person) not guilty. **2** *refl.* **a** conduct oneself in a specified way (*we acquitted ourselves well*). **b** (foll. by *of*) discharge (a duty or responsibility).

ac·quit·tal /əkwít'l/ *n.* **1** the process of freeing or being freed from a charge, esp. by a judgment of not guilty. **2** performance of a duty.

ac·quit·tance /əkwít'ns/ *n.* **1** payment of or release from a debt. **2** a written receipt attesting settlement of a debt.

a·cre /áykər/ *n.* **1** a measure of land, 4,840 sq. yds., 4047 sq. m. **2** (in *pl.*) a large area. □□ **a·cred** *adj.* (also in *comb.*).

acre Old English *æcer* (denoting the amount of land a yoke of oxen could plough in a day), of Germanic origin; related to Dutch *akker* and German *Acker* 'field,' from an Indo-European root shared by Sanskrit *ajra* 'field,' Latin *ager*, and Greek *agros*.

a·cre·age /áykərij, áykrij/ *n.* **1** a number of acres. **2** an extent of land.

ac·rid /ákrid/ *adj.* (**acrider, acridest**) **1** bitterly pungent; irritating; corrosive. **2** bitter in temper or manner. □□ **a·crid·i·ty** /–ríditee/ *n.* **ac·rid·ly** *adv.*

ac·ri·mo·ni·ous /ákrimṓneeəs/ *adj.* bitter in manner or temper. □□ **ac·ri·mo·ni·ous·ly** *adv.*

ac·ri·mo·ny /ákrimōnee/ *n.* (*pl.* **·nies**) bitterness of temper or manner; ill feeling.

ac·ro·bat /ákrəbat/ *n.* a performer of spectacular gymnastic feats. □□ **ac·ro·bat·ic** /–bátik/ *adj.* **ac·ro·bat·i·cal·ly** *adv.*

ac•ro•bat•ics /ákrəbátiks/ *n.pl.* **1** acrobatic feats. **2** (as *sing.*) the art of performing these. **3** a skill requiring ingenuity (*mental acrobatics*).

ac•ro•gen /ákrəjən/ *n. Bot.* any nonflowering plant having a perennial stem with the growing point at its apex, e.g., a fern or moss. ▫▫ **a•crog•e•nous** /əkrójinəs/ *adj.*

ac•ro•nym /ákrənim/ *n.* a word formed from the initial letters of other words (e.g., *laser, NATO*).

a•crop•e•tal /əkrópit'l/ *adj. Bot.* developing from below upwards. ▫▫ **a•crop•e•tal•ly** *adv.*

ac•ro•pho•bi•a /ákrəfṓbeeə/ *n. Psychol.* an abnormal dread of heights. ▫▫ **ac•ro•pho•bic** /–fṓbik/ *adj.*

a•crop•o•lis /əkrópəlis/ *n.* a citadel of an ancient Greek city.

a•cross /əkráws, əkrós/ *prep. & adv.* • *prep.* **1** to or on the other side of (*lives across the river*). **2** from one side to another side of (*a bridge across the river*). **3** at or forming an angle (esp. a right angle) with (*deep cuts across his legs*). • *adv.* **1** to or on the other side (*ran across*). **2** from one side to another (*a blanket stretched across*). **3** forming a cross (*with cuts across*). **4** (of a crossword clue or answer) read horizontally. ▫ **across the board** applying to all.
▶Avoid pronouncing **across** with a *t*-sound at the end of the word; many regard this as uneducated pronunciation.

a•cros•tic /əkráwstik, əkrós–/ *n.* **1** a poem in which certain letters in each line form a word or words. **2** a word puzzle constructed in this way.

a•cryl•ic /əkrílik/ *adj. & n.* • *adj.* **1** made with a synthetic polymer derived from acrylic acid. **2** *Chem.* of or derived from acrylic acid. • *n.* an acrylic fiber.

a•cryl•ic ac•id *n.* a pungent liquid organic acid.

ACT *abbr.* American College Test.

act /akt/ *n. & v.* • *n.* **1** something done; an action. **2** the process of doing something (*caught in the act*). **3 a** a piece of entertainment. **b** the performer(s) of this. **4** a pretense (*it was all an act*). **5** a main division of a play or opera. **6 a** a written ordinance of a legislative body. **b** a document attesting a legal transaction. **7** (often in *pl.*) the recorded decisions or proceedings of a committee, etc. **8** (**Acts**) (in full **Acts of the Apostles**) the New Testament book relating the growth of the early Church. • *v.* **1** *intr.* behave. **2** *intr.* perform actions or functions; take action (*act as referee; we must act quickly*). **3** *intr.* (also foll. by *on*) exert energy or influence (*alcohol acts on the brain*). **4** *intr.* **a** perform a part in a play, movie, etc. **b** pretend. **5** *tr.* **a** perform the part of (*acts the fool*). **b** perform (a play, etc.). **c** portray (an incident) by actions. **d** feign. ▫ **act for** be the representative of. **act out 1** translate (ideas, etc.) into action. **2** *Psychol.* represent (one's subconscious desires, etc.) in action. **act up** *colloq.* misbehave; give trouble. **get one's act together** *sl.* become properly organized. **get in on the act** *sl.* become a participant (esp. for profit). **put on an act** *colloq.* carry out a pretense.

act•ing /ákting/ *n. & attrib.* • *n.* **1** the art or occupation of an actor. **2** in senses of ACT *v.* • *attrib.adj.* serving temporarily or on behalf of another or others (*acting manager*).

ac•ti•nide /áktinīd/ *n. Chem.* any of the series of 15 radioactive elements having increasing atomic numbers from actinium to lawrencium.

ac•tin•i•um /aktíneeəm/ *n. Chem.* a radioactive metallic element of the actinide series, occurring naturally in pitchblende. ¶ Symb.: **Ac.**

ac•ti•nom•e•ter /áktinómitər/ *n.* an instrument for measuring the intensity of radiation, esp. ultraviolet radiation.

ac•tin•o•mor•phic /áktinəmáwrfik/ *adj. Biol.* radially symmetrical.

ac•tion /ákshən/ *n. & v.* • *n.* **1** the fact or process of doing or acting (*put ideas into action*). **2** forcefulness or energy as a characteristic (*a woman of action*). **3** the exertion of energy or influence (*the action of acid on metal*). **4** something done; a deed or act (*not aware of his own actions*). **5 a** a series of events represented in a story, play, etc. **b** *sl.* exciting activity (*arrived late and missed the action*). **6 a** armed conflict; fighting (*killed in action*). **b** an occurrence of this. **7 a** the way in which a machine, instrument, etc., works (*explain the action of an air pump*). **b** the mechanism that makes a machine, instrument, etc., work. **c** the mode or style of movement of an animal or human (usu. described in some way) (*a runner with good action*). **8** a legal process; a lawsuit (*bring an action*). **9** (in *imper.*) a word of command to begin, esp. used by a film director, etc. • *v.tr.* bring a legal action against. ▫ **out of action** not working.

ac•tion•a•ble /ákshənəbəl/ *adj.* giving cause for legal action.

ac•tion paint•ing *n.* an aspect of abstract expressionism with paint applied by the artist's random or spontaneous gestures.

ac•ti•vate /áktivayt/ *v.tr.* **1** make active; bring into action. **2** *Chem.* cause reaction in; excite (a substance, molecules, etc.). **3** *Physics* make radioactive. ▫▫ **ac•ti•va•tion** /–váyshən/ *n.* **ac•ti•va•tor** *n.*

ac•tive /áktiv/ *adj. & n.* • *adj.* **1 a** consisting in or marked by action; energetic; (*leads an active life*). **b** able to move about or accomplish practical tasks. **2** working. **3** originating action; not merely passive (*active support*). **4** radioactive. **5** *Gram.* designating the voice that attributes the action of a verb to the person or thing from which it logically proceeds (e.g., of the verbs in *guns kill; we saw him*) • *n. Gram.* the active form or voice of a verb. ▫▫ **ac•tive•ly** *adv.* **ac•tive•ness** *n.*

ac•tive serv•ice *n.* service in the armed forces during a war.

ac•tiv•ism /áktivizəm/ *n.* a policy of vigorous action in a cause, esp. in politics. ▫▫ **ac•tiv•ist** *n.*

ac•tiv•i•ty /aktívitee/ *n.* (*pl.* **•ties**) **1 a** the condition of being active or moving about. **b** the exertion of energy. **2** (often in *pl.*) a particular occupation or pursuit (*outdoor activities*). **3** = RADIOACTIVITY.

act of God *n.* the operation of uncontrollable natural forces.

ac•tor /áktər/ *n.* **1** the performer of a part in a play, movie, etc. **2** a person whose profession is performing such parts.

ac•tress /áktris/ *n.* a female actor.

ac•tu•al /ákchōōəl/ *adj.* (usu. *attrib.*) **1** existing in fact; real (often as distinct from ideal). **2** existing now. ▫▫ **ac•tu•al•ize** *v.tr.* **ac•tu•al•i•za•tion** /–lizáyshən/ *n.* ▶Redundant use, as in *tell me the actual facts*, is disputed, but common.

ac•tu•al•i•ty /ákchōō–álitee/ *n.* (*pl.* **•ties**) **1** reality. **2** (in *pl.*) existing conditions.

ac•tu•al•ly /ákchōōəlee/ *adv.* **1** as a fact; really (*time actually worked on a job*). **2** emphasizing that something someone has said or done is surprising (*he actually refused!*).

ac•tu•ar•y /ákchōōeree/ *n.* (*pl.* **•ies**) an expert in statistics, esp. one who calculates insurance risks. ▫▫ **ac•tu•ar•i•al** /–chōōáireeəl/ *adj.* **ac•tu•ar•i•al•ly** *adv.*

ac•tu•ate /ákchōō–ayt/ *v.tr.* **1** communicate motion to (a machine, etc.). **2** cause the operation of (an electrical device, etc.). **3** cause (a person) to act. ▫▫ **ac•tu•a•tion** /–áyshən/ *n.* **ac•tu•a•tor** *n.*

a•cu•i•ty /əkyṓōitee/ *n.* sharpness; acuteness.

a•cu•men /ákyəmən/ *n.* keen insight or discernment.

a•cu•mi•nate /əkyṓōminət, –nayt/ *adj. Biol.* tapering to a point.

ac•u•pres•sure /ákyəpreshər/ *n.* a form of therapy in

which symptoms are relieved by applying pressure with the fingers to specific points on the body.

ac·u·punc·ture /ákyəpungkchər/ *n.* a method (orig. Chinese) of treating various conditions by pricking the skin or tissues with needles. □□ **ac·u·punc·tur·ist** *n.*

a·cute /əkyóot/ *adj. & n.* • *adj.* (**acuter, acutest**) **1 a** (of senses, etc.) keen; penetrating. **b** (of pain) intense; severe; sharp. **2** shrewd; perceptive. **3** (of a disease) coming sharply to a crisis; severe. **4** (of a difficulty) critical; serious. **5 a** (of an angle) less than 90°. **b** sharp; pointed. **6** (of a sound) shrill. • *n.* = ACUTE ACCENT. □□ **a·cute·ly** *adv.* **a·cute·ness** *n.*

a·cute ac·cent *n.* a mark (´) placed over letters in some languages to show quality, vowel length, pronunciation (e.g., *maté*), etc.

AD *abbr.* (of a date) of the Christian era.
▶Strictly, AD should precede a date (e.g., AD 410), but uses such as *the tenth century* AD are well established.

ad /ad/ *n. colloq.* an advertisement.

ad·age /ádij/ *n.* a traditional maxim; a proverb.

a·da·gio /ədaázheeō/ *adv., adj., & n. Mus.* • *adv. & adj.* in slow time. • *n.* an adagio movement or passage.

Ad·am /ádəm/ *n.* the first man, in the biblical and Koranic traditions.

ad·a·mant /ádəmənt/ *adj.* stubbornly resolute □□ **ad·a·mance** *n.* **ad·a·mant·ly** *adv.*

Ad·am's ap·ple *n.* a projection of the thyroid cartilage of the larynx.

a·dapt /ədápt/ *v.* **1** *tr.* **a** (foll. by *to*) fit; adjust (one thing to another). **b** (foll. by *to, for*) make suitable for a purpose. **c** alter or modify (esp. a text). **2** *intr. & refl.* (usu. foll. by *to*) become adjusted to new conditions. □□ **a·dap·tive** *adj.* ▶Avoid confusing **adapt** with **adopt**. Trouble sometimes arises because in *adapting* to new conditions an animal or plant can be said to *adopt* something, e.g., a new color or behavior pattern.

a·dapt·a·ble /ədáptəbəl/ *adj.* **1** able to adapt oneself to new conditions. **2** that can be adapted. □□ **a·dapt·a·bil·i·ty** /–bílitee/ *n.* **a·dapt·a·bly** *adv.*

ad·ap·ta·tion /ádaptáyshən/ *n.* **1** the act or process of adapting or being adapted. **2** a thing that has been adapted.

a·dapt·er /ədáptər/ *n.* (also **a·dap·tor**) **1** a device for making equipment compatible. **2** a person who adapts.

ad·ax·i·al /adákseeəl/ *adj. Bot.* facing toward the stem of a plant, esp. of the upper side of a leaf (cf. ABAXIAL).

ADD *abbr.* attention deficit disorder.

add /ad/ *v.tr.* **1** join (one thing to another) as an increase or supplement. **2** put together (numbers) to find their combined value. **3** say in addition. □ **add in** include. **add to** increase (*this adds to our difficulties*). **add up 1** find the total of. **2** (foll. by *to*) amount to (*adds up to a disaster*). **3** *colloq.* make sense. □□ **add·er** *adj.*

ad·den·dum /ədéndəm/ *n.* (*pl.* **addenda** /–də/) a thing (usu. something omitted) to be added, esp. (in *pl.*) as additional matter at the end of a book.

ad·der /ádər/ *n.* any of various small venomous snakes.

ad·dict *v. & n.* • *v.tr. & refl.* /ədíkt/ (usu. foll. by *to*) devote or apply habitually or compulsively; make addicted. • *n.* /ádikt/ **1** a person addicted to a substance or a habit (*drug addict*). **2** *colloq.* an enthusiastic devotee of a pastime (*movie addict*).

ad·dict·ed /ədíktid/ *adj.* (foll. by *to*) **1** dependent on; unable to do without (*addicted to heroin*; *addicted to smoking*). **2** devoted (*addicted to football*).

ad·dic·tion /ədíkshən/ *n.* the fact or process of being addicted.

ad·dic·tive /ədíktiv/ *adj.* (of a drug, habit, etc.) causing addiction.

ad·di·tion /ədíshən/ *n.* **1** the act or process of adding or being added. **2** a person or thing added (*a useful addition to the team*). □ **in addition** moreover; furthermore; as well.

ad·di·tion·al /ədíshənəl/ *adj.* added; extra; supplementary. □□ **ad·di·tion·al·ly** *adv.*

ad·di·tive /áditiv/ *n.* a thing added (*food additive*).

ad·dle /ád'l/ *v. & adj.* • *v.* **1** *tr.* muddle; confuse. **2** *intr.* (of an egg) become addled. • *adj.* muddled; unsound.

ad·dled /ád'ld/ *adj.* **1** (of an egg) rotten, producing no chick. **2** muddled.

ad·dress /ədrés/ *n. & v.* • *n.* **1** (also /ádres/) **a** the place where a person lives or an organization is situated. **b** particulars of this, esp. for postal purposes. **c** *Computing* the location of an item of stored information. **2** a discourse delivered to an audience. **3** skill; desxterity; readiness. • *v.tr.* **1** write directions for delivery on (an envelope, package, etc.). **2** direct in speech or writing (remarks, a protest, etc.). **3** speak or write to, esp. formally (*addressed the audience*). **4** direct one's attention to. **5** *Golf* take aim at or prepare to hit (the ball)

ad·dress·ee /ádresée/ *n.* the person to whom something is addressed.

ad·duce /ədóos, ədyóos/ *v.tr.* cite as an instance or as proof or evidence. □□ **ad·duc·i·ble** *adj.*

ad·e·nine /ád'neen, –in/ *n.* a purine derivative found in all living tissue as a component base of DNA or RNA.

ad·e·noids /ád'noydz/ *n.pl. Med.* a mass of enlarged lymphatic tissue between the back of the nose and the throat, often hindering speaking and breathing in the young. □□ **ad·e·noi·dal** /–nóyd'l/ *adj.*

ad·e·no·ma /ád'nốmə/ *n.* (*pl.* **adenomas** or **adenomata** /–mətə/) a glandlike benign tumor.

a·den·o·sine /ədénəseen/ *n.* a compound of adenine and ribose present in all living tissue in a combined form (see AMP, ATP).

a·dept *adj. & n.* • *adj.* /ədépt/ (foll. by *at, in*) thoroughly proficient. • *n.* /ádept/ a skilled performer; an expert. □□ **a·dept·ly** *adv.* **a·dept·ness** *n.*

ad·e·quate /ádikwət/ *adj.* **1** sufficient; satisfactory. **2** (foll. by *to*) proportionate. **3** barely sufficient. □□ **ad·e·qua·cy** *n.* **ad·e·quate·ly** *adv.*

ad fin. /ad fin/ *abbr.* at or near the end. [L ad finem]

ADHD *abbr.* attention deficit hyperactivity disorder.

ad·here /ədhéer/ *v.intr.* **1** (usu. foll. by *to*) (of a substance) stick fast to a surface, another substance, etc. **2** (foll. by *to*) behave according to (*adhered to our plan*). **3** (foll. by *to*) give support or allegiance.

ad·her·ent /ədhéerənt, –hér–/ *n. & adj.* • *n.* **1** a supporter of a party, person, etc. **2** a devotee of an activity. • *adj.* (often foll. by *to*) (of a substance) sticking fast. □□ **ad·her·ence** /–rəns/ *n.*

ad·he·sion /ədhéezhən/ *n.* **1** the act or process of adhering. **2** the capacity of a substance to stick fast. **3** *Med.* an unnatural union of surfaces due to inflammation. **4** the maintenance of contact between the wheels of a vehicle and the road. **5** the giving of support or allegiance. ▶More common in physical senses (e.g., *the glue has good adhesion*), with *adherence* used in abstract senses (e.g., *adherence to principles*).

ad·he·sive /ədhéesiv, –ziv/ *adj. & n.* • *adj.* enabling surfaces or substances to adhere to one another. • *n.* an adhesive substance. □□ **ad·he·sive·ly** *adv.*

ad·hib·it /ədhíbit/ *v.tr.* (**adhibited, adhibiting**) **1** affix. **2** apply or administer (a remedy). □□ **ad·hi·bi·tion** /ádhibíshən/ *n.*

ad hoc /ád hók/ *adv. & adj.* formed or done for a particular purpose only (*an ad hoc committee*).

ad ho·mi·nem /ad hốminem, hó–/ *adv. & adj.* relating to or associated with a particular person.

a·dieu /ədyóó, ədóó/ *int. & n.* • *int.* good-bye. • *n.* (*pl.* **adieus** or **adieux** /ədyóóz, ədóoz/) a good-bye.

ad in·fi·ni·tum /ad ínfinítəm/ *adv.* without limit; forever.

ad·i·os /áadee–ós, ádee–/ *int.* good-bye.

ad·i·po·cere /ádipōseér/ *n.* a grayish fatty or soapy substance generated in dead bodies subjected to moisture.

ad·i·pose /ádipōs/ *adj.* of or characterized by fat. ▫▫ **ad·i·pos·i·ty** /–pósitee/ *n.*

ad·ja·cent /əjáysənt/ *adj.* (often foll. by *to*) lying near or adjoining. ▫▫ **ad·ja·cen·cy** /–sənsee/ *n.*

ad·jec·tive /ájiktiv/ *n.* a word or phrase naming an attribute, added to or grammatically related to a noun. ▫▫ **ad·jec·ti·val** /ájiktívəl/ *adj.* **ad·jec·ti·val·ly** *adv.*

ad·join /əjóyn/ *v.tr.* (often as **adjoining** *adj.*) be next to and joined with.

ad·journ /əjə́rn/ *v.* **1** *tr.* **a** put off; postpone. **b** break off (a meeting, discussion, etc.) with the intention of resuming later. **2** *intr.* (of persons at a meeting): **a** break off proceedings and disperse. **b** (foll. by *to*) transfer the meeting to another place. ▫▫ **ad·journ·ment** *n.*

ad·judge /əjúj/ *v.tr.* **1** adjudicate (a matter). **2** (often foll. by *that* + clause, or *to* + infin.) pronounce judicially. **3** (foll. by *to*) award judicially.

ad·ju·di·cate /əjóódikayt/ *v.* **1** *intr.* act as judge in a competition, court, tribunal, etc. **2** *tr.* decide judicially regarding (a claim, etc.). ▫▫ **ad·ju·di·ca·tion** /–dikáyshən/ *n.* **ad·ju·di·ca·tive** *adj.* **ad·ju·di·ca·tor** *n.*

ad·junct /ájungkt/ *n.* **1** (foll. by *to, of*) a subordinate or incidental thing. **2** an assistant. ▫▫ **ad·junc·tive** /əjúngktiv/ *adj.*

ad·jure /əjóór/ *v.tr.* (usu. foll. by *to* + infin.) charge or request (a person) solemnly or earnestly, esp. under oath. ▫▫ **ad·ju·ra·tion** /ájōōráyshən/ *n.*

ad·just /əjúst/ *v.* **1** *tr.* **a** arrange; put in the correct order or position. **b** regulate, esp. by a small amount. **2** *tr.* (usu. foll. by *to*) make suitable. **3** *tr.* harmonize (discrepancies). **4** *tr.* assess (loss or damages). **5** *intr.* (usu. foll. by *to*) make oneself suited to; become familiar with. ▫▫ **ad·just·a·ble** *adj.* **ad·just·a·bil·i·ty** /əjústəbílitee/ *n.* **ad·just·er** *n.* **ad·just·ment** *n.*

ad·ju·tant /ájət'nt/ *n.* **1 a** *Mil.* an officer who assists superior officers by communicating orders, conducting correspondence, etc. **b** an assistant. **2** a giant Indian stork.

ad lib /ád líb/ *v., adj., adv., & n.* • *v.intr.* (**ad libbed, ad libbing**) speak or perform without preparation; improvise. • *adj.* improvised. • *adv.* as one pleases; to any desired extent. • *n.* something spoken or played extempore.

ad lib·i·tum /ad líbitəm/ *adv.* = AD LIB *adv.*

ad li·tem /ad lítem/ *adj.* (of a guardian, etc.) appointed for a lawsuit.

ad·man /ádman/ *n.* (*pl.* **admen**) *colloq.* a person who produces advertisements commercially.

ad·min·is·ter /ədmínistər/ *v.* **1** *tr.* attend to the running of (business affairs, etc.). **2** *tr.* **a** be responsible for the implementation of (the law, punishment, etc.). **b** *Eccl.* perform the rites of (a sacrament). **c** (usu. foll. by *to*) direct the taking of (an oath). **3** *tr.* **a** provide; apply (a remedy). **b** give; deliver (a rebuke). **4** *intr.* act as administrator. ▫▫ **ad·min·is·tra·ble** *adj.*

ad·min·is·trate /ədmínistrayt/ *v.tr. & intr.* administer (esp. business affairs).

ad·min·is·tra·tion /ədmínistráyshən/ *n.* **1** management of a business. **2** the management of public affairs; government. **3** the government in power. **4 a** a President's period of office. **b** a President's advisers, cabinet officials, and their subordinates. **5** *Law* the management of another person's estate. **6** (foll. by *of*) **a** the administering of justice, an oath, etc. **b** application of remedies.

ad·min·is·tra·tive /ədmínistráytiv, –trətiv/ *adj.* concerning or relating to the management of affairs. ▫▫ **ad·min·is·tra·tive·ly** *adv.*

ad·min·is·tra·tor /ədmínistraytər/ *n.* (*fem.* **ad·min·i·stra·trix** /ədmínistrətriks/) **1** a person who administers a business or public affairs. **2** a person capable of organizing. **3** *Law* a person appointed to manage the estate of a person who has died intestate.

ad·mi·ra·ble /ádmərəbəl/ *adj.* **1** deserving admiration. **2** excellent. ▫▫ **ad·mi·ra·bly** *adv.*

ad·mi·ral /ádmərəl/ *n.* **1 a** the commander in chief of a country's navy. **b** a naval officer of high rank, the commander of a fleet or squadron. **2** any of various butterflies (*red admiral*).

---

admiral Middle English (denoting an emir or Saracen commander): from Old French *amiral, admirail,* via medieval Latin from Arabic *'amīr* 'commander' (from *'amara* 'to command'). The ending *-al* was from Arabic *-al-* in the sense 'of the' used in forming titles (e.g. *'amīr-al-'umarā* 'ruler of rulers'), later assimilated to the familiar Latinate suffix -AL.

---

ad·mi·ral·ty /ádmərəltee/ *n.* (*pl.* **·ties**) *Law* trial and decision of maritime questions and offenses.

ad·mi·ra·tion /ádmiráyshən/ *n.* **1** pleased contemplation. **2** respect; warm approval. **3** an object of this (*was the admiration of the whole town*).

ad·mire /ədmír/ *v.tr.* **1** regard with approval, respect, or satisfaction. **2** express one's admiration of.

ad·mir·er /ədmírər/ *n.* **1** a person's suitor. **2** a person who admires.

ad·mir·ing /ədmíring/ *adj.* showing admiration. ▫▫ **ad·mir·ing·ly** *adv.*

ad·mis·si·ble /ədmísibəl/ *adj.* **1** (of an idea) worth considering. **2** *Law* allowable as evidence. **3** (foll. by *to*) capable of being admitted. ▫▫ **ad·mis·si·bil·i·ty** /–bílitee/ *n.*

ad·mis·sion /ədmíshən/ *n.* **1** an acknowledgment (*admission of error*). **2 a** the right of entering. **b** a charge for this. **3** a person admitted to a hospital.

▶**Admission** traditionally referred to the price paid for entry or the right to enter: *Admission was $5.* **Admittance** more often referred to physical entry: *We were denied admittance by a large man with a forbidding scowl.* In the sense of 'permission or right to enter,' these words have become almost interchangeable, although **admittance** is more formal and technical.

ad·mit /ədmít/ *v.* (**admitted, admitting**) **1** *tr.* **a** (often foll. by *to be,* or *that* + clause) acknowledge; recognize as true. **b** accept as valid. **2** *intr.* (foll. by *to*) acknowledge responsibility for (a deed, fault, etc.). **3** *tr.* **a** allow (a person) entrance or access. **b** allow (a person) to be a member of (a group, etc.) or to share in (a privilege, etc.). **c** (of a hospital, etc.) bring in (a person) for inpatient treatment. **4** *tr.* (of an enclosed space) have room for. **5** *intr.* (foll. by *of*) allow as possible.

ad·mit·tance /ədmít'ns/ *n.* the right of admitting.

ad·mit·ted·ly /ədmítidlee/ *adv.* as an acknowledged fact.

ad·mix·ture /admíkschər/ *n.* **1** a thing added. **2** the act of adding this.

ad·mon·ish /ədmónish/ *v.tr.* **1** reprove. **2** (foll. by *to* + infin., or *that* + clause) urge. **3** give earnest advice to. **4** (foll. by *of*) warn. ▫▫ **ad·mon·ish·ment** *n.* **ad·mo·ni·tion** /ádmənishən/ *n.* **ad·mon·i·to·ry** *adj.*

ad nau·se·am /ad náwzeeəm/ *adv.* to an excessive or disgusting degree.

a·do /ədóó/ *n.* (*pl.* **ados**) fuss; busy activity; trouble.

a·do·be /ədóbee/ *n.* **1** a sun-dried brick of clay and straw. **2** the clay used for making such bricks.

ad·o·les·cent /ádəlésənt/ *adj. & n.* • *adj.* between childhood and adulthood. • *n.* an adolescent person. ▫▫ **ad·o·les·cence** /–səns/ *n.*

A·don·is /ədónis, ədṓ–/ *n.* a handsome young man.

a·dopt /ədópt/ *v.tr.* **1** take (a person) into a relationship, esp. another's child as one's own. **2** choose to follow (a course of action, etc.). **3** take over (a name, idea, etc.). **4** accept; formally approve (a report, etc.). ▫▫ **a·dop·tion** /–dópshən/ *n.*

▶See note at ADAPT.

a·dop·tive /ədóptiv/ *adj.* due to adoption (*adoptive son*).

a·dor·a·ble /ədáwrəbəl/ *adj.* **1** deserving adoration. **2** *colloq.* delightful; charming. ▫▫ **a·dor·a·bly** *adv.*

a·dore /ədáwr/ *v.tr.* **1** regard with honor and deep affection. **2** worship as divine. **3** *colloq.* like very much. ▫▫ **ad·o·ra·tion** /ádəráyshən/ *n.* **a·dor·ing** *adj.* **a·dor·ing·ly** *adv.*

a·dor·er /ədáwrər/ *n.* **1** a worshiper. **2** an ardent admirer.

a·dorn /ədáwrn/ *v.tr.* **1** add beauty or luster to; be an ornament to. **2** furnish with ornaments; decorate. ▫▫ **a·dorn·ment** *n.*

ADP *abbr.* automatic data processing.

ad rem /ad rém/ *adv. & adj.* to the point; to the purpose.

ad·re·nal /ədréenəl/ *adj. & n.* • *adj.* **1** at or near the kidneys. **2** of the adrenal glands. • *n.* (in full **adrenal gland**) either of two ductless glands above the kidneys, secreting adrenaline.

a·dren·a·line /ədrénəlin/ = EPINEPHRINE.

a·drift /ədrift/ *adv. & predic.adj.* **1** drifting. **2** at the mercy of circumstances.

a·droit /ədróyt/ *adj.* dexterous; skillful. ▫▫ **a·droit·ly** *adv.* **a·droit·ness** *n.*

ad·sorb /adsáwrb, –záwrb/ *v.tr.* (usu. of a solid) hold (molecules) to its surface, causing a thin film to form. ▫▫ **ad·sorb·a·ble** *adj.* **ad·sorb·ent** *adj. & n.* **ad·sorp·tion** *n.* (also **ad·sorb·tion**).

ad·sorb·ate /adsáwrbayt, –bit, –záwr–/ *n.* a substance adsorbed.

ad·u·late /ájəlayt/ *v.tr.* flatter obsequiously. ▫▫ **ad·u·la·tion** /–láyshən/ *n.* **ad·u·la·to·ry** /–lətáwree/ *adj.*

a·dult /ədúlt, ádult/ *adj. & n.* • *adj.* **1** mature; grown-up. **2 a** of or for adults. **b** *euphem.* sexually explicit (*adult films*) • *n.* **1** an adult person. **2** *Law* a person who has reached the age of majority. ▫▫ **a·dult·hood** *n.*

a·dul·ter·ate /ədúltərayt/ *v.tr.* debase (esp. foods) by adding other substances. ▫▫ **a·dul·ter·a·tion** /–ráyshən/ *n.* **a·dul·ter·a·tor** *n.*

a·dul·ter·er /ədúltərər/ *n.* (*fem.* **adulteress** /–təris/) a person who commits adultery.

a·dul·ter·y /ədúltəree/ *n.* voluntary sexual intercourse between a married person and a person other than his or her spouse. ▫▫ **a·dul·ter·ous** /ədúltərəs/ *adj.*

ad·um·brate /ádumbrayt/ *v.tr.* **1** indicate faintly. **2** represent in outline. **3** foreshadow; typify. **4** overshadow. ▫▫ **ad·um·bra·tion** /–bráyshən/ *n.*

ad·vance /ədváns/ *v., n., & adj.* • *v.* **1** *tr. & intr.* move or put forward. **2** *intr.* make progress. **3** *tr.* **a** pay (money) before it is due. **b** lend (money). **4** *tr.* give active support to (a person, cause, or plan). **5** *tr.* put forward (a claim or suggestion). **6** *tr.* cause (an event) to occur at an earlier date. **7** *tr.* raise (a price). **8** *intr.* rise (in price). **9** *tr.* (as **advanced** *adj.*) **a** far on in progress. **b** ahead of the times. • *n.* **1** an act of going forward. **2** progress. **3** a payment made before the due time. **4** a loan. **5** (esp. in *pl.*; often foll. by *to*) an amorous approach. **6** a rise in price. • *attrib.adj.* done or supplied beforehand (*advance warning*). ▫ **advance on** approach threateningly. **in advance** ahead in place or time.

ad·vance·ment /ədvánsmənt/ *n.* the promotion of a person, cause, or plan.

ad·van·tage /ədvántij/ *n. & v.* • *n.* **1** a beneficial feature. **2** benefit; profit (*to your advantage*). **3** (often foll. by *over*) a better position. **4** (in tennis) the next point won after deuce. • *v.tr.* **1** be beneficial to. **2** further; promote. ▫ **take advantage of 1** make good use of (a favorable circumstance). **2** exploit (a person), esp. unfairly. **3** *euphem.* seduce. ▫▫ **ad·van·ta·geous** /ádvəntáyjəs/ *adj.* **ad·van·ta·geous·ly** *adv.*

ad·vec·tion /ədvékshən/ *n.* **1** *Meteorol.* transfer of heat by the horizontal flow of air. **2** horizontal flow of air or water. ▫▫ **ad·vec·tive** *adj.*

Ad·vent /ádvent/ *n.* **1** the season before Christmas. **2** the coming or second coming of Christ. **3** (**advent**) the arrival of an important person or thing.

Ad·vent cal·en·dar *n.* a calendar for Advent, usu. of cardboard with flaps to open each day revealing a picture or scene.

Ad·vent·ist /ádvéntist/ *n.* a member of a Christian sect that believes in the imminent second coming of Christ. ▫▫ **Ad·vent·ism** *n.*

ad·ven·ti·tious /ádventíshəs/ *adj.* **1** accidental; casual. **2** added from outside. **3** *Biol.* formed accidentally or under unusual conditions. ▫▫ **ad·ven·ti·tious·ly** *adv.*

ad·ven·ture /ədvénchər/ *n. & v.* • *n.* **1** an unusual and exciting experience. **2** a daring enterprise. **3** enterprise (*the spirit of adventure*). **4** a commercial speculation. • *v.intr.* **1** (often foll. by *into, upon*) dare to go. **2** (foll. by *on, upon*) dare to undertake. **3** engage in adventure. ▫▫ **ad·ven·ture·some** *adj.*

ad·ven·tur·er /ədvénchərər/ *n.* **1** a person who seeks adventure. **2** a financial speculator.

ad·ven·tur·ism /ədvénchərizəm/ *n.* a tendency to take risks, esp. in foreign policy. ▫▫ **ad·ven·tur·ist** *n.*

ad·ven·tur·ous /ədvénchərəs/ *adj.* **1** rash; venturesome; enterprising. **2** characterized by adventures. ▫▫ **ad·ven·tur·ous·ly** *adv.* **ad·ven·tur·ous·ness** *n.*

ad·verb /ádvərb/ *n.* a word or phrase that modifies or qualifies another word or a group of words, expressing a relation of place, time, manner, degree, etc. (e.g., *gently, quite, then, there*). ▫▫ **ad·ver·bi·al** /ədvə́rbeeəl/ *adj.*

ad·ver·sar·i·al /ádvərsáireeəl/ *adj.* **1** involving conflict. **2** opposed; hostile.

ad·ver·sar·y /ádvərseree / *n.* (*pl.* **·ies**) **1** an enemy. **2** an opponent in a sport.

ad·verse /advə́rs, ád–/ *adj.* (often foll. by *to*) **1** contrary; hostile. **2** harmful. ▫▫ **ad·verse·ly** *adv.*

▶**Adverse** means 'hostile, unfavorable, opposed,' and is usually applied to situations, conditions, or events, not people, e.g., *The dry weather has had an adverse effect on the garden.* **Averse** is related in origin and also has the sense of 'opposed,' but is usually employed to describe a person's attitude, e.g., *I would not be averse to making the repairs myself.*

ad·ver·si·ty /ədvə́rsitee/ *n.* (*pl.* **·ties**) **1** adverse fortune. **2** a misfortune.

ad·vert /ədvə́rt/ *v.intr.* (foll. by *to*) *literary* refer in speaking or writing.

ad·ver·tise /ádvərtīz/ *v.* **1** *tr.* promote (goods or services) publicly to promote sales. **2** *tr.* make generally or publicly known. **3** *intr.* (foll. by *for*) seek by public notice. ▫▫ **ad·ver·tis·er** *n.*

ad·ver·tise·ment /ádvərtīzmənt/ *n.* a public notice, esp. one advertising goods or services.

ad·vice /ədvís/ *n.* **1** words offered as a recommendation about future action. **2** information given.

ad·vis·a·ble /ədvízəbəl/ *adj.* **1** to be recommended. **2** expedient. ▫▫ **ad·vis·a·bil·i·ty** /–bilitee/ *n.*

ad·vise /ədvíz/ *v.* **1** *tr.* (also *absol.*) give advice to. **2** *tr.* recommend (*they advise caution*). **3** *tr.* inform; notify.

ad·vised /ədvízd/ *adj.* deliberate; considered. ▫▫ **ad·vis·ed·ly** /–zidlee/ *adv.*

ad•vis•er /ədvízər/ *n.* (also **ad•vis•or**) a person who advises, esp. one appointed to do so.
▶Either spelling of the word is acceptable, although **adviser** may be seen as less formal, while **advisor** suggests an official position.

ad•vi•so•ry /ədvízəree/ *adj.* **1** giving advice; constituted to give advice (*an advisory body*). **2** consisting in giving advice.

ad•vo•ca•cy /ádvəkəsee/ *n.* **1** (usu. foll. by *of*) verbal support or argument for a cause, policy, etc. **2** the function of an advocate.

ad•vo•cate *n. & v.* •*n.* /ádvəkət/ **1** (foll. by *of*) a person who supports or speaks in favor. **2** a person who pleads for another. **3** a professional pleader in a court of justice. •*v.tr.* /ádvəkayt/ **1** recommend or support by argument (a cause, policy, etc.). **2** plead for; defend. ▫▫ **ad•vo•cate•ship** *n.* **ad•voc•a•to•ry** /advókətáwree, ádvəkə–, ádvəkaytəree/ *adj.*

adze /adz/ *n. & v.* • (also **adz**) *n.* a tool for cutting away the surface of wood, like an ax with an arched blade at right angles to the handle. •*v.tr.* dress or cut with an adze.

ad•zu•ki /ədzóōkee/ *n.* **1** an annual leguminous plant, *Vigna angularis*, native to China and Japan. **2** the small, round, dark red edible bean of this plant.

ae•gis /éejis/ *n.* ▫ **under the aegis of** under the auspices of.

ae•o•li•an harp /eeṓleean/ *n.* a stringed instrument or toy that produces musical sounds when the wind passes through it.

Ae•o•li•an mode /eeṓleeən/ *n. Mus.* the mode represented by the natural diatonic scale A–A.

ae•on var. of EON.

aer•ate /áirayt/ *v.tr.* **1** expose to the mechanical or chemical action of the air. **2** *Brit.* = CARBONATE. ▫▫ **aer•a•tion** /–ráyshən/ *n.* **aer•a•tor** *n.*

aer•i•al /áireeəl/ *n. & adj.* •*n.* = ANTENNA 2. •*adj.* **1** by or from or involving aircraft (*aerial photography*). **2 a** existing, moving, or happening in the air. **b** of or in the atmosphere; atmospheric. ▫▫ **aer•i•al•ly** *adv.*

aer•i•al•ist /áireeəlist/ *n.* a high-wire or trapeze artist.

aer•ie /áiree, áree/ *n.* (also **eyrie**) **1** a nest of a bird of prey, esp. an eagle, built high up. **2** a house, etc., perched high up.

aer•i•form /áirifawrm/ *adj.* **1** of the form of air; gaseous. **2** unsubstantial; unreal.

aero- /áirō/ *comb.form* **1** air. **2** aircraft.

aer•o•bat•ics /áirəbátiks/ *n.pl.* **1** feats of expert and usu. spectacular flying and maneuvering of aircraft. **2** (as *sing.*) a performance of these.

aer•obe /áirōb/ *n.* a microorganism usu. growing in the presence of oxygen, or needing oxygen for growth.

aer•o•bic /airṓbik/ *adj.* **1** existing or active only in the presence of oxygen. **2** of or relating to aerobes. **3** of or relating to aerobics.

aer•o•bics /airṓbiks/ *n.pl.* vigorous exercises designed to increase the body's heart rate and oxygen intake.

aer•o•bi•ol•o•gy /áirōbīóləjee/ *n.* the study of airborne microorganisms, pollen, spores, etc.

aer•o•dy•nam•ics /áirōdīnámiks/ *n.pl.* (usu. treated as *sing.*) the study of the interaction between the air and solid bodies moving through it. ▫▫ **aer•o•dy•nam•ic** *adj.* **aer•o•dy•nam•i•cal•ly** *adv.* **aer•o•dy•nam•i•cist** /–misist/ *n.*

aer•o•em•bo•lism /áirōémbəlizəm/ *n.* a condition caused by the sudden lowering of air pressure and formation of bubbles in the blood.

aer•o•gram /áirəgram/ *n.* an airmail letter in the form of a single sheet that is folded and sealed.

aer•o•lite /áirəlīt/ *n.* a stony meteorite.

aer•ol•o•gy /airóləjee/ *n.* the study of the upper levels of the atmosphere. ▫▫ **aer•o•log•i•cal** /áirəlójikəl/ *adj.*

aer•o•nau•tics /áirənáwtiks/ *n.pl.* (usu. treated as *sing.*) the science or practice of motion or travel in the air. ▫▫ **aer•o•nau•tic** *adj.* **aer•o•nau•ti•cal** *adj.*

ae•ron•o•my /airónəmee/ *n.* the science, esp. the physics and chemistry, of the upper atmosphere.

aer•o•plane esp. *Brit.* var. of AIRPLANE.

aer•o•sol /áirəsawl, –sol/ *n.* **1** a container used to hold a substance packed under pressure with a device for releasing it as a fine spray. **2** a system of colloidal particles dispersed in a gas (e.g., fog or smoke).

aer•o•space /áirōspays/ *n.* **1** the earth's atmosphere and outer space. **2** the technology of aviation in this region.

aes•thete /és–theet/ *n.* (also **es•thete**) a person who has or professes to have a special appreciation of beauty.

aes•thet•ic /es–thétik/ *adj. & n.* (also **es•thet•ic**) •*adj.* **1** concerned with beauty or the appreciation of beauty. **2** having such appreciation. **3** in accordance with good taste. •*n.* **1** (in *pl.*) the philosophy of the beautiful. **2** a set of principles of good taste and the appreciation of beauty. ▫▫ **aes•thet•i•cal•ly** *adv.* **aes•thet•i•cism** /–tisizəm/ *n.*

aesthetic late 18th cent. (in the sense 'relating to perception by the senses'): from Greek *aisthētikos*, from *aisthēta* 'perceptible things,' from *aisthesthai* 'perceive.' The sense 'concerned with beauty' was coined in German in the mid-18th cent. and adopted into English in the early 19th cent., but its use was controversial until much later in the century.

a•far /əfáar/ *adv.* at or to a distance.

AFB *abbr.* Air Force Base.

AFC *abbr.* American Football Conference.

af•fa•ble /áfəbəl/ *adj.* approachable and friendly. ▫▫ **af•fa•bil•i•ty** /–bílitee/ *n.* **af•fa•bly** *adv.*

af•fair /əfáir/ *n.* **1** a concern; a business (*that is my affair*). **2** a celebrated or notorious happening. **3** = LOVE AFFAIR. **4** (in *pl.*) **a** ordinary pursuits of life. **b** business dealings. **c** public matters (*current affairs*).

af•fect[1] /əfékt/ *v.tr.* **1** produce an effect on. **2** touch the feelings of (*affected me deeply*).
▶Both **affect** and **effect** are both verbs and nouns, but only **effect** is common as a noun, usually meaning 'a result, consequence, impression, etc.,' e.g., *My father's warnings had no effect on my adventurousness.* As verbs they are used differently. **Affect** means 'to produce an effect upon,' e.g., *Smoking during pregnancy can affect the baby's development.* **Effect** means 'to bring about,' e.g., *The negotiators effected an agreement despite many difficulties.*

af•fect[2] /əfékt/ *v.tr.* **1** pretend to feel (*affected indifference*). **2** (foll. by *to* + infin.) pretend. **3** assume the manner of (*affect the freethinker*).

af•fect[3] /áfekt/ *n. Psychol.* a feeling, emotion, or desire, esp. as leading to action.

af•fec•ta•tion /áfektáyshən/ *n.* **1** an assumed or contrived manner of behavior, esp. in order to impress. **2** (foll. by *of*) a studied display. **3** pretense.

af•fect•ed /əféktid/ *adj.* **1** artificially assumed; pretended (*an affected air of innocence*). **2** (of a person) full of affectation. ▫▫ **af•fect•ed•ly** *adv.*

af•fec•tion /əfékshən/ *n.* (often foll. by *for, toward*) goodwill; fond feeling.

af•fec•tion•ate /əfékshənət/ *adj.* loving; tender. ▫▫ **af•fec•tion•ate•ly** *adv.*

af•fec•tive /əféktiv/ *adj.* concerning the affections; emotional. ▫▫ **af•fec•tiv•i•ty** /áfektívitee/ *n.*

af•fi•ance /əfíəns/ *v.tr.* (usu. in *passive*) *literary* promise solemnly to give (a person) in marriage.

af•fi•da•vit /áfidáyvit/ *n.* a written statement confirmed under oath, for use as evidence in court.

af•fil•i•ate *v. & n.* •*v.* /əfíleeayt/ **1** *tr.* (usu. in *passive*; foll. by *to, with*) attach or connect (a person or society) with a larger organization. **2** *tr.* (of an institution) adopt (persons as members, societies as branches, etc.). **3** *intr.* **a** (foll. by *to*) associate oneself with a society. **b** (foll. by *with*) associate oneself with a political party. •*n.* /əfíleeət, –leeayt/ an affiliated person or organization.

af•fil•i•a•tion /əfíleeáyshən/ *n.* the act or process of affiliating or being affiliated.

af•fined /əfínd/ *adj.* related; connected.

af•fin•i•ty /əfínitee/ *n.* (*pl.* **•ties**) **1** a natural attraction to a person or thing. **2** relationship, esp. by marriage. **3** resemblance in structure between animals, plants, or languages. **4** a similarity of character suggesting a relationship. **5** *Chem.* the tendency of certain substances to combine with others.

af•firm /əfə́rm/ *v.* **1** *tr.* assert strongly; state as a fact. **2** *intr.* **a** *Law* make an affirmation. **b** make a formal declaration.

af•fir•ma•tion /áfərmáyshən/ *n.* **1** the act or process of affirming or being affirmed. **2** *Law* a solemn declaration by a person who declines to take an oath.

af•firm•a•tive /əfə́rmətiv/ *adj. & n.* •*adj.* **1** asserting that a thing is so. **2** (of a vote) expressing approval. •*n.* **1** an affirmative statement, reply, or word. **2** (prec. by *the*) a positive or affirming position. ▫▫ **af•firm•a•tive•ly** *adv.*

af•firm•a•tive ac•tion *n.* action favoring those who often suffer from discrimination.

af•fix *v. & n.* •*v.tr.* /əfíks/ **1** (usu. foll. by *to, on*) attach; fasten. **2** add in writing. **3** impress (a seal or stamp). •*n.* /áfiks/ **1** an appendage; an addition. **2** *Gram.* an addition placed at the beginning (*prefix*) or end (*suffix*) of a root, stem, or word to modify its meaning. ▫▫ **af•fix•a•tion** /áfiksáyshən/ *n.*

af•flict /əflíkt/ *v.tr.* inflict suffering on. ▫ **afflicted with** suffering from.

af•flic•tion /əflíkshən/ *n.* **1** physical or mental distress. **2** a cause of this.

af•flu•ent /áflōōənt/ *adj.* **1** wealthy; rich. **2** abundant. ▫▫ **af•flu•ence** *n.* **af•flu•ent•ly** *adv.*

af•ford /əfáwrd/ *v.tr.* **1** (prec. by *can* or *be able to*) **a** have enough money, means, time, etc., for; be able to spare (*can afford $50; can we afford to buy a new television?*). **b** be in a position to do something (*can't afford to let him think so*). **2** provide (*affords a view of the sea*). ▫▫ **af•ford•a•ble** *adj.* **af•ford•a•bil•i•ty** *n.*

af•for•est /əfáwrist, əfór–/ *v.tr.* **1** convert into forest. **2** plant with trees. ▫▫ **af•for•est•a•tion** /–stáyshən/ *n.*

af•fray /əfráy/ *n.* a breach of the peace by fighting or rioting in public.

af•fri•cate /áfrikət/ *n. Phonet.* a combination of a stop, or plosive, with an immediately following fricative or spirant, e.g., ch.

af•front /əfrúnt/ *n. & v.* •*n.* an open insult (*feel it an affront*). •*v.tr.* **1** insult openly. **2** offend the modesty or self-respect of.

Af•ghan /áfgan/ *n. & adj.* •*n.* **1 a** a native or inhabitant of Afghanistan. **b** a person of Afghan descent. **2** the official language of Afghanistan. **3** (**afghan**) a knitted or crocheted shawl or throw. •*adj.* of or relating to Afghanistan or its people or language.

Af•ghan hound *n.* a tall hunting dog with long silky hair.

a•fi•cio•na•do /əfísheeənaádō, əfísee–/ *n.* (*pl.* **•dos**) a devotee of a sport or pastime.

a•field /əféeld/ *adv.* away from home; to or at a distance (esp. **far afield**).

a•fire /əfír/ *adv. & predic.adj.* **1** on fire. **2** intensely roused or excited.

a•flame /əfláym/ *adv. & predic.adj.* = AFIRE.

a•float /əflṓt/ *adv. & predic.adj.* **1** floating in water or air. **2** at sea; on board ship. **3** out of debt or difficulty. **4** in general circulation; current.

a•foot /əfŏŏt/ *adv. & predic.adj.* in operation; progressing.

a•fore /əfáwr/ *prep. & adv. archaic & dial.* before; previously; in front (of).

afore- /əfáwr/ *comb.form* before; previously (*aforementioned; aforesaid*).

a•fore•thought /əfáwrthawt/ *adj.* premeditated (following a noun: *malice aforethought*).

a•foul /əfówl/ *adv.* ▫ **run afoul of** come into conflict with.

a•fraid /əfráyd/ *predic.adj.* **1** frightened. **2** reluctant for fear of the consequences (*afraid to go in*). ▫ **be afraid** (foll. by *that* + clause) *colloq.* admit or declare with regret (*I'm afraid there's none left*).

a•fresh /əfrésh/ *adv.* anew; with a fresh beginning.

Af•ri•can /áfrikən/ *n. & adj.* •*n.* **1** a native of Africa. **2** a person of African descent. •*adj.* of or relating to Africa.

Af•ri•ca•na /áfrikaánə/ *n.pl.* things connected with Africa.

Af•ri•can-A•mer•i•can *n. & adj.* •*n.* an American citizen of African origin or descent. •*adj.* of or relating to American blacks or their culture.

▶See note at BLACK.

Af•ri•can vi•o•let *n.* a tropical plant, *Saintpaulia ionantha*, with heart-shaped velvety leaves and blue, purple, or pink flowers.

Af•ri•kaans /áfrikaáns/ *n.* the language of the Afrikaner people.

Af•ri•ka•ner /áfrikaánər/ *n.* an Afrikaans-speaking white person in S. Africa, esp. one of Dutch descent.

Af•ro /áfrō/ *adj. & n.* •*adj.* (of a hairstyle) full and bushy, as naturally grown originally by blacks. •*n.* (*pl.* **•ros**) an Afro hairstyle.

Afro- /áfrō/ *comb.form* African (*Afro-Asian*).

Af•ro-A•mer•i•can /áfrōəmérikən/ *adj. & n.* = AFRICAN-AMERICAN.

▶See note at BLACK.

aft /aft/ *adv. Naut. & Aeron.* at or toward the stern or tail.

af•ter /áftər/ *prep., conj., adv., & adj.* •*prep.* **1 a** following in time; later than (*after midnight*). **b** in specifying time (*a quarter after eight*). **2** in view of (*after your behavior tonight what do you expect?*). **3** in spite of (*after all my efforts I'm no better off*). **4** behind (*shut the door after you*). **5** in pursuit or quest of (*run after them*). **6** about; concerning (*asked after her*). **7** in allusion to (*named him William after his uncle*). **8** in imitation of (*a painting after Rubens*). **9** next in importance to (*the best book on the subject after mine*). **10** according to (*after a fashion*). •*conj.* in or at a time later than that when (*left after we arrived*). •*adv.* **1** later in time (*soon after*). **2** behind in place (*followed on after*). •*adj.* **1** later; following (*in after years*). **2** *Naut.* nearer the stern (*after mast*). ▫ **after all 1** in spite of all that has happened or has been said, etc. (*after all, what does it matter?*). **2** in spite of one's exertions, expectations, etc. (*so you have come after all!*).

af•ter•birth /áftərbərth/ *n. Med.* the placenta and fetal membranes discharged from the womb after childbirth.

af•ter•burn•er /áftərbərnər/ *n.* an auxiliary burner in a jet engine to increase thrust.

af•ter•care /áftərkair, –ker/ *n.* care of a patient after a stay in the hospital or of a person on release from prison.

af•ter•ef•fect /áftərəfékt/ *n.* an effect that follows after an interval or after the primary action of something.

af·ter·glow /áftərglō/ *n.* a light or radiance remaining after its source has disappeared or been removed.

af·ter·im·age /áftərímij/ *n.* an image retained by a sense organ, esp. the eye, and producing a sensation after the cessation of the stimulus.

af·ter·life /áftərlīf/ *n.* **1** life after death. **2** life at a later time.

af·ter·math /áftərmath/ *n.* consequences; aftereffects.

af·ter·most /áftərmōst/ *adj.* **1** last. **2** *Naut.* farthest aft.

af·ter·noon /áftərnóōn/ *n.* the time from noon to evening (*this afternoon*; *during the afternoon*).

af·ter·shave /áftərshayv/ *n.* an astringent lotion for use after shaving.

af·ter·shock /áftərshok/ *n.* a lesser shock following the main shock of an earthquake.

af·ter·taste /áftərtáyst/ *n.* a taste remaining after eating or drinking.

af·ter-tax /áftərtáks/ *adj.* (of income) after the deduction of taxes.

af·ter·thought /áftərthawt/ *n.* an item or thing that is thought of or added later.

af·ter·ward /áftərwərd/ *adv.* (also **af·ter·wards**) later; subsequently.

af·ter·word /áftərwərd/ *n.* concluding remarks in a book.

Ag *symb. Chem.* the element silver.

a·gain /əgén/ *adv.* **1** another time; once more. **2** as in a previous position or condition (*back again*; *healthy again*). **3** in addition (*as much again*). **4** further; besides (*again, what about the children?*). **5** on the other hand (*I might, and again I might not*).

a·gainst /əgénst/ *prep.* **1** in opposition to (*fight against the invaders*; *arson is against the law*). **2** into collision or in contact with (*ran against a rock*; *lean against the wall*). **3** to the disadvantage of (*his age is against him*). **4** in contrast to (*against a dark background*). **5** in anticipation of or preparation for (*protected against the cold*). **6** as a compensating factor to (*income against expenditure*). **7** in return for (*issued against a later payment*).

a·gam·ic /əgámik/ *adj.* characterized by the absence of sexual reproduction.

ag·a·mo·gen·e·sis /əgáməjénisis, ágəmō–/ *n. Biol.* asexual reproduction. ▫▫ **agamogenetic** /–jinétik/ *adj.*

ag·a·pan·thus /ágəpánthəs/ *n.* any African plant of the genus *Agapanthus*, esp. the ornamental African lily, with blue or white flowers.

a·gape[1] /əgáyp/ *adv.* & *predic.adj.* gaping; openmouthed, esp. with wonder.

a·ga·pe[2] /əgaápay, ágə–/ *n.* **1** a Christian feast in token of fellowship. **2** love for one's fellow humans, esp. as distinct from erotic love.

a·gar /áygaar/ *n.* a gelatinous substance obtained from any of various kinds of red seaweed and used in food, microbiological media, etc.

ag·a·ric /ágərik, əgár–/ *n.* any fungus of the family Agaricaceae, with cap and stalk, including the common edible mushroom.

ag·ate /ágət/ *n.* any of several varieties of hard usu. streaked chalcedony.

a·ga·ve /əgaávee, əgáy–/ *n.* any plant of the genus *Agave*, e.g., the aloe.

a·gaze /əgáyz/ *adv.* gazing.

age /ayj/ *n.* & *v.* • *n.* **1 a** the length of time that a person or thing has existed. **b** a particular point in or part of one's life (*old age*; *voting age*). **2 a** *colloq.* (often in *pl.*) a long time (*took an age to answer*; *have been waiting for ages*). **b** a distinct period of the past (*golden age*; *Middle Ages*). **c** *Geol.* a period of time. **d** a generation. **3** the latter part of life; old age (*the infirmity of age*). • *v.* (*pres. part.* **aging, ageing**) **1** *intr.* show signs of advancing age (*has aged a lot recently*). **2** *intr.* grow old. **3** *intr.* mature. **4** *tr.* cause or allow to age. ▫ **come of age** reach adult status.

aged *adj.* **1** /ayjd/ **a** of the age of (*aged ten*). **b** that has been subjected to aging. **2** /áyjid/ having lived long; old.

age·ism /áyjizəm/ *n.* (also **ag·ism**) prejudice or discrimination on the grounds of age. ▫▫ **age·ist** *adj.* & *n.* (also **ag·ist**).

age·less /áyjlis/ *adj.* **1** never growing or appearing old or outmoded. **2** eternal; timeless.

a·gen·cy /áyjənsee/ *n.* (*pl.* **·cies**) **1 a** the business or establishment of an agent (*employment agency*). **b** the function of an agent. **2 a** active operation; action. **b** intervening action (*fertilized by the agency of insects*). **c** action personified (*an invisible agency*). **3** a specialized department, as of a government.

a·gen·da /əjéndə/ *n.* **1** (*pl.* **agendas**) a list of items of business to be considered at a meeting. **2** a series of things to be done. **3** an ideology or underlying motivation.

a·gent /áyjənt/ *n.* **1 a** a person who acts for another in business, politics, etc. (*insurance agent*). **b** a spy. **2** a person or thing that exerts power or produces an effect.

A·gent Or·ange *n.* a dioxin-containing herbicide used as a defoliant by the US during the Vietnam War.

a·gent pro·vo·ca·teur /aázhon prəvókətőr/ *n.* (*pl.* **agents provocateurs** *pronunc.* same) a person employed to detect suspected offenders by tempting them to overt self-incriminating action.

age-old *adj.* having existed for a very long time.

ag·glom·er·ate *v., n.,* & *adj.* • *v.tr.* & *intr.* /əglóməráyt/ **1** collect into a mass. **2** accumulate in a disorderly way. • *n.* /əglómərət/ a mass or collection of things. • *adj.* /əglómərət/ collected into a mass. ▫▫ **ag·glom·er·a·tion** /–ráyshən/ *n.* **ag·glom·er·a·tive** /əglómərətiv/ *adj.*

ag·glu·ti·nate /əglóōt'nayt/ *v.* **1** *tr.* unite as with glue. **2** *tr.* & *intr. Biol.* cause or undergo adhesion (of bacteria, erythrocytes, etc.). ▫▫ **ag·glu·ti·na·tion** /–náyshən/ *n.* **ag·glu·ti·na·tive** /əglóōt'nətiv, –aytiv/ *adj.*

ag·gran·dize /əgrándīz/ *v.tr.* **1** increase the power, rank, or wealth of. **2** cause to appear greater than is the case. ▫▫ **ag·gran·dize·ment** /–dizmənt/ *n.*

ag·gra·vate /ágrəvayt/ *v.tr.* **1** increase the seriousness of (an illness, offense, etc.). **2** *disp.* annoy; exasperate (a person). ▫▫ **ag·gra·va·tion** /–váyshən/ *n.*

▶**Aggravate** is used informally to mean 'to annoy or exasperate,' rather than 'to make worse or more serious.' An example of more correct usage is *Heavy lifting aggravated the strain on my back.*

ag·gre·gate *n., adj.,* & *v.* • *n.* /ágrigət/ **1** a collection of, or the total of, disparate elements. **2** pieces of crushed stone, gravel, etc., used in making concrete. **3 a** *Geol.* a mass of minerals formed into solid rock. **b** a mass of particles. • *adj.* /ágrigət/ **1** (of disparate elements) collected into one mass. **2** constituted by the collection of many units into one body. • *v.* /ágrigayt/ *tr.* & *intr.* collect together; combine into one mass. ▫ **in the aggregate** as a whole. ▫▫ **ag·gre·ga·tion** /–gáyshən/ *n.* **ag·gre·ga·tive** /–gáytiv/ *adj.*

ag·gres·sion /əgréshən/ *n.* **1** the act or practice of attacking without provocation. **2** an unprovoked attack. **3** forcefulness. **4** *Psychol.* hostile or destructive tendency or behavior.

ag·gres·sive /əgrésiv/ *adj.* **1** of a person: **a** given to aggression. **b** forceful. **2** (of an act) offensive; hostile. **3** of aggression. ▫▫ **ag·gres·sive·ly** *adv.* **ag·gres·sive·ness** *n.*

ag·gres·sor /əgrésər/ *n.* a person who attacks without provocation.

ag·grieved /əgreévd/ *adj.* having a grievance. ▫▫ **ag·griev·ed·ly** /–vidlee/ *adv.*

a·ghast /əgást/ *adj.* (usu. *predic.*) filled with dismay.

aghast late Middle English: past participle of the obsolete verb *agast, gast* 'frighten,' from Old English *gǣsten*. The spelling with *gh* (originally Scots) became general by about 1700, probably influenced by GHOST; compare with GHASTLY.

ag·ile /ájəl, ájīl/ *adj.* nimble; active. ▫▫ **ag·ile·ly** *adv.* **a·gil·i·ty** /əjílitee/ *n.*

ag·ing /áyjing/ *n.* (also **age·ing**) **1** growing old. **2** giving the appearance of advancing age.

ag·i·tate /ájitayt/ *v.* **1** *tr.* disturb or excite. **2** *intr.* stir up interest or concern, esp. publicly (*agitated for tax reform*). **3** *tr.* shake or move. ▫▫ **ag·i·tat·ed·ly** *adv.*

ag·i·ta·tion /ájitáyshən/ *n.* **1** agitating or being agitated. **2** mental anxiety.

a·gi·ta·to /ájitaátō/ *adv. & adj. Mus.* in an agitated manner.

ag·i·ta·tor /ájitaytər/ *n.* **1** a person who agitates, esp. publicly for a cause, etc. **2** an apparatus for shaking or mixing liquid, etc.

ag·it·prop /ájitprop/ *n.* the dissemination of Communist political propaganda, esp. in plays, movies, books, etc.

a·glow /əglṓ/ *adv. & adj.* • *adv.* glowingly. • *predic.adj.* glowing.

ag·ma /ágmə/ *n.* **1** the sound represented by the pronunciation /ng/. **2** a symbol (ŋ) used for this sound.

ag·nos·tic /agnóstik/ *n. & adj.* • *n.* a person who believes that nothing is known of the existence or nature of God, or of anything beyond material phenomena. • *adj.* of or relating to agnostics. ▫▫ **ag·nos·ti·cist** *n.*

Ag·nus De·i /ágnəs dáyee, dée–ī, aányoos/ *n.* **1** a figure of a lamb bearing a cross or flag, as an emblem of Christ. **2** the prayer in the Mass beginning with the words "Lamb of God."

a·go /əgṓ/ *adv.* earlier; before the present (*ten years ago; long ago*).

a·gog /əgóg/ *adv. & adj.* • *adv.* eagerly; expectantly. • *predic.adj.* eager; expectant.

à·go·go /əgṓgō/ *adv.* in abundance (*whiskey àgogo*). [F]

ag·o·nis·tic /ágənístik/ *adj.* polemical; combative. ▫▫ **ag·o·nis·ti·cal·ly** *adv.*

ag·o·nize /ágənīz/ *v.* **1** *intr.* (often foll. by *over*) undergo (esp. mental) anguish. **2** *tr.* (as **agonized** *adj.*) expressing agony (*an agonized look*). ▫▫ **ag·o·niz·ing·ly** *adv.*

ag·o·ny /ágənee/ *n.* (*pl.* **·nies**) **1** extreme suffering. **2** a severe struggle.

ag·o·ra·phobe /ágərəfōb/ *n.* a person who suffers from agoraphobia.

ag·o·ra·pho·bi·a /ágərəfṓbeeə/ *n. Psychol.* an abnormal fear of open spaces or public places. ▫▫ **ag·o·ra·pho·bic** *adj. & n.*

a·grar·i·an /əgráireeən/ *adj.* **1** of or relating to the land or its cultivation. **2** relating to the ownership of land.

a·gree /əgrée/ *v.intr.* (**agrees, agreed, agreeing**) **1** hold a similar opinion (*I agree with you*). **2** (often foll. by *to*, or *to* + infin.) consent (*agreed to the arrangement; agreed to go*). **3** *intr.* (often foll. by *with*) **a** become or be in harmony. **b** suit; be good for (*caviar didn't agree with him*). **c** *Gram.* have the same number, gender, case, or person as. **4** (foll. by *on*) decide by mutual consent (*agreed on a compromise*).

▶Note the distinction between *agreeing to* something like a plan, scheme, or project; and *agreeing with* somebody: *I agree to the repayment schedule suggested. Danielle agrees with Eric that we should all go hiking on Saturday. Humid weather does not agree with me. Agree with* is also used regarding two things that go together: *That story does not agree with the facts. The verb must agree with the noun in person and number.*

a·gree·a·ble /əgréeəbəl/ *adj.* **1** pleasing. **2** (of a person) willing to agree (*was agreeable to going*). **3** conformable. ▫▫ **a·gree·a·ble·ness** *n.* **a·gree·a·bly** *adv.*

a·gree·ment /əgréemənt/ *n.* **1** the act of agreeing; the holding of the same opinion. **2** mutual understanding. **3** an arrangement between parties as to a course of action, etc. **4** *Gram.* having the same number, gender, case, or person. **5** mutual conformity of things; harmony.

ag·ri·busi·ness /ágribiznis/ *n.* **1** agriculture conducted on strictly commercial principles, esp. using advanced technology. **2** an organization engaged in this.

ag·ri·cul·ture /ágrikulchər/ *n.* the science or practice of cultivating the soil, raising crops, and rearing animals. ▫▫ **ag·ri·cul·tur·al** /–kúlchərəl/ *adj.* **ag·ri·cul·tur·al·ist** *n.* **ag·ri·cul·tur·al·ly** *adv.* **ag·ri·cul·tur·ist** *n.*

agro- /ágrō/ *comb.form* agricultural (*agrochemical*).

ag·ro·chem·i·cal /ágrōkémikəl/ *n.* a chemical used in agriculture.

a·gron·o·my /əgrónəmee/ *n.* the science of soil management and crop production. ▫▫ **ag·ro·nom·ic** /ágrənómik/ *adj.* **a·gron·o·mist** /–grón–/ *n.*

a·ground /əgrównd/ *predic.adj. & adv.* (of a ship) on or on to the bottom of shallow water (*be aground; run aground*).

a·gue /áygyoo/ *n.* **1** *hist.* a malarial fever, with cold, hot, and sweating stages. **2** a shivering fit. ▫▫ **a·gued** *adj.* **a·gu·ish** *adj.*

AH *abbr.* in the year of the Hegira (AD 622); of the Muslim era.

ah /aa/ *int.* expressing surprise, pleasure, resignation, etc.

a·ha /aahaá, əhaá/ *int.* expressing surprise, triumph, mockery, irony, etc.

a·head /əhéd/ *adv.* **1** further forward in space or time. **2** in the lead; further advanced (*ahead on points*). **3** in the line of one's forward motion (*road construction ahead*). **4** straight forward.

a·hem /əhém/ *int.* used to attract attention, gain time, or express disapproval.

a·him·sa /əhímsaa/ *n.* (in the Hindu, Buddhist, etc., traditions) respect for all living things and avoidance of violence in both thought and deed.

a·hoy /əhóy/ *int. Naut.* a call used in hailing.

AI *abbr.* **1** artificial insemination. **2** artificial intelligence.

aid /ayd/ *n. & v.* • *n.* **1** help. **2** financial or material help, esp. given by one country to another. **3** a person or thing that helps. • *v.tr.* **1** (often foll. by *to* + infin.) help. **2** promote or encourage (*sleep will aid recovery*).

aide /ayd/ *n.* **1** an aide-de-camp. **2** an assistant.

aide-de-camp /áyd–dəkámp/ *n.* (*pl.* **aides-de-camp** *pronunc.* same) an officer acting as a confidential assistant to a senior officer.

AIDS /aydz/ *n.* acquired immune deficiency syndrome, a fatal disorder caused by a virus transmitted in the blood and other bodily fluids, marked by severe loss of resistance to infection.

ai·ki·do /íkeedō/ *n.* a Japanese form of self-defense making use of the attacker's own movements without causing injury.

ail /ayl/ *v.* **1** *tr. archaic* trouble or afflict (*what ails him?*). **2** *intr.* be ill.

ai·ler·on /áylərən/ *n.* a hinged surface in the trailing edge of an airplane wing, used to control lateral balance and to initiate banking for turns, etc.

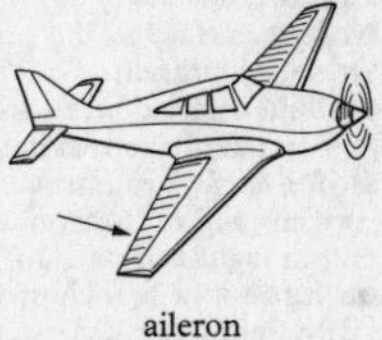
aileron

See page xii for the *Key to Pronunciation*.

ail·ing /áyling/ *adj.* **1** ill, esp. chronically. **2** in poor condition.

ail·ment /áylmənt/ *n.* an illness, esp. a minor or chronic one.

aim /aym/ *v.* & *n.* •*v.* **1** *intr.* intend or try (*aim at winning; aim to win*). **2** *tr.* direct or point (a weapon, remark, etc.). **3** *intr.* take aim. **4** *intr.* (foll. by *at, for*) seek to attain or achieve. •*n.* **1** a purpose; a design; an object aimed at. **2** the directing of a weapon, missile, etc., at an object. □ **take aim** direct a weapon, etc., at an object.

aim·less /áymlis/ *adj.* without purpose. □□ **aim·less·ly** *adv.* **aim·less·ness** *n.*

ain't /aynt/ *contr. colloq.* **1** am not; are not; is not (*she ain't nice*). **2** has not; have not (*we ain't seen him*). ▶Although this form has been used for hundreds of years, it is generally thought incorrect, and should be avoided in formal contexts.

air /air/ *n.* & *v.* •*n.* **1** an invisible gaseous substance surrounding the earth, a mixture mainly of oxygen and nitrogen. **2 a** the earth's atmosphere. **b** the free space in the atmosphere (*in the open air*). **c** the atmosphere as a place where aircraft operate. **3 a** a distinctive characteristic (*an air of absurdity*). **b** one's manner, esp. a confident one (*with a triumphant air*). **c** (esp. in *pl.*) an affected manner; pretentiousness (*gave himself airs*). **4** *Mus.* a melody. **5** a breeze or light wind. •*v.tr.* **1** esp. *Brit.* warm (washed laundry) to dry, esp. at a fire or in a heated closet. **2** expose (a room, etc.) to the open air; ventilate. **3** express publicly (an opinion, grievance, etc.). **4** broadcast, esp. a radio or television program. □ **in the air** (of opinions, feelings, etc.) prevalent; gaining currency. **on** (or **off**) **the air** in (or not in) the process of broadcasting. **up in the air** (of projects, etc.) uncertain; not decided. **walk on air** feel elated.

air bag *n.* a safety device that fills with nitrogen on impact to protect the occupants of a vehicle in a collision.

air base /áir bays/ *n.* a base for the operation of military aircraft.

air blad·der *n.* a bladder or sac filled with air in fish or some plants.

air·borne /áirbawrn/ *adj.* **1** transported by air. **2** (of aircraft) in the air after taking off.

air brake *n.* **1** a brake worked by air pressure. **2** a movable flap or spoiler on an aircraft to reduce its speed.

air·brush /áirbrush/ *n.* & *v.* •*n.* an artist's device for spraying paint by means of compressed air •*v.tr.* paint with an airbrush.

air-con·di·tion·ing *n.* a system for regulating the humidity, ventilation, and temperature in a building. □□ **air-con·di·tioned** *adj.* **air con·di·tion·er** *n.*

air·craft /áirkraft/ *n.* (*pl.* same) a machine capable of flight, esp. an airplane or helicopter.

air·craft car·ri·er *n.* a warship that carries and serves as a base for airplanes.

air cush·ion *n.* **1** an inflatable cushion. **2** the layer of air supporting a hovercraft or similar vehicle.

Aire·dale /áirdayl/ *n.* a large terrier of a rough-coated breed.

air·fare /áirfair/ *n.* the price of a passenger ticket for travel by aircraft.

air·field /áirfeeld/ *n.* an area of land where aircraft take off and land, are maintained, etc.

air·foil /áirfoyl/ *n.* a structure with curved surfaces (e.g., a wing, fin, or horizontal stabilizer) designed to give lift in flight.

air force *n.* a branch of the armed forces concerned with fighting or defense in the air.

air·frame /áirfraym/ *n.* the body of an aircraft as distinct from its engine(s).

air·freight /áirfrayt/ *n.* & *v.* •*n.* cargo carried by an aircraft. •*v.tr.* transport by air.

air·glow /áirglō/ *n.* radiation from the upper atmosphere, detectable at night.

air gun *n.* a gun using compressed air to propel pellets.

air·head /áirhed/ *n. sl.* a silly or stupid person.

air·ing /áiring/ *n.* **1** exposure to fresh air, esp. for exercise. **2** esp. *Brit.* exposure (of laundry, etc.) to warm air. **3** public expression of an opinion, etc. **4** a broadcast.

air·less /áirlis/ *adj.* **1** stuffy. **2** without wind or breeze. □□ **air·less·ness** *n.*

air·lift /áirlift/ *n.* & *v.* •*n.* the transport of troops, supplies, or passengers by air, esp. in a blockade or other emergency. •*v.tr.* transport in this way.

air·line /áirlīn/ *n.* an organization providing a regular public service of air transport on one or more routes.

air·lin·er /áirlīnər/ *n.* a passenger aircraft, esp. a large one.

air·lock /áirlok/ *n.* **1** a stoppage of the flow in a pump or pipe, caused by an air bubble. **2** a compartment with controlled pressure and parallel sets of doors, to permit movement between areas at different pressures.

air·mail /áirmayl/ *n.* & *v.* •*n.* **1** a system of transporting mail by air. **2** mail carried by air. •*v.tr.* send by airmail.

air·man /áirmən/ *n.* (*pl.* **·men**) **1** a pilot or member of the crew of an aircraft. **2** a member of the USAF below commissioned rank.

air mat·tress *n.* an inflatable mattress.

air·plane /áirplayn/ *n.* a powered heavier-than-air flying vehicle with fixed wings.

air·play /áirplay/ *n.* broadcasting (of recorded music).

air pock·et *n.* an apparent downdraft in the air causing an aircraft to drop suddenly.

air·port /áirpawrt/ *n.* a complex of runways and buildings for the takeoff, landing, and maintenance of civil aircraft, with facilities for passengers.

air pow·er *n.* the ability to defend and attack by means of aircraft, missiles, etc.

air raid *n.* an attack by aircraft.

air ri·fle *n.* a rifle using compressed air to propel pellets.

air·ship /áirship/ *n.* a power-driven aircraft that is lighter than air.

air·sick /áirsik/ *adj.* affected with nausea due to travel in an aircraft. □□ **air·sick·ness** *n.*

air·space /áirspays/ *n.* the air available to aircraft to fly in, esp. the part subject to the jurisdiction of a particular country.

air·speed /áirspeed/ *n.* the speed of an aircraft relative to the air through which it is moving.

air·strip /áirstrip/ *n.* a strip of ground suitable for the takeoff and landing of aircraft but usu. without other facilities.

air·tight /áirtīt/ *adj.* **1** not allowing air to pass through. **2** having no visible or apparent weaknesses (*an airtight alibi*).

air·time /áirtīm/ *n.* time allotted for a broadcast.

air-traf·fic con·trol·ler *n.* an airport official who controls air traffic by giving radio instructions to pilots concerning route, altitude, takeoff, and landing.

air·waves /áirwayvz/ *n.pl. colloq.* radio waves used in broadcasting.

air·way /áirway/ *n.* **1 a** a recognized route followed by aircraft. **b** (often in *pl.*) = AIRLINE. **2** *Med.* the passage through which air passes into the lungs.

air·wom·an /áirwŏŏmən/ *n.* (*pl.* **·women**) **1** a woman pilot or member of the crew of an aircraft. **2** a member of the USAF or WRAF below commissioned rank.

air·wor·thy /áirwərthee/ *adj.* (of an aircraft) fit to fly.

air·y /áiree/ *adj.* (**airier, airiest**) **1** well ventilated; breezy. **2** flippant; superficial. **3 a** light as air. **b** graceful; delicate. **4** insubstantial; ethereal; immaterial. ▫▫ **air·i·ly** *adv.* **air·i·ness** *n.*

aisle /īl/ *n.* **1** part of a church parallel to the nave, choir, or transept. **2** a passage between rows of pews, seats, etc. **3** a passageway. ▫▫ **aisled** *adj.*

aitch /aych/ *n.* the name of the letter H.

aitch·bone /áychbōn/ *n.* the buttock or rump bone.

a·jar /əjaár/ *adv. & predic.adj.* (of a door) slightly open.

AK *abbr.* Alaska (in official postal use).

a.k.a. *abbr.* also known as.

AKC *abbr.* American Kennel Club.

a·kim·bo /əkímbō/ *adv.* (of the arms) with hands on the hips and elbows turned outwards.

a·kin /əkín/ *predic.adj.* **1** related by blood. **2** of similar or kindred character.

AL *abbr.* Alabama (in official postal use).

Al *symb. Chem.* the element aluminum.

Ala. *abbr.* Alabama.

à la /aá laa/ *prep.* after the manner of (*à la russe*).

al·a·bas·ter /áləbastər/ *n. & adj.* • *n.* a translucent usu. white form of gypsum, often carved into ornaments. • *adj.* **1** of alabaster. **2** like alabaster in whiteness or smoothness.

à la carte /aá laa kaárt/ *adv. & adj.* ordered as separately priced item(s) from a menu, not as part of a set meal.

a·lack /əlák/ *int.* (also **a·lack-a-day** /əlákəday) *archaic* an expression of regret or surprise.

a·lac·ri·ty /əlákritee/ *n.* briskness or cheerful readiness.

à la mode /aá laa mṓd/ *adv. & adj.* **1** in fashion; fashionable. **2** served with ice cream.

a·lar /áylər/ *adj.* **1** relating to wings. **2** winglike or wing-shaped. **3** axillary.

a·larm /əlaárm/ *n. & v.* • *n.* **1** a warning of danger, etc. **2 a** a warning sound or device. **b** = ALARM CLOCK. **3** frightened expectation of danger or difficulty. • *v.tr.* **1** frighten or disturb. **2** arouse to a sense of danger.

a·larm clock *n.* a clock with a device that can be made to sound at a time set in advance.

a·larm·ing /əlaárming/ *adj.* disturbing; frightening. ▫▫ **a·larm·ing·ly** *adv.*

a·larm·ist /əlaármist/ *n. & adj.* • *n.* a person given to spreading needless alarm. • *adj.* creating needless alarm. ▫▫ **a·larm·ism** *n.*

a·lar·um /əlaárəm/ *n. archaic* = ALARM.

Alas. *abbr.* Alaska.

a·las /əlás/ *int.* an expression of grief, pity, or concern.

a·late /áylayt/ *adj.* having wings or winglike appendages.

alb /alb/ *n.* a usu. white vestment reaching to the feet, worn by some Christian priests at church ceremonies.

al·ba·core /álbəkawr/ *n.* **1** a long-finned tuna, *Thunnus alalunga*. **2** any of various other related fish.

Al·ba·ni·an /albáyneeən, awl–/ *n. & adj.* • *n.* **1 a** a native or inhabitant of Albania in SE Europe. **b** a person of Albanian descent. **2** the language of Albania. • *adj.* of or relating to Albania or its people or language.

al·ba·tross /álbətraws, –tros/ *n.* **1 a** any long-winged stout-bodied bird of the family Diomedeidae, inhabiting the Pacific Ocean. **b** a source of frustration or guilt. **2** *Golf* = DOUBLE EAGLE.

---

albatross late 17th cent.: alteration (influenced by Latin *albus* 'white') of 16th-cent. *alcatras*, applied to various seabirds including the frigate bird and pelican, from Spanish and Portuguese *alcatraz*, from Arabic *al-ġaṭṭās* 'the diver.'

---

al·be·do /albeédō/ *n.* (*pl.* **·dos**) the proportion of light or radiation reflected by a surface, esp. of a planet or moon.

al·be·it /áwlbeéit/ *conj. formal* though (*he tried, albeit without success*).

al·bi·no /albínō/ *n.* (*pl.* **·nos**) a person or animal having a congenital absence of pigment in the skin and hair (which are white), and the eyes (which are usu. pink). ▫▫ **al·bi·nism** /álbinizəm/ *n.*

al·bum /álbəm/ *n.* **1** a blank book for the insertion of photographs, stamps, etc. **2** a long-playing phonograph, audio cassette, or compact disc recording.

al·bu·men /albyoómin/ *n.* **1** egg white. **2** *Bot.* the substance found between the skin and embryo of many seeds.

al·bu·min /albyoómin/ *n.* any of a class of water-soluble proteins found in egg white, milk, blood, etc. ▫▫ **al·bu·mi·nous** *adj.*

al·bu·mi·nu·ri·a /albyoóminoóreeə, –nyoór–/ *n.* the presence of albumin in the urine, usu. as a symptom of kidney disease.

al·che·my /álkəmee/ *n.* (*pl.* **·mies**) **1** the medieval forerunner of chemistry, esp. seeking to turn base metals into gold or silver. **2** a miraculous transformation or the means of achieving this. ▫▫ **al·chem·i·cal** /–kémikəl/ *adj.* **al·che·mist** *n.*

al·co·hol /álkəhawl, –hol/ *n.* **1** (in full **ethyl alcohol**) a colorless volatile flammable liquid forming the intoxicating element in wine, beer, liquor, etc., and also used as a solvent, as fuel, etc. Also called ETHANOL. **2** any liquor containing this. **3** *Chem.* any of a large class of organic compounds that contain one or more hydroxyl groups attached to carbon atoms.

---

alcohol mid-16th cent.: French (earlier form of *alcool*), or from medieval Latin, from Arabic *al-kuḥl* 'the kohl.' In early use the term denoted powders, specifically kohl, and especially those obtained by sublimation; later 'a distilled or rectified spirit' (mid-17th cent).

---

al·co·hol·ic /álkəháwlik, –hól–/ *adj. & n.* • *adj.* of, relating to, containing, or caused by alcohol. • *n.* a person suffering from alcoholism.

al·co·hol·ism /álkəhawlízəm, –ho–/ *n.* **1** an addiction to the consumption of alcoholic liquor. **2** the diseased condition resulting from this.

al·cove /álkōv/ *n.* a recess, esp. in the wall of a room or of a garden.

al den·te /aal déntay, al déntee/ *adj.* (of pasta, etc.) cooked so as to be still firm when bitten.

al·der /áwldər/ *n.* any tree of the genus *Alnus*, related to the birch, with catkins and toothed leaves.

al·der·man /áwldərmən/ *n.* (*pl.* **·men**; *fem.* **alderwoman**, *pl.* **·women**) an elected municipal official serving on the governing council of a city. ▫▫ **al·der·man·ic** /–mánik/ *adj.*

ale /ayl/ *n.* **1** beer. **2** a similar beverage with a more pronounced, often bitter taste.

a·le·a·tor·ic /áyleeətáwrik, –tór–/ *adj.* depending on chance.

a·le·a·to·ry /áyleeətawree/ *adj.* = ALEATORIC.

a·lee /əlée/ *adv. & predic.adj.* **1** on the lee or sheltered side of a ship. **2** to leeward.

ale·house /áylhows/ *n.* a tavern.

a·lem·bic /əlémbik/ *n. hist.* an apparatus formerly used in distilling.

a·leph /aálif/ *n.* the first letter of the Hebrew alphabet.

a·lert /əlárt/ *adj., n., & v.* • *adj.* **1** vigilant; ready to take action. **2** quick (esp. of mental faculties); attentive. • *n.* a warning call or alarm. • *v.tr.* (often foll. by *to*) make alert; warn (*were alerted to the danger*). ▫ **on the alert** on the lookout against danger or attack. ▫▫ **a·lert·ly** *adv.* **a·lert·ness** *n.*

Al·eut /aleeóot, əlóot/ *n.* **1 a** a N. American people native to the Aleutian Islands and the western Alaskan Peninsula. **b** a member of this people. **2** the language of this people. ▫▫ **A·leu·tian** *adj.*

Al·ex·an·dri·an /áligzándreeən/ *adj.* **1** of or characteristic of Alexandria in Egypt. **2 a** belonging to or akin to the schools of literature and philosophy of Alexandria. **b** (of a writer) derivative or imitative; fond of recondite learning.

al·ex·an·drine /áligzándrin, –dreen/ *adj. & n.* • *adj.* (of a line of verse) having six iambic feet. • *n.* an alexandrine line.

a·lex·i·a /əlékseeə/ *n.* the inability to see words or to read, caused by a condition of the brain.

al·fal·fa /alfálfə/ *n.* a leguminous plant, *Medicago sativa*, with cloverlike leaves and flowers used for fodder.

al·fres·co /alfréskō/ *adv. & adj.* in the open air (*we lunched alfresco*; *an alfresco lunch*).

al·ga /álgə/ *n.* (*pl.* **algae** /áljee/ also **algas**) (usu. in *pl.*) a nonflowering stemless water plant, esp. seaweed and phytoplankton. ▫▫ **al·gal** *adj.*

al·ge·bra /áljibrə/ *n.* the branch of mathematics that uses letters to represent numbers and quantities in formulae and equations. ▫▫ **al·ge·bra·ic** /áljibráyik/ *adj.* **al·ge·bra·i·cal·ly** *adv.*

---

algebra late Middle English: from Italian, Spanish, and medieval Latin, from Arabic *al-jabr* 'the reunion of broken parts,' 'bone-setting,' from *jabara* 'reunite, restore.' The original sense, 'the surgical treatment of fractures,' probably came via Spanish, in which it survives; the mathematical sense comes from the title of a book, '*ilm al-jabr wa'l-muḳābala* 'The Science of Restoring What Is Missing and Equating Like with Like,' by the mathematician al-K̲wārizmī (see ALGORITHM).

-algia /áljə/ *comb.form Med.* denoting pain in a part specified by the first element (*neuralgia*). ▫▫ **-algic** *comb.form* forming adjectives.

al·gi·cide /áljəsīd/ *n.* a preparation for destroying algae.

al·gid /áljid/ *adj. Med.* cold; chilly. ▫▫ **al·gid·i·ty** /aljíditee/ *n.*

al·gin·ic ac·id /aljínik/ *n.* an insoluble carbohydrate found (chiefly as salts) in many brown seaweeds.

Al·gol /álgawl, –gol/ *n.* a high-level computer programming language.

Al·gon·qui·an /algóngkweeən/ *n.* any of the languages or dialects used by the Algonquin peoples.

Al·gon·quin /algóngkwən/ *n.* **1** a N. American people native to the Ottawa River valley and the northern St. Lawrence River valley. **2** a member of this people.

al·go·rithm /álgəri<u>th</u>əm/ *n. Math.* a set of rules used for calculation or problem-solving. ▫▫ **al·go·rith·mic** /álgərí<u>th</u>mik/ *adj.*

a·li·as /áyleeəs/ *adv. & n.* • *adv.* also known as. • *n.* a false name.

al·i·bi /álibī/ *n.* (*pl.* **alibis**) **1** a claim or piece of evidence that one was elsewhere when an act, usu. a criminal one, is alleged to have taken place. **2** an excuse of any kind.

▶The chief meaning of this Latin word is 'evidence that when something took place one was elsewhere,' e.g., *He has no alibi for the evening in question.* It is also used informally, however, to mean 'an excuse, pretext, or justification'; many consider this incorrect.

al·ien /áyleeən/ *adj. & n.* • *adj.* **1 a** (often foll. by *to*) unfamiliar; not in accordance; unfriendly; hostile; repugnant (*army discipline was alien to him*; *struck an alien note*). **b** different or separated. **2** from a foreign country. **3** of or relating to beings supposedly from other worlds. **4** *Bot.* (of a plant) introduced from elsewhere and naturalized. • *n.* **1** a foreigner, esp. one who is not a naturalized citizen of the country where he or she is living. **2** a being supposedly from another world. **3** *Bot.* an alien plant. ▫▫ **al·ien·ness** *n.*

al·ien·ate /áyleeənayt/ *v.tr.* **1 a** cause (a person) to become hostile. **b** (often foll. by *from*) cause (a person) to feel estranged from (friends, society, etc.). **2** transfer ownership of (property) to another person, etc. ▫▫ **al·ien·a·tion** /áyleeənáyshən/ *n.*

al·i·form /álifawrm/ *adj.* wing-shaped.

a·light[1] /əlít/ *v.intr.* **1** esp. *Brit.* **a** descend from a vehicle. **b** dismount from a horse. **2** come to earth from the air. **3** (foll. by *on*) find by chance; notice.

a·light[2] /əlít/ *predic.adj.* **1** on fire; burning. **2** lighted up; excited.

a·lign /əlín/ *v.tr.* **1** put in a straight line or bring into line (*three books were neatly aligned on the shelf*). **2** (usu. foll. by *with*) bring (oneself, etc.) into alliance with (a cause, policy, political party, etc.). ▫▫ **a·lign·ment** *n.*

a·like /əlík/ *adj. & adv.* • *adj.* (usu. *predic.*) similar; like one another; indistinguishable. • *adv.* in a similar way or manner (*all were treated alike*).

al·i·men·ta·ry /áliméntəree/ *adj.* of, relating to, or providing nourishment.

al·i·men·tary ca·nal *n. Anat.* the passage along which food is passed from the mouth to the anus during digestion.

al·i·men·ta·tion /álimentáyshən/ *n.* **1** nourishment. **2** maintenance; support.

al·i·mo·ny /álimōnee/ *n.* money payable to a spouse after divorce or legal separation.

A-line /áylīn/ *adj.* (of a garment) having a narrow waist or shoulders and somewhat flared skirt.

al·i·phat·ic /álifátik/ *adj. Chem.* of, denoting, or relating to organic compounds in which carbon atoms form open chains, not aromatic rings.

al·i·quot /álikwot/ *adj. & n.* • *adj.* (of a part or portion) contained by the whole an integral or whole number of times. • *n.* **1** an aliquot part; an integral factor. **2** a known fraction of a whole; a sample.

a·live /əlív/ *adj.* (usu. *predic.*) **1** (of a person, animal, plant, etc.) living. **2 a** (of a thing) continuing; in operation or action (*kept his interest alive*). **b** provoking interest (*the topic is still very much alive*). **3** lively; active. **4** charged with an electric current; connected to a source of electricity. **5** (foll. by *to*) alert or responsive to. **6** (foll. by *with*) **a** swarming or teeming with. **b** full of. ▫▫ **a·live·ness** *n.*

al·ka·li /álkəlī/ *n.* (*pl.* **alkalis**) **1 a** any of a class of substances that liberate hydroxide ions in water, usu. form caustic or corrosive solutions, turn litmus blue, and have a pH of more than 7, e.g., sodium hydroxide. **b** any other substance with similar but weaker properties, e.g., sodium carbonate. **2** *Chem.* any substance that reacts with or neutralizes hydrogen ions.

al·ka·line /álkəlīn/ *adj.* of, relating to, or having the nature of an alkali. ▫▫ **al·ka·lin·i·ty** /álkəlínitee/ *n.*

al·ka·loid /álkəloyd/ *n.* any of a series of nitrogenous organic compounds of plant origin, many of which are used as drugs, e.g., morphine, quinine.

al·ka·lo·sis /álkəlṓsis/ *n. Med.* an excessive alkaline condition of the body fluids or tissues.

al·kane /álkayn/ *n. Chem.* any of a series of saturated aliphatic hydrocarbons having the general formula C_nH_{2n+2}, including methane, ethane, and propane.

al·kene /álkeen/ *n. Chem.* any of a series of unsaturated aliphatic hydrocarbons containing a double bond and having the general formula C_nH_{2n}.

al·kyd /álkid/ *n.* any of the group of synthetic resins derived from various alcohols and acids.

al·kyl /álkil/ *n. Chem.* any radical derived from an alkane by the removal of a hydrogen atom.

all /awl/ *adj., n., & adv.* • *adj.* **1 a** the whole amount, quantity, or extent of (*waited all day*; *all his life*; *we all know why*). **b** (with *pl.*) the entire number of (*all the others left*; *all ten men*). **2** any whatever (*beyond all doubt*). **3** greatest possible (*with all speed*). • *n.* **1 a** all the persons or things concerned (*all were present*). **b** everything (*that is all*). **2** (foll. by *of*) **a** the whole of (*take all of it*). **b** every one of (*all of us*). **c** *colloq.* as much as (*all of six feet tall*). **d** *colloq.* in a state of (*all of a dither*). **3** one's whole strength or resources (prec. by *my*, *your*, etc.). **4** (in games) on both sides (*the score was two all*). • *adv.* **1 a** entirely (*dressed all in black*; *all around the room*). **b** as an intensifier (*a book all about ships*; *stop all this grumbling*). **2** (foll. by *the* + compar.) **a** to that extent (*if they go, all the better*). **b** in the full degree to be expected (*that makes it all the worse*). □ **all along** all the time (*he was joking all along*). **all and sundry** everyone. **all but** very nearly (*it was all but impossible*). **all for** *colloq.* strongly in favor of. **all in** *colloq.* exhausted. **all in all** everything considered. **all manner of** many different kinds of. **all one** (or **the same**) a matter of indifference (*it's all one to me*). **all over 1** completely finished. **2** in or on all parts of (esp. the body) (*went hot and cold all over*). **3** *colloq.* typically (*that is you all over*). **4** *sl.* effusively attentive to (a person). **all the same** nevertheless; in spite of this (*he was innocent but was punished all the same*). **all set** *colloq.* ready to start. **all there** *colloq.* mentally alert. **all together** all at once; all in one place or in a group (*they came all together*) (cf. ALTOGETHER). **all told** in all. **all very well** *colloq.* an expression used to imply skepticism about a favorable or consoling remark (*your plan is all very well in theory, but it won't work*). **all the way** the whole distance; completely. **at all** (with *neg.* or *interrog.*) to any extent (*did not swim at all*; *did you like it at all?*). **in all** in total number (*there were 10 people in all*).

al·la bre·ve /álə brév, aálaa brévay/ *n. Mus.* a time signature indicating 2 half-note beats in a bar.

al·la cap·pel·la var. of A CAPPELLA.

Al·lah /álə, aálaa/ *n.* the name of God in Islam.

all-A·mer·i·can *adj.* **1** representing the whole of (or only) America or the US. **2** truly American (*all-American boy*). **3** *Sports* recognized as one of the best in a particular sport.

all-a·round *adj.* **1** versatile, having many uses or abilities (*an all-around artist*; *a lightweight, all-around saw*). **2** in many or all respects *her all-around excellence*).

al·lay /əláy/ *v.tr.* **1** diminish (fear, suspicion, etc.). **2** relieve or alleviate (pain, hunger, etc.).

all clear *n.* a signal that danger or difficulty is over.

al·le·ga·tion /áligáyshən/ *n.* **1** an assertion, esp. an unproved one. **2** the act or an instance of alleging.

al·lege /əléj/ *v.tr.* **1** declare to be the case, esp. without proof. **2** advance as an argument. □□ **al·leged** *adj.*

al·leg·ed·ly /əléjidlee/ *adv.* as is alleged or said to be the case.

al·le·giance /əléejəns/ *n.* **1** loyalty (to a person or cause, etc.). **2** the duty of a subject to his or her sovereign or government.

al·le·gor·i·cal /áligáwrikəl, –gór–/ *adj.* consisting of or relating to allegory; by means of allegory. □□ **al·le·gor·i·cal·ly** *adv.*

al·le·go·rize /áligərīz/ *v.tr.* treat as or by means of an allegory. □□ **al·le·go·ri·za·tion** /–rizáyshən/ *n.*

al·le·go·ry /áligawree/ *n.* (*pl.* **·ries**) **1** a story, picture, etc., in which the meaning is represented symbolically. **2** the use of such symbols. **3** a symbol.

al·le·gret·to /áligrétō/ *adv., adj.,* & *n. Mus.* • *adv.* & *adj.* in a fairly brisk tempo. • *n.* (*pl.* **·tos**) an allegretto passage or movement.

al·le·gro /əléggrō, əláy–/ *adv., adj.,* & *n. Mus.* • *adv.* & *adj.* in a brisk tempo. • *n.* (*pl.* **·gros**) an allegro passage or movement.

al·lele /əléel/ *n.* one of the (usu. two) alternative forms of a gene. □□ **al·lel·ic** /əléelik/ *adj.*

al·le·lu·ia /álilóoyə/ *int.* & *n.* (also **al·le·lu·ya, hal·le·lu·jah** /hál–) • *int.* God be praised. • *n.* **1** praise to God. **2** a song of praise to God.

Al·len screw /álən/ *n.* a screw with a hexagonal socket in the head.

Al·len wrench /álən/ *n.* a hexagonal wrench designed to fit into and turn an Allen screw.

al·ler·gen /álərjən/ *n.* any substance that causes an allergic reaction. □□ **al·ler·gen·ic** /–jénik/ *adj.*

al·ler·gic /ələ́rjik/ *adj.* **1** (foll. by *to*) **a** having an allergy to. **b** *colloq.* having a strong dislike for (a person or thing). **2** caused by or relating to an allergy.

al·ler·gy /álərjee/ *n.* (*pl.* **·gies**) **1** *Med.* a condition of reacting adversely to certain substances. **2** *colloq.* an antipathy or dislike. □□ **al·ler·gist** *n.*

al·le·vi·ate /əléeveeayt/ *v.tr.* lessen or make less severe (pain, suffering, etc.). □□ **al·le·vi·a·tion** /–áyshən/ *n.*

al·ley /álee/ *n.* (*pl.* **·leys**) **1** (also **al·ley·way**) **a** a narrow street. **b** a narrow passageway between or behind buildings. **2** a path in a park or garden. **3** an enclosure for bowling, etc.

All Fools' Day *n.* = APRIL FOOL'S DAY.

al·li·a·ceous /álee–áyshəs/ *adj.* **1** of or relating to the genus Allium. **2** tasting or smelling like onion or garlic.

al·lied /əlíd, álīd/ *adj.* **1** united or associated in an alliance. **2** connected or related.

al·li·ga·tor /áligaytər/ *n.* **1** a large reptile of the crocodile family native to the Americas and China, with a head broader and shorter than that of the crocodile. **2** (in general use) any of several large members of the crocodile family. **3** the skin of such an animal or material resembling it.

al·li·ga·tor clip *n.* a clip with teeth for gripping.

al·li·ga·tor pear *n.* an avocado.

al·lit·er·ate /əlítərayt/ *v.* **1** *intr.* **a** contain alliteration. **b** use alliteration in speech or writing. **2** *tr.* construct or pronounce (a phrase, etc.) with alliteration. □□ **al·lit·er·a·tive** /əlítəraytiv, –rətiv/ *adj.*

al·lit·er·a·tion /əlítəráyshən/ *n.* the occurrence of the same letter or sound at the beginning of adjacent or closely connected words (e.g., *calm, cool, and collected*).

al·li·um /áleeəm/ *n.* any plant of the genus *Allium*, usu. bulbous and strong smelling, e.g., onion and garlic.

allo- /álō, əló/ *comb.form* other (*allophone*; *allogamy*).

al·lo·cate /áləkayt/ *v.tr.* (usu. foll. by *to*) assign, apportion, or devote to (a purpose, person, or place). □□ **al·lo·ca·ble** /–kəbəl/ *adj.* **al·lo·ca·tion** /–káyshən/ *n.*

al·lo·cu·tion /áləkyóoshən/ *n.* formal or hortatory speech or manner of address.

al·log·a·my /əlógəmee/ *n. Bot.* cross-fertilization in plants.

al·lo·path /áləpath/ *n.* one who practices allopathy.

al·lop·a·thy /əlópəthee/ *n.* the treatment of disease with drugs, etc., having opposite effects to the symptoms (cf. HOMEOPATHY). □□ **al·lo·path·ic** /áləpáthik/ *adj.*

al·lo·phone /áləfōn/ *n. Linguistics* any of the variant sounds forming a single phoneme. □□ **al·lo·phon·ic** /–fónik/ *adj.*

al·lot /əlót/ *v.tr.* (**allotted, allotting**) **1** give or apportion to (a person) as a share or task; distribute officially to (*they allotted us each a pair of boots*). **2** (foll. by *to*) give or distribute officially (*money allotted to each charity*).

al·lot·ment /əlótmənt/ *n.* **1** a share allotted. **2** the action of allotting.

al·lo·trope /álətrōp/ *n.* any of two or more different physical forms in which an element can exist.

all out *adj.* involving all one's strength; at full speed (also (with hyphen) *attrib.*: *an all-out effort*).

al·low /əlów/ *v.* **1** *tr.* permit (*smoking is not allowed*). **2** *tr.* give or provide; permit (a person) to have (a limited quantity or sum) (*we were allowed $500 a year*). **3** *tr.*

provide or set aside for a purpose; add or deduct in consideration of something (*allow 10% for inflation*). **4** *tr.* **a** admit; concede (*he allowed that it was so*). **b** be of the opinion. **5** *refl.* permit oneself; indulge oneself in (conduct) (*allowed herself to be persuaded*). **6** *intr.* (foll. by *of*) admit of. **7** *intr.* (foll. by *for*) take into consideration; make addition or deduction corresponding to (*allowing for waste*). ▫▫ **al·low·a·ble** *adj.*

al·low·ance /əlówəns/ *n.* & *v.* • *n.* **1** an amount or sum allowed to a person, esp. regularly. **2** an amount allowed in reckoning. **3** a deduction or discount. **4** (foll. by *of*) tolerance of. • *v.tr.* **1** make an allowance to (a person). **2** supply in limited quantities.

al·loy /áloy, əlóy/ *n.* & *v.* • *n.* **1** a mixture of two or more chemical elements, at least one of which is a metal. **2** an inferior metal mixed esp. with gold or silver. • *v.tr.* **1** mix (metals). **2** debase (a pure substance) by admixture.

all-pur·pose *adj.* suitable for many uses.

all right *adj., adv.* & *int.* • *adj.* (*predic.*) satisfactory; safe and sound. • *adv.* satisfactorily (*it worked out all right*). • *int.* **1** expressing consent or assent to a proposal or order. **2** as an intensifier (*that's the one all right*). ▶Although found widely, **alright** remains nonstandard, even where standard spelling leads to awkwardness, e.g., *I wanted to make sure it was all all right.*

all-right *attrib.adj. colloq.* fine; acceptable (*an all-right guy*).

All Saints' Day *n.* a Christian festival in honor of all the saints, held (in the Western Church) on Nov. 1.

All Souls' Day *n.* a festival in some Christian churches with prayers for the souls of the dead, held on Nov. 2.

all·spice /áwlspīs/ *n.* **1** the aromatic spice obtained from the ground berry of the pimento plant, *Pimenta dioica.* **2** the berry of this. **3** any of various other aromatic shrubs.

all-time *adj.* (of a record, etc.) hitherto unsurpassed.

al·lude /əlóód/ *v.intr.* (foll. by *to*) **1** refer, esp. indirectly, covertly, or briefly, to. **2** mention.

al·lure /əlóór/ *v.* & *n.* • *v.tr.* attract, charm, or fascinate. • *n.* attractiveness; personal charm; fascination. ▫▫ **al·lure·ment** *n.* **al·lur·ing** *adj.*

al·lu·sion /əlóózhən/ *n.* a reference, esp. a passing or indirect one. ▶Often confused with *illusion.* ▫▫ **al·lu·sive** /əlóósiv/ *adj.*

al·lu·vi·on /əlóóveeən/ *n.* **1** the wash of the sea against the shore, or of a river against its banks. **2 a** a large overflow of water. **b** matter deposited by this, esp. alluvium. **3** the formation of new land by the movement of the sea or of a river. ▫▫ **al·lu·vi·al** *adj.*

al·lu·vi·um /əlóóveeəm/ *n.* (*pl.* **alluviums** or **alluvia** /–ə/) a deposit of usu. fine fertile soil left during a time of flood, esp. in a river valley or delta.

al·ly /álī/ *n.* & *v.* • *n.* (*pl.* **·lies**) **1** a government formally cooperating or united with another for a special purpose, esp. by a treaty. **2** a person or organization that cooperates with or helps another. • *v.tr.* also /əlí/ (**·lies, ·lied**) (often foll. by *with*) combine or unite in alliance.

al·ma ma·ter /áalmə máatər/ *n.* (also **Al·ma Ma·ter**) **1** the university, school, or college one attends or attended. **2** the official anthem or song of a university, school, or college.

al·ma·nac /áwlmənak, ál–/ *n.* an annual calendar of months and days, usu. with astronomical data and other information.

al·might·y /áwlmítee/ *adj.* & *adv.* • *adj.* **1** having complete power; omnipotent. **2** (**the Almighty**) God. **3** *sl.* very great (*an almighty crash*). • *adv. sl.* extremely; very much.

al·mond /áamənd, ám–/ *n.* **1** the oval nutlike seed of the fruit from the tree *Prunus dulcis.* **2** the tree itself, of the rose family and related to the peach and plum.

al·most /áwlmōst/ *adv.* all but; very nearly.

alms /aamz/ *n.pl. hist.* the charitable donation of money or food to the poor.

alms·house /áamz–hows/ *n.* esp. *Brit. hist.* a house founded by charity for the poor.

al·oe /álō/ *n.* **1** any plant of the genus *Aloe*, usu. having toothed fleshy leaves. **2** (in *pl.*) (in full **bitter aloes**) a strong laxative obtained from the bitter juice of various species of aloe. **3** (also **A·mer·i·can al·oe**) an agave native to Central America.

a·loft /əláwft, əlóft/ *predic.adj.* & *adv.* **1** high up; overhead. **2** upwards.

a·lo·ha /əlṓhaa, aa–/ *int.* a Hawaiian salutation at meeting or parting.

a·lone /əlṓn/ *predic.adj.* & *adv.* **1 a** without others present. **b** without others' help. **c** lonely and isolated (*felt alone*). **2** (often foll. by *in*) standing by oneself in an opinion, etc. (*was alone in thinking this*). **3** only; exclusively (*you alone can help me*). ▫▫ **a·lone·ness** *n.*

a·long /əláwng, əlóng/ *prep.* & *adv.* • *prep.* **1** from one end to the other end of (*a handkerchief with lace along the edge*). **2** on or through any part of the length of (*was walking along the road*). **3** beside or through the length of (*shelves stood along the wall*). • *adv.* **1** onward; into a more advanced state (*come along*). **2** at or to a particular place; arriving (*I'll be along soon*). **3** in company with a person, esp. oneself (*bring a book along*). **4** beside or through part or the whole length of a thing. ▫ **along with** together with.

a·long·shore /əláwngsháwr, əlóng–/ *adv.* along or by the shore.

a·long·side /əláwngsíd, əlóng–/ *adv.* & *prep* • *adv.* at or to the side (of a ship, pier, etc.). • *prep.* close to the side of; next to. ▫ **alongside of** side by side with.

a·loof /əlóóf/ *adj.* & *adv.* • *adj.* distant; unsympathetic. • *adv.* away; apart (*he kept aloof from his colleagues*). ▫▫ **a·loof·ly** *adv.* **a·loof·ness** *n.*

a·loud /əlówd/ *adv.* **1** audibly; not silently or in a whisper. **2** *archaic* loudly.

alp /alp/ *n.* **1** a high mountain. **2** (**the Alps**) the high range of mountains in Switzerland and adjoining countries.

al·pac·a /alpákə/ *n.* **1** a S. American mammal, *Lama pacos*, related to the llama, with long shaggy hair. **2** the wool from the animal. **3** fabric made from the wool, with or without other fibers.

al·pen·horn /álpənhawrn/ *n.* a long wooden horn used by Alpine herdsmen to call their cattle.

al·pha /álfə/ *n.* **1** the first letter of the Greek alphabet (Α, α). **2** a beginning; something that is primary or first.

al·pha·bet /álfəbet/ *n.* the set of letters used in writing a language.

al·pha·bet·i·cal /álfəbétikəl/ *adj.* (also **al·pha·bet·ic** /–bétik) **1** of or relating to an alphabet. **2** in the order of the letters of the alphabet. ▫▫ **al·pha·bet·i·cal·ly** *adv.*

al·pha·bet·ize /álfəbətīz/ *v.tr.* arrange (words, names, etc.) in alphabetical order. ▫▫ **al·pha·bet·i·za·tion** /–izáyshən/ *n.*

al·pha·nu·mer·ic /álfənōōmérik, –nyōō–/ *adj.* containing both alphabetical and numerical symbols.

al·pha par·ti·cle *n.* (also **al·pha ray**) *n.* a helium nucleus emitted by a radioactive substance, orig. regarded as a ray.

al·pine /álpīn/ *adj.* & *n.* • *adj.* **1 a** of or relating to high mountains. **b** growing or found on high mountains. **2** (**Alpine**) of or relating to the Alps. • *n.* a plant native or suited to a high mountain habitat.

al·read·y /áwlrédee/ *adv.* **1** before the time in question (*I knew that already*). **2** as early or as soon as this (*already it was past four o'clock*).

al·right /áwlrít/ *adj., adv., & int. disp.* = ALL RIGHT. ▶See note at ALL RIGHT.

Al·sa·tian /alsáyshən/ *n.* a native of Alsace, a region of E. France.

al·so /áwlsō/ *adv.* in addition; likewise; besides.

al·so-ran *n.* **1** a horse or dog, etc., not among the winners in a race. **2** an undistinguished person.

al·tar /áwltər/ *n.* **1** a table or flat-topped block, often of stone, for sacrifice or offering to a deity. **2** a table at which a Christian service, esp. the Eucharist, is celebrated.

al·tar·piece /áwltərpees/ *n.* a piece of art, esp. a painting, set above an altar.

alt·az·i·muth /altázimәth/ *n.* a telescope or other instrument mounted so as to allow both vertical and horizontal movement, esp. one used for measuring the altitude and azimuth of celestial bodies.

al·ter /áwltər/ *v.* **1** *tr. & intr.* make or become different; change. **2** *tr.* castrate or spay. ▫▫ **al·ter·a·ble** *adj.* **al·ter·a·tion** /–ráyshən/ *n.*

al·ter·cate /áwltərkayt/ *v.intr.* (often foll. by *with*) dispute hotly; wrangle. ▫▫ **al·ter·ca·tion** /–káyshən/ *n.*

al·ter e·go /áwltər éegō, égō/ *n.* (*pl.* **alter egos**) **1** an intimate and trusted friend. **2** a person's secondary or alternative personality.

al·ter·nate *v., adj., & n.* • *v.* /áwltərnayt, ál–/ **1** *intr.* (often foll. by *with*) (of two things) succeed each other by turns (*elation alternated with depression*). **2** *intr.* (foll. by *between*) change repeatedly (between two conditions) (*the patient alternated between hot and cold fevers*). **3** *tr.* (often foll. by *with*) cause (two things) to succeed each other by turns (*the band alternated fast and slow tunes*). • *adj.* /áwltərnət, ál–/ **1** (with noun in *pl.*) every other (*comes on alternate days*). **2** (of things of two kinds) each following and succeeded by one of the other kind (*alternate joy and misery*). **3** (of a sequence, etc.) consisting of alternate things. **4** = ALTERNATIVE. • *n.* /áwltərnət, ál–/ something or someone that is an alternative; a deputy or substitute. ▫▫ **al·ter·nate·ly** *adv.*

▶In both American and British English **alternate** means 'every other,' e.g., *There will be a dance on alternate Saturdays,* and **alternative** means 'available as another choice,' e.g., *an alternative route*. In American usage, however, **alternate** can also be used to mean 'available as another choice,' e.g., *An alternate plan called for construction to begin immediately rather than waiting for spring.*

al·ter·nate an·gles *n.pl.* two angles, not adjoining one another, that are formed on opposite sides of a line that intersects two other lines.

al·ter·nat·ing cur·rent *n.* an electric current that reverses its direction at regular intervals.

al·ter·na·tion /áwltərnáyshən, ál–/ *n.* the action or result of alternating.

al·ter·na·tive /awltə́rnətiv, al–/ *adj. & n.* • *adj.* **1** (of one or more things) available or usable instead of another (*an alternative route*). **2** (of two things) mutually exclusive. **3** of or relating to practices that offer a substitute for conventional ones (*alternative theater*). • *n.* any of two or more possibilities. ▫▫ **al·ter·na·tive·ly** *adv.*

▶See note at ALTERNATE.

al·ter·na·tor /áwltərnaytər, ál–/ *n.* a generator that produces an alternating current.

alt·horn /ált–hawrn/ *n. Mus.* an instrument of the saxhorn family, esp. the alto or tenor saxhorn in E flat.

al·though /awlthṓ/ *conj.* = THOUGH *conj.* 1–3.

al·tim·e·ter /altímitər, áltimeetər/ *n.* an instrument for showing height above sea or ground level, esp. one fitted in an aircraft.

al·ti·tude /áltitood, –tyood/ *n.* the height of an object in relation to a given point, esp. sea level or the horizon. ▫▫ **al·ti·tu·di·nal** /–tóodin'l, –tyóo–/ *adj.*

al·to /áltō/ *n.* (*pl.* **·tos**) **1** = CONTRALTO. **2** = COUNTERTENOR. **3** (*attrib.*) denoting the member of a family of instruments pitched next below a soprano of its type.

al·to·geth·er /áwltəgéthər/ *adv.* **1** totally; completely (*you are altogether wrong*). **2** on the whole (*altogether it had been a good day*). **3** in total.

▶**Altogether** and **all together** are used in different contexts. **Altogether** means 'in total,' e.g., *The hotel has twenty rooms altogether. Altogether, I spent five years on the island.* **All together** means 'all at once' or 'all in one place or in one group,' e.g., *The packages arrived all together. We managed to get three bedrooms all together* (i.e., near each other).

al·to-re·lie·vo /áltōrileévō/ *n.* (also **al·to·ri·lie·vo** /áltōrilyáyvō/) (*pl.* **·vos**) *Sculpture* **1** a form of relief in which the sculptured shapes stand out from the background to at least half their actual depth. **2** a sculpture characterized by this.

al·tru·ism /áltrooizəm/ *n.* **1** regard for others as a principle of action. **2** unselfishness; concern for other people. ▫▫ **al·tru·ist** *n.* **al·tru·is·tic** /–ístik/ *adj.* **al·tru·is·ti·cal·ly** *adv.*

a·lum /áləm/ *n.* a double sulfate of aluminum and potassium.

a·lu·mi·na /əlóominə/ *n.* the compound aluminum oxide occurring naturally as corundum and emery.

a·lu·mi·num /əlóominəm/ *n.* (*Brit.* **aluminium** /ályəmíneeəm/) a silvery light and malleable metallic element resistant to tarnishing by air. ¶ Symb.: **Al**.

a·lum·nus /əlúmnəs/ *n.* (*pl.* **alumni** /–nī/; *fem.* **alumna**, *pl.* **alumnae** /–nee, nī/) a former pupil or student of a particular school, college, or university.

al·ve·o·lar /alvéeələr/ *adj.* **1** of an alveolus. **2** *Phonet.* (of a consonant) pronounced with the tip of the tongue in contact with the ridge of the upper teeth, e.g., *n, s, t*.

al·ve·o·lus /alvéeələs/ *n.* (*pl.* **alveoli** /–lī/) **1** a small cavity, pit, or hollow. **2** any of the many tiny air sacs of the lungs which allow for rapid gaseous exchange. **3** the bony socket for the root of a tooth. **4** the cell of a honeycomb. ▫▫ **al·ve·o·late** *adj.*

al·ways /áwlwayz/ *adv.* **1** at all times (*they are always late*). **2** whatever the circumstances (*I can always sleep on the floor*). **3** repeatedly; often (*they are always complaining*). **4** forever (*I am with you always*).

a·lys·sum /álisəm/ *n.* any plant of the genus *Alyssum*, usu. having yellow or white flowers.

Alz·hei·mer's dis·ease /áalts–hīmərz, álts–, áwlts–, áwlz–/ *n.* a serious disorder of the brain manifesting itself in premature senility.

AM *abbr.* **1** amplitude modulation. **2** Master of Arts.

Am *symb. Chem.* the element americium.

am *1st person sing. present* of BE.

a.m. *abbr.* (also **A.M.** or **AM**) between midnight and noon.

AMA *abbr.* American Medical Association.

a·mal·gam /əmálgəm/ *n.* **1** a mixture or blend. **2** an alloy of mercury with one or more other metals, used esp. in dentistry.

a·mal·ga·mate /əmálgəmayt/ *v.* **1** *tr. & intr.* combine or unite to form one structure, organization, etc. **2** *intr.* (of metals) alloy with mercury. ▫▫ **a·mal·ga·ma·tion** /–máyshən/ *n.*

a·man·u·en·sis /əmányoo–énsis/ *n.* (*pl.* **amanuenses** /–seez/) **1** a person who writes from dictation or copies manuscripts. **2** a literary assistant.

am·a·ret·to /amərétō/ *n.* an almond-flavored liqueur.

am·a·ryl·lis /ámərílis/ *n. Amaryllis belladonna*, a bulbous lily-like plant with white, pink, or red flowers.

a·mass /əmás/ *v.tr.* **1** gather or heap together. **2** accumulate (esp. riches). ▫▫ **a·mass·er** *n.* **a·mass·ment** *n.*

See page xii for the *Key to Pronunciation*.

the sick or injured to and from a hospital. **2** *hist.* a mobile hospital following an army.

am·a·teur /ámәchŏŏr, –chәr, –tәr, –tɔ́r/ *n. & adj.* • *n.* **1** a person who engages in a pursuit as a pastime rather than a profession. **2** *derog.* a person who does something unskillfully. • *adj.* for or done by amateurs; unskillful (*amateur athletics; did an amateur job*). ▫▫ **am·a·teur·ism** *n.*

am·a·teur·ish /ámәchŏŏr, –chәrish, tәr–, –tɔ́r–/ *adj.* characteristic of an amateur, esp. unskillful or inexperienced. ▫▫ **am·a·teur·ish·ly** *adv.* **am·a·teur·ish·ness** *n.*

am·a·to·ry /ámәtawree/ *adj.* of or relating to sexual love or desire.

a·maze /әmáyz/ *v.tr.* (often foll. by *at*, or *that* + clause, or *to* + infin.) surprise greatly. ▫▫ **a·maze·ment** *n.* **a·maz·ing** *adj.* **a·maz·ing·ly** *adv.* **a·maz·ing·ness** *n.*

Am·a·zon /ámәzon, –zәn/ *n.* **1** a member of a mythical race of female warriors. **2** (**amazon**) a very tall or athletic woman. ▫▫ **Am·a·zo·ni·an** /–zṓneeәn/ *adj.*

am·bas·sa·dor /ambásәdәr, –dawr/ *n.* **1** an accredited diplomat sent by a nation on a mission to, or as its permanent representative in, a foreign country. **2** a representative or promoter of a specified thing (*an ambassador of peace*). ▫▫ **am·bas·sa·do·ri·al** /–dáwreeәl/ *adj.* **am·bas·sa·dor·ship** *n.*

am·ber /ámbәr/ *n. & adj.* • *n.* **1 a** a yellowish translucent fossilized resin deriving from extinct trees and used in jewelry. **b** the honey-yellow color of this. **2** a yellow traffic signal meaning caution. • *adj.* made of or colored like amber.

am·ber·gris /ámbәrgris, –grees/ *n.* a strong-smelling waxlike secretion of the intestine of the sperm whale, used in perfume manufacture.

am·bi·dex·trous /ámbidékstrәs/ *adj.* able to use the right and left hands equally well. ▫▫ **am·bi·dex·ter·i·ty** /–stéritee/ *n.* **am·bi·dex·trous·ly** *adv.* **am·bi·dex·trous·ness** *n.*

am·bi·ence /ámbeeәns, aaNbeeáɴs/ *n.* (also **am·bi·ance**) the surroundings or atmosphere of a place.

am·bi·ent /ámbeeәnt/ *adj.* surrounding.

am·bi·gu·i·ty /ámbigyŏŏitee/ *n.* (*pl.* **·ties**) **1** double meaning. **2** an expression able to be interpreted in more than one way (e.g., *fighting dogs should be avoided*).

am·big·u·ous /ambígyŏŏәs/ *adj.* having an obscure or double meaning. ▫▫ **am·big·u·ous·ly** *adv.* **am·big·u·ous·ness** *n.*

am·bit /ámbit/ *n.* the extent or bounds of something.

am·bi·tion /ambíshәn/ *n.* **1** the determination to achieve success or distinction, usu. in a chosen field. **2** the object of this determination.

am·bi·tious /ambíshәs/ *adj.* **1** full of ambition. **2** showing ambition (*an ambitious attempt*). ▫▫ **am·bi·tious·ly** *adv.* **am·bi·tious·ness** *n.*

am·biv·a·lence /ambívәlәns/ *n.* **1** the coexistence in one person's mind of opposing feelings, esp. love and hate, in a single context. **2** uncertainty over a course of action or decision. ▫▫ **am·biv·a·lent** *adj.* **am·biv·a·lent·ly** *adv.*

am·bi·vert /ámbivert/ *n. Psychol.* a person who fluctuates between being an introvert and an extrovert. ▫▫ **am·bi·ver·sion** /–vérzhәn/ *n.*

am·ble /ámbәl/ *v. & n.* • *v.intr.* **1** move at an easy pace. **2** (of a horse, etc.) move by lifting the two feet on one side together. **3** ride an ambling horse; ride at an easy pace. • *n.* an easy pace; the gait of an ambling horse.

am·bro·sia /ambrṓzhә/ *n.* **1** (in Greek and Roman mythology) the food of the gods. **2** anything very pleasing to taste or smell. **3** a dessert made with oranges and shredded coconut. ▫▫ **am·bro·sial** *adj.* **am·bro·sian** *adj.*

am·bu·lance /ámbyәlәns/ *n.* **1** a vehicle for conveying

am·bu·lant /ámbyәlәnt/ *adj. Med.* **1** (of a patient) able to walk about; not confined to bed. **2** (of treatment) not confining a patient to bed.

am·bu·la·to·ry /ámbyәlәtawree/ *adj. & n.* • *adj.* **1** = AMBULANT. **2** of or adapted for walking. • *n.* (*pl.* **·ries**) a place for walking, esp. in a monastery.

am·bush /ámbŏŏsh/ *n. & v.* • *n.* **1** a surprise attack by persons (e.g., troops) in a concealed position. **2 a** the concealment of troops, etc., to make such an attack. **b** the place where they are concealed. • *v.tr.* attack by means of an ambush.

a·me·ba var. of AMOEBA.

a·mel·io·rate /әméelyәrayt/ *v.tr. & intr.* make or become better; improve. ▫▫ **a·mel·io·ra·tion** /–ráyshәn/ *n.* **a·mel·io·ra·tive** *adj.* **a·mel·io·ra·tor** *n.*

a·men /aámén, áy–/ *int. & n.* • *int.* **1** uttered at the end of a prayer or hymn, etc., meaning 'so be it.' **2** (foll. by *to*) expressing agreement or assent (*amen to that*). • *n.* an utterance of 'amen' (sense 1).

a·me·na·ble /әméenәbәl, әmén–/ *adj.* **1** responsive; tractable. **2** (of a person) responsible to law. ▫▫ **a·me·na·bil·i·ty** /–bílitee/ *n.* **a·me·na·bly** *adv.*

a·mend /әménd/ *v.tr.* **1** make minor improvements in (a text or a written proposal). **2** correct an error or errors in (a document). ▶Often confused with *emend*, a more technical word used in the context of textual correction. ▫▫ **a·mend·a·ble** *adj.* **a·mend·er** *n.*

a·mend·ment /әméndmәnt/ *n.* **1** a minor change in a document (esp. a legal or statutory one). **2** an article added to the US Constitution.

a·mends /әméndz/ *n.* ▫ **make amends** (often foll. by *for*) compensate (for).

a·men·i·ty /әménitee, әmée–/ *n.* (*pl.* **·ties**) **1** (usu. in *pl.*) a pleasant or useful feature. **2** pleasantness (of a place, person, etc.).

a·men·or·rhe·a /ayménәréeә/ *n. Med.* an abnormal absence of menstruation.

Am·er·a·sian /amәráyzhәn/ *n.* a person of American and Asian descent.

a·merce /әmɔ́rs/ *v.tr.* **1** *Law* punish by fine. **2** punish arbitrarily. ▫▫ **a·merce·ment** *n.* **a·merce·a·ble** *adj.*

A·mer·i·can /әmérikәn/ *adj. & n.* • *adj.* **1** of, relating to, or characteristic of the United States or its inhabitants. **2** (usu. in *comb.*) of or relating to the continents of America (*Latin-American*). • *n.* **1** a native or citizen of the United States. **2** (usu. in *comb.*) a native or inhabitant of the continents of America (*North Americans*). **3** (also **A·mer·i·can Eng·lish**) the English language as it is used in the United States.

A·mer·i·ca·na /әmérikánә, –kaánә, –káynә/ *n.pl.* things connected with America, esp. with the United States.

A·mer·i·can In·di·an *n.* a member of the aboriginal peoples of America or their descendants. ▶See note at INDIAN.

A·mer·i·can·ism /әmérikәnizәm/ *n.* **1 a** a word or phrase peculiar to or originating from the United States. **b** a thing or feature characteristic of or peculiar to the United States. **2** attachment to or sympathy for the United States.

A·mer·i·can·ize /әmérikәnīz/ *v.* **1** *tr.* **a** make American in character. **b** naturalize as an American. **2** *intr.* become American in character. ▫▫ **A·mer·i·can·i·za·tion** /–nizáyshәn/ *n.*

am·er·i·ci·um /ámәrísheeәm/ *n. Chem.* an artificially made transuranic radioactive metallic element. ¶ Symb.: **Am**.

Am·er·in·di·an /ámәrindeeәn/ *adj. & n.* (also **Am·er·ind** /ámәrínd/) = AMERICAN INDIAN. ▫▫ **Am·er·in·dic** /–ríndik/ *adj.*

am·e·thyst /ámithist/ *n.* a precious stone of a violet or purple variety of quartz. ▫▫ **am·e·thys·tine** /–thísteen/ *adj.*

a·mi·a·ble /áymeeəbəl/ *adj.* friendly and pleasant in temperament. ▫▫ **a·mi·a·bil·i·ty** /–bilitee/ *n.* **a·mi·a·bly** *adv.*

amiable late Middle English (originally in the senses 'kind,' and 'lovely, lovable'): via Old French from late Latin *amicabilis* 'amicable.' The current sense, influenced by modern French *aimable* 'trying to please,' dates from the mid-18th cent.

am·i·ca·ble /ámikəbəl/ *adj.* showing a friendly spirit. ▫▫ **am·i·ca·bly** *adv.*

am·ice /ámis/ *n.* a white linen cloth worn on the neck and shoulders by a priest celebrating the Eucharist.

a·mid /əmíd/ *prep.* (also **a·midst** /əmídst/) **1** in the middle of. **2** in the course of.

am·ide /áymīd, ám–/ *n. Chem.* a compound formed from ammonia.

a·mid·ships /əmídships/ *adv.* (also **a·mid·ship**) in or into the middle of a ship.

a·mi·go /əmeégō/ *n.* (*pl.* **·gos**) a friend, esp. in Spanish-speaking areas.

a·mine /əmeén, ámeen/ *n. Chem.* a compound formed from ammonia.

a·mi·no ac·id /əmeénō/ *n. Biochem.* any of a group of organic compounds containing both the carboxyl and amino groups, occurring naturally in plant and animal tissues and forming the basic constituents of proteins.

a·mir var. of EMIR.

a·miss /əmís/ *predic.adj. & adv.* •*predic.adj.* wrong (*something was amiss*).• *adv.* wrong (*everything went amiss*). ▫ **take amiss** be offended by.

am·i·trip·ty·line /ámitríptileen/ *n. Pharm.* an antidepressant drug that has a mild tranquilizing action.

am·i·ty /ámitee/ *n.* friendship; friendly relations.

am·me·ter /ám–meetər/ *n.* an instrument for measuring electric current in amperes.

am·mo /ámō/ *n. colloq.* ammunition.

am·mo·nia /əmṓnyə/ *n.* **1** a colorless gas with a characteristic pungent smell. **2** (in general use) a solution of ammonia gas in water.

am·mo·ni·a·cal /ámənīəkəl/ *adj.* of or containing ammonia or sal ammoniac.

am·mo·ni·at·ed /əmṓneeaytid/ *adj.* combined or treated with ammonia.

am·mo·nite /ámənīt/ *n.* any extinct cephalopod mollusk of the order Ammonoidea, with a flat coiled spiral shell found as a fossil.

am·mo·ni·um /əmṓneeəm/ *n.* the univalent ion NH_4^+, formed from ammonia.

am·mu·ni·tion /ámyənishən/ *n.* **1** a supply of projectiles (esp. bullets, shells, and grenades). **2** points used or usable to advantage in an argument.

am·ne·sia /amneézhə/ *n.* a partial or total loss of memory. ▫▫ **am·ne·si·ac** /–zeeak, –zheeak/ *n.* **am·ne·sic** *adj. & n.*

am·nes·ty /ámnistee/ *n. & v.* •*n.* (*pl.* **·ties**) a general pardon, esp. for political offenses. •*v.tr.* (**·ties, ·tied**) grant an amnesty to.

am·ni·o·cen·te·sis /ámneeōsenteésis/ *n.* (*pl.* **amniocenteses** /–seez/) *Med.* the sampling of amniotic fluid to determine certain abnormalities in an embryo.

am·ni·on /ámneeən/ *n.* (*pl.* **amnia** /–neeə/) *Zool. & Physiol.* the innermost membrane that encloses the embryo of a reptile, bird, or mammal. ▫▫ **am·ni·ot·ic** /ámneeótik/ *adj.*

a·moe·ba /əmeébə/ *n.* (also **a·me·ba**) (*pl.* **amoebas** or **amoebae** /–bee/) any usu. aquatic protozoan of the genus *Amoeba*, esp. *A. proteus*, capable of changing shape. ▫▫ **a·moe·bic** *adj.* **a·moe·boid** *adj.*

a·mok /əmúk, əmók/ *adv.* (also **a·muck** /əmúk/) ▫ **run amok** run about wildly in an uncontrollable violent rage.

a·mong /əmúng/ *prep.* (also **a·mongst** /əmúngst/) **1** surrounded by; in the company of. **2** in the number of (*among us were those who disagreed*). **3** in the class or category of (*is among the richest men alive*). **4** between; shared by (*had $5 among us*). **5** with one another; by the reciprocal action of (*talked among themselves*). ▶See note at BETWEEN.

a·mor·al /áymáwrəl, –mór–/ *adj.* **1** not concerned with morality (cf. IMMORAL). **2** having no moral principles. ▫▫ **a·mor·al·ism** *n.* **a·mo·ral·i·ty** /–rálitee/ *n.* ▶See note at IMMORAL.

a·mo·ro·so /áməróśō/ *adv. & adj. Mus.* in a loving or tender manner.

am·o·rous /ámərəs/ *adj.* **1** showing, feeling, or inclined to sexual love. **2** of or relating to sexual love. ▫▫ **am·o·rous·ly** *adv.* **am·o·rous·ness** *n.*

a·mor·phous /əmáwrfəs/ *adj.* **1** shapeless. **2** vague; ill-organized. **3** *Mineral. & Chem.* having neither definite form nor structure. ▫▫ **a·mor·phous·ly** *adv.* **a·mor·phous·ness** *n.*

am·or·tize /ámərtīz, əmáwr–/ *v.tr. Commerce* **1** gradually extinguish (a debt) by money regularly put aside. **2** gradually write off the initial cost of (assets). ▫▫ **am·or·ti·za·tion** /–tizáyshən/ *n.*

a·mount /əmównt/ *n. & v.* •*n.* a quantity, esp. the total of a thing or things in number, size, value, extent, etc. (*a large amount of money*). •*v.intr.* (foll. by *to*) **1** be equivalent to in number, size, significance, etc. (*amounted to $100*). **2** (of a person) become (*might one day amount to something*).

a·mour /əmóór/ *n.* a love affair, esp. a secret one.

a·mour pro·pre /aámoorr práwprə/ *n.* self-respect.

amp[1] /amp/ *n. Electr.* an ampere.

amp[2] /amp/ *n. colloq.* an amplifier.

am·per·age /ámpərij/ *n. Electr.* the strength of an electric current in amperes.

am·pere /ámpeer/ *n. Electr.* the SI base unit of electric current.

am·per·sand /ámpərsand/ *n.* the sign & (= *and*).

am·phet·a·mine /amfétəmeen, –min/ *n.* a synthetic drug used esp. as a stimulant.

amphi- /ámfee/ *comb.form* **1** both. **2** of both kinds. **3** on both sides. **4** around.

am·phib·i·an /amfíbeeən/ *adj. & n.* •*adj.* **1** living on land and in water. **2** *Zool.* of or relating to the class Amphibia. **3** (of a vehicle) able to operate on land and water. •*n.* **1** *Zool.* any vertebrate of the class Amphibia, with an aquatic gill-breathing larval stage followed by a terrestrial lung-breathing adult stage, including frogs, toads, and salamanders. **2** (in general use) a creature living on land and in water. **3** an amphibian vehicle.

amphibian mid-17th cent. (in the sense 'having two modes of existence or of doubtful nature'): from modern Latin *amphibium* 'an amphibian,' from Greek *amphibion* (noun use of *amphibios* 'living both in water and on land,' from *amphi* 'both' + *bios* 'life').

am·phib·i·ous /amfíbeeəs/ *adj.* **1** living on land and in water. **2** relating to or suited for land and water. **3** *Mil.* **a** (of a military operation) involving forces landed from the sea. **b** (of forces) trained for such operations. ▫▫ **am·phib·i·ous·ly** *adv.*

am·phi·the·a·ter /ámfitheeətər/ *n.* **1** a round, usu. unroofed building with tiers of seats surrounding a central space. **2** a semicircular gallery in a theater. **3** a large circular hollow. **4** the scene of a contest.

am·pho·ra /ámfərə/ *n.* (*pl.* **amphorae** /–ree/ or **amphoras**) a Greek or Roman vessel with two handles and a narrow neck.
am·pi·cil·lin /ámpisílin/ *n. Pharm.* a semisynthetic penicillin used esp. in treating infections of the urinary and respiratory tracts.
am·ple /ámpəl/ *adj.* (**ampler, amplest**) **1 a** plentiful; abundant; extensive. **b** *euphem.* (esp. of a person) large; stout. **2** enough or more than enough. ▫▫ **am·ple·ness** *n.* **am·ply** *adv.*
am·pli·fi·er /ámplifīər/ *n.* an electronic device for increasing the strength of electrical signals, esp. for conversion into sound in radio, etc., equipment.
am·pli·fy /ámplifī/ *v.* (**·fies, ·fied**) **1** *tr.* increase the volume or strength of (sound, electrical signals, etc.). **2** *tr.* add detail to (a story, etc.). ▫▫ **am·pli·fi·ca·tion** /–fikáyshən/ *n.*
am·pli·tude /ámplitood, –tyood/ *n.* **1** *Physics* the maximum extent of a vibration from the position of equilibrium. **2** *Electr.* the maximum departure of the value of an alternating current or wave from the average value.
am·pli·tude mod·u·la·tion *n. Electr.* **1** the modulation of a wave by variation of its amplitude. **2** the system using such modulation.
am·poule /ámpyool, –pool/ *n.* (also **am·pule** or **am·pul**) a small capsule in which measured quantities of liquids or solids, esp. for injecting, are sealed ready for use.
am·pul·la /ampóolə/ *n.* (*pl.* **ampullae** /–ee/) **1** a Roman globular flask with two handles. **2** a vessel for sacred uses.
am·pu·tate /ámpyətayt/ *v.tr.* cut off by surgical operation (a part of the body, esp. a limb). ▫▫ **am·pu·ta·tion** /–táyshən/ *n.* **am·pu·ta·tor** *n.*
am·pu·tee /ámpyətée/ *n.* a person who has lost a limb, etc., by amputation.
am·trac /ámtrak/ *n.* (also **am·track**) an amphibious tracked vehicle used for landing assault troops on a shore.
Am·trak /ámtrak/ *n. Trademark* US passenger railroad system.
amu *abbr.* atomic mass unit.
a·muck var. of AMOK.
am·u·let /ámyəlit/ *n.* an ornament worn as a charm against evil.
a·muse /əmyóoz/ *v.* **1** *tr.* cause (a person) to laugh or smile. **2** *tr.* & *refl.* (often foll. by *with*, *by*) interest or occupy; keep (a person) entertained. ▫▫ **a·mus·ing** *adj.* **a·mus·ing·ly** *adv.*
a·muse·ment /əmyóozmənt/ *n.* **1** something that amuses, esp. a pleasant diversion, game, or pastime. **2** the state of being amused.
a·muse·ment park *n.* a park with rides such as a merry-go-round, Ferris wheel, roller coaster, etc.
a·myg·da·loid nu·cle·us /əmígdəloyd/ *n.* a roughly almond-shaped mass of gray matter deep inside each cerebral hemisphere.
am·yl·ase /ámilays, –layz/ *n. Biochem.* any of several enzymes that convert starch and glycogen into simple sugars.
a·my·o·troph·ic lat·er·al scle·ro·sis /aymīətrófik, –tró–/ *n.* an incurable degenerative disease of the nervous system marked by increasing muscle weakness and eventual paralysis. Also called **Lou Gehrig's disease**.
an /an, ən/ *adj.* the form of the indefinite article (see A[1]) used before words beginning with a vowel sound (*an egg*; *an hour*).
▶Now less often used before aspirated words beginning with *h* and stressed on a syllable other than the first (so *a hotel*, not *an hotel*).
an- /ən, an/ *prefix* not; without (*anarchy*) (cf. A-).
-ana /ánə, aánə, áynə/ *suffix* forming plural nouns meaning 'things associated with' (*Victoriana*; *Americana*).
An·a·bap·tism /ánəbáptizəm/ *n.* the doctrine that baptism should only be administered to believing adults. ▫▫ **An·a·bap·tist** *n.*
an·a·bol·ic /ánəbólik/ *adj. Biochem.* of or relating to anabolism.
an·a·bol·ic ste·roid *n.* any of a group of synthetic steroid hormones used to increase muscle size.
a·nab·o·lism /ənábəlizəm/ *n. Biochem.* the synthesis of complex molecules in living organisms from simpler ones together with the storage of energy; constructive metabolism (opp. CATABOLISM).
an·a·branch /ánəbranch/ *n.* a stream that leaves a river and reenters it lower down.
a·nach·ro·nism /ənákrənizəm/ *n.* **1 a** the attribution of a custom, event, etc., to a period to which it does not belong. **b** a thing attributed in this way. **2** an old-fashioned or out-of-date person or thing. ▫▫ **a·nach·ro·nis·tic** /–nístik/ *adj.* **a·nach·ro·nis·ti·cal·ly** *adv.*
an·a·co·lu·thon /ánəkəlóothon/ *n.* (*pl.* **anacolutha** /–thə/) a sentence or construction that lacks grammatical sequence (e.g., *while in the garden the door banged shut*). ▫▫ **an·a·co·lu·thic** *adj.*
an·a·con·da /ánəkóndə/ *n.* a large nonpoisonous snake that kills its prey by constriction.
an·a·cru·sis /ánəkróosis/ *n.* (*pl.* **anacruses** /–seez/) **1** (in poetry) an unstressed syllable at the beginning of a verse. **2** *Mus.* an unstressed note or notes before the first bar line.
an·aer·obe /ánərōb, anáirōb/ *n.* an organism that grows without air. ▫▫ **an·aer·o·bic** *adj.*
an·a·gram /ánəgram/ *n.* a word or phrase formed by transposing the letters of another word or phrase. ▫▫ **an·a·gram·mat·ic** /–mátik/ *adj.* **an·a·gram·mat·i·cal** *adj.* **an·a·gram·ma·tize** /–grámətīz/ *v.tr.*
a·nal /áynəl/ *adj.* **1** relating to or situated near the anus. **2** = ANAL RETENTIVE. ▫▫ **a·nal·ly** *adv.*
an·a·lects /ánəlekts/ *n.pl.* (also **an·a·lec·ta** /ánəléktə/) a collection of short literary extracts.
an·a·lep·tic /ánəléptik/ *adj.* & *n.* • *adj.* restorative. • *n.* a restorative medicine or drug.
an·al·ge·si·a /ánəljéezeeə, –seeə/ *n.* the absence or relief of pain.
an·al·ge·sic /ánəljéezik, –sik/ *adj.* & *n.* • *adj.* relieving pain. • *n.* an analgesic drug.
an·a·log /ánəlog/ *n.* **1** an analogous or parallel thing. **2** (*attrib.*) (of a computer or electronic process) using physical variables, e.g., voltage, weight, or length, to represent numbers (cf. DIGITAL).
a·nal·o·gize /ənáləjīz/ *v.* **1** *tr.* represent or explain by analogy. **2** *intr.* use analogy.
a·nal·o·gous /ənáləgəs/ *adj.* (usu. foll. by *to*) partially similar or parallel; showing analogy. ▫▫ **a·nal·o·gous·ly** *adv.*
an·a·logue var. of ANALOG.
a·nal·o·gy /ənáləjee/ *n.* (*pl.* **·gies**) **1** (usu. foll. by *to*, *with*, *between*) correspondence or partial similarity. **2** *Biol.* the resemblance of function between organs essentially different. **3** = ANALOG 1. ▫▫ **an·a·log·i·cal** /ánəlójikəl/ *adj.* **an·a·log·i·cal·ly** *adv.*
a·nal re·ten·tive *adj.* (of a person) excessively orderly and fussy (supposedly owing to aspects of toilet training in infancy).
a·nal·y·sand /ənálisand/ *n.* a person undergoing psychoanalysis.
a·nal·y·sis /ənálisis/ *n.* (*pl.* **analyses** /–seez/) **1 a** a detailed examination of the elements or structure of a substance, etc. **b** a statement of the result of this. **2** *Chem.* the determination of the constituent parts of a mixture or compound. **3** psychoanalysis.

an·a·lyst /ánəlist/ *n.* **1** a person skilled in (esp. chemical) analysis. **2** a psychoanalyst.

an·a·lyt·ic /ánəlítik/ *adj.* of or relating to analysis.

an·a·lyt·i·cal /ánəlítikəl/ *adj.* using analytic methods. ▫▫ **an·a·lyt·i·cal·ly** *adv.*

an·a·lyt·i·cal ge·om·e·try *n.* geometry using coordinates.

an·a·lyze /ánəlīz/ *v.tr.* **1** examine in detail the constitution or structure of. **2** *Chem.* ascertain the constituents of (a sample of a mixture or compound). **3** find or show the essence or structure of (a book, music, etc.). **4** psychoanalyze. ▫▫ **an·a·lyz·a·ble** *adj.* **an·a·lyz·er** *n.*

an·a·pest /ánəpest/ *n. Prosody* a foot consisting of two short or unstressed syllables followed by one long or stressed syllable. ▫▫ **an·a·pes·tic** /–péstik/ *adj.*

a·naph·o·ra /ənáfərə/ *n.* **1** *Rhet.* the repetition of a word or phrase at the beginning of successive clauses. **2** *Gram.* the use of a word referring to or replacing a word used earlier in a sentence (e.g., *do* in *I like it and so do they*). ▫▫ **an·a·phor·ic** /ánəfórik/ *adj.*

an·aph·ro·dis·i·ac /anáfrədeézeeak, –díz–/ *adj. & n.* • *adj.* tending to reduce sexual desire. • *n.* an anaphrodisiac drug.

an·a·phy·lax·is /ánəfiláksis/ *n.* (*pl.* **anaphylaxes** /–seez/) *Med.* hypersensitivity of tissues to a dose of antigen, as a reaction against a previous dose. ▫▫ **an·a·phy·lac·tic** /–láktik/ *adj.*

an·ar·chism /ánərkizəm/ *n.* the doctrine that all government should be abolished.

an·ar·chist /ánərkist/ *n.* an advocate of anarchism or of political disorder. ▫▫ **an·ar·chis·tic** *adj.*

an·ar·chy /ánərkee/ *n.* **1** disorder, esp. political or social. **2** lack of government in a society. ▫▫ **an·ar·chic** /ənaárkik/ *adj.* **an·ar·chi·cal** *adj.* **an·ar·chi·cal·ly** *adv.*

A·na·sa·zi /onəsaázee/ *n.* **1 a** a prehistoric N. American people native to the southwestern US. **b** a member of this people. **2** the language of this people.

an·as·tig·mat·ic /ánəstigmátik/ *adj.* free from astigmatism.

a·nas·to·mose /ənástəmōz, –mōs/ *v.intr.* link by anastomosis.

a·nas·to·mo·sis /ənástəmṓsis/ *n.* (*pl.* **anastomoses** /–seez/) a cross-connection of arteries, branches, rivers, etc.

a·nas·tro·phe /ənástrəfee/ *n. Rhet.* the inversion of the usual order of words or clauses.

a·nath·e·ma /ənáthəmə/ *n.* (*pl.* **anathemas**) **1** a detested thing or person (*is anathema to me*). **2 a** an ecclesiastical curse, excommunicating a person or denouncing a doctrine. **b** a cursed thing or person. **c** a strong curse.

a·nath·e·ma·tize /ənáthəmətīz/ *v.tr. & intr.* curse.

an·a·tom·i·cal /ánətómikəl/ *adj.* **1** of or relating to anatomy. **2** structural. ▫▫ **an·a·tom·i·cal·ly** *adv.*

a·nat·o·mize /ənátəmīz/ *v.tr.* **1** examine in detail. **2** dissect.

a·nat·o·my /ənátəmee/ *n.* (*pl.* **·mies**) **1** the science of the bodily structure of animals and plants. **2** this structure. **3** *colloq.* a human body. **4** analysis.

ANC *abbr.* African National Congress.

an·ces·tor /ánsestər/ *n.* (*fem.* **ancestress** /–stris/) **1** any (esp. remote) person from whom one is descended. **2** an early type of animal or plant from which others have evolved. **3** an early prototype.

an·ces·tral /anséstrəl/ *adj.* belonging to or inherited from one's ancestors.

an·ces·try /ánsestree/ *n.* (*pl.* **·tries**) one's (esp. remote) family descent.

an·chor /ángkər/ *n. & v.* • *n.* **1** a heavy metal weight used to moor a ship to the seafloor or a balloon to the ground. **2** (in full **anchorman, anchorperson, anchorwoman**) **a** a person who plays a vital part, as the end member of a tug-of-war team, the last member of a relay team, etc. **b** a news broadcaster who introduces segments and reads the main portion of the news. • *v.* **1** *tr.* secure (a ship or balloon) by means of an anchor. **2** *tr.* fix firmly. **3** *intr.* be moored by means of an anchor. ▫ **cast** (or **come to**) **anchor** let the anchor down. **weigh anchor** take the anchor up.

an·chor·age /ángkərij/ *n.* a place where a ship may be anchored.

an·cho·rite /ángkərīt/ *n.* (*fem.* **anchoress** /–ris/) **1** a hermit; a religious recluse. **2** a person of secluded habits. ▫▫ **an·cho·ret·ic** /–rétik/ *adj.* **an·cho·rit·ic** /–rítik/ *adj.*

an·chor·man /ángkərmən/ *n.* (*pl.* **·men**) = ANCHOR *n.* 2.

an·cho·vy /ánchṓvee/ *n.* (*pl.* **·vies**) any of various small silvery fish of the herring family usu. preserved in salt and oil and having a strong taste.

an·cien ré·gime /onsyáN rezheém/ *n.* (*pl.* **anciens régimes** *pronunc.* same) **1** the political and social system in France before the Revolution of 1789. **2** any superseded regime.

an·cient /áynshənt/ *adj. & n.* • *adj.* **1** of long ago. **2** having existed long. • *n.* **1** *archaic* an old man. **2** (*pl.*) the people of ancient times, esp. the Greeks and Romans. ▫▫ **an·cient·ness** *n.*

an·cient his·to·ry *n.* **1** the history of the ancient civilizations of the Mediterranean area and the Near East before the fall of the Western Roman Empire in 476. **2** something already long familiar.

an·cil·lar·y /ánsəleree/ *adj. & n.* • *adj.* **1** providing essential support to a central service or industry. **2** (often foll. by *to*) subordinate. • *n.* (*pl.* **·ies**) **1** an ancillary worker. **2** something which is ancillary.

and /and, ənd/ *conj.* **1 a** connecting words, clauses, or sentences, that are to be taken jointly (*cakes and pastries; buy and sell*). **b** implying progression (*better and better*). **c** implying causation (*do that and I'll hit you*). **d** implying great duration (*he cried and cried*). **e** implying a great number (*miles and miles*). **f** implying addition (*two and two are four*). **g** implying variety (*there are books and books*). **2** *colloq.* to (*try and open it*). **3** in relation to (*Britain and the US*).

an·dan·te /aandaántay/ *adv., adj., & n. Mus.* • *adv. & adj.* in a moderately slow tempo. • *n.* an andante passage or movement.

an·dan·ti·no /aándaanteénō/ *adv., adj., & n. Mus.* • *adv. & adj.* somewhat quicker than andante. • *n.* (*pl.* **·nos**) an andantino passage or movement.

and·i·ron /ándīrn/ *n.* a metal stand (usu. one of a pair) for supporting burning wood in a fireplace; a firedog.

an·dro·gen /ándrəjən/ *n.* a male sex hormone or other substance capable of developing and maintaining certain male sexual characteristics. ▫▫ **an·dro·gen·ic** /–jénik/ *adj.*

an·drog·y·nous /andrójinəs/ *adj.* **1** hermaphroditic. **2** not clearly male or female; exhibiting the appearance or attributes of both sexes. **3** *Bot.* with stamens and pistils in the same flower or inflorescence. ▫▫ **an·drog·y·ny** *n.*

an·droid /ándroyd/ *n.* a robot with a human form or appearance.

an·ec·dote /ánikdōt/ *n.* a short account of an entertaining or interesting incident. ▫▫ **an·ec·do·tal** /–dṓt'l/ *adj.*

a·ne·mi·a /əneémeeə/ *n.* a deficiency in the blood, usu. of red cells or their hemoglobin, resulting in pallor and weariness.

a·ne·mic /əneémik/ *adj.* **1** relating to or suffering from anemia. **2** pale; lacking in vitality.

an·e·mom·e·ter /ánimómitər/ *n.* an instrument for measuring the force of the wind.

an•e•mom•e•try /ánimómitree/ *n.* the measurement of the force, direction, etc., of the wind. ▫▫ **an•e•mo•met•ric** /–məmétrik/ *adj.*

a•nem•o•ne /ənémənee/ *n.* a plant akin to the buttercup, with flowers of various vivid colors.

an•er•oid /ánəroyd/ *adj. & n.* • *adj.* (of a barometer) that measures air pressure by its action on the elastic lid of an evacuated box. • *n.* an aneroid barometer.

an•es•the•sia /ánis–theézhə/ *n.* the absence of sensation, esp. artificially induced before surgery. ▫▫ **an•es•the•si•ol•o•gy** /–zeeóləjee/ *n.*

an•es•thet•ic /ánis–thétik/ *adj. & n.* • *n.* a substance that produces insensibility to pain, etc. • *adj.* producing partial or complete insensibility to pain, etc.

an•es•the•tist /ənés–thətist/ *n.* a specialist in the administration of anesthetics.

an•es•the•tize /ənés–thətīz/ *v.tr.* **1** administer an anesthetic to. **2** deprive of physical or mental sensation. ▫▫ **an•es•the•ti•za•tion** /–tizáyshən/ *n.*

an•eu•rysm /ányərizəm/ *n.* (also **an•eu•rism**) an excessive localized enlargement of an artery. ▫▫ **an•eu•rys•mal** /–rízməl/ *adj.* (also **an•eu•ris•mal**).

a•new /ənóō, ənyóō/ *adv.* **1** again. **2** in a different way.

an•gel /áynjəl/ *n.* **1 a** a spiritual being believed to act as an attendant or messenger of God. **b** a representation of this in human form with wings. **c** an attendant spirit (*guardian angel*). **2 a** a very virtuous person. **b** an obliging person. **3** *sl.* a financial backer of an enterprise, esp. in the theater. **4** an unexplained radar echo.

an•gel dust *n. sl.* the hallucinogenic drug phencyclidine hydrochloride.

an•gel•fish /áynjəlfish/ *n.* any of various fish, esp. *Pterophyllum scalare*, with large dorsal and ventral fins.

an•gel food cake *n.* a very light sponge cake.

an•gel•ic /anjélik/ *adj.* **1** like or relating to angels. **2** having characteristics attributed to angels, esp. beauty or innocence. ▫▫ **an•gel•i•cal•ly** *adv.*

an•ge•lus /ánjiləs/ *n.* **1** a Roman Catholic devotion said at morning, noon, and sunset. **2** a bell rung to announce this.

an•ger /ánggər/ *n. & v.* • *n.* extreme displeasure. • *v.tr.* make angry.

an•gi•na /anjínə, ánjənə/ *n.* **1** an attack of intense constricting pain often causing suffocation. **2** (in full **angina pectoris** /péktəris/) pain in the chest brought on by exertion, owing to an inadequate blood supply to the heart.

an•gi•o•gram /ánjeeəgram/ *n.* an X-ray taken by angiography.

an•gi•og•ra•phy /anjeeáagrəfee/ *n.* the visualization by X-ray of blood vessels following injection with a substance that is opaque to X-rays.

an•gi•o•sperm /ánjeeəspərm/ *n.* any plant producing flowers and reproducing by seeds enclosed within a carpel. ▫▫ **an•gi•o•sper•mous** /–spármәs/ *adj.*

An•gle /ánggəl/ *n.* (usu. in *pl.*) a member of a tribe from Schleswig, Germany, that settled in Eastern Britain in the 5th c. ▫▫ **An•gli•an** *adj.*

an•gle[1] /ánggəl/ *n. & v.* • *n.* **1 a** the space between two meeting lines or surfaces. **b** the inclination of two lines or surfaces to each other. **2 a** a corner. **b** a sharp projection. **3 a** the direction from which a photograph, etc., is taken. **b** the aspect from which a matter is considered. **c** an approach, technique, etc. • *v.* **1** *tr. & intr.* point in a particular direction. **2** *tr.* present (information) from a particular point of view.

an•gle[2] /ánggəl/ *v.intr.* **1** (often foll. by *for*) fish with hook and line. **2** (foll. by *for*) seek an objective by devious or calculated means.

an•gle brack•ets *n.pl.* brackets in the form <> (see BRACKET *n.* 3).

an•gled /ánggəld/ *adj.* **1** placed at an angle to something else. **2** presented to suit a particular point of view. **3** having an angle.

an•gler /ángglər/ *n.* a person who fishes with a hook and line.

an•gler•fish /ángglərfish/ *n.* any of various fishes that prey upon small fish, attracting them by filaments arising from the dorsal fin: also called FROGFISH.

An•gli•can /ánglikən/ *adj. & n.* • *adj.* of or relating to the Church of England. • *n.* a member of an Anglican Church. ▫▫ **An•gli•can•ism** *n.*

An•gli•cism /ánglisizəm/ *n.* **1** a peculiarly English word or custom. **2** Englishness. **3** preference for what is English.

An•gli•cize /ánglisīz/ *v.tr.* make English in form or character.

An•glo /áŋgglō/ *n.* (*pl.* **•glos**) **1** a person of British or northern European origin. **2** a white, English-speaking person not of Hispanic descent.

Anglo- /áŋgglō/ *comb.form* **1** English (*Anglo-Catholic*). **2** of English origin (*an Anglo-American*). **3** English or British and (*an Anglo-American agreement*).

An•glo•cen•tric /áŋgglōséntrik/ *adj.* considered in terms of England.

An•glo-French /áŋgglōfrénch/ *adj. & n.* • *adj.* **1** English or British and French. **2** of Anglo-French. • *n.* the French language as retained and separately developed in England after the Norman Conquest.

An•glo•phile /áŋggləfīl/ *n. & adj.* (also **An•glo•phil** /–fil/) • *n.* a person who greatly admires England or the English. • *adj.* being an Anglophile.

An•glo•phobe /áŋggləfōb/ *n. & adj.* • *n.* a person who greatly hates or fears England or the English. • *adj.* being an Anglophobe.

An•glo•pho•bi•a /áŋggləfóbeeə/ *n.* intense hatred or fear of England or the English.

an•glo•phone /áŋggləfōn/ *adj. & n.* • *adj.* English-speaking. • *n.* an English-speaking person.

An•glo-Sax•on /áŋgglōsáksən/ *adj. & n.* • *adj.* **1** of the English Saxons before the Norman Conquest. **2** of the Old English people as a whole before the Norman Conquest. **3** of English descent. • *n.* **1** an Anglo-Saxon person. **2** the Old English language. **3** *colloq.* plain (esp. crude) English.

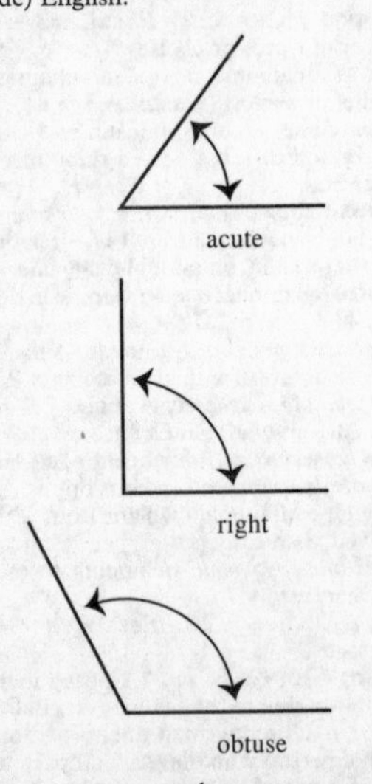

angles

an·go·ra /anggáwrə/ *n.* **1** a fabric made from the hair of the angora goat or rabbit. **2** a long-haired variety of cat, goat, or rabbit.

an·go·ra wool *n.* a mixture of sheep's wool and angora rabbit hair.

an·gos·tu·ra /ánggəstŏŏrə, –styŏŏrə/ *n.* (in full **angostura bark**) an aromatic bitter bark used as a flavoring, and formerly as a tonic and to reduce fever.

an·gry /ánggree/ *adj.* (**angrier, angriest**) **1** feeling or showing anger. **2** (of a sore, etc.) inflamed; painful. **3** suggesting anger (*an angry sky*). ◻◻ **an·gri·ly** *adv.*

angst /aangkst/ *n.* **1** anxiety. **2** a feeling of guilt or remorse.

ang·strom /ángstrəm/ *n.* (also **ångström** /áwngström/) a unit of length equal to 10^{-10} meter.

an·guish /ánggwish/ *n.* severe misery or suffering.

an·guished /ánggwisht/ *adj.* suffering or expressing anguish.

an·gu·lar /ánggyələr/ *adj.* **1 a** having angles or sharp corners. **b** (of a person) having sharp features. **c** awkward in manner. **2** forming an angle. **3** measured by angle. ◻◻ **an·gu·lar·i·ty** /–láritee/ *n.* **an·gu·lar·ly** *adv.*

an·hy·drous /anhídrəs/ *adj. Chem.* without water, esp. water of crystallization.

an·i·line /ánillin, –līn/ *n.* a colorless oily liquid, used in the manufacture of dyes, drugs, and plastics.

an·i·line dye *n.* **1** any of numerous dyes made from aniline. **2** any synthetic dye.

an·i·ma /ánimə/ *n. Psychol.* **1** the inner personality (opp. PERSONA). **2** Jung's term for the feminine part of a man's personality (opp. ANIMUS).

an·i·mad·vert /ánimadvárt/ *v.intr.* (foll. by *on*) criticize; censure (conduct, a fault, etc.). ◻◻ **an·i·mad·ver·sion** /–várzhən/ *n.*

an·i·mal /ánimәl/ *n.* & *adj.* • *n.* **1** a living organism which feeds on organic matter, usu. one with specialized sense organs and a nervous system. **2** such an organism other than human beings. **3** a brutish or uncivilized person. **4** *colloq.* a person or thing of any kind (*no such animal*). • *adj.* **1** characteristic of animals. **2** of animals as distinct from vegetables (*animal charcoal*). **3** characteristic of the physical needs of animals; carnal; sensual.

an·i·mal·ism /ánimәlizәm/ *n.* **1** the nature and activity of animals. **2** the belief that humans are not superior to other animals. **3** sensuality.

an·i·mate *adj.* & *v.* • *adj.* /ánimәt/ **1** having life. **2** lively. • *v.tr.* /ánimayt/ **1** enliven; make lively. **2** give life to. **3** inspire; actuate. **4** encourage. **5** produce using animation.

an·i·mat·ed /ánimaytid/ *adj.* **1** lively; vigorous. **2** having life. **3** (of a movie, etc.) using techniques of animation. ◻◻ **an·i·mat·ed·ly** *adv.* **an·i·ma·tor** *n.* (in sense 3).

an·i·ma·tion /ánimáyshən/ *n.* **1** vivacity; ardor. **2** the state of being alive. **3** *Cinematog.* the technique of filming successive drawings or positions of puppets, etc., to create an illusion of movement when the film is shown as a sequence.

an·i·mism /ánimizәm/ *n.* the attribution of a living soul to plants, inanimate objects, and natural phenomena. ◻◻ **an·i·mist** *n.* **an·i·mis·tic** /–místik/ *adj.*

an·i·mos·i·ty /ánimósitee/ *n.* (*pl.* **·ties**) a spirit or feeling of strong hostility.

an·i·mus /ánimәs/ *n.* **1** a display of animosity. **2** ill feeling. **3** a motivating spirit or feeling. **4** *Psychol.* Jung's term for the masculine part of a woman's personality (opp. ANIMA).

an·i·on /ánīən/ *n.* a negatively charged ion; an ion that is attracted to the anode in electrolysis (opp. CATION).

an·i·on·ic /ánīónik/ *adj.* **1** of an anion or anions. **2** having an active anion.

an·ise /ánis/ *n.* an umbelliferous plant, *Pimpinella anisum*, having aromatic seeds (see ANISEED).

an·i·seed /ániseed/ *n.* the seed of the anise, used to flavor liqueurs and candy.

ankh /angk/ *n.* a device consisting of a looped bar with a shorter crossbar, used in ancient Egypt as a symbol of life.

ankh

an·kle /ángkəl/ *n.* **1** the joint connecting the foot with the leg. **2** the part of the leg between this and the calf.

an·klet /ángklit/ *n.* an ornament or fetter worn around the ankle.

an·ky·lose /ángkilōs/ *v.tr.* & *intr.* (of bones or a joint) stiffen or unite by ankylosis.

an·ky·lo·sis /ángkilṓsis/ *n.* **1** the abnormal stiffening and immobility of a joint by fusion of the bones. **2** such fusion. ◻◻ **an·ky·lot·ic** /–lótik/ *adj.*

an·nal·ist /ánәlist/ *n.* a writer of annals. ◻◻ **an·nal·is·tic** /–lístik/ *adj.*

an·nals /ánәlz/ *n.pl.* **1** a narrative of events year by year. **2** historical records.

an·neal /əneel/ *v.* & *n.* • *v.tr.* **1** heat (metal or glass) and allow it to cool slowly, esp. to toughen it. **2** toughen. • *n.* treatment by annealing. ◻◻ **an·neal·er** *n.*

an·ne·lid /án'lid/ *n.* any segmented worm of the phylum Annelida, e.g., earthworms, lugworms, etc.

an·nex *v.* & *n.* • *v.tr.* /anéks, áneks/ **1** add as a subordinate part. **2** incorporate (territory of another) into one's own. **3** add as a condition. **4** *colloq.* take without right. • *n.* (*Brit.* also **annexe** /áneks, ániks/) **1** a separate or added building. **2** an addition to a document. ◻◻ **an·nex·a·tion** /–sáyshən/ *n.*

an·ni·hi·late /ənīəlayt/ *v.tr.* **1** completely destroy. **2** defeat utterly; make insignificant or powerless. ◻◻ **an·ni·hi·la·tor** *n.*

an·ni·hi·la·tion /ənīəláyshən/ *n.* the act or process of annihilating.

an·ni·ver·sa·ry /ánivə́rsəree/ *n.* (*pl.* **·ries**) **1** the date on which an event took place in a previous year. **2** the celebration of this.

An·no Dom·i·ni /ánō dómini, –nee/ *adv.* in the year of our Lord; in the year of the Christian era.

an·no·tate /ánōtayt/ *v.tr.* add explanatory notes to (a book, document, etc.). ◻◻ **an·no·tat·a·ble** *adj.* **an·no·ta·tion** /–táyshən/ *n.* **an·no·ta·tor** *n.*

an·nounce /ənówns/ *v.* **1** *tr.* (often foll. by *that*) make publicly known. **2** *tr.* make known the arrival or imminence of (a guest, dinner, etc.). **3** be a sign of.

an·nounce·ment /ənównsmənt/ *n.* **1** the action of announcing; something announced. **2** an official communication or statement. **3** an advertisement.

an·nounc·er /ənównsər/ *n.* a person who announces, esp. introducing programs or describing sports events in broadcasting.

an·noy /ənóy/ *v.tr.* **1** cause slight anger or mental distress to. **2** (in *passive*) be somewhat angry. **3** harass repeatedly. ◻◻ **an·noy·er** *n.* **an·noy·ing** *adj.*

an·noy·ance /ənóyəns/ *n.* **1** irritation; vexation. **2** something that annoys.

an·nu·al /ányōōəl/ *adj.* & *n.* • *adj.* **1** reckoned by the year. **2** occurring every year. **3** living or lasting for one year. • *n.* **1** a book, etc., published once a year. **2** a plant that lives only for a year or less. ◻◻ **an·nu·al·ly** *adv.*

an·nu·al·ized /ányōōəlīzd/ *adj.* (of rates of interest, inflation, etc.) calculated on an annual basis, as a projection from figures obtained for a shorter period.

an·nu·i·ty /ənṓōitee, ənyṓō–/ *n.* (*pl.* **·ties**) **1** a yearly grant or allowance. **2** an investment of money entitling the investor to a series of equal annual sums.

---

an•nul /ənúl/ *v.tr.* (**annulled, annulling**) **1** declare (a marriage, etc.) invalid. **2** cancel; abolish. ▫▫ **an•nul•ment** *n.*

an•nu•lar /ányələr/ *adj.* ring-shaped; forming a ring. ▫▫ **an•nu•lar•ly** *adv.*

an•nu•late /ányələt, –layt/ *adj.* having rings; marked with or formed of rings. ▫▫ **an•nu•la•tion** /–láyshən/ *n.*

an•nu•lus /ányələs/ *n.* (*pl.* **annuli** /–lī/) esp. *Math. & Biol.* a ring.

an•nun•ci•ate /ənúnseeayt/ *v.tr.* **1** proclaim. **2** indicate as coming or ready.

an•nun•ci•a•tion /ənúnseeáyshən/ *n.* **1** (**Annunciation**) **a** the announcing of the Incarnation, related in Luke 1:26–38. **b** the festival commemorating this on March 25. **2 a** the act or process of announcing. **b** an announcement.

an•nus mi•ra•bi•lis /ánəs mirábilis/ *n.* a remarkable or auspicious year.

an•ode /ánōd/ *n. Electr.* **1** the positively charged electrode by which electrons leave an electric device. **2** the negatively charged electrode of a device supplying current, e.g., a primary cell. ▫▫ **an•od•al** *adj.* **an•od•ic** /ənódik/ *adj.*

an•ode ray *n.* a beam of particles emitted from the anode of a high vacuum tube.

an•o•dize /ánədīz/ *v.tr.* coat (a metal, esp. aluminum) with a protective oxide layer by electrolysis. ▫▫ **an•o•diz•er** *n.*

an•o•dyne /ánədīn/ *adj.* **1** able to relieve pain. **2** mentally soothing.

a•noint /ənóynt/ *v.tr.* **1** apply oil or ointment to, esp. as a religious ceremony. **2** (usu. foll. by *with*) smear; rub. ▫▫ **a•noint•er** *n.*

a•nom•a•lous /ənóməlәs/ *adj.* having an irregular or deviant feature; abnormal. ▫▫ **a•nom•a•lous•ly** *adv.* **a•nom•a•lous•ness** *n.*

a•nom•a•ly /ənóməlee/ *n.* (*pl.* **•lies**) **1** an anomalous circumstance or thing; an irregularity. **2** irregularity of motion, behavior, etc.

an•o•mie /ánəmee/ *n.* (also **an•o•my**) lack of the usual social or ethical standards in an individual or group. ▫▫ **a•nom•ic** /ənómik/ *adj.*

a•non /ənón/ *adv. archaic* or *literary* soon; shortly.

anon. /ənón/ *abbr.* anonymous; an anonymous author.

an•o•nym /ánənim/ *n.* **1** an anonymous person or publication. **2** a pseudonym.

a•non•y•mous /ənónimәs/ *adj.* **1** of unknown name. **2** of unknown or undeclared source or authorship. **3** without character; featureless; impersonal. ▫▫ **an•o•nym•i•ty** /ánənímitee/ *n.* **a•non•y•mous•ly** *adv.*

a•noph•e•les /ənófileez/ *n.* any of various mosquitoes of the genus *Anopheles*, many of which are carriers of the malarial parasite.

an•o•rak /ánərak/ *n.* a waterproof jacket, usu. with a hood, of a kind orig. used in polar regions.

an•o•rex•i•a /ánəréksееə/ *n.* **1** a lack or loss of appetite for food. **2** (in full **anorexia ner•vo•sa** /nərvṓsə/) a psychological illness characterized by an obsessive desire to lose weight by refusing to eat.

an•o•rex•ic /ánəréksik/ *adj. & n.* • *adj.* **1** characterized by a lack of appetite, esp. in anorexia nervosa. **2** *colloq.* extremely thin. • *n.* a person with anorexia.

an•oth•er /ənúthər/ *adj. & pron.* • *adj.* **1** an additional (*have another piece of cake*). **2** a person comparable to (*another Lincoln*). **3** a different (*quite another matter*). **4** some or any other (*will not do another person's work*). • *pron.* **1** an additional one (*have another*). **2** a different one (*take this book away and bring me another*). **3** some or any other one (*I love another*).

an•ov•u•lant /anóvyələnt/ *n. & adj. Pharm.* • *n.* a drug preventing ovulation. • *adj.* preventing ovulation.

an•swer /ánsər/ *n. & v.* • *n.* **1** something said or done in reaction to a question, statement, or circumstance. **2** the solution to a problem. • *v.* **1** *tr.* make an answer to (*answer me*). **2** *intr.* (often foll. by *to*) make an answer. **3** *tr.* respond to the summons or signal of (*answer the door*). **4** *tr.* be satisfactory for (a purpose or need). **5** *intr.* (foll. by *for, to*) be responsible (*you will answer to me for your conduct*). **6** *intr.* (foll. by *to*) correspond, esp. to a description. **7** *intr.* be satisfactory or successful.

an•swer•a•ble /ánsərəbəl/ *adj.* **1** (usu. foll. by *to, for*) responsible (*answerable to them for any accident*). **2** that can be answered.

an•swer•ing ma•chine *n.* a tape recorder which supplies a recorded answer to a telephone call and usu. records incoming messages.

an•swer•ing serv•ice *n.* a business that receives and answers telephone calls for its clients.

ant /ant/ *n.* any small insect of a widely distributed hymenopterous family, living in complex social colonies, and proverbial for industry.

ant- /ant/ assim. form of ANTI- before a vowel or *h* (*Antarctic*).

ant•ac•id /antásid/ *n. & adj.* • *n.* a substance that prevents or corrects acidity, esp. in the stomach. • *adj.* having these properties.

an•tag•o•nism /antágənizəm/ *n.* active opposition or hostility.

an•tag•o•nist /antágənist/ *n.* **1** an opponent or adversary. **2** *Biol.* a substance, muscle, or organ that partially or completely opposes the action of another. ▫▫ **an•tag•o•nis•tic** *adj.* **an•tag•o•nis•ti•cal•ly** *adv.*

an•tag•o•nize /antágənīz/ *v.tr.* **1** evoke hostility or opposition in. **2** (of one force, etc.) counteract or tend to neutralize (another).

Ant•arc•tic /antaárktik/ *adj. & n.* • *adj.* of the south polar regions. • *n.* this region.

Ant•arc•tic Cir•cle *n.* the parallel of latitude 66° 32′ S., forming an imaginary line around this region.

an•te /ántee/ *n. & v.* • *n.* **1** a stake put up by a player in poker, etc., before receiving cards. **2** an amount to be paid in advance. • *v.tr.* (**antes, anted**) **1** put up as an ante. **2 a** bet; stake. **b** (foll. by *up*) pay.

ante- /ántee/ *prefix* forming nouns and adjectives meaning 'before; preceding' (*anteroom*; *antenatal*).

ant•eat•er /ánteetər/ *n.* any of various mammals feeding on ants and termites.

an•te•bel•lum /ánteebéləm/ *adj.* occurring or existing before a particular war, esp. the US Civil War.

an•te•ced•ent /ántiseéd'nt/ *n. & adj.* • *n.* **1** a preceding thing or circumstance. **2** *Gram.* a word, phrase, clause, or sentence, to which another word refers. **3** (in *pl.*) history, esp. of a person. • *adj.* **1** (often foll. by *to*) previous. **2** presumptive; a priori. ▫▫ **an•te•ced•ence** /–d'ns/ *n.* **an•te•ced•ent•ly** *adv.*

an•te•cham•ber /ánteechaymbər/ *n.* a small room leading to a main one.

an•te•date /ántidáyt/ *v. & n.* • *v.tr.* **1** occur at a date earlier than. **2** assign an earlier date to (a document, event, etc.). • *n.* a date earlier than the actual one.

an•te•di•lu•vi•an /ánteediloóveeən/ *adj.* **1** of or belonging to the time before the Biblical flood. **2** *colloq.* very old or out of date.

an•te•lope /ántilōp/ *n.* (*pl.* same or **antelopes**) any of various deerlike ruminants of the family Bovidae, esp. abundant in Africa and typically tall, slender, graceful, and swift-moving with upward-pointing horns.

an•te•na•tal /ánteenáyt'l/ *adj.* **1** existing or occurring before birth; prenatal. **2** relating to the period of pregnancy.

an•ten•na /anténə/ *n.* **1** (*pl.* **antennae** /–ee/) *Zool.* one of a pair of mobile appendages on the heads of insects, crustaceans, etc., sensitive to touch and taste. **2** (*pl.*

antennas) a metal rod, wire, or other structure by which signals are transmitted or received as part of a radio or television transmission or receiving system.

an·te·pe·nul·ti·mate /ánteepinúltimət/ *adj.* last but two.

an·te·ri·or /anteéreeər/ *adj.* **1** nearer the front. **2** (often foll. by *to*) earlier; prior. ▫▫ **an·te·ri·or·i·ty** /–reeáwritee/ *n.* **an·te·ri·or·ly** *adv.*

an·te·room /ánteeroom, –room/ *n.* a small room leading to a main one.

ant·he·li·on /ant–héeleeən, anthée–/ *n.* (*pl.* **anthelia** /–liə/) a luminous halo projected on a cloud or fog bank opposite to the Sun.

an·them /ánthəm/ *n.* **1** an elaborate choral composition usu. based on a passage of scripture. **2** a solemn hymn of praise, etc., esp. = NATIONAL ANTHEM.

an·ther /ánthər/ *n. Bot.* the apical portion of a stamen containing pollen. ▫▫ **an·ther·al** *adj.*

ant·hill /ánt–hil/ *n.* a moundlike nest built by ants or termites.

an·thol·o·gize /anthóləjīz/ *v.tr. & intr.* compile or include in an anthology.

an·thol·o·gy /anthóləjee/ *n.* (*pl.* **·gies**) a published collection of passages from literature, songs, reproductions of paintings, etc. ▫▫ **an·thol·o·gist** *n.*

anthology mid-17th cent.: via French or medieval Latin from Greek *anthologia*, from *anthos* 'flower' + *-logia* 'collection' (from *legein* 'gather'). In Greek, the word originally denoted a collection of the 'flowers' of verse, i.e. small choice poems or epigrams, by various authors.

an·thra·cene /ánthrəseen/ *n.* a colorless crystalline aromatic hydrocarbon obtained by the distillation of crude oils and used in the manufacture of chemicals.

an·thra·cite /ánthrəsīt/ *n.* coal of a hard variety burning with little flame and smoke. ▫▫ **an·thra·cit·ic** /–sítik/ *adj.*

an·thrax /ánthraks/ *n.* a disease of sheep and cattle transmissible to humans.

anthropo- /ánthrəpō/ *comb.form* human; humankind.

an·thro·po·cen·tric /ánthrəpōséntrik/ *adj.* regarding humankind as the center of existence. ▫▫ **an·thro·po·cen·trist** *n.*

an·thro·poid /ánthrəpoyd/ *adj. & n.* • *adj.* **1** resembling a human being in form. **2** *colloq.* (of a person) apelike. • *n.* a being that is human in form only.

an·thro·pol·o·gy /ánthrəpóləjee/ *n.* **1** the study of humankind. **2** the study of the structure and evolution of human beings as animals. ▫▫ **an·thro·po·log·i·cal** /–pəlójikəl/ *adj.* **an·thro·pol·o·gist** *n.*

an·thro·pom·e·try /ánthrəpómitree/ *n.* the scientific study of the measurements of the human body. ▫▫ **an·thro·po·met·ric** /–pəmétrik/ *adj.*

an·thro·po·mor·phic /ánthrəpəmáwrfik/ *adj.* of or characterized by anthropomorphism. ▫▫ **an·thro·po·mor·phi·cal·ly** *adv.*

an·thro·po·mor·phism /ánthrəpəmáwrfizəm/ *n.* the attribution of a human form or personality to a god, animal, or thing. ▫▫ **an·thro·po·mor·phize** *v.tr.*

an·thro·po·mor·phous /ánthrəpəmáwrfəs/ *adj.* human in form.

an·thro·poph·a·gy /ánthrəpófəjee/ *n.* cannibalism. ▫▫ **an·thro·poph·a·gous** *adj.*

an·ti /ántee, –tī/ *prep. & n.* • *prep.* (also *absol.*) opposed to (*is anti everything; seems to be rather anti*). • *n.* (*pl.* **antis**) a person opposed to a particular policy, etc.

anti- /ántee/ *prefix* (also **ant-** before a vowel or *h*) forming nouns and adjectives meaning: **1** opposed to; against (*antivivisectionism*). **2** preventing (*antiscorbutic*). **3** the opposite of (*anticlimax*). **4** rival (*antipope*). **5** unlike the conventional form (*antihero*). **6** *Physics* the antiparticle of a specified particle (*antiproton*).

an·ti·a·bor·tion /ánteeəbáwrshən, ántī–/ *adj.* opposing abortion. ▫▫ **an·ti·a·bor·tion·ist** *n.*

an·ti·air·craft /ánteeáirkraft, ántī–/ *adj.* (of a gun, missile, etc.) used to attack enemy aircraft.

an·ti·bal·lis·tic mis·sile /ánteebəlístik, ántī–/ *n.* a missile designed for intercepting and destroying a ballistic missile while in flight.

an·ti·bi·o·sis /ánteebīṓsis, ántī–/ *n.* an antagonistic association between two organisms (esp. microorganisms), in which one is adversely affected (cf. SYMBIOSIS).

an·ti·bi·ot·ic /ántibīótik, ántī–/ *n. Pharm.* any of various substances (e.g., penicillin) produced by microorganisms or made synthetically, that can inhibit or destroy susceptible microorganisms.

an·ti·bod·y /ántibodee, ántī–/ *n.* (*pl.* **·ies**) any of various blood proteins produced in response to and then counteracting antigens.

an·tic /ántik/ *n.* **1** (usu. in *pl.*) absurd or foolish behavior. **2** an absurd or silly action.

An·ti·christ /ánteekrīst, ántī–/ *n.* an archenemy of Christ.

an·tic·i·pate /antísipayt/ *v.tr.* **1** deal with or use before the proper time. **2** *disp.* expect (*did not anticipate any difficulty*). **3** forestall (a person or thing). **4** look forward to. ▫▫ **an·tic·i·pa·tor** *n.* **an·tic·i·pa·to·ry** *adj.*

▶**Anticipate** in the sense 'expect, foresee' is well-established in informal use (e.g., *He anticipated a restless night*), but is regarded as incorrect by some people. The formal sense, 'deal with or use before the proper time,' is illustrated by the sentence *The doctor anticipated the possibility of a relapse by prescribing new medications.*

an·tic·i·pa·tion /antísipáyshən/ *n.* the act or process of anticipating.

an·ti·cli·max /ánteeklīmaks, ántī–/ *n.* a disappointingly trivial conclusion to something significant, esp. where a climax was expected. ▫▫ **an·ti·cli·mac·tic** /–máktik/ *adj.*

an·ti·co·ag·u·lant /ánteekō–ágyələnt, ántī–/ *n.* any drug or agent that retards or inhibits coagulation, esp. of the blood.

an·ti·con·vul·sant /ánteekənvúlsənt, ántī–/ *n.* any drug or agent that prevents or reduces the severity of convulsions, esp. as in epilepsy.

an·ti·cy·clone /ánteesīklōn, ántī–/ *n.* a system of winds rotating outwards from an area of high barometric pressure. ▫▫ **an·ti·cy·clon·ic** /–klónik/ *adj.*

an·ti·de·pres·sant /ánteedipresənt, ántī–/ *n.* any drug or agent that alleviates depression.

an·ti·dote /ántidōt/ *n.* **1** a medicine, etc., taken or given to counteract poison. **2** anything that counteracts something unpleasant or evil. ▫▫ **an·ti·dot·al** *adj.*

an·ti·freeze /ántifreez, ántee–/ *n.* a substance (usu. ethylene glycol) added to water to lower its freezing point, esp. in the radiator of a motor vehicle.

an·ti·gen /ántijən/ *n.* a foreign substance (e.g., toxin) that causes the body to produce antibodies. ▫▫ **an·ti·gen·ic** /–jénik/ *adj.*

an·ti·grav·i·ty /ánteegrávitee, ántī–/ *n. Physics* a hypothetical force opposing gravity.

an·ti·he·ro /ánteeheerō, ántī–/ *n.* (*pl.* **·roes**) a central character in a story or drama who noticeably lacks conventional heroic attributes.

an·ti·his·ta·mine /ánteehístəmin, –meen, ántī–/ *n.* a substance that counteracts the effects of histamine, used esp. in the treatment of allergies.

an·ti·in·flam·ma·to·ry /anteeinflámətōree, ántī–/ *adj.* & *n.* • *adj.* reducing inflammation. • *n.* (*pl.* **·ries**) an anti-inflammatory medication.

an·ti·knock /ánteenók, ántī–/ *n.* a substance added to motor fuel to prevent premature combustion.

an·ti·lock /ánteelók, ántī–/ *attrib. adj.* (of brakes) designed to prevent locking and skidding.

an·ti·log·a·rithm /ánteeláwgərithəm, –lóg–, ántī–/ *n.* the number to which a logarithm belongs (*100 is the common antilogarithm of 2*).

an·ti·ma·cas·sar /ánteeməkásər/ *n.* a covering put over furniture, esp. over the back of a chair as protection or as an ornament.

an·ti·mat·ter /ánteematər, ántī–/ *n. Physics* matter composed solely of antiparticles.

an·ti·mo·ny /ántimōnee/ *n. Chem.* a brittle silvery white metallic element used esp. in alloys. ¶ Symb.: **Sb**. ▫▫ **an·ti·mo·ni·al** /–mṓneeəl/ *adj.* **an·ti·mo·ni·al** *adj.* **an·ti·mo·ni·ous** /–mṓneeəs/ *adj.*

an·ti·node /ánteenōd, ántī–/ *n. Physics* the position of maximum displacement in a standing wave system.

an·tin·o·my /antínəmee/ *n.* (*pl.* **·mies**) **1** a contradiction between two beliefs or conclusions that are in themselves reasonable; a paradox. **2** a conflict between two laws or authorities.

an·ti·nov·el /ánteenovəl, ántī–/ *n.* a novel in which the conventions of the form are studiously avoided.

an·ti·nu·cle·ar /ánteenóōkleeər, –nyóō–, ántī–/ *adj.* opposed to the development of nuclear weapons or nuclear power.

an·ti·ox·i·dant /ántee–óksid'nt, ántī–/ *n.* an agent that inhibits oxidation, esp. used to reduce deterioration of products stored in air.

an·ti·par·ti·cle /ánteepaartikəl, ántī–/ *n. Physics* an elementary particle having the same mass as a given particle but opposite electric or magnetic properties.

an·ti·pas·to /ánteepaástō/ *n.* (*pl.* **·tos** or **antipasti** /–tee/) an hors d'oeuvre, esp. in an Italian meal.

an·tip·a·thy /antípəthee/ *n.* (*pl.* **·thies**) a strong aversion or dislike.

an·ti·per·son·nel /ánteepérsənél, ántī–/ *adj.* (of a bomb, mine, etc.) designed to kill or injure people rather than to damage buildings or equipment.

an·ti·per·spi·rant /ánteepérspirənt, ántī–/ *n.* & *adj.* • *n.* a substance applied to the skin to prevent perspiration. • *adj.* that acts as an antiperspirant.

an·ti·phon /ántifon/ *n.* **1** a hymn or psalm, the parts of which are sung or recited alternately by two groups. **2** a versicle or phrase from this.

an·tiph·o·nal /antífənəl/ *adj.* & *n.* • *adj.* **1** sung or recited alternately by two groups. **2** responsive; answering. • *n.* a collection of antiphons. ▫▫ **an·tiph·o·nal·ly** *adv.*

an·tiph·o·ny /antífənee/ *n.* (*pl.* **·nies**) **1** antiphonal singing or chanting. **2** a response or echo.

an·ti·pode /ántipōd/ *n.* (usu. foll. by *of, to*) the exact opposite.

an·tip·o·des /antípədeez/ *n.pl.* **1 a** (also **Antipodes**) a place diametrically opposite another, esp. Australasia as the region on the opposite side of the earth from Europe. **b** places diametrically opposite each other. **2** (usu. foll. by *of, to*) the exact opposite. ▫▫ **an·tip·o·dal** *adj.* **an·tip·o·de·an** /–deéən/ *adj.* & *n.*

an·ti·pope /ánteepōp, ántī–/ *n.* a person set up as pope in opposition to one (held by others to be) canonically chosen.

an·ti·pro·ton /ánteeprṓton, ántī–/ *n. Physics* the negatively charged antiparticle of a proton.

an·ti·py·ret·ic /ánteepīrétik, ántī–/ *adj.* preventing or reducing fever.

an·ti·quar·i·an /ántikwáireeən/ *adj.* & *n.* • *adj.* **1** of or dealing in antiques or rare books. **2** of the study of antiquities. • *n.* an antiquary. ▫▫ **an·ti·quar·i·an·ist** *n.*

an·ti·quar·y /ántikweree/ *n.* (*pl.* **·ies**) a student or collector of antiques or antiquities.

an·ti·quat·ed /ántikwaytid/ *adj.* old-fashioned; out of date.

an·tique /anteék/ *n.* & *adj.* • *n.* an object of considerable age, esp. an item of furniture or the decorative arts having a high value. • *adj.* **1** of or existing from an early date. **2** old-fashioned; archaic. **3** of ancient times.

an·tiq·ui·ty /antíkwitee/ *n.* (*pl.* **·ties**) **1** ancient times, esp. the period before the Middle Ages. **2** great age (*a city of great antiquity*). **3** (usu. in *pl.*) physical remains or relics from ancient times, esp. buildings and works of art. **4** (in *pl.*) customs, events, etc., of ancient times.

an·ti-Sem·ite /ánteesémīt, ántī–/ *n.* a person hostile to or prejudiced against Jews. ▫▫ **an·ti-Se·mit·ic** /–simítik/ *adj.* **an·ti-Sem·i·tism** /–sémitizəm/ *n.*

an·ti·sep·sis /ántisépsis/ *n.* the process of using antiseptics to eliminate undesirable microorganisms.

an·ti·sep·tic /ántiséptik/ *adj.* & *n.* • *adj.* **1** counteracting sepsis, esp. by preventing the growth of disease-causing microorganisms. **2** free from contamination. **3** lacking character. • *n.* an antiseptic agent. ▫▫ **an·ti·sep·ti·cal·ly** *adv.*

an·ti·se·rum /ántiseerəm/ *n.* (*pl.* **antisera** /–rə/) a blood serum containing antibodies against specific antigens, injected to treat specific diseases.

an·ti·so·cial /ánteesṓshəl, ántī–/ *adj.* **1** contrary to normal social instincts or practices. **2** not sociable. **3** opposed to the existing social order.

an·tith·e·sis /antíthisis/ *n.* (*pl.* **antitheses** /–seez/) **1** (foll. by *of, to*) the direct opposite. **2** (usu. foll. by *of, between*) contrast or opposition between two things.

an·ti·thet·i·cal /ántithétikəl/ *adj.* (also **an·ti·thet·ic**) **1** contrasted; opposite. **2** connected with, containing, or using antithesis. ▫▫ **an·ti·thet·i·cal·ly** *adv.*

an·ti·tox·in /ánteetóksin/ *n.* an antibody that counteracts a toxin. ▫▫ **an·ti·tox·ic** *adj.*

an·ti·trust /ánteetrúst, ántī–/ *adj.* (of a law, etc.) opposed to or controlling trusts or other monopolies.

an·ti·type /ánteetīp/ *n.* **1** that which is represented by a type or symbol. **2** a person or thing of the opposite type. ▫▫ **an·ti·typ·i·cal** /–típikəl/ *adj.*

an·ti·vi·ral /ánteevírəl, ántī–/ *adj.* effective against viruses.

an·ti·viv·i·sec·tion·ism /ánteevívisékshənizəm, ántī–/ *n.* opposition to vivisection. ▫▫ **an·ti·viv·i·sec·tion·ist** *n.*

ant·ler /ántlər/ *n.* **1** each of the branched horns of a stag or other (usu. male) deer. **2** a branch of this. ▫▫ **ant·lered** *adj.*

ant li·on *n.* any of various dragonflylike insects, the larvae of which dig pits in which to trap ants and other insects for food.

an·to·no·ma·sia /ántənəmáyzhə/ *n.* **1** the substitution of an epithet or title, etc., for a proper name (e.g., the Maid of Orleans for Joan of Arc). **2** the use of a proper name to express a general idea (e.g., a Scrooge for a miser).

an·to·nym /ántənim/ *n.* a word opposite in meaning to another in the same language (e.g., *bad* and *good*) (opp. SYNONYM). ▫▫ **an·ton·y·mous** /antónimәs/ *adj.*

an·trum /ántrəm/ *n.* (*pl.* **antra** /–trə/) *Anat.* a natural chamber or cavity in the body, esp. in a bone. ▫▫ **an·tral** *adj.*

ants·y /ántsee/ *adj. colloq.* impatient; fidgety; restless.

a·nus /áynəs/ *n. Anat.* the excretory opening at the end of the alimentary canal.

an·vil /ánvil/ *n.* a block (usu. of iron) with a flat top, concave sides, and often a pointed end, on which metals are worked in forging.

anvil

anx·i·e·ty /angzíətee/ *n.* (*pl.* **·ties**) **1** the state of being anxious. **2** concern about an imminent danger, difficulty, etc. **3** (foll. by *for*, or *to* + infin.) anxious desire.

anx·ious /ángkshəs/ *adj.* **1** uneasy in the mind. **2** causing or marked by anxiety (*an anxious moment*). **3** (foll. by *for*, or *to* + infin.) earnestly or uneasily wanting (*anxious to please*). □□ **anx·ious·ly** *adv.* **anx·ious·ness** *n.*

▶**Anxious** and **eager** both mean 'looking forward to something,' but they have different connotations. **Eager** suggests enthusiasm about something, a positive outlook: *I'm eager to get started on my vacation.* **Anxious** implies worry about something: *I'm anxious to get started before it rains.*

an·y /énee/ *adj., pron., & adv.* • *adj.* **1** (with *interrog.*, *neg.*, or conditional expressed or implied) **a** one, no matter which, of several (*cannot find any answer*). **b** some, no matter how much or many or of what sort (*if any books arrive*; *have you any sugar?*). **2** a minimal amount of (*hardly any difference*). **3** whichever is chosen (*any fool knows that*). **4 a** a significant (*did not stay for any length of time*). **b** a very large (*has any amount of money*). • *pron.* **1** any one (*did not know any of them*). **2** any number (*are any of them yours?*). **3** any amount (*is there any left?*). • *adv.* (usu. with *neg.* or *interrog.*) at all (*is that any good?*).

an·y·bod·y /éneebudee, –bodee/ *n. & pron.* **1 a** a person, no matter who. **b** a person of any kind. **c** whatever person is chosen. **2** a person of importance.

an·y·how /éneehow/ *adv.* **1** anyway. **2** in a disorderly manner or state.

an·y·one /éneewun/ *pron.* anybody.

▶**Anyone** is written as two words only to emphasize singularity, e.g., *Any one of us could do the job.* Otherwise it is written as one word (e.g., *Anyone who wants to come is welcome*).

an·y·place /éneeplays/ *adv.* anywhere.

an·y·thing /éneething/ *pron.* **1** a thing, no matter which. **2** a thing of any kind. **3** whatever thing is chosen. □ **anything but** not at all (*was anything but honest*).

an·y·way /éneeway/ *adv.* (also *dial.* **anyways** /éneewayz/) **1** in any way or manner. **2** in any case. **3** to resume (*anyway, as I was saying*).

an·y·where /éneehwair, –wair/ *adv. & pron.* • *adv.* in or to any place. • *pron.* any place (*anywhere will do*).

An·zac /ánzak/ *n.* **1** a soldier in the Australian and New Zealand Army Corps (1914–18). **2** any person from Australia or New Zealand.

A-OK *abbr. colloq.* excellent; in good order.

a·or·ta /ayáwrtə/ *n.* (*pl.* **aortas**) the main artery, giving rise to the arterial network through which oxygenated blood is supplied to the body from the heart. □□ **a·or·tic** *adj.*

a·pace /əpáys/ *adv. literary* swiftly; quickly.

A·pach·e /əpáchee/ *n.* a member of a N. American Indian tribe of the southwestern US.

a·part /əpaárt/ *adv.* **1** separately; not together (*stand apart from the crowd*). **2** into pieces (*came apart in my hands*). **3 a** to or on one side. **b** out of consideration (placed after noun: *joking apart*). **4** to or at a distance. □ **apart from** excepting; not considering.

a·part·heid /əpaártayt, –tīd/ *n.* (esp. as formerly in S. Africa) a policy or system of segregation or discrimination on grounds of race.

a·part·ment /əpaártmənt/ *n.* **1** a set of rooms forming one residence, usu. in a building containing a number of these, and usu. rented.

ap·a·thet·ic /ápəthétik/ *adj.* having no emotion. □□ **ap·a·thet·i·cal·ly** *adv.*

ap·a·thy /ápəthee/ *n.* (often foll. by *toward*) lack of interest or feeling.

a·pa·to·sau·rus /əpátəsáwrəs/ *n.* a large herbivorous dinosaur of the late Jurassic period, with a long neck and tail. Formerly called **brontosaurus**.

ape /ayp/ *n. & v.* • *n.* **1** any of the various primates of the family Pongidae, characterized by the absence of a tail. **2** (in general use) any monkey. **3 a** an imitator. **b** an apelike person. • *v.tr.* imitate; mimic. □ **go ape** *sl.* **1** become crazy. **2** be emotional or enthusiatic.

a·per·çu /aapersv/ *n.* **1** a summary or survey. **2** an insight.

a·per·i·ent /əpéereeənt/ *adj. & n.* • *adj.* laxative. • *n.* a laxative medicine.

a·pe·ri·od·ic /áypeereeódik/ *adj.* not periodic; irregular.

a·pe·ri·tif /əpériteéf/ *n.* an alcoholic drink taken before a meal to stimulate the appetite.

ap·er·ture /ápərchər/ *n.* **1** an opening; a gap. **2** a space through which light passes in an optical or photographic instrument.

a·pex /áypeks/ *n.* (*pl.* **apexes** or **apices** /áypiseez/) **1** the highest point. **2** a climax. **3** the vertex of a triangle or cone. **4** a tip or pointed end.

a·phaer·e·sis /əférisis/ *n.* (also **a·pher·e·sis**) (*pl.* **aphaereses, aphereses** /–seez/) the omission of a letter or syllable at the beginning of a word as a morphological development (e.g., in the derivation of adder from naddre).

a·pha·sia /əfáyzhə/ *n. Med.* the loss of ability to understand or express speech, owing to brain damage. □□ **a·pha·sic** /–zik/ *adj. & n.*

a·phe·li·on /əféeleeən, ap–héeleeən/ *n.* (*pl.* **aphelia** /–leeə/) the point in a body's orbit where it is furthest from the sun (opp. PERIHELION).

aph·e·sis /áfisis/ *n.* (*pl.* **apheses** /–seez/) the gradual loss of an unstressed vowel at the beginning of a word (e.g., of e from esquire to form squire). □□ **a·phet·ic** /əfétik/ *adj.* **a·phet·i·cal·ly** *adv.*

a·phid /áyfid, áfid/ *n.* any small homopterous insect which feeds by sucking sap from leaves, stems, or roots of plants; a plant louse.

a·phis /áyfis, áfis/ *n.* (*pl.* **aphides** /áyfideez/) an aphid, esp. of the genus *Aphis* including the greenfly.

aph·o·rism /áfərizəm/ *n.* **1** a short pithy maxim. **2** a brief statement of a principle. □□ **aph·o·ris·tic** *adj.*

aph·ro·dis·i·ac /áfrədéezeeak, –díz–/ *adj. & n.* • *adj.* that arouses sexual desire. • *n.* an aphrodisiac drug.

a·pi·ar·y /áypee–eree/ *n.* (*pl.* **·ies**) a place where bees are kept. □□ **a·pi·a·rist** *n.*

a·pi·cal /áypikəl, áp–/ *adj.* of, at, or forming an apex. □□ **a·pi·cal·ly** *adv.*

a·pi·ces *pl.* of APEX.

a·pi·cul·ture /áypikulchər/ *n.* beekeeping. □□ **a·pi·cul·tur·al** /–kúlchərəl/ *adj.* **a·pi·cul·tur·ist** *n.*

a·piece /əpées/ *adv.* for each one (*had five dollars apiece*).

ap·ish /áypish/ *adj.* **1** of or like an ape. **2** silly. □□ **ap·ish·ly** *adv.* **ap·ish·ness** *n.*

a·plen·ty /əpléntee/ *adv.* in plenty.

a·plomb /əplóm, əplúm/ *n.* assurance; self-confidence.

ap·ne·a /ápneeə, apnéeə/ *n. Med.* a temporary cessation of breathing.

APO *abbr.* Army post office.

apo- /ápə/ *prefix* **1** away from (*apogee*). **2** separate (*apocarpous*).

a·poc·a·lypse /əpókəlips/ *n.* **1** (**the Apocalypse**) Revelation, the last book of the New Testament. **2** a grand or violent event resembling those described in the Apocalypse.

a·poc·a·lyp·tic /əpókəlíptik/ *adj.* **1** of or resembling the Apocalypse. **2** revelatory.

A·poc·ry·pha /əpókrifə/ *n.pl.* **1** the books included in the Septuagint and Vulgate versions of the Old Testament but not in the Hebrew Bible. ▶Modern Bibles sometimes include them in the Old Testament or as an appendix, and sometimes omit them. **2** (**apocrypha**) writings not considered genuine.

a·poc·ry·phal /əpókrifəl/ *adj.* **1** of doubtful authenticity. **2** invented; mythical (*an apocryphal story*). **3** of or belonging to the Apocrypha.

ap·o·gee /ápəjee/ *n.* **1** the point in a celestial body's orbit where it is farthest from the earth (opp. PERIGEE). **2** the most distant or highest point.

a·po·lit·i·cal /áypəlítikəl/ *adj.* not interested in or concerned with politics.

a·pol·o·get·ic /əpóləjétik/ *adj. & n.* • *adj.* **1** regretfully acknowledging an offense. **2** diffident. **3** of reasoned defense. • *n.* (usu. in *pl.*) a reasoned defense. ▫▫ **a·pol·o·get·i·cal·ly** *adv.*

ap·o·lo·gi·a /ápəlṓjeeə/ *n.* a formal defense of one's opinions or conduct.

a·pol·o·gist /əpóləjist/ *n.* a person who defends something by argument.

a·pol·o·gize /əpóləjīz/ *v.intr.* (often foll. by *for*) make an apology.

a·pol·o·gy /əpóləjee/ *n.* (*pl.* **·gies**) **1** a regretful acknowledgement of an offense or failure. **2** an assurance that no offense was intended. **3** an explanation or defense. **4** (foll. by *for*) a poor specimen of (*this apology for a letter*).

ap·o·plec·tic /ápəpléktik/ *adj.* **1** of or liable to apoplexy. **2** *colloq.* overcome with anger (*apoplectic with rage*).

ap·o·plex·y /ápəpleksee/ *n.* a sudden loss of consciousness, voluntary movement, and sensation caused by blockage or rupture of a brain artery; a stroke.

a·pos·ta·sy /əpóstəsee/ *n.* (*pl.* **·sies**) **1** renunciation of a belief or faith. **2** abandonment of principles or of a party. **3** an instance of apostasy.

a·pos·tate /əpóstayt/ *n. & adj.* • *n.* a person who renounces a former belief, adherence, etc. • *adj.* engaged in apostasy.

a·pos·ta·tize /əpóstətīz/ *v.intr.* renounce a former belief, adherence, etc.

a pos·te·ri·o·ri /áy posteéeree–áwree, –áwrī/ *adj. & adv.* • *adj.* (of reasoning) inductive; empirical; proceeding from effects to causes. • *adv.* inductively; empirically; from effects to causes (opp. A PRIORI).

a·pos·tle /əpósəl/ *n.* **1** (**Apostle**) **a** any of the chosen twelve first sent out to preach the Christian Gospel. **b** the first successful Christian missionary in a country or to a people. **2** a leader or outstanding figure, esp. of a reform movement (*apostle of temperance*). **3** a messenger or representative.

ap·os·tol·ic /ápəstólik/ *adj.* **1** of or relating to the Apostles. **2** of the Pope regarded as the successor of St. Peter. **3** of the character of an Apostle.

ap·os·tol·ic suc·ces·sion *n.* the uninterrupted transmission of spiritual authority from the Apostles through successive popes and bishops.

a·pos·tro·phe[1] /əpóstrəfee/ *n.* a punctuation mark used to indicate: **1** the omission of letters or numbers (e.g., *can't*; *he's*). **2** the possessive case (e.g., *Harry's book*).

▶The apostrophe is used **1.** to indicate missing letters or numbers: *Hallowe'en, the summer of '63;* **2.** in forming some possessives; see note at POSSESSIVE; **3.** in forming some plurals; see note at PLURAL.

a·pos·tro·phe[2] /əpóstrəfee/ *n.* an exclamatory passage in a speech or poem, addressed to a person. ▫▫ **a·pos·tro·phize** *v.tr. & intr.*

a·poth·e·car·y /əpóthəkeree/ *n.* (*pl.* **·ies**) *archaic* a pharmacist licensed to dispense medicines.

ap·o·thegm /ápəthem/ *n.* a terse saying or maxim; an aphorism. ▫▫ **ap·o·theg·mat·ic** /–thegmátik/ *adj.*

ap·o·them /ápəthem/ *n. Geom.* a line from the center of a regular polygon at right angles to any of its sides.

a·poth·e·o·sis /əpóthee–ṓsis/ *n.* (*pl.* **apotheoses** /–seez/) **1** elevation to divine status; deification. **2** a glorification of a thing (*apotheosis of the dance*).

ap·o·tro·pa·ic /ápətrōpáyik/ *adj.* supposedly having the power to avert an evil influence or bad luck.

ap·pall /əpáwl/ *v.tr.* (also **ap·pal**) (**appalled, appalling**) **1** greatly dismay. **2** (as **appalling** *adj.*) *colloq.* shocking; unpleasant; bad. ▫▫ **ap·pall·ing·ly** *adv.*

Ap·pa·loo·sa /ápəlóósə/ *n.* a horse of a N. American breed having dark spots on a light background.

ap·pa·rat·chik /aápəraátchik/ *n.* (*pl.* **apparatchiks** or *Russ.* **apparatchiki** /–kee/) **1 a** a member of the administrative system of a Communist party. **b** a Communist agent or spy. **2 a** a member of a political party in any country who blindly executes policy; a zealous functionary. **b** an official of a public or private organization.

ap·pa·rat·us /ápərátəs, –ráytəs/ *n.* **1** the equipment needed for a particular purpose or function. **2** a political or other complex organization. **3** (in full **apparatus crit·i·cus**) a collection of variants and annotations accompanying a printed text and usu. appearing below it.

ap·par·el /əpárəl/ *n.* clothing; dress.

ap·par·ent /əpárənt/ *adj.* **1** readily visible or perceivable. **2** seeming. ▫▫ **ap·par·ent·ly** *adv.*

ap·pa·ri·tion /ápəríshən/ *n.* a sudden or dramatic appearance, esp. of a ghost or phantom; a visible ghost.

ap·peal /əpeél/ *v. & n.* • *v.* **1** *intr.* make an earnest request; plead (*appealed for calm*). **2** *intr.* be attractive or of interest. **3** *intr.* (foll. by *to*) resort to or cite for support. **4** *Law* **a** *intr.* apply (to a higher court) for a reconsideration of the decision of a lower court. **b** *tr.* refer to a higher court to review (a case). **5** *intr. Sports* call on an umpire or referee to reverse a decision. • *n.* **1** the act or an instance of appealing. **2** a formal or urgent request for public support, esp. financial, for a cause. **3** *Law* the referral of a case to a higher court. **4** attractiveness; appealing quality (*sex appeal*).

ap·peal·ing /əpeéling/ *adj.* attractive; likable. ▫▫ **ap·peal·ing·ly** *adv.*

ap·pear /əpeér/ *v.intr.* **1** become or be visible. **2** be evident (*a new problem then appeared*). **3** seem; have the appearance of being (*you appear to be right*). **4** present oneself publicly or formally, esp. on stage or as the accused or counsel in a court of law. **5** be published (*it appeared in the papers*).

ap·pear·ance /əpeérəns/ *n.* **1** the act or an instance of appearing. **2** an outward form as perceived, esp. visually (*neaten up one's appearance*; *gives the appearance of trying hard*). **3** a semblance. ▫ **make** (or **put in**) **an appearance** be present, esp. briefly.

ap·pease /əpeéz/ *v.tr.* **1** make calm or quiet, esp. conciliate (a potential aggressor) by making concessions. **2** satisfy (an appetite, scruples). ▫▫ **ap·pease·ment** *n.* **ap·peas·er** *n.*

ap·pel·lant /əpélənt/ *n. Law* a person who appeals to a higher court.

ap·pel·late /əpélət/ *adj. Law* (esp. of a court) concerned with appeals.

ap·pel·la·tion /ápəláyshən/ *n. formal* a name or title; nomenclature.

ap·pend /əpénd/ *v.tr.* attach, affix, add, esp. to a written document, etc.

ap·pend·age /əpéndij/ *n.* **1** something attached; an addition. **2** *Zool.* a limb or other projecting part of a body.

ap·pen·dec·to·my /ápəndéktəmee/ *n.* (also **ap·pen·di·cec·to·my** /–diséktəmee/) (*pl.* **·mies**) the surgical removal of the appendix.

ap·pen·di·ci·tis /əpéndisítis/ *n.* inflammation of the appendix.

ap·pen·dix /əpéndiks/ *n.* (*pl.* **appendices** /–diseez/; **appendixes**) **1** (in full **vermiform appendix**) *Anat.* a small outgrowth of tissue forming a tube-shaped sac attached to the lower end of the large intestine. **2** subsidiary matter at the end of a book or document.

ap·per·ceive /ápərséev/ *v.tr.* **1** be conscious of perceiving. **2** *Psychol.* compare (a perception) to previously held ideas so as to extract meaning from it. ▫▫ **ap·per·cep·tion** /–sépshən/ *n.* **ap·per·cep·tive** *adj.*

ap·per·tain /ápərtáyn/ *v.intr.* (foll. by *to*) **1** relate. **2** belong as a possession or right. **3** be appropriate.

ap·pe·tite /ápitīt/ *n.* **1** a natural desire to satisfy bodily needs, esp. for food or sexual activity. **2** (usu. foll. by *for*) an inclination or desire. ▫▫ **ap·pe·ti·tive** /ápitítiv/ *adj.*

ap·pe·tiz·er /ápitīzər/ *n.* a small amount to stimulate an appetite.

ap·pe·tiz·ing /ápitīzing/ *adj.* stimulating an appetite. ▫▫ **ap·pe·tiz·ing·ly** *adv.*

ap·plaud /əpláwd/ *v.* **1** *intr.* express strong approval or praise, esp. by clapping. **2** *tr.* express approval of (a person or action).

ap·plause /əpláwz/ *n.* **1** an expression of approbation, esp. from an audience, etc., by clapping. **2** emphatic approval.

ap·ple /ápəl/ *n.* **1** a rounded edible fruit with a crisp flesh. **2** the tree bearing this. ▫ **apple of one's eye** a cherished person or thing.

ap·ple·jack /ápəljak/ *n.* an alcoholic beverage made by distilling or freezing fermented apple cider.

ap·pli·ance /əplíəns/ *n.* a device or piece of equipment used for a specific task, esp. a household device for washing, drying, cooking, etc.

ap·pli·ca·ble /áplikəbəl, əplíkə–/ *adj.* **1** that may be applied. **2** having reference; appropriate. ▫▫ **ap·pli·ca·bil·i·ty** *n.*

ap·pli·cant /áplikənt/ *n.* a person who applies for something, esp. a job.

ap·pli·ca·tion /áplikáyshən/ *n.* **1** the act of applying. **2** a formal request for employment, membership, etc. **3 a** relevance. **b** the use to which something can or should be put. **4** sustained effort; diligence.

ap·pli·ca·tor /áplikaytər/ *n.* a device for applying a substance to a surface.

ap·plied /əplíd/ *adj.* (of a subject of study) put to practical use as opposed to being theoretical.

ap·pli·qué /áplikáy/ *n., adj., & v.* • *n.* ornamental work in which fabric is cut out and attached to the surface of another fabric to form pictures or patterns. • *adj.* executed in appliqué. • *v.tr.* (**appliqués, appliquéd, appliquéing**) decorate with appliqué; make using appliqué technique.

ap·ply /əplí/ *v.* (**·plies, ·plied**) **1** *intr.* make a formal request for something to be done, given, etc. (*apply for a job*). **2** *intr.* have relevance (*does not apply in this case*). **3** *tr.* **a** make use of as relevant or suitable (*apply the rules*). **b** operate (*apply the hand brake*). **4** *tr.* **a** put or spread on (*applied the ointment to the cut*). **b** administer (*applied common sense to the problem*). **5** *refl.* devote oneself (*applied myself to the task*).

ap·pog·gia·tu·ra /əpójətŏŏrə/ *n. Mus.* a grace note performed before an essential note of a melody and normally taking half or less than half its time value.

ap·point /əpóynt/ *v.tr.* **1** assign a post to (*appoint him governor*). **2** fix; decide on (a time, place, etc.) (*8:30 was the appointed time*). **3** (as **appointed** *adj.*) equipped; furnished (*a badly appointed hotel*). ▫▫ **ap·point·ee** /–tée/ *n.* **ap·poin·tive** *adj.*

ap·point·ment /əpóyntmənt/ *n.* **1** an arrangement to meet at a specific time and place. **2 a** a post available for applicants, or recently filled. **b** a person appointed. **3** (usu. in *pl.*) **a** furniture; fittings. **b** equipment.

ap·por·tion /əpáwrshən/ *v.tr.* share out; assign as a share. ▫▫ **ap·por·tion·ment** *n.*

ap·po·site /ápəzit/ *adj.* (often foll. by *to*) **1** apt; well chosen. **2** well expressed. ▫▫ **ap·po·site·ly** *adv.* **ap·po·site·ness** *n.*

ap·po·si·tion /ápəzíshən/ *n.* **1** placing side by side; juxtaposition. **2** *Gram.* the placing of a word next to another, esp. the addition of one noun to another, in order to qualify or explain the first (e.g., *William the Conqueror*). ▫▫ **ap·po·si·tion·al** *adj.*

ap·prais·al /əpráyzəl/ *n.* the act or an instance of appraising.

ap·praise /əpráyz/ *v.tr.* **1** estimate the quality of (*appraised her skills*). **2** set a price on; value. ▫▫ **ap·prais·er** *n.* **ap·prais·ive** *adj.*

▶**Appraise,** meaning 'evaluate,' should not be confused with **apprise,** which means 'inform': *The painting was appraised at $3 million. They gasped when apprised of this valuation.*

ap·pre·ci·a·ble /əpréeshəbəl/ *adj.* large enough to be noticed; significant; considerable (*appreciable progress has been made*). ▫▫ **ap·pre·ci·a·bly** *adv.*

ap·pre·ci·ate /əpréesheeáyt/ *v.* **1** *tr.* **a** esteem highly; value. **b** be grateful for (*we appreciate your sympathy*). **c** be sensitive to (*appreciate the nuances*). **2** *tr.* (often foll. by *that* + clause) understand; recognize. **3 a** *intr.* (of property, etc.) rise in value. **b** *tr.* raise in value. ▫▫ **ap·pre·cia·tive** /–shətiv, –shee–áytiv/ *adj.* **ap·pre·cia·tive·ly** *adv.* **ap·pre·ci·a·tor** *n.*

ap·pre·ci·a·tion /əpréeshee–áyshən/ *n.* **1** favorable recognition. **2** sensitive understanding (*a quick appreciation of the problem*). **3** an increase in value.

ap·pre·hend /áprihénd/ *v.tr.* **1** understand; perceive (*apprehend your meaning*). **2** seize; arrest (*apprehended the criminal*). ▫▫ **ap·pre·hen·si·ble** /áprihénsibəl/ *adj.*

ap·pre·hen·sion /áprihénshən/ *n.* **1** uneasiness; dread. **2** understanding; perception. **3** arrest; capture.

ap·pre·hen·sive /áprihénsiv/ *adj.* uneasily fearful; dreading. ▫▫ **ap·pre·hen·sive·ly** *adv.* **ap·pre·hen·sive·ness** *n.*

ap·pren·tice /əpréntis/ *n. & v.* • *n.* **1** a person who is learning a trade by being employed in it for an agreed period at low wages. **2** a beginner; a novice. • *v.tr.* engage as an apprentice. ▫▫ **ap·pren·tice·ship** *n.*

ap·prise /əpríz/ *v.tr.* inform.

ap·proach /əprṓch/ *v. & n.* • *v.* **1** *tr.* come near or nearer to (a place or time). **2** *intr.* come near or nearer in space or time. **3** *tr.* make a tentative proposal to. **4** *tr.* **a** be similar in character, quality, etc., to. **b** approximate to. **5** *tr.* attempt to influence or bribe. **6** *tr.* set about, tackle (a task, etc.). **7** *intr. Golf* play an approach shot. • *n.* **1** an act or means of approaching. **2** an approximation. **3** a way of dealing with a person or thing (*needs a new approach*). **4** (usu. in *pl.*) a sexual advance. **5** *Golf* a stroke from the fairway to the green. **6** *Aeron.* the final descent of a flight before landing.

ap·proach·a·ble /əprṓchəbəl/ *adj.* **1** friendly; easy to talk to. **2** able to be approached. ▫▫ **ap·proach·a·bil·i·ty** /–bílitee/ *n.*

ap·pro·ba·tion /áprəbáyshən/ *n.* approval; consent. ▫▫ **ap·pro·ba·to·ry** /əprṓbətawree/ *adj.*

ap·pro·pri·ate *adj. & v.* • *adj.* /əprṓpreeət/ **1** suitable or proper. **2** belonging or particular to. • *v.tr.* /əprṓpreeayt/ **1** take possession of. **2** devote (money, etc.) to special purposes. ▫▫ **ap·pro·pri·ate·ly** *adv.* **ap·pro·pri·ate·ness** *n.* **ap·pro·pri·a·tor** *n.*

ap·pro·pri·a·tion /əprṓpreeáyshən/ *n.* **1** an act or instance of appropriating. **2** something appropriated, as money officially set aside for a specific use.

ap•prov•al /əpro͞ovəl/ *n.* **1** the act of approving. **2** consent; a favorable opinion. ▫ **on approval** (of goods supplied) to be returned if not satisfactory.

ap•prove /əpro͞ov/ *v.* **1** *tr.* confirm; sanction (*approved her application*). **2** *intr.* give or have a favorable opinion. **3** *tr.* commend. ▫▫ **ap•prov•ing•ly** *adv.*

approx. *abbr.* **1** approximate. **2** approximately.

ap•prox•i•mate *adj. & v.* • *adj.* /əpróksimət/ fairly correct or accurate; near to the actual. • *v.tr. & intr.* /əpróksimayt/ bring or come near (esp. in quality, number, etc.), but not exactly. ▫▫ **ap•prox•i•mate•ly** /–mətlee/ *adv.* **ap•prox•i•ma•tion** /–máyshən/ *n.*

ap•pur•te•nance /əpə́rt'nəns/ *n.* (usu. in *pl.*) a belonging; an appendage.

APR *abbr.* annual or annualized percentage rate.

Apr. *abbr.* April.

a•près-ski /áprayskée, aáprayˊ–/ *n. & adj.* • *n.* the evening, esp. its social activities, following a day's skiing. • *attrib.adj.* (of clothes, drinks, etc.) appropriate to social activities following skiing.

ap•ri•cot /áprikot, áypri–/ *n. & adj.* • *n.* **1 a** a juicy soft fruit, smaller than a peach, of an orange-yellow color. **b** the tree, *Prunus armeniaca*, bearing it. **2** the ripe fruit's orange-yellow color. • *adj.* orange-yellow.

A•pril /áypril/ *n.* the fourth month of the year.

A•pril Fool's (or **Fools'**) **Day** *n.* April 1, traditionally an occasion for playing tricks on people in many Western countries.

a pri•o•ri /aá pree–áwree, áy prī–áwrī/ *adj. & adv.* • *adj.* **1** (of reasoning) deductive; proceeding from causes to effects (opp. A POSTERIORI). **2** (of concepts, knowledge, etc.) logically independent of experience (opp. EMPIRICAL). **3** not submitted to critical investigation. • *adv.* **1** in an a priori manner. **2** as far as one knows. ▫▫ **a•pri•o•rism** /aypríərizəm/ *n.*

a•pron /áyprən/ *n.* **1** a garment covering and protecting the front of a person's clothes. **2** *Theatr.* the part of a stage in front of the curtain. **3** the paved area of an airfield used for maneuvering or loading aircraft. **4** an endless conveyor belt. ▫▫ **a•proned** *adj.*

a•pron strings *n.pl.* ▫ **tied to a person's apron strings** dominated by or dependent on that person.

ap•ro•pos /áprəpṓ/ *adj., adv., & prep* • *adj.* to the point; appropriate. • *adv.* **1** appropriately. **2** by the way; incidentally. • *prep.* (foll. by *of*) in respect to; concerning.

apse /aps/ *n.* a large semicircular or polygonal recess, esp. at the eastern end of a church.

ap•sis /ápsis/ *n.* (*pl.* **apsides** /–sideez/) either of two points in the orbit of a planet or satellite that are nearest to or farthest from the body around which it moves. ▫▫ **ap•si•dal** /ápsid'l/ *adj.*

apt /apt/ *adj.* **1** appropriate. **2** (foll. by *to* + infin.) having a tendency. **3** clever; quick to learn (*an apt pupil*). ▫▫ **apt•ly** *adv.* **apt•ness** *n.*

ap•ti•tude /áptito͞od, –tyo͞od/ *n.* **1** a natural talent (*an aptitude for drawing*). **2** ability or suitability.

aq•ua /ákwə, aákwə/ *n.* the color aquamarine.

aq•ua•cul•ture /ákwəkulchər, aákwə–/ *n.* (also **aq•ui•cul•ture**) the cultivation or rearing of aquatic plants or animals. ▫▫ **aquacultural** *adj.* **aquaculturist** *n.*

Aq•ua-Lung /ákwəlung, aákwə–/ *n. Trademark* a portable breathing apparatus for divers, consisting of cylinders of compressed air strapped on the back, feeding air through a mask or mouthpiece.

aq•ua•ma•rine /ákwəməréen, aákwə–/ *n.* **1** a light bluish green beryl. **2** its color.

aq•ua•naut /ákwənawt, aákwə–/ *n.* an underwater swimmer or explorer.

aq•ua•plane /ákwəplayn, aákwə–/ *n. & v.* • *n.* a board for riding on water, pulled by a speedboat. • *v.intr.* ride on an aquaplane.

a•quar•i•um /əkwáireeəm/ *n.* (*pl.* **aquariums** or **aquaria** /–reeə/) an artificial environment designed for keeping live aquatic plants and animals.

A•quar•i•us /əkwáireeəs/ *n.* **1** a constellation, traditionally regarded as portraying the figure of a water carrier. **2 a** the eleventh sign of the zodiac (the Water Carrier). **b** a person born when the sun is in this sign. ▫▫ **A•quar•i•an** *adj. & n.*

a•quat•ic /əkwátik, əkwótik/ *adj. & n.* • *adj.* **1** growing or living in or near water. **2** (of a sport) played in or on water. • *n.* **1** an aquatic plant or animal. **2** (in *pl.*) aquatic sports.

aq•ua•tint /ákwətint, aákwə–/ *n.* **1** a print resembling a watercolor, produced from a copper plate etched with nitric acid. **2** the process of producing this.

aq•ua•vit /aákwəveet, ákwə–/ *n.* an alcoholic liquor made from potatoes, etc., and usu. flavored with caraway seeds.

aq•ua vi•tae /aákwə vítee, vée–/ *n.* a strong alcoholic liquor, esp. brandy.

aq•ue•duct /ákwidukt/ *n.* an artificial channel for conveying water, esp. in the form of a bridge supported by tall columns across a valley.

a•que•ous /áykweeəs, ák–/ *adj.* **1** of, containing, or like water. **2** *Geol.* produced by water (*aqueous rocks*).

a•que•ous hu•mor *n. Anat.* the clear fluid in the eye between the lens and the cornea.

aq•ui•fer /ákwifər/ *n. Geol.* a layer of rock or soil able to hold much water.

aq•ui•line /ákwilīn/ *adj.* **1** like an eagle. **2** (of a nose) curved like an eagle's beak.

AR *abbr.* Arkansas (in official postal use).

Ar *symb. Chem.* the element argon.

Ar•ab /árəb/ *n. & adj.* • *n.* **1** a member of a Semitic people inhabiting originally Saudi Arabia and the neighboring countries, now the Middle East generally. **2** = ARABIAN 2. • *adj.* of Arabia or the Arabs (esp. with ethnic reference).

ar•a•besque /árəbésk/ *n.* **1** *Ballet* a posture with one leg extended horizontally backward, torso extended forward, and arms outstretched. **2** a design of intertwined leaves, scrolls, etc.

A•ra•bi•an /əráybeeən/ *adj. & n.* • *adj.* of or relating to Arabia. • *n.* **1** a native of Arabia. ¶ Now less common than *Arab* in this sense. **2** a horse of a breed orig. native to Arabia.

Ar•a•bic /árəbik/ *n. & adj.* • *n.* the Semitic language of the Arabs. • *adj.* of or relating to Arabia (esp. with reference to language or literature).

Ar•a•bic nu•mer•al *n.* any of the numerals 0, 1, 2, 3, 4, 5, 6, 7, 8, and 9 (cf. ROMAN NUMERAL).

ar•a•ble /árəbəl/ *adj.* **1** (of land) suitable for crop production. **2** (of crops) that can be grown on arable land.

Ar•a•by /árəbee/ *n. poet.* Arabia.

a•rach•nid /əráknid/ *n.* an arthropod having four pairs of walking legs and simple eyes, e.g., scorpions, spiders, mites, and ticks. ▫▫ **a•rach•ni•dan** *adj. & n.*

a•rach•noid /əráknoyd/ *n. Anat.* (in full **arachnoid membrane**) one of the three membranes (see MENINX) that surround the brain and spinal cord of vertebrates.

a•rach•no•pho•bi•a /əráknəfṓbeeə/ *n.* an abnormal fear of spiders. ▫▫ **a•rach•no•phobe** /əráknəfōb/ *n.*

Ar•a•ma•ic /árəmáyik/ *n. & adj.* • *n.* a branch of the Semitic family of languages, esp. the language of Syria used as a lingua franca in the Near East. • *adj.* of or in Aramaic.

A•rap•a•ho /ərápəhō/ *n.* **1 a** a N. American people native to the central plains of Canada and the US. **b** a member of this people. **2** the language of this people.

ar•bi•ter /aárbitər/ *n.* **1 a** an arbitrator in a dispute. **b** a judge; an authority (*arbiter of taste*). **2** a person who has entire control of something.

ar·bi·trage /aárbitraazh, –trij/ *n.* the buying and selling of stocks or bills of exchange to take advantage of varying prices in different markets.
ar·bi·tra·geur /aárbitraazhőr/ *n.* (also **ar·bi·trag·er** /aárbitraazhər/) a person who engages in arbitrage.
ar·bi·trar·y /aárbitreree/ *adj.* **1** based on or derived from uninformed opinion or random choice; capricious. **2** despotic. ▫▫ **ar·bi·trar·i·ly** *adv.* **ar·bi·trar·i·ness** *n.*
ar·bi·trate /aárbitrayt/ *v.tr. & intr.* decide by arbitration.
ar·bi·tra·tion /aárbitráyshən/ *n.* the settlement of a dispute by an arbitrator.
ar·bi·tra·tor /aárbitraytər/ *n.* a person appointed to settle a dispute; an arbiter.
ar·bor[1] /aárbər/ *n.* **1** an axle or spindle on which something revolves. **2** a device holding a tool in a lathe, etc.
ar·bor[2] /aárbər/ *n.* a shady alcove with the sides and roof formed by trees or climbing plants; a bower. ▫▫ **ar·bored** *adj.*
ar·bo·ra·ceous /aárbəráyshəs/ *adj.* **1** treelike. **2** wooded.
Ar·bor Day /aárbər/ *n.* a day dedicated annually to tree planting in the US, Australia, and other countries.
ar·bo·re·al /aarbáwreeəl/ *adj.* of, living in, or connected with trees.
ar·bo·re·tum /aárbəreétəm/ *n.* (*pl.* **arboretums** or **arboreta** /–tə/) a botanical garden devoted to trees, shrubs, etc.
ar·bor·i·za·tion /aárbərizáyshən/ *n.* a treelike arrangement, esp. in anatomy.
ar·bor vi·tae /aárbər vítee/ *n.* any of the evergreen conifers of the genus *Thuja*, native to N. Asia and N. America, usu. of pyramidal shape.
arc /aark/ *n. & v.* •*n.* **1** part of the circumference of a circle or any other curve. **2** *Electr.* a luminous discharge between two electrodes. •*v.intr.* (**arced** /aarkt/; **arcing** /aárking/) form an arc.
ar·cade /aarkáyd/ *n.* **1** a passage with an arched roof. **2** any covered walk, esp. with shops along one or both sides. **3** *Archit.* a series of arches supporting or set along a wall. ▫▫ **ar·cad·ed** *adj.*
Ar·ca·di·an /aarkáydeeən/ *n. & adj.* •*n.* an idealized peasant or country dweller, esp. in poetry. •*adj.* simple and poetically rural. ▫▫ **Ar·ca·di·an·ist** *n.*
ar·cane /aarkáyn/ *adj.* mysterious; secret; understood by few. ▫▫ **ar·cane·ly** *adv.*
ar·ca·num /aarkáynəm/ *n.* (*pl.* **arcana** /–nə/) (usu. in *pl.*) a mystery; a profound secret.
arch[1] /aarch/ *n. & v.* •*n.* **1** a curved structure as an opening or a support for a bridge, roof, floor, etc. **2** any arch-shaped curve, as on the inner side of the foot, the eyebrows, etc. •*v.* **1** *tr.* provide with or form into an arch. **2** *intr.* form an arch.
arch[2] /aarch/ *adj.* self-consciously or affectedly playful or teasing. ▫▫ **arch·ly** *adv.* **arch·ness** *n.*
arch- /aarch/ *comb.form* **1** chief; superior (*archbishop*; *archduke*). **2** preeminent of its kind (esp. in unfavorable senses) (*archenemy*).
ar·chae·ol·o·gy /aárkee–óləjee/ *n.* (also **ar·che·ol·o·gy**) the study of human history and prehistory through the excavation of sites and the analysis of physical remains. ▫▫ **ar·chae·o·log·i·cal** *adj.* **ar·chae·ol·o·gist** *n.*
ar·cha·ic /aarkáyik/ *adj.* **1 a** antiquated. **b** (of a word, etc.) no longer in ordinary use, though retained for special purposes. **2** primitive. **3** of an early period of art or culture, esp. the 7th–6th c. BC in Greece. ▫▫ **ar·cha·i·cal·ly** *adv.*
ar·cha·ism /aárkeeizəm, –kay–/ *n.* **1** the retention or imitation of the obsolete, esp. in language or art. **2** an archaic word. ▫▫ **ar·cha·is·tic** *adj.*
arch·an·gel /aárkaynjəl/ *n.* **1** an angel of the highest rank. **2** a member of the eighth order of the nine ranks of heavenly beings. ▫▫ **arch·an·gel·ic** /–anjélik/ *adj.*
arch·bish·op /aárchbíshəp/ *n.* the chief bishop of a province. ▫▫ **arch·bish·op·ric** /aárchbíshəprik/ *n.*
arch·dea·con /aárchdeékən/ *n.* a cleric in various churches ranking below a bishop. ▫▫ **arch·dea·con·ry** *n.* (*pl.* **·ries**).
arch·di·o·cese /aárchdíəsis, –seez/ *n.* the diocese of an archbishop. ▫▫ **arch·di·oc·e·san** /aárchdiósisən/ *adj.*
arch·duke /aárchdóók, –dyóók/ *n.* (*fem.* **archduchess** /–dúchis/) *hist.* the chief duke (esp. of Austria). ▫▫ **arch·du·cal** *adj.* **arch·duch·y** /–dúchee/ *n.* (*pl.* **·ies**).
arch·en·e·my /aárchénəmee/ *n.* (*pl.* **·mies**) **1** a chief enemy. **2** the Devil.
ar·che·ol·o·gy var. of ARCHAEOLOGY.
arch·er /aárchər/ *n.* **1** a person who shoots with a bow and arrows. **2** (**the Archer**) the zodiacal sign or constellation Sagittarius.
ar·cher·y /aárchəree/ *n.* shooting with a bow and arrows, esp. as a sport.
ar·che·type /aárkitīp/ *n.* **1** an original model. **2** a typical specimen. ▫▫ **ar·che·typ·al** *adj.* **ar·che·typ·i·cal** /–típikəl/ *adj.*
ar·chi·di·ac·o·nal /aárkidīákənəl/ *adj.* of or relating to an archdeacon. ▫▫ **ar·chi·di·ac·o·nate** /–nət, –nayt/ *n.*
ar·chi·e·pis·co·pal /aárkee–ipískəpəl/ *adj.* of or relating to an archbishop. ▫▫ **ar·chi·e·pis·co·pate** /–pət/ *n.*
Ar·chi·me·de·an /aárkimeédeeən/ *adj.* of or associated with the Greek mathematician Archimedes.
Ar·chi·me·de·an screw *n.* a device of ancient origin for raising water by means of a spiral inside a tube.
ar·chi·pel·a·go /aárkipéləgō/ *n.* (*pl.* **·gos** or **·goes**) a group of islands.
ar·chi·tect /aárkitekt/ *n.* **1** a designer who prepares plans for buildings, ships, etc., and supervises their construction. **2** (foll. by *of*) a person who brings about a specified thing (*the architect of the tax reform bill*).
ar·chi·tec·ton·ic /aárkitektónik/ *adj. & n.* •*adj.* **1** of architecture. **2** of the systematization of knowledge. •*n.* (in *pl.*; usu. treated as *sing.*) **1** the scientific study of architecture. **2** the study of the systematization of knowledge.
ar·chi·tec·ture /aárkitekchər/ *n.* **1** the art or science of designing and constructing buildings. **2** the style of a building as regards design and construction. **3** buildings or other structures collectively. ▫▫ **ar·chi·tec·tur·al** /–tékchərəl/ *adj.* **ar·chi·tec·tur·al·ly** *adv.*
ar·chi·trave /aárkitrayv/ *n.* **1** (in classical architecture) a main beam resting across the tops of columns. **2** the molded frame around a doorway or window.
ar·chive /aárkīv/ *n. & v.* •*n.* (usu. in *pl.*) **1** a collection of esp. public or corporate documents or records. **2** the place where these are kept. •*v.tr.* **1** place or store in an archive. **2** *Computing* transfer (data) to a less frequently used file or less easily accessible medium. ▫▫ **ar·chi·val** /aarkívəl/ *adj.*
ar·chi·vist /aárkivist, aárkī–/ *n.* a person who maintains archives.
arch·lute /aárchlóót/ *n.* a bass lute with an extended neck and unstopped bass strings.
arch·way /aárchway/ *n.* **1** a vaulted passage. **2** an arched entrance.
arc lamp *n.* (also **arc light**) a light source using an electric arc.
Arc·tic /aárktik, aártik/ *adj. & n.* •*adj.* **1** of the north polar regions. **2** (**arctic**) *colloq.* (esp. of weather) very cold. •*n.* the Arctic regions.
Arc·tic Cir·cle *n.* the parallel of latitude 66° 33′ N., forming an imaginary line around this region.
arc weld·ing *n.* a method of using an electric arc to melt metals to be welded.

ar·dent /aárd'nt/ *adj.* eager; zealous; fervent; passionate. ▫▫ **ar·den·cy** /–d'nsee/ *n.* **ar·dent·ly** *adv.*

ar·dor /aárdər/ *n.* zeal; burning enthusiasm; passion.

ar·du·ous /aárjōōəs/ *adj.* **1** (of a task, etc.) hard to achieve or overcome; laborious. **2** (of an action, etc.) strenuous. ▫▫ **ar·du·ous·ly** *adv.* **ar·du·ous·ness** *n.*

are[1] *2nd sing. present* & *1st, 2nd, 3rd pl. present* of BE.

are[2] /aar/ *n.* a metric unit of measure, equal to 100 square meters.

ar·e·a /áireeə/ *n.* **1** the extent or measure of a surface (*over a large area*). **2** a region or tract (*the southern area*). **3** a space allocated for a specific purpose (*dining area*). **4** scope or range. ▫▫ **ar·e·al** *adj.*

ar·e·a code *n.* a three-digit number that identifies one of the telephone service regions into which the US, Canada, etc., are divided and which is dialed when calling from one area to another.

a·re·ca /əreékə, árikə/ *n.* any tropical palm of the genus *Areca*, native to Asia.

a·re·na /əreénə/ *n.* **1** the central part of an amphitheater, etc., where contests take place. **2** a scene of conflict; a sphere of action or discussion.

ar·e·na·ceous /árináyshəs/ *adj.* **1** (of rocks) containing sand; having a sandy texture. **2** sandlike. **3** (of plants) growing in sand.

aren't /aarnt, aárənt/ *contr.* **1** are not. **2** (in *interrog.*) am not (*aren't I coming too?*).

a·re·o·la /əreéələ/ *n.* (*pl.* **areolae** /–lee) *Anat.* a circular pigmented area, esp. that surrounding a nipple. ▫▫ **a·re·o·lar** *adj.*

a·rête /aráyt/ *n.* a sharp mountain ridge.

ar·gent /aárjənt/ *n.* & *adj. Heraldry* silver; silvery white.

Ar·gen·tine /aárjənteen, –tīn/ *adj.* & *n.* (also **Ar·gen·tin·i·an** /–tíneeən/) • *adj.* of or relating to Argentina. • *n.* **1** a native or citizen of Argentina. **2** a person of Argentine descent. **3** (**the Argentine**) Argentina.

ar·gil /aárjil/ *n.* clay, esp. that used in pottery. ▫▫ **ar·gil·la·ceous** /–jiláyshəs/ *adj.*

ar·gon /aárgon/ *n. Chem.* an inert gaseous element of the noble gas group. ¶ Symb.: **Ar**.

ar·go·sy /aárgəsee/ *n.* (*pl.* **·sies**) *poet.* **1** a large merchant ship, orig. esp. from Ragusa (now Dubrovnik) or Venice. **2** an opulent or abundant supply.

ar·got /aárgō, –gət/ *n.* the jargon of a group or class.

ar·gu·a·ble /aárgyōōəbəl/ *adj.* open to dispute. ▫▫ **ar·gu·a·bly** *adv.*

ar·gue /aárgyōō/ *v.* (**argues, argued, arguing**) **1** *intr.* exchange views or opinions, esp. heatedly or contentiously. **2** *tr.* & *intr.* (often foll. by *that* + clause) maintain by reasoning. **3** *intr.* (foll. by *for, against*) reason (*argued against joining*). **4** *tr.* treat by reasoning (*argue the point*). ▫▫ **ar·gu·er** *n.*

ar·gu·ment /aárgyəmənt/ *n.* **1** an exchange of views, esp. a contentious or prolonged one. **2** (often foll. by *for, against*) a reason advanced (*an argument for abolition*). **3** a summary of the line of reasoning of a book.

ar·gu·men·ta·tion /aárgyəmentáyshən/ *n.* **1** methodical reasoning. **2** debate.

ar·gu·men·ta·tive /aárgyəméntətiv/ *adj.* **1** fond of arguing; quarrelsome. **2** using methodical reasoning. ▫▫ **ar·gu·men·ta·tive·ly** *adv.* **ar·gu·men·ta·tive·ness** *n.*

Ar·gus /aárgəs/ *n.* a watchful guardian.

a·ri·a /aáreeə/ *n. Mus.* a long accompanied song for solo voice in an opera.

ar·id /árid/ *adj.* **1 a** (of ground, climate, etc.) dry. **b** too dry to support vegetation. **2** uninteresting. ▫▫ **a·rid·i·ty** /ərídítee/ *n.* **ar·id·ly** *adv.* **ar·id·ness** *n.*

Ar·ies /áireez/ *n.* (*pl.* same) **1** a constellation, traditionally regarded as portraying the figure of a ram. **2 a** the first sign of the zodiac (the Ram). **b** a person born when the sun is in this sign. ▫▫ **Ar·i·an** /–reeən/ *adj.* & *n.*

a·right /ərít/ *adv.* rightly.

ar·il /áril/ *n. Bot.* an extra seed covering, e.g., around a yew seed. ▫▫ **ar·il·late** *adj.*

a·rise /ərīz/ *v.intr.* (*past* **arose** /ərṓz; *past part.* **arisen** /arízən/) **1** originate. **2** (usu. foll. by *from, out of*) result (*accidents can arise from carelessness*). **3** come to one's notice; emerge (*the question of payment arose*). **4** rise.

ar·is·toc·ra·cy /áristókrəsee/ *n.* (*pl.* **·cies**) **1** the highest class in society; the nobility. **2 a** government by a privileged group. **b** a nation governed in this way.

▶**Aristocracy, oligarchy**, and **plutocracy** are sometimes confused. All mean some form of rule by a small elite. **Aristocracy** is rule by a traditional elite, held to be made up of 'the best' people, and is usually hereditary. **Oligarchy** is literally rule by a few. **Plutocracy** is rule by the (necessarily few) very rich.

a·ris·to·crat /ərístəkrat, áris–/ *n.* a member of the aristocracy.

a·ris·to·crat·ic /arístəkrátik/ *adj.* **1** of or relating to the aristocracy. **2 a** distinguished in manners or bearing. **b** grand; stylish. ▫▫ **a·ris·to·crat·i·cal·ly** *adv.*

Ar·is·to·te·lian /áristəteéleeən, ərís–/ *n.* & *adj.* • *n.* a disciple or student of the Greek philosopher Aristotle. • *adj.* of or concerning Aristotle.

a·rith·me·tic *n.* & *adj.* • *n.* /əríthmətik/ **1** the science of numbers. **2** the use of numbers; computation. • *adj.* /árithmétik/ (also **ar·ith·met·i·cal** /–métikəl/) of or concerning arithmetic. ▫▫ **a·rith·me·ti·cian** /əríthmətíshən/ *n.*

a·rith·me·tic mean *n.* an average calculated by adding quantities and dividing the total by the number of quantities.

a·rith·me·tic pro·gres·sion *n.* **1** an increase or decrease by a constant quantity (e.g., 1, 2, 3, 4, etc., 9, 7, 5, 3, etc.). **2** a sequence of numbers showing this.

Ariz. *abbr.* Arizona.

Ark. *abbr.* Arkansas.

ark /aark/ *n.* **1** = NOAH'S ARK 1. **2** *archaic* a chest or box.

Ark of the Cov·e·nant *n.* a chest or box containing the tablets of the Ten Commandments.

arm[1] /aarm/ *n.* **1** each of the upper limbs of the human body from the shoulder to the hand. **2 a** the forelimb of an animal. **b** the flexible limb of an invertebrate animal (e.g., an octopus). **3 a** the sleeve of a garment. **b** the side part of a chair, etc., used to support a sitter's arm. **c** a thing resembling an arm in branching from a main stem (*an arm of the sea*). **4** a control; a means of reaching (*arm of the law*) **5** a division of a larger group (*the pacifist arm of the movement*). ▫ **an arm and a leg** a large sum of money. **arm in arm** (of two or more persons) with arms linked. **at arm's length 1** as far as an arm can reach. **2** far enough to avoid undue familiarity. ▫▫ **arm·ful** *n.* (*pl.* **·fuls**). **arm·less** *adj.*

arm[2] /aarm/ *n.* & *v.* • *n.* **1** (usu. in *pl.*) **a** a weapon. **b** = FIREARM. **2** (in *pl.*) the military profession. **3** a branch of the military (e.g., infantry, cavalry, artillery). **4** (in *pl.*) heraldic devices (*coat of arms*). • *v.tr.* & *refl.* **1** supply with weapons. **2** supply with tools or other requisites or advantages (*armed with the truth*). **3** make a bomb, etc.) able to explode. ▫ **under arms** ready for war or battle. **up in arms** (usu. foll. by *against, about*) actively rebelling. ▫▫ **arm·less** *adj.*

ar·ma·da /aarmaádə/ *n.* a fleet of warships, esp. those sent by Spain against England in 1588.

ar·ma·dil·lo /aármədílō/ *n.* (*pl.* **·los**) a nocturnal insect-eating mammal ranging from the south-

armadillo

ern US to S. America, with a body covered in bony plates.

Ar·ma·ged·don /aármagéd'n/ *n.* **1** (in the New Testament) the last battle between good and evil before the Day of Judgment. **2** a bloody battle or struggle on a huge scale.

ar·ma·ment /aármamənt/ *n.* **1** (often in *pl.*) military weapons and equipment, esp. guns on a warship. **2** the process of equipping for war.

ar·ma·men·tar·i·um /aármamentáireeəm/ *n.* (*pl.* **armamentaria** /–reeə/) **1** a set of medical equipment or drugs. **2** the resources available to a person engaged in a task.

ar·ma·ture /aármachŏor/ *n.* **1** the rotating coil or coils of a generator or electric motor. **2** a piece of soft iron placed in contact with the poles of a horseshoe magnet to preserve its power. Also called **keeper**. **3** *Biol.* the protective covering of an animal or plant. **4** a metal framework on which a sculpture is molded.

arm·band /aármband/ *n.* a band worn around the upper arm to hold up a shirtsleeve or as a form of identification, etc.

arm·chair /aármcháir/ *n.* **1** a comfortable chair with side supports for the arms. **2** (*attrib.*) theoretical rather than active (*an armchair critic*).

Ar·me·ni·an /aarmeéneeən/ *n.* & *adj.* • *n.* **1 a** a native of Armenia, an ancient kingdom corresponding to an area in modern Armenia, Turkey, and Iran. **b** a person of Armenian descent. **2** the language of Armenia. • *adj.* of or relating to Armenia, its language, or the Christian Church established there *c.*300.

arm·hole /aármhōl/ *n.* each of two holes in a garment through which the arms are put, usu. into a sleeve.

ar·mil·lar·y /aarmíleree/ *adj.* relating to bracelets.

ar·mi·stice /aármistis/ *n.* a stopping of hostilities by agreement of the opposing sides; a truce.

Ar·mis·tice Day *n.* former name of Veteran's Day, the anniversary of the World War I armistice of Nov. 11, 1918.

arm·let /aármlit/ *n.* a band worn around the arm.

ar·moire /aarmwaár/ *n.* a tall, upright, often ornate cupboard or wardrobe.

ar·mor /aármər/ *n.* & *v.* • *n.* **1** a defensive covering, usu. of metal, formerly worn to protect the body in fighting. **2 a** (in full **armor plate**) a protective metal covering for an armed vehicle, ship, etc. **b** armored fighting vehicles collectively. **3** a protective covering or shell on certain animals and plants. • *v.tr.* (usu. as **armored** *adj.*) provide with a protective covering (*armored car*).

ar·mor·er *n.* /aármərər/ **1** a maker or repairer of arms or armor. **2** an official in charge of a ship's or a regiment's arms.

ar·mor·y[1] /aárməree/ *n.* (*pl.* **·ies**) **1** a place where arms are kept. **2** an array of weapons, defensive resources, etc. **3** a place where arms are manufactured.

ar·mor·y[2] /aárməree/ *n.* (*pl.* **·ies**) heraldry. ▫▫ **ar·mo·ri·al** /aarmóreeəl/ *adj.*

arm·pit /aármpit/ *n.* the hollow under the arm at the shoulder.

arm·rest /aármrest/ *n.* = ARM[1] 3b.

arm-twist·ing *n. colloq.* (persuasion by) the use of physical force or moral pressure.

arm wres·tling *n.* a trial of strength in which each party tries to force the other's arm down onto a table on which their elbows rest.

ar·my /aármee/ *n.* (*pl.* **·mies**) **1** an organized force armed for fighting on land. **2** (prec. by *the*) the military profession. **3** (often foll. by *of*) a very large number (*an army of helpers*). **4** an organized body regarded as working for a particular cause.

ar·ni·ca /aárnikə/ *n.* **1** a plant of the genus *Arnica*, having yellow daisy-like flower heads. **2** a medicine prepared from this, used for bruises, etc.

a·ro·ma /ərṓmə/ *n.* a fragrance; a distinctive and pleasing smell, often of food.

a·ro·ma·ther·a·py /ərṓməthérəpee/ *n.* the use of plant extracts and essential oils in massage. ▫▫ **a·ro·ma·ther·a·peu·tic** /–pyŏotik/ *adj.* **a·ro·ma·ther·a·pist** *n.*

ar·o·mat·ic /árəmátik/ *adj.* & *n.* • *adj.* **1** fragrant. **2** *Chem.* of organic compounds having an unsaturated ring, esp. a benzene ring. • *n.* an aromatic substance. ▫▫ **ar·o·mat·i·cal·ly** *adv.* **ar·o·ma·tic·i·ty** /árəmətísitee/ *n.*

a·ro·ma·tize /ərṓmətīz/ *v.tr. Chem.* convert (a compound) into an aromatic structure. ▫▫ **a·ro·ma·ti·za·tion** /–tizáyshən/ *n.*

a·rose *past* of ARISE.

a·round /ərównd/ *adv.* & *prep.* • *adv.* **1** on every side; on all sides. **2** in various places; here and there (*fool around; shop around*). **3** *colloq.* **a** in existence; available. **b** near at hand. **4** approximately. **5** with circular motion. **6** with return to the starting point or an earlier state. **7 a** with rotation, or change to an opposite position. **b** with change to an opposite opinion, etc. **8** to, at, or affecting all or many points of an area or the members of a company, etc. **9** in every direction from a center or within a radius. **10** by a circuitous way. **11 a** to a person's house, etc. **b** to a more prominent or convenient position. **12** measuring (a specified distance) in girth. • *prep.* **1** on or along the circuit of. **2** on every side of; enveloping. **3** here and there; in or near (*chairs around the room*). **4** (of amount, time, etc.) about; at a time near to (*come around four o'clock*). **5** so as to encircle or enclose. **6** at or to points on the circumference of. **7** with successive visits to. **8** in various directions from or with regard to. **9** having as an axis of revolution or as a central point. **10 a** so as to double or pass in a curved course. **b** having passed in this way (*be around the corner*). **c** in the position that would result from this. **11** so as to come close from various sides but not into contact. **12** at various places in or around. ▫ **around the bend** see BEND[1]. **have been around** *colloq.* be widely experienced.

a·rouse /ərówz/ *v.tr.* **1** induce (esp. a feeling, emotion, etc.). **2** awake from sleep. **3** stir into activity. **4** stimulate sexually. ▫▫ **a·rous·a·ble** *adj.* **a·rous·al** *n.*

ar·peg·gi·o /aarpéjeeō/ *n.* (*pl.* **·os**) *Mus.* the notes of a chord played in succession, either ascending or descending.

arr. *abbr.* **1** *Mus.* arranged by. **2** arrives.

ar·rack /árək/ *n.* (also **ar·ak** /ərák/) an alcoholic liquor, esp. distilled from rice and various palms.

ar·raign /əráyn/ *v.tr.* **1** indict before a court; formally accuse. **2** find fault with; call into question (an action or statement). ▫▫ **ar·raign·ment** *n.*

ar·range /əráynj/ *v.* **1** *tr.* put into the required order. **2** *tr.* plan or provide for. **3** *intr.* take measures; make plans; give instructions. **4** *intr.* come to an agreement. **5** *tr. Mus.* adapt (a composition) for performance with instruments or voices other than those originally specified. ▫▫ **ar·range·a·ble** *adj.* **ar·rang·er** *n.*

ar·range·ment /əráynjmənt/ *n.* **1** the act or process of arranging or being arranged. **2** the manner in which a thing is arranged. **3** something arranged. **4** (in *pl.*) plans; preparations (*make your own arrangements*). **5** *Mus.* a composition arranged for performance by different instruments or voices.

ar·rant /árənt/ *attrib.adj.* utter (*arrant nonsense*). ▫▫ **ar·rant·ly** *adv.*

ar·ray /əráy/ *n.* & *v.* • *n.* **1** an imposing or well-ordered series or display. **2** an ordered arrangement, esp. of troops (*battle array*). **3** *Computing* an ordered set of related elements. •*v.tr.* **1** deck; adorn. **2** set in order; marshal (forces).

ar·rears /əre͞erz/ *n.pl.* an amount still outstanding or uncompleted. □ **in arrears** (or **arrear**) late, esp. in payment. □□ **ar·rear·age** *n.*

ar·rest /ərést/ *v. & n.* •*v.tr.* **1 a** seize (a person) and take into custody, esp. by legal authority. **b** seize (a ship) by legal authority. **2** stop or check (esp. a process or moving thing). **3** attract (a person's attention). •*n.* **1** the act of arresting or being arrested. **2** a stoppage or check (*cardiac arrest*). □□ **ar·rest·ing·ly** *adv.*

ar·ri·val /ərívəl/ *n.* **1** the act of arriving. **2** a person or thing that has arrived.

ar·rive /ərív/ *v.intr.* (often foll. by *at, in*) **1** reach a destination; come to the end of a journey or a specified part of a journey. **2** (foll. by *at*) reach (a conclusion, decision, etc.). **3** *colloq.* establish one's reputation or position. **4** *colloq.* (of a child) be born. **5** (of a time) come (*her birthday arrived at last*).

ar·ri·viste /áreeve͞est/ *n.* an ambitious or ruthlessly self-seeking person.

ar·ro·gant /árəgənt/ *adj.* aggressively assertive or presumptuous. □□ **ar·ro·gance** *n.* **ar·ro·gant·ly** *adv.*

ar·ro·gate /árəgayt/ *v.tr.* **1** (often foll. by *to oneself*) claim (power, responsibility, etc.) without justification. **2** (often foll. by *to*) attribute unjustly (to a person). □□ **ar·ro·ga·tion** /–gáyshən/ *n.*

ar·row /árō/ *n.* **1** a sharp pointed wooden or metal stick shot from a bow as a weapon. **2** a drawn or printed, etc., representation of an arrow indicating a direction. □□ **ar·row·y** *adj.*

ar·row·head /árōhed/ *n.* **1** the pointed end of an arrow. **2** a decorative device resembling an arrowhead.

ar·row·root /árōro͞ot, –ro͝ot/ *n.* a plant of the family Marantaceae from which a starch is prepared and used for nutritional and medicinal purposes.

ar·roy·o /əróyō/ *n.* (*pl.* **·os**) **1** a brook or stream, esp. in an arid region. **2** a gully.

ar·se·nal /áarsənəl/ *n.* **1** a store of weapons. **2** a government establishment for the storage and manufacture of weapons and ammunition. **3** resources regarded collectively.

ar·se·nic /áarsənik/ *n.* **1** a nonscientific name for arsenic trioxide, a highly poisonous substance used in weed killers, rat poison, etc. **2** *Chem.* a brittle semimetallic element, used in semiconductors and alloys. ¶ Symb.: **As.** □□ **ar·se·ni·ous** /aarse͞eniəs/ *adj.*

ar·sen·i·cal /aarsénikəl/ *adj. & n.* •*adj.* of or containing arsenic. •*n.* a drug containing arsenic.

ar·son /áarsən/ *n.* the act of maliciously setting fire to property. □□ **ar·son·ist** *n.*

art /aart/ *n.* **1 a** human creative skill or its application. **b** work exhibiting this. **2 a** (in *pl.*; prec. by *the*) the various branches of creative activity, e.g., painting, music, writing, considered collectively. **b** any one of these branches. **3** creative activity, esp. painting and drawing, resulting in visual representation (*interested in music but not art*). **4** human skill or workmanship as opposed to the work of nature. **5** (often foll. by *of*) a skill, aptitude, or knack (*the art of writing clearly*). **6** (in *pl.*; usu. prec. by *the*) those branches of learning (esp. languages, literature, and history) associated with creative skill as opposed to scientific, technical, or vocational skills.

art dec·o /dékō/ *n.* a decorative art style of the period 1910–30, characterized by precise and boldly delineated geometric motifs, shapes, and strong colors.

ar·te·ri·al /aarte͞ereeəl/ *adj.* **1** of or relating to an artery (*arterial blood*). **2** (esp. of a road) main, important, esp. linking large cities or towns.

ar·te·ri·ole /aarte͞ereeōl/ *n.* a small branch of an artery leading into capillaries.

ar·te·ri·o·scle·ro·sis /aarte͞ereeōsklərṓsis/ *n.* the loss of elasticity and thickening of the walls of the arteries, esp. in old age. □□ **ar·te·ri·o·scle·rot·ic** /–rótik/ *adj.*

ar·ter·y /áartəree/ *n.* (*pl.* **·ies**) **1** any of the muscular-walled tubes forming part of the blood circulation system of the body (cf. VEIN). **2** a main road or railroad line. □□ **ar·te·ri·tis** /–rítis/ *n.*

ar·te·sian well /aarte͞ezhən/ *n.* a well bored so that natural pressure produces a constant supply of water.

art·ful /áartfo͝ol/ *adj.* **1** (of a person or action) crafty; deceitful. **2** skillful; clever. □□ **art·ful·ly** *adv.* **art·ful·ness** *n.*

ar·thri·tis /aarthrítis/ *n.* inflammation of a joint. □□ **ar·thrit·ic** /–thrítik/ *adj. & n.*

ar·thro·pod /áarthrəpod/ *n. Zool.* any invertebrate animal of the phylum Arthropoda, with a segmented body, jointed limbs, and an external skeleton.

ar·thro·scope /árthrəskōp/ *n.* an endoscope for viewing the interior of a joint, as the knee. □□ **ar·thro·scop·ic** *adj.* **ar·thros·co·py** *n.*

ar·ti·choke /áartichōk/ *n.* **1** a European plant, *Cynara scolymus*, allied to the thistle. **2** (in full **globe artichoke**) the flower head of the artichoke, the bracts of which have edible bases.

ar·ti·cle /áartikəl/ *n. & v.* •*n.* **1** (often in *pl.*) an item or commodity (*a collection of odd articles*). **2** a nonfictional essay, esp. in a newspaper, magazine, etc. **3 a** a particular part (*an article of faith*). **b** a separate clause or portion of any document (*articles of apprenticeship*). **4** *Gram.* the definite or indefinite article. •*v.tr.* bind by articles of apprenticeship.

ar·tic·u·lar /aartíkyələr/ *adj.* of or relating to the joints.

ar·tic·u·late *adj. & v.* •*adj.* /aartíkyələt/ **1** able to speak fluently and coherently. **2** (of sound or speech) having clearly distinguishable parts. **3** having joints. •*v.* /aartíkyəlayt/ **1** *tr.* **a** pronounce (words) clearly and distinctly. **b** express (an idea, etc.) coherently. **2** *intr.* speak distinctly. **3** *tr.* (usu. in *passive*) connect by joints. **4** *intr.* (often foll. by *with*) form a joint. □□ **ar·tic·u·late·ly** *adv.* **ar·tic·u·late·ness** *n.* **ar·tic·u·la·tor** *n.*

ar·tic·u·la·tion /aartíkyəláyshən/ *n.* **1 a** the act of speaking. **b** articulate utterance; speech. **2 a** the act or a mode of jointing. **b** a joint.

ar·ti·fact /áartifakt/ *n.* **1** a product of human art and workmanship. **2** *Archaeol.* a product of prehistoric or aboriginal workmanship. □□ **ar·ti·fac·tu·al** /–fákcho͞oəl/ *adj.*

ar·ti·fice /áartifis/ *n.* **1** cunning. **2** an instance of this.

ar·tif·i·cer /aartífisər/ *n.* **1** an inventor. **2** a craftsman.

ar·ti·fi·cial /áartifishəl/ *adj.* **1** produced by human art or effort rather than originating naturally (*an artificial lake*). **2** not real; imitation; fake (*artificial flowers*). **3** affected; insincere (*an artificial smile*). □□ **ar·ti·fi·ci·al·i·ty** /–sheeálitee/ *n.* **ar·ti·fi·cial·ly** *adv.*

ar·ti·fi·cial in·sem·i·na·tion *n.* the injection of semen into the vagina or uterus other than by sexual intercourse.

ar·ti·fi·cial in·tel·li·gence *n.* the application of computers to areas normally regarded as requiring human intelligence.

ar·ti·fi·cial kid·ney *n.* an apparatus that performs the functions of the human kidney (outside the body), when one or both organs are damaged.

ar·ti·fi·cial res·pi·ra·tion *n.* the restoration or initiation of breathing by manual or mechanical or mouth-to-mouth methods.

ar·til·ler·y /aartíləree/ *n.* (*pl.* **·ies**) **1** large-caliber guns used in warfare on land. **2** a branch of the armed forces that uses these. □□ **ar·til·ler·ist** *n.*

ar·til·ler·y·man /aartíləreeman/ *n.* (*pl.* **·men**) a member of the artillery.

ar·ti·o·dac·tyl /aartéeōdáktil/ *adj. & n.* • *adj.* of or relating to the order Artiodactyla of ungulate mammals with two main toes on each foot, including camels, pigs, and ruminants. • *n.* an animal of this order.
ar·ti·san /áartizən, –sən/ *n.* a skilled, esp. manual, worker or craftsman.
art·ist /áartist/ *n.* **1** a painter. **2** a person who practices any of the arts. **3** a professional performer, esp. a singer or dancer. **4** *colloq.* a practicer of a specified activity (*con artist*). ▫▫ **art·ist·ry** *n.*
ar·tis·tic /aartístik/ *adj.* **1** having natural skill in art. **2** made or done with art. **3** of art or artists. ▫▫ **ar·tis·ti·cal·ly** *adv.*
art·less /áartlis/ *adj.* **1** guileless. **2** not displaying art. ▫▫ **art·less·ly** *adv.*
art nou·veau /áart noovó/ *n.* an art style of the late 19th century characterized by flowing lines and natural organic forms.
arts and crafts *n.pl.* decorative design and handcrafts.
art·sy-craft·sy /ártsee–kráftsee/ *adj.* quaintly artistic.
art·work /áartwərk/ *n.* the illustrations in a printed work.
art·y /áartee/ *adj.* (**artier, artiest**) *colloq.* pretentiously artistic. ▫▫ **art·i·ness** *n.*
ar·um lil·y *n.* = CALLA.
Ar·y·an /áireeən/ *n. & adj.* • *n.* **1** a member of the peoples speaking any of the languages of the Indo-European (esp. Indo-Iranian) family. **2** the parent language of this family. **3** *improperly* (in Nazi ideology) a Caucasian not of Jewish descent. • *adj.* of or relating to Aryan or the Aryans.
AS *abbr.* American Samoa (in official postal use).
As *symb. Chem.* the element arsenic.
as /az, *unstressed* əz/ *adv., conj., & pron.* • *adv. & conj.* (*adv.* as antecedent in main sentence; *conj.* in relative clause expressed or implied) ... to the extent to which ... is or does, etc. (*I am as tall as he is; am not so tall as he; as many as six; as recently as last week*). • *conj.* (with relative clause expressed or implied) **1** (with antecedent *so*) expressing result or purpose (*came early so as to meet us*). **2** (with antecedent adverb omitted) having concessive force (*good as it is* = although it is good). **3** (without antecedent adverb) **a** in the manner in which (*do as you like*). **b** in the capacity or form of (*I speak as your friend; as a matter of fact*). **c** during or at the time that (*came up as I was speaking*). **d** for the reason that (*as you are here, we can talk*). • *rel.pron.* (with verb of relative clause expressed or implied) **1** that; who; which (*I had the same trouble as you; he is a writer, as is his wife; such countries as France*). **2** (with sentence as antecedent) a fact that (*he lost, as you know*). ▫ **as for** with regard to (*as for you, I think you are wrong*). **as if** (or **though**) as would be the case if (*acts as if she were in charge; looks as though we've won*). **as it is** in the existing circumstances. **as it were** in a way; to a certain extent (*he is, as it were, infatuated*). **as of 1** on and after (a specified date). **2** as at (a specified time). **as to** with respect to (*as to you, I think you are wrong*). **as yet** until now or a particular time in the past (usu. with *neg: have received no news as yet*).
▶See note at LIKE.
a.s.a.p. *abbr.* (also **ASAP**) as soon as possible.
as·bes·tos /asbéstəs, az–/ *n.* a fibrous silicate mineral that is not flammable. ▫▫ **as·bes·tine** /–tin/ *adj.*
as·bes·to·sis /ásbestósis, áz–/ *n.* a lung disease resulting from the inhalation of asbestos particles.
as·cend /əsénd/ *v.* **1** *intr.* move upward. **2** *intr.* slope upward. **3** *tr.* climb. **4** *intr.* rise in rank or status. **5** *intr.* (of sound) rise in pitch. ▫ **ascend the throne** become king or queen.
as·cend·an·cy /əséndənsee/ *n.* (also **as·cend·en·cy**) (often foll. by *over*) a superior position.
as·cend·ant /əséndənt/ *adj. & n.* • *adj.* **1** rising. **2** *Astron.* rising toward the zenith. **3** *Astrol.* just above the eastern horizon. **4** predominant • *n. Astrol.* the point of the sun's apparent path that is ascendant at a given time.
as·cend·er /əséndər/ *n.* **1 a** a part of a letter that extends above the main part (as in b and d). **b** a letter having this. **2** a person or thing that ascends.
as·cen·sion /əsénshən/ *n.* **1** the act or instance of ascending. **2** (**Ascension**) the ascent of Christ into heaven. ▫▫ **as·cen·sion·al** *adj.*
as·cent /əsént/ *n.* **1** the act or instance of ascending. **2 a** an upward movement or rise. **b** advancement or progress (*the ascent of mammals*). **3** a way by which one may ascend; an upward slope (*a steep ascent*).
as·cer·tain /ásərtáyn/ *v.tr.* find out as a definite fact. ▫▫ **as·cer·tain·a·ble** *adj.* **as·cer·tain·ment** *n.*
as·ce·sis /əséesis/ *n.* the practice of self-discipline.
as·cet·ic /əsétik/ *n. & adj.* • *n.* a person who practices severe self-discipline and abstains from pleasure, esp. for religious or spiritual reasons. • *adj.* relating to or characteristic of ascetics. ▫▫ **as·cet·i·cal·ly** *adv.* **as·cet·i·cism** /–tisizəm/ *n.*
ASCII /áskee/ *abbr. Computing* American Standard Code for Information Interchange.
as·ci·tes /əsíteez/ *n.* (*pl.* same) *Med.* the accumulation of fluid in the abdominal cavity, causing swelling.
a·scor·bic ac·id /əskáwrbik/ *n.* a vitamin found in citrus fruits and green vegetables, a deficiency of which results in scurvy. Also called **vitamin C**.
as·cot /áskot, –kət/ *n.* a scarf-like item of neckwear with broad ends worn looped to lie flat one over the other against the chest.
as·cribe /əskríb/ *v.tr.* usu. foll. by *to*) **1** attribute or impute (*ascribes his well-being to a sound constitution*). **2** (usu. *be ascribed to*) attribute a text, quotation, or work of art to (a person or period). ▫▫ **a·scrib·a·ble** *adj.*
as·crip·tion /əskrípshən/ *n.* **1** the act or an instance of ascribing. **2** a preacher's words ascribing praise to God at the end of a sermon.
ASEAN /áseeən/ *abbr.* Association of South East Asian Nations.
a·sep·sis /aysépsis/ *n.* the absence of harmful bacteria, viruses, or other microorganisms.
a·sep·tic /ayséptik/ *adj.* free from contamination caused by harmful bacteria, viruses, or other microorganisms.
a·sex·u·al /ayséksho͞oəl/ *adj. Biol.* **1** without sex or sexual organs. **2** (of reproduction) not involving the fusion of gametes. ▫▫ **a·sex·u·al·i·ty** /–sho͞oálitee/ *n.* **a·sex·u·al·ly** *adv.*
ash[1] /ash/ *n.* **1** (often in *pl.*) the powdery residue left after the burning of any substance. **2** (*pl.*) the remains of the human body after cremation.
ash[2] /ash/ *n.* **1** any tree of the genus *Fraxinus*, with silvery-gray bark and hard wood. **2** its wood.
ash blond *n.* (also **ash blonde**) **1** a very pale blond color. **2** a person with hair of this color.
ash·en /áshən/ *adj.* **1** of or resembling ashes. **2** ash colored; gray or pale.
Ash·ke·naz·i /áashkənáazee/ *n.* (*pl.* **Ashkenazim** /–zim/) a Jew of eastern European ancestry (cf. SEPHARDI). ▫▫ **Ash·ke·naz·ic** *adj.*
ash·lar /áshlər/ *n.* **1** a large square-cut stone used in building. **2** masonry made of ashlars.
a·shore /əsháwr/ *adv.* toward or on the shore.
ash·ram /áashrəm/ *n. Ind.* a place of religious retreat for Hindus; a hermitage.

---

ash·tray /áshtray/ *n.* a small receptacle for cigarette ashes, butts, etc.

Ash Wednes·day *n.* the first day of Lent (from the custom of marking the foreheads of penitents with ashes on that day).

ash·y /áshee/ *adj.* (**ashier, ashiest**) **1** = ASHEN. **2** covered with ashes.

A·sian /áyzhən, –shən/ *n. & adj.* • *n.* **1** a native of Asia. **2** a person of Asian descent. • *adj.* of or relating to Asia or its people, customs, or languages.
▶See note at ORIENTAL.

A·si·at·ic /áyzheeátik, –shee–, –zee–/ *n. & adj.* • *n. offens.* an Asian. • *adj.* Asian.

A-side /áy–sīd/ *n.* the side of a phonograph record regarded as the main one.

a·side /əsíd/ *adv. & n.* • *adv.* **1** to or on one side. **2** out of consideration (*joking aside*). • *n.* **1** a remark in a play intended for the audience but supposedly unheard by the other characters in the play. **2** an incidental remark. □ **aside from** apart from. **set aside 1** put to one side. **2** keep for future use. **3** reject. **4** annul. **5** remove (land) from agricultural production for fallow, forestry, or other use. **take aside** engage (a person) esp. in a private conversation.

as·i·nine /ásinīn/ *adj.* stupid. □□ **as·i·nin·i·ty** /–nínitee/ *n.*

ask /ask/ *v.* **1** *tr.* call for an answer to or about. **2** *tr.* seek to obtain from another person. **3** *tr.* (usu. foll. by *out* or *over*, or *to* (a function, etc.)) invite. **4** *intr.* (foll. by *for*) seek to obtain, meet, or be directed to. □ **ask after** inquire about (esp. a person). **ask for it** *sl.* invite trouble. **for the asking** for nothing. **if you ask me** *colloq.* in my opinion. □□ **ask·er** *n.*

a·skance /əskáns/ *adv.* sideways or squinting. □ **look askance at** regard with suspicion or disapproval.

a·skew /əskyóó/ *adv. & predic.adj.* • *adv.* obliquely; awry. • *predic.adj.* oblique; awry.

a·slant /əslánt/ *adv. & prep* • *adv.* at a slant. • *prep.* obliquely across.

a·sleep /əsléep/ *predic.adj. & adv.* **1** in or into a state of sleep (*he fell asleep*). **2** (of a limb, etc.) numb. **3** *euphem.* dead.

ASM *abbr.* air-to-surface missile.

a·so·cial /áysṓshəl/ *adj.* **1** not social; antisocial. **2** hostile to others.

asp /asp/ *n.* **1** a small viper, *Vipera aspis*, native to southern Europe. **2** a small venomous snake, *Naja haje*, native to North Africa and Arabia.

as·par·a·gus /əspárəgəs/ *n.* **1** any plant of the genus *Asparagus*. **2** one species of this, *A. officinalis*, with edible young shoots and leaves.

as·par·tame /əspaártaym/ *n.* a sweet, low-calorie substance used as a sweetener instead of sugar.

as·pect /áspekt/ *n.* **1 a** a particular component or feature of a matter (*only one aspect of the problem*). **b** a particular way in which a matter may be considered. **2 a** a facial expression; a look (*a cheerful aspect*). **b** the appearance of a person or thing (*has a frightening aspect*). **3** the side of a building or location facing a particular direction (*southern aspect*).

as·pect ra·tio *n.* **1** *Aeron.* the ratio of the span to the mean chord of an airfoil. **2** *Telev.* the ratio of picture width to height.

as·pen /áspən/ *n.* a poplar tree, *Populus tremula*, with tremulous leaves.

as·per·i·ty /əspéritee/ *n.* (*pl.* **·ties**) **1** harshness of temper or tone. **2** roughness.

as·per·sion /əspérzhən/ *n.* □ **cast aspersions on** attack the reputation of.

as·phalt /ásfalt/ *n. & v.* • *n.* **1** a dark bituminous pitch occurring naturally or made from petroleum. **2** a mixture of this with sand, gravel, etc., for surfacing roads. • *v.tr.* surface with asphalt. □□ **as·phal·tic** /–fáltik/ *adj.*

as·pho·del /ásfədel/ *n.* **1** any plant of the genus *Asphodelus*, of the lily family. **2** *poet.* an immortal flower growing in Elysium.

as·phyx·i·a /asfíkseeə/ *n.* a lack of oxygen in the blood, causing unconsciousness or death; suffocation. □□ **as·phyx·i·ant** *adj. & n.*

as·phyx·i·ate /asfíkseeayt/ *v.tr.* cause (a person) to have asphyxia; suffocate. □□ **as·phyx·i·a·tion** /–áyshən/ *n.*

as·pic /áspik/ *n.* a savory meat jelly used as a garnish.

as·pi·dis·tra /áspidístrə/ *n.* a foliage plant with broad tapering leaves, often grown as a houseplant.

as·pir·ant /áspirənt, əspírənt/ *adj. & n.* • *adj.* aspiring. • *n.* a person who aspires.

as·pi·rate /áspirət/ *adj., n., & v. Phonet.* • *adj.* **1** pronounced with an exhalation of breath. **2** blended with the sound of *h*. • *n.* **1** a consonant pronounced in this way. **2** the sound of *h*. • *v.* also /áspiráyt/ **1 a** *tr.* pronounce with a breath. **b** *intr.* make the sound of *h*. **2** *tr.* draw (fluid) by suction from a vessel or cavity.

as·pi·ra·tion /áspiráyshən/ *n.* **1** an ambition. **2** the act of drawing breath. **3** the action of aspirating.

as·pi·ra·tor /áspiraytər/ *n.* an apparatus for aspirating fluid.

as·pire /əspír/ *v.intr.* **1** have ambition. **2** *poet.* rise high.

as·pi·rin /ásprin/ *n.* (*pl.* same or **aspirins**) **1** a white powder, acetylsalicylic acid, used to relieve pain and reduce fever. **2** a tablet of this.

a·squint /əskwínt/ *predic.adj. & adv.* **1** to one side; from the corner of an eye. **2** with a squint.

ass[1] /as/ *n.* **1 a** either of two kinds of four-legged long-eared mammals of the horse genus *Equus*, *E. africanus* of Africa and *E. hemionus* of Asia. **b** (in general use) a donkey. **2** a stupid person.

ass[2] /as/ (*Brit.* **arse** /aars/) *n. coarse sl.* the buttocks.
▶usually considered a taboo word.

as·sa·i /así/ *adv. Mus.* very (*adagio assai*).

as·sail /əsáyl/ *v.tr.* make a concerted attack on. □□ **as·sail·a·ble** *adj.*

as·sail·ant /əsáylənt/ *n.* a person who attacks another.

as·sas·sin /əsásin/ *n.* a killer, esp. of a political or religious leader.

as·sas·si·nate /əsásinayt/ *v.tr.* kill for political or religious motives. □□ **as·sas·si·na·tion** /–náyshən/ *n.*

as·sault /əsáwlt/ *n. & v.* • *n.* **1** a violent attack. **2 a** *Law* an act that threatens physical harm to a person. **b** *euphem.* an act of rape. **3** (*attrib.*) relating to an assault (*assault troops*). **4** a vigorous start made to a lengthy task. **5** a final rush on a fortified place. • *v.tr.* **1** make an assault on. **2** *euphem.* rape. □□ **as·sault·er** *n.*

as·say /əsáy, ásay/ *n. & v.* • *n.* **1** the testing of a metal or ore to determine its ingredients and quality. **2** *Chem.* etc., the determination of the content or strength of a substance. • *v.* **1** *tr.* make an assay of (a metal or ore). **2** *tr. Chem.* etc. perform a concentration on (a substance). **3** *tr.* show (content) on being assayed. **4** *intr.* make an assay. □□ **as·say·er** *n.*

as·sem·blage /əsémblij/ *n.* **1** the act of bringing or coming together. **2** a collection of things or gathering of people.

as·sem·ble /əsémbəl/ *v.* **1** *tr. & intr.* gather together; collect. **2** *tr.* arrange in order. **3** *tr.* esp. *Mech.* fit together the parts of.

as·sem·bler /əsémblər/ *n.* **1** a person who assembles a machine or its parts. **2** *Computing* **a** a program for converting instructions written in low-level symbolic code into machine code. **b** the low-level symbolic code itself.

as·sem·bly /əsémblee/ *n.* (*pl.* **·blies**) **1** the act of gathering together. **2 a** a group of persons gathered together, esp. as a deliberative or legislative body. **b** a gathering of the entire membership of a school. **3** the assembling of a machine or structure or its parts. **4** *Mil.* a call to assemble, given by drum or bugle.

as·sem·bly lan·guage *n. Computing* the low-level symbolic code converted by an assembler.

as·sem·bly line *n.* machinery arranged in stages by which a product is progressively assembled.

as·sent /əsént/ *v. & n.* • *v.intr.* (usu. foll. by *to*) **1** express agreement (*assented to my view*). **2** consent (*assented to my request.* • *n.* **1** mental acceptance or agreement (*nod of assent*). **2** consent or sanction, esp. official.

as·sert /əsə́rt/ *v.* **1** *tr.* state clearly. **2** *refl.* insist on one's rights. **3** *tr.* vindicate a claim to.

as·ser·tion /əsə́rshən/ *n.* **1** a forthright statement. **2** the act of asserting. **3** (also **self-assertion**) insistence on the recognition of one's rights.

as·ser·tive /əsə́rtiv/ *adj.* **1** tending to assert oneself; forthright; positive. **2** dogmatic. ▫▫ **as·ser·tive·ly** *adv.* **as·ser·tive·ness** *n.*

as·sess /əsés/ *v.tr.* **1 a** estimate the size or quality of. **b** estimate the value of (a property) for taxation. **2 a** fix the amount of (a tax, etc.) and impose it on a person or community. **b** fine or tax (a person, community, etc.) at a specific amount. ▫▫ **as·sess·a·ble** *adj.* **as·sess·ment** *n.*

as·ses·sor /əsésər/ *n.* a person who assesses taxes or estimates the value of property for taxation purposes.

as·set /áset/ *n.* **1 a** a useful or valuable quality. **b** a person or thing possessing such a quality. **2** (usu. in *pl.*) property and possessions, regarded as having value in meeting debts, commitments, etc.

as·sev·er·ate /əsévərayt/ *v.tr.* declare solemnly. ▫▫ **as·sev·er·a·tion** /–ráyshən/ *n.*

ass·hole /ás–hōl/ *n.* **1** the anus. **2** *offens.* a term of contempt for a person.

as·si·du·i·ty /ásidóoitee, –dyóo–/ *n.* (*pl.* **·ties**) constant or close attention to what one is doing.

as·sid·u·ous /əsíjooəs/ *adj.* persevering; hardworking. ▫▫ **as·sid·u·ous·ly** *adv.* **as·sid·u·ous·ness** *n.*

as·sign /əsín/ *v. & n.* • *v.tr.* **1 a** allot as a share or responsibility. **b** appoint to a position, task, etc. **2** fix (a time, place, etc.) for a specific purpose. **3** (foll. by *to*) ascribe to (a reason, date, etc.). **4** (foll. by *to*) transfer formally to. • *n.* a person to whom property or rights are legally transferred. ▫▫ **as·sign·a·ble** *adj.*

as·sig·na·tion /ásignáyshən/ *n.* **1 a** an appointment to meet. **b** a secret appointment, esp. between illicit lovers. **2** the act of assigning.

as·sign·ee /ásīnée/ *n.* **1** a person appointed to act for another. **2** an assign.

as·sign·ment /əsínmənt/ *n.* **1** something assigned, esp. a task allotted to a person. **2** the act of assigning. **3 a** a legal transfer. **b** the document effecting this.

as·sim·i·late /əsímilayt/ *v.* **1** *tr.* **a** absorb (food, etc.) into the body. **b** absorb (information, etc.) into the mind. **c** absorb (people) into a larger group. **2** *tr.* cause to resemble. ▫▫ **as·sim·i·la·ble** /əsímələbəl/ *adj.* **as·sim·i·la·tion** /–láyshən/ *n.* **as·sim·i·la·tive** *adj.* **as·sim·i·la·tor** *n.* **as·sim·i·la·to·ry** /–lətáwree/ *adj.*

As·sin·i·boin /əsínəboyn/ *n.* **1 a** a N. American people native to northeastern Montana and adjoining parts of Canada. **b** a member of this people. **2** the language of this people.

as·sist /əsíst/ *v. & n.* • *v.tr.* help (a person, process, etc.). • *n. Sports* a player's action of helping a teammate to put out a runner (as in baseball) or score (as in basketball). ▫▫ **as·sis·tance** *n.*

as·sis·tant /əsístənt/ *n.* **1** a helper. **2** (often *attrib.*) a person who assists.

as·so·ci·ate *v., n., & adj.* • *v.* /əsṓsheeayt, –see–/ **1** *tr.* connect in the mind. **2** *tr.* join or combine. **3** *refl.* make oneself a partner; declare oneself in agreement. **4** *intr.* combine for a common purpose. **5** *intr.* meet frequently or have dealings. • *n.* /əsṓsheeət, –see–/ **1** a business partner or colleague. **2** a friend or companion. **3** a subordinate member of a body, institute, etc. • *adj.* /əsṓshiət, əsṓsee–/ **1** joined in companionship, function, or dignity. **2** allied; in the same group or category. **3** of less than full status. ▫▫ **as·so·ci·ate·ship** *n.*

as·so·ci·a·tion /əsṓseeáyshən/ *n.* **1** a group of people organized for a joint purpose. **2** the act or an instance of associating. **3** fellowship; human contact or cooperation. **4** a mental connection between ideas. ▫▫ **as·so·ci·a·tion·al** *adj.*

as·so·ci·a·tive /əsṓsheeətiv, –see–/ *adj.* **1** of or involving association. **2** *Math.* involving the condition that a group of quantities connected by operators gives the same result whatever their grouping, as long as their order remains the same, e.g., $(a \times b) \times c = a \times (b \times c)$.

as·so·nance /ásənəns/ *n.* the resemblance of sound between two syllables in nearby words (e.g., *fat black cat*).

as·sort /əsáwrt/ *v.* **1** *tr.* classify in groups. **2** *intr.* suit; harmonize with.

as·sort·ed /əsáwrtid/ *adj.* **1** of various kinds put together; miscellaneous. **2** sorted into groups. **3** matched (*ill-assorted; poorly assorted*).

as·sort·ment /əsáwrtmənt/ *n.* a mixed collection.

as·suage /əswáyj/ *v.tr.* **1** soothe (a person, pain, etc.). **2** appease or relieve (an appetite or desire). ▫▫ **as·suage·ment** *n.*

as·sume /əsóom/ *v.tr.* **1** accept as being true, without proof, for the purpose of argument or action. **2** pretend (ignorance, etc.). **3** undertake (an office or duty). **4** take or put on oneself or itself (an aspect, attribute, etc.). **5** arrogate, usurp, or seize (credit, power, etc.).

as·sumed /əsóomd/ *adj.* **1** false; adopted (*went under an assumed name*). **2** supposed; accepted (*assumed income*).

as·sum·ing /əsóoming/ *adj.* (of a person) taking too much for granted; arrogant; presumptuous.

as·sump·tion /əsúmpshən/ *n.* **1** the act or an instance of assuming. **2 a** the act or an instance of accepting without proof. **b** a thing assumed in this way. **3** arrogance. **4** (**Assumption**) the reception of the Virgin Mary bodily into heaven, according to Roman Catholic and Orthodox Christian belief.

as·sur·ance /əshóorəns/ *n.* **1** a positive declaration that a thing is true. **2** a solemn promise or guarantee. **3** esp. *Brit.* insurance. **4** certainty. **5 a** self-confidence. **b** impudence.

as·sure /əshóor/ *v.tr.* **1 a** make (a person) sure; convince (*assured him of my sincerity*). **b** tell (a person) confidently (*assured him the bus went to Baltimore*). **2 a** make certain of; ensure the happening, etc., of (*will assure her success*). **b** make safe (against overthrow, etc.). **3** *Brit.* insure. **4** (as **assured** *adj.*) **a** guaranteed. **b** self-confident. ▫▫ **as·sur·er** *n.*

▶See note at INSURE.

as·sur·ed·ly /əshóoridlee/ *adv.* certainly.

as·sur·ed·ness /əshóoridnis/ *n.* certainty; (self-)assurance.

AST *abbr.* Atlantic Standard Time.

as·ta·tine /ástəteen, –tin/ *n. Chem.* a radioactive element, the heaviest of the halogens, which occurs naturally. ¶ Symb.: **At.**

as·ter /ástər/ *n.* a plant of the genus *Aster*, with bright daisylike flowers.

as·ter·isk /ástərisk/ *n.* & *v.* •*n.* a symbol (*) used in printing and writing to mark words, etc., for reference, to stand for omitted matter, etc. •*v.tr.* mark with an asterisk.
▶Avoid pronouncing this word "as-tuhr-riks,"; many regard this as uneducated.

a·stern /əstə́rn/ *adv. Naut.* & *Aeron.* **1** aft; away to the rear. **2** backward.

as·ter·oid /ástəroyd/ *n.* **1** any of the small celestial bodies revolving around the sun. **2** *Zool.* a starfish. ▫▫ **as·ter·oi·dal** /ástəróyd'l/ *adj.*

as·the·ni·a /asthéeneeə/ *n. Med.* loss of strength; debility.

asth·ma /ázmə, ás–/ *n.* a respiratory disease, often with paroxysms of difficult breathing.

asth·mat·ic /azmátik, as–/ *adj.* & *n.* •*adj.* relating to or suffering from asthma. •*n.* a person suffering from asthma. ▫▫ **asth·mat·i·cal·ly** *adv.*

a·stig·ma·tism /əstígmətizəm/ *n.* a defect in the eye or in a lens resulting in distorted images, as light rays are prevented from meeting at a common focus. ▫▫ **as·tig·mat·ic** /ástigmátik/ *adj.*

a·stir /əstə́r/ *predic.adj.* & *adv.* **1** in motion. **2** awake and out of bed (*astir early*; *already astir*). **3** excited.

as·ton·ish /əstónish/ *v.tr.* amaze; surprise greatly. ▫▫ **as·ton·ish·ing** *adj.* **as·ton·ish·ing·ly** *adv.* **as·ton·ish·ment** *n.*

as·tound /əstównd/ *v.tr.* shock with alarm or surprise; amaze. ▫▫ **as·tound·ing** *adj.* **as·tound·ing·ly** *adv.*

as·tral /ástrəl/ *adj.* **1** of or connected with the stars. **2** consisting of stars.

a·stray /əstráy/ *adv.* & *predic.adj.* **1** in or into error or sin (esp. **lead astray**). **2** out of the right way. ▫ **go astray** be lost or misled.

a·stride /əstríd/ *adv.* & *prep* •*adv.* **1** with a leg on each side. **2** with legs apart. •*prep.* with a leg on each side of.

as·trin·gent /əstrínjənt/ *adj.* & *n.* •*adj.* **1** causing the contraction of body tissues. **2** checking bleeding. **3** severe; austere. •*n.* an astringent substance or drug. ▫▫ **as·trin·gen·cy** /–jənsee/ *n.* **as·trin·gent·ly** *adv.*

astro- /ástrō/ *comb.form* **1** relating to the stars. **2** relating to outer space.

as·tro·labe /ástrəlayb/ *n.* an instrument, usu. consisting of a disk and pointer, formerly used to make astronomical measurements and as an aid in navigation.

as·trol·o·gy /əstróləjee/ *n.* the study of the movements and relative positions of celestial bodies interpreted as an influence on human affairs. ▫▫ **as·trol·o·ger** *n.* **as·tro·log·i·cal** /ástrəlójikəl/ *adj.* **as·trol·o·gist** *n.*

as·tro·naut /ástrənawt/ *n.* a person trained to travel in a spacecraft. ▫▫ **as·tro·nau·ti·cal** /–náwtikəl/ *adj.*

as·tro·nau·tics /ástrənáwtiks/ *n.* the science of space travel.

as·tro·nom·i·cal /ástrənómikəl/ *adj.* (also **as·tro·nom·ic**) **1** of or relating to astronomy. **2** extremely large; too large to contemplate. ▫▫ **as·tro·nom·i·cal·ly** *adv.*

as·tro·nom·i·cal u·nit *n.* a unit of measurement in astronomy equal to the mean distance from the center of the earth to the center of the sun.

as·tron·o·my /əstrónəmee/ *n.* the scientific study of celestial bodies and other matter beyond earth's atmosphere. ▫▫ **as·tron·o·mer** *n.*

as·tro·phys·ics /ástrōfíziks/ *n.* a branch of astronomy concerned with the physics of celestial bodies. ▫▫ **as·tro·phys·i·cal** *adj.* **as·tro·phys·i·cist** /–zisist/ *n.*

As·tro·turf /ástrōtərf/ *n.propr.* an artificial grass surface, esp. for sports fields.

as·tute /əstóot, əstyóot/ *adj.* **1** shrewd. **2** crafty. ▫▫ **as·tute·ly** *adv.* **as·tute·ness** *n.*

a·sun·der /əsúndər/ *adv. literary* apart.

a·sy·lum /əsíləm/ *n.* **1** sanctuary; protection (*seek asylum*). **2** *hist.* any of various kinds of institution offering shelter to distressed individuals, esp. the mentally ill.

a·sym·me·try /aysímitree/ *n.* lack of symmetry. ▫▫ **a·sym·met·ric** /–métrik/ *adj.* **a·sym·met·ri·cal** *adj.* **a·sym·met·ri·cal·ly** /–métrikəlee/ *adv.*

a·symp·to·mat·ic /áysimptəmátik/ *adj.* producing or showing no symptoms.

a·syn·chro·nous /aysíngkrənəs/ *adj.* not synchronous. ▫▫ **a·syn·chro·nous·ly** *adv.*

At *symb. Chem.* the element astatine.

at /at, *unstressed* ət/ *prep.* **1** expressing position (*wait at the corner*; *is at school*; *at a distance*). **2** expressing a point in time (*see you at three*). **3** expressing a point in a scale or range (*at boiling point*; *at his best*). **4** expressing engagement or concern in a state or activity (*at work*; *at odds*). **5** expressing a value or rate (*sell at $10 each*). **6 a** with or with reference to; in terms of (*at a disadvantage*; *good at soccer*; *sick at heart*). **b** by means of (*drank it at a gulp*). **7** expressing: **a** motion toward (*went at them*). **b** aim toward or pursuit of (*aim at the target*; *guess at the truth*; *laughed at us*). ▫ **at that** moreover (*found one, and a good one at that*).

at·a·rac·tic /átəráktik/ *adj.* & *n.* (also **at·a·rax·ic** /–ráksik/)•*adj.* calming or tranquilizing. •*n.* a tranquilizing drug.

at·a·rax·y /átəraksee/ *n.* (also **at·a·rax·i·a** /–rákseeə/) calmness or tranquility; imperturbability.

at·a·vism /átəvizəm/ *n.* **1** a resemblance to remote ancestors rather than to parents in plants or animals. **2** reversion to an earlier type. ▫▫ **at·a·vis·tic** *adj.* **at·a·vis·ti·cal·ly** *adv.*

a·tax·i·a /ətákseeə/ *n. Med.* the loss of full control of bodily movements. ▫▫ **a·tax·ic** *adj.*

ate *past* of EAT.

at·el·ier /átəlyáy/ *n.* a workshop or artist's studio.

a tem·po /aa témpō/ *adv. Mus.* in the previous tempo.

a·the·ism /áytheeizəm/ *n.* the theory or belief that God does not exist. ▫▫ **a·the·ist** *n.* **a·the·is·tic** *adj.* **a·the·is·ti·cal** *adj.*

a·the·mat·ic /áytheemátik/ *adj.* **1** *Mus.* not based on the use of themes. **2** *Gram.* (of a verb form) having a suffix attached to the stem without a correcting (thematic) vowel.

ath·e·nae·um /áthinéeəm/ *n.* (also **ath·e·ne·um**) **1** an institution for literary or scientific study. **2** a library.

ath·er·o·scle·ro·sis /áthərōsklərṓsis/ *n.* a form of arteriosclerosis characterized by the degeneration of the arteries because of a buildup of fatty deposits. ▫▫ **ath·er·o·scle·rot·ic** /–rótik/ *adj.*

ath·lete /áthleet/ *n.* a skilled performer in sports and physical activities, esp. *Brit.* in track and field events.

ath·lete's foot *n.* a fungal foot condition.

ath·let·ic /athlétik/ *adj.* **1** of or relating to athletes or athletics. **2** muscular or physically powerful. ▫▫ **ath·let·i·cal·ly** *adv.* **ath·let·i·cism** /–tisizəm/ *n.*

ath·let·ics /athlétiks/ *n.pl.* (usu. treated as *sing.*) **1 a** physical exercises. **b** the practice of these. **2** physical sports and games of any kind.

a·thwart /əthwáwrt/ *adv.* & *prep* •*adv.* **1** across from side to side (usu. obliquely). **2** perversely or in opposition. •*prep.* **1** from side to side of. **2** in opposition to.

At·lan·tic Time *n.* the standard time used in the most eastern parts of Canada and in parts of the Caribbean.

at·las /átləs/ *n.* a book of maps or charts.

ATM *abbr.* automated teller machine.

at·man /aátmən/ *n. Hinduism* **1** the real self. **2** the supreme spiritual principle.

at•mos•phere /átməsfeer/ *n.* **1 a** the envelope of gases surrounding the earth, any other planet, or any substance. **b** the air in any particular place. **2** the pervading tone or mood of a place or situation. **3** *Physics* a unit of pressure equal to mean atmospheric pressure at sea level. □□ **at•mos•pher•ic** /–férik, –féer–/ *adj.* **at•mos•pher•i•cal•ly** *adv.*

at•mos•pher•ics /átməsfériks, –féer–/ *n.pl.* **1** electrical disturbance in the atmosphere. **2** interference with telecommunications caused by this.

at•oll /átawl, átol, áy–/ *n.* a ring-shaped coral reef enclosing a lagoon.

at•om /átəm/ *n.* **1** the smallest particle of a chemical element that can take part in a chemical reaction. **2** this particle as a source of nuclear energy.

at•om bomb *n.* a bomb involving the release of energy by nuclear fission.

a•tom•ic /ətómik/ *adj.* **1** concerned with or using atomic energy or atomic bombs. **2** of or relating to an atom or atoms. □□ **a•tom•i•cal•ly** *adv.*

a•tom•ic bomb *n.* = ATOM BOMB.

a•tom•ic clock *n.* a clock in which the time scale is regulated by the vibrations of an atomic or molecular system, such as cesium.

a•tom•ic en•er•gy *n.* nuclear energy.

a•tom•ic mass *n.* the mass of an atom measured in atomic mass units.

a•tom•ic mass u•nit *n.* a unit of mass used to express atomic and molecular weight.

a•tom•ic num•ber *n.* the number of protons in the nucleus of an atom, which is characteristic of a chemical element and determines its place in the periodic table.

a•tom•ic par•ti•cle *n.* any one of the particles of which an atom is constituted.

a•tom•ic phys•ics *n.* the branch of physics concerned with the structure of the atom and the characteristics of the elementary particles of which it is composed.

a•tom•ic pow•er *n.* nuclear power.

a•tom•ic struc•ture *n.* the structure of an atom as being a central positively charged nucleus surrounded by negatively charged orbiting electrons.

a•tom•ic the•o•ry *n.* **1** the concept of an atom as being composed of elementary particles. **2** the theory that all matter is made up of small indivisible particles called atoms.

a•tom•ic weight *n.* the ratio of the average mass of one atom of an element to one twelfth of the mass of an atom of carbon-12. Also called **relative atomic mass.**

at•om•ize /átəmīz/ *v.tr.* reduce to atoms or fine particles. □□ **at•om•i•za•tion** *n.*

at•om•iz•er /átəmīzər/ *n.* an instrument for emitting liquids as a fine spray.

a•ton•al /áytṓn'l/ *adj. Mus.* not written in any key or mode. □□ **a•to•nal•i•ty** /–nálitee/ *n.*

a•tone /ətṓn/ *v.intr.* (usu. foll. by *for*) make amends; expiate for (a wrong).

a•tone•ment /ətṓnmənt/ *n.* **1** expiation; reparation for a wrong or injury. **2** the reconciliation of God and humans. **3** (**the Atonement**) the expiation by Christ of humankind's sin.

a•ton•ic /ətónik/ *adj.* **1** without accent or stress. **2** *Med.* lacking bodily tone. □□ **at•o•ny** /átənee/ *n.*

a•top /ətóp/ *adv. & prep* • *adv.* on the top. • *prep.* on the top of.

ATP *abbr.* adenosine triphosphate.

at•ra•bil•ious /átrəbílyəs/ *adj.* melancholy; ill-tempered.

a•tri•um /áytreeəm/ *n.* (*pl.* **atriums** or **atria** /–treeə/) **1 a** the central court of an ancient Roman house. **b** a central court rising through several stories with galleries and rooms opening off at each level. **c** (in a modern house) a central hall or courtyard with rooms opening off it. **2** *Anat.* a cavity in the body, esp. one of the two upper cavities of the heart, receiving blood from the veins. □□ **a•tri•al** *adj.*

a•tro•cious /ətrṓshəs/ *adj.* **1** very bad or unpleasant (*atrocious weather*). **2** extremely savage or wicked (*atrocious cruelty*). □□ **a•tro•cious•ly** *adv.*

a•troc•i•ty /ətrósitee/ *n.* (*pl.* **•ties**) **1** an extremely evil or cruel act. **2** extreme wickedness.

at•ro•phy /átrəfee/ *v. & n.* • *v.* (**•phies, •phied**) **1** *intr.* waste away through undernourishment or lack of use. **2** *tr.* cause to atrophy. • *n.* the process of atrophying.

at•ro•pine /átrəpeen, –pin/ *n.* a poisonous alkaloid found in deadly nightshade, used in medicine.

at•tach /ətách/ *v.* **1** *tr.* fasten; affix; join. **2** *tr.* (in *passive*; foll. by *to*) be very fond of or devoted to (*am deeply attached to her*). **3** *tr.* attribute; assign (some function, quality, or characteristic) (*attaches great importance to it*). **4 a** *tr.* include (*attach no conditions to the agreement*). **b** *intr.* (foll. by *to*) be an attribute or characteristic (*great prestige attaches to the job*). **5** *refl.* join; take part (*climbers attached themselves to the expedition*). **6** *tr.* appoint for special or temporary duties. **7** *tr. Law* seize (a person or property) by legal authority. □□ **at•tach•a•ble** *adj.*

at•ta•ché /atasháy/ *n.* a person appointed to an ambassador's staff (*military attaché; press attaché*).

at•ta•ché case *n.* a small flat rectangular case for carrying documents, etc.

at•tached /ətácht/ *adj.* **1** fixed; connected; enclosed. **2** (of a person) involved in a long-term relationship, esp. engagement or marriage.

at•tach•ment /ətáchmənt/ *n.* **1** a thing attached or to be attached. **2** affection; devotion. **3** a means of attaching. **4** the act of attaching. **5** legal seizure.

at•tack /əták/ *v. & n.* • *v.* **1** *tr.* act against with force. **2** *tr.* seek to hurt or defeat. **3** *tr.* criticize adversely. **4** *tr.* act harmfully upon (*a virus attacking the nervous system*). **5** *tr.* vigorously apply oneself to (*attacked his meal with gusto*). **6** *intr.* make an attack. **7** *intr.* be in a mode of attack. • *n.* **1** the act of attacking. **2** an offensive operation. **3** *Mus.* the action of beginning a piece, passage, etc. **4** gusto; vigor. **5** a sudden occurrence of an illness. **6** a player or players seeking to score goals, etc.; offensive players. □□ **at•tack•er** *n.*

at•tain /ətáyn/ *v.* **1** *tr.* reach (a goal, etc.). **2** *tr.* accomplish (an aim, distinction, etc.). **3** *intr.* (foll. by *to*) arrive at by conscious development. □□ **at•tain•a•ble** *adj.* **at•tain•a•bil•i•ty** *n.*

at•tain•ment /ətáynmənt/ *n.* **1** something achieved. **2** the act of attaining.

at•tar /átaar/ *n.* (also **ot•to** /ótō/) a fragrant essential oil, esp. from rose petals.

at•tempt /ətémpt/ *v. & n.* • *v.tr.* seek to achieve or master (a task, action, etc.) (*attempted to explain*). • *n.* an endeavor (*an attempt to succeed*).

at•tend /əténd/ *v.* **1** *tr.* **a** be present at (*attended the meeting*). **b** go regularly to (*attends the local school*). **2** *intr.* **a** be present (*many members failed to attend*). **b** be present in a serving capacity. **3 a** *tr.* escort (*the king was attended by soldiers*). **b** *intr.* (foll. by *on*) wait on. **4** *intr.* **a** apply one's mind (*attend to what I am saying*). **b** (foll. by *to*) deal with (*shall attend to the matter myself*). **5** *tr.* follow as a result from (*the error was attended by serious consequences*). □□ **at•tend•er** *n.*

at•tend•ance /əténdəns/ *n.* **1** the act of attending. **2** the number of people present (*a high attendance*).

at·tend·ant /əténdənt/ *n. & adj.* •*n.* a person employed to wait on others. •*adj.* **1** accompanying. **2** waiting on.

at·tend·ee /átendée/ *n.* a person who attends (a meeting, etc.).

at·ten·tion /aténshən/ *n. & int* •*n.* **1** the act or faculty of applying one's mind (*attract his attention*). **2 a** consideration (*give attention to the problem*). **b** care (*give special attention to your handwriting*). **3** (in *pl.*) **a** ceremonious politeness (*he paid his attentions to her*). **b** wooing (*he was the subject of her attentions*). **4** *Mil.* an erect attitude of readiness (*stand at attention*). •*int.* (in full **stand to attention!**) *Mil.* an order to assume an attitude of attention.

at·ten·tion def·i·cit hy·per·ac·tiv·i·ty dis·or·der *n.* (also **attention deficit disorder**) a behavioral disorder occurring primarily in children, including such symptoms as poor concentration, hyperactivity, and learning difficulties. ¶ Abbr.: **ADHD**.

at·ten·tive /aténtiv/ *adj.* **1** paying attention. **2** assiduously polite. ▫▫ **at·ten·tive·ly** *adv.* **at·ten·tive·ness** *n.*

at·ten·u·ate *v. & adj.* •*v.tr.* /aténydoayt/ **1** make thin. **2** reduce in force, value, or virulence. •*adj.* /aténydoət/ **1** slender. **2** tapering gradually. **3** rarefied. ▫▫ **at·ten·u·at·ed** *adj.* **at·ten·u·a·tion** /–áyshən/ *n.* **at·ten·u·a·tor** *n.*

at·test /atést/ *v.* **1** *tr.* certify the validity of. **2** *intr.* (foll. by *to*) bear witness to. ▫▫ **at·test·a·ble** *adj.* **at·tes·tor** *n.*

At·tic /átik/ *adj.* of or relating to ancient Athens or Attica, or the form of Greek spoken there.

at·tic /átik/ *n.* **1** the uppermost story in a house, usu. under the roof. **2** a room in the attic area.

at·tire /ətír/ *v. & n.* •*v.tr. formal* dress, esp. in fine clothes or formal wear. •*n.* clothes, esp. fine or formal.

at·ti·tude /átitood, –tyood/ *n.* **1 a** a settled opinion. **b** behavior reflecting this. **2 a** a bodily posture. **b** a pose adopted for dramatic effect. ▫▫ **at·ti·tu·di·nal** /–tóod'nəl, –tyóod–/ *adj.*

at·tor·ney /ətárnee/ *n.* (*pl.* **·neys**) **1** a person, esp. a lawyer, appointed to act for another in business or legal matters. **2** a lawyer. ▫▫ **at·tor·ney·ship** *n.*

at·tor·ney gen·er·al *n.* the chief legal officer in the US, England, and other countries.

at·tract /ətrákt/ *v.tr.* **1** (also *absol.*) draw to oneself or itself. **2** be attractive to. **3** (of a magnet, etc.) exert a pull on (an object). ▫▫ **at·tract·a·ble** *adj.* **at·trac·tor** *n.*

at·trac·tion /ətrákshən/ *n.* **1 a** the power of attracting (*the attraction of foreign travel*). **b** a person or thing that attracts by arousing interest (*the fair is a big attraction*). **2** *Physics* the force by which bodies attract or approach each other (opp. REPULSION).

at·trac·tive /ətráktiv/ *adj.* **1** attracting or capable of attracting (*an attractive proposition*). **2** aesthetically pleasing. ▫▫ **at·trac·tive·ly** *adv.* **at·trac·tive·ness** *n.*

at·trib·ute *v. & n.* •*v.tr.* /ətríbyoot/ (foll. by *to*) **1** regard as belonging or appropriate (*a poem attributed to Shakespeare*). **2** ascribe; regard as the effect of a stated cause (*the delays were attributed to the heavy traffic*). •*n.* /átribyoot/ **1 a** a quality ascribed to a person or thing. **b** a characteristic quality. **2** a material object recognized as appropriate to a person, office, or status. ▫▫ **at·trib·ut·a·ble** /ətríbyootəbəl/ *adj.* **at·tri·bu·tion** /–byóoshən/ *n.*

at·trib·u·tive /ətríbyətiv/ *adj. Gram.* (of an adjective or noun) preceding the word described and expressing an attribute, as *old* in *the old dog* and *expiration* in *expiration date* (opp. PREDICATIVE). ▫▫ **at·trib·u·tive·ly** *adv.*

at·tri·tion /ətríshən/ *n.* **1** the act or process of gradually wearing out. **2** abrasion.

at·tune /ətóon, ətyóon/ *v.tr.* **1** adjust (a person or thing) to a situation. **2** bring (an orchestra, instrument, etc.) into musical accord.

atty. *abbr.* attorney.

Atty. Gen. *abbr.* Attorney General.

ATV *abbr.* all-terrain vehicle.

a·typ·i·cal /áytípikəl/ *adj.* not conforming to a type. ▫▫ **a·typ·i·cal·ly** *adv.*

Au *symb. Chem.* the element gold.

au·burn /áwbərn/ *adj.* reddish brown (usu. of a person's hair).

---

auburn late Middle English: from Old French *auborne*, *alborne*, from Latin *alburnus* 'whitish,' from *albus* 'white.' The original sense was 'yellowish white,' but the word became associated with *brown* because in the 16th and 17th centuries it was often written *abrune* or *abroun*.

---

auc·tion /áwkshən/ *n. & v.* •*n.* a sale of goods in which articles are sold to the highest bidder. •*v.tr.* sell at auction.

auc·tion·eer /áwkshənéer/ *n.* a person who conducts auctions professionally, by calling for bids and declaring goods sold. ▫▫ **auc·tion·eer·ing** *n.*

au·da·cious /awdáyshəs/ *adj.* **1** daring; bold. **2** impudent. ▫▫ **au·da·cious·ly** *adv.* **au·da·cious·ness** *n.* **au·dac·i·ty** /awdásitee/ *n.*

au·di·ble /áwdibəl/ *adj.* capable of being heard. ▫▫ **au·di·bil·i·ty** *n.* **au·di·bly** *adv.*

au·di·ence /áwdeeəns/ *n.* **1 a** the assembled listeners or spectators at an event. **b** the people addressed by a movie, play, etc. **2** a formal interview with a person in authority.

au·di·o /áwdeeō/ *n.* (usu. *attrib.*) sound or the reproduction of sound.

audio- /áwdeeō/ *comb.form* hearing or sound.

au·di·o·cas·sette /áwdeeōkəsét/ *n.* an audiotape enclosed within a cassette.

au·di·o fre·quen·cy *n.* a frequency capable of being perceived by the human ear.

au·di·ol·o·gy /áwdeeóləjee/ *n.* the science of hearing. ▫▫ **au·di·ol·o·gist** *n.*

au·di·om·e·ter /áwdeeómitər/ *n.* an instrument for testing hearing.

au·di·o·phile /áwdeeōfil/ *n.* a high-fidelity sound enthusiast.

au·di·o·tape /áwdeeōtayp/ *n.* **1 a** magnetic tape on which sound can be recorded. **b** a length of this. **2** a sound recording on tape.

au·di·o·vis·u·al /áwdeeōvízhyooəl/ *adj.* using both sight and sound.

au·dit /áwdit/ *n. & v.* •*n.* an official examination of accounts. •*v.tr.* (**audited, auditing**) **1** conduct an audit of. **2** attend (a class) informally, without working for a grade or credit.

au·di·tion /awdíshən/ *n. & v.* •*n.* a test of a performer's ability or suitability, usu. for a particular role. •*v.* assess or be assessed.

au·di·tor /áwditər/ *n.* **1** a person who audits accounts. **2** a person who audits a class. **3** a listener. ▫▫ **au·di·to·ri·al** /–táwreeəl/ *adj.*

au·di·to·ri·um /áwditáwreeəm/ *n.* (*pl.* **auditoriums** or **auditoria** /–reeə/) the part of a theater, etc., in which the audience sits.

au·di·to·ry /áwditawree/ *adj.* **1** concerned with hearing. **2** received by the ear.

au fait /ō fáy/ *predic.adj.* (usu. foll. by *with*) having current knowledge (*au fait with the arrangements*).

Aug. *abbr.* August.

au·ger /áwgər/ *n.* a tool resembling a large corkscrew, for boring holes.

aught /awt/ *n.* (also **ought**) *archaic* (usu. implying *neg.*) anything at all.

aug·ment /awgmént/ *v.tr. & intr.* increase. ▫▫ **aug·ment·er** *n.*

aug·men·ta·tion /áwgmentáyshən/ *n.* **1** enlargement; growth; increase. **2** *Mus.* the lengthening of the time values of notes in melodic parts.

aug·ment·a·tive /awgméntətiv/ *adj.* having the property of increasing.

au grat·in /ṓ gratáN/ *adj. Cooking* cooked with a crisp brown crust, usu. of breadcrumbs or melted cheese.

au·gur /áwgər/ *v. & n.* •*v.* **1** *intr.* (of an event, circumstance, etc.) suggest a specified outcome (usu. **augur well** or **ill**). **2** *tr.* **a** foresee; predict. **b** portend. •*n.* an ancient Roman religious official who observed natural signs, esp. the behavior of birds, interpreting these as an indication of divine approval or disapproval of a proposed action. ▫▫ **au·gu·ral** *adj.*

au·gu·ry /áwgyəree/ *n.* (*pl.* **·ries**) **1** an omen. **2** the interpretation of omens.

Au·gust /áwgəst/ *n.* the eighth month of the year.

au·gust /awgúst/ *adj.* inspiring reverence. ▫▫ **au·gust·ly** *adv.* **au·gust·ness** *n.*

Au·gus·tan /awgústən/ *adj.* connected with the reign of the Roman emperor Augustus, esp. as an outstanding period of Latin literature.

Au·gus·tin·i·an /áwgəstíneeən/ *adj. & n.* •*adj.* **1** of or relating to St. Augustine or his doctrines. **2** belonging to a religious order observing a rule derived from St. Augustine's writings. •*n.* one of the order of Augustinian friars.

auk /awk/ *n.* any sea diving bird of the family Alcidae, with heavy body, short wings, and black and white plumage, e.g., the puffin.

auld lang syne /áwld lang zīn, sīn/ *n.* times long past.

au na·tu·rel /ṓ nachərél/ *predic.adj. & adv.* naked.

aunt /ant, aant/ *n.* **1** the sister of one's father or mother. **2** an uncle's wife. **3** *colloq.* an unrelated woman friend of a child or children.

au pair /ō páir/ *n.* a young foreign person, esp. a woman, helping with housework, etc., in exchange for room, board, and pocket money.

au·ra /áwrə/ *n.* (*pl.* **aurae** /–ree/ or **auras**) **1** the distinctive atmosphere diffused by or attending a person, place, etc. **2** (in mystic or spiritualistic use) a supposed subtle emanation, surrounding the body of a living creature. **3** a subtle emanation or aroma from flowers, etc. **4** *Med.* premonitory symptom(s) in epilepsy, etc.

au·ral[1] /áwrəl/ *adj.* of or relating to or received by the ear. ▫▫ **au·ral·ly** *adv.*

au·ral[2] /áwrəl/ *adj.* of, relating to, or resembling an aura; atmospheric.

au·re·ate /áwreeət/ *adj.* **1** golden, gold colored. **2** resplendent.

au·re·ole /áwreeōl/ *n.* (also **au·re·o·la** /awreéələ/) **1** a halo or circle of light. **2** a corona around the sun or moon.

au re·voir /ṓ rəvwaár/ *int. & n.* good-bye.

au·ri·cle /áwrikəl/ *n. Anat.* **1 a** a small muscular pouch on the surface of each atrium of the heart. **b** the atrium itself. **2** the external ear of animals.

au·ric·u·la /awríkyələ/ *n.* a primrose, *Primula auricula*, with leaves shaped like bears' ears.

au·ric·u·lar /awríkyələr/ *adj.* **1** of or relating to the ear or hearing. **2** of or relating to the auricle of the heart. **3** shaped like an auricle.

au·rochs /áwroks, ówroks/ *n.* (*pl.* same) an extinct wild ox, *Bos primigenius*, ancestor of domestic cattle.

au·ro·ra /awráwrə/ *n.* (*pl.* **auroras** or **aurorae** /–ree/) **1** a luminous electrical atmospheric phenomenon, usu. of streamers of light in the sky above the northern or southern magnetic pole. **2** *poet.* the dawn. ▫▫ **au·ro·ral** *adj.*

au·ro·ra aus·tra·lis /awstráylis/ *n.* a southern occurrence of aurora.

au·ro·ra bo·re·al·is /báwree–ális/ *n.* a northern occurrence of aurora.

aus·cul·ta·tion /áwskəltáyshən/ *n.* the act of listening to sounds from the heart, lungs, etc., as a part of medical diagnosis. ▫▫ **aus·cul·ta·to·ry** /–kúltətawree/ *adj.*

aus·pice /áwspis/ *n.* **1** (in *pl.*) patronage (esp. **under the auspices of**). **2** a forecast.

aus·pi·cious /awspíshəs/ *adj.* **1** of good omen; favorable. **2** prosperous. ▫▫ **aus·pi·cious·ly** *adv.* **aus·pi·cious·ness** *n.*

Aus·sie /áwsee, –zee/ *n. & adj.* (also **Ossie, Ozzie**) •*n. colloq.* an Australian. •*adj.* Australian.

aus·tere /awsteér/ *adj.* (**austerer, austerest**) **1** severely simple. **2** morally strict. **3** harsh; stern. ▫▫ **aus·tere·ly** *adv.*

aus·ter·i·ty /awstéritee/ *n.* (*pl.* **·ties**) **1** sternness; moral severity. **2** severe simplicity. **3** (esp. in *pl.*) an austere practice.

aus·tral /áwstrəl/ *adj.* **1** southern. **2** (**Austral**) of Australia or Australasia.

Aus·tral·a·sian /áwstrəláyzhən, –shən/ *adj.* of or relating to Australasia, a region consisting of Australia and islands of the SW Pacific.

Aus·tral·ian /awstráylyən/ *n. & adj.* •*n.* **1** a native or inhabitant of Australia. **2** a person of Australian descent. •*adj.* of or relating to Australia. ▫▫ **Aus·tral·ian·ism** *n.*

Austro- /áwstrō/ *comb.form* Austrian; Austrian and (*Austro-Hungarian*).

au·then·tic /awthéntik/ *adj.* **1** of undisputed origin; genuine. **2** reliable or trustworthy. **3** *Mus.* (of a mode) containing notes between the final and an octave higher. ▫▫ **au·then·ti·cal·ly** *adv.* **au·then·tic·i·ty** /áwthentísitee/ *n.*

au·then·ti·cate /awthéntikayt/ *v.tr.* **1** establish the truth or genuineness of. **2** validate. ▫▫ **au·then·ti·ca·tion** /–káyshən/ *n.* **au·then·ti·ca·tor** *n.*

au·thor /áwthər/ *n. & v.* •*n.* (*fem.* **authoress** /áwthris, áwthərés/) **1** a writer, esp. of books. **2** the originator of an event, condition, etc. (*the author of all my woes*). •*v.tr.* be the author of. ▫▫ **au·tho·ri·al** /awtháwriəl/ *adj.*

---

author Middle English (in the sense 'a person who invents or causes something'): from Old French *autor*, from Latin *auctor*, from *augere* 'increase, originate, promote.' The spelling with *th* arose in the 15th cent., and perhaps became established under the influence of *authentic*.

---

au·thor·i·tar·i·an /ətháwritáireeən, əthór–/ *adj.* **1** favoring, encouraging, or enforcing strict obedience to authority, as opposed to individual freedom. **2** tyrannical or domineering. ▫▫ **au·thor·i·tar·i·an·ism** *n.*

au·thor·i·ta·tive /ətháwritáytiv, əthór–/ *adj.* **1** being recognized as true or dependable. **2** (of a person, behavior, etc.) commanding or self-confident. **3** official; supported by authority (*an authoritative document*). **4** having or claiming influence through recognized knowledge or expertise. ▫▫ **au·thor·i·ta·tive·ly** *adv.* **au·thor·i·ta·tive·ness** *n.*

au·thor·i·ty /ətháwritee, əthór–/ *n.* (*pl.* **·ties**) **1 a** the power or right to enforce obedience. **b** (often foll. by *for*, or *to* + infin.) delegated power. **2** (esp. in *pl.*) a person or body having authority, esp. political or administrative. **3 a** an influence exerted on opinion because of recognized knowledge or expertise. **b** such an influence expressed in a book, etc. (*an authority on vintage cars*). **c** an expert in a subject.

au·thor·ize /áwthərīz/ *v.tr.* **1** sanction. **2** (foll. by *to* + infin.) **a** give authority. **b** commission (a person or body) (*authorized to trade*). □□ **au·thor·i·za·tion** /–rizáyshən/ *n.*

au·thor·ship /áwthərship/ *n.* **1** the origin of a written work. **2** the occupation of writing.

au·tism /áwtizəm/ *n.* a mental condition characterized by complete self-absorption and a reduced ability to respond to the outside world. □□ **au·tis·tic** /awtístik/ *adj.*

au·to /áwtō/ *n.* (*pl.* **·tos**) *colloq.* an automobile.

auto- /áwtō/ *comb.form* (usu. **aut-** before a vowel) **1** self (*autism*). **2** one's own (*autobiography*). **3** by oneself (*autosuggestion*). **4** automatic (*automobile*).

au·to·bahn /áwtōbaan/ *n.* a German, Austrian, or Swiss highway.

au·to·bi·og·ra·phy /áwtōbīógrəfee/ *n.* (*pl.* **·phies**) **1** a personal account of one's own life. **2** this as a process or literary form. □□ **au·to·bi·og·ra·pher** *n.* **au·to·bi·o·graph·ic** /–bīəgráfik/ *adj.* **au·to·bi·o·graph·i·cal** *adj.*

au·toch·thon /awtókthən/ *n.* (*pl.* **autochthons** or **autochthones** /–thəneez/) (in *pl.*) the original or earliest known inhabitants of a country; aboriginals. □□ **au·toch·tho·nous** *adj.*

au·to·clave /áwtōklayv/ *n.* **1** a strong vessel used for chemical reactions at high pressures and temperatures. **2** a sterilizer using high pressure steam.

au·toc·ra·cy /awtókrəsee/ *n.* (*pl.* **·cies**) **1** absolute government by one person. **2** the power exercised by such a person. **3** an autocratic country or society.

au·to·crat /áwtəkrat/ *n.* **1** an absolute ruler. **2** a dictatorial person. □□ **au·to·crat·ic** /–krátik/ *adj.* **au·to·crat·i·cal·ly** *adv.*

au·to·cross /áwtōkraws, –kros/ *n.* automobile racing on a challenging course that usu. includes twisting turns and obstacles.

auto-da-fé /áwtōdaafáy/ *n.* (*pl.* **autos-da-fé** /áwtōz–/) **1** a sentence of punishment by the Spanish Inquisition. **2** the execution of such a sentence.

au·to·di·dact /áwtōdídakt, –dákt/ *n.* a self-taught person. □□ **au·to·di·dac·tic** /–dáktik/ *adj.*

au·to·er·o·tism /áwtō–érətizəm/ *n.* (also **au·to·e·rot·i·ci·sm** /–irótisizəm/) *Psychol.* masturbation. □□ **au·to·e·rot·ic** /–irótik/ *adj.*

au·to·fo·cus /áwtōfōkəs/ *n.* a device for focusing a camera, etc., automatically.

au·tog·a·my /awtógəmee/ *n. Bot.* self-fertilization in plants. □□ **au·tog·a·mous** *adj.*

au·tog·e·nous /awtójinəs/ *adj.* arising from within or from a thing itself; self-produced.

au·to·gi·ro /áwtōjírō/ *n.* (also **au·to·gy·ro**) (*pl.* **·ros**) an early form of helicopter with freely rotating horizontal vanes and a propeller.

au·to·graft /áwtōgraft/ *n. Surgery* a graft of tissue from one point to another of the same person's body.

au·to·graph /áwtəgraf/ *n. & v.* • *n.* **1 a** a signature, esp. that of a celebrity. **b** handwriting. **2** a manuscript in an author's handwriting. **3** a document signed by its author. • *v.tr.* **1** sign (a photograph etc.). **2** write (a letter, etc.) by hand.

au·to·gy·ro var. of AUTOGIRO.

Au·to·harp /áwtōhaarp/ *n. Trademark* a kind of zither with a mechanical device to allow the playing of chords.

au·to·im·mune /áwtōimyóōn/ *adj. Med.* (of a disease) caused by antibodies produced against substances naturally present in the body. □□ **au·to·im·mu·ni·ty** *n.*

au·to·in·tox·i·ca·tion /áwtōintóksikáyshən/ *n. Med.* poisoning by a toxin formed within the body itself.

au·tol·y·sis /awtólisis/ *n.* the destruction of cells by their own enzymes. □□ **au·to·lyt·ic** /áwtəlítik/ *adj.*

Au·to·mat /áwtəmat/ *n. Trademark* a cafeteria containing coin-operated machines dispensing food and drink.

au·to·mate /áwtəmayt/ *v.tr.* convert to or operate by automation (*the ticket office has been automated*).

au·to·mat·ed tel·ler ma·chine *n.* an electronic machine that allows customers to perform banking transactions such as depositing or withdrawing funds, etc. ¶ Abbr.: **ATM**

au·to·mat·ic /áwtəmátik/ *adj. & n.* • *adj.* **1** (of a device or its function) designed to work by itself, without direct human intervention. **2 a** done spontaneously, without conscious thought or intention (*an automatic reaction*). **b** necessary and inevitable (*an automatic penalty*). **3** *Psychol.* performed unconsciously or subconsciously. **4** (of a firearm) that continues firing until the ammunition is exhausted or the pressure on the trigger is released. **5** (of a motor vehicle or its transmission) using gears that change automatically according to speed and acceleration. • *n.* **1** an automatic device. **2** *colloq.* a vehicle with automatic transmission. □□ **au·to·mat·i·cal·ly** *adv.* **au·to·ma·tic·i·ty** /áwtəmətísitee/ *n.*

au·to·mat·ic pi·lot *n.* a device for automatically keeping an aircraft on a set course.

au·to·ma·tion /áwtəmáyshən/ *n.* **1** the use of automatic equipment to save labor. **2** the automatic control of the manufacture of a product through its successive stages.

au·tom·a·tism /awtómətizəm/ *n.* **1** *Psychol.* the performance of actions unconsciously or subconsciously. **2** involuntary action. **3** unthinking routine.

au·tom·a·tize /awtómətīz/ *v.tr.* **1** make (a process, etc.) automatic. **2** subject (a business, enterprise, etc.) to automation. □□ **au·tom·a·ti·za·tion** *n.*

au·tom·a·ton /awtómətən, –ton/ *n.* (*pl.* **automata** /–tə/ or **automatons**) **1** an automated device with concealed motive power; a robot. **2** a person who behaves in a mechanical or unemotional way.

au·to·mo·bile /áwtəməbeel/ *n.* a motor vehicle for road use with an enclosed passenger compartment; a car.

au·to·mo·tive /áwtəmṓtiv/ *adj.* concerned with motor vehicles.

au·to·nom·ic /áwtənómik/ *adj.* esp. *Physiol.* functioning involuntarily.

au·to·nom·ic nerv·ous sys·tem *n.* the part of the nervous system responsible for control of the bodily functions not consciously directed, e.g., heartbeat.

au·ton·o·mous /awtónəməs/ *adj.* **1** having self-government. **2** acting independently or having the freedom to do so. □□ **au·ton·o·mous·ly** *adv.*

au·ton·o·my /awtónəmee/ *n.* (*pl.* **·mies**) **1** the right of self-government. **2** personal freedom. **3** freedom of the will. **4** a self-governing community. □□ **au·ton·o·mist** *n.*

au·to·pi·lot /áwtōpīlət/ *n.* an automatic pilot.

au·top·sy /áwtopsee/ *n.* (*pl.* **·sies**) **1** a postmortem examination. **2** any critical analysis.

au·to·ra·di·o·graph /áwtōráydeeəgraf/ *n.* a photograph of an object, produced by radiation from radioactive material in the object. □□ **au·to·ra·di·o·graph·ic** *adj.* **au·to·ra·di·og·ra·phy** /áwtōráydiógrəfee/ *n.*

au·to·save *n. & v.* • *n.* a software facility that automatically saves a computer user's work at regular intervals. • *v.tr.* save (keyed work) automatically.

au·to·sug·ges·tion /áwtōsəgjéschən/ *n.* a hypnotic or

subconscious suggestion made by a person to himself or herself and affecting behavior.

au·tot·o·my /awtótəmee/ *n. Zool.* the casting off of a part of the body when threatened, e.g., the tail of a lizard.

au·to·tox·in /áwtōtóksin/ *n.* a poisonous substance originating within an organism. ▫▫ **au·to·tox·ic** *adj.*

au·to·trans·form·er /áwtōtransfáwrmər/ *n.* an electrical transformer that has a single coil winding, part of which is common to both primary and secondary circuits.

au·to·type /áwtətīp/ *n.* **1** a facsimile. **2 a** a photographic printing process for monochrome reproduction. **b** a print made by this process.

au·tumn /áwtəm/ *n.* **1** the third season of the year, when crops and fruits are gathered, and leaves fall. Also called FALL. **2** *Astron.* the period from the autumnal equinox to the winter solstice.

au·tum·nal /awtúmnəl/ *adj.* **1** of, characteristic of, or appropriate to autumn (*autumnal colors*). **2** occurring in autumn (*autumnal equinox*).

au·tum·nal e·qui·nox *n.* the time in fall (about September 22) when the sun crosses the celestial equator, and day and night are of equal length.

aux·il·ia·ry /awgzílyəree/ *adj. & n.* • *adj.* **1** (of a person or thing) that gives help. **2** (of services or equipment) subsidiary; additional. • *n.* (*pl.* **·ries**) **1** an auxiliary person or thing. **2** (in *pl.*) *Mil.* auxiliary troops.

aux·il·ia·ry verb *n. Gram.* one used in forming tenses, moods, and voices of other verbs.

aux·in /áwksin/ *n.* a plant hormone that regulates growth.

AV *abbr.* audiovisual (teaching aids, etc.).

a·vail /əváyl/ *v. & n.* • *v.* **1** *tr.* help; benefit. **2** *refl.* (foll. by *of*) profit by; take advantage of. **3** *intr.* **a** provide help. **b** be of use, value, or profit. • *n.* (usu. in *neg.* or *interrog.* phrases) use; profit (*to no avail*).

a·vail·a·ble /əváyləbəl/ *adj.* (often foll. by *to, for*) **1** capable of being used; at one's disposal. **2** within one's reach. **3** (of a person) **a** free. **b** able to be contacted. ▫▫ **a·vail·a·bil·i·ty** *n.* **a·vail·a·ble·ness** *n.* **a·vail·a·bly** *adv.*

av·a·lanche /ávəlanch/ *n.* **1** a mass of snow and ice tumbling rapidly down a mountain. **2** a sudden arrival of anything in large quantities (*an avalanche of work*).

a·vant-garde /avóɴ-gaárd/ *n. & adj.* • *n.* pioneers or innovators. • *adj.* (of ideas, etc.) new; progressive. ▫▫ **a·vant-gard·ism** *n.* **a·vant-gard·ist** *n.*

av·a·rice /ávəris/ *n.* extreme greed for money or material gain. ▫▫ **av·a·ri·cious** /–ríshəs/ *adj.* **av·a·ri·cious·ly** *adv.* **av·a·ri·cious·ness** /–ríshəsnis/ *n.*

a·vast /əvást/ *int. Naut.* stop; cease.

av·a·tar /ávətaar/ *n.* **1** (in Hindu mythology) the descent of a deity or released soul to earth in bodily form. **2** incarnation. **3** a manifestation or phase.

Ave. *abbr.* Avenue.

a·venge /əvénj/ *v.tr.* **1** inflict retribution on behalf of. **2** take vengeance for (an injury). ▫ **be avenged** avenge oneself. ▫▫ **a·veng·er** *n.*

av·e·nue /ávənoo, –nyoo/ *n.* **1** a broad road or street, often with trees at regular intervals along its sides. **2** a way of dealing with something.

a·ver /əvə́r/ *v.tr.* (**averred, averring**) *formal* assert; affirm.

av·er·age /ávərij, ávrij/ *n., adj., & v.* • *n.* **1 a** the usual amount, extent, or rate. **b** the ordinary standard. **2** an amount obtained by dividing the total of given amounts by the number of amounts in the set. • *adj.* **1 a** usual; typical. **b** mediocre; undistinguished. **2** estimated by average. • *v.tr.* **1** amount on average to. **2** do on average. **3 a** estimate the average of. **b** estimate the general standard of. ▫ **average out at** result in an average of. **on average** as an average rate or estimate.

---

average late 15th cent.: from French *avarie* 'damage to ship or cargo,' earlier 'customs duty,' from Italian *avaria*, from Arabic *'awār* 'damage to goods'; the suffix *-age* is on the pattern of *damage.* Originally denoting a charge or customs duty payable by the owner of goods to be shipped, the term later denoted the financial liability from goods lost or damaged at sea, and specifically the equitable apportionment of this between the owners of the vessel and the cargo (late 16th cent.); this gave rise to the general sense of the equalizing out of gains and losses by calculating the mean (mid-18th cent.).

---

a·ver·ment /əvə́rmənt/ *n.* an affirmation, esp. *Law* one with an offer of proof.

a·verse /əvə́rs/ *predic.adj.* (usu. foll. by *to*; also foll. by *from*) opposed; disinclined (*not averse to helping*). ▶See note at ADVERSE.

a·ver·sion /əvə́rzhən, –shən/ *n.* **1** (usu. foll. by *to, from, for*) a strong dislike or disinclination (*an aversion to exercise*). **2** the object of such feelings.

a·ver·sion ther·a·py *n.* therapy designed to make a patient give up an undesirable habit by causing him or her to associate it with an unpleasant effect.

a·vert /əvə́rt/ *v.tr.* (often foll. by *from*) **1** turn away (one's eyes or thoughts). **2** prevent (an undesirable occurrence). ▫▫ **a·vert·a·ble** *adj.* **a·vert·i·ble** *adj.*

a·vi·an /áyveeən/ *adj.* of or relating to birds.

a·vi·ar·y /áyvee–eree/ *n.* (*pl.* **·ies**) a large enclosure or building for keeping birds.

a·vi·ate /áyveeayt/ *v.* **1** *intr.* fly in an airplane. **2** *tr.* pilot (an airplane).

a·vi·a·tion /áyveeáyshən/ *n.* **1** the skill or practice of operating aircraft. **2** aircraft manufacture.

a·vi·a·tor /áyveeaytər/ *n.* (*fem.* **aviatrix** /áyveeáytriks/) a person who pilots an aircraft.

a·vi·cul·ture /áyvikulchər/ *n.* the rearing and keeping of birds. ▫▫ **a·vi·cul·tur·ist** /–kúlchərist/ *n.*

av·id /ávid/ *adj.* eager; enthusiastic. ▫▫ **a·vid·i·ty** /əvíditee/ *n.* **av·id·ly** *adv.*

a·vi·fau·na /áyvifawnə/ *n.* birds of a region or country collectively.

a·vi·on·ics /áyveeóniks/ *n.pl.* (treated as *sing.*) electronics as applied to aviation.

a·vi·ta·min·o·sis /ayvītəminṓsis/ *n. Med.* a condition resulting from a deficiency of one or more vitamins.

av·o·ca·do /ávəkaádō, aávə–/ *n.* (*pl.* **·dos**) **1** (also **av·o·ca·do pear**) a pear-shaped fruit with a smooth oily edible flesh and a large stone. **2** the tropical evergreen tree, *Persea americana*, native to Central America, bearing this fruit. Also called **alligator pear**. **3** the light green color of the flesh of this fruit.

av·o·ca·tion /ávōkáyshən/ *n.* **1** a minor occupation. **2** *colloq.* a vocation or calling.

av·o·cet /ávəset/ *n.* any wading bird of the genus *Recurvirostra* with long legs and a long slender upward-curved bill and usu. black and white plumage.

a·void /əvóyd/ *v.tr.* **1** refrain or keep away from (a thing, person, or action). **2** escape; evade. **3** *Law* **a** nullify. **b** quash (a sentence). ▫▫ **a·void·a·ble** *adj.* **a·void·a·bly** *adv.* **a·void·ance** *n.* **a·void·er** *n.*

av·oir·du·pois /ávərdəpóyz/ *n.* (in full **avoirdupois weight**) a system of weights based on a pound of 16 ounces or 7,000 grains.

a·vow /əvów/ *v.tr.* admit. ▫▫ **a·vow·al** *n.* **a·vow·ed·ly** /əvówidlee/ *adv.*

a•vun•cu•lar /əvúngkyələr/ *adj.* like or of an uncle; kind and friendly.

AWACS /áywaks/ *n.* a long-range radar system for detecting enemy aircraft.

a•wait /əwáyt/ *v.tr.* **1** wait for. **2** (of an event or thing) be in store for.

a•wake /əwáyk/ *v. & adj.* •*v.* (*past* **awoke** /əwṓk; *past part.* **awoken** /əwṓkən/) **1** *intr.* **a** cease to sleep. **b** become active. **2** *intr.* (foll. by *to*) become aware of. **3** *tr.* rouse from sleep. •*predic.adj.* **1 a** not asleep. **b** vigilant. **2** (foll. by *to*) aware of.

a•wak•en /əwáykən/ *v.* **1** *tr. & intr.* = AWAKE *v.* **2** *tr.* (often foll. by *to*) make aware.

a•ward /əwáwrd/ *v. & n.* •*v.tr.* **1** give or order to be given as a payment, compensation, or prize. **2** grant; assign.•*n.* **1** a payment, compensation, or prize awarded. **2** a judicial decision. ▫▫ **a•ward•er** *n.*

a•ware /əwáir/ *predic.adj.* **1** (often foll. by *of*, or *that* + clause) conscious; not ignorant; having knowledge. **2** well-informed. ▶Also found in *attrib.* use in sense 2, as in *a very aware person*; this is disputed. ▫▫ **a•ware•ness** *n.*

a•wash /əwósh, əwáwsh/ *predic.adj.* **1** level with the surface of water, so that it just washes over. **2** carried or washed by the waves; flooded or as if flooded.

a•way /əwáy/ *adv., adj., & n.* •*adv.* **1** to or at a distance from the place, person, or thing in question (*go away; give away; they are away*). **2** toward or into nonexistence (*sounds die away*). **3** constantly; persistently. **4** without delay. •*adj. Sports* played at an opponent's field, etc. •*n. Sports* an away game or win. ▫ **away with** (as *imper.*) take away; let us be rid of.

awe /aw/ *n. & v.* •*n.* reverential fear or wonder. •*v.tr.* inspire with awe.

a•weigh /əwáy/ *predic.adj. Naut.* (of an anchor) clear of the sea or river bed.

awe-in•spir•ing *adj.* causing awe or wonder; amazing. ▫▫ **awe-in•spir•ing•ly** *adv.*

awe•some /áwsəm/ *adj.* **1** inspiring awe. **2** *sl.* excellent. ▫▫ **awe•some•ly** *adv.* **awe•some•ness** *n.*

awe•strick•en /áwstrikən/ *adj.* (also **awe•struck** /–struk/) struck or affected by awe.

aw•ful /áwfŏŏl/ *adj.* **1** *colloq.* **a** unpleasant (*awful weather*). **b** poor in quality (*awful writing*). **c** (*attrib.*) excessive; remarkably large (*an awful lot of money*). **2** *poet.* inspiring awe. ▫▫ **aw•ful•ness** *n.*

aw•ful•ly /áwfəlee, –flee/ *adv.* **1** *colloq.* in an unpleasant or horrible way. **2** *colloq.* very.

a•while /əhwíl, əwíl/ *adv.* for a short time.

awk•ward /áwkwərd/ *adj.* **1** ill-adapted for use. **2** clumsy or bungling. **3 a** embarrassed (*felt awkward about it*). **b** embarrassing (*an awkward situation*). ▫▫ **awk•ward•ly** *adv.* **awk•ward•ness** *n.*

awk•ward age *n.* adolescence.

awl /awl/ *n.* a small pointed tool used for piercing holes, esp. in leather.

awn /awn/ *n.* a stiff bristle growing from the grain sheath of grasses. ▫▫ **awne** *adj.*

awn•ing /áwning/ *n.* a sheet of canvas or similar material stretched on a frame and used to shade a window, doorway, or other area from the sun or rain.

a•woke *past* of AWAKE.

a•wo•ken *past part.* of AWAKE.

AWOL /áywawl/ *abbr.* absent without leave.

a•wry /ərí/ *adv. & adj.* •*adv.* **1** crookedly or askew. **2** improperly or amiss. •*predic.adj.* crooked; unsound. ▫ **go awry** go wrong.

ax /aks/ *n. & v.* (also **axe**) •*n.* **1** a chopping tool, usu. with a steel edge at a right angle to a wooden handle. **2** the drastic cutting or elimination of expenditure, staff, etc. •*v.tr.* (**axing**) **1** use an ax. **2** cut (esp. costs or services) drastically. **3** remove or dismiss. ▫ **an ax to grind** a private reason for doing or being involved in something.

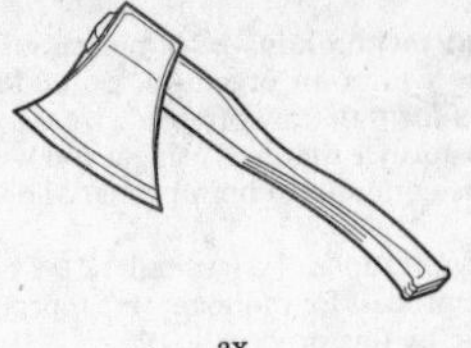
ax

ax•el /áksəl/ *n.* a jumping movement in figure skating, similar to a loop but from one foot to the other.

ax•es *pl.* of AXIS.

ax•i•al /ákseeəl/ *adj.* **1** forming or belonging to an axis. **2** around or along an axis (*axial rotation*). ▫▫ **ax•i•al•ly** *adv.*

ax•il /áksil/ *n.* the upper angle between a leaf and stem it springs from, or between a branch and trunk.

ax•il•la /aksílə/ *n.* (*pl.* **axillae** /–ee/) **1** *Anat.* the armpit. **2** an axil.

ax•il•lar•y /áksiléree/ *adj.* **1** *Anat.* of or relating to the armpit. **2** *Bot.* in or growing from the axil.

ax•i•om /ákseeəm/ *n.* **1** an established or widely accepted principle. **2** esp. *Geom.* a self-evident truth.

ax•i•o•mat•ic /ákseeəmátik/ *adj.* **1** self-evident. **2** relating to or containing axioms. ▫▫ **ax•i•o•mat•i•cal•ly** *adv.*

ax•is /áksis/ *n.* (*pl.* **axes** /–seez/) **1 a** an imaginary line about which a body rotates or about which a plane figure is conceived as generating a solid. **b** a line that divides a regular figure symmetrically. **2** *Math.* a fixed reference line for the measurement of coordinates, etc. **3 a** an agreement or alliance between two or more countries forming a center for an eventual larger grouping of nations sharing an ideal or objective. **b** (**the Axis**) the alliance of Germany and Italy formed before and during World War II, later extended to include Japan and other countries; these countries as a group.

ax•le /áksəl/ *n.* a rod or spindle on which a wheel or group of wheels is fixed.

ax•on /ákson/ *n. Anat. & Zool.* a long threadlike part of a nerve cell, conducting impulses from the cell body.

a•ya•tol•lah /íətṓlə/ *n.* a Shiite religious leader in Iran.

aye /ī/ *adv. & n.* (also **ay**) •*adv.* **1** *archaic* or *dial.* yes. **2** (as **aye aye**) *Naut.* a response accepting an order. •*n.* an affirmative answer, esp. in voting.

aye-aye /í–ī/ *n.* an arboreal nocturnal lemur, *Daubentonia madagascariensis*, native to Madagascar.

AZ *abbr.* Arizona (in official postal use).

a•zal•ea /əzáylyə/ *n.* any of various flowering deciduous shrubs of the genus *Rhododendron*, with large pink, purple, white, or yellow flowers.

a•ze•o•trope /əzéeətrōp, áyzee–/ *n. Chem.* a mixture of liquids in which the boiling point remains constant during distillation at a given pressure, without change in composition. ▫▫ **az•e•o•trop•ic** /əzéeətrópik/ *adj.*

az•i•muth /ázimǝth/ *n.* **1** the angular distance from a north or south point of the horizon to the intersection with the horizon of a vertical circle passing through a given celestial body. **2** the horizontal angle or direction of a compass bearing.

a•zi•muth•al pro•jec•tion /ázimǝl/ *n.* a map projection in which a region of the earth is projected onto a plane tangential to the surface, usually at the pole or equator.

a•zo•ic /ayzṓik/ *adj.* **1** having no trace of life. **2** *Geol.* (of an age, etc.) having left no organic remains.

AZT *n. Trademark* azidothymidine, a drug used against the AIDS virus.

Az•tec /áztek/ *n. & adj.* • *n.* **1** a member of the native people dominant in Mexico before the Spanish conquest of the 16th century. **2** the language of the Aztecs. • *adj.* of the Aztecs or their language.

az•ure /á<u>zh</u>ər/ *n. & adj.* • *n.* **1** a deep sky-blue color. **2** *poet.* the clear sky. • *adj.* of the color azure.

az•y•gous /ayzígəs/ *adj. & n. Anat.* • *adj.* (of any organic structure) single; not existing in pairs. • *n.* an organic structure occurring singly.

B

B[1] /bee/ *n.* (also **b**) (*pl.* **Bs** or **B's**) **1** the second letter of the alphabet. **2** *Mus.* the seventh note of the diatonic scale of C major. **3** the second hypothetical person or example. **4** the second highest class or category. **5** *Algebra* (usu. **b**) the second known quantity. **6** a human blood type of the ABO system.

B[2] *symb. Chem.* the element boron.

B[3] *abbr.* (also **B.**) **1** Bachelor. **2** bel(s). **3** *Chess* bishop. **4** black (pencil lead). **5** *Baseball* base; baseman.

b. *abbr.* born.

BA *abbr.* Bachelor of Arts.

Ba *symb. Chem.* the element barium.

baa /baa/ *v.intr.* (**baas, baaed** or **baa'd**) (esp. of a sheep) bleat.

ba·ba /ba̋abaa/ *n.* (in full **baba au rhum** /ō rúm/) a small rich sponge cake, usu. soaked in rum syrup.

Bab·bitt /bábit/ *n.* (also **bab·bitt**) **1** (in full **Babbitt metal**) any of a group of soft alloys of tin, antimony, copper, and usu. lead, used for lining bearings, etc., to diminish friction. **2** (**babbitt**) a bearing lining made of this. [I. *Babbitt*, Amer. inventor d. 1862]

bab·ble /bábəl/ *v. & n.* • *v.* **1** *intr.* **a** talk in an incoherent manner. **b** chatter excessively. **c** (of a stream, etc.) murmur. **2** *tr.* divulge through chatter. • *n.* **1 a** incoherent speech. **b** idle or childish talk. **2** the murmur of voices, water, etc. ▫▫ **bab·bler** *n.*

babe /bayb/ *n.* **1** *literary* a baby. **2** an innocent or helpless person (*babes in the woods*). **3** sometimes *derog. sl.* a young woman (often as a form of address). **4** a sexually attractive young woman.

ba·bel /báybəl, báb-/ *n.* **1** a confused noise, esp. of voices. **2** a noisy assembly. **3** a scene of confusion.

ba·boon /baboo̅n/ *n.* any of various large Old World monkeys of the genera *Papio* and *Mandrillus*, having a long snout, large teeth, and callosities on the buttocks.

ba·bush·ka /bəbo͝oshkə/ *n.* **1** a headscarf tied under the chin. **2** an elderly or grandmotherly Russian woman.

ba·by /báybee/ *n. & v.* • *n.* (*pl.* **-bies**) **1** a very young child or infant. **2** an unduly childish person. **3** the youngest member of a family, team, etc. **4** (often *attrib.*) **a** a young or newly born animal. **b** a thing that is small of its kind (*baby rose*). **5** *sl.* a young woman; sweetheart (often as a form of address). **6** one's own responsibility, invention, etc., regarded in a personal way. • *v.tr.* (**-bies, -bied**) **1** treat like a baby. **2** pamper. ▫▫ **ba·by·hood** *n.* **ba·by·ish** *adj.* **ba·by·ish·ly** *adv.*

ba·by boom *n. colloq.* a temporary marked increase in the birthrate. ▫ **baby boomer** *n.* a person born during a baby boom, esp. after World War II.

ba·by car·riage *n.* a four-wheeled carriage for a baby, pushed by a person on foot.

ba·by grand *n.* the smallest size of grand piano.

ba·by-sit *v.intr.* (**-sitting**; *past and past part.* **-sat**) look after a child while the parents are out. ▫▫ **ba·by-sit·ter** *n.*

ba·by talk *n.* childish talk used by or to young children.

bac·ca·lau·re·ate /bákəláwreeət/ *n.* **1** the college or university degree of bachelor. **2** an examination intended to qualify successful candidates for higher education.

bac·ca·rat /baakəra̋a, bá-/ *n.* a gambling card game played against the dealer.

bac·cha·nal /bakənál, bákənəl/ *n.* **1** a wild and drunken revelry. **2** a drunken reveler. **3** a priest, worshiper, or follower of Bacchus, the Greek or Roman god of wine.

Bac·cha·na·li·a /bákənáylyə/ *n.pl.* **1** the Roman festival of Bacchus. **2** (**bacchanalia**) a drunken revelry. ▫▫ **Bac·cha·na·li·an** *adj. & n.*

bac·chant /bəkánt, -ka̋ant, bákənt/ *n.* (*pl.* **bacchants** or **bacchantes** /bəkánteez/; *fem.* **bacchante** /bəkántee, -ka̋ant-/) **1** a priest, worshiper, or follower of Bacchus. **2** a drunken reveler. ▫▫ **bacchantic** *adj.*

bach·e·lor /báchələr, báchlər/ *n.* **1** an unmarried man. **2** a man or woman who has taken the degree of Bachelor of Arts or Science, etc. ▫▫ **bach·e·lor·hood** *n.*

bac·il·lar·y /básəleree, bəsíləree/ *adj.* relating to or caused by bacilli.

ba·cil·li·form /bəsílifawrm/ *adj.* rod-shaped.

ba·cil·lus /bəsíləs/ *n.* (*pl.* **bacilli** /-lī/) **1** any rod-shaped bacterium. **2** (usu. in *pl.*) any pathogenic bacterium.

back /bak/ *n., adv., v., & adj.* • *n.* **1 a** the rear surface of the human body from the shoulders to the hips. **b** the corresponding upper surface of an animal's body. **c** the spine (*fell and broke his back*). **2 a** any surface regarded as corresponding to the human back, e.g., of the head or hand, or of a chair. **b** the part of a garment that covers the back. **3 a** the less important part of something functional, e.g., of a knife or a piece of paper (*write it on the back*). **b** the part normally away from the spectator or the direction of motion or attention, e.g., of a car, house, or room (*stood at the back*). **4 a** a defensive player in some games. **b** this position. • *adv.* **1** to the rear; away from what is considered to be the front (*go back a little*; *ran off without looking back*). **2 a** in or into an earlier position or condition (*came back late*; *ran back to the car*; *put it back on the shelf*). **b** in return (*pay back*). **3** in or into the past (*back in June*; *three years back*). **4** at a distance (*stand back from the road*). **5** in check (*hold him back*). **6** (foll. by *of*) behind (*in the back of the house*). • *v.* **1** *tr.* **a** help with moral or financial support. **b** bet on the success of (a horse, etc.). **2** *tr. & intr.* move, or cause (a vehicle, etc.) to move, backward. **3** *tr.* **a** put or serve as a back, background, or support to. **b** *Mus.* accompany. **4** *tr.* lie at the back of (*a beach backed by steep cliffs*). **5** *intr.* (of the wind) move around to a counterclockwise direction. • *adj.* **1** situated behind (*back teeth*; *back entrance*). **2** of or relating to the past (*back pay*; *back issue*). **3** reversed (*back flow*). ▫ **at the back of one's mind** remembered but not consciously thought of. **back and forth** to and fro. **back down** withdraw one's claim; concede defeat in an argument, etc. **back off 1** draw back; retreat. **2** abandon one's intention, stand, etc. **back out** (often foll. by *of*) withdraw from a commitment. **back up 1** give support to. **2** *Computing* make a spare copy of (data, a disk, etc.). **3** (of running water) accumulate behind an obstruction. **4** reverse (a vehicle) into a desired position. **5** form a line of vehicles, etc. **get off a person's back** stop troubling a person. **go back on** fail to honor (a promise or commitment). **know like the back of one's hand** be entirely familiar with. **put one's back into** approach (a task, etc.) with vigor. **turn one's back on 1** abandon. **2** ignore. **with one's back to** (or **up against**) **the wall** in a desperate situation; hard-pressed. ▫▫ **back•er** *n.* (in sense 1 of *v.*). **back•less** *adj.*

back•ache /bákayk/ *n.* a (usu. prolonged) pain in one's back.

back•bite /bákbīt/ *v.tr.* slander; speak badly of. ▫▫ **back•bit•er** *n.*

back•board /bákbawrd/ *n.* **1** a board placed at the back of anything. **2** *Basketball* the board behind the basket.

back•bone /bákbōn/ *n.* **1** the spine. **2** the main support of a structure or system. **3** firmness of character.

back•break•ing /bákbrayking/ *adj.* (esp. of manual work) extremely hard.

back•coun•try /bák-kuntree/ *n.* an area away from settled districts.

back•date /bákdáyt/ *v.tr.* put an earlier date on (an agreement, etc.) than the actual one.

back door *n.* **1** the door at the back of a building. **2** a secret means of gaining an objective.

back•door /bákdáwr/ *adj.* clandestine; underhand (*backdoor deal*).

back•drop /bákdrop/ *n.* **1** *Theatr.* a painted cloth at the back of the stage as a main part of the scenery. **2** the background to a situation.

back•fill /bákfil/ *v.tr. & intr.* refill an excavated hole with the material dug out of it.

back•fire /bákfīr/ *v. & n.* • *v.intr.* **1** undergo a mistimed explosion in the cylinder or exhaust of an internal combustion engine. **2** (of a plan, etc.) have the opposite effect to what was intended. • *n.* an instance of backfiring.

back-for•ma•tion *n.* **1** the formation of a word from its seeming derivative (e.g., *laze* from *lazy*). **2** a word formed in this way.

back•gam•mon /bákgámən/ *n.* a game for two played on a board with pieces moved according to throws of the dice.

back•ground /bákgrownd/ *n.* **1** part of a scene, picture, or description that serves as a setting to the chief figures or objects and foreground. **2** an inconspicuous position (*kept in the background*). **3** a person's education, knowledge, or social circumstances. **4** explanatory information.

back•hand /bák-hand/ *n. Tennis,* etc. **1** a stroke played with the back of the hand turned toward the opponent. **2** (*attrib.*) of or made with a backhand (*backhand volley*).

back•hand•ed /bák-hándid/ *adj.* **1** (of a blow, etc.) delivered with the back of the hand, or in a direction opposite to the usual one. **2** indirect; ambiguous (*a backhanded compliment*). **3** = BACKHAND.

back•hoe *n.* a mechanical excavator that draws toward itself a bucket attached to a hinged boom.

back•ing /báking/ *n.* **1 a** support. **b** a body of supporters. **c** material used to form a back or support. **2** musical accompaniment.

back•lash /báklash/ *n.* **1** a marked adverse reaction. **2 a** a sudden recoil or reaction between parts of a mechanism. **b** excessive play between such parts.

back•list /báklist/ *n.* a publisher's list of books published before the current season and still in print.

back•lit /báklit/ *adj.* (esp. in photography) illuminated from behind.

back•log /báklawg, -log/ *n.* accumulation of uncompleted work, etc.

back num•ber *n.* **1** an issue of a periodical earlier than the current one. **2** *sl.* an out-of-date person or thing.

back•pack /bákpak/ *n. & v.* • *n.* a bag slung by straps from both shoulders and resting on the back. • *v.intr.* travel with a backpack. ▫▫ **back•pack•er** *n.*

back•ped•al /bákped'l/ *v.* (**-pedaled, -pedaling**) **1** pedal backward on a bicycle, etc. **2** reverse one's previous action or opinion.

back•scat•ter /bákskatər/ *n.* the scattering of radiation in a reverse direction.

back•scratch•er /bákskrachər/ *n.* **1** a rod terminating in a clawed hand for scratching one's own back. **2** a person who exchanges mutual services with another for gain.

back•seat /bákseét/ *n.* **1** a seat in the rear. **2** an inferior position or status.

back•seat driv•er *n.* a person who is eager to advise without responsibility (orig. of a passenger in a car, etc.).

back•sheesh var. of BAKSHEESH.

back•side /báksīd/ *n. colloq.* the buttocks.

back•slash /bákslash/ *n.* a reverse slash (\).

back•slide /bákslīd/ *v.intr.* (*past* **-slid** /-slid/; *past part.* **-slid** or **-slidden** /-slid'n/) relapse into bad ways or error. ▫▫ **back•slid•er** *n.*

back•space /bákspays/ *v.intr.* move a typewriter carriage or computer cursor back one or more spaces.

back•spin /bákspin/ *n.* a backward spin imparted to a ball causing it to fly off at an angle on hitting a surface.

back•stage /bákstáyj/ *adv. & adj.* • *adv.* **1** *Theatr.* out of view of the audience. **2** not known to the public. • *adj.* that is backstage; concealed.

back•stairs /bákstairz/ *n.pl.* **1** stairs at the back of a building. **2** (also **back•stair**) (*attrib.*) denoting underhand or clandestine activity.

back•stitch /bákstich/ *n. & v.* • *n.* a stitch bringing the thread back to the preceding stitch. • *v.tr. & intr.* sew using a backstitch or stitches.

back•stop /bákstaap/ *n.* **1** *Baseball* a fence or screen positioned behind home plate. **2** something that provides support or reinforcement.

back street *n.* a street away from the main streets.

back-street *adj.* denoting illicit activity (*a back-street drug deal*).

back•stroke /bákstrōk/ *n.* a swimming stroke performed on the back with the arms lifted out of the water in a backward circular motion and the legs extended in a kicking action.

back talk *n. colloq.* the practice of replying rudely or impudently.

back to back *adv.* **1** (of two people) facing in opposite directions with backs touching (*we stood back to back*). **2** consecutively (*the games were played back to back*).

back-to-na•ture *adj.* (usu. *attrib.*) applied to a movement or enthusiast for the reversion to a simpler way of life.

back•track /báktrak/ *v.intr.* **1** retrace one's steps. **2** reverse one's previous action or opinion.

back•up /bákup/ *n.* **1** moral or technical support (*called for extra backup*). **2** a reserve. **3** *Computing* (often *attrib.*) **a** the procedure for making security copies of data (*backup facilities*). **b** the copy itself (*made a backup*). **4** a line of vehicles, etc.

back•ward /bákwərd/ *adv. & adj.* • *adv.* (also **back•wards**) **1** away from one's front (*lean backward*). **2 a** with the back foremost (*walk backward*). **b** in reverse of the usual way (*count backward*). **3 a** into a worse state (*new policies are taking us backward*). **b** into the past (*looked backward over the years*). **c** back toward the starting point (*rolled the film backward*). • *adj.* **1** directed to the rear or starting point (*a backward look*). **2** reversed. **3** mentally retarded or slow. **4** reluctant; shy; unassertive. ▫ **backward and forward** to and fro. **bend** (or **fall** or **lean**) **over backward** (often foll. by *to* + infin.) *colloq.* make every effort. **know**

backward and forward be entirely familiar with. ▫▫ **back•ward•ness** *n.*

back•wash /bákwosh, -wawsh/ *n.* **1 a** receding waves created by the motion of a ship, etc. **b** a backward current of air created by a moving aircraft. **2** repercussions.

back•wa•ter /bákwawtər, -wotər/ *n.* **1** a place or condition remote from the center of activity or thought. **2** stagnant water.

back•woods /bákwŏŏdz/ *n.pl.* **1** uncleared forest land. **2** any remote or sparsely inhabited region.

back•woods•man /bakwŏŏdzmən/ *n.* (*pl.* **-men**) **1** an inhabitant of backwoods. **2** an uncouth person.

back•yard /bakyaárd/ *n.* a yard at the back of a house, etc. ▫ **in one's own backyard** *colloq.* near at hand.

ba•cla•va var. of BAKLAVA.

ba•con /báykən/ *n.* cured meat from the back or sides of a pig. ▫ **bring home the bacon** *colloq.* **1** succeed in one's undertaking. **2** supply material provision or support.

bac•te•ri•a *pl.* of BACTERIUM.

bac•te•ri•cide /bakteérisīd/ *n.* a substance capable of destroying bacteria. ▫▫ **bac•te•ri•cid•al** /-rísīd'l/ *adj.*

bac•te•ri•ol•o•gy /bákteereeóləjee/ *n.* the study of bacteria. ▫▫ **bac•te•ri•o•log•i•cal** /-reeəlójikəl/ *adj.* **bac•te•ri•ol•o•gist** /-óləjist/ *n.*

bac•te•ri•o•phage /bakteéreeəfayj/ *n.* a virus parasitic on a bacterium.

bac•te•ri•o•sta•sis /bakteéreeōstáysis/ *n.* the inhibition of the growth of bacteria without destroying them. ▫▫ **bac•te•ri•o•stat•ic** /–státik/ *adj.*

bac•te•ri•um /bakteéreeəm/ *n.* (*pl.* **bacteria** /-reeə/) a member of a large group of unicellular microorganisms lacking organelles and an organized nucleus, some of which can cause disease. ▫▫ **bac•te•ri•al** *adj.*

Bac•tri•an cam•el /báktreeən/ *n.* a camel, *Camelus bactrianus*, native to central Asia, with two humps.

bad /bad/ *adj., n., & adv.* •*adj.* (**worse** /wərs/; **worst** /wərst/) **1** inferior; inadequate; defective (*bad work*; *a bad driver*; *bad light*). **2 a** unpleasant (*bad weather*; *bad news*). **b** unfortunate (*bad business*). **3** harmful (*is bad for you*). **4 a** (of food) decayed. **b** polluted (*bad air*). **5** ill; injured (*am feeling bad today*; *a bad leg*). **6** *colloq.* regretful; ashamed (*feels bad about it*). **7** (of an unwelcome thing) serious; severe (*a bad mistake*). **8 a** morally unsound or offensive (*a bad man*; *bad language*). **b** disobedient; badly behaved (*a bad child*). **9** not valid (*a bad check*). **10** (**badder, baddest**) *sl.* good; excellent. •*n.* **1 a** ill fortune (*take the bad with the good*). **b** ruin; a degenerate condition (*go to the bad*). **2** the debit side of an account (*$500 to the bad*). **3** (as *pl.*; prec. by *the*) bad people. •*adv. colloq.* badly (*took it bad*). ▫ **in a bad way** ill; in trouble (*looked in a bad way*). **too bad** *colloq.* (of circumstances, etc.) regrettable but now beyond retrieval. ▫▫ **bad•ness** *n.*

▶Confusion in the use of **bad** and **good** vs. **badly** and **well** usually has to do with verbs called copulas, such as **feel** or **seem**: Thus, standard usage calls for *I feel bad* and *I feel well,* but *I feel badly,* to a precise speaker or writer, means 'I do not have a good sense of touch.' See note at GOOD.

bad blood *n.* ill feeling.

bad break *n. colloq.* **1** a piece of bad luck. **2** a mistake or blunder.

bad debt *n.* a debt the creditor cannot recover.

bade see BID.

bad faith *n.* intent to deceive.

badge /baj/ *n.* **1** a distinctive emblem worn as a mark of office, membership, achievement, licensed employment, etc. **2** any feature or sign that reveals a characteristic condition or quality.

badg•er /bájər/ *n. & v.* •*n.* an omnivorous gray-coated nocturnal mammal of the family Mustelidae with a white stripe flanked by black stripes on its head, which lives in sets. •*v.tr.* pester; harass; tease.

bad•i•nage /bád'naázh/ *n.* humorous or witty conversation.

bad•lands /bádlandz/ *n.pl.* extensive uncultivable eroded tracts in arid areas.

bad lot *n.* a person of bad character.

bad•ly /bádlee/ *adv.* (**worse** /wərs/; **worst** /wərst/) **1** in a bad manner (*works badly*). **2** *colloq.* very much (*wants it badly*). **3** severely (*was badly defeated*).

bad•min•ton /bádmint'n/ *n.* a game with rackets in which a shuttlecock is volleyed back and forth across a net.

bad-mouth *v.tr.* criticize someone or something; speak disloyally of.

bad news *n. colloq.* an unpleasant or troublesome person or thing.

bad-tem•pered /bádtémpərd/ *adj.* irritable; easily annoyed.

baf•fle /báfəl/ *v. & n.* •*v.tr.* **1** confuse or perplex. **2 a** frustrate or hinder (plans, etc.). **b** restrain or regulate the progress of (fluid, etc.). •*n.* (also **baf•fle-board, baf•fle-plate**) a device used to restrain the flow of fluid, gas, etc., or to limit the emission of sound, light, etc. ▫▫ **baf•fle•ment** *n.* **baf•fling** *adj.* **baf•fling•ly** *adv.*

bag /bag/ *n. & v.* •*n.* **1** a receptacle of flexible material with an opening at the top. **2 a** (usu. in *pl.*) a piece of luggage (*put the bags in the trunk*). **b** a woman's handbag. **3** (in *pl.*; usu. foll. by *of*) *colloq.* a large amount; plenty (*bags of money*). **4** *sl.derog.* a woman, esp. regarded as unattractive or unpleasant. **5** (usu. in *pl.*) baggy folds of skin under the eyes. •*v.* (**bagged, bagging**) **1** *tr.* put in a bag. **2** *colloq. tr.* **a** secure; get hold of (*bagged the best seat*). **b** *colloq.* steal. **c** shoot (game). **3 a** *intr.* hang loosely; bulge. **b** *tr.* cause to do this. ▫ **bag and baggage** with all one's belongings. **bag** (or **whole bag**) **of tricks** *colloq.* a set of ingenious plans or resources. **in the bag** *colloq.* achieved; as good as secured. ▫▫ **bag•ful** *n.* (*pl.* **-fuls**).

bag•a•telle /bágətél/ *n.* **1** a game in which small balls are struck into numbered holes on a board, with pins as obstructions. **2** a mere trifle. **3** *Mus.* a short piece of music, esp. for the piano.

ba•gel /báygəl/ *n.* a hard bread roll in the shape of a ring.

bag•gage /bágij/ *n.* **1** everyday belongings packed up in suitcases, etc., for traveling; luggage. **2** the portable equipment of an army. **3** past experiences or long-held ideas perceived as burdensome encumbrances.

bag•gage car *n.* a car on a passenger train used for luggage, trunks, etc.

bag•gy /bágee/ *adj.* (**baggier, baggiest**) **1** hanging in loose folds. **2** puffed out. ▫▫ **bag•gi•ness** *n.*

bag la•dy *n.* (*pl.* **-dies**) a homeless woman who carries her possessions around in shopping bags.

bag•man /bágmən/ *n.* (*pl.* **-men**) *sl.* an agent who collects or distributes illicitly gained money.

bagn•io /baányō/ *n.* (*pl.* **-os**) **1** a brothel. **2** *hist.* a prison in the Orient.

bag•pipe /bágpīp/ *n.* (usu. in *pl.*) a musical instrument consisting of a windbag that is squeezed by the player's arm to force air into reeded pipes.

bagpipes

ba•guette /bagét/ *n.* a long narrow French loaf.

bah /baa/ *int.* an expression of contempt or disbelief.

Ba•ha•'i /bəhaá-ee, -hī́/ *n.* (*pl.*

Baha'is) a member of a monotheistic religion founded in 1863 as a branch of Babism (an offshoot of Islam), emphasizing religious unity and world peace. □□ **Ba·ha·'ism** *n.*

Ba·ha·mi·an /bəháymeeən, –haá–/ *n.* & *adj.* • *n.* **1** a native or inhabitant of the Bahamas in the W. Indies. **2** a person of Bahamian descent. • *adj.* of or relating to the Bahamas.

bail[1] /bayl/ *n.* & *v.* • *n.* **1** money, etc., required as security for the temporary release of a prisoner pending trial. **2** a person or persons giving such security. • *v.tr.* (usu. foll. by *out*) **1** release or secure the release of (a prisoner) on payment of bail. **2** release from a difficulty; come to the rescue of. □ **forfeit** (or *colloq.* **jump**) **bail** fail to appear for trial after being released on bail. **go** (or **stand**) **bail** (often foll. by *for*) act as surety (for an accused person).

bail[2] /bayl/ *n.* & *v.* • *n.* **1** the bar on a typewriter holding the paper against the platen. **2** an arched usu. wire handle, as of a pail. **3** a bar separating horses in an open stable.

bail[3] /bayl/ *v.tr.* **1** (usu. foll. by *out*) scoop water out of (a boat, etc.). **2** scoop (water, etc.) out. □ **bail out** (of a pilot, etc.) make an emergency parachute descent from an aircraft.

bai·ley /báylee/ *n.* (*pl.* **-leys**) **1** the outer wall of a castle. **2** a court enclosed by it.

bail·iff /báylif/ *n.* an official in a court of law who keeps order, looks after prisoners, etc.

bail·i·wick /báyliwik/ *n.* **1** *Law* the district or jurisdiction of a bailiff. **2** *joc.* a person's sphere of operations or particular area of interest.

bail·ment /báylmənt/ *n.* the act of delivering goods, etc., for a (usu. specified) purpose.

bail·out /báylowt/ *n.* a rescue from a dire situation (*a financial bailout for an ailing company*).

bails·man /báylzmən/ *n.* (*pl.* **·men**) a person who provides bail for another.

bain-ma·rie /báɴmareé/ *n.* (*pl.* **bains-marie** *pronunc.* same) a cooking utensil consisting of a vessel of hot water in which a receptacle can be slowly and gently heated.

bait /bayt/ *n.* & *v.* • *n.* **1** food used to entice a prey. **2** an allurement; something intended to tempt or entice. • *v.tr.* **1 a** harass or annoy (a person). **b** torment (a chained animal). **2** put bait on or in (a hook, trap, etc.) to entice a prey.

baize /bayz/ *n.* a coarse usu. green woolen material resembling felt used as a covering or lining, esp. on the tops of billiard and card tables.

bake /bayk/ *v.* & *n.* • *v.* **1 a** *tr.* cook (food) by dry heat in an oven or on a hot surface, without direct exposure to a flame. **b** *intr.* undergo the process of being baked. **2** *intr. colloq.* **a** (usu. as **be baking**) (of weather, etc.) be very hot. **b** (of a person) become hot. **3 a** *tr.* harden (clay, etc.) by heat. **b** *intr.* (of clay, etc.) be hardened by heat. • *n.* **1** the act or an instance of baking. **2** a batch of baking. **3** a gathering at which baked food is eaten.

baked A·las·ka /əlaáskə/ *n.* sponge cake and ice cream in a meringue covering.

baked beans *n.pl.* baked white beans usu. cooked with salt pork and brown sugar or molasses.

Ba·ke·lite /báykəlīt, báyklīt/ *n.* *Trademark* any of various thermosetting resins or plastics made from formaldehyde and phenol and used for cables, buttons, etc.

bak·er /báykər/ *n.* a person who bakes and sells bread, cakes, etc., esp. professionally.

bak·er's doz·en *n.* thirteen (so called from the former bakers' custom of adding an extra loaf to a dozen sold; the exact reason for this is unclear).

bak·er·y /báykəree/ *n.* (*pl.* **-ies**) a place where bread and cakes are made or sold.

bak·ing pow·der *n.* a mixture of sodium bicarbonate, cream of tartar, etc., used instead of yeast in baking.

bak·ing so·da *n.* sodium bicarbonate.

ba·kla·va /baákləvaá/ *n.* (also **ba·cla·va**) a rich dessert of flaky pastry, honey, and nuts, originating in Turkey.

bak·sheesh /báksheésh/ *n.* (also **back·sheesh**) (esp. in the Middle East) a small sum of money given as a gratuity, a bribe, or as alms.

bal·a·cla·va /báləklaávə/ *n.* (in full **balaclava helmet**) a tight woolen garment covering the whole head and neck except for the eyes, nostrils, and mouth.

bal·a·lai·ka /báləlíkə/ *n.* a guitarlike musical instrument having a triangular body and 2–4 strings, popular in Russia and other Slavic countries.

balalaika

bal·ance /báləns/ *n.* & *v.* • *n.* **1** an apparatus for weighing. **2 a** a counteracting weight or force. **b** (in full **balance wheel**) the regulating device in a clock, etc. **3 a** an even distribution of weight or amount. **b** stability of body or mind (*regained his balance*). **4** a preponderating weight or amount (*the balance of opinion*). **5 a** an agreement between or the difference between credits and debits in an account. **b** the difference between an amount due and an amount paid (*will pay the balance next week*). **c** an amount left over; the rest. **6** *Art* harmony of design and proportion. **7** (**the Balance**) the zodiacal sign or constellation Libra. • *v.* **1** *tr.* (foll. by *with, against*) offset or compare (one thing) with another (*must balance the advantages with the disadvantages*). **2** *tr.* counteract, equal, or neutralize the weight or importance of. **3 a** *tr.* bring into or keep in equilibrium (*balanced a book on her head*). **b** *intr.* be in equilibrium (*balanced on one leg*). **4** *tr.* (usu. as **balanced** *adj.*) establish equal or appropriate proportions of elements in (*a balanced diet*). **5** *tr.* weigh (arguments, etc.) against each other. **6 a** *tr.* compare debits and credits of (an account). **b** *intr.* (of an account) have credits and debits equal. □ **in the balance** uncertain; at a critical stage. **on balance** all things considered. **strike a balance** choose a moderate course or compromise. □□ **bal·anc·er** *n.*

bal·ance beam *n.* a narrow horizontal bar raised off the floor, on which a gymnast balances while performing exercises.

bal·ance of pay·ments *n.* the difference in value between payments into and out of a country.

bal·ance of pow·er *n.* **1** a situation in which the chief nations of the world have roughly equal power. **2** the power held by a small group when larger groups are of equal strength.

bal·ance of trade *n.* the difference in value between imports and exports.

bal·ance sheet *n.* a statement giving the balance of an account.

ba·la·ta /balótə/ *n.* **1** any of several latex-yielding trees of Central America, esp. *Manilkara bidentata*. **2** the dried sap of this used in manufacturing.

bal·co·ny /bálkənee/ *n.* (*pl.* **-nies**) **1** a platform on the outside of a building, with access from an upper-floor window or door. **2 a** a tier of seats in a gallery in a theater, etc. **b** the upstairs seats in a movie theater, etc. □□ **bal·co·nied** *adj.*

bald /bawld/ *adj.* **1** with the scalp wholly or partly lacking hair. **2** not covered by the usual hair, feathers, leaves, etc. **3** *colloq.* with the surface worn away (*a bald tire*). **4 a** blunt; unelaborated (*a bald statement*). **b** undisguised (*the bald effrontery*). ▫▫ **bald·ing** *adj.* (in senses 1–3). **bald·ly** *adv.* (in sense 4). **bald·ness** *n.*

bald ea·gle *n.* a white-headed eagle (*Haliaeetus leucocephalus*), used as the emblem of the United States.

bal·der·dash /báwldərdash/ *n.* senseless talk or writing; nonsense.

bal·dric /báwldrik/ *n. hist.* a belt for a sword, bugle, etc., hung from the shoulder across the body to the opposite hip.

bale /bayl/ *n. & v.* •*n.* **1** a bundle of merchandise or hay, etc., tightly wrapped and bound with cords or hoops. **2** the quantity in a bale as a measure, esp. 500 lb. of cotton. •*v.tr.* make up into bales.

ba·leen whale /bəleén/ *n.* any of various whales of the suborder Mysticeti, having plates of whalebone in the mouth for straining plankton from the water.

bale·ful /báylfool/ *adj.* **1** gloomy; menacing. **2** harmful; malignant; destructive. ▫▫ **bale·ful·ly** *adv.*

Ba·li·nese /baálineéz/ *n. & adj.* •*n.* (*pl.* same) **1** a native of Bali, an island in Indonesia. **2** the language of Bali. •*adj.* of or relating to Bali or its people or language.

balk /bawk/ *v. & n.* •*v.* **1** *intr.* **a** refuse to go on. **b** (often foll. by *at*) hesitate. **2** *tr.* **a** thwart; hinder. **b** disappoint. **3** *tr.* **a** let slip (a chance, etc.). **b** ignore; shirk. •*n.* **1** a stumbling block. **2** a roughly-squared timber beam. **3** *Baseball* an illegal motion made by a pitcher.

Bal·kan /báwlkən/ *adj. & n.* •*adj.* **1** of or relating to the region of SE Europe bounded by the Adriatic, the Aegean, and the Black Sea. **2** of or relating to its peoples or countries. •*n.* (**the Balkans**) the Balkan countries.

Bal·kan·ize /báwlkənīz/ *v.tr.* divide a region or body into smaller mutually hostile states or groups.

balk·y /báwkee/ *adj.* (**·ier, ·iest**) reluctant; perverse. ▫▫ **balk·i·ness** *n.*

ball[1] /bawl/ *n. & v.* •*n.* **1** a solid or hollow sphere, esp. for use in a game. **2 a** a ball-shaped object (*ball of wool*). **b** a rounded part of the body (*ball of the foot*). **3** a solid nonexplosive missile for a cannon, etc. **4** a single delivery of a ball in cricket, etc., or passing of a ball in soccer. **5** *Baseball* a pitched ball that is not swung at by the batter and that does not pass through the strike zone. **6** (in *pl.*) *coarse sl.* **a** the testicles. **b** courage. ▶Sense 6 is usually considered a taboo use. •*v.* **1** *tr.* squeeze or wind into a ball. **2** *intr.* form into a ball or balls. **3** *tr. & intr. coarse sl.* have sexual intercourse. ▫ **the ball is in your**, etc., **court** you, etc., must be next to act. **on the ball** *colloq.* alert. **play ball 1** start or continue a ballgame. **2** *colloq.* cooperate. **start**, etc., **the ball rolling** set an activity in motion.

ball[2] /bawl/ *n.* **1** a formal social gathering for dancing. **2** *sl.* an enjoyable time (esp. *have a ball*).

bal·lad /bálәd/ *n.* **1** a poem or song narrating a popular story. **2** a slow sentimental or romantic song.

ballad late 15th century (denoting a light, simple song): from Old French *balade*, from Provençal *balada* 'dance, song to dance to,' from *balar* 'to dance,' from late Latin *ballare*, from Greek *ballizein* 'to dance.' The sense 'narrative poem' dates from the mid-18th century.

bal·lade /balaád/ *n.* **1** a poem of one or more triplets of stanzas with a repeated refrain and an envoy. **2** *Mus.* a short lyrical piece, esp. for piano.

bal·lad·eer /bálədeér/ *n.* a singer or composer of ballads.

ball-and-sock·et joint *n. Anat.* a joint in which a rounded end lies in a concave cup or socket, allowing freedom of movement.

bal·last /báləst/ *n. & v.* •*n.* **1** any heavy material placed in a ship or the basket of a balloon, etc., to secure stability. **2** coarse stone, etc., used to form the bed of a railroad track or road. •*v.tr.* **1** provide with ballast. **2** afford stability or weight to.

ball bear·ing *n.* **1** a bearing in which the two halves are separated by a ring of small metal balls that reduce friction. **2** one of these balls.

ball·boy /báwlboy/ *n.* (*fem.* **ballgirl** /-gərl/) a boy or girl who retrieves balls that go out of play during a game.

ball cock *n.* a floating ball on a hinged arm, whose movement controls the water level in a toilet tank, etc.

bal·le·ri·na /báləreénə/ *n.* a female ballet dancer.

bal·let /baláy, bálay/ *n.* **1 a** a dramatic or representational style of dancing and mime, using set steps and techniques and usu. (esp. in classical ballet) accompanied by music. **b** a particular piece or performance of ballet. **c** the music for this. **2** a company performing ballet. ▫▫ **bal·let·ic** /balétik/ *adj.*

ball game *n.* **1** any game played with a ball, esp. a game of baseball. **2** *colloq.* a particular affair or concern (*a whole new ball game*).

bal·lis·tic /bəlístik/ *adj.* **1** of or relating to projectiles. **2** moving under the force of gravity only. ▫ **go ballistic** *colloq.* become furious.

bal·lis·tic mis·sile *n.* a missile that is initially powered and guided but falls under gravity onto its target.

bal·lis·tics /bəlístiks/ *n.pl.* (usu. treated as *sing.*) the science of projectiles and firearms.

bal·loon /bəloón/ *n. & v.* •*n.* **1** a small inflatable rubber pouch with a neck, used as a child's toy or as decoration. **2** a large bag inflatable with hot air or gas to make it rise in the air, often carrying a basket for passengers. **3** a balloon shape enclosing the words or thoughts of characters in a comic strip. **4** a large globular drinking glass. •*v.* **1** *intr. & tr.* swell out or cause to swell out like a balloon. **2** *intr.* travel by balloon. ▫▫ **bal·loon·ist** *n.*

bal·lot /bálət/ *n. & v.* •*n.* **1** a process of voting. **2** the total of votes recorded in a ballot. **3** the drawing of lots. **4** a paper or ticket, etc., used in voting. •*v.* (**balloted, balloting**) **1** *tr.* **1** (of an organization) elicit a secret vote from members on a particular issue. **2** *intr.* cast one's vote on a particular issue.

bal·lot box *n.* a sealed box into which voters put completed ballot papers.

ball·park /báwlpaark/ *n.* **1** a baseball field. **2** (*attrib.*) *colloq.* approximate; rough (*a ballpark figure*). ▫ **in the (right) ballpark** *colloq.* close to one's objective; approximately correct.

ball·point /báwlpoint/ *n.* (in full **ballpoint pen**) a pen with a tiny ball as its writing point.

ball·room /báwlroom, -room/ *n.* a large hall for dancing.

ball·room danc·ing *n.* formal social dancing.

bal·ly·hoo /báleehoo/ *n.* **1** a loud noise or fuss; a confused state or commotion. **2** extravagant or sensational publicity.

balm /baam/ *n.* **1** an aromatic ointment for anointing, soothing, or healing. **2** a fragrant and medicinal exudation from certain trees and plants. **3** a soothing influence. **4** any aromatic herb, esp. one of the genus *Melissa*. **5** a pleasant perfume or fragrance.

balm·y /baámee/ *adj.* (**balmier, balmiest**) **1** (of the weather) pleasantly warm. **2** yielding balm. **3** *sl.* stupid; crazy; foolish.

bal·ne·ol·o·gy /bálneeóləjee/ *n.* the scientific study of bathing and medicinal springs. ▫▫ **bal·ne·o·log·i·cal** /–neeəlójikəl/ *adj.* **bal·ne·ol·o·gist** *n.*

ba·lo·ney /bəlónee/ *n.* (also **bo·lo·ney**) (*pl.* **-neys**) *sl.* **1** humbug; nonsense. **2** = BOLOGNA.

bal·sa /báwlsə/ *n.* **1** (in full **balsa wood**) a tough lightweight wood used for making models, etc. **2** the tropical American tree, *Ochroma lagopus*, from which it comes.

bal·sam /báwlsəm/ *n.* **1** an aromatic resinous exudation obtained from various trees and shrubs and used as a base for certain fragrances and medical preparations. **2** an ointment, esp. one composed of a substance dissolved in oil or turpentine. **3** any of various trees or shrubs that yield balsam. **4** any of several flowering plants of the genus *Impatiens*. □□ **bal·sam·ic** /-sámik/ *adj.*

bal·sam fir *n.* a N. American tree (*Abies balsamea*) that yields balsam.

bal·sam pop·lar *n.* any of various N. American poplars, esp. *Populus balsamifera*, yielding balsam.

Bal·tic /báwltik/ *n. & adj.* •*n.* **1 a** an almost landlocked sea of NE Europe. **b** the lands bordering this sea. **2** an Indo-European branch of languages comprising Old Prussian, Lithuanian, and Latvian. •*adj.* of or relating to the Baltic or the Baltic branch of languages.

bal·us·ter /báləstər/ *n.* each of a series of often ornamental short posts or pillars supporting a rail or coping, etc.

▶Often confused with *banister*.

baluster early 17th century: from French *balustre*, from Italian *balaustro*, from *balaust(r)a* 'wild pomegranate flower' (via Latin from Greek *balaustion*), so named because part of the pillar resembles the curving calyx tube of the flower.

bal·us·trade /báləstráyd/ *n.* a railing supported by balusters.

balustrade

bam·bi·no /bambeénō/ *n.* (*pl.* **bambini** /-nee/) *colloq.* a young child.

bam·boo /bambóō/ *n.* **1** a mainly tropical giant woody grass of the subfamily Bambusidae. **2** its hollow jointed stem, used as a stick or to make furniture.

bam·boo shoot *n.* a young shoot of bamboo, eaten as a vegetable.

bam·boo·zle /bambóōzəl/ *v.tr. colloq.* cheat; hoax; mystify. □□ **bam·boo·zle·ment** *n.* **bam·boo·zler** *n.*

ban /ban/ *v. & n.* •*v.tr.* (**banned, banning**) forbid; prohibit. •*n.* a formal or authoritative prohibition (*a ban on smoking*).

ba·nal /bənál, báynəl, bənaál/ *adj.* trite; feeble; commonplace. □□ **ba·nal·i·ty** /-nálitee/ *n.* (*pl.* **-ties**).

ba·nan·a /bənánə/ *n.* **1** a long curved fruit with soft pulpy flesh and yellow skin when ripe, growing in clusters. **2** (in full **banana tree**) the tropical and subtropical treelike plant, *Musa sapientum*, bearing this. □ **go bananas** *sl.* become crazy or angry.

ba·nan·a re·pub·lic *n. derog.* a small nation, esp. in Central America, dependent on one crop or the influx of foreign capital.

ba·nan·a split *n.* a dessert made with split bananas, ice cream, sauce, whipped cream, etc.

band[1] /band/ *n. & v.* •*n.* **1** a flat, thin strip or loop of material put around something, esp. to hold it together or decorate it (*headband; rubber band*). **2 a** a strip of material forming part of a garment (*hatband; waistband*). **b** a stripe of a different color or material in or on an object. **3 a** a range of frequencies or wavelengths in a spectrum (esp. of radio frequencies). **b** a range of values within a series. **4** a plain or simple ring, esp. without a gem. **5** *Mech.* a belt connecting wheels or pulleys. •*v.tr.* **1** put a band on. **2 a** mark with stripes. **b** (as **banded** *adj.*) *Bot. & Zool.* marked with colored bands or stripes.

band[2] /band/ *n. & v.* •*n.* **1** an organized group of people having a common object, esp. of a criminal nature (*band of cutthroats*). **2 a** a group of musicians who play together (*brass band; rock band*). **b** *colloq.* an orchestra. •*v.tr. & intr.* form into a group for a purpose (*band together for mutual protection*).

band·age /bándij/ *n. & v.* •*n.* **1** a strip of material for binding up a wound, etc. **2** a piece of material used as a blindfold. •*v.tr.* bind (a wound, etc.) with a bandage.

Band-Aid /bándayd/ *n.* **1** *Trademark* an adhesive bandage with a gauze pad in the center for covering minor wounds. **2** (**band-aid**) a stopgap solution.

ban·dan·na /bandánə/ *n.* a large handkerchief or neckerchief, often having a colorful pattern.

b. & b. *abbr.* (also **B. & B.**) bed and breakfast.

ban·deau /bandṓ/ *n.* (*pl.* **bandeaux** /-dōz/) **1** a narrow band worn around the head. **2** a narrow covering for the breasts.

ban·de·ril·la /bándəreéə, -rílyə/ *n.* a decorated dart thrust into a bull's neck or shoulders during a bullfight.

ban·de·role /bándərṓl/ *n.* (also **ban·de·rol**) **1 a** a long narrow flag with a cleft end, flown at a masthead. **b** an ornamental streamer on a knight's lance. **2 a** a ribbonlike scroll. **b** a stone band resembling a banderole, bearing an inscription.

ban·di·coot /bándikoot/ *n.* **1** any of the insect- and plant-eating marsupials of the family Peramelidae. **2** (in full **bandicoot rat**) *Ind.* a destructive rat, *Bandicota benegalensis*.

ban·dit /bándit/ *n.* (*pl.* **bandits** or **banditti** /-dítee/) **1** a robber or murderer, esp. a member of a band. **2** an outlaw. □□ **ban·dit·ry** *n.*

band·mas·ter /bándmastər/ *n.* the conductor of a band.

ban·do·lier /bándəleér/ *n.* (also **ban·do·leer**) a shoulder belt with loops or pockets for cartridges.

band saw *n.* a mechanical saw with a blade formed by an endless toothed band.

band·stand /bándstand/ *n.* a platform, usu. covered, for a band to play on.

band·wag·on /bándwagən/ *n.* a wagon used for carrying a band in a parade, etc. □ **climb** (or **jump**) **on the bandwagon** join a party, cause, or group that seems likely to succeed.

band·width /bándwidth, -with/ *n.* the range of frequencies within a given band (see BAND[1] *n.* 3a).

ban·dy[1] /bándee/ *adj.* (**bandier, bandiest**) **1** (of the legs) curved so as to be wide apart at the knees. **2** (also **ban·dy-leg·ged** /-légəd, -legd/) having bandy legs.

ban·dy[2] /bándee/ *v.tr.* (**-dies, -died**) **1** (often foll. by *about*) **a** pass (a story, rumor, etc.) back and forth. **b** throw or pass (a ball, etc.) back and forth. **2** (often foll. by *about*) discuss disparagingly (*bandied his name about*). **3** (often foll. by *with*) exchange (blows, insults, etc.) (*don't bandy words with me*).

bane /bayn/ *n.* the cause of ruin or trouble (esp. *the bane of one's life*). □□ **bane·ful** *adj.*

bang /bang/ *n., v., & adv.* •*n.* **1 a** a loud short sound. **b** an explosion. **c** the report of a gun. **2 a** a sharp blow. **b** the sound of this. **3** (in *pl.*) a fringe of hair cut straight across the forehead. •*v.* **1** *tr. & intr.* strike or shut noisily (*banged on the table*). **2** *tr. & intr.* make or cause to make the sound of a blow or an explosion. **3** *tr.* cut (hair) in bangs. •*adv.* with a bang or sudden impact. □ **go with a bang** go successfully.

ban·gle /bánggəl/ *n.* a rigid ornamental bracelet worn around the arm.

bang-up *adj. sl.* first-class; excellent (esp. *bang-up job*).

ban·ian var. of BANYAN.

ban·ish /bánish/ *v.tr.* **1** formally expel. **2** dismiss from one's presence or mind. ▫▫ **ban·ish·ment** *n.*

ban·is·ter /bánistər/ *n.* (also **ban·nis·ter**) **1** the uprights and handrail at the side of a staircase. **2** an upright supporting a handrail. ▶Often confused with *baluster.*

ban·jo /bánjō/ *n.* (*pl.* **-jos** or **-joes**) a stringed musical instrument with a neck and head like a guitar and an open-backed body consisting of parchment stretched over a metal hoop.

bank[1] /bangk/ *n.* & *v.* •*n.* **1 a** the sloping edge of land by a river. **b** the area of ground alongside a river (*had a picnic on the bank*). **2** a raised shelf of ground; a slope. **3** an elevation in the sea or a river bed. **4** the artificial slope of a road, etc., enabling vehicles to maintain speed around a curve. **5** a mass of cloud, fog, snow, etc. •*v.* **1** *tr.* & *intr.* (often foll. by *up*) heap or rise into banks. **2** *tr.* heap up (a fire) tightly so that it burns slowly. **3 a** *intr.* (of a vehicle or aircraft or its occupant) travel with one side higher than the other in rounding a curve. **b** *tr.* cause (a vehicle or aircraft) to do this.

bank[2] /bangk/ *n.* & *v.* •*n.* **1 a** a financial establishment that uses money deposited by customers for investment, pays it out when required, makes loans at interest, etc. **b** a building in which this business takes place. **2** = PIGGY BANK. **3 a** the money or tokens held by the banker in some gambling games. **b** the banker in such games. **4** a place for storing anything for future use (*data bank*). •*v.* **1** *tr.* deposit in a bank. **2** *intr.* engage in business as a banker. **3** *intr.* (often foll. by *at, with*) keep money (at a bank). ▫ **bank on** rely on (*I'm banking on your help*).

bank[3] /bangk/ *n.* **1** a row of similar objects, esp. of keys, lights, or switches. **2** a tier of oars.

bank·card /bángk-kard/ *n.* a bank-issued credit card or automated teller machine card.

bank·er /bángkər/ *n.* **1** a person who manages or owns a bank. **2** a keeper of the bank or dealer in some gambling games.

bank·ing /bángking/ *n.* the business transactions of a bank.

bank·note /bángknōt/ *n.* a banker's promissory note payable to the bearer on demand, and serving as money.

bank·roll /bángkrōl/ *n.* & *v.* •*n.* **1** a roll of paper currency. **2** funds. •*v.tr. colloq.* support financially.

bank·rupt /bángkrupt/ *adj., n.,* & *v.* •*adj.* **1** insolvent; declared in law unable to pay debts. **2** undergoing the legal process resulting from this. •*n.* **1** an insolvent person whose estate is administered and disposed of for the benefit of the creditors. **2** an insolvent debtor. •*v.tr.* make bankrupt. ▫▫ **bank·rupt·cy** /-ruptsee/ *n.* (*pl.* **-cies**).

bank state·ment *n.* a printed statement of transactions and balance issued periodically to the holder of a bank account.

ban·ner /bánər/ *n.* **1 a** a large rectangular sign bearing a slogan or design and usu. carried on two side poles or a crossbar in a demonstration or procession. **b** a long strip of cloth, etc., bearing a slogan. **2** a flag on a pole used as the standard of a king, knight, etc. **3** (*attrib.*) excellent; outstanding (*a banner year in sales*).

ban·ner·et /bánəret/ *n.* **1** a small banner. **2** (also /-rit/) *hist.* a knight who commanded his own troops in battle under his own banner. **3** *hist.* a knighthood given on the battlefield for courage.

ban·nis·ter var. of BANISTER.

banns /banz/ *n.pl.* a notice, read in church, announcing an intended marriage and giving the opportunity for objections.

ban·quet /bángkwit/ *n.* & *v.* •*n.* **1** an elaborate feast. **2** a dinner for many people followed by speeches. •*v.* (**banqueted, banqueting**) **1** *intr.* hold a banquet. **2** *tr.* entertain with a banquet.

ban·quette /bangkét/ *n.* an upholstered bench along a wall.

ban·shee /bánshee, -shée/ *n.* (in Irish folklore) a female spirit whose wailing warns of a death in a house.

ban·tam /bántəm/ *n.* **1** any of several small breeds of domestic fowl, of which the male is very aggressive. **2** a small but aggressive person.

ban·tam·weight /bántəmwayt/ *n.* **1** a weight in certain sports intermediate between flyweight and featherweight. **2** an athlete of this weight.

ban·ter /bántər/ *n.* & *v.* •*n.* good-humored teasing. •*v.* talk in a good-humored way.

Ban·tu /bántoo/ *n.* & *adj.* •*n.* (*pl.* same or **Bantus**) **1** often *offens.* **a** a large group of Negroid peoples of central and southern Africa. **b** a member of any of these peoples. **2** the group of languages spoken by them. •*adj.* of or relating to these peoples or languages.

ban·yan /bányən/ *n.* (also **ban·ian**) an Indian fig tree, *Ficus benghalensis*, the branches of which hang down and root themselves.

---

banyan late 16th century: from Portuguese, from Gujarati *vāṇiyo* 'man of the trading caste,' from Sanskrit. Originally denoting a Hindu trader or merchant, the term was applied by Europeans in the mid-17th century to a particular tree under which such traders had built a pagoda.

---

ban·zai /baanzí/ *int.* a Japanese battle cry.

bap·tism /báptizəm/ *n.* **1** the religious rite, symbolizing admission to the Christian Church, of sprinkling the forehead with water, or (usu. only with adults) by immersion, generally accompanied by name giving. **2** the act of baptizing or being baptized. ▫▫ **bap·tis·mal** /-tízməl/ *adj.*

bap·tism of fire *n.* **1** initiation into battle. **2** a painful new undertaking or experience.

bap·tist /báptist/ *n.* **1** a person who baptizes, esp. John the Baptist. **2** (**Baptist**) a member of a Protestant Christian denomination advocating baptism by total immersion, esp. of adults.

bap·tize /báptíz/ *v.tr.* **1** (also *absol.*) administer baptism to. **2** give a name or nickname to; christen.

bar[1] /baar/ *n., v.,* & *prep.* •*n.* **1** a long rod or piece of rigid wood, metal, etc. **2 a** something resembling a bar (*bar of soap; candy bar*). **b** the heating element of an electric heater. **c** = CROSSBAR. **d** *Mil.* a metal or cloth strip worn as part of an officer's insignia. **e** a sandbank or shoal as at the mouth of a harbor or an estuary. **3 a** a barrier of any shape. **b** a restriction (*a bar to promotion*). **4 a** a counter across which alcohol or refreshments are served. **b** a room in which alcohol is served and customers may sit and drink. **c** an establishment selling alcoholic drinks to be consumed on the premises. **d** a small store or stall serving refreshments (*snack bar*). **5** an enclosure in which a defendant stands in a court of law. **6** *Mus.* any of the sections of usu. equal time value into which a musical composition is divided by vertical lines across the staff. **7** (**the Bar**) *Law* **a** lawyers collectively. **b** the profession of lawyers. •*v.tr.* (**barred, barring**) **1 a** fasten with a bar or bars. **b** (usu. foll. by *in, out*) shut or keep in or out. **2** obstruct (*bar his progress*). **3** (usu. foll. by *from*) exclude (*bar them from attending*). **4** mark with stripes. •*prep.* except (*all were there bar a few*). ▫ **bar none** with no exceptions. **be called to the Bar** be admitted as a lawyer. **behind bars** in prison.

bar[2] /baar/ *n.* esp. *Meteorol.* a unit of pressure, 10^5 newtons per square meter, approx. one atmosphere.

barb /baarb/ *n.* & *v.* • *n.* **1** a secondary, backward facing projection from an arrow, fishhook, etc. **2** a deliberately hurtful remark. **3** a beardlike filament at the mouth of some fish. • *v.tr.* **1** provide (an arrow, etc.) with a barb or barbs. **2** (as **barbed** *adj.*) (of a remark, etc.) deliberately hurtful.

Bar·ba·di·an /baarbáydeeən/ *n.* & *adj.* • *n.* **1** a native or inhabitant of Barbados in the W. Indies. **2** a person of Barbadian descent. • *adj.* of or relating to Barbados or its people.

bar·bar·i·an /baarbáireeən/ *n.* & *adj.* • *n.* **1** an uncultured or brutish person. **2** a member of a primitive community. • *adj.* **1** rough and uncultured. **2** uncivilized.

bar·bar·ic /-bárik/ *adj.* **1** brutal; cruel (*flogging is a barbaric punishment*). **2** rough and uncultured; unrestrained. **3** of or like barbarians and their art or taste; primitive. □□ **bar·bar·i·cal·ly** *adv.*

bar·ba·rism /baárbərizəm/ *n.* **1 a** the absence of culture and civilized standards; ignorance and rudeness. **b** an example of this. **2** a solecism. **3** anything considered to be in bad taste.

bar·bar·i·ty /baarbáritee/ *n.* (*pl.* **-ties**) **1** savage cruelty. **2** an example of this.

bar·ba·rous /baárbərəs/ *adj.* **1** uncivilized. **2** cruel. **3** coarse and unrefined. □□ **bar·ba·rous·ly** *adv.* **bar·ba·rous·ness** *n.*

Bar·ba·ry ape /baárbəree/ *n.* a macaque, *Macaca sylvanus*, of N. Africa and Gibraltar.

bar·be·cue /baárbikyoo/ *n.* & *v.* • *n.* **1 a** a meal cooked on an open fire out of doors, esp. meat grilled on a metal appliance. **b** a party at which such a meal is cooked. **2 a** the metal appliance used for the preparation of a barbecue. **b** a fireplace, usu. of brick, containing such an appliance. • *v.tr.* (**barbecues, barbecued, barbecuing**) cook (esp. meat) on a barbecue. ¶ Abbr.: **BBQ**

barbecue mid-17th century: from Spanish *barbacoa*, perhaps from Arawak *barbacoa* 'wooden frame on posts.' The original sense was 'wooden framework for sleeping on, or for storing meat or fish to be dried.'

bar·be·cue sauce *n.* a highly seasoned sauce containing vinegar, spices, and usu. chilies, in which meat, etc., may be cooked.

barbed wire *n.* wire bearing sharp pointed spikes close together, used in fencing or as an obstruction.

bar·bel /baárbəl/ *n.* **1** any large European freshwater fish of the genus *Barbus*, with fleshy filaments hanging from its mouth. **2** such a filament.

bar·bell /baárbel/ *n.* an iron bar with a series of weighted disks at each end, used for weightlifting exercises.

bar·ber /baárbər/ *n.* a men's hairdresser.

bar·ber pole *n.* a spirally painted striped red and white pole hung outside barbers' shops as a business sign.

bar·ber·ry /baárberee/ *n.* (*pl.* **-ries**) **1** any shrub of the genus *Berberis*, with spiny shoots, yellow flowers, and ovoid red berries. **2** its berry.

bar·ber·shop /bárbərshop/ *n.* **1** a barber's place of business. **2** (often *attrib.*) a popular style of close harmony singing for four male voices (*barbershop quartet*).

bar·bi·can /baárbikən/ *n.* the outer defense of a city, castle, etc., esp. a double tower above a gate or drawbridge.

bar·bi·tal /baárbitawl, -tal/ *n.* a sedative drug.

bar·bi·tu·rate /baarbítchərət, -rayt/ *n.* any derivative of barbituric acid used in the preparation of sedative and sleep-inducing drugs.

bar·bi·tu·ric ac·id /baárbitóorik, -tyóor-/ *n. Chem.* an organic acid from which various sedatives are derived.

bar·bule /baárbyool/ *n.* a minute filament projecting from the barb of a feather.

barb·wire /baárbwīr/ *n.* = BARBED WIRE.

bar·ca·role /baárkərōl/ *n.* **1** a song sung by Venetian gondoliers. **2** music in imitation of this.

bar chart *n.* a chart using bars to represent quantity.

bar code *n.* a machine-readable code in the form of a pattern of stripes printed on and identifying a commodity.

bard[1] /baard/ *n.* **1** *hist.* a Celtic minstrel. **2** *poet.* a poet, esp. one treating heroic themes. **3 the Bard** (or **the Bard of Avon**) Shakespeare. □□ **bard·ic** *adj.*

bard[2] /baard/ *n.* & *v.* • *n.* a strip of fat placed on meat or game before roasting. • *v.tr.* cover (meat, etc.) with bards.

bare /bair/ *adj.* & *v.* • *adj.* **1** (esp. of part of the body) unclothed or uncovered (*with bare head*). **2** without appropriate covering or contents: **a** (of a tree) leafless. **b** empty (*bare rooms; the cupboard was bare*). **c** (of a floor) uncarpeted. **3 a** undisguised (*the bare truth*). **b** unadorned (*bare facts*). **4** (*attrib.*) **a** scanty (*a bare majority*). **b** mere (*bare necessities*). • *v.tr.* **1** uncover (*bared his teeth*). **2** reveal (*bared his soul*). □ **bare of** without. **with one's bare hands** without using tools or weapons. □□ **bare·ness** *n.*

bare·back /báirbak/ *adj.* & *adv.* on an unsaddled horse, donkey, etc.

bare bones *n.pl.* the minimum essential facts, ingredients, etc.

bare·faced /báirfáyst/ *adj.* undisguised; impudent (*barefaced lie*). □□ **bare·fac·ed·ly** /-fáysidlee/ *adv.*

bare·foot /báirfoot/ *adj.* & *adv.* (also **bare·foot·ed** /-footid/) with nothing on the feet.

bare·head·ed /báirhédid/ *adj.* & *adv.* without a covering for the head.

bare·ly /báirlee/ *adv.* **1** only just; scarcely (*barely escaped*). **2** scantily (*barely furnished*).

barf /baarf/ *v.* & *n. sl.* • *v.intr.* vomit or retch. • *n.* vomit.

bar·fly /baárflī/ *n.* (*pl.* **-flies**) *colloq.* a person who frequents bars.

bar·gain /baárgin/ *n.* & *v.* • *n.* **1 a** an agreement on the terms of a transaction or sale. **b** this seen from the buyer's viewpoint (*a bad bargain*). **2** something acquired or offered cheaply. • *v.intr.* (often foll. by *with, for*) discuss the terms of a transaction. □ **bargain for** (or *colloq.* **on**) (usu. with *neg.* actual or implied) expect (*didn't bargain for bad weather*). □□ **bar·gain·er** *n.*

bar·gain base·ment *n.* (also *attrib.*) a part of a store where goods are sold cheaply because they are old or imperfect.

barge /baarj/ *n.* & *v.* • *n.* **1** a long flat-bottomed boat for carrying freight on canals, etc. **2** a long ornamental boat used for pleasure or ceremony. **3** a boat used by the chief officers of a warship. • *v.intr.* **1** (often foll. by *around*) lurch or rush clumsily about. **2** (foll. by *in, into*) **a** interrupt rudely (*barged in while we were kissing*). **b** collide with (*barged into her*).

barge·pole /baárjpōl/ *n.* a long pole used for punting barges, etc.

bar·ite /báirīt, bár-/ *n.* a mineral form of barium sulfate.

bar·i·tone /báritōn/ *n.* **1 a** the second-lowest adult male singing voice. **b** a singer with this voice. **c** a part written for it. **2** an instrument that is second-lowest in pitch in its family.

bar·i·um /báireeəm, bár-/ *n. Chem.* a white reactive soft metallic element. ¶ Symb.: **Ba**.

bark[1] /baark/ *n.* & *v.* • *n.* **1** the sharp explosive cry of a dog, fox, etc. **2** a sound resembling this. • *v.* **1** *intr.* give a bark. **2** *tr.* & *intr.* speak or utter sharply or brusquely. □ **bark up the wrong tree** pursue a mistaken line of thought or course of action.

bark[2] /baark/ *n.* & *v.* • *n.* the tough protective outer sheath of the trunks, branches, and twigs of trees or woody shrubs. • *v.tr.* graze or scrape (one's shin, etc.).

bark[3] /baark/ *n.* a ship or boat.

bar·keep·er /baárkeepər/ *n.* (also **bar·keep**) a person who owns or serves drinks in a bar.

bark·en·tine /baárkənteen/ *n.* (also **bar·quen·tine, bar·quan·tine**) a sailing ship with the foremast square-rigged and the remaining (usu. two) masts fore-and-aft rigged.

bar·ley /baárlee/ *n.* **1** any of various hardy awned cereals of the genus *Hordeum* widely used as food and in malt liquors and spirits such as whiskey. **2** the grain produced from this (cf. PEARL BARLEY).

bar·ley·corn /baárleekawrn/ *n.* **1** the grain of barley. **2** a former unit of measure (about a third of an inch) based on the length of a grain of barley.

bar·ley wa·ter *n.* a drink made from water and a boiled barley mixture.

barm /baarm/ *n.* the froth on fermenting malt liquor.

bar·maid /baármayd/ *n.* a woman serving drinks in a bar, restaurant, etc.

bar mitz·vah /baar mítsvə/ *n.* **1** the religious initiation ceremony of a Jewish boy who has reached the age of 13. **2** the boy undergoing this ceremony.

barn[1] /baarn/ *n.* **1** a large farm building for storing grain, housing livestock, etc. **2** a large shed for storing road or railroad vehicles.

barn[2] /baarn/ *n.* *Physics* a unit of area, 10^{-24} square centimeters, used esp. in particle physics. ¶ Symb.: **b**.

bar·na·cle /baárnəkəl/ *n.* **1** any of various small marine crustaceans of the class Cirripedia which in adult form cling to rocks, ships' hulls, etc. **2** a tenacious attendant or follower who cannot easily be shaken off. □□ **bar·na·cled** *adj.*

barn burn·er (or **barn·burn·er**) *n.* *colloq.* something or someone that has a sensational effect or stirs excited interest.

barn dance *n.* **1** an informal social gathering for country dancing, orig. in a barn. **2** a dance for a number of couples forming a line or circle, with couples moving along it in turn.

barn owl *n.* a kind of owl, *Tyto alba*, frequenting barns.

barn·storm /baárnstawrm/ *v.intr.* **1** tour rural districts giving theatrical performances (formerly often in barns). **2** make a rapid tour, esp. for political meetings. □□ **barn·storm·er** *n.*

barn·yard /baárnyaard/ *n.* the area around a barn.

bar·o·graph /bárəgraf/ *n.* a barometer equipped to record its readings.

ba·rom·e·ter /bərómitər/ *n.* **1** an instrument measuring atmospheric pressure, esp. in forecasting the weather and determining altitude. **2** anything that reflects changes in circumstances, etc. □□ **bar·o·met·ric** /bárəmétrik/ *adj.* **bar·o·met·ri·cal** /bárəmétrikəl/ *adj.*

bar·on /bárən/ *n.* **1** a member of the lowest order of a nobility. **2** a powerful or influential person; a magnate (*sugar baron*). **3** *hist.* a person who held lands or property from the sovereign or a powerful overlord. □□ **ba·ro·ni·al** /bərṓneeəl/ *adj.* **bar·o·ny** /bárənee/ *n.*

bar·on·age /bárənij/ *n.* **1** barons or nobles collectively. **2** an annotated list of barons or peers.

bar·on·ess /bárənis/ *n.* **1** a woman holding the rank of baron. **2** the wife or widow of a baron.

bar·on·et /bárənit, -nét/ *n.* a member of the lowest hereditary titled British order. □□ **bar·on·et·cy** /bárənitsee, -nét-/ *n.* (*pl.* **-cies**)

ba·roque /bərók/ *adj.* & *n.* • *adj.* **1** highly ornate and extravagant in style, esp. of European art, etc., of the 17th and 18th c. **2** of or relating to this period. • *n.* **1** the baroque style. **2** baroque art collectively.

barque /baark/ *n.* (also **bark**) **1** a sailing ship with the rear mast fore-and-aft rigged and the remaining (usu. two) masts square-rigged. **2** *poet.* any boat.

bar·rack /bárək/ *n.* (usu. in *pl.*, often treated as *sing.*) **1** a building or complex used to house soldiers. **2** any building used to accommodate large numbers of people. **3** a large building of a bleak or plain appearance.

bar·ra·cou·ta /bárəkṓōtə/ *n.* (*pl.* same or **barracoutas**) a long slender fish, *Thyrsites atun*, usu. found in southern oceans.

bar·ra·cu·da /bárəkṓōdə/ *n.* (*pl.* same or **barracudas**) a large and voracious tropical marine fish of the family Sphyraenidae.

bar·rage /bəraáz͟h/ *n.* **1** a concentrated artillery bombardment over a wide area. **2** a rapid succession of questions or criticisms. **3** /baárij/ an artificial barrier, esp. in a river.

bar·rage bal·loon *n.* a large anchored balloon, often with netting suspended from it, used as a defense against low-flying aircraft.

bar·ra·try /bárətree/ *n.* **1** fraud or gross negligence of a ship's master or crew at the expense of its owners or users. **2** trade in the sale of church or state appointments. □□ **bar·ra·trous** *adj.*

barre /baar/ *n.* a horizontal bar at waist level used in dance exercises.

bar·ré /baaráy/ *n.* *Mus.* a method of playing a chord on the guitar, etc., with a finger laid across the strings at a particular fret, raising their pitch.

bar·rel /bárəl/ *n.* **1** a cylindrical container usu. bulging out in the middle, traditionally made of wooden staves with metal hoops around them. **2** the contents of this. **3** a measure of capacity, usu. varying from 30 to 40 gallons. **4** a cylindrical tube forming part of an object such as a gun. □ **over a barrel** *colloq.* in a helpless position; at a person's mercy.

bar·rel-chest·ed *adj.* having a large rounded chest.

bar·rel or·gan *n.* a mechanical musical instrument in which a rotating pin-studded cylinder acts on a series of pipe valves, strings, or metal tongues.

bar·rel vault *n.* *Archit.* a vault forming a half-cylinder.

bar·ren /bárən/ *adj.* (**barrener, barrenest**) **1** unable to bear young, fruit, etc. **2** meager; unprofitable. **3** dull; unstimulating. **4** (foll. by *of*) lacking in (*barren of wit*). □□ **bar·ren·ly** *adv.* **bar·ren·ness** *n.*

bar·rette /bərét/ *n.* a typically bar-shaped clip or ornament for the hair.

bar·ri·cade /bárikáyd/ *n.* & *v.* • *n.* a barrier, esp. one improvised across a street, etc. • *v.tr.* block or defend with a barricade.

bar·ri·er /báreeər/ *n.* **1** an obstacle that bars advance or access. **2** an obstacle or circumstance that keeps people or things apart (*class barriers*; *a language barrier*).

bar·ri·er reef *n.* a coral reef separated from the shore by a broad deep channel.

bar·ring /baáring/ *prep.* except; not including.

bar·ri·o /baáreeō, bár-/ *n.* (*pl.* **-os**) **1** (in Spanish-speaking countries) a division or district of a city or town. **2** (in the US) the Spanish-speaking quarter or neighborhood of a town or city.

bar·ris·ter /báristər/ *n.* (in full **barrister-at-law**) **1** *Brit.* a person called to the Bar and entitled to practice as an advocate in the higher courts. **2** a lawyer.

bar·room /bárōōm, -rŏŏm/ *n.* an establishment where alcoholic drinks are served over a counter.

bar·row[1] /bárō/ *n.* **1** a metal frame with two wheels used for transporting luggage, etc. **2** = WHEELBARROW.

bar·row[2] /bárō/ *n.* *Archaeol.* an ancient grave mound or tumulus.

bar·tend·er /baártendər/ *n.* a person who mixes and serves drinks at a tavern, bar, etc.

bar·ter /baártər/ *v. & n.* •*v.* **1** *tr.* exchange (goods or services) without using money. **2** *intr.* make such an exchange. •*n.* trade by exchange of goods.

bar·y·on /báreeon/ *n.* *Physics* an elementary particle that is of equal mass to or greater mass than a proton. □□ **bar·y·on·ic** /-ónik/ *adj.*

bar·y·sphere /bárisfeer/ *n.* the dense interior of the earth, including the mantle and core, enclosed by the lithosphere.

ba·sal /báysəl, -zəl/ *adj.* **1** of, at, or forming a base. **2** fundamental.

ba·sal me·tab·o·lism *n.* the chemical processes occurring in an organism at complete rest.

ba·salt /bəsáwlt, báysawlt/ *n.* **1** a dark volcanic rock whose strata sometimes form columns. **2** a kind of black stoneware resembling basalt. □□ **ba·sal·tic** /-sáwltik/ *adj.*

base[1] /bays/ *n. & v.* •*n.* **1 a** a part that supports from beneath or serves as a foundation. **b** a notional structure on which something depends (*power base*). **2** a principle or starting point. **3** esp. *Mil.* a place from which activity is directed. **4 a** a main or important ingredient. **b** a substance, e.g., water, in combination with which pigment forms paint, etc. **5** a substance used as a foundation for makeup. **6** *Chem.* a substance capable of combining with an acid to form a salt and water and usu. producing hydroxide ions when dissolved in water. **7** *Math.* a number in terms of which other numbers or logarithms are expressed (see RADIX). **8** *Baseball*, etc. one of the four stations that must be reached in turn to score a run. •*v.tr.* **1** (usu. foll. by *on, upon*) establish (*a theory based on speculation*). **2** (foll. by *at, in*, etc.) station (*troops were based in Kuwait*).

base[2] /bays/ *adj.* **1** cowardly; despicable. **2** menial. **3** alloyed (*base coin*). **4** (of a metal) low in value. □□ **base·ly** *adv.* **base·ness** *n.*

base·ball /báysbawl/ *n.* **1** a game played with two teams of nine, a bat and ball, and a circuit of four bases that must be completed to score. **2** the ball used in this game.

base·board /báysbawrd/ *n.* a narrow board, etc., along the bottom of the wall of a room.

base hit *n.* *Baseball* a fair ball that enables the batter to get on base without benefit of an opponent's error and without forcing out another player already on base.

base·less /báyslis/ *adj.* unfounded; groundless. □□ **base·less·ly** *adv.* **base·less·ness** *n.*

base·line /bájslīn/ *n.* **1** a line used as a base or starting point. **2** (in tennis, basketball, etc.) the line marking each end of a court. **3** *Baseball* either of the lines leading from home plate to first and third bases and determining the boundaries of fair territory.

base·man /báysmən/ *n.* (*pl.* **-men**) *Baseball* a fielder stationed near a base.

base·ment /báysmənt/ *n.* the lowest floor of a building, usu. at least partly below ground level.

base on balls *n.* *Baseball* advancement to first base by a player who has been pitched four balls while at bat.

ba·ses *pl.* of BASE[1], BASIS.

base u·nit *n.* a unit that is defined arbitrarily and not by combinations of other units.

bash /bash/ *v. & n.* •*v.* **1** *tr.* **a** strike bluntly or heavily. **b** (often foll. by *up*) *colloq.* attack or criticize violently. **c** (often foll. by *down, in*, etc.) damage or break by striking forcibly. **2** *intr.* (foll. by *into*) collide with. •*n.* a heavy blow.

bash·ful /báshfŏŏl/ *adj.* **1** shy; self-conscious. **2** sheepish. □□ **bash·ful·ly** *adv.* **bash·ful·ness** *n.*

BASIC /báysik/ *n.* a computer programming language using familiar English words and designed for beginners (acronym for *B*eginners' *A*ll-purpose *S*ymbolic *I*nstruction *C*ode).

ba·sic /báysik/ *adj. & n.* •*adj.* **1** forming or serving as a base. **2** fundamental. **3 a** simplest or lowest in level (*basic requirements*). **b** vulgar (*basic humor*). **4** *Chem.* having the properties of or containing a base. •*n.* (usu. in *pl.*) the fundamental facts or principles.

ba·si·cal·ly *adv.* **1** fundamentally. **2** (qualifying a clause) in fact; actually.

bas·il /bázəl, báyzəl/ *n.* an aromatic herb of the genus *Ocimum*, esp. *O. basilicum* (in full **sweet basil**), whose leaves are used as a flavoring in cooking.

ba·sil·i·ca /bəsílikə/ *n.* **1** an ancient Roman public hall with an apse and colonnades. **2** a similar building used as a Christian church. **3** a church having special privileges from the Pope. □□ **ba·sil·i·can** *adj.*

bas·i·lisk /básilisk, báz-/ *n.* **1** a mythical reptile with a lethal breath and look. **2** any small American lizard of the genus *Basiliscus*, with a crest from its back to its tail.

ba·sin /báysən/ *n.* **1** a wide, shallow, open container, esp. a fixed one for holding water. **2** a hollow, rounded depression. **3** any sheltered area of water where boats can moor safely. **4** a round valley. **5** an area drained by rivers and tributaries. □□ **ba·sin·ful** *n.* (*pl.* **-fuls**).

ba·sis /báysis/ *n.* (*pl.* **bases** /-seez/) **1** the foundation or support of esp. an idea or argument. **2** the determining principle (*on a purely friendly basis*).

bask /bask/ *v.intr.* **1** sit or lie back lazily in warmth and light. **2** (foll. by *in*) derive great pleasure (from) (*basking in glory*).

bas·ket /báskit/ *n.* **1** a container made of interwoven cane, etc. **2** a container resembling this. **3** the amount held by a basket. **4** the goal in basketball, or a goal scored. □□ **bas·ket·ful** *n.* (*pl.* **-fuls**).

bas·ket·ball /báskitbawl/ *n.* **1** a game between two teams, usu. of five, in which points are scored by making the ball drop through hooped nets fixed high up at each end of the court. **2** the ball used in this game.

bas·ket case *n.* **1** a person who cannot function because of tension, stress, etc. **2** *offens.* a person, esp. a soldier, who has lost all four limbs.

bas·ket·ry /báskitree/ *n.* **1** the art of making baskets. **2** baskets collectively.

bas·ket weave *n.* a weave resembling that of a basket.

bas·ket·work /báskitwərk/ *n.* **1** material woven in the style of a basket. **2** the art of making this.

bas mitz·vah /bas mítsvə/ *n.* (also **bat mitz·vah**) **1** the religious initiation ceremony of a Jewish girl who has reached the age of 12 or 13. **2** the girl undergoing this ceremony.

Basque /bask/ *n.* **1** a member of a people of the Western Pyrenees. **2** the language of this people.

bas-re·lief /baá-rileéf, bás-/ *n.* (also **low relief**) sculpture or carving in which the figures project slightly from the background.

bass[1] /bays/ *n. & adj.* •*n.* **1 a** the lowest adult male singing voice. **b** a singer with this voice. **c** a part written for it. **2** the lowest part in harmonized music. **3 a** an instrument that is the lowest in pitch in its family. **b** its player. **4** *colloq.* a bass guitar or double bass. **5** the low-frequency output of a radio, CD player, etc., corresponding to the bass in music. •*adj.* **1** lowest in musical pitch. **2** deep-sounding. □□ **bass·ist** *n.* (in sense 3b).

bass[2] /bas/ *n.* (*pl.* same or **basses**) any of various edible fishes including the common European perch and several N. American marine and freshwater fishes, esp. *Morone saxatilis* and *Micropterus salmoides*.

bass³ /bas/ *n.* = BAST.

bass clef *n.* a clef placing F below middle C on the second highest line of the staff.

bas·set /básit/ *n.* (in full **basset hound**) a hunting dog of a breed with a long body, short legs, and big ears.

bas·si·net /básinét/ *n.* a child's wicker cradle, usu. with a hood.

bas·so /básō, baá-/ *n.* (*pl.* **-sos** or **bassi** /-see/) a singer with a bass voice.

bas·soon /bəsóōn/ *n.* a bass instrument of the oboe family. ▫▫ **bas·soon·ist** *n.*

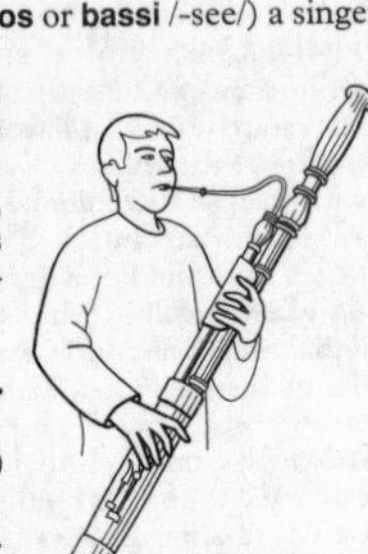
bassoon

bas·so pro·fun·do /básō, baá–, prōfóōndō/ *n.* a bass singer with an exceptionally low range.

bas·so-re·lie·vo /básō-rileévō/ *n.* (also **bas·so-ri·lie·vo** /básō-reelyáyvō/) (*pl.* **·vos**) = BAS-RELIEF.

bass·wood /báswood/ *n.* **1** the American linden, *Tilia americana*. **2** the wood of this tree.

bast /bast/ *n.* the inner bark of linden, or other flexible fibrous bark, used as fiber in matting, etc.

bas·tard /bástərd/ *n.* & *adj.* •*n.* **1** a person born of parents not married to each other. **2** *sl.* **a** an unpleasant or despicable person. **b** a person of a specified kind (*poor bastard*). **3** *sl.* a difficult or awkward thing. •*adj.* **1** illegitimate. **2** (of things): **a** unauthorized; counterfeit. **b** hybrid. ▫▫ **bas·tar·dy** *n.* (in sense 1 of *n.*).

---

bastard Middle English: via Old French from medieval Latin *bastardus*, probably from *bastum* 'packsaddle'; compare with Old French *fils de bast*, literally 'packsaddle son' (i.e., the son of a mule driver who uses a packsaddle for a pillow and is gone by morning).

---

bas·tard·ize /bástərdīz/ *v.tr.* **1** declare (a person) illegitimate. **2** corrupt; debase. ▫▫ **bas·tard·i·za·tion** *n.*

baste¹ /bayst/ *v.tr.* moisten (meat) with gravy or melted fat during cooking.

baste² /bayst/ *v.tr.* stitch loosely together in preparation for sewing; tack.

bas·ti·na·do /bástináydō, -naá-/ *n.* punishment by beating with a stick on the soles of the feet.

bas·tion /báschən, -teeən/ *n.* **1** a projecting part of a fortification built at an angle of, or against the line of, a wall. **2** a thing regarded as protecting (*bastion of freedom*).

bat¹ /bat/ *n.* & *v.* •*n.* **1** an implement with a handle and a flat or curved surface, used for hitting balls in games. **2** a batter described in some way (*a hot bat*). •*v.* (**batted, batting**) **1** *tr.* hit with or as with a bat. **2** *intr.* take a turn at using a bat. ▫ **bat around 1** *sl.* drift or putter aimlessly. **2** discuss (an idea or proposal). **3** *Baseball* have each player in a lineup bat in the course of a single inning. **right off the bat** immediately.

bat² /bat/ *n.* any mouselike nocturnal mammal of the order Chiroptera, capable of flight by means of membranous wings extending from its forelimbs. ▫ **have bats in the belfry** be eccentric or crazy. **like a bat out of hell** very fast.

bat³ /bat/ *v.tr.* (**batted, batting**) ▫ **not** (or **never**) **bat an eye** *colloq.* show no reaction.

batch /bach/ *n.* & *v.* •*n.* **1** a number of things or persons forming a group. **2** an installment (*sent off the latest batch*). **3** the loaves produced at one baking. **4** (*attrib.*) using or dealt with in batches, not as a continuous flow (*batch production*). •*v.tr.* arrange or deal with in batches.

bate /bayt/ *v.* **1** *tr.* moderate; restrain. **2** *tr.* diminish; deduct. **3** *intr.* diminish; abate.

ba·teau /batṓ/ *n.* (*pl.* **bateaux** /-tōz/) a light riverboat, esp. of the flat-bottomed kind used in Canada and the southern US.

bat·ed /báytid/ *adj.* ▫ **with bated breath** very anxiously.

bath /bath/ *n.* & *v.* •*n.* (*pl.* **baths** /baṯẖz, baths/) **1 a** = BATHTUB. **b** a bathtub with its contents (*your bath is ready*). **2** the act or process of immersing the body for washing or therapy (*take a bath*). **3 a** a vessel containing liquid in which something is immersed, e.g., a film for developing. **b** this with its contents. •*v. Brit.* **1** *tr.* wash (esp. a person) in a bath. **2** *intr.* take a bath. ▫ **take a bath** sl. suffer a large financial loss.

bathe /baṯẖ/ *v.* **1** *intr.* immerse oneself in water, esp. to wash oneself or (*Brit.*) to swim. **2** *tr.* **a** wash (esp. a person) in a bath. **b** treat with liquid for cleansing or medicinal purposes. **3** *tr.* (of sunlight, etc.) envelop. ▫▫ **bath·er** *n.*

bath·house /báth-hows/ *n.* a building with baths for public use.

ba·thing suit (also *Brit.* **ba·thing cos·tume**) *n.* a garment worn for swimming.

ba·thom·e·ter /bəthómitər/ *n.* an instrument used to measure the depth of water.

ba·thos /báythaws, -thos/ *n.* **1** (esp. in a work of literature) an effect of anticlimax created by an unintentional lapse in mood from the sublime to the absurd or trivial. ▫▫ **ba·thet·ic** /bəthétik/ *adj.* **ba·thot·ic** /bəthótik/ *adj.*

bath·robe /báthrōb/ *n.* a loose robe or dressing gown, worn before and after bathing or for lounging.

bath·room /báthrōōm, -rŏŏm/ *n.* **1** a room containing a toilet. **2** a room containing a bath and usu. other washing facilities.

bath salts *n.pl.* soluble salts used for softening or scenting bathwater.

bath·tub /báthtəb/ *n.* a tub, usu. installed in a bathroom, used for immersing and washing the body.

bath·y·scaphe /báthiskaf/ *n.* a manned vessel for deep-sea diving.

bath·y·sphere /báthisfeer/ *n.* a spherical vessel for deep-sea observation.

ba·tik /bəteék, bátik/ *n.* a method (orig. used in Indonesia) of producing colored designs on textiles by applying wax to the parts to be left uncolored.

ba·tiste /bateést/ *n.* & *adj.* •*n.* a fine linen or cotton cloth. •*adj.* made of batiste.

bat mitz·vah /bat mítsvə/ var. of BAS MITZVAH.

ba·ton /bətón, ba-, bát'n/ *n.* **1** a thin stick used by a conductor to direct an orchestra, etc. **2** *Sports* a short stick or tube carried and passed on in a relay race. **3** a long stick carried and twirled by a drum major.

bat·tal·ion /bətályən/ *n.* **1** a large body of men ready for battle, esp. an infantry unit forming part of a brigade. **2** a large group of people pursuing a common aim or sharing a major undertaking.

bat·ten /bát'n/ *n.* & *v.* •*n.* a long flat strip of squared lumber or metal, esp. used to hold something in place or as a fastening against a wall, etc. •*v.tr.* strengthen or fasten with battens. ▫ **batten down the hatches 1** *Naut.* secure a ship's tarpaulins. **2** prepare for a difficulty or crisis.

bat·ter¹ /bátər/ *v.* **1 a** *tr.* strike repeatedly with hard blows. **b** *intr.* (often foll. by *against*, *at*, etc.) pound heavily and insistently. **2** *tr.* (often in *passive*) handle roughly, esp. over a long period. ▫▫ **bat·ter·er** *n.*

bat·ter² /bátər/ *n.* a fluid mixture of flour, egg, and milk or water, used in cooking, esp. for cakes, etc., and for coating food before frying.

bat·ter[3] /bátər/ *n. Sports* a player batting, esp. in baseball.

bat·ter[4] /bátər/ *n. & v.* • *n.* **1** a wall, etc., with a sloping face. **2** a receding slope. • *v.intr.* have a receding slope.

bat·tered /bátərd/ *adj.* injured by repeated blows or punishment.

bat·ter·ing ram *n. hist.* a heavy beam, orig. with an end in the form of a carved ram's head, used in breaching fortifications.

bat·ter·y /bátəree/ *n.* (*pl.* **-ies**) **1** a usu. portable container of a cell or cells carrying an electric charge, as a source of current. **2** a set of similar units of equipment, esp. connected. **3** a series of tests, esp. psychological. **4 a** a fortified emplacement for heavy guns. **b** an artillery unit of guns, soldiers, and vehicles. **5** *Law* an act involving unlawful touching of another (see ASSAULT).

bat·ting /báting/ *n.* cotton wadding prepared in sheets for use in quilts, etc.

bat·ting or·der *n. Sports* the order in which batters or batsmen take their turns.

bat·tle /bát'l/ *n. & v.* • *n.* **1** a prolonged fight, esp. between large organized armed forces. **2** a contest (*a battle of wits*). • *v.* **1** *intr.* fight persistently (*battled against the elements*). **2** *tr.* fight (one's way, etc.). ◻◻ **bat·tler** *n.*

bat·tle-ax *n.* **1** a large ax used in ancient warfare. **2** *colloq.* a formidable or domineering older woman.

bat·tle cruis·er *n.* a heavily armed ship faster and more lightly armored than a battleship.

bat·tle cry *n.* a cry or slogan of participants in a battle or contest.

bat·tle·dore /bát'ldawr/ *n. hist.* **1 a** (in full **battledore and shuttlecock**) a game similar to badminton played with a shuttlecock and rackets. **b** the racket used in this. **2** a kind of wooden utensil like a paddle, formerly used in washing, baking, etc.

bat·tle fa·tigue *n.* = COMBAT FATIGUE.

bat·tle·field /bát'lfeeld/ *n.* (also **bat·tle·ground** /-grownd/) the piece of ground on which a battle is or was fought.

bat·tle·ment /bát'lmənt/ *n.* (usu. in *pl.*) **1** a parapet with recesses along the top of a wall, as part of a fortification. **2** a section of roof enclosed by this. ◻◻ **bat·tle·ment·ed** *adj.*

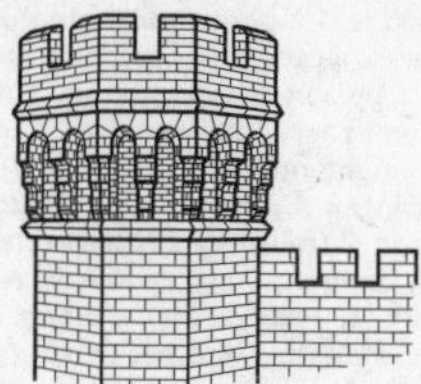

battlement

bat·tle roy·al *n.* (*pl.* **battles royal**) **1** a battle in which several combatants or all available forces engage; a free fight. **2** a heated argument.

bat·tle·ship /bát'lship/ *n.* a warship of the class with the heaviest armor and the largest guns.

bat·tue /batóō, –työō/ *n.* **1 a** the driving of game toward hunters by beaters. **b** a hunt arranged in this way. **2** wholesale slaughter.

bat·ty /bátee/ *adj.* (**battier, battiest**) *sl.* crazy. ◻◻ **bat·ti·ly** *adv.* **bat·ti·ness** *n.*

bau·ble /báwbəl/ *n.* **1** a showy trinket or toy of little value. **2** a baton formerly used as an emblem by jesters.

baud /bawd/ *n.* (*pl.* same or **bauds**) *Computing*, etc. **1** a unit used to express the speed of electronic code signals, corresponding to one information unit per second. **2** (loosely) a unit of data transmission speed of one bit per second.

baux·ite /báwksīt/ *n.* a claylike mineral containing varying proportions of alumina, the chief ore of aluminum. ◻◻ **baux·it·ic** /-sítik/ *adj.*

bawd·y /báwdee/ *adj.* (**bawdier, bawdiest**) (esp. humorously) indecent; raunchy. ◻◻ **bawd·i·ly** *adv.* **bawd·i·ness** *n.*

bawl /bawl/ *v.* **1** *tr.* speak or call out noisily. **2** *intr.* weep loudly. ◻ **bawl out** *colloq.* reprimand angrily.

bay[1] /bay/ *n.* **1** a broad inlet of the sea within a curve of land. **2** a recess in a mountain range.

bay[2] /bay/ *n.* **1** (in full **bay laurel**) a laurel, *Laurus nobilis*, having deep green leaves and purple berries. **2** (in *pl.*) a wreath made of bay leaves, for a victor or poet.

bay[3] /bay/ *n.* **1** a space created by a window line projecting outward from a wall. **2** a recess. **3** an area specially allocated (*loading bay*).

bay[4] /bay/ *adj. & n.* • *adj.* (esp. of a horse) dark reddish brown. • *n.* a bay horse with a black mane and tail.

bay[5] /bay/ *v. & n.* • *v.* **1** *intr.* (esp. of a large dog) bark or howl loudly and plaintively. **2** *tr.* bay at. • *n.* the sound of baying, esp. in chorus from hounds in close pursuit. ◻ **at bay 1** cornered; apparently unable to escape. **2** in a desperate situation. **hold** (or **keep**) **at bay** hold off (a pursuer).

bay·ber·ry /báyberee/ *n.* (*pl.* **-ries**) any of various N. American plants of the genus *Myrica*, having aromatic leaves and bearing berries covered in a wax coating.

bay leaf *n.* the aromatic (usu. dried) leaf of the bay tree, used in cooking.

bay·o·net /báyənét/ *n. & v.* • *n.* **1** a stabbing blade attachable to the muzzle of a rifle. **2** an electrical or other fitting engaged by being pushed into a socket and twisted. • *v.tr.* (**bayoneted, bayoneting**) stab with a bayonet.

bay·ou /bī́-ōō/ *n.* a marshy offshoot of a river, etc., in the southern US.

bay rum *n.* a perfume, esp. for the hair, distilled orig. from bayberry leaves in rum.

bay win·dow *n.* a window built to project outward from an outside wall.

ba·zaar /bəza'ar/ *n.* **1** a market in an Eastern or Middle Eastern country. **2** a fund-raising sale of goods, esp. for charity.

ba·zoo·ka /bəzóōkə/ *n.* a tubular short-range rocket launcher used against tanks.

BB *abbr.* a shot pellet about .18 inch in diameter, for use in a BB gun or air gun.

BBC *abbr.* British Broadcasting Corporation.

BC *abbr.* **1** (of a date) before Christ. **2** British Columbia.

BCE *abbr.* (of a date) before the Common Era.

bdel·li·um /déleeəm/ *n.* **1** any of various trees, esp. of the genus *Commiphora*, yielding resin. **2** this fragrant resin used in perfumes.

Be *symb. Chem.* the element beryllium.

be /bee/ *v. & v.aux.* (*sing. present* **am** /am, əm/; **are** /aar, ər/; **is** /iz/; *pl. present* **are**; *1st and 3rd sing. past* **was** /wuz, woz, wəz/; *2nd sing. past and pl. past* **were** /wər/; *present subj.* **be**; *past subj.* **were**; *pres. part.* **being**; *past part.* **been** /bin/) • *v.intr.* **1** (often prec. by *there*) exist; live (*there is a house on the corner*). **2 a** take place (*dinner is at eight*). **b** occupy a position in space (*he is in the garden*). **3** remain; continue (*let it be*). **4** linking subject and predicate, expressing: **a** identity (*today is Thursday*). **b** condition (*he is ill today*). **c** state or quality (*he is very kind*). **d** opinion (*I am against hanging*). **e** total (*two and two are four*). **f** cost or significance (*it is $5 to enter*). • *v.aux.* **1** with a past participle to form the passive mood (*it was done*). **2** with a present participle to form continuous tenses (*we are coming*). **3** with an infinitive to express duty or commitment, intention, possibility, destiny, or hypothesis (*he is to come at four; if I were to die*). □ **be about** occupy oneself with (*is about his business*). **be off** *colloq.* go away; leave. **be that as it may** see MAY. **-to-be** of the future (in *comb.*: *bride-to-be*).

beach /beech/ *n.* & *v.* • *n.* a pebbly or sandy shore. • *v.tr.* run or haul up (a boat, etc.) on to a beach.

beach ball *n.* a large inflated ball for games on the beach.

beach•comb•er /béechkōmər/ *n.* **1** a vagrant who lives by searching beaches for articles of value. **2** a long wave rolling in from the sea.

beach•head /béech-hed/ *n. Mil.* a fortified position established on a beach by landing forces.

bea•con /béekən/ *n.* **1** a fire or light set up in a prominent position as a warning, etc. **2** a visible guiding point or device (e.g., a lighthouse). **3** a radio transmitter whose signal helps fix the position of a ship or aircraft.

bead /beed/ *n.* & *v.* • *n.* **1 a** a small usu. rounded and perforated piece of glass, stone, etc., for threading with others. **b** (in *pl.*) a string of beads; a rosary. **2** a drop of liquid. **3** a small knob in the foresight of a gun. **4** the inner edge of a pneumatic tire. • *v.* **1** *tr.* furnish or decorate with beads. **2** *intr.* form or grow into beads. □ **draw a bead on** take aim at. □□ **bead•ed** *adj.*

bead•ing /béeding/ *n.* **1** decoration in the form of or resembling a row of beads, esp. looped edging. **2** the inner edge of a pneumatic tire.

bead•y /béedee/ *adj.* (**beadier, beadiest**) **1** (of the eyes) small, round, and bright. **2** covered with beads or drops. □□ **bead•i•ly** *adv.* **bead•i•ness** *n.*

bead•y-eyed *adj.* with beady eyes.

bea•gle /béegəl/ *n.* a small hound of a breed with a short coat, orig. used for hunting hares.

beak /beek/ *n.* **1 a** a bird's horny projecting jaws; a bill. **b** the similar projecting jaw of other animals, e.g., a turtle. **2** *sl.* a hooked nose. **3** *Naut. hist.* the projection at the prow of a warship. □□ **beaked** *adj.* **beak•y** *adj.*

beak•er /béekər/ *n.* **1** a tall drinking vessel, usu. of plastic and tumbler-shaped. **2** a lipped cylindrical glass vessel for scientific experiments. **3** *archaic* or *literary* a large drinking vessel with a wide mouth.

be-all and end-all *n. colloq.* the feature of an activity or way of life that is of greater importance than any other.

beam /beem/ *n.* & *v.* • *n.* **1** a long sturdy piece of squared timber or metal spanning an opening or room, usu. to support the structure above. **2 a** a ray or shaft of light. **b** a directional flow of particles or radiation. **3** a bright look or smile. **4 a** a series of radio or radar signals as a guide to a ship or aircraft. **b** the course indicated by this (*off beam*). **5** the crossbar of a balance. **6 a** a ship's breadth at its widest point. **b** the width of a person's hips (esp. *broad in the beam*). **7** the side of a ship (*land on the port beam*). **8** the chief timber of a plow. • *v.* **1** *tr.* emit or direct (light, radio waves, etc.). **2** *intr.* **a** shine. **b** look or smile radiantly. □ **off** (*or* **off the**) **beam** *colloq.* mistaken. **on the beam** *colloq.* on the right track.

bean /been/ *n.* & *v.* • *n.* **1 a** any kind of leguminous plant with edible seeds in long pods. **b** one of these seeds. **2** a similar seed of coffee and other plants. **3** *sl.* the head. **4** (in *pl.*; with *neg.*) *sl.* anything at all (*doesn't know beans about it*). • *v.tr. sl.* hit on the head.

bean•bag /béenbag/ *n.* **1** a small bag filled with dried beans and used esp. in children's games. **2** (in full **bean•bag chair**) a large cushion filled usu. with polystyrene beads and used as a seat.

bean curd *n.* a soft cheeselike cake or paste made from soybeans, used esp. in Asian cooking. Also called **tofu.**

bean•ie /béenee/ *n.* a small close-fitting cap worn on the back of the head.

bean•pole /béenpōl/ *n.* **1** a stick for supporting bean plants. **2** *colloq.* a tall thin person.

bean sprout *n.* a sprout of a bean seed, esp. of the mung bean, used as food.

bear[1] /bair/ *v.* (*past* **bore** /bor/; *past part.* **borne, born** /bawrn/)

▶In the passive *born* is used with reference to birth (e.g., *was born in July*), except for *borne by* foll. by the name of the mother (e.g., *was borne by Sarah*). **1** *tr.* carry, bring, or take (*bear gifts*). **2** *tr.* show; be marked by; have as an attribute or characteristic (*bear marks of violence; bears no relation to the case*). **3** *tr.* **a** produce; yield (fruit, etc.). **b** give birth to (*has borne a son; was born last week*). **4** *tr.* **a** sustain (a weight, responsibility, cost, etc.). **b** stand; endure (an ordeal, difficulty, etc.). **5** *tr.* (usu. with *neg.* or *interrog.*) **a** tolerate; put up with (*can't bear him; how can you bear it?*). **b** admit of; be fit for (*does not bear thinking about*). **6** *tr.* carry in thought or memory (*bear a grudge*). **7** *intr.* veer in a given direction (*bear left*). □ **bear down** exert downward pressure. **bear down on** approach rapidly or purposefully. **bear fruit** have results. **bear hard on** oppress. **bear in mind** remember and take into account. **bear on** (or **upon**) be relevant to. **bear out** support or confirm (an account or the person giving it). **bear up** raise one's spirits; not despair. **bear with** treat forbearingly; tolerate patiently. **bear witness** testify.

bear[2] /bair/ *n.* **1** any large heavy mammal of the family Ursidae. **2** a rough, unmannerly, or uncouth person. **3** *Stock Exch.* a person who sells shares hoping to buy them back later at a lower price. **4** = TEDDY.

bear•a•ble /báirəbəl/ *adj.* that may be endured or tolerated.

bear•bait•ing /báirbayting/ *n. hist.* an entertainment involving setting dogs to attack a captive bear.

beard /beerd/ *n.* & *v.* • *n.* **1** hair growing on the chin and lower cheeks. **2** a similar tuft or part on an animal (esp. a goat). • *v.tr.* oppose openly; defy. □□ **beard•ed** *adj.* **beard•less** *adj.*

bear•er /báirər/ *n.* **1** a person or thing that bears, carries, or brings. **2** a carrier of equipment on an expedition, etc. **3** a person who possesses and presents a check or other order to pay money.

bear hug *n.* a tight embrace.

bear•ing /báiring/ *n.* **1** a person's bodily attitude or outward behavior. **2** (foll. by *on, upon*) relation or relevance to (*his comments have no bearing on the subject*). **3** endurability (*beyond bearing*). **4** a part of a machine that supports a rotating or other moving part. **5** direction or position relative to a fixed point. **6** (in *pl.*) **a** one's position relative to one's surroundings. **b** awareness of this (*get one's bearings; lose one's bearings*).

bear•ish /báirish/ *adj.* **1** like a bear, esp. in temper. **2** *Stock Exch.* causing or associated with a fall in prices.

bear•skin /báirskin/ *n.* **1** the skin of a bear. **2** a tall furry hat worn ceremonially by some regiments.

beast /beest/ *n.* **1** an animal other than a human being, esp. a wild quadruped. **2 a** a brutal person. **b** *colloq.* an objectionable or unpleasant person or thing. **3** (prec. by *the*) a human being's brutish or uncivilized characteristics (*saw the beast in him*).

beast•ie /béestee/ *n.* a small animal.

beast•ly /béestlee/ *adj.* (**beastlier, beastliest**) **1** *colloq.* objectionable; unpleasant. **2** like a beast; brutal. □□ **beast•li•ness** *n.*

beast of bur·den *n.* an animal used for carrying loads.
beast of prey *n.* an animal that hunts animals for food.
beat /beet/ *v., n., & adj.* •*v.* (*past* **beat**; *past part.* **beat·en** /béet'n/) **1** *tr.* **a** strike (a person or animal) persistently. **b** strike (a thing) repeatedly, e.g., to remove dust from (a carpet, etc.), or to sound (a drum, etc.). **2** *intr.* (foll. by *against, at, on,* etc.) **a** pound or knock repeatedly (*beat at the door*). **b** = *beat down* 3. **3** *tr.* **a** overcome; surpass. **b** complete an activity before (another person, etc.). **4** *tr.* (often foll. by *up*) stir (eggs, etc.) vigorously into a frothy mixture. **5** *tr.* (often foll. by *out*) shape (metal, etc.) by blows. **6** *intr.* (of the heart, a drum, etc.) pulsate rhythmically. **7** *tr.* (often foll. by *out*) **a** indicate (a tempo or rhythm) by gestures, tapping, etc. **b** sound (a signal, etc.) by striking a drum or other means (*beat a tattoo*). **8 a** *intr.* (of a bird's wings) move up and down. **b** *tr.* cause (wings) to move in this way. **9** *tr.* make (a path, etc.) by trampling. **10** *tr.* strike (bushes, etc.) to rouse game. •*n.* **1 a** a main accent or rhythmic unit in music or verse (*three beats to the bar*). **b** the indication of rhythm by a conductor's movements (*watch the beat*). **c** the tempo or rhythm of a piece of music as indicated by the repeated fall of the main beat. **d** (in popular music) a strong rhythm. **2 a** a stroke or blow. **b** a measured sequence of strokes (*the beat of the waves on the rocks*). **c** a throbbing movement or sound (*the beat of his heart*). **3 a** a route or area allocated to a police officer, etc. **b** a person's habitual round. •*predic.adj. sl.* exhausted; tired out. □ **beat around (or about) the bush** discuss a matter without coming to the point. **beat down 1 a** bargain with (a seller) to lower the price. **b** cause a seller to lower (the price). **2** strike (a resisting object) until it falls (*beat the door down*). **3** (of the sun, rain, etc.) radiate heat or fall continuously and vigorously. **beat it** *sl.* go away. **beat off** drive back (an attack, etc.). **beat a retreat** withdraw; abandon an undertaking. **beat a person to it** arrive or achieve something before another person. **beat up** give a beating to, esp. with punches and kicks. □□ **beat·a·ble** *adj.* **beat·er** *n.* **beat·ing** *n.*
beat·en /béet'n/ *adj.* **1** outwitted; defeated. **2** exhausted; dejected. **3** (of gold or any other metal) shaped by a hammer. **4** (of a path, etc.) well-trodden; much used. □ **off the beaten track** (or **path**) **1** in or into an isolated place. **2** unusual.
beat gen·er·a·tion *n.* the members of a movement of young people esp. in the 1950s who rejected conventional society in their dress, habits, and beliefs.
be·a·tif·ic /béeətífik/ *adj.* **1** *colloq.* blissful (*a beatific smile*). **2 a** of or relating to blessedness. **b** making blessed.
be·at·i·fi·ca·tion /beeátifikáyshən/ *n. RC Ch.* the act of formally declaring a dead person "blessed."
be·at·i·fy /beeátifī/ *v.tr.* (**-fies, -ied**) **1** *RC Ch.* announce the beatification of. **2** make happy.
be·at·i·tude /beeátitood, -tyood/ *n.* **1** blessedness. **2** (in *pl.*) the declarations of blessedness in Matt. 5: 3–11.
beat·nik /béetnik/ *n.* a member of the beat generation.
beat-up *adj. colloq.* in a state of disrepair.
beau /bō/ *n.* (*pl.* **beaux** or **beaus** /bōz, bō/) **1** an admirer; a boyfriend. **2** a dandy.
Beau·fort scale /bṓfərt/ *n.* a scale of wind speed ranging from 0 (calm) to 12 (hurricane).
beau geste /bō zhést/ *n.* (*pl.* **beaux gestes** *pronunc.* same) a generous or gracious act.
beau id·eal /bṓ īdéeəl/ *n.* (*pl.* **beau ideals** /bṓ īdéeəlz/) the highest type of excellence or beauty.
Beau·jo·lais /bṓzhəlay/ *n.* a red or white burgundy wine from the Beaujolais district of France.
beau monde /bō mónd, máwnd/ *n.* fashionable society.
beaut /byoot/ *n. sl.* an excellent, outstanding, or beautiful person or thing.
beau·te·ous /byóoteeəs/ *adj. poet.* beautiful.
beau·ti·cian /byootíshən/ *n.* **1** a person who gives beauty treatment. **2** a person who works in a beauty salon.
beau·ti·ful /byóotifool/ *adj.* **1** delighting the aesthetic senses (*a beautiful voice*). **2** pleasant; enjoyable (*had a beautiful time*). **3** excellent (*a beautiful specimen*). □□ **beau·ti·ful·ly** *adv.*
beau·ti·fy /byóotifī/ *v.tr.* (**-fies, -ied**) make beautiful; adorn. □□ **beau·ti·fi·ca·tion** /-fikáyshən/ *n.*
beau·ty /byóotee/ *n.* (*pl.* **-ties**) **1 a** a combination of qualities that pleases the senses. **b** a combination of qualities that pleases the intellect (*the beauty of the argument*). **2** *colloq.* **a** an excellent specimen (*what a beauty!*). **b** an attractive feature; an advantage (*that's the beauty of it!*).
beau·ty par·lor *n.* (also **beau·ty sa·lon**) an establishment in which hairdressing, manicure, makeup, etc., are offered to women.
beau·ty queen *n.* the woman judged most beautiful in a competition.
beau·ty sleep *n.* sleep before midnight, supposed to be health-giving.
beau·ty spot *n.* **1** a place known for its beauty. **2** a small natural or artificial mark such as a mole on the face, considered to enhance another feature.
beaux *pl.* of BEAU.
beaux arts /bōz áar/ *n.pl.* **1** fine arts. **2** (*attrib.*) relating to the rules and conventions of the École des Beaux-Arts in Paris (later called Académie des Beaux Arts).
bea·ver /béevər/ *n.* (*pl.* same or **beavers**) **1** any large amphibious broad-tailed rodent of the genus *Castor*, native to N. America, Europe, and Asia, and able to cut down trees and build dams. **2** its soft light-brown fur. **3** a hat of this.
be·bop /béebop/ *n.* a type of jazz originating in the 1940s and characterized by complex harmony and rhythms. □□ **be·bop·per** *n.*
be·calm /bikáam/ *v.tr.* (usu. in *passive*) deprive (a sailing ship) of wind.
be·came *past* of BECOME.
be·cause /bikáwz, -kúz/ *conj.* for the reason that; since. □ **because of** on account of; by reason of.
beck /bek/ *n.* □ **at a person's beck and call** having constantly to obey a person's orders.
beck·et /békit/ *n. Naut.* a contrivance such as a hook, bracket, or rope loop, for securing loose ropes, tackle, or spars.
beck·on /békən/ *v.* **1** *tr.* **a** attract the attention of; summon by gesture. **b** entice. **2** *intr.* (usu. foll. by *to*) make a signal to attract a person's attention; summon a person by doing this.
be·come /bikúm/ *v.* (*past* **became** /bikáym/; *past part.* **become**) **1** *intr.* (foll. by compl.) begin to be (*became president; will become famous*). **2** *tr.* **a** look well on; suit (*blue becomes him*). **b** befit (*it ill becomes you to complain*). **3** *intr.* (as **becoming** *adj.*) **a** flattering the appearance. **b** suitable; decorous. □ **become of** happen to (*what will become of me?*). □□ **be·com·ing·ly** *adv.*
bed /bed/ *n. & v.* •*n.* **1 a** a piece of furniture used for sleeping on. **b** a mattress, with or without coverings. **2** any place used by a person or animal for sleep or rest. **3 a** a garden plot. **b** a place where other things may be grown (*osier bed*). **4** the use of a bed: **a** *colloq.* for sexual intercourse. **b** for rest. **5** something flat, forming a support or base as in: **a** the bottom of the sea or a river. **b** the foundations of a road or railroad. **6** a stratum, such as a layer of oysters, etc. •*v.* (**bedded, bedding**) **1** *tr. & intr.* (usu. foll. by *down*) put or go to bed. **2** *tr. colloq.* have sexual intercourse with. **3** *tr.*

(usu. foll. by *out*) plant in a garden bed. **4** *tr.* cover up or fix firmly in something. **5 a** *tr.* arrange as a layer. **b** *intr.* be or form a layer. □ **go to bed 1** retire for the night. **2** have sexual intercourse. **3** (of a newspaper) go to press. **make the bed** arrange the bed for use. **put to bed 1** cause to go to bed. **2** make (a newspaper) ready for press.

bed and break·fast *n.* **1** one night's lodging and breakfast. **2** an establishment that provides this.

be·daz·zle /bidázəl/ *v.tr.* **1** dazzle. **2** confuse (a person).

bed·bug /bédbug/ *n.* a flat, wingless, bloodsucking insect, *Cimex lectularius*, infesting beds and houses.

bed·cham·ber /bédchaymbər/ *n. archaic* a bedroom.

bed·clothes /bédklōthz, -klōz/ *n.pl.* coverings for a bed, such as sheets, blankets, etc.

bed·ding /béding/ *n.* **1** a mattress and bedclothes. **2** litter for cattle, horses, etc. **3** a bottom layer. **4** *Geol.* the stratification of rocks.

be·deck /bidék/ *v.tr.* adorn.

be·dev·il /bidévəl/ *v.tr.* (**bedeviled, bedeviling**) **1** plague; afflict. **2** confound; confuse. **3** possess as if with a devil.

bed·fel·low /bédfelō/ *n.* **1** a person who shares a bed. **2** an associate.

bed·lam /bédləm/ *n.* a scene of uproar and confusion.

bed lin·en *n.* sheets and pillowcases.

Bed·ou·in /bédōōin/ *n. & adj.* (also **Bed·u·in**) • *n.* (*pl.* same) a nomadic Arab of the desert. • *adj.* of or relating to the Bedouin.

bed·pan /bédpan/ *n.* a receptacle used by a bedridden patient for urine and feces.

bed·post /bédpōst/ *n.* any of the four upright supports of a bedstead.

be·drag·gled /bidrágəld/ *adj.* **1** wet and soiled from rain or mud. **2** dirty and disheveled (*bedraggled refugees*).

bed·rid·den /bédrid'n/ *adj.* confined to bed by infirmity.

bed·rock /bédrok/ *n.* solid rock underlying alluvial deposits, etc.

bed·roll /bédrōl/ *n.* portable bedding rolled into a bundle.

bed·room /bédrōōm, -rŏŏm/ *n.* **1** a room for sleeping in. **2** (*attrib.*) of or referring to sexual relations (*bedroom comedy*).

bed·side /bédsīd/ *n.* **1** the space beside esp. a patient's bed. **2** (*attrib.*) of or relating to the side of a bed (*bedside lamp*).

bed·side man·ner *n.* (of a doctor) an approach or attitude to a patient.

bed·sore /bédsawr/ *n.* a sore developed by an invalid because of pressure caused by lying in bed.

bed·spread /bédspred/ *n.* a cloth used to cover a bed when not in use.

bed·stead /bédsted/ *n.* the framework of a bed.

bed·time /bédtīm/ *n.* **1** the usual time for going to bed. **2** (*attrib.*) of or relating to bedtime (*bedtime story*).

bed·wet·ting /bédweting/ *n.* involuntary urination during the night.

bee /bee/ *n.* **1** any four-winged insect of the superfamily Apoidea which collects nectar and pollen, produces wax and honey, and lives in large communities. **2** any insect of a similar type. **3** (usu. **busy bee**) a busy person. **4** a meeting for communal work or amusement (*spelling bee*). □ **a bee in one's bonnet** an obsession.

beech /beech/ *n.* **1** (also **beech tree**) any large forest tree of the genus *Fagus*, having smooth gray bark and glossy leaves. **2** (also **beech·wood**) its wood.

bee-eat·er *n.* any brightly plumaged insect-eating bird of the family Meropidae with a long, slender curved bill.

beef /beef/ *n. & v.* • *n.* **1** the flesh of the ox, bull, or cow for eating. **2** *colloq.* well-developed male muscle. **3** (*pl.* **beeves** /beevz/ or **beefs**) a cow, bull, or ox fattened for beef; its carcass. **4** (*pl.* **beefs**) *sl.* a complaint; a protest. • *v.intr. sl.* complain. □ **beef up** *sl.* strengthen; reinforce.

beef·cake /béefkayk/ *n. sl.* well-developed male muscles, esp. when photographed and displayed for admiration.

beef·steak /béefstáyk/ *n.* a thick slice of lean beef, esp. from the rump.

beef·y /béefee/ *adj.* (**beefier, beefiest**) **1** like beef. **2** solid; muscular. □□ **beef·i·ly** *adv.* **beef·i·ness** *n.*

bee·hive /béehīv/ *n.* **1** an artificial habitation for bees. **2** a busy place. **3** anything resembling a wicker beehive in being domed.

bee·keep·ing /béekeeping/ *n.* the occupation of keeping bees. □□ **bee·keep·er** *n.*

bee·line /béelīn/ *n.* a straight line between two places. □ **make a beeline for** hurry directly to.

been *past part.* of BE.

beep /beep/ *n. & v.* • *n.* **1** the sound of an automobile horn. **2** any similar short high-pitched noise. • *v.intr.* emit a beep.

beep·er /béepər/ *n.* an electronic device that receives signals and emits a beep to summon the person carrying it to the telephone, etc.

beer /beer/ *n.* **1 a** an alcoholic drink made from yeast-fermented malt, etc., flavored with hops. **b** a glass, can, or bottle of this. **2** any of several other fermented drinks, e.g., ginger beer.

beer gar·den *n.* an outdoor bar where beer is sold.

beest·ings /béestingz/ *n.pl.* (also treated as *sing.*) the first milk (esp. of a cow) after giving birth.

bees·wax /béezwaks/ *n. & v.* • *n.* **1** the wax secreted by bees to make honeycombs. **2** this wax refined and used to polish wood. • *v.tr.* polish (furniture, etc.) with beeswax.

beet /beet/ *n.* any plant of the genus *Beta*, with an edible root (see BEETROOT, SUGAR BEET).

bee·tle[1] /béet'l/ *n.* **1** any insect of the order Coleoptera, with modified front wings forming hard protective cases closing over the back wings. **2** *colloq.* any similar insect. **3** *sl.* a type of compact rounded Volkswagen car.

bee·tle[2] /béet'l/ *adj. & v.* • *adj.* (esp. of the eyebrows) projecting; shaggy; scowling. • *v.intr.* (usu. as **beetling** *adj.*) (of brows, cliffs, etc.) project; overhang threateningly.

bee·tle[3] /béet'l/ *n. & v.* • *n.* **1** a tool with a heavy head and a handle, used for ramming, crushing, driving wedges, etc. **2** a machine used for heightening the luster of cloth by pressure from rollers. • *v.tr.* **1** ram, crush, drive, etc., with a beetle. **2** finish (cloth) with a beetle.

bee·tle-browed *adj.* with shaggy, projecting, or scowling eyebrows.

beet·root /béetrōōt, -rŏŏt/ *n.* esp. *Brit.* **1** a beet, *Beta vulgaris*, with an edible spherical dark red root. **2** this root used as a vegetable.

beeves *pl.* of BEEF.

be·fall /bifáwl/ *v.* (*past* **befell** /bifél/; *past part.* **befallen** /bifáwlən/) *poet.* **1** *intr.* happen (*so it befell*). **2** *tr.* happen to (a person, etc.) (*what has befallen her?*).

be·fit /bifít/ *v.tr.* (**befitted, befitting**) **1** be fitted or appropriate for; suit. **2** be incumbent on. □□ **be·fit·ting** *adj.*

be·fore /bifáwr/ *conj., prep., & adv.* • *conj.* **1** earlier than the time when (*crawled before he walked*). **2** rather than that (*would starve before he stole*). • *prep.* **1 a** in front of (*before her in the line*). **b** ahead of (*crossed the line before him*). **c** under the impulse of (*recoil before the attack*). **d** awaiting (*the future before them*). **2** earlier than; preceding (*Lent comes before Easter*). **3** rather than (*death *before dishonor*). **4 a** in the presence of (*appear before the judge*). **b** for the attention of (*a plan put before the committee*). • *adv.* **1 a** earlier; already (*heard it before*). **b** in the past (*happened long before*). **2** ahead (*go before*). **3** on the front (*hit before and behind*).

be•fore•hand /bifáwrhand/ *adv.* in anticipation; in advance (*had prepared the meal beforehand*).

be•foul /bifówl/ *v.tr. poet.* **1** make foul or dirty. **2** defile.

be•friend /bifrénd/ *v.tr.* act as a friend to; help.

be•fud•dle /bifúd'l/ *v.tr.* **1** make drunk. **2** confuse. ▫▫ **be•fud•dle•ment** *n.*

beg /beg/ *v.* (**begged, begging**) **1 a** *intr.* (usu. foll. by *for*) ask for (esp. food, money, etc.) (*begged for alms*). **b** *tr.* ask for (food, money, etc.) as a gift. **c** *intr.* live by begging. **2** *tr. & intr.* (usu. foll. by *for*, or *to* + infin.) ask earnestly or humbly. **3** *tr.* ask formally for (*I beg your pardon*). **4** *intr.* (of a dog, etc.) sit up with the front paws raised expectantly. **5** *tr.* take or ask leave (to do something) (*I beg to differ*). ▫ **beg off** decline to take part in or attend. **beg the question 1** assume the truth of an argument or proposition to be proved. **2** *disp.* pose the question. **3** *colloq.* evade a difficulty. **go begging** (of a chance or a thing) not be taken; be unwanted.

be•gan *past* of BEGIN.

be•get /bigét/ *v.tr.* (**begetting;** *past* **begot** /bigót/; *archaic* **begat** /bigát/; *past part.* **begotten** /bigót'n/) *literary* **1** (usu. of a father, sometimes of a father and mother) procreate. **2** give rise to; cause (*beget strife*). ▫▫ **be•get•ter** *n.*

beg•gar /bégər/ *n. & v.* • *n.* **1** a person who begs, esp. one who lives by begging. **2** a poor person. **3** *colloq.* a person; a fellow (*poor beggar*). • *v.tr.* **1** reduce to poverty. **2** exhaust the resources of (*it beggars description*).

beg•gar•ly /bégərlee/ *adj.* **1** poverty-stricken; needy. **2** intellectually poor. **3** mean; sordid. **4** ungenerous.

beg•gar•y /bégəree/ *n.* extreme poverty.

be•gin /bigín/ *v.* (**beginning;** *past* **began** /bigán/; *past part.* **begun** /bigún/) **1** *tr.* perform the first part of; start (*begin work; begin crying; begin to understand*). **2** *intr.* come into being; arise: **a** in time (*the season began last week*). **b** in space (*your jurisdiction begins beyond the river*). **3** *tr.* (usu. foll. by *to* + infin.) start at a certain time (*then began to feel ill*). **4** *intr.* be begun (*the meeting will begin at 7*). **5** *intr.* **a** start speaking (*"No," he began*). **b** be the first to do something (*who wants to begin?*).

be•gin•ner /bigínər/ *n.* a person just beginning to learn a skill, etc.

be•gin•ning /bigíning/ *n.* **1** the time or place at which anything begins. **2** a source or origin. **3** the first part.

be•gone /bigáwn, –gón/ *int. poet.* go away at once!

be•go•nia /bigṓnyə/ *n.* any plant of the genus *Begonia*, with brightly colored sepals and no petals.

be•got *past* of BEGET.

be•got•ten *past part.* of BEGET.

be•grudge /bigrúj/ *v.tr.* **1** resent; be dissatisfied at. **2** envy (a person) the possession of. ▫▫ **be•grudg•ing•ly** *adv.*

be•guile /bigíl/ *v.tr.* **1** charm; amuse. **2** divert attention pleasantly from (work, etc.). **3** (often foll. by *of*, *out of*, or *into* + verbal noun) delude; cheat (*beguiled him into paying*). ▫▫ **be•guil•ing** *adj.* **be•guil•ing•ly** *adv.*

be•guine /bigéen/ *n.* **1** a popular dance of W. Indian origin. **2** its rhythm.

be•gun *past part.* of BEGIN.

be•half /biháf/ *n.* ▫ **on** (also **in**) **behalf of** (or **on a person's behalf**) **1** in the interests of (a person, principle, etc.). **2** as representative of (*acting on behalf of my client*).

be•have /biháyv/ *v.* **1** *intr.* **a** act or react (in a specified way) (*behaved well*). **b** conduct oneself properly. **2** *refl.* show good manners (*behaved herself*).

be•hav•ior /biháyvyər/ *n.* **1 a** the way one conducts oneself; manners. **b** the treatment of others; moral conduct. **2** the way in which a machine, chemical substance, etc., acts or works. ▫▫ **be•hav•ior•al** *adj.*

be•hav•ior•al sci•ence *n.* the scientific study of human and animal behavior (see BEHAVIORISM).

be•hav•ior•ism /biháyvyərizəm/ *n. Psychol.* the theory that human behavior is determined by conditioning rather than by thoughts or feelings, and that psychological disorders are best treated by altering behavior patterns. ▫▫ **be•hav•ior•ist** *n.* **be•hav•ior•is•tic** /-rístik/ *adj.*

be•head /bihéd/ *v.tr.* cut off the head of (a person).

be•held *past* and *past part.* of BEHOLD.

be•he•moth /bihéeməth, béeə-/ *n.* an enormous creature or thing.

be•hest /bihést/ *n. literary* a command; an entreaty (*went at his behest*).

be•hind /bihínd/ *prep., adv., & n.* • *prep.* **1 a** in, toward, or to the rear of. **b** on the farther side of (*behind the bush*). **c** hidden by (*something behind that alibi*). **2 a** in the past in relation to (*trouble is behind me now*). **b** late in relation to (*behind schedule*). **3** inferior to; weaker than (*behind the others in math*). **4 a** in support of (*she's right behind us*). **b** responsible for; giving rise to (*the person behind the project; the reasons behind his resignation*). **5** in the tracks of; following. • *adv.* **1 a** in or to or toward the rear; farther back (*the street behind*). **b** on the farther side (*a high wall with a field behind*). **2** remaining after the departure of most others (*stay behind*). **3** (usu. foll. by *with*) **a** in arrears (*behind with the rent*). **b** late in accomplishing a task, etc. (*working too slowly and getting behind*). **4** in a weak position; backward (*behind in Latin*). **5** following (*his dog running behind*). • *n. colloq.* the buttocks. ▫ **behind the times** old-fashioned.

be•hind-the-scenes *adj.* secret, using secret information (*a behind-the-scenes investigation*).

be•hold /bihṓld/ *v.tr.* (*past & past part.* **beheld** /bihéld/) *literary* (esp. in *imper.*) see; observe. ▫▫ **be•hold•er** *n.*

be•hold•en /bihṓldən/ *predic.adj.* (usu. foll. by *to*) under obligation.

be•hoove /bihóov/ *v.tr.* /-hṓv/) (prec. by *it* as subject; foll. by *to* + infin.) **1** be incumbent on. **2** (usu. with *neg.*) befit (*ill behooves him to protest*).

beige /bayzh/ *n. & adj.* • *n.* a pale sandy fawn color. • *adj.* of this color.

be•ing /béeing/ *n.* **1** existence. **2** the nature or essence (of a person, etc.) (*his whole being revolted*). **3** a human being. **4** anything that exists or is imagined.

be•jew•eled /bijóoəld/ *adj.* adorned with jewels.

bel /bel/ *n.* a unit used in the comparison of power levels in electrical communication or intensities of sound (cf. DECIBEL).

be•la•bor /biláybər/ *v.tr.* **1 a** thrash; beat. **b** attack verbally. **2** argue or elaborate (a subject) in excessive detail.

be•lat•ed /biláytid/ *adj.* coming late. ▫▫ **be•lat•ed•ly** *adv.* **be•lat•ed•ness** *n.*

be•lay /biláy/ *v. & n.* • *v.* **1** *tr.* fix (a running rope) around a cleat, pin, rock, etc., to secure it. **2** *tr. & intr.* (usu. in *imper.*) *Naut. sl.* stop; enough! (esp. *belay there!*). • *n.* **1** an act of belaying. **2** a spike of rock, etc., used for belaying.

bel can•to /bel kántō, káan-/ *n.* **1** a lyrical style of operatic singing using a full rich broad tone. **2** (*attrib.*) characterized by this type of singing.

belch /belch/ *v. & n.* • *v.* **1** *intr.* emit wind noisily from the stomach through the mouth. **2** *tr.* (of a chimney, volcano, gun, etc.) send (smoke, etc.) out or up. • *n.* an act of belching.

---

be·lea·guer /bileégər/ *v.tr.* **1** besiege. **2** vex; harass.

bel·fry /bélfree/ *n.* (*pl.* **-fries**) **1** a bell tower or steeple housing bells. **2** a space for hanging bells in a church tower. □ **have bats in the belfry** see BAT[2].

Bel·gian /béljən/ *n. & adj.* • *n.* **1** a native or inhabitant of Belgium. **2** a person of Belgian descent. • *adj.* of or relating to Belgium.

be·lie /bilí/ *v.tr.* (**belying**) **1** give a false notion of (*its appearance belies its age*). **2 a** fail to fulfill (a promise, etc.). **b** fail to justify (a hope, etc.).

be·lief /bileéf/ *n.* **1 a** a person's religion; religious conviction (*has no belief*). **b** a firm opinion (*my belief is that he did it*). **c** an acceptance (of a fact, idea, etc.) (*belief in the afterlife*). **2** (usu. foll. by *in*) trust or confidence. □ **beyond belief** incredible.

be·lieve /bileév/ *v.* **1** *tr.* accept as true or as conveying the truth (*I believe it; don't believe him*). **2** *tr.* think; suppose (*I believe it's raining*). **3** *intr.* (foll. by *in*) **a** have faith in the existence of (*believes in God*). **b** have confidence in (*believes in alternative medicine*). **c** have trust in the advisability of (*believes in telling the truth*). **4** *intr.* have faith. □□ **be·liev·a·ble** *adj.* **be·liev·a·bil·i·ty** /-leévəbílitee/ *n.*

be·liev·er /bileévər/ *n.* **1** an adherent of a specified religion. **2** a person who believes (*a great believer in exercise*).

be·lit·tle /bilít'l/ *v.tr.* **1** disparage; depreciate. **2** make small; dwarf.

bell[1] /bel/ *n. & v.* • *n.* **1** a hollow object in the shape of a deep upturned cup, made to sound a clear musical note when struck (either externally or by means of a clapper inside). **2 a** a sound or stroke of a bell. **b** (prec. by a numeral) *Naut.* the time as indicated every half hour of a watch by the striking of the ship's bell one to eight times. **3** anything that sounds like or functions as a bell. **4 a** any bell-shaped part, e.g., of a musical instrument. **b** the corolla of a flower when bell-shaped. • *v.tr.* provide with a bell or bells. □ **ring a bell** *colloq.* revive a distant recollection.

bell[2] /bel/ *n. & v.* • *n.* the cry of a stag or buck at rutting time. • *v.intr.* make this cry.

bel·la·don·na /béladónə/ *n.* **1** deadly nightshade. **2** *Med.* a drug prepared from this.

bell-bot·tom *n.* **1** a marked flare below the knee (of a pants leg). **2** (in *pl.*) pants with bell-bottoms. □□ **bell-bot·tomed** *adj.*

bell bu·oy *n.* a buoy equipped with a warning bell rung by the motion of the sea.

belle /bel/ *n.* a beautiful woman.

belle é·poque /bél epúk/ *n.* the period of settled and comfortable life preceding World War I.

belles let·tres /bel-létrə/ *n.pl.* (also treated as *sing.*) writings or studies of a literary nature, esp. essays and criticisms. □□ **bel·let·rist** /bel-létrist/ *n. & adj.*

bell·hop /bélhop/ *n.* a person who carries luggage, runs errands, etc., in a hotel or club.

bel·li·cose /bélikōs/ *adj.* eager to fight; warlike. □□ **bel·li·cos·i·ty** /-kósitee/ *n.*

bel·lig·er·ent /bilíjərənt/ *adj. & n.* • *adj.* **1** engaged in war or conflict. **2** given to constant fighting. • *n.* a nation or person engaged in war or conflict. □□ **bel·lig·er·ence** (also **bel·lig·er·en·cy**) *n.* **bel·lig·er·ent·ly** *adv.*

bell jar *n.* a bell-shaped glass cover or container for use in a laboratory.

bell met·al *n.* an alloy of copper and tin for making bells (the tin content being greater than in bronze).

bel·low /bélō/ *v. & n.* • *v.* **1** *intr.* **a** emit a deep loud roar. **b** cry or shout with pain. **2** *tr.* utter loudly and usu. angrily. • *n.* a bellowing sound.

bel·lows /bélōz/ *n.pl.* (also treated as *sing.*) **1** a device with an air bag that emits a stream of air when squeezed, esp. (in full **pair of bellows**) a kind with two handles used for blowing air onto a fire. **2** an expandable component, e.g., joining the lens to the body of a camera.

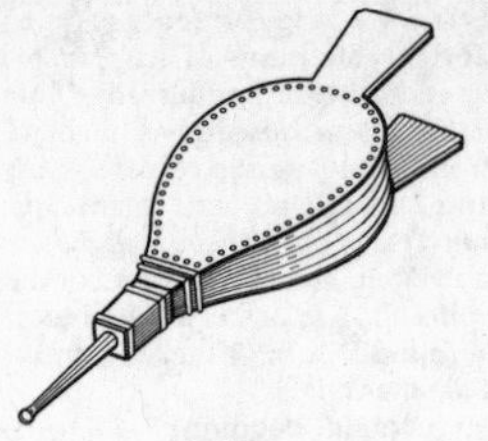

bellows

bell pep·per *n.* a sweet pepper of the genus *Capsicum*, with a bell shape.

bells and whis·tles *n.pl. colloq.* attractive but unnecessary additional features, esp. in computing.

bell·weth·er /bélwethər/ *n.* **1** the leading sheep of a flock, with a bell on its neck. **2** a ringleader.

bel·ly /bélee/ *n.* (*pl.* **-lies**) **1** the part of the human body below the chest, containing the stomach and bowels. **2** the stomach, esp. representing the body's need for food. **3** the front of the body from the waist to the groin. **4** the underside of a four-legged animal. **5** a cavity or bulging part of anything. □ **go belly up** *colloq.* fail financially. □□ **bel·ly·ful** *n.* (*pl.* **-fuls**).

bel·ly·ache /béleeayk/ *n. & v.* • *n. colloq.* a stomach pain. • *v.intr. sl.* complain persistently. □□ **bel·ly·ach·er** *n.*

bel·ly but·ton *n. colloq.* the navel.

bel·ly dance *n.* a Middle Eastern dance performed by a woman, involving voluptuous movements of the belly. □□ **bel·ly danc·er** *n.* **bel·ly danc·ing** *n.*

bel·ly·flop /béleeflop/ *n.* a dive in which the body lands with the belly flat on the water.

bel·ly laugh *n.* a loud unrestrained laugh.

be·long /biláwng, -lóng/ *v.intr.* **1** (foll. by *to*) **a** be the property of. **b** be rightly assigned to as a duty, right, part, member, characteristic, etc. **c** be a member of (a club, etc.). **2** have the right qualities to be a member of a particular group (*he's nice but just doesn't belong*). **3** (foll. by *in, under*) **a** be rightly placed or classified. **b** fit a particular environment.

be·long·ings /biláwngingz, -lóng-/ *n.pl.* one's movable possessions or luggage.

be·lov·ed /bilúvid, -lúvd/ *adj. & n.* • *adj.* much loved. • *n.* a much loved person.

be·low /biló/ *prep. & adv.* • *prep.* **1** lower in position (down a slope, etc.) than. **2** at or to a greater depth than (*below 500 feet*). **3** lower or less than in amount or degree (*below freezing*). **4** lower in position or importance than. **5** unworthy of. • *adv.* **1** at or to a lower point or level. **2 a** downstairs (*lives below*). **b** downstream. **3** (of a text reference) later in a book (*as noted below*). **4** on the lower side (*looks similar above and below*).

belt /belt/ *n. & v.* • *n.* **1** a strip of leather or other material worn around the waist or across the chest. **2** a belt worn as a sign of rank or achievement. **3 a** a circular band used as a driving medium in machinery. **b** a conveyor belt. **c** a flexible strip carrying machine gun cartridges. **4** a strip of color or texture, etc., differing from that on each side. **5** a distinct region or extent (*cotton belt*). **6** *sl.* a heavy blow. • *v.* **1** *tr.* put a belt around. **2** *tr.* (often foll. by *on*) fasten with a belt. **3** *tr.* **a** beat with a belt. **b** *sl.* hit hard. **4** *intr. sl.* rush (usu. with compl.: *belted along; belted home*). □ **below the belt** unfair or unfairly. **belt out** *sl.* sing or utter loudly and forcibly. **tighten one's belt** live more frugally. **under**

one's belt 1 (of food) eaten. **2** securely acquired (*has a degree under her belt*). ▫▫ **belt·er** *n.* (esp. in sense of *belt out*).

belt·way /béltway/ *n.* **1** a highway skirting a metropolitan region. **2** (**the Beltway**) the interstate highway skirting Washington DC.

be·lu·ga /bəlóōgə/ *n.* **1 a** a large kind of sturgeon, *Huso huso*. **b** caviar obtained from it. **2** a white whale.

bel·ve·dere /bélvideer/ *n.* a summerhouse or open-sided gallery, usu. at rooftop level.

be·ly·ing *pres. part.* of BELIE.

be·moan /bimṓn/ *v.tr.* express regret or sorrow over; lament.

be·muse /bimyóōz/ *v.tr.* bewilder (a person). ▫▫ **be·mus·ed·ly** /-zidlee/ *adv.* **be·muse·ment** *n.*

bench /bench/ *n.* **1** a long seat of wood or stone. **2** a worktable, e.g., for a carpenter or mechanic. **3** (prec. by *the*) **a** the office of judge or magistrate. **b** a judge's seat in a court of law. **c** a court of law. **d** judges and magistrates collectively. **4** *Sports* an area to the side of a field with seating where coaches and players not taking part can watch the game. ▫ **on the bench 1** appointed a judge or magistrate. **2** *Sports* acting as substitute or reserve.

bench·mark /bénchmaark/ *n.* **1** a surveyor's mark cut in a wall, etc., used for reference in measuring altitudes. **2** a standard or point of reference.

bench test *n.* & *v.* esp. *Computing* •*n.* a test made by benchmarking. •*v.tr.* (**bench-test**) run a series of tests on (a computer, etc.) before its use.

bend[1] /bend/ *v.* & *n.* •*v.* (*past* **bent**; *past part.* **bent** exc. in *bended knee*) **1 a** *tr.* force or adapt into a curve or angle. **b** *intr.* (of an object) be altered in this way. **2** *intr.* move in a curved course (*the road bends to the left*). **3** *intr.* & *tr.* (often foll. by *down*, *over*, etc.) incline or cause to incline from the vertical. **4** *tr.* interpret or modify (a rule). **5** *tr.* & *refl.* (foll. by *to*, *on*) direct or devote (oneself or one's attention, energies, etc.). **6** *tr.* turn (one's steps or eyes) in a new direction. **7** *tr.* (in *passive*; foll. by *on*) be determined (*was bent on selling*). **8 a** *intr.* stoop or submit (*bent before his master*). **b** *tr.* force to submit. •*n.* **1** a curve in a road, stream, etc. **2** a departure from a straight course. **3** a bent part of anything. **4** (in *pl.*; prec. by *the*) *colloq.* sickness due to too rapid decompression on rising from deep water. ▫▫ **bend·a·ble** *adj.* **bend·y** *adj.* (**bendier, bendiest**)

bend[2] /bend/ *n.* **1** *Naut.* any of various knots for tying ropes. **2** *Heraldry* **a** a diagonal stripe from top right to bottom left of a shield. **b** (**bend sinister**) a diagonal stripe from top left to bottom right, as a sign of bastardy.

bend·er /béndər/ *n. sl.* a wild drinking spree.

be·neath /bineéth/ *prep.* & *adv.* •*prep.* **1** too demeaning for (*beneath him to reply*). **2** below; under. •*adv.* underneath.

Ben·e·dic·tine /bénidíktin/ *n.* a monk or nun of an order following the rule of St. Benedict.

ben·e·dic·tion /bénidíkshən/ *n.* **1** the utterance of a blessing. **2** the state of being blessed.

ben·e·fac·tion /bénifákshən/ *n.* **1** a donation or gift. **2** an act of giving or doing good.

ben·e·fac·tor /bénifaktər/ *n.* (*fem.* **benefactress** /-tris/) a person who gives support (esp. financial) to a person or cause.

ben·e·fice /bénifis/ *n.* **1** an income from a church office. **2** the property attached to a church office. ▫▫ **ben·e·ficed** *adj.*

be·nef·i·cent /binéfisənt/ *adj.* doing good; actively kind. ▫▫ **be·nef·i·cence** /-səns/ *n.* **be·nef·i·cent·ly** *adv.*

ben·e·fi·cial /bénifíshəl/ *adj.* advantageous; having benefits. ▫▫ **ben·e·fi·cial·ly** *adv.*

ben·e·fi·ci·ar·y /bénifíshee-e-ree, -físhəree/ *n.* (*pl.* **-ies**) **1** a person who receives benefits under a will, etc. **2** a holder of a benefice.

ben·e·fit /bénifit/ *n.* & *v.* •*n.* **1** a favorable or helpful factor or circumstance; advantage; profit. **2** (often in *pl.*) payment made under insurance, etc. **3** a public performance or game of which the proceeds go to a particular charitable cause. •*v.* (**benefited, benefiting**; also **benefitted, benefitting**) **1** *tr.* bring advantage to. **2** *intr.* (often foll. by *from*, *by*) receive an advantage or gain. ▫ **the benefit of the doubt** a concession that a person is innocent, correct, etc., although doubt exists.

be·nev·o·lent /binévələnt/ *adj.* **1** wishing to do good; actively helpful. **2** charitable (*benevolent fund*). ▫▫ **be·nev·o·lence** /-ləns/ *n.* **be·nev·o·lent·ly** *adv.*

be·night·ed /binítid/ *adj.* **1** intellectually or morally ignorant. **2** overtaken by darkness.

be·nign /binín/ *adj.* **1** gentle; kindly. **2** salutary. **3** (of the climate, etc.) mild. **4** *Med.* not malignant. ▫▫ **be·nig·ni·ty** /binígnitee/ *n.* (*pl.* **-ties**) **be·nign·ly** *adv.*

be·nig·nant /binígnənt/ *adj.* **1** kindly, esp. to inferiors. **2** salutary; beneficial. **3** *Med.* = BENIGN 4. ▫▫ **be·nig·nan·cy** /-nənsee/ *n.* **be·nig·nant·ly** *adv.*

bent[1] /bent/ *past* and *past part.* of BEND[1] *v. adj.* & *n.* •*adj.* **1** curved or having an angle. **2** (foll. by *on*) determined to do or have. •*n.* **1** an inclination or bias. **2** (foll. by *for*) a talent (*a bent for mimicry*).

bent[2] /bent/ *n.* **1 a** any stiff grass of the genus *Agrostis*. **b** any of various grasslike reeds, rushes, or sedges. **2** a stiff stalk of a grass.

bent·wood /béntwŏŏd/ *n.* wood that is artificially shaped for use in making furniture.

ben·zene /bénzeen/ *n.* a colorless carcinogenic volatile liquid found in coal tar, etc. ▫▫ **ben·ze·noid** /-zənoyd/ *adj.*

benzene ring *n.* the hexagonal unsaturated ring of six carbon atoms in the benzene molecule.

ben·zine /bénzeen/ *n.* (also **ben·zin** /-zin/) a mixture of liquid hydrocarbons obtained from petroleum.

ben·zo·in /bénzōin/ *n.* a fragrant gum resin obtained from various E. Asian trees of the genus *Styrax*, and used in the manufacture of perfumes and incense.

be·queath /bikwéeth, -kwéeth/ *v.tr.* **1** leave to a person by a will. **2** hand down to posterity. ▫▫ **be·queath·al** *n.* **be·queath·er** *n.*

be·quest /bikwést/ *n.* **1** the act or an instance of bequeathing. **2** a thing bequeathed.

be·rate /biráyt/ *v.tr.* scold; rebuke.

be·reave /biréev/ *v.tr.* (esp. as **bereaved** *adj.*) (foll. by *of*) deprive of a relation, etc., esp. by death. ▫▫ **be·reave·ment** *n.*

be·reft /biréft/ *adj.* (foll. by *of*) deprived (*bereft of hope*).

be·ret /bəráy/ *n.* a round flattish visorless cap of felt or cloth.

ber·ga·mot /bə́rgəmot/ *n.* **1** an aromatic herb, esp. *Mentha citrata*. **2** an oily perfume extracted from the rind of the fruit of the citrus tree *Citrus bergamia*. **3** the tree itself.

ber·i·ber·i /béreebéree/ *n.* a disease causing inflammation of the nerves due to a deficiency of vitamin B_1.

ber·ke·li·um /bərkéeleeəm, bə́rkleeəm/ *n. Chem.* a transuranic radioactive metallic element. ¶ Symb.: **Bk**.

berm /bərm/ *n.* a narrow path or grass strip beside a road, canal, etc.

Ber·mu·da onion /bərmyóōdə/ *n.* a large yellow-skinned onion with a mild flavor.

Ber·mu·da shorts /bərmyóōdə/ *n.pl.* (also **Ber·mu·das**) shorts reaching almost to the knees.

ber·ry /béree/ *n.* (*pl.* **-ries**) **1** any small roundish juicy fruit without a stone. **2** *Bot.* a fruit with its seeds enclosed in a pulp (e.g., a banana). **3** any of various kernels or seeds (e.g., coffee bean).

ber•serk /bərsə́rk, -zə́rk/ *adj.* (esp. in **go berserk**) wild; in a violent rage.

berth /bərth/ *n. & v.* • *n.* **1** a fixed bunk on a ship, train, etc., for sleeping in. **2** a ship's place at a wharf. **3** adequate sea room. **4** *colloq.* a situation or appointment. **5** the proper place for anything. • *v.* **1** *tr.* moor (a ship) in its berth. **2** *tr.* provide a sleeping place for. **3** *intr.* (of a ship) come to its mooring place. □ **give a wide berth to** stay away from.

ber•yl /béril/ *n.* **1** a kind of transparent precious stone, esp. pale green, blue, or yellow. **2** a mineral species that includes this, emerald, and aquamarine.

be•ryl•li•um /bəríleeəm/ *n. Chem.* a hard white metallic element used in the manufacture of light corrosion-resistant alloys. ¶ Symb.: **Be**.

be•seech /biseéch/ *v.tr.* (*past* and *past part.* **besought** /-sáwt/ or **beseeched**) **1** (foll. by *for*, or *to* + infin.) entreat. **2** ask earnestly for. □□ **be•seech•ing** *adj.*

be•set /bisét/ *v.tr.* (**besetting**; *past* and *past part.* **beset**) **1** harass persistently (*beset by worries*). **2** hem in (a person, etc.).

be•side /bisíd/ *prep.* **1** at the side of. **2** compared with. **3** irrelevant to (*beside the point*). **4** = BESIDES. □ **beside oneself** overcome with worry, etc.

be•sides /bisídz/ *prep. & adv.* • *prep.* in addition to. • *adv.* also; as well; moreover.

be•siege /biseéj/ *v.tr.* **1** lay siege to. **2** harass. □□ **be•sieg•er** *n.*

be•smirch /bismə́rch/ *v.tr.* **1** soil; discolor. **2** dishonor; sully the reputation or name of.

be•som /beézəm/ *n.* a broom made of twigs tied around a stick.

be•sot•ted /bisótid/ *adj.* **1** intoxicated. **2** confused. **3** infatuated.

be•sought *past* and *past part.* of BESEECH.

be•spat•ter /bispátər/ *v.tr.* **1** spatter (an object) all over. **2** spatter (liquid, etc.). **3** overwhelm with abuse, etc.

be•speak /bispeék/ *v.tr.* (*past* **bespoke** /-spṓk/; *past part.* **bespoken** /-spṓkən/ or as *adj.* **bespoke**) **1** engage in advance. **2** order (goods). **3** be evidence of (*bespeaks a kind heart*).

best /best/ *adj., adv., n., & v.* • *adj.* (*superl.* of GOOD) of the most excellent or outstanding or desirable kind (*my best work*; *the best thing to do would be to confess*). • *adv.* (*superl.* of WELL[1]). **1** in the best manner (*does it best*). **2** to the greatest degree (*like it best*). **3** most usefully (*is best ignored*). • *n.* **1** that which is best (*the best is yet to come*). **2** the chief merit or advantage (*brings out the best in him*). **3** (foll. by *of*) a winning majority of (a certain number of games, etc., played) (*the best of five*). • *v.tr. colloq.* defeat, outwit, outbid, etc. □ **as best one can** as well as possible under the circumstances. **at best** on the most optimistic view. **be for** (or **all for**) **the best** be desirable in the end. **the best part of** most of. **do one's best** do all one can. **get the best of** defeat; outwit. **had best** would find it wisest to.

bes•tial /béschəl, beés-/ *adj.* **1** brutish; cruel; savage. **2** sexually depraved; lustful. **3** of or like a beast. □□ **bes•tial•ize** *v.tr.* **bes•tial•ly** *adv.*

bes•ti•al•i•ty /béscheeálitee, beés-/ *n.* (*pl.* **-ties**) **1** bestial behavior or an instance of this. **2** sexual intercourse between a person and an animal.

bes•ti•ar•y /béschee-eree, beés-/ *n.* (*pl.* **-ies**) a moralizing medieval treatise on real and imaginary beasts.

be•stir /bistə́r/ *v.refl.* (**bestirred, bestirring**) exert or rouse (oneself).

best man *n.* the bridegroom's chief attendant at a wedding.

be•stow /bistṓ/ *v.tr.* **1** (foll. by *on, upon*) confer (a gift, right, etc.). **2** deposit. □□ **be•stow•al** *n.*

be•strew /bistrṓō/ *v.tr.* (*past part.* **bestrewed** or **bestrewn** /-strṓōn/) **1** (foll. by *with*) cover or partly cover (a surface). **2** scatter (things) about. **3** lie scattered over.

be•stride /bistríd/ *v.tr.* (*past* **bestrode** /-strṓd/; *past part.* **bestridden** /-stríd'n/) **1** sit astride on. **2** stand astride over.

best•sell•er *n.* a book or other item that has sold in large numbers.

bet /bet/ *v. & n.* • *v.* (**betting**; *past* and *past part.* **bet** or **betted**) **1** *intr.* (foll. by *on* or *against* with ref. to the outcome) risk a sum of money, etc., against another's on the basis of the outcome of an uncertain event. **2** *tr.* risk (an amount) on such an outcome (*bet $10 on a horse race*). **3** *tr.* risk a sum of money against (a person). **4** *tr. colloq.* feel sure (*bet they've forgotten it*). • *n.* **1** the act of betting (*make a bet*). **2** the money, etc. staked (*put a bet on*). **3** *colloq.* an opinion (*my bet is that he won't come*). **4** *colloq.* a choice or course of action (*she's our best bet*). □ **you bet** *colloq.* you may be sure.

be•ta /báytə, beé-/ *n.* **1** the second letter of the Greek alphabet (Β, β). **2** the second member of a series.

be•ta-block•er *n. Pharm.* a drug that prevents the stimulation of increased cardiac action, used to reduce high blood pressure.

be•take /bitáyk/ *v.refl.* (*past* **betook** /bitṓōk/; *past part.* **betaken** /bitáykən/) (foll. by *to*) go to (a place or person).

be•ta par•ti•cle *n.* (also **be•ta ray**) a fast-moving electron emitted by radioactive decay of substances (orig. regarded as rays).

be•ta•tron /báytətron, beé-/ *n. Physics* an apparatus for accelerating electrons in a circular path by magnetic induction.

be•tel /beét'l/ *n.* the leaf of the Asian evergreen climbing plant *Piper betle*, chewed in parts of Asia with the areca nut.

be•tel nut *n.* the areca nut.

bête noire /bet nwaár/ *n.* (*pl.* **bêtes noires** *pronunc.* same) a person or thing one particularly dislikes or fears; a bugbear.

be•tide /bitíd/ *v. poet.* (only in infin. and 3rd sing. subj.) **1** *tr.* happen to (*woe betide him*). **2** *intr.* happen (*whate'er may betide*).

be•to•ken /bitṓkən/ *v.tr.* **1** be a sign of; indicate. **2** augur.

be•took *past* of BETAKE.

be•tray /bitráy/ *v.tr.* **1** place (a person, one's country, etc.) in the power of an enemy. **2** be disloyal to (another person, etc.). **3** reveal involuntarily (*his shaking hand betrayed his fear*). **4** lead into error. □□ **be•tray•al** *n.* **be•tray•er** *n.*

be•troth /bitrṓth, -tráwth/ *v.tr.* (usu. as **betrothed** *adj.*) bind with a promise to marry. □□ **be•troth•al** *n.*

bet•ter /bétər/ *adj., adv., n., & v.* • *adj.* (*compar.* of GOOD). **1** of a more excellent or outstanding or desirable kind (*a better product*). **2** partly or fully recovered from illness (*feeling better*). • *adv.* (*compar.* of WELL[1]). **1** in a better manner (*she sings better*). **2** to a greater degree (*like it better*). **3** more usefully or advantageously (*is better forgotten*). • *n.* **1** that which is better (*the better of the two*). **2** (usu. in *pl.*; prec. by *my*, etc.) one's superior in ability or rank (*take notice of your betters*). • *v.* **1** *tr.* improve on; surpass. **2** *tr.* make better; improve. **3** *refl.* improve one's position, etc. □ **the better part of** most of. **get the better of** defeat; outwit; win an advantage over. **go one better 1** outbid, etc., by one. **2** outdo another person. **had better** would find it wiser to. □□ **bet•ter•ment** *n.*

bet•ter half *n. colloq.* one's wife or husband.

bet·ting /béting/ *n.* **1** gambling by risking money on an unpredictable outcome. **2** the odds offered in this.
bet·tor /bétər/ *n.* (also **bet·ter**) a person who bets.
be·tween /bitwe͞en/ *prep. & adv.* • *prep.* **1 a** at or to a point in the area or interval bounded by two or more other points in space, time, etc. (*stopped between Boston and Providence; we must meet between now and Friday*). **b** along the extent of such an interval (*there are five shops between here and the main road; works best between five and six; the numbers between 10 and 20*). **2** separating, physically or conceptually (*the distance between here and the moon; the difference between right and wrong*). **3 a** by combining the resources of (*between us we could afford it*). **b** as the joint resources of (*$5 between them*). **c** by joint or reciprocal action (*an agreement between us*). **4** to and from (*runs between New York and LA*). **5** taking one and rejecting the other of (*decide between eating here and going out*). • *adv.* (also **in between**) at a point or in the area bounded by two or more other points in space, time, sequence, etc. (*not fat or thin but in between*).
▶**1. Between** is used in speaking of only two things, people, etc.: *We must choose between two equally unattractive alternatives.* **Among** is used when more than two are involved: *Agreement on landscaping was reached among all the neighbors.* But where there are more than two parties involved, **between** may be proper to emphasize the relationship of pairs within the group or the sense 'shared by': *There is close friendship between the members of the club; relations between the United States, Canada, and Mexico.* **2.** *Between you and I, between you and he*, etc., are incorrect; **between** should be followed only by the objective case: *me, her, him, them.*
be·twixt /bitwíkst/ *prep. & adv. archaic* between. □ **betwixt and between** *colloq.* neither one thing nor the other.
bev·el /bévəl/ *n. & v.* • *n.* **1** a slope from the horizontal or vertical in carpentry and stonework. **2** (in full **bevel square**) a tool for marking angles in carpentry and stonework. • *v.* (**beveled, beveling** or **bevelled, bevelling**) **1** *tr.* reduce (a square edge) to a sloping edge. **2** *intr.* slope at an angle; slant.
bev·el gear *n.* a gear working another gear at an angle to it by means of beveled wheels.

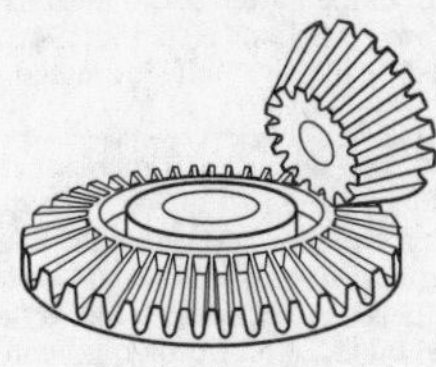

bevel gears

bev·er·age /bévərij, bévrij/ *n.* a drink (*hot beverage; alcoholic beverage*).
bev·y /bévee/ *n.* (*pl.* **-ies**) **1** a flock of quails or larks. **2** a company or group (orig. of women).
be·wail /biwáyl/ *v.tr.* **1** greatly regret or lament. **2** wail over; mourn for.
be·ware /biwáir/ *v.* (only in *imper.* or *infin.*) **1** *intr.* (often foll. by *of*, or *that, lest*, etc. + clause) be cautious; take heed (*beware of the dog; told us to beware; beware that you don't fall*). **2** *tr.* be cautious of (*beware the Ides of March*).
be·wil·der /biwíldər/ *v.tr.* perplex or confuse. □□ **be·wil·dered·ly** *adv.* **be·wil·der·ing** *adj.* **be·wil·der·ment** *n.*
be·witch /biwích/ *v.tr.* **1** enchant; greatly delight. **2** cast a spell on. □□ **be·witch·ing** *adj.* **be·witch·ing·ly** *adv.*
be·yond /biyónd/ *prep., adv., & n.* • *prep.* **1** at or to the farther side of (*beyond the river*). **2** outside the scope, range, or understanding of (*beyond repair; beyond a joke; it is beyond me*). **3** more than. • *adv.* **1** at or to the farther side. **2** farther on. • *n.* (prec. by *the*) the unknown after death.
bez·el /bézəl/ *n.* **1** the sloped edge of a chisel. **2** the oblique faces of a cut gem. **3** a groove holding a watch crystal or gem.
Bi *symb. Chem.* the element bismuth.
bi- /bī/ *comb.* form (often **bin-** before a vowel) forming nouns and adjectives meaning: **1** having two; a thing having two (*bilateral; biplane*). **2 a** occurring twice in every one or once in every two (*biweekly*). **b** lasting for two (*biennial*). **3** doubly; in two ways (*biconcave*). **4** *Chem.* a substance having a double proportion of the acid, etc., indicated by the simple word (*bicarbonate*).
bi·an·nu·al /bī́-ányo͞oəl/ *adj.* occurring, appearing, etc., twice a year. □□ **bi·an·nu·al·ly** *adv.*
▶see note at BIENNIAL.
bi·as /bī́əs/ *n. & v.* • *n.* **1** (often foll. by *toward, against*) a predisposition or prejudice. **2** *Statistics* a systematic distortion of a statistical result due to a factor not allowed for in its derivation. **3** an edge cut obliquely across the weave of a fabric. • *v.tr.* (**biased, biasing; biassed, biassing**) **1** (esp. as **biased** *adj.*) influence (usu. unfairly); prejudice. **2** give a bias to. □ **on the bias** obliquely; diagonally.
bi·ath·lon /bī-áthlon, -lən/ *n. Sports* an athletic contest comprising skiing and shooting or cycling and running. □□ **bi·ath·lete** *n.*
bib /bib/ *n.* **1** a piece of cloth or plastic fastened round a child's neck to keep the clothes clean while eating. **2** the top front part of an apron, overalls, etc.
bi·be·lot /be͞eblō/ *n.* a small curio or artistic trinket.
Bi·ble /bī́bəl/ *n.* **1 a** the Christian scriptures consisting of the Old and New Testaments. **b** the Jewish scriptures. **c** (**bible**) any copy of these (*three bibles on the table*). **2** (**bible**) *colloq.* any authoritative book (*the woodworker's bible*).
Bi·ble belt *n.* the area of the southern and central US where fundamentalist Protestant beliefs prevail.
bib·li·cal /bíblikəl/ *adj.* **1** of, concerning, or contained in the Bible. **2** resembling the language of the Authorized Version of the Bible. □□ **bib·li·cal·ly** *adv.*
biblio- /bíbleeō/ *comb.form* denoting a book or books.
bib·li·og·ra·phy /bíbleeógrəfee/ *n.* (*pl.* **-phies**) **1 a** a list of the books referred to in a scholarly work. **b** a list of the books of a specific author or publisher, or on a specific subject, etc. **2 a** the history or description of books, including authors, editions, etc. **b** any book containing such information. □□ **bib·li·og·ra·pher** *n.* **bib·li·o·graph·ic** /-leeəgráfik/ *adj.* **bib·li·o·graph·i·cal** *adj.*
bib·li·o·phile /bíbleeōfīl/ *n.* a person who collects or is fond of books.
bib·u·lous /bíbyələs/ *adj.* given to drinking alcohol.
bi·cam·er·al /bīkámərəl/ *adj.* (of a parliament or legislative body) having two chambers. □□ **bi·cam·er·al·ism** *n.*
bi·car·bo·nate /bīkaárbənit/ *n.* **1** *Chem.* any acid salt of carbonic acid. **2** (in full **bicarbonate of soda**) sodium bicarbonate used as an antacid or in baking powder.
bi·cen·ten·ar·y /bī́senténəree, bīséntəneree/ *n. & adj.* esp. *Brit.* = BICENTENNIAL.
bi·cen·ten·ni·al /bī́senténeeəl/ *n. & adj.* • *n.* **1** a two-hundredth anniversary. **2** a celebration of this. • *adj.* **1** lasting two hundred years or occurring every two hundred years. **2** of or concerning a bicentennial.
bi·ceps /bī́seps/ *n.* (*pl.* same) a muscle having two heads

or attachments at one end, esp. the muscle that bends the elbow.

bick•er /bíkər/ *v.intr.* quarrel pettily; wrangle.

bi•con•cave /bīkónkayv, bíkonkáyv/ *adj.* (esp. of a lens) concave on both sides.

bi•con•vex /bīkónveks, bíkonvéks/ *adj.* (esp. of a lens) convex on both sides.

bi•cul•tur•al /bíkúlchərəl/ *adj.* having or combining two cultures.

bi•cus•pid /bíkúspid/ *adj. & n.* •*adj.* having two cusps or points. •*n.* the premolar tooth in humans.

bi•cy•cle /bísikəl, -sīkəl/ *n. & v.* •*n.* a vehicle with two wheels held in a frame one behind the other, propelled by pedals and steered with handlebars attached to the front wheel. •*v.intr.* ride a bicycle. ▫▫ **bi•cy•clist** /-klist/ *n.*

bid /bid/ *v. & n.* •*v.* (**bidding**; *past* **bid**, *archaic* **bade** /bayd, bad/; *past part.* **bid**, *archaic* **bidden** /bíd'n/) **1** *tr. & intr.* (*past* and *past part.* **bid**) (often foll. by *for, against*) **a** offer (a certain price) (*did not bid for the vase; bid against the dealer; bid $20*). **b** offer to do work, etc., for a stated price. **2** *tr. archaic* or *literary* **a** command (*bid the soldiers to shoot*). **b** invite (*bade her to start*). **3** *tr. archaic* or *literary* utter (greeting or farewell) to (*I bade him welcome*). **4** (*past* and *past part.* **bid**) *Cards* **a** *intr.* state before play how many tricks one intends to make. **b** *tr.* state (one's intended number of tricks). •*n.* **1 a** an offer (of a price) (*a bid of $5*). **b** an offer (to do work, supply goods, etc.) at a stated price; a tender. **2** *Cards* a statement of the number of tricks a player proposes to make. **3** an attempt (*a bid for power*). ▫ **make a bid for** try to gain (*made a bid for freedom*). ▫▫ **bid•der** *n.*

bid•ding /bíding/ *n.* **1** the offers at an auction. **2** *Cards* the act of making a bid or bids. **3** a command, request, or invitation.

bid•dy /bídee/ *n.* (*pl.* **-dies**) *sl. derog.* a woman (esp. *old biddy*).

bide /bīd/ *v.tr.* ▫ **bide one's time** await one's best opportunity.

bi•det /beedáy/ *n.* a low oval basinlike bathroom fixture used esp. for washing the genital area.

bi•en•ni•al /bí-éneeəl/ *adj. & n.* •*adj.* **1** lasting two years. **2** recurring every two years (cf. BIANNUAL). •*n.* **1** *Bot.* a plant that takes two years to grow from seed to fruition and die. **2** an event celebrated or taking place every two years.

▶**Biennial** means 'lasting or occurring every two years': *Congressional elections are a biennial phenomenon.* A *biennial plant* is one that lives a two-year cycle, flowering and producing seed in the second year. **Biannual** means 'twice a year': *The solstice is a biannual event.*

bi•en•ni•um /bī-éneeəm/ *n.* (*pl.* **bi•en•ni•ums** or **bi•en•ni•a** /–neeə/) a period of two years.

bier /beer/ *n.* a movable frame on which a coffin or a corpse is placed.

bi•fo•cal /bífṓkəl/ *adj. & n.* •*adj.* having two focuses, esp. of a lens with a part for distant vision and a part for near vision. •*n.* (in *pl.*) bifocal eyeglasses.

bi•fur•cate /bífərkayt/ *v. & adj.* •*v.tr. & intr.* divide into two branches; fork. •*adj.* forked; branched.

bi•fur•ca•tion /bífərkáyshən/ *n.* **1 a** a division into two branches. **b** either or both of such branches. **2** the point of such a division.

big /big/ *adj. & adv.* •*adj.* (**bigger, biggest**) **1 a** of considerable size, amount, intensity, etc. (*a big mistake; a big helping*). **b** of a large or the largest size (*big toe; big drum*). **2** important; significant; outstanding (*my big chance*). **3 a** grown up (*a big boy now*). **b** elder (*big sister*). **4** *colloq.* **a** boastful (*big words*). **b** often *iron.* generous (*big of him*). **c** ambitious (*big ideas*). **d** popular (*when disco was big*). **5** (usu. foll. by *with*) advanced in pregnancy; fecund (*big with child; big with consequences*). •*adv. colloq.* in a big manner, esp.: **1** effectively (*went over big*). **2** boastfully (*talk big*). **3** ambitiously (*think big*). ▫ **in a big way 1** on a large scale. **2** *colloq.* with great enthusiasm, display, etc. **talk big** boast. ▫▫ **big•gish** *adj.* **big•ness** *n.*

big•a•my /bígəmee/ *n.* (*pl.* **-mies**) the crime of marrying when one is lawfully married to another person. ▫▫ **big•a•mist** *n.* **big•a•mous** *adj.*

Big Ap•ple *n. sl.* New York City.

big band *n.* a large jazz or swing orchestra.

big bang the•o•ry *n.* the theory that the universe began with the explosion of dense matter.

Big Broth•er *n.* an all-powerful supposedly benevolent dictator (from Orwell's *1984*).

big busi•ness *n.* large-scale financial dealings and the businesses involved in them.

big deal! *int. sl. iron.* I am not impressed.

Big Dip•per *n.* a constellation of seven bright stars in Ursa Major in the shape of a dipper.

Big•foot *n.* = SASQUATCH.

big game *n.* large animals hunted for sport.

big•head /bíghed/ *n. colloq.* a conceited person. ▫▫ **big•head•ed** *adj.*

big•heart•ed /bighártid/ *adj.* generous.

big•horn /bíghawrn/ *n.* (in full **bighorn sheep**) an American sheep, *Ovis canadensis*, esp. native to the Rocky Mountains.

bight /bīt/ *n.* **1** a curve or recess in a coastline, river, etc. **2** a loop of rope.

big•mouth /bígmowth/ *n. colloq.* a boastful or talkative person; a gossipmonger.

big•ot /bígət/ *n.* an obstinate and intolerant believer in a religion, political theory, etc. ▫▫ **big•ot•ry** *n.*

big•ot•ed /bígətid/ *adj.* prejudiced and intolerant.

big top *n.* the main tent in a circus.

big wheel *n.* **1** a Ferris wheel. **2** *sl.* = BIGWIG.

big•wig /bígwig/ *n. colloq.* an important person.

bike /bīk/ *n. & v.* •*n. colloq.* a bicycle or motorcycle. •*v.intr.* ride a bicycle or motorcycle.

bik•er /bíkər/ *n.* a cyclist, esp. a motorcyclist.

bi•ki•ni /bikéenee/ *n.* a very brief two-piece swimsuit for women.

---

bikini 1940s: named after Bikini atoll in the Pacific, where an atom bomb was tested in 1946 (because of the supposed "explosive" effect created by the garment).

---

bi•ki•ni briefs *n.pl.* women's or men's scanty briefs.

bi•lat•er•al /bīlátərəl/ *adj.* **1** of, on, or with two sides. **2** affecting or between two parties, countries, etc. (*bilateral negotiations*). ▫▫ **bi•lat•er•al•ly** *adv.*

bil•ber•ry /bílberee/ *n.* (*pl.* **-ries**) **1** a hardy dwarf shrub, *Vaccinium myrtillus*, of N. Europe, growing on heaths and mountains, and having dark blue berries. **2** the berry of this species.

bile /bīl/ *n.* **1** a bitter greenish brown alkaline fluid that aids digestion and is secreted by the liver and stored in the gallbladder. **2** peevish anger.

bile duct *n.* the duct that conveys bile from the liver and the gallbladder to the duodenum.

bilge /bilj/ *n.* **1 a** the almost flat part of a ship's bottom, inside or out. **b** (in full **bilgewater**) dirty water that collects inside the bilge. **2** *sl.* nonsense.

bil•i•ar•y /bílee-eree/ *adj.* of the bile.

bi•lin•gual /bílinggwəl/ *adj. & n.* •*adj.* **1** able to speak two languages. **2** spoken, written, or conducted in two languages. •*n.* a bilingual person. ▫▫ **bi•lin•gual•ism** *n.*

bil•ious /bílyəs/ *adj.* **1** affected by a disorder of the bile. **2** bad-tempered. ▫▫ **bil•ious•ness** *n.*

bil•i•ru•bin /bíleeróobin/ *n.* the orangish yellow pigment occurring in bile and causing jaundice when accumulated in blood.

bilk /bilk/ *v.tr. sl.* **1** cheat. **2** give the slip to. **3** avoid paying (a creditor or debt).

bill[1] /bil/ *n. & v.* • *n.* **1 a** a statement of charges for goods supplied or services rendered. **b** the amount owed (*ran up a bill of $300*). **2** a draft of a proposed law. **3 a** a poster; a placard. **b** = HANDBILL. **4 a** a printed list, esp. a theater program. **b** the entertainment itself (*top of the bill*). **5** a piece of paper money (*ten-dollar bill*). • *v.tr.* **1** put in the program; announce. **2** (foll. by *as*) advertise. **3** send a note of charges to. □□ **bill·a·ble** *adj.*

bill[2] /bil/ *n. & v.* • *n.* **1** the beak of a bird. **2** the muzzle of a platypus. **3** a narrow promontory. • *v.intr.* (of doves, etc.) stroke a bill with a bill. □ **bill and coo** exchange caresses. □□ **billed** *adj.* (usu. in *comb.*).

bill[3] /bil/ *n.* = BILLHOOK.

bill·board /bílbawrd/ *n.* a large outdoor board for advertisements, etc.

bil·let[1] /bílit/ *n. & v.* • *n.* **1 a** a place where troops, etc., are lodged. **b** a written order requiring a householder to lodge the bearer. **2** *colloq.* a situation; a job. • *v.tr.* (**billeted, billeting**) **1** (usu. foll. by *on, in, at*) quarter (soldiers, etc.). **2** (of a householder) provide (a soldier, etc.) with board and lodging.

bil·let[2] /bílit/ *n.* **1** a thick piece of firewood. **2** a small metal bar.

bill·fold /bílfōld/ *n.* a wallet for keeping paper money.

bill·hook /bílhŏŏk/ *n.* a sickle-shaped tool with a sharp inner edge, used for pruning, lopping, etc.

bil·liards /bílyərdz/ *n.* **1** any of several games played on an oblong cloth-covered table, esp. one in which balls are struck into pockets around the edge of the table. **2** (**billiard**) (in *comb.*) used in billiards (*billiard ball*).

bil·lion /bílyən/ *n. & adj.* • *n.* (*pl.* same or (in sense 3) **billions**) (in *sing.* prec. by *a* or *one*) **1** a thousand million (1,000,000,000 or 10^9). **2** *Brit.* a million million (1,000,000,000,000 or 10^{12}). **3** (in *pl.*) *colloq.* a very large number (*billions of friends*). • *adj.* that amount to a billion. □□ **bil·lionth** *adj. & n.*

bil·lion·aire /bílyənáir/ *n.* a person possessing over a billion dollars, pounds, etc.

bill of ex·change *n. Econ.* a written order to pay a sum of money on a given date.

bill of fare *n.* a menu.

bill of goods *n.* **1** a shipment of merchandise, often for resale. **2** *colloq.* an article that is misrepresented, fraudulent, etc. (*at first it seemed a bargain, but we were being sold a bill of goods*).

bill of health *n.* **1** *Naut.* a certificate regarding infectious disease on a ship at the time of sailing. **2** (**clean bill of health**) **a** such a certificate stating that there is no disease. **b** a declaration that a person or thing examined has been found to be healthy.

bill of lad·ing *n. Naut.* **1** a detailed list of a ship's cargo. **2** = WAYBILL.

Bill of Rights *n.* **1** *Law* (in the US) the original constitutional amendments of 1791. **2** *Law* the English constitutional settlement of 1689. **3** a statement of the rights of a class of people.

bill of sale *n. Econ.* a certificate of transfer of personal property, esp. as a security against debt.

bil·low /bílō/ *n. & v.* • *n.* **1** a wave. **2** a soft upward-curving flow. **3** any large soft mass. • *v.intr.* move in billows. □□ **bil·low·y** *adj.*

bil·ly goat /bíligōt/ *n.* (also **bil·ly**) a male goat.

bim·bo /bímbō/ *n.* (*pl.* **-bos** or **-boes**) *sl.* usu. *derog.* **1** a foolish person. **2** an empty-headed woman, esp. an attractive one.

bi·me·tal·lic /bímitálik/ *adj.* made of two metals.

bi·mil·le·nar·y /bīmílənereé, –milénəree/ *adj. & n.* (also **bi·mil·len·ni·al** /–léneeəl/) • *adj.* of or relating to a two-thousandth anniversary. • *n.* (*pl.* **-ies**) a bimillenary year or festival.

bi·month·ly /bīmúnthlee/ *adj., adv., & n.* • *adj.* occurring twice a month or every two months. • *adv.* twice a month or every two months. • *n.* (*pl.* **-lies**) a bimonthly periodical.

▶Often avoided, because of the ambiguity of meaning, in favor of *every two months* and *twice a month.*

bin /bin/ *n. & v.* • *n.* a large receptacle for storage or display, or for depositing trash, garbage, etc. • *v.tr.* (**binned, binning**) *colloq.* store or put in a bin.

bin- /bin, bīn/ *prefix* var. of BI- before a vowel.

bi·na·ry /bínəree/ *adj. & n.* • *adj.* **1 a** dual. **b** of or involving pairs. **2** of the arithmetical system using 2 as a base. • *n.* (*pl.* **-ries**) **1** something having two parts. **2** a binary number. **3** a binary star.

bi·na·ry code *n. Computing* a coding system using the binary digits 0 and 1.

bi·na·ry com·pound *n. Chem.* a compound having two elements or radicals.

bi·na·ry num·ber *n.* (also **bi·na·ry dig·it**) one of two digits (usu. 0 or 1) in a binary system of notation.

bi·na·ry star *n.* a system of two stars orbiting each other.

bi·na·ry sys·tem *n.* a system in which information can be expressed by combinations of the digits 0 and 1.

bi·nate /bínayt/ *adj. Bot.* **1** growing in pairs. **2** composed of two equal parts.

bin·au·ral /bínáwrəl/ *adj.* **1** of or used with both ears. **2** recorded using two microphones for recording and two channels for transmitting.

bind /bīnd/ *v. & n.* • *v.* (*past* and *past part.* **bound** /bownd/) (see also BOUNDEN). **1** *tr.* (often foll. by *to, on, together*) tie or fasten tightly. **2** *tr.* **a** restrain; put in bonds. **b** (as **-bound** *adj.*) constricted; obstructed (*snowbound*). **3** *tr.* esp. *Cooking* cause (ingredients) to cohere. **4** *tr.* fasten or hold together as a single mass. **5** *tr.* compel; impose a duty on. **6** *tr.* **a** edge with braid, etc. **b** fasten (the pages of a book) in a cover. **7** *tr.* constipate. **8** *tr.* (in *passive*) be required by an obligation or duty (*am bound to answer*). **9** *tr.* (often foll. by *up*) **a** put a bandage or other covering around. **b** fix together with something put around (*bound her hair*). • *n. colloq.* a nuisance; a restriction. □ **be bound up with** be closely associated with.

bind·er /bíndər/ *n.* **1** a cover for sheets of paper, for a book, etc. **2** a substance that acts cohesively. **3** a reaping machine that binds grain into sheaves. **4** a bookbinder. **5** a temporary agreement providing insurance coverage until a policy is issued.

bind·er·y /bíndəree/ *n.* (*pl.* **-ies**) a workshop or factory for binding books.

bind·ing /bínding/ *n. & adj.* • *n.* something that binds, esp. the covers, glue, etc., of a book. • *adj.* (often foll. by *on*) obligatory.

binge /binj/ *n. & v. sl.* • *n.* a period of uncontrolled eating, drinking, etc. • *v.intr.* indulge in uncontrolled eating, drinking, etc. □□ **bing·er** *n.*

bin·go /bínggō/ *n. & int.* • *n.* a game for any number of players, each having a card of squares with numbers that are marked off as numbers are randomly drawn by a caller. • *int.* expressing sudden surprise, satisfaction, etc.

bin·na·cle /bínəkəl/ *n.* a housing for a ship's compass.

bin·oc·u·lar /bīnókyələr/ *adj.* adapted for or using both eyes.

bin·oc·u·lars /binókyələrz/ *n.pl.* an optical instrument with a lens for each eye, for viewing distant objects.

bi·no·mi·al /bīnómeeəl/ *n. & adj.* • *n.* **1** an algebraic expression of the sum or the difference of two terms. **2** a two-part name, esp. in taxonomy. • *adj.* consisting of two terms.

bi·o / bī́-ō/ *n. & adj.* •*n.* **1** biology. **2** (*pl.* **bios**) biography. •*adj.* biological.
bio- /bī́-ō/ *comb.form* **1** life (*biography*). **2** biological (*biomathematics*). **3** of living beings (*biophysics*).
bi·o·ac·tive /bī́-ōáktiv/ *adj.* (of foods, cosmetic compounds, etc.) having an effect on or interacting with living tissue. ▫▫ **bi·o·ac·tiv·i·ty** *n.*
bi·o·chem·is·try /bī́-ōkémistree/ *n.* the study of the chemical and physicochemical processes of living organisms. ▫▫ **bi·o·chem·i·cal** *adj.* **bi·o·chem·ist** *n.*
bi·o·de·grad·a·ble /bī́-ōdigráydəbəl/ *adj.* capable of being decomposed by bacteria or other living organisms. ▫▫ **bi·o·de·grad·a·bil·i·ty** *n.* **bi·o·deg·ra·da·tion** /bī́-ōdégrədáyshən/ *n.*
bi·o·di·ver·si·ty *n.* /bī́-ōdivə́rsitee/ diversity of plant and animal life.
bi·o·en·gi·neer·ing /bī́-ō-énjinéering/ *n.* **1** the application of engineering techniques to biological processes. **2** the use of artificial tissues, organs, or organ components to replace damaged or absent parts of the body. ▫▫ **bi·o·en·gi·neer** *n. & v.*
bi·o·feed·back /bī́-ōféedbak/ *n.* the technique of using the feedback of a normally automatic bodily response to a stimulus in order to acquire voluntary control of that response.
bi·o·gas /bī́-ōgas/ *n.* gaseous fuel, esp. methane, produced by fermentation of organic matter.
bi·o·gen·e·sis /bī́-ōjénisis/ *n.* **1** the synthesis of substances by living organisms. **2** the hypothesis that a living organism arises only from another similar living organism. ▫▫ **bi·o·ge·net·ic** /–jinétik/ *adj.*
bi·o·gen·ic /bī́-ōjénik/ *adj.* produced by living organisms.
bi·og·ra·phy /bīógrəfee/ *n.* (*pl.* **-phies**) **1 a** a written account of a person's life. **b** such writing as a branch of literature. **2** the course of a living being's life. ▫▫ **bi·og·ra·pher** *n.* **bi·o·graph·i·cal** *adj.*
bi·o·haz·ard /bī́-ōházərd/ *n.* a risk to human health or the environment arising from biological work, esp. with microorganisms.
bi·o·log·i·cal /bī́əlójikəl/ *adj.* **1** of or relating to biology or living organisms. **2** related genetically, not by marriage, adoption, etc. ▫▫ **bi·o·log·i·cal·ly** *adv.*
bi·o·log·i·cal clock *n.* an innate mechanism controlling the rhythmic physiological activities of an organism.
bi·o·log·i·cal war·fare *n.* warfare involving the use of toxins or microorganisms.
bi·ol·o·gy /bīóləjee/ *n.* **1** the study of living organisms. **2** the plants and animals of a particular area. ▫▫ **bi·ol·o·gist** *n.*
bi·o·lu·mi·nes·cence /bī́-ōlóominésəns/ *n.* the emission of light by living organisms such as the firefly and glowworm. ▫▫ **bi·o·lu·mi·nes·cent** *adj.*
bi·o·mass /bī́-ōmas/ *n.* the total quantity or weight of organisms in a given area or volume.
bi·ome /bī́-ōm/ *n.* **1** a large naturally occurring community of flora and fauna adapted to the particular conditions in which they occur, e.g., tundra. **2** the geographical region containing such a community.
bi·o·me·chan·ics /bī́-ōmikániks/ *n.* the study of the mechanical laws relating to the movement or structure of living organisms.
bi·on·ics /bīóniks/ *n.pl.* (treated as *sing.*) the study of mechanical systems that function like living organisms or parts of living organisms.
bi·o·nom·ics /bī́ənómiks/ *n.pl.* (treated as *sing.*) the study of the mode of life of organisms in their natural habitat and their adaptations to their surroundings; ecology. ▫▫ **bi·o·nom·ic** *adj.*
bi·o·phys·ics /bī́-ōfiziks/ *n.* the science of the application of the laws of physics to biological phenomena. ▫▫ **bi·o·phys·i·cal** *adj.* **bi·o·phys·i·cist** *n.*
bi·op·sy /bī́opsee/ *n.* (*pl.* **-sies**) the examination of tissue removed from a living body to discover the presence, cause, or extent of a disease.
bi·o·rhythm /bī́-ōri*th*əm/ *n.* **1** any of the recurring cycles of biological processes thought to affect a person's emotional, intellectual, and physical activity. **2** any periodic change in the behavior or physiology of an organism.
bi·o·sphere /bī́-ōsfeer/ *n.* the regions of the earth's crust and atmosphere occupied by living organisms.
bi·o·syn·the·sis /bī́-ōsínthisis/ *n.* the production of organic molecules by living organisms. ▫▫ **bi·o·syn·thet·ic** /-thétik/ *adj.*
bi·o·ta /bī-ṓtə/ *n.* the animal and plant life of a region.
bi·o·tech·nol·o·gy /bī́-ōteknóləjee/ *n.* the exploitation of biological processes for industrial and other purposes, esp. genetic manipulation of microorganisms.
bi·ot·ic /bīótik/ *adj.* **1** relating to life or to living things. **2** of biological origin.
bi·o·tin /bī́ətin/ *n.* a vitamin of the B complex, found in egg yolk, liver, and yeast, and involved in metabolism. Also called **vitamin H**.
bi·par·ti·san /bīpaártizən, -sən/ *adj.* of or involving two parties. ▫▫ **bi·par·ti·san·ship** *n.*
bi·par·tite /bīpaártīt/ *adj.* **1** consisting of two parts. **2** shared by or involving two parties. **3** *Law* (of a contract, etc.) drawn up in two corresponding parts or between two parties.
bi·ped /bīped/ *n. & adj.* •*n.* a two-footed animal. •*adj.* two-footed. ▫▫ **bi·ped·al** *adj.*
bi·plane /bīplayn/ *n.* a type of airplane having two sets of wings, one above the other.
bi·po·lar /bīpṓlər/ *adj.* having two poles or extremities. ▫▫ **bi·po·lar·i·ty** /-láritee/ *n.*
bi·po·lar dis·or·der *n.* a psychiatric illness characterized by manic episodes, usually alternating with periods of depression.
birch /bərch/ *n. & v.* •*n.* **1** any tree of the genus *Betula*, bearing catkins, and found predominantly in northern temperate regions. **2** (in full **birchwood**) the hard fine-grained pale wood of these trees. **3** (in full **birch rod**) a bundle of birch twigs used for flogging. •*v.tr.* beat with a birch (in sense 3).
bird /bərd/ *n.* **1** a feathered vertebrate with a beak, two wings, and two feet, egg-laying and usu. able to fly. **2** a game bird. **3** *colloq.* a person (*a wily old bird*). ▫ **a bird in the hand** something secured or certain. **birds of a feather** people of like character. **for** (or **strictly for**) **the birds** *colloq.* trivial; uninteresting.
bird·brain /bə́rdbrayn/ *n. colloq.* a stupid or flighty person. ▫▫ **bird·brained** *adj.*
bird·cage /bə́rdkayj/ *n.* **1** a cage for birds usu. made of wire or cane. **2** an object of a similar design.
bird call *n.* **1** a bird's natural call. **2** an instrument imitating this.
bird·ie /bə́rdee/ *n. & v.* •*n.* **1** *colloq.* a little bird. **2** *Golf* a score of one stroke less than par for any hole. •*v.tr.* (**birdies, birdied, birdying**) *Golf* play (a hole) in a birdie.
bird·lime /bə́rdlīm/ *n.* sticky material painted on twigs to trap small birds.
bird of par·a·dise *n.* any bird of the family Paradiseidae, the males having very beautiful brilliantly colored plumage.
bird of prey *n.* a bird that hunts animals for food.
bird's-eye view *n.* a general view from above.
bird-watch·er *n.* a person who observes birds in their natural surroundings. ▫▫ **bird-watch·ing** *n.*
bi·reme /bī́reem/ *n. hist.* an ancient Greek warship, with two banks of oarsmen on each side.

bi•ret•ta /birétə/ *n.* a square cap with three flat projections on top, worn by clergymen.

birth /bərth/ *n.* & *v.* • *n.* **1** the emergence of an infant or other young from the body of its mother. **2** *rhet.* the beginning of something (*the birth of socialism*). **3 a** origin; descent; ancestry (*of noble birth*). **b** noble birth; inherited position. • *v.tr. colloq.* **1** give birth to. **2** assist (a woman) to give birth. □ **give birth** bear a child, etc. **give birth to 1** produce (young) from the womb. **2** cause to begin.

birth cer•tif•i•cate *n.* an official document identifying a person by name, and place and date of birth.

birth con•trol *n.* the control of the number of children one conceives.

birth con•trol pill *n.* an oral contraceptive.

birth•day /bórthday/ *n.* **1** the day on which a person, etc., was born. **2** the anniversary of this. □ **in one's birthday suit** *joc.* naked.

birth de•fect *n.* a physical, mental, or biochemical abnormality present at birth.

birth•mark /bórthmaark/ *n.* an unusual brown or red mark on a person's body at or from birth.

birth•place /bórthplays/ *n.* the place where a person was born.

birth rate *n.* the number of live births per thousand of a given population per year.

birth•right /bórthrīt/ *n.* a right of possession or privilege one has from birth.

birth•stone /bórthstōn/ *n.* a gemstone popularly associated with the month of one's birth.

bis•cuit /bískit/ *n.* & *adj.* • *n.* **1** a small bread or cake leavened with baking soda or baking powder. **2** *Brit.* **a** = COOKIE. **b** = CRACKER. **3** fired unglazed pottery. **4** a light brown color. • *adj.* light brown.

biscuit Middle English: from Old French *bescuit*, based on Latin *bis* 'twice' + *coctus*, past participle of *coquere* 'to cook' (so named because originally biscuits were cooked in a twofold process: first baked and then dried out in a slow oven so that they would keep).

bi•sect /bísékt/ *v.tr.* divide into two (equal) parts. □□ **bi•sec•tion** /-sékshən/ *n.*

bi•sex•u•al /bísékshōōəl/ *adj.* & *n.* • *adj.* **1** sexually attracted to persons of both sexes. **2** *Biol.* having characteristics of both sexes. • *n.* a bisexual person. □□ **bi•sex•u•al•i•ty** /-sékshoo-álitee, -séksyoo-álitee/ *n.*

bish•op /bíshəp/ *n.* **1** a senior member of the Christian clergy empowered to confer holy orders. **2** a chess piece with the top sometimes shaped like a miter.

bish•op•ric /bíshəprik/ *n.* **1** the office of a bishop. **2** a diocese.

bis•muth /bízməth/ *n. Chem.* **1** a brittle reddish-tinged metallic element, occurring naturally and used in alloys. ¶ Symb.: **Bi**. **2** any compound of this element used medicinally.

bi•son /bísən/ *n.* (*pl.* same) either of two wild humpbacked shaggy-haired oxen of the genus *Bison*, native to N. America (*B. bison*) or Europe (*B. bonasus*).

bisque /bisk/ *n.* a rich shellfish soup.

bis•ter /bístər/ *n.* & *adj.* • *n.* **1** a brownish pigment made from the soot of burned wood. **2** the brownish color of this. • *adj.* of this color.

bis•tro /béestrō, bís-/ *n.* (*pl.* **-tros**) a small restaurant.

bi•sul•fate /bīsúlfayt/ *n. Chem.* a salt or ester of sulfuric acid.

bit[1] /bit/ *n.* **1** a small piece or quantity (*a bit of cheese*). **2** (prec. by *a*) **a** a fair amount (*sold quite a bit*). **b** *colloq.* somewhat (*am a bit tired*). **c** (foll. by *of*) *colloq.* rather (*a bit of an idiot*). **3** a short time or distance (*wait a bit; move up a bit*). **4** *sl.* an amount equal to 12 $^1/_2$ cents (esp. in the phrase *two bits*). □ **bit by bit** gradually. **not a bit** not at all. **to bits** into pieces.

bit[2] /bit/ *n.* **1** a metal mouthpiece on a bridle, used to control a horse. **2** a tool or piece for boring or drilling. **3** the cutting or gripping part of a plane, pliers, etc. □ **take the bit between one's teeth 1** take decisive personal action. **2** escape from control.

bit[3] /bit/ *n. Computing* a unit of information; a 0 or 1 in binary notation.

bitch /bich/ *n.* & *v.* • *n.* **1** a female dog or other canine animal. **2** *sl.offens.* a spiteful woman. **3** *sl.* a very unpleasant or difficult thing. • *v.intr. colloq.* **1** (often foll. by *about*) speak scathingly. **2** complain.

bitch•y /bíchee/ *adj.* (**bitchier, bitchiest**) *sl.* spiteful; bad-tempered. □□ **bitch•i•ness** *n.*

bite /bīt/ *v.* & *n.* • *v.* (*past* **bit** /bit/; *past part.* **bitten** /bít'n/) **1** *tr.* cut or puncture using the teeth. **2** *tr.* (often foll. by *off*, etc.) detach with the teeth. **3** *tr.* (of an insect, snake, etc.) wound with a sting, fangs, etc. **4** *intr.* (of a wheel, screw, etc.) grip; penetrate. **5** *intr.* accept bait. **6** *intr.* have a (desired) adverse effect. **7** *tr.* (in *passive*) **a** take in; swindle. **b** (foll. by *by*, *with*, etc.) be infected by (enthusiasm, etc.). **8** *tr.* (as **bitten** *adj.*) cause a smarting pain to (*frostbitten*). **9** *intr.* (foll. by *at*) snap at. • *n.* **1** an act of biting. **2** a wound or sore made by biting. **3 a** a mouthful of food. **b** a snack or light meal. **4** the taking of bait by a fish. **5** pungency. **6** incisiveness; sharpness. □ **bite the bullet** *sl.* behave bravely or stoically. **bite the dust** *sl.* **1** die. **2** fail; break down. **bite the hand that feeds one** hurt a benefactor. **bite a person's head off** *colloq.* respond fiercely or angrily. **bite off more than one can chew** take on a commitment one cannot fulfill. □□ **bit•er** *n.*

bit•ing /bíting/ *adj.* **1** stinging; intensely cold (*a biting wind*). **2** sharp; effective (*biting sarcasm*). □□ **bit•ing•ly** *adv.*

bit part *n.* a minor part in a play or a movie.

bits and pieces *n.pl.* an assortment of small items.

bit•ter /bítər/ *adj.* & *n.* • *adj.* **1** having a sharp pungent taste; not sweet. **2 a** caused by or showing mental pain or resentment (*bitter memories; bitter rejoinder*). **b** painful or difficult to accept (*bitter disappointment*). **3 a** harsh; virulent (*bitter animosity*). **b** piercingly cold. • *n.* **1** *Brit.* beer strongly flavored with hops and having a bitter taste. **2** (in *pl.*) liquor with a bitter flavor used as an additive in cocktails. □ **to the bitter end** to the very end in spite of difficulties. □□ **bit•ter•ly** *adv.* **bit•ter•ness** *n.*

bit•tern /bítərn/ *n.* any of a group of wading birds of the heron family.

bit•ter pill *n.* something unpleasant that has to be accepted.

bit•ter•sweet /bítərsweet/ *adj.* & *n.* • *adj.* **1** sweet with a bitter aftertaste. **2** arousing pleasure tinged with pain or sorrow. • *n.* **a** sweetness with a bitter aftertaste. **b** pleasure tinged with pain or sorrow.

bit•ty /bítee/ *adj. colloq.* tiny (esp. in phrs. **little bitty, itty-bitty**).

bi•tu•men /bītóomin, -tyóo-, bi-/ *n.* any of various tarlike mixtures of hydrocarbons derived from petroleum and used for road surfacing and roofing.

bi•tu•mi•nous /bītóominəs, -tyóo-, bi-/ *adj.* of, relating to, or containing bitumen.

bi•tu•mi•nous coal *n.* a form of coal burning with a smoky flame.

bi•valve /bívalv/ *n.* & *adj.* • *n.* any of a group of aquatic mollusks of the class Bivalvia, with laterally compressed bodies enclosed within two hinged shells, e.g., oysters, clams, etc. • *adj.* **1** with a hinged double shell. **2** *Biol.* having two valves, e.g., of a peapod.

biv•ou•ac /bívoo-ak, bívwak/ *n.* & *v.* • *n.* a temporary open encampment without tents. • *v.intr.* (**bivou-**

acked, bivouacking) camp in a bivouac, esp. overnight.

bi·week·ly /bíweeklee/ *adv., adj., & n.* • *adv.* **1** every two weeks. **2** twice a week. • *adj.* produced or occurring biweekly. • *n.* (*pl.* **-lies**) a biweekly periodical.
▶See the note at *bimonthly*.

bi·year·ly /bíyeerlee/ *adv. & adj.* • *adv.* **1** every two years. **2** twice a year. • *adj.* produced or occurring biyearly.
▶See the note at *bimonthly*.

biz /biz/ *n. colloq.* business (*the music biz*).

bi·zarre /bizaar/ *adj.* strange; eccentric; grotesque. ▫▫ **bi·zarre·ly** *adv.*

Bk *symb. Chem.* the element berkelium.

blab /blab/ *v. & n.* • *v.* (**blabbed, blabbing**) **1** *intr.* **a** talk foolishly or indiscreetly. **b** reveal secrets. **2** *tr.* reveal (a secret, etc.) by indiscreet talk. • *n.* a person who blabs.

blab·ber /blábər/ *n. & v.* • *n.* (also **blab·ber·mouth** /blábərmowth/) a person who blabs. • *v.intr.* (often foll. by *on*) talk foolishly or inconsequentially, esp. at length.

black /blak/ *adj., n., & v.* • *adj.* **1** very dark; having no color from the absorption of incident light (like coal or soot). **2** completely dark from the absence of a source of light (*black night*). **3 a** of the human group having dark-colored skin. **b** of or relating to black people (*black rights*). **4** (of the sky, a cloud, etc.) heavily overcast. **5** angry; threatening (*a black look*). **6** implying disgrace or condemnation (*in his black books*). **7** sinister; deadly (*black-hearted*). **8** depressed; sullen (*a black mood*). **9** portending trouble or difficulty (*things looked black*). **10** (of hands, clothes, etc.) dirty; soiled. **11** (of humor or its representation) macabre (*black comedy*). **12** (of coffee or tea) without milk. **13** dark in color as distinguished from a lighter variety (*black bear*). • *n.* **1** a black color or pigment. **2** black clothes or material (*dressed in black*). **3 a** (in a game or sport) a black piece, ball, etc. **b** the player using such pieces. **4** the credit side of an account (*in the black*). **5** a member of a dark-skinned race. • *v.tr.* **1** make black (*blacked his face*). **2** polish with black polish, paste, etc. ▫ **black out 1 a** effect a blackout on. **b** undergo a blackout. **2** obscure windows, etc., or extinguish all lights for protection esp. against an air attack. ▫▫ **black·ish** *adj.* **black·ly** *adv.* **black·ness** *n.*
▶**Black**, designating Americans of African heritage, became a widely used and accepted term in the 1960s and 1970s, replacing **Negro.** It is not usually capitalized: *black Americans.* Through the 1980s, the more formal **African American** replaced **black** in much usage, but both are widely acceptable. **Afro-American,** an earlier alternative to **black**, is heard mostly in anthropological and cultural contexts. 'Colored people', common earlier in the twentieth century, is now regarded as derogatory, although the phrase survives in the full name of the NAACP. An inversion, 'people of color' has come to be used for all non-white ethnic groups: *a gathering spot for African Americans and other people of color interested in studying their cultures.*

black and blue *adj.* discolored by bruises.

black and white *n. & adj.* • *n.* writing or print (*down in black and white*). • *adj.* **1** (of film, etc.) not in color. **2** consisting of extremes only; oversimplified (*interpreted the problem in black and white terms*).

black art *n.* (prec. by *the*) = BLACK MAGIC.

black·ball /blákbawl/ *v.tr.* **1** reject (a candidate) in a ballot (orig. by voting with a black ball). **2** exclude; ostracize.

black belt *n.* **1** a black belt worn by an expert in judo, karate, etc. **2** a person qualified to wear this.

black·ber·ry /blákberee/ *n.* (*pl.* **-ries**) **1** a climbing thorny rosaceous shrub, *Rubus fruticosus*, bearing white or pink flowers and purplish-black berries. **2** the edible berry of this plant.

black·bird /blákbərd/ *n.* **1** a common Eurasian thrush, *Turdus merula*, the male of which is black with an orange beak. **2** any of various birds with black plumage.

black·board /blákbawrd/ *n.* a board with a smooth usu. dark surface for writing on with chalk.

black box *n.* **1** a flight recorder in an aircraft. **2** any complex piece of equipment with contents that are mysterious to the user.

black·cur·rant /blák-kərənt, -kúr-/ *n.* **1** a widely cultivated shrub, *Ribes nigrum*, bearing flowers in racemes. **2** the small dark edible berry of this plant.

Black Death *n.* (usu. prec. by *the*) a widespread epidemic of bubonic plague in Europe in the 14th c.

black e·con·o·my *n.* a part of a country's economic activity that is unrecorded and untaxed by its government.

black·en /blákən/ *v.* **1** *tr. & intr.* make or become black or dark. **2** *tr.* speak evil of; defame (*blacken someone's character*).

black Eng·lish *n.* the form of English spoken by many African-Americans, esp. as an urban dialect of the US.

black eye *n.* bruised skin around the eye resulting from a blow.

black-eyed Su·san *n.* any of several flowers, esp. of the genus *Rudbeckia*, with yellow colored petals and a dark center.

black·fly /blákflī/ *n.* (*pl.* **-flies**) **1** any of various small biting flies of the family Simuliidae. **2** any of various thrips or aphids infesting plants.

Black·foot /blákfoot/ *n.* **1 a** a N. American people native to Montana and adjoining parts of Canada. **b** a member of this people. **2** the language of this people.

black·guard /blágaard, -ərd/ *n.* a villain; a scoundrel.

black·head /blák-hed/ *n.* a black-topped pimple on the skin.

black hole *n.* a region of space possessing a strong gravitational field from which matter and radiation cannot escape.

black ice *n.* thin hard transparent ice.

black·jack /blákjak/ *n.* **1** a card game in which players try to acquire cards with a face value totaling 21 and no more. **2** a flexible, usu. lead-filled bludgeon. **3** a pirate's black flag.

black light *n. Physics* the invisible ultraviolet or infrared radiations of the electromagnetic spectrum.

black·list /bláklist/ *n. & v.* • *n.* a list of persons under suspicion, in disfavor, etc. • *v.tr.* put the name of (a person) on a blacklist.

black lung *n.* a chronic lung disease caused by the inhalation of coal dust.

black mag·ic *n.* magic involving invocation of evil spirits.

black·mail /blákmayl/ *n. & v.* • *n.* **1 a** an extortion of payment in return for not disclosing a secret, etc. **b** any payment extorted in this way. **2** the use of threats or moral pressure. • *v.tr.* **1** extort or try to extort money, etc., from (a person) by blackmail. **2** threaten; coerce. ▫▫ **black·mail·er** *n.*

black mark *n.* a mark of discredit.

black mar·ket *n.* an illicit traffic in officially controlled or scarce commodities. ▫▫ **black mar·ke·teer** *n.*

Black Mus·lim *n.* a member of an exclusively African-American Islamic sect proposing a separate African-American community.

Black Na·tion·al·ism *n.* advocacy of civil rights and separatism for African-Americans and occas. blacks in other countries.

black·out /blákowt/ *n.* **1** a temporary or complete loss of vision, consciousness, or memory. **2** a loss of power, radio reception, etc. **3** a compulsory period of darkness as a precaution against air raids. **4** a temporary suppression of the release of information, esp. from police or government sources.

Black Pan·ther *n.* one of a group of extremist activists for African-American civil rights in the US.

black pep·per *n.* pepper made by grinding the whole dried berry, including the husk, of the pepper plant.

black rasp·ber·ry *n.* **1** a N. American shrub, *Rubus occidentalis.* **2** the edible fruit of this shrub.

black sheep *n. colloq.* a disreputable member of a family, etc.; a misfit.

black·shirt /blákshərt/ *n.* a member of a fascist organization.

black·smith /bláksmith/ *n.* **1** a smith who works in iron. **2** a smith who shoes horses.

black·thorn /blákthawrn/ *n.* **1** a thorny rosaceous shrub, *Prunus spinosa,* bearing white flowers before small blue-black fruits. Also called **sloe**. **2** a cudgel or walking stick made from its wood.

black tie *n.* **1** a black bow tie worn with a dinner jacket. **2** *colloq.* formal evening dress.

black·top /bláktop/ *n.* a type of surfacing material for roads.

black·wa·ter fe·ver /blákwawtər/ *n.* a complication of malaria in which blood cells are rapidly destroyed, resulting in dark urine.

black wid·ow *n.* a venomous spider, *Latrodectus mactans,* of which the female has an hourglass-shaped red mark on her abdomen.

blad·der /bládər/ *n.* **1 a** any of various membranous sacs in some animals, containing urine (**urinary bladder**), bile (**gallbladder**), or air (**swim bladder**). **b** this or part of it or a similar object prepared for various uses. **2** an inflated pericarp or vesicle in various plants. **3** anything inflated and hollow.

blad·der·wrack /bládərak/ *n.* a common brown seaweed, *Fucus vesiculosus,* with fronds containing air bladders that give buoyancy.

blade /blayd/ *n.* **1 a** the flat part of a knife, chisel, etc., that forms the cutting edge. **b** a flat piece of metal with a sharp edge or edges used in a razor. **2** the flattened functional part of an oar, spade, propeller, skate, snowplow, etc. **3** the flat, narrow leaf of grass and cereals. □□ **blad·ed** *adj.* (also in *comb.*).

blah /blaa/ *n. & adj. colloq.* •*n.* (usu. **the blahs**) a lethargic, dissatisfied feeling of malaise. •*adj.* dull; insipid.

blame /blaym/ *v. & n.* •*v.tr.* **1** assign fault or responsibility to. **2** (foll. by *on*) assign the responsibility for (an error or wrong) to a person, etc. (*blamed his death on a poor diet*). •*n.* **1** responsibility for a bad result (*shared the blame equally*). **2** the act of blaming or attributing responsibility (*she got all the blame*). □ **be to blame** (often foll. by *for*) be responsible; deserve censure (*she is not to blame for the accident*).

blame·ful /bláymfo͝ol/ *adj.* deserving blame; guilty. □□ **blame·ful·ly** *adv.*

blame·less /bláymlis/ *adj.* innocent; free from blame. □□ **blame·less·ly** *adv.*

blame·wor·thy /bláymwər*th*ee/ *adj.* deserving blame. □□ **blame·wor·thi·ness** *n.*

blanch /blanch/ *v.* **1** *tr.* make white or pale by extracting color. **2** *intr. & tr.* grow or make pale from shock, fear, etc. **3** *tr. Cooking* **a** peel (almonds, etc.) by scalding. **b** immerse (vegetables or meat) briefly in boiling water. **4** *tr.* whiten (a plant) by depriving it of light.

blanc·mange /bləmaánj/ *n.* a sweet opaque gelatinous dessert made with flavored cornstarch and milk.

bland /bland/ *adj.* **1 a** mild; not irritating. **b** tasteless; unstimulating; insipid. **2** gentle in manner; smooth. □□ **bland·ly** *adv.* **bland·ness** *n.*

bland·ish /blándish/ *v.tr.* flatter; coax; cajole.

bland·ish·ment /blándishmənt/ *n.* (usu. in *pl.*) flattery.

blank /blangk/ *adj., n., & v.* •*adj.* **1 a** (of paper) not written or printed on. **b** (of a document) with spaces left for a signature or details. **2 a** empty (*a blank space*). **b** unrelieved; plain; undecorated (*a blank wall*). **3 a** having or showing no interest or expression (*a blank stare*). **b** void of incident or result. **c** puzzled; nonplussed. **d** having (temporarily) no knowledge (*my mind went blank*). **4** (with neg. import) complete; downright (*blank despair*). **5** *euphem.* used in place of an adjective regarded as coarse or abusive. •*n.* **1 a** a space left to be filled in a document. **b** a document having blank spaces to be filled. **2** a cartridge containing gunpowder but no bullet. **3** an empty space or period of time. •*v.tr.* (usu. foll. by *off, out*) screen; obscure (*clouds blanked out the sun*). □ **draw a blank** elicit no response; fail. □□ **blank·ly** *adv.* **blank·ness** *n.*

blank check *n.* **1** a check with the amount left for the payee to fill in. **2** *colloq.* unlimited freedom of action (cf. CARTE BLANCHE).

blan·ket /blángkit/ *n., adj., & v.* •*n.* **1** a large piece of woolen or other material used esp. as a bed covering or to wrap up a person or an animal for warmth. **2** (usu. foll. by *of*) a thick mass or layer that covers something (*blanket of fog; blanket of silence*). •*attrib.adj.* covering all cases or classes; inclusive (*blanket condemnation; blanket agreement*). •*v.tr.* (**blanketed, blanketing**) **1** cover with or as if with a blanket (*snow blanketed the land*). **2** stifle (*blanketed all discussion*).

blank·e·ty-blank /blángkətee blangk/ *adj. colloq.* used euphemistically to replace a word considered coarse or vulgar (*blankety-blank taxes!*).

blank verse *n.* unrhymed verse, esp. that which uses iambic pentameters.

blare /blair/ *v. & n.* •*v.* **1** *tr. & intr.* sound or utter loudly. **2** *intr.* make the sound of a trumpet. •*n.* a loud sound resembling that of a trumpet.

blar·ney /blaárnee/ *n.* **1** cajoling talk; flattery. **2** nonsense.

bla·sé /blaazáy/ *adj.* **1** indifferent because of over-familiarity. **2** tired of pleasure; surfeited.

blas·pheme /blasféem, blásfeem/ *v.* **1** *intr.* talk profanely, making use of religious names, etc. **2** *tr.* talk profanely about; revile. □□ **blas·phem·er** *n.*

blas·phe·my /blásfəmee/ *n.* (*pl.* **-mies**) **1** profane talk. **2** an instance of this. □□ **blas·phe·mous** *adj.* **blas·phe·mous·ly** *adv.*

blast /blast/ *n. & v.* •*n.* **1** a strong gust of air. **2 a** a destructive wave of highly compressed air spreading outward from an explosion. **b** such an explosion. **3** the single loud note of a wind instrument, car horn, etc. **4** *colloq.* a severe reprimand. **5** a strong current of air used in smelting, etc. •*v.* **1** *tr.* blow up (rocks, etc.) with explosives. **2** *tr.* **a** wither, shrivel, or blight (a plant, animal, limb, etc.) (*blasted oak*). **b** ruin (*blasted her hopes*). **c** strike with divine anger. **3** *intr. & tr.* make or cause to make a loud noise (*blasted away on his trumpet*). **4** *tr. colloq.* reprimand severely. **5** *colloq.* **a** *tr.* shoot; shoot at. **b** *intr.* shoot. □ **at full blast** *colloq.* working at maximum speed, etc. **blast off** (of a rocket, etc.) take off from a launching site.

-blast /blast/ *comb.form Biol.* an embryonic cell (cf. -CYTE).

blast·ed /blástid/ *attrib.adj.* damned; annoying (*that blasted job!*).

blast fur·nace *n.* a smelting furnace into which compressed hot air is driven.

blast·off /blástawf/ *n.* the launching of a rocket, etc.

blas·tu·la /bláschələ/ *n.* (*pl.* **blastulas** or **blastulae**

/-lee/) *Biol.* an animal embryo at an early stage of development when it is a hollow ball of cells.

bla·tant /bláyt'nt/ *adj.* **1** flagrant; unashamed (*blatant attempt to steal*). **2** offensively noisy or obtrusive. ◻◻ **blatancy** /-t'nsee/ *n.* **bla·tant·ly** *adv.*

blath·er /bláthər/ *n.* & *v.* (also **bleth·er** /bléthər/) •*n.* foolish chatter. •*v.intr.* chatter foolishly.

blaze[1] /blayz/ *n.* & *v.* •*n.* **1** a bright flame or fire. **2 a** a bright glaring light. **b** a full light (*a blaze of publicity*). **3** a violent outburst (of passion, etc.). **4 a** a glow of color (*roses were a blaze of scarlet*). **b** a bright display (*a blaze of glory*). •*v.intr.* **1** burn with a bright flame. **2** be brilliantly lit. **3** be consumed with anger, excitement, etc. **4 a** show bright colors (*blazing with jewels*). **b** emit light (*stars blazing*). ◻ **blaze away** (often foll. by *at*) **1** fire continuously with rifles, etc. **2** work enthusiastically. **like blazes** *sl.* **1** with great energy. **2** very fast. ◻◻ **blaz·ing** *adj.* **blaz·ing·ly** *adv.*

blaze[2] /blayz/ *n.* & *v.* •*n.* **1** a white mark on an animal's face. **2** a mark made on a tree by slashing the bark. •*v.tr.* mark (a tree or a path) by slashing bark. ◻ **blaze a trail 1** mark out a path or route. **2** be the first to do, invent, or study something; pioneer.

blaz·er /bláyzər/ *n.* **1** a man's or woman's sports jacket not worn with matching trousers. **2** a colored jacket worn as part of a uniform.

bla·zon /bláyzən/ *v.tr.* **1** proclaim (esp. *blazon abroad*). **2** *Heraldry* **a** describe or paint (arms). **b** inscribe or paint (an object) with arms, names, etc.

bleach /bleech/ *v.* & *n.* •*v.tr.* & *intr.* whiten by exposure to sunlight or by a chemical process. •*n.* **1** a bleaching substance. **2** the process of bleaching.

bleach·er /bléechər/ *n.* **1 a** a person who bleaches. **b** a vessel or chemical used in bleaching. **2** (usu. in *pl.*) an inexpensive, uncovered bench seat at a sports field or arena.

bleak /bleek/ *adj.* **1** bare; exposed; windswept. **2** unpromising; dreary (*bleak prospects*). ◻◻ **bleak·ly** *adv.* **bleak·ness** *n.*

blear /bleer/ *adj.* & *v.* •*adj.* **1** (of the eyes or the mind) dim; dull; filmy. **2** indistinct. •*v.tr.* make dim or obscure; blur.

blear·y /bléeree/ *adj.* (**blearier, bleariest**) **1** (of the eyes) dim, as from sleep or fatigue. **2** indistinct; blurred. ◻◻ **blear·i·ly** *adv.*

blear·y-eyed *adj.* having bleary eyes.

bleat /bleet/ *v.* & *n.* •*v.* **1** *intr.* (of a sheep, goat, or calf) make a weak, wavering cry. **2** *intr.* & *tr.* (often foll. by *out*) speak or say feebly, foolishly, or plaintively. •*n.* **1** the sound made by a sheep, goat, etc. **2** a weak, plaintive, or foolish cry.

bleed /bleed/ *v.* & *n.* •*v.* (*past* and *past part.* **bled** /bled/) **1** *intr.* emit blood. **2** *tr.* draw blood from surgically. **3** *tr.* extort money from. **4** *intr.* (often foll. by *for*) suffer wounds or violent death (*bled for the Revolution*). **5** *intr.* **a** (of a plant) emit sap. **b** (of dye) come out in water. **6** *tr.* **a** allow (fluid or gas) to escape from a closed system through a valve, etc. **b** treat (such a system) in this way. •*n.* an act of bleeding (cf. NOSEBLEED). ◻ **one's heart bleeds** usu. *iron.* one is very sorrowful.

bleed·er /bléedər/ *n. colloq.* a hemophiliac.

bleed·ing heart *n.* **1** *colloq.* a dangerously or foolishly soft-hearted person. **2** any of various plants, esp. *Dicentra spectabilis* having heart-shaped crimson flowers hanging from an arched stem.

bleep /bleep/ *n.* & *v.* •*n.* **1** an intermittent high-pitched sound made electronically. **2** a sound of this type used in broadcasting as a substitute for a censored word or phrase. •*v.* **1** *intr.* & *tr.* make or cause to make such a sound, esp. as a signal. **2** *tr.* substitute a bleep or bleeps for a censored word or phrase.

blem·ish /blémish/ *n.* & *v.* •*n.* **1** a small mark or flaw that spoils the appearance of something. **2** moral defect or fault; a flaw (*not a blemish on his character*). •*v.tr.* spoil the beauty or perfection of (*spots blemished her complexion*).

blench /blench/ *v.intr.* flinch; quail.

blend /blend/ *v.* & *n.* •*v.* **1** *tr.* **a** mix together to produce a desired flavor, etc. **b** produce by this method (*blended whiskey*). **2** *intr.* form a harmonious compound; become one. **3 a** *tr.* & *intr.* (often foll. by *with*) mingle or be mingled (*blends well with the locals*). **b** *tr.* (often foll. by *in, with*) mix thoroughly. **4** *intr.* (esp. of colors): **a** pass imperceptibly into each other. **b** go well together; harmonize. •*n.* **1 a** a mixture, esp. of various sorts of a substance. **b** a combination (of different abstract or personal qualities). **2** a portmanteau word.

blend·er /bléndər/ *n.* **1** a mixing machine used in food preparation for liquefying, chopping, or puréeing. **2 a** a thing that blends. **b** a person who blends.

bless /bles/ *v.tr.* (*past* and *past part.* **blessed,** *poet.* **blest** /blest/) **1** pronounce words, esp. in a religious rite, asking for divine favor. **2 a** consecrate. **b** sanctify by the sign of the cross. **3** call (God) holy; adore. **4** attribute one's good fortune to (an auspicious time, one's fate, etc.); thank (*bless the day I met her*). **5** (usu. in *passive*; often foll. by *with*) make happy or successful (*they were truly blessed*). ◻ **(God) bless you! 1** an exclamation of endearment, gratitude, etc. **2** an exclamation made to a person who has just sneezed.

---

bless Old English *blēdsian, blētsian,* based on *blōd* 'blood' (i.e., originally perhaps 'mark or consecrate with blood'). The meaning was influenced by its being used to translate Latin *benedicere* 'to praise, worship,' and later by association with **bliss**.

---

bless·ed /blésid, blest/ *adj.* (also *poet.* **blest**) **1 a** consecrated (*Blessed Sacrament*). **b** revered. **2** /blest/ (usu. foll. by *with*) often *iron.* fortunate (in the possession of) (*blessed with children*). **3** *euphem.* cursed; damned (*blessed nuisance!*). **4 a** in paradise. **b** *RC Ch.* a title given to a dead person as an acknowledgment of his or her holy life. **5** bringing happiness; blissful (*blessed ignorance*). ◻◻ **bless·ed·ly** *adv.*

bless·ed·ness /blésidnis/ *n.* **1** happiness. **2** the enjoyment of divine favor.

bless·ing /blésing/ *n.* **1** the act of declaring, seeking, or bestowing favor *his mother gave him her blessing*). **2** grace said before or after a meal. **3** a gift of God, nature, etc.; a thing one is glad of.

blew *past* of BLOW[1].

blight /blīt/ *n.* & *v.* •*n.* **1** any plant disease caused by mildews, rusts, smuts, fungi, or insects. **2** any insect or parasite causing such a disease. **3** any obscure force that is harmful. **4** an unsightly or neglected urban area. •*v.tr.* **1** affect with blight. **2** harm; destroy.

blimp /blimp/ *n.* **1 a** a small nonrigid airship. **b** a barrage balloon. **2** *derog. sl.* a fat person. ◻◻ **blimp·ish** *adj.*

blind /blīnd/ *adj., v., n.,* & *adv.* •*adj.* **1** lacking the power of sight. **2 a** without foresight, discernment, intellectual perception, or adequate information. **b** (often foll. by *to*) unwilling or unable to appreciate (a factor, circumstance, etc.) (*blind to argument*). **3** not governed by purpose or reason (*blind forces*). **4** reckless (*blind hitting*). **5 a** concealed (*blind driveway*). **b** (of a door, window, etc.) walled up. **c** closed at one end. **6** *Aeron.* (of flying) without direct observation, using instruments only. •*v.* **1** *tr.* deprive of sight (*blinded by tears*). **2** *tr.* (often foll. by *to*) rob of judgment; deceive (*blinded them to the danger*). •*n.* **1** a screen for a window (*Venetian blind*). **2** something designed or used to hide the truth. **3** any obstruction to sight or light. •*adv.* blindly (*fly blind*). ◻ **turn a** (or **one's**) **blind eye to** pretend not to notice. ◻◻ **blind·ly** *adv.* **blind·ness** *n.*

blind al·ley *n.* **1** a dead end. **2** a course of action leading nowhere.

blind date *n.* **1** a social engagement between two people who have not previously met. **2** either of the couple on a blind date.

blind·er /blíndər/ *n. colloq.* (in *pl.*) either of a pair of screens or flaps attached to a horse's bridle to prevent it from seeing sideways.

blind·fold /blíndfōld/ *v., n., adj., & adv.* •*v.tr.* deprive (a person) of sight by covering the eyes, esp. with a tied cloth. •*n.* a bandage or cloth used to blindfold. •*adj. & adv.* (usu. **blindfolded**) **1** with the eyes covered. **2** without care or circumspection (*went into it blindfolded*).

blind man's buff *n.* (or **blind man's bluff**) a game in which a blindfolded player tries to catch others while being pushed around by them.

blind·side /blīndsīd/ *v.tr.* **1** strike or attack unexpectedly from one's blind side. **2** spring a disagreeable surprise upon.

blind spot *n.* **1** *Anat.* the point of entry of the optic nerve on the retina, insensitive to light. **2** an area in which a person lacks understanding or impartiality.

blind-stitch *n. & v.* •*n.* sewing visible on one side only. •*v.tr. & intr.* sew with this stitch.

blink /blingk/ *v. & n.* •*v.* **1** *intr.* shut and open the eyes quickly. **2** *intr.* (often foll. by *at*) look with eyes opening and shutting. **3** *tr.* **a** (often foll. by *back*) prevent (tears) by blinking. **b** (often foll. by *away, from*) clear (dust, etc.) from the eyes by blinking. **4** *tr.* (foll. by *at*) *& intr.* ignore. **5** *intr.* **a** shine with an intermittent light. **b** cast a momentary gleam. **6** *tr.* blink with (eyes). •*n.* **1** an act of blinking. **2** a momentary gleam or glimpse. □ **on the blink** *sl.* out of order, esp. intermittently.

blink·er /blíngkər/ *n. & v.* •*n.* **1** a device that blinks. **2** = BLINDER. •*v.tr.* **1** obscure with blinders. **2** (as **blinkered** *adj.*) having narrow views.

blip /blip/ *n. & v.* •*n.* **1** a quick popping sound, as of dripping water or an electronic device. **2** a small image of an object on a radar screen. **3** a minor deviation or error. •*v.intr.* (**blipped, blipping**) make a blip.

bliss /blis/ *n.* **1 a** perfect joy or happiness. **b** enjoyment; gladness. **2** a state of blessedness. □□ **bliss·ful** *adj.* **bliss·ful·ly** *adv.* **bliss·ful·ness** *n.*

blis·ter /blístər/ *n. & v.* •*n.* **1** a small bubble on the skin filled with serum and caused by burning, etc. **2** a similar swelling on any other surface. •*v.* **1** *tr.* raise a blister on. **2** *intr.* come up in a blister or blisters. **3** *tr.* attack sharply (*blistered them with his criticisms*).

blis·ter pack *n.* packaging consisting of a transparent plastic attached to cardboard, used to hold and display a product in a store. Also called **bubble pack**.

blithe /blīth/ *adj.* **1** *poet.* gay; joyous. **2** careless; casual (*with blithe indifference*). □□ **blithe·ly** *adv.* **blithe·ness** *n.* **blithe·some** /blīthsəm/ *adj.*

blith·er·ing /blíthəring/ *attrib. adj. colloq.* **1** senselessly talkative. **2** utter; hopeless (*blithering idiot*).

blitz /blits/ *n. & v. colloq.* •*n.* **1** an intensive or sudden attack. **2** (**the Blitz**) the German air raids on London in 1940 during World War II. **3** *Football* a charge of the passer by the defensive linebackers or backs. •*v.tr.* attack, damage, or destroy by a blitz.

blitz·krieg /blítskreeg/ *n.* an intense military campaign intended to bring about a swift victory.

bliz·zard /blízərd/ *n.* a severe snowstorm with high winds.

bloat /blōt/ *v.* **1** *tr. & intr.* inflate; swell (*bloated with gas*). **2** *tr.* (as **bloated** *adj.*) **a** swollen. **b** puffed up with pride or wealth (*bloated plutocrat*). **3** *tr.* cure (a herring) by salting and smoking lightly.

blob /blob/ *n.* **1** a small roundish mass; a drop of matter. **2** a drop of liquid. **3** a spot of color.

bloc /blok/ *n.* a combination of governments, groups, etc., sharing a common purpose.

block /blok/ *n. & v.* •*n.* **1** a large solid piece of hard material, esp. rock, stone, or wood, usu. with flat surfaces on each side (*block of ice; block of marble*). **2** a flat-topped base for chopping food, hammering on, etc. **3** a group of buildings bounded by (usu. four) streets. **4** an obstruction. **5** a pulley or system of pulleys mounted in a case. **6** (in *pl.*) any of a set of solid cubes used as a child's toy. **7** *Printing* a piece of wood or metal engraved for printing on paper or fabric. **8** *sl.* the head (*knock his block off*). **9 a** the area between streets in a town or suburb. **b** the length of such an area (*lives three blocks away*). **10** a large quantity of things treated as a unit, esp. shares, seats in a theater, etc. •*v.tr.* **1 a** (often foll. by *up, off*) obstruct (a passage, etc.) (*you are blocking my view*). **b** put obstacles in the way of (progress, etc.). **2** restrict the use or conversion of (currency or any other asset). **3** *Sports* stop or impede. □ **block in 1** sketch roughly; plan. **2** park one's car in such a way as to prevent another car from moving away. **block out 1 a** shut out (light, noise, etc.). **b** exclude from memory, as being too painful. **2** sketch roughly; plan. □□ **block·er** *n.*

block·ade /blokáyd/ *n. & v.* •*n.* **1** the surrounding or blocking of a place, esp. a port, by an enemy to prevent entry and exit of supplies, etc. **2** anything that prevents access or progress. •*v.tr.* **1** subject to a blockade. **2** obstruct (a passage, etc.). □ **run a blockade** enter or leave a blockaded port by evading the blockading force. □□ **block·ad·er** *n.*

block·age /blókij/ *n.* **1** an obstruction. **2** a blocked state.

block and tack·le *n.* a system of pulleys and ropes, esp. for lifting.

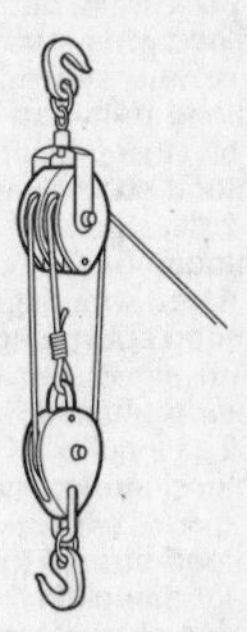
block and tackle

block·bust·er /blókbustər/ *n. sl.* **1** something of great power or size, esp. an epic or extremely popular movie or book. **2** a huge aerial bomb.

block·head /blókhed/ *n.* a stupid person. □□ **block·head·ed** *adj.*

block·house /blókhows/ *n.* **1** a reinforced concrete shelter used as an observation point, etc. **2** *hist.* a one-story timber building with loopholes, used as a fort. **3** a house made of squared logs.

blond /blond/ *adj. & n.* •*adj.* **1** (of hair) light-colored; fair. **2** (of the complexion, esp. as an indication of race) light-colored. •*n.* a person with fair hair and skin. □□ **blond·ish** *adj.* **blond·ness** *n.*

blonde /blond/ *adj. & n.* •*adj.* (of a woman or a woman's hair) blond. •*n.* a blond-haired woman.

blood /blud/ *n. & v.* •*n.* **1** a liquid, usually red and circulating in the arteries and veins of vertebrates, that carries oxygen to and carbon dioxide from the tissues of the body. **2** a corresponding fluid in invertebrates. **3** bloodshed, esp. killing. **4** passion; temperament. **5** race; parentage (*of the same blood*). •*v.tr.* initiate (a person) by experience. □ **in one's blood** inherent in one's character. **make a person's blood boil** infuriate. **new** (or **fresh**) **blood** new members admitted to a group, esp. as an invigorating force.

blood bank *n.* a place where supplies of blood or plasma for transfusion are stored.

blood bath *n.* a massacre.

blood broth·er *n.* a brother by birth or by the ceremonial mingling of blood.
blood count *n.* **1** the counting of the number of corpuscles in a specific amount of blood. **2** the number itself.
blood·cur·dling /blúdkərdling/ *adj.* horrifying.
blood do·nor *n.* a person who gives blood for transfusion.
blood·ed /blúdid/ *adj.* **1** (of horses, etc.) of good pedigree. **2** (in *comb.*) having blood or a disposition of a specified kind (*cold-blooded*; *red-blooded*).
blood feud *n.* a feud between families involving killing or injury.
blood group *n.* any one of the various types of human blood determining compatibility in transfusion.
blood·hound /blúdhownd/ *n.* a large hound of a breed used in tracking and having a very keen sense of smell.
blood·less /blúdlis/ *adj.* **1** without blood. **2** unemotional. **3** pale. **4** without bloodshed (*a bloodless coup*). **5** feeble. ▫▫ **blood·less·ly** *adv.* **blood·less·ness** *n.*
blood·let·ting /blúdleting/ *n.* **1** the surgical removal of some of a patient's blood. **2** bloodshed.
blood·line /blúdlīn/ *n.* a line of descent; pedigree; descent.
blood·mo·bile /blúdmōbēel/ *n.* a van, truck, or bus equipped and staffed to take blood from donors.
blood mon·ey *n.* **1** money paid to the next of kin of a person who has been killed. **2** money paid to a hired murderer. **3** money paid for information about a murder.
blood or·ange *n.* an orange with red or red-streaked pulp.
blood poi·son·ing *n.* a diseased state caused by the presence of microorganisms in the blood.
blood pres·sure *n.* the pressure of the blood in the circulatory system, often measured for diagnosis.
blood re·la·tion *n.* (also **blood rel·a·tive**) a relative by blood, not by marriage or adoption.
blood·shed /blúdshed/ *n.* **1** the spilling of blood. **2** slaughter.
blood·shot /blúdshot/ *adj.* (of an eyeball) inflamed; tinged with blood.
blood sport *n.* sport involving the wounding or killing of animals, esp. hunting.
blood·stained /blúdstaynd/ *adj.* **1** stained with blood. **2** guilty of bloodshed.
blood·stone /blúdstōn/ *n.* a type of green chalcedony spotted or streaked with red, often used as a gemstone.
blood·stream /blúdstreem/ *n.* blood in circulation.
blood·suck·er /blúdsukər/ *n.* **1** an animal or insect that sucks blood, esp. a leech. **2** an extortioner. ▫▫ **blood·suck·ing** *adj.*
blood sug·ar *n.* the amount of glucose in the blood.
blood·thirst·y /blúdthərstee/ *adj.* (**bloodthirstier, bloodthirstiest**) eager for bloodshed. ▫▫ **blood·thirst·i·ly** *adv.* **blood·thirst·i·ness** *n.*
blood type *n.* see BLOOD GROUP.
blood ves·sel *n.* a vein or artery carrying blood.
blood·y /blúdee/ *adj.* & *v.* • *adj.* (**bloodier, bloodiest**) **1 a** of or like blood. **b** running or smeared with blood. **2 a** involving bloodshed (*bloody battle*). **b** sanguinary; cruel (*bloody butcher*). **3** esp. *Brit. coarse sl.* expressing annoyance or antipathy, or as an intensive (*a bloody shame*). **4** red. • *v.tr.* (**-ies, -ied**) make bloody; stain with blood. ▫▫ **blood·i·ly** *adv.* **blood·i·ness** *n.*
Blood·y Mar·y *n.* a drink composed of vodka and tomato juice.
bloom[1] /bloōm/ *n.* & *v.* • *n.* **1 a** a flower, esp. one cultivated for its beauty. **b** the state of flowering (*in bloom*). **2** a state of perfection or loveliness (*in full bloom*). **3 a** (of the complexion) a flush; a glow. **b** a delicate powdery surface deposit on plums, leaves, etc., indicating freshness. **c** a cloudiness on a shiny surface. **4** an overgrowth of algae, plankton, etc. • *v.* **1** *intr.* be in flower. **2** *intr.* **a** come into, or remain in, full beauty. **b** be in a healthy, vigorous state. **3** *intr.* become overgrown with algae, plankton, etc. (esp. of a lake or stream). ▫ **take the bloom off** make stale.
bloom[2] /bloōm/ *n.* & *v.* • *n.* a mass of iron hammered or squeezed into a thick bar. • *v.tr.* make into bloom.
bloom·er /blōōmər/ *n.* a plant or person that blooms (in a specified way) (*early autumn bloomer; late bloomer*).
bloo·mers /blōōmərz/ *n.pl.* **1** women's loose almost knee-length underpants. **2** *colloq.* any women's underpants. **3** *hist.* women's loose trousers, gathered at the knee or (orig.) the ankle.
bloom·ing /blōōming/ *adj.* flourishing; healthy.
bloop·er /blōōpər/ *n. colloq.* an embarrassing error.
blos·som /blósəm/ *n.* & *v.* • *n.* **1** a flower or a mass of flowers, esp. of a fruit tree. **2** the state or time of flowering (*in blossom*). **3** a promising stage (*the blossom of youth*). • *v.intr.* **1** open into flower. **2** mature; thrive. ▫▫ **blos·som·y** *adj.*
blot /blot/ *n.* & *v.* • *n.* **1** a stain of ink, etc. **2** a disgraceful act or quality. **3** any disfigurement or blemish. • *v.* (**blotted, blotting**) **1 a** *tr.* spot or stain, esp. with ink. **b** *intr.* (of a pen, etc.) make blots. **2** *tr.* **a** use blotting paper, etc., to absorb excess liquid, esp. ink, from. **b** (of blotting paper, etc.) soak up (esp. ink). **3** *tr.* disgrace (*blotted his reputation*). ▫ **blot out 1** obliterate; obscure. **2** destroy.
blotch /bloch/ *n.* & *v.* • *n.* **1** a discolored or inflamed patch on the skin. **2** an irregular patch of ink or color. • *v.tr.* cover with blotches. ▫▫ **blotch·y** *adj.* (**blotchier, blotchiest**).
blot·ter /blótər/ *n.* a sheet or sheets of blotting paper, usu. inserted into a frame.
blot·ting pa·per *n.* unsized absorbent paper used for soaking up excess ink.
blouse /blows, blowz/ *n.* & *v.* • *n.* **1** a woman's upper garment, usu. buttoned and collared. **2** the upper part of a military uniform. • *v.tr.* make (a shirt, etc.) fall loosely like a blouse.
blous·on /blówson, blōōzon/ *n.* a short blouse-shaped jacket.
blow[1] /blō/ *v.* & *n.* • *v.* (*past* **blew** /bloō/; *past part.* **blown** /blōn/) **1 a** *intr.* (of the wind or impersonally) move along; act as an air current (*it was blowing hard*). **b** *intr.* be driven by an air current (*paper blew along*). **c** *tr.* drive with an air current (*blew the door open*). **2 a** *tr.* send out (esp. air) by breathing (*blew cigarette smoke*). **b** *intr.* send a directed air current from the mouth. **3** *tr.* & *intr.* sound or be sounded by blowing (*the whistle blew*). **4** *tr.* **a** direct an air current at (*blew the embers*). **b** (foll. by *off*, *away*, etc.) clear of by means of an air current. **5** *tr.* clear (the nose) of mucus by blowing. **6** *intr.* puff; pant. **7** *sl.* **a** *tr.* depart suddenly from (*blew the town yesterday*). **b** *intr.* depart suddenly. **8** *tr.* shatter or send flying by an explosion (*blew them to smithereens*). **9** *tr.* make or shape (glass or a bubble) by blowing air in. **10** *tr.* & *intr.* melt from overloading (*the fuse has blown*). **11** *intr.* (of a whale) eject air and water through a blowhole. **12** *tr.* break into (a safe, etc.) with explosives. **13** *tr. sl.* **a** spend recklessly (*blew $20 on a meal*). **b** bungle (an opportunity, etc.) (*he's blown his chances*). **c** reveal (a secret, etc.). **14** *tr.* (of flies) deposit eggs in. • *n.* **1** an act of blowing (e.g., one's nose). **2 a** a gust of air. **b** exposure to fresh air. ▫ **blow hot and cold** *colloq.* vacillate. **blow in 1** break inward by an explosion. **2** *colloq.* arrive unexpectedly. **blow a person's mind** *sl.* impress or affect someone very strongly. **blow off 1** escape or allow (steam, etc.) to escape forcibly. **2** *sl.* renege on (an obligation) (*I decided to blow off studying so I could go to the party*). **blow out 1 a** extinguish by blow-

ing. **b** send outward by an explosion. **2** (of a tire) burst. **3** (of a fuse, etc.) melt. **blow over** fade away without serious consequences. **blow one's own horn** praise oneself. **blow one's top** (or **stack**) *colloq.* explode in rage. **blow up 1 a** shatter or destroy by an explosion. **b** erupt. **2** *colloq.* lose one's temper. **3** inflate (a tire, etc.). **4** *colloq.* enlarge (a photograph, etc.). **5** exaggerate.. □□ **blow·y** *adj.* (**blowier, blowiest**).

blow[2] /blō/ *n.* **1** a hard stroke with a hand or weapon. **2** a sudden shock or misfortune. □ **come to blows** end up fighting.

blow[3] /blō/ *v. & n. archaic* • *v.intr.* (*past* **blew** /bloo/; *past part.* **blown** /blōn/) burst into or be in flower. • *n.* blossoming; bloom (*in full blow*).

blow-by-blow *attrib.adj.* (of a description, etc.) giving all the details in sequence.

blow-dry *v.tr.* arrange (the hair) while drying it with a hand-held dryer. □□ **blow-dry·er** *n.*

blow·er /blṓər/ *n.* **1** in senses of BLOW[1] *v.* **2** a device for creating a current of air.

blow·fish /blṓfish/ *n.* any of several kinds of fish able to inflate their bodies when frightened, etc.

blow·fly /blṓflī/ *n.* (*pl.* **-flies**) a meat fly; a bluebottle.

blow·gun /blṓgun/ *n.* a tube used esp. by primitive peoples for propelling darts by blowing.

blow·hard /blṓhaard/ *n. & adj. colloq.* • *n.* a boastful person. • *adj.* boastful; blustering.

blow·hole /blṓhōl/ *n.* **1** the nostril of a whale, on the top of its head. **2** a hole (esp. in ice) for breathing or fishing through. **3** a vent for smoke, etc., in a tunnel, etc.

blown *past part.* of BLOW[1].

blow·out /blṓ-owt/ *n. colloq.* **1** a burst tire. **2** a melted fuse. **3** a large party. **4** *Sports* victory by a wide margin.

blow·pipe /blṓpīp/ *n.* **1** = BLOWGUN. **2** a tube used to intensify the heat of a flame by blowing air or other gas through it. **3** a tube used in glass blowing.

blow·torch /blṓtawrch/ *n.* a portable device with a very hot flame used for burning off paint, soldering, etc.

blow-up *n.* **1** *colloq.* an enlargement (of a photograph, etc.). **2** an explosion. **3** an argument or outburst of anger.

blowz·y /blówzee/ *adj.* (**blowzier, blowziest**) **1** coarse-looking; red-faced. **2** disheveled.

BLT *abbr.* (*pl.* **BLT's** or **BLTs**) a bacon, lettuce, and tomato sandwich.

blub·ber /blúbər/ *n. & v.* • *n.* whale fat. • *v.* **1** *intr.* sob loudly. **2** *tr.* sob out (words). □□ **blub·ber·er** *n.* **blub·ber·y** *adj.*

bludg·eon /blújən/ *n. & v.* • *n.* a club with a heavy end. • *v.tr.* **1** beat with a bludgeon. **2** coerce.

blue /bloo/ *adj., n., & v.* • *adj.* (**bluer, bluest**) **1** having a color like that of a clear sky. **2** sad; gloomy (*feel blue*). **3** pornographic (*a blue film*). **4** with bluish skin through cold, anger, etc. • *n.* **1** a blue color or pigment. **2** blue clothes or material (*dressed in blue*). **3** (usu. **Blue**) **a** a soldier in the Union army in the US Civil War. **b** the Union army. **4** (prec. by *the*) the clear sky. • *v.tr.* (**blues, blued, bluing** or **blueing**) make blue. □ **once in a blue moon** very rarely. **out of the blue** unexpectedly.

blue ba·by *n.* a baby with a blue complexion from lack of oxygen in the blood due to a congenital defect of the heart or major vessels.

blue·bell /blóobel/ *n.* **1** any of a number of plants with blue bell-shaped flowers, esp. a North American flower of the genus *Mertensia.* **2** a European liliaceous plant, *Hyacinthoides nonscripta*, with clusters of bell-shaped blue flowers on a stem arising from a rhizome.

blue·ber·ry /blóoberee/ *n.* (*pl.* **-ries**) **1** any of several plants of the genus *Vaccinium*, with an edible fruit. **2** the small blue-black fruit of these plants.

blue·bird /blóobərd/ *n.* any of various N. American songbirds of the thrush family, esp. of the genus *Sialia*, with distinctive blue plumage usu. on the back or head.

blue blood *n.* **1** noble birth. **2** a person of noble birth. □□ **blue-blood·ed** *adj.*

blue book *n.* **1** a listing of socially prominent people. **2** a blank book used for college examinations. **3** a reference book listing the prices of used cars.

blue·bot·tle /blóobot'l/ *n.* a large buzzing fly, *Calliphora vomitoria*, with a metallic blue body. Also called BLOWFLY.

blue cheese *n.* cheese produced with veins of blue mold.

blue-chip *adj. attrib.* (of stock) of reliable investment, though less secure than gilt-edged stock.

blue-col·lar *attrib.adj.* of workers who wear work clothes and perform manual labor.

blue crab *n.* an edible bluish-green crab, *Callinectes sapidus*, of the Atlantic and Gulf coasts.

blue·fish /blóofish/ *n.* a voracious marine fish, *Pomatomus saltatrix*, inhabiting tropical and temperate waters and popular as a game fish.

blue·grass /blóogras/ *n.* **1** any of several bluish green grasses, esp. Kentucky bluegrass, *Poa pratensis.* **2** a kind of unamplified country music characterized by virtuosic playing of banjos, guitars, etc.

blue-green al·ga = CYANOBACTERIUM.

blue·gum /blóogum/ *n.* any tree of the genus *Eucalyptus*, esp. *E. regnans*, with blue-green aromatic leaves.

blue jay *n.* a crested jay, *Cyanocitta cristata*, common to N. America, with a blue back and head.

blue jeans *n.pl.* pants made of blue denim.

blue mold *n.* a bluish fungus growing on food and other organic matter.

blue-pen·cil *v.tr.* (**-penciled, -penciling**; also **-pencilled, -pencilling**) edit (a manuscript, etc.).

blue·print /blóoprint/ *n.* **1** a print of the final stage of engineering, esp. plans in white on a blue background. **2** a detailed plan.

blue rib·bon *n.* a high honor, esp. awarded for finishing first in a competition.

blue roan *adj. & n.* • *adj.* black mixed with white. • *n.* a blue roan animal.

blues /blooz/ *n.pl.* **1** (prec. by *the*) a bout of depression. **2** (prec. by *the*; often treated as *sing.*) predominantly melancholic music of African-American folk origin, often in a twelve-bar sequence. □□ **blues·y** *adj.* (in sense 2).

blue·stock·ing /blóostoking/ *n.* usu. *derog.* an intellectual or literary woman.

blue whale *n.* a rorqual, *Balaenoptera musculus*, the largest known living mammal.

bluff[1] /bluf/ *v. & n.* • *v.* **1** *intr.* make a pretense of strength or confidence to gain an advantage. **2** *tr.* mislead by bluffing. • *n.* an act of bluffing. □ **call a person's bluff** challenge a person thought to be bluffing.

bluff[2] /bluf/ *adj. & n.* • *adj.* **1** (of a cliff, or a ship's bows) having a vertical or steep broad front. **2** (of a person or manner) blunt; frank; hearty. • *n.* a steep cliff or headland. □□ **bluff·ly** *adv.* (in sense 2 of *adj.*). **bluff·ness** *n.* (in sense 2 of *adj.*).

blu·ing /blóoing/ *n.* (also **blueing**) blue powder used to whiten laundry.

blun·der /blúndər/ *n. & v.* • *n.* a clumsy or foolish mistake. • *v.* **1** *intr.* make a blunder. **2** *tr.* deal incompetently with. **3** *intr.* move about clumsily. □□ **blun·der·er** *n.* **blund·er·ing·ly** *adv.*

blun·der·buss /blúndərbus/ *n. hist.* a short large-bored gun firing balls or slugs.

blunt /blunt/ *adj. & v.* • *adj.* **1** (of a knife, pencil, etc.) lacking a sharp edge or point. **2** (of a person or manner) direct; outspoken. • *v.tr.* make blunt or less sharp. □□ **blunt·ly** *adv.* (in sense 2 of *adj.*). **blunt·ness** *n.*

blur /blər/ *v. & n.* • *v.* (**blurred, blurring**) **1** *tr. & intr.* make or become unclear or less distinct. **2** *tr.* smear; partially efface. • *n.* something that appears or sounds indistinct or unclear. □□ **blur·ry** *adj.* (**blur·ri·er, blur·ri·est**).

blurb /blərb/ *n.* a description of a book as promotion by its publishers.

blurt /blərt/ *v.tr.* (usu. foll. by *out*) utter abruptly, thoughtlessly, or tactlessly.

blush /blush/ *v. & n.* • *v.intr.* **1 a** develop a pink tinge in the face from embarrassment or shame. **b** (of the face) redden in this way. **2** feel embarrassed or ashamed. • *n.* **1** the act of blushing. **2** a pink tinge.

blush·er /blúshər/ *n.* a cosmetic used to give a usu. reddish or pinkish color to the face.

blus·ter /blústər/ *v. & n.* • *v.intr.* **1** behave pompously and boisterously. **2** (of the wind, etc.) blow fiercely. • *n.* **1** noisily self-assertive talk. **2** empty threats. □□ **blus·ter·er** *n.* **blus·ter·y** *adj.*

blvd. *abbr.* boulevard.

B mov·ie *n.* a supporting movie in a theater's program, esp. one considered to be of poor quality.

bo·a /bṓə/ *n.* **1** any large nonpoisonous snake from tropical America, esp. of the genus *Boa*, which kills its prey by crushing it in its coils. **2** any snake that is similar in appearance, such as Old World pythons. **3** a long scarflike fashion accessory, often made of feathers, worn around the neck.

boar /bawr/ *n.* **1** the tusked wild pig, *Sus scrofa*, from which domestic pigs are descended. **2** an uncastrated male pig. **3** its flesh. **4** a male guinea pig, etc.

board /bawrd/ *n. & v.* • *n.* **1 a** a flat thin piece of sawn lumber, usu. long and narrow. **b** a piece of material resembling this, made from compressed fibers. **c** a thin slab of wood or a similar substance, often with a covering, used for any of various purposes (*chessboard*; *ironing board*). **d** thick stiff cardboard used in bookbinding. **2** the provision of regular meals for payment. **3** the directors of a company; any other specially constituted administrative body. **4** (in *pl.*) the stage of a theater (cf. *tread the boards*). • *v.* **1** *tr.* **a** go on board (a ship, etc.). **b** force one's way on board (a ship, etc.) in attack. **2 a** *intr.* receive meals or meals and lodging, for payment. **b** *tr.* provide (a lodger, etc.) with regular meals. **3** *tr.* (usu. foll. by *up*) cover with boards; seal. □ **go by the board** be neglected, omitted, or discarded. **on board** on or on to a ship, aircraft, oil rig, etc.

board·er /báwrdər/ *n.* **1** a person who boards (see BOARD *v.* 2a), esp. a pupil at a boarding school. **2** a person who boards a ship, esp. an enemy.

board·ing·house /báwrdinghows/ *n.* an establishment providing board and lodging.

board·ing school /báwrding sko͞ol/ *n.* a school where pupils reside during the school term.

board·room /báwrdro͞om, -ro͝om/ *n.* a room in which a board of directors, etc., meets regularly.

board·walk /báwrdwawk/ *n.* **1** a wooden walkway across sand, marsh, etc. **2** a promenade, esp. of wooden planks, along a beach.

boast /bōst/ *v. & n.* • *v.* **1** *intr.* declare one's achievements, possessions, or abilities with indulgent pride and satisfaction. **2** *tr.* own or have as something praiseworthy, etc. (*boasts magnificent views*). • *n.* **1** an act of boasting. **2** something one is proud of. □□ **boast·er** *n.* **boast·ing·ly** *adv.*

boast·ful /bṓstfo͝ol/ *adj.* given to or characterized by boasting. □□ **boast·ful·ly** *adv.* **boast·ful·ness** *n.*

boat /bōt/ *n. & v.* • *n.* **1** a small vessel propelled on water by an engine, oars, or sails. **2** (in general use) a ship of any size. **3** a boat-shaped jug used for holding sauce, etc. • *v.intr.* travel in a boat, esp. for pleasure. □ **in the same boat** sharing the same adverse circumstances.

boat·house /bṓt-hows/ *n.* a shed at the edge of a river, lake, etc., for housing boats.

boat·ing /bṓting/ *n.* rowing or sailing in boats as a sport or form of recreation.

boat peo·ple *n.pl.* refugees who have left a country by sea.

boat·swain /bṓs'n/ *n.* (also **bo'sun, bo·sun, bo's'n**) a ship's officer in charge of equipment and the crew.

bob[1] /bob/ *v. & n.* • *v.intr.* (**bobbed, bobbing**) **1** move quickly up and down. **2** (usu. foll. by *back, up*) **a** bounce buoyantly. **b** emerge suddenly; become active again. **3** curtsy. **4** (foll. by *for*) try to catch with the mouth alone (an apple, etc., floating or hanging). • *n.* **1** a jerking or bouncing movement, esp. upward. **2** a curtsy.

bob[2] /bob/ *n. & v.* • *n.* **1** a short hairstyle for women and children. **2** a weight on a pendulum, plumb line, or kite tail. **3** = BOBSLED. **4** a horse's docked tail. • *v.* (**bobbed, bobbing**) **1** *tr.* cut (a woman's or child's hair) so that it hangs clear of the shoulders. **2** *intr.* ride on a bobsled.

bob·bin /bóbin/ *n.* **1** a cylinder or cone holding thread, etc. **2** a spool or reel.

bob·ble /bóbəl/ *n. & vb.* • *n.* **1** a small woolly or tufted ball as a decoration or trimming. **2** a fumble, esp. of a baseball or football. • *vb.tr.* to fumble or juggle (a ball).

bob·by pin /bóbeepin/ *n.* a flat, closed hairpin.

bob·by socks *n.pl.* (also **bob·by sox**) short socks reaching just above the ankle.

bob·cat /bóbkat/ *n.* a small N. American lynx, *Lynx rufus*, with a spotted reddish brown coat and a short tail.

bob·sled /bóbsled/ (also *Brit.* **bobsleigh** /bóbslay/) *n.* a mechanically steered and braked sled used for racing down a steep ice-covered run. □□ **bob·sled·ding** *n.*

bob·white /bóbhwít, bóbwít/ *n.* an American quail of the genus *Colinus*.

bock /bok/ *n.* a strong dark German beer.

bo·da·cious /bōdáyshəs/ *adj. sl.* **1** remarkable; excellent. **2** bold; audacious.

bode /bōd/ *v.tr.* **1** portend, promise. **2** foresee; foretell (evil). □ **bode well** (or **ill**) show good (or bad) signs for the future.

bo·de·ga /bōdáygə/ *n.* **1** a grocery store in a Spanish-speaking neighborhood. **2** a wineshop.

bo·dh·isatt·va /bṓdisútvə/ *n.* in Mahayana Buddhism, one who is able to reach nirvana but delays doing so in order to help suffering beings.

bod·ice /bódis/ *n.* **1** the part of a woman's dress above the waist. **2** a woman's vest, esp. a laced vest worn as an outer garment.

bod·i·ly /bód'lee/ *adj. & adv.* • *adj.* of or concerning the body. • *adv.* **1** as a whole (*threw them bodily*). **2** as a person.

bod·kin /bódkin/ *n.* **1** a blunt thick needle with a large eye. **2** a long pin for fastening hair. **3** a small pointed instrument.

bod·y /bódee/ *n. & v.* • *n.* (*pl.* **-ies**) **1** the physical structure, including the bones, flesh, and organs, of a person or an animal. **2** the trunk apart from the head and the limbs. **3 a** the main or central part of a thing (*body of the car*). **b** the majority (*body of opinion*). **4 a** a group of persons regarded collectively (*governing body*). **b** (usu. foll. by *of*) a collection (*body of facts*). **5** a quantity (*body of water*). **6** a piece of matter (*heavenly body*). **7** *colloq.* a person. **8** a substantial quality of flavor, tone, etc. • *v.tr.* (**-ies, -ied**) (usu. foll. by *forth*) give body or substance to. □□ **-bodied** *adj.* (in *comb.*) (*able-bodied*).

bod·y·build·ing /bódeebílding/ *n.* the practice of strengthening the body, esp. enlarging the muscles, by exercise.

bod·y·guard /bódeegaard/ *n.* a person or group of persons escorting and protecting another person.

bod·y lan·guage *n.* the process of communicating through conscious or unconscious gestures and poses.

bod·y pol·i·tic *n.* the nation or government as a corporate body.

bod·y shop *n.* a workshop where repairs to the bodies of vehicles are carried out.

bod·y stock·ing *n.* a woman's undergarment that covers the torso and legs.

bod·y·suit /bódeesoot/ *n.* a close-fitting one-piece stretch garment for women.

bod·y·work /bódeewərk/ *n.* the outer shell of a vehicle.

Boer /bōr, bawr/ *n.* a South African of Dutch descent.

bog /bog, bawg/ *n.* & *v.* •*n.* **1** wet spongy ground. **2** a stretch of such ground. •*v.tr.* (**bogged, bogging**) (foll. by *down*; usu. in *passive*) impede (*bogged down by difficulties*). ▫▫ **bog·gy** *adj.* (**boggier, boggiest**). **bog·gi·ness** *n.*

bo·gey[1] /bṓgee/ *n.* (*pl.* **-geys**) *Golf* a score of one stroke more than par for any hole.

bo·gey[2] /bṓgee/ *n.* (also **bo·gy**) (*pl.* **-geys** or **-gies**) **1** an evil spirit. **2** an awkward thing or circumstance.

bo·gey·man /bóogeeman, bṓgee-, bóogee-/ *n.* (also **bo·gy·man, boog·ey·man, boog·ie·man**) (*pl.* **-men**) a person (real or imaginary) causing fear or difficulty.

bog·gle /bógəl/ *v.intr. colloq.* **1** be baffled (esp. *the mind boggles*). **2** (usu. foll. by *about, at*) hesitate.

bo·gus /bṓgəs/ *adj.* sham; spurious. ▫▫ **bo·gus·ly** *adv.* **bo·gus·ness** *n.*

bo·gy·man var. of BOGEYMAN.

Bo·he·mi·an /bōhéemeeən/ *n.* & *adj.* •*n.* **1** a native of Bohemia, a former kingdom in central Europe corresponding to part of the modern Czech Republic; Czech. **2** (also **bohemian**) a socially unconventional person. •*adj.* **1** of or characteristic of Bohemia or its people. **2** socially unconventional.

boil[1] /boyl/ *v.* & *n.* •*v.* **1** *intr.* **a** (of a liquid) start to bubble up and turn into vapor; reach a temperature at which this happens. **b** (of a vessel) contain boiling liquid (*the kettle is boiling*). **2 a** *tr.* bring (a liquid or vessel) to a temperature at which it boils. **b** *tr.* cook (food) by boiling. **c** *intr.* (of food) be cooked by boiling. **d** *tr.* subject to the heat of boiling water, e.g., to clean. **3** *intr.* **a** (of the sea, etc.) undulate or seethe like boiling water. **b** (of a person or feelings) be agitated by anger. •*n.* the act or process of boiling; boiling point (*at a boil*). ▫ **boil down 1** reduce volume by boiling. **2** reduce to essentials. **3** (foll. by *to*) is basically. **boil over 1** spill over in boiling. **2** lose one's temper.

boil[2] /boyl/ *n.* an inflamed pus-filled swelling caused by infection of a hair follicle, etc.

boil·er /bóylər/ *n.* **1** a fuel-burning apparatus for heating a hot water supply. **2** a tank for heating water to steam under pressure.

boil·ing /bóyling/ *adj.* (also **boil·ing hot**) *colloq.* very hot.

boil·ing point /bóyling poynt/ *n.* the temperature at which a liquid starts to boil.

bois·ter·ous /bóystərəs/ *adj.* **1** (of a person) rough; noisily exuberant. **2** (of the weather, etc.) stormy. ▫▫ **bois·ter·ous·ly** *adv.* **bois·ter·ous·ness** *n.*

bok choy /bok chóy/ *n.* a Chinese vegetable resembling cabbage.

bo·la /bṓlə/ *n.* (also **bo·las**) (esp. in S. America) a weapon consisting of a number of balls connected by strong cord, thrown to entangle the limbs of the quarry.

bold /bōld/ *adj.* **1** confidently assertive; adventurous. **2** impudent. **3** vivid; distinct (*bold colors*). **4** *Printing* (in full **boldface** or **-faced**) printed in a thick black typeface. ▫▫ **bold·ly** *adv.* **bold·ness** *n.*

bo·le·ro /bōláirō, bə-/ *n.* (*pl.* **-ros**) **1** a Spanish dance or music in simple triple time. **2** a woman's short open jacket.

boll /bōl/ *n.* a rounded capsule containing seeds, esp. flax or cotton.

bol·lard /bólərd/ *n.* a short post on a wharf or ship for securing a rope.

boll wee·vil *n.* a small American or Mexican weevil, *Anthonomus grandis*, whose larvae destroy cotton bolls.

bo·lo·gna /bəlṓnee, -nyə/ *n.* a large smoked sausage made of beef, veal, pork, and other meats, and sold ready for eating.

bo·lom·e·ter /bōlómitər/ *n.* a sensitive electrical instrument for measuring radiant energy. ▫▫ **bo·lo·met·ric** /bṓləmétrik/ *adj.*

bo·lo·ney var. of BALONEY.

Bol·she·vik /bṓlshəvik, ból-/ *n.* **1** *hist.* a member of the radical faction of the Russian Social Democratic party, which became the Communist party in 1918. **2** a Russian communist. **3** (in general use) any revolutionary socialist. ▫▫ **Bol·she·vism** *n.* **Bol·she·vist** *n.*

bol·ster /bṓlstər/ *n.* & *v.* •*n.* **1** a long thick pillow. **2** a pad or support, esp. in a machine. •*v.tr.* (usu. foll. by *up*) **1** reinforce (*bolstered our morale*). **2** prop up.

bolt[1] /bōlt/ *n.*, *v.*, & *adv.* •*n.* **1** a sliding bar and socket used to fasten a door, etc. **2** a large usu. metal pin with a head, used to hold things together. **3** a discharge of lightning. **4** a sudden escape for freedom. **5** an arrow for shooting from a crossbow. **6** a roll of fabric (orig. as a measure). •*v.* **1** *tr.* fasten or lock with a bolt. **2** *tr.* (foll. by *in, out*) keep from leaving or entering by bolting a door. **3** *tr.* fasten together with bolts. **4** *intr.* dash suddenly away. **5** *tr.* gulp down (food) unchewed. **6** *intr.* (of a plant) go to seed. •*adv.* (usu. in **bolt upright**) rigidly; stiffly. ▫ **a bolt from the blue** a complete surprise. ▫▫ **bolt·er** *n.* (in sense 4 of *v.*).

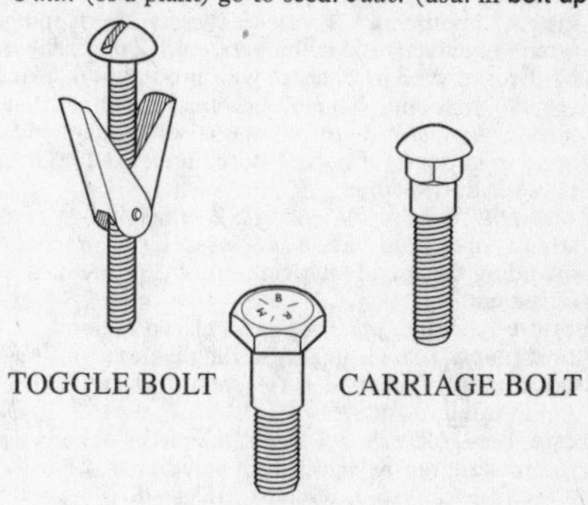

bolt, 2

bolt[2] /bōlt/ *v.tr.* sift (flour, etc.).

bomb /bom/ *n.* & *v.* •*n.* **1 a** a container with explosive gas, etc., designed to explode on impact or by means of a mechanism, lit fuse, etc. **b** an ordinary object fitted with an explosive device (*letter bomb*). **2** (prec. by *the*) the atomic or hydrogen bomb. **3** *colloq.* a failure (esp. a theatrical one). •*v.* **1** *tr.* drop bombs on. **2** *intr.* throw bombs. **4** *intr. sl.* fail badly. **5** *intr. colloq.* go very quickly.

bom·bard /bombaárd/ *v.tr.* **1** attack with heavy guns or bombs. **2** (often foll. by *with*) subject to persistent questioning, etc. **3** *Physics* direct a stream of high-speed particles at (a substance). □□ **bom·bard·ment** *n.*

bom·bar·dier /bómbərdéer/ *n.* a member of a bomber crew responsible for sighting and releasing bombs.

bom·bast /bómbast/ *n.* pompous or extravagant language. □□ **bom·bas·tic** /-bástik/ *adj.* **bom·bas·ti·cal·ly** *adv.*

bombe /bonb/ *n. Cooking* a dome-shaped dish or confection, freq. frozen.

bomb·er /bómər/ *n.* **1** an aircraft equipped to carry and drop bombs. **2** a person using bombs, esp. illegally.

bomb·er jack·et *n.* a short esp. leather jacket tightly gathered at the waist and cuffs.

bomb·shell /bómshel/ *n.* **1** an overwhelming surprise or disappointment. **2** an artillery bomb. **3** *sl.* a very attractive woman (*blonde bombshell*).

bo·na fide /bṓnə fīd, fīdee, bónə/ *adj. & adv.* • *adj.* genuine; sincere. • *adv.* genuinely; sincerely.

bo·na fides /bónaa féedes, fīdeez, bónə, (*esp.* for 2) bṓnə fīdz/ *n.* **1** esp. *Law* an honest intention; sincerity. **2** (as *pl.*) *colloq.* documentary evidence of acceptability.

bo·nan·za /bənánzə/ *n.* **1** a source of wealth or prosperity. **2** a large output (esp. of a mine). **3 a** prosperity; good luck. **b** a run of good luck.

bon·bon /bónbon/ *n.* a piece of candy, esp. with a chocolate or fondant coating.

bond /bond/ *n. & v.* • *n.* **1 a** a thing that ties another down or together. **b** (usu. in *pl.*) a thing restraining bodily freedom (*broke his bonds*). **2** (often in *pl.*) **a** a uniting force (*sisterly bond*). **b** a restraint; a responsibility (*bonds of duty*). **3** a binding engagement (*his word is his bond*). **4** *Commerce* a debenture. **5** adhesiveness. **6** *Law* a deed by which a person is bound to make payment to another. • *v.* **1** *tr.* **a** lay (bricks) overlapping. **b** bind together (resin with fibers, etc.). **2** *intr.* adhere; hold together. **3** *tr.* connect with a bond. **4** *tr.* place (goods) in bond. **5 a** *intr.* become emotionally attached. **b** *tr.* link by an emotional or psychological bond. □ **in bond** (of goods) stored until the importer pays the duty owing.

bond·age /bóndij/ *n.* **1** slavery. **2** subjection to constraint, obligation, etc. **3** sadomasochistic practices, including the use of physical restraints or mental enslavement.

bond·ed /bóndid/ *adj.* (of goods) placed in bond.

bond pa·per *n.* high-quality writing paper.

bonds·man /bóndzmən/ *n.* (*pl.* **-men**) **1** a slave. **2** a person in thrall to another.

bone /bōn/ *n. & v.* • *n.* **1** any of the pieces of hard tissue making up the skeleton in vertebrates. **2** (in *pl.*) **a** the skeleton, esp. as remains after death. **b** the body, esp. as a seat of intuitive feeling (*felt it in my bones*). **3 a** the material of which bones consist. **b** a similar substance such as ivory. **4** a thing made of bone. **5** (in *pl.*) the essential part of a thing (*the bare bones*). **6** (in *pl.*) **a** dice. **b** flat bone or wood clappers held between the fingers and used as a simple rhythm instrument. **7** a strip of stiffening in a corset, etc. • *v.tr.* **1** take out the bones from (meat or fish). **2** stiffen (a garment) with bone, etc. □ **bone up** (often foll. by *on*) *colloq.* study (a subject) intensively. **have a bone to pick** (usu. foll. by *with*) have a cause for dispute (with another person). **make no bones about 1** admit or allow without fuss. **2** not hesitate or scruple. □□ **bone·less** *adj.*

bone chi·na *n.* fine china made of clay mixed with the ash from bones.

bone-dry *adj.* quite dry.

bone·head /bṓnhed/ *n. sl.* a stupid person. □□ **bone·head·ed** *adj.*

bone·meal /bṓnmeel/ *n.* crushed or ground bones used esp. as a fertilizer.

bone of con·ten·tion *n.* a source or ground of dispute.

bon·er /bṓnər/ *n. sl.* **1** a stupid mistake. **2** *coarse sl.* an erection of the penis.

bon·fire /bónfīr/ *n.* a large open-air fire.

bong /bong, bawng/ *n.* a water pipe for smoking marijuana or the like.

bon·go /bónggō/ *n.* (*pl.* **-gos** or **-goes**) either of a pair of small connected drums usu. held between the knees and played with the fingers.

bon·ho·mie /bónəmée/ *n.* good-natured friendliness. □□ **bon·ho·mous** *adj.*

bo·ni·to /bənéetō/ *n.* (*pl.* **-tos**) any of several fish similar to the tuna and striped like mackerel.

bonk /bongk/ *v. & n.* • *v.* **1** *tr.* hit sharply. **2** *intr.* bang; bump. • *n.* an instance of bonking (*a bonk on the head*).

bon·kers /bóngkərz/ *adj. sl.* crazy.

bon mot /bawn mṓ/ *n.* (*pl.* **bons mots** *pronunc.* same or /-mṓz/) a witty saying.

bon·net /bónit/ *n.* **1 a** a woman's or child's hat tied under the chin and usu. with a brim framing the face. **b** a soft round brimless hat like a beret worn by men and boys in Scotland. **c** *colloq.* any hat. **2** *Brit.* a hinged cover over the engine of a motor vehicle; a hood. **3** the ceremonial feathered headdress of a Native American.

bon·sai /bónsī, -zī/ *n.* (*pl.* same) **1** the art of cultivating ornamental artificially dwarfed varieties of trees and shrubs. **2** a tree or shrub grown by this method.

bo·nus /bṓnəs/ *n.* **1** an unsought or unexpected extra benefit. **2** a gratuity to employees beyond their normal pay.

bon vi·vant /báwn veevaán/ *n.* (*pl.* **bon vivants** or **bons vivants** *pronunc.* same) a person indulging in good living.

bon vo·yage /báwn vwaayaázh/ *int.* an expression of good wishes to a departing traveler.

bon·y /bṓnee/ *adj.* (**bonier, boniest**) **1** (of a person) thin with prominent bones. **2** having many bones. **3** of or like bone. **4** (of a fish) having bones rather than cartilage. □□ **bon·i·ness** *n.*

boo /boo/ *int., n., & v.* • *int.* **1** an expression of disapproval. **2** a sound intended to surprise. • *n.* an utterance of *boo*, esp. as an expression of disapproval to a performer, etc. • *v.* (**boos, booed**) **1** *intr.* utter a boo or boos. **2** *tr.* jeer at (a performer, etc.) by booing.

boob[1] /boob/ *n.* a simpleton.

boob[2] /boob/ *n. sl.* a woman's breast.

boo·boo /bóoboo/ *n. sl.* **1** a mistake. **2** (esp. by or to a child) a minor injury.

boob tube *n. sl.* (usu. prec. by *the*) television; one's television set.

boo·by /bóobee/ *n.* (*pl.* **-bies**) **1** a stupid person. **2** a small gannet of the genus *Sula*.

boo·by prize *n.* a prize given to the least successful competitor in a contest.

boo·by trap *n. & v.* • *n.* **1** a trap intended as a practical joke; e.g., an object placed on top of a door. **2** *Mil.* an apparently harmless device intended to kill or injure anyone touching it. • *v.tr.* (**booby-trap**) (**-trapped, -trapping**) place a booby trap or traps in or on.

boog·ey·man var. of BOGEYMAN.

boog·ie /bóogee/ *v. & n.* • *v.intr.* (**boogies, boogied, boogying**) *sl.* **1** dance to rock music. **2** leave, esp. quickly. • *n.* **1** = BOOGIE-WOOGIE. **2** *sl.* a dance to rock music.

boog·ie·man var. of BOGEYMAN.

boog·ie-woog·ie /bóogeewóogee, bóogeewóogee/ *n.* a style of playing blues or jazz on the piano, marked by a persistent bass rhythm.

book /book/ *n. & v.* • *n.* **1 a** a written or printed work consisting of pages fixed together along one side and bound in covers. **b** a literary composition intended for publication (*is working on her book*). **2** a bound set of blank sheets for writing on. **3** a set of tickets, stamps, matches, checks, etc., bound up together. **4** (in *pl.*) a set of records or accounts. **5** a main division of a literary work, or of the Bible. **6** a libretto, script of a play, etc. **7** *colloq.* a magazine. **8** a telephone directory. **9** a record of bets made and money paid out at a racetrack by a bookmaker. • *v.* **1** *tr.* **a** engage (a seat, etc.) in advance; make a reservation for. **b** engage (a guest, etc.) for some occasion. **2** *tr.* **a** take the personal details of (esp. a criminal offender). **b** enter in a book or list. **3** *tr.* issue an airline, etc., ticket to. **4** *intr.* make a reservation (*no need to book*). □ **go by the book** proceed according to the rules. **in my book** in my opinion. **make book** take bets and pay out winnings on a race, game, etc. **one for the books** an event worthy of being recorded. **on the books** contained in a list of members, etc. **throw the book at** *colloq.* charge or punish to the utmost.

book·bind·er /bŏŏkbīndər/ *n.* a person who binds books professionally. □□ **book·bind·ing** *n.*

book·case /bŏŏk-kays/ *n.* a set of shelves for books in the form of a cabinet.

booked *adj.* (also **booked up**) with all places reserved.

book·end /bŏŏkend/ *n.* a usu. ornamental prop used to keep a row of books upright.

book·ie /bŏŏkee/ *n. colloq.* = BOOKMAKER.

book·ing /bŏŏking/ *n.* the act or an instance of booking or reserving a seat, a room in a hotel, etc.; a reservation (see BOOK *v.* 1).

book·ish /bŏŏkish/ *adj.* **1** studious; fond of reading. **2** acquiring knowledge from books. **3** (of language, etc.) literary. □□ **book·ish·ly** *adv.* **book·ish·ness** *n.*

book·keep·er /bŏŏk-keepər/ *n.* a person who keeps accounts for a business, etc. □□ **book·keep·ing** *n.*

book learn·ing *n.* theory, as opposed to practical knowledge.

book·let /bŏŏklit/ *n.* a small book, usu. paperback.

book·mak·er /bŏŏkmaykər/ *n.* a person who takes bets, calculates odds, and pays out winnings. □□ **book·mak·ing** *n.*

book·mark /bŏŏkmaark/ *n.* a strip of card, etc., used to mark one's place in a book.

book·plate /bŏŏkplayt/ *n.* a decorative label stuck in the front of a book bearing the owner's name.

book·sell·er /bŏŏkselər/ *n.* a dealer in books.

book·shop /bŏŏkshop/ *n.* esp. *Brit.* = BOOKSTORE.

book·store /bŏŏkstawr/ *n.* a store where books are sold.

book val·ue *n.* the value of a commodity as entered in a book of accounts (opp. *market value*).

book·worm /bŏŏkwərm/ *n.* **1** *colloq.* a person devoted to reading. **2** the larva of a moth or beetle that feeds on the paper and glue used in books.

Bool·e·an /bŏŏleeən/ *adj.* denoting a system of algebraic notation to represent logical propositions.

Bool·e·an log·ic *n.* the use of the logical operators 'and,' 'or,' and 'not' in retrieving information from a computer database.

boom[1] /bōōm/ *n.* & *v.* • *n.* a deep resonant sound. • *v.tr.* make or speak with a boom.

boom[2] /bōōm/ *n.* & *v.* • *n.* a period of prosperity or sudden activity in commerce. • *v.intr.* be suddenly prosperous or successful.

boom[3] /bōōm/ *n.* **1** *Naut.* a pivoted spar to which the foot of a sail is attached, allowing the angle of the sail to be changed. **2** a long pole over a movie or television stage set, carrying microphones, cameras, etc.

boom box *n. sl.* a portable radio, often with a cassette and/or CD player.

boo·mer·ang /bōōmərang/ *n.* & *v.* • *n.* a curved flat missile used by Australian Aboriginals to kill prey, and often able to return to the thrower. • *v.intr.* **1** act as a boomerang. **2** (of a plan or action) backfire.

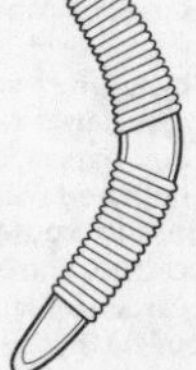

boomerang

boom town *n.* a town undergoing sudden growth due to a boom.

boon[1] /bōōn/ *n.* an advantage; a blessing.

boon[2] /bōōn/ *adj.* intimate; favorite (usu. *boon companion*).

boon·docks /bōōndoks/ *n.pl. sl.* rough, remote, or isolated country.

boon·dog·gle /bōōndogəl, -daw-/ *n.* **1** work or activity that is wasteful or pointless but gives the appearance of having value. **2** a public project of questionable merit that typically involves political patronage and graft.

boon·ies /bōōneez/ *n.pl.* (prec. by *the*) *sl.* = BOONDOCKS.

boor /bŏŏr/ *n.* a rude clumsy person. □□ **boor·ish** *adj.* **boor·ish·ly** *adv.* **boor·ish·ness** *n.*

boost /bōōst/ *v.* & *n.* • *v.tr.* **1 a** promote (a person, scheme, commodity, etc.) by praise or advertising; increase or assist (*boosted his spirits; boost sales*). **b** push from below (*boosted me up into the tree*). **2 a** raise the voltage of (an electric circuit, etc.). **b** amplify (a radio signal). • *n.* an act, process, or result of boosting; a push.

boost·er /bōōstər/ *n.* **1** a device for increasing electrical power or voltage. **2** an auxiliary engine or rocket used to give initial acceleration. **3** *Med.* a dose of an immunizing agent renewing the effect of an earlier one.

boost·er ca·bles *n.pl.* = JUMPER CABLES.

boot[1] /bōōt/ *n.* & *v.* • *n.* **1** an outer covering for the foot, reaching above the ankle. **2** *colloq.* a firm kick. **3** (prec. by *the*) *colloq.* dismissal (*gave them the boot*). **4** *Mil.* a navy or marine recruit. • *v.tr.* **1** kick, esp. hard. **2** (often foll. by *out*) dismiss (a person) forcefully. **3** (usu. foll. by *up*) put (a computer) in a state of readiness (cf. BOOTSTRAP 2). □□ **boot·ed** *adj.*

boot[2] /bōōt/ *n.* □ **to boot** as well; to the good.

boot camp *n. Mil.* a camp for training navy or marine recruits.

boot·ee /bōōtee/ *n.* (also **boot·ie**) **1** a soft shoe worn by a baby. **2** a woman's short boot.

booth /bōōth/ *n.* (*pl.* **booths** /bōō<u>th</u>z, bōōths/) **1** a small temporary roofed structure used esp. for the sale or display of goods at a market, fair, etc. **2** a compartment for various purposes, e.g., telephoning or voting. **3** a set of a table and benches in a restaurant or bar.

boot·jack /bōōtjak/ *n.* a device for holding a boot by the heel to ease withdrawal of the leg.

boot·lace /bōōtlays/ *n.* a cord or leather thong for lacing boots.

boot·leg /bōōtleg/ *adj.*, *v.*, & *n.* • *adj.* (esp. of liquor) smuggled; illicitly sold. • *v.tr.* (**-legged, -legging**) make, distribute, or smuggle (illicit goods, esp. alcohol, computer software, etc.). • *n.* **1** illicitly made or sold liquor. **2** an illicitly made recording. □□ **boot·leg·ger** *n.*

boot·less /bōōtlis/ *adj.* unavailing; useless.

boot·lick·er /bōōtlikər/ *n. colloq.* a person who behaves obsequiously.

boot·strap /bōōtstrap/ *n.* **1** a loop at the back of a boot used to pull it on. **2** *Computing* a technique of loading a program through a few initial instructions that enable the introduction of the rest of the program from an input device.

boo·ty /bōōtee/ *n.* **1** plunder gained esp. in war or by piracy. **2** *colloq.* something gained or won.

booze /bōōz/ *n.* & *v. colloq.* • *n.* **1** alcohol, esp. hard liquor. **2** the drinking of this (*nights lost to booze*). • *v.intr.*

drink alcohol, esp. excessively or habitually. ▫▫ **booz·er** *n.*

bop[1] /bop/ *n.* = BEBOP.

bop[2] /bop/ *v. & n. colloq.* • *v.tr.* (**bopped, bopping**) hit; punch lightly. • *n.* a light blow or hit.

bor·age /báwrij, bór-/ *n.* any plant of the genus *Borago,* esp. *Borago officinalis,* native to Europe, with bright blue flowers and leaves used as flavoring.

bo·rate /báwrayt/ *n.* a salt or ester of boric acid.

bo·rax /báwraks/ *n.* **1** the mineral salt sodium borate. **2** the purified form of this, used in making glass and china, and as an antiseptic. ▫▫ **bo·rac·ic** /bərásik/ *adj.*

bor·del·lo /bawrdélō/ *n.* (*pl.* **-los**) a brothel.

bor·der /báwrdər/ *n. & v.* • *n.* **1** the edge or boundary of anything, or the part near it. **2 a** the line separating two political or geographical areas, esp. countries. **b** the district on each side of this. **3** a distinct edging around anything, esp. for strength or decoration. **4** a long narrow bed of flowers or shrubs. • *v.* **1** *tr.* be a border to. **2** *tr.* provide with a border. **3** *intr.* (usu. foll. by *on, upon*) **a** adjoin; come close to being. **b** approximate; resemble.

bord·er·land /báwrdərland/ *n.* **1** the district near a border. **2** an intermediate condition between two extremes. **3** an area for debate.

bord·er·line /báwrdərlīn/ *n. & adj.* • *n.* **1** the line dividing two (often extreme) conditions. **2** a line marking a boundary. • *adj.* **1** on the borderline. **2** verging on an extreme condition; only just acceptable.

bore[1] /bawr/ *v. & n.* • *v.* **1** *tr.* make a hole in, esp. with a revolving tool. **2** *tr.* hollow out (a tube, etc.). **3** *tr.* make (a hole) by boring or excavation. **4** *intr.* drill a well, mine, etc. • *n.* **1** the hollow of a firearm barrel or of a cylinder in an internal combustion engine. **2** the caliber of this. **3** ; eq BOREHOLE.

bore[2] /bawr/ *n. & v.* • *n.* a tiresome or dull person or thing. • *v.tr.* weary by tedious talk or dullness. ▫▫ **bore·dom** *n.*

bore[3] *past* of BEAR[1].

bo·re·al /báwreeəl/ *adj.* of the north or northern regions.

bore·hole /báwrhōl/ *n.* a deep narrow hole, esp. one made in the earth to find water, oil, etc.

bor·er /báwrər/ *n.* **1** any of several worms, mollusks, insects, or insect larvae that bore into wood, other plant material, or rock. **2** a tool for boring.

bo·ric /báwrik/ *adj.* of or containing boron.

bo·ric ac·id *n.* an acid derived from borax, used as a mild antiseptic and in the manufacture of heat-resistant glass and enamels.

bor·ing /báwring/ *adj.* that makes one bored; dull. ▫▫ **bor·ing·ly** *adv.* **bor·ing·ness** *n.*

born /bawrn/ *adj.* **1** existing as a result of birth. **2 a** being such or likely to become such by natural ability or quality (*a born leader*). **b** (usu. foll. by *to* + infin.) having a specified destiny (*born to lose*). **3** (in *comb.*) of a certain status by birth (*French-born*). ▫ **in all one's born days** *colloq.* in one's life so far. **not born yesterday** *colloq.* not stupid; shrewd.

▶**Born** refers to birth (e.g., *born in Detroit in 1947*). **Borne**, meaning 'carried,' is used in the expression *borne by* followed by the name of the mother (e.g., *the baby borne by Sarah*), as well as in other senses (e.g., *a litter borne by slaves*).

born-a·gain *attrib.*adj. converted (esp. to fundamentalist Christianity).

borne /bawrn/ **1** *past part.* of BEAR[1]. **2** (in *comb.*) carried or transported by (*airborne*).

bo·ron /báwron/ *n. Chem.* a nonmetallic brown amorphous element extracted from borax and boric acid and mainly used for hardening steel. ¶ Symb.: **B**.

bo·ro·sil·i·cate /báwrōsílikit, –kayt/ *n.* any of many substances containing boron, silicon, and oxygen generally used in glazes and enamels and in the production of glass.

bor·ough /bə́rō, búrō/ *n.* **1** an incorporated municipality in certain states. **2** each of five political divisions of New York City. **3** (in Alaska) a county equivalent.

bor·row /bórō, báwrō/ *v.* **1 a** *tr.* acquire temporarily with the promise or intention of returning. **b** *intr.* obtain money in this way. **2** *tr.* use (an idea, etc.) originated by another. ▫▫ **bor·row·er** *n.* **bor·row·ing** *n.*

bor·rowed time *n.* an unexpected extension, esp. of life (*living on borrowed time*).

borscht /bawrsht/ *n.* (also **borsch** /bawrsh, bawrshch/) a highly seasoned Russian or Polish soup of esp. beets and cabbage and served with sour cream.

bor·zoi /báwrzoy/ *n.* a large Russian wolfhound of a breed with a narrow head and silky, usu. white, coat.

bos·cage /bóskij/ *n.* (also **bos·kage**) **1** a mass of trees or shrubs. **2** a wood or thicket.

bo's'n var. of BOATSWAIN.

bos·om /bŏŏzəm/ *n.* **1 a** a person's breast or chest, esp. a woman's. **b** *colloq.* each of a woman's breasts. **c** the enclosure formed by a person's breast and arms. **2** an emotional center.

boss[1] /baws, bos/ *n. & v.* • *n.* **1** a person in charge. **2** a person who controls or dominates a political organization. • *v.tr.* **1** (usu. foll. by *around*) give constant peremptory orders to. **2** be the master or manager of. ▫▫ **boss·y** *adj.* (**bossier, bossiest**) *colloq.* **boss·i·ly** *adv.* **boss·i·ness** *n.*

boss[2] /baws, bos/ *n.* **1** a round knob or other protuberance, esp. in ornamental work. **2** *Archit.* a piece of ornamental carving, etc., covering the point where the ribs in a vault or ceiling cross.

bos·sa no·va /bósə nṓvə, báwsə/ *n.* **1** a dance like the samba, originating in Brazil. **2** a piece of music for this or in its rhythm.

bo·sun (also **bo'sun**) var. of BOATSWAIN.

bot·a·ny /bót'nee/ *n.* **1** the study of plants. **2** the plant life of a particular area or time. ▫▫ **bo·tan·ic** /bətánik/ *adj.* **bo·tan·i·cal** *adj.* **bo·tan·i·cal·ly** *adv.* **bot·a·nist** /bót'nist/ *n.*

botch /boch/ *v. & n.* • *v.tr.* **1** bungle. **2** repair clumsily. • *n.* bungled or spoiled work (*made a botch of it*). ▫▫ **botch·er** *n.*

bot·fly /bótflī/ *n.* (*pl.* **-flies**) any dipterous fly of the genus *Oestrus,* with a stout hairy body.

both /bōth/ *adj., pron., & adv.* • *adj. & pron.* the two; not only one (*both boys; the boys are both here*).

▶Widely used with *of,* esp. when followed by a pronoun (e.g., *both of us*) or a noun implying separate rather than collective consideration, e.g., *both of the boys* suggests *each boy* rather than the two together. • *adv.* with equal truth in two cases (*both the boy and his sister are here*).

▶Avoid using **both** when you mean **each**: *Q: Would you like vanilla or chocolate? A: May I have a little of each?* (not "of both"); *Each child* (not "Both children") *claimed the toy.*

both·er /bóthər/ *v., n., & int.* • *v.* **1** *tr.* **a** worry; disturb. **b** *refl.* be concerned. **2** *intr.* **a** (often foll. by *to* + infin.) worry or trouble oneself (*don't bother about that*). **b** (foll. by *with*) be concerned. • *n.* **1 a** a person or thing that causes worry. **b** a minor nuisance. **2** trouble; fuss. • *int.* expressing annoyance or impatience. ▫ **cannot be bothered** will not make the effort needed.

both·er·some /bóthərsəm/ *adj.* troublesome.

bo-tree /bṓtree/ *n.* the Indian fig tree, *Ficus religiosa,* regarded as sacred by Buddhists.

bot·tle /bót'l/ *n. & v.* • *n.* **1** a container, usu. of glass or plastic and with a narrow neck, for storing liquid. **2** the amount that will fill a bottle. **3** a container used in feeding a baby (esp. formula or milk). 4 = HOT-WATER BOTTLE. •*v.tr.* 1 put into bottles or jars. 2 (foll. by *up*) **a** conceal or restrain for a time (esp. a feeling). **b** keep (an enemy force, etc.) contained or entrapped. □ **hit the bottle** *sl.* drink heavily.

bot·tle-feed *v.tr.* (*past* and *past part.* **-fed**) feed (a baby) with milk, formula, etc., by means of a bottle.

bot·tle·neck /bót'lnek/ *n.* 1 a point at which the flow of traffic, production, etc., is constricted. 2 a narrow place causing constriction.

bot·tle-nosed dol·phin /bót'l-nōzd/ *n.* a dolphin, *Tursiops truncatus*, with a bottle-shaped snout.

bot·tom /bótəm/ *n., adj., & v.* •*n.* 1 **a** the lowest point or part (*bottom of the stairs*). **b** the part on which a thing rests (*bottom of a frying pan*). **c** the underneath part (*scraped the bottom of the car*). **d** the farthest or innermost part (*bottom of the yard*). 2 *colloq.* **a** the buttocks. **b** the seat of a chair, etc. 3 **a** the less important or successful end of a class, etc. (*at the bottom of the list of requirements*). **b** a person occupying this place (*he's always the bottom of the class*). **c** *Baseball* the second half of an inning. 4 the basis (*he's at the bottom of it*). 5 the essential character. 6 *Naut.* a ship, esp. a cargo ship. •*adj.* 1 lowest (*bottom button*). 2 last (*got the bottom score*). •*v.* 1 *tr.* put a bottom on (a chair, pot, etc.). 2 *intr.* (of a ship) reach or touch the bottom. 3 *tr.* work out. 4 *tr.* (usu. foll. by *on*) base (an argument, etc.) (*reasoning bottomed on logic*). 5 *tr.* touch the bottom or lowest point of. □ **at bottom** basically; essentially. **bet one's bottom dollar** *sl.* stake everything. **bottom falls out** collapse occurs. **bottom out** reach the lowest level. **bottoms up!** a call to drain one's glass. **get to the bottom of** fully investigate and explain. □□ **bot·tom·most** /bótəm-mōst/ *adj.*

bot·tom·less /bótəmlis/ *adj.* 1 without a bottom. 2 (of a supply, etc.) inexhaustible.

bot·tom line *n. colloq.* the underlying or ultimate truth; the ultimate, esp. financial, criterion.

bot·u·lism /bóchəlizəm/ *n.* poisoning caused by a toxin produced by the bacillus *Clostridium botulinum* growing in spoiled food.

bou·clé /bōōkláy/ *n.* 1 a looped or curled yarn (esp. wool). 2 a fabric made of this.

bou·doir /bóódwaar/ *n.* a woman's private room or bedroom.

bouf·fant /bōōfaánt/ *adj.* (of a dress, hair, etc.) puffed out.

bou·gain·vil·le·a /bóógənvílyə, -veéə/ *n.* (also **bou·gain·vil·la·ea**) any widely cultivated tropical plant of the genus *Bougainvillaea*, with large colored bracts.

bough /bow/ *n.* a branch of a tree.

bought *past* and *past part.* of BUY.

bou·gie /bóózhee/ *n.* 1 *Med.* a thin flexible surgical instrument for exploring, dilating, etc. the passages of the body. 2 a wax candle.

bouil·la·baisse /bóólyəbés, bōōyəbáys/ *n. Cooking* a rich, spicy fish stew, orig. from Provence.

bouil·lon /bóólyən, -yon, bōōyóN/ *n.* a clear soup; broth.

boul·der /bốldər/ *n.* a large stone worn smooth by erosion.

boule[1] /bōōl/ *n.* (also **boules** *pronunc.* same) a French form of lawn bowling, played on rough ground with usu. metal balls.

bou·le[2] /bóólee/ *n.* a legislative body of an ancient Greek city or of modern Greece.

boules var. of BOULE[1].

boul·e·vard /bóóləvaard/ *n.* 1 a broad tree-lined avenue. 2 a broad main road.

bounce /bowns/ *v. & n.* •*v.* 1 **a** *intr.* (of a ball, etc.) rebound. **b** *tr.* cause to rebound. **c** *tr. & intr.* bounce repeatedly. 2 *intr. sl.* (of a check) be returned by a bank when there are insufficient funds to meet it. 3 *intr.* **a** (foll. by *about, up*) (of a person, dog, etc.) jump or spring energetically. **b** (foll. by *in, out*, etc.) rush angrily, enthusiastically, etc. (*bounced out in a fury*). •*n.* 1 **a** a rebound. **b** the power of rebounding. 2 *colloq.* **a** self-confidence (*has a lot of bounce*). **b** liveliness. □ **bounce back** regain one's good health, spirits, etc. □□ **bounc·y** *adj.* (**bouncier, bounciest**) **bounc·i·ly** *adv.* **bounc·i·ness** *n.*

bounc·er /bównsər/ *n. sl.* a person employed to eject troublemakers from a nightclub, etc.

bounc·ing /bównsing/ *adj.* 1 (esp. of a baby) big and healthy. 2 boisterous.

bound[1] /bownd/ *v. & n.* •*v.intr.* 1 **a** spring; leap (*bounded out of bed*). **b** move with leaping strides. 2 (of a ball, etc.) recoil; bounce. •*n.* 1 a leap. 2 a bounce.

bound[2] /bownd/ *n. & v.* •*n.* (usu. in *pl.*) 1 a restriction (*beyond the bounds of possibility*). 2 a boundary. •*v.tr.* 1 (esp. in *passive*; foll. by *by*) limit (*views bounded by prejudice*). 2 be the boundary of. □ **out of bounds** 1 outside designated limits, a restricted area, etc. 2 beyond what is acceptable.

bound[3] /bownd/ *adj.* 1 (usu. foll. by *for*) ready to start or having started (*bound for stardom*). 2 (in *comb.*) moving in a specified direction (*northbound*).

bound[4] /bownd/ *past* and *past part.* of BIND. □ **bound to** certain to (*he's bound to come*).

bound·a·ry /bówndəree, -dree/ *n.* (*pl.* **-ries**) a line marking the limits of an area, territory, etc.

bound·en du·ty /bówndən/ *n.* solemn responsibility.

bound·less /bówndlis/ *adj.* unlimited (*boundless enthusiasm*). □□ **bound·less·ly** *adv.* **bound·less·ness** *n.*

boun·te·ous /bównteeəs/ *adj. poet.* = BOUNTIFUL 1. □□ **boun·te·ous·ly** *adv.* **boun·te·ous·ness** *n.*

boun·ti·ful /bówntifōōl/ *adj.* 1 generous; liberal. 2 ample. □□ **boun·ti·ful·ly** *adv.*

boun·ty /bówntee/ *n.* (*pl.* **-ties**) 1 liberality. 2 a gift or reward, made usu. by a government.

boun·ty hunt·er *n.* a person who pursues a criminal or seeks an achievement for the sake of the reward.

bou·quet /bōōkáy, bō-/ *n.* 1 a bunch of flowers, esp. for carrying at a wedding or other ceremony. 2 the scent of wine, etc. 3 a favorable comment; a compliment.

bour·bon /bə́rbən/ *n.* whiskey distilled from corn and rye.

bour·geois /bóórzhwaá/ *adj. & n.* often *derog.* •*adj.* 1 **a** conventionally middle class. **b** unimaginative. **c** selfishly materialistic. 2 upholding the interests of the capitalist class. •*n.* (*pl.* same) a bourgeois person. □□ **bour·geoi·sie** /bóórzhwaázee/ *n.*

bourn /bawrn, bōōrn/ *n.* (also **bourne**) a small stream.

bourse /bōōrs/ *n.* 1 a stock exchange, esp. on the European continent. 2 a money market.

bout /bowt/ *n.* (often foll. by *of*) 1 a short period of intense activity of a specified kind (*a bout of strenuous exercise; a drinking bout*). 2 an attack of illness or strong emotion (*a severe bout of flu*). 3 **a** a wrestling or boxing match. **b** a trial or contest of strength.

bou·tique /bōōteék/ *n.* a small shop or department of a store, esp. one selling fashionable clothes or accessories.

bou·ton·niere /bóótəneér, -tənyáir/ *n.* (also **bou·ton·nière**) a flower or spray of flowers worn in a buttonhole.

bou·zou·ki /bōōzóókee/ *n.* a Greek form of mandolin.

bo·vine /bốvīn, -veen/ *adj.* 1 of or relating to cattle. 2 slow-moving; unimaginative. □□ **bo·vine·ly** *adv.*

bow[1] /bō/ *n. & v.* •*n.* 1 **a** a slipknot with a double loop. **b** a ribbon, shoelace, etc., tied with this. **c** a decoration in the form of a bow. 2 a device for shooting arrows with a taut string joining the ends of a curved piece of wood, etc. 3 a rod with horsehair stretched along its length, used for playing the violin, cello, etc. **4** a shallow curve or bend. • *v.tr.* (also *absol.*) use a bow on (a violin, etc.).

bow[2] /bow/ *v. & n.* • *v.* **1** *intr.* incline the head or trunk, in acknowledgment of applause, etc. **2** *intr.* submit (*bowed to the inevitable*). **3** *tr.* cause to incline or submit (*bowed his head; bowed his will to hers*). **4** *tr.* (foll. by *in, out*) usher or escort obsequiously. • *n.* an inclining of the head or body. □ **bow down 1** bend or kneel in submission or reverence. **2** (usu. in *passive*) crush (*was bowed down by care*). **bow out 1** make one's exit (esp. formally). **2** retire or retreat gracefully. **take a bow** acknowledge applause.

bow[3] /bow/ *n. Naut.* the forward end of a boat or ship.

bowd·ler·ize /bówdlərīz/ *v.tr.* expurgate (a book, etc.). □□ **bowd·ler·ism** *n.* **bowd·ler·i·za·tion** /-rizáyshən/ *n.*

bow·el /bówəl/ *n.* **1** the intestine. **2** (in *pl.*) the depths (*the bowels of the earth*).

bow·el move·ment *n.* discharge from the bowels.

bow·er /bówər/ *n. & v.* • *n.* **1** a secluded place enclosed by foliage; an arbor. **2** *poet.* a boudoir. • *v.tr. poet.* embower.

bow·er·bird /bówərbərd/ *n.* any of various birds of the Ptilonorhyncidae family, native to Australia and New Guinea, the males of which construct elaborate bowers of feathers, grasses, shells, etc., during courtship.

bow·er·y /bówəree, bówree/ *n.* (also **Bowery**) (*pl.* **-ies**) a district known as a neighborhood of drunks and derelicts.

bow·head /bṓhed/ *n.* an Arctic whale, *Balaena mysticetus.*

bow·ie /bṓōee, bṓ-/ *n.* (in full **bowie knife**) a long knife with a blade double-edged at the point.

bowl[1] /bōl/ *n.* **1 a** a usu. round deep basin used for food or liquid. **b** the quantity a bowl holds. **c** the contents of a bowl. **2 a** any deep-sided container shaped like a bowl (*toilet bowl*). **b** the bowl-shaped part of a tobacco pipe, spoon, balance, etc. **3** a bowl-shaped region or building, esp. an amphitheater (*Hollywood Bowl*). **4** *Sports* a post-season football game between invited teams or as a championship. □□ **bowl·ful** *n.* (*pl.* **-fuls**).

bowl[2] /bōl/ *n. & v.* • *n.* **1 a** a wooden or hard rubber ball, slightly asymmetrical, used in the game of lawn bowling. **b** a large ball with indents for gripping, used in tenpin bowling. **c** a wooden ball or disk used in playing skittles. **2** esp. *Brit.* (in *pl.*; usu. treated as *sing.*) lawn bowling. **3** a spell or turn of bowling in cricket. • *v.* **1 a** *tr.* roll (a hoop, etc.) along the ground. **b** *intr.* play lawn bowling or skittles. **2** *intr.* (often foll. by *along*) go along rapidly, esp. on wheels (*the cart bowled along the road*). □ **bowl over 1** knock down. **2** *colloq.* **a** impress greatly. **b** overwhelm. □□ **bowl·er** *n.*

bow·legs /bṓlegz/ *n.pl.* legs that curve outward at the knee. □□ **bow·leg·ged** /bṓlegid/ *adj.*

bowl·er /bṓlər/ *n.* (in full **bowler hat**) a man's hard felt hat with a round dome-shaped crown.

bow·line /bṓlin/ *n. Naut.* a knot for forming a non-slipping loop at the end of a rope.

bowl·ing /bṓling/ *n.* the games of tenpins, skittles, or bowls as a sport or recreation.

bowl·ing al·ley *n.* **1** a long, smooth, wooden lane for bowling. **2** a building containing a number of these.

bowl·ing ball *n.* a hard ball with holes drilled in it for gripping, used in tenpin bowling.

bowl·ing green *n.* a lawn used for playing bowls.

bow·man[1] /bṓmən/ *n.* (*pl.* **-men**) an archer.

bow·man[2] /bówmən/ *n.* (*pl.* **-men**) the rower nearest the bow of esp. a racing boat.

bow saw *n. Carpentry* a narrow saw stretched like a bowstring on a light frame.

bow·sprit /bówsprit/ *n. Naut.* a spar running out from a ship's bow for supporting various jibs or stays.

bow tie *n.* a necktie in the form of a bow (see BOW[1] *n.* 1a).

bow-wow /bów-wów/ *int. & n.* • *int.* an imitation of a dog's bark. • *n.* **1** *colloq.* a dog. **2** a dog's bark.

box[1] /boks/ *n. & v.* • *n.* **1** a container, usu. with flat sides and of firm material, esp. for holding solids. **2** the amount that will fill a box. **3** a separate compartment, e.g., in a theater. **4** an enclosure or receptacle for a special purpose (*cash box*). **5** a facility for receiving replies to an advertisement. **6** (prec. by *the*) *colloq.* television (*what's on the box?*). **7** a space or area of print on a page, enclosed by a border. **8** a protective casing for a piece of mechanism. **9** (prec. by *the*) *Soccer colloq.* the penalty area. **10** *Baseball* one of several areas occupied by the batter, catcher, pitcher, and first and third base coaches. • *v.tr.* **1** put in or provide with a box. **2** (foll. by *in, up*) confine. □□ **box·ful** *n.* (*pl.* **-fuls**). **box·like** *adj.*

box[2] /boks/ *v.* **1 a** *tr.* fight (an opponent) at boxing. **b** *intr.* practice boxing. **2** slap (esp. a person's ears).

box[3] /boks/ *n.* **1 a** any small evergreen tree or shrub of the genus *Buxus*, esp. *B. sempervirens*, often used in hedging. **b** any of various trees in Australasia, esp. those of several species of *Eucalyptus*. **2** = BOXWOOD.

box cam·er·a *n.* a simple box-shaped hand camera.

box·car /bókskaar/ *n.* an enclosed railroad freight car, usu. with sliding doors on the sides.

box el·der *n.* the American ash-leaved maple, *Acer negundo.*

box·er /bóksər/ *n.* **1** a person who practices boxing, esp. for sport. **2** a medium-sized dog of a breed with a smooth brown coat and puglike face.

box·er shorts *n.pl.* (also **box·ers**) men's underwear similar to shorts.

box·ing /bóksing/ *n.* the practice of fighting with the fists, esp. in padded gloves as a sport.

box·ing glove *n.* each of a pair of heavily padded gloves used in boxing.

box kite *n.* a kite in the form of a long box open at each end.

box lunch *n.* a lunch packed in a box.

box of·fice *n.* **1** an office for booking seats and buying tickets at a theater, movie theater, etc. **2** the commercial aspect of the arts and entertainment (often *attrib.*: *a box-office failure*).

box pleat *n.* a pleat consisting of two parallel creases forming a raised band.

box score *n. Sports* printed information about a game in which players for both teams are listed with statistics about their performances.

box seat *n.* a seat in a box enclosure, as at a theater, sports arena, etc.

box spring *n.* a set of vertical springs housed in a frame under a mattress or upholstered chair.

box·wood /bókswŏŏd/ *n.* **1** the wood of the box used esp. by engravers for the fineness of its grain and for its hardness. **2** = BOX[3] 1.

boy /boy/ *n. & int.* • *n.* **1** a male child or youth. **2** a young man. **3** a male servant, attendant, etc. **4** (**the boys**) *colloq.* a group of men mixing socially. • *int.* expressing pleasure, surprise, etc. □□ **boy·hood** *n.* **boy·ish** *adj.* **boy·ish·ly** *adv.* **boy·ish·ness** *n.*

boy·cott /bóykot/ *v. & n.* • *v.tr.* **1** combine in refusing relations with (a person, group, country, etc.). **2** refuse to handle (goods). • *n.* such a refusal.

boy·friend /bóyfrend/ *n.* a person's regular male companion or lover.

Boyle's law /boylz/ *n.* the law that the pressure of a given mass of gas is inversely proportional to its volume at a constant temperature.

boy scout *n.* **1** (also **Boy Scout**) a member of an organization of boys, esp. the Boy Scouts of America, that promotes character, outdoor activities, community service, etc. **2** a boy or man who demonstrates the qualities associated with a Boy Scout.

boy·sen·ber·ry /bóyzənberee/ *n.* (*pl.* **-ries**) **1** a hybrid of several species of bramble. **2** the large red edible fruit of this plant.

bo·zo /bṓzō/ *n.* (*pl.* **-zos**) *sl.* a stupid or obnoxious person.

BP *abbr.* **1** boiling point. **2** blood pressure. **3** before the present (era).

bps *abbr.* (also **BPS**) *Computing* bits per second.

Br *symb. Chem.* the element bromine.

bra /braa/ *n.* (*pl.* **bras**) *colloq.* = BRASSIERE.

brace /brays/ *n.* & *v.* • *n.* **1 a** a device that clamps or fastens tightly. **b** a strengthening piece of iron or lumber in building. **2** (in *pl.*) *Brit.* = SUSPENDER 1. **3** (in *pl.*) a wire device for straightening the teeth. **4** (*pl.* same) a pair. **5** a rope attached to the yard of a ship for trimming the sail. **6** a connecting mark { or } used in printing. • *v.tr.* **1** fasten tightly; give strength to. **2** make steady by supporting. **3** (esp. as **bracing** *adj.*) invigorate; refresh. **4** (often *refl.*) prepare for a difficulty, shock, etc. ▫▫ **brac·ing·ly** *adv.*

brace and bit *n.* a revolving tool with a D-shaped central handle for boring.

brace·let /bráyslit/ *n.* **1** an ornamental band, hoop, or chain worn on the wrist or arm. **2** *sl.* a handcuff.

brac·er /bráysər/ *n. colloq.* a tonic, esp. an alcoholic drink.

bra·chi·al /bráykeeəl, brák–/ *adj.* **1** of or relating to the arm (*brachial artery*). **2** like an arm.

bra·chi·ate /bráykeeit, –ayt, brák–/ *v.* & *adj.* • *v.intr.* (of certain apes and monkeys) move by using the arms to swing from branch to branch. • *adj. Biol.* **1** having arms. **2** having paired branches on alternate sides. ▫▫ **bra·chiation** /–áyshən/ *n.* **brachiator** *n.*

brace and bit

bra·chi·o·pod /bráykeeəpod, brák-/ *n.* any marine invertebrate of the phylum Brachiopoda (esp. a fossil one) having a bivalved shell and a ciliated feeding arm.

bra·chi·o·sau·rus /bráykeeəsáwrəs, brák-/ *n.* any huge plant-eating dinosaur of the genus *Brachiosaurus* with forelegs longer than its hind legs.

bra·chyl·o·gy /brəkíləjee/ *n.* (*pl.* **·gies**) **1** conciseness of expression. **2** an instance of this.

brack·en /brákən/ *n.* **1** any large coarse fern, esp. *Pteridium aquilinum*, abundant in tropical and temperate areas. **2** a mass of such ferns.

brack·et /brákit/ *n.* & *v.* • *n.* **1** a support attached to and projecting from a vertical surface. **2** a shelf fixed with such a support to a wall. **3** each of a pair of marks ( ) (**parentheses**), [ ] (**square brackets**) or (**angle brackets**) used to enclose words or figures. **4** a group classified as containing similar elements or falling between given limits (*income bracket*). • *v.tr.* (**bracketed, bracketing**) **1 a** combine (names, etc.) within brackets. **b** imply a connection or equality between. **2** enclose in brackets as parenthetic or spurious.

brack·ish /brákish/ *adj.* (of water, etc.) slightly salty.

bract /brakt/ *n.* a modified leaf, with a flower or an inflorescence in its axil.

brad /brad/ *n.* a thin flat nail with a head in the form of a slight enlargement at the top.

brad·y·car·di·a /brádikaárdeeə/ *n. Med.* abnormally slow heart action.

brag /brag/ *v.* & *n.* • *v.* (**bragged, bragging**) **1** *intr.* talk boastfully. **2** *tr.* boast about. • *n.* **1** a card game like poker. **2** a boastful statement; boastful talk.

brag·ga·do·ci·o /brágədṓsheeō/ *n.* empty boasting; a boastful manner of speech and behavior.

brag·gart /brágərt/ *n.* & *adj.* • *n.* a person given to bragging. • *adj.* boastful.

Brah·ma /braámə/ *n.* **1** the Hindu Creator. **2** the supreme divine reality in Hindu belief.

Brah·man[1] /braámən/ *n.* (also **brahman**) (*pl.* **-mans**) a member of the highest Hindu caste, whose members are traditionally eligible for the priesthood.

Brah·man[2] /bráymən, braámən/ *n.* (also **brahman**) any of various breeds of Indian cattle, esp. a US breed of humped, heat-resistant, grayish cattle.

brah·ma·pu·tra /braáməpṓōtrə/ *n.* **1** any bird of a large Asian breed of domestic fowl. **2** this breed.

Brah·min /braámin/ *n.* **1** = BRAHMAN. **2** (esp. in New England) a socially or culturally superior person.

braid /brayd/ *n.* & *v.* • *n.* **1** a woven band used for edging or trimming. **2** a length of hair, straw, etc. in three or more interlaced strands. • *v.tr.* **1** weave or intertwine (hair or thread). **2** trim or decorate with braid.

Braille /brayl/ *n.* a system of writing and printing for the blind, in which characters are represented by patterns of raised dots.

brain /brayn/ *n.* & *v.* • *n.* **1** an organ of soft nervous tissue contained in the skull of vertebrates, functioning as the coordinating center of sensation and of intellectual and nervous activity. **2** (in *pl.*) the substance of the brain, esp. as food. **3 a** a person's intellectual capacity (*has a weak brain*). **b** (often in *pl.*) intelligence; high intellectual capacity (*has a brain; has brains*). **c** *colloq.* a clever person. **4** (in *pl.*; prec. by *the*) *colloq.* **a** the cleverest person in a group. **b** a person who originates a complex plan or idea (*the brains behind the robbery*). **5** an electronic device with functions comparable to those of a brain. • *v.tr.* **1** dash out the brains of. **2** strike hard on the head. ▫ **on the brain** *colloq.* obsessively in one's thoughts.

brain death *n.* irreversible brain damage causing the end of independent respiration, regarded as indicative of death.

brain drain *n. colloq.* the loss of skilled personnel by emigration.

brain·pan /bráynpan/ *n. colloq.* the skull.

brain·pow·er /bráynpowr/ *n.* mental ability or intelligence.

brain stem *n.* the central trunk of the brain, upon which the cerebrum and cerebellum are set, and which continues downward to form the spinal cord.

brain·storm /bráynstawrm/ *n.* & *v.* • *n.* **1** a violent or excited outburst often as a result of a sudden mental disturbance. **2** a sudden bright idea. **3** a concerted intellectual treatment of a problem by discussing spontaneous ideas about it. • *v.intr.* discuss ideas spontaneously and openly.

brain·teas·er /bráynteezər/ *n. colloq.* a puzzle or problem.

brain trust *n.* a group of experts, official or unofficial, who advise on policy and strategy.

brain·wash /bráynwosh, -wawsh/ *v.tr.* subject (a person) to a prolonged process by which ideas at variance with those already held are implanted in the mind. ▫▫ **brain·wash·ing** *n.*

brain wave *n.* **1** (usu. in *pl.*) an electrical impulse in the brain. **2** *colloq.* = BRAINSTORM 3.

brain·y /bráynee/ *adj.* (**brainier, brainiest**) intellectually clever or active.

braise /brayz/ *v.tr.* fry lightly and then stew slowly with a little liquid in a closed container.

brake[1] /brayk/ *n.* & *v.* • *n.* **1** (often in *pl.*) a device for

checking the motion of a mechanism, esp. a wheel or vehicle, or for keeping it at rest. **2** anything that hinders something (*put a brake on their enthusiasm*). • *v.* **1** *intr.* apply a brake. **2** *tr.* retard or stop with a brake.
brake[2] /brayk/ *n.* **1** a toothed instrument for crushing flax and hemp. **2** (in full **brake harrow**) a heavy kind of harrow for breaking up large lumps of earth.
brake[3] *archaic past* of BREAK[1].
brake drum *n.* a cylinder attached to a wheel on which the brake shoe presses to brake.
brake horse·pow·er *n.* the power of an engine reckoned in terms of the force needed to brake it.
brake lin·ing *n.* a strip of material that increases the friction of the brake shoe.
brake·man /bráykmən/ *n.* (*pl.* **·men**) **1** a railroad worker responsible for maintenance on a journey. **2** a person in charge of brakes.
brake shoe *n.* a long curved block that presses on the brake drum to brake.
bram·ble /brámbəl/ *n.* **1** any of various thorny shrubs bearing fleshy red or black berries, esp. (*Brit.*) the blackberry bush, *Rubus fructicosus*. **2** any of various other rosaceous shrubs with similar foliage, esp. the dog rose (*Rosa canina*). ▫▫ **bram·bly** *adj.*
bran /bran/ *n.* grain husks separated from the flour.
branch /branch/ *n.* & *v.* • *n.* **1** a limb extending from a tree or bough. **2** a lateral extension or subdivision, esp. of a river or railroad. **3** a subdivision of a family, knowledge, etc. **4** a local division or office, etc., of a large business, library, etc. • *v.intr.* (often foll. by *off*) **1** diverge from the main part. **2** divide into branches. **3** (of a tree) bear or send out branches. ▫ **branch out** extend one's field of interest. ▫▫ **branched** *adj.* **branch·let** *n.*
brand /brand/ *n.* & *v.* • *n.* **1 a** a particular make of goods. **b** an identifying trademark, label, etc. **2** (usu. foll. by *of*) a special or characteristic kind (*brand of humor*). **3** an identifying mark burned on livestock, etc., with a hot iron. **4** an iron used for this. **5** a piece of burning, smoldering, or charred wood. **6** a stigma; a mark of disgrace. **7** *poet.* a torch. • *v.tr.* **1** mark with a hot iron. **2** stigmatize; mark with disgrace (*they branded him a liar; was branded for life*). **3** impress unforgettably on one's mind. **4** assign a trademark or label to.
brand·ish /brándish/ *v.tr.* wave as a threat or in display.
brand·ling /brándling/ *n.* a red earthworm, *Eisenia foetida*, with rings of a brighter color, which is often found in manure and used as bait.
brand-name *attrib.adj.* having an identifying trademark, label, etc., esp. one that is well-known.
brand-new *adj.* completely new.
bran·dy /brándee/ *n.* (*pl.* **-dies**) a strong alcoholic spirit distilled from wine or fermented fruit juice.
brash /brash/ *adj.* **1** vulgarly or overly self-assertive. **2** hasty; rash. **3** impudent. ▫▫ **brash·ly** *adv.* **brash·ness** *n.*
brass /bras/ *n.* & *adj.* • *n.* **1** a yellow alloy of copper and zinc. **2 a** a decorated piece of brass. **b** brass objects collectively. **3** *Mus.* brass wind instruments. **4** (in full **top brass**) *colloq.* persons in authority or of high rank. **5** *colloq.* effrontery (*then had the brass to demand money*). • *adj.* made of brass.
brass band *n.* a group of musicians playing brass instruments, sometimes also with percussion.
bras·se·rie /brásəree/ *n.* a restaurant, orig. one serving beer with food.
bras·si·ca /brásikə/ *n.* any cruciferous plant of the genus *Brassica*, having tap roots and erect branched stems, including cabbage, rutabaga, broccoli, etc.
bras·siere /brəzéer/ *n.* an undergarment worn by women to support the breasts.
brass knuck·les *n.pl.* a metal guard worn over the knuckles in fighting, esp. to increase the effect of the blows.
brass ring *n. sl.* an opportunity for wealth or success; a rich prize.
brass tacks *n.pl. sl.* actual details; real business (*get down to brass tacks*).
brass·y /brásee/ *adj.* (**brassier, brassiest**) **1** impudent. **2** pretentious; showy. **3** loud and blaring. **4** of or like brass. ▫▫ **brass·i·ly** *adv.* **brass·i·ness** *n.*
brat /brat/ *n.* usu. *derog.* a child, esp. a badly-behaved one. ▫▫ **brat·ty** *adj.*
brat·wurst /brátwərst, -vöorst/ *n.* a type of small pork sausage.
bra·va·do /brəvaádō/ *n.* a bold manner or a show of boldness.
brave /brayv/ *adj., n., & v.* • *adj.* **1** able or ready to face and endure danger or pain. **2** splendid (*make a brave show*). • *n.* a Native American warrior. • *v.tr.* defy; encounter bravely. ▫▫ **brave·ly** *adv.*
brav·er·y /bráyvəree/ *n.* **1** brave conduct. **2** a brave nature.
bra·vo[1] /braávō/ *int.* & *n.* • *int.* expressing approval of a performer, etc. • *n.* (*pl.* **-vos**) a cry of bravo.
bra·vo[2] /braávō/ *n.* (*pl.* **-voes** or **-vos**) a hired thug or killer.
bra·vu·ra /brəvöörə, -vyöörə/ *n.* (often *attrib.*) **1** a brilliant or ambitious action or display. **2 a** a style of music requiring exceptional ability. **b** a passage of this kind. **3** bravado.
brawl /brawl/ *n.* & *v.* • *n.* a noisy quarrel or fight. • *v.intr.* quarrel noisily or roughly. ▫▫ **brawl·er** *n.*
brawn /brawn/ *n.* **1** muscular strength. **2** muscle; lean flesh.
brawn·y /bráwnee/ *adj.* (**brawnier, brawniest**) muscular; strong.
bray /bray/ *n.* & *v.* • *n.* **1** the cry of a donkey. **2** a sound like this cry. • *v.* **1** *intr.* make a braying sound. **2** *tr.* utter harshly.
braze[1] /brayz/ *v.tr.* solder with a nonferrous material at a high temperature.
braze[2] /brayz/ *v.tr.* **1 a** make of brass. **b** cover or ornament with brass. **2** make hard like brass.
bra·zen /bráyzən/ *adj.* & *v.* • *adj.* **1** (also **bra·zen-faced**) flagrant and shameless; insolent. **2** made of brass. **3** of or like brass. • *v.tr.* (foll. by *out*) face or undergo defiantly. ▫▫ **bra·zen·ly** *adv.* **bra·zen·ness** *n.*
bra·zier /bráyzhər/ *n.* a portable heater consisting of a pan or stand for holding lighted coals.
Bra·zil /brəzíl/ *n.* **1** a tall tree, *Bertholletia excelsa*, forming large forests in S. America. **2** (in full **Brazil nut**) a large three-sided edible nut from this tree.
bra·zil·wood /brəzílwŏŏd/ *n.* a hard red wood from any tropical tree of the genus *Caesalpinia*, that yields dyes.
breach /breech/ *n.* & *v.* • *n.* **1** (often foll. by *of*) the breaking of a law, contract, etc. **2 a** a breaking of relations. **b** a quarrel. **3 a** a broken state. **b** a gap. • *v.tr.* **1** break through; make a gap in. **2** break (a law, contract, etc.).
breach of prom·ise *n.* the breaking of a promise, esp. a promise to marry.
breach of the peace *n.* a violation of the public peace by any disturbance or riot, etc.
bread /bred/ *n.* & *v.* • *n.* **1** baked dough made of flour usu. leavened with yeast and moistened. **2 a** necessary food. **b** (also **daily bread**) one's livelihood. **3** *sl.* money. • *v.tr.* coat with breadcrumbs for cooking.
bread and but·ter *n.* **1** bread spread with butter. **2 a** one's livelihood. **b** routine work to ensure an income. ▫▫ **bread-and-butter** *adj.*
bread bas·ket *n.* **1** a basket for bread. **2** *sl.* the stomach.
bread·crumb /brédkrum/ *n.* **1** a small fragment of bread. **2** (in *pl.*) bread crumbled for use in cooking.

bread·fruit /brédfrōōt/ *n.* **1** a tropical evergreen tree, *Artocarpus altilis,* bearing edible usu. seedless fruit. **2** the fruit of this tree, which when roasted becomes soft like new bread.

bread·line /brédlīn/ *n.* a line of people waiting to receive free food.

breadth /bredth/ *n.* **1** the distance or measurement from side to side of a thing. **2** a piece (of cloth, etc.) of standard or full breadth. **3** extent; distance; room. **4** (usu. foll. by *of*) freedom from prejudice or intolerance (esp. *breadth of mind* or *view*).

bread·win·ner /brédwinər/ *n.* a person who earns the money to support a family.

break /brayk/ *v. & n.* • *v.* (*past* **broke** /brōk/ or *archaic* **brake** /brayk/; *past part.* **broken** /brṓkən/ or *archaic* **broke**) **1** *tr. & intr.* **a** separate into pieces under a blow or strain. **b** make or become inoperative (*the toaster has broken*). **c** sustain an injury involving the fracture of a bone in (part of the body). **d** cause a cut or graze in the skin. **2 a** *tr.* cause an interruption in (*broke our journey; broke the silence*). **b** *intr.* have an interval between periods of work (*we broke for coffee*). **3** *tr.* fail to keep (a law, promise, etc.). **4 a** *tr. & intr.* make or become subdued or weakened; yield or cause to yield (*broke his spirit; he broke under the strain*). **b** *tr.* weaken the effect of (a fall, blow, etc.). **c** *tr.* tame or discipline (an animal); accustom (a horse) to saddle and bridle, etc. **d** *tr.* defeat; destroy (*broke the enemy's power*). **e** *tr.* defeat the object of (a strike). **5** *tr.* surpass (a record). **6** *intr.* (foll. by *with*) cease association with (another person, etc.). **7** *tr.* **a** be no longer subject to (a habit). **b** (foll. by *of*) cause (a person) to be free of a habit (*broke them of their addiction*). **8** *tr. & intr.* reveal or be revealed (*broke the news; the story broke on Friday*). **9** *intr.* **a** (of the weather) change suddenly. **b** (of waves) curl over and dissolve into foam. **c** (of the day) dawn. **d** (of clouds) move apart. **e** (of a storm) begin violently. **10** *tr. Electr.* disconnect (a circuit). **11** *intr.* **a** (of the voice) change with emotion. **b** (of a boy's voice) change in register, etc., at puberty. **12** *tr.* **a** (often foll. by *up*) divide (a set, etc.) into parts, e.g., by selling to different buyers. **b** change (a bill, etc.) for coins or smaller denominations. **13** *tr.* ruin financially (see also BROKE *predic.adj.*). **14** *tr.* penetrate (e.g., a safe) by force. **15** *tr.* decipher (a code). **16** *tr.* make (a path, etc.) by separating obstacles. **17** *intr.* burst forth (*the sun broke through the clouds*). **18** *Mil.* **a** *intr.* (of troops) disperse in confusion. **b** *tr.* make a rupture in (ranks). **19 a** *intr.* (usu. foll. by *free, loose, out,* etc.) escape from constraint by a sudden effort. **b** *tr.* escape or emerge from (prison, cover, etc.). **20** *tr. Tennis,* etc. win a game against (an opponent's service). **21** *intr. Boxing,* etc. (of two fighters) come out of a clinch. **22** *intr.* (of a thrown or bowled ball) change direction abruptly. **23** *intr. Billiards,* etc. disperse the balls at the beginning of a game. • *n.* **1 a** an act or instance of breaking. **b** a point where something is broken; a gap. **2** an interval; an interruption; a pause in work. **3** a sudden dash. **4** *colloq.* **a** a piece of good luck; a fair chance. **b** (also **bad break**) an unfortunate remark or action; a blunder. **5** a change in direction of a thrown or bowled ball. **6** *Billiards,* etc. **a** a series of points scored during one turn. **b** the opening shot that disperses the balls. **7** *Electr.* a discontinuity in a circuit. □ **break away** make or become free or separate (see also BREAKAWAY). **break down 1 a** fail in mechanical action; cease to function. **b** (of human relationships, etc.) collapse. **c** fail in (esp. mental) health. **d** be overcome by emotion. **2 a** demolish. **b** suppress (resistance). **c** force (a person) to yield under pressure. **3** analyze into components (see also BREAKDOWN). **break even** emerge from a transaction, etc., with neither profit nor loss. **break the ice 1** begin to overcome formality or shyness. **2** make a start. **break in 1** enter premises by force. **2** interrupt. **3 a** accustom to a habit, etc. **b** wear until comfortable. **c** = BREAK 4c. **break into 1** enter forcibly or violently. **2 a** suddenly begin; burst forth with (a song, laughter, etc.). **b** suddenly change one's pace for (a faster one) (*broke into a gallop*). **3** interrupt. **break new ground** innovate; start on something new. **break off 1** detach by breaking. **2** bring to an end. **3** cease talking, etc. **break open** open forcibly. **break out 1** escape by force. **2** begin suddenly (*then violence broke out*). **3** (foll. by *in*) become covered in (a rash, etc.). **4** exclaim. **5 a** open up (a receptacle) and remove its contents. **b** remove (articles) from a place of storage. **break up 1** break into small pieces. **2** disperse. **3 a** terminate a relationship; disband. **b** cause to do this. **4 a** upset or be upset. **b** excite or be excited. **c** convulse or be convulsed (see also BREAKUP). □□ **break·a·ble** *adj. & n.*

break·age /bráykij/ *n.* **1 a** a broken thing. **b** damage caused by breaking. **2** an act or instance of breaking.

break·a·way /bráykəway/ *n.* **1** the act or an instance of breaking away or seceding. **2** (*attrib.*) that breaks away or has broken away.

break danc·ing *n.* an energetic style of street-dancing, developed by African-Americans.

break·down /bráykdown/ *n.* **1 a** a mechanical failure. **b** a loss of (esp. mental) health. **2** a collapse (*breakdown of communication*). **3** a detailed analysis (of statistics, etc.).

break·er /bráykər/ *n.* **1** a person or thing that breaks something. **2** a person who breaks in a horse. **3** a heavy wave that breaks.

break·fast /brékfəst/ *n. & v.* • *n.* the first meal of the day. • *v.intr.* have breakfast.

break-in *n.* an illegal forced entry into premises.

break·ing and en·ter·ing *n.* the illegal entering of a building with intent to commit a felony.

break·ing point *n.* the point of greatest strain, at which a thing breaks or a person gives way.

break·neck /bráyknek/ *attrib.adj.* (of speed) dangerously fast.

break of day *n.* dawn.

break·out /brákyowt/ *n.* a forcible escape.

break point *n.* **1** a place or time at which an interruption or change is made. **2** *Computing* (usu. **breakpoint**) a place in a program where the sequence of instructions is interrupted, esp. by another program. **3** *Tennis* a point that would win the game for the player(s) receiving service (*three break points*).

break·through /bráykthrōō/ *n.* **1** a major advance or discovery. **2** an act of breaking through an obstacle, etc.

break·up /bráykup/ *n.* **1** disintegration; collapse. **2** dispersal. **3** the end of a relationship.

break·wa·ter /bráykwawtər, -wotər/ *n.* a barrier built out into the sea to break the force of waves.

bream /breem/ *n.* (*pl.* same) **1** a yellowish arch-backed European freshwater fish, *Abramis brama.* **2** (in full **sea bream**) **a** a similarly shaped marine fish of the family Sparidae, of the NE Atlantic. **b** an Atlantic porgy, *Archosargus rhomboidalis.*

breast /brest/ *n. & v.* • *n.* **1 a** either of two milk-secreting organs on the upper front of a woman's body. **b** the corresponding part of a man's body. **2 a** the chest. **b** the corresponding part of an animal. **3** the part of a garment that covers the breast. • *v.tr.* **1** face; meet in full opposition (*breast the wind*). **2** contend with (*prepared to breast the difficulties of the journey*). **3** reach the top of (a hill). □ **make a clean breast of** confess fully. □□ **breast·ed** *adj.* (also in *comb.*).

breast·bone /bréstbōn/ *n.* a thin flat vertical bone and cartilage in the chest connecting the ribs.
breast-feed *v.tr.* (*past* and *past part.* **-fed**) feed (a baby) from the breast.
breast·plate /bréstplayt/ *n.* armor covering the breast.
breast·stroke /bréststrōk/ *n.* a stroke made while swimming face down by extending arms forward and sweeping them back in unison.
breast·work /bréstwərk/ *n.* a low temporary defense or parapet.
breath /breth/ *n.* **1 a** the air taken into or expelled from the lungs. **b** one respiration of air. **c** an exhalation of air that can be seen, smelled, or heard (*bad breath*). **2 a** a slight movement of air. **b** a whiff of perfume, etc. **3** a whisper; a murmur. **4** the power of breathing; life (*is there breath in him?*). □ **below** (or **under**) **one's breath** in a whisper. **breath of fresh air 1** a small amount of or a brief time in the fresh air. **2** a refreshing change. **catch one's breath 1** cease breathing momentarily in surprise, etc. **2** rest after exercise to restore normal breathing. **draw breath** breathe; live. **hold one's breath 1** cease breathing temporarily. **2** *colloq.* wait in eager anticipation. **take a person's breath away** astound; delight.
Breath·a·lyz·er /bréthəlīzər/ *n. Trademark* an instrument for measuring alcohol in the breath of a driver.
breathe /breeth/ *v.* **1** *intr.* take air into and expel it from the lungs. **2** *intr.* be or seem alive (*is she breathing?*). **3** *tr.* **a** utter; say (*breathed her forgiveness*). **b** express (*breathed defiance*). **4** *intr.* take a breath; pause. **5** *tr.* send out or take in (as if) with breathed air (*breathed enthusiasm into them*). **6** *intr.* (of wine, fabric, etc.) be exposed to fresh air. □ **breathe down a person's neck** follow or check up on a person, esp. menacingly. **breathe new life into** revitalize; refresh. **breathe one's last** die. **not breathe a word** remain silent about something; keep secret.
breath·er /brée̱thər/ *n. colloq.* a brief pause for rest.
breath·ing /brée̱thing/ *n.* **1** the process of taking air into and expelling it from the lungs. **2** *Phonet.* a sign in Greek indicating that an initial vowel is aspirated (**rough breathing**) or not aspirated (**smooth breathing**).
breath·less /bréthlis/ *adj.* **1** out of breath. **2** (as if) holding the breath because of excitement, etc. **3** still. □□ **breath·less·ly** *adv.* **breath·less·ness** *n.*
breath·tak·ing /bréthtayking/ *adj.* awe-inspiring. □□ **breath·tak·ing·ly** *adv.*
breath test *n.* a test of a person's alcohol consumption, using a Breathalyzer.
breath·y /bréthee/ *adj.* (**breathier, breathiest**) (of a singing voice, etc.) containing the sound of breathing. □□ **breath·i·ly** *adv.* **breath·i·ness** *n.*
brec·ci·a /brécheeə/ *n.* & *v.* • *n.* a rock of angular stones, etc., cemented by finer material. • *v.tr.* form into breccia. □□ **brec·ci·ate** /-eeayt/ *v.tr.* **brec·ci·a·tion** *n.*
bred /bred/ *past* and *past part.* of BREED.
breech /breech/ *n.* **1** the part of a cannon behind the bore. **2** the back part of a rifle or gun barrel.
breech birth *n.* (also **breech de·liv·er·y**) the delivery of a baby with the buttocks or feet foremost.
breech·es /brichiz/ *n.pl.* (also **pair of breeches** *sing.*) short trousers, esp. fastened below the knee.
breech·load·er /bréchlōdər/ *n.* a gun loaded at the breech, not through the muzzle. □□ **breech-load·ing** *adj.*
breed /breed/ *v.* & *n.* • *v.* (*past* and *past part.* **bred** /bred/) **1** *tr.* & *intr.* bear; generate (offspring). **2** *tr.* & *intr.* propagate or cause to propagate; raise (livestock). **3** *tr.* **a** yield; result in (*war breeds famine*). **b** spread (*discontent bred by rumor*). **4** *intr.* arise; spread (*disease breeds in poor sanitation*). **5** *tr.* bring up; train (*Hollywood breeds stars*). **6** *tr. Physics* create (fissile material) by nuclear reaction. • *n.* **1** a stock of animals or plants within a species, having a similar appearance, and usu. developed by deliberate selection. **2** a race; a lineage. **3** a sort; a kind. □□ **breed·er** *n.*
breed·er re·ac·tor *n.* a nuclear reactor that can create more fissile material than it consumes.
breed·ing /bréeding/ *n.* **1** the process of developing or propagating (animals, plants, etc.). **2** generation; childbearing. **3** the result of training or education; behavior. **4** good manners (*has no breeding*).
breeze /breez/ *n.* & *v.* • *n.* **1** a gentle wind. **2** a wind blowing from land at night or sea during the day. **3** *colloq.* an easy task. • *v.intr.* (foll. by *in, out, along,* etc.) *colloq.* come or go in a casual manner.
breez·y /bréezee/ *adj.* (**breezier, breeziest**) **1 a** windswept. **b** pleasantly windy. **2** *colloq.* lively; jovial. **3** *colloq.* careless (*breezy indifference*). □□ **breez·i·ly** *adv.* **breez·i·ness** *n.*
breth·ren see BROTHER.
Bre·ton /brétən, brətáwN/ *n.* & *adj.* • *n.* **1** a native of Brittany. **2** the Celtic language of Brittany. • *adj.* of or relating to Brittany or its people or language.
breve /brev, breev/ *n.* **1** *Mus.* a note having the time value of two whole notes. **2** a written or printed mark (˘) indicating a short or unstressed vowel.
bre·vet /brəvét, brévit/ *n.* (often *attrib.*) a document conferring a privilege, esp. a rank in the army, without the appropriate pay (*was promoted by brevet; brevet major*).
bre·vi·ar·y /bréevee-eree, brév-/ *n.* (*pl.* **-ies**) *RC Ch.* a book containing the service for each day.
brev·i·ty /brévitee/ *n.* **1** conciseness. **2** shortness (of time, etc.) (*the brevity of happiness*).
brew /broo/ *v.* & *n.* • *v.* **1** *tr.* **a** make (beer, etc.) by infusion, boiling, and fermentation. **b** make (tea, coffee, etc.) by infusion or (punch, etc.) by mixture. **2** *intr.* undergo either of these processes (*the tea is brewing*). **3** *intr.* (of trouble, a storm, etc.) gather force; threaten. **4** *tr.* bring about; concoct. • *n.* **1** an amount (of beer, etc.) brewed at one time (*this year's brew*). **2** what is brewed (*a strong brew*). **3** the process of brewing. □□ **brew·er** *n.*
brew·er·y /bróoəree, bróoree/ *n.* (*pl.* **-ies**) a place where beer, etc., is brewed commercially.
bri·ar var. of BRIER[1] and BRIER[2].
bribe /brīb/ *v.* & *n.* • *v.tr.* (often foll. by *to* + infin.) persuade to act improperly in one's favor by a gift of money, services, etc. • *n.* money or services offered in the process of bribing. □□ **brib·er·y** *n.*
bric-à-brac /bríkəbrak/ *n.* (also **bric-a-brac, bric·a·brac**) miscellaneous furnishings, etc., of no great value.
brick /brik/ *n., v.,* & *adj.* • *n.* **1 a** a small block of fired or sun-dried clay, used in building. **b** the material used to make these. **c** a similar block of concrete, etc. **2** a brick-shaped solid object (*a brick of ice cream*). **3** *sl.* a generous or loyal person. • *v.tr.* (foll. by *in, up, over*) close or block with brickwork. • *adj.* **1** built of brick (*brick wall*). **2** of a dull red color.
brick·bat /bríkbat/ *n.* **1** a piece of brick, esp. when used as a missile. **2** an uncomplimentary remark.
brick·lay·er /bríklayər/ *n.* a worker who builds with bricks. □□ **brick·lay·ing** *n.*
brick·work /bríkwərk/ *n.* **1** building in brick. **2** a wall, etc., made of brick.
brick·yard /bríkyaard/ *n.* a place where bricks are made.
brid·al /bríd'l/ *adj.* of or concerning a bride or a wedding.
bride /brīd/ *n.* a woman on her wedding day and for some time before and after it.

bride·groom /brídgrōōm, -grōōm/ *n.* a man on his wedding day and for some time before and after it.

brides·maid /brídzmayd/ *n.* a girl or woman attending a bride on her wedding day.

bridge[1] /brij/ *n. & v.* •*n.* **1 a** a structure carrying a road, path, railroad, etc., across a stream, ravine, road, etc. **b** anything providing a connection between different things. **2** the superstructure on a ship from which the officers direct operations. **3** the upper bony part of the nose. **4** *Mus.* an upright piece of wood on a violin, etc., over which the strings are stretched. **5** = BRIDGEWORK. •*v.tr.* **1 a** be a bridge over (*a fallen tree bridges the stream*). **b** make a bridge over. **2** span as if with a bridge (*bridged their differences with understanding*).

bridge[2] /brij/ *n.* a card game derived from whist.

bridge·head /bríjhed/ *n. Mil.* a fortified position held on the enemy's side of a river or other obstacle.

bridge·work /bríjwərk/ *n. Dentistry* a dental structure used to cover a gap, joined to the teeth on either side.

bri·dle /bríd'l/ *n. & v.* •*n.* the headgear used to control a horse, consisting of leather straps and a metal bit. •*v.* **1** *tr.* put a bridle on (a horse, etc.). **2** *tr.* bring under control.

bridle

bri·dle path *n.* a rough path or road suitable for horseback riding.

Brie /bree/ *n.* a kind of soft ripened cheese.

brief /breef/ *adj., n., & v.* •*adj.* **1** of short duration. **2** concise in expression. **3** brusque. **4** scanty (*wearing a brief skirt*). •*n.* **1** (in *pl.*) women's or men's brief underpants. **2** *Law* a summary of the facts and legal points of a case drawn up for the court or counsel. **3** instructions given for a task, etc. •*v.tr.* instruct (an employee, etc.) in preparation for a task (*briefed him for the interview*) (cf. DEBRIEF). □ **in brief** in short. □□ **brief·ing** *n.* **brief·ly** *adv.* **brief·ness** *n.*

brief·case /bréefkays/ *n.* a flat rectangular case for carrying documents, etc.

bri·er[1] /bríər/ *n.* (also **bri·ar**) any prickly bush, esp. of a wild rose.

bri·er[2] /bríər/ *n.* (also **bri·ar**) **1** a white heath, *Erica arborea*, native to S. Europe. **2** a tobacco pipe made from its root.

brig /brig/ *n.* **1** a two-masted square-rigged ship with an additional lower fore-and-aft sail on the gaff and a boom to the mainmast. **2** a prison, esp. in the navy.

Brig. *abbr.* Brigadier.

bri·gade /brigáyd/ *n.* **1** *Mil.* **a** a subdivision of an army. **b** an infantry unit consisting usu. of three battalions and forming part of a division. **c** a corresponding armored unit. **2** an organized or uniformed band of workers (*fire brigade*). **3** *colloq.* any group of people with a characteristic in common.

brig·a·dier gen·er·al *n.* an officer ranking between colonel and major general.

brig·and /brígənd/ *n.* a member of a robber band living by pillage and ransom. □□ **brig·and·age** *n.* **brig·and·ry** *n.*

brig·an·tine /brígənteen/ *n.* a two-masted sailing ship with a square-rigged foremast and a fore-and-aft rigged mainmast.

bright /brīt/ *adj. & adv.* •*adj.* **1** emitting or reflecting much light. **2** (of color) intense. **3** clever (*a bright idea; a bright child*). **4** cheerful. •*adv.* esp. *poet.* brightly (*the moon shone bright*). □□ **bright·ish** *adj.* **bright·ly** *adv.* **bright·ness** *n.*

bright·en /brít'n/ *v.tr. & intr.* (often foll. by *up*) make or become brighter.

bright-eyed *adj.* **1** having bright eyes. **2** alert; eager. □ **bright-eyed and bushy-tailed** *colloq.* alert and energetic.

Bright's dis·ease /brīts/ *n.* inflammation of the kidney from any of various causes; nephritis.

brill /bril/ *n.* a European flatfish, *Scophthalmus rhombus*, resembling a turbot.

bril·liance /brílyəns/ *n.* **1** great brightness; radiant quality. **2** outstanding talent or intelligence.

bril·liant /brílyənt/ *adj. & n.* •*adj.* **1** very bright; sparkling. **2** outstandingly talented or intelligent. •*n.* a diamond of the finest cut with many facets. □□ **bril·liant·ly** *adv.*

brim /brim/ *n. & v.* •*n.* **1** the edge or lip of a cup, etc., or of a hollow. **2** the projecting edge of a hat. •*v.tr. & intr.* (**brimmed, brimming**) fill or be full to the brim. □ **brim over** overflow. □□ **brimmed** *adj.* (usu. in *comb.*).

brim·ful /brímfōōl/ *adj.* (also **brim·full**) (often foll. by *of*) filled to the brim.

brim·stone /brímstōn/ *n.* **1** the element sulfur. **2** a butterfly, *Gonepteryx rhamni*, or moth, *Opisthograptis luteolata*, having yellow wings.

brin·dled /brínd'ld/ *adj.* (also **brin·dle**) brownish or tawny with streaks of other color(s) (esp. of domestic animals).

brine /brīn/ *n.* **1** water saturated or strongly impregnated with salt. **2** sea water.

bring /bring/ *v.tr.* (*past* and *past part.* **brought** /brawt/) **1 a** come conveying esp. by carrying or leading. **b** come with. **2** cause to come (*what brings you here?*). **3** result in (*war brings misery*). **4** produce as income. **5 a** prefer (a charge). **b** initiate (legal action). **6** cause to become or to reach a particular state (*brought them to their senses*). **7** adduce (evidence, an argument, etc.). □ **bring about 1** cause to happen. **2** turn (a ship) around. **bring around 1** restore to consciousness. **2** persuade. **bring back** call to mind. **bring down 1** cause to fall. **2** lower (a price). **3** *sl.* make unhappy or less happy. **4** *colloq.* damage the reputation of; demean. **bring forth** produce. **bring forward 1** move to an earlier time. **2** transfer from the previous page or account. **3** draw attention to. **bring home to** cause to realize fully (*brought home to me that I was wrong*). **bring the house down** receive rapturous applause. **bring in 1** introduce (legislation, a custom, etc.). **2** yield as income or profit. **bring into play** activate. **bring off** achieve successfully. **bring on 1** cause to happen or appear. **2** accelerate the progress of. **bring out 1** make evident. **2** publish. **bring through** aid (a person) through adversity. **bring to 1** restore to consciousness (*brought him to*). **2** check the motion of. **bring to bear** (usu. foll. by *on*) direct and concentrate (forces). **bring to light** reveal. **bring to pass** cause to happen. **bring up 1** rear (a child). **2** vomit. **3** call attention to. **bring upon oneself** be responsible for (something one suffers). □□ **bring·er** *n.*

brink /bringk/ *n.* **1** the extreme edge of land before a precipice, etc. **2** the furthest point before something dangerous or exciting is discovered. □ **on the brink of** about to experience or suffer.

brink·man·ship /bríngkmənship/ *n.* the art or policy of pursuing a dangerous course to the brink of catastrophe before desisting, esp. in politics.

brin·y /brínee/ *adj.* (**brinier, briniest**) of brine or the sea; salty. □□ **brin·i·ness** *n.*

bri·o /brée-ō/ *n.* dash; vigor; vivacity.

bri·oche /bree-ósh, brée-ōsh, -osh/ *n.* a small rounded sweet roll made with a light yeast dough.

bri·quette /brikét/ *n.* (also **bri·quet**) a block of compressed coal dust or charcoal used as fuel.

brisk /brisk/ *adj. & v.* •*adj.* **1** quick; lively (*a brisk pace*). **2** enlivening; fresh (*a brisk wind*). •*v.tr. & intr.* (often foll. by *up*) make or grow brisk. □□ **brisk·ly** *adv.* **brisk·ness** *n.*

bris·ket /brískit/ *n.* an animal's breast, esp. as a cut of meat.

bris·ling /brízling, brís-/ *n.* (*pl.* same or **brislings**) a small herring or sprat.

bris·tle /brísəl/ *n. & v.* •*n.* **1** a short stiff hair, esp. one of those on an animal's back. **2** this, or an artificial substitute, used in clumps to make a brush. •*v.* **1 a** *intr.* (of the hair) stand upright. **b** *tr.* make (the hair) do this. **2** *intr.* show irritation or defensiveness. **3** *intr.* (usu. foll. by *with*) be abundant (in). □□ **bris·tly** /bríslee/ *adj.* (**bristlier, bristliest**)

Brit /brit/ *n. colloq.* a British person.

Bri·tan·nia /britányə/ *n.* the personification of Britain, esp. as a helmeted woman with shield and trident.

Brit·i·cism /brítisizəm/ *n.* (also **Brit·ish·ism** /-tishizəm/) an idiom used in Britain but not in other English-speaking countries.

Brit·ish /brítish/ *adj. & n.* •*adj.* **1** of or relating to Great Britain or the United Kingdom, or to its people or language. **2** of the British Commonwealth or (formerly) the British Empire (*British subject*). •*n.* **1** (prec. by *the*; treated as *pl.*) the British people. **2** = BRITISH ENGLISH.

Brit·ish Eng·lish *n.* English as used in Great Britain, as distinct from that used elsewhere.

Brit·ish·er /brítishər/ *n.* a British subject.

Brit·on /brítən/ *n.* **1** one of the people of S. Britain before the Roman conquest. **2** a native or inhabitant of Great Britain or (formerly) of the British Empire.

brit·tle /brít'l/ *adj. & n.* •*adj.* hard and fragile; apt to break. •*n.* a brittle confection made from nuts and hardened melted sugar. □□ **brit·tle·ness** *n.*

brit·tle star *n.* an echinoderm of the class Ophiuroidea, with long brittle arms radiating from a central body.

broach /brōch/ *v. & n.* •*v.tr.* **1** raise (a subject) for discussion. **2** pierce (a cask) to draw liquor. **3** open and start using contents of (a box, etc.). •*n.* **1** a bit for boring. **2** a roasting spit.

broad /brawd/ *adj. & n.* •*adj.* **1** large in extent from one side to the other; wide. **2** in breadth (*2 meters broad*). **3** extensive (*broad acres*). **4** full and clear (*broad daylight*). **5** explicit; unmistakable (*broad hint*). **6** general (*a broad inquiry*). **7** principal (*the broad facts*). **8** tolerant; liberal (*take a broad view*). **9** somewhat coarse (*broad humor*). **10** (of speech) markedly regional (*broad Brooklyn accent*). •*n.* **1** the broad part of something (*broad of the back*). **2** *sl.* a woman. □□ **broad·ness** *n.*

broad bean *n.* **1** a kind of bean, *Vicia faba*, with pods containing large edible flat seeds. **2** one of these seeds.

broad·cast /bráwdkast/ *v., n., adj., & adv.* •*v.* (*past* **broadcast** or **broadcasted**; *past part.* **broadcast**) **1** *tr.* **a** transmit by radio or television. **b** disseminate (information) widely. **2** *intr.* undertake or take part in a radio or television transmission. **3** *tr.* scatter (seed, etc.) over a large area. •*n.* a radio or television program or transmission. •*adj.* **1** transmitted by radio or television. **2** widely disseminated. •*adv.* over a large area. □□ **broad·cast·er** *n.* **broad·cast·ing** *n.*

broad·cloth /bráwdklawth, -kloth/ *n.* a fine cloth of wool, cotton, or silk.

broad·en /bráwdən/ *v.tr. & intr.* make or become broader.

broad·loom /bráwdlōōm/ *adj.* (esp. of carpet) woven in broad widths.

broad·ly /bráwdlee/ *adv.* widely (*grinned broadly*). □ **broadly speaking** disregarding minor exceptions.

broad-mind·ed *adj.* tolerant in one's views. □□ **broad-mind·ed·ly** *adv.* **broad-mind·ed·ness** *n.*

broad·side /bráwdsīd/ *n.* **1** the firing of all guns from one side of a ship. **2** a vigorous verbal onslaught.

broad spec·trum *adj.* (of a medicinal substance) effective against a large variety of microorganisms.

broad·sword /bráwdsawrd/ *n.* a sword with a broad blade, for cutting rather than thrusting.

broad·way /bráwdway/ *n.* **1** a large open or main road. **2** (as **Broad·way**) a principal thoroughfare in New York City, noted for its theaters, and the center of U.S. commercial theater production.

bro·cade /brōkáyd/ *n.* a rich fabric with a silky finish woven with a raised pattern.

broc·co·li /brókəlee/ *n.* a vegetable related to cabbage with a loose cluster of greenish flower buds.

bro·chette /brōshét/ *n.* a skewer on which chunks of meat are cooked.

bro·chure /brōshóor/ *n.* a pamphlet of descriptive information.

brogue[1] /brōg/ *n.* **1** a strong outdoor shoe with perforated bands. **2** a rough shoe of untanned leather.

brogue[2] /brōg/ *n.* a marked accent, esp. Irish.

broil /broyl/ *v.* **1** *tr.* cook (meat) on a rack or a grill. **2** *tr. & intr.* make or become very hot, esp. from the sun.

broil·er /bróylər/ *n.* **1** a young chicken raised for broiling or roasting. **2 a** a device on a stove for radiating heat downward. **b** a grill, griddle, etc., for broiling.

broke /brōk/ *past* of BREAK. •*predic.adj. colloq.* having no money. □ **go for broke** *sl.* risk everything in a strenuous effort.

bro·ken /brókən/ *past part.* of BREAK. •*adj.* **1** that has been broken. **2** (of a person) reduced to despair. **3** spoken falteringly and with many mistakes (*broken English*). **4** interrupted. **5** uneven. □□ **bro·ken·ly** *adv.* **bro·ken·ness** *n.*

bro·ken-down *adj.* **1** worn out. **2** out of order.

bro·ken·heart·ed /brókənhaártid/ *adj.* overwhelmed with sorrow.

bro·ken home *n.* a family in which the parents are divorced or separated.

bro·ker /brókər/ *n.* **1** an agent who buys and sells for others. **2** a member of the stock exchange dealing in stocks and bonds. □□ **bro·ker·ing** *n.*

bro·ker·age /brókərij/ *n.* **1** a broker's fee or commission. **2** a broker's business.

bro·me·li·ad /brōméeleead/ *n.* any plant of the family Bromeliaceae (esp. of the genus *Bromelia*), native to the New World, having short stems with rosettes of stiff leaves, e.g., pineapple.

bro·mic /brómik/ *adj. Chem.* of or containing bromine.

bro·mic ac·id *n.* a strong acid used as an oxidizing agent.

bro·mide /brómīd/ *n.* **1** *Chem.* any binary compound of bromine. **2** *Pharm.* a preparation of usu. potassium bromide, used as a sedative. **3** a trite remark.

bro·mine /brómeen/ *n. Chem.* a liquid element with a choking irritating smell, used in the manufacture of chemicals for photography and medicine. ¶ Symb.: **Br.**

bron·chi *pl.* of BRONCHUS.

bron·chi·al /bróngkeeəl/ *adj.* of or relating to the bronchi or bronchioles.

bron·chi·al tube *n.* a bronchus or any tube branching from it.

bron·chi·ole /bróngkeeōl/ *n.* any of the minute divisions of a bronchus. □□ **bron·chi·o·lar** /-ōlər, -kíə-/ *adj.*

bron·chi·tis /brongkítis/ *n.* inflammation of the mucous membrane in the bronchial tubes. □□ **bron·chit·ic** /-kítik/ *adj. & n.*

broncho- /bróngkō/ *comb.form* bronchi.

bron·cho·scope /bróngkəskōp/ *n.* a usu. fiber-optic instrument for inspecting the bronchi. □□ **bronchoscopy** /–kóskəpee/ *n.*

bron·chus /bróngkəs/ *n.* (*pl.* **bronchi** /-kī/) any of the major air passages of the lungs. □□ **bron·chi·al** /bróngkeeəl/ *adj.*

bron·co /bróngkō/ *n.* (*pl.* **-cos**) a wild or half-tamed horse of western N. America.

bron·to·sau·rus /bróntəsáwrəs/ *n.* (also **bron·to·saur** /bróntəsawr/) a large plant-eating dinosaur of the genus *Brontosaurus*, with a long tail and trunk-like legs. Now more correctly APATOSAURUS.

Bronx cheer /brongks/ *n. colloq.* = RASPBERRY 3a.

bronze /bronz/ *n. & adj.* • *n.* **1** an alloy of copper and tin. **2** its brownish color. **3** a thing made of bronze, esp. as a work of art. • *adj.* made of or colored like bronze.

Bronze Age *n.* the period when weapons and tools were usu. made of bronze.

brooch /brōch, brōōch/ *n.* an ornament fastened to clothing with a hinged pin.

brood /brōōd/ *n. & v.* • *n.* **1** the young of an animal (esp. a bird) produced at one hatching or birth. **2** *colloq.* the children in a family. **3** a group of related things. **4** bee or wasp larvae. **5** (*attrib.*) kept for breeding (*brood mare*). • *v.* **1** *intr.* (often foll. by *on*, *over*, etc.) worry or ponder (esp. resentfully). **2 a** *intr.* sit as a hen on eggs to hatch them. **b** *tr.* sit on (eggs) to hatch them. □□ **brood·ing·ly** *adv.*

brood·er /brōōdər/ *n.* **1** a heated house for chicks, piglets, etc. **2** a person who broods.

brook[1] /brŏŏk/ *n.* a small stream. □□ **brook·let** /-lət/ *n.*

brook[2] /brŏŏk/ *v.tr.* (usu. with *neg.*) *formal* tolerate.

brook trout *n.* the speckled trout (*Salvelinus fontinalis*), a game fish of N. America.

broom /brōōm, brŏŏm/ *n.* **1** a long-handled brush of bristles, twigs, etc., for sweeping. **2** any of various shrubs, esp. *Cytisus scoparius*, bearing bright yellow flowers.

Bros. *abbr.* Brothers (esp. in the name of a business).

broth /brawth, broth/ *n. Cooking* **1** a thin soup of meat or fish stock. **2** unclarified meat, fish or vegetable stock.

broth·el /bróthəl/ *n.* a house, etc., where prostitution takes place.

broth·er /brú<u>th</u>ər/ *n.* **1** a man or boy in relation to other sons and daughters of his parents. **2 a** a close male friend or associate. **b** a male fellow member of a labor union, etc. **3** (*pl.* also **brethren** /bré<u>th</u>rin/) **a** a member of a male religious order. **b** a fellow member of a religion, etc. **4** a fellow human being. □□ **broth·er·less** *adj.* **broth·er·ly** *adj. & adv.* **broth·er·li·ness** *n.*

broth·er·hood /brú<u>th</u>ərhŏŏd/ *n.* **1 a** the relationship between brothers. **b** brotherly friendliness. **2 a** an association or community of people linked by a common interest, etc. **b** its members collectively. **3** a labor union.

broth·er-in-law *n.* (*pl.* **brothers-in-law**) **1** the brother of one's wife or husband. **2** the husband of one's sister. **3** the husband of one's sister-in-law.

brought *past* and *past part.* of BRING.

brou·ha·ha /brōōhaahaa/ *n.* commotion; uproar.

brow /brow/ *n.* **1** the forehead. **2** (usu. in *pl.*) an eyebrow. **3** the summit of a hill or pass. **4** the edge of a cliff, etc. □□ **-browed** *adj.* (in *comb.*)

brow·beat /brówbeet/ *v.tr.* (*past* **-beat**; *past part.* **-beaten**) intimidate with stern looks and words. □□ **brow·beat·er** *n.*

brown /brown/ *adj.*, *n.*, *& v.* • *adj.* **1** having the color as of dark wood or rich soil. **2** dark-skinned or suntanned. **3** (of bread) made from a dark flour. • *n.* **1** a brown color or pigment. **2** brown clothes or material (*dressed in brown*). • *v.tr. & intr.* make or become brown. □□ **brown·ish** *adj.* **brown·ness** *n.* **brown·y** *adj.*

brown bag·ging *n.* taking one's lunch to work, etc., in a brown paper bag.

brown bear *n.* a N. American brown bear, *Ursus arctos*.

Brown·i·an mo·tion /brówniən/ *n. Physics* the erratic random movement of microscopic particles in a liquid, gas, etc., as a result of continuous bombardment from molecules of the surrounding medium.

Brown·ie /brównee/ *n.* **1** a member of the junior branch of the Girl Scouts. **2** (**brownie**) *Cooking* a small square of rich, usu. chocolate, cake with nuts.

Brown·ie point *n. colloq.* a notional credit for something done to win favor.

brown·nose /brównnōz/ *v.intr. coarse sl.* ingratiate oneself; be servile. □□ **brown·nos·er** *n.*

brown·out /brównowt/ *n.* a period during which electrical voltage is reduced to avoid a blackout, resulting in lowered illumination.

brown rice *n.* unpolished rice with only the husk of the grain removed.

Brown shirt *n.* a Nazi; a member of a fascist organization.

brown·stone /brównstōn/ *n.* **1** a reddish brown sandstone used for building. **2** a building faced with this.

brown sug·ar *n.* unrefined or partially refined sugar.

browse /browz/ *v. & n.* • *v.* **1** *intr. & tr.* read or survey desultorily. **2** *intr.* (often foll. by *on*) feed (on leaves, etc.). **3** *tr.* crop and eat. **4** *intr. & tr. Computing*, etc. read or survey (data files, etc.), esp. via a network. • *n.* **1** young shoots, etc., as fodder for cattle. **2** an act of browsing. □□ **brows·er** *n.*

bruin /brōōin/ *n.* a bear.

bruise /brōōz/ *n. & v.* • *n.* **1** an injury appearing as an area of discolored skin on a human or animal body, caused by impact. **2** an area of damage on a fruit, etc. • *v.* **1** *tr.* inflict a bruise on. **2** *intr.* be susceptible to bruising. **3** *tr.* crush or pound.

bruis·er /brōōzər/ *n. colloq.* a large tough-looking person.

bruit /brōōt/ *v.tr.* (often foll. by *abroad*, *about*) spread (a report or rumor).

brume /brōōm/ *n.* mist; fog.

brunch /brunch/ *n.* a late-morning meal eaten as the first meal of the day.

bru·nette /brōōnét/ *n. & adj.* (also *masc.* **bru·net**) • *n.* a woman with dark hair. • *adj.* (of a woman) having dark hair.

brunt /brunt/ *n.* the chief impact of an attack, task, etc. (esp. *bear the brunt of*).

brush /brush/ *n. & v.* • *n.* **1** an implement with bristles, hair, wire, etc., set into a block or projecting from the end of a handle, for any of various purposes, esp. cleaning or scrubbing, painting, arranging the hair, etc. **2** the application of a brush; brushing. **3 a** (usu. foll. by *with*) a short encounter (*a brush with the law*). **b** a skirmish. **4 a** the bushy tail of a fox. **b** a brushlike tuft. **5** *Electr.* a piece of carbon or metal serving as an electrical contact. **6 a** undergrowth; small trees and shrubs. **b** such wood cut or broken. **c** land covered with brush. • *v.* **1** *tr.* **a** sweep or scrub or put in order with a brush. **b** treat (a surface) with a brush so as to change its nature or appearance. **2** *tr.* **a** remove (dust, etc.) with a brush. **b** apply (a liquid preparation) to a surface with a brush. **3** *tr. & intr.* graze or touch in passing. **4** *intr.* perform a brushing action or motion. □ **brush aside** dismiss curtly or lightly. **brush off** rebuff; dismiss abruptly. **brush over** paint lightly. **brush up** (often foll. by *on*) revive one's former knowledge of (a subject). □□ **brush·y** *adj.*

brush-off *n.* a rebuff.

brush·wood /brúshwŏŏd/ *n.* **1** cut or broken twigs, etc. **2** undergrowth.

brush·work /brúshwərk/ *n.* **1** manipulation of the brush in painting. **2** a painter's style in this.

brusque /brusk/ *adj.* abrupt or offhand in manner or speech. □□ **brusque·ly** *adv.* **brusque·ness** *n.*

brus·sels sprout /brúsəlz/ *n.* **1** a vegetable related to cabbage with small compact cabbage-like buds borne close together along a tall single stem. **2** any of these buds used as a vegetable.

brut /brōōt/ *adj.* (of wine) very dry; unsweetened.

bru·tal /brōōt'l/ *adj.* **1** savagely cruel. **2** harsh; merciless. □□ **bru·tal·i·ty** /-tálitee/ *n.* (*pl.* **-ties**). **bru·tal·ly** *adv.*

bru·tal·ism /brōōt'lizəm/ *n.* **1** brutality. **2** a heavy plain style of architecture, etc. □□ **bru·tal·ist** *n. & adj.*

bru·tal·ize /brōōt'līz/ *v.tr.* **1** make brutal. **2** treat brutally. □□ **bru·tal·i·za·tion** /-lizáyshən/ *n.*

brute /brōōt/ *n. & adj.* • *n.* **1 a** a savagely violent person or animal. **b** *colloq.* a cruel, unpleasant, or insensitive person. **2** an animal as opposed to a human being. • *adj.* **1** not possessing the capacity to reason. **2 a** merely physical (*brute force*). **b** harsh, fundamental, or inescapable (*brute necessities*). □□ **brut·ish** *adj.* **brut·ish·ness** *n.*

brux·ism /brúksizəm/ *n.* the involuntary or habitual grinding or clenching of the teeth.

bry·o·ny /bríənee/ *n.* (*pl.* **-nies**) any climbing plant of the genus *Bryonia*, esp. *B. dioica*, bearing greenish white flowers and red berries.

bry·o·phyte /bríəfīt/ *n.* any plant of the phylum Bryophyta, including mosses and liverworts.

bry·o·zo·an /bríəzṓən/ *n. & adj.* • *n.* any aquatic invertebrate animal of the phylum Bryozoa, forming colonies attached to rocks, seaweeds, etc. • *adj.* of or relating to the phylum Bryozoa.

BS *abbr.* **1** Bachelor of Science. **2** Bachelor of Surgery. **3** *coarse sl.* bullshit.

B-side /beésīd/ *n.* the side of a phonograph record regarded as less important.

BTU *abbr.* (also **B.t.u.**) British thermal unit(s).

bub /bub/ *n. colloq.* a boy or a man, often used as a form of address.

bub·ble /búbəl/ *n. & v.* • *n.* **1 a** a thin sphere of liquid enclosing air, etc. **b** an air-filled cavity in a liquid or a solidified liquid such as glass or amber. **2** the sound or appearance of boiling. **3** a semicylindrical or domed cavity. • *v.intr.* **1** rise in or send up bubbles. **2** make the sound of boiling. □ **bubble over** (often foll. by *with*) be exuberant with laughter, excitement, anger, etc.

bub·ble bath *n.* **1** a preparation for adding to bath water to make it foam. **2** a bath with this added.

bub·ble gum *n.* chewing gum that can be blown into bubbles.

bub·ble mem·o·ry *n. Computing* a type of memory that stores data as a pattern of magnetized regions in a thin layer of magnetic material.

bub·ble wrap *n.* a clear plastic packaging material containing numerous small air cushions designed to protect fragile objects in shipping.

bub·bly /búblee/ *adj. & n.* • *adj.* (**bubblier, bubbliest**) **1** having or resembling bubbles. **2** exuberant. • *n. colloq.* champagne.

bu·bo /byṓōbō, bṓō-/ *n.* (*pl.* **-boes**) a swollen inflamed lymph node in the armpit or groin.

bu·bon·ic plague /byōōbónik, bōō-/ *n.* a contagious bacterial disease characterized by fever, delirium, and the formation of buboes.

buc·cal /búkəl/ *adj.* **1** of or relating to the cheek. **2** of or in the mouth.

buc·ca·neer /búkənéer/ *n.* **1** a pirate. **2** an unscrupulous adventurer. □□ **buc·ca·neer·ing** *n. & adj.*

buck[1] /buk/ *n. & v.* • *n.* **1** the male of various animals, esp. the deer, hare, or rabbit. **2** (*attrib.*) **a** male (*buck antelope*). **b** *Mil.* of the lowest rank (*buck private*). • *v.* **1** *intr.* (of a horse) jump upwards with back arched and feet drawn together. **2** *tr. & intr.* (usu. foll. by *up*) *colloq.* make or become more cheerful.

buck[2] /buk/ *n. sl.* a dollar. □ **a fast buck** easy money.

buck[3] /buk/ *n. sl.* an article placed as a reminder before a player whose turn it is to deal at poker. □ **pass the buck** *colloq.* shift responsibility (to another).

buck[4] /buk/ *n.* **1** a sawhorse. **2** a vaulting horse.

buck·board /búkbawrd/ *n.* a horse-drawn vehicle with the body formed by a plank fixed to the axles.

buck·et /búkit/ *n.* **1 a** a roughly cylindrical open container, used for carrying, catching, or holding water, etc. **b** the amount contained in this. **2** (in *pl.*) large quantities of liquid (*wept buckets*). **3** a compartment on the outer edge of a waterwheel. **4** the scoop of a dredger or a grain elevator. □□ **buck·et·ful** *n.* (*pl.* **-fuls**).

buck·et seat *n.* a seat with a rounded back to fit one person, esp. in a car.

buck·eye /búkī/ *n.* **1** any shrub or tree of the genus *Aesculus* of the horse chestnut family, with large sticky buds and showy red or white flowers. **2** the shiny brown nutlike seed of this plant.

buck·horn /búkhawrn/ *n.* horn of a buck as a material for knife handles, etc.

buck·hound /búkhownd/ *n.* a small kind of staghound.

buck·le /búkəl/ *n. & v.* • *n.* **1** a flat frame with a hinged pin, used for joining the ends of a belt, strap, etc. **2** a similarly shaped ornament. • *v.* **1** *tr.* (often foll. by *up*, *on*, etc.) fasten with a buckle. **2** *tr. & intr.* give way or cause to give way under longitudinal pressure. □ **buckle down** make a determined effort.

buck·ler /búklər/ *n. hist.* a small round shield held by a handle.

buck·ram /búkrəm/ *n.* a coarse linen or other cloth stiffened with gum or paste, and used as interfacing or in bookbinding.

buck·saw /búksaw/ *n.* a two-handed saw set in an H-shaped frame and used for sawing wood.

buck·shot /búkshot/ *n.* large-sized lead shot.

buck·skin /búkskin/ *n.* **1 a** the skin of a buck. **b** leather made from a buck's skin. **2** a thick smooth cloth.

buck·thorn /búkthawrn/ *n.* any thorny shrub of the genus *Rhamnus*, esp. *R. cathartica* with berries formerly used as a cathartic.

buck·tooth /búktōōth/ *n.* (*pl.* **-teeth**) an upper tooth that projects.

buck·wheat /búkhweet, -weet/ *n.* any cereal plant of the genus *Fagopyrum*, esp. *F. esculentum* with seeds used for fodder and for flour.

bu·col·ic /byōōkólik/ *adj.* of or concerning shepherds, the pastoral life, etc.; rural.

bud[1] /bud/ *n. & v.* • *n.* **1 a** an immature knoblike shoot from which a stem, leaf, or flower develops. **b** a flower or leaf that is not fully open. **2** *Biol.* an asexual outgrowth from a parent organism that separates to form a new individual. • *v.* (**budded, budding**) **1** *intr. Bot. & Zool.* form a bud. **2** *intr.* begin to develop. **3** *tr. Hort.* graft a bud (of a plant) on to another plant.

bud[2] /bud/ *n. colloq.* (as a form of address) = BUDDY.

Bud·dha /bṓōdə, bṓōdə/ *n.* **1** a title given to successive teachers of Buddhism, esp. to its founder, Gautama. **2** a statue or picture of the Buddha.

Bud·dhism /bŏŏdizəm, bōōd-/ *n.* a widespread religion or philosophy, founded by Gautama Buddha in India in the 5th c. BC, which teaches that elimination of the self and earthly desires is the highest goal. ▫▫ **Bud·dhist** *n. & adj.*

bud·dle·ia /búdleeə/ *n.* any shrub of the genus *Buddleia*, with fragrant flowers attractive to butterflies.

bud·dy /búdee/ *n. & v. colloq.* • *n.* (*pl.* **-dies**) (often as a form of address) a close friend or companion. • *v.intr.* (**-ies, -ied**) (often foll. by *up*) become friendly.

budge /buj/ *v.* (usu. with *neg.*) **1** *intr.* **a** make the slightest movement. **b** change one's opinion. **2** *tr.* cause or compel to budge (*nothing will budge him*).

budg·er·i·gar /búјəreegaar/ *n.* a small parakeet, *Melopsittacus undulatus*, native to Australia, and often kept as a cage bird.

budg·et /bújit/ *n. & v.* • *n.* **1** the amount of money needed or available (*a budget of $200*). **2 a** the usu. annual estimate of national revenue and expenditure. **b** an estimate or plan of expenditure in relation to income for a business, etc. **c** a private person's or family's similar estimate. **3** (*attrib.*) inexpensive. • *v.tr. & intr.* (**budgeted, budgeting**) (often foll. by *for*) allow or arrange for in a budget (*have budgeted for a new car*). ▫ **on a budget** avoiding expense; cheap. ▫▫ **budg·et·ar·y** *adj.*

buff /buf/ *adj., n., & v.* • *adj.* **1** of a yellowish beige color. **2** *sl.* fit; with well-defined muscles. • *n.* **1** a yellowish beige color. **2** *colloq.* an enthusiast (*railroad buff*). **3** *colloq.* the human skin unclothed. **4 a** a velvety dull yellow ox leather. **b** (*attrib.*) made of this. • *v.tr.* **1** polish (metal, fingernails, etc.). **2** make (leather) velvety like buff, by removing the surface. ▫ **in the buff** *colloq.* naked.

buf·fa·lo /búfəlō/ *n. & v.* • *n.* (*pl.* same or **-loes**) **1** a N. American bison, *Bison bison*. **2** either of two species of ox, *Synceros caffer*, native to Africa, or *Bubalus arnee*, native to Asia, with heavy backswept horns. • *v.* (**-loes, -loed**) *sl.* overawe; outwit.

buf·fa·lo wings *n.pl.* fried chicken wings coated in hot, spicy sauce and served with blue cheese dressing.

buff·er /búfər/ *n. & v.* • *n.* **1** a device that protects against or reduces the effect of an impact. **2** *Biochem.* a substance that maintains the hydrogen ion concentration of a solution when an acid or alkali is added. **3** *Computing* a temporary memory area for data to aid its transfer between programs operating at different speeds, etc. • *v.tr.* **1** act as a buffer to. **2** *Biochem.* treat with a buffer.

buff·er zone *n.* **1** a neutral area between two warring groups. **2** any area separating those in conflict.

buf·fet¹ /bŏŏfáy, bə-/ *n.* a meal consisting of several dishes set out from which guests serve themselves.

buf·fet² /búfit/ *v. & n.* • *v.* (**buffeted, buffeting**) **1** *tr.* **a** strike or knock repeatedly (*wind buffeted the trees*). **b** strike with the hand or fist. **2** *tr.* (of fate, etc.) treat badly; plague (*buffeted by misfortune*). **3 a** *intr.* struggle; fight one's way (through difficulties, etc.). **b** *tr.* contend with (waves, etc.). • *n.* **1** a blow, esp. of the hand. **2** a shock.

buf·fet·ing /búfiting/ *n.* **1** a beating; repeated blows. **2** *Aeron.* an irregular oscillation, caused by air eddies, of any part of an aircraft.

buf·fo /bŏŏfō/ *n. & adj.* • *n.* (*pl.* **·fos**) a comic actor, esp. in Italian opera. • *adj.* comic; burlesque.

buf·foon /bəfŏŏn/ *n.* **1** a jester; a mocker. **2** a stupid person. ▫▫ **buf·foon·er·y** *n.* **buf·foon·ish** *adj.*

bug /bug/ *n. & v.* • *n.* **1 a** any of various hemipterous insects with mouthparts modified for piercing and sucking. **b** *colloq.* any small insect. **2** *sl.* a microorganism or a disease caused by it. **3** a concealed microphone. **4** *sl.* an error in a computer program or system, etc. **5** *sl.* an obsession, enthusiasm, etc. • *v.* (**bugged, bugging**) **1** *tr.* conceal a microphone in. **2** *tr. sl.* annoy; bother. **3** *intr.* (often foll. by *out*) *sl.* leave quickly.

bug·a·boo /búgabōō/ *n.* a bogey (see BOGEY²) or bugbear.

bug·bear /búgbair/ *n.* **1** a cause of annoyance or anger. **2** an object of baseless fear.

bug-eyed *adj.* with bulging eyes.

bug·ger /búgər/ *n. & v.* • *n.* **1** a person who commits buggery. • *v.tr.* **1** *coarse sl.* as an exclamation of annoyance (*bugger the thing!*). **2** commit buggery with.

bug·ger·y /búgəree/ *n.* anal intercourse.

bug·gy /búgee/ *n.* (*pl.* **-gies**) **1** a light, horse-drawn vehicle for one or two people. **2** a small, sturdy motor vehicle (*beach buggy*; *dune buggy*). **3** a baby carriage.

bu·gle¹ /byŏŏgəl/ *n.* (also **bu·gle horn**) a brass instrument like a small trumpet without valves, used esp. for military signals. ▫▫ **bu·gler** /byŏŏglər/ *n.*

bu·gle² /byŏŏgəl/ *n.* a blue-flowered mat-forming European plant, *Ajuga reptans*.

bu·gle³ /byŏŏgəl/ *n.* a tube-shaped bead sewn on a dress, etc., for ornament.

bu·gloss /byŏŏglaws, -glos/ *n.* any of various bristly plants related to borage, esp. of the genus *Anchusa* with bright blue tubular flowers.

build /bild/ *v. & n.* • *v.tr.* (*past* and *past. part.* **built** /bilt/) **1 a** construct (a house, vehicle, fire, road, model, etc.) by putting parts or material together. **b** commission, finance, and oversee the building of (*the board has built two new schools*). **2 a** (often foll. by *up*) establish, develop, make, or accumulate gradually (*built the business up from nothing*). **b** (often foll. by *on*) base (hopes, theories, etc.) (*ideas built on a false foundation*). **3** (as **built** *adj.*) having a specified build (*sturdily built*; *brick-built*). • *n.* **1** the proportions of the body (*a slim build*). **2** a style of construction. ▫ **build in** incorporate as part of a structure. **build up 1** increase in size or strength. **2** praise; boost. **3** gradually become established.

build·er /bíldər/ *n.* **1** a contractor for building houses, etc. **2** a person engaged as a construction worker, etc., on a building site.

build·ing /bílding/ *n.* **1** a permanent fixed structure forming an enclosure and providing protection from the elements, etc. **2** the constructing of such structures.

build·up /bíldəp/ *n.* **1** a favorable description in advance. **2** a gradual approach to a climax or maximum.

built-in *adj.* **1** forming an integral part of a structure. **2** forming an integral part of a person's character (*built-in integrity*).

built-up *adj.* **1** (of a locality) densely covered by houses, etc. **2** increased in height, etc., by the addition of parts. **3** composed of separately prepared parts.

bulb /bulb/ *n.* **1 a** a fleshy-leaved storage organ of some plants sending roots downward and leaves upward. **b** a plant grown from this. **2** = LIGHTBULB (see LIGHT¹). **3** any object or part shaped like a bulb.

bul·bous /búlbəs/ *adj.* **1** shaped like a bulb; fat or bulging. **2** having a bulb or bulbs. **3** (of a plant) growing from a bulb.

Bul·gar·i·an /bulgáireeən/ *n. & adj.* • *n.* **1 a** a native or inhabitant of Bulgaria. **b** a person of Bulgarian descent. **2** the language of Bulgaria. • *adj.* of or relating to Bulgaria or its people or language.

bulge /bulj/ *n. & v.* • *n.* **1 a** a convex part of an otherwise flat or flatter surface. **b** an irregular swelling; a lump. **2** *colloq.* a temporary increase in quantity or number. • *v.* **1** *intr.* swell outwards. **2** *intr.* be full or re-plete. **3** *tr.* swell (a bag, cheeks, etc.) by stuffing. ▫▫ **bulg·y** *adj.*

bul·gur /búlgər/ *n.* (also **bul·gar, bul·ghur**) whole wheat that has been partially boiled then dried.

bu·lim·a·rex·i·a /boolímərékseeə, –léemə–, byoo–/ *n.* = BULIMIA 2. ▫▫ **bu·lim·a·rex·ic** *adj. & n.*

bu·lim·i·a /booléemeeə/ *n. Med.* **1** insatiable overeating. **2** (in full **bulimia nervosa**) an emotional disorder in which bouts of extreme overeating are followed by self-induced vomiting, etc. ▫▫ **bu·lim·ic** *adj. & n.*

bulk /bulk/ *n. & v.* • *n.* **1 a** a size; magnitude (esp. large). **b** a large mass. **c** a large quantity. **2** a large shape or body (*jacket barely covered his bulk*). **3** (usu. prec. by *the*; treated as *pl.*) the greater part or number (*the bulk of the applicants are women*). **4** roughage. • *v.* **1** *intr.* seem in respect to size or importance (*bulks large in his reckoning*). **2** *tr.* (often foll. by *out*) make (a book, a textile yarn, etc.) seem thicker by suitable treatment (*bulked it with irrelevant stories*). ▫ **in bulk** in large quantities.

bulk·head /búlk-hed/ *n.* **1** an upright partition separating the compartments in a ship, vehicle, etc. **2** an embankment or retaining wall, esp. along a waterfront.

bulk·y /búlkee/ *adj.* (**bulkier, bulkiest**) **1** taking up much space; large. **2** awkwardly large; unwieldy. ▫▫ **bulk·i·ly** *adv.* **bulk·i·ness** *n.*

bull[1] /bool/ *n.* **1 a** an uncastrated male bovine animal. **b** a male of the whale, elephant, and other large animals. **2** (**the Bull**) the zodiacal sign or constellation Taurus. **3** *Stock Exch.* a person who buys shares hoping to sell them at a higher price later (cf. BEAR[3]).

bull[2] /bool/ *n.* a papal edict.

bull[3] /bool/ *n.* **1** (also **Irish bull**) an expression containing a contradiction in terms. **2** *sl.* **a** unnecessary routine tasks or discipline. **b** nonsense. **c** trivial or insincere talk or writing.

bull·dog /bóoldawg, -dog/ *n.* a dog of a sturdy breed with a large head and smooth hair.

bull·doze /bóoldōz/ *v.tr.* **1** clear with a bulldozer. **2** *colloq.* **a** intimidate. **b** make (one's way) forcibly.

bull·doz·er /bóoldōzər/ *n.* a powerful tractor with a broad curved vertical blade at the front for clearing ground.

bul·let /bóolit/ *n.* **1** a small round or cylindrical missile with a pointed end, fired from a rifle, revolver, etc. **2** *Printing* a round black dot used as a marker (•).

bul·le·tin /bóolitin/ *n.* **1** a short official statement of news. **2** a regular periodical issued by an organization.

---

bulletin mid-17th century (denoting an official warrant in some European countries) from French, from Italian *bullettino*, diminutive of *bulletta* 'passport,' diminutive of *bulla* 'official seal on a document.'

---

bul·le·tin board *n.* **1** a board for posting notices, information, etc. **2** *Computing* a public computer file serving the function of a bulletin board.

bul·let·proof /bóolitproof/ *adj.* (of a material) designed to resist the penetration of bullets.

bull·fight /bóolfit/ *n.* a sport of baiting and (usu.) killing bulls as a public spectacle. ▫▫ **bull·fight·er** *n.* **bull·fight·ing** *n.*

bull·finch /bóolfinch/ *n.* a European finch, *Pyrrhula pyrrhula*, with a short stout beak and bright plumage.

bull·frog /bóolfrawg, -frog/ *n.* a large frog, *Rana catesbiana*, native to eastern N. America, with a deep croak.

bull·head /bóolhed/ *n.* any of various freshwater catfishes of N. America.

bull·head·ed /bóolhédid/ *adj.* obstinate; impetuous; blundering. ▫▫ **bull·head·ed·ly** *adv.* **bull·head·ed·ness** *n.*

bull·horn /bóolhawrn/ *n.* an electronic device for amplifying the voice so it can be heard at a distance.

bul·lion /bóolyən/ *n.* a metal (esp. gold or silver) in bulk before coining, or valued by weight.

bull·ish /bóolish/ *adj.* **1** like a bull, esp. in size or temper. **2 a** *Stock Exch.* causing or associated with a rise in prices. **b** optimistic. ▫▫ **bull·ish·ly** *adv.* **bull·ish·ness** *n.*

bull mar·ket *n. Stock Exch.* a market with shares rising in price.

bul·lock /bóolək/ *n.* a castrated bull.

bull pen *n.* (also **bull·pen**) **1** *Baseball* **a** an area in which relief pitchers warm up during a game. **b** the relief pitchers on a team. **2** a large holding cell for prisoners awaiting court appearances. **3** *colloq.* an open, unpartitioned area for several workers.

bull·ring /bóolring/ *n.* an arena for bullfights.

bull ses·sion *n.* an informal group discussion.

bull's-eye *n.* **1 a** the center of a target. **b** a shot that hits this. **2** a large hard peppermint-flavored candy. **3** a hemisphere or thick disk of glass in a ship's deck or side to admit light. **4** a small circular window. **5 a** a hemispherical lens. **b** a lantern fitted with this. **6** a boss of glass at the center of a blown glass sheet.

bull·shit /bóolshit/ *n. & v. coarse sl.* • *n.* **1** (often as *int.*) nonsense. **2** trivial or insincere talk or writing. • *v.intr.* (**-shitted, -shitting**) talk nonsense; bluff. ▫▫ **bull·shit·ter** *n.*

bull ter·ri·er *n.* a short-haired dog of a breed that is a cross between a bulldog and a terrier.

bul·ly[1] /bóolee/ *n. & v.* • *n.* (*pl.* **-lies**) a person who uses strength or power to coerce others by fear. • *v.tr.* (**-ies, -ied**) **1** persecute by force or threats. **2** (foll. by *into* + verbal noun) pressure (a person) to do something (*bullied him into agreeing*).

bul·ly[2] /bóolee/ *adj. & int. colloq.* • *adj.* very good. • *int.* (foll. by *for*) expressing admiration or approval, or *iron.* (*bully for them!*).

bul·ly·boy /bóoleeboy/ *n.* a hired thug.

bul·rush /bóolrush/ *n.* **1** a rushlike water plant, *Scirpus lacustris*, used for weaving. **2** *Bibl.* a papyrus plant.

bul·wark /bóolwərk/ *n.* **1** a defensive wall, esp. of earth; a breakwater. **2** a person, principle, etc., that acts as a defense. **3** (usu. in *pl.*) a ship's side above deck.

bum /bum/ *n., v., & adj. sl.* • *n.* a habitual loafer or tramp; a lazy dissolute person. • *v.* (**bummed, bumming**) **1** *intr.* (often foll. by *about, around*) loaf or wander around. **2** *tr.* cadge. • *attrib.adj.* **1** of poor quality. **2** not entirely functional (*bum ankle*).

bum·ble /búmbəl/ *v.intr.* **1** (foll. by *on*) speak in a rambling way. **2** (often as **bumbling** *adj.*) move or act ineptly. **3** make a buzz or hum. ▫▫ **bum·bler** *n.*

bum·ble·bee /búmbəlbee/ *n.* any large humming bee of the genus *Bombus*.

bum·mer /búmər/ *n. sl.* **1** a bum; a loafer. **2** an unpleasant occurrence.

bump /bump/ *n., v., & adv.* • *n.* **1** a dull-sounding blow or collision. **2** a swelling or dent caused by this. **3** an uneven patch on a road, field, etc. **4** *Phrenol.* any of various prominences on the skull thought to indicate different mental faculties. • *v.* **1 a** *tr.* hit or come against with a bump. **b** *intr.* (of two objects) collide. **2** *intr.* (foll. by *against, into*) hit with a bump; collide with. **3** *tr.* (often foll. by *against, on*) hurt or damage by striking (*bumped my head on the ceiling*). **4** *intr.* (usu. foll. by *along*) move with much jolting (*bumped along the road*). **5** *tr.* displace, esp. by seniority. • *adv.* with a bump; suddenly; violently. ▫ **bump into** *colloq.* meet by chance. **bump off** *sl.* murder. **bump up** *colloq.* increase (prices, etc.).

bump·er /búmpər/ *n.* **1** a horizontal device fixed across the front or back of a vehicle to reduce damage in a collision or as trim. **2** (usu. *attrib.*) an unusually large or fine example (*a bumper crop*).

bump·er car *n.* each of a number of small electrically-driven cars in an enclosure at an amusement park, driven around and bumped into each other.

bump·er stick·er *n.* a strip of paper backed with adhesive that may be affixed to an automobile bumper, usu. bearing a joke, political slogan, advertisement, etc.

bump·kin /búmpkin/ *n.* a rustic or socially inept person.

bump·tious /búmpshəs/ *adj.* offensively self-assertive or conceited. ▫▫ **bump·tious·ly** *adv.* **bump·tious·ness** *n.*

bump·y /búmpee/ *adj.* (**bumpier, bumpiest**) **1** having many bumps (*a bumpy road*). **2** affected by bumps (*a bumpy ride*). ▫▫ **bump·i·ly** *adv.* **bump·i·ness** *n.*

bum rap *n. sl.* imprisonment on a false charge.

bum's rush *n. sl.* forcible ejection.

bum steer *n. sl.* false information.

bun /bun/ *n.* **1** a small often sweet bread roll. **2** hair worn in the shape of a bun. **3** (in *pl.*) *sl.* the buttocks. ▫ **have a bun in the oven** *sl.* be pregnant.

bunch /bunch/ *n. & v.* • *n.* **1** a cluster of things growing or fastened together. **2** a collection; a set (*best of the bunch*). **3** *colloq.* a group; a gang. • *v.* **1** *tr.* make into a bunch; gather into close folds. **2** *intr.* form into a group or crowd. ▫▫ **bunch·y** *adj.*

bun·co /búngkō/ *n. & v.* (also **bun·ko**) *sl.* • *n.* (*pl.* **-cos**) a swindle, esp. by card sharping or a confidence trick. • *v.tr.* (**-oes, -oed**) swindle; cheat.

bun·combe var. of BUNKUM.

bun·dle /búndəl/ *n. & v.* • *n.* **1** a collection of things tied or fastened together. **2** a set of nerve fibers, etc., banded together. **3** *sl.* a large amount of money. • *v.* **1** *tr.* **a** (usu. foll. by *up*) tie in or make into a bundle (*bundled up my exercise things*). **b** sell (a product) together with another one in a single transaction. **2** *tr.* (usu. foll. by *into*) throw or push, esp. quickly or confusedly (*bundled the papers into the drawer*). **3** *tr.* (usu. foll. by *out, off, away,* etc.) send away hurriedly or unceremoniously (*bundled them off the premises*). ▫ **bundle up** dress warmly or cumbersomely.

bung /bung/ *n. & v.* • *n.* a stopper for closing a hole in a container. • *v.tr.* stop with a bung. ▫ **bunged up** closed; blocked.

bun·ga·low /búnggəlō/ *n.* a one-storied house.

bun·gee /búnjee/ *n.* (in full **bungee cord**) elasticized cord or rope.

bun·gee jump·ing *n.* the sport of jumping from a height while secured by a bungee from the ankles or a harness.

bun·gle /búnggəl/ *v. & n.* • *v.* **1** *tr.* mismanage or fail at (a task). **2** *intr.* work badly or clumsily. • *n.* a bungled attempt; bungled work. ▫▫ **bun·gler** *n.*

bun·ion /búnyən/ *n.* a swelling on the foot, esp. at the first joint of the big toe.

bunk[1] /bungk/ *n. & v.* • *n.* a shelflike bed against a wall. • *v.intr.* **1** sleep in a bunk. **2** occupy sleeping quarters.

bunk[2] /bungk/ *n. sl.* = BUNKUM.

bunk bed *n.* each of two or more beds one above the other, forming a unit.

bun·ker /búngkər/ *n. & v.* • *n.* **1** a large container or compartment for storing fuel. **2** a reinforced underground shelter. **3** a hollow filled with sand, used as an obstacle in a golf course. • *v.tr.* **1** fill the fuel bunkers of (a ship, etc.). **2** (usu. in *passive*) trap in a bunker (in sense 3).

bunk·house /búngk-hows/ *n.* a house where workers, etc., are lodged.

bun·kum /búngkəm/ *n.* (also **bun·combe**) nonsense; humbug.

bun·ny /búnee/ *n.* (*pl.* **-nies**) a child's name for a rabbit.

Bun·sen burn·er /búnsən/ *n.* an adjustable gas burner used in scientific work as a source of heat.

bunt /bunt/ *v. & n.* • *v.* **1** *tr. & intr.* push with the head or horns; butt. **2** *tr. Baseball* to tap or push (a ball) with the bat without swinging. • *n.* an act of bunting.

bunt·ing[1] /búnting/ *n.* any of numerous seed-eating birds of the family Emberizidae, related to the finches.

bunt·ing[2] /búnting/ *n.* flags and other decorations.

bunt·ing[3] /búnting/ *n.* a baby's hooded sleeping bag made of soft fabric.

bu·oy /bo͞o-ee, boy/ *n. & v.* • *n.* **1** an anchored float serving as a navigation mark or to show reefs, etc. **2** a lifebuoy. • *v.tr.* **1** (usu. foll. by *up*) **a** keep afloat. **b** sustain the spirits of (a person, etc.); encourage. **2** (often foll. by *out*) mark with a buoy or buoys.

buoy·an·cy /bóyənsee/ *n.* **1** the capacity to be or remain buoyant. **2** resilience. **3** cheerfulness.

buoy·ant /bóyənt/ *adj.* **1 a** able or apt to keep afloat or rise to the top of a liquid or gas. **b** (of a liquid or gas) able to keep something afloat. **2** lighthearted. ▫▫ **bu·oy·ant·ly** *adv.*

bur /bər/ *n.* var. of BURR.

bur·ble /bárbəl/ *v. & n.* • *v.intr.* **1** speak ramblingly. **2** make a murmuring noise. • *n.* a murmuring noise.

bur·bot /bárbət/ *n.* an eellike, bearded freshwater fish, *Lota lota.*

bur·den /bárdən/ *n. & v.* • *n.* **1** a load. **2** an oppressive duty, obligation, expense, emotion, etc. **3** the bearing of loads (*beast of burden*). **4** a ship's carrying capacity. • *v.tr.* load with a burden; oppress. ▫▫ **bur·den·some** *adj.*

bur·den of proof *n.* the obligation to prove one's case.

bur·dock /bárdok/ *n.* any plant of the genus *Arctium*, with prickly flowers and docklike leaves.

bu·reau /byo͝orō/ *n.* (*pl.* **bureaus** or **bureaux** /-rōz/) **1** a chest of drawers. **2** an office or department for transacting specific business.

bu·reauc·ra·cy /byo͝orókrəsee/ *n.* (*pl.* **-cies**) **1 a** government by central administration. **b** a nation or organization so governed. **2** the officials of such a government. **3** conduct typical of such officials.

bu·reau·crat /byo͝orəkrat/ *n.* **1** an official in a bureaucracy. **2** an officious administrator. ▫▫ **bu·reau·crat·ic** /-krátik/ *adj.* **bu·reau·crat·i·cal·ly** *adv.*

bu·reauc·ra·tize /byo͝orókrətīz/ *v.tr.* govern by or transform into a bureaucratic system. ▫▫ **bu·reauc·ra·ti·za·tion** /-tizáyshən/ *n.*

bu·rette /byo͝orét/ *n.* (also **bu·ret**) a graduated glass tube with a stopcock for measuring small volumes of liquid in chemical analysis.

burg /bərg/ *n.* a town or city.

bur·gee /bərjée/ *n.* a triangular or swallow-tailed flag bearing the colors or emblem of a yacht club.

bur·geon /bárjən/ *v.intr. literary* **1** begin to grow rapidly; flourish. **2** put forth young shoots; bud.

burg·er /bárgər/ *n.* **1** *colloq.* a hamburger. **2** (in *comb.*) a certain kind of hamburger or variation of it (*beefburger; veggieburger*).

bur·gess /bárjis/ *n. hist.* a borough magistrate or legislator in colonial Maryland or Virginia.

burgh·er /bárgər/ *n.* a citizen of a town on the European continent.

bur·glar /bárglər/ *n.* a person who commits burglary.

bur·glar·ize /bárglərīz/ *v.* **1** *tr.* commit burglary against (a building or person). **2** *intr.* commit burglary.

bur·gla·ry /bárgləree/ *n.* (*pl.* **-ries**) **1** entry into a building illegally with intent to commit theft, do bodily harm, or do damage. **2** an instance of this.

bur·gle /bárgəl/ *v.tr. & intr.* = BURGLARIZE.

bur·grave /bárgrayv/ *n. hist.* the ruler of a town or castle.

bur·gun·dy /bə́rgəndee/ *n.* (*pl.* **-dies**) **1 a** the wine (usu. red) of Burgundy in E. France. **b** a similar wine from another place. **2** the dark red color of Burgundy wine.

bur·i·al /béreeəl/ *n.* **1 a** the burying of a dead body. **b** a funeral. **2** *Archaeol.* a grave or its remains.

bu·rin /byŏŏrin, bə́r-/ *n.* **1** a steel tool for engraving on copper or wood. **2** *Archaeol.* a flint tool with a chisel point.

Bur·kitt's lym·pho·ma /bə́rkits/ *n. Med.* a malignant tumor of the lymphatic system, esp. affecting children of Central Africa.

burl /bərl/ *n.* **1** a knot or lump in wool or cloth. **2** a rounded knotty growth on a tree.

bur·lap /bə́rlap/ *n.* **1** coarse canvas esp. of jute used for sacking, etc. **2** a similar lighter material for use in dressmaking or furnishing.

bur·lesque /bərlésk/ *n., adj., & v.* • *n.* **1 a** comic imitation, parody. **b** a performance or work of this kind. **c** bombast; mock-seriousness. **2** a variety show, often including striptease. • *adj.* of or in the nature of burlesque. • *v.tr.* (**burlesques, burlesqued, burlesquing**) make or give a burlesque of.

bur·ly /bə́rlee/ *adj.* (**burlier, burliest**) of stout sturdy build; big and strong.

Bur·mese /bə́rmeez/ *n. & adj.* • *n.* (*pl.* same) **1 a** a native or inhabitant of Burma (also called Myanmar) in SE Asia. **b** a person of Burmese descent. **2** a member of the largest ethnic group of Burma. **3** the language of this group. **4** a breed of short-coated domestic cat. • *adj.* of or relating to Burma or its people or language.

burn /bərn/ *v. & n.* • *v.* (*past* and *past part.* **burned** or **burnt**) **1** *tr. & intr.* be or cause to be consumed or destroyed by fire. **2** *intr.* **a** blaze or glow with fire. **b** be in the state characteristic of fire. **3** *tr. & intr.* be or cause to be injured or damaged by fire or great heat or by radiation. **4** *tr. & intr.* use or be used as a source of heat, light, or other energy. **5** *tr. & intr.* char in cooking (*burned the vegetables*; *the vegetables are burning*). **6** *tr.* produce (a hole, a mark, etc.) by fire or heat. **7** *tr.* **a** subject (clay, chalk, etc.) to heat for a purpose. **b** harden (bricks) by fire. **c** make (lime or charcoal) by heat. **8** *tr.* color, tan, or parch with heat or light. **9** *tr. & intr.* put or be put to death by fire or electrocution. **10** *tr.* **a** cauterize; brand. **b** (foll. by *in*) imprint by burning. **11** *tr. & intr.* make or be hot; give or feel a sensation or pain of or like heat. **12** *tr. & intr.* (often foll. by *with*) make or be passionate; feel or cause to feel great emotion (*burn with shame*). **13** *intr.* (foll. by *into*) (of acid, etc.) gradually penetrate (into) causing disintegration. • *n.* **1** a mark or injury caused by burning. **2** the ignition of a rocket engine in flight, giving extra thrust. □ **burn one's bridges** commit oneself irrevocably. **burn the candle at both ends** exhaust one's resources by undertaking too much. **burn down 1 a** destroy (a building) by burning. **b** (of a building) be destroyed by fire. **2** burn less vigorously as fuel fails. **burn a hole in one's pocket** (of money) be quickly spent. **burn low** (of fire) be nearly out. **burn the midnight oil** read or work late into the night. **burn out 1** be reduced to nothing by burning. **2** fail or cause to fail by burning. **3** (usu. *refl.*) suffer physical or emotional exhaustion. **4** consume the contents of by burning. **5** make (a person) homeless by burning his or her house. **burn up 1** get rid of by fire. **2** begin to blaze. **3** *sl.* be or make furious.

burned-out *adj.* physically or emotionally exhausted.

burn·er /bə́rnər/ *n.* the part of a gas stove, lamp, etc., that emits and shapes the flame. □ **on the back** (or **front**) **burner** *colloq.* receiving little (or much) attention.

burn·ing /bə́rning/ *adj.* **1** ardent; intense (*burning desire*). **2** hotly discussed; exciting; vital, urgent (*burning question*). **3** flagrant (*burning shame*). □□ **burn·ing·ly** *adv.*

bur·nish /bə́rnish/ *v.tr.* polish by rubbing.

bur·noose /bərnŏŏs/ *n.* (also **bur·nous**) an Arab or Moorish hooded cloak.

burn·out /bə́rnowt/ *n.* **1** physical or emotional exhaustion. **2** depression; disillusionment.

burnt /bərnt/ *past* and *past part.* of BURN.

burnt of·fer·ing *n.* **1** an offering burned on an altar as a sacrifice. **2** *joc.* overcooked food.

burp /bərp/ *v. & n. colloq.* • *v.* **1** *intr.* belch. **2** *tr.* make (a baby) belch. • *n.* a belch.

burr /bər/ *n. & v.* • *n.* **1 a** a whirring sound. **b** a rough sounding of the letter *r.* **2 a** a rough edge left on cut or punched metal or paper. **b** a surgeon's or dentist's small drill. **3 a** a prickly clinging seedcase or flowerhead. **b** any plant producing these. • *v.* **1** *tr.* pronounce with a burr. **2** *intr.* make a whirring sound.

bur·ri·to /bəreétō/ *n.* (*pl.* **-tos**) a tortilla rolled around a meat or bean filling.

bur·ro /bə́rō, bŏŏrō, búrō/ *n.* (*pl.* **-ros**) a small donkey used as a pack animal.

bur·row /bə́rō, búrō/ *n. & v.* • *n.* a hole or tunnel dug by a small animal as a dwelling. • *v.* **1** *intr.* make or live in a burrow. **2** *tr.* make (a hole, etc.) by digging. **3** *intr.* hide oneself. **4** *intr.* (foll. by *into*) investigate; search.

bur·sa /bə́rsə/ *n.* (*pl.* **bursae** /-see/ or **bursas**) *Anat.* a fluid-filled sac or cavity to lessen friction. □□ **bur·sal** *adj.*

bur·sar /bə́rsər/ *n.* a treasurer, esp. the person in charge of the funds and other property of a college.

bur·si·tis /bərsítis/ *n.* inflammation of a bursa.

burst /bərst/ *v. & n.* • *v.* (*past* and *past part.* **burst**) **1 a** *intr.* break suddenly and violently apart by expansion of contents or internal pressure. **b** *tr.* cause to do this. **c** *tr.* send (a container, etc.) violently apart. **2 a** *tr.* open forcibly. **b** *intr.* come open or be opened forcibly. **3 a** *intr.* (usu. foll. by *in, out*) make one's way suddenly or by force. **b** *tr.* break away from or through (*the river burst its banks*). **4** *tr. & intr.* fill or be full to overflowing. **5** *intr.* appear or come suddenly (*burst into flame*; *sun burst out*). **6** *intr.* (foll. by *into*) suddenly begin to shed or utter (esp. *burst into tears* or *laughter* or *song*). **7** *intr.* be as if about to burst because of effort, excitement, etc. **8** *tr.* suffer bursting of (*burst a blood vessel*). • *n.* **1** the act of or an instance of bursting; a split. **2** a sudden issuing forth (*burst of flame*). **3** a sudden outbreak (*burst of applause*). **4 a** a short sudden effort; a spurt. **b** a gallop. **5** an explosion. □ **burst out 1** suddenly begin (*burst out laughing*). **2** exclaim.

bur·y /béree/ *v.tr.* (**-ies, -ied**) **1** place (a dead body) in the earth, in a tomb, or in the sea. **2** lose by death (*has buried three husbands*). **3 a** put under ground (*bury alive*). **b** hide in the earth. **c** cover up; submerge. **4 a** put out of sight (*buried his face in his hands*). **b** consign to obscurity (*the idea was buried*). **c** put away; forget. **5** involve deeply (*buried himself in his work*). □ **bury the hatchet** cease to quarrel.

bus /bus/ *n. & v.* • *n.* (*pl.* **buses** or **busses**) **1** a large passenger vehicle, esp. one serving the public on a fixed route. **2** *colloq.* an automobile, airplane, etc. **3** *Computing* a defined set of conductors carrying data and control signals within a computer. • *v.* (**buses** or **busses, bused** or **bussed, busing** or **bussing**) **1** *intr.* go by bus. **2** *tr.* transport by bus, esp. children to more distant schools to promote racial integration.

bus·boy /búsboy/ *n.* an assistant to a restaurant waiter who performs such chores as filling water glasses and removing dirty dishes from diners' tables.

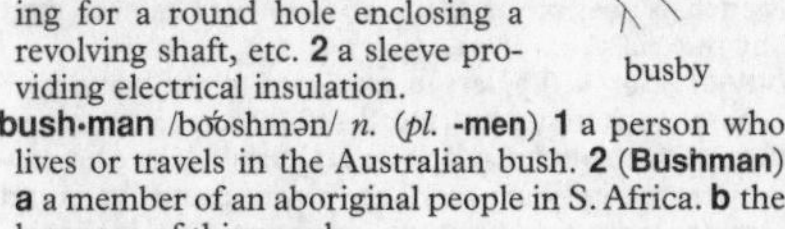
busby

bus•by /búzbee/ *n.* (*pl.* **-bies**) a tall fur hat worn by some military, esp. British, units.
bush /bŏŏsh/ *n.* **1** a shrub or clump of shrubs. **2** a thing resembling this. **3** a wild, uncultivated area (*the Australian bush*).
bush•ba•by *n.* (*pl.* **-bies**) a small African tree-climbing lemur; a galago.
bushed /bŏŏsht/ *adj. colloq.* tired out.
bush•el /bŏŏshəl/ *n.* a measure of capacity for grain, fruit, etc. (64 pints; *Brit.* 8 gallons, or 36.4 liters).
bush•ing /bŏŏshing/ *n.* **1** a metal lining for a round hole enclosing a revolving shaft, etc. **2** a sleeve providing electrical insulation.
bush•man /bŏŏshmən/ *n.* (*pl.* **-men**) **1** a person who lives or travels in the Australian bush. **2** (**Bushman**) **a** a member of an aboriginal people in S. Africa. **b** the language of this people.
bush•whack /bŏŏsh-hwak, -wak/ *v.* **1** *intr.* **a** clear woods and bush country. **b** live or travel in bush country. **2** *tr.* ambush.
bush•whack•er /bŏŏsh-hwakər, -wakər/ *n.* **1 a** a person who clears woods and bush country. **b** a person who lives or travels in bush country. **2** a guerrilla fighter (orig. in the American Civil War).
bush•y /bŏŏshee/ *adj.* (**bushier, bushiest**) **1** growing thickly like a bush. **2** having many bushes. **3** covered with bush. ▫▫ **bush•i•ness** *n.*
busi•ness /bíznis/ *n.* **1** one's regular occupation, profession, or trade. **2** a thing that is one's concern. **3 a** a task or duty. **b** a reason for coming (*what is your business?*). **4** serious activity (*get down to business*). **5** *derog.* a matter (*sick of the whole business*). **6** a thing or series of things to be dealt with (*the business of the day*). **7** buying and selling; trade; dealings, esp. of a commercial nature (*good stroke of business*). **8** a commercial firm. **9** *Theatr.* action on stage. **10** a difficult matter (*what a business*). ▫ **has no business to** has no right to. **in business 1** trading. **2** able to begin operations. **in the business of 1** engaged in. **2** intending to (*we are not in the business of surrendering*). **like nobody's business** *colloq.* extraordinarily. **mind one's own business** not meddle.
busi•ness card *n.* a card printed with one's name and professional details.
busi•ness•like /bízníslik/ *adj.* efficient; practical.
busi•ness•man /bíznismən/ *n.* (*pl.* **-men**; *fem.* **businesswoman,** *pl.* **-women**) a man or woman engaged in trade or commerce, esp. at a senior level.
busi•ness per•son *n.* a businessman or businesswoman.
busk /busk/ *v.intr.* play music or otherwise perform for donations in the streets or subways. ▫▫ **busk•er** *n.*
bus•man /búsmən/ *n.* (*pl.* **-men**) the driver of a bus.
bus•man's hol•i•day *n.* leisure time spent in an activity similar to one's regular work.
bust[1] /bust/ *n.* **1 a** the human chest, esp. that of a woman; the bosom. **b** the circumference of the body at bust level (*a 36-inch bust*). **2** a sculpture of a person's head, shoulders, and chest.
bust[2] /bust/ *v., n., & adj. colloq.* • *v.* (*past* and *past part.* **busted** or **bust**) **1** *tr. & intr.* burst; break. **2** *tr.* reduce (a soldier, etc.) to a lower rank; dismiss. **3** *tr.* **a** raid; search. **b** arrest. • *n.* **1** a sudden failure; a bankruptcy. **2 a** a police raid. **b** an arrest. • *adj.* (also **bust•ed**) **1** broken; burst; collapsed. **2** bankrupt. **3** arrested. ▫ **bust up 1** bring or come to collapse; explode. **2** (of a couple) separate. **go bust** become bankrupt; fail.
bus•tard /bústərd/ *n.* any large terrestrial bird of the family Otididae, with long neck, long legs, and stout tapering body.
bust•er /bústər/ *n.* **1** *sl.* buddy; fellow (used esp. as a disrespectful form of address). **2** a violent gale.
bus•tier /bŏŏstyáy, bústeeay/ *n.* a strapless close-fitting bodice.
bus•tle[1] /búsəl/ *v. & n.* • *v.* **1** *intr.* (often foll. by *about*) **a** work, etc., showily, energetically, and officiously. **b** hasten. **2** *tr.* make (a person) hurry or work hard (*bustled him into his overcoat*). **3** *intr.* (as **bustling** *adj.*) *colloq.* full of activity. • *n.* excited activity; a fuss.
bus•tle[2] /búsəl/ *n. hist.* a pad or frame worn under a skirt and puffing it out behind.
bust•y /bústee/ *adj.* (**bustier, bustiest**) (of a woman) having a prominent bust.
bus•y /bízee/ *adj., & v.* • *adj.* (**busier, busiest**) **1** (often foll. by *in, with, at,* or pres. part.) occupied or engaged in work, etc., with the attention concentrated. **2** full of activity or detail; fussy (*a busy evening; a picture busy with detail*). **3** employed continuously; unresting. **4** meddlesome; prying. **5** (of a telephone line) in use. • *v.tr.* (**-ies, -ied**) (often *refl.*) keep busy; occupy. ▫▫ **bus•ily** /bízilee/ *adv.*
bus•y•bod•y /bízeebodee, -budee/ *n.* (*pl.* **-ies**) a meddlesome person.
bus•y sig•nal *n.* an intermittent buzzing sound indicating that a telephone line is in use.
but /but, bət/ *conj., prep., adv., pron., & n.* • *conj.* **1 a** nevertheless; however (*tried hard but did not succeed*). **b** on the other hand; on the contrary (*I am old but you are young*). **2** (prec. by *can,* etc.; in *neg.* or *interrog.*) except; other than; otherwise than (*cannot choose but do it; what could we do but run?*). **3** without the result that (*it never rains but it pours*). **4** prefixing an interruption to the speaker's train of thought (*the weather is ideal – but is that a cloud on the horizon?*). • *prep.* except; apart from; other than (*everyone went but me*). • *adv.* **1** only; no more than; only just (*we can but try; is but a child; had but arrived*). **2** introducing emphatic repetition; definitely (*wanted to see nobody, but nobody*). • *rel.pron.* who not; that not (*there is not a man but feels pity*). • *n.* an objection (*ifs and buts*). ▫ **but for** without the help or hindrance, etc., of (*but for you I'd be rich by now*). **but one** (or **two,** etc.) excluding one (or two, etc.) from the number (*next door but one; last but one*). **but then** (or **yet**) however; on the other hand (*I won, but then the others were beginners*).
bu•tane /byŏŏtayn/ *n. Chem.* a gaseous hydrocarbon of the alkane series used in liquefied form as fuel.
butch /bŏŏch/ *adj.* masculine; tough-looking.
butch•er /bŏŏchər/ *n. & v.* • *n.* **1** a person who prepares or sells meat. **2** a person who kills indiscriminately or brutally. • *v.tr.* **1** slaughter or cut up (an animal) for food. **2** kill wantonly or cruelly. **3** ruin through incompetence.
butch•er•y /bŏŏchəree/ *n.* (*pl.* **-ies**) **1** needless or cruel slaughter. **2** the butcher's trade. **3** a slaughterhouse.
but•ler /bútlər/ *n.* the principal manservant of a household.
butt[1] /but/ *v. & n.* • *v.* **1** *tr. & intr.* push with the head or horns. **2 a** *intr.* (usu. foll. by *against, upon*) touch with one end flat; meet end to end; abut. **b** *tr.* (usu. foll. by *against*) place (lumber, etc.) with the end flat against a wall, etc. • *n.* **1** a push with the head. **2** a join of two edges. ▫ **butt in** interrupt; meddle. **butt out 1** stop interrupting. **2** stop doing something.
butt[2] /but/ *n.* **1** (often foll. by *of*) an object (of ridicule, etc.) (*the butt of his jokes*). **2 a** a mound behind a target. **b** (in *pl.*) a shooting range. **c** a target.
butt[3] /but/ *n.* **1** (also **butt end**) the thicker end, esp. of a tool or a weapon (*gun butt*). **2 a** the stub of a cigar

or a cigarette. **b** (also **butt end**) a remnant. **3** *sl.* the buttocks.

butt[4] /but/ *n.* a cask, esp. as a measure of wine or ale.

butte /byo͞ot/ *n.* a high, isolated, steep-sided hill.

but·ter /bútər/ *n.* & *v.* • *n.* **1** a fatty substance made by churning cream and used as a spread or in cooking. **2** a substance of a similar consistency or appearance (*peanut butter*). • *v.tr.* spread, cook, or serve with butter (*butter the bread*; *buttered rum*). □ **butter up** *colloq.* flatter excessively.

but·ter·ball /bútərbawl/ *n. sl.* a fat person or animal.

but·ter bean *n.* **1** the flat, dried, white lima bean. **2** a yellow-podded bean.

but·ter cream *n.* (also **but·ter ic·ing**) a mixture of butter, confectioner's sugar, etc., used as a filling or a topping for a cake.

but·ter·cup /bútərkup/ *n.* any common yellow-flowered plant of the genus *Ranunculus*.

but·ter·fat /bútərfat/ *n.* the essential fats of pure butter.

but·ter·fin·gers /bútərfinggərz/ *n. colloq.* a clumsy person prone to drop things.

but·ter·fly /bútərflī/ *n.* (*pl.* **-flies**) **1** any diurnal insect of the order Lepidoptera, with four usu. brightly colored wings held erect when at rest. **2** (in *pl.*) *colloq.* a nervous sensation felt in the stomach.

but·ter·fly net *n.* a fine net on a ring attached to a pole, used for catching butterflies.

but·ter·fly stroke *n.* a stroke in swimming, with both arms raised out of the water and lifted forward together.

but·ter knife *n.* (*pl.* **knives**) a blunt knife used for cutting butter at table.

but·ter·milk /bútərmilk/ *n.* a slightly acid liquid left after churning butter.

but·ter·nut /bútərnut/ *n.* **1** a N. American tree, *Juglans cinerea*. **2** the oily nut of this tree.

but·ter·scotch /bútərskoch/ *n.* **1** a brittle candy made from butter, brown sugar, etc. **2** this flavor in dessert toppings, puddings, etc.

but·ter·y[1] /bútəree/ *n.* (*pl.* **-ies**) a pantry.

but·ter·y[2] /bútəree/ *adj.* like, containing, or spread with butter. □□ **but·ter·i·ness** *n.*

but·tock /bútək/ *n.* (usu. in *pl.*) **1** each of two fleshy protuberances on the lower rear part of the human trunk. **2** the corresponding part of an animal.

but·ton /bút'n/ *n.* & *v.* • *n.* **1** a small disk or knob sewn on to a garment, either to fasten it by being pushed through a buttonhole, or as an ornament or badge. **2** a knob on a piece of equipment which is pressed to operate it. **3 a** a small round object (*chocolate buttons*). **b** (*attrib.*) anything resembling a button (*button nose*). **4 a** a bud. **b** a button mushroom. **5** *Fencing* a terminal knob on a foil making it harmless. • *v.* **1** *tr.* & *intr.* fasten with buttons. **2** *tr.* supply with buttons. □ **button one's lip** *sl.* remain silent. **button up 1** fasten with buttons. **2** *colloq.* complete satisfactorily. **3** *colloq.* become silent. **on the button** *sl.* precisely. □□ **but·toned** *adj.* **but·ton·less** *adj.*

but·ton·hole /bút'nhōl/ *n.* & *v.* • *n.* a slit made in a garment to receive a button for fastening. • *v.tr. colloq.* accost and detain (a reluctant listener).

but·tress /bútris/ *n.* & *v.* • *n.* **1 a** a projecting support built against a wall. **b** a source of help or encouragement. **2** a projecting portion of a hill or mountain. • *v.tr.* (often foll. by *up*) **1** support with a buttress. **2** support by argument, etc.

bux·om /búksəm/ *adj.* (esp. of a woman) plump; busty.

buy /bī/ *v.* & *n.* • *v.* (**buys, buying**; *past* and *past part.* **bought** /bawt/) **1** *tr.* **a** obtain in exchange for money, etc. **b** (usu. in *neg.*) serve to obtain (*money can't buy happiness*). **2** *tr.* **a** procure (the loyalty, etc.) of a person by bribery, promises, etc. **b** win over (a person) in this way. **3** *tr.* get by sacrifice, great effort, etc. (*dearly bought*). **4** *tr. sl.* accept; believe in; approve of. **5** *absol.* be a buyer for a store, etc. (*buys for Macy's*). • *n. colloq.* a purchase (*a good buy*). □ **buy the farm** die. **buy in 1** buy a supply of. **2** withdraw (an item) at auction because of failure to reach the reserve price. **buy into 1** obtain a share in (an enterprise) by payment. **2** *colloq.* support, embrace (an idea, etc.). **buy it** (usu. in *past*) *sl.* be killed. **buy off** get rid of (a claim, a claimant, a blackmailer) by payment. **buy out** pay (a person) to give up an ownership, etc. **buy time** delay an event, conclusion, etc., temporarily. **buy up 1** buy as much as possible of. **2** absorb (another business, etc.) by purchase.

buy·er /bíər/ *n.* **1** a person employed to select and purchase stock for a store, etc. **2** a purchaser; a customer.

buy·er's mar·ket *n.* (also **buy·ers' mar·ket**) an economic position in which goods are plentiful and cheap and buyers have the advantage.

buy·out /bíowt/ *n.* the purchase of a controlling share in a company, etc.

buzz /buz/ *n.* & *v.* • *n.* **1** the hum of a bee, etc. **2** the sound of a buzzer. **3 a** a confused low sound as of people talking; a murmur. **b** a stir (*a buzz of excitement*). **c** *colloq.* a rumor. **4** *sl.* a telephone call. **5** *sl.* a thrill; a euphoric sensation. • *v.* **1** *intr.* make a humming sound. **2 a** *tr.* & *intr.* signal or signal to with a buzzer. **b** *tr. sl.* telephone. **3** *intr.* **a** (often foll. by *about*) move or hover busily. **b** (of a place) have an air of excitement or purposeful activity. **4** *tr. Aeron. colloq.* fly fast and very close to (another aircraft, the ground, etc.). □ **buzz off** *sl.* go or hurry away.

buz·zard /búzərd/ *n.* **1** a turkey vulture. **2** a European hawk, esp. of the genus *Butea*, with broad wings well adapted for soaring.

buzz·er /búzər/ *n.* **1** an electrical device that makes a buzzing noise. **2** a whistle or siren.

buzz saw *n.* a circular saw.

buzz·word /búzwərd/ *n. sl.* **1** a fashionable piece of jargon. **2** a catchword; a slogan.

by /bī/ *prep., adv.,* & *n.* • *prep.* **1** near; beside (*stand by the door*; *sit by me*). **2** through the agency, means, instrumentality, or causation of (*bought by a millionaire*; *a poem by Frost*; *went by bus*; *succeeded by persisting*; *divide four by two*). **3** not later than (*by next week*). **4 a** past; beyond (*drove by the zoo*). **b** passing through; via (*went by Paris*). **5** in the circumstances of (*by day*). **6** to the extent of (*missed by a foot*). **7** according to; using as a standard or unit (*judge by appearances*; *paid by the hour*). **8** with the succession of (*worse by the minute*). **9** concerning; in respect of (*did our duty by them*). **10** used in mild oaths (orig. = as surely as one believes in) (*by God*). **11** placed between specified lengths in two directions (*three feet by two*). **12** avoiding; ignoring (*passed us by*). **13** inclining to (*north by northwest*). • *adv.* **1** near (*sat by, watching*). **2** aside; in reserve (*put $5 by*). **3** past (*marched by*). • *n.* (*pl.* **byes**) = BYE. □ **by and by** before long; eventually. **by and large** on the whole; everything considered. **by the by** (or **bye**) incidentally; parenthetically.

by- /bī/ *prefix* (also **bye-**) subordinate; incidental; secondary (*by-effect*; *byroad*).

bye[1] /bī/ *n.* **1** the status of an unpaired competitor in a sport, who proceeds to the next round as if having won. **2** *Golf* one or more holes remaining unplayed after the match has been decided.

bye[2] /bī/ *int. colloq.* = GOOD-BYE.

bye- *prefix* var. of BY-.

bye-bye /bíbí, bəbí/ *int. colloq.* = GOOD-BYE.

bye·law *n.* var. of BYLAW.

Bye·lo·rus·sian var. of BELORUSSIAN.

by·gone /bígawn, -gon/ *adj. & n.* • *adj.* past; antiquated (*bygone years*). • *n.* (in *pl.*) past offenses (*let bygones be bygones*).
by·law /bílaw/ *n.* (also **bye·law**) a regulation made by an organization for its members.
by·line /bílīn/ *n.* **1** a line in a newspaper, etc., naming the writer of an article. **2** a secondary line of work.
by·name /bínaym/ *n.* a sobriquet; a nickname.
by·pass /bípas/ *n. & v.* • *n.* **1** a road passing around a town or its center. **2 a** a secondary channel or pipe, etc., to allow a flow when the main one is closed or blocked. **b** an alternative passage for the circulation of blood during a surgical operation on the heart. • *v.tr.* **1** avoid; go around. **2** provide with a bypass.
by·prod·uct /bíprodəkt/ *n.* **1** an incidental product of the manufacture of something else. **2** a secondary result.
by·road /bírōd/ *n.* a minor road.
By·ron·ic /bīrónik/ *adj.* **1** characteristic of Lord Byron, English poet d. 1824, or his romantic poetry. **2** (of a man) handsomely dark, mysterious, or moody.
by·stand·er /bístandər/ *n.* a person who stands by but does not take part.
byte /bīt/ *n. Computing* a group of eight binary digits, often used to represent one character.
by·way /bíway/ *n.* **1** a small seldom-traveled road. **2** a minor activity.
by·word /bíwərd/ *n.* **1** a person or thing cited as a notable example (*is a byword for luxury*). **2** a familiar saying.
Byz·an·tine /bízənteen, -tīn, bizántin/ *adj. & n.* • *adj.* **1** of Byzantium or the E. Roman Empire. **2** (of a political situation, etc.): **a** extremely complicated. **b** inflexible. **3** *Archit. & Painting* of a highly decorated style developed in the Eastern Empire. • *n.* a citizen of Byzantium or the E. Roman Empire.

C

C¹ /see/ *n.* (also **c**) (*pl.* **Cs** or **C's**) **1** the third letter of the alphabet. **2** *Mus.* the first note of the diatonic scale of C major. **3** the third hypothetical person or example. **4** the third highest class or category. **5** *Algebra* (usu. **c**) the third known quantity. **6** (as a Roman numeral) 100. **7** (**c**) the speed of light in a vacuum. **8** (also ©) copyright.

C² *symb. Chem.* the element carbon.

C³ *abbr.* (also **C.**) **1** Cape. **2** Celsius; centigrade. **3** Coulomb(s); capacitance.

c. *abbr.* **1** century; centuries. **2** chapter. **3** cent(s). **4** cold. **5** cubic. **6** *Baseball* catcher. **7** centi-. **8** circa; about.

CA *abbr.* **1** California (in official postal use). **2** *Sc. & Can.* chartered accountant.

Ca *symb. Chem.* the element calcium.

ca. *abbr.* circa, about.

cab /kab/ *n.* **1** a taxi. **2** the driver's compartment in a truck, train, crane, etc.

ca·bal /kəbál/ *n.* **1** a secret intrigue. **2** a political clique or faction.

cab·a·la /kábələ, kəbaálə/ *n.* (also **cab·ba·la, kab·ba·la**) **1** the Jewish mystical tradition. **2** mystic interpretation; any esoteric doctrine or occult lore. □□ **cab·a·lism** *n.* **cab·a·list** *n.* **cab·a·lis·tic** /–lístik/ *adj.*

ca·ba·na /kəbánə, –baányə/ *n.* a shelter, bathhouse, etc., at a beach or swimming pool.

cab·a·ret /kabəráy/ *n.* **1** an entertainment in a nightclub or restaurant while guests eat or drink at tables. **2** such a nightclub, etc.

cab·bage /kábij/ *n.* **1** any of several cultivated varieties of *Brassica oleracea*, with thick green or purple leaves forming a round heart or head. **2** this head usu. eaten as a vegetable. □□ **cab·bag·y** *adj.*

cab·bage white *n.* a butterfly, *Pieris brassicae*, whose caterpillars feed on cabbage leaves.

cab·ba·la var. of CABALA.

cab·by /kábee/ *n.* (also **cab·bie**) (*pl.* **·bies**) *colloq.* a cabdriver.

ca·ber /káybər/ *n.* a roughly trimmed tree trunk used in the Scottish Highland sport of tossing the caber.

cab·in /kábin/ *n. & v.* • *n.* **1** a small shelter or house. **2** a room or compartment in an aircraft or ship for passengers or crew. **3** a driver's cab. • *v.tr.* (**cabined, cabining**) confine in a small place; cramp.

cab·i·net /kábinit/ *n.* **1 a** a cupboard or case with drawers, shelves, etc., for storing or displaying articles. **b** a piece of furniture housing a radio or television set, etc. **2** (**Cabinet**) the committee of senior advisers responsible for counseling the head of state on government policy.

cab·in fe·ver *n.* a state of restlessness and irritability from having been confined or in a remote location for an extended period.

ca·ble /káybəl/ *n. & v.* • *n.* **1** a thick rope of wire or hemp. **2** an encased group of insulated wires for transmitting electricity or electrical signals. **3** a cablegram. **4** *Naut.* **a** the chain of an anchor. **b** (in full **cable length**) a measure of 720 feet (US Navy) or 608 feet (Brit. Navy). **5** (in full **cable-stitch**) a knitted stitch resembling twisted rope. • *v.* **1 a** *tr.* transmit (a message) by cablegram. **b** *tr.* inform (a person) by cablegram. **c** *intr.* send a cablegram. **2** *tr.* furnish or fasten with a cable or cables.

ca·ble car *n.* **1** a small cabin (often one of a series) suspended on an endless cable and drawn up and down a mountainside, etc., by an engine at one end. **2** a vehicle drawn along a cable railway.

ca·ble·gram /káybəlgram/ *n.* a telegraph message sent by undersea cable, etc.

ca·ble-read·y *adj.* (of a TV, VCR, etc.) designed for direct connection to a coaxial cable TV system.

ca·ble·way /káybəlway/ *n.* a transporting system with a usu. elevated cable.

cab·man /kábmən/ *n.* (*pl.* **·men**) a cabdriver.

cab·o·chon /kábəshon/ *n.* a gem polished but not faceted.

ca·boo·dle /kəbóōd'l/ *n.* □ **the whole (kit and) caboodle** *sl.* the whole lot (of persons or things).

ca·boose /kəbóōs/ *n.* a car on a freight train for workers, often the final car.

cab·ri·ole /kábreeōl/ *n.* a kind of curved leg characteristic of Queen Anne and Chippendale furniture.

cab·ri·o·let /kábreeōláy/ *n.* **1** a light, two-wheeled carriage with a hood, drawn by one horse. **2** an automobile with a folding top.

ca·ca·o /kəkaá–ō, –káyō/ *n.* (*pl.* **·os**) **1** a seed pod from which cocoa and chocolate are made. **2** a small, widely cultivated evergreen tree, *Theobroma cacao*, bearing these.

cache /kash/ *n. & v.* • *n.* **1** a hiding place for treasure, provisions, ammunition, etc. **2** what is hidden in a cache. • *v.tr.* put in a cache.

ca·chet /kasháy/ *n.* **1** a distinguishing mark or seal. **2** prestige. **3** *Med.* a flat capsule enclosing a dose of unpleasant-tasting medicine.

ca·cique /kəséek/ *n.* **1** a native tribal chief of the West Indies or Mexico. **2** a political boss in Spain or Latin America.

cack·le /kákəl/ *n. & v.* • *n.* **1** a clucking sound as of a hen or a goose. **2** a loud, silly laugh. **3** noisy inconsequential talk. • *v.* **1** *intr.* emit a cackle. **2** *intr.* talk noisily and inconsequentially. **3** *tr.* utter or express with a cackle.

ca·cog·ra·phy /kəkógrəfee/ *n.* **1** bad handwriting. **2** bad spelling. □□ **ca·cog·ra·pher** *n.* **cac·o·graph·ic** /kákəgráfik/ *adj.* **cac·o·graph·i·cal** *adj.*

ca·col·o·gy /kəkóləjee/ *n.* **1** bad choice of words. **2** bad pronunciation.

ca·coph·o·ny /kəkófənee/ *n.* (*pl.* **·nies**) **1** a harsh discordant mixture of sound. **2** dissonance; discord. □□ **ca·coph·o·nous** *adj.*

cac·tus /káktəs/ *n.* (*pl.* **cacti** /–tī/ or **cactuses**) any succulent plant of the family Cactaceae, with a thick fleshy stem and usu. spines but no leaves. □□ **cac·ta·ceous** /–táyshəs/ *adj.*

CAD /kad/ *abbr.* computer-aided design.

cad /kad/ *n.* a person (esp. a man) who behaves dishonorably. □□ **cad·dish** *adj.* **cad·dish·ly** *adv.* **cad·dish·ness** *n.*

ca·dav·er /kədávər/ *n.* esp. *Med.* a corpse. □□ **ca·dav·er·ic** /–dávərik/ *adj.*

ca·dav·er·ous /kədávərəs/ *adj.* **1** corpselike. **2** deathly pale.

cad•die /kádee/ *n. & v.* (also **cad•dy**) • *n.* (*pl.* **•dies**) a person who assists a golfer during a game, by carrying clubs, etc. • *v.intr.* (**caddies, caddied, caddying**) act as caddie.

caddie mid 17th century (originally Scots): from French *cadet*. The original term denoted a gentleman who joined the army without a commission, intending to learn the profession and follow a military career, later coming to mean 'odd-job man.' The current sense dates from the late 18th century.

cad•dis fly /kádisflī/ *n.* (*pl.* **flies**) any small, hairy-winged nocturnal insect of the order Trichoptera, living near water.

cad•dis•worm /kádiswərm/ *n.* (also **cad•dis**) the aquatic larva of the caddis fly.

cad•dy[1] /kádee/ *n.* (*pl.* **•dies**) a small container, esp. a box for holding tea.

cad•dy[2] var. of CADDIE.

ca•dence /káyd'ns/ *n.* **1** a fall in pitch of the voice, esp. at the end of a phrase or sentence. **2** intonation; tonal inflection. **3** *Mus.* the close of a musical phrase. **4** rhythm; the measure or beat of sound or movement. ▫▫ **ca•denced** *adj.*

ca•den•za /kədénzə/ *n. Mus.* a virtuosic passage for a solo instrument or voice, usu. near the close of a movement of a concerto, sometimes improvised.

ca•det /kədét/ *n.* **1** a young trainee in the armed services or police force. **2** a business trainee. **3** a younger son. ▫▫ **ca•det•ship** *n.*

cadge /kaj/ *v.* **1** *tr.* get or seek by begging. **2** *intr.* beg. ▫▫ **cadg•er** *n.*

cad•mi•um /kádmeeəm/ *n.* a soft, bluish-white metallic element occurring naturally with zinc ores, and used in the manufacture of solders and in electroplating. ¶ Symb.: **Cd**.

ca•dre /kádree, kaádray/ *n.* **1** a basic unit, esp. of servicemen, forming a nucleus for expansion when necessary. **2 a** a group of activists in a communist or any revolutionary party. **b** a member of such a group.

ca•du•ce•us /kədóōseeəs, –shəs, –dyóō–/ *n.* (*pl.* **caducei** /–see–ī/) **1** an ancient Greek or Roman herald's wand, usu. with two serpents twined around it, carried by the messenger god Hermes or Mercury. **2** this used as a symbol of the medical profession.

caduceus

Cae•no•zo•ic var. of CENOZOIC.

Caer•phil•ly /kairfílee, kaar–/ *n.* a kind of mild white cheese orig. made in Caerphilly in Wales.

Cae•sar /séezər/ *n.* **1** the title of the Roman emperors, esp. from Augustus to Hadrian. **2** an autocrat. ▫▫ **Cae•sar•e•an, Cae•sar•i•an** /–záireeən/ *adj.*

Cae•sar•e•an (also **Cae•sar•i•an**) var. of CESAREAN.

cae•su•ra /sizhóorə, –zóorə/ *n.* (*pl.* **caesuras** or **caesurae** /–zhóoree, –zóoree/) *Prosody* a pause near the middle of a line. ▫▫ **cae•su•ral** *adj.*

CAF *abbr.* cost and freight.

café /kafáy/ *n.* (also **ca•fe**) **1** a small coffeehouse; a simple restaurant. **2** a bar.

café au lait /kafáy ō láy/ *n.* **1** coffee with milk. **2** the color of this.

caf•e•te•ri•a /káfitéereeə/ *n.* a restaurant in which customers collect their meals on trays at a counter and usu. pay before sitting down to eat.

caf•feine /káfeen, kaféen/ *n.* an alkaloid drug with stimulant action, found in tea leaves and coffee beans.

caf•tan /káftan/ *n.* (also **kaf•tan**) **1** a long, usu. belted tunic worn in countries of the Near East. **2 a** a long, loose dress. **b** a loose shirt or top.

cage /kayj/ *n. & v.* • *n.* **1** a structure of bars or wires, esp. for confining animals or birds. **2** any similar open framework, as an enclosed platform for passengers in a freight elevator, etc. • *v.tr.* place or keep in a cage.

cag•ey /káyjee/ *adj.* (also **cag•y**) (**cagier, cagiest**) *colloq.* cautious and uncommunicative; wary. ▫▫ **cag•i•ly** *adv.* **cag•i•ness** *n.* (also **cag•ey•ness**).

ca•hoots /kəhóōts/ *n.pl.* ▫ **in cahoots** (often foll. by *with*) *sl.* in collusion.

CAI *abbr.* computer-assisted (or -aided) instruction.

cai•man /káymən/ *n.* (also **cay•man**) any of various S. American alligatorlike reptilians, esp. of the genus *Caiman*.

Cain /kayn/ *n.* (in the Bible) the eldest son of Adam and Eve and murderer of his brother Abel. ▫ **raise Cain** make a disturbance; create trouble.

Cai•no•zo•ic var. of CENOZOIC.

cairn /kairn/ *n.* **1** a mound of rough stones as a monument or landmark. **2** (in full **cairn terrier**) a small terrier of a breed with short legs, a longish body, and a shaggy coat.

cais•son /káyson, –sən/ *n.* **1** a watertight chamber in which underwater construction work can be done. **2** a floating vessel used as a floodgate in docks. **3** an ammunition chest or wagon.

ca•jole /kəjṓl/ *v.tr.* (often foll. by *into*, *out of*) persuade by flattery, deceit, etc. ▫▫ **ca•jole•ment** *n.* **ca•jol•er** *n.* **ca•jol•er•y** *n.*

cake /kayk/ *n. & v.* • *n.* **1 a** a mixture of flour, butter, eggs, sugar, etc., baked in the oven. **b** a quantity of this baked in a flat round or ornamental shape and often iced and decorated. **2** other food in a flat round shape (*fish cake*). **3** a flattish compact mass (*a cake of soap*). • *v.* **1** *tr. & intr.* form into a compact mass. **2** *tr.* (usu. foll. by *with*) cover (with a hard or sticky mass) (*boots caked with mud*). ▫ **have one's cake and eat it too** *colloq.* enjoy both of two mutually exclusive alternatives. **a piece of cake** *colloq.* something easily achieved.

CAL *abbr.* computer-assisted learning.

Cal *abbr.* large calorie(s).

Cal. *abbr.* California.

cal *abbr.* small calorie(s).

cal•a•bash /káləbash/ *n.* **1 a** an evergreen tree, *Crescentia cujete*, native to tropical America, bearing fruit in the form of large gourds. **b** a gourd from this tree. **2** the shell of this or a similar gourd used as a vessel, etc.

cal•a•boose /káləbóōs/ *n. sl.* a prison.

ca•la•ma•ri /kaaləmaáree, ka–/ *n.* (*pl.* **•ries**) any cephalopod mollusk with a long, tapering, penlike horny internal shell, esp. a squid of the genus *Loligo*.

cal•a•mine /káləmīn/ *n.* **1** a pink powder consisting of zinc carbonate and ferric oxide used as a lotion or ointment. **2** a zinc mineral, usu. zinc carbonate.

ca•lam•i•ty /kəlámitee/ *n.* (*pl.* **•ties**) **1** a disaster, a great misfortune. **2 a** adversity. **b** deep distress. ▫▫ **ca•lam•i•tous** *adj.* **ca•lam•i•tous•ly** *adv.*

calc- /kalk/ *comb. form* lime or calcium.

cal•ca•ne•us /kalkáyneeəs/ *n.* (also **cal•ca•ne•um** /–neeəm/) (*pl.* **calcanei** /–nee–ī/ or **calcanea** /–neeə/) the bone forming the heel.

cal•car•e•ous /kalkáireeəs/ *adj.* (also **cal•car•i•ous**) of or containing calcium carbonate; chalky.

cal•ce•o•lar•i•a /kálseeəláireeə/ *n. Bot.* any plant of the genus *Calceolaria*, native to S. America, with slipper-shaped flowers.

See page xii for the *Key to Pronunciation*.

cal·cif·er·ol /kalsífərōl, –rol/ *n.* one of the D vitamins, routinely added to dairy products, essential for the deposition of calcium in bones. Also called ERGOCALCIFEROL, *vitamin* D_2.
cal·cif·er·ous /kalsífərəs/ *adj.* yielding calcium salts, esp. calcium carbonate.
cal·ci·fy /kálsifī/ *v.tr. & intr.* (**·fies, ·fied**) **1** harden or become hardened by deposition of calcium salts; petrify. **2** convert or be converted to calcium carbonate. ▫▫ **cal·cif·ic** /–sífik/ *adj.* **cal·ci·fi·ca·tion** *n.*
cal·cine /kálsīn, –sin/ *v.* **1** *tr.* **a** reduce, oxidize, or desiccate by strong heat. **b** burn to ashes; consume by fire; roast. **c** reduce to calcium oxide by roasting or burning. **2** *tr.* consume or purify as if by fire. **3** *intr.* undergo any of these. ▫▫ **cal·ci·na·tion** /–sináyshən/ *n.*
cal·cite /kálsīt/ *n.* natural crystalline calcium carbonate.
cal·ci·um /kálseeəm/ *n.* a soft, gray metallic element of the alkaline earth group occurring naturally in limestone, marble, chalk, etc., that is important in industry and essential for normal growth in living organisms. ¶ Symb.: **Ca**.
cal·ci·um car·bon·ate /kálseeəm kaárbənayt/ *n.* a white, insoluble solid occurring naturally as chalk, limestone, marble, and calcite, and used in the manufacture of lime and cement.
calc-spar /kálkspaar/ *n.* = CALCITE.
cal·cu·late /kálkyəlayt/ *v.* **1** *tr.* ascertain or determine beforehand, esp. by mathematics or by reckoning. **2** *tr.* plan deliberately. **3** *intr.* (foll. by *on, upon*) rely on; make an essential part of one's reckoning. **4** *tr. dial.* suppose; believe. ▫▫ **cal·cu·la·tion** *n.* **cal·cu·la·tive** /–lətiv/ *adj.*
cal·cu·lat·ed /kálkyəlaytid/ *adj.* **1** (of an action) done with awareness of the likely consequences. **2** (foll. by *to* + infin.) designed or suitable; intended. ▫▫ **cal·cu·lat·ed·ly** *adv.*
cal·cu·lat·ing /kálkyəlayting/ *adj.* (of a person) shrewd; scheming. ▫▫ **cal·cu·lat·ing·ly** *adv.*
cal·cu·la·tor /kálkyəlaytər/ *n.* **1** a device (esp. a small electronic one) used for making mathematical calculations. **2** a person or thing that calculates.
cal·cu·lus /kálkyələs/ *n.* (*pl.* **calculi** /–lī/ or **calculuses**) **1** *Math.* **a** a particular method of calculation or reasoning (*calculus of probabilities*). **b** the infinitesimal calculi of integration or differentiation (see INTEGRAL CALCULUS, DIFFERENTIAL CALCULUS). **2** *Med.* a stone or concretion of minerals formed within the body. ▫▫ **cal·cu·lous** *adj.* (in sense 2).
cal·de·ra /kaldáirə/ *n.* a large volcanic depression.
cal·dron var. of CAULDRON.
Cal·e·do·ni·an /kálidóneeən/ *adj. & n.* • *adj.* **1** of or relating to Scotland. **2** *Geol.* of a mountain-forming period in Europe in the Paleozoic era. • *n.* a Scotsman.
cal·en·dar /kálindər/ *n. & v.* • *n.* **1** a system by which the beginning, length, and subdivisions of the year are fixed. **2** a chart or series of pages showing the days, weeks, and months of a particular year, or giving special seasonal information. **3** a timetable or program of appointments, special events, etc. • *v.tr.* register or enter in a calendar or timetable, etc. ▫▫ **ca·len·dric** /–léndrik/ *adj.* **ca·len·dri·cal** *adj.*
cal·en·der /kálindər/ *n. & v.* • *n.* a machine in which cloth, paper, etc., is pressed by rollers to glaze or smooth it. • *v.tr.* press in a calender.
ca·len·du·la /kəlénjələ/ *n.* any plant of the genus *Calendula*, with large yellow or orange flowers.
calf[1] /kaf/ *n.* (*pl.* **calves** /kavz/) **1** a young bovine animal, used esp. of domestic cattle. **2** the young of some other large mammals, e.g., elephant, deer, and whale. ▫▫ **calf·hood** *n.* **calf·ish** *adj.* **calf·like** *adj.*
calf[2] /kaf/ *n.* (*pl.* **calves** /kavz/) the fleshy hind part of the human leg below the knee. ▫▫ **-calved** /kavd/ *adj.* (in *comb.*).
calf·skin /káfskin/ *n.* calf leather.
cal·i·ber /kálibər/ *n.* (*Brit.* **calibre**) **1 a** the internal diameter of a gun or tube. **b** the diameter of a bullet or shell. **2** strength or quality of character; ability; importance (*we need someone of your caliber*). ▫▫ **cal·i·bered** *adj.* (also in *comb.*).
cal·i·brate /kálibrayt/ *v.tr.* **1** mark (a gauge) with a standard scale of readings. **2** correlate the readings of (an instrument) with a standard. **3** determine the caliber of (a gun). **4** determine the correct capacity or value of. ▫▫ **cal·i·bra·tion** /–bráyshən/ *n.* **cal·i·bra·tor** *n.*
cal·i·co /kálikō/ *n. & adj.* • *n.* (*pl.* **·coes** or **·cos**) **1** a printed cotton fabric. **2** *Brit.* a cotton cloth, esp. plain white or unbleached. • *adj.* **1** made of calico. **2** multicolored; piebald.
Calif. *abbr.* California.
cal·i·for·ni·um /kálifáwrneeəm/ *n. Chem.* a transuranic radioactive metallic element produced artificially from curium. ¶ Symb.: **Cf**.
cal·i·per /kálipər/ *n.* (in *pl.*) (also **cal·i·per com·pas·ses**) compasses with bowed legs for measuring the diameter of convex bodies, or with out-turned points for measuring internal dimensions.
ca·liph /káylif, kál–/ *n.* esp. *hist.* the chief Muslim civil and religious ruler, regarded as the successor of Muhammad. ▫▫ **cal·iph·ate** *n.*
cal·is·then·ics /kálisthéniks/ *n.pl.* (also esp. *Brit.* **cal·lis·then·ics**) gymnastic exercises to achieve bodily fitness and grace of movement. ▫▫ **cal·is·then·ic** *adj.*
calk var. of CAULK.
call /kawl/ *v. & n.* • *v.* **1** *intr.* **a** (often foll. by *out*) cry; shout; speak loudly. **b** (of a bird or animal) emit its characteristic note or cry. **2** *tr.* communicate or converse with by telephone or radio. **3** *tr.* **a** bring to one's presence by calling; summon (*will you call the children?*). **b** arrange for (a person or thing) to come or be present (*called a taxi*). **4** *intr.* (often foll. by *at, on*) pay a brief visit (*called at the house; come and call on me*). **5** *tr.* **a** order to take place; fix a time for (*called a meeting*). **b** direct to happen; announce (*call a halt*). **6 a** *intr.* require one's attention (*duty calls*). **b** *tr.* urge; invite; nominate (*call to run for office*). **7** *tr.* name; describe as (*call her Jennifer*). **8** *tr.* consider; regard or estimate as (*I call that silly*). **9** *tr.* rouse from sleep (*call me at 8*). **10** *intr.* guess the outcome of tossing a coin, etc. **11** *intr.* (foll. by *for*) order; require; demand (*called for silence*). **12** *intr.* (foll. by *on, upon*) invoke; appeal to; request or require (*called on us to be quiet*). **13** *tr. Cards* specify (a suit or contract) in bidding. • *n.* **1** a shout or cry; an act of calling. **2 a** the characteristic cry of a bird or animal. **b** an imitation of this. **c** an instrument for imitating it. **3** a brief visit (*paid them a call*). **4 a** an act of telephoning. **b** a telephone conversation. **5 a** an invitation or summons to appear or be present. **b** an appeal or invitation (from a specific source or discerned by a person's conscience, etc.) to follow a certain profession, set of principles, etc. **6** (foll. by *for*, or *to* + infin.) a duty, need, or occasion (*no call for violence*). **7** (foll. by *for, on*) a demand (*not much call for it these days; a call on one's time*). **8** a signal on a bugle, etc.; a signaling whistle. **9** *Stock Exch.* an option of buying stock at a fixed price at a given date. **10** *Cards* **a** a player's right or turn to make a bid. **b** a bid made. ▫ **call away** divert; distract. **call down 1** invoke. **2** reprimand. **call forth** elicit. **call in 1** withdraw from circulation. **2** seek the advice or services of. **call in** (or **into**) **question** dispute; doubt the validity of. **call into play** give scope for; make use of. **call a person names** abuse a person verbally. **call off 1** cancel (an arrangement, etc.). **2** order (an attacker or pursuer) to desist. **call of nature** a

need to urinate or defecate. **call out 1** summon (troops, etc.) to action. **2** order (workers) to strike. **call the shots** (or **tune**) be in control; take the initiative. **call to account** see ACCOUNT. **call to mind** recollect; cause one to remember. **call to order 1** request to be orderly. **2** declare (a meeting) open. **call up 1** reach by telephone. **2** imagine; recollect. **3** summon, esp. to serve on active military duty. **on call 1** (of a doctor, etc.) available if required but not formally on duty. **2** (of money lent) repayable on demand. **within call** near enough to be summoned by calling.

cal·la /kálə/ *n.* (in full **calla lily**) a tall, lilylike plant, *Zantedeschia aethiopica,* with white spathe and spadix.

call·er /káwlər/ *n.* a person who calls, esp. one who pays a visit or makes a telephone call.

cal·lig·ra·phy /kəlígrəfee/ *n.* **1** handwriting, esp. when fine or pleasing. **2** the art of handwriting. ▫▫ **cal·lig·ra·pher** *n.* **cal·li·graph·ic** /káligráfik/ *adj.* **cal·lig·ra·phist** *n.*

---

calligraphy mid-19th century (as a noun): from Greek *kalligraphia,* from *kalligraphos* 'person who writes beautifully,' from *kallos* 'beauty' + *graphein* 'write.' The verb dates from the late 19th century.

---

call·ing /káwling/ *n.* **1** a profession or occupation. **2** an inwardly felt call or summons; a vocation.

call·ing card /káwling kaard/ *n.* **1** a card with a person's name, etc., sent or left in lieu of a formal visit. **2** evidence of someone's presence; an identifying mark, etc., left behind (by someone). **3** a card used to charge a telephone call to a number other than that from which the call is placed.

cal·lis·then·ics esp. *Brit.* var. of CALISTHENICS.

cal·los·i·ty /kəlósitee/ *n.* (*pl.* **·ties**) a hard, thick area of skin usu. occurring in parts of the body subject to pressure or friction.

cal·lous /káləs/ *adj.* **1** unfeeling; insensitive. **2** (of skin) hardened or hard. ▫▫ **cal·lous·ly** *adv.* (in sense 1). **cal·lous·ness** *n.*

cal·low /kálō/ *adj.* inexperienced; immature. ▫▫ **cal·low·ly** *adv.* **cal·low·ness** *n.*

cal·lus /káləs/ *n.* **1** a hard, thick area of skin or tissue. **2** a hard tissue formed around bone ends after a fracture. **3** *Bot.* a new protective tissue formed over a wound.

calm /kaam/ *adj., n., & v.* • *adj.* **1** tranquil; quiet; windless (*a calm sea; a calm night*). **2** (of a person or disposition) settled; not agitated (*remained calm throughout the ordeal*). **3** self-assured; confident (*his calm assumption that we would wait*). • *n.* **1** a state of being calm; stillness; serenity. **2** a period without wind or storm. • *v.tr. & intr.* (often foll. by *down*) make or become calm. ▫▫ **calm·ly** *adv.* **calm·ness** *n.*

cal·or·ic /kəláwrik, –lór–/ *adj.* of heat or calories.

cal·o·rie /káləree/ *n.* (also **cal·o·ry**) (*pl.* **·ries**) a unit of quantity of heat: **1** (in full **small calorie**) the amount needed to raise the temperature of 1 gram of water through 1°C. ¶ Abbr.: **cal. 2** (in full **large calorie**) the amount needed to raise the temperature of 1 kilogram of water through 1°C, often used to measure the energy value of foods. ¶ Abbr.: **Cal.**

cal·o·rif·ic /kálərífik/ *adj.* producing heat. ▫▫ **cal·o·rif·i·cal·ly** *adv.*

cal·trop /káltrəp/ *n.* (also **cal·trap**) **1** *hist.* a four-spiked iron ball thrown on the ground to impede cavalry horses. **2** any creeping plant of the genus *Tribulus,* with woody carpels usu. having hard spines.

cal·u·met /kályəmét/ *n.* a Native American ceremonial peace pipe.

ca·lum·ni·ate /kəlúmneeayt/ *v.tr.* slander. ▫▫ **ca·lum·ni·a·tion** /–neeáyshən/ *n.* **ca·lum·ni·a·tor** *n.* **ca·lum·ni·a·to·ry** /–ətáwree/ *adj.*

cal·um·ny /káləmnee/ *n. & v.* • *n.* (*pl.* **·nies**) **1** slander; malicious representation. **2** an instance of this. • *v.tr.* (**·nies, ·nied**) slander. ▫▫ **ca·lum·ni·ous** /–lúmneeəs/ *adj.*

cal·va·dos /kálvədōs/ *n.* (also **Cal·va·dos**) an apple brandy.

Cal·va·ry /kálvəree/ *n.* the place where Christ was crucified.

calve /kav/ *v.* **1** *intr.* give birth to a calf. **2** *tr.* (esp. in *passive*) give birth to (a calf).

calves *pl.* of CALF[1], CALF[2].

Cal·vin·ism /kálvinizəm/ *n.* the theology of the French theologian J. Calvin (d. 1564) or his followers, in which predestination and justification by faith are important elements. ▫▫ **Cal·vin·ist** *n.* **Cal·vin·is·tic** *adj.*

ca·lyp·so /kəlípsō/ *n.* (*pl.* **·sos**) a W. Indian song in African rhythm, usu. improvised on a topical theme.

ca·lyx /káyliks, kál–/ *n.* (*pl.* **calyxes** or **calyces** /–liseez/) **1** *Bot.* the sepals collectively, forming the protective layer of a flower in bud. **2** *Biol.* any cuplike cavity or structure.

cam /kam/ *n.* a projection on a rotating part in machinery, shaped to impart reciprocal or variable motion to the part in contact with it.

ca·ma·ra·de·rie /ka͡amərа́adəree/ *n.* mutual trust and sociability among friends.

cam·ber /kámbər/ *n. & v.* • *n.* **1** the slightly convex or arched shape of the surface of a ship's deck, aircraft wing, etc. **2** the slight sideways inclination of the front wheel of a motor vehicle. • *v.* **1** *intr.* (of a surface) have a camber. **2** *tr.* give a camber to; build with a camber.

Cam·bo·di·an /kambṓdeeən/ *n. & adj.* • *n.* **1 a** a native or national of Cambodia (Kampuchea) in SE Asia. **b** a person of Cambodian descent. **2** the language of Cambodia. • *adj.* of or relating to Cambodia or its people or language. Also called KAMPUCHEAN.

Cam·bri·an /kámbreeən/ *adj. & n.* • *adj.* **1** Welsh. **2** *Geol.* of or relating to the first period in the Paleozoic era, marked by the occurrence of many forms of invertebrate life (including trilobites and brachiopods). • *n.* this period or system.

cam·bric /kámbrik/ *n.* a fine white linen or cotton fabric.

cam·cord·er /kámkawrdər/ *n.* a combined video camera and sound recorder.

came *past* of COME.

cam·el /káməl/ *n.* **1** either of two kinds of large, cud-chewing mammals having slender, cushion-footed legs and one hump (**Arabian camel,** *Camelus dromedarius*) or two humps (**Bactrian camel,** *Camelus bactrianus*). **2** a fawn color. **3** an apparatus for providing additional buoyancy to ships, etc.; a pontoon.

cam·el (or **cam·el's**) **hair** *n.* **1** a fabric made from the hair of a camel. **2** fine, soft hair from a squirrel's tail, used in artists' brushes.

ca·mel·lia /kəme͞elyə/ *n.* any evergreen shrub of the genus *Camellia,* native to E. Asia, with shiny leaves and showy flowers.

Cam·em·bert /káməmbair/ *n.* a kind of soft, creamy French cheese, usu. with a strong flavor.

cam·e·o /kámeeō/ *n.* (*pl.* **·os**) **1 a** a small piece of onyx or other hard stone carved in relief with a background of a different color. **b** a similar relief design using other materials. **2 a** a short descriptive literary sketch or acted scene. **b** a small character part in a play or film, usu. played by a distinguished actor.

cam·er·a /kámrə, kámərə/ *n.* **1** an apparatus consisting of a lightproof box to hold light-sensitive film, a lens, and a shutter mechanism, either for taking still photographs or for motion-picture film. **2** *Telev.* a piece of equipment that forms an optical image and converts it into electrical impulses for transmission or storage. □ **in camera 1** *Law* in a judge's private room. **2** privately; not in public.

cam·er·a ob·scu·ra /obskyŏŏrə/ *n.* an internally darkened box with an aperture for projecting the image of an external object on a screen inside it.

cam·er·a-read·y *adj. Printing* (of copy) in a form suitable for immediate photographic reproduction.

cam·i·sole /kámisōl/ *n.* an upper-body undergarment, often embroidered.

cam·o·mile var. of CHAMOMILE.

cam·ou·flage /káməflaazh/ *n. & v.* •*n.* **1 a** the disguising, by the military, of people, vehicles, aircraft, ships, and installations by painting them or covering them to make them blend with their surroundings. **b** such a disguise. **2** the natural coloring of an animal that enables it to blend in with its surroundings. **3** a misleading or evasive precaution or expedient. •*v.tr.* hide or disguise by means of camouflage.

camouflage World War I: from French, from *camoufler* 'to disguise' (originally thieves' slang), from Italian *camuffare* 'disguise, deceive, ' perhaps by association with French *camouflet* 'whiff of smoke in the face.'

camp[1] /kamp/ *n. & v.* •*n.* **1** a place where troops are lodged or trained. **2** temporary overnight lodging in tents, etc., in the open. **3 a** temporary accommodation of various kinds, usu. consisting of huts or tents, for detainees, homeless persons, and other emergency use. **b** a complex of buildings for vacation accommodation. **4** the adherents of a particular party or doctrine regarded collectively (*the Republican camp was jubilant*). •*v.intr.* **1** set up or spend time in a camp (in senses 1 and 2 of *n.*). **2** (often foll. by *out*) lodge in temporary quarters or in the open. □□ **camp·ing** *n.*

camp[2] /kamp/ *adj., n., & v. colloq.* •*adj.* **1** done in an exaggerated way for effect. **2** affected; effeminate. •*n.* a camp manner or style. •*v.intr. & tr.* behave or do in a camp way. □ **camp it up** overact; behave affectedly. □□ **camp·y** *adj.* (**campier, campiest**). **camp·i·ly** *adv.* **camp·i·ness** *n.*

cam·paign /kampáyn/ *n. & v.* •*n.* **1** an organized course of action for a particular purpose, esp. to arouse public interest (e.g., before a political election). **2 a** a series of military operations in a definite area or to achieve a particular objective. **b** military service in the field (*on campaign*). •*v.intr.* conduct or take part in a campaign. □□ **cam·paign·er** *n.*

campaign early 17th century (denoting a tract of open country): from French *campagne* 'open country,' via Italian from late Latin *campania*, from *campus* 'level ground.' The change in sense arose from the army's practice of 'taking the field' (i.e., moving from fortress or town, etc., to open country) at the onset of summer.

cam·pa·ni·le /kámpənéelee, –néel/ *n.* a bell tower (usu. freestanding), esp. in Italy.

cam·pa·nol·o·gy /kámpənóləjee/ *n.* **1** the study of bells. **2** the art or practice of bell ringing. □□ **cam·pa·nol·o·ger** *n.* **cam·pa·no·log·i·cal** /–nəlójikəl/ *adj.* **cam·pa·nol·o·gist** *n.*

camp·er /kámpər/ *n.* **1** a person who camps out or lives temporarily in a tent, hut, etc., esp. for recreation. **2** a large motor vehicle with accommodation for camping out.

cam·phor /kámfər/ *n.* a white, translucent, crystalline volatile substance with aromatic smell and bitter taste, used to make celluloid and in medicine. □□ **cam·phor·ic** /–fórik/ *adj.*

cam·pi·on /kámpeeən/ *n.* **1** any plant of the genus *Silene*, with usu. pink or white notched flowers. **2** any of several similar cultivated plants of the genus *Lychnis*.

camp·site /kámpsīt/ *n.* a place suitable for camping; a site used by campers.

cam·pus /kámpəs/ *n.* (*pl.* **campuses**) **1** the grounds of a university or college. **2** a college or university, esp. as a teaching institution.

cam·shaft /kámshaft/ *n.* a shaft with one or more cams attached to it.

Can. *abbr.* Canada; Canadian.

can[1] /kan, kən/ *v.aux.* (*3rd sing. present* **can**; *past* **could** /kŏŏd/) (foll. by infin. without *to*, or *absol.*; present and past only in use) **1 a** be able to; know how to (*I can run fast; can he?; can you speak German?*). **b** be potentially capable of (*you can do it if you try*). **2** be permitted to (*can we go to the party?*).

▶**Can** is properly used to mean 'be able': *I can solve any problem on this list.* **May** means 'be permitted or have approval': *May I leave now? You may take anything you like.*

can[2] /kan/ *n. & v.* •*n.* **1** a metal vessel for liquid. **2** a metal container in which food or drink is hermetically sealed to enable storage over long periods. **3** (prec. by *the*) *sl.* **a** prison (*sent to the can*). **b** *sl.* toilet. **4** *sl.* the buttocks. •*v.tr.* (**canned, canning**) **1** put or preserve in a can. **2** record on film or tape for future use. □ **in the can** *colloq.* completed; ready (orig. of filmed or recorded material). □□ **can·ner** *n.*

Can·a·da goose *n.* a wild goose, *Branta canadensis*, with a brownish-gray body and white cheeks and breast.

ca·nal /kənál/ *n.* **1** an artificial waterway for inland navigation or irrigation. **2** any of various tubular ducts in a plant or animal, for carrying food, liquid, or air.

can·al·ize /kánəlīz/ *v.tr.* **1** make a canal through. **2** convert (a river) into a canal. **3** provide with canals. **4** give the desired direction or purpose to. □□ **ca·nal·i·za·tion** *n.*

can·a·pé /kánəpay, –pee/ *n.* a small piece of bread or pastry with a savory food on top, often served as an hors d'oeuvre.

ca·nard /kənaárd/ *n.* an unfounded rumor or story.

ca·nar·y /kənáiree/ *n.* (*pl.* **·ies**) **1** any of various small finches of the genus *Serinus*, esp. *S. canaria*, a songbird native to the Canary Islands, with mainly yellow plumage. **2** *hist.* a sweet wine from the Canary Islands.

ca·nas·ta /kənástə/ *n.* **1** a card game using two packs and resembling rummy, the aim being to collect sets (or melds) of cards. **2** a set of seven cards in this game.

can·can /kánkan/ *n.* a lively stage dance with high kicking.

can·cel /kánsəl/ *v.* (**canceled, canceling**; esp. *Brit.* **cancelled, cancelling**) **1** *tr.* **a** withdraw or revoke (a previous arrangement). **b** discontinue (an arrangement in progress). **2** *tr.* obliterate or delete (writing, etc.). **3** *tr.* mark or pierce (a ticket, stamp, etc.) to invalidate it. **4** *tr.* annul; make void; abolish. **5** (often foll. by *out*) **a** *tr.* (of one factor or circumstance) neutralize or counterbalance (another). **b** *intr.* (of two factors or circumstances) neutralize each other. **6** *tr. Math.* strike out (an equal factor) on each side of an equation or from the numerator and denominator of a fraction. □□ **can·cel·er** *n.*

can·cel·la·tion /kánsəláyshən/ *n.* (also **can·cel·a·tion**) **1** the act or an instance of canceling or being canceled. **2** something that has been canceled, esp. a booking or reservation.

can·cer /kánsər/ *n.* **1 a** any malignant growth or tumor from an abnormal and uncontrolled division of body cells. **b** a disease caused by this. **2** an evil influence or corruption spreading uncontrollably. **3** (**Cancer**) **a** a constellation, traditionally regarded as contained in the figure of a crab. **b** the fourth sign of the zodiac (the Crab). **c** a person born when the sun is in this sign. □ **Tropic of Cancer** see TROPIC. □□ **Can·cer·i·an** /–séreeən/ *n. & adj.* (in sense 3). **can·cer·ous** *adj.*

cancer Old English, from Latin, 'crab or creeping ulcer,' translating Greek *karkinos*, which is said to have been applied to such tumors because the swollen veins around them resembled the limbs of a crab. *Canker* was the usual form until the 17th century.

can·de·la /kandeélə, –délə/ *n.* the SI unit of luminous intensity. ¶ Abbr.: **cd.**

can·de·la·brum /kánd'laábrəm/ *n.* (also **can·de·la·bra** /–brə/) (*pl.* **candelabra, candelabrums, candelabras**) a large branched candlestick or lamp holder.

can·did /kándid/ *adj.* **1** frank; not hiding one's thoughts. **2** (of a photograph) taken informally, usu. without the subject's knowledge. □□ **can·did·ly** *adv.* **can·did·ness** *n.*

can·di·da /kándidə/ *n.* any yeastlike parasitic fungus of the genus *Candida*, esp. *C. albicans* causing thrush.

can·di·date /kándidət, –dayt/ *n.* **1** a person who seeks or is nominated for an office, award, etc. **2** a person or thing likely to gain some distinction or position. **3** a person entered for an examination. □□ **can·di·da·cy** /–dəsee/ *n.* **can·di·da·ture** /–dəchər/ *n. Brit.*

can·dle /kánd'l/ *n.* **1** a cylinder or block of wax or tallow with a central wick, for giving light when burning. **2** = CANDLEPOWER. □ **cannot hold a candle to** cannot be compared with; is much inferior to.

Can·dle·mas /kándəlməs/ *n.* a feast with blessing of candles (Feb. 2), commemorating the Purification of the Virgin Mary.

can·dle·pow·er /kánd'lpowr/ *n.* a unit of luminous intensity.

can·dle·stick /kánd'lstik/ *n.* a holder for one or more candles.

can·dle·wick /kánd'lwik/ *n.* **1** a thick soft cotton yarn. **2** material made from this, usu. with a tufted pattern.

can·dor /kándər/ *n.* candid behavior or action; frankness.

C. & W. *abbr.* country-and-western.

can·dy /kándee/ *n. & v.* • *n.* (*pl.* **·dies**) a sweet confection, usu. containing sugar, chocolate, etc. • *v.tr.* (**·dies, ·died**) (usu. as **candied** *adj.*) preserve by coating and impregnating with a sugar syrup (*candied fruit*).

can·dy-strip·er *n.* a hospital volunteer, esp. a teenager, who wears a brightly-striped uniform.

can·dy·tuft /kándeetuft/ *n.* any of various plants of the genus *Iberis*, native to W. Europe, with white, pink, or purple flowers in tufts.

cane /kayn/ *n. & v.* • *n.* **1 a** the hollow jointed stem of giant reeds or grasses (*bamboo cane*). **b** the solid stem of slender palms (*malacca cane*). **2** = SUGAR CANE. **3** material of cane used for wickerwork, etc. **4 a** a cane used as a walking stick or a support for a plant or an instrument of punishment. **b** any slender walking stick. • *v.tr.* **1** beat with a cane. **2** weave cane into (a chair, etc.). □□ **can·er** *n.* (in sense 2 of *v.*). **can·ing** *n.*

cane sug·ar *n.* sugar obtained from sugar cane.

ca·nine /káynīn/ *adj. & n.* • *adj.* **1** of a dog or dogs. **2** of or belonging to the family Canidae, including dogs, wolves, foxes, etc. • *n.* **1** a dog. **2** (in full **canine tooth**) a pointed tooth between the incisors and premolars.

can·is·ter /kánistər/ *n.* **1** a small container, usu. of metal and cylindrical, for storing sugar, etc. **2 a** a cylinder of shot, tear gas, etc., that explodes on impact. **b** such cylinders collectively.

can·ker /kángkər/ *n. & v.* • *n.* **1 a** a destructive fungus disease of trees and plants. **b** an open wound in the stem of a tree or plant. **2** *Zool.* an ulcerous ear disease of animals, esp. cats and dogs. **3** *Med.* an ulceration, esp. of the lips. **4** a corrupting influence. • *v.tr.* **1** consume with canker. **2** corrupt. **3** (as **cankered** *adj.*) soured; malignant; crabbed. □□ **can·ker·ous** *adj.*

can·ker·worm /kángkərwərm/ *n.* any caterpillar of various wingless moths that consume the buds and leaves of shade and fruit trees in N. America.

can·na·bis /kánəbis/ *n.* **1** any hemp plant of the genus *Cannabis*, esp. Indian hemp. **2** a preparation of parts of this used as an intoxicant or hallucinogen.

canned /kand/ *adj.* **1** supplied in a can (*canned fruit*). **2** prerecorded (*canned laughter; canned music*). **3** *sl.* drunk.

can·nel /kánəl/ *n.* (in full **cannel coal**) a bituminous coal burning with a bright flame.

can·nel·lo·ni /kánəlṓnee/ *n.pl.* tubes or rolls of pasta stuffed with meat or a vegetable mixture.

can·ner·y /kánəree/ *n.* (*pl.* **·ies**) a factory where food is canned.

can·ni·bal /kánibəl/ *n. & adj.* • *n.* **1** a person who eats human flesh. **2** an animal that feeds on flesh of its own species. • *adj.* of or like a cannibal. □□ **can·ni·bal·ism** *n.* **can·ni·bal·is·tic** *adj.* **can·ni·bal·is·ti·cal·ly** *adv.*

can·ni·bal·ize /kánibəlīz/ *v.tr.* use (a machine, etc.) as a source of spare parts for others. □□ **can·ni·bal·i·za·tion** *n.*

can·non /kánən/ *n. & v.* • *n.* **1** *hist.* (*pl.* same) a large, heavy gun installed on a carriage or mounting. **2** an automatic aircraft gun firing shells. **3** *Billiards Brit.* = CAROM. • *v.intr. Brit.* (usu. foll. by *against, into*) collide heavily or obliquely.

can·non·ade /kánənáyd/ *n. & v.* • *n.* a period of continuous heavy gunfire. • *v.tr.* bombard with a cannonade.

can·non·ball /kánənbawl/ *n. & v.* • *n.* **1** a large, usu. metal ball fired by a cannon. **2** *Tennis* a very rapid serve. **3** a very fast vehicle, etc., esp. an express train. • *v.intr.* travel with great force, momentum, and speed.

can·non fod·der *n.* soldiers regarded merely as material to be expended in war.

can·not /kánot, kanót/ *v.aux.* can not.

can·nu·la /kányələ/ *n.* (*pl.* **cannulas** or **cannulae** /–lee/) *Surgery* a small tube for inserting into the body to allow fluid to enter or escape.

can·ny /kánee/ *adj.* (**cannier, canniest**) **1 a** shrewd; worldly-wise. **b** thrifty. **c** circumspect. **2** sly; dryly humorous. □□ **can·ni·ly** *adv.* **can·ni·ness** *n.*

ca·noe /kənóō/ *n. & v.* • *n.* a small, narrow boat with pointed ends usu. propelled by paddling. • *v.intr.* (**canoes, canoed, canoeing**) travel in a canoe. □□ **ca·noe·ist** *n.*

can of worms *n. colloq.* unwanted complications (*let's not open a can of worms*)

can·ol·a oil /kənṓlə/ *n.* cooking oil derived from the seed of a variety of the rape plant.

can·on /kánən/ *n.* **1 a** a general law, rule, principle, or criterion. **b** a church decree or law. **2** (*fem.* **canoness**) **a** a member of a cathedral chapter. **b** a member of certain Roman Catholic orders. **3 a** a collection or list of sacred books, etc., accepted as genuine. **b** the recognized genuine works of a particular author; a list of these. **c** a list of literary or artistic works considered to be permanently established as being of the highest quality. **4** *Eccl.* the part of the Mass containing the words of consecration. **5** *Mus.* a piece with different parts taking up the same theme successively.

ca·non·i·cal /kənónikəl/ *adj.* **1 a** according to canon law. **b** included in the canon of Scripture. **2** authoritative; standard; accepted. **3** of a cathedral chapter or a member of it. **4** *Mus.* in canon form. ▫▫ **ca•non•i•cal•ly** *adv.*

can•on•ize /kánənīz/ *v.tr.* **1 a** declare officially to be a saint, usu. with a ceremony. **b** regard as a saint. **2** admit to the canon of Scripture. **3** sanction by church authority. ▫▫ **can•on•i•za•tion** *n.*

can•on law *n.* ecclesiastical law.

can o•pen•er *n.* a device for opening cans (in sense 2 of *n.*).

can•o•py /kánəpee/ *n.* (*pl.* **•pies**) **1 a** a covering hung or held up over a throne, bed, person, etc. **b** the sky. **c** an overhanging shelter. **2** *Archit.* a rooflike projection over a niche, etc. **3** the uppermost layers of foliage, etc., in a forest. **4 a** the expanding part of a parachute. **b** the cover of an aircraft's cockpit.

canst /kanst/ *archaic 2nd person sing.* of CAN[1].

cant[1] /kant/ *n.* & *v.* • *n.* **1** insincere pious or moral talk. **2** ephemeral or fashionable catchwords. **3** language peculiar to a class, profession, sect, etc.; jargon. • *v.intr.* use cant.

cant[2] /kant/ *n.* & *v.* • *n.* **1 a** a slanting surface, e.g., of a bank. **b** a bevel of a crystal, etc. **2** an oblique push or movement that upsets or partly upsets something. **3** a tilted position. • *v.* **1** *tr.* push or pitch out of level; tilt. **2** *intr.* take or lie in a slanting position. **3** *tr.* impart a bevel to.

can't /kant/ *contr.* can not.

can•ta•bi•le /kantaábilay/ *adv., adj.,* & *n. Mus.* • *adv.* & *adj.* in a smooth singing style. • *n.* a cantabile passage or movement.

can•ta•loupe /kánt'lōp/ *n.* a small, round ribbed variety of melon with orange flesh.

can•tan•ker•ous /kantángkərəs/ *adj.* bad-tempered; quarrelsome. ▫▫ **can•tan•ker•ous•ly** *adv.* **can•tan•ker•ous•ness** *n.*

can•ta•ta /kəntaátə/ *n. Mus.* a short narrative or descriptive composition with vocal solos and usu. chorus and orchestral accompaniment.

can•teen /kanteén/ *n.* **1 a** a restaurant for employees in an office or factory, etc. **b** a store selling provisions or liquor in a barracks or camp. **2** *Brit.* a case or box of cutlery. **3** a soldier's or camper's water flask.

can•ter /kántər/ *n.* & *v.* • *n.* a gentle gallop. • *v.* **1** *intr.* (of a horse or its rider) go at a canter. **2** *tr.* make (a horse) canter.

can•ter•bur•y /kántərberee/ *n.* (*pl.* **•ies**) a piece of furniture with partitions for holding music, etc.

can•thar•i•des /kanthárideez/ *n.pl.* a preparation made from dried bodies of a beetle *Lytta vesicatoria*, causing blistering of the skin and formerly used in medicine and as an aphrodisiac. Also called SPANISH FLY.

can•thus /kánthəs/ *n.* (*pl.* **canthi** /–thī/) the outer or inner corner of the eye, where the upper and lower lids meet.

can•ti•cle /kántikəl/ *n.* a song or chant with a biblical text.

can•ti•le•na /kánt'leénə/ *n. Mus.* a simple or sustained melody.

can•ti•le•ver /kánt'leevər, –evər/ *n.* & *v.* • *n.* **1** a long bracket or beam, etc., projecting from a wall to support a balcony, etc. **2** a beam or girder fixed at only one end. • *v.intr.* **1** project as a cantilever. **2** be supported by cantilevers.

can•ti•na /kanteénə/ *n.* esp. *SW US* a tavern, bar, etc.

can•to /kántō/ *n.* (*pl.* **•tos**) a division of a long poem.

can•ton *n.* & *v.* • *n.* **1** /kánton/ **a** a subdivision of a country. **b** a state of the Swiss confederation. **2** /kántən/ *Heraldry* a square division, less than a quarter, in the upper (usu. dexter) corner of a shield. • *v.tr.* **1** /kantón, –tṓn *Brit.*/ put (troops) into quarters. **2** /kantón/ divide into cantons. ▫▫ **can•ton•al** /kánt'nəl, kantónəl/ *adj.*

Can•ton•ese /kántəneéz/ *adj.* & *n.* • *adj.* of Canton or the Cantonese dialect of Chinese. • *n.* (*pl.* same) **1** a native of Canton. **2** the dialect of Chinese spoken in SE China and Hong Kong.

can•ton•ment /kantónmənt, –tṓn–/ *n.* **1** quarters assigned to troops. **2** a permanent military station in India.

can•tor /kántər/ *n.* **1** the leader of the singing in church; a precentor. **2** the precentor in a synagogue.

Ca•nuck /kənúk/ *n.* & *adj. sl.* often *derog.* • *n.* **1** a Canadian, esp. a French Canadian. **2** a Canadian horse or pony. • *adj.* Canadian, esp. French Canadian.

can•vas /kánvəs/ *n.* & *v.* • *n.* **1 a** a strong coarse kind of cloth made from hemp or flax or other coarse yarn and used for sails and tents, etc., and as a surface for oil painting. **b** a piece of this. **2** a painting on canvas, esp. in oils. **3** an open kind of canvas used as a basis for tapestry and embroidery. **4** *sl.* the floor of a boxing or wrestling ring. • *v.tr.* (**canvased, canvasing**; esp. *Brit.* **canvassed, canvassing**) cover with canvas. ▫ **under canvas 1** in a tent or tents. **2** with sails spread.

can•vas•back /kánvəsbak/ *n.* a wild duck, *Aythya valisineria*, of N. America, with back feathers the color of unbleached canvas.

can•vass /kánvəs/ *v.* & *n.* • *v.* **1 a** *intr.* solicit votes. **b** *tr.* solicit votes from (electors in a constituency). **2** *tr.* **a** ascertain opinions of. **b** seek business from. **c** discuss thoroughly. • *n.* the process of or an instance of canvassing, esp. of electors. ▫▫ **can•vass•er** *n.*

can•yon /kányən/ *n.* a deep gorge, often with a stream or river.

cap /kap/ *n.* & *v.* • *n.* **1 a** a covering for the head, often of soft fabric and with a visor. **b** a head covering worn in a particular profession (*nurse's cap*). **c** esp. *Brit.* a cap awarded as a sign of membership of a sports team. **d** an academic mortarboard or soft hat. **2 a** a cover like a cap in shape or position (*kneecap; toecap*). **b** a device to seal a bottle or protect the point of a pen, lens of a camera, etc. **3** = MOBCAP. **4** = PERCUSSION CAP. **5** = CROWN *n.* 9b. • *v.tr.* (**capped, capping**) **1 a** put a cap on. **b** cover the top or end of. **c** set a limit to (expenditure, etc.). **2** esp. *Brit.* award a sports cap to. **3 a** lie on top of; form the cap of. **b** surpass; excel. **c** improve on (a story, quotation, etc.), esp. by producing a better or more apposite one. ▫ **cap in hand** humbly. **set one's cap for** try to attract as a suitor. ▫▫ **cap•ful** *n.* (*pl.* **•fuls**). **cap•ping** *n.*

cap. *abbr.* **1** capital. **2** capital letter. **3** chapter.

ca•pa•bil•i•ty /káypəbílitee/ *n.* (*pl.* **•ties**) **1** (often foll. by *of, for, to*) ability; power; the condition of being capable. **2** an undeveloped or unused faculty.

ca•pa•ble /káypəbəl/ *adj.* **1** competent; able; gifted. **2** (foll. by *of*) **a** having the ability or fitness or necessary quality for. **b** susceptible or admitting of (explanation or improvement, etc.). ▫▫ **ca•pa•bly** *adv.*

ca•pa•cious /kəpáyshəs/ *adj.* roomy; able to hold much.

ca•pac•i•tance /kəpásit'ns/ *n. Electr.* **1** the ability of a system to store an electric charge. **2** the ratio of the change in an electric charge in a system to the corresponding change in its electric potential. ¶ Symb.: **C**.

ca•pac•i•tor /kəpásitər/ *n. Electr.* a device of one or more pairs of conductors separated by insulators used to store an electric charge.

ca•pac•i•ty /kəpásitee/ *n.* (*pl.* **•ties**) **1 a** the power of containing, receiving, experiencing, or producing (*capacity for heat, pain,* etc.). **b** the maximum amount that can be contained or produced, etc. **c** the volume, e.g., of the cylinders in an internal combustion engine. **d** (*attrib.*) fully occupying the available space, resources, etc. (*a capacity audience*). **2 a** mental power. **b** a faculty or talent. **3** a position or function (*in a civil capacity; in my capacity as a critic*). **4** legal competence. **5** *Electr.* capacitance. □ **to capacity** fully; using all resources (*working to capacity*). □□ **ca·pac·i·ta·tive** /–táytiv/ *adj.* (also **ca·pac·i·tive**) (in sense 5).

ca·par·i·son /kəpárisən/ *n.* & *v.* •*n.* **1** (usu. in *pl.*) a horse's trappings. **2** equipment; finery. •*v.tr.* put caparisons on; adorn richly.

cape[1] /kayp/ *n.* **1** a sleeveless cloak. **2** a short, sleeveless cloak as a fixed or detachable part of a longer cloak or coat.

cape[2] /kayp/ *n.* **1** a headland or promontory. **2** (**the Cape**) **a** the Cape of Good Hope. **b** the S. African province containing it. **c** Cape Cod, Massachusetts.

cap·e·lin /kápəlin, káplin/ *n.* (also **cap·lin** /káplin/) a small smeltlike fish, *Mallotus villosus*, of the N. Atlantic, used as food and as bait for catching cod, etc.

ca·per[1] /káypər/ *v.* & *n.* •*v.intr.* jump or run about playfully. •*n.* **1** a playful jump or leap. **2 a** a fantastic proceeding; a prank. **b** *sl.* any activity or occupation.

ca·per[2] /káypər/ *n.* **1** a bramblelike S. European shrub, *Capparis spinosa*. **2** (in *pl.*) its flower buds cooked and pickled for use as flavoring, esp. for a savory sauce.

cap·il·lar·y /kápəleree/ *adj.* & *n.* •*adj.* **1** of or like a hair. **2** (of a tube) of hairlike internal diameter. **3** of one of the delicate ramified blood vessels intervening between arteries and veins. •*n.* (*pl.* **·ies**) **1** a capillary tube. **2** a capillary blood vessel.

cap·il·lar·y ac·tion *n.* the tendency of a liquid in a capillary tube or absorbent material to rise and fall as a result of surface tension. Also called **capillarity**.

cap·i·tal[1] /kápit'l/ *n., adj.,* & *int.* •*n.* **1** the most important town or city of a country, state, or region, usu. its seat of government and administrative center. **2 a** the money or other assets with which a company starts in business. **b** accumulated wealth, esp. as used in further production. **c** money invested or lent at interest. **3** capitalists generally. **4** a capital letter. •*adj.* **1 a** principal; most important. **b** *colloq.* excellent; first-rate. **2 a** involving or punishable by death (*capital punishment*). **b** (of an error, etc.) vitally harmful; fatal. **3** (of letters of the alphabet) large in size and of the form used to begin sentences and names, etc. •*int.* expressing approval or satisfaction. □ **make capital out of** use to one's advantage. **with a capital** — emphatically such (*art with a capital A*). □□ **cap·i·tal·ly** *adv.*

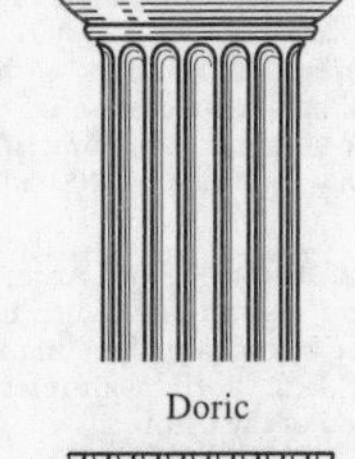

Doric

Ionic

Corinthian

capital

cap·i·tal[2] /kápit'l/ *n. Archit.* the head or cornice of a pillar or column.

cap·i·tal gain *n.* a profit from the sale of investments or property.

cap·i·tal·ism /kápit'lizəm/ *n.* **1 a** an economic system in which the production and distribution of goods depend on invested private capital and profit making. **b** the possession of capital or wealth. **2** *Polit.* the dominance of private owners of capital and production for profit.

cap·i·tal·ist /kápit'list/ *n.* & *adj.* •*n.* **1** a person using or possessing capital; a rich person. **2** an advocate of capitalism. •*adj.* of or favoring capitalism. □□ **cap·i·tal·is·tic** *adj.* **cap·i·tal·is·ti·cal·ly** *adv.*

cap·i·tal·ize /kápit'līz/ *v.* **1** *tr.* **a** convert into or provide with capital. **b** calculate or realize the present value of an income. **c** reckon (the value of an asset) by setting future benefits against the cost of maintenance. **2** *tr.* **a** write (a letter of the alphabet) as a capital. **b** begin (a word) with a capital letter. **3** *intr.* (foll. by *on*) use to one's advantage; profit from. □□ **cap·i·tal·i·za·tion** *n.*

Cap·i·tol /kápit'l/ *n.* **1** the building in Washington, D.C., in which the U.S. Congress meets. **2** (as **capitol**) a building in which a state legislature meets.

ca·pit·u·late /kəpíchəlayt/ *v.intr.* surrender, esp. on stated conditions. □□ **ca·pit·u·la·tor** *n.* **ca·pit·u·la·to·ry** /–lətáwree/ *adj.*

ca·pit·u·la·tion /kəpíchəláyshən/ *n.* **1** the act of capitulating; surrender. **2** a statement of the main divisions of a subject. **3** an agreement or set of conditions.

cap'n /káp'm/ *n. sl.* captain.

ca·po /káypō/ *n.* (in full **ca·po·tas·to** /–tástō /) (*pl.* **capos** or **capotastos**) *Mus.* a device secured across the neck of a fretted instrument to raise equally the tuning of all strings by the required amount.

ca·pon /káypon, –pən/ *n.* a domestic cock castrated and fattened for eating. □□ **ca·pon·ize** *v.tr.*

cap·puc·ci·no /kápoochéenō/ *n.* (*pl.* **·nos**) espresso coffee with milk made frothy with pressurized steam.

ca·pric·ci·o /kəpréecheeō/ *n.* (*pl.* **·os**) **1** a lively and usu. short musical composition. **2** a painting, etc., representing a fantasy or a mixture of real and imaginary features.

ca·price /kəprées/ *n.* **1 a** an unaccountable or whimsical change of mind or conduct. **b** a tendency to this. **2** a work of lively fancy in painting, drawing, or music; a capriccio.

ca·pri·cious /kəpríshəs, –prée–/ *adj.* **1** guided by or given to caprice. **2** irregular; unpredictable. □□ **ca·pri·cious·ly** *adv.* **ca·pri·cious·ness** *n.*

Cap·ri·corn /káprikawrn/ *n.* (also **Cap·ri·cor·nus** /–káwrnəs/) **1** a constellation, traditionally regarded as contained in the figure of a goat's horns. **2 a** the tenth sign of the zodiac (the Goat). **b** a person born when the sun is in this sign. □□ **Cap·ri·corn·i·an** *n.* & *adj.*

cap·rine /káprīn, –rin/ *adj.* of or like a goat.

cap·ri·ole /kápreeōl/ *n.* & *v.* •*n.* **1** a leap or caper. **2** a trained horse's high leap and kick without advancing. •*v.* **1** *intr.* (of a horse or its rider) perform a capriole. **2** *tr.* make (a horse) capriole.

ca·pris /kəpréez/ *n.pl.* (also **ca·pri pants**) women's close-fitting tapered trousers that end above the ankle.

caps. *abbr.* capital letters.

cap·si·cum /kápsikəm/ *n.* **1** any plant of the genus *Capsicum*, having edible capsular fruits containing many seeds, esp. *C. annuum* yielding chili and sweet peppers. **2** the fruit of any of these plants.

cap·sid[1] /kápsid/ *n.* any bug of the family Capsidae, esp. one that feeds on plants.

cap·sid[2] /kápsid/ *n.* the protein coat or shell of a virus.

cap·size /kápsīz, –síz/ *v.* **1** *tr.* upset or overturn (a boat). **2** *intr.* be capsized.

cap·stan /kápstən/ *n.* **1** a thick revolving cylinder with a vertical axis, for winding an anchor cable or a halyard, etc. **2** a motor-driven revolving spindle on a tape recorder, that guides the tape past the head.

cap·sule /kápsəl, –sōōl/ *n.* **1** a small gelatinous case enclosing a dose of medicine and swallowed with it. **2** a detachable compartment of a spacecraft or nose cone of a rocket. **3** an enclosing membrane in the body. **4 a** a dry fruit that releases its seeds when ripe. **b** the spore-producing part of mosses and liverworts. **5** *Biol.* an enveloping layer surrounding certain bacteria. **6** (*attrib.*) concise; highly condensed (*a capsule history of jazz*). ▫▫ **cap·su·lar** *adj.* **cap·su·late** *adj.*

Capt. *abbr.* Captain.

cap·tain /káptin/ *n.* & *v.* • *n.* **1 a** a chief or leader. **b** the leader of a team, esp. in sports. **c** a powerful or influential person (*captain of industry*). **2 a** the person in command of a merchant or passenger ship. **b** the pilot of a civil aircraft. **3 a** an army or air force officer next above lieutenant. **b** a navy officer in command of a warship; one ranking below commodore or rear admiral and above commander. **c** a police officer in charge of a precinct, ranking below chief. **4** a supervisor of waiters or bellboys. **5 a** a great soldier or strategist. **b** an experienced commander. • *v.tr.* be captain of; lead. ▫▫ **cap·tain·cy** *n.* (*pl.* **·cies**). **cap·tain·ship** *n.*

cap·tion /kápshən/ *n.* & *v.* • *n.* **1** a title or brief explanation appended to an illustration, cartoon, etc. **2** wording appearing on a motion-picture or television screen as part of a movie or broadcast. **3** the heading of a chapter or article, etc. **4** *Law* a certificate attached to or written on a document. • *v.tr.* provide with a caption.

---

caption late Middle English (in the sense 'seizing, capture'): from Latin *captio(n-)*, from *capere* 'take, seize.' The early senses 'arrest,' 'warrant for arrest' gave rise to 'statement of where, when, and by whose authority a warrant was issued' (late 17th century): this was usually appended to a legal document, hence the sense 'heading or appended wording' (late 18th century).

---

cap·tious /kápshəs/ *adj.* given to finding fault or raising petty objections. ▫▫ **cap·tious·ly** *adv.* **cap·tious·ness** *n.*

cap·ti·vate /káptivayt/ *v.tr.* **1** overwhelm with charm or affection. **2** fascinate. ▫▫ **cap·ti·vat·ing** *adj.* **cap·ti·vat·ing·ly** *adv.* **cap·ti·va·tion** /–váyshən/ *n.*

cap·tive /káptiv/ *n.* & *adj.* • *n.* a person or animal that has been taken prisoner or confined. • *adj.* **1 a** taken prisoner. **b** kept in confinement or under restraint. **2 a** unable to escape. **b** in a position of having to comply (*captive audience*; *captive market*). **3** of or like a prisoner (*captive state*).

cap·tiv·i·ty /kaptívitee/ *n.* (*pl.* **·ties**) **1** the condition or circumstances of being a captive. **2** a period of captivity.

cap·tor /káptər, –tawr/ *n.* a person who captures (a person, place, etc.).

cap·ture /kápchər/ *v.* & *n.* • *v.tr.* **1 a** take prisoner; seize as a prize. **b** obtain by force or trickery. **2** portray in permanent form (*could not capture the likeness*). **3** *Physics* absorb (a subatomic particle). **4** (in board games) make a move that secures the removal of (an opposing piece) from the board. **5** cause (data) to be stored in a computer. • *n.* **1** the act of capturing. **2** a thing or person captured. ▫▫ **cap·tur·er** *n.*

cap·u·chin /kápyəchin, –shin, kəpyōō–/ *n.* **1** (**Capuchin**) a Franciscan friar of the new rule of 1529. **2** any monkey of the genus *Cebus* of S. America, with cowl-like head hair.

cap·y·ba·ra /kápəbaárə/ *n.* a very large semiaquatic rodent, *Hydrochoerus hydrochaeris*, native to S. America.

car /kaar/ *n.* **1** a road vehicle with an enclosed passenger compartment, powered by an internal-combustion engine; an automobile. **2** a vehicle that runs on rails, esp. a railroad car or a streetcar. **3** a railroad car of a specified type (*dining car*). **4** the passenger compartment of an elevator, cable railway, balloon, etc. **5** *poet.* a wheeled vehicle; a chariot. ▫▫ **car·ful** *n.* (*pl.* **·fuls**).

car·a·bi·ner /karəbeénər/ *n.* a coupling link with a safety closure, used by rock climbers.

car·a·cal /kárəkal/ *n.* a lynx, *Felis caracal*, native to N. Africa and SW Asia.

car·a·cole /kárəkōl/ *n.* & *v.* • *n.* a horse's half turn to the right or left. • *v.* **1** *intr.* (of a horse or its rider) perform a caracole. **2** *tr.* make (a horse) caracole.

car·a·cul var. of KARAKUL.

ca·rafe /kəráf/ *n.* a glass container for water or wine, esp. at a table or bedside.

car·a·mel /kárəmel, –məl, kaármәl/ *n.* **1 a** sugar or syrup heated until it turns brown, then used as a flavoring or to color spirits, etc. **b** a kind of soft toffee made with sugar, butter, etc., melted and further heated. **2** the light-brown color of caramel.

car·a·mel·ize /kárəməlīz, kaármə–/ *v.* **1 a** *tr.* convert (sugar or syrup) into caramel. **b** *intr.* (of sugar or syrup) be converted into caramel. **2** *tr.* coat or cook (food) with caramelized sugar or syrup. ▫▫ **car·a·mel·i·za·tion** /–lizáyshən/ *n.*

car·a·pace /kárəpays/ *n.* the hard upper shell of a turtle or a crustacean.

car·at /kárət/ *n.* **1** a unit of weight for precious stones, now equivalent to 200 milligrams. **2** *Brit.* var. of KARAT.

---

carat from French, from Italian *carato*, from Arabic *ķīrāṭ* (a unit of weight), from Greek *keration* 'fruit of the carob' (also denoting a unit of weight), diminutive of *keras* 'horn,' with reference to the elongated seed pod of the carob.

---

car·a·van /kárəvan/ *n.* **1** a covered or enclosed wagon or truck; van. **2** a company of merchants or pilgrims, etc., traveling together, esp. across a desert in Asia or N. Africa. **3** a covered cart or carriage. ▫▫ **car·a·van·ner** *n.*

car·a·van·sa·ry /kárəvánsəree, –rī/ *n.* (also **car·a·van·se·rai**) a Near Eastern inn with a central court where caravans (see CARAVAN 2) may rest.

car·a·way /kárəway/ *n.* an umbelliferous plant, *Carum carvi*, bearing clusters of tiny white flowers.

car·a·way seed *n.* the fruit of the caraway plant used as flavoring and as a source of oil.

car·bide /kaárbīd/ *n.* *Chem.* a binary compound of carbon.

car·bine /kaárbeen, –bīn/ *n.* a lightweight firearm, usu. a rifle, orig. for cavalry use.

carbo- /kaárbō/ *comb. form* carbon (*carbohydrate*; *carbolic*; *carboxyl*).

car·bo·hy·drate /kaárbəhídrayt, –bō–/ *n.* *Biochem.* any of a large group of energy-producing organic compounds containing carbon, hydrogen, and oxygen, e.g., starch, glucose, and other sugars.

car·bol·ic /kaarbólik/ *n.* (in full **carbolic acid**) phenol, esp. when used as a disinfectant.

car·bon /kaárbən/ *n.* **1** a nonmetallic element occurring naturally as diamond, graphite, and charcoal, and in all organic compounds. ¶ Symb.: **C**. **2 a** = CARBON COPY. **b** = CARBON PAPER. **3** a rod of carbon in an arc lamp.

carbon 14 *n.* a long-lived radioactive carbon isotope of mass 14, used in radiocarbon dating, and as a tracer in biochemistry.
car·bo·na·do /kaárbənáydō/ *n.* (*pl.* **·dos**) a dark opaque or impure kind of diamond used as an abrasive, for drills, etc.
car·bo·nate /kaárbənayt/ *n.* & *v.* • *n. Chem.* a salt of carbonic acid. • *v.tr.* **1** impregnate with carbon dioxide; aerate. **2** convert into a carbonate. □□ **car·bo·na·tion** /–náyshən/ *n.*
car·bon cop·y *n.* **1** a copy made with carbon paper. **2** a person or thing identical or similar to another (*is a carbon copy of his father*).
car·bon dat·ing *n.* the determination of the age of an organic object from the ratio of isotopes, which changes as carbon 14 decays.
car·bon di·ox·ide *n.* a colorless, odorless gas occurring naturally in the atmosphere and formed by respiration. ¶ Chem. formula: CO_2.
car·bon·ic /kaarbónik/ *adj. Chem.* containing carbon.
car·bon·ic ac·id *n.* a very weak acid formed from carbon dioxide dissolved in water.
car·bon·if·er·ous /kaárbənífərəs/ *adj.* & *n.* • *adj.* **1** producing coal. **2** (**Carboniferous**) *Geol.* of or relating to the fifth period in the Paleozoic era, with evidence of the first reptiles and coal-forming swamp forests. • *n.* (**Carboniferous**) *Geol.* this period or system.
car·bon·ize /kaárbənīz/ *v.tr.* **1** convert into carbon by heating. **2** reduce to charcoal or coke. **3** coat with carbon. □□ **car·bon·i·za·tion** /–nizáyshən/ *n.*
car·bon mon·ox·ide *n.* a colorless, odorless toxic gas formed by the incomplete burning of carbon. ¶ Chem. formula: CO.
car·bon pa·per *n.* a thin carbon-coated paper used between two sheets of paper when writing to make a copy onto the bottom sheet.
car·bon·yl /kaárbənil/ *n.* (used *attrib.*) *Chem.* the divalent radical CO.
car·bo·run·dum /kaábərúndəm/ *n.* a compound of carbon and silicon used esp. as an abrasive.
car·box·yl /kaarbóksil/ *n. Chem.* the univalent acid radical (-COOH), present in most organic acids. □□ **car·box·yl·ic** /–boksílik/ *adj.*
car·boy /kaárboy/ *n.* a large bottle often protected by a frame, used for containing liquids.
car·bun·cle /kaárbungkəl/ *n.* **1** a severe abscess in the skin. **2** a bright red gem. □□ **car·bun·cu·lar** /–búngkyələr/ *adj.*
car·bu·ra·tion /kaárbəráyshən, –byə–/ *n.* the process of charging air with a spray of liquid hydrocarbon fuel, esp. in an internal combustion engine.
car·bu·re·tor /kaárbəráytter, –byə–/ *n.* (also **car·bu·ra·tor**) an apparatus for carburation of fuel and air in an internal combustion engine.
car·ca·jou /kaárkəjōō, –kəzhōō/ *n.* = WOLVERINE.
car·cass /kaárkəs/ *n.* (also *Brit.* **car·case**) **1** the dead body of an animal, esp. for cutting up as meat. **2** the bones of a cooked bird. **3** *derog.* the human body, living or dead. **4** the skeleton, framework of a building, ship, etc. **5** worthless remains.
car·cin·o·gen /kaarsínəjən, kaársinəjen/ *n.* any substance that produces cancer.
car·cin·o·gen·ic /kaársinəjénik/ *adj.* having the potential to cause cancer.
car·ci·no·ma /kaársinómə/ *n.* (*pl.* **carcinomas** or **carcinomata** /–mətə/) a cancer, esp. one arising in epithelial tissue. □□ **car·ci·no·ma·tous** *adj.*
card[1] /kaard/ *n.* & *v.* • *n.* **1** thick, stiff paper or thin pasteboard. **2 a** a flat piece of this, esp. for writing or printing on. **b** = POSTCARD. **c** a card used to send greetings, issue an invitation, etc. (*birthday card*). **d** = CALLING CARD. **e** = BUSINESS CARD. **f** a ticket of admission or membership. **3 a** = PLAYING CARD. **b** a similar card in a set designed for board games, etc. **c** (in *pl.*) card playing; a card game. **4 a** a program of events at boxing matches, races, etc. **b** a scorecard. **c** a list of holes on a golf course, on which a player's scores are entered. **5** *colloq.* a person, esp. an odd or amusing one. **6** a small rectangular piece of plastic issued by a bank, retail establishment, etc., with personal (often machine-readable) data on it, chiefly to obtain cash or credit (*credit card; do you have a card?*). • *v.tr.* **1** fix to a card. **2** write on a card, esp. for indexing. **3** ask for proof of age, as at a bar. □ **in the cards** possible or likely. **put** (or **lay**) **one's cards on the table** reveal one's resources, intentions, etc.
card[2] /kaard/ *n.* & *v.* • *n.* a toothed instrument, wire brush, etc., for raising a nap on cloth or for disentangling fibers before spinning. • *v.tr.* brush, comb, cleanse, or scratch with a card. □□ **card·er** *n.*
car·da·mom /kaárdəməm/ *n.* (also **car·da·mum**) **1** an aromatic SE Asian plant, *Elettaria cardamomum*. **2** the seed capsules of this used as a spice.
card·board /kaárdbawrd/ *n.* & *adj.* • *n.* pasteboard or stiff paper, esp. for making cards or boxes. • *adj.* **1** made of cardboard. **2** flimsy; insubstantial.
card-car·ry·ing *adj.* being a registered member of an organization, esp. a political party or labor union.
car·di·ac /kaárdeeak/ *adj.* & *n.* • *adj.* of or relating to the heart. • *n.* a person with heart disease.
car·di·gan /kaárdigən/ *n.* a knitted sweater fastening down the front, usu. with long sleeves.

---

cardigan mid-19th century (Crimean War): named after James Thomas Brudenel, 7th Earl of Cardigan (1797–1868), leader of the famous Charge of the Light Brigade; his troops first wore such garments.

---

car·di·nal /kaárd'nəl/ *n.* & *adj.* • *n.* **1** (as a title **Cardinal**) a leading dignitary of the RC Church, one of the college electing the Pope. **2** any small American songbird of the genus *Richmondena*, the males of which have scarlet plumage. • *adj.* **1** chief; fundamental; on which something hinges. **2** of deep scarlet (like a cardinal's cassock). □□ **car·di·nal·ate** /–nəlayt/ *n.* (in sense 1 of *n.*). **car·di·nal·ly** *adv.* **car·di·nal·ship** *n.* (in sense 1 of *n.*).
car·di·nal num·ber *n.* a number denoting quantity (one, two, three, etc.), as opposed to ordinal numbers (first, second, third, etc.).
cardio- /kaárdeeō/ *comb. form* heart (*cardiogram; cardiology*).
car·di·o·gram /kaárdeeəgram/ *n.* a record of muscle activity within the heart, made by a cardiograph.
car·di·o·graph /kaárdeeəgraf/ *n.* an instrument for recording heart muscle activity. □□ **car·di·og·ra·pher** /–deeógrəfər/ *n.* **car·di·og·ra·phy** *n.*
car·di·ol·o·gy /kaárdeeóləjee/ *n.* the branch of medicine concerned with diseases and abnormalities of the heart. □□ **car·di·ol·o·gist** *n.*
car·di·o·pul·mo·nar·y re·sus·ci·ta·tion /kardeeōpóólməneree/ *n.* emergency medical procedures for restoring normal heartbeat and breathing to victims of heart failure, drowning, etc. ¶ Abbr.: **CPR**.
car·di·o·vas·cu·lar /kaárdeeōváskyələr/ *adj.* of or relating to the heart and blood vessels.
car·doon /kaardóón/ *n.* a thistlelike plant, *Cynara cardunculus*, allied to the globe artichoke, with leaves used as a vegetable.
card·shark /kaárdshaark/ *n.* **1** a person who is an expert cardplayer. **2** a cardsharp.
card·sharp /kaárdshaarp/ *n.* (also **card·sharp·er**) a swindler at card games.

---

care /kair/ *n.* & *v.* • *n.* **1** worry; anxiety. **2** an occasion for this. **3** serious attention; heed; caution; pains (*assembled with care*; *handle with care*). **4** protection; charge. **5** a thing to be done or seen to. • *v.intr.* **1** (usu. foll. by *about*, *for*, *whether*) feel concern or interest. **2** (usu. foll. by *for*, *about*) feel liking, affection, regard, or deference (*don't care for jazz*; *she cares for him a great deal*). **3** (foll. by *to* + infin.) wish or be willing (*do not care to be seen with him*; *would you care to try them?*). □ **care for** provide for; look after. **care of** at the address of (*sent it care of his sister*). **for all one cares** *colloq.* denoting uninterest or unconcern (*I could be dying for all you care*). **have a care** take care; be careful. **I** (etc.) **couldn't** (freq. **could**) **care less** *colloq.* an expression of complete indifference. **take care 1** be careful. **2** (foll. by *to* + infin.) not fail nor neglect. **take care of 1** look after; keep safe. **2** deal with. **3** dispose of.

ca·reen /kəréen/ *v.* **1** *tr.* turn (a ship) on one side for cleaning, caulking, or repair. **2 a** *intr.* tilt; lean over. **b** *tr.* cause to do this. **3** *intr.* swerve about; career. ▶Sense 3 is infl. by *career* (v.). □□ **ca·reen·age** *n.*

ca·reer /kəréer/ *n.* & *v.* • *n.* **1 a** one's advancement through life, esp. in a profession. **b** the progress through history of a group or institution. **2** a profession or occupation, esp. as offering advancement. **3** (*attrib.*) **a** pursuing or wishing to pursue a career (*career woman*). **b** working permanently in a specified profession (*career diplomat*). • *v.intr.* **1** move or swerve about wildly. **2** go swiftly.

care·free /káirfree/ *adj.* free from anxiety or responsibility; lighthearted. □□ **care·free·ness** *n.*

care·ful /káirfōōl/ *adj.* **1** painstaking; thorough. **2** cautious. **3** done with care and attention. **4** (usu. foll. by *that* + clause, or *to* + infin.) taking care; not neglecting. **5** (foll. by *for*, *of*) concerned for; taking care of. □□ **care·ful·ly** *adv.* **care·ful·ness** *n.*

care·giv·er /káirgivər/ *n.* a person who provides care for children, the sick, the elderly, etc.

care·less /káirlis/ *adj.* **1** not taking care nor paying attention. **2** unthinking; insensitive. **3** done without care; inaccurate. **4** lighthearted. **5** (foll. by *of*) not concerned about; taking no heed of. **6** effortless; casual. □□ **care·less·ly** *adv.* **care·less·ness** *n.*

ca·ress /kərés/ *v.* & *n.* • *v.tr.* **1** touch or stroke gently or lovingly; kiss. **2** treat fondly or kindly. • *n.* a loving or gentle touch or kiss.

car·et /kárət/ *n.* a mark (‸) indicating a proposed insertion in printing or writing.

care·tak·er /káirtaykər/ *n.* **1 a** a person employed to look after something, esp. a house in the owner's absence. **b** *Brit.* a janitor. **2** (*attrib.*) exercising temporary authority (*caretaker government*).

care·worn /káirwawrn/ *adj.* showing the effects of prolonged worry.

car·go /kaárgō/ *n.* (*pl.* **·goes** or **·gos**) **1 a** goods carried on a ship or aircraft. **b** a load of such goods. **2 a** goods carried in a motor vehicle. **b** a load of such goods.

Car·ib /kárib/ *n.* & *adj.* • *n.* **1** an aboriginal inhabitant of the southern W. Indies or the adjacent coasts. **2** the language of this people. • *adj.* of or relating to this people.

Car·ib·be·an /káribéeən, kəríbeeən/ *n.* & *adj.* • *n.* the part of the Atlantic between the southern W. Indies and Central America. • *adj.* **1** of or relating to this region. **2** of the Caribs or their language or culture.

car·i·bou /káribōō/ *n.* (*pl.* same) a N. American reindeer.

---

caribou mid-17th century: from Canadian French, from Micmac *γalipu*, literally 'snow-shoveler,' because the caribou scrapes away snow to feed on the vegetation underneath.

---

car·i·ca·ture /kárikəchər, –chŏŏr/ *n.* & *v.* • *n.* **1** a grotesque usu. comic representation of a person by exaggeration of characteristic traits, in a picture, writing, or mime. **2** a ridiculously poor or absurd imitation or version. • *v.tr.* make or give a caricature of. □□ **car·i·ca·tur·al** /–chŏŏrəl/ *adj.* **car·i·ca·tur·ist** *n.*

car·ies /káireez/ *n.* (*pl.* same) decay and crumbling of a tooth or bone.

car·il·lon /kárilon, –lən/ *n.* **1** a set of bells sounded either from a keyboard or mechanically. **2** a tune played on bells. **3** an organ stop imitating a peal of bells.

ca·ri·na /kəréenə/ *n.* (*pl.* **carinas** or **carinae** /–nee/) *Biol.* a keel-shaped structure, esp. the ridge of a bird's breastbone. □□ **ca·ri·nal** *adj.*

car·ing /káiring/ *adj.* **1** compassionate. **2** involving the care of the sick, elderly, or disabled.

car·i·o·gen·ic /káireeōjénik/ *adj.* causing caries.

car·i·ous /káireeəs/ *adj.* (of bones or teeth) decayed.

car·jack·ing /kárjaking/ *n.* theft of an automobile whose driver is forced to leave the vehicle or is kept captive while the thief drives. □□ **car·jack** *v.tr.* **car·jack·er** *n.*

car·load /kaárlōd/ *n.* **1** a quantity that can be carried in a car. **2** the minimum quantity of goods for which a lower rate is charged for transport.

Car·lo·vin·gi·an var. of CAROLINGIAN.

Car·mel·ite /kaármilīt/ *n.* & *adj.* • *n.* **1** a friar of the Order of Our Lady of Mount Carmel, following a rule of extreme asceticism. **2** a nun of a similar order. • *adj.* of or relating to the Carmelites.

car·min·a·tive /kaarmínətiv, kaárminaytiv/ *adj.* & *n.* • *adj.* relieving flatulence. • *n.* a carminative drug.

car·mine /kaármin, –mīn/ *adj.* & *n.* • *adj.* of a vivid crimson color. • *n.* this color.

car·nage /kaárnij/ *n.* great slaughter, esp. of human beings in battle.

car·nal /kaárnəl/ *adj.* **1** of the body or flesh; worldly. **2** sensual; sexual. □□ **car·nal·i·ty** /–aálitee/ *n.* **car·nal·ize** *v.tr.* **car·nal·ly** *adv.*

car·nal knowl·edge *n.* *Law* sexual intercourse.

car·nas·si·al /kaarnáseeəl/ *adj.* & *n.* • *adj.* (of a carnivore's upper premolar and lower molar teeth) adapted for shearing flesh. • *n.* such a tooth.

car·na·tion[1] /kaarnáyshən/ *n.* **1** any of several cultivated varieties of clove-scented pink, with variously colored showy flowers (see also CLOVE[1] 2). **2** this flower.

car·na·tion[2] /kaarnáyshən/ *n.* & *adj.* • *n.* a rosy pink color. • *adj.* of this color.

car·nau·ba /kaarnówbə, –náwbə, –nŏŏbə/ *n.* **1** a fan palm, *Copernicia cerifera*, native to NE Brazil. **2** (in full **carnauba wax**) the yellowish leaf wax of this tree used as a polish, etc.

car·nel·ian /kaarnéelyən/ *n.* (also **cor·nel·ian** /kawr–/) a dull red or reddish-white variety of chalcedony.

car·ni·val /kaárnivəl/ *n.* **1 a** the festivities usual during the period before Lent in Roman Catholic countries. **b** any festivities, esp. those occurring at a regular date. **2** merrymaking; revelry. **3** a traveling fair or circus.

car·ni·vore /kaárnivawr/ *n.* **1 a** any mammal of the order Carnivora, with powerful jaws and teeth adapted for stabbing, tearing, and eating flesh. **b** any other flesh-eating mammal. **2** any flesh-eating plant.

car·niv·o·rous /kaarnívərəs/ *adj.* **1** (of an animal) feeding on other animals. **2** (of a plant) digesting trapped insects or other animal substances. **3** of or relating to the order Carnivora. □□ **car·niv·o·rous·ly** *adv.* **car·niv·o·rous·ness** *n.*

car·ob /kárəb/ *n.* **1** an evergreen tree, *Ceratonia siliqua*, native to the Mediterranean, bearing edible pods. **2** its bean-shaped edible seed pod sometimes used as a substitute for chocolate.

car·ol /kárəl/ *n.* & *v.* •*n.* a joyous song, esp. a Christmas hymn. •*v.* (**caroled, caroling**; esp. *Brit.* **carolled, carolling**) **1** *intr.* sing carols, esp. outdoors at Christmas. **2** *tr.* & *intr.* sing joyfully. ▫▫ **car·ol·er** *n.* (also esp. *Brit.* **car·ol·ler**).

Car·o·lin·gi·an /kárəlínjən, –jeeən/ *adj.* & *n.* (also **Car·lo·vin·gi·an** /kaárləvínjeeən/) •*adj.* of or relating to the second Frankish dynasty, founded by Charlemagne (d. 814). •*n.* a member of the Carolingian dynasty.

car·om /kárəm/ *n.* & *v.* *Billiards* •*n.* the hitting of two balls by the one ball on one shot. •*v.intr.* **1** make a carom. **2** (usu. foll. by *off*) strike and rebound.

car·o·tene /kárəteen/ *n.* any of several orange-colored plant pigments found in carrots, tomatoes, etc., acting as a source of vitamin A.

ca·rot·id /kərótid/ *n.* & *adj.* •*n.* each of the two main arteries carrying blood to the head and neck. •*adj.* of or relating to either of these arteries.

ca·rouse /kərówz/ *v.* & *n.* •*v.intr.* **1** have a noisy or lively drinking party. **2** drink heavily. •*n.* a noisy or lively drinking party. ▫▫ **ca·rous·al** *n.* **ca·rous·er** *n.*

car·ou·sel /kárəsél, –zél/ *n.* (also **car·rou·sel**) **1** a merry-go-round. **2** a rotating delivery or conveyor system, esp. for passengers' luggage at an airport.

carp[1] /kaarp/ *n.* (*pl.* same) any freshwater fish of the family Cyprinidae, esp. *Cyprinus carpio*, often bred for use as food.

carp[2] /kaarp/ *v.intr.* (usu. foll. by *at*) find fault; complain pettily. ▫▫ **carp·er** *n.*

car·pal /kaárpəl/ *adj.* & *n.* •*adj.* of or relating to the bones in the wrist. •*n.* any of the bones forming the wrist.

car·pal tun·nel syn·drome *n.* a disorder of the hand caused by compression of a major nerve where it passes over the carpal bones through a passage at the front of the wrist, alongside the flexor tendons of the hand.

car·pel /kaárpəl/ *n.* *Bot.* the female reproductive organ of a flower, consisting of a stigma, style, and ovary. ▫▫ **car·pel·lar·y** *adj.*

car·pen·ter /kaárpintər/ *n.* & *v.* •*n.* a person skilled in woodwork, esp. of a structural kind (cf. JOINER). •*v.* **1** *intr.* do carpentry. **2** *tr.* make by means of carpentry. **3** *tr.* (often foll. by *together*) construct; fit together.

---

carpenter Middle English: from Anglo-Norman French, from Old French *carpentier, charpentier*, from late Latin *carpentarius (artifex)* 'carriage(-maker),' from *carpentum* 'wagon,' of Gaulish origin; related to *car*

---

car·pen·ter ant *n.* any large ant of the genus *Camponotus*, boring into wood to nest.

car·pen·try /kaárpintree/ *n.* **1** the work or occupation of a carpenter. **2** work constructed by a carpenter.

car·pet /kaárpit/ *n.* & *v.* •*n.* **1 a** thick fabric for covering a floor or stairs. **b** a piece of this fabric. **2** an expanse or layer resembling a carpet in being smooth, soft, bright, or thick (*carpet of snow*). •*v.tr.* **1** cover with or as with a carpet. **2** *colloq.* reprimand; reprove. ▫ **on the carpet 1** *colloq.* being reprimanded. **2** under consideration. **sweep under the carpet** conceal (a problem or difficulty) in the hope that it will be forgotten.

car·pet·bag /kaárpitbag/ *n.* a traveling bag of a kind orig. made of carpetlike material.

car·pet·bag·ger /kaárpitbagər/ *n.* **1** a political candidate in an area where the candidate has no local connections (orig. a Northerner in the South after the Civil War). **2** an unscrupulous opportunist, esp. an outsider.

car·pool /kárpōōl/ *n.* & *v.* •*n.* (also **car pool**) **1** an arrangement by which a group of commuters travel to and from their destination in a single vehicle, often with the members taking turns as driver. **2** the commuters taking part in such an arrangement (*there are four people in our carpool*). •*v.intr.* (also **car-pool**) participate in or organize a carpool.

car·port /kaárpawrt/ *n.* a shelter with a roof and open sides for a car, usu. beside a house.

car·pus /kaárpəs/ *n.* (*pl.* **carpi** /–pī/) the small bones between the forelimb and metacarpus in terrestrial vertebrates, forming the wrist in humans.

car·ra·geen /kárəgeen/ *n.* (also **car·ra·gheen**) an edible red seaweed, *Chondrus crispus*, of the N. hemisphere.

car·rel /kárəl/ *n.* **1** a small cubicle for a reader in a library. **2** *hist.* a small enclosure or study in a cloister.

car·riage /kárij/ *n.* **1** a wheeled vehicle, esp. one with four wheels and pulled by horses. **2** the part of a machine (e.g., a typewriter) that carries other parts into the required position. **3** a gun carriage. **4** a manner of carrying oneself; one's bearing or deportment.

car·ri·er /káreeər/ *n.* **1** a person or thing that carries. **2** a person or company undertaking to convey goods or passengers for payment. **3** a part of a bicycle, etc., for carrying luggage or a passenger. **4** an insurance company. **5** a person or animal that may transmit a disease or a hereditary characteristic without suffering from or displaying it. **6** = AIRCRAFT CARRIER. **7** a substance used to support or convey a pigment, a catalyst, radioactive material, etc. **8** *Physics* a mobile electron or hole that carries a charge in a semiconductor.

car·ri·er pig·eon *n.* a pigeon trained to carry messages tied to its neck or leg.

car·ri·on /káriən/ *n.* **1** dead putrefying flesh. **2** something vile or filthy.

car·rot /kárət/ *n.* **1 a** an umbelliferous plant, *Daucus carota*, with a tapering orange-colored root. **b** this root as a vegetable. **2** a means of enticement or persuasion. **3** (in *pl.*) *sl.* a red-haired person. ▫▫ **car·rot·y** *adj.*

car·rou·sel var. of CAROUSEL.

car·ry /káree/ *v.* & *n.* •*v.* (**·ries, ·ried**) **1** *tr.* support or hold up, esp. while moving. **2** *tr.* convey with one from one place to another. **3** *tr.* have on one's person (*carry a watch*). **4** *tr.* conduct or transmit (*pipe carries water; wire carries electric current*). **5** *tr.* take (a process, etc.) to a specified point (*carry into effect; carry a joke too far*). **6** *tr.* (foll. by *to*) continue or prolong (*carry modesty to excess*). **7** *tr.* involve; imply; have as a feature or consequence (*carries a two-year guarantee; principles carry consequences*). **8** *tr.* (in reckoning) transfer (a figure) to a column of higher value. **9** *tr.* hold in a specified way (*carry oneself erect*). **10** *tr.* **a** (of a newspaper or magazine) publish; include in its contents, esp. regularly. **b** (of a radio or television station) broadcast, esp. regularly. **11** *tr.* (of a retailing outlet) keep a regular stock of (particular goods for sale) (*have stopped carrying that brand*). **12** *intr.* **a** (of sound, esp. a voice) be audible at a distance. **b** (of a missile) travel; penetrate. **13** *tr.* (of a gun, etc.) propel to a specified distance. **14** *tr.* **a** win victory or acceptance for (a proposal, etc.). **b** win acceptance from (*carried the audience with them*). **c** win; capture (a prize, a fortress, etc.). **d** gain (a state or district) in an election. **e** *Golf* cause the ball to pass beyond (a bunker, etc.). **15** *tr.* **a** endure the weight of; support (*columns carry the dome*). **b** be the chief cause of the effectiveness of; be the driving force in (*you carry the sales department*). **16** *tr.* be pregnant with (*is carrying twins*). **17** *tr.* **a** (of a motive, money, etc.) cause or enable (a person) to go to a specified place. **b** (of a journey) bring (a person) to a specified point. •*n.* (*pl.* **·ries**) **1** an act of carrying. **2** *Golf* the distance a ball travels before reaching the ground. **3** a portage between rivers, etc. **4** the range of a gun, etc. □ **carry all before one** succeed; overcome all opposition. **carry away 1** remove. **2** inspire; affect emotionally or spiritually. **3** deprive of self-control (*got carried away*). **carry back** take (a person) back in thought to a past time. **carry conviction** be convincing. **carry the day** be victorious or successful. **carry forward** transfer to a new page or account. **carry it off** (or **carry it off well**) do well under difficulties. **carry off 1** take away, esp. by force. **2** win (a prize). **3** (esp. of a disease) kill. **4** render acceptable or passable. **carry on 1** continue (*carry on eating*; *carry on, don't mind me*). **2** engage in (a conversation or a business). **3** *colloq.* behave strangely or excitedly. **4** (often foll. by *with*) *Brit. colloq.* flirt or have a love affair. **5** advance (a process) by a stage. **carry out** put (ideas, instructions, etc.) into practice. **carry over 1** = *carry forward.* **2** postpone (work, etc.). **carry through 1** complete successfully. **2** bring safely out of difficulties. **carry weight** be influential or important. **carry with one** bear in mind.

car·ry·ing-on (or **car·ry·ings-on**) *n. sl.* **1** a state of excitement or fuss. **2** salacious or improper behavior. **3** a flirtation or love affair.

car·ry·out /káreeowt/ *n. & adj.* • *n.* **1** food prepared and packaged for consumption elsewhere than the place of sale. **2** an establishment that sells such food. • *adj.* of or designating such foods.

car·sick /kaársik/ *adj.* affected with nausea caused by the motion of a car. □□ **car·sick·ness** *n.*

cart /kaart/ *n. & v.* • *n.* **1** a strong vehicle with two or four wheels for carrying loads, usu. drawn by a horse. **2** a light vehicle for pulling by hand. **3** a light vehicle with two wheels for driving in, drawn by a single horse. • *v.tr.* **1** convey in or as in a cart. **2** *sl.* carry (esp. a cumbersome thing) with difficulty or over a long distance (*carted it all the way home*). □ **put the cart before the horse 1** reverse the proper order or procedure. **2** take an effect for a cause. □□ **cart·er** *n.* **cart·ful** *n.* (*pl.* **·fuls**).

cart·age /kaártij/ *n.* the price paid for carting.

carte blanche /kaárt blónsh, blánch/ *n.* full discretionary power given to a person.

car·tel /kaartél/ *n.* **1** an informal association of manufacturers or suppliers to maintain prices at a high level, and control production, marketing arrangements, etc. **2** a political combination between parties. □□ **car·tel·ize** /kaártəlīz/ *v.tr. & intr.*

Car·te·sian /kaartéezhən/ *adj. & n.* • *adj.* of or relating to R. Descartes, 17th-c. French philosopher and mathematician. • *n.* a follower of Descartes. □□ **Car·te·sian·ism** *n.*

Car·te·sian co·or·di·nates *n.pl.* a system for locating a point by reference to its distance from two or three axes intersecting at right angles.

Car·thu·sian /kaarthóozhən/ *n. & adj.* • *n.* a monk of a contemplative order founded by St. Bruno in 1084. • *adj.* of or relating to this order.

car·ti·lage /kaárt'lij/ *n.* gristle; a firm flexible connective tissue forming the infant skeleton, which is mainly replaced by bone in adulthood. □□ **car·ti·lag·i·nous** /–lájinəs/ *adj.*

car·ti·la·gi·nous fish /kaárt'lájinəs/ *n.* a fish of the class Selachii, including sharks and rays, with a skeleton of cartilage.

car·tog·ra·phy /kaartógrəfee/ *n.* the science or practice of map drawing. □□ **car·tog·ra·pher** *n.* **car·to·graph·ic** /–təgráfik/ *adj.* **car·to·graph·i·cal** *adj.*

car·ton /kaárt'n/ *n.* a light box or container, esp. one made of cardboard.

car·toon /kaartóon/ *n. & v.* • *n.* **1** a humorous drawing in a newspaper, magazine, etc., esp. as a topical comment. **2** a sequence of drawings, often with speech indicated, telling a story; comic strip. **3** a filmed sequence of drawings using the technique of animation. **4** a full-size drawing as an artist's preliminary design for a painting, tapestry, mosaic, etc. • *v.* **1** *tr.* draw a cartoon of. **2** *intr.* draw cartoons. □□ **car·toon·ist** *n.*

car·touche /kaartóosh/ *n.* **1** *Archit.* a scroll-like ornament. **2** *Archaeol.* an oval ring enclosing Egyptian hieroglyphs, usu. representing the name and title of a king.

car·tridge /kaártrij/ *n.* **1** a case containing a charge of propelling explosive for firearms or blasting, with a bullet or shot if for small arms. **2** a spool of film, magnetic tape, etc., in a sealed container ready for insertion. **3** a component carrying the stylus on the pickup head of a record player. **4** an ink container for insertion in a pen.

cart·wheel /kaárt–hweel, –weel/ *n.* **1** the (usu. spoked) wheel of a cart. **2** a circular sideways handspring with the arms and legs extended.

carve /kaarv/ *v.* **1** *tr.* produce or shape (a statue, representation in relief, etc.) by cutting into a hard material (*carved a figure out of rock*; *carved it in wood*). **2** *tr.* **a** cut patterns, designs, letters, etc., in (hard material). **b** (foll. by *into*) form a pattern, design, etc., from (*carved it into a bust*). **c** (foll. by *with*) cover or decorate (material) with figures or designs cut in it. **3** *tr.* (*absol.*) cut (meat, etc.) into slices for eating. □ **carve out 1** take from a larger whole. **2** establish (a career, etc.) purposefully (*carved out a name for themselves*). **carve up** divide into several pieces; subdivide (territory, etc.).

Car·ver /kaárvər/ *n.* (in full **Carver chair**) a chair with arms, a rush seat, and a back having horizontal and vertical spindles.

car·ver /kaárvər/ *n.* **1** a person who carves. **2 a** a carving knife. **b** (in *pl.*) a knife and fork for carving.

carv·ing /kaárving/ *n.* a carved object, esp. as a work of art.

car·y·at·id /káreeátid/ *n.* (*pl.* **caryatids** or **caryatides** /–deez/) *Archit.* a pillar in the form of a draped female figure, supporting an entablature.

Cas·a·no·va /kásənóvə/ *n.* a man notorious for seducing women.

Cas·bah /kázbaa, kaáz–/ *n.* (also **Kas·bah**) **1** the citadel of a N. African city. **2** an Arab quarter near this.

cas·cade /kaskáyd/ *n. & v.* • *n.* **1** a small waterfall, esp. forming one in a series or part of a large broken waterfall. **2** a succession of electrical devices or stages in a process. **3** a quantity of material, etc., draped in descending folds. • *v.intr.* fall in or like a cascade.

case[1] /kays/ *n.* **1** an instance of something occurring. **2** a state of affairs, hypothetical or actual. **3 a** an instance of a person receiving professional guidance, e.g., from a doctor or social worker. **b** this person or the circumstances involved. **4** a matter under official investigation, esp. by the police. **5** *Law* a cause or suit for trial. **6 a** the sum of the arguments on one side, esp. in a lawsuit (*that is our case*). **b** a set of arguments, esp. in relation to persuasiveness (*have a good case*). **c** a valid set of arguments (*have no case*). **7** *Gram.* **a** the relation of a word to other words in a sentence. **b** a form of a noun, adjective, or pronoun expressing this. **8** the position or circumstances in which one is. □ **as the case may be** according to the situation. **in any case** whatever the truth is; whatever may happen. **in case 1** in the event that; if. **2** lest; in provision against a stated or implied possibility (*take an umbrella in case it rains*; *took it in case*). **in case of** in the event of. **in the case of** as regards. **in no case** under no circumstances. **in that case** if that is true; should that happen. **is** (or **is not**) **the case** is (or is not) so.

case[2] /kays/ *n. & v.* • *n.* **1** a container or covering serving to enclose or contain. **2** a container with its contents. **3** the outer protective covering of a watch, book, seed vessel, sausage, etc. **4** *Brit.* an item of luggage, esp. a suitcase. **5** *Printing* a partitioned receptacle for type. **6** a glass box for showing specimens, curiosities, etc. • *v.tr.* **1** enclose in a case. **2** (foll. by *with*) surround. **3** *sl.* reconnoiter (a house, etc.), esp. with a view to robbery.

case•bound /káysbownd/ *adj.* (of a book) in a hard cover.

case-hard•en *v.tr.* **1** harden the surface of, esp. give a steel surface to (iron) by carbonizing. **2** make callous.

case his•to•ry *n.* information about a person for use in professional treatment, e.g., by a doctor.

ca•sein /káyseen, káyseein/ *n.* the main protein in milk, esp. in coagulated form as in cheese.

case law *n.* the law as established by the outcome of former cases.

case•load /káyslōd/ *n.* the cases with which a lawyer, doctor, etc., is concerned at one time.

case•ment /káysmənt/ *n.* **1** a window or part of a window hinged vertically to open like a door. **2** *poet.* a window.

case-sen•si•tive *adj. Computing* distinguishing upper- and lower-case letters.

case stud•y *n.* **1** an attempt to understand a person, institution, etc., from collected information. **2** a record of such an attempt. **3** the use of a particular instance as an examplar of general principles.

case•work /káyswərk/ *n.* social work concerned with individuals, esp. involving understanding of the client's family and background. ▫▫ **case•work•er** *n.*

cash /kash/ *n.* & *v.* • *n.* **1** money in coins or bills, as distinct from checks or orders. **2** (also **cash down**) money paid as full payment at the time of purchase, as distinct from credit. **3** *colloq.* wealth. • *v.tr.* give or obtain cash for (a note, check, etc.). ▫ **cash in 1** obtain cash for. **2** *colloq.* (usu. foll. by *on*) profit (from); take advantage (of). **3** (in full **cash in one's chips**) *colloq.* die. ▫▫ **cash•a•ble** *adj.* **cash•less** *adj.*

cash and car•ry *n.* **1** a system in which goods are paid for in cash and taken away by the purchaser. **2** a store where this system operates.

cash cow *n.* a business, product, etc., generating steady profits that are usu. used to fund other enterprises.

cash crop *n.* a crop produced for sale, not for use as food, etc.

cash•ew /káshōō, kashōō/ *n.* **1** a bushy evergreen tree, *Anacardium occidentale*, native to Central and S. America, bearing kidney-shaped nuts attached to fleshy fruits. **2** (in full **cashew nut**) the edible nut of this tree.

cash flow *n.* the movement of money into and out of a business, as a measure of profitability, or as affecting liquidity.

cash•ier[1] /kashéer/ *n.* a person dealing with cash transactions in a store, bank, etc.

cash•ier[2] /kashéer/ *v.tr.* dismiss from service, esp. from the armed forces with disgrace.

cash•mere /kázhmeer, kásh–/ *n.* **1** a fine soft wool, esp. that of a Kashmir goat. **2** a material made from this.

cash reg•is•ter *n.* a machine in a store, etc., with a drawer for money, recording the amount of each sale, totaling receipts, etc.

cas•ing /káysing/ *n.* **1** a protective or enclosing cover or shell. **2** the material for this.

ca•si•no /kəséenō/ *n.* (*pl.* **•nos**) a public room or building for gambling.

cask /kask/ *n.* **1** a large barrellike container made of wood, metal, or plastic, esp. one for alcoholic liquor. **2** its contents. **3** its capacity.

cas•ket /káskit/ *n.* **1 a** a coffin, esp. a rectangular one. **b** a small wooden box for cremated ashes. **2** a small, often ornamental box or chest for jewels, letters, etc.

cas•sa•va /kəsaávə/ *n.* **1 a** any plant of the genus *Manihot*, esp. the cultivated varieties *M. esculenta* (**bitter cassava**) and *M. dulcis* (**sweet cassava**), having starchy tuberous roots. **b** the roots themselves. **2** a starch or flour obtained from these roots. Also called TAPIOCA, MANIOC.

cas•se•role /kásərōl/ *n.* & *v.* • *n.* **1** a covered dish, usu. of earthenware or glass, in which food is cooked, esp. slowly in the oven. **2** food cooked in a casserole. • *v.tr.* cook in a casserole.

cas•sette /kəsét, ka–/ *n.* a sealed case containing a length of tape, ribbon, etc., ready for insertion in a machine, esp.: **1** a length of magnetic tape wound on to spools, ready for insertion in a tape recorder. **2** a length of photographic film, ready for insertion in a camera.

cas•sia /káshə/ *n.* **1** any tree of the genus *Cassia*, bearing leaves from which senna is extracted. **2** the cinnamonlike bark of this tree used as a spice.

cas•sis /kasées/ *n.* a syrupy liqueur flavored with black currants and produced mainly in Burgundy.

cas•sock /kásək/ *n.* a long, close-fitting, usu. black or red garment worn by clergy, members of choirs, etc. ▫▫ **cas•socked** *adj.*

cas•sou•let /kasōōláy/ *n.* a stew of meat and beans.

cas•so•war•y /kásəwairee/ *n.* (*pl.* **•ies**) any large flightless Australasian bird of the genus *Casuarius*, with a heavy body and a bony crest on its forehead.

cast /kast/ *v.* & *n.* • *v.* (*past* and *past part.* **cast**) **1** *tr.* throw, esp. deliberately or forcefully. **2** *tr.* (often foll. by *on, over*) **a** direct or cause to fall (one's eyes, a glance, light, a shadow, a spell, etc.). **b** express (doubts, aspersions, etc.). **3** *tr.* throw out (a fishing line) into the water. **4** *tr.* let down (an anchor, etc.). **5** *tr.* **a** throw off; get rid of. **b** shed (skin, etc.), esp. in the process of growth. **c** (of a horse) lose (a shoe). **6** *tr.* record, register, or give (a vote). **7** *tr.* **a** shape (molten metal or plastic material) in a mold. **b** make (a product) in this way. **8** *tr. Printing* make (type). **9** *tr.* **a** (usu. foll. by *as*) assign (an actor) to play a particular character. **b** allocate roles in (a play, motion picture, etc.). **10** *tr.* (foll. by *in, into*) arrange or formulate (facts, etc.) in a specified form. **11** *tr.* & *intr.* reckon; add up; calculate (accounts or figures). **12** *tr.* calculate and record details of (a horoscope). • *n.* **1 a** the throwing of a missile, etc. **b** the distance reached by this. **2** a throw or a number thrown at dice. **3** a throw of a net, fishing line, etc. **4** *Fishing* **a** that which is cast, esp. the line with hook and fly. **b** a place for casting (*a good cast*). **5 a** an object of metal, clay, etc., made in a mold. **b** a molded mass of solidified material, esp. plaster protecting a broken limb. **6** the actors taking part in a play, motion picture, etc. **7** form, type, or quality (*cast of features; cast of mind*). **8** a tinge or shade of color. **9 a** (in full **cast in the eye**) a slight squint. **b** a twist or inclination. **10 a** a mass of earth excreted by a worm. **b** a mass of indigestible food thrown up by a hawk, owl, etc. **11** the form into which any work is thrown or arranged. ▫ **cast adrift** leave to drift. **cast aside** give up using; abandon. **cast away 1** reject. **2** (in *passive*) be shipwrecked (cf. CASTAWAY). **cast down** depress; deject (cf. DOWNCAST). **cast loose** detach; detach oneself. **cast lots** see LOT. **cast off 1** abandon. **2** *Knitting* take the stitches off the needle by looping each over the next to finish the edge. **3** *Naut.* **a** set a ship free from a mooring, etc. **b** loosen and throw off (rope, etc.). **4** *Printing* estimate the space that will be taken in print by manuscript copy. **cast on** *Knitting* make the first row of loops on the needle. **cast out** expel. **cast up 1** (of the sea) deposit on the shore. **2** add up (figures, etc.).

cas·ta·net /kástənét/ *n.* (usu. in *pl.*) a small concave piece of hardwood, ivory, etc., in pairs held in the hands and clicked together by the fingers as a rhythmic accompaniment, esp. by Spanish dancers.

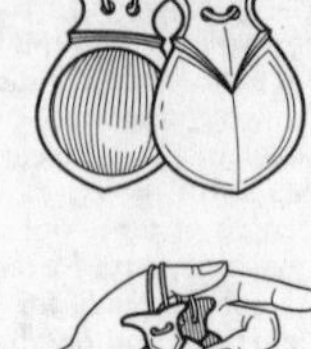
castanets

cast·a·way /kástəway/ *n.* & *adj.* • *n.* a shipwrecked person. • *adj.* **1** shipwrecked. **2** cast aside; rejected.

caste /kast/ *n.* **1** any of the Hindu hereditary classes, distinguished by relative degrees of purity or pollution, whose members are socially equal with one another and often follow the same occupations. **2** a more or less exclusive social class. **3** a system of such classes. **4** the position it confers. **5** *Zool.* a form of social insect having a particular function. □ **lose caste** descend in the social order.

cas·tel·lat·ed /kástəlaytid/ *adj.* **1** having battlements. **2** castlelike. □□ **cas·tel·la·tion** /–láyshən/ *n.*

cast·er /kástər/ *n.* (also *Brit.* **cas·tor**) **1** a small swiveled wheel (often one of a set) fixed to a leg (or the underside) of a piece of furniture. **2** a small container with holes in the top for sprinkling the contents. **3** a person who casts. **4** a machine for casting type.

cas·ti·gate /kástigayt/ *v.tr.* rebuke or punish severely. □□ **cas·ti·ga·tion** /–gáyshən/ *n.* **cas·ti·ga·tor** *n.*

cast·ing /kásting/ *n.* an object made by casting, esp. of molten metal.

cast i·ron *n.* & *adj.* • *n.* a hard alloy of iron, carbon, and silicon cast in a mold. • *adj.* (**cast-iron**) **1** made of cast iron. **2** hard; unchallengeable; unchangeable.

cas·tle /kásəl/ *n.* & *v.* • *n.* **1 a** a large fortified building or group of buildings; a stronghold. **b** a formerly fortified mansion. **2** *Chess* = ROOK². • *v. Chess* **1** *intr.* make a special move (once only in a game on each side) in which the king is moved two squares along the back rank and the nearer rook is moved to the square passed over by the king. **2** *tr.* move (the king) by castling. □ **castles in the air** (or **in Spain**) a visionary unattainable scheme; a daydream. □□ **cas·tled** *adj.*

cast·off /kástawf/ *n.* a cast-off thing; esp. a garment.

cast-off /kástawf/ *adj.* abandoned, discarded.

cas·tor /kástər/ *n.* **1** an oily substance secreted by beavers and used in medicine and perfumes. **2** a beaver.

cas·tor oil /kástər/ *n.* **1** an oil from the seeds of a plant, *Ricinus communis*, used as a purgative and lubricant. **2** (in full **castor-oil plant**) this plant.

cas·trate /kástrayt/ *v.tr.* **1** remove the testicles of; geld. **2** deprive of vigor. □□ **cas·tra·tion** /–tráyshən/ *n.* **cas·tra·tor** *n.*

cas·tra·to /kastraátō/ *n.* (*pl.* **castrati** /–tee/) *hist.* a male singer castrated in boyhood so as to retain a soprano or alto voice.

cas·u·al /kázhōōəl/ *adj.* & *n.* • *adj.* **1** accidental; due to chance. **2** not regular nor permanent; temporary; occasional (*casual work*; *a casual affair*). **3 a** unconcerned; uninterested (*was very casual about it*). **b** made or done without great care or thought (*a casual remark*). **c** acting carelessly or unmethodically. **4** (of clothes) informal. • *n.* **1** a casual worker. **2** (usu. in *pl.*) casual clothes or shoes. □□ **cas·u·al·ly** *adv.* **cas·u·al·ness** *n.*

cas·u·al·ty /kázhōōəltee/ *n.* (*pl.* **·ties**) **1** a person killed or injured in a war or accident. **2** a thing lost or destroyed.

cas·u·ist /kázhōōist/ *n.* **1** a person, esp. a theologian, who resolves problems of conscience, duty, etc., often with clever but false reasoning. **2** a sophist or quibbler. □□ **cas·u·is·tic** *adj.* **cas·u·is·ti·cal** *adj.* **cas·u·is·ti·cal·ly** *adv.* **cas·u·ist·ry** /kázhōōəstree/ *n.*

CAT /kat/ *abbr.* **1** *Med.* computerized axial tomography. **2** clear-air turbulence.

cat /kat/ *n.* & *v.* • *n.* **1** a small, soft-furred, four-legged domesticated animal, *Felis catus* or *F. domestica*. **2** any wild animal of the genus *Felis*, e.g., a lion, tiger, or leopard. **3** a catlike animal of any other species (*civet cat*). **4** *colloq.* a malicious or spiteful woman. **5** *sl.* a jazz enthusiast. **6** *Naut.* = CATHEAD. **7** = CAT-O'-NINE-TAILS. • *v.tr.* (also *absol.*) (**catted, catting**) *Naut.* raise (an anchor) from the surface of the water to the cathead.

cata- /kátə/ *prefix* (usu. **cat-** before a vowel or *h*) **1** down; downward (*catadromous*). **2** wrongly; badly (*catachresis*).

ca·tab·o·lism /kətábəlizəm/ *n. Biochem.* the breakdown of complex molecules in living organisms to form simpler ones with the release of energy; destructive metabolism (opp. ANABOLISM). □□ **cat·a·bol·ic** /kátəbólik/ *adj.*

cat·a·chre·sis /kátəkreésis/ *n.* (*pl.* **catachreses** /–seez/) an incorrect use of words. □□ **cat·a·chres·tic** /–kréstik/ *adj.*

cat·a·clysm /kátəklizəm/ *n.* **1 a** a violent, esp. social or political, upheaval or disaster. **b** a great change. **2** a great flood or deluge. □□ **cat·a·clys·mal** /–klízməl/ *adj.* **cat·a·clys·mic** *adj.* **cat·a·clys·mi·cal·ly** *adv.*

cat·a·comb /kátəkōm/ *n.* (often in *pl.*) **1** an underground cemetery, esp. a Roman subterranean gallery with recesses for tombs. **2** a similar underground construction; a cellar.

ca·tad·ro·mous /kətádrəməs/ *adj.* (of a fish, e.g., the eel) that swims down rivers to the sea to spawn.

cat·a·falque /kátəfawk, –fawlk/ *n.* a decorated wooden framework for supporting the coffin of a distinguished person during a funeral or while lying in state.

cat·a·lase /kát'lays, –layz/ *n. Biochem.* an enzyme that catalyzes the reduction of hydrogen peroxide.

cat·a·lep·sy /kát'lepsee/ *n.* a trance or seizure with loss of sensation and consciousness accompanied by rigidity of the body. □□ **cat·a·lep·tic** /–léptik/ *adj.* & *n.*

cat·a·log /kát'lawg, –log/ *n.* & *v.* (also **cat·a·logue**) • *n.* **1** a list of items (e.g., articles for sale, books held by a library), usu. in alphabetical or other systematic order and often with a description of each. **2** an extensive list (*a catalog of crimes*). **3** a listing of a university's courses, etc. • *v.tr.* (**catalogs, cataloged, cataloging; catalogues, catalogued, cataloguing**) **1** make a catalog of. **2** enter in a catalog. □□ **cat·a·log·er** *n.* (also **cat·a·logu·er**).

ca·tal·pa /kətálpə/ *n.* any tree of the genus *Catalpa*, with heart-shaped leaves, trumpet-shaped flowers, and long pods.

ca·tal·y·sis /kətálisis/ *n.* (*pl.* **catalyses** /–seez/) *Chem.* & *Biochem.* the acceleration of a chemical or biochemical reaction by a catalyst.

cat·a·lyst /kát'list/ *n.* **1** *Chem.* a substance that, without itself undergoing any permanent chemical change, increases the rate of a reaction. **2** a person or thing that precipitates a change.

cat·a·lyt·ic con·vert·er *n.* a device incorporated in the exhaust system of a motor vehicle, with a catalyst for converting pollutant gases into harmless products.

cat·a·lyze /kát'līz/ *v.tr.* (*Brit.* **catalyse**) *Chem.* produce (a reaction) by catalysis.

cat·a·ma·ran /kátəmərán/ *n.* **1** a boat with twin hulls in parallel. **2** a raft of yoked logs or boats.

cat·a·mite /kátəmīt/ *n.* the passive partner in sodomy.

cat·a·moun·tain /kátəmowntin/ *n.* (also **cat·a-moun·tain, cat·a·mount**) a lynx, leopard, puma, or other wild cat.

cat·a·nan·che /kátənángkee/ *n.* any composite plant of the genus *Catananche*, with blue or yellow flowers.

cat·a·plex·y /kátəpleksee/ *n.* sudden temporary paralysis due to fright, etc. ▫▫ **cat·a·plec·tic** /–pléktik/ *adj.*

cat·a·pult /kátəpult, –pŏŏlt/ *n.* & *v.* • *n.* **1** a mechanical device for launching a glider, an aircraft from the deck of a ship, etc. **2** *hist.* a military machine worked by a lever and ropes for hurling large stones, etc. **3** *Brit.* = SLINGSHOT. • *v.* **1** *tr.* **a** hurl from or launch with a catapult. **b** fling forcibly. **2** *intr.* leap or be hurled forcibly.

cat·a·ract /kátərakt/ *n.* **1 a** a large waterfall or cascade. **b** a downpour; a rush of water. **2** *Med.* a condition in which the lens of the eye becomes progressively opaque, resulting in blurred vision.

ca·tarrh /kətaar/ *n.* **1** inflammation of the mucous membrane of the nose, air passages, etc. **2** a watery discharge in the nose or throat due to this. ▫▫ **ca·tarrh·al** *adj.*

ca·tas·tro·phe /kətástrəfee/ *n.* **1** a great and usu. sudden disaster. **2** a disastrous end; ruin. **3** an event producing a subversion of the order of things. ▫▫ **cat·a·stroph·ic** /kátəstrófik/ *adj.* **cat·a·stroph·i·cal·ly** /kátəstrófikəlee/ *adv.*

ca·tas·tro·phism /kətástrəfizəm/ *n.* *Geol.* the theory that changes in the earth's crust have occurred in sudden violent and unusual events. ▫▫ **ca·tas·tro·phist** *n.*

cat·a·to·ni·a /kátətóneeə/ *n.* **1** schizophrenia with intervals of catalepsy and sometimes violence. **2** catalepsy. ▫▫ **cat·a·ton·ic** /–tónik/ *adj.* & *n.*

cat·boat /kátbōt/ *n.* a sailboat with a single mast placed well forward and carrying only one sail.

cat bur·glar *n.* a burglar who enters by climbing to an upper story.

cat·call /kátkawl/ *n.* & *v.* • *n.* a shrill whistle of disapproval made at sporting events, stage performances, meetings, etc. • *v.* **1** *intr.* make a catcall. **2** *tr.* make a catcall at.

catch /kach/ *v.* & *n.* • *v.* (*past* and *past part.* **caught** /kawt/) **1** *tr.* **a** lay hold of so as to restrain or prevent from escaping; capture in a trap, in one's hands, etc. **b** (also **catch hold of**) get into one's hands so as to retain, operate, etc. (*caught hold of the handle*). **2** *tr.* detect or surprise (a person, esp. in a wrongful or embarrassing act) (*caught me in the act; caught him smoking*). **3** *tr.* intercept and hold (a moving thing) in the hands, etc. (*catch the ball; a bowl to catch the drips*). **4** *tr.* **a** contract (a disease) by infection or contagion. **b** acquire (a quality or feeling) from another's example (*caught her enthusiasm*). **5** *tr.* **a** reach in time and board (a train, bus, etc.). **b** be in time to see, etc. (a person or thing about to leave or finish)(*if you hurry you'll catch them; caught the end of the performance*). **6** *tr.* **a** apprehend with the senses or the mind (esp. a thing occurring quickly or briefly) (*didn't catch what he said*). **b** (of an artist, etc.) reproduce faithfully. **7 a** *intr.* become fixed or entangled; be checked (*the bolt began to catch*). **b** *tr.* cause to do this (*caught her sleeve on a nail*). **c** *tr.* (often foll. by *on*) hit; deal a blow to (*caught him on the nose; caught his elbow on the table*). **8** *tr.* draw the attention of; captivate (*caught his eye*). **9** *intr.* begin to burn. **10** *tr.* (often foll. by *up*) reach or overtake (a person, etc., ahead). **11** *tr.* check suddenly (*caught his breath*). **12** *tr.* (foll. by *at*) grasp or try to grasp. • *n.* **1 a** an act of catching. **b** *Baseball* a chance or act of catching the ball. **2 a** an amount of a thing caught, esp. of fish. **b** a thing or person caught or worth catching, esp. in marriage. **3 a** a question, trick, etc., intended to deceive, incriminate, etc. **b** an unexpected or hidden difficulty or disadvantage. **4** a device for fastening a door or window, etc. **5** *Mus.* a round, esp. with words arranged to produce a humorous effect. ▫ **catch it** *sl.* be punished or in trouble. **catch on** *colloq.* **1** (of a practice, fashion, etc.) become popular. **2** (of a person) understand what is meant. **catch up 1 a** (often foll. by *with*) reach a person, etc., ahead (*he caught up with us*). **b** (often foll. by *with, on*) make up arrears (of work, etc.) (*must catch up with my correspondence*). **2** snatch or pick up hurriedly. **3** (often in *passive*) **a** involve; entangle (*caught up in suspicious dealings*). **b** fasten up (*hair caught up in a ribbon*). ▫▫ **catch·a·ble** *adj.*

catch·all /káchawl/ *n.* (often *attrib.*) **1** something designed to be all-inclusive. **2** a container for odds and ends.

catch-as-catch-can *n.* **1** a style of wrestling with few holds barred. **2** using any method available.

catch·er /káchər/ *n.* *Baseball* a fielder positioned behind home plate.

catch·fly /káchflī/ *n.* (*pl.* **·flies**) any plant of the genus *Silene* or *Lychnis* with a sticky stem.

catch·ing /káching/ *adj.* **1 a** (of a disease) infectious. **b** (of a practice, habit, etc.) likely to be imitated. **2** attractive; captivating.

catch·line /káchlīn/ *n.* *Printing* a short line of type, esp. at the head of copy or as a running headline.

catch·ment /káchmənt/ *n.* **1** the collection of rainfall. **2** an opening or basin for storm water, etc.

catch·pen·ny /káchpenee/ *adj.* intended merely to sell quickly; superficially attractive.

catch·phrase /káchfrayz/ *n.* a phrase in frequent use.

catch-22 /káchtwenteetóō/ *n.* (often *attrib.*) *colloq.* a circumstance that presents a dilemma because of mutually conflicting or dependent conditions.

catch·up var. of KETCHUP.

catch·weight /káchwayt/ *adj.* & *n.* • *adj.* unrestricted as regards weight. • *n.* unrestricted weight, as a weight category in sports.

catch·word /káchwərd/ *n.* **1** a word or phrase in common (often temporary) use; a topical slogan. **2** a word so placed as to draw attention.

catch·y /káchee/ *adj.* (**catchier, catchiest**) (of a tune) easy to remember; attractive. ▫▫ **catch·i·ly** *adv.* **catch·i·ness** *n.*

cat·e·chism /kátikizəm/ *n.* **1 a** a summary of the principles of a religion in the form of questions and answers. **b** a book containing this. **2** a series of questions put to anyone. ▫▫ **cat·e·chis·mal** /–kízməl/ *adj.*

cat·e·chist /kátikist/ *n.* a religious teacher, esp. one using a catechism.

cat·e·chize /kátikīz/ *v.tr.* **1** instruct by means of question and answer, esp. from a catechism. **2** put questions to; examine. ▫▫ **cat·e·chiz·er** *n.*

cat·e·gor·i·cal /kátigáwrikəl, –gór–/ *adj.* (also **cat·e·gor·ic**) unconditional; absolute; explicit; direct (*a categorical refusal*). ▫▫ **cat·e·gor·i·cal·ly** *adv.*

cat·e·go·rize /kátigərīz/ *v.tr.* place in a category or categories. ▫▫ **cat·e·go·ri·za·tion** *n.*

cat·e·go·ry /kátigawree, –goree/ *n.* (*pl.* **·ries**) a class or division. ▫▫ **cat·e·go·ri·al** /–gáwreeəl/ *adj.*

cat·e·nate /kát'nayt/ *v.tr.* connect like links of a chain. ▫▫ **cat·e·na·tion** /–náyshən/ *n.*

ca·ter /káytər/ *v.* **1 a** *intr.* (often foll. by *for*) provide food. **b** *tr.* provide food and service (*cater a party*). **2** *intr.* (foll. by *for, to*) provide what is desired or needed by. **3** *intr.* (foll. by *to*) pander to (esp. low tastes).

cat·er·cor·nered /kátərkáwrnərd/ *adj.* & *adv.* (also **cat·er·cor·ner, cat·ty-cor·nered** /kátee–/, **kitty-corner** /kítee–/) • *adj.* placed or situated diagonally. • *adv.* diagonally.

ca·ter·er /káytərər/ *n.* a person who supplies food for social events, esp. professionally.

ca·ter·ing /káytəring/ *n.* the profession or work of a caterer.

cat·er·pil·lar /kátərpilər/ *n.* **1 a** the larva of a butterfly or moth. **b** (in general use) any similar larva of various insects. **2** (**Caterpillar**) **a** (in full **Caterpillar track** *or* **tread**) *Trademark* a continuous belt of linked pieces passing around the wheels of a tractor, etc., for travel on rough ground. **b** a vehicle with these tracks, e.g., a tractor or tank.

caterpillar late Middle English: perhaps from a variant of Old French *chatepelose*, literally 'hairy cat, ' influenced by obsolete *piller* 'ravager.' The association with 'cat' is found in other languages, e.g., Swiss *teufelskatz* (literally 'devil's cat'), Lombard *gatta* (literally 'cat'). Compare with French *chaton*, English *catkin*, resembling hairy caterpillars.

cat·er·waul /kátərwawl/ *v. & n.* • *v.intr.* make the shrill howl of a cat. • *n.* a caterwauling noise.

cat·fish /kátfish/ *n.* any of various esp. freshwater fish, usu. having whiskerlike barbels around the mouth.

cat·gut /kátgut/ *n.* a material used for the strings of musical instruments and surgical sutures, made of the dried twisted intestines of sheep or horses, but not cats.

Cath. *abbr.* **1** cathedral. **2** Catholic.

ca·thar·sis /kəthaársis/ *n.* (*pl.* **catharses** /–seez/) **1** an emotional release in drama or art. **2** *Psychol.* the process of freeing repressed emotion by association with the cause, and elimination by abreaction. **3** *Med.* purging of the bowels.

ca·thar·tic /kəthaártik/ *adj. & n.* • *adj.* **1** effecting catharsis. **2** purgative. • *n.* a cathartic drug. ▫▫ **ca·thar·ti·cal·ly** *adv.*

cat·head /kát–hed/ *n. Naut.* a horizontal beam from each side of a ship's bow for raising and carrying the anchor.

ca·the·dral /kəthéédrəl/ *n.* the principal church of a diocese, containing the bishop's throne.

cath·e·ter /káthitər/ *n. Med.* a tube for insertion into a body cavity for introducing or removing fluid.

cath·e·ter·ize /káthitərīz/ *v.tr. Med.* insert a catheter into.

cath·e·tom·e·ter /káthitómitər/ *n.* a telescope mounted on a graduated scale along which it can slide, used for accurate measurement of small vertical distances.

cath·ode /káthōd/ *n. Electr.* **1** the negatively charged electrode by which electrons enter or leave a system. **2** the positively charged electrode of a device supplying current, e.g., a battery (opp. ANODE). ▫▫ **cath·o·dal** *adj.* **cath·o·dic** /kəthódik/ *adj.*

cath·ode ray *n.* a beam of electrons emitted from the cathode of a high-vacuum tube.

cath·ode-ray tube *n.* a high-vacuum tube in which cathode rays produce a luminous image on a fluorescent screen. ¶ Abbr.: **CRT**.

cath·o·lic /káthəlik, káthlik/ *adj. & n.* • *adj.* **1** of interest or use to all; universal. **2** all-embracing; of wide sympathies or interests (*has catholic tastes*). **3** (**Catholic**) **a** of the Roman Catholic religion. **b** including all Christians. **c** including all of the Western Church. • *n.* (**Catholic**) a Roman Catholic. ▫▫ **ca·thol·i·cal·ly** /kəthóliklee/ *adv.* **Ca·thol·i·cism** /kəthólisizəm/ *n.* **cath·o·lic·i·ty** /káthəlísitee/ *n.* **ca·thol·ic·ly** *adv.*

ca·thol·i·cize /kəthólisīz/ *v.tr. & intr.* **1** make or become catholic. **2** (**Catholicize**) make or become a Roman Catholic.

cat·i·on /kátīən/ *n.* a positively charged ion; an ion that is attracted to the cathode in electrolysis (opp. ANION).

cat·kin /kátkin/ *n.* a spike of usu. downy or silky male or female flowers hanging from a willow, hazel, etc.

cat·nap /kátnap/ *n. & v.* • *n.* a short sleep. • *v.intr.* (· **napped**, ·**napping**) have a catnap.

cat·nip /kátnip/ *n.* a white-flowered plant, *Nepeta cataria*, having a pungent smell attractive to cats.

cat-o'-nine-tails *n. hist.* a rope whip with nine knotted lashes for flogging sailors, soldiers, or criminals.

CAT scan /kat/ *n.* an X-ray image made using computerized axial tomography. ▫▫ **CAT scan·ner** *n.*

cat's cradle *n.* a child's game in which a loop of string is held between the fingers and patterns are formed.

cat's-eye *n.* a precious stone of Sri Lanka and Malabar.

cat's-paw *n.* **1** a person used as a tool by another. **2** a slight breeze rippling the surface of the water.

cat·sup /kátsəp, kéchəp, kách–/ var. of KETCHUP.

cat·tail /kát–tayl/ *n.* any tall, reedlike marsh plant of the genus *Typha*, esp. *T. latifola*, with long, flat leaves and brown, velvety flower spikes. (Also called **bulrush** and **reed mace**.)

cat·tish /kátish/ *adj.* = CATTY. ▫▫ **cat·tish·ly** *adv.* **cat·tish·ness** *n.*

cat·tle /kát'l/ *n.pl.* **1** bison, buffalo, yaks, or domesticated bovine animals, esp. of the genus *Bos*. **2** *archaic* livestock.

cat·tle·man /kát'lmən/ *n.* (*pl.* **·men**) a person who breeds or rears cattle.

catt·ley·a /kátleeə/ *n.* any epiphytic orchid of the genus *Cattleya*, with handsome violet, pink, or yellow flowers.

cat·ty /kátee/ *adj.* (**cattier, cattiest**) **1** sly; spiteful; deliberately hurtful in speech. **2** catlike. ▫▫ **cat·ti·ly** *adv.* **cat·ti·ness** *n.*

CATV *abbr.* community antenna television.

cat·walk /kátwawk/ *n.* **1** a narrow footway along a bridge, above a theater stage, etc. **2** a narrow platform or gangway used in fashion shows, etc.

Cau·ca·sian /kawkáyzhən/ *adj. & n.* • *adj.* **1** of or relating to the white or light-skinned division of mankind. **2** of or relating to the Caucasus, a region in SE Europe. • *n.* a Caucasian person.

cau·cus /káwkəs/ *n.* **1 a** a meeting of the members of a political party, esp. in a legislature or convention, to decide policy. **b** a bloc of such members. **c** this system as a political force. **2** often *derog.* (esp. in the UK) **a** a usu. secret meeting of a group within a larger organization or party. **b** such a group.

cau·dal /káwd'l/ *adj.* **1** of or like a tail. **2** of the posterior part of the body. ▫▫ **cau·dal·ly** *adv.*

cau·dil·lo /kawdéélyō, –déeyō, kowthéélyō, –théeyō/ *n.* (*pl.* **·los**) (in Spanish-speaking countries) a military or political leader.

caught *past* and *past part.* of CATCH.

caul /kawl/ *n.* **1** the inner membrane enclosing a fetus. **2** part of this occasionally found on a child's head at birth, thought to bring good luck.

caul·dron /káwldrən/ *n.* (also **cal·dron**) a large, deep, bowl-shaped vessel for boiling over an open fire; an ornamental vessel resembling this.

cau·li·flow·er /káwliflowr, kól–/ *n.* **1** a variety of cabbage with a large immature flower head of small usu. creamy-white flower buds. **2** the flower head eaten as a vegetable.

cau·li·flow·er ear *n.* an ear deformed by repeated blows, esp. in boxing.

caulk /kawk/ *v.tr.* (also **calk**) **1** stop up (the seams of a boat, etc.) with oakum, etc., and waterproofing material, or by driving plate junctions together. **2** make (esp. a boat) watertight by this method. ▫▫ **caulk·er** *n.*

caus·al /káwzəl/ *adj.* **1** of, forming, or expressing a cause or causes. **2** relating to, or of the nature of, cause and effect. ▫▫ **caus·al·ly** *adv.*

cau·sal·i·ty /kawzálitee/ *n.* **1** the relation of cause and effect. **2** the principle that everything has a cause.

cau·sa·tion /kawzáyshən/ *n.* **1** the act of causing or producing an effect. **2** = CAUSALITY.

caus·a·tive /káwzətiv/ *adj.* **1** acting as cause. **2** (foll. by *of*) producing; having as effect. **3** *Gram.* expressing cause. ▫▫ **caus·a·tive·ly** *adv.*

cause /kawz/ *n. & v.* •*n.* **1 a** that which produces an effect, or gives rise to an action, phenomenon, or condition. **b** a person or thing that occasions something. **c** a reason or motive; a ground that may be held to justify something (*no cause for complaint*). **2** a reason adjudged adequate (*show cause*). **3** a principle, belief, or purpose that is advocated or supported (*faithful to the cause*). **4 a** a matter to be settled at law. **b** an individual's case offered at law (*plead a cause*). **5** the side taken by any party in a dispute. •*v.tr.* **1** be the cause of; produce; make happen (*caused a commotion*). **2** (foll. by *to* + infin.) induce (*caused me to smile; caused it to be done*). ▫ **in the cause of** to maintain, defend, or support (*in the cause of justice*). ▫▫ **caus·a·ble** *adj.* **cause·less** *adj.* **caus·er** *n.*

'cause /kawz, kuz/ *conj. & adv. colloq.* = BECAUSE.

cause cé·lè·bre /káwz selébrə/ *n.* (*pl.* **causes célèbres** *pronunc.* same) a trial or case that attracts much attention.

cau·se·rie /kōzreé, kōzə–/ *n.* (*pl.* **causeries** *pronunc.* same) an informal article or talk, esp. on a literary subject.

cause·way /káwzway/ *n.* **1** a raised road or track across low or wet ground or a stretch of water. **2** a raised path by a road.

caus·tic /káwstik/ *adj. & n.* •*adj.* **1** that burns or corrodes organic tissue. **2** sarcastic; biting. **3** *Chem.* strongly alkaline. **4** *Physics* formed by the intersection of reflected or refracted parallel rays from a curved surface. •*n.* **1** a caustic substance. **2** *Physics* a caustic surface or curve. ▫▫ **caus·ti·cal·ly** *adv.* **caus·tic·i·ty** /–tísitee/ *n.*

cau·ter·ize /káwtərīz/ *v.tr. Med.* burn or coagulate (tissue) with a heated instrument or caustic substance, esp. to stop bleeding. ▫▫ **cau·ter·i·za·tion** *n.*

cau·tion /káwshən/ *n. & v.* •*n.* **1** attention to safety; prudence; carefulness. **2 a** esp. *Brit.* a warning, esp. a formal one in law. **b** a formal warning and reprimand. **3** *colloq.* an amusing or surprising person or thing. •*v.tr.* **1** (often foll. by *against*, or *to* + infin.) warn or admonish. **2** esp. *Brit.* issue a caution to.

cau·tion·ar·y /káwshəneree/ *adj.* that gives or serves as a warning (*a cautionary tale*).

cau·tious /káwshəs/ *adj.* careful; prudent; attentive to safety. ▫▫ **cau·tious·ly** *adv.* **cau·tious·ness** *n.*

cav·al·cade /kávəlkáyd/ *n.* a procession or formal company of riders, motor vehicles, etc.

cav·a·lier /kávəleér/ *n. & adj.* •*n.* **1** *hist.* (**Cavalier**) a supporter of Charles I in the English Civil War. **2** a courtly gentleman, esp. as a lady's escort. **3** *archaic* a horseman. •*adj.* offhand; supercilious; blasé. ▫▫ **cav·a·lier·ly** *adv.*

cav·al·ry /kávəlree/ *n.* (*pl.* **·ries**) (usu. treated as *pl.*) soldiers on horseback or in armored vehicles.

cav·al·ry·man /kávəlrimən/ *n.* (*pl.* **·men**) a soldier of a cavalry regiment.

cave /kayv/ *n. & v.* •*n.* a large hollow in the side of a cliff, hill, etc., or underground. •*v.intr.* explore caves, esp. interconnecting or underground. ▫ **cave in 1 a** (of a wall, earth over a hollow, etc.) subside; collapse. **b** cause (a wall, earth, etc.) to do this. **2** yield or submit under pressure; give up. ▫▫ **cave·like** *adj.* **cav·er** *n.*

ca·ve·at /kávee–aat, kaá–, –at/ *n.* **1** a warning or proviso. **2** *Law* a process in court to suspend proceedings.

ca·ve·at emp·tor /émptawr/ *n.* the principle that the buyer alone is responsible if dissatisfied (from the Latin 'let the buyer beware').

cave bear *n.* a large extinct bear of the Pleistocene epoch, whose bones have been found in caves throughout Europe.

cave-in *n.* a collapse, submission, etc.

cave dwell·er *n.* **1** = CAVEMAN. **2** *sl.* a person who lives in an apartment building in a big city.

cave·man /káyvman/ *n.* (*pl.* **·men**) **1** (*fem.* **cavewoman,** *pl.* **·women**) a prehistoric human living in a cave. **2** a primitive or crude person, esp. a man who behaves roughly toward women.

cav·ern /kávərn/ *n.* **1** a cave, esp. a large or dark one. **2** a dark, cavelike place, e.g., a room. ▫▫ **cav·ern·ous** *adj.* **cav·ern·ous·ly** *adv.*

cav·i·ar /kávee–aár/ *n.* (also **cav·i·are**) the pickled roe of sturgeon or other large fish, eaten as a delicacy.

cav·il /kávil/ *v. & n.* •*v.intr.* (**caviled, caviling;** esp. *Brit.* **cavilled, cavilling**) (usu. foll. by *at*, *about*) make petty objections; carp. •*n.* a trivial objection. ▫▫ **cav·il·er** *n.*

cav·ing /káyving/ *n.* exploring caves as a sport or pastime.

cav·i·ty /kávitee/ *n.* (*pl.* **·ties**) **1** a hollow within a solid body. **2** a decayed part of a tooth.

cav·i·ty wall *n.* a wall built with two thicknesses of masonry separated by a space in between, for insulation and to prevent water penetration.

ca·vort /kəváwrt/ *v.intr. sl.* caper excitedly; gambol; prance.

ca·vy /káyvee/ *n.* (*pl.* **·vies**) any small rodent of the family Caviidae, native to S. America and having a sturdy body and vestigial tail, including guinea pigs.

caw /kaw/ *n. & v.* •*n.* the harsh cry of a crow or similar bird. •*v.intr.* utter this cry.

cay /kee, kay/ *n.* a low insular bank or reef of coral, sand, etc. (cf. KEY[2]).

cay·enne /kī–én, kay–/ *n.* (in full **cayenne pepper**) a pungent red powder obtained from various plants of the genus *Capsicum* and used for seasoning.

cay·man var. of CAIMAN.

CB *abbr.* **1** citizens' band. **2** *Mil.* construction battalion.

Cb *symb. Chem.* the element columbium.

CBC *abbr.* complete blood count.

CBE *abbr.* Commander of the Order of the British Empire.

CBI *abbr.* computer-based instruction.

CBS *abbr.* Columbia Broadcasting System.

CC *abbr.* **1** city council. **2** county clerk. **3** circuit court.

cc *abbr.* (also **c.c.**) **1** cubic centimeter(s). **2** (carbon) copy; copies.

CCU *abbr.* **1** cardiac care unit. **2** coronary care unit. **3** critical care unit.

CD *abbr.* **1** compact disc. **2** certificate of deposit. **3** congressional district. **4** civil defense. **5** diplomatic corps (*corps diplomatique*).

Cd *symb. Chem.* the element cadmium.

cd *abbr.* candela(s).

CDC *abbr.* Centers for Disease Control (and Prevention).

Cdr. *abbr. Mil.* commander.

Cdre. *abbr.* commodore.

CD-ROM /seédeeróm/ *abbr.* compact disc read-only memory, a medium for data storage and distribution.

CDT *abbr.* central daylight time.

CE *abbr.* **1** Church of England. **2** civil engineer. **3** (with dates) Common Era.

Ce *symb. Chem.* the element cerium.

cease /sees/ *v. & n.* •*v.tr. & intr.* stop; bring or come to an end (*ceased breathing*). •*n.* (in **without cease**) unendingly.

cease-fire *n.* **1** an order to stop firing. **2** a period of truce; a suspension of hostilities.

See page xii for the *Key to Pronunciation.*

cease·less /séeslis/ *adj.* without end; not ceasing. □□ **cease·less·ly** *adv.*

ce·cro·pi·a moth /sikrṓpeeə/ *n.* a large N. American silk moth with boldly marked reddish-brown wings.

ce·cum /séekəm/ *n.* (*pl.* **·ca** /–kə/) a blind-ended pouch at the junction of the small and large intestines. □□ **ce·cal** *adj.*

ce·dar /séedər/ *n.* **1** any spreading evergreen conifer of the genus *Cedrus*, bearing tufts of small needles and cones of papery scales. **2** any of various similar conifers yielding timber.

cede /seed/ *v.tr.* give up one's rights to or possession of.

ce·dil·la /sidílə/ *n.* **1** a mark written under the letter *c*, esp. in French, to show that it is sibilant (as in *façade*). **2** a similar mark under *s* in Turkish and other Eastern languages.

ceil·ing /séeling/ *n.* **1 a** the upper interior surface of a room or other similar compartment. **b** the material forming this. **2** an upper limit on prices, wages, performance, etc. **3** *Aeron.* the maximum altitude a given aircraft can reach.

cel·an·dine /séləndīn, –deen/ *n.* either of two yellow-flowered plants, the greater celandine, *Chelidonium majus*, and the lesser celandine, *Ranunculus ficaria*.

-cele /seel/ *comb. form* (also **-coele**) *Med.* swelling; hernia (*gastrocele*).

ce·leb /siléb/ *n. colloq.* a celebrity; a star.

cel·e·brant /sélibrənt/ *n.* a person who performs a rite, esp. a priest at the Eucharist.

cel·e·brate /sélibrayt/ *v.* **1** *tr.* mark (a festival or special event) with festivities, etc. **2** *tr.* perform publicly and duly (a religious ceremony, etc.). **3 a** *tr.* officiate at (the Eucharist). **b** *intr.* officiate, esp. at the Eucharist. **4** *intr.* engage in festivities, usu. after a special event, etc. **5** *tr.* (esp. as **celebrated** *adj.*) honor publicly; make widely known. □□ **cel·e·bra·tion** /–bráyshən/ *n.* **cel·e·bra·tor** *n.* **cel·e·bra·to·ry** /–brətáwree, səlébrətáwree/ *adj.*

ce·leb·ri·ty /silébritee/ *n.* (*pl.* **·ties**) **1** a well-known person. **2** fame.

ce·ler·i·ty /siléritee/ *n. archaic* or *literary* swiftness (esp. of a living creature).

cel·er·y /séləree/ *n.* an umbelliferous plant, *Apium graveolens*, with closely packed succulent leafstalks used as a vegetable.

ce·les·ta /siléstə/ *n. Mus.* a small keyboard instrument resembling a glockenspiel, with hammers striking steel plates suspended over wooden resonators, giving an ethereal bell-like sound.

ce·leste /silést/ *n. Mus.* **1** an organ and harmonium stop with a soft tremulous tone. **2** = CELESTA.

ce·les·tial /siléschəl/ *adj.* **1** heavenly; divinely good or beautiful; sublime. **2** of the sky; of the part of the sky commonly observed in astronomy, etc. □□ **ce·les·tial·ly** *adv.*

ce·les·tial e·qua·tor *n.* the great circle of the sky in the plane perpendicular to the earth's axis.

ce·les·tial sphere *n.* an imaginary sphere of which the observer is the center and in which celestial objects are represented as lying.

cel·i·bate /sélibət/ *adj.* & *n.* • *adj.* **1** committed to abstention from sexual relations and from marriage, esp. for religious reasons. **2** abstaining from sexual relations. • *n.* a celibate person. □□ **cel·i·ba·cy** /–bəsee/ *n.*

cell /sel/ *n.* **1** a small room, esp. in a prison or monastery. **2** a small compartment, e.g., in a honeycomb. **3** *Biol.* **a** the structural and functional usu. microscopic unit of an organism, consisting of cytoplasm and a nucleus enclosed in a membrane. **b** an enclosed cavity in an organism, etc. **4** a small group as a nucleus of political activity, esp. of a subversive kind. **5** *Electr.* a vessel for containing electrodes within an electrolyte for current generation or electrolysis. □□ **celled** *adj.* (also in *comb.*).

cel·lar /sélər/ *n.* & *v.* • *n.* **1** a room below ground level in a house, used for storage, etc. **2** a stock of wine in a cellar (*has a good cellar*). • *v.tr.* store or put in a cellar.

cel·lo /chélō/ *n.* (*pl.* **·los**) a bass instrument of the violin family, held upright on the floor between the legs of the seated player. □□ **cel·list** *n.*

cel·lo·phane /séləfayn/ *n. formerly Trademark* a thin transparent wrapping material made from viscose.

cell·phone /sélfōn/ *n.* a small, portable radiotelephone having access to a cellular telephone system.

cel·lu·lar /sélyələr/ *adj.* **1** of or having small compartments or cavities. **2** of open texture; porous. **3** *Physiol.* of or consisting of cells. □□ **cel·lu·lar·i·ty** /–láritee/ *n.*

cel·lu·lar tel·e·phone (or **phone**) *n.* a system of mobile radiotelephone transmission with an area divided into "cells" each served by its own small transmitter.

cel·lu·lite /sélyəlīt/ *n.* a lumpy form of fat, esp. on the hips and thighs of women, causing puckering of the skin.

cel·lu·loid /sélyəloyd/ *n.* **1** a transparent flammable plastic made from camphor and cellulose nitrate. **2** motion-picture film.

cel·lu·lose /sélyəlōs, –lōz/ *n.* **1** *Biochem.* a carbohydrate forming the main constituent of plant cell walls, used in the production of textile fibers. **2** (in general use) a paint or lacquer consisting of esp. cellulose acetate or nitrate in solution. □□ **cel·lu·lo·sic** /–lṓsik/ *adj.*

Cel·si·us /sélseeəs/ *adj.* of or denoting a temperature on the Celsius scale.

Cel·si·us scale *n.* a scale of temperature on which water freezes at 0° and boils at 100° under standard conditions.

Celt /kelt, selt/ *n.* (also **Kelt**) a member of a group of W. European peoples, including the pre-Roman inhabitants of Britain and Gaul and their descendants, esp. in Ireland, Wales, Scotland, Cornwall, Brittany, and the Isle of Man.

celt /kelt/ *n. Archaeol.* a stone or metal prehistoric implement with a chisel edge.

Celt·ic /kéltik, séltik/ *adj.* & *n.* • *adj.* of or relating to the Celts. • *n.* a group of languages spoken by Celtic peoples, including Gaelic, Welsh, Cornish, and Breton. □□ **Celt·i·cism** /–tisizəm/ *n.*

Celtic cross *n.* a Latin cross with a circle around the center.

ce·ment /simént/ *n.* & *v.* • *n.* **1** a powdery substance made by calcining lime and clay, mixed with water to form mortar or used in concrete **2** any similar substance that hardens and fastens on setting. **3** a uniting factor or principle. **4** a substance for filling cavities in teeth. • *v.tr.* **1 a** unite with or as with cement. **b** establish or strengthen (a friendship, etc.). **2** apply cement to. **3** line or cover with cement. □□ **ce·men·ta·tion** *n.* **ce·ment·er** *n.*

cem·e·ter·y /sémiteree/ *n.* (*pl.* **·ies**) a burial ground, esp. one not in a churchyard.

ce·no·taph /sénətaf/ *n.* a tomblike monument, esp. a war memorial, to a person whose body is elsewhere.

Ce·no·zo·ic /séenəzṓik, sén–/ (also **Cai·no·zo·ic** /kī́nə–/, **Caenozoic** /séenə–/) *adj.* & *n. Geol.* • *adj.* of or relating to the most recent era of geological time, which began 70,000,000 years ago, marked by the evolution and development of mammals, birds, and flowers. • *n.* this era (cf. MESOZOIC, PALEOZOIC).

cen·ser /sénsər/ *n.* a vessel in which incense is burned, esp. during a religious procession or ceremony.

cen·sor /sénsər/ *n.* & *v.* • *n.* **1** an official authorized to examine printed matter, movies, news, etc., before public release, and to suppress any parts on the grounds of obscenity, a threat to security, etc. **2** *Rom.Hist.* either of two annual magistrates responsible for holding censuses and empowered to supervise public morals. • *v.tr.* **1** act as a censor of. **2** make deletions or changes in. ▶As a verb, often confused with *censure.* ▫▫ **cen·so·ri·al** /–sáwreeəl/ *adj.* **cen·sor·ship** *n.*

▶Both **censor** and **censure** are both verbs and nouns, but **censor** is used to mean 'to cut unacceptable parts out of a book, movie, etc.' or 'a person who does this,' while **censure** means 'to criticize harshly' or 'harsh criticism:' *The censure of her friends caused her to regret her actions.*

cen·so·ri·ous /sensáwreeəs/ *adj.* severely critical; fault-finding; quick or eager to criticize. ▫▫ **cen·so·ri·ous·ly** *adv.* **cen·so·ri·ous·ness** *n.*

cen·sure /sénshər/ *v.* & *n.* • *v.tr.* criticize harshly; reprove.

▶Often confused with *censor.* • *n.* harsh criticism; expression of disapproval. ▫▫ **cen·sur·a·ble** *adj.*

▶see note at CENSOR.

cen·sus /sénsəs/ *n.* (*pl.* **censuses**) the official count of a population or of a class of things, often with various statistics noted.

cent /sent/ *n.* **1 a** a monetary unit valued at one-hundredth of a dollar or other metric unit. **b** a coin of this value. **2** *colloq.* a very small sum of money. **3** see PERCENT.

cen·taur /séntawr/ *n.* a creature in Greek mythology with the head, arms, and torso of a man and the body and legs of a horse.

cen·te·nar·i·an /séntináireeən/ *n.* & *adj.* • *n.* a person a hundred or more years old. • *adj.* a hundred or more years old.

cen·ten·ar·y /senténəree, séntəneree/ *n.* & *adj.* • *n.* (*pl.* **·ies**) = CENTENNIAL *n.* • *adj.* **1** of or relating to a centenary. **2** occurring every hundred years.

cen·ten·ni·al /senténeeəl/ *adj.* & *n.* • *adj.* **1** lasting for a hundred years. **2** occurring every hundred years. • *n.* **1** a hundredth anniversary. **2** a celebration of this.

cen·ter /séntər/ *n.* & *v.* • *n.* **1** the middle point, esp. of a line, circle, or sphere, equidistant from the ends or from any point on the circumference or surface. **2** a pivot or axis of rotation. **3 a** a place or group of buildings forming a central point in a district, city, etc., or a main area for an activity (*shopping center; town center*). **b** (with preceding word) a piece or set of equipment for a number of connected functions (*music center*). **4** a point of concentration or dispersion; a nucleus or source. **5** a political party or group holding moderate opinions. **6** the filling in a chocolate, candy, etc. **7** *Sports* **a** the middle player in a line or group in many games. **b** a kick or hit from the side to the center of the playing area. **8** (*attrib.*) of or at the center. • *v.* **1** *intr.* (foll. by *in, on; disp.* foll. by *around*) have as its main center. **2** *tr.* place in the center. **3** *tr.* mark with a center. **4** *tr.* (foll. by *in,* etc.) concentrate. **5** *tr. Sports* kick or hit (the ball) from the side to the center of the playing area. ▫▫ **centered** *adj.* (often in *comb.*). **cen·ter·most** *adj.*

cen·ter·board /séntərbawrd/ *n.* a retractable keel, as for a small sailboat.

cen·ter·fold /séntərfōld/ *n.* a printed and usu. illustrated sheet folded to form the center spread of a magazine, etc.

cen·ter·ing /séntəring/ *n.* a temporary frame used to support an arch, dome, etc., while under construction.

cen·ter of grav·i·ty (or **mass**) *n.* the point at which the weight of a body may be considered to act.

cen·ter·piece /séntərpees/ *n.* **1** an ornament for the middle of a table. **2** a principal item.

cen·tes·i·mal /sentésiməl/ *adj.* reckoning or reckoned by hundredths. ▫▫ **cen·tes·i·mal·ly** *adv.*

centi- /séntee/ *comb. form* **1** one-hundredth, esp. of a unit in the metric system (*centigram; centiliter*). **2** hundred. ¶ Abbr.: **c**.

cen·ti·grade /séntigrayd/ *adj.* **1** = CELSIUS. **2** having a scale of a hundred degrees. ▶In sense 1 *Celsius* is usually preferred in technical use..

cen·ti·gram /séntigram/ *n.* (also a metric unit of mass, equal to one-hundredth of a gram.

cen·ti·li·ter /séntileetər/ *n.* a metric unit of capacity, equal to one-hundredth of a liter.

cen·time /sɴtéem/ *n.* **1** a monetary unit valued at one-hundredth of a franc. **2** a coin of this value.

cen·ti·me·ter /séntimeetər/ *n.* a metric unit of length, equal to one-hundredth of a meter.

cen·ti·pede /séntipeed/ *n.* any arthropod of the class Chilopoda, with a wormlike body of many segments each with a pair of legs.

cen·tral /séntrəl/ *adj.* **1** of, at, or forming the center. **2** from the center. **3** chief; essential; most important. ▫▫ **cen·tral·i·ty** /–trálitee/ *n.* **cen·tral·ly** *adv.*

Cen·tral A·mer·i·ca *n.* the isthmus joining N. and S. America, usually comprising the countries from Guatemala and Belize south to Panama.

cen·tral·ize /séntrəlīz/ *v.* **1** *tr.* & *intr.* bring or come to a center. **2** *tr.* **a** concentrate (administration) at a single center. **b** subject (a government) to this system. ▫▫ **cen·tral·i·za·tion** *n.*

cen·tral nerv·ous sys·tem *n. Anat.* the complex of nerve tissues that controls the activities of the body, in vertebrates the brain and spinal cord.

cen·tral proc·es·sing u·nit *n.* (also **cen·tral proc·es·sor**) the principal operating part of a computer. ¶ Abbr.: **CPU**.

cen·trif·u·gal /sentrífyəgəl, –trífə–/ *adj.* moving or tending to move from a center (cf. CENTRIPETAL). ▫▫ **cen·trif·u·gal·ly** *adv.*

cen·trif·u·gal force *n.* an apparent force that acts outward on a body moving about a center.

cen·tri·fuge /séntrifyōōj/ *n.* & *v.* • *n.* a machine with a rapidly rotating device designed to separate liquids from solids or other liquids (e.g., cream from milk). • *v.tr.* **1** subject to the action of a centrifuge. **2** separate by centrifuge. ▫▫ **cen·trif·u·ga·tion** /–fyəgáyshən, –fə–/ *n.*

cen·trip·e·tal /sentrípit'l/ *adj.* moving or tending to move toward a center (cf. CENTRIFUGAL). ▫▫ **cen·trip·e·tal·ly** *adv.*

cen·trip·e·tal force *n.* the force acting on a body causing it to move about a center.

cen·trist /séntrist/ *n. Polit.* often *derog.* a person who holds moderate views. ▫▫ **cen·trism** *n.*

cen·tu·ri·on /sentyŏŏreeən, –tyŏŏr–/ *n.* the commander of a century in the ancient Roman army.

cen·tu·ry /sénchəree/ *n.* (*pl.* **·ries**) **1 a** a period of one hundred years. **b** any of the centuries calculated from the birth of Christ (*twentieth century* = 1901–2000; *fifth century* BC = 500–401 BC). **2 a** a score, etc., of a hundred in a sporting event, esp. a hundred runs by one batsman in cricket. **b** a group of a hundred things. **3 a** a company in the ancient Roman army, orig. of 100 men. **b** an ancient Roman political division for voting. **century**

▶In modern use, **century** is often calculated as, e.g., 1900–1999.

cen·tu·ry plant *n.* a plant, *Agave americana*, flowering once in many years and yielding sap from which tequila is distilled: also called AMERICAN ALOE.

CEO *abbr.* chief executive officer.

cep /sep/ *n.* an edible mushroom, *Boletus edulis*, with a stout stalk and brown smooth cap.

ce·phal·ic /sifálik/ *adj.* of or in the head.

-cephalic /sifálik/ *comb. form* = -CEPHALOUS.

ceph·a·lo·pod /séfələpod/ *n.* any mollusk of the class Cephalopoda, having a distinct tentacled head, e.g., octopus, squid, and cuttlefish.

ceph·a·lo·tho·rax /séfəlōtháwraks/ *n.* (*pl.* **·thoraxes** or **·thoraces** /–tháwrəseez/) *Anat.* the fused head and thorax of a spider, crab, or other arthropod.

-cephalous /séfələs/ *comb. form* -headed (*brachycephalous*).

Ce·pheid /séefeeid, séf–/ *n.* (in full **Cepheid variable**) *Astron.* any of a class of variable stars with a regular cycle of brightness that can be used to measure distances.

ce·ram·ic /sirámik/ *adj.* & *n.* • *adj.* **1** made of (esp.) clay and permanently hardened by heat (*a ceramic bowl*). **2** of or relating to ceramics (*the ceramic arts*). • *n.* **1** a ceramic article or product. **2** a substance, esp. clay, used to make ceramic articles.

ce·ram·ics /sirámiks/ *n.pl.* **1** ceramic products collectively (*exhibition of ceramics*). **2** (usu. treated as *sing.*) the art of making ceramic articles.

ce·re·al /séereeəl/ *n.* & *adj* • *n.* **1** (usu. in *pl.*) **a** any kind of grain used for food. **b** any grass producing this, e.g., wheat, corn, rye, etc. **2** a breakfast food made from a cereal and requiring no cooking. • *adj.* of edible grain or products of it.

cer·e·bel·lum /séribéləm/ *n.* (*pl.* **cerebellums** or **cerebella** /–lə/) the part of the brain at the back of the skull in vertebrates, which coordinates and regulates muscular activity. □□ **cer·e·bel·lar** *adj.*

ce·re·bral /séribrəl, səréé–/ *adj.* **1** of the brain. **2** intellectual rather than emotional. □□ **ce·re·bral·ly** *adv.*

ce·re·bral hem·i·sphere *n.* each of the two halves of the vertebrate cerebrum.

ce·re·bral pal·sy *n. Med.* spastic paralysis from brain damage before or at birth, with jerky or uncontrolled movements.

cer·e·bra·tion /séribráyshən/ *n.* working of the brain. □□ **cer·e·brate** /–brayt/ *v.intr.*

cerebro- /séribrō, səréé–/ *comb. form* brain (*cerebrospinal*).

ce·re·bro·spi·nal /séribrōspínəl, səréé–/ *adj.* of the brain and spine.

ce·re·bro·vas·cu·lar /séribrōváskyələr, səréé–/ *adj.* of the brain and its blood vessels.

ce·re·brum /séribrəm, səréé–/ *n.* (*pl.* **cerebrums** or **cerebra** /–brə/) the principal part of the brain in vertebrates, located in the front area of the skull, which integrates complex sensory and neural functions.

cer·e·mo·ni·al /sérimóneeəl/ *adj.* & *n.* • *adj.* **1** with or concerning ritual or ceremony. **2** formal (*a ceremonial bow*). • *n.* **1** a system of rites, etc., to be used esp. at a formal or religious occasion. **2** the formalities or behavior proper to any occasion (*the ceremonial of a presidential appearance*). □□ **cer·e·mo·ni·al·ism** *n.* **cer·e·mo·ni·al·ist** *n.* **cer·e·mo·ni·al·ly** *adv.*

cer·e·mo·ni·ous /sérimóneeəs/ *adj.* **1** excessively polite; punctilious. **2** having or showing a fondness for ritualistic observance or formality. □□ **cer·e·mo·ni·ous·ly** *adv.* **cer·e·mo·ni·ous·ness** *n.*

cer·e·mo·ny /sérimōnee/ *n.* (*pl.* **·nies**) **1** a formal religious or public occasion, esp. celebrating a particular event or anniversary. **2** formalities, esp. of an empty or ritualistic kind (*ceremony of exchanging compliments*). **3** excessively polite behavior (*bowed low with great ceremony*). □ **stand on ceremony** insist on the observance of formalities. **without ceremony** informally.

ce·ri·um /séereeəm/ *n. Chem.* a silvery metallic element of the lanthanide series occurring naturally in various minerals and used in the manufacture of lighter flints. ¶ Symb.: **Ce**.

cero- /séerō/ *comb. form* wax (cf. CEROGRAPHY).

ce·rog·ra·phy /seerógrəfee/ *n.* the technique of engraving or designing on or with wax.

cert. /sərt/ *abbr.* **1** a certificate. **2** certified.

cer·tain /sə́rt'n/ *adj.* & *pron.* • *adj.* **1 a** (often foll. by *of*, or *that* + clause) confident; convinced (*certain that I put it here*). **b** (often foll. by *that* + clause) indisputable; known for sure (*it is certain that he is guilty*). **2** (often foll. by *to* + infin.) **a** that may be relied on to happen (*it is certain to rain*). **b** destined (*certain to become a star*). **3** definite; unfailing; reliable (*a certain indication of the coming storm*; *his touch is certain*). **4** (of a person, place, etc.) that might be specified, but is not (*a certain lady*; *of a certain age*). **5** some though not much (*a certain reluctance*). **6** (of a person, place, etc.) existing, though probably unknown to the reader or hearer (*a certain John Smith*). • *pron.* (as *pl.*) some but not all (*certain of them were wounded*). □ **for certain** without doubt. **make certain** = *make sure* (see SURE).

cer·tain·ly /sə́rt'nlee/ *adv.* **1** undoubtedly; definitely. **2** confidently. **3** (in affirmative answer to a question or command) yes; by all means.

cer·tain·ty /sə́rt'ntee/ *n.* (*pl.* **·ties**) **1 a** an undoubted fact. **b** a certain prospect (*his return is a certainty*). **2** (often foll. by *of*, or *that* + clause) an absolute conviction (*has a certainty of his own worth*). **3** (often foll. by *to* + infin.) a thing or person that may be relied on (*a certainty to win the Derby*). □ **for a certainty** beyond the possibility of doubt.

cer·ti·fi·a·ble /sə́rtifīəbəl/ *adj.* **1** able or needing to be certified. **2** *colloq.* insane.

cer·tif·i·cate *n.* & *v.* • *n.* /sərtífikət/ a formal document attesting a fact, esp. birth, marriage, death, a medical condition, a level of achievement, a fulfillment of requirements, ownership of shares, etc. • *v.tr.* /sərtífikayt/ (esp. as **certificated** *adj.*) provide with or license or attest by a certificate. □□ **cer·ti·fi·ca·tion** /sə́rtifikáyshən/ *n.*

cer·tif·i·cate of de·pos·it a certificate issued by a bank to a depositor, stating the amount of money on deposit, usu. at a specified rate of interest and for a specified time period. ¶ Abbr.: **CD**.

cer·ti·fied check *n.* a check the validity of which is guaranteed by a bank.

cer·ti·fied pub·lic ac·count·ant *n.* a member of an officially accredited professional body of accountants.

cer·ti·fy /sə́rtifī/ *v.tr.* (**·fies**, **·fied**) **1** make a formal statement of; attest; attest to (*certified that he had witnessed the crime*). **2** declare by certificate (that a person is qualified or competent) (*certified as a trained bookkeeper*). **3** officially declare insane (*he should be certified*).

cer·ti·tude /sə́rtitōōd, –tyōōd/ *n.* a feeling of absolute certainty or conviction.

ce·ru·le·an /sərṓōleeən/ *adj.* & *n. literary* • *adj.* deep blue like a clear sky. • *n.* this color.

ce·ru·men /sərṓōmen/ *n.* the yellow waxy substance in the outer ear. □□ **ce·ru·mi·nous** *adj.*

cer·ve·lat /sə́rvəlaa, –lat/ *n.* a kind of smoked pork or beef sausage.

cer·vi·cal /sə́rvikəl/ *adj. Anat.* **1** of or relating to the neck (*cervical vertebrae*). **2** of or relating to the cervix.

cer·vi·cal screen·ing *n.* examination of a large number of apparently healthy women for cervical cancer.

cer·vi·cal smear *n.* a specimen of cellular material from the neck of the womb for detection of cancer.

cer·vine /sə́rvīn/ *adj.* of or like a deer.

cer·vix /sə́rviks/ *n.* (*pl.* **cervices** /–viseez/ or **cervixes**) *Anat.* **1** the neck. **2** any necklike structure, esp. the neck of the womb.

Ce·sar·e·an /sizáireeən/ *adj.* & *n.* (also **Ce·sar·i·an, Cae·sar·e·an, Cae·sar·i·an**) • *adj.* (of a birth) effected by cesarean section. • *n.* a cesarean section.

ce·sar·e·an sec·tion *n.* (also **C-section**) an operation for delivering a child by cutting through the wall of the abdomen (Julius Caesar supposedly having been born this way).

ce·si·um /séezeeəm/ *n.* (*Brit.* **caesium**) a soft, silver-white element of the alkali metal group, occurring naturally in a number of minerals, and used in photoelectric cells. ¶ Symb.: **Cs**.

ces·sa·tion /sesáyshən/ *n.* **1** a ceasing (*cessation of the truce*). **2** a pause (*resumed fighting after the cessation*).

ces·sion /séshən/ *n.* **1** (often foll. by *of*) the ceding or giving up (of rights, property, and esp. of territory by a nation). **2** the territory, etc., so ceded.

cess·pool /séspōōl/ *n.* **1** an underground container for the temporary storage of liquid waste or sewage. **2** a center of corruption, depravity, etc.

ces·tode /séstōd/ *n.* (also **ces·toid** /séstoyd/) any flatworm of the class Cestoda, including tapeworms.

ce·ta·ce·an /sitáyshən/ *n.* & *adj.* • *n.* any marine mammal of the order Cetacea with streamlined hairless body and dorsal blowhole for breathing, including whales, dolphins, and porpoises. • *adj.* of cetaceans. ▫▫ **ce·ta·ceous** /–táyshəs/ *adj.*

ce·tane /séetayn/ *n. Chem.* a colorless liquid hydrocarbon of the alkane series used in standardizing ratings of diesel fuel.

ce·tane num·ber *n.* a measure of the ignition properties of diesel fuel.

Cey·lon moss /silón, say–/ *n.* a red seaweed, *Gracilaria lichenoides*, from E. India.

Cf *symb. Chem.* the element californium.

cf. *abbr.* compare.

c.f. *abbr.* **1** carried forward. **2** *Baseball* center fielder.

CFA *abbr.* chartered financial analyst.

CFC *abbr. Chem.* chlorofluorocarbon, any of various usu. gaseous compounds of carbon, hydrogen, chlorine, and fluorine, used in refrigerants, aerosol propellants, etc., and thought to be harmful to the ozone layer in the earth's atmosphere.

cfm *abbr.* cubic feet per minute.

cfs *abbr.* cubic feet per second.

cg *abbr.* centigram(s).

cgs *abbr.* centimeter-gram-second.

ch. *abbr.* **1** church. **2** chapter. **3** *Chess* check.

c.h. *abbr.* (also **C.H.**) **1** clearing house. **2** courthouse.

cha var. of CHAR[3].

Cha·blis /shablée, sháblee/ *n.* (*pl.* same /–leez/) a type of dry white wine.

cha-cha /chaáchaa/ (also **cha-cha-cha** /chaáchaachaá/) *n.* & *v.* • *n.* **1** a ballroom dance with a Latin-American rhythm. **2** music for or in the rhythm of a cha-cha. • *v.intr.* (**cha-chas, cha-chaed** /–chaad/, **cha-chaing** /–chaa–ing/) dance the cha-cha.

chad·or /chaadáwr/ *n.* (also **chad·ar, chud·dar**) a large piece of cloth worn in some countries by Muslim women, wrapped around the body to leave only the face exposed.

chafe /chayf/ *v.* & *n.* • *v.* **1** *tr.* & *intr.* make or become sore or damaged by rubbing. **2** *tr.* rub (esp. the skin to restore warmth or sensation). **3** *tr.* & *intr.* make or become annoyed; fret (*was chafed by the delay*). • *n.* **1 a** an act of chafing. **b** a sore resulting from this. **2** a state of annoyance.

chaf·er /cháyfər/ *n.* any of various large, slow-moving beetles of the family Scarabeidae, esp. the cockchafer.

chaff /chaf/ *n.* & *v.* • *n.* **1** the husks of grain or other seed separated by winnowing or threshing. **2** chopped hay and straw used as fodder. **3** lighthearted joking; banter. **4** worthless things; rubbish. • *v.tr.* **1** tease; banter. **2** chop (straw, etc.). ▫ **separate the wheat from the chaff** distinguish good from bad. ▫▫ **chaff·y** *adj.*

chaf·fer /cháfər/ *v.* & *n.* • *v.intr.* haggle; bargain. • *n.* bargaining; haggling. ▫▫ **chaf·fer·er** *n.*

chaf·ing dish /cháyfing/ *n.* **1** a cooking pot with an outer pan of hot water, used for keeping food warm. **2** a dish with an alcohol lamp, etc., for cooking at table.

cha·grin /shəgrin/ *n.* & *v.* • *n.* acute vexation or mortification. • *v.tr.* affect with chagrin.

chain /chayn/ *n.* & *v.* • *n.* **1 a** a connected flexible series of esp. metal links as decoration or for a practical purpose. **b** something resembling this (*formed a human chain*). **2** (in *pl.*) **a** fetters used to confine prisoners. **b** any restraining force. **3** a sequence, series, or set (*chain of events*; *mountain chain*). **4** a group of associated hotels, shops, newspapers, etc. **5** esp. *Brit.* a badge of office in the form of a chain worn around the neck (*mayoral chain*). **6** a measure of length (66 or 100 ft.). **7** *Chem.* a group of (esp. carbon) atoms bonded in sequence in a molecule. • *v.tr.* **1** (often foll. by *up*) secure or confine with a chain. **2** confine or restrict (a person) (*is chained to the office*).

chain gang *n.* a team of convicts chained together and forced to work in the open air.

chain let·ter *n.* one of a sequence of letters the recipient of which is requested to send copies to a specific number of other people.

chain mail *n.* armor made of interlaced rings.

chain re·ac·tion *n.* **1** *Physics* a self-sustaining nuclear reaction, esp. one in which a neutron from a fission reaction initiates a series of these reactions. **2** *Chem.* a self-sustaining molecular reaction in which intermediate products initiate further reactions. **3** a series of events, each caused by the previous one.

chain saw *n.* a motor-driven saw with teeth on an endless chain.

chain-smok·er *n.* a person who smokes continually, esp. one who lights a cigarette, etc., from the stub of the last one smoked.

chain·wheel /cháynhweel, –weel/ *n.* a wheel transmitting power by a chain fitted to its edges; a sprocket.

chair /chair/ *n.* & *v.* • *n.* **1** a separate seat for one person, of various forms, usu. having a back and four legs. **2 a** a professorship (*offered the chair in physics*). **b** a seat of authority, esp. on a board of directors. **3 a** a chairperson. **b** the seat or office of a chairperson (*will you take the chair?*; *I'm in the chair*). **4** = ELECTRIC CHAIR. **5** *hist.* = *sedan chair*. • *v.tr.* **1** act as chairperson of or preside over (a meeting). **2** *Brit.* carry (a person) aloft in a chair or in a sitting position, in triumph. **3** install in a chair, esp. as a position of authority. ▫ **take a chair** sit down.

chair·la·dy /cháirlaydee/ *n.* (*pl.* **·dies**) = *chairwoman* (see CHAIRMAN).

chair·lift /cháirlift/ *n.* a series of chairs on an endless cable for carrying passengers up and down a mountain, etc.

chair·man /cháirmən/ *n.* (*pl.* **·men**; *fem.* **chairwoman**, *pl.* **·women**) **1** a person chosen to preside over a meeting. **2** the permanent president of a committee, a board of directors, (*Brit.*) a firm, etc. **3** the master of ceremonies at an entertainment, etc. **4** *hist.* either of two sedan bearers. ▫▫ **chair·man·ship** *n.*

chair·per·son /cháirpərsən/ *n.* a chairman or chairwoman (used as a neutral alternative).

chaise /shayz/ *n.* **1** esp. *hist.* a horse-drawn carriage for one or two persons, esp. one with an open top and two wheels. **2** = POST CHAISE.

chaise longue /sháyz lóng, shéz/ *n.* a reclining chair with a lengthened seat forming a leg rest.

chal·ced·o·ny /kalséd'nee/ *n.* a type of quartz occurring in several different forms, e.g., onyx, agate, tiger's eye, etc. ▫▫ **chal·ce·don·ic** /kálsidónik/ *adj.*

Chal·de·an /kaldéeən/ *n.* & *adj.* • *n.* **1 a** a native of ancient Chaldea or Babylonia. **b** the language of the Chaldeans. **2** an astrologer. **3** a member of the Uniat (formerly Nestorian) sect in Iran, etc. • *adj.* **1** of or relating to ancient Chaldea or its people or language. **2** of or relating to astrology. **3** of or relating to the Uniat sect.

cha·let /shaláy, shálay/ *n.* **1** a small suburban house or bungalow, esp. with an overhanging roof. **2** a small, usu. wooden hut or house at a ski resort, beach, etc. **3** a Swiss hut or wooden cottage with overhanging eaves.

chal·ice /chális/ *n.* **1** a wine cup used in the Communion service. **2** *literary* a goblet.

chalk /chawk/ *n.* & *v.* • *n.* **1** a white, soft, earthy limestone (calcium carbonate) formed from the skeletal remains of sea creatures. **2 a** a similar substance (calcium sulfate), sometimes colored, used for writing or drawing. **b** a piece of this (*a box of chalk*). **3** a series of strata consisting mainly of chalk. • *v.tr.* **1** rub, mark, draw, or write with chalk. **2** (foll. by *up*) **a** write or record with chalk. **b** register (a success, etc.). **c** *Brit.* charge (to an account). ▫ **chalk out** sketch or plan a thing to be accomplished. **chalk something up** ascribe something to a particular cause.

chalk·board /cháwkbawrd/ *n.* = BLACKBOARD.

chalk stripe *n.* a pattern of thin white stripes on a dark background.

chalk·y /cháwkee/ *adj.* (**chalkier, chalkiest**) **1 a** abounding in chalk. **b** white as chalk. **2** like or containing chalk stones. ▫▫ **chalk·i·ness** *n.*

chal·lenge /chálinj/ *n.* & *v.* • *n.* **1 a** a summons to take part in a contest or a trial of strength, etc., esp. to a duel. **b** a summons to prove or justify something. **2** a demanding or difficult task (*rose to the challenge of the new job*). **3** an act of disputing or denying a statement, claim, etc. **4** *Law* an objection made to a jury member. **5** a call to respond, esp. a sentry's call for a password, etc. **6** an invitation to a sporting contest, esp. one issued to a reigning champion. • *v.tr.* **1** (often foll. by *to* + infin.) **a** invite to take part in a contest, game, debate, duel, etc. **b** invite to prove or justify something. **2** dispute; deny (*I challenge that remark*). **3 a** stretch; stimulate (*challenges him to produce his best*). **b** (as **challenging** *adj.*) demanding; stimulatingly difficult. **4** (of a sentry) call to respond. **5** claim (attention, etc.). **6** *Law* object to (a jury member, evidence, etc.). ▫▫ **chal·lenge·a·ble** *adj.* **chal·leng·er** *n.*

chal·lis /shálee/ *n.* a lightweight, soft clothing fabric.

cham·ber /cháymbər/ *n.* **1 a** a hall used by a legislative or judicial body. **b** the body that meets in it. **c** any of the houses of a legislature (*the House chamber*). **2** (in *pl.*) a judge's room used for hearing cases not needing to be taken in court. **3** *poet.* or *archaic* a room, esp. a bedroom. **4** *Mus.* (*attrib.*) of or for a small group of instruments (*chamber orchestra*; *chamber music*). **5** an enclosed space in machinery, etc. (esp. the part of a gun bore that contains the charge).

cham·ber·lain /cháymbərlin/ *n.* an officer managing the household of a sovereign or a great noble. ▫▫ **cham·ber·lain·ship** *n.*

cham·ber·maid /cháymbərmayd/ *n.* **1** a housemaid at a hotel, etc. **2** a housemaid.

cham·ber of com·merce *n.* an association to promote local commercial interests.

cham·ber pot *n.* a receptacle for urine, etc., used in a bedroom.

Cham·ber·tin /shoNbertáN/ *n.* a high-quality dry red wine.

cham·bray /shámbray/ *n.* a cotton, silk, or linen gingham cloth with a white weft and a colored warp.

cha·me·le·on /kəméelyən/ *n.* **1** any of a family of small lizards having grasping tails, long tongues, protruding eyes, and the power of changing color. **2** a variable or inconstant person. ▫▫ **cha·me·le·on·ic** /–leeónik/ *adj.*

cham·fer /chámfər/ *v.* & *n.* • *v.tr.* bevel symmetrically (a right-angled edge or corner). • *n.* a beveled surface at an edge or corner.

cham·ois /shámee/ *n.* (*pl.* same /–eez/) **1** an agile goat antelope, *Rupicapra rupicapra*, native to the mountains of Europe and Asia. **2** (in full **chamois leather**) **a** soft pliable leather from sheep, goats, deer, etc. **b** a piece of this for polishing, etc.

cham·o·mile /kámәmīl, –meel/ *n.* (also **cam·o·mile**) any aromatic plant of the genus *Anthemis* or *Matricaria*, with daisylike flowers.

champ[1] /champ/ *v.* & *n.* • *v.* **1** *tr.* & *intr.* munch or chew noisily. **2** *tr.* (of a horse, etc.) work (the bit) noisily between the teeth. **3** *intr.* fret with impatience (*is champing to be away*). • *n.* a chewing noise or motion. ▫ **champ at the bit** be restlessly impatient.

champ[2] /champ/ *n. sl.* a champion.

cham·pagne /shampáyn/ *n.* **1 a** a white sparkling wine from Champagne in France. **b** a similar wine from elsewhere. **2** a pale cream or straw color.

cham·pi·on /chámpeeən/ *n.* & *v.* • *n.* **1** (often *attrib.*) a person (esp. in a sport or game), an animal, plant, etc., that has defeated or surpassed all rivals in a competition, etc. **2 a** a person who fights or argues for a cause or on behalf of another person. **b** *hist.* a knight, etc., who fought in single combat on behalf of a king, etc. • *v.tr.* support the cause of; defend; argue in favor of.

cham·pi·on·ship /chámpeeənship/ *n.* **1** (often in *pl.*) a contest for the position of champion in a sport, etc. **2** the position of champion over all rivals. **3** the advocacy or defense (of a cause, etc.).

chance /chans/ *n.*, *adj.*, & *v.* • *n.* **1 a** a possibility (*just a chance we will catch the train*). **b** (often in *pl.*) probability (*the chances are against it*). **2** a risk (*have to take a chance*). **3 a** an undesigned occurrence (*just a chance that they met*). **b** the absence of design or discoverable cause (*here merely because of chance*). **4** an opportunity (*didn't have a chance to speak to him*). **5** the way things happen; fortune; luck (*we'll just leave it to chance*). **6** (often **Chance**) the course of events regarded as a power; fate (*blind Chance rules the universe*). • *adj.* fortuitous; accidental (*a chance meeting*). • *v.* **1** *tr. colloq.* risk (*we'll chance it and go*). **2** *intr.* (often foll. by *that* + clause, or *to* + infin.) happen without intention (*it chanced that I found it*; *I chanced to find it*). ▫ **by any chance** as it happens; perhaps. **by chance** without design; unintentionally. **chance on** (or **upon**) happen to find, meet, etc. **the off chance** the slight possibility. **on the chance** (often foll. by *of*, or *that* + clause) in view of the possibility. **stand a chance** have a prospect of success, etc. **take a chance** (or **chances**) behave riskily; risk failure. **take a** (or **one's**) **chance on** (or **with**) consent to take the consequences of; trust to luck.

chan·cel /chánsəl/ *n.* the part of a church near the altar, usu. enclosed by a screen or separated from the nave by steps.

chan·cel·ler·y /chánsələree, chánslə–/ *n.* (*pl.* **·ies**) **1 a** the position, office, staff, department, etc., of a chancellor. **b** the official residence of a chancellor. **2** an office attached to an embassy or consulate.

chan·cel·lor /chánsələr, chánslər/ *n.* **1** a government official of various kinds; the head of the government in some European countries, e.g., Germany. **2 a** the chief administrator at certain universities. **b** *Brit.* the nonresident honorary head of a university. □□ **chan·cel·lor·ship** *n.*

chan·cer·y /chánsəree/ *n.* (*pl.* **·ies**) **1** (**Chancery**) *Brit. Law* the Lord Chancellor's court, a division of the High Court of Justice. **2** an office attached to an embassy or consulate. □ **in chancery** *sl.* (of a boxer or wrestler) with the head held under the opponent's arm and being pummeled.

chan·cre /shángkər/ *n.* a painless ulcer developing in venereal disease, etc.

chanc·y /chánsee/ *adj.* (**chancier, chanciest**) subject to chance; uncertain; risky. □□ **chanc·i·ly** *adv.* **chanc·i·ness** *n.*

chan·de·lier /shándəléer/ *n.* an ornamental branched hanging support for several candles or electric lightbulbs.

chan·dler /chándlər/ *n.* a dealer in candles, oil, soap, paint, groceries, etc. □□ **chan·dler·y**

change /chaynj/ *n.* & *v.* •*n.* **1 a** the act or an instance of making or becoming different. **b** an alteration or modification (*the change in her expression*). **2 a** money given in exchange for money in larger units or a different currency. **b** money returned as the balance of that given in payment. **c** = SMALL CHANGE. **3** a new experience; variety (*fancied a change*; *for a change*). **4 a** the substitution of one thing for another; an exchange (*change of scene*). **b** a set of clothes, etc., put on in place of another. **5** (in full **change of life**) *colloq.* the menopause. **6** (usu. in *pl.*) the different orders in which a peal of bells can be rung. •*v.* **1** *tr.* & *intr.* undergo, show, or subject to change; make or become different (*the toupee changed his appearance*; *changed from an introvert into an extrovert*). **2** *tr.* **a** take or use another instead of; go from one to another (*change one's socks*; *changed his doctor*; *changed trains*). **b** (usu. foll. by *for*) give up or get rid of in exchange (*changed the car for a van*). **3** *tr.* **a** give or get change in smaller denominations for (*can you change a ten-dollar bill?*). **b** (foll. by *for*) exchange (a sum of money) for (*changed his dollars for pounds*). **4** *tr.* & *intr.* put fresh clothes or coverings on (*changed the baby as he was wet*; *changed into something loose*). **5** *tr.* (often foll. by *with*) give and receive; exchange (*changed places with him*; *we changed places*). **6** *intr.* change trains, etc. (*changed at Grand Central Station*). □ **change color** blanch or flush. **change hands 1** pass to a different owner. **2** substitute one hand for another. **change one's mind** adopt a different opinion or plan. **change of heart** a conversion to a different view. **change step** begin to keep step with the opposite leg when marching, etc. **change the subject** begin talking of something different, esp. to avoid embarrassment. **change one's tune 1** voice a different opinion from that expressed previously. **2** change one's style of language or manner, esp. from an insolent to a respectful tone. □□ **change·ful** *adj.* **chang·er** *n.*

change·a·ble /cháynjəbəl/ *adj.* **1** irregular; inconstant. **2** that can change or be changed. □□ **change·a·bil·i·ty** *n.* **change·a·ble·ness** *n.* **change·a·bly** *adv.*

change·less /cháynjlis/ *adj.* unchanging. □□ **change·less·ly** *adv.* **change·less·ness** *n.*

change·ling /cháynjling/ *n.* a child believed to be substituted for another by stealth, esp. an elf child left by fairies.

change·o·ver /cháynjōvər/ *n.* a change from one system or situation to another.

chan·nel /chánəl/ *n.* & *v.* •*n.* **1 a** a length of water wider than a strait, joining two larger areas, esp. seas. **b** (**the Channel**) the English Channel between Britain and France. **2** a medium of communication; an agency for conveying information (*through the usual channels*). **3** *Broadcasting* **a** a band of frequencies used in radio and television transmission, esp. as used by a particular station. **b** a service or station using this. **4** the course in which anything moves; a direction. **5 a** a natural or artificial hollow bed of water. **b** the navigable part of a waterway. **6** a tubular passage for liquid. **7** *Electronics* a lengthwise strip on recording tape, etc. **8** a groove or a flute, esp. in a column. •*v.tr.* (**channeled, channeling**; esp. *Brit.* **channelled, channelling**) **1** guide; direct (*channeled them through customs*). **2** form channels in; groove.

chant /chant/ *n.* & *v.* •*n.* **1 a** a spoken singsong phrase, esp. one performed in unison by a crowd, etc. **b** a repetitious singsong way of speaking. **2** *Mus.* **a** a short musical passage in two or more phrases used for singing unmetrical words, e.g., psalms, canticles. **b** the psalm or canticle so sung. **c** a song, esp. monotonous or repetitive. •*v.tr.* & *intr.* **1** talk or repeat monotonously (*a crowd chanting slogans*). **2** sing or intone (a psalm, etc.).

chant·er /chántər/ *n. Mus.* the melody pipe, with finger holes, of a bagpipe.

chan·teuse /shaantőz/ *n.* a female singer of popular songs.

chant·ey /shántee, chán–/ *n.* (also **chant·y, shan·ty**) (*pl.* **chanteys, ·ies**) (in full **sea chantey**) a song with alternating solo and chorus, of a kind orig. sung by sailors while hauling ropes, etc.

Chan·til·ly /shantílee, shóNteeyée/ *n.* **1** a delicate kind of bobbin lace. **2** sweetened or flavored whipped cream.

chant·y var. of CHANTEY.

Cha·nuk·kah var. of HANUKKAH.

cha·os /káyos/ *n.* **1 a** utter confusion. **b** *Math.* the unpredictable and apparently random behavior of a deterministic system that is extremely sensitive to infinitesimal changes in initial parameters. **2** the formless matter supposed to have existed before the creation of the universe. □□ **cha·ot·ic** /kayótik/ *adj.* **cha·ot·i·cal·ly** *adv.*

chap[1] /chap/ *v.* & *n.* •*v.* (**chapped, chapping**) **1** *intr.* (esp. of the skin; also of dry ground, etc.) crack in fissures, esp. because of exposure and dryness. **2** *tr.* (of the wind, cold, etc.) cause to chap. •*n.* (usu. in *pl.*) **1** a crack in the skin. **2** an open seam.

chap[2] /chap/ *n.* esp. *Brit. colloq.* a man; a boy; a fellow.

chap·ar·ral /shápərál, cháp–/ *n.* dense, tangled brushwood; undergrowth.

chape /chayp/ *n.* **1** the metal cap of a scabbard point. **2** the back piece of a buckle attaching it to a strap, etc. **3** a sliding loop on a belt or strap.

chap·el /chápəl/ *n.* **1 a** a place for private Christian worship in a large church or esp. a cathedral, with its own altar and dedication. **b** a place of Christian worship attached to a private house or institution. **2** a building or room in which funeral services are held. **3** *Brit.* a place of worship for certain Protestant denominations. **4** an Anglican church subordinate to a parish church. **5** the members or branch of a printers' union.

chap·er·on /shápərōn/ *n.* & *v.* (also **chap·er·one**) •*n.* **1** a person, esp. an older woman, who ensures propriety by accompanying a young unmarried woman on social occasions. **2** a person who takes charge of esp. young people in public. •*v.tr.* act as a chaperon to. □□ **chap·er·on·age** /shápərōnij/ *n.*

chap·lain /cháplin/ *n.* a member of the clergy attached to a private chapel, institution, ship, regiment, etc. □□ **chap·lain·cy** *n.* (*pl.* **·cies**).

chap·let /cháplit/ *n.* **1** a garland or circlet for the head.

2 a string of 55 beads (one-third of the rosary number) for counting prayers, or as a necklace. **3** a bead molding. ▫▫ **chap·let·ed** *adj.*

chaps /chaps/ *n.pl.* a cowboy's leather leggings worn over the trousers as protection for the front of the legs.

chap·ter /cháptər/ *n.* **1** a main division of a book. **2** a period of time (in a person's life, a nation's history, etc.). **3** a series or sequence (*a chapter of misfortunes*). **4 a** the canons of a cathedral or other religious community or knightly order. **b** a meeting of these. **5** *Brit.* an Act of Parliament numbered as part of a session's proceedings. **6** a local branch of a society. ▫ **chapter and verse** an exact reference or authority.

chap·ter house *n.* a building used for the meetings of a chapter.

char[1] /chaar/ *v.tr. & intr.* (**charred, charring**) **1** make or become black by burning; scorch. **2** burn or be burned to charcoal.

char[2] /chaar/ *n. & v. Brit. colloq.* •*n.* = CHARWOMAN. •*v.intr.* (**charred, charring**) work as a charwoman.

char[3] /chaar/ *n.* (also **charr**) (*pl.* same) any small troutlike fish of the genus *Salvelinus*.

char·a·banc /shárəbang/ *n. Brit. hist.* an early form of tour bus.

char·ac·ter /káriktər/ *n. & v.* •*n.* **1** the collective qualities or characteristics, esp. mental and moral, that distinguish a person or thing. **2 a** moral strength (*has a weak character*). **b** reputation, esp. good reputation. **3 a** a person in a novel, play, etc. **b** a part played by an actor; a role. **4** *colloq.* a person, esp. an eccentric or outstanding individual (*he's a real character*). **5 a** a printed or written letter, symbol, or distinctive mark (*Chinese characters*). **b** *Computing* any of a group of symbols representing a letter, etc. **6** a written description of a person's qualities; a testimonial. **7** a characteristic (esp. of a biological species). •*v.tr. archaic* inscribe; describe. ▫ **in** (or **out of**) **character** consistent (or inconsistent) with a person's character. ▫▫ **char·ac·ter·less** *adj.*

char·ac·ter·is·tic /káriktərístik/ *adj. & n.* •*adj.* typical; distinctive (*with characteristic expertise*). •*n.* **1** a characteristic feature or quality. **2** *Math.* the whole number or integral part of a logarithm. ▫▫ **char·ac·ter·is·ti·cal·ly** *adv.*

char·ac·ter·ize /káriktərīz/ *v.tr.* **1 a** describe the character of. **b** (foll. by *as*) describe as. **2** be characteristic of. **3** impart character to. ▫▫ **char·ac·ter·i·za·tion** *n.*

cha·rade /shəráyd/ *n.* **1 a** (usu. in *pl.*, treated as *sing.*) a game of guessing a word from a written or acted clue given for each syllable and for the whole. **b** one such clue. **2** an absurd pretense.

char·coal /chaárkōl/ *n.* **1 a** an amorphous form of carbon consisting of a porous black residue from partially burned wood, bones, etc. **b** a piece of this used for drawing. **2** a drawing in charcoal. **3** (in full **charcoal gray**) a dark gray color.

chard /chaard/ *n.* (in full **Swiss chard**) a kind of beet, *Beta vulgaris cicla*, with edible broad, white leafstalks and green leaves.

Char·don·nay /shaárd'náy/ *n.* **1** a variety of white grape used for making champagne and other wines. **2** the vine on which this grape grows. **3** a wine made from Chardonnay grapes.

charge /chaarj/ *v. & n.* •*v.* **1** *tr.* **a** ask (an amount) as a price (*charges $5 a ticket*). **b** ask (a person) for an amount as a price (*you forgot to charge me*). **2** *tr.* **a** (foll. by *to, up to*) debit the cost of to (a person or account) (*charge it to my account; charge it up to me*). **b** debit (a person or an account) (*bought a new car and charged the company*). **3** *tr.* **a** (often foll. by *with*) accuse (of an offense) (*charged him with theft*). **b** (foll. by *that* + clause) make an accusation that. **4** *tr.* (foll. by *to* + infin.) instruct or urge. **5** (foll. by *with*) **a** *tr.* entrust with. **b** *refl.* undertake. **6 a** *intr.* make a rushing attack; rush headlong. **b** *tr.* make a rushing attack on; throw oneself against. **7** *tr.* (often foll. by *up*) **a** give an electric charge to (a body). **b** store energy in (a battery). **8** *tr.* (often foll. by *with*) load or fill (a vessel, gun, etc.) to the full or proper extent. **9** *tr.* (usu. as **charged** *adj.*) **a** (foll. by *with*) saturated with (*air charged with vapor*). **b** (usu. foll. by *with*) pervaded (with strong feelings, etc.) (*atmosphere charged with emotion; a charged atmosphere*). •*n.* **1 a** a price asked for goods or services. **b** a financial liability or commitment. **2** an accusation, esp. against a prisoner brought to trial. **3 a** a task, duty, or commission. **b** care, custody, responsible possession. **c** a person or thing entrusted; a minister's congregation. **4 a** an impetuous rush or attack, esp. in a battle. **b** the signal for this. **5** the appropriate amount of material to be put into a receptacle, mechanism, etc., at one time, esp. of explosive for a gun. **6 a** a property of matter that is a consequence of the interaction between its constituent particles and exists in a positive or negative form, causing electrical phenomena. **b** the quantity of this carried by a body. **c** energy stored chemically for conversion into electricity. **d** the process of charging a battery. **7** an exhortation; directions; orders. **8** a burden or load. **9** *Heraldry* a device; a bearing. ▫ **free of charge** gratis. **in charge** having command. **take charge** (often foll. by *of*) assume control or direction. ▫▫ **charge·a·ble** *adj.*

charge ac·count *n.* a credit account at a store, etc.

charge card *n.* a credit card for which the account must be paid in full when a statement is issued.

charg·er[1] /chaárjər/ *n.* **1 a** a cavalry horse. **b** *poet.* any horse. **2** an apparatus for charging a battery. **3** a person or thing that charges.

charg·er[2] /chaárjər/ *n.* a large, flat dish; a platter.

char·i·ot /cháreeət/ *n. & v.* •*n.* **1** *hist.* **a** a two-wheeled vehicle drawn by horses, used in ancient warfare and racing. **b** a four-wheeled carriage with back seats only. **2** *poet.* a stately or triumphal vehicle. •*v.tr. literary* convey in or as in a chariot.

chariot

char·i·ot·eer /cháreeətéer/ *n.* a chariot driver.

cha·ris·ma /kərízmə/ *n.* (*pl.* **charismata** /–mətə/) the ability to inspire followers with devotion and enthusiasm.

char·is·mat·ic /kárizmátik/ *adj.* **1** having charisma; inspiring enthusiasm. **2** (of Christian worship) characterized by spontaneity, ecstatic utterances, etc. ▫▫ **char·is·mat·i·cal·ly** *adv.*

char·is·mat·ic move·ment *n.* a fundamentalist Christian movement emphasizing talents thought to be conferred by the Holy Spirit, such as speaking in tongues and healing of the sick.

char·i·ta·ble /cháritəbəl/ *adj.* **1** generous in giving to those in need. **2** of, relating to, or connected with a charity or charities. **3** apt to judge favorably of persons, acts, and motives. ▫▫ **char·i·ta·ble·ness** *n.* **char·i·ta·bly** *adv.*

char·i·ty /cháritee/ *n.* (*pl.* **·ties**) **1 a** giving voluntarily to those in need; almsgiving. **b** the help, esp. money, so given. **2** an institution or organization for helping those in need. **3 a** kindness; benevolence. **b** tolerance in judging others. **c** love of one's fellow men.

char·la·dy /chaárlaydee/ *n.* (*pl.* **·dies**) = CHARWOMAN.

char·la·tan /shaárlətən/ *n.* a person falsely claiming a special knowledge or skill. ▫▫ **char·la·tan·ism** *n.* **char·la·tan·ry** *n.*

Charles·ton /chaárlstən/ *n.* & *v.* •*n.* a lively American dance of the 1920s with side kicks from the knee. •*v.intr.* dance the Charleston.

char·ley horse /chaárlee/ *n. sl.* stiffness or cramp in an arm or leg.

charm /chaarm/ *n.* & *v.* •*n.* **1 a** the power or quality of giving delight or arousing admiration. **b** fascination; attractiveness. **c** (usu. in *pl.*) an attractive or enticing quality. **2** a trinket on a bracelet, etc. **3 a** an object, act, or word(s) supposedly having occult or magic power; a spell. **b** a thing worn to avert evil, etc.; an amulet. **4** *Physics* a property of matter manifested by some elementary particles. •*v.tr.* **1** delight; captivate (*charmed by the performance*). **2** influence or protect as if by magic (*leads a charmed life*). **3 a** gain by charm (*charmed agreement out of him*). **b** influence by charm (*charmed her into consenting*). **4** cast a spell on; bewitch. ▫ **like a charm** perfectly; wonderfully (*worked like a charm; fits like a charm*). ▫▫ **charm·er** *n.* **charm·less** *adj.*

charm·ing /chaárming/ *adj.* **1** delightful; attractive; pleasing. **2** (often as *int.*) *iron.* expressing displeasure or disapproval. ▫▫ **charm·ing·ly** *adv.*

char·nel house /chaárnəlhows/ *n.* a house or vault in which dead bodies or bones are piled.

chart /chaart/ *n.* & *v.* •*n.* **1** a geographical map or plan, esp. for navigation by sea or air. **2** a sheet of information in the form of a table, graph, or diagram. **3** (usu. in *pl.*) *colloq.* a listing of the currently most popular music recordings. •*v.tr.* make a chart of; map.

chart·bust·er /chaártbustər/ *n. colloq.* a best-selling popular song, recording, etc.

char·ter /chaártər/ *n.* & *v.* •*n.* **1 a** a written grant of rights, by the sovereign or legislature, esp. the creation of a borough, company, university, etc. **b** a written constitution or description of an organization's functions, etc. **2** a contract to hire an aircraft, ship, etc., for a special purpose. •*v.tr.* **1** grant a charter to. **2** hire (an aircraft, ship, etc.). ▫▫ **char·ter·er** *n.*

char·ter mem·ber *n.* an original member of a society, corporation, etc.

Chart·ism /chaártizəm/ *n. hist.* the principles of the UK Parliamentary reform movement of 1837–48. ▫▫ **Chart·ist** *n.*

char·treuse /shaartrṓoz, –trṓos/ *n.* **1** (**Chartreuse**) a pale green or yellow liqueur of brandy and aromatic herbs, etc. **2** the pale yellow or pale green color of this.

char·wom·an /chaárwŏŏmən/ *n.* (*pl.* **·women**) a woman employed as a cleaner in houses or offices.

char·y /cháiree/ *adj.* (**charier, chariest**) **1** cautious; wary (*chary of employing such people*). **2** sparing; ungenerous (*chary of giving praise*). **3** shy. ▫▫ **char·i·ly** *adv.* **char·i·ness** *n.*

chase[1] /chays/ *v.* & *n.* •*v.* **1** *tr.* pursue in order to catch. **2** *tr.* (foll. by *from, out of, to,* etc.) drive. **3** *intr.* **a** (foll. by *after*) hurry in pursuit of (a person). **b** (foll. by *around,* etc.) *colloq.* act or move about hurriedly. **4** *tr. Brit.* (usu. foll. by *up*) *colloq.* pursue (overdue work, payment, etc., or the person responsible for it). **5** *tr. colloq.* **a** try to attain. **b** court persistently and openly. •*n.* **1** pursuit. **2** *Brit.* unenclosed hunting land. **3** (prec. by *the*) hunting, esp. as a sport. **4** = STEEPLECHASE.

chase[2] /chays/ *v.tr.* emboss or engrave (metal).

chase[3] /chays/ *n.* **1** the part of a gun enclosing the bore. **2** a trench or groove cut to receive a pipe, etc.

chas·er /cháysər/ *n.* **1** a person or thing that chases. **2** a horse for steeplechasing. **3** *colloq.* a drink taken after another of a different kind, e.g., beer after liquor.

chasm /kázəm/ *n.* **1** a deep fissure or opening in the earth, rock, etc. **2** a wide difference of feeling, interests, etc.; a gulf. **3** *archaic* a hiatus. ▫▫ **chas·mic** *adj.*

chas·sé /shasáy/ *n.* & *v.* •*n.* a gliding step in dancing. •*v.intr.* (**chasséd; chasséing**) make this step.

chas·sis /shásee, chás–/ *n.* (*pl.* same /–siz/) **1** the base frame of a motor vehicle, carriage, etc. **2** a frame to carry radio, etc., components.

chaste /chayst/ *adj.* **1** abstaining from extramarital, or from all, sexual intercourse. **2** (of behavior, speech, etc.) pure, virtuous, decent. ▫▫ **chaste·ly** *adv.* **chaste·ness** *n.*

chas·ten /cháysən/ *v.tr.* **1** (esp. as **chastening, chastened** *adjs.*) subdue; restrain (*a chastening experience; chastened by his failure*). **2** discipline; punish. **3** moderate. ▫▫ **chas·ten·er** *n.*

chas·tise /chastíz, chástīz/ *v.tr.* **1** rebuke or reprimand severely. **2** punish, esp. by beating. ▫▫ **chas·tise·ment** *n.* **chas·tis·er** *n.*

chas·ti·ty /chástitee/ *n.* **1** being chaste. **2** sexual abstinence; virginity. **3** simplicity of style or taste.

chas·ti·ty belt *n. hist.* a garment designed to prevent a woman from having sexual intercourse.

chas·u·ble /cházəbəl, cházyə–, chás–/ *n.* a loose, sleeveless, often ornate outer vestment worn by a priest celebrating Mass or the Eucharist.

chat /chat/ *v.* & *n.* •*v.intr.* (**chatted, chatting**) talk in a light familiar way. •*n.* **1** informal conversation or talk. **2** an instance of this.

châ·teau /shatṓ/ *n.* (*pl.* **châteaus** or **châteaux** /–tṓz/) a large French country house or castle, often giving its name to wine made in its neighborhood.

cha·teau·bri·and /shatṓbreé–óN/ *n.* a thick fillet of beef steak usu. served with a béarnaise sauce.

chat·e·laine /shát'layn/ *n.* the mistress of a large house.

chat·tel /chát'l/ *n.* (usu. in *pl.*) a moveable possession; any possession or piece of property other than real estate or a freehold. ▫ **goods and chattels** personal possessions.

chat·ter /chátər/ *v.* & *n.* •*v.intr.* **1** talk quickly, incessantly, trivially, or indiscreetly. **2** (of a bird) emit short, quick notes. **3** (of the teeth) click repeatedly together (usu. from cold). •*n.* chattering talk or sounds. ▫▫ **chat·ter·er** *n.* **chat·ter·y** *adj.*

chat·ter·box /chátərboks/ *n.* a talkative person.

chat·ty /chátee/ *adj.* (**chattier, chattiest**) **1** fond of chatting; talkative. **2** resembling chat; informal and lively (*a chatty letter*). ▫▫ **chat·ti·ly** *adv.* **chat·ti·ness** *n.*

chauf·feur /shṓfər, –fṓr/ *n.* & *v.* •*n.* (*fem.* **chauffeuse** /–fṓz/) a person employed to drive a private or rented automobile or limousine. •*v.tr.* drive (a car or a person) as a chauffeur.

chau·vin·ism /shṓvinizəm/ *n.* **1** exaggerated or aggressive patriotism. **2** excessive or prejudiced support or loyalty for one's cause or group or sex (*male chauvinism*).

chau·vin·ist /shṓvinist/ *n.* **1** a person exhibiting chauvinism. **2** (in full **male chauvinist**) a man showing excessive loyalty to men and prejudice against women. ▫▫ **chau·vin·is·tic** /–nístik/ *adj.* **chau·vin·is·ti·cal·ly** /–nístikəlee/ *adv.*

Ch.E. *abbr.* chemical engineer.

cheap /cheep/ *adj.* & *adv.* •*adj.* **1** low in price; worth more than its cost (*a cheap vacation; cheap labor*). **2** charging low prices; offering good value (*a cheap restaurant*). **3** of poor quality; inferior (*cheap housing*). **4 a** costing little effort or acquired by discreditable means and hence of little worth (*cheap popularity; a cheap joke*). **b** contemptible; despicable (*a cheap crim-*

inal). • *adv.* cheaply (*got it cheap*). □ **feel cheap** feel ashamed or contemptible. **on the cheap** cheaply. □□ **cheap·ish** *adj.* **cheap·ly** *adv.* **cheap·ness** *n.*

cheap·en /chéepən/ *v.tr. & intr.* make or become cheap or cheaper; depreciate; degrade.

cheap·skate /chéepskayt/ *n. colloq.* a stingy person.

cheat /cheet/ *v. & n.* • *v.* **1** *tr.* **a** (often foll. by *into, out of*) deceive or trick (*cheated into parting with his savings*). **b** (foll. by *of*) deprive of (*cheated of a chance to reply*). **2** *intr.* gain unfair advantage by deception or breaking rules, esp. in a game or examination. **3** *tr.* avoid (something undesirable) by luck or skill (*cheated the bad weather*). **4** *tr. archaic* divert attention from; beguile (time, tedium, etc.). • *n.* **1** a person who cheats. **2** a trick, fraud, or deception. **3** an act of cheating. □ **cheat on** *colloq.* be sexually unfaithful to. □□ **cheat·ing·ly** *adv.*

cheat·er /chéetər/ *n.* **1** a person who cheats. **2** (in *pl.*) *sl.* eyeglasses.

check[1] /chek/ *v., n., & int.* • *v.* **1** *tr.* (also *absol.*) **a** examine the accuracy, quality, or condition of. **b** (often foll. by *that* + clause) make sure; verify; establish to one's satisfaction (*checked that the doors were locked; checked the train times*). **2** *tr.* **a** stop or slow the motion of; curb; restrain (*progress was checked by bad weather*). **b** *colloq.* find fault with; rebuke. **3** *tr. Chess* move a piece into a position that directly threatens (the opposing king). **4** *intr.* agree or correspond when compared. **5** *tr.* mark with a check mark, etc. **6** *tr.* deposit (luggage, etc.) for storage or dispatch. **7** *intr.* (of hounds) pause to ensure or regain scent. • *n.* **1** a means or act of testing or ensuring accuracy, quality, satisfactory condition, etc. **2 a** a stopping or slowing of motion; a restraint on action. **b** a rebuff or rebuke. **c** a person or thing that restrains. **3** *Chess* (also as *int.*) **a** the exposure of a king to direct attack from an opposing piece. **b** an announcement of this by the attacking player. **4** a bill in a restaurant. **5** a token of identification for left luggage, etc. **6** *Cards* a counter used in various games, esp. a poker chip. **7** a temporary loss of the scent in hunting. **8** a crack or flaw in lumber. **9** = CHECK MARK. *int.* expressing assent or agreement. □ **check in 1** arrive or register at a hotel, airport, etc. **2** record the arrival of. **check into** register one's arrival at (a hotel, etc.). **check off** mark on a list, etc., as having been examined or dealt with. **check on** examine carefully or in detail; ascertain the truth about; keep a watch on (a person, work done, etc.). **check out 1** (often foll. by *of*) leave a hotel, etc., with due formalities. **2** *colloq.* investigate; examine for authenticity or suitability. **check over** examine for errors; verify. **check through** inspect or examine exhaustively; verify successive items of. **check up** ascertain; verify; make sure. **check up on** = *check on*. **in check** under control; restrained. □□ **check·a·ble** *adj.*

check[2] /chek/ *n.* **1** a pattern of small squares. **2** fabric having this pattern.

check[3] /chek/ *n.* (*Brit.* **cheque**) **1** a written order to a bank to pay the stated sum from the drawer's account. **2** the printed form on which such an order is written.

check·book /chékbo͝ok/ *n.* a book of blank checks with a register for recording checks written.

checked /chekt/ *adj.* having a pattern of small squares.

check·er[1] /chékər/ *n.* **1** a person or thing that verifies or examines, esp. in a factory, etc. **2** a cashier in a supermarket, etc.

check·er[2] /chékər/ *n. & v.* (*Brit.* **chequer**) • *n.* **1** (often in *pl.*) a pattern of squares often alternately colored. **2 a** (in *pl.*) a game for two played with 12 pieces each on a checkerboard. **b** each of the usu. red or black disk-shaped playing pieces in a game of checkers. • *v.tr.* **1** mark with checkers. **2** variegate; break the uniformity of. **3** (as **checkered** *adj.*) with varied fortunes (*a checkered career*).

check·er·board /chékərbawrd/ *n.* **1** a checkered board, identical to a chessboard, used in the game of checkers. **2** a pattern or design resembling it.

check·ing ac·count /chéking/ *n.* an account at a bank against which checks can be drawn by the account depositor.

check mark *n.* a mark (√) to denote correctness, check items, etc.

check·mate /chékmayt/ *n. & v.* • *n.* **1** (also as *int.*) *Chess* **a** check from which a king cannot escape. **b** an announcement of this. **2** a final defeat or deadlock. • *v.tr.* **1** *Chess* put into checkmate. **2** defeat; frustrate.

check·out /chékowt/ *n.* **1** an act of checking out. **2** a point at which goods are paid for in a supermarket, etc.

check·point /chékpoynt/ *n.* a place, esp. a barrier or manned entrance, where documents, vehicles, etc., are inspected.

check·rein /chékrayn/ *n.* a rein attaching one horse's rein to another's bit, or preventing a horse from lowering its head.

check·up /chékup/ *n.* a thorough (esp. medical) examination.

ched·dar /chédər/ *n.* (in full **cheddar cheese**) a kind of firm smooth cheese orig. made in Cheddar in S. England.

cheek /cheek/ *n. & v.* • *n.* **1 a** the side of the face below the eye. **b** the side wall of the mouth. **2** esp. *Brit.* impertinence; cool confidence (*had the cheek to ask for more*). **3** *sl.* either buttock. **4 a** either of the side posts of a door, etc. **b** either of the sidepieces of various parts of machines arranged in lateral pairs. • *v.tr.* speak impertinently to. □ **cheek by jowl** close together; intimate. **turn the other cheek** accept attack, etc., meekly; refuse to retaliate.

cheek·bone /chéekbōn/ *n.* the bone below the eye.

cheek·y /chéekee/ *adj.* (**cheekier, cheekiest**) impertinent; impudent. □□ **cheek·i·ly** *adv.* **cheek·i·ness** *n.*

cheep /cheep/ *n. & v.* • *n.* the weak shrill cry of a young bird. • *v.intr.* make such a cry.

cheer /cheer/ *n. & v.* • *n.* **1** a shout of encouragement or applause. **2** mood; disposition (*full of good cheer*). **3** cheerfulness; joy. **4** (in *pl.*; as *int.*) *colloq.* **a** expressing good wishes on parting. **b** expressing good wishes before drinking. **c** expressing gratitude. • *v.* **1** *tr.* **a** applaud with shouts. **b** (usu. foll. by *on*) urge or encourage with shouts. **2** *intr.* shout for joy. **3** *tr.* gladden; comfort. □ **cheer up** make or become less depressed.

cheer·ful /chéerfo͝ol/ *adj.* **1** in good spirits; noticeably happy (*a cheerful disposition*). **2** bright; pleasant (*a cheerful room*). **3** willing; not reluctant. □□ **cheer·ful·ly** *adv.* **cheer·ful·ness** *n.*

cheer·lead·er /chéerleedər/ *n.* a person who leads cheers of applause, etc., esp. at a sports event.

cheer·less /chéerlis/ *adj.* gloomy; dreary; miserable. □□ **cheer·less·ly** *adv.* **cheer·less·ness** *n.*

cheer·y /chéeree/ *adj.* (**cheerier, cheeriest**) lively; in good spirits; genial; cheering. □□ **cheer·i·ly** *adv.* **cheer·i·ness** *n.*

cheese[1] /cheez/ *n.* **1 a** a food made from the pressed curds of milk. **b** a complete cake of this with rind. **2** *Brit.* a conserve having the consistency of soft cheese (*lemon cheese*).

cheese[2] /cheez/ *n.* (also **big cheese**) *sl.* an important person.

cheese·burg·er /chéezbərgər/ *n.* a hamburger with cheese on it.

cheese·cake /chéezkayk/ *n.* **1** a rich dessert cake made with cream cheese, etc. **2** *sl.* the portrayal of women in a sexually attractive manner.

cheese·cloth /chéezklawth, –kloth/ *n.* thin loosely woven cloth, used orig. for wrapping cheese.
chees·y /chéezee/ *adj.* (**cheesier**, **cheesiest**) **1** like cheese in taste, smell, appearance, etc. **2** *sl.* inferior; cheap and nasty. ▫▫ **chees·i·ness** *n.*
chee·tah /chéetə/ *n.* a swift-running feline, *Acinonyx jubatus*, with a leopardlike spotted coat.
chef /shef/ *n.* a cook, esp. the chief cook in a restaurant, etc.
chef d'oeu·vre /shaydṓvrə/ *n.* (*pl.* **chefs d'oeuvre** *pronunc.* same) a masterpiece.
cheiro- *comb. form* var. of CHIRO-.
che·la[1] /kéelə/ *n.* (*pl.* **chelae** /–lee/) a prehensile claw of crabs, lobsters, scorpions, etc.
che·la[2] /cháylə/ *n.* **1** (in esoteric Buddhism) a novice qualifying for initiation. **2** a disciple; a pupil.
che·late /kéelayt/ *n.* & *adj.* • *n.* *Chem.* a usu. organometallic compound containing a bonded ring of atoms including a metal atom. • *adj.* **1** *Chem.* of a chelate. **2** *Zool.* & *Anat.* of or having chelae.
che·lo·ni·an /kilṓneeən/ *n.* & *adj.* • *n.* any reptile of the order Chelonia, including turtles, terrapins, and tortoises, having a shell of bony plates covered with horny scales. • *adj.* of or relating to this order.
chem. *abbr.* **1** chemical. **2** chemist. **3** chemistry.
chemi- *comb. form* var. of CHEMO-.
chem·i·cal /kémikəl/ *adj.* & *n.* • *adj.* of, made by, or employing chemistry or chemicals. • *n.* a substance obtained or used in chemistry. ▫▫ **chem·i·cal·ly** *adv.*
chem·i·cal war·fare *n.* warfare using poison gas and other chemicals.
chemico- /kémikō/ *comb. form* chemical; chemical and (*chemico-physical*).
chem·i·lum·i·nes·cence /kémilōōminésəns/ *n.* the emission of light during a chemical reaction. ▫▫ **chem·i·lu·mi·nes·cent** /–nésənt/ *adj.*
che·mise /shəméez/ *n. hist.* a woman's loose-fitting undergarment or dress hanging straight from the shoulders.
chem·i·sorp·tion /kémisáwrpshən/ *n.* adsorption by chemical bonding.
chem·ist /kémist/ *n.* **1** a person practicing or trained in chemistry. **2** *Brit.* **a** a dealer in medicinal drugs, usu. also selling other medical goods and toiletries. **b** an authorized dispenser of medicines.
chem·is·try /kémistree/ *n.* (*pl.* **·tries**) **1** the study of the elements and the compounds they form and the reactions they undergo. **2** any complex (esp. emotional) change or process (*the chemistry of fear*). **3** *colloq.* a person's personality or temperament.
chemo- /kéemō/ *comb.* form (also **chemi-** /kémee/) chemical.
che·mo·syn·the·sis /kéemōsínthisis/ *n.* the synthesis of organic compounds by energy derived from chemical reactions.
che·mo·ther·a·py /kéemōthérəpee/ *n.* the treatment of disease, esp. cancer, by use of chemical substances. ▫▫ **che·mo·ther·a·pist** *n.*
chem·ur·gy /kémərjee, kimə́r–/ *n.* the chemical and industrial use of organic raw materials. ▫▫ **chem·ur·gic** /–ə́rjik/ *adj.*
che·nille /shənéel/ *n.* **1** a tufty, velvety cord or yarn, used in trimming furniture, etc. **2** fabric made from this.
cheong·sam /chawngsám/ *n.* a Chinese woman's garment with a high neck and slit skirt.
cheque *Brit.* var. of CHECK[3].
cheq·uer *Brit.* var. of CHECKER[2].
cher·ish /chérish/ *v.tr.* **1** protect or tend (a child, plant, etc.) lovingly. **2** hold dear; cling to (hopes, feelings, etc.).
Cher·o·kee /chérəkee/ *n.* & *adj.* • *n.* **1 a** a N. American people formerly inhabiting much of the southern US. **b** an individual of this people. **2** the language of this people. • *adj.* of or relating to the Cherokees or their language.
che·root /shərṓōt/ *n.* a cigar with both ends open.
cher·ry /chéree/ *n.* & *adj.* • *n.* (*pl.* **·ries**) **1 a** a small, soft, round stone fruit. **b** any of several trees of the genus *Prunus* bearing this or grown for its ornamental flowers. **2** (in full **cherry wood**) the wood of a cherry. **3** *coarse sl.* **a** hymen. **b** virginity. • *adj.* of a light red color.
cher·ry pick·er *n. colloq.* a hydraulic crane with a platform or bucket attached, for raising and lowering people for work on telephone cables, power lines, etc.
cher·ry to·ma·to *n.* a miniature tomato.
cher·so·nese /kə́rsəneez, –nees/ *n.* a peninsula, esp. the Thracian peninsula west of the Hellespont.
cher·ub /chérəb/ *n.* **1** (*pl.* **cherubim** /–bim/) an angelic being of the second order of the celestial hierarchy. **2** (*pl.* usu. **cherubs**) **a** a representation of a winged child or the head of a winged child. **b** a beautiful or innocent child. ▫▫ **che·ru·bic** /chirṓōbik/ *adj.* **che·ru·bi·cal·ly** /chirṓōbikəlee/ *adv.*
cher·vil /chə́rvil/ *n.* an umbelliferous plant, *Anthriscus cerefolium*, with small white flowers, used as an herb for flavoring.
Chesh·ire /chéshər/ *n.* (in full **Cheshire cheese**) a kind of firm crumbly cheese, orig. made in Cheshire. ▫ **like a Cheshire cat** with a broad fixed grin.
chess /ches/ *n.* a game for two with 16 pieces each, played on a chessboard.
chess·board /chésbawrd/ *n.* a checkered board of 64 squares on which chess and checkers are played.
chess·man /chésman, –mən/ *n.* (*pl.* **·men**) a piece used in playing chess.
chest /chest/ *n.* **1** a large strong box, esp. for storage or transport. **2 a** the part of a human or animal body enclosed by the ribs. **b** the front surface of the body from neck to waist. **3** a small cabinet for medicines, toiletries, etc. **4 a** the treasury or financial resources of an institution. **b** the money available from it. ▫ **get a thing off one's chest** *colloq.* disclose a fact, secret, etc., to relieve one's anxiety about it; say what is on one's mind. **play one's cards close to one's chest** *colloq.* be cautious or secretive about. ▫▫ **-chest·ed** *adj.* (in *comb.*).
ches·ter·field /chéstərfeeld/ *n.* **1** a sofa with arms and back of the same height and curved outward at the top. **2** (also **Ches·ter·field**) a plain overcoat usu. with a velvet collar.
chest·nut /chésnut/ *n.* & *adj.* • *n.* **1 a** a glossy, hard, brown edible nut. **b** the tree *Castanea sativa*, bearing flowers in catkins and nuts enclosed in a spiny fruit. **2** any other tree of the genus *Castanea*, esp. the American chestnut *C. dentata*. **3** = HORSE CHESTNUT. **4** (in full **chestnut wood**) the heavy wood of any chestnut tree. **5** a horse of a reddish-brown or yellowish-brown color. **6** *colloq.* a stale joke or anecdote. **7** a small hard patch on a horse's leg. **8** a reddish-brown color. • *adj.* of the color chestnut.
chest·y /chéstee/ *adj.* (**chestier, chestiest**) **1** *colloq.* having a large chest or prominent breasts. **2** *sl.* arrogant.
Chet·nik /chétnik/ *n. hist.* a member of a guerrilla force in the Balkans, esp. during World Wars I and II.
che·val glass /shəválglas/ *n.* a tall mirror swung on an upright frame.
chev·a·lier /shévəléer/ *n.* **1 a** a member of certain orders of knighthood, and of modern French orders, as the Legion of Honor. **b** *archaic* or *hist.* a knight. **2** *Brit. hist.* the title of James and Charles Stuart, pretenders to the British throne.

che·vet /shəváy/ *n.* the apsidal end of a church, sometimes with an attached group of apses.
chè·vre /shévrə/ *n.* a variety of goat cheese.
chev·ron /shévrən/ *n.* **1** a badge in a V shape on the sleeve of a uniform indicating rank or length of service. **2** *Heraldry & Archit.* a bent bar of an inverted V shape. **3** any V-shaped line or stripe.

chevron

chev·ro·tain /shévrətayn/ *n.* (also **chev·ro·tin** /–tin/) any small deerlike animal of the family Tragulidae, native to Africa and SE Asia, having small tusks. Also called MOUSE DEER.
chew /choo/ *v. & n.* • *v.tr.* (also *absol.*) work (food, etc.) between the teeth; crush or indent with the teeth. • *n.* **1** an act of chewing. **2** something for chewing, esp. a chewy candy. □ **chew the cud** reflect; ruminate. **chew the fat** (or **rag**) *sl.* **1** chat. **2** grumble. **chew on 1** work continuously between the teeth (*chewed on a piece of string*). **2** think about; meditate on. **chew out** *colloq.* reprimand. **chew over 1** discuss; talk over. **2** think about; meditate on. □□ **chew·a·ble** *adj.* **chew·er** *n.*
chew·ing gum *n.* flavored gum for chewing, typically sold in packets of individually wrapped thin strips.
chew·y /chóoee/ *adj.* (**chewier, chewiest**) **1** needing much chewing. **2** suitable for chewing. □□ **chew·i·ness** *n.*
Chey·enne /shīán, –én/ *n. & adj.* • *n.* **1 a** a N. American people formerly living between the Missouri and Arkansas rivers. **b** a member of this people. **2** the language of this people. • *adj.* of or relating to the Cheyenne or their language.
chi /kī/ *n.* the twenty-second letter of the Greek alphabet (Χ, χ).
Chi·an·ti /keeaántee, keeán–/ *n.* (*pl.* **Chiantis**) a dry, red Italian wine.
chi·a·ro·scu·ro /keeaárəskóorō/ *n.* **1** the treatment of light and shade in drawing and painting. **2** the use of contrast in literature, etc. **3** (*attrib.*) half-revealed.
chic /sheek/ *adj. & n.* • *adj.* (**chicer, chicest**) stylish; elegant (in dress or appearance). • *n.* stylishness; elegance. □□ **chic·ly** *adv.*
chi·cane /shikáyn/ *n. & v.* • *n.* **1** chicanery. **2** an artificial barrier or obstacle on an automobile racecourse. **3** *Bridge* a hand without trumps, or without cards of one suit. • *v. archaic* **1** *intr.* use chicanery. **2** *tr.* (usu. foll. by *into*, *out of*, etc.) cheat (a person).
chi·can·er·y /shikáynəree/ *n.* (*pl.* **·ies**) **1** clever but misleading talk; a false argument. **2** trickery; deception.
Chi·ca·no /chikaánō/ *n.* (*pl.* **·nos**; *fem.* **Chicana**, *pl.* **·nas**) an American of Mexican origin.
chi·chi /shéeshee/ *adj. & n.* • *adj.* **1** (of a thing) frilly; showy. **2** (of a person or behavior) fussy; affected. • *n.* **1** overrefinement; pretentiousness; fussiness. **2** a frilly, showy, or pretentious object.
chick /chik/ *n.* **1** a young bird, esp. one newly hatched. **2** *sl.* a young woman.
chick·a·dee /chíkədee/ *n.* any of various small birds of the titmouse family, esp. *Parus atricapillus* with a distinctive black crown and throat.
Chick·a·saw /chíkəsaw/ *n.* **1 a** a N. American people native to Mississippi and Alabama. **b** a member of this people. **2** the language of this people.
chick·en /chíkin/ *n., adj., & v.* • *n.* (*pl.* same or **chickens**) **1** a common breed of domestic fowl. **2 a** a domestic fowl prepared as food. **b** its flesh. **3** *colloq.* a pastime testing courage, usu. recklessly. • *adj. colloq.* cowardly. • *v.intr.* (foll. by *out*) *colloq.* withdraw from or fail in some activity through fear or lack of nerve.
chick·en feed *n.* **1** food for poultry. **2** *colloq.* an unimportant amount, esp. of money.
chick·en·heart·ed /chíkinhaartəd/ *adj.* easily frightened; lacking nerve or courage.
chick·en pox *n.* an infectious disease, esp. of children, with a rash of small blisters. Also called **varicella**.
chick·en wire *n.* a light wire netting with a hexagonal mesh.
chick·pea /chíkpee/ *n.* **1** a leguminous plant, *Cicer arietinum*, with short, swollen pods containing yellow, beaked seeds. **2** this seed used as a vegetable.
chic·le /chíkəl/ *n.* the milky juice of the sapodilla tree, used in the manufacture of chewing gum.
chic·o·ry /chíkəree/ *n.* (*pl.* **·ries**) **1** a blue-flowered plant, *Cichorium intybus*, cultivated for its salad leaves and its root. **2** its root, roasted and ground for use with or instead of coffee. **3** = ENDIVE.
chide /chīd/ *v.tr. & intr.* (*past* **chided** or **chid** /chid/; *past part.* **chided** or **chid** or **chidden** /chíd'n/) *archaic* or *literary* scold; rebuke. □□ **chid·er** *n.* **chid·ing·ly** *adv.*
chief /cheef/ *n. & adj.* • *n.* **1 a** a leader or ruler. **b** the head of a tribe, clan, etc. **2** the head of a department; the highest official. **3** *Heraldry* the upper third of a shield. • *adj.* (usu. *attrib.*) **1** first in position, importance, influence, etc. (*chief engineer*). **2** prominent; leading. □□ **chief·dom** *n.*
chief ex·ec·u·tive of·fi·cer *n.* the highest ranking executive in a corporation, organization, etc. ¶ Abbr.: **CEO.**
chief jus·tice *n.* **1** the presiding judge in a court having several judges. **2** (**Chief Justice of the United States**) the presiding judge of the US Supreme Court.
chief·ly /chéeflee/ *adv.* above all; mainly but not exclusively.
chief of staff *n.* the senior staff officer of a service or command.
chief·tain /chéeftən/ *n.* (*fem.* **chieftainess** /–tənis/) the leader of a tribe, clan, etc. □□ **chief·tain·cy** /–tənsee/ *n.* (*pl.* **·cies**). **chief·tain·ship** *n.*
chif·fon /shifón, shífon/ *n. & adj.* • *n.* a light, diaphanous fabric of silk, nylon, etc. • *adj.* **1** made of chiffon. **2** (of a pie filling, dessert, etc.) light-textured.
chif·fo·nier /shífənéer/ *n.* **1** a tall chest of drawers. **2** a movable low cupboard with a sideboard top.
chig·ger /chígər/ *n.* **1** (also *chigoe*)a tropical parasitic flea of the genus *Tunga*. **2** any harvest mite of the genus *Leptotrombidium*, with parasitic larvae.
chi·gnon /shéenyon, sheenyón/ *n.* a coil or knot of hair worn at the back of the head.
chi·hua·hua /chiwaáwə/ *n.* a very small dog of a smooth-haired, large-eyed breed originating in Mexico.
chil·blain /chílblayn/ *n.* a painful, itchy swelling of the skin, usu. on a hand, foot, etc., caused by exposure to cold and by poor circulation. □□ **chil·blained** *adj.*
child /chīld/ *n.* (*pl.* **children** /chíldrən/) **1 a** a young human being below the age of puberty. **b** an unborn or newborn human being. **2** one's son or daughter (at any age). **3** (foll. by *of*) a descendant, follower, adherent, or product of (*children of Israel*; *child of God*; *child of nature*). **4** a childish person. □□ **child·less** *adj.* **child·less·ness** *n.*

child·bear·ing /chíldbairing/ *n.* the act of giving birth to a child or children.
child·birth /chíldbərth/ *n.* the act of giving birth to a child.
child care *n.* the care of children, esp. by someone other than a parent, as at a day-care center, etc.
child·hood /chíldhood/ *n.* the state or period of being a child.
child·ish /chíldish/ *adj.* **1** of, like, or proper to a child. **2** immature, silly. □□ **child·ish·ly** *adv.* **child·ish·ness** *n.*
child·like /chíldlīk/ *adj.* having the good qualities of a child as innocence, frankness, etc.
child·proof /chíldproof/ *adj.* that cannot be damaged nor operated by a child.
chil·dren *pl.* of CHILD.
Chil·e·an /chíleeən, chiláyən/ *n. & adj.* •*n.* **1** a native or national of Chile in S. America. **2** a person of Chilean descent. •*adj.* of or relating to Chile.
Chil·e salt·pe·ter /chílee/ *n.* (also **Chil·e ni·ter**) naturally occurring sodium nitrate.
chil·i /chílee/ *n.* (*pl.* **·ies**) a small, hot-tasting dried red pod of a capsicum, *Capsicum frutescens,* used as seasoning and in curry powder, cayenne pepper, etc.
chil·i·ad /kíleead/ *n.* **1** a thousand. **2** a thousand years.
chil·i·asm /kíleeazəm/ *n.* the doctrine of or belief in Christ's prophesied reign of 1,000 years on earth (see MILLENNIUM).
chil·i pow·der *n.* a powder made of dried chilies, garlic, herbs, spices, etc., used as a seasoning.
chill /chil/ *n., v., & adj.* •*n.* **1 a** an unpleasant cold sensation; lowered body temperature. **b** a feverish cold (*catch a chill*). **2** unpleasant coldness (of air, water, etc.). **3 a** a depressing influence (*cast a chill over*). **b** a feeling of fear or dread accompanied by coldness. **4** coldness of manner. •*v.* **1** *tr. & intr.* make or become cold. **2** *tr.* depress; dispirit. **3** *tr.* cool (food or drink); preserve by cooling. **4** *intr. sl.* = *chill out.* **5** *tr.* harden (molten metal) by contact with cold material. *adj.* = CHILLY. □ **chill out** become calm or less agitated. **take the chill off** warm slightly. □□ **chill·er** *n.* **chill·ing·ly** *adv.* **chill·ness** *n.*
chill·y /chílee/ *adj.* (**chillier, chilliest**) **1** (of the weather or an object) somewhat cold. **2** (of a person or animal) feeling somewhat cold; sensitive to the cold. **3** unfriendly; unemotional. □□ **chill·i·ness** *n.*
chime /chīm/ *n. & v.* •*n.* **1 a** a set of attuned bells. **b** the series of sounds given by this. **c** (usu. in *pl.*) a set of attuned bells as a door bell. **2** agreement; correspondence; harmony. •*v.* **1 a** *intr.* (of bells) ring. **b** *tr.* sound (a bell or chime) by striking. **2** *tr.* show (the hour) by chiming. **3** *intr.* (usu. foll. by *together, with*) be in agreement; harmonize. □ **chime in 1** interject a remark. **2** join in harmoniously. **3** (foll. by *with*) agree with. □□ **chim·er** *n.*
chi·me·ra /kīmeerə, kee–/ (also **chi·mae·ra**) *n.* **1** (in Greek mythology) a fire-breathing female monster with a lion's head, a goat's body, and a serpent's tail. **2** a fantastic or grotesque product of the imagination; a bogey. **3** any fabulous beast with parts taken from various animals. **4** *Biol.* **a** an organism containing genetically different tissues, formed by grafting, mutation, etc. **b** a nucleic acid formed by laboratory manipulation. □□ **chi·mer·ic** /–mérik/ *adj.* **chi·mer·i·cal** *adj.* **chi·mer·i·cal·ly** *adv.*
chim·ney /chímnee/ *n.* (*pl.* **·neys**) **1** a vertical channel conducting smoke or combustion gases, etc., up and away from a fire, furnace, etc. **2** the part of this that projects above a roof. **3** a glass tube protecting the flame of a lamp. **4** a narrow vertical crack in a rock face, often used by mountaineers to ascend.
chim·ney sweep *n.* a person whose job is removing soot from inside chimneys.
chimp /chimp/ *n. colloq.* = CHIMPANZEE.
chim·pan·zee /chímpanzeé, chimpánzee/ *n.* a small African anthropoid ape, *Pan troglodytes.*
chin /chin/ *n.* the front of the lower jaw. □ **chin up** *colloq.* cheer up. **keep one's chin up** *colloq.* remain cheerful, esp. in adversity. **take on the chin 1** suffer a severe blow from (a misfortune, etc.). **2** endure courageously. □□ **-chinned** *adj.* (in *comb.*).
chi·na /chínə/ *n. & adj.* •*n.* **1** a kind of fine white or translucent ceramic ware, porcelain, etc. **2** things made from ceramic, esp. household tableware. **3** *Brit. rhyming sl.* one's 'mate,' i.e., husband or wife (short for *china plate*). •*adj.* made of china.
chi·na clay *n.* kaolin.
Chi·na·town /chínətown/ *n.* a district of any non-Chinese city in which the population is predominantly Chinese.
chinch /chinch/ *n.* (in full **chinch bug**) **1** a small insect, *Blissus leucopterus,* that destroys the shoots of grasses and grains. **2** a bedbug.
chin·chil·la /chinchílə/ *n.* **1 a** any small rodent of the genus *Chinchilla,* native to S. America, having soft, silver-gray fur and a bushy tail. **b** its highly valued fur. **2** a breed of cat or rabbit.
chin-chin /chínchín/ *int. Brit. colloq.* a toast; a greeting or farewell.
chine /chīn/ *n. & v.* •*n.* **1 a** a backbone, esp. of an animal. **b** a joint of meat containing all or part of this. **2** a ridge or arête. •*v.tr.* cut (meat) across or along the backbone.
Chi·nese /chīneéz/ *adj. & n.* •*adj.* **1** of or relating to China. **2** of Chinese descent. •*n.* **1** the Chinese language. **2** (*pl.* same) **a** a native or national of China. **b** a person of Chinese descent.
Chi·nese cab·bage *n.* a lettucelike cabbage, *Brassica chinensis.*
Chi·nese lan·tern *n.* **1** a collapsible paper lantern. **2** a plant, *Physalis alkekengi,* bearing white flowers and globular orange fruits enclosed in an orange-red, papery calyx.
Chink /chingk/ *n. sl. offens.* a Chinese person. □□ **Chink·y** *adj.*
chink[1] /chingk/ *n.* **1** an unintended crack that admits light or allows an attack; a flaw. **2** a narrow opening; a slit.
chink[2] /chingk/ *v. & n.* •*v.* **1** *intr.* make a slight ringing sound, as of glasses or coins striking together. **2** *tr.* cause to make this sound. •*n.* this sound.
chin·less /chínlis/ *adj. colloq.* weak or feeble in character.
chi·no /cheénō/ *n.* (*pl.* **·nos**) **1** a cotton twill fabric, usu. khaki-colored. **2** (in *pl.*) a garment, esp. trousers, made from this.
Chino- /chínō/ *comb. form* = SINO-.
Chi·nook /shənóok, chə–/ *n.* **1 a** a N. American people native to the northwestern coast of the US. **b** a member of this people. **2** the language of this people and other nearby peoples. **3** (**chinook**) **a** a warm, dry wind that blows east of the Rocky Mountains. **b** a warm, wet southerly wind west of the Rocky Mountains. □□ **Chi·nook·an** *adj.*
chintz /chints/ *n. & adj.* •*n.* a printed, multicolored cotton fabric with a glazed finish. •*adj.* made from or upholstered with this fabric.
chintz·y /chíntsee/ *adj.* (**chintzier, chintziest**) **1** like chintz. **2** gaudy; cheap. **3** characteristic of the decor associated with chintz soft furnishings. □□ **chintz·i·ly** *adv.* **chintz·i·ness** *n.*
chin-up *n.* an exercise in which the chin is raised up to the level of an overhead horizontal bar that one grasps.

chip /chip/ *n. & v.* •*n.* **1** a small piece removed by or in the course of chopping, cutting, or breaking, esp. from hard material such as wood or stone. **2** the place where such a chip has been made. **3 a** = POTATO CHIP. **b** (usu. in *pl.*) a strip of potato, deep fried (*fish and chips*). **4** a counter used in some gambling games to represent money. **5** *Electronics* = MICROCHIP. **6** *Brit.* **a** a thin strip of wood, straw, etc., used for weaving hats, baskets, etc. **b** a basket made from these. **7** (in soccer, golf, and other sports) a short shot, kick, or pass with the ball describing an arc. •*v.* (**chipped, chipping**) **1** *tr.* (often foll. by *off, away*) cut or break (a piece) from a hard material. **2** *intr.* (foll. by *at, away at*) cut pieces off (a hard material) to alter its shape, break it up, etc. **3** *intr.* (of stone, china, etc.) be susceptible to being chipped; be apt to break at the edge (*will chip easily*). **4** *tr.* (also *absol.*) *Soccer, etc., & Golf* strike or kick (the ball) with a chip (cf. sense 7 of *n.*). **5** *tr.* (usu. as **chipped** *adj.*) cut into chips. □ **chip in** *colloq.* **1** interrupt or contribute abruptly to a conversation (*chipped in with a reminiscence*). **2** contribute (money or resources). **a chip off the old block** a child who resembles a parent, esp. in character. **a chip on one's shoulder** *colloq.* a disposition or inclination to feel resentful or aggrieved. **have had one's chips** *Brit. colloq.* be unable to avoid defeat, punishment, etc. **in the chips** *sl.* moneyed; affluent. **when the chips are down** *colloq.* in times of discouragement or disappointment.

chip·board /chípbawrd/ *n.* a rigid sheet or panel made from compressed wood chips and resin.

chip·munk /chípmungk/ *n.* any ground squirrel of the genus *Tamias* or *Eutamias*, having alternate light and dark stripes running down the body.

Chip·pen·dale /chípəndayl/ *adj.* **1** (of furniture) designed or made by the English cabinetmaker Thomas Chippendale (d. 1779). **2** in the ornately elegant style of Chippendale's furniture.

chip·per /chípər/ *adj. colloq.* **1** cheerful. **2** smartly dressed.

Chip·pe·wa /chípəwaw, –wə, –waa, –way/ *n.* = OJIBWA.

chip·py[1] /chípee/ *adj.* (**chippier, chippiest**) marked by belligerence or aggression, esp. in the play of ice hockey.

chip·py[2] /chípee/ *n.* (also **chip·pie**) (*pl.* **·pies**) **1** *derog.* a promiscuous female; a prostitute. **2** *Brit. colloq.* a fish-and-chip store.

chip shot = CHIP *n.* 7.

chi·ral /kírəl/ *adj. Chem.* (of a crystal, etc.) not superimposable on its mirror image. □□ **chi·ral·i·ty** /–rálitee/ *n.*

chiro- /kírō/ (also **cheiro-**) *comb. form* of the hand.

chi·rog·ra·phy /kīrógrəfee/ *n.* handwriting; calligraphy.

chi·ro·man·cy /kírəmansee/ *n.* palmistry.

chi·rop·o·dy /kirópədee/ = PODIATRY. □□ **chi·rop·o·dist** *n.*

chi·ro·prac·tic /kírəpráktik/ *n.* the diagnosis and manipulative treatment of mechanical disorders of the joints, esp. of the spinal column. □□ **chi·ro·prac·tor** *n.*

chi·rop·ter·an /kīróptərən/ *n.* any member of the order Chiroptera, with membraned limbs serving as wings, including bats and flying foxes. □□ **chi·rop·ter·ous** *adj.*

chirp /chərp/ *v. & n.* •*v.* **1** *intr.* (usu. of small birds, grasshoppers, etc.) utter a short, sharp, high-pitched note. **2** *tr. & intr.* (esp. of a child) speak or utter in a lively or jolly way. •*n.* a chirping sound. □□ **chirp·er** *n.*

chirp·y /chə́rpee/ *adj. colloq.* (**chirpier, chirpiest**) cheerful; lively. □□ **chirp·i·ly** *adv.* **chirp·i·ness** *n.*

chir·rup /chírəp/ *v. & n.* •*v.intr.* (**chirruped, chirruping**) (esp. of small birds) chirp, esp. repeatedly; twitter. •*n.* a chirruping sound. □□ **chir·rup·y** *adj.*

chis·el /chízəl/ *n. & v.* •*n.* a hand tool with a squared, beveled blade for shaping wood, stone, or metal. •*v.* **1** *tr.* (**chiseled, chiseling**; esp. *Brit.* **chiselled, chiselling**) cut or shape with a chisel. **2** *tr.* (as **chiseled** *adj.*) (of facial features) sharply defined. **3** *tr. & intr. sl.* cheat; swindle. □□ **chis·el·er** *n.*

chit[1] /chit/ *n.* **1** *derog.* or *joc.* a young, small, or frail girl or woman (esp. a chit of a girl). **2** a young child.

chit[2] /chit/ *n.* **1** a note of requisition; a note of a sum owed, esp. for food or drink. **2** esp. *Brit.* a note or memorandum.

chit·chat /chítchat/ *n. & v. colloq.* •*n.* light conversation; gossip. •*v.intr.* (**·chatted, ·chatting**) talk informally; gossip.

chi·tin /kít'n/ *n. Chem.* a polysaccharide forming the major constituent in the exoskeleton of arthropods and in the cell walls of fungi. □□ **chi·tin·ous** *adj.*

chi·ton /kít'n, –ton/ *n.* **1** a long, woolen tunic worn by ancient Greeks. **2** any marine mollusk of the class Amphineura, having a shell of overlapping plates.

chit·ter·lings /chítlinz/ *n.* (also **chit·lings, chit·lins**) the small intestines of pigs, etc., esp. as cooked for food.

chiv·al·rous /shívəlrəs/ *adj.* **1** (usu. of a male) gallant; honorable; courteous. **2** involving or showing chivalry. □□ **chiv·al·rous·ly** *adv.*

chiv·al·ry /shívəlree/ *n.* **1** the medieval knightly system with its religious, moral, and social code. **2** the combination of qualities expected of an ideal knight, esp. courage, honor, courtesy, justice, and readiness to help the weak. **3** a man's courteous behavior, esp. toward women. □□ **chiv·al·ric** *adj.*

chive /chīv/ *n.* a small alliaceous plant, *Allium schoenoprasum*, having purple-pink flowers and dense tufts of long tubular leaves, which are used as an herb.

chla·myd·i·a /kləmídeeə/ *n.* (*pl.* **chlamydiae** /–dee–ee/) any parasitic bacterium of the genus *Chlamydia*, some of which cause diseases such as trachoma, and nonspecific urethritis.

chlor- var. of CHLORO-.

chlo·ride /kláwrīd/ *n. Chem.* any compound of chlorine with another element or group.

chlo·ri·nate /kláwrinayt/ *v.tr.* **1** impregnate or treat with chlorine. **2** *Chem.* cause to react or combine with chlorine. □□ **chlo·ri·na·tor** *n.*

chlo·ri·na·tion /kláwrináyshən/ *n.* **1** the treatment of water with chlorine to disinfect it. **2** *Chem.* a reaction in which chlorine is introduced into a compound.

chlo·rine /kláwreen/ *n. Chem.* a poisonous, greenish-yellow gaseous element of the halogen group occurring naturally in salt, seawater, rock salt, etc., and used for purifying water, bleaching, and the manufacture of many organic chemicals. ¶ Symb.: **Cl**.

chloro- /kláwrō/ *comb. form* (also **chlor-** esp. before a vowel) **1** *Bot. & Mineral.* green. **2** *Chem.* chlorine.

chlo·ro·fluor·o·car·bon *n.* see CFC.

chlo·ro·form /kláwrəfawrm/ *n. & v.* •*n.* a colorless, volatile, sweet-smelling liquid used as a solvent and formerly used as a general anesthetic. ¶ Chem. formula: $CHCl_3$. •*v.tr.* render (a person) unconscious with this.

chlo·ro·phyll /kláwrəfil/ *n.* the green pigment found in most plants, responsible for light absorption to provide energy for photosynthesis. □□ **chlo·ro·phyl·lous** /–filəs/ *adj.*

chlo·ro·plast /kláwrōplast/ *n.* a plastid containing chlorophyll, found in plant cells undergoing photosynthesis.

chlo·ro·sis /klərṓsis/ *n.* **1** *hist.* a severe form of anemia from iron deficiency esp. in young women, causing a greenish complexion (cf. GREENSICK). **2** *Bot.* a reduction or loss of the normal green coloration of plants. □□ **chlo·rot·ic** /–rótik/ *adj.*

chock /chok/ *n., v., & adv.* •*n.* a block or wedge of wood to check motion, esp. of a cask or a wheel. •*v.tr.* **1** fit or make fast with chocks. **2** (usu. foll. by *up*) *Brit.* cram full. • *adv.* as closely or tightly as possible.

choc·o·late /cháwkələt, cháwklət, chók–/ *n.* & *adj.* • *n.* **1 a** a food preparation in the form of a paste or solid block made from roasted and ground cacao seeds, usually sweetened. **b** a candy made of or coated with this. **c** a drink made with chocolate. **2** a deep brown color. • *adj.* **1** made from or of chocolate. **2** chocolate-colored. ▫▫ **choc·o·lat·y** *adj.* (also **choc·o·lat·ey**).

chocolate early 17th century (in the sense 'a drink made with chocolate'): from French *chocolat* or Spanish *chocolate*, from Nahuatl *chocolatl* 'food made from cacao seeds,' influenced by unrelated *cacaua-atl* 'drink made from cacao.'

Choc·taw /chóktaw/ *n.* (*pl.* same or **Choctaws**) **1 a** a N. American people orig. from Alabama. **b** an individual of this people. **c** the language of this people. **2** (in skating) a step from one edge of a skate to the other edge of the other skate in the opposite direction.

choice /choys/ *n.* & *adj.* • *n.* **1 a** the act or an instance of choosing. **b** a thing or person chosen (*not a good choice*). **2** a range from which to choose. **3** (usu. foll. by *of*) the élite; the best. **4** the power or opportunity to choose (*what choice have I?*). • *adj.* of superior quality; carefully chosen. ▫▫ **choice·ly** *adv.* **choice·ness** *n.*

choir /kwīr/ *n.* **1** a regular group of singers, esp. taking part in church services. **2** the part of a cathedral or large church between the altar and the nave, used by the choir and clergy. **3** a company of singers, birds, angels, etc. (*a heavenly choir*). **4** *Mus.* a group of instruments of one family playing together (*a clarinet choir*).

choir·boy /kwīrboy/ *n.* (*fem.* **choirgirl**) a child who sings in a church or cathedral choir.

choir loft *n.* a church gallery in which the choir is situated.

choke[1] /chōk/ *v.* & *n.* • *v.* **1** *tr.* hinder or impede the breathing of (a person or animal), esp. by constricting the windpipe or (of gas, smoke, etc.) by being unbreathable. **2** *intr.* suffer a hindrance or stoppage of breath. **3** *tr.* & *intr.* make or become speechless from emotion. **4** *tr.* retard the growth of or kill (esp. plants) by the deprivation of light, air, nourishment, etc. **5** *tr.* (often foll. by *back*) suppress (feelings) with difficulty. **6** *tr.* block or clog (a passage, tube, etc.). **7** *tr.* enrich the fuel mixture in (an internal combustion engine) by reducing the intake of air. • *n.* **1** the valve in the carburetor of an internal combustion engine that controls the intake of air, esp. to enrich the fuel mixture. **2** *Electr.* an inductance coil used to smooth the variations of an alternating current or to alter its phase. ▫ **choke down** swallow with difficulty. **choke up 1** become overly anxious or emotionally affected (*got all choked up over that sad movie*). **2** block (a channel, etc.).

choke[2] /chōk/ *n.* the center part of an artichoke.

choke·ber·ry /chṓkberee/ *n.* (*pl.* **·ries**) *Bot.* **1** any rosaceous shrub of the genus *Aronia.* **2** its scarlet berrylike fruit.

choke chain (or **col·lar**) *n.* a chain looped around a dog's neck to exert control by pressure on its windpipe when the dog pulls.

chok·er /chṓkər/ *n.* **1** a close-fitting necklace or ornamental neckband. **2** a clerical or other high collar.

chole- /kṓlee/ *comb. form* (also **chol–** esp. before a vowel) *Med.* & *Chem.* bile.

chol·er /kólər/ *n.* **1** *hist.* one of the four humors, bile. **2** *poet.* or *archaic* anger; irascibility.

chol·er·a /kólərə/ *n. Med.* an infectious and often fatal disease of the small intestine caused by the bacterium *Vibrio cholerae*, resulting in severe vomiting and diarrhea. ▫▫ **chol·e·ra·ic** /–ráyik/ *adj.*

chol·er·ic /kólərik, kəlérik/ *adj.* irascible; angry. ▫▫ **chol·er·i·cal·ly** *adv.*

cho·les·ter·ol /kəléstərawl, –rōl/ *n. Biochem.* a sterol found in most body tissues, including the blood, where high concentrations promote arteriosclerosis.

chomp /chomp/ *v.tr.* = CHAMP[1].

choo-choo /chóōchōō/ *n. colloq.* (esp. as a child's word) a railroad train or locomotive, esp. a steam engine.

choose /chōōz/ *v.* (*past* **chose** /chōz/; *past part.* **chosen** /chṓzən/) **1** *tr.* select out of a greater number. **2** *intr.* (usu. foll. by *between, from*) take or select one or another. **3** *tr.* (usu. foll. by *to* + infin.) decide; be determined (*chose to stay behind*). **4** *tr.* (foll. by *complement*) select as (*was chosen king*). **5** *tr. Theol.* (esp. as **chosen** *adj.*) destine to be saved (*God's chosen people*). ▫ **nothing** (or **little**) **to choose between them** they are equivalent. ▫▫ **choos·er** *n.*

choos·y /chóōzee/ *adj.* (**choosier, choosiest**) *colloq.* fastidious. ▫▫ **choos·i·ly** *adv.* **choos·i·ness** *n.*

chop[1] /chop/ *v.* & *n.* • *v.tr.* (**chopped, chopping**) **1** (usu. foll. by *off, down*, etc.) cut or fell by a blow, usu. with an axe. **2** (often foll. by *up*) cut (esp. meat or vegetables) into small pieces. **3** strike (esp. a ball) with a short heavy edgewise blow. **4** *colloq.* dispense with; shorten or curtail. • *n.* **1** a cutting blow, esp. with an axe. **2** a thick slice of meat (esp. pork or lamb) usu. including a rib. **3** a short, sharp, edgewise stroke or blow in tennis, karate, boxing, etc. **4** the broken motion of water, usu. owing to the action of the wind against the tide. **5** (prec. by *the*) *Brit. sl.* **a** dismissal from employment. **b** the action of killing or being killed.

chop[2] /chop/ *n.* (usu. in *pl.*) the jaw of an animal, etc.

chop·per /chópər/ *n.* **1** a person or thing that chops. **2** a butcher's cleaver. **3** *colloq.* a helicopter. **4** *colloq.* a type of bicycle or motorcycle with high handlebars. **5** (in *pl.*) *sl.* teeth.

chop·py /chópee/ *adj.* (**choppier, choppiest**) (of the sea, the weather, etc.) fairly rough. ▫▫ **chop·pi·ly** *adv.* **chop·pi·ness** *n.*

chop shop *n. colloq.* a garage in which stolen cars are dismantled so that the parts can be sold separately.

chop·stick /chópstik/ *n.* each of a pair of small thin sticks of wood or ivory, etc., held both in one hand as eating utensils by the Chinese, Japanese, etc.

chop su·ey /chopsóō–ee/ *n.* (*pl.* **·eys**) a Chinese-style dish of meat stewed and fried with bean sprouts, bamboo shoots, onions, and served with rice.

cho·ral /káwrəl/ *adj.* of, for, or sung by a choir or chorus. ▫▫ **cho·ral·ly** *adv.*

cho·rale /kərál, –ráal/ *n.* (also **cho·ral**) **1** a stately and simple hymn tune; a harmonized version of this. **2** a choir or choral society.

chord[1] /kawrd/ *n. Mus.* a group of (usu. three or more) notes sounded together, as a basis of harmony. ▫▫ **chord·al** *adj.*

chord[2] /kawrd/ *n.* **1** *Math.* & *Aeron.*, etc. a straight line joining the ends of an arc, the wings of an airplane, etc. **2** *Anat.* = CORD. ▫ **strike a chord 1** recall something to a person's memory. **2** elicit sympathy. **touch the right chord** appeal skillfully to the emotions. ▫▫ **chord·al** *adj.*

chor·date /káwrdayt/ *n.* & *adj.* • *n.* any animal of the phylum Chordata, possessing a notochord at some stage during its development. • *adj.* of or relating to the chordates.

chore /chawr/ *n.* a tedious or routine task, esp. domestic.

cho·re·a /kawréėə/ *n. Med.* a disorder characterized by jerky involuntary movements affecting esp. the shoulders, hips, and face.

cho·re·o·graph /káwreeəgraf/ *v.tr.* compose the choreography for (a ballet, etc.). ▫▫ **cho·re·og·ra·pher** /–reeógrəfər/ *n.*

cho·re·og·ra·phy /káwreeógrəfee/ *n.* **1** the design or arrangement of a ballet or other staged dance. **2** the sequence of steps and movements in dance. **3** the written notation for this. ▫▫ **cho·re·o·graph·ic** /–reeəgráfik/ *adj.* **cho·re·o·graph·i·cal·ly** *adv.*

cho·re·ol·o·gy /káwreeóləjee/ *n.* the study and description of the movements of dancing. ▫▫ **cho·re·ol·o·gist** *n.*

cho·ri·on /káwreeən/ *n.* the outermost membrane surrounding an embryo of a reptile, bird, or mammal. ▫▫ **cho·ri·on·ic** /–reeónik/ *adj.*

chor·is·ter /káwristər, kór–/ *n.* **1** a member of a choir, esp. a choirboy. **2** the leader of a church choir.

chor·tle /cháwrt'l/ *v.* & *n.* • *v.intr. colloq.* chuckle gleefully. • *n.* a gleeful chuckle.

cho·rus /káwrəs/ *n.* & *v.* • *n.* (*pl.* **choruses**) **1** a group (esp. a large one) of singers; a choir. **2** a piece of music composed for a choir. **3** the refrain or the main part of a popular song, in which a chorus participates. **4** any simultaneous utterance by many persons, etc. (*a chorus of disapproval followed*). **5** a group of singers and dancers performing in concert in a musical comedy, opera, etc. **6** *Gk Antiq.* **a** in Greek tragedy, a group of performers who comment together in voice and movement on the main action. **b** an utterance of the chorus. **7** esp. in Elizabethan drama, a character who speaks the prologue and other linking parts of the play. **8** the part spoken by this character. • *v.tr.* & *intr.* (of a group) speak or utter simultaneously. ▫ **in chorus** (uttered) together; in unison.

cho·rus girl *n.* a young woman who sings or dances in the chorus of a musical comedy, etc.

chose *past* of CHOOSE.

cho·sen *past part.* of CHOOSE.

chow /chow/ *n.* **1** *sl.* food. **2** *offens.* a Chinese. **3** (in full **chow chow**) **a** a dog of a Chinese breed with long hair and bluish-black tongue. **b** this breed.

chow·der /chówdər/ *n.* a rich soup or stew usu. containing fresh fish, clams, or corn with potatoes, onions, etc.

chow mein /chów máyn/ *n.* a Chinese–style dish of fried noodles with shredded meat or shrimp, etc., and vegetables.

Chr. *abbr.* Chronicles (Old Testament).

chres·tom·a·thy /krestóməthee/ *n.* (*pl.* **·thies**) a selection of passages from an author or authors, designed to help in learning a language.

chrism /krízəm/ *n.* a consecrated oil or unguent used esp. for anointing in Roman Catholic, Anglican, and Orthodox Christian rites.

chris·om /krízəm/ *n.* **1** = CHRISM. **2** (in full **chrisom cloth**) *hist.* a white robe put on a child at baptism, and used as its shroud if it died within the month.

Christ /krīst/ *n.* & *int.* • *n.* **1** the title, also now treated as a name, given to Jesus of Nazareth, believed by Christians to have fulfilled the Old Testament prophecies of a coming Messiah. **2** the Messiah as prophesied in the Old Testament. • *int. sl.* expressing surprise, anger, etc. ▫▫ **Christ·hood** *n.* **Christ·like** *adj.* **Christ·ly** *adj.*

Chris·ta·del·phi·an /krístədélfeeən/ *n.* & *adj.* • *n.* a member of a Christian sect rejecting the doctrine of the Trinity and expecting a second coming of Christ on Earth. • *adj.* of or adhering to this sect and its beliefs.

chris·ten /krísən/ *v.tr.* **1** give a Christian name to at baptism as a sign of admission to a Christian church. **2** give a name to anything, esp. formally or with a ceremony. **3** *colloq.* use for the first time. ▫▫ **chris·ten·er** *n.* **chris·ten·ing** *n.*

Chris·ten·dom /krísəndəm/ *n.* Christians worldwide, regarded as a collective body.

Chris·tian /kríschən/ *adj.* & *n.* • *adj.* **1** of Christ's teachings or religion. **2** believing in or following the religion based on the teachings of Jesus Christ. **3** showing the qualities associated with Christ's teachings. **4** *colloq.* (of a person) kind; fair; decent. • *n.* **1** **a** a person who has received Christian baptism. **b** an adherent of Christ's teachings. **2** a person exhibiting Christian qualities. ▫▫ **Chris·tian·ize** *v.tr.* & *intr.* **Chris·tian·i·za·tion** *n.*

Chris·tian e·ra *n.* the era calculated from the traditional date of Christ's birth.

Chris·ti·an·i·ty /krischeeánitee/ *n.* **1** the Christian religion; its beliefs and practices. **2** being a Christian; Christian quality or character. **3** = CHRISTENDOM.

Chris·tian name *n.* a forename, esp. as given at baptism.

Chris·tian Sci·ence *n.* a Christian sect believing in the power of healing by prayer alone. ▫▫ **Chris·tian Sci·en·tist** *n.*

chris·tie /krístee/ *n.* (also **chris·ty**) (*pl.* **·ties**) *Skiing* a sudden turn in which the skis are kept parallel, used for changing direction fast or stopping short.

Christ·mas /krísməs/ *n.* (*pl.* **Christmases**) **1** (also **Christ·mas Day**) the annual festival of Christ's birth, celebrated on Dec. 25. **2** the season in which this occurs; the time immediately before and after Dec. 25. ▫▫ **Christ·mas·sy** *adj.*

Christ·mas rose a white-flowered, winter-blooming evergreen, *Helleborus niger*.

chro·ma /krṓmə/ *n.* purity or intensity of color.

chro·mat·ic /krōmátik/ *adj.* **1** of or produced by color; in (esp. bright) colors. **2** *Mus.* **a** of or having notes not belonging to a diatonic scale. **b** (of a scale) ascending or descending by semitones. ▫▫ **chro·mat·i·cal·ly** *adv.* **chro·mat·i·cism** /–tisizəm/ *n.*

chro·ma·tic·i·ty /krṓmətísitee/ *n.* the quality of color regarded independently of brightness.

chro·ma·tid /krṓmətid/ *n.* either of two threadlike strands into which a chromosome divides longitudinally during cell division.

chro·ma·tin /krṓmətin/ *n.* the material in a cell nucleus that stains with basic dyes and consists of protein, RNA, and DNA, of which eukaryotic chromosomes are composed.

chromato– /krṓmətō/ *comb. form* (also **chromo–** /krṓmō/) color.

chro·ma·tog·ra·phy /krṓmətógrəfee/ *n. Chem.* the separation of the components of a mixture by slow passage through or over a material which adsorbs them differently. ▫▫ **chro·mat·o·graph** /–mátəgraf/ *n.* **chro·mat·o·graph·ic** *adj.*

chrome /krōm/ *n.* **1** chromium, esp. as plating. **2** (in full **chrome yellow**) a yellow pigment obtained from lead chromate.

chro·mite /krṓmīt/ *n.* **1** *Mineral.* a black mineral of chromium and iron oxides, which is the principal ore of chromium. **2** *Chem.* a salt of bivalent chromium.

chro·mi·um /krṓmeeəm/ *n. Chem.* a hard, white metallic transition element, occurring naturally as chromite and used as a shiny decorative electroplated coating. ¶ Symb.: **Cr**.

chromo–[1] /krṓmō/ *comb. form Chem.* chromium.

chromo–[2] *comb. form* var. of CHROMATO–.

chro·mo·lith·o·graph /krṓmōlíthəgraf/ *n.* & *v.* • *n.* a colored picture printed by lithography. • *v.tr.* print or produce by this process. ▫▫ **chro·mo·li·thog·ra·pher** /–lithógrəfər/ *n.* **chro·mo·lith·o·graph·ic** *adj.* **chro·mo·li·thog·ra·phy** /–lithógrəfee/ *n.*

chro·mo·some /krṓməsōm/ *n. Biochem.* one of the

threadlike structures, usu. found in the cell nucleus, that carry the genetic information in the form of genes. ▫▫ **chro•mo•so•mal** *adj.*

chro•mo•sphere /krṓməsfeer/ *n.* a gaseous layer of the sun's atmosphere between the photosphere and the corona. ▫▫ **chro•mo•spher•ic** /–sféerik, –sfér–/ *adj.*

Chron. *abbr.* Chronicles (Old Testament).

chron•ic /krónik/ *adj.* **1** persisting for a long time (usu. of an illness or a personal or social problem). **2** having a chronic complaint. **3** *colloq. disp.* habitual; inveterate (*a chronic liar*). **4** *Brit. colloq.* very bad; intense; severe. ▫▫ **chron•i•cal•ly** *adv.* **chro•nic•i•ty** /kronísitee/ *n.*

▶**Chronic** is often used to mean 'habitual, inveterate,' e.g., *a chronic liar.* Some consider this use incorrect. The precise meaning of **chronic** is 'persisting for a long time' and it is used chiefly of illnesses or other problems, e.g., *More than one million people in the United States have chronic bronchitis.*

chron•i•cle /kronikəl/ *n. & v.* •*n.* **1** a register of events in order of their occurrence. **2** a narrative; a full account. **3** (**Chronicles**) the name of two of the historical books of the Old Testament or Hebrew bible. •*v.tr.* record (events) in the order of their occurrence. ▫▫ **chron•i•cler** *n.*

chrono– /krṓnō/ *comb. form* time.

chron•o•graph /krónəgraf, krṓnə–/ *n.* **1** an instrument for recording time with extreme accuracy. **2** a stopwatch. ▫▫ **chron•o•graph•ic** *adj.*

chron•o•log•i•cal /krónəlójikəl/ *adj.* **1** (of a number of events) arranged or regarded in the order of their occurrence. **2** of or relating to chronology. ▫▫ **chron•o•log•i•cal•ly** *adv.*

chro•nol•o•gy /krənóləjee/ *n.* (*pl.* **•gies**) **1** the study of historical records to establish the dates of past events. **2 a** the arrangement of events, dates, etc., in the order of their occurrence. **b** a table or document displaying this. ▫▫ **chro•nol•o•gist** *n.* **chro•nol•o•gize** *v.tr.*

chro•nom•e•ter /krənómitər/ *n.* a time–measuring instrument, esp. one keeping accurate time at all temperatures and used in navigation.

chro•nom•e•try /krənómitree/ *n.* the science of accurate time measurement. ▫▫ **chron•o•met•ric** /krónəmétrik/ *adj.* **chron•o•met•ri•cal** *adj.* **chron•o•met•ri•cal•ly** *adv.*

chrys•a•lis /krísəlis/ *n.* (also **chrysalid**) (*pl.* **chrysalides** /krisálideez/ or **chrysalises**) **1 a** a quiescent pupa of a butterfly or moth. **b** the hard outer case enclosing it. **2** a preparatory or transitional state.

chry•san•the•mum /krisánthəməm/ *n.* any composite plant of the genus *Chrysanthemum*, having brightly colored flowers.

chub /chub/ *n.* a thick–bodied, coarse–fleshed river fish, *Leuciscus cephalus*.

chub•by /chúbee/ *adj.* (**chubbier, chubbiest**) plump and rounded (esp. of a person or a part of the body). ▫▫ **chub•bi•ly** *adv.* **chub•bi•ness** *n.*

chuck[1] /chuk/ *v. & n.* •*v.tr.* **1** *colloq.* fling or throw carelessly or with indifference. **2** *colloq.* give up; reject; abandon; jilt (*chucked my job*; *chucked her boyfriend*). **3** touch playfully, esp. under the chin. •*n.* a playful touch under the chin. ▫ **chuck it** *sl.* stop; desist. **chuck out** *colloq.* **1** expel (a person) from a gathering, etc. **2** get rid of; discard.

chuck[2] /chuk/ *n. & v.* •*n.* **1** a cut of beef between the neck and the ribs. **2** a device for holding a workpiece in a lathe or a tool in a drill. •*v.tr.* fix (wood, a tool, etc.) to a chuck.

chuck•le /chúkəl/ *v. & n.* •*v.intr.* laugh quietly or inwardly. •*n.* a quiet or suppressed laugh. ▫▫ **chuck•ler** *n.*

chuck wag•on *n.* a wagon for storing food and preparing meals on a ranch, etc.

chuff /chuf/ *v.intr.* (of a steam engine, etc.) work with a regular sharp puffing sound.

chug /chug/ *v. & n.* •*v.intr.* (**chugged, chugging**) **1** emit a regular muffled explosive sound, as of an engine running slowly. **2** move with this sound. •*n.* a chugging sound.

chuk•ker /chúkər/ *n.* (also **chuk•ka**) each of the periods of play into which a game of polo is divided.

chum /chum/ *n. & v.* •*n. colloq.* (esp. among schoolchildren) a close friend. •*v.intr.* (often foll. by *with*) *Brit.* share rooms. ▫ **chum up** (often foll. by *with*) become a close friend (of). ▫▫ **chum•my** *adj.* (**chummier, chummiest**). **chum•mi•ly** *adv.* **chum•mi•ness** *n.*

chump /chump/ *n.* **1 a** *colloq.* a foolish person. **b** an easily deceived person; a sucker. **2** *Brit.* the thick end, esp. of a loin of lamb or mutton (*chump chop*). **3** a short thick block of wood.

chunk /chungk/ *n.* **1** a thick, solid slice or piece of something firm or hard. **2** a substantial amount or piece.

chunk•y /chúngkee/ *adj.* (**chunkier, chunkiest**) **1** containing or consisting of chunks. **2** short and thick; small and sturdy. **3** (of clothes) made of a thick material. ▫▫ **chunk•i•ness** *n.*

Chun•nel /chúnəl/ *n. colloq.* a tunnel under the English Channel linking England and France.

church /chərch/ *n. & v.* •*n.* **1** a building for public (usu. Christian) worship. **2** a meeting for public worship in such a building (*go to church*; *met after church*). **3** (**Church**) the body of all Christians. **4** (**Church**) the clergy or clerical profession (*went into the Church*). **5** (**Church**) an organized Christian group or society of any time, country, or distinct principles of worship (*the Baptist Church*; *Church of England*). **6** institutionalized religion as a political or social force (*church and state*). •*v.tr.* bring to church for a service of thanksgiving.

---

church Old English *cir(i)ce, cyr(i)ce*, related to Dutch *kerk* and German *Kirche*, based on medieval Greek *kurikon*, from Greek *kuriakon (dōma)* 'Lord's (house),' from *kurios* 'master or lord.'

---

church•go•er /chə́rchgōər/ *n.* a person who goes to church, esp. regularly. ▫▫ **church•go•ing** *n. & adj.*

church•man /chə́rchmən/ *n.* (*pl.* **•men**) **1** a member of the clergy or of a church. **2** a supporter of the church.

Church of Eng•land *n.* the English Church, recognized by the British government and having the British sovereign as its head.

church•y /chə́rchee/ *adj.* **1** obtrusively or intolerantly devoted to the Church or opposed to religious dissent. **2** like a church. ▫▫ **church•i•ness** *n.*

church•yard /chə́rchyaard/ *n.* the enclosed ground around a church, esp. as used for burials.

churl /chərl/ *n.* an ill-bred person.

churl•ish /chə́rlish/ *adj.* surly; mean. ▫▫ **churl•ish•ly** *adv.* **churl•ish•ness** *n.*

churn /chərn/ *n. & v.* •*n.* **1** a machine for making butter by agitating milk or cream. **2** *Brit.* a large milk can. •*v.* **1** *tr.* agitate (milk or cream) in a churn. **2** *tr.* produce (butter) in this way. **3** *tr.* (usu. foll. by *up*) cause distress to; upset; agitate. **4** *intr.* (of a liquid) seethe; foam violently (*the churning sea*). **5** *tr.* agitate or move (liquid) vigorously, causing it to foam. ▫ **churn out** produce routinely or mechanically, esp. in large quantities.

chute[1] /shōōt/ *n.* **1** a sloping channel or slide, with or without water, for conveying things to a lower level. **2** a slide into a swimming pool. **3** a cataract or cascade of water; a steep descent in a riverbed producing a swift current.

chute[2] /shōōt/ *n. colloq.* parachute. ▫▫ **chut·ist** *n.*

chut·ney /chútnee/ *n.* (*pl.* **·neys**) a pungent orig. Indian condiment made of fruits or vegetables, vinegar, spices, sugar, etc.

chutz·pah /khŏŏtspə/ *n.* (also **chutzpa**) *sl.* shameless audacity; gall.

CI *abbr.* Channel Islands.

Ci *abbr.* curie(s).

CIA *abbr.* Central Intelligence Agency.

cia·o /chow/ *int. colloq.* **1** good–bye. **2** hello.

ci·bo·ri·um /sibáwreeəm/ *n.* (*pl.* **ciboria** /–reeə/) a vessel with an arched cover used to hold the Eucharist.

ci·ca·da /sikáydə, –kaádə/ *n.* (also **ci·ca·la** /sikaálə/) (*pl.* **cicadas** or **cicadae** /–dee/) any transparent–winged large insect of the family Cicadidae, the males of which make a loud, rhythmic, chirping sound.

cic·a·trix /síkətriks, sikáy–/ *n.* (also **cic·a·trice** /síkətris/) (*pl.* **cicatrices** /–tríseez/) **1** any mark left by a healed wound; a scar. **2** *Bot.* **a** a mark on a stem, etc., left when a leaf or other part becomes detached. **b** a scar on the bark of a tree. ▫▫ **cic·a·tri·cial** /–tríshəl/ *adj.*

cic·e·ly /sísəlee/ *n.* (*pl.* **·lies**) any of various umbelliferous plants, esp. sweet cicely (*Myrrhis odorata*).

cic·e·ro·ne /chíchərṓnee, sísə–/ *n.* (*pl.* **ciceroni** *pronunc.* same) a guide who gives information about antiquities, places of interest, etc., to sightseers.

CID *abbr.* (in the UK) Criminal Investigation Department.

–cide /sīd/ *suffix* forming nouns meaning: **1** a person or substance that kills (*regicide; insecticide*). **2** the killing of (*infanticide; suicide*).

ci·der /sídər/ *n.* **1** *US* a usu. unfermented drink made from crushed apples. **2** *Brit.* (also **cy·der**) an alcoholic drink made from fermented apple juice.

ci–de·vant /seédəvóɴ/ *adj. & adv.* that has been (with person's earlier name or status); former or formerly.

c.i.f. *abbr.* cost, insurance, freight (as being included in a price).

cig /sig/ *n. colloq.* cigarette; cigar.

ci·gar /sigaár/ *n.* a cylinder of tobacco rolled in tobacco leaves for smoking.

cig·a·rette /sígərét/ *n.* (also **cig·a·ret**) **1** a thin cylinder of finely cut tobacco rolled in paper for smoking. **2** a similar cylinder containing a narcotic or medicated substance.

cig·a·ril·lo /sígərílō/ *n.* (*pl.* **·los**) a small cigar.

cil·i·um /síleeəm/ *n.* (*pl.* **cilia** /–leeə/) **1** a short, minute, hairlike vibrating structure on the surface of some cells, causing currents in the surrounding fluid. **2** an eyelash. ▫▫ **cil·i·ar·y** *adj.* **cil·i·ate** /–ayt, –ət/ *adj.* **cil·i·at·ed** *adj.* **cil·i·a·tion** *n.*

C. in C. *abbr.* commander in chief.

cinch /sinch/ *n. & v.* •*n.* **1** *colloq.* **a** a sure thing; a certainty. **b** an easy task. **2** a firm hold. **3** a girth for a saddle or pack. •*v.tr.* **1 a** tighten as with a cinch (*cinched at the waist with a belt*). **b** secure a grip on. **2** *sl.* make certain of. **3** put a cinch (sense 3) on.

cin·cho·na /singkṓnə/ *n.* **1 a** any evergreen tree or shrub of the genus *Cinchona*, native to S. America. **b** the bark of this tree, containing quinine. **2** any drug from this bark formerly used as a tonic and to stimulate the appetite. ▫▫ **cin·cho·nic** /–kónik/ *adj.* **cin·cho·nine** /síngkəneen/ *n.*

cinc·ture /síngkchər/ *n. literary* a girdle, belt, or border.

cin·der /síndər/ *n.* **1** the residue of coal or wood, etc., that has stopped giving off flames but still has combustible matter in it. **2** slag. **3** (in *pl.*) ashes. ▫ **burned to a cinder** made useless by burning. ▫▫ **cin·der·y** *adj.*

cin·der block *n.* a concrete building block, usu. made from cinders mixed with sand and cement.

Cin·der·el·la /síndərélə/ *n.* **1** a person or thing of unrecognized or disregarded merit or beauty. **2** a neglected or despised member of a group.

cine– /sínə/ *comb. form* pertaining to film or movies (*cinephotography*).

cin·e·aste /síneeast/ *n.* (also **cin·e·ast**) **1** a person who makes films, esp. professionally. **2** a movie lover.

cin·e·ma /sínəmə/ *n.* **1 a** films collectively. **b** the production of films as an art or industry; cinematography. **2** *Brit.* a theater where motion pictures are shown.

cin·e·mat·o·graph /sínəmátəgraf/ (also **kinematograph** /kín–/) *n.* a movie camera.

cin·e·ma·tog·ra·phy /sínəmətógrəfee/ *n.* the art of making motion pictures. ▫▫ **cin·e·ma·tog·ra·pher** *n.* **cin·e·mat·o·graph·ic** /–mátəgráfik/ *adj.* **cin·e·mat·o·graph·i·cal·ly** *adv.*

cin·e·ma ve·ri·té /seénemaá véreetáy/ *n. Cinematog.* **1** the art or process of making realistic (esp. documentary) films that avoid artificiality and artistic effect. **2** such films collectively.

cin·e·plex /sínipleks/ *n.* a multiplex cinema.

cin·e·rar·y /sínəreree/ *adj.* of ashes.

cin·na·bar /sínəbaar/ *n.* **1** a bright red mineral form of mercuric sulfide from which mercury is obtained. **2** vermilion.

cin·na·mon /sínəmən/ *n.* **1** an aromatic spice from the peeled, dried, and rolled bark of a SE Asian tree. **2** any tree of the genus *Cinnamomum*, esp. *C. zeylanicum* yielding the spice. **3** yellowish–brown.

ci·pher /sífər/ *n. & v.* (*Brit.* **cipher** or **cypher**) •*n.* **1 a** a secret or disguised way of writing. **b** a thing written in this way. **c** the key to it. **2** the arithmetical symbol (0) denoting no amount but used to occupy a vacant place in decimal, etc., numeration (as in 12.05). **3** a person or thing of no importance. **4** the interlaced initials of a person or company, etc.; a monogram. •*v.* **1** *tr.* put into secret writing; encipher. **2 a** *tr.* (usu. foll. by *out*) work out by arithmetic; calculate. **b** *intr. archaic* do arithmetic.

cir. *abbr.* (also **circ.**) **1** circle. **2** circuit. **3** circular. **4** circulation. **5** circumference.

cir·ca /sə́rkə/ *prep.* (preceding a date) about.

cir·ca·di·an /sərkáydeeən/ *adj. Physiol.* occurring or recurring about once per day.

Cir·ce /sə́rsee/ *n.* a dangerously attractive enchantress.

cir·cle /sə́rkəl/ *n. & v.* •*n.* **1 a** a round plane figure whose circumference is everywhere equidistant from its center. **b** the line enclosing a circle. **2** a roundish enclosure or structure. **3** a ring. **4** a curved upper tier of seats in a theater, etc. (*dress circle*). **5** a circular route. **6** *Archaeol.* a group of (usu. large embedded) stones arranged in a circle. **7** persons grouped around a center of interest. **8** a set or class or restricted group (*literary circles; not done in the best circles*). **9** a period or cycle (*the circle of the year*). **10** (in full **vicious circle**) **a** an unbroken sequence of reciprocal cause and effect. **b** the fallacy of proving a proposition from another which depends on the first for its own proof. •*v.* **1** *intr.* (often foll. by *around, about*) move in a circle. **2** *tr.* **a** revolve around. **b** form a circle around. ▫ **circle back** move in a wide loop toward the starting point. **come full circle** return to the starting point. **go around in circles** make no progress despite effort. **run around in circles** *colloq.* be fussily busy with little result. ▫▫ **cir·cler** *n.*

cir·clet /sə́rklit/ *n.* **1** a small circle. **2** a circular band, esp. of gold or jeweled, etc., as an ornament.

cir·cuit /sə́rkit/ *n.* **1 a** a line or course enclosing an area; the distance around; the circumference. **b** the area enclosed. **2** *Electr.* **a** the path of a current. **b** the apparatus through which a current passes. **3 a** the journey of a judge in a particular district to hold courts. **b** this district. **c** the lawyers following a circuit. **4** a chain of theaters, etc., under a single management. **5** *Brit.* an automobile racing track. **6 a** a sequence of sporting events (*the US tennis circuit*). **b** a sequence of athletic exercises. **7** a roundabout journey. **8 a** a group of local Methodist churches forming a minor administrative unit. **b** the journey of an itinerant minister within this.

cir·cuit board *n. Electronics* a board of nonconductive material on which integrated circuits, printed circuits, etc., are mounted or etched.

cir·cu·i·tous /sərkyóō–itəs/ *adj.* **1** indirect (and usu. long). **2** going a long way around. ▫▫ **cir·cu·i·tous·ly** *adv.* **cir·cu·i·tous·ness** *n.*

cir·cuit·ry /sə́rkitree/ *n.* (*pl.* **·ries**) **1** a system of electric circuits. **2** the equipment forming this.

cir·cu·lar /sə́rkyələr/ *adj. & n.* • *adj.* **1 a** having the form of a circle. **b** moving or taking place along a circle; indirect; circuitous (*circular route*). **2** *Logic* (of reasoning) depending on a vicious circle. **3** (of a letter or advertisement, etc.) printed for distribution to a large number of people. • *n.* a circular letter, leaflet, etc. ▫▫ **cir·cu·lar·i·ty** /–láritee/ *n.* **cir·cu·lar·ly** *adv.*

cir·cu·lar·ize /sə́rkyələrīz/ *v.tr.* **1** distribute circulars to. **2** seek opinions of (people) by means of a questionnaire. ▫▫ **cir·cu·lar·i·za·tion** *n.*

cir·cu·late /sə́rkyəlayt/ *v.* **1** *intr.* go around from one place or person, etc., to the next and so on; be in circulation. **2** *tr.* **a** cause to go around; put into circulation. **b** give currency to (a report, etc.). **c** circularize. **3** *intr.* be actively sociable at a party, gathering, etc. ▫▫ **cir·cu·la·tive** *adj.* **cir·cu·la·tor** *n.*

cir·cu·la·tion /sə́rkyəláyshən/ *n.* **1 a** movement back and forth, or from and back to a starting point, esp. of a fluid in a confined area or circuit. **b** the movement of blood from and to the heart. **c** a similar movement of sap, etc. **2 a** the transmission or distribution (of news or information or books, etc.). **b** the number of copies sold, esp. of journals and newspapers. **3 a** currency, coin, etc. **b** the movement or exchange of this in a country, etc. ▫ **in** (or **out of**) **circulation** participating (or not participating) in activities, etc.

cir·cu·la·to·ry /sə́rkyələtawree/ *adj.* of or relating to the circulation of blood or sap.

circum. *abbr.* circumference.

cir·cum·cise /sə́rkəmsīz/ *v.tr.* **1** cut off the foreskin, as a Jewish or Muslim rite or a surgical operation. **2** cut off the clitoris (and sometimes the labia), usu. as a religious rite.

cir·cum·ci·sion /sə́rkəmsízhən/ *n.* **1** the act or rite of circumcising or being circumcised. **2** (**Circumcision**) *Eccl.* the feast of the Circumcision of Christ, Jan. 1.

cir·cum·fer·ence /sərkúmfərəns/ *n.* **1** the enclosing boundary, esp. of a circle or other figure enclosed by a curve. **2** the distance around. ▫▫ **cir·cum·fer·en·tial** /–fərénshəl/ *adj.* **cir·cum·fer·en·tial·ly** *adv.*

cir·cum·flex /sə́rkəmfleks/ *n. & adj.* • *n.* (in full **circumflex accent**) a mark (ŋ) placed over a vowel in some languages to indicate a contraction, length, or a special quality. • *adj. Anat.* curved, bending around something else (*circumflex nerve*).

cir·cum·lo·cu·tion /sə́rkəmlōkyóōshən/ *n.* **1 a** a roundabout expression. **b** evasive talk. **2** the use of many words where fewer would do; verbosity. ▫▫ **circum·lo·cu·tion·al** *adj.* **cir·cum·lo·cu·tion·ar·y** *adj.* **circum·lo·cu·tion·ist** *n.* **cir·cum·loc·u·to·ry** /–lókyətáwree/ *adj.*

cir·cum·nav·i·gate /sə́rkəmnávigayt/ *v.tr.* sail around (esp. the world). ▫▫ **cir·cum·nav·i·ga·tion** /–gáyshən/ *n.* **cir·cum·nav·i·ga·tor** *n.*

cir·cum·scribe /sə́rkəmskrīb/ *v.tr.* **1** (of a line, etc.) enclose or outline. **2** lay down the limits of; confine; restrict. **3** *Geom.* draw (a figure) around another, touching it at points but not cutting it (cf. INSCRIBE). ▫▫ **cir·cum·scrib·a·ble** *adj.* **cir·cum·scrib·er** *n.* **cir·cum·scrip·tion** /–skrípshən/ *n.*

cir·cum·spect /sə́rkəmspekt/ *adj.* wary; cautious; taking everything into account. ▫▫ **cir·cum·spec·tion** /–spékshən/ *n.* **cir·cum·spect·ly** *adv.*

cir·cum·stance /sə́rkəmstans/ *n.* **1 a** a fact, occurrence, or condition, esp. (in *pl.*) the time, place, manner, cause, occasion, etc., or surroundings of an act or event. **b** (in *pl.*) the external conditions that affect or might affect an action. **2** (often foll. by *that* + clause) an incident, occurrence, or fact, as needing consideration (*the circumstance that he left early*). **3** (in *pl.*) one's state of financial or material welfare (*in reduced circumstances*). **4** ceremony; fuss (*pomp and circumstance*). ▫ **in** (or **under**) **the** (or **these**) **circumstances** the state of affairs being what it is. **in** (or **under**) **no circumstances** not at all; never. ▫▫ **cir·cum·stanced** *adj.*

cir·cum·stan·tial /sə́rkəmstánshəl/ *adj.* **1** given in full detail (*a circumstantial account*). **2** (of evidence, a legal case, etc.) tending to establish a conclusion by inference from known facts hard to explain otherwise. **3 a** depending on circumstances. **b** adventitious; incidental. ▫▫ **cir·cum·stan·ti·al·i·ty** /–sheeálitee/ *n.* **cir·cum·stan·ti·al·ly** *adv.*

cir·cum·vent /sə́rkəmvént/ *v.tr.* **1 a** evade (a difficulty); find a way around. **b** baffle; outwit. **2** entrap (an enemy) by surrounding. ▫▫ **cir·cum·ven·tion** /–vénshən/ *n.*

cir·cus /sə́rkəs/ *n.* (*pl.* **circuses**) **1** a traveling show of performing animals, acrobats, clowns, etc. **2** *colloq.* **a** a scene of lively action; a disturbance. **b** a group of people in a common activity, esp. sports. **3** *Brit.* an open space in a town or city, where several streets converge (*Piccadilly Circus*). **4** a circular hollow surrounded by hills. **5** *Rom.Antiq.* **a** a rounded or oval arena with tiers of seats, for equestrian and other sports and games. **b** a performance given there (*bread and circuses*).

cir·rho·sis /sirṓsis/ *n.* a chronic disease of the liver marked by the degeneration of cells and the thickening of surrounding tissues, as a result of alcoholism, hepatitis, etc. ▫▫ **cir·rhot·ic** /sirótik/ *adj.*

cir·ri·ped /síriped/ *n.* (also **cir·ri·pede** /síripeed/) any marine crustacean of the class Cirripedia, having a valved shell and usu. sessile when adult, e.g., a barnacle.

cirro- /sírō/ *comb. form* cirrus (cloud).

cir·rus /sírəs/ *n.* (*pl.* **cirri** /–rī/) **1** *Meteorol.* a form of white wispy cloud, esp. at high altitude. **2** *Bot.* a tendril. **3** *Zool.* a long, slender appendage or filament. ▫▫ **cir·rose** *adj.* **cir·rous** *adj.*

cis·al·pine /sisálpīn/ *adj.* on the southern side of the Alps.

cis·at·lan·tic /sísətlántik/ *adj.* (from the speaker's point of view) on this side of the Atlantic.

cis·co /sískō/ *n.* (*pl.* **·coes**) any of various freshwater whitefish of the genus *Coregonus*, native to N. America.

cis·lu·nar /sislóōnər/ *adj.* between the earth and the moon.

cist[1] /sist, kist/ *n.* (also **kist** /kist/) *Archaeol.* a coffin or burial chamber made from stone or a hollowed tree.

cist[2] /sist/ *n. Gk. Antiq.* a box used for sacred utensils.

Cis·ter·cian /sistə́rshən/ *n. & adj.* • *n.* a monk or nun of an order founded in 1098 as a stricter branch of the Benedictines. • *adj.* of the Cistercians.

cis·tern /sístərn/ *n.* **1** a tank or container for storing water, etc. **2** an underground reservoir for rainwater.

cit. *abbr.* **1** citation. **2** cited. **3** citizen.

cit·a·del /sítəd'l, –del/ *n.* **1** a fortress, usu. on high ground protecting or dominating a city. **2** a meeting hall of the Salvation Army.

ci·ta·tion /sītáyshən/ *n.* **1** the citing of a book or other source; a passage cited. **2** a mention in an official dispatch. **3** a note accompanying an award, describing the reasons for it.

cite /sīt/ *v.tr.* **1** adduce as an instance. **2** quote (a passage, book, or author) in support of an argument, etc. **3** mention in an official dispatch. **4** summon to appear in a court of law. ▫▫ **cit·a·ble** *adj.*

cit·i·fied /sítifīd/ *adj.* (also **cit·y·fied**) usu. *derog.* citylike or urban in appearance or behavior.

cit·i·zen /sítizən/ *n.* **1** a member of a nation or commonwealth, either native or naturalized (*American citizen*). **2** (usu. foll. by *of*) **a** an inhabitant of a city. **b** a freeman of a city. **3** a civilian. ▫▫ **cit·i·zen·hood** *n.* **cit·i·zen·ry** *n.* **cit·i·zen·ship** *n.*

cit·i·zen's ar·rest *n.* an arrest by an ordinary person without a warrant, allowable in certain cases.

cit·i·zen·ship /sítizənship/ *n.*. **2>** the character of a person, regarding his or her behavior as a member of society (*a youth group that promoted good citizenship*).

cit·ric ac·id *n.* a sharp-tasting, water-soluble organic acid found in the juice of lemons and other sour fruits.

cit·ron /sítrən/ *n.* **1** a shrubby tree, *Citrus medica*, bearing large lemonlike fruits with thick fragrant peel. **2** this fruit.

cit·ron·el·la /sítrənélə/ *n.* **1** any fragrant grass of the genus *Cymbopogon*, native to S. Asia. **2** the scented oil from these, used in insect repellent, and in perfume and soap manufacture.

cit·rus /sítrəs/ *n.* **1** any tree of the genus *Citrus*, including citron, lemon, lime, orange, and grapefruit. **2** (in full **citrus fruit**) a fruit from such a tree. ▫▫ **cit·rous** *adj.*

cit·y /sítee/ *n.* (*pl.* **·ies**) **1 a** a large town. **b** *US* a state-chartered municipal corporation occupying a definite area. **c** *Brit.* (strictly) a town created a city by charter and containing a cathedral. **2** (**the City**) **a** the major center of a region. **b** the part of London governed by the Lord Mayor and the Corporation. **c** the business part of this. **d** *Brit.* commercial circles; high finance. ▫▫ **cit·y·ward** *adj.* & *adv.* **cit·y·wards** *adv.*

---

city Middle English: from Old French *cite*, from Latin *civitas*, from *civis* 'citizen.' Originally denoting a town, and often used as a Latin equivalent to Old English *burh* 'borough,' the term was later applied to foreign and ancient cities and to the more important English boroughs. The connection between city and cathedral grew up under the Norman kings, as the episcopal sees (many of which had been established in villages) were removed to the chief borough of the diocese.

---

cit·y·fied var. of CITIFIED.

cit·y hall *n.* municipal offices or officers.

cit·y·scape /síteeskayp/ *n.* **1** a view of a city (actual or depicted). **2** city scenery.

cit·y-state *n.* esp. *hist.* a city that with its surrounding territory forms an independent state.

civ·et /sívit/ *n.* **1** (in full **civet cat**) any catlike animal of the mongoose family, esp. *Civettictis civetta* of Central Africa, having well-developed anal scent glands. **2** a strong musky perfume obtained from the secretions of these scent glands.

civ·ic /sívik/ *adj.* **1** of a city; municipal. **2** of or proper to citizens (*civic virtues*). **3** of citizenship; civil. ▫▫ **civ·i·cal·ly** *adv.*

civ·ic cen·ter *n.* **1** *Brit.* the area where municipal offices and other public buildings are situated; the buildings themselves. **2** a municipal building with space for conventions, sports events, etc., and other public facilities, often publicly supported.

civ·ics /síviks/ *n.pl.* (usu. treated as *sing.*) the study of the rights and duties of citizenship.

civ·il /sívəl/ *adj.* **1** of or belonging to citizens. **2** of ordinary citizens and their concerns, as distinct from military or naval or ecclesiastical matters. **3** polite; obliging; not rude. **4** *Law* relating to civil law (see below), not criminal or political matters (*civil court; civil lawyer*). **5** (of the length of a day, year, etc.) fixed by custom or law, not natural or astronomical. **6** occurring within a community or among fellow citizens; internal (*civil unrest*). ▫▫ **civ·il·ly** *adv.*

civ·il de·fense *n.* the organization and training of civilians for the protection of lives and property during and after attacks in wartime, natural disasters, emergencies, etc.

civ·il dis·o·be·di·ence *n.* the refusal to comply with certain laws or to pay taxes, etc., as a peaceful form of political protest.

civ·il en·gi·neer *n.* an engineer who designs or maintains roads, bridges, dams, etc. ▫▫ **civ·il en·gi·neer·ing** *n.*

ci·vil·ian /sivílyən/ *n.* & *adj.* • *n.* a person not in the armed services or the police force. • *adj.* of or for civilians.

ci·vil·ian·ize /sivílyənīz/ *v.tr.* make civilian in character or function. ▫▫ **ci·vil·ian·i·za·tion** *n.*

ci·vil·i·ty /sivílitee/ *n.* (*pl.* **·ties**) **1** politeness. **2** an act of politeness.

civ·i·li·za·tion /sívilәzáyshən/ *n.* **1** an advanced stage or system of social development. **2** those peoples of the world regarded as having this. **3** a people or nation (esp. of the past) regarded as an element of social evolution (*ancient civilizations; the Inca civilization*). **4** making or becoming civilized.

civ·i·lize /sívilīz/ *v.tr.* **1** bring out of a barbarous or primitive stage of society. **2** enlighten; refine and educate. ▫▫ **civ·i·liz·a·ble** *adj.* **civ·i·liz·er** *n.*

civ·il law *n.* **1** law concerning private rights (opp. CRIMINAL LAW). **2** *hist.* Roman or nonecclesiastical law.

civ·il lib·er·ty *n.* (often in *pl.*) freedom of action and speech subject to the law.

civ·il rights *n.pl.* the rights of citizens to political and social freedom and equality.

civ·il serv·ant *n.* a member of the civil service.

civ·il serv·ice *n.* the permanent professional branches of governmental administration, excluding military and judicial branches and elected politicians.

civ·il war *n.* a war between citizens of the same country.

civ·vies /síveez/ *n.pl. sl.* civilian clothes.

Cl *symb. Chem.* the element chlorine.

cl *abbr.* **1** centiliter(s). **2** class.

clack /klak/ *v.* & *n.* • *v.intr.* **1** make a sharp sound as of boards struck together. **2** chatter, esp. loudly. • *n.* **1** a clacking sound. **2** clacking talk. ▫▫ **clack·er** *n.*

clad[1] /klad/ *adj.* **1** clothed. **2** provided with cladding.

clad[2] /klad/ *v.tr.* (**cladding**; *past* and *past part.* **cladded** or **clad**) provide with cladding.

clad·ding /kláding/ *n.* a covering or coating on a structure or material, etc.

clade /klayd/ *n. Biol.* a group of organisms evolved from a common ancestor.

claim /klaym/ *v.* & *n.* • *v.tr.* **1 a** (often foll. by *that* + clause) demand as one's due or property. **b** (usu. *absol.*) submit a request for payment under an insurance policy. **2 a** represent oneself as having or achieving (*claim victory*). **b** (foll. by *to* + infin.) profess (*claimed to be the owner*). **c** assert; contend (*claim that one knows*). **3** have as a consequence (*the fire claimed many victims*). **4** (of a thing) deserve (one's attention, etc.). •*n.* **1 a** a demand or request for something considered one's due (*lay claim to*; *put in a claim*). **b** an application for compensation under the terms of an insurance policy. **2** (foll. by *to, on*) a right or title to a thing (*his only claim to fame*; *have many claims on my time*). **3** a contention or assertion. **4** a thing claimed. **5** *Mining* a piece of land allotted or taken. ▫▫ **claim·a·ble** *adj.* **claim·er** *n.*

claim·ant /kláymənt/ *n.* a person making a claim, esp. in a lawsuit or for a government benefit.

clair·voy·ance /klairvóyəns/ *n.* **1** the supposed faculty of perceiving things or events in the future or beyond normal sensory contact. **2** exceptional insight.

clair·voy·ant /klairvóyənt/ *n.* & *adj.* •*n.* a person having clairvoyance. •*adj.* having clairvoyance. ▫▫ **clair·voy·ant·ly** *adv.*

clam /klam/ *n.* & *v.* •*n.* **1** any bivalve mollusk, esp. the edible N. American hard or round clam (*Mercenaria mercenaria*) or the soft or long clam (*Mya arenaria*). **2** *colloq.* a shy or withdrawn person. •*v.intr.* (**clammed, clamming**) **1** dig for clams. **2** (foll. by *up*) *colloq.* refuse to talk.

clam·bake /klámbayk/ *n.* a picnic at the seashore typically featuring clams, lobsters, and ears of corn steamed over hot stones beneath a layer of seaweed.

clam·ber /klámbər/ *v.* & *n.* •*v.intr.* climb with hands and feet, esp. with difficulty or laboriously. •*n.* a difficult climb.

clam·my /klámee/ *adj.* (**clammier, clammiest**) **1** unpleasantly damp and sticky or slimy. **2** (of weather) cold and damp. ▫▫ **clam·mi·ly** *adv.* **clam·mi·ness** *n.*

clam·or /klámər/ *n.* & *v.* (*Brit.* **clamour**) •*n.* **1** loud or vehement shouting or noise. **2** a protest or complaint; an appeal or demand. •*v.* **1** *intr.* make a clamor. **2** *tr.* utter with a clamor. ▫▫ **clam·or·ous** *adj.* **clam·or·ous·ly** *adv.* **clam·or·ous·ness** *n.*

clamp /klamp/ *n.* & *v.* •*n.* a device, esp. a brace or band of iron, etc., for strengthening other materials or holding things together. •*v.tr.* **1** strengthen or fasten with a clamp. **2** place or hold firmly. **3** immobilize (an illegally parked car) by fixing a clamp to one of its wheels. ▫ **clamp down 1** (often foll. by *on*) be rigid in enforcing a rule, etc. **2** (foll. by *on*) try to suppress.

clamp

clamp·down /klámpdown/ *n.* severe restriction or suppression.

clan /klan/ *n.* **1** a group of people with a common ancestor, esp. in the Scottish Highlands. **2** a large family as a social group. **3** a group with a strong common interest. **4 a** a genus, species, or class. **b** a family or group of animals, e.g., elephants.

clan·des·tine /klandéstin/ *adj.* surreptitious; secret. ▫▫ **clan·des·tine·ly** *adv.* **clan·des·tin·i·ty** /–tínitee/ *n.*

clang /klang/ *n.* & *v.* •*n.* a loud, resonant, metallic sound as of a bell or hammer, etc. •*v.* **1** *intr.* make a clang. **2** *tr.* cause to clang.

clang·er /klángər/ *n. Brit. sl.* a mistake or blunder. ▫ **drop a clanger** commit a conspicuous indiscretion.

clang·or /klánggər/ *n.* **1** a prolonged or repeated clanging noise. **2** an uproar or commotion. ▫▫ **clang·or·ous** *adj.* **clang·or·ous·ly** *adv.*

clank /klangk/ *n.* & *v.* •*n.* a sound as of heavy pieces of metal meeting or a chain rattling. •*v.* **1** *intr.* make a clanking sound. **2** *tr.* cause to clank. ▫▫ **clank·ing·ly** *adv.*

clap[1] /klap/ *v.* & *n.* •*v.* (**clapped, clapping**) **1 a** *intr.* strike the palms of one's hands together as a signal or repeatedly as applause. **b** *tr.* strike (the hands) together in this way. **2** *tr.* **a** *Brit.* applaud or show one's approval of (esp. a person) in this way. **b** slap with the palm of the hand as a sign of approval or encouragement. **3** *tr.* (of a bird) flap (its wings) audibly. **4** *tr.* put or place quickly or with determination (*clapped him in prison*; *clap a tax on whiskey*). •*n.* **1** the act of clapping, esp. as applause. **2** an explosive sound, esp. of thunder. **3** a slap; a pat. ▫ **clap eyes on** *colloq.* see.

clap[2] /klap/ *n. coarse sl.* venereal disease, esp. gonorrhea.

clap·per /klápər/ *n.* the tongue or striker of a bell. ▫ **like the clappers** *Brit. sl.* very fast or hard.

clap·trap /kláptrap/ *n.* **1** insincere or pretentious talk; nonsense. **2** language used or feelings expressed only to gain applause.

claque /klak/ *n.* a group of people hired to applaud in a theater, etc.

clar·et /klárət/ *n.* & *adj.* •*n.* **1** red wine, esp. from Bordeaux. **2** a deep purplish-red. •*adj.* claret-colored.

clar·i·fy /klárifī/ *v.* (**·fies, ·fied**) **1** *tr.* & *intr.* make or become clearer. **2** *tr.* **a** free (liquid, butter, etc.) from impurities. **b** make transparent. **c** purify. ▫▫ **clar·i·fi·ca·tion** *n.* **clar·i·fi·er** *n.*

clar·i·net /klárinét/ *n.* **1 a** a woodwind instrument with a single-reed mouthpiece, a cylindrical tube with a flared end, holes, and keys. **b** its player. **2** an organ stop with a quality resembling a clarinet. ▫▫ **clar·i·net·ist** *n.* (also **clar·i·net·tist**)

clar·i·on /kláreeən/ *n.* & *adj.* •*n.* **1** a clear, rousing sound. **2** *hist.* a shrill, narrow-tubed war trumpet. **3** an organ stop with the quality of a clarion. •*adj.* clear and loud.

clar·i·ty /kláritee/ *n.* the state or quality of being clear, esp. of sound or expression.

clash /klash/ *n.* & *v.* •*n.* **1 a** a loud, jarring sound as of metal objects being struck together. **b** a collision, esp. with force. **2 a** a conflict or disagreement. **b** a discord of colors, etc. •*v.* **1 a** *intr.* make a clashing sound. **b** *tr.* cause to clash. **2** *intr.* collide; coincide awkwardly. **3** *intr.* (often foll. by *with*) **a** come into conflict or be at variance. **b** (of colors) be discordant. ▫▫ **clash·er** *n.*

clasp /klasp/ *n.* & *v.* •*n.* **1 a** a device with interlocking parts for fastening. **b** a buckle or brooch. **c** a metal fastening on a book cover. **2 a** an embrace; a person's reach. **b** a grasp or handshake. **3** a bar of silver on a medal ribbon with the name of the battle, etc., at which the wearer was present. •*v.* **1** *tr.* fasten with or as with a clasp. **2** *tr.* **a** grasp; hold closely. **b** embrace, encircle. **3** *intr.* fasten a clasp. ▫ **clasp hands** shake hands with fervor or affection. **clasp one's hands** interlace one's fingers. ▫▫ **clasp·er** *n.*

clasper /kláspər/ *n.* (in *pl.*) the appendages of some male fish and insects used to hold the female in copulation.

class /klas/ *n.* & *v.* •*n.* **1** any set of persons or things grouped together, or graded or differentiated from others esp. by quality (*first class*; *economy class*). **2 a** a division or order of society (*upper class*; *professional classes*). **b** a caste system; a system of social classes. **c** (**the classes**) *archaic* the rich or educated. **3** *colloq.* distinction or high quality in appearance, behavior, etc.; stylishness. **4 a** a group of students taught together. **b** the occasion when they meet. **c** their course of instruction. **5** all the college or school students of the same standing or graduating in a given year (*the class of 1990*). **6** (in conscripted armies) all the recruits born in a given year (*the 1950 class*). **7** *Brit.* a division of candidates according to merit in an examination. **8** *Biol.* a grouping of organisms, the next major rank below a division or phylum. • *v.tr.* assign to a class or category. □ **in a class of its** (or **one's**) **own** unequaled. **no class** *colloq.* a lack of quality or distinction, esp. in behavior.

class-con·scious *adj.* aware of and reacting to social divisions or one's place in a system of social class. □□ **class-con·scious·ness** *n.*

clas·sic /klásik/ *adj.* & *n.* • *adj.* **1 a** of the first class; of acknowledged excellence. **b** remarkably typical; outstandingly important (*a classic case*). **c** having enduring worth; timeless. **2 a** of ancient Greek and Latin literature, art, or culture. **b** (of style in art, music, etc.) simple, harmonious, well-proportioned; in accordance with established forms (cf. ROMANTIC). **3** having literary or historic associations (*classic ground*). **4** (of clothes) made in a simple elegant style not much affected by changes in fashion. • *n.* **1** a classic writer, artist, work, or example. **2 a** an ancient Greek or Latin writer. **b** (in *pl.*) the study of ancient Greek and Latin literature and history. **3** a garment in classic style. ▶Traditionally, **classic** means 'typical; excellent as an example; timeless' and **classical** means 'of (esp. Greek or Roman) antiquity.' Thus: *John Ford directed many classic Westerns. The museum was built in the classical style.* Great art is considered **classic**, not **classical**, unless it is created in the forms of antiquity. *Classical music* is formal and sophisticated music adhering to certain stylistic principles, esp. those of the late 18th century, but *a classic folk song* is one that well expresses its culture. A *classical education* exposes a student to *classical* literature, disciplines, and languages (especially Latin and Greek), but the study of Greek and Latin languages and their literature is also referred to as *classics*, as in *he majored in classics at college.*

clas·si·cal /klásikəl/ *adj.* **1 a** of ancient Greek or Latin literature or art. **b** (of language) having the form used by the ancient standard authors (*classical Latin*; *classical Hebrew*). **c** based on the study of ancient Greek and Latin (*a classical education*). **d** learned in classical studies. **2 a** (of music) serious or conventional; following traditional principles and intended to be of permanent rather than ephemeral value (cf. POPULAR, LIGHT). **b** of the period *c.*1750–1800 (cf. ROMANTIC). **3 a** in or following the restrained style of classical antiquity (cf. ROMANTIC). **b** (of a form or period of art, etc.) representing an exemplary standard; having a long-established worth. **4** *Physics* relating to the concepts that preceded relativity and quantum theory. □□ **clas·si·cal·ism** *n.* **clas·si·cal·ist** *n.* **clas·si·cal·i·ty** /–kálitee/ *n.* **clas·si·cal·ly** *adv.*

clas·si·cism /klásisizəm/ *n.* **1** the following of a classic style. **2 a** classical scholarship. **b** the advocacy of a classical education. **3** an ancient Greek or Latin idiom. □□ **clas·si·cist** *n.*

clas·si·cize /klásisīz/ *v.* **1** *tr.* make classic. **2** *intr.* imitate a classical style.

clas·si·fied /klásifīd/ *adj.* **1** arranged in classes or categories. **2** (of information, etc.) designated as officially secret. **3** *Brit.* (of a road) assigned to a category according to its importance. **4** (of newspaper advertisements) arranged in columns according to various categories.

clas·si·fy /klásifī/ *v.tr.* (**·fies, ·fied**) **1 a** arrange in classes or categories. **b** assign (a thing) to a class or category. **2** designate as officially secret or not for general disclosure. □□ **clas·si·fi·a·ble** *adj.* **clas·si·fi·ca·tion** *n.* **clas·si·fi·ca·to·ry** /klásifikətáwree, kləsífi–, klásifikáytəree/ *adj.* **clas·si·fi·er** *n.*

class·less /kláslis/ *adj.* making or showing no distinction of classes (*classless society*; *classless accent*). □□ **class·less·ness** *n.*

class·mate /klásmayt/ *n.* a fellow member of a class, esp. at school.

class·room /klásrōōm, –rŏŏm/ *n.* a room in which a class of students is taught, esp. in a school.

class·y /klásee/ *adj.* (**classier, classiest**) *colloq.* superior; stylish. □□ **class·i·ly** *adv.* **class·i·ness** *n.*

clat·ter /klátər/ *n.* & *v.* • *n.* **1** a rattling sound as of many hard objects struck together. **2** noisy talk. • *v.* **1** *intr.* **a** make a clatter. **b** fall or move, etc., with a clatter. **2** *tr.* cause (plates, etc.) to clatter.

clause /klawz/ *n.* **1** *Gram.* a distinct part of a sentence, including a subject and predicate. **2** a single statement in a treaty, law, bill, or contract. □□ **claus·al** *adj.*

claus·tro·pho·bi·a /kláwstrəfṓbeeə/ *n.* an abnormal fear of confined places. □□ **claus·tro·phobe** /–rəfōb/ *n.*

claus·tro·pho·bic /kláwstrəfṓbik/ *adj.* **1** suffering from claustrophobia. **2** inducing claustrophobia. □□ **claus·tro·pho·bi·cal·ly** *adv.*

clave[1] /klayv/ *n. Mus.* a hardwood stick used in pairs to make a hollow sound when struck together.

clave[2] *past* of CLEAVE[2].

clav·i·chord /klávikawrd/ *n.* a small keyboard instrument with a very soft tone.

clav·i·cle /klávikəl/ *n.* the collarbone. □□ **cla·vic·u·lar** /kləvíkyələr/ *adj.*

cla·vier /kləvéer, kláveeər, kláyveeər/ *n. Mus.* **1** any keyboard instrument. **2** its keyboard.

claw /klaw/ *n.* & *v.* • *n.* **1 a** a pointed horny nail on an animal's or bird's foot. **b** a foot armed with claws. **2** the pincers of a shellfish. **3** a device for grappling, holding, etc. • *v.* **1** *tr.* & *intr.* scratch, maul, or pull (a person or thing) with claws. **2** *intr.* (often foll. by *at*) grasp, clutch, or scrabble at as with claws. □ **claw back** regain laboriously or gradually. □□ **clawed** *adj.* (also in *comb.*). **claw·er** *n.* **claw·less** *adj.*

claw ham·mer *n.* a hammer with one side of the head forked for extracting nails.

clay /klay/ *n.* **1** a stiff, sticky earth, used for making bricks, pottery, ceramics, etc. **2** *poet.* the substance of the human body. **3** (in full **clay pipe**) a tobacco pipe made of clay. □□ **clay·ey** *adj.* **clay·ish** *adj.* **clay·like** *adj.*

clay pig·eon *n.* a breakable disk thrown up from a trap as a target for shooting.

-cle /kəl/ *suffix* forming (orig. diminutive) nouns (*article*; *particle*).

clean /kleen/ *adj., adv., v.,* & *n.* • *adj.* **1** (often foll. by *of*) free from dirt or contaminating matter; unsoiled. **2** clear; unused or unpolluted; preserving what is regarded as the original state (*clean air*; *clean page*). **3** free from obscenity or indecency. **4 a** attentive to personal hygiene and cleanliness. **b** (of animals) house-trained. **5** complete; clear-cut; unobstructed; even. **6 a** (of a ship, aircraft, or car) streamlined; smooth. **b** well-formed; slender and shapely (*clean-limbed*; *the car has clean lines*). **7** adroit; skillful (*clean fielding*). **8** (of a nuclear weapon) producing relatively little fallout. **9 a** free from ceremonial defilement or from disease. **b** (of food) not prohibited. **10 a** free from any record of a crime, offense, etc. (*a clean driving record*). **b** colloq. (of an alcoholic or drug addict) not possessing or using alcohol or drugs. **c** *sl.* not carrying a weapon or incriminating material; free from suspicion. **11** (of a taste, smell, etc.) sharp; fresh; distinctive. • *adv.* **1** completely; outright; simply (*cut clean through*; *clean forgot*). **2** in a clean manner. • *v.* **1** *tr.* (also foll. by *of*) & *intr.* make or become clean. **2** *tr.* eat all the food on (one's plate). **3** *tr. Cooking* remove the innards of (fish or fowl). **4** *intr.* make oneself clean. • *n.* esp. *Brit.* the act or process of cleaning or being cleaned (*give it a clean*). □ **clean out 1** clean or clear thoroughly. **2** *sl.* empty or deprive (esp. of money). **clean up 1 a** clear (a mess) away. **b** (also *absol.*) make (things) neat. **c** make (oneself) clean. **2** restore order or morality to. **3** *sl.* **a** acquire as gain or profit. **b** make a gain or profit. **come clean** *colloq.* own up; confess everything. **make a clean breast of** see BREAST. **make a clean sweep of** see SWEEP. □□ **clean·a·ble** *adj.* **clean·ish** *adj.* **clean·ness** *n.*

clean-cut *adj.* **1** sharply outlined. **2** neatly groomed.

clean·er /kléenər/ *n.* **1** a person employed to clean the interior of a building. **2** (usu. in *pl.*) a commercial establishment for cleaning clothes. **3** a device or substance for cleaning. □ **take to the cleaners** *sl.* **1** defraud or rob (a person) of all his or her money. **2** criticize severely.

clean-liv·ing *adj.* of upright character.

clean·ly /kléenlee/ *adv.* **1** in a clean way. **2** efficiently; without difficulty.

cleanse /klenz/ *v.tr.* **1** usu. *formal* make clean. **2** (often foll. by *of*) purify from sin or guilt.

cleans·er /klénzər/ *n.* **1** one that cleanses. **2** an agent, as a lotion or an abrasive powder, used for cleansing.

clean slate *n.* freedom from commitments or imputations; the removal of these from one's record.

clean·up /kléenup/ *n.* **1** an act of cleaning up. **2** *sl.* a huge profit. **3** *Baseball* the fourth position in the batting order.

clear /kleer/ *adj., adv., & v.* • *adj.* **1** free from dirt or contamination. **2** (of weather, the sky, etc.) not dull or cloudy. **3 a** transparent. **b** lustrous; shining. **c** (of the complexion) fresh and unblemished. **4** (of soup) not containing solid ingredients. **5 a** distinct; easily perceived by the senses. **b** unambiguous; easily understood (*make a thing clear; make oneself clear*). **c** manifest; not confused nor doubtful (*clear evidence*). **6** that discerns or is able to discern readily and accurately (*clear thinking; clear-sighted*). **7** (usu. foll. by *about, on,* or *that* + clause) confident; convinced; certain. **8** (of a conscience) free from guilt. **9** (of a road, etc.) unobstructed; open. **10 a** net; without deduction (*a clear $1,000*). **b** complete (*three clear days*). **11** (often foll. by *of*) free; unhampered; unencumbered by debt, commitments, etc. **12** (foll. by *of*) not obstructed by. • *adv.* **1** clearly (*speak loud and clear*). **2** completely (*he got clear away*). **3** apart; out of contact (*keep clear; stand clear of the doors*). **4** (foll. by *to*) all the way. • *v.* **1** *tr. & intr.* make or become clear. **2 a** *tr.* (often foll. by *of*) free from prohibition or obstruction. **b** *tr. & intr.* make or become empty or unobstructed. **c** *tr.* free (land) for cultivation or building by cutting down trees, etc. **d** *tr.* cause people to leave (a room, etc.). **3** *tr.* (often foll. by *of*) show or declare (a person) to be innocent (*cleared them of complicity*). **4** *tr.* approve (a person) for special duty, access to information, etc. **5** *tr.* pass over or by safely or without touching, esp. by jumping. **6** *tr.* make (an amount of money) as a net gain or to balance expenses. **7** *tr.* pass (a check) through a clearinghouse. **8** *tr.* pass through (a customs office, etc.). **9** *tr.* remove (an obstruction, an unwanted object, etc.) (*clear them out of the way*). **10** *tr.* (also *absol.*) *Sports* send (the ball, puck, etc.) out of one's defensive zone. **11** *intr.* (often foll. by *away, up*) (of physical phenomena) disappear; gradually diminish (*mist cleared by lunchtime*). **12** *tr.* (often foll. by *off*) discharge (a debt). □ **clear the air 1** make the air less sultry. **2** disperse an atmosphere of suspicion, tension, etc. **clear away 1** remove completely. **2** remove the remains of a meal from the table. **clear the decks** prepare for action, esp. fighting. **clear off 1** get rid of. **2** *colloq.* go away. **clear out 1** empty. **2** remove. **3** *colloq.* go away. **clear one's throat** cough slightly to make one's voice clear. **clear up 1** tidy up. **2** solve (a mystery, etc.); remove (a difficulty, etc.). **3** (of weather) become fine. **clear the way 1** remove obstacles. **2** stand aside. **clear (something) with** get approval or authorization for a thing from (a person). **in the clear** free from suspicion or difficulty. **out of a clear (blue) sky** as a complete surprise. □□ **clear·a·ble** *adj.* **clear·er** *n.* **clear·ly** *adv.* **clear·ness** *n.*

clear·ance /kléerəns/ *n.* **1** the removal of obstructions, etc., esp. removal of buildings, persons, etc., so as to clear land. **2** clear space allowed for the passing of two objects or two parts in machinery, etc. **3** special authorization or permission (esp. for an aircraft to take off or land, or for access to information, etc.). **4 a** the clearing of a person, ship, etc., by customs. **b** a certificate showing this. **5** the clearing of checks.

clear·ing /kléering/ *n.* **1** in senses of CLEAR *v.* **2** an area in a forest cleared for cultivation.

clear·ing·house /kléeringhows/ *n.* **1** a bankers' establishment where checks and bills from member banks are exchanged, so that only the balances need be paid in cash. **2** an agency for collecting and distributing information, etc.

clear·sto·ry var. of CLERESTORY.

cleat /kleet/ *n.* **1** a piece of metal, wood, etc., bolted on for fastening ropes to, or to strengthen woodwork, etc. **2** a projecting piece on a spar, gangway, athletic shoe, etc., to give footing or prevent slipping. **3** a wedge.

cleav·age /kléevij/ *n.* **1** the hollow between a woman's breasts, esp. as exposed by a low-cut garment. **2** a division or splitting. **3** the splitting of rocks, crystals, etc., in a preferred direction.

cleave[1] /kleev/ *v.* (*past* **cleaved** or **cleft** /kleft/ or **clove** /klōv/; *past part.* **cleaved** or **cleft** or **cloven** /klṓvən/) *literary* **1 a** *tr.* chop or break apart; split, esp. along the grain or the line of cleavage. **b** *intr.* come apart in this way. **2** *tr.* make one's way through (air or water). □□ **cleav·a·ble** *adj.*

cleave[2] /kleev/ *v.intr.* (*past* **cleaved** or **clove** /klōv/ or **clave** /klayv/) (foll. by *to*) *literary* stick fast; adhere.

cleav·er /kléevər/ *n.* a tool for cleaving, esp. a heavy chopping tool used by butchers.

clef /klef/ *n. Mus.* any of several symbols placed at the beginning of a staff, indicating the pitch of the notes written on it.

cleft[1] /kleft/ *adj.* split; partly divided.

cleft[2] /kleft/ *n.* a split or fissure; a space or division made by cleaving.

cleft pal·ate *n.* a congenital split in the lip or the roof of the mouth.

clem·a·tis /klémətis, klәmátis/ *n.* any erect or climbing plant of the genus *Clematis*, bearing white, pink, or purple flowers and feathery seeds, e.g., old man's beard.

clem·ent /klémənt/ *adj.* **1** mild (*clement weather*). **2** merciful. □□ **clem·en·cy** /–mənsee/ *n.*

clem·en·tine /kléməntīn, –teen/ *n.* a small citrus fruit, thought to be a hybrid between a tangerine and sweet orange.

clench /klench/ *v. & n.* • *v.tr.* **1** close (the teeth or fingers) tightly. **2** grasp firmly. **3** = CLINCH *v.* 4. • *n.* **1** a clenching action. **2** a clenched state.

clere·sto·ry /kléerstawree/ *n.* (also **clear·sto·ry**) (*pl.* **·ries**) **1** an upper row of windows in a cathedral or large church, above the level of the aisle roofs. **2** a raised section of the roof of a railroad car, with windows or ventilators.

cler·gy /klə́rjee/ *n.* (*pl.* **·gies**) (usu. treated as *pl.*) **1** (usu. prec. by *the*) the body of all persons ordained for religious duties. **2** a number of such persons (*ten clergy were present*).

cler·gy·man /klə́rjeemən/ *n.* (*pl.* **·men;** *fem.* **clergywoman,** *pl.* **·women**) a member of the clergy.

cler·ic /klérik/ *n.* a member of the clergy.

cler·i·cal /klérikəl/ *adj.* **1** of the clergy or clergymen. **2** of or done by a clerk or clerks. ◻◻ **cler·i·cal·ism** *n.* **cler·i·cal·ist** *n.* **cler·i·cal·ly** *adv.*

cler·i·cal er·ror *n.* an error made in copying or writing out.

clerk /klərk/ *n.* & *v.* •*n.* **1** a person employed in an office, bank, etc., to keep records, accounts, etc. **2** a secretary, agent, or record keeper of a municipality (*town clerk*), court, etc. **3** a lay officer of a church (*parish clerk*), college chapel, etc. **4** *Brit.* a senior official in Parliament. **5** a person who works at the sales counter of a store, at a hotel desk, etc. **6** *archaic* a clergyman. •*v.intr.* work as a clerk. ◻◻ **clerk·dom** *n.* **clerk·ess** *n.* **clerk·ly** *adj.* **clerk·ship** *n.*

clev·er /klévər/ *adj.* (**cleverer, cleverest**) **1 a** skillful; talented; quick to understand and learn. **b** showing good sense or wisdom; wise. **2** adroit; dextrous. **3** (of the doer or the thing done) ingenious; cunning. ◻◻ **clev·er·ly** *adv.* **clev·er·ness** *n.*

---

clever Middle English (in the sense 'quick to catch hold,' only recorded in this period): perhaps of Dutch or Low German origin, and related to CLEAVE[2]. In the late 16th century the term came to mean (probably through dialect use) 'manually skilfull'; the sense 'possessing mental agility' dates from the early 18th century.

---

clev·is /klévis/ *n.* **1** a U-shaped piece of metal at the end of a beam for attaching tackle, etc. **2** a connection in which a bolt holds one part that fits between the forked ends of another.

clew /klo͞o/ *n.* & *v.* •*n.* **1** *Naut.* **a** a lower or after corner of a sail. **b** a set of small cords suspending a hammock. **2** *archaic* **a** a ball of thread or yarn, esp. with reference to the legend of Theseus and the labyrinth. **b** *Brit.* = CLUE. •*v.tr. Naut.* **1** (foll. by *up*) draw the lower ends of (a sail) to the upper yard or the mast ready for furling. **2** (foll. by *down*) let down (a sail) by the clews in unfurling.

cli·ché /kleesháy/ *n.* (also **cli·che**) **1** a hackneyed phrase or opinion. **2** *Brit.* a metal casting of a stereotype or electrotype.

click /klik/ *n.* & *v.* •*n.* **1** a slight, sharp sound, as of a switch being operated. **2** a sharp nonvocal suction, used as a speech sound in some languages. **3** a catch in machinery acting with a slight, sharp sound. **4** (of a horse) an action causing a hind foot to touch the shoe of a forefoot. •*v.* **1 a** *intr.* make a click. **b** *tr.* cause (one's tongue, heels, etc.) to click. **2** *intr. colloq.* **a** become clear or understandable (often prec. by *it* as subject: *when I saw them it all clicked*). **b** be successful; secure one's object. **c** (foll. by *with*) become friendly, esp. with a person of the opposite sex. **d** come to an agreement. ◻◻ **click·er** *n.*

cli·ent /klíənt/ *n.* **1** a person using the services of a lawyer, architect, social worker, or other professional person. **2** a customer. ◻◻ **cli·ent·ship** *n.*

cli·en·tele /klíəntél, kléeon–/ *n.* **1** clients collectively. **2** customers, esp. of a store or restaurant. **3** the patrons of a theater, etc.

cli·ent-serv·er *attrib.adj. Computing* relating to a computer system in which a central server provides data to a number of networked workstations.

cliff /klif/ *n.* a steep rock face, as at the edge of the sea. ◻◻ **cliff·like** *adj.* **cliff·y** *adj.*

cliff-hang·er *n.* a story, etc., with a strong element of suspense; a suspenseful ending to an episode of a serial. ◻◻ **cliff-hang·ing** *adj.*

cli·mac·ter·ic /klīmáktərik, klīmaktérik/ *n.* & *adj.* •*n.* **1** *Med.* the period of life when fertility and sexual activity are in decline. **2** a supposed critical period in life (esp. occurring at intervals of seven years). •*adj.* **1** *Med.* occurring at the climacteric. **2** constituting a crisis; critical.

cli·mate /klímit/ *n.* **1** the prevailing weather conditions of an area. **2** a region with particular weather conditions. **3** the prevailing trend of opinion or public feeling. ◻◻ **cli·mat·ic** /–mátik/ *adj.* **cli·mat·i·cal** *adj.* **cli·mat·i·cal·ly** *adv.*

cli·ma·tol·o·gy /klímətóləjee/ *n.* the scientific study of climate. ◻◻ **cli·ma·to·log·i·cal** /–təlójikəl/ *adj.* **cli·ma·tol·o·gist** *n.*

cli·max /klímaks/ *n.* & *v.* •*n.* **1** the event or point of greatest intensity or interest; a culmination or apex. **2** a sexual orgasm. **3** *Rhet.* **a** a series arranged in order of increasing importance, etc. **b** the last term in such a series. **4** *Ecol.* a state of equilibrium reached by a plant community. •*v.tr.* & *intr. colloq.* bring or come to a climax.

climb /klīm/ *v.* & *n.* •*v.* **1** *tr.* & *intr.* (often foll. by *up*) ascend, mount, go or come up, esp. by using one's hands. **2** *intr.* (of a plant) grow up a wall, tree, trellis, etc., by clinging with tendrils or by twining. **3** *intr.* make progress from one's own efforts, esp. in social rank, intellectual or moral strength, etc. **4** *intr.* (of an aircraft, the sun, etc.) go upward. **5** *intr.* slope upward. •*n.* **1** an ascent by climbing. **2 a** a place, esp. a hill, climbed or to be climbed. **b** a recognized route up a mountain, etc. ◻ **climb down 1** descend with the help of one's hands. **2** withdraw from a stance taken up in argument, negotiation, etc. ◻◻ **climb·a·ble** *adj.*

clime /klīm/ *n. literary* **1** a region. **2** a climate.

clinch /klinch/ *v.* & *n.* •*v.* **1** *tr.* confirm or settle (an argument, bargain, etc.) conclusively. **2** *intr. Boxing & Wrestling* (of participants) become too closely engaged. **3** *intr. colloq.* embrace. **4** *tr.* secure (a nail or rivet) by driving the point sideways when through. **5** *tr. Naut.* fasten (a rope) with a particular half hitch. •*n.* **1 a** a clinching action. **b** a clinched state. **2** *colloq.* an (esp. amorous) embrace. **3** *Boxing & Wrestling* an action or state in which participants become too closely engaged.

clinch·er /klínchər/ *n. colloq.* a remark or argument that settles a matter conclusively.

cline /klīn/ *n. Biol.* the graded sequence of differences within a species, etc. ◻◻ **clin·al** *adj.*

cling /kling/ *v.intr.* (*past* and *past part.* **clung** /klung/) **1** (foll. by *to*) adhere, stick, or hold on (by means of stickiness, suction, grasping, or embracing). **2** (foll. by *to*) remain persistently or stubbornly faithful (to a friend, habit, idea, etc.). **3** maintain one's grasp; keep hold; resist separation. ◻ **cling together** remain in one body or in contact. ◻◻ **cling·er** *n.* **cling·ing·ly** *adv.*

cling·y /klíngee/ *adj.* (**clingier, clingiest**) liable to cling. ◻◻ **cling·i·ness** *n.*

clin·ic /klínik/ *n.* **1** a private or specialized hospital. **2** a place or occasion for giving specialist medical treatment or advice (*eye clinic*; *fertility clinic*). **3** a gathering at a hospital bedside for the teaching of medicine or surgery. **4** a conference or short course on a particular subject (*golf clinic*). ◻◻ **cli·ni·cian** /klinishən/ *n.*

clin·i·cal /klínikəl/ *adj.* **1** *Med.* **a** of or for the treatment of patients. **b** taught or learned at the hospital bedside. **2** dispassionate; coldly detached. ◻◻ **clin·i·cal·ly** *adv.*

clink[1] /klingk/ *n.* & *v.* •*n.* a sharp ringing sound. •*v.* **1** *intr.* make a clink. **2** *tr.* cause (glasses, etc.) to clink.

clink[2] /klingk/ *n.* (often prec. by *in*) *sl.* prison.

clink·er /klíngkər/ *n.* **1** a mass of slag or lava. **2** a stony residue from burned coal.

cli·nom·e·ter /klīnómitər/ *n. Surveying* an instrument for measuring slopes.

clip[1] /klip/ *n.* & *v.* •*n.* **1** a device for holding things together or for attachment to an object as a marker, esp. a paper clip or a device worked by a spring. **2** a piece of jewelry fastened by a clip. **3** a set of attached cartridges for a firearm. • *v.tr.* (**clipped, clipping**) **1** fix with a clip. **2** grip tightly.

clip[2] /klip/ *v. & n.* • *v.tr.* (**clipped, clipping**) **1** cut with shears or scissors, esp. cut short or trim (hair, wool, etc.). **2** trim or remove the hair or wool of (a person or animal). **3** *colloq.* hit smartly. **4 a** curtail; diminish; cut short. **b** omit (a letter, etc.) from a word; omit letters or syllables of (words pronounced). **5** *Brit.* remove a small piece of (a ticket) to show that it has been used. **6** cut (an extract) from a newspaper, etc. **7** *sl.* swindle; rob. • *n.* **1** an act of clipping, esp. shearing or haircutting. **2** *colloq.* a smart blow, esp. with the hand. **3** a short sequence from a motion picture. **4** the quantity of wool clipped from a sheep, flock, etc. **5** *colloq.* speed, esp. rapid. □ **clip a person's wings** prevent a person from pursuing ambitions or acting effectively. □□ **clip·pa·ble** *adj.*

clip·board /klípbawrd/ *n.* a small board with a spring clip for holding papers, etc., and providing support for writing.

clip·per /klípər/ *n.* **1** (usu. in *pl.*) any of various instruments for clipping hair, fingernails, hedges, etc. **2** a fast sailing ship, esp. one with raking bows and masts. **3** a fast horse.

clip·ping /klíping/ *n.* a piece clipped or cut from something, esp. from a newspaper.

clique /kleek, klik/ *n.* a small exclusive group of people. □□ **cli·quey** *adj.* (**cliquier, cliquiest**). **cli·quish** *adj.* **cli·quish·ness** *n.* **cli·quism** *n.*

clit·o·ris /klítəris, klí–/ *n.* a small erectile part of the female genitals at the upper end of the vulva. □□ **clit·o·ral** *adj.*

clo·a·ca /klō–áykə/ *n.* (*pl.* **cloacae** /–áysee/) **1** the genital and excretory cavity at the end of the intestinal canal in birds, reptiles, etc. **2** a sewer. □□ **clo·a·cal** *adj.*

cloak /klōk/ *n. & v.* • *n.* **1** an outdoor overgarment, usu. sleeveless, hanging loosely from the shoulders. **2** a covering (*cloak of snow*). **3** *Brit.* (in *pl.*) = CLOAKROOM. • *v.tr.* **1** cover with a cloak. **2** conceal; disguise. □ **under the cloak of** using as a pretext or for concealment.

cloak-and-dag·ger *adj.* involving intrigue and espionage.

cloak·room /klṓkrōōm, –rōōm/ *n.* a room where outdoor clothes or luggage may be left.

clob·ber /klóbər/ *v.tr. sl.* **1** hit repeatedly; beat up. **2** defeat. **3** criticize severely.

cloche /klōsh/ *n.* **1** a small translucent cover for protecting or forcing outdoor plants. **2** (in full **cloche hat**) a woman's close-fitting, bell-shaped hat.

cloche

clock /klok/ *n. & v.* • *n.* **1** an instrument for measuring time, driven mechanically or electrically and indicating hours, minutes, etc., by hands on a dial or by displayed figures. **2 a** any measuring device resembling a clock. **b** *colloq.* a speedometer, taximeter, or stopwatch. **3** time taken as an element in competitive sports, etc. (*ran against the clock*). • *v.tr.* **1** *colloq.* **a** (often foll. by *up*) attain or register (a stated time, distance, or speed, esp. in a race). **b** time (a race) with a stopwatch. **2** *sl.* hit, esp. on the head. □ **around the clock** all day and (usu.) night. **clock in** (or **on**) register one's arrival at work, esp. by means of an automatic recording clock. **clock off** (or **out**) register one's departure similarly.

clock·wise /klókwīz/ *adj. & adv.* in a curve corresponding in direction to the movement of the hands of a clock.

clock·work /klókwərk/ *n.* **1** a mechanism like that of a mechanical clock, with a spring and gears. **2** (*attrib.*) **a** driven by clockwork. **b** regular; mechanical. □ **like clockwork** smoothly; regularly; automatically.

clod /klod/ *n.* **1** a lump of earth, clay, etc. **2** *sl.* a silly or foolish person. □□ **clod·dy** *adj.*

clod·dish /klódish/ *adj.* loutish; foolish; clumsy. □□ **clod·dish·ly** *adv.* **clod·dish·ness** *n.*

clod·hop·per /klódhopər/ *n.* **1** (usu. in *pl.*) *colloq.* a large heavy shoe. **2** = CLOD 2.

clod·hop·ping /klódhoping/ *adj.* = CLODDISH.

clog /klawg, klog/ *n. & v.* • *n.* **1** a shoe with a thick wooden sole. **2** *archaic* an encumbrance or impediment. • *v.* (**clogged, clogging**) **1** (often foll. by *up*) **a** *tr.* obstruct, esp. by accumulation of glutinous matter. **b** *intr.* become obstructed. **2** *tr.* impede; hamper. **3** *tr. & intr.* (often foll. by *up*) fill with glutinous or choking matter.

clog·gy /klawgee, klógee/ *adj.* (**cloggier, cloggiest**) **1** lumpy; knotty. **2** sticky.

cloi·son·né /klóyzənáy, klwaá–/ *n.* **1** an enamel finish produced by forming areas of different colors separated by strips of wire placed edgeways on a metal backing. **2** this process.

clois·ter /klóystər/ *n. & v.* • *n.* **1** a covered walk, often with a wall on one side and a colonnade open to a quadrangle on the other, esp. in a convent, monastery, college, or cathedral. **2** monastic life or seclusion. **3** a convent or monastery. • *v.tr.* seclude or shut up usu. in a convent or monastery. □□ **clois·tral** *adj.*

clomp var. of CLUMP *v.* 2.

clone /klōn/ *n. & v.* • *n.* **1 a** a group of organisms produced asexually from one stock or ancestor. **b** one such organism. **2** a person or thing regarded as identical with another. • *v.tr.* propagate as a clone. □□ **clon·al** *adj.*

clonk /klongk, klawngk/ *n. & v.* • *n.* an abrupt heavy sound of impact. • *v.* **1** *intr.* make such a sound. **2** *tr. colloq.* hit.

clop /klop/ *n. & v.* • *n.* the sound made by a horse's hooves. • *v.intr.* (**clopped, clopping**) make this sound.

close[1] /klōs/ *adj., adv., & n.* • *adj.* **1** (often foll. by *to*) situated at only a short distance or interval. **2 a** having a strong or immediate relation or connection (*close friend; close relative*). **b** in intimate friendship or association (*were very close*). **c** corresponding almost exactly (*close resemblance*). **d** fitting tightly (*close cap*). **e** (of hair, etc.) short; near the surface. **3** in or almost in contact (*close combat; close proximity*). **4** dense; compact; with no or only slight intervals (*close texture; close writing; close formation*). **5** in which competitors are almost equal (*close contest*). **6** leaving no gaps or weaknesses; rigorous (*close reasoning*). **7** concentrated; searching (*close examination; close attention*). **8** (of air, etc.) stuffy or humid. **9 a** closed; shut. **b** shut up; under secure confinement. **10** limited or restricted to certain persons, etc. (*close corporation; close scholarship*). **11 a** hidden; secret; covered. **b** secretive. **12** (of a danger, etc.) directly threatening; narrowly avoided (*that was close*). **13** niggardly. **14** (of a vowel) pronounced with a relatively narrow opening of the mouth. • *adv.* **1** (often foll. by *by, to*) at only a short distance or interval (*they live close by; close to the church*). **2** closely; in a close manner (*shut close*). • *n.* an enclosed space. □ **at close quarters** very close together. **close to the wind** see SAIL. □□ **close·ly** *adv.* **close·ness** *n.* **clos·ish** *adj.*

close[2] /klōz/ *v.* & *n.* •*v.* **1 a** *tr.* shut (a lid, box, door, room, house, etc.). **b** *intr.* become shut (*the door closed slowly*). **c** *tr.* block up. **2 a** *tr.* & *intr.* bring or come to an end. **b** *intr.* finish speaking (*closed with an expression of thanks*). **c** *tr.* settle (a bargain, etc.). **3 a** *intr.* end the day's business. **b** *tr.* end the day's business at (a store, office, etc.). **4** *tr.* & *intr.* bring or come closer or into contact (*close ranks*). **5** *tr.* make (an electric circuit, etc.) continuous. **6** *intr.* (often foll. by *with*) come within striking distance; grapple. **7** *intr.* (foll. by *on*) (of a hand, box, etc.) grasp or entrap. •*n.* **1** a conclusion; an end. **2** *Mus.* a cadence. □ **close down** (of a store, factory, etc.) discontinue business, esp. permanently. **close one's eyes 1** (foll. by *to*) pay no attention. **2** die. **close in 1** enclose. **2** come nearer. **3** (of days) get successively shorter with the approach of the winter solstice. **close off** prevent access to by blocking or sealing the entrance. **close out** discontinue; terminate; dispose of (a business). **close up 1** (often foll. by *to*) move closer. **2** shut, esp. temporarily. **3** block up. **4** (of an aperture) grow smaller. □□ **clos·a·ble** *adj.* **clos·er** *n.*

closed /klōzd/ *adj.* **1** not giving access; shut. **2** (of a store, etc.) having ceased business temporarily. **3** (of a society, system, etc.) self-contained; not communicating with others. **4** (of a sport, etc.) restricted to specified competitors, etc.

closed-cap·tioned *adj.* (of a television program) broadcast with captions visible only to viewers with a decoding device attached to their television set.

closed syl·la·ble *n.* a syllable ending in a consonant.

close·fist·ed /klōsfistid/ *adj.* miserly.

close-fit·ting *adj.* (of a garment) fitting close to the body.

close-knit *adj.* tightly bound or interlocked; closely united in friendship.

close·mouthed /klōsmówthd/ *adj.* reticent.

clos·et /klózit/ *n.* & *v.* •*n.* **1** a small or private room. **2** a cupboard or recess. **3** (*attrib.*) secret; covert (*closet homosexual*). •*v.tr.* (**closeted, closeting**) shut away, esp. in private conference or study. □ **come out of the closet** stop hiding something about oneself, esp. one's homosexuality.

close-up *n.* **1** a photograph, etc., taken at close range and showing the subject on a large scale. **2** an intimate description.

clo·sure /klṓzhər/ *n.* **1** the act or process of closing. **2** a closed condition. **3** something that closes or seals, e.g., a cap or tie.

clot /klot/ *n.* & *v.* •*n.* **1 a** a thick mass of coagulated liquid, esp. of blood exposed to air. **b** a mass of material stuck together. **2** *Brit. colloq.* a silly or foolish person. •*v.tr.* & *intr.* (**clotted, clotting**) form into clots.

cloth /klawth, kloth/ *n.* (*pl.* **cloths** /kloths, klothz/) **1** woven or felted material. **2** a piece of this. **3** a piece of cloth for a particular purpose; a tablecloth, dishcloth, etc. **4** woolen woven fabric as used for clothes. **5 a** profession or status, esp. of the clergy, as shown by clothes (*respect due to his cloth*). **b** (prec. by *the*) the clergy.

clothe /klōth/ *v.tr.* (*past* and *past part.* **clothed** or *formal* **clad**) **1** put clothes on; provide with clothes. **2** cover as with clothes or a cloth.

clothes /klōz, klōthz/ *n.pl.* **1** garments worn to cover the body and limbs. **2** bedclothes.

clothes·horse /klṓz–hawrs, klṓthz–/ *n.* **1** a frame for airing washed clothes. **2** *colloq.* an affectedly fashionable person.

clothes·line /klṓzlīn, klōthz–/ *n.* a rope or wire, etc., on which washed clothes are hung to dry.

clothes·pin /klṓzpin, klṓthz–/ *n.* a clip or forked device for securing clothes to a clothesline.

cloth·ier /klṓtheeər/ *n.* a seller of clothes.

cloth·ing /klṓthing/ *n.* clothes collectively.

clo·ture /klṓchər/ *n.* & *v.* •*n.* the legislative procedure for ending debate and taking a vote. •*v.tr.* apply cloture to.

cloud /klowd/ *n.* & *v.* •*n.* **1** a visible mass of condensed watery vapor floating in the atmosphere high above the general level of the ground. **2** a mass of smoke or dust. **3** (foll. by *of*) a great number of insects, birds, etc., moving together. **4 a** a state of gloom, trouble, or suspicion. **b** a frowning or depressed look (*a cloud on his brow*). **5** a local dimness or a vague patch of color in or on a liquid or a transparent body. •*v.* **1** *tr.* cover or darken with clouds or gloom or trouble. **2** *intr.* (often foll. by *over, up*) become overcast or gloomy. **3** *tr.* make unclear. □ **in the clouds 1** unreal; imaginary; mystical. **2** (of a person) abstracted; inattentive. **on cloud nine** *colloq.* extremely happy. **under a cloud** out of favor; discredited; under suspicion. **with one's head in the clouds** daydreaming; unrealistic. □□ **cloud·less** *adj.* **cloud·less·ly** *adv.* **cloud·let** *n.*

cloud·burst /klówdbərst/ *n.* a sudden violent rainstorm.

cloud·scape /klówdskayp/ *n.* **1** a picturesque grouping of clouds. **2** a picture or view of clouds.

cloud·y /klówdee/ *adj.* (**cloudier, cloudiest**) **1 a** (of the sky) covered with clouds; overcast. **b** (of weather) characterized by clouds. **2** not transparent; unclear. □□ **cloud·i·ly** *adv.* **cloud·i·ness** *n.*

clout /klowt/ *n.* & *v.* •*n.* **1** a heavy blow. **2** *colloq.* influence; power of effective action esp. in politics or business. **3** a nail with a large, flat head. •*v.tr.* hit hard.

clove[1] /klōv/ *n.* **1 a** a dried flower bud of a tropical plant, *Eugenia aromatica*, used as a pungent aromatic spice. **b** this plant. **2** (in full **clove gillyflower** *or* **clove pink**) a clove-scented pink, *Dianthus caryophyllus*, the original of the carnation and other double pinks.

clove[2] /klōv/ *n.* any of the small bulbs making up a compound bulb of garlic, shallot, etc.

clove[3] *past* of CLEAVE.

clo·ven /klṓv'n/ *adj.* split; partly divided.

clo·ven hoof *n.* (also **clo·ven foot**) the divided hoof of ruminant quadrupeds (e.g., oxen, sheep, goats); also ascribed to the god Pan, and so to the Devil. □□ **clo·ven-foot·ed** /–fŏŏtid/ *adj.* **clo·ven-hoofed** /–hŏŏft/ *adj.*

clo·ver /klṓvər/ *n.* any leguminous fodder plant of the genus *Trifolium*, having dense flower heads and leaves each consisting of usu. three leaflets. □ **in clover** in ease and luxury.

clo·ver·leaf /clṓvərleef/ *n.* a junction of roads intersecting at different levels with connecting sections forming the pattern of a four-leaf clover.

clown /klown/ *n.* & *v.* •*n.* **1** a comic entertainer, esp. in a pantomime or circus, usu. with traditional costume and makeup. **2** a silly, foolish, or playful person. •*v.* **1** *intr.* (often foll. by *about, around*) behave like a clown; act foolishly or playfully. **2** *tr.* perform (a part, an action, etc.) like a clown. □□ **clown·er·y** *n.* **clown·ish** *adj.* **clown·ish·ly** *adv.* **clown·ish·ness** *n.*

cloy /kloy/ *v.tr.* (usu. foll. by *with*) satiate or sicken with an excess of sweetness, richness, etc. □□ **cloy·ing·ly** *adv.*

CLU *abbr.* chartered life underwriter.

club /klub/ *n.* & *v.* •*n.* **1** a heavy stick with a thick end, used as a weapon, etc. **2** a stick used in a game, esp. a stick with a head used in golf. **3 a** a playing card of a suit denoted by a black trefoil. **b** (in *pl.*) this suit. **4** an association of persons united by a common interest, usu. meeting periodically for a shared activity (*tennis club*; *yacht club*). **5 a** an organization or premises offering members social amenities, meals, and temporary residence, etc. **b** a nightclub. **6** an organization offering subscribers certain benefits (*book club*). **7** a group of persons, nations, etc., having something in common. **8** = CLUBHOUSE. • *v.* (**clubbed, clubbing**) **1** *tr.* beat with or as with a club. **2** *intr.* (foll. by *together, with*) combine for joint action, esp. making up a sum of money for a purpose. ▫▫ **club·ber** *n.*

club·by /klúbee/ *adj.* (**clubbier, clubbiest**) sociable; friendly.

club·foot /klúbfŏŏt/ *n.* a congenitally deformed foot. ▫▫ **club·foot·ed** *adj.*

club·house /klúbhows/ *n.* the premises used by a club.

club·man /klúbmən, –man/ *n.* (*pl.* **·men**; *fem.* **·woman,** *pl.* **·women**) a member of one or more social clubs.

club sand·wich *n.* a sandwich with two layers of filling between three slices of toast or bread.

club so·da *n.* = SODA *n.* 2.

cluck /kluk/ *n.* & *v.* • *n.* **1** a guttural cry like that of a hen. **2** *sl.* a silly or foolish person (*dumb cluck*). • *v.intr.* emit a cluck or clucks.

clue /klōō/ *n.* & *v.* • *n.* **1** a fact or idea that serves as a guide, or suggests a line of inquiry, in a problem or investigation. **2** a piece of evidence, etc., in the detection of a crime. **3** a verbal formula serving as a hint as to what is to be inserted in a crossword. **4 a** the thread of a story. **b** a train of thought. • *v.tr.* (**clues, clued, clueing** or **cluing**) provide a clue to. ▫ **clue in** (or *Brit.* **up**) *sl.* inform. **not have a clue** *colloq.* be ignorant or incompetent.

clue·less /klṓōlis/ *adj. colloq.* ignorant; stupid. ▫▫ **clue·less·ly** *adv.* **clue·less·ness** *n.*

clump /klump/ *n.* & *v.* • *n.* **1** (foll. by *of*) a cluster of plants, esp. trees or shrubs. **2** an agglutinated mass of blood cells, etc. • *v.* **1 a** *intr.* form a clump. **b** *tr.* heap or plant together. **2** *intr.* (also **clomp** /klomp/) walk with heavy tread. **3** *tr. colloq.* hit. ▫▫ **clump·y** *adj.* (**clumpier, clumpiest**).

clum·sy /klúmzee/ *adj.* (**clumsier, clumsiest**) **1** awkward in movement or shape; ungainly. **2** difficult to handle or use. **3** tactless. ▫▫ **clum·si·ly** *adv.* **clum·si·ness** *n.*

clung *past* and *past part.* of CLING.

clunk /klungk/ *n.* & *v.* • *n.* a dull sound as of thick pieces of metal meeting. • *v.intr.* make such a sound.

clus·ter /klústər/ *n.* & *v.* • *n.* **1** a close group or bunch of similar things growing together. **2** a close group or swarm of people, animals, faint stars, gems, etc. **3** a group of successive consonants or vowels. • *v.* **1** *tr.* bring into a cluster or clusters. **2** *intr.* be or come into a cluster or clusters. **3** *intr.* (foll. by *around*) gather; congregate.

clus·tered /klústərd/ *adj.* **1** growing in or brought into a cluster. **2** *Archit.* (of pillars, columns, or shafts) several close together, or disposed around or half detached from a pier.

clutch[1] /kluch/ *v.* & *n.* • *v.* **1** *tr.* seize eagerly; grasp tightly. **2** *intr.* (foll. by *at*) snatch suddenly. • *n.* **1 a** a tight grasp. **b** (foll. by *at*) grasping. **2** (in *pl.*) grasping hands, esp. as representing a cruel or relentless grasp or control. **3 a** (in a motor vehicle) a device for connecting and disconnecting the engine to the transmission. **b** the pedal operating this. **c** an arrangement for connecting or disconnecting working parts of a machine. **4** a critical situation in a game, etc. (*always comes through in the clutch*).

clutch[2] /kluch/ *n.* **1** a set of eggs for hatching. **2** a brood of chickens.

clut·ter /klútər/ *n.* & *v.* • *n.* **1** a crowded and untidy collection of things. **2** an untidy state. • *v.tr.* (often foll. by *up, with*) crowd untidily; fill with clutter.

Cm *symb. Chem.* the element curium.

cm *abbr.* centimeter(s).

Cmdr. *abbr.* commander.

Cmdre. *abbr.* commodore.

cni·dar·i·an /nidáireeən/ *n.* an aquatic invertebrate animal of the phylum Cnidaria (formerly Coelenterata), typically having a simple tube-shaped or cup-shaped body and tentacles with stinging hairs and including jellyfish, corals, and sea anenomes.

cnr. *abbr.* corner.

CNS *abbr.* central nervous system.

CO *abbr.* **1** Colorado (in official postal use). **2** commanding officer. **3** conscientious objector. **4** carbon monoxide.

Co *symb. Chem.* the element cobalt.

Co. *abbr.* **1** company. **2** county.

c/o *abbr.* care of.

co- /kō/ *prefix* added to: **a** nouns, with the sense 'joint, mutual, common' (*coauthor*; *coequality*). **b** adjectives and adverbs, with the sense 'jointly, mutually' (*cobelligerent*; *coequal*; *coequally*). **c** verbs, with the sense 'together with another or others' (*cooperate*; *coauthor*).

coach /kōch/ *n.* & *v.* • *n.* **1** a passenger bus, usu. comfortably equipped for longer journeys. **2** a railroad car. **3** a horse-drawn carriage, usu. closed, esp. a stagecoach. **4 a** an instructor or trainer in sport. **b** a private tutor. **5** economy-class seating in an aircraft. • *v.* **1** *tr.* **a** train or teach (a pupil, sports team, etc.) as a coach. **b** give hints to; prime with facts. **2** *intr.* travel by stagecoach (*in the old coaching days*).

coach house *n.* an outbuilding for carriages.

coach·work /kṓchwərk/ *n.* the bodywork of a road or rail vehicle.

co·ad·ju·tor /kō-ájətər, kṓəjṓō–/ *n.* an assistant, esp. an assistant bishop.

co·ag·u·lant /kō-ágyələnt/ *n.* a substance that produces coagulation.

co·ag·u·late /kō-ágyəlayt/ *v.tr.* & *intr.* **1** change from a fluid to a solid or semisolid state. **2** clot; curdle. **3** set; solidify. ▫▫ **co·ag·u·la·ble** *adj.* **co·ag·u·la·tive** /–láytiv, –lətiv/ *adj.* **co·ag·u·la·tor** *n.*

co·ag·u·la·tion /kṓ-agyəláyshən/ *n.* the process by which a liquid changes to a semisolid mass.

coal /kōl/ *n.* & *v.* • *n.* **1 a** a hard black or blackish rock, mainly carbonized plant matter, found in underground seams and used as a fuel and in the manufacture of gas, tar, etc. **b** *Brit.* a piece of this for burning. **2** a red-hot piece of coal, wood, etc., in a fire. • *v.* **1** *intr.* take in a supply of coal. **2** *tr.* put coal into (an engine, fire, etc.). ▫ **coals to Newcastle** something brought or sent to a place where it is already plentiful. **haul** (or **rake**) **over the coals** reprimand. ▫▫ **coal·y** *adj.*

co·a·lesce /kṓəlés/ *v.intr.* **1** come together and form one whole. **2** combine in a coalition. ▫▫ **co·a·les·cence** *n.* **co·a·les·cent** *adj.*

coal·face /kṓlfays/ *n.* an exposed surface of coal in a mine.

coal·field /kṓlfeeld/ *n.* an extensive area with strata containing coal.

coal·hole /kṓlhōl/ *n.* a hole, as from a sidewalk, leading to a coal bin.

co·a·li·tion /kṓəlíshən/ *n.* **1** *Polit.* a temporary alliance for combined action, esp. of distinct parties forming a government, or of nations. **2** fusion into one whole. ▫▫ **co·a·li·tion·ist** *n.*

coal tar *n.* a thick, black, oily liquid distilled from coal and used as a source of benzene.

coam·ing /kṓming/ *n.* a raised border around the hatches, etc., of a ship to keep out water.

coarse /kawrs/ *adj.* **1 a** rough or loose in texture or grain; made of large particles. **b** (of a person's features) rough or large. **2** lacking refinement or delicacy; crude; obscene (*coarse humor*). **3** rude; uncivil. **4** inferior; common. ▫▫ **coarse·ly** *adv.* **coarse·ness** *n.* **coars·ish** *adj.*

coars·en /káwrsən/ *v.tr. & intr.* make or become coarse.

coast /kōst/ *n. & v.* •*n.* **1 a** the border of the land near the sea; the seashore. **b** (**the Coast**) the Pacific coast of the US. **2 a** a run, usu. downhill, on a bicycle without pedaling or in a motor vehicle without using the engine. **b** a toboggan slide or slope. •*v.intr.* **1** ride or move, usu. downhill, without use of power; freewheel. **2** make progress without much effort. **3** slide down a hill on a toboggan or other sled. □ **the coast is clear** there is no danger of being observed or caught. □□ **coast·al** *adj.*

coast·er /kṓstər/ *n.* **1** a ship that travels along the coast from port to port. **2** a small tray or mat for a bottle or glass.

Coast Guard /kṓst gaard/ *n.* the U.S. military service that protects coastal waters, aids shipping and pleasure craft, and enforces maritime laws.

coast·line /kṓstlīn/ *n.* the line of the seashore, esp. with regard to its shape (*a rugged coastline*).

coast-to-coast *adj., adv.* across an island or continent.

coat /kōt/ *n. & v.* •*n.* **1** an outer garment with sleeves and often extending below the hips; an overcoat or jacket. **2 a** an animal's fur, hair, etc. **b** *Physiol.* a structure, esp. a membrane, enclosing or lining an organ. **c** a skin, rind, or husk. **d** a layer of a bulb, etc. **3 a** a layer or covering. **b** a covering of paint, etc., laid on a surface at one time. •*v.tr.* **1** (usu. foll. by *with, in*) **a** apply a coat of paint, etc., to; provide with a layer or covering. **b** (as **coated** *adj.*) covered with. **2** (of paint, etc.) form a covering to. □□ **coat·ed** *adj.* (also in *comb.*).

coat hang·er *n.* see HANGER.

co·a·ti /kō-áatee/ *n.* (*pl.* **coatis**) (also **coatimundi**) any raccoonlike, carnivorous mammal of the genus *Nasua*, with a long, flexible snout and a long, usu. ringed tail.

coat·ing /kṓting/ *n.* a thin layer or covering of paint, etc.

coat of arms *n.* the heraldic bearings or shield of a person, family, or corporation.

coat of mail *n.* a jacket covered with mail or composed of mail.

coat·tail /kṓttayl/ *n.* **1** the back flap of a man's jacket or coat. **2** (in *pl.*) **a** the back skirts of a dress coat, cutaway, etc. **b** *Polit.* (of a party candidate) popularity such as to attract votes for other party candidates.

coax /kōks/ *v.tr.* **1** (usu. foll. by *into*, or *to* + infin.) persuade (a person) gradually or by flattery. **2** (foll. by *out of*) obtain (a thing from a person) by coaxing. **3** manipulate (a thing) carefully or slowly. □□ **coax·er** *n.* **co·ax·ing·ly** *adv.*

co·ax·i·al /kō-ákseeəl/ *adj.* **1** having a common axis. **2** *Electr.* (of a cable or line) transmitting by means of two concentric conductors separated by an insulator. □□ **co·ax·i·al·ly** *adv.*

cob /kob/ *n.* **1** = CORN COB. **2** a sturdy riding or driving horse with short legs. **3** a male swan.

co·balt /kṓbawlt/ *n. Chem.* a silvery-white, magnetic metallic element occurring naturally as a mineral in combination with sulfur and arsenic, and used in many alloys. ¶ Symb.: **Co.** □□ **co·bal·tic** /kōbáwltik/ *adj.* **co·bal·tous** /kōbáwltəs/ *adj.*

co·balt blue *n.* **1** a pigment containing a cobalt salt. **2** the deep-blue color of this.

cob·ble[1] /kóbəl/ *n. & v.* •*n.* (in full **cobblestone**) a small rounded stone of a size used for paving. •*v.tr.* pave with cobbles.

cob·ble[2] /kóbəl/ *v.tr.* **1** mend or patch up (esp. shoes). **2** (often foll. by *together*) join or assemble roughly.

cob·bler /kóblər/ *n.* **1** a person who mends shoes, esp. professionally. **2** an iced drink of wine, etc., sugar, and lemon (*sherry cobbler*). **3** a fruit pie with a rich, thick biscuit crust, usu. only on the top.

COBOL /kṓbawl/ *n. Computing* a programming language designed for use in commerce (acronym of *co*mmon *b*usiness *o*riented *l*anguage).

co·bra /kṓbrə/ *n.* any venomous snake of the genus *Naja*, native to Africa and Asia, with a neck dilated like a hood when excited.

cob·web /kóbweb/ *n.* **1 a** a fine network of threads spun by a spider from a liquid secreted by it, used to trap insects, etc. **b** the thread of this. **2** anything compared with a cobweb, esp. in flimsiness of texture. **3** a trap or insidious entanglement. □□ **cob·webbed** *adj.* **cob·web·by** *adj.*

co·ca /kṓkə/ *n.* **1** a S. American shrub, *Erythroxylum coca*. **2** its dried leaves, chewed as a stimulant.

Co·ca-Co·la /kṓkəkṓlə/ *n. Trademark* a carbonated soft drink flavored with extract of cola nuts.

co·caine /kōkáyn/ *n.* a drug derived from coca or prepared synthetically, used as a local anesthetic and as a stimulant.

coc·cus /kókəs/ *n.* (*pl.* **cocci** /kóksī, kókī/) any spherical or roughly spherical bacterium. □□ **coc·cal** *adj.* **coc·coid** *adj.*

coc·cyx /kóksiks/ *n.* (*pl.* **coccyges** /–sijeez/ or **coccyxes**) the small triangular bone at the base of the spinal column in humans and some apes, representing a vestigial tail. □□ **coc·cyg·e·al** /koksíjeeəl/ *adj.*

coch·le·a /kókleeə/ *n.* (*pl.* **cochleas** or **cochleae** /–leeee/) the spiral cavity of the internal ear. □□ **coch·le·ar** *adj.*

cock /kok/ *n. & v.* •*n.* **1** a male bird, esp. of a domestic fowl. **2** *coarse sl.* the penis. **3 a** a firing lever in a gun which can be raised to be released by the trigger. **b** the cocked position of this (*at full cock*). **4** a tap or valve controlling flow. ▶In sense 2 usually considered a taboo word. •*v.tr.* **1** raise or make upright or erect. **2** turn or move (the eye or ear) attentively or knowingly. **3** set aslant, or turn up the brim of (a hat). **4** raise the cock of (a gun). □ **at half cock** only partly ready. **knock into a cocked hat** defeat utterly.

cock·ade /kokáyd/ *n.* a rosette, etc., worn in a hat as a badge of office or party, or as part of a livery. □□ **cock·ad·ed** *adj.*

cock-and-bull sto·ry *n.* an absurd or incredible account.

cock·a·tiel /kókəteél/ *n.* (also **cock·a·teel**) *Austral.* a small, delicately colored crested parrot, *Nymphicus hollandicus*.

cock·a·too /kókətóo/ *n.* any of several parrots of the family Cacatuinae, having powerful beaks and erectile crests.

cock·a·trice /kókətris, –trīs/ *n.* **1** = BASILISK 1. **2** *Heraldry* a fabulous animal, a cock with a serpent's tail.

cock·chaf·er /kókchayfər/ *n.* a large nocturnal beetle, *Melolontha melolontha*, which feeds on leaves and whose larva feeds on roots of crops, etc.

cock·crow /kókkrō/ *n.* dawn.

cock·er /kókər/ *n.* (in full **cocker spaniel**) a small spaniel of a breed with a silky coat.

cock·er·el /kókrəl/ *n.* a young cock.

cock·eyed /kókíd/ *adj. colloq.* **1** crooked; askew; not level. **2** (of a scheme, etc.) absurd; not practical. **3** drunk. **4** squinting.

cock·fight /kókfīt/ *n.* a fight between cocks as sport. □□ **cock·fight·ing** *n.*

cock·le[1] /kókəl/ *n.* **1 a** any edible mollusk of the genus *Cardium*, having a chubby, ribbed bivalve shell. **b** (in full **cockleshell**) its shell. **2** (in full **cockleshell**) a small shallow boat. □ **warm the cockles of one's heart** make one contented; be satisfying.

cock·le[2] /kókəl/ *v. & n.* •*v.* **1** *intr.* pucker; wrinkle. **2** *tr.* cause to cockle. •*n.* a pucker or wrinkle in paper, glass, etc.

cock·ney /kóknee/ *n. & adj.* •*n.* (*pl.* **-neys**) **1** a native of East London, esp. one born within hearing of Bow Bells (of the Bow church in London's East End district). **2** the dialect or accent typical of this area. • *adj.* of or characteristic of cockneys or their dialect or accent.

cock•pit /kókpit/ *n.* **1** a compartment for the pilot (or the pilot and crew) of an aircraft or spacecraft. **2** a similar compartment for the driver in a racing car. **3** a space for the helmsman in some small yachts.

cock•roach /kókrōch/ *n.* any of various flat brown insects, esp. *Blatta orientalis*, infesting kitchens, bathrooms, etc.

cocks•comb /kókskōm/ *n.* the crest or comb of a cock.

cock•sure /kókshŏŏr/ *adj.* **1** presumptuously or arrogantly confident. **2** (foll. by *of, about*) absolutely sure. ▫▫ **cock•sure•ly** *adv.* **cock•sure•ness** *n.*

cock•tail /kóktayl/ *n.* **1** a usu. alcoholic drink made by mixing various spirits, fruit juices, etc. **2** a dish of mixed ingredients (*fruit cocktail; shellfish cocktail*). **3** any hybrid mixture.

cock•y /kókee/ *adj.* (**cockier, cockiest**) **1** conceited; arrogant. **2** saucy; impudent. ▫▫ **cock•i•ly** *adv.* **cock•i•ness** *n.*

co•co /kṓkō/ *n.* (*pl.* **cocos**) a tall tropical palm tree, *Cocos nucifera*, bearing coconuts.

co•coa /kṓkō/ *n.* **1** a powder made from crushed cacao seeds, often with other ingredients. **2** a hot drink made from this.

co•coa but•ter *n.* a fatty substance obtained from cocoa beans and used for candy, cosmetics, etc.

co•co•nut /kṓkənut/ *n.* (also **co•coa•nut**) **1 a** a large ovate brown seed of the coco, with a hard shell and edible lining enclosing a milky juice. **b** its edible lining. **c** = COCO. **2** *sl.* the human head.

co•coon /kəkṓŏn/ *n.* & *v.* • *n.* **1 a** a silky case spun by many insect larvae for protection as pupae. **b** a similar structure made by other animals. **2** a protective covering, esp. to prevent corrosion of metal equipment. • *v.* **1** *tr.* & *intr.* wrap in or form a cocoon. **2** *tr.* spray with a protective coating.

co•cotte /kəkót, kawkáwt/ *n.* **1** a small fireproof dish for cooking and serving an individual portion of food. **2** a deep cooking pot with a tight-fitting lid and handles.

COD *abbr.* **1** cash on delivery. **2** collect on delivery.

cod /kod/ *n.* (*pl.* same) any large marine fish of the family Gadidae, used as food, esp. *Gadus morhua*.

co•da /kṓdə/ *n.* **1** *Mus.* the concluding passage of a piece or movement, usu. forming an addition to the basic structure. **2** *Ballet* the concluding section of a dance. **3** a concluding event or series of events.

cod•dle /kód'l/ *v.tr.* **1 a** treat as an invalid; protect attentively. **b** *Brit.* (foll. by *up*) strengthen by feeding. **2** cook (an egg) in water below boiling point. ▫▫ **cod•dler** *n.*

code /kōd/ *n.* & *v.* • *n.* **1** a system of words, letters, figures, or symbols, used to represent others for secrecy or brevity. **2** a system of prearranged signals, esp. used to ensure secrecy in transmitting messages. **3** *Computing* a piece of program text. **4 a** a systematic collection of statutes, a body of laws so arranged as to avoid inconsistency and overlapping. **b** a set of rules on any subject. **5 a** the prevailing morality of a society or class (*code of honor*). **b** a person's standard of moral behavior. • *v.tr.* put (a message, program, etc.) into code. ▫▫ **cod•er** *n.*

co•deine /kṓdeen/ *n.* an alkaloid derived from morphine and used to relieve pain.

co•de•pend•en•cy / kṓdipéndənsee/ *n.* addiction to a supportive role in a relationship. ▫▫ **co•de•pend•ent** /–dənt/ *adj.* & *n.*

co•de•ter•mi•na•tion /kṓditərmináyshən/ *n.* cooperation between management and workers in decision making.

co•dex /kṓdeks/ *n.* (*pl.* **codices** /kṓdiseez, kód–/) **1** an ancient manuscript text in book form. **2** a collection of pharmaceutical descriptions of drugs, etc.

cod•fish /kódfish/ *n.* = COD.

codg•er /kójər/ *n.* (usu. in **old codger**) *colloq.* a person, esp. an old or strange one.

co•di•ces *pl.* of CODEX.

cod•i•cil /kódisil/ *n.* an addition explaining, modifying, or revoking a will or part of one. ▫▫ **cod•i•cil•la•ry** /kódisílәree/ *adj.*

cod•i•fy /kódifī, kṓd–/ *v.tr.* (**-fies, -fied**) arrange (laws, etc.) systematically into a code. ▫▫ **cod•i•fi•ca•tion** /–fikáyshən/ *n.* **cod•i•fi•er** *n.*

cod•ling /kódling/ *n.* a small codfish.

cod-liv•er oil *n.* an oil pressed from the fresh liver of cod, which is rich in vitamins D and A.

cod•piece /kódpees/ *n. hist.* an appendage like a small bag or flap at the front of a man's breeches to cover the genitals.

co•ed /kó-ed, –éd/ *n.* & *adj. colloq.* • *n.* **1** a coeducational system or institution. **2** a female student at a coeducational institution. • *adj.* coeducational.

co•ed•u•ca•tion /kóejŏŏkáyshən/ *n.* the education of pupils of both sexes together. ▫▫ **co•ed•u•ca•tion•al** *adj.*

co•ef•fi•cient /kṓifíshənt/ *n.* **1** *Math.* a quantity placed before and multiplying an algebraic expression (e.g., *4* in *4xʸ*). **2** *Physics* a multiplier or factor that measures some property (*coefficient of expansion*).

coe•la•canth /seéləkanth/ *n.* a large bony marine fish, *Latimeria chalumnae*, formerly thought to be extinct, having a trilobed tail fin and fleshy pectoral fins.

-coele *comb. form* var. of -CELE.

coe•len•ter•ate /seeléntərayt, –tərit/ = CNIDARIAN.

co•en•zyme /kō-énzīm/ *n. Biochem.* a nonproteinaceous compound that assists in the action of an enzyme.

co•e•qual /kō-eékwəl/ *adj.* & *n. archaic* or *literary* • *adj.* equal with one another. • *n.* an equal. ▫▫ **co•e•qual•i•ty** /kṓ-eekwólitee/ *n.* **co•e•qual•ly** *adv.*

co•erce /kō-ə́rs/ *v.tr.* (often foll. by *into*) persuade or restrain (an unwilling person) by force (*coerced you into signing*). ▫▫ **co•er•ci•ble** *adj.*

co•er•cion /kō-ə́rzhən, –shən/ *n.* **1** the act or process of coercing. **2** government by force. ▫▫ **co•er•cive** /–siv/ *adj.* **co•er•cive•ly** *adv.* **co•er•cive•ness** *n.*

Coeur d'A•lene /kərd'láyn/ *n.* **1 a** a N. American people native to northern Idaho. **b** a member of this people. **2** the language of this people.

co•e•val /kō-eévəl/ *adj.* & *n.* • *adj.* **1** having the same age or date of origin. **2** living or existing at the same epoch. **3** having the same duration. • *n.* a coeval person; a contemporary. ▫▫ **co•e•val•i•ty** /–válitee/ *n.* **co•e•val•ly** *adv.*

co•ex•ist /kṓigzíst/ *v.intr.* (often foll. by *with*) **1** exist together (in time or place). **2** (esp. of nations) exist in mutual tolerance though professing different ideologies, etc. ▫▫ **co•ex•ist•ence** *n.* **co•ex•ist•ent** *adj.*

co•ex•ten•sive /kṓiksténsiv/ *adj.* extending over the same space or time.

cof•fee /káwfee, kófee/ *n.* **1 a** a drink made from the roasted and ground beanlike seeds of a tropical shrub. **b** a cup of this. **2 a** any shrub of the genus *Coffea*, yielding berries containing one or more seeds. **b** these seeds raw, or roasted and ground. **3** a pale brown color, as of coffee mixed with milk.

cof•fee break *n.* a short rest from work during which refreshments are usually taken.

cof•fee cake *n.* a type of cake or sweetened bread, often served with coffee.

cof•fee•house /káwfeehows, kóf–/ *n.* a place serving coffee and other refreshments, and often providing informal entertainment.

cof•fee ta•ble *n.* a small low table.

cof•fer /káwfər, kóf–/ *n.* **1** a box, esp. a large strongbox for valuables. **2** (in *pl.*) a treasury or store of funds. **3** a sunken panel in a ceiling, etc. ▫▫ **cof•fered** *adj.*

cof•fer•dam /káwfərdam, kóf–/ *n.* a watertight enclosure pumped dry to permit work below the waterline on building bridges, etc., or for repairing a ship.

cof•fin /káwfin, kóf–/ *n. & v.* •*n.* a long, narrow, usu. wooden box in which a corpse is buried or cremated.

cog /kawg, kog/ *n.* **1** each of a series of projections on the edge of a wheel or bar transferring motion by engaging with another series. **2** an unimportant member of an organization, etc. ▫▫ **cogged** *adj.*

co•gent /kṓjənt/ *adj.* (of arguments, reasons, etc.) convincing; compelling. ▫▫ **co•gen•cy** /–jənsee/ *n.* **co•gent•ly** *adv.*

cog•i•tate /kójitayt/ *v.tr. & intr.* ponder; meditate. ▫▫ **cog•i•ta•tion** /–táyshən/ *n.* **cog•i•ta•tive** *adj.* **cog•i•ta•tor** *n.*

co•gnac /káwnyak, kón–/ *n.* a high-quality brandy, properly that distilled in Cognac in W. France.

cog•nate /kógnayt/ *adj. & n.* •*adj.* **1** related to or descended from a common ancestor. **2** *Philol.* (of a word) having the same linguistic family or derivation (as another); representing the same original word or root (e.g., English *father*, German *Vater*, Latin *pater*). •*n.* **1** a relative. **2** a cognate word. ▫▫ **cog•nate•ly** *adv.* **cog•nate•ness** *n.*

cog•nate ob•ject *n. Gram.* an object that is related in origin and sense to the verb governing it (as in *live a good life*).

cog•ni•tion /kognishən/ *n.* **1** *Philos.* knowing, perceiving, or conceiving as an act or faculty distinct from emotion and volition. **2** a result of this; a perception, sensation, notion, or intuition. ▫▫ **cog•ni•tion•al** *adj.* **cog•ni•tive** /kógnitiv/ *adj.*

cog•ni•za•ble /kógnizəbəl, kón–, kogní–/ *adj.* **1** perceptible; recognizable; clearly identifiable. **2** within the jurisdiction of a court. ▫▫ **cog•ni•za•bly** *adv.*

cog•ni•zance /kógnizəns/ *n.* **1** knowledge or awareness; perception; notice. **2** the sphere of one's observation or concern. **3** *Law* the right of a court to deal with a matter. **4** *Heraldry* a distinctive device or mark. ▫ **have cognizance of** know, esp. officially.

cog•ni•zant /kógnizənt/ *adj.* (foll. by *of*) having knowledge or being aware of.

cog•no•men /kognṓmen/ *n.* **1** a nickname. **2** an ancient Roman's personal name or epithet, as in Marcus Tullius *Cicero*, Publius Cornelius Scipio *Africanus*.

cog rail•way *n.* a railway with a cogged third rail designed to mesh with a cogwheel on a locomotive to prevent slippage on steep slopes.

cog•wheel /kóghweel, –weel/ *n.* a wheel with cogs.

co•hab•it /kōhábit/ *v.intr.* (**cohabited, cohabiting**) live together, esp. as husband and wife without being married to one another. ▫▫ **co•hab•i•tant** *n.* **co•hab•i•ta•tion** *n.* **co•hab•i•tee** /–tée/ *n.* **co•hab•i•ter** *n.*

co•here /kōhéer/ *v.intr.* **1** (of parts or a whole) stick together; remain united. **2** (of reasoning, etc.) be logical or consistent.

co•her•ent /kōhéerənt, –hér–/ *adj.* **1** (of a person) able to speak intelligibly and articulately. **2** (of speech, an argument, etc.) logical and consistent; easily followed. **3** cohering; sticking together. **4** *Physics* (of waves) having a constant phase relationship. ▫▫ **co•her•ence** /–rəns/ *n.* **co•her•en•cy** *n.* **co•her•ent•ly** *adv.*

co•he•sion /kōhéezhən/ *n.* **1 a** the act or condition of sticking together. **b** a tendency to cohere. **2** *Chem.* the force with which molecules cohere. ▫▫ **co•he•sive** /–héesiv/ *adj.* **co•he•sive•ly** /–héesivlee/ *adv.* **co•he•sive•ness** /–héesivnis/ *n.*

co•ho /kṓhō/ *n.* (also **co•hoe**) (*pl.* same or **-hos** or **-hoes**) a silver salmon, *Oncorhynchus kisutch*, of the N. Pacific.

co•hort /kṓhawrt/ *n.* **1** an ancient Roman military unit, equal to one-tenth of a legion. **2** a band of warriors. **3 a** persons banded or grouped together, esp. in a common cause. **b** a group of persons with a common statistical characteristic. **4** a companion or colleague.

coif /koyf/ *n. hist.* **1** a close-fitting cap, esp. as worn by nuns under a veil. **2** a protective metal skullcap worn under armor. **3** = COIFFURE.

coif•feur /kwaafṓr/ *n.* (*fem.* **coiffeuse** /–fṓz/) a hairdresser.

coif•fure /kwaafyŏŏr/ *n. & v.* •*n.* (also **coif**) the way hair is arranged; a hairstyle. •*v.tr.* to provide with a coiffure.

coil[1] /koyl/ *n. & v.* •*n.* **1** anything arranged in a joined sequence of concentric circles. **2** a length of rope, a spring, etc., arranged in this way. **3** a single turn of something coiled, e.g., a snake. **4** an intrauterine contraceptive device in the form of a coil. **5** *Electr.* a device consisting of a coiled wire for converting low voltage to high voltage, esp. for transmission to the spark plugs of an internal combustion engine. •*v.* **1** *tr.* arrange in a series of concentric loops or rings. **2** *tr. & intr.* twist or be twisted into a circular or spiral shape. **3** *intr.* move sinuously.

coil[2] /koyl/ *n.* ▫ **this mortal coil** the difficulties of earthly life (with ref. to Shakesp. *Hamlet* III. i. 67).

coin /koyn/ *n. & v.* •*n.* **1** a piece of flat, usu. round metal stamped and issued by authority as money. **2** (*collect.*) metal money. •*v.tr.* **1** make (coins) by stamping. **2** make (metal) into coins. **3** invent or devise (esp. a new word or phrase). ▫ **coin money** make much money quickly. **to coin a phrase** *iron.* introducing a banal remark or cliché. ▫▫ **coin•er** *n.*

coin•age /kóynij/ *n.* **1** the act or process of coining. **2 a** coins collectively. **b** a system or type of coins in use (*decimal coinage*; *bronze coinage*). **3** an invention, esp. of a new word or phrase.

co•in•cide /kṓinsíd/ *v.intr.* **1** occur at or during the same time. **2** occupy the same portion of space. **3** (often foll. by *with*) be in agreement; have the same view.

co•in•ci•dence /kō-ínsidəns/ *n.* **1 a** occurring or being together. **b** an instance of this. **2** a remarkable concurrence of events or circumstances without apparent causal connection. **3** *Physics* the presence of ionizing particles, etc., in two or more detectors simultaneously, or of two or more signals simultaneously in a circuit.

co•in•ci•dent /kō-ínsidənt/ *adj.* **1** occurring together in space or time. **2** (foll. by *with*) in agreement; harmonious. ▫▫ **co•in•ci•dent•ly** *adv.*

co•in•ci•den•tal /kō-ínsidént'l/ *adj.* **1** in the nature of or resulting from a coincidence. **2** happening or existing at the same time. ▫▫ **co•in•ci•den•tal•ly** *adv.*

coir /kóyər/ *n.* fiber from the outer husk of the coconut, used for ropes, matting, etc.

co•i•tus /kṓitəs, kō-ée–/ *n. Med.* sexual intercourse. ▫▫ **co•i•tal** *adj.*

co•i•tus in•ter•rup•tus /íntərúptəs/ *n.* sexual intercourse in which the penis is withdrawn before ejaculation.

Coke /kōk/ *n. Trademark* Coca-Cola.

coke[1] /kōk/ *n. & v.* •*n.* **1** a solid substance left after the gases have been extracted from coal. **2** a residue left after the incomplete combustion of gasoline, etc. •*v.tr.* convert (coal) into coke.

coke[2] /kōk/ *n. sl.* cocaine.

Col. *abbr.* **1** colonel. **2** Colossians (New Testament).

col /kol/ *n.* **1** a depression in the summit line of a chain of mountains, generally affording a pass from one slope to another. **2** *Meteorol.* a low-pressure region between anticyclones.

col. *abbr.* column.

COLA /kṓlə/ *abbr.* **1** cost-of-living adjustment. **2** cost-of-living allowance.

co·la /kṓlə/ *n.* (also **kola**) **1** any small tree of the genus *Cola*, native to W. Africa, bearing seeds containing caffeine. **2** a carbonated drink usu. flavored with these seeds.

col·an·der /kúləndər, kól–/ *n.* a perforated vessel used to strain off liquid in cooking.

col·chi·cum /kólchikəm, kólkee–/ *n.* **1** any liliaceous plant of the genus *Colchicum*, esp. meadow saffron. **2** its dried corm or seed. Also called AUTUMN CROCUS.

cold /kōld/ *adj., n., & adv.* • *adj.* **1** of or at a low or relatively low temperature, esp. when compared with the human body. **2** not heated; cooled after being heated. **3** (of a person) feeling cold. **4** lacking ardor, friendliness, or affection; undemonstrative; apathetic. **5** depressing; uninteresting (*cold facts*). **6 a** dead. **b** *colloq.* unconscious. **7** *colloq.* at one's mercy (*had me cold*). **8** (of soil) slow to absorb heat. **9** (of a scent in hunting) having become weak. **10** (in children's games) far from finding or guessing what is sought. **11** without preparation or rehearsal. • *n.* **1 a** the prevalence of a low temperature, esp. in the atmosphere. **b** cold weather; a cold environment (*went out into the cold*). **2** an infection in which the mucous membrane of the nose and throat becomes inflamed, causing running at the nose, sneezing, sore throat, etc. • *adv.* completely; entirely (*was stopped cold mid-sentence*). □ **catch a cold** become infected with a cold. **cold call** sell goods or services by making unsolicited calls on prospective customers by telephone or in person. **in cold blood** without feeling or passion; deliberately; ruthlessly. **out in the cold** ignored; neglected. **throw** (or **pour**) **cold water on** be discouraging or depreciatory about. □□ **cold·ish** *adj.* **cold·ly** *adv.* **cold·ness** *n.*

cold-blood·ed /kṓldblúdid/ *adj.* **1** (of fish, etc.) having a body temperature varying with that of the environment. **2 a** callous; deliberately cruel. **b** without excitement or sensibility, dispassionate. □□ **cold-blood·ed·ly** *adv.* **cold-blood·ed·ness** *n.*

cold cream *n.* ointment for cleansing and softening the skin.

cold cuts *n.pl.* slices of cold cooked meats.

cold feet *n.pl. colloq.* loss of nerve or confidence.

cold frame *n.* an unheated frame with a glass top for growing small plants.

cold front *n.* the boundary of an advancing mass of cold air, esp. the trailing edge of the warm sector of a low-pressure system.

cold fu·sion *n.* hypothetical nuclear fusion at room temperature esp. as a possible energy source.

cold-heart·ed /kṓldhaártid/ *adj.* lacking affection or warmth; unfriendly. □□ **cold-heart·ed·ly** *adv.* **cold-heart·ed·ness** *n.*

cold shoul·der *n.* a show of intentional unfriendliness.

cold sore *n.* inflammation and blisters in and around the mouth, caused by a viral infection.

cold stor·age *n.* **1** storage in a refrigerator or other cold place for preservation. **2** a state in which something (esp. an idea) is put aside temporarily.

cold sweat *n.* a state of sweating induced by fear or illness.

cold tur·key *n. sl.* the abrupt and complete withdrawal from taking a drug to which one is addicted.

cold war *n.* a state of hostility between nations without actual fighting.

cole /kōl/ *n.* (usu. in *comb.*) **1** cabbage. **2** = RAPE[2].

co·le·op·ter·on /kóleeóptərən/ *n.* any insect of the order Coleoptera, with front wings modified into sheaths to protect the hind wings, e.g., a beetle or weevil. □□ **co·le·op·ter·an** *adj.* **co·le·op·ter·ist** *n.* **co·le·op·ter·ous** *adj.*

cole·slaw /kṓlslaw/ *n.* a dressed salad of sliced raw cabbage, carrot, onion, etc.

co·le·us /kṓleeəs/ *n.* any plant of the genus *Coleus*, having variegated colored leaves.

col·ic /kólik/ *n.* a severe spasmodic abdominal pain. □□ **col·ick·y** *adj.*

col·i·se·um /kóliséeəm/ *n.* (also **col·os·se·um**) a large stadium or amphitheater.

co·li·tis /kəlítis/ *n.* inflammation of the lining of the colon.

coll. *abbr.* **1** collect. **2** collection. **3** collateral. **4** college.

col·lab·o·rate /kəlábərayt/ *v.intr.* (often foll. by *with*) **1** work jointly, esp. in a literary or artistic production. **2** cooperate traitorously with an enemy. □□ **col·lab·o·ra·tion** /–ráyshən/ *n.* **col·lab·o·ra·tion·ist** *n. & adj.* **col·lab·o·ra·tive** /–ráytiv, –rətiv/ *adj.* **col·lab·o·ra·tor** *n.*

col·lage /kəlaázh/ *n.* **1** a form of art in which various materials (e.g., photographs, pieces of paper, matchsticks) are arranged and glued to a backing. **2** a work of art done in this way. **3** a collection of unrelated things. □□ **col·lag·ist** *n.*

col·la·gen /kóləjən/ *n.* a protein found in animal connective tissue, yielding gelatin on boiling.

col·lapse /kəláps/ *n. & v.* • *n.* **1** the tumbling down or falling in of a structure; folding up; giving way. **2** a sudden failure of a plan, undertaking, etc. **3** a physical or mental breakdown. • *v.* **1 a** *intr.* undergo or experience a collapse. **b** *tr.* cause to collapse. **2** *intr. colloq.* lie or sit down and relax, esp. after prolonged effort (*collapsed into a chair*). **3 a** *intr.* (of furniture, etc.) be foldable into a small space. **b** *tr.* fold (furniture) in this way. □□ **col·laps·i·ble** *adj.* **col·laps·i·bil·i·ty** /–səbílitee/ *n.*

col·lar /kólər/ *n. & v.* • *n.* **1** the part of a shirt, dress, coat, etc., that goes around the neck, either upright or turned over. **2** a band of linen, lace, etc., completing the upper part of a costume. **3** a band of leather or other material put around an animal's (esp. a dog's) neck. **4** a restraining or connecting band, ring, or pipe in machinery. **5** a colored marking resembling a collar around the neck of a bird or animal. • *v.tr.* **1** seize (a person) by the collar or neck. **2** capture; apprehend. **3** *colloq.* accost. **4** *sl.* take, esp. illicitly. □□ **col·lared** *adj.* (also in *comb.*). **col·lar·less** *adj.*

col·lar·bone /kólərbōn/ *n.* either of two bones joining the breastbone and the shoulder blades; the clavicle.

col·late /kəláyt, kólayt, kṓ–/ *v.tr.* **1** analyze and compare (texts, statements, etc.) to identify points of agreement and difference. **2** arrange (pages) in proper sequence. **3** assemble (information) from different sources. □□ **col·la·tor** *n.*

col·lat·er·al /kəlátərəl/ *n. & adj.* • *n.* **1** security pledged as a guarantee for repayment of a loan. **2** a person having the same descent as another but by a different line. • *adj.* **1** descended from the same stock but by a different line. **2** side by side; parallel. **3 a** additional but subordinate. **b** contributory. **c** connected but aside from the main subject, course, etc. □□ **col·lat·er·al·i·ty** /–rálitee/ *n.* **col·lat·er·al·ly** *adv.*

col·la·tion /kəláyshən, ko–/ *n.* **1** the act or an instance of collating. **2** a light informal meal.

col·league /kóleeg/ *n.* a fellow official or worker, esp. in a profession or business.

col·lect /kəlékt/ *v., adj., & adv.* • *v.* **1** *tr. & intr.* bring or come together; assemble; accumulate. **2** *tr.* systematically seek and acquire (books, stamps, etc.), esp. as a continuing hobby. **3 a** *tr.* obtain (taxes, contributions, etc.) from a number of people. **b** *intr. colloq.* receive money. **4** *tr.* call for; fetch (*went to collect the laundry*). **5 a** *refl.* regain control of oneself esp. after a shock. **b** *tr.* concentrate (one's energies, thoughts, etc.). **c** *tr.* (as **collected** *adj.*) calm and cool; not perturbed nor distracted. **6** *tr.* infer; gather; conclude. • *adj. & adv.* to be paid for by the receiver (of a telephone call, parcel, etc.). ▫▫ **col·lect·a·ble** *adj.* **col·lect·ed·ly** *adv.*

col·lect·i·ble /kəléktibəl/ *adj. & n.* • *adj.* worth collecting. • *n.* an item sought by collectors.

col·lec·tion /kəlékshən/ *n.* **1** the act or process of collecting or being collected. **2** a group of things collected together (e.g., works of art, literary items, or specimens), esp. systematically. **3** (foll. by *of*) an accumulation; a mass or pile (*a collection of dust*). **4 a** the collecting of money, esp. in church or for a charitable cause. **b** the amount collected. **5** the regular removal of mail, esp. from a public mailbox, for dispatch.

col·lec·tive /kəléktiv/ *adj. & n.* • *adj.* **1** formed by or constituting a collection. **2** taken as a whole; aggregate (*our collective opinion*). **3** of or from several or many individuals; common. • *n.* **1 a** any cooperative enterprise. **b** its members. **2** = COLLECTIVE NOUN. ▫▫ **col·lec·tive·ly** *adv.* **col·lec·tive·ness** *n.* **col·lec·tiv·i·ty** /kólektívitee/ *n.*

col·lec·tive bar·gain·ing *n.* negotiation of wages, etc., by an organized body of employees.

col·lec·tive noun *n. Gram.* a noun that is grammatically singular and denotes a collection or number of individuals (e.g., *assembly, family, troop*).

col·lec·tiv·ism /kəléktivizəm/ *n.* the theory and practice of the collective ownership of land and the means of production. ▫▫ **col·lec·tiv·ist** *n.* **col·lec·tiv·is·tic** /–vístik/ *adj.*

col·lec·tor /kəléktər/ *n.* **1** a person who collects, esp. things of interest as a hobby. **2** a person who collects money, etc., due (*tax collector; ticket collector*).

col·lec·tor's i·tem *n.* (also **col·lec·tor's piece**) a valuable object, esp. one of interest to collectors.

col·lege /kólij/ *n.* **1** an establishment for further or higher education, sometimes part of a university. **2** an establishment for specialized professional education (*business college; college of music; naval college*). **3** the students and teachers in a college. **4** *Brit.* a public school. **5** an organized body of persons with shared functions and privileges (*electoral college*). ▫▫ **col·le·gial** /kəléejəl/ *adj.*

col·le·giate /kəléejət/ *adj.* constituted as or belonging to a college; corporate. ▫▫ **col·le·giate·ly** *adv.*

col·lide /kəlíd/ *v.intr.* (often foll. by *with*) **1** come into abrupt or violent impact. **2** be in conflict.

col·lie /kólee/ *n.* **1** a sheepdog orig. of a Scottish breed, with a long pointed nose and usu. dense, long hair. **2** this breed.

col·lier /kólyər/ *n.* **1** a coal miner. **2** a coal-carrying ship.

col·lier·y /kólyəree/ *n.* (*pl.* **-ies**) a coal mine and its associated buildings.

col·li·gate /kóligayt/ *v.tr.* bring into connection (esp. isolated facts by a generalization). ▫▫ **col·li·ga·tion** /–gáyshən/ *n.*

col·lin·e·ar /kəlíneeər/ *adj. Geom.* (of points) lying in the same straight line. ▫▫ **col·lin·e·ar·i·ty** /–neeáiritee/ *n.* **col·lin·e·ar·ly** *adv.*

col·lins /kólinz/ *n.* (also **Col·lins**) an iced drink made of gin or whiskey, etc., with soda water, lemon or lime juice, and sugar.

col·li·sion /kəlízhən/ *n.* **1** a violent impact of a moving body, esp. a vehicle or ship, with another or with a fixed object. **2** the clashing of opposed interests or considerations. ▫▫ **col·li·sion·al** *adj.*

col·li·sion course *n.* a course or action that is bound to cause a collision or conflict.

col·lo·cate /kóləkayt/ *v.tr.* **1** place together or side by side. **2** arrange; set in a particular place. **3** (often foll. by *with*) *Linguistics* juxtapose (a word, etc.) with another. ▫▫ **col·lo·ca·tion** /–káyshən/ *n.*

col·loid /kóloyd/ *n. Chem.* a substance consisting of ultramicroscopic particles suspended in a liquid or other medium. ▫▫ **col·loi·dal** /kəlóyd'l/ *adj.*

col·lo·qui·al /kəlṓkweeəl/ *adj.* belonging to or proper to ordinary or familiar conversation, not formal or literary. ▫▫ **col·lo·qui·al·ly** *adv.*

col·lo·qui·al·ism /kəlṓkweeəlizəm/ *n.* **1** a colloquial word or phrase. **2** the use of colloquialisms.

col·lo·qui·um /kəlṓkweeəm/ *n.* (*pl.* **colloquiums** or **colloquia** /–kweeə/) an academic conference or seminar.

col·lo·quy /kóləkwee/ *n.* (*pl.* **-quies**) **1** the act of conversing. **2** a conversation.

col·lude /kəlóód/ *v.intr.* come to an understanding or conspire together, esp. for a fraudulent purpose. ▫▫ **col·lud·er** *n.*

col·lu·sion /kəlóózhən/ *n.* **1** a secret understanding, esp. for a fraudulent purpose. **2** *Law* such an understanding between ostensible opponents in a lawsuit. ▫▫ **col·lu·sive** /–lóósiv/ *adj.* **col·lu·sive·ly** *adv.*

Colo. *abbr.* Colorado.

col·o·bus /kóləbəs/ *n.* any leaf-eating monkey of the genus *Colobus*, native to Africa, having shortened or absent thumbs.

co·logne /kəlṓn/ *n.* (in full **cologne water**) eau de cologne or a similar scented toilet water.

co·lon[1] /kṓlən/ *n.* a punctuation mark (:), used esp. to introduce a quotation or a list of items or to separate clauses when the second expands or illustrates the first; also between numbers in a statement of proportion (as in 10:1) and in Biblical references (as in Exodus 3:2)

co·lon[2] /kṓlən/ *n. Anat.* the lower and greater part of the large intestine, from the cecum to the rectum. ▫▫ **co·lon·ic** /kəlónik/ *adj.*

colo·nel /kárnəl/ *n.* **1** an army, air force, or marine officer, immediately below a brigadier general in rank. **2** = LIEUTENANT COLONEL. ▫▫ **colo·nel·cy** *n.* (*pl.* **-cies**).

colonel mid-16th century: from obsolete French *coronel* (earlier form of *colonel*), from Italian *colonnello* 'column of soldiers,' from *colonna* 'column,' from Latin *columna*. The form *coronel*, the source of the modern pronunciation, was usual until the mid-17th century.

co·lo·ni·al /kəlṓneeəl/ *adj. & n.* • *adj.* **1** of, relating to, or characteristic of a colony or colonies. **2** (esp. of architecture or furniture) built or designed in, or in a style characteristic of, the period of the British colonies in America before independence. • *n.* **1** a native or inhabitant of a colony. **2** a house built in colonial style. ▫▫ **co·lo·ni·al·ly** *adv.*

co·lo·ni·al·ism /kəlṓneeəlizəm/ *n.* **1** a policy of acquiring or maintaining colonies. **2** *derog.* this policy regarded as the esp. economic exploitation of weak or backward peoples by a larger power. ▫▫ **co·lo·ni·al·ist** *n.*

col·o·nist /kólənist/ *n.* a settler in or inhabitant of a colony.

col·o·nize /kólənīz/ *v.* **1** *tr.* **a** establish a colony or colonies in (a country or area). **b** settle as colonists. **2** *intr.* establish or join a colony. **3** *tr. Biol.* (of plants and animals) become established (in an area). ▫▫ **col·o·ni·za·tion** *n.* **col·o·niz·er** *n.*

col·on·nade /kólənáyd/ *n.* a row of columns, esp. supporting an entablature or roof. ▫▫ **col·on·nad·ed** *adj.*

col·o·ny /kólənee/ *n.* (*pl.* **-nies**) **1 a** a group of settlers in a new country (whether or not already inhabited) fully or partly subject to the mother country. **b** the settlement or its territory. **2 a** people of one nationality or race or occupation in a city, esp. if living more or less in isolation or in a special quarter. **b** a separate or segregated group (*nudist colony*). **3** *Biol.* a collection of animals, plants, etc., connected, in contact, or living close together.

col·o·phon /kóləfon, –fən/ *n.* **1** a publisher's device or imprint, esp. on the title page. **2** a tailpiece in a manuscript or book, often ornamental, giving the writer's or printer's name, the date, etc.

col·or /kúlər/ *n.* & *v.* • *n.* **1 a** the sensation produced on the eye by rays of light when resolved as by a prism, selective reflection, etc., into different wavelengths. **b** perception of color; a system of colors. **2** one, or any mixture, of the constituents into which light can be separated as in a spectrum or rainbow, sometimes including (loosely) black and white. **3** a coloring substance, esp. paint. **4** the use of all colors, not only black and white, as in photography and television. **5 a** pigmentation of the skin, esp. when dark. **b** this as a ground for prejudice or discrimination. **6** ruddiness of complexion (*a healthy color*). **7** (in *pl.*) appearance or aspect (*see things in their true colors*). **8** (in *pl.*) **a** a colored ribbon or uniform, etc., worn to signify membership of a school, club, team, etc. **b** the flag of a regiment or ship. **c** a national flag. **9** quality, mood, or variety in music, literature, speech, etc.; distinctive character or timbre. **10** a pretext (*under color of*). • *v.* **1** *tr.* apply color to, esp. by painting or dyeing or with colored pens or pencils. **2** *tr.* influence (*an attitude colored by experience*). **3** *tr.* **a** misrepresent, exaggerate, esp. with spurious detail (*a highly colored account*). **b** disguise. **4** *intr.* take on color; blush. □ **show one's true colors** reveal one's true character or intentions. **under false colors** falsely; deceitfully. **with flying colors** see FLYING.

Col·o·rad·o po·ta·to bee·tle /kólərádō, –raădō/ *n.* a yellow and black striped beetle, *Leptinotarsa decemlineata*, the larva of which is highly destructive to the potato plant.

col·or·a·tion /kúləráyshən/ *n.* **1** coloring; a scheme or method of applying color. **2** the natural (esp. variegated) color of living things or animals.

col·o·ra·tu·ra /kúlərətŏŏrə, –tyŏŏr–/ *n.* **1** elaborate ornamentation of a vocal melody. **2** a singer (esp. a soprano) skilled in coloratura singing.

col·or-blind *adj.* **1** unable to distinguish certain colors. **2** ignoring racial prejudice. □□ **col·or-blind·ness** *n.*

col·ored /kúlərd/ *adj.* & *n.* • *adj.* **1** having color(s). **2** (also **Colored**) often *offens.* wholly or partly of nonwhite descent. • *n.* (also **Colored**) a colored person. ▶see note at BLACK.

col·or·fast /kúlərfast/ *adj.* dyed in colors that will not fade nor be washed out. □□ **col·or·fast·ness** *n.*

col·or·ful /kúlərfŏŏl/ *adj.* **1** having much or varied color; bright. **2** full of interest; vivid; lively. □□ **col·or·ful·ly** *adv.*

col·or·if·ic /kúlərífik/ *adj.* **1** producing color. **2** highly colored.

col·or·ing /kúləring/ *n.* **1** the process of or skill in using color(s). **2** the style in which a thing is colored, or in which an artist uses color. **3** facial complexion.

col·or·ist /kúlərist/ *n.* a person who uses color, esp. in art.

col·or·ize /kúlərīz/ *v.tr.* (**colorized, colorizing**) add color to (orig. black-and-white movie film) using computer technology.

col·or·less /kúlərlis/ *adj.* **1** without color. **2** lacking character or interest. **3** dull or pale in hue. **4** neutral; impartial; indifferent. □□ **color·less·ly** *adv.*

col·or scheme *n.* an arrangement or planned combination of colors esp. in interior design.

co·los·sal /kəlósəl/ *adj.* **1** of immense size; huge, gigantic. **2** *colloq.* remarkable; splendid. □□ **co·los·sal·ly** *adv.*

co·los·sus /kəlósəs/ *n.* (*pl.* **colossi** /–sī/ or **colossuses**) **1** a statue much bigger than life size. **2** a gigantic person, animal, building, etc. **3** an imperial power personified.

co·los·to·my /kəlóstəmee/ *n.* (*pl.* **-mies**) *Surgery* an operation on the colon to make an opening in the abdominal wall to provide an artificial anus.

co·los·trum /kəlóstrəm/ *n.* the first secretion from the mammary glands occurring after giving birth.

col·pos·co·py /kolpóskəpee/ *n.* (*pl.* **-pies**) examination of the vagina and the neck of the womb.

colt /kōlt/ *n.* a young, uncastrated male horse, usu. less than four years old. □□ **colt·hood** *n.* **colt·ish** *adj.* **colt·ish·ly** *adv.* **colt·ish·ness** *n.*

colts·foot /kṓltsfŏŏt/ *n.* (*pl.* **coltsfoots**) a wild composite plant, *Tussilago farfara*, with large leaves and yellow flowers.

col·u·brine /kóləbrīn, kólyə–/ *adj.* **1** snakelike. **2** of the subfamily Colubrinae of nonpoisonous snakes.

co·lum·bine /kóləmbīn/ *n.* any plant of the genus *Aquilegia*, esp. *A. canadensis*, having purple-blue flowers.

co·lum·bi·um /kəlúmbiəm/ *n. Chem.* = NIOBIUM.

col·umn /kóləm/ *n.* **1** *Archit.* an upright cylindrical pillar often slightly tapering and usu. supporting an entablature or arch. **2** a structure or part shaped like a column. **3** a vertical cylindrical mass of liquid or vapor. **4 a** a vertical division of a page, chart, etc., containing a sequence of figures or words. **b** the figures or words themselves. **5** a part of a newspaper regularly devoted to a particular subject. **6** *Mil.* an arrangement of troops in successive lines, with a narrow front. □□ **co·lum·nar** /kəlúmnər/ *adj.* **col·umned** *adj.*

col·um·nist /kóləmnist, –mist/ *n.* a journalist contributing regularly to a newspaper.

co·ma /kṓmə/ *n.* (*pl.* **comas**) a prolonged deep unconsciousness.

Co·man·che /kəmánchee/ *n.* **1 a** a N. American people native to the western plains. **b** a member of this people. **2** the language of this people.

com·a·tose /kṓmətōs, kóm–/ *adj.* **1** in a coma. **2** drowsy.

comb /kōm/ *n.* & *v.* • *n.* **1** a toothed strip of rigid material for tidying and arranging the hair. **2** a part of a machine having a similar design or purpose. **3** the red, fleshy crest of a fowl, esp. a cock. **4** a honeycomb. • *v.tr.* **1** arrange or tidy (the hair) by drawing a comb through. **2** curry (a horse). **3** dress (wool or flax) with a comb. **4** search (a place) thoroughly. □□ **combed** *adj.*

com·bat *n.* & *v.* • *n.* /kómbat, kúm–/ **1** a fight; an armed encounter or conflict; fighting; battle. **2** a struggle, contest, or dispute. • *v.* /kəmbát, kómbat/ (**combated, combating**) **1** *intr.* engage in combat. **2** *tr.* oppose; strive against.

com·bat·ant /kəmbát'nt, kómbət'nt/ *n.* & *adj.* • *n.* a person engaged in fighting. • *adj.* **1** fighting. **2** for fighting.

com·bat fa·tigue *n.* a mental disorder caused by stress in wartime combat.

com·bat·ive /kəmbátiv/ *adj.* ready to fight; pugnacious. □□ **com·bat·ive·ly** *adv.* **com·bat·ive·ness** *n.*

comb·er /kṓmər/ *n.* **1** a person or thing that combs, esp. a machine for combing cotton or wool very fine. **2** a long curling wave; a breaker.

com·bi·na·tion /kómbináyshən/ *n.* **1** the act or an instance of combining; the process of being combined. **2** a combined state (*in combination with*). **3** a combined set of things or people. **4** a sequence of numbers or letters used to open a combination lock. ▫▫ **com·bi·na·tion·al** *adj.* **com·bi·na·tive** /kómbinàytiv, kəmbínə–/ *adj.*

com·bi·na·tion lock *n.* a lock that can be opened only by rotating a dial or set of dials through a specific sequence of movements.

com·bine *v. & n.* • *v.* /kəmbín/ **1** *tr. & intr.* join together; unite for a common purpose. **2** *tr.* possess (qualities usually distinct) together (*combines charm and authority*). **3 a** *intr.* coalesce in one substance. **b** *tr.* cause to do this. **c** *intr.* form a chemical compound. **4** /kómbīn/ *tr.* harvest (crops, etc.) by means of a combine harvester. • *n.* /kómbīn/ a combination of esp. commercial interests to control prices, etc. ▫▫ **com·bin·a·ble** /kəmbínəbəl/ *adj.*

com·bine har·ves·ter /kómbīn/ *n.* a mobile machine that reaps and threshes in one operation.

com·bin·ing form *n. Gram.* a linguistic element used in combination with another element to form a word (e.g., *Anglo-* = English, *bio-* = life, *-graphy* = writing). ▶In this dictionary, *combining form* is used of an element that contributes to the particular sense of words (as with both elements of *biography*), as distinct from a prefix or suffix that adjusts the sense of or determines the function.

com·bo /kómbō/ *n.* (*pl.* **-bos**) *sl.* a small jazz or dance band.

com·bus·ti·ble /kəmbústibəl/ *adj. & n.* • *adj.* capable of or used for burning. • *n.* a combustible substance. ▫▫ **com·bus·ti·bil·i·ty** /–bílitee/ *n.*

com·bus·tion /kəmbúschən/ *n.* **1** burning; consumption by fire. **2** *Chem.* the development of light and heat from the chemical combination of a substance with oxygen. ▫▫ **com·bus·tive** /–bústiv/ *adj.*

com·bus·tion cham·ber *n.* a space in which combustion takes place, e.g., of gases in a boiler-furnace or fuel in an internal-combustion engine.

Comdr. *abbr.* commander.

come /kum/ *v.intr.* (*past* **came** /kaym/; *past part.* **come**) **1** move, be brought toward, or reach a place thought of as near or familiar to the speaker or hearer (*come and see me; the books have come*). **2** reach or be brought to a specified situation or result (*you'll come to no harm; have come to believe it*). **3** extend to a specified point (*the road comes within a mile of us*). **4** traverse or accomplish (with compl.: *have come a long way*). **5** get to be in a certain condition (*how did you come to break your leg?*). **6** take or occupy a specified position (*it comes on the third page*). **7** become perceptible or known (*the church came into sight; it will come to me*). **8** be available (*comes in three sizes*). **9** become (with compl.: *come loose*). **10** (foll. by *of*) **a** be descended from (*comes of a rich family*). **b** be the result of (*that comes of complaining*). **11** *colloq.* play the part of; behave like (with compl.: *don't come the bully with me*). **12** *sl.* have a sexual orgasm. **13** (in *subj.*) *colloq.* when a specified time is reached (*come next month*). **14** (as *int.*) expressing caution or reserve (*come now, it cannot be that bad*). ▫ **as they come** typically or supremely so (*is as tough as they come*). **come about** happen; take place. **come across 1 a** be effective or understood. **b** appear or sound in a specified way. **2** (foll. by *with*) *sl.* hand over what is wanted. **3** meet or find by chance (*came across an old jacket*). **come again** *colloq.* **1** make a further effort. **2** (as *imper.*) what did you say? **come along 1** make progress; move forward. **2** (as *imper.*) hurry up. **come and go 1** pass to and fro; be transitory. **2** pay brief visits. **come apart** fall or break into pieces; disintegrate. **come around 1** pay an informal visit. **2** recover consciousness. **3** be converted to another person's opinion. **4** (of a date or regular occurrence) recur; be imminent again. **come at 1** reach; discover; get access to. **2** attack (*came at me with a knife*). **come away 1** become detached or broken off (*came away in my hands*). **2** (foll. by *with*) be left with a feeling, impression, etc. **come back 1** return. **2** recur to one's memory. **3** become fashionable or popular again. **4** reply; retort. **come before** be dealt with by (a judge, etc.). **come between 1** interfere with the relationship of. **2** separate; prevent contact between. **come by 1** pass; go past. **2** call on a visit (*come by tomorrow*). **3** acquire (*came by a new bicycle*). **come down 1** come to a place or position regarded as lower. **2** lose position or wealth (*has come down in the world*). **3** be handed down by tradition or inheritance. **4** be reduced; show a downward trend (*prices are coming down*). **5** (foll. by *against, in favor of, on the side of*) reach a decision or recommendation (*the report came down against change*). **6** (foll. by *to*) signify basically; be dependent on (a factor) (*it comes down to who is willing to go*). **7** (foll. by *on*) criticize harshly; punish. **8** (foll. by *with*) begin to suffer from (a disease). **come for 1** come to collect or receive. **2** attack (*came for me with a hammer*). **come forward 1** advance. **2** offer oneself for a task, post, etc. **come in 1** enter a house or room. **2** take a specified position in a race, etc. (*came in third*). **3** become fashionable or seasonable. **4 a** have a useful role or function. **b** (with compl.) prove to be (*came in very handy*). **c** have a part to play (*where do I come in?*). **5** be received (*news has just come in*). **6** begin speaking, esp. in radio transmission. **7** be elected; come to power. **8** (foll. by *for*) receive; be the object of (*came in for much criticism*). **9** (foll. by *on*) join (an enterprise, etc.). **10** (of a tide) turn to high tide. **11** (of a train, ship, or aircraft) approach its destination. **come into 1** see senses 2, 7 of *v.* **2** receive, esp. as heir. **come off 1** *colloq.* (of an action) succeed; be accomplished. **2** (with compl.) fare; turn out (*came off badly; came off the winner*). **3** be detached or detachable (from). **4** fall (from). **5** be reduced or subtracted from (*$5 came off the price*). **come off it** (as *imper.*) *colloq.* an expression of disbelief or refusal to accept another's opinion, behavior, etc. **come on 1** continue to come. **2** (foll. by *to*) make sexual advances. **3** make progress; thrive (*is really coming on*). **4** appear on the stage, field of play, etc. **5** be heard or seen on television, on the telephone, etc. **6** arise to be discussed. **7** (as *imper.*) expressing encouragement. **8** = *come upon*. **come out 1** emerge; become known (*it came out that he had left*). **2** appear or be published (*comes out every Saturday*). **3 a** declare oneself; make a decision (*came out in favor of joining*). **b** openly declare that one is a homosexual. **4 a** be satisfactorily visible in a photograph, etc., or present in a specified way (*the dog didn't come out; he came out badly*). **b** (of a photograph) be produced satisfactorily or in a specified way (*only three have come out*). **5** attain a specified result in an examination, etc. **6** (of a stain, etc.) be removed. **7** make one's début in society. **8** (foll. by *in*) be covered with (*came out in spots*). **9** (of a problem) be solved. **10** (foll. by *with*) declare openly; disclose. **come over 1** come from some distance or nearer to the speaker (*came over from Paris; come over here*). **2** change sides or one's opinion. **3** (of a feeling, etc.) overtake or affect (a person). **come through 1** be successful; survive. **2** be received by telephone. **3** survive or overcome (a difficulty) (*came through the ordeal*). **come to 1** recover consciousness. **2** *Naut.* bring a vessel to a stop. **3** reach in total; amount to. **4** *refl.* recover consciousness. **5** have as a destiny; reach (*what is the world coming to?*). **come to nothing** have no useful result in the end; fail. **come to pass** occur. **come to rest** cease moving. **come to that** *colloq.* in fact; if that is the case. **come under 1** be classified as or among. **2** be subject to (influence or authority). **come up 1** come to a place or position regarded as higher. **2** attain wealth or position (*come up in the world*). **3** (of an issue, problem, etc.) arise; be mentioned or discussed. **4** (often foll. by *to*) **a** approach a person, esp. to talk. **b** (foll. by *to, on*) approach a specified time, etc. (*is coming up to eight o'clock*). **5** (foll. by *to*) match (a standard, etc.). **6** (foll. by *with*) produce (an idea, etc.), esp. in response to a challenge. **7** (of a plant, etc.) spring up out of the ground. **8** become brighter (e.g., with polishing). **come up against** be faced with. **come upon 1** meet or find by chance. **2** attack by surprise. **come what may** no matter what happens. **have it coming to one** *colloq.* be about to get one's deserts. **how come?** *colloq.* how did that happen? **if it comes to that** in that case. **to come** future; in the future (*the year to come; many problems were still to come*).

come·back /kúmbak/ *n.* **1** a return to a previous (esp. successful) state. **2** *sl.* a retaliation.

co·me·di·an /kəmeédeeən/ *n.* **1** a humorous entertainer. **2** an actor in comedy. **3** *sl.* an amusing person.

co·me·di·enne /kəmeédee-én/ *n.* a female comedian.

come·down /kúmdown/ *n.* **1** a loss of status; decline. **2** a disappointment.

com·e·dy /kómidee/ *n.* (*pl.* **-dies**) **1 a** a play, film, etc., of an amusing character, usu. with a happy ending. **b** the genre consisting of works of this kind (cf. TRAGEDY). **2** an amusing incident or series of incidents in everyday life. **3** humor, esp. in a work of art. □□ **co·me·dic** /kəmeédik/ *adj.*

com·e·dy of man·ners *n.* satirical portrayal of social behavior, esp. of the upper classes.

come-hith·er *attrib.adj. colloq.* enticing; flirtatious.

come·ly /kúmlee/ *adj.* (**comelier, comeliest**) pleasant to look at. □□ **come·li·ness** /kúmleenis/ *n.*

come-on *n. sl.* a lure or enticement.

com·er /kúmər/ *n.* **1** a person who comes, esp. as an applicant, participant, etc. (*offered the job to the first comer*). **2** *colloq.* a person likely to be a success.

com·et /kómit/ *n.* a hazy object usu. with a nucleus of ice and dust surrounded by gas and with a tail pointing away from the sun, moving in an eccentric orbit around the sun. □□ **com·et·ar·y** *adj.*

come·up·pance /kumúpəns/ *n. colloq.* one's deserved fate (*got his comeuppance*).

com·fort /kúmfərt/ *n. & v.* •*n.* **1** consolation; relief in affliction. **2 a** a state of physical well-being (*live in comfort*). **b** (usu. in *pl.*) things that make life easy or pleasant. **3** a cause of satisfaction (*a comfort to me that you are here*). **4** a person who consoles or helps one (*he's a comfort to her in her old age*). •*v.tr.* **1** soothe in grief; console. **2** make comfortable. □□ **com·fort·ing** *adj.* **com·fort·ing·ly** *adv.* **com·fort·less** *adj.*

com·fort·a·ble /kúmftəbəl, –fərtəbəl/ *adj.* **1 a** such as give comfort or ease (*a comfortable pair of shoes*). **b** (of a person) relaxing to be with; congenial. **2** free from discomfort; at ease. **3** *colloq.* having an adequate standard of living. **4** having an easy conscience (*did not feel comfortable about refusing him*). **5** with a wide margin (*a comfortable win*). □□ **com·fort·a·bly** *adv.*

com·fort·er /kúmfərtər/ *n.* **1** a person who comforts. **2** a warm quilt.

com·frey /kúmfree/ *n.* (*pl.* **-freys**) any of various plants of the genus *Symphytum*, esp. *S. officinale*, having large, hairy leaves and clusters of usu. white or purple bell-shaped flowers.

com·fy /kúmfee/ *adj.* (**comfier, comfiest**) *colloq.* comfortable. □□ **com·fi·ly** *adv.* **com·fi·ness** *n.*

com·ic /kómik/ *adj. & n.* •*adj.* **1** of, or in the style of, comedy (*comic opera*). **2** causing or meant to cause laughter; funny. •*n.* **1** a professional comedian. **2** (*pl.*) section or page of a newspaper featuring several comic strips. □□ **com·i·cal** *adj.*

com·i·cal /kómikəl/ *adj.* funny; causing laughter. □□ **com·i·cal·i·ty** /–kálitee/ *n.* **com·i·cal·ly** *adv.*

com·ic book *n.* a magazine in the form of comic strips.

com·ic op·er·a *n.* **1** an opera with much spoken dialogue, usu. with humorous treatment. **2** this genre.

com·ic strip *n.* a horizontal series of drawings in a comic book, newspaper, etc., telling a story.

com·ing /kúming/ *adj. & n.* •*attrib.adj.* **1** approaching; next (*in the coming week*). **2** of potential importance (*a coming man*). •*n.* arrival; approach.

com·i·ty /kómitee/ *n.* (*pl.* **-ties**) **1** civility; considerate behavior toward others. **2** an association of nations, etc., for mutual benefit.

com·ma /kómə/ *n.* a punctuation mark (,) indicating a pause between parts of a sentence, or dividing items in a list, string of figures, etc.

com·mand /kəmánd/ *v. & n.* •*v.tr.* **1** (also *absol.*; often foll. by *to* + infin., or *that* + clause) give formal order or instructions to (*commands us to obey; commands that it be done*). **2** (also *absol.*) have authority over. **3 a** (often *refl.*) restrain; master. **b** gain the use of; have at one's disposal (skill, resources, etc.). **4** deserve and get (sympathy, respect, etc.). **5** *Mil.* dominate (a strategic position) from a superior height; look down over. •*n.* **1** an order; an instruction. **2** mastery; control (*a good command of languages*). **3** the exercise or tenure of authority, esp. naval or military (*has command of this ship*). **4** *Mil.* **a** a body of troops, etc. (*Artillery Command*). **b** a district under a commander (*Western Command*). **5** *Computing* **a** an instruction causing a computer to perform one of its basic functions. **b** a signal initiating such an operation. □ **in command of** commanding. **under command of** commanded by.

com·man·dant /kóməndánt, –daánt/ *n.* a commanding officer. □□ **com·man·dant·ship** *n.*

com·man·deer /kóməndeér/ *v.tr.* **1** seize (men or goods) for military purposes. **2** take possession of without authority.

com·mand·er /kəmándər/ *n.* a person who commands, esp. a naval officer next in rank below captain.

com·mand·er-in-chief *n.* (*pl.* **commanders in chief**) the supreme commander, esp. of a nation's forces.

com·mand·ing /kəmánding/ *adj.* **1** dignified; exalted; impressive. **2** (of a hill, etc.) giving a wide view. **3** (of an advantage, a position, etc.) controlling; superior (*has a commanding lead*). □□ **com·mand·ing·ly** *adv.*

com·mand·ment /kəmándmənt/ *n.* a divine command.

com·man·do /kəmándō/ *n.* (*pl.* **-dos**) *Mil.* **1 a** a unit of amphibious shock troops. **b** a member of such a unit. **2 a** a party of men called out for military service. **b** a body of troops.

com·mand per·for·mance *n.* a theatrical or film performance given at the request of a head of state or sovereign.

com·mem·o·rate /kəmémərayt/ *v.tr.* **1** celebrate in speech or writing. **2 a** preserve in memory by some celebration. **b** (of a plaque, etc.) be a memorial of. □□ **com·mem·o·ra·tion** /kəmémәráyshən/ *n.* **com·mem·o·ra·tive** /–ráytiv, –rətiv/ *adj.* **com·mem·o·ra·tor** *n.*

com·mence /kəméns/ *v.tr. & intr. formal* begin.

com·mence·ment /kəménsmənt/ *n. formal* **1** a beginning. **2** a ceremony of degree conferment.

com·mend /kəménd/ *v.tr.* **1** (often foll. by *to*) entrust; commit (*commends his soul to God*). **2** praise. **3** recommend (*method commends itself*).

com·mend·a·ble /kəméndəbəl/ *adj.* praiseworthy. □□ **com·mend·a·bly** *adv.*

com·men·da·tion /kóməndáyshən/ *n.* **1** an act of

commending or recommending (esp. a person to another's favor). **2** praise.

com·mend·a·to·ry /kəméndətawree/ *adj.* commending; recommending.

com·men·sal /kəménsəl/ *adj. & n. Biol.* • *adj.* of, relating to, or exhibiting commensalism. • *n.* a commensal organism. ▫▫ **com·men·sal·ly** *adv.*

com·men·sal·ism /kəménsəlizəm/ *n. Biol.* an association between two organisms in which one benefits and the other derives no benefit or harm.

com·men·su·ra·ble /kəménsərəbəl, –shərə–/ *adj.* **1** (often foll. by *with, to*) measurable by the same standard. **2** (foll. by *to*) proportionate to. **3** *Math.* (of numbers) in a ratio equal to the ratio of integers. ▫▫ **com·men·su·ra·bil·i·ty** *n.* **com·men·su·ra·bly** *adv.*

com·men·su·rate /kəménsərət, –shərət/ *adj.* **1** (usu. foll. by *with*) having the same size, duration, etc. **2** (often foll. by *to, with*) proportionate. ▫▫ **com·men·su·rate·ly** *adv.*

com·ment /kóment/ *n. & v.* • *n.* **1 a** a remark, esp. critical (*passed a comment on her hat*). **b** commenting; criticism (*his behavior aroused much comment*). **2** an explanatory note (e.g., on a written text). • *v.intr.* **1** (often foll. by *on, upon,* or *that* + clause) make (esp. critical) remarks (*commented on her choice of friends*). **2** (often foll. by *on, upon*) write explanatory notes. ▫ **no comment** *colloq.* I decline to answer your question. ▫▫ **com·ment·er** *n.*

com·men·tar·y /kóménteree/ *n.* (*pl.* **-ies**) **1** a set of explanatory or critical notes on a text, etc. **2** a descriptive spoken account (esp. on radio or television) of an event as it happens.

com·men·ta·tor /kóməntaytər/ *n.* **1** a person who provides a commentary on an event, etc. **2** the writer of a commentary. **3** a person who writes or speaks on current events.

com·merce /kómərs/ *n.* financial transactions, esp. the buying and selling of merchandise, on a large scale.

com·mer·cial /kəmə́rshəl/ *adj. & n.* • *adj.* **1** of, engaged in, or concerned with, commerce. **2** having profit as a primary aim rather than artistic, etc., value; philistine. • *n.* a television or radio advertisement. ▫▫ **com·mer·ci·al·i·ty** /–sheeálitee/ *n.* **com·mer·cial·ly** *adv.*

com·mer·cial·ism /kəmə́rshəlizəm/ *n.* **1** the principles and practice of commerce. **2** (esp. excessive) emphasis on financial profit as a measure of worth.

com·mer·cial·ize /kəmə́rshəlīz/ *v.tr.* **1** exploit or spoil for gaining profit. **2** make commercial. ▫▫ **com·mer·cial·i·za·tion** *n.*

com·mie /kómee/ *n. sl. derog.* (also **Com·mie**) a Communist.

com·min·a·to·ry /kəmínətawree, kóminə–/ *adj.* threatening.

com·min·gle /kəmínggəl/ *v.tr. & intr. literary* mingle together.

com·mi·nute /kómənoot, –nyoot/ *v.tr.* **1** reduce to small fragments. **2** divide (property) into small portions. ▫▫ **com·mi·nu·tion** /–nóoshən, –nyóo–/ *n.*

com·mis·er·ate /kəmízərayt/ *v. intr.* (usu. foll. by *with*) express or feel pity. ▫▫ **com·mis·er·a·tion** /–ráyshən/ *n.* **com·mis·er·a·tive** /–ráytiv/ *adj.*

com·mis·sar·y /kómiseree/ *n.* (*pl.* **-ies**) **1** *Mil.* **a** a store for the supply of food, etc., to soldiers. **b** an officer responsible for the supply of food, etc., to soldiers. **2 a** a restaurant in a movie studio, etc. **b** the food supplied. **3** a deputy or delegate. ▫▫ **com·mis·sar·i·al** *adj.*

com·mis·sion /kəmíshən/ *n. & v.* • *n.* **1 a** the authority to perform a task or certain duties. **b** a person or group entrusted esp. by a government with such authority. **c** an instruction or duty given to such a group or person (*their commission was to simplify the procedure*). **2** an order for something, esp. a work of art, to be produced specially. **3** *Mil.* **a** a warrant conferring the rank of officer in the army, navy, marines, or air force. **b** the rank so conferred. **4 a** the authority to act as agent for a company, etc., in trade. **b** a percentage paid to the agent from the business obtained (*his wages are low, but he gets 20 percent commission*). **5** the act of committing (a crime, sin, etc.). **6** the office or department of a commissioner. • *v.tr.* **1** authorize or empower by a commission. **2 a** give (an artist, etc.) a commission for a piece of work. **b** order (a work) to be written. **3** *Naut.* **a** give (an officer) the command of a ship. **b** prepare (a ship) for active service. **4** bring (a machine, equipment, etc.) into operation. ▫ **in commission** (of a warship, etc.) manned, armed, and ready for service. **out of commission** (esp. of a ship) not in service; not in working order.

com·mis·sion·er /kəmíshənər/ *n.* **1** a person appointed by a commission to perform a specific task. **2** a person appointed as a member of a government commission. **3** a representative of the supreme authority in a district, department, etc.

com·mit /kəmít/ *v.tr.* (**committed, committing**) **1** (usu. foll. by *to*) entrust or consign for: **a** safe keeping (*I commit him to your care*). **b** treatment, usu. destruction (*committed the book to the flames*). **c** official custody as a criminal or as insane (*you could be committed for such behavior*). **2** perpetrate, do (esp. a crime, sin, or blunder). **3** pledge, involve, or bind (esp. oneself) to a certain course or policy. **4** (as **committed** *adj.*) (often foll. by *to*) **a** morally dedicated or politically aligned (*a committed Christian*; *committed to the cause*). **b** obliged (to take certain action). ▫ **commit to memory** memorize. ▫▫ **com·mit·ta·ble** *adj.* **com·mit·ter** *n.*

com·mit·ment /kəmítmənt/ *n.* **1** an engagement or obligation that restricts freedom of action. **2** the process or an instance of committing oneself.

com·mit·tal /kəmít'l/ *n.* **1** the act of committing a person to an institution, esp. prison or a psychiatric hospital. **2** the burial of a dead body.

com·mit·tee /kəmítee/ *n.* **1** a body of persons appointed for a specific function by, and usu. out of, a larger body. **2** such a body appointed by a legislature, etc., to consider the details of proposed legislation.

com·mode /kəmód/ *n.* **1** a chest of drawers. **2 a** = TOILET 1. **b** (also **night commode**) a bedside table with a cupboard containing a chamber pot.

com·mo·di·ous /kəmódeeəs/ *adj.* roomy and comfortable. ▫▫ **com·mo·di·ous·ly** *adv.* **com·mo·di·ous·ness** *n.*

com·mod·i·ty /kəmóditee/ *n.* (*pl.* **-ties**) **1** *Commerce* an article or raw material that can be bought and sold. **2** a useful thing.

com·mo·dore /kómədawr/ *n.* **1** a naval officer above a captain and below a rear admiral. **2** the commander of a squadron or other division of a fleet. **3** the president of a yacht club.

com·mon /kómən/ *adj. & n.* • *adj.* **1 a** occurring often (*a common mistake*). **b** ordinary; of ordinary qualities; without special rank or position (*common soldier; the common people*). **2 a** shared by, coming from, or done by, more than one (*common knowledge*; *by common consent*). **b** belonging to, open to, or affecting, the whole community (*common land*). **3** *derog.* low-class; inferior (*a common little man*). **4** of the most familiar type (*common cold*). **5** *Math.* belonging to two or more quantities (*common factor*). **6** *Gram.* (of gender) referring to individuals of either sex (e.g., *teacher*). **7** *Mus.* having two or four beats, esp. four quarter notes, in a bar. • *n.* a piece of open public land, esp. in a village or town. ▫ **in common 1** in joint use; shared. **2** of joint interest (*have little in common*). **in common with** in the same way as. ▫▫ **com·mon·ly** *adv.* **com·mon·ness** *n.*

com·mon·al·i·ty /kómənálitee/ *n.* (*pl.* **-ties**) **1** the sharing of an attribute. **2** a common occurrence. **3** = COMMONALTY.

com·mon de·nom·i·na·tor *n.* **1** a common multiple of the denominators of several fractions. **2** a common feature of members of a group.

com·mon·er /kómənər/ *n.* one of the common people, as opposed to the aristocracy.

Com·mon E·ra *n.* the Christian era.

com·mon ground *n.* a point or argument accepted by both sides in a dispute.

com·mon law *n.* law derived from custom and judicial precedent (cf. CASE LAW, STATUTE LAW).

Com·mon Mar·ket *n.* the European Economic Community.

com·mon noun *n.* (also **common name**) *Gram.* a name denoting a class of objects or a concept as opposed to a particular individual (e.g., *boy, chocolate, beauty*).

com·mon·place /kómənplays/ *adj.* & *n.* •*adj.* lacking originality; trite. •*n.* **1 a** an everyday saying; a platitude. **b** an ordinary topic of conversation. **2** anything usual or trite. ▫▫ **com·mon·place·ness** *n.*

com·mons /kómənz/ *n.pl.* **1** ***US*** a dining hall at a university, etc. **2** *New Eng.* a central public park or ground in a town, etc. **3** the common people.

com·mon sense *n.* sound practical sense, esp. in everyday matters. ▫▫ **com·mon·sen·si·cal** /kómənsénsikəl/ *adj.*

com·mon stock *n.* ordinary shares of stock in a company, entitling their holder to dividends that vary in amount. (cf. PREFERRED STOCK).

com·mon·wealth /kómənwelth/ *n.* **1** an independent state or community, esp. a democratic republic. **2** (**the Commonwealth**) **a** (in full **the British Commonwealth of Nations**) an international association consisting of the UK together with nations that were previously part of the British Empire. **b** a part of the title of Puerto Rico and some of the states of the US.

com·mo·tion /kəmṓshən/ *n.* **1** a confused and noisy disturbance or outburst. **2** loud and confusing noise.

com·mu·nal /kəmyṓōnəl, kómyə–/ *adj.* **1** relating to or benefiting a community; for common use (*communal baths*). **2** between different esp. ethnic or religious communities (*communal violence*). ▫▫ **com·mu·nal·i·ty** /–nálitee/ *n.* **com·mu·nal·ize** *v.tr.* **com·mu·nal·i·za·tion** *n.* **com·mu·nal·ly** *adv.*

com·mu·nal·ism /kəmyṓōnəlizəm, kómyənə–/ *n.* **1** a principle of political organization based on federated communes. **2** the principle of communal ownership, etc.

com·mune[1] /kómyōōn/ *n.* **1 a** a group of people sharing living accommodation, goods, etc. **b** a communal settlement, esp. for the pursuit of shared interests. **2 a** the smallest French territorial division for administrative purposes. **b** a similar division elsewhere.

com·mune[2] /kəmyṓōn/ *v.intr.* **1** (usu. foll. by *with*) speak intimately **2** feel in close touch (with nature, etc.) (*communed with the hills*).

com·mu·ni·ca·ble /kəmyṓōnikəbəl/ *adj.* (esp. of a disease) able to be passed on. ▫▫ **com·mu·ni·ca·bil·i·ty** *n.* **com·mu·ni·ca·bly** *adv.*

com·mu·ni·cant /kəmyṓōnikənt/ *n.* a person who receives Holy Communion.

com·mu·ni·cate /kəmyṓōnikayt/ *v.* **1** *tr.* **a** transmit or pass on by speaking or writing. **b** transmit (heat, motion, etc.). **c** pass on (an infectious illness). **d** impart (feelings, etc.) nonverbally. **2** *intr.* (often foll. by *with*) succeed in conveying information, evoking understanding, etc. (*she communicates well*). **3** *intr.* (often foll. by *with*) relate socially. **4** *intr.* (often foll. by *with*) (of a room, etc.) have a common door (*my room communicates with yours*). ▫▫ **com·mu·ni·ca·tor** *n.*

com·mu·ni·ca·tion /kəmyṓōnikáyshən/ *n.* **1 a** the act of imparting, esp. news. **b** an instance of this. **c** the information, etc., communicated. **2** a means of connecting different places. **3** social intercourse. **4** (in *pl.*) the science and practice of transmitting information.

com·mu·ni·ca·tive /kəmyṓōnikáytiv, –kətiv/ *adj.* **1** open; talkative; informative. **2** ready to communicate. ▫▫ **com·mu·ni·ca·tive·ly** *adv.*

com·mun·ion /kəmyṓōnyən/ *n.* **1** a sharing, esp. of thoughts, etc.; fellowship. **2** participation; a sharing in common (*communion of interests*). **3** (**Communion, Holy Communion**) **a** the Eucharist. **b** participation in the Communion service. **4** a body or group within the Christian faith (*the Methodist communion*).

com·mu·ni·qué /kəmyṓōnikáy/ *n.* an official communication, esp. a news report.

com·mu·nism /kómyənizəm/ *n.* **1** a political theory advocating a society in which all property is publicly owned and each person is paid and works according to his or her needs and abilities. **2** (usu. **Communism**) **a** the communistic form of society established in the former USSR and elsewhere. **b** any movement or political doctrine advocating communism, esp. Marxism. **3** = COMMUNALISM.

com·mu·nist /kómyənist/ *n.* & *adj.* •*n.* **1** a person advocating or practicing communism. **2** (**Communist**) a member of a Communist party. •*adj.* of or relating to communism (*a communist play*). ▫▫ **com·mu·nis·tic** /–nístik/ *adj.*

com·mu·ni·tar·i·an /kəmyṓōnitáireeən/ *n.* & *adj.* •*n.* a member of a communistic community. •*adj.* of or relating to such a community.

com·mu·ni·ty /kəmyṓōnitee/ *n.* (*pl.* **-ties**) **1** all the people living in a specific locality. **2** a body of people having a religion, a profession, etc., in common (*the immigrant community*). **3** fellowship; similarity (*community of intellect*). **4** a monastic, socialistic, etc., body practicing common ownership. **5** joint ownership or liability (*community of goods*). **6** (prec. by *the*) the public.

com·mu·ni·ty cen·ter *n.* a place providing social, etc., facilities for a neighborhood.

com·mu·ni·ty col·lege *n.* a college offering courses to a local community or region.

com·mu·ni·ty serv·ice *n.* unpaid work performed in service to the community, esp. as part of a criminal sentence.

com·mut·a·ble /kəmyṓōtəbəl/ *adj.* **1** convertible into money; exchangeable. **2** *Law* (of a punishment) able to be commuted. **3** within commuting distance. ▫▫ **com·mut·a·bil·i·ty** *n.*

com·mu·ta·tion /kómyətáyshən/ *n.* **1** the act or process of commuting or being commuted (in legal and exchange senses). **2** *Math.* the reversal of the order of two quantities.

com·mu·ta·tive /kəmyṓōtətiv/ *adj.* **1** relating to or involving substitution. **2** *Math.* unchanged in result by the interchange of the order of quantities.

com·mu·ta·tor /kómyətaytər/ *n.* *Electr.* a device for reversing electric current.

com·mute /kəmyṓōt/ *v.* **1** *intr.* travel to and from one's daily work, usu. in a city, esp. by car or train. **2** *tr.* *Law* (usu. foll. by *to*) change (a judicial sentence, etc.) to another less severe. **3** *tr.* (often foll. by *into, for*) change (one kind of payment) for another. **4** *tr.* **a** exchange; interchange. **b** change (to another thing).

com·mut·er /kəmyṓōtər/ *n.* a person who travels some distance to work, usu. in a city, esp. by car or train.

---

comp /komp/ *n. colloq.* compensation (workmen's comp).

com·pact[1] *adj., v., & n.* • *adj.* /kəmpákt, kóm–/ **1** closely or neatly packed together. **2** (of a piece of equipment, a room, etc.) well-fitted and practical though small. **3** (of style, etc.) condensed. **4** (esp. of the human body) small but well-proportioned. • *v.tr.* /kəmpákt/ **1** join or press firmly together. **2** condense. • *n.* /kómpakt/ **1** a small, flat case for face powder, a mirror, etc. **2** a medium-sized automobile. ▫▫ **com·pac·tion** /–pákshən/ *n.* **com·pact·ly** *adv.* **com·pact·ness** *n.* **com·pac·tor** *n.*

com·pact[2] /kómpakt/ *n.* an agreement or contract between two or more parties.

com·pact disc /kómpakt/ *n.* a disk on which information or sound is recorded digitally and reproduced by reflection of laser light. ¶ Abbr: **CD.**

com·pan·ion[1] /kəmpányən/ *n.* **1 a** (often foll. by *in, of*) a person who accompanies, associates with, or shares with, another. **b** a person employed to live with and assist another. **2** a handbook or reference book. **3** a thing that matches another.

com·pan·ion[2] /kəmpányən/ *n. Naut.* **1** a raised frame on a quarterdeck used for lighting the cabins, etc., below. **2** = COMPANIONWAY.

com·pan·ion·a·ble /kəmpányənəbəl/ *adj.* agreeable as a companion; sociable. ▫▫ **com·pan·ion·a·ble·ness** *n.* **com·pan·ion·a·bly** *adv.*

com·pan·ion·ate /kəmpányənit/ *adj.* **1** well-suited; (of clothes) matching. **2** of or like a companion.

com·pan·ion·ship /kəmpányənship/ *n.* good fellowship; friendship.

com·pan·ion·way /kəmpányənway/ *n. Naut.* a staircase to a ship's cabin.

com·pa·ny /kúmpənee/ *n.* (*pl.* **-nies**) **1 a** a number of people assembled. **b** guests or a guest (*am expecting company*). **2** companionship, esp. of a specific kind (*enjoys low company; do not care for his company*). **3 a** a commercial business. **b** (usu. **Co.**) the partner or partners not named in the title of a firm (*Smith and Co.*). **4** a troupe of actors or entertainers. **5** *Mil.* a subdivision of an infantry battalion. **6** a ship's crew. ▫ **in company** not alone. **in company with** together with. **keep company** (often foll. by *with*) associate habitually. **keep a person company** accompany a person; be sociable. **part company** (often foll. by *with*) cease to associate.

com·pa·ra·ble /kómpərəbəl/ *adj.* **1** (often foll. by *with*) able to be compared. **2** (often foll. by *to*) fit to be compared; worth comparing. ▶Use with *to* and *with* corresponds to the senses at *compare*; *to* is more common. ▫▫ **com·pa·ra·bil·i·ty** *n.* **com·pa·ra·ble·ness** *n.* **com·pa·ra·bly** *adv.*

com·par·a·tive /kəmpárətiv/ *adj. & n.* • *adj.* **1** perceptible by comparison; relative (*in comparative comfort*). **2** estimated by comparison (*the comparative merits of the two ideas*). **3** of or involving comparison (*a comparative study*). **4** *Gram.* (of an adjective or adverb) expressing a higher degree of a quality, but not the highest possible (e.g., *braver, more fiercely*) (cf. POSITIVE, SUPERLATIVE). • *n. Gram.* **1** the comparative expression or form of a word. **2** a word in the comparative. ▫▫ **com·par·a·tive·ly** *adv.*

com·pare /kəmpáir/ *v. & n.* • *v.* **1** *tr.* (usu. foll. by *to*) express similarities in; liken (*compared the landscape to a painting*). **2** *tr.* (often foll. by *to, with*) estimate the similarity or dissimilarity of (*compared radio with television; that lacks quality compared to this*). ▶In current use *to* and *with* are generally interchangeable, but *with* often implies a greater element of formal analysis, as in *compared my account with yours*. **3** *intr.* (often foll. by *with*) bear comparison (*compares favorably with the rest*). • *n. literary* comparison (*beyond compare*). ▫ **compare notes** exchange ideas or opinions. ▶Traditionally, **compare to** is used when similarities are noted in dissimilar things: *He compares life to a box of chocolates.* To **compare with** is to look for either differences or similarities, usually in similar things: *Let's compare the movie with the book on which it was based.* In practice, however, this distinction is rarely maintained. See also note at **contrast.**

com·par·i·son /kəmpárisən/ *n.* **1** the act or an instance of comparing. **2** a simile or semantic illustration. **3** capacity for being likened; similarity (*there's no comparison*). **4** (in full **degrees of comparison**) *Gram.* the positive, comparative, and superlative forms of adjectives and adverbs. ▫ **bear** (or **stand**) **comparison** (often foll. by *with*) be able to be compared favorably. **beyond comparison 1** totally different in quality. **2** greatly superior; excellent.

com·part·ment /kəmpaártmənt/ *n.* **1** a space within a larger space, separated from the rest by partitions **2** *Naut.* a watertight division of a ship. ▫▫ **com·part·men·ta·tion** /–mentáyshən/ *n.*

com·part·men·tal /kómpaartméntʼl/ *adj.* consisting of or relating to compartments or a compartment. ▫▫ **com·part·men·tal·ly** *adv.*

com·part·men·tal·ize /kəmpaartméntʼlīz, kómpaart–/ *v.tr.* divide into compartments or categories. ▫▫ **com·part·men·tal·i·za·tion** *n.*

com·pass /kúmpəs, kóm–/ *n. & v.* • *n.* **1** (in full **magnetic compass**) an instrument showing the direction of magnetic north and bearings from it. **2** (often *pl.*) an instrument for taking measurements and describing circles, with two arms connected at one end by a movable joint. **3** a circumference or boundary. **4** area; extent; scope; range. • *v.tr. literary* **1** hem in. **2** grasp mentally. ▫▫ **com·pass·a·ble** *adj.*

com·pass card *n.* a circular rotating card showing the 32 principal bearings, forming the indicator of a magnetic compass.

com·pas·sion /kəmpáshən/ *n.* pity inclining one to help or be merciful.

com·pas·sion·ate /kəmpáshənət/ *adj.* sympathetic; pitying. ▫▫ **com·pas·sion·ate·ly** *adv.*

com·pat·i·ble /kəmpátəbəl/ *adj.* **1** (often foll. by *with*) **a** able to coexist; well-suited; mutually tolerant. **b** consistent (*their views are not compatible with their actions*). **2** (of equipment, etc.) capable of being used in combination. ▫▫ **com·pat·i·bil·i·ty** *n.* **com·pat·i·bly** *adv.*

com·pa·tri·ot /kəmpáytreeət, –ot/ *n.* a fellow countryman. ▫▫ **com·pa·tri·ot·ic** /–reeótik/ *adj.*

com·pel /kəmpél/ *v.tr.* (**compelled, compelling**) **1** (usu. foll. by *to* + infin.) force, constrain. **2** bring about (an action) by force (*compel submission*). **3** (as **compelling** *adj.*) rousing strong interest, attention, conviction, or admiration. ▫▫ **com·pel·la·ble** *adj.* **com·pel·ling·ly** *adv.*

com·pen·di·ous /kəmpéndeeəs/ *adj.* (esp. of a book, etc.) comprehensive but fairly brief.

com·pen·di·um /kəmpéndeeəm/ *n.* (*pl.* **compendiums** or **compendia** /–deeə/) **1** a summary or abstract of a larger work. **2** an abridgment.

com·pen·sate /kómpənsayt/ *v.* **1** *tr.* (often foll. by *for*) recompense (a person) (*compensated him for his loss*). **2** *intr.* (usu. foll. by *for*) make amends (*compensated for the insult*). **3** *tr.* counterbalance. **4** *intr. Psychol.* offset a disability or frustration by development in another direction. ▫▫ **com·pen·sa·tor** *n.* **com·pen·sa·to·ry** /–pénsətáwree/ *adj.*

com·pen·sa·tion /kómpensáyshən/ *n.* **1 a** the act of compensating. **b** the process of being compensated. **2** something, esp. money, given as a recompense. **3** a salary or wages. ▫▫ **com·pen·sa·tion·al** *adj.*

com·pete /kəmpeét/ *v.intr.* **1** (often foll. by *with, against* a person, *for* a thing) strive for superiority or supremacy (*compete for the victory*). **2** (often foll. by *in*) take part (in a contest, etc.).

com·pe·tence /kómpit'ns/ *n.* (also **com·pe·ten·cy** /kómpitənsee/) **1** (often foll. by *for*, or *to* + infin.) ability; the state of being competent. **2** an income large enough to live on, usu. unearned. **3** *Law* the legal capacity (of a court, a magistrate, etc.) to deal with a matter.

com·pe·tent /kómpit'nt/ *adj.* **1** (usu. foll. by *to* + infin. or *for*) properly qualified or skilled (*not competent to drive*); adequately capable. **2** *Law* (of a judge, court, or witness) legally qualified or qualifying. ▫▫ **com·pe·tent·ly** *adv.*

com·pe·ti·tion /kómpətishən/ *n.* **1** (often foll. by *for*) competing, esp. in an examination, in trade, etc. **2** an event or contest in which people compete. **3 a** the people competing against a person. **b** the opposition they represent.

com·pet·i·tive /kəmpétitiv/ *adj.* **1** involving, offered for, or by competition (*competitive contest*). **2** (of prices, etc.) low enough to compare well with those of rival traders. **3** (of a person) having a strong urge to win. ▫▫ **com·pet·i·tive·ly** *adv.* **com·pet·i·tive·ness** *n.*

com·pet·i·tor /kəmpétitər/ *n.* **1** a person who competes. **2** a rival, esp. in business or commerce.

com·pi·la·tion /kómpiláyshən/ *n.* **1 a** the act of compiling. **b** the process of being compiled. **2** something compiled, esp. a book, etc., composed of separate articles, stories, etc.

com·pile /kəmpíl/ *v.tr.* **1 a** collect (material) into a list, volume, etc. **b** make up (a volume, etc.) from such material. **2** accumulate (a large number of) (*compiled a score of 160*). **3** *Computing* produce (a machine-coded form of a high-level program).

com·pil·er /kəmpílər/ *n.* **1** *Computing* a program for translating a high-level programming language into machine code. **2** a person who compiles.

com·pla·cent /kəmpláysənt/ *adj.* **1** smugly self-satisfied. **2** calmly content. ▶Often confused with *complaisant*. ▫▫ **com·pla·cence** *n.* **com·pla·cen·cy** /kəmpláysənsee/ *n.* **com·pla·cent·ly** *adv.*

▶**Complacent** means 'smugly self-satisfied:' *After four consecutive championships the team became complacent.* **Complaisant**, a much rarer word, means 'deferential, willing to please:' *Once released from the pen, the barking dogs become peaceful and complaisant.*

com·plain /kəmpláyn/ *v.intr.* **1** (often foll. by *about, at,* or *that* + clause) express dissatisfaction. **2** (foll. by *of*) **a** announce that one is suffering from (an ailment) (*complained of a headache*). **b** state a grievance concerning (*complained of the delay*). **3** make a mournful sound; groan, creak under a strain. ▫▫ **com·plain·er** *n.* **com·plain·ing·ly** *adv.*

com·plain·ant /kəmpláynənt/ *n. Law* a plaintiff.

com·plaint /kəmpláynt/ *n.* **1** an act of complaining. **2** a grievance. **3** an ailment or illness. **4** *Law* the plaintiff's case in a civil action.

com·plai·sant /kəmpláysənt/ *adj.* **1** deferential. **2** willing to please; acquiescent. ▶Often confused with *complacent*. ▫▫ **com·plai·sance** /–səns/ *n.*

▶see note at COMPLACENT.

com·pleat *archaic* var. of COMPLETE.

com·ple·ment *n.* & *v.* • *n.* /kómplimənt/ **1 a** something that completes. **b** one of two things that go together. **2** (often **full complement**) the full number needed to man a ship, etc. **3** *Gram.* a word or phrase added to a verb to complete the predicate of a sentence. **4** *Math.* any element not belonging to a specified set or class. **5** *Geom.* the amount by which an angle is less than 90° (cf. SUPPLEMENT). • *v.tr.* /kómpliment/ **1** complete; round out or off. **2** form a complement to (*the scarf complements her dress*). ▫▫ **com·ple·men·tal** /–mént'l/ *adj.*

com·ple·men·tar·i·ty /kómplimentáritee/ *n.* (*pl.* **-ties**) **1** a complementary relationship or situation. **2** *Physics* the concept that a single model may not be adequate to explain atomic systems in different experimental conditions.

com·ple·men·ta·ry /kómpliméntəree/ *adj.* **1** completing; forming a complement. **2** (of two or more things) complementing each other. ▫▫ **com·ple·men·ta·ri·ly** /–táirəlee/ *adv.* **com·ple·men·ta·ri·ness** *n.*

▶**Complementary** means 'forming a complement or addition, completing': *I purchased a suit with a complementary tie and handkerchief.* It can be confused with **complimentary**, for which one sense is 'given freely, as a courtesy': You must pay for the suit, but the tie and handkerchief are complimentary.

com·ple·men·ta·ry an·gle *n.* either of two angles making up 90°.

com·ple·men·ta·ry med·i·cine *n.* any of a range of medical therapies, such as acupuncture and osteopathy, that fall beyond the scope of scientific medicine but may be used alongside it in the treatment of disease.

com·plete /kəmpleét/ *adj.* & *v.* • *adj.* **1** having all its parts; entire. **2** finished. **3** of the maximum extent or degree (*a complete surprise; a complete stranger*). **4** (also **com·pleat** after Walton's *Compleat Angler*) *joc.* accomplished (*the complete horseman*). • *v.tr.* **1** finish. **2 a** make whole or perfect. **b** make up the amount of (*completes the quota*). **3** fill in the answers to (a questionnaire, etc.). **4** (usu. *absol.*) *Law* conclude a sale of property. ▫ **complete with** having (as an important accessory) (*comes complete with instructions*). ▫▫ **com·plete·ly** *adv.* **com·plete·ness** *n.* **com·ple·tion** /–pleéshən/ *n.*

com·plex *n.* & *adj.* • *n.* /kómpleks/ **1** a building, a series of rooms, a network, etc. made up of related parts. **2** *Psychol.* a related group of usu. repressed feelings or thoughts which cause abnormal behavior or mental states (*inferiority complex; Oedipus complex*). **3** (in general use) a preoccupation or obsession (*has a complex about punctuality*). **4** *Chem.* a compound in which molecules or ions form coordinate bonds to a metal atom or ion. • *adj.* /kəmpléks, kómpleks/ **1** consisting of related parts; composite. **2** complicated (*a complex problem*). **3** *Math.* containing real and imaginary parts (cf. IMAGINARY). ▫▫ **com·plex·i·ty** /–pléksitee/ *n.* (*pl.* **-ties**). **com·plex·ly** *adv.*

com·plex·ion /kəmplékshən/ *n.* **1** the natural color, texture, and appearance, of the skin, esp. of the face. **2** an aspect; a character (*puts a different complexion on the matter*). ▫▫ **com·plex·ioned** *adj.* (also in *comb.*)

com·plex sen·tence *n.* a sentence containing a subordinate clause or clauses.

com·pli·ance /kəmplíəns/ *n.* **1** the act or an instance of complying. **2** *Mech.* **a** the capacity to yield under an applied force. **b** the degree of such yielding. **3** unworthy acquiescence.

com·pli·ant /kəmplíənt/ *adj.* yielding; obedient. ▫▫ **com·pli·ant·ly** *adv.*

com·pli·cate /kómplikayt/ *v.tr.* & *intr.* **1** (often foll. by *with*) make or become difficult, confused, or complex. **2** (as **complicated** *adj.*) complex; intricate. ▫▫ **com·pli·cat·ed·ly** *adv.* **com·pli·cat·ed·ness** *n.*

com·pli·ca·tion /kómplikáyshn/ *n.* **1 a** an involved or confused condition or state. **b** a complicating circumstance; a difficulty. **2** *Med.* a secondary disease or condition aggravating a previous one.

com·plic·i·ty /kəmplísitee/ *n.* partnership in a crime or wrongdoing.

com·pli·ment *n. & v.* •*n.* /kómplimənt/ **1 a** a spoken or written expression of praise. **b** an act or circumstance implying praise (*their success was a compliment to their efforts*). **2** (in *pl.*) **a** formal greetings, esp. as a written accompaniment to a gift, etc. (*with the compliments of the management*). **b** praise (*my compliments to the cook*). •*v.tr.* /kómpliment/ **1** (often foll. by *on*) congratulate; praise. **2** (often foll. by *with*) present as a mark of courtesy (*complimented her with his attention*). □ **pay a compliment to** praise. **return the compliment 1** give a compliment in return for another. **2** retaliate or recompense in kind.

com·pli·men·ta·ry /kómpliméntəree/ *adj.* **1** expressing a compliment; praising. **2** (of a ticket for a play, etc.) given free of charge.

▶See note at COMPLEMENTARY.

com·pline /kómplin, –plīn/ (also **com·plin**) *n. Eccl.* the last of the canonical hours of prayer.

com·ply /kəmplī́/ *v.intr.* (**-plies, -plied**) (often foll. by *with*) act in accordance (with a wish, command, etc.).

com·po·nent /kəmpṓnənt/ *n. & adj.* •*n.* **1** a part of a larger whole. **2** *Math.* one of two or more vectors equivalent to a given vector. •*adj.* being part of a larger whole (*component parts*). □□ **com·po·nen·tial** /kómpənénshəl/ *adj.*

com·port /kəmpáwrt/ *v.refl. literary* conduct oneself; behave. □□ **com·port·ment** *n.*

com·pose /kəmpṓz/ *v.* **1 a** *tr.* construct or create (a work of art, esp. literature or music). **b** *intr.* compose music. **2** *tr.* constitute; make up (*six tribes which composed the German nation*). ▶Preferred to *comprise* in this sense. **3** *tr.* order; arrange (*composed the group for the photographer*). **4** *tr.* **a** (often *refl.*) calm; settle (*compose your expression*). **b** (as **composed** *adj.*) calm; settled. **5** *tr.* settle (a dispute, etc.). **6** *tr. Printing* **a** set up (type) to form words and blocks of words. **b** set up (a manuscript, etc.) in type. □ **composed of** made up of; consisting of. □□ **com·pos·ed·ly** /–zidlee/ *adv.*

▶Both **compose** and **comprise** can be used to mean 'to constitute or make up' but **compose** is preferred in this sense, e.g., *Citizens who have been been chosen at random and screened for prejudices compose a jury.* **Comprise** is correctly used to mean 'to be composed of, consist of,' e.g., *Each crew comprises a commander, a gunner, and a driver.* The usage "is comprised of" is avoided by careful speakers and writers.

com·pos·er /kəmpṓzər/ *n.* a person who composes (esp. music).

com·pos·ite /kəmpózit/ *adj., n., & v.* •*adj.* **1** made up of various parts; blended. **2** (esp. of a synthetic building material) made up of recognizable constituents. **3** *Archit.* of the fifth classical order of architecture, consisting of elements of the Ionic and Corinthian orders. **4** *Bot.* of the plant family Compositae. •*n.* composite thing or plant. •*v.tr. Polit.* amalgamate (two or more similar resolutions). □□ **com·pos·ite·ly** *adv.* **com·pos·ite·ness** *n.*

com·po·si·tion /kómpəzíshən/ *n.* **1 a** the act of putting together; formation or construction. **b** something so composed; a mixture. **c** the constitution of such a mixture; the nature of its ingredients. **2 a** a literary or musical work. **b** the act or art of producing such a work. **c** an essay, esp. written by a schoolchild. **d** an artistic arrangement (of parts of a picture, subjects for a photograph, etc.). **3** mental constitution; character (*jealousy is not in his composition*). **4** (often *attrib.*) a compound artificial substance. **5** *Printing* the setting-up of type. **6** *Gram.* the formation of words into a compound word. **7** *Law* **a** a compromise, esp. a legal agreement to pay a sum in lieu of a larger sum, or other obligation (*made a composition with his creditors*). **b** a sum paid in this way. □□ **com·po·si·tion·al** *adj.* **com·po·si·tion·al·ly** *adv.*

com·pos·i·tor /kəmpózitər/ *n. Printing* a person who sets up type for printing.

com·post /kómpōst/ *n. & v.* •*n.* **1 a** mixed manure, esp. of organic origin. **b** a loam soil or other medium with added compost, used for growing plants. **2** a mixture of ingredients (*a rich compost of lies and innuendo*). •*v.tr.* **1** treat (soil) with compost. **2** make (manure, vegetable matter, etc.) into compost.

com·post heap (or **pile**) *n.* a layered structure of garden refuse, soil, etc., which decays to become compost.

com·po·sure /kəmpṓzhər/ *n.* a tranquil manner; calmness.

com·pote /kómpōt/ *n.* fruit preserved or cooked in syrup.

com·pound[1] *n., adj., & v.* •*n.* /kómpownd/ **1** a mixture of two or more things, qualities, etc. **2** (also **compound word**) a word made up of two or more existing words. **3** *Chem.* a substance formed from two or more elements chemically united in fixed proportions. •*adj.* /kómpownd/ **1 a** made up of several ingredients. **b** consisting of several parts. **2** combined; collective. **3** *Zool.* consisting of individual organisms. •*v.* /kəmpównd/ **1** *tr.* mix or combine (ingredients, ideas, motives, etc.) (*grief compounded with fear*). **2** *tr.* increase or complicate (difficulties, etc.) (*anxiety compounded by discomfort*). **3** *tr.* make up or concoct (a composite whole). **4** *tr.* (also *absol.*) settle (a debt, dispute, etc.) by concession or special arrangement. **5** *tr. Law* **a** condone (a liability or offense) in exchange for money, etc. **b** forbear from prosecuting (a felony) from private motives. **6** *intr.* (usu. foll. by *with, for*) *Law* come to terms with a person, for forgoing a claim, etc., for an offense. □□ **com·pound·a·ble** /–pówndəbəl/ *adj.*

com·pound[2] /kómpownd/ *n.* enclosure or fenced-in space.

com·pound eye *n.* an eye consisting of numerous visual units, as found in insects and crustaceans.

com·pound frac·ture *n.* an injury in which a broken bone pierces the skin, causing a risk of infection.

com·pound in·ter·est *n.* interest payable on capital and its accumulated interest (cf. SIMPLE INTEREST).

com·pound in·ter·val *n. Mus.* an interval exceeding one octave.

com·pound leaf *n.* a leaf consisting of several or many leaflets.

com·pound sen·tence *n.* a sentence with more than one main, independent clause.

com·pre·hend /kómprihénd/ *v.tr.* **1** grasp mentally; understand. **2** include; take in.

com·pre·hen·si·ble /kómprihénsibəl/ *adj.* **1** that can be understood; intelligible. **2** that can be included or contained. □□ **com·pre·hen·si·bil·i·ty** /–bílitee/ *n.* **com·pre·hen·si·bly** *adv.*

com·pre·hen·sion /kómprihénshən/ *n.* **1** the act or capability of understanding, esp. writing or speech. **2** inclusion.

com·pre·hen·sive /kómprihénsiv/ *adj.* **1** complete; including all or nearly all elements, aspects, etc. (*a comprehensive grasp of the subject*). **2** of or relating to understanding (*the comprehensive faculty*). **3** (of motor-vehicle insurance) providing complete protection. □□ **com·pre·hen·sive·ly** *adv.* **com·pre·hen·sive·ness** *n.*

com·press *v. & n.* •*v.tr.* /kəmprés/ **1** squeeze together. **2** bring into a smaller space or shorter extent. •*n.* /kómpres/ a pad pressed on to part of the body to relieve inflammation, stop bleeding, etc. □□ **com·press·i·ble** /kəmprésəbəl/ *adj.* **com·press·i·bil·i·ty** *n.* **com·pres·sive** /kəmprésiv/ *adj.*

com•pres•sion /kəmpréshən/ *n.* **1** the act of compressing or being compressed. **2** the reduction in volume (causing an increase in pressure) of the fuel mixture in an internal combustion engine before ignition.
com•pres•sor /kəmprésər/ *n.* an instrument or device for compressing, esp. a machine used for increasing the pressure of air or other gases.
com•prise /kəmprīz/ *v.tr.* **1** include; comprehend. **2** consist of; be composed of (*the book comprises 350 pages*). **3** *disp.* make up, compose. ▫▫ **com•pris•a•ble** *adj.*
▶See note at COMPOSE.
com•pro•mise /kómprəmīz/ *n. & v.* •*n.* **1** the settlement of a dispute by mutual concession. **2** (often foll. by *between*) an intermediate state between conflicting opinions, actions, etc., reached by mutual concession. •*v.* **1** *intr.* settle a dispute by mutual concession. **2** *tr.* bring into disrepute or danger esp. by indiscretion or folly. ▫▫ **com•pro•mis•er** *n.* **com•pro•mis•ing•ly** *adv.*
comp•trol•ler /kəntrṓlər/ *n.* a controller (used in the title of some financial officers).
com•pul•sion /kəmpúlshən/ *n.* **1** a constraint; an obligation. **2** *Psychol.* an irresistible urge to a form of behavior, esp. against one's conscious wishes. ▫ **under compulsion** because one is compelled.
com•pul•sive /kəmpúlsiv/ *adj.* **1** compelling. **2** *Psychol.* resulting or acting from compulsion against one's conscious wishes. **3** irresistible (*compulsive viewing*). ▫▫ **com•pul•sive•ly** *adv.* **com•pul•sive•ness** *n.*
com•pul•so•ry /kəmpúlsəree/ *adj.* **1** required by law or a rule. **2** essential; necessary. ▫▫ **com•pul•so•ri•ly** *adv.*
com•punc•tion /kəmpúngkshən/ *n.* (usu. with *neg.*) **1** the pricking of the conscience. **2** a slight regret; a scruple.
com•pu•ta•tion /kompyŏŏtayshən/ *n.* **1** the act or an instance of reckoning; calculation. **2** the use of a computer. **3** a result obtained by calculation. ▫▫ **com•pu•ta•tion•al** *adj.* **com•pu•ta•tion•al•ly** *adv.*
com•pute /kəmpyŏŏt/ *v.* **1** *tr.* (often foll. by *that* + clause) reckon or calculate (a number, an amount, etc.). **2** *intr.* make a reckoning, esp. using a computer. ▫▫ **com•put•a•bil•i•ty** /–təbílitee/ *n.* **com•put•a•ble** *adj.*
com•put•er /kəmpyŏŏtər/ *n.* **1** a usu. electronic device for storing and processing data (usu. in binary form), according to instructions given to it in a variable program. **2** a person who computes or makes calculations.
com•put•er•ize /kəmpyŏŏtərīz/ *v.tr.* **1** equip with a computer; install a computer in. **2** store, perform, or produce by computer. ▫▫ **com•put•er•i•za•tion** *n.*
com•put•er-lit•er•ate *adj.* able to use computers; familiar with the operation of computers.
com•put•er vi•rus *n.* a hidden code within a computer program intended to corrupt a system or destroy data stored in it.
com•rade /kómrad, –rid/ *n.* **1** (also **com•rade in arms**) **a** a coworker, friend, or companion. **b** a fellow soldier, etc. **2** *Polit.* a fellow socialist or communist. ▫▫ **com•rade•ly** *adj.* **com•rade•ship** *n.*
con[1] /kon/ *n. & v. sl.* •*n.* a confidence trick. •*v.tr.* (**conned, conning**) swindle; deceive (*conned him into thinking he had won*).
con[2] /kon/ *n., prep., & adv.* •*n.* (usu. in *pl.*) a reason against. •*prep. & adv.* against (cf. PRO[2]).
con[3] /kon/ *n. sl.* a convict.
con bri•o /kón brée-ō, káwn/ *adv. Mus.* with vigor.
con•cat•e•nate /konkát'nayt/ *v. & adj.* •*v.tr.* link together (a chain of events, things, etc.). •*adj.* joined; linked. ▫▫ **con•cat•e•na•tion** /–náyshən/ *n.*
con•cave /kónkáyv/ *adj.* having an outline or surface curved like the interior of a circle or sphere (cf. CONVEX). ▫▫ **con•cave•ly** *adv.* **con•cav•i•ty** /–kávitee/ *n.*
con•ceal /kənséel/ *v.tr.* **1** (often foll. by *from*) keep secret (*concealed her motive from him*). **2** not allow to be seen; hide. ▫▫ **con•ceal•er** *n.* **con•ceal•ment** *n.*
con•cede /kənséed/ *v.tr.* **1 a** (often foll. by *that* + clause) admit (a defeat, etc.) to be true (*conceded that his work was inadequate*). **b** admit defeat in. **2** (often foll. by *to*) grant or surrender (a right, points in a game, etc.). **3** *Sports* allow an opponent to score (a goal, etc.) or to win (a match), etc. ▫▫ **con•ced•er** *n.*
con•ceit /kənséet/ *n.* **1** personal vanity; pride. **2** *literary* **a** a far-fetched comparison. **b** a fanciful notion.
con•ceit•ed /kənséetid/ *adj.* vain; proud. ▫▫ **con•ceit•ed•ly** *adv.* **con•ceit•ed•ness** *n.*
con•ceiv•a•ble /kənséevəbəl/ *adj.* capable of being grasped or imagined; understandable. ▫▫ **con•ceiv•a•bil•i•ty** /–bílitee/ *n.* **con•ceiv•a•bly** *adv.*
con•ceive /kənséev/ *v.* **1** *intr.* become pregnant. **2** *tr.* become pregnant with (a child). **3** *tr.* (often foll. by *that* + clause) **a** imagine; fancy; think. **b** (usu. in *passive*) formulate; express (a belief, a plan, etc.).
con•cen•trate /kónsəntrayt/ *v. & n.* •*v.* **1** *intr.* (often foll. by *on, upon*) focus one's attention or mental ability. **2** *tr.* bring together (troops, power, attention, etc.) to one point. **3** *tr.* increase the strength of (a liquid, etc.) by removing water or any other diluting agent. **4** *tr.* (as **concentrated** *adj.*) (of hate, etc.) intense; strong. •*n.* **1** a concentrated substance. **2** a concentrated form of esp. food. ▫▫ **con•cen•tra•tor** *n.*
con•cen•tra•tion /kónsəntráyshən/ *n.* **1 a** the act or power of concentrating (*needs to develop concentration*). **b** an instance of this (*interrupted my concentration*). **2** something concentrated. **3** something brought together; a gathering. **4** the weight of substance in a given weight or volume of material.
con•cen•tra•tion camp *n.* a camp for the detention of political prisoners, etc., esp. in Nazi Germany.
con•cen•tric /kənséntrik/ *adj.* (often foll. by *with*) (esp. of circles) having a common center (cf. ECCENTRIC). ▫▫ **con•cen•tri•cal•ly** *adv.* **con•cen•tric•i•ty** /kónsentrísitee/ *n.*
con•cept /kónsept/ *n.* **1** a general notion; an abstract idea (*the concept of evolution*). **2** *colloq.* an idea or invention to help sell or publicize a commodity (*a new concept in swimwear*). **3** *Philos.* an idea or mental picture of a group or class of objects formed by combining all their aspects.
con•cep•tion /kənsépshən/ *n.* **1 a** the act or an instance of conceiving; the process of being conceived. **b** the faculty of conceiving in the mind; apprehension; imagination. **2** an idea or plan, esp. as being new or daring (*the whole conception showed originality*). ▫▫ **con•cep•tion•al** *adj.* **con•cep•tive** /kənséptiv/ *adj.*
con•cep•tu•al /kənsépchŏŏəl/ *adj.* of mental conceptions or concepts. ▫▫ **con•cep•tu•al•ly** *adv.*
con•cep•tu•al•ize /kənsépchŏŏəlīz/ *v.tr.* form a concept or idea of. ▫▫ **con•cep•tu•al•i•za•tion** *n.*
con•cern /kənsə́rn/ *v. & n.* •*v.tr.* **1 a** be relevant or important to (*this concerns you*). **b** relate to; be about. **2** (usu. *refl.*; often foll. by *with, in, about*, or *to* + infin.) interest or involve oneself. **3** worry; cause anxiety to. •*n.* **1 a** anxiety; worry (*felt a deep concern*). **b** solicitous regard; care; consideration. **2 a** a matter of interest or importance to one (*no concern of mine*). **b** (usu. in *pl.*) affairs; private business. **3** a business; a firm. ▫ **have a concern in** have an interest or share in. **have no concern with** have nothing to do with. **to whom it may concern** to those who have a proper interest in the matter (as an address to the reader of a testimonial, reference, etc.).

con•cerned /kənsə́rnd/ *adj.* **1** involved; interested (*concerned with proving his innocence*). **2** (often foll. by *that, about, at, for,* or *to* + infin.) troubled; anxious (*concerned about her*). □ **as** (or **so**) **far as I am concerned** as regards my interests. **be concerned** (often foll. by *in*) take part. **I am not concerned** it is not my business. □□ **con•cern•ed•ly** /–sə́rnidlee/ *adv.* **con•cern•ed•ness** /–sə́rnidnis/ *n.*

con•cern•ing /kənsə́rning/ *prep.* about; regarding.

con•cert *n.* & *v.* • *n.* /kónsərt/ **1 a** a musical performance of usu. several separate compositions. **b** a comedy, etc., performance in a large hall. **2** agreement; harmony. **3** a combination of voices or sounds. • *v.tr.* /kənsə́rt/ arrange (by mutual agreement or coordination). □ **in concert 1** (often foll. by *with*) acting jointly and accordantly. **2** (*predic.*) (of a musician) in a performance.

con•cert•ed /kənsə́rtid/ *adj.* **1** jointly arranged or planned (*a concerted effort*). **2** *Mus.* arranged in parts for voices or instruments.

con•cert grand *n.* the largest size of grand piano.

con•cer•ti•na /kónsərtéenə/ *n.* a musical instrument held in the hands and stretched and squeezed like bellows, having reeds and a set of buttons at each end to control the valves.

concertina

con•cert•mas•ter /kónsərtmástər/ *n.* the leading first-violin player in some orchestras.

con•cer•to /kəncháirtō/ *n.* (*pl.* **concerti** /–tee/ or **-tos**) *Mus.* a composition for a solo instrument or instruments accompanied by an orchestra.

con•cert pitch *n.* **1** *Mus.* the internationally agreed pitch whereby the A above middle C = 440 Hz. **2** a state of unusual readiness, efficiency, and keenness (for action, etc.).

con•ces•sion /kənséshən/ *n.* **1 a** the act or an instance of conceding. **b** a thing conceded. **2** a reduction in price for a certain category of person. **3 a** the right to use land or other property. **b** the right to sell goods, esp. in a particular territory. **c** the land or property used or given. □□ **con•ces•sion•ar•y** *adj.* (also **con•ces•sion•al**).

con•ces•sive /kənsésiv/ *adj.* **1** of or tending to concession. **2** *Gram.* **a** (of a preposition or conjunction) introducing a phrase or clause which might be expected to preclude the action of the main clause, but does not (e.g., *in spite of, although*). **b** (of a phrase or clause) introduced by a concessive preposition or conjunction.

conch /kongk, konch/ *n.* (*pl.* **conchs** /kongks/ or **conches** /kónchiz/) **1** a thick, heavy spiral shell of various marine gastropod mollusks of the family Strombidae. **2** any of these gastropods.

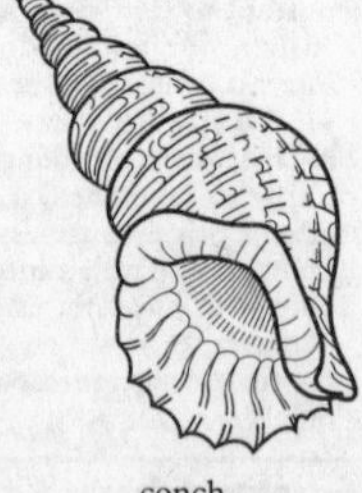

conch

con•cierge /konseeáirzh, káwnsyáirzh/ *n.* **1** a hotel worker who arranges tours, transportation, etc., for guests. **2** (esp. in France) a doorkeeper or porter for an apartment building, etc.

con•cil•i•ate /kənsíleeayt/ *v.tr.* **1** make calm and amenable; pacify. **2** gain (esteem or goodwill). □□ **con•cil•i•a•tion** /kənsílee-áyshən/ *n.* **con•cil•i•a•tor** *n.* **con•cil•i•a•to•ry** /–síleeətáwree/ *adj.*

con•cise /kənsís/ *adj.* (of speech, writing, style, or a person) brief but comprehensive in expression. □□ **con•cise•ly** *adv.* **con•cise•ness** *n.* **con•ci•sion** /kənsízhən/ *n.*

con•clave /kónklayv, kóng–/ *n.* **1** a private meeting. **2** *RC Ch.* **a** the assembly of cardinals for the election of a pope. **b** the meeting place for a conclave.

con•clude /kənklóod/ *v.* **1** *tr.* & *intr.* bring or come to an end. **2** *tr.* (often foll. by *from,* or *that* + clause) infer (from given premises). **3** *tr.* settle; arrange (a treaty, etc.). **4** *intr.* decide.

con•clu•sion /kənklóozhən/ *n.* **1** a final result; a termination. **2** a judgment reached by reasoning. **3** a summing-up. **4** a settling; an arrangement (*the conclusion of peace*). **5** *Logic* a proposition that is reached from given premises. □ **in conclusion** lastly; to conclude.

con•clu•sive /kənklóosiv/ *adj.* decisive; convincing. □□ **con•clu•sive•ly** *adv.* **con•clu•sive•ness** *n.*

con•coct /kənkókt/ *v.tr.* **1** make by mixing ingredients. **2** invent (a story, a lie, etc.). □□ **con•coct•er** *n.* **con•coc•tion** /–kókshən/ *n.* **con•coct•or** *n.*

con•com•i•tant /kənkómit'nt/ *adj.* & *n.* • *adj.* going together; associated (*concomitant circumstances*). • *n.* an accompanying thing. □□ **con•com•i•tance** /kənkómit'ns/ *n.* **con•com•i•tan•cy** *n.* **con•com•i•tant•ly** *adv.*

con•cord /kónkawrd, kóng–/ *n.* **1** agreement or harmony between people or things. **2** a treaty. **3** *Mus.* a chord that is pleasing or satisfactory in itself. **4** *Gram.* agreement between words in gender, number, etc.

con•cord•ance /kənkáwrd'ns/ *n.* **1** agreement. **2** an alphabetical list of the important words used in a book or by an author.

con•cord•ant /kənkáwrd'nt/ *adj.* **1** (often foll. by *with*) agreeing; harmonious. **2** *Mus.* in harmony. □□ **con•cord•ant•ly** *adv.*

con•course /kónkawrs/ *n.* **1** a crowd. **2** a coming together; a gathering (*a concourse of ideas*). **3** an open central area in a large public building.

con•crete /kónkreet, kóng–, konkréet, kong–/ *adj., n.,* & *v.* • *adj.* **1 a** existing in a material form; real. **b** specific; definite (*concrete evidence; a concrete proposal*). **2** *Gram.* (of a noun) denoting a material object. • *n.* (often *attrib.*) a composition of gravel, sand, cement, and water, used for building. • *v.* **1** *tr.* **a** cover with concrete. **b** embed in concrete. **2** /konkréet, kong–/ **a** *tr.* & *intr.* form into a mass; solidify. **b** *tr.* make concrete instead of abstract. □□ **con•crete•ly** *adv.*

con•cre•tion /kənkréeshən/ *n.* **1 a** a hard, solid concreted mass. **b** the forming of this by coalescence. **2** *Med.* a stony mass formed within the body. **3** *Geol.* a small, round mass of rock particles embedded in limestone or clay. □□ **con•cre•tion•ar•y** *adj.*

con•cu•bine /kóngkyəbīn/ *n.* **1** a woman who lives with a man as his wife. **2** (among polygamous peoples) a secondary wife.

con•cu•pis•cence /konkyóopisəns/ *n. formal* sexual desire. □□ **con•cu•pis•cent** /–sənt/ *adj.*

con•cur /kənkə́r/ *v.intr.* (**concurred, concurring**) **1** happen together; coincide. **2** (often foll. by *with*) **a** agree in opinion. **b** express agreement. **3** combine together for a cause; act in combination.

con•cur•rent /kənkə́rənt, –kúr–/ *adj.* **1** (often foll. by *with*) **a** existing or in operation at the same time (*served two concurrent sentences*). **b** existing or acting together. **2** *Geom.* (of three or more lines) meeting at or tending toward one point. **3** agreeing; harmonious. ▫▫ **con·cur·rence** /–rəns/ *n.* **con·cur·rent·ly** *adv.*

con·cus·sion /kənkúshən/ *n.* **1** *Med.* temporary unconsciousness or incapacity due to injury to the head. **2** violent shaking; shock.

con·demn /kəndém/ *v.tr.* **1** express utter disapproval of; censure. **2 a** find guilty; convict. **b** (usu. foll. by *to*) sentence to (a punishment, esp. death). **c** bring about the conviction of (*his looks condemn him*). **3** pronounce (a building, etc.) unfit for use or habitation. **4** (usu. foll. by *to*) doom or assign (to something unwelcome or painful) (*condemned to spending hours at the kitchen sink*). **5 a** declare (smuggled goods, property, etc.) to be forfeited. **b** pronounce incurable. ▫▫ **con·dem·na·ble** /–démnəbəl/ *adj.* **con·dem·na·tion** /kóndemnáyshən/ *n.* **con·dem·na·to·ry** /–démnətáwree/ *adj.*

con·den·sa·tion /kóndensáyshən/ *n.* **1** the act of condensing. **2** any condensed material (esp. water on a cold surface). **3** an abridgment. **4** *Chem.* the combination of molecules with the elimination of water or other small molecules.

con·dense /kəndéns/ *v.* **1** *tr.* make denser or more concentrated. **2** *tr.* express in fewer words; make concise. **3** *tr.* & *intr.* reduce or be reduced from a gas or vapor to a liquid or solid. ▫▫ **con·den·sa·ble** *adj.*

con·densed milk *n.* milk thickened by evaporation and sweetened.

con·dens·er /kəndénsər/ *n.* **1** an apparatus or vessel for condensing vapor. **2** *Electr.* = CAPACITOR. **3** a lens or system of lenses for concentrating light.

con·de·scend /kóndisénd/ *v.intr.* **1** (usu. foll. by *to* + infin.) be gracious enough (to do a thing) esp. while showing one's sense of dignity or superiority (*condescended to attend the meeting*). **2** (foll. by *to*) behave as if one is on equal terms with (an inferior), while maintaining an attitude of superiority. **3** (as **condescending** *adj.*) patronizing; kind to inferiors. ▫▫ **con·de·scend·ing·ly** *adv.* **con·de·scen·sion** /kóndisénshən/ *n.*

con·dign /kəndín/ *adj.* (of a punishment, etc.) severe and well-deserved. ▫▫ **con·dign·ly** *adv.*

con·di·ment /kóndimənt/ *n.* a seasoning or relish for food.

con·di·tion /kəndíshən/ *n.* & *v.* • *n.* **1** a stipulation; something upon the fulfillment of which something else depends. **2 a** the state of being or fitness of a person or thing (*arrived in bad condition*). **b** an ailment or abnormality (*a heart condition*). **3** (in *pl.*) circumstances, esp. those affecting the functioning or existence of something (*working conditions are good*). **4** *Gram.* a clause expressing a condition. • *v.tr.* **1 a** bring into a good or desired state or condition. **b** make fit (esp. dogs or horses). **2** teach or accustom to adopt certain habits, etc. (*conditioned by society*). **3** govern; determine. **4 a** impose conditions on. **b** be essential to. **5** test the condition of (textiles, etc.). ▫ **in** (or **out of**) **condition** in good (or bad) condition. **in no condition to** certainly not fit to. **on condition that** with the stipulation that.

con·di·tion·al /kəndíshənəl/ *adj.* & *n.* • *adj.* **1** (often foll. by *on*) dependent; not absolute; containing a condition or stipulation (*a conditional offer*). **2** *Gram.* (of a clause, mood, etc.) expressing a condition. • *n.* *Gram.* **1** a conditional clause, etc. **2** the conditional mood. ▫▫ **con·di·tion·al·i·ty** /–nálitee/ *n.* **con·di·tion·al·ly** *adv.*

con·di·tion·er /kəndíshənər/ *n.* an agent that conditions, esp. a substance applied to the hair.

con·do /kóndō/ *n.* (*pl.* **-dos**) *colloq.* a condominium.

con·dole /kəndṓl/ *v.intr.* (foll. by *with*) express sympathy with a person over a loss, grief, etc.
▶Often confused with *console.* ▫▫ **con·do·la·to·ry** /kəndṓlətawree/ *adj.*

con·do·lence /kəndṓləns/ *n.* (often in *pl.*) an expression of sympathy (*sent my condolences*).

con·dom /kóndom/ *n.* a rubber sheath worn on the penis during sexual intercourse as a contraceptive or to prevent infection.

con·do·min·i·um /kóndəmíneeəm/ *n.* **1** a building or complex containing apartments that are individually owned. **2** joint sovereignty.

con·done /kəndṓn/ *v.tr.* **1** forgive or overlook (an offense or wrongdoing). **2** approve or sanction, usu. reluctantly. **3** (of an action) atone for (an offense); make up for. ▫▫ **con·do·na·tion** /kóndənáyshən/ *n.* **con·don·er** *n.*

con·dor /kóndawr/ *n.* **1** (in full **Andean condor**) a large vulture, *Vultur gryphus*, of S. America, having black plumage with a white neck ruff. **2** (in full **California condor**) a small vulture, *Gymnogyps californianus*, of California.

con·duce /kəndṓṓs, –dyṓṓs/ *v.intr.* (foll. by *to*) contribute to (a result).

con·du·cive /kəndṓṓsiv, –dyṓṓ–/ *adj.* (often foll. by *to*) contributing or helping (toward something).

con·duct *n.* & *v.* • *n.* /kóndukt/ **1** behavior (esp. in its moral aspect). **2** the action or manner of directing or managing (business, war, etc.). **3** leading; guidance. • *v.* /kəndúkt/ **1** *tr.* lead or guide (a person). **2** *tr.* direct or manage (business, etc.). **3** *tr.* (also *absol.*) be the conductor of (an orchestra, etc.). **4** *tr.* *Physics* transmit (heat, electricity, etc.) by conduction. **5** *refl.* behave. ▫▫ **con·duct·i·ble** /kəndúktibəl/ *adj.* **con·duct·i·bil·i·ty** *n.* **con·duc·tive** *adj.* **con·duc·tive·ly** *adv.*

con·duct·ance /kəndúktəns/ *n.* *Physics* the power of a specified material to conduct electricity.

con·duc·tion /kəndúkshən/ *n.* **1** the transmission of heat or electricity through a substance. **2** the transmission of impulses along nerves. **3** the conducting of liquid through a pipe, etc.

con·duc·tiv·i·ty /kónduktívitee/ *n.* the conducting power of a specified material.

con·duc·tor /kəndúktər/ *n.* **1** a person who directs the performance of an orchestra or choir, etc. **2 a** an official in charge of a train. **b** a person who collects fares in a bus, etc. **3** *Physics* **a** a thing that conducts or transmits heat or electricity. **b** = LIGHTNING ROD. **4** a guide or leader. **5** a manager or director. ▫▫ **con·duc·tor·ship** *n.*

con·duit /kóndōoit, –dyōoit, –dit/ *n.* **1** a channel or pipe for conveying liquids. **2 a** a tube or trough for protecting insulated electric wires. **b** a length or stretch of this.

cone /kōn/ *n.* **1** a solid figure with a circular (or other curved) plane base, tapering to a point. **2** a thing of a similar shape, e.g., as used to mark off areas of roads. **3** the dry fruit of a conifer. **4** a cone-shaped wafer for holding ice cream. **5** any of the minute cone-shaped structures in the retina. **6** a conical mountain esp. of volcanic origin. **7** (in full **cone shell**) any marine gastropod mollusk of the family Conidae.

Con·es·to·ga /konəstṓgə/ *n.* **1** a N. American people native to the northeastern US. **2** a member of this people.

con·fab /kónfab/ *n.* & *v.* *colloq.* • *n.* a conversation; a chat. • *v.intr.* (**confabbed, confabbing**) = CONFABULATE.

con·fab·u·late /kənfábyəlayt/ *v.intr.* **1** converse; chat. **2** *Psychol.* fabricate imaginary experiences as compensation for the loss of memory. ▫▫ **con·fab·u·la·tion** /–láyshən/ *n.* **con·fab·u·la·to·ry** /–lətáwree/ *adj.*

con·fec·tion /kənfékshən/ *n.* **1** a dish or delicacy made with sweet ingredients. **2** mixing; compounding.

con·fec·tion·er /kənfékshənər/ *n.* a maker or retailer of confectionery.

confectioners' sugar *n.* very fine powdered sugar.

con•fec•tion•er•y /kənfékshəneree/ *n.* candy and other confections.

con•fed•er•a•cy /kənfédərəsee/ *n.* (*pl.* **-cies**) **1** a league or alliance, esp. of confederate nations. **2** a league for an unlawful or evil purpose; a conspiracy. **3** the condition or fact of being confederate; alliance; conspiracy. **4** (**the Confederacy**) = CONFEDERATE STATES OF AMERICA.

con•fed•er•ate *adj.*, *n.*, *& v.* • *adj.* /kənfédərət/ esp. *Polit.* allied; joined by an agreement or treaty. • *n.* /kənfédərət/ **1** an ally, esp. (in a bad sense) an accomplice. **2** (**Confederate**) a supporter of the Confederate States of America. • *v.* /kənfédərayt/ (often foll. by *with*) **1** *tr.* bring (a person, state, or oneself) into alliance. **2** *intr.* come into alliance.

Con•fed•er•ate States of A•mer•i•ca *n.pl.* the eleven Southern states that seceded from the US in 1860–61.

con•fed•er•a•tion /kənfédəráyshən/ *n.* **1** a union or alliance of nations, etc. **2** the act or an instance of confederating; the state of being confederated.

con•fer /kənfə́r/ *v.* (**conferred, conferring**) **1** *tr.* (often foll. by *on*, *upon*) grant or bestow (a title, degree, favor, etc.). **2** *intr.* (often foll. by *with*) consult. □□ **con•fer•ment** *n.* **con•fer•ra•ble** *adj.* **con•fer•ral** *n.*

con•fer•ence /kónfərəns, –frəns/ *n.* **1** consultation; discussion. **2** a meeting for discussion, esp. a regular one held by an association or organization. □ **in conference** engaged in discussion.

con•fer•ence call *n.* a telephone call in which three or more people are connected.

con•fess /kənfés/ *v.* **1 a** *tr.* (also *absol.*) acknowledge or admit (a fault, wrongdoing, etc.). **b** *intr.* (foll. by *to*) admit to (*confessed to having lied*). **2** *tr.* admit reluctantly (*confessed it would be difficult*). **3 a** *tr.* (also *absol.*) declare (one's sins) to a priest. **b** *tr.* (of a priest) hear the confession of. **c** *refl.* declare one's sins to a priest.

con•fess•ed•ly /kənfésidlee/ *adv.* by one's own or general admission.

con•fes•sion /kənféshən/ *n.* **1 a** confessing or acknowledgment of a fault, wrongdoing, a sin to a priest, etc. **b** an instance of this. **c** a thing confessed. **2** (in full **confession of faith**) **a** a declaration of one's religious beliefs. **b** a statement of one's principles. □□ **con•fes•sion•ar•y** *adj.*

con•fes•sion•al /kənféshənəl/ *n.* & *adj.* • *n.* an enclosed stall in a church in which a priest hears confessions. • *adj.* **1** of or relating to confession. **2** denominational.

con•fes•sor /kənfésər/ *n.* **1** a person who makes a confession. **2** a priest who hears confessions and gives spiritual counsel. **3** a person who avows a religion in the face of its suppression, but does not suffer martyrdom.

con•fet•ti /kənfétee/ *n.* small bits of colored paper thrown during celebrations, etc.

con•fi•dant /kónfidánt, –daánt/ *n.* (*fem.* **confidante** *pronunc.* same) a person trusted with knowledge of one's private affairs.

con•fide /kənfíd/ *v.* **1** *tr.* (usu. foll. by *to*) tell (a secret, etc.) in confidence. **2** *tr.* (foll. by *to*) entrust (an object of care, a task, etc.) to. **3** *intr.* (foll. by *in*) **a** have trust or confidence in. **b** talk confidentially to.

con•fi•dence /kónfidəns/ *n.* **1** firm trust. **2 a** a feeling of reliance or certainty. **b** a sense of self-reliance; boldness. **3 a** something told confidentially. **b** the telling of private matters with mutual trust. □ **in confidence** as a secret. **in a person's confidence** trusted with a person's secrets. **take into one's confidence** confide in.

con•fi•dence game *n.* a swindle in which the victim is persuaded to trust the swindler.

con•fi•dence man *n.* (*pl.* **-men**) a man who robs by means of a confidence game.

con•fi•dent /kónfid'nt/ *adj.* **1** feeling or showing confidence; self-assured; bold. **2** (often foll. by *of*, or *that* + clause) assured; trusting. □□ **con•fi•dent•ly** *adv.*

con•fi•den•tial /kónfidénshəl/ *adj.* **1** spoken or written in confidence. **2** entrusted with secrets (*a confidential secretary*). **3** confiding. □□ **con•fi•den•ti•al•i•ty** /–sheeálitee/ *n.* **con•fi•den•tial•ly** *adv.*

con•fig•u•ra•tion /kənfígyəráyshən/ *n.* **1 a** an arrangement of parts or elements in a particular form or figure. **b** the form, shape, or figure resulting from such an arrangement. **2** *Physics* the distribution of electrons among the energy levels of an atom, or of nucleons among the energy levels of a nucleus, as specified by quantum numbers. **3** *Chem.* the fixed three-dimensional relationship of the atoms in a molecule. □□ **con•fig•u•ra•tion•al** *adj.* **con•fig•ure** *v.tr.* (in sense 1).

con•fine *v.* & *n.* • *v.tr.* /kənfín/ (often foll. by *in*, *to*, *within*) **1** keep or restrict (within certain limits, etc.). **2** hold captive; imprison. • *n.* /kónfin/ (usu. in *pl.*) a limit or boundary (*within the confines of the town*).

con•fine•ment /kənfínmənt/ *n.* **1** the act or an instance of confining; the state of being confined. **2** the time of a woman's giving birth.

con•firm /kənfə́rm/ *v.tr.* **1** provide support for the truth or correctness of; make definitely valid (*confirmed my suspicions*; *confirmed his arrival time*). **2** ratify (a treaty, title, etc.); make formally valid. **3** (foll. by *in*) encourage (a person) in (an opinion, etc.). **4** establish more firmly (power, possession, etc.). **5** administer the religious rite of confirmation to. □□ **con•firm•a•tive** *adj.* **con•firm•a•to•ry** *adj.*

con•fir•ma•tion /kónfərmáyshən/ *n.* **1 a** the act or an instance of confirming; the state of being confirmed. **b** an instance of this. **2** a religious rite confirming a baptized person as a church member.

con•firmed /kənfə́rmd/ *adj.* firmly settled in some habit or condition (*a confirmed bachelor*).

con•fis•cate /kónfiskayt/ *v.tr.* **1** take or seize by authority. **2** appropriate to the public treasury (by way of a penalty). □□ **con•fis•ca•ble** /kənfískəbəl/ *adj.* **con•fis•ca•tion** /–káyshən/ *n.* **con•fis•ca•tor** *n.*

con•fla•gra•tion /kónfləgráyshən/ *n.* a great and destructive fire.

con•flate /kənfláyt/ *v.tr.* blend or fuse together. □□ **con•fla•tion** /–fláyshən/ *n.*

con•flict *n.* & *v.* • *n.* /kónflikt/ **1 a** a state of opposition or hostilities. **b** a fight or struggle. **2** (often foll. by *of*) **a** the clashing of opposed principles, etc. **b** an instance of this. **3** *Psychol.* **a** the opposition of incompatible wishes or needs in a person. **b** an instance of this. **c** the distress resulting from this. • *v.intr.* /kənflíkt/ **1** clash; be incompatible. **2** (often foll. by *with*) struggle or contend. **3** (as **conflicting** *adj.*) contradictory. □ **in conflict** conflicting. □□ **con•flic•tion** /–flíkshən/ *n.* **con•flic•tu•al** /kənflíkchōōəl/ *adj.*

con•flu•ence /kónflōōəns/ *n.* **1** a place where two rivers meet. **2 a** a coming together. **b** a crowd of people.

con•flu•ent /kónflōōənt/ *adj.* & *n.* • *adj.* flowing together; uniting. • *n.* a stream joining another.

con•flux /kónfluks/ *n.* = CONFLUENCE.

con•form /kənfáwrm/ *v.* **1** *intr.* comply with rules or custom. **2** *intr.* & *tr.* (often foll. by *to*) be or make accordant or suitable. **3** *tr.* (often foll. by *to*) make similar. **4** *intr.* (foll. by *to*, *with*) comply with. □□ **con•form•er** *n.*

con•form•a•ble /kənfáwrməbəl/ *adj.* **1** (often foll. by *to*) similar. **2** (often foll. by *with*) consistent. **3** (often foll. by *to*) adapted. **4** tractable. □□ **con•form•a•bil•i•ty** *n.* **con•form•a•bly** *adv.*

con•for•ma•tion /kónfawrmáyshən/ *n.* **1** the way in which a thing is formed. **2** (often foll. by *to*) adjustment in form or character; adaptation. **3** *Chem.* any spatial arrangement of atoms in a molecule from the rotation of part of the molecule about a single bond.

con·form·ist /kənfáwrmist/ *n.* & *adj.* • *n.* a person who conforms to an established practice. • *adj.* (of a person) conventional. ▫▫ **con·form·ism** *n.*

con·form·i·ty /kənfáwrmitee/ *n.* **1** (often foll. by *to*, *with*) action or behavior in accordance with established practice. **2** (often foll. by *to, with*) likeness; agreement.

con·found /kənfównd/ *v.* & *int.* • *v.tr.* **1** throw into perplexity. **2** confuse (in one's mind). **3** *archaic* defeat; overthrow. • *int.* expressing annoyance (*confound you!*).

con·found·ed /kənfówndid/ *adj. colloq.* damned (*a confounded nuisance!*). ▫▫ **con·found·ed·ly** *adv.*

con·front /kənfrúnt/ *v.tr.* **1 a** face in hostility or defiance. **b** face up to and deal with (a problem, etc.). **2** (of a difficulty, etc.) present itself to. **3** (foll. by *with*) **a** bring (a person) face to face with (a circumstance). **b** set (a thing) face to face with (another) for comparison. **4** meet or stand facing. ▫▫ **con·fron·ta·tion** /kónfruntáyshən/ *n.* **con·fron·ta·tion·al** /kónfruntáyshənəl/ *adj.*

Con·fu·cian /kənfyóoshən/ *adj.* & *n.* • *adj.* of or relating to Confucius, Chinese philosopher d. 479 BC, or his philosophy. • *n.* a follower of Confucius. ▫▫ **Con·fu·cian·ism** *n.* **Con·fu·cian·ist** *n.*

con·fuse /kənfyóoz/ *v.tr.* **1 a** disconcert; perplex. **b** embarrass. **2** mistake (one for another). **3** make indistinct (*that point confuses the issue*). **4** (as **confused** *adj.*) **a** mentally decrepit. **b** puzzled; perplexed. **5** (often as **confused** *adj.*) throw into disorder (*a confused jumble of clothes*). ▫▫ **con·fus·a·bil·i·ty** *n.* **con·fus·a·ble** *adj.* **con·fus·ed·ly** /kənfyóozidlee/ *adv.* **con·fus·ing** *adj.* **con·fus·ing·ly** *adv.*

con·fu·sion /kənfyóozhən/ *n.* **1 a** the act of confusing (*the confusion of fact and fiction*). **b** a misunderstanding (*confusions arise from a lack of communication*). **2 a** a confused state. **b** (foll. by *of*) a disorderly jumble (*a confusion of ideas*). **3 a** a civil commotion (*confusion broke out at the announcement*). **b** an instance of this.

con·fute /kənfyóot/ *v.tr.* **1** prove (a person) to be in error. **2** prove (an argument) to be false. ▫▫ **con·fu·ta·tion** /kónfyootáyshən/ *n.*

con·ga /kónggə/ *n.* **1** a Latin American dance of African origin, usu. with several persons in a single line, one behind the other. **2** (also **con·ga drum**) a tall, narrow, low-toned drum beaten with the hands.

con·geal /kənjéel/ *v.tr.* & *intr.* **1** make or become semisolid by cooling. **2** (of blood, etc.) coagulate. ▫▫ **con·geal·a·ble** *adj.* **con·geal·ment** *n.*

con·ge·la·tion /kónjiláyshən/ *n.* **1** the process of congealing. **2** a congealed state. **3** a congealed substance.

con·gen·ial /kənjéenyəl/ *adj.* **1** (often foll. by *with, to*) (of a person, character, etc.) pleasant because akin to oneself in temperament or interests. **2** (often foll. by *to*) agreeable. ▫▫ **con·ge·ni·al·i·ty** /–jéeneeálitee/ *n.* **con·gen·ial·ly** *adv.*

con·gen·i·tal /kənjénitəl/ *adj.* **1** (esp. of a disease, defect, etc.) existing from birth. **2** that is (or as if) such from birth (*a congenital liar*). ▫▫ **con·gen·i·tal·ly** *adv.*

con·ger /kónggər/ *n.* (in full **conger eel**) any large marine eel of the family Congridae.

con·ge·ries /kənjéereez, kónjə–/ *n.* (*pl.* same) a disorderly collection.

con·gest /kənjést/ *v.tr.* (esp. as **congested** *adj.*) affect with congestion. ▫▫ **con·ges·tive** *adj.*

con·ges·tion /kənjés-chən/ *n.* abnormal accumulation, crowding, or obstruction.

con·glom·er·ate *adj.*, *n.*, & *v.* • *adj.* /kənglómərət/ gathered into a rounded mass. • *n.* /kənglómərət/ **1** a number of things or parts forming a heterogeneous mass. **2** a group or corporation formed by the merging of separate and diverse firms. • *v.tr.* & *intr.* /kənglóməráyt/ collect into a coherent mass. ▫▫ **con·glom·er·a·tion** /–ráyshən/ *n.*

Con·go·lese /kónggəléez/ *adj.* & *n.* • *adj.* of or relating to the Republic of the Congo in Central Africa, or the region surrounding the Zaire (formerly Congo) River. • *n.* (*pl.* same) a native of either of these regions.

con·grat·u·late /kəngráchəlayt, –gráj–, kəng–/ *v.tr.* & *refl.* (often foll. by *on*, *upon*) **1** *tr.* express pleasure at the happiness or excellence of (a person) (*congratulated them on their success*). **2** *refl.* think oneself fortunate or clever. ▫▫ **con·grat·u·la·to·ry** /–lətáwree/ *adj.*

con·grat·u·la·tion /kəngráchəláyshən –gráj–, kəng–/ *n.* **1** congratulating. **2** (also as *int.*; usu. in *pl.*) an expression of this.

con·gre·gate /kónggrigayt/ *v.intr.* & *tr.* collect or gather into a crowd or mass.

con·gre·ga·tion /kónggrigáyshən/ *n.* **1** the process of congregating; collection into a crowd or mass. **2** a crowd or mass gathered together. **3 a** a body assembled for religious worship. **b** a body of persons regularly attending a particular church, etc.

con·gre·ga·tion·al /kónggrigáyshənəl/ *adj.* **1** of a congregation. **2** (**Congregational**) of or adhering to Congregationalism.

Con·gre·ga·tion·al·ism /kónggrigáyshənəlizəm/ *n.* a system of ecclesiastical organization whereby individual churches are largely self-governing. ▫▫ **Con·gre·ga·tion·al·ist** *n.* **Con·gre·ga·tion·al·ize** *v.tr.*

con·gress /kónggris/ *n.* **1** a formal meeting of delegates for discussion. **2** (**Congress**) a national legislative body, esp. that of the US. **3** a society or organization. **4** meeting. ▫▫ **con·gres·sion·al** /kəngréshən'l/ *adj.*

Con·gres·sion·al Med·al of Hon·or *n.* = MEDAL OF HONOR.

con·gress·man /kónggrismən/ *n.* (*pl.* **-men**; *fem.* **congresswoman**, *pl.* **-women**) a member of the US Congress, esp. of the US House of Representatives.

con·gru·ence /kónggrooəns, kəngróo–/ *n.* (also **con·gru·en·cy** /–ənsee/) **1** agreement; consistency. **2** *Geom.* the state of being congruent.

con·gru·ent /kónggrooənt, kəngróo–/ *adj.* **1** (often foll. by *with*) suitable; agreeing. **2** *Geom.* (of figures) coinciding exactly when superimposed. ▫▫ **con·gru·ent·ly** *adv.*

con·gru·ous /kónggrooəs/ *adj.* (often foll. by *with*) suitable; fitting. ▫▫ **con·gru·i·ty** /–gróoitee/ *n.* **con·gru·ous·ly** *adv.*

con·ic /kónik/ *adj.* of a cone.

con·i·cal /kónikəl/ *adj.* cone-shaped. ▫▫ **con·i·cal·ly** *adv.*

co·ni·fer /kónifər, kṓ–/ *n.* any evergreen tree of a group usu. bearing cones, including pines, yews, cedars, and redwoods. ▫▫ **co·nif·er·ous** /kənífərəs/ *adj.*

con·jec·ture /kənjékchər/ *n.* & *v.* • *n.* **1 a** the formation of an opinion on incomplete information; guessing. **b** an opinion or conclusion reached in this way. **2 a** (in textual criticism) the guessing of a reading not in the text. **b** a proposed reading. • *v.* **1** *tr.* & *intr.* guess. **2** *tr.* (in textual criticism) propose (a reading). ▫▫ **con·jec·tur·al** /kənjékchərəl/ *adj.* **con·jec·tur·al·ly** *adv.*

con·join /kənjóyn/ *v.tr.* & *intr.* join; combine.

con·joint /kənjóynt/ *adj.* associated, conjoined. ▫▫ **con·joint·ly** *adv.*

con·ju·gal /kónjəgəl/ *adj.* of marriage or the relation between husband and wife. ▫▫ **con·ju·gal·i·ty** /–gálitee/ *n.* **con·ju·gal·ly** *adv.*

con·ju·gate *v.*, *adj.*, & *n.* • *v.* /kónjəgayt/ **1** *tr.* *Gram.* give the different forms of (a verb). **2** *intr.* **a** unite sexually. **b** (of gametes) become fused. • *adj.* /kónjəgət,

–gayt/ **1** joined together, esp. as a pair. **2** *Gram.* derived from the same root. **3** *Biol.* fused. • *n.* /kónjəgət, –gayt/ a conjugate word or thing. ▫▫ **con·ju·ga·tion** /kónjəgáyshən/ *n.* **con·ju·ga·tion·al** *adj.*

con·junct /kənjúngkt/ *adj.* joined together; combined; associated.

con·junc·tion /kənjúngkshən/ *n.* **1 a** the action of joining; the condition of being joined. **b** an instance of this. **2** *Gram.* a word used to connect clauses or sentences or words in the same clause (e.g., *and, but, if*). **3 a** a combination (of events or circumstances). **b** a number of associated persons or things. ▫ **in conjunction with** together with. ▫▫ **con·junc·tion·al** *adj.*

con·junc·ti·va /kónjungktívə, kənjúngktivə/ *n.* (*pl.* **conjunctivas** or **conjunctivae** /–vee/) *Anat.* the mucous membrane that covers the front of the eye and lines the inside of the eyelids. ▫▫ **con·junc·ti·val** *adj.*

con·junc·tive /kənjúngktiv/ *adj.* **1** serving to join. **2** *Gram.* of the nature of a conjunction. ▫▫ **con·junc·tive·ly** *adv.*

con·junc·ti·vi·tis /kənjúngktivítis/ *n.* inflammation of the conjunctiva.

con·junc·ture /kənjúngkchər/ *n.* a combination of events; a state of affairs.

con·jure /kónjər/ *v.* **1** *tr.* call upon (a spirit) to appear. **2** *tr.* (usu. foll. by *out of, away, to*, etc.) cause to appear or disappear as if by magic. **3** *intr.* perform marvels. **4** *tr.* /kənjóor/ (often foll. by *to* + infin.) appeal solemnly to (a person). ▫ **conjure up 1** bring into existence or cause to appear as if by magic. **2** evoke.

con·jur·er /kónjərər, kún–/ *n.* (also **con·jur·or**) a person who conjures.

conk[1] /kongk/ *v.intr.* (usu. foll. by *out*) *colloq.* **1** (of a machine, etc.) break down. **2** (of a person) become exhausted and give up; faint; die.

conk[2] /kongk/ *v.tr. sl.* hit on the head, etc.

con man *n.* (*pl.* **men**) = CONFIDENCE MAN.

con mo·to /kón mṓtō, káwn/ *adv. Mus.* with movement.

Conn. *abbr.* Connecticut.

conn /kon/ *n.* & *v. Naut.* • *v.tr.* direct the steering of (a ship). • *n.* **1** the act of conning. **2** the responsibility or station of one who conns.

con·nect /kənékt/ *v.* **1 a** *tr.* (often foll. by *to, with*) join (one thing with another). **b** *tr.* join (two things) (*a track connected the two villages*). **c** *intr.* be joined or joinable (*the two parts do not connect*). **2** *tr.* (often foll. by *with*) associate mentally or practically (*did not connect the two ideas*). **3** *intr.* (foll. by *with*) (of a train, etc.) be synchronized at its destination with another train, etc., so that passengers can transfer. **4** *tr.* put into communication by telephone. **5 a** *tr.* (usu. in *passive*; foll. by *with*) unite or associate with others in relationships, etc. (*am connected with the royal family*). **b** *intr.* form a logical sequence; be meaningful. **6** *intr. colloq.* hit or strike effectively. ▫▫ **con·nect·a·ble** *adj.* **con·nect·or** *n.*

con·nect·ed /kənéktid/ *adj.* **1** joined in sequence. **2** (of ideas, etc.) coherent. **3** related or associated. ▫▫ **con·nect·ed·ly** *adv.* **con·nect·ed·ness** *n.*

con·nec·tion /kənékshən/ *n.* **1 a** the act of connecting; the state of being connected. **b** an instance of this. **2** the point at which two things are connected. **3 a** a link (*a radio formed the only connection with the outside world*). **b** a telephone link (*got a bad connection*). **4** arrangement or opportunity for catching a connecting train, etc.; the train, etc., itself (*missed the connection*). **5** *Electr.* **a** the linking up of an electric current by contact. **b** a device for effecting this. **6** (often in *pl.*) a relative or associate, esp. one with influence (*has connections in the State Department*). **7** a relation of ideas; a context. **8** *sl.* **a** a transaction involving illegal drugs. **b** a supplier of narcotics. ▫ **in connection with** with reference to. **in this** (or **that**) **connection** with reference to this (or that).

con·nec·tive /kənéktiv/ *adj.* & *n.* • *adj.* serving or tending to connect. • *n.* something that connects.

con·nec·tive tis·sue *n. Anat.* a fibrous tissue that supports, binds, or separates more specialized tissue.

conn·ing tow·er /kóning/ *n.* **1** the superstructure of a submarine which contains the periscope. **2** the armored pilothouse of a warship.

con·nive /kənív/ *v.intr.* **1** (foll. by *at*) disregard or tacitly consent to (a wrongdoing). **2** (usu. foll. by *with*) conspire. ▫▫ **con·niv·er** *n.*

con·nois·seur /kónəsṓr/ *n.* (often foll. by *of, in*) an expert judge in matters of taste. ▫▫ **con·nois·seur·ship** *n.*

con·note /kənṓt/ *v.tr.* **1** (of a word, etc.) imply in addition to the literal or primary meaning. **2** (of a fact) imply as a consequence or condition. **3** mean; signify. ▫▫ **con·no·ta·tion** /kónətáyshən/ *n.* **con·no·ta·tive** /kónətaytiv, kənṓtətiv/ *adj.*

▶**Connote** means 'suggest': *"Mother" connotes warmth, concern, and security.* **Denote** refers to the literal meaning: *"Mother" denotes a female who has given birth.*

con·nu·bi·al /kənóobeeəl, kənyóo–/ *adj.* of or relating to marriage or the relationship of husband and wife. ▫▫ **con·nu·bi·al·i·ty** /–beeálitee/ *n.* **con·nu·bi·al·ly** *adv.*

con·quer /kóngkər/ *v.tr.* **1 a** overcome and control by military force. **b** *absol.* be victorious. **2** overcome (a habit, disability, etc.) by effort. **3** climb (a mountain) successfully. ▫▫ **con·quer·a·ble** *adj.* **con·quer·or** *n.*

con·quest /kóngkwest/ *n.* **1** the act or an instance of conquering; the state of being conquered. **2 a** conquered territory. **b** something won. **3** a person whose affection has been won. ▫ **make a conquest of** win the affections of.

con·quis·ta·dor /konkwístədawr, kongkéestə–/ *n.* (*pl.* **conquistadores** /–dáwrez/ or **conquistadors**) a conqueror, esp. one of the Spanish conquerors of Mexico and Peru in the 16th c.

con·san·guin·e·ous /kónsanggwíneeəs/ *adj.* descended from the same ancestor. ▫▫ **con·san·guin·i·ty** *n.*

con·science /kónshəns/ *n.* **1** a moral sense of right and wrong. **2** an inner feeling as to the goodness or otherwise of one's behavior (*has a guilty conscience*). ▫ **in all conscience** *colloq.* by any reasonable standard. **on one's conscience** causing one feelings of guilt. ▫▫ **con·science·less** *adj.*

con·sci·en·tious /kónshee-énshəs/ *adj.* (of a person or conduct) diligent and scrupulous. ▫▫ **con·sci·en·tious·ly** *adv.* **con·sci·en·tious·ness** *n.*

con·sci·en·tious ob·jec·tor *n.* a person who for reasons of conscience objects to conforming to a requirement, esp. that of military service.

con·scious /kónshəs/ *adj.* & *n.* • *adj.* **1** awake and aware of one's surroundings and identity. **2** (usu. foll. by *of*, or *that* + clause) aware (*conscious of his inferiority*). **3** (of actions, emotions, etc.) realized or recognized by the doer; intentional (*made a conscious effort not to laugh*). **4** (in *comb.*) aware of; concerned with (*appearance-conscious*). • *n.* (prec. by *the*) the conscious mind. ▫▫ **con·scious·ly** *adv.*

con·scious·ness /kónshəsnis/ *n.* **1** the state of being conscious. **2 a** awareness; perception (*no consciousness of being ridiculed*). **b** (in *comb.*) awareness of (*class consciousness*). **3** the totality of a person's thoughts and feelings, or of a class of these (*moral consciousness*).

con·script *v.* & *n.* • *v.tr.* /kənskrípt/ enlist by conscription. • *n.* /kónskript/ a person enlisted by conscription.

con·scrip·tion /kənskrípshən/ *n.* compulsory enlistment for government service, esp. military service.

con·se·crate /kónsikrayt/ *v.tr.* **1** make or declare sacred. **2** (in Christian belief) make (bread and wine) into the body and blood of Christ. **3** (foll. by *to*) devote (one's life, etc.) to (a purpose). **4** ordain (esp. a bishop) to a sacred office. ▫▫ **con·se·cra·tion** /–kráyshən/ *n.* **con·se·cra·tor** *n.* **con·se·cra·to·ry** /–krətáwree/ *adj.*

con·sec·u·tive /kənsékyətiv/ *adj.* **1 a** following continuously. **b** in unbroken or logical order. **2** *Gram.* expressing consequence. ▫▫ **con·sec·u·tive·ly** *adv.* **con·sec·u·tive·ness** *n.*

con·sen·sus /kənsénsəs/ *n.* (often foll. by *of*) **1 a** general agreement (of opinion, testimony, etc.). **b** an instance of this. **2** (*attrib.*) majority view; collective opinion (*consensus politics*). ▫▫ **con·sen·su·al** /kənsénshōōəl/ *adj.* **con·sen·su·al·ly** *adv.*

con·sent /kənsént/ *v.* & *n.* • *v.intr.* (often foll. by *to*) give permission; agree. • *n.* voluntary agreement; permission; compliance.

con·sent·ing a·dult *n.* an adult who consents to something, esp. a sexual act.

con·se·quence /kónsikwens, –kwəns/ *n.* **1** the result or effect of an action or condition. **2 a** importance (*of no consequence*). **b** social distinction (*persons of consequence*). ▫ **in consequence** as a result. **take the consequences** accept the results of one's choice or action.

con·se·quent /kónsikwənt/ *adj.* & *n.* • *adj.* **1** (often foll. by *on, upon*) following as a result or consequence. **2** logically consistent. • *n.* **1** a thing that follows another. **2** *Logic* the second part of a conditional proposition, dependent on the antecedent.

con·se·quen·tial /kónsikwénshəl/ *adj.* **1** following as a result or consequence. **2** resulting indirectly (*consequential damage*). **3 a** significant. **b** (of a person) self-important. ▫▫ **con·se·quen·ti·al·i·ty** /–sheeálitee/ *n.* **con·se·quen·tial·ly** *adv.*

con·se·quent·ly /kónsikwentlee/ *adv.* & *conj.* as a result; therefore.

con·serv·an·cy /kənsərvənsee/ *n.* (*pl.* **-cies**) **1** a body concerned with the preservation of natural resources. **2** conservation; official preservation (of forests, etc.).

con·ser·va·tion /kónsərváyshən/ *n.* preservation, esp. of the natural environment. ▫ **conservation of energy** (or **mass** or **momentum**, etc.) *Physics* the principle that the total quantity of energy, etc., of any system not subject to external action remains constant. ▫▫ **con·ser·va·tion·al** *adj.* **con·ser·va·tion·ist** *n.*

con·serv·a·tive /kənsərvətiv/ *adj.* & *n.* • *adj.* **1 a** averse to rapid change. **b** (of views, taste, etc.) avoiding extremes (*conservative in her dress*). **2** (of an estimate, etc.) purposely low; moderate. **3** (**Conservative**) of or characteristic of Conservatives or the British Conservative Party. **4** tending to conserve. • *n.* **1** a conservative person. **2** (**Conservative**) a supporter or member of the British Conservative Party. ▫▫ **con·serv·a·tism** *n.* **con·serv·a·tive·ly** *adv.*

con·serv·a·to·ry /kənsərvətawree/ *n.* (*pl.* **-ries**) a greenhouse for tender plants, esp. one attached to and communicating with a house.

con·serve /kənsərv/ *v.* & *n.* • *v.tr.* **1** store up; keep from harm or damage, esp. for later use. **2** *Physics* maintain a quantity of (heat, etc.). **3** preserve (food, esp. fruit), usu. with sugar. • *n.* /also kónsərv/ **1** fruit, etc., preserved in sugar. **2** fresh fruit jam.

con·sid·er /kənsídər/ *v.tr.* (often *absol.*) **1** contemplate mentally, esp. in order to reach a conclusion. **2** examine the merits of (a candidate, claim, etc.). **3** give attention to. **4** take into account. **5** (foll. by *that* + clause) have the opinion. **6** (foll. by *compl.*) believe (*consider it to be genuine*). **7** (as **considered** *adj.*) formed after careful thought (*a considered opinion*). ▫ **all things considered** taking everything into account.

con·sid·er·a·ble /kənsídərəbəl/ *adj.* **1** enough in amount or extent to need consideration. **2** much; a lot of (*considerable pain*). **3** notable (*considerable achievement*). ▫▫ **con·sid·er·a·bly** *adv.*

con·sid·er·ate /kənsídərət/ *adj.* thoughtful toward other people; careful not to cause hurt or inconvenience. ▫▫ **con·sid·er·ate·ly** *adv.*

con·sid·er·a·tion /kənsídəráyshən/ *n.* **1** the act of considering; careful thought. **2** being considerate. **3** a fact or a thing taken into account. **4** compensation; a payment or reward. **5** *Law* (in a contractual agreement) anything given or promised or forborne by one party in exchange for the promise or undertaking of another. ▫ **in consideration of** in return for; on account of. **take into consideration** include as a factor, reason, etc. **under consideration** being considered.

con·sid·er·ing /kənsídəring/ *prep., conj.,* & *adv.* • *prep.* & *conj.* in view of; taking into consideration. • *adv. colloq.* taking everything into account (*not so bad, considering*).

con·sign /kənsín/ *v.tr.* (often foll. by *to*) **1** deliver to a person's possession or trust. **2** commit decisively or permanently (*consigned it to the trash can*). **3** transmit or send (goods). ▫▫ **con·sign·ee** /kónsīnée/ *n.* **con·sign·ment** *n.* **con·sign·or** *n.*

con·sist /kənsíst/ *v.intr.* **1** (foll. by *of*) be composed; have specified ingredients or elements. **2** (foll. by *in, of*) have its essential features as specified (*its beauty consists in the use of color*). **3** (usu. foll. by *with*) harmonize; be consistent.

con·sist·en·cy /kənsístənsee/ *n.* (*pl.* **-cies**) (also **con·sist·ence**) **1** the degree of density, esp. of thick liquids. **2** conformity with other or earlier attitudes, practice, etc. **3** the state or quality of holding or sticking together and retaining shape.

con·sist·ent /kənsístənt/ *adj.* (usu. foll. by *with*) **1** compatible or in harmony. **2** (of a person) constant to the same principles. ▫▫ **con·sist·ent·ly** *adv.*

con·so·la·tion /kónsəláyshən/ *n.* **1** the act or an instance of consoling; the state of being consoled. **2** a consoling thing, person, or circumstance. ▫▫ **con·sol·a·to·ry** /kənsṓlətawree, –sól–/ *adj.*

con·so·la·tion prize *n.* a prize given to a competitor who just fails to win a main prize.

con·sole[1] /kənsṓl/ *v.tr.* comfort, esp. in grief or disappointment.

▶Often confused with *condole.* ▫▫ **con·sol·a·ble** *adj.* **con·sol·er** *n.* **con·sol·ing·ly** *adv.*

con·sole[2] /kónsōl/ *n.* **1** a panel or unit accommodating switches, controls, etc. **2** a cabinet for television, etc. **3** *Mus.* a cabinet with the keyboards, stops, pedals, etc., of an organ. **4** a bracket supporting a shelf, etc.

con·sol·i·date /kənsólidayt/ *v.* **1** *tr.* & *intr.* make or become strong or solid. **2** *tr.* strengthen (one's position, etc.). **3** *tr.* combine (territories, companies, debts, etc.) into one whole. ▫▫ **con·sol·i·da·tion** /–dáyshən/ *n.* **con·sol·i·da·tor** *n.* **con·sol·i·da·to·ry** *adj.*

con·som·mé /kónsəmáy/ *n.* a clear soup made with meat stock.

con·so·nance /kónsənəns/ *n.* **1** agreement; harmony. **2** *Prosody* a recurrence of similar-sounding consonants. **3** *Mus.* a harmonious combination of notes; a harmonious interval.

con·so·nant /kónsənənt/ *n.* & *adj.* • *n.* **1** a speech sound in which the breath is at least partly obstructed, and which to form a syllable must be combined with a vowel. **2** a letter or letters representing this. • *adj.* (foll. by *with, to*) **1** consistent; in agreement or harmony. **2** similar in sound. **3** *Mus.* making a concord. ▫▫ **con·so·nan·tal** /–nánt'l/ *adj.* **con·so·nant·ly** *adv.*

con·sort[1] *n.* & *v.* • *n.* /kónsawrt/ **1** a wife or husband, esp. of royalty (*prince consort*). **2** a companion or associate. **3** a ship sailing with another. • *v.* /kənsórt/ **1** *intr.* (usu. foll. by *with, together*) **a** keep company; associate. **b** harmonize. **2** *tr.* class or bring together.

con•sort[2] /kónsawrt/ *n. Mus.* a group of players or instruments, esp. playing early music (*recorder consort*).

con•sor•ti•um /kənsáwrsheeəm, –teeəm/ *n.* (*pl.* **consortia** /–sheeə, –teeə/ or **consortiums**) an association, esp. of several business companies.

con•spec•tus /kənspéktəs/ *n.* **1** a general or comprehensive survey. **2** a summary or synopsis.

con•spic•u•ous /kənspíkyooəs/ *adj.* **1** clearly visible; striking to the eye. **2** remarkable of its kind (*conspicuous extravagance*). ▫▫ **con•spic•u•ous•ly** *adv.* **con•spic•u•ous•ness** *n.*

con•spir•a•cy /kənspírəsee/ *n.* (*pl.* **-cies**) **1** a secret plan to commit a crime or do harm; a plot. **2** the act of conspiring.

con•spir•a•tor /kənspírətər/ *n.* a person who takes part in a conspiracy. ▫▫ **con•spir•a•to•ri•al** /–táwreeəl/ *adj.* **con•spir•a•to•ri•al•ly** *adv.*

con•spire /kənspír/ *v.intr.* **1** combine secretly to plan and prepare an unlawful or harmful act. **2** (often foll. by *against*, or *to* + infin.) (of events or circumstances) seem to be working together, esp. disadvantageously.

con•sta•ble /kónstəbəl, kún–/ *n.* esp. *Brit.* a police officer.

con•stab•u•lar•y /kənstábyəleree/ *n.* & *adj.* • *n.* **1** (*pl.* **-ies**) a police force. **2** armed police organized as a military unit. • *attrib.adj.* of or concerning the police force.

con•stan•cy /kónstənsee/ *n.* **1** the quality of being unchanging and dependable; faithfulness. **2** firmness; endurance.

con•stant /kónstənt/ *adj.* & *n.* • *adj.* **1** continuous (*constant attention*). **2** occurring frequently (*constant complaints*). **3** (often foll. by *to*) unchanging; faithful; dependable. • *n.* **1** anything that does not vary. **2** *Math.* & *Physics* a quantity or number that remains the same. ▫▫ **con•stant•ly** *adv.*

con•stel•la•tion /kónstəláyshən/ *n.* **1** a group of stars that form an imaginary pattern representing an object, animal, or person. **2** one of the 88 areas into which the sky is divided by astronomers. **3** a group of associated persons, etc. ▫▫ **con•stel•late** /kónstəlayt/ *v.tr.*

con•ster•na•tion /kónstərnáyshən/ *n.* anxiety or dismay.

con•sti•pate /kónstipayt/ *v.tr.* (esp. as **constipated** *adj.*) affect with constipation.

con•sti•pa•tion /kónstipáyshən/ *n.* **1** difficulty in emptying the bowels. **2** a restricted state.

con•stit•u•en•cy /kənstíchooənsee/ *n.* (*pl.* **-cies**) **1** a body of voters in a specified area who elect a representative member to a legislative body. **2** the area represented in this way. **3** a body of customers, supporters, etc.

con•stit•u•ent /kənstíchooənt/ *adj.* & *n.* • *adj.* **1** composing or helping to make up a whole. **2** able to make or change a (political, etc.) constitution (*constituent assembly*). **3** electing. • *n.* **1** a member of a constituency. **2** a component part.

con•sti•tute /kónstitoot, tyoot/ *v.tr.* **1** be the components or essence of; make up; form. **2 a** be equivalent or tantamount to (*this constitutes a warning*). **b** formally establish (*constitute a precedent*). **3** give legal or constitutional form to.

con•sti•tu•tion /kónstitóoshən, –tyóo–/ *n.* **1** the act or method of constituting; composition. **2 a** the body of fundamental principles according to which a nation, state, or other organization is acknowledged to be governed. **b** a (usu. written) record of this. **c** (**Constitution**) the US Constitution. **3** a person's physical state as regards health, strength, etc. **4** a person's psychological makeup.

con•sti•tu•tion•al /kónstitóoshənəl, –tyóo–/ *adj.* & *n.* • *adj.* **1** of or consistent with a political constitution (*constitutional duties of office*). **2** inherent in the physical or mental constitution. • *n.* a walk taken regularly to maintain or restore good health. ▫▫ **con•sti•tu•tion•al•i•ty** /–nálitee/ *n.* **con•sti•tu•tion•al•ize** *v.tr.* **con•sti•tu•tion•al•ly** *adv.*

con•strain /kənstráyn/ *v.tr.* **1** compel. **2 a** confine forcibly; imprison. **b** restrict severely. **3** bring about by compulsion. **4** (as **constrained** *adj.*) forced; embarrassed (*a constrained manner*). ▫▫ **con•strain•ed•ly** /–nidlee/ *adv.*

con•straint /kənstráynt/ *n.* **1** the act or result of constraining or being constrained; restriction of liberty. **2** something that constrains; a limitation on motion or action. **3** the restraint of natural feelings or their expression; a constrained manner.

con•strict /kənstríkt/ *v.tr.* **1** make narrow or tight; compress. **2** *Biol.* cause (organic tissue) to contract. ▫▫ **con•stric•tion** /–stríkshən/ *n.* **con•stric•tive** *adj.*

con•stric•tor /kənstríktər/ *n.* **1** any snake that kills by compressing. **2** *Anat.* any muscle that contracts an organ or part of the body.

con•struct *v.* & *n.* • *v.tr.* /kənstrúkt/ make by fitting parts together; build; form. • *n.* /kónstrukt/ **1** a thing constructed, esp. by the mind. **2** *Linguistics* a group of words forming a phrase. ▫▫ **con•struct•or** *n.*

con•struc•tion /kənstrúkshən/ *n.* **1** the act or a mode of constructing. **2** a thing constructed. **3** an interpretation or explanation. **4** *Gram.* an arrangement of words according to syntactical rules. ▫▫ **con•struc•tion•al** *adj.* **con•struc•tion•al•ly** *adv.*

con•struc•tive /kənstrúktiv/ *adj.* **1 a** of construction; tending to construct. **b** tending to form a basis for ideas (*constructive criticism*). **2** helpful; positive (*a constructive approach*). **3** derived by inference (*constructive permission*). **4** belonging to the structure of a building. ▫▫ **con•struc•tive•ly** *adv.* **con•struc•tive•ness** *n.*

con•strue /kənstróo/ *v.tr.* (**construes, construed, construing**) **1** interpret. **2** (often foll. by *with*) combine (words) grammatically (*"rely" is construed with "on"*). **3** analyze the syntax of (a sentence). **4** translate word for word. ▫▫ **con•stru•a•ble** *adj.* **con•stru•al** *n.*

con•sub•stan•tial /kónsəbstánshəl/ *adj. Theol.* of the same substance (esp. of the three persons of the Trinity). ▫▫ **con•sub•stan•ti•al•i•ty** /–sheeálitee/ *n.*

con•sub•stan•ti•a•tion /kónsəbstánsheeáyshən/ *n. Theol.* the doctrine of the real substantial presence of the body and blood of Christ in and with the bread and wine in the Eucharist.

con•sul /kónsəl/ *n.* **1** an official appointed by a government to live in a foreign city and protect the government's citizens and interests there. **2** *Hist.* either of two annually elected chief magistrates in ancient Rome. ▫▫ **con•su•lar** *adj.* **con•sul•ship** *n.*

con•su•late /kónsələt/ *n.* **1** the building officially used by a consul. **2** the office, position, or period of office of consul.

con•sult /kənsúlt/ *v.* & *n.* **1** *tr.* seek information or advice from. **2** *intr.* (often foll. by *with*) refer to a person for advice, etc. **3** *tr.* seek permission or approval from (a person) for a proposed action. **4** *tr.* take into account (feelings, interests, etc.). • *n.* /kónsult/ = CONSULTATION 1, 2. ▫▫ **con•sul•ta•tive** /–súltətiv/ *adj.*

con•sult•ant /kənsúlt'nt/ *n.* a person providing professional advice, etc., esp. for a fee.

con•sul•ta•tion /kónsəltáyshən/ *n.* **1** a meeting arranged to consult. **2** the act or an instance of consulting. **3** a conference.

con•sult•ing /kənsúlting/ *attrib.adj.* giving professional advice to others working in the same field or subject (*consulting physician*).

con•sume /kənsóóm/ *v.tr.* **1** eat or drink. **2** completely destroy. **3** (often as **consumed** *adj.*) possess or entirely take up (foll. by *with*: *consumed with rage*). **4** use up. ▫▫ **con•sum•a•ble** *adj. & n.* **con•sum•ing•ly** *adv.*

con•sum•er /kənsóómər/ *n.* **1** a person who consumes, esp. one who uses a product. **2** a purchaser of goods or services.

con•sum•er goods *n.pl.* goods bought and used by consumers, rather than by manufacturers for producing other goods.

con•sum•er•ism /kənsóómərizəm/ *n.* the protection or promotion of consumers' interests in relation to the producer. ▫▫ **con•sum•er•ist** *adj. & n.*

con•sum•mate *v. & adj.* • *v.tr.* /kónsəmayt/ **1** complete; make perfect. **2** complete (a marriage) by sexual intercourse. • *adj.* /kənsúmit, kónsəmit/ complete; perfect; fully skilled. ▫▫ **con•sum•mate•ly** *adv.* **con•sum•ma•tor** *n.*

con•sum•ma•tion /kónsəmáyshən/ *n.* **1** completion, esp. of a marriage by sexual intercourse. **2** a desired end or goal; perfection.

con•sump•tion /kənsúmpshən/ *n.* **1** the act or an instance of consuming; the process of being consumed. **2** an amount consumed. **3** the purchase and use of goods, etc. **4** a wasting disease, esp. pulmonary tuberculosis.

con•sump•tive /kənsúmptiv/ *adj.* **1** of or tending to consumption. **2** tending to or affected with pulmonary tuberculosis. ▫▫ **con•sump•tive•ly** *adv.*

cont. *abbr.* **1** contents. **2** continued.

con•tact *n. & v.* • *n.* /kóntakt/ **1** the state or condition of touching, meeting, or communicating. **2** a person who is or may be communicated with for information, assistance, etc. **3** *Electr.* **a** a connection for the passage of a current. **b** a device for providing this. **4** a person likely to carry a contagious disease through being associated with an infected person. **5** (usu. in *pl.*) *colloq.* a contact lens. • *v.tr.* /kóntakt, kəntákt/ **1** get into communication with (a person). **2** begin correspondence or personal dealings with. ▫▫ **con•tact•a•ble** *adj.*

con•tact lens *n.* a small lens placed on the eyeball to correct the vision.

con•tact sport *n.* a sport in which participants necessarily come into bodily contact with one another.

con•ta•gion /kəntáyjən/ *n.* **1 a** the communication of disease from one person to another by bodily contact. **b** a contagious disease. **2** a contagious or harmful influence. **3** moral corruption, esp. when tending to be widespread.

con•ta•gious /kəntáyjəs/ *adj.* **1 a** (of a person) likely to transmit disease by contact. **b** (of a disease) transmitted in this way. **2** (of emotions, reactions, etc.) likely to affect others (*contagious enthusiasm*). ▫▫ **con•ta•gious•ly** *adv.* **con•ta•gious•ness** *n.*

con•tain /kəntáyn/ *v.tr.* **1** hold or be capable of holding within itself; include; comprise. **2** (of measures) be equal to (*a gallon contains eight pints*). **3** prevent (an enemy, difficulty, etc.) from moving or extending. **4** control or restrain (feelings, etc.). ▫▫ **con•tain•a•ble** *adj.*

con•tain•er /kəntáynər/ *n.* **1** a vessel, box, etc., for holding things. **2** a large boxlike receptacle for the transport of goods, esp. one readily transferable from one form of transport to another (also *attrib.*: *container cargo*).

con•tain•ment /kəntáynmənt/ *n.* the action or policy of preventing the expansion of a hostile country or influence.

con•tam•i•nate /kəntáminayt/ *v.tr.* **1** pollute. **2** infect; corrupt. ▫▫ **con•tam•i•nant** /–minənt/ *n.* **con•tam•i•na•tion** /–náyshən/ *n.* **con•tam•i•na•tor** *n.*

con•tem•plate /kóntəmplayt/ *v.* **1** *tr.* survey with the eyes or in the mind. **2** *tr.* regard (an event) as possible. **3** *tr.* intend (*contemplate leaving tomorrow*). **4** *intr.* meditate. ▫▫ **con•tem•pla•tion** /–pláyshən/ *n.* **con•tem•pla•tor** *n.*

con•tem•pla•tive /kəntémplətiv, kóntəmpláy–/ *adj.* of or given to (esp. religious) contemplation; meditative. ▫▫ **con•tem•pla•tive•ly** *adv.*

con•tem•po•ra•ne•ous /kəntémpəráyneeəs/ *adj.* (usu. foll. by *with*) **1** existing or occurring at the same time. **2** of the same period. ▫▫ **con•tem•po•ra•ne•i•ty** /–pərənáyitee, –neé–/ *n.* **con•tem•po•ra•ne•ous•ly** *adv.*

con•tem•po•rar•y /kəntémpəreree/ *adj. & n.* • *adj.* **1** living or occurring at the same time. **2** approximately equal in age. **3** following modern ideas or fashion in style or design. • *n.* (*pl.* **-ies**) **1** a person or thing living or existing at the same time as another. **2** a person of roughly the same age as another. ▫▫ **con•tem•po•rar•i•ly** /–rérilee/ *adv.* **con•tem•po•rar•i•ness** *n.*

con•tempt /kəntémpt/ *n.* **1** a feeling that a person or a thing is beneath consideration or worthless, or deserving scorn or reproach. **2** the condition of being held in contempt. **3** (in full **contempt of court**) disobedience to or disrespect for a court of law and its officers. ▫ **beneath contempt** utterly despicable. **hold in contempt** despise.

con•tempt•i•ble /kəntémptibəl/ *adj.* deserving contempt; despicable. ▫▫ **con•tempt•i•bil•i•ty** /–bilitee/ *n.* **con•tempt•i•bly** *adv.*

con•temp•tu•ous /kəntémpchóóəs/ *adj.* (often foll. by *of*) showing contempt; scornful. ▫▫ **con•temp•tu•ous•ly** *adv.* **con•temp•tu•ous•ness** *n.*

con•tend /kənténd/ *v.* **1** *intr.* (usu. foll. by *with*) strive; fight. **2** *intr.* compete. **3** *tr.* (usu. foll. by *that* + clause) maintain. ▫▫ **con•tend•er** *n.*

con•tent[1] /kəntént/ *adj., v., & n.* • *predic.adj.* **1** satisfied; adequately happy. **2** (foll. by *to* + infin.) willing. • *v.tr.* make content; satisfy. • *n.* a contented state; satisfaction. ▫ **to one's heart's content** to the full extent of one's desires. ▫▫ **con•tent•ment** *n.*

con•tent[2] /kóntent/ *n.* **1** (usu. in *pl.*) what is contained in something. **2** the amount of a constituent contained (*low sodium content*). **3** the substance dealt with (in a speech, etc.) as distinct from its form. **4** the capacity or volume of a thing.

con•tent•ed /kənténtid/ *adj.* (often foll. by *with*, or *to* + infin.) **1** happy; satisfied. **2** (foll. by *with*) willing to be content. ▫▫ **con•tent•ed•ly** *adv.* **con•tent•ed•ness** *n.*

con•ten•tion /kənténshən/ *n.* **1** a dispute or argument; rivalry. **2** a point contended for in an argument (*it is my contention that you are wrong*). ▫ **in contention** competing, esp. with a good chance of success.

con•ten•tious /kənténshəs/ *adj.* **1** argumentative; quarrelsome. **2** likely to cause argument; disputed; controversial. ▫▫ **con•ten•tious•ly** *adv.* **con•ten•tious•ness** *n.*

con•ter•mi•nous /kəntərminəs/ *adj.* (often foll. by *with*) **1** having a common boundary. **2** coextensive; coterminous. ▫▫ **con•ter•mi•nous•ly** *adv.*

con•test *n. & v.* • *n.* /kóntest/ **1** a competition. **2** a dispute; a controversy. • *v.tr.* /kəntést, kóntest/ **1** challenge or dispute (a decision, etc.). **2** debate (a point, statement, etc.). **3** compete for (a prize, parliamentary seat, etc.); compete in (an election). ▫▫ **con•test•a•ble** /kəntéstəbəl/ *adj.* **con•test•er** /kəntéstər/ *n.*

con•test•ant /kəntéstənt/ *n.* a person who takes part in a contest or competition.

con•text /kóntekst/ *n.* **1** parts that immediately precede and follow a word or passage and clarify its meaning. **2** the circumstances relevant to something under consideration. ▫▫ **con•tex•tu•al** /kəntéks-chóóəl/ *adj.*

con·tex·tu·al·ize /kəntéks-chōōəlīz/ *v.tr.* place in a context; study in context. ▫▫ **con·tex·tu·al·i·za·tion** *n.* **con·tex·tu·al·ly** *adv.*

con·tig·u·ous /kəntígyōōəs/ *adj.* (usu. foll. by *with, to*) touching, esp. along a line; in contact. ▫▫ **con·ti·gu·i·ty** /kóntigyōōitee/ *n.* **con·tig·u·ous·ly** *adv.*

con·ti·nent[1] /kóntinənt/ *n.* **1** any of the main continuous expanses of land (Europe, Asia, Africa, N. and S. America, Australia, Antarctica). **2** continuous land; a mainland.

con·ti·nent[2] /kóntinənt/ *adj.* **1** able to control movements of the bowels and bladder. **2** exercising self-restraint, esp. sexually. ▫▫ **con·ti·nence** /–nəns/ *n.* **con·ti·nent·ly** *adv.*

con·ti·nen·tal /kóntinént'l/ *adj.* & *n.* •*adj.* of or characteristic of a continent. •*n.* an inhabitant of mainland Europe. ▫▫ **con·ti·nen·tal·ly** *adv.*

con·ti·nen·tal break·fast *n.* a light breakfast of coffee, rolls, etc.

con·ti·nen·tal drift *n. Geol.* the hypothesis that the continents are moving slowly over the surface of the earth.

con·ti·nen·tal shelf *n.* an area of shallow seabed between the shore of a continent and the deeper ocean.

con·tin·gen·cy /kəntínjənsee/ *n.* (*pl.* **-cies**) **1** a future event regarded as likely to occur, or as influencing present action. **2** something that is dependent on another uncertain event. **3** uncertainty of occurrence. **4 a** one thing incident to another. **b** an incidental or unanticipated expense, etc.

con·tin·gent /kəntínjənt/ *adj.* & *n.* •*adj.* **1** (usu. foll. by *on, upon*) dependent (on an uncertain event or circumstance). **2** associated. **3** (usu. foll. by *to*) incidental. **4 a** that may or may not occur. **b** fortuitous. **5** true only under existing or specified conditions. •*n.* a body forming part of a larger group. ▫▫ **con·tin·gent·ly** *adv.*

con·tin·u·al /kəntínyōōəl/ *adj.* constantly or frequently recurring; always happening. ▫▫ **con·tin·u·al·ly** *adv.*
▶In precise usage, **continual** means 'frequent, repeating at intervals' and **continuous** means 'going on without pause or interruption': *We suffered from the continual attacks of mosquitoes. The waterfall's continuous flow creates an endless roar.*

con·tin·u·ance /kəntínyōōəns/ *n.* **1** a state of continuing in existence or operation. **2** the duration of an event or action. **3** *Law* a postponement or adjournment.

con·tin·u·a·tion /kəntínyōō-áyshən/ *n.* **1** the act or an instance of continuing; the process of being continued. **2** a part that continues something else.

con·tin·ue /kəntínyōō/ *v.* (**continues, continued, continuing**) **1** *tr.* (often foll. by verbal noun, or *to* + infin.) maintain, not stop (an action, etc.). **2 a** *tr.* (also *absol.*) resume or prolong (a narrative, journey, etc.). **b** *intr.* recommence after a pause. **3** *tr.* be a sequel to. **4** *intr.* remain in existence or in a specified state (*the weather continued fine*). **5** *tr. Law* postpone or adjourn (proceedings). ▫▫ **con·tin·u·a·ble** *adj.* **con·tin·u·er** *n.*

con·ti·nu·i·ty /kóntinōōitee, –nyōō–/ *n.* (*pl.* **-ties**) **1** the state of being continuous. **2** an unbroken succession. **3** a logical sequence.

con·tin·u·o /kəntínyōō-ō/ *n.* (*pl.* **-os**) *Mus.* an accompaniment providing a bass line, usu. played on a keyboard instrument.

con·tin·u·ous /kəntínyōōəs/ *adj.* unbroken; uninterrupted; connected throughout in space or time. ▫▫ **con·tin·u·ous·ly** *adv.* **con·tin·u·ous·ness** *n.*
▶See note at CONTINUAL.

con·tin·u·um /kəntínyōōəm/ *n.* (*pl.* **continua** /–yōōə/ or **continuums**) anything seen as having a continuous, not discrete, structure (*space-time continuum*).

con·tort /kəntáwrt/ *v.tr.* twist or force out of normal shape. ▫▫ **con·tor·tion** /kəntáwrshən/ *n.*

con·tor·tion·ist /kəntáwrshənist/ *n.* an entertainer who adopts contorted postures.

con·tour /kóntōōr/ *n.* & *v.* •*n.* **1** an outline, esp. representing or bounding the shape or form of something. **2** the outline of a natural feature, e.g., a coast or mountain mass. **3** a line separating differently colored parts of a design. •*v.tr.* **1** mark with contour lines. **2** carry (a road or railroad) around the side of a hill.

con·tour line *n.* a line on a map joining points of equal altitude.

contra- /kóntrə/ *comb. form* **1** against; opposite (*contradict*). **2** *Mus.* (of instruments, organ stops, etc.) pitched an octave below (*contrabassoon*).

con·tra·band /kóntrəband/ *n.* & *adj.* •*n.* **1** goods that have been smuggled, or imported or exported illegally. **2** prohibited trade; smuggling. **3** (in full **contraband of war**) goods forbidden to be supplied by neutrals to belligerents. •*adj.* **1** forbidden to be imported or exported (at all or without payment of duty). **2** concerning traffic in contraband (*contraband trade*).

con·tra·bass /kóntrəbays/ *n. Mus.* = DOUBLE BASS.

con·tra·cep·tion /kóntrəsépshən/ *n.* the intentional prevention of pregnancy.

con·tra·cep·tive /kóntrəséptiv/ *adj.* & *n.* •*adj.* preventing pregnancy. •*n.* a contraceptive device or drug.

con·tract *n.* & *v.* •*n.* /kóntrakt/ **1** a written or spoken agreement, esp. one intended to be enforceable by law. **2** a document recording this. **3** *Bridge*, etc., an undertaking to win the number of tricks bid. •*v.* /kəntrákt, kóntrakt/ **1** *tr.* & *intr.* make or become smaller. **2 a** *intr.* (usu. foll. by *with*) make a contract. **b** *intr.* (usu. foll. by *for*, or *to* + infin.) enter formally into a business or legal arrangement. **c** *tr.* (often foll. by *out*) arrange (work) to be done by contract. **3** *tr.* catch or develop (a disease). **4** *tr.* incur (a debt, etc.). **5** *tr.* shorten (a word) by combination or elision. **6** *tr.* draw (one's muscles, brow, etc.) together. ▫▫ **con·trac·tive** /kəntráktiv/ *adj.*

con·tract bridge *n.* a form of bridge, in which only tricks bid and won count toward the game.

con·trac·tile /kəntrákt'l, tīl/ *adj.* capable of or producing contraction. ▫▫ **con·trac·til·i·ty** /kóntraktílitee/ *n.*

con·trac·tion /kəntrákshən/ *n.* **1** the act of contracting. **2** *Med.* (usu. in *pl.*) shortening of the uterine muscles during childbirth. **3** shrinking; diminution. **4 a** a shortening of a word by combination or elision. **b** a contracted word or group of words.

con·trac·tor /kóntraktər, kəntrák–/ *n.* a person who undertakes a contract, esp. to conduct building operations, etc.

con·trac·tu·al /kəntrákchōōəl/ *adj.* of or in the nature of a contract. ▫▫ **con·trac·tu·al·ly** *adv.*

con·tra·dict /kóntrədíkt/ *v.tr.* **1** deny (a statement). **2** express the opposite of a statement made by (a person). **3** be in opposition to or in conflict with. ▫▫ **con·tra·dic·tion** /kóntrədíkshən/ *n.* **con·tra·dic·tor** *n.*

con·tra·dic·to·ry /kóntrədíktəree/ *adj.* **1** expressing a denial or opposite statement. **2** (of statements, etc.) mutually opposed or inconsistent. **3** (of a person) inclined to contradict. **4** *Logic* (of two propositions) so related that one and only one must be true.

con·tra·dis·tinc·tion /kóntrədistíngkshən/ *n.* a distinction made by contrasting.

con·trail /kóntrayl/ *n.* a condensation trail, esp. from an aircraft.

con·tra·in·di·cate /kóntrəíndikayt/ *v.tr. Med.* act as an indication against (the use of a particular substance or treatment). ▫▫ **con·tra·in·di·ca·tion** /–káyshən/ *n.*

con·tral·to /kəntráltō/ *n.* (*pl.* **-tos**) **1 a** the lowest female singing voice. **b** a singer with this voice. **2** a part written for contralto.

con·trap·tion /kəntrápshən/ *n.* often *derog.* or *joc.* a machine or device, esp. a strange or cumbersome one.

con·tra·pun·tal /kóntrəpúnt'l/ *adj. Mus.* of or in counterpoint. ◻◻ **con·tra·pun·tal·ly** *adv.* **con·tra·pun·tist** *n.*

con·trar·y /kóntreree/ *adj., n., & adv.* • *adj.* **1** (usu. foll. by *to*) opposed in nature or tendency. **2** /kəntráiree/ *colloq.* perverse; self-willed. **3** (of a wind) unfavorable. **4** mutually opposed. **5** opposite in position or direction. • *n.* (*pl.* **-ies**) (prec. by *the*) the opposite. • *adv.* (foll. by *to*) in opposition or contrast (*contrary to expectations it rained*). ◻ **on the contrary** intensifying a denial of what has just been implied or stated. **to the contrary** to the opposite effect. ◻◻ **con·trar·i·ly** /–trérilee/ *adv.* **con·trar·i·ness** /–tréreenis/ *n.*

con·trast *n. & v.* • *n.* /kóntrast/ **1 a** a juxtaposition or comparison showing striking differences. **b** a difference so revealed. **2** (often foll. by *to*) a thing or person having qualities noticeably different from another. **3 a** the degree of difference between tones in a television picture or a photograph. **b** the change of apparent brightness or color of an object caused by the juxtaposition of other objects. • *v.* /kəntrást, kóntrast/ (often foll. by *with*) **1** *tr.* distinguish or set together so as to reveal a contrast. **2** *intr.* have or show a contrast. ◻◻ **con·trast·ing·ly** /–trást–/ *adv.* **con·tras·tive** /–trástiv/ *adj.*

▶**Contrast** means 'note the differences.' **Compare,** though, means 'note the similarities.'

con·tra·vene /kóntrəvéen/ *v.tr.* **1** infringe (a law or code of conduct). **2** (of things) conflict with.

con·tra·ven·tion /kóntrəvénshən/ *n.* **1** infringement. **2** an instance of this.

con·tre·temps /kóntrətóɴ/ *n.* **1** an awkward or unfortunate occurrence. **2** an unexpected mishap.

con·trib·ute /kəntríbyoot/ *v.* (often foll. by *to*) **1** *tr.* give (money, an idea, help, etc.) toward a common purpose. **2** *intr.* help to bring about a result, etc. (*contributed to their downfall*). **3** *tr.* (also *absol.*) supply (an article, etc.) for publication with others in a journal, etc. ◻◻ **con·trib·u·tive** *adj.* **con·trib·u·tor** /kəntríbyətər/ *n.*

con·tri·bu·tion /kóntribyóoshən/ *n.* **1** the act of contributing. **2** something contributed. **3** an article, etc., contributed to a publication.

con·trib·u·to·ry /kəntríbyətawree/ *adj.* **1** that contributes. **2** operated by means of contributions (*contributory pension plan*).

con·trite /kəntrít, kóntrīt/ *adj.* **1** completely penitent. **2** feeling guilt. **3** (of an action) showing a contrite spirit. ◻◻ **con·trite·ly** *adv.* **con·trite·ness** *n.* **con·tri·tion** /kəntríshən/ *n.*

con·triv·ance /kəntrívəns/ *n.* **1** something contrived, esp. a mechanical device or a plan. **2** an act of contriving, esp. deceitfully. **3** inventive capacity.

con·trive /kəntrív/ *v.tr.* **1** devise. **2** (often foll. by *to* + infin.) manage. ◻◻ **con·triv·a·ble** *adj.* **con·triv·er** *n.*

con·trived /kəntrívd/ *adj.* planned so carefully as to seem unnatural; forced.

con·trol /kəntrṓl/ *n. & v.* • *n.* **1** command (*under the control of*). **2** the power of restraining, esp. self-restraint. **3** a means of restraint. **4** (usu. in *pl.*) a means of regulating prices, etc. **5** (usu. in *pl.*) switches and other devices by which a machine is controlled (also *attrib.*: *control panel*). **6 a** a place where something is controlled or verified. **b** a person or group that controls something. **7** (also *attrib.*: *control group*) a standard of comparison for checking the results of a survey or experiment. • *v.tr.* (**controlled, controlling**) **1** have control or command of. **2** regulate. **3** restrain (*told him to control himself*). **4** serve as control to. **5** check; verify. ◻ **in control** (often foll. by *of*) directing an activity. **out of control** no longer subject to containment, restraint, or guidance. **under control** being dealt with successfully. ◻◻ **con·trol·la·bil·i·ty** *n.* **con·trol·la·ble** *adj.* **con·trol·la·bly** *adv.*

con·trol·ler /kəntrṓlər/ *n.* **1** a person or thing that controls. **2** a person in charge of expenditure. ◻◻ **con·trol·ler·ship** *n.*

con·trol·ling in·ter·est *n.* a means of determining the policy of a business, etc., esp. by ownership of a majority of the stock.

con·trol tow·er *n.* a tall building at an airport, etc., from which air traffic is controlled.

con·tro·ver·sial /kóntrəvə́rshəl/ *adj.* **1** causing or subject to controversy. **2** of controversy. **3** given to controversy. ◻◻ **con·tro·ver·sial·ism** *n.* **con·tro·ver·sial·ist** *n.* **con·tro·ver·sial·ly** *adv.*

con·tro·ver·sy /kóntrəvərsee/ *n.* (*pl.* **-sies**) a prolonged argument or dispute, esp. when conducted publicly.

con·tro·vert /kóntrəvə́rt/ *v.tr.* **1** dispute; deny. **2** argue about; discuss. ◻◻ **con·tro·vert·i·ble** *adj.*

con·tu·ma·cious /kóntoomáyshəs, –tyoo–/ *adj.* stubbornly or willfully disobedient. ◻◻ **con·tu·ma·cious·ly** *adv.* **con·tu·ma·cy** /kóntoomәsee, –tyoo–/ *n.*

con·tu·me·ly /kóntoomәlee, –toomlee, –tóo, –tyóo/ *n.* **1** insolent or reproachful language or treatment. **2** disgrace. ◻◻ **con·tu·me·li·ous** /kóntooméeleeəs, –tyoo–/ *adj.* **con·tu·me·li·ous·ly** *adv.*

con·tuse /kəntóoz, –tyóoz/ *v.tr.* bruise. ◻◻ **con·tu·sion** /–zhən/ *n.*

co·nun·drum /kənúndrəm/ *n.* **1** a riddle, esp. one with a pun in its answer. **2** a puzzling question.

con·ur·ba·tion /kónərbáyshən/ *n.* an extended urban area, esp. one consisting of several towns and merging suburbs.

con·va·lesce /kónvəlés/ *v.intr.* recover one's health after illness.

con·va·les·cent /kónvəlésənt/ *adj. & n.* • *adj.* **1** recovering from an illness. **2** of or for persons in convalescence. • *n.* a convalescent person. ◻◻ **con·va·les·cence** /–səns/ *n.*

con·vec·tion /kənvékshən/ *n.* transference of heat by upward movement of the heated and less dense medium. ◻◻ **con·vec·tion·al** *adj.* **con·vec·tive** *adj.*

con·vec·tor /kənvéktər/ *n.* a heating appliance that circulates warm air by convection.

con·vene /kənvéen/ *v.* **1** *tr.* summon or arrange. **2** *intr.* assemble. **3** *tr.* summon (a person) before a tribunal. ◻◻ **con·ven·a·ble** *adj.* **con·ven·er** *n.* **con·ve·nor** *n.*

con·ven·ience /kənvéenyəns/ *n. & v.* • *n.* **1** the quality of being convenient; suitability. **2** material advantage. **3** an advantage (*a great convenience*). **4** a useful thing. • *v.tr.* afford convenience to; suit; accommodate. ◻ **at one's convenience** at a time or place that suits one. **at one's earliest convenience** as soon as one can.

con·ven·ience store *n.* a store that stocks basic household goods and groceries, usu. having extended opening hours.

con·ven·ient /kənvéenyənt/ *adj.* **1** (often foll. by *for, to*) **a** serving one's comfort or interests. **b** suitable. **c** free of trouble or difficulty. **2** available or occurring at a suitable time or place (*a convenient moment*). **3** well situated for some purpose. ◻◻ **con·ven·ient·ly** *adv.*

con·vent /kónvent, –vənt/ *n.* **1** a religious community, esp. of nuns, under vows. **2** the premises occupied by this. **3** (in full **convent school**) a school attached to and run by a convent.

con·ven·tion /kənvénshən/ *n.* **1 a** general agreement, esp. agreement on social behavior, etc., by implicit consent of the majority. **b** a custom or customary practice. **2 a** a formal assembly for a common purpose. **b** an assembly of the delegates of a political party to select candidates for office. **3 a** a formal agreement. **b** an agreement between nations, esp. one less formal than a treaty. **4** *Cards* an accepted method of play (in leading, bidding, etc.) used to convey information to a partner. **5** the act of convening.

con•ven•tion•al /kənvénshənəl/ *adj.* **1** depending on or according to convention. **2** (of a person) attentive to social conventions. **3** usual. **4** not spontaneous nor sincere nor original. **5** (of weapons or power) nonnuclear. **6** *Art* following tradition rather than nature. ▫▫ **con•ven•tion•al•ism** *n.* **con•ven•tion•al•ist** *n.* **con•ven•tion•al•i•ty** /–shənálitee/ *n.* (*pl.* **-ties**). **con•ven•tion•al•ize** *v.tr.* **con•ven•tion•al•ly** *adv.*

con•verge /kənvə́rj/ *v.intr.* **1** come together as if to meet or join. **2** (of lines) tend to meet at a point. **3** (foll. by *on, upon*) approach from different directions. ▫▫ **con•ver•gence** /–jəns/ *n.* **con•ver•gen•cy** *n.* **con•ver•gent** /–jənt/ *adj.*

con•ver•sant /kənvə́rsənt, kónvərs–/ *adj.* (foll. by *with*) well acquainted with a subject or person, etc. ▫▫ **con•ver•sance** /–və́rsəns/ *n.* **con•ver•san•cy** *n.*

con•ver•sa•tion /kónvərsáyshən/ *n.* **1** the informal exchange of ideas by spoken words. **2** an instance of this.

con•ver•sa•tion•al /kónvərsáyshənəl/ *adj.* **1** of or in conversation. **2** fond of or good at conversation. **3** colloquial. ▫▫ **con•ver•sa•tion•al•ly** *adv.*

con•ver•sa•tion•al•ist /kónvərsáyshənəlist/ *n.* one who is good at or fond of conversing.

con•verse[1] /kənvə́rs/ *v.intr.* (often foll. by *with*) engage in conversation. ▫▫ **con•vers•er** /kənvə́rsər/ *n.*

con•verse[2] /kənvə́rs, kónvərs/ *adj. & n.* • *adj.* opposite; contrary; reversed. • *n.* /kónvərs/ **1** something that is opposite or contrary. **2** a statement formed from another statement by the transposition of certain words, e.g., *some philosophers are men* from *some men are philosophers*. **3** *Math.* a theorem whose hypothesis and conclusion are the conclusion and hypothesis of another. ▫▫ **con•verse•ly** *adv.*

con•ver•sion /kənvə́rzhən, –shən/ *n.* **1** the act or an instance of converting or the process of being converted, esp. in belief or religion. **2 a** an adaptation of a building for new purposes. **b** a converted building. **3** transposition; inversion. **4** *Theol.* the turning of sinners to God. **5** *Football* the scoring of an extra point or points after scoring a touchdown.

con•vert *v. & n.* • *v.* /kənvə́rt/ **1** *tr.* (usu. foll. by *into*) change in form, character, or function. **2** *tr.* cause (a person) to change beliefs, etc. **3** *tr.* change (money, etc.) into others of a different kind. **4** *tr.* make structural alterations in (a building) to serve a new purpose. **5** *tr.* (also *absol.*) *Football* score an extra point or points after a touchdown. **6** *intr.* be converted or convertible (*the sofa converts into a bed*). • *n.* /kónvərt/ (often foll. by *to*) a person who has been converted to a different belief, opinion, etc. ▫ **convert to one's own use** wrongfully make use of (another's property).

con•vert•er /kənvə́rtər/ *n.* (also **con•ver•tor**) **1** a person or thing that converts. **2** *Electr.* **a** an electrical apparatus for the interconversion of alternating current and direct current. **b** *Electronics* an apparatus for converting a signal from one frequency to another.

con•vert•i•ble /kənvə́rtibəl/ *adj. & n.* • *adj.* **1** that may be converted. **2** (of currency, etc.) that may be converted into other forms, esp. into gold or US dollars. **3** (of a car) having a folding or detachable roof. **4** (of terms) synonymous. • *n.* a car with a folding or detachable top. ▫▫ **con•vert•i•bil•i•ty** *n.* **con•vert•i•bly** *adv.*

con•vex /kónveks, kənvéks/ *adj.* having an outline or surface curved like the exterior of a circle or sphere (cf. CONCAVE). ▫▫ **con•vex•i•ty** /–véksitee/ *n.* **con•vex•ly** *adv.*

convex and concave

con•vey /kənváy/ *v.tr.* **1** transport or carry (goods, passengers, etc.). **2** communicate (an idea, meaning, etc.). **3** *Law* transfer the title to (property). **4** transmit (sound, smell, etc.). ▫▫ **con•vey•a•ble** *adj.*

con•vey•ance /kənváyəns/ *n.* **1 a** the act or process of carrying. **b** the communication (of ideas, etc.). **c** transmission. **2** a means of transport; a vehicle. **3** *Law* **a** the transfer of property from one owner to another. **b** a document effecting this. ▫▫ **con•vey•anc•er** *n.* (in sense 3). **con•vey•anc•ing** *n.* (in sense 3).

con•vey•or /kənváyər/ *n.* (also **con•vey•er**) a person or thing that conveys.

con•vey•or belt *n.* an endless moving belt for conveying articles or materials, esp. in a factory.

con•vict *v. & n.* • *v.tr.* /kənvíkt/ **1** (often foll. by *of*) prove to be guilty (of a crime, etc.). **2** declare guilty by the verdict of a jury or the decision of a judge. • *n.* /kónvikt/ **1** a person found guilty of a criminal offense. **2** a person serving a prison sentence.

con•vic•tion /kənvíkshən/ *n.* **1 a** the act or process of proving or finding guilty. **b** an instance of this (*has two previous convictions*). **2 a** the action or resulting state of being convinced. **b** a firm belief or opinion. **c** an act of convincing.

con•vince /kənvíns/ *v.tr.* **1** (often foll. by *of*, or *that* + clause) persuade (a person) to believe or realize. **2** (as **convinced** *adj.*) firmly persuaded (*a convinced pacifist*). ▫▫ **con•vinc•er** *n.* **con•vin•ci•ble** *adj.*

con•vinc•ing /kənvínsing/ *adj.* **1** able to or such as to convince. **2** substantial (*a convincing victory*). ▫▫ **con•vinc•ing•ly** *adv.*

con•viv•i•al /kənvíveeəl/ *adj.* **1** sociable and lively. **2** festive (*a convivial atmosphere*). ▫▫ **con•viv•i•al•i•ty** /–veeálitee/ *n.* **con•viv•i•al•ly** *adv.*

con•vo•ca•tion /kónvəkáyshən/ *n.* **1** the act of calling together. **2** a large formal gathering of people, esp. a formal ceremony at a university, as for giving awards. ▫▫ **con•vo•ca•tion•al** *adj.*

con•voke /kənvṓk/ *v.tr. formal* call (people) together; summon to assemble.

con•vo•lut•ed /kónvəlōōtid/ *adj.* **1** coiled; twisted. **2** complex; intricate. ▫▫ **con•vo•lut•ed•ly** *adv.*

con•vo•lu•tion /kónvəlōōshən/ *n.* **1** coiling; twisting. **2** a coil or twist. **3** complexity. **4** a sinuous fold in the surface of the brain. ▫▫ **con•vo•lu•tion•al** *adj.*

con•voy /kónvoy/ *n. & v.* • *n.* **1** a group of ships or vehicles traveling together or under escort. **2** a supply of provisions, etc., under escort. **3** the act of traveling or moving in a group or under escort. • *v.tr.* **1** (of a warship) escort (a merchant or passenger vessel). **2** escort, esp. with armed force.

con•vulse /kənvúls/ *v.tr.* **1** (usu. in *passive*) affect with convulsions. **2** cause to laugh uncontrollably. **3** shake violently; agitate; disturb. ▫▫ **con•vul•sive** *adj.* **con•vul•sive•ly** *adv.*

con•vul•sion /kənvúlshən/ *n.* **1** (usu. in *pl.*) violent irregular motion of a limb or limbs or the body caused by involuntary contraction of muscles. **2** a violent disturbance, esp. an earthquake. **3** (in *pl.*) uncontrollable laughter. ▫▫ **con•vul•sion•ar•y** *adj.*

coo /kōō/ *n. & v.* • *n.* a soft murmuring sound like that of a dove or pigeon. • *v.* (**coos, cooed**) **1** *intr.* make the sound of a coo. **2** *intr. & tr.* talk or say in a soft or amorous voice. ▫▫ **coo•ing•ly** *adv.*

cook /kŏŏk/ *v. & n.* • *v.* **1** *tr.* prepare (food) by heating it. **2** *intr.* (of food) undergo cooking. **3** *tr. colloq.* falsify (accounts, etc.); alter to produce a desired result. **4** *tr. sl.* ruin; spoil. **5** *tr. & intr. colloq.* do or proceed successfully. **6** *intr.* (as **be cooking**) *colloq.* be happening or about to happen (*went to find out what was cooking*). •*n.* a person who cooks. □ **cook a person's goose** ruin a person's chances. **cook up** *colloq.* invent or concoct (a story, excuse, etc.). □□ **cook·a·ble** *adj.*

cook·book /kŏŏkbŏŏk/ *n.* a book containing recipes and other information about cooking.

cook·er /kŏŏkər/ *n.* a container or device for cooking food.

cook·er·y /kŏŏkəree/ *n.* (*pl.* **-ies**) the art or practice of cooking.

cook·ie /kŏŏkee/ *n.* (also **cooky**) (*pl.* **cookies**) a small sweet cake. □ **that's the way the cookie crumbles** *colloq.* that is how things turn out; that is the unalterable state of affairs. cooking

cook·ing /kŏŏking/ *n.* **1** the art or process by which food is cooked. **2** (*attrib.*) suitable for or used in cooking (*cooking apple; cooking utensils*).

cook·out /kŏŏkowt/ *n.* a gathering with an open-air cooked meal; a barbecue.

cook·ware /kŏŏkwair/ *n.* utensils for cooking.

cook·y var. of COOKIE.

cool /kōōl/ *adj., n., & v.* •*adj.* **1** of or at a fairly low temperature, fairly cold (*a cool day; a cool bath*). **2** suggesting or achieving coolness (*cool colors; cool clothes*). **3 a** (of a person) calm; unexcited. **b** (of an act) done without emotion. **4** lacking enthusiasm. **5** unfriendly; lacking cordiality (*got a cool reception*). **6** (of jazz playing) restrained; relaxed. **7** calmly audacious (*a cool customer*). **8** (prec. by *a*) *colloq.* not less than (*cost me a cool thousand*). **9** *sl.* excellent; marvelous. •*n.* **1** coolness. **2** cool air; a cool place. **3** *sl.* calmness; composure (*keep one's cool; lose one's cool*). •*v.* (often foll. by *down, off*) **1** *tr. & intr.* make or become cool. **2** *intr.* (of anger, emotions, etc.) lessen; become calmer. □ **cool one's heels** see HEEL[1]. **cool it** *sl.* relax, calm down. □□ **cool·ish** *adj.* **cool·ly** /kōōl-lee/ *adv.* **cool·ness** *n.*

cool·ant /kōōlənt/ *n.* a cooling agent, esp. fluid, to remove heat from an engine, nuclear reactor, etc.

cool·er /kōōlər/ *n.* **1** a vessel in which a thing is cooled. **2 a** a refrigerated room. **b** an insulated container for keeping foods, etc., cold. **3** a long drink, esp. a spritzer. **4** *sl.* prison or a prison cell.

cool·head·ed /kōōlhédid/ *adj.* not easily excited.

cool·ing-off pe·ri·od *n.* an interval to allow for a change of mind before commitment to action.

cool·ing tow·er *n.* a tall structure for cooling hot water before reuse, esp. in industry.

coon /kōōn/ *n.* a raccoon.

coon's age *n.sl.* a long time.

coop /kōōp/ *n. & v.* •*n.* **1** a cage placed over sitting or fattening fowls. **2** building for keeping chickens, etc. **3** a small place of confinement, esp. a prison. •*v.tr.* **1** put or keep (a fowl) in a coop. **2** (often foll. by *up, in*) confine (a person) in a small space.

co-op /kṓ-op/ *n. colloq.* **1** a cooperative business or enterprise. **2** = COOPERATIVE 4.

co·op·er·ate /kō-ópərayt/ *v.intr.* (also **co-operate**) **1** (often foll. by *with*) work or act together; assist. **2** (of things) concur in producing an effect. □□ **co·op·er·ant** /–rənt/ *adj.* **co·op·er·a·tion** /–áyshən/ *n.* **co·op·er·a·tor** *n.*

co·op·er·a·tive /kō-ópərətiv, –óprə–/ *adj. & n.* (also **co-operative**) •*adj.* **1** of or affording cooperation. **2** willing to cooperate. **3** *Econ.* (of a farm, shop, or other business) owned and run jointly by its members, with profits shared among them. **4** (of an apartment building) with individual units owned by their occupiers. •*n.* a cooperative farm or society or business. □□ **co·op·er·a·tive·ly** *adv.* **co·op·er·a·tive·ness** *n.*

co-opt /kō-ópt, kṓ-opt/ *v.tr.* appoint to membership of a body by invitation of the existing members. □□ **co-op·tion** /–ópshən/ *n.* **co-op·tive** *adj.*

co·or·di·nate *v., adj., & n.* (also **co-ordinate**) •*v.* /kō-áwrd'nayt/ **1** *tr.* bring (various parts, movements, etc.) into a proper or required relation. **2** *intr.* work or act together effectively. **3** *tr.* make coordinate; organize; classify. •*adj.* /kō-áwrd'nət/ **1** equal in rank or importance. **2** in which the parts are coordinated; involving coordination. **3** *Gram.* (of parts of a compound sentence) equal in status. **4** *Chem.* denoting a type of covalent bond in which one atom provides both the shared electrons. •*n.* /kō-áwrd'nət/ **1** *Math.* each of a system of magnitudes used to fix the position of a point, line, or plane. **2** a person or thing equal in rank or importance. **3** (in *pl.*) matching items of clothing. □□ **co·or·di·na·tion** /–d'náyshən/ *n.* **co·or·di·na·tive** *adj.* **co·or·di·na·tor** *n.*

coot /kōōt/ *n.* **1** any black aquatic bird of the genus *Fulica*, esp. *F. atra* with a white plate on the forehead. **2** *colloq.* a stupid person.

coot·ie /kṓōtee/ *n. sl.* a body louse.

cop /kop/ *n. & v. sl.* •*n.* a policeman. •*v.tr.* (**copped, copping**) **1** catch or arrest (an offender). **2** take; seize. □ **cop out 1** withdraw; give up an attempt. **2** go back on a promise. **3** escape. **cop a plea** *sl.* = PLEA-BARGAIN.

cop·a·cet·ic /kṓpəsétik/ *adj. sl.* excellent; in good order.

co·part·ner /kṓpaártnər/ *n.* a partner or associate, esp. when sharing equally. □□ **co·part·ner·ship** *n.*

cope[1] /kōp/ *v.intr.* **1** (foll. by *with*) deal effectively with a person or task. **2** deal with a situation or problem (*could no longer cope*).

cope[2] /kōp/ *n. Eccl.* a long, cloaklike vestment worn by a priest or bishop.

co·peck var. of KOPECK.

Co·per·ni·can sys·tem /kəpə́rnikən/ *n.* (also **Co·per·ni·can the·o·ry**) *Astron.* the theory that the planets (including the earth) move around the sun (cf. PTOLEMAIC SYSTEM).

cope·stone /kṓpstōn/ *n.* **1** a stone used in a coping. **2** a finishing touch.

cop·i·a·ble /kópeeəbəl/ *adj.* that can or may be copied.

cop·i·er /kópeeər/ *n.* a machine or person that copies (esp. documents).

co·pi·lot /kṓpīlət/ *n.* a second pilot in an aircraft.

cop·ing /kṓping/ *n.* the top (usu. sloping) course of masonry in a wall or parapet.

co·pi·ous /kṓpeeəs/ *adj.* **1** abundant; plentiful. **2** producing much. **3** providing much information. **4** profuse in speech. □□ **co·pi·ous·ly** *adv.* **co·pi·ous·ness** *n.*

co·pol·y·mer /kṓpólimər/ *n. Chem.* a polymer with units of more than one kind. □□ **co·pol·y·mer·ize** *v.tr. & intr.*

cop-out *n.* **1** a cowardly or feeble evasion. **2** an escape; a way of escape.

cop·per[1] /kópər/ *n., adj., & v.* •*n.* **1** *Chem.* a malleable, red-brown metallic element used esp. for electrical cables and apparatus. ¶ Symb.: **Cu. 2** a bronze coin. •*adj.* made of or colored like copper. •*v.tr.* cover with copper.

cop·per[2] /kópər/ *n. sl.* a policeman.

cop·per beech *n.* a variety of beech with copper-colored leaves.

cop·per·head /kópərhed/ *n.* **1** a venomous viper, *Agkistrodon contortrix*, native to N. America. **2** a venomous cobra, *Denisonia superba*, native to Australia.

cop·per·plate /kópərplayt/ *n. & adj.* •*n.* **1 a** a polished copper plate for engraving or etching. **b** a print made from this. **2** an ornate style of handwriting. • *adj.* of or in copperplate writing.

cop·per·y /kópəree/ *adj.* of or like copper, esp. in color.

cop·pice /kópis/ *n.* & *v.* • *n.* an area of undergrowth and small trees, grown for periodic cutting. • *v.tr.* cut back (young trees) periodically to stimulate growth of shoots. ▫▫ **cop·piced** *adj.*

cop·ra /kóprə/ *n.* the dried kernels of the coconut.

co·pro·duc·tion /kṓprədúkshən/ *n.* a production of a play, broadcast, etc., jointly by more than one company.

copse /kops/ *n.* **1** = COPPICE. **2** (in general use) a small forest.

cop·ter /kóptər/ *n. colloq.* a helicopter.

cop·u·la /kópyələ/ *n.* (*pl.* **copulas** or **copulae** /–lee/) *Logic & Gram.* a connecting word, esp. a part of the verb *be* connecting a subject and predicate. ▫▫ **cop·u·lar** *adj.*

cop·u·late /kópyəlayt/ *v.intr.* (often foll. by *with*) have sexual intercourse. ▫▫ **cop·u·la·tion** /–láyshən/ *n.* **cop·u·la·to·ry** /–latáwree/ *adj.*

cop·y /kópee/ *n.* & *v.* • *n.* (*pl.* **-ies**) **1** a thing made to imitate or be identical to another. **2** a single specimen of a publication or issue. **3 a** matter to be printed. **b** material for a newspaper or magazine article (*scandals make good copy*). **c** the text of an advertisement. **4 a** a model to be copied. **b** a page written after a model (of penmanship). • *v.* (**-ies, -ied**) **1** *tr.* **a** make a copy of. **b** (often foll. by *out*) transcribe. **2** *intr.* make a copy, esp. clandestinely. **3** *tr.* (foll. by *to*) send a copy of (a letter) to a third party. **4** *tr.* do the same as; imitate.

cop·y·book /kópeebŏŏk/ *n.* **1** a book containing models of handwriting. **2** (*attrib.*) **a** tritely conventional. **b** accurate; exemplary.

cop·y·cat /kópeekat/ *n. colloq.* a person who copies another, esp. closely.

cop·y ed·i·tor *n.* a person who edits copy for printing.

cop·y desk *n.* the desk in a newspaper office at which copy is edited for printing.

cop·y·ist /kópee-ist/ *n.* **1** a person who makes (esp. written) copies. **2** an imitator.

cop·y·read·er /kópeereedər/ *n.* a person who reads and edits copy for a newspaper or book. ▫▫ **cop·y·read** *v.tr.*

cop·y·right /kópeerīt/ *n., adj.,* & *v.* • *n.* the exclusive legal right to print, publish, perform, film, or record literary, artistic, or musical material. • *adj.* (of such material) protected by copyright. • *v.tr.* secure copyright for (material).

cop·y·writ·er /kópeerītər/ *n.* a person who writes or prepares copy (esp. of advertising material) for publication. ▫▫ **cop·y·writ·ing** *n.*

co·quette /kōkét/ *n.* **1** a woman who flirts. **2** any crested hummingbird of the genus *Lophornis*. ▫▫ **co·quet·ry** /kṓkitree, kōkétree/ *n.* (*pl.* **-ries**). **co·quet·tish** *adj.* **co·quet·tish·ly** *adv.* **co·quet·tish·ness** *n.*

cor·al /káwrəl, kór;n–/ *n.* & *adj.* • *n.* **1 a** a hard calcareous substance secreted by various marine polyps for support and habitation. **b** any of these usu. colonial organisms. **2** the unimpregnated roe of a lobster or scallop. • *adj.* **1** like coral, esp. in color; pinkish or redish yellow. **2** made of coral.

cor·al·line /káwrəlin, –līn, kór;n–/ *n.* & *adj.* • *n.* **1** any seaweed of the genus *Corallina* having a calcareous jointed stem. **2** (in general use) the name of various plantlike compound organisms. • *adj.* **1** coral red. **2** of or like coral.

cor·al reef *n.* one formed by the growth of coral.

cor·al snake *n.* any of various brightly colored poisonous snakes, esp. *Micrurus fulvius*, native to the southeastern US.

cor·bel /káwrbəl, –bel/ *n.* & *v. Archit.* • *n.* **1** a projection of stone, timber, etc., jutting out from a wall to support a weight. **2** a short timber laid longitudinally under a beam to help support it. • *v.tr.* & *intr.* (**corbeled, corbeling**; esp. foll. by *out, off*) support or project on corbels.

cord /kawrd/ *n.* & *v.* • *n.* **1 a** long, thin, flexible material made from several twisted strands. **b** a piece of this. **2** *Anat.* a structure in the body resembling a cord (*spinal cord*). **3 a** ribbed fabric, esp. corduroy. **b** (in *pl.*) corduroy pants. **c** a cordlike rib on fabric. **4** *Electr.* a flexible insulated cable (*telephone cord*). **5** a measure of cut wood (usu. 128 cu.ft., 3.6 cubic meters). **6** a moral or emotional tie (*cords of affection*). • *v.tr.* **1** fasten or bind with cord. **2** (as **corded** *adj.*) **a** (of cloth) ribbed. **b** provided with cords. **c** (of muscles) standing out like taut cords. ▫▫ **cord·like** *adj.*

cord·age /káwrdij/ *n.* cords or ropes, esp. in the rigging of a ship.

cor·date /káwrdayt/ *adj.* heart-shaped.

cor·dial /káwrjəl/ *adj.* & *n.* • *adj.* **1** heartfelt; sincere. **2** warm; friendly. • *n.* a liqueur. ▫▫ **cor·dial·i·ty** /–jeálitee/ *n.* **cor·dial·ly** *adv.*

cor·dil·le·ra /káwrd'lyáirə, kawrdílərə/ *n.* a system or group of usu. parallel mountain ranges together with intervening plateaus, etc., esp. of the Andes and in Central America and Mexico.

cord·ite /káwrdīt/ *n.* a smokeless explosive made from cellulose nitrate and nitroglycerine.

cord·less /káwrdlis/ *adj.* (of an electrical appliance, telephone, etc.) working without a connection to an electrical supply or central unit.

cor·don /káwrd'n/ *n.* & *v.* • *n.* **1** a line or circle of police, soldiers, etc., esp. preventing access to or from an area. **2 a** an ornamental cord or braid. **b** the ribbon of a knightly order. **3** a fruit tree trained to grow as a single stem. • *v.tr.* (often foll. by *off*) enclose or separate with a cordon of police, etc.

cor·don bleu /káwrdawn blṓ/ *adj.* & *n. Cooking* • *adj.* of the highest class. • *n.* a cook of this class.

cor·du·roy /káwrdəroy/ *n.* **1** a thick cotton fabric with velvety ribs. **2** (in *pl.*) corduroy pants.

core /kawr/ *n.* & *v.* • *n.* **1** the horny central part of various fruits, containing the seeds. **2 a** the central or most important part of anything (also *attrib.*: *core curriculum*). **b** the central part, of different character from the surroundings. **3** the central region of the earth. **4** the central part of a nuclear reactor, containing the fissile material. **5** a magnetic structural unit in a computer, storing one bit of data (see BIT[4]). **6** the inner strand of an electric cable, rope, etc. **7** a piece of soft iron forming the center of an electromagnet or an induction coil. **8** an internal mold filling a space to be left hollow in a casting. • *v.tr.* remove the core from. ▫▫ **cor·er** *n.*

core mem·o·ry *n. Computing* the memory of a computer consisting of many cores.

co·re·op·sis /káwreeópsis/ *n.* any composite plant of the genus *Coreopsis*, having rayed usu. yellow flowers.

co·re·spond·ent /kṓ-rispóndənt/ *n.* a person cited in a divorce case as having committed adultery with the respondent.

cor·gi /káwrgee/ *n.* (*pl.* **corgis**) (in full **Welsh corgi**) **1** a dog of a short-legged breed with foxlike head. **2** this breed.

co·ri·an·der /káwreeándər/ *n.* **1** a plant, *Coriandrum sativum*, with leaves used for flavoring and small, round, aromatic fruits. **2** (also **co·ri·an·der seed**) the dried fruit used for flavoring curries, etc.

Co·rin·thi·an /kəríntheeən/ *adj.* & *n.* • *adj.* **1** of ancient Corinth in southern Greece. **2** *Archit.* of an order characterized by ornate decoration and flared capitals with acanthus leaves. • *n.* a native of Corinth.

cork /kawrk/ *n. & v.* • *n.* **1** the buoyant light-brown bark of the cork oak. **2** a bottle stopper of cork or other material. **3** a float of cork used in fishing, etc. **4** *Bot.* a protective layer of dead cells immediately below the bark of woody plants. **5** (*attrib.*) made of cork. • *v.tr.* (often foll. by *up*) **1** stop or confine. **2** restrain (feelings, etc.). **3** blacken with burned cork. □□ **cork·like** *adj.*

corked /kawrkt/ *adj.* **1** stopped with a cork. **2** (of wine) spoiled by a decayed cork. **3** blackened with burned cork.

cork·ing /káwrking/ *adj. sl.* strikingly large or splendid.

cork oak *n.* a S. European oak, *Quercus suber.*

cork·screw /káwrkskrōō/ *n. & v.* • *n.* **1** a device for pulling corks from bottles, consisting of a spiral metal rod that is inserted into the cork and a handle that extracts it. **2** (often *attrib.*) a thing with a spiral shape. • *v.tr. & intr.* move spirally; twist.

cork·y /káwrkee/ *adj.* (**corkier, corkiest**) **1** corklike. **2** (of wine) corked.

corm /kawrm/ *n. Bot.* an underground swollen stem base of some plants, e.g., crocus.

cor·mo·rant /káwrmərənt, –mərant/ *n.* any diving sea bird of the family Phalacrocoracidae, esp. *Phalacrocorax carbo* having lustrous black plumage.

corn[1] /kawrn/ *n. & v.* • *n.* **1 a** a tall-growing orig. N. American cereal plant, *Zea mays,* cultivated in many varieties, bearing kernels on a long ear (cob). **b** the cobs or kernels of this plant. **2** *colloq.* something corny or trite. • *v.tr.* (as **corned** *adj.*) sprinkled or preserved with salt or brine (*corned beef*).

corn[2] /kawrn/ *n.* a small area of horny usu. tender skin esp. on the toes, extending into subcutaneous tissue.

corn·ball /kórnbawl/ *n. & adj.* • *n.* an unsophisticated or mawkishly sentimental person. • *adj.* = CORNY *adj.* 1.

corn bread *n.* bread made with cornmeal.

corn·cob /káwrnkaab/ *n.* the cylindrical center of the corn ear to which rows of grains (kernels) are attached.

corn·cob pipe *n.* a tobacco pipe made from a corncob.

corn dol·ly *n.* a symbolic or decorative figure made of plaited straw, corn husks, etc.

cor·ne·a /káwrneeə/ *n.* the transparent circular part of the front of the eyeball. □□ **cor·ne·al** *adj.*

cor·nel·ian var. of CARNELIAN.

cor·ne·ous /káwrneeəs/ *adj.* hornlike; horny.

cor·ner /káwrnər/ *n. & v.* • *n.* **1** a place where converging sides or edges meet. **2** a projecting angle, esp. where two streets meet. **3** the internal space or recess formed by the meeting of two sides, esp. of a room. **4** a difficult position, esp. one from which there is no escape (*driven into a corner*). **5** a secluded or remote place. **6** a region or quarter, esp. a remote one (*from the four corners of the earth*). **7** the action or result of buying or controlling the whole available stock of a commodity, thereby dominating the market. **8** *Boxing & Wrestling* **a** an angle of the ring, esp. one where a contestant rests between rounds. **b** a contestant's supporters offering assistance at the corner between rounds. **9** *Soccer* a free kick or hit from a corner of the field after the ball has been kicked over the goal line by a defending player. • *v.* **1** *tr.* force (a person or animal) into a difficult or inescapable position. **2** *tr.* **a** establish a corner in (a commodity). **b** dominate (the market) in this way. **3** *intr.* (esp. of or in a vehicle) go around a corner. □ **just around the corner** *colloq.* very near; imminent.

cor·ner·stone /káwrnərstōn/ *n.* **1 a** a stone in a projecting angle of a wall. **b** a foundation stone. **2** an indispensable part or basis of something.

cor·net /kawrnét/ *Mus.* **1 a** a brass instrument resembling a trumpet but shorter and wider. **b** its player. **2** an organ stop with the quality of a cornet. □□ **cor·net·ist** or **cor·net·tist** *n.*

corn·flake /káwrnflayk/ *n.* **1** (in *pl.*) a breakfast cereal of toasted flakes made from cornmeal. **2** a flake of this cereal.

corn·flow·er /káwrnflowər/ *n.* any plant of the genus *Centaurea* growing among corn, esp. *C. cyanus,* with deep-blue flowers.

cor·nice /káwrnis/ *n.* **1** *Archit.* **a** an ornamental molding around the wall of a room just below the ceiling. **b** a horizontal molded projection crowning a building or structure. **2** *Mountaineering* an overhanging mass of hardened snow at the edge of a precipice. □□ **cor·niced** *adj.*

Cor·nish /káwrnish/ *adj. & n.* • *adj.* of or relating to the county of Cornwall in SW England. • *n.* the ancient Celtic language of Cornwall.

corn·meal /káwrnmeel/ *n.* meal ground from corn.

corn·row /kórnrō/ *n. & v.* • *n.* any of usu. several narrow plaits of hair braided close to the scalp. • *v.tr.* plait (hair) in cornrows.

corn·starch /káwrnstaarch/ *n.* fine-ground flour made from corn.

cor·nu·co·pi·a /káwrnəkṓpeeə, –nyə–/ *n.* **1 a** a symbol of plenty consisting of a goat's horn overflowing with flowers, fruit, etc. **b** an ornamental vessel shaped like this. **2** an abundant supply. □□ **cor·nu·co·pi·an** *adj.*

corn·y /káwrnee/ *adj.* (**cornier, corniest**) **1** *colloq.* **a** trite. **b** feebly humorous. **c** sentimental. **d** old-fashioned; out of date. **2** of or abounding in corn. □□ **corn·i·ly** *adv.* **corn·i·ness** *n.*

co·rol·la /kərólə, –rṓ–/ *n. Bot.* a whorl or whorls of petals forming the inner envelope of a flower.

cor·ol·lar·y /káwrəleree, kór–/ *n. & adj.* • *n.* (*pl.* **-ies**) **1 a** a proposition that follows from one already proved. **b** an immediate deduction. **2** (often foll. by *of*) a natural consequence or result. • *adj.* **1** supplementary; associated. **2** (often foll. by *to*) forming a corollary.

co·ro·na[1] /kərṓnə/ *n.* (*pl.* **coronas** or **coronae** /–nee/) **1 a** a small circle of light around the sun or moon. **b** the gaseous envelope of the sun, seen as an area of light around the moon's disk during a total solar eclipse. **2** a circular chandelier hung from a roof. **3** *Anat.* a crown or crownlike structure. □□ **cor·o·nal** /kərṓnəl, káwrən'l, kór–/ *adj.*

co·ro·na[2] /kərṓnə/ *n.* a long cigar with straight sides.

cor·o·nar·y /káwrəneree, kór–/ *adj. & n.* • *adj. Anat.* resembling or encircling like a crown. • *n.* (*pl.* **-ies**) **1** = CORONARY THROMBOSIS. **2** a heart attack.

cor·o·nar·y throm·bo·sis *n.* a blockage of the blood flow caused by a blood clot in a coronary artery.

cor·o·na·tion /káwrənáyshən, kór–/ *n.* the ceremony of crowning a sovereign or a sovereign's consort.

cor·o·ner /káwrənər, kór–/ *n.* an officer of a county, district, or municipality, holding inquests on deaths thought to be violent or accidental.

cor·o·net /káwrənit, –nét, kór–/ *n.* **1** a small crown. **2** a circlet of precious materials, esp. as a headdress. **3** a garland for the head. □□ **cor·o·net·ed** *adj.*

Corp. *abbr.* **1** corporal. **2** corporation.

cor·po·ra *pl.* of CORPUS.

cor·po·ral[1] /káwrpərəl, káwrprəl/ *n.* a noncommissioned army, air force, or marine officer ranking next below sergeant.

cor·po·ral[2] /káwrpərəl, káwrprəl/ *adj.* of or relating to the human body (cf. CORPOREAL). □□ **cor·po·ral·ly** *adv.*

cor·po·ral·i·ty /káwrpərálitee/ *n.* (*pl.* **-ties**) **1** material existence. **2** a body.

---

cor·po·ral pun·ish·ment *n.* punishment inflicted on the body, esp. by beating.

cor·po·rate /káwrpərət, káwrprit/ *adj.* **1** forming a corporation (*corporate body*). **2** forming one body of many individuals. **3** of or belonging to a corporation or group (*corporate responsibility*). **4** corporative. ▫▫ **cor·po·rate·ly** *adv.* **cor·po·rat·ism** *n.*

cor·po·rate raid·er *n.* a person who mounts an unwelcome takeover bid by buying up a company's shares on the stock market.

cor·po·ra·tion /káwrpəráyshən/ *n.* a group of people authorized to act as an individual, esp. in business.

cor·po·ra·tive /káwrpərətiv, –ráytiv/ *adj.* **1** of a corporation. **2** governed by or organized in corporations. ▫▫ **cor·po·ra·tiv·ism** *n.*

cor·po·re·al /kawrpáwreeəl/ *adj.* **1** bodily, physical, material, esp. as distinct from spiritual (cf. CORPORAL[2]). **2** *Law* consisting of material objects. ▫▫ **cor·po·re·al·i·ty** /–reeálitee/ *n.* **cor·po·re·al·ly** *adv.*

corps /kawr/ *n.* (*pl.* **corps** /kawrz/) **1** *Mil.* **a** a body of troops with special duties (*intelligence corps*; *Marine Corps*). **b** a main subdivision of an army in the field. **2** a body of people engaged in a special activity (*diplomatic corps*).

corpse /kawrps/ *n.* a dead (usu. human) body.

---

corpse Middle English (denoting the living body of a person or animal): alteration of archaic *corse* by association with Latin *corpus*, a change which also took place in French (Old French *cors* becoming *corps*). The *p* was originally silent, as in French; the final *e* was rare before the 19th century, but now distinguishes *corpse* from *corps*.

---

cor·pu·lent /káwrpyələnt/ *adj.* bulky in body; fat. ▫▫ **cor·pu·lence** /–ləns/ *n.* **cor·pu·len·cy** *n.*

cor·pus /káwrpəs/ *n.* (*pl.* **corpora** /káwrpərə/ or **corpuses**) **1** a body or collection of writings, texts, spoken material, etc. **2** *Anat.* a structure of a special character in the animal body.

cor·pus·cle /káwrpusəl/ *n.* a minute body or cell in an organism, esp. (in *pl.*) the red or white cells in the blood of vertebrates. ▫▫ **cor·pus·cu·lar** /kawrpúskyələr/ *adj.*

cor·pus de·lic·ti /káwrpəs dilíktī/ *n. Law* the facts and circumstances constituting a breach of a law.

cor·ral /kərál/ *n.* & *v.* • *n.* **1** a pen for cattle, horses, etc. **2** an enclosure for capturing wild animals. • *v.tr.* (**corralled, corralling**) **1** put or keep in a corral. **2** form (wagons) into a corral. **3** *colloq.* gather in; acquire.

cor·rect /kərékt/ *adj.* & *v.* • *adj.* **1** true; right; accurate. **2** (of conduct, manners, etc.) proper; right. **3** in accordance with good standards of taste, etc. • *v.tr.* **1** set right; amend (an error, omission, etc., or person). **2** mark the errors in (work). **3** substitute the right thing for (the wrong one). **4 a** admonish or rebuke (a person). **b** punish (a person or fault). **5** counteract (a harmful quality). **6** adjust (an instrument, etc.). ▫▫ **cor·rect·ly** *adv.* **cor·rect·ness** *n.* **cor·rec·tor** *n.*

cor·rec·tion /kərékshən/ *n.* **1 a** the act or process of correcting. **b** an instance of this. **2** a thing substituted for what is wrong. **3** a program of incarceration, parole, probation, etc., for dealing with convicted offenders. ▫▫ **cor·rec·tion·al** *adj.*

cor·rec·tive /kəréktiv/ *adj.* & *n.* • *adj.* serving or tending to correct or counteract something undesired. • *n.* a corrective measure or thing. ▫▫ **cor·rec·tive·ly** *adv.*

cor·re·late /káwrəlayt, kór–/ *v.* & *n.* • *v.* **1** *intr.* (foll. by *with*, *to*) have a mutual relation. **2** *tr.* (usu. foll. by *with*) bring into a mutual relation. • *n.* each of two related or complementary things.

cor·re·la·tion /káwrəláyshən, kór–/ *n.* **1** a mutual relation between two or more things. **2 a** interdependence of variable quantities. **b** a quantity measuring the extent of this. **3** the act of correlating. ▫▫ **cor·re·la·tion·al** *adj.*

cor·rel·a·tive /kərélətiv/ *adj.* & *n.* • *adj.* **1** (often foll. by *with*, *to*) having a mutual relation. **2** *Gram.* (of words) corresponding to each other and regularly used together (as *neither* and *nor*). • *n.* a correlative word or thing. ▫▫ **cor·rel·a·tive·ly** *adv.* **cor·rel·a·tiv·i·ty** /–tívitee/ *n.*

cor·re·spond /káwrispónd, kór–/ *v.intr.* **1 a** (usu. foll. by *to*) be analogous or similar. **b** (usu. foll. by *to*) agree in amount, position, etc. **c** (usu. foll. by *with*, *to*) be in harmony or agreement. **2** (usu. foll. by *with*) communicate by interchange of letters. ▫▫ **cor·re·spond·ing·ly** *adv.*

cor·re·spond·ence /káwrispóndəns, kór–/ *n.* **1** (usu. foll. by *with*, *to*, *between*) agreement, similarity, or harmony. **2 a** communication by letters. **b** letters sent or received.

cor·re·spond·ence course *n.* a course of study conducted by mail.

cor·re·spond·ent /káwrispóndənt, –kór–/ *n.* **1** a person who writes letters, esp. regularly. **2** a person employed to contribute material for a periodical or for broadcasting. **3** a person or firm having regular business relations with another, esp. in another country.

cor·ri·da /kawréedə, –thaa/ *n.* a bullfight.

cor·ri·dor /káwridər, –dor, kór–/ *n.* **1** a passage from which doors lead into rooms. **2** a strip of the territory of one nation passing through that of another, esp. to the sea. **3** a route to which aircraft are restricted, esp. over a foreign country.

cor·ri·gen·dum /káwrijéndəm, kór–/ *n.* (*pl.* **corrigenda** /–də/) a thing to be corrected in a printed book.

cor·ri·gi·ble /káwrijibəl, kór–/ *adj.* **1** capable of being corrected. **2** (of a person) submissive; open to correction. ▫▫ **cor·ri·gi·bly** *adv.*

cor·rob·o·rate /kəróbərayt/ *v.tr.* confirm or give support to (a statement or belief, or the person holding it). ▫▫ **cor·rob·o·ra·tion** /–ráyshən/ *n.* **cor·rob·o·ra·tive** /–rətiv, –ráytiv/ *adj.* **cor·rob·o·ra·tor** *n.*

cor·rode /kərṓd/ *v.* **1 a** *tr.* wear away, esp. by chemical action. **b** *intr.* be worn away; decay. **2** *tr.* destroy gradually (*optimism corroded by recent misfortunes*). ▫▫ **cor·rod·i·ble** *adj.*

cor·ro·sion /kərṓzhən/ *n.* **1** the process of corroding, esp. of a rusting metal. **2 a** damage caused by corroding. **b** a corroded area.

cor·ro·sive /kərṓsiv/ *adj.* & *n.* • *adj.* tending to corrode or consume. • *n.* a corrosive substance. ▫▫ **cor·ro·sive·ly** *adv.* **cor·ro·sive·ness** *n.*

cor·ru·gate /káwrəgayt, kór–/ *v.* **1** *tr.* (esp. as **corrugated** *adj.*) form into alternate ridges and grooves, esp. to strengthen (*corrugated iron*; *corrugated cardboard*). **2** *tr.* & *intr.* contract into wrinkles or folds. ▫▫ **cor·ru·ga·tion** /–gáyshən/ *n.*

cor·rupt /kərúpt/ *adj.* & *v.* • *adj.* **1** morally depraved; wicked. **2** influenced by or using bribery or fraudulent activity. **3** (of a text, language, etc.) harmed (esp. made suspect or unreliable) by errors or alterations. **4** rotten. • *v.* **1** *tr.* & *intr.* make or become corrupt or depraved. **2** *tr.* affect or harm by errors or alterations. **3** *tr.* infect; taint. ▫▫ **cor·rupt·er** *n.* **cor·rupt·i·ble** *adj.* **cor·rupt·i·bil·i·ty** *n.* **cor·rup·tive** *adj.* **cor·rupt·ly** *adv.* **cor·rupt·ness** *n.*

cor·rup·tion /kərúpshən/ *n.* **1** moral deterioration, esp. widespread. **2** use of corrupt practices, esp. bribery or fraud. **3 a** irregular alteration (of a text, language, etc.) from its original state. **b** an irregularly altered form of a word. **4** decomposition, esp. of a corpse or other organic matter.

cor·sage /kawrsaázh/ *n.* **1** a small bouquet worn by a woman. **2** the bodice of a woman's dress.

cor·sair /káwrsair/ *n.* **1** a pirate ship. **2** a pirate.

cor·set /káwrsit/ *n.* **1** a closely fitting undergarment worn by women to support the abdomen. **2** a similar garment worn by men and women because of injury, weakness, or deformity. ▫▫ **cor·set·ed** *adj.* **cor·se·try** *n.*

Cor·si·can /káwrsikən/ *adj.* & *n.* • *adj.* of or relating to Corsica. • *n.* **1** a native of Corsica. **2** the Italian dialect of Corsica.

cor·tege /kawrtéyzh/ *n.* (also **cortège**) **1** a procession, esp. for a funeral. **2** a train of attendants.

cor·tex /káwrteks/ *n.* (*pl.* **cortices** /–tiseez/ or **cortex·es**) **1** *Anat.* the outer part of an organ, esp. of the brain (**cerebral cortex**) or kidneys (**renal cortex**). **2** *Bot.* **a** an outer layer of tissue immediately below the epidermis. **b** bark. ▫▫ **cor·ti·cal** /káwrtikəl/ *adj.*

cor·ti·sone /káwrtisōn, –zōn/ *n. Biochem.* a steroid hormone used medicinally esp. against inflammation and allergy.

co·run·dum /kərúndəm/ *n. Mineral.* extremely hard crystallized alumina, used esp. as an abrasive, and varieties of which are used for gemstones.

cor·us·cate /káwrəskayt, kór–/ *v.intr.* **1** give off flashing light; sparkle. **2** be showy or brilliant. ▫▫ **cor·us·ca·tion** /–káyshən/ *n.*

cor·vine /káwrvīn, –vin/ *adj.* of or akin to the raven or crow.

cos[1] /kaws, kos/ *n.* a variety of lettuce with crisp narrow leaves forming a long, upright head.

cos[2] /kos, koz/ *abbr.* cosine.

Co·sa Nos·tra /kṓsə nṓstrə/ *n.* a US criminal organization resembling and related to the Mafia.

co·se·cant /kōséekant, –kənt/ *n. Math.* the ratio of the hypotenuse (in a right triangle) to the side opposite an acute angle; the reciprocal of sine.

co·sig·na·to·ry /kōsígnətáwree/ *n.* & *adj.* • *n.* (*pl.* **-ries**) a person or nation signing (a treaty, etc.) jointly with others. • *adj.* signing jointly.

co·sine /kṓsīn/ *n. Math.* the ratio of the side adjacent to an acute angle (in a right triangle) to the hypotenuse.

cos·met·ic /kozmétik/ *adj.* & *n.* • *adj.* **1** intended to adorn or beautify the body, esp. the face. **2** intended to improve only appearances; superficially improving or beneficial (*the reform was merely a cosmetic exercise*). **3** (of surgery or a prosthetic device) imitating, restoring, or enhancing the normal appearance. • *n.* (usu. **cosmetics**) a product applied to the body, esp. the face, to improve its appearance. ▫▫ **cos·met·i·cal·ly** *adv.*

cos·me·tol·o·gy /kosmətóləjee/ *n.* the art and technique of treating the skin, nails, and hair with cosmetic preparations. ▫▫ **cos·me·tol·o·gist** *n.*

cos·mic /kózmik/ *adj.* **1** of the universe or cosmos. **2** of or for space travel. ▫▫ **cos·mi·cal** *adj.* **cos·mi·cal·ly** *adv.*

cos·mog·o·ny /kozmógənee/ *n.* (*pl.* **-nies**) **1** the branch of science that deals with the origin of the universe; esp. the solar system. **2** a theory regarding this. ▫▫ **cos·mo·gon·ic** /–məgónik/ *adj.* **cos·mo·gon·i·cal** *adj.* **cos·mog·o·nist** /–móg–/ *n.*

cos·mog·ra·phy /kozmógrəfee/ *n.* (*pl.* **-phies**) a description or mapping of general features of the universe. ▫▫ **cos·mog·ra·pher** *n.* **cos·mo·graph·ic** /–məgráfik/ *adj.* **cos·mo·graph·i·cal** *adj.*

cos·mol·o·gy /kozmóləjee/ *n.* the science of the origin and development of the universe. ▫▫ **cos·mo·log·i·cal** /–məlójikəl/ *adj.* **cos·mol·o·gist** *n.*

cos·mo·naut /kózmənawt/ *n.* a Russian astronaut.

cos·mo·pol·i·tan /kózməpólit'n/ *adj.* & *n.* • *adj.* **1 a** of or from or knowing many parts of the world. **b** consisting of people from many or all parts. **2** free from national limitations or prejudices. **3** *Ecol.* (of a plant, animal, etc.) widely distributed. • *n.* **1** a cosmopolitan person. **2** *Ecol.* a widely distributed animal or plant. ▫▫ **cos·mo·pol·i·tan·ism** *n.*

cos·mos[1] /kózmōs, –məs, –mos/ *n.* **1** the universe, esp. as a well-ordered whole. **2 a** an ordered system of ideas, etc. **b** a sum total of experience.

cos·mos[2] /kózməs, -mos, -mōs/ *n.* any composite plant of the genus *Cosmos,* bearing single dahlialike blossoms of various colors.

Cos·sack /kósak/ *n.* & *adj.* • *n.* **1** a member of a people of southern Imperial Russia, Ukraine, and Siberia, orig. famous for their horsemanship and military skill. **2** a member of a Cossack military unit. • *adj.* of, relating to, or characteristic of the Cossacks.

cost /kawst/ *v.* & *n.* • *v.* (*past* and *past part.* **cost**) **1** *tr.* be obtainable for (a sum of money); have as a price (*what does it cost?*). **2** *tr.* involve as a loss or sacrifice (*it cost him his life*). **3** *tr.* (*past* and *past part.* **costed**) fix or estimate the cost or price of. **4** *colloq.* **a** *tr.* be costly to (*it'll cost you*). **b** *intr.* be costly. • *n.* **1** what a thing costs; the price paid or to be paid. **2** a loss or sacrifice; an expenditure of time, effort, etc. **3** (in *pl.*) legal expenses. ▫ **at all costs** (or **at any cost**) no matter what the cost or risk may be. **at cost** at the initial cost; at cost price; without profit to the seller. **at the cost of** at the expense of losing or sacrificing. **cost a person dearly** (or **dear**) involve someone in a serious loss or a heavy penalty.

co·star /kṓstaar/ *n.* & *v.* • *n.* a movie or stage star appearing with another or others of equal importance. • *v.* (**-starred, -starring**) **1** *intr.* take part as a costar. **2** *tr.* (of a production) include as a costar.

cost-ef·fec·tive *adj.* effective or productive in relation to its cost.

cos·tive /kóstiv/ *adj.* **1** constipated. **2** slow or reluctant in speech or action. ▫▫ **cos·tive·ly** *adv.* **cos·tive·ness** *n.*

cost·ly /kawstlee/ *adj.* (**costlier, costliest**) **1** costing much; expensive. **2** of great value. ▫▫ **cost·li·ness** *n.*

cost of liv·ing *n.* the level of prices, esp. of the basic necessities of life.

cos·tume /kóstōōm, –tyōōm/ *n.* & *v.* • *n.* **1** a style of dress, esp. that of a particular place, time, or class. **2** a set of clothes. **3** clothing for a particular activity (*dancing costume*). **4** an actor's clothes for a part. • *v.tr.* provide with a costume.

cos·tume jew·el·ry *n.* jewelry made with inexpensive materials or imitation gems.

cos·tume play *n.* (or **costume drama**) a play or television drama in which the actors wear historical costume.

cos·tum·er /kóstōōmər, –tyōō–/ *n.* a person who makes or deals in costumes, esp. for theatrical use.

cot[1] /kot/ *n.* **1** a small folding bed. **2** a hospital bed. **3** *Ind.* a light bedstead. **4** *Naut.* a kind of swinging bed hung from deck beams, formerly used by officers.

cot[2] /kot/ *n.* **1** a small shelter; a cote. **2** *poet.* a cottage.

cot[3] /kot/ *abbr. Math.* cotangent.

co·tan·gent /kōtánjənt/ *n. Math.* the ratio of the side adjacent to an acute angle (in a right triangle) to the opposite side.

cote /kōt/ *n.* a shelter, esp. for animals or birds; a shed or stall (*sheepcote*).

co·te·rie /kṓtəree/ *n.* **1** an exclusive group of people sharing interests. **2** a select circle in society.

co·ter·mi·nous /kōtə́rminəs/ *adj.* (often foll. by *with*) having the same boundaries or extent (in space, time, or meaning).

co·tid·al line /kōtíd'l/ *n.* a line on a map connecting points at which tidal levels (as high tide or low tide) occur simultaneously.

cot·tage /kótij/ *n.* **1** a small, simple house, esp. in the country. **2** a dwelling forming part of a farm establishment, used by a worker. ▫▫ **cot·tag·ey** *adj.*

cot·tage cheese *n.* soft white cheese made from curds of skimmed milk.

cot·tage in·dus·try *n.* a business activity partly or wholly carried on at home.

cot·ter /kótər/ *n.* **1** a bolt or wedge for securing parts of machinery, etc. **2** (in full **cotter pin**) a split pin that opens after passing through a hole.

cot·ton /kót'n/ *n. & v.* •*n.* **1** a soft, white fibrous substance covering the seeds of certain plants. **2 a** (in full **cotton plant**) such a plant, esp. any of the genus *Gossypium*. **b** cotton plants cultivated as a crop for the fiber or the seeds. **3** thread or cloth made from the fiber. **4** (*attrib.*) made of cotton. •*v.intr.* (foll. by *to*) be attracted by (a person). ▫ **cotton to** (or **on to**) *colloq.* **1** begin to be fond of or agreeable to. **2** begin to understand. ▫▫ **cot·ton·y** *adj.*

cot·ton can·dy *n.* a fluffy mass of spun sugar, usu. served on a stick or in a paper cone.

cot·ton gin *n.* a machine for separating cotton from its seeds.

cot·ton·mouth /kót'nmowth/ *n.* a venomous pit viper, *Agkistrodon piscivorus*, of swampy areas of the southeastern US, related to the coppermouth. Also called **water moccasin**.

cot·ton-pick·ing *adj. sl.* unpleasant; wretched.

cot·ton·tail /kót'ntayl/ *n.* any rabbit of the genus *Sylvilagus*, native to America, having a mainly white fluffy tail.

cot·ton·wood /kót'nwŏŏd/ *n.* **1** any of several poplars, native to N. America, having seeds covered in white cottony hairs. **2** any of several trees native to Australia, esp. a downy-leaved tree, *Bedfordia arborescens*.

cot·y·le·don /kót'lééd'n/ *n.* an embryonic leaf in seed-bearing plants.

couch[1] /kowch/ *n. & v.* •*n.* **1** an upholstered piece of furniture for several people; a sofa. **2** a long padded seat with a headrest at one end. •*v.* **1** *tr.* (foll. by *in*) express in words of a specified kind (*couched in simple language*). **2** *tr.* lay on or as on a couch. **3** *intr.* **a** (of an animal) lie, esp. in its lair. **b** lie in ambush.

couch[2] /kowch, kōōch/ *n.* (in full **couch grass**) any of several grasses of the genus *Agropyron*, esp. *A. repens*, having long, creeping roots.

cou·chette /kōōshét/ *n.* **1** a railroad car with seats convertible into sleeping berths. **2** a berth in this.

couch po·ta·to *n. sl.* a person who likes lazing at home, esp. watching television.

cou·gar /kóōgər/ *n.* a puma.

cough /kawf, kof/ *v. & n.* •*v.intr.* **1** expel air from the lungs with a sudden, sharp sound to remove an obstruction or congestion. **2** (of an engine, gun, etc.) make a similar sound. •*n.* **1** an act of coughing. **2** a condition of the respiratory organs causing coughing. **3** a tendency to cough. ▫ **cough out 1** eject by coughing. **2** say with a cough. **cough up 1** = *cough out*. **2** *sl.* bring out or give (money or information) reluctantly. **3** *sl.* confess.

cough drop *n.* a medicated lozenge to relieve a cough.

cough med·i·cine *n.* (also **cough syr·up**) a medicated liquid to relieve a cough.

could *past* of CAN[1].

couldn't /kóŏd'nt/ *contr.* could not.

cou·lomb /kóōlom/ *n. Electr.* the SI unit of electric charge. ¶ Symb.: **C**.

coun·cil /kównsəl/ *n.* **1 a** an advisory, deliberative, or administrative body of people. **b** a meeting of such a body. **2** the elected local legislative body of a town, city, or county. **3** a body of persons chosen as advisers. **4** an ecclesiastical assembly.

coun·cil·man /kównsəlmən/ *n.* (*pl.* **-men**; *fem.* **councilwoman**, *pl.* **-women**) a member of a council.

coun·cil·or /kównsələr, –slər/ *n.* (also **coun·cil·lor**) an elected member of a council, esp. a local one.

▶See note at COUNSELOR.

coun·sel /kównsəl/ *n. & v.* •*n.* **1** advice, esp. formally given. **2** consultation, esp. to seek or give advice. **3** (*pl.* same) an attorney or other legal adviser; a body of these in a case. **4** a plan of action. •*v.tr.* **1** (often foll. by *to* + infin.) advise (a person). **2 a** give advice to (a person) on personal problems, esp. professionally. **b** assist or guide (a person) in resolving personal difficulties. **3** (often foll. by *that*) recommend (a course of action). ▫▫ **coun·sel·ing** /kównsəling, –sling/ *n.*

coun·se·lor /kównsələr, –slər/ *n.* **1** an adviser. **2** a person trained to give guidance on personal problems. **3** a senior officer in the diplomatic service. **4** (also **coun·se·lor-at-law** *pl.* **counselors-at-law**) a lawyer, esp. one who gives advice in law.

▶A **counselor** is someone who gives advice or counsel, especially an attorney. A **councilor** is a member of a council, such as a town or city council. Confusion arises because many *counselors* sit on councils, and *councilors* are often called on to give counsel.

count[1] /kownt/ *v. & n.* •*v.* **1** *tr.* determine the total number or amount of, esp. by assigning successive numbers. **2** *intr.* repeat numbers in ascending order. **3 a** *tr.* (often foll. by *in*) include in one's reckoning or plan (*you can count me in*; *fifteen people, counting the guide*). **b** *intr.* be included in a reckoning or plan. **4** *tr.* consider (a thing or a person) to be (lucky, etc.). **5** *intr.* (often foll. by *for*) have value; matter (*his opinion counts for a great deal*). •*n.* **1 a** the act of counting (*after a count of fifty*). **b** the sum total of a reckoning (*pollen count*). **2** *Law* each charge in an indictment (*guilty on ten counts*). **3** a count of up to ten seconds by a referee when a boxer is knocked down. **4** *Polit.* the act of counting the votes after a general or local election. **5** one of several points under discussion. ▫ **count against** be reckoned to the disadvantage of. **count one's blessings** be grateful for what one has. **count one's chickens before they're hatched** be overoptimistic or hasty in anticipating good fortune. **count the cost** consider the risks before taking action. **count the days** (or **hours**, etc.) be impatient. **count down** recite numbers backward to zero, esp. as part of a rocket-launching procedure. **count on** depend on; rely on; expect confidently. **count out 1** count while taking from a stock. **2** complete a count of ten seconds over (a fallen boxer, etc.), indicating defeat. **3** (in children's games) select (a player) for dismissal or a special role by use of a counting rhyme, etc. **4** *colloq.* exclude from a plan or reckoning (*I'm too tired, count me out*). **count up** find the sum of. **down for the count 1** *Boxing* defeated by being unable to rise within ten seconds. **2 a** defeated or demoralized. **b** sound asleep. **keep count** take note of how many there have been, etc. **lose count** fail to take note of the number, etc. **not counting** excluding from the reckoning.

count[2] /kownt/ *n.* a noble of continental Europe corresponding in rank to a British earl. ▫▫ **count·ship** *n.*

count·a·ble /kówntəbəl/ *adj.* **1** that can be counted. **2** *Gram.* (of a noun) that can form a plural or be used with the indefinite article (e.g., *book*, *kindness*).

count·down /kówntdown/ *n.* **1 a** the act of counting down, esp. at the launching of a rocket, etc. **b** the procedures carried out during this time. **2** the final moments before any significant event.

coun·te·nance /kówntinəns/ *n. & v.* •*n.* **1** a person's face or facial expression (*his inscrutable countenance* *gave little away*. **2** composure. **3** moral support. • *v.tr.* **1** give approval to (an act, etc.). **2** (often foll. by *in*) encourage (a person or a practice).

coun·ter[1] /kówntər/ *n.* **1 a** a long, flat-topped fixture in a store, bank, etc., across which business is conducted. **b** a similar structure used for serving food, etc., in a cafeteria or bar. **2 a** a small disk used for keeping the score, etc., esp. in board games. **b** a token representing a coin. **c** something used in bargaining (*a counter in the struggle for power*). **3** an apparatus used for counting. **4** a person or thing that counts. □ **over the counter 1** (of stock) sold through a broker directly, not on an exchange. **2** by ordinary retail purchase. **under the counter** (esp. of the sale of scarce goods) surreptitiously, esp. illegally.

coun·ter[2] /kówntər/ *v., adv., adj., & n.* • *v.* **1** *tr.* **a** oppose; contradict (*countered our proposal with their own*). **b** meet by a countermove. **2** *intr.* **a** make a countermove. **b** make an opposing statement. **3** *intr. Boxing* give a return blow while parrying. • *adv.* **1** in the opposite direction (*ran counter to the fox*). **2** contrary (*her action was counter to my wishes*). • *adj.* **1** opposed; opposite. **2** duplicate; serving as a check. • *n.* **1** a parry; a countermove. **2** something opposite or opposed. □ **act** (or **go**) **counter to** disobey (instructions, etc.). **run counter to** act contrary to.

counter- /kówntər/ *comb. form* denoting: **1** retaliation, opposition, or rivalry (*counterthreat; countercheck*). **2** opposite direction (*countercurrent*). **3** correspondence, duplication, or substitution (*counterpart; countersign*).

coun·ter·act /kówntərákt/ *v.tr.* **1** hinder or oppose by contrary action. **2** neutralize. □□ **coun·ter·ac·tion** /–ákshən/ *n.* **coun·ter·ac·tive** *adj.*

coun·ter·at·tack *n. & v.* • *n.* /kówntərətak/ an attack in reply to an attack by an enemy or opponent. • *v.tr. & intr.* /kówntərəták/ attack in reply.

coun·ter·at·trac·tion /kówntərətrákshən/ *n.* **1** a rival attraction. **2** the attraction of a contrary tendency.

coun·ter·bal·ance *n. & v.* • *n.* /kówntərbaləns/ **1** a weight balancing another. **2** an argument, force, etc., balancing another. • *v.tr.* /kówntərbáləns/ act as a counterbalance to.

coun·ter·charge *n. & v.* • *n.* /kówntərchaarj/ a charge or accusation in return for one received. • *v.tr.* /kówntərcháarj/ make a countercharge against.

coun·ter·claim *n. & v.* • *n.* /kówntərklaym/ **1** a claim made against another claim. **2** *Law* a claim made by a defendant in a suit against the plaintiff. • *v.tr. & intr.* /kówntərkláym/ make a counterclaim (for).

coun·ter·clock·wise /kówntərklókwīz/ *adv. & adj.* • *adv.* in a curve opposite in direction to the movement of the hands of a clock. • *adj.* moving counterclockwise.

coun·ter·cul·ture /kówntərkulchər/ *n.* a way of life, etc., opposed to that usually considered normal.

coun·ter·es·pi·o·nage /kówntəréspeeənaazh, –nij/ *n.* action taken to frustrate enemy spying.

coun·ter·feit /kówntərfit/ *adj., n., & v.* • *adj.* **1** not genuine. **2** (of a claimant, etc.) pretended. • *n.* a forgery; an imitation. • *v.tr.* **1 a** imitate fraudulently (a coin, handwriting, etc.); forge. **b** make an imitation of. **2** simulate (feelings, etc.) (*counterfeited interest*). **3** resemble closely. □□ **coun·ter·feit·er** *n.*

coun·ter·in·tel·li·gence /kówntərintélijəns/ *n.* = COUNTERESPIONAGE.

coun·ter·mand *v. & n.* • *v.tr.* /kówntərmánd/ **1** *Mil.* **a** revoke (an order or command). **b** recall (forces, etc.) by a contrary order. **2** cancel an order for (goods, etc.). • *n.* /kówntərmand/ an order revoking a previous one.

coun·ter·meas·ure /kówntərmezhər/ *n.* an action taken to counteract a danger, threat, etc.

coun·ter·of·fen·sive /kówntərəfénsiv/ *n. Mil.* an attack made from a defensive position.

coun·ter·pane /kówntərpayn/ *n.* a bedspread.

coun·ter·part /kówntərpaart/ *n.* **1 a** a person or thing extremely like another. **b** a natural complement or equivalent. **2** *Law* one of two copies of a legal document.

coun·ter·point /kówntərpoynt/ *n. & v.* • *n.* **1** *Mus.* **a** the art of writing or playing a melody or melodies in conjunction with another, according to fixed rules. **b** a melody played in conjunction with another. **2** a contrasting argument, plot, idea, etc., used to set off the main element. • *v.tr.* **1** *Mus.* add counterpoint to. **2** set (an argument, plot, etc.) in contrast to (a main element).

coun·ter·poise *n. & v.* • *n.* /kówntərpoyz/ **1** a force, etc., equivalent to another on the opposite side. **2** a state of equilibrium. **3** a counterbalancing weight. • *v.tr.* /kówntərpóyz/ **1** counterbalance. **2** compensate. **3** bring into or keep in equilibrium.

coun·ter·pro·duc·tive /kówntərprədúktiv/ *adj.* having the opposite of the desired effect.

Coun·ter-Ref·or·ma·tion /kówntəréfərmáyshən/ *n. Hist.* the reform of the Roman Catholic Church in the 16th and 17th centuries that took place in response to the Protestant Reformation.

coun·ter·rev·o·lu·tion /kówntərévəlo͞oshən/ *n.* a revolution opposing a former one or reversing its results. □□ **coun·ter·rev·o·lu·tion·ar·y** *adj. & n.* (*pl.* **-ies**).

coun·ter·sign /kówntərsīn/ *v. & n.* • *v.tr.* **1** add a signature to (a document already signed by another). **2** ratify. • *n.* **1** a watchword or password spoken to a person on guard. **2** a mark used for identification, etc. □□ **coun·ter·sig·na·ture** /–sígnəchər/ *n.*

coun·ter·sink /kówntərsingk/ *v.tr.* (*past* and *past part.* **-sunk**) **1** enlarge and bevel (the rim of a hole) so that a screw or bolt can be inserted flush with the surface. **2** sink (a screw, etc.) in such a hole.

coun·ter·ten·or /kówntərtenər/ *n. Mus.* **1 a** the highest adult male singing voice, above tenor. **b** a singer with this voice. **2** a part written for countertenor.

coun·ter·top /kówntərtop/ *n.* a horizontal, flat work surface, as in a kitchen.

coun·ter·vail /kówntərváyl/ *v.* **1** *tr.* counterbalance. **2** *tr. & intr.* (often foll. by *against*) oppose forcefully and usu. successfully.

coun·ter·weight /kówntərwayt/ *n.* a counterbalancing weight.

count·ess /kówntis/ *n.* **1** the wife or widow of a count or an earl. **2** a woman holding the rank of count or earl.

count·ing·house /kówntinghows/ *n.* a place where accounts are kept.

count·less /kówntlis/ *adj.* too many to be counted.

coun·tri·fied /kúntrifīd/ *adj.* (also **coun·try·fied**) often *derog.* rural or rustic, esp. of manners, appearance, etc.

coun·try /kúntree/ *n.* (*pl.* **-tries**) **1 a** the territory of a nation with its own government; a nation. **b** a territory possessing its own language, people, culture, etc. **2** (often *attrib.*) rural districts as opposed to towns and cities or the capital. **3** the land of a person's birth or citizenship. **4 a** a territory, esp. an area of interest or knowledge. **b** a region associated with a particular person, esp. a writer (*Faulkner country*). **5** a national population, esp. as voters (*the country won't stand for it*).

coun·try and west·ern *n.* a form of popular music originating from folk music of the rural South and cowboy music of the West, usu. a mixture of ballads and dance tunes played on fiddle, banjo, guitar, and pedal steel guitar.

coun·try club *n.* a golfing and social club, often in a rural setting.

coun·try·fied var. of COUNTRIFIED.

coun·try·man /kúntreemən/ *n.* (*pl.* **-men**; *fem.* **country-woman**, *pl.* **-women**) **1** a person living in a rural area. **2 a** a person of one's own country or district. **b** (often in *comb.*) a person from a specified country or district (*north-countryman*).

coun·try mu·sic *n.* = COUNTRY AND WESTERN.

coun·try·side /kúntreesīd/ *n.* **1 a** a rural area. **b** rural areas in general. **2** the inhabitants of a rural area.

coun·ty /kówntee/ *n.* & *adj.* • *n.* (*pl.* **-ties**) **1** *US* a political and administrative division of a state. **2** any of the territorial divisions of some countries, forming the chief unit of local administration.

coun·ty seat *n.* the administrative capital of a county.

coup /ko͞o/ *n.* (*pl.* **coups** /ko͞oz/) **1** a notable or successful stroke or move. **2** = COUP D'ÉTAT.

coup de grâce /ko͞o də graás/ *n.* (*pl.* **coups de grâce** *pronunc.* same) a finishing stroke, esp. to kill a wounded animal or person.

coup d'état /ko͞o daytaá/ *n.* (*pl.* **coups d'état** *pronunc.* same) a violent or illegal seizure of power.

coupe /ko͞op/ *n.* (also **coupé** /koopáy/) a two-door car with a hard top.

cou·ple /kúpəl/ *n.* & *v.* • *n.* **1** (usu. foll. by *of*; often as *sing.*) **a** two (*a couple of girls*). **b** about two (*a couple of hours*). **2** (often as *sing.*) **a** a married, engaged, or similar pair. **b** a pair of partners in a dance, a game, etc. **3** (in *pl.*) a pair of joined collars used for holding hounds together. • *v.* **1** *tr.* fasten or link together; connect (esp. railroad car). **2** *tr.* (often foll. by *together*, *with*) associate in thought or speech (*papers coupled their names*). **3** *intr.* copulate. **4** *tr. Physics* connect (oscillators) with a coupling.

cou·pler /kúplər/ *n.* **1** *Mus.* **a** a device in an organ for connecting two manuals, or a manual with pedals, so that they both sound when only one is played. **b** (also **octave coupler**) a similar device for connecting notes with their octaves above or below. **2** anything that connects two things, esp. a transformer used for connecting electric circuits.

cou·plet /kúplit/ *n. Prosody* two successive lines of verse, usu. rhyming and of the same length.

cou·pling /kúpling/ *n.* **1 a** a link connecting a railroad car, etc. **b** a device for connecting parts of machinery. **2** *Physics* a connection between two systems, causing one to oscillate when the other does so. **3** (an act of) sexual intercourse.

cou·pon /ko͞opon, kyo͞o–/ *n.* **1** a form in a newspaper that may be filled in as an application for a purchase, information, etc. **2** a voucher for a discount on a purchase. **3 a** a detachable ticket entitling the holder to a ration of food, clothes, etc., esp. in wartime. **b** a similar ticket entitling the holder to payment, goods, services, etc.

cour·age /kárij, kúr–/ *n.* the ability to disregard fear; bravery. □ **courage of one's convictions** the courage to act on one's beliefs. **lose courage** become less brave. **pluck up** (or **take**) **courage** muster one's courage. **take one's courage in both hands** nerve oneself to a venture.

cou·ra·geous /kəráyjəs/ *adj.* brave; fearless. □□ **cou·ra·geous·ly** *adv.* **cou·ra·geous·ness** *n.*

cour·i·er /ko͞oreeər, kár–, kúr–/ *n.* **1** a person employed, usu. by a travel company, to guide and assist a group of tourists. **2** a special messenger.

course /kawrs/ *n.* & *v.* • *n.* **1** a continuous onward movement or progression. **2 a** a line along which a person or thing moves; a direction taken (*has changed course*; *the course of the winding river*). **b** a correct or intended direction or line of movement. **c** the direction taken by a ship or aircraft. **3 a** the ground on which a race (or other sport involving extensive linear movement) takes place. **b** a series of fences, hurdles, or other obstacles to be crossed in a race, etc. **4 a** a series of lectures, lessons, etc., in a particular subject. **b** a book for such a course (*A Modern French Course*). **5** any of the successive parts of a meal. **6** *Med.* a sequence of medical treatment, etc. (*prescribed a course of antibiotics*). **7** a line of conduct. **8** *Archit.* a continuous horizontal layer of brick, stone, etc., in a building. **9** a channel in which water flows. **10** the pursuit of game (esp. hares) with hounds, esp. greyhounds, by sight rather than scent. • *v.* **1** *intr.* (esp. of liquid) run, esp. fast (*blood coursed through his veins*). **2** *tr.* (also *absol.*) **a** use (hounds) to hunt. **b** pursue (hares, etc.) in hunting. □ **the course of nature** ordinary events or procedure. **in the course of** during. **in the course of time** as time goes by; eventually. **a matter of course** the natural or expected thing. **of course** naturally; as is or was to be expected; admittedly. **on** (or **off**) **course** following (or deviating from) the desired direction or goal. **run** (or **take**) **its course** (esp. of an illness) complete its natural development. □□ **cours·er** *n.* (in sense 2 of *v.*).

court /kawrt/ *n.* & *v.* • *n.* **1** (in full **court of law**) **a** a judge or assembly of judges or other persons acting as a tribunal in civil and criminal cases. **b** = COURTROOM. **2 a** an enclosed quadrangular area for games, which may be open or covered (*tennis court*; *squash court*). **b** an area marked out for lawn tennis, etc. **3 a** a small enclosed street in a town, having a yard surrounded by houses, and adjoining a larger street. **b** the name of a large house, block of apartments, street, etc. (*Grosvenor Court*). **c** a subdivision of a building, usu. a large hall extending to the ceiling with galleries and staircases. **4 a** the establishment, retinue, and courtiers of a sovereign. **b** a sovereign and his or her councilors, constituting a ruling power. **c** a sovereign's residence. **d** an assembly held by a sovereign; a state reception. **5** attention paid to a person whose favor, love, or interest is sought (*paid court to her*). • *v.tr.* **1 a** try to win the affection or favor of (a person). **b** pay amorous attention to (*courting couples*). **2** seek to win (applause, fame, etc.). **3** invite (misfortune) by one's actions (*you are courting disaster*). □ **go to court** take legal action. **in court** appearing as a party or an advocate in a court of law. **out of court 1** (of a plaintiff) not entitled to be heard. **2** before a hearing or judgment can take place.

cour·te·ous /kárteeəs/ *adj.* polite, kind, or considerate. □□ **cour·te·ous·ly** *adv.* **cour·te·ous·ness** *n.*

cour·te·san /káwrtizán/ *n. literary* a prostitute, esp. one with wealthy or upper-class clients.

cour·te·sy /kártisee/ *n.* (*pl.* **-sies**) **1** courteous behavior. **2** a courteous act. □ **by courtesy** by favor, not by right. **by courtesy of** with the formal permission of (a person, etc.).

court·house /káwrthows/ *n.* **1** a building in which a judicial court is held. **2** a building containing the administrative offices of a county.

cour·ti·er /káwrteeər/ *n.* a person who attends or frequents a sovereign's court.

court·ly /káwrtlee/ *adj.* (**courtlier**, **courtliest**) **1** polished or refined in manners. **2** obsequious. **3** punctilious. □□ **court·li·ness** *n.*

court-mar·tial /káwrt maárshəl/ *n.* & *v.* • *n.* (*pl.* **courts-martial**) a judicial court for trying members of the armed services. • *v.tr.* try by a court-martial.

court or·der *n.* a direction issued by a court or a judge, usu. requiring a person to do or not do something.

court re·port·er *n.* a stenographer who makes a verbatim record and transcription of the proceedings in a court of law.

court·room /káwrtro͞om, –ro͝om/ *n.* the place or room in which a court of law meets.

court·ship /káwrtship/ *n.* **1 a** courting with a view to marriage. **b** the courting behavior of male animals, birds, etc. **c** a period of courting. **2** an attempt to gain advantage by flattery, attention, etc.

court·yard /káwrtyaard/ *n.* an area enclosed by walls or buildings, often opening off a street.

cous·cous /ko͞oskoo͞s/ *n.* **1** a type of N. African semolina in granules made from crushed durum wheat. **2** a spicy dish made by steaming or soaking such granules and adding meat, vegetables, or fruit.

cous·in /kúzən/ *n.* **1** (also **first cousin, cous·in-ger·man,** *pl.* **cousins-german**) the child of one's uncle or aunt. **2** (usu. in *pl.*) applied to the people of kindred races or nations (*our British cousins*).

cou·ture /ko͞oto͝or, –tyo͝or/ *n.* the design and manufacture of fashionable clothes; = HAUTE COUTURE.

co·va·lent /kōváylənt/ *adj. Chem.* of or designating chemical bonds formed by the sharing of electrons by two atoms in a molecule. ▫▫ **co·va·lence** *n.* **co·va·len·cy** *n.* **co·va·lent·ly** *adv.*

co·va·lent bond *n. Chem.* a bond formed by sharing of electrons usu. in pairs by two atoms in a molecule.

cove /kōv/ *n.* & *v.* •*n.* **1** a small, esp. sheltered, bay or creek. **2** a sheltered recess. **3** *Archit.* a concave arch or arched molding, esp. one formed at the junction of a wall with a ceiling. •*v.tr. Archit.* provide (a room, ceiling, etc.) with a cove.

cov·en /kúvən/ *n.* an assembly of witches.

cov·e·nant /kúvənənt/ *n.* & *v.* •*n.* **1** an agreement; a contract. **2** *Law* **a** a contract drawn up under a seal, esp. undertaking to make regular payments to a charity. **b** a clause of a covenant. **3** (**Covenant**) *Bibl.* the agreement between God and the Israelites (see ARK OF THE COVENANT). •*v.tr.* & *intr.* agree, esp. by legal covenant. ▫▫ **cov·e·nan·tal** /–nánt'l/ *adj.* **cov·e·nan·tor** *n.* **covenanter** *n.*

cov·er /kúvər/ *v.* & *n.* •*v.tr.* **1 a** (often foll. by *with*) protect or conceal by means of a cloth, lid, etc. **b** prevent the perception or discovery of; conceal (*to cover my embarrassment*). **2 a** extend over; occupy the whole surface of (*covered in dirt; covered with writing*). **b** (often foll. by *with*) strew thickly or thoroughly (*covered the floor with straw*). **c** lie over; be a covering to (*the blanket scarcely covered him*). **3 a** protect; clothe. **b** (as **covered** *adj.*) wearing a hat; having a roof. **4** include; comprise; deal with (*the talk covered recent discoveries*). **5** travel (a specified distance) (*covered sixty miles*). **6** *Journalism* **a** report (events, a meeting, etc.). **b** investigate as a reporter. **7** be enough to defray (expenses, a bill, etc.). **8 a** *refl.* take precautionary measures so as to protect oneself (*had covered myself by saying I might be late*). **b** (*absol.*; foll. by *for*) deputize or stand in for (a colleague, etc.) (*will you cover for me?*). **9** *Mil.* **a** aim a gun, etc., at. **b** (of a fortress, guns, etc.) command (a territory). **c** stand behind (a person in the front rank). **d** protect (an exposed person, etc.) by being able to return fire. •*n.* **1** something that covers or protects, esp.: **a** a lid. **b** the binding of a book. **c** either board of this. **d** an envelope or the wrapping of a mailed package (*under separate cover*). **e** the outer case of a pneumatic tire. **f** (in *pl.*) bedclothes. **2** a hiding place; a shelter. **3** woods or undergrowth sheltering game or covering the ground (see COVERT *n.* 1). **4 a** a pretense; a screen (*under cover of humility*). **b** a spy's pretended identity or activity. **c** *Mil.* a supporting force protecting an advance party from attack. **5** a place setting at table, esp. in a restaurant. ▫ **break cover** (of game or a hunted person) leave a place of shelter, esp. vegetation. **cover one's tracks** conceal evidence of what one has done. **cover up 1** completely cover or conceal. **2** conceal (circumstances, etc., esp. illicitly) (also *absol.*: *refused to cover up for them*). **from cover to cover** from beginning to end of a book, etc. **take cover** use a natural or prepared shelter against an attack.

cov·er·age /kúvərij/ *n.* **1** an area or an amount covered. **2** *Journalism* the amount of press, etc., publicity received by a particular story, person, etc. **3** a risk covered by an insurance policy. **4** an area reached by a particular broadcasting station or advertising medium.

cov·er·all /kúvərawl/ *n.* & *adj.* •*n.* **1** something that covers entirely. **2** (usu. in *pl.*) a full-length protective outer garment often zipped up the front. •*attrib.adj.* covering entirely (*a coverall term*).

cov·er charge *n.* an extra charge levied per head in a restaurant, nightclub, etc.

cov·er girl *n.* a female model whose picture appears on magazine covers, etc.

cov·er·ing /kúvəring/ *n.* something that covers, esp. a bedspread, blanket, etc., or clothing.

cov·er·let /kúvərlit/ *n.* a bedspread.

cov·er let·ter *n.* (also **cov·er·ing let·ter**) an explanatory letter sent with an enclosure.

co·vert /kṓvərt, kú–/ *adj.* & *n.* •*adj.* secret or disguised (*a covert glance; covert operations*). •*n.* **1** a shelter, esp. a thicket hiding game. **2** a feather covering the base of a bird's flight feather. ▫▫ **co·vert·ly** *adv.* **co·vert·ness** *n.*

cov·et /kúvit/ *v.tr.* desire greatly (esp. something belonging to another person). ▫▫ **cov·et·a·ble** *adj.*

cov·et·ous /kúvitəs/ *adj.* (usu. foll. by *of*) **1** greatly desirous (esp. of another person's property). **2** grasping; avaricious. ▫▫ **cov·et·ous·ly** *adv.* **cov·et·ous·ness** *n.*

cov·ey /kúvee/ *n.* (*pl.* **-eys**) **1** a brood of partridges. **2** a small party or group of people or things.

cov·ing *n.* = COVE *n.* 3.

cow[1] /kow/ *n.* **1** a fully grown female of any bovine animal, esp. of the genus *Bos*, used as a source of milk and beef. **2** the female of other large animals, esp. the elephant, whale, and seal. ▫ **till the cows come home** *colloq.* an indefinitely long time.

cow[2] /kow/ *v.tr.* (usu. in *passive*) intimidate or dispirit (*cowed by ill-treatment*).

cow·ard /kówərd/ *n.* a person who is easily frightened or intimidated by danger or pain.

cow·ard·ice /kówərdis/ *n.* a lack of bravery.

cow·ard·ly /kówərdlee/ *adj.* **1** of or like a coward; lacking courage. **2** (of an action) done against one who cannot retaliate. ▫▫ **cow·ard·li·ness** *n.*

cow·bell /kówbel/ *n.* **1** a bell worn around a cow's neck for easy location of the animal. **2** a similar bell used as a percussion instrument.

cow·boy /kówboy/ *n.* **1** (*fem.* **cowgirl**) a person who herds and tends cattle, esp. in the western US. **2** this as a conventional figure in American folklore, esp. in films. **3** *colloq.* an unscrupulous or reckless person in business.

cow·catch·er /kówkachər/ *n.* a peaked metal frame at the front of a locomotive for pushing aside obstacles on the line.

cow·er /kowər/ *v.intr.* **1** crouch or shrink back, esp. in fear; cringe. **2** stand or squat in a bent position.

cow·hand /kówhand/ *n.* = COWBOY 1.

cow·herd /kówhərd/ *n.* a person who tends cattle.

cow·hide /kówhīd/ *n.* **1 a** a cow's hide. **b** leather made from this. **2** a leather whip made from cowhide.

cowl /kowl/ *n.* **1** the hood of a monk's habit. **2** a loose hood. **3** a monk's hooded habit. ▫▫ **cowled** *adj.* (in sense 1).

cow·lick /kówlik/ *n.* a projecting lock of hair.

co·work·er /kṓ-wərkər/ *n.* a person who works in collaboration with another.

cow pars·ley *n.* a tall hedgerow plant, *Anthriscus sylvestris*, having lacelike umbels of flowers resembling Queen Anne's lace.

cow·pea /kówpee/ *n.* **1** a plant of the pea family, *Vigna unguiculata*, grown esp. in the southern US for forage and green manure. **2** its edible seed. (Also called **black-eyed pea**).

cow·poke /kówpōk/ *n.* = COWBOY 1.

cow·pox /kówpoks/ *n.* a disease of cows, of which the virus was formerly used in vaccination against smallpox.

cow·punch·er /kówpunchər/ *n.* = COWBOY 1.

cow·rie /kówree/ *n.* (also **cow·ry**) (*pl.* **-ries**) **1** any gastropod mollusk of the family Cypraeidae, having a smooth, glossy, and usu. brightly colored shell. **2** its shell, esp. used as money in parts of Africa and S. Asia.

cow·shed /kówshed/ *n.* **1** a shed for cattle that are not at pasture. **2** a milking shed.

cow·slip /kówslip/ *n.* **1** a primula, *Primula veris*, with fragrant yellow flowers and growing in pastures. **2** a marsh marigold.

cox /koks/ *n.* & *v.* • *n.* a coxswain, esp. of a racing boat. • *v.* **1** *intr.* act as a cox (*coxed for Harvard*). **2** *tr.* act as cox for (*coxed the winning boat*).

cox·comb /kókskōm/ *n.* an ostentatiously conceited man; a dandy.

cox·swain /kóksən, –swayn/ *n.* & *v.* • *n.* a person who steers and directs the crew, esp. in a rowing boat. • *v.* **1** *intr.* act as a coxswain. **2** *tr.* act as a coxswain of. ▫▫ **cox·swain·ship** *n.*

coy /koy/ *adj.* (**coyer, coyest**) **1** archly or affectedly shy. **2** irritatingly reticent (*always coy about her age*). **3** (esp. of a girl) modest or shy. ▫▫ **coy·ly** *adv.* **coy·ness** *n.*

coy·o·te /kīyṓtee, kíyōt/ *n.* (*pl.* same or **coyotes**) a wolflike wild dog, *Canis latrans*, native to N. America.

coy·pu /kóypōō/ *n.* (*pl.* **coypus**) = NUTRIA 1.

co·zy /kṓzee/ *adj.*, *n.*, & *v.* • *adj.* (**cozier, coziest**) **1** comfortable and warm. **2** *derog.* complacent; self-serving. **3** warm and friendly. • *n.* (*pl.* **-zies**) a cover to keep something hot, esp. a teapot or a boiled egg. • *v.tr.* (**-zies, -zied**) (often foll. by *along*) *colloq.* reassure, esp. deceptively. ▫ **cozy up to** *colloq.* **1** ingratiate oneself with. **2** snuggle up to. ▫▫ **co·zi·ly** *adv.* **co·zi·ness** *n.*

cp. *abbr.* compare.

CPA *abbr.* certified public accountant.

cpd *abbr.* compound.

CPI *abbr.* consumer price index.

Cpl. *abbr.* corporal.

CPR *abbr.* cardiopulmonary resuscitation.

cps *abbr.* (also **c.p.s.**) **1** *Computing* characters per second. **2** cycles per second.

Cpt. *abbr.* captain.

CPU *abbr. Computing* central processing unit.

Cr *symb. Chem.* the element chromium.

crab[1] /krab/ *n.* **1 a** any of numerous ten-footed crustaceans having the first pair of legs modified as pincers. **b** the flesh of a crab, esp. *Cancer pagurus*, as food. **2** (**the Crab**) the zodiacal sign or constellation Cancer. **3** (in full **crab louse**) (often in *pl.*) a parasitic louse, *Phthirus pubis*, infesting hairy parts of the body. ▫▫ **crab·like** *adj.*

crab[2] /krab/ *n.* **1** (in full **crab apple**) a small sour, applelike fruit. **2** (in full **crab tree** or **crab apple tree**) any of several trees bearing this fruit. **3** a sour person.

crab[3] /krab/ *v.* (**crabbed, crabbing**) *colloq.* **1** *tr.* & *intr.* criticize adversely or captiously; grumble. **2** *tr.* spoil (*the mistake crabbed his chances*).

crab·bed /krábid/ *adj.* **1** irritable or morose. **2** (of handwriting) ill-formed and hard to decipher. **3** perverse or cross-grained. **4** difficult to understand. ▫▫ **crab·bed·ly** *adv.* **crab·bed·ness** *n.*

crab·by /krábee/ *adj.* (**crabbier, crabbiest**) = CRABBED 1,3. ▫▫ **crab·bi·ly** *adv.* **crab·bi·ness** *n.*

crab·grass /krábgras/ *n.* a creeping grass infesting lawns.

crack /krak/ *n.*, *v.*, & *adj.* • *n.* **1 a** a sudden sharp or explosive noise (*the crack of a whip*; *a loud crack of thunder*). **b** (in a voice) a sudden harshness or change in pitch. **2** a sharp blow (*a crack on the head*). **3 a** a narrow opening between two surfaces, esp. ones that have broken or been moved apart (*the door opened a tiny crack*). **b** a partial fracture, with the parts still joined (*a hairline crack down the middle of the glass*). **4** *colloq.* a mischievous or malicious remark or aside (*a nasty crack about my age*). **5** *colloq.* an attempt (*I'll have a crack at it*). **6** the exact moment (*the crack of noon*). **7** *sl.* a potent hard crystalline form of cocaine that is inhaled or smoked. • *v.* **1** *tr.* & *intr.* break without a complete separation of the parts (*cracked the window*). **2** *intr.* & *tr.* make or cause to make a sudden sharp or explosive sound. **3** *intr.* & *tr.* break or cause to break with a sudden, sharp sound. **4** *intr.* & *tr.* give way or cause to give way (under torture, etc.); yield. **5** *intr.* (of the voice, esp. of an adolescent boy or a person under strain) become dissonant; break. **6** *tr. colloq.* find a solution to (a problem, code, etc.). **7** *tr.* say (a joke, etc.). **8** *tr. colloq.* hit sharply or hard (*cracked her head on the ceiling*). **9** *tr. Chem.* decompose (heavy oils) to produce lighter hydrocarbons (such as gasoline). **10** *tr.* break (wheat) into coarse pieces. • *attrib.adj. colloq.* excellent; first-rate (*a crack shot*). ▫ **crack a bottle** open a bottle, esp. of wine, and drink it. **crack down on** *colloq.* take severe measures against. **crack up** *colloq.* **1** collapse under strain. **2** burst into laughter. **3** repute (*not all it's cracked up to be*). **get cracking** *colloq.* begin promptly and vigorously. **have a crack at** *colloq.* attempt.

crack·down /krákdown/ *n. colloq.* severe measures (esp. against lawbreakers, etc.).

cracked /krakt/ *adj.* **1** having cracks. **2** (*predic.*) *sl.* crazy.

cracked wheat *n.* grains of wheat that have been crushed into small pieces.

crack·er /krákər/ *n.* **1** a thin, dry biscuit often eaten with cheese. **2** a firework exploding with a sharp noise. **3** (usu. in *pl.*) an instrument for cracking (*nutcrackers*). **4** a paper cylinder both ends of which are pulled at Christmas, etc., making a sharp noise and releasing a small toy, etc. **5** *offens.* = POOR WHITE.

crack·er-bar·rel *adj.* (of philosophy, etc.) unsophisticated.

crack·er·jack /krákərjak/ *adj. sl.* exceptionally fine or expert.

crack·ers /krákərz/ *predic.adj. sl.* crazy.

crack·le /krákəl/ *v.* & *n.* • *v.intr.* make a repeated slight cracking sound (*radio crackled*; *fire was crackling*). • *n.* **1** such a sound. **2 a** paintwork, china, or glass decorated with a pattern of minute surface cracks. **b** the smooth surface of such paintwork, etc. ▫▫ **crack·ly** *adj.*

crack·ling /krákling/ *n.* the crisp skin of roast pork.

crack·pot /krákpot/ *n.* & *adj. sl.* • *n.* an eccentric or impractical person. • *adj.* mad; unworkable (*a crackpot scheme*).

-cracy /krəsee/ *comb. form* denoting a particular form of government, rule, or influence (*aristocracy*; *bureaucracy*).

cra·dle /kráyd'l/ *n.* & *v.* • *n.* **1 a** a child's bed, esp. one mounted on rockers. **b** a place in which a thing begins, esp. a civilization, etc., or is nurtured in its infancy (*cradle of democracy*). **2** a framework resembling a cradle, esp.: **a** that on which a ship, a boat, etc., rests during construction or repairs. **b** that on which a worker is suspended to work on a ceiling, a ship, the vertical side of a building, etc. **c** the part of a telephone on which the receiver rests when not in use. • *v.tr.* **1** contain or shelter as if in a cradle (*cradled his head in her arms*). **2** place in a cradle. □ **from the cradle** from infancy. **from the cradle to the grave** from infancy till death.

cra·dle-rob·ber *n. sl.* a person amorously attached to a much younger person.

craft /kraft/ *n.* & *v.* • *n.* **1** skill, esp. in practical arts. **2 a** (esp. in *comb.*) a trade or an art (*statecraft; handicraft; priestcraft; the craft of pottery*). **b** the members of a craft. **3** (*pl.* **craft**) **a** a boat or vessel. **b** an aircraft or spacecraft. **4** cunning or deceit. • *v.tr.* make in a skillful way(*crafted a poem*).

crafts·man /kráftsmən/ *n.* (*pl.* **-men**; *fem.* **craftswoman**, *pl.* **-women**) **1** a skilled worker. **2** a person who practices a handicraft. □□ **crafts·man·ship** *n.*

craft·y /kráftee/ *adj.* (**craftier, craftiest**) cunning; artful; wily. □□ **craft·i·ly** *adv.* **craft·i·ness** *n.*

crag /krag/ *n.* a steep or rugged rock.

crag·gy /krágee/ *adj.* (**craggier, craggiest**) **1** (esp. of a person's face) rugged; rough-textured. **2** (of a landscape) having crags. □□ **crag·gi·ly** *adv.* **crag·gi·ness** *n.*

cram /kram/ *v.* (**crammed, cramming**) **1** *tr.* **a** fill to bursting; stuff (*the room was crammed*). **b** (foll. by *in*, *into*) force (a thing) into (*cram the sandwiches into the bag*). **2** *tr.* & *intr.* prepare for an examination by intensive study. **3** *tr.* (often foll. by *with*) feed (poultry, etc.) to excess. **4** *tr.* & *intr. colloq.* eat greedily. □ **cram in** push in to bursting point (*crammed in another five minutes' work*).

cramp /kramp/ *n.* & *v.* • *n.* **1 a** a painful involuntary contraction of a muscle or muscles. **b** = WRITER'S CRAMP. **2** (also **cramp i·ron**) a metal bar with bent ends for holding masonry, etc., together. **3** a portable tool for holding two planks, etc., together; a clamp. **4** a restraint. • *v.tr.* **1** affect with cramp. **2** confine narrowly. **3** restrict (energies, etc.). **4** (as **cramped** *adj.*) **a** (of handwriting) small and difficult to read. **b** (of a room, etc.) uncomfortably crowded; lacking space. **5** fasten with a cramp. □ **cramp a person's style** prevent a person from acting freely or naturally. **cramp up** confine narrowly.

cram·pon /krámpon/ *n.* (also **cram·poon** /–pōōn/) (usu. in *pl.*) **1** an iron plate with spikes fixed to a boot for walking on ice, climbing, etc. **2** a metal hook for lifting timber, rock, etc.; a grappling iron.

cran·ber·ry /kránberee/ *n.* (*pl.* **-ries**) **1** any evergreen shrub of the genus *Vaccinium*, esp. *V. macrocarpon* of America and *V. oxycoccos* of Europe, yielding small, red, acid berries. **2** a berry from this used in cooking.

crane /krayn/ *n.* & *v.* • *n.* **1** a machine for moving heavy objects, usu. by suspending them from a projecting beam. **2** any tall wading bird of the family Gruidae, with long legs, long neck, and straight bill. **3** a moving platform supporting a television camera or movie camera. • *v.tr.* **1** (also *absol.*) stretch out (one's neck) in order to see something. **2** *tr.* move (an object) by a crane.

crane fly *n.* (*pl.* **flies**) any fly of the family Tipulidae, having two wings and long legs, resembling a large mosquito.

cra·ni·al /kráyneeəl/ *adj.* of or relating to the skull.

cranio- /kráyneeō/ *comb. form* cranium.

cra·ni·ol·o·gy /kráyneeóləjee/ *n.* the scientific study of the shape and size of the human skull. □□ **cra·ni·o·log·i·cal** /–neeəlójikəl/ *adj.* **cra·ni·ol·o·gist** *n.*

cra·ni·om·e·try /kráyneeómitree/ *n.* the scientific measurement of skulls. □□ **cra·ni·o·met·ric** /–neeəmétrik/ *adj.*

cra·ni·ot·o·my /kráyneeótəmee/ *n.* (*pl.* **-mies**) **1** surgical removal of a portion of the skull. **2** surgical perforation of the skull of a dead fetus to ease delivery.

cra·ni·um /kráyneeəm/ *n.* (*pl.* **craniums** or **crania** /–neeə/) **1** the skull. **2** the part of the skeleton that encloses the brain.

crank[1] /krangk/ *n.* & *v.* • *n.* **1** part of an axle or shaft bent at right angles for interconverting reciprocal and circular motion. **2** an elbow-shaped connection in bell hanging. • *v.tr.* **1** cause to move by means of a crank. **2 a** bend into a crank shape. **b** furnish or fasten with a crank. □ **crank up 1** start (a car engine) by turning a crank. **2** *sl.* increase (speed, etc.) by intensive effort.

crank[2] /krangk/ *n.* **1** an eccentric person. **2** a bad-tempered person. □□ **crank·y** /krángkee/ *adj.* (**crankier, crankiest**). **crank·i·ly** *adv.* **crank·i·ness** *n.*

crank[3] /krangk/ *adj. Naut.* liable to capsize.

crank·case /krángk-kays/ *n.* a case enclosing a crankshaft.

crank·shaft /krángkshaft/ *n.* a shaft driven by a crank (see CRANK[1] *n.* 1).

cran·ny /kránee/ *n.* (*pl.* **-nies**) a chink; a crevice. □□ **cran·nied** /–need/ *adj.*

crap /krap/ *n.* & *v. coarse sl.* • *n.* **1** (often as *int.*) nonsense; rubbish. **2** feces. • *v.intr.* (**crapped, crapping**) defecate.

▶Usually considered a taboo word. □ **crap out 1** be unsuccessful. **2** withdraw from a game, etc. □□ **crap·py** /krápee/ *adj.* (**crappier, crappiest**).

crape /krayp/ *n.* **1** crepe, usu. of black silk or imitation silk, formerly used for mourning clothes. **2** a band of this formerly worn as a sign of mourning. □□ **crap·y** *adj.*

craps /kraps/ *n.pl.* a gambling game played with dice. □ **shoot craps** play craps.

crap·shoot /krápshōōt/ *n. sl.* a venture marked by uncertainty and risk.

crap·u·lent /krápyələnt/ *adj.* **1** given to indulging in alcohol. **2** resulting from drunkenness. **3 a** drunk. **b** suffering from the effects of drunkenness. □□ **crap·u·lence** /–ləns/ *n.* **crap·u·lous** *adj.*

crash /krash/ *v.*, *n.*, & *adv.* • *v.* **1** *intr.* & *tr.* make or cause to make a loud smashing noise (*the cymbals crashed*). **2** *tr.* & *intr.* throw, drive, move, or fall with a loud smashing noise. **3** *intr.* & *tr.* **a** collide or cause (a vehicle) to collide violently with another vehicle, obstacle, etc. **b** fall or cause (an aircraft) to fall violently on to the land or the sea. **4** *intr.* (usu. foll. by *into*) collide violently (*crashed into the window*). **5** *intr.* undergo financial ruin. **6** *tr. colloq.* enter without permission (*crashed the party*). **7** *intr. colloq.* be heavily defeated (*crashed to a 4– 0 defeat*). **8** *intr. Computing* (of a machine or system) fail suddenly. **9** *intr.* (often foll. by *out*) *sl.* sleep for a night, esp. in an improvised setting. • *n.* **1 a** a loud and sudden smashing noise. **b** a breakage (esp. of china, etc.). **2 a** a violent collision, esp. of one vehicle with another or with an object. **b** the violent fall of an aircraft on to the land or sea. **3** ruin, esp. financial. **4** *Computing* a sudden failure which puts a system out of action. **5** (*attrib.*) done rapidly or urgently (*a crash course in first aid*). • *adv.* with a crash (*the window went crash*).

crash-dive *v.* & *n.* • *v.* **1** *intr.* **a** (of a submarine or its pilot) dive hastily and steeply in an emergency. **b** (of an aircraft or pilot) dive and crash. **2** *tr.* cause to crash-dive. • *n.* such a dive.

crash hel·met *n.* a helmet worn to protect the head in a crash.

crash-land *v.* **1** *intr.* (of an aircraft or its pilot) land hurriedly with a crash, usu. without lowering the undercarriage. **2** *tr.* cause (an aircraft) to crash-land. ▫▫ **crash land·ing** *n.*

crass /kras/ *adj.* **1** grossly stupid. **2** gross (*crass stupidity*). ▫▫ **cras·si·tude** *n.* **crass·ly** *adv.* **crass·ness** *n.*

-crat /krat/ *comb. form* a member or supporter of a particular form of government or rule (*autocrat; democrat*).

crate /krayt/ *n.* & *v.* •*n.* **1** a large wickerwork basket or slatted wooden case, etc., for packing esp. fragile goods for transportation. **2** *sl.* an old airplane or other vehicle. •*v.tr.* pack in a crate. ▫▫ **crate·ful** *n.* (*pl.* **-fuls**).

cra·ter /kráytər/ *n.* & *v.* •*n.* **1** the mouth of a volcano. **2** a bowl-shaped cavity, esp. that made by an explosion. **3** *Astron.* a hollow with a raised rim on the surface of a planet or moon, caused by impact. •*v.tr.* form a crater in. ▫▫ **cra·ter·ous** *adj.*

cra·vat /krəvát/ *n.* a scarf worn by men inside an open-necked shirt. ▫▫ **cra·vat·ted** *adj.*

cravat mid-17th century: from French *cravate*, from *Cravate* 'Croat' (from German *Krabat*, from Croat *Hrvat*), because of the scarf worn by Croatian mercenaries in France.

crave /krayv/ *v.* **1** *tr.* **a** long for (*craved affection*). **b** beg for (*craves a blessing*). **2** *intr.* (foll. by *for*) long for; beg for (*craved for comfort*). ▫▫ **crav·er** *n.*

cra·ven /kráyvən/ *adj.* & *n.* •*adj.* (of a person, behavior, etc.) cowardly; abject. •*n.* a cowardly person. ▫▫ **cra·ven·ly** *adv.* **cra·ven·ness** *n.*

crav·ing /kráyving/ *n.* (usu. foll. by *for*) a strong desire or longing.

craw /kraw/ *n. Zool.* the crop of a bird or insect. ▫ **stick in one's craw** be unacceptable.

crawl /krawl/ *v.* & *n.* •*v.intr.* **1** move slowly, esp. on hands and knees. **2** (of a snake, etc.) move slowly with the body close to the ground, etc. **3** walk or move slowly (*the train crawled into the station*). **4** (often foll. by *to*) *colloq.* behave obsequiously or ingratiatingly in the hope of advantage. **5** (often foll. by *with*) be covered or filled with crawling or moving things or people. **6** (esp. of the skin) feel a creepy sensation. **7** swim with a crawl stroke. •*n.* **1** an act of crawling. **2** a slow rate of movement. **3** a high-speed swimming stroke with alternate overarm movements and rapid straight-legged kicks. ▫▫ **crawl·y** *adj.* (in senses 5, 6 of *v.*).

crawl·er /kráwlər/ *n.* **1** (usu. in *pl.*) a baby's overall for crawling in. **2** anything that crawls, esp. an insect. **3** *sl.* a person who behaves obsequiously in the hope of advantage.

cray·fish /kráyfish/ *n.* (also **craw·dad** or **craw·fish**) (*pl.* same) **1** a small, lobsterlike freshwater crustacean. **2** a large marine spiny lobster.

cray·on /kráyon/ *n.* & *v.* •*n.* **1** a stick or pencil of colored chalk, wax, etc., used for drawing. **2** a drawing made with this. •*v.tr.* draw with crayons.

craze /krayz/ *v.* & *n.* •*v.* **1** *tr.* (usu. as **crazed** *adj.*) make insane (*crazed with grief*). **2 a** *tr.* produce fine surface cracks on (pottery glaze, etc.). **b** *intr.* develop such cracks. •*n.* **1 a** a usu. temporary enthusiasm (*a craze for hula hoops*). **b** the object of this. **2** an insane fancy or condition.

cra·zy /kráyzee/ *adj.* (**crazier, craziest**) **1** *colloq.* insane or mad; foolish. **2** *colloq.* (usu. foll. by *about*) extremely enthusiastic. **3** *sl.* exciting; unrestrained. **4** (*attrib.*) (of paving, etc.) made of irregular pieces fitted together. ▫ **like crazy** *colloq.* = *like mad* (see MAD). ▫▫ **cra·zi·ly** *adv.* **cra·zi·ness** *n.*

creak /kreek/ *n.* & *v.* •*n.* a harsh scraping or squeaking sound. •*v.intr.* **1** make a creak. **2 a** move with a creaking noise. **b** move stiffly and awkwardly. **c** show weakness under strain. ▫▫ **creak·ing·ly** *adv.*

creak·y /kréekee/ *adj.* (**creakier, creakiest**) **1** liable to creak. **2** stiff or frail. ▫▫ **creak·i·ly** *adv.* **creak·i·ness** *n.*

cream /kreem/ *n.*, *v.*, & *adj.* •*n.* **1 a** the fatty content of milk. **b** this eaten (often whipped) with a dessert, as a cake filling, etc. (*strawberries and cream; cream cake*). **2** the part of a liquid that gathers at the top. **3** (usu. prec. by *the*) the best or choicest part of something. **4** a creamlike preparation, esp. a cosmetic (*hand cream*). **5** a very pale yellow or off-white color. **6 a** a dish like or made with cream. **b** a soup or sauce containing milk or cream. **c** a full-bodied, mellow, sweet sherry. **d** a chocolate-covered usu. fruit-flavored fondant confection. •*v.* **1** *tr.* (usu. foll. by *off*) **a** take the cream from (milk). **b** take the best or a specified part from. **2** *tr.* work (butter, etc.) to a creamy consistency. **3** *tr.* treat (the skin, etc.) with cosmetic cream. **4** *tr.* add cream to (coffee, etc.). **5** *intr.* (of milk or any other liquid) form a cream or scum. **6** *tr. colloq.* defeat soundly or by a wide margin (esp. in a sporting contest). •*adj.* pale yellow; off-white.

cream cheese *n.* a soft, rich cheese made from unskimmed milk and cream.

cream·er /kréemər/ *n.* **1** a flat dish used for skimming the cream off milk. **2** a machine used for separating cream from milk. **3** a small pitcher for cream.

cream·er·y /kréeməree/ *n.* (*pl.* **-ies**) **1** a factory producing butter and cheese. **2** a dairy.

cream of tar·tar *n.* crystallized potassium hydrogen tartrate, used in medicine, baking powder, etc.

cream puff *n.* **1** a cake made of puff pastry filled with custard or whipped cream. **2** *colloq.* an ineffectual or effeminate person. **3** a second-hand car or other item maintained in excellent condition.

cream·y /kréemee/ *adj.* (**creamier, creamiest**) **1** like cream in consistency or color. **2** rich in cream. ▫▫ **cream·i·ly** *adv.* **cream·i·ness** *n.*

crease /krees/ *n.* & *v.* •*n.* **1 a** a line in paper, etc., caused by folding. **b** a fold or wrinkle. **2** an area near the goal in ice hockey or lacrosse into which the puck or the ball must precede the players. •*v.* **1** *tr.* make creases in (material). **2** *intr.* become creased (*linen creases badly*).

cre·ate /kree-áyt/ *v.* **1** *tr.* **a** bring into existence (*poverty creates resentment*). **b** (of a person or persons) make or cause (*create a diversion*). **2** *tr.* originate (*an actor creates a part*). **3** *tr.* invest (a person) with a rank (*created him a lord*). ▫▫ **cre·at·a·ble** *adj.*

cre·a·tion /kree-áyshən/ *n.* **1 a** the act of creating. **b** an instance of this. **2 a** (usu. **the Creation**) the creating of the universe regarded as an act of God. **b** (usu. **Creation**) everything so created; the universe. **3** a product of human intelligence, esp. of imaginative thought or artistic ability. **4 a** the act of investing with a title or rank. **b** an instance of this.

cre·a·tion·ism /kree-áyshənizəm/ *n. Theol.* a theory attributing all matter, biological species, etc., to separate acts of creation, rather than to evolution. ▫▫ **cre·a·tion·ist** *n.*

cre·a·tive /kree-áytiv/ *adj.* **1** inventive and imaginative. **2** creating or able to create. ▫▫ **cre·a·tive·ly** *adv.* **cre·a·tive·ness** *n.* **cre·a·tiv·i·ty** /–aytívitee, –ətív–/ *n.*

cre·a·tor /kree-áytər/ *n.* **1** a person who creates. **2** (as **the Creator**) God.

crea·ture /kréechər/ *n.* **1 a** an animal, as distinct from a human being. **b** any living being (*we are all fellow creatures on this planet*). **c** a fictional or imaginary being (*a creature from outer space*). **2** a person of a specified kind (*poor creature*). **3** a person owing status to and obsequiously subservient to another. **4** anything created. ▫▫ **crea·ture·ly** *adj.*

crea·ture com·forts *n.pl.* material comforts such as good food, warmth, etc.

crea·ture of hab·it *n.* a person set in an unvarying routine.

crèche /kresh/ *n.* a representation of a Nativity scene.
cred•al see CREED.
cre•dence /kreéd'ns/ *n.* belief. □ **give credence to** believe.
cre•den•tial /kridénshəl/ *n.* (usu. in *pl.*) **1** evidence of a person's achievements or trustworthiness, usu. in the form of certificates, references, etc. **2** a letter or letters of introduction.
cre•den•za /kridénzə/ *n.* a sideboard or cupboard.
cred•i•bil•i•ty /krédibílitee/ *n.* **1** the condition of being credible or believable. **2** reputation; status.
cred•i•bil•i•ty gap *n.* an apparent difference between what is said and what is true.
cred•i•ble /krédibəl/ *adj.* **1** (of a person or statement) believable or worthy of belief. **2** (of a threat, etc.) convincing. □□ **cred•i•bly** *adv.*
cred•it /krédit/ *n.* & *v.* •*n.* **1** (usu. of a person) a source of honor, pride, etc. (*a credit to the school*). **2** the acknowledgment of merit (*must give her credit*). **3** a good reputation (*his credit stands high*). **4 a** belief or trust (*I place credit in that*). **b** something believable or trustworthy (*that statement has credit*). **5 a** a person's financial standing; the sum of money at a person's disposal in a bank, etc. **b** the power to obtain goods, etc., before payment. **6** (usu. in *pl.*) an acknowledgment of a contributor's services to a film, etc. **7** a reputation for solvency and honesty in business. **8 a** (in bookkeeping) the acknowledgment of being paid by an entry on the credit side of an account. **b** the sum entered. **c** the credit side of an account. **9** a certification indicating that a student has completed a course. •*v.tr.* **1** believe (*cannot credit it*). **2** (usu. foll. by *to, with*) **a** enter on the credit side of an account. **b** ascribe a good quality or achievement to (*he was credited with the improved sales*). □ **credit a person with** ascribe (a good quality) to a person. **do credit to a person** or **do a person credit** enhance the reputation of a person. **get credit for** be given credit for. **give a person credit for 1** enter (a sum) to a person's credit. **2** ascribe (a good quality) to a person. **give credit to** believe. **on credit** with an arrangement to pay later. **to one's credit** in one's praise or commendation.
cred•it•a•ble /kréditəbəl/ *adj.* (often foll. by *to*) bringing credit or honor. □□ **cred•it•a•bil•i•ty** *n.* **cred•it•a•bly** *adv.*
cred•it card *n.* a card from a bank, etc., authorizing the obtaining of goods on credit.
cred•i•tor /kréditər/ *n.* **1** a person to whom a debt is owing (cf. DEBTOR). **2** a person or company that gives credit for money or goods.
cred•it un•ion *n.* a cooperative association that makes low-interest loans to its members.
cre•do /kreéydō, kráy–/ *n.* (*pl.* **-dos**) a statement of belief; a creed.
cred•u•lous /kréjələs/ *adj.* **1** too ready to believe; gullible. **2** (of behavior) showing such gullibility. □□ **cre•du•li•ty** /kridóolitee, –dyóo–/ *n.* **cred•u•lous•ly** *adv.* ▶See note at INCREDIBLE.
Cree /kree/ *n.* & *adj.* •*n.* (*pl.* same or **Crees**) **1 a** a N. American people of E. and central Canada. **b** a member of this people. **2** the language of this people. •*adj.* of or relating to the Crees or their language.
creed /kreed/ *n.* **1** a set of principles or opinions, esp. as a philosophy of life (*his creed is moderation in everything*). **2** (also **the Creed**) a brief formal summary of Christian belief. □□ **creed•al** /kreéd'l/ *adj.* **cred•al** *adj.*
Creek /kreek/ *n.* **1 a** a confederacy of N. American peoples that formerly occupied much of Alabama and Georgia. **b** a member of these peoples. **2** the language used by these peoples.
creek /kreek, krik/ *n. Regional* a stream. □ **up shit creek** *coarse sl.* = *up the creek.* **up the creek** *sl.* in difficulties.
creel /kreel/ *n.* a large wicker basket for fish.
creep /kreep/ *v.* & *n.* •*v.intr.* (*past* and *past part.* **crept** /krept/) **1** move with the body prone and close to the ground. **2** (often foll. by *in, out, up,* etc.) come, go, or move slowly and stealthily or timidly. **3** enter slowly (into a person's affections, awareness, etc.) (*a feeling crept over her*). **4** *colloq.* act obsequiously in the hope of advancement. **5** (of a plant) grow along the ground or up a wall. **6** (as **creeping** *adj.*) developing slowly and steadily (*creeping inflation*). **7** (of the flesh) feel as if insects, etc., were creeping over it, as a result of fear, etc. •*n.* **1 a** the act of creeping. **b** an instance of this. **2** (in *pl.*; prec. by *the*) *colloq.* a feeling of revulsion or fear (*gives me the creeps*). **3** *sl.* an unpleasant person. □ **creep up on** approach (a person) stealthily or unnoticed.
creep•er /kreépər/ *n.* **1** *Bot.* any climbing or creeping plant. **2** any bird that climbs, esp. a tree creeper. **3** *sl.* a soft-soled shoe.
creep•y /kreépee/ *adj.* (**creepier, creepiest**) **1** *colloq.* having or producing a creeping of the flesh (*a creepy movie*). **2** given to creeping. □□ **creep•i•ly** *adv.* **creep•i•ness** *n.*
creep•y-crawl•y /kreépeekráwlee/ *n.* & *adj. colloq.* •*n.* (*pl.* **-ies**) an insect, worm, etc. •*adj.* creeping and crawling.
cre•mate /kreémayt, krimáyt/ *v.tr.* consume (a corpse, etc.) by fire. □□ **cre•ma•tion** /krimáyshən/ *n.* **cre•ma•tor** *n.*
cre•ma•to•ri•um /kreémətáwreeəm/ *n.* (*pl.* **crematoriums** or **crematoria** /–reeə/) a place for cremating corpses in a furnace.
cre•ma•to•ry /kreémətawree, krém–/ *adj.* & *n.* •*adj.* of or relating to cremation. •*n.* (*pl.* **-ries**) = CREMATORIUM.
crème /krem/ *n.* **1** = CREAM *n.* 6a. **2** a name for various creamy liqueurs (*crème de cassis*).
crème de la crème /krem də laa krém/ *n.* the best part; the elite.
crème de menthe /krem də maánt, ménth, mínt/ *n.* a peppermint-flavored liqueur.
cren•el•ate /krénəlayt/ *v.tr.* provide (a tower, etc.) with battlements or loopholes. □□ **cren•el•a•tion** /–láyshən/ *n.*
Cre•ole /kreé-ōl/ *n.* & *adj.* •*n.* **1 a** a descendant of European (esp. Spanish) settlers in the W. Indies or Central or S. America. **b** a white descendant of French settlers, esp. in Louisiana. **c** a person of mixed European and black descent. **2** a mother tongue formed from the contact of a European language (esp. English, French, or Portuguese) with another (esp. African) language. •*adj.* **1** of or relating to a Creole or Creoles. **2** (usu. **creole**) of Creole origin or production (*creole cooking*).
cre•o•sote /kreéəsōt/ *n.* & *v.* •*n.* **1** (in full **creosote oil**) a dark-brown oil distilled from coal tar, used as a wood preservative. **2** a colorless oily fluid distilled from wood tar, used as an antiseptic. •*v.tr.* treat with creosote.
crepe /krayp/ *n.* (also **crêpe**) **1** a fine, often gauzelike fabric with a wrinkled surface. **2** a thin pancake, usu. with a savory or sweet filling. **3** (also **crepe rub•ber**) a very hard-wearing wrinkled sheet rubber used for the soles of shoes, etc. □□ **crep•ey** *adj.* **crep•y** *adj.*
crêpe pa•per *n.* thin crinkled paper.
crêpe su•zette /sóozét/ (also **crêpe Su•zette**) a small dessert pancake flamed in alcohol at the table.
crept *past* and *past part.* of CREEP.
cre•pus•cu•lar /kripúskyələr/ *adj.* **1 a** of twilight. **b** dim. **2** *Zool.* appearing or active in twilight.
cre•scen•do /krishéndō/ *n., adv., adj.,* & *v.* •*n.* (*pl.* **-dos** or **crescendi** /–dee/) **1** *Mus.* a passage gradually

increasing in loudness. **2 a** progress toward a climax (*a crescendo of emotions*). **b** *disp.* a climax. • *adv. & adj. Mus.* with a gradual increase in loudness. • *v.intr.* (**-does, -doed**) increase gradually in loudness or intensity.

cres·cent /krésənt/ *n.* **1** the curved sickle shape of the waxing or waning moon. **2** anything of this shape. **3 a** the crescent-shaped emblem of Islam or Turkey. **b** (**the Crescent**) the world or power of Islam.

cress /kres/ *n.* any of various cruciferous plants usu. with pungent edible leaves.

crest /krest/ *n. & v.* • *n.* **1 a** a comb or tuft on a bird's or animal's head. **b** something resembling this. **c** a helmet; the top of a helmet. **2** the top of a mountain, wave, etc. **3** *Heraldry* **a** a device above the shield and helmet of a coat of arms. **b** such a device reproduced on writing paper, etc. **4 a** a line along the top of the neck of some animals. **b** the hair growing from this; a mane. **5** *Anat.* a ridge along the surface of a bone. • *v.* **1** *tr.* reach the crest of (a hill, wave, etc.). **2** *tr.* **a** provide with a crest. **b** serve as a crest to. **3** *intr.* (of a wave) form into a crest. □ **on the crest of a wave** at the most favorable moment in one's progress. □□ **crest·ed** *adj.* (also in *comb.*). **crest·less** *adj.*

crest·fal·len /kréstfawlən/ *adj.* **1** dejected. **2** with a fallen or drooping crest.

cre·ta·ceous /kritáyshəs/ *adj. & n.* • *adj.* **1** of the nature of chalk. **2** (**Cretaceous**) *Geol.* of or relating to the last period of the Mesozoic era. • *n. Geol.* this era or system.

cre·tin /kreétin/ *n.* **1** a person who is deformed and mentally retarded as the result of a thyroid deficiency. **2** *colloq.* a stupid person. □□ **cre·tin·ism** *n.* **cre·tin·ize** *v.tr.* **cre·tin·ous** *adj.*

cre·vasse /krəvás/ *n.* **1** a deep open crack, esp. in a glacier. **2** a breach in a river levee.

crev·ice /krévis/ *n.* a narrow opening or fissure in a rock, etc.

crew /kroo/ *n. & v.* • *n.* (often treated as *pl.*) **1 a** a body of people manning a ship, aircraft, train, etc. **b** such a body as distinguished from the captain or officers. **c** a body of people working together. **2** *colloq.* a company of people (*a motley crew*). • *v.* **1** *tr.* supply or act as a crew or member of a crew for. **2** *intr.* act as a crew or member of a crew.

crew cut *n.* a very short haircut.

crew·el /króoəl/ *n.* a thin worsted yarn used for tapestry and embroidery.

crew neck *n.* a close-fitting round neckline, esp. on a sweater.

crib /krib/ *n. & v.* • *n.* **1** a child's bed with barred or latticed sides. **2** a barred rack for animal fodder. **3** *colloq.* **a** a translation of a text for the use of students. **b** plagiarized work, etc. **4** a small house or cottage. **5** a framework lining the shaft of a mine. **6** *colloq.* **a** cribbage. **b** a set of cards given to the dealer at cribbage by all the players. • *v.tr.* (also *absol.*) (**cribbed, cribbing**) **1** *colloq.* copy (another person's work) unfairly or without acknowledgment. **2** confine in a small space. **3** *colloq.* pilfer; steal. □□ **crib·ber** *n.*

crib·bage /kríbij/ *n.* a card game for two, three, or four players.

crib death *n.* = SUDDEN INFANT DEATH SYNDROME.

crick /krik/ *n. & v.* • *n.* a sudden painful stiffness in the neck, etc. • *v.tr.* produce a crick in.

crick·et[1] /kríkit/ *n. & v.* • *n.* a game played on a grass field with two teams of 11 players taking turns to bowl at a wicket defended by a batting player of the other team. • *v.intr.* play cricket. □□ **crick·et·er** *n.*

crick·et[2] /kríkit/ *n.* any of various grasshopperlike insects of the order Orthoptera.

cried *past* and *past part.* of CRY.

cri·er /kríər/ *n.* (also **cry·er**) **1** a person who cries. **2** an officer who makes public announcements in a court of justice.

crime /krīm/ *n.* **1 a** an offense punishable by law. **b** illegal acts as a whole (*resorted to crime*). **2** an evil act (*a crime against humanity*). **3** *colloq.* a shameful act (*a crime to tease them*).

crime of pas·sion *n.* a crime, esp. murder, committed in a fit of sexual jealousy.

crime wave *n.* a sudden increase in crime.

crim·i·nal /kríminəl/ *n. & adj.* • *n.* a person who has committed a crime. • *adj.* **1** of, involving, or concerning crime (*criminal records*). **2** having committed a crime. **3** *Law* relating to or expert in criminal law (*criminal code; criminal lawyer*). **4** *colloq.* scandalous; deplorable. □□ **crim·i·nal·i·ty** *n.* /–nálitee/ **crim·i·nal·ly** *adv.*

crim·i·nal law *n.* law concerned with punishment of offenders (opp. CIVIL LAW).

crim·i·nol·o·gy /kríminóləjee/ *n.* the scientific study of crime. □□ **crim·i·no·log·i·cal** /–nəlójikəl/ *adj.* **crim·i·nol·o·gist** *n.*

crimp /krimp/ *v. & n.* • *v.tr.* **1** compress into small folds or ridges; frill. **2** corrugate. **3** make waves in (the hair) with a hot iron. • *n.* a crimped thing or form. □ **put a crimp in** *sl.* thwart; interfere with. □□ **crimp·er** *n.* **crimp·y** *adj.* **crimp·i·ness** *n.*

crim·son /krímzən/ *adj., n., & v.* • *adj.* of a rich, deep red inclining to purple. • *n.* this color. • *v.tr. & intr.* make or become crimson.

cringe /krinj/ *v. & n.* • *v.intr.* **1** shrink back in fear; cower. **2** (often foll. by *to*) behave obsequiously. • *n.* the act or an instance of cringing. □□ **cring·er** *n.*

crin·kle /kríngkəl/ *n. & v.* • *n.* a wrinkle or crease in paper, cloth, etc. • *v.* **1** *intr.* form crinkles. **2** *tr.* form crinkles in. □□ **crin·kly** *adj.*

crin·o·line /krínəlin/ *n.* **1** a stiffened or hooped petticoat formerly worn to make a long skirt stand out. **2** a stiff fabric of horsehair, etc., used for linings, hats, etc.

crip·ple /krípəl/ *n. & v.* • *n.* usu. *offens.* a person who is permanently lame. • *v.tr.* **1** cause someone to become unable to move or walk properly (*crippled by polio*). **2** disable; impair. **3** weaken or damage seriously (*crippled by the loss of funding*). □□ **crip·pler** *n.*

cri·sis /krísis/ *n.* (*pl.* **crises** /–seez/) **1 a** a time of intense difficulty or danger. **b** a time when a difficult or important decision must be made. **c** a severe problem or breakdown. **2** the turning point of a disease when an important change takes place, indicating recovery or death.

crisp /krisp/ *adj., n., & v.* • *adj.* **1** hard but brittle. **2 a** (of air) bracing. **b** (of a style or manner) lively; brisk and decisive. **c** (of features, etc.) neat and clear-cut. **d** (of paper) stiff and crackling. • *n.* a thing overdone in roasting, etc. (*burned to a crisp*). • *v.tr. & intr.* make or become crisp. □□ **crisp·ly** *adv.* **crisp·ness** *n.*

crisp·bread /kríspbred/ *n.* **1** a thin, crisp cracker of crushed rye, etc. **2** these collectively (*a box of crispbread*).

crisp·er /kríspər/ *n.* a compartment in a refrigerator for storing fruit and vegetables.

crisp·y /kríspee/ *adj.* (**crispier, crispiest**) **1** crisp; brittle. **2** brisk. □□ **crisp·i·ness** *n.*

criss·cross /krískráws, –krós/ *n., adj., adv., & v.* • *n.* **1** a pattern of crossing lines. **2** the crossing of lines or currents, etc. • *adj.* crossing; in cross lines (*crisscross marking*). • *adv.* crosswise; at cross purposes. • *v.* **1** *intr.* **a** intersect repeatedly. **b** move crosswise. **2** *tr.* mark or make with a crisscross pattern.

cri·te·ri·on /krīteéreeən/ *n.* (*pl.* **criteria** /–reeə/ or **criterions**) a principle or standard that a thing is judged by. □□ **cri·te·ri·al** *adj.*

▶**Criterion** is singular; the plural of this word is **criteria.** *There are several criteria* is correct usage; "the only criteria" is not.

crit·ic /krítik/ *n.* **1** a person who censures. **2** a person who reviews literary, artistic, or musical works, etc. **3** a person engaged in textual criticism.

crit·i·cal /krítikəl/ *adj.* **1 a** making or involving adverse judgments. **b** expressing or involving criticism. **2** skillful at or engaged in criticism. **3** providing textual criticism (*a critical edition of Frost*). **4 a** of or at a crisis; involving risk or suspense (*in a critical condition*). **b** decisive; crucial (*at the critical moment*). ▫▫ **crit·i·cal·i·ty** /–kálitee/ *n.* (in sense 5). **crit·i·cal·ly** *adv.* **crit·i·cal·ness** *n.*

crit·i·cal mass *n. Physics* the amount of fissile material needed to maintain a nuclear chain reaction.

crit·i·cism /krítisizəm/ *n.* **1 a** finding fault. **b** a statement expressing this. **2 a** the work of a critic. **b** an article, essay, etc., expressing or containing an analytical evaluation of something.

crit·i·cize /krítisīz/ *v.tr.* (also *absol.*) **1** find fault with. **2** discuss critically. ▫▫ **crit·i·ciz·a·ble** *adj.* **crit·i·ciz·er** *n.*

cri·tique /kritéek/ *n. & v.* •*n.* a critical essay or analysis; an instance or the process of formal criticism. •*v.tr.* (**critiques, critiqued, critiquing**) discuss critically.

crit·ter /krítər/ *n. dial.* or *joc.* a creature.

croak /krōk/ *n. & v.* •*n.* **1** a deep, hoarse sound as of a frog. **2** a sound resembling this. •*v.* **1 a** *intr.* utter a croak. **b** *tr.* utter with a croak or in a dismal manner. **2** *sl.* **a** *intr.* die. **b** *tr.* kill.

croak·y /krókee/ *adj.* (**croakier, croakiest**) (of a voice) croaking; hoarse. ▫▫ **croak·i·ly** *adv.* **croak·i·ness** *n.*

Cro·at /kró-at/ *n. & adj.* •*n.* **1 a** a native of Croatia in the former Yugoslavia. **b** a person of Croatian descent. **2** the Slavonic dialect of the Croats (cf. SERBO-CROAT). •*adj.* of or relating to the Croats or their dialect.

Cro·a·tian /krō-áyshən/ *n. & adj.* = CROAT.

cro·chet /krōsháy/ *n. & v.* •*n.* **1** a handicraft in which yarn is made up into a patterned fabric by means of a hooked needle. **2** work made in this way. •*v.* (**crocheted** /–sháyd/; **crocheting** /–sháying/) **1** *tr.* make by crocheting. **2** *intr.* do crochet. ▫▫ **cro·chet·er** *n.*

crock[1] /krok/ *n.* **1** an earthenware pot or jar. **2** a broken piece of earthenware.

crock[2] /krok/ *n. colloq.* nonsense; exaggeration (*his explanation is just a crock*).

crock·er·y /krókəree/ *n.* earthenware or china dishes, plates, etc.

croc·o·dile /krókədīl/ *n.* **1** any large tropical amphibious reptile of the order Crocodilia, with long jaws. **2** leather from its skin, used to make bags, shoes, etc. ▫▫ **croc·o·dil·i·an** /–díleeən/ *adj.*

croc·o·dile tears *n.pl.* insincere grief.

cro·cus /krókəs/ *n.* (*pl.* **crocuses**) any dwarf plant of the genus *Crocus*, growing from a corm and having brilliant usu. yellow or purple flowers.

Croe·sus /kréesəs/ *n.* a person of great wealth.

crois·sant /krwaasaáɴ, krəsánt/ *n.* a crescent-shaped roll made of rich yeast pastry.

Cro-Mag·non /krōmágnən, –mányən/ *adj. Anthropol.* of a tall, broad-faced European race of late Paleolithic times.

crone /krōn/ *n.* **1** a withered old woman. **2** an old ewe.

cro·ny /krónee/ *n.* (*pl.* **-nies**) a close friend or companion.

crook /kro͝ok/ *n. & v.* •*n.* **1** the hooked staff of a shepherd or bishop. **2 a** a bend, curve, or hook. **b** anything hooked or curved. **3** *colloq.* **a** a rogue; a swindler. **b** a professional criminal. •*v.tr. & intr.* bend; curve.

crook·ed /kro͝okid/ *adj.* **1 a** not straight or level; bent. **b** deformed; bent with age. **2** *colloq.* not straightforward; dishonest. ▫▫ **crook·ed·ly** *adv.* **crook·ed·ness** *n.*

croon /kro͞on/ *v. & n.* •*v.tr. & intr.* hum or sing in a low subdued voice. •*n.* such singing. ▫▫ **croon·er** *n.*

crop /krop/ *n. & v.* •*n.* **1 a** the produce of cultivated plants. **b** the season's yield of this (*a good crop*). **2** a group or an amount appearing at one time (*this year's crop of students*). **3** (in full **hunting crop**) the stock or handle of a whip. **4 a** a style of hair cut very short. **b** the cropping of hair. **5** *Zool.* **a** the pouch in a bird's gullet where food is prepared for digestion. **b** a similar organ in other animals. **6** a piece cut off or out of something. •*v.* (**cropped, cropping**) **1** *tr.* **a** cut off. **b** bite off (the tops of plants). **2** *tr.* cut (hair, cloth, edges of a book, etc.) short. **3** *tr.* gather or reap (produce). **4** *tr.* (foll. by *with*) sow or plant (land) with a crop. **5** *intr.* (of land) bear a crop. ▫ **crop up 1** (of a subject, circumstance, etc.) appear or come to one's notice unexpectedly. **2** *Geol.* appear at the surface.

crop cir·cle *n.* an area of standing crops that has been flattened in the form of a circle without an apparent reason.

crop-dust·ing *n.* the sprinkling of powdered insecticide or fertilizer on crops, esp. from the air.

crop·per /krópər/ *n.* a crop-producing plant of specified quality (*a good cropper; a heavy cropper*). ▫ **come a cropper** *sl.* **1** fall heavily. **2** fail badly.

cro·quet /krōkáy/ *n. & v.* •*n.* **1** a game played on a lawn, with wooden balls which are driven through a series of hoops with mallets. **2** the act of croqueting a ball. •*v.tr.* (**croqueted** /–káyd/; **croqueting** /–káying/) drive away (one's opponent's ball in croquet) by placing one's own against it and striking one's own.

cro·quette /krōkét/ *n.* a fried, breaded roll or ball of mashed potato or ground meat, etc.

cro·sier /krózhər/ *n.* (also **cro·zier**) **1** a hooked staff carried by a bishop. **2** a crook.

cross /kraws, kros/ *n., v., & adj.* •*n.* **1** an upright post with a transverse bar, as used in antiquity for crucifixion. **2 a** (**the Cross**) the cross on which Christ was crucified. **b** a representation of this as an emblem of Christianity. **c** = SIGN OF THE CROSS. **3** a staff surmounted by a cross and borne in a religious procession. **4 a** a thing or mark shaped like a cross, esp. two short intersecting lines (+ or x). **b** a monument in the form of a cross. **5** a cross-shaped decoration indicating rank in some orders of knighthood or awarded for personal valor. **6 a** an intermixture of animal breeds or plant varieties. **b** an animal or plant resulting from this. **7** (foll. by *between*) a mixture of two things. **8** a crosswise movement. **9** a trial or affliction (*bear one's crosses*). •*v.* **1** *tr.* (often foll. by *over*; also *absol.*) go across or to the other side of (a road, river, sea, etc.). **2 a** *intr.* intersect or be across one another (*the roads cross near the bridge*). **b** *tr.* cause to do this; place crosswise (*cross one's legs*). **3** *tr.* draw a line or lines across. **4** *tr.* (foll. by *off, out, through*) cancel or obliterate or remove from a list with lines drawn across. **5** *tr.* (often *refl.*) make the sign of the cross on or over. **6** *intr.* **a** pass in opposite or different directions. **b** (of letters between two correspondents) each be dispatched before receipt of the other. **c** (of telephone lines) become wrongly interconnected so that intrusive calls can be heard. **7** *tr.* **a** cause to interbreed. **b** cross-fertilize (plants). **8** *tr.* thwart or frustrate (*crossed in love*). **9** *tr. sl.* cheat. •*adj.* **1** (often foll. by *with*) peevish; angry. **2** (usu. *attrib.*) transverse; reaching from side to side. **3** (usu. *attrib.*) intersecting. **4** (usu. *attrib.*) contrary; opposed; reciprocal. ▫ **at cross purposes** misunderstanding one another. **cross one's fingers** (or **keep one's fingers crossed**) **1** put one finger across another as a sign of hoping for good luck. **2** trust in good luck. **cross one's heart** make a solemn pledge, esp. by crossing one's front. **cross one's mind** (of a thought, etc.) occur to one, esp. transiently. **cross a person's palm** (usu. foll. by *with*) **1** pay a person for a favor. **2** bribe. **cross the path of 1** meet with (a person). **2** thwart. **cross swords** (often foll. by *with*) have an argument or dispute. **cross wires** (or **get one's wires crossed**) **1** become wrongly connected by telephone. **2** have a misunderstanding. □□ **cross·ly** *adv.* **cross·ness** *n.*

cross- /kraws, kros/ *comb. form.* **1** denoting movement or position across something (*cross-channel*). **2** denoting interaction (*cross-cultural*; *cross-fertilize*). **3 a** passing from side to side; transverse (*crossbar*; *crosscurrent*). **b** having a transverse part (*crossbow*). **4** describing the form or figure of a cross (*crossroads*).

cross·bar /kráwsbaar, krós–/ *n.* a horizontal bar, held on a pivot or between two upright bars, e.g., of a bicycle or of a football goal.

cross·bill /kráwsbil, krós–/ *n.* a finch of the genus *Loxia*, having a bill with crossed mandibles for opening pine cones.

cross·bones /kráwsbōnz, krós;n–/ *n.* a representation of two crossed leg or arm bones, usu. below a skull, as an emblem of piracy or death.

cross·bow /kráwsbō, krós–/ *n.* esp. *hist.* a bow fixed across a wooden stock, with a mechanism for drawing and releasing the string.

cross·breed *n.* & *v.* • *n.* /kráwsbreed, krós–/ **1** a breed of animals or plants produced by crossing. **2** an individual animal or plant of a crossbreed. • *v.tr.* /kráwsbreéd, krós–/ (*past* and *past part.* **-bred**) produce by crossing.

cross-check *v.* & *n.* • *v.tr.* /kráws-chék, krós–/ check by an alternative method, or by several methods. • *n.* /kráws-chek, krós–/ an instance of cross-checking.

cross-coun·try /kráwskúntree, krós–/ *adj.* & *adv.* **1** across open country. **2** not keeping to main or direct roads.

cross-dress *v.intr.* wear clothing typically worn by members of the opposite sex.

crosse /kraws, kros/ *n.* a stick with a triangular net at the end for conveying the ball in lacrosse.

cross-ex·am·ine /kráwsigzámin, krós–/ *v.tr.* examine (esp. a witness in a court of law) to check or extend testimony already given. □□ **cross-ex·am·i·na·tion** /–náyshən/ *n.* **cross-ex·am·in·er** *n.*

cross-eyed /kráwsíd, krós–/ *adj.* (as a disorder) having one or both eyes turned permanently inward toward the nose.

cross-fer·ti·lize /kráwsfért'līz, krós–/ *v.tr.* **1** fertilize (an animal or plant) from another. **2** help by the interchange of ideas, etc. □□ **cross-fer·ti·li·za·tion** /–fértəlīzáyshən/ *n.*

cross·fire /kráwsfīr, krós–/ *n.* (also **cross fire**) **1** firing in two crossing directions simultaneously. **2 a** an attack or criticism from several sources at once. **b** a lively or combative exchange of views, etc.

cross·hair /kráws-hair, krós–/ *n.* a fine wire at the focus of an optical instrument, gun, sight, etc.

cross·hatch /kráws-hách, krós–/ *v.tr.* (in drawing or graphics) shade an area with intersecting sets of parallel lines.

cross·ing /kráwsing, krós–/ *n.* **1** a place where things (esp. roads) cross. **2** a place at which one may cross a street, etc. (*pedestrian crossing*). **3** a journey across water (*had a smooth crossing*). **4** the intersection of a church nave and transepts. **5** *Biol.* mating.

cross-leg·ged /kráwslégid, –légd, krós–/ *adj.* with one leg crossed over the other.

cross-match /kráwsmách, krós–/ *v.tr. Med.* test the compatibility of (a donor's and a recipient's blood). □□ **cross-match·ing** *n.* **cross·match** *n.*

cross·o·ver /kráwsōvər, krós–/ *n.* & *adj.* • *n.* a point or place of crossing from one side to the other. • *adj.* having a crossover.

cross·piece /kráwspees, krós–/ *n.* a beam or bar fixed or placed across something else.

cross-pol·li·nate /kráwspólinayt, krós–/ *v.tr.* pollinate (a plant) from another. □□ **cross-pol·li·na·tion** /–náyshən/ *n.*

cross-ques·tion /kráwskwés-chən, krós–/ *v.tr.* = CROSS-EXAMINE.

cross-ref·er·ence /kráwsréfərəns, krós–/ *n.* & *v.* • *n.* a reference from one part of a book, etc., to another. • *v.tr.* provide with cross-references.

cross·road /kráwsrōd, krós–/ *n.* **1** (usu. in *pl.*) an intersection of roads. **2** a road that crosses a main road or joins two main roads. □ **at the crossroads** at a critical point in one's life.

cross sec·tion /kráws-sékshən, krós–/ *n.* **1 a** a cutting of a solid at right angles to an axis. **b** a plane surface produced in this way. **c** a representation of this. **2** a representative sample. **3** *Physics* a quantity expressing the probability of interaction between particles. □□ **cross-sec·tion·al** *adj.*

cross-stitch /kráws-stich, krós–/ *n.* & *v.* • *n.* **1** a stitch formed of two stitches crossing each other. **2** needlework done using this stitch. • *v.intr.* & *tr.* work in cross-stitch.

cross·talk /kráws-tawk, krós–/ *n.* (also **cross talk**) unwanted transfer of signals between communication channels.

cross·walk /kráwswawk, krós–/ *n.* a pedestrian crossing.

cross·ways /kráwswayz, krós–/ *adv.* = CROSSWISE.

cross·wind /kráwswind, krós–/ *n.* a wind blowing across one's direction of travel.

cross·wise /kráwswīz, krós–/ *adj.* & *adv.* **1** in the form of a cross; intersecting. **2** transverse or transversely.

cross·word /kráwswərd, krós–/ *n.* (also **cross·word puz·zle**) a puzzle of a grid of squares and blanks into which words crossing vertically and horizontally have to be filled in according to provided clues.

---

crossword said to have been invented by the journalist Arthur Wynne, whose puzzle (called a 'word cross') appeared in a Sunday newspaper, the *New York World*, on December 21, 1913.

---

crotch /kroch/ *n.* a place where something forks, esp. the legs of the human body or a garment.

crotch·et·y /króchitee/ *adj.* peevish; irritable. □□ **crotch·et·i·ness** *n.*

cro·ton /krṓt'n/ *n.* **1** any small trees or shrub of the genus *Croton*, producing a capsulelike fruit. **2** any small tree or shrub of the genus *Codiaeum*, esp. *C. variegatum*, with colored ornamental leaves.

cro·ton oil *n.* a powerful purgative obtained from the fruit of *Croton tiglium*.

crouch /krowch/ *v.* & *n.* • *v.intr.* lower the body with the limbs close to the chest; be in this position. • *n.* an act of crouching; a crouching position.

croup /kroop/ *n.* an inflammation of the larynx and trachea in children, with a hard cough. □□ **croup·y** *adj.*

croup·i·er /kroopeeər, –eeay/ *n.* **1** the person in charge of a gaming table, raking in and paying out money, etc. **2** the assistant chairperson at a public dinner, seated at the foot of the table.

crou·ton /krooton/ *n.* a small piece of fried or toasted bread served with soup or used as a garnish.

Crow /krō/ *n.* **1 a** a N. American people native to eastern Montana. **b** a member of this people. **2** the language of this people.

crow[1] /krō/ *n.* **1** any large, black bird of the genus *Corvus,* having a powerful black beak. **2** any similar bird of the family Corvidae. □ **as the crow flies** in a straight line. **eat crow** submit to humiliation.

crow[2] /krō/ *v. & n.* •*v.intr.* **1** (*past* **crowed**) (of a cock) utter its characteristic loud cry. **2** (of a baby) utter happy cries. **3** (usu. foll. by *over*) express unrestrained gleeful satisfaction. •*n.* **1** the cry of a cock. **2** a happy cry of a baby.

crow·bar /kŕōbaar/ *n.* an iron bar with a flattened end, used as a lever.

crowd /krowd/ *n. & v.* •*n.* **1** a large number of people gathered together. **2** a mass of spectators; an audience. **3** *colloq.* a particular set of people. **4** (prec. by *the*) the mass or multitude of people. **5** a large number (of things). •*v.* **1 a** *intr.* come together in a crowd. **b** *tr.* cause to do this. **c** *intr.* force one's way. **2** *tr.* **a** (foll. by *into*) force or compress into a confined space. **b** (often foll. by *with*; usu. in *passive*) fill or make abundant with (*was crowded with tourists*). **3** *tr.* **a** come aggressively close to. **b** *colloq.* harass or pressure (a person). □ **crowd out** exclude by crowding. □□ **crowd·ed·ness** *n.*

crow·foot /kŕōfŏŏt/ *n.* (*pl.* **crowfoots** for 1 & 2, **crowfeet** for 3 & 4) **1** any of various plants of the genus *Ranunculus,* esp. buttercup, often characterized by divided leaves that resemble a crow's foot. **2** any of various other plants whose leaves, etc., bear a similar resemblance. **3** *Mil.* a caltrop. **4** a three-legged antislip support for a motion-picture camera's tripod.

crown /krown/ *n. & v.* •*n.* **1** a monarch's ornamental headdress. **2** (**the Crown**) **a** the monarch as head of state. **b** the power or authority residing in the monarchy. **3 a** a wreath worn on the head, esp. as an emblem of victory. **b** an award or distinction gained by a victory or achievement, esp. in sport. **4** a crown-shaped device or ornament. **5** the top part of a thing, esp. of the head or a hat. **6 a** the highest or central part of an arched or curved thing (*crown of the road*). **b** a thing that completes or forms the summit. **7** the part of a plant just above and below the ground. **8** the upper part of a cut gem above the girdle. **9 a** the part of a tooth projecting from the gum. **b** an artificial replacement or covering for this. •*v.tr.* **1** put a crown on (a person or a person's head). **2** invest (a person) with a royal crown or authority. **3** be a crown to; rest on the top of. **4 a** (often as **crowning** *adj.*) be or cause to be the consummation, reward, or finishing touch to (*the crowning glory*). **b** bring (efforts) to a happy issue. **5** fit a crown to (a tooth). **6** *sl.* hit on the head.

crown jew·els *n.pl.* the regalia and other jewelry worn by the sovereign on certain state occasions.

crown prince *n.* a male heir to a sovereign throne.

crown prin·cess *n.* **1** the wife of a crown prince. **2** a female heir to a sovereign throne.

crow's-foot *n.* (*pl.* **-feet**) **1** (usu. in *pl.*) a wrinkle at the outer corner of a person's eye. **2** *Mil.* a caltrop.

crow's nest *n.* a barrel or platform fixed at the masthead of a sailing vessel as a shelter for a lookout.

cro·zier var. of CROSIER.

cru·ces *pl.* of CRUX.

cru·cial /kŕōōshəl/ *adj.* **1** decisive; critical. **2** *colloq. disp.* very important. **3** *sl.* excellent. □□ **cru·ci·al·i·ty** /–sheeálitee/ *n.* (*pl.* **-ties**). **cru·cial·ly** *adv.*

▶**Crucial** is used in formal contexts to mean 'decisive, critical,', e.g., *The testimony of the only eyewitness was crucial to the case.* Its broader use to mean 'very important,' as in *It is crucial to get good light for your photographs,* should be restricted to informal contexts.

cru·ci·ble /kŕōōsibəl/ *n.* **1** a melting pot for metals, etc. **2** a severe test or trial.

cru·cif·er·ous /krōōsífərəs/ *adj. Bot.* of the family Cruciferae, having flowers with four petals arranged in a cross.

cru·ci·fix /kŕōōsifiks/ *n.* a model or image of a cross with a figure of Christ on it.

cru·ci·fix·ion /kŕōōsifikshən/ *n.* **1 a** crucifying or being crucified. **b** an instance of this. **2** (**Crucifixion**) **a** the crucifixion of Christ. **b** a representation of this.

cru·ci·form /kŕōōsifawrm/ *adj.* cross-shaped.

cru·ci·fy /kŕōōsifī/ *v.tr.* (**-fies, -fied**) **1** put to death by fastening to a cross. **2 a** cause extreme pain to. **b** persecute; torment. **c** *sl.* defeat thoroughly in an argument, match, etc.

crud /krud/ *n. sl.* **1 a** unwanted impurities, grease, etc. **b** something disgusting or undesirable. **c** a corrosive deposit in a nuclear reactor. **2** an unpleasant person. **3** nonsense. □□ **crud·dy** *adj.* (**cruddier, cruddiest**).

crude /krōōd/ *adj. & n.* •*adj.* **1 a** in the natural or raw state; not refined. **b** unpolished; lacking finish. **2 a** (of an action or statement or manners) rude; blunt. **b** offensive; indecent. **3 a** *Statistics* (of numerical totals) not adjusted or corrected. **b** rough (*a crude estimate*). •*n.* natural mineral oil. □□ **crude·ly** *adv.* **crude·ness** *n.* **cru·di·ty** *n.*

cru·di·tés /kŕōōditáy/ *n.pl.* an hors d'oeuvre of mixed raw vegetables, often served with a sauce into which they are dipped.

cru·el /kŕōōəl/ *adj.* (**crueler, cruelest**) **1** indifferent to or gratified by another's suffering. **2** causing pain or suffering; esp. deliberately. □□ **cru·el·ly** *adv.*

cru·el·ty /kŕōōəltee/ *n.* (*pl.* **-ties**) **1** a cruel act or attitude; indifference to another's suffering. **2** a succession of cruel acts; a continued cruel attitude (*suffered much cruelty*). **3** *Law* physical or mental harm inflicted (whether or not intentional), esp. as a ground for divorce.

cru·el·ty-free *adj.* (of cosmetics, etc.) produced without involving cruelty to animals in the development or manufacturing process.

cru·et /kŕōōit/ *n.* a small container for oil or vinegar for use at the table.

cruise /krōōz/ *v. & n.* •*v.* **1** *intr.* make a journey by sea calling at a series of ports, esp. for pleasure. **2** *intr.* sail about in an area without a precise destination. **3** *intr.* **a** (of a motor vehicle or aircraft) travel at a moderate or economical speed. **b** (of a vehicle or its driver) travel at random. **4** *intr.* achieve an objective, win a race, etc., with ease. **5** *intr. & tr. sl.* walk or drive about (the streets, etc.) in search of a sexual (esp. homosexual) partner. •*n.* a cruising voyage, esp. as a vacation.

cruise con·trol *n.* a device on a motor vehicle that maintains a constant speed and relieves the operator of the need to depress the accelerator.

cruise mis·sile *n.* a low-flying missile that is guided to its target by an on-board computer.

cruis·er /kŕōōzər/ *n.* **1** a warship of high speed and medium armament. **2** = CABIN CRUISER. **3** a police patrol car.

crumb /krum/ *n. & v.* •*n.* **1 a** a small fragment, esp. of bread. **b** a small particle (*a crumb of comfort*). **2** the soft inner part of a loaf of bread. **3** *sl.* an objectionable person. •*v.tr.* **1** cover with breadcrumbs. **2** break into crumbs.

crum·ble /krúmbəl/ *v. & n.* •*v.* **1** *tr. & intr.* break or fall into fragments. **2** *intr.* (of power, a reputation, etc.) gradually disintegrate. •*n.* a crumbly or crumbled substance.

crum·bly /krúmblee/ *adj.* (**crumblier, crumbliest**) consisting of, or apt to fall into, crumbs or fragments. □□ **crum·bli·ness** *n.*

crumb·y /krúmee/ *adj.* (**crumbier, crumbiest**) **1** like or covered in crumbs. **2** *colloq.* = CRUMMY.
crum·horn var. of KRUMMHORN.
crum·my /krúmee/ *adj.* (**crummier, crummiest**) *colloq.* dirty; squalid; inferior; worthless. ▫▫ **crum·mi·ness** *n.*
crum·pet /krúmpit/ *n.* a soft, flat cake of a yeast mixture cooked on a griddle and eaten toasted and buttered.
crum·ple /krúmpəl/ *v.* & *n.* •*v.* **1** *tr.* & *intr.* (often foll. by *up*) **a** crush or become crushed into creases. **b** ruffle; wrinkle. **2** *intr.* (often foll. by *up*) collapse; give way. •*n.* a crease or wrinkle. ▫▫ **crum·ply** *adj.*
crunch /krunch/ *v.* & *n.* •*v.* **1** *tr.* **a** crush noisily with the teeth. **b** grind (gravel, dry snow, etc.) under foot, wheels, etc. **2** *intr.* (often foll. by *up, through*) make a crunching sound in walking, moving, etc. •*n.* **1** crunching; a crunching sound. **2** *colloq.* a decisive event or moment.
crunch·y /krúnchee/ *adj.* (**crunchier, crunchiest**) hard and crispy. ▫▫ **crunch·i·ly** *adv.* **crunch·i·ness** *n.*
cru·sade /kro͞osáyd/ *n.* & *v.* •*n.* **1 a** any of several medieval military expeditions made by Europeans to recover the Holy Land from the Muslims. **b** a war instigated by the Roman Catholic Church for alleged religious ends. **2** a vigorous campaign in favor of a cause. •*v.intr.* engage in a crusade. ▫▫ **cru·sad·er** *n.*
crush /krush/ *v.* & *n.* •*v.tr.* **1** compress with force or violence, so as to break, bruise, etc. **2** reduce to powder by pressure. **3** crease or crumple. **4** defeat or subdue completely (*crushed by my reply*). •*n.* **1** an act of crushing. **2** a crowded mass of people. **3** *colloq.* **a** (usu. foll. by *on*) an infatuation. **b** the object of an infatuation (*who's the latest crush?*). ▫▫ **crush·a·ble** *adj.* **crush·er** *n.* **crush·ing** *adj.* (in sense 4 of *v.*). **crush·ing·ly** *adv.*
crust /krust/ *n.* & *v.* •*n.* **1 a** the hard outer part of a loaf of bread. **b** a piece of this with some soft bread attached. **c** a hard, dry scrap of bread. **2** the pastry covering of a pie. **3** a hard casing of a softer thing. **4** *Geol.* the outer portion of the earth. **5 a** a coating or deposit on the surface of anything. **b** a hard, dry formation on the skin; a scab. **6** a deposit of tartar formed in bottles of old wine. **7 a** *sl.* impudence (*you have a lot of crust!*). **b** a superficial hardness of manner. •*v.tr.* & *intr.* **1** cover or become covered with a crust. **2** form into a crust. ▫▫ **crus·tal** *adj.* (in sense 4 of *n.*).
crus·ta·cean /krustáyshən/ *n.* & *adj.* •*n.* any arthropod of the class Crustacea, having a hard shell and usu. aquatic, e.g., the crab, lobster, and shrimp. •*adj.* of or relating to crustaceans. ▫▫ **crus·ta·ceous** /–shəs/ *adj.*
crust·ed /krústid/ *adj.* **1 a** having a crust. **b** (of wine) having deposited a crust. **2** antiquated; venerable.
crust·y /krústee/ *adj.* (**crustier, crustiest**) **1** having a crisp crust (*a crusty loaf*). **2** irritable; curt. **3** hard; crustlike. ▫▫ **crust·i·ly** *adv.* **crust·i·ness** *n.*
crutch /kruch/ *n.* **1** a support for a lame person, usu. with a crosspiece at the top fitting under the armpit (*pair of crutches*). **2** any support or prop.
crux /kruks/ *n.* (*pl.* **cruxes** or **cruces** /kro͞oseez/) **1** the decisive point at issue. **2** a difficult matter; a puzzle.
cry /krī/ *v.* & *n.* •*v.* (**cries, cried**) **1** *intr.* (often foll. by *out*) make a loud or shrill sound, esp. to express pain, grief, etc., or to appeal for help. **2 a** *intr.* shed tears; weep. **b** *tr.* shed (tears). **3** *tr.* (often foll. by *out*) say or exclaim loudly or excitedly. **4** *intr.* (of an animal, esp. a bird) make a loud call. **5** *tr.* (of a hawker, etc.) proclaim (wares, etc.) in the street. •*n.* (*pl.* **cries**) **1** a loud inarticulate utterance of grief, pain, fear, joy, etc. **2** a loud excited utterance of words. **3** an urgent appeal. **4** a spell of weeping. **5 a** public demand; a strong movement of opinion. **b** a rallying call. **6** the natural utterance of an animal. **7** the street call of a hawker, etc. ▫ **cry one's eyes** (or **heart**) **out** weep bitterly. **cry out for** demand as a self-evident requirement or solution. **a far cry 1** a long way. **2** a very different thing. **for crying out loud** *colloq.* an exclamation of surprise or annoyance.
cry·ba·by /krībaybee/ *n.* (*pl.* **-babies**) a person who sheds tears frequently.
cry·er var. of CRIER.
cry·ing /krī-ing/ *attrib.adj.* (of an injustice or other evil) flagrant; demanding redress (*a crying shame*).
cryo- /krīō/ *comb. form* (extreme) cold.
cry·o·gen·ics /krīəjéniks/ *n.* the branch of physics dealing with very low temperatures. ▫▫ **cry·o·gen·ic** *adj.*
crypt /kript/ *n.* an underground room or vault, esp. used as a burial place.
cryp·tic /kríptik/ *adj.* **1 a** obscure in meaning. **b** (of a crossword clue, etc.) indicating the solution in a way that is not obvious. **c** secret; mysterious; enigmatic. **2** *Zool.* (of coloration, etc.) serving for concealment. ▫▫ **cryp·ti·cal·ly** *adv.*
crypto- /kríptō/ *comb. form* concealed; secret (*crypto-communist*).
cryp·to·gram /kríptəgram/ *n.* a text written in code.
cryp·tog·ra·phy /kriptógrəfee/ *n.* the art of writing or solving codes. ▫▫ **cryp·tog·ra·pher** *n.* **cryp·to·graph·ic** /–təgráfik/ *adj.* **cryp·to·graph·i·cal·ly** *adv.*
crys·tal /kríst'l/ *n.* & *adj.* •*n.* **1 a** a clear transparent mineral, esp. rock crystal. **b** a piece of this. **2** (in full **crystal glass**) **a** highly transparent glass. **b** articles made of this. **3** the glass over a watch face. **4** *Electronics* a crystalline piece of semiconductor. **5** *Chem.* **a** an aggregation of molecules with a definite internal structure and the external form of a solid enclosed by symmetrically arranged plane faces. **b** a solid whose constituent particles are symmetrically arranged. •*adj.* (usu. *attrib.*) made of, like, or clear as crystal. ▫ **crystal clear** unclouded; transparent.
crys·tal ball *n.* a glass globe used in crystal gazing.
crys·tal gaz·ing *n.* the process of concentrating one's gaze on a crystal ball supposedly in order to obtain a picture of future events, etc.
crys·tal·line /kríst'lin, –līn/ *adj.* **1** of, like, or clear as crystal. **2** *Chem.* & *Mineral.* having the structure and form of a crystal. ▫▫ **crys·tal·lin·i·ty** /–línitee/ *n.*
crys·tal·lize /kríst'līz/ *v.* **1** *tr.* & *intr.* form or cause to form crystals. **2** (often foll. by *out*) **a** *intr.* (of ideas or plans) become definite. **b** *tr.* make definite. **3** *tr.* & *intr.* coat or impregnate or become coated or impregnated with sugar (*crystallized fruit*). ▫▫ **crys·tal·liz·a·ble** *adj.* **crys·tal·li·za·tion** *n.*
crys·tal·log·ra·phy /kríst'lógrəfee/ *n.* the science of crystal form and structure. ▫▫ **crys·tal·log·ra·pher** *n.* **crys·tal·lo·graph·ic** /–ləgráfik/ *adj.*
Cs *symb. Chem.* the element cesium.
c/s *abbr.* cycles per second.
C-section *abbr.* of CESAREAN SECTION.
CST *abbr.* central standard time.
CT *abbr.* Connecticut (in official postal use).
Cu *symb. Chem.* the element copper.
cu. *abbr.* cubic.
cub /kub/ *n.* **1** the young of a fox, lion, etc. **2** an ill-mannered young man. **3** (**Cub**) (in full **Cub Scout**) a member of the junior branch of the Boy Scouts. **4** (in full **cub reporter**) *colloq.* an inexperienced newspaper reporter. **5** an apprentice.
Cu·ban /kyo͞obən/ *adj.* & *n.* •*adj.* of or relating to Cuba, an island republic in the Caribbean, or its people. •*n.* a native or national of Cuba.
cub·by /kúbee/ *n.* (*pl.* **-bies**) (in full **cubbyhole**) **1** a very small room. **2** a snug space. **3** a boxlike compartment for storage, etc.
cube /kyo͞ob/ *n.* & *v.* •*n.* **1** a solid contained by six equal

squares. **2** a cube-shaped block. **3** *Math.* the product of a number multiplied by its square. •*v.tr.* **1** find the cube of (a number). **2** cut (food for cooking, etc.) into small cubes. **3** tenderize (meat) by scoring it in a criss-cross pattern.

cube root *n.* the number which produces a given number when cubed.

cube steak *n.* a thin slice of steak that has been tenderized by cubing.

cu·bic /kyóobik/ *adj.* **1** cube-shaped. **2** of three dimensions. **3** involving the cube (and no higher power) of a number (*cubic equation*). **4** (*attrib.*) designating a unit of measure equal to the volume of a cube whose side is one of the linear unit specified (*cubic meter*). **5** *Crystallog.* having three equal axes at right angles.

cu·bi·cal /kyóobikəl/ *adj.* cube-shaped. □□ **cu·bi·cal·ly** *adv.*

cu·bi·cle /kyóobikəl/ *n.* **1** a small partitioned space, screened for privacy. **2** a small, separate sleeping compartment.

cu·bi·form /kyóobifawrm/ *adj.* cube-shaped.

cub·ism /kyóobizəm/ *n.* a style and movement in art, esp. painting, in which objects are represented geometrically. □□ **cub·ist** *n. & adj.*

cuck·old /kúkōld/ *n. & v.* •*n.* the husband of an adulteress. •*v.tr.* make a cuckold of. □□ **cuck·old·ry** *n.*

cuck·oo /kóokoo/ *n. & adj.* •*n.* any bird of the family Cuculidae, esp. *Cuculus canorus*, having a characteristic cry, and depositing its eggs in the nests of small birds. •*predic.adj. sl.* crazy; foolish.

cuck·oo clock *n.* a clock that strikes the hour with a sound like a cuckoo's call.

cu·cum·ber /kyóokumbər/ *n.* **1** a long, green, fleshy fruit, used in salads. **2** the climbing plant, *Cucumis sativus*, yielding this fruit.

cud /kud/ *n.* half-digested food returned from the first stomach of ruminants to the mouth for further chewing.

cud·dle /kúd'l/ *v. & n.* •*v.* **1** *tr.* hug; embrace; fondle. **2** *intr.* nestle together; lie close; kiss and fondle amorously. •*n.* a prolonged and fond hug. □□ **cud·dle·some** *adj.*

cud·dly /kúdlee/ *adj.* (**cuddlier, cuddliest**) tempting to cuddle; given to cuddling.

cudg·el /kújəl/ *n. & v.* •*n.* a short, thick stick used as a weapon. •*v.tr.* beat with a cudgel.

cue[1] /kyoo/ *n. & v.* •*n.* **1 a** the last words of an actor's speech serving as a signal to another actor to enter or speak. **b** a similar signal to a singer, etc. **2 a** a stimulus to perception, etc. **b** a signal for action. **c** a hint on how to behave in particular circumstances. **3** a facility for or an instance of cuing audio equipment (see sense 2 of *v.*). •*v.tr.* (**cues, cued, cuing** or **cueing**) **1** give a cue to. **2** put (a piece of audio equipment) in readiness to play a particular part of the recorded material. □ **cue in 1** insert a cue for. **2** give information to. **on cue** at the correct moment. **take one's cue from** follow the example or advice of.

cue[2] /kyoo/ *n. & v. Billiards*, etc. •*n.* a long, straight, tapering rod for striking the ball. •*v.* (**cues, cued, cuing** or **cueing**) **1** *tr.* strike (a ball) with a cue. **2** *intr.* use a cue. □□ **cue·ist** *n.*

cue ball *n. Billiards* the ball that is to be struck with the cue.

cue card *n. colloq.* a card or board displaying a television script to a speaker as an aid to memory.

cuff[1] /kuf/ *n.* **1 a** the end part of a sleeve. **b** a separate band of linen worn around the wrist so as to appear under the sleeve. **c** the part of a glove covering the wrist. **2** a turned-up hem on pants. **3** (in *pl.*) *colloq.* handcuffs. □□ **cuffed** *adj.* (also in *comb.*).

cuff[2] /kuf/ *v. & n.* •*v.tr.* strike with an open hand. •*n.* such a blow.

cuff link *n.* a device of two joined studs, etc., to fasten the sides of a cuff together.

Cu·fic var. of KUFIC.

cui·rass /kwirás/ *n. hist.* a piece of armor consisting of breastplate and backplate fastened together.

cui·sine /kwizéen/ *n.* a style or method of cooking, esp. of a particular country or establishment.

cul-de-sac /kúldəsak, kóol–/ *n.* (*pl.* **culs-de-sac** *pronunc.* same) **1** a street or passage closed at one end. **2** a route or course leading nowhere; a position from which one cannot escape. **3** *Anat.* = DIVERTICULUM.

cu·li·nar·y /kyóoləneree, kúl–/ *adj.* of or for cooking or the kitchen. □□ **cu·li·nar·i·ly** *adv.*

cull /kul/ *v. & n.* •*v.tr.* **1** select or gather (*knowledge culled from books*). **2** pick (flowers, fruit, etc.). **3** select (animals), esp. for killing. •*n.* **1** an act of culling. **2** an animal or animals culled. □□ **cull·er** *n.*

cul·mi·nate /kúlminayt/ *v.* **1** *intr.* (usu. foll. by *in*) reach its highest or final point. **2** *tr.* bring to its highest or final point. □□ **cul·mi·na·tion** /–náyshən/ *n.*

cu·lottes /kóolóts, kyóo–/ *n.pl.* women's (usu. short) trousers cut to resemble a skirt.

cul·pa·ble /kúlpəbəl/ *adj.* deserving blame. □□ **cul·pa·bil·i·ty** *n.* **cul·pa·bly** *adv.*

cul·prit /kúlprit/ *n.* a person accused of or guilty of an offense.

cult /kult/ *n.* **1** a system of religious worship esp. as expressed in ritual. **2 a** devotion to a person or thing (*the cult of aestheticism*). **b** a popular fashion. **3** (*attrib.*) denoting a person or thing popularized in this way (*cult film; cult figure*). □□ **cul·tic** *adj.* **cult·ism** *n.* **cult·ist** *n.*

cul·ti·var /kúltivaar/ *n. Bot.* a plant variety produced by cultivation.

cul·ti·vate /kúltivayt/ *v.tr.* **1 a** prepare and use (soil, etc.) for crops or gardening. **b** break up (the ground) with a cultivator. **2 a** raise or produce (crops). **b** culture (bacteria, etc.). **3 a** (often as **cultivated** *adj.*) apply oneself to improving or developing (the mind, etc.). **b** pay attention to or nurture; ingratiate oneself with. □□ **cul·ti·va·ble** *adj.* **cul·ti·vat·a·ble** *adj.* **cul·ti·va·tion** *n.*

cul·ti·va·tor /kúltivaytər/ *n.* a mechanical implement for breaking up the ground and uprooting weeds.

cul·tur·al /kúlchərəl/ *adj.* of or relating to the cultivation of the mind or manners, esp. through artistic or intellectual activity. □□ **cul·tur·al·ly** *adv.*

cul·ture /kúlchər/ *n. & v.* •*n.* **1 a** the arts and other manifestations of human intellectual achievement regarded collectively. **b** a refined understanding of this. **2** the customs, civilization, and achievements of a particular time or people (*studied Chinese culture*). **3** improvement by mental or physical training. **4 a** the cultivation of plants; the rearing of bees, etc. **b** the cultivation of the soil. **5** a quantity of microorganisms and the nutrient material supporting their growth. •*v.tr.* maintain (bacteria, etc.) in conditions suitable for growth.

culture Middle English (denoting a cultivated piece of land): the noun from French *culture* or directly from Latin *cultura* 'growing, cultivation'; the verb from obsolete French *culturer* or medieval Latin *culturare*, both based on Latin *colere* 'tend, cultivate.' In late Middle English the sense was 'the cultivation of the soil' and from this, in the early 16th century, arose the sense 'cultivation (of the mind, faculties, or manners).'

cul·tured /kúlchərd/ *adj.* having refined taste and manners and a good education.
cul·tured pearl *n.* a pearl formed by an oyster after the insertion of a foreign body into its shell.
cul·vert /kúlvərt/ *n.* an underground channel carrying water across a road, etc.
cum /kum/ *prep.* (usu. in *comb.*) with; combined with; also used as (*a bedroom-cum-study*).
cum·ber·some /kúmbərsəm/ *adj.* inconvenient in size, weight, or shape.
cum·brous /kúmbrəs/ *adj.* = CUMBERSOME.
cum·in /kúmin, kóo–, kyóo–/ *n.* **1** an umbelliferous plant, *Cuminum cyminum*, bearing aromatic seeds. **2** these seeds used as flavoring.
cum·mer·bund /kúmərbund/ *n.* a waist sash.

cummerbund early 17th century: from Urdu and Persian *kamar-band*, from *kamar* 'waist, loins' and *-bandi* 'band.' The sash was formerly worn in the Indian subcontinent by domestic workers and lower-caste office workers.

cum·quat var. of KUMQUAT.
cu·mu·la·tive /kyóomyələtiv, –láytiv/ *adj.* **1** increasing, increased, or formed by successive additions. **2** *Stock Exch.* (of shares) entitling holders to arrears of interest before any other distribution is made. ▫▫ **cu·mu·la·tive·ly** *adv.* **cu·mu·la·tive·ness** *n.*
cumulo- /kyóomyəlō/ *comb. form* cumulous (cloud).
cu·mu·lus /kyóomyələs/ *n.* (*pl.* **cumuli** /–lī/) a cloud formation consisting of rounded masses heaped on each other above a horizontal base. ▫▫ **cu·mu·lous** *adj.*
cu·ne·i·form /kyóoneeəfawrm, kyóoneeə–, kyóoni–/ *adj.* & *n.* • *adj.* **1** wedge-shaped. **2** of, relating to, or using the wedge-shaped writing in ancient Babylonian, etc., inscriptions. • *n.* cuneiform writing.
cun·ni·lin·gus /kúnilínggəs/ *n.* (also **cun·ni·linc·tus** /–língktəs/) oral stimulation of the female genitals.
cun·ning /kúning/ *adj.* & *n.* • *adj.* **1 a** skilled in ingenuity or deceit. **b** selfishly clever or crafty. **2** ingenious (*a cunning device*). **3** attractive; quaint. • *n.* **1** craftiness. **2** skill; ingenuity. ▫▫ **cun·ning·ly** *adv.* **cun·ning·ness** *n.*
cunt /kunt/ *n. coarse sl.* **1** the female genitals. **2** *offens.* a stupid person. ▶A highly taboo word.
cup /kup/ *n.* & *v.* • *n.* **1** a small bowl-shaped container for drinking from. **2 a** its contents (*a cup of tea*). **b** = CUPFUL. **3** a cup-shaped thing. **4** flavored wine, cider, etc., usu. chilled. **5** an ornamental cup-shaped trophy. **6** one's fate or fortune (*a bitter cup*). **7** either of the two cup-shaped parts of a brassiere. **8** the chalice used or the wine taken at the Eucharist. **9** *Golf* the hole on a putting green or the metal container in it. • *v.tr.* (**cupped, cupping**) **1** form (esp. one's hands) into the shape of a cup. **2** take or hold as in a cup. ▫ **one's cup of tea** *colloq.* what interests or suits one. **in one's cups** while drunk; drunk.
cup·board /kúbərd/ *n.* a recess or piece of furniture with a door and (usu.) shelves.
cup·cake /kúpkayk/ *n.* a small cake baked in a cup-shaped metal, foil, or paper container and often iced.
cup·ful /kúpfool/ *n.* (*pl.* **-fuls**) **1** the amount held by a cup, esp. a half-pint (8-ounce) measure in cooking. **2** a cup full of a substance. ▶A *cupful* is a measure, and so *three cupfuls* is a quantity regarded in terms of a cup; *three cups full* denotes the actual cups, as in *three cups full of water*. Sense 2 is an intermediate use.
Cu·pid /kyóopid/ *n.* **1** the Roman god of love represented as a naked winged boy with a bow and arrows. **2** (also **cupid**) a representation of Cupid.
cu·pid·i·ty /kyoopíditee/ *n.* greed for gain.
cu·po·la /kyóopələ/ *n.* **1 a** a rounded dome forming a roof or ceiling. **b** a small rounded dome adorning a roof. **2** a revolving dome protecting mounted guns.

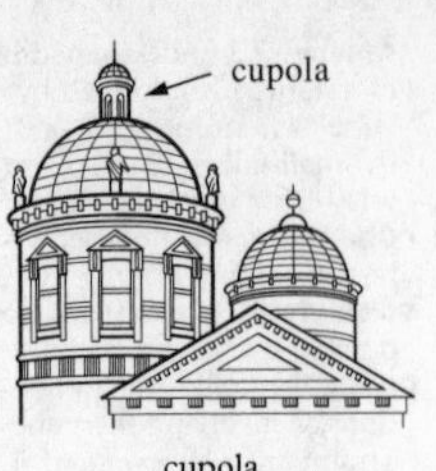

cupola

cu·pre·ous /kóopreeəs, kyóo–/ *adj.* of or like copper.
cu·pric /kóoprik, kyóo–/ *adj.* of copper, esp. divalent copper. ▫▫ **cu·prif·er·ous** /–prífərəs/ *adj.*
cu·prous /kóoprəs, kyóo–/ *adj.* of copper, esp. monovalent copper.
cur /kər/ *n.* **1** a worthless or snappy dog. **2** *colloq.* a contemptible person.
cur·a·ble /kyóorəbəl/ *adj.* that can be cured. ▫▫ **cur·a·bil·i·ty** *n.*
cu·ra·çao /kyóorəsō, –sów/ *n.* (also **curaçoa** /–sóə/) (*pl.* **-ços** or **curaçoas**) a liqueur of spirits flavored with the peel of bitter oranges.
cu·ra·cy /kyóorəsee/ *n.* (*pl.* **-cies**) a curate's office or the tenure of it.
cu·ra·re /kyooraáree, koo–/ *n.* a resinous bitter substance prepared from S. American plants of the genera *Strychnos* and *Chondodendron*, paralyzing the motor nerves.
cu·rate /kyóorət/ *n.* a member of the clergy engaged as assistant to a parish priest.
cu·ra·tor /kyooráytər, kyóorə–/ *n.* a keeper or custodian of a museum or other collection. ▫▫ **cu·ra·to·ri·al** /kyóorətáwreeəl/ *adj.* **cu·ra·tor·ship** *n.*
curb /kərb/ *n.* & *v.* • *n.* **1** a check or restraint. **2** a rim of concrete, stone, etc., along the side of a paved road. **3** a strap, etc., fastened to the bit and passing under a horse's lower jaw, used as a check. **4** an enclosing border or edging. • *v.tr.* **1** restrain. **2** put a curb on (a horse).
curd /kərd/ *n.* (often in *pl.*) a coagulated substance formed by the action of acids on milk, which may be eaten as food. ▫▫ **curd·y** *adj.*
cur·dle /kərd'l/ *v.tr.* & *intr.* make into or become curds, (of milk) turn sour; congeal. ▫ **make one's blood curdle** fill one with horror. ▫▫ **cur·dler** *n.*
cure /kyoor/ *v.* & *n.* • *v.* **1** *tr.* (often foll. by *of*) restore (a person or animal) to health (*was cured of pleurisy*). **2** *tr.* eliminate (a disease, evil, etc.). **3** *tr.* preserve by salting, drying, etc. **4** *tr.* **a** vulcanize (rubber). **b** harden (concrete or plastic). **5** *intr.* effect a cure. **6** *intr.* undergo a process of curing. • *n.* **1** restoration to health. **2** a thing that effects a cure. **3** a course of healing treatment. **4 a** the office or function of a curate. **b** a parish or other sphere of spiritual ministration. **5 a** the process of curing rubber or plastic. **b** (with qualifying adj.) the degree of this. ▫▫ **cur·a·tive** /kyóorətiv/ *adj.* & *n.* **cur·er** *n.*
cu·ré /kyooráy, kyóoray/ *n.* a parish priest in France, etc.
cure-all *n.* a panacea.
cu·rette /kyoorét/ *n.* & *v.* • *n.* a surgeon's small scraping instrument. • *v.tr.* & *intr.* clean or scrape with a curette. ▫▫ **cu·ret·tage** /kyooritaázh/ *n.*
cur·few /kárfyoo/ *n.* **1 a** a regulation requiring people to remain indoors between specified hours. **b** the hour designated as the beginning of such a restriction. **c** a daily signal indicating this. **2** the ringing of a bell at a fixed evening hour.
cu·ri·a /kyóoreeə/ *n.* (also **Curia**) (*pl.* **curiae**) the papal court; the government departments of the Vatican. ▫▫ **cu·ri·al** *adj.*
cu·rie /kyóoree/ *n.* **1** a unit of radioactivity. ¶ Abbr.: **Ci**.

2 a quantity of radioactive substance having this activity.

cu·ri·o /kyŏŏreeō/ *n.* (*pl.* **-os**) a rare or unusual object or person.

cu·ri·os·i·ty /kyŏŏreeósitee/ *n.* (*pl.* **-ties**) **1** inquisitiveness. **2** strangeness. **3** a strange, rare, or interesting object.

cu·ri·ous /kyŏŏreeəs/ *adj.* **1** inquisitive. **2** strange; surprising. ▫▫ **cu·ri·ous·ly** *adv.* **cu·ri·ous·ness** *n.*

cu·ri·um /kyŏŏreeəm/ *n.* an artificially made transuranic radioactive metallic element. ¶ Symb.: **Cm**.

curl /kərl/ *v. & n.* • *v.* **1** *tr. & intr.* (often foll. by *up*) bend or coil into a spiral. **2** *intr.* move in a spiral form. **3 a** *intr.* (of the upper lip) be raised slightly on one side in disapproval. **b** *tr.* cause (the lip) to do this. **4** *intr.* play curling. • *n.* **1** a lock of curled hair. **2** anything spiral or curved inward. **3 a** a curling movement or act. **b** the state of being curled. ▫ **curl up 1** lie or sit with the knees drawn up. **2** *colloq.* writhe with embarrassment or horror. **make a person's hair curl** *colloq.* shock or horrify a person. ▫▫ **curl·y** /kórlee/ *adj.* (**curlier, curliest**). **curl·i·ness** *n.*

curl·er /kórlər/ *n.* **1** a roller, etc., for curling the hair. **2** a player in the game of curling.

cur·lew /kórlōō, –lyōō/ *n.* any wading bird of the genus *Numenius* with a long, slender, down-curved bill.

curl·ing /kórling/ *n.* **1** in senses of CURL *v.* **2** a game played on ice, in which large, round, flat stones are slid across the surface.

cur·mudg·eon /kərmújən/ *n.* a bad-tempered person. ▫▫ **cur·mudg·eon·ly** *adj.*

cur·rant /kórənt, kúr–/ *n.* **1** a dried fruit of a small seedless variety of grape. **2 a** any of various shrubs of the genus *Ribes* producing red, white, or black berries. **b** a berry of these shrubs.

cur·ren·cy /kórənsee, kúr–/ *n.* (*pl.* **-cies**) **1 a** the money in general use in a country. **b** any other commodity used as a medium of exchange. **2** the condition of being current (e.g., of words or ideas). **3** the time during which something is current.

cur·rent /kórənt, kúr–/ *adj. & n.* • *adj.* **1** belonging to the present time; happening now (*current events*; *the current week*). **2** (of money, opinion, a rumor, a word, etc.) in general circulation or use. • *n.* **1** a body of water, air, etc., moving esp. through a stiller surrounding body. **2 a** an ordered movement of electrically charged particles. **b** a quantity representing the intensity of such movement. **3** (usu. foll. by *of*) a general tendency or course (of events, opinions, etc.).

cur·rent·ly /kórəntlee, kúr–/ *adv.* at the present time; now.

cur·ric·u·lum /kəríkyələm/ *n.* (*pl.* **curricula** /–lə/ or **curriculums**) **1** the subjects that are studied or prescribed for study in a school. **2** any program of activities. ▫▫ **cur·ric·u·lar** *adj.*

cur·ric·u·lum vi·tae /kəríkyələm vítee, véetī/ *n.* (*pl.* **curricula vitae**) a brief account of one's education, qualifications, and previous occupations.

cur·ry[1] /kóree, kúree/ *n. & v.* • *n.* (*pl.* **-ries**) a dish of meat, vegetables, etc., cooked in a sauce of hot-tasting spices, usu. served with rice. • *v.tr.* (**-ries, -ried**) prepare or flavor with a sauce of hot-tasting spices.

cur·ry[2] /kóree, kúree/ *v.tr.* (**-ries, -ried**) **1** groom (a horse) with a currycomb. **2** treat (tanned leather) to improve its properties. **3** thrash. ▫ **curry favor** ingratiate oneself.

cur·ry·comb /kóreekōm, kúree–/ *n. & v.* • *n.* a hand-held metal serrated device for grooming horses. • *v.tr.* use a currycomb on.

cur·ry pow·der *n.* a preparation of ground spices, such as turmeric, ginger, and coriander, for making curry.

curse /kərs/ *n. & v.* • *n.* **1** a solemn utterance intended to invoke a supernatural power to inflict destruction or punishment on a person or thing. **2** the evil supposedly resulting from a curse. **3** a violent exclamation of anger; a profane oath. **4** a thing that causes evil or harm. **5** (prec. by *the*) *colloq.* menstruation. **6** a sentence of excommunication. • *v.* **1** *tr.* **a** utter a curse against. **b** (in *imper.*) may God curse. **2** *tr.* (usu. in *passive*; foll. by *with*) afflict with (*cursed with blindness*). **3** *intr.* utter expletive curses; swear. **4** *tr.* excommunicate. ▫▫ **curs·er** *n.*

curs·ed /kórsid, kərst/ *adj.* damnable; abominable. ▫▫ **curs·ed·ly** *adv.* **curs·ed·ness** *n.*

cur·sive /kórsiv/ *adj. & n.* • *adj.* (of writing) done with joined characters. • *n.* cursive writing. ▫▫ **cur·sive·ly** *adv.*

cur·sor /kórsər/ *n.* *Computing* a movable indicator on a monitor screen identifying a particular position in the display.

cur·so·ry /kórsəree/ *adj.* hasty; hurried. ▫▫ **cur·so·ri·ly** *adv.* **cur·so·ri·ness** *n.*

curt /kərt/ *adj.* noticeably or rudely brief. ▫▫ **curt·ly** *adv.* **curt·ness** *n.*

cur·tail /kərtáyl/ *v.tr.* cut short; reduce. ▫▫ **cur·tail·ment** *n.*

cur·tain /kórtən/ *n. & v.* • *n.* **1** a piece of cloth, etc., hung up as a screen and usu. movable sideways or upward, esp. at a window or between the stage and auditorium of a theater. **2** *Theatr.* **a** the rise or fall of the stage curtain at the beginning or end of an act or scene. **b** = CURTAIN CALL. **3** a partition or cover. **4** (in *pl.*) *sl.* the end. • *v.tr.* **1** furnish or cover with a curtain or curtains. **2** (foll. by *off*) shut off with a curtain or curtains.

cur·tain call *n.* *Theatr.* an audience's summons to performer(s) to take a bow after the fall of the curtain.

curt·sy /kórtsee/ *n. & v.* (also **curt·sey**) • *n.* (*pl.* **-sies** or **-seys**) a woman's or girl's formal greeting made by bending the knees and lowering the body. • *v.intr.* (**-sies, -sied** or **-seys, -seyed**) make a curtsy.

curtsy early 16th century: variant of COURTESY. Both forms were used to denote the expression of respect or courtesy by a gesture, especially in phrases such as *do courtesy*, *make courtesy*, and from this arose the current use (late 16th century).

cur·va·ceous /kərváyshəs/ *adj. colloq.* (esp. of a woman) having a shapely curved figure.

cur·va·ture /kórvəchər/ *n.* **1** the act or state of curving. **2** a curved form. **3** *Geom.* **a** the deviation of a curved surface from a plane. **b** the quantity expressing this.

curve /kərv/ *n. & v.* • *n.* **1** a line or surface having along its length a regular deviation from being straight or flat. **2** a curved form or thing. **3** a curved line on a graph. **4** *Baseball* a ball caused to deviate by the pitcher's spin. • *v.tr. & intr.* bend or shape so as to form a curve. ▫▫ **curved** *adj.*

curve·ball /kórvbawl/ *n.* = CURVE *n.* 4.

curvi- /kórvee/ *comb. form* curved.

cur·vi·lin·e·ar /kórvilíneeər/ *adj.* contained by or consisting of curved lines. ▫▫ **cur·vi·lin·e·ar·ly** *adv.*

curv·y /kórvee/ *adj.* (**curvier, curviest**) **1** having many curves. **2** (of a woman's figure) shapely. ▫▫ **curv·i·ness** *n.*

cush·ion /kŏŏshən/ *n. & v.* • *n.* **1** a bag stuffed with soft material for sitting or leaning on, etc. **2** a means of protection against shock. **3** the elastic lining of the sides of a billiard table, from which the ball rebounds. • *v.tr.* **1** provide or protect with a cushion or cushions. **2** provide with a defense; protect. **3** mitigate the adverse effects of. **4** quietly suppress. **5** place or bounce (the ball) against the cushion in billiards. ▫▫ **cush·ion·y** *adj.*

cush·y /kŏŏshee/ *adj.* (**cushier, cushiest**) *colloq.* **1** (of a job, etc.) easy and pleasant. **2** (of a seat, surroundings, etc.) soft; comfortable. ▫▫ **cush·i·ness** *n.*

cusp /kusp/ *n.* **1** an apex or peak. **2** the horn of a crescent moon, etc. **3** *Astrol.* the initial point of a house. **4** a cone-shaped prominence on the surface of a tooth. ▫▫ **cus·pate** /kúspayt/ *adj.* **cusped** *adj.* **cus·pi·dal** /kúspid'l/ *adj.*

cus·pi·dor /kúspidawr/ *n.* a spittoon.

cuss /kus/ *n. & v. colloq.* •*n.* **1** a curse. **2** usu. *derog.* a person; a creature. •*v.tr. & intr.* curse.

cuss·word /kúswərd/ *n.* a swearword.

cus·tard /kústərd/ *n.* **1** a dish made with milk and eggs, usu. sweetened. **2** a sweet sauce made with milk and flavored cornstarch.

cus·to·di·an /kustṓdeeən/ *n.* a guardian or keeper, esp. of a public building, etc. ▫▫ **cus·to·di·an·ship** *n.*

cus·to·dy /kústədee/ *n.* **1** guardianship; protective care. **2** imprisonment. ▫ **take into custody** arrest. ▫▫ **cus·to·di·al** /kustṓdeeəl/ *adj.*

cus·tom /kústəm/ *n.* **1 a** the usual way of behaving or acting (*a slave to custom*). **b** a particular established way of behaving (*our customs seem strange to foreigners*). **2** *Law* established usage having the force of law. **3** (in *pl.*; also treated as *sing.*) **a** a duty levied on certain imported and exported goods. **b** the official department that administers this. **c** the area at a port, frontier, etc., where customs officials deal with incoming goods, etc.

cus·tom·ar·y /kústəmeree/ *adj.* usual; in accordance with custom. ▫▫ **cus·tom·ar·i·ly** *adv.* **cus·tom·ar·i·ness** *n.*

cus·tom-built *adj.* (also **cus·tom-made**) made to a customer's order.

cus·tom·er /kústəmər/ *n.* **1** a person who buys goods or services from a store or business. **2** a person one has to deal with (*an awkward customer*).

cus·tom·ize /kústəmīz/ *v.tr.* make to order or modify according to individual requirements.

cus·tom-made see CUSTOM-BUILT.

cut /kut/ *v. & n.* •*v.* (**cutting**; *past* and *past part.* **cut**) **1** *tr.* (also *absol.*) penetrate or wound with a sharp-edged instrument. **2** *tr. & intr.* (often foll. by *into*) divide or be divided with a knife, etc. **3** *tr.* **a** trim (hair, a hedge, etc.) by cutting. **b** detach (flowers, grain, etc.) by cutting. **c** reduce the length of (a book, movie, etc.). **4** *tr.* (foll. by *loose, open*, etc.) make loose, open, etc. by cutting. **5** *tr.* (esp. as **cutting** *adj.*) cause sharp physical or mental pain to (*a cutting remark*; *a cutting wind*). **6** *tr.* (often foll. by *down*) **a** reduce (wages, prices, time, etc.). **b** reduce or cease (services, etc.). **7** *tr.* **a** shape or fashion (a coat, gem, key, record, etc.) by cutting. **b** make (a path, tunnel, etc.) by removing material. **8** *tr.* perform; make (*cut a caper*; *cut a sorry figure*). **9** *tr.* (also *absol.*) cross; intersect (*the line cuts the circle at two points*). **10** *intr.* (foll. by *across, through*, etc.) traverse, esp. as a shorter way (*cut across the grass*). **11** *tr.* **a** ignore or refuse to recognize (a person). **b** renounce (a connection). **12** *tr.* deliberately fail to attend (a class, etc.). **13** *Cards* **a** *tr.* divide (a deck) into two parts. **b** *intr.* select a dealer, etc., by dividing the deck. **14** *Cinematog.* **a** *tr.* edit (a movie or tape). **b** *intr.* (often in *imper.*) stop filming or recording. **c** *intr.* (foll. by *to*) go quickly to (another shot). **15** *tr.* switch off (an engine, etc.). **16** *tr.* **a** hit (a ball) with a chopping motion. **b** *Golf* slice (the ball). **17** *tr.* dilute; adulterate. •*n.* **1** an act of cutting. **2** a division or wound made by cutting. **3** a stroke with a knife, sword, whip, etc. **4** a reduction (in prices, wages, etc.). **5** an excision of part of a play, movie, book, etc. **6** a wounding remark or act. **7** the way or style in which a garment, the hair, etc., is cut. **8** a piece of meat, etc., cut from a carcass. **9** *colloq.* commission; a share of profits. **10** *Tennis, etc.* a stroke made by cutting. **11** ignoring of or refusal to recognize a person. **12 a** an engraved block for printing. **b** a woodcut or other print. ▫ **a cut above** *colloq.* noticeably superior to. **be cut out** (foll. by *for*, or *to* + infin.) be suited (*was not cut out to be a teacher*). **cut across 1** transcend or take no account of (normal limitations, etc.) (*their concern cuts across normal rivalries*). **2** see sense 10 of *v.* **cut and run** *sl.* run away. **cut and thrust 1** a lively interchange of argument, etc. **2** the use of both the edge and the point of a sword. **cut back 1** reduce (expenditure, etc.). **2** prune (a tree, etc.). **3** *Cinematog.* repeat part of a previous scene for dramatic effect. **cut both ways 1** serve both sides of an argument, etc. **2** (of an action) have both good and bad effects. **cut corners** do a task, etc., perfunctorily or incompletely, esp. to save time. **cut down 1 a** bring or throw down by cutting. **b** kill by means of a sword or disease. **2** see sense 6 of *v.* **3** reduce the length of (*cut down the pants to make shorts*). **4** (often foll. by *on*) reduce one's consumption (*cut down on chocolate*). **cut a person down to size** *colloq.* ruthlessly expose the limitations of a person's importance, ability, etc. **cut one's eyeteeth** (or **teeth**) attain worldly wisdom. **cut in 1** interrupt. **2** pull in too closely in front of another vehicle (esp. having overtaken it). **3** give a share of profits, etc. to (a person). **4** connect (a source of electricity). **5** join in a card game by taking the place of a player who cuts out. **6** interrupt a dancing couple to take over from one partner. **cut into 1** make a cut in. **2** interfere with and reduce (*traveling cuts into my free time*). **cut it out** (usu. in *imper.*) *sl.* stop doing that (esp. quarreling). **cut loose 1** begin to act freely. **2** see sense 4 of *v.* **cut one's losses** abandon an unprofitable enterprise before losses become too great. **cut the mustard** *sl.* reach the required standard. **cut off 1** remove by cutting. **2 a** (often in *passive*) bring to an abrupt end or (esp. early) death. **b** intercept; interrupt; prevent from continuing (*cut off supplies*. **c** disconnect (a person engaged in a telephone conversation) (*was suddenly cut off*). **3 a** prevent from traveling or venturing out (*cut off by the snow*). **b** (as **cut off** *adj.*) isolated; remote (*felt cut off in the country*). **4 a** disinherit (*was cut off without a penny*). **b** sever a relationship (*was cut off from the children*). **cut out 1** remove from the inside by cutting. **2** make by cutting from a larger whole. **3** omit; leave out. **4** *colloq.* stop doing or using (*cut out chocolate*; *let's cut out the arguing*). **5** cease or cause to cease functioning (*the engine cut out*). **6** *colloq.* prepare; plan (*has his work cut out*). **cut short 1** interrupt; terminate prematurely (*cut short his visit*). **2** make shorter or more concise. **cut one's teeth on** acquire initial practice or experience from (something). **cut a tooth** have it appear through the gum. **cut up 1** cut into pieces. **2** destroy utterly. **3** criticize severely. **4** behave in a comical or unruly manner.

cut-and-dried *adj.* (also **cut-and-dry**) **1** completely decided; prearranged; inflexible. **2** (of opinions, etc.) ready-made; lacking freshness or imagination.

cu·ta·ne·ous /kyōōtáyneeəs/ *adj.* of the skin.

cut·a·way /kútəway/ *adj.* **1** (of a diagram, etc.) with some parts left out to reveal the interior. **2** (of a coat) with the front below the waist cut away.

cut·back /kútbak/ *n.* an instance or the act of cutting back, esp. a reduction in expenditure.

cute /kyōōt/ *adj. colloq.* **1 a** attractive; quaint. **b** affectedly attractive. **2** clever; ingenious. ▫▫ **cute·ly** *adv.* **cute·ness** *n.*

cu·ti·cle /kyṓōtikəl/ *n.* **1 a** the dead skin at the base of a fingernail or toenail. **b** the epidermis or other superficial skin. **2** *Bot.* a thin surface film on plants. ▫▫ **cu·tic·u·lar** /–tíkyələr/ *adj.*

cut·lass /kútləs/ *n.* a short sword with a slightly curved blade, formerly used by sailors.

cut·ler /kútlər/ *n.* a person who makes or deals in knives and similar utensils.

cut·ler·y /kútləree/ *n.* knives, forks, and spoons for use at table.

cut·let /kútlit/ *n.* **1** a small piece of veal, etc., for frying. **2** a flat cake of ground meat or nuts and breadcrumbs, etc.

cut·off /kútawf/ *n.* **1** the point at which something is cut off. **2** a device for stopping a flow. **3** a shortcut. **4** (in *pl.*) shorts made from jeans, etc., whose legs have been cut off.

cut·out /kútowt/ *n.* **1** a figure cut out of paper, etc. **2** a device that automatically breaks an electric circuit for safety.

cut rate *adj.* selling or sold at a reduced price.

cut·ter /kútər/ *n.* **1** a tailor, etc., who takes measurements and cuts cloth. **2** *Naut.* **a** a small, fast sailing ship. **b** a small boat carried by a large ship.

cut·throat /kút-thrōt/ *n.* & *adj.* • *n.* **1** a murderer. **2** a species of trout, *Salmo clarki*, with a red mark under the jaw. • *adj.* **1** (of competition) ruthless and intense. **2** (of a person) murderous. **3** (of a card game) three-handed.

cut·ting /kúting/ *n.* & *adj.* • *n.* a piece cut from a plant for propagation. • *adj.* see CUT *v.* 5. ▫▫ **cut·ting·ly** *adv.*

cut·ting edge *n.* the forefront; the vanguard.

cut·tle·bone /kút'lbōn/ *n.* the internal shell of the cuttlefish.

cut·tle·fish /kút'lfish/ *n.* any marine cephalopod mollusk of the genera *Sepia* and *Sepiola*, having ten arms and ejecting a black fluid when threatened or pursued.

cut·up /kútup/ *n.* a person who clowns around; prankster.

cut·worm /kútwərm/ *n.* any of various caterpillars that eat through the stems of young plants level with the ground.

c.v. *abbr.* curriculum vitae.

cwt. *abbr.* hundredweight.

cy·a·nide /sīənīd/ *n.* any of the highly poisonous salts or esters of hydrocyanic acid, esp. the potassium salt used in the extraction of gold and silver.

cy·a·no·bac·te·ri·um /sīənṓbaktéereeəm, sīánō–/ *n.* any prokaryotic organism of the division Cyanobacteria, capable of photosynthesizing. Also called BLUE-GREEN ALGA.

cy·a·no·co·bal·a·min /sīənṓkōbáləmin, sīánō–/ *n.* a vitamin of the B complex, found in foods of animal origin such as liver, fish, and eggs. Also called *vitamin* B_{12}.

cy·a·no·sis /sīənṓsis/ *n. Med.* a bluish discoloration of the skin due to the presence of oxygen-deficient blood. ▫▫ **cy·a·not·ic** /–nótik/ *adj.*

cy·ber·net·ics /sībərnétiks/ *n.pl.* (usu. treated as *sing.*) the science of communications and automatic control systems in both machines and living things. ▫▫ **cy·ber·net·ic** *adj.* **cy·ber·net·i·cist** /–tisist/ *n.*

cy·ber·space /sībərspays/ *n.* an environment in which information exchange by computer occurs.

cy·cad /síkad/ *n. Bot.* any of the palmlike plants of the order Cycadales (including fossil forms).

cy·cla·men /síkləmən, sík–/ *n.* **1** any plant of the genus *Cyclamen*, originating in Europe, having pink, red, or white flowers with reflexed petals. **2** the shade of color of the red or pink cyclamen flower.

cy·cle /síkəl/ *n.* & *v.* • *n.* **1 a** a recurrent round or period (of events, phenomena, etc.). **b** the time needed for one such round or period. **2 a** *Physics*, etc., a recurrent series of operations or states. **b** *Electr.* = HERTZ. **3** a series of songs, poems, etc., usu. on a single theme. **4** a bicycle, tricycle, or similar machine. • *v.intr.* **1** ride a bicycle, etc. **2** move in cycles.

cy·clic /síklik, sík–/ *adj.* **1 a** recurring in cycles. **b** belonging to a chronological cycle. **2** *Chem.* with constituent atoms forming a ring. **3** of a cycle of songs, etc. **4** *Bot.* (of a flower) with its parts arranged in whorls.

cy·cli·cal /síklikəl, sík–/ *adj.* = CYCLIC 1. ▫▫ **cy·cli·cal·ly** *adv.*

cy·clist /síklist/ *n.* a rider of a bicycle.

cyclo- /síklō/ *comb. form* circle, cycle, or cyclic (*cyclometer*; *cyclorama*).

cy·clom·e·ter /sīklómitər/ *n.* **1** an instrument for measuring circular arcs. **2** an instrument for measuring the distance traversed by a bicycle, etc.

cy·clone /síklōn/ *n.* **1** a system of winds rotating inward to an area of low barometric pressure; a depression. **2** a violent hurricane of limited diameter. ▫▫ **cy·clon·ic** /–klónik/ *adj.* **cy·clon·i·cal·ly** *adv.*

cy·clo·pe·di·a /síkləpéedeeə/ *n.* an encyclopedia. ▫▫ **cy·clo·pe·dic** *adj.*

cy·clo·tron /síklətron/ *n. Physics* an apparatus in which charged atomic and subatomic particles are accelerated by an alternating electric field while following an outward spiral or circular path in a magnetic field.

cyg·net /sígnit/ *n.* a young swan.

cyl·in·der /sílindər/ *n.* **1 a** a uniform solid or hollow body with straight sides and a circular section. **b** a thing of this shape, e.g., a container for liquefied gas. **2** a cylinder-shaped part of various machines, esp. a piston chamber in an engine. **3** *Printing* a metal roller. ▫▫ **cy·lin·dri·cal** /silíndrikəl/ *adj.* **cy·lin·dri·cal·ly** *adv.*

cym·bal /símbəl/ *n.* a percussion instrument of indefinite pitch consisting of a concave brass or bronze plate, struck with another or with a stick, etc., to make a ringing sound. ▫▫ **cym·bal·ist** *n.*

cymbals

cyn·ic /sínik/ *n.* & *adj.* • *n.* **1** a person who has little faith in human sincerity and goodness. **2** (**Cynic**) one of a school of ancient Greek philosophers founded by Antisthenes, marked by ostentatious contempt for ease and pleasure. • *adj.* **1** (**Cynic**) of the Cynics. **2** = CYNICAL. ▫▫ **cyn·i·cism** /–nisizəm/ *n.*

cyn·i·cal /sínikəl/ *adj.* **1** incredulous of human sincerity and goodness. **2** disregarding normal standards. **3** sneering; mocking. ▫▫ **cyn·i·cal·ly** *adv.*

cy·no·sure /sínəshoor, sín–/ *n.* **1** a center of attraction or admiration. **2** a guiding star.

cy·pher var. of CIPHER.

cy·press /sípres/ *n.* **1** any coniferous tree of the genus *Cupressus* or *Chamaecyparis*, with hard wood and dark foliage. **2** this, or branches from it, as a symbol of mourning.

Cyp·ri·ot /sípreeət/ *n.* & *adj.* (also **Cyp·ri·ote** /–ōt/) • *n.* a native or national of Cyprus. • *adj.* of Cyprus.

Cy·ril·lic /sirílik/ *adj.* & *n.* • *adj.* denoting the alphabet used by the Slavonic peoples of the Orthodox Church, now used for Russian, Bulgarian, Serbian, Ukrainian, and other Slavic languages. • *n.* this alphabet.

cyst /sist/ *n.* **1** *Med.* a sac containing morbid matter, a parasitic larva, etc. **2** *Biol.* **a** a hollow organ, bladder, etc., in an animal or plant, containing a liquid secretion. **b** a cell or cavity enclosing reproductive bodies, an embryo, parasite, microorganism, etc.

cys·tic /sístik/ *adj.* **1** of the urinary bladder. **2** of the gallbladder. **3** of the nature of a cyst.

cys·tic fi·bro·sis *n. Med.* a hereditary disease affecting the exocrine glands and usu. resulting in respiratory infections.

cys·ti·tis /sistítis/ *n.* an inflammation of the urinary bladder, usu. accompanied by frequent painful urination.

cysto- /sístō/ *comb. form* the urinary bladder (*cystoscope*; *cystotomy*).

-cyte /sīt/ *comb. form Biol.* a mature cell (*leukocyte*) (cf. -BLAST).

cyto- /sítō/ *comb. form Biol.* cells or a cell.

cy·to·ge·net·ics /sítōjinétiks/ *n.* the study of inheritance in relation to the structure and function of cells. □□ **cy·to·ge·net·ic** *adj.* **cy·to·ge·net·i·cal** *adj.* **cy·to·ge·net·i·cal·ly** *adv.* **cy·to·ge·net·i·cist** /–nétisist/ *n.*

cy·tol·o·gy /sītóləjee/ *n.* the study of cells. □□ **cy·to·log·i·cal** /sítəlójikəl/ *adj.* **cy·to·log·i·cal·ly** *adv.* **cy·tol·o·gist** *n.*

cy·to·plasm /sítəplazəm/ *n.* the protoplasmic content of a cell apart from its nucleus. □□ **cy·to·plas·mic** /–plázmik/ *adj.*

czar /zaar/ *n.* (also **tsar**) **1** *hist.* the title of the former emperor of Russia. **2** a person with great authority. □□ **czar·dom** *n.* **czar·ism** *n.* **czar·ist** *n.*

czar·e·vich /za'arivich/ *n.* (also **tsar·e·vich**) *hist.* the eldest son of an emperor of Russia.

cza·ri·na /zaare'enə/ *n.* (also **tsa·ri·na**) *hist.* the title of the former empress of Russia.

Czech /chek/ *n. & adj.* • *n.* **1** a native or national of the Czech Republic, Bohemia, or *(hist.)* Czechoslovakia. **2** the West Slavonic language of the Czech people. • *adj.* of or relating to the Czechs or their language.

Czech·o·slo·vak /chékəslṓvak, –vaak/ *n. & adj.* (also **Czech·o·slo·va·ki·an** /–sləva'akeeən/) • *n.* a native or national of Czechoslovakia, a former nation in central Europe including Bohemia, Moravia, and Slovakia. • *adj.* of or relating to Czechoslovaks or the former nation of Czechoslovakia.

D

D[1] /dee/ *n.* (also **d**) (*pl.* **ds** or **D's**) **1** the fourth letter of the alphabet. **2** *Mus.* the second note of the diatonic scale of C major. **3** (as a Roman numeral) 500. **4** = DEE. **5** the fourth highest class or category (of academic marks, etc.).

D[2] *symb. Chem.* the element deuterium.

d. *abbr.* **1** died. **2** departs. **3** delete. **4** daughter. **5** depth. **6** deci-.

'd *v. colloq.* (usu. after pronouns) had; would (*I'd; he'd*).

DA *abbr.* **1** district attorney. **2** *sl.* = DUCK'S ASS.

da *abbr.* deca-.

dab /dab/ *v. & n.* •*v.* (**dabbed, dabbing**) **1** *tr.* press (a surface) briefly with a cloth, etc., without rubbing. **2** *tr.* press (a sponge, etc.) lightly on a surface. **3** *tr.* (foll. by *on*) apply (a substance) by dabbing a surface. **4** *intr.* (usu. foll. by *at*) aim a feeble blow; tap. **5** *tr.* strike lightly; tap. •*n.* **1** a brief application of a cloth, etc., to a surface without rubbing. **2** a small amount applied in this way (*a dab of paint*). **3** a light blow. ▫▫ **dab·ber** *n.*

dab·ble /dábəl/ *v.* **1** *intr.* (usu. foll. by *in, at*) take a superficial interest (in a subject or activity). **2** *intr.* move the feet, hands, etc., about in (usu. a small amount of) liquid. **3** *tr.* wet partly; stain; splash. ▫▫ **dab·bler** *n.*

dace /days/ *n.* (*pl.* same) any small freshwater fish, esp. of the genus *Leuciscus*, related to the carp.

da·cha /daáchə/ *n.* a country house or cottage in Russia.

dachs·hund /daáks-hoont, daáksənt, –hoond, –ənd/ *n.* a dog of a short-legged, long-bodied breed.

dac·tyl /dáktil/ *n.* a metrical foot (¯˘˘) consisting of one long syllable followed by two short. ▫▫ **dac·tyl·ic** /daktílik/ *adj.*

dad /dad/ *n. colloq.* father.

Da·da /daádaa/ *n.* an early 20th-c. international movement in art, literature, music, and film, repudiating conventions. ▫▫ **Da·da·ism** /daádəizəm/ *n.* **Da·da·ist** *n. & adj.* **Da·da·is·tic** *adj.*

dad·dy /dádee/ *n.* (*pl.* **-dies**) *colloq.* **1** father. **2** (usu. foll. by *of*) the oldest or supreme example (*a daddy of a lie*).

dad·dy long·legs *n.* an arachnid of the order Opiliones, with long, thin, bent legs. Also called **harvestman**.

da·do /dáydō/ *n.* (*pl.* **-dos**) **1** the lower part of the wall of a room when visually distinct from the upper part. **2** the plinth of a column. **3** the cube of a pedestal between the base and the cornice.

daf·fo·dil /dáfədil/ *n.* **1 a** a bulbous plant, *Narcissus pseudonarcissus*, with a yellow trumpet-shaped crown. **b** any of various other plants of the genus *Narcissus*. **c** a flower of any of these plants. **2** a pale-yellow color.

daf·fy /dáfee/ *adj.* (**daffier, daffiest**) *sl.* = DAFT. ▫▫ **daf·fi·ly** *adv.* **daf·fi·ness** *n.*

daft /daft/ *adj. colloq.* **1** foolish; crazy. **2** (foll. by *about*) fond of; infatuated with. ▫▫ **daft·ly** *adv.* **daft·ness** *n.*

dag·ger /dágər/ *n.* **1** a short stabbing weapon with a pointed and edged blade. **2** *Printing* = OBELUS. ▫ **look daggers at** glare angrily at.

da·guerre·o·type /dəgérətīp/ *n.* **1** a photograph taken by an early photographic process employing an iodine-sensitized silvered plate and mercury vapor. **2** this process.

dahl·ia /dályə, daál–, dáyl–/ *n.* any garden plant of the genus *Dahlia*, cultivated for its many-colored flowers.

dai·ly /dáylee/ *adj., adv., & n.* •*adj.* **1** done, produced, or occurring every day or every weekday. **2** constant; regular. •*adv.* **1** every day; from day to day. **2** constantly. •*n.* (*pl.* **-lies**) *colloq.* a daily newspaper.

dain·ty /dayntee/ *adj. & n.* •*adj.* (**daintier, daintiest**) **1** delicately pretty. **2** delicate of build or in movement. **3** (of food) choice. **4** fastidious. •*n.* (*pl.* **-ties**) a choice delicacy. ▫▫ **dain·ti·ly** *adv.* **dain·ti·ness** *n.*

dai·qui·ri /dákəree, dí–/ *n.* (*pl.* **daiquiris**) a cocktail of rum, lime juice, etc.

dair·y /dáiree/ *n.* (*pl.* **-ies**) **1** a building or room for the storage, processing, and distribution of milk and its products. **2** a store where milk and milk products are sold. **3** (*attrib.*) **a** of, containing, or concerning milk and its products (and sometimes eggs). **b** used for dairy products (*dairy cow*).

da·is /dáyis, dí–/ *n.* a low platform, usu. at the upper end of a hall.

dai·sy /dáyzee/ *n.* (*pl.* **-sies**) **1 a** a small composite plant, *Bellis perennis*, bearing flowers each with a yellow disk and white rays. **b** any other plant with daisy-like flowers. **2** *sl.* a first-rate specimen of anything. ▫ **pushing up daisies** *sl.* dead and buried.

dai·sy wheel *n.* a disk of spokes extending radially from a central hub, each terminating in a printing character, used as a printer in word processors and typewriters.

Da·lai la·ma /daálī laámə/ *n.* the spiritual head of Tibetan Buddhism.

dale /dayl/ *n.* a valley, esp. a broad one.

dal·li·ance /dáleeəns, –yəns/ *n.* **1** a leisurely or frivolous passing of time. **2** an instance of lighthearted flirting.

dal·ly /dálee/ *v.intr.* (**-lies, -lied**) **1** delay; waste time, esp. frivolously. **2** (often foll. by *with*) play about; flirt; treat frivolously. ▫ **dally away** waste or fritter (one's time, life, etc.).

Dal·ma·tian /dalmáyshən/ *n.* a dog of a large, white, short-haired breed with dark spots.

dam[1] /dam/ *n. & v.* •*n.* **1** a barrier constructed to hold back water and raise its level, forming a reservoir or preventing flooding. **2** a barrier constructed in a stream by a beaver. **3** anything functioning as a dam does. **4** a causeway. •*v.tr.* (**dammed, damming**) **1** furnish or confine with a dam. **2** (often foll. by *up*) block up; obstruct.

dam[2] /dam/ *n.* the female parent of an animal, esp. a four-footed one.

dam·age /dámij/ *n. & v.* •*n.* **1** harm or injury. **2** (in *pl.*) *Law* a sum of money claimed or awarded in compensation for a loss or an injury. **3** the loss of what is desirable. **4** (prec. by *the*) *sl.* cost (*what's the damage?*). •*v.tr.* **1** inflict damage on. **2** (esp. as **damaging** *adj.*) detract from the reputation of (*a most damaging admission*). ▫▫ **dam·ag·ing·ly** *adv.*

dam·ask /dáməsk/ *n., adj., & v.* •*n.* **1 a** a figured woven fabric (esp. silk or linen) with a pattern visible on both sides. **b** twilled table linen with woven designs shown by the reflection of light. **2** a tablecloth made of this material. • *adj.* **1** made of or resembling damask. **2** velvety pink or vivid red. • *v.tr.* weave with figured designs.

dam•ask rose *n.* an old sweet-scented variety of rose, with very soft velvety petals, used to make attar.

dame /daym/ *n.* **1** (**Dame**) **a** (in the UK) honorific title given to a woman. **b** a woman holding this title. **2** *sl.* a woman.

dam•mit /dámit/ *int.* damn it.

damn /dam/ *v., n., adj., & adv.* • *v.tr.* **1** (often *absol.* or as *int.* of anger or annoyance, = *may God damn*) curse (a person or thing). **2** doom to hell; cause the damnation of. **3** condemn; censure (*a review damning the performance*). **4 a** (often as **damning** *adj.*) (of a circumstance, evidence, etc.) show or prove to be guilty. **b** be the ruin of. • *n.* **1** an uttered curse. **2** *sl.* a negligible amount (*not worth a damn*). • *adj. & adv. colloq.* = DAMNED. □ **damn with faint praise** commend so unenthusiastically as to imply disapproval. □□ **damn•ing•ly** *adv.*

dam•na•ble /dámnəbəl/ *adj.* hateful; annoying. □□ **dam•na•bly** *adv.*

dam•na•tion /damnáyshən/ *n. & int.* • *n.* eternal punishment in hell. • *int.* expressing anger.

damned /damd/ *adj. & adv. colloq.* • *adj.* damnable. • *adv.* extremely (*damned hot*). □ **do one's damnedest** do one's utmost.

damp /damp/ *adj., n., & v.* • *adj.* slightly wet. • *n.* **1** diffused moisture in the air, on a surface, or in a solid. **2** dejection; discouragement. **3** = FIREDAMP. • *v.tr.* **1** make damp; moisten. **2** (often foll. by *down*) **a** take the force out of (*damp one's enthusiasm*). **b** make spiritless. **c** make (a fire) burn less strongly by reducing the flow of air to it. **3** reduce or stop the vibration of (esp. the strings of a musical instrument). **4** quiet. □ **damp off** (of a plant) die from a fungus attack in damp conditions. □□ **damp•ly** *adv.* **damp•ness** *n.*

damp•en /dámpən/ *v.* **1** *v.tr. & intr.* make or become damp. **2** *tr.* make less forceful. □□ **damp•en•er** *n.*

damp•er /dámpər/ *n.* **1** a person or thing that discourages. **2** a device that reduces shock or noise. **3** a metal plate in a flue to control the draft. **4** *Mus.* a pad silencing a piano string. □ **put a damper on** take the enjoyment out of.

dam•sel /dámzəl/ *n. archaic* or *literary* a young unmarried woman.

dam•sel•fly /dámzəlflī/ *n.* (*pl.* **-flies**) any of various insects of the order Odonata, like a dragonfly but with its wings folded over the body when resting.

dam•son /dámzən, –sən/ *n. & adj.* • *n.* **1** (in full **damson plum**) **a** a small, dark-purple, plumlike fruit. **b** the small deciduous tree, *Prunus institia*, bearing this. **2** a dark-purple color. • *adj.* damson-colored.

dance /dans/ *v. & n.* • *v.* **1** *intr.* move rhythmically to music, alone or with a partner or in a set. **2** *intr.* skip or jump about; move in a lively way. **3** *tr.* **a** perform (a specified dance). **b** perform (a specified role) in a ballet, etc. **4** *intr.* move up and down (on water, in the field of vision, etc.). **5** *tr.* move (esp. a child) up and down. • *n.* **1 a** a piece of dancing; a sequence of steps in dancing. **b** a special form of this. **2** a single round or turn of a dance. **3** a social gathering for dancing. **4** a piece of music for dancing to or in a dance rhythm. **5** a dancing or lively motion. □□ **dance•a•ble** *adj.* **danc•er** *n.*

d. and c. *abbr.* dilatation and curettage.

dan•de•li•on /dánd'līən/ *n.* a composite plant, *Taraxacum officinale*, with jagged leaves and a large, bright-yellow flower on a hollow stalk.

dan•der[1] /dándər/ *n.* loose flakes of skin in a person's hair or an animal's fur.

dan•der[2] /dándər/ *n. colloq.* temper; indignation. □ **get one's dander up** become angry.

dan•di•fy /dándifī/ *v.tr.* (**•fies, •fied**) cause to resemble a dandy.

dan•dle /dánd'l/ *v.tr.* **1** dance (a child) on one's knees or in one's arms. **2** pamper; pet.

dan•druff /dándruf/ *n.* **1** dead skin in small scales among the hair. **2** the condition of having this.

dan•dy /dándee/ *n. & adj.* • *n.* (*pl.* **-dies**) **1** a man unduly devoted to style, smartness, and fashion in dress and appearance. **2** *colloq.* an excellent thing. • *adj.* (**dandier, dandiest**) *colloq.* very good of its kind; splendid. □□ **dan•dy•ish** *adj.* **dan•dy•ism** *n.*

Dane /dayn/ *n.* **1** a native or national of Denmark. **2** *hist.* a Viking invader of England in the 9th–11th c.

dan•ger /dáynjər/ *n.* **1** liability or exposure to harm. **2** a thing that causes or is likely to cause harm. **3** the status of a railroad signal directing a halt or caution. □ **in danger of** likely to incur or to suffer from.

dan•ger•ous /dáynjərəs/ *adj.* involving or causing danger. □□ **dan•ger•ous•ly** *adv.* **dan•ger•ous•ness** *n.*

dan•gle /dánggəl/ *v.* **1** *intr.* be loosely suspended, so as to be able to sway to and fro. **2** *tr.* hold or carry loosely suspended. **3** *tr.* hold out (a hope, temptation, etc.) enticingly. □□ **dan•gler** *n.*

Dan•ish /dáynish/ *adj. & n.* • *adj.* of Denmark or the Danes. • *n.* **1** the Danish language. **2** (prec. by *the*; treated as *pl.*) the Danish people.

Dan•ish pas•try *n.* (also **Danish**) a cake of sweetened yeast pastry topped with icing, fruit, nuts, etc.

dank /dangk/ *adj.* disagreeably damp and cold. □□ **dank•ly** *adv.* **dank•ness** *n.*

dap•per /dápər/ *adj.* **1** neat and precise, esp. in dress or movement. **2** sprightly. □□ **dap•per•ly** *adv.* **dap•per•ness** *n.*

dap•ple /dápəl/ *v. & n.* • *v.* **1** *tr.* mark with spots or rounded patches of color or shade. **2** *intr.* become marked in this way. *n.* **1** a dappled effect. **2** a dappled animal, esp. a horse.

dap•ple gray *n.* **1** (of an animal's coat) gray or white with darker spots. **2** a horse of this color.

D.A.R *abbr.* Daughters of the American Revolution.

dare /dair/ *v. & n.* • *v.tr.* (*3rd sing. present* usu. **dare** before an expressed or implied infinitive without *to*) **1** (foll. by infin. with or without *to*) venture (to); have the courage or impudence (to) (*dare he do it?*; *if they dare to come*; *how dare you?*). **2** (usu. foll. by *to* + infin.) defy or challenge (a person) (*I dare you to own up*). • *n.* **1** an act of daring. **2** a challenge, esp. to prove courage. □ **I daresay 1** (often foll. by *that* + clause) it is probable. **2** probably; I grant that much. □□ **dar•er** *n.*

dare•dev•il /dáirdevəl/ *n. & adj.* • *n.* a recklessly daring person. • *adj.* recklessly daring. □□ **dare•dev•il•ry** *n.* **dare•dev•il•try** *n.*

dar•ing /dáiring/ *n. & adj.* • *n.* adventurous courage. • *adj.* adventurous; bold; prepared to take risks. □□ **dar•ing•ly** *adv.*

dark /daark/ *adj. & n.* • *adj.* **1** with little or no light. **2** of a deep or somber color. **3** (of a person) with deep brown or black hair or skin. **4** gloomy; depressing; dismal (*dark thoughts*). **5** evil; sinister (*dark deeds*). **6** sullen; angry (*a dark mood*). **7** secret; mysterious (*the dark and distant past*; *keep it dark*). **8** ignorant; unenlightened. • *n.* **1** absence of light. **2** nightfall (*don't go out after dark*). **3** a lack of knowledge. **4** a dark area or color, esp. in painting. □ **in the dark** lacking information. □□ **dark•ish** *adj.* **dark•ly** *adv.* **dark•ness** *n.*

Dark Ag•es *n.pl.* (also **Dark Age**) (prec. by *the*) **1** the period of European history preceding the Middle Ages, esp. the 5th–10th c. **2** any period of supposed unenlightenment.

Dark Con•ti•nent *n.* (prec. by *the*) a name for Africa, esp. when little known to Europeans.

dark·en /daárkən/ *v.* **1** *tr.* make dark or darker. **2** *intr.* become dark or darker. □ **never darken a person's door** keep away permanently.
dark horse *n.* a little-known person who is unexpectedly successful.
dark·room /daárkrōōm, –rōōm/ *n.* a room for photographic work, with normal light excluded.
dar·ling /daárling/ *n.* & *adj.* •*n.* **1** a beloved or lovable person or thing. **2** a favorite. **3** *colloq.* a pretty or endearing person or thing. •*adj.* **1** beloved; lovable. **2** favorite. **3** *colloq.* charming or pretty.
darn[1] /daarn/ *v.* & *n.* •*v.tr.* **1** mend by interweaving yarn across a hole with a needle. **2** embroider with a large running stitch. •*n.* a darned area in material.
darn[2] /daarn/ *v.tr., int., adj.,* & *adv. colloq.* = DAMN (in imprecatory senses).
darned /daarnd/ *adj.* & *adv. colloq.* = DAMNED.
dart /daart/ *n.* & *v.* •*n.* **1** a small pointed missile used as a weapon or in a game. **2** (in *pl.*; usu. treated as *sing.*) an indoor game in which light feathered darts are thrown at a circular target to score points. **3** a sudden rapid movement. **4** *Zool.* a dartlike structure, such as an insect's sting. **5** a tapering tuck stitched in a garment. •*v.* **1** *intr.* (often foll. by *out, in, past,* etc.) move or go suddenly or rapidly (*darted into the store*). **2** *tr.* throw (a missile). **3** *tr.* direct suddenly (a glance, etc.).
dart·board /daártbawrd/ *n.* a circular board marked with numbered segments, used as a target in darts.
Dar·win·i·an /daarwíneeən/ *adj.* & *n.* •*adj.* of or relating to Darwin's theory of the evolution of species by the action of natural selection. •*n.* an adherent of this theory. □□ **Dar·win·ism** /daárwinizəm/ *n.* **Dar·win·ist** *n.*
dash /dash/ *v.* & *n.* •*v.* **1** *intr.* rush hastily or forcefully (*dashed up the stairs*). **2** *tr.* strike or fling with great force (*dashed it to the ground*). **3** *tr.* frustrate; daunt; dispirit (*dashed their hopes*). **4** *tr. colloq.* (esp. **dash it** *or* **dash it all**) = DAMN *v.* 1. •*n.* **1** a rush or onset; a sudden advance (*made a dash for shelter*). **2** a horizontal stroke in writing or printing to mark a pause or break in sense or to represent omitted letters or words. **3** impetuous vigor or the capacity for this. **4** showy appearance or behavior. **5** a sprinting race. **6** the longer signal of the two used in Morse code (cf. DOT *n.* 3). **7** a slight admixture, esp. of a liquid. **8** = DASHBOARD.
dash·board /dáshbawrd/ *n.* the surface below the windshield inside a motor vehicle or aircraft, containing instruments and controls.
da·shi·ki /daasheékee/ *n.* a loose, brightly colored shirt worn orig. by men in Africa.
dash·ing /dáshing/ *adj.* **1** spirited; lively. **2** stylish. □□ **dash·ing·ly** *adv.*
das·tard·ly /dástərdlee/ *adj.* cowardly; despicable.
DAT *abbr.* digital audiotape.
da·ta /dáytə, dátə, daá–/ *n.pl.* (also treated as *sing.*, although the singular form is strictly *datum*) **1** known facts or things used as a basis for inference or reckoning. **2** quantities or characters operated on by a computer, etc.

▶**Data** was originally the plural of the Latin word *datum*, 'something (e.g., a piece of information) given.' **Data** is now used as a singular where it means 'information': *This data was prepared for the conference.* It is used as a plural in technical contexts and when the collection of bits of information is stressed: *All recent data on hurricanes are being compared.*

da·ta·base /dáytəbays, dátə–/ *n.* a structured set of data held in a computer.
da·ta cap·ture *n.* the action or process of entering data into a computer.
da·ta pro·cess·ing *n.* a series of operations on data, esp. by a computer. □□ **da·ta proc·es·sor** *n.*
date[1] /dayt/ *n.* & *v.* •*n.* **1** a day of the month, esp. specified by a number. **2** a particular day or year, esp. when a given event occurred. **3** a statement (usu. giving the day, month, and year) in a document or inscription, etc., of the time of composition or publication. **4** the period to which a work of art, etc., belongs. **5** the time when an event happens or is to happen. **6** *colloq.* **a** an engagement or appointment, esp. with a person of the opposite sex. **b** a person with whom one has a social engagement. •*v.* **1** *tr.* mark with a date. **2** *tr.* **a** assign a date to (an object, event, etc.). **b** (foll. by *to*) assign to a particular time, period, etc. **3** *intr.* (often foll. by *from, back to,* etc.) have its origins at a particular time. **4** *intr.* become evidently out of date (*a design that does not date*). **5** *tr.* indicate or expose as being out of date (*that hat really dates you*). **6** *colloq.* **a** *tr.* make an arrangement with (a person) to meet socially. **b** *intr.* meet socially by agreement. □ **to date** until now.

---

date Middle English: via Old French from medieval Latin *data*, feminine past participle of *dare* 'give'; from the Latin formula used in dating letters, *data (epistola)* '(letter) given or delivered,' to record a particular time or place.

---

date[2] /dayt/ *n.* **1** a dark, oval, single-stoned fruit. **2** (in full **date palm**) the tall tree *Phoenix dactylifera*, native to W. Asia and N. Africa, bearing this fruit.
dat·ed /dáytid/ *adj.* **1** showing or having a date (*a dated letter*). **2** old-fashioned; out-of-date.
date·less *adj.* **1** having no date. **2** of immemorial age. **3** not likely to become out of date.
date·line /dáytlīn/ *n.* **1** (also **date line**; in full **international date line**) the line from north to south partly along the 180th meridian, to the east of which the date is a day earlier than it is to the west. **2** a line at the head of a dispatch or special article in a newspaper showing the date and place of writing.
date rape *n.* sexual assault involving two people who have met socially.
da·tive /dáytiv/ *n.* & *adj. Gram.* •*n.* the case of nouns and pronouns (and words in grammatical agreement with them) indicating an indirect object or recipient. •*adj.* of or in the dative.□□ **da·ti·val** /daytívəl/ *adj.* **da·tive·ly** *adv.*
da·tum /dáytəm, dátəm, daátəm/ *n.* (*pl.* **data**: see DATA). **1** a piece of information. **2** a thing known or granted; an assumption or premise from which inferences may be drawn. **3** a fixed starting point of a scale, etc.
daub /dawb/ *v.* & *n.* •*v.tr.* **1** spread (paint, plaster, or some other thick substance) crudely or roughly. **2** coat or smear (a surface) with paint, etc. **3 a** (also *absol.*) paint crudely or unskillfully. **b** lay (colors) on crudely and clumsily. •*n.* **1** paint or other substance daubed on a surface. **2** plaster, clay, etc., for coating a surface, esp. mixed with straw and applied to laths or wattles to form a wall. **3** a crude painting.
daugh·ter /dáwtər/ *n.* **1** a girl or woman in relation to either or both of her parents. **2** a female descendant. **3** (foll. by *of*) a female member of a family, nation, etc. **4** (foll. by *of*) a woman who is regarded as the spiritual descendant of, or as spiritually attached to, a person or thing. **5** a product or attribute personified as a daughter in relation to its source. **6** *Physics* a nuclide formed by the radioactive decay of another. **7** *Biol.* a cell, etc., formed by the division, etc., of another. □□ **daugh·ter·ly** *adj.*
daugh·ter-in-law *n.* (*pl.* **daughters-in-law**) the wife of one's son.
daunt /dawnt/ *v.tr.* discourage; intimidate. □□ **daunt·ing** *adj.* **daunt·ing·ly** *adv.*
daunt·less /dáwntlis/ *adj.* intrepid; persevering.

---

dau·phin /dáwfin, dōfáN/ *n. hist.* the eldest son of the king of France.

dav·en·port /dávənpawrt/ *n.* a large, heavily upholstered sofa.

da·vit /dávit, dáyvit/ *n.* a small crane on board a ship, esp. one of a pair for suspending or lowering a lifeboat.

Da·vy Jones /jṓnz/ *n. sl.* **1** (in full **Davy Jones's locker**) the bottom of the sea, esp. regarded as the grave of those drowned at sea. **2** the evil spirit of the sea.

daw·dle /dáwd'l/ *v. & n.* •*v.* **1** *intr.* **a** walk slowly and idly. **b** delay; waste time. **2** *tr.* (foll. by *away*) waste (time). •*n.* an act or instance of dawdling.

dawn /dawn/ *n. & v.* •*n.* **1** daybreak. **2** the beginning of something. •*v.intr.* **1** (of a day) begin; grow light. **2** begin to appear or develop. **3** (often foll. by *on, upon*) begin to become evident or understood (by a person). ▫▫ **dawn·ing** *n.*

day /day/ *n.* **1** the time between sunrise and sunset. **2** a period of 24 hours as a unit of time. **3** daylight (*clear as day*). **4** the time in a day during which work is normally done (*an eight-hour day*). **5 a** (also *pl.*) a period of the past or present (*the modern day; the old days*). **b** (prec. by *the*) the present time (*the issues of the day*). **6** the lifetime of a person or thing, esp. regarded as useful or productive (*have had my day; in my day things were different*). **7** a point of time (*will do it one day*). **8 a** the date of a specific festival. **b** a day associated with a particular event or purpose (*graduation day; payday; Christmas Day*). **9** a particular date; a date agreed on. **10** a day's endeavor, or the period of an endeavor, esp. as bringing success (*win the day*). ▫ **all in a day's work** part of normal routine. **at the end of the day** in the final reckoning, when all is said and done. **call it a day** end a period of activity, esp. resting content that enough has been done. **day after day** without respite. **day and night** all the time. **day by day** gradually. **day in, day out** routinely; constantly. **from day one** *colloq.* originally. **not one's day** a day of successive misfortunes for a person. **one of these days** before very long. **one of those days** a day when things go badly. **that will be the day** *colloq.* that will never happen. **this day and age** the present time or period.

day·break /dáybrayk/ *n.* the first appearance of light in the morning.

day care *n.* the supervision of young children, the elderly, etc., during the day.

day·dream /dáydreem/ *n. & v.* •*n.* a pleasant fantasy or reverie. •*v.intr.* indulge in this.

Day-Glo /dáyglō/ *n. & adj.* •*n. Trademark* a brand of fluorescent paint or other coloring. •*adj.* colored with or like this.

day·light /dáylīt/ *n.* **1** the light of day. **2** dawn (*before daylight*). **3 a** openness; publicity. **b** open knowledge. **4** a visible gap or interval. **5** (usu. in *pl.*) *sl.* one's life or consciousness (*beat the living daylights out of them*). ▫ **see daylight** begin to understand what was previously obscure.

day·light sav·ing time *n.* the achieving of longer evening daylight, esp. in summer, by setting the time an hour ahead of the standard time.

day·time /dáytīm/ *n.* the part of the day when there is natural light.

day-to-day *adj.* mundane; routine.

day-trip *n.* a trip or excursion completed in one day.

daze /dayz/ *v. & n.* •*v.tr.* stupefy; bewilder. •*n.* a state of confusion or bewilderment (*in a daze*). ▫▫ **daz·ed·ly** /–zidlee/ *adv.*

daz·zle /dázəl/ *v. & n.* •*v.* **1** *tr.* blind temporarily or confuse the sight of by an excess of light. **2** *tr.* impress or overpower (a person) with knowledge, ability, or any brilliant display or prospect. •*n.* bright confusing light. ▫▫ **daz·zle·ment** *n.* **daz·zler** *n.* **daz·zling** *adj.* **daz·zling·ly** *adv.*

dB *abbr.* decibel(s).

DC *abbr.* **1** (also **d.c.**) direct current. **2** District of Columbia.

DD *abbr.* doctor of divinity.

D day /déeday/ *n.* (also **D Day**) **1** the day (June 6, 1944) on which Allied forces invaded N. France. **2** the day on which an important operation is to begin or a change to take effect.

DDT *abbr.* dichlorodiphenyltrichloroethane, a colorless chlorinated hydrocarbon used as an insecticide.

de- /dee, di/ *prefix* **1** forming verbs and their derivatives: **a** down; away (*descend*). **b** completely (*declare; denude*). **2** added to verbs and their derivatives to form verbs and nouns implying removal or reversal (*decentralize; de-ice*).

dea·con /déekən/ *n. & v.* •*n.* **1** (in Episcopal churches) a minister of the third order, below bishop and priest. **2** (in various, esp. Protestant, churches) a lay officer attending to a congregation's secular affairs. **3** (in the early Christian church) an appointed minister of charity. •*v.tr.* appoint or ordain as a deacon.

dea·con·ess /déekənés, déekənis/ *n.* a woman in the early Christian church and in some modern churches with functions analogous to a deacon's.

de·ac·ti·vate /deeáktivayt/ *v.tr.* make inactive or less reactive. ▫▫ **de·ac·ti·va·tion** /–váyshən/ *n.*

dead /ded/ *adj., adv., & n.* •*adj.* **1** no longer alive. **2** *colloq.* extremely tired or unwell. **3** numb (*my fingers are dead*). **4** (foll. by *to*) insensitive to. **5** no longer effective or in use; extinct. **6** (of a match, of coal, etc.) no longer burning; extinguished. **7** inanimate. **8 a** lacking force or vigor. **b** (of sound) not resonant. **c** (of sparkling wine, etc.) no longer effervescent. **9 a** quiet; lacking activity (*the dead season*). **b** motionless; idle. **10 a** (of a microphone, telephone, etc.) not transmitting any sound. **b** (of a circuit, conductor, etc.) carrying or transmitting no current (*a dead battery*). **11** (of the ball in a game) out of play. **12** abrupt; complete (*come to a dead stop; in dead silence*). **13** without spiritual life. •*adv.* **1** absolutely; exactly; completely (*dead on target; dead level*). **2** *colloq.* very; extremely (*dead easy*). •*n.* (prec. by *the*) **1** (treated as *pl.*) those who have died. **2** a time of silence or inactivity (*the dead of night*). ▫ **dead as a doornail** see DOORNAIL. **dead from the neck up** *colloq.* stupid. **dead in the water** unable to move or to function. **dead to the world** *colloq.* fast asleep; unconscious. **dead weight** see DEADWEIGHT. **wouldn't be seen dead in** (or **with**, etc.) *colloq.* shall have nothing to do with; shall refuse to wear, etc. ▫▫ **dead·ness** *n.*

dead·beat /dédbeet/ *n.* **1** *colloq.* a penniless person. **2** *sl.* a person constantly in debt.

dead·bolt /dédbōlt/ *n.* a bolt engaged by turning a knob or key, rather than by spring action.

dead duck *n. sl.* **1** an unsuccessful or useless person or thing. **2** a person who is beyond help; one who is doomed.

dead·en /déd'n/ *v.* **1** *tr. & intr.* deprive of or lose vitality, force, brightness, sound, feeling, etc. **2** *tr.* (foll. by *to*) make insensitive.

dead end *n.* **1** a closed end of a road, passage, etc. **2** (often (with hyphen) *attrib.*) a situation offering no prospects of progress.

dead·eye /dédī/ *n.* **1** *Naut.* a circular wooden block with a groove around the circumference to take a lanyard, used singly or in pairs to tighten a shroud. **2** *colloq.* an expert marksman.

dead·head /dédhed/ *n. & v.* •*n.* **1** (**Deadhead**) a fan and follower of the rock group The Grateful Dead. **2** a boring or unenterprising person. **3** a passenger or member of an audience who has made use of a free ticket. • *v.* **1** *intr.* (of a commercial driver, etc.) complete a trip in an empty vehicle with no passengers or freight. **2** *tr.* remove faded flower heads from (a plant).

dead heat *n.* **1** a race in which two or more competitors finish in a tie. **2** the result of such a race.

dead let·ter *n.* **1** a law or practice no longer observed or recognized. **2** a letter that is undeliverable and unreturnable, esp. one with an incorrect address.

dead·line /dédlīn/ *n.* a time limit for the completion of an activity, etc.

dead·lock /dédlok/ *n. & v.* • *n.* **1** a situation, esp. one involving opposing parties, in which no progress can be made. **2** a type of lock requiring a key to open or close it. • *v.tr. & intr.* bring or come to a standstill.

dead·ly /dédlee/ *adj. & adv.* • *adj.* (**deadlier, deadliest**) **1 a** causing or able to cause fatal injury or serious damage. **b** poisonous. **2** intense; extreme (*deadly dullness*). **3** (of an aim, etc.) extremely accurate or effective. **4** deathlike (*deadly faintness*). **5** *colloq.* dreary; dull. • *adv.* **1** like death; as if dead (*deadly faint*). **2** extremely; intensely (*deadly serious*). ▫▫ **dead·li·ness** *n.*

dead·ly night·shade *n.* a poisonous plant, *Atropa belladonna*, with drooping purple flowers and black cherrylike fruit. Also called **belladonna**.

dead·ly sin *n.* a damning sin, esp. pride, covetousness, lust, gluttony, envy, anger, and sloth.

dead-on *adj.* exactly right.

dead·pan /dédpán/ *adj. & adv.* with a face or manner totally lacking expression or emotion.

dead reck·on·ing *n. Naut.* calculation of a ship's position from the log, compass, etc., when observations are impossible.

dead sol·diers *n.pl. colloq.* bottles (esp. of beer, liquor, etc.) after the contents have been drunk.

dead·weight /dédwáyt/ *n.* (also **dead weight**) **1 a** an inert mass. **b** a heavy burden. **2** a debt not covered by assets. **3** the total weight carried on a ship.

dead·wood /dédwood/ *n.* **1** dead trees or branches. **2** *colloq.* one or more useless people or things.

deaf /def/ *adj.* **1** wholly or partly without hearing (*deaf in one ear*). **2** (foll. by *to*) refusing to listen or comply. **3** insensitive to harmony, rhythm, etc. (*tone-deaf*). ▫ **deaf as a post** completely deaf. **fall on deaf ears** be ignored. **turn a deaf ear** (usu. foll. by *to*) be unresponsive. ▫▫ **deaf·ness** *n.*

deaf·en /défən/ *v.tr.* **1** (often as **deafening** *adj.*) overpower with sound. **2** deprive of hearing by noise, esp. temporarily. ▫▫ **deaf·en·ing·ly** *adv.*

deaf-mute *n.* a deaf and dumb person.

deal /deel/ *v. & n.* • *v.* (*past* and *past part.* **dealt** /delt/) **1** *intr.* **a** (foll. by *with*) take measures concerning (a problem, person, etc.), esp. in order to put something right. **b** (foll. by *with*) do business with; associate with. **c** (foll. by *with*) discuss or treat (a subject). **d** (often foll. by *by*) behave in a specified way toward a person (*dealt honorably by them*). **2** *intr.* (foll. by *in*) to sell or be concerned with commercially (*deals in insurance*). **3** *tr.* (often foll. by *out*) distribute or apportion to several people, etc. **4** *tr.* (also *absol.*) distribute (cards) to players. **5** *tr.* cause to be received; administer (*deal a heavy blow*). **6** *tr.* assign as a share or deserts to a person (*life dealt them much happiness*). **7** *tr.* (foll. by *in*) *colloq.* include (a person) in an activity (*you can deal me in*). • *n.* **1** (usu. **a good** *or* **great deal**) *colloq.* **a** a large amount (*a good deal of trouble*). **b** to a considerable extent (*is a great deal better*). **2** *colloq.* a business arrangement; a transaction. **3** a specified form of treatment (*gave them a bad deal*; *got a fair deal*). **4 a** the distribution of cards by dealing. **b** a player's turn to do this (*it's my deal*). **c** the round of play following this. **d** a set of hands dealt to players.

deal·er /déelər/ *n.* **1** a person or business dealing in (esp. retail) goods (*contact your dealer*; *car dealer*). **2** the player dealing at cards. **3** a person who sells illegal drugs. ▫▫ **deal·er·ship** *n.* (in sense 1).

deal·ings /déelingz/ *n.pl.* contacts or transactions. ▫ **have dealings with** associate with.

dealt *past* and *past part.* of DEAL[1].

dean /deen/ *n.* **1 a** a college or university official with disciplinary and advisory functions. **b** the head of a university faculty or department or of a medical school. **2** the head of the chapter of a cathedral or collegiate church. **3** = DOYEN.

dear /deer/ *adj., n., adv., & int.* • *adj.* **1 a** beloved or much esteemed. **b** as a merely polite or ironic form (*my dear man*). **2** used as a formula of address, esp. at the beginning of letters (*Dear Sir*). **3** (often foll. by *to*) precious; much cherished. **4** (usu. in *superl.*) earnest (*my dearest wish*). **5 a** high-priced relative to its value. **b** having high prices. **c** (of money) available as a loan only at a high rate of interest. • *n.* (esp. as a form of address) dear person. • *adv.* at great cost (*buy cheap and sell dear*). • *int.* expressing surprise, dismay, pity, etc. (*dear me!*; *oh dear!*). ▫▫ **dear·ly** *adv.* (esp. in sense 3 of *adj.*).

dearth /dərth/ *n.* scarcity or lack.

death /deth/ *n.* **1** the ending of life. **2** the event that terminates life. **3 a** the fact or process of being killed or killing (*stone to death*). **b** the fact or state of being dead. **4** the destruction or permanent cessation of something (*the death of our hopes*). **5** (usu. **Death**) a personification of death. ▫ **at death's door** close to death. **be the death of** be lethal or very harmful to. **catch one's death** *colloq.* catch a serious chill, etc. **do to death 1** kill. **2** overdo. **fate worse than death** *colloq.* a disastrous misfortune or experience. **like death warmed over** *sl.* very tired or ill. **to death** to the utmost; extremely (*bored to death*). ▫▫ **death·less** *adj.* **death·like** *adj.*

death·bed /déthbed/ *n.* a bed as the place where a person is dying or has died.

death·blow /déthblō/ *n.* **1** a blow or other action that causes death. **2** an event or circumstance that abruptly ends an activity, enterprise, etc.

death cap (or **cup**) *n.* a poisonous mushroom, *Amanita phalloides*.

death·ly /déthlee/ *adj. & adv.* • *adj.* (**deathlier, deathliest**) suggestive of death (*deathly silence*). • *adv.* in a deathly way (*deathly pale*).

death mask *n.* a cast taken of a dead person's face.

death row *n.* a prison block or section for prisoners sentenced to death.

death trap *n. colloq.* a dangerous building, vehicle, etc.

death wish *n. Psychol.* a desire (usu. unconscious) for the death of oneself or another.

deb /deb/ *n. colloq.* a debutante.

de·ba·cle /daybaákəl, –bákel, də–/ *n.* (also **débâcle**) **1 a** an utter defeat or failure. **b** a sudden collapse or downfall. **2** a confused rush or rout.

de·bar /deebaár/ *v.tr.* (**debarred, debarring**) (foll. by *from*) exclude from admission or from a right; prohibit from an action (*was debarred from entering*).

de·bark[1] /dibaárk/ *v.tr. & intr.* land from a ship.

de·bark[2] /déebaárk/ *v.tr.* remove the bark from (a tree).

de·base /dibáys/ *v.tr.* **1** lower in quality, value, or character. **2** depreciate (coin) by alloying, etc. ▫▫ **de·base·ment** *n.*

de·bat·a·ble /dibáytəbəl/ *adj.* **1** questionable; subject to dispute. **2** capable of being debated. ▫▫ **de·bat·a·bly** *adv.*

de·bate /dibáyt/ *v. & n.* • *v.* **1** *tr.* (also *absol.*) discuss or dispute about (an issue, proposal, etc.) esp. formally. **2 a** *tr.* consider; ponder (a matter). **b** *intr.* consider different sides of a question. • *n.* **1** a formal discussion on a particular matter. **2** debating; discussion (*open to debate*). ▫▫ **de•bat•er** *n.*

de•bauch /dibáwch/ *v.* & *n.* • *v.tr.* **1** corrupt morally. **2** make intemperate or sensually indulgent. **3** deprave or debase (taste or judgment). **4** (as **debauched** *adj.*) dissolute. **5** seduce (a woman). • *n.* **1** a bout of sensual indulgence. **2** debauchery.

deb•au•chee /díbawchée, –shée, déb–/ *n.* a person addicted to excessive sensual indulgence.

de•bauch•er•y /dibáwchəree/ *n.* excessive sensual indulgence.

de•ben•ture /dibénchər/ *n.* (in full **debenture bond**) a fixed-interest bond of a company, backed by general credit rather than specified assets.

de•bil•i•tate /dibílitayt/ *v.tr.* enfeeble; enervate. ▫▫ **de•bil•i•ta•tion** /–táyshən/ *n.*

de•bil•i•ty /dibílitee/ *n.* feebleness, esp. of health.

deb•it /débit/ *n.* & *v.* • *n.* **1** an entry in an account recording a sum owed. **2** the sum recorded. **3** the total of such sums. **4** the debit side of an account. • *v.tr.* (**debited, debiting**) **1** (foll. by *against*, *to*) enter (an amount) on the debit side of an account (*debited $500 against me*). **2** (foll. by *with*) enter (a person) on the debit side of an account (*debited me with $500*).

deb•it card *n.* a card issued by a bank allowing the holder to transfer deposited funds electronically, as to make a purchase.

deb•o•nair /débənáir/ *adj.* **1** carefree; cheerful; self-assured. **2** having pleasant manners.

de•bouch /dibówch, –bóosh/ *v.intr.* **1** (of troops or a stream) issue from a ravine, wood, etc., into open ground. **2** (often foll. by *into*) (of a river, road, etc.) merge into a larger body or area.

de•brief /deebréef/ *v.tr. colloq.* interrogate (a person) about a completed mission or undertaking. ▫▫ **de•brief•ing** *n.*

de•bris /dəbrée, day–, débree/ *n.* scattered fragments, esp. of something wrecked or destroyed.

debt /det/ *n.* **1** something that is owed, esp. money. **2** a state of obligation to pay something owed (*in debt*). ▫ **in a person's debt** under an obligation to a person.

debt•or /détər/ *n.* a person who owes a debt, esp. money.

de•bug /deebúg/ *v.tr.* (**debugged, debugging**) **1** *colloq.* remove concealed listening devices from (a room, etc.). **2** *colloq.* identify and remove defects from (a machine, computer program, etc.). **3** remove bugs from.

de•bunk /deebúngk/ *v.tr. colloq.* **1** show the good reputation of (a person, group, etc.) to be spurious. **2** expose the falseness of (a claim, etc.). ▫▫ **de•bunk•er** *n.*

de•but /daybyóo, dáybyoo/ *n.* (also **début**) **1** the first public appearance of a performer on stage, etc., or the opening performance of a show, etc. **2** the first appearance of a débutante in society.

deb•u•tante /débyətaant, dáybyoo–/ *n.* a (usu. wealthy) young woman making her social debut.

Dec. *abbr.* December.

deca- /dékə/ *comb.form* (also **dec-** before a vowel) **1** having ten. **2** tenfold. **3** ten (*decagram*; *decaliter*).

dec•ade /dékayd/ *n.* **1** a period of ten years. **2** a set, series, or group of ten.

dec•a•dence /dékəd'ns/ *n.* **1** moral or cultural deterioration. **2** decadent behavior; a state of decadence.

dec•a•dent /dékədənt/ *adj.* & *n.* • *adj.* **1 a** in a state of moral or cultural deterioration; showing or characterized by decadence. **b** of a period of decadence. **2** self-indulgent. • *n.* a decadent person. ▫▫ **dec•a•dent•ly** *adv.*

de•caf•fein•ate /deekáfinayt/ *v.tr.* **1** remove the caffeine from. **2** reduce the quantity of caffeine in (usu. coffee).

dec•a•gon /dékəgən/ *n.* a plane figure with ten sides and angles.

dec•a•he•dron /dékəhéedrən/ *n.* a solid figure with ten faces.

de•cal /déekal/ *n.* = DECALCOMANIA 2.

de•cal•ci•fy /deekálsifī/ *v.tr.* (**-fies, -fied**) remove lime or calcareous matter from (a bone, tooth, etc.). ▫▫ **de•cal•ci•fi•ca•tion** /–fikáyshən/ *n.*

de•cal•co•ma•ni•a /deekálkəmáyneeə/ *n.* **1** a process of transferring designs from specially prepared paper to the surface of glass, porcelain, etc. **2** a picture or design made by this process.

dec•a•li•ter /dékəleetər/ *n.* a metric unit of capacity, equal to 10 liters.

Dec•a•logue /dékəlawg, –log/ *n.* the Ten Commandments.

dec•a•me•ter /dékəmeetər/ *n.* a metric unit of length, equal to 10 meters.

de•camp /dikámp/ *v.intr.* **1** break up or leave a camp. **2** depart suddenly; abscond.

de•cant /dikánt/ *v.tr.* **1** gradually pour off (liquid) from one container to another, esp. without disturbing the sediment. **2** move as if by pouring.

de•cant•er /dikántər/ *n.* a stoppered glass container into which wine or brandy, etc., is decanted.

de•cap•i•tate /dikápitayt/ *v.tr.* **1** behead. **2** cut the head or end from. ▫▫ **de•cap•i•ta•tion** /–táyshən/ *n.*

dec•a•pod /dékəpod/ *n.* **1** any crustacean of the chiefly marine order Decapoda, characterized by five pairs of walking legs, e.g., shrimps, crabs, and lobsters. **2** any of various mollusks of the class Cephalopoda, having ten tentacles, e.g., squids and cuttlefish.

dec•a•syl•la•ble /dékəsiləbəl/ *n.* a metrical line of ten syllables. ▫▫ **dec•a•syl•lab•ic** /–silábik/ *adj.* & *n.*

de•cath•lon /dikáthlən, –lon/ *n.* an athletic contest in which each competitor takes part in ten events. ▫▫ **de•cath•lete** /–leet/ *n.*

de•cay /dikáy/ *v.* & *n.* • *v.* **1 a** *intr.* rot; decompose. **b** *tr.* cause to rot or decompose. **2** *intr.* & *tr.* decline or cause to decline in quality, power, wealth, energy, beauty, etc. **3** *intr. Physics* **a** (usu. foll. by *to*) (of a substance, etc.) undergo change by radioactivity. **b** undergo a gradual decrease in magnitude of a physical quantity. *n.* **1** a rotten state; a process of wasting away. **2** decline in health, quality, etc. **3** *Physics* **a** change into another substance, etc. by radioactivity. **b** a decrease in the magnitude of a physical quantity, esp. the intensity of radiation or amplitude of oscillation. **4** decayed tissue.

de•cease /diséés/ *n.* & *v. formal* esp. *Law* • *n.* death. • *v.intr.* die.

de•ceased /diséest/ *adj.* & *n. formal* • *adj.* dead. • *n.* (usu. prec. by *the*) a person who has died, esp. recently.

de•ce•dent /diséed'nt/ *n. Law* a deceased person.

de•ceit /diséet/ *n.* **1** the act or process of deceiving or misleading, esp. by concealing the truth. **2** a dishonest trick or stratagem. **3** willingness to deceive.

de•ceit•ful /diséetfool/ *adj.* **1** (of a person) using deceit. **2** (of an act, practice, etc.) intended to deceive. ▫▫ **de•ceit•ful•ly** *adv.* **de•ceit•ful•ness** *n.*

de•ceive /diséev/ *v.* **1** *tr.* make (a person) believe what is false; mislead purposely. **2** *tr.* be unfaithful to, esp. sexually. **3** *intr.* use deceit. ▫ **be deceived** be mistaken or deluded. **deceive oneself** persist in a mistaken belief. ▫▫ **de•ceiv•er** *n.*

de•cel•er•ate /deesélərayt/ *v.* **1** *intr.* & *tr.* begin or cause to begin to reduce speed. **2** *tr.* make slower. ▫▫ **de•cel•er•a•tion** /–ráyshən/ *n.*

De•cem•ber /disémbər/ *n.* the twelfth month of the year.

de•cen•cy /déesənsee/ *n.* (*pl.* **-cies**) **1** correct and tasteful standards of behavior as generally accepted. **2** conformity with current standards of behavior or propriety. **3** avoidance of obscenity. **4** (in *pl.*) the requirements of correct behavior.

de·cen·ni·al /diséneeəl/ *adj.* **1** lasting ten years. **2** recurring every ten years.

de·cent /deésənt/ *adj.* **1 a** conforming with current standards of behavior or propriety. **b** avoiding obscenity. **2** respectable. **3** acceptable; good enough. **4** kind; obliging; generous (*was decent enough to apologize*). □□ **de·cent·ly** *adv.*

de·cen·tral·ize /deeséntrəlīz/ *v.tr.* **1** transfer (powers, etc.) from a central to a local authority. **2** reorganize on the basis of greater local autonomy. □□ **de·cen·tral·ist** /–list/ *n.* & *adj.* **de·cen·tral·i·za·tion** *n.*

de·cep·tion /disépshən/ *n.* **1** the act or an instance of deceiving; the process of being deceived. **2** a thing that deceives.

de·cep·tive /diséptiv/ *adj.* apt to deceive; easily mistaken for something else or as having a different quality. □□ **de·cep·tive·ly** *adv.*

deci- /désee/ *comb. form* one-tenth (*deciliter; decimeter*).

dec·i·bel /désibel/ *n.* a unit (one-tenth of a bel) used in the comparison of two power levels relating to electrical signals or sound intensities. ¶ Abbr.: **dB**.

de·cide /disíd/ *v.* **1 a** *intr.* (often foll. by *on, about*) come to a resolution as a result of consideration. **b** *tr.* (usu. foll. by *to* + infin., or *that* + clause) have or reach as one's resolution about something (*decided to stay; decided that we should leave*). **2** *tr.* resolve or settle (a question, dispute, etc.). **3** *intr.* (usu. foll. by *between, for, against, in favor of*, or *that* + clause) give a judgment.

de·cid·ed /disídid/ *adj.* **1** (usu. *attrib.*) definite; unquestionable (*a decided difference*). **2** having clear opinions, resolute, not vacillating. □□ **de·cid·ed·ly** *adv.*

de·cid·u·ous /disíjōōəs/ *adj.* **1** (of a tree) shedding its leaves annually. **2** (of leaves, horns, teeth, etc.) shed periodically.

dec·i·gram /désigram/ *n.* a metric unit of mass, equal to 0.1 gram.

dec·i·li·ter /désileetər/ *n.* a metric unit of capacity, equal to 0.1 liter.

dec·i·mal /désiməl/ *adj.* & *n.* • *adj.* **1** (of a system of numbers, weights, measures, etc.) based on the number ten, in which the smaller units are related to the principal units as powers of ten (units, tens, hundreds, thousands, etc.). **2** of tenths or ten; reckoning or proceeding by tens. • *n.* a decimal fraction.

dec·i·mal·ize /désiməlīz/ *v.tr.* **1** express as a decimal. **2** convert to a decimal system. □□ **dec·i·mal·i·za·tion** *n.*

dec·i·mal point *n.* a period or dot placed before a numerator in a decimal fraction.

dec·i·mate /désimayt/ *v.tr.* **1** *disp.* destroy a large proportion of. **2** *orig. Mil.* kill or remove one in every ten of. □□ **dec·i·ma·tion** /–máyshən/ *n.*

▶The usual sense of **decimate** is now 'destroy a large proportion of': *the project would decimate the fragile wetland wilderness.* The original and literal sense is ' kill or remove one in ten of.' In any case, do not use **decimate** to mean 'defeat utterly.'

---

decimate late Middle English: from Latin *decimat-* 'taken as a tenth,' from the verb *decimare*, from *decimus* 'tenth.' In Middle English the term *decimation* denoted the levying of a tithe, and later it denoted the tax imposed by Cromwell on the Royalists (1655). The verb *decimate* originally alluded to the Roman punishment of executing one man in ten of a mutinous legion.

---

dec·i·me·ter /désimeetər/ *n.* a metric unit of length, equal to 0.1 meter.

de·ci·pher /disífər/ *v.tr.* **1** convert (a text written in cipher) into an intelligible script or language. **2** determine the meaning of (anything obscure or unclear). □□ **de·ci·pher·a·ble** *adj.* **de·ci·pher·ment** *n.*

de·ci·sion /disízhən/ *n.* **1** the act or process of deciding. **2** a conclusion or resolution reached after consideration (*have made my decision*). **3** (often foll. by *of*) **a** the settlement of a question. **b** a formal judgment. **4** resoluteness.

de·ci·sive /disísiv/ *adj.* **1** that decides an issue; conclusive. **2** able to decide quickly and effectively. □□ **de·ci·sive·ly** *adv.* **de·ci·sive·ness** *n.*

deck /dek/ *n.* & *v.* • *n.* **1 a** a platform in a ship covering all or part of the hull's area at any level and serving as a floor. **b** the accommodation on a particular deck of a ship. **2** the floor or compartment of a bus. **3** a component, usu. a flat horizontal surface, that carries a particular recording medium (such as a disk or tape) in sound-reproduction equipment. **4 a** a pack of cards. **b** *sl.* a packet of narcotics. **5** *sl.* the ground. **6 a** any floor or platform, esp. the floor of a pier or a platform for sunbathing. **b** a platformlike structure, usu. made of lumber and unroofed, attached to a house, etc. • *v.tr.* **1** (often foll. by *out*) decorate; adorn. **2** furnish with or cover as a deck. **3** *sl.* knock someone to the ground with a punch. □ **below deck** (or **decks**) in or into the space below the main deck. **on deck 1** in the open air on a ship's main deck. **2** ready for action, work, etc.

deck chair *n.* a folding chair of wood and canvas, of a kind used on deck on passenger ships.

-decker /dékər/ *comb. form* having a specified number of decks or layers (*double-decker*).

deck·hand /dékhand/ *n.* a person employed in cleaning and odd jobs on a ship's deck.

de·claim /dikláym/ *v.* **1** *intr.* & *tr.* speak or utter rhetorically or affectedly. **2** *intr.* practice oratory or recitation. **3** *intr.* (foll. by *against*) protest forcefully. **4** *intr.* deliver an impassioned (rather than reasoned) speech. □□ **dec·la·ma·tion** /dékləmáyshən/ *n.* **de·clam·a·to·ry** /diklámətawree/ *adj.*

dec·la·ra·tion /dékləráyshən/ *n.* **1** the act or process of declaring. **2 a** a formal, emphatic, or deliberate statement or announcement. **b** a statement asserting or protecting a legal right. **3** a written public announcement of intentions, terms of an agreement, etc.

de·clar·a·tive /diklárətiv/ *adj.* & *n.* • *adj.* **1 a** of the nature of, or making, a declaration. **b** *Gram.* (of a sentence) that takes the form of a simple statement. **2** *Computing* designating high-level programming languages which can be used to solve problems without requiring the programmer to specify an exact procedure to be followed. • *n.* **1** a declaratory statement or act. **2** *Gram.* a declarative sentence. □□ **de·clar·a·tive·ly** *adv.*

de·clare /dikláir/ *v.* **1** *tr.* announce openly or formally (*declare war; declare a dividend*). **2** *tr.* pronounce (a person or thing) to be something (*declared him to be an impostor; declared it invalid*). **3** *tr.* (usu. foll. by *that* + clause) assert emphatically. **4** *tr.* acknowledge possession of (dutiable goods, income, etc.). **5** *tr.* (as **declared** *adj.*) who admits to be such (*a declared atheist*). □ **declare oneself** reveal one's intentions or identity. **well, I declare** (or **I do declare**) an exclamation of incredulity, surprise, or vexation. □□ **de·clar·a·to·ry** /–klárətawree/ *adj.* **de·clar·er** *n.*

dé·clas·sé /dayklasáy/ *adj.* (*fem.* **déclassée**) that has fallen in social status.

de·clas·si·fy /deeklásifī/ *v.tr.* (**-fies, -fied**) declare (information, etc.) to be no longer secret. □□ **de·clas·si·fi·ca·tion** /–fikáyshən/ *n.*

de·clen·sion /diklénshən/ *n.* **1** *Gram.* **a** the variation of the form of a noun, pronoun, or adjective, by which its grammatical case, number, and gender are identified. **b** the class in which a noun, etc., is put according to the exact form of this variation. **2** deterioration; declining. ▫▫ **de·clen·sion·al** *adj.*

dec·li·na·tion /déklináyshən/ *n.* **1** a downward bend or turn. **2** *Astron.* the angular distance of a star, etc., north or south of the celestial equator. **3** *Physics* the angular deviation of a compass needle from true north. **4** a formal refusal. ▫▫ **dec·li·na·tion·al** *adj.*

de·cline /diklín/ *v.* & *n.* •*v.* **1** *intr.* deteriorate; lose strength or vigor; decrease. **2 a** *tr.* reply with formal courtesy that one will not accept (an invitation, etc.). **b** *tr.* refuse, esp. formally and courteously (*declined doing anything*). **c** *tr.* turn away from (a challenge, battle, discussion, etc.). **d** *intr.* give or send a refusal. **3** *intr.* slope downward. **4** *intr.* bend down; droop. **5** *tr. Gram.* state the forms of (a noun, pronoun, or adjective) corresponding to cases, number, and gender. **6** *intr.* (of a day, life, etc.) draw to a close. **7** *intr.* decrease in price, etc. **8** *tr.* bend down. •*n.* **1** gradual loss of vigor or excellence (*on the decline*). **2** decay; deterioration. **3** setting; the last part of the course (of the sun, of life, etc.). **4** a fall in price. ▫ **on the decline** in a declining state. ▫▫ **de·clin·a·ble** *adj.* **de·clin·er** *n.*

de·cliv·i·ty /diklívitee/ *n.* (*pl.* **-ties**) a downward slope. ▫▫ **de·cliv·i·tous** *adj.*

de·coct /dikókt/ *v.tr.* extract the essence from by decoction.

de·coc·tion /dikókshən/ *n.* **1** the liquor resulting from concentrating the essence of a substance by heating or boiling, esp. a medicinal preparation made from a plant. **2** the action or process of extracting the essence of something.

de·code /deekṓd/ *v.tr.* convert (a coded message) into intelligible language. ▫▫ **de·cod·a·ble** *adj.*

de·cod·er /deekṓdər/ *n.* **1** a person or thing that decodes. **2** an electronic device for analyzing signals and feeding separate amplifier channels.

de·col·late /dikólayt/ *v.tr. formal* **1** behead. **2** truncate. ▫▫ **de·col·la·tion** /déekəláyshən/ *n.*

dé·col·le·tage /dáykawltaázh/ *n.* a low neckline of a woman's dress, etc.

dé·col·le·té /daykawltáy/ *adj.* & *n.* •*adj.* **1** (of a dress, etc.) having a low neckline. **2** (of a woman) wearing a dress with a low neckline. •*n.* a low neckline.

de·col·o·nize /deekólənīz/ *v.tr.* (of a nation) withdraw from (a colony), leaving it independent. ▫▫ **de·col·o·ni·za·tion** *n.*

de·com·mis·sion /déekəmíshən/ *v.tr.* **1** close down (a nuclear reactor, etc.). **2** take (a ship) out of service.

de·com·pose /déekəmpṓz/ *v.* **1** *intr.* decay; rot. **2** *tr.* separate into its elements or simpler constituents. **3** *intr.* disintegrate; break up. ▫▫ **de·com·po·si·tion** /déekompəzíshən/ *n.*

de·com·press /déekəmprés/ *v.tr.* subject to decompression; relieve or reduce the compression on.

de·com·pres·sion /déekəmpréshən/ *n.* **1** release from compression. **2** a gradual reduction of air pressure on a person who has been subjected to high pressure (esp. underwater).

de·com·pres·sion cham·ber *n.* an enclosed space for subjecting a person to decompression.

de·com·pres·sor /déekəmprésər/ *n.* a device for reducing pressure in the engine of a motor vehicle.

de·con·ges·tant /déekənjéstənt/ *adj.* & *n.* •*adj.* that relieves (esp. nasal) congestion. •*n.* a medicinal agent that relieves nasal congestion.

de·con·se·crate /deekónsikrayt/ *v.tr.* transfer (esp. a building) from sacred to secular use. ▫▫ **de·con·se·cra·tion** /–kráyshən/ *n.*

de·con·struc·tion /déekənstrúkshən/ *n.* a method of critical analysis of philosophical and literary language. ▫▫ **de·con·struct** *v.tr.* **de·con·struc·tion·ism** *n.* **de·con·struc·tion·ist** *adj.* & *n.* **de·con·struc·tive** *adj.*

de·con·tam·i·nate /déekəntáminayt/ *v.tr.* remove contamination from. ▫▫ **de·con·tam·i·na·tion** /–náyshən/ *n.*

de·con·trol /déekəntrṓl/ *v.* & *n.* •*v.tr.* (**decontrolled, decontrolling**) release (a commodity, etc.) from controls or restrictions, esp. those imposed by the government. •*n.* the act of decontrolling.

de·cor /daykáwr, dáykawr/ *n.* (also **décor**) **1** the furnishing and decoration of a room, etc. **2** the decoration and scenery of a stage.

dec·o·rate /dékərayt/ *v.tr.* **1** provide with adornments. **2** provide (a room or building) with new paint, wallpaper, etc. **3** serve as an adornment to. **4** confer an award or distinction on.

dec·o·ra·tion /dékəráyshən/ *n.* **1** the process or art of decorating. **2** a thing that decorates or serves as an ornament. **3** a medal, etc., conferred as an honor. **4** (in *pl.*) flags, etc., put up on an occasion of public celebration.

Dec·o·ra·tion Day *n.* = Memorial Day.

dec·o·ra·tive /dékərətiv, dékrə–, –əray–/ *adj.* serving to decorate. ▫▫ **dec·o·ra·tive·ly** *adv.* **dec·o·ra·tive·ness** *n.*

dec·o·ra·tor /dékəraytər/ *n.* a person who decorates, esp. one who paints or papers houses professionally.

de·co·rum /dikáwrəm/ *n.* **1 a** seemliness; propriety. **b** behavior required by politeness or decency. **2** a particular requirement of this kind. **3** etiquette. ▫▫ **dec·o·rous** /dékərəs/ *adj.* **dec·o·rous·ly** *adv.*

de·cou·page /dáykoopaázh/ *n.* (also **découpage**) the decoration of surfaces with paper cutouts.

de·cou·ple /deekúpəl/ *v.tr.* **1** *Electr.* make the interaction between (oscillators, etc.) so weak that there is little transfer of energy between them. **2** separate; disengage; dissociate.

de·coy *n.* & *v.* •*n.* /déekoy, dikóy/ **1** a person or thing used to lure an animal or person into a trap or danger. **2** a bait or enticement. •*v.tr.* /dikóy/ (often foll. by *into, out of*) allure or entice, esp. by means of a decoy.

---

decoy mid-16th century (earlier as *coy*): from Dutch *de kooi* 'the decoy,' from Middle Dutch *de kouw* 'the cage,' from Latin *cavea* 'cage.' The meaning derives from the practice of using tamed ducks to lead wild ones along channels into captivity.

---

de·crease *v.* & *n.* •*v.tr.* & *intr.* /dikrées/ make or become smaller or fewer. •*n.* /déekrees/ **1** the act or an instance of decreasing. **2** the amount by which a thing decreases. ▫▫ **de·creas·ing·ly** *adv.*

de·cree /dikrée/ *n.* & *v.* •*n.* **1** an official order issued by a legal authority. **2** a judgment or decision of certain courts of law. •*v.tr.* (**decrees, decreed, decreeing**) ordain by decree.

dec·re·ment /dékrimənt/ *n.* **1** *Physics* the ratio of the amplitudes in successive cycles of a damped oscillation. **2** the amount lost by diminution or waste. **3** the act of decreasing.

de·crep·it /dikrépit/ *adj.* weakened or worn out by age, infirmity or long use. ▫▫ **de·crep·i·tude** *n.*

de·crim·i·nal·ize /deekríminəlīz/ *v.tr.* cease to treat as criminal. ▫▫ **de·crim·i·nal·i·za·tion** *n.*

de·cry /dikrí/ *v.tr.* (**-cries, -cried**) disparage; belittle. ▫▫ **de·cri·er** *n.*

ded·i·cate /dédikayt/ *v.tr.* **1** (foll. by *to*) devote (esp. oneself) to a special task or purpose. **2** (foll. by *to*) address (a book, etc.) as a compliment to a friend, patron, etc. **3** (often foll. by *to*) devote (a building, etc.) to a deity or purpose. **4** (as **dedicated** *adj.*) **a** (of a person) devoted to an aim or vocation. **b** (of equipment, esp. a computer) designed for a specific purpose. ▫▫ **ded·i·ca·tee** /–kaytée/ *n.* **ded·i·ca·tive** *adj.* **ded·i·ca·tor** *n.* **ded·i·ca·to·ry** /–kətáwree/ *adj.*

ded·i·ca·tion /dédikáyshən/ *n.* **1** the act or an instance of dedicating; the quality or process of being dedicated. **2** the words with which a book, etc., is dedicated. **3** a dedicatory inscription.

de·duce /didóós, –dyóós/ *v.tr.* (often foll. by *from*) infer; draw as a logical conclusion. ▫▫ **de·duc·i·ble** *adj.*

de·duct /didúkt/ *v.tr.* (often foll. by *from*) subtract, take away (an amount, portion, etc.).

de·duct·i·ble /didúktibəl/ *adj. & n.* • *adj.* that may be deducted, esp. from tax to be paid or taxable income. • *n.* part of an insurance claim to be paid by the insured.

de·duc·tion /didúkshən/ *n.* **1 a** the act of deducting. **b** an amount deducted. **2 a** the inferring of particular instances from a general law (cf. INDUCTION). **b** a conclusion deduced.

de·duc·tive /didúktiv/ *adj.* of or reasoning by deduction. ▫▫ **de·duc·tive·ly** *adv.*

dee /dee/ *n.* **1** the letter D. **2** a thing shaped like this.

deed /deed/ *n. & v.* • *n.* **1** a thing done intentionally or consciously. **2** a brave, skillful, or conspicuous act. **3** actual fact or performance (*kind in word and deed*). **4** *Law* a written or printed document often used for a legal transfer of ownership and bearing the disposer's signature. • *v.tr.* convey or transfer by legal deed.

dee·jay /déejáy/ *n. sl.* a disk jockey.

deem /deem/ *v.tr. formal* regard; consider; judge.

de·em·pha·size /dee-émfəsīz/ *v.tr.* **1** remove emphasis from. **2** reduce emphasis on.

deep /deep/ *adj., n., & adv.* • *adj.* **1 a** extending far down from the top (*deep hole*). **b** extending far in from the surface or edge (*deep border*). **2** (*predic.*) **a** extending to a specified depth (*water 6 feet deep*; *ankle-deep in mud*). **b** in a specified number of ranks one behind another (*soldiers drawn up six deep*). **3** situated far down or back (*hands deep in his pockets*). **4** coming or brought from far down or in (*deep sigh*). **5** low-pitched; full-toned; not shrill (*deep voice*). **6** intense; vivid; extreme (*deep disgrace*). **7** heartfelt; absorbing (*deep affection*). **8** (*predic.*) fully absorbed or overwhelmed (*deep in a book*). **9** profound; penetrating; not superficial (*deep thinker*; *deep insight*). • *n.* **1** (prec. by *the*) *poet.* the sea. **2** a deep part of the sea. **3** an abyss, pit, or cavity. **4** a deep state (*deep of the night*). • *adv.* deeply; far down or in (*dig deep*). ▫ **go off the deep end** *colloq.* give way to anger or emotion. **in deep water** (or **waters**) in trouble or difficulty. **jump** (or **be thrown**) **in at the deep end** face a difficult problem, undertaking, etc., with little experience of it. ▫▫ **deep·ly** *adv.* **deep·ness** *n.*

deep·en /déepən/ *v.tr. & intr.* make or become deep or deeper.

deep freeze *n.* **1** a refrigerator in which food can be quickly frozen and kept at a very low temperature. **2** a suspension of activity. ▫▫ **deep-freeze** *v.tr.* (**-froze, frozen**)

deep-fry *v.tr.* (**-fries, -fried**) fry (food) in an amount of fat or oil sufficient to cover it.

deep-root·ed *adj.* (esp. of convictions) firmly established.

deep sea *n.* the deeper parts of the ocean.

deep-seat·ed *adj.* (of emotion, disease, etc.) firmly established; profound.

Deep South *n.* (prec. by *the*) the region of the SE US, usu. including South Carolina, Georgia, Alabama, Mississippi, and Louisiana.

deep space *n.* the regions of outer space beyond the solar system.

deer /deer/ *n.* (*pl.* same) any four-hoofed grazing animal of the family Cervidae, the males of which usu. have deciduous branching antlers.

deer·fly /déerflī/ *n.* any bloodsucking fly of the genus *Chrysops.*

deer·stalk·er /déerstawkər/ *n.* **1** a soft cloth cap with peaks in front and behind and earflaps. **2** a person who stalks deer.

de·es·ca·late /dee-éskəlayt/ *v.tr.* reduce the level or intensity of. ▫▫ **de-es·ca·la·tion** /–láyshən/ *n.*

de·face /difáys/ *v.tr.* **1** spoil the appearance of. **2** make illegible. ▫▫ **de·face·a·ble** *adj.* **de·face·ment** *n.*

de fac·to /di fáktō, day/ *adv. & adj.* • *adv.* in fact, whether by right or not. • *adj.* that exists or is such in fact (*a de facto ruler*).

de·fal·cate /deefálkayt, –fáwl–/ *v.intr. formal* misappropriate property in one's charge, esp. money. ▫▫ **de·fal·ca·tor** *n.*

de·fame /difáym/ *v.tr.* attack the good reputation of. ▫▫ **def·a·ma·tion** /défəmáyshən/ *n.* **de·fam·a·to·ry** /difámətawree/ *adj.*

de·fault /difáwlt/ *n. & v.* • *n.* **1** failure to fulfill an obligation, esp. to appear, pay, or act in some way. **2** lack; absence. **3** a preselected option adopted by a computer program when no alternative is specified by the user or programmer. • *v.* **1** *intr.* fail to fulfill an obligation. **2** *tr.* declare (a party) in default and give judgment against that party. ▫ **win by default** win because an opponent fails to participate.

de·fea·si·ble /diféezibəl/ *adj.* **1** capable of annulment. **2** liable to forfeiture. ▫▫ **de·fea·si·bil·i·ty** *n.* **de·fea·si·bly** *adv.*

de·feat /diféet/ *v. & n.* • *v.tr.* **1** overcome in a battle or other contest. **2** frustrate; baffle. **3** reject (a motion, etc.) by voting. **4** *Law* annul. • *n.* the act or process of defeating or being defeated.

de·feat·ism /diféetizəm/ *n.* **1** an excessive readiness to accept defeat. **2** conduct conducive to this. ▫▫ **de·feat·ist** *n. & adj.*

def·e·cate /défikayt/ *v.intr.* discharge feces from the body. ▫▫ **def·e·ca·tion** /–káyshən/ *n.*

de·fect *n. & v.* • *n.* /déefekt, difékt/ **1** lack of something essential; imperfection. **2** a shortcoming. **3** a blemish. **4** the amount by which a thing falls short. • *v.intr.* /difékt/ abandon one's country or cause in favor of another. ▫▫ **de·fec·tion** /difékshən/ *n.* **de·fec·tor** *n.*

de·fec·tive /diféktiv/ *adj. & n.* • *adj.* **1** having a defect or defects; incomplete; faulty. **2** often *offens.* mentally subnormal. **3** (usu. foll. by *in*) lacking; deficient. **4** *Gram.* not having all the usual inflections. • *n.* often *offens.* a mentally defective person. ▫▫ **de·fec·tive·ly** *adv.* **de·fec·tive·ness** *n.*

de·fend /difénd/ *v.tr.* (also *absol.*) **1** (often foll. by *against, from*) resist an attack made on; protect. **2** uphold by argument. **3** conduct the case for (a defendant in a lawsuit). ▫▫ **de·fend·er** *n.*

de·fend·ant /diféndənt, –ant/ *n.* a person, etc., sued or accused in a court of law.

de·fen·es·tra·tion /déefenistráyshən/ *n. formal* or *joc.* the action of throwing (esp. a person) out of a window. ▫▫ **de·fen·es·trate** /deefénistrayt/ *v.tr.*

de·fense /diféns/ *n.* **1** the act of defending from or resisting attack. **2 a** a means of resisting attack. **b** a thing that protects. **c** the military resources of a country. **3** (in *pl.*) fortifications. **4 a** justification; vindication. **b** a speech or piece of writing used to this end. **5 a** the defendant's case in a lawsuit. **b** the counsel for the defendant. **6** /déefens/ **a** the action or role of defending one's goal, etc., against attack. **b** the players on a team who perform this role. ▫▫ **de·fense·less** *adj.* **de·fense·less·ly** *adv.* **de·fense·less·ness** *n.*

de·fense mech·an·ism *n.* **1** the body's reaction against disease organisms. **2** a usu. unconscious mental process to avoid conscious conflict or anxiety.

de·fen·si·ble /difénsibəl/ *adj.* **1** supportable by argument. **2** that can be easily defended militarily. ▫▫ **de·fen·si·bil·i·ty** *n.* **de·fen·si·bly** *adv.*

de·fen·sive /difénsiv/ *adj.* **1** done or intended for defense or to defend. **2** (of a person or attitude) concerned to challenge criticism. ▫ **on the defensive 1** expecting criticism. **2** in an attitude or position of defense. ▫▫ **de·fen·sive·ly** *adv.* **de·fen·sive·ness** *n.*

de·fer[1] /difə́r/ *v.tr.* (**deferred, deferring**) **1** postpone. **2** postpone the conscription of (a person). ▫▫ **de·fer·ment** *n.* **de·fer·ra·ble** *adj.* **de·fer·ral** *n.*

de·fer[2] /difə́r/ *v.intr.* (**deferred, deferring**) (foll. by *to*) yield or make concessions. ▫▫ **de·fer·rer** *n.*

def·er·ence /défərəns, défrəns/ *n.* **1** courteous regard; respect. **2** compliance with the advice or wishes of another. ▫ **in deference to** out of respect for.

def·er·en·tial /défərénshəl/ *adj.* showing deference; respectful. ▫▫ **def·er·en·tial·ly** *adv.*

de·fi·ance /difíəns/ *n.* **1** open disobedience; bold resistance. **2** a challenge to fight or maintain a cause, assertion, etc. ▫ **in defiance of** disregarding; in conflict with.

de·fi·ant /difíənt/ *adj.* **1** showing defiance. **2** openly disobedient. ▫▫ **de·fi·ant·ly** *adv.*

de·fib·ril·la·tion /deefibriláyshən/ *n. Med.* the stopping of the fibrillation of the heart. ▫▫ **de·fib·ril·la·tor** *n.*

de·fi·cien·cy /difishənsee/ *n.* (*pl.* **-cies**) **1** the state or condition of being deficient. **2** (usu. foll. by *of*) a lack or shortage. **3** a thing lacking. **4** the amount by which a thing, esp. revenue, falls short.

de·fi·cient /difishənt/ *adj.* **1** (usu. foll. by *in*) incomplete; not having enough of a specified quality or ingredient. **2** insufficient in quantity, force, etc. **3** (in full **mentally deficient**) incapable of adequate social or intellectual behavior through imperfect mental development. ▫▫ **de·fi·cient·ly** *adv.*

def·i·cit /défisit/ *n.* **1** the amount by which a thing (esp. a sum of money) is too small. **2** an excess of liabilities over assets (opp. SURPLUS).

de·file[1] /difíl/ *v.tr.* **1** make dirty; pollute. **2** corrupt. **3** desecrate. ▫▫ **de·file·ment** *n.* **de·fil·er** *n.*

de·file[2] /difíl/ *n.* & *v.* • *n.* also /deefil/ **1** a narrow way. **2** a gorge. • *v.intr.* march in file.

de·fine /difín/ *v.tr.* **1** give the exact meaning of (a word, etc.). **2** describe or explain the scope of. **3** make clear, esp. in outline (*well-defined image*). **4** mark out the limits of. **5** (of properties) make up the total character of. ▫▫ **de·fin·a·ble** *adj.* **de·fin·er** *n.*

def·i·nite /définit/ *adj.* **1** having exact and discernible limits. **2** clear and distinct; not vague. ▶See the note at DEFINITIVE. ▫▫ **def·i·nite·ness** *n.*

def·i·nite ar·ti·cle *n. Gram.* the word (*the* in English) preceding a noun and implying a specific or known instance (*the art of government*).

def·i·nite·ly /définitlee/ *adv.* & *int.* • *adv.* **1** in a definite manner. **2** without doubt. • *int. colloq.* yes; certainly.

def·i·ni·tion /défínishən/ *n.* **1 a** the act or process of defining. **b** a statement of the meaning of a word or the nature of a thing. **2** the degree of distinctness in the outline of an object or image.

de·fin·i·tive /difínitiv/ *adj.* **1** (of an answer, treaty, etc.) decisive; final. **2** (of an edition of a book, etc.) most authoritative. ▫▫ **de·fin·i·tive·ly** *adv.*

▶**Definitive** in the sense 'decisive, unconditional, final' is sometimes confused with **definite.** However, **definite** does not have the connotations of authority: a *definite no* is simply a firm refusal, whereas a *definitive no* is an authoritative judgment or decision that something is not the case.

de·flate /difláyt/ *v.* **1 a** *tr.* let air or gas out of. **b** *intr.* be emptied of air or gas. **2 a** *tr.* cause to lose confidence or conceit. **b** *intr.* lose confidence. **3** *Econ.* **a** *tr.* subject (a currency or economy) to deflation. **b** *intr.* pursue a policy of deflation. **4** *tr.* reduce the importance of; depreciate. ▫▫ **de·fla·tor** *n.*

de·fla·tion /difláyshən/ *n.* **1** the act or process of deflating or being deflated. **2** *Econ.* reduction of the amount of money in circulation to increase its value as a measure against inflation. ▫▫ **de·fla·tion·ar·y** *adj.* **de·fla·tion·ist** *n.*

de·flect /diflékt/ *v.* **1** *tr.* & *intr.* bend or turn aside from a straight course or intended purpose. **2** (often foll. by *from*) **a** *tr.* cause to deviate. **b** *intr.* deviate. ▫▫ **de·flec·tion** /diflékshən/ *n.*

de·flec·tor /difléktər/ *n.* a thing that deflects, esp. a device for deflecting a flow of air, etc.

de·flow·er /diflówr/ *v.tr.* **1** deprive of virginity. **2** ravage; spoil. **3** strip of flowers.

de·fo·li·ate /deefóleeayt/ *v.tr.* remove leaves from. ▫▫ **de·fo·li·ant** *n.* & *adj.* **de·fo·li·a·tion** /–áyshən/ *n.* **de·fo·li·a·tor** *n.*

de·form /difáwrm/ *v.* **1** *tr.* make ugly; deface. **2** *tr.* put out of shape. **3** *intr.* undergo deformation; be misshapened. ▫▫ **de·form·a·ble** *adj.* **de·for·ma·tion** /deefawrmáyshən/ *n.* **de·formed** *adj.*

de·form·i·ty /difáwrmitee/ *n.* (*pl.* **-ties**) **1** the state of being deformed; ugliness; disfigurement. **2** a malformation, esp. of body or limb.

de·fraud /difráwd/ *v.tr.* (often foll. by *of*) cheat by fraud. ▫▫ **de·fraud·er** *n.*

de·fray /difráy/ *v.tr.* provide money to pay (a cost). ▫▫ **de·fray·a·ble** *adj.* **de·fray·al** *n.* **de·fray·ment** *n.*

de·frock /deefrók/ *v.tr.* deprive (a person) of ecclesiastical status.

de·frost /difráwst, –fróst/ *v.* **1** *tr.* remove frost or ice from (a refrigerator, windshield of a motor vehicle, etc.). **2** *tr.* unfreeze (frozen food). **3** *intr.* become unfrozen. ▫▫ **de·frost·er** *n.*

deft /deft/ *adj.* neatly skillful or dexterous; adroit. ▫▫ **deft·ly** *adv.* **deft·ness** *n.*

de·funct /difúngkt/ *adj.* **1** no longer existing. **2** no longer used or in fashion. **3** dead or extinct.

de·fuse /deefyóoz/ *v.tr.* **1** remove the fuse from (an explosive device). **2** reduce the tension or potential danger in (a crisis, difficulty, etc.).

de·fy /difí/ *v.tr.* (**-fies, -fied**) **1** resist openly; refuse to obey. **2** present insuperable obstacles to (*defies solution*). **3** (foll. by *to* + infin.) challenge (a person) to do or prove something.

de·gen·er·ate *adj.*, *n.*, & *v.* • *adj.* /dijénərət/ **1** having lost the qualities that are normal and desirable or proper to its kind. **2** *Biol.* having changed to a lower type. • *n.* /dijénərət/ a degenerate person or animal. • *v.intr.* /dijénərayt/ become degenerate. ▫▫ **de·gen·er·a·cy** *n.* **de·gen·er·ate·ly** *adv.* **de·gen·er·a·tion** /dijénəráyshən/ *n.*

de·gen·er·a·tive /dijénərətiv/ *adj.* **1** of or tending to degeneration. **2** (of disease) characterized by progressive often irreversible deterioration.

de·grade /digráyd/ *v.tr.* **1** reduce to a lower rank, esp. as a punishment. **2** bring into dishonor or contempt. **3** *Chem.* reduce to a simpler molecular structure. **4** *Physics* reduce (energy) to a less convertible form. ▫▫ **de·grad·a·ble** *adj.* **deg·ra·da·tion** /dégrədáyshən/ *n.* **deg·ra·da·tive** /–dáytiv/ *adj.*

de·grad·ing /digráyding/ *adj.* humiliating. ▫▫ **de·grad·ing·ly** *adv.*

de·gree /digrée/ *n.* **1** a stage in an ascending or descending scale or process. **2** a stage in intensity or amount (*in some degree*). **3** relative condition (*each is good in its degree*). **4** *Math.* a unit of measurement of angles. **5** *Physics* a unit in a scale of temperature, hardness, etc. **6** *Med.* an extent of burns on a scale characterized by the destruction of the skin. **7** an academic rank conferred usu. after examination or after completion of a course. **8** a grade of crime or criminality (*murder in the* *first degree*). **9** a step in direct genealogical descent. **10** social or official rank. ▫ **by degrees** a little at a time; gradually. **to a degree** *colloq.* considerably.

de·gree-day *n.* a unit of measurement equal to one degree of variation between a standard temperature and the mean temperature on a given day.

de·hu·man·ize /deehyóómənīz/ *v.tr.* **1** deprive of human characteristics. **2** make impersonal or machine-like. ▫▫ **de·hu·man·i·za·tion** *n.*

de·hu·mid·i·fy /déehyoomídifī/ *v.tr.* (**-fies, -fied**) reduce the degree of humidity of; remove moisture from (esp. air). ▫▫ **de·hu·mid·i·fi·ca·tion** /–fikáyshən/ *n.* **de·hu·mid·i·fi·er** *n.*

de·hy·drate /deéhīdráyt/ *v.* **1** *tr.* **a** remove water from (esp. foods for preservation). **b** make dry, esp. make (the body) deficient in water. **c** render lifeless or uninteresting. **2** *intr.* lose water. ▫▫ **de·hy·dra·tion** /–dráyshən/ *n.* **de·hy·dra·tor** *n.*

de·i·fy /deéifī, dáyee–/ *v.tr.* (**-fies, -fied**) **1** make a god of. **2** regard or worship as a god. ▫▫ **de·i·fi·ca·tion** /–fikáyshən/ *n.*

deign /dayn/ *v. intr.* (foll. by *to* + infin.) think fit; condescend.

de·ism /deéizəm, dáy–/ *n.* belief in the existence of a god, based on reason rather than revelation (cf. THEISM). ▫▫ **de·ist** *n.* **de·is·tic** *adj.* **de·is·ti·cal** *adj.*

de·i·ty /deéitee, dáy–/ *n.* (*pl.* **-ties**) **1** a god or goddess. **2** divine status, quality, or nature. **3** (**the Deity**) God.

dé·jà vu /dáyzhaa vóó/ *n.* **1** *Psychol.* an illusory feeling of having already experienced a present situation. **2** something tediously familiar.

de·ject /dijékt/ *v.tr.* (usu. as **dejected** *adj.*) make sad or dispirited; depress. ▫▫ **de·ject·ed·ly** *adv.* **de·jec·tion** /dijékshən/ *n.*

de ju·re /dee jóóree, day jóóray/ *adj. & adv.* • *adj.* rightful. • *adv.* rightfully; by right.

Del·a·ware /déləwair/ *n.* **1 a** a N. American people native to the northeastern US. **b** a member of this people. **2** the language of this people. ▶Also called **Lenape** or **Lenni Lenape**.

de·lay /diláy/ *v. & n.* • *v.* **1** *tr.* postpone; defer. **2** *tr.* make late (*was delayed by the traffic lights*). **3** *intr.* loiter; be late (*don't delay!*). • *n.* **1** the act or an instance of delaying; the process of being delayed. **2** time lost by inaction or the inability to proceed. **3** a hindrance. ▫▫ **de·lay·er** *n.*

de·lec·ta·ble /diléktəbəl/ *adj.* esp. *literary* delightful; pleasant. ▫▫ **de·lec·ta·bly** *adv.*

de·lec·ta·tion /déelektáyshən/ *n. literary* pleasure; enjoyment (*sang for his delectation*).

del·e·gate *n. & v.* • *n.* /déligət/ **1** an elected representative sent to a conference. **2** a member of a committee or deputation. • *v.tr.* /déligayt/ **1** (often foll. by *to*) **a** commit (authority, etc.) to an agent or deputy. **b** entrust (a task) to another person. **2** send or authorize (a person) as a representative. ▫▫ **del·e·ga·ble** /–gəbəl/ *adj.* **del·e·ga·tor** *n.*

del·e·ga·tion /déligáyshən/ *n.* **1** a body of delegates. **2** the act or process of delegating or being delegated.

de·lete /diléet/ *v.tr.* remove or obliterate (written or printed matter), esp. by striking out. ▫▫ **de·le·tion** *n.*

del·e·te·ri·ous /délitéereeəs/ *adj.* harmful (to the mind or body). ▫▫ **del·e·te·ri·ous·ly** *adv.*

delft /delft/ *n.* (also **delft·ware** /délftwair/) glazed, usu. blue and white, earthenware, made in Delft in Holland.

del·i /délee/ *n.* (*pl.* **delis**) *colloq.* a delicatessen.

de·lib·er·ate *adj. & v.* • *adj.* /dilíbərət/ **1 a** intentional. **b** fully considered; not impulsive. **2** slow in deciding; cautious (*a ponderous and deliberate mind*). **3** (of movement, etc.) unhurried. • *v.* /dilíbərayt/ **1** *intr.* think carefully; take counsel (*the jury deliberated for an hour*). **2** *tr.* consider; discuss carefully. ▫▫ **de·lib·er·ate·ly** /dilíbərətlee/ *adv.* **de·lib·er·ate·ness** *n.*

de·lib·er·a·tion /dilíbəráyshən/ *n.* **1** careful consideration. **2** a debate; discussion. **3 a** caution and care. **b** (of movement) slowness or ponderousness.

de·lib·er·a·tive /dilíbərətiv, –ráytiv/ *adj.* of, or appointed for the purpose of, deliberation or debate.

del·i·ca·cy /délikəsee/ *n.* (*pl.* **-cies**) **1** the quality of being delicate. **2** a choice or expensive food.

del·i·cate /délikət/ *adj.* **1 a** fine in texture or structure; soft, slender, or slight. **b** (of color) subtle or subdued. **c** subtle; hard to appreciate. **2** (of a person) easily injured; susceptible to illness. **3 a** requiring careful handling; tricky (*a delicate situation*). **b** (of an instrument) highly sensitive. **4** deft. **5** (of a person) avoiding the immodest or offensive. **6** (esp. of actions) considerate. ▫▫ **del·i·cate·ly** *adv.* **del·i·cate·ness** *n.*

del·i·ca·tes·sen /délikətésən/ *n.* **1** a store selling cooked meats, cheeses, and unusual or foreign prepared foods. **2** (often *attrib.*) such foods collectively (*a delicatessen counter*).

de·li·cious /dilíshəs/ *adj.* **1** highly delightful and enjoyable to the taste or sense of smell. **2** (of a joke, etc.) very witty. ▫▫ **de·li·cious·ly** *adv.* **de·li·cious·ness** *n.*

de·light /dilít/ *v. & n.* • *v.* **1** *tr.* (often foll. by *with*, or *that* + clause, or *to* + infin.) please greatly. **2** *intr.* (often foll. by *in*, or *to* + infin.) take great pleasure; be highly pleased. • *n.* **1** great pleasure. **2** something giving pleasure. ▫▫ **de·light·ed** *adj.* **de·light·ed·ly** *adv.*

de·light·ful /dilítfool/ *adj.* causing delight; pleasant; charming. ▫▫ **de·light·ful·ly** *adv.* **de·light·ful·ness** *n.*

de·lim·it /dilímit/ *v.tr.* determine the limits or boundary of. ▫▫ **de·lim·i·ta·tion** /–táyshən/ *n.*

de·lin·e·ate /dilíneeayt/ *v.tr.* portray by drawing, etc., or in words. ▫▫ **de·lin·e·a·tion** /–áyshən/ *n.*

de·lin·quent /dilíngkwənt/ *n. & adj.* • *n.* an offender (*juvenile delinquent*). • *adj.* **1** guilty of a minor crime or a misdeed. **2** failing in one's duty. **3** in arrears. ▫▫ **de·lin·quen·cy** /dilíngkwənsee/ *n.* (*pl.* **-cies**) **de·lin·quent·ly** *adv.*

del·i·quesce /délikwés/ *v.intr.* **1** become liquid; melt. **2** *Chem.* dissolve in water absorbed from the air. ▫▫ **del·i·ques·cence** *n.* **del·i·ques·cent** *adj.*

de·lir·i·ous /dilíreeəs/ *adj.* **1** affected with delirium; temporarily or apparently mad; raving. **2** wildly excited; ecstatic. ▫▫ **de·lir·i·ous·ly** *adv.*

de·lir·i·um /dilíreeəm/ *n.* **1** an acutely disordered state of mind involving incoherent speech, hallucinations, and frenzied excitement. **2** great excitement; ecstasy.

de·lir·i·um tre·mens /treémənz, –menz/ *n.* a psychosis of chronic alcoholism involving tremors and hallucinations.

de·liv·er /dilívər/ *v.tr.* **1 a** distribute (letters, packages, ordered goods, etc.) to the addressee or the purchaser. **b** (often foll. by *to*) hand over (*delivered the boy safely to his teacher*). **2** (often foll. by *from*) save, rescue, or set free (*delivered him from his enemies*). **3 a** give birth to (*delivered a girl*). **b** (in *passive*; often foll. by *of*) give birth (*was delivered of a child*). **c** assist at the birth of (*delivered six babies that week*). **d** assist in giving birth (*delivered the baby successfully*). **4** (often *refl.*) utter or recite (an opinion, a speech, etc.) (*delivered himself of the observation; delivered the sermon well*). **5** (often foll. by *up, over*) abandon; resign; hand over (*delivered his soul up to God*). **6** launch or aim (a blow, a ball, or an attack). **7** *colloq.* = *deliver the goods*. ▫ **deliver the goods** *colloq.* carry out one's part of an agreement. ▫▫ **de·liv·er·a·ble** *adj.* **de·liv·er·er** *n.*

de·liv·er·ance /dilívərəns/ *n.* **1** the act or an instance of rescuing; the process of being rescued. **2** a rescue.

de·liv·er·y /dilívəree/ *n.* (*pl.* **-ies**) **1 a** the delivering of letters, etc. **b** something delivered. **2 a** the process of childbirth. **b** an act of this. **3** deliverance. **4** an act of throwing, as of a baseball. **5** the act of giving or surrendering (*delivery of the town to the enemy*). **6 a** the uttering of a speech, etc. **b** the manner or style of such a delivery. □ **take delivery of** receive (something purchased).

dell /del/ *n.* a small usu. wooded hollow or valley.

del·phin·i·um /delfíneeəm/ *n.* any ranunculaceous garden plant of the genus *Delphinium,* with tall spikes of usu. blue flowers.

del·ta /déltə/ *n.* **1** a triangular tract of deposited earth, alluvium, etc., at the mouth of a river, formed by its diverging outlets. **2** the fourth letter of the Greek alphabet (Δ, δ). □□ **del·ta·ic** /deltáyik/ *adj.*

del·ta wing *n.* the triangular swept-back wing of an aircraft.

del·toid /déltoyd/ *n.* (in full **deltoid muscle**) a thick triangular muscle covering the shoulder joint and used for raising the arm away from the body.

de·lude /dilóód/ *v.tr.* deceive or mislead.

del·uge /délyooj, –yoozh/ *n. & v.* • *n.* **1** a great flood. **2** (**the Deluge**) the biblical Flood (Gen. 6–8). **3** a great outpouring (of words, paper, etc.). **4** a heavy fall of rain. • *v.tr.* **1** flood. **2** inundate with a great number or amount (*deluged with complaints*).

de·lu·sion /dilóózhən/ *n.* **1** a false belief or impression. **2** *Psychol.* this as a symptom or form of mental disorder. □□ **de·lu·sion·al** *adj.*

de·lu·sions of gran·deur *n.pl.* a false idea of oneself as being important, noble, famous, etc.

de·lu·sive /dilóósiv/ *adj.* deceptive or unreal. □□ **de·lu·sive·ly** *adv.* **de·lu·sive·ness** *n.*

de·luxe /də lúks, lóóks/ *adj.* **1** luxurious or sumptuous. **2** of a superior kind.

delve /delv/ *v.* **1** *intr.* (often foll. by *in, into*) **a** search energetically (*delved into his pocket*). **b** research (*delved into his family history*). **2** *tr. & intr. poet.* dig. □□ **delv·er** *n.*

de·mag·net·ize /deemágnitīz/ *v.tr.* remove the magnetic properties of. □□ **de·mag·net·i·za·tion** /–tizáyshən/ *n.* **de·mag·net·iz·er** *n.*

dem·a·gogue /déməgog, –gawg/ *n.* (also **-gog**) a political agitator appealing to the basest instincts of a mob. □□ **dem·a·gog·ic** /–gójik, –gógik, –gṓ–/ *adj.* **dem·a·gogu·er·y** /–gógəree, –gáwg–/ *n.* **dem·a·go·gy** /–gójee, –gáw–/ *n.*

de·mand /dimánd/ *n. & v.* • *n.* **1** an insistent and peremptory request, made as of right. **2** *Econ.* the desire of purchasers or consumers for a commodity (*no demand for solid tires these days*). **3** an urgent claim (*care of her mother makes demands on her*). • *v.tr.* **1** (often foll. by *of, from,* or *to* + infin., or *that* + clause) ask for (something) insistently and urgently, as of right. **2** require or need (*a task demanding skill*). **3** insist on being told (*demanded the truth*). **4** (as **demanding** *adj.*) making demands; requiring skill, effort, etc. (*a demanding job*). □ **in demand** sought after. **on demand** as soon as a demand is made (*a check payable on demand*). □□ **de·mand·ing·ly** *adv.*

de·mar·ca·tion /déemaarkáyshən/ *n.* **1** the act of marking a boundary or limits. **2** the trade-union practice of strictly assigning specific jobs to different unions. □□ **de·mar·cate** /dimaárkayt, déemaar–/ *v.tr.*

de·mean /diméen/ *v.tr.* (usu. *refl.*) lower the dignity of.

de·mean·or /diméenər/ *n.* outward behavior or bearing.

de·ment·ed /diméntid/ *adj.* mad; crazy. □□ **de·ment·ed·ly** *adv.* **de·ment·ed·ness** *n.*

de·men·tia /diménshə/ *n. Med.* a chronic or persistent disorder of the mental processes due to brain disease or injury, marked by memory disorders, personality changes, impaired reasoning, etc.

de·mer·it /dimérit/ *n.* **1** a quality or action deserving blame; a fault. **2** a mark given to an offender.

de·mesne /dimáyn, –méen/ *n.* **1 a** a sovereign's or nation's territory; a domain. **b** land attached to a mansion, etc. **c** landed property; an estate. **2** (usu. foll. by *of*) a region or sphere. **3** *Law hist.* possession (of real property) as one's own. □ **held in demesne** (of an estate) occupied by the owner, not by tenants.

demi- /démee/ *prefix* **1** half; half-size. **2** partially or imperfectly such (*demigod*).

dem·i·god /démeegod/ *n.* (*fem.* **-goddess** /–godis/) **1 a** a partly divine being. **b** the offspring of a god or goddess and a mortal. **2** *colloq.* a person of compelling beauty, powers, or personality.

dem·i·john /démeejon/ *n.* a bulbous, narrow-necked, usu. wicker-covered bottle holding 3–10 gallons.

de·mil·i·ta·rize /deemílitərīz/ *v.tr.* remove a military organization or forces from (a frontier, a zone, etc.). □□ **de·mil·i·ta·ri·za·tion** *n.*

dem·i·monde /démeemond, –máwnd/ *n.* **1 a** *hist.* a class of women in 19th-c. France considered to be of doubtful social standing and morality. **b** a similar class of women in any society. **2** any group considered to be on the fringes of respectable society.

de·min·er·al·ize /deemínərəlīz/ *v.tr.* remove salts from (sea water, etc.). □□ **de·min·er·al·i·za·tion** *n.*

de·mise /dimíz/ *n. & v.* • *n.* **1** death (*left a will on her demise; the demise of the agreement*). **2** *Law* conveyance or transfer (of property, a title, etc.) by demising. • *v.tr.* *Law* **1** convey or grant (an estate) by will or lease. **2** transmit (a title, etc.) by death.

dem·i·tasse /démeetas, -taas/ *n.* **1** a small coffee cup. **2** its contents.

dem·o /démō/ *n.* (*pl.* **-os**) *colloq.* = DEMONSTRATION 3.

de·mo·bi·lize /deemṓbilīz/ *v.tr.* disband (troops). □□ **de·mo·bi·li·za·tion** *n.*

de·moc·ra·cy /dimókrəsee/ *n.* (*pl.* **-cies**) **1 a** a system of government by the whole population, usu. through elected representatives. **b** a nation so governed. **c** any organization governed on democratic principles. **2** a classless and tolerant form of society. **3 a** the principles of the Democratic party. **b** its members.

dem·o·crat /déməkrat/ *n.* **1** an advocate of democracy. **2** (**Democrat**) a member of the Democratic party.

dem·o·crat·ic /déməkrátik/ *adj.* **1** of, like, practicing, advocating, or constituting democracy or a democracy. **2** favoring social equality. □□ **dem·o·crat·i·cal·ly** *adv.*

Dem·o·crat·ic par·ty *n.* one of the two main US political parties, considered to support social reform and strong federal powers. (cf. REPUBLICAN PARTY).

de·moc·ra·tize /dimókrətīz/ *v.tr.* make (a nation, institution, etc.) democratic. □□ **de·moc·ra·ti·za·tion** *n.*

de·mod·u·late /deemójəlayt/ *v.tr. Physics* extract (a modulating signal) from its carrier. □□ **de·mod·u·la·tion** /–láyshən/ *n.* **de·mod·u·la·tor** *n.*

de·mog·ra·phy /dimógrəfee/ *n.* the study of the statistics of births, deaths, disease, etc. □□ **de·mog·ra·pher** *n.* **dem·o·graph·ic** /déməgráfik/ *adj.* **dem·o·graph·i·cal·ly** *adv.*

de·mol·ish /dimólish/ *v.tr.* **1 a** pull down (a building). **b** completely destroy or break. **2** overthrow (an institution). **3** refute (an argument, theory, etc.). **4** *joc.* eat up completely and quickly. □□ **de·mol·ish·er** *n.* **dem·o·li·tion** /déməlíshən/ *n.*

de·mon /déemən/ *n.* **1 a** an evil spirit or devil, esp. one thought to possess a person. **b** the personification of evil. **2** a malignant supernatural being; the Devil. **3** (often *attrib.*) a forceful, fierce, or skillful performer (*a demon player*). **4** a cruel or destructive person. □□ **de·mon·ize** /déemənīz/ *v.tr.*

de•mon•e•tize /deemónitīz, –mún–/ *v.tr.* withdraw (a coin, etc.) from use as money. ▫▫ **de•mon•e•ti•za•tion** *n.*

de•mo•ni•ac /dimṓneeak/ *adj. & n.* • *adj.* **1** fiercely energetic or frenzied. **2 a** supposedly possessed by an evil spirit. **b** of or concerning such possession. **3** of or like demons. • *n.* a person possessed by an evil spirit. ▫▫ **de•mo•ni•a•cal** /de͞eməníəkəl/ *adj.* **de•mo•ni•a•cal•ly** *adv.*

de•mon•ic /dimónik/ *adj.* **1** = DEMONIAC. **2** having or seeming to have supernatural genius or power.

de•mon•ism /de͞emənizəm/ *n.* belief in the power of demons.

de•mon•stra•ble /dimónstrəbəl/ *adj.* capable of being shown or logically proved. ▫▫ **de•mon•stra•bly** *adv.*

dem•on•strate /démənstrayt/ *v.* **1** *tr.* show evidence of (feelings, etc.). **2** *tr.* describe and explain (a scientific proposition, machine, etc.) by experiment, practical use, etc. **3** *tr.* **a** logically prove the truth of. **b** be proof of the existence of. **4** *intr.* take part in or organize a public demonstration. **5** *intr.* act as a demonstrator.

dem•on•stra•tion /démənstráyshən/ *n.* **1** (foll. by *of*) **a** the outward showing of feeling, etc. **b** an instance of this. **2** a public meeting, march, etc., for a political or moral purpose. **3 a** the exhibiting or explaining of specimens or experiments as a method of esp. scientific teaching. **b** an instance of this. **4** proof provided by logic, argument, etc. **5** *Mil.* a show of military force. ▫▫ **dem•on•stra•tion•al** *adj.*

de•mon•stra•tive /dimónstrətiv/ *adj. & n.* • *adj.* **1** given to or marked by an open expression of feeling, esp. of affection. **2** (usu. foll. by *of*) logically conclusive; giving proof (*the work is demonstrative of their skill*). **3 a** serving to point out or exhibit. **b** involving esp. scientific demonstration (*demonstrative technique*). **4** *Gram.* (of an adjective or pronoun) indicating the person or thing referred to (e.g., *this, that, those*). • *n. Gram.* a demonstrative adjective or pronoun. ▫▫ **de•mon•stra•tive•ly** *adv.*

dem•on•stra•tor /démənstraytər/ *n.* **1** a person who takes part in a political demonstration, etc. **2** a person who demonstrates, esp. machines, equipment, etc., to prospective customers. **3** a person who teaches by demonstration, esp. in a laboratory, etc.

de•mor•al•ize /dimáwrəlīz, –mór–/ *v.tr.* destroy (a person's) morale; make hopeless. ▫▫ **de•mor•al•i•za•tion** *n.* **de•mor•al•iz•ing** *adj.* **de•mor•al•iz•ing•ly** *adv.*

de•mote /dimṓt/ *v.tr.* reduce to a lower rank or class. ▫▫ **de•mo•tion** /–mṓshən/ *n.*

de•mur /dimə́r/ *v. & n.* • *v.intr.* (**demurred, demurring**) **1** (often foll. by *to, at*) raise scruples or objections. **2** *Law* put in a demurrer. • *n.* (also **de•mur•ral** /dimə́rəl/) (usu. in *neg.*) **1** an objection (*agreed without demur*). **2** the act or process of objecting.

de•mure /dimyŏŏr/ *adj.* (**demurer, demurest**) **1** quiet and reserved; modest. **2** affectedly shy and quiet; coy. **3** decorous (*a demure high collar*). ▫▫ **de•mure•ly** *adv.* **de•mure•ness** *n.*

de•mur•rer /dimə́rər, –múr–/ *n. Law* an objection raised or exception taken.

de•mys•ti•fy /deemístifī/ *v.tr.* (**•fies, •fied**) **1** clarify (obscure beliefs or subjects, etc.). **2** reduce or remove the irrationality in (a person). ▫▫ **de•mys•ti•fi•ca•tion** /–fikáyshən/ *n.*

de•my•thol•o•gize /de͞emithóləjīz/ *v.tr.* **1** remove mythical elements from (a legend, famous person's life, etc.). **2** reinterpret what some consider to be the mythological elements in (the Bible).

den /den/ *n.* **1** a wild animal's lair. **2** a place of crime or vice (*den of iniquity; opium den*). **3** a small private room for pursuing a hobby, etc.

de•nar•i•us /dináireeəs/ *n.* (*pl.* **denarii** /–ree-ī/) an ancient Roman silver coin.

de•na•tion•al•ize /deenáshənəlīz/ *v.tr.* **1** transfer (a nationalized industry or institution, etc.) from public to private ownership. **2 a** deprive (a nation) of its status or characteristics as a nation. **b** deprive (a person) of nationality or national characteristics. ▫▫ **de•na•tion•al•i•za•tion** *n.*

de•nat•u•ral•ize /deenáchərəlīz/ *v.tr.* **1** change the nature or properties of; make unnatural. **2** deprive of the rights of citizenship. **3** = DENATURE *v.* 1. ▫▫ **de•nat•u•ral•i•za•tion** *n.*

de•na•ture /de͞enáychər/ *v.tr.* **1** change the properties of (a protein, etc.) by heat, acidity, etc. **2** make (alcohol) unfit for drinking, esp. by the addition of another substance. ▫▫ **de•na•tur•a•tion** /de͞enaychəráyshən/ *n.*

den•drite /déndrīt/ *n.* **1** natural treelike or mosslike markings on stones or minerals. **2** *Anat.* a branching process of a nerve cell conducting signals to a cell body.

den•drit•ic /dendrítik/ *adj.* **1** of or like a dendrite. **2** treelike in shape or markings. ▫▫ **den•drit•i•cal•ly** *adv.*

den•dro•chro•nol•o•gy /déndrōkrənóləjee/ *n.* **1** a system of dating using the annual growth rings of trees. **2** the study of these growth rings. ▫▫ **den•dro•chron•o•log•i•cal** /–krónəlójikəl/ *adj.* **den•dro•chro•nol•o•gist** *n.*

den•drol•o•gy /dendróləjee/ *n.* the scientific study of trees. ▫▫ **den•dro•log•i•cal** /–drəlójikəl/ *adj.* **den•drol•o•gist** *n.*

den•gue /dénggay, –gee/ *n.* an infectious viral disease of the tropics causing a fever and acute pains in the joints.

de•ni•al /diníəl/ *n.* **1** the act or an instance of denying. **2** a refusal of a request or wish. **3** a statement that a thing is not true; a rejection (*denial of the accusation*). **4** a disavowal of a person as one's leader, etc. **5** = SELF-DENIAL.

de•nier /dényər, dənyáy, dəne͞er/ *n.* a unit of weight by which the fineness of silk, rayon, or nylon yarn is measured.

den•i•grate /dénigrayt/ *v.tr.* disparage the reputation of (a person). ▫▫ **den•i•gra•tion** /–gráyshən/ *n.* **den•i•gra•tor** *n.* **den•i•gra•to•ry** /–grətáwree/ *adj.*

den•im /dénim/ *n.* **1** (often *attrib.*) a usu. blue, hard-wearing, cotton twill fabric used for jeans, overalls, etc. (*a denim skirt*). **2** (in *pl.*) *colloq.* jeans, overalls, etc., made of this.

den•i•zen /dénizən/ *n.* **1** a foreigner admitted to certain rights in his or her adopted country. **2** a naturalized foreign word, animal, or plant. **3** (usu. foll. by *of*) an inhabitant or occupant.

de•nom•i•nate /dinóminayt/ *v.tr.* **1** give a name to. **2** call or describe (a person or thing) as.

de•nom•i•na•tion /dinómináyshən/ *n.* **1** a church or religious sect. **2** a class of units within a range or sequence of numbers, weights, money, etc. (*money of small denominations*). **3 a** a name or designation, esp. a characteristic or class name. **b** a class or kind having a specific name. **4** the rank of a playing card within a suit, or of a suit relative to others. ▫▫ **de•nom•i•na•tion•al** *adj.*

de•nom•i•na•tor /dinóminaytər/ *n. Math.* the number below the line in a vulgar fraction; a divisor.

de•note /dinṓt/ *v.tr.* **1** be a sign of; indicate. **2** (usu. foll. by *that* + clause) mean; convey. **3** stand as a name for; signify. ▫▫ **de•no•ta•tion** /de͞enōtáyshən/ *n.* **de•no•ta•tive** /de͞enōtáytiv, dinṓtətiv/ *adj.*
▶See note at CONNOTE.

de•noue•ment /daynōōmṓN/ *n.* (also **dénouement**) **1** the final unraveling of a plot or complicated situation. **2** the final scene in a play, novel, etc., in which the plot is resolved.

---

de•nounce /dinówns/ *v.tr.* **1** accuse publicly; condemn. **2** inform against. **3** give notice of the termination of (an armistice, treaty, etc.). ▫▫ **de•nounce•ment** *n.* **de•nounc•er** *n.*

dense /dens/ *adj.* **1** closely compacted in substance; thick (*dense fog*). **2** crowded together (*the population is less dense on the outskirts*). **3** *colloq.* stupid. ▫▫ **dense•ly** *adv.* **dense•ness** *n.*

den•si•ty /dénsitee/ *n.* (*pl.* **-ties**) **1** the degree of compactness of a substance. **2** *Physics* degree of consistency measured by the quantity of mass per unit volume. **3** the opacity of a photographic image. **4** a crowded state. **5** stupidity.

dent /dent/ *n.* & *v.* • *n.* **1** a slight mark or hollow in a surface. **2** a noticeable effect (*lunch made a dent in our funds*). • *v.tr.* **1** mark with a dent. **2** have (esp. an adverse) effect on (*the news dented our hopes*).

den•tal /dént'l/ *adj.* **1** of the teeth; of or relating to dentistry. **2** *Phonet.* (of a consonant) produced with the tip of the tongue against the upper front teeth (as *th*) or the ridge of the teeth (as *n*, *s*, *t*).

den•tal floss *n.* a thread used to clean between the teeth.

den•tate /déntayt/ *adj. Bot.* & *Zool.* toothed; serrated.

den•ti•frice /déntifris/ *n.* a paste or powder for cleaning the teeth.

den•tin /dént'n/ *n.* (also **den•tine** /–teen/) a hard, dense, bony tissue forming the bulk of a tooth.

den•tist /déntist/ *n.* a person who is qualified to treat the diseases and conditions that affect the mouth, jaws, teeth, etc. ▫▫ **den•tis•try** *n.*

den•ti•tion /dentíshən/ *n.* **1** the type, number, and arrangement of teeth in a species, etc. **2** the cutting of teeth; teething.

den•ture /dénchər/ *n.* a removable artificial replacement for one or more teeth carried on a removable plate or frame.

de•nude /dinóód, –nyóód/ *v.tr.* **1** make naked or bare. **2** (foll. by *of*) **a** strip of clothing, a covering, etc. **b** deprive of a possession or attribute. ▫▫ **den•u•da•tion** /déenoodáyshən, –nyoo–, dényoo–/ *n.*

de•nun•ci•a•tion /dinúnsee-áyshən, –shee–/ *n.* the act or an instance of denouncing. ▫▫ **de•nun•ci•ate** /–seeayt/ *v.tr.* **de•nun•ci•a•to•ry** /–seeətawree/ *adj.*

de•ny /diní/ *v.tr.* (**-nies, -nied**) **1** declare untrue or nonexistent (*denied the charge*). **2** repudiate or disclaim (*denied her signature*). **3** (often foll. by *to*) refuse (a person or thing, or something to a person) (*this was denied to me*; *denied him the satisfaction*). **4** refuse access to (a person sought) (*denied him his son*). ▫▫ **de•ni•er** *n.*

de•o•dor•ant /deeódərənt/ *n.* (often *attrib.*) a substance sprayed or rubbed on to the body or sprayed into the air to remove or conceal unpleasant smells.

de•o•dor•ize /deeódərīz/ *v.tr.* remove or destroy the (usu. unpleasant) smell of. ▫▫ **de•o•dor•i•za•tion** *n.* **de•o•dor•iz•er** *n.*

de•ox•y•gen•ate /deeóksijənayt/ *v.tr.* remove oxygen from. ▫▫ **de•ox•y•gen•a•tion** /–náyshən/ *n.*

de•ox•y•ri•bo•nu•cle•ic ac•id /déeokseerībōnookléeik, –kláyik, –nyoo–/ *n.* see DNA.

de•part /dipaárt/ *v.* **1** *intr.* **a** (usu. foll. by *from*) go away; leave (*the train departs from this platform*). **b** (usu. foll. by *for*) start; set out (*flights depart for New York every hour*). **2** *intr.* (usu. foll. by *from*) diverge; deviate (*departs from standard practice*). **3** **a** *intr.* die. **b** *tr. formal* or *literary* leave by death (*departed this life*).

de•part•ed /dipaártid/ *n.* (prec. by *the*) *euphem.* a particular dead person or dead people (*we are here to mourn the departed*).

de•part•ment /dipaártmənt/ *n.* **1** a separate part of a complex whole, esp.: **a** a branch of municipal or federal administration (*State Department*; *Department of Agriculture*). **b** a branch of study and its administration at a university, school, etc. (*the physics department*). **c** a section of a large store (*hardware department*). **2** *colloq.* an area of special expertise. **3** an administrative district in France and other countries.

de•part•men•tal /déepaartmént'l/ *adj.* of or belonging to a department. ▫▫ **de•part•men•tal•ize** *v.tr.* **de•part•men•tal•i•za•tion** *n.* **de•part•men•tal•ly** *adv.*

de•part•ment store *n.* a large retail establishment stocking many varieties of goods in different departments.

de•par•ture /dipaárchər/ *n.* **1** the act or an instance of departing. **2** (often foll. by *from*) a deviation (from the truth, a standard, etc.). **3** (often *attrib.*) the starting of a train, an aircraft, etc. (*the departure was late*; *departure lounge*). **4** a new course of action or thought (*driving a car is rather a departure for him*).

de•pend /dipénd/ *v.intr.* **1** (often foll. by *on*, *upon*) be controlled or determined by (*success depends on hard work*; *it depends how you tackle the problem*). **2** (foll. by *on*, *upon*) **a** be unable to do without (*depends on her mother*). **b** rely on (*I'm depending on you to come*). **3** (foll. by *on*, *upon*) be grammatically dependent on. ▫ **depend upon it!** you may be sure! **it** (or **it all** or **that**) **depends** expressing uncertainty or qualification in answering a question (*Will they come? It depends*).

de•pend•a•ble /dipéndəbəl/ *adj.* reliable. ▫▫ **de•pend•a•bil•i•ty** *n.* **de•pend•a•bly** *adv.*

de•pend•ence /dipéndəns/ *n.* **1** the state of being dependent, esp. on financial or other support. **2** reliance; trust (*shows great dependence on his judgment*).

de•pend•en•cy /dipéndənsee/ *n.* (*pl.* **-cies**) **1** a country or province controlled by another. **2** anything subordinate or dependent.

de•pend•ent /dipéndənt/ *adj.* & *n.* • *adj.* **1** (usu. foll. by *on*) depending, conditional, or subordinate. **2** unable to do without (esp. a drug). **3** maintained at another's cost. **4** *Math.* (of a variable) having a value determined by that of another variable. **5** *Gram.* (of a clause, phrase, or word) subordinate to a sentence or word. • *n.* **1** a person who relies on another, esp. for financial support. **2** a servant. ▫▫ **de•pend•ent•ly** *adv.*

de•pict /dipíkt/ *v.tr.* **1** represent in a drawing or painting, etc. **2** portray in words; describe (*the play depicts him as vain and petty*). ▫▫ **de•pic•tion** /–píkshən/ *n.*

dep•i•late /dépilayt/ *v.tr.* remove the hair from. ▫▫ **dep•i•la•tion** /–láyshən/ *n.*

de•pil•a•to•ry /dipílətawree/ *adj.* & *n.* • *adj.* capable of removing unwanted hair. • *n.* (*pl.* **•ries**) a cream or lotion that removes unwanted hair from the body.

de•plane /deepláyn/ *v.intr.* disembark from an airplane.

de•plete /dipléet/ *v.tr.* (esp. in *passive*) **1** reduce in numbers or quantity (*depleted forces*). **2** empty out; exhaust (*their energies were depleted*). ▫▫ **de•ple•tion** /–pléeshən/ *n.*

de•plor•a•ble /dipláwrəbəl/ *adj.* **1** exceedingly bad (*a deplorable meal*). **2** that can be deplored. ▫▫ **de•plor•a•bly** *adv.*

de•plore /dipláwr/ *v.tr.* **1** grieve over; regret. **2** be scandalized by; find exceedingly bad. ▫▫ **de•plor•ing•ly** *adv.*

de•ploy /diplóy/ *v.* **1** *Mil.* **a** *tr.* cause (troops) to spread out from a column into a line. **b** *intr.* (of troops) spread out in this way. **2** *tr.* bring (arguments, forces, etc.) into effective action. ▫▫ **de•ploy•ment** *n.*

de•po•lit•i•cize /déepəlítisīz/ *v.tr.* **1** make (a person, an organization, etc.) nonpolitical. **2** remove from political activity or influence. ▫▫ **de•po•lit•i•ci•za•tion** *n.*

de•pop•u•late /deepópyəlayt/ *v.* **1** *tr.* reduce the population of. **2** *intr.* decline in population. ▫▫ **de•pop•u•la•tion** /–láyshən/ *n.*

de•port /dipáwrt/ *v.tr.* **1** **a** remove (an immigrant or foreigner) forcibly to another country; banish. **b** exile (a native) to another country. **2** *refl.* conduct (oneself) or behave (in a specified manner) (*deported himself well*). ▫▫ **de·por·ta·tion** /–táyshən/ *n.*

de·por·tee /deépawrteé/ *n.* a person who has been or is being deported.

de·port·ment /dipáwrtmənt/ *n.* bearing, demeanor, or manners, esp. of a cultivated kind.

de·pose /dipṓz/ *v.* **1** *tr.* remove from office, esp. dethrone. **2** *intr. Law* (usu. foll. by *to*, or *that* + clause) bear witness, esp. on oath in court.

de·pos·it /dipózit/ *n. & v.* • *n.* **1 a** a sum of money placed in an account in a bank. **b** anything stored or entrusted for safekeeping, usu. in a bank. **2 a** a sum payable as a first installment on a time-payment purchase, or as a pledge for a contract. **b** a returnable sum payable on the short-term rental of a car, boat, etc. **3 a** a natural layer of sand, rock, coal, etc. **b** a layer of precipitated matter on a surface, e.g., on the inside of a kettle. • *v.tr.* (**deposited, depositing**) **1 a** put or lay down in a (usu. specified) place (*deposited the book on the floor*). **b** (of water, wind, etc.) leave (matter, etc.) lying in a displaced position. **2 a** store or entrust for keeping. **b** pay (a sum of money) into a bank account, esp. a deposit account. **3** pay (a sum) as a first installment or as a pledge for a contract.

dep·o·si·tion /dépəzíshən/ *n.* **1** the act or an instance of deposing, esp. a monarch. **2** *Law* **a** the process of giving sworn evidence. **b** an instance of this. **c** evidence given under oath. **3** the act or an instance of depositing.

de·pos·i·tor /dipózitər/ *n.* a person who deposits money, property, etc.

de·pos·i·to·ry /dipózitawree/ *n.* (*pl.* **-ries**) **1** a storehouse. **2** a store (of wisdom, knowledge, etc.).

de·pot /deépō, dépō/ *n.* **1** a storehouse. **2** *Mil.* a storehouse for equipment, etc. **3 a** a building for the servicing, parking, etc., of esp. buses, trains, or goods vehicles. **b** a railroad or bus station.

de·prave /dipráyv/ *v.tr.* pervert or corrupt, esp. morally. ▫▫ **dep·ra·va·tion** /dépraváyshən/ *n.* **de·praved** *adj.*

de·prav·i·ty /diprávitee/ *n.* (*pl.* **-ties**) **1** moral corruption; wickedness. **2** an instance of this; a wicked act.

dep·re·cate /déprikayt/ *v.tr.* **1** express disapproval of or a wish against; deplore (*deprecate hasty action*). **2** plead earnestly against. ▫▫ **dep·re·cat·ing·ly** *adv.* **dep·re·ca·tion** /–káyshən/ *n.* **dep·re·ca·to·ry** /–kətawree/ *adj.*

▶**Deprecate** means 'to express disapproval of, to deplore,' e.g., *The mainstream press began by deprecating the film's attitude towards terrorism,* while **depreciate** (apart from its financial senses) means 'to disparage or belittle,' e.g., *He is always depreciating his own skills out of a strong sense of humility.*

de·pre·ci·ate /dipreésheeayt/ *v.* **1** *tr. & intr.* diminish in value (*the car has depreciated*). **2** *tr.* disparage; belittle (*they are always depreciating his taste*). **3** *tr.* reduce the purchasing power of (money). ▫▫ **de·pre·ci·a·to·ry** /–sheeətáwree/ *adj.*

▶See note at DEPRECATE.

de·pre·ci·a·tion /dipreésheeáyshən/ *n.* **1** the amount of wear and tear (of a property, etc.) for which a reduction may be made in a valuation or a balance sheet. **2** *Econ.* a decrease in the value of a currency. **3** the act or an instance of depreciating; belittlement.

dep·re·da·tion /dépridáyshən/ *n.* (usu. in *pl.*) **1** ravaging or plundering. **2** an instance or instances of this.

de·press /diprés/ *v.tr.* **1** push or pull down; lower (*depressed the lever*). **2** make dispirited or dejected. **3** *Econ.* reduce the activity of (esp. trade). **4** (as **depressed** *adj.*) **a** dispirited or miserable. **b** *Psychol.* suffering from depression. ▫▫ **de·press·ing** *adj.* **de·press·ing·ly** *adv.*

de·pres·sant /diprésənt/ *adj. & n.* • *adj.* **1** that depresses. **2** *Med.* sedative. • *n.* **1** *Med.* an agent, esp. a drug, that sedates. **2** an influence that depresses.

de·pres·sion /dipréshən/ *n.* **1 a** *Psychol.* a state of extreme dejection or morbidly excessive melancholy, often with physical symptoms. **b** a reduction in vitality, vigor, or spirits. **2 a** a long period of financial and industrial decline; a slump. **b** (**the Depression**) the depression of 1929–34. **3** *Meteorol.* a lowering of atmospheric pressure, esp. the center of a region of minimum pressure or the system of winds around it. **4** a sunken place or hollow on a surface. **5 a** a lowering or sinking (often foll. by *of*). **b** pressing down.

de·pres·sive /diprésiv/ *adj. & n.* • *adj.* **1** tending to depress. **2** *Psychol.* involving or characterized by depression. • *n. Psychol.* a person suffering or with a tendency to suffer from depression.

de·pres·sur·ize /deepréshərīz/ *v.tr.* cause a drop in the pressure of the gas inside (a container), esp. to the ambient level. ▫▫ **de·pres·sur·i·za·tion** *n.*

dep·ri·va·tion /déprivayshən/ *n.* (usu. foll. by *of*) the act or an instance of depriving; the state of being deprived (*deprivation of liberty; suffered many deprivations*).

de·prive /diprív/ *v.tr.* **1** (usu. foll. by *of*) strip, dispossess; debar from enjoying. **2** (as **deprived** *adj.*) **a** (of a child, etc.) suffering from the effects of a poor or loveless home. **b** (of an area) with inadequate housing, facilities, employment, etc. ▫▫ **de·priv·al** *n.*

Dept. *abbr.* Department.

depth /depth/ *n.* **1 a** deepness (*the depth is not great at the edge*). **b** the measurement from the top down, from the surface inward, or from the front to the back (*depth of the drawer is 12 inches*). **2** difficulty; abstruseness. **3 a** sagacity; wisdom. **b** intensity of emotion, etc. **4** an intensity of color, darkness, etc. **5** (in *pl.*) **a** deep water, a deep place; an abyss. **b** a low, depressed state. **c** the lowest or inmost part (*the depths of the country*). **6** the middle (*the depth of winter*). ▫ **in depth** comprehensively, thoroughly, or profoundly. (cf. IN-DEPTH).

depth charge *n.* (also **depth bomb**) a bomb capable of exploding under water, esp. for dropping on a submerged submarine, etc.

dep·u·ta·tion /dépyootáyshən/ *n.* a group of people appointed to represent others.

de·pute *v.tr.* /dipyóot/ (often foll. by *to*) **1** appoint as a deputy. **2** delegate (a task, authority, etc.) (*deputed the leadership to her*).

dep·u·tize /dépyətīz/ *v.* **1** *intr.* (usu. foll. by *for*) act as a deputy or understudy. **2** *tr.* appoint as a deputy.

dep·u·ty /dépyətee/ *n.* (*pl.* **·ties**) **1** a person appointed or delegated to act for another or others (also *attrib.*: *deputy sheriff*). **2** *Polit.* a parliamentary representative in certain countries, e.g., France. ▫ **by deputy** by proxy.

de·rail /diráyl/ *v.tr.* (usu. in *passive*) cause (a train, etc.) to leave the rails. ▫▫ **de·rail·ment** *n.*

de·rail·leur /dəráylər/ *n.* a gear-shifting mechanism on a bicycle that moves the chain from one sprocket wheel to another.

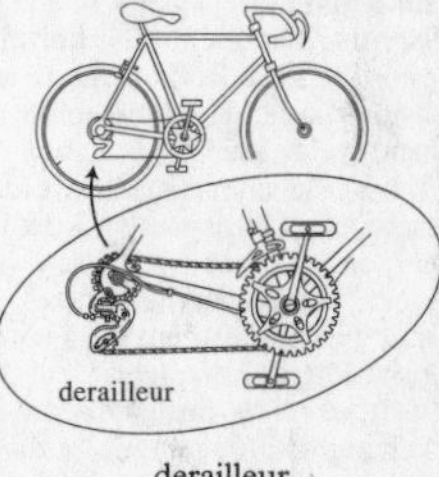

derailleur

de·range /diráynj/ *v.tr.* **1** throw into confusion; disorganize. **2** (esp. as **deranged** *adj.*) make insane (*deranged by the tragic events*). **3** disturb; interrupt. ▫▫ **de·range·ment** *n.*

framework over an oil well etc., holding the drilling machinery.

der•by /dórbee/ *n.* (*pl.* **-bies**) **1** any of several horse races that are run annually, esp. for three-year olds (*Kentucky Derby*). **2** a sporting contest, etc., esp. one open to all comers. **3** a bowler hat.

de•reg•u•late /dee-régyəlayt/ *v.tr.* remove regulations or restrictions from. ▫▫ **de•reg•u•la•tion** /–láyshən/ *n.*

der•e•lict /dérilikt/ *adj.* & *n.* • *adj.* **1** abandoned; ownerless (esp. of a ship at sea or an empty decrepit property). **2** (esp. of property) ruined; dilapidated. **3** negligent (of duty, etc.). • *n.* **1** a person without a home, a job, or property. **2** abandoned property, esp. a ship.

der•e•lic•tion /dérilíkshən/ *n.* **1** (usu. foll. by *of*) **a** neglect; failure to carry out one's obligations (*dereliction of duty*). **b** an instance of this. **2** the act or an instance of abandoning; the process of being abandoned. **3 a** the retreat of the sea exposing new land. **b** the land so exposed.

de•ride /diríd/ *v.tr.* laugh scornfully at; mock. ▫▫ **de•rid•er** *n.* **de•rid•ing•ly** *adv.*

de ri•gueur /də rigốr/ *predic.adj.* required by custom or etiquette (*evening dress is de rigueur*).

de•ri•sion /dirízhən/ *n.* ridicule; mockery (*bring into derision*).

de•ri•sive /dirísiv/ *adj.* scoffing; ironical; scornful (*derisive cheers*). ▫▫ **de•ri•sive•ly** *adv.* **de•ri•sive•ness** *n.*

de•ri•so•ry /dirísəree, zə–/ *adj.* **1** = DERISIVE. **2** so small or unimportant as to be ridiculous (*derisory costs*).

der•i•va•tion /dériváyshən/ *n.* **1** the act or an instance of deriving or obtaining from a source. **2 a** the formation of a word from another word or from a root. **b** a derivative. **c** the tracing of the origin of a word. **d** a statement or account of this. **3** extraction; descent. **4** *Math.* a sequence of statements showing that a formula, theorem, etc., is a consequence of previously accepted statements. ▫▫ **der•i•va•tion•al** *adj.*

de•riv•a•tive /dirívətiv/ *adj.* & *n.* • *adj.* derived from another source; not original (*his music is derivative*). • *n.* **1** something derived from another source, esp.: **a** a word derived from another or from a root (e.g., *quickly* from *quick*). **b** *Chem.* a chemical compound derived from another. **2** *Math.* a quantity measuring the rate of change of another. ▫▫ **de•riv•a•tive•ly** *adv.*

de•rive /dirív/ *v.* **1** *tr.* (usu. foll. by *from*) get, obtain, or form (*derived satisfaction from work*). **2** *intr.* (foll. by *from*) arise from, originate in, be descended or obtained from. **3** *tr.* gather or deduce (*derived the information from the clues*). **4** *tr.* **a** trace the descent of (a person). **b** show the origin of (a thing). **5** *tr.* (usu. foll. by *from*) show or state the origin or formation of (a word, etc.) (*derived the word from Latin*). **6** *tr. Math.* obtain (a function) by differentiation. ▫▫ **de•riv•a•ble** *adj.*

der•ma•ti•tis /dórmətítis/ *n.* inflammation of the skin.

der•ma•tol•o•gy /dórmətóləjee/ *n.* the study of skin disorders. ▫▫ **der•ma•to•log•i•cal** /–təlójikəl/ *adj.* **der•ma•tol•o•gist** *n.*

der•mis /dórmis/ *n.* (also **der•ma** /dórmə/) **1** (in general use) the skin. **2** *Anat.* the true skin, the thick layer of living tissue below the epidermis. ▫▫ **der•mal** *adj.*

der•o•gate /dérəgayt/ *v.intr.* (foll. by *from*) *formal* **1 a** take away a part from; detract from (a merit, a right, etc.). **b** disparage. **2** deviate from (correct behavior, etc.).

der•o•ga•tion /dérəgáyshən/ *n.* **1** (foll. by *of*) a lessening or impairment of (a law, authority, etc.). **2** deterioration; debasement.

de•rog•a•to•ry /dirógətawree/ *adj.* (often foll. by *to*) involving disparagement or discredit; insulting; depreciatory (*a derogatory remark*). ▫▫ **de•rog•a•to•ri•ly** *adv.*

der•rick /dérik/ *n.* **1** a kind of crane for moving or lifting heavy weights, having a movable pivoted arm. **2** the framework over an oil well etc., holding the drilling machinery.

der•ri•ere /déreeáir/ *n. colloq. euphem.* (also **derrière**) the buttocks.

der•ring-do /déringdóó/ *n. literary joc.* heroic courage or action.

der•vish /dórvish/ *n.* a member of any of several Muslim fraternities vowed to poverty and austerity.

de•sal•i•nate /deesálinayt/ *v.tr.* remove salt from (esp. sea water). ▫▫ **de•sal•i•na•tion** /–náyshən/ *n.*

des•cant *n.* & *v.* • *n.* /déskant/ **1** *Mus.* an independent treble melody above a basic melody, esp. of a hymn tune. **2** *poet.* a melody; a song. • *v.intr.* /diskánt/ **1** (foll. by *on*, *upon*) talk lengthily and prosily, esp. in praise of. **2** *Mus.* sing or play a descant.

de•scend /disénd/ *v.* **1** *tr.* & *intr.* go or come down (a hill, stairs, etc.). **2** *intr.* (of a thing) sink; fall (*rain descended heavily*). **3** *intr.* slope downward; lie along a descending slope (*fields descended to the beach*). **4** *intr.* (usu. foll. by *on*) **a** make a sudden attack. **b** make an unexpected and usu. unwelcome visit. **5** *intr.* (usu. foll. by *from*, *to*) (of property, qualities, rights, etc.) be passed by inheritance. **6** *intr.* **a** sink in rank, quality, etc. **b** (foll. by *to*) degrade oneself morally to (an unworthy act) (*descend to violence*). **7** *intr. Mus.* (of sound) become lower in pitch. **8** *intr.* (usu. foll. by *to*) proceed (in discourse or writing): **a** in time (to a subsequent event, etc.). **b** from the general (to the particular) (*now let's descend to details*). **9** *tr.* go along (a river, etc.) to the sea, etc. ▫ **be descended from** have as an ancestor. ▫▫ **de•scend•ent** *adj.*

de•scend•ant /diséndənt/ *n.* (often foll. by *of*) a person or thing descended from another (*a descendant of John Adams*).

de•scend•er /diséndər/ *n. Printing* a part of a letter that extends below the level of the base of a letter, as in *g* or *p*.

de•scent /disént/ *n.* **1 a** the act of descending. **b** an instance of this. **c** a downward movement. **2 a** a way or path, etc., by which one may descend. **b** a downward slope. **3 a** being descended; lineage; family origin. **b** the transmission of qualities, property, privileges, etc., by inheritance. **4 a** a decline; a fall. **b** a lowering (of pitch, temperature, etc.). **5** a sudden violent attack.

de•scram•ble /deeskrámbəl/ *v.tr.* **1** convert or restore (a signal) to intelligible form. **2** counteract the effects of (a scrambling device). **3** recover an original signal from (a scrambled signal). ▫▫ **de•scram•bler** *n.*

de•scribe /diskríb/ *v.tr.* **1 a** state the characteristics, appearance, etc., of, in spoken or written form (*described the landscape*). **b** (foll. by *as*) assert to be; call (*described him as a habitual liar*). **2 a** mark out or draw (esp. a geometrical figure). **b** move in (a specified way, esp. a curve) (*described a parabola through the air*). ▫▫ **de•scrib•a•ble** *adj.* **de•scrib•er** *n.*

de•scrip•tion /diskrípshən/ *n.* **1 a** the act or an instance of describing; the process of being described. **b** a spoken or written representation (of a person, object, or event). **2** a sort, kind, or class (*no food of any description*). ▫ **answers** (or **fits**) **the description** has the qualities specified.

de•scrip•tive /diskríptiv/ *adj.* **1** serving or seeking to describe (*a descriptive writer*). **2** describing or classifying without expressing feelings or judging (*a purely descriptive account*). ▫▫ **de•scrip•tive•ly** *adv.* **de•scrip•tive•ness** *n.*

de•scry /diskrí/ *v.tr.* (**-scries**, **-scried**) *literary* catch sight of; discern.

des•e•crate /désikrayt/ *v.tr.* **1** violate (a sacred place or thing) with violence, profanity, etc. **2** deprive (a church, a sacred object, etc.) of sanctity; deconsecrate. ▫▫ **des•e•cra•tion** /–kráyshən/ *n.* **des•e•cra•tor** *n.*

de•seg•re•gate /deeségrigayt/ *v.tr.* abolish racial

segregation in (schools, etc.) or of (people, etc.). □□ **de·seg·re·ga·tion** /–gáyshən/ *n.*

de·sen·si·tize /deesénsitiz/ *v.tr.* reduce or destroy the sensitiveness of (photographic materials, an allergic person, etc.). □□ **de·sen·si·ti·za·tion** *n.* **de·sen·si·tiz·er** *n.*

de·sert[1] /dizə́rt/ *v.* **1** *tr.* abandon; give up; leave (*desert a sinking ship*). **2** *tr.* forsake or abandon (a cause or a person, etc.). **3** *tr.* fail (*his memory deserted him*). **4** *intr. Mil.* run away (esp. from military service). **5** *tr.* (as **deserted** *adj.*) empty; abandoned (*a deserted house*). □□ **de·sert·er** *n.* (in sense 4 of *v.*). **de·ser·tion** /–zə́rshən/ *n.*

des·ert[2] /dézərt/ *n. & adj.* • *n.* a dry, barren, often sand-covered area of land; an uninteresting or barren subject, period, etc. (*a cultural desert*). • *adj.* **1** uninhabited; desolate. **2** uncultivated; barren.

des·ert[3] /dizə́rt/ *n.* **1** (in *pl.*) **a** acts or qualities deserving reward or punishment. **b** such reward or punishment (*has gotten his just deserts*). **2** the fact of being worthy of reward or punishment; deservingness.

de·serve /dizə́rv/ *v.tr.* **1** (often foll. by *to* + infin.) show conduct or qualities worthy of (reward, punishment, etc.). **2** (as **deserved** *adj.*) rightfully merited or earned (*a deserved win*). □□ **de·serv·ed·ly** /–vidlee/ *adv.*

de·serv·ing /dizə́rving/ *adj.* meritorious. □ **deserving of** showing conduct or qualities worthy of (praise, blame, help, etc.). □□ **de·serv·ing·ly** *adv.*

des·ic·cant /désikənt/ *n. Chem.* a hygroscopic substance used as a drying agent.

des·ic·cate /désikayt/ *v.tr.* remove the moisture from (esp. food for preservation). □□ **des·ic·ca·tion** /–káyshən/ *n.* **des·ic·ca·tive** *adj.*

des·ic·ca·tor /désikaytər/ *n.* **1** an apparatus for desiccating. **2** *Chem.* an apparatus containing a drying agent to remove the moisture from specimens.

de·sid·er·a·tum /disídəráytəm, –raátəm/ *n.* (*pl.* **desiderata** /–tə/) something lacking but needed or desired.

de·sign /dizín/ *n. & v.* • *n.* **1 a** a preliminary plan or sketch for making something. **b** the art of producing these. **2** a scheme of lines or shapes forming a pattern or decoration. **3** a plan, purpose, or intention. **4 a** the general arrangement or layout of a product. **b** an established version of a product (*our most popular designs*). • *v.* **1** *tr.* produce a design for (a thing). **2** *tr.* intend, plan, or purpose (*designed to offend*). **3** *absol.* be a designer. □ **by design** on purpose. **have designs on** plan to harm or appropriate.

des·ig·nate *v. & adj.* • *v.tr.* /dézignayt/ **1** (often foll. by *as*) appoint to an office or function (*designated him as postmaster general*). **2** specify (*at designated times*). **3** (often foll. by *as*) describe as; entitle; style. **4** serve as the name or distinctive mark of (*English uses French words to designate ballet steps*). • *adj.* /dézignət/ (placed after noun) appointed to an office but not yet installed (*bishop designate*). □□ **des·ig·na·tor** *n.*

des·ig·nat·ed driv·er *n.* one in a group who abstains from alcohol in order to drive the others safely.

des·ig·nat·ed hit·ter *n. Baseball* a batter in the lineup who hits for the pitcher. ¶ Abbr.: **DH**.

des·ig·na·tion /dézignáyshən/ *n.* **1** a name, description, or title. **2** the act or process of designating.

de·sign·ed·ly /dizínidlee/ *adv.* by design; on purpose.

de·sign·er /dizínər/ *n.* **1** a person who makes artistic designs or plans for construction, e.g., for clothing, theater sets. **2** (*attrib.*) (of clothing, etc.) bearing the name or label of a famous designer.

de·sign·er drug *n.* a synthetic analog, not itself illegal, of an illegal drug.

de·sign·ing /dizíning/ *adj.* crafty, artful, or scheming. □□ **de·sign·ing·ly** *adv.*

de·sir·a·ble /dizírəbəl/ *adj.* **1** worth having or wishing for (*it is desirable that nobody should smoke*). **2** arousing sexual desire. □□ **de·sir·a·bil·i·ty** *n.* **de·sir·a·ble·ness** *n.* **de·sir·a·bly** *adv.*

de·sire /dizír/ *n. & v.* • *n.* **1 a** an unsatisfied longing or craving. **b** a request (*expressed a desire to rest*). **2** lust. **3** something desired (*her heart's desire*). • *v.tr.* **1** (often foll. by *to* + infin., or *that* + clause) long for; crave. **2** request.

de·sir·ous /dizírəs/ *predic.adj.* **1** (usu. foll. by *of*) ambitious; desiring. **2** (usu. foll. by *to* + infin., or *that* + clause) hoping (*desirous to do the right thing*).

de·sist /dizíst/ *v.intr.* (often foll. by *from*) *literary* abstain; cease.

desk /desk/ *n.* **1** a piece of furniture with a flat or sloped surface for writing on, and often drawers. **2** a counter which separates the customer from the assistant. **3** a section of a newspaper office, etc., dealing with a specified topic (*the sports desk*). **4** *Mus.* a music stand in an orchestra regarded as a unit of two players.

desk·top /désktop/ *n.* **1 a** the working surface of a desk. **b** the working area for manipulating windows, icons, etc., in some computer software environments. **2** (*attrib.*) (esp. of a microcomputer) suitable for use at an ordinary desk.

desk·top pub·lish·ing *n.* the production of printed matter with a desktop computer and printer.

des·o·late *adj. & v.* • *adj.* /désələt/ **1** left alone; solitary. **2** (of a building or place) uninhabited; neglected; barren; dreary; empty (*a desolate beach*). **3** forlorn; wretched (*was left desolate and weeping*). • *v.tr.* /désəlayt/ **1** depopulate or devastate; lay waste to. **2** (esp. as **desolated** *adj.*) make forlorn (*desolated by grief*). □□ **des·o·late·ly** /–lətlee/ *adv.* **des·o·late·ness** *n.* **des·o·la·tion** /désəláyshən/ *n.*

de·spair /dispáir/ *n. & v.* • *n.* the complete loss or absence of hope. • *v.intr.* **1** (often foll. by *of*) lose or be without hope. **2** (foll. by *of*) lose hope about (*his life is despaired of*). □ **be the despair of** be the cause of despair by badness or unapproachable excellence (*he's the despair of his parents*). □□ **de·spair·ing·ly** *adv.*

des·patch var. of DISPATCH.

des·per·a·do /déspəraádō/ *n.* (*pl.* **-does** or **-dos**) a desperate or reckless person, esp. a criminal.

des·per·ate /déspərət, –prit/ *adj.* **1** reckless from despair. **2 a** extremely dangerous or serious (*a desperate situation*). **b** staking all on a small chance (*a desperate remedy*). **3** very bad (*desperate poverty*). **4** (usu. foll. by *for*) needing or desiring very much (*desperate for recognition*). □□ **des·per·ate·ly** *adv.* **des·per·ate·ness** *n.* **des·per·a·tion** /–ráyshən/ *n.*

des·pi·ca·ble /déspikəbəl, dispík–/ *adj.* vile; contemptible, esp. morally. □□ **des·pi·ca·bly** *adv.*

de·spise /dispíz/ *v.tr.* look down on as inferior, worthless, or contemptible. □□ **de·spis·er** *n.*

de·spite /dispít/ *prep.* in spite of.

de·spoil /dispóyl/ *v.tr. literary* (often foll. by *of*) plunder; deprive. □□ **de·spoil·ment** *n.* **de·spo·li·a·tion** /dispṓleeáyshən/ *n.*

de·spond /dispónd/ *v. & n.* • *v.intr.* lose heart or hope; be dejected. • *n. archaic* despondency.

de·spond·ent /dispóndənt/ *adj.* in low spirits; dejected. □□ **de·spond·ence** /–dəns/ *n.* **de·spond·en·cy** *n.* **de·spond·ent·ly** *adv.*

des·pot /déspət/ *n.* **1** an absolute ruler. **2** a tyrant. □□ **des·pot·ic** /–spótik/ *adj.* **des·pot·i·cal·ly** *adv.* **des·pot·ism** /déspətizəm/ *n.*

des·sert /dizə́rt/ *n.* the sweet course of a meal, served at or near the end.

---

de·sta·bi·lize /deestáybilīz/ *v.tr.* **1** render unstable. **2** subvert (esp. a foreign government). □□ **de·sta·bi·li·za·tion** *n.*

des·ti·na·tion /déstináyshən/ *n.* a place to which a person or thing is going.

des·tine /déstin/ *v.tr.* (often foll. by *to*, *for*, or *to* + infin.) preordain; intend. □ **be destined to** be fated to.

des·ti·ny /déstinee/ *n.* (*pl.* **-nies**) **1 a** fate. **b** this regarded as a power. **2** what is destined to happen to a particular person, etc. (*it was their destiny*).

des·ti·tute /déstitōōt, –tyōōt/ *adj.* **1** without food, shelter, etc.; completely impoverished. **2** (usu. foll. by *of*) lacking. □□ **des·ti·tu·tion** /–tōōshən, –tyōō–/ *n.*

de·stroy /distróy/ *v.tr.* **1** pull or break down. **2** end the existence of (*destroyed her confidence*). **3** kill (esp. a sick or savage animal). **4** make useless. **5** ruin financially, professionally, or in reputation. **6** defeat (*destroyed the enemy*).

de·stroy·er /distróyər/ *n.* **1** a person or thing that destroys. **2** *Naut.* a fast warship with guns and torpedoes used to protect other ships.

de·struct /distrúkt/ *v.* & *n.* esp. *Astronaut.* • *v.* **1** *tr.* destroy (one's own rocket, etc.) deliberately, esp. for safety reasons. **2** *intr.* be destroyed in this way. • *n.* an act of destructing.

de·struct·i·ble /distrúktibəl/ *adj.* able to be destroyed.

de·struc·tion /distrúkshən/ *n.* **1** the act or an instance of destroying; the process of being destroyed. **2** a cause of ruin (*greed was their destruction*).

de·struc·tive /distrúktiv/ *adj.* **1** (often foll. by *to*, *of*) destroying or tending to destroy (*a destructive child*). **2** negative in attitude or criticism. □□ **de·struc·tive·ly** *adv.* **de·struc·tive·ness** *n.*

des·ue·tude /déswitōōd, –tyōōd/ *n.* a state of disuse.

des·ul·to·ry /désəltáwree, déz–/ *adj.* **1** going constantly from one subject to another, esp. in a halfhearted way. **2** disconnected; unmethodical; superficial. □□ **des·ul·to·ri·ly** *adv.* **des·ul·to·ri·ness** *n.*

de·tach /ditách/ *v.tr.* **1** (often foll. by *from*) unfasten or disengage and remove. **2** *Mil.* send (a ship, officer, etc.) on a separate mission. **3** (as **detached** *adj.*) **a** impartial; unemotional (*a detached viewpoint*). **b** (esp. of a house) not joined to another or others. □□ **de·tach·a·ble** *adj.* **de·tach·ed·ly** /ditáchidlee/ *adv.*

de·tach·ment /ditáchmənt/ *n.* **1 a** a state of aloofness or indifference. **b** disinterested independence of judgment. **2 a** the act or process of detaching or being detached. **b** an instance of this. **3** *Mil.* a separate group or unit used for a specific purpose.

de·tail /ditáyl, déetayl/ *n.* & *v.* • *n.* **1 a** a small or subordinate particular. **b** such a particular, considered (ironically) to be unimportant (*the truth is just a detail*). **2 a** small items or particulars regarded collectively (*has an eye for detail*). **b** the treatment of them (*the detail was insufficient*). **3** (often in *pl.*) a number of particulars (*filled in the details*). **4 a** a minor decoration on a building, in a picture, etc. **b** a small part of a picture, etc., shown alone. **5** *Mil.* **a** the distribution of orders for the day. **b** a small detachment of soldiers, etc., for special duty. • *v.tr.* **1** give particulars of. **2** relate circumstantially. **3** *Mil.* assign for special duty. **4** (as **detailed** *adj.*) **a** (of a picture, story, etc.) having many details. **b** itemized (*a detailed list*).

de·tain /ditáyn/ *v.tr.* **1** keep in confinement or under restraint. **2** delay. □□ **de·tain·ment** *n.*

de·tain·ee /déetaynée/ *n.* a person detained in custody.

de·tect /ditékt/ *v.tr.* **1 a** (often foll. by *in*) reveal the guilt of. **b** discover (a crime). **2** perceive the existence of (*detected a smell of burning*). **3** *Physics* use an instrument to observe (a signal, radiation, etc.). □□ **de·tect·a·ble** *adj.* **de·tec·tor** *n.*

de·tec·tion /ditékshən/ *n.* **1** the act or an instance of detecting; the process or an instance of being detected. **2** the work of a detective.

de·tec·tive /ditéktiv/ *n.* & *adj.* • *n.* (often *attrib.*) a person, esp. a member of a police force, employed to investigate crime. • *adj.* serving to detect.

dé·tente /daytóNt/ *n.* an easing of strained relations, esp. between nations.

de·ten·tion /diténshən/ *n.* **1** detaining or being detained. **2 a** being kept in school after hours as a punishment. **b** an instance of this. **3** custody; confinement.

de·ter /ditə́r/ *v.tr.* (**deterred, deterring**) **1** (often foll. by *from*) discourage or prevent (a person) through fear or dislike of the consequences. **2** check or prevent (a thing, process, etc.).

de·ter·gent /ditə́rjənt/ *n.* & *adj.* • *n.* a cleansing agent, esp. a synthetic substance (usu. other than soap) used with water as a means of removing dirt, etc. • *adj.* cleansing, esp. in the manner of a detergent.

de·te·ri·o·rate /ditéereeərayt/ *v.tr.* & *intr.* make or become bad or worse. □□ **de·te·ri·o·ra·tion** /–ráyshən/ *n.* **de·te·ri·o·ra·tive** *adj.*

de·ter·mi·nant /ditə́rminənt/ *adj.* & *n.* • *adj.* serving to determine or define. • *n.* **1** a determining factor, element, word, etc. **2** *Math.* a quantity obtained by the addition of products of the elements of a square matrix according to a given rule.

de·ter·mi·nate /ditə́rminət/ *adj.* **1** limited in time, space, or character. **2** of definite scope or nature. □□ **de·ter·mi·na·cy** /–nəsee/ *n.* **de·ter·mi·nate·ly** *adv.*

de·ter·mi·na·tion /ditə́rmináyshən/ *n.* **1** firmness of purpose; resoluteness. **2** the process of deciding, determining, or calculating. **3 a** the conclusion of a dispute by the decision of an arbitrator. **b** the decision reached.

de·ter·mine /ditə́rmin/ *v.* **1** *tr.* find out or establish precisely. **2** *tr.* decide or settle. **3** *tr.* be a decisive factor in regard to. **4** *intr.* & *tr.* make or cause (a person) to make a decision (*what determined you to do it?*). □ **be determined** be resolved (*was determined not to give up*). □□ **de·ter·mi·na·ble** *adj.*

de·ter·mined /ditə́rmind/ *adj.* **1** showing determination. **2** fixed in scope or character; settled; determinate. □□ **de·ter·mined·ly** *adv.* **de·ter·mined·ness** *n.*

de·ter·min·er /ditə́rminər/ *n.* **1** a person or thing that determines. **2** *Gram.* any of a class of words (e.g., *a*, *the*, *every*) that determine the kind of reference a noun or noun substitute has.

de·ter·min·ism /ditə́rminizəm/ *n.* *Philos.* the doctrine that all events, including human action, are determined by causes regarded as external to the will. □□ **de·ter·min·ist** *n.* **de·ter·min·is·tic** *adj.*

de·ter·rent /ditə́rənt, –túr–/ *adj.* & *n.* • *adj.* that deters. • *n.* a deterrent thing or factor. □□ **de·ter·rence** /–rəns/ *n.*

de·test /ditést/ *v.tr.* hate; loathe. □□ **de·tes·ta·tion** /déetestáyshən/ *n.*

de·test·a·ble /ditéstəbəl/ *adj.* intensely disliked; hateful. □□ **de·test·a·bly** *adv.*

de·throne /deethrṓn/ *v.tr.* **1** remove from the throne; depose. **2** remove from a position of authority. □□ **de·throne·ment** *n.*

det·o·nate /dét'nayt/ *v.intr.* & *tr.* explode with a loud noise. □□ **det·o·na·tion** /dét'náyshən/ *n.* **det·o·na·tive** *adj.* **det·o·na·tor** *n.*

de·tour /déetōōr, ditṓōr/ *n.* & *v.* • *n.* **1** a divergence from a direct or intended route. **2** an alternative route, when a road is temporarily closed to traffic. • *v.intr.* & *tr.* make or cause to make a detour.

de·tox·i·fy /deetóksifī/ *v.tr.* remove the poison from. □□ **de·tox·i·fi·ca·tion** /–fikáyshən/ *n.*

de·tract /ditrákt/ *v.tr.* (usu. foll. by *from*) take away (a part of something); reduce; diminish. ◻◻ **de·trac·tion** /–trákshən/ *n.* **de·trac·tor** *n.*

det·ri·ment /détrimənt/ *n.* **1** harm; damage. **2** something causing this. ◻◻ **det·ri·men·tal** /détriméntʼl/ *adj.* **det·ri·men·tal·ly** *adv.*

de·tri·tus /ditrítəs/ *n.* **1** matter produced by erosion. **2** debris. ◻◻ **de·tri·tal** /ditrítʼl/ *adj.*

deuce /do͞os, dyo͞os/ *n.* **1** the two on dice or playing cards. **2** (in tennis) the score of 40 all, at which two consecutive points are needed to win.

deu·te·ri·um /do͞oteéreeəm, dyo͞o–/ *n. Chem.* a stable isotope of hydrogen with a mass about double that of the usual isotope.

Deutsche mark /dóych, dóychə/ *n.* (also **Deut·sche·mark**) the chief monetary unit of Germany.

de·val·ue /deeványo͞o/ *v.tr.* (**devalues, devalued, devaluing**) **1** reduce the value of. **2** *Econ.* reduce the value of (a currency) in relation to other currencies or to gold (opp. REVALUE). ◻◻ **de·val·u·a·tion** *n.*

dev·as·tate /dévəstayt/ *v.tr.* **1** cause great destruction to. **2** (often in *passive*) overwhelm with shock or grief. ◻◻ **dev·as·ta·tion** /–táyshən/ *n.* **dev·as·ta·tor** *n.*

dev·as·tat·ing /dévəstayting/ *adj.* **1** crushingly effective; overwhelming. **2** *colloq.* **a** incisive; savage (*devastating accuracy*). **b** extremely impressive or attractive (*she wore a devastating black silk dress*). ◻◻ **dev·as·tat·ing·ly** *adv.*

de·vel·op /divéləp/ *v.* (**developed, developing**) **1** *tr. & intr.* **a** make or become bigger or fuller or more elaborate or systematic. **b** bring or come to an active or visible state or to maturity. **2 a** *tr.* begin to suffer from (*developed a rattle*). **b** *intr.* come into existence (*a fault developed in the engine*). **3** *tr.* **a** construct on (land). **b** convert (land) to a new purpose. **4** *tr.* treat (photographic film, etc.) to make the image visible. ◻◻ **de·vel·op·a·ble** /divéləpəbəl/ *adj.* **de·vel·op·er** *n.*

de·vel·op·ment /divéləpmənt/ *n.* **1** the act or an instance of developing; the process of being developed. **2 a** a stage of growth or advancement. **b** a thing that has developed (*the latest developments*). **3** a full-grown state. **4** the process of developing a photograph. **5** a developed area of land.

de·vel·op·men·tal /divéləpméntʼl/ *adj.* **1** incidental to growth (*developmental diseases*). **2** evolutionary. ◻◻ **de·vel·op·men·tal·ly** *adv.*

de·vi·ant /deéveeənt/ *adj. & n.* • *adj.* that deviates from the normal. • *n.* a deviant person or thing. ◻◻ **de·vi·ance** /–veeəns/ *n.* **de·vi·an·cy** *n.*

de·vi·ate *v. & n.* • *v.intr.* /deéveeayt/ (often foll. by *from*) turn aside or diverge (from a course of action, truth, etc.); digress. • *n.* /déeveeət/ a deviant, esp. a sexual pervert. ◻◻ **de·vi·a·tor** *n.* **de·vi·a·to·ry** /–veeətáwree/ *adj.*

de·vi·a·tion /deéveeáyshən/ *n.* **1 a** deviating; digressing. **b** an instance of this. **2** *Polit.* a departure from accepted (esp. Communist) party doctrine. **3** *Statistics* the amount by which a single measurement differs from the mean.

de·vice /divís/ *n.* **1 a** a thing made or adapted for a particular purpose. **b** an explosive contrivance. **2** a plan, scheme, or trick. **3 a** an emblematic or heraldic design. **b** a drawing or design. ◻ **leave a person to his or her own devices** leave a person to do as he or she wishes.

---

device Middle English: from Old French *devis*, based on Latin *divis-* 'divided,' from the verb *dividere*. The original sense was 'desire or intention,' found now only in *leave a person to his or her own devices* (which has become associated with sense 2).

---

dev·il /dévəl/ *n. & v.* • *n.* **1** (usu. **the Devil**) (in Christian and Jewish belief) the supreme spirit of evil; Satan. **2 a** an evil spirit; a demon. **b** a personified evil force or attribute. **3 a** a wicked or cruel person. **b** a mischievously energetic, clever, or self-willed person. **4** *colloq.* a person; a fellow (*lucky devil*). **5** fighting spirit; mischievousness (*the devil is in him tonight*). **6** *colloq.* something awkward (*this door is a devil to open*). **7** (**the devil** or **the Devil**) *colloq.* used as an exclamation of surprise or annoyance (*who the devil are you?*). **8** a literary hack exploited by an employer. • *v.* (**deviled, deviling; devilled, devilling**) **1** *tr.* cook (food) with hot seasoning. **2** *tr.* harass; worry. ◻ **between the devil and the deep blue sea** in a dilemma. **a devil of** *colloq.* considerable, difficult, or remarkable. **devil take the hindmost** a motto of selfish competition. **the devil to pay** trouble to be expected. **like the devil** with great energy. **speak of the devil** said when a person appears just after being mentioned.

---

devil Old English *dēofol* (related to Dutch *duivel* and German *Teufel*), via late Latin from Greek *diabolos* 'accuser, slanderer' (used in Greek to translate Hebrew *śāṭān* 'Satan'), from *diaballein* 'to slander,' from *dia* 'across' + *ballein* 'to throw.'

---

dev·il·ish /dévəlish/ *adj. & adv.* • *adj.* **1** of or like a devil; wicked. **2** mischievous. • *adv. colloq.* very; extremely. ◻◻ **dev·il·ish·ly** *adv.* **dev·il·ish·ness** *n.*

dev·il-may-care *adj.* cheerful and reckless.

dev·il·ment /dévəlmənt/ *n.* mischief; wild spirits.

dev·il·ry /dévilree/ *n.* (also **dev·il·try** /–tree/) (*pl.* **·ries**) **1 a** reckless mischief. **b** an instance of this. **2 a** black magic. **b** the Devil and his works.

dev·il's ad·vo·cate *n.* a person who tests a proposition by arguing against it.

de·vi·ous /deéveeəs/ *adj.* **1** (of a person, etc.) not straightforward. **2** circuitous. **3** erring. ◻◻ **de·vi·ous·ly** *adv.* **de·vi·ous·ness** *n.*

de·vise /divíz/ *v. & n.* • *v.tr.* **1** plan or invent by careful thought. **2** *Law* leave (real estate) by will (cf. BEQUEATH). • *n.* **1** the act or an instance of devising. **2** *Law* a devising clause in a will. ◻◻ **de·vis·a·ble** *adj.* **de·vi·see** /–zeé/ *n.* (in sense 2 of *v.*). **de·vis·er** *n.* **de·vi·sor** *n.* (in sense 2 of *v.*).

de·vi·tal·ize /deevítʼlīz/ *v.tr.* take away strength and vigor from. ◻◻ **de·vi·tal·i·za·tion** *n.*

de·void /divóyd/ *predic.adj.* (foll. by *of*) quite lacking or free from.

dev·o·lu·tion /deévəló͞oshən/ *n.* **1** the delegation of power, esp. by central government to local or regional administration. **2 a** descent or passing on through a series of stages. **b** descent by natural or due succession from one to another of property or qualities. **3** the lapse of an unexercised right to an ultimate owner. ◻◻ **dev·o·lu·tion·ar·y** *adj.* **dev·o·lu·tion·ist** *n.*

de·volve /divólv/ *v.* **1** (foll. by *on, upon*, etc.) **a** *tr.* pass (work or duties) to (a deputy, etc.). **b** *intr.* (of work or duties) pass to (a deputy, etc.). **2** *intr.* (foll. by *on, to, upon*) *Law* (of property, etc.) fall by succession to. ◻◻ **de·volve·ment** *n.*

De·vo·ni·an /divṓneeən/ *adj. & n.* • *adj. Geol.* of or relating to the fourth period of the Paleozoic era. • *n.* this period or system.

de·vote /divṓt/ *v.tr. & refl.* (foll. by *to*) apply or give over to (a particular activity or purpose or person).

de·vot·ed /divṓtid/ *adj.* very loving or loyal. ◻◻ **de·vot·ed·ly** *adv.* **de·vot·ed·ness** *n.*

dev·o·tee /dévəteé, –táy/ *n.* **1** (usu. foll. by *of*) a zealous enthusiast or supporter. **2** a zealously pious person.

de·vo·tion /divṓshən/ *n.* **1** (usu. foll. by *to*) enthusiastic attachment or loyalty (to a person or cause); great love. **2 a** religious worship. **b** (in *pl.*) prayers. **c** devoutness; religious fervor. □□ **de·vo·tion·al** *adj.*

de·vour /divówr/ *v.tr.* **1** eat hungrily or greedily. **2** (of fire, etc.) engulf; destroy. **3** take in greedily with the eyes or ears (*devoured book after book*). **4** absorb the attention of (*devoured by anxiety*).

de·vout /divówt/ *adj.* **1** earnestly religious. **2** earnestly sincere (*devout hope*). □□ **de·vout·ly** *adv.* **de·vout·ness** *n.*

dew /dōō, dyōō/ *n.* & *v.* •*n.* **1** atmospheric vapor condensing in small drops on cool surfaces at night. **2** glistening moisture resembling this. **3** freshness; refreshing quality. •*v.tr.* wet with or as with dew. □□ **dew·y** /dōō-ee, dyōō-ee/ *adj.* (**dewier, dewiest**)

dew·ber·ry /dōōberee, dyōō–/ *n.* (*pl.* **-ries**) **1** a bluish fruit like the blackberry. **2** the shrub, *Rubus caesius*, bearing this.

dew·claw /dōōklaw, dyōō–/ *n.* **1** a rudimentary inner toe found on some dogs. **2** a false hoof on a deer, etc.

dew·drop /dōōdrop, dyōō–/ *n.* a drop of dew.

Dew·ey sys·tem /dōō-ee, dyōō-ee/ *n.* a decimal system of library classification.

dew·fall /dōōfawl, dyōō–/ *n.* **1** the time when dew begins to form. **2** the formation of dew.

dew·lap /dōōlap, dyōō–/ *n.* **1** a loose fold of skin hanging from the throat of cattle, dogs, etc. **2** similar loose skin around the throat of an elderly person.

dew point *n.* the temperature at which dew forms.

dex·ter /dékstər/ *adj.* esp. *Heraldry* on or of the right-hand side (the observer's left) of a shield, etc.

dex·ter·i·ty /dekstéritee/ *n.* **1** skill in handling. **2** manual or mental adroitness. **3** right-handedness.

dex·ter·ous /dékstrəs, –stərəs/ *adj.* (also **dex·trous** /–strəs/) having or showing dexterity. □□ **dex·ter·ous·ly** *adv.* **dex·ter·ous·ness** *n.*

dex·trose /dékstrōs/ *n. Chem.* a form of glucose.

DH *abbr. Baseball* designated hitter.

di- /dī/ *comb. form* **1** twice, two-, double. **2** *Chem.* containing two atoms, molecules, or groups of a specified kind (*dichromate*; *dioxide*).

dia. *abbr.* diameter.

dia- /díə/ *prefix* (also **di-** before a vowel) **1** through (*diaphanous*). **2** apart (*diacritical*). **3** across (*diameter*).

di·a·be·tes /díəbeétis, –teez/ *n.* **1** any disorder of the metabolism with excessive thirst, increased urine production, and high blood sugar. **2** (in full **diabetes mellitus**) the most common form of diabetes.

di·a·be·tic /díəbétik/ *adj.* & *n.* •*adj.* **1** of or relating to or having diabetes. **2** for use by diabetics. •*n.* a person suffering from diabetes.

di·a·bol·ic /díəbólik/ *adj.* (also **di·a·bol·i·cal** /–bólikəl/) **1** of the Devil. **2** devilish; inhumanly cruel or wicked. **3** fiendishly clever or cunning or annoying. **4** *colloq.* disgracefully bad; outrageous. □□ **di·a·bol·i·cal·ly** *adv.*

di·ab·o·lism /dīábəlizəm/ *n.* **1 a** belief in or worship of the Devil. **b** sorcery. **2** devilish conduct or character.

di·a·crit·ic /díəkrítik/ *n.* & *adj.* •*n.* a sign used to indicate different sounds or values of a letter. •*adj.* = DIACRITICAL.

di·a·crit·i·cal /díəkritikəl/ *adj.* & *n.* •*adj.* distinguishing; distinctive. •*n.* (in full **diacritical mark** or **sign**) = DIACRITIC *n.*

di·a·dem /díədem/ *n.* & *v.* •*n.* **1** a crown or headband worn as a sign of sovereignty. **2** a wreath worn around the head. **3** sovereignty. **4** a crowning distinction. •*v.tr.* (esp. as **diademed** *adj.*) adorn with or as with a diadem.

di·aer·e·sis /dī-érəsis/ *n.* (also **di·er·e·sis**) (*pl.* **-ses** /–seez/) a mark (as in *naïve*) over a vowel to indicate that it is sounded separately.

di·ag·nose /díəgnṓs, –nṓz/ *v.tr.* make a diagnosis of (a disease, a mechanical fault, etc.). □□ **di·ag·nos·a·ble** *adj.*

di·ag·no·sis /díəgnṓsis/ *n.* (*pl.* **diagnoses** /–seez/) **1 a** the identification of a disease by means of a patient's symptoms. **b** an instance or formal statement of this. **2 a** the identification of the cause of a mechanical fault, etc. **b** an instance of this. **3 a** the distinctive characterization in precise terms of a genus, species, etc. **b** an instance of this.

di·ag·nos·tic /díəgnóstik/ *adj.* & *n.* •*adj.* of or assisting diagnosis. •*n.* a symptom. □□ **di·ag·nos·ti·cal·ly** *adv.* **di·ag·nos·ti·cian** /–nostíshən/ *n.*

di·ag·nos·tics /díəgnóstiks/ *n.* **1** (treated as *pl.*) *Computing* mechanisms used to identify faults in hardware or software. **2** (treated as *sing.*) the science of diagnosing disease.

di·ag·o·nal /dīágənəl/ *adj.* & *n.* •*adj.* **1** crossing a straight-sided figure from corner to corner. **2** slanting; oblique. •*n.* a straight line joining two nonadjacent corners. □□ **di·ag·o·nal·ly** *adv.*

di·a·gram /díəgram/ *n.* & *v.* •*n.* **1** a drawing showing the general scheme or outline of an object and its parts. **2** a graphic representation of the course or results of an action or process. •*v.tr.* (**diagramed, diagraming** or **diagrammed, diagramming**) represent by means of a diagram. □□ **di·a·gram·mat·ic** /–grəmátik/ *adj.* **di·a·gram·mat·i·cal·ly** *adv.*

di·al /díəl/ *n.* & *v.* •*n.* **1** the face of a clock or watch. **2** a plate with a scale for measuring weight, volume, etc., indicated by a pointer. **3** a movable disk on a telephone, with finger holes and numbers for making a connection. **4 a** a plate or disk, etc., on a radio or television set for selecting wavelength or channel. **b** a similar selecting device on other equipment. •*v.* **1** *tr.* (also *absol.*) select (a telephone number) by means of a dial or set of buttons (*dialed 911*). **2** *tr.* measure, indicate, or regulate by means of a dial. □□ **di·al·er** *n.*

di·a·lect /díəlekt/ *n.* **1** a form of speech peculiar to a particular region. **2** a subordinate variety of a language with nonstandard vocabulary, pronunciation, or grammar. □□ **di·a·lec·tal** /–lékt'l/ *adj.* **di·a·lec·tol·o·gy** /–tóləjee/ *n.* **di·a·lec·tol·o·gist** /–tóləjist/ *n.*

di·a·lec·tic /díəléktik/ *n.* & *adj.* •*n.* **1** (often in *pl.*) **a** the art of investigating the truth of opinions; the testing of truth by discussion. **b** logical disputation. **2** *Philos.* **a** inquiry into metaphysical contradictions and their solutions. **b** the existence or action of opposing social forces, etc. •*adj.* **1** of or relating to logical disputation. **2** fond of or skilled in logical disputation. □□ **di·a·lec·ti·cian** /díəlektíshən/ *n.*

di·a·lec·ti·cal /díəléktikəl/ *adj.* of dialectic or dialectics. □□ **di·a·lec·ti·cal·ly** *adv.*

di·a·logue /díəlawg, –log/ *n.* (also **di·a·log**) **1 a** conversation. **b** conversation in written form. **2 a** a discussion, esp. one between representatives of two groups. **b** a conversation; a talk (*long dialogues between the two main characters*).

di·al tone *n.* a sound indicating that a caller may start to dial a telephone.

di·al·y·sis /dīálisis/ *n.* (*pl.* **dialyses** /–seez/) **1** *Chem.* the separation of particles in a liquid by differences in their ability to pass through a membrane into another liquid. **2** *Med.* the clinical purification of blood by this technique.

di·am·e·ter /dīámitər/ *n.* **1 a** a straight line passing from side to side through the center of a circle or sphere. **b** the length of this line. **2** a transverse measurement; width; thickness. **3** a unit of linear measurement of magnifying power (*a lens magnifying 2000 diameters*).

di·a·met·ri·cal /díəmétrikəl/ *adj.* (also **di·a·met·ric**) **1** of or along a diameter. **2** (of opposition, difference, etc.) complete. □□ **di·a·met·ri·cal·ly** *adv.*

dia·mond /dímənd, díə–/ *n.*, *adj.*, & *v.* •*n.* **1** a precious stone of pure crystallized carbon, the hardest naturally occurring substance. **2** a rhombus. **3 a** a playing card of a suit denoted by a red rhombus. **b** (in *pl.*) this suit. **4** a glittering particle or point (of frost, etc.). **5** a tool with a small diamond for cutting glass. **6** *Baseball* **a** the space delimited by the bases. **b** the entire field. • *adj.* **1** made of or set with diamonds or a diamond. **2** rhombus-shaped. • *v.tr.* adorn with or as with diamonds.

dia·mond·back /dímәndbak, díә–/ *n.* **1** an edible freshwater terrapin, *Malaclemys terrapin*, native to N. America, with diamond-shaped markings on its shell. **2** any rattlesnake of the genus *Crotalus*, native to N. America, with diamond-shaped markings.

di·an·thus /dīánthәs/ *n.* any flowering plant of the genus *Dianthus*, e.g., a carnation or pink.

di·a·pa·son /díәpáyzәn, –sәn/ *n. Mus.* **1** the compass of a voice or musical instrument. **2** a fixed standard of musical pitch. **3** (in full **open** or **stopped diapason**) either of two main organ stops extending through the organ's whole compass. **4 a** a combination of notes or parts in a harmonious whole. **b** a melodious succession of notes, esp. a grand swelling burst of harmony. **5** an entire compass, range, or scope.

dia·per /dípәr, díәpәr/ *n. & v.* • *n.* **1** a piece of toweling or other absorbent material wrapped around a baby to retain urine and feces. **2 a** a linen or cotton fabric with a small diamond pattern. **b** this pattern. **3** a similar ornamental design of diamonds, etc., for panels, walls, etc. • *v.tr.* decorate with a diaper pattern.

diaper Middle English: from Old French *diapre*, from medieval Latin *diasprum*, from medieval Greek *diaspros* (adjective), from *dia* 'across' + *aspros* 'white.' The term seems originally to have denoted a costly fabric, but after the 15th century it was used of a fabric woven with a repeating diamond pattern. This sort of fabric came to be used as a wrap for babies.

di·aph·a·nous /dīáfәnәs/ *adj.* (of fabric, etc.) light and delicate, and almost transparent.

di·a·phragm /díәfram/ *n.* **1** a muscular partition separating the thorax from the abdomen in mammals. **2** a partition in animal and plant tissues. **3** a disk pierced by one or more holes in optical and acoustic systems, etc. **4** a device for varying the effective aperture of the lens in a camera, etc. **5** a thin contraceptive cap fitting over the cervix. **6** a thin sheet of material used as a partition, etc. ▫▫ **di·a·phrag·mat·ic** /–fragmátik/ *adj.*

di·a·rist /díәrist/ *n.* a person who keeps a diary.

di·ar·rhe·a /díәréeә/ *n.* a condition of excessively frequent and loose bowel movements. ▫▫ **di·ar·rhe·al** *adj.*

di·a·ry /díәree/ *n.* (*pl.* **-ries**) **1** a daily record of events or thoughts. **2** a book for this or for noting future engagements.

Di·as·po·ra /dīáspәrә/ *n.* **1** (prec. by *the*) **a** the dispersion of the Jews among the Gentiles mainly in the 8th–6th C. BC. **b** Jews dispersed in this way. **2** (also **diaspora**) **a** any group of people similarly dispersed. **b** their dispersion.

di·a·stase /díәstays, –stayz/ *n. Biochem.* = AMYLASE.

di·as·to·le /dīástәlee/ *n. Physiol.* the period between two contractions of the heart when the heart muscle relaxes and allows the chambers to fill with blood (cf. SYSTOLE). ▫▫ **di·as·tol·ic** /díәstólik/ *adj.*

di·a·tom /díәtom/ *n.* a unicellular alga found as plankton and forming fossil deposits. ▫▫ **di·a·to·ma·ceous** /–máyshәs/ *adj.*

di·a·tom·ic /díәtómik/ *adj.* consisting of two atoms.

di·a·ton·ic /díәtónik/ *adj. Mus.* **1** (of a scale, interval, etc.) involving only notes proper to the prevailing key without chromatic alteration. **2** (of a melody or harmony) constructed from such a scale.

di·a·tribe /díәtrīb/ *n.* a forceful verbal attack.

di·az·e·pam /dīázipam/ *n.* a tranquilizing muscle-relaxant drug with anticonvulsant properties used to relieve anxiety, tension, etc.

dib·ble /díbәl/ *n. & v.* • *n.* a hand tool for making holes in the ground for seeds or young plants. • *v.* **1** *tr.* sow or plant with a dibble. **2** *tr.* prepare (soil) with a dibble. **3** *intr.* use a dibble.

dibs /dibz/ *n.pl. sl.* rights; claim (*I have dibs on the last slice of pizza*).

dice /dīs/ *n. & v.* • *n.pl.* **1 a** small cubes with faces bearing 1–6 spots used in games of chance. **b** (treated as *sing.*) one of these cubes (see DIE[2]). **2** a game played with one or more such cubes. **3** food cut into small cubes for cooking. • *v.* **1 a** *intr.* play dice. **b** *intr.* take great risks; gamble (*dicing with death*). **c** *tr.* (foll. by *away*) gamble away. **2** *tr.* cut (food) into small cubes. **3** *tr.* mark with squares. ▫ **no dice** *sl.* no success or prospect of it.

dic·ey /dísee/ *adj.* (**dicier, diciest**) *sl.* risky; unreliable.

di·chot·o·my /dīkótәmee/ *n.* (*pl.* **-mies**) **1 a** a division into two, esp. a sharply defined one. **b** the result of such a division. **2** binary classification. **3** *Bot. & Zool.* repeated bifurcation. ▫▫ **di·chot·o·mize** *v.* **di·chot·o·mous** *adj.*

dick[1] /dik/ *n. coarse sl.* the penis.
▶Usually considered a taboo word.

dick[2] /dik/ *n. sl.* a detective.

dick·ens /díkinz/ *n.* (usu. prec. by *how, what, why*, etc., *the*) *colloq.* (esp. in exclamations) deuce; the Devil (*what the dickens are you doing here?*).

Dick·en·si·an /dikénzeeәn/ *adj. & n.* • *adj.* **1** of or relating to Charles Dickens, Engl. novelist d. 1870, or his work. **2** resembling or reminiscent of the situations, poor social conditions, or comically repulsive characters described in Dickens's work. • *n.* an admirer or student of Dickens or his work.

dick·er /díkәr/ *v. & n.* • *v.* **1 a** *intr.* bargain; haggle. **b** *tr.* barter; exchange. **2** *intr.* dither; hesitate. • *n.* a deal; a barter.

dick·ey /díkee/ *n.* (also **dick·y**) (*pl.* **-eys** or **-ies**) *colloq.* a false shirtfront.

di·cot·y·le·don /díkot'léed'n/ *n.* any flowering plant having two cotyledons. ▫▫ **di·cot·y·le·don·ous** *adj.*

dic·ta *pl.* of DICTUM.

dic·tate *v. & n.* • *v.* /díktayt, diktáyt/ **1** *tr.* say or read aloud (words to be written down or recorded). **2 a** *tr.* prescribe or lay down authoritatively. **b** *intr.* give orders. • *n.* /díktayt/ (usu. in *pl.*) an authoritative instruction (*dictates of conscience*).

dic·ta·tion /diktáyshәn/ *n.* **1 a** the saying of words to be written down or recorded. **b** an instance of this. **c** the material that is dictated. **2 a** authoritative prescription. **b** an instance of this. **c** a command.

dic·ta·tor /díktaytәr, diktáy–/ *n.* **1** a ruler with unrestricted authority. **2** a person with supreme authority in any sphere. **3** a domineering person. **4** a person who dictates for transcription.

dic·ta·to·ri·al /díktәtáwreeәl/ *adj.* **1** of or like a dictator. **2** imperious; overbearing. ▫▫ **dic·ta·to·ri·al·ly** *adv.*

dic·ta·tor·ship /diktáytәrship/ *n.* **1** a nation ruled by a dictator. **2 a** the position, rule, or period of rule of a dictator. **b** rule by a dictator. **3** absolute authority in any sphere.

dic·tion /díkshәn/ *n.* **1** the manner of enunciation in speaking or singing. **2** the choice of words or phrases.

dic·tion·ar·y /díkshәneree/ *n.* (*pl.* **-ies**) **1** a book that lists and explains the words of a language or gives equivalent words in another language. **2** a reference book on any subject, the items of which are arranged in alphabetical order.

dic·tum /díktəm/ *n.* (*pl.* **dicta** /–tə/ or **dictums**) **1** a formal utterance or pronouncement. **2** a saying or maxim.

did *past* of DO[1].

di·dac·tic /dīdáktik/ *adj.* **1** meant to instruct. **2** (of a person) tediously pedantic. □□ **di·dac·ti·cal·ly** *adv.* **di·dac·ti·cism** /–tisizəm/ *n.*

did·dle /díd'l/ *v. colloq.* **1** *tr.* cheat; swindle. **2** *intr.* waste time.

did·dly /dídlee/ *n.* (also **diddly squat**) *sl.* the slightest amount (*he hasn't done diddly to help us out*).

did·ger·i·doo /díjəreedōō/ *n.* (also **did·jer·i·doo**) an Australian Aboriginal musical wind instrument of long tubular shape.

didn't /díd'nt/ *contr.* did not.

di·do /dídō/ *n.* (*pl.* **-does** or **-dos**) *colloq.* an antic; a caper; a prank.

die[1] /dī/ *v.* (**dies, died, dying** /dí-ing/) **1** *intr.* (often foll. by *of*) cease to live (*died of hunger*). **2** *intr.* **a** come to an end; fade away (*the project died within six months*). **b** cease to function (*the engine died*). **c** (of a flame) go out. **3** *intr.* (foll. by *on*) die or cease to function while in the presence or charge of (a person). **4** *intr.* (usu. foll. by *of, from, with*) be exhausted or tormented (*nearly died of boredom*). **5** *tr.* suffer (a specified death) (*died a natural death*). □ **be dying** (foll. by *for*, or *to* + infin.) wish for longingly or intently (*am dying to see you*). **die away** become weaker or fainter to the point of extinction. **die back** (of a plant) decay from the tip toward the root. **die down** become less loud or strong. **die hard** die reluctantly, not without a struggle (*old habits die hard*). **die off** die one after another. **die out** become extinct. **never say die** keep up courage, not give in.

die[2] /dī/ *n.* **1** *sing.* of DICE *n.* 1a. **2** (*pl.* **dies**) **a** an engraved device for stamping a design on coins, medals, etc. **b** a device for stamping, cutting, or molding material into a particular shape. □ **the die is cast** an irrevocable step has been taken.

▶**Dice** is now standard in general use for both the singular and plural.

die cast·ing *n.* the process or product of casting from metal molds. □□ **die cast** *v.tr.* (*past* and *past part.* **cast**)

die-hard /díhaard/ *n. & adj.* • *n.* a conservative or stubborn person. • *adj.* stubborn; strongly devoted.

di·er·e·sis var. of DIAERESIS.

die·sel /deézəl/ *n.* **1** (in full **diesel engine**) an internal combustion engine in which the heat produced by the compression of air in the cylinder ignites the fuel. **2** a vehicle driven by a diesel engine. **3** fuel for a diesel engine.

di·et[1] /díət/ *n. & v.* • *n.* **1** the kinds of food that a person or animal habitually eats. **2** a special course of food to which a person is restricted. **3** a regular occupation or series of activities to which one is restricted or which form one's main concern, usu. for a purpose (*a diet of light reading and fresh air*). • *v.* (**dieted, dieting**) **1** *intr.* restrict oneself to small amounts or special kinds of food, esp. to control one's weight. **2** *tr.* restrict (a person or animal) to a special diet. □□ **di·et·er** *n.*

di·et[2] /díət/ *n.* **1** a legislative assembly in certain countries. **2** *hist.* a national or international conference, esp. of a federal government or confederation.

di·e·tar·y /díəteree/ *adj.* of or relating to a diet.

di·e·tet·ic /díətétik/ *adj.* of or relating to diet.

di·e·tet·ics /díətétiks/ *n.pl.* (usu. treated as *sing.*) the scientific study of diet and nutrition.

di·e·ti·tian /díətíshən/ *n.* (also **di·e·ti·cian**) an expert in dietetics.

dif·fer /dífər/ *v.intr.* **1** (often foll. by *from*) be unlike or distinguishable. **2** (often foll. by *with*) disagree.

dif·fer·ence /dífrəns/ *n.* **1** the state or condition of being different or unlike. **2** a point in which things differ. **3** a degree of unlikeness. **4 a** the quantity by which amounts differ; a deficit (*will have to make up the difference*). **b** the remainder left after subtraction. **5 a** a disagreement, quarrel, or dispute. **b** the grounds of disagreement (*put aside their differences*). **6** a notable change (*the difference in his behavior is remarkable*). □ **make a** (or **all the**, etc.) **difference** (often foll. by *to*) have a significant effect or influence. **make no difference** (often foll. by *to*) have no effect.

dif·fer·ent /dífrənt/ *adj.* **1** (often foll. by *from, to, than*) unlike; distinguishable in nature, form, or quality. **2** distinct; separate; not the same one. **3** *colloq.* unusual (*wanted to do something different*). **4** of various kinds; assorted; several; miscellaneous (*available in different colors*). □□ **dif·fer·ent·ly** *adv.* **dif·fer·ent·ness** *n.*

▶Many traditional critics regard **different than** as an improper substitute for **different from**: *My opinion is quite different from his.* But **different than** now appears widely in good writing, as well as in informal contexts.

dif·fer·en·tial /dífərénshəl/ *adj. & n.* • *adj.* **1 a** of, exhibiting, or depending on a difference. **b** varying according to circumstances. **2** *Math.* relating to infinitesimal differences. **3** constituting a specific difference; distinctive; relating to specific differences (*differential diagnosis*). **4** *Physics & Mech.* concerning the difference of two or more motions, pressures, etc. • *n.* **1** a difference between individuals of the same kind. **2** a difference between rates of interest, etc. **3** *Math.* **a** an infinitesimal difference between successive values of a variable. **b** a function expressing this as a rate of change with respect to another variable. **4** (in full **differential gear**) a gear allowing a vehicle's driven wheels to revolve at different speeds in cornering. □□ **dif·fer·en·tial·ly** *adv.*

dif·fer·en·tial cal·cu·lus *n. Math.* a method of calculating rates of change, maximum or minimum values, etc. (cf. INTEGRAL CALCULUS).

dif·fer·en·ti·ate /dífərénsheeayt/ *v.* **1** *tr.* constitute a difference between or in. **2** *tr. &* (often foll. by *between*) *intr.* find differences (between); discriminate. **3** *tr. & intr.* make or become different in the process of development. **4** *tr. Math.* transform (a function) into its derivative. □□ **dif·fer·en·ti·a·tion** /–sheeáyshən/ *n.* **dif·fer·en·ti·a·tor** *n.*

dif·fi·cult /dífikult, –kəlt/ *adj.* **1 a** needing much effort or skill. **b** troublesome; perplexing. **2** (of a person): **a** not easy to please or satisfy. **b** uncooperative; troublesome. **3** characterized by hardships or problems.

dif·fi·cul·ty /dífikultee, –kəl–/ *n.* (*pl.* **-ties**) **1** the state or condition of being difficult. **2 a** a difficult thing; a problem or hindrance. **b** (often in *pl.*) a cause of distress or hardship.

dif·fi·dent /dífidənt/ *adj.* **1** shy; lacking self-confidence. **2** excessively reticent. □□ **dif·fi·dence** /–dəns/ *n.* **dif·fi·dent·ly** *adv.*

dif·fract /difrákt/ *v. Physics* undergo or cause diffraction.

dif·frac·tion /difrákshən/ *n. Physics* the process in which a beam of light or other system of waves is spread out as a result of passing through a narrow aperture or across an edge, often accompanied by interference between the waveforms produced.

dif·fuse *adj. & v.* • *adj.* /difyōōs/ **1** spread out; not concentrated. **2** not concise; long-winded; verbose. • *v.tr. & intr.* /difyōōz/ **1** disperse or be dispersed from a center. **2** spread or be spread widely. **3** *Physics* intermingle by diffusion. □□ **dif·fuse·ly** /difyōōslee/ *adv.* **dif·fuse·ness** /difyōōsnis/ *n.* **dif·fus·i·ble** /difyōōzibəl/ *adj.* **dif·fu·sive** /difyōōsiv/ *adj.*

dif·fus·er /difyóozər/ *n.* (also **dif·fu·sor**) **1** a person or thing that diffuses. **2** *Engin.* a duct for broadening an airflow and reducing its speed.

dif·fu·sion /difyóozhən/ *n.* **1** the act or an instance of diffusing; the process of being diffused. **2** *Physics & Chem.* the interpenetration of substances by the natural movement of their particles.

dig /dig/ *v. & n.* •*v.* (**digging**; *past* and *past part.* **dug** /dug/) **1** *intr.* break up and remove or turn over soil, ground, etc. **2** *tr.* **a** break up and displace (the ground, etc.) in this way. **b** (foll. by *up*) break up the soil of (fallow land). **3** *tr.* make (a hole, grave, tunnel, etc.) by digging. **4** *tr.* (often foll. by *up, out*) **a** obtain or remove by digging. **b** find or discover after searching. **5** *tr.* (also *absol.*) excavate (an archaeological site). **6** *tr. sl.* like, appreciate, or understand. **7** *tr. & intr.* (foll. by *in, into*) thrust or poke into. **8** *intr.* make one's way by digging (*dug through the mountainside*). **9** *intr.* (usu. foll. by *into*) investigate or study closely; probe. •*n.* **1** a piece of digging. **2** a thrust or poke (*a dig in the ribs*). **3** *colloq.* (often foll. by *at*) a pointed remark. **4** an archaeological excavation. **5** (in *pl.*) *colloq.* living quarters. □ **dig in** *colloq.* begin eating. □□ **dig·ger** *n.*

di·gest *v. & n.* •*v.tr.* /dijést, dī–/ **1** assimilate (food) in the stomach and bowels. **2** understand and assimilate mentally. **3** *Chem.* treat (a substance) with heat, enzymes, or a solvent in order to decompose it, extract the essence, etc. **4 a** reduce to a systematic or convenient form; summarize. **b** think over; arrange in the mind. **5** bear without resistance; tolerate; endure. •*n.* /díjest/ **1** a methodical summary, esp. of a body of laws. **2 a** a compendium or summary of information; a résumé. **b** a regular or occasional synopsis of current literature or news. □□ **di·gest·er** *n.* **di·gest·i·ble** *adj.* **di·gest·i·bil·i·ty** *n.*

di·ges·tion /dijés-chən, dī–/ *n.* **1** the process of digesting. **2** the capacity to digest food (*has a weak digestion*). **3** digesting a substance by means of heat, enzymes, or a solvent.

di·ges·tive /dijéstiv, dī–/ *adj. & n.* •*adj.* **1** of or relating to digestion. **2** aiding or promoting digestion. •*n.* a substance that aids digestion.

dig·it /díjit/ *n.* **1** any numeral from 0 to 9. **2** *Anat. & Zool.* a finger, thumb, or toe.

dig·it·al /díjit'l/ *adj.* **1** of or using a digit or digits. **2** (of a clock, watch, etc.) that gives a reading by means of displayed digits instead of hands. **3** (of a computer) operating on data represented as a series of usu. binary digits or in similar discrete form. **4 a** (of a recording) with sound information represented in digits for more reliable transmission. **b** (of a recording medium) using this process. □□ **dig·i·tal·ize** *v.tr.* **dig·it·al·ly** *adv.*

dig·it·al au·di·o·tape *n.* magnetic tape on which sound is recorded digitally. ¶ Abbr.: **d.a.t.**

dig·i·tal·is /díjitális/ *n.* a drug prepared from the dried leaves of foxgloves and containing substances that stimulate the heart muscle.

dig·i·tize /díjitīz/ *v.tr.* convert (data, etc.) into digital form, esp. for a computer. □□ **dig·i·ti·za·tion** *n.*

dig·ni·fied /dígnifīd/ *adj.* having or expressing dignity.

dig·ni·fy /dígnifī/ *v.tr.* (**-fies, -fied**) **1** give dignity to. **2** ennoble; make worthy or illustrious. **3** give the form or appearance of dignity to (*dignified the house with the name of mansion*).

dig·ni·tar·y /dígniteree/ *n.* (*pl.* **-ies**) a person holding high rank or office.

dig·ni·ty /dígnitee/ *n.* (*pl.* **-ties**) **1** a composed and serious manner. **2** the state of being worthy of honor or respect. **3** worthiness; excellence. **4** a high rank or position. **5** high regard or estimation. **6** self-respect.

di·graph /dígraf/ *n.* a group of two letters representing one sound, as in *ph* and *ey.*

di·gress /dīgrés/ *v.intr.* depart from the main subject. □□ **di·gres·sion** /–greshən/ *n.* **di·gres·sive** *adj.*

digs see DIG *n.* 5.

di·hed·ral /dīhéedrəl/ *adj.* having or contained by two plane faces.

dike[1] /dīk/ *n. & v.* (also **dyke**) •*n.* **1** a long wall or embankment built to prevent flooding, esp. from the sea. **2** a ditch. **3 a** a low wall, esp. of turf. **b** a causeway. **4** a barrier or obstacle; a defense. •*v.tr.* provide or defend with a dike or dikes.

dike[2] var. of DYKE[2].

di·lap·i·dat·ed /dilápidaytid/ *adj.* in a state of disrepair or ruin. □□ **di·lap·i·da·tion** *n.*

dil·a·ta·tion /dilətáyshən, dī–/ *n.* **1** the widening or expansion of a hollow organ or cavity. **2** the process of dilating.

dil·a·ta·tion and cu·ret·tage *n.* an operation in which the cervix is expanded and the womb lining scraped off with a curette.

di·late /dīláyt, dílayt/ *v.* **1** *tr. & intr.* make or become wider or larger. **2** *intr.* (often foll. by *on, upon*) speak or write at length. □□ **di·la·tion** /–láyshən/ *n.*

dil·a·to·ry /dílətawree/ *adj.* given to or causing delay. □□ **dil·a·to·ri·ness** *n.*

dil·do /díldō/ *n.* (*pl.* **-dos** or **-does**) an object shaped like an erect penis and used for sexual stimulation.

di·lem·ma /dilémə/ *n.* **1** a situation in which a choice has to be made between two equally undesirable alternatives. **2** a state of indecision between two alternatives. **3** a difficult situation. **4** an argument forcing an opponent to choose either of two unfavorable alternatives.

▶**Dilemma** should be used with regard to situations in which a difficult choice has to be made between undesirable alternatives, as in *You see his dilemma? He would have to give up either his childhood home or his dreams of traveling.* It is imprecise to use **dilemma** to mean simply 'a difficult situation.'

dil·et·tante /dílitaant/ *n. & adj.* •*n.* (*pl.* **dilettantes** or **dilettanti** /–tee/) **1** a person who studies a subject superficially. **2** a person who enjoys the arts. •*adj.* trifling; not thorough; amateurish. □□ **dil·et·tant·ism** *n.*

dil·i·gence /dílijəns/ *n.* **1** careful and persistent application or effort. **2** industriousness.

dil·i·gent /dílijənt/ *adj.* **1** careful and steady in application to one's work or duties. **2** showing care and effort. □□ **dil·i·gent·ly** *adv.*

dill /dil/ *n.* **1** an umbelliferous herb, *Anethum graveolens,* with yellow flowers and aromatic seeds. **2** the leaves or seeds of this plant used esp. for flavoring.

dil·ly /dílee/ *n.* (*pl.* **-lies**) *sl.* a remarkable or excellent person or thing.

dil·ly·dal·ly /díleedálee/ *v.intr.* (**-lies, -lied**) *colloq.* **1** dawdle; loiter. **2** vacillate.

di·lute /dilóot, dī–/ *v. & adj.* •*v.tr.* **1** reduce the strength of (a fluid) by adding water or another solvent. **2** weaken or reduce the strength or forcefulness of. •*adj.* also /dī–/ **1** diluted. **2** (of a color) washed out; low in saturation. **3** *Chem.* **a** (of a solution) having relatively low concentration of solute. **b** (of a substance) in solution (*dilute sulfuric acid*). □□ **di·lu·tion** /–lóoshən/ *n.*

dim /dim/ *adj. & v.* •*adj.* (**dimmer, dimmest**) **1 a** only faintly luminous or visible; not bright. **b** obscure; ill-defined. **2** not clearly perceived or remembered. **3** *colloq.* stupid. **4** (of the eyes) not seeing clearly. •*v.* (**dimmed, dimming**) **1** *tr. & intr.* make or become dim. **2** *tr.* switch (headlights) to low beam. □ **take a dim view of** *colloq.* **1** disapprove of. **2** feel gloomy about. □□ **dim·ly** *adv.* **dim·ness** *n.*

dime /dīm/ *n.* a ten-cent coin. □ **a dime a dozen** very cheap or commonplace. **turn on a dime** *colloq.* make a sharp turn in a vehicle.

di·men·sion /diménshən, dī–/ *n. & v.* • *n.* **1** a measurable extent of any kind, as length, breadth, depth. **2** (in *pl.*) size; scope; extent. **3** an aspect or facet. • *v.tr.* (usu. as **dimensioned** *adj.*) mark the dimensions on (a diagram, etc.). □□ **di·men·sion·al** *adj.* (also in *comb.*). **di·men·sion·less** *adj.*

di·mer /dímər/ *n. Chem.* a compound consisting of two identical molecules linked together (cf. MONOMER). □□ **di·mer·ic** /–mérik/ *adj.*

di·min·ish /dimínish/ *v.* **1** *tr. & intr.* make or become smaller or less. **2** *tr.* lessen the reputation of.

di·min·ished /dimínisht/ *adj.* **1** reduced; made smaller or less. **2** *Mus.* (of an interval) less by a semitone than the corresponding minor or perfect interval.

di·min·u·en·do /dimínyoo͞-éndō/ *adv. & n. Mus.* • *adv.* with a gradual decrease in loudness. • *n.* (*pl.* **-dos**) a passage to be played in this way.

dim·i·nu·tion /diminoo͞shən, –nyoo͞–/ *n.* **1 a** the act or an instance of diminishing. **b** the amount by which something diminishes. **2** *Mus.* the repetition of a passage in notes shorter than those originally used.

di·min·u·tive /dimínyətiv/ *adj. & n.* • *adj.* **1** tiny. **2** *Gram.* (of a word or suffix) implying smallness, either actual or imputed in token of affection, scorn, etc. (e.g., *-let*, *-kins*). • *n. Gram.* a diminutive word or suffix.

dim·mer /dímər/ *n.* **1** a device for varying the brightness of an electric light. **2** (in *pl.*) **a** small parking lights on a motor vehicle. **b** headlights on low beam.

dim·ple /dímpəl/ *n. & v.* • *n.* a small hollow in the flesh, esp. in the cheeks or chin. • *v.* **1** *intr.* produce or show dimples. **2** *tr.* produce dimples in (a cheek, etc.). □□ **dim·ply** *adj.*

dim sum /dim súm/ *n.* (also **dim sim** /sim/) a meal or course of savory Cantonese-style snacks.

dim·wit /dímwit/ *n. colloq.* a stupid person.

dim·wit·ted *adj. colloq.* stupid; unintelligent.

din /din/ *n.* a prolonged loud and distracting noise.

dine /dīn/ *v.* **1** *intr.* eat dinner. **2** *tr.* give dinner to. □ **dine out** dine away from home.

din·er /dínər/ *n.* **1** a person who dines, esp. in a restaurant. **2** a railroad dining car. **3** a small restaurant.

di·nette /dīnét/ *n.* **1** a small room or part of a room used for eating meals. **2** (in full **dinette set**) table and chairs designed for such a room.

ding[1] /ding/ *v. & n.* • *v.intr.* make a ringing sound. • *n.* a ringing sound, as of a bell.

ding[2] /ding/ *v. & n.* • *v.tr.* cause surface damage; dent. • *n.* nick; minor surface damage; dent.

ding-a-ling /díngəling/ *n.* a foolish, flighty, or eccentric person.

ding·bat /díngbat/ *n. sl.* **1** a stupid or eccentric person. **2** *Printing* an ornamental design in typography.

din·ghy /díngee, dínggee/ *n.* (*pl.* **-ghies**) **1** a small boat carried by a ship. **2** a small pleasure boat. **3** a small inflatable rubber boat.

din·go /dínggō/ *n.* (*pl.* **-goes**) a wild Australian dog, *Canis dingo*.

din·gy /dínjee/ *adj.* (**dingier, dingiest**) dirty-looking; drab; dull-colored. □□ **din·gi·ness** *n.*

din·ing car *n.* a railroad car equipped as a restaurant.

din·ing room *n.* a room in which meals are eaten.

dink·y /díngkee/ *adj.* (**dinkier, dinkiest**) *colloq.* trifling; insignificant.

din·ner /dínər/ *n.* **1** the main meal of the day, taken either at midday or in the evening. **2** a formal evening meal.

din·ner jack·et *n.* a man's, usu. black, formal jacket for evening wear.

di·no·saur /dínəsawr/ *n.* **1** an extinct reptile of the Mesozoic era. **2** a large, unwieldy system or organization, esp. one not adapting to new conditions. □□ **di·no·sau·ri·an** *adj. & n.*

dint /dint/ *n.* □ **by dint of** by force or means of.

di·o·cese /díəsis, –sees, –seez/ *n.* a district under the pastoral care of a bishop. □□ **di·oc·e·san** /dīósisən/ *adj.*

di·ode /díōd/ *n. Electronics* **1** a semiconductor allowing the flow of current in one direction only and having two terminals. **2** a thermionic valve having two electrodes.

di·op·trics /dīóptriks/ *n. Optics* the part of optics dealing with refraction.

di·o·ram·a /díərámə, –raámə/ *n.* **1** a scenic painting in which changes in color and direction of illumination simulate a sunrise, etc. **2** a small representation of a scene with three-dimensional figures, viewed through a window, etc. **3** a small-scale model or movie set.

di·ox·ide /dīóksīd/ *n. Chem.* an oxide containing two atoms of oxygen (*carbon dioxide*).

DIP /dip/ *n. Computing* a form of integrated circuit consisting of a small plastic or ceramic slab with two parallel rows of pins (acronym for *d*ual *i*n-line *p*ackage).

dip /dip/ *v. & n.* • *v.* (**dipped, dipping**) **1** *tr.* put or let down briefly into liquid, etc. **2** *intr.* **a** go below a surface or level (*the sun dipped below the horizon*). **b** (of a level of income, activity, etc.) decline slightly (*profits dipped in May*). **3** *intr.* extend downward; take or have a downward slope (*the road dips after the curve*). **4** *intr.* go under water and emerge quickly. **5** *intr.* (foll. by *into*) **a** read briefly from (a book, etc.). **b** take a cursory interest in (a subject). **6** (foll. by *into*) **a** *intr.* put a hand, ladle, etc., into a container to take something out. **b** *tr.* put (a hand, etc.) into a container to do this. **c** *intr.* spend from or make use of one's resources (*dipped into our savings*). **7** *tr. & intr.* lower or be lowered, esp. in salute. **8** *tr.* color (a fabric) by immersing it in dye. **9** *tr.* wash (sheep) by immersion in a vermin-killing liquid. **10** *tr.* make (a candle) by immersing a wick briefly in hot tallow. • *n.* **1** an act of dipping or being dipped. **2** a liquid into which something is dipped. **3** a brief swim in the ocean, lake, etc. **4** a brief downward slope in a road, etc. **5** a sauce or dressing into which food is dipped before eating. **6** a depression in the skyline.

diph·the·ri·a /difthéereeə, dip–/ *n.* an acute infectious bacterial disease with inflammation of a mucous membrane esp. of the throat.

diph·thong /dífthawng, –thong, díp–/ *n.* **1** a speech sound in one syllable in which the articulation begins as for one vowel and moves as for another (as in *coin*, *loud*, and *side*). **2 a** a digraph representing the sound of a diphthong or single vowel (as in *feat*). **b** a compound vowel character; a ligature (as *æ*).

di·plod·o·cus /diplódəkəs, dī–/ *n.* a giant plant-eating dinosaur with a long neck and tail.

dip·loid /díployd/ *adj. & n. Biol.* • *adj.* (of an organism or cell) having two complete sets of chromosomes per cell. • *n.* a diploid cell or organism.

di·plo·ma /diplṓmə/ *n.* (*pl.* **diplomas**) **1** a certificate of qualification awarded by a college, etc. **2** a document conferring an honor or privilege. **3** (*pl.* also **diplomata** /–mətə/) a state paper; an official document; a charter.

di·plo·ma·cy /diplṓməsee/ *n.* **1 a** the management of international relations. **b** expertise in this. **2** the art of dealing with people in a tactful and effective way.

dip·lo·mat /dípləmat/ *n.* **1** an official representing a country abroad; a member of a diplomatic service. **2** a tactful person.

dip·lo·mat·ic /dípləmátik/ *adj.* **1 a** of or involved in diplomacy. **b** skilled in diplomacy. **2** tactful. **3** (of an edition, etc.) exactly reproducing the original. ▫▫ **dip·lo·mat·i·cal·ly** *adv.*

dip·lo·mat·ic im·mu·ni·ty *n.* the exemption of diplomatic staff abroad from arrest, taxation, etc.

di·pole /dípōl/ *n.* **1** *Physics* two equal and oppositely charged or magnetized poles separated by a distance. **2** *Chem.* a molecule in which a concentration of positive charges is separated from a concentration of negative charges. **3** an aerial consisting of a horizontal metal rod with a connecting wire at its center.

dip·per /dípər/ *n.* **1** a diving bird, *Cinclus cinclus.* **2** a ladle.

dip·py /dípee/ *adj.* (**dippier, dippiest**) *sl.* crazy; silly.

dip·so /dípsō/ *n.* (*pl.* **-sos**) *colloq.* a dipsomaniac.

dip·so·ma·ni·a /dípsəmáyneeə/ *n.* an abnormal craving for alcohol. ▫▫ **dip·so·ma·ni·ac** /–máyneeak/ *n.*

dip·stick /dípstik/ *n.* a graduated rod for measuring the depth of a liquid, esp. in a vehicle's engine.

DIP switch *n.* an arrangement of switches on a printer for selecting a printing mode.

dip·ter·ous /díptərəs/ *adj.* **1** (of an insect) of the order Diptera, having two membranous wings, e.g.; the fly, gnat, or mosquito. **2** *Bot.* having two winglike appendages.

dip·tych /díptik/ *n.* **1** a painting on two hinged panels which may be closed like a book. **2** an ancient writing tablet consisting of two hinged leaves with waxed inner sides.

dire /dīr/ *adj.* **1 a** calamitous; dreadful. **b** ominous (*dire warnings*). **2** urgent (*in dire need*). ▫▫ **dire·ly** *adv.*

di·rect /dirékt, dī–/ *adj., adv., & v.* • *adj.* **1** extending or moving in a straight line or by the shortest route; not crooked or circuitous. **2 a** straightforward; going straight to the point. **b** frank; not ambiguous. **3** without intermediaries or the intervention of other factors (*a direct approach*). **4** (of descent) lineal; not collateral. **5** complete; greatest possible (*the direct opposite*). • *adv.* **1** without an intermediary or intervening factor (*dealt with them direct*). **2** frankly; without evasion. **3** by a direct route (*send it direct to Chicago*). • *v.tr.* **1** control; guide; govern the movements of. **2** (foll. by *to* + infin., or *that* + clause) give a formal order or command to. **3** (foll. by *to*) **a** address (a letter, etc.). **b** tell or show (a person) the way to a destination. **4** (foll. by *at, to, toward*) **a** point, aim, or cause (a blow or missile) to move in a certain direction. **b** point or address (one's attention, a remark, etc.). **5** guide as an adviser, as a principle, etc. **6 a** (also *absol.*) supervise the performing, staging, etc., of (a movie, play, etc.). **b** supervise the performance of (an actor, etc.). **7** (also *absol.*) guide the performance of (a group of musicians). ▫▫ **di·rect·ness** *n.*

di·rect ac·cess *n.* the facility of retrieving data immediately from any part of a computer file.

di·rect ad·dress *n. Computing* an address (see ADDRESS *n.* 1c) which specifies the location of data to be used in an operation.

di·rect cur·rent *n.* (Abbr.: **DC, d.c.**) an electric current flowing in one direction only.

di·rec·tion /dirékshən, dī–/ *n.* **1** the act or process of directing; supervision. **2** (usu. in *pl.*) an order or instruction, esp. each of a set guiding the use of equipment, etc. **3 a** the course or line along which a person or thing moves or looks, or which must be taken to reach a destination. **b** (in *pl.*) guidance on how to reach a destination or how to do something (*give me directions to your house; directions for making puff pastry*). **c** the point to or from which a person or thing moves or looks. **4** the tendency or scope of a theme, subject, or inquiry. ▫▫ **di·rec·tion·less** *adj.*

di·rec·tion·al /dirékshənəl, dī–/ *adj.* **1** of or indicating direction. **2** *Electronics* **a** concerned with the transmission of radio or sound waves in a particular direction. **b** (of equipment) designed to receive radio or sound waves most effectively from a particular direction or directions. ▫▫ **di·rec·tion·al·i·ty** /–álitee/ *n.* **di·rec·tion·al·ly** *adv.*

di·rec·tion find·er *n.* a device for determining the source of radio waves, esp. as an aid in navigation.

di·rec·tive /diréktiv, dī–/ *n. & adj.* • *n.* a general instruction from one in authority. • *adj.* serving to direct.

di·rect·ly /diréktlee, dī–/ *adv.* **1 a** at once; without delay. **b** presently; shortly. **2** exactly; immediately (*directly opposite; directly after lunch*). **3** in a direct manner.

di·rect ob·ject *n. Gram.* the primary object of the action of a transitive verb.

di·rec·tor /diréktər, dī–/ *n.* **1** a person who directs or controls something. **2** a member of the managing board of a commercial company. **3** a person who directs a movie, etc. **4** = CONDUCTOR 1. ▫▫ **di·rec·to·ri·al** /–táwreeəl/ *adj.* **di·rec·tor·ship** *n.* (esp. in sense 2).

di·rec·to·rate /diréktərət, dī–/ *n.* **1** a board of directors. **2** the office of director.

di·rec·to·ry /diréktəree, dī–/ *n.* (*pl.* **-ries**) **1** a book listing a particular group of individuals or organizations with various details. **2** a computer file listing other files or programs, etc.

dirge /dərj/ *n.* **1** a lament for the dead. **2** any mournful song or lament.

dir·i·gi·ble /dírijibəl, diríj–/ *adj. & n.* • *adj.* capable of being guided. • *n.* a dirigible balloon or airship.

dirk /dərk/ *n.* a long dagger, esp. as formerly worn by Scottish Highlanders.

dirn·dl /dərnd'l/ *n.* **1** a woman's dress with close-fitting bodice, tight waistband, and full skirt. **2** a full skirt of this kind.

dirt /dərt/ *n.* **1** unclean matter that soils. **2 a** earth; soil. **b** earth; cinders, etc., used to make a surface for a road, etc. (usu. *attrib.*: *dirt track*). **3 a** foul or malicious words or talk. **b** scurrilous information; scandal; gossip; the lowdown. **4** excrement. **5** a dirty condition. **6** a person or thing considered worthless. ▫ **do a person dirt** *sl.* harm or injure a person's reputation maliciously. **eat dirt 1** suffer insults, etc., without retaliating. **2** make a humiliating confession. **treat like dirt** treat (a person) contemptuously.

dirt bike *n.* a motorcycle designed for use on unpaved roads and tracks, esp. in scrambling.

dirt cheap *adj. & adv. colloq.* extremely cheap.

dirt poor *adj.* extremely poor; lacking basic necessities.

dirt·y /dártee/ *adj. & v.* • *adj.* (**dirtier, dirtiest**) **1** soiled; unclean. **2** causing one to become dirty (*a dirty job*). **3** sordid; lewd (*dirty joke*). **4** unpleasant; nasty. **5** dishonest; unfair (*dirty play*). **6** (of weather) rough; stormy. **7** (of a color) not pure nor clear; dingy. **8** *colloq.* (of a nuclear weapon) producing considerable radioactive fallout. • *v.tr. & intr.* (**-ies, -ied**) make or become dirty. ▫▫ **dirt·i·ness** *n.*

dirt·y lin·en *n.* (also **dirty laundry** or **wash**) *colloq.* intimate secrets, esp. of a scandalous nature.

dirt·y look *n. colloq.* a look of disapproval, anger, or disgust.

dirt·y trick *n.* **1** a dishonorable and deceitful act. **2** (in *pl.*) underhanded political activity, esp. to discredit an opponent.

dirt·y word *n.* **1** an offensive or indecent word. **2** a word for something which is disapproved of (*profit is a dirty word*).

dirt·y work *n.* **1** unpleasant tasks. **2** dishonorable or illegal activity.

dis *v.tr. sl.* put (a person) down verbally; bad-mouth.

dis- /dis/ *prefix* forming nouns, adjectives, and verbs: **1** expressing negation (*dishonest*). **2** indicating reversal or absence of an action or state (*disengage*; *disbelieve*). **3** indicating removal of a thing or quality (*dismember*; *disable*). **4** indicating separation (*distinguish*; *dispose*). **5** indicating completeness or intensification of the action (*disembowel*; *disgruntled*). **6** indicating expulsion from (*disbar*).

dis·a·bil·i·ty /dìsəbílitee/ *n.* (*pl.* **-ties**) **1** physical incapacity. **2** a lack of some asset, quality, or attribute, that prevents one's doing something. **3** a legal disqualification.

dis·a·ble /disáybəl/ *v.tr.* **1** render unable to function. **2** (often as **disabled** *adj.*) deprive of or reduce the power to walk or do other normal activities, esp. by crippling. ▫▫ **dis·a·ble·ment** *n.*

dis·a·buse /dísəbyóoz/ *v.tr.* **1** (foll. by *of*) free from a mistaken idea. **2** disillusion; undeceive.

dis·ad·van·tage /dísədvántij/ *n.* & *v.* •*n.* **1** an unfavorable circumstance or condition. **2** damage to one's interest or reputation. •*v.tr.* cause disadvantage to. ▫ **at a disadvantage** in an unfavorable position or aspect.

dis·ad·van·taged /dísədvántijd/ *adj.* placed in unfavorable circumstances (esp. of a person lacking the normal social opportunities).

dis·ad·van·ta·geous /disádvəntáyjəs, dísad–/ *adj.* **1** involving disadvantage. **2** derogatory.

dis·af·fect·ed /dísəféktid/ *adj.* **1** disloyal, esp. to one's superiors. **2** estranged; no longer friendly. ▫▫ **dis·af·fec·tion** *n.*

dis·af·fil·i·ate /dísəfíleeayt/ *v.* **1** *tr.* end the affiliation of. **2** *intr.* end one's affiliation. **3** *tr.* & *intr.* detach. ▫▫ **dis·af·fil·i·a·tion** /–leeáyshən/ *n.*

dis·a·gree /dísəgrée/ *v.intr.* (**-agrees, -agreed, -agreeing**) (often foll. by *with*) **1** hold a different opinion. **2** quarrel. **3** (of factors or circumstances) not correspond. **4** have an adverse effect upon (a person's health, digestion, etc.). ▫▫ **dis·a·gree·ment** *n.*

dis·a·gree·a·ble /dísəgréeəbəl/ *adj.* **1** unpleasant. **2** bad-tempered. ▫▫ **dis·a·gree·a·bly** *adv.*

dis·al·low /dísəlów/ *v.tr.* refuse to allow or accept as valid; prohibit. ▫▫ **dis·al·low·ance** *n.*

dis·ap·pear /dísəpéer/ *v.intr.* **1** cease to be visible; pass from sight. **2** cease to exist or be in circulation or use (*rotary telephones had all but disappeared*). ▫▫ **dis·ap·pear·ance** *n.*

dis·ap·point /dísəpóynt/ *v.tr.* **1** (also *absol.*) fail to fulfill a desire or expectation of (a person). **2** frustrate (hopes, etc.). ▫ **be disappointed** (foll. by *with*, *at*, *in*, or *to* + infin., or *that* + clause) fail to have one's expectation, etc., fulfilled in some regard (*was disappointed in you*; *disappointed to be last*). ▫▫ **dis·ap·point·ed·ly** *adv.* **dis·ap·point·ing** *adj.* **dis·ap·point·ing·ly** *adv.*

dis·ap·point·ment /dísəpóyntmənt/ *n.* **1** an event, thing, or person that disappoints. **2** a feeling of distress, vexation, etc., resulting from this.

dis·ap·pro·ba·tion /disáprəbáyshən/ *n.* strong disapproval.

dis·ap·prove /dísəpróov/ *v.* **1** *intr.* (usu. foll. by *of*) have or express an unfavorable opinion. **2** *tr.* be displeased with. ▫▫ **dis·ap·prov·al** *n.* **dis·ap·prov·ing** *adj.* **dis·ap·prov·ing·ly** *adv.*

dis·arm /disaárm/ *v.* **1** *tr.* **a** take weapons away from (often foll. by *of*). **b** *Fencing*, etc., deprive of a weapon. **2** *tr.* deprive (a ship, etc.) of its means of defense. **3** *intr.* (of a nation, etc.) disband or reduce its military forces. **4** *tr.* remove the fuse from (a bomb, etc.). **5** *tr.* deprive of the power to injure. **6** *tr.* pacify or allay the hostility or suspicions of; mollify; placate. ▫▫ **dis·arm·er** *n.* **dis·arm·ing** *adj.* (esp. in sense 6). **dis·arm·ing·ly** *adv.*

dis·ar·ma·ment /disaármәmәnt/ *n.* the reduction by a nation of its military forces and weapons.

dis·ar·range /dísəráynj/ *v.tr.* bring into disorder.

dis·ar·ray /dísəráy/ *n.* & *v.* •*n.* (often prec. by *in*, *into*) disorder; confusion. •*v.tr.* throw into disorder.

dis·ar·tic·u·late /dísaartíkyəlayt/ *v.tr.* & *intr.* separate at the joints. ▫▫ **dis·ar·tic·u·la·tion** /–láyshən/ *n.*

dis·as·sem·ble /dísəsémbəl/ *v.tr.* take (a machine, etc.) to pieces. ▫▫ **dis·as·sem·bly** *n.*

dis·as·so·ci·ate /dísəsósheeayt, –seeayt/ *v.tr.* & *intr.* = DISSOCIATE. ▫▫ **dis·as·so·ci·a·tion** /–áyshən/ *n.*

dis·as·ter /dizástər/ *n.* **1** a great or sudden misfortune. **2 a** a complete failure. **b** a person or enterprise ending in failure. ▫▫ **dis·as·trous** *adj.* **dis·as·trous·ly** *adv.*

dis·a·vow /dísəvów/ *v.tr.* disclaim knowledge of, responsibility for, or belief in. ▫▫ **dis·a·vow·al** *n.*

dis·band /disbánd/ *v.* **1** *intr.* (of an organized group, etc.) cease to work or act together; disperse. **2** *tr.* cause (such a group) to disband. ▫▫ **dis·band·ment** *n.*

dis·bar /disbaár/ *v.tr.* (**disbarred, disbarring**) deprive (an attorney) of the right to practice. ▫▫ **dis·bar·ment** *n.*

dis·be·lieve /dísbiléev/ *v.* **1** *tr.* be unable or unwilling to believe (a person or statement). **2** *intr.* have no faith. ▫▫ **dis·be·lief** /–léef/ *n.* **dis·be·liev·er** *n.* **dis·be·liev·ing·ly** *adv.*

dis·burse /disbə́rs/ *v.* **1** *tr.* expend (money). **2** *tr.* defray (a cost). **3** *intr.* pay money. ▫▫ **dis·burse·ment** *n.*

disc var. of DISK.

dis·card *v.* & *n.* •*v.tr.* /diskaárd/ **1** reject or get rid of as unwanted or superfluous. **2** (also *absol.*) *Cards* remove or put aside (a card) from one's hand. •*n.* /dískaard/ (often in *pl.*) a discarded item, esp. a card in a card game.

dis·cern /disə́rn/ *v.tr.* **1** perceive clearly with the mind or the senses. **2** make out by thought or by gazing, listening, etc. ▫▫ **dis·cern·i·ble** *adj.* **dis·cern·i·bly** *adv.*

dis·cern·ing /disə́rning/ *adj.* having or showing good judgment or insight. ▫▫ **dis·cern·ment** *n.*

dis·charge *v.* & *n.* •*v.* /dischaárj/ **1** *tr.* **a** let go, or release, esp. from a duty, commitment, or period of confinement. **b** relieve (a bankrupt) of residual liability. **2** *tr.* dismiss from office, employment, etc. **3** *tr.* **a** fire (a gun, etc.). **b** (of a gun, etc.) fire (a bullet, etc.). **4 a** *tr.* (also *absol.*) pour out or cause to pour out (pus, liquid, etc.) (*the wound was discharging*). **b** *tr.* throw; eject (*discharged a stone at the gopher*). **c** *tr.* utter (abuse, etc.). **d** *intr.* (foll. by *into*) (of a river, etc.) flow into. **5** *tr.* **a** carry out; perform (a duty or obligation). **b** relieve oneself of (a financial commitment) (*discharged his debt*). **6** *tr. Law* cancel (an order of court). **7** *tr. Physics* release an electrical charge from. **8** *tr.* **a** relieve (a ship, etc.) of its cargo. **b** unload (a cargo). •*n.* /díschaarj, dischaárj/ **1** the act or an instance of discharging; the process of being discharged. **2** a dismissal. **3 a** a release, exemption, acquittal, etc. **b** a written certificate of release, etc. **4** an act of firing a gun, etc. **5 a** an emission (of pus, liquid, etc.). **b** the liquid or matter so discharged. **6** (usu. foll. by *of*) **a** the payment (of a debt). **b** the performance (of a duty, etc.). **7** *Physics* **a** the release of a quantity of electric charge from an object. **b** a flow of electricity through the air or other gas, esp. when accompanied by the emission of light. **c** the conversion of chemical energy in a cell into electrical energy. **8** the unloading (of a ship or a cargo). ▫▫ **dis·charg·er** *n.* (in sense 7 of *v.*).

dis·ci·ple /disípəl/ *n.* **1** a follower or pupil of a leader, teacher, philosophy, etc. (*a disciple of Zen Buddhism*). **2** any early believer in Christ, esp. one of the twelve Apostles. ▫▫ **dis·ci·ple·ship** *n.*

dis·ci·pli·nar·i·an /dísiplináireeən/ *n.* a person who upholds or practices firm discipline.

dis·ci·pli·nar·y /dísiplinéree/ *adj.* of, promoting, or enforcing discipline.

dis·ci·pline /dísiplin/ *n.* & *v.* •*n.* **1 a** control or order exercised over people or animals. **b** the system of rules used to maintain this control. **c** the behavior of groups subjected to such rules (*poor discipline in the ranks*). **2 a** mental, moral, or physical training. **b** adversity as used to bring about such training. **3** a branch of instruction or learning. **4** punishment. **5** *Eccl.* mortification by physical self-punishment, esp. scourging. •*v.tr.* **1** punish; chastise. **2** bring under control by training in obedience.

dis·claim /diskláym/ *v.tr.* **1** deny or disown. **2** (often *absol.*) *Law* renounce a legal claim to (property, etc.).

dis·claim·er /diskláymər/ *n.* a renunciation or disavowal, esp. of responsibility.

dis·close /disklṓz/ *v.tr.* **1** make known (*disclosed the truth*). **2** expose to view.

dis·clo·sure /disklṓzhər/ *n.* **1** the act or an instance of disclosing; the process of being disclosed. **2** something disclosed; a revelation.

dis·co /dískō/ *n.* & *v. colloq.* •*n.* (*pl.* **·cos**) = DISCOTHEQUE. •*v.intr.* (**·coes, ·coed**) **1** attend a discotheque. **2** dance to disco music (*discoed the night away*).

dis·cog·ra·phy /diskógrəfee/ *n.* (*pl.* **·phies**) **1** a descriptive catalog of recordings. **2** the study of recordings.

dis·coid /dískoyd/ *adj.* disk-shaped.

dis·col·or /diskúlər/ *v.tr.* & *intr.* spoil the color of; stain; tarnish. ▫▫ **dis·col·or·a·tion** *n.*

dis·com·bob·u·late /dískəmbóbyəlayt/ *v.tr. joc.* disturb; disconcert.

dis·com·fit /diskúmfit/ *v.tr.* **1** disconcert or baffle. **2** thwart. ▫▫ **dis·com·fi·ture** *n.*

dis·com·fort /diskúmfərt/ *n.* & *v.* •*n.* **1 a** a lack of ease; slight pain (*tight collar caused discomfort*). **b** mental uneasiness (*his presence caused her discomfort*). **2** a lack of comfort. •*v.tr.* make uneasy.

dis·com·mode /dískəmṓd/ *v.tr.* inconvenience (a person, etc.).

dis·com·pose /dískəmpṓz/ *v.tr.* disturb the composure of. ▫▫ **dis·com·po·sure** /–pṓzhər/ *n.*

dis·co mu·sic *n.* popular dance music characterized by a heavy bass rhythm.

dis·con·cert /dískənsə́rt/ *v.tr.* **1** (often as **disconcerted** *adj.*) disturb the composure of; fluster (*disconcerted by his expression*). **2** spoil or upset (plans, etc.). ▫▫ **dis·con·cert·ing** *adj.* **dis·con·cert·ing·ly** *adv.*

dis·con·nect /dískənékt/ *v.tr.* **1** (often foll. by *from*) break the connection of (things, ideas, etc.). **2** put (an electrical device) out of action by disconnecting the parts, esp. by pulling out the plug. ▫▫ **dis·con·nec·tion** *n.*

dis·con·nect·ed /dískənéktid/ *adj.* **1** not connected; detached; separated. **2** (of speech, writing, argument, etc.) incoherent and illogical.

dis·con·so·late /diskónsələt/ *adj.* **1** forlorn or inconsolable. **2** unhappy or disappointed. ▫▫ **dis·con·so·late·ly** *adv.*

dis·con·tent /dískəntént/ *n., adj.,* & *v.* •*n.* lack of contentment; restlessness, dissatisfaction. •*adj.* dissatisfied. •*v.tr.* (esp. as **discontented** *adj.*) make dissatisfied. ▫▫ **dis·con·tent·ed·ly** *adv.* **dis·con·tent·ment** *n.*

dis·con·tin·ue /dískəntínyoo/ *v.* (**-continues, -continued, -continuing**) **1** *intr.* & *tr.* cease or cause to cease to exist or be made (*a discontinued line*). **2** *tr.* give up; cease from (*discontinued his visits*). **3** *tr.* cease taking or paying (a newspaper, a subscription, etc.). ▫▫ **dis·con·tin·u·ance** *n.* **dis·con·tin·u·a·tion** *n.*

dis·con·tin·u·ous /dískəntínyooəs/ *adj.* lacking continuity in space or time; intermittent. ▫▫ **dis·con·ti·nu·i·ty** /–kontinoo-itee, –nyoo–/ *n.* **dis·con·tin·u·ous·ly** *adv.*

dis·cord *n.* & *v.* •*n.* /dískawrd/ **1** disagreement; strife. **2** harsh clashing noise; clangor. **3** *Mus.* **a** a lack of harmony between notes sounding together. **b** an unpleasing or unfinished chord needing to be completed by another. •*v.intr.* /diskáwrd/ **1** (usu. foll. by *with*) **a** disagree or quarrel. **b** be different or inconsistent. **2** jar; clash; be dissonant.

dis·cord·ant /diskáwrd'nt/ *adj.* (usu. foll. by *to, from, with*) **1** disagreeing; at variance. **2** (of sounds) not in harmony; dissonant. ▫▫ **dis·cord·ance** /–d'ns/ *n.* **dis·cord·ant·ly** *adv.*

dis·co·theque /dískəték/ *n.* **1** a club, etc., for dancing to recorded popular music. **2 a** the professional lighting and sound equipment used at a discotheque. **b** a business that provides this. **3** a party with dancing to popular music, esp. using such equipment.

dis·count *n.* & *v.* •*n.* /dískownt/ **1** a deduction from a bill or amount due. **2** a deduction from the amount of a bill of exchange, etc., by a person who gives value for it before it is due. **3** the act or an instance of discounting. •*v.tr.* /diskównt/ **1** disregard as unreliable or unimportant (*discounted his story*). **2** reduce the effect of (an event, etc.) by previous action. **3** deduct (esp. an amount from a bill, etc.). **4** give or get the present worth of (a bill not yet due). ▫ **at a discount 1** below the nominal or usual price (cf. PREMIUM). **2** not in demand; depreciated. ▫▫ **dis·count·er** *n.*

dis·coun·te·nance /diskówntinəns/ *v.tr.* **1** (esp. in *passive*) disconcert. **2** refuse to countenance; show disapproval of.

dis·cour·age /diskə́rij, –kúr–/ *v.tr.* **1** deprive of courage, confidence, or energy. **2** (usu. foll. by *from*) dissuade (*discouraged her from going*). **3** inhibit or seek to prevent (an action, etc.) by showing disapproval (*smoking is discouraged*). ▫▫ **dis·cour·age·ment** *n.* **dis·cour·ag·ing·ly** *adv.*

dis·course *n.* & *v.* •*n.* /dískawrs/ **1** *literary* **a** conversation; talk. **b** a dissertation or treatise on an academic subject. **c** a lecture or sermon. **2** *Linguistics* a connected series of utterances; a text. •*v.intr.* /diskórs/ **1** talk; converse. **2** (usu. foll. by *of, on, upon*) speak or write at length.

dis·cour·te·ous /diskə́rteeəs/ *adj.* impolite; rude. ▫▫ **dis·cour·te·ous·ly** *adv.*

dis·cour·te·sy /diskə́rtəsee/ *n.* (*pl.* **-sies**) **1** bad manners; rudeness. **2** an impolite act or remark.

dis·cov·er /diskúvər/ *v.tr.* **1** (often foll. by *that* + clause) **a** find out or become aware of. **b** be the first to find or find out (*who discovered America?*). **c** devise or pioneer (*discover new techniques*). **2** give (check) in a game of chess by removing one's own obstructing piece. **3** (in show business) find and promote as a new singer, actor, etc. ▫▫ **dis·cov·er·a·ble** *adj.* **dis·cov·er·er** *n.*

dis·cov·er·y /diskúvəree/ *n.* (*pl.* **-ies**) **1 a** the act or process of discovering or being discovered. **b** an instance of this (*the discovery of a new planet*). **2** a person or thing discovered.

dis·cred·it /diskrédit/ *n.* & *v.* •*n.* **1** harm to reputation (*brought discredit on the enterprise*). **2** a person or thing causing this (*he is a discredit to his family*). **3** lack of credibility (*throws discredit on her story*). **4** the loss of commercial credit. •*v.tr.* **1** harm the good reputation of. **2** cause to be disbelieved. **3** refuse to believe.

dis·cred·it·a·ble /diskréditəbəl/ *adj.* bringing discredit; shameful. ▫▫ **dis·cred·it·a·bly** *adv.*

dis·creet /diskréet/ *adj.* (**discreeter, discreetest**) **1 a** circumspect. **b** tactful; trustworthy. **2** unobtrusive (*a discreet touch of rouge*). ▫▫ **dis·creet·ly** *adv.*

▶**Discreet,** meaning 'prudent; cautious,' and **discrete,** meaning 'separate' are different words: *Be discreet and* *don't give away the surprise. I can see three discrete possibilities causing this problem.*

dis·crep·an·cy /diskrépənsee/ *n.* (*pl.* **-cies**) **1** difference; inconsistency. **2** an instance of this. ▫▫ **dis·crep·ant** *adj.*

dis·crete /diskréet/ *adj.* individually distinct; separate; discontinuous. ▫▫ **dis·crete·ly** *adv.* **dis·crete·ness** *n.* ▶See note at DISCREET.

dis·cre·tion /diskréshən/ *n.* **1** being discreet; discreet behavior (*treats confidences with discretion*). **2** prudence; self-preservation. **3** the freedom to act and think as one wishes (*it is within his discretion to leave*). **4** *Law* a court's freedom to decide a sentence, etc. ▫ **at the discretion of** to be settled or disposed of according to the judgment or choice of. **discretion is the better part of valor** reckless courage is often self-defeating. **use one's discretion** act according to one's own judgment. **age of discretion** the esp. legal age at which a person is able to manage his or her own affairs. ▫▫ **dis·cre·tion·ar·y** *adj.*

dis·crim·i·nate /diskríminayt/ *v.* **1** *intr.* (often foll. by *between*) make or see a distinction; differentiate. **2** *intr.* make a distinction, esp. unjustly. **3** *intr.* (foll. by *against*) select for unfavorable treatment. **4** *tr.* (usu. foll. by *from*) make or see or constitute a difference in or between. **5** *intr.* (esp. as **discriminating** *adj.*) observe distinctions carefully; have good judgment. **6** *tr.* mark as distinctive; be a distinguishing feature of. ▫▫ **dis·crim·i·na·tive** /–nətiv/ *adj.* **dis·crim·i·na·tor** *n.* **dis·crim·i·na·to·ry** /–nətáwree/ *adj.*

dis·crim·i·nat·ing /diskríminayting/ *adj.* **1** able to discern distinctions. **2** having good taste.

dis·crim·i·na·tion /diskríminάyshən/ *n.* **1** unfavorable treatment based on prejudice. **2** good taste or judgment in artistic matters, etc. **3** the power of discriminating or observing differences. **4** a distinction made with the mind or in action.

dis·cur·sive /diskə́rsiv/ *adj.* **1** rambling or digressive. **2** *Philos.* proceeding by argument or reasoning (opp. INTUITIVE). ▫▫ **dis·cur·sive·ly** *adv.* **dis·cur·sive·ness** *n.*

dis·cus /dískəs/ *n.* (*pl.* **discuses**) **1** a heavy, thick-centered disk thrown in ancient Greek games. **2** a similar disk thrown in modern field events.

discus thrower

dis·cuss /diskús/ *v.tr.* **1** hold a conversation about. **2** talk or write about a topic in detail; examine different ideas (*Chapter Two discusses problems*). ▫▫ **dis·cus·sant** *n.*

dis·cus·sion /diskúshən/ *n.* **1** a conversation, esp. on specific subjects; a debate (*had a discussion about what they should do*). **2** an examination by argument.

dis·dain /disdáyn/ *n.* & *v.* •*n.* scorn; contempt. •*v.tr.* **1** regard with disdain. **2** think oneself superior to; reject (*disdained his offer; disdained to enter; disdained answering*).

dis·dain·ful /disdáynfŏŏl/ *adj.* showing disdain or contempt. ▫▫ **dis·dain·ful·ly** *adv.*

dis·ease /dizéez/ *n.* **1** an unhealthy condition of the body or the mind. **2** a corresponding physical condition of plants. **3** a particular kind of disease with special symptoms or location.

dis·eased /dizéezd/ *adj.* **1** affected with disease. **2** abnormal; disordered.

dis·em·bark /dísimbaárk/ *v.tr.* & *intr.* put or go ashore or land from a ship or an aircraft. ▫▫ **dis·em·bar·ka·tion** *n.*

dis·em·bar·rass /dísimbárəs/ *v.tr.* **1** (usu. foll. by *of*) relieve (of a load, etc.). **2** free from embarrassment.

dis·em·bod·y /dísimbódee/ *v.tr.* (**-ies, -ied**) (esp. as **disembodied** *adj.*) separate or free from the body or a concrete form (*disembodied spirit*).

dis·em·bow·el /dísimbówəl/ *v.tr.* remove the bowels or entrails of.

dis·en·chant /dísinchánt/ *v.tr.* free from enchantment; disillusion. ▫▫ **dis·en·chant·ment** *n.*

dis·en·cum·ber /dísinkúmbər/ *v.tr.* free from encumbrance.

dis·en·fran·chise var. of DISFRANCHISE.

dis·en·gage /dísingáyj/ *v.* **1 a** *tr.* detach, loosen, or separate (parts, etc.) (*disengaged the clutch*). **b** *refl.* detach oneself; get loose (*disengaged ourselves from their company*). **2** *tr. Mil.* remove (troops) from a battle or a battle area. **3** *intr.* become detached. **4** *intr.* (as **disengaged** *adj.*) **a** unoccupied; free; vacant. **b** uncommitted.

dis·en·gage·ment /dísingáyjmənt/ *n.* **1 a** the act of disengaging. **b** an instance of this. **2** freedom from ties; detachment. **3** the dissolution of an engagement to marry. **4** ease of manner or behavior.

dis·en·tan·gle /dísintánggəl/ *v.* **1** *tr.* **a** unravel; untwist. **b** free from complications; extricate (*disentangled her from the difficulty*). **2** *intr.* become disentangled. ▫▫ **dis·en·tan·gle·ment** *n.*

dis·en·ti·tle /dísintít'l/ *v.tr.* (usu. foll. by *to*) deprive of any rightful claim.

dis·es·tab·lish /dísistáblish/ *v.tr.* **1** deprive (a church) of government support. **2** depose from an official position. **3** terminate the establishment of. ▫▫ **dis·es·tab·lish·ment** *n.*

dis·fa·vor /disfáyvər/ *n.* & *v.* •*n.* **1** disapproval or dislike. **2** the state of being disliked (*fell into disfavor*). •*v.tr.* regard or treat with disfavor.

dis·fig·ure /disfígyər/ *v.tr.* spoil the beauty of; deform; deface. ▫▫ **dis·fig·ure·ment** *n.*

dis·fran·chise /disfránchīz/ *v.tr.* (also **dis·en·fran·chise** /disinfránchīz/) **1 a** deprive (a person) of the right to vote. **b** deprive (a place) of the right to send a representative to parliament. **2** deprive (a person) of rights as a citizen or of a franchise held. ▫▫ **dis·fran·chise·ment** *n.*

dis·gorge /disgáwrj/ *v.tr.* **1** eject from the throat or stomach. **2** pour forth; discharge. ▫▫ **dis·gorge·ment** *n.*

dis·grace /disgráys/ *n.* & *v.* •*n.* **1** shame; ignominy (*brought disgrace on his family*). **2** a dishonorable, inefficient, or shameful person, thing, state of affairs, etc. (*the bus service is a disgrace*). •*v.tr.* **1** bring shame or discredit on. **2** degrade from a position of honor; dismiss from favor. ▫ **in disgrace** out of favor.

dis·grace·ful /disgráysfŏŏl/ *adj.* shameful; dishonorable; degrading. ▫▫ **dis·grace·ful·ly** *adv.*

dis·grun·tled /disgrúnt'ld/ *adj.* discontented; sulky. ▫▫ **dis·grun·tle·ment** *n.*

dis·guise /disgíz/ *v.* & *n.* •*v.tr.* **1** (often foll. by *as*) alter the appearance, sound, smell, etc., of, so as to conceal the identity; make unrecognizable. **2** misrepresent or cover up (*disguised their intentions*). •*n.* **1 a** a costume, false beard, makeup, etc., used to alter the appearance so as to conceal or deceive. **b** any action, manner, etc., used for deception. **2 a** the act or practice of disguising; the concealment of reality. **b** an instance of this. ▫ **in disguise 1** wearing a concealing costume, etc. **2** appearing to be the opposite (*a blessing in disguise*).

dis·gust /disgúst/ *n.* & *v.* •*n.* (usu. foll. by *at, for*) **1** strong aversion; repugnance. **2** strong distaste for (some item of) food, drink, medicine, etc.; nausea. • *v.tr.* cause disgust in. □ **in disgust** as a result of disgust (*left in disgust*). □□ **dis·gust·ed·ly** *adv.*

dis·gust·ing /disgústing/ *adj.* arousing aversion or indignation (*disgusting behavior*). □□ **dis·gust·ing·ly** *adv.*

dish /dish/ *n. & v.* • *n.* **1 a** a shallow container for cooking or serving food. **b** the food served in a dish (*all the dishes were delicious*). **c** a particular kind of food (*a meat dish*). **2** (in *pl.*) dirty plates, utensils, cooking pots, etc., after a meal. **3 a** a dish-shaped object, or cavity. **b** = SATELLITE DISH. **4** *sl.* a sexually attractive person. • *v.tr.* **1** put (food) into a dish ready for serving. **2** *colloq.* outmaneuver. **3** make concave or dish-shaped. □ **dish out** *sl.* distribute. **dish up 1** serve or prepare to serve (food). **2** *colloq.* seek to present (facts, argument, etc.) attractively. □□ **dish·ful** *n.* (*pl.* **-fuls**).

dis·har·mo·ny /dis-haármənee/ *n.* a lack of harmony; discord. □□ **dis·har·mo·ni·ous** /–mṓneeəs/ *adj.*

dish·cloth /díshklawth, –kloth/ *n.* a cloth for washing or drying dishes.

dis·heart·en /dis-haárt'n/ *v.tr.* cause to lose courage or confidence; make despondent. □□ **dis·heart·en·ing·ly** *adv.* **dis·heart·en·ment** *n.*

di·shev·eled /dishévəld/ *adj.* untidy; ruffled; disordered. □□ **di·shev·el** *v.tr.* **di·shev·el·ment** *n.*

dis·hon·est /disónist/ *adj.* fraudulent or insincere. □□ **dis·hon·est·ly** *adv.* **dis·hon·es·ty** /disónistee/ *n.* (*pl.* **-ties**)

dis·hon·or /disónər/ *n. & v.* • *n.* **1** a state of shame or disgrace. **2** something that causes dishonor. • *v.tr.* **1** treat without honor or respect. **2** disgrace (*dishonored his name*). **3** refuse to accept or pay (a check or a bill of exchange).

dis·hon·or·a·ble /disónərəbəl/ *adj.* **1** causing disgrace; ignominious. **2** unprincipled. □□ **dis·hon·or·a·bly** *adv.*

dish·pan /díshpan/ *n.* a large, deep, usu. circular pan for washing dishes.

dish·wash·er /díshwoshər, –wawshər/ *n.* **1** a machine for automatically washing dishes. **2** a person employed to wash dishes.

dish·wa·ter /díshwawtər, –woter/ *n.* water in which dishes have been washed. □ **dull as dishwater** extremely dull; boring.

dis·il·lu·sion /dísilóózhən/ *n. & v.* • *n.* freedom from illusions. • *v.tr.* disenchant. □□ **dis·il·lu·sion·ment** *n.*

dis·in·cline /dísinklín/ *v.tr.* (usu. foll. by *to* + infin. or *for*) **1** make unwilling or reluctant. **2** (as **disinclined** *adj.*) unwilling; averse. □□ **dis·in·cli·na·tion** /dísinklináyshən/ *n.*

dis·in·fect /dísinfékt/ *v.tr.* cleanse (a wound, a room, clothing, etc.) of infection, esp. with a disinfectant. □□ **dis·in·fect·ant** *n. & adj.* **dis·in·fec·tion** /–fékshən/ *n.*

dis·in·gen·u·ous /dísinjényóóəs/ *adj.* having secret motives; insincere. □□ **dis·in·gen·u·ous·ly** *adv.* **dis·in·gen·u·ous·ness** *n.*

dis·in·her·it /dísinhérit/ *v.tr.* reject as one's heir; deprive of the right of inheritance. □□ **dis·in·her·i·tance** *n.*

dis·in·te·grate /disíntigrayt/ *v.* **1** *tr. & intr.* **a** separate into component parts or fragments. **b** lose or cause to lose cohesion. **2** *intr. colloq.* deteriorate mentally or physically. **3** *intr. & tr. Physics* undergo or cause to undergo disintegration. □□ **dis·in·te·gra·tor** *n.*

dis·in·te·gra·tion /disíntigráyshən/ *n.* **1** the act or an instance of disintegrating. **2** *Physics* any process in which a nucleus emits a particle or particles or divides into smaller nuclei.

dis·in·ter /dísintér/ *v.tr.* (**disinterred, disinterring**) **1** remove (esp. a corpse) from the ground; unearth. **2** find after a protracted search (*disinterred the letter from the back of the drawer*). □□ **dis·in·ter·ment** *n.*

dis·in·ter·est /disíntrist, –íntərist/ *n.* **1** impartiality. **2** *disp.* lack of interest; unconcern.

dis·in·ter·est·ed /disíntristid, –íntəri–/ *adj.* **1** not influenced by one's own advantage. **2** *disp.* uninterested. □□ **dis·in·ter·est·ed·ly** *adv.* **dis·in·ter·est·ed·ness** *n.*

▶**Disinterested** means 'not having a personal interest, impartial': *A juror must be disinterested in the case being tried.* **Uninterested** means 'not interested; indifferent': *On the other hand, a juror must not be uninterested.*

dis·joint /disjóynt/ *v. & adj.* • *v.tr.* **1** take apart at the joints. **2** (as **disjointed** *adj.*) (esp. of conversation) incoherent. **3** disturb the working or connection of. • *adj.* (of two or more sets) having no elements in common. □□ **dis·joint·ed·ly** *adv.* **dis·joint·ed·ness** *n.*

disk /disk/ *n.* (also **disc**) **1 a** a flat thin circular object. **b** a round, flat or apparently flat surface (*the sun's disk*). **c** a mark of this shape. **2** a layer of cartilage between vertebrae. **3 a** a phonograph record. **b** = COMPACT DISK. **4 a** (in full **magnetic disk**) a computer storage device consisting of several flat, circular, magnetically coated plates formed into a rotatable disk. **b** (in full **optical disc** or **disk**) a smooth nonmagnetic disk for data recorded and read by laser.

disk brake *n.* (often **disc brake**) a brake employing the friction of pads against a disk.

disk drive *n. Computing* a mechanism for rotating a disk and reading or writing data from or to it.

disk·ette /diskét/ *n. Computing* = FLOPPY DISK.

disk har·row *n.* a harrow with cutting edges consisting of a row of concave disks set at an oblique angle.

disk jock·ey *n.* (also **disc jock·ey**) the presenter of a selection of phonograph records, compact discs, etc., of popular music.

dis·like /dislík/ *v. & n.* • *v.tr.* have an aversion or objection to; not like. • *n.* **1** a feeling of repugnance or not liking. **2** an object of dislike. □□ **dis·lik·a·ble** *adj.* (also **dis·like·a·ble**) .

dis·lo·cate /díslōkayt, dislṓ–/ *v.tr.* **1** disturb the normal connection of (esp. a joint in the body). **2** disrupt; put out of order. **3** displace. □□ **dis·lo·ca·tion** /díslōkáyshən/ *n.*

dis·lodge /dislój/ *v.tr.* remove from an established or fixed position. □□ **dis·lodg·ment** *n.* (also **dis·lodge·ment**) .

dis·loy·al /dislóyəl/ *adj.* (often foll. by *to*) **1** not loyal; unfaithful. **2** untrue to one's allegiance. □□ **dis·loy·al·ly** *adv.* **dis·loy·al·ty** *n.*

dis·mal /dízməl/ *adj.* **1** causing or showing gloom; miserable. **2** dreary or somber. **3** *colloq.* feeble or inept (*a dismal performance*). □□ **dis·mal·ly** *adv.*

dismal late Middle English: from earlier *dismal* (noun), denoting the two days in each month that in medieval times were believed to be unlucky, from Anglo-Norman French *dis mal*, from medieval Latin *dies mali* 'evil days.'

dis·man·tle /dismánt'l/ *v.tr.* **1** take to pieces; pull down. **2** deprive of defenses or equipment. **3** (often foll. by *of*) strip of covering or protection. □□ **dis·man·tle·ment** *n.* **dis·man·tler** *n.*

dis·may /dismáy/ *v. & n.* • *v.tr.* fill with consternation or anxiety; reduce to despair. • *n.* **1** consternation or anxiety. **2** depression or despair.

dis·mem·ber /dismémbər/ *v.tr.* **1** tear or cut the limbs from. **2** divide up (a country, etc.). □□ **dis·mem·ber·ment** *n.*

dis·miss /dismís/ *v.* **1 a** *tr.* cause to leave one's presence; disperse (an assembly or army). **b** *intr.* (of an assembly, etc.) break ranks. **2** *tr.* discharge from employment, office, etc., esp. dishonorably. **3** *tr.* put out of one's thoughts (*dismissed him from memory*). **4** *tr.*

treat summarily (*dismissed his application*). **5** *tr. Law* refuse further hearing to (a case). ▫▫ **dis·miss·al** *n.* **dis·miss·i·ble** *adj.*

dis·mis·sive /dismísiv/ *adj.* tending to dismiss from consideration. ▫▫ **dis·mis·sive·ly** *adv.* **dis·mis·sive·ness** *n.*

dis·mount *v. & n.* •*v.* /dismównt/ **1 a** *intr.* alight from a horse, bicycle, etc. **b** *tr.* (usu. in *passive*) throw from a horse; unseat. **2** *tr.* remove (a thing) from its mounting (esp. a gun from its carriage). •*n.* /dismównt, dís–/ the act of dismounting.

dis·o·be·di·ent /dísəbeédeeənt/ *adj.* disobeying; rebellious. ▫▫ **dis·o·be·di·ence** /–deeəns/ *n.* **dis·o·be·di·ent·ly** *adv.*

dis·o·bey /dísəbáy/ *v.tr.* (also *absol.*) fail or refuse to obey; disregard (orders); break (rules).

dis·o·blige /dísəblíj/ *v.tr.* **1** refuse to consider the convenience or wishes of. **2** (as **disobliging** *adj.*) uncooperative.

dis·or·der /disáwrdər/ *n. & v.* •*n.* **1** a lack of order; confusion. **2** a riot; a commotion. **3** *Med.* a usu. minor ailment or disease. •*v.tr.* **1** throw into confusion; disarrange. **2** *Med.* upset.

dis·or·der·ly /disáwrdərlee/ *adj.* **1** untidy; confused. **2** unruly; riotous. **3** *Law* contrary to public order or morality. ▫▫ **dis·or·der·li·ness** *n.*

dis·or·gan·ize /disáwrgənīz/ *v.tr.* **1** destroy the system or order of. **2** (as **disorganized** *adj.*) lacking organization or system. ▫▫ **dis·or·gan·i·za·tion** *n.*

dis·o·ri·ent /disáwreeənt/ *v.tr.* **1** confuse (a person) as to his or her bearings. **2** (often as **disoriented** *adj.*) confuse (a person) (*disoriented by his unexpected behavior*).

dis·o·ri·en·tate /disáwriəntayt/ *v.tr.* = DISORIENT. ▫▫ **dis·o·ri·en·ta·tion** /–táyshən/ *n.*

dis·own /disṓn/ *v.tr.* **1** refuse to recognize; repudiate. **2** renounce one's connection with or allegiance to.

dis·par·age /dispárij/ *v.tr.* **1** speak slightingly of; depreciate. **2** bring discredit on. ▫▫ **dis·par·age·ment** *n.* **dis·par·ag·ing·ly** *adv.*

dis·pa·rate /dispərət, dispár–/ *adj. & n.* •*adj.* essentially different in kind; without comparison or relation. •*n.* (in *pl.*) things so unlike that there is no basis for their comparison. ▫▫ **dis·pa·rate·ly** *adv.* **dis·pa·rate·ness** *n.* **dis·par·i·ty** /dispáritee/ *n.* (*pl.* **-ties**).

dis·pas·sion·ate /dispáshənət/ *adj.* free from passion; calm; impartial. ▫▫ **dis·pas·sion·ate·ly** *adv.* **dis·pas·sion·ate·ness** *n.*

dis·patch /dispách/ *v. & n.* (also **des·patch**) •*v.tr.* **1** send off to a destination or for a purpose. **2** perform (business, a task, etc.) promptly. **3** kill; execute. **4** *colloq.* eat (food, a meal, etc.) quickly. •*n.* **1** the act or an instance of sending. **2** the act or an instance of killing. **3** (also /díspach/) **a** an official written message on state or esp. military affairs. **b** a report sent in by a newspaper's correspondent. **4** promptness (*done with dispatch*). ▫▫ **dis·patch·er** *n.*

dis·pel /dispél/ *v.tr.* (**dispelled, dispelling**) dissipate; disperse; scatter.

dis·pen·sa·ble /dispénsəbəl/ *adj.* **1** able to be done without; unnecessary. **2** (of a law, etc.) able to be relaxed in special cases. ▫▫ **dis·pen·sa·bil·i·ty** *n.*

dis·pen·sa·ry /dispénsəree/ *n.* (*pl.* **-ries**) **1** a place where medicines, etc., are dispensed. **2** a public or charitable institution for medical advice and the dispensing of medicines.

dis·pen·sa·tion /dispensáyshən/ *n.* **1 a** the act or an instance of dispensing or distributing. **b** (foll. by *with*) the state of doing without (a thing). **c** something distributed. **2** (usu. foll. by *from*) exemption from a penalty, duty or religious observance; an instance of this. **3** a religious or political system obtaining in a nation, etc. **4 a** the ordering or management of the world by providence. **b** a specific example of such ordering (of a community, a person, etc.). ▫▫ **dis·pen·sa·tion·al** *adj.*

dis·pense /dispéns/ *v.* **1** *tr.* distribute; deal out. **2** *tr.* administer (a sacrament, justice, etc.). **3** *tr.* make up and give out (medicine, etc.) according to a doctor's prescription. **4** *tr.* (usu. foll. by *from*) grant a dispensation to (a person) from an obligation, esp. a religious observance. **5** *intr.* (foll. by *with*) **a** do without; render needless. **b** give exemption from (a rule).

dis·pens·er /dispénsər/ *n.* a person or thing that dispenses something, e.g., medicine, good advice, cash.

dis·perse /dispə́rs/ *v.* **1** *intr. & tr.* go, send, drive, or distribute in different directions or over a wide area. **2 a** *intr.* (of people at a meeting, etc.) leave and go their various ways. **b** *tr.* cause to do this. **3** *tr.* send to or station at separate points. **4** *tr.* disseminate. ▫▫ **dis·per·sal** *n.* **dis·pers·er** *n.* **dis·pers·i·ble** *adj.* **dis·per·sion** *n.* **dis·per·sive** *adj.*

dis·pir·it /dispírit/ *v.tr.* **1** (esp. as **dispiriting** *adj.*) make despondent; discourage. **2** (as **dispirited** *adj.*) dejected; discouraged. ▫▫ **dis·pir·it·ed·ly** *adv.* **dis·pir·it·ed·ness** *n.* **dis·pir·it·ing·ly** *adv.*

dis·place /displáys/ *v.tr.* **1** shift from its accustomed place. **2** remove from office. **3** take the place of; oust.

dis·placed per·son *n.* a person who is forced to leave his or her home country because of war, persecution, etc.; a refugee.

dis·place·ment /displáysmənt/ *n.* **1 a** the act or an instance of displacing; the process of being displaced. **b** an instance of this. **2** *Physics* the amount of a fluid displaced by a solid floating or immersed in it. **3** *Psychol.* **a** the substitution of one idea or impulse for another. **b** the unconscious transfer of strong unacceptable emotions from one object to another. **4** the amount by which a thing is shifted from its place.

dis·play /displáy/ *v. & n.* •*v.tr.* **1** expose to view; exhibit. **2** show ostentatiously. **3** reveal (*displayed his ignorance*). •*n.* **1** the act or an instance of displaying. **2** an exhibition or show. **3** ostentation; flashiness. **4** the distinct behavior of some animals used to attract a mate. **5 a** the presentation of signals or data on a visual display unit, etc. **b** the information so presented. ▫▫ **dis·play·er** *n.*

dis·please /displéez/ *v.tr.* make indignant or angry; offend; annoy. ▫ **be displeased** (often foll. by *at, with*) be indignant or dissatisfied; disapprove. ▫▫ **dis·pleas·ing** *adj.* **dis·pleas·ing·ly** *adv.*

dis·pleas·ure /displézhər/ *n.* disapproval; anger; dissatisfaction.

dis·port /dispáwrt/ *v.intr. & refl.* frolic; gambol; enjoy oneself.

dis·pos·a·ble /dispṓzəbəl/ *adj. & n.* •*adj.* **1** intended to be used once and then thrown away. **2** that can be got rid of, made over, or used. **3** (esp. of assets) at the owner's disposal. •*n.* a thing designed to be thrown away after one use. ▫▫ **dis·pos·a·bil·i·ty** *n.*

dis·pos·a·ble in·come *n.* income after taxes, etc., available for spending.

dis·pos·al /dispṓzəl/ *n.* (usu. foll. by *of*) **1** the act or an instance of disposing of something. **2** the arrangement, disposition, or placing of something. **3** control or management (of a person, business, etc.). **4** (esp. as **garbage disposal**) an electric device under a sink for grinding up food waste so it can be flushed down the drain. ▫ **at one's disposal 1** available for one's use. **2** subject to one's orders or decisions.

dis·pose /dispṓz/ *v.* **1** *tr.* (usu. foll. by *to*, or *to* + infin.) **a** make willing; incline (*disposed him to the idea*). **b** give a tendency to (*disposed to buckle*). **2** *tr.* place suitably (*disposed the pictures in sequence*). **3** *tr.* (as **disposed** *adj.*) have a specified mental inclination (usu. in *comb.*: *ill-disposed*). **4** *intr.* determine the course of events (*man *proposes, God disposes*). ▫ **dispose of 1 a** deal with. **b** get rid of. **c** finish. **d** kill. **e** distribute; dispense; bestow. **2** sell. **3** prove (a claim, an argument, an opponent, etc.) to be incorrect. **4** consume (food). ▫▫ **dis•pos•er** *n.*

dis•po•si•tion /díspəzíshən/ *n.* **1 a** (often foll. by *to*) a natural tendency; an inclination. **b** a person's temperament. **2 a** setting in order; arranging. **b** the relative position of parts; an arrangement. **3** (usu. in *pl.*) **a** *Mil.* the stationing of troops ready for attack or defense. **b** preparations; plans. **4 a** a bestowal by deed or will. **b** control; the power of disposing. **5** ordinance; dispensation.

dis•pos•sess /díspəzés/ *v.tr.* **1** oust (a person). **2** (usu. foll. by *of*) deprive. ▫▫ **dis•pos•ses•sion** /–zéshən/ *n.*

dis•proof /disprо́оf/ *n.* **1** something that disproves. **2 a** refutation. **b** an instance of this.

dis•pro•por•tion /díspropáwrshən/ *n.* **1** a lack of proportion. **2** an instance of this. ▫▫ **dis•pro•por•tion•al** *adj.* **dis•pro•por•tion•al•ly** *adv.*

dis•pro•por•tion•ate /dísprəpáwrshənət/ *adj.* **1** lacking proportion. **2** relatively too large, long, etc. ▫▫ **dis•pro•por•tion•ate•ly** *adv.* **dis•pro•por•tion•ate•ness** *n.*

dis•prove /disprо́оv/ *v.tr.* prove false. ▫▫ **dis•prov•a•ble** *adj.*

dis•put•a•ble /dispyо́оtəbəl/ *adj.* open to question; uncertain. ▫▫ **dis•put•a•bly** *adv.*

dis•pu•ta•tion /díspyətáyshən/ *n.* **1 a** disputing; debating. **b** an argument; a controversy. **2** a formal debate.

dis•pu•ta•tious /díspyətáyshəs/ *adj.* fond of or inclined to argument. ▫▫ **dis•pu•ta•tious•ly** *adv.* **dis•pu•ta•tious•ness** *n.*

dis•pute /dispyо́оt/ *v.* & *n.* • *v.* **1** *intr.* (usu. foll. by *with, against*) **a** debate; argue. **b** quarrel. **2** *tr.* discuss, esp. heatedly (*disputed whether it was true*). **3** *tr.* question the truth or correctness or validity of (a statement, alleged fact, etc.). **4** *tr.* contend for; strive to win (*disputed the crown*). **5** *tr.* resist (a landing, advance, etc.). *n.* **1** a controversy; a debate. **2** a quarrel. **3** a disagreement leading to industrial action. ▫ **beyond** (or **past** or **without**) **dispute 1** certainly; indisputably. **2** certain; indisputable. **in dispute 1** being argued about. **2** (of a workforce) involved in industrial action. ▫▫ **dis•pu•tant** /–spyо́оt'nt/ *n.* **dis•put•er** *n.*

dis•qual•i•fy /diskwólifī/ *v.tr.* (**-fies, -fied**) **1** (often foll. by *from*) debar from a competition or pronounce ineligible as a winner. **2** (often foll. by *for, from*) make or pronounce ineligible or unsuitable (*his age disqualifies him*). **3** (often foll. by *from*) incapacitate legally; pronounce unqualified (*disqualified from practicing as a doctor*). ▫▫ **dis•qual•i•fi•ca•tion** /diskwólifikáyshən/ *n.*

dis•qui•et /diskwíət/ *v.* & *n.* • *v.tr.* worry. • *n.* anxiety; unrest. ▫▫ **dis•qui•et•ing** *adj.* **dis•qui•et•ing•ly** *adv.*

dis•qui•e•tude /diskwíətood, –tyood/ *n.* a state of uneasiness; anxiety.

dis•qui•si•tion /dískwizíshən/ *n.* a long or elaborate treatise or discourse.

dis•re•gard /dísrigaárd/ *v.* & *n.* • *v.tr.* **1** pay no attention to; ignore. **2** treat as of no importance. • *n.* (often foll. by *of, for*) indifference; neglect.

dis•re•pair /dísripáir/ *n.* poor condition due to neglect.

dis•rep•u•ta•ble /disrépyətəbəl/ *adj.* **1** of bad reputation; discreditable. **2** not respectable in appearance; dirty; untidy. ▫▫ **dis•rep•u•ta•ble•ness** *n.* **dis•rep•u•ta•bly** *adv.*

dis•re•pute /dísripyо́оt/ *n.* a lack of good reputation or respectability; discredit.

dis•re•spect /dísrispékt/ *n.* a lack of respect; discourtesy. ▫▫ **dis•re•spect•ful** *adj.* **dis•re•spect•ful•ly** *adv.*

dis•robe /disrо́b/ *v.tr.* & *refl.* (also *absol.*) **1** undress. **2** divest (oneself or another) of office, authority, etc.

dis•rupt /disrúpt/ *v.tr.* **1** interrupt the flow or continuity of. **2** separate forcibly; shatter. ▫▫ **dis•rupt•er** *n.* (also **dis•rup•tor**). **dis•rup•tion** /–rúpshən/ *n.* **dis•rup•tive** *adj.* **dis•rup•tive•ly** *adv.* **dis•rup•tive•ness** *n.*

diss /dis/ var. of DIS.

dis•sat•is•fy /disátisfī/ *v.tr.* (**-fies, -fied**) (often as **dissatisfied** *adj.*) make discontented; fail to satisfy. ▫▫ **dis•sat•is•fac•tion** /–fákshən/ *n.* **dis•sat•is•fied•ly** *adv.*

dis•sect /disékt, dī–/ *v.tr.* **1** cut into pieces. **2** cut up (a plant or animal) to examine its parts, structure, etc., or (a corpse) for a post mortem. **3** analyze; criticize or examine in detail. ▫▫ **dis•sec•tion** /–sékshən/ *n.* **dis•sec•tor** *n.*

dis•sem•ble /disémbəl/ *v.* **1** *intr.* talk or act hypocritically. **2** *tr.* **a** disguise or conceal (a feeling, intention, act, etc.). **b** simulate (*dissembled grief in public*). ▫▫ **dis•sem•blance** *n.* **dis•sem•bler** *n.*

dis•sem•i•nate /diséminayt/ *v.tr.* scatter about; spread (esp. ideas) widely. ▫▫ **dis•sem•i•na•tion** /–náyshən/ *n.* **dis•sem•i•na•tor** *n.*

dis•sen•sion /disénshən/ *n.* disagreement giving rise to discord.

dis•sent /disént/ *v.* & *n.* • *v.intr.* (often foll. by *from*) **1** think differently; disagree; express disagreement. **2** differ in religious opinion, esp. from the doctrine of an established or orthodox church. • *n.* **1 a** a difference of opinion. **b** an expression of this. **2** the refusal to accept the doctrines of an established or orthodox church; nonconformity. ▫▫ **dis•sent•er** *n.* **dis•sent•ing** *adj.*

dis•ser•ta•tion /dísərtáyshən/ *n.* a detailed discourse on a subject, esp. one submitted in partial fulfillment of the requirements of a degree or diploma.

dis•serv•ice /dis-sə́rvis/ *n.* an ill turn; a harmful action.

dis•si•dent /dísid'nt/ *adj.* & *n.* • *adj.* disagreeing, esp. with an established government, system, etc. • *n.* a dissident person. ▫▫ **dis•si•dence** /dísid'ns/ *n.*

dis•sim•i•lar /disímilər/ *adj.* (often foll. by *to*) unlike; not similar. ▫▫ **dis•sim•i•lar•i•ty** /–láritee/ *n.* (*pl.* **-ties**).

dis•sim•i•late /disímilayt/ *v.* (often foll. by *to*) *Phonet.* **1** *tr.* change (a sound or sounds in a word) to another when the word originally had the same sound repeated, as in *cinnamon*, orig. *cinnamom*. **2** *intr.* (of a sound) be changed in this way. ▫▫ **dis•sim•i•la•tion** /–láyshən/ *n.* **dis•sim•i•la•tory** /–lətáwree/ *adj.*

dis•sim•u•late /disímyəlayt/ *v.tr.* & *intr.* dissemble. ▫▫ **dis•sim•u•la•tion** /–láyshən/ *n.*

dis•si•pate /dísipayt/ *v.* **1 a** *intr.* disperse or scatter (*the cloud of smoke dissipated*). **b** *intr.* (of a feeling or other intangible thing) disappear or be dispelled (*her concern for him had wholly dissipated*) **3** *tr.* cause (a feeling or other intangible thing) to disappear or disperse (*he wanted to dissipate his anger*). **3** *tr.* squander (money, energy, or resources). **4** *intr.* (as **dissipated** *adj.*) dissolute. ▫▫ **dis•si•pa•tive** *adj.* **dis•si•pa•tor** *n.*

dis•si•pa•tion /dísipáyshən/ *n.* **1** intemperate or dissolute living. **2** (usu. foll. by *of*) wasteful expenditure (*dissipation of resources*). **3** scattering, dispersion, or disintegration. **4** a frivolous amusement.

dis•so•ci•ate /disо́sheeayt, –seeayt/ *v.tr.* & *intr.* (usu. foll. by *from*) disconnect or become disconnected. ▫▫ **dis•so•ci•a•tion** /disо́seeáyshən, –shee–/ *n.* **dis•so•ci•a•tive** /–sheeətiv, –seeətiv/ *adj.*

dis•so•lute /dísəloot/ *adj.* lax in morals; licentious. ▫▫ **dis•so•lute•ly** *adv.* **dis•so•lute•ness** *n.*

dis•so•lu•tion /dísəlо́оshən/ *n.* **1** disintegration; decomposition. **2** (usu. foll. by *of*) the undoing or relaxing of a bond, esp.: **a** a marriage. **b** a partnership. **c** an alliance. **3** the dismissal or dispersal of an assembly, esp. of a parliament at the end of its term. **4** death.

5 bringing or coming to an end; fading away; disappearance. **6** dissipation; debauchery.

dis·solve /dizólv/ *v. & n.* • *v.* **1** *tr. & intr.* make or become liquid, esp. by immersion or dispersion in a liquid. **2** *intr. & tr.* disappear or cause to disappear gradually. **3 a** *tr.* dismiss (an assembly, esp. parliament). **b** *intr.* (of an assembly) be dissolved (cf. DISSOLUTION 3). **4** *tr.* annul (a partnership, marriage, etc.). **5** *intr.* (of a person) become emotionally overcome. **6** *intr.* (often foll. by *into*) *Cinematog.* change gradually (from one picture into another). • *n. Cinematog.* the act or process of dissolving a picture. □□ **dis·solv·a·ble** *adj.*

dis·so·nant /dísənənt/ *adj.* **1** *Mus.* harsh-toned; inharmonious. **2** incongruous. □□ **dis·so·nance** /–nəns/ *n.* **dis·so·nant·ly** *adv.*

dis·suade /diswáyd/ *v.tr.* (often foll. by *from*) discourage (a person); persuade against. □□ **dis·sua·sion** /–swáyzhən/ *n.* **dis·sua·sive** *adj.*

dis·taff /dístaf/ *n.* **a** a cleft stick holding wool or flax wound for spinning by hand. **b** the corresponding part of a spinning wheel.

dis·taff side *n.* the female branch of a family.

dis·tance /dístəns/ *n. & v.* • *n.* **1** remoteness. **2 a** a space or interval between two things. **b** the length of this (*a distance of twenty miles*). **3** a distant point or place. **4** aloofness; reserve. **5** a remoter field of vision (*in the distance*). **6** an interval of time (*can't remember at this distance*). **7 a** the full length of a race, etc. **b** *Boxing* the scheduled length of a fight. • *v.tr.* (often *refl.*) **1** place far off (*distanced herself from them*). **2** leave far behind in a race or competition. □ **at a distance** far off. **go the distance 1** *Boxing* complete a fight without being knocked out. **2** complete a hard task; endure an ordeal. **keep one's distance** maintain one's reserve.

dis·tant /dístənt/ *adj.* **1 a** far away in space or time. **b** (usu. *predic.*; often foll. by *from*) at a specified distance (*three miles distant*). **2** remote in position, time, etc. (*distant prospect; distant relation*). **3** reserved; cool (*a distant nod*). **4** abstracted (*a distant stare*). **5** faint; vague (*a distant memory*). □□ **dis·tant·ly** *adv.*

dis·taste /distáyst/ *n.* (usu. foll. by *for*) dislike; aversion. □□ **dis·taste·ful** *adj.* **dis·taste·ful·ly** *adv.* **dis·taste·ful·ness** *n.*

dis·tem·per[1] /distémpər/ *n. & v.* • *n.* **1** a kind of paint using glue or size instead of an oil base. **2** a method of mural and poster painting using this. • *v.tr.* paint with distemper.

dis·tem·per[2] /distémpər/ *n.* a disease of esp. dogs, causing fever, coughing, and catarrh.

dis·tend /disténd/ *v.tr. & intr.* swell out by pressure from within (*distended stomach*). □□ **dis·ten·si·ble** /–sténsibəl/ *adj.* **dis·ten·si·bil·i·ty** /–sténsibílitee/ *n.* **dis·ten·sion** /–sténshən/ *n.*

dis·till /distíl/ *v.* **1** *tr. Chem.* purify (a liquid) by vaporizing then condensing it and collecting the result. **2** *tr.* **a** *Chem.* extract the essence of (a plant, etc.) usu. by heating it in a solvent. **b** extract the essential meaning of (an idea, etc.). **3** *tr.* make (whiskey, essence, etc.) by distilling raw materials. **4** *tr.* (foll. by *off, out*) *Chem.* drive (the volatile constituent) off or out by heat. **5** *tr. & intr.* come as or give forth in drops; exude. **6** *intr.* undergo distillation. □□ **dis·til·late** /dístilit, –áyt/ *n.* **dis·til·la·tion** /dístiláyshən/ *n.* **dis·til·la·to·ry** *adj.*

dis·till·er /distílər/ *n.* a person who distills, esp. a manufacturer of alcoholic liquor.

dis·till·er·y /distíləree/ *n.* (*pl.* **-ies**) a place where alcoholic liquor is distilled.

dis·tinct /distíngkt/ *adj.* **1** (often foll. by *from*) **a** not identical; separate; individual. **b** different in kind or quality; unlike. **2 a** clearly perceptible. **b** clearly understandable. **3** unmistakable (*a distinct impression of being watched*). □□ **dis·tinct·ly** *adv.* **dis·tinct·ness** *n.*

dis·tinc·tion /distíngkshən/ *n.* **1 a** the act or an instance of discriminating or distinguishing. **b** the difference made by distinguishing. **2 a** something that differentiates, e.g., a mark, name, or title. **b** the fact of being different. **3** special consideration or honor. **4** excellence; eminence. **5** a grade in an examination denoting great excellence (*passed with distinction*).

dis·tinc·tive /distíngktiv/ *adj.* distinguishing; characteristic. □□ **dis·tinc·tive·ly** *adv.* **dis·tinc·tive·ness** *n.*

dis·tin·guish /distínggwish/ *v.* **1** *tr.* (often foll. by *from*) **a** see or point out the difference of (*cannot distinguish one from the other*). **b** constitute such a difference (*the mole distinguishes him from his twin*). **c** draw distinctions between; differentiate. **2** *tr.* characterize (*distinguished by her greed*). **3** *tr.* discover by listening, looking, etc. (*could distinguish two voices*). **4** *tr.* (usu. *refl.*; often foll. by *by*) make prominent or noteworthy. **5** *tr.* (often foll. by *into*) divide; classify. **6** *intr.* (foll. by *between*) make or point out a difference between. □□ **dis·tin·guish·a·ble** *adj.*

dis·tin·guished /distínggwisht/ *adj.* **1** (often foll. by *for, by*) of high standing; eminent; famous. **2** having an air of distinction, dignity, etc.

dis·tort /distáwrt/ *v.tr.* **1 a** put out of shape; make crooked or unshapely. **b** distort the appearance of, esp. by curved mirrors, etc. **2** misrepresent. □□ **dis·tort·ed·ly** *adv.* **dis·tort·ed·ness** *n.* **dis·tor·tion** /distáwrshən/ *n.*

dis·tract /distrákt/ *v.tr.* **1** (often foll. by *from*) draw away the attention of. **2** bewilder; perplex. **3** (as **distracted** *adj.*) troubled or distraught. **4** amuse, esp. in order to take the attention from pain. □□ **dis·tract·ed·ly** *adv.*

dis·trac·tion /distrákshən/ *n.* **1 a** the act of distracting, esp. the mind. **b** something that distracts. **2** a relaxation; an amusement. **3** a lack of concentration. **4** confusion; perplexity. **5** frenzy; madness. □ **to distraction** almost to a state of madness.

dis·trait /distráy/ *adj.* (*fem.* **distraite** /–stráyt/) not paying attention; distraught.

dis·traught /distráwt/ *adj.* distracted with worry, fear, etc.; extremely agitated.

dis·tress /distrés/ *n. & v.* • *n.* **1** severe pain, sorrow, anguish, etc. **2** the lack of money or comforts. **3** breathlessness; exhaustion. • *v.tr.* **1** subject to distress. **2** cause anxiety to; make unhappy. □ **in distress 1** suffering or in danger. **2** (of a ship, aircraft, etc.) in danger or damaged. □□ **dis·tress·ful** *adj.* **dis·tress·ing·ly** *adv.*

dis·tressed /distrést/ *adj.* **1** suffering from distress. **2** impoverished (*in distressed circumstances*). **3** (of furniture, leather, etc.) having simulated marks of age and wear.

dis·trib·u·tar·y /distríbyəteree/ *n.* (*pl.* **-ies**) a branch of a river or glacier that does not return to the main stream after leaving it (as in a delta).

dis·trib·ute /distríbyōōt/ *v.tr.* **1** give shares of; deal out. **2** spread about; scatter. **3** divide into parts; arrange; classify. □□ **dis·trib·ut·a·ble** *adj.*

dis·tri·bu·tion /dístribyóōshən/ *n.* **1** the act or an instance of distributing; the process of being distributed. **2** *Econ.* **a** the dispersal of goods, etc., among consumers, brought about by commerce. **b** the extent to which different groups, classes, or individuals share in the total production or wealth of a community. **3** *Statistics* the way in which a characteristic is spread over members of a class. □□ **dis·tri·bu·tion·al** *adj.*

dis·tri·bu·tive /distríbyətiv/ *adj. & n.* • *adj.* **1** of, concerned with, or produced by distribution. **2** *Logic & Gram.* (of a pronoun, etc.) referring to each individual of a class, not to the class collectively (e.g., *each*, *either*). •*n. Gram.* a distributive word. ▫▫ **dis·tri·bu·tive·ly** *adv.*

dis·trib·u·tor /distríbyətər/ *n.* **1** a person or thing that distributes. **2** an agent who supplies goods. **3** *Electr.* a device in an internal combustion engine for passing current to each spark plug in turn.

dis·trict /dístrikt/ *n. & v.* •*n.* **1** (often *attrib.*) a territory marked off for special administrative purposes. **2** an area which has common characteristics; a region (*the wine-growing district*). •*v.tr.* divide into districts.

dis·trict at·tor·ney *n.* the prosecuting officer of a district.

dis·trust /distrúst/ *n. & v.* •*n.* a lack of trust; doubt; suspicion. •*v.tr.* have no trust or confidence in; doubt. ▫▫ **dis·trust·ful** *adj.* **dis·trust·ful·ly** *adv.*

dis·turb /distə́rb/ *v.tr.* **1** break the rest, calm, or quiet of; interrupt. **2 a** agitate; worry (*your story disturbs me*). **b** irritate. **3** move from a settled position; disarrange (*the papers had been disturbed*). **4** (as **disturbed** *adj.*) *Psychol.* emotionally or mentally unstable or abnormal. ▫▫ **dis·turb·er** *n.* **dis·turb·ing** *adj.* **dis·turb·ing·ly** *adv.*

dis·turb·ance /distə́rbəns/ *n.* **1** the act or an instance of disturbing; the process of being disturbed. **2** a tumult; an uproar. **3** agitation; worry. **4** an interruption.

dis·un·ion /disyóonyən/ *n.* a lack of union; separation; dissension. ▫▫ **dis·u·nite** /dísyoonít/ *v.tr. & intr.* **dis·u·ni·ty** *n.*

dis·use *n. & v.* •*n.* /disyóos/ **1** lack of use or practice; discontinuance. **2** a disused state. •*v.tr.* /disyóoz/ (esp. as **disused** *adj.*) cease to use.

ditch /dich/ *n. & v.* •*n.* **1** a long, narrow excavated channel, esp. for drainage or to mark a boundary. **2** a watercourse, stream, etc. •*v.* **1** *intr.* make or repair ditches. **2** *tr.* provide with ditches; drain. **3** *tr. sl.* leave in the lurch; abandon. **4** *tr. colloq.* **a** bring (an aircraft) down on water in an emergency. **b** drive (a vehicle) into a ditch. **5** *intr. colloq.* (of an aircraft) make a forced landing on water. **6** *tr. sl.* defeat; frustrate. **7** *tr.* derail (a train). ▫▫ **ditch·er** *n.*

dith·er /dí*th*ər/ *v. & n.* •*v.intr.* hesitate; be indecisive. •*n. colloq.* **1** a state of agitation or apprehension. **2** a state of hesitation; indecisiveness. ▫ **in a dither** *colloq.* in a state of extreme agitation or vacillation. ▫▫ **dith·er·er** *n.* **dith·er·y** *adj.*

dit·sy /dítsee/ *adj.* (also **ditzy; ditsier** or **ditzier, ditsiest** or **ditziest**) *colloq.* silly; foolishly giddy; scatterbrained.

dit·to /dítō/ *n. & v.* •*n.* (*pl.* **-tos**) **1** (in accounts, lists, etc.) the aforesaid; the same. ▶Often represented by " under the word or sum to be repeated. **2** *colloq.* (replacing a word or phrase to avoid repetition) the same (*came in late last night and ditto the night before*). **3** a similar thing; a duplicate. •*v.tr.* (**-toes, -toed**) repeat (another's action or words).

dit·to marks *n.pl.* quotation marks representing 'ditto.'

dit·ty /dítee/ *n.* (*pl.* **-ties**) a short simple song.

ditz /dits/ *n. sl.* a ditsy person.

dit·zy var. of DITSY.

di·u·re·sis /díəréesis/ *n. Med.* an increased excretion of urine.

di·u·ret·ic /díərétik/ *adj. & n.* •*adj.* causing increased output of urine. •*n.* a diuretic drug.

di·ur·nal /dī-ə́rnəl/ *adj.* **1** of or during the day; not nocturnal. **2** daily; of each day. **3** *Astron.* occupying one day. **4** *Zool.* (of animals) active in the daytime. **5** *Bot.* (of plants) open only during the day. ▫▫ **di·ur·nal·ly** *adv.*

div. *abbr.* division.

di·va /déevə/ *n.* (*pl.* **divas** or **dive** /–vay/) a great or famous woman singer; a prima donna.

di·va·lent /díváylənt/ *adj. Chem.* **1** having a valence of two; bivalent. **2** having two valencies. ▫▫ **di·va·lence** *n.*

di·van /diván, dī–/ *n.* **1** a long, low, padded seat set against a wall; a backless sofa. **2** a bed consisting of a base and mattress, usu. with no board at either end.

di·var·i·cate /dīvárikayt, dee–/ *v.intr.* diverge; branch; separate widely. ▫▫ **di·var·i·cate** /–kət/ *adj.* **di·var·i·ca·tion** /–káyshən/ *n.*

dive /dīv/ *v. & n.* •*v.* (**dived** or **dove** /dōv/) **1** *intr.* plunge head first into water, esp. as a sport. **2** *intr.* **a** *Aeron.* (of an aircraft) plunge steeply downward at speed. **b** *Naut.* (of a submarine) submerge. **c** (of a person) plunge downward. **3** *intr.* (foll. by *into*) *colloq.* **a** put one's hand into (a pocket, handbag, vessel, etc.) quickly and deeply. **b** occupy oneself suddenly and enthusiastically with (a subject, meal, etc.). **4** *tr.* (foll. by *into*) plunge (a hand, etc.) into. •*n.* **1** an act of diving; a plunge. **2 a** the submerging of a submarine. **b** the steep descent of an aircraft. **3** a sudden darting movement. **4** *colloq.* a disreputable nightclub, etc. **5** *Boxing sl.* a pretended knockout (*took a dive in the second round*). ▫ **dive in** *colloq.* help oneself (to food).

dive-bomb *v.tr.* bomb (a target) while diving in an aircraft. ▫▫ **dive-bomb·er** *n.*

div·er /dívər/ *n.* **1** a person who dives. **2 a** a person who wears a diving suit to work under water for long periods. **b** a pearl diver, etc. **3** any of various diving birds, esp. large waterbirds of the family Gaviidae.

di·verge /dīvə́rj/ *v.* **1** *intr.* **a** proceed in a different direction or in different directions from a point. **b** take a different course or different courses (*their interests diverged*). **2** *intr.* **a** (often foll. by *from*) depart from a set course. **b** differ markedly. **3** *tr.* cause to diverge; deflect. ▫▫ **di·ver·gence** /–jəns/ *n.* **di·ver·gen·cy** *n.* **di·ver·gent** *adj.* **di·ver·gent·ly** *adv.*

di·vers /dívərz/ *adj. archaic* or *literary* more than one; sundry; several.

di·verse /dívə́rs, di–/ *adj.* unlike in nature or qualities; varied. ▫▫ **di·verse·ly** *adv.*

di·ver·si·fy /divə́rsifī, dī–/ *v.* (**-fies, -fied**) **1** *tr.* make diverse; vary. **2** *tr. Commerce* **a** spread (investment) over several enterprises or products, esp. to reduce the risk of loss. **b** introduce a spread of investment in (an enterprise, etc.). **3** *intr.* (often foll. by *into*) esp. *Commerce* (of a firm, etc.) expand the range of products handled. ▫▫ **di·ver·si·fi·ca·tion** /–fikáyshən/ *n.*

di·ver·sion /divə́r*zh*ən, dī–/ *n.* **1 a** the act of diverting. **b** an instance of this. **2 a** the diverting of attention deliberately. **b** a stratagem for this purpose. **3** a recreation or pastime. ▫▫ **di·ver·sion·ar·y** *adj.*

di·ver·si·ty /divə́rsitee, dī–/ *n.* (*pl.* **-ties**) **1** being diverse; variety. **2** a different kind; a variety.

di·vert /divə́rt, dī–/ *v.tr.* **1** (often foll. by *from, to*) **a** deflect. **b** distract. **2** (often as **diverting** *adj.*) entertain; amuse. ▫▫ **di·vert·ing·ly** *adv.*

di·ver·tic·u·lum /dívərtíkyələm/ *n.* (*pl.* **diverticula** /–lə/) *Anat.* a blind tube forming at weak points in a cavity or passage, esp. of the alimentary tract. ▫▫ **di·ver·tic·u·lo·sis** /–lṓsis/ *n.*

di·ver·ti·men·to /divə́rtiméntō, diváir–/ *n.* (*pl.* **divertimenti** /–tee/ or **-os**) *Mus.* a light and entertaining composition.

di·ver·tisse·ment /divə́rtismənt, deevairteesmóN/ *n.* **1** a diversion; an entertainment. **2** a short ballet, etc., between acts or longer pieces.

di·vest /divést, dī–/ *v.tr.* **1** (usu. foll. by *of*; often *refl.*) unclothe; strip (*divested himself of his jacket*). **2** deprive; dispossess; free; rid. ▫▫ **di·vest·ment** *n.*

di·vide /divíd/ *v. & n.* •*v.* **1** *tr. & intr.* (often foll. by *in, into*) separate or be separated into parts; break up; split. **2** *tr. & intr.* (often foll. by *out*) distribute; deal; share.

3 *tr.* **a** cut off; separate; part. **b** mark out into parts (*a ruler divided into inches*). **c** specify different kinds of; classify (*people can be divided into two types*). **4** *tr.* cause to disagree (*religion divided them*). **5** *Math.* **a** *tr.* find how many times (a number) contains another (*divide 20 by 4*). **b** *intr.* (of a number) be contained in (a number) without a remainder (*4 divides into 20*). **c** *intr.* be susceptible of division (*10 divides by 2 and 5*). **d** *tr.* find how many times (a number) is contained in another (*divide 4 into 20*). **6** *intr. Math.* do division. • *n.* **1** a dividing or boundary line (*the divide between rich and poor*). **2** a watershed.

div•i•dend /dívidend/ *n.* **1 a** a sum of money paid by a company to shareholders. **b** a similar sum payable to winners in a betting pool or to members of a cooperative. **c** an individual's share of a dividend. **2** *Math.* a number to be divided. **3** a benefit from any action (*their long training paid dividends*).

di•vid•er /divídər/ *n.* **1** a screen, piece of furniture, etc., dividing a room into two parts. **2** (in *pl.*) a measuring compass, esp. with a screw for making fine adjustments.

div•i•na•tion /dívináyshən/ *n.* **1** supposed insight into the future or the unknown gained by supernatural means. **2 a** a skillful and accurate forecast. **b** a good guess. □□ **di•vin•a•to•ry** /–vínətáwree/ *adj.*

di•vine /divín/ *adj., v., & n.* • *adj.* (**diviner, divinest**) **1 a** of, from, or like God or a god. **b** sacred (*divine service*). **2 a** more than humanly excellent, gifted, or beautiful. **b** *colloq.* excellent; delightful. • *v.* **1** *tr.* discover by guessing, intuition, inspiration, or magic. **2** *tr.* foresee; predict; conjecture. **3** *intr.* practice divination. **4** *intr.* dowse. • *n.* **1** a cleric, usu. an expert in theology. **2** (**the Divine**) providence or God. □□ **di•vine•ly** *adv.* **di•vin•er** *n.* **div•i•nize** /dívinīz/ *v.tr.*

di•vin•ing rod /divíning/ *n.* = DOWSING ROD.

di•vin•i•ty /divínitee/ *n.* (*pl.* **-ties**) **1** the state or quality of being divine. **2 a** a god; a divine being. **b** (as **the Divinity**) God. **3** the study of religion.

di•vis•i•ble /divízibəl/ *adj.* **1** capable of being divided, physically or mentally. **2** (foll. by *by*) *Math.* containing (a number) several times without a remainder (*15 is divisible by 3*). □□ **di•vis•i•bil•i•ty** /–bílitee/ *n.*

di•vi•sion /divízhən/ *n.* **1** the act or an instance of dividing; the process of being divided. **2** *Math.* the process of dividing one number by another. **3** disagreement or discord (*division of opinion*). **4** *Parl.* the separation of members of a legislative body into two sets for counting votes. **5 a** one of two or more parts into which a thing is divided. **b** the point at which a thing is divided. **6** a major unit of administration or organization, esp.: **a** a group of army brigades or regiments. **b** *Sports* a grouping of teams within a league. **7** a district defined for administrative purposes. □□ **di•vi•sion•al** *adj.* **di•vi•sion•al•ly** *adv.*

di•vi•sive /divísiv/ *adj.* tending to divide, esp. in opinion; causing disagreement. □□ **di•vi•sive•ly** *adv.* **di•vi•sive•ness** *n.*

di•vi•sor /divízər/ *n. Math.* **1** a number by which another is to be divided. **2** a number that divides another without a remainder.

di•vorce /diváwrs/ *n. & v.* • *n.* **1 a** the legal dissolution of a marriage. **b** a legal decree of this. **2** a severance or separation (*a divorce between thought and feeling*). • *v.* **1 a** *tr.* (usu. as **divorced** *adj.*) (often foll. by *from*) legally dissolve the marriage of (*a divorced couple*; *he wants to get divorced from her*). **b** *intr.* separate by divorce (*they divorced*). **c** *tr.* end one's marriage with (*divorced him*). **2** *tr.* (often foll. by *from*) detach; separate (*divorced from reality*).

di•vor•cé /divawrsáy/ *n.* a divorced man.

di•vor•cée /divawrsáy/ *n.* a divorced woman.

div•ot /dívət/ *n.* a piece of turf cut out by a golf club in making a stroke.

di•vulge /divúlj, dī–/ *v.tr.* disclose; reveal (a secret, etc.). □□ **di•vul•ga•tion** /–vulgáyshən/ *n.* **di•vulge•ment** *n.* **di•vul•gence** *n.*

div•vy /dívee/ *n. & v. colloq.* • *n.* (*pl.* **-vies**) a distribution. • *v.tr.* (**-vies, -vied**) (often foll. by *up*) share out.

Dix•ie /díksee/ *n.* the southern states of the US.

dix•ie /díksee/ *n.* a large iron cooking pot used by campers, etc.

Dix•ie•land /díkseeland/ *n.* **1** = DIXIE. **2** a kind of jazz with a strong, two-beat rhythm and collective improvisation.

diz•zy /dízee/ *adj. & v.* • *adj.* (**dizzier, dizziest**) **1 a** giddy; unsteady. **b** lacking mental stability; confused. **2** causing giddiness. • *v.tr.* **1** make dizzy. **2** bewilder. □□ **diz•zi•ly** *adv.* **diz•zi•ness** *n.*

DJ *abbr.* **1** disk jockey. **2** district judge.

dl *abbr.* deciliter(s).

dm *abbr.* decimeter(s).

DMZ *abbr.* demilitarized zone.

DNA *abbr.* deoxyribonucleic acid, the self-replicating material present in nearly all living organisms, esp. as a constituent of chromosomes, which is the carrier of genetic information.

do[1] /doo/ *v. & n.* • *v.* (*3rd sing. present* **does** /duz/; *past* **did** /did/; *past part.* **done** /dun/) **1** *tr.* perform; carry out; achieve; complete (work, etc.) (*did his homework*). **2** *tr.* **a** produce; make (*she was doing a painting*). **b** provide (*do you do lunches?*). **3** *tr.* bestow; grant; have a specified effect on (*do me a favor*). **4** *intr.* act; behave; proceed (*do as I do*). **5** *tr.* work at; study; be occupied with (*what does your father do?*). **6 a** *intr.* be suitable or acceptable; suffice (*a sandwich will do until we get home*). **b** *tr.* satisfy; be suitable for (*that hotel will do me nicely*). **7** *tr.* deal with; put in order (*I must do my hair*). **8** *intr.* **a** fare; get on (*he did badly in the test*). **b** perform; work (*could do better*). **9** *tr.* **a** solve; work out (*we did the puzzle*). **b** (prec. by *can* or *be able to*) be competent at (*can you do cartwheels?*). **10** *tr.* **a** traverse (a certain distance) (*we did fifty miles today*). **b** travel at a specified speed (*he overtook us doing about eighty*). **11** *tr. colloq.* act or behave like (*did a Houdini*). **12** *intr.* **a** *colloq.* finish (*are you done annoying me?*). **b** (as **done** *adj.*) be over (*the day is done*). **13** *tr.* produce or give a performance of (*we've never done* Pygmalion). **14** *tr.* cook, esp. to the right degree (*the potatoes aren't done yet*). **15** *intr.* be in progress (*what's doing?*). **16** *tr. colloq.* visit; see the sights of (*we did all the art galleries*). **17** *tr. colloq.* **a** (often as **done** *adj.*; often foll. by *in*) exhaust; tire out (*the climb has done me in*). **b** beat up; defeat; kill. **c** ruin (*now you've done it*). **18** *tr.* (foll. by *into*) translate or transform (*the book was done into French*). **19** *tr. sl.* rob (*they did a liquor store downtown*). **20** *tr. sl.* undergo (a specified term of imprisonment) (*he did two years for fraud*). **21** *tr. coarse sl.* have sexual intercourse with. **22** *tr. sl.* take (a drug). • *v.aux.* **1 a** (except with *be, can, may, ought, shall, will*) in questions and negative statements (*do you understand?*; *I don't smoke*). **b** (except with *can, may, ought, shall, will*) in negative commands (*don't be silly*; *do not come tomorrow*). **2** *ellipt.* or in place of verb or verb and object (*you know her better than I do*). **3** forming emphatic present and past tenses (*I do want to*). **4** in inversion for emphasis (*rarely does it happen*). • *n.* (*pl.* **dos** or **do's**) *colloq.* an elaborate event, party, or operation. □ **do away with** *colloq.* **1** abolish. **2** kill. **do for 1** be satisfactory or sufficient for. **2** *colloq.* (esp. as **done for** *adj.*) destroy; ruin; kill (*he knew he was done for*). **do in 1** *sl.* **a** kill. **b** ruin; do injury to. **2** *colloq.* exhaust; tire out. **do nothing for** (or **to**) *colloq.* detract from the appearance or quality of. **do or die** persist regardless of danger. **do a**

person out of *colloq.* unjustly deprive a person of; swindle out of (*he was done out of his pension*). **do over 1** *sl.* attack; beat up. **2** *colloq.* redecorate; refurbish. **3** *colloq.* do again. **dos and don'ts** rules of behavior. **do something for** (or **to**) *colloq.* enhance the appearance or quality of (*that carpet does something for the room*). **do up 1** fasten; secure. **2** *colloq.* **a** refurbish; renovate. **b** adorn; dress up. **do with** (prec. by *could*) would be glad to have; would profit by (*I could do with a rest*). **do without** manage without; forgo (also *absol.*: *we shall just have to do without*). **have nothing to do with 1** have no connection or dealings with (*our problem has nothing to do with the latest news; after the disagreement he had nothing to do with his father*). **2** be no business or concern of (*the decision has nothing to do with her*). **have to do** (or **something to do**) **with** be connected with (*his limp has to do with a car accident*).

do[2] /dō/ *n.* (also **doh**) *Mus.* **1** (in tonic sol-fa) the first and eighth notes of a major scale. **2** the note C in the fixed-do system.

do. *abbr.* ditto.

DOA *abbr.* dead on arrival (at a hospital, etc.).

do·a·ble /dőoəbəl/ *adj.* that can be done.

Do·ber·man /dőbərmən/ *n.* (in full **Doberman pinscher** /pínshər/) a large dog of a German breed with a smooth coat.

doc /dok/ *n. colloq.* doctor.

do·cent /dősənt/ *n.* a person who serves as a well-informed guide, as in a museum.

doc·ile /dósəl/ *adj.* submissive; easily managed. ▫▫ **doc·ile·ly** *adv.* **do·cil·i·ty** /–sílitee/ *n.*

dock[1] /dok/ *n. & v.* •*n.* **1** an artificially enclosed body of water for the loading, unloading, and repair of ships. **2** (in *pl.*) a range of docks with wharves and offices; a dockyard. **3** a ship's berth; a wharf. •*v.* **1** *tr. & intr.* bring or come into a dock. **2 a** *tr.* join (spacecraft) together in space. **b** *intr.* (of spacecraft) be joined. **3** *tr.* provide with a dock or docks.

dock[2] /dok/ *n.* the enclosure in a criminal court for the accused. ▫ **in the dock** on trial.

dock[3] /dok/ *n.* any weed of the genus *Rumex*, with broad leaves.

dock[4] /dok/ *v. & n.* •*v.tr.* **1 a** cut short (an animal's tail). **b** cut short the tail of (an animal). **2 a** (often foll. by *from*) deduct (a part) from wages, supplies, etc. **b** reduce (wages, etc.) in this way. •*n.* the solid, bony part of an animal's tail.

dock·age /dókij/ *n.* **1** the charge made for using docks. **2** dock accommodation. **3** the berthing of vessels in docks.

dock·et /dókit/ *n. & v.* •*n.* **1** a list of causes for trial or persons having causes pending. **2** a list of things to be done. •*v.tr.* label with a docket.

dock·side /dóksīd/ *n.* the area adjacent to a dock.

dock·yard /dókyaard/ *n.* an area with docks and equipment for building and repairing ships.

doc·tor /dóktər/ *n. & v.* •*n.* **1 a** a medical practitioner; a physician. **b** a dentist. **c** a veterinarian. **2** a person who holds a doctorate. **3** *colloq.* a person who carries out repairs. •*v. colloq.* **1 a** *tr.* treat medically. **b** *intr.* (esp. as **doctoring** *n.*) practice as a physician. **2** *tr.* patch up (machinery, etc.); mend. **3** *tr.* adulterate. **4** *tr.* tamper with; falsify. **5** *tr.* confer a degree of doctor on. ▫ **(just) what the doctor ordered** *colloq.* something beneficial or desirable. ▫▫ **doc·tor·ly** *adj.*

doc·tor·al /dóktərəl/ *adj.* of or for a degree of doctor.

doc·tor·ate /dóktərət/ *n.* the highest university degree in any faculty, often honorary.

Doc·tor of Phi·los·o·phy *n.* a doctorate in a discipline other than education, law, medicine, or sometimes theology.

doc·tri·naire /dóktrináir/ *adj. & n.* •*adj.* seeking to apply a theory or doctrine in all circumstances without regard to practical considerations. •*n.* a doctrinaire person. ▫▫ **doc·tri·nair·ism** *n.*

doc·tri·nal /dóktrinəl/ *adj.* of or inculcating a doctrine or doctrines. ▫▫ **doc·tri·nal·ly** *adv.*

doc·trine /dóktrin/ *n.* **1** what is taught; a body of instruction. **2 a** a principle of religious or political, etc., belief. **b** a set of such principles; dogma. ▫▫ **doc·trin·ism** *n.* **doc·trin·ist** *n.*

doc·u·dra·ma /dókyōōdraamə, –dramə/ *n.* a dramatized television movie based on real events.

doc·u·ment *n. & v.* •*n.* /dókyəmənt/ a piece of written or printed matter that provides a record or evidence of events, an agreement, ownership, identification, etc. •*v.tr.* /dókyəment/ **1** prove by or provide with documents or evidence. **2** record in a document.

doc·u·men·ta·ry /dókyəméntəree/ *adj. & n.* •*adj.* **1** consisting of documents (*documentary evidence*). **2** providing a factual record or report. •*n.* (*pl.* **-ries**) a documentary film, etc.

doc·u·men·ta·tion /dókyəmentáyshən/ *n.* **1** the accumulation, classification, and dissemination of information. **2** the material collected or disseminated. **3** the collection of documents relating to a process or event.

dod·der /dódər/ *v.intr.* tremble or totter, esp. from age. ▫▫ **dod·der·er** *n.* **dod·der·y** *adj.*

dodeca- /dődekə/ *comb. form* twelve.

do·dec·a·gon /dōdékəgon/ *n.* a plane figure with twelve sides.

do·dec·a·he·dron /dődekəhéedrən/ *n.* a solid figure with twelve faces. ▫▫ **do·dec·a·he·dral** *adj.*

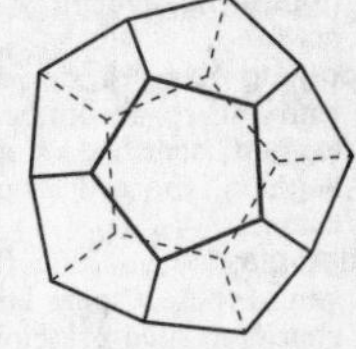

dodecahedron

dodge /doj/ *v. & n.* •*v.* **1** *intr.* (often foll. by *about, behind, around*) move quickly to one side or quickly change position, to elude a pursuer, blow, etc. (*dodged behind the chair*). **2** *tr.* **a** evade by cunning or trickery (*dodged paying the fare*). **b** elude (a pursuer, opponent, blow, etc.) by a sideward movement, etc. •*n.* **1** a quick movement to avoid or evade something. **2** a clever trick or expedient. ▫▫ **dodg·er** *n.*

dodg·y /dójee/ *adj.* (**dodgier, dodgiest**) *colloq.* awkward; unreliable; tricky.

do·do /dődō/ *n.* (*pl.* **-does** or **-dos**) **1** any large flightless bird of the extinct family Raphidae, formerly native to Mauritius. **2** an old-fashioned, stupid, or idle person.

doe /dō/ *n.* a female deer, reindeer, hare, or rabbit.

do·er /dőoər/ *n.* **1** a person who does something. **2** one who acts rather than merely talking or thinking.

does *3rd sing. present* of DO[1].

doe·skin /dőskin/ *n.* **1 a** the skin of a doe fallow deer. **b** leather made from this. **2** a fine cloth resembling it.

doesn't /dúzənt/ *contr.* does not.

doff /dawf, dof/ *v.tr. literary* take off (one's hat, clothing).

dog /dawg, dog/ *n. & v.* •*n.* **1** any four-legged, flesh-eating animal of the genus *Canis*, of many breeds, domesticated and wild, kept as pets or for work or sport. **2** the male of the dog, or of the fox or wolf. **3 a** *colloq.* a despicable person. **b** *colloq.* a person or fellow of a specified kind (*a lucky dog*). **c** *sl.* a horse that is difficult to handle. **e** *sl. derog.* an unattractive or slovenly woman. **4** a mechanical device for gripping. **5** *sl.*

something poor; a failure. **6** = FIREDOG. • *v.tr.* (**dogged, dogging**) follow closely and persistently; pursue; track. □ **go to the dogs** *sl.* deteriorate, be ruined. **put on the dog** *colloq.* behave pretentiously. □□ **dog•like** *adj.*

dog days *n.pl.* the hottest period of the year.

doge /dōj/ *n. hist.* the chief magistrate of Venice or Genoa.

dog-eared *adj.* (of a book, etc.) with the corners worn or battered with use.

dog-eat-dog *adj. colloq.* ruthlessly competitive.

dog•fight /dáwgfit, dóg–/ *n.* **1** a close combat between fighter aircraft. **2** uproar; a fight like that between dogs.

dog•fish /dáwgfish, dóg–/ *n.* (*pl.* same or **dogfishes**) any of various small sharks, esp. of the families Scyliorhinidae or Squalidae.

dog•ged /dáwgid, dóg–/ *adj.* tenacious; grimly persistent. □□ **dog•ged•ly** *adv.* **dog•ged•ness** *n.*

dog•ger•el /dáwgərəl, dóg–/ *n.* poor or trivial verse.

dog•gie var. of DOGGY *n.*

dog•gie bag *n.* (also **dog•gy bag**) a bag given to a customer in a restaurant or to a guest at a party, etc., for putting leftovers in to take home.

dog•gone /dáwg-gon, dóg–/ *adj., adv., & int. sl.* • *adj. & adv.* damned. • *int.* expressing annoyance.

dog•gy /dáwgee, dógee/ *n.* (also **dog•gie**) (*pl.* **-gies**) a little dog; a pet name for a dog.

dog•house /dáwghows, dóg–/ *n.* a dog's shelter. □ **in the doghouse** *sl.* in disgrace or disfavor.

do•gie /dṓgee/ *n.* a motherless or neglected calf.

dog in the man•ger *n.* a person who prevents others from using something, although that person has no use for it.

dog•leg /dáwgleg, dóg–/ *n., adj., & v.* • *n.* something with a sharp, abrupt bend, as a road. • *adj.* (also **dog-leg•ged**) bent like a dog's hind leg. • *v.intr.* (**-legged, -legging**) proceed around a dogleg or on a dogleg course.

dog•ma /dáwgmə, dóg–/ *n.* **1 a** a principle, tenet, or system of these, esp. as laid down by the authority of a church. **b** such principles collectively. **2** an arrogant declaration of opinion.

dog•mat•ic /dawgmátik, dog–/ *adj.* **1 a** (of a person) given to asserting or imposing personal opinions; arrogant. **b** intolerantly authoritative. **2 a** of or in the nature of dogma; doctrinal. **b** based on a priori principles, not on induction. □□ **dog•mat•i•cal•ly** *adv.*

dog•ma•tism /dáwgmətizəm, dóg–/ *n.* a tendency to be dogmatic. □□ **dog•ma•tist** *n.*

do-good•er /dōōgŏŏdər/ *n.* a well-meaning but unrealistic philanthropist or reformer.

dog pad•dle *n.* an elementary swimming stroke like that of a dog. □□ **dog-pad•dle** *v.intr.*

dog's life *n.* a life of misery or harassment.

dogs of war *n.pl. poet.* the havoc accompanying war.

Dog Star *n.* the chief star of the constellation Canis Major or Minor, esp. Sirius.

dog tag *n.* **1** a usu. metal plate attached to a dog's collar, giving owner's address, etc. **2** an identification tag, esp. as worn by a member of the military.

dog-tired *adj.* tired out.

dog•wood /dáwgwŏŏd, dóg–/ *n.* **1** any of various shrubs of the genus *Cornus*, esp. the wild cornel with dark red branches, greenish-white flowers, and purple berries. **2** any of various similar trees. **3** the wood of the dogwood.

doh var. of DO².

doi•ly /dóylee/ *n.* (*pl.* **-lies**) a small ornamental mat of paper, lace, etc., on a plate for cakes, etc.

do•ing /dōōing/ *n.* **1 a** (usu. in *pl.*) an action (*famous for his doings*; *it was my doing*). **b** activity; effort (*it takes a lot of doing*). **2** *colloq.* a scolding; a beating. **3** (in *pl.*) *sl.* things needed; adjuncts; things whose names are not known (*have we got all the doings?*).

do-it-your•self *adj. & n.* • *adj.* (of work, esp. building, painting, decorating, etc.) done or to be done by an amateur at home. • *n.* such work.

Dol•by /dṓlbee/ *n. Trademark* an electronic noise-reduction system used esp. in tape recording to reduce hiss.

dol•ce vi•ta /dṓlchay véetə/ *n.* a life of pleasure and luxury.

dol•drums /dṓldrəmz/ *n.pl.* (usu. prec. by *the*) **1** low spirits. **2** a period of inactivity. **3** an equatorial ocean region of calms, sudden storms, and light unpredictable winds.

dole /dōl/ *n. & v.* • *n.* **1** (usu. prec. by *the*) *Brit. colloq.* benefit claimable by the unemployed from the government. **2 a** charitable distribution. **b** a charitable (esp. sparing, niggardly) gift of food, clothes, or money. • *v.tr.* (usu. foll. by *out*) deal out sparingly. □ **on the dole** *colloq.* receiving welfare, etc., payments from the government.

dole•ful /dṓlfōōl/ *adj.* **1** mournful; sad. **2** dreary; dismal. □□ **dole•ful•ly** *adv.* **dole•ful•ness** *n.*

doll /dol/ *n. & v.* • *n.* **1** a small model of a human figure as a child's toy. **2 a** *colloq.* a pretty but silly young woman. **b** *sl.* a young woman, esp. an attractive one. **3** a ventriloquist's dummy. • *v.tr. & intr.* (foll. by *up*; often *refl.*) dress up smartly.

dol•lar /dólər/ *n.* **1** the chief monetary unit in the US, Canada, and Australia. **2** the chief monetary unit of certain countries in the Pacific, West Indies, SE Asia, Africa, and S. America.

---

dollar from early Flemish or Low German *daler*, from German *Taler*, formerly spelled *Thaler*, short for *Joachimsthaler*, a coin from the silver mine of Joachimsthal ('Joachim's valley'), now Jáchymov in the Czech Republic. Originally denoting a German *thaler* coin, the term was later applied to a Spanish coin used in the Spanish American colonies. The Spanish coin was also widely used in the British North American colonies at the time of the Revolutionary War and its name was adopted as the name of the US monetary unit in the late 18th century.

---

dol•lar sign *n.* the sign ($), used to indicate currency in dollars.

doll•house /dólhows/ *n.* **1** a miniature toy house for dolls. **2** a very small house.

dol•lop /dóləp/ *n. & v.* • *n.* a shapeless lump of food, etc. • *v.tr.* (usu. foll. by *out*) serve out in large, shapeless quantities.

dol•ly /dólee/ *n.* (*pl.* **-lies**) **1** a child's name for a doll. **2** a movable platform on wheels used for moving heavy objects, typically film or television cameras.

dol•man sleeve /dōlmən/ *n.* a loose sleeve cut in one piece with the body of the coat, etc.

dol•men /dōlmən/ *n.* a megalithic tomb with a large, flat stone laid on upright ones.

do•lo•mite /dṓləmīt, dól–/ *n.* a mineral or rock of calcium magnesium carbonate. □□ **dol•o•mit•ic** /–mítik/ *adj.*

do•lor /dōlər/ *n. literary* sorrow; distress.

do•lor•ous /dṓlərəs/ *adj. literary* or *joc.* **1** distressing; painful; doleful; dismal. **2** distressed; sad. □□ **dol•or•ous•ly** *adv.*

dol•phin /dólfin/ *n.* **1** any of various porpoiselike aquatic mammals of the family Delphinidae having a slender, beaklike snout. **2** a fish of the genus *Coryphaena*, caught as a food fish. **3** a pile or buoy for mooring. **4** a structure for protecting the pier of a bridge.

dolt /dōlt/ *n.* a stupid person. □□ **dolt•ish** *adj.* **dolt•ish•ness** *n.*

Dom /dom/ *n.* **1** a title prefixed to the names of some Roman Catholic dignitaries, and Benedictine and

Carthusian monks. **2** the Portuguese equivalent of Don (see DON[1] 2a, b).

do•main /dōmáyn/ *n.* **1** an area under one rule; a realm. **2** an estate or lands under one control. **3** a sphere of control or influence.

dome /dōm/ *n. & v.* • *n.* **1 a** a rounded vault as a roof, with a circular, elliptical, or polygonal base. **b** the revolving, openable hemispherical roof of an observatory. **2 a** a natural vault or canopy (of the sky, trees, etc.). **b** the rounded summit of a hill, etc. **3** *Geol.* a dome-shaped structure. **4** *sl.* the head. • *v.tr.* (usu. as **domed** *adj.*) cover with or shape as a dome. □□ **dome•like** *adj.*

do•mes•tic /dəméstik/ *adj. & n.* • *adj.* **1** of the home, household, or family affairs. **2 a** of one's own country, not foreign or international. **b** homegrown or homemade. **3** (of an animal) kept by or living with humans. **4** fond of home life. • *n.* a household servant. □□ **do•mes•ti•cal•ly** *adv.*

do•mes•ti•cate /dəméstikayt/ *v.tr.* **1** tame (an animal) to live with humans. **2** accustom to home life and management. **3** naturalize (a plant or animal). □□ **do•mes•ti•ca•ble** /–kəbəl/ *adj.* **do•mes•ti•ca•tion** /–káyshən/ *n.*

do•mes•tic•i•ty /dṓməstísitee/ *n.* **1** the state of being domestic. **2** domestic or home life.

do•mes•tic sci•ence *n.* the study of household management.

dom•i•cile /dómisīl, –sil, dṓ–/ *n. & v.* (also **dom•i•cil** /–sil/) • *n.* **1** a dwelling place; one's home. **2** *Law* **a** a place of permanent residence. **b** the fact of residing. **3** the place at which a bill of exchange is made payable. • *v.tr.* **1** (usu. as **domiciled** *adj.*) (usu. foll. by *at*, *in*) establish or settle in a place. **2** (usu. foll. by *at*) make (a bill of exchange) payable at a certain place.

dom•i•nant /dóminənt/ *adj. & n.* • *adj.* **1** dominating; prevailing; most influential. **2** (of a high place) prominent; overlooking others. **3 a** (of an allele) expressed even when inherited from only one parent. **b** (of an inherited characteristic) appearing in an individual even when its allelic counterpart is also inherited (cf. RECESSIVE). • *n.* *Mus.* the fifth note of the diatonic scale of any key. □□ **dom•i•nance** /dóminəns/ *n.* **dom•i•nant•ly** *adv.*

dom•i•nate /dóminayt/ *v.* **1** *tr.* & (foll. by *over*) *intr.* exercise control over (*fear dominated them for years*; *dominates over his friends*). **2** *intr.* (of a person, sound, feature of a scene, etc.) be the most influential or conspicuous. **3** *tr.* & (foll. by *over*) *intr.* (of a building, etc.) overlook. □□ **dom•i•na•tion** /dóminteam/ *n.* **dom•i•na•tor** *n.*

dom•i•neer /dómineér/ *v.intr.* (often as **domineering** *adj.*) behave in an arrogant and overbearing way. □□ **dom•i•neer•ing•ly** *adv.*

Do•min•i•can /dəmínikən/ *adj. & n.* • *adj.* **1** of or relating to St. Dominic or the order of preaching friars which he founded. **2** of or relating to either of two female religious orders founded on Dominican principles. • *n.* a Dominican friar, nun, or sister.

do•min•ion /dəmínyən/ *n.* **1** sovereignty; control. **2** the territory of a sovereign or government; a domain.

dom•i•no /dóminō/ *n.* (*pl.* **-noes** or **-nos**) **1 a** a small oblong tile marked with 0–6 dots in each half. **b** (in *pl.*, usu. treated as *sing.*) a game played with these. **2** a loose cloak with a mask for the upper part of the face.

dom•i•no the•o•ry *n.* the theory that a political event, etc., in one country will cause similar events in neighboring countries, like a row of falling dominoes.

don[1] /don/ *n.* **1** a university teacher, esp. a senior member of a college at Oxford or Cambridge. **2** (**Don**) **a** a Spanish title prefixed to a forename. **b** a Spanish gentleman; a Spaniard.

don[2] /don/ *v.tr.* (**donned, donning**) put on (clothing).

do•nate /dṓnayt, dōnáyt/ *v.tr.* give or contribute (money, etc.), esp. to a charity. □□ **do•na•tor** *n.*

do•na•tion /dōnáyshən/ *n.* **1** the act or an instance of donating. **2** something, esp. money, donated.

done /dun/ *past part.* of DO[1]. *adj.* **1** *colloq.* socially acceptable (*the done thing*). **2** (often with *in*, *up*) *colloq.* tired out. **3** (esp. as *int.* in reply to an offer, etc.) accepted. □ **be done with** be finished with. **done for** *colloq.* in serious trouble. **have done** have ceased or finished. **have done with** be rid of; have finished dealing with.

do•nee /dōneé/ *n.* the recipient of a gift.

don•gle /dáwnggəl, dóng–/ *n.* *Computing sl.* a security attachment required by a computer to enable protected software to be used.

don•jon /dónjən, dún–/ *n.* the great tower or innermost keep of a castle.

Don Juan /don wáan, hwáan, jṓōən/ *n.* a seducer of women; a libertine.

don•key /dóngkee, dúng–, dáwng–/ *n.* (*pl.* **-keys**) **1** a domestic ass. **2** *colloq.* a stupid or foolish person.

do•nor /dṓnər/ *n.* **1** a person who gives or donates something (e.g., to a charity). **2** one who provides blood for a transfusion, semen for insemination, or an organ or tissue for transplantation.

do•nor card *n.* an official card authorizing use of organs for transplant, carried by the donor.

don't /dōnt/ *contr. & n.* • *contr.* do not. • *n.* a prohibition (*dos and don'ts*).

▶The use of **don't** as a singular is now generally regarded as uneducated, although it was once standard and is now often employed informally for effect, e.g., "It don't mean a thing to me."

do•nut var. of DOUGHNUT.

doo•dad /dṓōdad/ *n.* **1** a fancy article; a trivial ornament. **2** a gadget or thingamajig.

doo•dle /dṓōd'l/ *v. & n.* • *v.intr.* scribble or draw, esp. absentmindedly. • *n.* a scrawl or drawing so made. □□ **doo•dler** *n.*

doo•dle•bug /dṓōd'lbug/ *n.* **1** any of various insects, esp. the larva of an ant lion. **2** an unscientific device for locating minerals. **3** *colloq.* a robot bomb.

doo•hick•ey /dṓōhikee/ *n.* (*pl.* **-eys** or **-ies**) *colloq.* a small object, esp. mechanical.

doom /dōōm/ *n. & v.* • *n.* **1 a** a grim fate or destiny. **b** death or ruin. **2 a** a condemnation; a judgment or sentence. **b** the Last Judgment (*the crack of doom*). • *v.tr.* **1** (usu. foll. by *to*) condemn or destine (*doomed to destruction*). **2** (esp. as **doomed** *adj.*) consign to misfortune or destruction.

dooms•day /dṓōmzday/ *n.* the day of the Last Judgment.

door /dawr/ *n.* **1 a** a hinged, sliding, or revolving barrier for closing and opening an entrance to a building, room, cupboard, etc. **b** this as representing a house, etc. (*lives two doors away*). **2 a** an entrance or exit; a doorway. **b** a means of access or approach. □ **close the door to** exclude the opportunity for. **lay** (or **lie**) **at the door of** impute (or be imputable) to. **leave the door open** ensure that an option remains available. **next door to 1** in the next house to. **2** nearly, near to. **open the door to** create an opportunity for. **out of doors** in or into the open air. □□ **doored** *adj.* (also in *comb.*).

door•bell /dáwrbel/ *n.* a bell in a house, etc., rung by visitors outside to signal their arrival.

door•frame /dáwrfraym/ *n.* the framework of a doorway.

door•keep•er /dáwrkeepər/ *n.* = DOORMAN 1.

See page xii for the *Key to Pronunciation*.

door·knob /dáwrnob/ *n.* a knob for turning to release the latch of a door.

door·man /dáwrman, –mən/ *n.* (*pl.* **-men**) a person on duty at the door to a large building.

door·mat /dáwrmat/ *n.* **1** a mat at an entrance for wiping one's shoes. **2** a feebly submissive person.

door·nail /dáwrnayl/ *n.* a nail with which doors were studded for strength or ornament. □ **dead as a doornail** completely or unmistakably dead.

door·post /dáwrpōst/ *n.* each of the uprights of a doorframe.

door prize *n.* a prize awarded usu. by lottery at a dance, party, charity event, etc.

door·step /dáwrstep/ *n.* & *v.* •*n.* a step leading up to the outer door of a house, etc. •*v.intr.* (**-stepped, -stepping**) go from door to door selling, canvassing, etc. □ **on one's** (or **the**) **doorstep** very close.

door·stop /dáwrstop/ *n.* a device for keeping a door open or to prevent it from striking a wall, etc., when opened.

door-to-door *adj.* (of selling, etc.) done at each house in turn.

door·way /dáwrway/ *n.* an opening filled by a door.

door·yard /dáwryaard/ *n.* a yard or garden near the door of a house.

doo·zy /dóozee/ *n.* (*pl.* **doozies**) *colloq.* one that is outstanding of its kind (*that mistake was a doozy*).

dope /dōp/ *n.* & *v.* •*n.* **1** a varnish applied to the cloth surface of airplane parts. **2** a thick liquid used as a lubricant, etc. **3** a substance added to gasoline, etc., to increase its effectiveness. **4 a** *sl.* a narcotic. **b** a drug, etc., given to a horse or greyhound, or taken by an athlete, to affect performance. **5** *sl.* a stupid person. **6** *sl.* **a** information about a subject, esp. if not generally known. **b** misleading information. •*v.* **1** *tr.* administer dope to; drug. **2** *tr.* apply dope to. **3** *intr.* take addictive drugs. □ **dope out** *sl.* discover. □□ **dop·er** *n.*

dope·y /dópee/ *adj.* (also **dop·y**) (**dopier, dopiest**) *colloq.* **1 a** half asleep. **b** stupefied by or as if by a drug. **2** stupid; silly. □□ **dop·i·ly** *adv.* **dop·i·ness** *n.*

dop·pel·gäng·er /dópəlgangər/ *n.* an apparition or double of a living person.

Dop·pler ef·fect /dóplər/ *n.* (also **Dop·pler shift**) *Physics* an increase (or decrease) in the frequency of sound, light, or other waves as the source and observer move toward (or away) from each other.

dop·y var. of DOPEY.

Dor·ic /dáwrik, dór–/ *adj.* & *n.* •*adj.* **1** (of a dialect) broad; rustic. **2** *Archit.* of the oldest, sturdiest, and simplest of the Greek orders. •*n.* **1** rustic English or esp. Scots. **2** *Archit.* the Doric order. **3** the dialect of the Dorians in ancient Greece.

dork /dawrk/ *n. sl.* a dull, slow-witted, or oafish person. □□ **dork·y** *adj.*

dorm /dawrm/ *n. colloq.* dormitory.

dor·mant /dáwrmənt/ *adj.* **1** lying inactive; sleeping. **2 a** (of a volcano, etc.) temporarily inactive. **b** (of potential faculties, etc.) in abeyance. **3** (of plants) alive but not actively growing. □□ **dor·man·cy** *n.*

dor·mer /dáwrmər/ *n.* (in full **dormer window**) a projecting upright window in a sloping roof.

dor·mi·to·ry /dáwrmitáwree/ *n.* (*pl.* **-ries**) **1** a sleeping room with several beds, esp. in a school or institution. **2** a university or college hall of residence or hostel.

dor·mouse /dáwrmows/ *n.* (*pl.* **dormice** /–mīs/) any small, mouselike hibernating rodent of the family Gliridae.

dor·sal /dáwrsəl/ *adj. Anat., Zool.,* & *Bot.* **1** of, on, or near the back (cf. VENTRAL). **2** ridge-shaped. □□ **dor·sal·ly** *adv.*

do·ry /dáwree/ *n.* (*pl.* **-ries**) a flat-bottomed fishing boat with high sides.

DOS /dos, daws/ *n. Computing* a software operating system for personal computers (abbr. of *d*isk *o*perating *s*ystem).

dos·age /dósij/ *n.* **1** the giving of medicine in doses. **2** the size of a dose.

dose /dōs/ *n.* & *v.* •*n.* **1** an amount of a medicine or drug taken at one time. **2** a quantity of something administered or allocated (e.g., work, praise, punishment, etc.). **3** the amount of ionizing radiation received by a person or thing. **4** *sl.* a venereal infection. •*v.tr.* **1** treat (a person or animal) with doses of medicine. **2** give a dose or doses to.

do·sim·e·ter /dōsímitər/ *n.* a device used to measure an absorbed dose of ionizing radiation. □□ **do·si·met·ric** /–métrik/ *adj.* **do·sim·e·try** *n.*

dos·si·er /dósee-ay, dáw–/ *n.* a set of documents, esp. about a person, event, or subject.

dot /dot/ *n.* & *v.* •*n.* **1 a** a small spot, speck, or mark. **b** such a mark as part of an *i* or *j*, as a full stop, etc. **c** a decimal point. **2** *Mus.* a dot used to denote the lengthening of a note or rest, or to indicate staccato. **3** the shorter signal of the two used in Morse code (cf. DASH *n.* 6). **4** a tiny or apparently tiny object (*a dot on the horizon*). •*v.tr.* (**dotted, dotting**) **1 a** mark with a dot or dots. **b** place a dot over (a letter). **2** *Mus.* mark (a note or rest) to show that the time value is increased by half. **3** (often foll. by *about*) scatter like dots. **4** partly cover as with dots (*an ocean dotted with ships*). □ **dot the i's and cross the t's** *colloq.* **1** be minutely accurate; emphasize details. **2** add the final touches to a task. **on the dot** exactly on time.

dot·age /dótij/ *n.* feeble-minded senility (*in his dotage*).

do·tard /dótərd/ *n.* a person who is feeble-minded, esp. from senility.

dote /dōt/ *v.intr.* **1** (foll. by *on, upon*) be foolishly or excessively fond of. **2** be silly or feeble-minded, esp. from old age.

dot ma·trix print·er *n. Computing* a printer with characters formed from dots printed by configurations of the tips of small wires.

dot·ted line *n.* a line of dots on a document.

dot·ty /dótee/ *adj.* (**dottier, dottiest**) *colloq.* **1** feeble-minded; silly. **2** eccentric. **3** absurd. **4** (foll. by *about, on*) infatuated with; obsessed by. □□ **dot·ti·ly** *adv.* **dot·ti·ness** *n.*

dou·ble /dúbəl/ *adj., adv., n.,* & *v.* •*adj.* **1 a** consisting of two parts or things. **b** consisting of two identical parts. **2** twice as much or many (*double the amount*). **3** having twice the usual size, quantity, strength, etc. (*double whiskey*). **4** designed for two people (*double bed*). **5 a** having some part double. **b** (of a flower) having more than one circle of petals. **c** (of a domino) having the same number of pips on each half. **6** having two different roles or interpretations, esp. implying confusion or deceit (*leads a double life*). **7** *Mus.* lower in pitch by an octave (*double bassoon*). •*adv.* **1** at or to twice the amount, etc. (*counts double*). **2** two to-

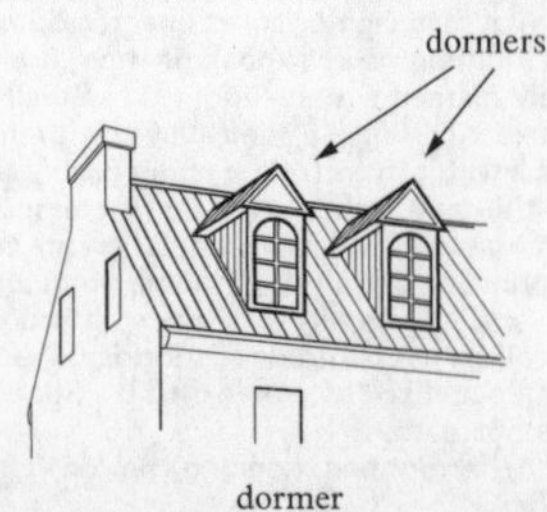

dormer

gether (*sleep double*). •*n.* **1 a** a double quantity or thing; twice as much or many. **b** *colloq.* a double measure of liquor. **2 a** a person who looks exactly like another. **b** an understudy. **c** a wraith. **3** (in *pl.*) *Sports* (esp. tennis) a game between two pairs of players. **4** *Sports* a pair of victories over the same team, a pair of championships at the same game, etc. **5** a system of betting in which the winnings and stake from the first bet are transferred to a second. **6** *Bridge* the doubling of an opponent's bid. **7** *Darts* a hit on the narrow ring enclosed by the two outer circles of a dartboard. **8** a sharp turn, esp. of the tracks of a hunted animal, or the course of a river. •*v.* **1** *tr. & intr.* make or become twice as much or many; increase twofold; multiply by two. **2** *tr.* amount to twice as much as. **3 a** *tr.* fold or bend (paper, cloth, etc.) over on itself. **b** *intr.* become folded. **4 a** *tr.* (of an actor) play (two parts) in the same piece. **b** *intr.* (often foll. by *for*) be understudy, etc. **5** *intr.* (usu. foll. by *as*) play a twofold role. **6** *intr.* turn sharply in flight or pursuit. **7** *tr. Naut.* sail around (a headland). **8** *tr. Bridge* make a call increasing the value of the points to be won or lost on (an opponent's bid). **9** *Mus.* **a** *intr.* (often foll. by *on*) play two or more musical instruments (*the clarinettist doubles on tenor sax*). **b** *tr.* add the same note in a higher or lower octave to (a note). **10** *tr.* clench (a fist). **11** *intr.* move at twice the usual speed; run. **12** *Billiards* **a** *intr.* rebound. **b** *tr.* cause to rebound. □ **double back** take a new direction opposite to the previous one. **double or nothing** a gamble to decide whether a player's loss or debt be doubled or canceled. **double up 1 a** bend or curl up. **b** cause to do this. **2** be overcome with pain or laughter. **3** share or assign to a room, quarters, etc., with another or others. **4** fold or become folded. **5** use winnings from a bet as stake for another. **on the double** running; hurrying. □□ **dou·bler** *n.* **dou·bly** *adv.*

dou·ble a·gent *n.* one who spies simultaneously for two rival countries, etc.

dou·ble-bar·reled *adj.* **1** (of a gun) having two barrels. **2** twofold.

dou·ble bass *n.* **1** the largest and lowest-pitched instrument of the violin family. **2** (also **dou·ble bass·ist**) its player.

dou·ble-blind *adj. & n.* •*adj.* (of a test or experiment) in which neither the tester nor the subject has knowledge of identities, etc., that might lead to bias. •*n.* such a test or experiment.

dou·ble boil·er *n.* a saucepan with a detachable upper compartment heated by boiling water in the lower one.

dou·ble-breast·ed *adj.* (of a coat, etc.) having two fronts overlapping across the body.

dou·ble chin *n.* a chin with a fold of loose flesh below it. □□ **dou·ble-chinned** *adj.*

dou·ble-cross *v. & n.* •*v.tr.* deceive or betray (a person one is supposedly helping). •*n.* an act of double-crossing. □□ **dou·ble-cross·er** *n.*

dou·ble-deal·ing *n. & adj.* •*n.* deceit. •*adj.* practicing deceit. □□ **dou·ble-deal·er** *n.*

dou·ble-deck·er *n.* **1** esp. *Brit.* a bus having an upper and lower deck. **2** *colloq.* anything consisting of two layers.

dou·ble Dutch *n.* a synchronized jump-rope game using two outstretched ropes swung in opposite directions.

dou·ble ea·gle *n.* **1** a figure of a two-headed eagle. **2** *Golf* a score of three strokes under par at any hole.

dou·ble en·ten·dre /dúbəl aantaándrə, dööblaan taáNdrə/ *n.* **1** a word or phrase open to two interpretations, one usu. risqué or indecent. **2** humor using such words or phrases.

dou·ble ex·po·sure *n. Photog.* the accidental or deliberate repeated exposure of a plate, film, etc.

dou·ble fea·ture *n.* a movie program with two full-length films.

dou·ble-head·er /dúbəlhedər/ *n.* **1** a train pulled by two locomotives coupled together. **2** two games (esp. baseball) played in succession.

dou·ble he·lix *n.* a pair of parallel helices with a common axis, esp. in the structure of the DNA molecule.

dou·ble in·dem·ni·ty *n.* a clause in a life-insurance policy providing double payment to the beneficiary if the insured person dies accidentally.

dou·ble-joint·ed *adj.* having joints that allow unusual bending.

dou·ble knit *n.* (of fabric) knit of two joined layers for extra thickness.

dou·ble neg·a·tive *n. Gram.* a negative statement containing two negative elements (e.g., *didn't say nothing*). ▶Considered ungrammatical in standard English.

dou·ble-park *v.tr. & intr.* park (a vehicle) alongside one that is already parked at the roadside.

dou·ble play *n. Baseball* putting out two runners.

dou·ble pneu·mo·nia *n.* pneumonia affecting both lungs.

dou·ble stand·ard *n.* **1** a rule or principle applied more strictly to some people than to others. **2** bimetallism.

dou·blet /dúblit/ *n.* **1** either of a pair of similar things. **2** *hist.* a man's short, close-fitting jacket.

dou·ble take *n.* a delayed reaction to a situation, etc., immediately after one's first reaction.

dou·ble-talk *n.* verbal expression that is ambiguous or misleading.

dou·ble·think /dúbəlthingk/ *n.* the capacity to accept contrary opinions at the same time.

dou·bloon /dublóōn/ *n. hist.* a Spanish gold coin.

doubt /dowt/ *n. & v.* •*n.* **1** a feeling of uncertainty; an undecided state of mind (*be in no doubt about; have no doubt that*). **2** (often foll. by *of, about*) an inclination to disbelieve. **3** an uncertain state of things. **4** a lack of full proof or clear indication (*benefit of the doubt*). •*v.* **1** *tr.* (often foll. by *whether, if, that* + clause; also foll. (after *neg.* or *interrog.*) by *but, but that*) feel uncertain or undecided about (*I doubt that you are right*). **2** *tr.* hesitate to believe. **3** *intr.* (often foll. by *of*) feel uncertain or undecided; have doubts (*never doubted of success*). □ **beyond doubt** certainly. **in doubt** open to question. **no doubt** certainly; probably; admittedly. **without doubt** (or **a doubt**) certainly. □□ **doubt·er** *n.*

doubt·ful /dówtfōōl/ *adj.* **1** feeling doubt. **2** causing doubt. **3** unreliable (*a doubtful ally*). □□ **doubt·ful·ly** *adv.*

doubt·ing Thom·as /tóməs/ *n.* a skeptical person.

doubt·less /dówtlis/ *adv.* (often qualifying a sentence) **1** certainly; no doubt. **2** probably. □□ **doubt·less·ly** *adv.*

douche /dōōsh/ *n. & v.* •*n.* **1** a jet of liquid applied to a body part for cleansing or medicinal purposes. **2** a device for producing such a jet. •*v.* **1** *tr.* treat with a douche. **2** *intr.* use a douche.

dough /dō/ *n.* **1** a thick mixture of flour, etc., and liquid, for baking. **2** *sl.* money.

dough·boy /dōboy/ *n. colloq.* a US infantryman, esp. in World War I.

dough·nut /dōnut/ *n.* (also **do·nut**) a small fried cake of sweetened dough.

dough·ty /dówtee/ *adj.* (**doughtier, doughtiest**) *archaic* or *joc.* valiant.

Doug·las fir /dúgləs/ *n.* any large conifer of the genus *Pseudotsuga*, of Western N. America.

dour /dōōr, dowr/ *adj.* stern; obstinate. □□ **dour·ly** *adv.*

douse /dows/ *v.tr.* (also **dowse**) **1 a** throw water over. **b** plunge into water. **2** extinguish (a light).
dove[1] /duv/ *n.* **1** any bird of the family Columbidae, with short legs, small head, and large breast. **2** a gentle or innocent person. **3** *Polit.* an advocate of peace or peaceful policies. **4** a soft gray color.
dove[2] /dōv/ *past* and *past part.* of DIVE.
dove·cote /dúvkōt, –kot/ *n.* (also **dove·cot**) a shelter with nesting holes for domesticated pigeons.
dove·tail /dúvtayl/ *n.* & *v.* • *n.* **1** a joint formed by a mortise with a tenon shaped like a dove's spread tail. **2** such a tenon. • *v.* **1** *tr.* join together by means of a dovetail. **2** *tr.* & *intr.* (often foll. by *into*, *with*) fit readily together; combine neatly or compactly.

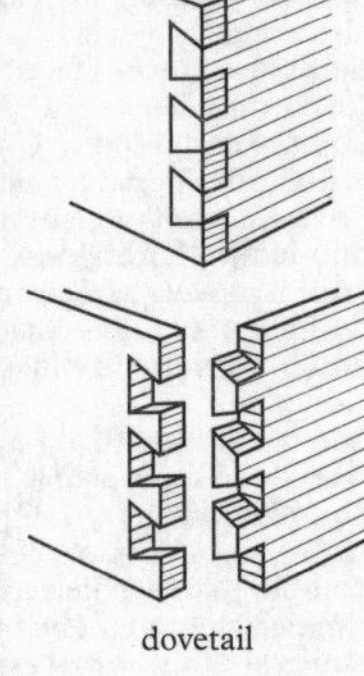
dovetail

dow·a·ger /dówəjər/ *n.* **1** a widow with a title or property derived from her late husband (*Queen dowager*; *dowager duchess*). **2** *colloq.* a dignified elderly woman.
dow·dy /dówdee/ *adj.* & *n.* • *adj.* (**dowdier**, **dowdiest**) **1** (of clothes) unattractively dull. **2** dressed in dowdy clothes. • *n.* (*pl.* **-dies**) a dowdy woman. ▫▫ **dow·di·ly** *adv.* **dow·di·ness** *n.*
dow·el /dówəl/ *n.* & *v.* • *n.* a headless peg holding together components of a structure. • *v.tr.* fasten with a dowel.
dow·el·ing /dówəling/ *n.* round rods for cutting into dowels.
dow·er /dowər/ *n.* & *v.* • *n.* **1** a widow's share for life of her husband's estate. **2** *archaic* a dowry. **3** a natural gift or talent. • *v.tr.* (foll. by *with*) endow with talent, etc.
Dow–Jones av·er·age /dowjṓnz/ *n.* (also **Dow–Jones in·dex**) a figure indicating the relative price of shares on the New York Stock Exchange.
down[1] /down/ *adv.*, *prep.*, *adj.*, *v.*, & *n.* • *adv.* **1** into or toward a lower place (*fall down*). **2** in a lower place or position (*blinds were down*). **3** to or in a place regarded as lower, esp. southward. **4 a** in or into a low or weaker position, mood, or condition (*hit a man when he's down*). **b** in a position of lagging or loss (*our team was three goals down*). **c** (of a computer system) out of action. **5** from an earlier to a later time (*customs handed down*). **6** to a finer or thinner consistency or a smaller amount or size (*water down*). **7** cheaper (*bread is down*; *stocks are down*). **8** into a more settled state (*calm down*). **9** in writing; in or into recorded or listed form (*copy it down*). **10** (of part of a larger whole) paid; dealt with (*$5 down*). **11** *Naut.* **a** with the current or wind. **b** (of a ship's helm) with the rudder to windward. **12** inclusively of the lower limit in a series (*read down to the third paragraph*). **13** (as *int.*) lie down, put (something) down, etc. **14** (of a crossword clue or answer) read vertically (*cannot do five down*). **15** downstairs, esp. after rising (*is not down yet*). **16** swallowed (*could not get the pill down*). **17** *Football* (of the ball) no longer in play. • *prep.* **1** downward along, through, or into. **2** from top to bottom of. **3** along (*walk down the road*). **4** at or in a lower part of (*situated down the river*). • *adj.* **1** directed downward. **2** *colloq.* unhappy; depressed. • *v.tr. colloq.* **1** knock or bring down. **2** swallow. • *n.* **1** an act of putting down (as an opponent in wrestling). **2** a reverse of fortune (*ups and downs*). **3** *colloq.* a period of depression. **4** *Football* **a** one of a series of plays (up to four) in which the offensive team must advance the ball 10 yards in order to keep the ball. **b** the declaring of the ball as no longer in play. ▫ **be down on** *colloq.* disapprove of; show animosity toward. **be down to 1** be attributable to. **2** be the responsibility of. **3** have used up everything except (*down to their last can of rations*). **down on one's luck** *colloq.* **1** temporarily unfortunate. **2** dispirited by misfortune. **down with** *int.* expressing rejection of a specified person or thing.
down[2] /down/ *n.* **1 a** the first covering of young birds. **b** a bird's under-plumage. **c** a layer of fine, soft feathers. **2** fine, soft hair esp. on the face. **3** short, soft hairs on some leaves, fruit, seeds, etc. **4** a fluffy substance, e.g., thistledown.
down-and-out *adj.* & *n.* • *adj.* (**down and out** when *predic.*) **1** penniless; destitute. **2** *Boxing* unable to resume the fight. • *n.* a destitute person.
down-at-the-heels *adj.* (also **down-at-heel, down-at-the-heel**) shabby; slovenly.
down·beat /dównbeet/ *n.* & *adj.* • *n. Mus.* an accented beat, usu. the first of the bar. • *adj.* **1** pessimistic; gloomy. **2** relaxed.
down·cast /dównkast/ *adj.* & *n.* • *adj.* **1** (of eyes) looking downward. **2** dejected. • *n.* a shaft dug in a mine for extra ventilation.
down·draft /dówndraft/ *n.* a downward draft, esp. one down a chimney into a room.
down·er /dównər/ *n. sl.* **1** a depressant or tranquilizing drug. **2** a depressing person or experience; a failure.
down·fall /dównfawl/ *n.* **1** a fall from prosperity or power. **2** the cause of this.
down·grade *v.* & *n.* • *v.tr.* /dówngráyd/ **1** make lower in rank or status. **2** speak disparagingly of. • *n.* /dówngrayd/ **1** a descending slope of a road or railroad. **2** a deterioration. ▫ **on the downgrade** in decline.
down·heart·ed /dównhaártid/ *adj.* dejected; in low spirits. ▫▫ **down·heart·ed·ly** *adv.* **down·heart·ed·ness** *n.*
down·hill *adv.*, *adj.*, & *n.* • *adv.* /dównhíl/ in a descending direction. • *adj.* /dównhil/ **1** sloping down; descending. **2** declining; deteriorating. • *n.* /dównhil/ **1** *Skiing* a downhill race. **2** a downward slope. **3** a decline. ▫ **go downhill** *colloq.* decline; deteriorate.
down in the mouth *adj. colloq.* looking unhappy.
down·load /dównlṓd/ *v.tr. Computing* transfer (data) from one storage device or system to another.
down-mar·ket *adj.* & *adv. colloq.* toward or relating to the cheaper sector of the market.
down pay·ment *n.* a partial payment made at the time of purchase.
down·play /dównpláy/ *v.tr.* play down; minimize the importance of.
down·pour /dównpawr/ *n.* a heavy fall of rain.
down·right /dównrīt/ *adj.* & *adv.* • *adj.* **1** plain; straightforward. **2** utter (*a downright lie*; *downright nonsense*). • *adv.* thoroughly (*downright rude*).
down·scale /dównskáyl/ *v.* & *adj.* • *v.tr.* reduce or restrict in size, scale, or extent. • *adj.* at the lower end of a scale; inferior.
down·shift /dównshift/ *v.intr.* & *tr.* shift (an automotive vehicle) into a lower gear.
down·side /dównsīd/ *n.* a downward movement of share prices, etc.
down·size /dównsīz/ *v.tr.* (**downsized, downsizing**) **1** reduce in size. **2** cut back on the number of employees in (a company).
Down's syn·drome /downz/ *n. Med.* (also **Down syn·drome**) a congenital disorder characterized by mental retardation and physical abnormalities (cf. MONGOLISM).
down·stage /dównstayj/ *n.*, *adj.*, & *adv. Theatr.* • *n.* the frontmost portion of the stage. • *adj.* & *adv.* at or to the front of the stage.

down·stairs *adv., adj., & n.* • *adv.* /dównstáirz/ **1** down a flight of stairs. **2** to or on a lower floor. • *adj.* /dównstairz/ (also **down·stair**) situated downstairs. • *n.* /dównstáirz/ the lower floor.
down·state /dównstáyt/ *adj., n., & adv.* • *adj.* of or in a southern part of a state. • *n.* a downstate area. • *adv.* in a downstate area.
down·stream /dównstreem/ *adv. & adj.* • *adv.* in the direction of the flow of a stream, etc. • *adj.* moving downstream.
down·time /dówntīm/ *n.* time during which a machine, esp. a computer, is out of action or unavailable for use.
down-to-earth *adj.* practical; realistic.
down·town /dówntówn/ *adj., n., & adv.* • *adj.* of or in the lower or more central part, or the business part, of a town or city. • *n.* a downtown area. • *adv.* in or into a downtown area.
down·trod·den /dówntród'n/ *adj.* oppressed; badly treated.
down·turn /dówntərn/ *n.* a decline, esp. in economic activity.
down un·der *adv. colloq.* (also **Down Un·der**) in the antipodes, esp. Australia.
down·ward /dównwərd/ *adv. & adj.* • *adv.* (also **down·wards**) toward what is lower, inferior, less important, or later. • *adj.* moving, extending, pointing, or leading downward. ▫▫ **down·ward·ly** *adv.*
down·wind /dównwind/ *adj. & adv.* in the direction in which the wind is blowing.
down·y /dównee/ *adj.* (**downier, downiest**) **1** of, like, or covered with down. **2** soft and fluffy.
dow·ry /dówree/ *n.* (*pl.* **-ries**) **1** property or money brought by a bride to her husband. **2** a talent; a natural gift.
dowse[1] /dowz/ *v.intr.* search for underground water or minerals by holding a stick or rod which dips abruptly when over the right spot. ▫▫ **dows·er** *n.*
dowse[2] var. of DOUSE.
dows·ing rod *n.* (also **di·vin·ing rod**) a stick or rod used in dowsing.
dox·ol·o·gy /doksóləjee/ *n.* (*pl.* **-gies**) a liturgical formula of praise to God.
doy·en /doyén, dóyən, dwaáyaN/ *n.* (*fem.* **doyenne** /doyén, dwaayén/) the senior member of a body of colleagues, esp. the senior ambassador at a court.
doz. *abbr.* dozen.
doze /dōz/ *v. & n.* • *v.intr.* sleep lightly; be half asleep. • *n.* a short, light sleep. ▫ **doze off** fall lightly asleep.
doz·en /dúzən/ *n.* **1** (prec. by *a* or a number) (*pl.* **dozen**) twelve (*a dozen eggs*). **2** a set or group of twelve. **3** *colloq.* about twelve; a fairly large indefinite number. **4** (in *pl.*; usu. foll. by *of*) *colloq.* very many (*dozens of mistakes*). ▫ **by the dozen** in large quantities.
doz·y /dōzee/ *adj.* (**dozier, doziest**) drowsy; tending to doze. ▫▫ **doz·i·ly** *adv.* **doz·i·ness** *n.*
DPT *abbr.* (vaccination against) diphtheria, pertussis, and tetanus.
Dr. *abbr.* **1** Doctor. **2** Drive. **3** debtor.
dr. *abbr.* **1** dram(s). **2** drachma(s).
drab[1] /drab/ *adj. & n.* • *adj.* (**drabber, drabbest**) **1** dull; uninteresting. **2** of a dull brownish color. • *n.* **1** drab color. **2** monotony. ▫▫ **drab·ly** *adv.* **drab·ness** *n.*
drab[2] /drab/ see DRIBS AND DRABS.
drach·ma /drákmə/ *n.* (*pl.* **drachmas** or **drachmai** /–mī/ or **drachmae** /–mee/) **1** the chief monetary unit of Greece. **2** a silver coin of ancient Greece.
dra·co·ni·an /drəkṓneeən, dray–/ *adj.* (also **dra·con·ic** /–kónik/) (esp. of laws) very harsh or severe.
draft /draft/ *n. & v.* • *n.* **1 a** a preliminary written version of a speech, document, etc. **b** a rough preliminary outline of a scheme. **c** a sketch of work to be carried out. **2 a** a written order for payment of money by a bank. **b** the drawing of money by means of this. **3** (foll. by *on*) a demand made on a person's confidence, friendship, etc. **4 a** a party detached from a larger group for a special purpose. **b** the selection of this. **5** compulsory military service. **6** a reinforcement. **7** a current of air in a confined space. **8** pulling; traction. **9** *Naut.* the depth of water needed to float a ship. **10** the drawing of liquor from a cask, etc. **11 a** a single act of drinking. **b** the amount drunk in this. **c** a dose of liquid medicine. **12 a** the drawing in of a fishing net. **b** the fish taken at one drawing. • *v.tr.* **1** prepare a draft of (a document, scheme, etc.). **2** select for a special purpose. **3** conscript for military service. ▫▫ **draft·ee** /–tee/ *n.* **draft·er** *n.*
draft beer *n.* beer drawn from a cask.
draft horse *n.* a horse used for pulling heavy loads.
drag /drag/ *v. & n.* • *v.* (**dragged, dragging**) **1** *tr.* pull along with effort. **2 a** *tr.* allow (one's feet, tail, etc.) to trail along the ground. **b** *intr.* trail along the ground. **c** *intr.* (of time, etc.) go or pass heavily or slowly or tediously. **3 a** *intr.* (usu. foll. by *for*) use a grapnel or drag (to find a drowned person or lost object). **b** *tr.* search the bottom of (a river, etc.) with grapnels, nets, or drags. **4** *tr.* (often foll. by *to*) *colloq.* take (a person to a place, etc., esp. against his or her will). **5** *intr.* (foll. by *on, at*) draw on (a cigarette, etc.). **6** *intr.* (often foll. by *on*) continue at tedious length. • *n.* **1 a** an obstruction to progress. **b** *Aeron.* the longitudinal retarding force exerted by air. **c** slow motion; impeded progress. **d** an iron shoe for retarding a horse-drawn vehicle downhill. **2** *colloq.* a boring or dreary person, duty, performance, etc. **3 a** a lure drawn before hounds as a substitute for a fox. **b** a hunt using this. **4** an apparatus for dredging or recovering drowned persons, etc. from under water. **5** = DRAGNET. **6** *sl.* a draw on a cigarette, etc. **7** *sl.* **a** women's clothes worn by men. **b** a party at which these are worn. **c** clothes in general. **8** an act of dragging. **9** sl. (in full **drag race**) an acceleration race between cars. **10** *sl.* influence; pull. **11** *sl.* a street or road (*the main drag*). ▫ **drag one's feet** (or **heels**) be deliberately slow or reluctant to act. **drag out** protract.
drag·net /drágnet/ *n* **1** a net drawn through a river or across ground to trap fish or game. **2** a systematic hunt for criminals, etc.
drag·on /drágən/ *n.* **1** a mythical monster like a reptile, usu. with wings and able to breathe out fire. **2** a fierce woman. **3** (in full **flying dragon**) a lizard, *Draco volans*, with a long tail and membranous winglike structures.
drag·on·fly /drágənflī/ *n.* (*pl.* **-flies**) any of various insects of the order Odonata, having a long, slender body and two pairs of large transparent wings.
dra·goon /drəgóon/ *n. & v.* • *n.* **1** a cavalryman (originally a mounted infantryman armed with a carbine). **2** a rough, fierce fellow. **3** a variety of pigeon. • *v.tr.* **1** (foll. by *into*) coerce into doing something. **2** persecute, esp. with troops.
drag queen *n. sl.* a male transvestite.
drag race *n.* = DRAG *n.* 9.
drag·ster /drágstər/ *n.* a car built or modified to take part in drag races.
drain /drayn/ *v. & n.* • *v.* **1** *tr.* draw off liquid from, esp.: **a** make (land, etc.) dry by providing an outflow for moisture. **b** (of a river) carry off the superfluous water of (a district). **c** remove purulent matter from (an abscess). **2** *tr.* (foll. by *off, away*) draw off (liquid), esp. by a pipe. **3** *intr.* (foll. by *away, off, through*) flow or trickle away. **4** *intr.* become dry as liquid flows away (*put it there to drain*). **5** *tr.* (often foll. by *of*) exhaust or deprive (a person or thing) of strength, resources, etc. **6** *tr.* **a** drink (liquid) to the dregs. **b** empty (a vessel)

by drinking the contents. • *n.* **1 a** a channel, conduit, or pipe carrying off liquid, esp. an artificial conduit for water or sewage. **b** a tube for drawing off the discharge from an abscess, etc. **2** a constant outflow, withdrawal, or expenditure (*a great drain on my resources*). □ **down the drain** *colloq.* lost; wasted.

drain•age /dráynij/ *n.* **1** the process or means of draining (*the land has poor drainage*). **2** a system of drains, artificial or natural. **3** what is drained off.

drain•board /dráynbawrd/ *n.* a sloping surface beside a sink, on which washed dishes, etc., are left to drain.

drain•er /dráynər/ *n.* **1** a device for draining; anything on which things are put to drain. **2** a person who drains.

drain•pipe /dráynpīp/ *n.* a pipe for carrying off water, sewage, etc., from a building.

drake /drayk/ *n.* a male duck.

dram /dram/ *n.* **1** a small drink of liquor. **2** apothecaries' weight or measure equivalent to one eighth of an ounce or (in full **fluid dram**) one eighth of a fluid ounce.

dra•ma /drámə, draámə/ *n.* **1** a play for acting on stage or for broadcasting. **2** the art of writing and presenting plays. **3** an exciting or emotional event, set of circumstances, etc. **4** dramatic quality (*the drama of the situation*).

dra•mat•ic /drəmátik/ *adj.* **1** of drama or the study of drama. **2** (of an event, circumstance, etc.) sudden and exciting or unexpected. **3** vividly striking. **4** (of a gesture, etc.) theatrical; overdone; absurd. □□ **dra•mat•i•cal•ly** *adv.*

dra•mat•ic i•ro•ny = TRAGIC IRONY.

dra•mat•ics /drəmátiks/ *n.pl.* (often treated as *sing.*) **1** the production and performance of plays. **2** exaggerated or showy behavior.

dram•a•tis per•so•nae /drámətis pərsṓnee, draámətis pərsṓnī/ *n.pl.* (often treated as *sing.*) **1** the characters in a play. **2** a list of these.

dram•a•tist /drámətist, draámə–/ *n.* a writer of dramas.

dram•a•tize /drámətīz, draámə–/ *v.* **1 a** *tr.* adapt (a novel, etc.) to form a stage play. **b** *intr.* admit of such adaptation. **2** *tr.* make a drama or dramatic scene of. **3** *tr.* (also *absol.*) express or react to in a dramatic way. □□ **dram•a•ti•za•tion** *n.*

drank *past* of DRINK.

drape /drayp/ *v.* & *n.* • *v.tr.* **1** hang, cover loosely, or adorn with cloth, etc. **2** arrange (clothes or hangings) carefully in folds. • *n.* **1** (often in *pl.*) a curtain or drapery. **2** a piece of drapery. **3** the way in which a garment or fabric hangs.

dra•per•y /dráypəree/ *n.* (*pl.* **-ies**) **1** clothing or hangings arranged in folds. **2** (often in *pl.*) a curtain or hanging.

dras•tic /drástik/ *adj.* having a strong or far-reaching effect; severe. □□ **dras•ti•cal•ly** *adv.*

drat /drat/ *v.* & *int. colloq.* • *v.tr.* (**dratted, dratting** (usu. as an exclam.)) curse; confound (*drat the thing!*). • *int.* expressing anger or annoyance. □□ **drat•ted** *adj.*

draw /draw/ *v.* & *n.* • *v.* (*past* **drew** /drōō/; *past part.* **drawn** /drawn/) **1** *tr.* pull or cause to move toward or after one. **2** *tr.* pull (a thing) up, over, or across. **3** *tr.* pull (curtains, etc.) open or shut. **4** *tr.* take (a person) aside, esp. to talk to. **5** *tr.* attract; bring to oneself or to something; take in (*drew a deep breath*). **6** *intr.* (foll. by *at, on*) suck smoke from (a cigarette, pipe, etc.). **7** *tr.* **a** (also *absol.*) take out; remove (e.g., a gun from a holster). **b** select by taking out (e.g., a playing card from a deck). **8** *tr.* obtain or take from a source (*draw a salary*). **9** *tr.* trace (a line, mark, furrow, or figure). **10 a** *tr.* produce (a picture) by tracing lines and marks. **b** *tr.* represent (a thing) by this means. **c** *absol.* make a drawing. **11** *tr.* (also *absol.*) finish (a contest or game) with neither side winning. **12** *intr.* make one's or its way; proceed; move; come (*drew near the bridge*). **13** *tr.* infer; deduce (a conclusion). **14** *tr.* **a** elicit; evoke. **b** bring about; entail (*draw criticism*). **15** *tr.* haul up (water) from a well. **16** *tr.* bring out or extract (liquid, etc., from a vessel or a wound). **17** *intr.* (of a chimney or pipe) promote or allow a draft. **18 a** *tr.* obtain by lot (*drew the winning number*). **b** *absol.* draw lots. **19** *intr.* (foll. by *on*) make a demand on a person, a person's skill, memory, imagination, etc. **20** *tr.* write out (a bill, check, or draft) (*drew a check on the bank*). **21** *tr.* (foll. by *up*)) frame (a document) in due form; compose. **22** *tr.* formulate or perceive (a comparison or distinction). **23** *tr.* (of a ship) require (a specified depth of water) to float in. **24** *tr.* disembowel (*draw the fowl before cooking it*). • *n.* **1** an act of drawing. **2 a** a person or thing that draws custom, attention, etc. **b** the power to attract attention. **3** the drawing of lots, esp. a raffle. **4** a drawn game. **5** a suck on a cigarette, etc. **6** the act of removing a gun from its holster in order to shoot (*quick on the draw*). **7** strain; pull. **8** the movable part of a drawbridge. □ **draw back** withdraw from an undertaking. **draw a person's fire** attract hostility, criticism, etc., away from a more important target. **draw in 1 a** (of successive days) become shorter. **b** (of a day) approach its end. **c** (of successive evenings or nights) start earlier because of the changing seasons. **2** persuade to join; entice. **draw in one's horns** become less assertive or ambitious; draw back. **draw the line at** set a limit (of tolerance, etc.) at. **draw out 1** prolong. **2** elicit. **3** induce to talk. **4** (of successive days) become longer. **5** lead out, detach, or array (troops).

draw•back /dráwbak/ *n.* a thing that impairs satisfaction; a disadvantage.

draw•bridge /dráwbrij/ *n.* a bridge, esp. over water, hinged at one end so that it may be raised to prevent passage or to allow ships, etc., to pass.

draw•er *n.* **1** /dráwər/ a person or thing that draws, esp. a person who draws a check, etc. **2** /drawr/ a boxlike storage compartment without a lid, sliding in and out of a frame, table, etc. (*chest of drawers*). **3** (in *pl.*) /drawrz/ an undergarment worn next to the body below the waist. □□ **draw•er•ful** *n.* (*pl.* **-fuls**).

draw•ing /dráwing/ *n.* **1 a** the art of representing by line. **b** delineation without color or with a single color. **c** the art of representing with pencils, pens, crayons, etc., rather than paint. **2** a picture produced in this way.

draw•ing board *n.* a board for spreading drawing paper on. □ **back to the drawing board** *colloq.* back to begin afresh (after earlier failure).

draw•ing room /dráwingrōōm, –rōōm/ *n.* **1** a room for comfortable sitting or entertaining in a private house. **2** a private compartment in a train.

drawl /drawl/ *v.* & *n.* • *v.* **1** *intr.* speak with drawn-out vowel sounds. **2** *tr.* utter in this way. • *n.* a drawling utterance or way of speaking. □□ **drawl•er** *n.*

drawn /drawn/ *past part.* of DRAW. *adj.* **1** looking strained from fear, anxiety, or pain. **2** (of butter) melted.

draw•sheet /dráwsheet/ *n.* a sheet that can be taken from under a patient without remaking the bed.

draw•string /dráwstring/ *n.* a string that can be pulled to tighten the mouth of a bag, the waist of a garment, etc.

dray[1] /dray/ *n.* a low cart without sides for heavy loads.

dray[2] var. of DREY.

dray horse *n.* a large, powerful horse.

dread /dred/ *v., n.,* & *adj.* • *v.tr.* **1** (foll. by *that,* or *to* + infin.) fear greatly. **2** shrink from; look forward to with great apprehension. **3** be in great fear of. • *n.* **1** great fear; apprehension; awe. **2** an object of fear or awe. • *adj.* **1** dreaded. **2** *archaic* awe-inspiring; revered.

dread•ful /drédfōōl/ *adj.* & *adv.* • *adj.* **1** terrible; inspiring fear or awe. **2** *colloq.* troublesome; disagreeable; very bad. • *adv. colloq.* dreadfully; very. ▫▫ **dread·ful·ly** *adv.* **dread·ful·ness** *n.*

dread·locks /drédloks/ *n.pl.* **1** a Rastafarian hairstyle in which the hair is twisted into tight braids or ringlets hanging down on all sides. **2** hair dressed in this way.

dread·nought /drédnawt/ *n.* (usu. **Dreadnought**) *Brit. hist.* a type of heavily armed battleship (from the name of the first, launched in 1906).

dream /dreem/ *n. & v.* • *n.* **1 a** a series of pictures or events in the mind of a sleeping person. **b** the act or time of seeing this. **c** (in full **waking dream**) a similar experience of one awake. **2** a daydream or fantasy. **3** an ideal, aspiration, or ambition, esp. of a nation. **4** a beautiful or ideal person or thing. **5** a state of mind without proper perception of reality (*goes about in a dream*). • *v.* (*past* and *past part.* **dreamed** or **dreamt** /dremt/) **1** *intr.* experience a dream. **2** *tr.* imagine in or as if in a dream. **3** (usu. with *neg.*) **a** *intr.* (foll. by *of*) contemplate the possibility of; have any conception or intention of (*would not dream of upsetting them*). **b** *tr.* (often foll. by *that* + clause) think of as a possibility (*never dreamed that he would come*). **4** *tr.* (foll. by *away*) spend (time) unprofitably. **5** *intr.* be inactive or unpractical. **6** *intr.* fall into a reverie. ▫ **dream up** imagine; invent. **like a dream** *colloq.* easily; effortlessly. ▫▫ **dream·ful** *adj.* **dream·less** *adj.* **dream·like** *adj.*

dream·boat /dreémbōt/ *n. colloq.* **1** a very attractive or ideal person, esp. of the opposite sex. **2** a very desirable or ideal thing.

dream·er /dreémər/ *n.* **1** a person who dreams. **2** a romantic or unpractical person.

dream·land /dreémland/ *n.* an ideal or imaginary land.

dream·y /dreémee/ *adj.* (**dreamier, dreamiest**) **1** given to daydreaming; fanciful; unpractical. **2** dreamlike; vague; misty. **3** *colloq.* delightful; marvelous. **4** *poet.* full of dreams. ▫▫ **dream·i·ly** *adv.* **dream·i·ness** *n.*

drear /dreer/ *adj. poet.* = DREARY.

drear·y /dreéree/ *adj.* (**drearier, dreariest**) dismal; dull; gloomy. ▫▫ **drear·i·ly** *adv.* **drear·i·ness** *n.*

dredge[1] /drej/ *v. & n.* • *v.* **1** *tr.* **a** (often foll. by *up*) bring up (lost or hidden material) as if with a dredge (*don't dredge all that up again*). **b** (often foll. by *away, up, out*) bring up or clear (mud, etc.) from a river, harbor, etc. with a dredge. **2** *tr.* clean (a harbor, river, etc.) with a dredge. **3** *intr.* use a dredge. • *n.* an apparatus used to scoop up oysters, specimens, etc., or to clear mud, etc., from a riverbed or seabed.

dredge[2] /drej/ *v.tr.* sprinkle with flour, sugar, etc.

dredg·er[1] /dréjər/ *n.* **1** a machine used for dredging rivers, etc.; a dredge. **2** a boat containing this.

dredg·er[2] /dréjər/ *n.* a container with a perforated lid used for sprinkling flour, sugar, etc.

dreg /dreg/ *n.* **1** (usu. in *pl.*) **a** a sediment; grounds, lees, etc. **b** a worthless part; refuse (*the dregs of humanity*). **2** a small remnant (*not a dreg*). ▫▫ **dreg·gy** *adj. colloq.*

drench /drench/ *v. & n.* • *v.tr.* **1** wet thoroughly (*was drenched by the rain*). **2** saturate; soak (in liquid). • *n.* a soaking; a downpour.

dress /dres/ *v. & n.* • *v.* **1 a** *tr.* clothe; array (*dressed in rags*). **b** *intr.* wear clothes of a specified kind or in a specified way (*dresses well*). **2** *intr.* **a** put on clothes. **b** put on formal or evening clothes, esp. for dinner. **3** *tr. Med.* **a** treat (a wound) with ointment, etc. **b** apply a dressing to (a wound). **4** *tr.* **a** clean and prepare (poultry, etc.) for cooking or eating. **b** add a dressing to (a salad, etc.). **5** *tr.* apply manure, etc., to a field, garden, etc. **6** *tr.* finish the surface of (fabric, building stone, etc.). **7** *tr.* groom (one's hair, a horse, etc.). **8** *Mil.* **a** *tr.* correct the alignment of (troops, etc.). **b** *intr.* (of troops) come into alignment. • *n.* **1** a one-piece woman's garment consisting of a bodice and skirt. **2** clothing, esp. a whole outfit, etc. **3** formal or ceremonial costume (*evening dress*). **4** an external covering; the outward form (*birds in their winter dress*). ▫ **dress down** *colloq.* **1** reprimand or scold. **2** dress casually, esp. for an informal affair. **dress rehearsal** the final rehearsal of a play, etc., wearing costume. **dress up 1** dress (oneself or another) elaborately for a special occasion. **2** dress in fancy dress. **3** decorate or adorn (*dress up the room*). **4** disguise (unwelcome facts) by embellishment.

dres·sage /drisaázh, dre–/ *n.* the training of a horse in obedience and deportment, esp. for competition.

dress cir·cle *n.* the first gallery in a theater, in which evening dress was formerly required.

dress code *n.* a set of rules, usu. written, describing acceptable dress, as at a school, restaurant, etc.

dress·er[1] /drésər/ *n.* a dressing table or chest of drawers; a bureau.

dress·er[2] /drésər/ *n.* **1** a person who assists actors to dress, takes care of their costumes, etc. **2** a person who dresses elegantly or in a specified way (*a snappy dresser*).

dress·ing /drésing/ *n.* **1** in senses of DRESS *v.* **2 a** an accompaniment to salads, usu. a mixture of oil with other ingredients; a sauce or seasoning (*French dressing*). **b** stuffing, esp. for poultry. **3 a** a bandage for a wound. **b** ointment, etc., used to dress a wound. **4** compost, etc., spread over land (*a top dressing of peat*).

dress·ing-down *n. colloq.* a scolding; a severe reprimand.

dress·ing gown *n.* = ROBE *n.* 2.

dress·ing room *n.* **1** a room for changing clothes, etc., in a theater, sports facility, etc. **2** a small room attached to a bedroom, containing clothes.

dress·ing ta·ble *n.* a table with mirror and drawers, used to sit at while applying makeup, etc.

dress·mak·er /drésmaykər/ *n.* a person who makes clothes professionally. ▫▫ **dress·mak·ing** *n.*

dress·y /drésee/ *adj.* (**dressier, dressiest**) **1 a** fond of smart clothes. **b** overdressed. **c** (of clothes) stylish or elaborate. **2** overelaborate. ▫▫ **dress·i·ness** *n.*

drew *past* of DRAW.

drib·ble /dríbəl/ *v. & n.* • *v.* **1** *intr.* allow saliva to flow from the mouth. **2** *intr. & tr.* flow or allow to flow in drops or a trickling stream. **3** *tr.* (also *absol.*) **a** *Basketball* bounce (the ball) repeatedly, esp. to retain control of it. **b** esp. *Soccer & Hockey* move (the ball, puck, etc.) forward with slight touches of the feet, the stick, etc. • *n.* **1** the act or an instance of dribbling. **2** a small trickling stream. ▫▫ **drib·bler** *n.* **drib·bly** *adj.*

dribs and drabs /dríbz ənd drábz/ *n.pl. colloq.* small scattered amounts (*did the work in dribs and drabs*).

dried *past* and *past part.* of DRY.

dri·er[1] *compar.* of DRY.

dri·er[2] /dríər/ *n.* (also **dry·er**) a machine for drying the hair, laundry, etc.

dri·est *superl.* of DRY.

drift /drift/ *n. & v.* • *n.* **1 a** a slow movement or variation. **b** such movement caused by a slow current. **2** the intention, meaning, scope, etc., of what is said, etc. (*didn't understand his drift*). **3** a large mass of snow, sand, etc., accumulated by the wind. **4** deviation of a ship, aircraft, etc., from its course. **5** *Geol.* material deposited by the wind, a current of water, etc. • *v.* **1** *intr.* be carried by or as if by a current of air or water. **2** *intr.* move or progress passively, casually, or aimlessly (*drifted into teaching*). **3 a** *tr. & intr.* pile or be piled by the wind into drifts. **b** *tr.* cover (a field, a road, etc.) with drifts. **4** *tr.* (of a current) carry. ▫▫ **drift·age** *n.*

drift·er /dríftər/ *n.* **1** an aimless or rootless person. **2** a boat used for drift-net fishing.

drift net *n.* a large net for herrings, etc., allowed to drift with the tide.

drift·wood /dríftwood/ *n.* wood, etc., driven or deposited by water.

drill[1] /dril/ *n. & v.* • *n.* **1** a pointed, esp. revolving, steel tool or machine used for boring cylindrical holes, sinking wells, etc. **2 a** esp. Mil. instruction or training in military exercises. **b** rigorous discipline or methodical instruction, esp. when learning or performing tasks. **c** routine procedure to be followed in an emergency (*fire drill*). **d** a routine or exercise (*drills in verb patterns*). **3** *colloq.* a recognized procedure (*you know the drill*). **4** a gastropod that bores into the shells of young oysters and other shellfish. • *v.* **1** *tr.* (also *absol.*) **a** (of a person or a tool) make a hole with a drill through or into (wood, metal, etc.). **b** make (a hole) with a drill. **2** *tr. & intr.* esp. *Mil.* subject to or undergo discipline by drill. **3** *tr.* impart (knowledge, etc.) by a strict method. **4** *tr. sl.* shoot with a gun (*drilled him full of holes*). ▫▫ **drill·er** *n.*

drill[2] /dril/ *n. & v.* • *n.* **1** a machine used for making furrows, sowing, and covering seed. **2** a small furrow for sowing seed in. **3** a ridge with such furrows on top. **4** a row of plants so sown. • *v.tr.* **1** sow (seed) with a drill. **2** plant (the ground) in drills.

drill[3] /dril/ *n.* a W. African baboon related to the mandrill.

drill[4] /dril/ *n.* a coarse twilled cotton or linen fabric.

drill·mas·ter /drílmastər/ *n.* **1** *Mil.* one who instructs or leads others (often recruits) in military drill. **2** a rigorous, exacting, or severe instructor.

drill press *n.* a drilling machine with a vertical bit that is lowered into the item being drilled.

drill rig *n.* (also **dril·ling rig**) a structure with equipment for drilling an oil well.

drill ser·geant *n.* **1** *Mil.* a noncommissioned officer who trains soldiers, esp. new recruits. **2** a strict disciplinarian.

drink /dringk/ *v. & n.* • *v.* (*past* **drank** /drangk/; *past part.* **drunk** /drungk/) **1 a** *tr.* swallow (a liquid). **b** *tr.* swallow the liquid contents of (a vessel). **c** *intr.* swallow liquid; take drafts (*drank from the stream*). **2** *intr.* take alcohol, esp. to excess (*I have heard that she drinks*). **3** *tr.* (of a plant, porous material, etc.) absorb (moisture). **4** *refl.* bring (oneself, etc.) to a specified condition by drinking (*drank himself into a stupor*). **5** *tr.* (usu. foll. by *away*) spend (wages, etc.) on drink (*drank away the money*). • *n.* **1 a** a liquid for drinking (*milk is a high-cholesterol drink*). **b** a draft or specified amount of this (*had a drink of milk*). **2 a** a portion, glass, etc., of alcohol (*have a drink*). **b** excessive indulgence in alcohol (*drink is his vice*). **3** (as **the drink**) *colloq.* the sea. ▫ **drink in** listen to closely or eagerly (*drank in his every word*). **drink to** toast; wish success to. **drink a person under the table** remain sober longer than one's drinking companion. **drink up** drink the whole of; empty. ▫▫ **drink·a·ble** *adj.* **drink·er** *n.*

drip /drip/ *v. & n.* • *v.* (**dripped, dripping**) **1** *intr. & tr.* fall or let fall in drops. **2** *intr.* (often foll. by *with*) be so wet as to shed drops (*dripped with sweat*). • *n.* **1 a** the act or an instance of dripping (*the steady drip of rain*). **b** a drop of liquid (*a drip of paint*). **c** a sound of dripping. **2** *colloq.* a stupid, dull, or ineffective person. **3** (in full **drip-feed**) *Med.* the drip-by-drip intravenous administration of a solution of salt, sugar, etc. **4** *Archit.* a projection, esp. from a windowsill, keeping the rain off the walls. ▫ **dripping wet** very wet.

drip-dry *v. & adj.* • *v.* (**·dries, ·dried**) **1** *intr.* (of fabric, etc.) dry crease-free when hung up to drip. **2** *tr.* leave (a garment, etc.) hanging up to dry. • *adj.* able to be drip-dried.

drip·ping /dríping/ *n.* (usu. *pl.*) fat melted from roasted meat and used for cooking or as a spread.

drip·py /drípee/ *adj.* (**drippier, drippiest**) **1** tending to drip. **2** *sl.* ineffectual; sloppily sentimental. ▫▫ **drip·pi·ly** *adv.* **drip·pi·ness** *n.*

drive /drīv/ *v. & n.* • *v.* (*past* **drove** /drōv/; *past part.* **driv·en** /drívən/) **1** *tr.* (usu. foll. by *away, back, in, out, to,* etc.) urge in some direction, esp. forcibly (*drove back the wolves*). **2** *tr.* **a** (usu. foll. by *to* + infin., or *to* + verbal noun) compel or constrain forcibly (*was driven to complain; drove her to stealing*). **b** (often foll. by *to*) force into a specified state (*drove him mad; driven to despair*). **c** (often *refl.*) urge to overwork (*drives himself too hard*). **3 a** *tr.* (also *absol.*) operate and direct the course of (a vehicle, a locomotive, etc.) (*drove a sports car; drives well*). **b** *tr. & intr.* convey or be conveyed in a vehicle (*drove them to the station; drove to the station in a bus*). **c** *tr.* (also *absol.*) be licensed or competent to drive (a vehicle) (*does he drive?*). **d** *tr.* (also *absol.*) urge and direct the course of (an animal drawing a vehicle or plow). **4** *tr.* (of wind, water, etc.) carry along, propel, send, or cause to go in some direction (*pure as the driven snow*). **5** *tr.* **a** (often foll. by *into*) force (a stake, nail, etc.) into place by blows (*drove the nail home*). **b** *Mining* bore (a tunnel, horizontal cavity, etc.). **6** *tr.* effect or conclude forcibly (*drove a hard bargain; drove her point home*). **7** *tr.* (of steam or other power) set or keep (machinery) going. **8** *intr.* (usu. foll. by *at*) work hard; dash, rush, or hasten. **9** *tr. Baseball & Tennis* hit (the ball) hard from a freely swung bat or racket. **10** *tr.* (often *absol.*) *Golf* strike (a ball) with a driver from the tee. **11** *tr. & intr.* herd cattle, etc.; deal in cattle, etc. **12** *tr.* chase or frighten (game, wild beasts, an enemy in warfare, etc.) from a large area to a smaller, to kill or capture; corner. • *n.* **1** an act of driving in a motor vehicle; a journey or excursion in such a vehicle (*went for a drive; lives an hour's drive from us*). **2 a** the capacity for achievement; motivation and energy (*lacks the drive needed to succeed*). **b** *Psychol.* an inner urge to attain a goal or satisfy a need (*unconscious emotional drives*). **3** a usu. landscaped street or road. **4** *Golf* a driving stroke of the club. **5** an organized effort to achieve a usu. charitable purpose (*a famine-relief drive*). **6 a** the transmission of power to machinery, the wheels of a motor vehicle, etc. (*belt drive; front-wheel drive*). **b** the position of a steering wheel in a motor vehicle (*left-hand drive*). **c** *Computing* = disk drive. **7** an act of driving game, cattle, an enemy, etc. ▫ **drive at** seek, intend, or mean (*what is he driving at?*). **drive out** take the place of; oust; exorcize; cast out. ▫▫ **driv·a·ble** *adj.*

drive-by *adj.* (of a crime, etc.) carried out from a moving vehicle.

drive-in *attrib.adj. & n.* • *attrib.adj.* (of a bank, movie theater, etc.) able to be used while sitting in one's car. • *n.* such a bank, movie theater, etc.

driv·el /drívəl/ *n. & v.* • *n.* silly nonsense; twaddle. • *v.* **1** *intr.* run at the mouth or nose; dribble. **2** *intr.* talk childishly or idiotically. **3** *tr.* (foll. by *away*) fritter; squander away. ▫▫ **driv·el·er** *n.*

driv·en *past part.* of DRIVE.

driv·er /drívər/ *n.* **1** (often in *comb.*) a person who drives a vehicle (*bus driver*). **2** *Golf* a club with a flat face and wooden head, used for driving from the tee. **3** *Electr.* a device or part of a circuit providing power for output. **4** *Mech.* a wheel, etc., receiving power directly and transmitting motion to other parts. **5** a person who herds cattle, etc. ▫ **in the driver's seat** in charge. ▫▫ **driv·er·less** *adj.*

drive·shaft /drívshaft/ *n.* a rotating shaft that transmits power to machinery.

drive·train /drívtrayn/ *n.* the components in an automotive vehicle that connect the transmission with the driving wheels.

drive·way /drívway/ *n.* a usu. private road from a public street, etc., to a house, garage, etc.

driv·ing *adj.* **1** (of rain or snow) falling and being blown by the wind with great force (*driving rain*). **2** having a strong and controlling influence (*she was the driving force behind the plan*).

driv·ing range *n. Golf* an area for practicing long-distance shots, usu. equipped with distance markers and with balls and clubs for rent.

driv·ing wheel *n.* **1** any of the large wheels of a locomotive, to which power is applied either directly or via coupling rods. **2** a wheel transmitting motive power in machinery.

driz·zle /drízəl/ *n. & v.* •*n.* very fine rain. •*v.intr.* (esp. of rain) fall in very fine drops. □□ **driz·zly** *adj.*

droll /drōl/ *adj.* **1** quaintly amusing. **2** odd; surprising. □□ **droll·er·y** *n.* (*pl.* **-ies**). **drol·ly** *adv.* **droll·ness** *n.*

-drome /drōm/ *comb. form* forming nouns denoting: **1** a place for running, racing, or other forms of movement (*hippodrome*). **2** a thing that runs or proceeds in a certain way (*palindrome*; *syndrome*).

drom·e·dar·y /drómideree, drúm–/ *n.* (*pl.* **-ies**) a one-humped camel bred for riding and racing.

drone /drōn/ *n. & v.* •*n.* **1** a nonworking male of certain bees, as the honeybee, whose sole function is to mate with fertile females. **2** an idler. **3** a deep humming sound. **4** a monotonous speech or speaker. **5 a** a pipe, esp. of a bagpipe, sounding a continuous note of fixed low pitch. **b** the note emitted by this. **6** a remote-controlled pilotless aircraft or missile. •*v.* **1** *intr.* make a deep humming sound. **2** *intr. & tr.* speak or utter monotonously. **3 a** *intr.* be idle. **b** *tr.* (often foll. by *away*) idle away (one's time, etc.).

drool /drōōl/ *v. & n.* •*v.intr.* **1** drivel; slobber. **2** (often foll. by *over*) show much pleasure or infatuation. •*n.* slobbering; driveling.

droop /drōōp/ *v. & n.* •*v.* **1** *intr. & tr.* hang or allow to hang down; languish, decline, or sag, esp. from weariness. **2** *intr.* **a** (of the eyes) look downward. **b** *poet.* (of the sun) sink. **3** *intr.* lose heart; be dejected; flag. •*n.* **1** a drooping attitude. **2** a loss of spirit or enthusiasm.

droop·y /drōōpee/ *adj.* (**droopier, droopiest**) **1** drooping. **2** dejected; gloomy. □□ **droop·i·ly** *adv.* **droop·i·ness** *n.*

drop /drop/ *n. & v.* •*n.* **1 a** a small, round or pear-shaped portion of liquid that hangs or falls or adheres to a surface (*drops of dew*). **b** a very small amount of usu. drinkable liquid (*just a drop left in the glass*). **c** a glass, etc., of alcoholic liquor (*take a drop with us*). **2 a** an abrupt fall or slope. **b** the amount of this (*a drop of fifteen feet*). **c** an act of falling or dropping. **d** a reduction in prices, temperature, etc. **e** a deterioration or worsening (*a drop in status*). **3** something resembling a drop, esp.: **a** a pendant or earring. **b** a crystal ornament on a chandelier, etc. **c** (often in *comb.*) a candy or lozenge (*lemon drop*). **4** something that drops or is dropped, esp.: **a** *Theatr.* a painted curtain or scenery let down on to the stage. **b** a platform or trapdoor on a gallows, the opening of which causes the victim to fall. **5** *Med.* **a** the smallest separable quantity of a liquid. **b** (in *pl.*) liquid medicine to be measured in drops (*eye drops*). **6** a minute quantity (*not a drop of pity*). **7** *sl.* **a** a hiding place for stolen or illicit goods. **b** a secret place where documents, etc., may be left or passed on in espionage. **8** a box for letters, etc. •*v.* (**dropped, dropping**) **1** *intr. & tr.* fall or let fall in drops (*tears dropped on to the book*). **2** *intr. & tr.* fall or allow to fall; relinquish; let go (*dropped the box*; *the egg dropped from my hand*). **3 a** *intr. & tr.* sink or cause to sink or fall to the ground from exhaustion, a blow, a wound, etc. **b** *intr.* die. **4 a** *intr. & tr.* cease or cause to cease; lapse or let lapse; abandon (*the connection dropped*; *drop everything and come at once*). **b** *tr. colloq.* cease to associate with. **5** *tr.* set down (a passenger, etc.) (*drop me at the station*). **6** *tr. & intr.* utter or be uttered casually (*dropped a hint*; *the remark dropped into the conversation*). **7** *tr.* send casually (*drop me a postcard*). **8 a** *intr. & tr.* fall or allow to fall in direction, amount, condition, degree, pitch, etc. (*his voice dropped*; *we dropped the price*). **b** *intr.* (of a person) jump down lightly; let oneself fall. **c** *tr.* remove (clothes, esp. pants) rapidly, allowing them to fall to the ground. **9** *tr. colloq.* lose (money, esp. in gambling). **10** *tr.* **a** omit (*drop this article*). **b** omit (a letter, esp. 'h,' a syllable, etc.) in speech. **11** *tr.* (as **dropped** *adj.*) in a lower position than usual (*dropped handlebars*; *dropped waist*). **12** *tr.* give birth to (esp. a lamb, a kitten, etc.). **13** *tr. Sports* lose (a game, a point, a contest, a match, etc.). **14** *tr. Aeron.* deliver (supplies, etc.) by parachute. **15** *tr. Football* **a** send (a ball) by a dropkick. **b** score points by a dropkick. **16** *tr. colloq.* dismiss or exclude (*was dropped from the team*). □ **at the drop of a hat** given the slightest excuse. **drop back** (or **behind** or **to the rear**) fall back; get left behind. **drop dead!** *sl.* an exclamation of intense scorn. **drop in** (or **by**) *colloq.* call casually as a visitor. **a drop in the ocean** (or **bucket**) a very small amount, esp. compared with what is needed or expected. **drop it!** *sl.* stop (talking about or referring to) that! **drop off 1** decline, esp. abruptly. **2** *colloq.* fall asleep. **3** = sense 5 of *v.* **drop out** *colloq.* cease to participate, esp. in a race, a course of study, or in conventional society. **ready to drop** extremely tired. □□ **drop·let** *n.*

drop cur·tain *n. Theatr.* a painted curtain or scenery.

drop·kick /drópkik/ *n. Football* a kick made by dropping the ball and kicking it on the bounce.

drop-leaf *adj.* (of a table, etc.) having a hinged flap.

drop·out /drópowt/ *n. colloq.* a person who has dropped out, esp. from school.

drop·per /drópər/ *n.* a device for administering liquid, esp. medicine, in drops.

drop·pings /drópingz/ *n.pl.* the dung of animals or birds.

drop shot *n.* (in tennis) a shot dropping abruptly over the net.

drop·sy /drópsee/ *n.* (*pl.* **-sies**) = EDEMA. □□ **drop·si·cal** /–sikəl/ *adj.*

dro·soph·i·la /drəsófilə/ *n.* any fruit fly of the genus *Drosophila*, used extensively in genetic research.

dross /draws, dros/ *n.* **1** rubbish; refuse. **2 a** the scum separated from metals in melting. **b** foreign matter mixed with anything; impurities. □□ **dross·y** *adj.*

drought /drowt/ *n.* **1** the continuous absence of rain; dry weather. **2** the prolonged lack of something. □□ **drought·y** *adj.*

drove[1] *past* of DRIVE.

drove[2] /drōv/ *n.* **1 a** a large number (of people, etc.) moving together; a crowd; a multitude; a shoal. **b** (in *pl.*) *colloq.* a great number (*people arrived in droves*). **2** a herd or flock being driven or moving together.

drown /drown/ *v.* **1** *tr. & intr.* kill or be killed by submersion in liquid. **2** *tr.* submerge; flood; drench (*drowned the fields in six feet of water*). **3** *tr.* (often foll. by *in*) deaden (grief, etc.) with drink (*drowned his sorrows*). **4** *tr.* (often foll. by *out*) make (a sound) inaudible by means of a louder sound. □ **like a drowned rat** *colloq.* extremely wet and bedraggled.

drowse /drowz/ *v. intr.* be dull and sleepy or half asleep.

drow·sy /drówzee/ *adj.* (**drowsier, drowsiest**) **1** half asleep. **2** lulling. **3** sluggish. □□ **drow·si·ly** *adv.* **drow·si·ness** *n.*

---

drub /drub/ *v.tr.* (**drubbed, drubbing**) **1** thump; belabor. **2** beat in a fight. ▫▫ **drub·bing** *n.*

drudge /druj/ *n. & v.* • *n.* a servile worker, esp. at menial tasks; a hack. • *v.intr.* (often foll. by *at*) work slavishly (at menial, hard, or dull work). ▫▫ **drudg·er·y** /drújəree/ *n.*

drug /drug/ *n. & v.* • *n.* **1** a medicinal substance. **2** a narcotic, hallucinogen, or stimulant, esp. one causing addiction. • *v.* (**drugged, drugging**) **1** *tr.* add a drug to (food or drink). **2** *tr.* **a** administer a drug to. **b** stupefy with a drug. **3** *intr.* take drugs as an addict.

drug ad·dict *n.* a person who is addicted to a narcotic drug.

drug·gie /drúgee/ *n. colloq.* (also **drug·gy**) (*pl.* **-gies**) a drug addict.

drug·gist /drúgist/ *n.* a pharmacist.

drug·store /drúgstawr/ *n.* a pharmacy also selling miscellaneous items, such as cosmetics.

Dru·id /dróoid/ *n.* (*fem.* **Druidess**) **1** an ancient Celtic priest, magician, or soothsayer of Gaul, Britain, or Ireland. **2** a member of a Welsh, etc., Druidic order. ▫▫ **Dru·id·ic** /–ídik/ *adj.* **Dru·id·ism** *n.*

drum /drum/ *n. & v.* • *n.* **1 a** a percussion instrument or toy made of a hollow cylinder or hemisphere covered at one or both ends with stretched skin or parchment and sounded by striking. **b** (often in *pl.*) percussion section (*the drums are playing too loud*). **c** a sound made by or resembling that of a drum. **2** something resembling a drum in shape, esp.: **a** a cylindrical container or receptacle for oil, etc. **b** a cylinder or barrel in machinery on which something is wound, etc. **c** *Archit.* a stone block forming a section of a shaft. **3** *Zool. & Anat.* the eardrum. • *v.* (**drummed, drumming**) **1** *intr. & tr.* play on a drum. **2** *tr. & intr.* beat, tap, or thump (knuckles, feet, etc.) continuously (on something). **3** *intr.* (of a bird or an insect) make a loud, hollow noise with quivering wings. ▫ **drum into** drive (a lesson) into (a person) by persistence. **drum out** *Mil.* dismiss with ignominy. **drum up** summon, gather, or call up (*needs to drum up more support*).

drum·beat /drúmbeet/ *n.* the sound of a drum being beaten.

drum brake *n.* a brake in which shoes on a vehicle press against the drum on a wheel.

drum·head /drúmhed/ *n.* **1** the skin or membrane of a drum. **2** an eardrum. **3** (*attrib.*) improvised (*drumhead court-martial*).

drum·lin /drúmlin/ *Geol.* a long, oval mound of boulder clay molded by glacial action.

drum ma·jor *n.* the leader of a marching band.

drum ma·jor·ette *n.* a female member of a baton-twirling parading group.

drum·mer /drúmər/ *n.* a person who plays a drum or drums.

drum·stick /drúmstik/ *n.* **1** a stick used for beating a drum. **2** the lower joint of the leg of a cooked chicken, turkey, etc.

drunk /drungk/ *adj. & n.* • *adj.* **1** rendered incapable by alcohol. **2** (often foll. by *with*) overcome with joy, success, power, etc. • *n.* **1** a habitually drunk person. **2** *sl.* a drinking bout; a period of drunkenness.

drunk·ard /drúngkərd/ *n.* a person who is drunk, esp. habitually.

drunk driv·er *n.* a person who drives a vehicle with an excess of alcohol in the blood. ▫▫ **drunk driv·ing** *adj.*

drunk·en /drúngkən/ *adj.* (usu. *attrib.*) **1** = DRUNK *adj.* 1. **2** caused by or exhibiting drunkenness (*a drunken brawl*). ▫▫ **drunk·en·ly** *adv.* **drunk·en·ness** *n.*

drupe /dróop/ *n.* any fleshy or pulpy fruit enclosing a stone containing one or a few seeds, e.g., an olive, plum, or peach.

drupe·let /dróoplit/ *n.* a small drupe usu. in an aggregate fruit, e.g., a blackberry or raspberry.

druse /drooz/ *n.* **1** a crust of crystals lining a rock cavity. **2** a cavity lined with this.

druth·ers /drúthərz/ *n.pl. colloq.* preference; choice (*if I had my druthers, I'd stay at home*).

dry /drī/ *adj., v., & n.* • *adj.* (**drier** /dríər/; **driest** /drí-ist/) **1** free from moisture, not wet, esp.: **a** with any moisture having evaporated, drained, or been wiped away (*the clothes are dry*). **b** (of the eyes) free from tears. **c** (of a climate, etc.) with insufficient rainfall; not rainy (*a dry spell*). **d** (of a river, well, etc.) dried up; not yielding water. **e** not connected with or for use without moisture (*dry shampoo*). **2** (of wine, etc.) not sweet (*dry sherry*). **3 a** meager, plain, or bare (*dry facts*). **b** uninteresting; dull (*dry as dust*). **4** (of a sense of humor, a joke, etc.) subtle, ironic, and quietly expressed; not obvious. **5** (of a country, legislation, etc.) prohibiting the sale of alcoholic drink. **6** (of toast, bread, etc.) without butter, etc. **7** (of provisions, groceries, etc.) solid; not liquid (*dry goods*). **8** impassive; unsympathetic; hard; cold. **9** (of a cow, etc.) not yielding milk. **10** *colloq.* thirsty or thirst-making (*feel dry; this is dry work*). • *v.* (**dries, dried**) **1** *tr. & intr.* make or become dry by wiping, evaporation, draining, etc. **2** *tr.* (usu. as **dried** *adj.*) preserve (food, etc.) by removing the moisture (*dried fruit*). **3** *intr.* (often foll. by *up*) *Theatr. colloq.* forget one's lines. • *n.* (*pl.* **dries**) a prohibitionist. ▫ **dry out 1** become fully dry. **2** (of a drug addict, alcoholic, etc.) undergo treatment to cure addiction. **dry up 1** make utterly dry. **2** (of a well, etc.) cease to yield water. **3** *colloq.* (esp. in *imper.*) cease talking. ▫▫ **dry·ish** *adj.* **dry·ly** *adv.* **dry·ness** *n.*

dry·ad /dríad, dríəd/ *n. Mythol.* a nymph inhabiting a tree; a wood nymph.

dry bat·ter·y *n. Electr.* an electric battery consisting of dry cells.

dry cell *n. Electr.* a cell in which the electrolyte is absorbed in a solid and cannot be spilled.

dry-clean *adj.* clean (clothes, etc.) with organic solvents without using water.

dry clean·er *n.* an individual or a business that specializes in dry cleaning.

dry cough *n.* a cough not producing phlegm.

dry-cure *v.tr.* cure (meat, etc.) without pickling in liquid.

dry dock *n.* an enclosed dock that can be drained of water to allow the inspection and repair of a ship.

dry·er var. of DRIER[2].

dry fly *n. Fishing* an artificial fly that is floated on the water's surface. ▫▫ **dry-fly** *adj., v.intr.* (**·flies, ·flied**).

dry goods *n.* fabric, thread, clothing, and related merchandise, esp. as distinct from hardware and groceries.

dry ice *n.* solid carbon dioxide.

dry·land *n.* land as opposed to the sea, etc.

dry meas·ure *n.* a measure of capacity for dry goods.

dry rot *n.* **1** a decayed state of wood when not ventilated, caused by certain fungi. **2** these fungi.

dry run *n. colloq.* a rehearsal.

dry·wall /dríwawl/ *n.* = PLASTERBOARD.

DST *abbr.* daylight saving(s) time.

DT *abbr.* (also **DT's** /deéteéz/) delirium tremens.

DTP *abbr.* desktop publishing.

du·al /dóoəl, dyóoəl/ *adj.* **1** of two; twofold. **2** divided in two; double (*dual ownership*). **3** *Gram.* (in some languages) denoting two persons or things (additional to singular and plural). ▫▫ **du·al·i·ty** /–álitee/ *n.* **du·al·ly** *adv.*

du·al in-line pack·age *n. Computing* see DIP.

du·al·ism /dóoəlizəm, dyóo–/ *n.* **1** being twofold; duality. **2** *Philos.* the theory that in any domain of reality there are two independent underlying principles, e.g., mind and matter, form and content. □□ **du·al·ist** *n.* **du·al·is·tic** *adj.* **du·al·is·ti·cal·ly** *adv.*

dub[1] /dub/ *v.tr.* (**dubbed, dubbing**) **1** make (a person) a knight by touching his shoulders with a sword. **2** give (a person) a nickname or title (*dubbed him a crank*).

dub[2] /dub/ *v.tr.* (**dubbed, dubbing**) **1** provide (a movie, etc.) with an alternative soundtrack, esp. in a different language. **2** add (sound effects or music) to a movie or a broadcast. **3** combine (soundtracks) into one. **4** transfer or make a copy of (a soundtrack).

du·bi·ous /dŏŏbeeəs, dyŏŏ–/ *adj.* **1** hesitating or doubting (*dubious about going*). **2** of questionable value or truth (*a dubious claim*). **3** unreliable; suspicious (*dubious company*). **4** of doubtful result (*a dubious undertaking*). □□ **du·bi·ous·ly** *adv.* **du·bi·ous·ness** *n.*

du·cal /dŏŏkəl, dyŏŏ–/ *adj.* of, like, or bearing the title of a duke.

duc·at /dúkət/ *n. hist.* a gold coin, formerly current in most European countries.

duch·ess /dúchis/ *n.* (as a title usu. **Duchess**) **1** a duke's wife or widow. **2** a woman holding the rank of duke in her own right.

duch·y /dúchee/ *n.* (*pl.* **-ies**) the territory of a duke or duchess; a dukedom.

duck[1] /duk/ *n.* (*pl.* same or **ducks**) **1** any waterfowl of the family Anatidae, esp. the domesticated form of the mallard or wild duck. **2** the female of this (opp. DRAKE). **3** the flesh of a duck as food. □ **like a duck to water** adapting very readily. **like water off a duck's back** *colloq.* (of remonstrances, etc.) producing no effect.

duck[2] /duk/ *v.* & *n.* • *v.* **1** *intr.* & *tr.* plunge, dive, or dip under water and emerge. **2** *intr.* & *tr.* bend (the head or the body) quickly to avoid a blow or being seen, or as a bow or curtsy; bob (*ducked out of sight*). **3** *tr.* & *intr. colloq.* avoid or dodge; withdraw (from) (*ducked out of the engagement*; *ducked the meeting*). **4** *intr. Bridge* lose a trick deliberately by playing a low card. • *n.* **1** a quick dip or swim. **2** a quick lowering of the head, etc. □□ **duck·er** *n.*

duck[3] /duk/ *n.* **1** a strong, untwilled linen or cotton fabric used for small sails and the outer clothing of sailors. **2** (in *pl.*) pants made of this (*white ducks*).

duck[4] /duk/ *n. colloq.* an amphibious landing craft.

duck·bill /dúkbil/ *n.* (also **duck-billed plat·y·pus**) = PLATYPUS.

duck·ling /dúkling/ *n.* **1** a young duck. **2** its flesh as food.

duck's ass *n. coarse sl.* a haircut with the hair on the back of the head shaped like a duck's tail (usu. abbr. as **DA**).

duck soup *n. sl.* an easy task.

duck·weed /dúkweed/ *n.* any of various aquatic plants, esp. of the genus *Lemna*, growing on the surface of still water.

duck·y /dúkee/ *adj. colloq.* fine; wonderful; splendid.

duct /dukt/ *n.* & *v.* • *n.* **1** a channel or tube for conveying fluid, cable, etc. **2** a tube in the body conveying secretions such as tears, etc. • *v.tr.* convey through a duct. □□ **duct·less** *adj.*

duc·tile /dúktəl, –tīl/ *adj.* **1** (of a metal) capable of being drawn into wire; pliable, not brittle. **2** (of a substance) easily molded. **3** (of a person) docile; gullible. □□ **duc·til·i·ty** /–tílitee/ *n.*

duct·ing /dúkting/ *n.* **1** a system of ducts. **2** material in the form of a duct or ducts.

duct·work /dúktwərk/ *n.* a series of interlinked ducts, as for a ventilation system.

dud /dud/ *n.* & *adj. sl.* • *n.* **1** a futile or ineffectual person or thing. **2** a counterfeit article. **3** a shell, etc., that fails to explode. **4** (in *pl.*) clothes. • *adj.* **1** useless; worthless; unsatisfactory or futile. **2** counterfeit.

dude /dŏŏd, dyŏŏd/ *n. sl.* **1** a fastidious aesthetic person, usu. male; a dandy. **2** a vacationer on a dude ranch. **3** a fellow; a guy.

dude ranch *n.* a cattle ranch converted to a vacation resort for tourists, etc.

dudg·eon /dújən/ *n.* a feeling of offense; resentment. □ **in high dudgeon** very angry or angrily.

due /dōō, dyōō/ *adj., n.,* & *adv.* • *adj.* **1** (*predic.*) owing or payable (*our thanks are due to him*; *$500 was due on the 15th*). **2** merited; fitting (*her due reward*). **3** proper; adequate. **4** (*predic.*; foll. by *to*) to be ascribed to (a cause, an agent, etc.) (*the discovery was due to Edison*). **5** (*predic.*) intended to arrive at a certain time (*a train is due at 7:30*). **6** (foll. by *to* + infin.) under an obligation or agreement to do something (*due to speak tonight*). • *n.* **1** a person's right; what is owed to a person (*a fair hearing is my due*). **2** (in *pl.*) **a** what one owes (*pays his dues*). **b** a legally demandable toll or fee (*harbor dues*). • *adv.* (of a point of the compass) exactly; directly (*went due east*). □ **due to** *disp.* because of; owing to (*was late due to an accident*) (cf. sense 4 of *adj.*). **fall** (or **become**) **due** (of a bill, etc.) be immediately payable. **in due course 1** at about the appropriate time. **2** in the natural order.

▶The use of **due to** meaning 'because of,' as in *we were late due to circumstances beyond our control,* is widely used and generally accepted, although some traditionalists hold that **due** is properly a predicate adjective and restrict its use to follow forms of the verb *to be,* e.g., *The collapse was due to flooding.*

du·el /dŏŏəl, dyŏŏəl/ *n.* & *v.* • *n.* **1** *hist.* a contest with deadly weapons between two people to settle a point of honor. **2** any contest between two people, causes, animals, etc. • *v.intr.* fight a duel or duels. □□ **du·el·er** *n.* **du·el·ist** *n.*

---

duel late 15th century: from Latin *duellum*, archaic and literary form of *bellum* 'war,' used in medieval Latin with the meaning 'combat between two persons,' partly influenced by *dualis* 'of two.' The original sense was 'single combat used to decide a judicial dispute'; the sense 'contest to decide a point of honor' dates from the early 17th century.

---

duen·de /dōō-énday/ *n.* **1** an evil spirit. **2** inspiration.

du·en·na /dōō-énə, dyōō–/ *n.* an older woman acting as a governess and companion in charge of girls, esp. in a Spanish family.

due proc·ess *n.* a course of legal proceedings in accordance with a state's or nation's legal system, such that individual rights are protected.

du·et /dōō-ét, dyōō–/ *n.* **1** *Mus.* **a** a performance by two voices, instrumentalists, etc. **b** a composition for two performers. **2** a dialogue. □□ **du·et·tist** *n.*

duff /duf/ *n. sl.* buttocks (*get off your duff!*).

duf·fel /dúfəl/ *n.* (also **duf·fle**) **1** a coarse woolen cloth with a thick nap. **2** a sportsman's or camper's equipment.

duf·fel bag *n.* a cylindrical canvas bag closed by a drawstring.

duf·fer /dúfər/ *n. sl.* an inefficient, useless, or stupid person.

duf·fle (or **duf·fel**) **coat** *n.* a hooded overcoat of heavy esp. woolen fabric, usu. fastened with toggles.

dug[1] *past* and *past part.* of DIG.

dug[2] /dug/ *n.* the udder, breast, teat, or nipple of a female animal.

du·gong /dŏŏgawng, –gong/ *n.* (*pl.* same or **dugongs**) a marine mammal, *Dugong dugon*, of Asian seas and coasts.

dug·out /dúgowt/ *n.* **1 a** a roofed shelter esp. for troops in trenches. **b** an underground air-raid or nuclear shelter. **c** *Baseball* a roofed seating area for players, facing the field. **2** a canoe made from a hollowed tree trunk.

duke /dōōk, dyōōk/ *n.* (as a title usu. **Duke**) **1 a** a person holding the highest hereditary title of the nobility. **b** a sovereign prince ruling a duchy or small state. **2** (usu. in *pl.*) *sl.* the hand; the fist (*put up your dukes!*).

duke·dom /dóōkdəm, dyóōk–/ *n.* **1** a territory ruled by a duke. **2** the rank of duke.

dul·cet /dúlsit/ *adj.* (esp. of sound) sweet and soothing.

dul·ci·fy /dúlsifī/ *v.tr.* (**·fies, ·fied**) *literary* **1** make gentle. **2** sweeten. ◻◻ **dul·ci·fi·ca·tion** /–fikáyshən/ *n.*

dul·ci·mer /dúlsimər/ *n.* a musical instrument with strings of graduated length stretched over a sounding board or box, played by being struck with hammers.

dull /dul/ *adj.* & *v.* • *adj.* **1** slow to understand; stupid. **2** tedious; boring. **3** (of the weather) overcast; gloomy. **4 a** (esp. of a knife edge, etc.) blunt. **b** (of color, light, sound, or taste) not bright, vivid, or keen. **5** (of a pain, etc.) usu. prolonged and indistinct (*a dull ache*). **6 a** sluggish; slow-moving. **b** listless; depressed. **7** (of the ears, eyes, etc.) without keen perception. • *v.tr.* & *intr.* make or become dull. ◻◻ **dull·ish** *adj.* **dull·ness** *n.* (also **dul·ness**). **dul·ly** *adv.*

dull·ard /dúlərd/ *n.* a stupid person.

dull-wit·ted *adj.* = DULL *adj.* 1.

du·ly /dóōlee, dyóō–/ *adv.* **1** in due time or manner. **2** rightly; properly; fitly.

dumb /dum/ *adj.* **1 a** (of a person) unable to speak. **b** (of an animal) naturally unable to speak (*our dumb friends*). **2** silenced by surprise, shyness, etc. **3** taciturn or reticent, esp. insultingly (*dumb insolence*). **4** (of an action, etc.) performed without speech. **5** (often in *comb.*) giving no sound; without voice or some other property normally belonging to things of the name (*a dumb piano*). **6** *colloq.* stupid; ignorant. **7** having no voice in government; inarticulate (*the dumb masses*). **8** (of a computer terminal, etc.) able only to transmit data to or receive data; not programmable (opp. INTELLIGENT). ◻◻ **dumb·ly** /dúmlee/ *adv.* **dumb·ness** /dúmnis/ *n.*

dumb·bell /dúmbel/ *n.* **1** a short bar with a weight at each end, used for exercise, muscle-building, etc. **2** *sl.* a stupid person.

dumb·found /dúmfównd/ *v.tr.* (also **dum·found**; esp. as **dumbfounded** *adj.*) strike dumb; confound; nonplus.

dum·bo /dúmbō/ *n.* (*pl.* **-bos**) *sl.* a stupid person; a fool.

dumb·struck /dúmstruk/ *adj.* greatly shocked or surprised and so lost for words.

dumb·wait·er /dúmwaytər/ *n.* **1** a small elevator for carrying food, plates, etc., between floors. **2** a movable table, esp. with revolving shelves, used in a dining room.

dum·dum /dúmdum/ *n.* (in full **dumdum bullet**) a kind of soft-nosed bullet that expands on impact and inflicts a severe wound.

dum·my /dúmee/ *n.* & *adj.* • *n.* (*pl.* **·mies**) **1** a model of a human being, esp.: **a** a ventriloquist's doll. **b** a figure used to model clothes in a store window, etc. **c** a target used for firearms practice. **2** (often *attrib.*) **a** a counterfeit object used to replace or resemble a real or normal one. **b** a prototype, esp. in publishing. **3** *colloq.* a stupid person. **4** a person taking no significant part; a figurehead. **5** an imaginary fourth player at whist, whose hand is turned up and played by a partner. **6** *Bridge* **a** the partner of the declarer, whose cards are exposed after the first lead. **b** this player's hand. **7** *Mil.* a blank round of ammunition. **8** *colloq.* a dumb person. • *adj.* sham; counterfeit. ◻ **dummy up** *sl.* keep quiet; give no information.

dump /dump/ *n.* & *v.* • *n.* **1 a** a place for depositing trash, garbage, etc. **b** a heap of trash, garbage, etc. **2** *colloq.* an unpleasant or dreary place. **3** *Mil.* a temporary store of ammunition, provisions, etc. **4** an accumulated pile of ore, earth, etc. **5** *Computing* **a** a printout of stored data. **b** the process or result of dumping data. • *v.tr.* **1** put down firmly or clumsily (*dumped the groceries on the table*). **2** deposit or dispose of (trash, etc.). **3** *colloq.* abandon; desert. **4** *Mil.* leave (ammunition, etc.) in a dump. **5** *Econ.* send (goods unsalable at a high price in the home market) to a foreign market for sale at a low price. **6** *Computing* **a** copy (stored data) to a different location. **b** reproduce the contents of (a store) externally. ◻ **dump on** *sl.* criticize or abuse; get the better of.

dump·ling /dúmpling/ *n.* **1** a small ball of boiled or steamed dough. **2** a dessert consisting of fruit enclosed in dough and baked.

dumps /dumps/ *n.pl. colloq.* depression; melancholy (*in the dumps*).

Dump·ster /dúmpstər/ *n. Trademark* a large trash receptacle designed to be hoisted and emptied into a truck.

dump truck *n.* a truck with a body that tilts or opens at the back for unloading.

dump·y /dúmpee/ *adj.* (**dumpier, dumpiest**) short and stout. ◻◻ **dump·i·ly** *adv.*

dun[1] /dun/ *adj.* & *n.* • *adj.* dull grayish brown. • *n.* **1** a dun color. **2** a dun horse.

dun[2] /dun/ *v.* & *n.* • *v.tr.* (**dunned, dunning**) make persistent demands on someone, esp. for payment of a debt. • *n.* **1** a debt collector or an insistent creditor. **2** a demand for payment.

dunce /duns/ *n.* a person slow at learning; a dullard.

dunce cap *n.* (also **dunce's cap**) a paper cone formerly put on the head of a dunce at school as a mark of disgrace.

dun·der·head /dúndərhed/ *n.* a stupid person. ◻◻ **dun·der·head·ed** *adj.*

dune /dōōn, dyōōn/ *n.* a mound or ridge of loose sand, etc., formed by the wind.

dung /dung/ *n.* & *v.* • *n.* the excrement of animals; manure. • *v.tr.* apply dung to; manure (land).

dun·ga·ree /dúnggəreé/ *n.* **1** (in *pl.*) **a** overalls, etc., usu. made of blue denim, worn esp. by workers. **b** blue jeans. **2** a coarse E. Indian calico.

dung bee·tle *n.* any of a family of beetles whose larvae develop in dung.

dun·geon /dúnjən/ *n.* a strong underground cell for prisoners.

dung·hill /dúnghil/ *n.* a heap of dung or refuse, esp. in a farmyard.

dunk /dungk/ *v.tr.* **1** dip (a doughnut, etc.) into milk, coffee, etc. before eating. **2** immerse; dip.

dunk shot *n. Basketball* a shot made by a player jumping up and thrusting the ball down through the basket.

dun·lin /dúnlin/ *n.* a long-billed sandpiper, *Calidris alpina*.

dun·nage /dúnij/ *n. Naut.* **1** mats, brushwood, etc., stowed under or among cargo to prevent wetting or chafing. **2** *colloq.* miscellaneous baggage.

dun·no /dənó/ *colloq.* (I) do not know.

du·o /dóō-ō, dyóō-ō/ *n.* (*pl.* **-os**) **1** a pair of actors, entertainers, singers, etc. **2** *Mus.* a duet.

du·o·dec·i·mal /dóō-ōdésiməl, dyóō–/ *adj.* & *n.* • *adj.* relating to or using a system of numerical notation that has 12 as a base. • *n.* **1** the duodecimal system. **2** duodecimal notation. ◻◻ **du·o·dec·i·mal·ly** *adv.*

du·o·de·num /dóōədeénəm, dyóō–, dōō-ód'nəm, dyōō–/ *n. Anat.* the first part of the small intestine immediately below the stomach. ◻◻ **du·o·de·nal** *adj.* **du·o·de·ni·tis** /–nítis/ *n.*

dupe /dōōp, dyōōp/ *n. & v.* • *n.* a victim of deception. • *v.tr.* make a fool of; cheat. ▫▫ **dup·er·y** *n.*

du·ple /dóōpəl, dyóō–/ *adj.* of two parts.

du·plex /dóōpleks, dyóō–/ *n. & adj.* • *n.* **1** an apartment on two levels. **2** a house subdivided for two families. • *adj.* **1** having two elements; twofold. **2 a** (of an apartment) two-story. **b** (of a house) for two families. **3** *Computing* (of a circuit) allowing the transmission of signals in both directions simultaneously.

du·pli·cate *adj., n., & v.* • *adj.* /dóōplikət, dyóō–/ **1** exactly like something already existing; copied (esp. in large numbers). **2 a** having two corresponding parts. **b** existing in two examples; paired. **c** doubled. • *n.* /dóōplikət, dyóō–/ **1 a** one of two identical things, esp. a copy of an original. **b** one of two or more specimens of a thing exactly or almost identical. **2** *Law* a second copy of a letter or document. **3** (in full **duplicate bridge** or **whist**) a form of bridge or whist in which the same hands are played successively by different players. • *v.tr.* /dóōplikayt, dyóō–/ **1** multiply by two; double. **2 a** make or be an exact copy of. **b** make or supply copies of (*duplicated the leaflet for distribution*). **3** repeat (an action, etc.), esp. unnecessarily. ▫ **in duplicate** consisting of two exact copies. ▫▫ **du·pli·ca·ble** /dóōplikəbəl, dyóō–/ *adj.* **du·pli·ca·tion** /–káyshən/ *n.*

du·pli·ca·tor /dóōplikaytər, dyóō–/ *n.* **1** a machine for making copies of a document, leaflet, etc. **2** a person or thing that duplicates.

du·plic·i·ty /dōōplísitee, dyōō–/ *n.* double-dealing; deceitfulness. ▫▫ **du·plic·i·tous** *adj.*

du·ra·ble /dóōrəbəl, dyóōr–/ *adj. & n.* • *adj.* **1** capable of lasting; hard-wearing. **2** (of goods) not for immediate consumption; able to be kept. • *n.* (in *pl.*) durable goods. ▫▫ **du·ra·bil·i·ty** *n.* **du·ra·bly** *adv.*

du·ra ma·ter /dóōrə máytər, maá–, dyóōrə/ *n. Anat.* the tough outermost membrane enveloping the brain and spinal cord (see MENINX).

du·ra·tion /dōōráyshən, dyōōr–/ *n.* **1** the length of time for which something continues. **2** a specified length of time (*after the duration of a minute*). ▫ **for the duration** **1** until the end of something obstructing normal activities, as a war. **2** for a very long time. ▫▫ **du·ra·tion·al** *adj.*

du·ress /dōōrés, dyóō–/ *n.* **1** compulsion, esp. imprisonment, threats, or violence, illegally used to force a person to act against his or her will (*under duress*). **2** imprisonment.

dur·ing /dóōring, dyóōr–/ *prep.* **1** throughout (*read during the meal*). **2** at some point in (*came in during the evening*).

du·rum /dóōrəm, dyóō–/ *n.* a kind of wheat, *Triticum turgidum*, yielding a flour used for pasta.

dusk /dusk/ *n.* **1** the darker stage of twilight. **2** shade; gloom.

dusk·y /dúskee/ *adj.* (**duskier, duskiest**) **1** shadowy; dim. **2** dark-colored, darkish. ▫▫ **dusk·i·ly** *adv.* **dusk·i·ness** *n.*

dust /dust/ *n. & v.* • *n.* **1 a** finely powdered earth, dirt, etc. **b** fine powder of any material (*pollen dust; gold dust*). **c** a cloud of dust. **2** a dead person's remains. **3** confusion or turmoil (*raised quite a dust*). **4** the ground; the earth (*kissed the dust*). • *v.* **1** *tr.* (also *absol.*) clear (furniture, etc.) of dust, etc., by wiping, brushing, etc. **2** *tr.* **a** sprinkle (esp. a cake) with powder, dust, sugar, etc. **b** sprinkle or strew (sugar, powder, etc.). **3** *tr.* make dusty. ▫ **dust off 1** remove the dust from. **2** use and enjoy again after a long period of neglect. **when the dust settles** when things quiet down. ▫▫ **dust·less** *adj.*

dust bowl *n.* an area denuded of vegetation by drought or erosion and reduced to desert.

dust·cov·er /dústkuvər/ *n.* **1** a cloth put over furniture to protect it from dust. **2** = DUST JACKET.

dust dev·il *n.* a whirlwind visible as a column of dust.

dust·er /dústər/ *n.* **1 a** a cloth for dusting furniture, etc. **b** a person or contrivance that dusts. **2** a woman's light, loose, full-length coat.

dust·ing pow·der *n.* talcum powder.

dust jack·et *n.* a usu. decorated paper cover used to protect a book from dirt, etc.

dust·pan /dústpan/ *n.* a small pan into which dust, etc., is brushed from the floor.

dust storm *n.* a storm with clouds of dust carried in the air.

dust·y /dústee/ *adj.* (**dustier, dustiest**) **1** full of, covered with, or resembling dust. **2** uninteresting. **3** (of a color) dull or muted. ▫▫ **dust·i·ly** *adv.* **dust·i·ness** *n.*

Dutch /duch/ *adj. & n.* • *adj.* of, relating to, or associated with the Netherlands. • *n.* **1** the language of the Netherlands. **2** (prec. by *the*; treated as *pl.*) the people of the Netherlands. ▫ **go Dutch** share expenses equally.

Dutch door *n.* a door divided into two parts horizontally allowing one part to be shut and the other open.

Dutch door

Dutch elm dis·ease *n.* a disease affecting elms caused by the fungus *Ceratocystis ulmi*, first found in the Netherlands.

Dutch·man /dúchmən/ *n.* (*pl.* **-men**; *fem.* **Dutchwoman**, *pl.* **-women**) **1 a** a native or national of the Netherlands. **b** a person of Dutch descent. **2** a Dutch ship.

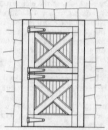

Dutch ov·en *n.* **1** a metal box the open side of which is turned toward a fire. **2** a covered cooking pot for braising, etc.

Dutch treat *n.* a party, outing, etc. to which each person makes a contribution.

Dutch un·cle *n.* a person giving advice with benevolent firmness.

du·ti·a·ble /dóōteeəbəl, dyóō–/ *adj.* liable to customs or other duties.

dut·i·ful /dóōtifōōl, dyóō–/ *adj.* doing or observant of one's duty; obedient. ▫▫ **dut·i·ful·ly** *adv.* **dut·i·ful·ness** *n.*

du·ty /dóōtee, dyóō–/ *n.* (*pl.* **-ties**) **1 a** a moral or legal obligation; a responsibility (*her duty to report it*). **b** the binding force of what is right (*strong sense of duty*). **c** what is required of one (*do one's duty*). **2** payment to the public revenue, esp.: **a** that levied on the import of goods (*customs duty*). **b** that levied on the transfer of property, licenses, etc. (*death duty*). **3** a job or function (*his duties as caretaker*). **4** the behavior due to a superior; deference; respect. ▫ **do duty for** serve as or pass for (something else). **on** (or **off**) **duty** engaged (or not engaged) in one's work.

du·ty-bound *adj.* obliged by duty.

du·ty-free *adj. & adv.* **1** exempt from payment of duty. **2** selling goods that are exempt from duty (*duty-free shop*).

du·vet /dōōváy/ *n.* a thick, soft quilt with a detachable cover, used instead of an upper sheet and blankets.

D.V.M. *abbr.* Doctor of Veterinary Medicine.

dwarf /dwawrf/ *n. & v.* • *n.* (*pl.* **dwarfs** or **dwarves** /dwawrvz/) **1 a** *Offens.* a person of abnormally small stature. **b** an animal or plant much below the ordinary size. **2** a small mythological being with supernatural powers. **3** (in full **dwarf star**) a small usu. dense star. **4** (*attrib.*) **a** of a kind very small in size (*dwarf bean*). **b** puny; stunted. • *v.tr.* **1** stunt in growth. **2** cause (something similar or comparable) to seem small or insignificant. ▫▫ **dwarf·ish** *adj.*

dweeb /dweeb/ *n. sl.* a studious or tedious person.

dwell /dwel/ *v. & n.* • *v.intr.* (*past* and *past part.* **dwelled** or **dwelt**) **1** *literary* (usu. foll. by *in, at, near, on,* etc.) live; reside (*dwelt in the forest*). **2** (of a horse) be slow in raising its feet; pause before taking a fence. • *n.* a slight, regular pause in the motion of a machine. ▫ **dwell on** (or **upon**) **1** write, brood, or speak at length on. **2** prolong (a note, a syllable, etc.). ▫▫ **dwell·er** *n.*

dwell·ing /dwéling/ *n.* (also **dwell·ing place**) *formal* a house; a residence; an abode.

dwin·dle /dwínd'l/ *v.intr.* **1** become gradually smaller; shrink. **2** lose importance; decline.

Dy *symb. Chem.* the element dysprosium.

dye /dī/ *n. & v.* • *n.* **1 a** a substance used to change the color of hair, fabric, wood, etc. **b** a color produced by this. **2** (in full **dyestuff**) a substance yielding a dye, esp. for coloring materials in solution. • *v.tr.* (**dyeing**) **1** impregnate with dye. **2** make (a thing) a specified color with dye (*dyed it yellow*). ▫▫ **dye·a·ble** *adj.*

dyed-in-the-wool *adj.* **1** out and out; inveterate. **2** (of a fabric) made of yarn dyed in its raw state.

dy·er /díər/ *n.* a person who dyes cloth, etc.

dye·stuff see DYE *n.* 2.

dy·ing /dí-ing/ *adj.* connected with, or at the time of, death (*his dying words*). ▫ **to one's dying day** for the rest of one's life.

dyke[1] var. of DIKE[1].

dyke[2] /dīk/ *n.* (also **dike**) *sl.* a lesbian.

dyn *abbr.* dyne(s).

dy·na·mic /dīnámik/ *adj. & n.* • *adj.* (also **dy·nam·i·cal**) **1** energetic; active; potent. **2** *Physics* **a** concerning motive force (opp. STATIC). **b** concerning force in actual operation. **3** of or concerning dynamics. **4** *Mus.* relating to the volume of sound. • *n.* **1** an energizing or motive force. **2** *Mus.* = DYNAMICS 3. ▫▫ **dy·nam·i·cal·ly** *adv.*

dy·nam·ics /dīnámiks/ *n.pl.* **1** (usu. treated as *sing.*) **a** *Mech.* the branch of mechanics concerned with the motion of bodies under the action of forces (cf. STATICS). **b** the branch of any science in which forces or changes are considered (*aerodynamics; population dynamics*). **2** the motive forces, physical or moral, affecting behavior and change in any sphere. **3** *Mus.* the varying degree of volume of sound in musical performance. ▫▫ **dy·nam·i·cist** /–məsist/ *n.* (in sense 1).

dy·na·mism /dínəmizəm/ *n.* energizing or dynamic action or power.

dy·na·mite /dínəmīt/ *n. & v.* • *n.* **1** a high explosive consisting of nitroglycerine mixed with an absorbent. **2** a potentially dangerous person, thing, or situation. **3** *sl.* a narcotic, esp. heroin. • *v.tr.* charge or shatter with dynamite. ▫▫ **dy·na·mit·er** *n.*

dy·na·mo /dínəmō/ *n.* (*pl.* **-mos**) **1** a machine converting mechanical into electrical energy, esp. by rotating coils of copper wire in a magnetic field. **2** *colloq.* an energetic person.

dy·nas·ty /dínəstee/ *n.* (*pl.* **-ties**) **1** a line of hereditary rulers. **2** a succession of leaders in any field. ▫▫ **dy·nas·tic** /–nástik/ *adj.* **dy·nas·ti·cal·ly** *adv.*

dyne /dīn/ *n. Physics* a unit of force that, acting on a mass of one gram, increases its velocity by one centimeter per second every second along the direction that it acts. ¶ Abbr.: **dyn.**

dys·en·ter·y /dísənteree/ *n.* a disease with inflammation of the intestines, causing severe diarrhea with blood and mucus. ▫▫ **dys·en·ter·ic** *adj.*

dys·func·tion /dísfúngkshən/ *n.* an abnormality or impairment of function. ▫▫ **dys·func·tion·al** *adj.*

dys·lex·i·a /dislékseeə/ *n.* an abnormal difficulty in reading and spelling, caused by a condition of the brain. ▫▫ **dys·lex·ic** *adj. & n.* **dys·lec·tic** /–léktik/ *adj. & n.*

dys·men·or·rhe·a /dísmenəréeə/ *n.* painful or difficult menstruation.

dys·pep·sia /dispépseeə/ *n.* indigestion.

dys·pha·sia /disfáyzhə, –zheeə/ *n. Med.* lack of coordination in speech, owing to brain damage. ▫▫ **dys·pha·sic** /–zik, –sik/ *adj.*

dys·pro·si·um /disprṓzeeəm/ *n. Chem.* a naturally occurring soft metallic element of the lanthanide series. ¶ Symb.: **Dy.**

E

E[1] /ee/ *n.* (also **e**) (*pl.* **Es** or **E's**) **1** the fifth letter of the alphabet. **2** *Mus.* the third note of the diatonic scale of C major.

E[2] *abbr.* (also **E.**) **1** east; eastern. **2** English. **3** energy.

e *symb.* **1** *Math.* the base of natural logarithms, equal to approx. 2.71828. **2** used on packaging (in conjunction with specification of weight, size, etc.) to indicate compliance with EEC regulations.

e- /ee, e/ *prefix* form of EX-[1] 1 before some consonants.

ea. *abbr.* each.

each /eech/ *adj. & pron.* • *adj.* every one of two or more persons or things, regarded and identified separately (*each person*; *five in each class*). • *pron.* each person or thing (*each of us*; *have two books each*).
▶See note at BOTH.

ea·ger /éegər/ *adj.* **1 a** full of keen desire; enthusiastic. **b** (of passions, etc.) keen; impatient. **2** keen; strongly desirous (*eager to learn*; *eager for news*). ▫▫ **ea·ger·ly** *adv.* **ea·ger·ness** *n.*
▶See note at ANXIOUS.

ea·gle /éegəl/ *n.* **1 a** any of various large birds of prey of the family Accipitridae, with keen vision and powerful flight. **b** a figure of an eagle, esp. as a symbol of the US. **2** *Golf* a score of two strokes under par at any hole. **3** *US* a gold coin worth ten dollars.

ea·gle eye *n.* keen sight; watchfulness. ▫▫ **eagle-eyed** *adj.*

Ea·gle Scout *n.* the highest rank a Boy Scout can attain.

ea·glet /éeglit/ *n.* a young eagle.

ear[1] /eer/ *n.* **1** the organ of hearing and balance in humans and other vertebrates, esp. the external part of this. **2** the faculty for discriminating sounds (*an ear for music*). **3** listening; attention. ▫ **all ears** listening attentively. **have** (or **keep**) **an ear to the ground** be alert to rumors or the trend of opinion. **out on one's ear** dismissed ignominiously. **up to one's ears** (often foll. by *in*) *colloq.* deeply involved or occupied. ▫▫ **eared** *adj.* (also in *comb.*). **ear·less** *adj.*

ear[2] /eer/ *n.* the seed-bearing head of a cereal plant.

ear·ache /éerayk/ *n.* a (usu. prolonged) pain in the ear.

ear·drum /éerdrum/ *n.* the membrane of the middle ear.

earl /ərl/ *n.* a British nobleman ranking between a marquess and a viscount (cf. COUNT[2]). ▫▫ **earl·dom** *n.*

ear·lobe /éerlōb/ *n.* the lower soft pendulous external part of the ear.

ear·ly /ə́rlee/ *adj., adv., & n.* • *adj. & adv.* (**earlier, earliest**) **1** before the due, usual, or expected time (*was early for my appointment*; *arrived early*). **2 a** not far on in the day or night, or in time (*early evening*; *at the earliest opportunity*). **b** prompt (*early payment appreciated*; *at your earliest convenience*). **3 a** not far on in a period, development, or process of evolution; being the first stage (*the early Egyptians*; *early spring*). **b** of the distant past (*early man*). **c** not far on in a sequence (*the early chapters*). **4 a** of childhood, esp. the preschool years (*early learning*). **b** (of a piece of writing, music, etc.) immature; youthful (*an early work*). **5** flowering, etc., before other varieties. • *n.* (*pl.* **-lies**) (usu. in *pl.*) an early fruit or vegetable, esp. potatoes. ▫▫ **ear·li·ness** *n.*

ear·mark /éermaark/ *n. & v.* • *n.* **1** an identifying mark. **2** an owner's mark on the ear of an animal. • *v.tr.* **1** set aside (money, etc.) for a special purpose. **2** mark (sheep, etc.) with such an identifying mark.

ear·muff /éermuf/ *n.* a wrap or cover for the ears, protecting them from cold, noise, etc.

earn /ərn/ *v.tr.* **1** (also *absol.*) **a** (of a person) obtain (income) in return for labor or services. **b** (of capital invested) bring in as interest or profit. **2 a** deserve; obtain as the reward for hard work or merit. **b** incur (a reproach, reputation, etc.).

ear·nest[1] *adj. & n.* • *adj.* intensely serious; not trifling or joking. • *n.* seriousness. ▫ **in** (or **in real**) **earnest** serious(ly), not joking(ly); with determination. ▫▫ **ear·nest·ly** *adv.* **ear·nest·ness** *n.*

ear·nest[2] /ə́rnist/ *n.* **1** money paid as an installment, esp. to confirm a contract, etc. **2** a token or foretaste (*in earnest of what is to come*).

earn·ings /ə́rningz/ *n.pl.* money earned.

ear·phone /éerfōn/ *n.* a device applied to the ear to aid hearing or receive radio or telephone communications.

ear·piece /éerpees/ *n.* the part of a telephone, etc., applied to the ear during use.

ear·plug /éerplug/ *n.* a piece of plastic, etc., placed in the ear to protect against cold air, water, or noise.

ear·ring /éering/ *n.* a piece of jewelry worn in or on (esp. the lobe of) the ear.

ear·shot /éershot/ *n.* the distance over which something can be heard (esp. *within* or *out of earshot*).

earth /ərth/ *n. & v.* • *n.* **1 a** (also **Earth**) one of the planets of the solar system orbiting about the sun between Venus and Mars; the planet on which we live. **b** land and sea, as distinct from sky. **2 a** dry land; the ground (*fell to earth*). **b** soil; clay; mold. **c** bodily matter (*earth to earth*). **3** *Relig.* the present abode of mankind, as distinct from heaven or hell; the world. **4** the hole of a badger, fox, etc. **5** (prec. by *the*) *colloq.* a huge amount; everything (*cost the earth*; *want the earth*). • *v.* **1** *tr.* (foll. by *up*) cover (the roots and lower stems of plants) with heaped-up earth. **2 a** *tr.* drive (a fox) to its earth. **b** *intr.* (of a fox, etc.) run to its earth. ▫ **come back** (or **down**) **to earth** return to reality. **gone to earth** in hiding. **on earth** *colloq.* **1** existing anywhere (*the happiest man on earth*). **2** as an intensifier (*what on earth?*). ▫▫ **earth·ward** *adj. & adv.* **earth·wards** *adv.*

earth·en /ə́rthən// *adj.* **1** made of earth. **2** made of baked clay.

earth·en·ware /ə́rthənwair/ *n. & adj.* • *n.* pottery, vessels, etc., made of clay fired to a porous state, which can be made impervious to liquids by the use of a glaze (cf. PORCELAIN). • *adj.* made of fired clay.

earth·ling /ə́rthling/ *n.* an inhabitant of the earth, esp. as regarded in fiction by outsiders.

earth·ly /ə́rthlee/ *adj.* **1 a** of the earth; terrestrial. **b** of human life on earth. **2** (usu. with *neg.*) *colloq.* remotely possible or conceivable (*is no earthly use*). ▫ **not an earthly** *colloq.* no chance whatever. ▫▫ **earth·li·ness** *n.*

earth·quake /ə́rthkwayk/ *n.* **1** a convulsion of the superficial parts of the earth due to the release of accumulated stress as a result of faults in strata or volcanic action. **2** a social, etc., disturbance.

earth sci·en·ces *n.pl.* the sciences concerned with the earth or part of it, or its atmosphere (e.g., geology, oceanography, meteorology).

earth-shat·ter·ing *adj. colloq.* having a traumatic or devastating effect. ◻◻ **earth-shat·ter·ing·ly** *adv.*

earth·work /árthwərk/ *n.* **1** an artificial bank of earth in fortification or road building, etc. **2** the process of excavating soil in civil engineering work.

earth·worm /árthwərm/ *n.* any of various annelid worms, esp. of the genus *Lumbricus* or *Allolobophora*, living and burrowing in the ground.

earth·y /árthee/ *adj.* (**earthier, earthiest**) **1** of or like earth or soil. **2** somewhat coarse or crude; unrefined (*earthy humor*). ◻◻ **earth·i·ly** *adv.* **earth·i·ness** *n.*

ear·wax /éerwaks/ *n.* a yellow waxy secretion produced by the ear. Also called **cerumen**.

ear·wig /éerwig/ *n.* any small elongate insect of the order Dermaptera, with a pair of terminal appendages in the shape of forceps.

ease /eez/ *n.* & *v.* • *n.* **1** absence of difficulty; facility; effortlessness (*did it with ease*). **2** freedom or relief from pain, embarrassment, or constraint. • *v.* **1** *tr.* relieve from pain or anxiety, etc. (often foll. by *of*: *eased my mind*; *eased me of the burden*). **2** *intr.* (often foll. by *off*, *up*) **a** become less painful or burdensome. **b** relax; begin to take it easy. **c** slow down; moderate one's behavior, habits, etc. **3** *intr. Meteorol.* become less severe (*the wind will ease tonight*). **4 a** *tr.* relax; slacken. **b** *tr.* & *intr.* (foll. by *through*, *into*, etc.) move or be moved carefully into place (*eased it into the hole*). **5** *intr.* (often foll. by *off*) *Stock Exch.* (of shares, etc.) descend in price or value. ◻ **at ease 1** free from anxiety or constraint. **2** *Mil.* **a** in a relaxed attitude, with the feet apart. **b** the order to stand in this way.

ea·sel /éezəl/ *n.* a standing frame, usu. of wood, for supporting an artist's work, a blackboard, etc.

easel

ease·ment /éezmənt/ *n. Law* a right of way or a similar right over another's land.

eas·i·ly /éezilee/ *adv.* **1** without difficulty. **2** by far (*easily the best*). **3** very probably (*it could easily snow*).

east /eest/ *n.*, *adj.*, & *adv.* • *n.* **1 a** the point of the horizon where the sun rises at the equinoxes. **b** the compass point corresponding to this. **c** the direction in which this lies. **2** (usu. **the East**) **a** the regions or countries lying to the east of Europe. **b** the formerly Communist nations of eastern Europe. **3** the eastern part of a country, town, etc. **4** (**East**) *Bridge* a player occupying the position designated "east." • *adj.* **1** toward, at, near, or facing east. **2** coming from the east (*east wind*). • *adv.* **1** toward, at, or near the east. **2** (foll. by *of*) further east than (*east of the Rockies*).

east·bound /éestbownd/ *adj.* traveling or leading eastward.

Eas·ter /éestər/ *n.* (also **Eas·ter Sun·day** or **Eas·ter Day**) the festival (held on a variable Sunday in March or April) commemorating Christ's resurrection.

east·er·ly /éestərlee/ *adj.*, *adv.*, & *n.* • *adj.* & *adv.* **1** in an eastern position or direction. **2** (of a wind) blowing from the east. • *n.* (*pl.* **-lies**) a wind blowing from the east.

east·ern /éestərn/ *adj.* **1** of or in the east; inhabiting the east. **2** lying or directed toward the east. **3** (**Eastern**) of or in the Far, Middle, or Near East. ◻◻ **east·ern·most** *adj.*

East·ern·er /éestərnər/ *n.* a native or inhabitant of the east; esp. in the US.

east·ern hem·i·sphere *n.* (also **East·ern Hem·i·sphere**) the half of the earth containing Europe, Asia, and Africa.

east-north·east *n.* the direction or compass point midway between east and northeast.

east-south·east *n.* the direction or compass point midway between east and southeast.

east·ward /éestwərd/ *adj.*, *adv.*, & *n.* • *adj.* & *adv.* (also **east·wards**) toward the east. • *n.* an eastward direction or region. ◻◻ **east·ward·ly** *adj.* & *adv.*

eas·y /éezee/ *adj.*, *adv.*, & *int.* (**easier, easiest**) • *adj.* **1** not difficult; achieved without great effort. **2** free from pain, discomfort, anxiety, etc. (*easy circumstances*). **3** free from embarrassment, awkwardness, or constraint (*an easy manner*). **4 a** not strict; tolerant. **b** compliant; obliging; easily persuaded (*an easy touch*). • *adv.* with ease; in an effortless or relaxed manner. • *int.* go carefully; move gently. ◻ **easy come easy go** *colloq.* what is easily obtained is soon lost or spent. **easy does it** *colloq.* go carefully. **easy on the eye** (or **ear**, etc.) *colloq.* pleasant to look at (or listen to, etc.). **go easy** (foll. by *with*, *on*) be sparing or cautious. **take it easy 1** proceed gently or carefully. **2** relax; avoid overwork. ◻◻ **eas·i·ness** *n.*

eas·y chair *n.* a large comfortable chair, usu. an armchair.

eas·y·go·ing /éezeegṓing/ *adj.* placid and tolerant; relaxed in manner; accepting things as they are.

eat /eet/ *v.* (*past* **ate** /ayt/, esp. *Brit.* /et/; *past part.* **eaten** /éet'n/) **1 a** *tr.* take into the mouth, chew, and swallow (food). **b** *intr.* consume food; take a meal. **c** *tr.* devour. **2** *intr.* (foll. by *away at*, *into*) **a** destroy gradually, esp. by corrosion, erosion, disease, etc. **b** begin to consume or diminish (resources, etc.). **3** *tr. colloq.* trouble; vex (*what's eating you?*). ◻ **eat dirt** see DIRT. **eat one's heart out** suffer from excessive longing or envy. **eat out of a person's hand** be entirely submissive to a person. **eat up 1** (also *absol.*) eat or consume completely. **2** use or deal with rapidly or wastefully (*eats up time*). **3** encroach upon or annex (*eating up the neighboring countries*). **4** absorb; preoccupy (*eaten up with pride*). **eat one's words** admit that one was wrong.

eat·er·y /éetəree/ *n.* (*pl.* **-ies**) *colloq.* a restaurant, esp. a diner, luncheonette, etc.

eats /eets/ *n.pl. colloq.* food.

eau de co·logne /ṓdəkəlṓn/ *n.* an alcohol-based perfume of a kind made orig. at Cologne, Germany.

eaves /eevz/ *n.pl.* the underside of a projecting roof.

eaves·drop /éevzdrop/ *v.intr.* (**-dropped, -dropping**) listen secretly to a private conversation. ◻◻ **eaves·drop·per** *n.*

---

eavesdrop early 17th cent.: back-formation from *eavesdropper* (late Middle English) 'a person who listens from under the eaves', from the obsolete noun *eavesdrop* 'the ground on to which water drips from the eaves', probably from Old Norse *upsardropi*, from *ups* 'eaves' + *dropi* 'a drop'.

---

ebb /eb/ *n.* & *v.* • *n.* **1** the movement of the tide out to sea (also *attrib.*: *ebb tide*). **2** the process of declining or diminishing; the state of being in decline. • *v.intr.* (often foll. by *away*) **1** (of tidewater) flow out to sea; recede; drain away. **2** decline; run low (*his life was ebbing away*).

E·bon·ics /eebóniks/ *n.pl.* the English used by Black Americans, regarded as a language in its own right.

eb·on·ite /ébənīt/ *n.* = VULCANITE.

eb·on·y /ébənee/ *n.* & *adj.* • *n.* (*pl.* **-ies**) **1** a heavy, hard, dark wood used for furniture. **2** any of various trees of the genus *Diospyros* producing this. • *adj.* **1** made of ebony. **2** black like ebony.

e·bul·lient /ibúlyənt, ibŏŏl–/ *adj.* exuberant; high-spirited. ▫▫ **e·bul·lience** /–yəns/ *n.* **e·bul·lien·cy** *n.* **e·bul·lient·ly** *adv.*

EC *abbr.* **1** European Community. **2** executive committee.

ec·cen·tric /iksέntrik, ek–/ *adj. & n.* • *adj.* **1** odd or capricious in behavior or appearance. **2 a** not placed or not having its axis, etc., placed centrally. **b** (often foll. by *to*) (of a circle) not concentric (to another). **c** (of an orbit) not circular. • *n.* **1** an eccentric person. **2** *Mech.* an eccentric contrivance for changing rotatory into backward-and-forward motion. ▫▫ **ec·cen·tri·cal·ly** *adv.* **ec·cen·tric·i·ty** /éksentrísitee/ *n.* (*pl.* **-ties**).

ec·cle·si·as·tic /iklééezeeástik/ *n. & adj.* • *n.* a priest or clergyman. • *adj.* = ECCLESIASTICAL. ▫▫ **ec·cle·si·as·ti·cism** /–tisizəm/ *n.*

ec·cle·si·as·ti·cal /ikléezeeástikəl/ *adj.* of the church or the clergy. ▫▫ **ec·cle·si·as·ti·cal·ly** *adv.*

ECG *abbr.* electrocardiogram.

ech·e·lon /éshəlon/ *n.* **1** a level or rank in an organization, in society, etc.; those occupying it (often in *pl.*: *the upper echelons*). **2** *Mil.* a formation of troops, ships, aircraft, etc., in parallel rows with the end of each row projecting further than the one in front (*in echelon*).

e·chid·na /ikídnə/ *n.* any of several egg-laying, insectivorous mammals native to Australia and New Guinea, with a covering of spines, and having a long snout and long claws. Also called **spiny anteater**.

e·chi·no·derm /ikínədərm/ *n.* any marine invertebrate of the phylum Echinodermata, usu. having a spiny skin, e.g., starfish and sea urchins.

e·chi·noid /ikínoyd/ *n.* a sea urchin.

ech·o /ékō/ *n. & v.* • *n.* (*pl.* **-oes** or **-os**) **1 a** the repetition of a sound by the reflection of sound waves. **b** the secondary sound produced. **2** a reflected radio or radar beam. **3** a close imitation or repetition of something already done. **4** a person who slavishly repeats the words or opinions of another. **5** (often in *pl.*) circumstances or events reminiscent of or remotely connected with earlier ones. • *v.* (**-oes, -oed**) **1** *intr.* **a** (of a place) resound with an echo. **b** (of a sound) be repeated; resound. **2** *tr.* repeat (a sound) by an echo. **3** *tr.* **a** repeat (another's words). **b** imitate the words, opinions, or actions of (a person). ▫▫ **ech·o·er** *n.* **ech·o·less** *adj.*

ech·o·car·di·o·gram /ékōkaárdeeəgram/ *n. Med.* a record produced by echocardiography.

ech·o·car·di·og·ra·phy /ékōkaárdeeógrəfee/ *n. Med.* the use of ultrasound waves to investigate the action of the heart. ▫▫ **ech·o·car·di·o·graph** /–deeəgraf/ *n.* **ech·o·car·di·og·ra·pher** *n.*

e·cho·ic /ekṓik/ *adj. Phonet.* (of a word) imitating the sound it represents; onomatopoeic.

ech·o sound·er *n.* sounding apparatus for determining the depth of the sea beneath a ship by measuring the time taken for an echo to be received. ▫▫ **echo-sound·ing** *n.*

ech·o·vi·rus /ékōvīrəs/ *n.* (also **ECHO vi·rus**) any of a group of enteroviruses sometimes causing mild meningitis, encephalitis, etc.

é·clair /aykláir/ *n.* a small, elongated light pastry filled with cream.

é·clat /ayklaá/ *n.* **1** brilliant display; dazzling effect. **2** social distinction; conspicuous success.

ec·lec·tic /ikléktik/ *adj. & n.* • *adj.* deriving ideas, tastes, style, etc., from various sources. • *n.* an eclectic person. ▫▫ **ec·lec·ti·cal·ly** *adv.* **ec·lec·ti·cism** /–tisizəm/ *n.*

e·clipse /iklíps/ *n. & v.* • *n.* **1** the obscuring of the reflected light from one celestial body by the passage of another between it and the eye or between it and its source of illumination. **2** a deprivation of light or the period of this. **3** a rapid or sudden loss of importance or prominence, esp. in relation to another or a newly arrived person or thing. • *v.tr.* **1** (of a celestial body) obscure the light from or to (another). **2** deprive of prominence or importance; outshine; surpass. ▫▫ **e·clips·er** *n.*

e·clip·tic /iklíptik/ *n. & adj.* • *n.* the sun's apparent path among the stars during the year. • *adj.* of an eclipse or the ecliptic.

ec·logue /éklawg, –log/ *n.* a short poem, esp. a pastoral dialogue.

eco- /ékō, éékō/ *comb. form* ecology; ecological.

e·co·cli·mate /ékōklīmit, éékō–/ *n.* climate considered as an ecological factor.

ecol. *abbr.* **1** ecological. **2** ecologist. **3** ecology.

E. co·li /éékṓlī/ *n.* a species of anaerobic bacteria in the large intestine of humans and other animals; it is toxic in large quantities (abbr. for **Esch·e·rich·i·a co·li**).

e·col·o·gy /ikóləjee/ *n.* **1** the branch of biology dealing with the relations of organisms to one another and to their physical surroundings. **2** (in full **human ecology**) the study of the interaction of people with their environment. ▫▫ **ec·o·log·i·cal** /ékəlójikəl, éékə–/ *adj.* **ec·o·log·i·cal·ly** *adv.* **e·col·o·gist** *n.*

econ. *abbr.* **1** economics. **2** economy.

ec·o·nom·ic /ékənómik, éékə–/ *adj.* **1** of or relating to economics. **2** maintained for profit. **3** adequate to repay or recoup expenditure with some profit (*an economic rent*). **4** considered or studied with regard to human needs (*economic geography*).

▶**Economic** means 'concerning economics': *He's rebuilding a solid economic base for the country's future.* **Economical** is commonly used to mean 'thrifty; avoiding waste': *Small cars should be inexpensive to buy and economical to run.*

ec·o·nom·i·cal /ékənómikəl, éékə–/ *adj.* sparing in the use of resources; avoiding waste. ▫▫ **ec·o·nom·i·cal·ly** *adv.*

▶See note at ECONOMIC.

ec·o·nom·ics /ékənómiks, éékə–/ *n.pl.* (often treated as *sing.*) **1 a** the science of the production and distribution of wealth. **b** the application of this to a particular subject (*the economics of publishing*). **2** the condition of a country, etc., as regards material prosperity.

e·con·o·mist /ikónəmist/ *n.* **1** an expert in or student of economics. **2** a person who manages financial or economic matters.

e·con·o·mize /ikónəmīz/ *v.intr.* **1** be economical; make economies; reduce expenditure. **2** (foll. by *on*) use sparingly; spend less on. ▫▫ **e·con·o·mi·za·tion** *n.* **e·con·o·miz·er** *n.*

e·con·o·my /ikónəmee/ *n.* (*pl.* **-mies**) **1 a** the wealth and resources of a community. **b** a particular kind of this (*a capitalist economy*). **c** the administration or condition of an economy. **2 a** the careful management of (esp. financial) resources; frugality. **b** (often in *pl.*) an instance of this (*made many economies*). **3** sparing use (*economy of language*). **4** (also **e·con·o·my class**) the cheapest class of air travel. **5** (*attrib.*) (also **e·con·o·my-size**) (of goods) consisting of a large quantity for a proportionally lower cost.

ec·o·sphere /ékōsfeer, éékə–/ *n.* the region of space including planets where conditions are such that living things can exist.

ec·o·sys·tem /ékōsistəm, éékō–/ *n.* a biological community of interacting organisms and their physical environment.

ec·ru /ékrōō, áykrōō/ *n.* the color of unbleached linen.

ec·sta·sy /ékstəsee/ *n.* (*pl.* **-sies**) **1** an overwhelming feeling of joy or rapture. **2** *sl.* methylene dioxymethamphetamine, a powerful stimulant and hallucinatory

---

drug. ▫▫ **ec·sta·tic** /ikstátik, ek–/ *adj.* **ec·stat·i·cal·ly** *adv.*

ECT *abbr.* electroconvulsive therapy.

ecto- /éktō/ *comb. form* outside.

ec·to·derm /éktōdərm/ *n. Biol.* the outermost layer of an animal embryo in early development.

ec·to·gen·e·sis /éktōjénisis/ *n. Biol.* the production of structures outside the organism. ▫▫ **ec·to·ge·net·ic** /–jinétik/ *adj.* **ec·to·gen·ic** /–jénik/ *adj.* **ec·tog·e·nous** /ektójinəs/ *adj.*

ec·to·morph /éktəmawrf/ *n.* a person with a lean body build. (cf. ENDOMORPH, MESOMORPH). ▫▫ **ec·to·mor·phic** *adj.* **ec·to·morph·y** *n.*

-ectomy /éktəmee/ *comb. form* denoting a surgical operation in which a part of the body is removed (*appendectomy*).

ec·top·ic preg·nan·cy *n.* a pregnancy occurring outside the uterus.

ec·to·plasm /éktəplazəm/ *n.* **1** the dense outer layer of the cytoplasm (cf. ENDOPLASM). **2** the supposed viscous substance exuding from the body of a spiritualistic medium during a trance. ▫▫ **ec·to·plas·mic** *adj.*

ec·u·men·i·cal /ékyōōménikəl/ *adj.* **1** of or representing the whole Christian world. **2** seeking or promoting worldwide Christian unity. ▫▫ **e·cu·men·i·cal·ism** *n.* (also **ec·u·me·nism** /ékyəminizəm, ikyōōmənizəm/) **ec·u·men·i·cal·ly** *adv.*

ec·ze·ma /éksimə, égzi–, igzée–/ *n.* inflammation of the skin, with itching and discharge from blisters. ▫▫ **ec·zem·a·tous** /igzémətəs, egzém–, –zée–/ *adj.*

ed. *abbr.* **1** edited by. **2** edition. **3** editor. **4** educated; education.

-ed[1] /əd, id/ *suffix* forming adjectives: **1** from nouns, meaning 'having, wearing, affected by, etc.' (*talented*; *trousered*; *diseased*). **2** from phrases of adjective and noun (*good-humored*; *three-cornered*).

-ed[2] /əd, id/ *suffix* forming: **1** the past tense and past participle of weak verbs (*needed*; *risked*). **2** participial adjectives (*escaped prisoner*; *a pained look*).

E·dam /éedəm, éedam/ *n.* a round Dutch cheese, usu. pale yellow with a red rind.

ed·dy /édee/ *n.* & *v.* • *n.* (*pl.* **-dies**) **1** a circular movement of water causing a small whirlpool. **2** a movement of wind, fog, or smoke resembling this. • *v.tr.* & *intr.* (**-dies, -died**) whirl around in eddies.

e·del·weiss /áyd'lvīs/ *n.* an Alpine plant, *Leontopodium alpinum*, with woolly white bracts around the flower heads.

e·de·ma /idéemə/ *n.* a condition characterized by an excess of watery fluid collecting in the cavities or tissues of the body. Also called **dropsy**.

E·den /éedən/ *n.* (also **Garden of Eden**) a place or state of great happiness; paradise (with reference to the biblical account of the abode of Adam and Eve).

e·den·tate /idéntayt/ *adj.* & *n.* • *adj.* having no or few teeth. • *n.* any mammal, esp. of the order Edentata, having no or few teeth, e.g., an anteater or sloth.

edge /ej/ *n.* & *v.* • *n.* **1** a boundary line or margin of an area or surface. **2** a narrow surface of a thin object. **3** the meeting line of two surfaces of a solid. **4 a** the sharpened side of the blade of a cutting instrument or weapon. **b** the sharpness of this (*the knife has lost its edge*). **5** the area close to a steep drop (*along the edge of the cliff*). **6** anything compared to an edge, esp. the crest of a ridge. **7 a** (as a personal attribute) incisiveness. **b** keenness; excitement (esp. as an element in an otherwise routine situation). **8** an advantage; superiority. • *v.* **1** *tr.* & *intr.* (often foll. by *in, into, out,* etc.) move gradually or furtively toward an objective (*they all edged toward the door*). **2** *tr.* **a** provide with an edge or border. **b** form a border to. **c** trim the edge of. **3** *tr.* sharpen (a knife, tool, etc.). ▫ **have the edge on** (or **over**) have a slight advantage over. **on edge 1** tense and restless or irritable. **2** eager; excited. **on the edge of** almost involved in or affected by. ▫▫ **edge·less** *adj.* **edg·er** *n.*

---

edge Old English *ecg* 'sharpened side of a blade,' of Germanic origin; related to Dutch *egge* and German *Ecke*, also to Old Norse *eggja* (see EGG[2]), from an Indo-European root shared by Latin *acies* 'edge' and Greek *akis* 'point.'

---

edge·wise /éjwīz/ *adv.* (also esp. *Brit.* **edgeways** /–wayz/) **1** with the edge uppermost or toward the viewer. **2** edge to edge. ▫ **get a word in edgewise** contribute to a conversation when the dominant speaker pauses briefly.

edg·ing /éjing/ *n.* something forming an edge or border, e.g., a fringe or lace.

edg·y /éjee/ *adj.* (**edgier, edgiest**) irritable; nervously anxious. ▫▫ **edg·i·ly** *adv.* **edg·i·ness** *n.*

ed·i·ble /édibəl/ *adj.* & *n.* • *adj.* fit or suitable to be eaten (cf. EATABLE). • *n.* (in *pl.*) food. ▫▫ **ed·i·bil·i·ty** *n.*

e·dict /éedikt/ *n.* an order proclaimed by authority. ▫▫ **e·dic·tal** /eedíkt'l/ *adj.*

ed·i·fice /édifis/ *n.* **1** a building, esp. a large imposing one. **2** a complex organizational or conceptual structure.

ed·i·fy /édifī/ *v.tr.* (**-fies, -fied**) (of a circumstance, experience, etc.) instruct and improve morally or intellectually. ▫▫ **ed·i·fi·ca·tion** /–fikáyshən/ *n.* **ed·i·fy·ing** *adj.* **ed·i·fy·ing·ly** *adv.*

---

edify Middle English: from Old French *edifier*, from Latin *aedificare* 'build,' from *aedis* 'dwelling' + *facere* 'make' (compare with EDIFICE). The word originally meant 'construct a building,' also 'strengthen,' hence to 'build up' morally or spiritually.

---

ed·it /édit/ *v.* & *n.* • *v.tr.* **1 a** assemble, prepare, modify, or condense (written material, esp. the work of another or others) for publication. **b** prepare an edition of (an author's work). **2** be in overall charge of the content and arrangement of (a newspaper, journal, etc.). **3** take extracts from and collate (movies, tape recordings, etc.) to form a unified sequence. **4 a** prepare (data) for processing by a computer. **b** alter (a text entered in a word processor, etc.). **5 a** reword to correct, or to alter the emphasis. **b** (foll. by *out*) remove (part) from a text, etc. • *n.* **1 a** a piece of editing. **b** an edited item. **2** a facility for editing.

e·di·tion /idíshən/ *n.* **1 a** one of the particular forms in which a literary work, etc., is published (*paperback edition*; *pocket edition*). **b** a copy of a book in a particular form (*a first edition*). **2** a whole number of copies of a book, newspaper, etc., issued at one time. **3** a particular version or instance of a broadcast, esp. of a regular program or feature. **4** a person or thing similar to or resembling another (*a miniature edition of her mother*).

ed·i·tor /éditər/ *n.* **1** a person who edits material for publication or broadcasting. **2** a person who directs the preparation of a newspaper or periodical, or a particular section of one (*sports editor*). **3** a person who selects or commissions material for publication. **4** a person who edits film, sound track, etc. **5** a computer program for modifying data. ▫▫ **ed·i·tor·ship** *n.*

ed·i·to·ri·al /éditáwreeəl/ *adj.* & *n.* • *adj.* **1** of or concerned with editing or editors. **2** written or approved by an editor. • *n.* a newspaper article written by or on behalf of an editor, esp. one giving an opinion on a topical issue. ▫▫ **ed·i·to·ri·al·ist** *n.* **ed·i·to·ri·al·ize** *v.intr.* **ed·i·to·ri·al·ly** *adv.*

EDP *abbr.* electronic data processing.

EDT *abbr.* eastern daylight time.

ed·u·cate /éjəkayt/ *v.tr.* (also *absol.*) **1** give intellectual, moral, and social instruction to (a pupil, esp. a child), esp. as a formal and prolonged process. **2** provide education for. **3** (often foll. by *in*, or *to* + infin.) train or instruct for a particular purpose. ▫▫ **ed·u·ca·ble** /–kəbəl/ *adj.* **ed·u·ca·bil·i·ty** /–kəbílitee/ *n.* **ed·u·cat·a·ble** *adj.* **ed·u·ca·tive** *adj.* **ed·u·ca·tor** *n.*

ed·u·cat·ed /éjəkaytid/ *adj.* **1** having had an education, esp. to a higher level than average. **2** resulting from a (good) education (*an educated accent*). **3** based on experience or study (*an educated guess*).

ed·u·ca·tion /éjəkáyshən/ *n.* **1 a** the act or process of educating or being educated; systematic instruction. **b** the knowledge gained from this. **2** a particular kind of or stage in education (*a classical education*; *further education*). **3 a** development of character or mental powers. **b** a stage in or aspect of this (*travel will be an education for you*). ▫▫ **ed·u·ca·tion·al** *adj.* **ed·u·ca·tion·al·ist** *n.* **ed·u·ca·tion·al·ly** *adv.* **ed·u·ca·tion·ist** *n.*

e·duce /idóos, idyóos/ *v.tr.* **1** bring out or develop from latent or potential existence; elicit. **2** infer; elicit a principle, number, etc., from data. ▫▫ **e·duc·i·ble** *adj.* **e·duc·tion** /idúkshen/ *n.* **e·duc·tive** /idúktiv/ *adj.*

Ed·ward·i·an /edwáwrdeeən, –wáar–/ *adj.* & *n.* • *adj.* of, characteristic of, or associated with the reign of King Edward VII of England (1901–10). • *n.* a person belonging to this period.

-ee /ee/ *suffix* forming nouns denoting: **1** the person affected by the verbal action (*addressee*; *employee*). **2** a person concerned with or described as (*absentee*; *refugee*). **3** an object of smaller size (*bootee*).

EEG *abbr.* electroencephalogram.

eel /eel/ *n.* **1** any of various snakelike fish, with slender body and poorly developed fins. **2** a slippery or evasive person or thing. ▫▫ **eel·like** *adj.* **eel·y** *adj.*

EEOC *abbr.* Equal Employment Opportunity Commission.

ee·rie /éeree/ *adj.* (**eerier, eeriest**) gloomy and strange; weird; frightening (*an eerie silence*). ▫▫ **ee·ri·ly** *adv.* **ee·ri·ness** *n.*

ef- /if, ef/ *prefix* assim. form of EX-[1] 1 before *f*.

ef·face /ifáys/ *v.* **1** *tr.* rub or wipe out (a mark, etc.). **2** *tr.* (in abstract senses) obliterate; wipe out (*effaced it from his memory*). **3** *tr.* utterly surpass; eclipse (*success has effaced all previous attempts*). **4** *refl.* treat or regard oneself as unimportant (*self-effacing*). ▫▫ **ef·face·ment** *n.*

ef·fect /ifékt/ *n.* & *v.* • *n.* **1** the result or consequence of an action, etc.; the significance or implication of this. **2** efficacy (*had little effect*). **3** an impression produced on a spectator, hearer, etc. (*my words had no effect*). **4** (in *pl.*) property; luggage. **5** (in *pl.*) the lighting, sound, etc., used to accompany a play, movie, broadcast, etc. **6** *Physics* a physical phenomenon, usually named after its discoverer (*Doppler effect*). **7** the state of being operative. • *v.tr.* **1** bring about; accomplish. **2** cause to exist or occur. ▫ **bring** (or **carry**) **into effect** accomplish. **for effect** to create an impression. **in effect** for practical purposes; in reality. **take effect** become operative.

▶See note at AFFECT.

ef·fec·tive /iféktiv/ *adj.* & *n.* • *adj.* **1** having a definite or desired effect. **2** powerful in effect; impressive. **3 a** actual; existing in fact rather than officially or theoretically (*took effective control in their absence*). **b** actually usable; realizable; equivalent in its effect (*effective money*; *effective demand*). **4** coming into operation (*effective as of May 1*). • *n.* a soldier available for service. ▫▫ **ef·fec·tive·ly** *adv.* **ef·fec·tive·ness** *n.*

ef·fec·tu·al /ifékchōōəl/ *adj.* **1** capable of producing the required result or effect; answering its purpose. **2** valid. ▫▫ **ef·fec·tu·al·i·ty** /–chōōálitee/ *n.* **ef·fec·tu·al·ly** *adv.* **ef·fec·tu·al·ness** *n.*

ef·fem·i·nate /iféminət/ *adj.* (of a man) feminine in appearance or manner; unmasculine. ▫▫ **ef·fem·i·na·cy** *n.* **ef·fem·i·nate·ly** *adv.*

ef·fer·vesce /éfərvés/ *v.intr.* **1** give off bubbles of gas; bubble. **2** (of a person) be lively. ▫▫ **ef·fer·ves·cence** *n.* **ef·fer·ves·cen·cy** *n.* **ef·fer·ves·cent** *adj.*

ef·fete /iféet/ *adj.* **1 a** feeble and incapable. **b** effeminate. **2** worn out; exhausted of its essential quality or vitality. ▫▫ **ef·fete·ness** *n.*

ef·fi·ca·cious /éfikáyshəs/ *adj.* (of a thing) producing or sure to produce the desired effect. ▫▫ **ef·fi·ca·cious·ly** *adv.* **ef·fi·ca·cious·ness** *n.* **ef·fi·ca·cy** /éfikəsee/ *n.*

ef·fi·cien·cy /ifíshənsee/ *n.* (*pl.* **-cies**) **1** the state or quality of being efficient. **2** *Mech. & Physics* the ratio of useful work performed to the total energy expended or heat taken in.

ef·fi·cient /ifíshənt/ *adj.* **1** productive with minimum waste or effort. **2** (of a person) capable; acting effectively. ▫▫ **ef·fi·cient·ly** *adv.*

ef·fi·gy /éfijee/ *n.* (*pl.* **-gies**) a sculpture or model of a person. ▫ **in effigy** in the form of a (usu. crude) representation of a person.

ef·flo·resce /éflərés/ *v.intr.* **1** burst out into flower. **2** *Chem.* **a** (of a substance) turn to a fine powder on exposure to air. **b** (of salts) come to the surface and crystallize on it. **c** (of a surface) become covered with salt particles. ▫▫ **ef·flo·res·cence** *n.* **ef·flo·res·cent** *adj.*

ef·flu·ence /éflōōəns/ *n.* **1** a flowing out (of light, electricity, etc.). **2** that which flows out.

ef·flu·ent /éflōōənt/ *adj.* & *n.* • *adj.* flowing forth or out. • *n.* **1** sewage or industrial waste discharged into a river, the sea, etc. **2** a stream or lake flowing from a larger body of water.

ef·flu·vi·um /iflóoveeəm/ *n.* (*pl.* **effluvia** /–veeə/) an unpleasant or noxious odor or exhaled substance affecting the lungs or the sense of smell, etc.

ef·fort /éfərt/ *n.* **1** strenuous physical or mental exertion. **2** a vigorous or determined attempt. **3** *Mech.* a force exerted. **4** *colloq.* the result of an attempt; something accomplished (*not bad for a first effort*). ▫▫ **ef·fort·less** *adj.* **ef·fort·less·ly** *adv.*

ef·fron·ter·y /ifrúntəree/ *n.* (*pl.* **-ies**) shameless insolence; impudent audacity (esp. *have the effrontery to*).

ef·ful·gent /ifúljənt/ *adj. literary* radiant; shining brilliantly. ▫▫ **ef·ful·gence** /–jəns/ *n.* **ef·ful·gent·ly** *adv.*

ef·fuse *adj.* & *v.* • *adj.* /ifyóos/ *Bot.* (of an inflorescence, etc.) spreading loosely. • *v.tr.* /ifyóoz/ **1** pour forth (liquid, light, etc.). **2** give out (ideas, etc.).

ef·fu·sion /ifyóozhən/ *n.* **1** a copious outpouring. **2** usu. *derog.* an unrestrained flow of speech or writing.

ef·fu·sive /ifyóosiv/ *adj.* gushing; demonstrative; exuberant (*effusive praise*). ▫▫ **ef·fu·sive·ly** *adv.* **ef·fu·sive·ness** *n.*

e.g., *abbr.* for example.

e·gal·i·tar·i·an /igálitáireeən/ *adj.* & *n.* • *adj.* **1** of or relating to the principle of equal rights and opportunities for all (*an egalitarian society*). **2** advocating this principle. • *n.* a person who advocates or supports egalitarian principles. ▫▫ **e·gal·i·tar·i·an·ism** *n.*

egg[1] /eg/ *n.* **1 a** the spheroidal reproductive body produced by females of animals such as birds, reptiles, fish, etc., enclosed in a protective layer and capable of developing into a new individual. **b** the egg of the domestic hen, used for food. **2** *Biol.* the female reproductive cell in animals and plants. **3** *colloq.* a person or thing qualified in some way (*a tough egg*). ▫ **have** (or **put**) **all one's eggs in one basket** *colloq.* risk everything on a single venture. **with egg on one's face** *colloq.* made to look foolish. ▫▫ **egg·less** *adj.* **egg·y** *adj.* (**eggier, eggiest**).

egg[2] /eg/ *v.tr.* (foll. by *on*) urge (*egged them on to do it*).

egg·head /éghed/ *n. colloq.* an intellectual; an expert.

egg·nog /égnog/ *n.* a drink made from a mixture of eggs, cream, and flavorings, often with alcohol.

egg·plant /égplant/ *n.* **1** a tropical plant, *Solanum melongena*, having erect or spreading branches bearing purple or white egg-shaped fruit. **2** this fruit eaten as a vegetable. **3** the dark purple color of this fruit.

egg·shell /égshel/ *n. & adj.* • *n.* **1** the shell of an egg. **2** anything very fragile. **3** a pale yellowish-white color. • *adj.* **1** (of china) thin and fragile. **2** (of paint) with a slight gloss finish.

e·go /éegō/ *n.* (*pl.* **-gos**) **1** *Metaphysics* a conscious thinking subject. **2** *Psychol.* the part of the mind that reacts to reality and has a sense of individuality. **3** self-esteem.

e·go·cen·tric /éegōséntrik, égō–/ *adj.* **1** centered in the ego. **2** self-centered; egoistic. □□ **e·go·cen·tri·cal·ly** *adv.* **e·go·cen·tric·i·ty** /–trísitee/ *n.*

e·go·ism /éegōizəm, égō–/ *n.* **1** an ethical theory that treats self-interest as the foundation of morality. **2** systematic selfishness. **3** self-opinionatedness. **4** = EGOTISM. □□ **e·go·ist** *n.* **e·go·is·tic** *adj.* **e·go·is·ti·cal** *adj.*
▶An **egoist** is someone who is self-centered or selfish, as in feelings or actions. An **egotist** is someone who makes these feelings known, as by constant bragging or self-praise.

e·go·ma·ni·a /éegōmáyneeə, égō–/ *n.* obsessive egotism or self-centeredness. □□ **e·go·ma·ni·ac** *n.* **e·go·ma·ni·a·cal** /–mənīəkəl/ *adj.*

e·go·tism /éegətizəm, égə–/ *n.* **1** the practice of talking about oneself. **2** an exaggerated opinion of oneself. □□ **e·go·tist** *n.* **e·go·tis·tic** *adj.* **e·go·tis·ti·cal** *adj.*

e·go trip *n. colloq.* activity, etc., devoted entirely to one's own interests or feelings.

e·gre·gious /igréejəs/ *adj.* outstandingly bad; shocking (*an egregious error*). □□ **e·gre·gious·ly** *adv.*

e·gress /éegres/ *n.* **1 a** going out. **b** the right of going out. **2** an exit; a way out.

e·gret /éegrit/ *n.* any of various herons of the genus *Egretta* or *Bulbulcus*, usu. having long white feathers in the breeding season.

E·gyp·tian /ijípshən/ *adj. & n.* • *adj.* **1** of or relating to Egypt in NE Africa. **2** of or for Egyptian antiquities (*Egyptian room*). • *n.* **1** a native of ancient or modern Egypt; a national of the Arab Republic of Egypt. **2** the Hamitic language used in ancient Egypt until the 3rd C. AD. □□ **E·gyp·tian·ize** *v.tr.* **E·gyp·tian·i·za·tion** *n.*

E·gyp·tol·o·gy /éejiptóləjee/ *n.* the study of the language, history, and culture of ancient Egypt. □□ **E·gyp·tol·o·gist** *n.*

ei·der /īdər/ *n.* **1** (in full **eider duck**) any of various large northern ducks, esp. of the genus *Somateria*. **2** = EIDERDOWN 1.

ei·der·down /īdərdown/ *n.* **1** small, soft feathers from the breast of the eider duck. **2** a quilt stuffed with down (orig. from the eider) or some other soft material, esp. as the upper layer of bedclothes.

eight /ayt/ *n.* **1** one more than seven, or two less than ten; the product of two units and four units. **2** a symbol for this (8, viii, VIII). **3** a figure resembling the form of 8. **4** a size, etc., denoted by eight. **5** an eight-oared rowing boat or its crew. **6** the time of eight o'clock (*is it eight yet?*).

eight·een /áyteen/ *n. & adj.* • *n.* **1** one more than seventeen, or eight more than ten; the product of two units and nine units. **2** a symbol for this (18, xviii, XVIII). **3** a size, etc., denoted by eighteen. **4** a set or team of eighteen individuals. • *adj.* that amount to eighteen. □□ **eight·eenth** *adj. & n.*

eight·een-wheel·er *n.* a large tractor-trailer with eighteen wheels.

eight·fold /áytfōld/ *adj. & adv.* **1** eight times as much or as many. **2** consisting of eight parts.

eighth /ayt-th, ayth/ *n.* **1** the position in a sequence corresponding to the number 8 in the sequence 1–8. **2** something occupying this position. **3** one of eight equal parts of a thing.

eighth note *n. Mus.* a note having the time value of an eighth of a whole note and represented by a large dot with a hooked stem. Also called esp. *Brit.* QUAVER.

eight·y /áytee/ *n. & adj.* • *n.* (*pl.* **-ies**) **1** the product of eight and ten. **2** a symbol for this (80, lxxx, LXXX). **3** (in *pl.*) the numbers from 80 to 89, esp. the years of a century or of a person's life. • *adj.* that amount to eighty. □□ **eight·i·eth** *adj. & n.* **eight·y·fold** *adj. & adv.*

ein·stein·i·um /īnstíneeəm/ *n. Chem.* a transuranic radioactive metallic element produced artificially from plutonium. ¶ Symb.: **Es.**

ei·ther /éethər, īthər/ *adj., pron., adv., & conj.* • *adj. & pron.* **1** one or the other of two (*either of you can go*). **2** each of two (*houses on either side of the road*). • *adv. & conj.* **1** as one possibility (*is either black or white*). **2** as one choice or alternative (*either come in or go out*). **3** (with *neg.* or *interrog.*) **a** any more than the other (*I didn't like it either*). **b** moreover (*there is no time to lose, either*). □ **either or** *n.* an unavoidable choice between alternatives. *adj.* involving such a choice.

e·jac·u·late *v. & n.* • *v.tr.* /ijákyəlayt/ (also *absol.*) **1** utter suddenly (words esp. of prayer or other emotion). **2** eject (fluid, etc., esp. semen) from the body. • *n.* /ijákyələt/ semen that has been ejaculated from the body. □□ **e·jac·u·la·tion** /–láyshən/ *n.* **e·jac·u·la·tor** *n.*

e·ject /ijékt/ *v.tr.* **1 a** send or drive out precipitately or by force, esp. from a building or other property; compel to leave. **b** dismiss from employment or office. **2 a** cause (the pilot, etc.) to be propelled from an aircraft or spacecraft in an emergency. **b** (*absol.*) (of the pilot, etc.) be ejected in this way (*they ejected at 1,000 feet*). **3** cause to be removed or drop out (e.g., a spent cartridge from a gun). **4** dispossess (a tenant, etc.) by legal process. **5** dart forth; emit. □□ **e·jec·tion** *n.*

e·jec·tor /ijéktər/ *n.* a device for ejecting.

eke /eek/ *v.tr.* □ **eke out 1** (foll. by *with, by*) supplement; make the best use of (defective means, etc.). **2** make (a livelihood) or support (an existence).

EKG *abbr.* electrocardiogram.

e·lab·o·rate *adj. & v.* • *adj.* /ilábərət/ **1** carefully or minutely worked out. **2** highly developed or complicated. • *v.* /ilábərayt/ **1 a** *tr.* work out or explain in detail. **b** *tr.* make more intricate or ornate. **c** *intr.* (often foll. by *on*) go into details (*I need not elaborate*). **2** *tr.* produce by labor. □□ **e·lab·o·rate·ly** *adv.* **e·lab·o·rate·ness** *n.* **e·lab·o·ra·tion** /–ráyshən/ *n.* **e·lab·o·ra·tor** *n.*

é·lan /aylóN, aylón/ *n.* vivacity; dash.

e·land /éelənd/ *n.* any antelope of the genus *Taurotragus*, native to Africa, having spirally twisted horns, esp. the largest of living antelopes *T. derbianus*.

e·lapse /iláps/ *v.intr.* (of time) pass by.

e·las·mo·sau·rus /ilázməsáwrəs/ *n.* a large extinct marine reptile with paddlelike limbs and tough crocodilelike skin.

e·las·tic /ilástik/ *adj. & n.* • *adj.* **1** able to resume its normal bulk or shape spontaneously after contraction, dilatation, or distortion. **2** springy. **3** (of a person or feelings) buoyant. **4** flexible; adaptable (*elastic conscience*). **5** *Econ.* (of demand) variable according to price. **6** *Physics* (of a collision) involving no decrease of kinetic energy. • *n.* **1** elastic cord or fabric, usu. woven with strips of rubber. **2** (in full **elastic band**) = RUBBER BAND. □□ **e·las·ti·cal·ly** *adv.* **e·las·tic·i·ty** /ilastísitee, eelas–/ *n.* **e·las·ti·cize** /ilástisīz/ *v.tr.*

e·late /iláyt/ *v.tr* **1** (esp. as **elated** *adj.*) inspirit; stimulate. **2** make proud. ▫▫ **e·lat·ed·ly** *adv.* **e·lat·ed·ness** *n.* **e·la·tion** /–láyshən/ *n.*

E lay·er /éelayər/ *n.* a layer of the ionosphere able to reflect medium-frequency radio waves.

el·bow /élbō/ *n. & v.* • *n.* **1 a** the joint between the forearm and the upper arm. **b** the part of the sleeve of a garment covering the elbow. **2** an elbow-shaped bend or corner; a short piece of piping bent through a right angle. • *v.tr.* (foll. by *in, out, aside,* etc.) **1** thrust or jostle (a person or oneself). **2** make (one's way) by thrusting or jostling. **3** nudge or poke with the elbow.

el·bow grease *n. colloq.* vigorous polishing; hard work.

el·bow·room /élbōrōōm/ *n.* plenty of room to move or work in.

eld·er[1] /éldər/ *adj. & n.* • *attrib.adj.* (of two indicated persons, esp. when related) senior; of a greater age (*my elder brother*). • *n.* (often prec. by *the*) **1** the older or more senior of two indicated (esp. related) persons (*which is the elder?; is my elder by ten years*). **2** (in *pl.*) **a** persons of greater age or seniority (*respect your elders*). **b** persons venerable because of age. **3** a person advanced in life. **4** *hist.* a member of a senate or governing body. **5** an official in the early Christian, Presbyterian, or Mormon churches. ▫▫ **eld·er·ship** *n.*

eld·er[2] /éldər/ *n.* any shrub or tree of the genus *Sambucus,* with white flowers and usu. blue-black or red berries.

eld·er·ber·ry /éldərberee/ *n.* (*pl.* **-ries**) the berry of the elder, esp. common elder (*Sambucus nigra*) used for making jelly, wine, etc.

eld·er·ly /éldərlee/ *adj. & n.* • *adj.* **1** somewhat old. **2** (of a person) past middle age. • *n.* (*collect.*) (prec. by *the*) elderly people. ▫▫ **eld·er·li·ness** *n.*

eld·est /éldist/ *adj. & n.* • *adj.* first-born or oldest surviving (member of a family, son, daughter, etc.). • *n.* (often prec. by *the*) the eldest of three or more indicated (*who is the eldest?*).

elec. *abbr.* **1** electric. **2** electrical. **3** electricity.

el·e·cam·pane /élikampáyn/ *n.* **1** a sunflowerlike plant, *Inula helenium,* with bitter aromatic leaves and roots. **2** an esp. candied confection flavored with this.

e·lect /ilékt/ *v. & adj.* • *v.tr.* **1** (usu. foll. by *to* + infin.) choose (*the principles they elected to follow*). **2** choose (a person) by vote (*elected a new chairman*). **3** *Theol.* (of God) choose (persons) in preference to others for salvation. • *adj.* **1** chosen. **2** select; choice. **3** *Theol.* chosen by God. **4** (after a noun designating office) chosen but not yet in office (*president elect*).

e·lec·tion /ilékshən/ *n.* **1** the process of electing or being elected. **2** the act or an instance of electing.

e·lec·tive /iléktiv/ *adj. & n.* • *adj.* **1 a** (of an office or its holder) filled or appointed by election. **b** (of authority) derived from election. **2** (of a body) having the power to elect. **3** having a tendency to act on or be concerned with some things rather than others (*elective affinity*). **4** (of a course of study) chosen by the student; optional. **5** (of a surgical operation, etc.) optional; not urgently necessary. • *n.* an elective course of study. ▫▫ **e·lec·tive·ly** *adv.*

e·lec·tor /iléktər/ *n.* **1** a person who has the right of voting. **2** a member of the electoral college. ▫▫ **e·lec·tor·ship** *n.*

e·lec·tor·al /iléktərəl/ *adj.* relating to or ranking as electors. ▫▫ **e·lec·tor·al·ly** *adv.*

e·lec·tor·al col·lege *n.* **1** a body of persons representing each of the states of the US, who cast votes for the election of the president and vice president. **2** a body of electors.

e·lec·tor·ate /iléktərət/ *n.* a body of electors.

E·lec·tra com·plex /iléktrə/ *n. Psychol.* a daughter's subconscious sexual attraction to her father and hostility toward her mother, corresponding to the Oedipus complex in a son.

e·lec·tric /iléktrik/ *adj. & n.* • *adj.* **1** of, worked by, or charged with electricity; producing or capable of generating electricity. **2** causing or charged with sudden and dramatic excitement (*the news had an electric effect; the atmosphere was electric*). • *n.* **1** an electric light, vehicle, etc. **2** (in *pl.*) electrical equipment. ▫▫ **e·lec·tri·cal·ly** *adv.*

e·lec·tri·cal /iléktrikəl/ *adj.* **1** of or concerned with or of the nature of electricity. **2** operating by electricity. **3** suddenly or dramatically exciting (*the effect was electrical*).

e·lec·tric chair *n.* a chair in which criminals sentenced to death are executed by electrocution.

e·lec·tric eel *n.* an eellike freshwater fish, *Electrophorus electricus,* native to S. America, that kills its prey by electric shock.

e·lec·tri·cian /ilektríshən, éelek–/ *n.* a person who installs or maintains electrical equipment, esp. professionally.

e·lec·tric·i·ty /ilektrísitee, éelek–/ *n.* **1** a form of energy resulting from the existence of charged particles (electrons, protons, etc.), either statically as an accumulation of charge or dynamically as a current. **2** the branch of physics dealing with electricity. **3** a supply of electric current for heating, lighting, etc. **4** a state of heightened emotion; excitement; tension.

e·lec·tri·fy /iléktrifī/ *v.tr.* (**-fies, -fied**) **1** charge (a body) with electricity. **2** convert to the use of electric power. **3** cause dramatic or sudden excitement in. ▫▫ **e·lec·tri·fi·ca·tion** /–fikáyshən/ *n.* **e·lec·tri·fi·er** *n.*

e·lec·tro /iléktrō/ *n. & v.* • *n.* (*pl.* **-tros**) **1** = ELECTROTYPE *n.* **2** = ELECTROPLATE *n.* • *v.tr.* (**-troes, -troed**) *colloq.* **1** = ELECTROTYPE *v.* **2** = ELECTROPLATE *v.*

electro- /iléktrō/ *comb. form Electr.* of, relating to, or caused by electricity (*electrocute; electromagnet*).

e·lec·tro·car·di·o·gram /iléktrōkaárdeeəgram/ *n.* a record of the heartbeat traced by an electrocardiograph.

e·lec·tro·car·di·o·graph /iléktrōkaárdeeəgraf/ *n.* an instrument recording the electric currents generated by a person's heartbeat. ▫▫ **e·lec·tro·car·di·o·graph·ic** *adj.* **e·lec·tro·car·di·og·ra·phy** /–deeógrəfee/ *n.*

e·lec·tro·con·vul·sive /iléktrōkənvúlsiv/ *adj.* (of a therapy) employing the use of the convulsive response to the application of electric shocks.

e·lec·tro·cute /iléktrəkyōōt/ *v.tr.* **1** injure or kill someone by electric shock. **2** execute (a convicted criminal) by means of the electric chair. ▫▫ **e·lec·tro·cu·tion** /–kyōōshən/ *n.*

e·lec·trode /iléktrōd/ *n.* a conductor through which electricity enters or leaves an electrolyte, gas, vacuum, etc.

e·lec·tro·dy·nam·ics /iléktrōdīnámiks/ *n.pl.* (usu. treated as *sing.*) the branch of mechanics concerned with electric current applied to motive forces. ▫▫ **e·lec·tro·dy·nam·ic** *adj.*

e·lec·tro·en·ceph·a·lo·gram /iléktrōinséfələgram/ *n.* a record of the brain's activity traced by an electroencephalograph.

e·lec·tro·en·ceph·a·lo·graph /iléktrōinséfələgraf/ *n.* an instrument recording the electrical activity of the brain. ▫▫ **e·lec·tro·en·ceph·a·log·ra·phy** /–lógrəfee/ *n.*

e·lec·trol·y·sis /ilektrólisis, éelek–/ *n.* **1** *Chem.* the decomposition of a substance by the application of an electric current. **2** *Med.* this process applied to the destruction of tumors, hair roots, etc. ▫▫ **e·lec·tro·lyt·ic** /iléktrōlítik/ *adj.* **e·lec·tro·lyt·i·cal** *adj.* **e·lec·tro·lyt·i·cal·ly** *adv.*

See page xii for the *Key to Pronunciation.*

e•lec•tro•lyte /iléktrəlīt/ *n.* **1** a substance that conducts electricity when molten or in solution, esp. in an electric cell or battery. **2** a solution of this.

e•lec•tro•lyze /iléktrəlīz/ *v.tr.* subject to or treat by electrolysis. ▫▫ **e•lec•tro•lyz•er** *n.*

e•lec•tro•mag•net /iléktrōmágnit/ *n.* a soft metal core made into a magnet by the passage of electric current through a coil surrounding it.

e•lec•tro•mag•net•ic /iléktrōmagnétik/ *adj.* having both an electrical and a magnetic character or properties. ▫▫ **e•lec•tro•mag•net•i•cal•ly** *adv.*

e•lec•tro•mag•net•ism /iléktrōmágnitizəm/ *n.* **1** the magnetic forces produced by electricity. **2** the study of this.

e•lec•tro•me•chan•i•cal /iléktrōmikánikəl/ *adj.* relating to the application of electricity to mechanical processes, devices, etc.

e•lec•trom•e•ter /ilektrómitər, éelek–/ *n.* an instrument for measuring electrical potential without drawing any current from the circuit. ▫▫ **e•lec•tro•met•ric** /–métrik/ *adj.* **e•lec•trom•e•try** *n.*

e•lec•tro•mo•tive /iléktrōmṓtiv/ *adj.* producing or tending to produce an electric current.

e•lec•tron /iléktron/ *n.* a stable elementary particle with a charge of negative electricity, found in all atoms and acting as the primary carrier of electricity in solids.

e•lec•tron•ic /ilektrónik, éelek–/ *adj.* **1 a** produced by or involving the flow of electrons. **b** of or relating to electrons or electronics. **2** (of a device) using electronic components. **3 a** (of music) produced by electronic means, and usu. recorded on tape. **b** (of a musical instrument) producing sounds by electronic means. ▫▫ **e•lec•tron•i•cal•ly** *adv.*

e•lec•tron•ic mail *n.* messages distributed by electronic means, esp. from one computer system to one or more recipients. Also called E-mail.

e•lec•tron•ics /ilektróniks, éelek–/ *n.pl.* (usu. treated as *sing.*) **1** a branch of physics and technology concerned with the behavior and movement of electrons in a vacuum, gas, semiconductor, etc. **2** the circuits used in this.

e•lec•tron mi•cro•scope *n.* a microscope with high magnification and resolution, employing electron beams in place of light and using electron lenses.

e•lec•tron•volt /iléktronvōlt/ *n.* a unit of energy equal to the work done on an electron in accelerating it through a potential difference of one volt. ¶ Abbr.: **eV**.

e•lec•tro•plate /iléktrəplayt/ *v. & n.* • *v.tr.* coat by electrolytic deposition with chromium, silver, etc. • *n.* electroplated articles. ▫▫ **e•lec•tro•plat•er** *n.*

e•lec•tro•scope /iléktrəskōp/ *n.* an instrument for detecting and measuring electricity, esp. as an indication of the ionization of air by radioactivity. ▫▫ **e•lec•tro•scop•ic** /–skópik/ *adj.*

e•lec•tro•shock /iléktrōshok/ *attrib.adj.* (of medical treatment) by means of electric shocks.

e•lec•tro•stat•ic /iléktrōstátik/ *adj.* of or relating to stationary electric charges or electrostatics.

e•lec•tro•tech•nol•o•gy /iléktrōteknóləjee/ *n.* the science of the application of electricity in technology. ▫▫ **e•lec•tro•tech•nic** /–téknik/ *adj.* **e•lec•tro•tech•ni•cal** *adj.* **e•lec•tro•tech•nics** *n.*

e•lec•tro•ther•a•py /iléktrōthérəpee/ *n.* the treatment of diseases by the use of electricity. ▫▫ **e•lec•tro•thera•peu•tic** /–pyṓotik/ *adj.* **e•lec•tro•ther•a•peu•ti•cal** *adj.* **e•lec•tro•ther•a•pist** *n.*

e•lec•tro•ther•mal /iléktrōthə́rməl/ *adj.* relating to heat electrically derived.

e•lec•tro•type /iléktrōtīp/ *v. & n.* • *v.tr.* copy by the electrolytic deposition of copper on a mold, esp. for printing. • *n.* a copy so formed.

el•e•gant /éligənt/ *adj.* **1** graceful in appearance or manner. **2** tasteful; refined. **3** (of a mode of life, etc.) of refined luxury. **4** ingeniously simple and pleasing. **5** excellent. ▫▫ **el•e•gance** /–gəns/ *n.* **el•e•gant•ly** *adv.*

el•e•gi•ac /élijíək, iléejeeak/ *adj. & n.* • *adj.* **1** (of a meter) used for elegies. **2** mournful. • *n.* (in *pl.*) verses in an elegiac meter. ▫▫ **el•e•gi•a•cal•ly** *adv.*

el•e•gize /élijīz/ *v.* **1** *intr.* (often foll. by *upon*) write an elegy. **2** *intr.* write in a mournful strain. **3** *tr.* write an elegy upon. ▫▫ **el•e•gist** *n.*

el•e•gy /élijee/ *n.* (*pl.* **-gies**) **1** a song of lament, esp. for the dead (sometimes vaguely used of other poems). **2** a poem in elegiac meter.

el•e•ment /élimənt/ *n.* **1** a component part or group; a contributing factor or thing. **2** *Chem. & Physics* any of the hundred or so substances that cannot be resolved by chemical means into simpler substances. **3 a** any of the four substances (earth, water, air, and fire) in ancient and medieval philosophy. **b** any of these as a being's natural abode or environment. **c** a person's appropriate or preferred sphere of operation. **4** *Electr.* a resistance wire that heats up in an electric heater, cooker, etc.; an electrode. **5** (in *pl.*) atmospheric agencies, esp. wind and storm. **6** (in *pl.*) the rudiments of learning or of a branch of knowledge. **7** (in *pl.*) the bread and wine of the Eucharist.

el•e•men•tal /éliméntʼl/ *adj. & n.* • *adj.* **1** of the four elements. **2** of the powers of nature (*elemental worship*). **3** comparable to a force of nature (*elemental grandeur; elemental tumult*). **4** uncompounded (*elemental oxygen*). **5** essential. • *n.* an entity or force thought to be physically manifested by occult means.

el•e•men•ta•ry /éliméntəree, –tree/ *adj.* **1 a** dealing with or arising from the simplest facts of a subject; rudimentary; introductory. **b** simple. **2** *Chem.* not decomposable.

el•e•men•ta•ry school *n.* a school in which elementary subjects are taught to young children.

el•e•phant /élifənt/ *n.* (*pl.* same or **elephants**) the largest living land animal, of which two species survive, the larger African (*Loxodonta africana*) and the smaller Indian (*Elephas maximus*), both with a trunk and long curved ivory tusks. ▫▫ **el•e•phan•toid** /–fantóyd/ *adj.*

el•e•phan•ti•a•sis /élifəntíəsis/ *n.* gross enlargement of the body, esp. the limbs, due to lymphatic obstruction, esp. by a nematode parasite.

el•e•phan•tine /élifánteen, –tīn, éləfən–/ *adj.* **1** of elephants. **2 a** huge. **b** clumsy; unwieldy.

el•e•vate /élivayt/ *v.tr.* **1** bring to a higher position. **2** raise; lift. **3** raise the axis of (a gun). **4** raise (a railroad, etc.) above ground level. **5** exalt in rank, etc. **6** (usu. as **elevated** *adj.*) **a** raise the spirits of; elate. **b** raise morally or intellectually (*elevated style*).

el•e•va•tion /éliváyshən/ *n.* **1 a** the process of elevating or being elevated. **b** the angle with the horizontal, esp. of a gun or of the direction of a heavenly body. **c** the height above a given level, esp. sea level. **d** a raised area; a swelling on the skin. **2 a** a drawing or diagram made by projection on a vertical plane (cf. PLAN). **b** a flat drawing of the front, side, or back of a house, etc. **3** *Ballet* **a** the capacity of a dancer to attain height in springing movements. **b** the action of tightening the muscles and uplifting the body. ▫▫ **el•e•va•tion•al** *adj.* (in sense 2).

el•e•va•tor /élivaytər/ *n.* **1** a hoisting machine. **2** *Aeron.* the movable part of a tailplane for changing the pitch of an aircraft. **3 a** a platform or compartment housed in a shaft for raising and lowering persons or things to different floors of a building or different levels of a mine, etc. **b** a place for lifting and storing quantities of grain. **4** that which elevates, esp. a muscle that raises a limb.

e·lev·en /ilévən/ *n. & adj.* •*n.* **1** one more than ten; the sum of six units and five units. **2** a symbol for this (11, xi, XI). **3** a size, etc., denoted by eleven. **4** a set or team of eleven individuals. **5** the time of eleven o'clock. •*adj.* that amount to eleven.

e·lev·enth /ilévənth/ *n. & adj.* •*n.* **1** the position in a sequence corresponding to the number 11 in the sequence 1–11. **2** something occupying this position. **3** one of eleven equal parts of a thing. **4** *Mus.* **a** an interval or chord spanning an octave and a third in the diatonic scale. **b** a note separated from another by this interval. •*adj.* that is the eleventh.

e·lev·enth hour *n.* the last possible moment.

elf /elf/ *n.* (*pl.* **elves** /elvz/) **1** a mythological being, esp. one that is small and mischievous. **2** a sprite or little creature. ▫▫ **elf·ish** *adj.* **elv·ish** *adj.*

elf·in /élfin/ *adj.* of elves; elflike; tiny; dainty.

e·lic·it /ilísit/ *v.tr.* **1** draw out; evoke (an admission, response, etc.). **2** draw forth (what is latent). ▫▫ **e·lic·i·ta·tion** *n.* **e·lic·i·tor** *n.*

e·lide /ilíd/ *v.tr.* omit (a vowel or syllable) by elision.

el·i·gi·ble /élijibəl/ *adj.* **1** (often foll. by *for*) fit or entitled to be chosen. **2** desirable or suitable, esp. as a partner in marriage. ▫▫ **el·i·gi·bil·i·ty** *n.*

e·lim·i·nate /iliminayt/ *v.tr.* **1 a** remove; get rid of. **b** kill; murder. **2** exclude from consideration; ignore as irrelevant. **3** exclude from further participation in a competition, etc., on defeat. ▫▫ **e·lim·i·na·tion** /–náyshən/ *n.* **e·lim·i·na·tor** *n.* **e·lim·i·na·to·ry** /–nətáwree/ *adj.*

e·li·sion /ilízhən/ *n.* **1** the omission of a vowel or syllable in pronouncing (as in *I'm, let's, e'en*). **2** the omission of a passage in a book, etc.

e·lite /ayléet, əléet/ *n. & adj.* •*n.* **1** (prec. by *the*) the best of a group. **2** a select group or class. •*adj.* of or belonging to an elite; exclusive.

e·lit·ism /ayléetizəm, əleet–/ *n.* **1** advocacy of or reliance on leadership or dominance by a select group. **2** a sense of belonging to an elite. ▫▫ **e·lit·ist** *n. & adj.*

e·lix·ir /iliksər/ *n.* **1** *Alchemy* **a** a preparation supposedly able to change metals into gold. **b** (in full **elixir of life**) a preparation supposedly able to prolong life indefinitely. **c** a supposed remedy for all ills. **2** *Pharm.* an aromatic solution used as a medicine or flavoring.

E·liz·a·be·than /ilízəbéethən/ *adj. & n.* •*adj.* of the time of England's Queen Elizabeth I (1558–1603) or of Queen Elizabeth II (1952–). •*n.* a person of the time of Queen Elizabeth I or II.

elk /elk/ *n.* (*pl.* same or **elks**) **1** a large deer, *Cervus canadensis*, native to North America. Also called **wapiti.** **2** a large deer, *Alces alces*, of N. Europe and Asia; a moose.

el·lipse /ilíps/ *n.* a regular oval, traced by a point moving in a plane so that the sum of its distances from two other points is constant, or resulting when a cone is cut by a plane that does not intersect the base (cf. HYPERBOLA).

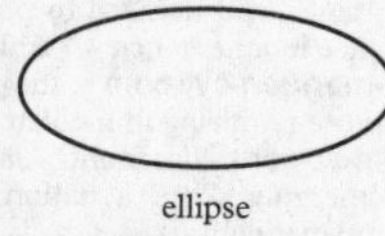

ellipse

el·lip·sis /ilípsis/ *n.* (*pl.* **ellipses** /–seez/) **1** the omission from a sentence of words needed to complete the construction or sense. **2** the omission of a sentence at the end of a paragraph. **3** a set of three dots, etc., indicating an omission.

el·lip·tic /ilíptik/ *adj.* (also **el·lip·ti·cal**) of, relating to, or having the form of an ellipse or ellipsis. ▫▫ **el·lip·ti·cal·ly** *adv.* **el·lip·tic·i·ty** /éliptísitee/ *n.*

elm /elm/ *n.* **1** any tree of the genus *Ulmus*, esp. *U. procera* with rough serrated leaves. **2** (in full **elmwood**) the wood of the elm. ▫▫ **elm·y** *adj.*

el·o·cu·tion /éləkyóoshən/ *n.* **1** the art of clear and expressive speech, esp. of distinct pronunciation and articulation. **2** a particular style of speaking. ▫▫ **el·o·cu·tion·ar·y** *adj.* **el·o·cu·tion·ist** *n.*

e·lon·gate /iláwnggayt, –long–/ *tr.* lengthen; prolong. ▫▫ **e·long·a·tion** /ilawnggáyshən, ilong–, éelawng–, éelong–/ *n.*

e·lon·gat·ed *adj.* **1** long in relation to its width. **2** that has been made longer.

e·lope /ilóp/ *v.intr.* **1** run away to marry secretly, esp. without parental consent. **2** run away with a lover. ▫▫ **e·lope·ment** *n.*

el·o·quence /éləkwəns/ *n.* **1** fluent and effective use of language. **2** rhetoric.

el·o·quent /éləkwənt/ *adj.* **1** possessing or showing eloquence. **2** (often foll. by *of*) clearly expressive or indicative. ▫▫ **el·o·quent·ly** *adv.*

else /els/ *adv.* **1** (prec. by indef. or interrog. pron.) besides; in addition (*someone else; nowhere else; who else*). **2** instead; other; different (*what else could I say?*). **3** otherwise; if not (*run, (or) else you will be late*).

else·where /éls-hwair, –wáir/ *adv.* in or to some other place.

e·lu·ci·date /ilóosidáyt/ *v.tr.* throw light on; explain. ▫▫ **e·lu·ci·da·tion** /–dáyshən/ *n.*

e·lude /ilóod/ *v.tr.* **1** escape adroitly from (a danger, difficulty, pursuer, etc.); dodge. **2** avoid compliance with (a law, request, etc.) or fulfillment of (an obligation). **3** (of a fact, solution, etc.) escape from or baffle (a person's memory or understanding). ▫▫ **e·lu·sion** /ilóozhən/ *n.* **e·lu·so·ry** /–lóosəree/ *adj.*

e·lu·sive /ilóosiv/ *adj.* **1** difficult to find or catch; tending to elude. **2** difficult to remember or recall. **3** (of an answer, etc.) avoiding the point raised; seeking to elude. ▫▫ **e·lu·sive·ly** *adv.* **e·lu·sive·ness** *n.*

E·ly·si·um /ilízeeəm, ilízh–/ *n.* **1** (also **E·ly·sian fields**) (in Greek mythology) the abode of the blessed after death. **2** a place or state of ideal happiness. ▫▫ **e·ly·si·an** or **E·ly·sian** *adj.*

el·y·tron /élitron/ *n.* (*pl.* **elytra** /–trə/) the outer hard, usu. brightly colored wing case of a coleopterous insect.

em /em/ *n.* *Printing* **1** a unit for measuring the amount of printed matter in a line, usually equal to the nominal width of capital M. **2** a unit of measurement equal to 12 points.

e·ma·ci·ate /imáysheeayt/ *v.tr.* (esp. as **emaciated** *adj.*) make abnormally thin or feeble. ▫▫ **e·ma·ci·a·tion** /–áyshən/ *n.*

E-mail /éemayl/ *n.* (also **e-mail**) = ELECTRONIC MAIL.

em·a·nate /émənayt/ *v.* **1** *intr.* (usu. foll. by *from*) (of an idea, rumor, etc.) issue; originate (from a source). **2** *intr.* (usu. foll. by *from*) (of gas, light, etc.) proceed; issue. **3** *tr.* emit; send forth. ▫▫ **em·a·na·tion** *n.*

e·man·ci·pate /imánsipayt/ *v.tr.* **1** free from restraint, esp. legal, social, or political. **2** (usu. as **emancipated** *adj.*) cause to be less inhibited by moral or social convention. **3** free from slavery. ▫▫ **e·man·ci·pa·tion** /–páyshən/ *n.* **e·man·ci·pa·tor** *n.* **e·man·ci·pa·to·ry** *adj.*

e·mas·cu·late *v. & adj.* •*v.tr.* /imáskyəlayt/ **1** deprive of force or vigor; make feeble or ineffective. **2** castrate. •*adj.* /imáskyələt/ **1** deprived of force or vigor. **2** castrated. **3** effeminate. ▫▫ **e·mas·cu·la·tion** /–láyshən/ *n.*

em·balm /embaám, im–/ *v.tr.* **1** preserve (a corpse) from decay orig. with spices, now by means of arterial injection. **2** preserve from oblivion. **3** give balmy fragrance to. ▫▫ **em·balm·er** *n.* **em·balm·ment** *n.*

em·bank·ment /embángkmənt, im–/ *n.* an earth or stone bank for keeping back water, or for carrying a road or railroad.

em•bar•go /embaárgō/ *n.* & *v.* •*n.* (*pl.* **-goes**) **1** an order of a government forbidding foreign ships to enter, or any ships to leave, its ports. **2** an official suspension of commerce or other activity (*be under an embargo*). **3** an impediment. •*v.tr.* (**-goes, -goed**) **1** place (ships, trade, etc.) under embargo. **2** seize (a ship, goods) for government service.

em•bark /embaárk, im–/ *v.* **1** *tr.* & *intr.* (often foll. by *for*) put or go on board a ship or aircraft (to a destination). **2** *intr.* (foll. by *on, upon*) engage in an activity or undertaking. ▫▫ **em•bar•ka•tion** *n.* (in sense 1).

em•bar•rass /embárəs, im–/ *v.tr.* **1 a** cause (a person) to feel awkward or self-conscious or ashamed. **b** (as **embarrassed** *adj.*) having or expressing a feeling of awkwardness or self-consciousness. **2** (as **embarrassed** *adj.*) encumbered with debts. **3** hamper; impede. ▫▫ **em•bar•rassed•ly** *adv.* **em•bar•rass•ing** *adj.* **em•bar•rass•ing•ly** *adv.* **em•bar•rass•ment** *n.*

em•bas•sy /émbəsee/ *n.* (*pl.* **-sies**) **1 a** the residence or offices of an ambassador. **b** the ambassador and staff attached to an embassy. **2** a deputation or mission to a foreign country.

em•bat•tle /embát'l, im–/ *v.tr.* **1 a** set (an army, etc.) in battle array. **b** fortify against attack. **2** provide (a building or wall) with battlements. **3** (as **embattled** *adj.*) **a** prepared or arrayed for battle. **b** involved in a conflict or difficult undertaking.

em•bed /embéd, im–/ *v.tr.* (also **im•bed**) (**-bedded, -bedding**) **1** (esp. as **embedded** *adj.*) fix firmly in a surrounding mass (*embedded in concrete*). **2** (of a mass) surround so as to fix firmly. **3** place in or as in a bed.

em•bel•lish /embélish, im–/ *v.tr.* **1** beautify; adorn. **2** add interest to (a narrative) with fictitious additions. ▫▫ **em•bel•lish•er** *n.* **em•bel•lish•ment** *n.*

em•ber /émbər/ *n.* **1** (usu. in *pl.*) a small piece of glowing coal or wood in a dying fire. **2** an almost extinct residue of a past activity, feeling, etc.

em•bez•zle /embézəl, im–/ *v.tr.* (also *absol.*) divert (money, etc.) fraudulently to one's own use. ▫▫ **em•bez•zle•ment** *n.* **em•bez•zler** *n.*

em•bit•ter /embítər, im–/ *v.tr.* **1** arouse bitter feelings in (a person). **2** make more bitter or painful. **3** render (a person or feelings) hostile. ▫▫ **em•bit•ter•ment** *n.*

em•bla•zon /embláyzən, im–/ *v.tr.* **1 a** portray conspicuously, as on a heraldic shield. **b** adorn (a shield) with heraldic devices. **2** adorn brightly and conspicuously. **3** celebrate, extol. ▫▫ **em•bla•zon•ment** *n.*

em•blem /émbləm/ *n.* **1** a symbol or representation typifying or identifying an institution, quality, etc. **2** (foll. by *of*) (of a person) the type (*the very emblem of courage*). **3** a heraldic device or symbolic object as a distinctive badge. ▫▫ **em•blem•at•ic** /–mátik/ *adj.* **em•blem•at•i•cal** *adj.* **em•blem•at•i•cal•ly** *adv.*

em•bod•y /embódee, im–/ *v.tr.* (**-ies, -ied**) **1** give a concrete or discernible form to (an idea, concept, etc.). **2** (of a thing or person) be an expression of (an idea, etc.). **3** express tangibly (*courage embodied in heroic actions*). **4** include; comprise. ▫▫ **em•bod•i•ment** *n.*

em•bold•en /embṓldən, im–/ *v.tr.* (often foll. by *to* + infin.) make bold; encourage.

em•bo•lism /émbəlizəm/ *n.* an obstruction of any artery by a clot of blood, air bubble, etc.

em•bo•lus /émbələs/ *n.* (*pl.* **emboli** /–lī/) an object causing an embolism.

em•boss /embós, im–/ *v.tr.* **1** carve or mold in relief. **2** form figures, etc., so that they stand out on (a surface). **3** make protuberant.

em•brace /embráys, im–/ *v.* & *n.* •*v.tr.* **1 a** hold (a person) closely in the arms, esp. as a sign of affection. **b** (*absol.* of two people) hold each other closely. **2** clasp; enclose. **3** accept eagerly (an offer, opportunity, etc.). **4** adopt (a course of action, doctrine, cause, etc.). **5** include; comprise. **6** take in with the eye or mind. •*n.* an act of embracing; holding in the arms. ▫▫ **em•brace•a•ble** *adj.* **em•brace•ment** *n.* **em•brac•er** *n.*

em•bra•sure /embráyzhər, im–/ *n.* **1** the beveling of a wall at the sides of a door or window. **2** a small opening in a parapet of a fortified building. ▫▫ **em•bra•sured** *adj.*

em•bro•ca•tion /émbrōkáyshən/ *n.* a liquid used for rubbing on the body to relieve muscular pain, etc.

em•broi•der /embróydər, im–/ *v.tr.* **1** (also *absol.*) **a** decorate (cloth, etc.) with needlework. **b** create (a design) in this way. **2** add interest to (a narrative) with fictitious additions. ▫▫ **em•broi•der•er** *n.*

em•broi•der•y /embróydəree, im–/ *n.* (*pl.* **-ies**) **1** the art of embroidering. **2** embroidered work; a piece of this.

em•broil /embróyl, im–/ *v.tr.* **1** (often foll. by *with*) involve (a person) in conflict or difficulties. **2** bring (affairs) into a state of confusion. ▫▫ **em•broil•ment** *n.*

em•bry•o /émbreeō/ *n.* (*pl.* **-os**) **1 a** an unborn or unhatched offspring. **b** a human offspring in the first eight weeks from conception. **2** a rudimentary plant contained in a seed. **3** a thing in a rudimentary stage. **4** (*attrib.*) undeveloped; immature. ▫ **in embryo** undeveloped. ▫▫ **em•bry•oid** /–breeoyd/ *adj.* **em•bry•on•ic** /émbreeónik/ *adj.* **em•bry•on•i•cal•ly** *adv.*

em•bry•o•gen•e•sis /émbreeōjénisis/ *n.* the formation of an embryo.

em•bry•ol•o•gy /émbreeóləjee/ *n.* the study of embryos. ▫▫ **em•bry•o•log•ic** /–breeəlójik/ *adj.* **em•bry•o•log•i•cal** *adj.* **em•bry•o•log•i•cal•ly** *adv.* **em•bry•ol•o•gist** *n.*

em•cee /émseé/ *n.* & *v. colloq.* •*n.* a master of ceremonies. •*v.tr.* & *intr.* (**emcees, emceed**) act as a master of ceremonies.

e•mend /iménd/ *v.tr.* edit (a text, etc.) to remove errors and corruptions. ▫▫ **e•men•da•tion** /éemendáyshən/ *n.*

em•er•ald /émərəld, émrəld/ *n.* **1** a bright-green precious stone, a variety of beryl. **2** (also **em•er•ald green**) the color of this.

e•merge /imə́rj/ *v.intr.* (often foll. by *from*) **1** come up or out into view, esp. when formerly concealed. **2** come up out of a liquid. **3** (of facts, circumstances, etc.) come to light; become known, esp. as a result of inquiry, etc. **4** become recognized or prominent (*emerged as a leading contender*). **5** (of a question, difficulty, etc.) become apparent. **6** survive (an ordeal, etc.) with a specified result (*emerged unscathed*). ▫▫ **e•mer•gence** *n.*

e•mer•gen•cy /imə́rjənsee/ *n.* (*pl.* **-cies**) **1** a sudden state of danger, conflict, etc., requiring immediate action. **2 a** a medical condition requiring immediate treatment. **b** a patient with such a condition. **3** (*attrib.*) characterized by or for use in an emergency.

e•mer•gen•cy med•i•cal tech•ni•cian *n.* a person trained and licensed to provide basic medical assistance in emergencies. ¶ Abbr.: **EMT.**

e•mer•gen•cy room *n.* the part of a hospital that treats those requiring immediate medical attention.

e•mer•gent /imə́rjənt/ *adj.* **1** becoming apparent; emerging. **2** (of a nation) newly formed or made independent.

e•mer•i•tus /iméritəs/ *adj.* retired and retaining one's title as an honor (*emeritus professor*).

em•er•y /éməree/ *n.* **1** a coarse corundum used for polishing metal, etc. **2** (*attrib.*) covered with emery.

em•er•y board *n.* a strip of thin wood or board coated with emery or another abrasive, used as a nail file.

e•met•ic /imétik/ *adj.* & *n.* •*adj.* that causes vomiting. •*n.* an emetic medicine.

em•i•grant /émigrənt/ *n.* & *adj.* •*n.* a person who emigrates. •*adj.* emigrating.

em•i•grate /émigrayt/ *v. intr.* leave one's own country to settle in another. ▫▫ **em•i•gra•tion** /–gráyshən/ *n.* **em•i•gra•to•ry** /–grətáwree/ *adj.*

▶To **emigrate** is to leave a country, especially one's own, intending to remain away. To **immigrate** is to enter a country, intending to remain there.

é·mi·gré /émigray/ *n.* (also **emigré**) an emigrant, esp. a political exile.

em·i·nence /éminəns/ *n.* **1** distinction; recognized superiority. **2** a piece of rising ground. **3** (**Eminence**) a title used in addressing or referring to a cardinal.

é·mi·nence grise /áymeenóɴs gréez/ *n.* (*pl.* **éminences grises** *pronunc.* same) **1** a person who exercises power or influence without holding office. **2** a confidential agent.

em·i·nent /éminənt/ *adj.* **1** distinguished; notable. **2** (of qualities) remarkable in degree. ▫▫ **em·i·nent·ly** *adv.*
▶**Eminent** means 'outstanding; famous': *The book was written by an eminent authority on folk art.* **Imminent** means 'about to happen': *War was imminent.* **Immanent**, often used in religious or philosophical contexts, means 'inherent': *He believed in the immanent unity of nature taught by the Hindus.*

em·i·nent do·main *n.* sovereign control over all property in a government jurisdiction.

e·mir /emeér/ *n.* a title of various Muslim rulers.

e·mir·ate /imeérit, –ayt, aymeér–, émərit/ *n.* the rank, domain, or reign of an emir.

em·is·sar·y /émiseree/ *n.* (*pl.* **-ies**) a person sent on a special, usu. diplomatic, mission.

e·mis·sion /imíshən/ *n.* **1** (often foll. by *of*) the process or an act of emitting. **2** a thing emitted.

e·mis·sive /imísiv/ *adj.* having the power to radiate light, heat, etc. ▫▫ **em·is·siv·i·ty** /éemisívitee/ *n.*

e·mit /imít/ *v.tr.* (**emitted, emitting**) **1 a** send out (heat, light, vapor, etc.). **b** discharge from the body. **2** utter (a cry, etc.). ▫▫ **e·mit·ter** *n.*

em·mer /émər/ *n.* a kind of wheat, *Triticum dicoccum*, grown mainly for fodder.

Em·my /émee/ *n.* (*pl.* **-mies**) one of the statuettes awarded annually to outstanding television programs and performers.

e·mol·lient /imólyənt/ *adj.* & *n.* • *adj.* that softens or soothes the skin. • *n.* an emollient agent. ▫▫ **e·mol·lience** /–yəns/ *n.*

e·mol·u·ment /imólyəmənt/ *n.* a salary, fee, or profit from employment or office.

e·mote /imṓt/ *v.intr. colloq.* show excessive emotion. ▫▫ **e·mot·er** *n.*

e·mo·tion /imṓshən/ *n.* a strong mental or instinctive feeling such as love or fear.

e·mo·tion·al /imṓshənəl/ *adj.* **1** of or relating to the emotions. **2** (of a person) liable to excessive emotion. **3** expressing or based on emotion (*an emotional appeal*). **4** likely to excite emotion (*an emotional issue*). ▫▫ **e·mo·tion·al·ize** *v.tr.* **e·mo·tion·al·ly** *adv.*

e·mo·tive /imṓtiv/ *adj.* **1** of or characterized by emotion. **2** tending to excite emotion. **3** arousing feeling; not purely descriptive. ▫▫ **e·mo·tive·ly** *adv.*

em·pan·el /empánəl, im–/ var. of IMPANEL.

em·pa·thize /émpəthīz/ *v. Psychol.* **1** *intr.* (usu. foll. by *with*) exercise empathy. **2** *tr.* treat with empathy.

em·pa·thy /émpəthee/ *n. Psychol.* the power of identifying oneself mentally with (and so fully comprehending) a person or object of contemplation. ▫▫ **em·pa·thet·ic** /–thétik/ *adj.* **em·pa·thet·i·cal·ly** *adv.* **em·path·ic** /empáthik/ *adj.* **em·path·i·cal·ly** *adv.*

em·per·or /émpərər/ *n.* the sovereign of an empire. ▫▫ **em·per·or·ship** *n.*

em·pha·sis /émfəsis/ *n.* (*pl.* **emphases** /–seez/) **1** special importance or prominence attached to a thing, fact, idea, etc. (*emphasis on economy*). **2** stress laid on a word or words to indicate special meaning or importance. **3** vigor or intensity of expression, feeling, action, etc.

em·pha·size /émfəsīz/ *v.tr.* **1** bring (a thing, fact, etc.) into special prominence. **2** lay stress on (a word in speaking).

em·phat·ic /emfátik/ *adj.* **1** (of language, tone, or gesture) forcibly expressive. **2** of words: **a** bearing the stress. **b** used to give emphasis. **3** expressing oneself with emphasis. **4** (of an action or process) forcible; significant. ▫▫ **em·phat·i·cal·ly** *adv.*

em·phy·se·ma /émfiséemə, –zéemə/ *n.* enlargement of the air sacs of the lungs causing breathlessness.

em·pire /émpīr/ *n.* **1** an extensive group of lands or countries under a single supreme authority, esp. an emperor. **2** supreme dominion. **3** a large commercial organization, etc., owned or directed by one person or group.

em·pir·ic /empírik, im–/ *adj.* & *n.* • *adj.* = EMPIRICAL. • *n. archaic* **1** a person who, in medicine or other branches of science, relies solely on observation and experiment. **2** a quack doctor. ▫▫ **em·pir·i·cism** /–sizəm/ *n.* (cf. RATIONALISM). **em·pir·i·cist** *n.*

em·pir·i·cal /empírikəl, im–/ *adj.* **1** based or acting on observation or experiment, not on theory. **2** *Philos.* regarding sense-data as valid information. **3** deriving knowledge from experience alone. ▫▫ **em·pir·i·cal·ly** *adv.*

em·place·ment /empláysmənt, im–/ *n.* **1** the act or an instance of putting in position. **2** a platform or defended position where a gun is placed for firing.

em·ploy /emplóy, im–/ *v.* & *n.* • *v.tr.* **1** use the services of (a person) in return for payment; keep (a person) in one's service. **2** (often foll. by *for, in, on*) use (a thing, time, energy, etc.) esp. to good effect. **3** (often foll. by *in*) keep (a person) occupied. • *n.* the state of being employed, esp. for wages. ▫ **in the employ of** employed by. ▫▫ **em·ploy·a·ble** *adj.* **em·ploy·a·bil·i·ty** *n.* **em·ploy·er** *n.*

em·ploy·ee /émplóyee, –ployée/ *n.* (also **em·ploy·e**) a person employed for wages or salary.

em·ploy·ment /emplóymənt, im–/ *n.* **1** the act of employing or the state of being employed. **2** a person's regular trade or profession.

em·po·ri·um /empáwreeəm/ *n.* (*pl.* **-ums** or **emporia** /–reeə/) **1** a large retail store selling a wide variety of goods. **2** a center of commerce; a market.

em·pow·er /empówər, im–/ *v.tr.* (foll. by *to* + infin.) **1** authorize; license. **2** give power to; make able. ▫▫ **em·pow·er·ment** *n.*

em·press /émpris/ *n.* **1** the wife or widow of an emperor. **2** a woman emperor.

emp·ty /émptee/ *adj.*, *v.*, & *n.* • *adj.* (**emptier, emptiest**) **1** containing nothing. **2** (of a space, place, house, etc.) unoccupied; uninhabited; deserted; unfurnished. **3** (of a transport vehicle, etc.) without a load, passengers, etc. **4 a** meaningless; hollow; insincere (*empty threats; an empty gesture*). **b** without substance or purpose (*an empty existence*). **c** (of a person) lacking sense or knowledge; vacant; foolish. **5** *colloq.* hungry. **6** (foll. by *of*) devoid; lacking. • *v.* (**-ties, -tied**) **1** *tr.* **a** make empty; remove the contents of. **b** (foll. by *of*) deprive of certain contents (*emptied the room of its chairs*). **c** remove (contents) from a container, etc. **2** *tr.* (often foll. by *into*) transfer (the contents of a container). **3** *intr.* become empty. **4** *intr.* (usu. foll. by *into*) (of a river) discharge itself (into the sea, etc.). • *n.* (*pl.* **-ties**) *colloq.* a container (esp. a bottle) left empty of its contents. ▫▫ **emp·ti·ly** *adv.* **emp·ti·ness** *n.*

emp·ty-hand·ed /émptee hándid/ *adj.* **1** bringing or taking nothing. **2** having achieved or obtained nothing.

EMT *abbr.* emergency medical technician.

See page xii for the *Key to Pronunciation*.

e•mu /éemyoo/ *n.* a large flightless bird, *Dromaius novaehollandiae*, native to Australia, and capable of running at high speed.

em•u•late /émyəlayt/ *v.tr.* **1** try to equal or excel. **2** imitate zealously. **3** rival. ◻◻ **em•u•la•tion** /–láyshən/ *n.* **em•u•la•tive** *adj.* **em•u•la•tor** *n.*

e•mul•si•fi•er /imúlsifiər/ *n.* **1** any substance that stabilizes an emulsion, esp. a food additive used to stabilize processed foods. **2** an apparatus used for producing an emulsion.

e•mul•si•fy /imúlsifi/ *v.tr.* (**-fies, -fied**) convert into an emulsion. ◻◻ **e•mul•si•fi•a•ble** *adj.* **e•mul•si•fi•ca•tion** /–fikáyshən/ *n.*

e•mul•sion /imúlshən/ *n.* **1** a fine dispersion of one liquid in another, esp. as paint, medicine, etc. **2** a mixture of a silver compound suspended in gelatin, etc., for coating plates or films. ◻◻ **e•mul•sion•ize** *v.tr.* **e•mul•sive** /–siv/ *adj.*

en /en/ *n. Printing* a unit of measurement equal to half an em.

en•a•ble /enáybəl/ *v.tr.* **1** (foll. by *to* + infin.) give (a person, etc.) the means or authority to do something. **2** make possible. **3** esp. *Computing* make (a device) operational. ◻◻ **en•a•bler** *n.*

en•act /enákt, in–/ *v.tr.* **1 a** (often foll. by *that* + clause) ordain; decree. **b** make (a bill, etc.) law. **2** play (a part or scene on stage or in life). ◻◻ **en•ac•tion** /–akshən/ *n.* **en•ac•tive** *adj.*

en•act•ment /enáktmənt, in–/ *n.* **1** a law enacted. **2** the process of enacting.

e•nam•el /inámәl/ *n. & v.* •*n.* **1** a glasslike opaque or semitransparent coating on metallic or other hard surfaces for ornament or as a preservative lining. **2 a** a smooth, hard coating. **b** a cosmetic simulating this. **3** the hard, glossy natural coating over the crown of a tooth. **4** painting done in enamel. •*v.tr.* **1** inlay or encrust (a metal, etc.) with enamel. **2** portray (figures, etc.) with enamel. ◻◻ **e•nam•el•er** *n.* **e•nam•el•work** *n.*

e•nam•el•ware /inámәlwair/ *n.* enameled kitchenware.

en•am•or /inámər/ *v.tr.* (usu. in *passive*; foll. by *of*) **1** inspire with love or liking. **2** charm; delight.

en•camp /enkámp/ *v.tr. & intr.* **1** settle in a military camp. **2** lodge in the open in tents.

en•camp•ment /enkámpmənt, in–/ *n.* **1** a place with temporary accommodations for troops or nomads. **2** the process of setting up a camp.

en•cap•su•late /enkápsəlayt, –syoo–, in–/ *v.tr.* **1** enclose in or as in a capsule. **2** summarize; express the essential features of. ◻◻ **en•cap•su•la•tion** /–láyshən/ *n.*

en•case /enkáys, in–/ *v.tr.* (also **in•case**) **1** put into a case. **2** surround as with a case. ◻◻ **en•case•ment** *n.*

en•caus•tic /enkáwstik, in–/ *adj. & n.* •*adj.* **1** (in painting, ceramics, etc.) using pigments mixed with hot wax, which are burned in as an inlay. **2** (of bricks and tiles) inlaid with differently colored clays burned in. •*n.* **1** the art of encaustic painting. **2** a painting done with this technique.

en•ceph•a•li•tis /enséfəlítis/ *n.* inflammation of the brain. ◻◻ **en•ceph•a•lit•ic** /–lítik/ *adj.*

encephalo- /enséfəlō/ *comb. form* brain.

en•ceph•a•lo•gram /enséfəlōgram/ *n.* an X-ray photograph of the brain.

en•ceph•a•lo•graph /enséfələgraf/ *n.* an instrument for recording the electrical activity of the brain.

en•ceph•a•lop•a•thy /enséfəlópəthee/ *n.* disease of the brain.

en•chain /encháyn, in–/ *v.tr.* **1** fetter. **2** hold fast (the attention, etc.). ◻◻ **en•chain•ment** *n.*

en•chant /enchánt, in–/ *v.tr.* **1** charm; delight. **2** bewitch. ◻◻ **en•chant•ed•ly** *adv.* **en•chant•ing** *adj.* **en•chant•ing•ly** *adv.* **en•chant•ment** *n.*

en•chant•er /enchántər, in–/ *n.* (*fem.* **enchantress**) a person who enchants, esp. by supposed use of magic.

en•chi•la•da /énchiláadə/ *n.* a tortilla with chili sauce and usu. a filling, esp. meat.

en•ci•pher /ensífər, in–/ *v.tr.* **1** write (a message, etc.) in cipher. **2** convert into coded form using a cipher. ◻◻ **en•ci•pher•ment** *n.*

en•cir•cle /ensúrkəl, in–/ *v.tr.* **1** (usu. foll. by *with*) surround; encompass. **2** form a circle around. ◻◻ **en•cir•cle•ment** *n.*

encl. *abbr.* **1** enclosed. **2** enclosure.

en•clave /énklayv, ón–/ *n.* **1** a portion of territory of one country surrounded by territory of another or others, as viewed by the surrounding territory. **2** a group of people who are culturally, intellectually, or socially distinct from those surrounding them.

en•close /enklṓz, in–/ *v.tr.* (also **in•close**) **1** (often foll. by *with, in*) **a** surround with a wall, fence, etc. **b** shut in on all sides. **2** fence in (common land) so as to make it private property. **3** put in a receptacle (esp. in an envelope together with a letter). **4** (usu. as **enclosed** *adj.*) seclude from the outside world.

en•clo•sure /enklṓzhər, in–/ *n.* (also **in•clo•sure**) **1** the act of enclosing, esp. of common land. **2** a thing enclosed with a letter.

en•code /enkṓd, in–/ *v.tr.* put (a message, etc.) into code or cipher. ◻◻ **en•cod•er** *n.*

en•co•mi•um /enkṓmeeəm/ *n.* (*pl.* **encomiums** or **encomia** /–meeə/) a formal or high-flown expression of praise.

en•com•pass /enkúmpəs, in–/ *v.tr.* **1** surround or form a circle about, esp. to protect or attack. **2** contain. ◻◻ **en•com•pass•ment** *n.*

en•core /óngkawr/ *n., v., & int.* •*n.* **1** a call by an audience or spectators for the repetition of an item, or for a further item. **2** such an item. •*v.tr.* **1** call for the repetition of (an item). **2** call back (a performer) for this. •*int.* also /–kór/ again; once more.

en•coun•ter /enkówntər, in–/ *v. & n.* •*v.tr.* **1** meet by chance or unexpectedly. **2** meet as an adversary. **3** meet with; experience (problems, opposition, etc.). •*n.* **1** a meeting by chance. **2** a meeting in conflict.

en•cour•age /enkə́rij, –kúr–, in–/ *v.tr.* **1** give courage, confidence, or hope to. **2** (foll. by *to* + infin.) urge; advise. **3** stimulate by help, reward, etc. **4** promote or assist (an enterprise, opinion, etc.). ◻◻ **en•cour•age•ment** *n.* **en•cour•ag•er** *n.* **en•cour•ag•ing** *adj.* **en•cour•ag•ing•ly** *adv.*

en•croach /enkrṓch, in–/ *v.intr.* **1** (foll. by *on, upon*) intrude, esp. on another's territory or rights. **2** advance gradually beyond due limits. ◻◻ **en•croach•er** *n.* **en•croach•ment** *n.*

en•crust /enkrúst, in–/ *v.* (also **in•crust**) **1** *tr.* cover with a crust. **2** *tr.* overlay with an ornamental crust of precious material. **3** *intr.* form a crust. ◻◻ **en•crust•ment** *n.*

en•crus•ta•tion var. of INCRUSTATION.

en•crypt /enkrípt, in–/ *v.tr.* **1** convert (data) into code, esp. to prevent unauthorized access. **2** conceal by this means. ◻◻ **en•cryp•tion** /–krípshən/ *n.*

en•cum•ber /enkúmbər, in–/ *v.tr.* **1** be a burden to. **2** hamper; impede. **3** burden (a person or estate) with debts, esp. mortgages. ◻◻ **en•cum•ber•ment** *n.*

en•cum•brance /enkúmbrəns, in–/ *n.* **1** a burden. **2** an impediment. **3** a mortgage or other charge on property. **4** an annoyance.

en•cyc•li•cal /ensíklikəl/ *n. & adj.* •*n.* a papal letter sent to all bishops of the Roman Catholic Church. •*adj.* (of a letter) for wide circulation.

en•cy•clo•pe•di•a /ensíkləpéedeeə/ *n.* (also **en•cy•clo•pae•di•a**) a book, often in several volumes, giving information on many subjects, or on many aspects of one subject, usu. arranged alphabetically.

en·cy·clo·pe·dic /ensíkləpeédik/ *adj.* (also **en·cy·clo·pae·dic**) (of knowledge or information) comprehensive.

en·cyst /ensíst, in–/ *v.tr. & intr. Biol.* enclose or become enclosed in a cyst.

end /end/ *n. & v.* •*n.* **1 a** the extreme limit. **b** an extremity of a line, or of the greatest dimension of an object. **c** the furthest point (*to the ends of the earth*). **2** the surface bounding a thing at either extremity; an extreme part. **3 a** conclusion; finish (*no end to his misery*). **b** the latter or final part. **c** death; destruction; downfall (*met an untimely end*). **d** result; outcome. **e** an ultimate state or condition. **4 a** a thing one seeks to attain; a purpose (*will do anything to achieve her ends*). **b** the object for which a thing exists. **5** a remnant; a piece left over (*a board end*). **6** (prec. by *the*) *colloq.* the limit of endurability. **7** the half of a sports field or court occupied by one team or player. **8** the part or share with which a person is concerned (*no problem at my end*). **9** *Football* a player at the extremity of the offensive or defensive line. •*v.* **1** *tr. & intr.* bring or come to an end. **2** *tr.* put an end to; destroy. **3** *intr.* (foll. by *in*) have as its result (*will end in tears*). **4** *intr.* (foll. by *by*) do or achieve eventually (*ended by marrying an heiress*). □ **at an end** exhausted or completed. **at the end of one's rope** having no patience or energy left to cope with something. **end it all** (or **end it**) *colloq.* commit suicide. **end of the road** the point at which a hope or endeavor has to be abandoned. **end to end** with the end of each of a series adjoining the end of the next. **end up** reach a specified state, action, or place eventually (*ended up making a fortune*). **in the end** finally; after all. **make ends** (or **both ends**) **meet** live within one's income. **no end** *colloq.* to a great extent; very much. **on end 1** upright (*hair stood on end*). **2** continuously (*for three weeks on end*). **put an end to 1** stop (an activity, etc.). **2** abolish; destroy.

en·dan·ger /endáynjər, in–/ *v.tr.* place in danger. □□ **en·dan·ger·ment** *n.*

en·dear /endeér, in–/ *v.tr.* (usu. foll. by *to*) make dear to or beloved by.

en·dear·ing /endeéring, in–/ *adj.* inspiring affection. □□ **en·dear·ing·ly** *adv.*

en·dear·ment /endeérmənt, in–/ *n.* **1** an expression of affection. **2** liking; affection.

en·deav·or /endévər, in–/ *v. & n.* •*v. intr.* (foll. by *to* + infin.) try earnestly. •*n.* (often foll. by *at*, or *to* + infin.) effort directed toward a goal; an earnest attempt.

en·dem·ic /endémik/ *adj. & n.* •*adj.* regularly or only found among a particular people or in a certain region. •*n.* an endemic disease or plant. □□ **en·dem·i·cal·ly** *adv.*

▶See note at EPIDEMIC.

end·game /éndgaym/ *n.* the final stage of a game (esp. chess), when few pieces remain.

end·ing /énding/ *n.* **1** an end or final part, esp. of a story. **2** an inflected final part of a word.

en·dive /éndīv, óndeev/ *n.* **1** a curly-leaved plant, *Cichorium endivia*, used in salads. **2** a chicory crown.

end·less /éndlis/ *adj.* **1** infinite; without end; eternal. **2** continual; incessant. **3** *colloq.* innumerable. **4** (of a belt, chain, etc.) having the ends joined for continuous action over wheels, etc. □□ **end·less·ly** *adv.*

end·most /éndmōst/ *adj.* nearest the end.

en·do·car·di·tis /éndōkaardítis/ *n.* inflammation of the lining of the heart.

en·do·crine /éndōkrin, –kreen, –krīn/ *adj.* (of a gland) secreting directly into the blood.

en·do·cri·nol·o·gy /éndōkrinóləjee/ *n.* the study of the structure and physiology of endocrine glands. □□ **en·do·crin·o·log·i·cal** /–nəlójikəl/ *adj.* **en·do·cri·nol·o·gist** *n.*

en·dog·a·my /endógəmee/ *n.* **1** *Anthropol.* marrying within the same tribe. **2** *Bot.* pollination from the same plant. □□ **en·dog·a·mous** *adj.*

en·dog·e·nous /endójinəs/ *adj.* growing or originating from within. □□ **en·do·gen·e·sis** /éndəjénisis/ *n.* **en·dog·e·ny** /endójinee/ *n.*

en·do·me·tri·um /éndōmeétreeəm/ *n. Anat.* the membrane lining the uterus. □□ **en·do·me·tri·tis** /éndōmitrítis/ *n.*

en·do·morph /éndōmawrf/ *n.* a person with a soft, round body build and a high proportion of fat tissue (cf. ECTOMORPH, MESOMORPH). □□ **en·do·mor·phic** *adj.*

en·do·plasm /éndōplazəm/ *n.* the inner fluid layer of the cytoplasm (cf. ECTOPLASM).

en·dor·phin /endáwrfin/ *n. Biochem.* any of a group of peptide neurotransmitters occurring naturally in the brain and having pain-relieving properties.

en·dorse /endáwrs, in–/ *v.tr.* (also **in·dorse**) **1 a** confirm (a statement or opinion). **b** declare one's approval of. **2** sign or write on the back of (a document), esp. the back of (a bill, check, etc.) as the payee or to specify another as payee. **3** write (an explanation or comment) on the back of a document. □□ **en·dors·a·ble** *adj.* **en·dor·see** /éndorseé/ *n.* **en·dors·er** *n.*

en·dorse·ment /endáwrsmənt, in–/ *n.* **1** the act or an instance of endorsing. **2** something with which a document, etc., is endorsed, esp. a signature.

en·do·scope /éndəskōp/ *n. Surgery* an instrument for viewing the internal parts of the body. □□ **en·do·scop·ic** /–skópik/ *adj.* **en·do·scop·i·cal·ly** *adv.*

en·do·skel·e·ton /éndōskélitən/ *n.* an internal skeleton, as found in vertebrates.

en·do·sperm /éndəspərm/ *n.* albumen enclosed with the germ in seeds.

en·dow /endów, in–/ *v.tr.* **1** bequeath or give a permanent income to (a person, institution, etc.). **2** (esp. as **endowed** *adj.*) (usu. foll. by *with*) provide (a person) with talent, ability, etc. □□ **en·dow·er** *n.*

en·dow·ment /endówmənt, in–/ *n.* **1** the act or an instance of endowing. **2** assets, esp. property or income, with which a person or body is endowed. **3** (usu. in *pl.*) skill, talent, etc., with which a person is endowed.

end·pa·per /éndpaypər/ *n.* a usu. blank leaf of paper at the beginning and end of a book, fixed to the inside of the cover.

en·due /endóō, –dyóō, in–/ *v.tr.* (also **in·due**) (foll. by *with*) invest or provide (a person) with qualities, powers, etc.

en·dur·ance /endóórəns, –dyóór–, in–/ *n.* **1** the power or habit of enduring (*beyond endurance*). **2** the ability to withstand prolonged strain (*endurance test*).

en·dure /endóór, –dyóór, in–/ *v.* **1** *tr.* undergo (a difficulty, hardship, etc.). **2** *tr.* **a** tolerate (a person) (*cannot endure him*). **b** (esp. with *neg.*; foll. by *to* + infin.) bear. **3** *intr.* (often as **enduring** *adj.*) remain in existence; last. **4** *tr.* submit to. □□ **en·dur·a·ble** *adj.* **en·dur·a·bil·i·ty** *n.*

end·ways /éndwayz/ *adv.* **1** with its end uppermost or foremost or turned toward the viewer. **2** end to end.

end·wise /éndwīz/ *adv.* = ENDWAYS.

ENE *abbr.* east-northeast.

en·e·ma /énimə/ *n.* (*pl.* **enemas** or **enemata** /inémətə/) **1** the injection of liquid or gas into the rectum, esp. to expel its contents. **2** a fluid or syringe used for this.

en·e·my /énəmee/ *n.* (*pl.* **-mies**) **1** a person or group actively opposing or hostile to another, or to a cause, etc. **2 a** a hostile nation or army, esp. in war. **b** a member of this. **c** a hostile ship or aircraft. **3** (usu. foll. by *of*, *to*) an adversary or opponent. **4** a thing that harms or injures. **5** (*attrib.*) of or belonging to an enemy (*destroyed by enemy action*).

en•er•get•ic /énərjétik/ *adj.* **1** strenuously active. **2** forcible; vigorous. **3** powerfully operative. ▫▫ **en•er•get•i•cal•ly** *adv.*

en•er•gize /énərjīz/ *v.tr.* **1** infuse energy into (a person or work). **2** provide energy for the operation of (a device). ▫▫ **en•er•giz•er** *n.*

en•er•gy /énərjee/ *n.* (*pl.* **-gies**) **1** force; vigor; capacity for activity. **2** (in *pl.*) individual powers in use (*devote your energies to this*). **3** *Physics* the capacity of matter or radiation to do work.

en•er•vate *v.* & *adj.* • *v.tr.* /énərvayt/ deprive of vigor or vitality. • *adj.* /inárvət/ enervated. ▫▫ **en•er•va•tion** /–váyshən/ *n.*

en•fant ter•ri•ble /aaNfaaN tereéblə/ *n.* a person who causes embarrassment by indiscreet or unruly behavior.

en•fee•ble /enfeébəl, in–/ *v.tr.* make feeble. ▫▫ **en•fee•ble•ment** *n.*

en•fi•lade /énfiláyd, –laád/ *n.* gunfire directed along a line from end to end.

en•fold /enfṓld, in–/ *v.tr.* (also **in•fold**) **1** (usu. foll. by *in, with*) wrap up; envelop. **2** clasp; embrace.

en•force /enfáwrs, in–/ *v.tr.* **1** compel observance of (a law, etc.). **2** (foll. by *on, upon*) impose (an action, conduct, one's will). **3** persist in (a demand or argument). ▫▫ **en•force•a•ble** *adj.* **en•force•ment** *n.*

en•fran•chise /enfránchīz, in–/ *v.tr.* **1** give (a person) the right to vote. **2** give (a town, city, etc.) municipal or parliamentary rights. **3** *hist.* free (a slave, etc.). ▫▫ **en•fran•chise•ment** *n.*

en•gage /en-gáyj, in–/ *v.* **1** *tr.* employ or hire (a person). **2** *tr.* **a** (usu. in *passive*) employ busily; occupy (*are you engaged tomorrow?*). **b** hold fast (a person's attention). **3** *tr.* (usu. in *passive*) bind by a promise, esp. of marriage. **4** *tr.* (usu. foll. by *to* + infin.) bind by a contract. **5** *tr.* arrange beforehand to occupy (a room, seat, etc.). **6** (usu. foll. by *with*) *Mech.* **a** *tr.* interlock (parts of a gear, etc.); cause (a part) to interlock. **b** *intr.* (of a part, gear, etc.) interlock. **7 a** *intr.* (usu. foll. by *with*) (of troops, etc.) come into battle. **b** *tr.* bring (troops) into battle. **c** *tr.* come into battle with (an enemy, etc.). **8** *intr.* take part (*engage in politics*).

en•ga•gé /ON-gazháy/ *adj.* (of a writer, artist, etc.) morally committed to a particular aim or cause.

en•gaged /en-gáyjd, in–/ *adj.* **1** under a promise to marry. **2 a** occupied; busy. **b** reserved; booked.

en•gage•ment /en-gáyjmənt, in–/ *n.* **1** the act or state of engaging or being engaged. **2** an appointment with another person. **3** a betrothal. **4** an encounter between hostile forces.

en•gag•ing /en-gáyjing, in–/ *adj.* attractive; charming. ▫▫ **en•gag•ing•ly** *adv.*

en•gen•der /enjéndər, in–/ *v.tr.* give rise to; bring about (a feeling, etc.).

en•gine /énjin/ *n.* **1** a mechanical contrivance consisting of several parts working together, esp. as a source of power. **2 a** a railroad locomotive. **b** = FIRE ENGINE. **c** = STEAM ENGINE.

▶An **engine** is a machine that (via combustion) converts fuel into energy, to drive something: *an automobile engine, a steam engine.* **Motor** is also used of a car's engine, but is also used of a wide range of machines that move something, like *electric motors.*

en•gi•neer /énjineér/ *n.* & *v.* • *n.* **1** a person qualified in a branch of engineering, esp. as a professional. **2** = CIVIL ENGINEER. **3** a person who makes or is in charge of engines. **4** the operator or supervisor of an engine, esp. a railroad locomotive. **5** a person who designs and constructs military works; a soldier trained for this purpose. **6** (foll. by *of*) a skillful or artful contriver. • *v.* **1** *tr.* arrange, contrive, or bring about. **2** *intr.* act as an engineer. **3** *tr.* construct or manage as an engineer.

en•gi•neer•ing /énjineéring/ *n.* the application of science to the design, building, and use of machines, constructions, etc.

Eng•lish /ingglish/ *adj.* & *n.* • *adj.* of or relating to England or its people or language. • *n.* **1** the language of England, now used in many varieties in the British Isles, the United States, and most Commonwealth or ex-Commonwealth countries, and often internationally. **2** (prec. by *the*; treated as *pl.*) the people of England. ▫▫ **Eng•lish•ness** *n.*

Eng•lish horn *n. Mus.* **1** an alto woodwind instrument of the oboe family. **2** its player.

Eng•lish muf•fin *n.* a flat, round, bread roll made from yeast dough, usu. served sliced, toasted, and buttered.

en•gorge /en-gáwrj, in–/ *v.tr.* **1** (in *passive*) **a** be crammed. **b** *Med.* be congested with blood. **2** devour greedily. ▫▫ **en•gorge•ment** *n.*

en•grain /en-gráyn, in–/ *v.tr.* **1** implant (a habit, belief, or attitude) ineradicably in a person (see also INGRAINED). **2** cause (dye, etc.) to sink deeply into a thing.

en•grained /en-gráynd, in–/ *adj.* inveterate (see also INGRAINED).

en•grave /en-gráyv, in–/ *v.tr.* **1** (often foll. by *on*) inscribe, cut, or carve (a text or design) on a hard surface. **2** (often foll. by *with*) inscribe or ornament (a surface) in this way. **3** cut (a design) as lines on a metal plate, block, etc., for printing. **4** (often foll. by *on*) impress deeply on a person's memory, etc. ▫▫ **en•grav•er** *n.*

en•grav•ing /en-gráyving, in–/ *n.* a print made from an engraved plate, block, or other surface.

en•gross /en-grṓs, in–/ *v.tr.* absorb the attention of; occupy fully (*engrossed in studying*). ▫▫ **en•gross•ing** *adj.*

en•gulf /en-gúlf, in–/ *v.tr.* (also **in•gulf**) **1** flow over and swamp; overwhelm. **2** swallow or plunge into a gulf. ▫▫ **en•gulf•ment** *n.*

en•hance /enháns, in–/ *v.tr.* heighten or intensify (qualities, powers, value, etc.); improve (something already of good quality). ▫▫ **en•hance•ment** *n.* **en•hanc•er** *n.*

e•nig•ma /inígmə/ *n.* **1** a puzzling thing or person. **2** a riddle or paradox. ▫▫ **en•ig•mat•ic** /énigmátik/ *adj.* **en•ig•mat•i•cal** *adj.* **en•ig•mat•i•cal•ly** *adv.*

en•join /enjóyn, in–/ *v.tr.* **1** (foll. by *to* + infin.) command or order (a person). **2** (usu. foll. by *from*) *Law* prohibit (a person) by order. ▫▫ **en•join•ment** *n.*

en•joy /enjóy, in–/ *v.tr.* **1** take delight or pleasure in. **2** have the use or benefit of. **3** experience (*enjoy good health*). ▫ **enjoy oneself** experience pleasure. ▫▫ **en•joy•ment** *n.*

en•joy•a•ble /enjóyəbəl, in–/ *adj.* pleasant; giving enjoyment. ▫▫ **en•joy•a•ble•ness** *n.* **en•joy•a•bly** *adv.*

en•kin•dle /enkíndəl, in–/ *v.tr. literary* **1 a** cause (flames) to flare up. **b** stimulate (feeling, passion, etc.). **2** inflame with passion.

en•large /enlaárj, in–/ *v.* **1** *tr.* & *intr.* make or become larger or wider. **2** *tr.* describe in greater detail. **3** *tr. Photog.* produce an enlargement of (a negative).

en•large•ment /enlaárjmənt, in–/ *n.* **1** the act or an instance of enlarging; the state of being enlarged. **2** *Photog.* a print that is larger than the negative from which it is produced.

en•larg•er /enlaárjər, in–/ *n. Photog.* an apparatus for enlarging or reducing negatives or positives.

en•light•en /enlī́t'n, in–/ *v.tr.* **1 a** (often foll. by *on*) instruct or inform (a person) about a subject. **b** (as **enlightened** *adj.*) well-informed; knowledgeable. **2** (esp. as **enlightened** *adj.*) free from prejudice or superstition.

en•light•en•ment /enlī́t'nmənt, in–/ *n.* **1** the act or an instance of enlightening; the state of being enlightened. **2** (**the Enlightenment**) the 18th-c. philosophy emphasizing reason and individualism rather than tradition.

en·list /enlíst, in–/ *v.* **1** *intr. & tr.* enroll in the armed services. **2** *tr.* secure as a means of help or support. ▫▫ **en·list·er** *n.* **en·list·ment** *n.*

en·liv·en /enlívən, in–/ *v.tr.* **1** give life or spirit to. **2** make cheerful; brighten (a picture or scene).

en masse /ON más/ *adv.* **1** all together. **2** in a mass.

en·mesh /enmésh, in–/ *v.tr.* entangle in or as in a net.

en·mi·ty /énmitee/ *n.* (*pl.* **-ties**) **1** the state of being an enemy. **2** a feeling of hostility.

en·no·ble /enṓbəl, in–/ *v.tr.* **1** make (a person) a noble. **2** make noble; elevate. ▫▫ **en·no·ble·ment** *n.*

en·nui /onwée/ *n.* mental weariness from lack of occupation or interest; boredom.

e·nol·o·gy /eenóləjee/ *n.* the study of wines. ▫▫ **e·no·log·i·cal** /éenəlójikəl/ *adj.* **e·nol·o·gist** *n.*

e·nor·mi·ty /ináwrmitee/ *n.* (*pl.* **-ties**) **1** extreme wickedness. **2** an act of extreme wickedness. **3** a serious error. **4** *disp.* great size; enormousness.

▶This word is imprecisely used to mean 'great size,' e.g., *it's difficult to recognize the enormity of the continent,* but the original and preferred meaning is 'extreme wickedness,' as in *the enormity of the crime.*

enormity late Middle English: via Old French from Latin *enormitas*, from *enormis*, from *e-* (variant of *ex-*) 'out of' + *norma* 'pattern, standard.' The word originally meant 'deviation from legal or moral rectitude' and 'transgression.' Current senses have been influenced by ENORMOUS.

e·nor·mous /ináwrməs/ *adj.* very large; huge. ▫▫ **e·nor·mous·ly** *adv.* **e·nor·mous·ness** *n.*

e·nough /inúf/ *adj., n., adv., & int.* • *adj.* as much or as many as required (*we have enough apples*). • *n.* an amount or quantity that is enough (*we have enough of everything now*). • *adv.* **1** to the required degree; adequately (*are you warm enough?*). **2** fairly (*she sings well enough*). **3** very; quite (*you know well enough what I mean*). • *int.* that is enough (in various senses, esp. to put an end to an action, thing said, etc.). ▫ **have had enough of** want no more of; be satiated with or tired of.

en pas·sant /ÓN pasÓN/ *adv.* by the way.

en·quire var. of INQUIRE.

en·quir·y var. of INQUIRY.

en·rage /enráyj, in–/ *v.tr.* (often foll. by *at, by, with*) make furious. ▫▫ **en·rage·ment** *n.*

en·rap·ture /enrápchər, in–/ *v.tr.* give intense delight to.

en·rich /enrích, in–/ *v.tr.* **1** make rich or richer. **2** make richer in quality, flavor, nutritive value, etc. **3** add to the contents of (a collection, museum, or book). ▫▫ **en·rich·ment** *n.*

en·roll /enrṓl, in–/ *v.* (also **en·rol**) (**enrolled, enrolling**) **1** *intr.* enter one's name on a list, esp. as a commitment to membership. **2** *tr.* **a** write the name of (a person) on a list. **b** (usu. foll. by *in*) incorporate (a person) as a member of a society, etc. ▫▫ **en·roll·ee** /–lée/ *n.*

en·roll·ment /enrṓlmənt, in–/ *n.* (also **en·rol·ment**) **1** the act or an instance of enrolling; the state of being enrolled. **2** the number of persons enrolled, esp. at a school or college.

en route /ON rŏŏt/ *adv.* (usu. foll. by *to, for*) on the way.

en·sconce /enskóns, in–/ *v.tr.* (usu. *refl.* or in *passive*) establish or settle comfortably, safely, or secretly.

en·sem·ble /onsómbəl/ *n.* **1 a** a thing viewed as the sum of its parts. **b** the general effect of this. **2** a set of clothes worn together; an outfit. **3** a group of actors, dancers, musicians, etc., performing together, esp. subsidiary dancers in ballet, etc.

en·shrine /enshrín, in–/ *v.tr.* **1** enclose in or as in a shrine. **2** serve as a shrine for. **3** preserve or cherish. ▫▫ **en·shrine·ment** *n.*

en·shroud /enshrówd, in–/ *v.tr. literary* **1** cover with or as with a shroud. **2** cover completely; hide from view.

en·sign /énsin, –sīn/ *n.* **1** a banner or flag, esp. the military or naval flag of a nation. **2 a** *hist.* the lowest commissioned infantry officer. **b** the lowest commissioned officer in the US Navy or US Coast Guard.

en·slave /ensláyv, in–/ *v.tr.* make (a person) a slave. ▫▫ **en·slave·ment** *n.* **en·slav·er** *n.*

en·snare /ensnáir, in–/ *v.tr.* catch in or as in a snare; entrap. ▫▫ **en·snare·ment** *n.*

en·sue /ensóō, in–/ *v.intr.* **1** happen afterward. **2** (often foll. by *from, on*) occur as a result.

en suite /ON swéet/ *adv.* forming a single unit (*bedroom with bathroom en suite*).

en·sure /enshóor, in–/ *v.tr.* **1** (often foll. by *that* + clause) make certain. **2** (usu. foll. by *to, for*) secure (a thing for a person, etc.). **3** (usu. foll. by *against*) make safe.

▶See note at INSURE.

en·swathe /enswáyth, in;n–/ *v.tr.* bind or wrap in or as in a bandage. ▫▫ **en·swathe·ment** *n.*

ENT *abbr.* ear, nose, and throat.

en·tab·la·ture /entáblәchər, in–/ *n. Archit.* the upper part of a classical building supported by columns or a colonnade, comprising architrave, frieze, and cornice.

en·tail /entáyl, in–/ *v.tr.* **1 a** necessitate or involve unavoidably (*the work entails much effort*). **b** give rise to; involve. **2** *Law* bequeath (property, etc.) so that it remains within a family. ▫▫ **en·tail·ment** *n.*

en·tan·gle /entánggəl, in–/ *v.tr.* **1** cause to get caught in a snare or among obstacles. **2** cause to become tangled. **3** involve in difficulties or illicit activities. **4** make (a thing) tangled or intricate; complicate.

en·tan·gle·ment /entánggəlmənt, in–/ *n.* **1** the act or condition of entangling or being entangled. **2** a thing that entangles. **3** a compromising (esp. amorous) relationship.

en·tente /aantaánt/ *n.* **1** also **entente cordiale** a friendly relationship between nations. **2** a group of nations in such a relation.

en·ter /éntər/ *v.* **1 a** *intr.* (often foll. by *into*) go or come in. **b** *tr.* go or come into. **c** *intr.* come on stage (as a direction: *enter Macbeth*). **2** *tr.* penetrate; go through; spread through (*a bullet entered his chest*). **3** *tr.* write (a name, details, etc.) in a list, book, etc. **4 a** *intr.* register or announce oneself as a competitor (*entered the long jump*). **b** *tr.* become a competitor in (an event). **c** *tr.* record the name of (a person, etc.) as a competitor (*entered two horses for the Kentucky Derby*). **5** *tr.* **a** become a member of (a society, etc.). **b** enroll as a member or prospective member of a society, school, etc.; admit or obtain admission for. **6** *tr.* make known; present for consideration (*entered a protest*). **7** *tr.* put into an official record. **8** *intr.* (foll. by *into*) **a** engage in (conversation, relations, an undertaking, etc.). **b** subscribe to; bind oneself by (an agreement, etc.). **c** form part of (one's calculations, plans, etc.). **9** *intr.* (foll. by *on, upon*) **a** begin; undertake; begin to deal with (a subject). **b** assume the functions of (an office). **c** assume possession of (property).

en·ter·ic /entérik/ *adj. & n.* • *adj.* of the intestines. • *n.* (in full **enteric fever**) typhoid. ▫▫ **en·ter·i·tis** /éntərítis/ *n.*

entero- /éntərō/ *comb. form* intestine.

en·ter·prise /éntərprīz/ *n.* **1** an undertaking, esp. a bold or difficult one. **2** (as a personal attribute) readiness to engage in such undertakings. **3** a business firm.

en·ter·pris·ing /éntərprīzing/ *adj.* **1** ready to engage in enterprises. **2** resourceful; imaginative; energetic. ▫▫ **en·ter·pris·ing·ly** *adv.*

en·ter·tain /éntərtáyn/ *v.tr.* **1** amuse; occupy agreeably. **2 a** receive or treat as a guest. **b** (*absol.*) receive guests (*they entertain a great deal*). **3** give attention or consideration to (an idea, feeling, or proposal).

en·ter·tain·er /éntərtáynər/ *n.* a person who entertains, esp. professionally on stage, etc.

en·ter·tain·ing /éntərtáyning/ *adj.* amusing; diverting.

en·ter·tain·ment /éntərtáynmənt/ *n.* **1** the act or an instance of entertaining; the process of being entertained. **2** a public performance or show. **3** diversions or amusements for guests, etc.

en·ter·tain·ment cen·ter *n.* a piece of furniture, usu. with several shelves to accommodate a television, video cassette recorder, stereo system, etc.

en·thrall /enthráwl, in–/ *v.tr.* (also **en·thral, in·thral, in·thrall**) (**-thralled, -thralling**) **1** (often as **enthralling** *adj.*) captivate; please greatly. **2** enslave. ▫▫ **en·thrall·ment** *n.*

en·throne /enthrṓn, in–/ *v.tr.* **1** install (a king, bishop, etc.) on a throne, esp. ceremonially. **2** exalt.

en·thuse /enthóōz, in–/ *v.intr. & tr. colloq.* be or make enthusiastic.

en·thu·si·asm /enthóōzeeazəm, in–/ *n.* **1** (often foll. by *for, about*) **a** strong interest or admiration. **b** great eagerness. **2** an object of enthusiasm.

en·thu·si·ast /enthóōzeeast, in–/ *n.* (often foll. by *for*) a person who is full of enthusiasm.

en·thu·si·as·tic /enthóōzeeástik, in–/ *adj.* having or showing enthusiasm. ▫▫ **en·thu·si·as·ti·cal·ly** *adv.*

en·tice /entís, in–/ *v.tr.* (often foll. by *from, into*, or *to* + infin.) persuade by the offer of pleasure or reward. ▫▫ **en·tice·ment** *n.* **en·tic·er** *n.* **en·tic·ing·ly** *adv.*

en·tire /entír, in–/ *adj.* **1** whole; complete. **2** not broken or decayed. **3** unqualified; absolute (*an entire success*). **4** in one piece; continuous.

en·tire·ly /entírlee, in–/ *adv.* **1** wholly; completely (*the stock is entirely exhausted*). **2** solely; exclusively.

en·tire·ty /entíərtee, in–/ *n.* (*pl.* **-ties**) **1** completeness. **2** (usu. foll. by *of*) the sum total. ▫ **in its entirety** in its complete form; completely.

en·ti·tle /entítəl, in–/ *v.tr.* **1 a** (usu. foll. by *to*) give (a person, etc.) a just claim. **b** (foll. by *to* + infin.) give (a person, etc.) a right. **2** give (a book, etc.) the title of. ▫▫ **en·ti·tle·ment** *n.*

en·ti·ty /éntitee/ *n.* (*pl.* **-ties**) **1** a thing with distinct existence, as opposed to a quality or relation. **2** a thing's existence regarded distinctly; a thing's essential nature.

en·tomb /entóōm, in–/ *v.tr.* **1** place in or as in a tomb. **2** serve as a tomb for. ▫▫ **en·tomb·ment** *n.*

en·to·mol·o·gy /éntəmóləjee/ *n.* the study of the forms and behavior of insects. ▫▫ **en·to·mo·log·i·cal** /–məlójikəl/ *adj.* **en·to·mol·o·gist** *n.*

en·tou·rage /óntooraázh/ *n.* **1** people attending an important person. **2** surroundings.

en·tr'acte /aantrákt, aán–/ *n.* **1** an interval between two acts of a play. **2** a piece of music or a dance performed during this.

en·trails /éntraylz, –trəlz/ *n.pl.* **1** the bowels and intestines of a person or animal. **2** the innermost parts (*entrails of the earth*).

en·trance[1] /éntrəns/ *n.* **1** the act or an instance of going or coming in. **2** a door, passage, etc., by which one enters. **3** right of admission. **4** the coming of an actor on stage.

en·trance[2] /entráns, in–/ *v.tr.* **1** enchant; delight. **2** put into a trance. **3** (often foll. by *with*) overwhelm with strong feeling. ▫▫ **en·trance·ment** *n.* **en·tranc·ing** *adj.* **en·tranc·ing·ly** *adv.*

en·trant /éntrənt/ *n.* a person who enters (esp. an examination, profession, etc.).

en·trap /entráp, in–/ *v.tr.* (**entrapped, entrapping**) **1** catch in or as in a trap. **2** (often foll. by *into* + verbal noun) beguile or trick (a person). ▫▫ **en·trap·per** *n.*

en·trap·ment /entrápmənt, in–/ *n.* **1** the act or an instance of entrapping; the process of being entrapped. **2** *Law* inducement to commit a crime, esp. by the authorities to secure a prosecution.

en·treat /entréet, in–/ *v.tr.* **1** (foll. by *to* + infin. or *that* + clause) ask (a person) earnestly. **2** ask earnestly for (a thing). ▫▫ **en·treat·ing·ly** *adv.*

en·treat·y /entréetee, in–/ *n.* (*pl.* **-ies**) an earnest request; a supplication.

en·tre·côte /óntrəkōt/ *n.* a boned steak cut off the sirloin.

en·trée /óntray/ *n.* (also **en·tree**) **1** *Cooking* esp. *US* the main dish of a meal. **2** the right or privilege of admission.

en·trench /entrénch, in–/ *v.* (also **intrench**) **1** *tr.* establish firmly (in a defensible position, in office, etc.). **2** *tr.* surround (a post, army, town, etc.) with a trench as a fortification. **3** *tr.* apply extra safeguards to (rights, etc., guaranteed by legislation). **4** *intr.* entrench oneself. **5** *intr.* (foll. by *upon*) encroach; trespass. ▫ **entrench oneself** adopt a well-defended position. ▫▫ **en·trench·ment** *n.*

en·tre·pre·neur /óntrəprənóōr/ *n.* a person who undertakes an enterprise or business, with the chance of profit or loss. ▫▫ **en·tre·pre·neur·i·al** *adj.* **en·tre·pre·neur·i·al·ly** *adv.* **en·tre·pre·neur·ship** *n.*

en·tro·py /éntrəpee/ *n.* **1** *Physics* a measure of the unavailability of a system's thermal energy for conversion into mechanical work. **2** *Physics* a measure of the disorganization or degradation of the universe. ▫▫ **en·tro·pic** /–trópik/ *adj.* **en·tro·pi·cal·ly** *adv.*

en·trust /entrúst, in–/ *v.tr.* (also **intrust**) **1** (foll. by *to*) give responsibility for (a person or a thing) to a person in whom one has confidence. **2** (foll. by *with*) assign responsibility for a thing to (a person).

en·try /éntree/ *n.* (*pl.* **-tries**) **1 a** the act or an instance of going or coming in. **b** the coming of an actor on stage. **c** ceremonial entrance. **2** liberty to go or come in. **3 a** a place of entrance; a door, gate, etc. **b** a lobby. **4** *Brit.* a passage between buildings. **5** the mouth of a river. **6 a** an item entered (in a diary, list, account book, etc.). **b** the recording of this. **7 a** a person or thing competing in a race, contest, etc. **b** a list of competitors.

en·twine /entwín, in–/ *v.* (also **in·twine** /in–/) **1** *tr. & intr.* (foll. by *with, about, around*) twine together (a thing with or around another). **2** *tr.* (as **entwined** *adj.*) entangled. **3** *tr.* interweave. ▫▫ **en·twine·ment** *n.*

e·nu·mer·ate /inóōmərayt, inyóō–/ *v.tr.* **1** specify (items); mention one by one. **2** count; establish the number of. ▫▫ **e·nu·mer·a·ble** *adj.* **e·nu·mer·a·tion** /–ráyshən/ *n.* **e·nu·mer·a·tive** /–raytiv, –rətiv/ *adj.*

e·nu·mer·a·tor /inóōməraytər, inyóō–/ *n.* **1** a person who enumerates. **2** a person employed in census taking.

e·nun·ci·ate /inúnseeayt/ *v.tr.* **1** pronounce (words) clearly. **2** express (a proposition or theory) in definite terms. **3** proclaim. ▫▫ **e·nun·ci·a·tion** /–áyshən/ *n.*

en·u·re·sis /ényooréesis/ *n. Med.* involuntary urination, esp. while sleeping. ▫▫ **en·u·ret·ic** /–rétik/ *adj. & n.*

en·vel·op /envéləp, in–/ *v.tr.* (**enveloped, enveloping**) (often foll. by *in*) **1** wrap up or cover completely. **2** make obscure; conceal. ▫▫ **en·vel·op·ment** *n.*

en•vel•ope /énvəlōp, ón–/ *n.* **1** a folded paper container, usu. with a sealable flap, for a letter, etc. **2** a wrapper or covering. **3** the structure within a balloon or airship containing the gas. **4** the outer metal or glass housing of a vacuum tube, electric light, etc.

en•ven•om /envénəm, in–/ *v.tr.* **1** put poison on or into; make poisonous. **2** infuse venom or bitterness into (feelings, words, or actions).

en•vi•a•ble /énveeəbəl/ *adj.* (of a person or thing) exciting or likely to excite envy. ▫▫ **en•vi•a•bly** *adv.*

en•vi•ous /énveeəs/ *adj.* (often foll. by *of*) feeling or showing envy. ▫▫ **en•vi•ous•ly** *adv.*

en•vi•ron•ment /envírənmənt, –víərn–, in–/ *n.* **1** physical surroundings and conditions, esp. as affecting people's lives. **2** conditions or circumstances of living. **3** *Ecol.* external conditions affecting the growth of plants and animals. **4** a structure designed to be experienced from inside as a work of art. **5** *Computing* the overall structure within which a user, computer, or program operates. ▫▫ **en•vi•ron•men•tal** /–ment'l/ *adj.* **en•vi•ron•men•tal•ly** *adv.*

en•vi•ron•men•tal•ist /envírənméntəlist, –víərn–, in–/ *n.* **1** a person who is concerned with or advocates the protection of the environment. **2** a person who considers that environment has the primary influence on the development of a person or group. ▫▫ **en•vir•on•men•tal•ism** *n.*

en•vi•ron•ment-friend•ly *adj.* not harmful to the environment.

en•vi•rons /envírənz, –víərnz, in–/ *n.pl.* a surrounding district, esp. around an urban area.

en•vis•age /envízij, in–/ *v.tr.* **1** have a mental picture of (a thing not yet existing). **2** contemplate or conceive, esp. as a possibility or desirable future event.

en•vi•sion /envízhən, in–/ *v.tr.* envisage; visualize.

en•voy /énvoy, ón–/ *n.* **1** a messenger or representative, esp. on a diplomatic mission. **2** (in full **envoy extraordinary**) a minister plenipotentiary, ranking below ambassador and above chargé d'affaires.

en•vy /énvee/ *n.* & *v.* •*n.* (*pl.* **-vies**) **1** a feeling of discontented or resentful longing aroused by another's better fortune, etc. **2** the object or ground of this feeling (*their house is the envy of the neighborhood*). •*v.tr.* (**-vies, -vied**) feel envy of (a person, circumstances, etc.) (*I envy you your position*). ▫▫ **en•vi•er** *n.*

en•zyme /énzīm/ *n. Biochem.* a protein acting as a catalyst in a specific biochemical reaction. ▫▫ **en•zy•mat•ic** /–zīmátik/ *adj.*

E•o•cene /éeəseen/ *adj.* & *n. Geol.* •*adj.* of or relating to the second epoch of the Tertiary period. •*n.* this epoch or system.

e•o•li•an /ee-ṓlee-ən/ *adj.* wind-borne.

e•o•lith•ic /éeəlíthik/ *adj. Archaeol.* of the period preceding the Paleolithic age.

e•on /éeon/ *n.* (also **aeon**) **1** a very long or indefinite period. **2** an age of the universe. **3** a billion years.

EPA *abbr.* Environmental Protection Agency.

ep•au•let /épəlét/ *n.* (also **ep•au•lette**) an ornamental shoulder piece on a coat, dress, etc., esp. on a uniform.

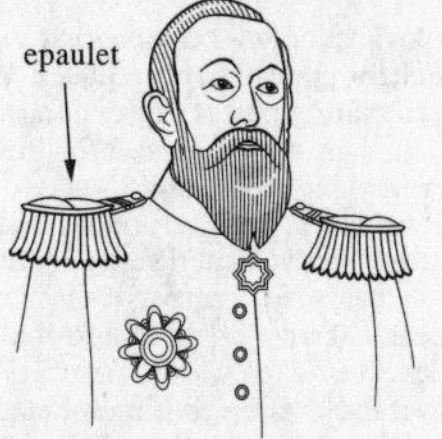

epaulet

é•pée /aypáy, épay/ *n.* a sharp-pointed dueling sword, used (with the end blunted) in fencing. ▫▫ **é•pée•ist** *n.*

e•pergne /ipárn, aypérn/ *n.* an ornament (esp. in branched form) for the center of a dinner-table, holding flowers or fruit.

e•phed•rine /ifédrin, éfədreen/ *n.* an alkaloid drug, causing constriction of the blood vessels and widening of the bronchial passages, used to relieve asthma, etc.

e•phem•er•a[1] /ifémərə/ *n.* (*pl.* **ephemera** or **ephemerae** /–ree/or **ephemeras**) **1 a** an insect living only a day or a few days. **b** any insect of the order Ephemeroptera, e.g., the mayfly. **2** = EPHEMERON 1.

e•phem•er•a[2] *pl.* of EPHEMERON 1.

e•phem•er•al /ifémərəl/ *adj.* **1** lasting or of use for only a short time; transitory. **2** lasting only a day. **3** (of an insect, flower, etc.) lasting a day or a few days. ▫▫ **e•phem•er•al•i•ty** /–rálitee/ *n.* **e•phem•er•al•ly** *adv.* **e•phem•er•al•ness** *n.*

e•phem•er•is /iféməris/ *n.* (*pl.* **ephemerides** /éfimérideez/) *Astron.* an astronomical almanac or table of the predicted positions of celestial bodies.

e•phem•er•ist /ifémərist/ *n.* a collector of ephemera.

e•phem•er•on /ifémərən/ *n.* **1** (*pl.* **ephemera** /–rə/) (usu. in *pl.*) **a** a thing (esp. a printed item) of short-lived interest or usefulness. **b** a short-lived thing. **2** (*pl.* **ephemerons**) = EPHEMERA[1] 1.

ep•ic /épik/ *n.* & *adj.* •*n.* **1** a long poem narrating the adventures or deeds of one or more heroic or legendary figures, e.g., the *Iliad*, *Paradise Lost*. **2** an imaginative work of any form, embodying a nation's conception of its history. **3** a book or motion picture based on an epic narrative or heroic in type or scale. **4** a subject fit for recital in an epic. •*adj.* **1** of or like an epic. **2** grand; heroic. ▫▫ **ep•i•cal** *adj.* **ep•i•cal•ly** *adv.*

ep•i•cene /épiseen/ *adj.* & *n.* •*adj.* **1** *Gram.* denoting either sex without change of gender. **2** of, for, or used by both sexes. **3** having characteristics of both sexes. **4** having no characteristics of either sex. **5** effete; effeminate. •*n.* an epicene person.

ep•i•cen•ter /épisentər/ *n.* **1** *Geol.* the point at which an earthquake reaches the earth's surface. **2** the central point of a difficulty. ▫▫ **ep•i•cen•tral** /–séntrəl/ *adj.*

ep•i•cure /épikyoor/ *n.* a person with refined tastes, esp. in food and drink. ▫▫ **ep•i•cur•ism** *n.*

Ep•i•cu•re•an /épikyooréeən, –kyóoree–/ *n.* & *adj.* •*n.* **1** a disciple or student of the Greek philosopher Epicurus. **2** (**epicurean**) a person devoted to (esp. sensual) enjoyment. •*adj.* **1** of or concerning Epicurus or his ideas. **2** (**epicurean**) characteristic of an epicurean.

ep•i•dem•ic /épidémik/ *n.* & *adj.* •*n.* **1** a widespread occurrence of a disease in a community at a particular time. **2** such a disease. **3** (foll. by *of*) a wide prevalence of something. •*adj.* in the nature of an epidemic (cf. ENDEMIC). ▫▫ **ep•i•dem•i•cal•ly** *adv.*

▶A disease that quickly affects a large number of people and then subsides is an **epidemic:** *Throughout the Middle Ages, successive epidemics of the plague killed millions.* **Epidemic** is also used as an adjective: *She studied the causes of epidemic cholera.* A disease that is continually present in a one area is **endemic:** *Malaria is endemic in hot, moist climates.*

ep•i•de•mi•ol•o•gy /épideemeeóləjee/ *n.* the study of the incidence and distribution of diseases. ▫▫ **ep•i•de•mi•o•log•i•cal** /–meeəlójikəl/ *adj.* **ep•i•de•mi•ol•o•gist** *n.*

ep•i•der•mis /épidármis/ *n.* **1** the outer cellular layer of the skin. **2** *Bot.* the outer layer of cells of leaves, stems, roots, etc. ▫▫ **ep•i•der•mal** *adj.*

ep•i•did•y•mis /épidídimis/ *n.* (*pl.* **epididymides**

/–didímideez/) *Anat.* a convoluted duct behind the testis, along which sperm passes to the vas deferens.

ep·i·du·ral /épidŏŏrəl, –dyŏŏr–/ *adj. & n.* • *adj.* **1** *Anat.* on or around the dura mater. **2** (of an anesthetic) introduced into the space around the dura mater of the spinal cord. • *n.* an epidural anesthetic, used esp. in childbirth.

ep·i·glot·tis /épiglótis/ *n. Anat.* a flap of cartilage at the root of the tongue, depressed during swallowing to cover the windpipe. □□ **ep·i·glot·tal** *adj.* **ep·i·glot·tic** *adj.*

ep·i·gram /épigram/ *n.* **1** a short poem with a witty ending. **2** a saying or maxim, esp a proverbial one. □□ **ep·i·gram·mat·ic** /–grəmátik/ *adj.*

ep·i·graph /épigraf/ *n.* an inscription.

ep·i·late /épilayt/ *v.tr.* remove hair from. □□ **ep·i·la·tion** /–láyshən/ *n.*

ep·i·lep·sy /épilepsee/ *n.* a nervous disorder with convulsions and often loss of consciousness. □□ **ep·i·lep·tic** /épiléptik/ *adj. & n.*

ep·i·logue /épilawg, –og/ *n.* (also **ep·i·log**) **1 a** the concluding part of a literary work. **b** an appendix. **2** a speech or short poem addressed to the audience by an actor at the end of a play.

ep·i·neph·rine /épinéfrin/ *n.* a hormone secreted by the adrenal glands, affecting circulation and muscular action, and causing excitement and stimulation. Also called **adrenaline**.

e·piph·a·ny /ipífənee/ *n.* (*pl.* **-nies**) **1** (**Epiphany**) **a** the manifestation of Christ to the Magi. **b** the festival commemorating this on January 6. **2** any manifestation of a god or demigod. □□ **ep·i·phan·ic** /épifánik/ *adj.*

ep·i·phyte /épifīt/ *n.* a plant growing but not parasitic on another, e.g., a moss. □□ **ep·i·phyt·ic** /–fítik/ *adj.*

e·pis·co·pa·cy /ipískəpəsee/ *n.* (*pl.* **-cies**) **1** government of a church by bishops. **2** (prec. by *the*) the bishops.

e·pis·co·pal /ipískəpəl/ *adj.* **1** of a bishop or bishops. **2** (of a Church) constituted on the principle of government by bishops. □□ **e·pis·co·pal·ism** *n.* **e·pis·co·pal·ly** *adv.*

E·pis·co·pal Church *n.* a Protestant Church in the US and Scotland, with elected bishops.

e·pis·co·pa·lian /ipískəpáyleeən/ *adj. & n.* • *adj.* **1** of or advocating government of a church by bishops. **2** of or belonging to an episcopal church or (**Episcopalian**) the Episcopal Church. • *n.* **1** an adherent of episcopacy. **2** (**Episcopalian**) a member of the Episcopal Church. □□ **e·pis·co·pa·lian·ism** *n.*

e·pis·co·pate /ipískəpət/ *n.* **1** the office or tenure of a bishop. **2** (prec. by *the*) the bishops collectively.

e·pi·si·ot·o·my /ipéezeeótəmee/ *n.* (*pl.* **-mies**) a surgical cut made at the opening of the vagina during childbirth.

ep·i·sode /épisōd/ *n.* **1** one event or a group of events as part of a sequence. **2** each of the parts of a serial story or broadcast. **3** an incident or set of incidents in a narrative. **4** an incident that is distinct but contributes to a whole (*a romantic episode in her life*). □□ **ep·i·sod·ic** /épisódik/ **ep·i·sod·i·cal** /–sódikəl/) *adj.* **ep·i·sod·i·cal·ly** *adv.*

e·pis·te·mol·o·gy /ipístimóləjee/ *n.* the theory of knowledge, esp. with regard to its methods and validation. □□ **e·pis·te·mo·log·i·cal** /–məlójikəl/ *adj.* **e·pis·te·mo·log·i·cal·ly** *adv.* **e·pis·te·mol·o·gist** *n.*

e·pis·tle /ipísəl/ *n.* **1** *formal* or *joc.* a letter, esp. a long one on a serious subject. **2** (**Epistle**) **a** any of the letters of the apostles in the New Testament. **b** an extract from an Epistle read in a church service. **3** a poem or other literary work in the form of a letter or series of letters.

e·pis·to·lar·y /ipístəleree/ *adj.* **1** in the style or form of a letter or letters. **2** of, carried by, or suited to letters.

ep·i·style /épistīl/ *n. Archit.* = ARCHITRAVE 1.

ep·i·taph /épitaf/ *n.* words written in memory of a person who has died, esp. as a tomb inscription.

ep·i·the·li·um /épitheéleeəm/ *n.* (*pl.* **epithelia** /–leeə/or **epitheliums**) the tissue forming the outer layer of the body surface and lining many hollow structures. □□ **ep·i·the·li·al** *adj.*

ep·i·thet /épithet/ *n.* **1** an adjective or other descriptive word expressing a quality or attribute. **2** such a word as a term of abuse.

e·pit·o·me /ipítəmee/ *n.* **1** a person or thing embodying a quality, class, etc. **2** a thing representing another in miniature. **3** a summary of a written work.

e·pit·o·mize /ipítəmīz/ *v.tr.* **1** be a perfect example of (a quality, etc.). **2** make an epitome of (a work).

ep·och /épək, éepok/ *n.* **1** a period of history or of a person's life marked by notable events. **2** the beginning of an era. **3** *Geol.* a division of a period, corresponding to a set of strata. □□ **ep·och·al** *adj.*

ep·o·nym /épənim/ *n.* **1** a person (real or imaginary) after whom a discovery, place, etc., is named. **2** the name given. □□ **ep·on·y·mous** /ipónimәs/ *adj.*

ep·ox·y /ipóksee/ *adj.* a resin used in adhesives, insulation, coatings, etc.

ep·si·lon /épsilon/ *n.* the fifth letter of the Greek alphabet (Ε, ϵ).

Ep·som salts /épsəm/ *n.pl.* a preparation of magnesium sulfate used as a purgative, etc.

eq·ua·ble /ékwəbəl/ *adj.* **1** even; not varying. **2** uniform and moderate. **3** (of a person) not easily angered. □□ **eq·ua·bil·i·ty** /–bílitee/ *n.* **eq·ua·bly** *adv.*

e·qual /éekwəl/ *adj., n., & v.* • *adj.* **1** (often foll. by *to, with*) the same in quantity, quality, size, rank, etc. **2** evenly balanced. **3** having the same rights (*human beings are essentially equal*). **4** uniform in application or effect. • *n.* a person or thing equal to another, esp. in rank, status, or characteristic quality (*he has no equal*). • *v.tr.* **1** be equal to in number, quality, etc. **2** achieve something that is equal to. □ **be equal to** have the ability or resources for. □□ **e·qual·i·ty** /ikwólitee/ *n.*

e·qual·ize /éekwəlīz/ *v.tr. & intr.* make or become equal. □□ **e·qual·i·za·tion** *n.*

e·qual·iz·er /éekwəlīzər/ *n.* **1** an equalizing score or goal, etc., in a game. **2** *sl.* a weapon, esp. a gun.

e·qual·ly /éekwəlee/ *adv.* **1** in an equal manner (*treated them all equally*). **2** to an equal degree (*is equally important*). ▶In sense 2 construction with *as* (*equally as important*) is often found, but is disputed.

e·qual op·por·tu·ni·ty *n.* (often in *pl.*) the opportunity or right to be employed, paid, etc., without discrimination on grounds of sex, race, etc.

e·qual sign *n.* (also **equals sign**) the symbol =.

e·qua·nim·i·ty /éekwənímitee, ékwə–/ *n.* mental composure; evenness of temper, esp. in misfortune.

e·quate /ikwáyt/ *v.* **1** *tr.* (usu. foll. by *to, with*) regard as equal or equivalent. **2** *intr.* (foll. by *with*) **a** be equal or equivalent to. **b** agree or correspond. □□ **e·quat·a·ble** *adj.*

e·qua·tion /ikwáyzhən/ *n.* **1** the process of equating or making equal; the state of being equal. **2** *Math.* a statement that two mathematical expressions are equal (indicated by the sign =). **3** *Chem.* a formula indicating a chemical reaction. □□ **e·qua·tion·al** *adj.*

e·qua·tor /ikwáytər/ *n.* **1** an imaginary line around the earth or other body, equidistant from the poles. **2** *Astron.* = CELESTIAL EQUATOR. □□ **e·qua·tor·i·al** /ékwətáwreeəl, éekwə–/ *adj.* **e·qua·to·ri·al·ly** *adv.*

eq·uer·ry /ékwəree/ *n.* (*pl.* **-ries**) **1** an officer of the British royal household attending members of the royal family. **2** *hist.* an officer of a prince's or noble's household in charge of the horses.

e·ques·tri·an /ikwéstreeən/ *adj. & n.* •*adj.* **1** of or relating to horses and horseback riding. **2** on horseback. •*n.* (*fem.* **equestrienne** /–tree-én/) a rider or performer on horseback. ▫▫ **e·ques·tri·an·ism** *n.*
equi- /éékwee, ékwi/ *comb. form* equal.
e·qui·an·gu·lar /éékweeángyələr, ékwee–/ *adj.* having equal angles.
e·qui·dis·tant /éékwidístənt, ékwi–/ *adj.* at equal distances. ▫▫ **e·qui·dis·tant·ly** *adv.*
e·qui·lat·er·al /éékwilátərəl, ékwi–/ *adj.* having all its sides equal in length.
e·quil·i·brist /ikwílibrist/ *n.* an acrobat, esp. on a high rope.
e·qui·lib·ri·um /éékwilíbreeəm, ékwi–/ *n.* (*pl.* **equilibriums** or **equilibria** /–reeə/) **1** a state of physical balance. **2** a state of mental or emotional equanimity. **3** a state in which the energy in a system is evenly distributed.
e·quine /éékwīn, ékwīn/ *adj.* of or like a horse.
e·qui·nox /éékwinoks, ékwi–/ *n.* the time or date (about March 20 *(vernal equinox)* and September 22 *(autumnal equinox)* each year) at which the sun crosses the celestial equator, when day and night are of equal length. ▫▫ **e·qui·noc·tial** /éékwinókshəl, ékwi–/ *adj.*
e·quip /ikwíp/ *v.tr.* (**equipped, equipping**) supply with what is needed. ▫▫ **e·quip·per** *n.*
eq·ui·page /ékwipij/ *n.* **1 a** requisites for an undertaking. **b** an outfit for a special purpose. **2** a carriage and horses with attendants.
e·quip·ment /ikwípmənt/ *n.* **1** the necessary articles, clothing, etc., for a purpose. **2** the process of equipping or being equipped.
e·qui·poise /éékwipoyz, ékwi–/ *n. & v.* •*n.* **1** equilibrium; a balanced state. **2** a counterbalancing thing. •*v.tr.* counterbalance.
eq·ui·ta·ble /ékwitəbəl/ *adj.* **1** fair; just. **2** *Law* valid in equity as distinct from law. ▫▫ **eq·ui·ta·ble·ness** *n.* **eq·ui·ta·bly** *adv.*
eq·ui·ta·tion /ékwitáyshən/ *n.* the art and practice of horsemanship and horseback riding.
eq·ui·ty /ékwitee/ *n.* (*pl.* **-ties**) **1** fairness. **2** the application of the principles of justice to correct or supplement the law. **3 a** the value of the shares issued by a company. **b** (in *pl.*) stocks and shares not bearing fixed interest. **4** the net value of a mortgaged property after the deduction of charges.
e·quiv·a·lent /ikwívələnt/ *adj. & n.* •*adj.* **1** (often foll. by *to*) equal in value, amount, etc. **2** corresponding. **3** (of words) having the same meaning. **4** having the same result. •*n.* an equivalent thing, amount, word, etc. ▫▫ **e·quiv·a·lence** /–ləns/ *n.* **e·quiv·a·len·cy** *n.*
e·quiv·o·cal /ikwívəkəl/ *adj.* **1** of double or doubtful meaning. **2** of uncertain nature. **3** (of a person, character, etc.) suspect. ▫▫ **e·quiv·o·cal·i·ty** /–kálitee/ *n.* **e·quiv·o·cal·ly** *adv.* **e·quiv·o·cal·ness** *n.*
e·quiv·o·cate /ikwívəkayt/ *v.intr.* use ambiguity to conceal the truth. ▫▫ **e·quiv·o·ca·tion** /–káyshən/ *n.* **e·quiv·o·ca·tor** *n.* **e·quiv·o·ca·to·ry** *adj.*
ER *abbr.* emergency room.
Er *symb. Chem.* the element erbium.
ERA *abbr.* **1** *Baseball* earned run average. **2** Equal Rights Amendment.
e·ra /éérə, érə/ *n.* **1** a system of chronology reckoning from a noteworthy event (*the Christian era*). **2** a distinct period of time, esp. regarded historically (*the pre-Roman era*). **3** a date at which an era begins.
e·rad·i·cate /irádikayt/ *v.tr.* root out; destroy completely. ▫▫ **e·rad·i·ca·ble** *adj.* **e·rad·i·ca·tion** /–káyshən/ *n.* **e·rad·i·ca·tor** *n.*
e·rase /iráys/ *v.tr.* **1** rub out. **2** remove all traces of (*erased it from my memory*). **3** remove recorded material from (a magnetic medium). ▫▫ **e·ras·a·ble** *adj.* **e·ra·sure** *n.*
e·ras·er /iráysər/ *n.* a thing that erases, esp. a piece of rubber or plastic used for removing pencil and ink marks.
er·bi·um /ərbeeəm/ *n. Chem.* a soft, silvery, metallic element of the lanthanide series. ¶ Symb.: **Er.**
ere /air/ *prep. & conj. poet.* or *archaic* before (of time) (*ere noon; ere they come*).
e·rect /irékt/ *adj. & v.* •*adj.* **1** upright; vertical. **2** enlarged and rigid, esp. in sexual excitement. **3** (of hair) bristling, standing up from the skin. •*v.tr.* **1** raise; set upright. **2** build. **3** establish (*erect a theory*). ▫▫ **e·rect·a·ble** *adj.* **e·rect·ly** *adv.* **e·rect·ness** *n.*
e·rec·tile /iréktʼl, –tīl/ *adj.* that can be erected or become erect.
e·rec·tion /irékshən/ *n.* **1** the act or an instance of erecting; the state of being erected. **2** a building or structure. **3** *Physiol.* an enlarged and erect state of erectile tissue, esp. of the penis.
er·e·mite /érimīt/ *n.* a hermit or recluse (esp. Christian). ▫▫ **er·e·mit·ic** /–mítik/ *adj.* **er·e·mit·i·cal** *adj.*
erg /ərg/ *n. Physics* a unit of work or energy.
er·go /ərgō, ér–/ *adv.* therefore.
er·go·nom·ics /ərgənómiks/ *n.* the study of the efficiency of persons in their working environment. ▫▫ **er·go·nom·ic** *adj.* **er·gon·o·mist** /ergónəmist/ *n.*
er·mine /ərmin/ *n.* (*pl.* same or **ermines**) **1** the stoat, esp. when in its white winter fur. **2** its white fur, used as trimming for the robes of judges, peers, etc.
erne /ern/ (also **ern**) a sea eagle.
e·rode /irṓd/ *v.tr.* & intr. wear away; destroy or be destroyed gradually. ▫▫ **e·rod·i·ble** *adj.* **e·ro·sion** /irṓzhən/ *n.* **e·ro·sive** *adj.*
e·rog·e·nous /irójinəs/ *adj.* **1** (esp. of a part of the body) sensitive to sexual stimulation. **2** giving rise to sexual desire or excitement.
e·rot·ic /irótik/ *adj.* of or causing sexual love, esp. tending to arouse sexual desire or excitement. ▫▫ **e·rot·i·cal·ly** *adv.*
e·rot·i·ca /irótikə/ *n.pl.* erotic literature or art.
e·rot·i·cism /irótisizəm/ *n.* **1** erotic nature or character. **2** the use of or response to erotic images or stimulation.
er·o·tism /érətizəm/ *n.* = EROTICISM.
eroto- /irótō, irṓ–/ *comb. form* erotic; eroticism.
e·ro·to·gen·ic /irótəjénik, irṓ–/ *adj.* = EROGENOUS.
e·ro·to·ma·ni·a /irótəmáyneeə, irṓ–/ *n.* **1** excessive or morbid erotic desire. **2** a preoccupation with sexual passion. ▫▫ **e·ro·to·ma·ni·ac** /–neeak/ *n.*
err /ər, er/ *v.intr.* **1** be mistaken or incorrect. **2** do wrong; sin. ▫ **err on the right side** act so that the least harmful of possible errors is the most likely to occur. **err on the side of** act with a specified bias.
▶Traditionally, this word rhymes with *her,* though the pronunciation that rhymes with *hair* is now common.
er·rand /érənd/ *n.* **1** a short journey, esp. on another's behalf, to take a message, collect goods, etc. **2** the object of such a journey.
er·rant /érənt/ *adj.* **1** erring; deviating from an accepted standard. **2** *literary* or *archaic* traveling in search of adventure (*knight errant*). ▫▫ **er·ran·cy** /–ənsee/ *n.* (in sense 1). **er·rant·ry** *n.* (in sense 2).
er·rat·ic /irátik/ *adj.* **1** inconsistently variable in conduct, opinions, etc. **2** uncertain in movement. ▫▫ **er·rat·i·cal·ly** *adv.*
er·ra·tum /iraátəm, irát–/ *n.* (*pl.* **errata** /–tə/) an error in printing or writing.
er·ro·ne·ous /irṓneeəs/ *adj.* incorrect; arising from error. ▫▫ **er·ro·ne·ous·ly** *adv.* **er·ro·ne·ous·ness** *n.*
er·ror /érər/ *n.* **1** a mistake. **2** the condition of being wrong in conduct or judgment. **3** a wrong opinion or

judgment. **4** the amount by which something is incorrect or inaccurate in a calculation or measurement.

er·satz /érzaats, –saats, erzaáts, –saáts/ *adj.* substitute; imitation (esp. of inferior quality).

Erse /ərs/ *adj. & n.* • *adj.* Irish or Highland Gaelic. • *n.* the Gaelic language.

erst·while /ə́rst-hwīl, –wīl/ *adj.* former; previous.

er·u·dite /éryədīt, érə–/ *adj.* **1** (of a person) learned. **2** (of writing, etc.) showing great learning. ◻◻ **er·u·dite·ly** *adv.* **er·u·di·tion** /–díshən/ *n.*

e·rupt /irúpt/ *v.intr.* **1** break out suddenly or dramatically. **2** (of a volcano) become active and eject lava, etc. **3 a** (of a rash, boil, etc.) appear on the skin. **b** (of the skin) produce a rash, etc. **4** (of the teeth) break through the gums. ◻◻ **e·rup·tion** /–rúpshən/ *n.* **e·rup·tive** *adj.*

er·y·the·ma /éritheéemə/ *n.* a superficial reddening of the skin, usu. in patches.

erythro- /iríthrō/ *comb. form* red.

e·ryth·ro·cyte /iríthrəsīt/ *n.* a red blood cell. ◻◻ **e·ryth·ro·cyt·ic** /–sítik/ *adj.*

Es *symb. Chem.* the element einsteinium.

-es[1] /iz/ *suffix* forming plurals of nouns ending in sibilant sounds (such words in *-e* dropping the *e*) (*kisses*; *cases*; *boxes*; *churches*).

-es[2] /iz, z/ *suffix* forming the 3rd person sing. present of verbs ending in sibilant sounds (such words in *-e* dropping the *e*) and ending in *-o* (but not *-oo*) (*goes*; *places*; *pushes*).

es·ca·late /éskəlayt/ *v.* **1** *intr. & tr.* increase or develop (usu. rapidly) by stages. **2** *tr.* cause to become more intense. ◻◻ **es·ca·la·tion** /–láyshən/ *n.*

es·ca·la·tor /éskəlaytər/ *n.* a moving staircase consisting of a circulating belt forming steps.

es·ca·lope /éskəlṓp/ *n.* a thin slice of meat without any bone, esp. veal.

es·ca·pade /éskəpáyd/ *n.* an act or incident involving excitement, daring, or adventure.

es·cape /iskáyp/ *v. & n.* • *v.* **1** *intr.* (often foll. by *from*) get free of the restriction or control of. **2** *intr.* (of a gas, liquid, etc.) leak. **3** *intr.* succeed in avoiding danger, punishment, etc. **4** *tr.* get completely free of (a person, grasp, etc.). **5** *tr.* elude (a commitment, danger, etc.). **6** *tr.* elude the notice or memory of (*the name escaped me*). **7** *tr.* (of words, etc.) issue unawares from (a person's lips). • *n.* **1** the act or an instance of escaping; avoidance of danger, injury, etc. **2** the state of having escaped (*a narrow escape*). **3** a means of escaping (often *attrib.*: *escape hatch*). **4** a leakage of gas, etc. **5** a temporary relief from reality or worry.

es·cape clause *n. Law* a clause specifying the conditions under which a contracting party is free from an obligation.

es·cap·ee /iskaypeé/ *n.* a person, esp. a prisoner, who has escaped.

es·cape·ment /iskáypmənt/ *n.* **1** the part of a clock or watch that connects and regulates the motive power. **2** the part of the mechanism in a piano that enables the hammer to fall back immediately after striking the string.

es·cape ve·loc·i·ty *n.* the minimum velocity needed to escape from the gravitational field of a body.

es·cap·ism /iskáypizəm/ *n.* the tendency to seek distraction and relief from reality, esp. in the arts or through fantasy. ◻◻ **es·cap·ist** *n. & adj.*

es·cap·ol·o·gy /éskəpóləjee/ *n.* the methods and techniques of escaping from confinement, esp. as a form of entertainment. ◻◻ **es·cap·ol·o·gist** *n.*

es·car·got /eskaargṓ/ *n.* an edible snail.

es·carp·ment /iskaárpmənt/ *n.* (also **es·carp**) *Geol.* a long, steep slope at the edge of a plateau, etc.

es·cha·tol·o·gy /éskətóləjee/ *n.* the part of theology concerned with death and final destiny. ◻◻ **es·cha·to·log·i·cal** /–təlójikəl/ *adj.* **es·cha·tol·o·gist** *n.*

es·chew /eschoó/ *v.tr. literary* avoid; abstain from. ◻◻ **es·chew·al** *n.*

es·cort *n. & v.* • *n.* /éskawrt/ **1** one or more persons, vehicles, ships, etc., accompanying a person, vehicle, etc., esp. for protection or security or as a mark of rank or status. **2** a person accompanying a person of the opposite sex socially. • *v.tr.* /iskáwrt/ act as an escort to.

es·cri·toire /éskritwaár/ *n.* a writing desk with drawers.

es·crow /éskrō/ *n. & v. Law* • *n.* **1** money, property, or a written bond, kept in the custody of a third party until a specified condition has been fulfilled. **2** the status of this (*in escrow*). • *v.tr.* place in escrow.

es·cu·do /eskoódō/ *n.* (*pl.* **-dos**) the principal monetary unit of Portugal and Chile.

es·cutch·eon /iskúchən/ *n.* **1** a shield or emblem bearing a coat of arms. **2** the protective plate around a keyhole or door handle.

ESE *abbr.* east-southeast.

-ese /eez/ *suffix* forming adjectives and nouns denoting: **1** an inhabitant or language of a country or city (*Japanese*; *Milanese*; *Viennese*). ▶Plural forms are the same. **2** often *derog.* character or style, esp. of language (*officialese*).

es·ker /éskər/ *n. Geol.* a long ridge of postglacial gravel in river valleys.

Es·ki·mo /éskimō/ *n. & adj.* • *n.* (*pl.* same or **-mos**) **1** a member of a people inhabiting N. Canada, Alaska, Greenland, and E. Siberia. **2** the language of this people. • *adj.* of or relating to the Eskimos or their language.

▶The term *Inuit* is preferred by the people themselves.

ESL *abbr.* English as a second language.

e·soph·a·gus /isófəgəs, ee–/ *n.* (*pl.* **esophagi** /–gī, –jī/) the part of the alimentary canal from the mouth to the stomach; the gullet. ◻◻ **e·so·pha·geal** /isófəjeéəl, eesəfájeeəl/ *adj.*

es·o·ter·ic /ésətérik/ *adj.* **1** intelligible only to those with special knowledge. **2** (of a belief, etc.) intended only for the initiated. ◻◻ **es·o·ter·i·cal** *adj.*

ESP *abbr.* extrasensory perception.

es·pa·drille /éspədríl/ *n.* a light canvas shoe with a plaited fiber sole.

es·pal·ier /ispályər, –yay/ *n.* **1** a latticework along which the branches of a tree or shrub are trained to grow flat against a wall, etc. **2** a tree or shrub trained in this way.

es·pe·cial /ispéshəl/ *adj.* **1** notable; exceptional. **2** attributed or belonging chiefly to one person or thing (*your especial charm*).

es·pe·cial·ly /ispéshəlee, espésh–/ *adv.* chiefly; much more than in other cases.

Es·pe·ran·to /éspəránto, –raán–/ *n.* an artificial universal language devised in 1887, based on roots common to the chief European languages. ◻◻ **Es·pe·ran·tist** *n.*

es·pi·o·nage /éspeeənaazh/ *n.* the practice of spying or of using spies.

es·pla·nade /ésplənaád, –náyd/ *n.* **1** a long, open level area for walking on, esp. beside the ocean. **2** a level space separating a fortress from a town.

es·pous·al /ispówzəl, –səl/ *n.* **1** (foll. by *of*) the espousing of a cause, etc. **2** *archaic* a marriage or betrothal.

es·pouse /ispówz/ *v.tr.* adopt or support (a cause, doctrine, etc.).

es·pres·so /esprésō/ *n.* (also **ex·pres·so** /eksprésō/) (*pl.* **-sos**) **1** strong, concentrated black coffee made under steam pressure. **2** a machine for making this.

es·prit /espreé/ *n.* sprightliness; wit.

es·prit de corps /espreé də káwr/ *n.* a feeling of devotion to and pride in the group one belongs to.

es·py /ispī́/ *v.tr.* (**-pies, -pied**) *literary* catch sight of.

Esq. *abbr.* esquire.

-esque /esk/ *suffix* forming adjectives meaning 'in the style of' or 'resembling' (*romanesque*; *Schumannesque*).

es•quire /éskwīr, iskwír/ *n.* **1** (usu. as abbr. **Esq.**) **a** a title appended to a man's surname when no other form of address is used, esp. as a form of address for letters. **b** a title placed after the name of an attorney (male or female), esp. in correspondence. **2** *archaic* = SQUIRE.

-ess /is/ *suffix* forming nouns denoting females (*actress*; *lioness*; *mayoress*).

es•say *n.* & *v.* • *n.* /ésay/ **1** a composition, usu. short and in prose, on any subject. **2** (often foll. by *at*, *in*) *formal* an attempt. • *v.tr.* /esáy/ *formal* attempt; try. □□ **es•say•ist** *n.*

es•sence /ésəns/ *n.* **1** fundamental nature or inherent characteristics. **2 a** an extract obtained by distillation, etc. **b** a perfume. **3** the constituent of a plant that determines its chemical properties. **4** an abstract entity; the reality underlying a phenomenon or all phenomena.

es•sen•tial /isénshəl/ *adj.* & *n.* • *adj.* **1** absolutely necessary; indispensable. **2** fundamental; basic. **3** of or constituting the essence of a person or thing. **4** (of a disease) with no known external stimulus or cause. • *n.* (esp. in *pl.*) a basic or indispensable element or thing. □□ **es•sen•tial•ly** *adv.*

es•sen•tial oil *n.* a volatile oil derived from a plant, etc., with its characteristic odor.

EST *abbr.* **1** eastern standard time. **2** electroshock treatment.

es•tab•lish /istáblish/ *v.tr.* **1** set up or consolidate (a business, system, etc.) on a permanent basis. **2** (foll. by *in*) settle (a person or oneself) in some capacity. **3** (esp. as **established** *adj.*) achieve permanent acceptance for (a custom, belief, practice, institution, etc.). **4** place beyond dispute (a fact, etc.). □□ **es•tab•lish•er** *n.*

es•tab•lish•ment /istáblishmənt/ *n.* **1** the act or an instance of establishing; the process of being established. **2 a** a business organization or public institution. **b** a place of business. **c** a residence. **3 a** the staff or equipment of an organization. **b** a household. **4** any organized body permanently maintained. **5** a church system organized by law. **6** (**the Establishment**) **a** the group in a society exercising authority or influence, and seen as resisting change. **b** any influential or controlling group (*the literary Establishment*).

es•tate /istáyt/ *n.* **1** a property consisting of an extensive area of land usu. with a large house. **2** *Brit.* a housing development. **3** all of a person's assets and liabilities, esp. at death. **4** a property where rubber, tea, grapes, etc., are cultivated. **5** (in full **estate of the realm**) a group or social class having specific political powers.

es•teem /istéem/ *v.* & *n.* • *v.tr.* **1** (usu. in *passive*) have a high regard for. **2** *formal* consider (*esteemed it an honor*). • *n.* high regard; favor (*held them in esteem*).

es•ter /éstər/ *n. Chem.* any of a class of organic compounds produced by replacing the hydrogen of an acid by an alkyl, etc., radical, many of which occur naturally as oils and fats. □□ **es•ter•i•fy** /estérifī/ *v.tr.*

es•thete var. of AESTHETE.

es•thet•ic var. of AESTHETIC.

es•ti•ma•ble /éstiməbəl/ *adj.* worthy of esteem.

es•ti•mate *n.* & *v.* • *n.* /éstimət/ **1** an approximate judgment. **2** a price specified as that likely to be charged for work to be undertaken. **3** opinion; judgment. • *v.tr.* (also *absol.*) /éstimayt/ **1** form an estimate of. **2** (foll. by *that* + clause) make a rough calculation.

es•ti•ma•tion /éstimáyshən/ *n.* **1** the process or result of estimating. **2** judgment of worth (*in my estimation*).

es•ti•val /éstəvəl, estívəl/ *adj.* (also **aes•ti•val**) *formal* belonging to or appearing in summer.

es•ti•vate /éstəvayt/ *v.intr.* (also **aes•ti•vate**) *Zool.* spend the summer or dry season in a state of torpor.

Es•to•ni•an /estóneeən/ *n.* & *adj* • *n.* **1 a** a native of Estonia, a Baltic republic. **b** a person of Estonian descent. **2** the language of Estonia. • *adj.* of or relating to Estonia or its people or language.

es•trange /istráynj/ *v.tr.* (usu. in *passive*; often foll. by *from*) cause to turn away in feeling or affection; alienate. □□ **es•trange•ment** *n.*

es•tro•gen /éstrəjən/ *n.* **1** any of various steroid hormones developing and maintaining female characteristics of the body. **2** this hormone produced artificially. □□ **es•tro•gen•ic** /–jénik/ *adj.*

es•trus /éstrəs/ *n.* (also **es•trum**) a recurring period of sexual receptivity in many female mammals. □□ **es•trous** *adj.*

es•tu•ar•y /és-chōōeree/ *n.* (*pl.* **-ies**) a wide tidal mouth of a river. □□ **es•tu•a•rine** /–ərīn, –əreen/ *adj.*

ET *abbr.* extraterrestrial.

ETA *abbr.* estimated time of arrival.

e•ta /áytə, éetə/ *n.* the seventh letter of the Greek alphabet (Η, η).

et al. /et ál/ *abbr.* and others.

etc. *abbr.* = ET CETERA.

et cet•er•a /et sétərə, sétrə/ *adv.* & *n.* (also **et•cet•er•a**) • *adv.* **1 a** and the rest; and similar things or people. **b** or similar things or people. **2** and so on. • *n.* (in *pl.*) the usual sundries or extras.

▶Avoid pronouncing this phrase "ek set-uhr-uh"; many regard this as uneducated.

etch /ech/ *v.* & *n.* • *v.* **1 a** *tr.* reproduce (a picture, etc.) by engraving a design on a metal plate with acid. **b** *tr.* engrave (a plate) in this way. **2** *intr.* practice this craft. **3** *tr.* (foll. by *on*, *upon*) impress deeply (esp. on the mind). • *n.* the action or process of etching. □□ **etch•er** *n.*

etch•ing /éching/ *n.* **1** a print made from an etched plate. **2** the art of producing these plates.

ETD *abbr.* estimated time of departure.

e•ter•nal /itárnəl/ *adj.* **1** existing always; without an end or (usu.) beginning in time. **2** essentially unchanging (*eternal truths*). **3** *colloq.* constant; seeming not to cease (*your eternal nagging*). □□ **e•ter•nal•ize** *v.tr.* **e•ter•nal•ly** *adv.*

e•ter•nal tri•an•gle *n.* a relationship of three people involving sexual rivalry.

e•ter•ni•ty /itárnitee/ *n.* (*pl.* **-ties**) **1** infinite or unending (esp. future) time. **2** *Theol.* endless life after death. **3** the state of being eternal. **4** *colloq.* (often prec. by *an*) a very long time.

eth•ane /éthayn/ *n. Chem.* a gaseous hydrocarbon of the alkane series, occurring in natural gas..

eth•a•nol /éthənawl, –nol/ *n. Chem.* = ALCOHOL 1.

e•ther /éethər/ *n.* **1** *Chem.* **a** a colorless volatile organic liquid used as an anesthetic or solvent. Also called **diethyl ether**. **b** any of a class of organic compounds with a similar structure to this, having an oxygen joined to two alkyl, etc., groups. **2** a clear sky; the upper regions of air. **3** *hist.* **a** a medium formerly assumed to permeate space. **b** a medium through which electromagnetic waves were formerly thought to be transmitted.

e•the•re•al /ithéereeəl/ *adj.* **1** extremely delicate and light in a way that seems too perfect for this world (*ethereal beauty*). **2** heavenly; celestial. □□ **e•the•re•al•ly** *adv.*

eth•ic /éthik/ *n.* & *adj.* • *n.* a set of moral principles (*the puritan ethic*). • *adj.* = ETHICAL.

eth•i•cal /éthikəl/ *adj.* **1** relating to morals. **2** morally correct; honorable. **3** (of a medicine or drug) not advertised to the general public, and usu. available only on a doctor's prescription. □□ **eth•i•cal•ly** *adv.*

eth·ics /éthiks/ *n.pl.* (also treated as *sing.*) **1** the science of morals in human conduct. **2 a** moral principles. **b** a set of these (*medical ethics*). ▫▫ **eth·i·cist** /éthisist/ *n.*

E·thi·o·pi·an /éetheeṓpeeən/ *n. & adj.* • *n.* **1** a native or national of Ethiopia in NE Africa. **2** a person of Ethiopian descent. • *adj.* of or relating to Ethiopia.

eth·nic /éthnik/ *adj. & n.* • *adj.* **1 a** (of a social group) having a common national or cultural tradition. **b** (of clothes, etc.) resembling those of a non-European exotic people. **2** denoting origin by birth or descent rather than nationality (*ethnic Turks*). **3** relating to race or culture (*ethnic group; ethnic origins*). • *n.* **1** a member of an (esp. minority) ethnic group. **2** (in *pl.*, usu. treated as *sing.*) = ETHNOLOGY. ▫▫ **eth·ni·cal·ly** *adv.* **eth·nic·i·ty** /–nísitee/ *n.*

eth·nic cleans·ing *n. euphem.* the practice of mass expulsion or killing of people from opposing ethnic or religious groups within a certain area.

ethno- /éthnō/ *comb. form* ethnic; ethnological.

eth·no·cen·tric /éthnōséntrik/ *adj.* evaluating other races and cultures by criteria specific to one's own. ▫▫ **eth·no·cen·tri·cal·ly** *adv.* **eth·no·cen·tric·i·ty** /–trísitee/ *n.* **eth·no·cen·trism** *n.*

eth·nog·ra·phy /ethnógrəfee/ *n.* the scientific description of races and cultures of mankind. ▫▫ **eth·nog·ra·pher** *n.* **eth·no·graph·ic** /–nəgráfik/ *adj.*

eth·nol·o·gy /ethnóləjee/ *n.* the comparative scientific study of human peoples. ▫▫ **eth·no·log·i·cal** *adj.* **eth·nol·o·gist** *n.*

e·thol·o·gy /eethóləjee/ *n.* **1** the science of animal behavior. **2** the science of character formation in human behavior. ▫▫ **e·tho·log·i·cal** /éethəlójikəl/ *adj.* **e·thol·o·gist** *n.*

e·thos /éethos/ *n.* the characteristic spirit or attitudes of a community, people, etc., or of a literary work.

eth·yl /éthil/ *n.* (*attrib.*) *Chem.* the univalent radical derived from ethane by removal of a hydrogen atom (*ethyl alcohol*).

eth·yl·ene /éthileen/ *n. Chem.* a gaseous hydrocarbon of the alkene series, occurring in natural gas and used in the manufacture of polyethylene. Also called **ethene**.

eth·yl·ene gly·col *n. Chem.* a colorless viscous hygroscopic liquid used as an antifreeze and in the manufacture of polyesters.

e·ti·o·late /éeteeəláyt/ *v.tr.* **1** make (a plant) pale by excluding light. **2** give a sickly hue to (a person).

e·ti·ol·o·gy /éeteeóləjee/ *n.* **1** the assignment of a cause or reason. **2** the philosophy of causation. **3** *Med.* the science of the causes of disease. ▫▫ **e·ti·o·log·i·cal** /–teeəlójikəl/ *adj.* **e·ti·o·log·i·cal·ly** /–teeəlójikəlee/ *adv.*

et·i·quette /étiket, –kit/ *n.* **1** the conventional rules of social behavior. **2 a** the customary behavior of members of a profession toward each other. **b** the unwritten code governing this (*medical etiquette*).

E·trus·can /itrúskən/ *adj. & n.* • *adj.* of ancient Etruria in Italy. • *n.* **1** a native of Etruria. **2** the language of Etruria.

et seq. *abbr.* (also **et seqq.**) and the following.

-ette /et/ *suffix* forming nouns meaning: **1** small (*kitchenette; cigarette*). **2** imitation or substitute (*leatherette; flannelette*). **3** often *offens.* female (*usherette; suffragette*).

é·tude /áytóōd, –tyóōd/ *n.* a short musical composition designed to improve the technique of the player.

et·y·mol·o·gy /étimóləjee/ *n.* (*pl.* **-gies**) **1 a** the sources of the formation of a word and the development of its meaning. **b** an account of these. **2** the branch of linguistic science concerned with etymologies. ▫▫ **et·y·mo·log·i·cal** /–məlójikəl/ *adj.* **et·y·mo·log·i·cal·ly** *adv.* **et·y·mol·o·gist** *n.*

EU *abbr.* European Union.

Eu *symb. Chem.* the element europium.

eu- /yoo/ *comb. form* well; easily.

eu·ca·lyp·tus /yóōkəlíptəs/ *n.* (also **eu·ca·lypt**) (*pl.* **eucalypti** /–tī/or **eucalyptuses** or **eucalypts**) any tree of the genus *Eucalyptus*, native to Australasia, cultivated for its wood and for the oil from its leaves.

Eu·cha·rist /yóōkərist/ *n.* **1** the Christian sacrament commemorating the Last Supper, in which bread and wine are consecrated and consumed. **2** the consecrated elements, esp. the bread (*receive the Eucharist*).

eu·clid·e·an /yōōklídeeən/ *adj.* (also **Eu·clid·e·an**) of or relating to Euclid, 3rd-c. BC Alexandrian geometrician.

eu·gen·ics /yōōjéniks/ *n.pl.* (also treated as *sing.*) the science of improving the population by controlled breeding for desirable inherited characteristics. ▫▫ **eu·gen·ic** *adj.* **eu·gen·i·cist** /yōōjénisist/ *n.*

eu·kar·y·ote /yōōkáreeōt/ *n.* (also **eu·car·y·ote**) *Biol.* an organism consisting of a cell or cells in which the genetic material is contained within a distinct nucleus (cf. PROKARYOTE). ▫▫ **eu·kar·y·ot·ic** /–reeótik/ *adj.*

eu·lo·gize /yóōləjīz/ *v.tr.* praise in speech or writing. ▫▫ **eu·lo·gist** /–jist/ *n.* **eu·lo·gis·tic** *adj.*

eu·lo·gy /yóōləjee/ *n.* (*pl.* **-gies**) **1 a** speech or writing in praise of a person. **b** an expression of praise. **2** a funeral oration in praise of a person.

---

eulogy late Middle English (in the sense 'high praise'): from medieval Latin *eulogium*, *eulogia* (from Greek *eulogia* 'praise'), apparently influenced by Latin *elogium* 'inscription on a tomb' (from Greek *elegia* 'elegy') . The current sense dates from the late 16th cent.

---

eu·nuch /yóōnək/ *n.* **1** a castrated man, esp. one formerly employed at an Oriental harem . **2** a person lacking effectiveness (*political eunuch*).

eu·on·y·mus /yoo-ónimәs/ *n.* any tree of the genus *Euonymus*, e.g., the spindle tree.

eu·phe·mism /yóōfimizəm/ *n.* **1** a mild or vague expression substituted for one thought to be too harsh or direct (e.g., *pass over* for *die*). **2** the use of such expressions. ▫▫ **eu·phe·mis·tic** *adj.* **eu·phe·mis·ti·cal·ly** *adv.* **eu·phe·mize** *v.tr. & intr.*

eu·pho·ni·ous /yōōfṓneeəs/ *adj.* **1** sounding pleasant; harmonious. **2** concerning euphony. ▫▫ **eu·pho·ni·ous·ly** *adv.*

eu·pho·ni·um /yōōfṓneeəm/ *n.* a brass wind instrument of the tuba family.

eu·pho·ny /yóōfənee/ *n.* (*pl.* **-nies**) **1 a** pleasantness of sound, esp. of a word or phrase. **b** a pleasant sound. **2** the tendency to make a phonetic change for ease of pronunciation. ▫▫ **eu·phon·ic** /–fónik/ *adj.*

eu·phor·bi·a /yōōfáwrbeeə/ *n.* any plant of the genus *Euphorbia*, including spurges.

eu·pho·ri·a /yōōfáwreeə/ *n.* a feeling of well-being, esp. one based on overconfidence or overoptimism. ▫▫ **eu·phor·ic** /–fáwrik, fór–/ *adj.* **eu·phor·i·cal·ly** *adv.*

eu·pho·ri·ant /yōōfáwreeənt/ *adj. & n.* • *adj.* inducing euphoria. • *n.* a euphoriant drug.

Eur·a·sian /yōōráyzhən/ *adj. & n.* • *adj.* **1** of mixed European and Asian parentage. **2** of Europe and Asia. • *n.* a Eurasian person.

eu·re·ka /yōōréekə/ *int. & n.* • *int.* I have found it! (announcing a discovery, etc.). • *n.* the exultant cry of 'eureka.'

eu·rhyth·mic var. of EURYTHMIC.

eu·rhyth·mics var. of EURYTHMICS.

Euro- /yóōrō/ *comb. form* Europe; European.

Eu·ro·dol·lar /yóōrōdolər/ *n.* a dollar held in a bank in Europe.

Eu·ro·pe·an /yóōrəpéeən/ *adj. & n.* • *adj.* **1** of or in Europe. **2 a** descended from natives of Europe. **b** originating in or characteristic of Europe. **3 a** happening in or extending over Europe. **b** concerning Europe as a whole rather than its individual countries. **4** of or relating to the European Economic Community. • *n.* **1 a** a native or inhabitant of Europe. **b** a person descended from natives of Europe. **c** a white person. **2** a person concerned with European matters. ◻◻ **Eu·ro·pe·an·ism** *n.* **Eu·ro·pe·an·ize** *v.tr. & intr.* **Eu·ro·pe·an·i·za·tion** *n.*

Eu·ro·pe·an Com·mu·ni·ty *n.* (also **European Economic Community**) an economic and political association of certain European countries as a unit with internal free trade and common external tariffs.

eu·ro·pi·um /yoorṓpeeəm/ *n. Chem.* a soft, silvery metallic element of the lanthanide series, occurring naturally in small quantities. ¶ Symb.: **Eu**.

eu·ryth·mic /yoorí<u>th</u>mik/ *adj.* (also **eu·rhyth·mic**) of or in harmonious proportion (esp. of architecture).

eu·ryth·mics /yoorí<u>th</u>miks/ *n.pl.* (also treated as *sing.*) (also **eu·rhyth·mics**) harmony of bodily movement, esp. as developed with music and dance into a system of education.

Eu·sta·chian tube /yoostáyshən, –keeən/ *n. Anat.* a tube leading from the pharynx to the cavity of the middle ear.

eu·sta·sy /yóostəsee/ *n.* a change in sea level throughout the world caused by tectonic movements, melting of glaciers, etc. ◻◻ **eu·stat·ic** /–státik/ *adj.*

eu·tha·na·sia /yóothənáy<u>zh</u>ə/ *n.* **1** the bringing about of a gentle and easy death in the case of incurable and painful disease. **2** such a death.

eu·troph·ic /yootrófik, –trṓfik/ *adj.* (of a lake, etc.) rich in nutrients and therefore supporting a dense plant population, which kills animal life by depriving it of oxygen. ◻◻ **eu·tro·phy** /yóotrəfee/ *n.*

EVA *abbr. Astronaut.* extravehicular activity.

e·vac·u·ate /ivákyoo-ayt/ *v.tr.* **1 a** remove (people) from a place of danger. **b** empty (a place) in this way. **2** make empty (a vessel of air, etc.). **3** (of troops) withdraw from (a place). **4 a** empty (the bowels or other bodily organ). **b** discharge (feces, etc.). ◻◻ **e·vac·u·a·tion** /–áyshən/ *n.*

e·vac·u·ee /ivákyoo-eé/ *n.* a person evacuated from a place of danger.

e·vade /iváyd/ *v.tr.* **1 a** escape from, avoid, esp. by guile or trickery. **b** avoid doing (one's duty, etc.). **c** avoid answering (a question). **2 a** fail to pay (tax due). **b** defeat the intention of (a law, etc.). **3** (of a thing) elude or baffle (a person). ◻◻ **e·vad·er** *n.*

e·val·u·ate /iványoo-ayt/ *v.tr.* **1** assess; appraise. **2 a** find or state the number or amount of. **b** find a numerical expression for. ◻◻ **e·val·u·a·tion** /–áyshən/ *n.* **e·val·u·a·tive** *adj.* **e·val·u·a·tor** *n.*

ev·a·nesce /évənés/ *v.intr.* fade from sight.

ev·a·nes·cent /évənésənt/ *adj.* quickly fading. ◻◻ **ev·a·nes·cence** /–səns/ *n.*

e·van·gel·i·cal /eévanjélikəl, évən–/ *adj. & n.* • *adj.* **1** of or according to the teaching of the gospel or the Christian religion. **2** of the Protestant school maintaining that the doctrine of salvation by faith in the Atonement is the essence of the gospel. • *n.* a member of the evangelical school. ◻◻ **e·van·gel·i·cal·ism** *n.* **e·van·gel·i·cal·ly** *adv.*

e·van·ge·lism /ivánjəlizəm/ *n.* **1** the preaching of the gospel. **2** zealous advocacy of a cause or doctrine.

e·van·ge·list /ivánjəlist/ *n.* **1** any of the writers of the four Gospels. **2** a preacher of the gospel. **3** a lay person doing missionary work. ◻◻ **e·van·ge·lis·tic** /ivánjəlístik/ *adj.*

e·van·ge·lize /ivánjəlīz/ *v.tr.* **1** (also *absol.*) preach the gospel to. **2** convert (a person) to Christianity. ◻◻ **e·van·ge·li·za·tion** *n.* **e·van·ge·liz·er** *n.*

e·vap·o·rate /ivápərayt/ *v.* **1** *intr.* turn from solid or liquid into vapor. **2** *intr. & tr.* lose or cause to lose moisture as vapor. **3** *intr. & tr.* disappear or cause to disappear. ◻◻ **e·vap·o·ra·tion** /–ráyshən/ *n.* **e·vap·o·ra·tor** *n.*

e·va·sion /iváy<u>zh</u>ən/ *n.* **1** the act of evading. **2 a** subterfuge or a prevaricating excuse. **b** an evasive answer.

e·va·sive /iváysiv/ *adj.* **1** seeking to evade something. **2** not direct in one's answers, etc. **3** enabling or effecting evasion. **4** (of a person) habitually practicing evasion. ◻◻ **e·va·sive·ly** *adv.* **e·va·sive·ness** *n.*

eve /eev/ *n.* **1** the evening or day before a church festival or any date or event. **2** the time just before anything (*the eve of the election*). **3** *archaic* evening.

e·ven /eévən/ *adj., adv., & v.* • *adj.* (**evener, evenest**) **1** level. **2 a** uniform in quality; constant. **b** equal in number or amount or value, etc. **c** equally balanced. **3** (usu. foll. by *with*) in the same plane or line. **4** (of a person's temper, etc.) equable; calm. **5 a** (of a number) divisible by two without a remainder. **b** bearing such a number (*no parking on even days*). **c** not involving fractions; exact. • *adv.* **1** used to invite comparison of the stated assertion, negation, etc., with an implied one that is less strong or remarkable (*never even opened* [let alone read] *the letter*). **2** used to introduce an extreme case (*even you must realize it*). **3** (sometimes foll. by *with* or *though*) in spite of; notwithstanding (*even with the delays, we arrived on time*). • *v. tr. & intr.* (often foll. by *up* or *out*) make or become even. ◻ **even as** at the very moment that. **even now 1** now as well as before. **2** at this very moment. **even so 1** notwithstanding that; nevertheless. **2** quite so. **3** in that case as well as in others. **get** (or **be**) **even with** have one's revenge on. **on an even keel 1** (of a ship or aircraft) not tilting or listing to one side. **2** (of a plan or person) functioning normally. ◻◻ **e·ven·ly** *adv.* **e·ven·ness** *n.*

e·ven·hand·ed /eévənhándid/ *adj.* impartial. ◻◻ **e·ven·hand·ed·ly** *adv.* **e·ven·hand·ed·ness** *n.*

eve·ning /eévning/ *n.* **1** the end part of the day, esp. from about 6 p.m. to bedtime (*this evening; during the evening; evening meal*). **2** this time spent in a particular way (*had a lively evening*). **3** a time compared with this, esp. the last part of a person's life.

eve·ning prim·rose *n.* any plant of the genus *Oenothera* with pale yellow flowers that open in the evening.

eve·ning star *n.* a planet, esp. Venus, conspicuous in the west after sunset.

e·ven·song /eévənsawng, –song/ *n.* a service of evening prayer esp. in the Anglican Church.

e·vent /ivént/ *n.* **1** a thing that happens. **2 a** the fact of a thing's occurring. **b** a result or outcome. **3** an item in a sports program, or the program as a whole. **4** *Physics* a single occurrence of a process. **5** something on the result of which money is staked. ◻ **in any event** whatever happens. **in the event** as it turns (or turned) out. **in the event of** if (a specified thing) happens. **in the event that** *disp.* if it happens that.

e·vent·ful /ivéntfool/ *adj.* marked by noteworthy events. ◻◻ **e·vent·ful·ly** *adv.* **e·vent·ful·ness** *n.*

e·ven·tide /eévəntīd/ *n. archaic* or *poet.* = EVENING.

e·ven·tu·al /ivénchooəl/ *adj.* occurring or existing in due course or at last. ◻◻ **e·ven·tu·al·ly** *adv.*

e·ven·tu·al·i·ty /ivénchoo-álitee/ *n.* (*pl.* **-ties**) a possible event or outcome.

e·ven·tu·ate /ivénchoo-ayt/ *v.intr. formal* **1** turn out in a specified way as the result. **2** (often foll. by *in*) result.

ev·er /évər/ *adv.* **1** at all times; always (*ever hopeful; ever after*). **2** at any time (*have you ever been to Paris?; as good as ever*). **3** as an emphatic word: **a** in any way; at all (*when will they ever learn?*). **b** (prec. by *as*) in any manner possible (*be as quick as ever you can*). **4** (in *comb.*)

constantly (*ever-present*). **5** (foll. by *so, such*) esp. *Brit. colloq.* very; very much (*is ever so easy*). **6** (foll. by compar.) constantly; increasingly (*grew ever larger*). □ **ever since** throughout the period since.

ev·er·green /évərgreen/ *adj. & n.* • *adj.* **1** always green or fresh. **2** (of a plant) retaining green leaves throughout the year. • *n.* an evergreen plant (cf. DECIDUOUS).

ev·er·last·ing /évərlásting/ *adj. & n.* • *adj.* **1** lasting forever. **2** lasting for a long time, esp. so as to become unwelcome. **3** (of flowers) keeping their shape and color when dried. • *n.* (**the everlasting**) eternity. □□ **ev·er·last·ing·ly** *adv.* **ev·er·last·ing·ness** *n.*

ev·er·more /évərmáwr/ *adv.* forever; always.

eve·ry /évree/ *adj.* **1** each single (*heard every word*). **2** each at a specified interval in a series (*comes every four days*). **3** all possible (*there is every prospect of success*). □ **every bit as** *colloq.* (in comparisons) quite as (*every bit as good*). **every now and again** (or **now and then**) from time to time. **every one** each one (see also EVERYONE). **every other** each second in a series (*every other day*). **every so often** occasionally. **every which way** *colloq.* **1** in all directions. **2** in a disorderly manner.

eve·ry·bod·y /évreebodee, –budee/ *pron.* every person. ▶**Everybody,** along with **everyone,**, traditionally used a singular pronoun of reference: *Everybody must sign his* (not *their*) *own name.* Because the use of *his* in this context is now perceived as sexist by some, a second option became popular: *Everybody must sign his or her own name.* But *his or her* is often awkward, and many feel that the plural simply makes more sense: *Everybody must sign their own name.* Although this violates logic, it is standard in British English and informal US usage. In some sentences, only *they* makes grammatical sense: *Everybody agreed to convict the defendant, and they so voted unanimously.*

eve·ry·day /évreedáy/ *adj.* **1** occurring every day. **2** suitable for or used on ordinary days. **3** commonplace; usual. **4** mundane; mediocre; inferior.

eve·ry·man /évreeman/ *n.* (also **Eve·ry·man**) the ordinary or typical human being; the "man in the street."

eve·ry·one /évreewun/ *pron.* everybody. ▶See note at EVERYBODY.

eve·ry·thing /évreething/ *pron.* **1** all things; all the things of a group or class. **2** *colloq.* a great deal (*gave me everything*). **3** an essential consideration (*speed is everything*).

eve·ry·where /évreehwair, –wair/ *adv.* **1** in every place. **2** *colloq.* in many places.

e·vict /ivíkt/ *v.tr.* expel (a tenant) from a property by legal process. □□ **e·vic·tion** /–víkshən/ *n.*

ev·i·dence /évidəns/ *n. & v.* • *n.* **1** (often foll. by *for, of*) the available facts, circumstances, etc., indicating whether or not a thing is true or valid. **2** *Law* **a** information tending to prove a fact or proposition. **b** statements or proofs admissible as testimony in a court of law. **3** clearness; obviousness. • *v.tr.* be evidence of. □ **in evidence** noticeable; conspicuous.

ev·i·dent /évidənt/ *adj.* **1** plain or obvious; manifest. **2** seeming; apparent (*his evident anxiety*).

ev·i·den·tial /évidénshəl/ *adj.* of or providing evidence. □□ **ev·i·den·tial·ly** *adv.*

ev·i·dent·ly /évidəntlee, –déntlee/ *adv.* **1** as shown by evidence. **2** seemingly; as it appears.

e·vil /éevəl/ *adj. & n.* • *adj.* **1** morally bad; wicked. **2** harmful or tending to harm. **3** disagreeable (*has an evil temper*). **4** unlucky; causing misfortune (*evil days*). • *n.* **1** an evil thing; an instance of something evil. **2** wickedness. □□ **e·vil·ly** *adv.* **e·vil·ness** *n.*

e·vil eye *n.* a gaze superstitiously believed to be able to cause harm.

e·vince /ivíns/ *v.tr.* **1** indicate or make evident. **2** show that one has (a quality). □□ **e·vin·ci·ble** *adj.*

e·vis·cer·ate /ivísərayt/ *v.tr. formal* **1** disembowel. **2** empty or deprive of essential contents. □□ **e·vis·cer·a·tion** /–ráyshən/ *n.*

e·voc·a·tive /ivókətiv/ *adj.* tending to evoke (esp. feelings or memories). □□ **e·voc·a·tive·ly** *adv.*

e·voke /ivṓk/ *v.tr.* **1** inspire or draw forth (memories, feelings, a response, etc.). **2** summon (a supposed spirit from the dead). □□ **ev·o·ca·tion** /évəkáyshən, éevō–/ *n.*

ev·o·lu·tion /évəlóoshən/ *n.* **1** gradual development. **2** a process by which species develop from earlier forms, as an explanation of their origins. **3** the appearance or presentation of events, etc., in due succession (*the evolution of the plot*). **4** a change in the disposition of troops or ships. **5** the giving off or evolving of gas, heat, etc. **6** an opening out. **7** the unfolding of a curve. □□ **ev·o·lu·tion·ar·y** *adj.*

ev·o·lu·tion·ist /évəlóoshənist/ *n.* a person who believes in evolution as explaining the origin of species. □□ **ev·o·lu·tion·ism** *n.*

e·volve /ivólv/ *v.* **1** *intr. & tr.* develop gradually by a natural process. **2** *tr.* devise (a theory, plan, etc.). **3** *intr. & tr.* unfold; open out. **4** *tr.* give off (gas, heat, etc.).

ewe /yoo/ *n.* a female sheep.

ew·er /yóoər/ *n.* a large water jug with a wide mouth.

ex[1] /eks/ *prep.* **1** (of goods) sold from (*ex factory*). **2** (of stocks or shares) without; excluding.

ex[2] /eks/ *n. colloq.* a former husband or wife.

ex- /eks/ *prefix* (also **e-** before some consonants, **ef-** before *f*) **1** forming verbs meaning: **a** out; forth (*exclude; exit*). **b** upward (*extol*). **c** thoroughly (*excruciate*). **d** bring into a state (*exasperate*). **e** remove or free from (*expatriate; exonerate*). **2** forming nouns from titles of office, status, etc., meaning 'formerly' (*ex-president; ex-wife*).

ex·ac·er·bate /igzásərbayt/ *v.tr.* **1** make (pain, anger, etc.) worse. **2** irritate (a person). □□ **ex·ac·er·ba·tion** /–báyshən/ *n.*

ex·act /igzákt/ *adj. & v.* • *adj.* **1** accurate; correct in all details (*an exact description*). **2** **a** precise. **b** (of a person) tending to precision. • *v.tr.* (often foll. by *from, of*) **1** demand and enforce payment of (money, etc.). **2** **a** demand; insist on. **b** (of circumstances) require urgently. □□ **ex·ac·ti·tude** *n.* **ex·act·ness** *n.*

ex·act·ing /igzákting/ *adj.* **1** making great demands. **2** calling for much effort. □□ **ex·act·ing·ly** *adv.*

ex·ac·tion /igzákshən/ *n.* **1** the act or an instance of exacting; the process of being exacted. **2** **a** an illegal or exorbitant demand. **b** a sum or thing exacted.

ex·act·ly /igzáktlee/ *adv.* **1** accurately; precisely; in an exact manner (*worked it out exactly*). **2** in exact terms (*exactly when did it happen?*). **3** (said in reply) quite so; I quite agree. **4** just; in all respects.

ex·ag·ger·ate /igzájərayt/ *v.tr.* **1** (also *absol.*) give an impression of (a thing) that makes it seem larger or greater, etc., than it really is. **2** enlarge or alter beyond normal or due proportions (*spoke with exaggerated politeness*). □□ **ex·ag·ger·at·ed·ly** *adv.* **ex·ag·ger·a·tion** /–ráyshən/ *n.* **ex·ag·ger·a·tor** *n.*

---

exaggerate mid-16th cent.: from Latin *exaggerat-* 'heaped up,' from the verb *exaggerare*, from *ex-* 'thoroughly' + *aggerare* 'heap up' (from *agger* 'heap'). The word originally meant 'pile up, accumulate,' later 'intensify praise or blame,' 'dwell on a virtue or fault,' giving rise to current senses.

---

ex·alt /igzáwlt/ *v.tr.* **1** raise in rank or power, etc. **2** praise highly. **3** (usu. as **exalted** *adj.*) **a** make lofty or noble (*exalted aims*). **b** make rapturously excited. **4** (as **ex-**

alted *adj.*) elevated in rank or character; eminent; celebrated. **5** stimulate to greater activity; intensify; heighten. □□ **ex·alt·ed·ly** *adv.* **ex·alt·ed·ness** *n.*

ex·al·ta·tion /égzawltáyshən/ *n.* **1** the act or an instance of exalting; the state of being exalted. **2** elation; rapturous emotion.

ex·am /igzám/ *n.* = EXAMINATION.

ex·am·i·na·tion /igzámináyshən/ *n.* **1** the act or an instance of examining; the state of being examined. **2** a detailed inspection. **3** the testing of the proficiency or knowledge of candidates for a qualification by questions. **4** an instance of examining or being examined medically. **5** *Law* the formal questioning of the accused or of a witness in court.

ex·am·ine /igzámin/ *v.* **1** *tr.* inquire into the nature or condition, etc., of. **2** *tr.* look closely at. **3** *tr.* test the proficiency of. **4** *tr.* check the health of (a patient). **5** *tr. Law* formally question (the accused or a witness) in court. **6** *intr.* (foll. by *into*) inquire. □□ **ex·am·in·a·ble** *adj.* **ex·am·in·ee** /–nee̅/ *n.* **ex·am·in·er** *n.*

ex·am·ple /igzaámpəl/ *n.* **1** a thing characteristic of its kind or illustrating a general rule. **2** a person, thing, or piece of conduct, regarded in terms of its fitness to be imitated (*must set him an example*). **3** a circumstance or treatment seen as a warning to others; a person so treated (*shall make an example of you*). **4** a problem or exercise designed to illustrate a rule.

ex·as·per·ate /igzaáspərayt/ *v.tr.* **1** (often as **exasperated** *adj.* or **exasperating** *adj.*) irritate intensely. **2** make (a pain, ill feeling, etc.) worse. □□ **ex·as·per·a·tion** /–ráyshən/ *n.*

ex ca·the·dra /éks kəthee̅drə/ *adj. & adv.* with full authority (esp. of a papal pronouncement).

ex·ca·vate /ékskəvayt/ *v.tr.* **1 a** make (a hole or channel) by digging. **b** dig out material from (the ground). **2** reveal or extract by digging. **3** (also *absol.*) *Archaeol.* dig systematically to explore (a site). □□ **ex·ca·va·tion** /–váyshən/ *n.* **ex·ca·va·tor** *n.*

ex·ceed /iksee̅d/ *v.tr.* **1** be more or greater than. **2** go beyond or do more than is warranted by (a set limit, esp. of one's instructions or rights). **3** surpass.

ex·ceed·ing /iksee̅ding/ *adj.* **1** surpassing in amount or degree. **2** preeminent.

ex·ceed·ing·ly /iksee̅ding-lee/ *adv.* **1** very; to a great extent. **2** surpassingly; preeminently.

ex·cel /iksél/ *v.* (**excelled, excelling**) (often foll. by *in, at*) **1** *tr.* be superior to. **2** *intr.* be preeminent (*excels at games*).

ex·cel·lence /éksələns/ *n.* **1** the state of excelling; surpassing merit or quality. **2** the activity, etc., in which a person excels.

Ex·cel·len·cy /éksələnsee/ *n.* (*pl.* **-cies**) (usu. prec. by *Your, His, Her, Their*) a title used in addressing or referring to certain high officials, e.g., ambassadors, governors, etc.

ex·cel·lent /éksələnt/ *adj.* extremely good. □□ **ex·cel·lent·ly** *adv.*

ex·cel·si·or /iksélseeər/ *n.* soft wood shavings used esp. for stuffing and packing.

ex·cept /iksépt/ *v., prep., & conj.* •*v.tr.* (often as **excepted** *adj.* placed after object) exclude from a general statement, condition, etc. (*present company excepted*). •*prep.* (often foll. by *for* or *that*) not including; other than (*all failed except her*). •*conj. archaic* unless (*except he be born again*).

▶See note at ACCEPT.

ex·cept·ing /iksépting/ *prep.* = EXCEPT *prep.*

ex·cep·tion /iksépshən/ *n.* **1** the act or an instance of excepting; the state of being excepted. **2** a thing that has been or will be excepted. **3** an instance that does not follow a rule. □ **take exception** (often foll. by *to*) object; be resentful (about). **with the exception of** except; not including.

ex·cep·tion·a·ble /iksépshənəbəl/ *adj.* open to objection. □□ **ex·cep·tion·a·bly** *adv.*

▶**Exceptionable** means 'open to objection,' e.g., *There was nothing exceptionable in the evidence,* and is usually found in negative contexts. It is sometimes confused with the much more common **exceptional,** meaning 'unusual, outstanding.'

ex·cep·tion·al /iksépshənəl/ *adj.* **1** forming an exception. **2** unusual; not typical. **3** unusually good; outstanding. □□ **ex·cep·tion·al·ly** *adv.*

▶See note at EXCEPTIONABLE.

ex·cerpt *n. & v.* •*n.* /éksərpt/ a short extract from a book, motion picture, piece of music, etc. •*v.tr.* /iksérpt/ (also *absol.*) **1** take an excerpt or excerpts from (a book, etc.). **2** take (an extract) from a book, etc. □□ **ex·cerpt·i·ble** *adj.* **ex·cerp·tion** /–sórpshən/ *n.*

ex·cess /iksés, ékses/ *n. & adj.* •*n.* **1** the state or an instance of exceeding. **2** the amount by which one quantity or number exceeds another. **3** exceeding of a proper or permitted limit. **4 a** the overstepping of the accepted limits of moderation, esp. intemperance in eating or drinking. **b** (in *pl.*) outrageous or immoderate behavior. **5** an extreme or improper degree or extent (*an excess of cruelty*). **6** part of an insurance claim to be paid by the insured. •*attrib.adj.* usu. /ékses/ **1** that exceeds a limited or prescribed amount (*excess weight*). **2** required as extra payment (*excess postage*).

ex·ces·sive /iksésiv/ *adj.* **1** too much or too great. **2** more than what is normal or necessary. □□ **ex·ces·sive·ly** *adv.* **ex·ces·sive·ness** *n.*

ex·change /ikscháynj/ *n. & v.* •*n.* **1** the act or an instance of giving one thing and receiving another in its place. **2 a** the giving of money for its equivalent in the money of the same or another country. **b** the fee or percentage charged for this. **3** the central telephone office of a district, where connections are effected. **4** a place where merchants, bankers, etc., gather to transact business. **5 a** an office where certain information is given or a service provided, usu. involving two parties. **b** an employment office. **6** a system of settling debts without the use of money, by bills of exchange (see BILL OF EXCHANGE). **7 a** a short conversation, esp. a disagreement or quarrel. **b** a sequence of letters between correspondents. **8** (*attrib.*) forming part of an exchange, e.g., of personnel between institutions (*an exchange student*). •*v.* **1** *tr.* (often foll. by *for*) give or receive (one thing) in place of another. **2** *tr.* give and receive as equivalents (e.g., things or people, blows, information, etc.). **3** *intr.* (often foll. by *with*) make an exchange. □ **in exchange** (often foll. by *for*) as a thing exchanged (for). □□ **ex·change·a·ble** *adj.*

ex·change rate *n.* the value of one currency in terms of another.

ex·cheq·uer /ikschékər/ *n.* **1** (in Great Britain) the former government department in charge of national revenue. ▶Its functions now belong to the Treasury, although the name formally survives. **2** a royal or national treasury. **3** the money of a private individual or group.

ex·cise[1] /éksīz/ *n. & v.* •*n.* **1** a duty or tax levied on goods and commodities produced or sold within the country of origin. **2** a tax levied on certain licenses. •*v.tr.* **1** charge excise on (goods). **2** force (a person) to pay excise.

ex·cise[2] /iksíz/ *v.tr.* **1** remove (a passage of a book, etc.). **2** cut out (an organ, etc.) by surgery. □□ **ex·ci·sion** /iksízhən/ *n.*

ex·cit·a·ble /iksítəbəl/ *adj.* **1** (esp. of a person) easily excited. **2** (of an organism, tissue, etc.) responding to a stimulus, or susceptible to stimulation. ▫▫ **ex•cit•a•bil•i•ty** *n.* **ex•cit•a•bly** *adv.*

ex•cite /iksít/ *v.tr.* **1 a** rouse the feelings or emotions of (a person). **b** bring into play; rouse up (feelings, faculties, etc.). **c** arouse sexually. **2** provoke; bring about (an action or active condition). **3** promote the activity of (an organism, tissue, etc.) by stimulus. **4** *Physics* put (an atom, etc.) into a state of higher energy. ▫▫ **ex•cit•ed•ly** *adv.* **ex•cite•ment** *n.* **ex•cit•er** *n.* (esp. in sense 4).

ex•cit•ing /iksíting/ *adj.* arousing great interest or enthusiasm; stirring. ▫▫ **ex•cit•ing•ly** *adv.*

ex•claim /ikskláym/ *v.* **1** *intr.* cry out suddenly, esp. in anger, surprise, pain, etc. **2** *tr.* (foll. by *that*) utter by exclaiming.

ex•cla•ma•tion /éksklәmáyshәn/ *n.* **1** the act or an instance of exclaiming. **2** words exclaimed.

ex•cla•ma•tion point *n.* a punctuation mark (!) indicating an exclamation.

ex•clam•a•to•ry /iksklámәtawree/ *adj.* of or serving as an exclamation.

ex•clude /iksklŏŏd/ *v.tr.* **1** shut or keep out (a person or thing) from a place, group, privilege, etc. **2** expel and shut out. **3** remove from consideration. **4** prevent the occurrence of; make impossible (*excluded all doubt*). ▫▫ **ex•clud•a•ble** *adj.* **ex•clud•er** *n.*

ex•clu•sion /iksklŏŏzhәn/ *n.* the act or an instance of excluding; the state of being excluded. ▫ **to the exclusion of** so as to exclude. ▫▫ **ex•clu•sion•ar•y** *adj.*

ex•clu•sive /iksklŏŏsiv/ *adj.* & *n.* • *adj.* **1** excluding other things. **2** (*predic.*; foll. by *of*) not including; except for. **3** tending to exclude others, esp. socially. **4** catering for few or select customers; high-class. **5 a** (of a commodity) not obtainable elsewhere. **b** (of a newspaper article) not published elsewhere. **6** (*predic.*; foll. by *to*) restricted or limited to; existing or available only in. **7** (of terms, etc.) excluding all but what is specified. **8** employed or followed or held to the exclusion of all else (*exclusive rights*). • *n.* an article or story published by only one newspaper or periodical. ▫▫ **ex•clu•sive•ly** *adv.* **ex•clu•siv•i•ty** /éksklooosívitee/ *n.*

ex•com•mu•ni•cate *v., adj., & n. Eccl.* • *v.tr.* /ékskәmyŏŏnikayt/ officially exclude (a person) from participation in the sacraments, or from formal communion with the church. • *adj.* /ékskәmyŏŏnikәt/ excommunicated. • *n.* /ékskәmyŏŏnikәt/ an excommunicated person. ▫▫ **ex•com•mu•ni•ca•tion** /–káyshәn/ *n.*

ex-con /ékskón/ *n. colloq.* an ex-convict.

ex•co•ri•ate /ekskáwreeayt/ *v.tr.* **1** remove part of the skin of (a person, etc.) by abrasion. **2** censure severely. ▫▫ **ex•co•ri•a•tion** /–áyshәn/ *n.*

ex•cre•ment /ékskrimәnt/ *n.* (in *sing.* or *pl.*) feces. ▫▫ **ex•cre•men•tal** /–mént'l/ *adj.*

ex•cres•cence /ikskrésәns/ *n.* **1** an abnormal or morbid outgrowth on the body or a plant. **2** an ugly addition. ▫▫ **ex•cres•cent** /–sәnt/ *adj.*

ex•cre•ta /ikskréetә/ *n.pl.* waste discharged from the body, esp. feces and urine.

ex•crete /ikskréet/ *v.tr.* (also *absol.*) (of an animal or plant) separate and expel (waste matter). ▫▫ **ex•cre•tion** /–kréeshәn/ *n.* **ex•cre•to•ry** /ékskrәtáwree/ *adj.*

ex•cru•ci•at•ing *adj.* causing acute mental or physical pain. ▫▫ **ex•cru•ci•at•ing•ly** *adv.*

ex•cul•pate /ékskulpayt, ikskúl–/ *v.tr. formal* **1** free from blame. **2** (foll. by *from*) clear (a person) of a charge. ▫▫ **ex•cul•pa•tion** /–páyshәn/ *n.* **ex•cul•pa•to•ry** /–kúlpәtáwree/ *adj.*

ex•cur•sion /ikskә́rzhәn/ *n.* a short journey for pleasure, with return to the starting point. ▫▫ **ex•cur•sion•ar•y** *adj.* **ex•cur•sion•ist** *n.*

ex•cuse *v. & n.* • *v.tr.* /ikskyŏŏz/ **1** attempt to lessen the blame attaching to (a person, act, or fault). **2** (of a fact) serve in mitigation of (a person or act). **3** obtain exemption for (a person or oneself). **4** (foll. by *from*) release (a person) from a duty, etc. (*excused from kitchen duties*). **5** overlook or forgive (a fault or offense). **6** (foll. by *for*) forgive (a person) for a fault. **7** not insist upon (what is due). **8** *refl.* apologize for leaving. • *n.* /ikskyŏŏs/ **1** a reason put forward to mitigate or justify an offense, fault, etc. **2** an apology. **3** (foll. by *for*) a poor or inadequate example of (*a pathetic excuse for a training video*). **4** the action of excusing; indulgence; pardon. ▫ **be excused** be allowed to leave a room, etc., e.g., to go to the bathroom. **excuse me** a polite apology for an interruption, etc., or for disagreeing. ▫▫ **ex•cus•a•ble** /–kyŏŏzәbәl/ *adj.* **ex•cus•a•bly** *adv.* **ex•cus•a•to•ry** /–kyŏŏzәtáwree/ *adj.*

ex•ec /igzék/ *n.* an executive.

ex•e•cra•ble /éksikrәbәl/ *adj.* abominable; detestable. ▫▫ **ex•e•cra•bly** *adv.*

ex•e•crate /éksikrayt/ *v.* **1** *tr.* express or feel abhorrence for. **2** *tr.* curse (a person or thing). **3** *intr.* utter curses. ▫▫ **ex•e•cra•tion** /–kráyshәn/ *n.*

ex•e•cute /éksikyoot/ *v.tr.* **1 a** carry out a sentence of death on (a condemned person). **b** kill as a political act. **2** carry into effect; perform (a plan, duty, command, operation, etc.). **3 a** carry out a design for (a product of art or skill). **b** perform (a musical composition, dance, etc.). **4** make (a legal instrument) valid by signing, sealing, etc. **5** put into effect (a judicial sentence, the terms of a will, etc.). ▫▫ **ex•e•cut•a•ble** *adj.*

ex•e•cu•tion /éksikyŏŏshәn/ *n.* **1** the carrying out of a sentence of death. **2** the act or an instance of carrying out or performing something. **3** technique or style of performance in the arts, esp. music. **4 a** seizure of the property or person of a debtor in default of payment. **b** a judicial writ enforcing a judgment. ▫▫ **ex•e•cu•tion•ar•y** *adj.*

ex•e•cu•tion•er /éksikyŏŏshәnәr/ *n.* an official who carries out a sentence of death.

ex•ec•u•tive /igzékyәtiv/ *n. & adj.* • *n.* **1** a person or body with managerial or administrative responsibility in a business organization, etc. **2** a branch of a government or organization concerned with executing laws, agreements, etc., or with other administration or management. • *adj.* **1** concerned with executing laws, agreements, etc., or with other administration or management. **2** relating to or having the function of executing. ▫▫ **ex•ec•u•tive•ly** *adv.*

ex•ec•u•tor /igzékyәtәr/ *n.* (*fem.* **executrix** /–triks/, *pl.* **-trices** /–tríseez/or **-trixes**) a person appointed by a testator to carry out the terms of his or her will. ▫▫ **ex•ec•u•tor•ship** *n.* **ex•ec•u•to•ry** *adj.*

ex•e•ge•sis /éksijéesis/ *n.* (*pl.* **exegeses** /–seez/) critical explanation of a text, esp. of Scripture. ▫▫ **ex•e•gete** /éksijeet/ *n.* **ex•e•get•ic** /–jétik/ *adj.* **ex•e•get•i•cal** *adj.*

ex•em•plar /igzémplәr, –plaar/ *n.* **1** a model or pattern. **2** a typical parallel instance.

ex•em•pla•ry /igzémplәree/ *adj.* **1** fit to be imitated; outstandingly good. **2 a** serving as a warning. **b** *Law* (of damages) exceeding the amount needed for simple compensation. **3** illustrative; representative.

ex•em•pli•fy /igzémplifī/ *v.tr.* (**-fies, -fied**) **1** illustrate by example. **2** be an example of. ▫▫ **ex•em•pli•fi•ca•tion** /–fikáyshәn/ *n.*

ex•empt /igzémpt/ *adj., n., & v.* • *adj.* **1** free from an obligation or liability, etc., imposed on others. **2** (foll. by *from*) not liable to. • *n.* a person who is exempt, esp. from payment of tax. • *v.tr.* (usu. foll. by *from*) free from an obligation, esp. one imposed on others. ▫▫ **ex•emp•tion** /–zémpshәn/ *n.*

ex•er•cise /éksәrsīz/ *n. & v.* • *n.* **1** activity requiring physical effort, done esp. as training or to sustain or improve health. **2** mental or spiritual activity, esp. as practice to develop a skill. **3** (often in *pl.*) a particular task or set of tasks devised as practice in a technique, etc. **4 a** the use or application of a mental faculty, right, etc. **b** practice of an ability, quality, etc. **5** (often in *pl.*) military drill or maneuvers. **6** (foll. by *in*) a process directed at or concerned with something specified (*was an exercise in public relations*). • *v.* **1** *tr.* use or apply (a faculty, right, influence, restraint, etc.). **2** *tr.* perform (a function). **3 a** *intr.* take (esp. physical) exercise; do exercises. **b** *tr.* provide (an animal) with exercise. **c** *tr.* train (a person). **4** *tr.* **a** tax the powers of. **b** perplex; worry.

ex•ert /igzə́rt/ *v.tr.* **1** exercise; bring to bear (a quality, influence, etc.). **2** *refl.* (often foll. by *for*, or *to* + infin.) use one's efforts or endeavors; strive. ▫▫ **ex•er•tion** /–zə́rshən/ *n.*

ex•e•unt /ékseeənt, –o͝ont/ *v.intr.* (as a stage direction) (actors) leave the stage.

ex•fo•li•ate /eksfṓleeayt/ *v.intr.* **1** (of bone, the skin, a mineral, etc.) come off in scales or layers. **2** (of a tree) throw off layers of bark. ▫▫ **ex•fo•li•a•tion** /–áyshən/ *n.*

ex•ha•la•tion /éks-həláyshən/ *n.* **1 a** an expiration of air. **b** a puff of breath. **2** a mist; vapor.

ex•hale /eks-háyl/ *v.* **1** *tr.* (also *absol.*) breathe out (esp. air or smoke) from the lungs. **2** *tr.* & *intr.* give off or be given off in vapor.

ex•haust /igzáwst/ *v.* & *n.* • *v.tr.* **1** consume or use up the whole of. **2** (often as **exhausted** *adj.* or **exhausting** *adj.*) tire out. **3** study or expound on (a subject) completely. **4** (often foll. by *of*) empty (a vessel, etc.) of its contents. **5** (often as **exhausted** *adj.*) drain of strength or resources; (of land) make barren. • *n.* **1 a** waste gases, etc., expelled from an engine after combustion. **b** (also **ex•haust pipe**) the pipe or system by which these are expelled. **c** the process of expulsion of these gases. **2 a** the production of an outward current of air by the creation of a partial vacuum. **b** an apparatus for this. ▫▫ **ex•haust•er** *n.* **ex•haust•i•ble** *adj.*

ex•haus•tion /igzáwschən/ *n.* **1** the action or process of draining or emptying something; the state of being depleted or emptied. **2** a total loss of strength or vitality. **3** the process of establishing a conclusion by eliminating alternatives.

ex•haus•tive /igzáwstiv/ *adj.* **1** thorough; comprehensive. **2** tending to exhaust a subject. ▫▫ **ex•haus•tive•ly** *adv.* **ex•haus•tive•ness** *n.*

ex•hib•it /igzíbit/ *v.* & *n.* • *v.tr.* **1** show or reveal publicly (for amusement, in competition, etc.). **2 a** show; display. **b** manifest (a quality). **3** submit for consideration. • *n.* **1** a thing or collection of things in an exhibition. **2** a document or other item produced in a court of law as evidence. ▫▫ **ex•hib•i•to•ry** *adj.*

ex•hi•bi•tion /éksibíshən/ *n.* **1** a display (esp. public) of works of art, industrial products, etc. **2** the act or an instance of exhibiting; the state of being exhibited.

ex•hi•bi•tion•ism /éksibíshənizəm/ *n.* **1** a tendency toward display or extravagant behavior. **2** *Psychol.* a mental condition characterized by the compulsion to display one's genitals in public. ▫▫ **ex•hi•bi•tion•ist** *n.*

ex•hib•i•tor /igzíbitər/ *n.* a person who provides an item or items for an exhibition.

ex•hil•a•rate /igzílərayt/ *v.tr.* (often as **exhilarating** *adj.* or **exhilarated** *adj.*) affect with great liveliness or joy; raise the spirits of. ▫▫ **ex•hil•a•ra•tion** /–ráyshən/ *n.*

ex•hort /igzáwrt/ *v.tr.* (often foll. by *to* + infin.) urge or advise strongly or earnestly. ▫▫ **ex•hor•ta•tion** /égzawrtáyshən/ *n.*

ex•hume /igzo͞om, –zyo͞om, eks-hyo͞om/ *v.tr.* dig out; unearth (esp. a buried corpse). ▫▫ **ex•hu•ma•tion** *n.*

ex hy•poth•e•si /éks hīpóthəsee/ *adv.* according to the hypothesis proposed.

ex•i•gen•cy /éksijənsee, igzíj–/ *n.* (*pl.* **-cies**) (also **ex•i•gence** /éksijəns/) **1** an urgent need or demand. **2** an emergency. ▫▫ **ex•i•gent** /éksijənt/ *adj.*

ex•ig•u•ous /igzígyo͞oəs, iksíg–/ *adj.* scanty; small. ▫▫ **ex•i•gu•i•ty** /éksigyo͞oitee/ *n.* **ex•ig•u•ous•ly** *adv.*

ex•ile /éksīl, égzīl/ *n.* & *v.* • *n.* **1** expulsion from one's native land or (**internal exile**) native town, etc. **2** long absence abroad, esp. enforced. **3** a person expelled or long absent from his or her native country. • *v.tr.* (foll. by *from*) officially expel (a person) from his or her native country or town, etc. ▫▫ **ex•il•ic** /–sílik, –zílik/ *adj.*

ex•ist /igzíst/ *v.intr.* **1** have a place as part of objective reality. **2 a** have being under specified conditions. **b** (foll. by *as*) exist in the form of. **3** (of circumstances, etc.) occur; be found. **4** live with no pleasure under adverse conditions. **5** continue in being; maintain life (*can hardly exist on this salary*). **6** be alive; live.

ex•ist•ence /igzístəns/ *n.* **1** the fact or condition of being or existing. **2** continued being; the manner of one's existing or living, esp. under adverse conditions (*a wretched existence*). **3** an existing thing. **4** all that exists.

ex•ist•ent /igzístənt/ *adj.* existing; actual; current.

ex•is•ten•tial /égzisténshəl/ *adj.* **1** of or relating to existence. **2** *Logic* (of a proposition, etc.) affirming or implying the existence of a thing. **3** *Philos.* concerned with existence, esp. with human existence as viewed by existentialism. ▫▫ **ex•is•ten•tial•ly** *adv.*

ex•is•ten•tial•ism /égzisténshəlizəm/ *n.* a philosophical theory emphasizing the existence of the individual person as a free and responsible agent determining his or her own development. ▫▫ **ex•is•ten•tial•ist** *n.*

ex•it /égzit, éksit/ *n.* & *v.* • *n.* **1** a passage or door by which to leave a room, building, etc. **2 a** the act of going out. **b** the right to go out. **3** a place where vehicles can leave a highway or major road. **4** the departure of an actor from the stage. **5** death. • *v.intr.* **1** go out of a room, building, etc. **2** (as a stage direction) (an actor) leaves the stage (*exit Macbeth*).

ex•it per•mit *n.* (or **visa**, etc.) authorization to leave a particular country.

ex•it poll *n.* a survey usu. of voters leaving voting booths, used to predict an election's outcome, analyze voting patterns, etc.

ex•o•crine /éksəkrin, –kreen, –krīn/ *adj.* (of a gland) secreting through a duct (cf. ENDOCRINE).

ex•o•dus /éksədəs/ *n.* **1** a mass departure of people. **2** (**Exodus**) *Bibl.* **a** the departure of the Israelites from Egypt. **b** the book of the Old Testament relating this.

ex of•fi•ci•o /eksəfísheeō/ *adv.* & *adj.* by virtue of one's office or status.

ex•og•a•my /eksógəmee/ *n.* **1** *Anthropol.* marriage of a man outside his own tribe. **2** *Biol.* the fusion of reproductive cells from distantly related or unrelated individuals. ▫▫ **ex•og•a•mous** *adj.*

ex•og•e•nous /eksójinəs/ *adj. Biol.* growing or originating from outside. ▫▫ **ex•og•e•nous•ly** *adv.*

ex•on•er•ate /igzónərayt/ *v.tr.* (often foll. by *from*) **1** free or declare free from blame, etc. **2** release from a duty, etc. ▫▫ **ex•on•er•a•tion** /–ráyshən/ *n.*

ex•or•bi•tant /igzáwrbit'nt/ *adj.* (of a price, demand, etc.) grossly excessive. ▫▫ **ex•or•bi•tance** /–təns/ *n.* **ex•or•bi•tant•ly** *adv.*

ex•or•cize /éksawrsīz, –sər–/ *v.tr.* **1** expel (a supposed evil spirit) by invocation, etc. **2** (often foll. by *of*) free (a person or place) of a supposed evil spirit. ▫▫ **ex•or•cism** /–sízəm/ *n.* **ex•or•cist** *n.*

ex•o•skel•e•ton /éksōskélit'n/ *n.* a rigid external covering for the body in certain animals, esp. arthropods. ▫▫ **ex•o•skel•e•tal** *adj.*

ex•ot•ic /igzótik/ *adj.* & *n.* • *adj.* **1** introduced from a foreign (esp. tropical) country (*exotic fruits*). **2** attractively or remarkably strange or unusual; bizarre. **3** (of a fuel, metal, etc.) of a kind newly brought into use. • *n.* an exotic person or thing. ▫▫ **ex·ot·i·cal·ly** *adv.*

ex·ot·i·ca /igzótikə/ *n.pl.* remarkably strange or rare objects.

ex·ot·ic danc·er *n.* a striptease dancer.

ex·pand /ikspánd/ *v.* **1** *tr. & intr.* increase in size or importance. **2** *intr.* (often foll. by *on*) give a fuller description or account. **3** *intr.* become more genial or effusive. **4** *tr.* set or write out in full. **5** *tr. & intr.* spread out flat. ▫▫ **ex·pand·a·ble** *adj.* **ex·pand·er** *n.*

ex·panse /ikspáns/ *n.* **1** a wide continuous area or extent of land, space, etc. **2** an amount of expansion.

ex·pan·sion /ikspánshən/ *n.* **1** the act or an instance of expanding; the state of being expanded. **2** enlargement of the scale or scope of (esp. commercial) operations. **3** increase in the amount of a country's territory or area of control. **4** an increase in the volume of fuel, etc., on combustion in the cylinder of an engine. **5** the action of making or becoming greater in area, bulk, capacity, etc. ▫▫ **ex·pan·sion·ar·y** *adj.* **ex·pan·sion·ist** *n.*

ex·pan·sive /ikspánsiv/ *adj.* **1** able or tending to expand. **2** extensive; wide-ranging. **3** (of a person, feelings, or speech) effusive; open. ▫▫ **ex·pan·sive·ly** *adv.* **ex·pan·sive·ness** *n.* **ex·pan·siv·i·ty** /–sívitee/ *n.*

ex·pa·ti·ate /ikspáysheeayt/ *v.intr.* (usu. foll. by *on, upon*) speak or write at length or in detail. ▫▫ **ex·pa·ti·a·tion** /–áyshən/ *n.*

ex·pa·tri·ate *adj., n., & v.* • *adj.* /ékspáytreeət/ **1** living abroad. **2** exiled. • *n.* /ekspáytreeət/ an expatriate person. • *v.tr.* /ekspáytreeayt/ **1** expel (a person) from his or her native country. **2** *refl.* withdraw (oneself) from one's citizenship or allegiance. ▫▫ **ex·pa·tri·a·tion** /–áyshən/ *n.*

ex·pect /ikspékt/ *v.tr.* **1** (often foll. by *to* + infin., or *that* + clause) **a** regard as likely. **b** (often foll. by *of*) look for as appropriate or one's due (from a person) (*I expect cooperation*). **2** *colloq.* (often foll. by *that* + clause) think; suppose (*I expect we'll be on time*). ▫ **be expecting** *colloq.* be pregnant. ▫▫ **ex·pect·a·ble** *adj.*

ex·pect·an·cy /ikspéktənsee/ *n.* (*pl.* **-cies**) **1** a state of expectation. **2** a prospect, esp. of future possession. **3** (foll. by *of*) a prospective chance.

ex·pect·ant /ikspéktənt/ *adj. & n.* • *adj.* **1** (often foll. by *of*) expecting. **2** having the expectation of possession, status, etc. **3** (*attrib.*) expecting a baby (said of the mother or father). • *n.* **1** one who expects. **2** a candidate for office, etc. ▫▫ **ex·pect·ant·ly** *adv.*

ex·pec·ta·tion /ékspektáyshən/ *n.* **1** the act or an instance of expecting or looking forward. **2** something expected or hoped for. **3** (foll. by *of*) the probability of an event. **4** (in *pl.*) one's prospects of inheritance.

ex·pec·to·rant /ikspéktərənt/ *adj. & n.* • *adj.* causing the coughing out of phlegm, etc. • *n.* an expectorant medicine.

ex·pec·to·rate /ikspéktərayt/ *v.tr.* (also *absol.*) cough or spit out (phlegm, etc.) from the chest or lungs. ▫▫ **ex·pec·to·ra·tion** /–ráyshən/ *n.*

ex·pe·di·ent /ikspeédeeənt/ *adj. & n.* • *adj.* **1** advantageous; advisable on practical rather than moral grounds. **2** suitable; appropriate. • *n.* a means of attaining an end. ▫▫ **ex·pe·di·ence** /–əns/ *n.* **ex·pe·di·en·cy** *n.* **ex·pe·di·ent·ly** *adv.*

ex·pe·dite /ékspidīt/ *v.tr.* **1** assist the progress of; hasten (an action, process, etc.). **2** accomplish (business) quickly. ▫▫ **ex·pe·dit·er** *n.*

ex·pe·di·tion /ékspidíshən/ *n.* **1** a journey or voyage for a particular purpose, esp. exploration, scientific research, or war. **2** the personnel or ships, etc., undertaking this. **3** promptness; speed. ▫▫ **ex·pe·di·tion·ar·y** /ékspidíshəneree/ *adj.*

ex·pe·di·tious /ékspidíshəs/ *adj.* **1** acting or done with speed and efficiency. **2** suited for speedy performance. ▫▫ **ex·pe·di·tious·ly** *adv.*

ex·pel /ikspél/ *v.tr.* (**expelled, expelling**) (often foll. by *from*) **1** deprive (a person) of the membership of or involvement in (a school, society, etc.). **2** force out or eject (a thing from its container, etc.). **3** order or force to leave a building, etc.

ex·pend /ikspénd/ *v.tr.* spend or use up (money, time, etc.).

ex·pend·a·ble /ikspéndəbəl/ *adj.* **1** that may be sacrificed or dispensed with, esp. to achieve a purpose. **2 a** not regarded as worth preserving or saving. **b** unimportant; insignificant. **3** not normally reused. ▫▫ **ex·pend·a·bil·i·ty** *n.*

ex·pend·i·ture /ikspéndichər/ *n.* **1** the process or an instance of spending or using up. **2** a thing (esp. a sum of money) expended.

ex·pense /ikspéns/ *n.* **1** cost incurred; payment of money. **2** (usu. in *pl.*) **a** costs incurred in doing a particular job, etc. (*will pay your expenses*). **b** an amount paid to reimburse this. **3** a thing that is a cause of much expense (*the house is a real expense to run*). ▫ **at the expense of** so as to cause loss or damage or discredit to.

ex·pense ac·count *n.* a list of an employee's expenses payable by the employer.

ex·pen·sive /ikspénsiv/ *adj.* **1** costing much. **2** making a high charge. **3** causing much expense (*has expensive tastes*). ▫▫ **ex·pen·sive·ly** *adv.* **ex·pen·sive·ness** *n.*

ex·pe·ri·ence /ikspeéreeəns/ *n. & v.* • *n.* **1** actual observation of or practical acquaintance with facts or events. **2** knowledge or skill resulting from this. **3 a** an event regarded as affecting one (*an unpleasant experience*). **b** the fact or process of being so affected (*learned by experience*). • *v.tr.* **1** have experience of; undergo. **2** feel or be affected by (an emotion, etc.).

ex·pe·ri·enced /ikspeéreeənst/ *adj.* **1** having had much experience. **2** skilled from experience (*an experienced driver*).

ex·pe·ri·en·tial /ikspeéree-énshəl/ *adj.* involving or based on experience. ▫▫ **ex·pe·ri·en·tial·ly** *adv.*

ex·per·i·ment /ikspérimənt/ *n. & v.* • *n.* **1** a procedure adopted on the chance of its succeeding, for testing a hypothesis, etc., or to demonstrate a known fact. **2** (foll. by *of*) a test or trial of. • *v.intr.* (often foll. by *on, with*) make an experiment. ▫▫ **ex·per·i·men·ta·tion** *n.* **ex·per·i·ment·er** *n.*

ex·per·i·men·tal /ikspérimént'l/ *adj.* **1** based on or making use of experiment (*experimental psychology*). **2 a** used in experiments. **b** serving or resulting from (esp. incomplete) experiment; tentative, provisional. **3** based on experience, not on authority or conjecture. ▫▫ **ex·per·i·men·tal·ism** *n.* **ex·per·i·men·tal·ist** *n.* **ex·per·i·men·tal·ly** *adv.*

ex·pert /ékspərt/ *adj. & n.* • *adj.* **1** (often foll. by *at, in*) having special knowledge or skill. **2** involving or resulting from this (*expert evidence; an expert piece of work*). • *n.* (often foll. by *at, in*) a person having special knowledge or skill. ▫▫ **ex·pert·ly** *adv.* **ex·pert·ness** *n.*

ex·per·tise /ékspərteéz/ *n.* expert skill, knowledge, or judgment.

ex·pert·ize /ékspərtīz/ *v.* **1** *intr.* give an expert opinion. **2** *tr.* give an expert opinion concerning.

ex·pi·ate /ékspeeayt/ *v.tr.* **1** pay the penalty for (wrongdoing). **2** make amends for. ▫▫ **ex·pi·a·tion** /–áyshən/ *n.* **ex·pi·a·to·ry** /–peeətawree/ *adj.*

ex·pi·ra·tion /ékspəráyshən/ *n.* **1** breathing out. **2** the end of the validity or duration of something.

ex·pire /ikspír/ *v.* **1** *intr.* (of a period of time, validity, etc.) come to an end. **2** *intr.* (of a document, authorization, etc.) cease to be valid. **3** *intr.* (of a person) die.

4 *tr.* (usu. foll. by *from*; also *absol.*) exhale (air, etc.) from the lungs.

ex·plain /ikspláyn/ *v.tr.* **1** make clear or intelligible (also *absol.*: *let me explain*). **2** (foll. by *that* + clause) say by way of explanation. **3** account for (one's conduct, etc.). □ **explain away** minimize the significance of (a difficulty or mistake) by explanation. □□ **ex·plain·a·ble** *adj.* **ex·plain·er** *n.*

ex·pla·na·tion /éksplənáyshən/ *n.* **1** the act or an instance of explaining. **2** a statement or circumstance that explains something. **3** a declaration made with a view to mutual understanding or reconciliation.

ex·plan·a·to·ry /iksplánətawree/ *adj.* serving or intended to serve to explain. □□ **ex·plan·a·to·ri·ly** *adv.*

ex·ple·tive /éksplətiv/ *n.* a swearword or other expression, used in an exclamation.

expletive late Middle English (as an adjective): from late Latin *expletivus*, from *explere* 'fill out,' from *ex-* 'out' + *plere* 'fill.' The general noun sense 'word used merely to fill out a sentence' (early 17th cent.) was applied specifically to an oath or swear word in the early 19th cent.

ex·pli·ca·ble /éksplikəbəl, iksplík–/ *adj.* that can be explained.

ex·pli·cate /éksplikayt/ *v.tr.* **1** develop the meaning of (an idea, principle, etc.). **2** explain (esp. a literary text). □□ **ex·pli·ca·tion** /–káyshən/ *n.* **ex·pli·ca·tive** /éksplikaytiv, iksplíkətiv/ *adj.* **ex·pli·ca·tor** *n.* **ex·pli·ca·to·ry** /éksplikətáwree, iksplík–/ *adj.*

ex·plic·it /iksplísit/ *adj.* **1** expressly stated; leaving nothing merely implied. **2** (of knowledge, a notion, etc.) definite; clear. **3** (of a person, book, etc.) outspoken. □□ **ex·plic·it·ly** *adv.* **ex·plic·it·ness** *n.*

ex·plode /iksplṓd/ *v.* **1 a** *intr.* (of gas, gunpowder, a bomb, a boiler, etc.) expand suddenly with a loud noise owing to a release of internal energy. **b** *tr.* cause (a bomb, etc.) to explode. **2** *intr.* give vent suddenly to emotion, esp. anger. **3** *intr.* (of a population, etc.) increase suddenly or rapidly. **4** *tr.* show (a theory, etc.) to be baseless. **5** *tr.* (as **exploded** *adj.*) (of a drawing, etc.) showing the components of a mechanism as if separated but in the normal relative positions.

ex·ploit *n.* & *v.* • *n.* /éksployt/ a daring feat. • *v.tr.* /iksplóyt/ **1** make use of (a resource, etc.); derive benefit from. **2** usu. *derog.* utilize or take advantage of (esp. a person) for one's own ends. □□ **ex·ploit·a·ble** *adj.* **ex·ploi·ta·tion** *n.* **ex·ploi·ta·tive** /iksplóytətiv/ *adj.* **ex·ploit·er** *n.* **ex·ploi·tive** *adj.*

ex·plo·ra·tion /éksploráyshən/ *n.* **1** an act or instance of exploring. **2** the process of exploring. □□ **ex·plo·ra·tion·al** *adj.*

ex·plor·a·to·ry /ikspláwrətawree/ *adj.* **1** (of discussion, etc.) preliminary. **2** of or concerning exploration or investigation (*exploratory surgery*).

ex·plore /ikspláwr/ *v.tr.* **1** travel through (a country, etc.) in order to learn about it. **2** inquire into. **3** *Surgery* examine (a part of the body) in detail. □□ **ex·plor·a·tive** /–rətiv/ *adj.* **ex·plor·er** /ikspláwrər/ *n.*

ex·plo·sion /iksplṓzhən/ *n.* **1** the act or an instance of exploding. **2** a loud noise caused by something exploding. **3 a** a sudden outburst of noise. **b** a sudden outbreak of feeling, esp. anger. **4** a rapid or sudden increase.

ex·plo·sive /iksplṓsiv/ *adj.* & *n.* • *adj.* **1** able or tending or likely to explode. **2** likely to cause a violent outburst, etc.; (of a situation, etc.) dangerously tense. • *n.* an explosive substance. □□ **ex·plo·sive·ly** *adv.* **ex·plo·sive·ness** *n.*

ex·po /ékspō/ *n.* (also **Ex·po**) (*pl.* **-pos**) a large international exhibition.

ex·po·nent /ikspṓnənt/ *n.* **1** a person who favors or promotes an idea, etc. **2** a representative or practitioner of an activity, profession, etc. **3** a person who explains or interprets something. **4** *Math.* a raised symbol or expression beside a numeral indicating how many times it is to be multiplied by itself (e.g., $2^3 = 2 \times 2 \times 2$).

ex·po·nen·tial /ékspənénshəl/ *adj.* **1** *Math.* of or indicated by a mathematical exponent. **2** (of an increase, etc.) more and more rapid. □□ **ex·po·nen·tial·ly** *adv.*

ex·port *v.* & *n.* • *v.tr.* /ekspáwrt, éks–/ send out (goods or services) esp. for sale in another country. • *n.* /ékspawrt/ **1** the process of exporting. **2 a** an exported article or service. **b** (in *pl.*) an amount exported (*exports exceeded $50 billion*). **3** (*attrib.*) suitable for export, esp. of better quality. □□ **ex·port·a·ble** *adj.* **ex·port·a·bil·i·ty** *n.* **ex·por·ta·tion** *n.* **ex·port·er** *n.*

ex·pose /ikspṓz/ *v.tr.* **1** leave uncovered or unprotected, esp. from the weather. **2** (foll. by *to*) **a** cause to be liable to or in danger of (*was exposed to great danger*). **b** lay open to the action or influence of; introduce to. **3** (as **exposed** *adj.*) **a** (foll. by *to*) open to; unprotected from (*exposed to the east*). **b** vulnerable; risky. **4** *Photog.* subject (film) to light, esp. by operation of a camera. **5** reveal the identity or fact of (esp. a person or thing disapproved of or guilty of crime, etc.). **6** disclose; make public. **7** exhibit; display. **8** put up for sale. □ **expose oneself** display one's body, esp. the genitals, publicly and indecently. □□ **ex·pos·er** *n.*

ex·pos·é /ekspōzáy/ *n.* (also **ex·pose**) **1** an orderly statement of facts. **2** the act or an instance of revealing something discreditable.

ex·po·si·tion /ékspəzíshən/ *n.* **1** an explanatory statement or account. **2** an explanation or commentary. **3** *Mus.* the part of a movement in which the principal themes are first presented. **4** a large public exhibition. □□ **ex·po·si·tion·al** *adj.*

ex·pos·i·tor /ikspózitər/ *n.* an expounder or interpreter. □□ **ex·pos·i·to·ry** *adj.*

ex·pos·tu·late /ikspóschəlayt/ *v.intr.* (often foll. by *with* a person) make a protest; remonstrate. □□ **ex·pos·tu·la·tion** /–láyshən/ *n.* **ex·pos·tu·la·to·ry** /–lətáwree/ *adj.*

ex·po·sure /ikspṓzhər/ *n.* **1** (foll. by *to*) the act or condition of exposing or being exposed. **2** the condition of being exposed to the elements, esp. in severe conditions (*died from exposure*). **3** the revelation of an identity or fact, esp. when concealed or likely to find disapproval. **4** *Photog.* **a** the action of exposing film, etc., to the light. **b** the duration of this action. **c** the area of film, etc., affected by it. **5** an aspect or outlook (*has a fine southern exposure*). **6** experience, esp. of a specified kind of work.

ex·pound /ikspównd/ *v.tr.* **1** set out in detail (a doctrine, etc.). **2** explain or interpret. □□ **ex·pound·er** *n.*

ex·press[1] /iksprés/ *v.tr.* **1** represent or make known (thought, feelings, etc.) in words or by gestures, conduct, etc. **2** *refl.* say what one thinks or means. **3** esp. *Math.* represent by symbols. **4** squeeze out (liquid or air). □□ **ex·press·er** *n.* **ex·press·i·ble** *adj.*

ex·press[2] /iksprés/ *adj., adv., n.,* & *v.* • *adj.* **1** operating at high speed. **2** also /ékspres/ definitely stated, not merely implied. **3 a** done, made, or sent for a special purpose. **b** (of messages or goods) delivered by a special messenger or service. • *adv.* **1** at high speed. **2** by express messenger or train. • *n.* **1** an express train or messenger. **2** a company undertaking the transport of packages, etc. • *v.tr.* send by express messenger or delivery. □□ **ex·press·ly** *adv.* (in senses 2 and 3a of *adj.*)

ex·pres·sion /ikspréshən/ *n.* **1** the act or an instance of expressing. **2 a** a word or phrase expressed. **b** manner or means of expressing in language; wording; diction.

3 *Math.* a collection of symbols expressing a quantity. 4 a person's facial appearance or intonation of voice, esp. as indicating feeling. 5 depiction of feeling, movement, etc., in art. 6 conveying of feeling in the performance of a piece of music. ◻◻ **ex•pres•sion•less** *adj.*

ex•pres•sion•ism /ikspréshənizəm/ *n.* a style of painting, music, drama, etc., in which an artist or writer seeks to express emotional experience rather than impressions of the external world. ◻◻ **ex•pres•sion•ist** *n. & adj.* **ex•pres•sion•is•tic** *adj.* **ex•pres•sion•is•ti•cal•ly** *adv.*

ex•pres•sive /iksprésiv/ *adj.* 1 full of expression (*an expressive look*). 2 (foll. by *of*) serving to express (*words expressive of contempt*). ◻◻ **ex•pres•sive•ly** *adv.* **ex•pres•sive•ness** *n.* **ex•pres•siv•i•ty** /–sívitee/ *n.*

ex•pres•so var. of ESPRESSO.

ex•press•way /iksprésway/ *n.* a divided highway for high-speed traffic.

ex•pro•pri•ate /eksprṓpreeayt/ *v.tr.* 1 take away (property) from its owner. 2 (foll. by *from*) dispossess. ◻◻ **ex•pro•pri•a•tion** /–áyshən/ *n.* **ex•pro•pri•a•tor** *n.*

ex•pul•sion /ikspúlshən/ *n.* the act or an instance of expelling; the process of being expelled.

ex•punge /ikspúnj/ *v.tr.* (foll. by *from*) erase; remove (esp. a passage from a book or a name from a list).

ex•pur•gate /ékspərgayt/ *v.tr.* remove matter thought to be objectionable from (a book, etc.). ◻◻ **ex•pur•ga•tion** /–gáyshən/ *n.* **ex•pur•ga•tor** *n.*

ex•quis•ite /ékskwizit, ikskwízit/ *adj. & n.* • *adj.* 1 extremely beautiful or delicate. 2 acute; keenly felt (*exquisite pleasure*). 3 **a** keen; highly sensitive or discriminating (*exquisite taste*). **b** elaborately devised or accomplished; consummate; perfect. • *n.* a person of refined (esp. affected) tastes. ◻◻ **ex•quis•ite•ly** *adv.*

ex•tant /ékstənt, ekstánt/ *adj.* (esp. of a document, etc.) still existing; surviving.

ex•tem•po•ra•ne•ous /ikstémpəráyneeəs/ *adj.* spoken or done without preparation. ◻◻ **ex•tem•po•ra•ne•ous•ly** *adv.*

ex•tem•po•rar•y /ikstémpəreree/ *adj.* = EXTEMPORANEOUS. ◻◻ **ex•tem•po•rar•i•ly** /–ráirəlee/ *adv.*

ex•tem•po•re /ikstémpəree/ *adj. & adv.* 1 without preparation. 2 offhand.

ex•tem•po•rize /ikstémpərīz/ *v.tr.* (also *absol.*) compose or produce (music, a speech, etc.) without preparation; improvise. ◻◻ **ex•tem•po•ri•za•tion** *n.*

ex•tend /iksténd/ *v.* 1 *tr. & intr.* lengthen or make larger in space or time. 2 **a** *tr.* stretch or lay out at full length. **b** *tr. & intr.* (often foll. by *over*) (cause to) stretch or span over a period of time. 3 *intr. & tr.* (foll. by *to, over*) reach or be or make continuous over a certain area. 4 *intr.* (foll. by *to*) have a certain scope (*the permit does not extend to camping*). 5 *tr.* offer or accord (an invitation, hospitality, kindness, etc.). 6 *tr.* (usu. *refl.* or in *passive*) tax the powers of (an athlete, horse, etc.) to the utmost. ◻◻ **ex•tend•a•ble** *adj.* **ex•tend•a•bil•i•ty** *n.* **ex•tend•i•ble** *adj.* **ex•tend•i•bil•i•ty** *n.*

ex•tend•ed fam•i•ly *n.* 1 a family group that includes relatives living in one household. 2 all the members of a family, including cousins, in-laws, etc.

ex•tend•er /ikstέndər/ *n.* 1 a person or thing that extends. 2 a substance added to paint, ink, glue, etc., to dilute its color or increase its bulk.

ex•ten•sion /iksténshən/ *n.* 1 the act or an instance of extending; the process of being extended. 2 prolongation; enlargement. 3 a part enlarging or added on to a main structure or building. 4 an additional part of anything. 5 a subsidiary telephone on the same line as the main one. 6 an additional period of time. 7 away from campus instruction by a university or college (*extension course*). 8 extent; range. ◻◻ **ex•ten•sion•al** *adj.*

ex•ten•sive /iksténsiv/ *adj.* 1 covering a large area in space or time. 2 having a wide scope; far-reaching. 3 *Agriculture* involving cultivation from a large area, with a minimum of special resources. ◻◻ **ex•ten•sive•ly** *adv.* **ex•ten•sive•ness** *n.*

ex•ten•sor /iksténsər/ *n.* (in full **extensor muscle**) *Anat.* a muscle that extends or straightens out part of the body (cf. FLEXOR).

ex•tent /ikstént/ *n.* 1 the space over which a thing extends. 2 the width or limits of application; scope (*to a great extent*).

ex•ten•u•ate /ikstényoo͞-ayt/ *v.tr.* (often as **extenuating** *adj.*) lessen the seeming seriousness of (guilt or an offense) by reference to some mitigating factor. ◻◻ **ex•ten•u•a•tion** /–áyshən/ *n.*

ex•te•ri•or /iksteéreeər/ *adj. & n.* • *adj.* 1 **a** of or on the outer side (opp. INTERIOR). **b** (foll. by *to*) situated on the outside of (a building, etc.). **c** coming from outside. 2 *Cinematog.* outdoor. • *n.* 1 the outward aspect or surface of a building, etc. 2 the apparent behavior or demeanor of a person. 3 *Cinematog.* an outdoor scene.

ex•ter•mi•nate /ikstə́rminayt/ *v.tr.* 1 destroy utterly (esp. something living). 2 get rid of; eliminate (a pest, disease, etc.). ◻◻ **ex•ter•mi•na•tion** /–náyshən/ *n.* **ex•ter•mi•na•tor** *n.* **ex•ter•mi•na•to•ry** /–nətáwree/ *adj.*

ex•ter•nal /ikstə́rnəl/ *adj. & n.* • *adj.* 1 **a** of or situated on the outside or visible part. **b** coming or derived from the outside or an outside source. 2 relating to a country's foreign affairs. 3 outside the conscious subject (*the external world*). 4 (of medicine, etc.) for use on the outside of the body. • *n.* (in *pl.*) 1 the outward features or aspect. 2 external circumstances. 3 inessentials. ◻◻ **ex•ter•nal•i•ty** /–nálitee/ *n.* (*pl.* **-ties**). **ex•ter•nal•ly** *adv.*

ex•ter•nal•ize /ikstə́rnəlīz/ *v.tr.* give or attribute external existence to. ◻◻ **ex•ter•nal•i•za•tion** *n.*

ex•tinct /ikstíngkt/ *adj.* 1 (of a family, class, or species) that has died out. 2 **a** (of fire, etc.) no longer burning. **b** (of a volcano) that no longer erupts. 3 (of life, hope, etc.) terminated; quenched.

ex•tinc•tion /ikstíngkshən/ *n.* 1 the act of making extinct; the state of being or process of becoming extinct. 2 the act of extinguishing; the state of being extinguished. 3 total destruction or annihilation. ◻◻ **ex•tinc•tive** *adj.*

ex•tin•guish /ikstínggwish/ *v.tr.* 1 cause (a flame, light, etc.) to die out; put out. 2 make extinct; annihilate; destroy. 3 put an end to; terminate; obscure utterly (a feeling, quality, etc.). 4 **a** abolish; wipe out (a debt). **b** *Law* render void. ◻◻ **ex•tin•guish•a•ble** *adj.*

ex•tin•guish•er /ikstínggwishər/ *n.* a person or thing that extinguishes, esp. = FIRE EXTINGUISHER.

ex•tir•pate /ékstərpayt/ *v.tr.* root out; destroy completely. ◻◻ **ex•tir•pa•tion** /–páyshən/ *n.* **ex•tir•pa•tor** *n.*

ex•tol /ikstṓl/ *v.tr.* (**extolled, extolling**) praise enthusiastically.

ex•tort /ikstáwrt/ *v.tr.* obtain by force, threats, persistent demands, etc.

ex•tor•tion /ikstáwrshən/ *n.* 1 the act or an instance of extorting, esp. money. 2 illegal exaction. ◻◻ **ex•tor•tion•er** *n.* **ex•tor•tion•ist** *n.*

ex•tor•tion•ate /ikstáwrshənət/ *adj.* (of a price, etc.) exorbitant. ◻◻ **ex•tor•tion•ate•ly** *adv.*

ex•tra /ékstrə/ *adj., adv., & n.* • *adj.* additional; more than is usual or necessary or expected. • *adv.* 1 more than usually. 2 additionally (*was charged extra*). • *n.* 1 an extra thing. 2 a thing for which an extra charge is made; such a charge. 3 a person engaged temporarily to fill out a scene in a motion picture or play, esp. as one of a crowd. 4 a special issue of a newspaper, etc.

extra- /ékstrə/ *comb. form* **1** outside; beyond (*extramarital*). **2** beyond the scope of (*extracurricular*).

ex·tract *v. & n.* • *v.tr.* /ikstrákt/ **1** remove or take out, esp. by effort or force (anything firmly rooted). **2** obtain (money, an admission, etc.) with difficulty or against a person's will. **3** obtain (a natural resource) from the earth. **4** select or reproduce for quotation or performance (a passage of writing, music, etc.). **5** obtain (juice, etc.) by suction, pressure, distillation, etc. **6** derive (pleasure, etc.). **7** *Math.* find (the root of a number). • *n.* /ékstrakt/ **1** a short passage taken from a book, piece of music, etc.; an excerpt. **2** a preparation containing the active principle of a substance in concentrated form (*malt extract*). □□ **ex·tract·a·ble** *adj.* **ex·trac·tor** /ikstráktər/ *n.*

ex·trac·tion /ikstrákshən/ *n.* **1** the act or an instance of extracting; the process of being extracted. **2** the removal of a tooth. **3** origin; lineage; descent (*of German extraction*). **4** something extracted; an extract.

ex·trac·tive /ikstráktiv/ *adj.* of or involving extraction, esp. extensive extracting of natural resources without provision for their renewal.

ex·tra·cur·ric·u·lar /ékstrəkəríkyələr/ *adj.* (of a subject of study) not included in the normal curriculum.

ex·tra·dite /ékstrədīt/ *v.tr.* hand over (a person accused or convicted of a crime) to the country, state, etc., in which the crime was committed. □□ **ex·tra·dit·a·ble** /ékstrədītəbəl/ *adj.* **ex·tra·di·tion** *n.*

ex·tra·mar·i·tal /ékstrəmárit'l/ *adj.* (esp. of sexual relations) occurring outside marriage. □□ **ex·tra·mar·i·tal·ly** *adv.*

ex·tra·ne·ous /ikstráyneeəs/ *adj.* **1** of external origin. **2** (often foll. by *to*) **a** separate from the object to which it is attached, etc. **b** external to; irrelevant or unrelated to. **c** inessential; superfluous. □□ **ex·tra·ne·ous·ly** *adv.* **ex·tra·ne·ous·ness** *n.*

ex·traor·di·nar·y /ikstráwrd'neree, ékstrəáwr–/ *adj.* **1** unusual or remarkable; out of the usual course. **2** unusually great (*an extraordinary talent*). **3** so exceptional as to provoke astonishment or admiration. **4** (of a meeting) specially convened. □□ **ex·traor·di·nar·i·ly** *adv.* **ex·traor·di·nar·i·ness** *n.*

ex·trap·o·late /ikstrápəlayt/ *v.tr.* (also *absol.*) **1** *Math. & Philos.* **a** calculate approximately from known values, data, etc. (others which lie outside the range of those known). **b** calculate on the basis of (known facts) to estimate unknown facts, esp. extend (a curve) on a graph. **2** infer more widely from a limited range of known facts. □□ **ex·trap·o·la·tion** /–láyshən/ *n.*

ex·tra·sen·so·ry /ékstrəsénsəree/ *adj.* derived by means other than the known senses, e.g., by telepathy, clairvoyance, etc.

ex·tra·sen·so·ry per·cep·tion *n.* a person's supposed faculty of perceiving by such means.

ex·tra·ter·res·tri·al /ékstrətəréstreeəl/ *adj. & n.* • *adj.* **1** outside the earth or its atmosphere. **2** (in science fiction) from outer space. • *n.* (in science fiction) a being from outer space.

ex·trav·a·gant /ikstrávəgənt/ *adj.* **1** spending (esp. money) excessively; immoderate or wasteful in use of resources. **2** exorbitant; costing much. **3** exceeding normal restraint or sense; unreasonable; absurd (*extravagant claims*). □□ **ex·tra·va·gance** /ikstrávəgəns/ *n.* **ex·trav·a·gant·ly** *adv.*

ex·trav·a·gan·za /ikstrávəgánzə/ *n.* **1** a fanciful literary, musical, or dramatic composition. **2** a spectacular theatrical or television production.

ex·treme /ikstréem/ *adj. & n.* • *adj.* **1** reaching a high or the highest degree; exceedingly great or intense (*in extreme danger*). **2 a** severe; stringent; lacking restraint or moderation (*an extreme reaction*). **b** (of a person, opinion, etc.) going to great lengths; advocating immoderate measures. **3** outermost (*the extreme edge*). **4** *Polit.* on the far left or right of a party. **5** utmost; last. • *n.* **1** (often in *pl.*) one or other of two things as remote or as different as possible. **2** a thing at either end of anything. **3** the highest degree of anything. **4** *Math.* the first or the last term of a ratio or series. □ **go to extremes** take an extreme course of action. **go to the other extreme** take a diametrically opposite course of action. **in the extreme** to an extreme degree. □□ **ex·treme·ly** *adv.*

ex·trem·ist /ikstréemist/ *n.* (also *attrib.*) a person who holds extreme or fanatical political or religious views. □□ **ex·trem·ism** *n.*

ex·trem·i·ty /ikstrémitee/ *n.* (*pl.* **-ties**) **1** the extreme point; the very end. **2** (in *pl.*) the hands and feet. **3** a condition of extreme adversity or difficulty.

ex·tri·cate /ékstrikayt/ *v.tr.* (often foll. by *from*) free or disentangle from a constraint or difficulty. □□ **ex·tri·ca·ble** *adj.* **ex·tri·ca·tion** /–káyshən/ *n.*

ex·trin·sic /ekstrínsik, –zik/ *adj.* **1** not inherent or intrinsic; not essential. **2** (often foll. by *to*) extraneous; lying outside; not belonging (to). **3** originating or operating from without. □□ **ex·trin·si·cal·ly** *adv.*

ex·tro·vert /ékstrəvərt/ *n. & adj.* • *n.* **1** *Psychol.* a person predominantly concerned with external things or objective considerations. **2** an outgoing or sociable person. • *adj.* typical or characteristic of an extrovert. □□ **ex·tro·ver·sion** /–vərzhən/ *n.* **ex·tro·vert·ed** *adj.*

ex·trude /ikstróod/ *v.tr.* **1** (foll. by *from*) thrust or force out. **2** shape metal, plastics, etc., by forcing them through a die. □□ **ex·tru·sion** /–tróozhən/ *n.* **ex·tru·sive** /–tróosiv/ *adj.*

ex·u·ber·ant /igzóobərənt/ *adj.* **1** lively; high-spirited. **2** (of a plant, etc.) prolific. **3** (of feelings, etc.) lavish; effusive. □□ **ex·u·ber·ance** /–rəns/ *n.* **ex·u·ber·ant·ly** *adv.*

ex·ude /igzóod, iksóod/ *v.* **1** *tr. & intr.* (of a liquid, moisture, etc.) escape or cause to escape gradually; ooze out; give off. **2** *tr.* emit (a smell). **3** *tr.* display (an emotion, etc.) freely or abundantly (*exuded displeasure*). □□ **ex·u·date** /éksyoodayt, éksə–/ *n.* **ex·u·da·tion** *n.*

ex·ult /igzúlt/ *v.intr.* (often foll. by *at*, *in*, *over*, or *to* + infin.) **1** be greatly joyful. **2** (often foll. by *over*) have a feeling of triumph (over a person). □□ **ex·ult·an·cy** /–tənsee/ *n.* **ex·ul·ta·tion** /égzultáyshən, éksul–/ *n.* **ex·ult·ant** *adj.* **ex·ult·ant·ly** *adv.* **ex·ult·ing·ly** *adv.*

-ey /ee/ *suffix* var. of -Y².

eye /ī/ *n. & v.* • *n.* **1 a** the organ of sight in humans and other animals. **b** the light-detecting organ in some invertebrates. **2** the eye characterized by the color of the iris (*has blue eyes*). **3** the region around the eye (*eyes red from crying*). **4** a glass or plastic ball serving as an artificial eye. **5** (in *sing.* or *pl.*) sight; the faculty of sight (*demonstrate to the eye*). **6** a particular visual faculty or talent; visual appreciation; perspicacity (*cast an expert eye over*). **7 a** (in *sing.* or *pl.*) a look, gaze, or glance, esp. as indicating the disposition of the viewer (*a friendly eye*). **b** (**the eye**) a flirtatious or sexually provocative glance. **8** mental awareness; consciousness. **9** a person or animal, etc., that sees on behalf of another. **10** = PRIVATE EYE. **11** a thing like an eye, esp.: **a** a spot on a peacock's tail. **b** the leaf bud of a potato. **12** the center of something circular, e.g., a flower or target. **13** the relatively calm region at the center of a storm or hurricane. **14** an aperture in an implement, esp. a needle, for the insertion of something, e.g., thread. **15** a ring or loop for a bolt or hook, etc., to pass through. • *v.tr.* (**eyes, eyed, eyeing** or **eying**) watch or observe closely, esp. admiringly or with curiosity or suspicion. □ **all eyes 1** watching intently. **2** general attention (*all eyes*

See page xii for the *Key to Pronunciation*.

were on us). **before one's** (or **one's very**) **eyes** right in front of one. **an eye for an eye** retaliation in kind (Exodus 21:24). **have an eye for 1** be quick to notice. **2** be partial to. **have eyes for** be interested in; wish to acquire. **have one's eye on** wish or plan to procure. **hit a person in the eye** (or **between the eyes**) *colloq.* be very obvious or impressive. **keep an eye on 1** pay attention to. **2** look after; take care of. **keep an eye open** (or **out**) (often foll. by *for*) watch carefully. **keep one's eyes open** (or **peeled**) watch out; be on the alert. **make eyes at** look amorously or flirtatiously at. **open a person's eyes** be enlightening or revealing to a person. **see eye to eye** (often foll. by *with*) be in full agreement. **under the eye of** under the supervision or observation of. **up to the** (or **one's**) **eyes in 1** deeply engaged or involved in; inundated with (*up to the eyes in work*). **2** to the utmost limit (*mortgaged up to the eyes*). **with one's eyes open** deliberately; with full awareness. **with one's eyes shut** (or **closed**) **1** easily; with little effort. **2** without awareness; unobservant. **with an eye to** with a view to; prudently considering. **with one eye on** directing one's attention partly to. **with one eye shut** *colloq.* easily; with little effort (*could do this with one eye shut*). □□ **eyed** *adj.* (also in *comb.*).

eye·ball /íbawl/ *n.* & *v.* •*n.* the ball of the eye within the lids and socket. •*v. sl.* **1** *tr.* look or stare at. **2** *intr.* look or stare. □ **eyeball to eyeball** *colloq.* confronting closely. **to** (or **up to**) **the eyeballs** *colloq.* completely.

eye·brow /íbrow/ *n.* the line of hair growing on the ridge above the eye socket. □ **raise one's eyebrows** show surprise, disbelief, or mild disapproval.

eye con·tact *n.* looking directly into another person's eyes.

eye·ful /íf o͝ol/ *n.* (*pl.* **-fuls**) *colloq.* **1** a long, steady look. **2** a visually striking person or thing. **3** anything thrown or blown into the eye.

eye·glass /íglas/ *n.* **1** a lens for correcting or assisting defective sight. **2** (in *pl.*) a pair of these, usu. set into a frame that rests on the nose and has side pieces that curve over the ears.

eye·lash /ílash/ *n.* each of the hairs growing on the edges of the eyelids. □ **by an eyelash** by a very small margin.

eye·let /ílit/ *n.* **1** a small hole in paper, leather, cloth, etc., for string or rope, etc., to pass through. **2** a metal ring reinforcement for this. **3** a form of decoration in embroidery.

eye lev·el *n.* the level seen by the eyes looking horizontally (*put it at eye level*).

eye·lid /ílid/ *n.* the upper or lower fold of skin closing to cover the eye.

eye·lin·er /ílīnər/ *n.* a cosmetic applied as a line around the eye.

eye·piece /ípees/ *n.* the lens or lenses at the end of a microscope, telescope, etc., to which the eye is applied.

eye·shade /íshayd/ *n.* a device, esp. a visor, to protect the eyes, esp. from strong light.

eye shad·ow *n.* a colored cosmetic applied to the skin around the eyes.

eye·shot /íshot/ *n.* seeing distance (*out of eyeshot*).

eye·sight /ísīt/ *n.* the faculty or power of seeing.

eye·sore /ísawr/ *n.* a visually offensive or ugly thing, esp. a building.

eye·strain /ístrayn/ *n.* fatigue of the (internal or external) muscles of the eye.

eye·tooth /íto͞oth/ *n.* a canine tooth just under or next to the eye, esp. in the upper jaw.

eye·wear /íwair/ *n.* spectacles, goggles, or lenses for improving eyesight or protecting the eyes.

eye·wit·ness /íwítnis/ *n.* a person who has seen a thing happen and can give evidence of it.

ey·rie var. of AERIE.

F

F[1] /ef/ *n.* (also **f**) (*pl.* **Fs** or **F's**) **1** the sixth letter of the alphabet. **2** *Mus.* the fourth note of the diatonic scale of C major.
F[2] *abbr.* (also **F.**) **1** Fahrenheit. **2** farad(s). **3** female.
F[3] *symb. Chem.* the element fluorine.
f *abbr.* (also **f.**) **1** female. **2** feminine. **3** following page, etc. **4** *Mus.* forte. **5** folio. **6** focal length (cf. F-NUMBER).
fa /faa/ *n. Mus.* **1** (in tonic sol-fa) the fourth note of a major scale. **2** the note F in the fixed-do system.
FAA *abbr.* Federal Aviation Administration.
fab /fab/ *adj. colloq.* fabulous; marvelous.
fa·ble /fáybəl/ *n. & v.* • *n.* **1 a** a story, esp. a supernatural one, not based on fact. **b** a tale, esp. with animals as characters, conveying a moral. **2** (*collect.*) myths and legendary tales (*in fable*). **3 a** a false statement; a lie. **b** a thing only supposed to exist. • *v.tr.* (as **fabled** *adj.*) celebrated in fable; famous; legendary.
fab·ric /fábrik/ *n.* **1 a** a woven material; a textile. **b** other material resembling woven cloth. **2** a structure or framework, esp. the walls, floor, and roof of a building. **3** (in abstract senses) the essential structure of a thing (*the fabric of society*).
fab·ri·cate /fábrikayt/ *v.tr.* **1** construct esp. from prepared components. **2** invent or concoct (a story, etc.). **3** forge (a document). ▫▫ **fab·ri·ca·tion** /fábrikáyshən/ *n.* **fab·ri·ca·tor** *n.*
fab·u·list /fábyəlist/ *n.* **1** a composer of fables. **2** a liar.
fab·u·lous /fábyələs/ *adj.* **1** incredible; exaggerated (*fabulous wealth*). **2** *colloq.* marvelous (*looking fabulous*). **3 a** celebrated in fable. **b** legendary; mythical. ▫▫ **fab·u·lous·ly** *adv.* **fab·u·lous·ness** *n.*
fa·çade /fəsáad/ *n.* **1** the face of a building, esp. its principal front. **2** an outward appearance or front, esp. a deceptive one.
face /fays/ *n. & v.* • *n.* **1** the front of the head from the forehead to the chin. **2 a** the expression of the facial features (*had a happy face*). **b** an expression of disgust; a grimace (*make a face*). **3** coolness; effrontery. **4** the surface of a thing, esp.: **a** the visible part of a celestial body. **b** a side of a mountain, etc. (*the north face*). **c** the (usu. vertical) surface of a coal seam, excavation, etc. **d** *Geom.* each surface of a solid. **e** the façade of a building. **f** the plate of a clock or watch. **5 a** the functional side of a tool, etc. **b** the distinctive side of a playing card. **c** the obverse of a coin. **6** = TYPEFACE. **7 a** the outward appearance or aspect (*the face of capitalism*). **b** outward show; disguise; pretense (*put on a brave face*). **8** a person, esp. conveying some quality or association (*a face from the past*). **9** credibility or respect; good reputation; dignity (*lose face*). • *v.* **1** *tr. & intr.* look or be positioned toward or in a certain direction (*facing the window; the room faces north*). **2** *tr.* be opposite (*facing page 20*). **3** *tr.* **a** meet resolutely or defiantly (*face one's critics*). **b** not shrink from (*face the facts*). **4** *tr.* present itself to (*the problem that faces us*). **5** *tr.* **a** cover the surface of (a thing) with a coating, etc. **b** put a facing on (a garment). **6** *intr. & tr.* turn or cause to turn in a certain direction. ▫ **face facts** (or **the facts**) recognize the truth. **face the music** *colloq.* stand up to unpleasant consequences, esp. criticism. **face to face** (often foll. by *with*) confronting each other. **face up to** accept bravely; confront. **in one's face 1** straight against one; as one approaches. **2** confronting. **in the face of 1** despite. **2** confronted by. **in your face** demanding attention. **let's face it** *colloq.* we must be honest or realistic about it. **on the face of it** as it would appear. **put a brave face on** accept difficulty, etc., cheerfully or with courage. **put one's face on** *colloq.* apply makeup to one's face. **put a new face on** alter the aspect of. **save face** preserve esteem. **save a person's face** enable a person to save face; forbear from humiliating a person. ▫▫ **faced** *adj.* (also in *comb.*). **facing** *adj.* (also in *comb.*).
face card *n. Cards* a king, queen, or jack.
face·less /fáyslis/ *adj.* **1** without identity. **2** lacking character. **3** without a face. ▫▫ **face·less·ly** *adv.* **face·less·ness** *n.*
face-lift *n.* **1** (also **face-lifting**) cosmetic surgery to remove wrinkles, etc. **2** a procedure to improve the appearance of a thing.
fac·er /fáysər/ *n. colloq.* **1** a blow in the face. **2** one that faces.
face-sav·ing *n.* preserving one's reputation, credibility, etc.
fac·et /fásit/ *n.* **1** a particular aspect of a thing. **2** one side of a many-sided thing, esp. a cut gem, a bone, etc. ▫▫ **fac·et·ed** *adj.* (also in *comb.*).

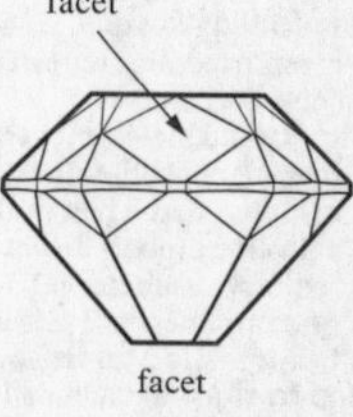

fa·ce·tious /fəséeshəs/ *adj.* **1** characterized by flippant or inappropriate humor. **2** intending to be amusing, esp. inappropriately. ▫▫ **fa·ce·tious·ly** *adv.* **fa·ce·tious·ness** *n.*
face val·ue *n.* **1** the nominal value as printed or stamped on money. **2** the superficial appearance or implication of a thing.
fa·cia var. of FASCIA.
fa·cial /fáyshəl/ *adj. & n.* • *adj.* of or for the face. • *n.* a beauty treatment for the face. ▫▫ **fa·cial·ly** *adv.*
-facient /fáyshənt/ *comb. form* forming adjectives and nouns indicating an action or state produced (*abortifacient*).
fa·ci·es /fáyshee-eez, –sheez/ *n.* (*pl.* same) **1** *Med.* the appearance or facial expression of an individual. **2** *Geol.* the character of rock, etc., expressed by its composition, fossil content, etc.
fac·ile /fásil/ *adj.* usu. *derog.* **1** easily achieved but of little value. **2** (of speech, writing, etc.) fluent; glib. ▫▫ **fac·ile·ly** *adv.* **fac·ile·ness** *n.*
fa·cil·i·tate /fəsílitayt/ *v.tr.* make easy or less difficult or more easily achieved. ▫▫ **fa·cil·i·ta·tion** /–táyshən/ *n.* **fa·cil·i·ta·tive** *adj.* **fa·cil·i·ta·tor** *n.*
fa·cil·i·ty /fəsílitee/ *n.* (*pl.* **-ties**) **1** ease; absence of difficulty. **2** dexterity; aptitude (*facility of expression*). **3** (esp. in *pl.*) an opportunity, the equipment, or the resources for doing something. **4** a plant, installation, or establishment. **5** *euphem.* (in *pl.*) a (public) toilet.
fac·ing /fáysing/ *n.* **1 a** a layer of material covering part of a garment, etc., for contrast or strength. **b** (in *pl.*)

the cuffs, collar, etc., of a military jacket. **2** an outer layer covering the surface of a wall, etc.

fac·sim·i·le /faksímilee/ *n.* & *v.* •*n.* **1** an exact copy, esp. of writing, a picture, etc. (often *attrib.*: *facsimile edition*). **2 a** production of an exact copy of a document, etc., by electronic scanning and transmission (see also FAX). **b** a copy produced in this way. •*v.tr.* (**facsimiled, facsimileing**) make a facsimile of.

fact /fakt/ *n.* **1** a thing that is known to have occurred, to exist, or to be true. **2** a datum of experience (often foll. by an explanatory clause or phrase: *the fact that fire burns*). **3** (usu. in *pl.*) a piece of evidence. **4** truth; reality. **5** a thing assumed as the basis for argument or inference. □ **before** (or **after**) **the fact** before (or after) the committing of a crime. **a fact of life** something that must be accepted. **facts and figures** precise details. **in** (or **in point of**) **fact 1** in reality; as a matter of fact. **2** (in summarizing) in short.

fac·tion[1] /fákshən/ *n.* **1** a small organized dissenting group within a larger one, esp. in politics. **2** a state of dissension within an organization. □□ **fac·tion·al** *adj.* **fac·tion·al·ize** *v.tr.* & *intr.* **fac·tion·al·ly** *adv.*

fac·tion[2] /fákshən/ *n.* a book, movie, etc., using real events as a basis for a fictional narrative or dramatization.

-faction /fákshən/ *comb. form* forming nouns of action from verbs ending in *-fy* (*petrifaction*; *satisfaction*).

fac·tious /fákshəs/ *adj.* of, characterized by, or inclined to faction. □□ **fac·tious·ly** *adv.* **fac·tious·ness** *n.*

fac·ti·tious /faktíshəs/ *adj.* **1** contrived; not genuine (*factitious value*). **2** not natural (*factitious joy*). □□ **fac·ti·tious·ly** *adv.* **fac·ti·tious·ness** *n.*

fac·toid /fáktoyd/ *n.* an assumption or speculation that is reported and repeated so often that it becomes accepted as fact.

fac·tor /fáktər/ *n.* & *v.* •*n.* **1** a circumstance, fact, or influence contributing to a result. **2** *Math.* a whole number, etc., that when multiplied with another produces a given number. **3** *Biol.* a gene, etc., determining hereditary character. •*v.tr.* **1** *Math.* resolve into factors or components. **2** *tr.* sell (one's receivable debts) to a factor. □□ **fac·tor·ize** /fáktərīz/ *v.tr.* & *intr.*

fac·to·ri·al /faktáwreeəl/ *n.* & *adj. Math.* •*n.* **1** the product of a number and all the whole numbers below it (*four factorial = 4 x 3 x 2 x 1*). ¶ **Symb.:** ! (as in 4!). **2** the product of a series of factors in an arithmetical progression. •*adj.* of a factor or factorial. □□ **fac·to·ri·al·ly** *adv.*

fac·to·ry /fáktəree/ *n.* (*pl.* **-ries**) **1** a building or buildings containing equipment for manufacturing machinery or goods. **2** (usu. *derog.*) a place producing mass quantities or a low quality of goods, etc. (*a degree factory*).

fac·to·tum /faktṓtəm/ *n.* (*pl.* **factotums**) an employee who does all kinds of work.

facts of life *n.pl.* (prec. by *the*) information about sexual functions and practices.

fac·tu·al /fákchōōəl/ *adj.* **1** based on or concerned with fact. **2** actual; true. □□ **fac·tu·al·i·ty** /–chōōálitee/ *n.* **fac·tu·al·ly** *adv.* **fac·tu·al·ness** *n.*

fac·tum /fáktəm/ *n.* (*pl.* **factums** or **facta** /–tə/) *Law* **1** an act or deed. **2** a statement of the facts.

fac·ul·ty /fákəltee/ *n.* (*pl.* **-ties**) **1** an aptitude or ability for a particular activity. **2** an inherent mental or physical power. **3 a** the teaching staff of a university, college, or secondary school. **b** a department of a university, etc., teaching a specific branch of learning (*faculty of modern languages*).

fad /fad/ *n.* **1** a craze. **2** a peculiar notion or idiosyncrasy. □□ **fad·dish** *adj.* **fad·dish·ly** *adv.* **fad·dish·ness** *n.* **fad·dism** *n.* **fad·dist** *n.*

fade /fayd/ *v.* & *n.* •*v.* **1** *intr.* & *tr.* lose or cause to lose color. **2** *intr.* lose freshness or strength; (of flowers, etc.) droop; wither. **3** *intr.* **a** (of color, light, etc.) grow pale or dim. **b** (of sound) grow faint. **4** *intr.* (of a feeling, etc.) diminish. **5** *intr.* (foll. by *away*, *out*) (of a person, etc.) disappear or depart gradually. **6** *tr.* (foll. by *in*, *out*) *Cinematog.* & *Broadcasting* **a** cause (a picture) to come gradually in or out of view on a screen, or to merge into another shot. **b** make (the sound) more or less audible. •*n.* the action or an instance of fading. □ **fade away** *colloq.* languish; grow thin. □□ **fad·er** *n.* (in sense 6 of *v.*).

fade-in *n. Cinematog.* & *Broadcasting* the action or an instance of fading in a picture or sound.

fade-out *n.* **1** *colloq.* disappearance; death. **2** *Cinematog.* & *Broadcasting* the action or an instance of fading out a picture or sound.

fa·er·ie /fáiree/ *n.* (also **fa·er·y**) *archaic* **1** fairyland; the fairies, esp. as represented by Spenser (*the Faerie Queene*). **2** (*attrib.*) visionary; imagined.

fag[1] /fag/ *n.* & *v.* •*n. sl.* a cigarette. •*v.* (**fagged, fagging**) *colloq. tr.* (often foll. by *out*) tire out; exhaust.

fag[2] /fag/ *n. sl.* often *offens.* a male homosexual.

fag·got /fágət/ *n. sl. offens.* a male homosexual.

fag·ot /fágət/ *n.* & *v.* •*n.* (also **fag·got**) **1** a bundle of sticks or twigs bound together as fuel. **2** a bundle of iron rods for heat treatment. •*v.tr.* (**fagoted, fagoting**) **1** bind in or make into fagots. **2** join by fagoting (see FAGOTING).

fag·ot·ing /fágəting/ *n.* (also **fag·got·ing**) **1** embroidery in which threads are fastened together like a fagot. **2** the joining of materials in a similar manner.

Fahr·en·heit /fárənhīt/ *adj.* of a scale of temperature on which water freezes at 32° and boils at 212° under standard conditions.

fa·ience /fī-óɴs, fay-/ *n.* decorated and glazed earthenware and porcelain.

fail /fayl/ *v.* & *n.* •*v.* **1** *intr.* not succeed. **2 a** *tr.* & *intr.* be unsuccessful in (an examination, etc.). **b** *tr.* (of a commodity, etc.) not pass (a test of quality). **c** *tr.* reject (a candidate, etc.); adjudge as unsuccessful. **3** *intr.* be unable to; neglect to (*failed to appear*). **4** *tr.* disappoint; let down. **5** *intr.* (of supplies, crops, etc.) be or become insufficient. **6** *intr.* become weaker; cease functioning (*the engine has failed*). **7** *intr.* **a** (of an enterprise) collapse. **b** become bankrupt. •*n.* a failure in an examination. □ **without fail** for certain; whatever happens.

failed /fayld/ *adj.* **1** not good enough (*a failed actor*). **2** deficient; broken down (*a failed crop*).

fail·ing /fáyling/ *n.* & *prep.* •*n.* a fault or shortcoming; a weakness, esp. in character. •*prep.* in default of; if not.

fail-safe *adj.* reverting to a safe condition in the event of a breakdown, etc.

fail·ure /fáylyər/ *n.* **1** lack of success. **2** an unsuccessful person, thing, or attempt. **3** nonperformance; nonoccurrence. **4** breaking down or ceasing to function (*heart failure*). **5** running short of supply, etc. **6** bankruptcy.

fain /fayn/ *adj.* & *adv. archaic* •*predic.adj.* (foll. by *to* + infin.) **1** willing under the circumstances to. **2** left with no alternative but to. •*adv.* gladly (esp. *would fain*).

faint /faynt/ *adj.*, *v.*, & *n.* •*adj.* **1** indistinct; pale; dim; not clearly perceived. **2** (of a person) weak or dizzy. **3** slight; remote (*a faint chance*). **4** halfhearted (*faint praise*). **5** timid (*a faint heart*). •*v.intr.* **1** lose consciousness. **2** become faint. •*n.* a sudden loss of consciousness. □ **not have the faintest** *colloq.* have no idea. □□ **faint·ness** *n.*

faint-heart·ed *adj.* cowardly; timid. □□ **faint-heart·ed·ly** *adv.* **faint-heart·ed·ness** *n.*

faint·ly /fáyntlee/ *adv.* **1** very slightly (*faintly amused*). **2** indistinctly; feebly.

fair[1] /fair/ *adj. & adv.* • *adj.* **1** just; equitable; in accordance with the rules. **2** blond; light or pale in color or complexion. **3 a** of (only) moderate quality or amount; average. **b** considerable; satisfactory (*a fair chance of success*). **4** (of weather) fine and dry; (of the wind) favorable. **5** clean; clear; unblemished (*fair copy*). **6** beautiful; attractive. • *adv.* in a fair manner (*play fair*). □ **fair and square** *adv. & adj.* **1** exactly. **2** straightforward; honest; aboveboard. **fair enough** *colloq.* that is reasonable or acceptable. **fair's fair** *colloq.* all involved should act fairly. **in a fair way to** likely to. □□ **fair·ish** *adj.* **fair·ness** *n.*

fair[2] /fair/ *n.* **1** a gathering of stalls, amusements, etc., for public entertainment. **2** a periodical gathering for the sale of goods, often with entertainments. **3** an exhibition of farm products, usu. held annually, with competitions, entertainments, etc. **4** an exhibition, esp. to promote particular products.

fair game *n.* a thing or person one may legitimately pursue, exploit, etc.

fair·ground /fáirgrownd/ *n.* an outdoor area where a fair is held.

fair·ly /fáirlee/ *adv.* **1** in a fair manner. **2** moderately (*fairly good*). **3** to a noticeable degree (*fairly narrow*). **4** utterly; completely (*fairly beside himself*). **5** actually (*fairly jumped for joy*).

fair-mind·ed *adj.* just; impartial. □□ **fair-mind·ed·ly** *adv.* **fair-mind·ed·ness** *n.*

fair play *n.* reasonable treatment or behavior.

fair·way /fáirway/ *n.* **1** a navigable channel. **2** the part of a golf course between a tee and its green, kept free of rough grass.

fair-weath·er friend *n.* a friend or ally who is unreliable in times of difficulty.

fair·y /fáiree/ *n. & adj.* • *n.* (*pl.* **-ies**) **1** a small imaginary being with magical powers. **2** *sl. derog.* a male homosexual. • *adj.* of fairies; fairylike; delicate; small. □□ **fair·y·like** *adj.*

fair·y·land /fáireeland/ *n.* **1** the imaginary home of fairies. **2** an enchanted region.

fair·y tale *n.* (also **fairy story**) **1** a tale about fairies or other fantastic creatures. **2** an incredible story; a fabrication.

fait ac·com·pli /fet aakawNplée, –komplée/ *n.* (*pl.* **faits accomplis** *pronunc.* same) a thing that has been done and is past altering.

faith /fayth/ *n.* **1** complete trust or confidence. **2** firm belief, esp. without logical proof. **3 a** religious belief. **b** spiritual apprehension of divine truth apart from proof. **c** things believed or to be believed. **4** duty or commitment to fulfill a trust, promise, etc. (*keep faith*). **5** (*attrib.*) concerned with a supposed ability to cure by faith rather than treatment.

faith·ful /fáythfool/ *adj.* **1** showing faith. **2** (often foll. by *to*) loyal; trustworthy. **3** accurate; true to fact (*a faithful account*). **4** thorough in performing one's duty; conscientious. **5** (**the Faithful**) the believers in a religion. □□ **faith·ful·ness** *n.*

faith·ful·ly /fáythfoolee/ *adv.* in a faithful manner. □ **yours faithfully** a formula for ending a business or formal letter.

faith heal·er *n.* one who uses religious faith and prayer to heal. □□ **faith heal·ing** *n.*

faith·less /fáythlis/ *adj.* **1** false; unreliable; disloyal. **2** without religious faith. □□ **faith·less·ly** *adv.* **faith·less·ness** *n.*

fa·ji·tas /faaheétəs, fə–/ *n.pl. Mexican Cooking* thin strips of fried or broiled meat, usu. seasoned with salsa.

fake /fayk/ *n., adj., & v.* • *n.* **1** a thing or person that is not genuine. **2** a trick. **3** *Sport* a feint. • *adj.* counterfeit; not genuine. • *v.tr.* **1** make (a false thing) appear genuine; forge; counterfeit. **2** make a pretense of having (a feeling, illness, etc.). **3** *Sport* feint. **4** improvise (*I'm not exactly sure, but I can fake it.*) □□ **fak·er** *n.* **fak·er·y** *n.*

fa·kir /fəkéer, fáykeer/ *n.* (also **fa·quir**) a Muslim or Hindu religious mendicant or ascetic.

fa·la·fel /fəlaáfəl/ *n.* (also **fe·la·fel**) (in Near Eastern countries) a spicy dish of fried patties made from mashed chick peas or beans.

fal·con /fálkən, fáwl–/ *n.* any diurnal bird of prey of the family Falconidae, sometimes trained to hunt small game for sport.

fal·con·er /fálkənər, fáwl–/ *n.* **1** a keeper and trainer of hawks. **2** a person who hunts with hawks.

fal·con·ry /fálkənree, fáwl–/ *n.* the breeding and training of hawks; the sport of hawking.

fall /fawl/ *v. & n.* • *v.intr.* (*past* **fell** /fel/; *past part.* **fallen** /fáwlən/) **1 a** descend rapidly from a higher to a lower level (*fell from the top floor*). **b** drop or be dropped (*supplies fell by parachute*). **2 a** (often foll. by *over* or *down*) cease to stand; come suddenly to the ground. **b** collapse forward or downward, esp. of one's own volition (*fell into my arms*). **3** become detached and descend or disappear. **4** take a downward direction: **a** (of hair, clothing, etc.) hang down. **b** (of ground, etc.) slope. **c** (foll. by *into*) (of a river, etc.) discharge into. **5 a** find a lower level; sink lower. **b** subside; abate. **6** (of a barometer, etc.) show a lower reading. **7** occur (*darkness fell*). **8** decline (*standards have fallen*). **9 a** (of the face) show dismay. **b** (of the eyes or a glance) look downward. **10 a** lose power or status (*the government will fall*). **b** lose esteem, moral integrity, etc. **11** commit sin, yield to temptation. **12** take or have a particular direction or place (*his eye fell on me*). **13 a** find a place; be naturally divisible (*the subject falls into three parts*). **b** (foll. by *under, within*) be classed among. **14** occur at a specified time (*Easter falls early this year*). **15** come by chance or duty (*it fell to me to answer*). **16 a** pass into a specified condition (*fall into decay*). **b** become (*fall asleep*). **17 a** (of a position, etc.) be overthrown or captured. **b** be defeated; fail. **18** die (*fall in battle*). **19** (foll. by *on, upon*) **a** attack. **b** meet with. **c** embrace or embark on avidly. **20** (foll. by *to* + verbal noun) begin (*fell to wondering*). **21** (foll. by *to*) lapse; revert (*revenues fall to the state*). • *n.* **1** the act or an instance of falling; a sudden rapid descent. **2** that which falls or has fallen, e.g., snow, etc. **3** the recorded amount of rainfall, etc. **4** a decline or diminution; depreciation in price, value, demand, etc. **5** downfall (*the fall of Rome*). **6 a** succumbing to temptation. **b** (**the Fall**) the biblical sin of Adam and its consequences. **7** (of material, land, light, etc.) a downward direction; a slope. **8** (also **Fall**) autumn. **9** (esp. in *pl.*) a waterfall, cataract, or cascade. □ **fall apart** (or **to pieces**) **1** break into pieces. **2** (of a situation, etc.) be reduced to chaos. **3** lose one's capacity to cope. **fall away 1** (of a surface) incline abruptly. **2** gradually vanish. **3** desert; revolt. **fall back** retreat. **fall back on** have recourse to in difficulty. **fall behind 1** lag. **2** be in arrears. **fall down** (often foll. by *on*) *colloq.* fail; fail to deliver (payment, etc.). **fall flat** fail to achieve expected success or evoke a desired response. **fall for** *colloq.* **1** be captivated or deceived by. **2** yield to the charms or merits of. **fall foul of** come into conflict with. **fall in 1 a** take one's place in military formation. **b** (as *int.*) the order to do this. **2** collapse inward. **fall into line 1** take one's place in the ranks. **2** conform with others. **fall into place** begin to make sense or cohere. **fall off 1** (of demand, etc.)

decrease. 2 withdraw. **fall out 1** quarrel. **2** (of the hair, etc.) become detached. **3** *Mil.* come out of formation. **fall over oneself** *colloq.* **1** be eager or competitive. **2** stumble through haste, confusion, etc. **fall short 1** be or become inadequate. **2** (of a missile, etc.) not reach its target. **fall short of** fail to reach or obtain. **fall through** come to nothing; miscarry.

fal·la·cy /fáləsee/ *n.* (*pl.* **-cies**) **1** a mistaken belief, esp. based on unsound argument. **2** faulty reasoning; misleading or unsound argument. ▫▫ **fal·la·cious** /fəláyshəs/ *adj.* **fal·la·cious·ly** *adv.* **fal·la·cious·ness** *n.*

fall·back /fáwlbak/ *n.* **1** (also *attrib.*) an alternative resource or plan that may be used in an emergency. **2** a reduction or retreat.

fall·en *past part.* of FALL *v. adj.* **1** (*attrib.*) having lost one's honor or reputation. **2** killed in war.

fall guy *sl.* **1** an easy victim. **2** a scapegoat.

fal·li·ble /fálibəl/ *adj.* **1** capable of making mistakes. **2** liable to be erroneous. ▫▫ **fal·li·bil·i·ty** *n.* **fal·li·bly** *adv.*

fall·ing star *n.* a meteor.

Fal·lo·pi·an tube /fəlṓpeeən/ *n. Anat.* either of two tubes in female mammals along which ova travel to the uterus.

fall·out /fáwlowt/ *n.* **1** radioactive debris caused by a nuclear explosion or accident. **2** the adverse side effects of a situation, etc.

fal·low[1] /fálō/ *adj. & n.* • *adj.* **1 a** (of land) plowed and harrowed but left unsown. **b** uncultivated. **2** (of an idea, etc.) potentially useful but not yet in use. • *n.* fallow or uncultivated land. ▫▫ **fal·low·ness** *n.*

fal·low[2] /fálō/ *adj.* of a pale brownish or reddish yellow.

false /fawls/ *adj. & adv.* • *adj.* **1** not according with fact; incorrect. **2 a** spurious; artificial (*false gods*; *false teeth*; *false modesty*). **b** acting as such, esp. deceptively (*a false lining*). **3** illusory (*a false economy*). **4** improperly so called (*false acacia*). **5** deceptive. **6** (foll. by *to*) deceitful, treacherous, or unfaithful. **7** illegal (*false imprisonment*). • *adv.* in a false manner (esp. *play false*). ▫▫ **false·ly** *adv.* **false·ness** *n.* **fal·si·ty** *n.* (*pl.* **-ties**).

false·hood /fáwls-hŏŏd/ *n.* **1** the state of being false, esp. untrue. **2** a false or untrue thing. **3 a** the act of lying. **b** a lie or lies.

fal·set·to /fawlsétō/ *n.* (*pl.* **-tos**) **1** a method of voice production used by male singers, esp. tenors, to sing notes higher than their normal range. **2** a singer using this method.

fals·ies /fáwlseez/ *n.pl. colloq.* padded material to increase the apparent size of the breasts.

fal·si·fy /fáwlsifī/ *v.tr.* (**-fies, -fied**) **1** fraudulently alter or make false (a document, evidence, etc.). **2** misrepresent. **3** make wrong; pervert. **4** show to be false. **5** disappoint (a hope, fear, etc.). ▫▫ **fal·si·fi·a·ble** *adj.* **fal·si·fi·ca·tion** *n.*

fal·ter /fáwltər/ *v.* **1** *intr.* stumble; go unsteadily. **2** *intr.* lose courage. **3** *tr. & intr.* speak hesitatingly. ▫▫ **fal·ter·er** *n.* **fal·ter·ing·ly** *adv.*

fame /faym/ *n.* **1** renown; the state of being famous. **2** reputation.

famed /faymd/ *adj.* (foll. by *for*) famous; much spoken of (*famed for its good food*).

fa·mil·ial /fəmílyəl, –leeəl/ *adj.* of, occurring in, or characteristic of a family or its members.

fa·mil·iar /fəmílyər/ *adj. & n.* • *adj.* **1 a** (often foll. by *to*) well known; no longer novel. **b** often encountered or experienced. **2** (foll. by *with*) knowing a thing well or in detail (*am familiar with all the problems*). **3** (often foll. by *with*) **a** well acquainted (with a person); intimate. **b** sexually intimate. **4** excessively informal. **5** unceremonious. **6** (of animals) tame. • *n.* **1** a close friend or associate. **2** (in full **familiar spirit**) a demon supposedly attending and obeying a witch, etc. ▫▫ **fa·mil·iar·ly** *adv.*

fa·mil·iar·i·ty /fəmíleeáritee, –yár–/ *n.* (*pl.* **-ties**) **1** the state of being well known. **2** (foll. by *with*) close acquaintance. **3** a close relationship. **4 a** sexual intimacy. **b** (in *pl.*) acts of physical intimacy. **5** informal behavior, esp. excessively so.

fa·mil·iar·ize /fəmílyərīz/ *v.tr.* **1** (foll. by *with*) make (a person) conversant or well acquainted. **2** make (a thing) well known. ▫▫ **fa·mil·iar·i·za·tion** *n.*

fam·i·ly /fámilee/ *n.* (*pl.* **-lies**) **1** a set of relations, living together or not. **2 a** the members of a household. **b** a person's children. **c** (*attrib.*) serving the needs of families (*family butcher*). **3 a** all the descendants of a common ancestor. **b** a group of peoples from a common stock. **4** all the languages ultimately derived from a particular early language, regarded as a group. **5** a brotherhood of persons or nations united by political or religious ties. **6** a group of objects distinguished by common features. **7** *Math.* a group of curves, etc., obtained by varying one quantity. **8** *Biol.* a group of related genera of organisms within an order in taxonomic classification. ▫ **in the** (or **a**) **family way** *colloq.* pregnant.

fam·i·ly plan·ning *n.* birth control.

fam·i·ly tree *n.* a chart showing relationships and lines of descent.

fam·ine /fámin/ *n.* **1** extreme scarcity of food. **2** a shortage of something specified (*water famine*).

fam·ish /fámish/ *v.tr. & intr.* (usu. in *passive*) **1** reduce or be reduced to extreme hunger. **2** *colloq.* (esp. as **famished** *adj.*) feel very hungry.

fa·mous /fáyməs/ *adj.* **1** (often foll. by *for*) celebrated; well known. **2** *colloq.* excellent. ▫▫ **fa·mous·ness** *n.*

fa·mous·ly /fáyməslee/ *adv.* **1** *colloq.* excellently (*got on famously*). **2** notably.

fan[1] /fan/ *n. & v.* • *n.* **1** an apparatus, usu. with rotating blades, giving a current of air for ventilation, etc. **2** a device, usu. folding and forming a semicircle when spread out, for agitating the air to cool oneself. **3** anything spread out like a fan. • *v.* (**fanned, fanning**) **1** *tr.* **a** blow a current of air on, with or as with a fan. **b** agitate (the air) with a fan. **2** *tr.* (of a breeze) blow gently on. **3** *tr.* winnow (grain). **4** *intr. & tr.* (usu. foll. by *out*) spread out in the shape of a fan. **5 a** *tr.* strike (a batter) out. **b** *intr.* strike out. ▫▫ **fan·like** *adj.*

fan[2] /fan/ *n.* a devotee of a particular activity, performer, etc.

fa·nat·ic /fənátik/ *n. & adj.* • *n.* a person filled with excessive and often misguided enthusiasm for something. • *adj.* excessively enthusiastic. ▫▫ **fa·nat·i·cal** *adj.* **fa·nat·i·cal·ly** *adv.* **fa·nat·i·cism** /–tisizəm/ *n.* **fa·nat·i·cize** /–tisīz/ *v.intr. & tr.*

fan belt *n.* a belt that drives a fan to cool the radiator in a motor vehicle.

fan·ci·er /fánseeər/ *n.* a connoisseur or follower of some activity or thing (*dog fancier*).

fan·ci·ful /fánsifŏŏl/ *adj.* **1** existing only in the imagination or fancy. **2** whimsical; capricious. **3** fantastically designed, etc. ▫▫ **fan·ci·ful·ly** *adv.* **fan·ci·ful·ness** *n.*

fan·cy /fánsee/ *n., adj., & v.* • *n.* (*pl.* **-cies**) **1** an individual taste or inclination. **2** a caprice or whim. **3** an arbitrary supposition. **4 a** the faculty of using imagination or of inventing imagery. **b** a mental image. • *adj.* (usu. *attrib.*) (**fancier, fanciest**) **1** ornamental; not plain. **2** capricious; whimsical; extravagant (*at a fancy price*). • *v.tr.* (**-cies, -cied**) **1** (foll. by *that* + clause) be inclined to suppose. **2** *Brit. colloq.* feel a desire for (*do you fancy a drink?*). ▫▫ **fan·ci·ly** *adv.* **fan·ci·ness** *n.*

fan·cy-free *adj.* without (esp. emotional) commitments.

fan·dan·go /fandánggō/ *n.* (*pl.* **-goes** or **-os**) **1 a** a lively Spanish dance for two. **b** the music for this. **2** nonsense; tomfoolery.

fan·fare /fánfair/ *n.* **1** a short showy or ceremonious sounding of trumpets, etc. **2** an elaborate display; a burst of publicity.

fang /fang/ *n.* **1** a canine tooth, esp. of a dog or wolf. **2** the tooth of a venomous snake, by which poison is injected. **3** the root of a tooth or its prong. **4** *colloq.* a person's tooth. ▫▫ **fanged** *adj.* (also in *comb.*).

fan·ny /fánee/ *n.* (*pl.* **-nies**) *sl.* the buttocks.

fan·ny pack *n.* a pouch for personal items, worn on a belt around the waist or hips.

fan·ta·sia /fantáyzhə, –zheeə, fántəzéeə/ *n.* a musical or other composition free in form and often in improvisatory style, or that is based on several familiar tunes.

fan·ta·size /fántəsīz/ *v.* **1** *intr.* have a fantasy or fanciful vision. **2** *tr.* imagine; create a fantasy about. ▫▫ **fan·ta·sist** *n.*

fan·tas·tic /fantástik/ *adj.* (also **fan·tas·ti·cal**) **1** *colloq.* excellent; extraordinary. **2** extravagantly fanciful. **3** grotesque or bizarre in design, etc. ▫▫ **fan·tas·ti·cal·i·ty** /–kálitee/ *n.* **fan·tas·ti·cal·ly** *adv.*

fan·ta·sy /fántəsee, –zee/ *n.* (*pl.* **-sies**) **1** the faculty of inventing images, esp. extravagant or visionary ones. **2** a fanciful mental image; a daydream. **3** a whimsical speculation. **4** a fantastic invention or composition. **5** fabrication; pretense; make-believe (*his account was pure fantasy*).

far /faar/ *adv. & adj.* (**farther, farthest** or **further, furthest**) • *adv.* **1** at or to or by a great distance (*far away; far off; far out*). **2** a long way (off) in space or time (*are you traveling far?; we talked far into the night*). **3** to a great extent or degree; by much (*far better; far too early*). • *adj.* **1** situated at or extending over a great distance in space or time; remote (*a far country*). **2** more distant (*the far end of the hall*). **3** extreme (*far right militants*). ▫ **as far as 1** to the distance of (a place). **2** to the extent that (*travel as far as you like*). **by far 1** by a great amount. **2** (as an intensifier) without doubt. **far and away** by a very large amount. **far and near** everywhere. **far and wide** over a large area. **far be it from me** (foll. by *to* + infin.) I am reluctant to (esp. express criticism, etc.). **far from** very different from; tending to the opposite of (*the problem is far from being solved*). **go far 1** achieve much. **2** contribute greatly. **3** be adequate. **go too far** go beyond the limits of what is reasonable, polite, etc. **how far** to what extent. **so far 1** to such an extent or distance; to this point. **2** until now. **so** (or **in so**) **far as** to the extent that. **so far so good** progress has been satisfactory up to now.

far·ad /fárəd, –ad/ *n. Electr.* a unit of capacitance, such that one coulomb of charge causes a potential difference of one volt. ¶ Abbr.: **F.**

far·a·day /fárədday/ *n.* (also **Faraday's constant**) *Electr.* the quantity of electric charge carried by one mole of electrons.

far·a·way /fáarəwáy/ *adj.* **1** remote; long past. **2** (of a look) dreamy. **3** (of a voice) sounding as if from a distance.

farce /faars/ *n.* **1 a** a broadly comic dramatic work based on ludicrously improbable events. **b** this branch of drama. **2** absurdly futile proceedings.

far·ci·cal /fáarsikəl/ *adj.* **1** extremely ludicrous or futile. **2** of or like farce. ▫▫ **far·ci·cal·ly** *adv.*

far cry *n.* a long way.

fare /fair/ *n. & v.* • *n.* **1 a** the price a passenger has to pay to be conveyed by bus, train, etc. **b** a passenger paying to travel in a public vehicle. **2** a range of food. • *v.intr.* **1** progress; get on (*how did you fare?*). **2** happen; turn out. **3** journey; go; travel.

Far East *n.* (prec. by *the*) China, Japan, and other countries of E. Asia. ▫▫ **Far East·ern** *adj.*

fare·well /fáirwél/ *int. & n.* • *int.* good-bye; adieu. • *n.* **1** leave-taking; departure (also *attrib.*: *a farewell kiss*). **2** parting good wishes.

far-fetched *adj.* (of an explanation, etc.) strained; unconvincing.

far-flung *adj.* **1** extending far; widely distributed. **2** remote; distant.

fa·ri·na /fəréenə/ *n.* **1** the flour or meal of cereal, nuts, or starchy roots. **2** a powdery substance.

farm /faarm/ *n. & v.* • *n.* **1** an area of land and its buildings used under one management for growing crops, rearing animals, etc. **2** a place or establishment for breeding a particular type of animal, growing fruit, etc. (*trout farm; mink farm*). **3** = FARMHOUSE. **4** a place with many tanks for the storage of oil or oil products. • *v.* **1 a** *tr.* use (land) for growing crops, rearing animals, etc. **b** *intr.* be a farmer; work on a farm. **2** *tr.* breed (fish, etc.) commercially. **3** *tr.* (often foll. by *out*) **a** delegate or subcontract (work) to others. **b** contract (the collection of taxes) to another for a fee. **c** arrange for (a person) to be looked after by another, with payment. **4** *tr.* lease the labor or services of (a person) for hire. **5** *tr.* contract to maintain and care for (a person, esp. a child) for a fixed sum. ▫▫ **farm·ing** *n.*

farm·er /fáarmər/ *n.* **1** a person who cultivates a farm. **2** a person to whom the collection of taxes is contracted for a fee. **3** a person who looks after children or performs other services for payment.

farm hand *n.* a worker on a farm.

farm·house /fáarmhows/ *n.* a dwelling place attached to a farm.

farm·land /fáarmland/ *n.* land used or suitable for farming.

farm·stead /fáarmsted/ *n.* a farm and its buildings.

farm·yard /fáarmyaard/ *n.* a yard attached to a farmhouse.

far·o /fáirō/ *n.* a gambling card game in which bets are placed on the order of appearance of the cards.

far-off *adj.* remote.

far-out *adj.* **1** distant. **2** avant-garde; unconventional.

far-reach·ing *adj.* **1** widely applicable. **2** having important consequences or implications.

far·ri·er /fáreeər/ *n.* a smith who shoes horses.

far·row /fárō/ *n. & v.* • *n.* **1** a litter of pigs. **2** the birth of a litter. • *v.tr.* (also *absol.*) (of a sow) produce (pigs).

far-see·ing /fáarséeing/ *adj.* shrewd in judgment; prescient.

Far·si /fáarsee/ *n.* the modern Persian language.

far·sight·ed /fáarsītid/ *adj.* **1** having foresight; prudent. **2** able to see clearly only what is comparatively distant. ▫▫ **far·sight·ed·ly** *adv.* **far·sight·ed·ness** *n.*

fart /faart/ *v. & n. coarse sl.* • *v.intr.* **1** emit intestinal gas from the anus. **2** (foll. by *around*) behave foolishly. • *n.* **1** an emission of intestinal gas from the anus. **2** an unpleasant person. ▶Usually considered a taboo word.

far·ther /fáarthər/ *adv. & adj.* (also **fur·ther** /fórthər/) • *adv.* **1** to or at a more advanced point in space or time (*unsafe to proceed farther*). **2** at a greater distance (*nothing was farther from his thoughts*). • *adj.* more distant or advanced (*on the farther side*). ▫▫ **far·ther·most** *adj.*

▶Traditionally, **farther, farthest** were used in referring to physical distance: *The falls were still two or three miles farther up the path.* **Further, furthest** were held to be restricted to figurative or abstract senses: *We decided to consider the matter further.* Although **farther, farthest** are still properly restricted to measurable distances, **further** is now common in both senses: *Put those plants the furthest from the window.*

far·thest /fáarthist/ *adj. & adv.* (also **fur·thest** /fúrthist/) • *adj.* most distant. • *adv.* to or at the greatest distance.

□ **at the farthest** (or **at farthest**) at the greatest distance; at the latest; at most.

far·thing /faárthing/ *n.* **1** (in the UK) a former coin and monetary unit worth a quarter of an old penny. **2** the least possible amount (*it doesn't matter a farthing*).

fas·ces /fáseez/ *n.pl.* **1** *Rom.Hist.* a bundle of rods with a projecting ax blade, carried as a symbol of a magistrate's power. **2** *hist.* (in Fascist Italy) emblems of authority.

fasces

fas·ci·a /fáyshə/ *n.* **1** a stripe or band. **2** *Archit.* **a** a long flat surface between moldings on the architrave in classical architecture. **b** a flat surface, usu. of wood, covering the ends of rafters. **3** /fásheeə/ *Anat.* a thin sheath of fibrous connective tissue. □□ **fas·ci·al** *adj.*

fas·ci·cle /fásikəl/ *n.* **1** (also **fas·ci·cule** /–kyool/) a separately published installment of a book. **2** a bunch or bundle.

fas·ci·nate /fásinayt/ *v.tr.* **1** capture the interest of; attract irresistibly. **2** paralyze (a victim) with fear. □□ **fas·ci·nat·ed** *adj.* **fas·ci·nat·ing** *adj.* **fas·ci·nat·ing·ly** *adv.* **fas·ci·na·tion** /–náyshən/ *n.* **fas·ci·na·tor** *n.*

Fas·cism /fáshizəm/ *n.* **1** the totalitarian principles and organization of the extreme right-wing nationalist movement in Italy (1922–43). **2** (also **fascism**) **a** any similar nationalist and authoritarian movement. **b** *disp.* any system of extreme right-wing or authoritarian views. □□ **Fas·cist** *n. & adj.* (also **fas·cist**). **Fas·cis·tic** *adj.* (also **fas·cis·tic**).

fash·ion /fáshən/ *n. & v.* • *n.* **1** the current popular custom or style, esp. in dress. **2** a manner of doing something (*in a peculiar fashion*). **3** (in *comb.*) in a specified manner (*in a peaceable fashion*). **4** fashionable society (*a woman of fashion*). • *v.tr.* (often foll. by *into*) make into a particular or the required form. □ **after** (or **in**) **a fashion** as well as is practicable, though not satisfactorily. **in** (or **out of**) **fashion** fashionable (or not fashionable).

fash·ion·a·ble /fáshənəbəl/ *adj.* **1** following, suited to, or influenced by the current fashion. **2** characteristic of or favored by those who are leaders of social fashion. □□ **fash·ion·a·ble·ness** *n.* **fash·ion·a·bly** *adv.*

fast[1] /fast/ *adj. & adv.* • *adj.* **1** rapid; quick-moving. **2** capable of high speed (*a fast car*). **3** enabling or causing or intended for high speed (*the fast lane*). **4** (of a clock, etc.) showing a time ahead of the correct time. **5** (of a field, etc., in a sport) likely to make the ball bounce quickly. **6 a** (of photographic film) needing only a short exposure. **b** (of a lens) having a large aperture. **7 a** firmly fixed or attached. **b** secure; firmly established (*a fast friendship*). **8** (of a color) not fading. **9** (of a person) immoral; dissipated. • *adv.* **1** quickly; in quick succession. **2** firmly; tightly (*stand fast*; *eyes fast shut*). **3** soundly; completely (*fast asleep*). **4** close; immediately (*fast on their heels*). **5** in a dissipated manner; extravagantly; immorally. □ **pull a fast one** (often foll. by *on*) *colloq.* try to deceive or gain an unfair advantage.

fast[2] /fast/ *v. & n.* • *v.intr.* abstain from all or some kinds of food or drink. • *n.* an act or period of fasting.

fast·back /fástbak/ *n.* **1** an automobile with the rear sloping continuously down to the bumper. **2** such a back.

fast breed·er *n.* (also **fast breeder reactor**) a reactor using fast neutrons to produce the same fissile material as it uses.

fast·en /fásən/ *v.* **1** *tr.* make or become fixed or secure. **2** *tr.* (foll. by *in, up*) lock securely; shut in. **3** *tr.* **a** (foll. by *on, upon*) direct (a look, thoughts, etc.) fixedly or intently. **b** focus or direct the attention fixedly upon (*fastened him with her eyes*). **4** *tr.* (foll. by *on, upon*) fix (a designation or imputation, etc.). **5** *intr.* (foll. by *on, upon*) **a** take hold of. **b** single out. □□ **fast·en·er** *n.*

fast·en·ing /fásəning/ *n.* a device that fastens something; a fastener.

fast food *n.* food that can be prepared and served quickly and easily, esp. in a snack bar or restaurant.

fas·tid·i·ous /fastídeeəs/ *adj.* **1** very careful in matters of choice or taste; fussy. **2** easily disgusted; squeamish. □□ **fas·tid·i·ous·ly** *adv.* **fas·tid·i·ous·ness** *n.*

fast·ness /fástnis/ *n.* **1** a stronghold or fortress. **2** the state of being secure.

fast-talk *v.tr. colloq.* persuade by rapid or deceitful talk.

fast track *n.* a course or situation leading to rapid advancement or promotion, as in a career.

fat /fat/ *n., adj., & v.* • *n.* **1** a natural oily or greasy substance occurring esp. in animal bodies. **2** the part of anything containing this. **3** excessive presence of fat in a person or animal. **4** *Chem.* any of a group of natural esters of glycerol and various fatty acids existing as solids at room temperature. **5** overabundance or excess. • *adj.* (**fatter, fattest**) **1** (of a person or animal) having excessive fat. **2** (of an animal) made plump for slaughter; fatted. **3** containing much fat. **4** greasy; oily; unctuous. **5** (of land or resources) fertile; rich; yielding abundantly. **6 a** thick; substantial in content (*a fat book*). **b** substantial as an asset or opportunity (*a fat check*). **7** *colloq. iron.* very little; not much (*a fat chance*). • *v.tr. & intr.* (**fatted, fatting**) make or become fat. □□ **fat·less** *adj.* **fat·ly** *adv.* **fat·ness** *n.* **fat·tish** *adj.*

fa·tal /fáytəl/ *adj.* **1** causing or ending in death (*a fatal accident*). **2** (often foll. by *to*) destructive; ruinous; ending in disaster (*was fatal to their chances; made a fatal mistake*). **3** fateful. □□ **fa·tal·ly** *adv.*

fa·tal·ism /fáyt'lizəm/ *n.* **1** the belief that all events are predetermined and therefore inevitable. **2** a submissive attitude to events as being inevitable. □□ **fa·tal·ist** *n.* **fa·tal·is·tic** *adj.* **fa·tal·is·ti·cal·ly** /–lístiklee/ *adv.*

fa·tal·i·ty /fətálətee, fay–/ *n.* (*pl.* **-ties**) **1 a** an occurrence of death by accident or in war, etc. **b** a person killed in this way. **2** a fatal influence. **3** a predestined liability to disaster. **4** subjection to or the supremacy of fate. **5** a disastrous event; a calamity.

fat cat *n. sl.* **1** a wealthy person, esp. as a benefactor. **2** a highly paid executive or official.

fate /fayt/ *n. & v.* • *n.* **1** a power regarded as predetermining events unalterably. **2 a** the future regarded as determined by such a power. **b** an individual's appointed lot. **c** the ultimate condition or end of a person or thing (*that sealed our fate*). **3** death; destruction. **4** (usu. **Fate**) a goddess of destiny. • *v.tr.* **1** (usu. in *passive*) preordain (*was fated to win*). **2** (as **fated** *adj.*) **a** doomed to destruction. **b** unavoidable; preordained; fateful.

fate·ful /fáytfool/ *adj.* **1** important; decisive; having far-reaching consequences. **2** controlled as if by fate. **3** causing or likely to cause disaster. **4** prophetic. □□ **fate·ful·ly** *adv.*

fat·head /fat-hed/ *n. colloq.* a stupid person. □□ **fat·head·ed** *adj.* **fat·head·ed·ness** *n.*

fa·ther /faáthər/ *n. & v.* • *n.* **1 a** a man in relation to a child born from his fertilization of an ovum. **b** a man who has continuous care of a child, esp. by adoption. **2** any male animal in relation to its offspring. **3** (usu. in *pl.*) a forefather. **4** an originator or early leader. **5** a person who deserves special respect (*the father of his country*). **6** (also **Father**) **a** (often as a title or form of address) a priest. **b** a religious leader. **7** (**the Father**) (in Christian belief) the first person of the Trinity. **8** (**Father**) a venerable person, esp. as a title in personifications (*Father Time*). **9** (usu. in *pl.*) the leading men or elders in a city, etc. (*city fathers*). • *v.tr.* **1** beget; be the father of. **2** behave as a father toward. **3** originate (a scheme, etc.). **4** appear as or admit that one is the father or originator of. **5** (foll. by *on*) assign the paternity of (a child, book, etc.) to a person. □□ **fa·ther·hood** *n.* **fa·ther·less** *adj.*

fa·ther-in-law *n.* (*pl.* **fathers-in-law**) the father of one's husband or wife.

fa·ther·land /faa͞thərland/ *n.* one's native country.

fa·ther·ly /faa͞thərlee/ *adj.* **1** like or characteristic of a father in affection, care, etc. (*fatherly concern*). **2** of or proper to a father. □□ **fa·ther·li·ness** *n.*

fath·om /fáthəm/ *n.* & *v.* • *n.* (*pl.* often **fathom** when prec. by a number) a measure of six feet, esp. used in taking depth soundings. • *v.tr.* **1** comprehend. **2** measure the depth of (water). □□ **fath·om·a·ble** *adj.* **fath·om·less** *adj.*

fa·tigue /fəteég/ *n.* & *v.* • *n.* **1** extreme tiredness after exertion. **2** weakness in materials, esp. metal, caused by repeated variations of stress. **3** a reduction in the efficiency of a muscle, organ, etc., after prolonged activity. **4 a** a nonmilitary duty in the army, often as a punishment. **b** (in full **fatigue party**) a group of soldiers ordered to do fatigues. **c** (in *pl.*) work clothing worn by soldiers on fatigue duty. • *v.tr.* (**fatigues, fatigued, fatiguing**) **1** cause fatigue in; tire; exhaust. **2** (as **fatigued** *adj.*) weary; listless.

fat·so /fátsō/ *n.* (*pl.* **-soes**) *sl. joc.* or *offens.* a fat person.

fat·ten /fát'n/ *v.* **1** *tr.* & *intr.* make or become fat. **2** *tr.* enrich (soil).

fat·ty /fátee/ *adj.* & *n.* • *adj.* (**fattier, fattiest**) **1** like fat; oily; greasy. **2** consisting of or containing fat; adipose. **3** marked by abnormal deposition of fat. • *n.* (*pl.* **-ties**) *colloq.* usu. *offens.* a fat person. □□ **fat·ti·ness** *n.*

fat·ty ac·id *n. Chem.* any of a class of organic compounds consisting of a hydrocarbon chain and a terminal carboxyl group.

fat·u·ous /fách͞ooəs/ *adj.* vacantly silly; purposeless; idiotic. □□ **fa·tu·i·ty** /fət͞ooitee, –ty͞oo–/ *n.* (*pl.* **-ties**). **fat·u·ous·ly** *adv.* **fat·u·ous·ness** *n.*

fat·wa /fátwaa/ *n.* (in Islamic countries) an authoritative ruling on a religious matter.

fau·cet /fáwsit/ *n.* a device by which a flow of liquid from a pipe or vessel can be controlled.

fault /fawlt/ *n.* & *v.* • *n.* **1** a defect or imperfection of character or of structure, appearance, etc. **2** a break in an electric circuit. **3** a transgression, offense, or thing wrongly done. **4 a** *Tennis*, etc., a service of the ball not in accordance with the rules. **b** (in show jumping) a penalty for an error. **5** responsibility for wrongdoing, error, etc. . **6** a defect regarded as the cause of something wrong (*the fault lies in the teaching methods*). **7** *Geol.* an extended break in the continuity of strata. • *v.* **1** *tr.* find fault with; blame. **2** *tr.* declare to be faulty. **3** *tr. Geol.* break the continuity of (strata). **4** *intr.* commit a fault. **5** *intr. Geol.* show a fault. □ **at fault** guilty; to blame. **find fault** (often foll. by *with*) make an adverse criticism; complain. **to a fault** (usu. of a commendable quality, etc.) excessively (*generous to a fault*).

fault·find·er /fáwltfindər/ *n.* a person given to continually finding fault. □□ **fault·find·ing** *n.* & *adj.*

fault·less /fáwltlis/ *adj.* without fault; free from defect or error. □□ **fault·less·ly** *adv.* **fault·less·ness** *n.*

fault·y /fáwltee/ (**faultier, faultiest**) *adj.* having faults; imperfect. □□ **fault·i·ly** *adv.* **fault·i·ness** *n.*

faun /fawn/ *n.* a Roman rural deity with a human face and torso and a goat's horns, legs, and tail.

fau·na /fáwnə/ *n.* (*pl.* **faunas** or **faunae** /–nee/) **1** the animal life of a region or geological period (cf. FLORA). **2** a treatise on or list of this. □□ **fau·nal** *adj.*

fauv·ism /fṓvizəm/ *n.* a style of painting with vivid use of color. □□ **fauv·ist** *n.*

faux /fō/ *adj.* imitation; counterfeit (*faux emeralds*).

faux pas /fō paá/ *n.* (*pl.* same, *pronunc.* /paaz/) **1** a tactless mistake; a blunder. **2** a social indiscretion.

fave /fayv/ *n.* & *adj. sl.* = FAVORITE.

fa·vor /fáyvər/ *n.* & *v.* • *n.* **1** an act of kindness (*did it as a favor*). **2** approval; goodwill; friendly regard (*gained their favor; look with favor on*). **3** partiality; too lenient or generous treatment. **4** aid; support (*under favor of night*). **5** a thing given or worn as a mark of favor or support, e.g., a badge or a knot of ribbons. **6** a small present or token given out, as at a party. • *v.tr.* **1** regard or treat with favor or partiality. **2** give support or approval to; promote; prefer. **3 a** be to the advantage of (a person). **b** facilitate (a process, etc.). **4** tend to confirm (an idea or theory). **5** (foll. by *with*) oblige (*favor me with a reply*). **6** (as **favored** *adj.*) **a** having special advantages. **b** preferred; favorite. **7** *colloq.* resemble in features. **8** treat gingerly or gently (*favored her injured wrist*). □ **in favor 1** meeting with approval. **2** (foll. by *of*) **a** in support of. **b** to the advantage of. **out of favor** lacking approval.

fa·vor·a·ble /fáyvərəbəl/ *adj.* **1 a** well-disposed; propitious. **b** approving. **2** giving consent (*a favorable answer*). **3** promising; auspicious (*a favorable aspect*). **4** (often foll. by *to*) helpful; suitable. □□ **fa·vor·a·ble·ness** *n.* **fa·vor·a·bly** *adv.*

fa·vor·ite /fáyvərit, fáyvrit/ *adj.* & *n.* • *adj.* preferred to all others (*my favorite book*). • *n.* **1** a particularly favored person. **2** *Sports* a competitor thought most likely to win.

fa·vor·it·ism /fáyvəritizəm, fáyvri–/ *n.* the unfair favoring of one person or group at the expense of another.

fawn[1] /fawn/ *n.*, *adj.*, & *v.* • *n.* **1** a deer in its first year. **2** a light yellowish brown. • *adj.* fawn colored. • *v.tr.* (also *absol.*) (of a deer) bring forth (young). □ **in fawn** (of a deer) pregnant.

fawn[2] /fawn/ *v.intr.* **1** (often foll. by *on*) (of a person) behave servilely; cringe. **2** (of an animal, esp. a dog) show extreme affection. □□ **fawn·ing** *adj.* **fawn·ing·ly** *adv.*

fax /faks/ *n.* & *v.* • *n.* **1** facsimile transmission (see FACSIMILE *n.* 2). **2 a** a copy produced by this. **b** a machine for transmitting and receiving these. • *v.tr.* transmit in this way.

fay /fay/ *n. literary* a fairy.

faze /fayz/ *v.tr.* (often as **fazed** *adj.*) *colloq.* disconcert; disorient.

FBI *abbr.* Federal Bureau of Investigation.

FCC *abbr.* Federal Communications Commission.

F clef *n.* = BASS CLEF.

FDA *abbr.* Food and Drug Administration.

FDIC *abbr.* Federal Deposit Insurance Corporation.

Fe *symb. Chem.* the element iron.

fe·al·ty /féealtee/ *n.* (*pl.* **-ties**) **1** *hist.* **a** a feudal tenant's or vassal's fidelity to a lord. **b** an acknowledgment of this. **2** allegiance.

fear /feer/ *n.* & *v.* • *n.* **1 a** an unpleasant emotion caused by exposure to danger, expectation of pain, etc. **b** a state of alarm (*be in fear*). **2** a cause of fear (*all fears removed*). **3** (often foll. by *of*) dread or fearful respect (for) (*had a fear of heights*). **4** anxiety for the safety of (*in fear of their lives*). **5** danger; likelihood (of something unwelcome) (*there is little fear of failure*). • *v.* **1 a** *tr.* feel fear about or toward. **b** *intr.* feel fear. **2** *intr.* (foll. by *for*) feel anxiety about (*feared for my life*). **3** *tr.* have uneasy expectation of (*fear the worst*). **4** *tr.* (usu. foll. by *that* + clause) apprehend with fear or regret (*I fear that you are wrong*). **5** *tr.* **a** (foll. by *to* + infin.) hesitate. **b** (foll. by verbal noun) shrink from; be apprehensive about (*he feared meeting his ex-wife*). **6** *tr.* show reverence toward. □ **for fear of** (or **that**) to avoid the risk of (or that). **never fear** there is no danger of that.

fear·ful /féerfool/ *adj.* **1** (usu. foll. by *of*, or *that* + clause) afraid. **2** terrible; awful. **3** *colloq.* extremely unwelcome or unpleasant. ▫▫ **fear·ful·ly** *adv.* **fear·ful·ness** *n.*

fear·less /féerlis/ *adj.* **1** courageous; brave. **2** (foll. by *of*) without fear. ▫▫ **fear·less·ly** *adv.* **fear·less·ness** *n.*

fear·some /féersəm/ *adj.* **1** appalling or frightening. **2** timid. ▫▫ **fear·some·ly** *adv.* **fear·some·ness** *n.*

fea·si·ble /féezibəl/ *adj.* **1** practicable; possible. **2** *disp.* likely; probable (*it is feasible that they will get the job*). ▫▫ **fea·si·bil·i·ty** /féezibílitee/ *n.* **fea·si·bly** *adv.*

▶The correct meaning of **feasible** is 'practicable' or 'possible,' e.g., *Walking at night was not feasible without the aid of a flashlight.* It should not be used to mean 'likely' or 'probable.'

feast /feest/ *n.* & *v.* • *n.* **1** a large or sumptuous meal. **2** a gratification to the senses or mind. **3 a** an annual religious celebration. **b** a day dedicated to a particular saint. • *v.* **1** *intr.* partake of a feast; eat and drink sumptuously. **2** *tr.* **a** regale. **b** pass (time) in feasting. ▫ **feast one's eyes on** take pleasure in beholding.

feat /feet/ *n.* a noteworthy act or achievement.

feath·er /féthər/ *n.* & *v.* • *n.* **1** any of the appendages growing from a bird's skin, with a horny hollow stem and fine strands. **2** one or more of these as decoration, etc. **3** (*collect.*) **a** plumage. **b** game birds. • *v.* **1** *tr.* cover or line with feathers. **2** *tr. Rowing* turn (an oar) so that it passes through the air edgewise. **3** *tr. Aeron.* & *Naut.* cause (blades) to rotate in such a way as to lessen the air or water resistance. ▫ **a feather in one's cap** an achievement to one's credit. **feather one's nest** enrich oneself. **in fine** (or **high**) **feather** *colloq.* in good spirits. ▫▫ **feath·ered** *adj.* (also in *comb.*). **feath·er·i·ness** *n.* **feath·er·less** *adj.* **feath·er·y** *adj.*

feath·er bed *n.* & *v.tr.* • *n.* a bed with a mattress stuffed with feathers. • *v.tr.* (**featherbed**) (**-bedded, -bedding**) provide with (esp. financial) advantages.

feath·er·bed·ding /féthərbeding/ *n.* the employment of excess staff, esp. due to union rules.

feath·er·brain /féthərbrayn/ *n.* (also **featherhead**) a silly or absent-minded person. ▫▫ **feath·er·brained** /féthərbraynd/ *adj.* (also **featherheaded**)

feath·er·edge /féthərej/ *n.* a fine edge produced by tapering a board, plank, or other object.

feath·er·ing /féthəring/ *n.* **1** bird's plumage. **2** the feathers of an arrow. **3** a featherlike structure in an animal's coat. **4** *Archit.* cusps in tracery.

feath·er·stitch /féthərstich/ *n.* ornamental zigzag sewing.

feath·er·weight /féthərwayt/ *n.* **1 a** any of various weight classes in certain sports intermediate between bantamweight and lightweight. **b** a boxer, etc., of this weight. **2** a very light person or thing. **3** (usu. *attrib.*) an unimportant thing.

fea·ture /féechər/ *n.* & *v.* • *n.* **1** a distinctive or characteristic part of a thing. **2** (usu. in *pl.*) (a distinctive part of) the face, esp. with regard to shape and visual effect. **3 a** a distinctive or regular article in a newspaper or magazine. **b** a special attraction at an event, etc. **4 a** (in full **feature film**) a full-length movie intended as the main item at a showing. **b** (in full **feature program**) a broadcast devoted to a particular topic. • *v.* **1** *tr.* make a special display or attraction of; give special prominence to. **2** *tr.* & *intr.* have as or be an important actor, participant, or topic in a movie, broadcast, etc. **3** *intr.* be a feature. ▫▫ **fea·tured** *adj.* (also in *comb.*).

Feb. *abbr.* February.

fe·brile /fébral, fée–/ *adj.* of or relating to fever; feverish. ▫▫ **fe·bril·i·ty** /fibrílitee/ *n.*

Feb·ru·ar·y /fébrooeree, fébyoo–/ *n.* (*pl.* **-ies**) the second month of the year.

fe·ces /féeseez/ *n.pl.* waste matter discharged from the bowels. ▫▫ **fe·cal** /féekəl/ *adj.*

feck·less /féklis/ *adj.* **1** feeble; ineffective. **2** unthinking; irresponsible (*feckless gaiety*). ▫▫ **feck·less·ly** *adv.* **feck·less·ness** *n.*

fec·u·lent /fékyələnt/ *adj.* **1** murky; filthy. **2** containing sediments or dregs. ▫▫ **fec·u·lence** *n.*

fe·cund /féekənd, fék–/ *adj.* **1** prolific; fertile. **2** fertilizing. ▫▫ **fe·cun·di·ty** /fikúnditee/ *n.*

Fed /fed/ *n. sl.* **1** a federal agent or official, esp. a member of the FBI. **2 a** the Federal Reserve System. **b** the Federal Reserve Board.

fed *past* and *past part.* of FEED.

fed·er·al /fédərəl/ *adj.* **1** of a system of government in which several states form a unity but remain independent in internal affairs. **2** relating to or affecting such a federation. **3 a** of or relating to central government (*federal laws*). **b** (also **Federal**) favoring centralized government. **4** (**Federal**) of or loyal to the Union army and federal government in the US Civil War. **5** comprising an association of largely independent units. ▫▫ **fed·er·al·ism** *n.* **fed·er·al·ist** *n.* **fed·er·al·ize** *v.tr.* **fed·er·al·i·za·tion** *n.* **fed·er·al·ly** *adv.*

fed·er·ate *v.* & *adj.* • *v.tr.* & *intr.* /fédərayt/ organize or be organized on a federal basis. • *adj.* /fédərət having a federal organization./

fed·er·a·tion /fédəráyshən/ *n.* **1** a federal group of states. **2** a federated society or group. **3** the act or an instance of federating. ▫▫ **fed·er·a·tion·ist** *n.*

fe·do·ra /fidáwrə/ *n.* a soft felt hat with a low crown creased lengthways.

fedora

fed up *adj.* (often foll. by *with*) discontented or bored (*am fed up with the rain*).

fee /fee/ *n.* & *v.* • *n.* **1** a payment made to a professional person or to a professional or public body in exchange for advice or services. **2** money paid as part of a special transaction, for a privilege, admission to a society, etc. (*enrollment fee*). **3** (in *pl.*) money regularly paid for continuing services. **4** *Law* an inherited estate, unlimited (**fee simple**) or limited (**fee tail**) as to the category of heir. • *v.tr.* (**fee'd** or **feed**) **1** pay a fee to. **2** engage for a fee.

fee·ble /féebəl/ *adj.* **1** weak; infirm. **2** lacking energy, force, or effectiveness. **3** dim; indistinct. **4** deficient in character or intelligence. ▫▫ **fee·ble·ness** *n.* **fee·blish** *adj.* **fee·bly** *adv.*

fee·ble·mind·ed /féebəlmíndid/ *adj.* **1** unintelligent. **2** mentally deficient. ▫▫ **fee·ble·mind·ed·ly** *adv.* **fee·ble·mind·ed·ness** *n.*

feed /feed/ *v.* & *n.* • *v.* (*past* and *past part.* **fed** /fed/) **1** *tr.* **a** supply with food. **b** put food into the mouth of. **2** *tr.* **a** give as food, esp. to animals. **b** graze (cattle). **3** *tr.* serve as food for. **4** *intr.* (usu. foll. by *on*) take food; eat. **5** *tr.* nourish; make grow. **6 a** *tr.* maintain supply of raw material, fuel, etc., to (a fire, machine, etc.). **b** *tr.* (foll. by *into*) supply (material) to a machine, etc. **c** *tr.* supply or send (an electronic signal) for broadcast, etc. **d** *intr.* (often foll. by *into*) (of a river, etc.) flow into another body of water. **e** *tr.* insert further coins into (a meter) to continue its function, validity, etc. **7** *intr.* (foll. by *on*) **a** be nourished by. **b** derive benefit from. **8** *tr.* use (land) as pasture. **9** *tr. Theatr. sl.* supply (an actor, etc.) with cues. **10** *tr. Sports* send passes to (a player) in a basketball game, soccer or hockey match, etc. **11** *tr.* gratify (vanity, etc.). **12** *tr.* provide (advice, information, etc.) to. • *n.* **1** an amount of food, esp. for animals. **2** the act or an instance of feeding; the giving of food. **3** *colloq.* a meal. **4** pasturage; green crops.

feed·back /féedbak/ *n.* **1** information about the result of an experiment, etc.; response. **2** *Electronics* **a** the return of a fraction of the output signal from one stage of a circuit, amplifier, etc., to the input of the same or a preceding stage. **b** a signal so returned. **3** *Biol.*, etc., the modification or control of a process or system by its results or effects.

feed bag *n.* a bag containing fodder, hung on a horse's head.

feed·er /féedər/ *n.* **1** a person or thing that feeds. **2** a person who eats in a specified manner. **3** a tributary stream. **4** a branch road, railroad line, etc., linking outlying districts with a main communication system. **5** *Electr.* a main conductor carrying electricity to a distribution point.

feel /feel/ *v.* & *n.* • *v.* (*past* and *past part.* **felt** /felt/) **1** *tr.* **a** examine or search by touch. **b** (*absol.*) have the sensation of touch (*was unable to feel*). **2** *tr.* perceive or ascertain by touch; have a sensation of (*could feel the warmth; felt that it was cold*). **3** *tr.* **a** undergo; experience (*shall feel my anger*). **b** exhibit or be conscious of (an emotion, sensation, conviction, etc.). **4 a** *intr.* have a specified feeling or reaction (*felt strongly about it*). **b** *tr.* be emotionally affected by (*felt the rebuke deeply*). **5** *tr.* (usu. foll. by *that* + clause) have a vague or unreasoned impression (*I feel that I am right*). **6** *tr.* consider; think (*I feel it is useful to go*). **7** *intr.* seem (*the air feels chilly*). **8** *intr.* be consciously; consider oneself (*I feel happy*). **9** *intr.* **a** (foll. by *with*) have sympathy with. **b** (foll. by *for*) have pity or compassion for. • *n.* **1** the act or an instance of feeling; testing by touch. **2** the sensation characterizing a material, situation, etc. **3** the sense of touch. □ **feel free** (often foll. by *to* + infin.) not be reluctant or hesitant (*do feel free to criticize*). **feel like** have a wish for; be inclined toward. **feel oneself** be fit or confident, etc. **feel out** investigate cautiously. **feel up to** be ready to face or deal with. **feel one's way** proceed carefully; act cautiously. **get the feel of** become accustomed to using.

feel·er /féelər/ *n.* **1** an organ in certain animals for testing things by touch or for searching for food. **2** a tentative proposal (*put out feelers*). **3** a person or thing that feels.

feel·ing /féeling/ *n.* & *adj.* • *n.* **1 a** the capacity to feel; a sense of touch (*lost all feeling in his arm*). **b** a physical sensation. **2 a** (often foll. by *of*) a particular emotional reaction (*a feeling of despair*). **b** (in *pl.*) emotional susceptibilities (*hurt my feelings*; *had strong feelings about it*). **c** intense emotion (*said it with such feeling*). **3** a particular sensitivity (*had a feeling for literature*). **4 a** an opinion or notion, esp. a vague or irrational one (*had a feeling she would be there*). **b** vague awareness (*had a feeling of safety*). **c** sentiment (*the general feeling was against it*). **5** readiness to feel sympathy or compassion. **6 a** the general emotional response produced by a work of art, piece of music, etc. **b** emotional commitment or sensibility in artistic execution (*played with feeling*). • *adj.* **1** sensitive; sympathetic. **2** showing emotion or sensitivity. □□ **feel·ing·less** *adj.* **feel·ing·ly** *adv.*

feet *pl.* of FOOT.

feign /fayn/ *v.* **1** *tr.* simulate; pretend to be affected by (*feign madness*). **2** *intr.* indulge in pretense.

feint /faynt/ *n.* & *v.* • *n.* **1** a sham attack or blow, etc. **2** pretense. • *v.intr.* make a feint.

feist·y /fístee/ *adj.* (**feistier, feistiest**) *sl.* **1** aggressive; exuberant. **2** touchy. □□ **feist·i·ness** *n.*

fe·la·fel var. of FALAFEL.

feld·spar /féldspaar/ *n. Mineral.* any of a group of aluminum silicates of potassium, sodium, or calcium. □□ **feld·spath·ic** /–spáthik/ *adj.* **feld·spath·oid** /féldspəthoyd, félspə–/ *n.*

fe·lic·i·tate /fəlísitayt/ *v.tr.* congratulate. □□ **fe·lic·i·ta·tion** /–táyshən/ *n.* (usu. in *pl.*).

fe·lic·i·tous /fəlísitəs/ *adj.* strikingly apt; pleasantly ingenious. □□ **fe·lic·i·tous·ly** *adv.* **fe·lic·i·tous·ness** *n.*

fe·lic·i·ty /fəlísitee/ *n.* (*pl.* **-ties**) **1** intense happiness; being happy. **2** a cause of happiness. **3 a** a capacity for apt expression. **b** an appropriate or well-chosen phrase. **4** a fortunate trait.

fe·line /féelīn/ *adj.* & *n.* • *adj.* **1** of or relating to the cat family. **2** catlike. • *n.* an animal of the cat family Felidae. □□ **fe·lin·i·ty** /filínitee/ *n.*

fell[1] *past* of FALL *v.*

fell[2] /fel/ *v.* & *n.* • *v.tr.* **1** cut down (esp. a tree). **2** strike or knock down (a person or animal). **3** stitch down (the edge of a seam) to lie flat. • *n.* an amount of timber cut.

fel·la·ti·o /filáysheeō, feláateeō/ *n.* oral stimulation of the penis. □□ **fel·late** /filáyt/ *v.tr.*

fell·er /félər/ *n.* = FELLOW 1, 2.

fel·low /félō/ *n.* **1** *colloq.* a man or boy (*poor fellow!*; *my dear fellow*). **2** *derog.* a person regarded with contempt. **3** (usu. in *pl.*) a comrade (*were separated from their fellows*). **4** a counterpart or match; the other of a pair. **5** an equal; one of the same class. **6** a contemporary. **7** a selected graduate receiving a stipend for a period of research. **8** a member of a learned society. **9** (*attrib.*) belonging to the same class or activity (*fellow soldier*).

fel·low feel·ing *n.* sympathy from common experience.

fel·low·ship /félōship/ *n.* **1** companionship; friendliness. **2** participation; sharing; community of interest. **3** a body of associates. **4** a brotherhood or fraternity. **5** a guild or corporation. **6** a financial grant to a scholar.

fel·low trav·el·er *n.* **1** a person who travels with another. **2** a sympathizer with the Communist Party.

fel·on /félən/ *n.* a person who has committed a felony.

fe·lo·ni·ous /filṓneeəs/ *adj.* **1** criminal. **2** *Law* **a** of or involving felony. **b** who has committed felony. □□ **fe·lo·ni·ous·ly** *adv.*

fel·o·ny /félənee/ *n.* (*pl.* **-nies**) a crime regarded by the law as grave, and usu. involving violence.

felt[1] /felt/ *n.* & *v.* • *n.* **1** a kind of cloth made by rolling and pressing wool, etc., or by weaving and shrinking it. **2** a similar material made from other fibers. • *v.* **1** *tr.* make into felt; mat together. **2** *tr.* cover with felt. **3** *intr.* become matted. □□ **felt·y** *adj.*

felt[2] *past* and *past part.* of FEEL.

fe·male /féemayl/ *adj.* & *n.* • *adj.* **1** of the sex that can bear offspring or produce eggs. **2** (of plants or their parts) fruit-bearing. **3** of or consisting of women, female animals, or female plants. **4** (of a screw, socket, etc.) hollow to receive a corresponding inserted part. • *n.* a female person, animal, or plant. □□ **fe·male·ness** *n.*

fem·i·nine /féminin/ *adj.* & *n.* • *adj.* **1** of or characteristic of women. **2** having qualities associated with women. **3** womanly; effeminate. **4** *Gram.* of or denoting the gender proper to women's names. • *n. Gram.* a feminine gender or word. □□ **fem·i·nine·ly** *adv.* **fem·i·nine·ness** *n.* **fem·i·nin·i·ty** /–nínitee/ *n.*

fem·i·nism /féminizəm/ *n.* **1** the advocacy of women's rights on the ground of the equality of the sexes. **2** *Med.* the development of female characteristics in a male person. □□ **fem·i·nist** *n.* (in sense 1).

fe·min·i·ty /feminitee/ *n.* = *femininity* (see FEMININE).

fem·i·nize /féminīz/ *v.tr.* & *intr.* make or become feminine or female. □□ **fem·i·ni·za·tion** *n.*

femme fa·tale /fém fətál, –taál, fay–/ *n.* (*pl.* **femmes fatales** *pronunc.* same) a seductively attractive woman.
fe·mur /féemər/ *n.* (*pl.* **femurs** or **femora** /fémərə/) *Anat.* the thigh bone, the thick bone between the hip and the knee. □□ **fem·o·ral** /fémərəl/ *adj.*
fen /fen/ *n.* a low marshy or flooded area of land.
fence /fens/ *n.* & *v.* • *n.* **1** a barrier or railing enclosing an area of ground. **2** a large upright obstacle in steeplechasing or show jumping. **3** *sl.* a receiver of stolen goods. **4** a guard or guide in machinery. • *v.* **1** *tr.* surround with or as with a fence. **2** *tr.* **a** (foll. by *in*, *off*) enclose or separate with or as with a fence. **b** (foll. by *up*) seal with or as with a fence. **3** *tr.* (foll. by *from*, *against*) screen; shield; protect. **4** *tr.* (foll. by *out*) exclude with or as with a fence; keep out. **5** *tr.* (also *absol.*) *sl.* deal in (stolen goods). **6** *intr.* practice the sport of fencing. **7** *intr.* (foll. by *with*) evade answering (a person or question). □ **sit on the fence** remain neutral or undecided in a dispute, etc. □□ **fenc·er** *n.*
fenc·ing /fénsing/ *n.* **1** a set or extent of fences. **2** material for making fences. **3** the art or sport of swordplay.
fend /fend/ *v.* **1** *intr.* (foll. by *for*) look after (esp. oneself). **2** *tr.* (usu. foll. by *off*) ward off.
fend·er /féndər/ *n.* **1** a low frame bordering a fireplace. **2** *Naut.* a piece of old timber, matting, etc., hung over a vessel's side to protect it against impact. **3 a** a thing used to keep something off, prevent a collision, etc. **b** a device or enclosure over or around the wheel of a motor vehicle, bicycle, etc.
fen·nel /fénəl/ *n.* **1** a yellow-flowered fragrant umbelliferous plant, *Foeniculum vulgare*, with leaves or leaf stalks used in salads, soups, etc. **2** the seeds of this used as flavoring.
fe·ral /féerəl, férəl/ *adj.* **1** untamed; uncultivated. **2** (of an animal) in a wild state after escape from captivity or domestication.
fer de lance /fáir də láns/ *n.* a large highly venomous snake, *Bothrops atrox*, native to Central and S. America.
fer·ment *n.* & *v.* • *n.* /fə́rment/ **1** agitation; excitement; tumult. **2 a** fermentation. **b** a fermenting agent. • *v.* /fərmént/ **1** *intr.* & *tr.* undergo or subject to fermentation. **2** *intr.* & *tr.* effervesce or cause to effervesce. **3** *tr.* excite; stir up. □□ **fer·ment·a·ble** *adj.* **fer·ment·er** /–méntər/ *n.*
fer·men·ta·tion /fə́rmentáyshən/ *n.* **1** the breakdown of a substance by microorganisms, such as yeasts and bacteria, esp. of sugar to ethyl alcohol in making beers, wines, and spirits. **2** agitation; excitement. □□ **fer·ment·a·tive** /–méntətiv/ *adj.*
fer·mi·um /fə́rmeeəm, fér–/ *n. Chem.* a transuranic radioactive metallic element produced artificially. ¶ Symb.: **Fm**.
fern /fərn/ *n.* (*pl.* same or **ferns**) any flowerless plant of the order Filicales, usu. having feathery fronds. □□ **fern·er·y** *n.* (*pl.* **-ies**). **fern·y** *adj.*
fe·ro·cious /fəróshəs/ *adj.* fierce; savage; wildly cruel. □□ **fe·ro·cious·ly** *adv.* **fe·ro·cious·ness** *n.*
fe·roc·i·ty /fərósitee/ *n.* (*pl.* **-ties**) **1** ferocious nature; the state of being ferocious. **2** a ferocious act.
-ferous /fərəs/ *comb. form* (usu. **–iferous**) forming adjectives with the sense 'bearing,' 'having' (*auriferous*; *odoriferous*). □□ **-ferously** *suffix forming adverbs.* **-ferousness** *suffix forming nouns.*
fer·rate /férayt/ *n. Chem.* a salt of (the hypothetical) ferric acid.
fer·ret /férit/ *n.* & *v.* • *n.* a small polecat, *Mustela putorius furo*, used in catching rabbits, rats, etc. • *v.* **1** *intr.* hunt with ferrets. **2** *intr.* rummage; search out. **3** *tr.* (often foll. by *about*, *away*, *out*, etc.) **a** clear out (holes or an area of ground) with ferrets. **b** take or drive away (rabbits, etc.) with ferrets. **4** *tr.* (foll. by *out*) search out (secrets, criminals, etc.). □□ **fer·ret·er** *n.* **fer·ret·y** *adj.*
fer·ric /férik/ *adj.* **1** of iron. **2** *Chem.* containing iron in a trivalent form (cf. FERROUS 2).
Fer·ris wheel /féris/ *n.* a carnival ride consisting of a tall revolving vertical wheel with passenger cars suspended on its outer edge.

ferris wheel

fer·rite /férīt/ *n. Chem.* **1** a magnetic subtance, a compound of ferric oxide and another metallic oxide. **2** an allotrope of pure iron occurring in low-carbon steel. □□ **fer·ri·tic** /ferítik/ *adj.*
ferro- /férō/ *comb. form Chem.* **1** iron, esp. in ferrous compounds (*ferrocyanide*). **2** (of alloys) containing iron (*ferromanganese*).
fer·rous /férəs/ *adj.* **1** containing iron (*ferrous and nonferrous metals*). **2** *Chem.* containing iron in a divalent form (cf. FERRIC 2).
fer·rule /férōōl/ *n.* **1** a ring or cap strengthening the end of a stick or tube. **2** a band strengthening or forming a joint.
fer·ry /féree/ *n.* & *v.* • *n.* (*pl.* **-ries**) **1** a boat or aircraft, etc., for conveying passengers and goods as a regular service. **2** the service itself or the place where it operates. • *v.* (**-ries**, **-ried**) **1** *tr.* & *intr.* convey in a boat, etc. across water. **2** *intr.* (of a boat, etc.) pass back and forth across water. **3** *tr.* transport from one place to another, esp. as a regular service. □□ **fer·ry·man** /–mən/ *n.* (*pl.* **-men**).
fer·tile /fə́rt'l/ *adj.* **1 a** (of soil) producing abundant vegetation or crops. **b** fruitful. **2 a** (of a seed, egg, etc.) capable of becoming a new individual. **b** (of animals and plants) able to conceive young or produce fruit. **3** (of the mind) inventive. **4** (of nuclear material) able to become fissile by the capture of neutrons. □□ **fer·til·i·ty** /–tílitee/ *n.*
fer·til·i·za·tion /fə́rt'lizáyshən/ *n.* **1** *Biol.* the fusion of male and female gametes during sexual reproduction to form a zygote. **2 a** the act or an instance of fertilizing. **b** the process of being fertilized.
fer·ti·lize /fə́rt'līz/ *v.tr.* **1** make (soil, etc.) fertile or productive. **2** cause (an egg, female animal, or plant) to develop a new individual by introducing male reproductive material. □□ **fer·ti·liz·a·ble** *adj.*
fer·ti·liz·er /fə́rt'līzər/ *n.* a chemical or natural substance added to soil to make it more fertile.
fer·vent /fə́rvənt/ *adj.* **1** ardent; impassioned; intense. **2** hot; glowing. □□ **fer·ven·cy** *n.* **fer·vent·ly** *adv.*
fer·vid /fə́rvid/ *adj.* **1** ardent; intense. **2** hot; glowing. □□ **fer·vid·ly** *adv.*
fer·vor /fə́rvər/ *n.* **1** vehemence; passion; zeal. **2** a glowing condition; intense heat.
fes·cue /féskyōō/ *n.* any grass of the genus *Festuca*, valuable for pasture and fodder.
fes·tal /fést'l/ *adj.* **1** joyous; merry. **2** engaging in holiday activities. **3** of a feast. □□ **fes·tal·ly** *adv.*
fes·ter /féstər/ *v.* **1** *tr.* & *intr.* make or become septic. **2** *intr.* cause continuing annoyance. **3** *intr.* rot; stagnate.
fes·ti·val /féstivəl/ *n.* (also *attrib.*) **1** a day or period of celebration. **2** a concentrated series of concerts, plays, etc., held regularly in a town, etc.
fes·tive /féstiv/ *adj.* **1** of or characteristic of a festival. **2** joyous. **3** fond of feasting; jovial. □□ **fes·tive·ly** *adv.* **fes·tive·ness** *n.*

fes·tiv·i·ty /festívitee/ *n.* (*pl.* **-ties**) **1** gaiety; rejoicing. **2 a** a festive celebration. **b** (in *pl.*) festive proceedings.

fes·toon /festóon/ *n. & v.* •*n.* a chain of flowers, leaves, ribbons, etc., hung in a curve as a decoration. •*v.tr.* (often foll. by *with*) adorn with or form into festoons; decorate elaborately. □□ **fes·toon·er·y** *n.*

fet·a /fétə/ *n.* a crumbly white ewe's milk or goat's milk cheese, made esp. in Greece.

fetch /fech/ *v. & n.* •*v.tr.* **1** go for and bring back (a person or thing) (*fetch a doctor*). **2** be sold for (a price) (*fetched $10*). **3** cause (blood, tears, etc.) to flow. **4** draw (breath). **5** *colloq.* give (a blow, slap, etc.) (*fetched him a slap on the face*). **6** excite the emotions of; delight or irritate. •*n.* **1** an act of fetching. **2** a dodge or trick. □ **fetch and carry** run backward and forward with things; be a servant. **fetch up** *colloq.* arrive; come to rest.

fetch·ing /féching/ *adj.* attractive. □□ **fetch·ing·ly** *adv.*

fête /fayt, fet/ *n. & v.* •*n.* **1** a festival. **2** *Brit.* an outdoor function with the sale of goods, amusements, etc. **3** a saint's day. •*v.tr.* honor or entertain lavishly.

fet·id /fétid, féetid/ *adj.* (also **foe·tid**) stinking. □□ **fet·id·ly** *adv.* **fet·id·ness** *n.*

fet·ish /fétish/ *n.* **1** *Psychol.* a thing abnormally stimulating or attracting sexual desire. **2 a** an object worshiped for its supposed inherent magical powers or as being inhabited by a spirit. **b** a thing evoking irrational devotion or respect. □□ **fet·ish·ism** *n.* **fet·ish·ist** *n.* **fet·ish·is·tic** /–shístik/ *adj.*

fetish early 17th cent. (originally denoting an object used by the peoples of West Africa as an amulet or charm): from French *fétiche*, from Portuguese *feitiço* 'charm, sorcery' (originally an adjective meaning 'made by art'), from Latin *factitius* (see FACTITIOUS).

fet·lock /fétlok/ *n.* part of the back of a horse's leg above the hoof where a tuft of hair grows.

fet·ter /fétər/ *n. & v.* •*n.* **1 a** a shackle for holding a prisoner by the ankles. **b** any shackle or bond. **2** (in *pl.*) captivity. **3** a restraint. •*v.tr.* **1** put into fetters. **2** restrict; impede.

fet·tle /fét'l/ *n. & v.* •*n.* condition or trim (*in fine fettle*). •*v.tr.* **1** trim or clean (the rough edge of a metal casting, pottery before firing, etc.). **2** line (a hearth, furnace, etc.) with loose sand or gravel.

fet·tuc·ci·ne /fetəchéenee/ *n.* (also **fet·tuc·ci·ni**) pasta in the form of long flat ribbons.

fe·tus /féetəs/ *n.* an unborn or unhatched offspring of a mammal, esp. a human one more than eight weeks after conception. □□ **fe·tal** *adj.* **fe·ti·cide** /–tisīd/ *n.*

feud /fyood/ *n. & v.* •*n.* **1** prolonged mutual hostility, esp. between two families, tribes, etc. **2** a prolonged or bitter quarrel or dispute. •*v.intr.* conduct a feud. □□ **feud·ist** *n.*

feu·dal /fyóod'l/ *adj.* **1** of, according to, or resembling the feudal system. **2** of a feud or fief. **3** outdated (*had a feudal attitude*). □□ **feu·dal·ism** *n.* **feu·dal·ist** *n.* **feu·dal·is·tic** *adj.*

feu·dal·i·ty /fyoodálitee/ *n.* (*pl.* **·ties**) **1** the feudal system or its principles. **2** a feudal holding; a fief.

feu·dal sys·tem *n.* the social system in medieval Europe whereby a vassal held land from a superior in exchange for allegiance and service.

fe·ver /féevər/ *n. & v.* •*n.* **1 a** an abnormally high body temperature, often with delirium, etc. **b** a disease characterized by this (*scarlet fever; typhoid fever*). **2** nervous excitement; agitation. •*v.tr.* (esp. as **fevered** *adj.*) affect with fever or excitement.

fe·ver·few /féevərfyoo/ *n.* an aromatic bushy European plant, *Chrysanthemum parthenium*, with feathery leaves and white daisylike flowers, formerly used to reduce fever.

fe·ver·ish /féevərish/ *adj.* **1** having the symptoms of a fever. **2** excited; fitful; restless. **3** (of a place) infested by fever; feverous. □□ **fe·ver·ish·ly** *adv.* **fe·ver·ish·ness** *n.*

few /fyoo/ *adj. & n.* •*adj.* not many (*few doctors smoke; visitors are few*). •*n.* (as *pl.*) **1** (prec. by *a*) some but not many (*a few of his friends were there*). **2** a small number; not many (*many are called but few are chosen*). **3** (prec. by *the*) **a** the minority. **b** the elect. □ **every few** once in every small group of (*every few days*). **few and far between** scarce. **no fewer than** as many as (a specified number). **not a few** a considerable number. **some few** some but not at all many.

▶**Fewer**, the comparative of *few*, properly refers to a countable quantity: *This has one-third fewer calories than regular sour cream.* Formally, **less** refers to uncountable, mass quantities: *less sand; less water in this glass than that; less time to work with.* Today informal speakers rarely use **fewer** for **less**, but often use **less** where **fewer** has been preferred: *There are less people in the room than there were before lunch.*

fey /fay/ *adj.* **1 a** strange; otherworldly; whimsical. **b** clairvoyant. **2** *Sc.* **a** fated to die soon. **b** overexcited or elated, as formerly associated with the state of mind of a person about to die. □□ **fey·ly** *adv.* **fey·ness** *n.*

fez /fez/ *n.* (*pl.* **fezzes**) a flat-topped conical red cap with a tassel, worn by men in some Muslim countries.

fez

ff *abbr. Mus.* fortissimo.

ff. *abbr.* **1** following pages, etc. **2** folios.

FHA *abbr.* Federal Housing Administration.

fi·an·cé /féeonsáy/ *n.* (*fem.* **fiancée** *pronunc.* same) a person to whom one is engaged to be married.

fi·as·co /feeáskō/ *n.* (*pl.* **-cos**) a ludicrous or humiliating failure or breakdown.

fi·at /féeət, –at, –aat, fíat, fíət/ *n.* **1** an authorization. **2** a decree or order.

fib /fib/ *n. & v.* •*n.* a trivial or venial lie. •*v.intr.* (**fibbed, fibbing**) tell a fib. □□ **fib·ber** *n.* **fib·ster** *n.*

fi·ber /fíbər/ *n.* **1** *Biol.* any of the threads or filaments forming animal or vegetable tissue and textile substances. **2** a piece of glass in the form of a thread. **3 a** a substance formed of fibers. **b** a substance that can be spun, woven, or felted. **4** the structure or character of something (*lacks moral fiber*). **5** dietary material that is resistant to the action of digestive enzymes; roughage. □□ **fi·bered** *adj.* (also in *comb.*). **fi·ber·less** *adj.* **fi·bri·form** /fíbrifawrm/ *adj.*

fi·ber·board /fíbərbawrd/ *n.* a building material made of wood or other plant fibers compressed into boards.

fi·ber·glass /fíbərglas/ *n.* **1** a textile fabric made from woven glass fibers. **2** a plastic reinforced by glass fibers.

fi·ber op·tics *n.* (treated as *sing.*) optics employing thin glass fibers, usu. for the transmission of light, esp. modulated to carry signals.

fi·bril /fíbril, fib–/ *n.* **1** a small fiber. **2** a subdivision of a fiber. □□ **fi·bril·lar** *adj.* **fi·bril·lar·y** *adj.*

fi·bril·late /fíbrilayt, fí–/ *v.* **1** *intr.* **a** (of a fiber) split up into fibrils. **b** (of a muscle, esp. in the heart) undergo a quivering movement in fibrils. **2** *tr.* break (a fiber) into fibrils. □□ **fi·bril·la·tion** /–láyshən/ *n.*

fi·broid /fíbroyd/ *adj. & n.* •*adj.* **1** of or characterized by fibrous tissue. **2** resembling or containing fibers. •*n.* a benign tumor of muscular and fibrous tissues, one or more of which may develop in the wall of the uterus.

fi·bro·sis /fībrósis/ *n. Med.* a thickening and scarring of connective tissue, usu. as a result of injury or disease. □□ **fi·brot·ic** /–brótik/ *adj.*

fi·brous /fībrəs/ *adj.* consisting of or like fibers. □□ **fi·brous·ness** *n.*

fib·u·la /fibyələ/ *n.* (*pl.* **fibulae** /–lee/or **fibulas**) *Anat.* the smaller and outer of the two bones between the knee and the ankle in terrestrial vertebrates. □□ **fib·u·lar** *adj.*

FICA /fīkə/ *abbr.* Federal Insurance Contributions Act.

fiche /feesh/ *n.* (*pl.* same or **fiches**) a microfiche.

fick·le /fikəl/ *adj.* inconstant or changeable, esp. in loyalty. □□ **fick·le·ness** *n.* **fick·ly** *adv.*

fic·tile /fiktəl, –tīl/ *adj.* **1** made of earth or clay by a potter. **2** of pottery.

fic·tion /fikshən/ *n.* **1** an invented idea or statement or narrative. **2** literature, esp. novels, describing imaginary events and people. **3** a conventionally accepted falsehood (*polite fiction*). **4** the act or process of inventing imaginary things. □□ **fic·tion·al** *adj.* **fic·tion·al·i·ty** /–nálitee/ *n.* **fic·tion·al·ize** *v.tr.* **fic·tion·al·i·za·tion** *n.* **fic·tion·al·ly** *adv.* **fic·tion·ist** *n.*

fic·ti·tious /fiktíshəs/ *adj.* **1** imaginary; unreal. **2** counterfeit; not genuine. **3** (of a name or character) assumed. **4** of or in novels. □□ **fic·ti·tious·ly** *adv.* **fic·ti·tious·ness** *n.*

fic·tive /fiktiv/ *adj.* **1** creating or created by imagination. **2** not genuine. □□ **fic·tive·ness** *n.*

fid·dle /fid'l/ *n. & v.* •*n.* **1** a stringed instrument played with a bow, esp. a violin. **2** *Brit. colloq.* an instance of cheating or fraud. **3** a fiddly task. •*v.* **1** *intr.* **a** (often foll. by *with*) play restlessly. **b** (often foll. by *about*) move aimlessly. **c** act idly or frivolously. **d** (usu. foll. by *with*) make minor adjustments; tinker. **2** *tr. Brit. sl.* **a** cheat; swindle. **b** falsify. **c** get by cheating. **3 a** *intr.* play the fiddle. **b** *tr.* play (a tune, etc.) on the fiddle. □ **as fit as a fiddle** in very good health. **play second** (or **first**) **fiddle** take a subordinate (or leading) role.

fid·dle-de-dee /fid'ldeedée/ *int. & n.* nonsense.

fid·dle-fad·dle /fid'lfad'l/ *n., v., int., & adj.* •*n.* trivial matters. •*v.intr.* fuss; trifle. •*int.* nonsense! *adj.* (of a person or thing) petty; fussy.

fid·dle·head /fid'lhed/ *n.* **1** a scroll like carving at a ship's bow. **2** the coiled frond of some ferns eaten as a vegetable.

fid·dler /fidlər/ *n.* **1** a fiddle player. **2** (in full **fiddler crab**) any small N. American crab of the genus *Uca*, the male having one of its claws enlarged and held in a position like a violinist's arm.

fid·dle·sticks /fid'lstiks/ *int.* nonsense!

fi·del·i·ty /fidélitee/ *n.* **1** (often foll. by *to*) faithfulness; loyalty. **2** strict conformity to truth or fact. **3** exact correspondence to the original. **4** precision in reproduction of sound or video (*high fidelity*).

fidg·et /fijit/ *v. & n.* •*v.* (**fidgeted, fidgeting**) **1** *intr.* move or act restlessly or nervously, usu. while maintaining basically the same posture. **2** *intr.* be uneasy; worry. **3** *tr.* make (a person) uneasy or uncomfortable. •*n.* **1** a person who fidgets. **2** (usu. in *pl.*) **a** bodily uneasiness seeking relief in spasmodic movements; such movements. **b** a restless mood. □□ **fidg·et·y** *adj.* **fidg·et·i·ness** *n.*

fi·du·ci·ar·y /fidóoshee-eree, –shəree, –dyóo–, fī–/ *adj. & n.* •*adj.* **1 a** of a trust, trustee, or trusteeship. **b** held or given in trust. **2** (of a paper currency) depending for its value on public confidence or securities. •*n.* (*pl.* **-ies**) a trustee.

fie /fī/ *int.* expressing disgust, shame, etc.

fief /feef/ *n.* **1** a piece of land held under the feudal system or in fee. **2** a person's sphere of operation or control.

fief·dom /féefdəm/ *n.* a fief.

field /feeld/ *n. & v.* •*n.* **1** an area of open land, esp. one used for pasture or crops. **2** an area rich in some natural product (*gas field; diamond field*). **3** a piece of land for a specified purpose, esp. **a** an area marked out for a game or sport (*football field*), or **b** an airfield. **4 a** the participants in a contest or sport. **b** all the competitors in a race or all except those specified. **5** *Cricket* **a** the side fielding. **b** a fielder. **6** an expanse of ice, snow, sea, sky, etc. **7 a** a battlefield. **b** the scene of a campaign. **c** (*attrib.*) (of artillery, etc.) light and mobile for use on campaign. **d** a battle. **8** an area of operation or activity; a subject of study. **9 a** the region in which a force is effective (*gravitational field; magnetic field*). **b** the force exerted in such an area. **10** a range of perception (*field of view; filled the field of the telescope*). **11** *Math.* a system subject to two operations analogous to those for the multiplication and addition of real numbers. **12** (*attrib.*) **a** (of an animal or plant) found in the countryside; wild (*field mouse*). **b** carried out or working in the natural environment, not in a laboratory, etc. (*field test*). **13** the background of a picture, coin, flag, etc. **14** *Computing* a part of a database record, representing an item of data. •*v.* **1** *Baseball, Cricket,* etc. **a** *intr.* act as a fielder. **b** *tr.* catch (and return) (the ball). **2** *tr.* select (a team or individual) to play in a game. **3** *tr.* deal with (a succession of questions, etc.). □ **play the field** *colloq.* avoid exclusive attachment to one person or activity, etc.

field day *n.* **1** wide scope for action or success; a time occupied with exciting events (*when crowds form, pickpockets have a field day*). **2** *Mil.* an exercise, esp. in maneuvering. **3** a day spent in exploration, scientific investigation, etc., in the natural environment. **4** an all-day sports or athletics meet, esp. at a school.

field·er /féeldər/ *n. Baseball,* etc. a member of the team that is fielding.

field glas·ses *n.pl.* binoculars for outdoor use.

field goal *n.* **1** *Football* a score of three points by a kick from the field. **2** *Basketball* a goal scored when the ball is in normal play.

field hock·ey *n.* a field game played between two teams with curved sticks and a small hard ball.

field hos·pi·tal *n.* a temporary hospital near a battlefield.

field mar·shal *n. Brit.* an army officer of the highest rank.

field mouse *n.* **1** a small rodent, *Apodemus sylvaticus*, with prominent ears and a long tail. **2** various similar rodents inhabiting fields.

field of vi·sion *n.* all that comes into view when the eyes are turned in some direction.

field·work /féeldwərk/ *n.* the practical work of a surveyor, collector of scientific data, sociologist, etc., conducted in the natural environment rather than a laboratory, office, etc. □□ **field·work·er** *n.*

fiend /feend/ *n.* **1 a** an evil spirit; a demon. **b** (prec. by *the*) the Devil. **2 a** a very wicked or cruel person. **b** a person causing mischief or annoyance. **3** (with a qualifying word) *sl.* a devotee or addict (*a fitness fiend*). **4** something difficult or unpleasant. □□ **fiend·ish** *adj.* **fiend·ish·ly** *adv.* **fiend·ish·ness** *n.* **fiend·like** *adj.*

fierce /feers/ *adj.* (**fiercer, fiercest**) **1** vehemently aggressive or frightening in temper or action; violent. **2** intense; ardent. **3** unpleasantly strong or intense (*fierce heat*). **4** (of a mechanism) not smooth or easy in action. □□ **fierce·ly** *adv.* **fierce·ness** *n.*

fier·y /fīree/ *adj.* (**fierier, fieriest**) **1 a** consisting of or flaming with fire. **b** (of an arrow, etc.) fire-bearing. **2** bright red. **3 a** hot as fire. **b** acting like fire; producing a burning sensation. **4 a** flashing; ardent (*fiery* *eyes*). **b** spirited; irritable (*fiery temper*). **c** (of a horse) mettlesome. ▫▫ **fier·i·ly** *adv.* **fier·i·ness** *n.*

fi·es·ta /fee-éstə/ *n.* **1** a holiday or festivity. **2** a religious festival in Spanish-speaking countries.

fife /fīf/ *n.* & *v.* • *n.* **1** a kind of small shrill flute used in military music. **2** its player. • *v.* **1** *intr.* play the fife. **2** *tr.* play (an air, etc.) on the fife. ▫▫ **fif·er** *n.*

fif·teen /fifteén/ *n.* & *adj.* • *n.* **1** one more than fourteen. **2** a symbol for this (15, xv, XV). **3** a size, etc., denoted by fifteen. **4** a team of fifteen players, esp. in rugby. • *adj.* that amount to fifteen. ▫▫ **fif·teenth** *adj.* & *n.*

fifth /fifth/ *n.* & *adj.* • *n.* **1** the position in a sequence corresponding to that of the number 5 in the sequence 1–5. **2** something occupying this position. **3** the fifth person, etc., in a race or competition. **4** any of five equal parts of a thing. **5** *Mus.* **a** an interval or chord spanning five consecutive notes in the diatonic scale (e.g., C to G). **b** a note separated from another by this interval. **6 a** a fifth of a gallon of liquor. **b** a bottle containing this. **7** (**the Fifth**) the Fifth Amendment to the US Constitution. • *adj.* that is the fifth. ▫ **take the Fifth** exercise the right guaranteed by the Fifth Amendment to the Constitution of refusing to answer questions in order to avoid incriminating oneself. ▫▫ **fifth·ly** *adv.*

fifth col·umn *n.* a group working for an enemy within a country at war, etc. ▫▫ **fifth col·umn·ist** *n.*

fifth gen·er·a·tion *n.* *Computing* a stage in computer design involving machines that make use of artificial intelligence.

fifth wheel *n.* **1** an extra wheel of a carriage. **2** a superfluous person or thing. **3** a horizontal turntable over the front axle of a carriage as an extra support to prevent its tipping. **4** a round coupling device to connect a tractor and trailer.

fif·ty /fiftee/ *n.* & *adj.* • *n.* (*pl.* **-ties**) **1** the product of five and ten. **2** a symbol for this (50, l (letter), L). **3** (in *pl.*) the numbers from 50 to 59, esp. the years of a century or of a person's life. **4** a set of fifty persons or things. **5** a large indefinite number (*have fifty things to tell you*). **6** a fifty-dollar bill. • *adj.* that amount to fifty. ▫▫ **fif·ti·eth** *adj.* & *n.* **fif·ty·fold** *adj.* & *adv.*

fif·ty-fif·ty *adj.* & *adv.* • *adj.* equal; with equal shares or chances (*on a fifty-fifty basis*). • *adv.* equally; half and half (*go fifty-fifty*).

fig[1] /fig/ *n.* **1 a** a soft pear-shaped fruit with many seeds, eaten fresh or dried. **b** (in full **fig tree**) any deciduous tree of the genus *Ficus*, esp. *F. carica*, having broad leaves and bearing figs. **2** a valueless thing (*don't care a fig for*).

fig[2] /fig/ *n.* & *v.* • *n.* **1** dress or equipment (*in full fig*). **2** condition or form (*in good fig*). • *v.tr.* (**figged, figging**) **1** (foll. by *out*) dress up (a person). **2** (foll. by *out, up*) make (a horse) lively.

fig. *abbr.* figure.

fight /fīt/ *v.* & *n.* • *v.* (*past* and *past part.* **fought** /fawt/) **1** *intr.* **a** (often foll. by *against, with*) contend or struggle in war, battle, single combat, etc. **b** (often foll. by *with*)) argue; quarrel. **2** *tr.* content with (an opponent) in this way. **3** *tr.* take part or engage in (a battle, war, duel, boxing match, etc.). **4** *tr.* contend about (an issue, an election); maintain (a lawsuit, cause, etc.) against an opponent. **5** *intr.* campaign or strive determinedly to achieve something. **6** *tr.* strive to overcome (disease, fire, fear, etc.). **7** *tr.* make (one's way) by fighting. **8** *tr.* cause (cocks or dogs) to fight. **9** *tr.* handle (troops, a ship, etc.) in battle. • *n.* **1 a** a combat, esp. unpremeditated, between two or more persons, animals, or parties. **b** a boxing match. **c** a battle. **d** an argument **2** a conflict or struggle; a vigorous effort in the face of difficulty. **3** power or inclination to fight (*has no fight left*). ▫ **fight back 1** counterattack. **2** suppress (one's feelings, tears, etc.). **fight down** suppress (one's feelings, tears, etc.). **fight for 1** fight on behalf of. **2** fight to secure (a thing). **fight off** repel with effort. **fight out** (usu. **fight it out**) setle (a dispute, etc.) by fighting. **fight shy of** avoid; be unwilling to approach (a person, task, etc.). **put up a fight** (or **make a fight of it**) offter resistance.

fight·er /fītər/ *n.* **1** a person or animal that fights. **2** a fast military aircraft designed for attacking other aircraft.

fight·ing chance *n.* an opportunity to succeed by great effort.

fig·ment /figmənt/ *n.* a thing invented or existing only in the imagination.

fig·u·ra·tion /figyəráyshən/ *n.* **1 a** the act of formation. **b** a mode of formation; a form. **c** a shape or outline. **2 a** ornamentation by designs. **b** *Mus.* ornamental patters of scales, arpeggios, etc.

fig·ur·a·tive /figyərətiv/ *adj.* **1 a** metaphorical, not literal. **b** metaphorically so called. **2** characterized by or addicted to figures of speech. **3** of pictorial or sculptural representation. **4** emblematic; serving as a type. ▫▫ **fig·ur·a·tive·ly** *adv.* **fig·ur·a·tive·ness** *n.*

fig·ure /figyər/ *n.* & *v.* • *n.* **1 a** the external form or shape of a thing. **b** bodily shape (*has a model's figure*). **2 a** a person as seen in outline but not identified. **b** a person as contemplated mentally (*a public figure*). **3** appearance as giving a certain impression (*cut a poor figure*). **4 a** a representation of the human form in drawing, sculpture, etc. **b** an image or likeness. **c** an emblem or type. **5** *Geom.* a two-dimensional space enclosed by a line or lines, or a three-dimensional space enclosed by a surface or surfaces. **6 a** a numerical symbol, esp. any of the ten in Arabic notation. **b** a number so expressed. **c** an amount of money; a value (*cannot put a figure on it*). **d** (in *pl.*) arithmetical calculations. **7** a diagram or illustrative drawing. **8** a decorative pattern. **9 a** a division of a set dance. **b** (in skating) a prescribed pattern of movements from a stationary position. **10** *Mus.* a short succession of notes producing a single impression. **11** (in full **figure of speech**) a recognized form of rhetorical expression, esp. metaphor or hyperbole. **12** *Gram.* a permitted deviation from the usual rules of construction, e.g., ellipsis. • *v.* **1** *intr.* appear or be mentioned, esp. prominently. **2** *tr.* represent in a diagram or picture. **3** *tr.* imagine; picture mentally. **4 a** *tr.* embellish with a pattern (*figured satin*). **b** *tr. Mus.* embellish with figures. **c** *intr.* perform a figure in skating or dancing. **5** *tr.* mark with numbers or prices. **6 a** *tr.* calculate. **b** *intr.* do arithmetic. **7** *tr.* be a symbol of; represent typically. **8 a** *tr.* understand; ascertain; consider. **b** *intr. colloq.* be likely or understandably (*that figures*). ▫ **figure on** count on; expect. **figure out 1** work out by arithmetic or logic. **2** estimate. **3** understand.

fig·ure-head /figyərhed/ *n* **1** a normal leader or head without real power. **2** a carving, usu. a bust or a full-length figure, at a ship's prow.

fig·ure skat·ing *n.* the sport of performing jumps and spins, etc., in a dancelike performance while ice skating, and also including skating in prescribed patterns from a stationary position. ▫▫ **fig·ure ska·ter** *n.*

fig·ur·ine /figyəreén/ *n.* a statuette.

fil·a·gree var. of FILIGREE.

fil·a·ment /filəmənt/ *n.* **1** a slender threadlike body or fiber (esp. in animal or vegetable structures). **2** a wire or thread in an electric bulb or vacuum tube, heated or made incandescent by an electric current. ▫▫ **fil·a·men·ta·ry** /–méntəree/ *adj.* **fil·a·ment·ed** *adj.* **fil·a·men·tous** /–méntəs/ *adj.*

fil·a·ri·a·sis /filəríəsis/ *n.* a disease common in the tropics, caused by the presence of parasitic nematode worms in the lymph vessels.
fil·bert /filbərt/ *n.* **1** the cultivated hazel, *Corylus maxima*, bearing edible ovoid nuts. **2** this nut.
filch /filch/ *v.tr.* pilfer; steal. ▫▫ **filch·er** *n.*
file[1] /fīl/ *n. & v.* •*n.* **1** a folder, box, etc., for holding loose papers. **2** a set of papers kept in this. **3** *Computing* a collection of (usu. related) data stored under one name. •*v.tr.* **1** place (papers) in a file or among (esp. public) records. **2** submit (a petition for divorce, an application for a patent, etc.). **3** (of a reporter) send (a story, information, etc.) to a newspaper. ▫▫ **fil·er** *n.*
file[2] /fīl/ *n. & v.* •*n.* a line of persons or things one behind another. •*v.intr.* walk in a file.
file[3] /fīl/ *n. & v.* •*n.* a tool with a roughened surface for smoothing or shaping wood, fingernails, etc. •*v.tr.* smooth or shape with a file. ▫ **file away** remove (roughness, etc.) with a file. ▫▫ **fil·er** *n.*
fi·let /filáy/ *n.* **1** a kind of net or lace with a square mesh. **2** a fillet of meat.
fi·let mi·gnon /filáy minyón/ *n.* a small tender piece of beef from the end of the tenderloin.
fil·i·al /fileeəl/ *adj.* of or due from a son or daughter. ▫▫ **fil·i·al·ly** *adv.*
fil·i·bus·ter /filibustər/ *n. & v.* •*n.* **1** the obstruction of progress in a legislative assembly, esp. by prolonged speaking. **2** a person who engages in filibuster. •*v.* **1** *intr.* act as filibuster. **2** *tr.* act in this way against (a motion, etc.). ▫▫ **fil·i·bus·ter·er** *n.*
fil·i·gree /filigree/ *n.* (also **fil·a·gree** /filə–/) **1** fine metal openwork. **2** anything delicate resembling this. ▫▫ **fil·i·greed** *adj.*
fil·ing /fīling/ *n.* (usu. in *pl.*) a particle rubbed off by a file.
Fil·i·pi·no /filipeénō/ *n. & adj.* •*n.* (*pl.* **-nos**; *fem.* **Filipina** /–nə/) a native or inhabitant of the Philippines, a group of islands in the SW Pacific. •*adj.* of or relating to the Philippines or the Filipinos.
fill /fil/ *v. & n.* •*v.* **1** *tr. & intr.* (often foll. by *with*) make or become full. **2** *tr.* occupy completely; spread over or through; pervade. **3** *tr.* block up (a cavity or hole in a tooth) with cement, amalgam, gold, etc. **4** *tr.* make level or raise the level of (low-lying land). **5** *tr.* appoint a person to hold (a vacant post). **6** *tr.* hold (a position); discharge the duties of (an office). **7** *tr.* carry out or supply (an order, commission, etc.). **8** *tr.* occupy (vacant time). **9** *intr.* (of a sail) be distended by wind. **10** *tr.* (usu. as **filling** *adj.*) (esp. of food) satisfy; satiate. **11** *tr.* satisfy; fulfill (a need or requirement). **12** *tr.* stock abundantly. •*n.* **1** (prec. by possessive) as much as one wants or can bear (*eat your fill*). **2** enough to fill something (*a fill of tobacco*). **3** earth, etc., used to fill a cavity. ▫ **fill the bill** be suitable or adequate. **fill in 1** add information to complete (a document, blank check, etc.). **2 a** complete (a drawing, etc.) within an outline. **b** fill (an outline) in this way. **3** fill (a hole, etc.) completely. **4** (often foll. by *for*) act as a substitute. **5** occupy oneself during (time between other activities). **6** *colloq.* inform (a person) more fully. **fill out 1** enlarge to the required size. **2** become enlarged or plump. **3** add information to complete (a document, etc.). **fill up 1** make or become completely full. **2** fill the fuel tank of (a car, etc.). **4** provide what is needed to occupy vacant parts or places or deal with deficiencies in.
fill·er /filər/ *n.* **1** material or an object used to fill a cavity or increase bulk. **2** an item filling space in a newspaper, etc. **3** paper for filling a binder or notebook. **4** a person or thing that fills.
fil·let /filit/ *n. & v.* •*n.* **1** (usu. /filáy/) **a** a fleshy boneless piece of meat from near the loins or the ribs. **b** (in full **fillet steak**) the tenderloin. **c** a boned longitudinal section of a fish. **2 a** a headband, ribbon, string, or narrow band, for binding the hair or worn around the head. **b** a band or bandage. **3 a** a thin narrow strip. **b** a raised rim or ridge. **4** *Archit.* **a** a narrow flat band separating two moldings. **b** a small band between the flutes of a column. •*v.tr.* (**filleted, filleting**) **1** (also /filáy, filay/) **a** remove bones from (fish or meat). **b** divide (fish or meat) into fillets. **2** bind or provide with a fillet or fillets. **3** encircle with an ornamental band. ▫▫ **fil·let·er** *n.*
fill·ing /filing/ *n.* **1** any material that is used to fill, esp.: **a** a piece of material used to fill a cavity in a tooth. **b** the edible substance between the bread in a sandwich or between the pastry crusts in a pie. **2** weft.
fill·ing sta·tion *n.* an establishment selling automotive fuel, etc., to motorists.
fil·lip /filip/ *n.* a stimulus or incentive.
fil·ly /filee/ *n.* (*pl.* **-lies**) **1** a young female horse, usu. before it is four years old. **2** *colloq.* a girl or young woman.
film /film/ *n. & v.* •*n.* **1** a thin coating or covering layer. **2** *Photog.* a strip or sheet of plastic or other flexible base coated with light-sensitive emulsion for exposure in a camera. **3 a** a representation of a story, episode, etc., on a film, with the illusion of movement; a movie. **b** a story represented in this way; a movie. **c** (in *pl.*) the movie industry. **4** a slight veil or haze, etc. **5** a dimness or morbid growth affecting the eyes. **6** a fine thread or filament. •*v.* **1 a** *tr.* make a photographic film of (a scene, person, etc.). **b** *tr.* (also *absol.*) make a movie or television film of (a book, etc.). **c** *intr.* be (well or ill) suited for reproduction on film. **2** *tr. & intr.* cover or become covered with or as with a film.
film·go·er /filmgōər/ *n.* a person who frequents movie theaters.
film·mak·er /filmaykər/ *n.* a person who makes motion pictures.
film·og·ra·phy /filmógrəfee/ *n.* (*pl.* **-phies**) a list of movies by one director, etc., or on one subject.
film·strip /filmstrip/ *n.* a series of transparencies in a strip for projection as still pictures.
film·y /filmee/ *adj.* (**filmier, filmiest**) **1** thin and translucent. **2** covered with or as with a film. ▫▫ **film·i·ly** *adv.* **film·i·ness** *n.*
fi·lo /féelō/ *n.* (also **phyllo**) dough that can be stretched into very thin layers; pastry made from this dough.
fils /fees/ *n.* (added to a surname to distinguish a son from a father) the son; junior (cf. PÈRE).
fil·ter /filtər/ *n. & v.* •*n.* **1** a porous device for removing impurities or solid particles from a liquid or gas passed through it. **2** = FILTER TIP. **3** a screen or attachment for absorbing or modifying light, X rays, etc. **4** a device for suppressing electrical or sound waves of frequencies not required. •*v.* **1** *tr. & intr.* pass or cause to pass through a filter. **2** *tr.* (foll. by *out*) remove (impurities, etc.) by means of a filter. **3** *intr.* (foll. by *through, into*, etc.) make way gradually. **4** *intr.* (foll. by *out*) leak or cause to leak.
fil·ter·a·ble /filtərəbəl/ *adj.* (also **fil·tra·ble** /filtrəbəl/) **1** *Med.* (of a virus) able to pass through a filter that retains bacteria. **2** that can be filtered.
fil·ter feed·ing *n. Zool.* feeding by filtering out plankton or nutrients suspended in water. ▫▫ **fil·ter feed·er** *n.*
fil·ter tip 1 a filter attached to a cigarette for removing impurities from the inhaled smoke. **2** a cigarette with this. ▫▫ **fil·ter-tipped** *adj.*
filth /filth/ *n.* **1** repugnant or extreme dirt. **2** vileness; corruption; obscenity. **3** foul or obscene language.
filth·y /filthee/ *adj. & adv.* •*adj.* (**filthier, filthiest**) **1** extremely or disgustingly dirty. **2** obscene. **3** vile; disgraceful. •*adv.* **1** filthily (*filthy dirty*). **2** *colloq.* extremely (*filthy rich*). ▫▫ **filth·i·ly** *adv.* **filth·i·ness** *n.*

filth·y lu·cre *n.* **1** dishonorable gain (Tit. 1:11). **2** *joc.* money.

fil·tra·ble var. of FILTERABLE.

fil·trate /filtrayt/ *v. & n.* •*v.tr.* filter. •*n.* filtered liquid. ▫▫ **fil·tra·tion** /–tráyshən/ *n.*

fin[1] /fin/ *n.* **1** an organ on various parts of the body of many aquatic vertebrates and some invertebrates, including fish and cetaceans, for propelling, steering, and balancing. **2** a small projecting surface or attachment on an aircraft, rocket, or automobile for ensuring aerodynamic stability. **3** an underwater swimmer's flipper. **4** a sharp lateral projection on the share or blade of a plow. **5** a finlike projection on any device, for improving heat transfer, etc. ▫▫ **fin·less** *adj.* **finned** *adj.* (also in *comb.*).

fin[2] /fin/ *n. sl. a five-dollar bill.*

fin·a·ble see FINE[2].

fi·na·gle /fináygəl/ *v.intr. & tr. colloq.* act or obtain dishonestly or deviously. ▫▫ **fi·na·gler** *n.*

fi·nal /fínəl/ *adj. & n.* •*adj.* **1** situated at the end; coming last. **2** conclusive; decisive; unalterable; putting an end to doubt. **3** concerned with the purpose or end aimed at. •*n.* **1** (also in *pl.*) the last or deciding heat or game in sports or in a competition. **2** the edition of a newspaper published latest in the day. **3** an examination at the end of an academic course. ▫▫ **fi·nal·ly** *adv.*

fi·na·le /finaalee, –nálee/ *n.* **1 a** the last movement of an instrumental composition. **b** a piece of music closing an act in an opera. **2** the close of a drama, etc. **3** a conclusion.

fi·nal·ist /fínəlist/ *n.* a competitor in the final of a competition, etc.

fi·nal·i·ty /finálitee, fə–/ *n.* (*pl.* **-ties**) **1** the quality or fact of being final. **2** the belief that something is final. **3** a final act, state, or utterance. **4** the principle of final cause viewed as operative in the universe.

fi·nal·ize /fínəlīz/ *v.tr.* **1** put into final form. **2** complete; bring to an end. **3** approve the final form or details of. ▫▫ **fi·nal·i·za·tion** *n.*

fi·nance /fináns, fī–, fínans/ *n. & v.* •*n.* **1** the management of (esp. public) money. **2** monetary support for an enterprise. **3** (in *pl.*) the money resources of a government, company, or person. •*v.tr.* provide capital for (a person or enterprise).

fi·nan·cial /finánshəl, fī–/ *adj.* of finance. ▫▫ **fi·nan·cial·ly** *adv.*

fin·an·cier /finənséer, fənan–, fínən–/ *n.* a person engaged in large-scale finance.

fin·back /finbak/ *n.* (or **fin whale**) a rorqual, *Balaenoptera physalus.*

finch /finch/ *n.* any small seed-eating passerine bird of the family Fringillidae (esp. one of the genus *Fringilla*), including crossbills, canaries, and chaffinches.

find /fīnd/ *v. & n.* •*v.tr.* (*past* and *past part.* **found** /fownd/) **1 a** discover by chance or effort (*found a key*). **b** become aware of. **2 a** get possession of by chance (*found a treasure*). **b** obtain; receive (*idea found acceptance*). **c** succeed in obtaining (*cannot find the money*). **d** summon up (*found courage to protest*). **3 a** seek out and provide (*will find you a book*). **b** supply; furnish (*each finds his own equipment*). **4** ascertain by study or calculation or inquiry (*could not find the answer*). **5 a** perceive or experience (*find no sense in it; find difficulty in breathing*). **b** (often in *passive*) recognize or discover to be present (*the word is not found in Shakespeare*). **c** regard or discover from experience (*finds Canada too cold*). **6** *Law* (of a jury, judge, etc.) decide and declare (*found him guilty*). **7** reach by a natural or normal process (*water finds its own level*). **8 a** (of a letter) reach (a person). **b** (of an address) be adequate to enable a letter, etc., to reach (a person). •*n.* **1** a discovery of treasure, minerals, etc. **2** a thing or person discovered, esp. when of value. ▫ **find oneself 1** discover that one is (*woke to find myself in the hospital*). **2** discover one's own talents, strengths, etc. **find out 1** discover or detect (a wrongdoer, etc.). **2** (often foll. by *about*) get information. **3** discover (*find out where we are*). **4** (often foll. by *about*) discover the truth, a fact, etc. (*he never found out*). **5** devise. **6** solve.
▶See note at LOCATE.

find·ing /fínding/ *n.* (often in *pl.*) a conclusion reached by an inquiry.

fine[1] /fīn/ *adj. & adv.* •*adj.* **1** of high quality. **2 a** excellent; of notable merit (*a fine painting*). **b** good; satisfactory (*that will be fine*). **c** fortunate (*has been a fine thing for him*). **d** well conceived or expressed (*a fine saying*). **3 a** pure; refined. **b** (of gold or silver) containing a specified proportion of pure metal. **4** of handsome appearance or size; imposing; dignified (*fine buildings*). **5** in good health (*I'm fine, thank you*). **6** (of weather, etc.) bright and clear with sunshine; free from rain. **7 a** thin; sharp. **b** in small particles. **c** worked in slender thread. **d** (esp. of print) small. **e** (of a pen) narrow-pointed. **8 a** capable of delicate perception or discrimination. **b** perceptible only with difficulty (*a fine distinction*). **9** (of wine or other goods) of a high standard; conforming to a specified grade. •*adv.* **1** finely. **2** *colloq.* very well (*suits me fine*). ▫▫ **fine·ly** *adv.* **fine·ness** *n.*

fine[2] /fīn/ *n. & v.* •*n.* a sum of money exacted as a penalty. •*v.tr.* punish by a fine (*fined him $5*). ▫ **in fine** to sum up; in short. ▫▫ **fin·a·ble** /fínəbəl/ *adj.*

fine arts *n.pl.* those appealing to the mind or to the sense of beauty, as poetry, music, and esp. painting, sculpture, and architecture.

fine print *n.* detailed printed information, esp. in legal documents, instructions, etc.

fin·er·y /fínəree/ *n.* showy dress or decoration.

fines herbes /feen áirb, feenz/ *n.pl.* mixed herbs used in cooking.

fi·nesse /finés/ *n. & v.* •*n.* **1** refinement. **2** subtle or delicate manipulation. **3** artfulness, esp. in handling a difficulty tactfully. **4** *Cards* an attempt to win a trick with a card that is not the highest held. •*v.* **1** *intr. & tr.* use or achieve by finesse. **2** *Cards* **a** *intr.* make a finesse. **b** *tr.* play (a card) by way of finesse. **3** *tr.* evade or trick by finesse.

fine-tooth comb *n.* a comb with narrow close-set teeth. ▫ **go over with a fine-tooth comb** check or search thoroughly.

fine-tune *v.tr.* make small adjustments to (a mechanism, etc.) in order to obtain the best possible results.

fin·ger /finggər/ *n. & v.* •*n.* **1** any of the terminal projections of the hand (including or excluding the thumb). **2** the part of a glove, etc. intended to cover a finger. **3 a** a finger-like object (*chicken finger*). **b** a long narrow structure. **4** *colloq.* a measure of liquor in a glass, based on the breadth of a finger. •*v.tr.* **1** touch, feel, or handle with the fingers. **2** *Mus.* **a** play (a passage) with fingers used in a particular way. **b** mark (music) with signs showing which fingers are to be used. **c** play upon (an instrument) with the fingers. **3** *sl.* indicate (a victim, or a criminal to the police). ▫ **have a finger in** (or **in the pie**) be (esp. officiously) concerned in (the matter). **lay a finger on** touch however slightly. **point the finger at** *colloq.* accuse; blame. **put one's finger on** locate or identify exactly. **put the finger on** *sl.* **1** inform against. **2** identify (an intended victim). **slip through one's fingers** escape. **twist** (or **wind** or **wrap**) **around one's finger** (or **little finger**) persuade (a person) without difficulty; dominate (a person) completely. ▫▫ **fin·gered** *adj.* (also in *comb.*). **fin·ger·less** *adj.*

fin·ger·board /finggərbawrd/ *n.* a flat strip at the top end of a stringed instrument, against which the strings are pressed to determine tones.

fin·ger bowl *n.* a small bowl for rinsing the fingers at the table.

fin·ger·ing /finggəring/ *n.* **1** a manner or technique of using the fingers, esp. to play an instrument. **2** an indication of this in a musical score.

fin·ger·nail /finggərnayl/ *n.* the nail at the tip of each finger.

fin·ger paint *n.* & *v.* • *n.* paint that can be applied with the fingers. • *v.intr.* apply paint with the fingers.

fin·ger·print /finggərprint/ *n.* & *v.* • *n.* **1** an impression made on a surface by the fine ridges on the fingertips. **2** a distinctive characteristic. • *v.tr.* record the fingerprints of (a person).

fin·ger·spell·ing /finggər-spéling/ *n.* a form of sign language in which individual letters are formed by the fingers to spell out words.

fin·ger·tip /finggərtip/ *n.* the tip of a finger. □ **have at one's fingertips** be thoroughly familiar with (a subject, etc.).

fin·i·al /fineeəl/ *n. Archit.* **1** an ornament finishing off the apex of a roof, pediment, gable, tower corner, canopy, etc. **2** the topmost part of a pinnacle.

fin·ick·y /finikee/ *adj.* **1** overly particular; fastidious. **2** needing much care or attention to detail. □□ **fin·ick·i·ness** *n.*

fin·is /finis, feenée, finis/ *n.* **1** (at the end of a book) the end. **2** the end of anything, esp. of life.

fin·ish /finish/ *v.* & *n.* • *v.* **1** *tr.* **a** (often foll. by *off*) bring to an end; come to the end of; complete. **b** (usu. foll. by *off*) *colloq.* kill; overcome completely. **c** (often foll. by *off, up*) consume or get through the whole or the remainder of (food or drink) (*finish your dinner*). **2** *intr.* **a** come to an end; cease. **b** reach the end, esp. of a race. **c** = *finish up*. **3** *tr.* **a** complete the manufacture of (cloth, woodwork, etc.) by surface treatment. **b** put the final touches to; make perfect or highly accomplished (*finished manners*). **c** prepare (a girl) for entry into fashionable society. • *n.* **1 a** the end; the last stage. **b** the point at which a race, etc., ends. **2** a method, material, or texture used for surface treatment of wood, cloth, etc. (*mahogany finish*). **3** what serves to give completeness. **4** an accomplished or completed state. □ **fight to the finish** fight until one party is completely beaten. **finish off** provide with an ending. **finish up** (often foll. by *in, by*) end in something, end by doing something (*the plan finished up in the wastebasket; finished up by apologizing*). **finish with** have no more to do with; complete one's use of or association with.

fin·ish·er /finishər/ *n.* **1** a person who finishes something. **2** a worker or machine doing the last operation in a manufacturing process. **3** *colloq.* a discomfiting thing, a crushing blow, etc.

fin·ish·ing school *n.* a private school where girls are prepared for entry into fashionable society.

fi·nite /fīnīt/ *adj.* **1** limited; bounded; not infinite. **2** *Gram.* (of a part of a verb) having a specific number and person. **3** not infinitely small. □□ **fi·nite·ly** *adv.* **fi·nite·ness** *n.* **fin·i·tude** /finitōōd, –tyōōd/ *n.*

fi·nit·ism /fīnītizəm/ *n.* belief in the finiteness of the world, God, etc. □□ **fi·nit·ist** /–tist/ *n.*

fink /fingk/ *n.* & *v. sl.* • *n.* **1** an unpleasant person. **2** an informer. **3** a strikebreaker. • *v.intr.* (foll. by *on*) inform on.

Finn /fin/ *n.* a native or inhabitant of Finland; a person of Finnish descent.

fin·nan /finən/ *n.* (in full **finnan haddie** or **haddock**) a haddock cured with the smoke of green wood, turf, or peat.

Finn·ish /finish/ *adj.* & *n.* • *adj.* of the Finns or their language. • *n.* the language of the Finns.

fin whale *n.* a large rorqual, *Balaenoptera physalus*, with a prominent dorsal fin.

fiord var. of FJORD.

fir /fər/ *n.* **1** (in full **fir tree**) any evergreen coniferous tree, esp. of the genus *Abies*, with needles borne singly on the stems (cf. PINE[1]). **2** the wood of the fir.

fire /fīr/ *n.* & *v.* • *n.* **1 a** the state or process of combustion, in which substances combine chemically with oxygen from the air and usu. give out bright light and heat. **b** the active principle operative in this. **c** flame or incandescence. **2** a conflagration; a destructive burning (*forest fire*). **3** burning fuel in a fireplace, furnace, etc. **4** firing of guns. **5 a** fervor; spirit; vivacity. **b** poetic inspiration; lively imagination. **c** vehement emotion. **6** burning heat; fever. **7** luminosity; glow (*St. Elmo's fire*). • *v.* **1 a** *tr.* discharge (a gun, etc.). **b** *tr.* propel (a missile) from a gun, etc. **c** *tr.* propel (a ball) with force or high speed. **d** *intr.* (often foll. by *at, into, on*) fire a gun or missile. **e** *tr.* produce (a broadside, salute, etc.) by discharge of guns. **f** *intr.* (of a gun, etc.) be discharged. **2** *tr.* cause (explosive) to explode. **3** *tr.* deliver or utter in rapid succession (*fired insults at us*). **4** *tr. sl.* dismiss (an employee) from a job. **5** *tr.* **a** set fire to with the intention of destroying. **b** kindle (explosives). **6** *intr.* catch fire. **7** *intr.* (of an internal combustion engine, or a cylinder in one) undergo ignition of its fuel. **8** *tr.* supply (a furnace, engine, boiler, or power station) with fuel. **9** *tr.* **a** stimulate (the imagination or emotion). **b** fill (a person) with enthusiasm. **10** *tr.* **a** bake or dry (pottery, bricks, etc.). **b** cure (tea or tobacco) by artificial heat. **11** *intr.* become heated or excited. **12** *tr.* cause to glow or redden. □ **fire away** *colloq.* begin; go ahead. **fire up 1** start up, as an engine. **2** show sudden anger. **on fire 1** burning. **2** excited. **under fire 1** being shot at. **2** being rigorously criticized or questioned. □□ **fire·less** *adj.* **fir·er** *n.*

fire and brim·stone *n.* the supposed torments of hell.

fire·arm /fīraarm/ *n.* (usu. in *pl.*) a gun, esp. a pistol or rifle.

fire·ball /fīrbawl/ *n.* **1** a large meteor. **2** a ball of flame, esp. from a nuclear explosion. **3** an energetic person.

fire·bomb /fīrbom/ *n.* an incendiary bomb.

fire·box /fīrboks/ *n.* **1** the fuel chamber of a steam engine or boiler. **2** an alarm box used to alert a fire department.

fire·brand /fīrbrand/ *n.* **1** a piece of burning wood. **2** a cause of trouble, esp. a person causing unrest.

fire·break /fīrbrayk/ *n.* an obstacle to the spread of fire in a forest, etc., esp. an open space.

fire·bug /fīrbug/ *n. colloq.* a pyromaniac.

fire·crack·er /fīrkrakər/ *n.* an explosive firework.

fire·damp /fīrdamp/ *n.* a miners' name for methane, which is explosive when mixed in certain proportions with air.

fire de·part·ment *n.* an organized body of firefighters trained and employed to extinguish fires.

fire·dog /fīrdawg, –dog/ *n.* a metal support for burning wood or for a grate or fire irons.

fire drill *n.* **1** a rehearsal of the procedures to be used in case of fire. **2** a primitive device for kindling fire with a stick and wood.

fire en·gine *n.* a vehicle carrying equipment for fighting large fires.

fire es·cape *n.* an emergency staircase or apparatus for escape from a building on fire.

fire ex·tin·guish·er *n.* an apparatus for discharging liquid chemicals, water, or foam to extinguish a fire.

fire·fight·er /fīrfītər/ *n.* a person whose task is to extinguish fires.

fire·fly /fīrflī/ *n.* (*pl.* **-flies**) any soft-bodied beetle of the family Lampyridae, emitting phosphorescent light, including glowworms.

fire•man /fírmən/ *n.* (*pl.* **-men**) **1** a member of a fire department; a person employed to extinguish fires. **2** a person who tends a furnace or the fire of a steam engine or steamship.

fire•place /fírplays/ *n. Archit.* **1** a place for a domestic fire, esp. a grate at the base of a chimney. **2** a structure surrounding this. **3** the area in front of this.

fire•plug /fírplug/ *n.* a hydrant for a fire hose.

fire•pow•er /fírpowər/ *n.* **1** the destructive capacity of guns, etc. **2** financial, intellectual, or emotional strength.

fire•proof /fírproof/ *adj. & v.* • *adj.* able to resist fire or great heat. • *v.tr.* make fireproof.

fire•side /fírsīd/ *n.* **1** the area around a fireplace. **2** a person's home or home life.

fire•side chat *n.* an informal talk.

fire•stone /fírstōn/ *n.* stone that resists fire, used for furnaces, etc.

fire storm *n.* **1** a high wind or storm following a very intense fire. **2** a sudden outburst, esp. of criticism, etc.

fire•wall /fírwawl/ *n.* **1** a wall or partition designed to inhibit or prevent the spread of fire. **2** *Computing* a part of a computer system or network designed to block unauthorized access while permitting outward communication.

fire•wa•ter /fírwawtər/ *n. colloq.* strong alcoholic liquor.

fire•wood /fírwood/ *n.* wood for use as fuel.

fire•work /fírwərk/ *n.* **1** a device containing combustible chemicals that cause explosions or spectacular effects. **2** (in *pl.*) **a** an outburst of passion, esp. anger. **b** a display of wit or brilliance.

fir•ing /fíring/ *n.* **1** the discharging of guns. **2** material for a fire; fuel. **3** the heating process that hardens clay into pottery, etc.

fir•ing line *n.* **1** the front line in a battle. **2** the leading part in an activity, etc.

fir•ing squad *n.* a group detailed to shoot a condemned person.

fir•kin /fə́rkin/ *n.* a small cask for liquids, butter, fish, etc.

firm[1] /fərm/ *adj., adv., & v.* • *adj.* **1 a** of solid or compact structure. **b** fixed; stable. **c** steady; not shaking. **2 a** resolute; determined. **b** not easily shaken (*firm belief*). **c** steadfast; constant (*a firm friend*). **3 a** (of an offer, etc.) not liable to cancellation after acceptance. **b** (of a decree, law, etc.) established; immutable. **4** *Commerce* (of prices or goods) maintaining their level or value. • *adv.* firmly (*stand firm*). • *v.* **1** *tr. & intr.* make or become firm, secure, compact, or solid. **2** *tr.* fix (plants) firmly in the soil. □□ **firm•ly** *adv.* **firm•ness** *n.*

firm[2] /fərm/ *n.* **1** a business concern. **2** the partners in such a concern.

fir•ma•ment /fə́rməmənt/ *n. literary* the sky regarded as a vault or arch. □□ **fir•ma•men•tal** /–mént'l/ *adj.*

firm•ware /fə́rmwair/ *n. Computing* a permanent kind of software programmed into a read-only memory.

first /fərst/ *adj., n., & adv.* • *adj.* **1 a** earliest in time or order. **b** coming next after a specified or implied time (*shall take the first train*; *the first robin of spring*). **2** foremost in position, rank, or importance (*first mate*). **3** *Mus.* performing the highest or chief of two or more parts for the same instrument or voice. **4** most willing or likely (*should be the first to admit the problem*). **5** basic or evident (*first principles*). • *n.* **1** (prec. by *the*) the person or thing first mentioned or occurring. **2** the first occurrence of something notable. **3** *Brit.* **a** a place in the first class in an examination. **b** a person having this. **4** the first day of a month. **5** first gear. **6 a** first place in a race. **b** the winner of this. **7** (in *pl.*) goods of the best quality. **8** first base. • *adv.* **1** before any other person or thing (*first of all*; *first and foremost*; *first come first served*). **2** before someone or something else (*must get this done first*). **3** for the first time (*when did you first see her?*). **4** in preference; sooner (*will see him damned first*). □ **at first** at the beginning. **first and last** taking one thing with another; on the whole. **first off** *colloq.* at first; first of all. **get to first base** achieve the first step toward an objective. **in the first place** as the first consideration.

first aid *n.* help given to an injured person until proper medical treatment is available.

first base *n. Baseball* **1** the base touched first by a base runner. **2 a** the fielder stationed nearest first base. **b** the position nearest first base.

first-born *adj. & n.* • *adj.* eldest. • *n.* the eldest child of a person.

first class *n.* **1** a set of persons or things grouped together as the best. **2** the best accommodations in a train, ship, etc. **3** the class of mail given priority in handling.

first-class *adj. & adv.* • *adj.* **1** belonging to or traveling by the first class. **2** of the best quality; very good. • *adv.* by the first class (*travels first-class*).

first cous•in see COUSIN.

first-day cov•er *n.* an envelope bearing a stamp or set of stamps postmarked on their first day of issue.

first-de•gree *adj. Med.* denoting burns that affect only the surface of the skin, causing reddening.

first gear *n.* the lowest gear in a series.

first•hand /fə́rst-hánd/ *attrib. adj. & adv.* from the original source; direct.

First La•dy *n.* the wife of the US President.

first•ly /fə́rstlee/ *adv.* (in enumerating topics, arguments, etc.) in the first place; first (cf. FIRST *adv.*). ▶See note at FIRST.

first mate *n.* (on a merchant ship) the officer second in command to the master.

first name *n.* a personal name other than a surname.

first per•son see PERSON 3.

first-rate *adj. & adv.* • *adj.* of the highest class; excellent. • *adv. colloq.* **1** very well (*feeling first-rate*). **2** excellently.

first thing *n. & adv.* • *n.* even the most elementary fact or principle (*does not know the first thing about it*). • *adv. colloq.* before anything else; very early in the morning (*shall do it first thing*). □ **first things first** the most important things before any others (*we must do first things first*).

firth /fərth/ *n.* **1** a narrow inlet of the sea. **2** an estuary.

fis•cal /fískəl/ *adj. & n.* • *adj.* of public revenue; of financial matters. • *n.* a legal official in some countries. □□ **fis•cal•ly** *adv.*

fis•cal year *n.* a year as reckoned for taxing or accounting.

fish[1] /fish/ *n. & v.* • *n.* (*pl.* same or **fishes**) **1** a vertebrate cold-blooded animal with gills and fins living wholly in water. **2** any animal living wholly in water, e.g., cuttlefish, shellfish, jellyfish. **3** the flesh of fish as food. **4** *colloq.* a person remarkable in some way (usu. unfavorable) (*an odd fish*). **5** (**the Fish** or Fishes) the zodiacal sign or constellation Pisces. • *v.* **1** *intr.* try to catch fish. **2** *tr.* fish for (a certain kind of fish) or in (a certain stretch of water). **3** *intr.* (foll. by *for*) **a** search for in water or a concealed place. **b** seek by indirect means (*fishing for compliments*). **4** *tr.* (foll. by *up*, *out*, etc.) retrieve with careful or awkward searching. □ **drink like a fish** drink excessively. **fish out of water** a person in an unsuitable or unwelcome environment or situation. **other fish to fry** other matters to attend to. ▫▫ **fish·like** *adj.*

fish[2] /fish/ *n. & v.* • *n.* **1** a flat plate of iron, wood, etc., to strengthen a beam or joint. **2** *Naut.* a piece of wood used to strengthen a mast, etc. • *v.tr.* **1** mend or strengthen (a spar, etc.) with a fish. **2** join (rails) with a fishplate.

fish·er /fishər/ *n.* **1** any animal that catches fish, esp. the marten, *Martes pennanti*, valued for its fur. **2** *archaic* a fisherman.

fish·er·man /fishərmən/ *n.* (*pl.* **-men**) **1** a person who catches fish. **2** a fishing boat.

fish·er·y /fishəree/ *n.* (*pl.* **-ies**) **1** a place where fish or other aquatic animals are caught or reared. **2** the occupation or industry of catching or rearing fish or other aquatic animals.

fish-eye lens *n. Photog.* a very wide-angle lens with a curved front.

fish·hook /fish-hŏŏk/ *n.* a barbed hook for catching fish.

fish·ing /fishing/ *n.* the activity of catching fish, for food or as recreation.

fish·ing rod *n.* a long tapering usu. jointed rod to which a fishing line is attached.

fish meal *n.* ground dried fish used as fertilizer or animal feed.

fish·net /fishnet/ *n.* (often *attrib.*) an open-meshed fabric (*fishnet stockings*).

fish·plate /fishplayt/ *n.* **a** a flat piece of iron, etc., connecting railroad rails. **b** a flat piece of metal with ends like a fish's tail, used to position masonry.

fish stick *n.* a small oblong piece of fish dipped in batter or breadcrumbs and fried.

fish sto·ry *n. colloq.* an exaggerated account.

fish·tail /fishtayl/ *n. & v.* • *n.* a device, etc., shaped like a fish's tail. • *v.intr.* move the tail of a vehicle from side to side.

fish·wife /fishwīf/ *n.* (*pl.* **-wives**) **1** an ill-mannered or noisy woman. **2** a woman who sells fish.

fish·y /fishee/ *adj.* (**fishier, fishiest**) **1 a** smelling or tasting like fish. **b** like that of a fish. **c** (of an eye) dull; vacant-looking. **d** consisting of fish (*a fishy repast*). **e** *joc.* or *poet.* abounding in fish. **2** *sl.* of dubious character; questionable; suspect. ▫▫ **fish·i·ness** *n.*

fis·sile /fisəl, –īl/ *adj.* **1** capable of undergoing nuclear fission. **2** tending to split.

fis·sion /fishən/ *n. & v.* • *n.* **1** *Physics* the spontaneous or impact-induced splitting of a heavy atomic nucleus, accompanied by a release of energy. **2** *Biol.* the division of a cell into new cells as a mode of reproduction. • *v.intr. & tr.* undergo or cause to undergo fission. ▫▫ **fis·sion·a·ble** *adj.*

fis·sure /fishər/ *n. & v.* • *n.* **1** an opening, usu. long and narrow, made esp. by cracking, splitting, or separation of parts. **2** *Bot. & Anat.* a narrow opening in an organ, etc., esp. a depression between convolutions of the brain. **3** a cleavage. • *v.tr. & intr.* split or crack.

fist /fist/ *n. & v.* • *n.* **1** a tightly closed hand. **2** *sl.* handwriting (*writes a good fist*; *I know his fist*). **3** *sl.* a hand (*give us your fist*). • *v.tr.* close into a fist. ▫ **make a good** (or **poor**, etc.) **fist** (foll. by *at, of*) *colloq.* make a good (or poor, etc.) attempt at. ▫▫ **fist·ed** *adj.* (also in *comb.*). **fist·ful** *n.* (*pl.* **-fuls**).

fist·fight /fistfīt/ *n.* a fight with bare fists.

fist·i·cuffs /fistikufs/ *n.pl.* fighting with the fists.

fis·tu·la /fischələ/ *n.* (*pl.* **fistulas** or **fistulae** /–lee/) **1** an abnormal or surgically made passage between a hollow organ and the body surface or between two hollow organs. **2** a natural pipe or spout in whales, insects, etc. ▫▫ **fis·tu·lar** *adj.* **fis·tu·lous** *adj.*

fit[1] /fit/ *adj., v., n., & adv.* • *adj.* (**fitter, fittest**) **1 a** (usu. foll. by *for*, or *to* + infin.) well suited. **b** (foll. by *to* + infin.) qualified; competent; worthy. **c** (foll. by *for*, or *to* + infin.) in a suitable condition; ready. **d** (foll. by *for*) good enough (*a dinner fit for a king*). **e** (foll. by *to* + infin.) sufficiently exhausted, troubled, or angry (*fit to drop*). **2** in good health or athletic condition. **3** proper; becoming; right (*it is fit that*). • *v.* (**fitted, fitting**) **1 a** *tr.* (also *absol.*) be of the right shape and size for (*the key doesn't fit the lock*; *these shoes don't fit*). **b** *tr.* make, fix, or insert (a thing) so that it is of the right size or shape (*fitted shelves in the alcoves*). **c** *intr.* (often foll. by *in, into*) (of a component) be correctly positioned (*that piece fits here*). **d** *tr.* find room for (*can't fit another person on the bench*). **2** *tr.* (foll. by *for*, or *to* + infin.) **a** make suitable; adapt. **b** make competent (*fitted him to be a priest*). **3** *tr.* (usu. foll. by *with*) supply; furnish (*fitted the boat with a new rudder*). **4** *tr.* fix in place (*fit a lock on the door*). **5** *tr.* try on (a garment). **6** *tr.* befit; become (*the punishment fits the crime*). • *n.* the way in which a garment, component, etc., fits (*a bad fit*; *a tight fit*). • *adv.* (foll. by *to* + infin.) *colloq.* in a suitable manner; appropriately (*was laughing fit to bust*). ▫ **fit the bill** = ***fill the bill***. **fit in 1** (often foll. by *with*) be compatible or accommodating (*tried to fit in with their plans*). **2** find space or time for (*the dentist fitted me in at the last minute*). **fit out** (or **up**) (often foll. by *with*) equip. **see** (or **think**) **fit** (often foll. by *to* + infin.) decide or choose (a specified course of action). ▫▫ **fit·ly** *adv.* **fit·ness** *n.*

fit[2] /fit/ *n.* **1** a sudden seizure of epilepsy, hysteria, apoplexy, fainting, or paralysis, with unconsciousness or convulsions. **2** a sudden brief attack of an illness or of symptoms (*fit of coughing*). **3** a sudden short bout or burst (*fit of energy*; *fit of giggles*). **4** *colloq.* an attack of strong feeling (*fit of rage*). **5** a capricious impulse; a mood (*when the fit was on him*). ▫ **by** (or **in**) **fits and starts** spasmodically. **give a person a fit** *colloq.* surprise or outrage him or her. **have a fit** *colloq.* be greatly surprised or outraged. **in fits** laughing uncontrollably.

fit·ful /fitfŏŏl/ *adj.* spasmodic or intermittent. ▫▫ **fit·ful·ly** *adv.* **fit·ful·ness** *n.*

fit·ted /fitid/ *adj.* **1** made or shaped to fill a space or cover something closely or exactly (*a fitted sheet*). **2** esp. *Brit.* built-in (*fitted cupboards*).

fit·ter /fitər/ *n.* **1** a person who supervises the cutting, fitting, altering, etc., of garments. **2** a mechanic who fits together and adjusts machinery.

fit·ting /fiting/ *n. & adj.* • *n.* **1** the process or an instance of having a garment, etc., fitted (*needed several fittings*). **2 a** (in *pl.*) the fixtures and furnishings of a building. **b** a piece of apparatus or a detachable part of a machine, fixture, etc. • *adj.* proper; becoming; right. ▫▫ **fit·ting·ly** *adv.* **fit·ting·ness** *n.*

five /fīv/ *n. & adj.* • *n.* **1** one more than four or one half of ten; the sum of three units and two units. **2** a symbol for this (5, v, V). **3** a size, etc., denoted by five. **4** a set or team of five individuals. **5** five o'clock (*is it five yet?*). **6** a card with five pips. **7** a five-dollar bill. • *adj.* that amount to five.

five·fold /fīvfōld/ *adj. & adv.* **1** five times as much or as many. **2** consisting of five parts. **3** amounting to five.

five o'clock shad·ow *n.* beard growth visible on a man's face in the latter part of the day.

fiv·er /fīvər/ *n. colloq.* **1** a five-dollar bill. **2** *Brit.* a five-pound note.

five-star *adj.* of the highest class.

fix /fiks/ *v. & n.* • *v.* **1** *tr.* make firm or stable; fasten; secure (*fixed a picture to the wall*). **2** *tr.* decide; settle; specify (a price, date, etc.). **3** *tr.* mend; repair. **4** *tr.* implant in the mind (*couldn't get the rules fixed in his head*). **5** *tr.* **a** (foll. by *on, upon*) direct steadily; set (one's eyes, gaze, attention, or affection). **b** attract and hold (a person's attention, eyes, etc.). **c** (foll. by *with*) single out with one's eyes, etc. **6** *tr.* place definitely; establish. **7** *tr.*

determine the exact nature, position, etc., of; refer (a thing or person) to a definite place or time; identify, locate. **8 a** *tr.* make (eyes, features, etc.) rigid. **b** *intr.* (of eyes, features, etc.) become rigid. **9** *tr. colloq.* prepare (food or drink) (*fixed me a drink*). **10 a** *tr.* congeal. **b** *intr.* become congealed. **11** *tr. colloq.* punish; kill; silence; deal with (a person). **12** *tr. colloq.* **a** secure the support of (a person) fraudulently, esp. by bribery. **b** arrange the result of (a race, match, etc.) fraudulently. **13** *sl.* **a** *tr.* inject (a person, esp. oneself) with a narcotic. **b** *intr.* take an injection of a narcotic. **14** *tr.* make (a color, photographic image, or microscope specimen) fast or permanent. **15** *tr.* (of a plant or microorganism) assimilate (nitrogen or carbon dioxide). **16** *tr.* castrate or spay (an animal). **17** *tr.* arrest changes or development in (a language or literature). **18** *tr.* determine the incidence of (liability, etc.). **19** (as **fixed** *adj.*) **a** permanently placed; stationary. **b** without moving; rigid; (of a gaze, etc.) steady or intent. **c** definite. **d** *sl.* dishonest; fraudulent. • *n.* **1** *colloq.* a dilemma or predicament. **2 a** the act of finding one's position by bearings or astronomical observations. **b** a position found in this way. **3** *sl.* a dose of a narcotic drug to which one is addicted. **4** *sl.* bribery. □ **be fixed** (usu. foll. by *for*) be disposed or affected (regarding) (*how are you fixed for Friday?*). **fix on** (or **upon**) choose; decide on. **fix up 1** arrange; organize; prepare. **2** accommodate. **3** (often foll. by *with*) provide (a person) with (*fixed me up with a job*). **4** restore; refurbish (*fixed up the old house*). □□ **fix·a·ble** *adj.* **fix·ed·ly** /fiksidlee/ *adv.* **fix·ed·ness** /fiksidnis/ *n.*

fix·ate /fiksáyt/ *v.tr.* **1** direct one's gaze on. **2** *Psychol.* **a** (usu. in *passive*; often foll. by *on, upon*) cause (a person) to acquire an abnormal attachment to persons or things (*was fixated on his son*). **b** arrest (the libido) at an immature stage, causing such attachment.

fix·a·tion /fiksáyshən/ *n.* **1** the act or an instance of being fixated. **2** an obsession; concentration on a single idea. **3** fixing or being fixed. **4** coagulation. **5** the process of assimilating a gas to form a solid compound.

fix·a·tive /fiksətiv/ *adj. & n.* • *adj.* tending to fix or secure. • *n.* a substance used to fix colors, hair, microscope specimens, etc.

fixed-do *attrib.adj. Mus.* applied to a system of sight-singing in which C is called 'do,' D is called 're,' etc., irrespective of the key in which they occur.

fix·er /fiksər/ *n.* **1** a person or thing that fixes. **2** *Photog.* a substance used for fixing a photographic image, etc.

fix·ings /fiksingz/ *n.pl.* **1** apparatus or equipment. **2** the trimmings for a dish. **3** the trimmings of a dress, etc.

fix·i·ty /fiksitee/ *n.* **1** a fixed state. **2** permanence.

fix·ture /fikschər/ *n.* **1 a** something fixed in position. **b** an attached appliance, apparatus, etc. (*an electrical fixture*). **c** (usu. *predic.*) *colloq.* a person or thing confined to or established in one place (*he seems to be a fixture*). **2** (in *pl.*) *Law* articles attached to a house or land and regarded as legally part of it.

fizz /fiz/ *v. & n.* • *v.intr.* **1** make a hissing or spluttering sound. **2** (of a drink) effervesce. • *n.* effervescence.

fiz·zle /fizəl/ *v. & n.* • *v.intr.* make a feeble hissing sound. • *n.* such a sound. □ **fizzle out** end feebly (*the party fizzled out at 10 o'clock*).

fizz·y /fizee/ *adj.* (**fizzier, fizziest**) effervescent; carbonated. □□ **fizz·i·ly** *adv.* **fizz·i·ness** *n.*

fjord /fyawrd/ *n.* (also **fiord**) a long narrow inlet of sea between high cliffs, as in Norway.

FL *abbr.* Florida (in official postal use).

fl. *abbr.* **1** floor. **2** floruit. **3** fluid.

Fla. *abbr.* Florida.

flab /flab/ *n. colloq.* fat; flabbiness.

flab·ber·gast /flábərgast/ *v.tr.* (esp. as **flabbergasted** *adj.*) *colloq.* overwhelm with astonishment.

flab·by /flábee/ *adj.* (**flabbier, flabbiest**) **1** (of flesh, etc.) hanging down; limp; flaccid. **2** (of language or character) feeble. □□ **flab·bi·ly** *adv.* **flab·bi·ness** *n.*

flac·cid /flásid, fláksid/ *adj.* **1 a** (of flesh, etc.) hanging loose or wrinkled; limp; flabby. **b** (of plant tissue) soft; less rigid. **2** relaxed; drooping. **3** lacking vigor; feeble. □□ **flac·cid·i·ty** /–síditee/ *n.* **flac·cid·ly** *adv.*

flack var. of FLAK.

flag[1] /flag/ *n. & v.* • *n.* **1** a piece of cloth, usu. oblong or square, attachable by one edge to a pole or rope and used as a country's emblem or as a standard, signal, etc. **2** a small toy, device, etc., resembling a flag. • *v.* (**flagged, flagging**) **1** *intr.* **a** grow tired; lose vigor; lag (*his energy flagged after the first lap*). **b** hang down; droop. **2** *tr.* **a** place a flag on or over. **b** mark out with or as if with a flag or flags (*they flagged the site of the accident*). **3** *tr.* (often foll. by *that*) **a** inform (a person) by flag signals. **b** communicate (information) by flagging. □ **flag down** signal to (a vehicle or driver) to stop.

flag[2] /flag/ *n. & v.* • *n.* (also **flag·stone**) **1** a flat usu. rectangular stone slab used for paving. **2** (in *pl.*) a pavement made of these. • *v.tr.* (**flagged, flagging**) pave with flags.

flag[3] /flag/ *n.* **1** any plant with a bladed leaf (esp. several of the genus *Iris*) growing on moist ground. **2** the long slender leaf of such a plant.

Flag Day *n.* June 14, the anniversary of the adoption of the Stars and Stripes as the official US flag in 1777.

flag·el·lant /flájələnt, fləjélənt/ *n. & adj.* • *n.* **1** a person who scourges himself or herself or others as a religious discipline. **2** a person who engages in flogging as a sexual stimulus. • *adj.* of or concerning flagellation.

flag·el·late[1] /flájəlayt/ *v.tr.* scourge; flog (cf. FLAGELLANT). □□ **flag·el·la·tion** /–láyshən/ *n.*

flag·el·late[2] /flájilit, –layt/ *adj. & n.* • *adj.* having flagella (see FLAGELLUM). • *n.* a protozoan having one or more flagella.

fla·gel·lum /fləjéləm/ *n.* (*pl.* **flagella** /–lə/) **1** *Biol.* a long lashlike appendage found principally on microscopic organisms. **2** *Bot.* a runner; a creeping shoot. □□ **fla·gel·lar** /–lər/ *adj.*

flag·on /flágən/ *n.* **1** a large bottle in which wine, cider, etc., are sold, usu. holding 1.13 liters. **2** a large vessel usu. with a handle, spout, and lid, to hold wine, etc.

flag·pole /flágpōl/ *n.* a pole on which a flag may be hoisted.

fla·grant /fláygrənt/ *adj.* (of an offense or an offender) glaring; notorious; scandalous. □□ **fla·gran·cy** /–grənsee/ *n.* **fla·grant·ly** *adv.*

flag·ship /flágship/ *n.* **1** a ship having an admiral on board. **2** something that is held to be the best or most important of its kind; a leader.

flag·staff /flágstaf/ *n.* = FLAGPOLE.

flag·stone /flágstōn/ *n.* = FLAG[2].

flag-wav·er *n.* a populist agitator; a patriotic chauvinist. □□ **flag-wav·ing** *n.*

flail /flayl/ *n. & v.* • *n.* a threshing tool consisting of a wooden staff with a short heavy stick swinging from it. • *v.* **1** *tr.* beat or strike with or as if with a flail. **2** *intr.* wave or swing wildly.

flair /flair/ *n.* **1** an instinct for selecting or performing what is excellent, useful, etc. **2** talent or ability, esp. artistic or stylistic.

flak /flak/ *n.* (also **flack**) **1** antiaircraft fire. **2** adverse criticism; abuse.

flake /flayk/ *n. & v.* • *n.* **1 a** a small thin light piece of snow. **b** a similar piece of another material. **2** a thin broad piece of material peeled or split off. **3** *Archaeol.* a piece of hard stone chipped off and used as a tool. **4** a natural division of the flesh of some fish. **5** the dogfish or other shark as food. **6** *sl.* a crazy or eccentric person. • *v.tr. & intr.* (often foll. by *away, off*) **1** take off or come away in flakes. **2** sprinkle with or fall in snowlike flakes. □ **flake out** *colloq.* **1** fall asleep or drop from exhaustion; faint. **2** act strangely.

flak jack•et *n.* a protective jacket reinforced with bulletproof material, worn by soldiers, etc.

flak•y /fláykee/ *adj.* (**flakier, flakiest**) **1** of or like flakes; separating easily into flakes. **2** *sl.* crazy; eccentric. □□ **flak•i•ly** *adv.* **flak•i•ness** *n.*

flam•bé /flaambáy/ *adj.* (of food) covered with alcohol and set alight briefly.

flam•boy•ant /flambóyənt/ *adj.* **1** ostentatious; showy. **2** floridly decorated. **3** gorgeously colored. □□ **flam•boy•ance** /–əns/ *n.* **flam•boy•ant•ly** *adv.*

flame /flaym/ *n. & v.* • *n.* **1 a** ignited gas (*the fire burned with a steady flame*). **b** one portion of this (*the flame flickered and died*). **c** (usu. in *pl.*) visible combustion (*burst into flames*). **2 a** a bright light; brilliant coloring. **b** a brilliant orange-red color. **3 a** strong passion, esp. love (*fan the flame*). **b** *colloq.* a boyfriend or girlfriend. • *v.* **1** *intr. & tr.* (often foll. by *away, forth, out, up*) emit or cause to emit flames. **2** *intr.* (often foll. by *out, up*) **a** (of passion) break out. **b** (of a person) become angry. **3** *intr.* shine or glow like flame (*leaves flamed in the autumn sun*). **4** *tr.* send (a signal) by means of flame. **5** *tr.* subject to the action of flame. □ **flame out** (of a jet engine) lose power through imperfect combustion in the combustion chamber. **go up in flames** be consumed by fire. □□ **flame•less** *adj.* **flame•like** *adj.* **flam•y** *adj.*

fla•men•co /fləméngkō/ *n.* (*pl.* **-cos**) **1** a style of music played (esp. on the guitar) and sung by Spanish gypsies. **2** a dance performed to this music.

flame•proof /fláymproōf/ *adj.* treated so as to be nonflammable.

flame•throw•er /fláymthrōər/ *n.* a weapon for throwing a spray of flame.

flam•ing /fláyming/ *adj.* **1** emitting flames. **2** very hot (*flaming day*). **3** *colloq.* **a** passionate (*a flaming argument*). **b** expressing annoyance, or as an intensifier (*that flaming idiot*). **4** bright colored (*flaming red hair*).

fla•min•go /fləmínggō/ *n.* (*pl.* **-gos** or **-goes**) any tall web-footed wading bird of the family Phoenicopteridae, with pink, scarlet, and black plumage.

flam•ma•ble /flámәbəl/ *adj.* easily set on fire; inflammable. □□ **flam•ma•bil•i•ty** *n.*

▶See note at INFLAMMABLE.

flan /flan/ *n.* **1 a** an open pastry case with a savory or sweet filling. **b** a custard topped with caramel glaze. **2** a disk of metal from which a coin, etc., is made.

flange /flanj/ *n. & v. Engin.* • *n.* a projecting flat rim, collar, or rib, used for strengthening or attachment. • *v.tr.* provide with a flange.

flank /flangk/ *n. & v.* • *n.* **1 a** the side of the body between the ribs and the hip. **b** the side of an animal carved as meat (*flank of beef*). **2** the side of a mountain, building, etc. **3** the right or left side of an army or other body of persons. • *v.tr.* **1** (often in *passive*) be situated at both sides of (*a road flanked by mountains*). **2** *Mil.* **a** guard or strengthen on the flank. **b** menace the flank of.

flank•er /flángkər/ *n.* **1** *Mil.* a fortification guarding or menacing the flank. **2** anything that flanks another thing. **3** *Football* an offensive back positioned outside the tackle and behind the line of scrimmage.

flan•nel /flánəl/ *n.* **1** a kind of woven wool fabric, usu. with a slight nap. **2** (in *pl.*) flannel garments, esp. underwear or trousers.

flap /flap/ *v. & n.* • *v.* (**flapped, flapping**) **1 a** *tr.* move (wings, the arms, etc.) up and down when flying, or as if flying. **b** *intr.* (of wings, the arms, etc.) move up and down. **2** *intr. colloq.* be agitated or panicky. **3** *intr.* (esp. of curtains, loose cloth, etc.) swing or sway about; flutter. **4** *tr.* (usu. foll. by *away, off*) strike (flies, etc.) with something broad; drive. **5** *intr. colloq.* (of ears) listen intently. • *n.* **1** a piece of cloth, wood, paper, etc., hinged or attached by one side only and often used to cover a gap, e.g., the folded part of an envelope, a table leaf. **2** one up-and-down motion of a wing, an arm, etc. **3** *colloq.* a state of agitation; panic (*don't get into a flap*). **4** a hinged or sliding section of a wing used to control lift and drag. **5** a light blow with something broad. **6** an open mushroom top. □□ **flap•py** *adj.*

flap•doo•dle /flápdōōd'l/ *n. colloq.* nonsense.

flap•jack /flápjak/ *n.* a pancake.

flap•per /flápər/ *n.* **1** a person or thing that flaps. **2** an instrument that is flapped to kill flies, scare birds, etc. **3** a person who panics easily. **4** *sl.* (in the 1920s) a young unconventional or lively woman.

flare /flair/ *v. & n.* • *v.* **1** *intr. & tr.* widen or cause to widen, esp. toward the bottom (*flared trousers*). **2** *intr. & tr.* burn or cause to burn suddenly with a bright unsteady flame. **3** *intr.* burst into anger; burst forth. • *n.* **1 a** a dazzling irregular flame or light. **b** a sudden outburst of flame. **2 a** a signal light used at sea. **b** a bright light used as a signal. **c** a flame dropped from an aircraft to illuminate a target, etc. **3** *Astron.* a sudden burst of radiation from a star. **4 a** a gradual widening, esp. of a skirt or trousers. **b** (in *pl.*) wide-bottomed trousers. **5** *Photog.* unnecessary illumination on a lens caused by internal reflection, etc. □ **flare up 1** burst into a sudden blaze. **2** become suddenly angry or active.

flare-up *n.* an outburst of flame, anger, activity, etc.

flash /flash/ *v. & n.* • *v.* **1** *intr. & tr.* emit or reflect or cause to emit or reflect light briefly, suddenly, or intermittently; gleam or cause to gleam. **2** *intr.* break suddenly into flame; give out flame or sparks. **3** *tr.* send or reflect like a sudden flame or blaze. **4** *intr.* **a** burst suddenly into view or perception (*the explanation flashed upon me*). **b** move swiftly (*the train flashed through the station*). **5** *tr.* **a** send (news, etc.) by radio, telegraph, etc. (*flashed a message to her*). **b** signal to (a person) by shining lights or headlights briefly. **6** *tr. colloq.* show ostentatiously (*flashed her engagement ring*). **7** *intr.* (of water) rush along; rise and flow. **8** *intr. sl.* indecently expose oneself. • *n.* **1** a sudden bright light or flame, e.g., of lightning. **2** a very brief time; an instant (*all over in a flash*). **3 a** a brief, sudden burst of feeling (*a flash of hope*). **b** a sudden display (of wit, understanding, etc.). **4** = NEWS FLASH. **5** *Photog.* = FLASHLIGHT 2. **6 a** a rush of water, esp. down a weir to take a boat over shallows. **b** a contrivance for producing this. **7** a bright patch of color. **8** *Cinematog.* the momentary exposure of a scene. □ **flash in the pan** a promising start followed by failure (from the priming of old guns).

flash•back /fláshbak/ *n.* a scene in a movie, novel, etc., set in a time earlier than the main action.

flash•board /fláshbawrd/ *n.* a board used for increasing the depth of water behind a dam.

flash bulb *n.* a bulb for a photographic flashlight.

flash burn *n.* a burn caused by sudden intense radiation, esp. from a nuclear explosion.

flash card *n.* a card containing a small amount of information, held up for pupils to see, as an aid to learning.

flash•cube /fláshkyōōb/ *n. Photog.* a set of four flash bulbs arranged as a cube and operated in turn.

flash•er /fláshər/ *n.* **1** *sl.* a person, esp. a man, who indecently exposes himself. **2 a** an automatic device for switching lights rapidly on and off. **b** a sign or signal using this. **3** a person or thing that flashes.

flash flood *n.* a sudden local flood due to heavy rain, etc.

flash·gun /fláshgun/ *n. Photog.* a device used to operate a photographic flashlight.

flash·ing /fláshing/ *n.* a usu. metallic strip used to prevent water penetration at the junction of a roof with a wall, chimney, etc.

flash·light /fláshlīt/ *n.* **1** a battery-operated portable light. **2** a light giving an intense flash, used for photographing by night, indoors, etc. **3** a flashing light used for signals and in lighthouses.

flash point *n.* **1** the temperature at which vapor from oil, etc., will ignite in air. **2** the point at which anger, indignation, etc., becomes uncontrollable.

flash·y /fláshee/ *adj.* (**flashier, flashiest**) showy; gaudy; cheaply attractive. ▫▫ **flash·i·ly** *adv.* **flash·i·ness** *n.*

flask /flask/ *n.* a narrow-necked bulbous bottle for wine, etc., or as used in chemistry.

flask Middle English (in the sense 'cask'): from medieval Latin *flasca*. From the mid-16th cent. the word denoted a case of horn, leather, or metal for carrying gunpowder. The sense 'glass container' (late 17th cent.) was influenced by Italian *fiasco*, from medieval Latin *flasco*. Compare with FLAGON.

flat[1] /flat/ *adj., adv., n., & v.* • *adj.* (**flatter, flattest**) **1 a** horizontally level (*a flat roof*). **b** even; smooth; unbroken; without projection or indentation (*a flat stomach*). **c** with a level surface and little depth; shallow (*a flat cap; a flat heel*). **2** unqualified; downright (*a flat refusal*). **3 a** dull; lifeless; monotonous (*spoke in a flat tone*). **b** dejected. **4** (of a carbonated drink) having lost its effervescence; stale. **5** *Mus.* **a** below true or normal pitch (*the violins are flat*). **b** (of a key) having a flat or flats in the signature. **c** (as **B, E,** etc., **flat**) a half step lower than B, E, etc. **6** *Photog.* lacking contrast. **7 a** (of paint, etc.) not glossy; matte. **b** (of a tint) uniform. **8** (of a tire) punctured; deflated. **9** (of a market, prices, etc.) inactive; sluggish. **10** of or relating to flat racing. • *adv.* **1** lying at full length; spread out (*lay flat on the floor; flat against the wall*). **2** *colloq.* **a** completely; absolutely (*flat broke*). **b** exactly (*in five minutes flat*). **3** *Mus.* below the true or normal pitch (*always sings flat*). • *n.* **1** the flat part of anything (*the flat of the hand*). **2** level ground, esp. a plain or swamp. **3** *Mus.* **a** a note lowered a half step below natural pitch. **b** the sign (♭) indicating this. **4** *colloq.* a flat tire. **5** a shallow planter box for starting seedlings. • *v.tr.* (**flatted, flatting**) **1** make flat; flatten (esp. in technical use). **2** *Mus.* make (a note) flat. ▫ **fall flat** fail to live up to expectations; not win applause. **flat out 1** at top speed. **2** without hesitation or delay. **3** using all one's strength, energy, or resources. ▫▫ **flat·ly** *adv.* **flat·ness** *n.* **flat·tish** *adj.*

flat[2] /flat/ *n.* esp. *Brit.* = APARTMENT 1. ▫▫ **flat·let** *n.*

flat·boat /flátbōt/ *n.* (or **flat-bot·tomed boat**) a boat with a flat bottom for transport in shallow water.

flat·car /flátkaar/ *n.* a railroad car without raised sides or ends.

flat·fish /flátfish/ *n.* (*pl.* usu. same) any marine fish of various families having an asymmetric appearance with both eyes on one side of a flattened body, including sole, turbot, plaice, etc.

flat·foot /flátfŏŏt/ *n.* **1** (*pl.* **flat feet**) a foot with a less than normal arch. **2** (*pl.* **-foots** or **-feet**) *sl.* a police officer.

flat-foot·ed /flátfŏŏtid/ *adj.* **1** having flat feet. **2** *colloq.* downright; positive. **3** *colloq.* unprepared; off guard (*was caught flat-footed*). ▫▫ **flat-foot·ed·ly** *adv.* **flat-foot·ed·ness** *n.*

flat·i·ron /flátīərn/ *n.* an iron heated externally and used for pressing clothes, etc.

flat·ten /flát'n/ *v.* **1** *tr. & intr.* make or become flat. **2** *tr. colloq.* **a** humiliate. **b** knock down. ▫ **flatten out** bring an aircraft parallel to the ground. ▫▫ **flat·ten·er** *n.*

flat·ter /flátər/ *v.tr.* **1** compliment unduly, esp. for gain or advantage. **2** (usu. *refl.*; usu. foll. by *that* + clause) congratulate or delude (oneself, etc.) (*I flatter myself that I can sing*). **3 a** (of a color, a style, etc.) make (a person) appear to the best advantage. **b** (esp. of a portrait, a painter, etc.) represent too favorably. **4** make (a person) feel honored. **5** inspire (a person) with hope, esp. unduly (*was flattered into thinking himself invulnerable*). **6** please or gratify (the ear, the eye, etc.). ▫▫ **flat·ter·er** *n.* **flat·ter·ing** *adj.* **flat·ter·ing·ly** *adv.*

flat·ter·y /flátəree/ *n.* (*pl.* **-ies**) **1** exaggerated or insincere praise. **2** the act or an instance of flattering.

flat·top *n.* **1** *Aeron. sl.* an aircraft carrier. **2** *sl.* a hairstyle in which the hair is cropped short so that it bristles up into a flat surface.

flat·u·lent /fláchələnt/ *adj.* **1 a** causing formation of gas in the alimentary canal. **b** caused by or suffering from this. **2** (of speech, etc.) inflated; pretentious. ▫▫ **flat·u·lence** *n.* **flat·u·lent·ly** *adv.*

fla·tus /fláytəs/ *n.* wind in or from the stomach or bowels.

flat·ware /flátwair/ *n.* **1** forks, knives, spoons, etc.; cutlery. **2** plates, saucers, etc. (cf. HOLLOWWARE).

flat·worm /flátwərm/ *n.* any worm of the phylum Platyhelminthes, having a flattened body and no body cavity or blood vessels, including turbellaria, flukes, etc.

flaunt /flawnt/ *v. & n.* • *v.tr. & intr.* **1** (often *refl.*) display ostentatiously; show off; parade (*liked to flaunt his gold cuff links; flaunted themselves before the crowd*). ▶Often confused with *flout*. **2** wave or cause to wave proudly (*flaunted the banner*). • *n.* an act or instance of flaunting.

▶**Flaunt** and **flout** are often confused because both suggest arrogance or showing off. However, **flaunt** means 'display ostentatiously,' e.g., *He liked to flaunt his wealth*, while **flout** means 'express contempt for or disobey (laws, convention, etc.),' e.g., *The fine is too low for those who flout the law so egregiously.*

flau·tist /fláwtist, flów–/ *n.* a flute player.

fla·vone /fláyvōn/ *n. Biochem.* any of a group of naturally occurring white or yellow pigments found in plants.

fla·vor /fláyvər/ *n. & v.* • *n.* **1** a distinctive mingled sensation of smell and taste (*a cheesy flavor*). **2** an indefinable characteristic quality (*music with a romantic flavor*). **3** (usu. foll. by *of*) a slight admixture of a quality (*the flavor of failure hangs over the enterprise*). **4** = FLAVORING. • *v.tr.* give flavor to; season. ▫ **flavor of the month** (or **week**) a temporary trend or fashion. ▫▫ **fla·vor·ful** *adj.* **fla·vor·less** *adj.* **fla·vor·some** *adj.*

fla·vor·ing /fláyvəring/ *n.* a substance used to flavor food or drink.

flaw /flaw/ *n. & v.* • *n.* **1** an imperfection; a blemish (*has a character without a flaw*). **2** a crack or similar fault (*the cup has a flaw*). **3** *Law* an invalidating defect in a legal matter. • *v.tr. & intr.* crack; damage; spoil. ▫▫ **flawed** *adj.* **flaw·less** *adj.* **flaw·less·ly** *adv.* **flaw·less·ness** *n.*

flax /flaks/ *n.* **1 a** a blue-flowered plant, *Linum usitatissimum*, cultivated for its textile fiber and its seeds (see LINSEED). **b** a plant resembling this. **2** flax fibers.

flax·en /fláksən/ *adj.* **1** of flax. **2** (of hair) colored like dressed flax; pale yellow.

flax·seed /flákseed/ *n.* linseed.

flay /flay/ *v.tr.* **1** strip the skin or hide off, esp. by beating. **2** criticize severely. **3** peel off (skin, bark, peel, etc.).

F layer /éf layər/ *n.* the highest and most strongly ionized region of the ionosphere.

flea /flee/ *n.* a small wingless jumping insect of the order Siphonaptera, feeding on blood. □ **a flea in one's ear** a sharp reproof.

flea·bag /fléebag/ *n. sl.* a shabby or unattractive place or thing.

flea-bit·ten *adj.* **1** bitten by or infested with fleas. **2** shabby.

flea col·lar *n.* an insecticidal collar for dogs and cats.

flea mar·ket *n.* a market selling secondhand goods, etc.

fleck /flek/ *n.* & *v.* • *n.* **1** a small patch of color or light (*eyes with green flecks*). **2** a small particle or speck. **3** a spot on the skin; a freckle. • *v.tr.* mark with flecks.

fled *past* and *past part.* of FLEE.

fledge /flej/ *v.* **1** *intr.* (of a bird) grow feathers. **2** *tr.* provide (an arrow) with feathers. **3** *tr.* bring up (a young bird) until it can fly. **4** *tr.* (as **fledged** *adj.*) **a** able to fly. **b** independent; mature. **5** *tr.* deck or provide with feathers or down.

fledg·ling /fléjling/ *n.* **1** a young bird. **2** an inexperienced person.

flee /flee/ *v.* (*past* and *past part.* **fled** /fled/) **1** *intr.* (often foll. by *from, before*) **a** run away. **b** seek safety by fleeing. **2** *tr.* run away from; leave abruptly; shun (*fled the room; fled his attentions*). **3** *intr.* vanish.

fleece /flees/ *n.* & *v.* • *n.* **1 a** the woolly covering of a sheep or a similar animal. **b** the amount of wool sheared from a sheep at one time. **2** something resembling a fleece, esp.: **a** a woolly or rough head of hair. **b** a soft warm fabric with a pile, used for lining coats, etc. **c** a white cloud, a blanket of snow, etc. • *v.tr.* **1** (often foll. by *of*) strip (a person) of money, valuables, etc.; swindle. **2** remove the fleece from (a sheep, etc.); shear. **3** cover as if with a fleece (*a sky fleeced with clouds*). □□ **fleeced** *adj.* (also in *comb.*).

fleec·y /fléesee/ *adj.* (**fleecier, fleeciest**) **1** of or like a fleece. **2** covered with a fleece. □□ **fleec·i·ness** *n.*

fleet[1] /fleet/ *n.* **1 a** a number of warships under one commander. **b** (prec. by *the*) all the warships and merchant ships of a nation. **2** a number of ships, aircraft, buses, trucks, taxis, etc., operating together or owned by one proprietor.

fleet[2] /fleet/ *adj.* swift; nimble. □□ **fleet·ly** *adv.* **fleet·ness** *n.*

Fleet Ad·mi·ral *n.* an admiral of the highest rank in the US Navy.

fleet·ing /fléeting/ *adj.* transitory; brief. □□ **fleet·ing·ly** *adv.*

Flem·ing /fléming/ *n.* **1** a native of medieval Flanders in the Low Countries. **2** a member of a Flemish-speaking people inhabiting N. and W. Belgium (see also WALLOON).

Flem·ish /flémish/ *adj.* & *n.* • *adj.* of or relating to Flanders. • *n.* the language of the Flemings.

flesh /flesh/ *n.* & *v.* • *n.* **1 a** the soft substance consisting of muscle and fat found between the skin and bones of an animal or a human. **b** plumpness; fat (*has put on flesh*). **c** *archaic* meat, esp. excluding poultry, game, and offal. **2** the body as opposed to the mind or the soul, esp. considered as sinful. **3** the pulpy substance of a fruit or a plant. **4 a** the visible surface of the human body. **b** (also **flesh col·or**) a yellowish pink color. **5** animal or human life. • *v.tr.* embody in flesh. □ **flesh out** make or become substantial. **in the flesh** in bodily form; in person. **the way of all flesh** experience common to all humankind. □□ **flesh·less** *adj.*

flesh and blood *n.* & *adj.* • *n.* **1** the body or its substance. **2** humankind. **3** human nature, esp. as being fallible. • *adj.* actually living, not imaginary or supernatural. □ **one's own flesh and blood** near relatives; descendants.

flesh·ly /fléshlee/ *adj.* (**fleshlier, fleshliest**) **1** (of desire, etc.) bodily; sensual. **2** mortal; not divine. **3** worldly.

flesh·pots /fléshpots/ *n.pl.* places providing luxurious or hedonistic living.

flesh·y /fléshee/ *adj.* (**fleshier, fleshiest**) **1** plump; fat. **2** of flesh; without bone. **3** (of plant or fruit tissue) pulpy. **4** like flesh. □□ **flesh·i·ness** *n.*

fleur-de-lis /flőrdəlée/ *n.* (also **fleur-de-lys**) (*pl.* **fleurs-** *pronunc.* same) **1** the iris flower. **2** *Heraldry* **a** a lily composed of three petals bound together near their bases. **b** the former royal arms of France.

fleur-de-lis

flew *past* of FLY[1].

flex /fleks/ *v.* **1** *tr.* & *intr.* bend (a joint, limb, etc.) or be bent. **2** *tr.* & *intr.* move (a muscle) or (of a muscle) be moved to bend a joint.

flex·i·ble /fléksibəl/ *adj.* **1** able to bend without breaking; pliable. **2** manageable. **3** adaptable; variable (*works flexible hours*). □□ **flex·i·bil·i·ty** *n.* **flex·i·bly** *adv.*

flex·ile /fléksəl, –sīl/ *adj. archaic* **1** supple; mobile. **2** tractable; manageable. **3** versatile. □□ **flex·il·i·ty** /–silitee/ *n.*

flex·i·time /fléksitīm/ *n.* var. of FLEXTIME.

flex·or /fléksər/ *n.* (in full **flexor muscle**) a muscle that bends part of the body (cf. EXTENSOR).

flex·time /flékstīm/ *n.* **1** a system of working a set number of hours with the starting and finishing times chosen within agreed limits by the employee. **2** the hours worked in this way.

flick /flik/ *n.* & *v.* • *n.* **1 a** a light, sharp blow with a whip, etc. **b** the sudden release of a bent finger or thumb, esp. to propel a small object. **2** a sudden movement or jerk. **3** a quick turn of the wrist in playing games, esp. in throwing or striking a ball. **4** a slight, sharp sound. **5** *colloq.* **a** a movie. **b** (in *pl.*; prec. by *the*) the movies. • *v.* **1** *tr.* (often foll. by *away, off*) strike or move with a flick (*flicked the ash off his cigar*). **2** *tr.* give a flick with (a whip, towel, etc.). **3** *intr.* make a flicking movement or sound.

flick·er[1] /flíkər/ *v.* & *n.* • *v.intr.* **1** (of light) shine unsteadily. **2** (of a flame) burn unsteadily, alternately flaring and dying down. **3 a** (of a flag, a reptile's tongue, an eyelid, etc.) move or wave back and forth; quiver; vibrate. **b** (of the wind) blow lightly and unsteadily. **4** (of hope, etc.) increase and decrease unsteadily. • *n.* a flickering movement, light, thought, etc.

flick·er[2] /flíkər/ *n.* any woodpecker of the genus *Colaptes*, a ground-feeder native to N. America.

fli·er /flíər/ *n.* (also **fly·er**) *colloq.* **1** an airman or airwoman. **2** a thing that flies in a specified way (*a poor flier*). **3** a fast-moving animal or vehicle. **4** an ambitious or outstanding person. **5** (usu. **fly·er**) a small handbill. **6** a speculative investment. **7** a flying jump.

flight[1] /flīt/ *n.* **1 a** the act or manner of flying through the air (*studied swallows' flight*). **b** the movement or passage of a projectile, etc., through the air (*the flight of an arrow*). **2 a** a journey made through the air or in space. **b** a timetabled journey made by an airline. **c** a military air unit of two or more aircraft. **3 a** a flock of birds, insects, etc. **b** a migration. **4** (usu. foll. by *of*) a series, esp. of stairs between floors, or of hurdles across a race track. **5** a mental or verbal excursion or sally (of wit, etc.) (*a flight of fancy*). **6** the trajectory and pace of a ball in games. **7** the distance that a bird, aircraft, or missile can fly. **8** (usu. foll. by *of*) a volley (*a flight* *of arrows*). **9** the tail of a dart. □ **in the first** (or **top**) **flight** taking a leading place. **take** (or **wing**) **one's flight** fly.

flight[2] /flīt/ *n.* **1 a** the act or manner of fleeing. **b** a hasty retreat. **2** *Econ.* the selling of currency, investments, etc., in anticipation of a fall in value (*flight from the dollar*). □ **put to flight** cause to flee. **take** (or **take to**) **flight** flee.

flight at·tend·ant *n.* an airline employee who attends to passengers' safety and comfort during flights.

flight deck *n.* **1** the deck of an aircraft carrier used for takeoff and landing. **2** the forward compartment occupied by the pilot, navigator, etc., in an aircraft.

flight·less /flítlis/ *adj.* (of a bird, etc.) naturally unable to fly.

flight·y /flítee/ *adj.* (**flightier, flightiest**) **1** frivolous; fickle; changeable. **2** crazy. □□ **flight·i·ly** *adv.* **flight·i·ness** *n.*

flim·flam /flímflam/ *n.* & *v.* • *n.* **1** a trifle; nonsense; idle talk. **2** humbug; deception. • *v.tr.* (**flimflammed, flimflamming**) cheat; deceive. □□ **flim·flam·mer** *n.*

flim·sy /flímzee/ *adj.* (**flimsier, flimsiest**) **1** insubstantial; easily damaged (*a flimsy structure*). **2** (of an excuse, etc.) unconvincing (*a flimsy pretext*). **3** paltry; trivial; superficial (*a flimsy play*). **4** (of clothing) thin (*a flimsy blouse*). □□ **flim·si·ly** *adv.* **flim·si·ness** *n.*

flinch /flinch/ *v.* & *n.* • *v.intr.* **1** draw back in pain or expectation of a blow, etc.; wince. **2** (often foll. by *from*) give way; shrink; turn aside (*flinched from his duty*). • *n.* an act or instance of flinching. □□ **flinch·ing·ly** *adv.*

fling /fling/ *v.* & *n.* • *v.* (*past* and *past part.* **flung** /flung/) **1** *tr.* throw or hurl (an object) forcefully. **2** *refl.* **a** (usu. foll. by *into*) rush headlong (into a person's arms, a train, etc.). **b** (usu. foll. by *into*) embark wholeheartedly (on an enterprise). **c** (usu. foll. by *on*) throw (oneself) on a person's mercy, etc. **3** *tr.* utter (words) forcefully. **4** *tr.* (usu. foll. by *out*) suddenly spread (the arms). **5** *tr.* (foll. by *on, off*) put on or take off (clothes) carelessly or rapidly. **6** *intr.* go angrily or violently; rush (*flung out of the room*). **7** *tr.* put or send suddenly or violently (*was flung into jail*). **8** *tr.* (foll. by *away*) discard thoughtlessly (*flung away their reputation*). • *n.* **1** an act or instance of flinging; a throw. **2 a** a spell of indulgence or wild behavior (*he's had his fling*). **b** *colloq.* an attempt (*give it a fling*). **3** a brief or casual romance. **4** an impetuous, whirling Scottish dance, esp. the Highland fling.

flint /flint/ *n.* **1 a** a hard gray stone of nearly pure silica occurring naturally as nodules or bands in chalk. **b** a piece of this, esp. as flaked or shaped to form a primitive tool or weapon. **2** a piece of hard alloy of rare earth metals used to give an igniting spark in a cigarette lighter, etc. **3** a piece of flint used with steel to produce fire. **4** anything hard and unyielding. □□ **flint·y** *adj.* (**flintier, flintiest**).

flint·lock /flíntlok/ *n. hist.* **1** an old type of gun fired by a spark from a flint. **2** the lock producing such a spark.

flip[1] /flip/ *v., n.,* & *adj.* • *v.* (**flipped, flipping**) **1** *tr.* **a** flick (a coin, ball, etc.) so that it spins in the air. **b** remove (a small object) from a surface with a flick of the fingers. **2** *tr.* **a** flick (a person's ear, cheek, etc.) lightly or smartly. **b** move (a whip, etc.) with a sudden jerk. **3** *tr.* turn or turn over. **4** *intr.* **a** make a flicking noise with the fingers. **b** (foll. by *at*) strike smartly at. **5** *intr.* move about with sudden jerks. **6** *intr. sl.* (often foll. by *out*) become suddenly angry, excited, or enthusiastic. • *n.* **1** a smart light blow; a flick. **2** a somersault, esp. while in the air. **3** an act of flipping over (*gave the stone a flip*). **4** *colloq.* **a** a short pleasure flight in an aircraft. **b** a quick tour, etc. • *adj. colloq.* glib; flippant. □ **flip one's lid** *sl.* **1** lose self-control. **2** go crazy. **flip through 1** turn over (cards, pages, etc.). **2 a** turn over the pages, etc., of, by a rapid movement of the fingers. **b** look cursorily through (a book, etc.).

flip[2] /flip/ *n.* a drink of heated beer and liquor.

flip chart *n.* a large pad erected on a stand and bound so that one page can be turned over at the top to reveal the next.

flip-flop /flípflop/ *n.* & *v.* • *n.* **1** a usu. rubber sandal with a thong between the big and second toe. **2** a backward somersault. **3** an electronic switching circuit changed from one stable state to another, or through an unstable state back to its stable state, by a triggering pulse. **4** an esp. sudden change of direction, attitude, policy, etc. • *v.intr.* (**-flopped, -flopping**) **1** move with a sound or motion suggested by "flip-flop." **2** to change direction, attitude, policy, etc., esp. suddenly.

flip·pant /flípənt/ *adj.* treating serious things lightly; disrespectful. □□ **flip·pan·cy** /–pənsee/ *n.* **flip·pant·ly** *adv.*

flip·per /flípər/ *n.* **1** a broadened limb of a tortoise, penguin, etc., used in swimming. **2** a flat rubber, etc., attachment worn on the foot for underwater swimming.

flip side *n. colloq.* the less important side of something (orig. of a phonograph record).

flirt /flərt/ *v.* & *n.* • *v.* **1** *intr.* (usu. foll. by *with*) behave in a frivolously amorous or sexually enticing manner. **2** *intr.* (usu. foll. by *with*) **a** superficially interest oneself (with an idea, etc.). **b** trifle (with danger, etc.). **3** *tr.* wave or move (a fan, a bird's tail, etc.) briskly. **4** *intr.* & *tr.* move or cause to move with a jerk. • *n.* **1** a person who indulges in flirting. **2** a quick movement; a sudden jerk. □□ **flir·ta·tion** *n.* **flir·ta·tious** *adj.* **flir·ta·tious·ly** *adv.* **flir·ta·tious·ness** *n.* **flirt·y** *adj.* (**flirtier, flirtiest**).

flit /flit/ *v.* & *n.* • *v.intr.* (**flitted, flitting**) **1** move lightly, softly, or rapidly (*flitted from one room to another*). **2** make short flights (*flitted from branch to branch*). • *n.* an act of flitting. □□ **flit·ter** *n.*

flit·ter /flítər/ *v.intr.* flit about; flutter.

float /flōt/ *v.* & *n.* • *v.* **1** *intr.* & *tr.* **a** rest or move or cause (a buoyant object) to rest or move on the surface of a liquid without sinking. **b** get afloat or set (a stranded ship) afloat. **2** *intr.* drift (*the clouds floated high up*). **3** *intr. colloq.* **a** move in a leisurely or casual way. **b** (often foll. by *before*) hover before the eye or mind (*the prospect of lunch floated before them*). **4** *intr.* (often foll. by *in*) move or be suspended freely in a liquid or a gas. **5** *tr.* **a** bring (a company, etc.) into being. **b** offer (stock, shares, etc.) on the stock market. **6** *Commerce* **a** *intr.* (of currency) be allowed to have a fluctuating exchange rate. **b** *tr.* cause (currency) to float. **c** *intr.* (of an acceptance) be in circulation. **7** *tr.* (of water, etc.) support; bear along (a buoyant object). **8** *intr.* & *tr.* circulate or cause (a rumor or idea) to circulate. **9** *tr.* put forward as a proposal. **10** waft (a buoyant object) through the air. • *n.* **1** a thing that floats, esp.: **a** a raft. **b** a cork or other buoyant object on a fishing line as an indicator of a fish biting. **c** a cork supporting the edge of a fishing net. **d** the hollow or inflated part or organ supporting a fish, etc., in the water. **e** a hollow structure fixed underneath an aircraft enabling it to float on water. **f** a floating device on the surface of water, fuel, etc., controlling the flow. **2** *Brit.* a small vehicle or cart, esp. one powered by electricity (*milk float*). **3** a platform mounted on a truck or trailer and carrying a display in a parade, etc. **4 a** an amount of money outstanding but not yet collected by a bank, etc., such as checks written but not yet collected on. **b** the time between the writing of a check, etc., and the actual collection of funds. **5** a tool used for smoothing plaster or concrete. □□ **float·a·ble** *adj.* **float·a·bil·i·ty** /–təbílitee/ *n.* **float·er** /flṓtər/ *n.*

float·a·tion var. of FLOTATION.

float·ing /flṓting/ *adj.* not settled in a definite place; variable (*the floating population*).

float·ing rib *n.* any of the lower ribs, which are not attached to the breastbone.

floc·cule /flókyōōl/ *n.* a small portion of matter resembling a tuft of wool.

floc·cu·lent /flókyələnt/ *adj.* **1** like tufts of wool. **2** downy. **3** *Chem.* (of precipitates) loosely massed. □□ **floc·cu·lence** /–ləns/ *n.*

flock[1] /flok/ *n.* & *v.* • *n.* **1 a** a number of animals of one kind, esp. birds, feeding or traveling together. **b** a number of domestic animals kept together. **2** a large crowd of people. **3 a** a Christian congregation or body of believers, esp. in relation to one minister. **b** a family of children, a number of pupils, etc. • *v.intr.* **1** congregate; mass. **2** (usu. foll. by *to*, *in*, *out*, *together*) go together in a crowd (*thousands flocked to the polls*).

flock[2] /flok/ *n.* **1** a lock or tuft of wool, cotton, etc. **2 a** (also in *pl.*; often *attrib.*) material for quilting and stuffing made of wool refuse or torn-up cloth (*a flock pillow*). **b** powdered wool or cloth.

floe /flō/ *n.* a sheet of floating ice.

flog /flawg, flog/ *v.* (**flogged, flogging**) **1** *tr.* **a** beat with a whip, stick, etc. **b** make work through violent effort (*flogged the engine*). **2** *sl.* sell or promote aggressively. **3** *tr.* (usu. foll. by *into*, *out of*) drive (a quality, knowledge, etc.) into or out of a person, esp. by physical punishment. □ **flog** (also **beat**) **a dead horse** waste energy on something unalterable. **flog to death** *colloq.* talk about at tedious length. □□ **flog·ger** *n.*

flood /flud/ *n.* & *v.* • *n.* **1 a** an overflowing or influx of water beyond its normal confines, esp. over land; an inundation. **b** the water that overflows. **2 a** an outpouring of water; a torrent (*a flood of rain*). **b** something resembling a torrent (*a flood of tears*). **c** an abundance or excess. **3** the inflow of the tide (also in *comb.*: *flood tide*). **4** *colloq.* a floodlight. **5** (**the Flood**) the flood described in Genesis. • *v.* **1** *tr.* **a** cover with or overflow in a flood (*rain flooded the cellar*). **b** overflow as if with a flood (*the market was flooded with foreign goods*). **2** *tr.* irrigate (*flooded the rice paddies*). **3** *tr.* deluge with water. **4** *intr.* (often foll. by *in*, *through*) arrive in great quantities. **5** *intr.* become inundated (*the bathroom flooded*). **6** *tr.* overfill (a carburetor) with fuel. **7** *intr.* experience a uterine hemorrhage. **8** *tr.* (of rain, etc.) fill (a river) to overflowing. □ **flood out** drive out (of one's home, etc.) with a flood.

flood·gate /flúdgayt/ *n.* **1** a gate opened or closed to admit or exclude water, esp. the lower gate of a lock. **2** (usu. in *pl.*) a last restraint holding back tears, etc.

flood·light /flúdlīt/ *n.* & *v.* • *n.* **1** a large powerful light (usu. one of several) to illuminate a building, stage, etc. **2** the illumination so provided. • *v.tr.* illuminate with floodlights.

flood·plain /flúdplayn/ *n.* flat terrain alongside a river that is subject to inundation when the river floods.

flood tide *n.* the periodical exceptional rise of the tide because of lunar or solar attraction.

flood·wa·ter /flúdwawtər, –wo–/ *n.* the water overflowing as the result of a flood.

floor /flawr/ *n.* & *v.* • *n.* **1 a** the lower surface of a room. **b** the boards, etc., of which it is made. **2 a** the bottom of the sea, a cave, etc. **b** any level area. **3** all the rooms, etc., on the same level of a building; a story. **4 a** (in a legislative assembly) the part of the house in which members sit and speak. **b** the right to speak next in debate (*gave him the floor*). **5** *Stock Exch.* the large central hall where trading takes place. **6** the minimum of prices, wages, etc. **7** *colloq.* the ground. • *v.tr.* **1** furnish with a floor; pave. **2** knock (a person) down. **3** *colloq.* confound; baffle. **4** *colloq.* get the better of. **5** serve as the floor of (*leopard skins floored the hall*). **6** cause a vehicle to accelerate rapidly. □ **from the floor** (of a speech, etc.) given by a member of the audience, not by those on the platform, etc. **take the floor 1** begin to dance. **2** speak in a debate. □□ **floor·less** *adj.*

floor·board /fláwrbawrd/ *n.* a long wooden board used for flooring.

floor·cloth /fláwrklawth, –kloth/ *n.* a thin canvas rug or similar light floor covering.

floor ex·er·cise *n.* a routine of gymnastic exercises performed without the use of apparatus.

floor·ing /fláwring/ *n.* the boards, etc., of which a floor is made.

floor lamp *n.* a lamp with a base that rests on the floor.

floor plan *n.* a diagram of the rooms, etc., on one floor of a building.

floor show *n.* an entertainment presented at a nightclub, etc.

floor·walk·er /fláwrwawkər/ *n.* a person employed in a retail store who assists customers and supervises other workers.

floo·zy /flṓōzee/ *n.* (also **floo·zie**) (*pl.* **-zies**) *colloq.* a girl or a woman, esp. a disreputable one.

flop /flop/ *v.*, *n.*, & *adv.* • *v.intr.* (**flopped, flopping**) **1** sway about heavily or loosely (*hair flopped over his face*). **2** move in an ungainly way (*flopped along in flippers*). **3** (often foll. by *down*, *on*, *into*) sit, kneel, lie, or fall awkwardly or suddenly. **4** *sl.* (esp. of a play, movie, etc.) fail; collapse (*flopped on Broadway*). **5** *sl.* sleep. **6** make a dull sound as of a soft body landing, or of a flat thing slapping water. • *n.* **1 a** a flopping movement. **b** the sound made by it. **2** *sl.* a failure. **3** *sl.* a place to sleep, esp. cheaply. **4** a piece of cow dung. • *adv.* with a flop.

flop·house /flóp-hows/ *n.* a cheap hotel or rooming house.

flop·py /flópee/ *adj.* & *n.* • *adj.* (**floppier, floppiest**) tending to flop; not firm or rigid. • *n.* (*pl.* **-pies**) (in full **floppy disk**) *Computing* a flexible removable magnetic disk for storing data. □□ **flop·pi·ly** *adv.* **flop·pi·ness** *n.*

flo·ra /fláwrə/ *n.* (*pl.* **floras** or **florae** /–ree/) the plants of a particular region or period (cf. FAUNA).

flo·ral /fláwrəl/ *adj.* **1** of flowers. **2** decorated with or depicting flowers. **3** of flora or floras. □□ **flo·ral·ly** *adv.*

Flor·en·tine /fláwrənteen, –tīn, flór–/ *adj.* & *n.* • *adj.* **1** of or relating to Florence in Italy. **2** (**florentine** /–teen/) (of a dish) served on a bed of spinach. • *n.* a native or citizen of Florence.

flo·res·cence /flawrésəns/ *n.* flowering.

flo·ret /fláwrit/ *n.* *Bot.* **1** each of the small flowers making up a composite flower head. **2** each of the flowering stems of a head of cauliflower, broccoli, etc. **3** a small flower.

flo·ri·ate /fláwriayt/ *v.tr.* decorate with flower designs, etc.

flo·ri·bun·da /fláwribúndə/ *n.* a plant, esp. a rose, bearing dense clusters of flowers.

flor·id /fláwrid, flór–/ *adj.* **1** ruddy (*a florid complexion*). **2** (of a book, music, etc.) elaborately ornate. **3** flowery. □□ **flo·rid·i·ty** *n.* **flor·id·ly** *adv.* **flor·id·ness** *n.*

flo·rist /fláwrist, flór–/ *n.* a person who deals in or grows flowers. □□ **flo·rist·ry** *n.*

flo·ru·it /fláwrōōit, flór–/ *v.* & *n.* • *v.intr.* (he or she) was alive and working; flourished (of a painter, writer, etc., whose exact dates are unknown). • *n.* the period or date at which a person lived or worked.

floss /flaws, flos/ *n.* & *v.* • *n.* **1** the rough silk enveloping a silkworm's cocoon. **2** untwisted silk thread used in embroidery. **3** = DENTAL FLOSS. • *v.tr.* (also *absol.*) clean (the teeth) with dental floss.

floss·y /fláwsee, flósee/ *adj.* (**flossier, flossiest**) **1** of or like floss. **2** *colloq.* fancy; showy.

flo·tage /flṓtij/ *n.* **1** the act or state of floating. **2 a** floating objects or masses; flotsam. **b** *Brit.* the right of appropriating flotsam. **3 a** ships, etc., afloat on a river. **b** the part of a ship above the water line. **4** buoyancy; floating power.

flo·ta·tion /flōtáyshən/ *n.* (also **float·a·tion**) **1** the process of launching or financing a commercial enterprise. **2** the separation of the components of crushed ore, etc., by their different capacities to float. **3** the capacity to float.

flo·til·la /flōtílə/ *n.* **1** a small fleet. **2** a fleet of small ships.

flot·sam /flótsəm/ *n.* wreckage found floating.

flot·sam and jet·sam *n.* **1** odds and ends; rubbish. **2** vagrants, etc.

flounce[1] /flowns/ *v.* & *n.* •*v.intr.* (often foll. by *away, off, out*) go or move with an agitated or impatient motion. •*n.* a flouncing movement.

flounce[2] /flowns/ *n.* & *v.* •*n.* a wide frill. •*v.tr.* trim with a flounce or flounces.

floun·der[1] /flówndər/ *v.* & *n.* •*v.intr.* **1** struggle in mud, or as if in mud, or when wading. **2** perform a task badly or without knowledge. •*n.* an act of floundering. ▫▫ **floun·der·er** *n.*

floun·der[2] /flówndər/ *n.* **1** an edible flatfish, *Pleuronectes flesus*, native to European shores. **2** any of various flatfish native to N. American shores.

flour /flowər/ *n.* & *v.* •*n.* **1** a meal or powder obtained by grinding and usu. sifting grain, esp. wheat. **2** any fine powder. •*v.tr.* **1** sprinkle with flour. **2** grind into flour. ▫▫ **flour·y** *adj.* (**flourier, flouriest**). **flour·i·ness** *n.*

flour·ish /flə́rish, flúr–/ *v.* & *n.* •*v.* **1** *intr.* **a** grow vigorously; thrive. **b** prosper. **c** be in one's prime. **d** be in good health. **e** (as **flourishing** *adj.*) successful; prosperous. **2** *intr.* (usu. foll. by *in, at, about*) spend one's life; be active (at a specified time) (*flourished in the Middle Ages*) (cf. FLORUIT). **3** *tr.* show ostentatiously. **4** *tr.* wave (a weapon, etc.) vigorously. •*n.* **1** an ostentatious gesture with a weapon, a hand, etc. **2** an ornamental curving decoration of handwriting. **3** a rhetorical embellishment. **4** *Mus.* **a** a fanfare played by brass instruments. **b** an ornate musical passage. **c** an extemporized addition played esp. at the beginning or end of a composition. ▫▫ **flour·ish·er** *n.*

flourish Middle English: from Old French *floriss-*, lengthened stem of *florir*, based on Latin *florere*, from *flos, flor-* 'a flower.' The noun senses 'ornamental curve' and 'florid expression' come from an obsolete sense of the verb, 'adorn' (originally with flowers).

flout /flowt/ *v.* **1** *tr.* express contempt for (the law, rules, etc.) by word or action; mock. **2** *intr.* (often foll. by *at*) mock or scoff.
▶See note at FLAUNT.

flow /flō/ *v.* & *n.* •*v.intr.* **1** glide along as a stream. **2 a** (of a liquid, esp. water) gush out; spring. **b** (of blood, liquid, etc.) be spilled. **3** (of blood, money, electric current, etc.) circulate. **4** (of people or things) come or go in large numbers or smoothly (*traffic flowed along the highway*). **5** (of talk, literary style, etc.) proceed easily and smoothly. **6** (of a garment, hair, etc.) hang easily or gracefully. **7** (often foll. by *from*) result from (*his failure flows from his diffidence*). **8** (esp. of the tide) be in flood. **9** (of wine) be poured out copiously. **10** (of a rock or metal) undergo a permanent change of shape under stress. **11** menstruate. **12** (foll. by *with*) *archaic* be plentifully supplied with (*land flowing with milk and honey*). •*n.* **1 a** a flowing movement in a stream. **b** the manner in which a thing flows (*a sluggish flow*). **c** a flowing liquid (*couldn't stop the flow*). **d** a copious outpouring (*a flow of complaints*). **e** a hardened mass that formerly flowed (*walked out onto the lava flow*). **2** the rise of a tide or a river (*ebb and flow*). **3** the gradual deformation of a rock or metal under stress. **4** menstruation.

flow chart 1 a diagram of the movement or action in a complex activity. **2** a graphical representation of a computer program in relation to its sequence of functions (as distinct from the data it processes).

flow·er /flowər/ *n.* & *v.* •*n.* **1** the part of a plant from which the fruit or seed is developed. **2** the reproductive organ in a plant containing one or more pistils or stamens or both, and usu. a corolla and calyx. **3** a blossom, esp. on a stem and used in bunches for decoration. **4** a plant cultivated or noted for its flowers. **5** (in *pl.*) ornamental phrases (*flowers of speech*). **6** the finest time, group, example, etc.; the peak. •*v.* **1** *intr.* (of a plant) produce flowers; bloom or blossom. **2** *intr.* reach a peak. **3** *tr.* cause or allow (a plant) to flower. **4** *tr.* decorate with worked flowers or a floral design. ▫ **the flower of** the best or best part of. **in flower** with the flowers out. ▫▫ **flow·ered** *adj.* (also in *comb.*). **flow·er·less** *adj.* **flow·er·like** *adj.*

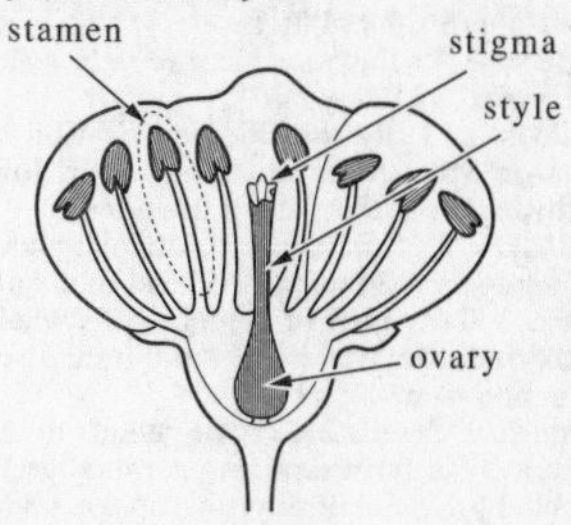

flower, 1

flow·er·et /flówərit/ *n.* a small flower.

flow·er girl *n.* a girl who carries flowers at a wedding as an attendant to the bride.

flow·er·y /flóweree/ *adj.* **1** decorated with flowers or floral designs. **2** (of literary style, etc.) highly embellished; ornate. **3** full of flowers (*a flowery meadow*). ▫▫ **flow·er·i·ness** *n.*

flow·ing /flṓing/ *adj.* **1** (of literary style, etc.) fluent; easy. **2** (of a line or contour) smoothly continuous; not abrupt. **3** (of hair, a garment, etc.) unconfined. ▫▫ **flow·ing·ly** *adv.*

flown *past part.* of FLY[1].

fl. oz. *abbr.* fluid ounce(s).

flu /flo͞o/ *n. colloq.* influenza.

flub /flub/ *v.* & *n. colloq.* •*v.tr.* & *intr.* (**flubbed, flubbing**) botch; bungle. •*n.* something badly or clumsily done.

fluc·tu·ate /flúkcho͞o-ayt/ *v.intr.* vary irregularly; vacillate; rise and fall. ▫▫ **fluc·tu·a·tion** /–áyshən/ *n.*

flue /flo͞o/ *n.* **1** a smoke duct in a chimney. **2** a channel for conveying heat.

flu·ent /flo͞oənt/ *adj.* **1 a** (of speech or literary style) flowing naturally and readily. **b** having command of a foreign language (*is fluent in German*). **c** able to speak quickly and easily. **2** flowing easily or gracefully (*the fluent line of her arabesque*). ▫▫ **flu·en·cy** /flo͞oənsee/ *n.* **flu·ent·ly** *adv.*

fluff /fluf/ *n.* & *v.* •*n.* **1** soft, light, feathery material coming off blankets, etc. **2** soft fur or feathers. **3** *sl.* **a** a mistake in delivering theatrical lines, in playing music, etc. **b** a mistake in playing a game. •*v.* **1** *tr.* & *intr.* (often foll. by *up*) shake into or become a soft mass. **2** *tr.* & *intr. colloq.* make a mistake in (a theatrical part, a game, playing music, etc.); blunder (*fluffed his opening line*). **3** *tr.* make into fluff. **4** *tr.* put a soft surface on (the flesh side of leather).

fluff·y /flúfee/ *adj.* (**fluffier, fluffiest**) **1** of or like fluff. **2** covered in fluff; downy. **3** nonintellectual; frivolous; superficial. ▫▫ **fluff·i·ly** *adv.* **fluff·i·ness** *n.*

flu·gel·horn /flóogəlhawrn/ *n.* (also **flue·gel·horn**) a valved brass wind instrument similar to a cornet.

flu·id /flóoid/ *n.* & *adj.* •*n.* **1** a substance, esp. a gas or liquid, lacking definite shape and capable of flowing and yielding to the slightest pressure. **2** a fluid part or secretion. •*adj.* **1** able to flow and alter shape freely. **2** constantly changing (*the situation is fluid*). **3** (of a clutch, coupling, etc.) in which liquid is used to transmit power. ▫▫ **flu·id·i·fy** /–idifī/ *v.tr.* (**-fies, -fied**). **flu·id·i·ty** /–íditee/ *n.* **flu·id·ly** *adv.* **flu·id·ness** *n.*

flu·id·ize /flóoidīz/ *v.tr.* cause (a finely divided solid) to acquire the characteristics of a fluid by the upward passage of a gas, etc. ▫▫ **flu·id·i·za·tion** /–dizáyshən/ *n.*

fluid ounce *n.* a unit of capacity equal to one-sixteenth of a pint (approx. 0.034 liter).

fluke[1] /flook/ *n.* **1** a lucky accident (*won by a fluke*). **2** a chance breeze. ▫▫ **fluk·y** *adj.*

fluke[2] /flook/ *n.* **1** any parasitic flatworm of the class Digenea or Monogenea, including liver flukes and blood flukes. **2** a flatfish, esp. a flounder.

fluke[3] /flook/ *n.* **1** *Naut.* a broad triangular plate on the arm of an anchor. **2** the barbed head of a lance, harpoon, etc. **3** *Zool.* either of the lobes of a whale's tail.

flum·mox /flúməks/ *v.tr. colloq.* confound; disconcert.

flung *past* and *past part.* of FLING.

flunk /flungk/ *v.* & *n. colloq.* •*v.* **1** *tr.* **a** fail (an examination, etc.). **b** fail (an examination candidate). **2** *intr.* (often foll. by *out*) fail utterly; give up. •*n.* an instance of flunking. ▫ **flunk out** be dismissed from school, etc., after failing an examination, course, etc.

flun·ky /flúngkee/ *n.* (also **flun·key**) (*pl.* **-kies** or **-keys**) usu. *derog.* **1** a liveried servant. **2** a toady. **3** a person who does menial work.

fluo·resce /floorés, flaw–/ *v.intr.* be or become fluorescent.

fluo·res·cence /floorésəns, flaw–/ *n.* **1** the visible or invisible radiation produced from certain substances as a result of incident radiation of a shorter wavelength such as X rays, ultraviolet light, etc. **2** the property of absorbing light of short (invisible) wavelength and emitting light of longer (visible) wavelength. ▫▫ **fluo·res·cent** *adj.*

fluo·res·cent lamp *n.* (also **fluorescent bulb**) a lamp or bulb radiating largely by fluorescence.

fluor·i·date /flooridayt, fláw–/ *v.tr.* add traces of fluoride to (drinking water, etc.). ▫▫ **fluor·i·da·tion** /flooridáyshən, fláw–/ *n.* (also **fluor·i·di·za·tion**)

fluor·ide /floorīd, fláw–/ *n.* any binary compound of fluorine.

fluor·i·nate /floorinayt, fláw–/ *v.tr.* **1** = FLUORIDATE. **2** introduce fluorine into (a compound). ▫▫ **fluor·i·na·tion** /–náyshən/ *n.*

fluor·ine /flooreen, fláw–/ *n.* a poisonous pale yellow gaseous element of the halogen group. ¶ Symb.: **f.**

fluo·rite /floorīt, fláw–/ *n.* a mineral form of calcium fluoride.

fluor·o·car·bon /floorōkaárbən, fláw–/ *n.* a compound formed by replacing one or more of the hydrogen atoms in a hydrocarbon with fluorine atoms.

fluor·o·scope /flooreskōp, fláw–/ *n.* an instrument with a fluorescent screen on which X-ray images may be viewed without taking and developing X-ray photographs.

flur·ry /flóree, flúree/ *n.* & *v.* •*n.* (*pl.* **-ries**) **1** a gust or squall (esp. of snow). **2** a sudden burst of activity. **3** nervous agitation (*a flurry of speculation*). •*v.tr.* (**-ries, -ried**) confuse by haste or noise; agitate.

flush[1] /flush/ *v.* & *n.* •*v.* **1** *intr.* **a** blush; redden (*he flushed with embarrassment*). **b** glow with a warm color (*sky flushed pink*). **2** *tr.* (usu. as **flushed** *adj.*) cause to glow, blush, or be elated (often foll. by *with*: *flushed with pride*). **3** *tr.* **a** cleanse (a drain, toilet, etc.) by a rushing flow of water. **b** (often foll. by *away, down*) dispose of (an object) in this way (*flushed away the cigarette*). **4** *intr.* rush out; spurt. **5** *tr.* flood (*the river flushed the meadow*). **6** *intr.* (of a plant) throw out fresh shoots. •*n.* **1 a** a blush. **b** a glow of light or color. **2 a** a rush of water. **b** the cleansing of a drain, toilet, etc., by flushing. **3 a** a rush of emotion. **b** the elation produced by a victory, etc. (*the flush of triumph*). **4** sudden abundance. **5** freshness; vigor (*in the first flush of womanhood*). **6 a** a feverish temperature. **b** facial redness, esp. caused by fever, alcohol, etc. ▫▫ **flush·er** *n.*

flush[2] /flush/ *adj.* & *v.* •*adj.* **1** (often foll. by *with*) in the same plane; level (*the sink is flush with the counter*). **2** (usu. *predic.*) *colloq.* **a** having plenty of money. **b** (of money) abundant; plentiful. **3** full to overflowing; in flood. •*v.tr.* **1** make (surfaces) level. **2** fill in (a joint) level with a surface. ▫▫ **flush·ness** *n.*

flush[3] /flush/ *n.* a hand of cards all of one suit.

flush[4] /flush/ *v.* **1** *tr.* cause (esp. a game bird) to fly up. **2** *intr.* (of a bird) fly up and away. ▫ **flush out 1** reveal. **2** drive out.

flust·er /flústər/ *v.* & *n.* •*v.* **1** *tr.* & *intr.* make or become nervous or confused (*was flustered by the noise*). **2** *tr.* confuse with drink; half-intoxicate. **3** *intr.* bustle. •*n.* a confused or agitated state.

flute /floot/ *n.* & *v.* •*n.* **1 a** a high-pitched woodwind instrument, having holes along it stopped by the fingers or keys, and held horizontally. **b** an organ stop having a similar sound. **c** any of various wind instruments resembling a flute. **d** a flute player. **2 a** *Archit.* an ornamental vertical groove in a column. **b** a trumpet-shaped frill on a dress, etc. **c** any similar cylindrical groove. **3** a tall narrow wineglass. •*v.* **1** *intr.* play the flute. **2** *intr.* speak, sing, or whistle in a fluting way. **3** *tr.* make flutes or grooves in. **4** *tr.* play (a tune, etc.) on a flute. ▫▫ **flute·like** *adj.* **flut·ing** *n.* **flut·ist** *n.* (cf. FLAUTIST). **flut·y** *adj.* (in sense 1a of *n.*).

flut·ter /flútər/ *v.* & *n.* •*v.* **1 a** *intr.* flap the wings in flying or trying to fly. **b** *tr.* flap (the wings). **2** *intr.* fall with a quivering motion. **3** *intr.* & *tr.* move or cause to move irregularly (*the wind fluttered the flag*). **4** *intr.* go about restlessly. **5** *tr.* agitate; confuse. **6** *intr.* (of a pulse or heartbeat) beat irregularly. **7** *intr.* tremble with excitement. •*n.* **1 a** the act of fluttering. **b** an instance of this. **2** a tremulous state of excitement; (*was in a flutter; caused a flutter with his behavior*). **3** an abnormally rapid but regular heartbeat. **4** *Electronics* a rapid variation of pitch, esp. of recorded sound (cf. WOW[2]). **5** a vibration. ▫▫ **flut·ter·y** *adj.*

flu·vi·al /flóoveeəl/ *adj.* of, found in, or produced by a river or rivers.

flux /fluks/ *n.* & *v.* •*n.* **1** a process of flowing or flowing out. **2** an issue or discharge. **3** continuous change (*in a state of flux*). **4** *Metallurgy* a substance mixed with a metal, etc., to promote fusion. **5** *Physics* **a** the rate of flow of any fluid across a given area. **b** the amount of fluid crossing an area in a given time. **6** *Physics* the amount of radiation or particles incident on an area in a given time. **7** *Electr.* the total electric or magnetic field passing through a surface. •*v.* **1** *tr.* & *intr.* make or become fluid. **2** *tr.* **a** fuse. **b** treat with a fusing flux.

fly[1] /flī/ *v.* & *n.* •*v.* (**flies**; *past* **flew** /floo/; *past part.* **flown** /flōn/) **1** *intr.* move through the air under control, esp. with wings. **2** (of an aircraft or its occupants): **a** *intr.*

travel through the air or through space. **b** *tr.* traverse (*flew the Atlantic*). **3** *tr.* **a** control the flight of (esp. an aircraft). **b** transport in an aircraft. **4 a** *tr.* cause to fly or remain aloft. **b** *intr.* (of a flag, hair, etc.) wave or flutter. **5** *intr.* pass or rise quickly through the air or over an obstacle. **6** *intr.* pass swiftly (*time flies*). **7** *intr.* **a** flee. **b** *colloq.* depart hastily. **8** *intr.* be forced off suddenly (*sent me flying*). **9** *intr.* (foll. by *at, upon*) **a** hasten or spring violently. **b** attack or criticize fiercely. **10** *tr.* flee from. **11** *intr. Baseball* hit a fly ball. • *n.* (*pl.* **-ies**) **1** an opening at the front of a pair of pants, closed with a zipper or buttons and covered with a flap. **2 a** a fabric cover pitched over a tent for extra protection from rain, etc. **b** a flap at the entrance of a tent. **3** (in *pl.*) the space over the proscenium in a theater. **4** the act or an instance of flying. **5** *Baseball* a batted ball hit high in the air. **6** a speed-regulating device in clockwork and machinery. □ **fly in the face of** openly disregard or disobey. **fly off the handle** *colloq.* lose one's temper suddenly and unexpectedly. □□ **fly·a·ble** *adj.*

fly[2] /flī/ *n.* (*pl.* **flies**) **1** any insect of the order Diptera with two usu. transparent wings. **2** any other winged insect. **3** a disease of plants or animals caused by flies. **4** a natural or artificial fly used as bait in fishing. □ **fly in the ointment** a minor irritation that spoils enjoyment. **fly on the wall** an unnoticed observer. **like flies** in large numbers.

fly·a·way /flíəway/ *adj.* (of hair, etc.) tending to fly out or up.

fly ball *n. Baseball* a batted ball hit high in the air.

fly-by-night *adj. & n.* • *adj.* **1** unreliable. **2** short-lived. • *n.* an unreliable person.

fly·catch·er /flíkachər/ *n.* any bird of the families Tyrannidae and Muscicapidae, catching insects, esp. in short flights from a perch.

fly·er var. of FLIER.

fly-fish *v.intr.* fish with a fly (sense 4 of FLY[2]).

fly·ing /flí-ing/ *adj. & n.* • *adj.* **1** fluttering or waving in the air. **2** hasty; brief (*a flying visit*). **3** designed for rapid movement. **4** (of an animal) able to make very long leaps by using winglike membranes, etc. • *n.* flight, esp. in an aircraft. □ **with flying colors** with distinction.

fly·ing but·tress *n.* a buttress slanting from a separate column, usu. forming an arch with the wall it supports.

fly·ing fish *n.* (*pl.* **fish** or **fishes**) any tropical fish of the family Exocoetidae, with winglike pectoral fins for gliding through the air.

fly·ing sau·cer *n.* any unidentified, esp. circular, flying object, popularly supposed to have come from space.

fly·ing squir·rel *n.* any of various squirrels, esp. of the genera *Glaucomys Pteromys*, with skin joining the fore and hind limbs for gliding from tree to tree.

fly·leaf /flíleef/ *n.* (*pl.* **-leaves**) a blank leaf at the beginning or end of a book.

fly·pa·per /flípaypər/ *n.* sticky treated paper for catching flies.

fly·sheet /flísheet/ *n.* a tract or circular of two or four pages.

fly swat·ter *n.* an implement for killing flies and other insects, usu. consisting of a flat mesh square attached to a handle.

fly·trap /flítrap/ *n.* any of various plants that catch flies, esp. the Venus flytrap.

fly·weight /flíwayt/ *n.* **1** a weight in certain sports intermediate between light flyweight and bantamweight. **2** a boxer, wrestler, etc., of this weight.

fly·wheel /flíhweel, –weel/ *n.* a heavy wheel on a revolving shaft used to regulate machinery or accumulate power.

FM *abbr.* **1** frequency modulation. **2** Field Marshal.

Fm *symb. Chem.* the element fermium.

f-number /éf numbər/ *n.* (also **f-stop**) *Photog.* the ratio of the focal length to the effective diameter of a lens.

foal /fōl/ *n. & v.* • *n.* the young of a horse or related animal. • *v.tr.* give birth to (a foal). □ **in** (or **with**) **foal** (of a mare, etc.) pregnant.

foam /fōm/ *n. & v.* • *n.* **1** a mass of small bubbles formed on or in liquid by agitation, fermentation, etc. **2** a froth of saliva or sweat. **3** a substance resembling these, e.g., rubber or plastic in a cellular mass. **4** the sea. • *v.intr.* **1** emit foam; froth. **2** run with foam. **3** (of a vessel) be filled and overflow with foam. □ **foam at the mouth** be very angry. □□ **foam·less** *adj.* **foam·y** *adj.* (**foamier, foamiest**).

foam rub·ber *n.* a light, spongy foam used for mattresses, pillows, cushions, etc.

fob[1] /fob/ *n. & v.* • *n.* **1** (in full **fob chain**) a chain attached to a watch for carrying in a waistcoat or pocket. **2** a small pocket for carrying a watch. **3** a tab on a key ring. • *v.tr.* (**fobbed, fobbing**) put in one's fob; pocket.

fob[2] /fob/ *v.tr.* (**fobbed, fobbing**) cheat; deceive. □ **fob off 1** (often foll. by *with* a thing) deceive into accepting something inferior. **2** (often foll. by *on to* a person) palm or pass off (an inferior thing).

fo·cal /fṓkəl/ *adj.* of, at, or in terms of a focus.

fo·cal length *n.* the distance between the center of a mirror or lens and its focus.

fo·cal point *n* = FOCUS *n.* 1.

fo'c's'le var. of FORECASTLE.

fo·cus /fṓkəs/ *n. & v.* • *n.* (*pl.* **focuses** or **foci** /fṓsī/) **1** *Physics* **a** the point at which rays or waves meet after reflection or refraction. **b** the point from which diverging rays or waves appear to proceed. **2 a** *Optics* the point at which an object must be situated for an image of it given by a lens or mirror to be well defined. **b** the adjustment of the eye or a lens necessary to produce a clear image. **c** a state of clear definition (*out of focus*). **3** the center of interest or activity (*focus of attention*). **4** *Geom.* one of the points from which the distances to any point of a given curve are connected by a linear relation. **5** *Med.* the principal site of an infection or other disease. **6** *Geol.* the place of origin of an earthquake. • *v.* (**focused, focusing** or **focussed, focussing**) **1** *tr.* bring into focus. **2** *tr.* adjust the focus of (a lens, the eye, etc.). **3** *tr. & intr.* (often foll. by *on*) concentrate or be concentrated on. **4** *intr. & tr.* converge or make converge to a focus. □□ **fo·cus·er** *n.*

fo·cus group *n.* a group that meets to discuss a particular problem, issue, etc.

fod·der /fódər/ *n. & v.* • *n.* dried hay or straw, etc., for cattle, etc. • *v.tr.* give fodder to.

foe /fō/ *n.* an enemy or opponent.

foet·id var. of FETID.

fog /fawg, fog/ *n. & v.* • *n.* **1** a thick cloud of water droplets or smoke suspended in the atmosphere at or near the earth's surface. **2** *Photog.* cloudiness on a developed negative, etc., obscuring the image. **3** an uncertain or confused position or state. • *v.* (**fogged, fogging**) **1** *tr.* **a** (often foll. by *up*) cover with fog or condensed vapor. **b** bewilder or confuse. **2** *intr.* (often foll. by *up*) become covered with fog or condensed vapor. **3** *tr. Photog.* make (a negative, etc.) obscure or cloudy. □ **in a fog** puzzled; at a loss.

fog bank *n.* a mass of fog at sea.

fo·gey var. of FOGY.

fog·gy /fáwgee, fógee/ *adj.* (**foggier, foggiest**) **1** (of the atmosphere) thick or obscure with fog. **2** of or like fog. **3** vague; confused; unclear. □ **not have the foggiest** *colloq.* have no idea at all. □□ **fog·gi·ness** *n.*

fog·horn /fáwghawrn, fóg–/ *n.* **1** a deep-sounding instrument for warning ships in fog. **2** *colloq.* a loud penetrating voice.

fo·gy /fṓgee/ *n.* (also **fo·gey**) (*pl.* **-gies** or **-geys**) a dull old-fashioned person (esp. *old fogy*). ▫▫ **fo·gy·ish** *adj.*

foi·ble /fóybəl/ *n.* a minor weakness or idiosyncrasy.

foie gras /fwaa graá/ *n. colloq.* = PÂTÉ DE FOIE GRAS.

foil[1] /foyl/ *v.tr.* frustrate; baffle; defeat.

foil[2] /foyl/ *n.* **1 a** metal hammered or rolled into a thin sheet (*tin foil*). **b** a sheet of this or another material attached to mirror glass as a reflector. **c** a leaf of foil placed under a precious stone, etc., to brighten or color it. **2** a person or thing that enhances the qualities of another by contrast.

foil[3] /foyl/ *n.* a light blunt-edged sword with a button on its point used in fencing.

foil[4] /foyl/ *n.* = HYDROFOIL.

foist /foyst/ *v.tr.* **1** (foll. by *on*, *upon*) impose (an unwelcome person or thing). **2** (foll. by *on*, *upon*) falsely fix the authorship of (a composition). **3** (foll. by *in*, *into*) introduce surreptitiously or unwarrantably.

fold[1] /fōld/ *v. & n.* •*v.* **1** *tr.* **a** bend or close (a flexible thing) over upon itself. **b** (foll. by *back*, *over*, *down*) bend a part of (a flexible thing) in the manner specified (*fold down the flap*). **2** *intr.* become or be able to be folded. **3** *tr.* (foll. by *away*, *up*) make compact by folding. **4** *intr. colloq.* **a** collapse; disintegrate. **b** (of an enterprise) fail; go bankrupt. **5** *tr.* (foll. by *about*, *around*) clasp (the arms); wrap; envelop. **6** *tr.* (foll. by *in*) mix (an ingredient with others) using a gentle cutting and turning motion. •*n.* **1** the act or an instance of folding. **2** a line made by or for folding. **3** a folded part. **4** a hollow among hills. **5** *Geol.* a curvature of strata. ▫▫ **fold·a·ble** *adj.*

fold[2] /fōld/ *n.* **1** = SHEEPFOLD. **2** a body of believers or members of a church.

fold·a·way /fṓldəway/ *adj.* adapted or designed to be folded away.

fold·er /fṓldər/ *n.* **1** a folding cover or holder for loose papers. **2** a folded leaflet.

fold·ing mon·ey *n. colloq.* paper money.

fo·li·a·ceous /fṓlee–áyshəs/ *adj.* **1** of or like leaves. **2** having organs like leaves. **3** laminated.

fo·li·age /fṓleeij/ *n.* **1** leaves; leafage. **2** a design in art resembling leaves.

fo·li·ar /fṓleeər/ *adj.* of or relating to leaves.

fo·li·ate *adj. & v.* •*adj.* /fṓleeət/ **1** leaflike. **2** having leaves. **3** (in *comb.*) having a specified number of leaflets (*trifoliate*). •*v.* /fṓleeayt/ **1** *intr.* split into laminae. **2** *tr.* number leaves (not pages) of (a volume) consecutively. ▫▫ **fo·li·a·tion** /–áyshən/ *n.*

fo·lic ac·id /fṓlik, fól–/ *n.* a vitamin of the B complex, found in leafy green vegetables, liver, and kidney, a deficiency of which causes pernicious anemia.

fo·li·o /fṓleeō/ *n. & adj.* •*n.* (*pl.* **-os**) **1** a leaf of paper, etc., esp. one numbered only on the front. **2 a** a leaf number of a book. **b** a page number of a book. **3** a sheet of paper folded once making two leaves of a book. **4** a book made of such sheets. •*adj.* (of a book) made of folios, of the largest size. ▫ **in folio** made of folios.

folk /fōk/ *n.* (*pl.* **folk** or **folks**) **1** (treated as *pl.*) people in general or of a specified class (*few folks about*; *townsfolk*). **2** (in *pl.*) (usu. **folks**) one's parents or relatives. **3** (treated as *sing.*) a people. **4** (treated as *sing.*) *colloq.* traditional music, esp. a style featuring acoustic guitar. **5** (*attrib.*) of popular origin; traditional (*folk art*).

folk dance *n.* **1** a dance of traditional origin. **2** the music for such a dance.

folk·lore /fṓklawr/ *n.* the traditional beliefs and stories of a people; the study of these. ▫▫ **folk·lor·ic** *adj.* **folk·lor·ist** *n.* **folk·lor·is·tic** *adj.*

folk mu·sic *n.* music that originates in traditional popular culture, typically of unknown authorship and transmitted orally from generation to generation.

folk sing·er *n.* a singer of folk songs.

folk song *n.* a song of popular or traditional origin or style.

folk·sy /fṓksee/ *adj.* (**folksier, folksiest**) **1** friendly; sociable; informal. **2 a** having the characteristics of folk art, culture, etc. **b** ostensibly or artificially folkish. ▫▫ **folk·si·ness** *n.*

folk tale *n.* a popular or traditional story.

fol·li·cle /fólikəl/ *n.* **1** a small sac or vesicle. **2** a small sac-shaped secretory gland or cavity. ▫▫ **fol·lic·u·lar** /folíkyələr/ *adj.*

fol·low /fólō/ *v.* **1** *tr.* or (foll. by *after*) *intr.* go or come after (a person or thing proceeding ahead). **2** *tr.* go along (a route, path, etc.). **3** *tr. & intr.* come after in order or time. **4** *tr.* take as a guide or leader. **5** *tr.* conform to (*follow your example*). **6** *tr.* practice (a trade or profession). **7** *tr.* undertake (a course of study, etc.). **8** *tr.* understand the meaning or tendency of (a speaker or argument). **9** *tr.* maintain awareness of the current state or progress of (events, etc., in a particular sphere). **10** *tr.* (foll. by *with*) provide with a sequel or successor. **11** *intr.* happen after something else; ensue. **12** *intr.* **a** be necessarily true as a result of something else. **b** (foll. by *from*) be a result of. **13** *tr.* strive after; aim at; pursue (*followed fame and fortune*). ▫ **follow out** carry out; adhere precisely to (instructions, etc.). **follow suit 1** *Cards* play a card of the suit led. **2** conform to another person's actions. **follow through 1** continue (an action, etc.) to its conclusion. **2** *Sports* continue the movement of a stroke after the ball has been struck. **follow up 1** (foll. by *with*) pursue; develop; supplement. **2** make further investigation of.

fol·low·er /fólōər/ *n.* **1** an adherent or devotee. **2** a person or thing that follows.

fol·low·ing /fólōing/ *prep., n., & adj.* •*prep.* coming after in time; as a sequel to. •*n.* a body of adherents or devotees. •*adj.* that follows or comes after.

fol·low-through *n.* the action of following through.

fol·low-up *n.* a subsequent or continued action, measure, experience, etc.

fol·ly /fólee/ *n.* (*pl.* **-lies**) **1** foolishness; lack of good sense. **2** a foolish act, behavior, idea, etc. **3** an ornamental building, usu. a tower or mock Gothic ruin. **4** (in *pl.*) *Theatr.* **a** a revue with glamorous female performers, esp. scantily clad. **b** the performers.

fo·ment /fōmént/ *v.tr.* **1** instigate or stir up (trouble, sedition, etc.). **2 a** bathe with warm or medicated liquid. **b** apply warmth to. ▫▫ **fo·ment·er** *n.*

fo·men·ta·tion /fṓmentáyshən/ *n.* **1** the act or an instance of fomenting. **2** materials prepared for application to a wound, etc.

fond /fond/ *adj.* **1** (foll. by *of*) having affection or a liking for. **2** affectionate; loving; doting. **3** (of beliefs, etc.) foolishly optimistic or credulous; naive. ▫▫ **fond·ly** *adv.* **fond·ness** *n.*

fon·dant /fóndənt/ *n.* a soft creamy candy of flavored sugar.

fon·dle /fónd'l/ *v.tr.* touch or stroke lovingly; caress. ▫▫ **fon·dler** *n.*

fon·due /fondóō, –dyóō/ *n.* **1** a dish of flavored melted cheese. **2** a dish of small pieces of food cooked at the table by dipping in hot melted chocolate, cheese, etc.

font[1] /font/ *n.* **1** a receptacle in a church for baptismal water. **2** the reservoir for oil in a lamp.

font[2] /font/ *n. Printing* a set of type of one face or size.

fon·ta·nel /fóntənél/ *n.* a membranous space in an infant's skull at the angles of the parietal bones.

food /fōōd/ *n.* **1** a nutritious substance, esp. solid in form, taken into an animal or a plant to maintain life and growth. **2** ideas as a resource for or stimulus to mental work (*food for thought*).

food chain *n. Ecol.* a series of organisms each dependent on the next for food.

food·stuff /fóódstuf/ *n.* any substance suitable as food.

fool[1] /fool/ *n., v., & adj.* • *n.* **1** a person who acts unwisely or imprudently; a stupid person. **2** *hist.* a jester; a clown. **3** a dupe. **4** (often foll. by *for*) a devotee or fan (*a fool for the ballet*). • *v.* **1** *tr.* deceive so as to cause to appear foolish. **2** *tr.* (foll. by *into* + verbal noun, or *out of*) trick; cause to do something foolish. **3** *tr.* play tricks on; dupe. **4** *intr.* act in a joking, frivolous, or teasing way. **5** *intr.* (foll. by *around*) behave in a playful or silly way. • *adj. colloq.* foolish; silly. □ **act** (or **play**) **the fool** behave in a silly way. **make a fool of** make (a person or oneself) look foolish; trick or deceive. **no** (or **nobody's**) **fool** a shrewd or prudent person.

fool[2] /fool/ *n.* esp. *Brit.* a dessert of usu. stewed fruit crushed and mixed with cream, custard, etc.

fool·har·dy /fóólhaardee/ *adj.* (**foolhardier, foolhardiest**) rashly or foolishly bold; reckless. □□ **fool·har·di·ly** *adv.* **fool·har·di·ness** *n.*

fool·ish /fóólish/ *adj.* (of a person, action, etc.) lacking good sense or judgment; unwise. □□ **fool·ish·ly** *adv.* **fool·ish·ness** *n.*

fool·proof /fóólproof/ *adj.* (of a procedure, mechanism, etc.) so straightforward or simple as to be incapable of misuse or mistake.

fool's gold *n.* iron pyrites.

foot /foot/ *n. & v.* • *n.* (*pl.* **feet** /feet/) **1 a** the lower extremity of the leg below the ankle. **b** the part of a sock, etc., covering the foot. **2 a** the lower or lowest part of a page, stairs, etc. **b** the lower end of a table. **c** the end of a bed where the user's feet normally rest. **3** the base, often projecting, of anything extending vertically. **4** a step, pace, or tread; a manner of walking (*fleet of foot*). **5** (*pl.* **feet** or **foot**) a unit of linear measure equal to 12 inches (30.48 cm). **6** *Prosody* **a** a group of syllables (one usu. stressed) constituting a metrical unit. **b** a similar unit of speech, etc. **7** *Brit. hist.* infantry (*a regiment of foot*). **8** *Zool.* the locomotive or adhesive organ of invertebrates. **9** *Bot.* the part by which a petal is attached. **10** a device on a sewing machine for holding the material steady as it is sewn. **11** (*pl.* **foots**) dregs; oil refuse. **12** (usu. in *pl.*) footlights. • *v.tr.* **1** (usu. as **foot it**) **a** traverse (esp. a long distance) by foot. **b** dance. **2** pay (a bill, esp. one considered large). □ **feet of clay** a fundamental weakness in a person otherwise revered. **get one's feet wet** begin to participate. **have one's** (or **both**) **feet on the ground** be practical. **have a foot in the door** have a prospect of success. **have one foot in the grave** be near death or very old. **my foot!** *int.* expressing strong contradiction. **on foot** walking; not riding, etc. **put one's foot down** *colloq.* **1** be firmly insistent or repressive. **2** accelerate a motor vehicle. **put one's foot in it** *colloq.* commit a blunder or indiscretion. **set foot in** (or **on**) enter; go into. □□ **foot·ed** *adj.* (also in *comb.*). **foot·less** *adj.*

foot·age /fóótij/ *n.* **1** length or distance in feet. **2** an amount of film made for showing, broadcasting, etc.

foot-and-mouth dis·ease *n.* a contagious viral disease of cattle, etc.

foot·ball /fóótbawl/ *n. & v.* • *n.* **1** any of several outdoor games between two teams played with a ball on a field with goals at each end. ▶In N. America this word generally refers to American football; elsewhere usu. soccer or rugby is meant. **2** a large inflated ball of a kind used in these. **3** a topical issue or problem that is the subject of continued argument or controversy. • *v.intr.* play football. □□ **foot·ball·er** *n.*

foot·board /fóótbawrd/ *n.* **1** a board to support the feet or a foot. **2** an upright board at the foot of a bed.

foot·bridge /fóótbrij/ *n.* a bridge for use by pedestrians.

foot·er /fóótər/ *n.* (in *comb.*) a person or thing of so many feet in length or height (*six-footer*).

foot·fall /fóótfawl/ *n.* the sound of a footstep.

foot·hill /fóót-hil/ *n.* (often in *pl.*) any of the low hills around the base of a mountain.

foot·hold /fóót-hōld/ *n.* **1** a place, esp. in climbing, where a foot can be supported securely. **2** a secure initial position or advantage.

foot·ing /fóóting/ *n.* **1** a foothold; a secure position (*lost his footing*). **2** the basis on which an enterprise is established or operates; the position or status of a person in relation to others (*on an equal footing*).

foot·lights /fóótlīts/ *n.pl.* a row of lights along the front of a stage.

foot·lock·er /fóólokər/ *n.* a small trunk usu. kept at the foot of a soldier's or camper's bunk to hold items of clothing or equipment.

foot·loose /fóótloos/ *adj.* free to go where or act as one pleases.

foot·man /fóótmən/ *n.* (*pl.* **-men**) a liveried servant.

foot·note /fóótnōt/ *n. & v.* • *n.* a note printed at the foot of a page. • *v.tr.* supply with a footnote or footnotes.

foot·path /fóótpath/ *n.* a trail or path for pedestrians (in the woods, etc.).

foot·print /fóótprint/ *n.* **1** the impression left by a foot or shoe. **2** *Computing* the area of desk space, etc., occupied by a computer or other piece of hardware. **3** the ground area covered by a communications satellite or affected by noise, etc., from aircraft.

foot·rest /fóótrest/ *n.* a support for the feet or a foot.

foot sol·dier *n.* a soldier who fights on foot.

foot·step /fóótstep/ *n.* **1** a step taken in walking. **2** the sound of this. □ **follow** (or **tread**) **in a person's footsteps** do as another person did before.

foot·stool /fóótstool/ *n.* a stool for resting the feet on when sitting.

foot·wear /fóótwair/ *n.* shoes, socks, etc.

foot·work /fóótwərk/ *n.* the use of the feet, esp. skillfully, in sports, dancing, etc.

fop /fop/ *n.* an affectedly elegant or fashionable man; a dandy. □□ **fop·per·y** *n.* **fop·pish** *adj.* **fop·pish·ly** *adv.* **fop·pish·ness** *n.*

for /fawr, fər/ *prep. & conj.* • *prep.* **1** in the interest or to the benefit of; intended to go to (*these flowers are for you; wish to see it for myself*). **2** in defense, support, or favor of (*fight for one's rights*). **3** suitable or appropriate to (*a dance for beginners; not for me to say*). **4** in respect of or with reference to; regarding (*usual for ties to be worn; don't care for him at all; ready for bed*). **5** representing or in place of (*here for my uncle*). **6** in exchange against (*swapped it for a bigger one*). **7 a** as the price of (*give me $5 for it*). **b** at the price of (*bought it for $5*). **c** to the amount of (*a bill for $100*). **8** as the penalty of (*fined them heavily for it*). **9** in requital of (*that's for upsetting my sister*). **10** as a reward for (*here's $5 for your trouble*). **11 a** with a view to; in the hope or quest of; in order to get (*go for a walk; did it for the money*). **b** on account of (*could not speak for laughing*). **12** corresponding to (*word for word*). **13** to reach; in the direction of; toward (*left for Rome*). **14** conducive or conducively to; in order to achieve (*take the pills for a sound night's sleep*). **15** starting at (a specified time) (*we set the meeting for eight*). **16** through or over (a distance or period); during (*walked for miles; sang for two hours*). **17** in the character of; as being (*for the last time; know it for a lie*). **18** because of; on account of (*could not see for tears*). **19** in spite of; notwithstanding (*for all your fine words*). **20** considering or making due allowance in respect of (*good for a beginner*). **21** in order to be (*gone for a soldier*). • *conj.* because; since; seeing that. □ **oh for** I wish I had (*oh for a strong black coffee*).

for·age /fáwrij, fór–/ *n. & v.* • *n.* **1** food for horses and cattle. **2** the act or an instance of searching for food. • *v.* **1** *intr.* go searching; rummage (esp. for food). **2** *tr.* obtain food from; plunder. **3** *tr.* **a** get by foraging. **b** supply with food. □□ **for·ag·er** *n.*

for·ay /fáwray, fór–/ *n. & v.* • *n.* **1** a sudden attack; a raid. **2** an attempt or venture, esp. into a field not one's own. • *v.intr.* make or go on a foray.

for·bade (also **for·bad**) *past* of FORBID.

for·bear¹ /fáwrbáir/ *v.intr. & tr.* (*past* **forbore** /–báwr/; *past part.* **forborne** /–báwrn/) (often foll. by *from*, or *to* + infin.) *literary* abstain or desist (from) (*could not forbear (from) speaking out; forbore to mention it*).

for·bear² var. of FOREBEAR.

for·bear·ance /fawrbáirəns/ *n.* patient self-control; tolerance.

for·bid /fərbíd, fawr–/ *v.tr.* (**forbidding**; *past* **forbade** /–bád, –báyd/or **forbad** /–bád/; *past part.* **forbidden** /–bíd'n/) **1** (foll. by *to* + infin.) order not (*I forbid you to go*). **2** refuse to allow (a thing, or a person to have a thing) (*I forbid it; was forbidden any wine*). **3** refuse a person entry to (*the gardens are forbidden to children*).

for·bid·den fruit *n.* something desired or enjoyed all the more because not allowed.

for·bid·ding /fərbíding, fawr–/ *adj.* uninviting; repellent; stern. □□ **for·bid·ding·ly** *adv.*

for·bore *past* of FORBEAR¹.

for·borne *past part.* of FORBEAR¹.

force /fawrs/ *n. & v.* • *n.* **1** power; exerted strength or impetus; intense effort. **2** coercion or compulsion, esp. with the use or threat of violence. **3** **a** military strength. **b** (in *pl.*) troops; fighting resources. **c** an organized body of people, esp. soldiers, police, or workers. **4** binding power; validity. **5** effect; precise significance (*the force of their words*). **6** **a** mental or moral strength; influence; efficacy (*force of habit*). **b** vividness of effect (*described with much force*). **7** *Physics* **a** an influence tending to cause the motion of a body. **b** the intensity of this. **8** a person or thing regarded as exerting influence (*is a force for good*). • *v.* **1** *tr.* constrain (a person) by force. **2** *tr.* make a way through or into by force. **3** *tr.* (usu. with *prep.* or *adv.*) drive or propel violently or against resistance (*the wind forced them back*). **4** *tr.* (foll. by *on, upon*) impose or press (on a person) (*forced their views on us*). **5** *tr.* **a** cause or produce by effort (*forced a smile*). **b** attain by strength or effort (*forced an entry; must force a decision*). **6** *tr.* strain or increase to the utmost; overstrain. **7** *tr.* artificially hasten the development or maturity of (a plant). **8** *tr.* seek or demand quick results from; accelerate the process of (*force the pace*). □ **force a person's hand** make a person act prematurely or unwillingly. **force the issue** render an immediate decision necessary. **in force 1** valid; effective. **2** in great strength or numbers. **join forces** combine efforts. □□ **force·a·ble** *adj.* **forc·er** *n.*

force-feed *v.tr.* (*past.* & *past part.* **-fed** /–fed/) force (esp. a prisoner) to take food.

force field *n.* (in science fiction) an invisible barrier of force.

force·ful /fáwrsfŏŏl/ *adj.* **1** vigorous; powerful. **2** (of speech) compelling; impressive. □□ **force·ful·ly** *adv.* **force·ful·ness** *n.*

force·meat /fáwrsmeet/ *n.* meat, etc., chopped and seasoned for use as a stuffing or a garnish.

for·ceps /fáwrseps/ *n.* (*pl.* same) surgical pincers, used for grasping and holding.

for·ci·ble /fáwrsibəl/ *adj.* done by or involving force; forceful. □□ **for·ci·ble·ness** *n.* **for·ci·bly** *adv.*

ford /fawrd/ *n. & v.* • *n.* a shallow place where a river or stream may be crossed by wading or in a vehicle. • *v.tr.* cross (water) at a ford. □□ **ford·a·ble** *adj.* **ford·less** *adj.*

fore /fawr/ *adj., n., int.* • *adj.* situated in front. • *n.* the front part, esp. of a ship; the bow. • *int. Golf* a warning to a person in the path of a ball. □ **come to the fore** take a leading part. **to the fore** in front; conspicuous.

fore and aft *adv. & adj.* • *adv.* at bow and stern; all over the ship. • *adj.* (**fore-and-aft**) (of a sail or rigging) set lengthwise, not on the yards.

fore·arm /fáwraarm/ *n.* **1** the part of the arm from the elbow to the wrist or the fingertips. **2** the corresponding part in a foreleg or wing.

fore·bear /fáwrbair/ *n.* (also **for·bear**) (usu. in *pl.*) an ancestor.

fore·bode /fawrbṓd/ *v.tr.* **1** betoken; be an advance warning of (an evil or unwelcome event). **2** have a presentiment of (usu. evil).

fore·bod·ing /fawrbṓding/ *n.* an expectation of trouble or evil; a presage or omen.

fore·cast /fáwrkast/ *v. & n.* • *v.tr.* (*past* and *past part.* **-cast** or **-casted**) predict; estimate or calculate beforehand. • *n.* a calculation or estimate of something future, esp. coming weather. □□ **fore·cast·er** *n.*

fore·cas·tle /fṓksəl/ *n.* (also **fo'c's'le**) *Naut.* the forward part of a ship.

fore·close /fawrklṓz/ *v.tr.* **1** (also *absol.*; foll. by *on*) stop (a mortgage) from being redeemable or (a mortgager) from redeeming, esp. as a result of defaults in payment. **2** exclude; prevent. **3** shut out; bar. □□ **fore·clo·sure** /–klṓzhər/ *n.*

fore·court /fáwrkawrt/ *n.* **1** an enclosed space in front of a building. **2** *Tennis* the part of the court between the service line and the net.

fore·doom /fawrdŏŏm/ *v.tr.* (often foll. by *to*) doom or condemn beforehand.

fore·fa·ther /fáwrfaa*th*ər/ *n.* (usu. in *pl.*) **1** an ancestor. **2** a member of a past generation of a family or people.

fore·fin·ger /fáwrfinggər/ *n.* the finger next to the thumb.

fore·foot /fáwrfŏŏt/ *n.* (*pl.* **-feet**) either of the front feet of a four-footed animal.

fore·front /fáwrfrunt/ *n.* **1** the foremost part. **2** the leading position.

fore·gath·er var. of FORGATHER.

fore·go¹ /fáwrgṓ/ *v.tr. & intr.* (**-goes**; *past* **-went** /–wént/; *past part.* **-gone** /–gón/) precede in place or time. □□ **fore·go·er** *n.*

fore·go² var. of FORGO.

fore·go·ing /fáwrgṓing/ *adj.* preceding; previously mentioned.

fore·gone con·clu·sion *n.* an easily foreseen or predictable result.

fore·ground /fáwrgrownd/ *n.* **1** the part of a view that is nearest the observer. **2** the most conspicuous position.

fore·hand /fáwrhand/ *n.* *Tennis*, etc. **1** a stroke played with the palm of the hand facing the opponent. **2** (*attrib.*) (also **fore·hand·ed**) of or made with a forehand.

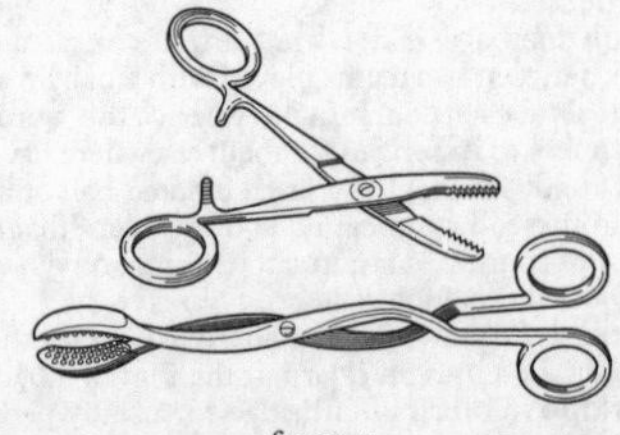

forceps

fore•head /fáwrid, –hed, fór–/ *n.* the part of the face above the eyebrows.
▶Traditionally, **forehead** was pronounced with the stress on the first syllable and with the *h* silent, so that it almost rhymed with *horrid.* But today many pronounce it sounding the *h* and giving the element *head* secondary stress.

for•eign /fáwrin, fór–/ *adj.* **1** of or from or situated in or characteristic of a country or a language other than one's own. **2** dealing with other countries (*foreign service*). **3** of another district, society, etc. **4** (often foll. by *to*) unfamiliar; strange; uncharacteristic (*his behavior is foreign to me*). **5** coming from outside (*a foreign body lodged in my eye*). ▫▫ **for•eign•ness** *n.*

for•eign•er /fáwrinər, fór–/ *n.* **1** a person born in or coming from a foreign country or place. **2** *dial.* a person not native to a place. **3 a** a foreign ship. **b** an imported animal or article.

for•eign ex•change *n.* **1** the currency of other countries. **2** dealings in these.

for•eign min•is•ter *n.* (also **foreign secretary**) (in some governments) a government minister in charge of his or her country's relations with other countries.

fore•leg /fáwrleg/ *n.* each of the front legs of a quadruped.

fore•limb /fáwrlim/ *n.* any of the front limbs of an animal.

fore•lock /fáwrlok/ *n.* a lock of hair growing just above the forehead.

fore•man /fáwrmən/ *n.* (*pl.* **-men**) **1** a worker with supervisory responsibilities. **2** the member of a jury who presides over its deliberations and speaks on its behalf.

fore•mast /fáwrmast, –məst/ *n.* the forward (lower) mast of a ship.

fore•most /fáwrmōst/ *adj. & adv.* • *adj.* **1** the chief or most notable. **2** the most advanced in position; the front. • *adv.* before anything else in position; in the first place (*first and foremost*).

fo•ren•sic /fərénsik, –zik/ *adj.* **1** of or used in connection with courts of law (*forensic science*). **2** *disp.* of or involving forensic science (*sent for forensic examination*). ▫▫ **fo•ren•si•cal•ly** *adv.*

fore•play /fáwrplay/ *n.* stimulation preceding sexual intercourse.

fore•run•ner /fáwr-runər/ *n.* **1** a predecessor. **2** an advance messenger.

fore•sail /fáwrsayl, –səl/ *n.* *Naut.* the principal sail on a foremast.

fore•see /fáwrsée/ *v.tr.* (*past* **-saw** /–sáw/; *past part.* **-seen** /–séen/) (often foll. by *that* + clause) see or be aware of beforehand. ▫▫ **fore•see•a•ble** *adj.* **fore•see•a•bil•i•ty** *n.*

fore•shad•ow /fáwrshádō/ *v.tr.* be a warning or indication of (a future event).

fore•short•en /fáwrsháwrt'n/ *v.tr.* show or portray (an object) with the apparent shortening due to visual perspective.

fore•sight /fáwrsīt/ *n.* **1** regard or provision for the future. **2** the process of foreseeing. **3** the front sight of a gun. **4** *Surveying* a sight taken forward. ▫▫ **fore•sight•ed** /–sítid/ *adj.* **fore•sight•ed•ly** *adv.* **fore•sight•ed•ness** *n.*

fore•skin /fáwrskin/ *n.* the fold of skin covering the end of the penis. Also called PREPUCE.

for•est /fáwrist, fór–/ *n. & v.* • *n.* **1 a** (often *attrib.*) a large area covered chiefly with trees and undergrowth. **b** the trees growing in it. **c** a large number or dense mass of vertical objects (*a forest of masts*). **2** a district formerly a forest but now cultivated. • *v.tr.* **1** plant with trees. **2** convert into a forest.

fore•stall /fáwrstáwl/ *v.tr.* **1** act in advance of in order to prevent. **2** anticipate (the action of another, or an event). **3** anticipate the action of. **4** deal with beforehand.

for•est•er /fáwristər, fór–/ *n.* **1** a person in charge of a forest or skilled in forestry. **2** a person or animal living in a forest.

for•est•ry /fáwristree, fór–/ *n.* **1** the science or management of forests. **2** wooded country; forests.

fore•taste *n. & v.* • *n.* /fáwrtayst/ partial enjoyment or suffering in advance; anticipation. • *v.tr.* /fáwrtáyst/ taste beforehand; anticipate the experience of.

fore•tell /fáwrtél/ *v.tr.* (*past* and *past part.* **-told** /–tṓld/) **1** tell of (an event, etc.) before it takes place; predict; prophesy. **2** presage; be a precursor of. ▫▫ **fore•tell•er** *n.*

fore•thought /fáwrthawt/ *n.* **1** care or provision for the future. **2** previous thinking or devising. **3** deliberate intention.

fore•to•ken *n. & v.* • *n.* /fáwrtōkən/ a sign of something to come. • *v.tr.* /fáwrtṓkən/ portend; indicate beforehand.

fore•told *past* and *past part.* of FORETELL.

for•ev•er /fərévər, fawr–/ *adv.* continually; persistently (*is forever complaining*).

fore•warn /fáwrwáwrn/ *v.tr.* warn beforehand.

fore•went *past* of FOREGO[1], FOREGO[2].

fore•wom•an /fáwrwŏŏmən/ *n.* (*pl.* **-women**) **1** a female worker with supervisory responsibilities. **2** a woman who presides over a jury's deliberations and speaks on its behalf.

fore•word /fáwrwərd/ *n.* introductory remarks at the beginning of a book, often by a person other than the author.

for•feit /fáwrfit/ *n., adj., & v.* • *n.* **1** a penalty for a breach of contract or neglect; a fine. **2 a** a trivial fine for a breach of rules in clubs, etc., or in a game. **b** (in *pl.*) a game in which forfeits are exacted. **3** something surrendered as a penalty. **4** the process of forfeiting. • *adj.* lost or surrendered as a penalty. • *v.tr.* (**forfeited, forfeiting**) lose the right to, be deprived of, or have to pay as a penalty. ▫▫ **for•feit•a•ble** *adj.* **for•fei•ture** /–fichər/ *n.*

for•fend /fawrfénd/ *v.tr.* **1** protect by precautions. **2** *archaic* avert; keep off.

for•gath•er /fáwrgá<u>th</u>ər/ *v.intr.* (also **fore•gath•er**) assemble; meet together; associate.

for•gave *past* of FORGIVE.

forge[1] /fawrj/ *v. & n.* • *v.tr.* **1 a** write (a document or signature) in order to pass it off as written by another. **b** make (money, etc.) in fraudulent imitation. **2** fabricate; invent. **3** shape (esp. metal) by heating and hammering. • *n.* **1** a blacksmith's workshop; a smithy. **2 a** a furnace or hearth for melting or refining metal. **b** a workshop containing this. ▫▫ **forge•a•ble** *adj.* **forg•er** *n.*

forge[2] /fawrj/ *v.intr.* move forward gradually or steadily. ▫ **forge ahead 1** take the lead in a race. **2** progress rapidly.

for•ger•y /fáwrjəree/ *n.* (*pl.* **-ies**) **1** the act or an instance of forging a document, etc. **2** a forged document.

for•get /fərgét/ *v.* (**forgetting**; *past* **forgot** /–gót/; *past part.* **forgotten** /–gót'n/ or esp. *US* **forgot**) **1** *tr.* & (often foll. by *about*) *intr.* lose the remembrance of; not remember (a person or thing). **2** *tr.* (foll. by clause or *to* + infin.) not remember; neglect (*forgot to come*; *forgot how to do it*). **3** *tr.* inadvertently omit to bring or mention or attend to. **4** *tr.* (also *absol.*) put out of mind; cease to think of (*forgive and forget*). ▫ **forget oneself 1** neglect one's own interests. **2** act unbecomingly or unworthily. ▫▫ **for•get•ta•ble** *adj.*

for·get·ful /fərgétfŏŏl/ *adj.* **1** apt to forget; absent-minded. **2** (often foll. by *of*) forgetting; neglectful. ▫▫ **for·get·ful·ly** *adj.* **for·get·ful·ness** *n.*

for·get-me-not *n.* any plant of the genus *Myosotis*, esp. *M. alpestris* with small yellow-eyed bright blue flowers.

for·give /fərgív/ *v.tr.* (also *absol.* or with double object) (*past* **forgave**; *past part.* **forgiven**) **1** cease to feel angry or resentful toward; pardon (an offender or offense)). **2** remit or let off (a debt or debtor). ▫▫ **for·giv·a·ble** *adj.* **for·giv·a·bly** *adv.* **for·giv·er** *n.*

for·give·ness /fərgívnis/ *n.* **1** the act of forgiving; the state of being forgiven. **2** readiness to forgive.

for·giv·ing /fərgíving/ *adj.* inclined readily to forgive. ▫▫ **for·giv·ing·ly** *adv.*

for·go /fáwrgṓ/ *v.tr.* (also **fore·go**) (**-goes**; *past* **-went** /–wént/; *past part.* **-gone** /–gáwn, –gón/) **1** abstain from; go without; relinquish. **2** omit or decline to take or use (a pleasure, advantage, etc.).

for·got *past* & esp. *US past part.* of FORGET.

for·got·ten *past part.* of FORGET.

fork /fawrk/ *n.* & *v.* • *n.* **1** an instrument with two or more prongs used in eating or cooking. **2** a similar much larger instrument used for digging, lifting, etc. **3** any pronged device or component (*tuning fork*). **4** a forked support for a bicycle wheel. **5 a** a divergence of anything, e.g., a stick, road, or a river, into two parts. **b** the place where this occurs. **c** either of the two parts (*take the left fork*). **6** a flash of forked lightning. • *v.* **1** *intr.* form a fork or branch by separating into two parts. **2** *intr.* take one or other road, etc., at a fork (*fork left for Danbury*). **3** *tr.* dig or lift, etc., with a fork. ▫ **fork out** (or **over** or **up**) *sl.* hand over or pay, usu. reluctantly.

forked /fawrkt/ *adj.* **1** having a fork or forklike end or branches. **2** divergent; cleft. **3** (in *comb.*) having so many prongs (*three-forked*).

forked light·ning *n.* a lightning flash in the form of a zigzag or branching line.

fork·lift /fáwrklift/ *n.* a vehicle with a horizontal fork in front for lifting and carrying loads.

for·lorn /fawrláwrn/ *adj.* **1** sad and abandoned or lonely. **2** in a pitiful state; of wretched appearance. ▫▫ **for·lorn·ly** *adv.* **for·lorn·ness** *n.*

form /fawrm/ *n.* & *v.* • *n.* **1 a** a shape; an arrangement of parts. **b** the outward aspect (esp. apart from color) or shape of a body. **2** a person or animal as visible or tangible (*the familiar form of the teacher*). **3** the mode in which a thing exists or manifests itself (*took the form of a book*). **4** a species, kind, or variety. **5 a** a printed document with blank spaces for information to be inserted. **b** a regularly drawn document. **6** a class or grade, as in some private schools or a British school. **7** a customary method; what is usually done (*common form*). **8** a set order of words; a formula. **9** behavior according to a rule or custom. **10** (prec. by *the*) correct procedure (*knows the form*). **11 a** (of an athlete, horse, etc.) condition of health and training (*is in top form*). **b** *Racing* details of previous performances. **12** general state or disposition (*was in great form*). **13** formality or mere ceremony. **14** *Gram.* **a** one of the ways in which a word may be spelled or pronounced or inflected. **b** the external characteristics of words apart from meaning. **15** arrangement and style in literary or musical composition. **16** *Philos.* the essential nature of a species or thing. **17** *Brit.* a long bench without a back. **18** a hare's lair. • *v.* **1** *tr.* make or fashion into a certain shape or form. **2** *intr.* take a certain shape; be formed. **3** *tr.* be the material of; make up or constitute (*together form a unit*; *forms part of the structure*). **4** *tr.* train or instruct. **5** *tr.* develop or establish as a concept, institution, or practice (*form an idea*; *formed an alliance*). **6** *tr.* (foll. by *into*) embody; organize. **7** *tr.* articulate (a word). **8** *tr.* & *intr.* (often foll. by *up*) esp. *Mil.* bring or be brought into a certain arrangement or formation. **9** *tr.* construct (a new word) by derivation, inflection, etc.

for·mal /fáwrməl/ *adj.* & *n.* • *adj.* **1** used or done or held in accordance with rules, convention, or ceremony (*formal dress*; *a formal occasion*). **2** ceremonial; required by convention (*a formal offer*). **3** precise or symmetrical (*a formal garden*). **4** prim or stiff in manner. **5** perfunctory; having the form without the spirit. **6** valid or correctly so called because of its form; explicit (*a formal agreement*). **7** in accordance with recognized forms or rules. **8** of or concerned with (outward) form or appearance, esp. as distinct from content or matter. • *n.* **1** evening dress. **2** an occasion on which evening dress is worn. ▫▫ **for·mal·ly** *adv.*

form·al·de·hyde /fawrmáldihīd/ *n.* a colorless pungent gas used as a disinfectant and preservative and in the manufacture of synthetic resins.

for·ma·lin /fáwrməlin/ *n.* a colorless solution of formaldehyde in water used as a preservative for biological specimens, etc.

for·mal·ism /fáwrməlizəm/ *n.* **1 a** excessive adherence to prescribed forms. **b** the use of forms without regard to inner significance. **2** *derog.* an artist's concentration on form at the expense of content. ▫▫ **for·mal·ist** *n.* **for·mal·is·tic** *adj.*

for·mal·i·ty /fawrmálitee/ *n.* (*pl.* **-ties**) **1 a** a formal or ceremonial act, requirement of etiquette, regulation, or custom. **b** a thing done simply to comply with a rule. **2** the rigid observance of rules or convention. **3** ceremony; elaborate procedure. **4** being formal; precision of manners.

for·mal·ize /fáwrməlīz/ *v.tr.* **1** give definite shape or legal formality to. **2** make ceremonious, precise, or rigid. ▫▫ **for·mal·i·za·tion** /–lizáyshən/ *n.*

for·mat /fáwrmat/ *n.* & *v.* • *n.* **1** the shape and size of a book, periodical, etc. **2** the style or manner of an arrangement or procedure. **3** *Computing* a defined structure for holding data in a record for processing or storage. • *v.tr.* (**formatted, formatting**) **1** arrange or put into a format. **2** *Computing* prepare (a storage medium) to receive data.

for·ma·tion /fawrmáyshən/ *n.* **1** the act or an instance of forming; the process of being formed. **2** a thing formed. **3** a structure or arrangement of parts. **4** a particular arrangement, e.g., of troops, aircraft in flight, etc. **5** *Geol.* an assemblage of rocks or series of strata having some common characteristic. ▫▫ **for·ma·tion·al** *adj.*

for·ma·tive /fáwrmətiv/ *adj.* serving to form or fashion; of formation. ▫▫ **for·ma·tive·ly** *adv.*

for·mer[1] /fáwrmər/ *attrib.adj.* **1** of or occurring in the past or an earlier period (*in former times*). **2** having been previously (*her former husband*). **3** (prec. by *the*; often *absol.*) the first or first mentioned of two.

▶When two previously mentioned items are referred to, the one named first is the **former**, the second the **latter:** *The menu offered coconut-crusted shrimp and barbecued ribs—the former decidedly sweet, the latter absolutely mild.* If there are three or more, **first, second, (etc.)** and **last** should be used, even if all are not mentioned: *Of winter, spring, and summer, I find the last most enjoyable.*

form·er[2] /fáwrmər/ *n.* **1** a person or thing that forms. **2** *Electr.* a frame or core for winding a coil on. **3** *Aeron.* a transverse strengthening member in a wing or fuselage. **4** esp. *Brit.* (in *comb.*) a pupil of a specified form in a school (*fourth-former*).

for·mer·ly /fáwrmərlee/ *adv.* in the past; in former times.

for·mic ac·id /fáwrmik/ *n.* a colorless irritant volatile acid emitted by some ants.

for·mi·da·ble /fáwrmidəbəl, *disp.* formídəbəl/ *adj.* **1** inspiring fear or dread. **2** inspiring respect or awe. **3** likely to be hard to overcome, resist, or deal with. ▫▫ **for·mi·da·ble·ness** *n.* **for·mi·da·bly** *adv.*

form·less /fáwrmlis/ *adj.* shapeless; without determinate or regular form. ▫▫ **form·less·ly** *adv.* **form·less·ness** *n.*

form let·ter *n.* a standardized letter to deal with frequently occurring matters.

for·mu·la /fáwrmyələ/ *n.* (*pl.* **formulas** or (esp. in senses 1, 2) **formulae** /–lee/) **1** *Chem.* a set of chemical symbols showing the constituents of a substance and their relative proportions. **2** *Math.* a mathematical rule expressed in symbols. **3 a** a fixed form of words, esp. one used on social or ceremonial occasions. **b** a rule unintelligently or slavishly followed. **c** a form of words embodying agreement, etc. **4 a** a list of ingredients; a recipe. **b** an infant's liquid food preparation. **5** a classification of racing car, esp. by the engine capacity. ▫▫ **for·mu·la·ic** /–láyik/ *adj.* **for·mu·lar·ize** /–lərīz/ *v.tr.* **for·mu·lize** *v.tr.*

for·mu·late /fáwrmyəlayt/ *v.tr.* **1** express in a formula. **2** express clearly and precisely. **3** create or devise (a plan, etc.). **4** develop or prepare following a formula. ▫▫ **for·mu·la·tion** /–láyshən/ *n.*

for·ni·cate /fáwrnikayt/ *v.intr.* (of people not married or not married to each other) have sexual intercourse voluntarily. ▫▫ **for·ni·ca·tion** /–kayshən/ *n.* **for·ni·ca·tor** *n.*

for·sake /fərsáyk, fawr–/ *v.tr.* (*past* **forsook** /–sŏŏk/; *past part.* **forsaken** /–sáykən/) **1** give up; renounce. **2** withdraw one's help, friendship, or companionship from; desert; abandon. ▫▫ **for·sak·en·ness** *n.* **for·sak·er** *n.*

for·sooth /fərsóoth, fawr–/ *adv. archaic* or *joc.* truly; in truth; no doubt.

for·swear /fáwrswáir/ *v.tr.* (*past* **forswore** /–swáwr/; *past part.* **forsworn** /–swáwrn/) **1** abjure; renounce on oath. **2** (in *refl.* or *passive*) swear falsely; commit perjury.

for·syth·i·a /fawrsítheeə/ *n.* any ornamental shrub of the genus *Forsythia* bearing bright yellow flowers in early spring.

fort /fawrt/ *n.* **1** a fortified building or position. **2** *hist.* a trading post, orig. fortified.

forte[1] /fawrt, fáwrtay/ *n.* a thing in which a person excels.

for·te[2] /fórtay/ *adj., adv., & n. Mus.* • *adj.* performed loudly. • *adv.* loudly. • *n.* a passage to be performed loudly.

for·te·pia·no /fórtaypyánō, –pyaánō/ *n* (*pl.* **-nos**) *Mus.* = PIANOFORTE esp. with ref. to an instrument of the 18th to early 19th c.

forth /fawrth/ *adv. archaic* except in set phrases and after certain verbs, esp. *bring, come, go,* and *set.* **1** forward; into view. **2** onward in time (*from this time forth; henceforth*). **3** forward. **4** out from a starting point (*set forth*). ▫ **and so forth** and so on; and the like.

forth·com·ing /fáwrthkúming/ *attrib.adj.* **1 a** about or likely to appear or become available. **b** approaching. **2** produced when wanted (*no reply was forthcoming*). **3** (of a person) informative; responsive. ▫▫ **forth·com·ing·ness** *n.*

forth·right /fáwrthrīt/ *adj. & adv.* • *adj.* **1** direct and outspoken. **2** decisive. • *adv.* in a direct manner; bluntly. ▫▫ **forth·right·ly** *adv.* **forth·right·ness** *n.*

forth·with /fáwrthwíth, –wíth/ *adv.* immediately; without delay.

for·ti·fi·ca·tion /fáwrtifikáyshən/ *n.* **1** the act or an instance of fortifying; the process of being fortified. **2** *Mil.* **a** the art or science of fortifying. **b** (usu. in *pl.*) defensive works fortifying a position.

for·ti·fy /fáwrtifī/ *v.tr.* (**-fies, -fied**) **1** provide or equip with defensive works. **2** strengthen or invigorate physically, mentally, or morally. **3** strengthen the structure of. **4** strengthen (wine) with alcohol. **5** increase the nutritive value of (food, esp. with vitamins). ▫▫ **for·ti·fi·a·ble** *adj.* **for·ti·fi·er** *n.*

for·tis·si·mo /fawrtísimō/ *adj., adv., & n. Mus.* • *adj.* performed very loudly. • *adv.* very loudly. • *n.* (*pl.* **-mos** or **fortissimi** /–mee/) a passage to be performed very loudly.

for·ti·tude /fáwrtitōōd, –tyōōd/ *n.* courage in pain or adversity.

fort·night /fáwrtnīt/ *n.* two weeks.

For·tran /fáwrtran/ *n.* (also **FORTRAN**) *Computing* a high-level programming language used esp. for scientific calculations (abbr. of *for*mula *tran*slation).

for·tress /fáwrtris/ *n.* a military stronghold, esp. a strongly fortified town.

for·tu·i·tous /fawrtóoitəs, –tyóo–/ *adj.* due to or characterized by chance. ▫▫ **for·tu·i·tous·ly** *adv.* **for·tu·i·tous·ness** *n.*

for·tu·nate /fáwrchənət/ *adj.* **1** lucky; prosperous. **2** auspicious; favorable.

for·tu·nate·ly /fáwrchənətlee/ *adv.* **1** luckily; successfully. **2** (qualifying a whole sentence) it is fortunate that.

for·tune /fáwrchən/ *n.* **1 a** chance or luck as a force in human affairs. **b** a person's destiny. **2** (**Fortune**) this force personified, often as a deity. **3** (in *sing.* or *pl.*) the good or bad luck that befalls a person or an enterprise. **4** good luck. **5** prosperity; a prosperous condition. **6** (also *colloq.* **small fortune**) great wealth; a huge sum of money. ▫ **make a** (or **one's**) **fortune** acquire wealth or prosperity. **tell a person's fortune** make predictions about a person's future.

for·tune hunt·er *n. colloq.* a person seeking wealth by marriage.

for·tune-tel·ler *n.* a person who claims to predict future events in a person's life. ▫▫ **for·tune-tell·ing** *n.*

for·ty /fáwrtee/ *n. & adj.* • *n.* (*pl.* **-ties**) **1** the product of four and ten. **2** a symbol for this (40, xl, XL). **3** (in *pl.*) the numbers from 40 to 49, esp. the years of a century or of a person's life. • *adj.* that amount to forty. ▫▫ **for·ti·eth** *adj. & n.* **for·ty·fold** *adj. & adv.*

for·ty-nin·er *n.* a seeker for gold, etc., esp. in the California gold rush of 1849.

for·ty winks *n.pl. colloq.* a short sleep.

fo·rum /fáwrəm/ *n.* **1** a place of or meeting for public discussion. **2** a periodical, etc., giving an opportunity for discussion. **3** a court or tribunal. **4** *hist.* a public square or marketplace in an ancient Roman city.

for·ward /fáwrwərd/ *adj., n., adv., & v.* • *adj.* **1** lying in one's line of motion. **2 a** onward or toward the front. **b** *Naut.* belonging to the fore part of a ship. **3** precocious; bold in manner; presumptuous. **4** *Commerce* relating to future produce, delivery, etc. (*forward contract*). **5 a** advanced; progressing toward or approaching maturity or completion. **b** (of a plant, etc.) well advanced or early. • *n.* an attacking player in soccer, hockey, etc. • *adv.* **1** to the front; into prominence. **2** in advance; ahead (*sent them forward*). **3** onward so as to make progress (*not getting any farther forward*). **4** toward the future; continuously onward (*from this time forward*). **5** (also **for·wards**) **a** in the direction one is facing. **b** in the normal direction of motion or of traversal. **c** with continuous forward motion (*rushing forward*). **6** *Naut. & Aeron.* in, near, or toward the bow or nose. • *v.tr.* **1 a** send (a letter, etc.) on to a further destination. **b** esp. *Brit.* dispatch (goods, etc.). **2** help to advance; promote. ▫▫ **for·ward·**

er *n.* **for•ward•ly** *adv.* **for•ward•ness** *n.* (esp. in sense 3 of *adj.*).

for•ward-look•ing *adj.* progressive; favoring change.

for•wards var. of FORWARD *adv.* 5.

for•went *past* of FORGO.

fos•sil /fósəl/ *n. & adj.* • *n.* **1** the remains or impression of a (usu. prehistoric) plant or animal in rock (often *attrib.*: *fossil shells*). **2** *colloq.* an antiquated or unchanging person or thing. • *adj.* **1** of or like a fossil. **2** antiquated. □□ **fos•sil•if•er•ous** /fósilífərəs/ *adj.* **fos•sil•ize** *v.tr. & intr.* **fos•sil•i•za•tion** *n.*

fos•sil fu•el *n.* a natural fuel such as coal or gas formed from the remains of living organisms.

fos•ter /fáwstər, fós–/ *v. & adj.* • *v.tr.* **1 a** promote the growth or development of. **b** encourage or harbor (a feeling). **2** (of circumstances) be favorable to. **3** bring up (a child that is not one's own by birth). **4** cherish; have affectionate regard for (an idea, scheme, etc.). • *adj.* **1** having a family connection by fostering and not by birth (*foster brother*; *foster parent*). **2** concerned with fostering a child (*foster care*; *foster home*). □□ **fos•ter•age** *n.* (esp. in sense 3 of *v.*). **fos•ter•er** *n.*

fought *past* and *past part.* of FIGHT.

foul /fowl/ *adj., n., adv., & v.* • *adj.* **1** offensive to the senses; loathsome; stinking. **2** dirty; soiled; filthy. **3** *colloq.* revolting; disgusting. **4 a** containing or charged with noxious matter (*foul air*). **b** clogged; choked. **5** disgustingly abusive or offensive (*foul language*; *foul deeds*). **6** unfair; against the rules of a game, etc. (*by fair means or foul*). **7** (of the weather) wet; rough; stormy. **8** (of a rope, etc.) entangled. **9** (of a ship's bottom) overgrown with weeds, barnacles, etc. • *n.* **1** *Sports* an unfair or invalid stroke or action. **2** *Baseball* a batted ball not hit into fair territory. **3** a collision or entanglement. **4** a foul thing. • *adv.* unfairly. • *v.* **1** *tr. & intr.* make or become foul or dirty. **2** *tr.* (of an animal) make dirty with excrement. **3 a** *tr. Sports* commit a foul against (a player). **b** *intr.* commit a foul. **4** *tr. & intr. Sports* hit a ball foul. **5 a** *tr.* (often foll. by *up*) cause (an anchor, cable, etc.) to become entangled or muddled. **b** *intr.* become entangled. **6** *tr.* jam or block (a crossing, railway line, or traffic). **7** *tr.* (usu. foll. by *up*) *colloq.* spoil or bungle. □□ **foul•ly** *adv.* **foul•ness** *n.*

fou•lard /fo͞oláard/ *n.* **1** a thin soft material of silk or silk and cotton. **2** an article made of this.

foul play *n.* **1** unfair play in games. **2** treacherous or violent activity, esp. murder.

foul shot *n.* = FREE THROW.

foul-up *n.* a muddled or bungled situation.

found[1] *past* and *past part.* of FIND.

found[2] /fownd/ *v.* **1** *tr.* **a** establish (esp. with an endowment). **b** originate or initiate (an institution). **2** *tr.* be the original builder or begin the building of (a town, etc.). **3** *tr.* lay the base of (a building, etc.). **4** (foll. by *on, upon*) **a** *tr.* construct or base (a story, theory, rule, etc.) according to a specified principle or ground. **b** *intr.* have a basis in.

found[3] /fownd/ *v.tr.* **1 a** melt and mold (metal). **b** fuse (materials for glass). **2** make by founding. □□ **found•er** *n.*

foun•da•tion /fowndáyshən/ *n.* **1 a** the solid ground or base on which a building rests. **b** (usu. in *pl.*) the lowest load-bearing part of a building, usu. below ground level. **2** a body or ground on which other parts are overlaid. **3** a basis or underlying principle (*the report has no foundation*). **4 a** the act or an instance of establishing or constituting (esp. an endowed institution). **b** such an institution, e.g., a college or hospital. **5** a cream used as a base to even out facial skin tone before applying other cosmetics. **6** (in full **foundation** garment) a woman's supporting undergarment, e.g., a corset. □□ **foun•da•tion•al** *adj.*

found•er[1] /fówndər/ *n.* a person who founds an institution.

found•er[2] /fówndər/ *v.* **1 a** *intr.* (of a ship) fill with water and sink. **b** *tr.* cause (a ship) to founder. **2** *intr.* (of a plan, etc.) fail. **3** *intr.* (of earth, a building, etc.) fall down or in. **4** *intr.* (of a horse or its rider) fall to the ground, fall from lameness, stick fast in mud, etc.

found•ing fa•ther *n.* a person associated with a founding, esp. (usu. *cap.*) an American statesman at the time of the Revolution.

found•ling /fówndling/ *n.* an abandoned infant of unknown parentage.

found•ry /fówndree/ *n.* (*pl.* **-ries**) a workshop for or a business of casting metal.

fount[1] /fownt/ *n. poet.* a spring or fountain; a source.

fount[2] /fownt, font/ *n. Brit.* = FONT[2].

foun•tain /fówntin/ *n.* **1 a** a jet or jets of water made to spout for ornamental purposes or for drinking. **b** a structure provided for this. **2** a structure for the constant public supply of drinking water. **3** a natural spring of water. **4** a source (in physical or abstract senses). **5** = SODA FOUNTAIN. **6** a reservoir for oil, ink, etc.

foun•tain•head /fównt'nhed/ *n.* an original source.

foun•tain pen *n.* a pen with a reservoir or cartridge holding ink.

four /fawr/ *n. & adj.* • *n.* **1** one more than three. **2** a symbol for this (4, iv, IV). **3** a size, etc., denoted by four. **4** a four-oared rowing boat or its crew. **5** four o'clock (*is it four yet?*). **6** a card with four pips. • *adj.* that amount to four. □ **on all fours** on hands and knees.

four-eyes *n. sl.* a person wearing glasses.

four-flush•er *n.* a bluffer; one who makes false claims.

four•fold /fáwrfōld/ *adj. & adv.* **1** four times as much or as many. **2** consisting of four parts. **3** amounting to four.

four-leaf clo•ver *n.* (also **four-leaved clover**) a clover leaf with four leaflets thought to bring good luck.

four-let•ter word *n.* any of several short words referring to sexual or excretory functions, regarded as coarse or offensive.

four-post•er *n.* a bed with a post at each corner supporting a canopy.

four•score /fáwrskáwr/ *n. archaic* eighty.

four•some /fáwrsəm/ *n.* **1** a group of four persons. **2 a** a golf match between two pairs with partners playing the same ball. **b** a golf match with four players.

four•square /fáwrskwáir/ *adj. & adv.* • *adj.* **1** solidly based. **2** steady; resolute; forthright. **3** square shaped. • *adv.* steadily; resolutely.

four-stroke *adj.* (of an internal combustion engine) having a cycle of four strokes (intake, compression, combustion, and exhaust).

four•teen /fáwrtéen/ *n. & adj.* • *n.* **1** one more than thirteen. **2** a symbol for this (14, xiv, XIV). **3** a size, etc., denoted by fourteen. • *adj.* that amount to fourteen. □□ **four•teenth** *adj. & n.*

fourth /fawrth/ *n. & adj.* • *n.* **1** the position in a sequence corresponding to that of the number 4 in the sequence 1–4. **2** something occupying this position. **3** the fourth person, etc., in a race or competition. **4** each of four equal parts of a thing; a quarter. **5** the fourth in a sequence of gears. **6** *Mus.* **a** an interval or chord spanning four consecutive notes in the diatonic scale (e.g., C to F). **b** a note separated from another by this interval. **7** (**Fourth**) the Fourth of July. • *adj.* that is the fourth. □□ **fourth•ly** *adv.*

fourth es•tate *n.* the press; journalism.

four-wheel drive *n.* drive powering all four wheels of a vehicle.

fowl /fowl/ *n. & v.* (*pl.* same or **fowls**) • *n.* **1** any domestic cock or hen kept for eggs and flesh. **2** the flesh of birds, esp. a domestic cock or hen, as food. • *v.intr.* catch or hunt wildfowl. ▫▫ **fowl·er** *n.* **fowl·ing** *n.*

Fox /foks/ *n.* **1 a** a N. American people native to the northeastern US. **b** a member of this people. **2** the language of this people.

fox /foks/ *n. & v.* • *n.* **1 a** any of various wild flesh-eating mammals of the dog family, esp. of the genus *Vulpes*, with a bushy tail, and red or gray fur. **b** the fur of a fox. **2** a cunning or sly person. **3** *sl.* an attractive young woman or man. • *v.* **1 a** *intr.* act craftily. **b** *tr.* deceive; baffle; trick. **2** *tr.* (usu. as **foxed** *adj.*) discolor (the leaves of a book, engraving, etc.) with brownish marks. ▫▫ **fox·ing** *n.* (in sense 2 of *v.*). **fox·like** *adj.*

fox·glove /fóksgluv/ *n.* any tall plant of the genus *Digitalis*, with erect spikes of purple or white flowers like glove fingers.

fox·hole /fóks-hōl/ *n.* **1** *Mil.* a hole in the ground used as a shelter. **2** a place of refuge or concealment.

fox·hound /fóks-hownd/ *n.* a kind of hound bred and trained to hunt foxes.

fox hunt /fóks-hunt/ *n. & v.* • *n.* **1** the hunting of foxes with hounds. **2** a particular group of people engaged in this. • *v.intr.* engage in a foxhunt. ▫▫ **fox·hunt·er** *n.* **fox·hunt·ing** *n. & adj.*

fox·tail /fókstayl/ *n.* any of several grasses of the genus *Alopecurus*, with brushlike spikes.

fox ter·ri·er *n.* a terrier of a short-haired breed.

fox·trot /fókstrot/ *n. & v.* • *n.* **1** a ballroom dance with slow and quick steps. **2** the music for this. • *v.intr.* (**foxtrotted, foxtrotting**) perform this dance.

fox·y /fóksee/ *adj.* (**foxier, foxiest**) **1** of or like a fox. **2** sly or cunning. **3** reddish brown. **4** (of paper) damaged, esp. by mildew. **5** *sl.* sexually attractive. ▫▫ **fox·i·ly** *adv.* **fox·i·ness** *n.*

foy·er /fóyər, fóyay, fwaáyay/ *n.* the entrance hall or other large area in a hotel, theater, etc.

Fr *symb. Chem.* the element francium.

Fr. *abbr.* (also **Fr**) **1** Father. **2** French.

fr. *abbr.* franc(s).

fra·cas /fráykəs/ *n.* (*pl.* same, *pronunc.* /–kaaz/) a noisy disturbance or quarrel.

frac·tion /frákshən/ *n.* **1** a numerical quantity that is not a whole number (e.g., 0.5, $^1/_2$). **2** a small, esp. very small, part, piece, or amount. **3** a portion of a mixture separated by distillation, etc.

frac·tion·al /frákshənəl/ *adj.* **1** of or relating to or being a fraction. **2** very slight; incomplete. **3** *Chem.* relating to the separation of parts of a mixture by making use of their different physical properties (*fractional crystallization; fractional distillation*). ▫▫ **frac·tion·al·ize** *v.tr.* **frac·tion·al·ly** *adv.* (esp. in sense 2).

frac·tious /frákshəs/ *adj.* **1** irritable; peevish. **2** unruly. ▫▫ **frac·tious·ly** *adv.* **frac·tious·ness** *n.*

frac·ture /frákchər/ *n. & v.* • *n.* **1 a** breakage or breaking, esp. of a bone or cartilage. **b** the result of breaking; a crack or split. **2** the surface appearance of a freshly broken rock or mineral. • *v.intr. & tr.* **1** *Med.* undergo or cause to undergo a fracture. **2** break or cause to break.

frag·ile /frájil, –jīl/ *adj.* **1** easily broken; weak. **2** of delicate frame or constitution; not strong. ▫▫ **frag·ile·ly** *adv.* **fra·gil·i·ty** /frəjílitee/ *n.*

frag·ment *n. & v.* • *n.* /frágmənt/ **1** a part broken off; a detached piece. **2** an isolated or incomplete part. **3** the remains of an otherwise lost or destroyed book or work of art. • *v.tr. & intr.* /fragmént/ break or separate into fragments. ▫▫ **frag·men·tal** /–mént'l/ *adj.* **frag·ment·ize** *v.tr.*

frag·men·tar·y /frágmənteree/ *adj.* **1** consisting of fragments. **2** disconnected. ▫▫ **frag·men·tar·i·ly** *adv.*

frag·men·ta·tion /frágməntáyshən/ *n.* the process or an instance of breaking into fragments.

fra·grance /fráygrəns/ *n.* (also **fra·gran·cy** (*pl.* **·cies**)) **1** sweetness of smell. **2** a sweet scent.

fra·grant /fráygrənt/ *adj.* sweet-smelling. ▫▫ **fra·grant·ly** *adv.*

frail /frayl/ *adj.* **1** fragile; delicate. **2** in weak health. **3** morally weak. **4** transient; insubstantial. ▫▫ **frail·ly** *adv.* **frail·ness** *n.*

frail·ty /fráyltee/ *n.* (*pl.* **-ties**) **1** the condition of being frail. **2** liability to err or yield to temptation. **3** a fault, weakness, or foible.

frame /fraym/ *n. & v.* • *n.* **1** a case or border enclosing a picture, window, door, etc. **2** the basic rigid supporting structure of anything, e.g., of a building, motor vehicle, or aircraft. **3** (in *pl.*) the structure of spectacles holding the lenses. **4** a human or animal body, esp. with reference to its size or structure. **5** a framed work or structure (*the frame of heaven*). **6 a** an established order, plan, or system (*the frame of society*). **b** construction; constitution; build. **7** a temporary state (esp. in **frame of mind**). **8** a single complete image or picture on a movie or video film or transmitted in a series of lines by television. **9 a** a triangular structure for positioning the balls in pool, etc. **b** the balls positioned in this way. **c** a round of play in bowling, etc. **10** *Hort.* a boxlike structure of glass, etc., for protecting plants. **11** a removable box of slats for the building of a honeycomb in a beehive. **12** *sl.* = FRAME-UP. • *v.tr.* **1 a** set in or provide with a frame. **b** serve as a frame for. **2** construct by a combination of parts or in accordance with a design or plan. **3** formulate the essentials of (a complex thing, idea, etc.). **4** (foll. by *to, into*) adapt or fit. **5** *colloq.* concoct a false charge or evidence against; devise a plot with regard to. **6** articulate (words). ▫▫ **fram·a·ble** *adj.* (also **frame·a·ble**) **frame·less** *adj.* **fram·er** *n.*

frame of ref·er·ence *n.* **1** a set of standards or principles governing behavior, thought, etc. **2** *Geom.* a system of geometrical axes for defining position.

frame-up *n. colloq.* a conspiracy, esp. to make an innocent person appear guilty.

frame·work /fráymwərk/ *n.* **1** an essential supporting structure. **2** a basic system.

franc /frangk/ *n.* the chief monetary unit of France, Belgium, Switzerland, Luxembourg, and several other countries.

fran·chise /fránchīz/ *n. & v.* • *n.* **1 a** the right to vote in governmental elections. **b** the principle of qualification for this. **2** full membership of a corporation or nation; citizenship. **3** authorization granted by a company to sell its goods or services in a particular way. **4** *hist.* legal immunity or exemption from a burden or jurisdiction. **5** a right or privilege granted to a person or corporation. **6** a professional sports team, esp. as part of a league. • *v.tr.* grant a franchise to. ▫▫ **fran·chi·see** /–zeé/ *n.* **fran·chis·er** *n.* (also **fran·chi·sor**) .

Fran·cis·can /fransískən/ *n. & adj.* • *n.* a friar, sister, or lay member of an order founded by St. Francis of Assisi (see also GREY FRIAR). • *adj.* of St. Francis or his order.

fran·ci·um /fránseeəm/ *n. Chem.* a radioactive metallic element occurring naturally in uranium and thorium ores. ¶ Symb.: **Fr**.

Franco- /frángkō/ *comb. form* **1** French; French and (*Franco-German*). **2** regarding France or the French (*Francophile*).

Fran·co·phile /frángkəfīl/ *n.* a person who is fond of France or the French.

fran·co·phone /frángkəfōn/ *n. & adj.* • *n.* a French-speaking person. • *adj.* French-speaking.

See page xii for the *Key to Pronunciation*.

fran·gi·ble /fránjibəl/ *adj.* breakable; fragile.

Frank /frangk/ *n.* **1** a member of the Germanic nation or coalition that conquered Gaul in the 6th c. **2** (in the Levant) a person of Western nationality. ▫▫ **Frank·ish** *adj.*

frank /frangk/ *adj., v., & n.* • *adj.* **1** candid; outspoken (*a frank opinion*). **2** undisguised; avowed (*frank admiration*). **3** ingenuous; open (*a frank face*). • *v.tr.* stamp (a letter) with an official mark to record the payment of postage. • *n.* **1** a franking mark. **2** a franked cover. ▫▫ **frank·er** *n.* **frank·ness** *n.*

Frank·en·stein /frángkənstīn/ *n.* (in full **Frankenstein's monster**) a thing that becomes terrifying to its maker; a monster (from a character in the 1818 novel by Mary Shelley; Frankenstein is not the name of the monster itself, as is often assumed).

frank·furt·er /frángkfərtər/ *n.* a seasoned sausage made of beef and pork.

frank·in·cense /frángkinsens/ *n.* an aromatic gum resin used for burning as incense.

Frank·lin stove /frángklin/ *n.* a cast-iron stove having the general shape of an open fireplace but often placed so as to be freestanding.

frank·ly /frángklee/ *adv.* **1** in a frank manner. **2** (qualifying a whole sentence) to be frank.

fran·tic /frántik/ *adj.* **1** wildly excited; frenzied. **2** characterized by great hurry or anxiety; desperate; violent. **3** *colloq.* extreme; very great. ▫▫ **fran·ti·cal·ly** *adv.* **fran·tic·ly** *adv.* **fran·tic·ness** *n.*

frap·pé /frapáy/ *adj. & n.* • *adj.* (esp. of wine) iced, cooled. • *n.* **1** an iced drink. **2** a soft semi-frozen drink or dessert.

frat /frat/ *n. colloq.* a student fraternity.

fra·ter·nal /frətérnəl/ *adj.* **1** of a brother or brothers. **2** suitable to a brother; brotherly. **3** (of twins) developed from separate ova and not necessarily similar. **4** of or concerning a fraternity (see FRATERNITY 3). ▫▫ **fra·ter·nal·ism** *n.* **fra·ter·nal·ly** *adv.*

fra·ter·ni·ty /frətérnitee/ *n.* (*pl.* **-ties**) **1** a male students' society in a university or college. **2** a group or company with common interests, or of the same professional class. **3** a religious brotherhood. **4** brotherliness.

frat·er·nize /frátərnīz/ *v.intr.* (often foll. by *with*) **1** associate; make friends. **2** (of troops) enter into friendly relations with enemy troops or the inhabitants of an occupied country. ▫▫ **frat·er·ni·za·tion** *n.*

frat·ri·cide /frátrisīd/ *n.* **1** the killing of one's brother or sister. **2** a person who does this. ▫▫ **frat·ri·cid·al** /–síd'l/ *adj.*

fraud /frawd/ *n.* **1** criminal deception. **2** a dishonest artifice or trick. **3** a person or thing not fulfilling what is claimed or expected of it.

fraud·u·lent /fráwjələnt/ *adj.* **1** characterized or achieved by fraud. **2** guilty of fraud. ▫▫ **fraud·u·lence** /–ləns/ *n.* **fraud·u·lent·ly** *adv.*

fraught /frawt/ *adj.* **1** (foll. by *with*) filled or attended with (*fraught with danger*). **2** *colloq.* causing or affected by great anxiety or distress.

fray[1] /fray/ *v.* **1** *tr. & intr.* wear through or become worn, esp. (of woven material) unweave at the edges. **2** *intr.* (of nerves, etc.) become strained.

fray[2] /fray/ *n.* conflict; fighting (*eager for the fray*).

fraz·zle /frázəl/ *n. & v. colloq.* • *n.* a worn or exhausted state (*burned to a frazzle*). • *v.tr.* (usu. as **frazzled** *adj.*) wear out; exhaust.

freak /freek/ *n. & v.* • *n.* **1** (also **freak of na·ture**) a monstrosity; an abnormally developed individual or thing. **2** (often *attrib.*) an abnormal, irregular, or bizarre occurrence (*a freak storm*). **3** *colloq.* **a** an unconventional person. **b** a person with a specified enthusiasm (*health freak*). **c** a person who undergoes hallucinations; a drug addict (see sense 2 of *v.*). **4 a** a caprice or vagary. **b** capriciousness. • *v.* (often foll. by *out*) *colloq.* **1** *intr. & tr.* become or make very angry. **2** *intr. & tr.* undergo or cause to undergo hallucinations, etc., esp. from use of narcotics. **3** *intr.* adopt a wildly unconventional lifestyle.

freak·ish /freékish/ *adj.* **1** of or like a freak. **2** bizarre; unconventional. ▫▫ **freak·ish·ly** *adv.* **freak·ish·ness** *n.*

freak·y /freékee/ *adj.* (**freakier, freakiest**) = FREAKISH. ▫▫ **freak·i·ly** *adv.* **freak·i·ness** *n.*

freck·le /frékəl/ *n. & v.* • *n.* (often in *pl.*) a light brown spot on the skin, usu. caused by exposure to the sun. • *v.* **1** *tr.* (usu. as **freckled** *adj.*) spot with freckles. **2** *intr.* be spotted with freckles. ▫▫ **freck·ly** /fréklee/ *adj.*

free /free/ *adj., adv., & v.* • *adj.* (**freer** /freéər/; **freest** /freéist/) **1** not in bondage to or under the control of another; having personal rights and social and political liberty. **2** (of a nation or its citizens) subject neither to foreign domination nor to despotic government; having national and civil liberty (*a free press; a free society*). **3 a** unrestricted; not restrained or fixed. **b** not confined or imprisoned. **c** released from ties or duties. **d** unrestrained as to action; independent (*set free*). **4** (foll. by *of, from*) **a** exempt from (*free of tax*). **b** not containing or subject to a specified (usu. undesirable) thing (*free of preservatives; free from disease*). **5** (foll. by *to* + infin.) able to take a specified action (*free to choose*). **6** unconstrained (*free gestures*). **7 a** costing nothing. **b** not subject to tax, duty, or fees. **8 a** clear of engagements (*are you free tomorrow?*). **b** not occupied or in use (*the bathroom is free now*). **c** clear of obstructions. **9** spontaneous; unforced (*free compliments*). **10** open to all comers. **11** lavish; profuse (*very free with their money*). **12** frank; unreserved. **13** (of a literary, sporting, etc., style) not observing the strict laws of form. **14** (of a translation) conveying the broad sense. **15** forward; impudent. **16** (of talk, stories, etc.) slightly indecent. **17** *Physics* **a** not modified by an external force. **b** not bound in an atom or molecule. **18** *Chem.* not combined (*free oxygen*). **19** (of power or energy) disengaged or available. • *adv.* **1** in a free manner. **2** without cost or payment. • *v.tr.* **1** make free; set at liberty. **2** (foll. by *of, from*) relieve from (something undesirable). **3** disengage; disentangle. ▫ **free and easy** informal; unceremonious. ▫▫ **free·ly** *adv.* **free·ness** *n.* ▶**Free** means 'without charge,' and a **gift** is 'something given without charge.' The expression "free gift" is therefore tautological.

-free /free/ *comb. form* free of or from (*duty-free; trouble-free*).

free·base /freébays/ *n. & v. sl.* • *n.* cocaine that has been purified by heating with ether, and is taken by inhaling the fumes or smoking the residue. • *v.tr.* purify (cocaine) for smoking or inhaling.

free·bie /freébee/ *n. colloq.* a thing provided free of charge.

free·boot·er /freébootər/ *n.* a pirate or buccaneer. ▫▫ **free·boot** *v.intr.*

free·born /freébawrn/ *adj.* inheriting a citizen's rights and liberty.

freed·man /freédmən/ *n.* (*pl.* **-men**) an emancipated slave.

free·dom /freédəm/ *n.* **1** the condition of being free or unrestricted. **2** personal or civic liberty. **3** the power of self-determination. **4** the state of being free to act (often foll. by *to* + infin.: *we have the freedom to leave*). **5** frankness; outspokenness. **6** (foll. by *from*) the condition of being exempt from or not subject to (a defect, burden, etc.). **7** (foll. by *of*) **a** full or honorary participation in (membership, privileges, etc.). **b** unrestricted use of (facilities, etc.). **8** a privilege possessed by a city or corporation. **9** facility or ease in action. **10** boldness of conception.

free·dom fight·er *n.* a person who takes part in violent resistance to an established political system, etc.
free en·ter·prise *n.* a system in which private business operates in competition and largely free of government control.
free fall *n.* movement under the force of gravity only, esp.: **1** the part of a parachute descent before the parachute opens. **2** the movement of a spacecraft in space without thrust from the engines.
free-for-all *n.* a free fight, unrestricted discussion, etc.
free-form *attrib.adj.* of an irregular shape or structure.
free·hand /frée̍hand/ *adj. & adv.* • *adj.* (of a drawing or plan, etc.) done by hand without special instruments. • *adv.* in a freehand manner.
free hand *n.* freedom to act at one's own discretion (see also FREEHAND).
free-hand·ed *adj.* generous. □□ **free-hand·ed·ly** *adv.* **free-hand·ed·ness** *n.*
free·hold /frée̍hōld/ *n. & adj.* • *n.* **1** tenure of land or property in fee simple or fee tail or for life. **2** esp. *Brit.* land or property or an office held by such tenure. • *adj.* held by or having the status of freehold. □□ **free·hold·er** *n.*
free·lance /frée̍lans/ *n., v., & adv.* • *n.* **1** (also **free·lanc·er**) a person, usu. self-employed, offering services on a temporary basis. **2** (*attrib.*) earn one's living in such a way (*a freelance editor*). • *v.intr.* act as a freelance. • *adv.* as a freelance.
free·load·er /frée̍lōdər/ *n. sl.* a person who eats, drinks, or lives at others' expense; a sponger. □□ **free·load** /–lṓd/ *v.intr.*
free love *n.* sexual relations according to choice and unrestricted by marriage.
free·man /frée̍mən/ *n.* (*pl.* **-men**) **1** a person who has the freedom of a city, company, etc. **2** a person who is not a slave.
free mar·ket *n.* a market in which prices are determined by unrestricted competition.
Free·ma·son /frée̍maysən/ *n.* a member of an international fraternity for mutual help, with elaborate secret rituals. □□ **Free·mason·ry** /frée̍maysənree/ *n.*
fre·er *compar.* of FREE.
free rad·i·cal *n. Chem.* an unchanged atom or group of atoms with one or more unpaired electrons.
free-range *adj.* (of hens, etc.) kept in natural conditions with freedom of movement.
free·si·a /fréezhə, –zeeə/ *n.* any bulbous plant of the genus *Freesia*, native to Africa, having fragrant flowers.
free speech *n.* the right to express opinions freely.
free-spok·en *adj.* speaking candidly; not concealing one's opinions.
fre·est *superl.* of FREE.
free-stand·ing *adj.* not supported by another structure.
free·style /frée̍stīl/ *adj. & n.* • *adj.* (of a contest) in which all styles are allowed, esp.: **1** *Swimming* in which any stroke may be used. **2** *Wrestling* with few restrictions on the holds permitted. • *n.* = CRAWL *n.* 3.
free·think·er /frée̍thíngkər/ *n.* a person who rejects dogma or authority. □□ **free·think·ing** *n. & adj.*
free throw *n. Basketball* an unhindered shot at the basket made by a player after a foul has been called against the opposing team.
free verse *n.* verse without a fixed metrical pattern.
free·ware /frée̍wair/ *n. Computing* software that is distributed free and without technical support to users.
free·way /frée̍way/ *n.* **1** an express highway, esp. with controlled access. **2** a toll-free highway.
free·wheel /frée̍weel/ *v.intr.* **1** move freely with gears disengaged, esp. downhill. **2** move or act without constraint or effort.
free will *n.* **1** the power of acting without the constraint of necessity or fate. **2** the ability to act at one's own discretion (*of my own free will*).
free world *n.* the noncommunist countries, esp. during the Cold War.
freeze /freez/ *v. & n.* • *v.* (*past* **froze** /frōz/; *past part.* **fro·zen** /frṓzən/) **1** *tr. & intr.* **a** turn or be turned into ice or another solid by cold. **b** (often foll. by *over, up*) make or become rigid as a result of the cold. **2** *intr.* be or feel very cold. **3** *tr. & intr.* cover or become covered with ice. **4** *intr.* (foll. by *to, together*) adhere by frost. **5** *tr.* preserve (food) by refrigeration below the freezing point. **6** *tr. & intr.* **a** make or become motionless or powerless through fear, etc. **b** react or cause to react with sudden detachment. **7** *tr.* stiffen or harden, injure or kill, by chilling (*frozen to death*). **8** *tr.* make (assets, etc.) unrealizable. **9** *tr.* fix or stabilize (prices, etc.) at a certain level. **10** *tr.* arrest (an action) at a stage of development. **11** *tr.* = FREEZE-FRAME *v.* • *n.* **1** a state of frost; a period of very cold weather. **2** the fixing or stabilization of prices, etc. **3** = FREEZE-FRAME *n.* □ **freeze out** *colloq.* exclude by competition or boycott, etc. **freeze up** obstruct or be obstructed by the formation of ice. □□ **freez·a·ble** *adj.* **fro·zen·ly** *adv.*

freeze Old English *frēosan* (in the phrase *hit frēoseth* 'it is freezing, it is so cold that water turns to ice'), of Germanic origin; related to Dutch *vriezen* and German *frieren*, from an Indo-European root shared by Latin *pruina* 'hoar frost' and FROST.

freeze-dry *v.tr.* (**-dries, -dried**) freeze and dry by the sublimation of ice in a high vacuum.
freeze-frame *n. & v.* • *n.* (also *attrib.*) the facility of stopping a videotape, etc. in order to view a motionless image; a film shot in which movement is arrested by repetition of a frame. • *v.tr.* use freeze-frame on (an image, etc.).
freez·er /frée̍zər/ *n.* a refrigerated compartment, cabinet, or room for preserving food at very low temperatures; = DEEP FREEZE *n.* 1.
freeze-up *n.* a period or conditions of extreme cold.
freez·ing point *n.* the temperature at which a liquid, esp. water, freezes.
freight /frayt/ *n. & v.* • *n.* **1** the transport of goods in containers or by air or land or, esp. *Brit.*, water. **2** goods transported; cargo. **3** a charge for transportation of goods. **4** the lease of a ship or aircraft for transporting goods. **5** a load or burden. • *v.tr.* **1** transport (goods) as freight. **2** load with freight. **3** lease out (a ship) for the carriage of goods and passengers.
freight car *n.* a railroad car used for transporting freight.
freight·er /fráytər/ *n.* **1** a ship or aircraft designed to carry freight. **2** a person who loads or charters and loads a ship. **3** a person who consigns goods for carriage inland. **4** a person whose business is to receive and forward freight.
French /french/ *adj. & n.* • *adj.* **1** of or relating to France or its people or language. **2** having the characteristics attributed to the French people. • *n.* **1** the language of France, also used in Belgium, Switzerland, Canada, and elsewhere. **2** (prec. by *the*; treated as *pl.*) the people of France. **3** *colloq.* bad language (*excuse my French*). **4** *colloq.* dry vermouth (*gin and French*). □□ **French·i·fy** /frénchifī/ *v.tr.* (**-fies, -fied**) **French·ness** *n.*
French bread *n.* white bread in a long crisp loaf.
French Ca·na·di·an *n. & adj.* • *n.* a Canadian whose principal language is French. • *adj.* of or relating to French-speaking Canadians.

French cuff *n.* a double cuff formed by turning back a long cuff and fastening it.
French curve *n.* a template used to draw curved lines.
French door *n.* a door with glass panes throughout its length.
French dress·ing *n.* **1** a sweet, creamy, orange salad dressing prepared from oil, tomato purée, and spices. **2** a salad dressing of vinegar and oil, and seasonings.
French fries *n.pl.* (also **French fried potatoes**) potatoes cut into strips and deep-fried.
French horn *n.* a coiled brass wind instrument with a wide bell.

French horn

French kiss *n.* a kiss with one partner's tongue inserted in the other's mouth.
French·man /frénchmən/ *n.* (*pl.* **-men**) a man who is French by birth or descent.
French toast *n.* bread dipped in egg and milk and sautéed.
French·wom·an /frénchwŏŏmən/ *n.* (*pl.* **-women**) a woman who is French by birth or descent.
fre·net·ic /frənétik/ *adj.* **1** frantic; frenzied. **2** fanatic. □□ **fre·net·i·cal·ly** *adv.*
fren·zy /frénzee/ *n.* & *v.* •*n.* (*pl.* **-zies**) **1** mental derangement; wild excitement or agitation. **2** delirious fury. •*v.tr.* (**-zies, -zied**) (usu. as **frenzied** *adj.*) drive to frenzy; infuriate. □□ **fren·zied·ly** *adv.*
Fre·on /fréeon/ *n.* *Trademark* a halogenated hydrocarbon containing fluorine, chlorine, and sometimes bromine, used in refrigerants, etc. (see also CFC).
fre·quen·cy /fréekwənsee/ *n.* (*pl.* **-cies**) **1** commonness of occurrence. **2 a** frequent occurrence. **b** the process of being repeated at short intervals. **3** *Physics* the rate of recurrence of a vibration, cycle, etc.; the number of repetitions in a given time.
fre·quen·cy mod·u·la·tion *n.* *Electronics* a modulation in which the frequency of the carrier wave is varied. ¶ Abbr.: **FM**.
fre·quent /fréekwənt/ *adj.* & *v.* •*adj.* **1** occurring often or in close succession. **2** habitual (*a frequent caller*). **3** found at short distances apart; abundant. **4** (of the pulse) rapid. •*v.tr.* /also frikwént/ attend or go to habitually. □□ **fre·quen·ta·tion** *n.* **fre·quent·er** /frikwéntər/ *n.* **fre·quent·ly** /fréekwəntlee/ *adv.*
fre·quen·ta·tive /frikwéntətiv/ *adj.* & *n.* *Gram.* •*adj.* expressing frequent repetition or intensity of action. •*n.* a verb or verbal form or conjugation expressing this (e.g., *chatter, twinkle*).
fres·co /fréskō/ *n.* (*pl.* **-cos** or **-coes**) **1** a painting done in watercolor on a wall or ceiling while the plaster is still wet. **2** this method of painting (esp. *in fresco*). □□ **fres·coed** *adj.*
fresh /fresh/ *adj., adv.,* & *n.* •*adj.* **1** newly made or obtained (*fresh sandwiches*). **2 a** other; different; not previously known or used (*start a fresh page*). **b** additional (*fresh supplies*). **3** (foll. by *from*) lately arrived from. **4** not stale or faded (*fresh memories*). **5** (of food) not preserved by salting, freezing, etc. **6** not salty (*fresh water*). **7 a** pure; untainted; invigorating (*fresh air*). **b** bright and pure in color (*a fresh complexion*). **8** (of the wind) brisk. **9** alert; vigorous (*never felt fresher*). **10** *colloq.* **a** cheeky. **b** amorously impudent. **11** young and inexperienced. •*adv.* recently (esp. in *comb.*: *fresh-baked*). •*n.* the fresh part of the day, etc. (*in the fresh of the morning*). □□ **fresh·ly** *adv.* **fresh·ness** *n.*
fresh·en /fréshən/ *v.* **1** *tr.* & *intr.* make or become fresh or fresher. **2** *intr.* & *tr.* (foll. by *up*) **a** wash, change one's clothes, etc. **b** revive; refresh; renew.
fresh·et /fréshit/ *n.* **1** a rush of fresh water flowing into the sea. **2** the flood of a river.
fresh·man /fréshmən/ *n.* (*pl.* **-men**) a first-year student at a high school, college, or university.
fresh·wa·ter /fréshwawtər, –wotər/ *adj.* **1** of or found in fresh water; not of the sea. **2** (esp. of a school or college) rustic or provincial.
fret[1] /fret/ *v.* (**fretted, fretting**) **1** *intr.* **a** be greatly and visibly worried or distressed. **b** be irritated or resentful. **2** *tr.* **a** cause anxiety or distress to. **b** irritate; annoy. **3** *tr.* wear or consume by gnawing or rubbing.
fret[2] /fret/ *n.* & *v.* •*n.* an ornamental pattern made of continuous combinations of straight lines joined usu. at right angles. •*v.tr.* (**fretted, fretting**) **1** embellish or decorate with a fret. **2** adorn (esp. a ceiling) with carved or embossed work.
fret[3] /fret/ *n.* each of a sequence of bars or ridges on the fingerboard of some stringed musical instruments (esp. the guitar) fixing the positions of the fingers to produce the desired notes. □□ **fret·less** *adj.*

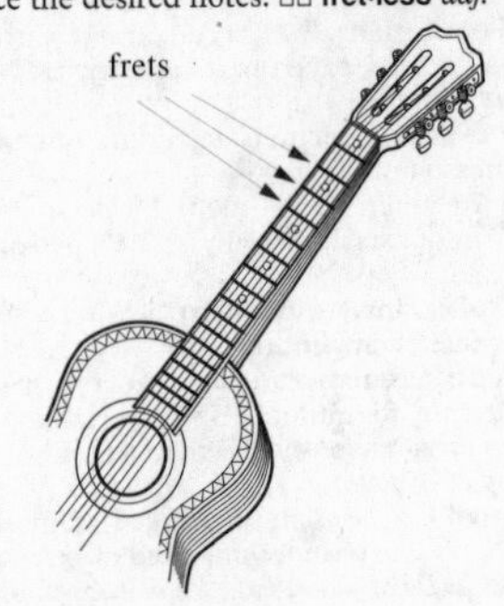

frets[3]

fret·ful /frétfŏŏl/ *adj.* visibly anxious or distressed. □□ **fret·ful·ly** *adv.* **fret·ful·ness** *n.*
fret·saw /frétsaw/ *n.* a saw consisting of a narrow blade stretched on a frame, for cutting thin wood in patterns.
fret·work /frétwərk/ *n.* ornamental work in wood, done with a fretsaw.
Freud·i·an /fróydeeən/ *adj.* & *n.* *Psychol.* •*adj.* of or relating to the Austrian psychologist Sigmund Freud (d. 1939) or his methods of psychoanalysis. •*n.* a follower of Freud or his methods. □□ **Freud·i·an·ism** *n.*
Freud·i·an slip *n.* an unintentional error regarded as revealing subconscious feelings.
Fri. *abbr.* Friday.
fri·a·ble /fríəbəl/ *adj.* easily crumbled. □□ **fri·a·bil·i·ty** *n.* **fri·a·ble·ness** *n.*
fri·ar /fríər/ *n.* a member of certain religious orders of men, esp. the four mendicant orders (Augustinians, Carmelites, Dominicans, and Franciscans).
fric·as·see /fríkəsée/ *n.* & *v.* •*n.* a dish of stewed or fried pieces of meat served in a thick white sauce. •*v.tr.* (**fricassees, fricasseed**) make a fricassee of.
fric·a·tive /fríkətiv/ *adj.* & *n.* *Phonet.* •*adj.* made by the friction of breath in a narrow opening. •*n.* a consonant made in this way, e.g., *f* and *th*.
fric·tion /fríkshən/ *n.* **1** the action of one object rubbing against another. **2** the resistance an object

encounters in moving over another. **3** a clash of wills, temperaments, or opinions. **4** (in *comb.*) of devices that transmit motion by frictional contact (*friction clutch*; *friction disk*). ▫▫ **fric·tion·al** *adj.* **fric·tion·less** *adj.*

Fri·day /fríday, –dee/ *n. & adv.* •*n.* the sixth day of the week, following Thursday. •*adv. colloq.* **1** on Friday. **2** (**Fridays**) on Fridays; each Friday.

fridge /frij/ *n. colloq.* = REFRIGERATOR.

friend /frend/ *n. & v.* •*n.* **1** a person with whom one enjoys mutual affection and regard (usu. exclusive of sexual or family bonds). **2** a sympathizer, helper, or patron (*no friend to virtue*). **3** a person who is not an enemy or who is on the same side (*friend or foe?*). **4 a** a person already mentioned (*my friend at the next table*). **b** a person known by sight. **c** used as a polite or ironic form of address. **5** (usu. in *pl.*) a regular contributor to an institution. **6** (**Friend**) a member of the Society of Friends; a Quaker. **7** a helpful thing or quality. •*v.tr.* befriend; help. ▫ **be friends with** be friendly with. ▫▫ **friend·ed** *adj.* **friend·less** *adj.*

friend·ly /fréndlee/ *adj. & adv.* •*adj.* (**friendlier, friendliest**) **1** acting as or like a friend; well-disposed; kindly. **2 a** (often foll. by *with*) on amicable terms. **b** not hostile. **3** characteristic of friends; showing or prompted by kindness. **4** favorably disposed; ready to approve or help. **5 a** (of a thing) serviceable; convenient; opportune. **b** = USER-FRIENDLY. •*adv.* in a friendly manner. ▫▫ **friend·li·ly** *adv.* **friend·li·ness** *n.*

friend·ly fire *n. Mil.* fire coming from one's own side, esp. as the cause of accidental injury to one's forces.

friend·ship /fréndship/ *n.* **1** being friends; the relationship between friends. **2** a friendly disposition felt or shown.

fri·er var. of FRYER.

frieze /freez/ *n.* **1** *Archit.* the part of an entablature between the architrave and the cornice. **2** *Archit.* a horizontal band of sculpture filling this. **3** a band of decoration elsewhere, esp. along a wall near the ceiling.

frig /frig/ *v. & n. coarse sl.* •*v.* (**frigged, frigging**) **1 a** *tr. & intr.* have sexual intercourse (with). **b** masturbate. **2** *tr.* (usu. as an exclamation) = FUCK *v.* 3. **3** *intr.* (foll. by *around, about*) mess around; fool around. **4** *intr.* (foll. by *off*) go away. •*n.* an act of frigging.

frig·ate /frígit/ *n.* **1 a** a naval vessel between a destroyer and a cruiser in size. **b** *Brit.* a similar ship between a corvette and a destroyer in size. **2** *hist.* a warship.

frig·ate bird *n.* any marine bird of the family Fregatidae, found in tropical seas, with a wide wingspan and deeply forked tail.

fright /frīt/ *n. & v.* •*n.* **1 a** sudden or extreme fear. **b** an instance of this (*gave me a fright*). **2** a person or thing looking grotesque or ridiculous. •*v.tr.* frighten.

fright·en /frítən/ *v.* **1** *tr.* fill with fright; terrify. **2** *tr.* (foll. by *away, off, out of, into*) drive or force by fright. **3** *intr.* become frightened (*I frighten easily*). ▫▫ **fright·en·ing** *adj.* **fright·en·ing·ly** *adv.*

fright·en·er /frít'nər/ *n.* a person or thing that frightens.

fright·ful /frítfo͝ol/ *adj.* **1 a** dreadful; shocking. **b** ugly. **2** *colloq.* extremely bad (*a frightful idea*). **3** *colloq.* very great; extreme. ▫▫ **fright·ful·ly** *adv.* **fright·ful·ness** *n.*

frig·id /fríjid/ *adj.* **1 a** lacking friendliness or enthusiasm. **b** dull; insipid. **c** chilling; depressing. **2** (of a woman) sexually unresponsive. **3** (esp. of climate or air) cold. ▫▫ **fri·gid·i·ty** /–jíditee/ *n.* **fri·gid·ly** *adv.* **fri·gid·ness** *n.*

fri·jo·les /freehṓlays/ *n.pl.* beans.

frill /fril/ *n. & v.* •*n.* **1 a** a strip of material with one side gathered or pleated and the other left loose with a fluted appearance, used as an ornamental edging. **b** a similar paper ornament on a lamb chop, etc. **c** a natural fringe of feathers, hair, etc., on esp. a bird or a plant. **2** (in *pl.*) **a** unnecessary embellishments or accomplishments. **b** airs; affectation (*put on frills*). •*v.tr.* **1** decorate with a frill. **2** form into a frill. ▫▫ **frilled** *adj.* **frill·y** /frílee/ *adj.* (**frillier, frilliest**). **frill·i·ness** *n.*

frilled liz·ard *n.* (also **frill-necked lizard**) a large N. Australian lizard, *Chlamydosaurus kingii*, with an erectile membrane round the neck.

fringe /frinj/ *n. & v.* •*n.* **1 a** an ornamental bordering of threads left loose or formed into tassels. **b** such a bordering made separately. **c** any border or edging. **2 a** *Brit.* a portion of the front hair hanging over the forehead; bangs. **b** a natural border of hair, etc., in an animal or plant. **3** an outer edge or margin; the outer limit of an area, population, etc. (often *attrib.*: *fringe theater*). **4** a thing, part, or area of minor importance. **5 a** a band of contrasting brightness or darkness produced by diffraction or interference of light. **b** a strip of false color in an optical image. **6** a fringe benefit. •*v.tr.* **1** adorn or encircle with a fringe. **2** serve as a fringe to. ▫▫ **fringe·less** *adj.*

fringe ben·e·fit *n.* an employee's benefit supplementing a money wage or salary.

frip·per·y /frípəree/ *n.* (*pl.* **-ies**) **1** showy, tawdry, or unnecessary ornament, esp. in dress. **2** empty display in literary style, etc. **3 a** knickknacks; trifles. **b** a knickknack or trifle.

Fris·bee /frízbee/ *n. Trademark* a molded plastic disk for skimmimg through the air as an outdoor game.

frisk /frisk/ *v. & n.* •*v.* **1** *intr.* leap or skip playfully. **2** *tr. sl.* feel over or search (a person) for a weapon, etc. (usu. rapidly). •*n.* **1** a playful leap or skip. **2** *sl.* the frisking of a person.

frisk·y /fráskee/ *adj.* (**friskier, friskiest**) lively; playful. ▫▫ **frisk·i·ly** *adv.* **frisk·i·ness** *n.*

frit·il·lar·y /frít'leree/ *n.* (*pl.* **-ies**) **1** any liliaceous plant of the genus *Fritillaria*, having pendent bell-like flowers. **2** any of various butterflies, esp. of the genus *Argynnis*, having reddish-brown wings checkered with black.

frit·ter[1] /frítər/ *v.tr.* (usu. foll. by *away*) waste (money, energy, etc.) triflingly.

frit·ter[2] /frítər/ *n.* a piece of fruit, meat, etc., coated in batter and deep-fried (*apple fritter*).

fritz /frits/ *n.* ▫ **on the fritz** *sl.* out of order; unsatisfactory.

friv·o·lous /frívələs/ *adj.* **1** not having any serious purpose or value (*frivolous lawsuits*). **2** (of a person) lacking seriousness; given to trifling; silly. ▫▫ **fri·vol·i·ty** /–vólitee/ *n.* (*pl.* **·ties**). **friv·o·lous·ly** *adv.* **friv·o·lous·ness** *n.*

frizz /friz/ *v. & n.* •*v.tr.* form (hair, etc.) into a mass of small curls. •*n.* **1 a** frizzed hair. **b** a row of curls. **2** a frizzed state. ▫▫ **friz·zi·ness** *n.* **friz·zy** /frízee/ *adj.* (**frizzier, frizziest**)

friz·zle[1] /frízəl/ *v.intr. & tr.* **1** fry, toast, or grill, with a sputtering noise. **2** (often foll. by *up*) burn or shrivel.

friz·zle[2] /frízəl/ *v. & n.* •*v.* **1** *tr.* form (hair) into tight curls. **2** *intr.* (often foll. by *up*) (of hair, etc.) curl tightly. •*n.* frizzled hair.

fro /frō/ *adv.* back (now only in *to and fro*: see TO).

frock /frok/ *n.* **1** esp. *Brit.* a woman's or girl's dress. **2 a** a monk's or priest's long gown with loose sleeves. **b** priestly office. **3** a smock.

frog[1] /frawg, frog/ *n.* **1** any of various small amphibians of the order Anura, having a tailless smooth-skinned body with legs developed for jumping. **2** (**Frog**) *sl. offens.* a French person. **3** a hollow in the top face of a brick for holding the mortar. **4** the nut of a violin bow, etc. □ **frog in the** (or **one's**) **throat** *colloq.* hoarseness. □□ **frog·gy** *adj.*

frog[2] /frawg, frog/ *n.* an elastic horny substance in the sole of a horse's foot.

frog[3] /frawg, frog/ *n.* **1** an ornamental coat fastening of a spindle-shaped button and loop. **2** an attachment to a belt to support a sword, bayonet, etc. □□ **frogged** *adj.* **frog·ging** *n.*

frog·man /fráwgman, fróg–, –mən/ *n.* (*pl.* **-men**) a person equipped with a rubber suit, flippers, and an oxygen supply for underwater swimming.

frog·march /fráwgmaarch, fróg–/ *v.* & *n.* •*v.tr.* **1** hustle (a person) forward holding and pinning the arms from behind. **2** carry (a person) in a frogmarch. •*n.* the carrying of a person face downward by four others each holding a limb.

frol·ic /frólik/ *v.* & *n.* •*v.intr.* (**frolicked, frolicking**) play about cheerfully; gambol. •*n.* **1** cheerful play. **2** a prank. **3** a merry party. **4** an outburst of gaiety. **5** merriment. □□ **frol·ick·er** *n.*

frol·ic·some /fróliksəm/ *adj.* merry; playful. □□ **frol·ic·some·ly** *adv.* **frol·ic·some·ness** *n.*

from /frum, from, frəm/ *prep.* expressing separation or origin, followed by: **1** a person, place, time, etc., that is the starting point of motion or action, or of extent in place or time (*rain comes from the clouds*; *dinner is served from 8*). **2** a place, object, etc., whose distance or remoteness is reckoned (*ten miles from Los Angeles*; *apart from its moral aspect*). **3 a** a source (*a man from Idaho*). **b** a giver or sender (*presents from their parents*). **4 a** a thing or person avoided, escaped, lost, etc. (*released him from prison*). **b** a person or thing deprived (*took his gun from him*). **5** a reason, cause, or motive (*died from fatigue*). **6** a thing distinguished or unlike (*know black from white*). **7** a lower limit (*tickets from $5*). **8** a state changed for another (*raised the penalty from a fine to imprisonment*). **9** an adverb or preposition of time or place (*from long ago*; *from under the bed*). **10** the position of a person who observes or considers (*saw it from the roof*). **11** a model (*painted it from nature*). □ **from now on** henceforward. **from time to time** occasionally.

frond /frond/ *n. Bot.* a large usu. divided leaf in esp. ferns and palms.

front /frunt/ *n., adj., & v.* •*n.* **1** the side or part normally nearer or toward the spectator or the direction of motion (*the front of the car*). **2** any face of a building, esp. that of the main entrance. **3** *Mil.* **a** the foremost line or part of an army, etc. **b** line of battle. **c** the part of the ground toward a real or imaginary enemy. **d** a scene of actual fighting. **e** the direction in which a formed line faces. **4 a** a sector of activity regarded as resembling a military front. **b** an organized political group. **5 a** demeanor; bearing. **b** outward appearance. **6** a forward or conspicuous position (*come to the front*). **7 a** a bluff. **b** a pretext. **8** a person, etc., serving to cover subversive or illegal activities. **9** *Meteorol.* the forward edge of an advancing mass of cold or warm air. **10** (prec. by *the*) the audience or auditorium of a theater. **11** a face. **12 a** the breast of a man's shirt. **b** a false shirtfront. **13** impudence. •*attrib.adj.* **1** of the front. **2** situated in front. •*v.* **1** *intr.* (foll. by *on, to, toward, upon*) have the front facing or directed. **2** *intr.* (foll. by *for*) *sl.* act as a front or cover for. **3** *tr.* furnish with a front (*fronted with stone*). **4** *tr.* lead (a band). **5** *tr.* **a** stand opposite to; front toward. **b** have its front on the side of (a street, etc.). □ **in front 1** in an advanced position. **2** facing the spectator. **in front of 1** ahead of. **2** in the presence of; confronting. □□ **front·ward** *adj. & adv.* **front·wards** *adv.*

front·age /frúntij/ *n.* **1** the front of a building. **2 a** land abutting on a street or on water. **b** the land between the front of a building and the road. **3** extent of front (*a store with little frontage*).

fron·tal /frúnt'l/ *adj.* **1 a** of, at, or on the front (*a frontal attack*). **b** of the front as seen by an onlooker (*a frontal view*). **2** of the forehead (*frontal bone*). □□ **front·al·ly** *adv.*

fron·tier /frúntéer/ *n.* **1 a** the border between two countries. **b** the district on each side of this. **2** the limits of attainment or knowledge in a subject. **3** the borders between settled and unsettled country.

fron·tiers·man /frúntéerzmən/ *n.* (*pl.* **-men**) a person living in the region of a frontier, esp. between settled and unsettled country.

fron·tis·piece /frúntispees/ *n.* an illustration facing the title page of a book or of one of its divisions.

front·line /frúntlīn/ *adj.* **1** *Mil.* relating to or located at a front line. **2** relating to the forefront of any activity.

front line *n. Mil.* = FRONT *n.* 3.

front man *n.* a person acting as a front or cover.

front of·fice *n.* **1** the executives or executive branch of an organization. **2** a main office.

fron·ton /frónton, –tón/ *n.* **1** a jai alai court. **2** a pediment.

front run·ner *n.* **1** the contestant most likely to succeed. **2** an athlete or horse running best when in the lead.

front-wheel drive *n.* an automobile drive system in which power is transmitted from the engine to the front wheels.

frost /frawst, frost/ *n.* & *v.* •*n.* **1 a** a deposit of white ice crystals formed on the gound or other surfaces when the temperature falls below freezing. **b** a consistent temperature below freezing point causing frost to form. **2** a chilling or dispiriting atmosphere. •*v.* **1** *intr.* (usu. foll. by *over, up*) become covered with frost. **2** *tr.* **a** cover with or as if with frost, powder, etc. **b** injure (a plant, etc.) with frost. **3** *tr.* give a roughened or finely granulated surface to (*frosted glass*). **4** *tr.* cover or decorate (a cake, etc.) with icing. □□ **frost·less** *adj.*

frost·bite /fráwstbīt, fróst–/ *n.* injury to body tissues, esp. the nose, fingers, or toes, due to freezing.

frost heave *n. Geol.* an upthrust of soil or pavement caused by the freezing of moist soil underneath.

frost·ing /fráwsting, fróst–/ *n.* **1** icing. **2** a rough surface on glass, etc.

frost·y /frawstee, fróstee/ *adj.* (**frostier, frostiest**) **1** cold with frost. **2** covered with or as with hoarfrost. **3** unfriendly in manner. □□ **frost·i·ly** *adv.* **frost·i·ness** *n.*

froth /frawth, froth/ *n.* & *v.* •*n.* **1 a** a collection of small bubbles; foam. **b** scum. **2 a** idle talk or ideas. **b** anything unsubstantial or of little worth. •*v.* **1** *intr.* emit or gather froth. **2** *tr.* cause (beer, etc.) to foam. □□ **froth·i·ly** *adv.* **froth·i·ness** *n.* **froth·y** *adj.* (**frothier, frothiest**).

frou·frou /fróofróo/ *n.* **1** a rustling, esp. of a dress. **2** a frilly ornamentation.

fro·ward /fróərd/ *adj. archaic* perverse; difficult to deal with. □□ **fro·ward·ly** *adv.* **fro·ward·ness** *n.*

frown /frown/ *v.* & *n.* •*v.* **1** *intr.* wrinkle one's brows, esp. in displeasure or deep thought. **2** *intr.* (foll. by *at, on, upon*) express disapproval. **3** *intr.* (of a thing) present a gloomy aspect. **4** *tr.* compel with a frown (*frowned them into silence*). **5** *tr.* express (defiance, etc.) with a frown. •*n.* **1** an action of frowning. **2** a look expressing severity, disapproval, or deep thought. □□ **frown·ing·ly** *adv.*

frowz·y /frówzee/ *adj.* (also **frows·y**) (**-ier, -iest**) **1** fusty. **2** slatternly; dingy. □□ **frowz·i·ness** *n.*

froze *past* of FREEZE.

fro·zen *past part.* of FREEZE.

fruc·tose /frúktōs, fróok–/ *n. Chem.* a simple sugar found in honey and fruits. Also called LEVULOSE.

fru·gal /fróogəl/ *adj.* **1** (often foll. by *of*) sparing or economical, esp. as regards food. **2** sparingly used or supplied; meager; costing little. ▫▫ **fru·gal·i·ty** /–gálitee/ *n.* **fru·gal·ly** *adv.* **fru·gal·ness** *n.*

fruit /froot/ *n. & v.* • *n.* **1 a** the usu. sweet and fleshy edible product of a plant or tree, containing seed. **b** (in *sing.*) these in quantity (*eats fruit*). **2** the seed of a plant or tree with its covering, e.g., an acorn, pea pod, cherry, etc. **3** (usu. in *pl.*) vegetables, grains, etc., used for food (*fruits of the earth*). **4** (usu. in *pl.*) the result of action, etc. (*fruits of his labors*). **5** *derog. sl.* a male homosexual. **6** *Bibl.* an offspring (*the fruit of the womb*). • *v.intr. & tr.* bear or cause to bear fruit. ▫▫ **fruit·ed** *adj.* (also in *comb.*).

fruit bat *n.* any large bat of the suborder Megachiroptera, feeding on fruit.

fruit·cake /fróotkayk/ *n.* **1** a cake containing dried fruit. **2** *sl.* an eccentric or mad person.

fruit fly *n.* (*pl.* **flies**) any of various flies, esp. of the genus *Drosophila*, having larvae that feed on fruit.

fruit·ful /fróotfool/ *adj.* **1** producing much fruit. **2** successful; beneficial; remunerative. **3** producing offspring, esp. prolifically. ▫▫ **fruit·ful·ly** *adv.* **fruit·ful·ness** *n.*

fru·i·tion /froo-íshən/ *n.* **1 a** the bearing of fruit. **b** the production of results. **2** the realization of aims or hopes. **3** enjoyment.

fruit·less /fróotlis/ *adj.* **1** not bearing fruit. **2** useless; unsuccessful. ▫▫ **fruit·less·ly** *adv.* **fruit·less·ness** *n.*

fruit·y /fróotee/ *adj.* (**fruitier, fruitiest**) **1 a** of fruit. **b** tasting or smelling like fruit. **2** (of a voice, etc.) of full rich quality. **3** *sl.* crazy; silly. **4** *offens. sl.* homosexual. ▫▫ **fruit·i·ly** *adv.* **fruit·i·ness** *n.*

frump /frump/ *n.* a dowdy, unattractive, old-fashioned woman. ▫▫ **frump·ish** *adj.* **frump·ish·ly** *adv.*

frump·y /frúmpee/ *adj.* (**frumpier, frumpiest**) dowdy, unattractive, and old-fashioned. ▫▫ **frump·i·ly** *adv.* **frump·i·ness** *n.*

frus·trate /frústrayt/ *v.tr.* **1** make (efforts) ineffective. **2** prevent (a person) from achieving a purpose. **3** (as **frustrated** *adj.*) **a** discontented because unable to achieve one's desire. **b** sexually unfulfilled. **4** disappoint (a hope). ▫▫ **frus·trat·ed·ly** /–stráytidlee/ *adv.* **frus·trat·ing** *adj.* **frus·trat·ing·ly** *adv.* **frus·tra·tion** /–stráyshən/ *n.*

fry[1] /frī/ *v. & n.* • *v.* (**fries, fried**) **1** *tr. & intr.* cook or be cooked in hot fat. **2** *tr. & intr. sl.* electrocute or be electrocuted. **3** *tr.* (as **fried** *adj.*) *sl.* drunk. **4** *intr. colloq.* be very hot. • *n.* (*pl.* **fries**) **1** a French fry. **2** a social gathering serving fried food. **3** a dish of fried food, esp. meat. **4** various internal parts of animals usu. eaten fried (*lamb's fry*). ▫ **out of the frying pan into the fire** from a bad situation to a worse one.

fry[2] /frī/ *n.pl.* **1** young or newly hatched fish. **2** the young of other creatures produced in large numbers, e.g., bees or frogs.

fry·er /fríər/ *n.* (also **fri·er**) **1** a person who fries. **2** a vessel for frying, esp. deep frying. **3** a young chicken suitable for frying.

fry·ing pan *n.* (also **fry pan**) a shallow pan used in frying.

FSH *abbr.* follicle-stimulating hormone.

FSLIC *abbr.* Federal Savings and Loan Insurance Corporation.

f-stop /éf stop/ var. of F-NUMBER.

Ft. *abbr.* Fort.

ft. *abbr.* foot, feet.

FTC *abbr.* Federal Trade Commission.

fuch·sia /fyóoshə/ *n.* any shrub of the genus *Fuchsia*, with drooping red or purple or white flowers.

fuck /fuk/ *v., int., & n. coarse sl.* • *v.* **1** *tr. & intr.* have sexual intercourse (with). **2** *intr.* (foll. by *around, about*) mess around; fool around. **3** *tr.* (usu. as an exclam.) curse; confound (*fuck the thing!*). **4** *intr.* (as **fucking** *adj., adv.*) used as an intensive to express annoyance, etc. • *int.* expressing anger or annoyance. • *n.* **1 a** an act of sexual intercourse. **b** a partner in sexual intercourse. **2** the slightest amount (*don't give a fuck*). ▫ **fuck off** go away. **fuck up** make a mess of. ▶A highly taboo word.

fuck-up *coarse sl. n.* a mess or muddle.

fud·dle /fúd'l/ *v. & n.* • *v.* **1** *tr.* confuse or stupefy, esp. with alcoholic liquor. **2** *intr.* tipple; booze. • *n.* **1** confusion. **2** intoxication.

fud·dy-dud·dy /fúdeedúdee/ *adj. & n. sl.* • *adj.* old-fashioned or quaintly fussy. • *n.* (*pl.* **-dies**) a fuddy-duddy person.

fudge /fuj/ *n. & v.* • *n.* **1** a soft toffee-like candy made with milk, sugar, butter, etc. **2** nonsense. **3** a piece of dishonesty or faking. **4** a piece of late news inserted in a newspaper page. • *v.* **1** *tr.* put together in a makeshift or dishonest way; fake. **2** *tr.* deal with incompetently. **3** *intr.* practice such methods.

fueh·rer var. of FÜHRER.

fu·el /fyóoəl/ *n. & v.* • *n.* **1** material burned or used as a source of heat or power. **2** food as a source of energy. **3** material used as a source of nuclear energy. **4** anything that sustains or inflames emotion or passion. • *v.* **1** *tr.* supply with fuel. **2** *tr.* inflame (an argument, feeling, etc.) (*liquor fueled his anger*). **3** *intr.* take in or get fuel.

fu·el cell *n.* a cell producing an electric current direct from a chemical reaction.

fu·el in·jec·tion *n.* the direct introduction of fuel under pressure into the combustion units of an internal combustion engine.

-fuge /fyooj/ *comb. form* forming adjectives and nouns denoting expelling or dispelling (*febrifuge; vermifuge*).

fu·gi·tive /fyóojitiv/ *adj. & n.* • *adj.* **1** fleeing. **2** transient; fleeting. **3** (of literature) of passing interest; ephemeral. **4** flitting; shifting. • *n.* **1** (often foll. by *from*) a person who flees. **2** an exile or refugee.

fugue /fyoog/ *n.* **1** *Mus.* a contrapuntal composition in which a short melody or phrase is introduced by one part and successively taken up by others and developed by interweaving the parts. **2** *Psychol.* loss of awareness of one's identity, often coupled with flight from one's usual environment.

füh·rer /fyóorər/ *n.* (also **fueh·rer**) a leader, esp. a tyrannical one.

ful·crum /fóolkrəm, fúl–/ *n.* (*pl.* **fulcra** /–rə/ or **fulcrums**) the point against which a lever is placed to get a purchase or on which it turns or is supported.

ful·fill /foolfil/ *v.tr.* (**fulfilled, fulfilling**) **1** carry out (a prophecy or promise). **2** satisfy (a desire or prayer). **3 a** execute; obey (a command or law). **b** perform; carry out (a task). **4** comply with (conditions). **5** answer (a purpose). **6** bring to an end; finish; complete (a period or piece of work). ▫ **fulfill oneself** develop one's gifts and character to the full. ▫▫ **ful·fill·ment** *n.*

full[1] /fool/ *adj., adv. & n.* • *adj.* **1** (often foll. by *of*) holding all its limits will allow (*the bucket is full; full of water*). **2** having eaten to one's limits or satisfaction. **3** abundant; copious; satisfying (*led a full life; the book is very full on this point*). **4** (foll. by *of*) having or holding an abundance of; showing marked signs of (*full of interest; full of mistakes*). **5** (foll. by *of*) **a** engrossed in thinking about (*full of himself*). **b** unable to refrain from talking about (*full of the news*). **6** complete; perfect (*full membership; full daylight; waited a full hour*). **7 a** (of tone or color) deep and clear. **b** (of light) intense. **c** (of motion, etc.) vigorous (*a full pulse; at full gallop*). **8** plump; rounded (*a full figure*). **9** (of clothes) made of much material arranged in folds. **10** (of the heart, etc.) overcharged with emotion. • *adv.* **1** very (*you know full well*). **2** quite; fully (*full six miles*). **3** exactly (*hit him full on the nose*). **4** more than sufficiently (*full early*). • *n.* **1** height; acme (*season is past the full*). **2** the state or time of full moon. **3** the whole; the complete amount. □ **full speed** (or **steam**) **ahead!** an order to proceed at maximum speed or to pursue a course of action energetically. **in full 1** without abridgment. **2** to or for the full amount (*paid in full*). **in full swing** at the height of activity. **in full view** entirely visible. **to the full** to the utmost extent.

full[2] /fŏŏl/ *v.tr.* cleanse and thicken (cloth).

full•back /fŏŏlbak/ *n.* **1** an offensive player in the backfield in football. **2** a defensive player, or a position near the goal, in soccer, field hockey, etc.

full-blood•ed *adj.* **1** vigorous; hearty; sensual. **2** not hybrid. □□ **full-blood•ed•ly** *adv.* **full-blood•ed•ness** *n.*

full-blown *adj.* fully developed.

full-bod•ied *adj.* rich in quality, tone, etc.

full-court press *n. Basketball* a defensive strategy in which the team with the ball is closely guarded the full length of the court.

ful•ler /fŏŏlər/ *n.* a person who fulls cloth.

ful•ler's earth *n.* a type of clay used in fulling cloth.

full-fledged *adj.* mature.

full-fron•tal *adj.* **1** (of nudity or a nude figure) with full exposure at the front. **2** unrestrained; explicit.

full-grown *adj.* having reached maturity.

full house *n.* **1** a maximum attendance at a theater, etc. **2** *Poker* a hand with three of a kind and a pair.

full-length *adj.* **1** not shortened. **2** (of a mirror, portrait, etc.) showing the whole height of the human figure.

full moon *n.* **1** the moon with its whole disk illuminated. **2** the time when this occurs.

full•ness /fŏŏlnis/ *n.* **1** being full. **2** (of sound, color, etc.) richness; volume; body. **3** all that is contained (in the world, etc.). □ **the fullness of time** the appropriate or destined time.

full-scale *adj.* not reduced in size; complete.

full-time *adj.* occupying or using the whole of the available working time.

ful•ly /fŏŏlee/ *adv.* **1** completely; entirely (*am fully aware*). **2** no less or fewer than (*fully 60*).

ful•mi•nate /fúlminayt, fŏŏl–/ *v.intr.* **1** (often foll. by *against*) express censure loudly and forcefully. **2** explode violently; flash like lightning (*fulminating mercury*). **3** *Med.* (of a disease or symptom) develop suddenly. □□ **ful•mi•na•tion** /–náyshən/ *n.*

ful•some /fŏŏlsəm/ *adj.* **1** disgusting by excess of flattery, servility, or expressions of affection; excessive; cloying. **2** *disp.* copious. □□ **ful•some•ly** *adv.* **ful•some•ness** *n.*

▶The earliest recorded use of **fulsome**, in the 13th century, had the meaning 'abundant,' but in modern use this is held by many to be incorrect. The correct current meaning is 'disgusting because overdone; excessive.' The word is still often used to mean 'abundant; copious,' but this use can give rise to ambiguity in such expressions as *fulsome praise*.

fum•ble /fúmbəl/ *v. & n.* • *v.* **1** *intr.* (often foll. by *at, with, for, after*) use the hands awkwardly; grope about. **2** *tr.* **a** handle clumsily or nervously. **b** *Football* drop (the ball). • *n.* an act of fumbling. □□ **fum•bler** *n.* **fum•bling•ly** *adv.*

fume /fyŏŏm/ *n. & v.* • *n.* **1** (usu. in *pl.*) exuded gas or smoke or vapor, esp. when harmful or unpleasant. **2** a fit of anger (*in a fume*). • *v.* **1 a** *intr.* emit fumes. **b** *tr.* give off as fumes. **2** *intr.* (often foll. by *at*) be affected by (esp. suppressed) anger (*was fuming at their inefficiency*). **3** *tr.* **a** fumigate. **b** subject to fumes (to darken tints in oak, photographic film, etc.). □□ **fum•y** *adj.* (in sense 1 of *n.*).

fu•mi•gate /fyŏŏmigayt/ *v.tr.* **1** disinfect or purify with fumes. **2** apply fumes to. □□ **fu•mi•gant** /–gənt/ *n.* **fu•mi•ga•tion** /–gáyshən/ *n.* **fu•mi•ga•tor** *n.*

fun /fun/ *n. & adj.* • *n.* **1** amusement, esp. lively or playful. **2** a source of this. **3** (in full **fun and games**) exciting or amusing goings-on. • *adj. disp. colloq.* amusing; enjoyable (*a fun thing to do*). □ **for fun** (or **for the fun of it**) not for a serious purpose. **have fun** enjoy oneself. **in fun** as a joke; not seriously. **make fun of** tease; ridicule.

fun•board /fúnbawrd/ *n.* a type of windsurfing board that is less stable but faster than a standard board.

func•tion /fúngkshən/ *n. & v.* • *n.* **1 a** an activity proper to a person or institution. **b** a mode of action or activity by which a thing fulfills its purpose. **c** an official or professional duty. **2 a** a public ceremony or occasion. **b** a social gathering, esp. a large, formal, or important one. **3** *Math.* a variable quantity regarded in relation to another or others in terms of which it may be expressed or on which its value depends (*x is a function of y and z*). **4** a part of a program that corresponds to a single value. • *v.intr.* fulfill a function; operate; be in working order. □□ **func•tion•less** *adj.*

func•tion•al /fúngkshənəl/ *adj.* **1** of or serving a function. **2** designed or intended to be practical rather than attractive. **3** *Physiol.* **a** (esp. of disease) of or affecting only the functions of an organ, etc., not structural or organic. **b** (of mental disorder) having no discernible organic cause. **c** (of an organ) having a function, not functionless or rudimentary. **4** *Math.* of a function. □□ **func•tion•al•i•ty** /–nálitee/ *n.* **func•tion•al•ly** *adv.*

func•tion•al•ism /fúngkshənəlizəm/ *n.* belief in or stress on the practical application of a thing. □□ **func•tion•al•ist** *n.*

func•tion•ar•y /fúngkshəneree/ *n.* (*pl.* **-ies**) a person who has to perform official functions or duties; an official.

fund /fund/ *n. & v.* • *n.* **1** a permanent stock of something ready to be drawn upon (*a fund of knowledge*). **2** a stock of money, esp. one set apart for a purpose. **3** (in *pl.*) money resources. • *v.tr.* **1** provide with money. **2** convert (a floating debt) into a more or less permanent debt at fixed interest. **3** put into a fund.

fun•da•men•tal /fúndəmént'l/ *adj. & n.* • *adj.* of, affecting, or serving as a base or foundation; essential; primary (*the fundamental rules*). • *n.* (usu. in *pl.*) a fundamental principle. □□ **fun•da•men•tal•ly** *adv.*

fun•da•men•tal•ism /fúndəméntəlizəm/ *n.* **1** (also **Fun•da•men•tal•ism**) strict maintenance of traditional Protestant beliefs. **2** strict maintenance of ancient or fundamental doctrines of any religion, esp. Islam. □□ **fun•da•men•tal•ist** *n.*

fund-rais•er *n.* a person who seeks financial support for a cause, enterprise, etc. □□ **fund-raising** *n.*

fu•ner•al /fyŏŏnərəl/ *n. & adj.* • *n.* **1 a** the burial or cremation of a dead person with its ceremonies. **b** a burial or cremation procession. **c** a burial or cremation service. **2** *sl.* one's (usu. unpleasant) concern (*that's your funeral*). • *attrib.adj.* of or used, etc., at a funeral (*funeral oration*).

fu•ner•al par•lor *n.* (also **funeral home**) an establishment where the dead are prepared for burial or cremation.

fu•ner•ar•y /fyŏŏnəreree/ *adj.* of or used at a funeral or funerals.

fu•ne•re•al /fyŏŏnéereeəl/ *adj.* **1** of or appropriate to a funeral. **2** dismal; dark. □□ **fu•ne•re•al•ly** *adv.*

fun•gi *pl.* of FUNGUS.

fun•gi•cide /fúnjisīd, fúnggi–/ *n.* a fungus-destroying substance. □□ **fun•gi•cid•al** /–sīd'l/ *adj.*

fun·goid /fúnggoyd/ *adj. & n.* • *adj.* resembling a fungus in texture or in rapid growth. • *n.* a fungoid plant.

fun·gous /fúnggəs/ *adj.* **1** having the nature of a fungus. **2** springing up like a mushroom; transitory.

fun·gus /fúnggəs/ *n.* (*pl.* **fungi** /–gī, –jī/or **funguses**) **1** any of a group of unicellular, multicellular, or multinucleate nonphotosynthetic organisms feeding on organic matter, which include molds, yeast, mushrooms, and toadstools. **2** anything similar usu. growing suddenly and rapidly. **3** *Med.* a spongy morbid growth. ▫▫ **fun·gal** /fúnggəl/ *adj.* **fun·gi·form** /fúnjifawrm, fúnggi–/ *adj.* **fun·giv·or·ous** /funjívərəs, funggív–/ *adj.*

fu·nic·u·lar /fyoonikyələr, fə–/ *adj. & n.* • *adj.* **1** (of a railway, esp. on a mountainside) operating by cable with ascending and descending cars counterbalanced. **2** of a rope or its tension. • *n.* a funicular railway.

funk[1] /fungk/ *n.* fear; panic. ▫ **in a funk** dejected.

funk[2] /fungk/ *n. sl.* **1** funky music. **2** a strong smell.

funk·y /fúngkee/ *adj.* (**funkier, funkiest**) *sl.* **1** (esp. of jazz or rock music) earthy, bluesy, with a heavy rhythmical beat. **2** fashionable. **3** odd; unconventional. **4** having a strong smell. ▫▫ **funk·i·ly** *adv.* **funk·i·ness** *n.*

fun·nel /fúnəl/ *n. & v.* • *n.* **1** a tube or pipe widening at the top, for pouring liquid, powder, etc., into a small opening. **2** a metal chimney on a steam engine or ship. **3** something resembling a funnel in shape or use. • *v.tr. & intr.* (**funneled, funneling; funnelled, funnelling**) guide or move through or as through a funnel. ▫▫ **funnel·like** *adj.*

fun·ny /fúnee/ *adj. & n.* • *adj.* (**funnier, funniest**) **1** amusing; comical. **2** strange; perplexing; hard to account for. **3** *colloq.* slightly unwell, eccentric, etc. • *n.* (*pl.* **-nies**) (usu. in *pl.*) *colloq.* **1** a comic strip in a newspaper. **2** a joke. ▫▫ **fun·ni·ly** *adv.* **fun·ni·ness** *n.*

fun·ny bone *n.* the part of the elbow over which the ulnar nerve passes.

fun·ny busi·ness *n.* **1** *sl.* misbehavior or deception. **2** comic behavior; comedy.

fun·ny farm *n. sl.* a mental hospital.

fun·ny mon·ey *n. colloq.* **1** counterfeit money. **2** foreign currency. **3** inflated currency.

fur /fər/ *n. & v.* • *n.* **1 a** the short fine soft hair of certain animals, distinguished from the longer hair. **b** the skin of such an animal with the fur on it. **2 a** the coat of certain animals as material for making, trimming, or lining clothes. **b** a trimming or lining made of the dressed coat of such animals, or of material imitating this. **c** a garment made of or trimmed or lined with fur. **3 a** a coating formed on the tongue in sickness. **b** a crust adhering to a surface, e.g., a deposit from wine. • *v.* (**furred, furring**) **1** *tr.* (esp. as **furred** *adj.*) **a** line or trim (a garment) with fur. **b** provide (an animal) with fur. **c** clothe (a person) with fur. **d** coat (a tongue, the inside of a kettle, etc.) with fur. **2** *intr.* (often foll. by *up*) (of a kettle, etc.) become coated with fur. ▫ **make the fur fly** *colloq.* cause a disturbance; stir up trouble.

fur·be·low /fárbilō/ *n. & v.* • *n.* **1** a gathered strip or pleated border of a skirt or petticoat. **2** (in *pl.*) *derog.* showy ornaments. • *v.tr.* adorn with a furbelow or furbelows.

fur·bish /fárbish/ *v.tr.* (often foll. by *up*) **1** remove rust from; polish; burnish. **2** give a new look to; renovate; revive (something antiquated).

fur·cate /fárkayt/ *adj. & v.* • *adj.* also /fúrkət/ forked; branched. • *v.intr.* form a fork; divide. ▫▫ **fur·ca·tion** /–káyshən/ *n.*

fu·ri·ous /fyooreeəs/ *adj.* **1** extremely angry. **2** full of fury. **3** raging; violent; intense. ▫ **fast and furious** *adv.* **1** rapidly. **2** eagerly; uproariously. • *adj.* (of mirth, etc.) eager; uproarious. ▫▫ **fu·ri·ous·ly** *adv.*

furl /fərl/ *v.* **1** *tr.* roll up and secure (a sail, umbrella, flag, etc.). **2** *intr.* become furled. **3** *tr.* **a** close (a fan). **b** fold up (wings). **c** draw away (a curtain).

fur·long /fárlawng, –long/ *n.* an eighth of a mile, 220 yards.

fur·lough /fárlō/ *n. & v.* • *n.* leave of absence, esp. granted to a member of the services or to a missionary. • *v.* **1** *tr.* grant furlough to. **2** *intr.* spend furlough. **3** lay off.

fur·nace /fárnis/ *n.* **1** an enclosed structure for intense heating by fire. **2** a very hot place.

fur·nish /fárnish/ *v.tr.* **1** provide (a house, etc.) with all necessary contents, esp. movable furniture. **2** (foll. by *with*) cause to have possession or use of. **3** provide; afford; yield.

fur·nished /fárnisht/ *adj.* (of a house, etc.) rented with furniture.

fur·nish·er /fárnishər/ *n.* **1** a person who sells furniture. **2** a person who furnishes.

fur·nish·ings /fárnishingz/ *n.pl.* the furniture and utensils, etc., in a house, room, etc.

fur·ni·ture /fárnichər/ *n.* **1** the movable equipment of a house, room, etc., e.g., tables, chairs, and beds. **2** *Naut.* a ship's equipment. **3** accessories, e.g., the handles and lock of a door. ▫ **part of the furniture** *colloq.* a person or thing taken for granted.

fu·ror /fyoorawr, –ər/ *n.* **1** an uproar; an outbreak of fury. **2** a wave of enthusiastic admiration; a craze.

fur·ri·er /fáreeər/ *n.* a dealer in furs.

fur·row /fárō, fúr–/ *n. & v.* • *n.* **1** a narrow trench made by a plow. **2** a rut, groove, or deep wrinkle. **3** a ship's track. • *v.tr.* **1** plow. **2 a** make furrows, grooves, etc., in. **b** mark with wrinkles.

fur·ry /fáree, fúree/ *adj.* (**furrier, furriest**) **1** of or like fur. **2** covered with or wearing fur. ▫▫ **fur·ri·ness** *n.*

fur·ther /fárthər/ *adv., adj., & v.* • *adv.* **1** = FARTHER. **2** to a greater extent; more (*will inquire further*). **3** in addition (*I may add further*). • *adj.* **1** = FARTHER. **2** more; additional (*threats of further punishment*). • *v.tr.* promote; favor (a scheme, undertaking, movement, or cause). ▫ **till further notice** (or **orders**) to continue until explicitly changed. ▫▫ **fur·ther·most** *adj.*

▶See note at FARTHER.

fur·ther·ance /fárthərəns/ *n.* furthering or being furthered; the advancement of a scheme, etc.

fur·ther·more /fárthərmáwr/ *adv.* in addition; besides.

fur·thest var. of FARTHEST.

fur·tive /fártiv/ *adj.* **1** done by stealth; clandestine; meant to escape notice. **2** sly; stealthy. **3** stolen; taken secretly. **4** thievish. ▫▫ **fur·tive·ly** *adv.* **fur·tive·ness** *n.*

fu·ry /fyooree/ *n.* (*pl.* **-ries**) **1 a** wild and passionate anger. **b** a fit of rage (*in a blind fury*). **c** impetuosity in battle, etc. **2** violence of a storm, disease, etc. **3** (**Fury**) (usu. in *pl.*) (in Greek mythology) each of three goddesses sent from Tartarus to avenge crime. **4** an avenging spirit. **5** an angry or spiteful woman. ▫ **like fury** *colloq.* with great force or effect.

fuse[1] /fyooz/ *v. & n.* • *v.* **1** *tr. & intr.* melt with intense heat. **2** *tr. & intr.* blend or amalgamate into one whole by or as by melting. **3** *tr.* provide (a circuit, plug, etc.) with a fuse. **4** *Brit.* **a** *intr.* (of an appliance) cease to function when a fuse blows. **b** *tr.* cause (an appliance) to do this. • *n.* a device or component for protecting an electric circuit, containing a strip of wire of easily melted metal and placed in the circuit so as to break it by melting when an excessive current passes through.

fuse[2] /fyooz/ *n. & v.* (also **fuze**) • *n.* **1** a device for igniting a bomb or explosive charge, consisting of a tube or cord, etc., filled or saturated with combustible matter. **2** a component in a shell, mine, etc., designed to detonate an explosive charge. •*v.tr.* fit a fuse to. ▫▫ **fuse·less** *adj.*

fuse box *n.* a box housing the fuses for circuits in a building.

fu·se·lage /fyóosəlaázh, –lij, –zə–/ *n.* the body of an airplane.

fu·si·ble /fyóozibəl/ *adj.* that can be easily fused or melted.

fu·sil·ier /fyóozileér/ *n.* (also **fu·sil·eer**) *hist.* a soldier armed with a light musket.

fu·sil·lade /fyóosiláyd, –laád, –zi–/ *n.* **1 a** a continuous discharge of firearms. **b** a wholesale execution by this means. **2** a sustained outburst of criticism, etc.

fu·sion /fyóozhən/ *n.* **1** the act or an instance of fusing or melting. **2** a fused mass. **3** the blending of different things into one. **4** a coalition. **5** *Physics* = NUCLEAR FUSION.

fuss /fus/ *n.* & *v.* •*n.* **1** excited commotion; bustle. **2 a** excessive concern about a trivial thing. **b** abundance of petty detail. **3** a sustained protest or dispute. **4** a person who fusses. •*v. intr.* **1** make a fuss. **2** busy oneself restlessly with trivial things. **3** move fussily. ▫ **make a fuss** complain vigorously. **make a fuss over** treat (a person or animal) with great or excessive attention. ▫▫ **fuss·er** *n.*

fuss·budg·et /fúsbəjət/ *n.* a person who habitually frets over minor matters.

fuss·pot /fúspot/ *n. colloq.* a person given to fussing.

fuss·y /fúsee/ *adj.* (**fussier, fussiest**) **1** inclined to fuss. **2** full of unnecessary detail or decoration. **3** fastidious. ▫▫ **fuss·i·ly** *adv.* **fuss·i·ness** *n.*

fus·tian /fúschən/ *n.* & *adj.* •*n.* **1** thick twilled cotton cloth with a short nap, usu. dyed in dark colors. **2** bombast. •*adj.* **1** made of fustian. **2** bombastic. **3** worthless.

fus·ty /fústee/ *adj.* (**fustier, fustiest**) **1** stale-smelling; musty. **2** stuffy. **3** antiquated; old-fashioned. ▫▫ **fus·ti·ly** *adv.* **fus·ti·ness** *n.*

fu·tile /fyóot'l, –tīl/ *adj.* **1** useless; ineffectual. **2** frivolous. ▫▫ **fu·tile·ly** *adv.* **fu·til·i·ty** /–tílitee/ *n.*

fu·ton /fóoton/ *n.* **1** a Japanese quilted mattress rolled out on the floor for use as a bed. **2** a type of low wooden bed using this kind of mattress.

fu·ture /fyóochər/ *adj.* & *n.* •*adj.* **1 a** going or expected to happen or be or become (*his future career*). **b** that will be something specified (*my future wife*). **c** that will be after death (*a future life*). **2 a** of time to come (*future years*). **b** *Gram.* (of a tense or participle) describing an event yet to happen. •*n.* **1** time to come (*past, present, and future*). **2** what will happen in the future (*the future is uncertain*). **3** the future condition of a person, country, etc. **4** a prospect of success, etc. (*there's no future in it*). **5** *Gram.* the future tense. **6** (in *pl.*) *Stock Exch.* **a** goods and stocks sold for future delivery. **b** contracts for these. ▫ **for the future** from now onward. **in future** = *for the future.*

fu·ture per·fect *n. Gram.* a tense expressing expected completion in the future *will have done.*

fu·ture shock *n.* inability to cope with rapid progress.

fu·tur·ism /fyóochərizəm/ *n.* a movement in art, literature, music, etc., with violent departure from traditional forms so as to express movement and growth.

fu·tur·ist /fyóochərist/ *n.* (often *attrib.*) **1** an adherent of futurism. **2** a believer in human progress. **3** a student of the future. **4** *Theol.* one who believes that biblical prophecies, esp. those of the Apocalypse, have yet to be fulfilled.

fu·tur·is·tic /fyóochərístik/ *adj.* **1** suitable for the future; ultramodern. **2** of futurism. **3** relating to the future. ▫▫ **fu·tur·is·ti·cal·ly** *adv.*

fu·tu·ri·ty /fyootóoritee, –tyóor–, chóor–/ *n.* (*pl.* **-ties**) **1** future time. **2** (in *sing.* or *pl.*) future events.

fuze var. of FUSE².

fuzz /fuz/ *n.* **1** fluff. **2** fluffy or frizzled hair. **3** *sl.* **a** the police. **b** a policeman.

fuzz·y /fúzee/ *adj.* (**fuzzier, fuzziest**) **1 a** like fuzz. **b** fluffy. **c** frizzy. **2** blurred; indistinct. ▫▫ **fuzz·i·ly** *adv.* **fuzz·i·ness** *n.*

G

G[1] /jee/ *n.* (also **g**) (*pl.* **Gs** or **G's**) **1** the seventh letter of the alphabet. **2** *Mus.* the fifth note in the diatonic scale of C major.

G[2] *abbr.* **1** gauss. **2** giga-. **3** gravitational constant. **4** *sl.* = GRAND *n.* 2.

g *abbr.* (also **g.**) **1** gelding. **2** gram(s). **3** gravity.

GA *abbr.* Georgia (in official postal use).

Ga *symb. Chem.* the element gallium.

Ga. *abbr.* Georgia (US).

gab /gab/ *n. & v. colloq.* •*n.* talk; chatter. •*v.intr.* talk incessantly; chatter. □ **gift of gab** the facility of speaking eloquently.

gab·ar·dine /gábərdéen/ *n.* (also **gab·er·dine**) **1** a smooth durable twilled cloth esp. of worsted or cotton. **2** *Brit.* a garment made of this, esp. a raincoat.

gab·ble /gábəl/ *v. & n.* •*v.* **1** *intr.* talk volubly or inarticulately. **2** *tr.* utter too fast. •*n.* fast unintelligible talk. □□ **gab·bler** *n.*

gab·by /gábee/ *adj.* (**gabbier, gabbiest**) *colloq.* talkative.

gab·er·dine /gábərdéen/ *n.* var. of GABARDINE.

ga·bi·on /gáybeeən/ *n.* a cylindrical wicker or metal basket for filling with earth or stones, used in engineering or (formerly) in fortification. □□ **ga·bi·on·age** *n.*

ga·ble /gáybəl/ *n.* **1 a** the triangular upper part of a wall at the end of a ridged roof. **b** (in full **gable end**) a gable-topped wall. **2** a gable-shaped canopy over a window or door. □□ **ga·bled** *adj.* (also in *comb.*).

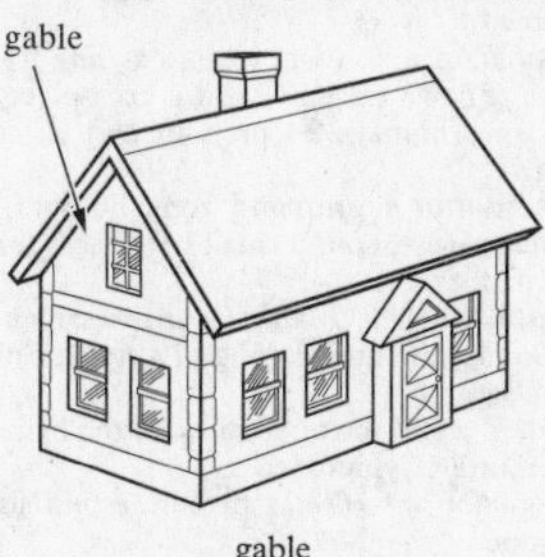

gable

gad[1] /gad/ *v.intr.* (**gadded, gadding**) (foll. by *about*) go about idly or in search of pleasure.

gad[2] /gad/ *int.* (also **by gad**) an expression of surprise or emphatic assertion (esp. a euphemism for 'God'.

gad·a·bout /gádəbowt/ *n.* a person who gads about; an idle pleasure seeker.

gad·fly /gádflī/ *n.* (*pl.* **-flies**) **1** a cattle-biting fly. **2** an irritating person.

gadg·et /gájit/ *n.* any small and usu. ingenious mechanical or electronic device or tool. □□ **gadg·et·ry** *n.*

gad·o·lin·i·um /gád'líneeəm/ *n. Chem.* a soft silvery metallic element of the lanthanide series. ¶ Symb.: **Gd.**

gad·wall /gádwawl/ *n.* a brownish gray freshwater duck, *Anas strepera.*

gad·zooks /gadzóoks/ *int. archaic* an expression of surprise, etc.

Gael /gayl/ *n.* **1** a Scottish Celt. **2** a Gaelic-speaking Celt.

Gael·ic /gáylik, gálik/ *n. & adj.* •*n.* any of the Celtic languages spoken in Ireland, Scotland, and the Isle of Man. •*adj.* of or relating to the Celts or the Celtic languages.

Gael·tacht /gáyltəkht/ *n.* any of the regions in Ireland where the vernacular language is Irish.

gaff /gaf/ *n. & v.* •*n.* **1 a** a stick with an iron hook for landing large fish. **b** a barbed fishing spear. **2** a spar to which the head of a fore-and-aft sail is bent. •*v.tr.* seize (a fish) with a gaff.

gaffe /gaf/ *n.* a blunder; an indiscreet act or remark.

gaf·fer /gáfər/ *n.* **1** an old fellow. **2** *colloq.* the chief electrician in a movie or television production unit.

gag /gag/ *n. & v.* •*n.* **1** a piece of cloth, etc., thrust into or held over the mouth to prevent speaking or crying out. **2** a joke or comic scene. **3** an actor's interpolation in a dramatic dialogue. **4** a thing or circumstance restricting free speech. **5** a joke or hoax. •*v.* (**gagged, gagging**) **1** *tr.* apply a gag to. **2** *tr.* deprive of free speech. **3 a** *intr.* choke or retch. **b** *tr.* cause to do this. **4** *intr. Theatr.* make gags.

ga·ga /gáagaa/ *adj. sl.* **1** senile. **2** fatuous; slightly crazy.

gage[1] /gayj/ *n.* **1** a pledge; a thing deposited as security. **2 a** a challenge to fight. **b** a symbol of this, esp. a glove thrown down.

▶See note at GAUGE.

gage[2] var. of GAUGE.

gag·gle /gágəl/ *n.* **1** a flock of geese. **2** *colloq.* a disorderly group of people.

gag·man /gágman/ *n.* a deviser, writer, or performer of theatrical gags.

gag·ster /gágstər/ *n.* = GAGMAN.

gai·e·ty /gáyətee/ *n.* **1** the state of being merry; mirth. **2** merrymaking. **3** a bright appearance.

gai·ly /gáylee/ *adv.* **1** in a lighthearted manner. **2** with a bright appearance.

gain /gayn/ *v. & n.* •*v.* **1** *tr.* obtain or secure (usu. something desired or favorable). **2** *tr.* acquire (a sum) as profits; earn. **3** *tr.* obtain as an increment or addition (*gain weight*). **4** *intr.* (foll. by *in*) make a specified advance or improvement (*gained in stature*). **5** *intr. & tr.* (of a clock, etc.) become fast, or be fast by (a specified amount of time). **6** *intr.* (often foll. by *on, upon*) come closer to a person or thing pursued. **7** *tr.* **a** bring over to one's views. **b** (foll. by *over*) win by persuasion, etc. **8** *tr.* reach (a desired place). •*n.* **1** something gained, achieved, etc. **2** an increase of possessions, etc.; a profit or improvement. **3** the acquisition of wealth. **4** (in *pl.*) sums of money acquired by trade, etc.; winnings. **5** an increase in amount. □ **gain ground** see GROUND[1]. □□ **gain·a·ble** *adj.* **gain·er** *n.*

gain·ful /gáynfool/ *adj.* **1** (of employment) paid. **2** lucrative. □□ **gain·ful·ly** *adv.* **gain·ful·ness** *n.*

gain·say /gáynsáy/ *v.tr.* (*past* and *past part.* **gainsaid** /–séd/) deny; contradict.

'gainst /genst/ *prep. poet* = AGAINST.

gait /gayt/ *n.* **1** a manner of walking; one's bearing or carriage as one walks. **2** the manner of forward motion of a runner, horse, vehicle, etc.

gait·er /gáytər/ *n.* a covering of cloth, leather, etc., covering the lower leg and part of the foot, used to protect against snow, mud, etc. □□ **gait·ered** *adj.*

gal /gal/ *n. sl.* a girl or woman.
gal. *abbr.* gallon(s).
ga·la /gáylə, gaálə, gálə/ *n.* (often *attrib.*) a festive or special occasion (*a gala performance*).
ga·lac·ta·gogue /gəláktəgawg/ *adj. & n.* • *adj.* inducing a flow of milk. • *n.* a galactagogue substance.
ga·lac·tic /gəláktik/ *adj.* of or relating to a galaxy, esp. the Milky Way.
ga·la·go /gəláygō, –laá–/ *n.* (*pl.* **-gos**) any small tree-climbing primate of the genus *Galago*, found in southern Africa, with large eyes and ears and a long tail. Also called BUSHBABY.
Gal·a·had /gáləhad/ *n.* a person characterized by nobility, integrity, courtesy, etc.
gal·ax·y /gáləksee/ *n.* (*pl.* **-ies**) **1** any of many independent systems of stars, dust, etc., held together by gravitational attraction. **2** (**the Galaxy**) the galaxy of which the solar system is a part. **3** (**the Galaxy**) the Milky Way.
gale /gayl/ *n.* **1** a very strong wind, esp. one of 32–63 m.p.h. **2** an outburst, esp. of laughter.
ga·len·i·cal /gəlénikəl/ *adj.* (also **ga·len·ic** /–lénik/) • *adj.* **1** of or relating to Galen, a Greek physician of the 2nd c. AD, or his methods. **2** made of natural as opposed to synthetic components.
Gal·i·le·an[1] /gáliláyən, –léeən/ *adj.* of or relating to Galileo, Italian astronomer d. 1642, or his methods.
Gal·i·le·an[2] /gálileéən/ *adj. & n.* • *adj.* **1** of Galilee in Palestine. **2** Christian. • *n.* **1** a native of Galilee. **2** a Christian. **3** (prec. by *the*) *derog.* Christ.
gall[1] /gawl/ *n.* **1** *sl.* impudence. **2** asperity; rancor. **3** bitterness; anything bitter (*gall and wormwood*). **4** the bile of animals. **5** the gallbladder and its contents.
gall[2] /gawl/ *n. & v.* • *n.* **1** a sore on the skin made by chafing. **2 a** mental soreness or vexation. **b** a cause of this. **3** a place rubbed bare. • *v.tr.* **1** rub sore; injure by rubbing. **2** vex; annoy; irritate. ▫▫ **gall·ing·ly** *adv.*
gall[3] /gawl/ *n.* **1** a growth produced by insects or fungus, etc., on plants and trees, esp. on oak. **2** (*attrib.*) of insects producing galls.
gal·lant *adj. & n.* • *adj.* /gálənt/ **1** brave, esp. in dealing with adversity; chivalrous. **2 a** (of a ship, horse, etc.) grand; stately. **b** *archaic* finely dressed. **3** /gálənt, gəlánt, –laánt/ **a** markedly attentive to women. **b** concerned with sexual love. • *n.* /gálənt, gəlánt, –laánt/ **1** a ladies' man; a paramour. **2** *archaic* a man of fashion; a fine gentleman. ▫▫ **gal·lant·ly** /gáləntlee/ *adv.*
gal·lant·ry /gáləntree/ *n.* (*pl.* **-ries**) **1** bravery; dashing courage. **2** courtesy to women. **3** a polite act or speech.
gall·blad·der *n.* the vessel storing bile after its secretion by the liver and before release into the intestine.
gal·le·on /gáleeən/ *n. hist.* **1** a ship of war (usu. Spanish). **2** a large Spanish merchant ship. **3** a vessel shorter and higher than a galley.
gal·le·ri·a /gáləréeə/ *n.* a collection of small shops under a single roof.
gal·ler·y /gáləree/ *n.* (*pl.* **-ies**) **1** a room or building for showing works of art. **2** a balcony, esp. a platform projecting from the inner wall of a church, etc. (*minstrels' gallery*). **3 a** the highest balcony in a theater. **b** its occupants. **4 a** a covered space for walking in, partly open at the side. **b** a long narrow passage in the thickness of a wall or supported on corbels, open toward the interior of the building. **5** a long narrow room or corridor. **6** *Mil. & Mining* a horizontal underground passage. **7** a group of spectators at a golf match, etc. ▫ **play to the gallery** seek to win approval by appealing to popular taste. ▫▫ **gal·ler·ied** *adj.*
gal·ler·y·ite /gáləree-īt/ *n.* a person occupying a seat in a gallery; a spectator at a play, tennis match, etc.
gal·ley /gálee/ *n.* (*pl.* **-leys**) **1** *hist.* **a** a low flat single-decked vessel using sails and oars, and usu. rowed by slaves or criminals. **b** an ancient Greek or Roman warship with one or more banks of oars. **2** a ship's or aircraft's kitchen. **3** *Printing* (in full **galley proof**) a proof in the form of long single-column strips, not in sheets or pages.
gal·ley slave *n.* **1** *hist.* a person condemned to row in a galley. **2** a drudge.
gal·liard /gályaard/ *n. hist.* **1** a lively dance usu. in triple time for two persons. **2** the music for this.
Gal·lic /gálik/ *adj.* **1** French or typically French. **2** of the Gauls. ▫▫ **Gal·li·cize** /–lisīz/ *v.tr. & intr.*
gal·lic ac·id /gálik/ *n. Chem.* an acid extracted from gallnuts, etc., formerly used in making ink.
gal·li·pot /gálipot/ *n.* a small pot of earthenware, metal, etc., used for ointments, etc.
gal·li·um /gáleeəm/ *n. Chem.* a soft bluish white metallic element occurring naturally in coal, bauxite, and kaolin. ¶ Symb.: **Ga**.
gal·li·vant /gálivant/ *v.intr. colloq.* **1** gad about. **2** flirt.
Gallo- /gálō/ *comb. form* **1** French; relating to France. **2** Gaul (*Gallo-Roman*).
gal·lon /gálən/ *n.* **1 a** a measure of capacity equivalent to four quarts (3785 cc). **b** (in full **imperial gallon**) *Brit.* a measure of capacity equal to eight pints and equivalent to four quarts (4546 cc). **2** (usu. in *pl.*) *colloq.* a large amount. ▫▫ **gal·lon·age** *n.*
gal·loon /gəlóon/ *n.* a narrow braid of gold, silver, silk, cotton, nylon, etc., for trimming dresses, etc.
gal·lop /gáləp/ *n. & v.* • *n.* **1** the fastest pace of a horse or other quadruped, with all the feet off the ground together in each stride. **2** a ride at this pace. • *v.* (**galloped, galloping**) **1 a** *intr.* go at the pace of a gallop. **b** *tr.* make (a horse, etc.) gallop. **2** *intr.* (foll. by *through*, *over*) read or talk at great speed. **3** *intr.* progress rapidly (*galloping inflation*). ▫▫ **gal·lop·er** *n.*
gal·lo·way /gáləway/ *n.* **1** an animal of a breed of hornless black beef cattle from Galloway in SW Scotland. **2** this breed.
gal·lows /gálōz/ *n.pl.* (usu. treated as *sing.*) **1** a structure, usu. of two uprights and a crosspiece, for the hanging of criminals. **2** (prec. by *the*) execution by hanging.
gal·lows hu·mor *n.* grim and ironic humor.
gall·stone /gáwlstōn/ *n.* a small hard mass forming in the gallbladder.
Gal·lup poll /gáləp/ *n. Trademark* an assessment of public opinion by the questioning of a statistically representative sample.
gall wasp *n.* a gall-forming insect of the hymenopteran superfamily Cynipoidea.
ga·loot /gəlóot/ *n. colloq.* a person, esp. a strange or clumsy one.
gal·op /gáləp/ *n. & v.* • *n.* **1** a lively dance in duple time. **2** the music for this. • *v.intr.* (**galoped, galoping**) perform this dance.
ga·lore /gəláwr/ *adj.* in abundance (placed after noun: *flowers galore*).
ga·losh /gəlósh/ *n.* (usu. in *pl.*) a waterproof overshoe of rubber.
ga·lumph /gəlúmf/ *v.intr. colloq.* **1** move clumsily. **2** go prancing in triumph.
gal·van·ic /galvánik/ *adj.* **1 a** sudden and remarkable (*a galvanic effect*). **b** full of energy. **2** producing an electric current by chemical action. ▫▫ **gal·van·i·cal·ly** *adv.*
gal·va·nism /gálvənizəm/ *n.* **1** electricity produced by chemical action. **2** the use of electricity for medical purposes. ▫▫ **gal·va·nist** *n.*
gal·va·nize /gálvənīz/ *v.tr.* **1** (often foll. by *into*) rouse forcefully, esp. by shock or excitement. **2** stimulate by or as if by electricity. **3** coat (iron) with zinc (usu. without the use of electricity) as a protection against rust. ▫▫ **gal·va·ni·za·tion** *n.* **gal·va·niz·er** *n.*

gal·va·nom·e·ter /gálvənómitər/ *n.* an instrument for detecting and measuring small electric currents. ▫▫ **gal·va·no·met·ric** /–nəmétrik/ *adj.*

gam·bit /gámbit/ *n.* **1** a chess opening in which a player sacrifices a piece or pawn to secure an advantage. **2** an opening move in a discussion, etc. **3** a trick or device.

gam·ble /gámbəl/ *v.* & *n.* • *v.* **1** *intr.* play games of chance for money, esp. for high stakes. **2** *tr.* **a** bet (a sum of money) in gambling. **b** (often foll. by *away*) lose (assets) by gambling. **3** *intr.* take great risks in the hope of substantial gain. **4** *intr.* (foll. by *on*) act in the hope of (*gambled on fine weather*). • *n.* **1** a risky undertaking or attempt. **2** an act of gambling. ▫▫ **gam·bler** *n.*

gam·bol /gámbəl/ *v.* & *n.* • *v.intr.* (**gamboled, gamboling**; also **gambolled, gambolling**) skip or frolic playfully. • *n.* a playful frolic.

gam·brel /gámbrəl/ *n.* (in full **gambrel roof**) a roof with gables and with each face having two slopes, the lower one steeper.

game[1] /gaym/ *n., adj.,* & *v.* • *n.* **1** a form or spell of play or sport, esp. a competitive one played according to rules. **2** a single portion of play forming a scoring unit in some contests, e.g., bridge or tennis. **3** (in *pl.*) **a** *Brit.* athletics or sports as organized in a school, etc. **b** a meeting for athletic, etc., contests (*Olympic Games*). **4** a winning score in a game; the state of the score in a game. **5** the equipment for a game. **6** one's level of achievement in a game, as specified (*has a strong game*). **7 a** a piece of fun (*was only playing a game with you*). **b** (in *pl.*) jokes; tricks (*none of your games!*). **8** a scheme, etc., regarded as a game (*so that's your game*). **9** a policy or line of action. **10** (*collect.*) **a** wild animals or birds hunted for sport or food. **b** the flesh of these. **11** a hunted animal. • *adj.* **1** eager and willing. **2** (foll. by *for*, or *to* + infin.) having the spirit or energy. • *v.intr.* esp. *Brit.* play at games of chance for money; gamble. ▫ **the game is up** the scheme is revealed. **off** (or **on**) **one's game** playing badly (or well). **play the game** behave fairly. ▫▫ **game·ly** *adv.* **game·ness** *n.* **game·ster** *n.*

game[2] /gaym/ *adj.* (of a leg, arm, etc.) lame; crippled.

game·cock /gáymkok/ *n.* (also **game·fowl** /–fowl/) a cock bred and trained for cockfighting.

game·keep·er /gáymkeepər/ *n.* a person employed to breed and protect game, usu. for a large estate.

game plan *n.* **1** a winning strategy worked out in advance for a particular game. **2** a plan of campaign, esp. in politics.

game point *n.* *Tennis*, etc., a point that, if won, would win the game.

games·man·ship /gáymzmənship/ *n.* the art or practice of winning games or other contests by gaining a psychological advantage over an opponent.

game·some /gáymsəm/ *adj.* merry; sportive. ▫▫ **game·some·ly** *adv.* **game·some·ness** *n.*

gam·ete /gámeet, gəméet/ *n.* *Biol.* a mature germ cell able to unite with another in sexual reproduction. ▫▫ **ga·met·ic** /gəmétik/ *adj.*

game theory *n.* (also **games theory**) the mathematical analysis of conflict in war, economics, games of skill, etc.

gameto- /gəméetō/ *comb. form Biol.* gamete.

ga·me·to·cyte /gəméetəsīt/ *n.* *Biol.* any cell that is in the process of developing into one or more gametes.

gam·e·to·gen·e·sis /gəméetəjénisis/ *n.* *Biol.* the process by which cells undergo meiosis to form gametes.

ga·me·to·phyte /gəméetəfīt/ *n.* the gamete-producing form of a plant that has alternation of generations between this and the asexual form. ▫▫ **ga·me·to·phyt·ic** /–fitik/ *adj.*

game war·den *n.* an official locally supervising game and hunting.

gam·in /gámin/ *n.* **1** a street urchin. **2** an impudent child.

gam·ine /gámeen/ *n.* **1** a girl gamin. **2** a girl with mischievous or boyish charm.

gam·ma /gámə/ *n.* **1** the third letter of the Greek alphabet (Γ, γ). **2** the third member of a series.

gam·ma ra·di·a·tion *n.* (also **gamma rays**) electromagnetic radiation of very short wavelength.

gam·mon[1] /gámən/ *n.* & *v.* • *n.* **1** the bottom piece of a side of bacon including a hind leg. **2** esp. *Brit.* the ham of a pig cured like bacon. • *v.tr.* cure (bacon).

gam·mon[2] /gámən/ *n.* & *v.* • *n.* a victory in backgammon in which the opponent removes no pieces from the board. • *v.tr.* defeat in this way.

gam·ut /gámət/ *n.* **1** the whole series or range or scope of anything (*the whole gamut of crime*). **2** *Mus.* **a** the whole series of notes used in medieval or modern music. **b** a major diatonic scale.

gam·y /gáymee/ *adj.* (**gamier, gamiest**) **1** having the flavor or scent of game kept till it is high. **2** scandalous; sensational. **3** = GAME[1] *adj.* ▫▫ **gam·i·ly** *adv.* **gam·i·ness** *n.*

gan·der /gándər/ *n.* **1** a male goose. **2** *sl.* a glance (*take a gander*).

gang /gang/ *n.* **1 a** a band of persons acting or going about together. **b** *colloq.* such a band pursuing antisocial purposes. **2** a set of workers, slaves, or prisoners. ▫ **gang up** *colloq.* **1** (often foll. by *with*) act in concert. **2** (foll. by *on*) combine against.

gang·bus·ter /gángbustər/ *n.* & *adj.* *colloq.* • *n.* a police officer or other person who takes part in breaking up criminal gangs. • *adj.* very successful, esp. commercially (*the restaurant did a gangbuster business*).

gang·land /gángland, –lənd/ *n.* the world of organized crime.

gan·gling /gánggling/ *adj.* (of a person) loosely built; lanky.

gan·gli·on /gánggleeən/ *n.* (*pl.* **ganglia** /–leeə/or **ganglions**) **1 a** an enlargement or knot on a nerve, etc., containing an assemblage of nerve cells. **b** a mass of gray matter in the central nervous system forming a nerve nucleus. **2** *Med.* a cyst, esp. on a tendon sheath. ▫▫ **gan·gli·on·at·ed** *adj.* **gan·gli·on·ic** /–leeónik/ *adj.*

gang·ly /gángglee/ *adj.* (**ganglier, gangliest**) = GANGLING.

gang·plank /gángplangk/ *n.* a movable plank usu. with cleats nailed on it for boarding or disembarking from a ship, etc.

gan·grene /gánggreen/ *n.* & *v.* • *n.* **1** *Med.* death and decomposition of a part of the body tissue, usu. resulting from obstructed circulation. **2** moral corruption. • *v.tr.* & *intr.* affect or become affected with gangrene. ▫▫ **gan·gre·nous** /gánggrinəs/ *adj.*

gang·ster /gángstər/ *n.* a member of a gang of violent criminals. ▫▫ **gang·ster·ism** *n.*

gang·way /gángway/ *n.* & *int.* • *n.* **1 a** an opening in the bulwarks for a gangplank by which a ship is entered or left. **b** a bridge laid from ship to shore. **c** a passage on a ship. **2** a temporary bridge on a building site, etc. • *int.* make way!

gan·ja /gaánjə/ *n.* marijuana.

gan·net /gánit/ *n.* **1** any sea bird of the genus *Morus*, which catches fish by plunge-diving. **2** *Brit. sl.* a greedy person. ▫▫ **gan·net·ry** *n.* (*pl.* **-ries**).

gant·let var. of GAUNTLET 2.

gan·try /gántree/ *n.* (*pl.* **-tries**) **1** an overhead structure supporting a traveling crane, or railroad or road signals. **2** a structure supporting a space rocket prior to launching.

See page xii for the *Key to Pronunciation*.

gap /gap/ *n.* **1** an unfilled space or interval; a break in continuity. **2** a wide (usu. undesirable) divergence in views, etc. (*generation gap*). **3** a gorge or pass. ▫▫ **gap·py** *adj.*

gape /gayp/ *v.* & *n.* • *v.intr.* **1 a** open one's mouth wide, esp. in amazement. **b** be or become wide open. **2** (foll. by *at*) gaze curiously or wondrously. **3** split. **4** yawn. • *n.* **1** an openmouthed stare. **2** a yawn. **3** a rent or opening. ▫▫ **gap·ing·ly** *adv.*

ga·rage /gəraázh, –raáj/ *n.* & *v.* • *n.* **1** a building for the storage of a motor vehicle or vehicles. **2** an establishment selling gasoline, etc., or repairing and selling motor vehicles. • *v.tr.* keep (a motor vehicle) in a garage. ▫ **garage sale** a sale of miscellaneous household goods held in the garage or yard of a private house.

ga·ram ma·sa·la /gaárəm məsaáalə/ *n.* a mixture of spices used in Indian cooking.

garb /gaarb/ *n.* & *v.* • *n.* **1** clothing, esp. of a distinctive kind. **2** the way a person is dressed. • *v.tr.* **1** (usu. in *passive* or *refl.*) put (esp. distinctive) clothes on (a person). **2** attire.

gar·bage /gaárbij/ *n.* **1 a** refuse; filth. **b** domestic waste, esp. food wastes. **2** offensive or inferior literature, etc. **3** nonsense. **4** incomprehensible or meaningless data.

gar·ble /gaárbəl/ *v.tr.* **1** unintentionally distort (messages, etc.). **2 a** mutilate in order to misrepresent. **b** make (usu. unfair) selections from (statements, etc.). ▫▫ **gar·bler** *n.*

gar·board /gaárbərd/ *n.* (in full **garboard strake**) the first range of planks or plates laid on a ship's bottom next to the keel.

gar·den /gaárd'n/ *n.* & *v.* • *n.* **1 a** a piece of ground used for growing esp. flowers or vegetables. **b** a piece of ground, usu. partly grassed and adjoining a private house, used for growing flowers, fruit, or vegetables, and as a place of recreation. **2** (esp. in *pl.*) ornamental grounds laid out for public enjoyment. **3** (*attrib.*) **a** (of plants) cultivated, not wild. **b** for use in a garden (*garden seat*). **4** (usu. in *pl.* prec. by a name) *Brit.* a street, square, etc. (*Onslow Gardens*). **5** an especially fertile region. **6** a large public hall. • *v.intr.* cultivate or work in a garden. ▫▫ **gar·den·ing** *n.*

gar·den·er /gaárdnər/ *n.* a person who gardens or is employed to tend a garden.

gar·de·nia /gaardeényə/ *n.* any tree or shrub of the genus *Gardenia*, with large white or yellow flowers and usu. a fragrant scent.

gar·fish /gaárfish/ *n.* (*pl.* same) = GAR.

gar·gan·tu·an /gaargánchōōən/ *adj.* enormous; gigantic.

gar·gle /gaárgəl/ *v.* & *n.* • *v.* **1** *tr.* (also *absol.*) wash (one's mouth and throat) with a liquid kept in motion by breathing through it. **2** *intr.* make a sound as when doing this. • *n.* a liquid used for gargling.

gar·goyle /gaárgoyl/ *n.* a grotesque carved human or animal face or figure projecting from the gutter of a building as a spout.

gar·ish /gáirish/ *adj.* **1** obtrusively bright. **2** gaudy; over-decorated. ▫▫ **gar·ish·ly** *adv.* **gar·ish·ness** *n.*

gar·land /gaárlənd/ *n.* & *v.* • *n.* **1** a wreath of flowers, leaves, etc., worn on the head or hung as a decoration. **2** a prize or distinction. • *v.tr.* **1** adorn with garlands. **2** crown with a garland.

gar·lic /gaárlik/ *n.* **1** any of various alliaceous plants, esp. *Allium sativum*. **2** the strong-smelling pungent bulb of this plant, used in cooking. ▫▫ **gar·lick·y** *adj.*

gar·ment /gaármənt/ *n.* **1 a** an article of dress. **b** (in *pl.*) clothes. **2** the outward and visible covering of anything.

gar·ner /gaárnər/ *v.* & *n.* • *v.tr.* **1** collect. **2** store; deposit. • *n.* *literary* a storehouse or granary.

gar·net /gaárnit/ *n.* a vitreous silicate mineral, esp. a transparent deep red kind used as a gem.

gar·nish /gaárnish/ *v.* & *n.* • *v.tr.* decorate or embellish (esp. food). • *n.* (also **gar·nish·ing**) a decoration or embellishment, esp. to food.

gar·nish·ee /gaárnisheé/ *v.* & *n.* *Law* • *v.tr.* (**garnishees, garnisheed**) **1** legally seize (money, etc.). **2** serve notice on (a person) for the purpose of seizing money. • *n.* a person garnished.

ga·rotte var. of GARROTE.

gar·ret /gárit/ *n.* **1** a top floor or attic room, esp. a dismal or unfurnished one. **2** an attic.

gar·ri·son /gárisən/ *n.* & *v.* • *n.* **1** the troops stationed in a fortress, etc., to defend it. **2** the building occupied by them. • *v.tr.* **1** provide (a place) with or occupy as a garrison. **2** place on garrison duty.

gar·rote /gərót/ *v.* & *n.* (also **ga·rotte; gar·rotte**) • *v.tr.* kill by strangulation, esp. with an iron or wire collar, etc. • *n.* the apparatus used for this.

gar·ru·lous /gárələs, gáryə–/ *adj.* **1** talkative, esp. on trivial matters. **2** wordy. ▫▫ **gar·ru·li·ty** /gəróōlitee/ *n.* **gar·ru·lous·ly** *adv.* **gar·ru·lous·ness** *n.*

gar·ter /gaártər/ *n.* **1** a band worn to keep a sock or stocking up. **2** a strap hanging from a girdle, etc., for holding up a stocking.

gar·ter belt *n.* a belt with hanging straps for holding up stockings.

gar·ter snake *n.* any harmless snake of the genus *Thamnophis*, native to N. America, having lengthwise stripes.

gas /gas/ *n.* & *v.* • *n.* (*pl.* **gases**) **1** any airlike substance that moves freely to fill any space available, irrespective of its quantity. **2** such a substance used as a domestic or industrial fuel (also *attrib.*: *gas stove*). **3** nitrous oxide or another gas used as an anesthetic (esp. in dentistry). **4** a gas or vapor used in warfare. **5** *colloq.* **a** gasoline. **b** a motor vehicle's accelerator. **6** *sl.* pointless idle talk. **7** *sl.* an amusing thing or person. • *v.* (**gases, gassed, gassing**) **1** *tr.* expose to gas, esp. to kill or make unconscious. **2** *intr.* give off gas. **3** *tr.* (usu. foll. by *up*) *colloq.* fill (the tank of a motor vehicle) with gasoline. **4** *intr. colloq.* talk idly.

gas·bag /gásbag/ *n.* **1** a container of gas for a balloon or airship. **2** *sl.* an idle talker.

gas cham·ber *n.* an airtight chamber that can be filled with poisonous gas to kill people or animals.

gas·e·ous /gáseeəs, gáshəs/ *adj.* of or like gas. ▫▫ **gas·e·ous·ness** *n.*

gas field *n.* an area yielding natural gas.

gas-guz·zler *n. colloq.* a motor vehicle that gets relatively poor gas mileage.

gash /gash/ *n.* & *v.* • *n.* **1** a long deep slash or wound. **2 a** a cleft such as might be made by a slashing cut. **b** the act of making such a cut. • *v.tr.* make a gash in.

gas·ket /gáskit/ *n.* a sheet or ring of rubber, etc., shaped to seal the junction of metal surfaces. ▫ **blow a gasket** *sl.* lose one's temper.

gas·light /gáslīt/ *n.* **1** a jet of burning gas, usu. heating a mantle, to provide light. **2** light emanating from this.

gas mask *n.* a respirator used as a defense against poison gas.

gas·o·line /gásəleén/ *n.* (also **gas·o·lene**) a volatile flammable liquid blended from petroleum and natural gas and used as a fuel.

gasp /gasp/ *v.* & *n.* • *v.* **1** *intr.* catch one's breath with an open mouth as in astonishment. **2** *intr.* (foll. by *for*) strain to obtain by gasping (*gasped for air*). **3** *tr.* (often foll. by *out*) utter with gasps. *n.* a convulsive catching of breath.

gas·ser /gásər/ *n.* **1** *colloq.* an idle talker. **2** *sl.* a very attractive or impressive person or thing.

gas sta·tion *n.* a service station.

gas·sy /gásee/ *adj.* (**gassier, gassiest**) **1 a** of or like gas.

b full of gas. **2** *colloq.* (of talk, etc.) pointless; verbose. ▫▫ **gas·si·ness** *n.*

gas·trec·to·my /gastréktəmee/ *n.* (*pl.* **-mies**) a surgical operation in which the whole or part of the stomach is removed.

gas·tric /gástrik/ *adj.* of the stomach.

gas·tric juice *n.* a thin clear virtually colorless acid fluid secreted by the stomach glands and active in promoting digestion.

gas·tri·tis /gastrítis/ *n.* inflammation of the lining of the stomach.

gastro- /gástrō/ *comb. form* (also **gastr-** before a vowel) stomach.

gas·tro·en·ter·ic /gástrōentérik/ *adj.* of or relating to the stomach and intestines.

gas·tro·en·ter·i·tis /gástrō-éntərítis/ *n.* inflammation of the stomach and intestines.

gas·tro·nome /gástrənōm/ *n.* a gourmet.

gas·tron·o·my /gastrónəmee/ *n.* the practice, study, or art of eating and drinking well. ▫▫ **gas·tro·nom·ic** /gástrənómik/ *adj.* **gas·tro·nom·i·cal** *adj.* **gas·tro·nom·i·cal·ly** *adv.*

gas·tro·pod /gástrəpod/ *n.* any mollusk of the class Gastropoda that moves along by means of a large muscular foot, e.g., a snail, slug, etc. ▫▫ **gas·trop·o·dous** /gastrópədəs/ *adj.*

gas·tro·scope /gástrəskōp/ *n.* an optical instrument used for inspecting the interior of the stomach.

gas·works /gáswərks/ *n.* a place where gas is manufactured and processed.

gat[1] /gat/ *n. sl.* a revolver or other firearm.

gat[2] /gat/ *n. archaic past* of GET *v.*

gate /gayt/ *n. & v.* • *n.* **1** a barrier, usu. hinged, used to close an opening made for entrance and exit through a wall, fence, etc. **2** such an opening, esp. in the wall of a city, enclosure, or large building. **3** a means of entrance or exit. **4** a numbered place of access to aircraft at an airport. **5 a** an electrical signal that causes or controls the passage of other signals. **b** an electrical circuit with an output that depends on the combination of several inputs. **6** a device regulating the passage of water in a lock, etc. **7 a** the number of people entering by payment at the gates of a sports stadium, etc. **b** (in full **gate money**) the proceeds taken for admission. **8** = STARTING GATE. • *v.tr.* (as **gated** *adj.*) (of a road) having a gate or gates to control the movement of traffic or animals.

ga·teau /gatṓ, gaa–/ *n.* (*pl.* **gateaus** or **gateaux** /–tṓz/) any of various rich cakes, usu. containing cream or fruit.

gate·crash·er /gáytkrashər/ *n.* an uninvited guest at a party, etc. ▫▫ **gate·crash** *v.tr. & intr.*

gate·fold /gáytfōld/ *n.* a page in a book or magazine, etc., that folds out to be larger than the page format.

gate·house /gáyt-hows/ *n.* **1** a house standing by a gateway, esp. to a large house or park. **2** *hist.* a room over a city gate, often used as a prison.

gate·keep·er /gáytkeepər/ *n.* an attendant at a gate, controlling entrance and exit.

gate·leg /gáytleg/ *n.* (in full **gateleg table**) a table with hinged legs that swing out from the frame to support folding leaves that make the surface of table larger. ▫▫ **gate·legged** *adj.*

gate·way /gáytway/ *n.* **1** an entrance with or opening for a gate. **2** a frame or structure built over a gate. **3** an entrance or exit.

gath·er /gáthər/ *v. & n.* • *v.* **1** *tr. & intr.* bring or come together; assemble. **2** *tr.* (usu. foll. by *up*) **a** bring together from scattered places. **b** take up together from the ground, etc. **c** draw into a smaller compass. **3** *tr.* acquire by gradually collecting. **4** *tr.* **a** pick a quantity of (flowers, etc.). **b** collect (grain, etc.) as a harvest. **5** *tr.* (often foll. by *that* + clause) infer or understand. **6** *tr.* be affected by the accumulation or increase of (*gather speed*). **7** *tr.* (often foll. by *up*) summon up (one's thoughts, energy, etc.) for a purpose. **8** *tr.* gain or recover (one's breath). **9** *tr.* **a** draw (material, or one's brow) together in folds or wrinkles. **b** pucker or draw together (part of a dress) by running a thread through. **10** *intr.* come to a head; develop a purulent swelling. • *n.* (in *pl.*) a part of a garment that is gathered or drawn in. ▫ **gather way** (of a ship) begin to move. ▫▫ **gath·er·er** *n.*

gath·er·ing /gáthəring/ *n.* **1** an assembly or meeting. **2** a purulent swelling. **3** a group of leaves taken together in bookbinding.

Gat·ling /gátling/ *n.* (in full **Gatling gun**) an early machine gun with clustered barrels.

ga·tor /gáytər/ *n.* (also **ga·ter**) *colloq.* an alligator.

gauche /gōsh/ *adj.* **1** socially awkward. **2** tactless. ▫▫ **gauche·ly** *adv.* **gauche·ness** *n.*

gau·che·rie /gṓshəree/ *n.* **1** gauche manners. **2** a gauche action.

gau·cho /gówchō/ *n.* (*pl.* **-chos**) a cowboy from the S. American pampas.

gaud /gawd/ *n.* a gaudy thing; a showy ornament.

gaud·y /gáwdee/ *adj.* (**gaudier, gaudiest**) tastelessly bright or showy. ▫▫ **gaud·i·ly** *adv.* **gaud·i·ness** *n.*

gauge /gayj/ *n. & v.* (also **gage**) • *n.* **1** a standard measure, esp.: **a** the capacity of a barrel. **b** the fineness of a textile. **c** the diameter of a bullet. **d** the thickness of sheet metal. **2** any of various instruments for measuring this, or for measuring other dimensions or properties. **3** the distance between a pair of rails or the wheels on one axle. **4** the capacity, extent, or scope of something. **5** a means of estimating. **6** *Naut.* a relative position with respect to the wind. • *v.tr.* **1** measure exactly (esp. objects of standard size). **2** determine the capacity or content of. **3** estimate or form a judgment of (a person, situation, etc.). ▫▫ **gaug·er** *n.*

Gaul /gawl/ *n.* **1** a native or inhabitant of ancient Gaul. **2** a native or inhabitant of France.

Gaul·ish /gáwlish/ *adj. & n.* • *adj.* of or relating to the ancient Gauls. • *n.* their language.

gaunt /gawnt/ *adj.* **1** lean; haggard. **2** grim or desolate in appearance. ▫▫ **gaunt·ly** *adv.* **gaunt·ness** *n.*

gaunt·let[1] /gáwntlit/ *n.* **1** a stout glove with a long loose wrist. **2** *hist.* an armored glove. **3** a challenge (esp. in **throw down the gauntlet**).

gaunt·let[2] /gáwntlit/ *n.* ▫ **run the gauntlet 1** be subjected to harsh criticism. **2** pass between two rows of people and receive blows from them, as a punishment or ordeal.

gauss /gows/ *n.* (*pl.* same or **gausses**) a unit of magnetic induction, equal to one ten-thousandth of a tesla.

Gauss·i·an dis·tri·bu·tion /gówseeən/ *n. Statistics* = NORMAL DISTRIBUTION

gauze /gawz/ *n.* **1** a thin transparent fabric of silk, cotton, etc. **2** a fine mesh of wire, etc. **3** a slight haze.

gauz·y /gáwzee/ *adj.* (**gauzier, gauziest**) **1** like gauze; thin and translucent. **2** flimsy; delicate. ▫▫ **gauz·i·ly** *adv.* **gauz·i·ness** *n.*

gave *past* of GIVE.

gav·el /gávəl/ *n. & v.* • *n.* a small hammer used by an auctioneer, or for calling a meeting, courtroom, etc., to order.

ga·votte /gəvót/ *n.* **1** an old French dance in moderately quick 4/4 time. **2** the music for this.

gawk /gawk/ *v. & n.* • *v.intr. colloq.* stare stupidly. • *n.* an awkward or bashful person. ▫▫ **gawk·ish** *adj.*

gawk·y /gáwkee/ *adj.* (**gawkier, gawkiest**) awkward or ungainly. ▫▫ **gawk·i·ly** *adv.* **gawk·i·ness** *n.*

---

gay /gay/ *adj. & n.* • *adj.* **1** lighthearted and carefree. **2 a** homosexual. **b** intended for or used by homosexuals (*a gay bar*).
▶Generally informal in use, but often favored by esp. male homosexuals with ref. to themselves. **3** brightly colored (*a gay scarf*). • *n.* a homosexual, esp. male. ▫▫ **gay·ness** *n.*

ga·za·ni·a /gəzáyneeə/ *n.* any herbaceous plant of the genus *Gazania,* with showy yellow or orange daisy-shaped flowers.

gaze /gayz/ *v. & n.* • *v.intr.* (foll. by *at, into,* etc.) look fixedly. • *n.* a fixed or intent look. ▫▫ **gaz·er** *n.*

ga·ze·bo /gəzéebō/ *n.* (*pl.* **-bos** or **-boes**) a summerhouse or turret designed to give a wide view.

ga·zelle /gəzél/ *n.* any of various small graceful soft-eyed antelopes of Asia or Africa, esp. of the genus *Gazella.*

ga·zette /gəzét/ *n.* a newspaper.

gaz·et·teer /gázitéer/ *n.* a geographical index or dictionary.

gaz·pa·cho /gəspaáchō/ *n.* (*pl.* **-chos**) a Spanish soup made with tomatoes, oil, garlic, onions, etc., and served cold.

gazebo

GB *abbr.* Great Britain.

GDP *abbr.* gross domestic product.

GDR *abbr. hist.* German Democratic Republic.

gear /geer/ *n. & v.* • *n.* **1** (often in *pl.*) a set of toothed wheels that work together to transmit and control motion from an engine, esp. to the road wheels of a vehicle. **2** a particular function or state of adjustment of engaged gears (*second gear*). **3** a mechanism of wheels, levers, etc., usu. for a special purpose (*winding gear*). **4** a particular apparatus or mechanism, as specified (*landing gear*). **5** equipment or tackle for a special purpose. **6** *colloq.* **a** clothing, esp. when modern or fashionable. **b** possessions in general. **7** goods; household utensils. **8** rigging. **9** a harness for a draft animal. • *v.* **1** *tr.* (foll. by *to*) adjust or adapt to suit a special purpose or need. **2** *tr.* (often foll. by *up*) equip with gears. **3** *tr.* (foll. by *up*) make ready or prepared. **4** *tr.* put (machinery) in gear. **5** *intr.* **a** *Brit.* be in gear. **b** (foll. by *with*) work smoothly with. ▫ **be geared** (or **all geared**) **up** *colloq.* be ready or enthusiastic. **in gear** with a gear engaged. **out of gear 1** with no gear engaged. **2** out of order.

gear·box /géerboks/ *n.* **1** the casing that encloses a set of gears. **2** a set of gears with its casing, esp. in a motor vehicle; a transmission.

gear·ing /géering/ *n.* a set or arrangement of gears in a machine.

gear·shift /géershift/ *n.* a lever used to engage or change gear, esp. in a motor vehicle.

gear·wheel /géerhweel, –weel/ *n.* **1** a toothed wheel in a set of gears. **2** (in a bicycle) the cogwheel driven directly by the chain.

geck·o /gékō/ *n.* (*pl.* **-os** or **-oes**) any of various house lizards found in warm climates, with adhesive feet for climbing vertical surfaces.

gee[1] /jee/ *int.* (also **gee whiz**) /wiz/) *colloq.* a mild expression of surprise, etc.

gee[2] /jee/ *int.* (often foll. by *up*) a command to a horse, etc., to go faster.

gee[3] /jee/ *n. sl.* (usu. in *pl.*) a thousand dollars.

geek /geek/ *n. sl.* **1** a person who is socially inept or tediously conventional. **2** a carnival performer who bites the heads off live chickens.

geese *pl.* of GOOSE.

gee·zer /géezər/ *n. sl.* a person, esp. an old man.

Gei·ger count·er /gígər/ *n.* a device for measuring radioactivity by detecting and counting ionizing particles.

gei·sha /gáyshə, gée–/ *n.* (*pl.* same or **geishas**) a Japanese hostess trained in entertaining men with dance and song.

gel /jel/ *n. & v.* • *n.* **1** a semisolid colloidal suspension or jelly, of a solid dispersed in a liquid. **2** a gelatinous hair-styling preparation. • *v.intr.* (**gelled, gelling**) form a gel.

gel·a·tin /jélətin/ *n.* (also **gel·a·tine** /–teen/) a virtually colorless, tasteless, transparent, water-soluble protein derived from collagen and used in food, photography, etc. ▫▫ **ge·lat·i·nize** /jilát'nīz/ *v.tr. & intr.* **ge·lat·i·ni·za·tion** /jilát'nizáyshən/ *n.*

ge·lat·i·nous /jilát'nəs/ *adj.* **1** of or like gelatin. **2** of a jellylike consistency. ▫▫ **ge·lat·i·nous·ly** *adv.*

ge·la·tion /jiláyshən/ *n.* solidification by freezing.

ge·la·to /jəlaátō/ *n.* a kind of Italian ice cream.

geld /geld/ *v.tr.* **1** deprive (usu. a male animal) of the ability to reproduce. **2** castrate or spay; excise the testicles or ovaries of.

geld·ing /gélding/ *n.* a gelded animal, esp. a male horse.

gel·ig·nite /jélignīt/ *n.* an explosive made from nitroglycerine, cellulose nitrate, sodium or potassium nitrate, and wood pulp.

gem /jem/ *n. & v.* • *n.* **1** a precious or semi-precious stone, esp. when cut and polished or engraved. **2** an object or person of great beauty or worth. • *v.tr.* (**gemmed, gemming**) adorn with or as with gems. ▫▫ **gem·like** *adj.*

Ge·ma·ra /gimaárə, -nee/ *n.* a rabbinical commentary forming the second part of the Talmud.

gem·i·nate *adj. & v.* • *adj.* /jéminət/ combined in pairs. • *v.tr.* /jéminayt/ **1** double; repeat. **2** arrange in pairs. ▫▫ **gem·i·na·tion** *n.*

Gem·i·ni /jéminī, –nee/ *n.* **1** a constellation, traditionally regarded as contained in the figures of twins. **2 a** the third sign of the zodiac (the Twins). **b** a person born when the sun is in this sign. ▫▫ **Gem·i·ne·an** /jémineéən, –nīən/ *n. & adj.*

gem·ma /jémə/ *n.* (**pl. gemmae** /–mee/) a small cellular body that separates from a mother plant and starts a new one; an asexual spore.

gem·ol·o·gy /jemóləjee/ *n.* (also **gem·mol·o·gy**) the study of gems. ▫▫ **gem·ol·o·gist** or **gem·mol·o·gist** *n.*

gem·stone /jémstōn/ *n.* a precious stone used as a gem.

Gen. *abbr.* General.

-gen /jən/ *comb. form Chem.* that which produces (*hydrogen; antigen*).

gen·darme /zhondaárm/ *n.* **1** a police officer, esp. in France. **2** a soldier, mounted or on foot, employed in police duties, esp. in France.

gen·der /jéndər/ *n.* **1 a** the grammatical classification of nouns and related words, roughly corresponding to the two sexes and sexlessness. **b** each of the classes of nouns (see MASCULINE, FEMININE, NEUTER, COMMON *adj.* 6). **2** (of nouns and related words) the property of belonging to such a class. **3** *colloq.* a person's sex.

gen·der ben·der *n.* a person or thing not conforming to sexual stereotypes.

gene /jeen/ *n.* a unit of heredity composed of DNA or RNA and forming part of a chromosome, etc., that determines a particular characteristic of an individual.

ge·ne·a·log·i·cal /jéeneeəlójikəl/ *adj.* **1** of or concerning genealogy. **2** tracing family descent. ▫▫ **ge·ne·a·log·i·cal·ly** *adv.*

ge·ne·al·o·gy /jéeneeáləjee/ *n.* (*pl.* **-gies**) **1 a** a line of descent traced continuously from an ancestor. **b** an account of this. **2** the study and investigation of lines of descent. **3** a plant's or animal's line of development from earlier forms. ▫▫ **ge·ne·al·o·gist** *n.* **ge·ne·al·o·gize** *v.tr. & intr.*

gen·er·a *pl.* of GENUS.

gen·er·al /jénərəl/ *adj. & n.* • *adj.* **1 a** completely or almost universal. **b** including or affecting all or nearly all parts or cases of things. **2** prevalent; widespread; usual. **3** not partial, particular, local, or sectional. **4** not limited in application; relating to whole classes or all cases. **5** including points common to the individuals of a class and neglecting the differences (*a general term*). **6** not restricted or specialized (*general knowledge*). **7 a** roughly corresponding. **b** sufficient for practical purposes. **8** not detailed (*a general resemblance*). **9** vague; indefinite (*spoke only in general terms*). **10** chief or principal; having overall authority (*general manager; Secretary General*). • *n.* **1 a** an army officer ranking next above lieutenant general. **b** = BRIGADIER GENERAL, LIEUTENANT GENERAL, MAJOR GENERAL. **2** a commander of an army. **3** a tactician or strategist of specified merit (*a great general*). **4** the head of a religious order, e.g., of the Jesuits or the Salvation Army. ▫ **in general 1** as a normal rule; usually. **2** for the most part. ▫▫ **gen·er·al·ness** *n.*

gen·er·al e·lec·tion *n.* the election of representatives to a legislature from constituencies throughout the country.

gen·er·al·is·si·mo /jénərəlísimō/ *n.* (*pl.* **-mos**) the commander of a combined military force in some countries consisting of army, navy, and air force units.

gen·er·al·ist /jénərəlist/ *n.* a person competent in several different fields or activities (opp. SPECIALIST).

gen·er·al·i·ty /jénərálitee/ *n.* (*pl.* **-ties**) **1** a statement or principle, etc. having general validity or force. **2** applicability to a whole class of instances. **3** vagueness; lack of detail. **4** (foll. by *of*) the main body or majority.

gen·er·al·i·za·tion /jénərəlizáyshən/ *n.* **1** a general notion or proposition obtained by inference from particular cases. **2** the act of generalizing.

gen·er·al·ize /jénərəlīz/ *v.* **1** *intr.* **a** speak in general or indefinite terms. **b** form general principles or notions. **2** *tr.* reduce to a general statement, principle, or notion. **3** *tr.* give a general character to. **4** *tr.* infer (a law or conclusion) by induction. **5** *tr. Math. & Philos.* express in a general form; extend the application of. **6** *tr.* bring into general use. ▫▫ **gen·er·al·iz·a·ble** *adj.* **gen·er·al·iz·a·bil·i·ty** *n.* **gen·er·al·iz·er** *n.*

gen·er·al·ly /jénərəlee/ *adv.* **1** usually; in most cases. **2** in a general sense; without regard to particulars or exceptions (*generally speaking*). **3** for the most part; extensively (*not generally known*). **4** in most respects (*they were generally well-behaved*).

gen·er·al prac·ti·tion·er *n.* a doctor working in the community and treating cases of all kinds in the first instance.

gen·er·al·ship /jénərəlship/ *n.* **1** the art or practice of exercising military command. **2** military skill; strategy. **3** skillful management; tact; diplomacy.

gen·er·al store *n.* a store, usu. located in a rural area, that carries a wide variety of items, as food, clothing, etc., without being divided into departments.

gen·er·ate /jénərayt/ *v.tr.* **1** bring into existence. **2** produce (electricity). ▫▫ **gen·er·a·ble** /–rəbəl/ *adj.*

gen·er·a·tion /jénəráyshən/ *n.* **1** all the people born at a particular time, regarded collectively (*my generation; the next generation*). **2** a single step in descent or pedigree (*have known them for three generations*). **3** a stage in (esp. technological) development (*fourth-generation computers*). **4** the average time in which children are ready to take the place of their parents (usu. figured at about 30 years). **5** production by natural or artificial process, esp. the production of electricity or heat. **6 a** procreation; the propagation of species. **b** the act of begetting or being begotten. ▫▫ **gen·er·a·tion·al** *adj.*

gen·er·a·tion gap *n.* difference of outlook or opinion between those of different generations.

Gen·er·a·tion X *n.* term used for people born from about 1965 to 1975 (fr. a novel by Douglas Coupland).

gen·er·a·tive /jénərətiv, –raytiv/ *adj.* **1** of or concerning procreation. **2** able to produce; productive.

gen·er·a·tor /jénəraytər/ *n.* **1** a machine for converting mechanical into electrical energy. **2** an apparatus for producing gas, steam, etc.

ge·ner·ic /jinérik/ *adj.* **1** characteristic of or relating to a class; general. **2** *Biol.* characteristic of or belonging to a genus. **3** (of goods, esp. a drug) having no brand name. ▫▫ **ge·ner·i·cal·ly** *adv.*

gen·er·ous /jénərəs/ *adj.* **1** giving or given freely. **2** magnanimous; noble-minded. **3** ample; abundant (*a generous portion*). ▫▫ **gen·er·os·i·ty** /–rósitee/ *n.* **gen·er·ous·ly** *adv.*

gen·e·sis /jénisis/ *n.* **1** the origin, or mode of formation, of a thing. **2** (**Genesis**) the first book of the Old Testament.

gene ther·a·py *n. Med.* the introduction of normal genes into cells in place of defective or missing ones in order to correct genetic disorders.

ge·net·ic /jinétik/ *adj.* **1** of genetics or genes; inherited. **2** of, in, or concerning origin; causal. ▫▫ **ge·net·i·cal·ly** *adv.*

ge·net·ic code *n. Biochem.* the means by which genetic information is stored as sequences of nucleotide bases in the chromosomal DNA.

ge·net·ic en·gi·neer·ing *n.* the deliberate modification of the characteristics of an organism by the manipulation of DNA.

ge·net·ic fin·ger·print·ing *n.* (also **genetic profiling**) the analysis of characteristic patterns in DNA as a means of identifying individuals.

ge·net·ics /jinétiks/ *n.pl.* (usu. treated as *sing.*) the study of heredity and the variation of inherited characteristics. ▫▫ **ge·net·i·cist** /–tisist/ *n.*

Ge·ne·va bands /jinéevə/ *n.pl.* two white cloth strips attached to the collar of some Protestants' clerical dress.

ge·nial[1] /jéeneeəl/ *adj.* **1** jovial; sociable. **2** (of the climate) mild and warm. **3** cheering; enlivening. ▫▫ **ge·ni·al·i·ty** /–neeálitee/ *n.* **gen·ial·ly** *adv.*

ge·ni·al[2] /jiníəl/ *adj. Anat.* of or relating to the chin.

-genic /jénik/ *comb. form* forming adjectives meaning: **1** producing (*carcinogenic*). **2** well suited to (*photogenic*). **3** produced by (*iatrogenic*).

ge·nie /jéenee/ *n.* (*pl.* usu. **genii** /jéenee-ī/) a jinni, goblin, or familiar spirit of Arabian folklore.

ge·ni·i *pl.* of GENIE, GENIUS.

gen·i·tal /jénit'l/ *adj. & n.* • *adj.* of or relating to animal reproduction. • *n.* (in *pl.*) the external reproductive organs.

gen·i·ta·li·a /jénitáyleeə/ *n.pl.* the genitals.

gen·i·tive /jénitiv/ *n. & adj. Gram.* • *n.* the case of nouns and pronouns (and words in grammatical agreement with them) corresponding to *of, from,* and other prepositions and indicating possession or close association. • *adj.* of or in the genitive. ▫▫ **gen·i·ti·val** /–tívəl/ *adj.* **gen·i·ti·val·ly** *adv.*

genito- /jénitō/ *comb. form* genital.

gen·ius /jéenyəs/ *n.* (*pl.* **geniuses** or **genii** /–nee-ī/) (*pl.* **geniuses**) **1** an exceptional intellectual or creative power. **2** a person having this.

gen·o·cide /jénəsīd/ *n.* the deliberate extermination of a people or nation. ▫▫ **gen·o·cid·al** /–sīd'l/ *adj.*

ge·nome /jéenōm/ *n.* **1** the haploid set of chromosomes of an organism. **2** the genetic material of an organism.

gen·o·type /jéenətīp/ *n. Biol.* the genetic constitution of an individual. ▫▫ **gen·o·typ·ic** /–típik/ *adj.*

-genous *comb. form* forming adjectives meaning 'produced' (*endogenous*).

gen·re /zhónrə/ *n.* **1** a kind or style, esp. of art or literature (e.g., novel, drama, satire). **2** (in full **genre painting**) the painting of scenes from ordinary life.

gens /jenz/ *n.* (*pl.* **gentes** /jénteez/) **1** *Rom.Hist.* a group of families sharing a name and claiming a common origin. **2** *Anthropol.* a number of people sharing descent through the male line.

gent /jent/ *n. colloq.* (often *joc.*) **1** a gentleman. **2** (**the Gents**) *Brit. colloq.* a men's public toilet.

gen·teel /jentéel/ *adj.* **1** polite, refined, respectable. **2** often *iron.* of or appropriate to the upper classes; polite or refined in an affected way. ▫▫ **gen·teel·ly** *adv.* **gen·teel·ness** *n.*

gen·tes *pl.* of **gens**

gen·tian /jénshən/ *n.* any plant of the genus *Gentiana* or *Gentianella*, found esp. in mountainous regions, and having usu. vivid blue flowers.

gen·tile /jéntīl/ *adj. & n.* (also **Gentile**) • *adj.* **1** not Jewish. **2** (in the Mormon Church) not Mormon. • *n.* **1** a person who is not Jewish. **2** (in the Mormon Church) a person who is not Mormon.

gen·til·i·ty /jentílitee/ *n.* **1** social superiority. **2** good manners.

gen·tle /jént'l/ *adj.* (**gentler, gentlest**) **1** mild or kind in temperament. **2** moderate; not severe or drastic (*a gentle rebuke; a gentle breeze*). **3** (of birth, pursuits, etc.) honorable; of or fit for people of good social position. **4** quiet; requiring patience (*gentle art*). ▫▫ **gen·tle·ness** *n.* **gent·ly** *adv.*

gent·le·man /jént'lmən/ *n.* (*pl.* **-men**) **1** a man (in polite or formal use). **2** a chivalrous or well-bred man. **3** a man of good social position or of wealth and leisure (*country gentleman*). **4** esp. *Brit.* a man of gentle birth attached to a royal household (*gentleman in waiting*). **5** (in *pl.* as a form of address) a male audience or the male part of an audience.

gen·tle·man·ly /jént'lmənlee/ *adj.* like a gentleman in looks or behavior; befitting a gentleman. ▫▫ **gen·tle·man·li·ness** *n.*

gen·tle·man's (or **-men's**) **a·gree·ment** *n.* an agreement that is binding in honor but not legally enforceable.

gen·tle·wom·an /jént'lwŏŏmən/ *n.* (*pl.* **-women**) *archaic* a woman of good birth.

gen·too /jéntōō/ *n.* a penguin, *Pygoscelis papua*, with a white triangular patch above the eye, breeding on subantarctic islands.

gen·tri·fi·ca·tion /jéntrifikáyshən/ *n.* the social advancement of an inner urban area by the refurbishing of buildings and arrival of affluent middle-class residents, usu. displacing poorer inhabitants. ▫▫ **gen·tri·fy** /–fī/ *v.tr.* (**-fies, -fied**).

gen·try /jéntree/ *n.pl.* the people next below the nobility in position and birth.

gen·u·flect /jényəflekt/ *v.intr.* bend the knee, esp. in worship or as a sign of respect. ▫▫ **gen·u·flec·tion** /–flékshən/ *n.* **gen·u·flec·tor** *n.*

gen·u·ine /jényōō-in/ *adj.* **1** actually coming from its stated or reputed source; authentic. **2** properly so called; not a sham. ▫▫ **gen·u·ine·ly** *adv.* **gen·u·ine·ness** *n.*

ge·nus /jéenəs/ *n.* (*pl.* **genera** /jénərə/) **1** *Biol.* a taxonomic grouping of organisms having common characteristics, usu. containing multiple species. **2** a kind or class having common characteristics.

-geny /jənee/ *comb. form* forming nouns meaning 'mode of production or development of' (*ontogeny, pathogeny*).

geo- /jée-ō/ *comb. form* earth.

ge·o·bot·a·ny /jéeōbót'nee/ *n.* the study of the geographical distribution of plants.▫▫ **ge·o·bot·a·nist** *n.*

ge·o·cen·tric /jéeōséntrik/ *adj.* **1** considered as viewed from the center of the earth. **2** having the earth as the center. ▫▫ **ge·o·cen·tri·cal·ly** *adv.*

ge·o·chem·is·try /jéeōkémistree/ *n.* the chemistry of the earth and its rocks, minerals, etc. ▫▫ **ge·o·chem·i·cal** /–mikəl/ *adj.* **ge·o·chem·ist** /–mist/ *n.*

ge·ode /jée-ōd/ *n.* **1** a small cavity lined with crystals or other mineral matter. **2** a rock containing such a cavity. ▫▫ **ge·od·ic** /jee-ódik/ *adj.*

ge·o·des·ic /jéeədéezik, –désik/ *adj.* (also **ge·o·det·ic** /–détik/) **1** of or relating to geodesy. **2** of, involving, or consisting of a geodesic line.

ge·o·des·ic dome *n.* a dome constructed of short struts along geodesic lines.

ge·o·des·ic line *n.* the shortest possible line between two points on a curved surface.

ge·od·e·sy /jeeódisee/ *n.* the branch of mathematics dealing with the shape and area of the earth. ▫▫ **ge·od·e·sist** *n.*

ge·o·det·ic var. of GEODESIC.

ge·o·graph·ic /jéeəgráfik/ *adj.* (also **ge·o·graph·i·cal** /–gráfikəl/) of or relating to geography. ▫▫ **ge·o·graph·i·cal·ly** *adv.*

ge·o·graph·ic in·for·ma·tion sys·tem(s) *n.* a computerized system utilizing precise locational data for mapping, navigation, etc. ¶ Abbr.: **GIS**.

ge·og·ra·phy /jeeógrəfee/ *n.* **1** the study of the earth's physical features, resources, and climate, and the physical aspects of its population. **2** the main physical features of an area. **3** the layout or arrangement of any set of constituent elements. ▫▫ **ge·og·ra·pher** *n.*

geol. *abbr.* **1** geologic. **2** geological. **3** geologist. **4** geology.

ge·ol·o·gy /jeeóləjee/ *n.* **1** the science of the earth, including the composition, structure, and origin of its rocks. **2** this science applied to any other planet. **3** the geological features of a district. ▫▫ **ge·o·log·ic** /jéeəlójik/ *adj.* **ge·o·log·i·cal** *adj.* **ge·o·log·i·cal·ly** *adv.* **ge·ol·o·gist** /–óləjist/ *n.*

geom. *abbr.* **1** geometric. **2** geometrical. **3** geometry.

ge·o·mag·net·ism /jéeōmágnitizəm/ *n.* the study of the magnetic properties of the earth. ▫▫ **ge·o·mag·net·ic** /–magnétik/ *adj.*

ge·om·e·ter /jeeómitər/ *n.* **1** a person skilled in geometry. **2** (also **ge·om·e·trid**) any moth, esp. of the family Geometridae, having twiglike larvae that move in a looping fashion, seeming to measure the ground.

ge·o·met·ric /jeeəmétrik/ *adj.* (also **ge·o·met·ri·cal**) **1** of or like geometry. **2** (of a design, etc.) characterized by or decorated with regular lines and shapes. ▫▫ **ge·o·met·ri·cal·ly** *adv.*

ge·o·met·ric pro·gres·sion *n.* a progression of numbers with a constant ratio between each number and the one before (as 1, 3, 9, 27, 81).

ge·om·e·try /jeeómitree/ *n.* **1** the branch of mathematics concerned with the properties and relations of points, lines, surfaces, and solids. **2** the relative arrangement of objects or parts. ▫▫ **ge·om·e·tri·cian** /jéeəmitríshən/ *n.*

ge·o·mor·phol·o·gy /jéeōmawrfóləjee/ *n.* the study of the physical features of the surface of the earth and their relation to its geological structures. ▫▫ **ge·o·mor·pho·log·i·cal** /–fəlójikəl/ *adj.* **ge·o·mor·phol·o·gist** *n.*

ge·oph·a·gy /jeeófəjee/ *n.* the practice in some cultures of eating earth, esp. clay, to supplement diet.

ge·o·phys·ics /jée-ōfíziks/ *n.* the physics of the earth. ▫▫ **ge·o·phys·i·cal** *adj.* **ge·o·phys·i·cist** /–zisist/ *n.*

ge·o·pol·i·tics /jée-ōpólitiks/ *n.* **1** the politics of a country as determined by its geographical features. **2** the study of this. ▫▫ **ge·o·po·lit·i·cal** /–pəlítikəl/ *adj.* **ge·o·po·lit·i·cal·ly** *adv.* **ge·o·pol·i·ti·cian** /–tíshən/ *n.*

Geor·gian[1] /jáwrjən/ *adj. & n.* • *adj.* of or relating to the state of Georgia. • *n.* a native of Georgia.

Geor·gian[2] /jáwrjən/ *adj.* **1** of or characteristic of the time of Kings George I–IV (1714–1830) of England. **2** of or characteristic of the time of Kings George V and VI (1910–52).

Geor·gian[3] /jáwrjən/ *adj. & n.* • *adj.* of or relating to Georgia in the Caucasus. • *n.* **1** a native of Georgia; a person of Georgian descent. **2** the language of Georgia.

ge·o·sphere /jéeəsfeer/ *n.* **1** the solid surface of the earth. **2** any of the almost spherical concentric regions of the earth and its atmosphere.

ge·o·sta·tion·ar·y /jée-ōstáyshəneree/ *adj.* = GEOSYNCHRONOUS.

ge·o·stroph·ic /jée-ōstrófik/ *adj. Meteorol.* depending upon the rotation of the Earth.

ge·o·syn·chro·nous /jée-ōsíngkrənəs/ *adj.* (of an artificial satellite of the earth) moving in an orbit equal to the earth's period of rotation, so as to remain above one place. Also called **geostationary**.

ge·o·ther·mal /jée-ōthə́rməl/ *adj.* relating to, originating from, or produced by the internal heat of the earth.

ge·ot·ro·pism /jeeótrəpizəm/ *n.* plant growth in relation to gravity. ▫ **negative geotropism** the tendency of stems, etc., to grow away from the center of the Earth. **positive geotropism** the tendency of roots to grow toward the center of the Earth. ▫▫ **ge·o·tro·pic** /jeeətrṓpik, -otrópik/ *adj.*

ge·ra·ni·um /jəráyneeəm/ *n.* **1** any herb or shrub of the genus *Geranium* bearing fruit shaped like the bill of a crane. **2** (in general use) a cultivated pelargonium.

ger·bil /jə́rbil/ *n.* a mouselike desert rodent of the subfamily Gerbillinae, with long hind legs.

ger·i·at·ric /jéreeátrik/ *adj. & n.* • *adj.* **1** of or relating to old people. **2** *colloq.* old; outdated. • *n.* an old person, esp. one receiving special care.

ger·i·at·rics /jéreeátriks/ *n.pl.* (usu. treated as *sing.*) a branch of medicine dealing with the health and care of old people. ▫▫ **ger·i·a·tri·cian** /–ətríshən/ *n.*

germ /jərm/ *n.* **1** a microorganism, esp. one that causes disease. **2 a** a portion of an organism capable of developing into a new one; the rudiment of an animal or plant. **b** an embryo of a seed (*wheat germ*). **3** an original idea, etc., from which something may develop.

Ger·man /jə́rmən/ *n. & adj.* • *n.* **1** a native or inhabitant of Germany; a person of German descent. **2** the language of Germany, also used in Austria and Switzerland. • *adj.* of or relating to Germany or its people or language.

ger·man /jə́rmən/ *adj.* (placed after *brother*, *sister*, or *cousin*) **1** having the same parents. **2** having the same grandparents on one side.

ger·mane /jərmáyn/ *adj.* (usu. foll. by *to*) relevant (to a subject under consideration). ▫▫ **ger·mane·ly** *adv.* **ger·mane·ness** *n.*

Ger·man·ic /jərmánik/ *adj. & n.* • *adj.* **1** having German characteristics. **2** *hist.* of the Germans. **3** of the Scandinavians, Anglo-Saxons, or Germans. **4** of the languages or language group called Germanic. • *n.* **1** the branch of Indo-European languages including English, German, Dutch, and the Scandinavian languages. **2** the (unrecorded) early language from which other Germanic languages developed.

ger·man·ic /jərmánik/ *adj. Chem.* of or containing germanium, esp. in its tetravalent state.

Ger·man·ist /jə́rmənist/ *n.* an expert in or student of the language, literature, and civilization of Germany, or Germanic languages.

ger·ma·ni·um /jərmáyneeəm/ *n. Chem.* a lustrous brittle semimetallic element occurring naturally in sulfide ores and used in semiconductors. ¶ Symb.: **Ge.**

Ger·man·ize /jə́rmənīz/ *v.tr. & intr.* adopt or cause to adopt German customs, etc. ▫▫ **Ger·man·i·za·tion** *n.* **Ger·man·i·zer** *n.*

Ger·man mea·sles *n.* a contagious disease, rubella, with symptoms like mild measles.

Ger·man shep·herd *n.* **1** a large breed of dog used esp. in police work and as guide dogs for the blind. **2** a dog of this breed.

ger·mi·cide /jə́rmisīd/ *n.* a substance destroying germs, esp. those causing disease. ▫▫ **ger·mi·cid·al** /sī́d'l/ *adj.*

ger·mi·nal /jə́rminəl/ *adj.* **1** relating to or of the nature of a germ or germs (see GERM 1). **2** in the earliest stage of development. **3** productive of new ideas. ▫▫ **ger·mi·nal·ly** *adv.*

ger·mi·nate /jə́rminayt/ *v.* **1 a** *intr.* sprout, bud, or put forth shoots. **b** *tr.* cause to sprout or shoot. **2 a** *tr.* cause (ideas, etc.) to originate. **b** *intr.* come into existence. ▫▫ **ger·mi·na·tion** /–náyshən/ *n.*

ger·on·tol·o·gy /jərontóləjee/ *n.* the scientific study of old age, the process of aging, and the special problems of old people. ▫▫ **ge·ron·to·log·i·cal** /–təlójikəl/ *adj.* **ger·on·tol·o·gist** *n.*

ger·ry·man·der /jérimándər/ *v.tr.* **1** manipulate the boundaries of (an electoral district, etc.) so as to give undue influence to some party or class. **2** manipulate (a situation, etc.) to gain advantage. ▫▫ **ger·ry·man·der·er** *n.*

ger·und /jérənd/ *n. Gram.* a form of a verb functioning as a noun, orig. in Latin ending in *-ndum* (declinable), in English ending in *-ing* and used distinctly as a part of a verb (e.g., *do you mind my asking?*).

ge·run·dive /jərúndiv/ *n. Gram.* a form of a Latin verb, ending in *-ndus* (declinable) and functioning as an adjective meaning 'that should or must be done,' etc.

ge·stalt /gəshtaált, –staált, –shtáwlt, –stawlt/ *n. Psychol.* an organized whole that is perceived as more than the sum of its parts. ▫▫ **ge·stalt·ism** *n.* **ge·stalt·ist** *n.*

Ge·sta·po /gestaápō, –shtaá–/ *n.* the German secret police under Nazi rule.

ges·tate /jéstáyt/ *v.tr.* **1** carry (a fetus) in gestation. **2** develop (an idea, etc.).

ges·ta·tion /jestáyshən/ *n.* **1 a** the process of carrying or being carried in the womb between conception and birth. **b** this period. **2** the private development of a plan, idea, etc.

ges·tic·u·late /jestíkyəlayt/ *v.* **1** *intr.* use gestures instead of or in addition to speech. **2** *tr.* express with gestures. ▫▫ **ges·tic·u·la·tion** /–láyshən/ *n.* **ges·tic·u·la·tive** *adj.* **ges·tic·u·la·to·ry** /–lətáwree/ *adj.*

ges·ture /jés-chər/ *n. & v.* • *n.* **1** a significant movement of a limb or the body. **2** the use of such movements, esp. as a rhetorical device. **3** an action to evoke a response or convey intention, usu. friendly. • *v.tr. & intr.* gesticulate. ▫▫ **ges·tur·al** *adj.*

ge·sund·heit /gəzŏŏnt-hīt/ *int.* expressing a wish of good health, esp. to a person who has sneezed.

get /get/ *v.* (**getting**; *past* **got** /got/; *past part.* **got** /got/, *gotten* /gót'n/) **1** *tr.* come into the possession of (*get a job; got a new car*). **2** *tr.* fetch; obtain (*get my book for me; got $200 a week*). **3** *tr.* go to catch (a bus, train, etc.). **4** *tr.* prepare (a meal, etc.). **5** *intr. & tr.* reach or cause to reach a certain state; become or cause to become (*get rich; get one's feet wet*). **6** *tr.* obtain as a result of calculation. **7** *tr.* contract (a disease, etc.). **8** *tr.* establish or be in communication with via telephone or radio; receive (a radio signal). **9** *tr.* experience or suffer; have inflicted on one; receive as one's lot or penalty (*got four years in prison*). **10 a** *tr.* succeed in bringing, placing, etc. (*get it onto the agenda; flattery will get you nowhere*). **b** *intr. & tr.* succeed or cause to succeed in coming or going (*will get you there somehow; got absolutely nowhere*). **11** *tr.* (prec. by *have*) **a** possess (*haven't got a penny*). **b** (foll. by *to* + infin.) be bound (*have got to see you*). **12** *tr.* (foll. by *to* + infin.) induce (*got them to help me*). **13** *tr. colloq.* understand (a person or an argument) (*have you got that?; do you get me?*). **14** *tr. colloq.* inflict punishment or retribution on, esp. in retaliation (*I'll get you for that*). **15** *tr. colloq.* **a** annoy. **b** affect emotionally. **c** attract; obsess. **d** amuse. **16** *tr.* (foll. by *to* + infin.) develop an inclination as specified (*am getting to like it*). **17** *intr.* (foll. by verbal noun) begin (*get going*). **18** *tr.* (esp. in *past* or *perfect*) catch in an argument; corner. **19** *tr.* establish (an idea) in one's mind. □ **get about** (or **around**) **1** travel extensively; go from place to place. **2** manage to walk (esp. after illness). **3** (of news) be circulated. **get across 1** manage to communicate (an idea). **2** (of an idea) be communicated successfully. **get ahead** be or become successful. **get along** (or **on**) (foll. by *together, with*) live harmoniously. **get around 1** successfully coax or cajole (a person) esp. to secure a favor. **2** evade (a law, etc.). **get around to** deal with (a task, etc.) in due course. **get at 1** reach; get hold of. **2** *colloq.* imply (*what are you getting at?*). **3** *colloq.* try to upset or irritate. **get away 1** escape. **2** (foll. by *with*) escape blame or punishment for. **get back at** *colloq.* retaliate against. **get by** *colloq.* **1** just manage, even with difficulty. **2** be acceptable. **get down 1** descend (from a vehicle, ladder, etc.). **2** record in writing. **get a person down** depress or deject him or her. **get down to** begin working on or discussing. **get even** (often foll. by *with*)achieve revenge; act in retaliation. **get his** (or **hers**, etc.) *sl.* **1** be killed. **2** be avenged. **get hold (or ahold) of 1** grasp (physically). **2** make contact with (a person). **3** acquire. **get in 1** enter. **2** be elected. **get into** become interested or involved in. **get it** *sl.* **1** understand. **2** be punished or in trouble. **get it into one's head** (foll. by *that* & clause) firmly believe or maintain. **get off 1** *colloq.* be acquitted; escape with little or no punishment. **2** leave. **3** alight; alight from (a bus, etc.). **get a person off** *colloq.* cause a person to be acquitted. **get off on** *sl.* be excited or aroused by. **get on 1** make progress; manage. **2** enter (a bus, etc.). **get on to** *colloq.* **1** make contact with. **2** become aware of. **get out 1** leave or escape. **2** manage to go outdoors. **3** alight from a vehicle. **4** become known. **5** succeed in uttering, publishing, etc. **get out of 1** avoid or escape (a duty, etc.). **2** abandon (a habit) gradually. **get over 1** recover from (an illness, upset, etc.). **2** overcome (a difficulty). **3** manage to communicate (an idea, etc.). **get a thing over** (or **over with**) complete (a tedious task) promptly. **get one's own back** *colloq.* have one's revenge. **get rid of** see RID. **get somewhere** make progress. **get there** *colloq.* **1** succeed. **2** understand what is meant. **get through 1** pass or assist in passing (an examination, an ordeal, etc.). **2** finish or use up (esp. resources). **3** make contact by telephone. **4** (foll. by *to*) succeed in making (a person) listen or understand. **get to 1** reach. **2** = *get down to*. **get together** gather; assemble. **get up 1** rise or cause to rise from sitting, etc., or from bed after sleeping or an illness. **2** ascend or mount, e.g., on horseback. **3** (of fire, wind, or the sea) begin to be strong or agitated. **4** prepare or organize. **5** enhance or refine one's knowledge of (a subject). **6** work up (a feeling, e.g., anger). **7** produce or stimulate (*get up steam; get up speed*). **8** (often *refl.*) dress or arrange elaborately; make presentable; arrange the appearance of. **9** (foll. by *to*) esp. *Brit. colloq.* indulge or be involved in (*always getting up to mischief*). **have got it bad** *sl.* be obsessed or affected emotionally. □□ **get·ta·ble** *adj.*

get·a·way /gétəway/ *n.* an escape, esp. after committing a crime.

get-rich-quick *adj.* designed to make a lot of money fast.

get-to·geth·er *n. colloq.* a social gathering.

get-up *n. colloq.* a style or arrangement of dress, etc., esp. an elaborate one.

gew·gaw /gyóogaw, góo–/ *n.* a gaudy plaything or ornament; a bauble.

gey·ser /gízər/ *n.* **1** an intermittently gushing hot spring that throws up a tall column of water. **2** /géezər/ *Brit.* an apparatus for heating water.

Gha·na·ian /gaáneeən/ *adj. & n.* • *adj.* of or relating to Ghana in W. Africa. • *n.* a native or inhabitant of Ghana; a person of Ghanaian descent.

ghast·ly /gástlee/ *adj. & adv.* (**ghastlier, ghastliest**) • *adj.* **1** horrible; frightful. **2** *colloq.* objectionable; unpleasant. **3** deathlike; pallid. • *adv.* in a ghastly or sickly way (*ghastly pale*). □□ **ghast·li·ly** *adv.* **ghast·li·ness** *n.*

Gha·zi /gaázee/ *n.* (*pl.* **Ghazis**) a Muslim fighter against non-Muslims.

ghee /gee/ *n.* (also **ghi**) clarified butter esp. from the milk of a buffalo or cow.

gher·kin /gárkin/ *n.* a small variety of cucumber, or a young green cucumber, used for pickling.

ghet·to /gétō/ *n.* (*pl.* **-tos**) **1** a part of a city, esp. a slum area, occupied by a minority group or groups. **2** *hist.* the Jewish quarter in a city. **3** a segregated group or area.

ghi var. of GHEE.

ghost /gōst/ *n. & v.* • *n.* **1** the supposed apparition of a dead person or animal. **2** a mere semblance (*not a ghost of a chance*). **3** a secondary image produced by defective television reception or by a telescope. • *v.* **1** *intr.* (often foll. by *for*) act as ghostwriter. **2** *tr.* act as ghostwriter of (a work). □□ **ghost·like** *adj.*

ghost·ing /gṓsting/ *n.* the appearance of a "ghost" (see GHOST *n.* 3) in a television picture.

ghost·ly /gṓstlee/ *adj.* (**ghostlier, ghostliest**) like a ghost. □□ **ghost·li·ness** *n.*

ghost town *n.* a once-thriving town with few or no remaining inhabitants.

ghost·write /gṓstrīt/ *v.tr. & intr.* act as ghostwriter (of).

ghost·writ·er *n.* a person who writes on behalf of the credited author of a work.

ghoul /gool/ *n.* **1** a person morbidly interested in death, etc. **2** an evil spirit or phantom. **3** a spirit in Muslim folklore preying on corpses. □□ **ghoul·ish** *adj.* **ghoul·ish·ly** *adv.* **ghoul·ish·ness** *n.*

GHQ *abbr.* General Headquarters.

GI /jée-í/ *n. & adj.* • *n.* an enlisted soldier in the US armed forces, esp. the army. • *adj.* of, for, or characteristic of US soldiers.

gi·ant /jíənt/ *n. & adj.* • *n.* **1** an imaginary or mythical being of human form but superhuman size. **2** an abnormally tall or large person, animal, or plant. **3** a person of exceptional ability, importance, courage, etc. **4** a large star. • *attrib.adj.* **1** gigantic; monstrous. **2** (of a plant or animal) of a very large kind. □□ **gi·ant·ism** *n.* **gi·ant-like** *adj.*

gib·ber /jíbər/ *v. & n.* • *v.intr.* chatter incoherently. • *n.* such speech.

gib·ber·el·lin /jíbərélin/ *n.* one of a group of plant hormones that stimulate the growth of leaves and shoots.

gib·ber·ish /jíbərish/ *n.* unintelligible or meaningless speech; nonsense.

gib•bet /jíbit/ *n. hist.* **1** a gallows. **2** an upright post with an arm on which the bodies of executed criminals were left hanging in chains, irons, or an iron cage as a warning or deterrent to others.

gib•bon /gíbən/ *n.* any small ape of the genus *Hylobates,* native to SE Asia.

gib•bous /gíbəs/ *adj.* **1** convex or protuberant. **2** (of a moon or planet) having the bright part greater than a semicircle and less than a circle.

gibe /jīb/ *v. & n.* (also **jibe**) •*v.intr.* (often foll. by *at*) jeer; mock. •*n.* an instance of gibing. ◻◻ **gib•er** *n.* ▶See note at JIBE.

gib•lets /jíblits/ *n.pl.* the liver, gizzard, neck, etc., of a bird, usu. removed and kept separate when the bird is prepared for cooking.

gid•dy /gídee/ *adj. & v.* •*adj.* (**giddier, giddiest**) **1** having a sensation of whirling and a tendency to fall, stagger, or spin around. **2 a** overexcited. **b** excitable; frivolous. **3** tending to make one giddy. •*v.tr. & intr.* (**-dies, -died**) make or become giddy. ◻◻ **gid•di•ly** *adv.* **gid•di•ness** *n.*

gift /gift/ *n. & v.* •*n.* **1** a thing given. **2** a natural ability or talent. **3** the power to give (*in his gift*). **4** the act or an instance of giving. **5** *colloq.* an easy task. •*v.tr.* bestow as a gift. ◻ **look a gift horse in the mouth** (usu. *neg.*) find fault with what has been given.

gift cer•tif•i•cate *n.* a certificate used as a gift and exchangeable for goods.

gift•ed /gíftid/ *adj.* exceptionally talented or intelligent. ◻◻ **gift•ed•ness** *n.*

gift-wrap *v.tr.* (**wrapped, wrapping**) wrap attractively as a gift.

gig[1] /gig/ *n.* **1** a light two-wheeled one-horse carriage. **2** a light ship's boat for rowing or sailing. **3** a rowing boat esp. for racing.

gig[2] /gig/ *n. & v. colloq.* •*n.* an engagement of an entertainer, esp. a musician, usu. for a single appearance. •*v.intr.* (**gigged, gigging**) perform a gig.

gig[3] /gig/ *n.* a kind of fishing spear.

giga- /gígə, jígə/ *comb. form* denoting a factor of 10^9.

gig•a•bit /gígəbit, jígə–/ *n. Computing* a unit of information equal to one billion (10^9) bits.

gig•a•byte /gígəbīt, jígə–/ *n. Computing* a unit of information equal to one billion (10^9) bytes.

gi•ga•me•ter /gígəmeetər, jígə–/ *n.* a metric unit equal to 10^9) meters.

gi•gan•tic /jīgántik/ *adj.* **1** very large; enormous. **2** like or suited to a giant. ◻◻ **gi•gan•ti•cal•ly** *adv.*

gi•gan•tism /jīgántizəm/ *n.* abnormal largeness.

gig•gle /gígəl/ *v. & n.* •*v.intr.* laugh in half-suppressed spasms. •*n.* such a laugh. ◻◻ **gig•gler** *n.* **gig•gly** *adj.* (**gigglier, giggliest**).

GIGO /gígō/ *n. Computing abbr.* *g*arbage *i*n, *g*arbage *o*ut, an informal rule stating that the quality of the data input determines the quality of the results.

gig•o•lo /jígəlō, zhíg–/ *n.* (*pl.* **-los**) **1** a young man paid by an older woman to be her escort or lover. **2** a professional male dancing partner or escort.

Gi•la mon•ster /heelə/ *n.* a large venomous lizard, *Heloderma suspectum,* of the southwestern US, having orange, yellow, and black scales like beads.

gild[1] /gild/ *v.tr.* (*past part.* **gilded** or as adj. in sense 1 **gilt**) **1** cover thinly with gold. **2** tinge with a golden color or light. ◻ **gild the lily** try to improve what is already beautiful or excellent. ◻◻ **gild•er** *n.*

gild[2] var. of GUILD.

gild•ing /gílding/ *n.* **1** the act of applying gilt. **2** material used in applying gilt.

gill[1] /gil/ *n.* (usu. in *pl.*) **1** the respiratory organ in fishes and other aquatic animals. **2** the vertical radial plates on the underside of mushrooms and other fungi. **3** the flesh below a person's jaws and ears. ◻◻ **gilled** *adj.* (also in *comb.*).

gill[2] /jil/ *n.* a unit of liquid measure, equal to a quarter of a pint.

gilt[1] /gilt/ *adj. & n.* •*adj.* **1** covered thinly with gold. **2** gold-colored. •*n.* gold or a goldlike substance applied in a thin layer to a surface.

gilt[2] /gilt/ *n.* a young unbred sow.

gim•bals /gímbəlz, jím–/ *n.pl.* a contrivance, usu. of rings and pivots, for keeping a stove or instruments such as a compass and chronometer horizontal at sea, in the air, etc.

gim•crack /jímkrak/ *adj. & n.* •*adj.* showy but flimsy and worthless. •*n.* a cheap showy ornament; a knickknack. ◻◻ **gim•crack•er•y** *n.* **gim•crack•y** *adj.*

gim•let /gímlit/ *n.* a small tool with a screw tip for boring holes.

gim•mick /gímik/ *n. colloq.* a trick or device, esp. to attract publicity or trade. ◻◻ **gim•mick•ry** *n.* **gim•mick•y** *adj.*

gimp[1] /gimp/ *n.* (also **guimp, gymp**) **1** a twist of silk, etc., with cord or wire running through it, used esp. as trimming. **2** fishing line of silk, etc., bound with wire.

gimp[2] /gimp/ *n. & v. sl.* •*n.* a lame person or leg. •*v.intr.* walk with a lame gait. ◻◻ **gimp•y** *adj.*

gin[1] /jin/ *n.* an alcoholic spirit distilled from grain or malt and flavored with juniper berries.

gin[2] /jin/ *n.* **1** a machine for separating cotton from its seeds. **2** a snare or trap. ◻◻ **gin•ner** *n.*

gin•ger /jínjər/ *n., adj., & v.* •*n.* **1 a** a hot spicy root usu. powdered for use in cooking, or preserved in syrup, or candied. **b** the plant, *Zingiber officinale,* of SE Asia, having this root. **2** a light reddish yellow color. •*adj.* of a ginger color. •*v.tr.* **1** flavor with ginger. **2** (foll. by *up*) rouse or enliven. ◻◻ **gin•ger•y** *adj.*

gin•ger ale *n.* a carbonated nonalcoholic clear drink flavored with ginger extract.

gin•ger•bread /jínjərbred/ *n.* a cake made with molasses or syrup and flavored with ginger.

gin•ger•ly /jínjərlee/ *adv. & adj.* •*adv.* in a cautious manner. •*adj.* showing great caution.

gin•ger•snap /jínjərsnap/ *n.* a thin brittle cookie flavored with ginger.

ging•ham /gíng-əm/ *n.* a plain-woven cotton cloth, esp. checked.

gin•gi•va /jinjívə, jínjivə/ *n.* (*pl.* **gingivae** /–vee/) the gums. ◻◻ **gin•gi•val** /–jívəl, -jivəl/ *adj.*

gin•gi•vi•tis /jínjivítis/ *n.* inflammation of the gums.

gink•go /gíngkgō/ *n.* (also **ging•ko**) (*pl.* **-gos** or **-goes**) an orig. Chinese and Japanese tree, *Ginkgo biloba,* with fan-shaped leaves and yellow flowers. Also called MAIDENHAIR TREE.

gin rum•my *n.* a form of the card game rummy.

gin•seng /jínseng/ *n.* **1** any of several medicinal plants of the genus *Panax,* found in E. Asia and N. America. **2** the root of this.

Gip•sy var. of GYPSY.

gi•raffe /jiráf/ *n.* (*pl.* same or **giraffes**) a ruminant mammal, *Giraffa camelopardalis* of Africa, the tallest living animal, with a long neck and forelegs and a skin of dark patches separated by lighter lines.

gir•an•dole /jírəndōl/ *n.* **1** a revolving cluster of fireworks. **2** a branched candle bracket or candlestick. **3** an earring or pendant with a large central stone surrounded by small ones.

gird[1] /gərd/ *v.tr.* (*past* and *past part.* **girded** or **girt**) **1** encircle or secure with a belt or band. **2** secure (clothes) on the body with a girdle or belt. **3** enclose or encircle. **4** (foll. by *around*) place (cord, etc.) around. ◻ **gird** (or **gird up**) **one's loins** prepare for action.

gird[2] /gərd/ *v. & n.* • *v.intr.* (foll. by *at*) jeer or gibe. • *n.* a gibe or taunt.

gird·er /gə́rdər/ *n.* a large iron beam or compound structure for bearing loads.

girdle /gə́rd'l/ *n. & v.* • *n.* **1** a belt or cord worn around the waist. **2** a woman's corset extending from waist to thigh. **3** the bony support for a limb (*pelvic girdle*). • *v.tr.* surround with a girdle.

girl /gərl/ *n.* **1** a female child. **2** *colloq.* a young woman. **3** *colloq.* a girlfriend. **4** *derog.* a female servant. ▫▫ **girl·hood** *n.*

girl·friend /gə́rlfrend/ *n.* **1** a regular female companion or lover. **2** a female friend.

girl·ish /gə́rlish/ *adj.* of or like a girl. ▫▫ **girl·ish·ly** *adv.* **girl·ish·ness** *n.*

Girl Scout *n.* a member of an organization of girls, esp. the Girl Scouts of America, that promotes character, outdoor activities, community service, etc.

gi·ro /jírō/ *n. & v.* • *n.* (*pl.* **-ros**) **1** a system of credit transfer between banks, post offices, etc., in Europe. **2** a payment by giro. • *v.tr.* (**-roes, -roed**) pay by giro.

girt[1] *past part.* of GIRD[1].

girt[2] var. of GIRTH.

girth /gərth/ *n.* (also **girt** /gərt/) **1** the distance around a thing. **2** a band around the body of a horse to secure the saddle, etc.

GIS *abbr.* geographic information system(s).

gist /jist/ *n.* the substance or essence of a matter.

give /giv/ *v. & n.* • *v.* (*past* **gave** /gayv/; *past part.* **given** /gívən/) **1** *tr.* (also *absol.*) hand over as a present (*gave them her old curtains*). **2** *tr.* **a** transfer the ownership of; bequeath (*gave him $1000 in her will*). **b** transfer, esp. temporarily or for safe keeping; hand over (*gave him the dog to hold*). **c** administer (medicine). **d** deliver (a message) (*give her my best wishes*). **3** *tr.* (usu. foll. by *for*) **a** pay (*gave him $30 for the bicycle*). **b** sell (*gave him the bicycle for $30*). **4** *tr.* **a** confer; grant (a benefit, an honor, etc.). **b** accord; bestow (one's affections, confidence, etc.). **c** administer (one's approval, blame, etc.); offer (esp. something unpleasant) (*gave him a talking-to; gave him my blessing*). **d** pledge (*gave his word*). **5** *tr.* **a** perform (an action, etc.) (*gave him a kiss; gave a jump*). **b** utter (*gave a shriek*). **6** *tr.* allot; assign (*was given the contract*). **7** *tr.* (in *passive*; foll. by *to*) be inclined to or fond of (*is given to speculation*). **8** *tr.* yield as a product or result (*the lamp gives a bad light; the field gives fodder for twenty cows*). **9** *intr.* **a** yield to pressure; become relaxed; lose firmness (*this elastic doesn't give properly*). **b** collapse (*the roof gave under the pressure*). **10** *intr.* (usu. foll. by *of*) grant; bestow (*gave freely of his time*). **11** *tr.* **a** commit, consign, or entrust (*gave him into custody; give her into your care*). **b** sanction the marriage of (a daughter, etc.). **12** *tr.* devote; dedicate (*gave his life to croquet*). **13** *tr.* (usu. *absol.*) *colloq.* tell what one knows (*What happened? Come on, give!*). **14** *tr.* show; hold out (*gives no sign of life*). **15** *tr. Theatr.* read, recite etc. (*gave them Hamlet's soliloquy*). **16** *tr.* impart; be a source of (*gave its name to the battle*). **17** *tr.* allow (esp. a fixed amount of time) (*can give you five minutes*). **18** *tr.* (usu. foll. by *for*) value (something) (*gives nothing for their opinions*). **19** *tr.* concede (*I give you the victory*). **20** *tr.* deliver (a judgment, etc.) authoritatively (*gave his verdict*). **21** *tr.* toast (a person, cause, etc.) (*I give you our President*). **22** *tr.* provide (a party etc.) as host (*gave a banquet*). • *n.* **1** capacity to yield under pressure. **2** ability to adapt (*no give in his attitudes*). ▫ **give and take** *v.tr.* exchange (words, blows, or concessions). *n.* an exchange of words, etc. **give as good as one gets** retort adequately in words or blows. **give away 1** transfer as a gift. **2** hand over (a bride) ceremonially to a bridegroom. **3** expose to detection. **give back** return (something) to its previous owner or in exchange. **give chase** pursue a person, animal, etc. **give the game away** reveal a secret. **give a hand** = *lend a hand* (see HAND). **give a person his or her due** acknowledge, esp. grudgingly, a person's abilities, etc. **give in** cease fighting or arguing. **give me** I prefer (*give me the Greek islands*). **give off** emit (vapor, etc.). **give oneself** (of a woman) yield sexually. **give oneself airs** act pretentiously. **give oneself up to 1** abandon oneself to. **2** addict oneself to. **give onto** (or **into**) (of a window, corridor, etc.) overlook or lead into. **give or take** *colloq.* add or subtract (a specified amount or number) in estimating. **give out 1** announce; emit. **2** break down from exhaustion, etc. **3** run short. **give rise to** cause. **give a person to understand** inform authoritatively. **give up 1** resign; surrender. **2** part with. **3** deliver (a wanted person, etc.). **4** pronounce incurable or insoluble. **5** cease (an activity). **give up the ghost** *archaic* or *colloq.* die. **give way** see WAY. **give a person what for** *colloq.* scold severely. **not give a damn** *colloq.* not care at all. **what gives?** *colloq.* what is the news? ▫▫ **giv·er** *n.*

give·a·way /gívəway/ *n. colloq.* **1** an inadvertent betrayal or revelation. **2** an act of giving away. **3** a free gift; a low price.

giv·en /gívən/ *adj. & n.* • *adj.* **1** granted; specified (*a given number of people*). **2** *Law* (of a document) signed and dated (*given this day the 30th of June*). • *n.* a known fact or situation.

giz·mo /gízmō/ *n.* (also **gis·mo**) (*pl.* **-mos**) *sl.* a gadget.

giz·zard /gízərd/ *n.* **1** the second part of a bird's stomach, for grinding food. **2** a muscular stomach of some fish, insects, mollusks, and other invertebrates.

gla·bel·la /gləbélə/ *n.* (*pl.* **glabellae** /–lee/) the smooth part of the forehead above and between the eyebrows. ▫▫ **gla·bel·lar** *adj.*

gla·cé /glasáy/ *adj.* **1** (of fruit, esp. cherries) preserved in sugar. **2** (of cloth, leather, etc.) smooth; polished.

gla·cial /gláyshəl/ *adj.* **1** of ice; icy. **2** *Geol.* characterized or produced by the presence or agency of ice. **3** *colloq.* exceptionally slow. **4** *Chem.* forming icelike crystals upon freezing (*glacial acetic acid*). ▫▫ **gla·cial·ly** *adv.*

gla·cier /gláyshər/ *n.* a mass of land ice formed by the accumulation of snow on high ground.

gla·ci·ol·o·gy /gláysheeóləjee, –see–/ *n.* the science of the internal dynamics and effects of glaciers. ▫▫ **gla·ci·o·log·i·cal** /–əlójikəl/ *adj.* **gla·ci·ol·o·gist** *n.*

glad /glad/ *adj.* (**gladder, gladdest**) **1** (*predic.*) pleased (*shall be glad to come*). **2 a** filled with or expressing joy (*a glad expression*). **b** (of news, events, etc.) giving joy (*glad tidings*). ▫▫ **glad·ly** *adv.* **glad·ness** *n.* **glad·some** *adj. poet.*

glade /glayd/ *n.* an open space in a wood or forest.

glad·i·a·tor /gládee-aytər/ *n. hist.* **1** a man trained to fight in an arena at ancient Roman shows. **2** a person defending or opposing a cause; a controversialist. ▫▫ **glad·i·a·to·ri·al** /–deeətáwreeəl/ *adj.*

glad·i·o·lus /gládeeṓləs/ *n.* (*pl.* **gladioli** /–lī/ or **gladioluses**) a plant of the genus *Gladiolus* with sword-shaped leaves and brightly colored flower spikes.

glad rags *n.pl. colloq.* best clothes.

Glad·stone bag /gládstōn, –stən/ *n.* a suitcase that opens flat into two equal compartments.

Glag·o·lit·ic /glágəlítik/ *adj.* of or relating to the alphabet ascribed to St. Cyril and formerly used in writing some Slavonic languages.

glair /glair/ *n.* (also **glaire**) **1** white of egg. **2** an adhesive preparation made from this, used in bookbinding, etc. ▫▫ **glair·e·eous** *adj.* **glair·y** *adj.*

glaive /glayv/ *n. archaic poet.* **1** a broadsword. **2** any sword.

glam·or·ize /glámərīz/ *v.tr.* (also **glam·our·ize**) make glamorous or attractive. □□ **glam·or·i·za·tion** *n.*

glam·our /glámər/ *n.* (also **glam·or**) **1** physical attractiveness, esp. when achieved by makeup, etc. **2** alluring or exciting beauty or charm (*the glamour of New York*). □□ **glam·or·ous** *adj.* **glam·or·ous·ly** *adv.*

glance /glans/ *v. & n.* •*v.* **1** *intr.* cast a momentary look (*glanced up at the sky*). **2** *intr.* (esp. of a weapon) bounce (off an object). **3** *intr.* (of talk or a talker) pass quickly over a subject (*glanced over the question of payment*). **4** *intr.* (of a bright object or light) flash or gleam (*the sun glanced off the knife*). **5** *tr.* (esp. of a weapon) strike (an object) obliquely. •*n.* **1** a brief look. **2** a flash or gleam (*a glance of sunlight*). □ **at a glance** immediately upon looking. **glance over** (or **through**) read cursorily. □□ **glanc·ing·ly** *adv.*

gland[1] /gland/ *n.* **1 a** an organ in an animal body secreting substances for use in the body or for ejection. **b** a structure resembling this, such as a lymph gland. **2** *Bot.* a secreting cell or group of cells on the surface of a plant structure.

gland[2] /gland/ *n.* a sleeve used to produce a seal around a moving shaft.

glan·du·lar /glánjələr/ *adj.* of or relating to a gland or glands.

glan·du·lar fe·ver *n.* an infectious viral disease characterized by swelling of the lymph glands and prolongued lassitude. Also called **infectious mononucleosis.**

glans /glanz/ *n.* (*pl.* **glandes** /glándeez/) the rounded part forming the end of the penis or clitoris.

glare[1] /glair/ *v. & n.* •*v.* **1** *intr.* look fiercely. **2** *intr.* shine dazzlingly. **3** *tr.* express (hate, defiance, etc.) by a look. •*n.* **1 a** strong fierce light, esp. sunshine. **b** oppressive public attention (*the glare of fame*). **2** a fierce look. □□ **glar·y** *adj.*

glare[2] /glair/ *adj.* (esp. of ice) smooth and glassy.

glar·ing /gláiring/ *adj.* **1** obvious; conspicuous (*a glaring error*). **2** shining oppressively. **3** staring fiercely. □□ **glar·ing·ly** *adv.*

glas·nost /glaásnəst, –nawst/ *n.* (in the former Soviet Union) the policy of more open government and wider dissemination of information.

glass /glas/ *n., v., & adj.* •*n.* **1 a** (often *attrib.*) a hard, brittle, usu. transparent or shiny substance, made by fusing sand with soda and lime and sometimes other ingredients. **b** a substance of similar properties. **2** (often *collect.*) an object or objects made from glass, esp.: **a** a drinking vessel. **b** esp. *Brit.* a mirror. **c** an hourglass. **d** a window. **e** a greenhouse (*rows of lettuce under glass*). **f** glass ornaments. **g** a barometer. **h** *Brit.* a glass disk covering a watch face. **i** a magnifying lens. **j** a monocle. **3** (in *pl.*) **a** eyeglasses. **b** field glasses; opera glasses. **4** the amount of liquid contained in a glass; a drink (*have another glass*). •*v.tr.* (usu. as **glassed** *adj.*) fit with glass. •*adj.* of or made from glass. □□ **glass·ful** *n.* (*pl.* **-fuls**). **glass·like** *adj.*

glass ceil·ing *n.* a barrier to advancement in a profession, esp. affecting women and minorities, that is not officially acknowledged.

glass·house /glás-hows/ *n.* **1** a building where glass is made. **2** *Brit.* a greenhouse.

glass·ine /glaéen/ *n.* a glossy transparent paper.

glass·wort /gláswərt/ *n.* any plant of the genus *Salicornia* or *Salsola* formerly burned for use in glassmaking.

glass·y /glásee/ *adj.* (**glassier, glassiest**) **1** of or resembling glass, esp. in smoothness. **2** (of the eye, the expression, etc.) abstracted; dull; fixed (*fixed her with a glassy stare*). □□ **glass·i·ly** *adv.* **glass·i·ness** *n.*

Glau·ber's salt /glówbərz/ *n.* (also **Glau·ber's salts**) a crystalline hydrated form of sodium sulfate used esp. as a laxative.

glau·co·ma /glawkṓmə, glou–/ *n.* an eye condition involving increased pressure within the eyeball, causing gradual loss of sight.

glau·cous /gláwkəs/ *adj.* **1** of a dull grayish green or blue. **2** covered with a powdery bloom as of grapes.

glaze /glayz/ *v. & n.* •*v.* **1** *tr.* **a** fit (a window, picture, etc.) with glass. **b** provide (a building) with glass windows. **2** *tr.* **a** cover (pottery, etc.) with a glaze. **b** fix (paint) on pottery with a glaze. **3** *tr.* cover (pastry, meat, etc.) with a glaze. **4** *intr.* (often foll. by *over*) (of the eyes) become fixed or glassy. **5** *tr.* cover (cloth, paper, etc.) with a glaze or other similar finish. **6** *tr.* give a glassy surface to, e.g., by rubbing. •*n.* **1** a vitreous substance, used to glaze pottery. **2** a smooth shiny coating on food. **3** a thin topcoat of transparent paint used to modify the tone of the underlying color. **4** a smooth surface formed by glazing.

gla·zier /gláyzhər/ *n.* a person whose trade is glazing windows, etc.

glaz·ing /gláyzing/ *n.* **1** the act or an instance of glazing. **2** windows (see also DOUBLE GLAZING). **3** material used to produce a glaze.

gleam /gleem/ *n. & v.* •*n.* **1** a faint light (*a gleam of sunlight*). **2** a faint, sudden, or temporary show (*not a gleam of hope*). •*v.intr.* **1** emit gleams. **2** shine with a faint brightness. **3** (of a quality) be indicated (*amusement gleamed in his eyes*).

glean /gleen/ *v.* **1** *tr.* collect or scrape together (news, facts, gossip, etc.) in small quantities. **2 a** *tr.* (also *absol.*) gather (ears of grain, etc.) after the harvest. **b** *tr.* strip (a field, etc.) after a harvest. □□ **glean·er** *n.*

glebe /gleeb/ *n.* **1** a piece of land serving as part of a clergyman's benefice and providing income. **2** *poet.* earth; land; a field.

glee /glee/ *n.* **1** mirth; delight. **2** a song for three or more voices, singing different parts simultaneously.

glee club *n.* a chorus for singing part-songs or other usu. short choral works.

glee·ful /gléefŏŏl/ *adj.* joyful. □□ **glee·ful·ly** *adv.*

glen /glen/ *n.* a narrow valley.

glen·gar·ry /glengáree/ *n.* (*pl.* **-ries**) a brimless Scottish cap with a cleft down the center and usu. two ribbons hanging at the back.

gle·noid cav·i·ty /gléenoyd/ *n.* a shallow depression on a bone, esp. the scapula and temporal bone, receiving the projection of another bone to form a joint.

glib /glib/ *adj.* (**glibber, glibbest**) fluent and voluble but insincere and shallow. □□ **glib·ly** *adv.* **glib·ness** *n.*

glide /glīd/ *v. & n.* •*v.* **1** *intr.* move with a smooth continuous motion. **2** *intr.* (of an aircraft) fly without engine power. **3** *intr.* of time, etc.: **a** pass gently and imperceptibly. **b** (often foll. by *into*) pass and change gradually and imperceptibly (*night glided into day*). **4** *intr.* move quietly or stealthily. **5** *tr.* cause to glide (*breezes glided the boat on its course*). **6** *tr.* traverse or fly in a glider. •*n.* **1 a** the act of gliding. **b** an instance of this. **2** *Phonet.* a gradually changing sound made in passing from one position of the speech organs to another. **3** a gliding dance or dance step. **4** a flight in a glider.

glid·er /glídər/ *n.* **1** an aircraft that flies without an engine. **2** a person or thing that glides.

glim·mer /glímər/ *v. & n.* •*v.intr.* shine faintly. •*n.* **1** a feeble light. **2** (usu. foll. by *of*) a faint gleam (of hope, understanding, etc.). **3** a glimpse.

glim·mer·ing /glíməring/ *n.* **1** = GLIMMER *n.* **2** an act of glimmering.

glimpse /glimps/ *n. & v.* •*n.* **1** a momentary view (*caught a glimpse of her*). **2** a faint and transient appearance (*glimpses of the truth*). • *v. tr.* see faintly (*glimpsed his face in the crowd*).

glint /glint/ *v. & n.* • *v.intr. & tr.* flash or cause to flash; glitter; sparkle (*eyes glinted with amusement; the sword glinted fire*). • *n.* a brief flash of light.

glis·san·do /glisaándō/ *n.* (*pl.* **glissandi** /–dee/or **-dos**) *Mus.* a continuous slide of adjacent notes upward or downward.

glis·ten /glísən/ *v. & n.* • *v.intr.* shine; glitter. • *n.* a glitter; a sparkle.

glis·ter /glístər/ *v. & n. archaic* • *v.intr.* sparkle; glitter. • *n.* a sparkle.

glitch /glich/ *n. colloq.* a sudden irregularity or malfunction.

glit·ter /glítər/ *v. & n.* • *v.intr.* **1** shine, esp. with a bright reflected light; sparkle. **2** (usu. foll. by *with*) **a** be showy (*glittered with diamonds*). **b** be flashily brilliant (*glittering rhetoric*). • *n.* **1** a gleam; a sparkle. **2** showiness; splendor. **3** tiny pieces of sparkling material used for decoration. ▫▫ **glit·ter·y** *adj.*

glitz /glits/ *n. sl.* extravagant but superficial display; show business glamour.

glitz·y /glítsee/ *adj.* (**glitzier, glitziest**) *sl.* extravagant; ostentatious; tawdry.

gloam·ing /glṓming/ *n. poet.* twilight; dusk.

gloat /glōt/ *v. & n.* • *v.intr.* (often foll. by *over*) contemplate with malice, triumph, etc. (*gloated over his collection*). • *n.* **1** the act of gloating. **2** a look of triumphant satisfaction.

glob /glob/ *n.* a mass or lump of semiliquid substance.

glob·al /glṓbəl/ *adj.* **1** worldwide (*global conflict*). **2** relating to or embracing a group of items, etc.; total. ▫▫ **glob·al·ly** *adv.*

glob·al warm·ing *n.* the increase in temperature of the earth's atmosphere caused by the greenhouse effect.

globe /glōb/ *n.* **1 a** (prec. by *the*) the planet earth. **b** a planet, star, or sun. **c** any spherical body. **2** a spherical representation of the earth or of the constellations with a map on the surface. **3** a golden sphere as an emblem of sovereignty. **4** any spherical glass vessel. ▫▫ **globe·like** *adj.* **glo·boid** *adj. & n.* **glo·bose** /–bōs/ *adj.*

globe·fish /glṓbfish/ *n.* = PUFFER 2.

glob·u·lar /glóbyələr/ *adj.* **1** globe-shaped; spherical. **2** composed of globules.

glob·ule /glóbyōōl/ *n.* a small globe or round particle; a drop.

glock·en·spiel /glókənspeel, –shpeel/ *n.* a musical instrument consisting of a series of bells or metal bars or tubes struck by hammers.

glom /glom/ *v. sl.* (**glommed, glomming**) **1** *tr.* steal; grab. **2** *intr.* (usu. foll. by *on to*) steal; grab.

glom·er·ate /glómərət/ *adj. Bot. & Anat.* compactly clustered.

glo·mer·u·lus /glōméryələs/ *n.* (*pl.* **glomeruli** /–lī/) a cluster of small organisms, tissues, or blood vessels, esp. a group of capillaries in the kidney. ▫▫ **glo·mer·u·lar** *adj.*

gloom /glōōm/ *n. & v.* • *n.* **1** darkness; obscurity. **2** melancholy; despondency. **3** *poet.* a dark place. • *v.* **1** *intr.* be gloomy or melancholy. **2** *intr.* (of the sky, etc.) be dull or threatening. **3** *intr.* appear obscurely. **4** *tr.* make dark or dismal.

gloom·y /glṓōmee/ *adj.* (**gloomier, gloomiest**) **1** dark; unlighted. **2** depressed; sullen. **3** dismal; depressing. ▫▫ **gloom·i·ly** *adv.* **gloom·i·ness** *n.*

glop /glop/ *n. sl.* a liquid or sticky mess, esp. unappealing or inedible food.

Glo·ri·a /gláwreeə/ *n.* **1** any of various doxologies beginning with *Gloria*, esp. the hymn beginning with *Gloria in excelsis Deo* (Glory be to God in the highest). **2** an aureole.

glo·ri·fy /gláwrifī/ *v.tr.* (**-fies, -fied**) **1** make glorious. **2** transform into something more splendid. **3** extol; praise. **4** (as **glorified** *adj.*) seeming to be better than in reality (*just a glorified office boy*). ▫▫ **glo·ri·fi·ca·tion** *n.*

glo·ri·ous /gláwreeəs/ *adj.* **1** possessing glory. **2** conferring glory. **3** *colloq.* splendid; magnificent; delightful (*a glorious day*). ▫▫ **glo·ri·ous·ly** *adv.*

glo·ry /gláwree/ *n. & v.* • *n.* (*pl.* **-ries**) **1** high renown or fame. **2** adoring praise (*Glory to the Lord*). **3** resplendent majesty or magnificence (*the glory of Versailles*). **4** a thing that brings renown or praise. **5** the bliss and splendor of heaven. **6** an aureole; a halo. • *v.intr.* pride oneself; exult (*glory in their skill*). ▫ **glory be! 1** a devout ejaculation. **2** *colloq.* an exclamation of surprise or delight.

gloss[1] /glaws, glos/ *n. & v.* • *n.* **1 a** surface shine or luster. **b** an instance of this. **2 a** deceptively attractive appearance. **b** an instance of this. **3** (in full **gloss paint**) paint formulated to give a hard glossy finish (cf. MATTE). • *v.tr.* make glossy. ▫ **gloss over 1** seek to conceal beneath a false appearance. **2** conceal by mentioning briefly.

gloss[2] /glaws, glos/ *n. & v.* • *n.* **1 a** an explanatory word or phrase inserted between the lines or in the margin of a text. **b** a comment, explanation, interpretation, or paraphrase. **2** a misrepresentation of another's words. **3 a** a glossary. **b** an interlinear translation or annotation. • *v.* **1** (also **gloze**) *tr.* **a** add a gloss or glosses to (a text, word, etc.). **b** read a different sense into; explain away. **2** *intr.* (often foll. by *on*) make (esp. unfavorable) comments. **3** *intr.* write or introduce glosses.

glos·sa·ry /gláwsəree, glós–/ *n.* (*pl.* **-ries**) (also **gloss**) an alphabetical list of terms relating to a specific subject or text.

glos·seme /gláwseem, glós–/ *n.* any meaningful feature of a language that cannot be analyzed into smaller meaningful units.

glos·si·tis /glawsítis, glo–/ *n.* inflammation of the tongue.

glos·so·la·ryn·ge·al /gláwsōlarínjeeəl, glós–/ *adj.* of the tongue and larynx.

gloss·y /gláwsee, glós–/ *adj. & n.* • *adj.* (**glossier, glossiest**) **1** having a shine. **2** (of paper, etc.) smooth and shiny. **3** (of a magazine, etc.) printed on such paper. • *n.* (*pl.* **-ies**) *colloq.* **1** a glossy magazine. **2** a photograph with a glossy surface. ▫▫ **gloss·i·ly** *adv.* **gloss·i·ness** *n.*

glot·tal /glót'l/ *adj.* of or produced by the glottis.

glot·tis /glótis/ *n.* the space at the upper end of the windpipe and between the vocal cords.

glove /gluv/ *n. & v.* • *n.* **1** a covering for the hand, worn esp. for protection against cold or dirt, and usu. having separate fingers. **2** a padded protective glove, esp.: **a** a boxing glove. **b** *Baseball* a fielder's glove. • *v.tr.* cover or provide with a glove. ▫▫ **glov·er** *n.*

glove box *n.* **1** a box for gloves. **2** a closed chamber with sealed-in gloves for handling radioactive material, etc. **3** = GLOVE COMPARTMENT.

glove com·part·ment *n.* a recess or cabinet for small articles in the dashboard of a motor vehicle.

glow /glō/ *v. & n.* • *v.intr.* **1 a** throw out light and heat without flame. **b** shine like something heated in this way. **2** (of the cheeks) redden, esp. from cold or exercise. **3 a** (of the body) be heated. **b** express or experience strong emotion (*glowed with pride*). **4** show a warm color (*the painting glows with warmth*). **5** (as **glowing** *adj.*) expressing pride or satisfaction (*a glowing report*). • *n.* **1** a glowing state. **2** a bright warm color. **3** ardor; passion. **4** a feeling induced by good health, exercise, etc. ▫▫ **glow·ing·ly** *adv.*

glow·er /glowr/ *v. & n.* • *v.intr.* stare or scowl. • *n.* a glowering look.

glow·worm /glṓwərm/ *n.* any beetle of the genus *Lampyris* whose wingless female emits light from the abdomen.

glox·in·i·a /gloksíneeə/ *n.* any tropical plant of the genus *Gloxinia,* native to S. America, with large bell flowers of various colors.

glu·ca·gon /glóōkəgon/ *n.* a hormone formed in the pancreas that aids the breakdown of glycogen to glucose in the liver.

glu·cose /glóōkōs/ *n.* **1** a simple sugar containing six carbon atoms, found mainly in the form of dextrose. Glucose is an important energy source in living organisms and obtainable from some carbohydrates by hydrolysis. ¶ Chem. formula: $C_6H_{12}O_6$. **2** a syrup containing glucose sugars from the incomplete hydrolysis of starch.

glu·co·side /glóōkəsīd/ *n.* a compound giving glucose and other products upon hydrolosis. ▫▫ **glu·co·sid·ic** /–sídik/ *adj.*

glue /glōō/ *n. & v.* • *n.* an adhesive substance used for sticking objects or materials together. • *v.tr.* (**glues, glued, gluing** or **glueing**) **1** fasten or join with glue. **2** keep or put very close (*an eye glued to the keyhole*). ▫▫ **glue·like** *adj.* **glu·er** *n.* **glue·y** /glóō-ee/ *adj.* (**gluier, gluiest**).

glug /glug/ *n. & v.* • *n.* a hollow, usu. repetitive gurgling sound. • *v.intr.* make a gurgling sound as of water from a bottle.

glum /glum/ *adj.* (**glummer, glummest**) looking or feeling dejected; sullen; displeased. ▫▫ **glum·ly** *adv.* **glum·ness** *n.*

glut /glut/ *v. & n.* • *v.tr.* (**glutted, glutting**) **1** feed (a person, one's stomach, etc.) or indulge (an appetite, a desire, etc.) to the full. **2** fill to excess. **3** *Econ.* overstock (a market). • *n.* **1** *Econ.* supply that exceeds demand. **2** full indulgence.

glu·ten /glóōtən/ *n.* a mixture of proteins present in cereal grains.

glu·te·us /glóōteeəs/ *n.* (*pl.* **glutei** /–teeī/) any of the three muscles in each buttock. ▫▫ **glu·te·al** *adj.*

glu·ti·nous /glóōt'nəs/ *adj.* sticky; like glue.

glut·ton /glút'n/ *n.* **1** an excessively greedy eater. **2** *colloq.* a person insatiably eager (*a glutton for work*). **3** the European wolverine, *Gulo gulo.* ▫ **glutton for punishment** a person eager to take on hard tasks. ▫▫ **glut·ton·ous** *adj.*

glut·ton·y /glút'nee/ *n.* habitual greed or excess in eating.

glyc·er·ide /glísərīd/ *n.* any fatty acid ester of glycerol.

glyc·er·in /glísərin/ *n.* (also **glyc·er·ine**) = GLYCEROL.

glyc·er·ol /glísərawl, –rol/ *n.* a colorless sweet viscous liquid formed as a byproduct in the manufacture of soap, used as an emollient and laxative, in explosives, etc.

gly·cine /glíseen/ *n.* the simplest naturally occuring amino acid, a general consitituent of proteins.

glyco- /glíkō/ *comb. form* sugar.

gly·co·gen /glíkəjən/ *n.* a polysaccharide serving as a store of carbohydrates, esp. in animal tissues, and yielding glucose on hydrolysis.

gly·co·gen·e·sis /glíkəjénisis/ *n.* the formation of glycogen from sugar.

gly·col /glíkawl, -kol/ *n.* an alcohol, esp. ethylene glycol. ▫▫ **gly·col·ic** /–kólik/ *adj.* **gly·col·lic** *adj.*

gly·col·y·sis /glīkólisis/ *n. Biochem.* the breakdown of glucose by enzymes.

gly·co·pro·tein /glíkōprṓteen/ *n.* any of a group of compounds consisting of a protein combined with a carbohydrate.

gly·co·side /glíkəsīd/ *n.* any compound giving sugar and other products on hydrolysis. ▫▫ **gly·co·sid·ic** /–sídik/ *adj.*

gly·cos·u·ri·a /glíkəsyóōreeə, –shóōr–/ *n.* a condition characterized by an excess of sugar in the urine, associated with diabetes, kidney disease, etc. ▫▫ **gly·cos·u·ric** *adj.*

glyp·tic /glíptik/ *adj.* of or concerning carving, esp. on precious stones.

glyp·tog·ra·phy /gliptógrəfee/ *n.* the art or scientific study of engraving gems.

GM *abbr.* **1** General Motors. **2** general manager.

gm *abbr.* gram(s).

G-man /jéeman/ *n.* (*pl.* **G-men**) *colloq.* an FBI agent.

GMT *abbr.* Greenwich Mean Time.

gnarled /naarld/ *adj.* (also **gnarl·y** /naárlee/) (of a tree, hands, etc.) knobbly; twisted; rugged.

gnash /nash/ *v.* **1** *tr.* grind (the teeth). **2** *intr.* (of the teeth) strike together.

gnat /nat/ *n.* **1** any small two-winged biting fly of the genus *Culex*, esp. *C. pipiens.* **2** an insignificant annoyance. **3** a tiny thing.

gnaw /naw/ *v.* (*past part.* **gnawed** or **gnawn**) **1 a** *tr.* bite persistently. **b** *intr.* (often foll. by *at, into*) bite; nibble. **2 a** *intr.* (often foll. by *at, into*) (of a destructive agent, pain, fear, etc.) consume; torture. **b** *tr.* consume, torture, etc., with pain, fear, etc. (*was gnawed by doubt*). **3** *tr.* (as **gnawing** *adj.*) persistent; worrying.

gneiss /nīs/ *n.* a usu. coarse-grained metamorphic rock principally of feldspar, quartz, and ferromagnesian minerals.

GNMA /jínee may/ *n.* Government National Mortgage Association.

gnoc·chi /nyáwkee/ *n.pl.* an Italian dish of small dumplings usu. made from potato, semolina flour, etc., or from spinach and cheese.

gnome[1] /nōm/ *n.* **1 a** a dwarfish legendary creature supposed to guard the earth's treasures underground. **b** a figure of a gnome, esp. as a garden ornament. **2** (esp. in *pl.*) *colloq.* a person with sinister influence, esp. financial (*gnomes of Zurich*). ▫▫ **gnom·ish** *adj.*

gnome[2] /nōm, nṓmee/ *n.* a maxim; a aphorism.

gno·mic /nṓmik/ *adj.* of, consisting of, or using aphorisms.

gnos·tic /nóstik/ *adj. & n.* • *adj.* **1** relating to knowledge, esp. esoteric mystical knowledge. **2** (**Gnostic**) concerning the Gnostics. • *n.* (**Gnostic**) (usu. in *pl.*) a Christian heretic of the 1st–3rd c. claiming mystical knowledge. ▫▫ **Gnos·ti·cism** /–tisizəm/ *n.*

GNP *abbr.* gross national product.

gnu /nōō, nyōō/ *n.* any antelope of the genus *Connochaetes*, native to S. Africa, with a large erect head and brown stripes on the neck and shoulders. Also called WILDEBEEST.

go[1] /gō/ *v., n., & adj.* • *v.* (*3rd sing. present* **goes** /gōz/; *past* **went** /went/; *past part.* **gone** /gon/) **1** *intr.* **a** start moving or be moving from one place or point in time to another. **b** (foll. by *to* + infin., or *and* + verb) proceed in order to (*went to find him*). **c** (foll. by *and* + verb) *colloq.* expressing annoyance (*you went and told him*). **2** *intr.* (foll. by verbal noun) make a special trip for; participate in (*went skiing*). **3** *intr.* lie in a certain direction (*the road goes to the shore*). **4** *intr.* leave (*they had to go*). **5** *intr.* move, work, etc. (*the clock doesn't go*). **6** *intr.* **a** make a specified movement (*go like this*). **b** make a sound (of a specified kind) (*the gun went bang*). **c** *colloq.* say (*so he goes to me, "Why didn't you like it?"*). **7** *intr.* be in a specified state (*go hungry*). **8** *intr.* **a** pass into a specified condition (*gone bad*). **b** *colloq.* die. **c** proceed or escape in a specified condition (*the crime went unnoticed*). **9** *intr.* (of time or distance) pass; elapse; be traversed (*ten days to go before Easter*). **10** *intr.* **a** have a specified content or wording (*the tune goes like this*). **b** be current or accepted (*so the story goes*). **c** be suitable; fit (*the shoes don't go with the hat*). **d** be regularly kept (*the forks go here*). **e** fit (*this won't go into the cupboard*). **11** *intr.* **a** turn out; proceed (*things went well*). **b** be successful (*make the party go*). **c** progress (*we've still got a long way to go*). **12** *intr.* **a** be sold (*went cheap*). **b** (of money) be spent (*$200 went on a new jacket*). **13** *intr.* **a** be relinquished or abolished (*the car will have to go*). **b** fail; decline (*his sight is going*). **14** *intr.* be acceptable or permitted (*anything goes*). **15** *intr.* be guided by; judge or act on (*have nothing to go on*). **16** *intr.* attend or travel to regularly (*goes to school*). **17** *intr.* (foll. by pres. part.) *colloq.* proceed (often foolishly) to do (*went running to the police*). **18** *intr.* proceed to a certain point (*will go so far and no further*). **19** *intr.* (of a number) be capable of being contained in another (*6 into 5 won't go*). **20** *tr. Cards* bid; declare (*has gone two spades*). **21** *intr.* be allotted or awarded (*the job went to his rival*). **22** *intr.* (foll. by *to, toward*) amount to (*12 inches go to make a foot*). **23** *intr.* (in *imper.*) begin motion (a starter's order in a race) (*ready, set, go!*). **24** *intr.* refer or appeal (*go to him for help*). **25** *intr.* take up a specified profession (*went on the stage*). **26** *intr.* (usu. foll. by *by, under*) be known or called (*goes by the name of Droopy*). **27** *tr. colloq.* proceed to (*go jump in the lake*). **28** *intr.* (foll. by *for*) apply to (*that goes for me too*). • *n.* (*pl.* **goes**) **1** the act of going. **2** spirit; animation (*she has a lot of go in her*). **3** vigorous activity (*it's all go*). **4** *colloq.* a success (*made a go of it*). **5** *colloq.* a turn; an attempt (*I'll have a go; it's my go*). **6** permission; approval; go-ahead (*gave us a go on the new project*). • *adj. colloq.* functioning properly (*all systems are go*). □ **from the word go** *colloq.* from the very beginning. **give it a go** *colloq.* make an effort to succeed. **go about 1** busy oneself with. **2** be socially active. **3** (foll. by *pres. part.*) make a habit of doing (*goes about telling lies*). **4** *Naut.* change to an opposite tack. **go ahead** proceed without hesitation. **go all the way 1** win a contest, one's ultimate goal, etc. **2** engage in sexual intercourse. **go along with** agree to; take the same view as. **go around 1** spin, revolve. **2** be long enough to encompass. **3** (of food, etc.) suffice for everybody. **4** (usu. foll. by *to*) visit informally. **5** (foll. by *with*) be regularly in the company of. **6** = *go about* 3. **7** = *go on* 4. **go at** take in hand energetically; attack. **go away** depart, esp. from home for a vacation, etc. **go back 1** return. **2** extend backward (in time or space). **3** (foll. by *to*) have a history extending back to. **go back on** fail to keep (one's word etc.). **go bail** see BAIL[1]. **go begging** see BEG. **go by 1** pass. **2** be dependent on. **go by default** see DEFAULT. **go down 1 a** (of an amount) become less (*the coffee has gone down a lot*). **b** subside (*the flood went down*). **c** decrease in price. **2 a** (of a ship) sink. **b** (of the sun) set. **3** (usu. foll. by *to*) be continued to a specified point. **4** fail; (of a computer network, etc.) cease to function. **5** be recorded in writing. **6** be swallowed. **7** (often foll. by *with*) be received (in a specified way). **8** fall (before a conqueror). **go Dutch** see DUTCH. **go far** be very successful. **go for 1** go to fetch. **2** be accounted as (*went for nothing*). **3** prefer; choose (*that's the one I go for*). **4** *colloq.* strive to attain (*go for it!*). **5** *colloq.* attack (*the dog went for him*). **go for broke** see BROKE. **go great guns** see GUN. **go halves** (or **shares**) (often foll. by *with*) share equally. **go in 1** enter a room, house, etc. **2** (usu. foll. by *for*) enter as a competitor. **3** (of the sun, etc.) become obscured by cloud. **go in for** take as one's object, style, etc. **going, going, gone!** an auctioneer's announcement that bidding is closing or closed. **go into 1** enter (a profession, etc.). **2** take part in. **3** investigate. **4** allow oneself to pass into (hysterics, etc.). **5** dress oneself in (mourning, etc.). **go a long way 1** have a great effect. **2** (of food, money, etc.) last a long time; buy much. **3** = *go far*. **go off 1** explode. **2** leave the stage. **3** gradually cease to be felt. **4** (esp. of foodstuffs) deteriorate; decompose. **5** go to sleep; become unconscious. **6** die. **7** be gotten rid of by sale, etc. **8** sound, as an alarm, etc. **go off well** (or **badly**, etc.) (of an enterprise, etc.) be received or accomplished well (or badly, etc.). **go on 1** continue; persevere (*went on trying*). **2** *colloq.* **a** talk at great length. **b** (foll. by *at*) admonish (*went on and on at him*). **3** (foll. by *to* + infin.) proceed (*went on to become a star*). **4** happen. **5** conduct oneself (*shameful, the way they went on*). **6** *Theatr.* appear on stage. **7** (of a garment) be large enough for its wearer. **8** take one's turn to do something. **9** *colloq.* use as evidence (*police don't have anything to go on*). **10** *colloq.* (esp. in *neg.*) **a** concern oneself about. **b** care for (*don't go much on red hair*). **go out 1** leave a room, house, etc. **2** be broadcast. **3** be extinguished. **4** (often foll. by *with*) be courting. **5** (of a government) leave office. **6** cease to be fashionable. **7** (usu. foll. by *to*) depart, esp. to a colony, etc. **8** *colloq.* lose consciousness. **9** (of workers) strike. **10** (usu. foll. by *to*) (of the heart, etc.) expand with sympathy, etc., toward (*my heart goes out to them*). **11** *Golf* play the first nine holes in a round. **12** *Cards* be the first to dispose of one's hand. **13** (of a tide) turn to low tide. **go over 1** inspect the details of; rehearse. **2** (often foll. by *to*) change one's allegiance or religion. **3** (of a play, etc.) be received in a specified way (*went over well in Dallas*). **go through 1** be dealt with or completed. **2** discuss in detail; scrutinize in sequence. **3** perform (a ceremony, a recitation, etc.). **4** undergo. **5** *colloq.* use up; spend (money, etc.). **6** make holes in. **7** (of a book) be successively published (in so many editions). **go through with** not leave unfinished. **go to blazes** (or **hell**, etc.) *sl.* an exclamation of dismissal, contempt, etc. **go together 1** match; fit. **2** be courting. **go to it!** *colloq.* begin work! **go to show** (or **prove**) serve to demonstrate (or prove). **go under** sink. **go up 1** increase in price. **2** be consumed (in flames, etc.). **go well** (often foll. by *with*) turn out well. **go with 1** be harmonious with. **2** agree to. **3 a** be a pair with. **b** be courting. **4** follow the drift of. **go without** manage without (also *absol.*: *we shall just have to go without*). **go with the tide** (or **times**) do as others do. **have a go at** attempt; try. **on the go** *colloq.* **1** in constant motion. **2** constantly working. **to go** (of food, etc.) to be eaten or drunk off the premises. **who goes there?** a sentry's challenge.

go[2] /gō/ *n.* a Japanese board game of territorial possession and capture.

goad /gōd/ *n. & v.* • *n.* **1** a spiked stick used for urging cattle forward. **2** anything that torments, incites, or stimulates. • *v.tr.* **1** urge on with a goad. **2** (usu. foll. by *into*) irritate; stimulate (*goaded him into retaliating*).

goal /g ōl/ *n.* **1** the object of a person's ambition or effort; a destination; an aim (*fame is his goal*; *Washington was our goal*). **2 a** *Football* a pair of posts with a crossbar between which the ball has to be kicked to score a field goal. **b** *Soccer, Ice Hockey, etc.* a cage or basket used similarly. **c** a point or points won (*scored 3 goals*). **3** a point marking the end of a race. □ **in goal** in the position of goalkeeper. □□ **goal·less** *adj.*

goal·ie /gṓlee/ *n. colloq.* = GOALKEEPER.

goal·keep·er /gṓlkeepər/ *n.* a player stationed to protect the goal in various sports.

goal line *n. Football, Soccer,* etc., a line between each pair of goalposts, extended to form the end boundary of a field of play (cf. TOUCHLINE).

goal·post /gṓlpōst/ *n.* either of the two upright posts of a goal. □ **move the goalposts** alter the basis or scope of a procedure during its course to fit adverse cirucmstances encountered.

goal·tend·er /gṓltendər/ *n.* a hockey goalkeeper.

goat /gōt/ *n.* **1 a** a hardy shorthaired domesticated mammal, *Capra aegagrus*, having horns and (in the male) a beard, and kept for its milk and meat. **b** either of two similar mammals, the mountain goat and the Spanish goat. **2** any other mammal of the genus *Capra*. **3** a lecherous man. **4** (**the Goat**) the zodiacal sign or constellation Capricorn. **5** a scapegoat. □ **get a person's goat** *colloq.* irritate a person. □□ **goat·ish** *adj.* **goat·y** *adj.*

goat·ee /gōtée/ *n.* a small pointed beard like that of a goat.

goat·herd /gṓt-hərd/ *n.* a person who tends goats.

goats·beard /gōtsbeerd/ *n.* **1** a meadow plant, *Tragopogon pratensis*. **2** a herbaceous plant, *Aruncus dioicus*, with long spikes of white flowers.

goat·skin /gṓtskin/ *n.* **1** the skin of a goat. **2** a garment or bottle made out of goatskin.

gob[1] /gob/ *n.* & *v. sl.* • *n.* **1** a lump or clot of slimy matter. **2** (in *pl.*) large amounts (*gobs of cash*) • *v.intr.* (**gobbed, gobbing**) spit.

gob[2] /gob/ *n. sl.* a sailor.

gob·ble[1] /góbəl/ *v.tr.* & *intr.* eat hurriedly and noisily. □□ **gob·bler** *n.*

gob·ble[2] /góbəl/ *v.intr.* **1** (of a male turkey) make a characteristic swallowing sound in the throat. **2** make such a sound when speaking, esp. when excited, angry, etc.

gob·ble·dy·gook /góbəldeegook/ *n.* (also **gob·ble·de·gook**) *colloq.* pompous or unintelligible jargon.

gob·bler /góblər/ *n. colloq.* a male turkey.

Gob·e·lin /góbəlin, gṓbəlin, gawblán/ *n.* (in full **Gobelin tapestry**) **1** a tapestry made at the Gobelins factory in Paris. **2** a tapestry imitating this.

gob·let /góblit/ *n.* **1** a drinking vessel with a foot and a stem, usu. of glass. **2** *archaic* a metal or glass bowl-shaped drinking cup without handles.

gob·lin /góblin/ *n.* a mischievous, ugly, dwarflike creature of folklore.

go·by /gṓbee/ *n.* (*pl.* **-bies**) any small marine fish of the family Gobiidae, having ventral fins joined to form a sucker or disk.

go-cart *n.* **1** a handcart; a stroller. **2** = GO-KART.

god /god/ *n.* **1 a** (in many religions) a superhuman being or spirit worshiped as having power over nature, human fortunes, etc. **b** an image, idol, animal, or other object worshiped as divine or symbolizing a god. **2** (**God**) (in Christian and other monotheistic religions) the creator and ruler of the universe. **3 a** an adored, admired, or influential person. **b** something worshiped like a god (*makes a god of success*). **4** *Theatr.* (in *pl.*) **a** the gallery. **b** the people sitting in it. □ **for God's sake!** see SAKE[1]. **God the Father, Son, and Holy Spirit** (or **Ghost**) (in the Christian tradition) the Persons of the Trinity. **in God's name** an appeal for help. **in the name of God** an expression of surprise or annoyance. **my** (or **oh**) **God!** an exclamation of surprise, anger, etc. **play God** assume importance or superiority. **thank God!** an exclamation of pleasure or relief. **with God** dead and in heaven. □□ **god·hood** *n.* **god·ship** *n.* **god·ward** *adj.* & *adv.* **god·wards** *adv.*

god·child /gódchīld/ *n.* a person in relation to a godparent.

god·damn /gódám/ *adj.* (or **god·dam** or **god·damned** /–dámd/) *sl.* accursed.

god·daugh·ter /góddawtər/ *n.* a female godchild.

god·dess /gódis/ *n.* **1** a female deity. **2** a woman who is adored.

go·det /gōdét, gōdáy/ *n.* a triangular piece of material inserted in a dress, glove, etc.

go-devil *n.* **1** a crude sled, used chiefly for dragging logs. **2** a jointed apparatus for cleaning pipelines.

god·fa·ther /gódfaathər/ *n.* **1** a male godparent. **2** a person directing an illegal organization, esp. the Mafia.

god·for·sak·en /gódfərsaykən/ *adj.* devoid of all merit; dismal; dreary.

god·head /gódhed/ *n.* (also **God·head**) **1 a** the state of being God or a god. **b** divine nature. **2** a deity. **3** (**the Godhead**) God.

god·less /gódlis/ *adj.* **1** impious; wicked. **2** without a god. **3** not recognizing a god or gods. □□ **god·less·ness** *n.*

god·like /gódlīk/ *adj.* **1** resembling God or a god. **2** befitting to a god.

god·ly /gódlee/ *adj.* religious; pious; devout. □□ **god·li·ness** *n.*

god·moth·er /gódmuthər/ *n.* a female godparent.

god·par·ent /gódpairənt/ *n.* a person who presents a child at baptism, promising to take responsibility for the child's religious education.

god·send /gódsend/ *n.* an unexpected but welcome event or acquisition.

god·son /gódsun/ *n.* a male godchild.

God·speed /gódspéed/ *int.* an expression of good wishes to a person starting a journey.

god·wit /gódwit/ *n.* any wading bird of the genus *Limosa*, with long legs and a long straight or slightly upcurved bill.

go·er /gṓər/ *n.* **1** a person or thing that goes (*a slow goer*). **2** (often in *comb.*) a person who attends (*a churchgoer*).

goes *3rd sing. present* of GO[1].

go·est /gṓist/ *archaic 2nd sing. present* of GO 1.

go·eth /gṓith/ *archaic 3rd sing. present* of GO 1.

go·fer /gṓfər/ *n. sl.* a person who runs errands, esp. on a movie set or in an office.

gof·fer /gófər/ *v.* & *n.* • *v.tr.* make wavy, flute, or crimp (a lace edge, a trimming, etc.) with heated irons. • *n.* an iron used for goffering.

go-get·ter *n. colloq.* an aggressively enterprising person.

gog·gle /gógəl/ *v.*, *adj.*, & *n.* • *v.* **1** *intr.* **a** (often foll. by *at*) look with wide-open eyes. **b** (of the eyes) be rolled about; protrude. **2** *tr.* turn (the eyes) sideways or from side to side. • *adj.* (usu. *attrib.*) (of the eyes) protuberant or rolling. • *n.* **1** (in *pl.*) **a** eyeglasses for protecting the eyes from glare, dust, water, etc. **b** *colloq.* eyeglasses. **2** (in *pl.*) a sheep disease; the staggers. **3** a goggling expression.

go-go *adj. colloq.* **1** (of a dancer, music, etc.) in pop music style, lively, and rhythmic. **2** unrestrained; energetic. **3** (of investment) speculative.

Goi·del /góyd'l/ *n.* a Celt who speaks Irish Gaelic, Scottish Gaelic, or Manx. □□ **goi·del·ic** /–délik/ *n.*

go·ing /gṓing/ *n.* & *adj.* • *n.* **1 a** the act or process of going. **b** an instance of this. **2 a** the condition of the ground for walking, riding, etc. **b** progress affected by this (*found the going hard*). • *adj.* **1** in or into action (*set the clock going*). **2** esp. *Brit.* existing; available (*there's hot soup going*). **3** current; prevalent (*the going rate*). □ **get going** start steadily talking, working, etc. (*can't stop him when he gets going*). **going for one** *colloq.* acting in one's favor (*he's got a lot going for him*). **going on fifteen**, etc. approaching one's fifteenth, etc., birthday. **going to** intending or intended to; about to (*it's going to sink!*). **while the going is good** while conditions are favorable.

go·ing con·cern *n.* a thriving business.

go·ing-o·ver *n.* **1** *colloq.* an inspection or overhaul. **2** *sl.* a beating. **3** *colloq.* a scolding.

goi·ter /góytər/ *n.* (*Brit.* **goitre**) *Med.* a swelling of the

neck resulting from enlargement of the thyroid gland. □□ **goit·rous** /–trus/ *adj.*
go-kart *n.* a miniature racing car.
gold /gōld/ *n. & adj.* • *n.* **1** a yellow, malleable, ductile, high density metallic element resistant to chemical reaction, occurring naturally in quartz veins and gravel, and precious as a monetary medium, in jewelry, etc. ¶ Symb.: **Au. 2** the color of gold. **3 a** coins or articles made of gold. **b** wealth. **4** something precious, beautiful, or brilliant (*all that glitters is not gold*). **5** = GOLD MEDAL. **6** the bull's-eye of an archery target. • *adj.* **1** made wholly or chiefly of gold. **2** colored like gold.
gold brick *n. sl.* **1** a thing with only a surface appearance of value. **2** a lazy person.
gold dig·ger *n.* **1** *sl.* **a** a woman who wheedles money out of men. **b** a woman who strives to marry a rich man. **2** a person who digs for gold.
gold dust *n.* **1** gold in fine particles as often found naturally. **2** a plant, *Alyssum saxatile*, with many small yellow flowers.
gold·en /gṓldən/ *adj.* **1 a** made or consisting of gold. **b** yielding gold. **2** colored like gold (*golden hair*). **3** precious; valuable (*a golden memory*).
gold·en age *n.* **1** a supposed past age when people were happy and innocent. **2** the period of a nation's greatest prosperity, literary merit, etc.
gold·en-ag·er *n.* an old person.
gold·en boy (or **girl**) *colloq. n.* a popular or successful person.
gold·en calf *n.* wealth as an object of worship (Exod. 32).
gold·en ea·gle *n.* a large eagle, *Aquila chrysaetos*, with yellow-tipped head feathers.
Gold·en Fleece *n.* (in Greek mythology) a fleece of gold sought and won by Jason.
gold·en goose *n.* a continuing source of wealth or profit.
gold·en old·ie *n. colloq.* an old hit record or movie, etc., that is still well known and popular.
gold·en re·triev·er *n.* a retriever with a thick, golden-colored coat.
gold·en·rod /gṓldənrod/ *n.* any plant of the genus *Solidago* with a rodlike stem and small bright yellow flowerheads.
gold·en rule *n.* a basic principle of action, esp. "do unto others as you would have them do unto you".
Gold·en State *n.* California.
gold·finch /gṓldfinch/ *n.* any of various brightly colored songbirds of the genus *Carduelis*.
gold·fish /gṓldfish/ *n.* a small reddish golden Chinese carp kept for ornament, *Carassius auratus*.
gold·fish bowl *n.* **1** a globular glass container for goldfish. **2** a situation lacking privacy.
gold leaf *n.* gold beaten into a very thin sheet.
gold med·al *n.* a medal of gold, usu. awarded as first prize.
gold mine *n.* **1** a place where gold is mined. **2** *colloq.* a source of wealth.
gold plate *n.* **1** vessels made of gold. **2** material plated with gold. □□ **gold-plate** *v.tr.*
gold rush *n.* a rush to a newly discovered gold field.
gold·smith /gṓldsmith/ *n.* a worker in gold; a manufacturer of gold articles.
gold stand·ard *n.* a system by which the value of a currency is defined in terms of gold.
golf /golf, gawlf/ *n. & v.* • *n.* a game in which a small hard ball is driven with clubs into a series of 18 or 9 holes with the fewest possible strokes. • *v.intr.* play golf.
golf ball *n.* **1** a ball used in golf. **2** a small ball used in some electric typewriters to carry the type.
golf cart *n.* **1** a cart used for carrying golf clubs. **2** a motorized cart for golfers and equipment.
golf club *n.* **1** a club used in golf. **2** an association for playing golf. **3** the premises used by a golf club.
golf course *n.* the course on which golf is played.
golf·er /gólfər/ *n.* a golf player.
Gol·gi bod·y /gáwljee/ *n.* (also **Gol·gi ap·pa·rat·us**) *Biol.* an organelle of vesicles and folded membranes within the cytoplasm of most eukaryotic cells, involved esp. in the secretion of substances.
gol·li·wog /góleewog/ *n.* a black-faced brightly dressed soft doll with fuzzy hair.
gol·ly[1] /gólee/ *int.* expressing surprise.
gol·ly[2] /gólee/ *n.* (*pl.* **-lies**) *colloq.* = GOLLIWOG.
-gon *comb. form* forming nouns denoting plane figures with a specified number of angles (*hexagon; polygon*).
go·nad /gṓnad/ *n.* an animal organ producing gametes, e.g., the testis or ovary. □□ **go·nad·al** /–nád'l/ *adj.*
go·nad·o·troph·ic hor·mone /gōnádətrṓfik, -trófik/ *n.* (also **go·nad·o·trop·ic** /–trṓpik, -trópik/) *Biochem.* any of various hormones stimulating the activity of the gonads.
go·nad·o·tro·phin /gōnádətrṓfin, -trófin/ *n.* (also **go·na·do·tro·pin**) =. gonadtrophic hormone
gon·do·la /góndələ, gondṓlə/ *n.* **1** a light flat-bottomed boat used on Venetian canals, worked by one oar at the stern. **2** a car suspended from an airship or balloon. **3** a car attached to a ski lift.

gondola, 1

gon·do·lier /góndəlēer/ *n.* the oarsman on a gondola.
gone /gawn, gon/ *adj.* **1 a** lost; hopeless. **b** dead. **2** *colloq.* pregnant for a specified time (*three months gone*). **3** *sl.* completely enthralled or entranced. □ **be gone** depart. **gone on** *sl.* infatuated with.
gon·er /gáwnər, gón–/ *n. sl.* a person or thing that is doomed, ended, irrevocably lost, etc.; a dead person.
gong /gawng, gong/ *n.* **1** a metal disk with a turned rim, giving a resonant note when struck. **2** a saucer-shaped bell. **3** *Brit. sl.* a medal.
go·ni·om·e·ter /gṓneeómitər/ *n.* an instrument for measuring angles. □□ **go·ni·om·e·try** *n.* **go·ni·o·met·ric** /–neeəmétrik/ *adj.* **go·ni·o·met·ri·cal** *adj.*
gon·o·coc·cus /gónəkókəs/ *n.* (*pl.* **gonococci** /–kókī, -kóksī/) a bacterium, *Neisseria gonorrhoeae*, that causes gonorrhea. □□ **gon·o·coc·cal** *adj.*
gon·or·rhe·a /gónərēeə/ *n.* a venereal disease with inflammatory discharge from the urethra or vagina.
goo /goo/ *n.* **1** a sticky or viscous substance. **2** sickly sentiment.
good /good/ *adj., n., & adv.* • *adj.* (**better, best**) **1** having the right or desired qualities. **2 a** (of a person) efficient; competent (*good at math*). **b** (of a thing) reliable; efficient (*good brakes*). **c** (of health, etc.) strong (*good eyesight*). **3 a** kind (*good of you to come*). **b** morally excellent (*a good deed*). **c** charitable (*good works*). **d** well-behaved (*a good child*). **4** enjoyable, agreeable (*a good party*). **5** thorough; considerable (*a good wash*). **6 a** not less than (*waited a good hour*). **b** considerable in number, quality, etc. (*a good many people*). **7** beneficial (*good for you*). **8 a** valid; sound (*a good reason*). **b** financially sound (*his credit is good*). **9** in exclamations of surprise (*good heavens!*). **10** right; proper (*thought it good to have a try*). **11** fresh; eatable. **12** (sometimes patronizing) commendable; worthy (*good old George*). **13** well shaped; attractive (*good

looks). **14** in courteous greetings and farewells (*good afternoon*). • *n.* **1** (only in *sing.*) what is beneficial or morally right (*only good can come of it*). **2** (only in *sing.*) a desirable end or object (*a future good*). **3** (in *pl.*) **a** movable property or merchandise. **b** *Brit.* things to be transported, as distinct from passengers; freight. **c** (prec. by *the*) *colloq.* what one has undertaken to supply (esp. deliver the goods). **d** (prec. by *the*) *sl.* the real thing; the genuine article. **4** proof, esp. of guilt. **5** (as *pl.*; prec. by *the*) virtuous people. • *adv. colloq.* well (*doing pretty good*). □ **as good as** practically (*he as good as told me*). **be so good as** (or **be good enough**) **to** (often in a request) be kind and do (a favor) (*be so good as to open the window*). **be (a certain amount) to the good** have as net profit or advantage. **do good** show kindness. **do a person good** be beneficial to. **for good (and all)** finally; permanently. **good and** *colloq.* used as an intensifier before an adj. or adv. (*was good and angry*). **good for 1** beneficial to. **2** able to perform; inclined for (*good for a ten-mile walk*). **3** able to be trusted to pay (*is good for $100*). **good for you!** (or **him!**, **her!**, etc.) exclamation of approval toward a person. **have a good mind** see MIND. **have the goods on a person** *sl.* have information that gives one an advantage over a person. **have a good time** enjoy oneself. **in a person's good books** see BOOK. **in good faith** with honest or sincere intentions. **in good time 1** with no risk of being late. **2** (also **all in good time**) in due course but without haste. **make good 1** make up for; compensate for. **2** fulfill (a promise); effect (a purpose). **3** demonstrate the truth of (a statement). **4** gain and hold (a position). **5** replace or restore (a thing lost or damaged). **6** (*absol.*) accomplish what one intended. **to the good** as profit or benefit. □□ **good·ish** *adj.*

▶The adverb corresponding to the adjective **good** is **well:** *She is a good swimmer who performs well in meets.* Confusion sometimes arises because **well** is also an adjective meaning 'healthy, fine,' and **good** is widely accepted as an informal substitute: *I feel well* (vs. informal "I feel good"). See note at BAD.

good-bye /gŏŏdbī́/ *int. & n.* (also **good·bye, good-by** or **goodby**) • *int.* expressing good wishes on parting, ending a telephone conversation, etc. • *n.* (*pl.* **good-byes**) the saying of "good-bye"; a parting; a farewell.

Good Fri·day *n.* the Friday before Easter commemorating the crucifixion of Christ.

good-heart·ed *adj.* kindly; well-meaning.

good-hu·mored /gŏŏdhyŏŏmərd/ *adj.* genial; cheerful. □□ **good-hu·mored·ly** *adv.*

good-look·ing *adj.* handsome; attractive.

good·ly /gŏŏdlee/ *adj.* (**goodlier, goodliest**) **1** comely; handsome. **2** of imposing size, etc.

good-na·tured /gŏŏdnáychərd/ *adj.* kind; patient. □□ **good-na·tured·ly** *adv.*

good·ness /gŏŏdnis/ *n. & int.* • *n.* **1** excellence, esp. moral. **2** kindness (*had the goodness to wait*). **3** what is beneficial in a thing (*vegetables with all the goodness boiled out*). • *int.* (as a substitution for "God") expressing surprise, anger, etc.

good·wife /gŏŏdwīf/ *n.* (*pl.* **-wives**) *archaic* the mistress of a household.

good·will /gŏŏdwíl/ *n.* **1** kindly feeling. **2** the established reputation of a business, etc., as enhancing its value. **3** cheerful consent or acquiescence.

good will *n.* the intention and hope that good will result (see also GOODWILL).

good word *n.* (often in phr. **put in a good word for**) words in recommendation or defense.

good·y /gŏŏdee/ *n. & int.* • *n.* (also **good·ie**) (*pl.* **-ies**) **1** (usu. in *pl.*) something good or attractive, esp. to eat. **2** *colloq.* a good or favored person, esp. a hero in a story, movie, etc. **3** = GOODY-GOODY *n.* • *int.* expressing childish delight.

good·y-good·y *n. & adj.* • *n.* a smug or obtrusively virtuous person. • *adj.* obtrusively or smugly virtuous.

goo·ey /gŏŏ-ee/ *adj.* (**gooier, gooiest**) *sl.* **1** viscous; sticky. **2** sickly; sentimental.

goof /gŏŏf/ *n. & v. sl.* • *n.* **1** a foolish person. **2** a mistake. • *v.* **1** *tr.* bungle. **2** *intr.* blunder. **3** *intr.* (often foll. by *off*) idle.

goof·ball /gŏŏfbawl/ *n. sl.* a silly, ridiculous, or inept person.

goof·y /gŏŏfee/ *adj.* (**goofier, goofiest**) *sl.* stupid; silly. □□ **goof·i·ly** *adv.* **goof·i·ness** *n.*

goo·gol /gŏŏgawl/ *n.* ten raised to the hundredth power (10^{100}).

▶Not in formal use.

gook /gŏŏk, gŏŏk/ *n. sl. offens.* a foreigner, esp. a person from E. Asia.

goon /gŏŏn/ *n. sl.* **1** a stupid person. **2** a person hired by racketeers, etc., to terrorize opponents.

goos·an·der /gŏŏsándər/ *n.* a large diving duck, *Mergus merganser*, with a narrow serrated bill; a common merganser.

goose /gŏŏs/ *n. & v.* • *n.* (*pl.* **geese** /gees/) **1 a** any of various large water birds of the family Anatidae, with short legs, webbed feet, and a broad bill. **b** the female of this (opp. GANDER). **c** the flesh of a goose as food. **2** *colloq.* a simpleton. • *v.tr. sl.* poke (a person) between the buttocks.

goose·ber·ry /gŏŏsberee, –bəree, gŏŏz–/ *n.* (*pl.* **-ries**) **1** a round edible yellowish green berry. **2** the thorny shrub, *Ribes grossularia*, bearing this fruit.

goose bumps *n.pl.* (also **goose flesh**) a bristling state of the skin produced by cold or fright.

goose egg *n.* a zero score in a game.

goose·foot /gŏŏsfŏŏt/ *n.* (*pl.* **-foots**) any plant of the genus *Chenopodium*, having leaves shaped like the foot of a goose.

goose step *n.* a military marching step in which the knees are kept stiff.

GOP *abbr.* Grand Old Party (the Republican Party).

go·pher[1] /gṓfər/ *n.* **1** (in full **pocket gopher**) any burrowing rodent of the family Geomyidae, native to N. America. **2** a N. American ground squirrel. **3** a tortoise, *Gopherus polyphemus*, native to the southern US.

go·pher[2] /gṓfər/ *n.* **1** *Bibl.* a tree from the wood of which Noah's ark was made. **2** (in full **gopher wood**) a tree, *Cladrastis lutea*, yielding yellowish timber.

go·ral /gáwrəl/ *n.* a goat antelope, *Nemorhaedus goral*, native to mountainous regions of N. India, having short horns curving to the rear.

Gor·di·an knot /gáwrdeeən/ *n.* **1** an intricate knot. **2** a difficult problem or task. □ **cut the Gordian knot** solve a problem by force or by evasion.

Gor·don set·ter /gáwrd'n/ *n.* **1** a setter of a black and tan breed, used as a gun dog. **2** this breed.

gore[1] /gawr/ *n.* **1** blood shed and clotted. **2** slaughter; carnage.

gore[2] /gawr/ *v.tr.* pierce with a horn, tusk, etc.

gore[3] /gawr/ *n. & v.* • *n.* **1** a wedge-shaped piece in a garment. **2** a triangular piece in an umbrella, etc. **3** a small, triangular piece of land. • *v.tr.* shape with a gore.

gorge /gawrj/ *n. & v.* • *n.* **1** a narrow opening between hills or a rocky ravine. **2** an act of gorging. **3** the contents of the stomach. • *v.* **1** *intr.* feed greedily. **2** *tr.* **a** (often *refl.*) satiate. **b** devour greedily. □ **one's gorge rises at** one is sickened by.

gor·geous /gáwrjəs/ *adj.* **1** richly colored; sumptuous. **2** *colloq.* very pleasant (*gorgeous weather*). **3** *colloq.* strikingly beautiful. □□ **gor·geous·ly** *adv.*

gor·get /górjit/ *n.* **1** *hist.* **a** a piece of armor for the throat. **b** a woman's wimple. **2** a patch of color on the throat of a bird, insect, etc.

Gor·gon /gáwrgən/ *n.* **1** (in Greek mythology) each of three snake-haired sisters (esp. Medusa) with the power to turn anyone who looked at them to stone. **2** a frightening or repulsive person, esp. a woman.

gor·gon·ize /gáwrgənīz/ *v.tr.* **1** stare at like a gorgon. **2** paralyze with terror, etc.

Gor·gon·zo·la /gáwrgənzṓlə/ *n.* a type of rich cheese with bluish green veins.

go·ril·la /gərílə/ *n.* the largest anthropoid ape, *Gorilla gorilla*, native to Central Africa, having a large head, short neck, and prominent mouth.

gor·mand·ize /gáwrməndīz/ *v. & n.* • *v.* **1** *intr. & tr.* eat or devour voraciously. **2** *intr.* indulge in good eating. • *n.* = gourmandise. ▫▫ **gor·mand·iz·er** *n.*

gorse /gawrs/ *n.* any spiny yellow-flowered shrub of the genus *Ulex*.

gor·y /gáwree/ *adj.* (**gorier, goriest**) **1** involving bloodshed; bloodthirsty (*a gory movie*). **2** covered in gore.

gosh /gosh/ *int.* expressing surprise.

gos·ling /gózling/ *n.* a young goose.

gos·pel /góspəl/ *n.* **1** the teaching or revelation of Christ. **2** (**Gospel**) **a** the record of Christ's life and teaching in the first four books of the New Testament. **b** each of these books. **c** a portion from one of them read at a service. **d** a similar book in the Apocrypha. **3** a thing regarded as absolutely true (*take my word as gospel*). **4** a principle one acts on or advocates. **5** (in full **gospel music**) African-American evangelical religious singing.

gos·pel truth *n.* something considered to be unquestionably true.

gos·sa·mer /gósəmər/ *n. & adj.* • *n.* **1** a filmy substance of small spiders' webs. **2** delicate filmy material. **3** a thread of gossamer. • *adj.* light and flimsy.

gos·sip /gósip/ *n. & v.* • *n.* **1 a** unconstrained talk or writing esp. about persons or social incidents. **b** idle talk; groundless rumor. **2** an informal chat, esp. about persons or social incidents. **3** a person who indulges in gossip. • *v.intr.* (**gossiped, gossiping**) talk or write gossip.

gos·sip col·umn *n.* a section of a newspaper devoted to gossip about well-known people. ▫▫ **gos·sip col·umn·ist** *n.*

gos·sip·mon·ger /gósipmongər/ *n.* a perpetrator of gossip.

got *past* and *past part.* of GET.

Goth /goth/ *n.* a member of a Germanic tribe that invaded the Roman Empire in the 3rd–5th c.

Goth·ic /góthik/ *adj. & n.* • *adj.* **1** of the Goths or their language. **2** in the style of architecture prevalent in W. Europe in the 12th–16th c., characterized by pointed arches. **3** (of a novel, etc.) in a style popular in the 18th–19th c., with supernatural events. **4** *Printing* (of type) old-fashioned German, black letter, or sans serif. • *n.* **1** the Gothic language. **2** Gothic architecture. **3** *Printing* Gothic type. ▫▫ **Goth·i·cism** /–thisizəm/ *n.* **Goth·i·cize** /–thisīz/ *v.tr. & intr.*

got·ta /gótə/ *colloq.* have got to (*we gotta go*).

got·ten *past part.* of GET.

gouache /gwaash, gōō-áash/ *n.* **1** a method of painting in opaque pigments ground in water and thickened with a gluelike substance. **2** these pigments. **3** a picture painted in this way.

Gou·da /gṓōdə, gów–/ *n.* a flat round usu. Dutch cheese with a yellow rind.

gouge /gowj/ *n. & v.* • *n.* **1** a chisel with a concave blade, used in woodworking, sculpture, and surgery. **2** an indentation or groove made with or as with this. • *v.* **1** *tr.* cut with or as with a gouge. **2** *tr.* **a** (foll. by *out*) force out (esp. an eye with the thumb) with or as with a gouge. **b** force out the eye of (a person). **3** *tr. colloq.* swindle; extort money from; overcharge. ▫▫ **goug·er** *n.*

gou·lash /gṓōlaash, –lash/ *n.* a highly seasoned Hungarian dish of meat and vegetables, usu. flavored with paprika.

gourd /gŏŏrd/ *n.* **1 a** any of various fleshy usu. large fruits with a hard skin. **b** any of various climbing or trailing plants of the family Cucurbitaceae bearing this fruit. Also called **cucurbit**. **2** the hollow hard skin of the gourd fruit, dried and used as a drinking vessel, percussion instrument, etc. ▫▫ **gourd·ful** *n.* (*pl.* **-fuls**).

gour·mand /gŏŏrmaánd/ *n. & adj.* • *n.* **1** a glutton. **2** *disp.* a gourmet. • *adj.* gluttonous; fond of eating, esp. to excess. ▫▫ **gour·mand·ism** *n.*

gour·met /gŏŏrmáy/ *n.* a connoisseur of good or delicate food.

gout /gowt/ *n.* **1** a disease with inflammation of the smaller joints, esp. the toe, as a result of excess uric acid salts in the blood. **2 a** a drop, esp. of blood. **b** a splash or spot. ▫▫ **gout·y** *adj.*

Gov. *abbr.* **1** Government. **2** Governor.

gov. *abbr.* governor.

gov·ern /gúvərn/ *v.* **1 a** *tr.* rule or control with authority; conduct the policy and affairs of. **b** *intr.* be in government. **2 a** *tr.* influence or determine (a person or a course of action). **b** *intr.* be the predominating influence. **3** *tr.* be a standard or principle for. **4** *tr.* check or control (esp. passions). **5** *tr. Gram.* (esp. of a verb or preposition) have (a noun or pronoun or its case) depending on it. ▫▫ **gov·ern·a·ble** *adj.* **gov·ern·a·bil·i·ty** *n.*

gov·ern·ance /gúvərnəns/ *n.* **1** the act or manner of governing. **2** the office of governing. **3** sway; control.

gov·ern·ess /gúvərnis/ *n.* a woman employed to teach children in a private household.

gov·ern·ment /gúvərnmənt/ *n.* **1** the act or manner of governing. **2** the system by which a nation is governed. **3 a** a body of persons governing a nation. **b** (usu. **Government**) a particular party in office. **4** the nation as an agent. ▫▫ **gov·ern·men·tal** /–mént'l/ *adj.* **gov·ern·men·tal·ly** *adv.*

gov·er·nor /gúvərnər/ *n.* **1** a person who governs; a ruler. **2** the executive head of each state of the US. **3** *hist.* an official governing a province, town, etc. **4** an officer commanding a fortress or garrison. **5** the head or a member of a governing body of an institution. **6** *Mech.* an automatic regulator controlling the speed of an engine, etc. ▫▫ **gov·er·nor·ate** /–rət, –rayt/ *n.* **gov·er·nor·ship** *n.*

Govt. *abbr.* Government.

gown /gown/ *n. & v.* • *n.* **1** a loose flowing garment, esp. a long dress worn by a woman. **2** the official robe of an alderman, judge, cleric, etc. **3** a surgeon's robe, worn during surgery. • *v.tr.* (usu. as **gowned** *adj.*) attire in a gown.

goy /goy/ *n.* (*pl.* **goyim** /góyim/or **goys**) *sl.* sometimes *derog.* a Jewish name for a non-Jew. ▫▫ **goy·ish** *adj.* (also **goy·isch**).

GP *abbr.* **1** general practitioner. **2** Grand Prix.

GPA *abbr.* grade point average.

GPO *abbr.* **1** General Post Office. **2** Government Printing Office.

gr *abbr.* (also **gr.**) **1** gram(s). **2** grain(s). **3** gross. **4** gray.

grab /grab/ *v. & n.* • *v.* (**grabbed, grabbing**) **1** *tr.* **a** seize suddenly. **b** capture; arrest. **2** *tr.* take greedily or unfairly. **3** *tr. sl.* attract the attention of; impress. **4** *intr.* (foll. by *at*) make a sudden snatch at. **5** *intr.* (of brakes) act harshly or jerkily. • *n.* **1** a sudden attempt to seize. **2** a mechanical device for clutching. **3** the practice of grabbing. □ **up for grabs** *sl.* easily obtainable. □□ **grab·ber** *n.*

grab bag *n.* **1** a container from which one removes a mystery gift. **2** a miscellaneous group of items.

grab·ble /grábəl/ *v.intr.* **1** grope about; feel for something. **2** (often foll. by *for*) sprawl on all fours; scramble (for something).

grab·by /grábee/ *adj. colloq.* tending to grab; greedy; grasping.

grace /grays/ *n.* & *v.* •*n.* **1** attractiveness, esp. in elegance of proportion or manner. **2** courteous good will (*had the grace to apologize*). **3** an attractive feature (*social graces*). **4 a** (in Christian belief) the unmerited favor of God. **b** the state of receiving this. **c** a divinely given talent. **5** goodwill; favor (*fall from grace*). **6** delay granted as a favor (*a year's grace*). **7** a short thanksgiving before or after a meal. **8** (**Grace**) (in Greek mythology) each of three beautiful sister goddesses, bestowers of beauty and charm. **9** (**Grace**) (prec. by *His, Her, Your*) forms of description or address for a duke, duchess, or archbishop. •*v.tr.* **1** enhance or embellish. **2** confer honor on (*graced us with his presence*). □ **with good** (or **bad**) **grace** as if willingly (or reluctantly).

grace·ful /gráysfōōl/ *adj.* having or showing grace or elegance. □□ **grace·ful·ly** *adv.* **grace·ful·ness** *n.*

grace·less /gráyslis/ *adj.* lacking elegance or charm. □□ **grace·less·ly** *adv.*

grace pe·ri·od *n.* a period of time allowed beyond when a payment becomes due before one incurs penalties.

gra·cious /gráyshəs/ *adj.* & *int.* •*adj.* **1** indulgent and beneficent to others. **2** (of God) merciful; benign. **3** kindly; courteous. •*int.* expressing surprise. □□ **gra·cious·ly** *adv.* **gra·cious·ness** *n.*

gra·cious liv·ing *n.* an elegant way of life.

grad /grad/ *n. colloq.* = GRADUATE *n.* 1.

gra·date /gráydayt/ *v.* **1** *v.intr.* & *tr.* pass or cause to pass by gradations from one shade to another. **2** *tr.* arrange in steps or grades of size, etc.

gra·da·tion /graydáyshən/ *n.* (usu. in *pl.*) **1** a stage of transition or advance. **2 a** a certain degree in rank, intensity, etc. **b** an arrangement in such degrees. **3** (of paint, etc.) the gradual passing from one shade, tone, etc., to another.

grade /grayd/ *n.* & *v.* •*n.* **1 a** a certain degree in rank, merit, proficiency, quality, etc. **b** a class of persons or things of the same grade. **2** a mark indicating the quality of a student's work. **3** a class in school, concerned with a particular year's work and usu. numbered from the first upwards. **4 a** a gradient or slope. **b** the rate of ascent or descent. **5 a** a variety of cattle produced by crossing native stock with a superior breed. **b** a group of animals at a similar level of development. •*v.* **1** *tr.* arrange in or allocate to grades; class; sort. **2** *intr.* pass gradually between grades, or into a grade. **3** *tr.* give a grade to (a student). **4** *tr.* blend so as to affect the grade of color with tints passing into each other. □ **make the grade** *colloq.* reach the desired standard.

grade cross·ing *n.* a crossing of a roadway, etc., with a railroad track at the same level.

grade point *n.* the numerical equivalent of a scholastic letter grade.

grade point av·er·age *n.* an average scholastic grade calculated by dividing the total of grade point values by the total number of course credits.

grad·er /gráydər/ *n.* **1** a person or thing that grades. **2** (in *comb.*) a pupil of a specified grade in a school (*third grader*).

grade school *n.* elementary school.

gra·di·ent /gráydeeənt/ *n.* **1 a** a stretch of road, railroad, etc., that slopes. **b** the amount of such a slope. **2** the rate of rise or fall of temperature, pressure, etc., in passing from one region to another.

grad·u·al /grájōōəl/ *adj.* **1** taking place or progressing by degrees. **2** not rapid or steep. □□ **grad·u·al·ly** *adv.* **grad·u·al·ness** *n.*

grad·u·al·ism /grájōōəlizəm/ *n.* a policy of gradual reform rather than sudden change or revolution. □□ **grad·u·al·ist** *n.*

grad·u·ate *n.* & *v.* •*n.* /grájōōət/ **1** a person who has been awarded an academic degree (also *attrib.*: *graduate student*). **2** a person who has completed a course of study. •*v.* /grájōō-áyt/ **1** *intr.* take an academic degree. **2** *intr.* **a** (foll. by *from*) be a graduate of a specified university. **b** (foll. by *in*) be a graduate in a specified subject. **3** *tr.* send out as a graduate from a university, etc. **4** *intr.* **a** (foll. by *to*) move up to (a higher grade of activity, etc.). **b** (foll. by *as, in*) gain specified qualifications. **5** *tr.* mark out in degrees. **6** *tr.* arrange in gradations; apportion (e.g., tax) according to a scale. **7** *intr.* (foll. by *into, away*) pass by degrees.

▶The traditional use is "to be graduated from": *She will be graduated from medical school in June.* It is now more common to say "graduate from": *He will graduate from high school next year.* Avoid using *graduate* as a transitive verb, as in "He graduated high school last week."

grad·u·ate school *n.* a division of a university for advanced work by graduates.

grad·u·a·tion /grájōōáyshən/ *n.* **1** the act of graduating. **2** a ceremony at which degrees are conferred. **3** each or all of the marks on a vessel or instrument indicating degrees of quantity, etc.

Grae·cism var. of GRECISM.

Grae·cize var. of GRECIZE.

Graeco- var. of GRECO-.

Grae·co-Ro·man var. of GRECO-ROMAN.

graf·fi·to /grəféetō/ *n.* (*pl.* **graffiti** /–tee/) **1** (usu. in *pl.*) a piece of writing or drawing scribbled, scratched, or sprayed on a surface.

▶The plural form *graffiti* is sometimes used with a singular verb, even though it is not a mass noun in this sense, and so properly a plural construction is needed, e.g., *graffiti are an art form.*

graft[1] /graft/ *n.* & *v.* •*n.* **1** *Bot.* **a** a shoot or scion inserted into a slit of stock, from which it receives sap. **b** the place where a graft is inserted. **2** *Surgery* a piece of living tissue, organ, etc., transplanted surgically. **3** *Brit. sl.* hard work. •*v.* **1** *tr.* **a** (often foll. by *into, on, together*, etc.) insert (a scion) as a graft. **b** insert a graft on (a stock). **2** *intr.* insert a graft. **3** *tr. Surgery* transplant (living tissue). **4** *tr.* (foll. by *in, on*) insert or fix (a thing) permanently to another. **5** *intr. Brit. sl.* work hard. □□ **graft·er** *n.*

graft[2] /graft/ *n.* & *v. colloq.* •*n.* **1** practices, esp. bribery, used to secure illicit gains in politics or business. **2** such gains. •*v.intr.* seek or make such gains. □□ **graft·er** *n.*

gra·ham crack·er /gram, gráyəm/ *n.* a crisp, slightly sweet cracker made from whole wheat flour.

Grail /grayl/ *n.* (in full **Holy Grail**) (in medieval legend) the cup or platter used by Christ at the Last Supper.

grain /grayn/ *n.* & *v.* •*n.* **1** a fruit or seed of a cereal. **2 a** (*collect.*) wheat or any related grass used as food. **b** (*collect.*) their fruit. **c** any particular species of a cereal crop. **3 a** a small hard particle of salt, sand, etc. **b** a discrete particle or crystal, usu. small, in a rock or metal. **c** a piece of solid propellant for use in a rocket engine. **4** the smallest unit of weight in the troy system (480 grains = 1 ounce), and in the avoirdupois system (437.5 grains = 1 ounce). **5** the smallest possible quantity (*a grain of truth*). **6 a** roughness of surface. **b** *Photog.* a granular appearance on a photograph or negative. **7** the texture of wood, stone, etc. **8 a** a pattern of lines of fiber in wood or paper. **b** lamination or planes of cleavage in stone, coal, etc. **9** nature; tendency. • *v.* **1** *tr.* paint in imitation of the grain of wood or marble. **2** *tr.* give a granular surface to. **3** *tr. & intr.* form into grains. □ **against the grain** (often in the phrase **go against the grain**) contrary to one's natural inclination or feeling. **in grain** thorough; genuine; by nature; downright; indelible. □□ **grained** *adj.* (also in *comb.*).

grain•y /gráynee/ *adj.* (**grainier, grainiest**) **1** granular. **2** resembling the grain of wood. **3** *Photog.* having a granular appearance. □□ **grain•i•ness** *n.*

gral•la•to•ri•al /grálətáwreeəl/ *adj. Zool.* of or relating to wading birds.

gram[1] /gram/ *n.* a metric unit of mass equal to one-thousandth of a kilogram.

gram[2] /gram/ *n.* any of various beans used as food, esp. the chickpea.

-gram /gram/ *comb. form* forming nouns denoting a thing written or recorded (*anagram*; *epigram*). □□ **-grammatic** /grəmátik/ *comb. form* forming adjectives.

gram•i•na•ceous /gráminàyshəs/ *adj.* = GRAMINEOUS.

gra•min•e•ous /grəmíneeəs/ *adj.* of or like grass; grassy.

gram•ma•logue /gráməlawg, -log/ *n.* a word represented by a single shorthand sign.

gram•mar /grámər/ *n.* **1** the study or rules of a language's inflections or other means of showing the relation between words. **2** application of the rules of grammar (*bad grammar*). **3** a book on grammar. **4** the rudiments of an art or science. **5** *Brit. colloq.* = GRAMMAR SCHOOL. □□ **gram•mar•less** *adj.*

gram•mar•i•an /grəmáireeən/ *n.* an expert in grammar or linguistics; a philologist.

gram•mar school *n.* **1** *US* an elementary school. **2** *Brit.* esp. *hist.* a selective state-supported secondary school with a mainly academic curriculum. **3** *Brit. hist.* a school founded in or before the 16th c. for teaching Latin, later becoming a secondary school teaching academic subjects.

gram•mat•i•cal /grəmátikəl/ *adj.* **1** of or relating to grammar. **2** conforming to the rules of grammar. □□ **gram•mat•i•cal•ly** *adv.*

gram•o•phone /gráməfōn/ *n.* = PHONOGRAPH. □□ **gram•o•phon•ic** /–fónik/ *adj.*

gram•pus /grámpəs/ *n.* (*pl.* **grampuses**) a dolphin, *Grampus griseus*, with a blunt snout and long pointed black flippers.

gran /gran/ *n. colloq.* grandmother (cf. GRANNY).

gra•na•ry /gránəree, gráy–/ *n.* (*pl.* **-ries**) **1** a storehouse for threshed grain. **2** a region producing, and esp. exporting, much grain.

grand /grand/ *adj. & n.* • *adj.* **1 a** imposing; dignified. **b** solemn in conception or expression. **2** main (*grand staircase*). **3** (**Grand**) of the highest rank, esp. in official titles (*Grand Inquisitor*). **4** *colloq.* excellent; enjoyable (*had a grand time*). **5** belonging to high society (*the grand folk at the manor*). **6** (in *comb.*) in family relationships, denoting the second degree of ascent or descent (*granddaughter*). • *n.* **1** = GRAND PIANO. **2** (*pl.* same) *sl.* a thousand dollars or pounds sterling. □□ **grand•ly** *adv.* **grand•ness** *n.*

gran•dad /grándad/ *n.* (also **grand•dad**) *colloq.* **1** grandfather. **2** an elderly man.

gran•dam /grándam/ *n.* **1** (also **gran•dame**) *archaic* grandmother. **2** an old woman. **3** an ancestress.

grand•child /gránchīld, gránd–/ *n.* (*pl.* **-children**) a child of one's son or daughter.

grand•dad•dy /grándadee/ *n.* (also **gran•dad•dy**) (*pl.* **-dies**) **1** *colloq.* a grandfather. **2** the original and usu. most venerated of its kind (*the granddaddy of symphony orchestras*).

grand•daugh•ter /grándawtər/ *n.* a female grandchild.

grande dame /grONd daám/ *n.* a dignified woman of high rank.

gran•dee /grandeé/ *n.* **1** a Spanish or Portuguese nobleman of the highest rank. **2** a person of high rank or eminence.

gran•deur /gránjər, –jōōr/ *n.* **1** majesty; splendor; dignity of appearance or bearing. **2** high rank; eminence. **3** nobility of character.

grand•fa•ther /gránfaaṯhər, gránd–/ *n.* a male grandparent. □□ **grand•fa•ther•ly** *adj.*

grand•fa•ther clock *n.* a floor-standing pendulum clock in a tall wooden case.

gran•di•flo•ra /grándiflàwrə/ *adj.* bearing large flowers.

gran•dil•o•quent /grandíləkwənt/ *adj.* **1** pompous in language. **2** given to boastful talk. □□ **gran•dil•o•quence** /–kwəns/ *n.* **gran•dil•o•quent•ly** *adv.*

gran•di•ose /grándeeṓs/ *adj.* **1** producing an imposing effect. **2** planned on an ambitious scale. □□ **gran•di•ose•ly** *adv.* **gran•di•os•i•ty** /–deeósitee/ *n.*

grand ju•ry *n. Law* a jury selected to determine whether there is enough evidence regarding a charge to merit a trial.

grand lar•ceny *n. Law* larceny in which the value of the stolen property exceeds a certain legally established limit.

grand•ma /gránmaa, gránd–/ *n. colloq.* grandmother.

grand mal /grON maál, gránd mál/ *n.* a serious form of epilepsy with loss of consciousness (cf. PETIT MAL).

grand•ma•ma /gránməmaá, –maamə, gránd–/ *n. archaic colloq.* = GRANDMA.

grand•moth•er /gránmuṯhər, gránd–/ *n.* a female grandparent. □□ **grand•moth•er•ly** *adj.*

grand•moth•er clock *n.* a clock like a grandfather clock but in a shorter case.

grand•pa /gránpaa, gránd–/ *n. colloq.* grandfather.

grand•pa•pa /gránpəpaá, –paapə, gránd–/ *n. archaic colloq.* = GRANDPA.

grand•par•ent /gránpairənt, gránd–/ *n.* a parent of one's father or mother.

grand pi•a•no *n.* a large full-toned piano standing on three legs, with the body, strings, and soundboard arranged horizontally and in line with the keys.

Grand Prix /grON preé/ *n.* any of several important international automobile or motorcycle racing events.

grand siècle /grON syéklə/ *n.* the classical or golden age, esp. the 17th c. in France.

grand slam *n.* **1 a** *Sports* the winning of all of a group of four major championships. **b** one of the events involved. **2** *Bridge* the winning of all 13 tricks. **3** *Baseball* a home run hit with three runners on base.

grand•son /gránsun, gránd–/ *n.* a male grandchild.

grand•stand /gránstand, gránd;n–/ *n. & v.* • *n.* the main seating area, usu. roofed, for spectators at a racetrack or sports stadium. • *v.intr.* seek to attract applause or favorable attention from spectators or the media (*a politician who will grandstand to get votes*).

grand to•tal *n.* the final amount after everything is added up; the sum of other totals.

grange /graynj/ *n.* **1** esp. *Brit.* a country house with farm buildings. **2** (**Grange**) a social and fraternal organization of farmers. **3** *archaic* a barn.

gran•i•fer•ous /grəníferəs/ *adj.* producing grain.

gran•ite /gránit/ *n.* a coarse, granular crystalline igneous rock of quartz, mica, etc., used for building. □□ **gra•nit•ic** /grənítik/ *adj.* **gran•it•oid** *adj. & n.*

gra•niv•o•rous /grənívərəs/ *adj.* feeding on grain. □□ **gra•ni•vore** /gránivawr/ *n.*

gran•ny /gránee/ *n.* (also **gran•nie**) (*pl.* **-nies**) *colloq.* grandmother.

Gran·ny Smith /gránee smíth/ *n.* an orig. Australian green variety of apple.
gra·no·la /grənṓlə/ *n.* a breakfast food consisting typically of a mixture of rolled oats, nuts, dried fruits, and brown sugar.
grant /grant/ *v.* & *n.* • *v.tr.* **1 a** consent to fulfill (a request, etc.) (*granted all he asked*). **b** allow (a person) to have (a thing). **c** (as **granted**) *colloq.* apology accepted. **2** give formally; transfer legally. **3** (often foll. by *that* + clause) concede, esp. as a basis for argument. • *n.* **1** the process of granting or a thing granted. **2** a sum of money given, esp. by the government, for any of various purposes, as to finance education. **3** *Law* **a** a legal conveyance by written instrument. **b** formal conferment. □ **take for granted 1** assume something to be true or valid. **2** cease to appreciate through familiarity. □□ **grant·a·ble** *adj.* **gran·tee** /–tée/ *n.* (esp. in sense 2 of *v.*). **grant·er** *n.* **gran·tor** /–tór/ *n.* (esp. in sense 2 of *v.*).
gran·u·lar /grányələr/ *adj.* **1** of grains or granules. **2** having a granulated surface. □□ **gran·u·lar·i·ty** /–láritee/ *n.*
gran·u·late /grányəlayt/ *v.* **1** *tr.* & *intr.* form into grains (*granulated sugar*). **2** *tr.* roughen the surface of. **3** *intr.* (of a wound, etc.) form small prominences as the beginning of healing; heal; join. □□ **gran·u·la·tion** /–láyshən/ *n.* **gran·u·la·tor** *n.*
gran·ule /grányoōl/ *n.* a small grain.
gran·u·lo·met·ric /grányəlōmétrik/ *adj.* relating to the distribution of grain sizes in sand, etc.
grape /grayp/ *n.* **1** a berry (usu. green, purple, or black) growing in clusters on a vine, eaten as fruit and used in making wine. **2** (prec. by *the*) *colloq.* wine. □□ **grap·y** *adj.* (also **grap·ey**).
grape·fruit /gráypfroōt/ *n.* (*pl.* same) a large round yellow citrus fruit with an acid juicy pulp.
grape·vine /gráypvīn/ *n.* **1** any of various vines of the genus *Vitis*. **2** *colloq.* the means of transmission of unofficial information or rumor (*heard it through the grapevine*).
graph[1] /graf/ *n.* & *v.* • *n.* a diagram showing the relation between usu. two variables, each measured along one of a pair of axes. • *v.tr.* plot on a graph.
graph[2] /graf/ *n. Linguistics* a visual symbol, esp. a letter or letters, representing a unit of sound or other feature of speech.
-graph /graf/ *comb. form* forming nouns meaning: **1** a thing written or drawn, etc., in a specified way (*autograph*). **2** an instrument that records (*seismograph*).
graph·eme /gráfeem/ *n. Linguistics* **1** a class of letters, etc., representing a unit of sound. **2** a feature of a written expression that cannot be analyzed into smaller meaningful units. □□ **gra·phe·mat·ic** /–mátik/ *adj.* **gra·phe·mic** /grəféemik/ *adj.* **gra·phe·mi·cal·ly** *adv.*
-grapher /grəfər/ *comb. form* forming nouns denoting a person concerned with a subject (*geographer; radiographer*).
graph·ic /gráfik/ *adj.* & *n.* • *adj.* **1** of or relating to the visual or descriptive arts, esp. writing and drawing. **2** vividly descriptive. **3** = GRAPHICAL. • *n.* a product of the graphic arts (cf. GRAPHICS). □□ **graph·i·cal·ly** *adv.*
-graphic /gráfik/ *comb. form* (also **-graphical** /gráfikəl/) forming adjectives corresponding to nouns in *-graphy* (see -graphy). □□ **-graphically** /gráfiklee/ *comb. form* forming adverbs.
graph·i·cal /gráfikəl/ *adj.* **1** of or in the form of graphs (see GRAPH[1]). **2** graphic. □□ **graph·i·cal·ly** *adv.*
graph·i·cal us·er in·ter·face *n. Computing* a visual way of interacting with a computer using items such as windows, icons, and menus. ¶ Abbr.: **GUI**.
graph·ic arts *n.* the visual and technical arts involving design, drawing, printing, the use of color, etc.
graph·ic e·qual·iz·er *n.* a device for the separate control of the strength and quality of selected frequency bands.
graph·ics /gráfiks/ *n.pl.* (usu. treated as *sing.*) **1** the products of the graphic arts, esp. commercial design or illustration. **2** the use of diagrams in calculation and design. **3** (in full **computer graphics**) *Computing* a mode of processing and output in which a significant part of the information is in pictorial form.
graph·ite /gráfīt/ *n.* a crystalline allotropic form of carbon used as a solid lubricant, in pencil leads, etc. Also called PLUMBAGO. □□ **gra·phit·ic** /–fítik/ *adj.* **graph·i·tize** /–fitīz/ *v.tr.* & *intr.*
graph·ol·o·gy /grəfóləjee/ *n.* **1** the study of handwriting esp. as a supposed guide to character. **2** a system of graphic formulae. **3** *Linguistics* the study of systems of writing. □□ **graph·o·log·i·cal** /gráfəlójikəl/ *adj.* **graph·ol·o·gist** *n.*
-graphy /grəfee/ *comb. form* forming nouns denoting: **1** a descriptive science (*bibliography; geography*). **2** a technique of producing images (*photography; radiography*). **3** a style or method of writing, drawing, etc. (*calligraphy*).
grap·nel /grápnəl/ *n.* **1** a device with iron claws, attached to a rope and used for dragging or grasping. **2** a small anchor with several flukes.

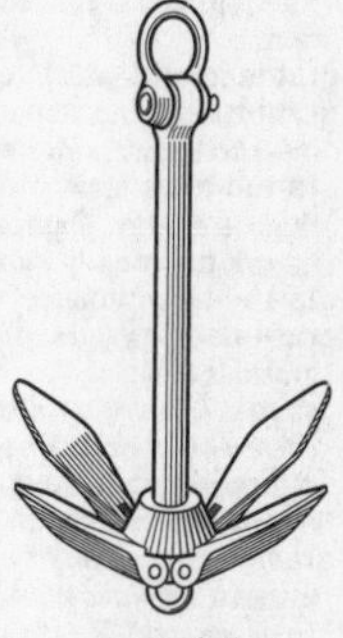
grapnel, 2

grap·ple /grápəl/ *v.* & *n.* • *v.* **1** *intr.* (often foll. by *with*) fight at close quarters. **2** *intr.* (foll. by *with*) try to manage a difficult problem, etc. **3** *tr.* **a** grip with the hands. **b** seize with or as with a grapnel. • *n.* **1 a** a hold or grip in or as in wrestling. **b** a contest at close quarters. **2** a clutching instrument. □□ **grap·pler** *n.*
grasp /grasp/ *v.* & *n.* • *v.* **1** *tr.* **a** clutch at; seize. **b** hold firmly. **2** *intr.* (foll. by *at*) try to seize. **3** *tr.* understand or realize (a fact or meaning). • *n.* **1** a firm hold. **2** (foll. by *of*) **a** mastery or control (*a grasp of the situation*). **b** a mental hold (*a grasp of the facts*). □ **grasp at straws** see STRAW. □□ **grasp·a·ble** *adj.* **grasp·er** *n.*
grasp·ing /grásping/ *adj.* avaricious; greedy. □□ **grasp·ing·ly** *adv.* **grasp·ing·ness** *n.*
grass /gras/ *n.* & *v.* • *n.* **1 a** vegetation belonging to a group of small plants with green blades that are eaten by cattle, horses, etc. **b** any species of this. **c** any plant of the family Gramineae, which includes cereals, reeds, and bamboos. **2** pasture land. **3** a lawn. **4** *sl.* marijuana. • *v.tr.* **1** cover with turf. **2** *tr.* provide with pasture. □ **out to grass 1** to pasture. **2** in retirement. □□ **grass·less** *adj.* **grass·like** *adj.*
grass·hop·per /grás-hoppər/ *n.* a jumping and chirping plant-eating insect of the order Saltatoria.
grass·land /grásland/ *n.* a large open area covered with grass, esp. one used for grazing.
grass roots *n.pl.* **1** a fundamental level or source. **2** ordinary people; the rank and file of an organization, esp. a political party.
grass snake *n.* **1** the common greensnake, *Opheodrys vernalis*. **2** *Brit.* the common ringed snake, *Natrix natrix*.
grass wid·ow (or **widower**) *n.* a person whose husband (or wife) is away for a prolonged period.
grass·y /grásee/ *adj.* (**grassier, grassiest**) **1** covered

with or abounding in grass. **2** resembling grass. **3** of grass. □□ **grass·i·ness** *n.*

grate[1] /grayt/ *v.* **1** *tr.* reduce to small particles by rubbing on a serrated surface. **2** *intr.* (often foll. by *against, on*) rub with a harsh scraping sound. **3** *tr.* utter in a harsh tone. **4** *intr.* **a** sound harshly. **b** have an irritating effect. **5** *tr.* grind (one's teeth). **6** *intr.* creak.

grate[2] /grayt/ *n.* **1** the recess of a fireplace. **2** a metal frame confining fuel in a grate.

grate·ful /gráytfŏŏl/ *adj.* **1** feeling or showing gratitude. **2** pleasant, acceptable. □□ **grate·ful·ly** *adv.* **grate·ful·ness** *n.*

grat·er /gráytər/ *n.* a device for reducing cheese or other food to small particles.

grat·i·fy /grátifī/ *v.tr.* (**-fies, -fied**) **1 a** please; delight. **b** please by compliance; assent to the wish of. **2** yield to (a feeling or desire). □□ **grat·i·fi·ca·tion** *n.* **grat·i·fi·er** *n.* **gra·ti·fy·ing** *adj.* **gra·ti·fy·ing·ly** *adv.*

grat·ing[1] /gráyting/ *adj.* **1** sounding harsh. **2** having an irritating effect. □□ **grat·ing·ly** *adv.*

grat·ing[2] /gráyting/ *n.* **1** a framework of parallel or crossed metal bars. **2** *Optics* a set of parallel wires, lines ruled on glass, etc., for producing spectra by diffraction.

grat·is /grátis, graá–/ *adv. & adj.* free; without charge.

grat·i·tude /grátitŏŏd, –tyŏŏd/ *n.* being thankful; readiness to return kindness.

gra·tu·i·tous /grətŏŏitəs, tyŏŏ–/ *adj.* **1** given or done free of charge. **2** uncalled-for; lacking good reason. □□ **gra·tu·i·tous·ly** *adv.* **gra·tu·i·tous·ness** *n.*

gra·tu·i·ty /grətŏŏitee, –tyŏŏ–/ *n.* (*pl.* **-ties**) a tip.

grat·u·la·to·ry /gráchələtáwree/ *adj.* expressing congratulations.

grave[1] /grayv/ *n.* **1** a trench dug in the ground to receive a body or coffin for burial. **2** (prec. by *the*) death. □ **turn in one's grave** (of a dead person) be likely to have been shocked or angry if still alive.

grave[2] /grayv/ *adj. & n.* • *adj.* **1 a** serious; weighty; important (*a grave matter*). **b** dignified; solemn; somber (*a grave look*). **2** extremely threatening (*grave danger*). • *n.* /graav/ = GRAVE ACCENT. □□ **grave·ly** *adv.* **grave·ness** *n.*

grave[3] /grayv/ *v.tr.* (*past part.* **graven** or **graved**) **1** (foll. by *in, on*) fix indelibly (on one's memory). **2** engrave.

grave[4] /grayv/ *v.tr.* clean (a ship's bottom) by burning off accretions and by tarring.

grave[5] /grávay/ *adj. & adv.* • *adj.* slow and solemn. • *adv.* slowly and solemnly.

grave ac·cent *n.* /graav, grayv/ a mark (`) placed over a vowel in some languages to denote pronunciation, length, etc., orig. indicating low or falling pitch.

grav·el /grávəl/ *n. & v.* • *n.* **1 a** a mixture of coarse sand and small waterworn or pounded stones, used for paths and roads. **b** *Geol.* a stratum of this. **2** *Med.* aggregations of crystals formed in the urinary tract. • *v.tr.* (**graveled, graveling**; also **gravelled, gravelling**) **1** lay or strew with gravel. **2** perplex; puzzle.

grave·lax var. of GRAVLAX.

gra·vel·ly /grávəlee/ *adj.* **1** of or like gravel. **2** having or containing gravel. **3** (of a voice) deep and rough sounding.

grav·en *past part.* of GRAVE[3].

grav·en im·age *n.* an idol.

grav·er /gráyvər/ *n.* **1** an engraving tool; a burin. **2** an engraver; a carver.

Graves' dis·ease /grayvz/ *n.* a type of goiter with characteristic swelling of the neck and protrusion of the eyes, resulting from an overactive thyroid gland.

grave·stone /gráyvstōn/ *n.* a stone (usu. inscribed) marking a grave.

grave·yard /gráyvyaard/ *n.* a burial ground.

grave·yard shift *n.* a work shift that usu. starts about midnight and ends about eight in the morning.

gra·vim·e·ter /grəvímitər/ *n.* an instrument for measuring the difference in the force of gravity from one place to another.

grav·i·met·ric /grávimétrik/ *adj.* of or relating to the measurement of weight.

gra·vim·e·try /grəvímitree/ *n.* the measurement of weight.

grav·i·tate /grávitayt/ *v.* intr. **1** (foll. by *to, toward*) be attracted to some source of influence. **2** sink by or as if by gravity.

grav·i·ta·tion /grávitáyshən/ *n. Physics* **1** a force of attraction between any particle of matter in the universe and any other. **2** the effect of this, esp. the falling of bodies to the earth.

grav·i·ta·tion·al /grávitáyshənəl/ *adj.* of or relating to gravitation. □□ **grav·i·ta·tion·al·ly** *adv.*

grav·i·ty /grávitee/ *n.* **1 a** the force that attracts a body to the center of the earth or other celestial body. **b** the degree of intensity of this measured by acceleration. **c** gravitational force. **2** the property of having weight. **3 a** importance; seriousness. **b** solemnity; sobriety.

grav·lax /graávlaaks/ *n.* (also **grave·lax**) filleted salmon cured by marination in salt, sugar, and dill.

gra·vure /grəvyŏŏr/ *n.* = PHOTOGRAVURE.

gra·vy /gráyvee/ *n.* (*pl.* **-vies**) **1 a** the juices exuding from meat during and after cooking. **b** sauce for food, made by thickening these. **2** *colloq.* something valuable that is unexpected or unearned.

gra·vy train *n. sl.* a source of easy financial benefit.

gray[1] /gray/ *adj., n., & v.* (also **grey**) • *adj.* **1** of a color intermediate between black and white. **2 a** (of the weather, etc.) dull; dismal. **b** bleak; (of a person) depressed. **3 a** (of hair) turning white with age, etc. **b** (of a person) having gray hair. **4** anonymous; nondescript. • *n.* **1 a** a gray color or pigment. **b** gray clothes or material (*dressed in gray*). **2** a gray or white horse. • *v.tr. & intr.* make or become gray. □□ **gray·ish** *adj.* **gray·ly** *adv.* **gray·ness** *n.*

gray[2] /gray/ *n. Physics* the SI unit of the absorbed dose of ionizing radiation, corresponding to one joule per kilogram. ¶ Abbr.: **Gy.**

gray a·re·a *n.* **1** a situation sharing features of more than one category and not clearly attributable to any one category. **2** an area in economic decline.

gray·ling /gráyling/ *n.* any silver-gray freshwater fish of the genus *Thymallus*, with a long high dorsal fin.

gray mat·ter *n.* **1** the darker tissues of the brain and spinal cord consisting of nerve cell bodies and branching dendrites. **2** *colloq.* intelligence.

graze[1] /grayz/ *v.* **1** *intr.* (of cattle, etc.) eat growing grass. **2** *tr.* **a** feed (cattle, etc.) on growing grass. **b** feed on (grass). **3** *intr.* pasture cattle. □□ **graz·er** *n.*

graze[2] /grayz/ *v. & n.* • *v.* **1** *tr.* scrape (the skin) so as to break the surface with only minor bleeding. **2 a** *tr.* touch lightly in passing. **b** *intr.* (foll. by *against, along,* etc.) move with a light passing contact. • *n.* an act or instance of grazing.

graz·ing /gráyzing/ *n.* grassland suitable for pasturage.

grease /grees/ *n. & v.* • *n.* **1** oily or fatty matter esp. as a lubricant. **2** the melted fat of a dead animal. • *v.tr.* also /greez/ lubricate with grease. □ **grease the palm of** *colloq.* bribe. **like greased lightning** *colloq.* very fast.

grease·gun *n.* a device for pumping grease under pressure to a particular point.

grease mon·key *n. sl.* a mechanic who works on motor vehicles.

grease·paint /gréespaynt/ *n.* a waxy composition used as makeup for actors.

greas·er /greésər/ *n.* **1** *sl.* a member of a gang of young street toughs. **2** *sl. offens.* a Mexican or Spanish-American.

greas·y /gréesee, gréezee/ *adj.* (**greasier, greasiest**) **1 a** of or like grease. **b** smeared with grease. **c** containing or having too much grease. **2 a** slippery. **b** (of a person or manner) unpleasantly unctuous. **c** objectionable. ▫▫ **greas·i·ly** *adv.* **greas·i·ness** *n.*

greas·y spoon *n. sl.* an inexpensive small restaurant that serves fried food and that is often dirty.

great /grayt/ *adj. & n.* • *adj.* **1 a** of a size, amount, extent, or intensity considerably above the average. **b** also with implied surprise, contempt, etc. (*great stuff!*). **c** reinforcing other words denoting size, quantity, etc. (*a great big hole*). **2** important; worthy or most worthy of consideration. **3** grand; imposing (*a great occasion*). **4 a** (esp. of a public or historic figure) distinguished. **b** (**the Great**) as a title denoting the most important person of the name (*Alexander the Great*). **5 a** (of a person) remarkable in ability, character, etc. (*a great thinker*). **b** (of a thing) outstanding of its kind (*the Great Depression*). **6** (foll. by *at*) skilled; well-informed. **7** doing a thing habitually or extensively (*a great reader*). **8** (also **great·er**) the larger of the species, etc. (*great auk*). **9** (**Greater**) (of a city, etc.) including adjacent urban areas (*Greater Boston*). **10** *colloq.* **a** very enjoyable or satisfactory; (*had a great time*). **b** (as an exclam.) fine; very good. **11** (in *comb.*) denoting one degree further removed upwards or downwards (*great-uncle*). • *n.* a great or outstanding person or thing. ▫ **great and small** all classes or types. **great deal** see DEAL[1]. **the great majority** by far the most. **to a great extent** largely. ▫▫ **great·ness** *n.*

Great Brit·ain *n.* England, Wales, and Scotland.
▶**Great Britain** is the name for the island that comprises England, Scotland, and Wales. The *United Kingdom* includes these and Northern Ireland. The *British Isles* include the United Kingdom and surrounding, smaller islands. The all-encompassing adjective *British* is unlikely to offend anyone from any of these places. *Welsh, Scottish,* and *English* should be used with care; it is safest to use *British* if unsure.

Great Di·vide *n.* (prec. by *the*) **1** a vast continental divide or watershed between two drainage systems, esp. that along the Rocky Mountains of N. America. **2** the boundary between life and death.

great·heart·ed /gráyt-haártəd/ *adj.* magnanimous; having a noble or generous mind. ▫▫ **great·heart·ed·ness** *n.*

Great Lakes *n.pl.* (prec. by *the*) the Lakes Superior, Huron, Michigan, Erie, and Ontario, along the boundary of the US and Canada.

great·ly /gráytlee/ *adv.* by a considerable amount; much (*greatly admired; greatly superior*).

great tit *n.* a Eurasian songbird, *Parus major*, with black and white head markings.

Great War *n.* World War I (1914–18).

greave /greev/ *n.* (usu. in *pl.*) armor for the shin.

grebe /greeb/ *n.* any diving bird of the family Podicipedidae, with a long neck.

Gre·cian /gréeshən/ *adj.* (of architecture or facial outline) following Greek models or ideals.

Gre·cism /gréesizəm/ *n.* (also **Grae·cism**) **1** a Greek idiom, esp. as imitated in another language. **2 a** the Greek spirit, style, mode of expression, etc. **b** the imitation of these.

Greco- /grékō/ *comb. form* (also **Graeco-**) Greek; Greek and.

Gre·co-Ro·man /gréekō-rṓmən, grékō–/ *adj.* **1** of or relating to the Greeks and Romans. **2** *Wrestling* denoting a style attacking only the upper part of the body.

greed /greed/ *n.* an excessive desire, esp. for food or wealth.

greed·y /gréedee/ *adj.* (**greedier, greediest**) **1** having or showing an excessive appetite for food. **2** wanting wealth to excess. **3** (foll. by *for*, or *to* + infin.) very keen or eager. ▫▫ **greed·i·ly** *adv.* **greed·i·ness** *n.*

Greek /greek/ *n. & adj.* • *n.* **1 a** a native or inhabitant of modern Greece; a person of Greek descent. **b** a native or citizen of any of the ancient states of Greece. **2** the Indo-European language of Greece. • *adj.* of Greece or its people or language. ▫▫ **Greek·ness** *n.*

green /green/ *adj., n., & v.* • *adj.* **1** of the color between blue and yellow in the spectrum. **2** covered with leaves or grass. **3** (of fruit, etc., or wood) unripe or unseasoned. **4** not dried, smoked, or tanned. **5** inexperienced; naive. **6 a** (of the complexion) sickly-hued. **b** jealous; envious. **7** young; flourishing. **8** not worn out (*a green old age*). **9** (also **Green**) concerned with protection of the environment as a political principle. • *n.* **1** a green color or pigment. **2** green clothes or material. **3 a** a piece of common grassy land (*village green*). **b** a grassy area used for a special purpose (*putting green*). **c** *Golf* a putting green. **4** (in *pl.*) green vegetables. **5** (also **Green**) a member or supporter of an environmentalist group or party. **6** *sl.* low-grade marijuana. **7** *sl.* money. **8** green foliage or growing plants. • *v. tr. & intr.* make or become green. ▫▫ **green·ish** *adj.* **green·ness** *n.*

green·back /gréenbak/ *n.* a US legal tender note.

green bean *n.* the green pods of a young kidney bean, eaten as a vegetable. Also STRING BEAN.

Green Be·ret *n. Mil.* a member of the U.S. Army Special Forces.

green·bot·tle /gréenbot'l/ *n.* any fly of the genus *Lucilia*, esp. *L. sericata* which lays eggs in the flesh of sheep.

green card *n.* **1** a work and residence permit issued to permanent resident aliens in the US. **2** *Brit.* an international insurance document for motorists.

green·er·y /gréenəree/ *n.* green foliage or growing plants.

green-eyed mon·ster *n.* jealousy.

green·finch /gréenfinch/ *n.* a European finch, *Carduelis chloris*, with green and yellow plumage.

green·fly /gréenflī/ *n.* (*pl.* **-flies**) **1** a green aphid. **2** these collectively.

green·gage /gréengayj/ *n.* a roundish green fine-flavored variety of plum.

green·gro·cer /gréengrṓsər/ *n.* a retailer of fruit and vegetables.

green·horn /gréenhawrn/ *n.* an inexperienced person; a new recruit.

green·house /gréenhows/ *n.* a light structure with the sides and roof mainly of glass, for rearing delicate plants or hastening the growth of plants.

green·house ef·fect *n.* the trapping of the sun's warmth in the lower atmosphere caused by an increase in carbon dioxide.

green·house gas *n.* any of various gases, esp. carbon dioxide, that contribute to the greenhouse effect.

green·ing /gréening/ *n.* any variety of apple that is green when ripe.

green·keep·er var. of GREENSKEEPER.

green light *n.* **1** a signal to proceed on a road, etc. **2** *colloq.* permission to go ahead with a project.

green·room /gréenrōōm/ *n.* a room in a theater for actors and actresses who are off stage.

green·sand /gréensand/ *n.* **1** a greenish kind of sandstone, often imperfectly cemented. **2** a stratum largely formed of this sandstone.

green·sick /gréensik/ *adj.* affected with chlorosis. ▫▫ **green·sick·ness** *n.*

greens·keep·er /gréenzkeepər/ *n.* the keeper of a golf course.
green·stone /gréenstōn/ *n.* a greenish igneous rock containing feldspar and hornblende.
green·stuff /gréenstuf/ *n.* vegetation; green vegetables.
green·sward /gréenswawrd/ *n. archaic* or *literary* **1** grassy turf. **2** an expanse of this.
green tea *n.* tea made from dried, not fermented, leaves.
green thumb *n.* skill in growing plants.
Green·wich Mean Time /grénich, grínij/ *n.* (also **Green·wich Time**) the local time on the meridian of Greenwich, England, used as an international basis for reckoning time.
green·wood /gréenwŏŏd/ *n.* a wood in summer, esp. as the scene of outlaw life.
green·y /gréenee/ *adj.* greenish (*greeny-yellow*).
greet /greet/ *v.tr.* **1** address politely or welcomingly on meeting or arrival. **2** receive in a specified way. **3** (of a sight, etc.) become apparent to or noticed by. ▫▫ **greet·er** *n.*
greet·ing /gréeting/ *n.* **1** the act of welcoming. **2** words, gestures, etc., used to greet a person. **3** (often in *pl.*) an expression of goodwill.
greet·ing card *n.* a decorative card sent to convey greetings.
gre·gar·i·ous /grigáireeəs/ *adj.* **1** fond of company. **2** living in flocks or communities. ▫▫ **gre·gar·i·ous·ly** *adv.* **gre·gar·i·ous·ness** *n.*
Gre·go·ri·an cal·en·dar /grigáwreeən/ *n.* the calendar introduced in 1582 by Pope Gregory XIII.
Gre·go·ri·an chant /grigáwreeən/ *n.* plainsong ritual music, named after Pope Gregory I.
grem·lin /grémlin/ *n. colloq.* an imaginary mischievous sprite regarded as responsible for mechanical faults.
gre·nade /grináyd/ *n.* a small bomb thrown by hand (**hand grenade**) or shot from a rifle.
gren·a·dier /grénədéer/ *n. hist.* a soldier armed with grenades.
gren·a·dine /grénədéen/ *n.* a syrup of pomegranates, etc., used in mixed drinks.
gres·so·ri·al /gresáwreeəl/ *adj. Zool.* **1** walking. **2** adapted for walking.
grew *past* of GROW.
grey var. of GRAY.
Grey Fri·ar *n.* a Franciscan friar.
grey·hound /gráyhownd/ *n.* **1** a dog of a tall slender breed capable of high speed. **2** this breed.
grey·lag /gráylag/ *n.* (in full **greylag goose**) a wild goose, *Anser anser*, native to Europe.
grid /grid/ *n.* **1** a framework of spaced parallel bars. **2** a system of numbered squares printed on a map and forming the basis of map references. **3** a network of lines, electrical power connections, etc. **4** a pattern of lines marking the starting places on a motor-racing track. **5** an arrangement of city streets in a rectangular pattern. ▫▫ **grid·ded** *adj.*
grid·dle /grid'l/ *n.* & *v.* •*n.* a circular iron plate placed over a fire or otherwise heated for baking, etc. •*v.tr.* cook with a griddle.
grid·i·ron /grídīərn/ *n.* **1** a cooking utensil of metal bars for broiling or grilling. **2** = GRID 5.
grid·lock /grídlok/ *n.* **1** a traffic jam affecting a network of streets. **2** a complete standstill in progress. ▫▫ **grid·locked** *adj.*
grief /greef/ *n.* **1** intense sorrow or mourning. **2** the cause of this. ▫ **come to grief** meet with disaster. **good grief!** an exclamation of surprise, etc.
griev·ance /gréevəns/ *n.* a real or fancied cause for complaint.
grieve /greev/ *v.* **1** *tr.* cause great distress to. **2** *intr.* suffer grief, esp. at another's death.
griev·ous /gréevəs/ *adj.* **1** (of pain, etc.) severe. **2** causing suffering. **3** injurious. **4** flagrant; heinous. ▫▫ **griev·ous·ly** *adv.* **griev·ous·ness** *n.*
▶Do not pronounce this word as though it had an extra syllable, as "gree-vee-uhs."
grif·fin /grífin/ *n.* (also **gryph·on**) a mythical creature with an eagle's head and wings and a lion's body.
grif·fon /grífən/ *n.* **1** a dog of a small terrierlike breed with coarse or smooth hair. **2** (in full **griffon vulture**) a large S. European vulture, *Gyps fulvus*.
grill[1] /gril/ *n.* & *v.* •*n.* **1** = GRIDIRON 1. **2** food cooked on a grill. **3** (in full **grill room**) a restaurant serving grilled food. •*v.* **1** *tr.* & *intr.* cook or be cooked under a boiler or on a gridiron. **2** *tr.* & *intr.* subject or be subjected to extreme heat. **3** *tr.* subject to severe questioning. ▫▫ **grill·ing** *n.* (in sense 3 of *v.*).
grill[2] var. of GRILLE.
grille /gril/ *n.* (also **grill**) **1** a grating or latticed screen, used as a partition or to allow discreet vision. **2** a metal grid protecting the radiator of a motor vehicle.
grill·work /grílwərk/ *n.* metal fashioned to form a grille (*a balcony of ornate grillwork*).
grim /grim/ *adj.* (**grimmer, grimmest**) **1** of a stern or forbidding appearance. **2** harsh; severe. **3** ghastly; joyless (*has a grim truth in it*). **4** unpleasant; unattractive. ▫ **like grim death** with great determination. ▫▫ **grim·ly** *adv.* **grim·ness** *n.*
grim·ace /grímas, grimáys/ *n.* & *v.* •*n.* a distortion of the face made in disgust, etc., or to amuse. •*v.intr.* make a grimace.
grime /grīm/ *n.* & *v.* •*n.* dirt ingrained in a surface. •*v.tr.* blacken with grime.
grim·y /grímee/ *adj.* (**grimier, grimiest**) covered with grime. ▫▫ **grim·i·ly** *adv.* **grim·i·ness** *n.*
grin /grin/ *v.* & *n.* •*v.* (**grinned, grinning**) **1** *intr.* smile broadly, showing the teeth. **2** *tr.* express by grinning. •*n.* the act of grinning. ▫ **grin and bear it** take misfortune stoically. ▫▫ **grin·ning·ly** *adv.*
grind /grīnd/ *v.* & *n.* •*v.* (*past* and *past part.* **ground** /grownd/) **1 a** *tr.* reduce to small particles by crushing. **b** *intr.* (of a machine, etc.) move with a crushing action. **2 a** *tr.* reduce, sharpen, or smooth by friction. **b** *tr.* & *intr.* rub or rub together gratingly. **3** *tr.* (often foll. by *down*) oppress (*grinding poverty*). **4** *intr.* **a** (often foll. by *away*) work or study hard. **b** (foll. by *out*) produce with effort. **c** (foll. by *on*) (of a sound) continue gratingly. **5** *tr.* turn the handle of e.g., a barrel organ, etc. **6** *intr. sl.* (of a dancer) rotate the hips. •*n.* **1** the act of grinding. **2** *colloq.* hard dull work (*the daily grind*). **3** the size of ground particles. ▫ **grind to a halt** stop laboriously. ▫▫ **grind·ing·ly** *adv.*
grind·er /gríndər/ *n.* **1** a person or thing that grinds, esp. a machine (often in *comb.*: *coffee grinder*). **2** a molar tooth. **3** *US dial.* a submarine sandwich.
grind·stone /grīndstōn/ *n.* **1** a thick revolving disk used for grinding. **2** a kind of stone used for this. ▫ **keep one's nose to the grindstone** work hard and continuously.
grip /grip/ *v.* & *n.* •*v.* (**gripped, gripping**) **1 a** *tr.* grasp tightly. **b** *intr.* take a firm hold, esp. by friction. **2** *tr.* (of a feeling or emotion) deeply affect (a person). **3** *tr.* compel the attention of (*a gripping story*). •*n.* **1 a** a firm hold. **b** a manner of grasping. **2** the power of holding attention. **3 a** mental or intellectual understanding. **b** effective control of a situation. (*lose one's grip*). **4 a** a part of a machine that grips or holds something. **b** a part by which a tool, weapon, etc., is held in the hand. **5** a traveling bag. **6** an assistant in a theater, movie studio, etc. ▫ **come** (or **get**) **to grips with** begin to deal with. **get a grip (on oneself)** recover one's self-control. ▫▫ **grip·ping·ly** *adv.*

gripe /grīp/ *v. & n.* •*v.* **1** *intr. colloq.* complain. **2** *tr.* affect with gastric pain. •*n.* **1** (usu. in *pl.*) gastric or intestinal pain; colic. **2** *colloq.* **a** a complaint. **b** the act of griping. **3** a grip or clutch. **4** (in *pl.*) *Naut.* lashings securing a boat in its place. □□ **grip·er** *n.* **grip·ing·ly** *adv.*

gris·e·o·ful·vin /grízeeəfŏŏlvin/ *n.* an antibiotic used against fungal infections of the hair and skin.

gris·ly /grízlee/ *adj.* (**grislier, grisliest**) causing horror or fear. □□ **gris·li·ness** *n.*

grist /grist/ *n.* **1** grain to grind. **2** malt crushed for brewing. □ **grist to the** (or **a person's**) **mill** a source of profit or advantage.

gris·tle /grísəl/ *n.* tough flexible tissue in vertebrates. □□ **gris·tly** /grislee/ *adj.*

grit /grit/ *n. & v.* •*n.* **1** particles of stone or sand, esp. as causing discomfort, etc. **2** coarse sandstone. **3** *colloq.* pluck; endurance. •*v.* (**gritted, gritting**) **1** *tr.* spread grit on (icy roads, etc.). **2** *tr.* clench (the teeth). **3** *intr.* make a grating sound. □□ **grit·ter** *n.* **grit·ty** *adj.* (**grittier, grittiest**). **grit·ti·ness** *n.*

grits /grits/ *n.pl.* coarsely ground grain, esp. hominy prepared by boiling, then sometimes frying.

griz·zled /grízəld/ *adj.* having, or streaked with, gray hair.

griz·zly /grízlee/ *adj. & n.* •*adj.* (**grizzlier, grizzliest**) gray, grayish, gray-haired. •*n.* (*pl.* **-ies**) (in full **grizzly bear**) a large variety of brown bear found in N. America.

groan /grōn/ *v. & n.* •*v.* **1 a** *intr.* make a deep sound expressing pain, grief, or disapproval. **b** *tr.* utter with groans. **2** *intr.* (usu. foll. by *under, beneath, with*) be loaded or oppressed. •*n.* the sound made in groaning. □□ **groan·er** *n.*

groat /grōt/ *n. hist.* a silver coin worth four old English pence.

gro·cer /grṓsər/ *n.* a dealer in food and household provisions.

gro·cer·y /grṓsəree/ *n.* (*pl.* **-ies**) **1** a grocer's store. **2** (in *pl.*) provisions, esp. food.

grog /grog/ *n.* a drink of liquor (orig. rum) and water.

grog·gy /grógee/ *adj.* (**groggier, groggiest**) unsteady from being dazed or semiconscious. □□ **grog·gi·ly** *adv.* **grog·gi·ness** *n.*

grog·ram /grógrəm, grṓ–/ *n.* a coarse fabric of silk, mohair and wool, or a mixture of these.

groin[1] /groyn/ *n. & v.* •*n.* **1** the depression between the belly and the thigh. **2** *Archit.* **a** an edge formed by intersecting vaults. **b** an arch supporting a vault. •*v.tr.* *Archit.* build with groins.

groin[2] /groyn/ *n.* (also **groyne**) a wooden framework or low broad wall built out from a shore to check erosion of a beach.

grom·met /grómit/ *n.* **1** a metal, plastic, or rubber eyelet placed in a hole to protect or insulate a rope or cable, etc., passed through it. **2** a tube passed through the eardrum in surgery to make a connection with the middle ear.

groom /grōōm/ *n. & v.* •*n.* **1** = BRIDEGROOM. **2** a person employed to take care of horses. •*v.tr.* **1 a** curry or tend (a horse). **b** give a neat appearance to (a person, etc.). **2** (of an ape or monkey, etc.) clean and comb the fur of (its fellow) with the fingers. **3** prepare or train (a person) for a particular purpose or activity (*was groomed for the top job*).

groove /grōōv/ *n. & v.* •*n.* **1 a** a channel or hollow, esp. one made to guide motion or receive a corresponding ridge. **b** a spiral track cut in a phonograph record. **2** an established routine or habit. •*v.* **1** *tr.* make a groove in. **2** *intr. sl.* enjoy oneself. ▶Often with ref. to popular music or jazz; now largely disused in general contexts.. □ **in the groove** *sl.* doing or performing well.

groov·y /grṓōvee/ *adj.* (**groovier, grooviest**) *sl.* or *joc.* fashionable and exciting. □□ **groov·i·ly** *adv.*

grope /grōp/ *v. & n.* •*v.* **1** *intr.* (usu. foll. by *for*) feel about or search blindly. **2** *intr.* (foll. by *for, after*) search mentally. **3** *tr.* feel (one's way) toward something. **4** *tr. sl.* fondle clumsily for sexual pleasure. •*n.* the process or an instance of groping. □□ **grop·er** *n.* **grop·ing·ly** *adv.*

gros·grain /grṓgrayn/ *n.* a corded fabric of silk, rayon, etc.

gros point /grō póynt, pwáN/ *n.* cross-stitch embroidery on canvas.

gross /grōs/ *adj., v., & n.* •*adj.* **1** overfed; repulsively fat. **2** (of a person, manners, or morals) noticeably coarse or indecent. **3** flagrant; conspicuously wrong (*gross negligence*). **4** total; without deductions (*gross income*). **5 a** luxuriant; rank. **b** thick; solid; dense. **6** (of the senses, etc.) dull. **7** *sl.* repulsive; disgusting. •*v.tr.* produce or earn as gross profit or income. •*n.* (*pl.* same) twelve dozen. □ **gross out** *sl.* disgust, esp. by repulsive behavior. □□ **gross·ly** *adv.* **gross·ness** *n.*

gross do·mes·tic prod·uct *n.* the total value of goods produced and services provided in a country in one year.

gross na·tion·al prod·uct *n.* the gross domestic product plus the total of net income from abroad.

gro·tesque /grōtésk/ *adj. & n.* •*adj.* **1** comically or repulsively distorted; monstrous; unnatural. **2** incongruous; absurd. •*n.* **1** a decorative form interweaving human and animal features. **2** a comically distorted figure or design. **3** *Printing* a family of sans serif typefaces. □□ **gro·tesque·ly** *adv.* **gro·tesque·ness** *n.* **gro·tes·quer·ie** /–téskəree/ *n.*

grot·to /grótō/ *n.* (*pl.* **-toes** or **-tos**) **1** a cave or cavern. **2** an artificial ornamental cave, esp. one in a park or garden. □□ **grot·toed** *adj.*

grouch /growch/ *v. & n. colloq.* •*v.intr.* grumble. •*n.* **1** a discontented person. **2** a fit of grumbling.

grouch·y /grówchee/ *adj.* (**grouchier, grouchiest**) *colloq.* discontented; grumpy. □□ **grouch·i·ly** *adv.* **grouch·i·ness** *n.*

ground[1] /grownd/ *n. & v.* •*n.* **1 a** the surface of the earth, esp. as contrasted with the air around it. **b** a part of this specified in some way (*low ground*). **2** soil; earth (*stony ground*). **3 a** a position, area, or distance on the earth's surface. **b** the extent of a subject dealt with (*the book covers a lot of ground*). **4** (often in *pl.*) a motive or reason (*ground for concern*). **5** an area of a special kind or designated for special use (often in *comb.*: *fishing-grounds*). **6** (in *pl.*) an area of sometimes enclosed land attached to a house, etc. **7** an area or basis for consideration, agreement, etc. (*common ground*; *on firm ground*). **8 a** (in painting) the prepared surface giving the predominant color or tone. **b** (in embroidery, ceramics, etc.) the undecorated surface. **9** (in full **ground bass**) *Mus.* a short theme in the bass constantly repeated with the upper parts of the music varied. **10** (in *pl.*) solid particles, esp. of coffee, forming a residue. **11** *Electr.* the connection to the ground that completes an electrical circuit. **12** the bottom of the sea. **13** (*attrib.*) **a** (of animals) living on or in the ground; (of fish) living at the bottom of water; (of plants) dwarfish. **b** relating to the ground (*ground staff*). •*v.* **1** *tr.* **a** refuse authority for (a pilot or an aircraft) to fly. **b** restrict (esp. a child) from certain activities, esp. as a form of punishment. **2 a** *tr.* run (a ship) aground. **b** *intr.* (of a ship) run aground. **3** *tr.* (foll. by *in*) instruct thoroughly (in a subject). **4** *tr.* (often as **grounded** *adj.*) (foll. by *on*) base (a conclusion, etc.) on. **5** *tr.* *Electr.* connect to the ground. **6** *intr.* alight on the ground. **7** *tr.* place (esp. weapons) on the ground.

□ **break new** (or **fresh**) **ground** treat a subject previously not dealt with. **gain ground 1** advance steadily. **2** (foll. by *on*) catch (a person) up. **get in on the ground floor** become part of an enterprise in its early stages. **get off the ground** *colloq.* make a successful start. **give** (or **lose**) **ground 1** retreat; decline. **2** lose the advantage. **go to ground 1** (of a fox, etc.) enter its burrow, etc. **2** (of a person) become inaccessible for a prolonged period. **hold one's ground** not give way. **on the ground** at the point of production or operation. **thin on the ground** not numerous.

ground[2] *past* and *past part.* of GRIND.

ground ball *n. Baseball* a ball batted so that it bounces or rolls on the ground. Also **grounder**.

ground·break·ing /grówndbrayking/ *adj.* innovative; pioneering.

ground con·trol *n.* the personnel directing the landing, etc., of aircraft or spacecraft.

ground cov·er *n.* plants covering the surface of the soil, esp. low-growing spreading plants that inhibit the growth of weeds.

ground glass *n.* **1** glass made nontransparent by grinding, etc. **2** glass ground to a powder.

ground·hog /grówndhawg, –hog/ *n.* a woodchuck.

ground·ing /grównding/ *n.* basic training or instruction in a subject.

ground·less /grówndlis/ *adj.* without motive or foundation. □□ **ground·less·ly** *adv.* **ground·less·ness** *n.*

ground·ling /grówndling/ *n.* **1 a** a creeping or dwarf plant. **b** an animal that lives near the ground, at the bottom of a lake, etc., esp. a groundfish. **2** a person on the ground as opposed to one in an aircraft. **3** a spectator or reader of inferior taste (with ref. to Shakesp. *Hamlet* III. ii. 11).

grounds·keep·er /grówndzkeepər, grównz–/ *n.* a person who maintains the grounds of a sizable property, as a golf course or park.

ground speed *n.* an aircraft's speed relative to the ground.

ground·swell /grówndswel/ *n.* an increasingly forceful presence.

ground swell *n.* **1** a heavy sea caused by a distant or past storm or an earthquake. **2** = GROUNDSWELL.

ground·wa·ter /grówndwáwtər,–wotər/ *n.* water found in soil or in pores, crevices, etc., in rock.

ground·work /grówndwərk/ *n.* **1** preliminary or basic work. **2** a foundation or basis.

ground ze·ro *n.* the point on the ground under an exploding bomb.

group /grōōp/ *n.* & *v.* • *n.* **1** a number of persons or things located close together, or classed together. **2** a number of people working together or sharing beliefs. **3** a number of commercial companies under common ownership. **4** an ensemble playing popular music. **5** a division of an air force or air fleet. • *v.* **1** *tr.* & *intr.* form or be formed into a group. **2** *tr.* (often foll. by *with*) place in a group or groups. **3** *tr.* form (colors, figures, etc.) into a well-arranged and harmonious whole. **4** *tr.* classify. □□ **group·age** *n.*

group dy·nam·ics *n. Psychol.* the field of social psychology concerned with the nature, development, and interactions of human groups.

group·er /grṓōpər/ *n.* any marine fish of the family Serranidae, with heavy body, big head, and wide mouth.

group·ie /grṓōpee/ *n. sl.* an ardent follower of a touring pop group.

group·ing /grṓōping/ *n.* **1** a process or system of allocation to groups. **2** the formation or arrangement so produced.

group ther·a·py *n.* therapy in which patients with a similar condition are brought together to assist one another psychologically.

grouse[1] /grows/ *n.* (*pl.* same) **1** any of various game birds of the family Tetraonidae, with a plump body. **2** the flesh of a grouse used as food.

grouse[2] /grows/ *v.* & *n. colloq.* • *v.intr.* grumble or complain pettily. • *n.* a complaint. □□ **grous·er** *n.*

grout /growt/ *n.* & *v.* • *n.* a thin fluid mortar for filling gaps in tiling, etc. • *v.tr.* provide or fill with grout. □□ **grout·er** *n.*

grove /grōv/ *n.* a small wood or group of trees.

grov·el /gróvəl/ *v.intr.* (**groveled, groveling**; also **grovelled, grovelling**) **1** behave obsequiously in seeking favor or forgiveness. **2** lie prone in abject humility. □□ **grov·el·er** *n.* **grov·el·ing** *adj.* **grov·el·ing·ly** *adv.*

grow /grō/ *v.* (*past* **grew** /grōō/; *past part.* **grown** /grōn/) **1** *intr.* increase in size, height, quantity, degree, or in any way regarded as measurable (e.g., authority or reputation) (often foll. by *in*: *grew in stature*). **2** *intr.* **a** develop or exist as a living plant or natural product. **b** develop in a specific way or direction (*began to grow sideways*). **c** germinate; sprout. **3** *intr.* be produced; come naturally into existence. **4** *intr.* (as **grown** *adj.*) fully matured. **5** *intr.* **a** become gradually (*grow rich*). **b** (foll. by *to* + infin.) come by degrees (*grew to like it*). **6** *intr.* (foll. by *into*) **a** become; having grown or developed (*will grow into a fine athlete*). **b** become large enough for (*will grow into the coat*). **7** *intr.* (foll. by *on*) become gradually more favored by. **8** *tr.* **a** produce (plants, etc.) by cultivation. **b** bring forth. **c** cause or allow (a beard, etc.) to develop. **9** *tr.* (in *passive*; foll. by *over, up*) be covered with a growth. □ **grow out of 1** become too large to wear (a garment). **2** become too mature to retain (a childish habit, etc.). **3** be the result of. **grow up 1** advance to maturity. **2** (of a custom) arise. □□ **grow·a·ble** *adj.*

grow·er /grṓər/ *n.* **1** (often in *comb.*) a person growing produce (*fruit-grower*). **2** a plant that grows in a specified way (*a fast grower*).

grow·ing pains *n.pl* **1** early difficulties in the development of an enterprise, etc. **2** neuralgic pain in children's legs due to fatigue, etc.

growl /growl/ *v.* & *n.* • *v.intr.* **1 a** (often foll. by *at*) (esp. of a dog) make a low guttural sound, usu. of anger. **b** murmur angrily. **2** rumble. • *n.* **1** a growling sound. **2** an angry murmur. **3** a rumble.

growl·er /grówlər/ *n.* a person or thing that growls, esp. *sl.* a dog.

grown *past part.* of GROW.

grown-up *adj.* & *n.* • *adj.* adult. • *n.* an adult person.

growth /grōth/ *n.* **1** the act or process of growing. **2** an increase in size or value. **3** something that has grown or is growing. **4** *Med.* a morbid formation. **5** the cultivation of produce.

grub /grub/ *n.* & *v.* • *n.* **1** the larva of an insect. **2** *colloq.* food. • *v.* (**grubbed, grubbing**) **1** *tr.* & *intr.* dig superficially. **2** *tr.* **a** clear (the ground) of roots and stumps. **b** clear away (roots, etc.). **3** *tr.* (foll. by *up, out*) **a** fetch by digging (*grubbing up weeds*). **b** extract (information, etc.) by searching in books, etc. **4** *intr.* search; rummage. □□ **grub·ber** *n.*

grub·by /grúbee/ *adj.* (**grubbier, grubbiest**) **1** dirty; grimy. **2** of or infested with grubs. □□ **grub·bi·ly** *adv.* **grub·bi·ness** *n.*

grub·stake /grúbstayk/ *n.* & *v.* • *n.* material or provisions supplied to an enterprise in return for a share in the resulting profits (orig. in prospecting for ore). • *v.tr.* provide with a grubstake. □□ **grub·stak·er** *n.*

grudge /gruj/ *n.* & *v.* • *n.* a persistent feeling of ill will or resentment, esp. one due to an insult or injury (*bears a grudge against me*). • *v.tr.* **1** be resentfully unwilling to give or allow (a thing). **2** reluctant to do (a thing) (*grudged paying so much*).

gru·el /gróoəl/ *n.* a liquid food of oatmeal, etc., boiled in milk or water.

gru·el·ing /gróoəling/ *adj.* & *n.* (also **gruel·ling**) • *adj.* extremely demanding, severe, or tiring. • *n.* a harsh or exhausting experience; punishment. □□ **gruel·ing·ly** *adv.*

grue·some /gróosəm/ *adj.* horrible; grisly; disgusting. □□ **grue·some·ly** *adv.* **grue·some·ness** *n.*

gruff /gruf/ *adj.* **1 a** (of a voice) low and harsh. **b** (of a person) having a gruff voice. **2** surly; laconic; rough-mannered. □□ **gruff·ly** *adv.* **gruff·ness** *n.*

grum·ble /grúmbəl/ *v.* & *n.* • *v.* **1** *intr.* **a** (often foll. by *at, about, over*) complain peevishly. **b** be discontented. **2** *intr.* **a** utter a dull inarticulate sound; murmur; growl faintly. **b** rumble. **3** *tr.* (often foll. by *out*) utter complainingly. **4** *intr.* (as **grumbling** *adj.*) *colloq.* giving intermittent discomfort (*a grumbling appendix*). • *n.* **1** a complaint. **2 a** a dull inarticulate sound. **b** a rumble. □□ **grum·bler** *n.* **grum·bling** *adj.* **grum·bling·ly** *adv.* **grum·bly** *adj.*

grump /grump/ *n. colloq.* **1** a grumpy person. **2** (in *pl.*) a fit of sulks. □□ **grump·ish** *adj.* **grump·ish·ly** *adv.*

grump·y /grúmpee/ *adj.* (**grumpier, grumpiest**) morosely irritable. □□ **grump·i·ly** *adv.* **grump·i·ness** *n.*

grunge /grunj/ *n. sl.* **1** grime; dirt. **2** an aggressive style of rock music characterized by a raucous guitar sound. **3** a style of clothing and appearance marked by studied dishevelment. □□ **grun·gy** *adj.*

grun·ion /grúnyən/ *n.* a California marine fish, *Leuresthes tenuis*.

grunt /grunt/ *n.* & *v.* • *n.* **1** a low guttural sound made by a pig. **2** a sound resembling this. • *v.* **1** *intr.* (of a pig) make a grunt. **2** *intr.* (of a person) make a low inarticulate sound resembling this, esp. to express discontent, fatigue, etc. **3** *tr.* utter with a grunt.

grunt·er /grúntər/ *n.* a person or animal that grunts, esp. a pig.

gryph·on var. of GRIFFIN.

GSA *abbr.* **1** General Services Administration. **2** Girl Scouts of America.

G-string /jéestring/ *n.* **1** *Mus.* a string sounding the note G. **2** a narrow strip of cloth covering only the genitals and attached to a string around the waist.

G suit /jéesoot/ *n.* a garment with inflatable pressurized pouches, worn to withstand high acceleration.

GT *n.* a high-performance two-door automobile.

gua·ca·mo·le /gwaákəmólee/ *n.* a dish of mashed avocado mixed with chopped onion, tomatoes, chili peppers, and seasoning.

guai·ac var. of GUAIACUM^2.

guai·a·cum /gwíəkəm/ *n.* **1** any tree of the genus *Guaiacum*, native to tropical America. **2** (also **guai·ac** /gwíak/) **a** the hard dense oily timber of some of these, esp. *G. officinale*. Also called LIGNUM VITAE. **b** the resin from this used medicinally.

gua·nine /gwaáneen/ *n. Biochem.* a purine derivative found in all living organisms as a component base of DNA and RNA.

gua·no /gwaánō/ *n.* & *v.* (*pl.* **-nos**) • *n.* **1** the excrement of seabirds, used as fertilizer. **2** artificial manure. • *v.tr.* (**-noes, -noed**) fertilize with guano.

Gua·ra·ni /gwaárənée/ *n.* **1** a member of a S. American Indian people. **2** the language of this people.

guar·an·tee /gárəntée/ *n.* & *v.* • *n.* **1 a** a formal promise or assurance, esp. that an obligation will be fulfilled or that something is of a specified quality and durability. **b** a document giving such an undertaking. **2** = GUARANTY. **3** a person making a guaranty or giving a security. • *v.tr.* (**guarantees, guaranteed**) **1 a** give or serve as a guarantee for. **b** assure the permanence, etc., of. **c** provide with a guarantee. **2** (foll. by *that* + clause, or *to* + infin.) give a promise. **3 a** (foll. by *to*) secure the possession of (a thing) for a person. **b** make (a person) secure against a risk or in possession of a thing. ▶**Guarantee** and **guaranty** are interchangeable for both noun and verb, although the latter is now rare as a verb. **Warranty** is widely used their place. *Warrantee* means 'person to whom a warranty is made'; it is not a spelling variant of *warranty*.

guar·an·tor /gárəntáwr, –tər/ *n.* a person who gives a guarantee or guaranty.

guar·an·ty /gárəntee/ *n.* (*pl.* **-ties**) **1** a written or other undertaking to answer for the payment of a debt or for the performance of an obligation by another person liable in the first instance. **2** a thing serving as security for a guaranty.

guard /gaard/ *v.* & *n.* • *v.* **1** *tr.* (often foll. by *from, against*) watch over and defend or protect from harm. **2** *tr.* keep watch by (a door, etc.) so as to control entry or exit. **3** *tr.* supervise (prisoners, etc.). **4** *tr.* provide (machinery) with a protective device. **5** *tr.* keep (thoughts or speech) in check. **6** *tr.* provide with safeguards. **7** *intr.* (foll. by *against*) take precautions. • *n.* **1** a state of vigilance or watchfulness. **2** a person who protects or keeps watch. **3** a body of soldiers, etc. serving to protect a place or person. **4** a person who keeps watch over prisoners. **5** a part of an army detached for some purpose (*advance guard*). **6** (in *pl.*) (usu. **Guards**) any of various bodies of troops nominally employed to guard a ruler. **7** a thing that protects. **8** (often in *comb.*) a device fitted to a machine, etc., to prevent injury (*fire guard*). □ **be on** (or **keep** or **stand**) **guard** (of a sentry, etc.) keep watch. **lower one's guard** reduce vigilance against attack. **off** (or **off one's**) **guard** unprepared for some surprise or difficulty. **on** (or **on one's**) **guard** prepared for all contingencies.

guard·ed /gaárdid/ *adj.* (of a remark, etc.) cautious. □□ **guard·ed·ly** *adv.*

guard·house /gaárdhows/ *n.* a building used to accommodate a military guard or to detain military prisoners temporarily.

guard·i·an /gaárdeeən/ *n.* **1** a defender, protector or keeper. **2** a person who looks after and is legally responsible for someone who is unable to manage his or her own affairs, esp. a child whose parents have died. □□ **guard·i·an·ship** *n.*

guard·i·an an·gel *n.* a spirit conceived as watching over a person or place.

guard·rail /gaárdrayl/ *n.* a rail, e.g., a handrail, fitted as a support or to prevent an accident.

guards·man /gaárdzmən/ *n.* (*pl.* **-men**) a soldier belonging to a body of guards.

gua·va /gwaávə/ *n.* **1** a small tropical American tree, *Psidium guajava*, bearing an edible pale yellow fruit with pink juicy flesh. **2** this fruit.

gu·ber·na·to·ri·al /góobərnətáwreeəl, gyóo–/ *adj.* of or relating to a governor.

gudg·eon /gújən/ *n.* **1** a pivot or spindle on which a bell or other object swings or rotates. **2** the tubular part of a hinge into which the pin fits to unite the joint. **3** a socket at the stern of a boat, into which a rudder is fitted. **4** a pin holding two blocks of stone, etc., together.

guel·der rose /géldər/ *n.* a deciduous shrub, *Viburnum opulus*, with round bunches of creamy white flowers. Also called SNOWBALL BUSH.

guer·don /gərdən/ *n.* & *v. poet.* • *n.* a reward or recompense. • *v.tr.* give a reward to.

guer·ril·la /gərílə/ *n.* (also **gue·ril·la**) a member of a small independent group taking part in irregular fighting, esp. against larger regular forces.

---

guer·ril·la war *n.* (also **warfare**) fighting by or with guerrillas.

guess /ges/ *v.* & *n.* • *v.* **1** *tr.* (often *absol.*) estimate without calculation or measurement, or on the basis of inadequate data. **2** *tr.* form a hypothesis or opinion about; think likely (*cannot guess how you did it*). **3** *tr.* conjecture or estimate correctly (*you have to guess the weight*). **4** *intr.* (foll. by *at*) make a conjecture about. • *n.* an estimate or conjecture. □ **I guess** *colloq.* I suppose. □□ **guess·er** *n.*

guess-rope var. of GUEST-ROPE.

guess·ti·mate /géstimət/ *n.* (also **gues·ti·mate**) *colloq.* an estimate based on a mixture of guesswork and calculation.

guess·work /géswərk/ *n.* the process of or results got by guessing.

guest /gest/ *n.* & *v.* • *n.* **1** a person invited to visit another's house or have a meal, etc., at the expense of the inviter. **2** a person lodging at a hotel, boarding house, etc. **3 a** an outside performer invited to take part with a regular body of performers. **b** a person who takes part by invitation in a radio or television program (often *attrib.*: *guest commentator*). **4** (*attrib.*) **a** serving or set aside for guests (*guest room*). **b** acting as a guest (*guest speaker*). **5** an organism living in close association with another. • *v.intr.* be a guest on a radio or television show. □ **be my guest** *colloq.* make what use you wish of the available facilities. □□ **guest·ship** *n.*

guest·house /gésthows/ *n.* a private house offering paid accommodation.

guest of hon·or *n.* the most important guest at an occasion.

guest-rope /géstrōp, gésrōp/ *n.* (also **guess-rope**) **1** a second rope fastened to a boat in tow to steady it. **2** a rope slung outside a ship to give a hold for boats coming alongside.

guff /guf/ *n. sl.* empty talk; nonsense.

guf·faw /gufáw/ *n.* & *v.* • *n.* a loud or boisterous laugh. • *v.* **1** *intr.* utter a guffaw. **2** *tr.* say with a guffaw.

guid·ance /gíd'ns/ *n.* **1 a** advice or information aimed at resolving a problem, difficulty, etc. **b** leadership or direction. **2** the process of guiding or being guided.

guide /gīd/ *n.* & *v.* • *n.* **1** a person who leads or shows the way, or directs the movements of a person or group. **2** a person who conducts travelers on tours, etc. **3** a professional mountain climber in charge of a group. **4** an adviser. **5** a directing principle or standard (*one's feelings are a bad guide*). **6** a book with essential information on a subject, esp. = GUIDEBOOK. **7** a thing marking a position or guiding the eye. **8** *Mech.* **a** a bar, rod, etc., directing the motion of something. **b** a gauge, etc., controlling a tool. **9** (**Guide**) *Brit.* a member of an organization similar to the Girl Scouts. • *v.tr.* **1 a** act as guide to; lead or direct. **b** arrange the course of (events). **2** be the principle, motive, or ground of (an action, judgment, etc.). **3** direct the affairs of (a government, etc.).

guide·book /gídbŏŏk/ *n.* a book of information about a place for visitors.

guid·ed mis·sile *n.* a missile directed to its target by remote control or by equipment within itself.

guide dog *n.* a dog trained to guide a blind person.

guide·line /gídlīn/ *n.* a principle or criterion guiding or directing action.

guide·way /gídway/ *n.* a groove or track that guides movement.

guild /gild/ *n.* (also **gild**) **1** an association of people for mutual aid or the pursuit of a common goal. **2** a medieval association of craftsmen or merchants.

guild·er /gíldər/ *n.* **1** the chief monetary unit of the Netherlands. **2** *hist.* a gold coin of the Netherlands and Germany.

guild·hall /gíldháwl/ *n.* the meeting place of a guild or corporation.

guilds·man /gíldzmən/ *n.* (*pl.* **·men**; *fem.* **guildswoman**, *pl.* **·women**) a member of a guild.

guile /gīl/ *n.* cunning or sly behavior. □□ **guile·ful** *adj.* **guile·less** *adj.* **guile·less·ly** *adv.*

guil·le·mot /gíləmot/ *n.* any fast-flying sea bird of the genus *Uria* or *Cepphus*, nesting on cliffs or islands.

guil·lo·tine /gílətéen, géeə–/ *n.* & *v.* • *n.* **1** a machine with a heavy knife blade dropping vertically in grooves, used for beheading. **2** a device for cutting paper, metal, etc. • *v.tr.* use a guillotine on.

guilt /gilt/ *n.* **1** the fact of having committed a specified or implied offense. **2 a** culpability. **b** the feeling of this.

guilt com·plex *n. Psychol.* a mental obsession with the idea of having done wrong.

guilt·less /gíltlis/ *adj.* **1** (often foll. by *of*) innocent. **2** (foll. by *of*) not having knowledge or possession of. □□ **guilt·less·ly** *adv.*

guilt·y /gíltee/ *adj.* (**guiltier, guiltiest**) **1** culpable of or responsible for a wrong. **2** conscious of or affected by guilt (*a guilty conscience*). **3** concerning guilt (*a guilty secret*). **4** (often foll. by *of*) **a** having committed a (specified) offense. **b** *Law* adjudged to have committed a specified offense, esp. by a verdict in a trial. □□ **guilt·i·ly** *adv.*

guimp var. of GIMP[1].

guin·ea /gínee/ *n.* **1** *Brit. hist.* the sum of 21 old shillings, used esp. in determining professional fees. **2** *hist.* a former British gold coin worth 21 shillings, first coined for the African trade.

guin·ea fowl *n.* any African fowl of the family Numididae, esp. *Numida meleagris*, with slate-colored white-spotted plumage.

guin·ea pig *n.* **1** a domesticated S. American cavy, *Cavia porcellus*, kept as a pet or for research in biology, etc. **2** a person or thing used as a subject for experiment.

guise /gīz/ *n.* **1** an assumed appearance (*in the guise of*). **2** external appearance.

gui·tar /gitaar/ *n.* a usu. six-stringed musical instrument, played by plucking with the fingers or a plectrum. □□ **gui·tar·ist** *n.*

gulch /gulch/ *n.* a ravine, esp. one in which a torrent flows.

gulf /gulf/ *n.* **1** a stretch of sea consisting of a deep inlet with a narrow mouth. **2** (**the Gulf**) **a** the Gulf of Mexico. **b** the Persian Gulf. **3** a deep hollow. **4** a wide difference of feelings, opinion, etc.

Gulf Stream *n.* a warm current flowing from the Gulf of Mexico to Newfoundland where it is deflected into the Atlantic Ocean.

gull[1] /gul/ *n.* any of various long-winged sea birds of the family Laridae.

gull[2] /gul/ *v.tr.* (usu. in *passive*; foll. by *into*) dupe; fool.

Gul·lah /gúlə/ *n.* **1** a member of a group of African-Americans living on the coast of S. Carolina. **2** the Creole language spoken by them.

gul·let /gúlit/ *n.* **1** the food passage extending from the mouth to the stomach; the esophagus. **2** the throat.

gul·li·ble /gúlibəl/ *adj.* easily persuaded or deceived. □□ **gul·li·bil·i·ty** *n.*

gul·ly /gúlee/ *n.* (*pl.* **-lies**) **1** a waterworn ravine. **2** a gutter or drain.

gulp /gulp/ *v.* & *n.* • *v.* **1** *tr.* swallow hastily, greedily, or with effort. **2** *intr.* swallow with difficulty. **3** *tr.* (foll. by *down, back*) stifle; suppress (esp. tears). • *n.* **1** an act of gulping (*drained it in one gulp*). **2** an effort to swallow. **3** a large mouthful of a drink.

gum[1] /gum/ *n.* & *v.* • *n.* **1 a** a viscous secretion of some trees and shrubs that hardens on drying but is soluble in water. **b** an adhesive substance made from this. **2** chewing gum. **3** = GUMDROP. **4** = GUM ARABIC. **5** = GUM TREE. •*v.* (**gummed, gumming**) **1** *tr.* smear or cover with gum. **2** *tr.* fasten with gum. □ **gum up 1** (of a mechanism, etc.) become clogged or obstructed with stickiness. **2** *colloq.* interfere with the smooth running of (*gum up the works*).

gum[2] /gum/ *n.* (usu. in *pl.*) the firm flesh around the roots of the teeth.

gum[3] /gum/ *n. colloq.* (in oaths) God (*by gum!*).

gum ar·a·bic *n.* a gum exuded by some kinds of acacia and used as an emulsifier, in glue, and as the binder for watercolor paints.

gum·bo /gúmbō/ *n.* (*pl.* **-bos**) **1** okra. **2** a soup thickened with okra pods. **3** (**Gumbo**) a patois of African-Americans and Creoles spoken esp. in Louisiana.

gum·drop /gúmdrop/ *n.* a soft candy made with gelatin or gum arabic.

gum·ma /gúmə/ *n.* (*pl.* **gummas** or **gummata** /–mətə/) *Med.* a small soft swelling occurring in the connective tissue of the liver, brain, testes, and heart, and characteristic of the late stages of syphilis. □□ **gum·ma·tous** *adj.*

gum·my[1] /gúmee/ *adj.* (**gummier, gummiest**) **1** sticky. **2** exuding gum. □□ **gum·mi·ness** *n.*

gum·my[2] /gúmee/ *adj.* (**gummier, gummiest**) toothless.

gump·tion /gúmpshən/ *n. colloq.* **1** resourcefulness; initiative. **2** common sense.

gum·shoe /gúmshoo͞/ *n.* **1** *sl.* a detective. **2** a galosh.

gum tree *n.* a tree exuding gum, esp. a eucalyptus.

gun /gun/ *n.* & *v.* •*n.* **1** any kind of weapon consisting of a metal tube, from which bullets or other missiles are propelled with great force by a contained explosion. **2** a starting pistol. **3** a device for discharging insecticide, grease, electrons, etc., in the required direction (often in *comb.*: *grease gun*). **4** a gunman. **5** the firing of a gun. •*v.* (**gunned, gunning**) **1** *tr.* (usu. foll. by *down*) shoot (a person) with a gun. **2** *tr. colloq.* accelerate (an engine or vehicle). **3** *intr.* go shooting. **4** *intr.* (foll. by *for*) seek out determinedly to attack. □ **go great guns** *colloq.* proceed vigorously or successfully. **jump the gun** *colloq.* start before a signal is given, or before an agreed time. **stick to one's guns** *colloq.* maintain one's position under attack.

gun·boat /gúnbōt/ *n.* a small vessel with heavy guns.

gun·boat di·plo·ma·cy *n.* political negotiation supported by the threat of military force.

gun car·riage *n.* a wheeled support for a gun.

gun dog *n.* a dog trained to follow hunters using guns.

gun·fight /gúnfīt/ *n.* a fight with firearms. □□ **gun·fight·er** *n.*

gun·fire /gúnfīr/ *n.* **1** the firing of a gun, esp. repeatedly. **2** the noise from this.

gung-ho /gúnghṓ/ *adj.* enthusiastic; eager.

gunk /gungk/ *n. sl.* viscous or liquid material.

gun·man /gúnmən/ *n.* (*pl.* **-men**) a man armed with a gun, esp. in committing a crime.

gun·met·al /gúnmetəl/ *n.* **1** a dull bluish gray color. **2** an alloy of copper and tin or zinc (formerly used for guns).

gun·nel var. of GUNWALE.

gun·ner /gúnər/ *n.* **1** an artillery soldier (esp. *Brit.* as an official term for a private). **2** *Naut.* a warrant officer in charge of a battery, magazine, etc. **3** a member of an aircraft crew who operates a gun. **4** a person who hunts game with a gun.

gun·ner·y /gúnəree/ *n.* **1** the construction and management of large guns. **2** the firing of guns.

gun·ny /gúnee/ *n.* (*pl.* **-nies**) **1** coarse sacking, usu. of jute fiber. **2** (also **gunnysack**) a sack made of this.

gun·point /gúnpoynt/ *n.* □ **at gunpoint** threatened with a gun or an ultimatum.

gun·pow·der /gúnpowdər/ *n.* **1** an explosive made of saltpeter, sulfur, and charcoal. **2** a fine green tea of granular appearance.

gun·pow·er /gúnpowər/ *n.* the strength or quantity of available guns.

gun·run·ner /gúnrunər/ *n.* a person engaged in the illegal sale or importing of firearms. □□ **gun·run·ning** *n.*

gun·sel /gúnsəl / *n. sl.* a criminal, esp. a gunman.

gun·ship /gúnship/ *n.* a heavily armed helicopter or other aircraft.

gun·shot /gúnshot/ *n.* **1** a shot fired from a gun. **2** the range of a gun (*within gunshot*).

gun·sling·er /gúnslingər/ *n. sl.* a gunman. □□ **gun·sling·ing** *n.*

gun·smith /gúnsmith/ *n.* a person who makes and repairs small firearms.

gun·stock /gúnstok/ *n.* the wooden mounting of the barrel of a gun.

gun·wale /gúnəl/ *n.* (also **gun·nel**) the upper edge of the side of a boat or ship.

gup·py /gúpee/ *n.* (*pl.* **-pies**) a freshwater fish, *Poecilia reticulata*, of the W. Indies and S. America, frequently kept in aquariums.

gur·gle /gə́rgəl/ *v.* & *n.* •*v.* **1** *intr.* make a bubbling sound as of water from a bottle. **2** *tr.* utter with such a sound. •*n.* a gurgling sound.

Gur·kha /gə́rkə/ *n.* **1** a member of the dominant Hindu people in Nepal. **2** a Nepalese soldier serving in the British army.

gu·ru /gōōroo͞/ *n.* **1** a Hindu spiritual teacher or head of a religious sect. **2 a** an influential teacher. **b** a revered mentor.

gush /gush/ *v.* & *n.* •*v.* **1** *tr.* & *intr.* emit or flow in a sudden and copious stream. **2** *intr.* speak or behave with effusiveness. •*n.* **1** a sudden or copious stream. **2** an effusive manner. □□ **gush·ing** *adj.* **gush·ing·ly** *adv.*

gush·er /gúshər/ *n.* **1** an oil well from which oil flows without being pumped. **2** an effusive person.

gush·y /gúshee/ *adj.* (**gushier, gushiest**) excessively effusive or sentimental.

gus·set /gúsit/ *n.* **1** a piece inserted into a garment, etc., to strengthen or enlarge a part. **2** a bracket strengthening an angle of a structure. □□ **gus·set·ed** *adj.*

gust /gust/ *n.* & *v.* •*n.* **1** a sudden strong rush of wind. **2** a burst of rain, fire, smoke, or sound. **3** a passionate or emotional outburst. •*v.intr.* blow in gusts.

gus·to /gústō/ *n.* (*pl.* **-toes**) zest; enjoyment or vigor in doing something.

gust·y /gústee/ *adj.* (**gustier, gustiest**) **1** characterized by or blowing in strong winds. **2** characterized by gusto. □□ **gust·i·ly** *adv.*

gut /gut/ *n.* & *v.* •*n.* **1** the intestine. **2** (in *pl.*) the bowel or entrails. **3** (in *pl.*) *colloq.* personal courage and determination; perseverance. **4** *colloq.* (in *pl.*) the belly as the source of appetite. **5** (in *pl.*) **a** the contents of anything. **b** the essence of a thing. **6 a** material for violin or racket strings or surgical use made from the intestines of animals. **b** material for fishing lines made from the silk glands of silkworms. **7** (*attrib.*) **a** instinctive (*a gut reaction*). **b** fundamental (*a gut issue*). •*v.tr.* (**gutted, gutting**) **1** remove or destroy the internal fittings of (a house, etc.). **2** take out the guts of (a fish, etc.). **3** extract the essence of (a book, etc.). □ **hate a person's guts** *colloq.* dislike a person intensely. **spill one's guts** *colloq.* reveal one's feelings, secrets, etc.

gut·less /gútlis/ *adj. colloq.* lacking courage or determination.

guts·y /gútsee/ *adj.* (**gutsier, gutsiest**) *colloq.* **1** courageous. **2** robust; hearty.

gut·ter /gútər/ *n.* & *v.* •*n.* **1** a shallow trough along the eaves of a house, or a channel at the side of a street, to carry off rainwater. **2** (prec. by *the*) a poor or degraded background or environment. **3** an open conduit. **4** a groove. • *v.intr.* **1** flow in streams. **2 a** (of a candle) melt away as the wax forms channels down the side. **b** (of a candle or flame) flicker and burn unsteadily.

gut·ter·ing /gútəring/ *n.* **1 a** the gutters of a building, etc. **b** a section or length of a gutter. **2** material for gutters.

gut·ter press *n.* esp. *Brit.* sensational journalism concerned esp. with the private lives of public figures.

gut·ter·snipe /gútərsnīp/ *n.* a street urchin.

gut·tur·al /gútərəl/ *adj.* & *n.* • *adj.* **1** throaty; harsh sounding. **2 a** *Phonet.* (of a consonant) produced in the throat or by the back of the tongue and palate. **b** (of a sound) coming from the throat. **c** of the throat. • *n. Phonet.* a guttural consonant (e.g., *k*, *g*).

guy[1] /gī/ *n.* & *v.* • *n.* **1** *colloq.* a man; a fellow. **2** (usu. in *pl.*) a person of either sex. • *v.tr.* ridicule.

guy[2] /gī/ *n.* & *v.* • *n.* a rope or chain to secure a tent or steady a crane load, etc. • *v.tr.* secure with a guy or guys.

guz·zle /gúzəl/ *v.tr.* & *intr.* eat, drink, or consume greedily. □□ **guz·zler** *n.*

gybe /jīb/ *v.* & *n.* var. of JIBE[2].

gym /jim/ *n. colloq.* **1** a gymnasium. **2** gymnastics.

gym·kha·na /jimkaánə/ *n.* a meeting for competition or display in a sport, esp. horse riding or automobile racing.

gym·na·si·um /jimnáyzeeəm/ *n.* (*pl.* **gymnasiums** or **gymnasia** /–zeeə/) **1** a room or building equipped for indoor sports, often including gymnastics. **2** a school in Germany or Scandinavia that prepares pupils for university entrance.

gym·nast /jímnast, –nəst/ *n.* an expert in gymnastics.

gym·nas·tic /jimnástik/ *adj.* of or involving gymnastics.

gym·nas·tics /jimnástiks/ *n.pl.* (also treated as *sing.*) **1** exercises developing or displaying physical agility and coordination. **2** other physical or mental agility.

gym·no·sperm /jímnəspərm/ *n.* any of various plants having seeds unprotected by an ovary, including conifers, cycads, and ginkgos. □□ **gym·no·sper·mous** *adj.*

gymp var. of GIMP[1].

gyneco- /gínikō, jínə;n–/ *comb. form* (*Brit.* **gynaeco-**) woman; women; female.

gyn·e·col·o·gy /gínikóləjee, jínə–/ *n.* the science of the physiological functions and diseases of women. □□ **gyn·e·co·log·i·cal** *adj.* **gy·ne·col·o·gist** /–kóləjist/ *n.*

gyn·e·co·mas·ti·a /gínikōmásteeə, jínə;n–/ *n. Med.* enlargement of a man's breasts, usu. due to hormone imbalance or hormone therapy.

gy·noe·ci·um /jineéseeəm, –shee;n–, gī;n–/ *n.* (also **gy·nae·ci·um**) (*pl.* **·cia** /–seeə, –sheeə/) *Bot.* the carpels of a flower taken collectively.

-gynous /jinəs, ginəs/ *comb. form Bot.* forming adjectives meaning 'having specified female organs or pistils' (*monogynous*).

gyp /jip/ *v.* & *n. sl.* • *v.tr.* (**gypped, gypping**) cheat; swindle. • *n.* a swindle.

gyp·sum /jípsəm/ *n.* a hydrated form of calcium sulfate occurring naturally and used to make plaster of Paris and in the building industry.

Gyp·sy /jípsee/ *n.* (also **Gip·sy**) (*pl.* **-sies**) **1** a member of a nomadic people of Asia, Europe and N. America, of Hindu origin with dark skin and hair, and speaking a language (Romany) related to Hindi. **2** (**gypsy**) a person resembling or living like a Gypsy.

gyp·sy moth *n.* a kind of tussock moth, *Lymantria dispar*, of which the larvae are very destructive to foliage.

gy·rate /jírayt/ *v.* & *adj.* • *v.intr.* (also /jīráyt/) go in a circle or spiral. • *adj. Bot.* arranged in rings or convolutions. □□ **gy·ra·tion** /–ráyshən/ *n.* **gy·ra·tor** *n.* **gy·ra·to·ry** /–rətáwree/ *adj.*

gyre /jīr/ *v.* & *n.* esp. *poet.* • *v.intr.* whirl or gyrate. • *n.* a gyration.

gy·ro[1] /jírō/ *n.* (*pl.* **-ros**) *colloq.* **1** = GYROSCOPE. **2** = GYROCOMPASS.

gy·ro[2] /jírō, jeérō/ *n.* (*pl.* **-ros**) a sandwich made with slices of spiced meat cooked on a spit and usu. topped with tomato, onions, or salad greens.

gyro- /jírō/ *comb. form* rotation.

gy·ro·com·pass /jírōkumpəs, –kom–/ *n.* a nonmagnetic compass giving true north and bearings from it by means of a gyroscope.

gy·ro·graph /jírəgraf/ *n.* an instrument for recording revolutions.

gy·ro·mag·net·ic /jírōmagnétik/ *adj.* **1** *Physics* of the magnetic and mechanical properties of a rotating charged particle. **2** (of a compass) combining a gyroscope and a normal magnetic compass.

gy·ro·plane /jírəplayn/ *n.* a form of aircraft deriving its lift mainly from freely rotating overhead vanes.

gy·ro·scope /jírəskōp/ *n.* a rotating wheel whose axis is free to turn but maintains a fixed direction unless perturbed, esp. used for stabilization or with the compass in an aircraft, ship, etc. □□ **gy·ro·scop·ic** /–skópik/ *adj.*

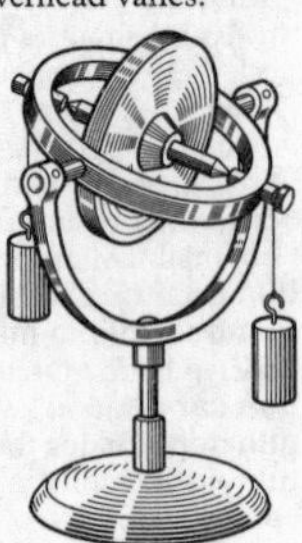
gyroscope

gy·ro·sta·bi·liz·er /jírōstáybilīzər/ *n.* a gyroscopic device for maintaining the equilibrium of a ship, aircraft, platform, etc.

gy·rus /jírəs/ *n.* (*pl.* **gyri** /–rī/) a fold or convolution, esp. of the brain.

gyt·tja /yíchə/ *n. Geol.* a lake deposit of a usu. black organic sediment.

H

H[1] /aych/ *n.* (also **h**) (*pl.* **Hs** or **H's**) **1** the eighth letter of the alphabet. **2** anything having the form of an H (esp. in *comb.*: *H-girder*).

H[2] *abbr.* (also **H.**) **1** (of a pencil lead) hard. **2** (water) hydrant. **3** *sl.* heroin.

H[3] *symb. Chem.* the element hydrogen.

h. *abbr.* **1** hecto-. **2** height. **3** *Baseball* hit; hits.. **4** hot.

Ha *symb. Chem.* the element hahnium.

ha[1] /haa/ *int.* (also **hah**) expressing surprise, suspicion, triumph, etc.

ha[2] *abbr.* hectare(s).

ha·be·as cor·pus /háybeeəs káwrpəs/ *n.* a writ requiring a person to be brought before a judge, esp. to investigate the lawfulness of his or her detention.

hab·er·dash·er /hábərdashər/ *n.* a dealer in men's clothing. □□ **hab·er·dash·er·y** *n.* (*pl.* **-ies**).

ha·bil·i·ment /həbílimənt/ *n.* (usu. in *pl.*) **1** clothes suited to a particular purpose. **2** *joc.* ordinary clothes.

hab·it /hábit/ *n.* **1** a settled or regular tendency (*has a habit of ignoring me*). **2** a practice that is hard to give up. **3** a mental constitution. **4** *colloq.* an addictive practice, esp. of taking drugs. **5 a** the dress of a particular class, esp. of a religious order. **b** (in full **riding habit**) a woman's riding dress.

hab·it·a·ble /hábitəbəl/ *adj.* that can be inhabited. □□ **hab·it·a·bil·i·ty** *n.* **hab·it·a·ble·ness** *n.* **hab·it·a·bly** *adv.*

hab·i·tant *n.* **1** /hábit'nt/ an inhabitant. **2** /ábeetóN/ **a** an early French settler in Canada or Louisiana. **b** a descendant of these early French settlers.

hab·i·tat /hábitat/ *n.* **1** the natural home of an organism. **2** a habitation.

hab·i·ta·tion /hábitáyshən/ *n.* **1** the process of inhabiting (*fit for human habitation*). **2** a dwelling.

hab·it-form·ing *adj.* causing addiction.

ha·bit·u·al /həbíchōōəl/ *adj.* **1** done constantly. **2** regular; usual. **3** given to a (specified) habit (*a habitual smoker*). □□ **ha·bit·u·al·ly** *adv.* **ha·bit·u·al·ness** *n.*

ha·bit·u·ate /həbíchōō-ayt/ *v.tr.* (often foll. by *to*) accustom. □□ **ha·bit·u·a·tion** /–áyshən/ *n.*

ha·bit·u·é /həbíchōō-áy/ *n.* a habitual visitor or resident.

ha·ček /haáchek/ *n.* (also **háček**) a diacritic mark (ˇ) placed over letters to modify the sound in some Slavic and Baltic languages.

ha·ci·en·da /haásee-éndə/ *n.* in Spanish-speaking countries: **1** an estate or plantation with a dwelling house. **2** a factory.

hack[1] /hak/ *v.* & *n.* • *v.* **1** *tr.* cut or chop roughly. **2** *tr.* strike illegally at the legs of (an opponent) during a game. **3** *intr.* deliver cutting blows. **4** *tr.* cut (one's way) through thick foliage, etc. **5** *tr. colloq.* gain unauthorized access to (data in a computer). **6** *tr. sl.* **a** cope with. **b** tolerate. **c** (often followed by *off* or as **hacked off** *adj.*) annoy; disconcert. • *n.* a wound, esp. from a kick.

hack[2] /hak/ *n., adj.,* & *v.* • *n.* **1 a** a horse for ordinary riding. **b** a horse let out for hire. **c** = JADE[2] 1. **2** a writer of mediocre literary work; *colloq.* usu. *derog.* a journalist. **3** a person hired to do dull routine work. **4** a taxi. • *attrib.adj.* **1** used as a hack. **2** commonplace (*hack work*). • *v.* **1** *intr.* ride on horseback at an ordinary pace. **2** *tr.* ride (a horse) in this way.

hack·er /hákər/ *n.* **1** a person or thing that cuts roughly. **2** *colloq.* **a** a person who is adept at programming computers. **b** a person who uses computers to gain unauthorized access to data. **3** a golfer who plays poorly.

hack·ing cough *n.* a short dry frequent cough.

hack·le /hákəl/ • *n.* **1** a long feather or series of feathers on the neck or saddle of a domestic fowl and other birds. **2** (in *pl.*) the erectile hairs along the back of a dog, which rise when it is angry or alarmed. □ **raise a person's hackles** cause a person to be angry.

hack·ney /háknee/ *n.* (*pl.* **-neys**) **1** a horse of average size for ordinary riding. **2** designating any of various vehicles for hire.

hack·neyed /hákneed/ *adj.* (of a phrase, etc.) made trite by overuse.

hack·saw /háksaw/ *n.* a saw with a narrow blade set in a frame, for cutting metal.

had *past* and *past part.* of HAVE.

had·dock /hádək/ *n.* (*pl.* same) a marine fish of the N. Atlantic, allied to cod, but smaller.

Ha·des /háydeez/ *n.* (in Greek mythology) the underworld; the abode of the spirits of the dead.

hadn't /hád'nt/ *contr.* had not.

had·ron /hádron/ *n. Physics* any strongly interacting elementary particle. □□ **had·ron·ic** /–drónik/ *adj.*

haf·ni·um /háfneeəm/ *n. Chem.* a silvery metallic element occurring naturally with zirconium, used in tungsten alloys for filaments and electrodes. ¶ Symb.: **Hf.**

haft /haft/ *n.* & *v.* • *n.* the handle of a dagger, knife, etc. • *v.tr.* provide with a haft.

hag /hag/ *n.* **1** an ugly old woman. **2** a witch.

hag·fish /hágfish/ *n.* a jawless fish with a rasplike tongue used for feeding on dead or dying fish.

hag·gard /hágərd/ *adj.* looking exhausted and distraught, esp. from fatigue or worry. □□ **hag·gard·ly** *adv.* **hag·gard·ness** *n.*

hag·gle /hágəl/ *v.* & *n.* • *v.intr.* (often foll. by *about, over*) bargain persistently. • *n.* a dispute or wrangle. □□ **hag·gler** *n.*

hagio- /hágeeō, háyjeeō/ *comb. form* of saints or holiness.

Hag·i·og·ra·pha /hágeeógrəfə, háyjee–/ *n.pl.* the twelve books comprising the last of the three major divisions of the Hebrew Scriptures, along with the Law and the Prophets.

hag·i·og·ra·pher /hágeeógrəfər, háyjee–/ *n.* **1** a writer of the lives of saints. **2** a writer of any of the Hagiographa.

hag·i·og·ra·phy /hágeeógrəfee, háyjee–/ *n.* the writing of the lives of saints. □□ **hag·i·o·graph·ic** /–geeəgráfik/ *adj.* **hag·i·o·graph·i·cal** *adj.*

hag·i·ol·a·try /hágeeólətree, háyjee–/ *n.* the worship of saints.

hag·i·ol·o·gy /hágióləjee/ *n.* literature dealing with the lives and legends of saints. □□ **hag·i·o·log·i·cal** /–geeəlójikəl/ *adj.* **hag·i·ol·o·gist** *n.*

hah var. of HA[1].

ha ha /haáhaá/ *int.* repr. laughter.

hahn·i·um /haániəm/ *n. Chem.* an artificially produced radioactive element. ¶ Symb.: **Ha.**

hai·ku /híkoo/ *n.* (*pl.* same) **1** a Japanese three-line poem of usu. 17 syllables. **2** an English imitation of this.

hail[1] /hayl/ *n. & v.* • *n.* **1** pellets of frozen rain falling in showers from cumulonimbus clouds. **2** (foll. by *of*) a barrage or onslaught (of missiles, curses, questions, etc.). • *v.* **1** *intr.* (prec. by *it* as subject) fall as hail (*it is hailing; if it hails*). **2 a** *tr.* pour down (blows, words, etc.). **b** *intr.* come down forcefully.

hail[2] /hayl/ *v., int., & n.* • *v.* **1** *tr.* greet enthusiastically. **2** *tr.* signal to (*hailed a taxi*). **3** *tr.* acclaim (*hailed him king; was hailed as a prodigy*). **4** *intr.* (foll. by *from*) have one's home or origins in (a place) (*hails from Mexico*). • *int. archaic* or *rhet.* expressing greeting. • *n.* **1** a greeting or act of hailing. **2** distance as affecting the possibility of hailing (*within hail; within hailing distance*).

Hail Mar·y *n.* the Ave Maria (see AVE).

hail·stone /háylstōn/ *n.* a pellet of hail.

hail·storm /háylstorm/ *n.* a period of heavy hail.

hair /hair/ *n.* **1 a** any of the fine threadlike strands growing from the skin of mammals, esp. from the human head. **b** these collectively (*his hair is falling out*). **c** a hairstyle or way of wearing the hair (*I like your hair today*). **2 a** an artificially produced hairlike strand, e.g., in a brush. **b** a mass of such hairs. **3** an elongated cell growing from the epidermis of a plant. **4** a very small quantity or extent (also *attrib.*: *a hair crack*). □ **get in a person's hair** *colloq.* annoy a person. **let one's hair down** *colloq.* abandon restraint. □□ **haired** *adj.* (also in *comb.*). **hair·less** *adj.* **hair·like** *adj.*

hair·ball /háirbawl/ *n.* (also **hair ball**) a compact ball of hair that accumulates in the stomach of a cat or other animal that grooms itself by licking its fur.

hair·breadth /háirbredth/ *n.* = HAIR'S BREADTH; (esp. *attrib.*: *a hairbreadth escape*).

hair·brush /háirbrush/ *n.* a brush for arranging or smoothing the hair.

hair·cloth /háirklawth, –kloth/ *n.* stiff cloth woven from hair.

hair·cut /háirkut/ *n.* **1** a cutting of the hair. **2** the style in which the hair is cut.

hair·do /háirdōō/ *n.* (*pl.* **-dos**) *colloq.* the style of a woman's hair.

hair·dress·er /háirdresər/ *n.* **1** a person who cuts and styles hair, esp. professionally. **2** the business or establishment of a hairdresser. □□ **hair·dress·ing** *n.*

hair dry·er *n.* (also **hair drier**) an electrical device for drying the hair by blowing warm air over it.

hair·line /háirlīn/ *n.* **1** the edge of a person's hair, esp. on the forehead. **2** a very thin line or crack, etc.

hair·net /háirnet/ *n.* a piece of fine mesh fabric for confining the hair.

hair of the dog *n.* further alcoholic drink to cure hangover from that drink.

hair·piece /háirpees/ *n.* a quantity or switch of detached hair used to augment a person's natural hair.

hair·pin /háirpin/ *n.* a U-shaped pin for fastening the hair.

hair·pin turn *n.* a sharp U-shaped bend in a road.

hair-rais·ing /háirrayzing/ *adj.* extremely alarming; terrifying.

hair's breadth *n.* a very small amount or margin.

hair·split·ting /háirspliting/ *adj. & n.* making overfine distinctions; quibbling. □□ **hair·split·ter** *n.*

hair spray *n.* a solution sprayed on the hair to keep it in place.

hair·spring /háirspring/ *n.* a fine spring regulating the balance wheel in a watch.

hair trig·ger *n.* a trigger of a firearm set for release at the slightest pressure.

hair-trig·ger *adj.* reacting to the slightest pressure or provocation; likely to prompt such a reaction.

hair·y /háiree/ *adj.* (**hairier, hairiest**) **1** covered with hair. **2** having the feel of hair. **3** *sl.* alarmingly unpleasant. □□ **hair·i·ly** *adv.* **hair·i·ness** *n.*

hajj /haj/ *n.* the Islamic pilgrimage to Mecca.

haj·ji /hájee/ *n.* (*pl.* **-jis**) a Muslim who has been to Mecca as a pilgrim: also (**Hajji**) used as a title.

hake /hayk/ *n.* any marine fish of the genus *Merluccius*, esp. *M. merluccius* with an elongate body and large head.

ha·lal /haala'al/ *v. & n.* (also **hal·lal**) • *v.tr.* (**halalled, halalling**) kill (an animal) as prescribed by Muslim law. • *n.* (often *attrib.*) meat prepared in this way.

hal·berd /hálbərd/ *n.* (also **hal·bert** /–bərt/) *hist.* a combined spear and battleax.

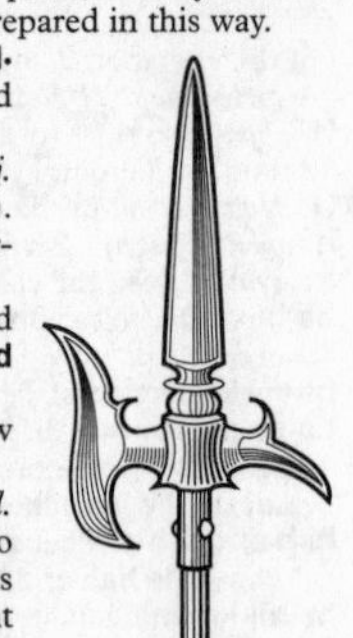
halberd

hal·cy·on /hálseeən/ • *adj.* **1** calm; peaceful (*halcyon days*). **2** (of a period) happy; prosperous.

hale[1] /hayl/ *adj.* strong and healthy (esp. in **hale and hearty**). □□ **hale·ness** *n.*

hale[2] /hayl/ *v.tr.* drag or draw forcibly.

half /haf/ *n., adj., & adv.* • *n.* (*pl.* **halves** /havz/) **1** either of two equal or corresponding parts into which a thing is or might be divided. **2** *colloq.* = HALFBACK. **3** either of two equal periods of play in sports. • *adj.* **1** of an amount or quantity equal to a half, or roughly a half (*half a pint*). **2** forming a half (*a half share*). • *adv.* **1** (often in *comb.*) to the extent of half (*half-frozen*). **2** to a certain extent (esp. in phrases: *half inclined to agree*). **3** (in reckoning time) by the amount of half (an hour, etc.) (*half past two*). □ **by half** (prec. by *too* + adj.) excessively (*too clever by half*). **by halves** incompletely (*never does things by halves*). **half a chance** *colloq.* the slightest opportunity (esp. **given half a chance**). **half measures** an unsatisfactory compromise or inadequate policy.

half-and-half *n.* a liquid of half cream and half milk.

half·back /háfbak/ *n.* (in some sports) a player between the linemen and fullbacks, or behind the forward line.

half-baked *adj.* **1** incompletely planned. **2** (of enthusiasm, etc.) only partly committed. **3** foolish.

half-blood *n.* **1** a person having one parent in common with another. **2** this relationship. **3** = HALF BREED. □□ **half-blooded** *adj.*

half breed *n.* often *offens.* a person of mixed race.

half broth·er *n.* a brother with only one parent in common.

half-doz·en *n.* *colloq.* six, or about six.

half·heart·ed /háfhaártid/ *adj.* lacking enthusiasm. □□ **half·heart·ed·ly** *adv.* **half·heart·ed·ness** *n.*

half hitch *n.* a knot formed by passing the end of a rope around its standing part and then through the loop.

half hour *n.* **1** (also **half an hour**) a period of 30 minutes. **2** a point of time 30 minutes after any hour o'clock. □□ **half-hourly** *adv.*

half-inch *n.* a unit of length half as large as an inch.

half-life *n.* the time taken for the radioactivity or some other property of a substance to fall to half its original value.

half-mast *n.* the position of a flag halfway down the mast, as a mark of respect for a person who has died. □ **at half-mast** often *joc.* (of a garment) having slipped down.

half moon *n.* **1** the moon when only half its illuminated surface is visible from earth. **2** the time when this occurs. **3** a semicircular object.

half note *n. Mus.* a note whose duration is one half of a whole note.

half sis·ter *n.* a sister with only one parent in common.

half step *n. Mus.* = SEMITONE.

half·time /háftīm/ *n. & adj.* • *n.* **1** the time at which half of a game is completed. **2** a short intermission occurring at this time. • *adj.* (**half-time**) working half the usual hours (*a half-time job*).

half·tone /háftōn/ *n.* a reproduction printed from a block (produced by photographic means) in which the various tones of gray are produced from small and large black dots.

half-truth *n.* a statement that conveys only part of the truth.

half·way /háfwáy/ *adv. & adj.* • *adv.* **1** at a point equidistant between two others (*we were halfway to Chicago*). **2** to some extent; more or less (*is halfway decent*). • *adj.* situated halfway (*reached a halfway point*).

half·way house *n.* a center for helping former drug addicts, prisoners, psychiatric patients, or others to adjust to life in general society.

half·wit /háfwit/ *n.* **1** *colloq.* an extremely stupid person. **2** a person who is mentally deficient. ▫▫ **half·wit·ted** /wítid/ *adj.*

hal·i·but /hálibət/ *n.* (*pl.* same) any of various large marine flatfishes commonly used as food.

hal·ide /hálīd, háyl–/ *n. Chem.* **1** a binary compound of a halogen with another group or element. **2** any organic compound containing a halogen.

hal·i·o·tis /háleeṓtis/ *n.* an edible gastropod mollusk with an ear-shaped shell lined with mother-of-pearl.

hal·ite /hálīt, háy–/ *n.* rock salt.

hal·i·to·sis /hálitṓsis/ *n.* = BAD BREATH.

hall /hawl/ *n.* **1 a** a space or passage into which the front entrance of a house, etc., opens. **b** a corridor or passage in a building. **2** a large room or building for meetings, meals, concerts, etc. **3** a university residence for students. **4** the building of a guild (*Fishmongers' Hall*).

hal·le·lu·jah var. of ALLELUIA.

hall·mark /háwlmaark/ *n. & v.* • *n.* **1** a mark used at Goldsmiths' Hall in London for marking the standard of gold, silver, and platinum. **2** any distinctive feature, esp. of excellence. • *v.tr.* **1** stamp with a hallmark. **2** designate as excellent.

Hall of Fame *n.* a building with memorials to individuals who excelled in a sport, etc.

hal·loo /həlṓō/ *int., n., & v.* • *int.* **1** inciting dogs to the chase. **2** calling attention. **3** expressing surprise. • *n.* the cry "halloo." • *v.* (**halloos, hallooed**) **1** *intr.* cry "halloo," esp. to dogs. **2** *intr.* shout to attract attention. **3** *tr.* urge on (dogs, etc.) with shouts.

hal·low /hálō/ *v.tr.* **1** make holy; consecrate. **2** honor as holy.

Hal·low·een /háləwéen/ *n.* (also **Hallowe'en**) the eve of All Saints' Day, Oct. 31, esp. as celebrated by children dressing in costumes and collecting treats door-to-door.

hal·lu·ces *pl.* of HALLUX.

hal·lu·ci·nate /həlṓōsinayt/ *v.* **1** *tr.* produce illusions in the mind of (a person). **2** *intr.* experience hallucinations. ▫▫ **hal·lu·ci·na·tor** *n.*

hal·lu·ci·na·tion /həlṓōsináyshən/ *n.* the apparent perception of an object not actually present. ▫▫ **hal·lu·ci·na·to·ry** /–sinətáwree/ *adj.*

hal·lu·ci·no·gen /həlṓōsinəjən/ *n.* a drug causing hallucinations. ▫▫ **hal·lu·ci·no·gen·ic** /–jénik/ *adj.*

hal·lux /háluks/ *n.* (*pl.* **halluces** /hályəseez/) **1** the big toe. **2** the innermost digit of the hind foot of vertebrates.

hall·way /háwlway/ *n.* an entrance hall or corridor.

halm var. of HAULM.

ha·lo /háylō/ *n. & v.* • *n.* (*pl.* **-loes**) **1** a disk or circle of light shown in art surrounding the head of a sacred person. **2** the glory associated with an idealized person, etc. **3** a circle of light around a luminous body, esp. the sun or moon. **4** a circle or ring. • *v.tr.* (**-loes, -loed**) surround with a halo.

hal·o·gen /háləjən/ *n. Chem.* any of the group of nonmetallic elements: fluorine, chlorine, bromine, iodine, and astatine, which form halides (e.g., sodium chloride) by simple union with a metal. ▫▫ **hal·o·gen·ic** /–jénik/ *adj.*

hal·o·gen·a·tion /háləjináyshən/ *n.* the introduction of a halogen atom into a molecule.

hal·on /háylon/ *n. Chem.* any of various gaseous compounds of carbon, bromine, and other halogens, used to extinguish fires.

hal·o·phyte /háləfīt/ *n.* a plant adapted to saline conditions.

halt[1] /hawlt/ *n. & v.* • *n.* **1** a stop (usu. temporary) (*come to a halt*). **2** a temporary stoppage on a march or journey. • *v.intr. & tr.* stop; come or bring to a halt.

halt[2] /hawlt/ *v. & adj.* • *v.intr.* **1** (esp. as **halting** *adj.*) lack smooth progress. **2** hesitate (*halt between two opinions*). **3** walk hesitatingly. **4** *archaic* be lame. • *adj. archaic* lame. ▫▫ **halt·ing·ly** *adv.*

halt·er /háwltər/ *n.* **1** a rope or strap with a noose or headstall for horses or cattle. **2 a** a strap around the back of a woman's neck holding her dress top and leaving her shoulders and back bare. **b** a dress top held by this.

hal·va /haalvaa/ *n.* (also **hal·vah**) a sweet confection of ground sesame seeds and honey.

halve /hav/ *v.tr.* **1** divide into two halves or parts. **2** reduce by half. **3** share equally. **4** *Golf* use the same number of strokes as one's opponent in (a hole or match).

halves *pl.* of HALF.

hal·yard /hályərd/ *n. Naut.* a rope or tackle for raising or lowering a sail or yard, etc.

ham /ham/ *n. & v.* • *n.* **1 a** the upper part of a pig's leg salted and dried or smoked for food. **b** the meat from this. **2** the back of the thigh. **3** *sl.* (often *attrib.*) an inexpert or unsubtle actor or piece of acting. **4** (in full **radio ham**) *colloq.* the operator of an amateur radio station. • *v.intr. & tr.* (often foll. by *up*) (**hammed, hamming**) *sl.* overact; act or treat emotionally or sentimentally.

---

ham Old English *ham, hom* (originally denoting the back of the knee), from a Germanic base meaning 'be crooked.' In the late 15th century the term came to denote the back of the thigh, hence that part of the animal used as food.

---

ham·burg·er /hámbərgər/ *n.* a patty of ground beef, usu. fried or grilled and eaten in a soft bread roll.

ham-fist·ed /hámfistid/ *adj. colloq.* clumsy. ▫▫ **ham-fist·ed·ly** *adv.* **ham-fist·ed·ness** *n.*

ham-hand·ed /hámhándid/ *adj. colloq.* = HAM-FISTED.

Ham·it·ic /həmítik/ *n. & adj.* • *n.* a group of African languages including ancient Egyptian and Berber. • *adj.* **1** of or relating to this group of languages. **2** of or relating to the Hamites, a group of peoples in Egypt and N. Africa, by tradition descended from Noah's son Ham (Gen. 10:6 ff.).

ham·let /hámlit/ *n.* a small village.

ham·mer /hámər/ *n. & v.* • *n.* **1 a** a tool with a heavy metal head at right angles to the handle, used for driving nails, etc. **b** a machine with a metal block serving the same purpose. **c** a similar contrivance, as for exploding the charge in a gun, etc. **2** an auctioneer's mallet, indicating by a rap that an article is sold. **3 a** a metal ball attached to a wire for throwing in an athletic contest. **b** the sport of throwing the hammer. • *v.* **1 a** *tr.* & *intr.* hit or beat with or as with a hammer. **b** *intr.* strike loudly. **2** *tr.* **a** drive in (nails) with a hammer. **b** fasten by hammering (*hammered the lid down*). **3** *tr.* (often foll. by *in*) inculcate (ideas, knowledge, etc.) forcefully. **4** *tr. colloq.* utterly defeat. **5** *intr.* (foll. by *away at*) work hard at. □ **come under the hammer** be sold at an auction. **hammer out 1** make flat or smooth by hammering. **2** work out the details of laboriously. **3** play (a tune, esp. on the piano) loudly or clumsily. □□ **ham•mer•ing** *n.* (esp. in sense 4 of *v.*). **ham•mer•less** *adj.*

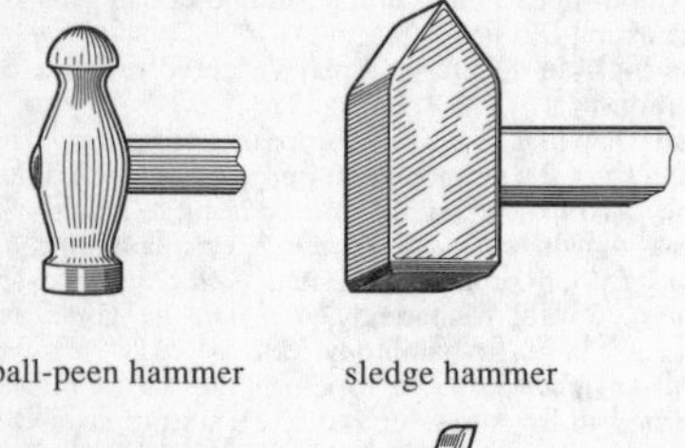

ball-peen hammer sledge hammer

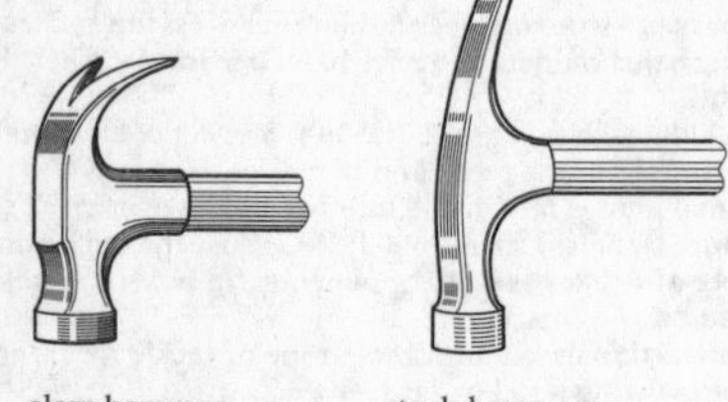

claw hammer tack hammer

hammer, 1a

ham•mer and sick•le *n.* the symbols of the industrial worker and the peasant used as the emblem of the former USSR and of international communism.

ham•mer•head /hámərhed/ *n.* a shark with a flattened head and eyes in lateral extensions of it.

ham•mer•lock /hámərlok/ *n. Wrestling* a hold in which the arm is twisted and bent behind the back.

ham•mer•toe /hámərtō/ *n.* a deformity in which the toe is bent permanently downward.

ham•mock /hámək/ *n.* a bed of canvas or rope network, suspended by cords.

ham•per[1] /hámpər/ *n.* a large basket, usu. with a hinged lid and containing laundry or food.

ham•per[2] /hámpər/ *v.tr.* **1** prevent the free movement or activity of. **2** impede; hinder.

ham•ster /hámstər/ *n.* any of various rodents of the subfamily Cricetinae having a short tail and large cheek pouches for storing food.

ham•string /hámstring/ *n.* & *v.* • *n. Anat.* **1** each of five tendons at the back of the knee in humans. **2** the great tendon at the back of the hock in quadrupeds. • *v.tr.* (*past* and *past part.* **hamstrung** or **hamstringed**) **1** cripple by cutting the hamstrings of (a person or animal). **2** prevent the activity of.

hand /hand/ *n.* & *v.* • *n.* **1 a** the end part of the human arm beyond the wrist. **b** in other primates, the end part of a forelimb, also used as a foot. **2 a** (often in *pl.*) control; custody (*is in good hands*). **b** agency or influence (*suffered at their hands*). **c** a share in an action. **3** the pointer of a clock or watch. **4** the right or left side or direction relative to a person or thing. **5 a** a skill (*a hand for making pastry*). **b** a person skillful in some respect. **6** a person who does or makes something, esp. distinctively (*a picture by the same hand*). **7** an individual's writing or the style of this. **8** a person as the source of information (*at first hand*). **9** a pledge of marriage. **10** a manual laborer, esp. in a factory, on a farm, or on board ship. **11 a** the playing cards dealt to a player. **b** the player holding these. **c** a round of play. **12** *colloq.* applause (*a big hand*). **13** the unit of measure of a horse's height, equal to 4 inches (10.16 cm). **14** a forehock of pork. **15** (*attrib.*) **a** operated or held in the hand (*hand drill*; *hand luggage*). **b** done by hand and not by machine (*hand-knitted*). • *v.tr.* **1** deliver; transfer. **2** convey verbally (*handed me a lot of abuse*). **3** *colloq.* give away too readily (*handed them the advantage*). □ **all hands 1** the entire crew of a ship. **2** the entire workforce. **at hand 1** close by. **2** about to happen. **by hand 1** by a person and not a machine. **2** delivered privately and not by the public mail. **from hand to mouth** satisfying only one's immediate needs. **get** (or **have** or **keep**) **one's hand in** become (or be or remain) practiced in something. **hand down 1** pass the ownership of to another. **2 a** transmit (a decision) from a higher court, etc. **b** express (an opinion or verdict). **hand in glove** in collusion or association. **hand in hand** in close association. **hand it to** *colloq.* acknowledge the merit of. **hand out 1** serve; distribute. **2** award, allocate (*the judges handed out stiff sentences*). **hand over** surrender possession of. **hands down** (esp. of winning) with no difficulty. **hands off** a warning not to touch or interfere with something. **hands on 1** *Computing* of or requiring personal operation at a keyboard. **2** involving or offering active participation rather than theory. **hands up!** an instruction to raise one's hands in surrender or to signify assent. **have a hand in** share or take part in. **have one's hands tied** *colloq.* be unable to act. **in hand 1** receiving attention. **2** in reserve. **3** under one's control. **lend** (or **give**) **a hand** assist in an action or enterprise. **off one's hands** no longer one's responsibility. **on hand** available. **on the one** (or **the other**) **hand** from one (or another) point of view. **out of hand 1** out of control. **2** peremptorily (*refused out of hand*). **put** (or **set**) **one's hand to** start work on; engage in. **to hand 1** within easy reach. **2** (of a letter) received. **turn one's hand to** undertake (as a new activity). □□ **hand•less** *adj.*

hand•bag /hándbag/ *n.* a small bag usu. with a handle or shoulder strap carried esp. by a woman and used to hold a wallet, cosmetics, etc.

hand•ball *n.* **1** /hándbawl/ one of several games with a ball thrown by hand among players or struck with an open hand against a wall. **2** /hándbáwl/ *Soccer* intentional touching of the ball with the hand or arm by a player other than a goalkeeper who is in the goal area, constituting a foul.

hand•bell /hándbel/ *n.* a small bell usu. tuned to a particular note and rung by hand, esp. one of a set giving a range of notes.

hand•bill /hándbil/ *n.* a printed notice distributed by hand.

hand•book /hándbo͝ok/ *n.* a short manual or guidebook.

hand•brake /hándbrayk/ *n.* a hand-operated brake.

hand•cart /hándkaart/ *n.* a small cart pushed or drawn by hand.

hand•clap /hándklap/ *n.* a clapping of the hands.

hand•craft /hándkraft/ *n.* & *v.* • *n.* = HANDICRAFT. • *v.tr.* make by handicraft.

hand•cuff /hándkuf/ *n.* & *v.* • *n.* (in *pl.*) a pair of lockable linked metal rings for securing a person's wrists. • *v.tr.* put handcuffs on.

-handed /hándid/ *adj.* (in *comb.*) **1** for or involving a specified number of hands (in various senses) (*two-handed*). **2** using chiefly the hand specified (*left-hand-*

ed). ▫▫ **-hand·ed·ly** *adv.* **-hand·ed·ness** *n.* (both in sense 2).

hand·ful /hánd fŏŏl/ *n.* (*pl.* **-fuls**) **1** a quantity that fills the hand. **2** a small number or amount. **3** *colloq.* a troublesome person or task.

hand gre·nade *n.* see GRENADE.

hand·gun /hándgun/ *n.* a small firearm held in and fired with one hand.

hand·hold /hándhōld/ *n.* something for the hands to grip on (in climbing, sailing, etc.).

hand·i·cap /hándeekap/ *n.* & *v.* •*n.* **1 a** a disadvantage imposed on a superior competitor in order to make a contest more equal. **b** a race or contest in which this is imposed. **2** the number of strokes by which a golfer normally exceeds par for the course. **3** a thing that makes progress difficult. **4** a physical or mental disability. •*v.tr.* (**handicapped, handicapping**) **1** impose a handicap on. **2** place at a disadvantage. ▫▫ **hand·i·cap·per** *n.*

hand·i·capped /hándeekapt/ *adj.* having a physical or mental disability.

hand·i·craft /hándeekraft/ *n.* work that requires both manual and artistic skill.

hand·i·work /hándeewərk/ *n.* work done or a thing made by hand.

hand·ker·chief /hángkərchif, –cheef/ *n.* (*pl.* **handkerchiefs** or **-chieves** /–cheevz/) a square of cotton, linen, silk, etc., for wiping one's nose, etc.

han·dle /hánd'l/ *n.* & *v.* •*n.* **1** the part by which a thing is held, carried, or controlled. **2** a fact that may be taken advantage of (*gave a handle to his critics*). **3** *colloq.* a personal title. **4** the feel of goods when handled. •*v.tr.* **1** touch, operate, or move with the hands. **2** manage or deal with (*knows how to handle people*). **3** deal in (goods). **4** discuss or write about (a subject). ▫▫ **han·dle·a·ble** *adj.* **han·dle·a·bil·i·ty** *n.* **han·dled** *adj.* (also in *comb.*).

han·dle·bar /hánd'lbaar/ *n.* (often in *pl.*) the steering bar of a bicycle, etc.

han·dle·bar mus·tache *n.* a thick mustache with curved ends.

han·dler /hándlər/ *n.* **1** a person who handles or deals in certain commodities. **2** a person who trains and looks after an animal (esp. a working or show dog).

hand·made /hándmáyd/ *adj.* made by hand and not by machine, esp. as designating superior quality.

hand·maid /hándmayd/ *n.* (also **hand·maid·en** /–máyd'n/) *archaic* a female servant or helper.

hand-me-down *n.* an article of clothing, etc., passed on from another person.

hand·out /hándowt/ *n.* **1** something given free to a needy person. **2** a statement given to the press, printed information given to a lecture audience, etc.

hand-o·ver-fist *adv. colloq.* with rapid progress.

hand·pick /hándpik/ *v.tr.* choose carefully or personally.

hand·rail /hándrayl/ *n.* a narrow rail for holding as a support on stairs, etc.

hand·saw /hándsaw/ *n.* a saw worked by one hand.

hand·set /hándset/ *n.* a telephone mouthpiece and earpiece forming one unit.

hand·shake /hándshayk/ *n.* the shaking of a person's hand by another's hand as a greeting, etc.

hand·some /hánsəm/ *adj.* (**handsomer, handsomest**) **1** (of a person) good-looking. **2** (of a building, etc.) imposing; attractive. **3 a** generous (*a handsome present*). **b** (of a price, fortune, etc., as assets gained) considerable. ▫▫ **hand·some·ness** *n.*

hand·some·ly /hánsəmlee/ *adv.* **1** generously. **2** finely; beautifully. **3** *Naut.* carefully.

hand·spring /hándspring/ *n.* an acrobatic flip in which one lands first on the hands and then on the feet.

hand·stand /hándstand/ *n.* balancing on one's hands with the feet in the air.

hand-to-hand *adj.* (of fighting) at close quarters.

hand·work /hándwərk/ *n.* work done with the hands. ▫▫ **hand·worked** *adj.*

hand·writ·ing /hándrīting/ *n.* **1** writing with a pen, pencil, etc. **2** a person's particular style of writing. ▫▫ **hand·writ·ten** /–rítən/ *adj.*

hand·y /hándee/ *adj.* (**handier, handiest**) **1** convenient to handle or use. **2** ready to hand. **3** clever with the hands. ▫▫ **hand·i·ly** *adv.* **hand·i·ness** *n.*

hand·y·man /hándeeman/ *n.* (*pl.* **-men**) a person able or employed to do occasional domestic repairs and minor renovations.

hang /hang/ *v.* & *n.* •*v.* (*past* and *past part.* **hung** /hung/except in sense 7) **1** *tr.* **a** secure or cause to be supported from above. **b** (foll. by *up, on, onto,* etc.) attach loosely by suspending from the top. **2** *tr.* set up (a door, gate, etc.) on its hinges. **3** *tr.* place (a picture) on a wall or in an exhibition. **4** *tr.* attach (wallpaper) to a wall. **5** *tr.* (foll. by *on*) *colloq.* attach the blame for (a thing) to (a person) (*you can't hang that on me*). **6** *tr.* (foll. by *with*) decorate by hanging decorations, etc. (*a hall hung with tapestries*). **7** *tr.* & *intr.* (*past* and *past part.* **hanged**) **a** suspend or be suspended by the neck until dead, esp. as a form of capital punishment. **b** as a mild oath (*hang the expense*). **8** *tr.* let droop (*hang one's head*). **9** *tr.* suspend (meat or game) from a hook and leave it until dry or tender. **10** *intr.* be hung (in various senses). **11** *intr.* remain static in the air. **12** *intr.* be present, esp. threateningly (*a hush hung over the room*). **13** *intr.* (foll. by *on*) **a** be dependent on (*everything hangs on the discussions*). **b** listen closely to (*hangs on their every word*). •*n.* **1** the way a thing hangs or falls. **2** a downward droop or bend. ▫ **get the hang of** *colloq.* understand the technique or meaning of. **hang around 1** loiter or dally. **2** (foll. by *with*) associate with (a person, etc.). **hang back 1** show reluctance to act or move. **2** remain behind. **hang heavily** (or **heavy**) (of time) pass slowly. **hang in** *colloq.* **1** persist; persevere. **2** linger. **hang it up** quit; retire; resign. **hang loose** *colloq.* relax; stay calm. **hang on** *colloq.* **1** continue or persevere. **2** (often foll. by *to*) retain one's grip. **3** (foll. by *to*) fail to give back. **4 a** wait for a short time. **b** (in telephoning) continue to listen during a pause in the conversation. **hang out 1** hang from a window, clothesline, etc. **2** protrude or cause to protrude downwards. **3** (foll. by *of*) lean out of (a window, etc.). **4** *sl.* be often present. **5** (foll. by *with*) *sl.* be friends with. **hang together 1** make sense. **2** remain associated. **hang up 1** hang from a hook, peg, etc. **2** end a telephone conversation, esp. abruptly (*then he hung up on me*). ▶A person suspended by the neck until dead is **hanged,** although *hung* is common in informal usage. Pictures, draperies, decorations, Christmas stockings, and the like are **hung.**

hang·ar /hángər/ *n.* a building for housing aircraft, etc.

hang·dog /hángdawg, –dog/ *adj.* having a dejected or guilty appearance; shamefaced.

hang·er /hángər/ *n.* **1** a person or thing that hangs. **2** a shaped piece of wood or plastic, etc., from which clothes may be hung.

hang·er-on *n.* (*pl.* **hangers-on**) a follower or dependent.

hang glid·er *n.* a frame with a fabric airfoil stretched over it, from which the operator is suspended and controls flight by body movement. ▫ **hang gliding** *n.*

hang·ing /hánging/ *n.* & *adj.* •*n.* **1 a** the act of executing by hanging a person. **b** (*attrib.*) meriting or causing this (*a hanging offense*). **2** (usu. in *pl.*) draperies hung on a wall, etc. • *adj.* that hangs or is hung.

hang•man /hángmən/ *n.* (*pl.* **-men**) **1** an executioner who hangs condemned persons. **2** a game for two players, in which the tally of failed guesses is kept by drawing a representation of a figure hanging from a gallows.

hang•nail /hángnayl/ *n.* a piece of torn skin at the root of a fingernail.

hang•out /hángowt/ *n. sl.* a place one frequently visits.

hang•o•ver /hángōvər/ *n.* **1** a severe headache or other aftereffects caused by drinking an excess of liquor. **2** a survival from the past.

hang-up *n. sl.* an emotional problem or inhibition.

hank /hangk/ *n.* a coil of wool.

hank•er /hángkər/ *v.intr.* (foll. by *to* + infin., *for*, or *after*) long for; crave. □□ **hank•er•er** *n.* **hank•er•ing** *n.*

han•ky /hángkee/ *n.* (also **han•kie**) (*pl.* **-kies**) *colloq.* a handkerchief.

han•ky-pan•ky /hángkeepángkee/ *n. sl.* **1** naughtiness, esp. sexual misbehavior. **2** dishonest dealing; trickery.

han•som /hánsəm/ *n.* (in full **hansom cab**) *hist.* a two-wheeled horse-drawn cab.

Ha•nuk•kah /khaánəkə, haá–/ *n.* (also **Chanukkah**) the Jewish festival of lights, commemorating the purification of the Temple in 165 BC.

hap /hap/ *n. archaic* **1** chance; luck. **2** a chance occurrence.

hap•haz•ard /hápházərd/ *adj.* & *adv.* • *adj.* done, etc., by chance; random. • *adv.* at random. □□ **hap•haz•ard•ly** *adv.* **hap•haz•ard•ness** *n.*

hap•less /háplis/ *adj.* unlucky. □□ **hap•less•ly** *adv.* **hap•less•ness** *n.*

hap•loid /háployd/ *adj.* & *n. Biol.* • *adj.* (of an organism or cell) with a single set of chromosomes. • *n.* a haploid organism or cell.

hap•pen /hápən/ *v.intr.* **1** occur (by chance or otherwise). **2** (foll. by *to* + infin.) have the (good or bad) fortune to (*I happened to meet her*). **3** (foll. by *to*) be the (esp. unwelcome) fate or experience of (*what happened to you?*). **4** (foll. by *on*) encounter or discover by chance.

hap•pen•ing /hápəning/ *n.* & *adj.* • *n.* **1** an event or occurrence. **2** an improvised or spontaneous theatrical, etc., performance. • *adj. sl.* exciting, fashionable.

hap•pen•stance /hápənstans/ *n.* a thing that happens by chance.

hap•py /hápee/ *adj.* (**happier, happiest**) **1** feeling or showing pleasure or contentment. **2 a** fortunate. **b** (of words, behavior, etc.) apt; pleasing. **3** *colloq.* slightly drunk. **4** (in *comb.*) *colloq.* inclined to use excessively (*trigger-happy*). □□ **hap•pi•ly** *adv.* **hap•pi•ness** *n.*

hap•py-go-luck•y *adj.* cheerfully casual.

hap•py hour *n.* a period of the day when drinks are sold at reduced prices.

hap•py me•di•um *n.* a compromise; the avoidance of extremes.

ha•ra-ki•ri /hárəkeéree, haáree–/ *n.* ritual suicide by disembowelment with a sword, formerly practiced by samurai when disgraced or sentenced to death.

ha•rangue /həráng/ *n.* & *v.* • *n.* a lengthy and earnest speech. • *v.tr.* lecture or make a harangue to. □□ **ha•rangu•er** *n.*

ha•rass /hərás, hárəs/ *v.tr.* **1** trouble and annoy continually or repeatedly. **2** make repeated attacks on (an enemy or opponent). □□ **ha•rass•er** *n.* **ha•rass•ing•ly** *adv.* **ha•rass•ment** *n.*

▶Traditionally, the preferred pronunciation stresses the first syllable, as "HAR-uhs," but the pronunciation that puts the stress on the second syllable is more widespread; this is also true for *harassment.*

har•bin•ger /haárbinjər/ *n.* & *v.* • *n.* **1** a person or thing that announces or signals the approach of another. **2** a forerunner. • *v.tr.* announce the approach of.

har•bor /haárbər/ *n.* & *v.* • *n.* **1** a place of shelter for ships. **2** a place of refuge or protection. • *v.* **1** *tr.* give shelter to (a criminal or wanted person). **2** *tr.* keep in one's mind, esp. resentfully (*harbor a grudge*). **3** *intr.* come to anchor in a harbor.

hard /haard/ *adj.* & *adv.* • *adj.* **1** (of a substance, material, etc.) firm and solid; unyielding to pressure; not easily cut. **2 a** difficult to understand or explain (*a hard problem*). **b** difficult to accomplish (*a hard decision*). **c** (foll. by *to* + infin.) not easy (*hard to believe*). **3** difficult to bear (*a hard life*). **4** unfeeling; severely critical. **5** (of a season or the weather) severe. **6** harsh or unpleasant to the senses (*a hard voice*). **7 a** strenuous; enthusiastic; intense (*a hard worker*). **b** severe; uncompromising (*a hard bargain*). **c** *Polit.* extreme; most radical (*the hard right*). **8 a** (of liquor) strongly alcoholic. **b** (of drugs) potent and addictive. **c** (of radiation) highly penetrating. **d** (of pornography) highly suggestive and explicit. **9** (of water) containing mineral salts that make lathering difficult. **10** established; not disputable (*hard data*). **11** *Stock Exch.* (of currency, prices, etc.) not likely to fall in value. **12** (of a consonant) guttural (as *c* in *cat*, *g* in *go*). **13** (of a shape, boundary, etc.) clearly defined; unambiguous. • *adv.* **1** strenuously; intensely (*try hard*). **2** with difficulty or effort (*hard-earned*). **3** so as to be hard or firm (*the jelly set hard*). □ **be hard on 1** be difficult for. **2** be severe in one's treatment of. **3** be unpleasant to (the senses). **be hard put** (usu. foll. by *to* + infin.) find it difficult. **hard by** near; close by. **a hard case 1** *colloq.* an intractable person. **2** a case of hardship. □□ **hard•ish** *adj.* **hard•ness** *n.*

hard and fast *adj.* (of a rule or a distinction made) definite; unalterable; strict.

hard•back /haárdbak/ *adj.* & *n.* • *adj.* (of a book) bound in stiff covers. • *n.* a hardback book.

hard•ball /haárdbawl/ *n.* **1** = BASEBALL. **2** *sl.* uncompromising methods or dealings, esp. in politics.

hard•bit•ten /haárdbítən/ *adj. colloq.* tough and cynical.

hard•board /haárdbawrd/ *n.* stiff board made of compressed and treated wood pulp.

hard-boiled *adj.* **1** (of an egg) boiled until the white and the yolk are solid. **2** (of a person) tough; shrewd.

hard cash *n.* negotiable coins and paper money.

hard cop•y *n.* printed material produced by computer, usu. on paper, suitable for ordinary reading.

hard core *n.* **1** an irreducible nucleus. **2** *colloq.* **a** the most active or committed members of a society, etc. **b** a conservative or reactionary minority.

hard-core *adj.* blatant; uncompromising, esp.: **1** (of pornography) explicit; obscene. **2** (of drug addiction) relating to hard drugs, esp. heroin.

hard•cov•er /hárdkəvər/ *adj.* & *n.* • *adj.* bound between rigid boards (*a hardcover edition*). • *n.* a hardcover book.

hard disk *n. Computing* a rigid nonremovable magnetic disk with a large data storage capacity.

hard drive *n. Computing* = HARD DISK.

hard•en /haárdən/ *v.* **1** *tr.* & *intr.* make or become hard. **2** *intr.* & *tr.* become, or make (one's attitude, etc.), less sympathetic. **3** *intr.* (of prices, etc.) cease to fall or fluctuate. □□ **hard•en•er** *n.*

hard•en•ing /haárdəning/ *n.* **1** the process of becoming hard. **2** (in full **hardening of the arteries**) *Med.* = ARTERIOSCLEROSIS.

hard hat *n.* **1** a protective helmet worn on building sites, etc. **2** *colloq.* a reactionary person.

hard•head•ed /haárdhédid/ *adj.* practical; realistic; not sentimental. □□ **hard•head•ed•ly** *adv.* **hard•head•ed•ness** *n.*

hard-heart·ed /haárdhaártid/ *adj.* unfeeling; unsympathetic. ▫▫ **hard-heart·ed·ly** *adv.* **hard-heart·ed·ness** *n.*
hard-hit·ting *adj.* aggressively critical.
har·di·hood /haárdeehood/ *n.* boldness; daring.
hard line *n.* unyielding adherence to a policy. ▫▫ **hard-liner** *n.* a person who adheres rigidly to a policy.
hard luck *n.* worse fortune than one deserves.
hard·ly /haárdlee/ *adv.* **1** scarcely (*we hardly knew them*). **2** only with difficulty (*could hardly speak*). **3** harshly.
hard-nosed *adj. colloq.* realistic; uncompromising.
hard nut *n. sl.* a tough, aggressive person. ▫ **a hard nut to crack** *colloq.* a difficult problem.
hard-pressed *adj.* **1** closely pursued. **2** burdened with urgent business.
hard sell *n.* aggressive salesmanship or advertising.
hard·ship /haárdship/ *n.* **1** severe suffering. **2** the circumstance causing this.
hard stuff *n. sl.* strong liquor, esp. whiskey.
hard·tack /haárdtak/ *n.* a hard biscuit, formerly given to sailors as rations.
hard up *adj.* **1** short of money. **2** (foll. by *for*) at a loss for; lacking.
hard·ware /haárdwair/ *n.* **1** tools and household articles. **2** heavy machinery or armaments. **3** the mechanical and electronic components of a computer, etc.
hard·wear·ing /haárdwáiring/ *adj.* able to stand much wear.
hard-wired *adj.* involving or achieved by permanently connected circuits designed to perform a specific function.
hard·wood /haárdwood/ *n.* the wood from a deciduous broad-leaved tree.
hard·work·ing /haárdwərking/ *adj.* diligent.
har·dy /haárdee/ *adj.* (**hardier, hardiest**) **1** capable of enduring difficult conditions. **2** (of a plant) able to grow in the open air all year round. ▫▫ **har·di·ness** *n.*
hare /hair/ *n.* **1** any of various mammals of the family Leporidae, like a large rabbit, with tawny fur, long ears, short tail and hind legs longer than forelegs. **2** (in full **electric hare**) a dummy hare propelled by electricity, used in greyhound racing.
hare·bell /háirbel/ *n.* **1** a plant with slender stems and pale blue bell-shaped flowers. **2** = BLUEBELL.
hare·brained /háirbraynd/ *adj.* rash; foolish; wild.
hare·lip /háirlíp/ *n.* a congenital fissure of the upper lip. ▫▫ **hare·lipped** *adj.*
har·em /háirəm, hár–/ *n.* **1** the women of a Muslim household. **2** their quarters.
har·i·cot /árikō/ *n.* **1** (in full **haricot vert** /ver/) a variety of French bean with small white seeds. **2** the dried seed of this used as a vegetable.
hark /haark/ *v.intr.* (usu. in *imper.*) *archaic* listen attentively. ▫ **hark back** revert to a topic discussed earlier.
hark·en var. of HEARKEN.
har·le·quin /haárlikwin/ *n.* & *adj.* •*n.* (**Harlequin**) a mute character in pantomime, usu. masked and dressed in a diamond-patterned costume. •*adj.* in varied colors.
har·lot /haárlət/ *n. archaic* a prostitute. ▫▫ **har·lot·ry** *n.*
harm /haarm/ *n.* & *v.* •*n.* hurt; damage. •*v.tr.* cause harm to. ▫ **out of harm's way** in safety.
harm·ful /haármfool/ *adj.* causing or likely to cause harm. ▫▫ **harm·ful·ly** *adv.* **harm·ful·ness** *n.*
harm·less /haármlis/ *adj.* **1** not likely to cause harm. **2** inoffensive. ▫▫ **harm·less·ly** *adv.* **harm·less·ness** *n.*
har·mon·ic /haarmónik/ *adj.* & *n.* •*adj.* **1** of or characterized by harmony. **2** *Mus.* **a** of or relating to harmony. **b** (of a tone) produced by vibration of a string, etc., in an exact fraction of its length. •*n. Mus.* an overtone accompanying at a fixed interval (and forming a note with) a fundamental. ▫▫ **har·mon·i·cal·ly** *adv.*
har·mon·i·ca /haarmónikə/ *n.* a small rectangular wind instrument held against the lips to produce different notes by blowing or sucking.
har·mo·ni·ous /haarmṓneeəs/ *adj.* **1** pleasant sounding; tuneful. **2** forming a pleasing or consistent whole. **3** free from disagreement. ▫▫ **har·mo·ni·ous·ly** *adv.* **har·mo·ni·ous·ness** *n.*
har·mo·ni·um /haarmṓneeəm/ *n.* a keyboard instrument in which the notes are produced by air driven through metal reeds by bellows operated by the feet.
har·mo·nize /haármənīz/ *v.* **1** *tr.* add notes to (a melody) to produce harmony. **2** *tr.* & *intr.* (often foll. by *with*) bring into or be in harmony. **3** *intr.* make or form a pleasing or consistent whole. ▫▫ **har·mo·ni·za·tion** *n.*
har·mo·ny /haármənee/ *n.* (*pl.* **-nies**) **1 a** a combination of simultaneously sounded musical notes to produce chords and chord progressions, esp. as having a pleasing effect. **b** the study of this. **2 a** an apt or aesthetic arrangement of parts. **b** the pleasing effect of this. **3** agreement; concord. ▫ **in harmony 1** (of singing, etc.) producing chords; not discordant. **2** (often foll. by *with*) in agreement.
har·ness /haárnis/ *n.* & *v.* •*n.* **1** the equipment of straps and fittings by which a horse is fastened to a cart, etc., and controlled. **2** a similar arrangement for fastening a thing to a person's body, for restraining a young child, etc. •*v.tr.* **1 a** put a harness on. **b** (foll. by *to*) attach by a harness. **2** make use of (natural resources) esp. to produce energy. ▫ **in harness** in the routine of daily work.
harp /haarp/ *n.* & *v.* •*n.* a musical instrument, roughly triangular in shape, consisting of a frame supporting a graduated series of parallel strings, played by plucking with the fingers. •*v.intr.* (foll. by *on*) talk repeatedly and tediously on a particular subject. ▫▫ **harp·ist** *n.*
har·poon /haarpoon/ *n.* & *v.* •*n.* a barbed spearlike missile with a rope attached, for killing whales, etc. •*v.tr.* spear with a harpoon. ▫▫ **har·poon·er** *n.*
har·poon gun *n.* a gun for firing a harpoon.
harp seal *n.* a Greenland seal, *Phoca groenlandica*, with a harp-shaped dark mark on its back.
harp·si·chord /haárpsikawrd/ *n.* a keyboard instrument with horizontal strings that are plucked mechanically. ▫▫ **harp·si·chord·ist** *n.*
har·py /haárpee/ *n.* (*pl.* **-pies**) **1** (in Greek and Roman mythology) a monster with a woman's head and body and bird's wings and claws. **2** a grasping unscrupulous person.
har·ri·dan /hárid'n/ *n.* a bad-tempered woman.
har·ri·er[1] /háreeər/ *n.* **1** a hound used for hunting hares. **2** a cross-country runner or group of runners.
har·ri·er[2] /háreeər/ *n.* any bird of prey of the genus *Circus*, with long wings for swooping over the ground.
har·row /hárō/ *n.* & *v.* •*n.* a heavy frame with iron teeth dragged over plowed land to break up clods, remove weeds, cover seed, etc. •*v.tr.* **1** draw a harrow over (land). **2** (usu. as **harrowing** *adj.*) upset or distress greatly. ▫▫ **har·row·er** *n.* **har·row·ing·ly** *adv.*
har·ry /háree/ *v.tr.* (**-ries, -ried**) **1** ravage or despoil. **2** harass; worry.
harsh /haarsh/ *adj.* **1** unpleasantly rough or sharp. **2** severe; cruel. ▫▫ **harsh·en** *v.tr.* & *intr.* **harsh·ly** *adv.* **harsh·ness** *n.*
hart /haart/ *n.* esp. *Brit.* the male of the deer.
har·te·beest /haártəbeest, haártbeest/ *n.* any large African antelope of the genus *Alcelaphus*, with ringed horns bent back at the tips.
harts·horn /haárts-hawrn/ *n. archaic* **1** an ammonious substance obtained from the horns of a hart. **2** (in full **spirit of hartshorn**) an aqueous solution of ammonia.

har·um-scar·um /háirəmskáirəm/ *adj. & n. colloq.* • *adj.* wild and reckless. • *n.* such a person.

har·vest /haárvist/ *n. & v.* • *n.* **1 a** the process of gathering in crops, etc. **b** the season when this takes place. **2** the season's yield. **3** the product of any action. • *v.tr.* **1** gather as a harvest. **2** experience (consequences). ▫▫ **har·vest·a·ble** *adj.*

har·vest·er /haárvistər/ *n.* **1** a reaper. **2** a reaping machine.

har·vest·man /haárvistmən/ *n.* (*pl.* **-men**) an arachnid of the family Opilionidae, with very long thin legs.

has *3rd sing. present* of HAVE.

has-been /házbin/ *n. colloq.* a person who has lost a former importance.

hash[1] /hash/ *n. & v.* • *n.* **1** a dish of cooked meat and potatoes cut into small pieces and recooked. **2 a** a mixture; a jumble. **b** a mess. • *v.tr.* (often foll. by *out*) settle by conferring or debating. ▫ **make a hash of** *colloq.* make a mess of; bungle.

hash[2] /hash/ *n. colloq.* hashish.

hash·ish /hásheesh, hashe̍esh/ *n.* a resinous product of the top leaves and tender parts of hemp, smoked or chewed for its narcotic effects.

Ha·sid /khaásid, kháw–, haá–/ *n.* (*pl.* **Hasidim** /–sídim, –se̍e–/) a member of any of several mystical Jewish sects, esp. one founded in the 18th c. ▫▫ **Ha·sid·ic** /–sídik/ *adj.*

hasn't /házənt/ *contr.* has not.

hasp /hasp/ *n. & v.* • *n.* a hinged metal clasp that fits over a staple and can be secured by a padlock. • *v.tr.* fasten with a hasp.

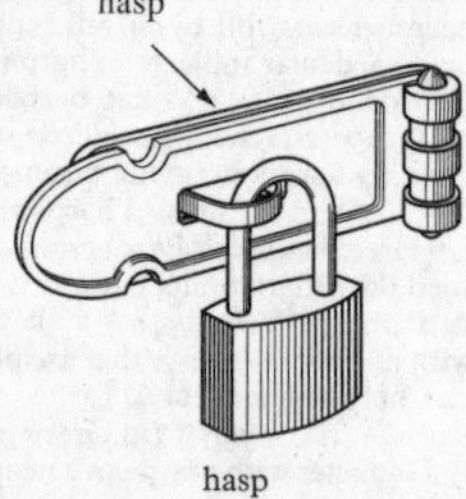

hasp

has·sle /hásəl/ *n. & v. colloq.* • *n.* **1** a prolonged trouble or inconvenience. **2** an argument or involved struggle. • *v.* **1** *tr.* harass; annoy. **2** *intr.* argue; quarrel.

has·sock /hásək/ *n.* a thick firm cushion for kneeling on, esp. in church.

haste /hayst/ *n. & v.* • *n.* **1** urgency of movement or action. **2** excessive hurry. • *v.intr. archaic* = HASTEN. ▫ **in haste** quickly; hurriedly. **make haste** hurry.

has·ten /háysən/ *v.* **1** *intr.* make haste; hurry. **2** *tr.* cause to occur sooner.

hast·y /háystee/ *adj.* (**hastier, hastiest**) **1** hurried; acting quickly. **2** said or done too quickly; rash. **3** quick-tempered. ▫▫ **hast·i·ly** *adv.* **hast·i·ness** *n.*

hat /hat/ *n.* **1** a covering for the head, often with a brim and worn out of doors. **2** *colloq.* a person's occupation or capacity, esp. one of several (*wearing his managerial hat*). ▫ **keep it under one's hat** *colloq.* keep it secret. **out of a hat** by random selection. **pass the hat** collect contributions of money. **take off one's hat to** (or **hats off to**) *colloq.* acknowledge admiration for. **throw one's hat in the ring** take up a challenge. ▫▫ **hat·ful** *n.* (*pl.* **-fuls**). **hat·less** *adj.*

hat·band /hátband/ *n.* a band of ribbon around a hat above the brim.

hat·box /hátboks/ *n.* a box to hold a hat.

hatch[1] /hach/ *n.* **1** an opening between two rooms, e.g., between a kitchen and a dining room for serving food. **2** an opening in an aircraft, spacecraft, etc. **3** *Naut.* **a** = HATCHWAY. **b** a trapdoor for this.

hatch[2] /hach/ *v. & n.* • *v.* **1** *intr.* **a** (often foll. by *out*) (of a young bird or fish, etc.) emerge from the egg. **b** (of an egg) produce a young animal. **2** *tr.* incubate (an egg). **3** *tr.* (also foll. by *up*) devise (a plot, etc.). • *n.* **1** the act or an instance of hatching. **2** a brood hatched.

hatch[3] /hach/ *v.tr.* mark (a surface) with close parallel lines.

hatch·back /háchbak/ *n.* a car with a sloping back hinged at the top to form a door.

hatch·er·y /háchəree/ *n.* (*pl.* **-ies**) a place for hatching eggs, esp. of fish or poultry.

hatch·et /háchit/ *n.* a light short-handled ax.

hatch·et job *n. colloq.* a fierce destructive critique of a person, esp. in print.

hatch·et man *n. colloq.* **1** a hired killer. **2** a person employed to harm or dismiss another.

hatch·ing /háching/ *n. Art & Archit.* close parallel lines forming shading.

hatch·way /háchway/ *n.* an opening in a ship's deck for lowering cargo into the hold.

hate /hayt/ *v. & n.* • *v.tr.* **1** dislike intensely. **2** *colloq.* **a** dislike. **b** (foll. by verbal noun or *to* + infin.) be reluctant (to do something). • *n.* **1** hatred. **2** *colloq.* a hated person or thing. ▫▫ **hate·a·ble** *adj.* (also **hat·a·ble**).

hate·ful /háytfool/ *adj.* arousing hatred. ▫▫ **hate·ful·ly** *adv.* **hate·ful·ness** *n.*

hat·pin /hátpin/ *n.* a long pin, often decorative, for securing a hat to the head.

ha·tred /háytrid/ *n.* intense dislike or ill will.

hat·stand /hátstand/ *n.* a stand with hooks on which to hang hats.

hat·ter /hátər/ *n.* a maker or seller of hats.

hat trick *n. Sports* the scoring of three goals, etc., in a single game, match, etc., by one player.

haugh·ty /háwtee/ *adj.* (**haughtier, haughtiest**) arrogantly self-admiring. ▫▫ **haugh·ti·ly** *adv.* **haugh·ti·ness** *n.*

haul /hawl/ *v. & n.* • *v.* **1** *tr.* pull forcibly. **2** *tr.* transport by truck, cart, etc. **3** *intr.* turn a ship's course. **4** *tr. colloq.* (usu. foll. by *up*) bring for reprimand. • *n.* **1** the act of hauling. **2** an amount acquired. **3** a distance to be traversed (*a short haul*). ▫▫ **haul·er** /háwlər/ *n.*

haul·age /háwlij/ *n.* **1** the commercial transport of goods. **2** a charge for this.

haulm /hawm/ *n.* (also **halm**) **1** a stalk or stem. **2** the stalks or stems collectively of peas, beans, potatoes, etc., without the pods, etc.

haunch /hawnch/ *n.* **1** the fleshy part of the buttock with the thigh, esp. in animals. **2** the leg and loin of a deer, etc., as food.

haunt /hawnt/ *v. & n.* • *v.tr.* **1** (of a ghost) visit (a place) regularly. **2** frequent (a place). **3** (of a memory, etc.) be persistently in the mind of. • *n.* **1** (often in *pl.*) a place frequented by a person. **2** a place frequented by animals, esp. for food and drink. ▫▫ **haunt·er** *n.*

haunt·ing /háwnting/ *adj.* (of a melody, etc.) wistful; evocative. ▫▫ **haunt·ing·ly** *adv.*

Hau·sa /hówzə/ *n. & adj.* • *n.* (*pl.* same or **Hausas**) **1 a** a people of W. Africa and the Sudan. **b** a member of this people. **2** the Hamitic language of this people, widely used in W. Africa. • *adj.* of or relating to this people or language.

haute cou·ture /ốt kootóor/ *n.* high fashion.

haute cui·sine /ốt kwize̍en/ *n.* cooking of a high standard.

hau·teur /hōtőr/ *n.* haughtiness of manner.

have /hav/ *v. & n.* • *v.* (*3rd sing. present* **has** /haz/; *past* and *past part.* **had** /had/) • *v.tr.* **1** hold in possession as one's property or at one's disposal (*has a car*). **2** hold in a certain relationship (*has a sister*). **3** contain as a part or quality (*house has two floors*). **4 a** undergo; experience; (*has a headache*). **b** be subjected to a specified state (*had my car stolen*). **c** cause or invite (a person or thing) to be in a particular state or take a particular action (*had him dismissed; had my hair cut*). **5 a** engage in (an activity) (*had an argument*). **b** hold (a meeting, party, etc.). **6** eat or drink (*had a beer*). **7** (usu. in *neg.*) accept or tolerate (*I won't have it*). **8 a** let (a feeling, etc.) be present (*have nothing against them*). **b** show or feel (mercy, pity, etc.) toward another person (*have pity on him*). **c** (foll. by *to* + infin.) show by action that one is influenced by (a feeling etc.) (*have the goodness to leave now*). **9 a** give birth to (offspring). **b** conceive mentally (an idea, etc.). **10** receive; obtain (*had a letter from him*). **11** be burdened with or committed to (*has a job to do*). **12 a** have obtained (a qualification) (*has several degrees*). **b** know (a language) (*has no Latin*). **13** *sl.* **a** get the better of (*I had him there*). **b** (usu. in *passive*) cheat (*you were had*). **14** *coarse sl.* have sexual intercourse with. • *v.aux.* (with *past part.* or *ellipt.*, to form the perfect, pluperfect, and future perfect tenses, and the conditional mood) (*have worked; had seen; will have been*). • *n.* (usu. in *pl.*) *colloq.* a person who has wealth or resources. □ **had better** would find it prudent to. **have got to** *colloq.* = *have to*. **have had it** *colloq.* **1** have missed one's chance. **2** (of a person) have passed one's prime; (of a thing) be worn out or broken. **3** have been killed, defeated, etc. **4** have suffered or endured enough. **have it 1** (foll. by *that* + clause) express the view that. **2** win a decision in a vote, etc. **3** have found the answer, etc. **have it in for** *colloq.* be hostile toward. **have it out** (often foll. by *with*) *colloq.* attempt to settle a dispute by discussion or argument. **have on 1** be wearing (clothes). **2** be committed to (an engagement). **have out** get (a tooth, etc.) extracted (*had her tonsils out*). **have to** be obliged to; must.

ha•ven /háyvən/ *n.* **1** a harbor or port. **2** a place of refuge.

have-not *n.* (usu. in *pl.*) *colloq.* a person lacking wealth or resources.

haven't /hávənt/ *contr.* have not.

hav•er•sack /hávərsak/ *n.* a stout bag carried on the back or over the shoulder.

hav•oc /hávək/ *n.* great confusion or disorder. □ **play havoc with** *colloq.* cause great confusion or difficulty to.

Ha•wai•ian /həwíən/ *n.* & *adj.* • *n.* **1 a** a native of Hawaii, an island or island group (comprising a US state) in the N. Pacific. **b** a person of Hawaiian descent. **2** the language of Hawaii. • *adj.* of or relating to Hawaii or its people or language.

haw•finch /háwfinch/ *n.* a large Old World finch of the genus *Coccothraustes*, with a thick beak for cracking seeds.

hawk[1] /hawk/ *n.* & *v.* • *n.* **1** any of various diurnal birds of prey of the family Accipitridae, having a characteristic curved beak and a long tail. **2** *Polit.* a person who advocates a warlike policy, esp. in foreign affairs. • *v. intr.* hunt game with a hawk. □□ **hawk•ish** *adj.* **hawk•ish•ness** *n.* **hawk•like** *adj.*

hawk[2] /hawk/ *v.tr.* carry around and offer goods for sale (*street vendors were hawking souvenirs*).

hawk[3] /hawk/ *v.* **1** *intr.* clear the throat noisily. **2** *tr.* (foll. by *up*) bring (phlegm, etc.) up from the throat.

hawk•er /háwkər/ *n.* a person who travels about selling goods.

hawk-eyed *adj.* keen-sighted.

hawk moth *n.* any moth of the family Sphingidae, having narrow forewings and a stout body.

hawks•bill /háwksbil/ *n.* (in full **hawksbill turtle**) a small turtle, *Eretmochelys imbricata*, yielding tortoiseshell.

hawk•weed /háwkweed/ *n.* any composite plant of the genus *Hieracium*, with yellow flowers.

haw•ser /háwzər/ *n. Naut.* a thick rope or cable for mooring a ship.

haw•thorn /háwthawrn/ *n.* a thorny shrub or tree with small dark red fruit.

hay /hay/ *n.* grass cut and dried for fodder. □ **make hay (while the sun shines)** seize opportunities for profit or enjoyment.

hay fe•ver *n.* a common allergy with respiratory symptoms, caused by pollen or dust.

hay•mak•er /háymaykər/ *n.* **1** a person who tosses and spreads hay to dry after mowing. **2** an apparatus for shaking and drying hay. **3** *sl.* a forceful punch. □□ **hay•mak•ing** *n.*

hay•rick /háyrik/ *n.* = HAYSTACK.

hay•seed /háyseed/ *n.* **1** grass seed obtained from hay. **2** *colloq.* a yokel.

hay•stack /háystak/ *n.* a packed pile of hay.

hay•wire /háywīr/ *adj. colloq.* **1** out of control. **2** (of a person) erratic.

haz•ard /házərd/ *n.* & *v.* • *n.* **1** a danger or risk. **2** a source of this. **3** chance. **4** *Golf* an obstruction in playing a shot, e.g., a bunker, water, etc. • *v.tr.* **1** venture (*hazard a guess*). **2** run the risk of. **3** expose to hazard.

haz•ard•ous /házərdəs/ *adj.* risky; dangerous. □□ **haz•ard•ous•ly** *adv.*

haze /hayz/ *n.* **1** obscuration of the atmosphere near the earth by fine particles of water, smoke, or dust. **2** mental obscurity or confusion.

ha•zel /háyzəl/ *n.* **1** a shrub or small tree bearing round brown edible nuts. **2** wood from the hazel. **3** a greenish brown color (esp. of the eyes).

ha•zel•nut /háyzəlnut/ *n.* the fruit of the hazel.

ha•zy /háyzee/ *adj.* (**hazier, haziest**) **1** misty. **2** vague; indistinct. **3** confused; uncertain. □□ **ha•zi•ly** *adv.* **ha•zi•ness** *n.*

Hb *symb.* hemoglobin.

H-bomb /áychbom/ *n.* = HYDROGEN BOMB.

HDTV *abbr.* high-definition television.

He *symb. Chem.* the element helium.

he /hee/ *pron.* & *n.* • *pron.* (*obj.* **him** /him/; *poss.* **his** /hiz/; *pl.* **they** /thay/) **1** the man or boy or male animal previously named or in question. **2** a person, etc., of unspecified sex (*if anyone comes he will have to wait*). • *n.* **1** a male; a man. **2** (in *comb.*) male (*he-goat*).
▶See note at EVERYBODY.

head /hed/ *n.*, *adj.*, & *v.* • *n.* **1** the upper part of the human body, or the foremost or upper part of an animal's body, containing the brain, mouth, and sense organs. **2 a** the head regarded as the seat of intellect. **b** intelligence (*use your head*). **c** mental aptitude (usu. foll. by *for*: *a good head for business*). **3** *colloq.* a headache. **4** a thing like a head in form or position, esp.: **a** the operative part of a tool. **b** the flattened top of a nail. **c** the ornamented top of a pillar. **d** a mass of flowers at the top of a stem. **e** the flat end of a drum. **f** the foam on top of a glass of beer. **g** the upper horizontal part of a window frame, etc. **5** life when regarded as vulnerable (*it cost him his head*). **6 a** a person in charge. **b** a position of leadership. **7** the forward part of something. **8** the upper end of something, e.g., a bed. **9** the top or highest part of something, e.g., a page. **10** a person regarded as a numerical unit (*$10 a head*). **11** (*pl.* same) **a** an individual animal as a unit. **b** (as *pl.*) a number of cattle (*20 head*). **12 a** the side of a coin bearing the image of a head. **b** (usu. in *pl.*) this side as a choice when tossing a coin. **13 a** the source of a river or stream. **b** the end of a lake at which a river enters it.

14 the height or length of a head as a measure. **15** the component of a machine that is in contact with or very close to what is being worked on, esp.: **a** the component on a tape recorder that touches the moving tape in play and converts the signals. **b** the part of a phonograph that holds the playing cartridge and stylus. **c** = PRINTHEAD. **16 a** a confined body of water or steam in an engine, etc. **b** the pressure exerted by this. **17** a promontory (esp. in place-names) (*Nags Head*). **18** *Naut.* **a** the bow of a ship. **b** a ship's latrine. **19** a main topic for consideration. **20** *Journalism* = HEADLINE *n.* **21** a culmination or crisis. **22** the fully developed top of a boil, etc. **23** *sl.* a habitual taker of drugs. • *attrib.adj.* chief or principal(*head gardener*; *head office*). • *v.* **1** *tr.* be at the head or front of. **2** *tr.* be in charge of (*headed a small team*). **3** *tr.* **a** provide with a head or heading. **b** (of an inscription, etc.) serve as a heading for. **4 a** *intr.* face or move in a specified direction (often foll. by *for*: *heading for trouble*). **b** *tr.* direct in a specified direction. **5** *tr.* *Soccer* strike (the ball) with the head. □ **come to a head** reach a crisis. **go out of one's head** go mad. **go to one's head 1** (of liquor) make one slightly drunk. **2** (of success) make one conceited. **head and shoulders** *colloq.* by a considerable amount. **head in the sand** refusal to acknowledge an obvious danger or difficulty. **head off 1** get ahead of so as to intercept and turn aside. **2** forestall. **head over heels 1** turning over completely in forward motion as in a somersault, etc. **2** utterly; completely (*head over heels in love*). **hold up one's head** be confident or unashamed. **in one's head 1** in one's imagination. **2** by mental process. **keep one's head** remain calm. **keep one's head down** *colloq.* remain inconspicuous in dangerous times. **lose one's head** lose self-control. **make head or tail of** (usu. with *neg.* or *interrog.*) understand at all. **off the top of one's head** *colloq.* impromptu. **out of one's head** *sl.* crazy. **over one's head 1** beyond one's ability to understand. **2** without one's knowledge or involvement. **3** with disregard for one's own (stronger) claim (*was promoted over their heads*). **put heads together** consult together. **put into a person's head** suggest to a person. □□ **head•ed** *adj.* (also in *comb.*). **head•less** *adj.*

head•ache /hédayk/ *n.* **1** a continuous pain in the head. **2** *colloq.* **a** a worrying problem. **b** a troublesome person. □□ **head•ach•y** *adj.*

head•band /hédband/ *n.* a band worn around the head as decoration or to keep the hair off the face.

head•board /hédbawrd/ *n.* an upright panel forming the head of a bed.

head•count /hédkownt/ *n.* **1** a counting of individual people. **2** a total number of people, esp. the number of people employed in a particular organization.

head•dress /héd-dres/ *n.* an ornamental covering or band for the head.

head•er /hédər/ *n.* **1** *Soccer* a shot made with the head. **2** *colloq.* a headlong fall. **3** line or lines of information printed at the top of the page throughout a document.

head•gear /hédgeer/ *n.* a hat, headdress, or head covering.

head-hunt•ing /hédhunting/ *n.* **1** the practice among some peoples of collecting the heads of dead enemies as trophies. **2** the practice of filling a (usu. senior) business position by approaching a suitable person employed elsewhere. □□ **head•hunt** *v.tr.* (also *absol.*). **head•hunt•er** *n.*

head•ing /héding/ *n.* **1 a** a title at the head of a page. **b** a division of a subject of discourse, etc. **2** a course of an aircraft, ship, etc.

head•lamp /hédlamp/ *n.* = HEADLIGHT.

head•land /hédlənd/ *n.* a promontory.

head•light /hédlīt/ *n.* **1** a strong light at the front of a motor vehicle or train engine. **2** the beam from this.

head•line /hédlīn/ *n.* & *v.* • *n.* **1** a heading at the top of an article or page, esp. in a newspaper. **2** (in *pl.*) the most important items of news in a newspaper or broadcast news bulletin. • *v.tr.* give a headline to.

head•lin•er /hédlīnər/ *n.* a star performer.

head•lock /hédlok/ *n.* *Wrestling* a hold with an arm around the opponent's head.

head•long /hédlawng, –lóng/ *adv.* & *adj.* **1** with head foremost. **2** in a rush.

head•mas•ter /hédmástər/ *n.* (*fem.* **headmistress** /–místris/) the person in charge of a school.

head-on *adj.* **1** with the front foremost (*a head-on crash*). **2** in direct confrontation.

head•phone /hédfōn/ *n.* (usu. in *pl.*) a pair of earphones joined by a band placed over the head, for listening to audio equipment, etc.

head•quar•ters /hédkwáwrtərz/ *n.* (as *sing.* or *pl.*) the administrative center of an organization.

head•rest /hédrest/ *n.* a support for the head, esp. on a seat or chair.

head•room /hédrōōm, –rōōm/ *n.* **1** the space or clearance between the top of a vehicle and the underside of a bridge, etc. **2** the space above a driver's or passenger's head in a vehicle.

head•scarf /hédskaarf/ *n.* a scarf worn around the head and tied under the chin, instead of a hat.

head•set /hédset/ *n.* a set of headphones, often with a microphone attached.

head•ship /hédship/ *n.* the position of chief or leader.

head shrink•er *n.* *sl.* a psychiatrist.

head•stall /hédstawl/ *n.* the part of a halter that fits around a horse's head.

head start *n.* an advantage granted or gained at an early stage.

head•stone /hédstōn/ *n.* a (usu. inscribed) stone set up at the head of a grave.

head•strong /hédstrawng, –strong/ *adj.* self-willed and obstinate.

head•wa•ter /hédwawtər, –wotər/ *n.* (in *sing.* or *pl.*) streams flowing at the sources of a river.

head•way /hédway/ *n.* **1** progress. **2** the rate of progress of a ship. **3** = HEADROOM 1.

head wind *n.* a wind blowing from directly in front.

head•word /hédwərd/ *n.* a word forming a heading.

head•y /hédee/ *adj.* (**headier, headiest**) **1** (of alcohol) potent; intoxicating. **2** (of success, etc.) likely to cause conceit. □□ **head•i•ly** *adv.* **head•i•ness** *n.*

heal /heel/ *v.* **1** *intr.* (often foll. by *up*) (of a wound or injury) become sound or healthy again. **2** *tr.* cause (a wound, disease, or person) to heal or be healed. **3** *tr.* put right (differences, etc.). □□ **heal•a•ble** *adj.* **heal•er** *n.*

health /helth/ *n.* **1** the state of being well in body or mind. **2** a person's mental or physical condition. **3** soundness (*the health of the nation*).

health food *n.* food thought to have health-giving qualities.

health•ful /hélthfōōl/ *adj.* conducive to good health.

health main•te•nance or•ga•ni•za•tion *n.* an organization that provides medical care to subscribers who have paid in advance, usu. through a health insurance plan.

health spa *n.* a resort, club, gym, etc., providing facilities for exercise and conditioning.

health•y /hélthee/ *adj.* (**healthier, healthiest**) **1** having or promoting good health. **2** beneficial; helpful. **3** of a satisfactory size or amount (*made a healthy profit*). □□ **health•i•ly** *adv.* **health•i•ness** *n.*

heap /heep/ *n.* & *v.* • *n.* **1** a collection of things lying haphazardly one on another. **2** (in *pl.*) *colloq.* a large number or amount (*heaps of time*). **3** *sl.* an old or dilapidated thing, esp. a motor vehicle. •*v.* **1** *tr. & intr.* collect or be collected in a heap. **2** *tr.* (foll. by *with*) load copiously. **3** *tr.* (foll. by *on, upon*) accord or offer copiously to. **4** *tr.* (as **heaping** *adj.*) (of a spoonful, etc.) with the contents piled above the brim.

hear /heer/ *v.* (*past* and *past part.* **heard** /herd/) **1** *tr.* (also *absol.*) perceive (sound, etc.) with the ear. **2** *tr.* listen to (*heard them on the radio*). **3** *tr.* listen judicially to and judge. **4** *intr.* (foll. by *about, of,* or *that* + clause) be told or informed. **5** *intr.* (foll. by *from*) be contacted by. **6** *tr.* be ready to obey (an order). **7** *tr.* grant (a prayer). □ **hear! hear!** *int.* expressing agreement (esp. with something said in a speech). **hear a person out** listen to all that a person says. **hear say** (or **tell**) (usu. foll. by *of,* or *that* + clause) be informed. □□ **hear·er** *n.*

hear·ing /heéring/ *n.* **1** the faculty of perceiving sounds. **2** earshot (*within hearing*). **3** an opportunity to state one's case (*give them a fair hearing*). **4** the listening to evidence in a court of law.

hear·ing aid *n.* a small device to amplify sound, worn by a partially deaf person.

heark·en /haárkən/ *v.intr.* (also **hark·en**) *archaic* or *literary* (foll. by *to*) listen.

hear·say /heérsay/ *n.* **1** rumor; gossip. **2** *Law* the report of another person's words by a witness, usu. disallowed as evidence in a court.

hearse /hərs/ *n.* a vehicle for conveying the coffin at a funeral.

heart /haart/ *n.* **1** a hollow muscular organ maintaining the circulation of blood by rhythmic contraction and dilation. **2** the breast. **3 a** the heart regarded as the center of thought and emotion. **b** a person's capacity for feeling emotion (*has no heart*). **4 a** courage (*take heart*). **b** one's mood (*change of heart*). **5 a** the central or innermost part of something. **b** the vital part (*the heart of the matter*). **6** the close compact head of cabbage, etc. **7 a** a heart-shaped thing. **b** a conventional representation of a heart. **8 a** a playing card of a suit denoted by a red figure of a heart. **b** (in *pl.*) this suit. □ **at heart 1** in one's inmost feelings. **2** basically; essentially. **break a person's heart** overwhelm a person with sorrow. **by heart** in or from memory. **close to** (or **near**) **one's heart 1** dear to one. **2** affecting one deeply. **from the heart** (or **the bottom of one's heart**) sincerely; profoundly. **heart to heart** *adj.* candidly; intimately. **in one's heart of hearts** in one's inmost feelings. **take to heart** be much affected or distressed by. **to one's heart's content** see CONTENT[1]. **with all one's heart** sincerely; with all goodwill. □□ **-heart·ed** *adj.*

heart·ache /haártayk/ *n.* mental anguish or grief.

heart at·tack *n.* a sudden occurrence of coronary thrombosis usu. resulting in the death of part of a heart muscle.

heart·beat /haártbeet/ *n.* a pulsation of the heart.

heart·break /haártbrayk/ *n.* overwhelming distress. □□ **heart·break·ing** *adj.* **heart·bro·ken** *adj.*

heart·break·er /haártbraykər/ *n.* **1** a person who is very attractive but irresponsible in emotional relationships. **2** a story or event that causes overwhelming distress.

heart·burn /haártbərn/ *n.* a burning sensation in the chest resulting from indigestion.

heart·en /haárt'n/ *v.tr. & intr.* make or become cheerful. □□ **heart·en·ing·ly** *adv.*

heart·felt /haártfélt/ *adj.* sincere; deeply felt.

hearth /haarth/ *n.* **1 a** the floor of a fireplace. **b** the area in front of a fireplace. **2** this symbolizing the home.

hearth·rug /haárthrug/ *n.* a rug laid before a fireplace.

heart·i·ly /haártilee/ *adv.* **1** in a hearty manner; with goodwill or courage. **2** to a great degree.

heart·land /haártland/ *n.* the central or most important part of a country or large area.

heart·less /haártlis/ *adj.* unfeeling; pitiless. □□ **heart·less·ly** *adv.* **heart·less·ness** *n.*

heart of gold *n.* a generous nature.

heart-rend·ing *adj.* very distressing. □□ **heart-rend·ing·ly** *adv.*

heart·sick /haártsik/ *adj.* very despondent. □□ **heart·sick·ness** *n.*

heart·strings /haártstringz/ *n.pl.* one's deepest feelings or emotions.

heart·throb /haárt-throb/ *n.* **1** beating of the heart. **2** *colloq.* a person for whom one has (esp. immature) romantic feelings.

heart-to-heart *adj. & n.* •*adj.* (of a conversation, etc.) candid; intimate. •*n.* a candid or personal conversation.

heart·warm·ing /haártwawrming/ *adj.* emotionally rewarding or uplifting.

heart·wood /haártwŏŏd/ *n.* the dense inner part of a tree trunk, yielding the hardest timber.

heart·y /haártee/ *adj.* (**heartier, heartiest**) **1** strong; vigorous. **2** spirited. **3** (of a meal or appetite) large. **4** warm; friendly. □□ **heart·i·ness** *n.*

heat /heet/ *n. & v.* •*n.* **1 a** the condition of being hot. **b** the sensation or perception of this. **c** high temperature of the body. **2** *Physics* **a** a form of energy arising from the random motion of the molecules of bodies, which may be transferred by conduction, convection, or radiation. **b** the amount of this needed to cause a specific process, or evolved in a process (*heat of formation*). **3** hot weather. **4 a** warmth of feeling. **b** anger or excitement. **5** (foll. by *of*) the most intense period of an activity (*in the heat of the battle*). **6** a (usu. preliminary or trial) round in a race or contest. **7** the receptive period of the sexual cycle, esp. in female mammals. **8** pungency of flavor. •*v.* **1** *tr. & intr.* make or become hot or warm. **2** *tr.* inflame; excite or intensify.

heat·ed /heétid/ *adj.* **1** angry; inflamed with passion or excitement. **2** made hot. □□ **heat·ed·ly** *adv.*

heat·er /heétər/ *n.* **1** a device for supplying heat to its environment. **2** a container with an element, etc., for heating the contents (*water heater*). **3** *sl.* a gun.

heat ex·haus·tion *n.* (also **heat prostration**) a condition caused by prolonged exposure to exercise in heat and characterized by faintness and nausea.

heath /heeth/ *n.* **1** an area of flattish uncultivated land with low shrubs. **2** a plant growing on a heath, esp. of the genus *Erica* or *Calluna*. □□ **heath·y** *adj.*

heath·en /heéthən/ *n. & adj.* •*n.* **1** a person who does not belong to a widely-held religion as regarded by those that do. **2** an unenlightened person; a person regarded as lacking culture or moral principles. **3** *Bibl.* a Gentile. •*adj.* **1** of or relating to heathens. **2** having no religion. □□ **heath·en·dom** *n.* **heath·en·ism** *n.*

heath·er /héthər/ *n.* **1** an evergreen shrub with purple bell-shaped flowers. **2** any of various shrubs growing esp. on moors and heaths. □□ **heath·er·y** *adj.*

heat·ing /heéting/ *n.* **1** the imparting or generation of heat. **2** equipment or devices used to provide heat, esp. to a building.

heat light·ning *n.* lightning seen as vivid flashes near the horizon, usu. without the sound of thunder.

heat-seek·ing *adj.* (of a missile, etc.) able to detect infrared radiation to guide it to its target.

heat·stroke /heétstrōk/ *n.* a feverish condition caused by excessive exposure to high temperature.

heat·wave /heétwayv/ *n.* a prolonged period of abnormally hot weather.

heave /heev/ *v. & n.* •*v.* (*past* and *past part.* **heaved** or esp. *Naut.* **hove** /hōv/) **1** *tr.* lift or haul with great effort. **2** *tr.* utter with effort or resignation. **3** *tr. colloq.*

throw. **4** *intr.* rise and fall rhythmically or spasmodically. **5** *intr.* retch. •*n.* an instance of heaving. □ **heave in sight** *Naut.* or *colloq.* come into view. **heave to** esp. *Naut.* bring or be brought to a standstill. □□ **heav·er** *n.*

heave-ho *int. & n.* •*int.* a sailors' cry, esp. on raising the anchor. •*n. sl.* (usu. prec. by *the* or *the old*) a dismissal or rejection.

heav·en /hévən/ *n.* **1** a place regarded in some religions as the abode of God and the angels, and of the good after death, often characterized as above the sky. **2** a place or state of supreme bliss. **3** *colloq.* something delightful. **4** (usu. **Heaven**) **a** God; Providence. **b** (in *sing.* or *pl.*) an exclamation or mild oath (*by Heaven!*). **5** (**the heavens**) esp. *poet.* the sky. □□ **heav·en·ward** *adj. & adv.* **heav·en·wards** *adv.*

heav·en·ly /hévənlee/ *adj.* **1** of heaven; divine. **2** of the heavens or sky. **3** *colloq.* very pleasing.

heav·en·ly bod·ies *n.pl.* the sun, stars, planets, etc.

heav·en-sent *adj.* providential; wonderfully opportune.

heav·y /hévee/ *adj., n., & adv.* •*adj.* (**heavier, heaviest**) **1 a** of great weight; difficult to lift. **b** (of a person) fat; overweight. **2** of great density. **3** abundant (*a heavy crop*). **4** severe; intense; extensive; excessive (*heavy fighting; a heavy sleep*). **5** doing something to excess (*a heavy drinker*). **6 a** striking or falling with force (*heavy blows; heavy rain*). **b** (of the sea) having large powerful waves. **7** (of machinery, artillery, etc.) very large of its kind; large in caliber, etc. (*heavy cruiser*). **8** causing a strong impact (*a heavy fall*). **9** needing much physical effort (*heavy work*). **10** (foll. by *with*) laden. **11** carrying heavy weapons (*the heavy brigade*). **12 a** (of a writing, music, etc.) serious or somber in tone or attitude. **b** (of an issue, etc.) grave; important. **13 a** (of food) hard to digest. **b** (of a literary work, etc.) hard to understand. **14** (of temperament) dignified; stern. **15** (of bread, etc.) too dense from not having risen. **16** (of ground) difficult to traverse or work. **17** hard to endure (*heavy demands*). **18 a** coarse; ungraceful (*heavy features*). **b** unwieldy. •*n.* (*pl.* **-ies**) **1** *colloq.* a large violent person. **2** a villainous or tragic role in a play, etc. •*adv.* heavily (esp. in *comb.*: *heavy-laden*). □□ **heav·i·ly** *adv.* **heav·i·ness** *n.* **heav·y·ish** *adj.*

heav·y-du·ty *adj.* **1** intended to withstand hard use. **2** serious; grave.

heav·y-foot·ed *adj.* awkward; ponderous.

heav·y go·ing *n.* slow or difficult progress.

heav·y-hand·ed /hévihándid/ *adj.* **1** clumsy. **2** overbearing; oppressive. □□ **heav·y-hand·ed·ly** *adv.* **heav·y-hand·ed·ness** *n.*

heav·y-heart·ed *adj.* sad; doleful.

heav·y in·dus·try *n.* industry producing metal, machinery, etc.

heav·y met·al *n.* **1** heavy guns. **2** metal of high density. **3** *colloq.* (often *attrib.*) a type of highly-amplified rock music with a strong beat.

heav·y wa·ter *n.* a substance composed entirely or mainly of deuterium oxide.

heav·y·weight /héveewayt/ *n.* **1 a** a weight in certain sports, variously defined for professional and amateur boxers, wrestlers, and weightlifters. **b** a sports participant of this weight. **2** a person, animal, or thing of above average weight. **3** *colloq.* a person of influence or importance.

He·brew /hēebrōō/ *n. & adj.* •*n.* **1** a member of a Semitic people historically centered in ancient Palestine. **2 a** the language of this people. **b** a modern form of this, used esp. in Israel. •*adj.* **1** of or in Hebrew. **2** of the Hebrews or the Jews.

heck /hek/ *int. colloq.* a mild exclamation of surprise or dismay.

heck·le /hékəl/ *v.tr.* **1** interrupt and harass (a public speaker). **2** dress (flax or hemp). □□ **heck·ler** *n.*

hec·tare /héktair/ *n.* a metric unit of square measure, equal to 100 ares (2.471 acres or 10,000 square meters). □□ **hec·tar·age** /–tərij/ *n.*

hec·tic /héktik/ *adj.* **1** busy and confused; excited. **2** having a fever; flushed. □□ **hec·ti·cal·ly** *adv.*

hecto- /héktə/ *comb. form* a hundred, esp. of a unit in the metric system. ¶ Abbr.: **ha.**

hec·to·gram /héktəgram/ *n.* a metric unit of mass, equal to one hundred grams.

hec·to·li·ter /héktəleetər/ *n.* a metric unit of capacity, equal to one hundred liters.

hec·to·me·ter /héktəmeetər, hektómitər/ *n.* a metric unit of length, equal to one hundred meters.

hec·tor /héktər/ *v.tr.* bully; intimidate.

he'd /heed/ *contr.* **1** he had. **2** he would.

hedge /hej/ *n. & v.* •*n.* **1** a fence or boundary formed by closely growing bushes or shrubs. **2** a protection against possible loss. •*v.* **1** *tr.* surround or bound with a hedge. **2** *tr.* (foll. by *in*) enclose. **3 a** *tr.* reduce one's risk of loss on (a bet or speculation) by compensating transactions on the other side. **b** *intr.* avoid a definite decision or commitment. **4** *intr.* make hedges. □□ **hedg·er** *n.*

hedge·hog /héjhawg, –hog/ *n.* a small nocturnal mammal having a piglike snout and a coat of spines, and rolling itself up into a ball for defense.

hedge·hop /héjhop/ *v.intr.* fly at a very low altitude.

hedge·row /héjrō/ *n.* a row of bushes forming a hedge.

he·don·ism /hēed'nizəm/ *n.* **1** belief in pleasure as the highest good and the proper aim of humans. **2** behavior based on this. □□ **he·don·ist** *n.* **he·don·is·tic** *adj.*

-hedron /hēedrən, hédrən/ *comb. form* (*pl.* **-hedra**) forming nouns denoting geometrical solids with various numbers or shapes of faces (*rhombohedron*). □□ **-hedral** *comb. form* forming adjectives.

hee·bie-jee·bies /hēebeejēebeez/ *n.pl.* (prec. by *the*) *sl.* a state of nervous depression or anxiety.

heed /heed/ *v. & n.* •*v.tr.* attend to; take notice of. •*n.* careful attention. □□ **heed·ful** *adj.* **heed·ful·ness** *n.* **heed·less** *adj.* **heed·less·ly** *adv.* **heed·less·ness** *n.*

hee-haw /hēehaw/ *n. & v.* •*n.* the bray of a donkey. •*v.intr.* emit a braying sound.

heel[1] /heel/ *n. & v.* •*n.* **1** the back part of the foot below the ankle. **2** the corresponding part in vertebrate animals. **3 a** the part of a sock, etc., covering the heel. **b** the part of a shoe or boot supporting the heel. **4** a thing like a heel in form or position. **5** *colloq.* an inconsiderate or untrustworthy person. •*v.* **1** *tr.* fit or renew a heel on (a shoe or boot). **2** *tr.* (of a dog) follow closely behind its owner. **3** *intr.* touch the ground with the heel, as in dancing. □ **at** (or **to**) **heel 1** (of a dog) close behind. **2** (of a person, etc.) under control. **at** (or **on**) **the heels of** following closely after (a person or event). **cool one's heels** be kept waiting. **take to one's heels** run away. **turn on one's heel** turn sharply around. □□ **heel·less** *adj.*

heel[2] /heel/ *v. & n.* •*v.* **1** *intr.* (of a ship, etc.) lean over owing to the pressure of wind or an uneven load (cf. LIST[2]). **2** *tr.* cause (a ship, etc.) to do this. •*n.* the act or amount of heeling.

heel[3] /heel/ *v.tr.* (foll. by *in*) set (a plant) temporarily in the ground at an angle and cover its roots.

heel·tap /hēeltap/ *n.* **1** a layer of leather, metal, etc., in a shoe heel. **2** liquor left at the bottom of a glass after drinking.

heft /heft/ *v.tr.* lift (something heavy), esp. to judge its weight.

heft·y /héftee/ *adj.* (**heftier, heftiest**) **1** (of a person) big and strong. **2** (of a thing) large; heavy; powerful; sizable; considerable. □□ **heft·i·ly** *adv.* **heft·i·ness** *n.*

He·ge·li·an /haygáyleeən, hijēe–/ *adj. & n.* •*adj.* of or relating to the German philosopher G.W.F. Hegel (d. 1831) or his philosophy of objective idealism. •*n.* an adherent of Hegel or his philosophy.

he·gem·o·ny /hijémənee, héjəmōnee/ *n.* leadership, esp. by one nation over others of a confederacy. ▫▫ **heg·e·mon·ic** *adj.*

he·gi·ra /hijírə, héjirə/ *n.* (also **he·ji·ra**) **1** (**Hegira**) Muhammad's departure from Mecca to Medina in AD 622. **2** the Muslim era reckoned from this date.

heif·er /héfər/ *n.* a young cow, esp. one that has not had more than one calf.

height /hīt/ *n.* **1** the measurement from base to top or (of a standing person) from head to foot. **2** the elevation above ground or a recognized level (usu. sea level). **3** any considerable elevation (*situated at a height*). **4 a** a high place or area. **b** rising ground. **5** the top of something. **6 a** the most intense part or period of anything (*the battle was at its height*). **b** an extreme instance or example (*the height of fashion*).

▶Avoid pronouncing **height** with a *-th* at the end; many regard this as uneducated.

height·en /hítən/ *v.tr. & intr.* make or become higher or more intense.

Heim·lich ma·neu·ver /hímlik/ *n.* an emergency procedure for assisting a choking victim in which one applies sudden upward pressure with the fist against the victim's upper abdomen in order to dislodge the object causing the choking.

hei·nous /háynəs/ *adj.* (of a crime or criminal) utterly odious or wicked. ▫▫ **hei·nous·ly** *adv.* **hei·nous·ness** *n.*

heir /air/ *n.* a person entitled to property or rank as the legal successor of its former owner. ▫▫ **heir·dom** *n.* **heir·less** *adj.* **heir·ship** *n.*

heir ap·par·ent *n.* an heir whose claim cannot be set aside by the birth of another heir.

heir·ess /áiris/ *n.* a female heir, esp. to great wealth.

heir·loom /áirlo͞om/ *n.* **1** a piece of personal property that has been in a family for several generations. **2** a piece of property received as part of an inheritance.

heist /hīst/ *n. & v. sl.* •*n.* a robbery. •*v.tr.* steal.

he·ji·ra var. of HEGIRA.

held *past* and *past part.* of HOLD.

heli- /hélee/ *comb. form* helicopter (*heliport*).

he·li·an·thus /heéleeánthəs/ *n.* any plant of the genus *Helianthus*, including the sunflower and Jerusalem artichoke.

hel·i·cal /hélikəl, heéli–/ *adj.* having the form of a helix. ▫▫ **hel·i·cal·ly** *adv.* **hel·i·coid** *adj. & n.*

hel·i·ces *pl.* of HELIX.

hel·i·cop·ter /hélikoptər/ *n.* a type of aircraft obtaining lift and propulsion from horizontally revolving overhead blades.

helio- /heéleeō/ *comb. form* the sun.

he·li·o·cen·tric /heéleeōséntrik/ *adj.* **1** regarding the sun as center. **2** considered as viewed from the sun's center. ▫▫ **he·li·o·cen·tri·cal·ly** *adv.*

he·li·o·graph /heéleeəgraf/ *n. & v.* •*n.* **1** a signaling apparatus reflecting sunlight in flashes from a movable mirror. **2** an apparatus for photographing the sun. •*v.tr.* send (a message) by heliograph. ▫▫ **he·li·og·ra·phy** /–leeógrəfee/ *n.*

he·li·o·trope /heéleeətrōp/ *n.* **1** a plant with fragrant purple flowers. **2** a light purple color.

hel·i·port /héleepawrt/ *n.* a place where helicopters take off and land.

he·li·um /heéleeəm/ *n. Chem.* a colorless, light, inert, gaseous element used in airships and balloons and as a refrigerant. ¶ Symb.: **He.**

he·lix /heéliks/ *n.* (*pl.* **helices** /–seez, hél–/) **1** a spiral curve (like a corkscrew) or a coiled curve (like a watch spring). **2** *Geom.* a curve that cuts a line on a solid cone or cylinder, at a constant angle with the axis.

hell /hel/ *n.* **1** in some religions, the abode of the dead, or of condemned sinners and devils. **2** a place or state of misery or wickedness. ▫ **for the hell of it** *colloq.* for fun. **give a person hell** *colloq.* scold or punish a person. **hell of** *colloq.* extreme or outstanding example of (*a hell of a mess*; *one hell of a party*). **hell for leather** at full speed. **like hell** *colloq.* **1** not at all. **2** exceedingly. **what the hell** *colloq.* it is of no importance.

he'll /heel/ *contr.* he will; he shall.

hell-bent *adj.* (foll. by *on*) recklessly determined.

hel·le·bore /hélibawr/ *n.* any evergreen plant having large white, green, or purplish flowers.

Hel·lene /héleen/ *n.* **1** a native of modern Greece. **2** an ancient Greek. ▫▫ **Hel·len·ic** /helénik/ *adj.*

Hel·len·ism /hélinizəm/ *n.* Greek character or culture (esp. of ancient Greece). ▫▫ **Hel·len·ize** *v.tr. & intr.* **Hel·len·i·za·tion** *n.*

Hel·len·ist /hélinist/ *n.* an expert on or admirer of Greek language or culture.

Hel·len·is·tic /hélinístik/ *adj.* of or relating to Greek history, language, and culture from 4th–1st c. BC.

hell·fire /hélfīr/ *n.* the fire or fires regarded as existing in hell.

hell·hole /hélhōl/ *n. colloq.* an oppressive or unbearable place.

hell·hound /hélhownd/ *n.* a fiend.

hell·ish /hélish/ *adj.* **1** of or like hell. **2** *colloq.* extremely unpleasant. ▫▫ **hell·ish·ly** *adv.* **hell·ish·ness** *n.*

hel·lo /heló, hə–/ *int., n. & v.* •*int.* **1** an expression of informal greeting. **2** a cry used to call attention. •*n.* (*pl.* **-los**) a cry of "hello." •*v.intr.* (**-loes, -loed**) cry "hello."

hell-rais·er *n.* a person who causes trouble or creates chaos.

Hell's An·gel *n.* a member of a gang of motorcyclists notorious for outrageous or violent behavior.

helm /helm/ *n. & v.* •*n.* **1** a tiller or wheel by which a ship's rudder is controlled. **2** the amount by which this is turned (*more helm needed*). •*v.tr.* steer or guide as if with a helm. ▫ **at the helm** in control; at the head (of an organization, etc.).

hel·met /hélmit/ *n.* any of various protective head coverings worn by soldiers, cyclists, etc. ▫▫ **hel·met·ed** *adj.*

helms·man /hélmzmən/ *n.* (*pl.* **-men**) a person who steers a vessel.

help /help/ *v. & n.* •*v.tr.* **1** provide (a person, etc.) with the means toward what is needed (*helped me with my work*). **2** (foll. by *up, down*, etc.) assist (a person) in moving, etc., as specified (*helped her into the chair*). **3** (often *absol.*) be of use to (a person) (*does that help?*). **4** contribute to alleviating (a pain or difficulty). **5** prevent or remedy (*it can't be helped*). **6** (usu. with *neg.*) **a** *tr.* refrain from (*could not help laughing*). **b** *refl.* refrain from acting (*couldn't help himself*). **7** *tr.* (often foll. by *to*) serve (a person with food) (*shall I help you to more rice?*). •*n.* **1** the act of helping or being helped (*we need your help*). **2** a person or thing that helps. **3** a domestic servant. ▫ **help oneself** (often foll. by *to*) **1** serve oneself (with food). **2** take without seeking help; take without permission. **help a person out** give a person help, esp. in difficulty. ▫▫ **help·er** *n.*

help·ful /hélpfo͝ol/ *adj.* (of a person or thing) giving help; useful. ▫▫ **help·ful·ly** *adv.* **help·ful·ness** *n.*

help·ing /hélping/ *n.* a portion of food, esp. at a meal.

help·less /hélplis/ *adj.* **1** unable to act without help. **2** lacking help or protection. ▫▫ **help·less·ly** *adv.* **help·less·ness** *n.*

help·line /hélplīn/ *n.* a telephone service providing help with problems.

See page xii for the *Key to Pronunciation.*

help•mate /hélpmayt/ *n.* a helpful companion (usu. a husband or wife).

hel•ter-skel•ter /héltərskéltər/ *adv. & adj.* •*adv.* in disorderly haste. •*adj.* characterized by disorderly haste.

hem[1] /hem/ *n. & v.* •*n.* the border of a piece of cloth, turned under and sewn down. •*v.tr.* (**hemmed, hemming**) turn down and sew in the edge of (a piece of cloth, etc.). □ **hem in** confine; restrict the movement of.

hem[2] /hem, həm/ *int., n., & v.* •*int.* (also **ahem**) calling attention or expressing hesitation by a slight cough or clearing of the throat. •*n.* an utterance of this. •*v.intr.* (**hemmed, hemming**) say *hem*; hesitate in speech. □ **hem and haw** hesitate in speaking.

he•mal /héeməl/ *adj. Anat.* **1** of or concerning the blood. **2** situated on the same side of the body as the heart and major blood vessels.

he-man *n.* (*pl.* **-men**) a masterful or virile man.

he•ma•tite /héemətīt, hém–/ *n.* a ferric oxide ore.

hemato- /héemətō, hém–/ *comb. form* blood.

he•mat•o•cele /himátəseel, héemətəseel, hém–/ *n. Med.* a swelling caused by blood collecting in a body cavity.

he•mat•ol•o•gy /héemətóləjee, hém–/ *n.* the study of the physiology of the blood and blood-forming organs. □□ **he•ma•to•log•i•cal** /–təlójikəl/ *adj.* **he•ma•tol•o•gist** *n.*

hemi- /hémee/ *comb. form* half.

hem•i•ple•gi•a /hémipléejə, –jeeə/ *n. Med.* paralysis of one side of the body. □□ **hem•i•ple•gic** *n. & adj.*

He•mip•ter•a /hemíptərə/ *n.pl.* an order of insects comprising the "true bugs," which have mouthparts adapted for piercing and sucking. □□ **he•mip•ter•an** *n. & adj.* **he•mip•ter•ous** *adj.*

hem•i•sphere /hémisfeer/ *n.* **1** half of a sphere. **2** a half of the earth, esp. as divided by the equator (into *northern* and *southern hemispheres*) or by a line passing through the poles (into *eastern* and *western hemisphere*). □□ **hem•i•spher•ic** /–sféerik, –sférik/ *adj.* **hem•i•spher•i•cal** *adj.*

hem•line /hémlīn/ *n.* the line or level of the lower edge of a skirt, dress, or coat.

hem•lock /hémlok/ *n.* **1** a poisonous umbelliferous plant, *Conium maculatum*, with fernlike leaves and small white flowers. **2** a poisonous potion obtained from this. **3** a coniferous North American tree of the genus *Tsuga*, with dark green foliage.

hemo- /héemō, hémmō/ *comb. form* = HEMATO-.

he•mo•glo•bin /héeməglṓbin, hém–/ *n.* a red oxygen-carrying substance containing iron, present in the red blood cells of vertebrates.

he•mo•phil•i•a /héeməfileeə, hém–/ *n. Med.* a usu. hereditary disorder causing one to tend to bleed severely from even a slight injury, through the failure of the blood to clot normally. □□ **he•mo•phil•ic** *adj.*

he•mo•phil•i•ac /héeməfileeak, –féelee–, hém–/ *n.* a person suffering from hemophilia.

hem•or•rhage /hémərij, hémrij/ *n. & v.* •*n.* **1** an escape of blood from a ruptured blood vessel, esp. when profuse. **2** an extensive, damaging loss, esp. of people or assets. •*v.intr.* undergo a hemorrhage. □□ **he•mor•rhag•ic** /hémərájik/ *adj.*

hem•or•rhoid /héməroyd/ *n.* (usu. in *pl.*) swollen veins at or near the anus.

he•mos•ta•sis /himóstəsis, héemōstáysis, hém–/ *n.* the stopping of the flow of blood. □□ **he•mo•stat•ic** /héeməstátik/ *adj.*

hemp /hemp/ *n.* **1** (in full **Indian hemp**) a herbaceous plant, *Cannabis sativa*, native to Asia. **2** its fiber extracted from the stem and used to make rope and strong fabrics. **3** any of several narcotic drugs made from the hemp plant (cf. CANNABIS, MARIJUANA).

hemp•en /hémpən/ *adj.* made from hemp.

hem•stitch /hémstich/ *n. & v.* •*n.* a decorative stitch used in sewing hems. •*v.tr.* hem with this stitch.

hen /hen/ *n.* **1** a female bird, esp. of a domestic fowl. **2** a female lobster or crab or salmon.

hence /hens/ *adv.* **1** from this time (*two years hence*). **2** for this reason (*hence we seem to be wrong*).

hence•forth /hénsfáwrth/ *adv.* (also **hence•for•ward** /–fáwrwərd/) from this time onward.

hench•man /hénchmən/ *n.* (*pl.* **-men**) **1** a faithful follower or political supporter, esp. one prepared to engage in crime or dishonest practices by way of service. **2** *hist.* a squire or page to a person of rank.

henge /henj/ *n.* a prehistoric monument consisting of a circle of massive stone or wood uprights.

hen•na /hénə/ *n.* **1** a tropical shrub, *Lawsonia inermis*, having small flowers. **2** the reddish dye from its shoots and leaves used to color hair.

hen•peck /hénpek/ *v.tr.* (of a woman) constantly harass (a man, esp. her husband).

hen•ry /hénree/ *n.* (*pl.* **-ries** or **henrys**) *Electr.* the SI unit of inductance that gives an electromotive force of one volt in a closed circuit with a uniform rate of change of current of one ampere per second. ¶ Abbr.: **H.**

hep var. of HIP[3].

hep•a•rin /hépərin/ *n. Biochem.* a substance produced in liver cells, etc., used as an anticoagulant.

he•pat•ic /hipátik/ *adj.* **1** of or relating to the liver. **2** dark brownish red.

hep•a•ti•tis /hépətítis/ *n.* inflammation of the liver.

hepta- /héptə/ *comb. form* seven.

hep•ta•gon /héptəgən/ *n.* a plane figure with seven sides and angles. □□ **hep•tag•o•nal** /–tágənəl/ *adj.*

hep•tath•lon /heptáthlon, –lən/ *n. Sports* a seven-event track and field competition, esp. for women.

her /hər/ *pron. & poss.pron.* •*pron. objective case* of SHE (*I like her*). •*poss.pron.* (*attrib.*) of or belonging to her (*her house; her own business*).

her•ald /hérəld/ *n. & v.* •*n.* **1** an official messenger bringing news. **2** a forerunner (*spring is the herald of summer*). •*v.tr.* proclaim the approach of; usher in.

he•ral•dic /heráldik/ *adj.* of or concerning heraldry. □□ **he•ral•di•cal•ly** *adv.*

her•ald•ry /hérəldree/ *n.* **1** the science or art of dealing with armorial bearings. **2** armorial bearings.

herb /ərb, hərb/ *n.* **1** any nonwoody seed-bearing plant that dies down to the ground after flowering. **2** any plant with leaves, seeds, or flowers used for flavoring, medicine, scent, etc. □□ **her•bif•er•ous** /–bífərəs/ *adj.* **herb•like** *adj.*

her•ba•ceous /hərbáyshəs, ər–/ *adj.* of or like herbs.

herb•al /ə́rbəl, hə́r–/ *adj. & n.* •*adj.* of herbs in medicinal and culinary use. •*n.* a book with descriptions and accounts of the properties of these.

herb•al•ist /ə́rbəlist, hə́r–/ *n.* **1** a dealer in medicinal herbs. **2** a person skilled in herbs, esp. an early botanical writer.

her•bar•i•um /hərbáireeəm, ər–/ *n.* (*pl.* **herbaria** /–reeə/) **1** a systematically arranged collection of dried plants. **2** a book, room, or building for these.

herb•i•cide /hə́rbisīd, ə́r–/ *n.* a substance toxic to plants.

her•biv•ore /hə́rbivawr, ə́r–/ *n.* an animal that feeds on plants. □□ **her•biv•o•rous** /–bívərəs/ *adj.*

Her•cu•le•an /hə́rkyəlée̍ən, –kyóóleeən/ *adj.* having or requiring great strength.

herd /hərd/ *n. & v.* •*n.* **1** a large number of animals, esp. cattle, feeding or traveling or kept together. **2** (often prec. by *the*) *derog.* a large number of people; a mob (*prefers not to follow the herd*). •*v.* **1** *intr. & tr.* go or cause to go in a herd (*herded together for warmth*). **2** *tr.* tend (sheep, cattle, etc.). □□ **herd•er** *n.*

herds·man /hə́rdzmən/ *n.* (*pl.* **-men**) the owner or keeper of herds.

here /heer/ *adv., n., & int.* • *adv.* **1** in or at or to this place. **2** indicating a person's presence or a thing offered (*here is your coat*). **3** at this point in the argument, situation, etc. • *n.* this place. • *int.* **1** calling attention (*here, where are you going with that*). **2** indicating one's presence in a roll call. □ **here goes!** *colloq.* an expression indicating the start of a bold or uncertain act. **here's to** I drink to the health of. **neither here nor there** of no relevance.

▶The use of **here** or **there** following a demonstrative, e.g., *this here gadget* or *that there field*, although common in dialect, is not regarded as standard, although a change in the position of the words, e.g., *this gadget here, that field there* removes objections.

here·a·bouts /heérəbówts/ *adv.* (also **here·a·bout**) near this place.

here·af·ter /heéráftər/ *adv. & n.* • *adv.* **1** from now on. **2** in the world to come (after death). • *n.* **1** the future. **2** life after death.

here·by /heérbí/ *adv.* by this means; as a result of this.

he·red·i·ta·ble /hiréditəbəl/ *adj.* that can be inherited.

he·red·i·tar·y /hirédíteree/ *adj.* **1** (of disease, instinct, etc.) able to be passed down from one generation to another. **2 a** descending by inheritance. **b** holding a position by inheritance. **3** the same as or resembling what one's parents had (*a hereditary hatred*). **4** of or relating to inheritance. □□ **he·red·i·tar·i·ly** *adv.*

he·red·i·ty /hiréditee/ *n.* **1** the passing on of physical or mental characteristics genetically from one generation to another. **2** these characteristics.

Her·e·ford /hə́rfərd, hérifərd/ *n.* an animal of a breed of red and white beef cattle.

here·in /heérín/ *adv. formal* in this matter, book, etc.

here·in·af·ter /heérináftər/ *adv.* esp. *Law formal* in a later part of this document.

her·e·sy /hérəsee/ *n.* (*pl.* **-sies**) **1 a** belief or practice contrary to the orthodox doctrine of esp. the Christian church. **b** an instance of this. **2 a** opinion contrary to what is normally accepted or maintained. **b** an instance of this.

her·e·tic /hérətik/ *n.* **1** the holder of an unorthodox opinion. **2** a person believing in or practicing religious heresy. □□ **he·ret·i·cal** /hirétikəl/ *adj.* **he·ret·i·cal·ly** *adv.*

here·to /heértóó/ *adv. formal* to this matter.

here·to·fore /heértəfáwr/ *adv. formal* before this time.

here·up·on /heérəpón, –páwn/ *adv.* after this; in consequence of this.

here·with /heérwíth, –wíth/ *adv.* with this (esp. of an enclosure in a letter, etc.).

her·it·a·ble /héritəbəl/ *adj.* **1** *Law* **a** (of property) capable of being inherited (cf. MOVABLE). **b** capable of inheriting. **2** *Biol.* (of a characteristic) transmissible from parent to offspring. □□ **her·it·a·bil·i·ty** *n.* **her·it·a·bly** *adv.*

her·it·age /héritij/ *n.* **1** anything that is or may be inherited. **2** inherited circumstances, benefits, etc. (*a heritage of confusion*). **3** a nation's historic buildings, monuments, traditions, countryside, etc., esp. when regarded as worthy of preservation.

her·maph·ro·dite /hərmáfrədīt/ *n. & adj.* • *n.* **1 a** *Zool.* an animal having both male and female sexual organs. **b** *Bot.* a plant having stamens and pistils in the same flower. **2** a human being in which both male and female sex organs are present, or in which the sex organs contain both ovarian and testicular tissue. • *adj.* combining both sexes. □□ **her·maph·ro·dit·ic** /–dítik/ *adj.* **her·maph·ro·dit·i·cal** *adj.* **her·maph·ro·dit·ism** *n.*

her·me·neu·tics /hə́rminóótiks, –nyóó–/ *n.pl.* (also treated as *sing.*) *Bibl.* interpretation, esp. of Scripture or literary texts. □□ **her·me·neu·tic** *adj.*

her·met·ic /hərmétik/ *adj.* (also **her·met·i·cal**) **1** with an airtight closure. **2** protected from outside agencies. □□ **her·met·i·cal·ly** *adv.* **her·me·tism** /hérmitizəm/ *n.*

her·mit /hə́rmit/ *n.* **1** an early Christian recluse. **2** any person living in solitude. □□ **her·mit·ic** /–mítik/ *adj.*

her·mit·age /hə́rmitij/ *n.* **1** a hermit's dwelling. **2** a monastery.

her·mit crab *n.* any crab of the family Paguridae that lives in a cast-off mollusk shell for protection.

her·ni·a /hə́rneeə/ *n.* (*pl.* **hernias** or **herniae** /–nee-ee/) the protrusion of part of an organ through the wall of the cavity containing it, esp. of the abdomen. □□ **her·ni·al** *adj.* **her·ni·at·ed** *adj.*

he·ro /heérō/ *n.* (*pl.* **-roes**) **1** a person noted or admired for nobility, courage, outstanding achievements, etc. **2** the chief male character in a poem, play, story, etc. **3** *Gk. Antiq.* a man of superhuman qualities, favored by the gods; a demigod. **4** *dial.* = SUBMARINE SANDWICH.

he·ro·ic /hirṓik/ *adj. & n.* • *adj.* **1 a** of or fit for a hero. **b** like a hero. **2 a** (of language) grand; dramatic. **b** (of a work of art) heroic in scale or subject. • *n.* (in *pl.*) **1** high-flown language or sentiments. **2** unduly bold behavior. □□ **he·ro·i·cal·ly** *adv.*

her·o·in /hérōin/ *n.* a highly addictive analgesic drug derived from morphine.

her·o·ine /hérōin/ *n.* **1** a woman admired for courage, outstanding achievements, etc. **2** the chief female character in a play, story, etc.

her·o·ism /hérōizəm/ *n.* heroic conduct or qualities.

her·on /hérən/ *n.* a large wading bird with long legs and a long S-shaped neck.

her·on·ry /hérənree/ *n.* (*pl.* **-ries**) a breeding colony of herons.

her·o-wor·ship *n.* idealization of an admired man.

her·pes /hə́rpeez/ *n.* a virus disease with outbreaks of blisters on the skin, etc. □□ **her·pet·ic** /–pétik/ *adj.*

her·pes sim·plex *n.* a viral infection that may produce blisters or conjunctivitis.

her·pes zos·ter /zóstər/ = SHINGLES.

her·pe·tol·o·gy /hə́rpitóləjee/ *n.* the study of reptiles. □□ **her·pe·tol·o·gist** *n.*

her·ring /héring/ *n.* a N. Atlantic fish, *Clupea harengus*, coming near the coast in large shoals to spawn.

her·ring·bone /héringbōn/ *n.* a stitch with a zigzag pattern.

hers /hərz/ *poss.pron.* the one or ones belonging to or associated with her (*it is hers; hers are over there*).

her·self /hərsélf/ *pron.* **1 a** *emphat. form* of SHE or HER (*she herself will do it*). **b** *refl. form* of HER (*she has hurt herself*). **2** in her normal state of body or mind (*does not feel quite herself today*).

hertz /herts/ *n.* (*pl.* same) a unit of frequency, equal to one cycle per second.

he's /heez/ *contr.* **1** he is. **2** he has.

hes·i·tant /hézit'nt/ *adj.* hesitating; irresolute. □□ **hes·i·tance** /–təns/ *n.* **hes·i·tan·cy** *n.* **hes·i·tant·ly** *adv.*

hes·i·tate /hézitayt/ *v.intr.* **1** show or feel indecision or uncertainty (*hesitated over her choice*). **2** (often foll. by *to* + infin.) be reluctant (*I hesitate to tell him*). □□ **hes·i·tat·ing·ly** *adv.* **hes·i·ta·tion** /–táyshən/ *n.*

hes·sian /héshən/ *n.* a strong coarse sacking made of hemp or jute.

het·er·o /hétərō/ *n.* (*pl.* **-os**) *colloq.* a heterosexual.

hetero- /hétərō/ *comb. form* other; different (often opp. HOMO-).

het·er·o·cy·clic /hétərōsíklik, –síklik/ *adj. Chem.* (of a compound) with a bonded ring of atoms of more than one kind.

het·er·o·dox /hétərədoks/ *adj.* (of a person, opinion, etc.) not orthodox. □□ **het·er·o·dox·y** *n.*

het·er·o·dyne /hétərədīn/ *adj. & v. Radio* • *adj.* relating to the production of a lower frequency from the combination of two almost equal high frequencies. • *v.intr.* produce a lower frequency in this way.

het·er·o·ge·ne·ous /hétərōjéeneeəs, –nyəs/ *adj.* **1** diverse in character. **2** varied in content. **3** *Math.* incommensurable through being of different kinds or degrees. ▫▫ **het·er·o·ge·ne·i·ty** /–jinéeitee/ *n.* **het·er·o·ge·ne·ous·ly** *adv.* **het·er·o·ge·ne·ous·ness** *n.*

het·er·ol·o·gous /hétərólәgəs/ *adj.* not homologous. ▫▫ **het·er·ol·o·gy** *n.*

het·er·o·mor·phic /hétərōmáwrfik/ *adj. Biol.* **1** of dissimilar forms. **2** (of insects) existing in different forms at different stages in their life cycle. ▫▫ **het·er·o·mor·phism** /hétərōmáwrfizəm/ *n.*

het·er·o·sex·u·al /hétərōsékshōōəl/ *adj. & n.* • *adj.* **1** feeling or involving sexual attraction to persons of the opposite sex. **2** concerning heterosexual relations or people. • *n.* a heterosexual person. ▫▫ **het·er·o·sex·u·al·i·ty** /–shōōálitee/ *n.* **het·er·o·sex·u·al·ly** *adv.*

heu·ris·tic /hyōōrístik/ *adj. & n.* • *adj.* **1** allowing or assisting to discover. **2** *Computing* proceeding to a solution by trial and error. • *n.* (in *pl.*, usu. treated as *sing.*) *Computing* the study and use of heuristic techniques in data processing. ▫▫ **heu·ris·ti·cal·ly** *adv.*

HEW *abbr. US hist.* Department of Health, Education, and Welfare (1953–79).

hew /hyōō/ *v.* (*past part.* **hewn** /hyōōn/or **hewed**) **1** *tr.* **a** (often foll. by *down, away, off*) chop or cut (a thing) with an ax, a sword, etc. **b** cut (a block of wood, etc.) into shape. **2** *intr.* (often foll. by *at, among*, etc.) strike cutting blows. **3** *intr.* (usu. foll. by *to*) conform.

hex /heks/ *v. & n.* • *v.* **1** *intr.* practice witchcraft. **2** *tr.* bewitch. • *n.* **1** a magic spell. **2** a witch.

hexa- /héksə/ *comb. form* six.

hex·ad /héksad/ *n.* a group of six.

hex·a·dec·i·mal /héksədésiməl/ *adj. & n.* esp. *Computing* • *adj.* relating to or using a system of numerical notation that has 16 rather than 10 as a base. • *n.* the hexadecimal system; hexadecimal notation. ▫▫ **hex·a·dec·i·mal·ly** *adv.*

hex·a·gon /héksəgən/ *n.* a plane figure with six sides and angles. ▫▫ **hex·a·gon·al** /–ságənəl/ *adj.*

hex·a·gram /héksəgram/ *n.* **1** a figure formed by two intersecting equilateral triangles. **2** a figure of six lines.

hex·a·he·dron /héksəhéedrən/ *n.* a solid figure with six faces. ▫▫ **hex·a·he·dral** *adj.*

hex·am·e·ter /heksámitər/ *n.* a line or verse of six metrical feet.

hex·ane /héksayn/ *n. Chem.* a liquid hydrocarbon of the alkane series.

hex·a·va·lent /héksəváylənt/ *adj.* having a valence of six; sexivalent.

hey /hay/ *int.* calling attention or expressing joy, surprise, inquiry, etc.

hey·day /háyday/ *n.* the flush or full bloom of youth, vigor, prosperity, etc.

HF *abbr.* high frequency.

Hf *symb. Chem.* the element hafnium.

Hg *symb. Chem.* the element mercury.

hg *abbr.* hectogram(s).

hgt. *abbr.* height.

H-hour /áychowr/ *n.* the hour at which a military operation is scheduled to begin.

HHS *abbr.* (Department of) Health and Human Services.

HI *abbr.* **1** Hawaii (also in official postal use). **2** the Hawaiian Islands.

hi /hī/ *int.* expression of greeting.

hi·a·tus /hīáytəs/ *n.* (*pl.* **hiatuses**) **1** a break or gap, esp. in a series, account, or chain of proof. **2** *Prosody & Gram.* a break between two vowels coming together but not in the same syllable, as in *though oft the ear.* ▫▫ **hi·a·tal** *adj.*

hi·ba·chi /həbaáchee/ *n.* a small charcoal-burning brazier for grilling food.

hi·ber·nate /híbərnayt/ *v.intr.* **1** (of some animals) spend the winter in a dormant state. **2** remain inactive. ▫▫ **hi·ber·na·tion** /–náyshən/ *n.* **hi·ber·na·tor** *n.*

Hi·ber·ni·an /hībárneeən/ *adj. & n. archaic poet.* • *adj.* of or concerning Ireland. • *n.* a native of Ireland.

hi·bis·cus /hibískəs/ *n.* any tree or shrub of the genus *Hibiscus*, cultivated for its large bright-colored flowers. Also called ROSE MALLOW.

hic /hik/ *int.* expressing the sound of a hiccup, esp. a drunken hiccup.

hic·cup /híkup/ *n. & v.* (also **hic·cough**) • *n.* **1** an involuntary spasm of the diaphragm and respiratory organs, with sudden closure of the glottis and characteristic coughlike sound. **2** a temporary or minor difficulty. • *v. intr.* make a hiccup or series of hiccups.

hick /hik/ *n. colloq.* a country dweller; a provincial.

hick·ey /híkee/ *n.* (*pl.* **-eys**) *colloq.* a reddish mark on the skin produced by a sucking kiss.

hick·o·ry /híkəree/ *n.* (*pl.* **-ries**) **1** a N. American tree yielding tough heavy wood and bearing nutlike edible fruits (see PECAN). **2** the wood of these trees.

hid *past* of HIDE[1].

hi·dal·go /hidálgō, eethaálgō/ *n.* (*pl.* **·gos**) a Spanish gentleman.

hid·den *past part.* of HIDE[1]

hide[1] /hīd/ *v.* (*past* **hid** /hid/; *past part.* **hidden** /hídən/or *archaic* **hid**) **1** *tr.* put or keep out of sight. **2** *intr.* conceal oneself. **3** *tr.* (usu. foll. by *from*) keep (a fact) secret (*hid his real motive from her*). **4** *tr.* conceal (a thing) from sight (*trees hid the house*). ▫▫ **hid·den** *adj.* **hid·er** *n.*

hide[2] /hīd/ *n.* **1** the skin of an animal, esp. when tanned or dressed. **2** *colloq.* the human skin (*I'll tan your hide*). ▫▫ **hid·ed** *adj.* (also in *comb.*).

hide-and-seek *n.* **1** a children's game in which one or more players seek a child or children hiding. **2** a process of attempting to find an evasive person or thing.

hide·a·way /hídəway/ *n.* a hiding place or place of retreat.

hide·bound /hídbownd/ *adj.* **1 a** narrow-minded; bigoted. **b** (of the law, rules, etc.) constricted by tradition. **2** (of cattle) with the skin clinging close as a result of bad feeding.

---

hidebound mid-16th century (as a noun denoting a condition of cattle): from HIDE[2] + BOUND[4]. The earliest sense of the adjective (referring to cattle) was extended to emaciated human beings, and then applied figuratively in the sense 'narrow, cramped, or bigoted in outlook.'

---

hid·e·ous /hídeeəs/ *adj.* **1** frightful, repulsive, or revolting, to the senses or the mind. **2** *colloq.* unpleasant. ▫▫ **hid·e·ous·ly** *adv.* **hid·e·ous·ness** *n.*

hide-out *n. colloq.* a hiding place.

hid·ey-hole /hídeehōl/ *n. colloq.* a hiding place.

hid·ing[1] /híding/ *n. colloq.* a thrashing.

hid·ing[2] /híding/ *n.* **1** the act of hiding. **2** the state of remaining hidden (*go into hiding*).

hie /hī/ *v.intr. & refl.* (**hies, hied, hieing** or **hying**) esp. *archaic* or *poet.* go quickly (*hie to your chamber; hied him to the chase*).

hi·er·ar·chy /híəraarkee/ *n.* (*pl.* **-chies**) **1 a** a system in which grades or classes of status or authority are ranked one above the other. **b** the hierarchical system (of government, management, etc.). **2 a** priestly government. **b** a priesthood organized in grades. ▫▫ **hi·er·ar·chic** *adj.* /–raárkik/ **hi·er·ar·chi·cal** *adj.*

hi·er·at·ic /híərátik/ *adj.* **1** of or concerning priests; priestly. **2** of the ancient Egyptian writing of abridged hieroglyphics as used by priests. □□ **hi·er·at·i·cal·ly** *adv.*
hiero- /híró/ *comb. form* sacred; holy.
hi·er·o·glyph /híraglif/ *n.* a picture of an object representing a word, syllable, or sound, as used in ancient Egyptian and other writing.
hi·er·o·glyph·ic /híraglífik/ *adj. & n.* • *adj.* **1** of or written in hieroglyphs. **2** symbolic. • *n.* (in *pl.*) hieroglyphs; hieroglyphic writing.
hi-fi /hífi/ *adj. & n. colloq.* • *adj.* of high fidelity. • *n.* (*pl.* **hi-fis**) a set of equipment for high fidelity sound reproduction.
hig·gle·dy-pig·gle·dy /hígəldeepígəldee/ *adv. & adj.* in confusion or disorder.
high /hī/ *adj., n., & adv.* • *adj.* **1 a** of great vertical extent (*a high building*). **b** (*predic.*; often in *comb.*) of a specified height (*one inch high*). **2** far above ground or sea level, etc. (*a high altitude*). **3** extending above the normal or average level (*high boots*). **4** of exalted, esp. spiritual, quality (*high principles*). **5** of exalted rank (*high society*). **6 a** great; intense (*high praise*; *high temperature*). **b** greater than normal (*high prices*). **c** extreme in religious or political opinion (*high Tory*). **7** *colloq.* (often foll. by *on*) intoxicated by alcohol or esp. drugs. **8** (of a sound or note) of high frequency; shrill; at the top end of the scale. **9** (of a period, an age, a time, etc.) at its peak (*high summer*; *High Renaissance*). • *n.* **1** a high, or the highest, level or figure. **2** an area of high barometric pressure. **3** *sl.* a euphoric drug-induced state. **4** top gear in a motor vehicle. **5** *colloq.* high school. • *adv.* **1** far up; aloft (*flew the flag high*). **2** in or to a high degree. **3** at a high price. **4** (of a sound) at or to a high pitch (*sang high*). □ **high old** *colloq.* most enjoyable (*a high old time*). **high opinion of** a favorable opinion of. **on high** in or to heaven or a high place. **on one's high horse** *colloq.* behaving superciliously or arrogantly. **run high 1** (of the sea) have a strong current with high tide. **2** (of feelings) be strong.
high and dry *adj.* **1** out of the current of events; stranded. **2** (of a ship) out of the water.
high·ball /híbawl/ *n.* a drink of liquor and soda, etc., served with ice in a tall glass.
high beam *n.* full, bright illumination from a motor vehicle's headlight.
high·born /híbáwrn/ *adj.* of noble birth.
high·boy /híboy/ *n.* a tall chest of drawers on legs.
high·brow /híbrow/ *adj. & n. colloq.* • *adj.* intellectual; cultural. • *n.* an intellectual or cultured person.
high chair *n.* an infant's chair with long legs and a tray, for use at meals.
high-class *adj.* of high quality.
high·er court *n. Law* a court that can overrule the decision of another.
high·er-up *n. colloq.* a person of higher rank.
high·fa·lu·tin /hífəloōt'n/ *adj.* (also **high·fa·lu·ting** /–ing/) *colloq.* absurdly pompous or pretentious.
high fi·del·i·ty *n.* the reproduction of sound with little distortion, giving a result very similar to the original.
high fi·nance *n.* financial transactions involving large sums.
high five *n.* a gesture of celebration or greeting in which two people slap each other's palms with their arms raised.
high-flown *adj.* (of language, etc.) extravagant; bombastic.
high-fly·er *n.* (also **high-flier**) **1** an ambitious person. **2** a person or thing with great potential for achievement. □□ **high-fly·ing** *adj.*
high fre·quen·cy *n.* a frequency, esp. in radio, of 3 to 30 megahertz.
high gear *n.* a gear such that the driven end of a transmission revolves faster (or slower) than the driving end.
high-grade *adj.* of high quality.
high-hand·ed /híhándid/ *adj.* disregarding others' feelings. □□ **high-hand·ed·ly** *adv.* **high-hand·ed·ness** *n.*
high-hat *adj., v. & n.* • *adj.* supercilious; snobbish. • *v.* (**-hatted, -hatting**) **1** *tr.* treat superciliously. **2** *intr.* assume a superior attitude. • *n.* = HI-HAT
high jinks *n.pl.* boisterous joking or merrymaking.
high jump *n.* an athletic event consisting of jumping as high as possible over a bar of adjustable height.
high·land /hílənd/ *n. & adj.* • *n.* (usu. in *pl.*) **1** an area of high land. **2** (**the Highlands**) the mountainous part of Scotland. • *adj.* of or in a highland or the Highlands. □□ **high·land·er** *n.*
high-lev·el *adj.* **1** (of negotiations, etc.) conducted by high-ranking people. **2** *Computing* (of a programming language) that is not machine-dependent and is usu. at a level of abstraction close to natural language.
high life *n.* (also **high living**) a luxurious existence ascribed to the upper classes.
high·light /hílīt/ *n. & v.* • *n.* **1** (in a painting, etc.) a light area, or one seeming to reflect light. **2** a moment or detail of vivid interest; an outstanding feature. **3** (usu. in *pl.*) a bright tint in the hair produced by bleaching. • *v.tr.* **1 a** draw attention to. **b** mark with a highlighter. **2** create highlights in (the hair).
high·light·er /hílītər/ *n.* a marker pen that overlays color on a printed word, etc., leaving it legible and emphasized.
high·ly /hílee/ *adv.* **1** in a high degree (*highly amusing*; *commend it highly*). **2** honorably; favorably (*think highly of him*). **3** in a high position or rank (*highly placed*).
high-mind·ed /hímíndid/ *adj.* **1** having high moral principles. **2** proud. □□ **high-mind·ed·ly** *adv.* **high-mind·ed·ness** *n.*
high·ness /hínis/ *n.* **1** the state of being high (cf. HEIGHT). **2** (**Highness**) a title used in addressing and referring to a prince or princess (*Her Highness*; *Your Royal Highness*).
high-oc·cu·pan·cy ve·hi·cle *n.* a commuter vehicle carrying several (or many) passengers.
high-oc·tane *adj.* (of gasoline, etc.) having good antiknock properties.
high-pitched *adj.* **1** (of a sound) high. **2** (of a roof) steep.
high-pow·ered *adj.* **1** having great power or energy. **2** important or influential.
high pres·sure *n.* **1** a high degree of activity or exertion. **2** a condition of the atmosphere with the pressure above average.
high priest *n.* **1** a chief priest, esp. in early Judaism. **2** the head of any cult.
high pro·file *n.* exposure to attention or publicity. □□ **high-pro·file** *adj.*
high-rise *adj. & n.* • *adj.* (of a building) having many stories. • *n.* such a building.
high-risk *adj.* (usu. *attrib.*) involving or exposed to danger (*high-risk sports*).
high roll·er *n. sl.* a person who gambles large sums or spends freely.
high school *n.* a secondary school.
high seas *n.pl.* open seas not within any country's jurisdiction.
high sign *n. colloq.* a surreptitious gesture indicating that all is well or that the coast is clear.
high-speed *adj.* **1** operating at great speed. **2** (of steel) suitable for cutting tools even when red-hot.

high spir·its *n.pl.* vivacity; energy; cheerfulness. ▫▫ **high-spirit·ed** *adj.* **high-spirit·ed·ness** *n.*
high-strung *adj.* very sensitive or nervous.
high·tail /hítayl/ *v.intr. colloq.* move at high speed, esp. in retreat.
high-tech *adj. & n.* • *adj.* **1** employing, requiring, or involved in high technology (*a high-tech security system*). **2** (of interior design, etc.) imitating styles more usual in industry, etc., esp. using steel, glass, or plastic in a functional way.*n.* = HIGH TECHNOLOGY.
high tech·nol·o·gy *n.* advanced technological development, esp. in electronics.
high ten·sion *n.* = HIGH-VOLTAGE.
high tide *n.* the time or level of the tide at its flow.
high time *n.* a time that is late or overdue (*it is high time they arrived*).
high tops *n.pl.* sports shoes or sneakers that cover the ankle.
high-volt·age *adj.* having enough electrical potential to injure or damage.
high·way /híway/ *n.* **1 a** a public road. **b** a main route (by land or water). **2** a direct course of action (*on the highway to success*).
high·way·man /híwaymən/ *n.* (*pl.* **-men**) *hist.* a robber of passengers, travelers, etc., usu. mounted.
high wire *n.* a high tightrope.
hi-hat *n.* a pair of foot-operated cymbals forming part of a drum set.
hi·jack /híjak/ *v. & n.* • *v.tr.* **1** seize control of (an aircraft in flight, etc.), esp. to force it to a different destination. **2** seize (goods) in transit. **3** take over (an organization, etc.) by force or subterfuge in order to redirect it. • *n.* an instance of hijacking. ▫▫ **hi·jack·er** *n.*
hike /hīk/ *n. & v.* • *n.* **1** a long walk, esp. in the wilderness with backpacks, etc. **2** an increase (of prices, etc.). • *v.* **1** *intr.* walk for a long distance, esp. with boots, backpack, etc. **2** (usu. foll. by *up*) *tr.* hitch up (clothing, etc.); hoist; shove. **3** *tr.* increase (prices, etc.). ▫ **take a hike** go away (used as an expression of annoyance). ▫▫ **hik·er** *n.*
hi·lar·i·ous /hiláireeəs/ *adj.* **1** exceedingly funny. **2** boisterously merry. ▫▫ **hi·lar·i·ous·ly** *adv.* **hi·lar·i·ous·ness** *n.* **hi·lar·i·ty** /–láritee/ *n.*
hill /hil/ *n.* **1** a naturally raised area of land, not as high as a mountain. **2** (often in *comb.*) a heap; a mound (*anthill*; *dunghill*). **3** a sloping piece of road. ▫ **over the hill** *colloq.* **1** past the prime of life; declining. **2** past the crisis.
hill·bil·ly /hílbilee/ *n.* (*pl.* **-lies**) *colloq.*, often *derog.* **1** a person from a remote or mountainous area, esp. in the Appalachian Mountains. **2** country music of or like that originating in the Appalachian region.
hill·ock /hílək/ *n.* a small hill or mound. ▫▫ **hill·ock·y** *adj.*
hill·side /hílsīd/ *n.* the sloping side of a hill.
hill·top /híltop/ *n.* the summit of a hill.
hill·y /hílee/ *adj.* (**hillier, hilliest**) having many hills. ▫▫ **hill·i·ness** *n.*
hilt /hilt/ *n.* the handle of a sword, dagger, etc. ▫ **up to the hilt** completely.
him /him/ *pron.* **1** *objective case* of HE (*I saw him*). **2** *colloq.* he (*it's him again*; *is taller than him*).
him·self /himsélf/ *pron.* **1 a** *emphat. form* of HE or HIM (*he himself will do it*). **b** *refl. form* of HIM (*he has hurt himself*). **2** in his normal state of body or mind (*does not feel quite himself today*). ▫ **be himself** act in his normal unconstrained manner.
hind[1] /hīnd/ *adj.* (esp. of parts of the body) situated at the back (*hind leg*).
hind[2] /hīnd/ *n.* a female deer (usu. a red deer), esp. in and after the third year.
hind·er[1] /híndər/ *v.tr.* (also *absol.*) impede; delay.
hind·er[2] /híndər/ *adj.* rear; hind (*the hinder part*).
Hin·di /híndee/ *n. & adj.* • *n.* **1** a group of spoken dialects of N. India. **2** a literary form of Hindustani with a Sanskrit-based vocabulary, an official language of India. • *adj.* of or concerning Hindi.
hind·most /híndmōst/ *adj.* farthest behind; most remote.
hind·quar·ters /híndkwáwrtərz/ *n.pl.* the hind legs and adjoining parts of a quadruped.
hin·drance /híndrəns/ *n.* **1** the act of hindering. **2** a thing that hinders; an obstacle.
hind·sight /híndsīt/ *n.* wisdom after the event.
Hin·du /híndoo/ *n. & adj.* • *n.* a follower of Hinduism. • *adj.* of or concerning Hindus or Hinduism.
Hin·du·ism /híndooizəm/ *n.* the main religious and social system of India, including belief in reincarnation and the worship of several gods.
Hin·du·sta·ni /híndoostaanee, –stánee/ *n. & adj.* • *n.* a language based on Western Hindi, with elements of Arabic, Persian, etc., used as a lingua franca in much of India. • *adj.* of or relating to Hindustan or its people, or Hindustani.
hinge /hinj/ *n. & v.* • *n.* **1 a** a movable joint by which a door is hung on a side post. **b** *Biol.* a natural joint performing a similar function, e.g., that of a bivalve shell. **2** a central point or principle on which everything depends. • *v.* **1** *intr.* (foll. by *on*) depend (on a principle, an event, etc.) (*all hinges on his acceptance*). **2** *tr.* attach with or as if with a hinge. ▫▫ **hinged** *adj.*

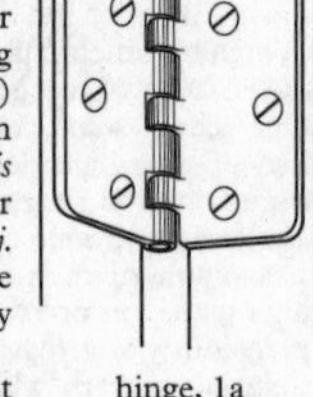
hinge, 1a

hin·ny /hínee/ *n.* (*pl.* **-nies**) the offspring of a female donkey and a male horse.
hint /hint/ *n. & v.* • *n.* **1** a slight or indirect indication or suggestion (*took the hint and left*). **2** a small piece of practical information (*handy hints on cooking*). **3** a very small trace; a suggestion (*a hint of perfume*). • *v.tr.* (often foll. by *that* + clause) suggest slightly (*hinted that they were wrong*). ▫ **hint at** give a hint of; refer indirectly to.
hin·ter·land /híntərland/ *n.* **1** the areas beyond a coastal district or a river's banks. **2** a remote area served by a port or other center.
hip[1] /hip/ *n.* a projection of the pelvis and upper thigh bone on each side of the body. ▫▫ **hipped** *adj.* (also in comb.).
hip[2] /hip/ *n.* the fruit of a rose, esp. a wild kind.
hip[3] /hip/ *adj.* (also **hep** /hep/) (**hipper, hippest** or **hepper, heppest**) *sl.* **1** following the latest fashion in music, clothes, etc. **2** understanding; aware (*he's hip to your games*). ▫▫ **hip·ness** *n.*
hip[4] /hip/ *int.* introducing a united cheer (*hip, hip, hooray*).
hip·bone /hípbōn/ *n.* a bone forming the hip, esp. the ilium.
hip-hop *n.* a style of urban youth rock music or the street subculture that surrounds it (typically including graffiti art, rap, and break dancing).
hip-hug·gers *n.pl.* trousers hanging from the hips.
hip joint *n.* the articulation of the head of the thigh bone with the ilium.
hip·pie /hípee/ *n.* (also **hip·py**) (*pl.* **-pies**) *colloq.* (esp. in the 1960s) a person with long hair, jeans, beads, etc., often associated with hallucinogenic drugs and a rejection of conventional values.
hip·po /hípō/ *n.* (*pl.* **-pos**) *colloq.* a hippopotamus.
Hip·po·crat·ic oath /hípəkrátik/ *n.* an oath taken by

doctors affirming their obligations and proper conduct.

hip·po·drome /hípədrōm/ *n.* an arena used for equestrian or other sporting events.

hip·po·pot·a·mus /hípəpótəməs/ *n.* (*pl.* **hippopotamuses** or **hippopotami** /–mī/) a large thick-skinned four-legged mammal, *Hippopotamus amphibius*, native to Africa, inhabiting rivers, lakes, etc.

hip·py[1] var. of HIPPIE.

hip·py[2] /hípee/ *adj.* having large hips.

hip·ster /hípstər/ *n. sl.* a person who is stylish or hip. ▫▫ **hip·ster·ism** *n.*

hire /hīr/ *v. & n.* •*v.tr.* **1** employ (a person). **2** procure the temporary use of (a thing) for an agreed payment. •*n.* hiring or being hired. ▫ **for hire** ready to be hired. ▫▫ **hir·a·ble** *adj.* (also **hire·a·ble**). **hir·er** *n.*

hire·ling /hírling/ *n.* usu. *derog.* a person who works for hire.

hir·sute /hərsoōt/ *adj.* hairy; shaggy. ▫▫ **hir·sute·ness** *n.*

his /hiz/ *poss.pron.* **1** (*attrib.*) of or belonging to him (*his house*). **2** the one or ones belonging to or associated with him (*it is his; his are over there*).

His·pan·ic /hispánik/ *adj. & n.* •*adj.* **1** of or being a person of Latin-American or Iberian descent in the US. **2** of or relating to Spain or to Iberia. **3** of Spain and other Spanish-speaking countries. •*n.* a Spanish-speaking person, esp. one of Latin-American descent, living in the US. ▫▫ **His·pan·i·cize** /–nisīz/ *v.tr.*

hiss /his/ *v. & n.* •*v.* **1** *intr.* (of a person, snake, etc.) make a sharp sibilant sound, esp. as a sign of disapproval (*audience booed and hissed*). **2** *tr.* express disapproval of (a person, etc.) by hisses. **3** *tr.* whisper (a threat, etc.) angrily (*"we'll see about that," he hissed*). •*n.* **1** a sharp sibilant sound as of the letter *s*, esp. as an expression of disapproval. **2** *Electronics* unwanted interference at audio frequencies.

his·ta·mine /hístəmin, –meen/ *n. Biochem.* an organic compound occurring in injured body tissues, etc., and also associated with allergic reactions. ▫▫ **his·ta·min·ic** /–mínik/ *adj.*

histo- /hístō/ *comb.form* (before a vowel also **hist-**) *Biol.* tissue.

his·to·gram /hístəgram/ *n. Statistics* a chart consisting of rectangles (usu. drawn vertically from a base line) whose areas and positions are proportional to the value or range of a number of variables.

his·tol·o·gy /históləjee/ *n.* the study of the structure of tissues. ▫▫ **his·to·log·i·cal** /hístəlójikəl/ *adj.* **his·tol·o·gist** /históləjist/ *n.*

his·tol·y·sis /histólisis/ *n.* the breaking down of tissues. ▫▫ **his·to·lyt·ic** /–təlítik/ *adj.*

his·to·ri·an /histáwreeən/ *n.* **1** a writer of history. **2** a person learned in or studying history.

his·tor·ic /histáwrik, –stór–/ *adj.* **1** important in history or potentially so (*a historic moment*). **2** *Gram.* (of a tense) normally used in the narration of past events. ▶**Historic** and *historical* denote different things. The former means 'important; notable': *historic leaders, historic battles.* The latter means 'relating to history': *historical writings*. An event can be either, depending on whether it is viewed as part of history or as extremely important. Note also that both of these words, traditionally preceded by *a,* are now often used with *an: a historic moment, an historic moment.*

his·tor·i·cal /histáwrikəl, –stór–/ *adj.* **1** of or concerning history (*historical evidence*). **2** belonging to history, not to prehistory or legend. **3** (of the study of a subject) based on an analysis of its development over a period. **4** belonging to the past, not the present. **5** (of a novel, a movie, etc.) dealing or professing to deal with historical events. **6** in connection with history (*of purely historical interest*). ▫▫ **his·tor·i·cal·ly** *adv.*

his·tor·i·cism /histáwrisizəm, –stór–/ *n.* **1** the theory that social and cultural phenomena are determined by history. **2** the belief that historical events are governed by laws. ▫▫ **his·tor·i·cist** *n.*

his·to·ric·i·ty /hístərísitee/ *n.* the historical genuineness of an event, etc.

his·to·ri·og·ra·phy /histáwreeógrəfee/ *n.* **1** the writing of history. **2** the study of historical writing. ▫▫ **his·to·ri·og·ra·pher** *n.* **his·to·ri·o·graph·ic** /–reeəgráfik/ *adj.* **his·to·ri·o·graph·i·cal** *adj.*

his·to·ry /hístəree/ *n.* (*pl.* **-ries**) **1** a continuous, usu. chronological, record of important or public events. **2 a** the study of past events, esp. human affairs. **b** the total accumulation of past events, esp. relating to human affairs or a particular nation, person, thing, etc. (*the history of astronomy*). **3** an eventful past (*this house has a history*). **4** a systematic account of a past event or events, etc. ▫ **make history** do something memorable.

history late Middle English (also as a verb): via Latin from Greek *historia* 'finding out, narrative, history,' from *histōr* 'learned, wise man,' from an Indo-European root shared by WIT[2].

his·tri·on·ic /hístreeónik/ *adj. & n.* •*adj.* (of behavior) theatrical; dramatic. •*n.* (in *pl.*) insincere and dramatic behavior designed to impress. ▫▫ **his·tri·on·i·cal·ly** *adv.*

hit /hit/ *v. & n.* •*v.* (**hitting**; *past* and *past part.* **hit**) **1** *tr.* **a** strike with a blow or a missile. **b** (of a moving body) strike (*the plane hit the ground*). **c** reach (a target, a person, etc.) with a directed missile (*hit the window with the ball*). **2** *tr.* cause to suffer or affect adversely. **3** *intr.* (often foll. by *at, against*) direct a blow. **4** *tr.* (often foll. by *against, on*) knock (a part of the body) (*hit his head on the door frame*). **5** *tr.* light upon (*he's hit the truth at last*) (see *hit on*). **6** *tr. colloq.* **a** encounter (*hit a snag*). **b** arrive at (*hit an all-time low*). **c** indulge in, esp. liquor, etc. (*hit the bottle*). **7** *tr. sl.* rob or kill. **8** *tr.* occur forcefully to (*the seriousness of the situation only hit him later*). **9** *tr. Sports* **a** propel (a ball, etc.) with a bat, etc. **b** score (runs, etc.) in this way. **c** (usu. foll. by *for*) strike (a ball or a pitcher, etc.) for a specific hit, result, etc. **10** *tr.* represent exactly. •*n.* **1 a** a blow; a stroke. **b** a collision. **2** a shot, etc., that hits its target. **3** *colloq.* a popular success in entertainment. **4** *sl.* **a** a murder or other violent crime. **b** a drug injection, etc. **7** a successful attempt. **8** *Baseball* = BASE HIT. ▫ **hit and run a** cause (accidental or willful) damage and escape or leave the scene before being discovered. **b** *Baseball* play in which a base runner begins running to the next base as the pitcher delivers the ball, which the batter then tries to hit. **hit back** retaliate. **hit below the belt 1** esp. *Boxing* foul with a low blow. **2** treat or behave unfairly. **hit it off** (often foll. by *with*) agree or be congenial. **hit the nail on the head** state the truth exactly. **hit on 1** (also **hit upon**) find (what is sought), esp. by chance. **2** *sl.* make sexual advances toward. **hit the road** (or **trail**) *sl.* depart. ▫▫ **hit·ter** *n.*

hitch /hich/ *v. & n.* •*v.* **1 a** *tr.* fasten with a loop, hook, etc. (*hitched the horse to the cart*). **b** *intr.* (often foll. by *in, onto,* etc.) become fastened in this way. **2** *tr.* move (a thing) with a jerk (*hitched the pillow into a comfortable position*). **3** *colloq.* **a** *intr.* = HITCHHIKE. **b** *tr.* obtain (a ride) by hitchhiking. •*n.* **1** a temporary obstacle. **2** an abrupt pull or push. **3** a noose or knot of various kinds. **4** *colloq.* a free ride in a vehicle. ▫ **get hitched** *colloq.* marry. **hitch up** lift (esp. clothing) with a jerk. ▫▫ **hitch·er** *n.*

hitch·hike /hích-hīk/ *v. & n.* •*v.intr.* travel by seeking free rides in passing vehicles. •*n.* a journey made by hitchhiking. □□ **hitch·hik·er** *n.*
hi-tech /hítek/ *adj.* = HIGH-TECH.
hith·er /híthər/ *adv.* usu. *formal* or *literary* to or toward this place.
hith·er·to /híthərtóō/ *adv.* until this time; up to now.
hit list *n. sl.* a list of prospective victims.
hit man *n.* (*pl.* **hit men**) *sl.* a hired assassin.
hit-or-miss *adj.* aimed or done carelessly.
hit pa·rade *n. colloq.* a list of the current best-selling records of popular music.
Hit·tite /hítīt/ *n. & adj.* •*n.* **1** a member of an ancient people of Asia Minor and Syria. **2** the extinct language of the Hittites. •*adj.* of or relating to the Hittites or their language.
HIV *abbr.* human immunodeficiency virus, a retrovirus causing AIDS.
hive /hīv/ *n.* **1** a beehive. **2** a busy swarming place.
hives /hīvz/ *n.pl.* a skin eruption, esp. one caused by an allergic reaction.
hiya /híyə/ *int. colloq.* a word used in greeting.
hl *abbr.* hectoliter(s).
hm *abbr.* hectometer(s).
HMO *abbr.* health maintenance organization.
Ho *symb. Chem.* the element holmium.
ho /hō/ *int.* an expression of surprise, triumph, or (often repeated as **ho! ho!**, etc.) derision.
hoa·gie /hṓgee/ *n.* (also **hoa·gy**) (*pl.* **-gies**) = SUBMARINE SANDWICH.
hoard /hawrd/ *n. & v.* •*n.* **1** a stock or supply (esp. of money) stored for future use. **2** an amassed store of facts, etc. •*v.* **1** *tr.* (often *absol.*; often foll. by *up*) amass (money, etc.) and put away. **2** *intr.* accumulate more than one's current requirements of food, etc., in a time of scarcity. □□ **hoard·er** *n.*
hoar·frost /háwrfrawst/ *n.* frozen water vapor deposited on vegetation, etc., in clear still weather.
hoarse /hawrs/ *adj.* **1** (of the voice) rough and deep. **2** having such a voice. □□ **hoarse·ly** *adv.* **hoars·en** *v.tr. & intr.* **hoarse·ness** *n.*
hoar·y /háwree/ *adj.* (**hoarier, hoariest**) **1 a** (of hair) gray or white with age. **b** having such hair. **2** old and trite (*a hoary joke*). □□ **hoar·i·ly** *adv.* **hoar·i·ness** *n.*
hoax /hōks/ *n. & v.* •*n.* a humorous or malicious deception. •*v.tr.* deceive (a person) with a hoax.
hob[1] /hob/ *n.* **1** a flat metal shelf at the side of a fireplace, used esp. for keeping things warm. **2** = HOBNAIL.
hob[2] /hob/ *n.* **1** a male ferret. **2** a hobgoblin.
hob·bit /hóbit/ *n.* a member of an imaginary race of half-sized people in stories by J.R.R. Tolkien.
hob·ble /hóbəl/ *v. & n.* •*v.* **1** *intr.* walk lamely; limp. **2** *tr.* tie together the legs of (a horse, etc.) to prevent it from straying. •*n.* **1** an uneven or infirm gait. **2** a rope, etc., used for hobbling a horse, etc. □□ **hob·bler** *n.*
hob·by /hóbee/ *n.* (*pl.* **-bies**) a favorite leisure time activity or occupation. □□ **hob·by·ist** *n.*
hob·by·horse /hóbeehawrs/ *n.* **1** a child's toy consisting of a stick with a horse's head. **2** a preoccupation; a favorite topic of conversation.
hob·gob·lin /hóbgoblin/ *n.* a mischievous imp; a bugbear.
hob·nail /hóbnayl/ *n.* a heavy-headed nail used for boot soles. □□ **hob·nailed** *adj.*
hob·nob /hóbnob/ *v.intr.* (**hobnobbed, hobnobbing**) (usu. foll. by *with*) mix socially or informally.
ho·bo /hṓbō/ *n.* (*pl.* **-boes** or **-bos**) a wandering worker; a tramp.
Hob·son's choice /hóbsənz/ *n.* a choice of taking the thing offered or nothing.
hock[1] /hok/ *n.* **1** the joint of a quadruped's hind leg between the knee and the fetlock. **2** a knuckle of pork; the lower joint of a ham.
hock[2] /hok/ *v. & n. colloq.* •*v.tr.* pawn; pledge. •*n.* a pawnbroker's pledge. □ **in hock 1** in pawn. **2** in debt.
hock·ey /hókee/ *n.* **1** = ICE HOCKEY. **2** = FIELD HOCKEY.
ho·cus /hṓkəs/ *v.tr.* (**hocussed, hocussing**; also **hocused, hocusing**) **1** take in; hoax. **2** stupefy (a person, animal, etc.) with drugs. **3** put a drug in someone's food or drink.
ho·cus-po·cus /hṓkəspṓkəs/ *n.* **1** deception; trickery. **2** a typical verbal formula used in conjuring.

hocus-pocus early 17th century: from *hax pax max Deus adimax*, a pseudo-Latin phrase used as a formula by magicians.

hod /hod/ *n.* **1** a V-shaped open trough on a pole used for carrying bricks, mortar, etc. **2** a portable receptacle for coal.
hodge·podge /hójpoj/ *n.* a confused mixture, a jumble.
hoe /hō/ *n. & v.* •*n.* a long-handled tool with a thin metal blade, used for weeding, etc. •*v.* (**hoes, hoed, hoeing**) **1** *tr.* weed (crops); loosen (earth); dig up or cut down with a hoe. **2** *intr.* use a hoe. □□ **hoer** *n.*
hoe·cake /hṓkayk/ *n.* a coarse cake of cornmeal orig. baked on the blade of a hoe.
hoe·down /hṓdown/ *n.* a lively dance or dance party, esp. one with square dancing.
hog /hawg, hog/ *n. & v.* •*n.* **1 a** a domesticated pig, esp. one over 120 pounds and reared for slaughter. **b** any of several other pigs of the family Suidae, e.g., a warthog. **2** *colloq.* a greedy person. •*v.* (**hogged, hogging**) *tr. colloq.* take greedily; hoard selfishly. □ **go the whole hog** *colloq.* do something completely or thoroughly. □□ **hog·ger** *n.* **hog·gish** *adj.* **hog·gish·ly** *adv.* **hog·gish·ness** *n.* **hog·like** *adj.*
ho·gan /hṓgaan, –gən/ *n.* a Navajo dwelling of logs, etc.
hog·back /háwgbak, hóg–/ *n.* (also **hog's back**) a steep-sided ridge of a hill.
hogs·head /háwgz-hed, hógz–/ *n.* **1** a large cask. **2** a liquid or dry measure, usu. about 63 gallons.
hog-tie *v.tr.* **1** secure by fastening the hands and feet or all four feet together. **2** restrain; impede.
hog·wash /háwgwosh, –wawsh, hóg–/ *n.* **1** *colloq.* nonsense; rubbish. **2** kitchen swill, etc., for pigs.
hog·weed /háwgweed, hóg–/ *n.* any of various coarse weeds of the genus *Heracleum*, esp. *H. sphondylium*.
ho-hum /hṓhúm/ *int.* expressing boredom.
hoi pol·loi /hóy pəlóy/ *n.* (often prec. by *the*: see note below) the masses; the common people.
▶The phrase **hoi polloi** is usually preceded by *the: The hoi polloi grew restless as candidate after candidate spoke.* Strictly speaking, the *the* is unnecessary because *hoi* means 'the' (in Greek). Perhaps because of confusion with *hoity-toity*, **hoi polloi** is sometimes wrongly taken to mean its opposite, 'the few, the elite.'
hoist /hoyst/ *v. & n.* •*v.tr.* **1** raise or haul up. **2** raise by means of ropes and pulleys, etc. •*n.* **1** an act of hoisting. **2** an apparatus for hoisting. **3** the part of a flag nearest the staff. □□ **hoist·er** *n.*
hoi·ty-toi·ty /hóyteetóytee/ *adj.* haughty; petulant; snobbish.
hok·ey /hṓkee/ *adj.* (also **hok·y**) (**hokier, hokiest**) *sl.* sentimental; melodramatic; artificial. □□ **hok·ey·ness** *n.*
ho·key-po·key /hṓkeepṓkee/ *n. colloq.* **1** = HOCUS-POCUS. **2** a communal dance that is performed in a circle with synchronized shaking of the limbs in turn.
ho·kum /hṓkəm/ *n. sl.* **1** sentimental, popular, sensational, or unreal situations, dialogue, etc., in a movie or play. **2** bunkum; rubbish.
Hol·arc·tic /hōlaárktik, –laártik/ *adj.* of or relating to

the geographical distribution of animals in the whole northern or Arctic region.

hold[1] /hōld/ *v. & n.* •*v.* (*past* and *past part.* **held** /held/) **1** *tr.* **a** grasp (esp. in the hands or arms). **b** (also *refl.*) sustain (a thing, oneself, one's head, etc.) in a particular position (*hold it to the light*). **c** grasp so as to control (*hold the reins*). **2** *tr.* (of a vessel, etc.) contain or be capable of containing (*the pitcher holds two pints*). **3** *tr.* possess or have, esp.: **a** be the owner or tenant of (land, property, etc.) (*holds the farm from the trust*). **b** gain or have gained (a degree, record, etc.) (*holds the long-jump record*). **c** have the position of (a job or office). **d** have (a specified card) in one's hand. **e** keep possession of (a place, a person's thoughts, etc.) esp. against attack (*held the fort against the enemy; held his place in her estimation*). **4** *intr.* remain unbroken (*the roof held under the storm*). **5** *tr.* observe; conduct (a meeting, festival, conversation, etc.). **6** *tr.* **a** keep (a person, etc.) in a specified condition, place, etc. (*held her prisoner*). **b** detain, esp. in custody (*hold him until I arrive*). **7** *tr.* **a** engross (a person or a person's attention) (*the book held him for hours*). **b** dominate (*held the stage*). **8** *tr.* (foll. by *to*) make (a person, etc.) adhere to (terms, a promise, etc.). **9** *intr.* (of weather) continue fine. **10** *tr.* (often foll. by *to* + infin., or *that* + clause) believe (*held it to be self-evident*). **11** *tr.* regard with a specified feeling (*held him in contempt*). **12** *tr.* **a** cease (*hold your fire*). **b** *colloq.* withhold (*hold the onions!*). **13** *tr.* keep or reserve (*will you hold our seats please?*). **14** *tr.* be able to drink (liquor) without apparent effect (*can hold his liquor*). **15** *tr.* (usu. foll. by *that* + clause) (of a judge, a court, etc.) lay down; decide. **16** *tr. Mus.* sustain (a note). •*n.* **1** a grasp (*catch hold of him*). **2** (often in *comb.*) a thing to hold by (*seized the handhold*). **3** (foll. by *on, over*) influence over (*has a strange hold over them*). **4** a manner of holding in wrestling, etc. **5** *archaic* a fortress. □ **hold (a thing) against (a person)** resent or regard it as discreditable to (a person). **hold back 1** impede the progress of. **2** keep (a thing) for oneself. **3** (often foll. by *from*) hesitate. **hold court** preside over one's admirers, etc. **hold dear** regard with affection. **hold down 1** repress. **2** *colloq.* be competent enough to keep (one's job, etc.). **hold everything!** (or **it!**) cease action or movement. **hold the fort 1** act as a temporary substitute. **2** cope in an emergency. **hold forth 1** offer (an inducement, etc.). **2** usu. *derog.* speak at length. **hold hands** grasp one another by the hand as a sign of affection or for support. **hold one's horses** *colloq.* stop; slow down. **hold the line 1** not yield. **2** maintain a telephone connection. **hold off 1** delay; not begin. **2** keep one's distance. **hold on 1** keep one's grasp on something. **2** wait a moment. **3** (when telephoning) not hang up. **hold out 1** stretch forth (a hand, etc.). **2** offer (an inducement, etc.). **3** maintain resistance. **4** persist or last. **hold out for** continue to demand. **hold out on** *colloq.* refuse something to (a person). **hold over** postpone. **hold together 1** cohere. **2** cause to cohere. **hold one's tongue** *colloq.* be silent. **hold up 1 a** support; sustain. **b** maintain (the head, etc.) erect. **2** exhibit; display. **3** arrest the progress of. **4** stop and rob by violence or threats. **hold water** (of reasoning) be sound; bear examination. **hold with** (usu. with *neg.*) *colloq.* approve of (*don't hold with motorcycles*). **on hold 1** temporarily deferred. **2** (of a telephone call or caller) holding on (see **hold on** 3 above). **take hold** (of a custom or habit) become established. **with no holds barred** with no restrictions. □□ **hold•a•ble** *adj.*

hold[2] /hōld/ *n.* a compartment or compartments in the lower part of a ship or aircraft in which the cargo is stored.

hold•er /hṓldər/ *n.* **1** (often in *comb.*) a device for holding something (*cigarette holder*). **2 a** the possessor of a title, etc. **b** the occupant of an office, etc.

hold•ing /hṓlding/ *n.* **1** land held by lease. **2** stocks, property, etc., held.

hold•ing com•pa•ny *n.* a company created to hold the shares of other companies, which it then controls.

hold•up /hṓldəp/ *n.* **1** a stoppage or delay by traffic, fog, etc. **2** a robbery conducted with the use of threats or violence.

hole /hōl/ *n. & v.* •*n.* **1 a** an empty space in a solid body. **b** an aperture in or through something. **2** an animal's burrow. **3** a cavity or receptacle for a ball in various sports or games. **4** *colloq.* a small, mean, or dingy abode. **5** *colloq.* an awkward situation. **6** *Golf* **a** a point scored by a player who gets the ball from tee to hole with the fewest strokes. **b** the terrain or distance from tee to hole. **7** a position from which an electron is absent, esp. acting as a mobile positive particle in a semiconductor. •*v.tr.* **1** make a hole or holes in. **2** put into a hole. **3** (also *absol.*; often foll. by *out*) send (a golf ball) into a hole. □ **hole up** *colloq.* hide oneself. **make a hole in** use a large amount of. □□ **hol•ey** *adj.*

hole in one *n. Golf* a shot that enters the hole from the tee.

hole in the wall *n.* a small dingy place.

hol•i•day /hóliday/ *n.* **1** a day of festivity or recreation when no work is done, esp. a religious festival, etc. **2** esp. *Brit.* (often in *pl.*) = VACATION. **3** (*attrib.*) (of clothes, etc.) festive.

ho•li•er-than-thou *adj. colloq.* self-righteous.

ho•li•ly /hṓlilee/ *adv.* in a holy manner.

ho•li•ness /hṓleenis/ *n.* **1** sanctity; the state of being holy. **2** (**Holiness**) a title used when referring to or addressing the Pope.

ho•lism /hṓlizəm/ *n.* (also **wholism**) **1** *Philos.* the theory that certain wholes are to be regarded as greater than the sum of their parts (cf. REDUCTIONISM). **2** *Med.* the treating of the whole person including mental and social factors rather than just the symptoms of a disease. □□ **ho•lis•tic** *adj.* **ho•lis•ti•cal•ly** *adv.*

hol•land /hólənd/ *n.* a smooth, hard-wearing, linen fabric.

hol•lan•daise sauce /hóləndáyz/ *n.* a creamy sauce of melted butter, egg yolks, and lemon juice or vinegar.

hol•ler /hólər/ *v. & n. colloq.* •*v.* **1** *intr.* make a loud cry or noise. **2** *tr.* express with a loud cry or shout. •*n.* a loud cry, noise, or shout.

hol•low /hólō/ *adj., n., & v.* •*adj.* **1 a** having a hole or cavity inside. **b** sunken (*hollow cheeks*). **2** (of a sound) echoing, as though made in or on a hollow container. **3** empty; hungry. **4** meaningless (*a hollow triumph*). **5** insincere; false (*a hollow laugh; hollow promises*). •*n.* **1** a hollow place; a hole. **2** a valley; a basin. •*v.tr.* (often foll. by *out*) make hollow; excavate. □□ **hol•low•ly** *adv.* **hol•low•ness** *n.*

hol•low•ware /hólōwair/ *n.* hollow articles of metal, china, etc., such as pots, kettles, pitchers, etc.

hol•ly /hólee/ *n.* (*pl.* **-lies**) an evergreen shrub, often with prickly usu. dark green leaves and red berries.

hol•ly•hock /hóleehok/ *n.* a tall plant, *Alcea rosea*, with large showy flowers of various colors.

Hol•ly•wood /hóleewŏŏd/ *n.* the American movie industry or its products, with its principal center at Hollywood, California.

holm /hōm/ *n.* (in full **holm oak**) an evergreen oak, *Quercus ilex*, with hollylike young leaves.

hol•mi•um /hṓlmeeəm/ *n. Chem.* a soft silvery metallic element of the lanthanide series. ¶ Symb.: **Ho**.

holo- /hólō/ *comb. form* whole (*Holocene; holocaust*).

hol•o•caust /hóləkawst/ *n.* **1** a case of large-scale destruction, esp. by fire or nuclear war. **2** (**the Holocaust**) the mass murder of the Jews by the Nazis in World War II.

Hol·o·cene /hóləseen/ *adj. & n. Geol.* • *adj.* of or relating to the most recent epoch of the Quaternary period with evidence of human development. • *n.* this period or system. Also called RECENT.

hol·o·gram /hóləgram/ *n. Physics* **1** a three-dimensional image formed by the interference of light beams from a coherent light source. **2** a photograph of the interference pattern, which when suitably illuminated produces a three-dimensional image.

hol·o·graph /hóləgraf/ *adj. & n.* • *adj.* wholly written by hand by the person named as the author. • *n.* a holograph document.

hol·og·ra·phy /həlógrəfee/ *n. Physics* the study or production of holograms. ▫▫ **hol·o·graph·ic** /hóləgráfik/ *adj.* **hol·o·graph·i·cal·ly** *adv.*

hol·ster /hṓlstər/ *n.* a leather case for a pistol or revolver.

ho·ly /hṓlee/ *adj.* (**holier, holiest**) **1** morally and spiritually excellent or perfect, and to be revered. **2** belonging to, devoted to, or empowered by God. **3** consecrated; sacred. **4** used as an intensive and in trivial exclamations (*holy smoke!*).

Ho·ly Ghost *n.* = HOLY SPIRIT.

Ho·ly Grail *n.* see GRAIL.

Ho·ly Land *n.* **1** W. Palestine, esp. Judaea. **2** a region similarly revered in non-Christian religions.

Ho·ly Ro·man Em·pire *n.* see ROMAN.

Ho·ly Spir·it *n.* the third person of the Christian Trinity, God as spiritually acting.

ho·ly war *n.* a war waged in support of a religious cause.

ho·ly wa·ter *n.* water dedicated to holy uses, or blessed by a priest.

Ho·ly Week *n.* the week before Easter.

hom·age /hómij/ *n.* acknowledgment of superiority; dutiful reverence (*pay homage to*).

hom·bre /ómbray/ *n.* a man.

Hom·burg /hómbərg/ *n.* a man's felt hat with a narrow curled brim and a lengthwise dent in the crown.

home /hōm/ *n., adj., adv., & v.* • *n.* **1 a** the place where one lives. **b** a dwelling house. **2** the members of a family collectively (*comes from a good home*). **3** the native land of a person or of a person's ancestors. **4** an institution for persons needing care, rest, or refuge (*nursing home*). **5** the place where a thing originates or is native or most common. **6 a** the finishing point in a race. **b** (in games) the place where one is free from attack. **c** *Baseball* home plate. • *attrib.adj.* **1 a** connected with one's home. **b** carried on, done, or made at home. **2 a** carried on or produced in one's own country (*the home market*). **b** dealing with the domestic affairs of a country. **3** *Sports* played on one's own field, etc. (*home game*). • *adv.* **1 a** to one's home or country (*go home*). **b** arrived at home (*is he home yet?*). **c** at home (*stay home*). **2 a** to the point aimed at (*the thrust went home*). **b** as far as possible (*drove the nail home*). • *v.* **1** *intr.* (esp. of a trained pigeon) return home (cf. HOMING 1). **2** *intr.* (often foll. by *on, in on*) (of a vessel, missile, etc.) be guided by a landmark, radio beam, etc. ▫ **at home 1** in one's own house or native land. **2** at ease as if in one's own home (*make yourself at home*). **3** (usu. foll. by *in, on, with*) familiar or well informed. **4** available to callers. **home away from home** a place other than one's home where one feels at home. ▫▫ **home·like** *adj.*

home·bod·y *n. colloq.* a person who likes to stay at home, esp. one who is perceived as unadventurous.

home·boy /hṓmboy/ *n. colloq.* a person from one's own town or neighborhood.

home·com·ing /hṓmkəming/ *n.* **1** arrival at home. **2** a high school, college, or university game, dance, or other event to which alumni are invited to visit.

home ec·o·nom·ics *n.* the study of household management.

home·grown /hṓmgrōn/ *adj.* grown or produced at home.

home·land /hṓmland/ *n.* **1** one's native land. **2** *hist.* an area in S. Africa formerly reserved for a particular African people.

home·less /hṓmlis/ *adj. & n.* • *adj.* lacking a home. • *n.* (prec. by *the*) homeless people. ▫▫ **home·less·ness** *n.*

home·ly /hṓmlee/ *adj.* (**homelier, homeliest**) **1** not attractive in appearance. **2 a** simple; plain. **b** unpretentious. **c** primitive. ▫▫ **home·li·ness** *n.*

home·made /hṓmayd/ *adj.* made at home.

home·mak·er /hṓmaykər/ *n.* a person, esp. a housewife, who manages a household.

home mov·ie *n.* a film made at home or of one's own activities.

ho·me·o·path /hṓmeeəpath/ *n.* a person who practices homeopathy.

ho·me·op·a·thy /hṓmeeópəthee/ *n.* the treatment of disease by minute doses of drugs that in a healthy person would produce symptoms of the disease (cf. ALLOPATHY). ▫▫ **hom·e·o·path·ic** /–meeəpáthik/ *adj.*

ho·me·o·therm /hṓmeeəthərm/ *n.* an organism that maintains its body temperature at a constant level, usu. above that of the environment, by its metabolic activity. ▫▫ **ho·me·o·ther·mal** *adj.* **ho·me·o·ther·mic** *adj.* **ho·me·o·ther·my** *n.*

home·own·er /hṓmōnər/ *n.* a person who owns his or her own home.

home page *n.* a hypertext document on the World Wide Web, serving as an introductory focus of information relating to an organization or an individual.

home plate *n. Baseball* a plate beside which the batter stands and which a runner must touch in order to score a run.

ho·mer /hṓmər/ *n. Baseball* a home run.

home rule *n.* the government of a country or region by its own citizens.

home run *n.* **1** *Baseball* a hit that allows the batter to make a complete circuit of the bases. **2** any singular success.

home·sick /hṓmsik/ *adj.* depressed by longing for one's home during absence from it. ▫▫ **home·sick·ness** *n.*

home·spun /hṓmspun/ *adj. & n.* • *adj.* **1 a** (of cloth) made of yarn spun at home. **b** (of yarn) spun at home. **2** plain; simple. • *n.* homespun cloth.

home·stead /hṓmsted/ *n.* **1** a house, esp. a farmhouse, and outbuildings. **2** an area of land (usu. 160 acres) granted to an early American settler as a home. ▫▫ **home·stead·er** *n.*

home stretch *n.* the concluding stretch of a racetrack.

home·style /hṓmstīl/ *adj.* (esp. of food) of a kind made or done at home; homey.

home town *n.* the town of one's birth or early life or present fixed residence.

home·ward /hṓmwərd/ *adv. & adj.* • *adv.* (also **home·wards** /–wərdz/) toward home. • *adj.* going or leading toward home.

home·work /hṓmwərk/ *n.* **1** work to be done at home, esp. by a school pupil. **2** preparatory work or study.

hom·ey /hṓmee/ *adj.* (also **hom·y**) (**homier, homiest**) suggesting home; cozy.

hom·i·cide /hómisīd, hṓ–/ *n.* **1** the killing of a human being by another. **2** a person who kills a human being. ▫▫ **hom·i·cid·al** /–síd'l/ *adj.*

hom·i·let·ic /hómilétik/ *adj.* of homilies.

hom·i·ly /hómilee/ *n.* (*pl.* **-lies**) **1** a sermon. **2** a tedious moralizing discourse. ▫▫ **hom·i·list** *n.*

hom·ing /hṓming/ *attrib. adj.* **1** (of a pigeon) trained to fly home; bred for long-distance racing. **2** (of a device) for guiding to a target, etc.

hom·i·nid /hóminid/ *n. & adj.* •*n.* any member of the primate family Hominidae, including humans. •*adj.* of or relating to this family.

hom·i·noid /hóminoyd/ *adj. & n.* •*adj.* like a human. •*n.* an animal resembling a human.

hom·i·ny /hóminee/ *n.* coarsely ground corn kernels soaked in lye then washed to remove the hulls.

ho·mo[1] /hṓmō/ *n.* any primate of the genus *Homo*, including modern humans.

ho·mo[2] /hṓmō/ *n.* (*pl.* **-mos**) *offens. colloq.* a homosexual.

homo- /hṓmō/ *comb. form* same (often opp. HETERO-).

ho·mo·ge·ne·ous /hṓməjéeneeəs, –yəs/ *adj.* **1** of the same kind. **2** consisting of parts all of the same kind. **3** *Math.* containing terms all of the same degree. ▫▫ **ho·mo·ge·ne·i·ty** /–jinéeitee/ *n.*

ho·mog·e·nize /həmójinīz/ *v.* **1** *tr. & intr.* make or become homogeneous. **2** *tr.* treat (milk) so that the fat droplets are emulsified and the cream does not separate. ▫▫ **ho·mog·e·ni·za·tion** *n.* **ho·mog·e·ni·zer** *n.*

ho·mo·graft /hṓməgraft, hóm–/ *n.* a graft of living tissue from one to another of the same species but different genotype.

ho·mo·graph /hóməgraf, hṓ–/ *n.* a word spelled like another but of different meaning or origin (e.g., POLE[1], POLE[2]).

ho·mol·o·gous /həmóləgəs/ *adj.* **1 a** having the same relation, relative position, etc. **b** corresponding. **2** *Biol.* (of organs, etc.) similar in position and structure but not necessarily in function.

ho·mo·logue /hóməlawg, –log, hṓ–/ *n.* (also **ho·mo·log**) a homologous thing.

hom·o·nym /hómənim/ *n.* **1** a word of the same spelling or sound as another but of different meaning. **2** a namesake. ▫▫ **ho·mon·y·mous** /həmónimәs/ *adj.*

ho·mo·pho·bi·a /hṓməfṓbeeə/ *n.* a hatred or fear of homosexuals. ▫▫ **ho·mo·phobe** /–əfōb/ *n.* **ho·mo·pho·bic** *adj.*

ho·mo·phone /hóməfōn, hṓ–/ *n.* **1** a word having the same sound as another but of different meaning or origin (e.g., *pair, pear*). **2** a symbol denoting the same sound as another.

ho·mo·phon·ic /hómōfónik, hṓ–/ *adj. Mus.* in unison; characterized by movement of all parts to the same melody. ▫▫ **ho·mo·phon·i·cal·ly** *adv.*

ho·mop·ter·an /həmóptərən/ *n.* any insect of the suborder Homoptera, including aphids and cicadas, with wings of uniform texture. ▫▫ **ho·mop·ter·ous** *adj.*

Ho·mo sa·pi·ens /hṓmō sáypee-enz/ *n.* modern humans regarded as a species.

ho·mo·sex·u·al /hṓməsékshoo͞əl/ *adj. & n.* •*adj.* **1** involving sexual attraction to persons of the same sex. **2** concerning homosexual relations or people. •*n.* a homosexual person. ▫▫ **ho·mo·sex·u·al·i·ty** /–shoo͞álitee/ *n.* **ho·mo·sex·u·al·ly** *adv.*

hom·y var. of HOMEY.

Hon. *abbr.* **1** Honorable. **2** Honorary.

hon /hun/ *n. colloq.* = HONEY 3.

hon·cho /hónchō/ *n. & v. sl.* •*n.* (*pl.* **-chos**) **1** a leader or manager; the person in charge. **2** an admirable man. •*v.tr.* (**-choes, -choed**) be in charge of; oversee.

honcho 1940s: from Japanese *hanchō* 'group leader,' a term brought back to the U.S. by servicemen stationed in Japan during the occupation following World War II.

hone /hōn/ *n. & v.* •*n.* **1** a whetstone, esp. for razors. **2** any of various stones used as material for this. •*v.tr.* sharpen on or as on a hone.

hon·est /ónist/ *adj. & adv.* •*adj.* **1** fair and just in character or behavior. **2** free of deceit and untruthfulness. **3** fairly earned (*an honest living*). **4** (of an act or feeling) showing fairness. **5** (of a thing) unadulterated; unsophisticated. •*adv. colloq.* genuinely; really. ▫ **make an honest woman of** *colloq.* marry (esp. a pregnant woman).

hon·est·ly /ónistlee/ *adv.* **1** in an honest way. **2** really (*I don't honestly know*).

hon·est-to-God *adj. & adv.* (also **honest-to-goodness**) *colloq.* •*adj.* genuine; real. •*adv.* genuinely; really.

hon·es·ty /ónistee/ *n.* **1** being honest. **2** truthfulness. **3** a plant of the genus *Lunaria* with flat round semitransparent seed pods.

hon·ey /húnee/ *n.* (*pl.* **-eys**) **1** a sweet sticky yellowish fluid made by bees and other insects from nectar collected from flowers. **2** the color of this. **3** (usu. as a form of address) darling; sweetheart.

hon·ey·bee /húneebee/ *n.* any of various bees of the genus *Apis*.

hon·ey·comb /húneekōm/ *n. & v.* •*n.* **1** a structure of hexagonal cells of wax, made by bees to store honey and eggs. **2** a pattern arranged hexagonally. •*v.tr.* **1** fill with cavities or tunnels. **2** mark with a honeycomb pattern.

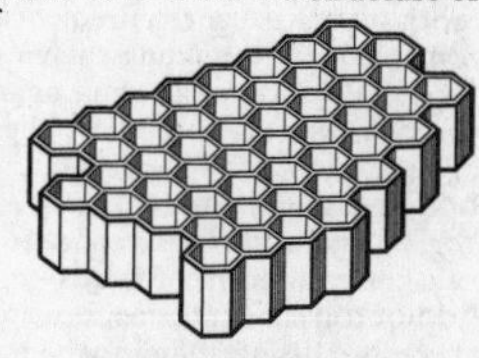

honeycomb, 1

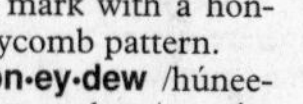

hon·ey·dew /húneedo͞o, –dyo͞o/ *n.* **1** a variety of melon with smooth pale skin and sweet green flesh. **2** a sweet sticky substance found on leaves and stems, excreted by aphids.

hon·eyed /húneed/ *adj.* **1** of or containing honey. **2** sweet.

hon·ey·moon /húneemo͞on/ *n. & v.* •*n.* **1** a vacation spent together by a newly married couple. **2** an initial period of enthusiasm or goodwill. •*v.intr.* (usu. foll. by *in, at*) spend a honeymoon. ▫▫ **hon·ey·moon·er** *n.*

hon·ey·suck·le /húneesukəl/ *n.* any climbing shrub of the genus *Lonicera* with fragrant yellow, pink, or red flowers.

honk /hawngk, hongk/ *n. & v.* •*n.* **1** the cry of a wild goose. **2** the harsh sound of a car horn. •*v.* **1** *intr.* emit or give a honk. **2** *tr.* cause to do this.

hon·ky /háwngkee, hóngkee/ *n.* (*pl.* **-kies**) *black sl. offens.* a white person.

hon·ky-tonk /háwngkeetawngk, hóngkeetongk/ *n. colloq.* **1** ragtime piano music. **2** a cheap or disreputable nightclub, bar, dancehall, etc.

hon·or /ónər/ *n. & v.* •*n.* **1** high respect; glory. **2** adherence to what is right or to a conventional standard of conduct. **3** nobleness of mind; magnanimity (*honor among thieves*). **4** a thing conferred as a distinction, esp. an official award for bravery or achievement. **5** (foll. by *of* + verbal noun, or *to* + infin.) privilege; special right (*had the honor of being invited*). **6 a** exalted position. **b** (**Honor**) (prec. by *your, his*, etc.) a title of respect given to or used in addressing a judge, a US mayor, and (in Irish or rustic speech) any person of rank. **7** (foll. by *to*) a person or thing that brings honor (*she is an honor to her profession*). **8 a** (of a woman) chastity. **b** the reputation for this. **9** (in *pl.*) **a** special distinction for proficiency in an examination. **b** a course of degree studies more specialized than for a standard course or degree. **10 a** *Bridge* the ace, king, queen, jack, and ten, esp. of trumps, or the four aces at no trumps. **b** *Whist* the ace, king, queen, and jack, esp. of trumps. **11** *Golf* the right of driving off first as having won the last hole (*it is my honor*). •*v.tr.* **1** respect highly. **2** confer honor on. **3** accept or pay (a bill or check) when due. **4** acknowledge. □ **do the honors** perform the duties of a host to guests, etc. **in honor of** as a celebration of. **on one's honor** (usu. foll. by *to* + infin.) under a moral obligation.

hon•or•a•ble /ónərəbəl/ *adj.* **1 a** worthy of honor. **b** bringing honor to its possessor. **c** showing honor. **d** consistent with honor. **e** *colloq.* (of the intentions of a man courting a woman) directed toward marriage. **2** (**Honorable**) a title given to certain government officials and members of Congress. □□ **hon•or•a•bly** *adv.*

hon•or•a•ble men•tion *n.* an award of merit to a candidate in an examination, a work of art, etc., not awarded a prize.

hon•o•rar•i•um /ónəráireeəm/ *n.* (*pl.* **honorariums** or **honoraria** /–reeə/) a voluntary payment for professional services rendered without the normal fee.

hon•or•ar•y /ónəreree/ *adj.* **1 a** conferred as an honor, without the usual requirements, functions, etc. (*honorary degree*). **b** holding such a title or position (*honorary colonel*). **2** (of an office or its holder) unpaid (*honorary treasurer*). **3** (of an obligation) depending on honor, not legally enforceable.

hon•or•if•ic /ónərífik/ *adj.* & *n.* •*adj.* **1** conferring honor. **2** (esp. of forms of speech) implying respect. •*n.* an honorific form of words. □□ **hon•or•if•i•cal•ly** *adv.*

hon•or roll *n.* a list of people who have attained an honor, esp. a list of students who have received academic honors.

hon•or sys•tem *n.* a system of examinations, etc., without supervision, relying on the honor of those concerned.

hooch /hōōch/ *n.* (also **hootch**) *colloq.* alcoholic liquor, esp. illicit whiskey.

hood[1] /hŏŏd/ *n.* & *v.* •*n.* **1 a** a covering for the head and neck, whether part of a cloak, etc., or separate. **b** a separate hoodlike garment worn over a university gown or a surplice to indicate the wearer's degree. **2** the cover over the engine of a motor vehicle. **3** a canopy to protect users of machinery or to remove fumes, etc. **4** the hoodlike part of a cobra, seal, etc. **5** a leather covering for a hawk's head. •*v.tr.* cover with a hood. □□ **hood•ed** *adj.* **hood•less** *adj.* **hood•like** *adj.*

hood[2] /hŏŏd/ *n. sl.* a gangster or gunman.

hood•lum /hŏŏdləm, hŏŏd–/ *n.* **1** a street hooligan; a young thug. **2** a gangster.

hoo•doo /hŏŏdōō/ *n.* & *v.* •*n.* **1 a** bad luck. **b** a thing or person that brings or causes this. **2** voodoo. **3** a fantastic rock pinnacle or column of rock formed by erosion, etc. •*v.tr.* (**hoodoos, hoodooed**) **1** make unlucky. **2** bewitch.

hood•wink /hŏŏdwingk/ *v.tr.* deceive; delude.

hoo•ey /hŏŏ-ee/ *n.* & *int. sl.* nonsense; humbug.

hoof /hŏŏf, hōōf/ *n.* (*pl.* **hoofs** or **hooves** /hōōvz/) the horny part of the foot of a horse, antelope, and other ungulates. □ **hoof it** *sl.* go on foot. **on the hoof** (of cattle) not yet slaughtered. □□ **hoofed** *adj.* (also in *comb.*).

hook /hŏŏk/ *n.* & *v.* •*n.* **1 a** a piece of metal or other material bent back at an angle or with a round bend, for catching hold or for hanging things on. **b** (in full **fishhook**) a bent piece of wire, usu. barbed and baited, for catching fish. **2** a curved cutting instrument (*reaping hook*). **3 a** a sharp bend, e.g., in a river. **b** a projecting point of land. **4 a** *Golf* a hooking stroke (see sense 5 of *v.*). **b** *Boxing* a short swinging blow with the elbow bent and rigid. •*v.* **1** *tr.* **a** grasp with a hook. **b** secure with a hook or hooks. **2** (often foll. by *on, up*) **a** *tr.* attach with or as with a hook. **b** *intr.* be attached with a hook. **3** *tr.* catch with or as with a hook. **4** *tr. sl.* steal. **5** *tr.* (also *absol.*) *Golf* strike (the ball) so that it deviates toward the striker. **6** *tr. Boxing* strike (one's opponent) with the elbow bent and rigid. □ **be hooked on** *sl.* be addicted to or captivated by. **by hook or by crook** by fair means or foul. **hook, line, and sinker** entirely. **off the hook 1** *colloq.* no longer in trouble. **2** (of a telephone receiver) not on its rest, and so preventing incoming calls. □□ **hook•less** *adj.* **hook•let** *n.* **hook•like** *adj.*

hook•ah /hŏŏkə/ *n.* an oriental tobacco pipe with a long tube passing through water for cooling the smoke as it is drawn through.

hooked /hŏŏkt/ *adj.* **1** hook-shaped (*hooked nose*). **2** furnished with a hook or hooks. **3** in senses of HOOK *v.*

hook•er /hŏŏkər/ *n. sl.* a prostitute.

hook•nose /hŏŏknōz/ *n.* an aquiline nose. □□ **hook-nosed** *adj.*

hook•up /hŏŏkəp/ *n.* a connection, esp. of broadcasting equipment.

hook•worm /hŏŏkwərm/ *n.* **1** any of various nematode worms, with hooklike mouthparts, infesting humans and animals. **2** a disease caused by one of these.

hook•y /hŏŏkee/ *n.* (also **hook•ey**) □ **play hooky** *sl.* play truant.

hoo•li•gan /hŏŏligən/ *n.* a young ruffian, esp. a member of a gang. □□ **hoo•li•gan•ism** *n.*

hoop[1] /hōōp/ *n.* & *v.* •*n.* **1** a circular band of metal, wood, etc., esp. for binding the staves of casks, etc., or for forming part of a framework. **2 a** a circular usu. wood or plastic band used as a toy. **b** a large ring usu. with paper stretched over it for circus performers to jump through. **3** an arch through which the balls are hit in croquet. **4** (in *pl.*) the game of basketball. **5** a band of contrasting color on a jockey's blouse, sleeves, or cap. •*v.tr.* **1** bind with a hoop or hoops. **2** encircle with or as with a hoop. □ **jump through hoops** perform a difficult or grueling series of tests at someone else's command.

hoop[2] var. of WHOOP.

hoop•la /hŏŏplaa/ *n.* **1** *sl.* commotion; excitement. **2** *sl.* pretentious nonsense.

hoo•poe /hŏŏpōō/ *n.* a salmon-pink bird, *Upupa epops*, with black and white wings and tail, a large erectile crest, and a long decurved bill.

hoo•ray /hŏŏráy/ *int.* = HURRAH.

hoose•gow /hŏŏsgow/ *n. sl.* a jail.

hoot /hōōt/ *n.* & *v.* •*n.* **1** an owl's cry. **2** the sound made by a vehicle's horn or a steam whistle. **3** a shout expressing scorn or disapproval. **4** *colloq.* **a** laughter. **b** a cause of this. **5** (also **two hoots**) *sl.* anything at all (*doesn't matter two hoots*). •*v.* **1** *intr.* **a** (of an owl) utter its cry. **b** (of a vehicle horn or steam whistle) make a hoot. **c** (often foll. by *at*) make loud sounds, esp. of scorn or *colloq.* merriment (*hooted with laughter*). **2** *tr.* **a** assail with scornful shouts. **b** (often foll. by *out, away*) drive away by hooting. **3** *tr.* sound (a vehicle horn or steam whistle).

hoot•en•an•ny /hŏŏt'nanee/ *n.* (*pl.* **-nies**) *colloq.* an informal gathering with folk music.

hoot•er /hŏŏtər/ *n.* **1** *sl.* a nose. **2** (*pl.*) *coarse sl.* a women's breasts.

hooves *pl.* of HOOF.

hop[1] /hop/ *v.* & *n.* •*v.* (**hopped, hopping**) **1** *intr.* (of a bird, etc.) spring with two or all feet at once. **2** *intr.* (of a person) jump on one foot. **3** *tr.* cross (a ditch, etc.) by hopping. **4** *tr. colloq.* **a** jump into (a vehicle). **b** obtain (a ride) in this way. **5** *tr.* (usu. as **hopping** *n.*) (esp. of aircraft) pass quickly from one (place of a specified type) to another (*island-hopping*). •*n.* **1** a hopping movement. **2** *colloq.* an informal dance. **3** a short flight in an aircraft. □ **hop in** (or **out**) *colloq.* get into (or out of) a car, etc. **hopping mad** *colloq.* very angry.

hop[2] /hop/ *n.* **1** a climbing plant, *Humulus lupulus*, cultivated for the cones borne by the female. **2** (in *pl.*) the ripe cones of this, used to give a bitter flavor to beer. **3** *sl.* opium or any other narcotic.

hope /hōp/ *n. & v.* • *n.* **1** (in *sing.* or *pl.*; often foll. by *of, that*) expectation and desire combined (*hope of getting the job*). **2 a** a person, thing, or circumstance that gives cause for hope. **b** ground of hope; promise. **3** what is hoped for. • *v.* **1** *intr.* (often foll. by *for*) feel hope. **2** *tr.* expect and desire. **3** *tr.* feel fairly confident. □ **hope against hope** cling to a mere possibility. **not a hope!** *colloq.* no chance at all. □□ **hop·er** *n.*

hope chest *n.* **1** a young woman's collection of clothes, linens, etc., in preparation for her marriage. **2** the chest in which it is stored.

hope·ful /hṓpfŏŏl/ *adj. & n.* • *adj.* **1** feeling hope. **2** causing or inspiring hope. **3** likely to succeed; promising. • *n.* (in full **young hopeful**) **1** a person likely to succeed. **2** *iron.* a person likely to be disappointed. □□ **hope·ful·ness** *n.*

hope·ful·ly /hṓpfŏŏlee/ *adv.* **1** in a hopeful manner. **2** *disp.* (qualifying a whole sentence) it is to be hoped. ▶Some object strongly to the use of **hopefully** as a sentence modifier, with the meaning 'it is to be hoped,' e.g., *Hopefully, all the details will be in this evening's newspapers.* However, this usage is not only common but long-established in English, as are similar uses of other sentence-modifying adverbs, such as *regrettably, unfortunately,* and *frankly.*

hope·less /hṓplis/ *adj.* **1** feeling no hope. **2** admitting no hope (*a hopeless case*). **3** inadequate; incompetent (*am hopeless at tennis*). □□ **hope·less·ly** *adv.* **hope·less·ness** *n.*

Ho·pi /hṓpee/ *n.* **1 a** a N. American people native to northeastern Arizona. **b** a member of this people. **2** the language of this people.

hop·per /hópər/ *n.* **1** a person who hops. **2** a hopping arthropod, esp. a flea or young locust. **3 a** a container tapering downward through which grain passes into a mill. **b** a similar contrivance in various machines. **4** a railway wagon able to discharge coal or other bulk material through its floor.

hop·ple /hópəl/ *v. & n.* • *v.tr.* fasten together the legs of (a horse, etc.) to prevent it from straying, etc. • *n.* an apparatus for this.

hop·scotch /hópskoch/ *n.* a children's game of hopping over squares or oblongs marked on the ground to retrieve a flat stone, etc.

horde /hawrd/ *n.* **1 a** usu. *derog.* a large group. **b** a moving swarm or pack (of insects, wolves, etc.). **2** a troop of nomads.

hore·hound /háwrhownd/ *n.* a herbaceous plant, *Marrubium vulgare*, with a white cottony covering on its stem and leaves.

ho·ri·zon /hərízən/ *n.* **1** the line at which the earth and sky appear to meet. **2** limit of mental perception, experience, interest, etc. □ **on the horizon** (of an event) just imminent or becoming apparent.

hor·i·zon·tal /háwrizónt'l, hór–/ *adj. & n.* • *adj.* **1 a** parallel to the plane of the horizon; at right angles to the vertical (*horizontal plane*). **b** (of machinery, etc.) having its parts working in a horizontal direction. **2 a** combining firms engaged in the same stage of production (*horizontal integration*). **b** involving social groups of equal status, etc. **3** of or at the horizon. • *n.* a horizontal line, plane, etc.

hor·i·zon·tal sta·bi·liz·er *n.* a horizontal airfoil at the tail of an aircraft.

hor·mone /háwrmōn/ *n.* **1** *Biochem.* a regulatory substance produced in an organism and transported in tissue fluids such as blood or sap to stimulate cells or tissues into action. **2** a synthetic substance with a similar effect. □□ **hor·mo·nal** /–mṓnəl/ *adj.*

horn /hawrn/ *n. & v.* • *n.* **1** a hard permanent outgrowth, often curved and pointed, on the head of cattle, giraffes, rhinoceroses, and other esp. hoofed mammals, found singly, in pairs, or one in front of the other. **2** each of two deciduous branched appendages on the head of (esp. male) deer. **3** a hornlike projection on the head of other animals, e.g., a snail's tentacle. **4** the substance of which horns are composed. **5** anything resembling or compared to a horn in shape. **6** *Mus.* **a** = FRENCH HORN. **b** a wind instrument played by lip vibration, orig. made of horn, now usu. of brass. **7** an instrument sounding a warning or other signal (*car horn*; *foghorn*). **8** a receptacle or instrument made of horn. **9** a horn-shaped projection. **10** the extremity of the visible moon or other crescent. **11** an arm or branch of a river, bay, etc. **12** *sl.* the telephone. • *v.tr.* **1** (esp. as **horned** *adj.*) provide with horns. **2** gore with the horns. □ **horn in** *sl.* **1** (usu. foll. by *on*) intrude. **2** interfere. **on the horns of a dilemma** faced with a decision that involves equally unfavorable alternatives. □□ **horn·ist** *n.* (in sense 6 of *n.*). **horn·less** *adj.* **horn·like** *adj.*

horn·bill /háwrnbil/ *n.* any bird of the family Bucerotidae, with a hornlike excrescence on its large red or yellow curved bill.

horn·blende /háwrnblend/ *n.* a dark brown, black, or green mineral occurring in many igneous and metamorphic rocks.

horned /hawrnd/ *adj.* having a horn.

horned owl *n.* an owl, *Bubo virginianus*, with hornlike feathers over the ears.

horned toad *n.* **1** an American lizard, *Phrynosoma cornutum*, covered with spiny scales. **2** any SE Asian toad of the family Pelobatidae, with horn-shaped extensions over the eyes.

hor·net /háwrnit/ *n.* a large wasp, *Vespa crabro.* □ **stir up a hornets' nest** provoke or cause trouble or opposition.

horn of plen·ty *n.* a cornucopia.

horn·pipe /háwrnpīp/ *n.* **1** a lively dance (esp. associated with sailors). **2** the music for this.

horn-rimmed *adj.* (esp. of eyeglasses) having rims made of horn or a substance resembling it.

horn·swog·gle /háwrnswogəl/ *v.tr. sl.* cheat; hoax.

horn·y /háwrnee/ *adj.* (**hornier, horniest**) **1** of or like horn. **2** hard like horn. **3** *sl.* sexually excited. □□ **horn·i·ness** *n.*

ho·rol·o·gy /hawróləjee/ *n.* the art of measuring time or making clocks, watches, etc.; the study of this. □□ **ho·rol·o·ger** *n.* **hor·o·log·ic** /háwrəlójik/ *adj.* **hor·o·log·i·cal** *adj.* **ho·rol·o·gist** /–ról əjist/ *n.*

hor·o·scope /háwrəskōp, hór–/ *n. Astrol.* **1** a forecast of a person's future based on a diagram showing the relative positions of the stars and planets at that person's birth. **2** such a diagram (*cast a horoscope*). **3** observation of the sky and planets at a particular moment, esp. at a person's birth. □□ **hor·o·scop·ic** /–skópik/ *adj.* **ho·ros·co·py** /həróskəpee/ *n.*

hor·ren·dous /həréndəs/ *adj.* horrifying; awful. □□ **hor·ren·dous·ly** *adv.* **hor·ren·dous·ness** *n.*

hor·ri·ble /háwribəl, hór–/ *adj.* **1** causing or likely to cause horror; hideous; shocking. **2** *colloq.* unpleasant; excessive (*horrible weather*). □□ **hor·ri·ble·ness** *n.* **hor·ri·bly** *adv.*

hor·rid /háwrid, hór–/ *adj.* **1** horrible; revolting. **2** *colloq.* unpleasant; disagreeable (*horrid weather*). **3** *archaic.* rough; bristling. □□ **hor·rid·ly** *adv.* **hor·rid·ness** *n.*

hor·ri·fic /hawrífik, hór–/ *adj.* horrifying. □□ **hor·ri·fi·cal·ly** *adv.*

hor·ri·fy /háwrifī, hór–/ *v.tr.* (**-fies, -fied**) arouse horror in; shock. ▫▫ **hor·ri·fi·ca·tion** *n.* **hor·ri·fy·ing** *adj.* **hor·ri·fy·ing·ly** *adv.*

hor·ror /háwrər, hór–/ *n.* & *adj.* • *n.* **1** a painful feeling of loathing and fear. **2 a** (often foll. by *of*) intense dislike. **b** (often foll. by *at*) *colloq.* intense dismay. **3 a** a person or thing causing horror. **b** *colloq.* a bad or mischievous person, etc. **4** (in *pl.*; prec. by *the*) a fit of horror or nervousness, esp. as in delirium tremens. **5** (in *pl.*) an exclamation of dismay. • *attrib.* adj. (of literature, movies, etc.) designed to attract by arousing pleasurable feelings of horror.

hors d'oeuvre /awrdőrvrə, –dörv/ *n.* an appetizer served at the beginning of a meal.

horse /hawrs/ *n.* & *v.* • *n.* **1 a** a solid-hoofed plant-eating quadruped, *Equus caballus*, with flowing mane and tail, used for riding and to carry and pull loads. **b** any other four-legged mammal of the genus *Equus*, including asses and zebras. **c** (*collect.*; as *sing.*) cavalry. **2** a vaulting block. **3** a supporting frame esp. with legs (*clothes-horse*). **4** *sl.* heroin. • *v.* **1** *intr.* (foll. by *around*) fool around. **2** *tr.* provide (a person or vehicle) with a horse or horses. **3** *intr.* mount or go on horseback. ▫ **from the horse's mouth** (of information, etc.) from the person directly concerned or another authoritative source. **to horse!** (as a command) mount your horses. ▫▫ **horse·less** *adj.* **horse·like** *adj.*

horse-and-bug·gy *adj.* old-fashioned; bygone.

horse·back /háwrsbak/ *n.* the back of a horse, esp. as sat on in riding. ▫ **on horseback** mounted on a horse.

horse chest·nut *n.* **1** any large ornamental tree of the genus *Aesculus*, with upright conical clusters of white or pink or red flowers. **2** the dark brown fruit of this.

horse·flesh /háwrsflesh/ *n.* **1** the flesh of a horse, esp. as food. **2** horses collectively.

horse·fly /háwrsflī/ *n.* (*pl.* **-flies**) any of various biting dipterous insects of the family Tabanidae troublesome esp. to horses.

horse·hair /háwrs-hair/ *n.* hair from the mane or tail of a horse, used for padding, etc.

horse·man /háwrsmən/ *n* (*pl.* **-men**) **1** a rider on horseback. **2** a skilled rider.

horse·man·ship /háwrsmənship/ *n.* the art of riding on horseback; skill in doing this.

horse·play /háwrsplay/ *n.* boisterous play.

horse·pow·er /háwrspowər/ *n.* (*pl.* same) **1** a unit of power equal to 550 foot-pounds per second (about 750 watts). **2** the power of an engine, etc., measured in terms of this.

horse race *n.* **1** a race between horses with riders. **2** any close contest. ▫▫ **horse rac·ing** *n.*

horse·rad·ish /háwrsradish/ *n.* **1** a cruciferous plant, *Armoracia rusticana*, with long lobed leaves. **2** the pungent root of this, scraped or grated as a condiment, often made into a sauce.

horse sense *n. colloq.* plain common sense.

horse·shoe /háwrs-sho͞o/ *n.* **1** an iron shoe for a horse shaped like the outline of the hard part of the hoof. **2** a thing of this shape. **3** (in *pl.*) a game in which horseshoes are thrown at a stake in the ground.

horse·shoe crab *n.* a large marine arthropod, *Limulus polyphemus*, with a horseshoe-shaped shell and a long tail-spine.

horse·tail /háwrstayl/ *n.* **1** the tail of a horse. **2** any cryptogamous plant of the genus *Equisetum*, like a horse's tail, with a hollow jointed stem and scalelike leaves.

horse-trad·ing *n.* **1** dealing in horses. **2** shrewd bargaining.

horse·whip /háwrs-hwip, –wip/ *n.* & *v.* • *n.* a whip for driving horses. • *v.tr.* (**-whipped, -whipping**) beat with a horsewhip.

horse·wom·an /háwrswo͝omən/ *n.* (*pl.* **-women**) **1** a woman who rides on horseback. **2** a skilled woman rider.

hors·ey /háwrsee/ *adj.* (also **hors·y**) (**horsier, horsiest**) **1** of or like a horse. **2** concerned with or devoted to horses or horse racing. **3** *colloq.* large and clumsy. ▫▫ **hors·i·ness** *n.*

hor·ta·tive /háwrtətiv/ *adj.* (also **hor·ta·to·ry** /háwrtətawree/) tending or serving to exhort. ▫▫ **hor·ta·tion** /hawrtáyshən/ *n.*

hor·ti·cul·ture /háwrtikúlchər/ *n.* the art of garden cultivation. ▫▫ **hor·ti·cul·tur·al** *adj.* **hor·ti·cul·tur·ist** *n.*

ho·san·na /hōzánə/ *n.* & *int.* a shout of adoration (Matt. 21: 9, 15, etc.).

hose /hōz/ *n.* & *v.* • *n.* **1** (also *Brit.* **hose-pipe**) a flexible tube conveying water for watering plants, putting out fires, etc. **2 a** (*collect.*; as *pl.*) stockings and socks (esp. in trade use). **b** *hist.* breeches (*doublet and hose*). • *v.tr.* **1** (often foll. by *down*) water or spray or drench with a hose. **2** provide with hose.

hose Old English *hosa*, of Germanic origin; related to Dutch *hoos* 'stocking, water-hose' and German *Hosen* 'trousers.' Originally as a singular, it denoted a covering for the leg, sometimes including the foot but sometimes reaching only as far as the ankle.

ho·sier /hṓzhər/ *n.* a dealer in hosiery.

ho·sier·y /hṓzhəree/ *n.* stockings and socks.

hos·pice /hóspis/ *n.* **1** a health-care facility or program for people who are terminally ill. **2** a lodging for travelers, esp. one kept by a religious order.

hos·pi·ta·ble /hóspitəbəl, hospít–/ *adj.* **1** giving welcome and entertainment to strangers or guests. **2** disposed to welcome something readily; receptive. ▫▫ **hos·pi·ta·bly** *adv.*

hos·pi·tal /hóspit'l/ *n.* **1** an institution providing medical and surgical treatment and nursing care for ill or injured people. **2** *hist.* a hospice.

hos·pi·tal·i·ty /hóspitálitee/ *n.* the friendly and generous reception and entertainment of guests or strangers.

hos·pi·tal·ize /hóspit'līz/ *v.tr.* send or admit to hospital. ▫▫ **hos·pi·tal·i·za·tion** *n.*

host[1] /hōst/ *n.* **1** (usu. foll. by *of*) a large number of people or things. **2** *archaic* an army.

host[2] /hōst/ *n.* & *v.* • *n.* **1** a person who receives or entertains another as a guest. **2** the landlord of an inn. **3** *Biol.* an animal or plant having a parasite or commensal. **4** an animal or person that has received a transplanted organ, etc. **5** the person who introduces and often interviews guests on a television or radio program. • *v.tr.* act as host to (a person) or at (an event).

host[3] /hōst/ *n.* the bread consecrated in the Eucharist.

hos·ta /hóstə/ *n.* any perennial garden plant of the genus *Hosta*, with green or variegated leaves and loose clusters of tubular lavender or white flowers.

hos·tage /hóstij/ *n.* **1** a person seized or held as security for the fulfillment of a condition. **2** a pledge or security. ▫ **a hostage to fortune** an acquisition, commitment, etc., regarded as endangered by unforeseen circumstances.

hos·tel /hóst'l/ *n.* inexpensive lodging for travelers, hikers, etc.

host·ess /hṓstis/ *n.* **1** a woman who receives or entertains a guest. **2** a woman employed to welcome and entertain customers at a nightclub, etc. **3** a stewardess on an aircraft, train, etc. (*air hostess*).

hos·tile /hóstəl, –tīl/ *adj.* **1** of an enemy. **2** (often foll. by *to*) unfriendly; opposed. ▫▫ **hos·tile·ly** *adv.*

hos·til·i·ty /hostílitee/ *n.* (*pl.* **-ties**) **1** being hostile; enmity. **2** a state of warfare. **3** (in *pl.*) acts of warfare. **4** opposition (in thought, etc.).

hos·tler /hóslər, ós;n–/ *n.* **1** = OSTLER. **2** a person who services vehicles or machines, esp. train engines, when they are not in use.

hot /hot/ *adj. & adv.* • *adj.* (**hotter, hottest**) **1 a** having a relatively high temperature. **b** (of food or drink) prepared by heating and served without cooling. **2** producing the sensation of heat (*hot flash*). **3** (of spices, etc.) pungent; piquant. **4** (of a person) feeling heat. **5 a** passionate; excited. **b** (often foll. by *for, on*) eager; keen (*in hot pursuit*). **c** lustful. **d** exciting. **6** (of news, etc.) fresh; recent. **7** *Hunting* (of the scent) fresh and strong. **8 a** (of a player) very skillful. **b** (of a competitor) strongly favored to win (*a hot favorite*). **c** (of a hit in ball games) difficult for an opponent to deal with. **d** *colloq.* currently popular or in demand. **9** (of music, esp. jazz) strongly rhythmical and emotional. **10 a** *sl.* (of goods) stolen, esp. easily identifiable and therefore difficult to dispose of. **b** *sl.* (of a person) wanted by the police. **11** *sl.* radioactive. **12** *colloq.* (of information) unusually reliable (*hot tip*). • *adv.* eagerly. □ **have the hots for** *sl.* be sexually attracted to. **hot under the collar** angry or embarrassed. **make it** (or **things**) **hot for a person** persecute a person. **not so hot** *colloq.* only mediocre. □□ **hot·ly** *adv.* **hot·ness** *n.* **hot·tish** *adj.*

hot air *n. sl.* empty boastful talk.

hot-air bal·loon *n.* a balloon (see BALLOON *n.* 2) consisting of a bag in which air is heated by burners located below it, causing it to rise.

hot·bed /hótbed/ *n.* **1** a bed of earth heated by fermenting manure. **2** (foll. by *of*) an environment promoting the growth of something (*a hotbed of vice; a hotbed of new music*).

hot-blood·ed *adj.* ardent; passionate.

hot·cake /hótkayk/ *n.* a pancake. □ **like hotcakes** quickly and in great quantity, esp. because of popularity (*the new CD is selling like hotcakes*).

hot·dog /hótdawg, –dog/ *v.intr. sl.* show off, esp. one's skills.

hot dog *n. & int.* **1 a** = FRANKFURTER. **b** a frankfurter sandwiched in a soft roll. **2** *sl.* a person who shows off skills. • *int. sl.* expressing approval.

ho·tel /hōtél/ *n.* an establishment providing accommodation and meals for payment.

ho·te·lier /ṓtelyáy, hōt'léer/ *n.* a hotel-keeper.

hot flash *n.* a sudden sensation of heat, esp. during menopause.

hot·foot /hótfŏŏt/ *adv., v., & adj.* • *adv.* in eager haste. • *v.tr.* hurry eagerly (esp. **hotfoot it**). • *adj.* acting quickly.

hot·head /hót-hed/ *n.* an impetuous person.

hot·head·ed /hót-hédid/ *adj.* impetuous; excitable. □□ **hot·head·ed·ness** *n.*

hot·house /hót-hows/ *n. & adj.* • *n.* **1** a heated building, usu. largely of glass, for rearing plants out of season or in a climate colder than is natural for them. **2** an environment that encourages the rapid growth or development of something. • *adj. (attrib.)* characteristic of something reared in a hothouse; sheltered; sensitive.

hot line *n.* a direct exclusive line of communication, esp. for emergencies.

hot plate *n.* a heated metal plate, etc. (or a set of these), for cooking food or keeping it hot.

hot po·ta·to *n. colloq.* a controversial or awkward matter or situation.

hot rod *n.* a motor vehicle modified to have extra power and speed.

hot seat *n. sl.* **1** a position of difficult responsibility. **2** the electric chair.

hot·shot /hótshot/ *n. & adj. colloq.* • *n.* an important or exceptionally able person. • *adj.* (*attrib.*) important; able; expert.

hot spot *n.* a lively or dangerous place.

hot spring *n.* a spring of naturally hot water.

hot stuff *n. colloq.* **1** a formidably capable person. **2** an important person or thing. **3** a sexually attractive person. **4** a spirited or passionate person. **5** a book, movie, etc. with a strongly erotic content.

hot-tem·pered *adj.* impulsively angry.

Hot·ten·tot /hót'ntot/ *n. & adj.* • *n.* **1** a member of a pastoral black people of SW Africa. **2** their language. • *adj.* of this people.

hot tub *n.* a tub of heated, circulating water for therapy or recreation, usu. able to accommodate several people.

hot wa·ter *n. colloq.* trouble or disgrace.

hot-wa·ter bot·tle *n.* (also **bag**) a container, usu. made of rubber, filled with hot water, esp. to warm a bed.

hot-wire *v.tr.* start the engine of a vehicle by bypassing the ignition system, usu. in order to steal it.

houm·mos var. of HUMMUS.

hound /hownd/ *n. & v.* • *n.* **1 a** a dog used for hunting, esp. one able to track by scent. **b** (**the hounds**) a pack of foxhounds. **2** *colloq.* a despicable man. **3** a person keen in pursuit of something (usu. in *comb.*: *newshound*). • *v.tr.* **1** harass or pursue relentlessly. **2** chase or pursue with a hound. **3** (foll. by *at*) set (a dog or person) on (a quarry). **4** urge on or nag (a person). □ **ride to hounds** go fox-hunting on horseback.

hound's-tooth *n.* a check pattern with notched corners suggestive of a canine tooth.

hour /owr/ *n.* **1** a twenty-fourth part of a day and night; 60 minutes. **2** a time of day; a point in time (*a late hour*). **3** (in *pl.*) this number of hours and minutes past midnight on the 24-hour clock (*assemble at 20:00 hours*). **4 a** a period set aside for some purpose (*lunch hour*). **b** (in *pl.*) a fixed period of time for work; use of a building, etc. (*office hours*). **5** a short indefinite period of time (*an idle hour*). **6** the present time (*question of the hour*). **7** a time for action, etc. (*the hour has come*). **8** the distance traversed in one hour by a means of transport stated or implied (*we are an hour from San Francisco*). **9** *RC Ch.* **a** prayers to be said at one of seven fixed times of day (*book of hours*). **b** any of these times. **10** (prec. by *the*) each time o'clock of a whole number of hours (*buses leave on the hour*). □ **after hours** after closing time.

hour·glass /ówrglas/ *n.* a reversible device with two connected glass bulbs containing sand that takes an hour to pass from the upper to the lower bulb.

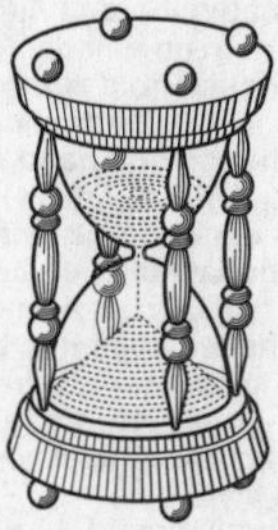

hourglass

hour·ly /ówrlee/ *adj. & adv.* • *adj.* **1** done or occurring every hour (*on an hourly basis*). **2** frequent; continual. **3** reckoned hour by hour (*hourly wage*). • *adv.* **1** every hour (*the train runs hourly*). **2** frequently; continually.

house *n. & v.* • *n.* /hows/ (*pl.* /hówziz, –siz/) **1 a** a building for human habitation. **b** (*attrib.*) (of an animal) kept in, frequenting, or infesting houses (*house cat; housefly*). **2** a building for a special purpose (*opera house; summer house*). **3** a building for keeping animals or goods (*henhouse*). **4 a** a religious community. **b** the buildings occupied by it. **5** esp. *Brit.* **a** a body of pupils living in the same building at a boarding school. **b** such a building. **c** a division of a day school for games, competitions, etc. **6** a family, esp. a royal family; a dynasty (*House of York*). **7** a business or institution. **8 a** a legislative or deliberative assembly. **b** the building where it meets. **c** (**the House**) the House of Representatives. **9 a** an audience in a theater, movie theater, etc. **b** a theater. **10** *Astrol.* a twelfth part of the heavens. **11** (*attrib.*) staying in a hospital as a member of the staff (*house surgeon*). **12 a** a place of public refreshment; a restaurant or inn (*coffeehouse*). **b** (*attrib.*) (of wine) selected by the management of a hotel, etc., to be offered at a special price. • *v.tr.* /howz/ **1** provide (a person, a population, etc.) with a house or other accommodation. **2** store (goods, etc.). **3** enclose or encase (a part or fitting). **4** fix in a socket, etc. □ **keep house** manage a household. **like a house on fire 1** vigorously; fast. **2** successfully. **on the house** at the management's expense; free. **play house** play at being a family in its home. **put** (or **set**) **one's house in order** make necessary reforms. **set up house** begin to live in a separate dwelling. □□ **house·ful** *n.* (*pl.* **-fuls**). **house·less** *adj.*

house ar·rest *n.* detention in one's own house, etc., not in prison.

house·boat /hówsbōt/ *n.* a boat fitted for living in.

house·bound /hówsbownd/ *adj.* unable to leave one's house due to illness, etc.

house·boy /hówsboy/ *n.* a boy or man who works as a servant in a house, hotel, etc.

house·break /hówsbrayk/ *v.tr.* train (a pet living indoors) to excrete outdoors.

house·break·ing /hówsbrayking/ *n.* the act of breaking into a building, esp. in daytime, to commit a crime. □□ **house·break·er** *n.*

house·bro·ken /hówsbrōkən/ *adj.* **1** (of animals) trained to urinate and defecate outside the house, or only in a special place. **2** *colloq.* well-mannered.

house·coat /hówskōt/ *n.* a woman's garment for informal wear in the house, usu. a long dresslike coat.

house·dress /hówsdres/ *n.* an inexpensive dress of simple design suitable for wear while doing housework.

house·fly /hówsflī/ *n.* a fly breeding in decaying organic matter and often entering houses.

house·guest /hówsgest/ *n.* a guest staying for some days in a private house.

house·hold /hóws-hōld/ *n.* **1** the occupants of a house regarded as a unit. **2** a house and its affairs.

house·hold·er /hóws-hōldər/ *n.* **1** a person who owns or rents a house. **2** the head of a household.

house·hold word *n.* (also **name**) **1** a familiar name or saying. **2** a familiar person or thing.

house·hus·band /hóws-həzbənd/ *n.* a husband who carries out the household duties traditionally carried out by a housewife.

house·keep·er /hówskeepər/ *n.* a person employed to manage a household.

house·keep·ing /hówskeeping/ *n.* **1** the management of household affairs. **2** money allowed for this. **3** operations of record keeping, etc., in an organization.

house lights *n.pl.* the lights in the auditorium of a theater.

house·maid /hówsmayd/ *n.* a female servant in a house.

house·man /hówsmən/ *n.* (*pl.* **-men**) = HOUSEBOY.

house mar·tin *n.* a black and white swallowlike bird, *Delichon arbica*, which builds a mud nest on house walls, etc.

house·moth·er /hówsməthər/ *n.* a woman in charge of a house, esp. of a home for children or a dormitory, etc.

house mu·sic *n.* a style of pop music typically using drum machines and synthesized bass lines with sparse repetitive vocals and a fast beat.

house of cards *n.* **1** an insecure scheme, etc. **2** a structure built (usu. by a child) out of playing cards.

house of God *n.* a church; a place of worship.

house of ill re·pute *n.* *archaic* a brothel.

House of Rep·re·sen·ta·tives *n.* the lower house of the US Congress and other legislatures.

house·par·ent /hówsparənt/ *n.* a housemother or housefather.

house·plant /hówsplant/ *n.* a plant grown indoors.

house·wares /hówswairz/ *n.pl.* small articles for furnishing a home, such as dishware, glassware, and small appliances.

house·warm·ing /hówswawrming/ *n.* a party celebrating a move to a new home.

house·wife /hówswīf/ *n.* (*pl.* **-wives**) a married woman managing a household. □□ **house·wife·ly** *adj.*

house·work /hówswərk/ *n.* regular work done in housekeeping, e.g., cleaning and cooking.

hous·ing /hówzing/ *n.* **1 a** dwelling houses collectively. **b** the provision of these. **2** shelter; lodging. **3** a rigid casing, esp. for moving or sensitive parts of a machine. **4** the hole or niche cut in one piece of wood to receive some part of another in order to join them.

hous·ing de·vel·op·ment *n.* a residential area in which the houses have all been planned and built at the same time.

HOV *abbr.* high-occupancy vehicle.

hove *past* of HEAVE.

hov·el /húvəl, hóv–/ *n.* a small miserable dwelling.

hov·er /húvər, hóvər/ *v.* & *n.* • *v.intr.* **1** (of a bird, helicopter, etc.) remain in one place in the air. **2** (often foll. by *about, around*) wait close at hand; linger. **3** remain undecided. • *n.* **1** hovering. **2** a state of suspense. □□ **hov·er·er** *n.*

hov·er·craft /húvərkraft, hóv–/ *n.* (*pl.* same) a vehicle or craft that travels over land or water on a cushion of air provided by a downward blast.

hov·er·port /húvərpawrt, hóv–/ *n.* a terminal for hovercraft.

how /how/ *adv., conj.,* & *n.* • *interrog.adv.* **1** by what means; in what way (*how do you do it?*). **2** in what condition, esp. of health (*how is the patient?*). **3 a** to what extent (*how far is it?*). **b** to what extent good or well, what . . . like (*how was the film?*). • *rel.* adv. in whatever way (*do it how you like*). • *conj. colloq.* that (*told us how he'd been in Canada*). *n.* the way a thing is done (*the how and why of it*). □ **how about 1** would you like. **2** what is to be done about. **3** what is the news about. **how are you? 1** what is your state of health? **2** = *how do you do?* **how come?** see COME. **how do you do?** a formal greeting. **how many** what number. **how much 1** what amount (*how much do I owe you?*). **2** what price (*how much is it?*). **how's that?** what is your explanation of that?

how·be·it /hówbeéit/ *adv. archaic* nevertheless.

how·dah /hówdə/ *n.* a seat, usu. with a canopy, for riding on the back of an elephant.

how·dy /hówdee/ *int.* = *how do you do?*

how·ev·er /hówévər/ *adv.* **1 a** in whatever way (*do it however you want*). **b** to whatever extent; no matter how (*however inconvenient*). **2** nevertheless. **3** *colloq.* (as an emphatic) in what way; by what means (*however did that happen?*).

how·itz·er /hówitsər/ *n.* a short cannon for high-angle firing of shells at low velocities.

howl /howl/ *n.* & *v.* • *n.* **1** a long, loud, doleful cry uttered by a dog, wolf, etc. **2** a prolonged wailing noise, e.g., as made by a strong wind. **3** a loud cry of pain or rage. **4** a yell of derision or merriment. **5** *Electronics* a howling noise in a loudspeaker due to electrical or acoustic feedback. • *v.* **1** *intr.* make a howl. **2** *intr.* weep loudly. **3** *tr.* utter (words) with a howl. □ **howl down** prevent (a speaker) from being heard by howls of derision.

howl·er /hówlər/ *n.* **1** *colloq.* a glaring mistake. **2** a S.

American monkey of the genus *Alouatta*. **3** a person or animal that howls.

howl·ing /hówling/ *adj.* **1** that howls. **2** *sl.* extreme (*a howling shame*).

how·so·ev·er /hówsō-évər/ *adv.* **1** in whatsoever way. **2** to whatsoever extent.

h.p. *abbr.* **1** horsepower. **2** high pressure.

HQ *abbr.* headquarters.

HR *abbr.* (also **H.R.**) **1** House of Representatives. **2** home run.

hr. *abbr.* hour.

HST *abbr.* Hawaii(an) Standard Time.

hub /hub/ *n.* **1** the central part of a wheel, rotating on or with the axle, and from which the spokes radiate. **2** a central point of interest, activity, etc.

hub·bub /húbub/ *n.* **1** a confused din. **2** a disturbance or riot.

hub·by /húbee/ *n.* (*pl.* **-bies**) *colloq.* a husband.

hub·cap /húbkap/ *n.* a cover for the hub of a vehicle's wheel.

hu·bris /hyóobris/ *n.* **1** arrogant pride or presumption. **2** (in Greek tragedy) excessive pride toward or defiance of the gods, leading to nemesis. ▫▫ **hu·bris·tic** *adj.*

huck·a·back /húkəbak/ *n.* a stout linen or cotton fabric with a rough surface, used for toweling.

huck·le·ber·ry /húkəlberee/ *n.* (*pl.* **-ries**) **1** any low-growing N. American shrub of the genus *Gaylussacia*. **2** the blue or black soft fruit of this plant.

huck·ster /húkstər/ *n.* & *v.* • *n.* **1** a mercenary person. **2** a publicity agent, esp. for broadcast material. **3** a peddler or hawker. • *v.* **1** *intr.* bargain; haggle. **2** *tr.* carry on a petty traffic in. **3** *tr.* adulterate.

HUD /hud/ *abbr.* (Department of) Housing and Urban Development.

hud·dle /húd'l/ *v.* & *n.* • *v.* **1** *tr.* & *intr.* (often foll. by *up*) crowd together; nestle closely. **2** *intr.* & *refl.* (often foll. by *up*) coil one's body into a small space. • *n.* **1** a confused mass of people or things. **2** *colloq.* a close or secret conference (esp. in **go into a huddle**). **3** *Football* a gathering of the players of one team to receive instructions about the next play.

hue /hyoo/ *n.* **1** a color or tint. **2** a variety or shade of color. ▫▫ **-hued** *adj.* **hue·less** *adj.*

hue and cry /hyoo/ *n.* a loud outcry.

huff /huf/ *v.* & *n.* • *v.* **1** *intr.* give out loud puffs of air, steam, etc. **2** *intr.* bluster loudly or threateningly. **3** *intr.* & *tr.* take or cause to take offense. **4** *tr. Checkers* remove (an opponent's man that could have made a capture) from the board as a forfeit. • *n.* a fit of petty annoyance. ▫ **in a huff** annoyed and offended.

huff·y /húfee/ *adj.* (**huffier, huffiest**) **1** apt to take offense. **2** offended. ▫▫ **huff·i·ly** *adv.* **huff·i·ness** *n.*

hug /hug/ *v.* & *n.* • *v.tr.* (**hugged, hugging**) **1** squeeze tightly in one's arms, esp. with affection. **2** (of a bear) squeeze (a person) between its forelegs. **3** keep close to (the curb, etc.). **4** cherish or cling to (prejudices, etc.). • *n.* **1** a strong clasp with the arms. **2** a squeezing grip in wrestling. ▫▫ **hug·ga·ble** *adj.*

huge /hyooj/ *adj.* **1** extremely large; enormous. **2** (of immaterial things) very great (*a huge success*). ▫▫ **huge·ness** *n.*

huge·ly /hyóojlee/ *adv.* **1** enormously (*hugely successful*). **2** very much (*enjoyed it hugely*).

Hu·gue·not /hyóogənot/ *n. hist.* a French Protestant.

huh /hə/ *int.* expressing disgust, surprise, etc.

hu·la /hóolə/ *n.* (also **hu·la-hu·la**) a native Hawaiian dance with undulating hips, and gestures symbolizing natural phenomena or historical or mythological subjects, often accompanied by chants and drums.

hu·la hoop *n.* a large hoop spun around the body by gyrating the hips, for play or exercise.

hu·la skirt *n.* a long grass skirt.

hulk /hulk/ *n.* **1 a** the body of a dismantled ship, used as a storage vessel, etc. **b** (in *pl.*) *hist.* this used as a prison. **2** *colloq.* a large clumsy-looking person or thing.

hulk·ing /húlking/ *adj. colloq.* bulky; large and clumsy.

hull[1] /hul/ *n.* & *v.* • *n.* the body or frame of a ship, airship, flying boat, etc. • *v.tr.* pierce the hull of (a ship) with gunshot, etc.

hull[2] /hul/ *n.* & *v.* • *n.* **1** the outer covering of a fruit, esp. the pod of peas and beans, the husk of grain, or the green calyx of a strawberry. **2** a covering. • *v.tr.* remove the hulls from (fruit, etc.).

hul·la·ba·loo /húləbəlóo/ *n.* (*pl.* **hullabaloos**) an uproar or clamor.

hum /hum/ *v.* & *n.* • *v.* (**hummed, humming**) **1** *intr.* make a low steady continuous sound like that of a bee. **2** *tr.* (also *absol.*) sing (a wordless tune) with closed lips. **3** *intr.* utter a slight inarticulate sound. **4** *intr. colloq.* be in an active state (*really made things hum*). • *n.* **1** a humming sound. **2** an unwanted low-frequency noise caused by variation of electric current, usu. the alternative frequency of a power source, in an amplifier, etc. ▫▫ **hum·ma·ble** *adj.* **hum·mer** *n.*

hu·man /hyóomən/ *adj.* & *n.* • *adj.* **1** of or belonging to the genus *Homo*. **2** consisting of human beings (*the human race*). **3** of or characteristic of people as opposed to God or animals or machines, esp. susceptible to weaknesses (*is only human*). **4** showing (esp. the better) qualities of man (*proved to be very human*). • *n.* a human being. ▫▫ **hu·man·ness** *n.*

▶See note at MAN.

hu·man be·ing *n.* any man or woman or child of the species *Homo sapiens*.

hu·mane /hyoomáyn/ *adj.* **1** benevolent; compassionate. **2** inflicting the minimum of pain. **3** (of a branch of learning) tending to civilize or confer refinement. ▫▫ **hu·mane·ly** *adv.* **hu·mane·ness** *n.*

hu·man in·ter·est *n.* (often *attrib.*) (in a newspaper story, etc.) reference to personal experience and emotions, etc.

hu·man·ism /hyóomənizəm/ *n.* **1** a system of thought concerned with human rather than divine or supernatural matters. **2** a belief or outlook emphasizing common human needs and concerned with human beings as responsible and progressive intellectual beings. **3** (often **Humanism**) literary culture, esp. that of the Renaissance humanists. ▫▫ **hu·man·ist** *n.*

hu·man·i·tar·i·an /hyoománitáireeən/ *n.* & *adj.* • *n.* **1** a person who seeks to promote human welfare. **2** a philanthropist. • *adj.* relating to humanitarians. ▫▫ **hu·man·i·tar·i·an·ism** *n.*

hu·man·i·ty /hyoománitee/ *n.* (*pl.* **-ties**) **1 a** the human race. **b** human beings collectively. **c** the fact or condition of being human. **2** humaneness. **3** (in *pl.*) human attributes. **4** (in *pl.*) learning or literature concerned with human culture.

hu·man·ize /hyóomənīz/ *v.tr.* **1** give a human character to. **2** make humane. ▫▫ **hu·man·i·za·tion** *n.*

hu·man·kind /hyóomənkínd/ *n.* human beings collectively.

hu·man·ly /hyóomənlee/ *adv.* **1** by human means (*if humanly possible*). **2** in a human manner. **3** from a human point of view. **4** with human feelings.

hu·man na·ture *n.* the general characteristics and feelings of human beings.

hu·man re·sourc·es *n.* = PERSONNEL.

hu·man rights *n.pl.* rights held to be justifiably belonging to any person.

hum·ble /húmbəl/ *adj.* & *v.* • *adj.* **1** having or showing a low estimate of one's own importance. **2** of low social or political rank (*humble origins*). **3** of modest pretensions, dimensions, etc. •*v.tr.* **1** make humble; abase. **2** lower the rank or status of. □ **eat humble pie** make a humble apology. □□ **hum·ble·ness** *n.* **hum·bly** *adv.*

hum·bug /húmbug/ *n.* & *v.* •*n.* **1** deceptive talk or behavior. **2** an impostor. •*v.* (**humbugged, humbugging**) **1** *intr.* behave like an impostor. **2** *tr.* deceive; hoax. □□ **hum·bug·ger·y** /–búgəree/ *n.*

hum·ding·er /húmdíngər/ *n. sl.* an excellent or remarkable person or thing.

hum·drum /húmdrum/ *adj.* **1** commonplace; dull. **2** monotonous.

hu·mec·tant /hyooméktənt/ *adj.* & *n.* •*adj.* retaining or preserving moisture. •*n.* a substance, esp. a food additive, used to reduce loss of moisture.

hu·mer·us /hyóomərəs/ *n.* (*pl.* **humeri** /–rī/) **1** the bone of the upper arm in humans. **2** the corresponding bone in other vertebrates. □□ **hu·mer·al** *adj.*

hu·mid /hyóomid/ *adj.* (of the air or climate) warm and damp. □□ **hu·mid·ly** *adv.*

hu·mid·i·fi·er /hyoomídifīər/ *n.* a device for keeping the atmosphere moist in a room.

hu·mid·i·fy /hyoomídifī/ *v.tr.* (**-fies, -fied**) make (air, etc.) humid or damp. □□ **hu·mid·i·fi·ca·tion** *n.*

hu·mid·i·ty /hyoomíditee/ *n.* (*pl.* **-ties**) **1** a humid state. **2** moisture. **3** the degree of moisture in the atmosphere.

hu·mi·dor /hyóomidawr/ *n.* a room or container for keeping cigars or tobacco moist.

hu·mil·i·ate /hyoomílee-ayt/ *v.tr.* injure the dignity or self-respect of. □□ **hu·mil·i·at·ing** *adj.* **hu·mil·i·at·ing·ly** *adv.* **hu·mil·i·a·tion** /–áyshən/ *n.* **hu·mil·i·a·tor** *n.*

hu·mil·i·ty /hyoomílitee/ *n.* **1** humbleness; meekness. **2** a humble condition.

hum·ming·bird /húmingbərd/ *n.* any tiny bird of the family Trochilidae that makes a humming sound by the vibration of its wings when it hovers.

hum·mock /húmək/ *n.* **1** a hillock or knoll. **2** a piece of rising ground, esp. in a marsh. **3** a hump or ridge in an ice field. □□ **hum·mock·y** *adj.*

hum·mus /hóoməs/ *n.* (also **houm·mos**) a thick sauce or spread made from chickpeas.

hu·mon·gous /hyoomónggəs, –múng–/ *adj.* (also **hu·mun·gous**) *sl.* extremely large.

hu·mor /hyóomər/ *n.* & *v.* •*n.* **1 a** the condition of being amusing or comical (less intellectual and more sympathetic than wit). **b** the expression of humor in literature, speech, etc. **2** (in full **sense of humor**) the ability to perceive or express humor. **3** a mood or state of mind (*bad humor*). **4** *hist.* each of the four chief fluids of the body (blood, phlegm, choler, melancholy), thought to determine a person's physical and mental qualities. •*v.tr.* indulge (a person or taste, etc.). □ **out of humor** displeased. □□ **-hu·mored** *adj.* **hu·mor·less** *adj.* **hu·mor·less·ly** *adv.* **hu·mor·less·ness** *n.*

---

humor Middle English: via Old French from Latin *humor* 'moisture', from *humere* (see HUMID). The original sense was 'bodily fluid' (surviving in *aqueous humor* and *vitreous humor*, fluids in the eyeball); it was used specifically for any of the cardinal humours (see sense 3), whence 'mental disposition' (thought to be caused by the relative proportions of the humours). This led, in the 16th cent., to the senses 'state of mind, mood' (see sense 2) and 'whim, fancy', hence *to humour someone* 'to indulge a person's whim'. Sense 1 dates from the late 16th cent.

---

hu·mor·ous /hyóomərəs/ *adj.* **1** showing humor or a sense of humor. **2** facetious; comic. □□ **hu·mor·ous·ly** *adv.* **hu·mor·ous·ness** *n.*

hump /hump/ *n.* & *v.* •*n.* **1** a rounded protuberance on the back of a camel, etc., or as an abnormality on a person's back. **2** a rounded raised mass of earth, etc. **3** a critical point in an undertaking, etc. •*v.tr.* **1 a** *colloq.* lift or carry (heavy objects, etc.) with difficulty. **b** esp. *Austral.* hoist up; shoulder (one's pack, etc.). **2** make hump-shaped. **3** *coarse sl.* have sexual intercourse with. ▶In sense 3 usually considered a taboo word. □ **over the hump** over the worst; well begun. □□ **humped** *adj.*

hump·back /húmpbak/ *n.* **1 a** a deformed back with a hump. **b** a person having this. **2** a baleen whale, *Megaptera novaeangliae*, with a dorsal fin forming a hump. □□ **hump·backed** *adj.*

hu·mus /hyóoməs/ *n.* the organic constituent of soil, usu. formed by the decomposition of plants and leaves.

Hun /hun/ *n.* **1** a member of a warlike Asiatic people who invaded Europe in the 4th–5th c. **2** *offens.* a German (esp. in military contexts). □□ **Hun·nish** *adj.*

hunch /hunch/ *v.* & *n.* •*v.* **1** *tr.* arch into a hump. **2** *tr.* thrust up to form a hump. •*n.* **1** *colloq.* an intuitive feeling. **2** *colloq.* a hint. **3** a hump.

hunch·back /húnchbak/ *n.* = HUMPBACK. □□ **hunch·backed** *adj.*

hun·dred /húndrəd/ *n.* & *adj.* •*n.* (*pl.* **hundreds** or (in sense 1) **hundred**) (in *sing.*, prec. by *a* or *one*) **1** the product of ten and ten. **2** a symbol for this (100, c, C). **3** a set of a hundred things. **4** (in *sing.* or *pl.*) *colloq.* a large number. **5** (in *pl.*) the years of a specified century (*the seventeen hundreds*). •*adj.* **1** that amount to a hundred. **2** used to express whole hours in the 24-hour system (*thirteen hundred hours*). □ **a** (or **one**) **hundred percent** *adv.* entirely. *adj.* **1** entire. **2** fully recovered. □□ **hun·dred·fold** *adj.* & *adv.* **hun·dredth** *adj.* & *n.*

hun·dred·weight /húndrədwayt/ *n.* (*pl.* same or **-weights**) **1** (in full **short hundredweight**) a unit of weight equal to 100 lb. (about 45.4 kg). **2** (in full **long hundredweight**) *Brit.* a unit of weight equal to 112 lb. (about 50.8 kg). **3** (in full **metric hundredweight**) a unit of weight equal to 50 kg.

hung *past* and *past part.* of HANG. □ **hung up on** have a psychological or emotional obsession or problem about *she's really hung up on her teacher.* ▶See note at HANG.

Hun·gar·i·an /hunggáireeən/ *n.* & *adj.* •*n.* **1 a** a native or inhabitant of Hungary in E. Europe. **b** a person of Hungarian descent. **2** the language of Hungary. •*adj.* of or relating to Hungary or its people or language.

hun·ger /húnggər/ *n.* & *v.* •*n.* **1** a feeling of discomfort, or (in extremes) an exhausted condition, caused by lack of food. **2** (often foll. by *for*) a strong desire. •*v.intr.* **1** (often foll. by *for*) have a craving or strong desire. **2** feel hunger.

hun·ger strike *n.* the refusal of food as a form of protest, esp. by prisoners.

hung ju·ry *n.* a jury unable to reach unanimous agreement after extended deliberations.

hung-o·ver *adj. colloq.* suffering from a hangover.

hun·gry /húnggree/ *adj.* (**hungrier, hungriest**) **1** feeling hunger; needing food. **2** eager; craving. □□ **hun·gri·ly** *adv.* **hun·gri·ness** *n.*

hunk /hungk/ *n.* **1 a** a large piece cut off (*a hunk of bread*). **b** a thick or clumsy piece. **2** *colloq.* **a** a sexually attractive man. **b** a very large person. □□ **hunk·y** *adj.* (**hunk·i·er, hunk·i·est**).

hunk·y-do·ry /húngkeedáwree/ *adj. colloq.* fine; going well.

hunt /hunt/ *v.* & *n.* •*v.* **1** *tr.* (also *absol.*) **a** pursue and kill (wild animals, esp. game), *Brit.* esp. on horseback and with hounds, for sport or food. **b** (of an animal) chase (its prey). **2** *intr.* (foll. by *after, for*) seek; search (*hunting for a pen*). **3** *intr.* oscillate. **4** *tr.* (foll. by *away*, etc.) drive off by pursuit. **5** *tr.* scour (a district) in pursuit of game. **6** *tr.* (as **hunted** *adj.*) (of a look, etc.)

expressing alarm or terror as of one being hunted. • *n.* **1** the practice of hunting. **2 a** an association of people engaged in hunting with hounds. **b** an area where hunting takes place. □ **hunt down** pursue and capture. **hunt out** find by searching.

hunt·er /húntər/ *n.* **1 a** (*fem.* **huntress**) a person or animal that hunts. **b** a horse used in hunting. **2** a person who seeks something. **3** a watch with a hinged cover protecting the glass.

hunt·ing /húnting/ *n.* the practice of pursuing and killing wild animals.

Hun·ting·ton's cho·re·a /húntingt'nz/ *n. Med.* chorea accompanied by a progressive dementia.

hunts·man /húntsmən/ *n.* (*pl.* **-men**) **1** a hunter. **2** a hunt official in charge of hounds.

hur·dle /hárd'l/ *n. & v.* • *n.* **1** *Track & Field* **a** each of a series of light frames to be cleared by runners in a race. **b** (in *pl.*) a hurdle race. **2** an obstacle or difficulty. **3** a portable rectangular frame used as a temporary fence, etc. • *v.* **1** *Track & Field* **a** *intr.* run in a hurdle race. **b** *tr.* clear (a hurdle). **2** *tr.* fence off, etc., with hurdles. □□ **hurd·ler** *n.*

hur·dy-gur·dy /hárdeegárdee/ *n.* (*pl.* **-dies**) **1** a musical instrument with a droning sound, played by turning a handle. **2** *colloq.* a barrel organ.

hurl /hərl/ *v. & n.* • *v.* **1** *tr.* throw with great force. **2** *tr.* utter (abuse, etc.) vehemently. • *n.* a forceful throw.

Hurl·er's syn·drome /hárlərz/ *n. Med.* a defect in metabolism resulting in mental retardation, a protruding abdomen, and deformities of the bones, including an abnormally large head. Also called **gargoylism**.

hurl·y-burl·y /hárleebárlee/ *n.* boisterous activity; commotion.

Hu·ron /hyóórən, –on/ *n.* **1 a** a N. American people native to the northeastern US and eastern Canada. **b** a member of this people. **2** the language of this people.

hur·rah /hŏŏraá/ *int., n., & v.* (also **hur·ray** /hŏŏráy/) • *int. & n.* an exclamation of joy or approval. • *v.intr.* cry or shout "hurrah" or "hurray."

hur·ri·cane /hárikayn, húr–/ *n.* a storm with violent wind, esp. a tropical cyclone.

hur·ri·cane lamp *n.* an oil lamp designed to resist a high wind.

hur·ry /hárее, húree/ *n. & v.* • *n.* (*pl.* **-ries**) **1 a** great haste. **b** (with *neg.* or *interrog.*) a need for haste (*what's the hurry?*). **2** (often foll. by *for*, or *to* + infin.) eagerness to get a thing done quickly. • *v.* (**-ries, -ried**) **1** *intr.* move or act with great or undue haste. **2** *tr.* (often foll. by *away*, *along*) cause to move or proceed in this way. **3** *tr.* (as **hurried** *adj.*) hasty; done rapidly owing to lack of time. □ **hurry up** (or **along**) make or cause to make haste. **in a hurry 1** hurrying; rushed; in a rushed manner. **2** *colloq.* easily or readily (*you will not beat that in a hurry; won't ask again in a hurry*). □□ **hur·ried·ly** *adv.* **hur·ried·ness** *n.*

hurt /hərt/ *v. & n.* • *v.* (*past* and *past part.* **hurt**) **1** *tr.* (also *absol.*) cause injury to. **2** *tr.* cause mental distress to. **3** *intr.* suffer pain (*my arm hurts*). • *n.* **1** bodily or material injury. **2** harm; wrong.

hurt·ful /hártfŏŏl/ *adj.* causing (esp. mental) hurt. □□ **hurt·ful·ly** *adv.* **hurt·ful·ness** *n.*

hur·tle /hárt'l/ *v.* **1** *intr. & tr.* move or hurl rapidly or with a clattering sound. **2** *intr.* come with a crash.

hus·band /húzbənd/ *n. & v.* • *n.* a married man, esp. in relation to his wife. • *v.tr.* manage thriftily. □□ **hus·band·er** *n.* **hus·band·hood** *n.* **hus·band·less** *adj.* **hus·band·ly** *adj.*

husband late Old English (in the senses 'male head of a household' and 'manager, steward,' from Old Norse *húsbóndi* 'master of a house,' from *hús* 'house' + *bóndi* 'occupier and tiller of the soil.' The original sense of the verb was 'till, cultivate.'

hus·band·ry /húzbəndree/ *n.* **1** farming. **2 a** management of resources. **b** careful management.

hush /hush/ *v., int., & n.* • *v. tr. & intr.* make or become silent or muted. • *int.* calling for silence. *n.* an expectant stillness or silence. □ **hush up** suppress public mention of (a scandal).

hush-hush /húsh-húsh/ *adj. colloq.* (esp. of an official plan or enterprise, etc.) highly secret or confidential.

hush mon·ey *n.* money paid to prevent the disclosure of a discreditable matter.

hush pup·py *n.* a deep-fried ball of cornmeal dough.

husk /husk/ *n. & v.* • *n.* **1** the dry outer covering of some fruits or seeds. **2** the worthless outside part of a thing. • *v.tr.* remove a husk from.

husk·y[1] /húskee/ *adj.* (**huskier, huskiest**) **1** (of a person or voice) dry in the throat; hoarse. **2** of or full of husks. **3** dry as a husk. **4** strong; hefty. □□ **husk·i·ly** *adv.* **husk·i·ness** *n.*

husk·y[2] /húskee/ *n.* (*pl.* **-ies**) a dog of a powerful breed used in the Arctic for pulling sledges.

hus·sar /həzaár, –saár/ *n.* a soldier of a light cavalry regiment.

hus·sy /húsee, –zee/ *n.* (*pl.* **-sies**) *derog.* an impudent or immoral girl or woman.

hust·ings /hústingz/ *n.* political campaigning, esp. the appearances and activities involved with a campaign.

hus·tle /húsəl/ *v. & n.* • *v.* **1** *tr.* push roughly. **2** *tr.* **a** (foll. by *into*, *out of*, etc.) force or deal with hurriedly or unceremoniously (*hustled them out of the room*). **b** (foll. by *into*) coerce hurriedly (*was hustled into agreeing*). **3** *intr.* push one's way; bustle. **4** *tr. sl.* **a** obtain by forceful action. **b** swindle. **5** *intr. sl.* engage in prostitution. • *n.* **1** an act of hustling. **2** *colloq.* a fraud or swindle.

hus·tler /húslər/ *n. sl.* **1** an aggressive and enterprising individual, esp. an unscrupulous one. **2** a prostitute.

hut /hut/ *n.* a small simple or crude house or shelter.

hutch /huch/ *n.* **1** a box or cage, usu. with a wire mesh front, for keeping small pet animals. **2** *derog.* a small house.

hwy. *abbr.* highway.

hy·a·cinth /híəsinth/ *n.* **1** any bulbous plant of the genus *Hyacinthus* with racemes of bell-shaped fragrant flowers. **2** = GRAPE HYACINTH. **3** the purplish blue color of the hyacinth flower. □□ **hy·a·cin·thine** /–sínthin, –in/ *adj.*

hy·a·lin /híəlin/ *n.* a clear glassy substance produced as a result of the degeneration of certain body tissues.

hy·a·line *adj. & n.* • /híəlin, –līn/ *adj.* glasslike; vitreous; transparent. • *n.* /híəleén, –lin/ *literary* a smooth sea, clear sky, etc.

hy·brid /híbrid/ *n. & adj.* • *n.* **1** *Biol.* the offspring of two plants or animals of different species or varieties. **2** often *offens.* a person of mixed racial origin. **3** a thing composed of incongruous elements. • *adj.* **1** bred as a hybrid from different species or varieties. **2** of mixed character; derived from incongruous elements or unlike sources. □□ **hy·brid·ism** *n.*

hy·brid·ize /híbridīz/ *v.* **1** *tr.* subject (a species, etc.) to cross-breeding. **2** *intr.* **a** produce hybrids. **b** (of an animal or plant) interbreed. □□ **hy·brid·i·za·tion** *n.*

hy·dra /hídrə/ *n.* **1** a freshwater polyp of the genus *Hydra* with tubular body and tentacles. **2** something that is hard to destroy.

hy·dran·gea /hīdráynjə, –dran–/ *n.* any shrub of the genus *Hydrangea* with large white, pink, or blue flowers.

hy·drant /hídrənt/ *n.* a pipe (esp. in a street) with a nozzle to which a hose can be attached for drawing water from a water main.

See page xii for the *Key to Pronunciation*.

hy·drate /hídrayt/ *n. & v.* •*n. Chem.* a compound of water with another compound or with an element. •*v.tr.* **1 a** combine chemically with water. **b** (as **hydrated** *adj.*) chemically bonded to water. **2** cause to absorb water. ▫▫ **hy·dra·ta·ble** *adj.* **hy·dra·tion** /–dráyshən/ *n.* **hy·dra·tor** *n.*

hy·drau·lic /hīdráwlik, –drólik/ *adj.* **1** (of water, oil, etc.) conveyed through pipes or channels, usu. by pressure. **2** (of a mechanism, etc.) operated by liquid moving in this manner (*hydraulic brakes*). **3** hardening under water (*hydraulic cement*). ▫▫ **hy·drau·li·cal·ly** *adv.* **hy·drau·lic·i·ty** /–lísitee/ *n.*

hy·drau·lics /hīdráwliks, –dróliks/ *n.pl.* (usu. treated as *sing.*) the science of the conveyance of liquids through pipes, etc., esp. as motive power.

hy·dra·zine /hídrəzeen/ *n. Chem.* a colorless alkaline liquid that is a powerful reducing agent and is used as a rocket propellant.

hy·dride /hídrīd/ *n. Chem.* a binary compound of hydrogen with an element, esp. with a metal.

hy·dro /hídrō/ *n.* (*pl.* **-dros**) *colloq.* a hydroelectric power plant.

hydro- /hídrō/ *comb. form* (also **hydr-** before a vowel) **1** having to do with water (*hydroelectric*). **2** *Med.* affected with an accumulation of serous fluid (*hydrocephalus*). **3** *Chem.* combined with hydrogen (*hydrochloric*).

hy·dro·car·bon /hídrəkaarbən/ *n. Chem.* a compound of hydrogen and carbon.

hy·dro·ceph·a·lus /hídrəséfələs/ *n. Med.* an abnormal amount of fluid within the brain, esp. in young children, which makes the head enlarge and can cause mental deficiency. ▫▫ **hy·dro·ce·phal·ic** /–sifálik/ *adj.*

hy·dro·chlo·ric ac·id /hídrəkláwrik/ *n. Chem.* a solution of the colorless gas hydrogen chloride in water.

hy·dro·chlo·ride /hídrəkláwrīd/ *n. Chem.* a compound of an organic base with hydrochloric acid.

hy·dro·cor·ti·sone /hídrəkáwrtizōn/ *n. Biochem.* a steroid hormone produced by the adrenal cortex, used medicinally to treat inflammation and rheumatism.

hy·dro·dy·nam·ics /hídrōdīnámiks/ *n.* the science of forces acting on or exerted by fluids (esp. liquids). ▫▫ **hy·dro·dy·nam·ic** *adj.* **hy·dro·dy·nam·i·cal** *adj.* **hy·dro·dy·nam·i·cist** /–misist/ *n.*

hy·dro·e·lec·tric /hídrōiléktrik/ *adj.* **1** generating electricity by waterpower. **2** (of electricity) generated in this way. ▫▫ **hy·dro·e·lec·tric·i·ty** /–trísitee/ *n.*

hy·dro·foil /hídrəfoyl/ *n.* **1** a boat equipped with a device consisting of planes for lifting its hull out of the water to increase its speed. **2** this device.

hy·dro·gen /hídrəjən/ *n. Chem.* a colorless gaseous element, the lightest of the elements and occurring in water and all organic compounds. ¶ Symb.: **H**. ▫▫ **hy·drog·e·nous** /–drójinəs/ *adj.*

hy·dro·gen·ate /hīdrójinayt, hídrəjənayt/ *v.tr.* charge with or cause to combine with hydrogen. ▫▫ **hy·dro·gen·a·tion** /–náyshən/ *n.*

hy·dro·gen bomb *n.* an immensely powerful bomb utilizing the explosive fusion of hydrogen nuclei: also called **H bomb**.

hy·dro·gen per·ox·ide *n.* a colorless viscous unstable liquid with strong oxidizing properties. ¶ Chem. formula: H_2O_2.

hy·drog·ra·phy /hīdrógrəfee/ *n.* the science of surveying and charting seas, lakes, rivers, etc. ▫▫ **hy·drog·ra·pher** *n.* **hy·dro·graph·ic** /hídrəgráfik/ *adj.* **hy·dro·graph·i·cal** *adj.* **hy·dro·graph·i·cal·ly** *adv.*

hy·droid /hídroyd/ *adj. & n. Zool.* any usu. polypoid hydrozoan of the order Hydroida, including the hydra.

hy·drol·o·gy /hīdróləjee/ *n.* the science of the properties of the earth's water, esp. of its movement in relation to land. ▫▫ **hy·dro·log·ic** /hídrəlójik/ *adj.* **hy·dro·log·i·cal** *adj.* **hy·dro·log·i·cal·ly** *adv.* **hy·drol·o·gist** /–róləjist/ *n.*

hy·drol·y·sis /hīdrólisis/ *n.* the chemical reaction of a substance with water, usu. resulting in decomposition. ▫▫ **hy·dro·lyt·ic** /hídrəlítik/ *adj.*

hy·dro·lyze /hídrəlīz/ *v.tr. & intr.* subject to or undergo the chemical action of water.

hy·dro·me·chan·ics /hídrōmikániks/ *n.* the mechanics of liquids; hydrodynamics.

hy·drom·e·ter /hīdrómitər/ *n.* an instrument for measuring the density of liquids. ▫▫ **hy·dro·met·ric** /hídrəmétrik/ *adj.* **hy·drom·e·try** *n.*

hy·drop·a·thy /hīdrópəthee/ *n.* the (medically unorthodox) treatment of disease by external and internal application of water. ▫▫ **hy·dro·path·ic** /hídrəpáthik/ *adj.* **hy·drop·a·thist** *n.*

hy·dro·phil·ic /hídrəfílik/ *adj.* **1** having an affinity for water. **2** wettable by water.

hy·dro·pho·bi·a /hídrəfóbeeə/ *n.* **1** a morbid aversion to water, esp. as a symptom of rabies in humans. **2** rabies, esp. in humans.

hy·dro·pho·bic /hídrəfóbik/ *adj.* **1** of or suffering from hydrophobia. **2 a** lacking an affinity for water. **b** not readily wettable.

hy·dro·plane /hídrəplayn/ *n. & v.* •*n.* **1** a light fast motorboat designed to skim over the surface of water. **2** a finlike attachment that enables a submarine to rise and submerge in water. •*v.intr.* (of a boat) skim over the surface of water with its hull lifted.

hy·dro·pon·ics /hídrəpóniks/ *n.* the process of growing plants in sand, gravel, or liquid, without soil and with added nutrients. ▫▫ **hy·dro·pon·ic** *adj.* **hy·dro·pon·i·cal·ly** *adv.*

hy·dro·sphere /hídrəsfeer/ *n.* the waters of the earth's surface.

hy·dro·stat·ic /hídrəstátik/ *adj.* of the equilibrium of liquids and the pressure exerted by liquid at rest. ▫▫ **hy·dro·stat·i·cal·ly** *adv.*

hy·dro·stat·ics /hídrəstátiks/ *n.pl.* (usu. treated as *sing.*) the branch of mechanics concerned with the hydrostatic properties of liquids.

hy·dro·ther·a·py /hídrəthérəpee/ *n.* the use of water in the treatment of disorders, usu. exercises in swimming pools. ▫▫ **hy·dro·ther·a·pist** *n.*

hy·dro·ther·mal /hídrəthə́rməl/ *adj.* of the action of heated water on the earth's crust. ▫▫ **hy·dro·ther·mal·ly** *adv.*

hy·drous /hídrəs/ *adj. Chem. & Mineral.* containing water.

hy·drox·ide /hīdróksīd/ *n. Chem.* a metallic compound containing oxygen and hydrogen either in the form of the hydroxide ion (OH^-) or the hydroxyl group (–OH).

hydroxy- /hīdróksee/ *comb. form Chem.* having a hydroxide ion or group.

hy·drox·yl /hīdróksil/ *n. Chem.* the univalent group containing hydrogen and oxygen, as -OH.

hy·dro·zo·an *n. & adj.* •*n.* any aquatic cnidarian of the class Hydrozoa of mainly marine polyp or medusoid forms, including hydra and Portuguese man-of-war.

hy·e·na /hī-éenə/ *n.* (also **hy·ae·na**) any carnivorous mammal of the order Hyaenidae.

---

hyena Middle English: via Latin from Greek *huaina*, feminine of *hus* 'pig.' The transference of the term was probably because the animal's mane was thought to resemble a hog's bristles.

---

hy·giene /híjeen/ *n.* **1 a** a study, or set of principles, of maintaining health. **b** conditions or practices conducive to maintaining health. **2** sanitary science.

hy·gi·en·ic /hījénik, hījéenik/ *adj.* clean and sanitary. ▫▫ **hy·gi·en·i·cal·ly** *adv.*

hy·gi·en·ics /hījéniks, hījeéeniks/ *n.pl.* (usu. treated as *sing.*) = HYGIENE 1a.

hy·gien·ist /hījénist, –jeé–, –híjeenist/ *n.* a specialist in the promotion and practice of cleanliness for the preservation of health.

hygro- /hígrō/ *comb. form* moisture.

hy·grom·e·ter /hīgrómitər/ *n.* an instrument for measuring the humidity of the air or a gas. □□ **hy·gro·met·ric** /hígrəmétrik/ *adj.* **hy·grom·e·try** *n.*

hy·ing *pres. part.* of HIE.

hy·men /hímən/ *n. Anat.* a membrane that partially closes the opening of the vagina and is usu. broken at the first occurrence of sexual intercourse.

hy·me·nop·ter·an /hímənóptərən/ *n.* an insect having four transparent wings, including bees, wasps, and ants. □□ **hy·me·nop·ter·ous** *adj.*

hymn /him/ *n. & v.* •*n.* a song of praise, esp. to God in Christian worship, usu. a metrical composition sung in a religious service. •*v.* **1** *tr.* praise in hymns. **2** *intr.* sing hymns.

hym·nal /hímnəl/ *n. & adj.* •*n.* a hymnbook. •*adj.* of hymns.

hym·no·dy /hímnədee/ *n.* (*pl.* **-dies**) **1 a** the singing of hymns. **b** the composition of hymns. **2** hymns collectively. □□ **hym·no·dist** *n.*

hy·os·cine /híəseen/ *n.* a poisonous alkaloid found in plants of the nightshade family, esp. of the genus *Scopolia,* and used as an antiemetic in motion sickness and a preoperative medication for examination of the eye. Also called **scopolamine.**

hype[1] /hīp/ *n. & v. sl.* •*n.* **1** extravagant or intensive publicity promotion. **2** cheating; a trick. •*v.tr.* **1** promote (a product) with extravagant publicity. **2** cheat; trick.

hype[2] /hīp/ *n. sl.* **1** a drug addict. **2** a hypodermic needle or injection. □ **hyped up** stimulated by or as if by a hypodermic injection.

hy·per /hípər/ *adj. sl.* excessively excited, nervous, stimulated, etc.

hyper- /hípər/ *prefix* meaning: **1** over; beyond; above (*hyperphysical*). **2** exceeding (*hypersonic*). **3** excessively; above normal (*hyperbole*; *hypersensitive*).

hy·per·ac·tive /hípəráktiv/ *adj.* (of a person, esp. a child) abnormally active. □□ **hy·per·ac·tiv·i·ty** /–tívitee/ *n.*

hy·per·bo·la /hīpə́rbələ/ *n.* (*pl.* **hyperbolas** or **hyperbolae** /–lee/) *Geom.* the plane curve of two equal branches, produced when a cone is cut by a plane that makes a larger angle with the base than the side of the cone (cf. ELLIPSE). □□ **hy·per·bol·ic** /hípərbólik/ *adj.*

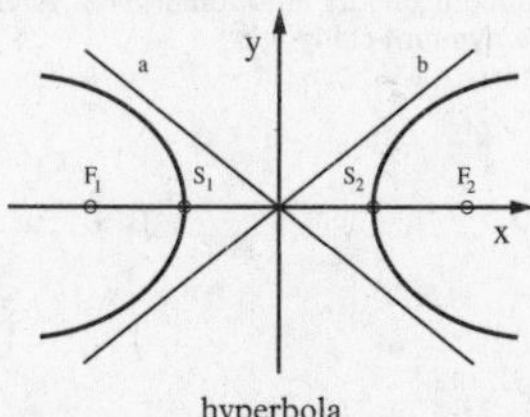

hyperbola

hy·per·bo·le /hīpə́rbəlee/ *n. Rhet.* an exaggerated statement not meant to be taken literally. □□ **hy·per·bol·i·cal** /hípərbólikəl/ *adj.* **hy·per·bol·i·cal·ly** *adv.*

hy·per·crit·i·cal /hípərkrítikəl/ *adj.* excessively critical, esp. of small faults.

hy·per·e·mi·a /hípəreéemeeə/ *n.* (*Brit.* **hyperaemia**) an excessive quantity of blood in the vessels supplying an organ or other part of the body. □□ **hy·per·e·mic** *adj.*

hy·per·es·the·sia /hípəris-theézhə/ *n.* (*Brit.* **hyperaesthesia**) an excessive physical sensibility, esp. of the skin. □□ **hy·per·es·thet·ic** /–thétik/ *adj.*

hy·per·gly·ce·mi·a /hípərglīseéemeeə/ *n.* an excess of glucose in the bloodstream, often associated with diabetes mellitus. □□ **hy·per·gly·ce·mic** *adj.*

hy·per·gol·ic /hípərgólik/ *adj.* (of a rocket propellant) igniting spontaneously on contact with an oxidant, etc.

hy·per·i·cum /hīpérikəm/ *n.* any shrub of the genus *Hypericum* with five-petaled yellow flowers.

hy·per·ki·ne·sia /hípərkineezha/ *n. Med.* muscle spasm. **2** *Psychiatry* a disorder of children marked by hyperactivity and inability to concentrate. □□ **hy·per·ki·net·ic** *adj.*

hy·per·phys·i·cal /hípərfízikəl/ *adj.* supernatural.

hy·per·sen·si·tive /hípərsénsitiv/ *adj.* excessively sensitive. □□ **hy·per·sen·si·tiv·i·ty** /–tívitee/ *n.*

hy·per·son·ic /hípərsónik/ *adj.* **1** relating to speeds of more than five times the speed of sound. **2** relating to sound frequencies above about a billion hertz.

hy·per·ten·sion /hípərténshən/ *n.* **1** abnormally high blood pressure. **2** a state of great emotional tension. □□ **hy·per·ten·sive** /–ténsiv/ *adj.*

hy·per·text /hípərtekst/ *n. Computing* computer software that links topics on the screen to related information, graphics, etc.

hy·per·ther·mi·a /hípərthə́rmeeə/ *n. Med.* the condition of having a body temperature greatly above normal.

hy·per·thy·roid·ism /hípərthíroydizəm/ *n. Med.* overactivity of the thyroid gland, resulting in an increased rate of metabolism. □□ **hy·per·thy·roid** *adj.*

hy·per·ton·ic /hípərtónik/ *adj.* **1** (of muscles) having high tension. **2** (of a solution) having a greater osmotic pressure than another solution. □□ **hy·per·to·ni·a** /–tṓneeə/ *n.* (in sense 1). **hy·per·to·nic·i·ty** /–tənísitee/ *n.*

hy·per·tro·phy /hīpə́rtrəfee/ *n.* enlargement of an organ or part. □□ **hy·per·troph·ic** /–trṓfik, –trófik/ *adj.* **hy·per·troph·ied** *adj.*

hy·per·ven·ti·la·tion /hípərvént'láyshən/ *n.* breathing at an abnormally rapid rate.

hy·phen /hífən/ *n. & v.* •*n.* the sign (-) used to join words semantically or syntactically (as in *pick-me-up, rock-forming*), to indicate the division of a word at the end of a line, or to indicate a missing or implied element (as in *man- and womankind*). •*v.tr.* **1** write (a compound word) with a hyphen. **2** join (words) with a hyphen.

hy·phen·ate /hífənayt/ *v.tr.* = HYPHEN *v.* □□ **hy·phen·a·tion** /–náyshən/ *n.*

hypno- /hípnō/ *comb. form* sleep; hypnosis.

hyp·no·gen·e·sis /hípnōjénisis/ *n.* the induction of a hypnotic state.

hyp·nol·o·gy /hipnóləjee/ *n.* the science of the phenomena of sleep. □□ **hyp·nol·o·gist** *n.*

hyp·no·sis /hipnṓsis/ *n.* **1** a state like sleep in which the subject acts only on external suggestion. **2** artificially produced sleep.

hyp·no·ther·a·py /hípnōthérəpee/ *n.* the treatment of disease by hypnosis.

hyp·not·ic /hipnótik/ *adj. & n.* •*adj.* **1** of or producing hypnosis. **2** (of a drug) soporific. •*n.* **1** a thing, esp. a drug, that produces sleep. **2** a person under or open to the influence of hypnotism. □□ **hyp·not·i·cal·ly** *adv.*

hyp·no·tism /hípnətizəm/ *n.* the practice of hypnosis. □□ **hyp·no·tist** *n.*

hyp·no·tize /hípnətīz/ *v.tr.* **1** produce hypnosis in. **2** fascinate; capture the mind of (a person). □□ **hyp·no·tiz·a·ble** *adj.*

hy·po[1] /hípō/ *n. Photog.* the chemical sodium thiosulfate (incorrectly called hyposulfite) used as a photographic fixer.

hy·po[2] /hípō/ *n.* (*pl.* **-pos**) *colloq.* = HYPODERMIC *n.*

hy·po·al·ler·gen·ic /hīpōalərjénik/ *adj.* having little likelihood of causing an allergic reaction (*hypoallergenic foods*; *hypoallergenic cosmetics*).

hy·po·chon·dri·a /hípəkóndreeə/ *n.* **1** abnormal anxiety about one's health. **2** morbid depression without real cause.

hy·po·chon·dri·ac /hípəkóndreeak/ *n. & adj.* •*n.* a person suffering from hypochondria. •*adj.* (also **hy·po·chon·dri·a·cal** /–dríəkəl/) of hypochondria.

hy·poc·ri·sy /hipókrisee/ *n.* (*pl.* **-sies**) **1** the assumption of moral standards to which one's own behavior does not conform; pretense. **2** an instance of this.

hyp·o·crite /hípəkrit/ *n.* a person given to hypocrisy. ▫▫ **hyp·o·crit·i·cal** /–krítikəl/ *adj.* **hyp·o·crit·i·cal·ly** *adv.*

hy·po·der·mic /hípədérmik/ *adj. & n.* •*adj. Med.* **1** of or relating to the area beneath the skin. **2 a** (of a drug, etc., or its application) injected beneath the skin. **b** (of a syringe, etc.) used to do this. •*n.* a hypodermic injection or syringe. ▫▫ **hy·po·der·mi·cal·ly** *adv.*

hy·po·gas·tri·um /hípəgástreeəm/ *n.* (*pl.* **hypogastria** /–treeə/) the part of the central abdomen that is situated below the region of the stomach. ▫▫ **hy·po·gas·tric** *adj.*

hy·po·ge·an /hípəjéeən/ *adj.* (also **hy·po·ge·al** /–jéeəl/) **1** (existing or growing) underground. **2** (of seed germination) with the seed leaves remaining below the ground.

hy·po·ge·um /hípəjéeəm/ *n.* (*pl.* **hypogea** /–jéeə/) an underground chamber.

hy·po·gly·ce·mi·a /hípōglīséemeeə/ *n.* a deficiency of glucose in the bloodstream. ▫▫ **hy·po·gly·ce·mic** *adj.*

hy·poid /hípoyd/ *n.* a gear with the pinion offset from the centerline of the wheel, to connect nonintersecting shafts.

hy·po·ma·ni·a /hípəmáyneeə/ *n.* a minor form of mania. ▫▫ **hy·po·man·ic** /–mánik/ *adj.*

hy·pos·ta·sis /hīpóstəsis/ *n.* (*pl.* **hypostases** /–seez/) **1** *Med.* an accumulation of fluid or blood in the lower parts of the body or organs under the influence of gravity, in cases of poor circulation. **2** *Metaphysics* an underlying substance, as opposed to attributes or to that which is unsubstantial. **3** *Theol.* **a** the person of Christ, combining human and divine natures. **b** each of the three persons of the Trinity. ▫▫ **hy·pos·ta·size** *v.tr.* (in senses 1, 2).

hy·po·stat·ic /hípəstátik/ *adj.* (also **hy·po·stat·i·cal**) *Theol.* relating to the three persons of the Trinity. ▫ **hypostatic union** the divine and human natures in Christ.

hy·po·style /hípəstīl/ *adj. Archit.* having a roof supported by pillars.

hy·po·tax·is /hípətáksis/ *n. Gram.* the subordination of one clause to another.

hy·po·ten·sion /hípətēnshən/ *n.* abnormally low blood pressure. ▫▫ **hy·po·ten·sive** *adj.*

hy·pot·e·nuse /hīpót'nōōs, –nyōōs/ *n.* the side opposite the right angle of a right-angled triangle.

hy·po·thal·a·mus /hípəthálәməs/ *n.* (*pl.* **-mi** /–mī/) *Anat.* the region of the brain that controls thirst, hunger, etc. ▫▫ **hy·po·tha·lam·ic** /–thəlámik/ *adj.*

hy·po·ther·mi·a /hípōthérmeeə/ *n. Med.* the condition of having an abnormally low body temperature.

hy·poth·e·sis /hīpóthisis/ *n.* (*pl.* **hypotheses** /–seez/) **1** a proposition made as a basis for reasoning. **2** a supposition made as a starting point for further investigation from known facts. **3** a groundless assumption.

hy·poth·e·size /hīpóthisīz/ *v.* **1** *intr.* frame a hypothesis. **2** *tr.* assume as a hypothesis. ▫▫ **hy·poth·e·sist** /–sist/ *n.* **hy·poth·e·siz·er** *n.*

hy·po·thet·i·cal /hípəthétikəl/ *adj.* **1** of or based on or serving as a hypothesis. **2** supposed but not necessarily real or true. ▫▫ **hy·po·thet·i·cal·ly** *adv.*

hy·po·thy·roid·ism /hípōthíroydizəm/ *n. Med.* subnormal activity of the thyroid gland, resulting in cretinism. ▫▫ **hy·po·thy·roid** *n. & adj.*

hy·po·ven·ti·la·tion /hípōvént'láyshən/ *n.* breathing at an abnormally slow rate.

hy·pox·i·a /hīpókseeə/ *n. Med.* a deficiency of oxygen reaching the tissues. ▫▫ **hy·pox·ic** *adj.*

hy·rax /híraks/ *n.* a small herbivorous mammal of the order Hyracoidea, with a compact body and a short tail, found in Africa and Arabia.

hys·sop /hísəp/ *n.* any small bushy aromatic herb of the genus *Hyssopus*, esp. *H. officinalis*, formerly used medicinally.

hys·ter·ec·to·my /hístəréktəmee/ *n.* (*pl.* **-mies**) the surgical removal of the uterus. ▫▫ **hys·ter·ec·to·mize** *v.tr.*

hys·te·ri·a /histéreeə, –stéer–/ *n.* **1** a wild uncontrollable emotion or excitement. **2** a functional disturbance of the nervous system, of psychoneurotic origin.

hys·ter·ic /histérik/ *n. & adj.* •*n.* **1** (in *pl.*) **a** a fit of hysteria. **b** *colloq.* overwhelming mirth or laughter (*we were in hysterics*). **2** a hysterical person. •*adj.* = HYSTERICAL.

---

hysteric mid-17th century (as an adjective): via Latin from Greek *husterikos* 'of the womb,' from *hustera* 'womb' (hysteria once being thought to be specific to women and associated with the womb).

---

hys·ter·i·cal /histérikəl/ *adj.* **1** of or affected with hysteria. **2** uncontrolledly emotional. **3** *colloq.* extremely funny. ▫▫ **hys·ter·i·cal·ly** *adv.*

Hz *abbr.* hertz.

I

I[1] /ī/ *n.* (also **i**) (*pl.* **Is** or **I's**) **1** the ninth letter of the alphabet. **2** (as a Roman numeral) 1.

I[2] /ī/ *pron.* (*obj.* **me**; *poss.* **my, mine**; *pl.* **we**) used by a speaker or writer to refer to himself or herself.

I[3] *symb. Chem.* the element iodine.

I[4] *abbr.* (also **I.**) **1** Island(s). **2** Isle(s).

IA *abbr.* Iowa (in official postal use).

i•amb /íamb/ *n. Prosody* a foot consisting of one short (or unstressed) followed by one long (or stressed) syllable.

i•am•bic /íambik/ *adj. & n. Prosody* • *adj.* of or using iambuses. • *n.* (usu. in *pl.*) iambic verse.

i•a•tro•gen•ic /íatrəjénik/ *adj.* (of a disease, etc.) caused by medical examination or treatment.

ib. var. of IBID.

I beam *n.* a girder of I-shaped section.

I•be•ri•an /ībeéreeən/ *adj. & n.* • *adj.* of ancient Iberia, the peninsula now comprising Spain and Portugal; of Spain and Portugal. • *n.* **1** a native of ancient Iberia. **2** any of the languages of ancient Iberia.

i•bex /íbeks/ *n.* (*pl.* same or **ibexes**) a wild goat, *Capra ibex*, esp. of mountainous areas of Europe, N. Africa, and Asia, with thick curved ridged horns.

ibid. /íbid/ *abbr.* (also **ib.**) in the same book or passage, etc.

i•bis /íbis/ *n.* (*pl.* same or **ibises**) any wading bird of the family Threskiornithidae with a curved bill, long neck, and long legs.

i•bu•pro•fen /íbyōōprṓfən/ *n.* an anti-inflammatory medication used to relieve pain and reduce fever.

ICBM *abbr.* intercontinental ballistic missile.

ICC *abbr.* **1** Interstate Commerce Commission. **2** International Claims Commission. **3** Indian Claims Commission.

ice /īs/ *n. & v.* • *n.* **1 a** frozen water, a brittle transparent crystalline solid. **b** a sheet of this on the surface of water (*fell through the ice*). **2** a frozen mixture of fruit juice or flavored water and sugar. **3** *sl.* diamonds. • *v.* **1** *tr.* mix with or cool in ice (*iced drinks*). **2** *tr. & intr.* (often foll. by *over, up*) **a** cover or become covered with ice. **b** freeze. **3** *tr.* cover (a cake, etc.) with icing. **4** *sl.* kill. □ **break the ice** do or say something to relieve the tension or get conversation going when people meet for the first time. **on ice 1** (of an entertainment, sport, etc.) performed by skaters. **2** *colloq.* held in reserve; awaiting further attention. **on thin ice** in a risky situation.

ice age *n.* a glacial period, esp. (the **Ice Age**) in the Pleistocene epoch.

ice•berg /ísbərg/ *n.* **1** a large floating mass of ice detached from a glacier or ice sheet and carried out to sea. **2** an unemotional or cold-blooded person. □ **the tip of the iceberg** a small perceptible part of something (esp. a difficulty) the greater part of which is hidden.

ice•berg let•tuce *n.* any of various crisp lettuces with a freely blanching head.

ice•bound /ísbownd/ *adj.* confined by ice.

ice•box /ísboks/ *n.* **1** a compartment in a refrigerator for making and storing ice. **2** *dated* a refrigerator.

ice•break•er /ísbraykər/ *n.* **1** a boat or ship used for breaking ice on a river, the sea, etc. **2** something that serves to relieve inhibitions, start a conversation, etc.

ice cap *n.* a permanent covering of ice, e.g., in polar regions.

ice cream *n.* a sweet creamy frozen food, usu. flavored.

ice cube *n.* a small block of ice made in a refrigerator.

ice hock•ey *n.* a form of hockey played on ice with a puck.

Ice•land•er /íslandər/ *n.* **1** a native or national of Iceland, an island in the N. Atlantic. **2** a person of Icelandic descent.

Ice•lan•dic /īslándik/ *adj. & n.* • *adj.* of or relating to Iceland. • *n.* the language of Iceland.

ice skate *n.* a boot with a blade attached to the sole, for skating on ice. □□ **ice-skate** *v.intr.* **ice-skat•er** *n.*

I Ching /eé chíng/ *n.* an ancient Chinese manual of divination based on symbolic trigrams and hexagrams.

ich•nog•ra•phy /iknógrəfee/ *n.* (*pl.* **-phies**) **1** the ground-plan of a building, map of a region, etc. **2** a drawing of this.

i•chor /íkawr, íkər/ *n.* **1** (in Greek mythology) fluid flowing like blood in the veins of the gods. **2** *poet.* bloodlike fluid. □□ **i•chor•ous** /íkərəs/ *adj.*

ichthyo- /íktheeō/ *comb. form* fish.

ich•thy•oid /íkthee-oyd/ *adj. & n.* • *adj.* fishlike. • *n.* any fishlike vertebrate.

ich•thy•o•lite /íktheeəlīt/ *n.* a fossil fish.

ich•thy•ol•o•gy /iktheeóləjee/ *n.* the study of fishes. □□ **ich•thy•ol•og•i•cal** /–theeəlójikəl/ *adj.* **ich•thy•ol•o•gist** *n.*

ich•thy•o•saur /íktheeəsáwr/ *n.* (also **ich•thy•o•saur•us** /íktheeəsáwrəs/) any extinct marine reptile of the order Ichthyosauria, with long head, tapering body, four flippers, and usu. a large tail.

ich•thy•o•sis /íktheeṓsis/ *n.* a skin disease that causes the epidermis to become dry and horny like fish scales. □□ **ich•thy•ot•ic** /–theeótik/ *adj.*

i•ci•cle /ísikəl/ *n.* a hanging tapering piece of ice, formed by the freezing of dripping water.

ic•ing /ísing/ *n.* **1** a coating of sugar, etc., on a cake or cookie. **2** the formation of ice on a ship or aircraft. □ **icing on the cake** an attractive though inessential addition or enhancement.

ick•y /íkee/ *adj. colloq.* (as a general term of disapproval) nasty; repulsive.

i•con /íkon/ *n.* (also **i•kon**) **1** a devotional painting or carving, usu. on wood, of Christ or another holy figure, esp. in the Eastern Church. **2** an image or statue. **3** *Computing* a symbol or graphic representation that appears on the monitor in a program, option, or window, esp. one of several for selection. **4** *Linguistics* a sign which has a characteristic in common with the thing it signifies.

i•con•ic /īkónik/ *adj.* **1** of or having the nature of an image or portrait. **2** (of a statue) following a conventional type. **3** *Linguistics* that is an icon. □□ **i•co•nic•i•ty** /íkənísitee/ *n.* (esp. in sense 3).

icono- /īkónō/ *comb. form* an image or likeness.

i•con•o•clasm /īkónəklazəm/ *n.* **1** the breaking of images. **2** the assailing of cherished beliefs.

i•con•o•clast /īkónəklast/ *n.* **1** a person who attacks cherished beliefs. **2** a person who destroys images used in religious worship, esp. *hist.* during the 8th–9th c. in the churches of the East, or as a Puritan of the

16th–17th c. ▫▫ **i·con·o·clas·tic** /–klástik/ *adj.* **i·con·o·clas·ti·cal·ly** *adv.*

i·co·nog·ra·phy /íkənógrəfee/ *n.* (*pl.* **-phies**) **1** the illustration of a subject by drawings or figures. **2 a** the study of portraits, esp. of an individual. **b** the study of artistic images or symbols. **3** a treatise on pictures or statuary. ▫▫ **i·co·nog·ra·pher** *n.* **i·con·o·graph·ic** /–nəgráfik/ *adj.* **i·con·o·graph·i·cal** *adj.* **i·con·o·graph·i·cal·ly** *adv.*

i·co·nol·o·gy /íkənóləjee/ *n.* **1** an artistic theory developed from iconography (see ICONOGRAPHY 2b). **2** symbolism.

i·co·sa·he·dron /íkōsəhéedrən, –íkós–/ *n.* a solid figure with twenty faces. ▫▫ **i·co·sa·he·dral** *adj.*

ic·ter·us /íktərəs/ *n. Med.* = JAUNDICE. ▫▫ **ic·ter·ic** /iktérik/ *adj.*

ic·tus /íktəs/ *n.* (*pl.* **ictuses** or same) **1** *Prosody* rhythmical or metrical stress. **2** *Med.* a stroke or seizure; a fit.

ICU *abbr.* intensive-care unit.

i·cy /ísee/ *adj.* (**icier, iciest**) **1** very cold. **2** covered with or abounding in ice. **3** (of a tone or manner) unfriendly; hostile (*an icy stare*). ▫▫ **i·ci·ly** *adv.* **i·ci·ness** *n.*

ID *abbr.* **1** identification, identity (*ID card*). **2** Idaho (in official postal use).

I'd /īd/ *contr.* **1** I had. **2** I should; I would.

id /id/ *n. Psychol.* the inherited instinctive impulses of the individual as part of the unconscious.

i·de·a /ídéeə/ *n.* **1** a conception or plan formed by mental effort (*have you any ideas?*). **2 a** a mental impression or notion; a concept. **b** a vague belief or fancy (*had an idea you were married*). **c** an opinion; an outlook or point of view (*had some funny ideas about marriage*). **3** an intention, purpose, or essential feature (*the idea is to make money*). **4** an archetype or pattern as distinguished from its realization in individual cases. ▫ **get** (or **have**) **ideas** *colloq.* be ambitious, rebellious, etc. **have no idea** *colloq.* **1** not know at all. **2** be completely incompetent. **not one's idea of** *colloq.* not what one regards as (*not my idea of a pleasant evening*). **put ideas into a person's head** suggest ambitions, etc., he or she would not otherwise have had. **that's an idea** *colloq.* that proposal, etc., is worth considering.

i·de·al /ídéeəl/ *adj.* & *n.* • *adj.* **1 a** answering to one's highest conception. **b** perfect or supremely excellent. **2 a** existing only in idea. **b** visionary. **3** embodying an idea. **4** relating to or consisting of ideas; dependent on the mind. • *n.* **1** a perfect type, or a conception of this. **2 a** an actual thing as a standard for imitation. **b** (often in *pl.*) a moral principle or standard of behavior. ▫▫ **i·de·al·ly** *adv.*

i·de·al gas *n.* a hypothetical gas consisting of molecules occupying negligible space and without attraction for each other, thereby obeying simple laws.

i·de·al·ism /ídéeəlizəm/ *n.* **1** the practice of forming or following after ideals, esp. unrealistically. **2** the representation of things in ideal or idealized form. **3** imaginative treatment. ▫▫ **i·de·al·ist** *n.* **i·de·al·is·tic** *adj.* **i·de·al·is·ti·cal·ly** *adv.*

i·de·al·ize /ídéeəlīz/ *v.tr.* **1** regard or represent (a thing or person) in ideal form or character. **2** exalt in thought to ideal perfection or excellence. ▫▫ **i·de·al·i·za·tion** *n.* **i·de·al·iz·er** *n.*

i·de·ate /ídeeayt/ *v. Psychol.* **1** *tr.* imagine; conceive. **2** *intr.* form ideas. ▫▫ **i·de·a·tion** /–áyshən/ *n.* **i·de·a·tion·al** /–áyshənəl/ *adj.* **i·de·a·tion·al·ly** /–áyshənəlee/ *adv.*

i·dée fixe /eeday féeks/ *n.* (*pl.* **idées fixes** *pronunc.* same) an idea that dominates the mind; an obsession.

i·den·ti·cal /īdéntikəl/ *adj.* **1** (often foll. by *with*) (of different things) agreeing in every detail. **2** (of one thing viewed at different times) one and the same. **3** (of twins) developed from a single fertilized ovum, therefore of the same sex and usu. very similar in appearance. **4** *Logic & Math.* expressing an identity. ▫▫ **i·den·ti·cal·ly** *adv.* **i·den·ti·cal·ness** *n.*
▶See note at SAME.

i·den·ti·fi·ca·tion /īdéntifikáyshən/ *n.* **1 a** the act or an instance of identifying; recognition; pinpointing. **b** association of oneself with the feelings, situation, characteristics, etc., of another person or group of people. **2** a means of identifying a person. **3** (*attrib.*) serving to identify (esp. the bearer) (*identification card*).

i·den·ti·fi·er /īdéntifīər/ *n.* **1** a person or thing that identifies. **2** *Computing* a sequence of characters used to identify or refer to a set of data.

i·den·ti·fy /īdéntifī/ *v.* (**-fies, -fied**) **1** *tr.* establish the identity of; recognize. **2** *tr.* establish or select by consideration or analysis of the circumstances (*identify the best method of solving the problem*). **3** *tr.* (foll. by *with*) associate (a person or oneself) inseparably or very closely (with a party, policy, etc.). **4** *tr.* (often foll. by *with*) treat (a thing) as identical. **5** *intr.* (foll. by *with*) **a** regard oneself as sharing characteristics of (another person). **b** associate oneself. ▫▫ **i·den·ti·fi·a·ble** /–fīəbəl/ *adj.* **i·den·ti·fi·a·bly** *adv.*

i·den·ti·ty /īdéntitee/ *n.* (*pl.* **-ties**) **1 a** the quality or condition of being a specified person or thing. **b** individuality; personality (*felt he had lost his identity*). **2** identification or the result of it (*a case of mistaken identity; identity card*). **3** the state of being the same in substance, nature, qualities, etc.; absolute sameness (*no identity of interests between them*).

i·den·ti·ty cri·sis *n.* a temporary period during which an individual experiences a feeling of loss or breakdown of identity.

id·e·o·gram /ídeeəgram/ *n.* a character symbolizing the idea of a thing without indicating the sequence of sounds in its name (e.g., a numeral, and many Chinese characters).

id·e·o·graph /ídeeəgraf/ *n.* = IDEOGRAM. ▫▫ **id·e·o·graph·ic** *adj.* **id·e·og·ra·phy** /ídeeógrəfee/ *n.*

i·de·o·logue /ídeeəlawg, –log, ídee–/ *n.* **1** a theorist; a visionary. **2** an adherent of an ideology.

i·de·ol·o·gy /ídeeóləjee, ídee–/ *n.* (*pl.* **-gies**) **1** the system of ideas at the basis of an economic or political theory (*Marxist ideology*). **2** the manner of thinking characteristic of a class or individual (*bourgeois ideology*). **3** visionary speculation. ▫▫ **i·de·o·log·i·cal** /–əlójikəl/ *adj.* **i·de·o·log·i·cal·ly** *adv.* **i·de·ol·o·gist** /–deeól–/ *n.*

ides /īdz/ *n.pl.* the eighth day after the nones in the ancient Roman calendar (the 15th day of March, May, July, October; the 13th of other months).

id·i·o·cy /ídeeəsee/ *n.* (*pl.* **-cies**) **1** utter foolishness; idiotic behavior or an idiotic action. **2** extreme mental imbecility.

id·i·om /ídeeəm/ *n.* **1** a group of words established by usage and having a meaning not deducible from those of the individual words (as in *at the drop of a hat, see the light*). **2** a form of expression peculiar to a language, person, or group of people. **3 a** the language of a people or country. **b** the specific character of this. **4** a characteristic mode of expression in music, art, etc.

id·i·o·mat·ic /ídeeəmátik/ *adj.* **1** relating to or conforming to idiom. **2** characteristic of a particular language. ▫▫ **id·i·o·mat·i·cal·ly** *adv.*

id·i·o·syn·cra·sy /ídeeōsíngkrəsee/ *n.* (*pl.* **-sies**) **1** a mental constitution, view or feeling, or mode of behavior, peculiar to a person. **2** anything highly individualized or eccentric. **3** a mode of expression peculiar to an author. ▫▫ **id·i·o·syn·crat·ic** /–krátik/ *adj.* **id·i·o·syn·crat·i·cal·ly** *adv.*

id·i·ot /ídeeət/ *n.* **1** *colloq.* a stupid person; an utter fool.

2 a person deficient in mind and permanently incapable of rational conduct. ▫▫ **id·i·ot·ic** /ideeótik/ *adj.* **id·i·ot·i·cal·ly** /ideeótiklee/ *adv.*

i·dle /íd'l/ *adj. & v.* • *adj.* (**idler, idlest**) **1** lazy; indolent. **2** not in use; not working; unemployed. **3** (of time, etc.) unoccupied. **4** having no special basis or purpose (*idle rumor; idle curiosity*). **5** useless. **6** (of an action, thought, or word) ineffective; worthless; vain. • *v.* **1 a** *intr.* (of an engine) run slowly while disconnected from a load or out of gear. **b** *tr.* cause (an engine) to idle. **2** *intr.* be idle. **3** *tr.* (foll. by *away*) pass (time, etc.) in idleness. ▫▫ **i·dle·ness** *n.* **i·dler** /ídlər/ *n.* **i·dly** *adv.*

i·dol /íd'l/ *n.* **1** an image of a deity, etc., used as an object of worship. **2** *Bibl.* a false god. **3** a person or thing that is the object of excessive or supreme adulation (*movie idol*).

i·dol·a·ter /ídólətər/ *n.* (*fem.* **idolatress** /–tris/) **1** a worshiper of idols. **2** (often foll. by *of*) a devoted admirer. ▫▫ **i·dol·a·trous** *adj.*

i·dol·a·try /ídólətree/ *n.* **1** the worship of idols. **2** great adulation.

i·dol·ize /íd'līz/ *v.* **1** *tr.* venerate or love extremely or excessively. **2** *tr.* make an idol of. **3** *intr.* practice idolatry. ▫▫ **i·dol·i·za·tion** *n.* **i·dol·iz·er** *n.*

i·dyll /íd'l/ *n.* (also **i·dyl**) **1** a short description in verse or prose of a picturesque scene or incident, esp. in rustic life. **2** an episode suitable for such treatment, usu. a love story. ▫▫ **i·dyl·list** *n.* **i·dyl·lize** *v.tr.*

i·dyl·lic /ídílik/ *adj.* **1** blissfully peaceful and happy. **2** of or like an idyll. ▫▫ **i·dyl·li·cal·ly** *adv.*

i.e. *abbr.* that is to say.

if /if/ *conj. & n.* • *conj.* **1** introducing a conditional clause: **a** on the condition or supposition that; in the event that (*if he comes I will tell him; if you are tired we will rest*). **b** (with past tense) implying that the condition is not fulfilled (*if I were you; if I knew I would say*). **2** even though (*I'll finish it, if it takes me all day*). **3** whenever (*if I am not sure I ask*). **4** whether (*see if you can find it*). **5 a** expressing wish or surprise (*if I could just try!; if it isn't my old hat!*). **b** expressing a request (*if you wouldn't mind opening the door?*). **6** with implied reservation, and perhaps not (*very rarely if at all*). **7** (with reduction of the protasis to its significant word) if there is or it is, etc. (*took little if any*). **8** despite being (*a useful if cumbersome device*). • *n.* a condition or supposition (*too many ifs about it*). ▫ **if only 1** even if for no other reason than (*I'll come if only to see her*). **2** (often *ellipt.*) an expression of regret (*if only I had thought of it; if only I could swim!*). **if so** if that is the case.

if·fy /ifee/ *adj.* (**iffier, iffiest**) *colloq.* uncertain; doubtful.

ig·loo /igloo/ *n.* a dome-shaped Eskimo dwelling, esp. one built of snow.

igloo

ig·ne·ous /igneeəs/ *adj.* **1** of fire; fiery. **2** *Geol.* (esp. of rocks) produced by volcanic or magmatic action.

ig·nite /ignít/ *v.* **1** *tr.* set fire to; cause to burn. **2** *intr.* catch fire. **3** *tr. Chem.* heat to the point of combustion or chemical change. **4** *tr.* provoke or excite (feelings, etc.). ▫▫ **ig·nit·a·ble** *adj.* **ig·nit·a·bil·i·ty** /–təbílitee/ *n.* **ig·nit·i·ble** *adj.* **ig·nit·i·bil·i·ty** /–tibílitee/ *n.*

ig·ni·ter /ignítər/ *n.* **1** a device for igniting a fuel mixture in an engine. **2** a device for causing an electric arc.

ig·ni·tion /ignishən/ *n.* **1** a mechanism for, or the action of, starting the combustion of fuel in the cylinder of an internal combustion engine. **2** the act or an instance of igniting or being ignited.

ig·no·ble /ignṓbəl/ *adj.* (**ignobler, ignoblest**) **1** dishonorable; mean; base. **2** of low birth, position, or reputation. ▫▫ **ig·no·bil·i·ty** *n.* **ig·no·bly** *adv.*

ig·no·min·i·ous /ignəmíneeəs/ *adj.* **1** causing or deserving ignominy. **2** humiliating. ▫▫ **ig·no·min·i·ous·ly** *adv.* **ig·no·min·i·ous·ness** *n.*

ig·no·min·y /ignəminee/ *n.* dishonor; infamy.

ig·no·ra·mus /ignəráyməs/ *n.* (*pl.* **ignoramuses** or **ignorami**) an ignorant person.

ignoramus late 16th cent. (as the endorsement made by a grand jury on an indictment considered backed by insufficient evidence to bring before a petty jury): Latin, literally 'we do not know' (in legal use 'we take no notice of it'), from *ignorare* (see IGNORE). The modern sense may derive from the name of a character in George Ruggle's *Ignoramus* (1615), a satirical comedy exposing lawyers' ignorance.

ig·no·rance /ignərəns/ *n.* (often foll. by *of*) lack of knowledge (about a thing).

ig·no·rant /ignərənt/ *adj.* **1 a** lacking knowledge or experience. **b** (foll. by *of, in*) uninformed (about a fact or subject). **2** *colloq.* ill-mannered; uncouth. ▫▫ **ig·no·rant·ly** *adv.*

ig·nore /ignáwr/ *v.tr.* **1** refuse to take notice of or accept. **2** intentionally disregard. ▫▫ **ig·nor·er** *n.*

i·gua·na /igwáanə/ *n.* any of various large arboreal lizards of the family Iguanidae, native to America, the W. Indies, and the Pacific islands, having a throat appendage and a spiny crest along the back.

i·guan·o·don /igwáanədon/ *n.* a large extinct plant-eating dinosaur of the genus *Iguanodon*, with forelimbs smaller than hind limbs.

IL *abbr.* Illinois (in official postal use).

il- /il/ *prefix* variant spelling of IN- assimilated before *l* (as in *illustrate, illuminate*).

il·e·um /íleeəm/ *n.* (*pl.* **ilea** /íleeə/) *Anat.* the third and last portion of the small intestine. ▫▫ **il·e·ac** *adj.*

il·i·ac /íleeak/ *adj.* of the lower body or ilium (*iliac artery*).

il·i·um /íleeəm/ *n.* (*pl.* **ilia** /íleeə/) **1** the bone forming the upper part of each half of the human pelvis. **2** the corresponding bone in animals.

ilk /ilk/ *n.* a family, class, or set (*not of the same ilk as you*).

Ill. *abbr.* Illinois.

ill. *abbr.* **1** illustrated. **2** illustration. **3** illustrator.

I'll /īl/ *contr.* I shall; I will.

ill /il/ *adj., adv., & n.* • *adj.* **1** (usu. *predic.*; often foll. by *with*) out of health; sick (*is ill; was taken ill with pneumonia; mentally ill people*). **2** (of health) unsound; disordered. **3** wretched; unfavorable (*ill fortune; ill luck*). **4** harmful (*ill effects*). **5** hostile; unkind (*ill feeling*). **6** *archaic* morally bad. **7** faulty; unskillful (*ill taste; ill management*). **8** (of manners or conduct) improper. • *adv.* **1** badly; wrongly (*ill-matched*). **2 a** imperfectly (*ill-provided*). **b** scarcely (*can ill afford to do it*). **3** unfavorably (*it would have gone ill with them*). • *n.* **1** injury; harm. **2** evil; the opposite of good. ▫ **ill at ease** embarrassed; uneasy. **speak ill of** say something unfavorable about.

ill-ad·vised *adj.* **1** (of a person) foolish or imprudent. **2** (of a plan, etc.) not well formed or considered. ▫▫ **ill-ad·vis·ed·ly** /–ədvízidlee/ *adv.*

ill-be·haved *adj.* having bad manners or conduct.

ill-bred *adj.* badly brought up; rude.

See page xii for the *Key to Pronunciation.*

il·le·gal /ileégəl/ *adj.* **1** not legal. **2** contrary to law. ▫▫ **il·le·gal·i·ty** /–gálitee/ *n.* (*pl.* **-ties**). **il·le·gal·ly** *adv.*

il·leg·i·ble /iléjibəl/ *adj.* not legible. ▫▫ **il·leg·i·bil·i·ty** *n.* **il·leg·i·bly** *adv.*

il·le·git·i·mate *adj.* & *n.* • *adj.* /ílijítimət/ **1** (of a child) born of parents not married to each other. **2** not authorized by law; unlawful. **3** improper. **4** wrongly inferred. **5** physiologically abnormal. • *n.* /ílijítimət/ a person whose position is illegitimate, esp. by birth. ▫▫ **il·le·git·i·ma·cy** /–məsee/ *n.* **il·le·git·i·mate·ly** *adv.*

ill-e·quipped *adj.* (often foll. by *to* + infin.) not adequately equipped or qualified.

ill-fat·ed *adj.* destined to or bringing bad fortune.

ill-found·ed *adj.* (of an idea, etc.) not well founded; baseless.

ill-got·ten *adj.* gained by wicked or unlawful means.

ill hu·mor *n.* moroseness; irritability. ▫▫ **ill-hu·mored** *adj.*

il·lib·er·al /ilíbərəl/ *adj.* **1** intolerant; narrow-minded. **2** without liberal culture. **3** not generous; stingy. ▫▫ **il·lib·er·al·i·ty** /–álitee/ *n.* (*pl.* **-ties**). **il·lib·er·al·ly** *adv.*

il·lic·it /ilísit/ *adj.* **1** unlawful; forbidden (*illicit dealings*). **2** secret; furtive (*an illicit romance*). ▫▫ **il·lic·it·ly** *adv.* **il·lic·it·ness** *n.*

il·lit·er·ate /ilítərət/ *adj.* & *n.* • *adj.* **1** unable to read. **2** uneducated. • *n.* an illiterate person. ▫▫ **il·lit·er·a·cy** *n.* **il·lit·er·ate·ly** *adv.* **il·lit·er·ate·ness** *n.*

ill-man·nered *adj.* having bad manners; rude.

ill na·ture *n.* churlishness; unkindness. ▫▫ **ill-na·tured** *adj.* **ill-na·tured·ly** *adv.*

ill·ness /ílnis/ *n.* **1** a disease, ailment, or malady. **2** the state of being ill.

il·log·i·cal /ilójikəl/ *adj.* devoid of or contrary to logic. ▫▫ **il·log·i·cal·i·ty** /–kálitee/ *n.* (*pl.* **-ties**). **il·log·i·cal·ly** *adv.*

ill-starred *adj.* unlucky; destined to failure.

ill tem·per *n.* moroseness. ▫▫ **ill-tem·pered** *adj.*

ill-timed *adj.* done or occurring at an inappropriate time.

ill-treat *v.tr.* treat badly; abuse. ▫▫ **ill-treat·ment** *n.*

il·lu·mi·nate /ilóominayt/ *v.tr.* **1** light up; make bright. **2** decorate (buildings, etc.) with lights as a sign of festivity. **3** decorate (an initial letter, a manuscript, etc.) with gold, silver, or brilliant colors. **4** help to explain (a subject, etc.). **5** enlighten spiritually or intellectually. **6** shed luster on. ▫▫ **il·lu·mi·nat·ing** *adj.* **il·lu·mi·nat·ing·ly** *adv.* **il·lu·mi·na·tion** /–náyshən/ *n.* **il·lu·mi·na·tive** /–náytiv, –nətiv/ *adj.* **il·lu·mi·na·tor** *n.*

il·lu·mine /ilóomin/ *v.tr. literary* **1** light up; make bright. **2** enlighten spiritually.

il·lu·sion /ilóozhən/ *n.* **1** deception; delusion. **2** a misapprehension of the true state of affairs. **3 a** the faulty perception of an external object. **b** an instance of this. **4** a figment of the imagination. **5** = OPTICAL ILLUSION. ▫ **be under the illusion** (foll. by *that* + clause) believe mistakenly. ▫▫ **il·lu·sion·al** *adj.*

il·lu·sion·ist /ilóozhənist/ *n.* a person who produces illusions; a magician. ▫▫ **il·lu·sion·ism** *n.* **il·lu·sion·is·tic** *adj.*

il·lu·so·ry /ilóosəree, –zəree/ *adj.* **1** deceptive (esp. as regards value or content). **2** having the character of an illusion. ▫▫ **il·lu·so·ri·ly** *adv.* **il·lu·so·ri·ness** *n.*

il·lus·trate /íləstrayt/ *v.tr.* **1 a** provide (a book, newspaper, etc.) with pictures. **b** elucidate (a description, etc.) by drawings or pictures. **2** serve as an example of. **3** explain or make clear, esp. by examples.

il·lus·tra·tion /íləstráyshən/ *n.* **1** a drawing or picture illustrating a book, magazine article, etc. **2** an example serving to elucidate. **3** the act or an instance of illustrating. ▫▫ **il·lus·tra·tion·al** *adj.*

il·lus·tra·tive /ilústrətiv, íləstray–/ *adj.* (often foll. by *of*) serving as an explanation or example. ▫▫ **il·lus·tra·tive·ly** *adv.*

il·lus·tra·tor /íləstraytər/ *n.* a person who makes illustrations, esp. for magazines, books, advertising copy, etc.

il·lus·tri·ous /ilústreeəs/ *adj.* distinguished; renowned. ▫▫ **il·lus·tri·ous·ly** *adv.* **il·lus·tri·ous·ness** *n.*

ill will *n.* bad feeling; animosity.

ill wind *n.* an unfavorable or untoward circumstance (with ref. to the proverb *it's an ill wind that blows nobody good*).

I'm /īm/ *contr.* I am.

im·age /ímij/ *n.* & *v.* • *n.* **1** a representation of the external form of an object, e.g., a statue (esp. of a saint, etc., as an object of veneration). **2** the character or reputation of a person or thing as generally perceived. **3** an optical appearance or counterpart produced by light or other radiation from an object reflected in a mirror, refracted through a lens, etc. **4** semblance; likeness. **5** a person or thing that closely resembles another (*is the image of his father*). **6** a typical example. **7** a simile or metaphor. **8 a** a mental representation. **b** an idea or conception. • *v.tr.* **1** make an image of; portray. **2** reflect; mirror. **3** describe or imagine vividly.

im·age·ry /ímijree/ *n.* **1** figurative illustration, esp. as used by an author for particular effects. **2** images collectively. **3** statuary; carving. **4** mental images collectively.

im·ag·i·na·ble /imájinəbəl/ *adj.* that can be imagined (*the greatest difficulty imaginable*). ▫▫ **i·mag·i·na·bly** *adv.*

im·ag·i·nar·y /imájinéree/ *adj.* **1** existing only in the imagination. **2** *Math.* being the square root of a negative quantity. ▫▫ **im·ag·i·nar·i·ly** *adv.*

▶**Imaginary** means 'product of the imagination; unreal'; **imaginative** means 'showing imagination; original.' Science fiction deals with imaginary people, places, and events; depending on the writer's ability, it may be more or less imaginative. Historical writing should not be imaginary, but the writer's approach, research, etc., may be quite imaginative.

im·ag·i·na·tion /imájináyshən/ *n.* **1** a mental faculty forming images or concepts of external objects not present to the senses. **2** the ability of the mind to be creative or resourceful. **3** the process of imagining.

im·ag·i·na·tive /imájinətiv/ *adj.* **1** having or showing in a high degree the faculty of imagination. **2** given to using the imagination. ▫▫ **im·ag·i·na·tive·ly** *adv.* **im·ag·i·na·tive·ness** *n.*

▶See note at IMAGINARY.

im·ag·ine /imájin/ *v.tr.* **1 a** form a mental image or concept of. **b** picture to oneself (something nonexistent or not present to the senses). **2** (often foll. by *to* + infin.) think or conceive (*imagined them to be soldiers*). **3** guess (*cannot imagine what they are doing*). **4** (often foll. by *that* + clause) suppose; be of the opinion (*I imagine you will need help*). ▫▫ **i·mag·in·er** *n.*

im·ag·in·ings /imájiningz/ *n.pl.* fancies; fantasies.

i·ma·go /imáygō, imaá–/ *n.* (*pl.* **-goes** or **imagines** /imájineez/) *Zool.* the final and fully developed stage of an insect after all metamorphoses, e.g., a butterfly or beetle.

i·mam /imaám/ *n.* **1** a leader of prayers in a mosque. **2** a title of various Islamic leaders, esp. of one succeeding Muhammad as leader of Islam. ▫▫ **i·mam·ate** /–mayt/ *n.*

im·bal·ance /imbáləns/ *n.* **1** lack of balance. **2** disproportion.

im·be·cile /ímbisil, –səl/ *n.* & *adj.* • *n.* **1** a person of abnormally weak intellect, esp. an adult with a mental age of about five. **2** *colloq.* a stupid person. • *adj.* mentally weak; stupid; idiotic. ▫▫ **im·be·cile·ly** *adv.* **im·be·cil·ic** /–sílik/ *adj.* **im·be·cil·i·ty** /–silitee/ *n.* (*pl.* **-ties**).

im·bibe /imbíb/ *v.tr.* **1** (also *absol.*) drink (esp. alcoholic liquor). **2 a** absorb or assimilate (ideas, etc.). **b** absorb (moisture, etc.). **3** inhale (air, etc.). ▫▫ **im·bib·er** *n.* **im·bi·bi·tion** /ìmbibíshən/ *n.*

im·bro·glio /imbrṓlyō/ *n.* (*pl.* **-glios**) **1** a confused or complicated situation. **2** a confused heap.

im·bue /imbyṓō/ *v.tr.* (**imbues, imbued, imbuing**) (often foll. by *with*) **1** inspire or permeate (with feelings, opinions, or qualities). **2** saturate. **3** dye.

IMF *abbr.* International Monetary Fund.

im·i·tate /ímitayt/ *v.tr.* **1** follow the example of; copy the action(s) of. **2** mimic. **3** make a copy of; reproduce. **4** be (consciously or not) like. ▫▫ **im·i·ta·ble** *adj.* **im·i·ta·tor** *n.*

im·i·ta·tion /ìmitáyshən/ *n.* & *adj.* • *n.* **1** the act or an instance of imitating or being imitated. **2** a copy. **3** *Mus.* the repetition of a phrase, etc., usu. at a different pitch, in another part or voice. • *adj.* made in imitation of something genuine; counterfeit; fake (*imitation leather*).

im·i·ta·tive /ímitaytiv/ *adj.* **1** (often foll. by *of*) imitating; following a model or example. **2** counterfeit. **3** of a word: **a** that reproduces a natural sound (e.g., *fizz*). **b** whose sound is thought to correspond to the appearance, etc., of the object or action described (e.g., *blob*). ▫▫ **im·i·ta·tive·ly** *adv.* **im·i·ta·tive·ness** *n.*

im·mac·u·late /imákyələt/ *adj.* **1** pure; spotless; perfectly clean or neat and tidy. **2** perfectly or extremely well executed (*an immaculate performance*). **3** free from sin or fault; innocent. ▫▫ **im·mac·u·la·cy** *n.* **im·mac·u·late·ly** *adv.* **im·mac·u·late·ness** *n.*

Im·mac·u·late Con·cep·tion *n. RC Ch.* the doctrine that God preserved the Virgin Mary from the taint of original sin from the moment she was conceived.

im·ma·nent /ímənənt/ *adj.* **1** (often foll. by *in*) indwelling; inherent. **2** (of the Supreme Being) permanently pervading the universe (opp. TRANSCENDENT). ▫▫ **im·ma·nence** /–nəns/ *n.* **im·ma·nen·cy** *n.* **im·ma·nent·ism** *n.* **im·ma·nent·ist** *n.*

▶See note at EMINENT.

im·ma·te·ri·al /ìmətéereeəl/ *adj.* **1** of no essential consequence; unimportant. **2** not material; incorporeal.

▶**Immaterial** and **irrelevant** are familiar in legal, especially courtroom, use. **Immaterial** means 'unimportant because not adding anything to the point.' **Irrelevant,** a much more common word, means 'beside the point, not speaking to the point.' Courts have long since ceased to demand precise distinctions, and evidence is often objected to as "immaterial, irrelevant, and incompetent (offered by a witness who is not qualified to offer it)."

im·ma·ture /ìməchṓōr, –tṓōr, –tyṓōr/ *adj.* **1** not mature or fully developed. **2** lacking emotional or intellectual development. **3** unripe. ▫▫ **im·ma·ture·ly** *adv.* **im·ma·tur·i·ty** *n.*

im·meas·ur·a·ble /imézhərəbəl/ *adj.* not measurable; immense. ▫▫ **im·meas·ur·a·bly** *adv.*

im·me·di·ate /iméedeeət/ *adj.* **1** occurring or done at once or without delay (*an immediate reply*). **2** nearest; next; not separated by others (*the immediate vicinity*; *the immediate future*; *my immediate neighbor*). **3** most pressing or urgent; of current concern (*our immediate concern was to get him to the hospital*). **4** (of a relation or action) having direct effect; without an intervening medium or agency (*the immediate cause of death*). **5** (of knowledge, reactions, etc.) intuitive; gained or exhibited without reasoning. ▫▫ **im·me·di·a·cy** *n.* **im·me·di·ate·ness** *n.*

im·me·di·ate·ly /iméedeeətlee/ *adv.* & *conj.* • *adv.* **1** without pause or delay. **2** without intermediary. • *conj. Brit.* as soon as.

im·me·mo·ri·al /ìmimáwreeəl/ *adj.* **1** ancient beyond memory or record. **2** very old. ▫▫ **im·me·mo·ri·al·ly** *adv.*

im·mense /iméns/ *adj.* **1** immeasurably large or great; huge. **2** very great; considerable (*made an immense difference*). **3** *colloq.* very good. ▫▫ **im·mense·ly** *adv.* **im·mense·ness** *n.* **im·men·si·ty** *n.*

im·merse /imə́rs/ *v.tr.* **1 a** (often foll. by *in*) dip; plunge. **b** cause (a person) to be completely under water. **2** (often *refl.* or in *passive*; often foll. by *in*) absorb or involve deeply. **3** (often foll. by *in*) bury; embed.

im·mer·sion /imə́rzhən, –shən/ *n.* **1** the act or an instance of immersing; the process of being immersed. **2** baptism by immersing the whole person in water. **3** mental absorption. **4** *Astron.* the disappearance of a celestial body behind another or in its shadow.

im·mi·grant /ímigrənt/ *n.* & *adj.* • *n.* a person who immigrates. • *adj.* **1** immigrating. **2** of or concerning immigrants.

im·mi·grate /ímigrayt/ *v.* **1** *intr.* come as a permanent resident to a country other than one's native land. **2** *tr.* bring in (a person) as an immigrant. ▫▫ **im·mi·gra·tion** /–gráyshən/ *n.* **im·mi·gra·to·ry** *adj.*

▶See note at EMIGRATE.

im·mi·nent /íminənt/ *adj.* **1** (of an event, esp. danger) impending; about to happen. **2** *archaic* overhanging. ▫▫ **im·mi·nence** /–nəns/ *n.* **im·mi·nent·ly** *adv.*

▶See note at EMINENT.

im·mis·ci·ble /imísibəl/ *adj.* (often foll. by *with*) that cannot be mixed. ▫▫ **im·mis·ci·bil·i·ty** *n.* **im·mis·ci·bly** *adv.*

im·mo·bile /imṓbəl, –beel, –bīl/ *adj.* **1** not moving. **2** not able to move or be moved. ▫▫ **im·mo·bil·i·ty** /–bílitee/ *n.*

im·mo·bi·lize /imṓbilīz/ *v.tr.* **1** make or keep immobile. **2** make (a vehicle or troops) incapable of being moved. **3** keep (a limb or patient) restricted in movement for healing purposes. **4** restrict the free movement of. **5** withdraw (coins) from circulation to support paper currency. ▫▫ **im·mo·bi·li·za·tion** *n.* **im·mo·bi·liz·er** *n.*

im·mod·er·ate /imódərət/ *adj.* excessive; lacking moderation. ▫▫ **im·mod·er·ate·ly** *adv.* **im·mod·er·ate·ness** *n.* **im·mod·er·a·tion** /–ráyshən/ *n.*

im·mod·est /imódist/ *adj.* **1** lacking modesty; forward; impudent. **2** lacking due decency. ▫▫ **im·mod·est·ly** *adv.* **im·mod·es·ty** *n.*

im·mo·late /íməlayt/ *v.tr.* **1** kill or offer as a sacrifice. **2** *literary* sacrifice (a valued thing). ▫▫ **im·mo·la·tion** /–láyshən/ *n.* **im·mo·la·tor** *n.*

im·mor·al /imáwrəl, imór–/ *adj.* **1** not conforming to accepted standards of morality (cf. AMORAL). **2** morally wrong (esp. in sexual matters). **3** depraved; dissolute. ▫▫ **im·mo·ral·i·ty** /–álitee/ *n.* (*pl.* **-ties**). **im·mor·al·ly** *adv.*

▶**Immoral** means 'failing to adhere to moral standards'; **amoral** means 'without moral standards.' An *immoral* person commits acts that violate society's moral norms; an *amoral* person is someone with no understanding of these norms, no sense of right and wrong.

im·mor·tal /imáwrt'l/ *adj.* & *n.* • *adj.* **1 a** living forever; not mortal. **b** divine. **2** unfading; incorruptible. **3** likely or worthy to be famous for all time. • *n.* **1 a** an immortal being. **b** (in *pl.*) the gods of mythology. **2** a person (esp. an author) of enduring fame. ▫▫ **im·mor·tal·i·ty** /–tálitee/ *n.* **im·mor·tal·ize** *v.tr.* **im·mor·tal·i·za·tion** *n.*

im·mov·a·ble /imṓōvəbəl/ *adj.* **1** that cannot be moved. **2** steadfast; unyielding. **3** emotionless. **4** not subject to change (*immovable law*). **5** motionless. ▫▫ **im·mov·a·bil·i·ty** *n.* **im·mov·a·bly** *adv.*

im·mune /imyṓōn/ *adj.* **1 a** (often foll. by *against, from, to*) protected against an infection owing to the pres-

---

ence of specific antibodies, or through inoculation or inherited or acquired resistance. **b** relating to immunity. **2** (foll. by *from, to*) free or exempt from or not subject to (some undesirable factor or circumstance).

im·mune res·ponse *n.* the reaction of the body to the introduction into it of an antigen.

im·mu·ni·ty /imyóonitee/ *n.* (*pl.* **-ties**) **1** *Med.* the ability of an organism to resist infection, by means of the presence of circulating antibodies and white blood cells. **2** freedom or exemption from an obligation, penalty, or unfavorable circumstance.

im·mu·nize /ímyənīz/ *v.tr.* make immune, esp. to infection, usu. by inoculation. ▫▫ **im·mu·ni·za·tion** *n.* **im·mu·niz·er** *n.*

immuno- /ímyənō/ *comb. form* immunity to infection.

im·mu·no·de·fi·cien·cy /imyənṓdifishənsee, imyóo–/ *n.* a reduction in a person's normal immune defenses.

im·mu·no·glob·u·lin /ímyənōglóbyəlin, imyóo–/ *n. Biochem.* any of a group of structurally related proteins that function as antibodies.

im·mu·nol·o·gy /imyənóləjee/ *n.* the scientific study of immunity. ▫▫ **im·mu·no·log·ic** /–nəlójik/ *adj.* **im·mu·no·log·i·cal** /–nəlójikəl/ *adj.* **im·mu·no·log·i·cal·ly** *adv.* **im·mu·nol·o·gist** /–nóləjist/ *n.*

im·mu·no·sup·pressed /imyənōsəprést, imyóo–/ *adj.* (of an individual) rendered partially or completely unable to react immunologically.

im·mu·no·sup·pres·sion /ímyənōsəpréshən, imyóo–/ *n. Biochem.* the partial or complete suppression of the immune response of an individual, esp. to maintain the survival of an organ after a transplant operation. ▫▫ **im·mu·no·sup·pres·sant** *n.*

im·mu·no·ther·a·py /imyənōthérəpee, imyóo–/ *n. Med.* the prevention or treatment of disease with substances that stimulate the immune response.

im·mure /imyóor/ *v.tr.* **1** enclose within walls; imprison. **2** *refl.* shut oneself away. ▫▫ **im·mure·ment** *n.*

im·mu·ta·ble /imyóotəbəl/ *adj.* **1** unchangeable. **2** not subject to variation in different cases. ▫▫ **im·mu·ta·bil·i·ty** /–bílitee/ *n.* **im·mu·ta·bly** *adv.*

imp /imp/ *n.* **1** a mischievous child. **2** a small mischievous devil or sprite.

imp Old English *impa, impe* 'young shoot, scion', *impian* 'to graft', based on Greek *emphuein* 'to implant'. In late Middle English, the noun denoted a descendant, especially of a noble family, and later a child of the devil or a person regarded as such; hence a 'little devil' or mischievous child (SENSE 1, early 17th cent.).

im·pact *n.* & *v.* • *n.* /ímpakt/ **1** (often foll. by *on, against*) the action of one body coming forcibly into contact with another. **2** an effect or influence, esp. when strong. • *v.* /impákt/ **1** *tr.* (often foll. by *in, into*) press or fix firmly. **2** *tr.* (as **impacted** *adj.*) **a** (of a tooth) wedged between another tooth and the jaw. **b** (of a fractured bone) with the parts crushed together. **c** (of feces) lodged in the intestine. **3** *intr.* **a** (foll. by *against, on*) come forcibly into contact with a (larger) body or surface. **b** (foll. by *on*) have a pronounced effect. ▫▫ **im·pac·tion** /–pákshən/ *n.*

im·pair /impáir/ *v.tr.* damage or weaken. ▫▫ **im·pair·ment** *n.*

im·pal·a /impaálə, –pálə/ *n.* (*pl.* same) a small antelope of S. and E. Africa, capable of long high jumps.

im·pale /impáyl/ *v.tr.* (foll. by *on, upon, with*) transfix or pierce with a sharp instrument. ▫▫ **im·pale·ment** *n.*

im·pal·pa·ble /impálpəbəl/ *adj.* **1** not easily grasped by the mind; intangible. **2** imperceptible to the touch. ▫▫ **im·pal·pa·bil·i·ty** /–bílitee/ *n.* **im·pal·pa·bly** *adv.*

im·pan·el /impán'l/ *v.tr.* (also **empanel**) (**-paneled, -paneling**) enroll or enter on a panel (those eligible for jury service). ▫▫ **im·pan·el·ment** *n.*

im·part /impaárt/ *v.tr.* (often foll. by *to*) **1** communicate (news, etc.). **2** give a share of (a thing).

im·par·tial /impaárshəl/ *adj.* treating all sides in a dispute, etc., equally; unprejudiced; fair. ▫▫ **im·par·ti·al·i·ty** /–sheeálitee/ *n.* **im·par·tial·ly** *adv.*

im·pas·sa·ble /impásəbəl/ *adj.* that cannot be traversed. ▫▫ **im·pas·sa·bil·i·ty** *n.* **im·pas·sa·ble·ness** *n.* **im·pas·sa·bly** *adv.*

im·passe /ímpas/ *n.* a position from which progress is impossible; deadlock.

im·pas·si·ble /impásibəl/ *adj.* **1** impassive. **2** incapable of feeling or emotion. **3** incapable of suffering injury. ▫▫ **im·pas·si·bil·i·ty** *n.* **im·pas·si·ble·ness** *n.* **im·pas·si·bly** *adv.*

im·pas·sioned /impáshənd/ *adj.* deeply felt; ardent (*an impassioned plea*).

im·pas·sive /impásiv/ *adj.* **1 a** deficient in or incapable of feeling emotion. **b** undisturbed by passion; serene. **2** without sensation. **3** not subject to suffering. ▫▫ **im·pas·sive·ly** *adv.* **im·pas·sive·ness** *n.* **im·pas·siv·i·ty** /–sívitee/ *n.*

im·pas·to /impástō, –paás–/ *n. Art* **1** the process of laying on paint thickly. **2** this technique of painting.

im·pa·tiens /impáyshənz/ *n.* any plant of the genus *Impatiens*, including several known popularly as touch-me-not.

im·pa·tient /impáyshənt/ *adj.* **1 a** (often foll. by *with, at*) lacking patience or tolerance. **b** (of an action) showing a lack of patience. **2** (often foll. by *for*, or *to* + infin.) restlessly eager. **3** (foll. by *of*) intolerant. ▫▫ **im·pa·tience** /–shəns/ *n.* **im·pa·tient·ly** *adv.*

im·peach /impéech/ *v.tr.* **1** charge (the holder of a public office) with misconduct. **2** *Brit.* charge with a crime against the government, esp. treason. **3** call in question; disparage (a person's integrity, etc.). ▫▫ **im·peach·a·ble** *adj.* **im·peach·ment** *n.*

im·pec·ca·ble /impékəbəl/ *adj.* **1** (of behavior, performance, etc.) faultless; exemplary. **2** not liable to sin. ▫▫ **im·pec·ca·bil·i·ty** *n.* **im·pec·ca·bly** *adv.*

im·pe·cu·ni·ous /impikyóoneeəs/ *adj.* having little or no money. ▫▫ **im·pe·cu·ni·ous·ness** *n.*

im·ped·ance /impéed'ns/ *n. Electr.* the total effective resistance of an electric circuit, etc., to alternating current, arising from ohmic resistance and reactance.

▶**impedance** is a specialized electrical term, while **impediment** is an everyday term meaning 'a hindrance or obstruction,', e.g., *Interpreting his handwriting was an impediment to getting business done.*

im·pede /impéed/ *v.tr.* retard by obstructing; hinder.

im·ped·i·ment /impédimənt/ *n.* **1** a hindrance or obstruction. **2** a defect in speech, e.g., a lisp or stammer. ▫▫ **im·ped·i·men·tal** /–mént'l/ *adj.*

im·pel /impél/ *v.tr.* (**impelled, impelling**) **1** drive, force, or urge into action. **2** drive forward; propel. ▫▫ **im·pel·lent** *adj.* & *n.* **im·pel·ler** *n.*

im·pend /impénd/ *v.intr.* **1** be about to happen. **2** (often foll. by *over*) **a** (of a danger) be threatening. **b** hang; be suspended. ▫▫ **im·pend·ing** *adj.*

im·pen·e·tra·ble /impénitrəbəl/ *adj.* **1** that cannot be penetrated. **2** inscrutable; unfathomable. **3** inaccessible to ideas, influences, etc. ▫▫ **im·pen·e·tra·bil·i·ty** *n.* **im·pen·e·tra·ble·ness** *n.* **im·pen·e·tra·bly** *adv.*

im·pen·i·tent /impénit'nt/ *adj.* not repentant or penitent. ▫▫ **im·pen·i·tence** *n.* **im·pen·i·ten·cy** *n.* **im·pen·i·tent·ly** *adv.*

im·per·a·tive /impérətiv/ *adj.* & *n.* • *adj.* **1** urgent. **2** obligatory. **3** commanding; peremptory. **4** *Gram.* (of a mood) expressing a command (e.g., *come here!*). • *n.* **1** *Gram.* the imperative mood. **2** a command. ▫▫ **im·per·a·tive·ly** *adv.* **im·per·a·tive·ness** *n.*

im·per·cep·ti·ble /impərséptibəl/ *adj.* **1** that cannot be perceived. **2** very slight, gradual, or subtle. ▫▫ **im·per·cep·ti·bil·i·ty** *n.* **im·per·cep·ti·bly** *adv.*

im·per·fect /impə́rfikt/ *adj. & n.* • *adj.* **1** not fully formed or done; faulty; incomplete. **2** *Gram.* (of a tense) denoting a (usu. past) action in progress but not completed at the time in question (e.g., *they were singing*). **3** *Mus.* (of a cadence) ending on the dominant chord. • *n.* the imperfect tense. ▫▫ **im·per·fect·ly** *adv.*

im·per·fec·tion /impərfékshən/ *n.* **1** incompleteness. **2 a** faultiness. **b** a fault or blemish.

im·pe·ri·al /impeéreeəl/ *adj.* **1** of or characteristic of an empire or comparable sovereign state. **2 a** of or characteristic of an emperor. **b** supreme in authority. **c** majestic; august. **d** magnificent. **3** (of nonmetric weights and measures) used or formerly used by statute in the UK (*imperial gallon*). ▫▫ **im·pe·ri·al·ly** *adv.*

im·pe·ri·al·ism /impeéreeəlizəm/ *n.* **1** an imperial rule or system. **2** usu. *derog.* a policy of acquiring dependent territories or extending a country's influence through trade, diplomacy, etc. ▫▫ **im·pe·ri·al·is·tic** *adj.* **im·pe·ri·al·is·ti·cal·ly** *adv.* **im·pe·ri·al·ize** *v.tr.*

im·pe·ri·al·ist /impeéreeəlist/ *n. & adj.* • *n.* usu. *derog.* an advocate or agent of imperial rule or of imperialism. • *adj.* of or relating to imperialism or imperialists.

im·per·il /impéril/ *v.tr.* (**imperiled, imperiling**) bring or put into danger.

im·pe·ri·ous /impeéreeəs/ *adj.* **1** overbearing; domineering. **2** urgent; imperative. ▫▫ **im·pe·ri·ous·ly** *adv.* **im·pe·ri·ous·ness** *n.*

im·per·ish·a·ble /impérishəbəl/ *adj.* that cannot or will not perish. ▫▫ **im·per·ish·a·bil·i·ty** *n.* **im·per·ish·a·ble·ness** *n.* **im·per·ish·a·bly** *adv.*

im·per·ma·nent /impə́rmənənt/ *adj.* not permanent; transient. ▫▫ **im·per·ma·nence** /–nəns/ *n.* **im·per·ma·nen·cy** *n.* **im·per·ma·nent·ly** *adv.*

im·per·me·a·ble /impə́rmeeəbəl/ *adj.* **1** that cannot be penetrated. **2** *Physics* that does not permit the passage of fluids. ▫▫ **im·per·me·a·bil·i·ty** *n.*

im·per·mis·si·ble /impərmísibəl/ *adj.* not allowable. ▫▫ **im·per·mis·si·bil·i·ty** *n.*

im·per·son·al /impə́rsənəl/ *adj.* **1** having no personality. **2** having or displaying no personal feeling or reference. **3** *Gram.* **a** (of a verb) used only with a formal subject (usu. *it*) and expressing an action not attributable to a definite subject (e.g., *it is snowing*). **b** (of a pronoun) = INDEFINITE 3. ▫▫ **im·per·son·al·i·ty** /–álitee/ *n.* **im·per·son·al·ly** *adv.*

im·per·son·ate /impə́rsənayt/ *v.tr.* **1** pretend to be (another person) for the purpose of entertainment or fraud. **2** act (a character). ▫▫ **im·per·son·a·tion** /–náyshən/ *n.* **im·per·son·a·tor** *n.*

im·per·ti·nent /impə́rt'nənt/ *adj.* **1** rude or insolent; lacking proper respect. **2** out of place; absurd. **3** esp. *Law* irrelevant; intrusive. ▫▫ **im·per·ti·nence** /–nəns/ *n.* **im·per·ti·nent·ly** *adv.*

im·per·turb·a·ble /impərtə́rbəbəl/ *adj.* not excitable; calm. ▫▫ **im·per·turb·a·bil·i·ty** *n.* **im·per·turb·a·ble·ness** *n.* **im·per·turb·a·bly** *adv.*

im·per·vi·ous /impə́rveeəs/ *adj.* (usu. foll. by *to*) **1** not responsive to an argument, etc. **2** not affording passage to a fluid. ▫▫ **im·per·vi·ous·ness** *n.*

im·pet·u·ous /impéchōōəs/ *adj.* **1** acting or done rashly or with sudden energy. **2** moving forcefully or rapidly. ▫▫ **im·pet·u·os·i·ty** /–ósitee/ *n.* **im·pet·u·ous·ly** *adv.* **im·pet·u·ous·ness** *n.*

im·pe·tus /ímpitəs/ *n.* **1** the force or energy with which a body moves. **2** a driving force or impulse.

im·pi·e·ty /impíətee/ *n.* (*pl.* **-ties**) **1** a lack of piety or reverence. **2** an act, etc. showing this.

im·pinge /impínj/ *v.tr.* (usu. foll. by *on, upon*) **1** make an impact; have an effect. **2** encroach.

im·pi·ous /impeeəs, impí–/ *adj.* **1** not pious. **2** wicked; profane. ▫▫ **im·pi·ous·ly** *adv.* **im·pi·ous·ness** *n.*

imp·ish /ímpish/ *adj.* of or like an imp; mischievous. ▫▫ **imp·ish·ly** *adv.* **imp·ish·ness** *n.*

im·plac·a·ble /implákəbəl/ *adj.* that cannot be appeased; inexorable. ▫▫ **im·plac·a·bil·i·ty** *n.* **im·plac·a·bly** *adv.*

im·plant *v. & n.* • *v.tr.* /implánt/ **1** (often foll. by *in*) insert or fix. **2** (often foll. by *in*) instill (a principle, idea, etc.) in a person's mind. **3** plant. **4** *Med.* **a** insert (tissue, etc.) in a living body. **b** (in *passive*) (of a fertilized ovum) become attached to the wall of the womb. • *n.* /ímplant/ **1** a thing implanted. **2** a thing implanted in the body. ▫▫ **im·plan·ta·tion** *n.*

im·plau·si·ble /impláwzibəl/ *adj.* not believable. ▫▫ **im·plau·si·bil·i·ty** *n.* **im·plau·si·bly** *adv.*

im·ple·ment *n. & v.* • *n.* /ímplimənt/ **1** a tool, instrument, or utensil. **2** (in *pl.*) equipment; articles of furniture, dress, etc. **3** *Law* performance of an obligation. • *v.tr.* /ímpliment/ **1 a** put (a decision, plan, etc.) into effect. **b** fulfill (an undertaking). **2** complete (a contract, etc.). ▫▫ **im·ple·men·ta·tion** *n.*

im·pli·cate *v. & n.* • *v.tr.* /ímplikayt/ **1** (often foll. by *in*) show (a person) to be concerned or involved (in a charge, crime, etc.). **2** (in *passive*; often foll. by *in*) be affected or involved. **3** lead to as a consequence or inference. • *n.* /ímplikət/ a thing implied. ▫▫ **im·pli·ca·tive** /ímplikaytiv, implíkə–/ *adj.* **im·pli·ca·tive·ly** *adv.*

---

implicate late Middle English: from Latin *implicatus* 'folded in', past participle of *implicare* (see IMPLY). The original sense was 'entwine, entangle'; compare with EMPLOY and IMPLY. The earliest modern sense (sense 2), dates from the early 17th cent., but appears earlier in IMPLICATION.

---

im·pli·ca·tion /implikáyshən/ *n.* **1** what is involved in or implied by something else. **2** the act of implicating or implying. ▫ **by implication** by what is implied or suggested rather than by formal expression.

im·plic·it /implísit/ *adj.* **1** implied though not plainly expressed. **2** (often foll. by *in*) virtually contained. **3** absolute; unquestioning; unreserved (*implicit obedience*). **4** *Math.* (of a function) not expressed directly in terms of independent variables. ▫▫ **im·plic·it·ly** *adv.* **im·plic·it·ness** *n.*

im·plode /implṓd/ *v.intr. & tr.* burst or cause to burst inward. ▫▫ **im·plo·sion** /–plṓzhən/ *n.* **im·plo·sive** /–plṓsiv/ *adj.*

im·plore /impláwr/ *v.tr.* **1** (often foll. by *to* + infin.) entreat (a person). **2** beg earnestly for. ▫▫ **im·plor·ing** *adj.* **im·plor·ing·ly** *adv.*

im·ply /implí/ *v.tr.* (**-plies, -plied**) **1** (often foll. by *that* + clause) strongly suggest the truth or existence of (a thing not expressly asserted). **2** insinuate; hint (*what are you implying?*). **3** signify. ▫▫ **im·plied** *adj.* **im·pli·ed·ly** *adv.*

▶See note at INFER.

---

imply late Middle English: from Old French *emplier*, from Latin *implicare*, from *in-* 'in' + *plicare* 'to fold'. The original sense was 'entwine, entangle'; in the 16th and 17th cents the word also meant 'employ'. Compare with EMPLOY and IMPLICATE.

---

im·po·lite /impəlít/ *adj.* ill-mannered; uncivil; rude. ▫▫ **im·po·lite·ly** *adv.* **im·po·lite·ness** *n.*

im·pol·i·tic /impólitik/ *adj.* **1** inexpedient; unwise. **2** not politic. ▫▫ **im·pol·i·tic·ly** *adv.*

im·pon·der·a·ble /impóndərəbəl/ *adj. & n.* • *adj.* that cannot be estimated or assessed in any definite way. • *n.* (usu. in *pl.*) something difficult or impossible to assess. ▫▫ **im·pon·der·a·bil·i·ty** *n.* **im·pon·der·a·bly** *adv.*

im·port *v. & n.* •*v.tr.* /impáwrt, ím–/ **1** bring in (esp. foreign goods or services) to a country. **2** (often foll. by *that* + clause) **a** imply; indicate; signify. **b** express; make known. •*n.* /impawrt/ **1** the process of importing. **2 a** an imported article or service. **b** (in *pl.*) an amount imported (*imports exceeded $50 billion*). **3** what is implied; meaning. **4** importance. ▫▫ **im·port·a·ble** *adj.* **im·por·ta·tion** *n.* **im·port·er** /–páwrtər/ *n.* (all in sense 1 of *v.*).

im·por·tant /impáwrt'nt/ *adj.* **1** (often foll. by *to*) of great effect or consequence; momentous. **2** (of a person) having high rank or status, or great authority. **3** pretentious; pompous. **4** (*absol.* in parenthetic construction) what is a more important point or matter (*they are willing and, more important, able*). ▶Use of *importantly* here is disputed. ▫▫ **im·por·tance** *n.* **im·por·tant·ly** *adv.* (see note above).

im·por·tu·nate /impáwrchənət/ *adj.* **1** making persistent or pressing requests. **2** (of affairs) urgent. ▫▫ **im·por·tu·nate·ly** *adv.* **im·por·tu·ni·ty** /–tóōnətee, –tyóō–/ *n.*

im·por·tune /ímpáwrtóōn, –tyōōn, impáwrchən/ *v.tr.* **1** solicit (a person) pressingly. **2** solicit for an immoral purpose.

im·pose /impṓz/ *v.* **1** *tr.* (often foll. by *on, upon*) require (a tax, duty, charge, or obligation) to be paid or undertaken (by a person, etc.). **2** *tr.* enforce compliance with. **3** *intr. & refl.* (foll. by *on, upon,* or *absol.*) demand the attention or commitment of (a person); take advantage of (*I do not want to impose on you any longer; I did not want to impose*). **4** *tr.* (often foll. by *on, upon*) palm (a thing) off on (a person).

im·pos·ing /impṓzing/ *adj.* impressive or formidable, esp. in appearance. ▫▫ **im·pos·ing·ly** *adv.*

im·po·si·tion /ímpəzíshən/ *n.* **1** the act or an instance of imposing; the process of being imposed. **2** an unfair or resented demand or burden. **3** a tax or duty.

im·pos·si·ble /impósibəl/ *adj.* **1** not possible; that cannot be done, occur, or exist (*it is impossible to alter them; such a thing is impossible*). **2** (loosely) not easy; not convenient; not easily believable. **3** *colloq.* (of a person or thing) outrageous; intolerable. ▫▫ **im·pos·si·bil·i·ty** /impósibílitee/ *n.* **im·pos·si·bly** *adv.*

impost /ímpōst/ *n.* a tax; duty; tribute.

im·pos·tor /impóstər/ *n.* (also **im·post·er**) **1** a person who assumes a false character or pretends to be someone else. **2** a swindler.

im·pos·ture /impós-chər/ *n.* fraudulent deception.

im·po·tent /ímpət'nt/ *adj.* **1 a** powerless; lacking all strength. **b** helpless. **c** ineffective. **2 a** (esp. of a male) unable, esp. for a prolonged period, to achieve a sexual erection or orgasm. **b** *colloq.* unable to procreate; infertile. ▫▫ **im·po·tence** /–t'ns/ *n.* **im·po·ten·cy** *n.* **im·po·tent·ly** *adv.*

im·pound /impównd/ *v.tr.* **1** confiscate. **2** take possession of. **3** shut up (animals) in a pound. ▫▫ **im·pound·er** *n.* **im·pound·ment** *n.*

im·pov·er·ish /impóvərish/ *v.tr.* (often as **impoverished** *adj.*) **1** make poor. **2** exhaust the strength or natural fertility of. ▫▫ **im·pov·er·ish·ment** *n.*

im·prac·ti·ca·ble /impráktikəbəl/ *adj.* **1** impossible in practice. **2** (of a road, etc.) impassable. **3** (of a person or thing) unmanageable. ▫▫ **im·prac·ti·ca·bil·i·ty** /–bílitee/ *n.* **im·prac·ti·ca·ble·ness** *n.* **im·prac·ti·ca·bly** *adv.*

im·prac·ti·cal /impráktikəl/ *adj.* **1** not practical. **2** not practicable. ▫▫ **im·prac·ti·cal·i·ty** /–kálitee/ *n.* **im·prac·ti·cal·ly** *adv.*

im·pre·ca·tion /ímprikáyshən/ *n.* **1** a spoken curse; a malediction. **2** the act of uttering an imprecation. ▫▫ **im·pre·ca·to·ry** /–kətáwree/ *adj.*

im·pre·cise /ímprisíś/ *adj.* not precise. ▫▫ **im·pre·cise·ly** *adv.* **im·pre·cise·ness** *n.* **im·pre·ci·sion** /–sízhən/ *n.*

im·preg·na·ble /imprégnəbəl/ *adj.* **1** (of a fortified position) that cannot be taken by force. **2** resistant to attack or criticism. ▫▫ **im·preg·na·bil·i·ty** /–bílitee/ *n.* **im·preg·na·bly** *adv.*

im·preg·nate /imprégnayt/ *v.tr.* **1** (often foll. by *with*) fill or saturate. **2** (often foll. by *with*) imbue; fill (with feelings, moral qualities, etc.). **3 a** make (a female) pregnant. **b** *Biol.* fertilize (a female reproductive cell or ovum). ▫▫ **im·preg·na·tion** /–náyshən/ *n.*

im·pre·sa·ri·o /ímprisaáreeō, –sáir–/ *n.* (*pl.* **-os**) an organizer of public entertainments, esp. the manager of an operatic, theatrical, or concert company.

im·press[1] *v. & n.* •*v.tr.* /imprés/ **1** (often foll. by *with*) **a** affect or influence deeply. **b** evoke a favorable opinion or reaction from (a person) (*was most impressed with your efforts*). **2** (often foll. by *on*) emphasize (an idea, etc.) (*must impress on you the need to be prompt*). **3** (often foll. by *on*) **a** imprint or stamp. **b** apply (a mark, etc.) with pressure. **4** make a mark or design on (a thing) with a stamp, seal, etc. •*n.* /ímpres/ **1** the act or an instance of impressing. **2** a mark made by a seal, stamp, etc. **3** a characteristic mark or quality. **4** = IMPRESSION 1. ▫▫ **im·pres·si·ble** /–présibəl/ *adj.*

im·press[2] /imprés/ *v.tr. hist.* **1** force (men) to serve in the army or navy. **2** seize (goods, etc.) for public service. ▫▫ **im·press·ment** *n.*

im·pres·sion /impréshən/ *n.* **1** an effect produced (esp. on the mind or feelings). **2** a notion or belief (esp. a vague or mistaken one) (*my impression is they are afraid*). **3** an imitation of a person or sound, esp. done to entertain. **4 a** the impressing of a mark. **b** a mark impressed. **5** an unaltered reprint from standing type or plates (esp. as distinct from *edition*).

im·pres·sion·a·ble /impréshənəbəl/ *adj.* easily influenced; susceptible to impressions. ▫▫ **im·pres·sion·a·bil·i·ty** /–bílitee/ *n.* **im·pres·sion·a·bly** *adv.*

im·pres·sion·ism /impréshənizəm/ *n.* **1** a style or movement in art concerned with expression of feeling by visual impression, esp. from the effect of light on objects. **2** a style of music or writing that seeks to describe a feeling or experience rather than achieve accurate depiction or systematic structure. ▫▫ **im·pres·sion·ist** *n.* **im·pres·sion·is·tic** /impréshənístik/ *adj.*

im·pres·sive /imprésiv/ *adj.* **1** impressing the mind or senses, esp. so as to cause approval or admiration. **2** (of language, a scene, etc.) tending to excite deep feeling. ▫▫ **im·pres·sive·ly** *adv.* **im·pres·sive·ness** *n.*

im·pri·ma·tur /ímprimaátər, –máytər, –tóōr/ *n.* **1** *RC Ch.* an official license to print (an ecclesiastical or religious book, etc.). **2** official approval.

im·print *v. & n.* •*v.tr.* /imprínt/ **1** (often foll. by *on*) impress or establish firmly, esp. on the mind. **2 a** (often foll. by *on*) make a stamp or impression of (a figure, etc.) on a thing. **b** make an impression on (a thing) with a stamp, etc. •*n.* /ímprint/ **1** an impression or stamp. **2** the printer's or publisher's name and other details printed in a book.

im·print·ing /imprínting/ *n. Zool.* the development in a young animal of recognition and trust for its own species.

im·pris·on /imprízən/ *v.tr.* **1** put into prison. **2** confine; shut up. ▫▫ **im·pris·on·ment** *n.*

im·prob·a·ble /impróbəbəl/ *adj.* **1** not likely to be true or to happen. **2** difficult to believe. ▫▫ **im·prob·a·bil·i·ty** *n.* **im·prob·a·bly** *adv.*

im·promp·tu /imprómptoo, –tyoo/ *adj., adv., & n.* •*adj. & adv.* extempore; unrehearsed. •*n.* **1** an extempore performance or speech. **2** a short piece of usu. solo instrumental music, often songlike.

im·prop·er /imprópər/ *adj.* **1 a** unseemly; indecent. **b** not in accordance with accepted rules of behavior.

2 inaccurate; wrong. **3** not properly so called. ▫▫ **im·prop·er·ly** *adv.*

im·prop·er frac·tion *n.* a fraction in which the numerator is greater than or equal to the denominator.

im·pro·pri·e·ty /imprəprī́ətee/ *n.* (*pl.* **-ties**) **1** lack of propriety; indecency. **2** an instance of improper conduct, etc. **3** incorrectness. **4** unfitness.

im·prove /improóv/ *v.* **1 a** *tr. & intr.* make or become better. **b** *intr.* (foll. by *on, upon*) produce something better than. **2** *absol.* (as **improving** *adj.*) giving moral benefit (*improving literature*). ▫▫ **im·prov·er** *n.*

---

improve early 16th cent. (as *emprowe* or *improwe*): from Anglo-Norman French *emprower* (based on Old French *prou* 'profit', ultimately from Latin *prodest* 'is of advantage'); *-owe* was changed to *-ove* under the influence of PROVE. The original sense was 'make a profit, increase the value of'; subsequently 'make greater in amount or degree', which led to sense 1 (early 17th cent.).

---

im·prove·ment /improóvmənt/ *n.* **1** the act or an instance of improving or being improved. **2** something that improves, esp. an addition or alteration that adds to value. **3** something that has been improved.

im·prov·i·dent /imprόvid'nt/ *adj.* **1** lacking foresight or care for the future. **2** not frugal. **3** heedless; incautious. ▫▫ **im·prov·i·dence** /–d'ns/ *n.* **im·prov·i·dent·ly** *adv.*

im·pro·vise /imprəvī́z/ *v.tr.* (also *absol.*) **1** compose or perform (music, verse, etc.) extempore. **2** provide or construct (a thing) extempore. ▫▫ **im·prov·i·sa·tion** /–izáyshən/ *n.* **im·prov·i·sa·tion·al** *adj.* **im·pro·vi·sa·to·ry** *adj.* **im·pro·vis·er** *n.*

im·pru·dent /improód'nt/ *adj.* rash; indiscreet. ▫▫ **im·pru·dence** /–d'ns/ *n.* **im·pru·dent·ly** *adv.*

im·pu·dent /impyəd'nt/ *adj.* **1** insolently disrespectful; impertinent. **2** shamelessly presumptuous. **3** unblushing. ▫▫ **im·pu·dence** /–d'ns/ *n.* **im·pu·dent·ly** *adv.*

im·pugn /impyóon/ *v.tr.* challenge or call in question (a statement, action, etc.). ▫▫ **im·pugn·a·ble** *adj.* **im·pugn·ment** *n.*

im·pulse /impuls/ *n.* **1** the act or an instance of impelling; a push. **2** an impetus. **3** a wave of excitation in a nerve. **4** a sudden desire or tendency to act without reflection (*did it on impulse*).

im·pul·sion /impúlshən/ *n.* **1** the act or an instance of impelling. **2** a mental impulse. **3** impetus.

im·pul·sive /impúlsiv/ *adj.* **1** (of a person or conduct, etc.) apt to be affected or determined by sudden impulse. **2** tending to impel. **3** *Physics* acting as an impulse. ▫▫ **im·pul·sive·ly** *adv.* **im·pul·sive·ness** *n.*

im·pu·ni·ty /impyóonitee/ *n.* exemption from punishment or from the injurious consequences of an action. ▫ **with impunity** without having to suffer the normal injurious consequences (of an action).

im·pure /impyóor/ *adj.* **1** mixed with foreign matter; adulterated. **2 a** dirty. **b** ceremonially unclean. **3** unchaste. **4** (of a color) mixed with another color. ▫▫ **im·pure·ly** *adv.* **im·pure·ness** *n.*

im·pu·ri·ty /impyóoritee/ *n.* (*pl.* **-ties**) **1** the quality or condition of being impure. **2** an impure thing or constituent.

im·pute /impyóot/ *v.tr.* (foll. by *to*) regard (esp. something undesirable) as being done or caused or possessed by. ▫▫ **im·put·a·ble** *adj.* **im·pu·ta·tion** *n.* **im·pu·ta·tive** /–tətiv/ *adj.*

IN *abbr.* Indiana (in official postal use).

In *symb. Chem.* the element indium.

in /in/ *prep., adv., & adj.* • *prep.* **1** expressing inclusion or position within limits of space, time, circumstance, etc. (*in Nebraska; in bed; in the rain*). **2** during the time of (*in the night; in 1989*). **3** within the time of (*will be back in two hours*). **4 a** with respect to (*blind in one eye; good in parts*). **b** as a kind of (*the latest thing in luxury*). **5** as a proportionate part of (*one in three failed; a gradient of one in six*). **6** with the form or arrangement of (*packed in tens; falling in folds*). **7** as a member of (*in the army*). **8** concerned with (*is in politics*). **9** as or regarding the content of (*there is something in what you say*). **10** within the ability of (*does he have it in him?*). **11** having the condition of; affected by (*in bad health; in danger*). **12** having as a purpose (*in search of; in reply to*). **13** by means of or using as material (*drawn in pencil; modeled in bronze*). **14 a** using as the language of expression (*written in French*). **b** (of music) having as its key (*symphony in C*). **15** (of a word) having as a beginning or ending (*words beginning in un-*). **16** wearing as dress (*in blue; in a suit*). **17** with the identity of (*found a friend in Mary*). **18** (of an animal) pregnant with (*in calf*). **19** into (with a verb of motion or change: *put it in the box; cut it in two*). **20** introducing an indirect object after a verb (*believe in; engage in; share in*). **21** forming adverbial phrases (*in any case; in reality; in short*). • *adv.* expressing position within limits, or motion to such a position: **1** into a room, house, etc. (*come in*). **2** at home, in one's office, etc. (*is not in*). **3** so as to be enclosed or confined (*locked in*). **4** in a publication (*is the advertisement in?*). **5** in or to the inward side (*rub it in*). **6 a** in fashion, season, or office (*long skirts are in; strawberries are not yet in*). **b** elected (*the Democrat got in*). **7** exerting favorable action or influence (*their luck was in*). **8** (of transport) at the platform, etc. (*the train is in*). **9** (of a season, harvest, order, etc.) having arrived or been received. **10** denoting effective action (*join in*). **11** (of the tide) at the highest point. **12** (in *comb.*) *colloq.* denoting prolonged or concerted action, esp. by large numbers (*sit-in; teach-in*). • *adj.* **1** internal; living in; inside (*in-patient*). **2** fashionable; esoteric (*the in thing to do*). **3** confined to or shared by a group of people (*in-joke*). ▫ **in for 1** about to undergo (esp. something unpleasant). **2** competing in or for. **3** involved in; committed to. **in on** sharing in; privy to (a secret, etc.). **in with** on good terms with.

in. *abbr.* inch(es).

in·a·bil·i·ty /inəbílitee/ *n.* **1** the state of being unable. **2** a lack of power or means.

in ab·sen·ti·a /in absénshə/ *adv.* in one's absence.

in·ac·ces·si·ble /inaksésibəl/ *adj.* **1** not accessible; that cannot be reached. **2** (of a person) not open to advances or influence; unapproachable. ▫▫ **in·ac·ces·si·bil·i·ty** *n.* **in·ac·ces·si·ble·ness** *n.* **in·ac·ces·si·bly** *adv.*

in·ac·cu·rate /inákyərət/ *adj.* not accurate. ▫▫ **in·ac·cu·ra·cy** *n.* (*pl.* **-cies**). **in·ac·cu·rate·ly** *adv.*

in·ac·tion /inákshən/ *n.* **1** lack of action. **2** sluggishness; inertness.

in·ac·tive /ináktiv/ *adj.* **1** not active or inclined to act. **2** passive. **3** indolent. ▫▫ **in·ac·tive·ly** *adv.* **in·ac·tiv·i·ty** /–tívitee/ *n.*

in·ad·e·quate /inádikwət/ *adj.* (often foll. by *to*) **1** not adequate; insufficient. **2** (of a person) incompetent; unable to deal with a situation. ▫▫ **in·ad·e·qua·cy** /–kwəsee/ *n.* (*pl.* **-cies**). **in·ad·e·quate·ly** *adv.*

in·ad·mis·si·ble /inədmísibəl/ *adj.* that cannot be admitted or allowed. ▫▫ **in·ad·mis·si·bil·i·ty** *n.*

in·ad·vert·ent /inədvə́rt'nt/ *adj.* **1** (of an action) unintentional. **2 a** not properly attentive. **b** negligent. ▫▫ **in·ad·vert·ence** /–t'ns/ *n.* **in·ad·vert·ent·ly** *adv.*

in·ad·vis·a·ble /inədvī́zəbəl/ *adj.* not advisable. ▫▫ **in·ad·vis·a·bil·i·ty** *n.*

in·al·ien·a·ble /ináyleeənəbəl/ *adj.* that cannot be transferred to another; not alienable. ▫▫ **in·al·ien·a·bil·i·ty** *n.* **in·al·ien·a·bly** *adv.*

in·am·o·ra·to /inámərаátō/ *n.* (*pl.* **-tos;** *fem.* **inamorata** /–tə/) a lover.

in·ane /ináyn/ *adj.* **1** silly; senseless. **2** empty; void. □□ **in·ane·ly** *adv.* **in·ane·ness** *n.* **in·an·i·ty** /–ánitee/ *n.* (*pl.* **-ties**).

in·an·i·mate /inánimət/ *adj.* **1** not animate; not endowed with (esp. animal) life. **2** lifeless; showing no sign of life. **3** spiritless; dull. □□ **in·an·i·mate·ly** *adv.* **in·an·i·ma·tion** /–máyshən/ *n.*

in·ap·pli·ca·ble /ináplikəbəl, ínəplík–/ *adj.* (often foll. by *to*) not applicable; unsuitable. □□ **in·ap·pli·ca·bil·i·ty** *n.* **in·ap·pli·ca·bly** *adv.*

in·ap·pro·pri·ate /ínəprṓpreeət/ *adj.* not appropriate. □□ **in·ap·pro·pri·ate·ly** *adv.* **in·ap·pro·pri·ate·ness** *n.*

in·apt /inápt/ *adj.* **1** not apt or suitable. **2** unskillful. □□ **in·ap·ti·tude** *n.* **in·apt·ly** *adv.* **in·apt·ness** *n.*

in·ar·gu·a·ble /inaárgyōōəbəl/ *adj.* that cannot be argued about or disputed. □□ **in·ar·gu·a·bly** *adv.*

in·ar·tic·u·late /inaartíkyələt/ *adj.* **1** unable to speak distinctly or express oneself clearly. **2** (of speech) not articulate; indistinctly pronounced. **3** dumb. **4** esp. *Anat.* not jointed. □□ **in·ar·tic·u·late·ly** *adv.* **in·ar·tic·u·late·ness** *n.*

in·as·much /inəzmúch/ *adv.* (foll. by *as*) **1** since; because. **2** to the extent that.

in·at·ten·tive /ínəténtiv/ *adj.* **1** not paying due attention; heedless. **2** neglecting to show courtesy. □□ **in·at·ten·tion** *n.* **in·at·ten·tive·ly** *adv.* **in·at·ten·tive·ness** *n.*

in·au·di·ble /ináwdibəl/ *adj.* that cannot be heard. □□ **in·au·di·bil·i·ty** *n.* **in·au·di·bly** *adv.*

in·au·gu·ral /ináwgyərəl/ *adj.* & *n.* • *adj.* **1** marking the beginning of an institution, activity, or period of office. **2** (of a lecture, etc.) given by a person being inaugurated. • *n.* an inaugural speech, etc.

in·au·gu·rate /ináwgyərayt/ *v.tr.* **1** admit (a person) formally to office. **2** initiate the public use of (a building, etc.). **3** begin; introduce. **4** enter with ceremony upon (an undertaking, etc.). □□ **in·au·gu·ra·tion** /–ráyshən/ *n.* **in·au·gu·ra·tor** *n.* **in·au·gu·ra·to·ry** /–rətáwree/ *adj.*

in·aus·pi·cious /inawspíshəs/ *adj.* **1** ill-omened; unpropitious. **2** unlucky. □□ **in·aus·pi·cious·ly** *adv.* **in·aus·pi·cious·ness** *n.*

in·be·tween *adj. attrib. colloq.* intermediate (*at an in-between stage*).

in·board /ínbawrd/ *adv.* & *adj.* • *adv.* within the sides of or toward the center of a ship, aircraft, or vehicle. • *adj.* situated inboard.

in·born /inbáwrn/ *adj.* existing from birth; implanted by nature.

in·bred /inbréd/ *adj.* **1** inborn. **2** produced by inbreeding.

in·breed·ing /inbreéding/ *n.* breeding from closely related animals or persons. □□ **in·breed** *v.tr.* & *intr.* (*past* and *past part.* **inbred**).

inc. *abbr.* **1** (esp. **Inc.**) incorporated. **2** incomplete.

In·ca /ingkə/ *n.* a member of a Native American people in Peru before the Spanish conquest. □□ **In·ca·ic** /ingkáyik/ *adj.* **In·can** *adj.*

in·cal·cu·la·ble /inkálkyələbəl/ *adj.* **1** too great for calculation. **2** that cannot be reckoned beforehand. **3** (of a person, character, etc.) unpredictable; uncertain. □□ **in·cal·cu·la·bil·i·ty** *n.* **in·cal·cu·la·bly** *adv.*

in·can·des·cent /inkandésənt/ *adj.* **1** glowing with heat. **2** shining brightly. **3** (of an electric or other light) produced by a glowing white-hot filament. □□ **in·can·desce** *v.* **in·can·des·cence** /–səns/ *n.* **in·can·des·cent·ly** *adv.*

in·can·ta·tion /ínkantáyshən/ *n.* **1 a** a magical formula. **b** the use of this. **2** a spell or charm.

in·ca·pa·ble /inkáypəbəl/ *adj.* **1** (often foll. by *of*) **a** not capable. **b** lacking the required quality or characteristic (favorable or adverse) (*incapable of hurting anyone*). **2** not capable of rational conduct or of managing one's own affairs (*drunk and incapable*). □□ **in·ca·pa·bil·i·ty** *n.* **in·ca·pa·bly** *adv.*

in·ca·pac·i·tate /ínkəpásitayt/ *v.tr.* **1** render incapable or unfit. **2** disqualify. □□ **in·ca·pac·i·tant** *n.* **in·ca·pac·i·ta·tion** /–táyshən/ *n.*

in·ca·pac·i·ty /ínkəpásitee/ *n.* (*pl.* **-ties**) **1** inability; lack of the necessary power or resources. **2** legal disqualification. **3** an instance of incapacity.

in·car·cer·ate /inkaársərayt/ *v.tr.* imprison or confine. □□ **in·car·cer·a·tion** /–ráyshən/ *n.* **in·car·cer·a·tor** *n.*

in·car·nate *adj.* & *v.* • *adj.* /inkaárnət, –nayt/ **1** (of a person, spirit, quality, etc.) embodied in flesh, esp. in human form (*is the devil incarnate*). **2** represented in a recognizable or typical form (*folly incarnate*). • *v.tr.* /inkaárnayt/ **1** embody in flesh. **2** put (an idea, etc.) into concrete form; realize. **3** (of a person, etc.) be the living embodiment of (a quality).

in·car·na·tion /ínkaarnáyshən/ *n.* **1 a** embodiment in (esp. human) flesh. **b** (**the Incarnation**) *Theol.* the embodiment of God the Son in human flesh as Jesus Christ. **2** a living type (of a quality, etc.).

in·cau·tious /inkáwshəs/ *adj.* heedless; rash. □□ **in·cau·tion** *n.* **in·cau·tious·ly** *adv.* **in·cau·tious·ness** *n.*

in·cen·di·ar·y /inséndee-eree/ *adj.* & *n.* • *adj.* **1** (of a substance or device, esp. a bomb) designed to cause fires. **2 a** of or relating to the malicious setting on fire of property. **b** guilty of this. **3** tending to stir up strife; inflammatory. • *n.* (*pl.* **-ies**) **1** an incendiary bomb or device. **2** an incendiary person. □□ **in·cen·di·a·rism** *n.*

in·cense[1] /ínsens/ *n.* & *v.* • *n.* **1** a gum or spice producing a sweet smell when burned. **2** the smoke of this, esp. in religious ceremonial. • *v.tr.* **1** treat or perfume (a person or thing) with incense. **2** burn incense to (a deity, etc.). □□ **in·cen·sa·tion** *n.*

incense Middle English (originally as *encense*): from Old French *encens* (noun), *encenser* (verb), from ecclesiastical Latin *incensum* 'something burnt, incense', neuter past participle of *incendere* 'set fire to', from *in-* 'in' + the base of *candere* 'to glow'.

in·cense[2] /inséns/ *v.tr.* (often foll. by *at, with, against*) enrage; make angry.

in·cen·tive /inséntiv/ *n.* & *adj.* • *n.* **1** (often foll. by *to*) a motive or incitement, esp. to action. **2** a payment or concession to stimulate greater output by workers. • *adj.* serving to motivate or incite.

in·cep·tion /insépshən/ *n.* a beginning.

in·ces·sant /insésənt/ *adj.* unceasing; continual; repeated. □□ **in·ces·san·cy** *n.* **in·ces·sant·ly** *adv.* **in·ces·sant·ness** *n.*

in·cest /insest/ *n.* sexual intercourse between persons regarded as too closely related to marry each other.

in·ces·tu·ous /inséschōōəs/ *adj.* **1** involving or guilty of incest. **2** (of human relations generally) excessively restricted or resistant to wider influence. □□ **in·ces·tu·ous·ly** *adv.* **in·ces·tu·ous·ness** *n.*

inch /inch/ *n.* & *v.* • *n.* **1** a unit of linear measure equal to one-twelfth of a foot (2.54 cm). **2 a** (as a unit of rainfall) a quantity that would cover a horizontal surface to a depth of 1 inch. **b** (of atmospheric or other pressure) an amount that balances the weight of a column of mercury 1 inch high. **3** (as a unit of map scale) so many inches representing 1 mile on the ground (*a 4-inch map*). **4** a small amount (usu. with *neg.*: *would not yield an inch*). • *v.tr.* & *intr.* move gradually in a specified way (*inched forward*). □ **every inch 1** entirely (*looked every inch a judge*). **2** the whole distance or area (*combed every inch of the garden*). **inch by inch** gradually.

in·cho·ate /inkṓit/ *adj.* & *v.* • *adj.* **1** just begun. **2** undeveloped; rudimentary; unformed. • *v.tr.* begin; originate. ▫▫ **in·cho·ate·ly** *adv.* **in·cho·ate·ness** *n.* **in·cho·a·tion** /–áyshən/ *n.* **in·cho·a·tive** /–kṓətiv/ *adj.*

▶**Inchoate** means 'just begun, rudimentary, undeveloped,' e.g., *All was as yet in an inchoate state,* but it is often used incorrectly to mean 'chaotic' or 'incoherent.' The *ch* is pronounced hard, like *k.*

in·ci·dence /ínsidəns/ *n.* **1** (often foll. by *of*) the fact, manner, or rate, of occurrence or action. **2** the range, scope, or extent of influence of a thing. **3** *Physics* the falling of a line, or of a thing moving in a line, upon a surface. **4** the act or an instance of coming into contact with a thing.

▶**Incidence** and **incidents** sound the same, but **incidence** is more often used in technical contexts, referring to the frequency with which something occurs: *Increased UV is likely to cause increased incidence of skin cancer. Incidents* is simply the plural of *incident,* an event: *The police are supposed to investigate any incidents of domestic violence.* The form "incidences" should be avoided.

in·ci·dent /ínsidənt/ *n. & adj.* •*n.* **1 a** an event or occurrence. **b** a minor or detached event attracting general attention or noteworthy in some way. **2** a hostile clash, esp. of troops of countries at war (*a frontier incident*). •*adj.* **1** (often foll. by *to*) apt or liable to happen; naturally attaching or dependent. **2** (often foll. by *on, upon*) (of light, etc.) falling or striking.

in·ci·den·tal /ínsidéntəl/ *adj.* **1** (often foll. by *to*) **a** having a minor role in relation to a more important thing, event, etc. **b** not essential. **c** casual; happening by chance. **2** (foll. by *to*) liable to happen.

in·ci·den·tal·ly /insidént'lee/ *adv.* **1** by the way; as an unconnected remark. **2** in an incidental way.

in·ci·den·tal mu·sic *n.* music used as a background to the action of a play, motion picture, broadcast, etc.

in·cin·er·ate /insínərayt/ *v.tr.* **1** consume (a body, etc.) by fire. **2** reduce to ashes. ▫▫ **in·cin·er·a·tion** /–ráyshən/ *n.*

in·cin·er·a·tor /insínəraytər/ *n.* a furnace or apparatus for burning, esp. refuse to ashes.

in·cip·i·ent /insípeeənt/ *adj.* **1** beginning. **2** in an initial stage. ▫▫ **in·cip·i·ence** /–əns/ *n.* **in·cip·i·en·cy** *n.* **in·cip·i·ent·ly** *adv.*

in·cise /insíz/ *v.tr.* **1** make a cut in. **2** engrave.

in·ci·sion /insízhən/ *n.* **1** a cut; a division produced by cutting; a notch. **2** the act of cutting into a thing.

in·ci·sive /insísiv/ *adj.* **1** mentally sharp; acute. **2** clear and effective. **3** cutting; penetrating. ▫▫ **in·ci·sive·ly** *adv.* **in·ci·sive·ness** *n.*

in·ci·sor /insízər/ *n.* a cutting tooth, esp. at the front of the mouth.

in·cite /insít/ *v.tr.* (often foll. by *to*) urge or stir up. ▫▫ **in·ci·ta·tion** *n.* **in·cite·ment** *n.* **in·cit·er** *n.*

in·clem·ent /inklémənt/ *adj.* (of the weather or climate) severe, esp. cold or stormy. ▫▫ **in·clem·en·cy** *n.* (*pl.* **-cies**). **in·clem·ent·ly** *adv.*

in·cli·na·tion /inklináyshən/ *n.* **1** (often foll. by *to*) a disposition or propensity. **2** (often foll. by *for*) a liking or affection. **3** a leaning, slope, or slant. **4** the difference of direction of two lines or planes, esp. as measured by the angle between them. **5** the dip of a magnetic needle.

in·cline *v. & n.* •*v.* /inklín/ **1** *tr.* (usu. in *passive*; often foll. by *to, for,* or *to* + infin.) **a** make (a person, feelings, etc.) willing or favorably disposed (*am inclined to think so; does not incline me to agree*). **b** give a specified tendency to (a thing) (*the door is inclined to bang*). **2** *intr.* **a** be disposed (*I incline to think so*). **b** (often foll. by *to, toward*) tend. **3** *intr. & tr.* lean or turn away from a given direction, esp. the vertical. **4** *tr.* bend (the head, body, or oneself) forward or downward. •*n.* /ínklin/ **1** a slope. **2** an inclined plane. ▫▫ **in·clin·er** *n.*

in·clude /inklóód/ *v.tr.* **1** comprise or reckon in as part of a whole; place in a class or category. **2** (as **including** *prep.*) if we include (*six members, including the chairperson*). **3** treat or regard as so included. **4** (as **included** *adj.*) shut in; enclosed. ▫ **include out** *colloq.* or *joc.* specifically exclude. ▫▫ **in·clud·a·ble** *adj.* **in·clud·i·ble** *adj.* **in·clu·sion** /–klóózhən/ *n.*

in·clu·sive /inklóósiv/ *adj.* **1** (often foll. by *of*) including, comprising. **2** with the inclusion of the extreme limits stated (*pages 7 to 26 inclusive*). **3** including all the normal services, etc. (*a hotel offering inclusive terms*). ▫▫ **in·clu·sive·ly** *adv.* **in·clu·sive·ness** *n.*

in·clu·sive lan·guage *n.* language that is deliberately nonsexist, esp. avoiding the use of masculine pronouns to cover both men and women.

in·cog·ni·to /inkogneétō, –kógni–/ *adj., adv., & n.* •*adj. & adv.* with one's name or identity kept secret (*was traveling incognito*). •*n.* (*pl.* **-tos**) **1** a person who is incognito. **2** the pretended identity or anonymous character of such a person.

in·co·her·ent /ínkōheérənt/ *adj.* **1** (of a person) unable to speak intelligibly. **2** (of speech, etc.) lacking logic or consistency. **3** *Physics* (of waves) having no definite or stable phase relationship. ▫▫ **in·co·her·ence** /–əns/ *n.* **in·co·her·en·cy** *n.* (*pl.* **-cies**). **in·co·her·ent·ly** *adv.*

in·come /ínkum/ *n.* the money or other assets received, esp. periodically or in a year, from one's business, lands, work, investments, etc.

in·come tax *n.* a tax levied on income.

in·com·ing /ínkuming/ *adj. & n.* •*adj.* **1** coming in (*incoming telephone calls*). **2** succeeding another person or persons (*the incoming tenant*). •*n.* **1** (usu. in *pl.*) revenue; income. **2** the act of arriving or entering.

in·com·men·su·rate /ínkəménsərət, –shərət/ *adj.* **1** (often foll. by *with, to*) out of proportion; inadequate. **2** = INCOMMENSURABLE. ▫▫ **in·com·men·su·rate·ly** *adv.* **in·com·men·su·rate·ness** *n.*

in·com·mode /ínkəmṓd/ *v.tr.* **1** hinder; inconvenience. **2** trouble; annoy.

in·com·mu·ni·ca·ble /ínkəmyóónikəbəl/ *adj.* that cannot be communicated or shared. ▫▫ **in·com·mu·ni·ca·bil·i·ty** *n.* **in·com·mu·ni·ca·bly** *adv.*

in·com·mu·ni·ca·do /ínkəmyōōnikaádō/ *adj.* without or deprived of the means of communication with others.

in·com·mu·ni·ca·tive /ínkəmyóónikətiv, –káytiv/ *adj.* not communicative; taciturn. ▫▫ **in·com·mu·ni·ca·tive·ly** *adv.* **in·com·mu·ni·ca·tive·ness** *n.*

in·com·mut·a·ble /ínkəmyóótəbəl/ *adj.* **1** not changeable. **2** not commutable. ▫▫ **in·com·mut·a·bly** *adv.*

in·com·pa·ra·ble /inkómpərəbəl/ *adj.* **1** without an equal; matchless. **2** (often foll. by *with, to*) not to be compared. ▫▫ **in·com·pa·ra·bil·i·ty** *n.* **in·com·pa·ra·ble·ness** *n.* **in·com·pa·ra·bly** *adv.*

in·com·pat·i·ble /ínkəmpátibəl/ *adj.* **1** opposed in character; discordant. **2** (often foll. by *with*) inconsistent. **3** (of persons) unable to live, work, etc., together in harmony. **4** (of drugs) not suitable for taking at the same time. **5** (of equipment, machinery, etc.) not capable of being used in combination. ▫▫ **in·com·pat·i·bil·i·ty** *n.* **in·com·pat·i·ble·ness** *n.* **in·com·pat·i·bly** *adv.*

in·com·pe·tent /inkómpit'nt/ *adj. & n.* •*adj.* **1** (often foll. by *to* + infin.) not qualified or able to perform a particular task or function (*an incompetent builder*). **2** showing a lack of skill (*an incompetent performance*). •*n.* an incompetent person. ▫▫ **in·com·pe·tence** /–t'ns/ *n.* **in·com·pe·ten·cy** *n.* **in·com·pe·tent·ly** *adv.*

in·com·plete /ínkəmpleét/ *adj.* not complete. ▫▫ **in·com·plete·ly** *adv.* **in·com·plete·ness** *n.*

in·com·pre·hen·si·ble /ínkomprihénsibəl/ *adj.* (often

foll. by *to*) that cannot be understood. ▫▫ **in•com•pre•hen•si•bil•i•ty** *n.* **in•com•pre•hen•si•ble•ness** *n.* **in•com•pre•hen•si•bly** *adv.*

in•com•pre•hen•sion /ínkomprihénshən/ *n.* failure to understand.

in•con•ceiv•a•ble /ínkənseévəbəl/ *adj.* **1** that cannot be imagined. **2** *colloq.* very remarkable. ▫▫ **in•con•ceiv•a•bil•i•ty** *n.* **in•con•ceiv•a•ble•ness** *n.* **in•con•ceiv•a•bly** *adv.*

in•con•clu•sive /ínkənklóosiv/ *adj.* (of an argument, evidence, or action) not decisive or convincing. ▫▫ **in•con•clu•sive•ly** *adv.* **in•con•clu•sive•ness** *n.*

in•con•gru•ous /inkónggrooəs/ *adj.* **1** out of place; absurd. **2** (often foll. by *with*) disagreeing; out of keeping. ▫▫ **in•con•gru•i•ty** /–gróoitee/ *n.* (*pl.* **-ties**). **in•con•gru•ous•ly** *adv.* **in•con•gru•ous•ness** *n.*

in•con•se•quent /inkónsikwənt/ *adj.* **1** not following naturally; irrelevant. **2** lacking logical sequence. **3** disconnected. ▫▫ **in•con•se•quence** /–kwəns/ *n.* **in•con•se•quent•ly** *adv.*

in•con•se•quen•tial /inkónsikwénshəl, ínkon–/ *adj.* **1** unimportant. **2** = INCONSEQUENT. ▫▫ **in•con•se•quen•ti•al•i•ty** /–sheeálitee/ *n.* (*pl.* **-ties**). **in•con•se•quen•tial•ly** *adv.* **in•con•se•quen•tial•ness** *n.*

in•con•sid•er•a•ble /ínkənsídərəbəl/ *adj.* **1** of small size, value, etc. **2** not worth considering. ▫▫ **in•con•sid•er•a•ble•ness** *n.* **in•con•sid•er•a•bly** *adv.*

in•con•sid•er•ate /ínkənsídərət/ *adj.* **1** (of a person or action) thoughtless; rash. **2** lacking in regard for the feelings of others. ▫▫ **in•con•sid•er•ate•ly** *adv.* **in•con•sid•er•ate•ness** *n.* **in•con•sid•er•a•tion** /–ráyshən/ *n.*

in•con•sist•ent /ínkənsístənt/ *adj.* **1** acting at variance with one's own principles or former conduct. **2** (often foll. by *with*) not in keeping; discordant; incompatible. ▫▫ **in•con•sist•en•cy** *n.* (*pl.* **-cies**). **in•con•sist•ent•ly** *adv.*

in•con•sol•a•ble /ínkənsṓləbəl/ *adj.* (of a person, grief, etc.) that cannot be consoled or comforted. ▫▫ **in•con•sol•a•bil•i•ty** /–bílitee/ *n.* **in•con•sol•a•ble•ness** *n.* **in•con•sol•a•bly** *adv.*

in•con•spic•u•ous /ínkənspíkyooəs/ *adj.* not conspicuous; not easily noticed. ▫▫ **in•con•spic•u•ous•ly** *adv.* **in•con•spic•u•ous•ness** *n.*

in•con•stant /inkónstənt/ *adj.* **1** (of a person) fickle; changeable. **2** frequently changing; variable; irregular. ▫▫ **in•con•stan•cy** *n.* (*pl.* **-cies**). **in•con•stant•ly** *adv.*

in•con•test•a•ble /ínkəntéstəbəl/ *adj.* that cannot be disputed. ▫▫ **in•con•test•a•bil•i•ty** /–bílitee/ *n.* **in•con•test•a•bly** *adv.*

in•con•ti•nent /inkóntinənt/ *adj.* **1** unable to control movements of the bowels or bladder or both. **2** lacking self-restraint (esp. in regard to sexual desire). **3** (foll. by *of*) unable to control. ▫▫ **in•con•ti•nence** /–nəns/ *n.*

in•con•tro•vert•i•ble /ínkontrəvə́rtibəl/ *adj.* indisputable; indubitable. ▫▫ **in•con•tro•vert•i•bly** *adv.*

in•con•ven•ience /ínkənveényəns/ *n.* & *v.* • *n.* **1** lack of suitability to personal requirements or ease. **2** a cause or instance of this. • *v.tr.* cause inconvenience to.

in•con•ven•ient /ínkənveényənt/ *adj.* **1** unfavorable to ease or comfort; not convenient. **2** awkward; troublesome. ▫▫ **in•con•ven•ient•ly** *adv.*

in•cor•po•rate *v.* & *adj.* • *v.* /inkáwrpərayt/ **1** *tr.* (often foll. by *in*, *with*) unite; form into one body or whole. **2** *intr.* become incorporated. **3** *tr.* combine (ingredients) into one substance. **4** *tr.* admit as a member of a company, etc. **5** *tr.* **a** constitute as a legal corporation. **b** (as **incorporated** *adj.*) forming a legal corporation. • *adj.* /inkáwrpərət/ **1** (of a company, etc.) formed into a legal corporation. **2** embodied. ▫▫ **in•cor•po•ra•tion** /–áyshən/ *n.* **in•cor•po•ra•tor** *n.*

in•cor•po•re•al /ínkawrpáwreeəl/ *adj.* **1** not composed of matter. **2** of immaterial beings. ▫▫ **in•cor•po•re•al•i•ty** /–reeálitee/ *n.* **in•cor•po•re•al•ly** *adv.*

in•cor•rect /ínkərékt/ *adj.* **1** not in accordance with fact; wrong. **2** (of style, etc.) improper; faulty. ▫▫ **in•cor•rect•ly** *adv.* **in•cor•rect•ness** *n.*

in•cor•ri•gi•ble /inkáwrijibəl, –kór–/ *adj.* **1** (of a person or habit) incurably bad or depraved. **2** not readily improved. ▫▫ **in•cor•ri•gi•bil•i•ty** *n.* **in•cor•ri•gi•ble•ness** *n.* **in•cor•ri•gi•bly** *adv.*

in•cor•rupt•i•ble /ínkərúptibəl/ *adj.* **1** that cannot be corrupted, esp. by bribery. **2** that cannot decay; everlasting. ▫▫ **in•cor•rupt•i•bil•i•ty** /–bílitee/ *n.* **in•cor•rupt•i•bly** *adv.*

in•crease *v.* & *n.* • *v.* /inkreés/ **1** *tr.* & *intr.* make or become greater in size, amount, etc., or more numerous. **2** *intr.* advance (in quality, attainment, etc.). **3** *tr.* intensify (a quality). • *n.* /ínkrees/ **1** the act or process of becoming greater or more numerous; growth; enlargement. **2** (of people, animals, or plants) growth in numbers; multiplication. **3** the amount or extent of an increase. ▫▫ **in•creas•a•ble** *adj.* **in•creas•er** *n.* **in•creas•ing•ly** *adv.*

in•cred•i•ble /inkrédibəl/ *adj.* **1** that cannot be believed. **2** *colloq.* hard to believe; amazing. ▫▫ **in•cred•i•bil•i•ty** *n.* **in•cred•i•ble•ness** *n.* **in•cred•i•bly** *adv.*

▶The adjective **incredible** means 'unbelievable' or 'not convincing' and can be applied to a situation, statement, policy, or threat to a person, e.g., *I find this testimony incredible.* **Incredulous** means 'disinclined to believe; skeptical' and is usually applied to a person's attitude, e.g., *You shouldn't wonder that I'm incredulous after all your lies.*

in•cred•u•lous /inkréjələs/ *adj.* (often foll. by *of*) unwilling to believe. ▫▫ **in•cre•du•li•ty** /ínkridóolitee, –dyóo–/ *n.* **in•cred•u•lous•ly** *adv.* **in•cred•u•lous•ness** *n.*

in•cre•ment /ínkrimənt/ *n.* an increase or addition, esp. one of a series on a fixed scale. ▫▫ **in•cre•men•tal** /–ment'l/ *adj.*

in•crim•i•nate /inkríminayt/ *v.tr.* **1** tend to prove the guilt of (*incriminating evidence*). **2** involve in an accusation. **3** charge with a crime. ▫▫ **in•crim•i•na•tion** /–náyshən/ *n.* **in•crim•i•na•to•ry** /–nətáwree/ *adj.*

in•crus•ta•tion /ínkrustáyshən/ *n.* **1** the process of encrusting or state of being encrusted. **2** a crust or hard coating, esp. of fine material. **3** a deposit on a surface.

in•cu•bate /íngkyəbayt/ *v.* **1** *tr.* sit on or artificially heat (eggs) in order to bring forth young birds, etc. **2** *tr.* cause the development of (bacteria, etc.) by creating suitable conditions. **3** *intr.* sit on eggs; brood.

in•cu•ba•tion /íngkyəbáyshən/ *n.* **1 a** the act of incubating. **b** brooding. **2** *Med.* (in full **in•cu•ba•tion pe•ri•od**) the period between exposure to an infection and the appearance of the first symptoms.

in•cu•ba•tor /íngkyəbaytər/ *n.* **1** an apparatus used to provide a suitable temperature and environment for a premature baby or one of low birthweight. **2** an apparatus used to hatch eggs or grow microorganisms.

in•cu•bus /íngkyəbəs/ *n.* (*pl.* **incubi** /–bī/ or **incubuses**) **1** an evil spirit supposed to descend on sleeping persons. **2** a nightmare. **3** a person or thing that oppresses like a nightmare.

in•cul•cate /inkúlkayt/ *v.tr.* (often foll. by *upon*, *in*) urge or impress (a fact, habit, or idea) persistently. ▫▫ **in•cul•ca•tion** /–káyshən/ *n.* **in•cul•ca•tor** *n.*

in•cum•ben•cy /inkúmbənsee/ *n.* (*pl.* **-cies**) the office, tenure, or sphere of an incumbent.

in•cum•bent /inkúmbənt/ *adj.* & *n.* • *adj.* **1** (foll. by *on*, *upon*) resting as a duty (*it is incumbent on you to warn them*). **2** (often foll. by *on*) lying; pressing. **3** currently holding office (*the incumbent president*). • *n.* the holder of an office or post, esp. an elected official.

in·cu·nab·u·lum /inkyənábyələm/ *n.* (*pl.* **incunabula** /–lə/) a book printed at an early date, esp. before 1501.

in·cur /inkə́r/ *v.tr.* (**incurred, incurring**) suffer, experience, or become subject to (something unpleasant) as a result of one's own behavior, etc. (*incurred huge debts*). □□ **in·cur·ra·ble** *adj.*

in·cur·a·ble /inkyŏŏrəbəl/ *adj.* & *n.* •*adj.* that cannot be cured. •*n.* a person who cannot be cured. □□ **in·cur·a·bil·i·ty** *n.* **in·cur·a·ble·ness** *n.* **in·cur·a·bly** *adv.*

in·cur·sion /inkə́rzhən, –shən/ *n.* an invasion or attack, esp. when sudden or brief. □□ **in·cur·sive** /–kə́rsiv/ *adj.*

in·cus /íngkəs/ *n.* (*pl.* **incudes** /–kyŏŏdeez/) the small anvil-shaped bone in the middle ear, in contact with the malleus and stapes.

Ind. *abbr.* **1** Independent. **2** Indiana. **3 a** India. **b** Indian.

in·debt·ed /indétid/ *adj.* (usu. foll. by *to*) owing gratitude or money. □□ **in·debt·ed·ness** *n.*

in·de·cent /indeésənt/ *adj.* **1** offending against recognized standards of decency. **2** unbecoming; highly unsuitable (*with indecent haste*). □□ **in·de·cen·cy** *n.* (*pl.* **-cies**). **in·de·cent·ly** *adv.*

in·de·cent ex·po·sure *n.* the intentional act of publicly and indecently exposing one's body, esp. the genitals.

in·de·ci·pher·a·ble /indisífərəbəl/ *adj.* that cannot be deciphered.

in·de·ci·sion /índisízhən/ *n.* lack of decision; hesitation.

in·de·ci·sive /índisísiv/ *adj.* **1** not decisive. **2** undecided; hesitating. □□ **in·de·ci·sive·ly** *adv.* **in·de·ci·sive·ness** *n.*

in·dec·o·rous /indékərəs/ *adj.* **1** improper. **2** in bad taste. □□ **in·dec·o·rous·ly** *adv.* **in·dec·o·rous·ness** *n.*

in·deed /indeéd/ *adv.* & *int.* •*adv.* **1** in truth; really; yes; that is so (*they are, indeed, a remarkable family*). **2** expressing emphasis or intensification (*indeed it is*). **3** admittedly (*there are indeed exceptions*). **4** in point of fact (*if indeed such a thing is possible*). •*int.* expressing irony, contempt, incredulity, etc.

in·de·fat·i·ga·ble /indifátigəbəl/ *adj.* (of a person, quality, etc.) that cannot be tired out; unwearying; unremitting. □□ **in·de·fat·i·ga·bil·i·ty** *n.* **in·de·fat·i·ga·bly** *adv.*

in·de·fen·si·ble /indifénsibəl/ *adj.* that cannot be defended or justified. □□ **in·de·fen·si·bil·i·ty** *n.* **in·de·fen·si·bly** *adv.*

in·de·fin·a·ble /indifínəbəl/ *adj.* that cannot be defined or exactly described. □□ **in·de·fin·a·bly** *adv.*

in·def·i·nite /indéfinit/ *adj.* **1** vague; undefined. **2** unlimited. **3** *Gram.* not determining the person, thing, time, etc., referred to. □□ **in·def·i·nite·ness** *n.*

in·def·i·nite ar·ti·cle *n. Gram.* the word (e.g., *a, an, some* in English) preceding a noun and implying lack of specificity (*bought me a book*; *government is an art*).

in·def·i·nite·ly /indéfinitlee/ *adv.* **1** for an unlimited time (*was postponed indefinitely*). **2** in an indefinite manner.

in·del·i·ble /indélibəl/ *adj.* **1** that cannot be rubbed out or (in abstract senses) removed. **2** (of ink, etc.) that makes indelible marks. □□ **in·del·i·bly** *adv.*

in·del·i·cate /indélikət/ *adj.* **1** coarse; unrefined. **2** tactless. **3** tending to indecency. □□ **in·del·i·ca·cy** *n.* (*pl.* **-cies**). **in·del·i·cate·ly** *adv.*

in·dem·ni·fy /indémnifī/ *v.tr.* (**-fies, -fied**) **1** protect or secure (a person) in respect of harm, a loss, etc. **2** (often foll. by *for*) secure (a person) against legal responsibility for actions. **3** (often foll. by *for*) compensate (a person) for a loss, expenses, etc. □□ **in·dem·ni·fi·ca·tion** /–fikáyshən/ *n.* **in·dem·ni·fi·er** *n.*

in·dem·ni·ty /indémnitee/ *n.* (*pl.* **-ties**) **1 a** compensation for loss incurred. **b** a sum paid for this, esp. a sum exacted by a victor in war, etc., as one condition of peace. **2** security against loss. **3** legal exemption from penalties, etc., incurred.

in·dent /indént/ *v.* & *n.* •*v.* **1** *tr.* start (a line of print or writing) farther from the margin than other lines, e.g., to mark a new paragraph. **2** *tr.* **a** divide (a document drawn up in duplicate) into its two copies with a zigzag line dividing them and ensuring identification. **b** draw up (usu. a legal document) in exact duplicate. **3** *tr.* make toothlike notches in. **4** *tr.* form deep recesses in (a coastline, etc.). •*n.* also /índent/ **1** indentation. **2** an indented line. **3** *Brit.* **a** an order (esp. from abroad) for goods. **b** an official requisition for stores. **4** an indenture. □□ **in·den·ta·tion** *n.* **in·dent·er** *n.* **in·den·tor** *n.*

in·den·tion /indénshən/ *n.* **1** the indenting of a line in printing or writing. **2** an indentation.

in·den·ture /indénchər/ *n.* & *v.* •*n.* **1** an indented document (see INDENT[1] *v.* 2). **2** (usu. in *pl.*) a sealed agreement or contract. **3** a formal list, certificate, etc. •*v.tr. hist.* bind (a person) by indentures, esp. as an apprentice. □□ **in·den·ture·ship** *n.*

in·de·pend·ence /indipéndəns/ *n.* (often foll. by *of, from*) the state of being independent.

In·de·pend·ence Day *n.* a day celebrating the anniversary of national independence; in the US July 4.

in·de·pend·ent /índipéndənt/ *adj.* & *n.* •*adj.* **1 a** (often foll. by *of*) not depending on authority or control. **b** self-governing. **2 a** not depending on another person for one's opinion or livelihood. **b** (of income or resources) making it unnecessary to earn one's living. **3** unwilling to be under an obligation to others. **4** *Polit.* (usu. **Independent**) not belonging to or supported by a party. **5** not depending on something else for its validity, efficiency, value, etc. (*independent proof*). **6** (of broadcasting, a school, etc.) not supported by public funds. •*n.* (usu. **Independent**) a person who is politically independent. □□ **in·de·pend·ent·ly** *adv.*

in-depth *attrib.adj.* thorough; done in depth.

in·de·scrib·a·ble /indiskríbəbəl/ *adj.* **1** too unusual or extreme to be described. **2** vague; indefinite. □□ **in·de·scrib·a·bil·i·ty** *n.* **in·de·scrib·a·bly** *adv.*

in·de·struct·i·ble /indistrúktibəl/ *adj.* that cannot be destroyed. □□ **in·de·struct·i·bil·i·ty** *n.*

in·de·ter·mi·na·ble /inditə́rminəbəl/ *adj.* **1** that cannot be ascertained. **2** (of a dispute, etc.) that cannot be settled. □□ **in·de·ter·mi·na·bly** *adv.*

in·de·ter·mi·nate /inditə́rminət/ *adj.* **1** not fixed in extent, character, etc. **2** left doubtful; vague. **3** *Math.* (of a quantity) not limited to a fixed value by the value of another quantity. □□ **in·de·ter·mi·na·cy** *n.* **in·de·ter·mi·nate·ly** *adv.* **in·de·ter·mi·nate·ness** *n.*

in·dex /índeks/ *n.* & *v.* •*n.* (*pl.* **indexes** or esp. in technical use **indices** /índiseez/) **1** an alphabetical list of names, subjects, etc., with references, usu. at the end of a book. **2** (in full **index number**) a number showing the variation of prices or wages as compared with a chosen base period (*retail price index*; *Dow Jones index*). **3** *Math.* **a** the exponent of a number. **b** the power to which it is raised. **4 a** a pointer, esp. on an instrument, showing a quantity, a position on a scale, etc. **b** an indicator of a trend, direction, tendency, etc. **c** (usu. foll. by *of*) a sign, token, or indication of something. **5** *Physics* a number expressing a physical property, etc., in terms of a standard (*refractive index*). **6** *Computing* a set of items each of which specifies one of the records of a file and contains information about its address. •*v.tr.* **1** provide (a book, etc.) with an index. **2** enter in an index. **3** relate (wages, etc.) to the value of a price index. ▫▫ **in·dex·a·tion** *n.* **in·dex·er** *n.* **in·dex·i·ble** /–déksibəl/ *adj.* **in·dex·i·cal** *adj.* **in·dex·less** *adj.*

▶The plural *indexes* is appropriate for all senses of **index.** In some technical contexts, the plural *indices* is employed.

in·dex fin·ger *n.* the forefinger.

in·di·a ink /indeeə/ *n.* a black liquid ink.

In·di·an /índeeən/ *n.* & *adj.* • *n.* **1 a** a native or national of India. **b** a person of Indian descent. **2** (in full **American Indian**) a member of the aboriginal peoples of America or their descendants. **3** any of the languages of the aboriginal peoples of America. • *adj.* **1** of or relating to India, or to the subcontinent comprising India, Pakistan, and Bangladesh. **2** of or relating to the aboriginal peoples of America.

▶**Indian,** meaning 'native of America before the arrival of Europeans,' is objected to by many who now favor **Native American.** There are others (including many members of this ethnic group), however, who see nothing wrong with *Indian* or *American Indian,* which are long-established and often used with pride. The terms *Amerind* and *Amerindian,* once proposed as alternatives to *Indian,* never gained wide use. Newer alternatives, not widely used or established, include *First Nation* (especially Canadian) and the more generic *aboriginal peoples.* It should be noted that *Indian* is held by many not to include some American groups, e.g., Aleuts and Inuit.

In·di·an el·e·phant *n.* the elephant, *Elephas maximus,* of India, which is smaller than the African elephant.

In·di·an sum·mer *n.* a period of unusually dry, warm weather sometimes occurring in late autumn.

in·di·cate /índikayt/ *v.tr.* (often foll. by *that* + clause) **1** point out; make known; show. **2** be a sign or symptom of; express the presence of. **3** (often in *passive*) suggest; call for; require or show to be necessary (*stronger measures are indicated*). **4** admit to or state briefly (*indicated his disapproval*). **5** (of a gauge, etc.) give as a reading.

in·di·ca·tion /índikáyshən/ *n.* **1 a** the act or an instance of indicating. **b** something that suggests or indicates; a sign or symptom. **2** something indicated or suggested, esp., in *Med.,* a remedy or treatment that is suggested by the symptoms. **3** a reading given by a gauge or instrument.

in·dic·a·tive /indíkətiv/ *adj.* & *n.* • *adj.* **1** (foll. by *of*) suggestive; serving as an indication. **2** *Gram.* (of a mood) denoting simple statement of a fact. • *n. Gram.* **1** the indicative mood. **2** a verb in this mood. ▫▫ **in·dic·a·tive·ly** *adv.*

in·di·ca·tor /índikaytər/ *n.* **1** a person or thing that indicates. **2** a device indicating the condition of a machine, etc. **3** a recording instrument attached to an apparatus.

in·di·ces *pl.* of INDEX.

in·dict /indít/ *v.tr.* accuse (a person) formally by legal process. ▫▫ **in·dict·ee** /–teé/ *n.* **in·dict·er** *n.*

in·dict·a·ble /indítəbəl/ *adj.* **1** (of an offense) rendering the person who commits it liable to be charged with a crime. **2** (of a person) so liable.

in·dict·ment /indítmənt/ *n.* **1** the act of indicting. **2 a** a formal accusation. **b** a legal process in which this is made. **c** a document containing a charge. **3** something that serves to condemn or censure.

in·dif·fer·ence /indífrəns/ *n.* **1** lack of interest or attention. **2** unimportance (*a matter of indifference*). **3** neutrality.

in·dif·fer·ent /indífrənt/ *adj.* **1** neither good nor bad; average; mediocre. **2 a** not especially good. **b** fairly bad. **3** (often prec. by *very*) decidedly inferior. **4** (foll. by *to*) having no partiality for or against; having no interest in or sympathy for. ▫▫ **in·dif·fer·ent·ly** *adv.*

in·dig·e·nous /indíjinəs/ *adj.* **1 a** (esp. of flora or fauna) originating naturally in a region. **b** (of people) originating or occurring in a particular place; native. **2** (foll. by *to*) belonging naturally to a place. ▫▫ **in·dig·e·nous·ly** *adv.* **in·dig·e·nous·ness** *n.*

in·di·gent /índijənt/ *adj.* needy; poor. ▫▫ **in·di·gence** /–jəns/ *n.*

in·di·gest·i·ble /índijéstibəl/ *adj.* **1** difficult or impossible to digest. **2** too complex or awkward to read or comprehend easily. ▫▫ **in·di·gest·i·bil·i·ty** *n.* **in·di·gest·i·bly** *adv.*

in·di·ges·tion /índijés-chən/ *n.* **1** difficulty in digesting food. **2** pain or discomfort caused by this. ▫▫ **in·di·ges·tive** *adj.*

in·dig·nant /indígnənt/ *adj.* feeling or showing scornful anger or a sense of injured innocence. ▫▫ **in·dig·nant·ly** *adv.*

in·dig·na·tion /índignáyshən/ *n.* anger or annoyance by what is perceived as unfair conduct or treatment.

in·dig·ni·ty /indígnitee/ *n.* (*pl.* **-ties**) **1** unworthy treatment. **2** a slight or insult. **3** the humiliating quality of something (*the indignity of my position*).

in·di·go /índigō/ *n.* (*pl.* **-gos**) **1** a natural blue dye obtained from the indigo plant. **2** any plant of the genus *Indigofera.* **3** (in full **indigo blue**) a color between blue and violet in the spectrum.

in·di·rect /índirékt, –dī–/ *adj.* **1** not going straight to the point. **2** (of a route, etc.) not straight. **3** not directly sought or aimed at (*an indirect result*). **4** (of lighting) from a concealed source and diffusely reflected. ▫▫ **in·di·rect·ly** *adv.* **in·di·rect·ness** *n.*

in·di·rect ob·ject *n. Gram.* a person or thing affected by a verbal action but not primarily acted on (e.g., *him* in *give him the book*).

in·dis·creet /índiskreét/ *adj.* **1** not discreet; revealing secrets. **2** injudicious; unwary. ▫▫ **in·dis·creet·ly** *adv.* **in·dis·creet·ness** *n.*

in·dis·cre·tion /índiskréshən/ *n.* **1** lack of discretion; indiscreet conduct. **2** an indiscreet action, remark, etc.

in·dis·crim·i·nate /índiskríminət/ *adj.* **1** making no distinctions. **2** confused; promiscuous. ▫▫ **in·dis·crim·i·nate·ly** *adv.* **in·dis·crim·i·nate·ness** *n.* **in·dis·crim·i·na·tion** /–náyshən/ *n.* **in·dis·crim·i·na·tive** *adj.*

in·dis·pen·sa·ble /índispénsəbəl/ *adj.* **1** (often foll. by *to, for*) that cannot be dispensed with; necessary. **2** (of a law, duty, etc.) that is not to be set aside. ▫▫ **in·dis·pen·sa·bil·i·ty** *n.* **in·dis·pen·sa·ble·ness** *n.* **in·dis·pen·sa·bly** *adv.*

in·dis·posed /índispṓzd/ *adj.* **1** slightly unwell. **2** averse or unwilling. ▫▫ **in·dis·po·si·tion** *n.*

in·dis·put·a·ble /índispyṓṓtəbəl/ *adj.* **1** that cannot be disputed. **2** unquestionable. ▫▫ **in·dis·put·a·bil·i·ty** *n.* **in·dis·put·a·ble·ness** *n.* **in·dis·put·a·bly** *adv.*

in·dis·sol·u·ble /índisólyəbəl/ *adj.* **1** that cannot be dissolved or decomposed. **2** lasting; stable (*an indissoluble bond*). ▫▫ **in·dis·sol·u·bil·i·ty** *n.* **in·dis·sol·u·bly** *adv.*

in·dis·tinct /índistíngkt/ *adj.* **1** not distinct. **2** confused; obscure. ▫▫ **in·dis·tinct·ly** *adv.* **in·dis·tinct·ness** *n.*

in·dis·tin·guish·a·ble /índistínggwishəbəl/ *adj.* (often foll. by *from*) not distinguishable. ▫▫ **in·dis·tin·guish·a·ble·ness** *n.* **in·dis·tin·guish·a·bly** *adv.*

in·dite /indít/ *v.tr. formal* or *joc.* **1** put (a speech, etc.) into words. **2** write (a letter, etc.).

in·di·um /índeeəm/ *n. Chem.* a soft, silvery-white metallic element occurring naturally in sphalerite, etc., used for electroplating and in semiconductors. ¶ Symb.: **In.**

in·di·vid·u·al /índivíjōōəl/ *adj.* & *n.* • *adj.* **1** single. **2** particular; special; not general. **3** having a distinct character. **4** characteristic of a particular person. **5** designed for use by one person. • *n.* **1** a single member of a class. **2** a single human being as distinct from a family or group. **3** *colloq.* a person (*a most unpleasant individual*).

in·di·vid·u·al·ism /indivíjōōəlizəm/ *n.* **1** the habit or principle of being independent and self-reliant. **2** a social theory favoring the free action of individuals. ▫▫ **in·di·vid·u·al·ist** *n.* **in·di·vid·u·al·is·tic** *adj.* **in·di·vid·u·al·is·ti·cal·ly** *adv.*

in·di·vid·u·al·i·ty /indivijōō-álitee/ *n.* (*pl.* **-ties**) **1** individual character, esp. when strongly marked. **2** (in *pl.*) individual tastes, etc. **3** separate existence.

in·di·vid·u·al·ize /indivíjōōəlīz/ *v.tr.* **1** give an individual character to. **2** specify. ▫▫ **in·di·vid·u·al·i·za·tion** *n.*

in·di·vid·u·al·ly /indivíjōōəlee/ *adv.* **1** personally; in an individual capacity. **2** in a distinctive manner. **3** one by one; not collectively.

in·di·vid·u·al re·tire·ment ac·count *n.* a savings plan in which money invested and interest earned are not taxed until retirement. ¶ Abbr.: **IRA**.

in·di·vis·i·ble /indivízibəl/ *adj.* **1** not divisible. **2** not distributable among a number. ▫▫ **in·di·vis·i·bil·i·ty** *n.*

Indo- /índō/ *comb. form* Indian; Indian and...(*Indo-Iranian*).

in·doc·tri·nate /indóktrinayt/ *v.tr.* teach (a person or group) systematically or for a long period to accept ideas uncritically. ▫▫ **in·doc·tri·na·tion** /–náyshən/ *n.* **in·doc·tri·na·tor** *n.*

In·do-Eu·ro·pe·an /índō-yŏŏrəpeéən/ *adj.* & *n.* • *adj.* **1** of or relating to the family of languages spoken over the greater part of Europe and Asia as far as N. India. **2** of or relating to the hypothetical parent language of this family. • *n.* **1** the Indo-European family of languages. **2** the hypothetical parent language of all languages belonging to this family.

in·do·lent /índələnt/ *adj.* lazy. ▫▫ **in·do·lence** /–ləns/ *n.* **in·do·lent·ly** *adv.*

in·dom·i·ta·ble /indómitəbəl/ *adj.* **1** that cannot be subdued; unyielding. **2** stubbornly persistent. ▫▫ **in·dom·i·ta·bil·i·ty** *n.* **in·dom·i·ta·bly** *adv.*

In·do·ne·sian /índəneézhən, –shən/ *n.* & *adj.* • *n.* **1** a native or national of Indonesia in SE Asia. **2** a person of Indonesian descent. • *adj.* of or relating to Indonesia or its people or language.

in·door /indáwr/ *adj.* situated, carried on, or used within a building or under cover (*indoor antenna*; *indoor games*).

in·doors /indáwrz/ *adv.* into or within a building.

in·du·bi·ta·ble /indōōbitəbəl, –dyōō–/ *adj.* that cannot be doubted. ▫▫ **in·du·bi·ta·bly** *adv.*

in·duce /indōōs, –dyōōs/ *v.tr.* **1** (often foll. by *to* + infin.) prevail on; persuade. **2** bring about; give rise to. **3** *Med.* bring on (labor) artificially, esp. by use of drugs. **4** *Electr.* produce (a current) by induction. **5** *Physics* cause (radioactivity) by bombardment. **6** infer; derive as a deduction. ▫▫ **in·duc·er** *n.* **in·duc·i·ble** *adj.*

in·duce·ment /indōōsmənt, –dyōōs–/ *n.* **1** (often foll. by *to*) an attraction that leads one on. **2** a thing that induces.

in·duct /indúkt/ *v.tr.* (often foll. by *to, into*) **1** introduce formally into possession of a benefice. **2** install into a room, office, etc. **3** introduce; initiate. **4** enlist (a person) for military service. ▫▫ **in·duc·tee** /indukteé/ *n.*

in·duc·tance /indúktəns/ *n. Electr.* the property of an electric circuit that causes an electromotive force to be generated by a change in the current flowing.

in·duc·tion /indúkshən/ *n.* **1** the act or an instance of inducting or inducing. **2** *Med.* the process of bringing on (esp. labor) by artificial means. **3** *Logic* **a** the inference of a general law from particular instances (cf. DEDUCTION). **b** *Math.* a means of proving a theorem by showing that, if it is true of any particular case, it is true of the next case in a series, and then showing that it is indeed true in one particular case. **c** (foll. by *of*) the production of (facts) to prove a general statement. **4** (often *attrib.*) a formal introduction to a new job, position, etc. (*attended an induction course*). **5** *Electr.* **a** the production of an electric or magnetic state by the proximity (without contact) of an electrified or magnetized body. **b** the production of an electric current in a conductor by a change of magnetic field. **6** the drawing of a fuel mixture into the cylinders of an internal combustion engine. **7** enlistment for military service.

in·duc·tive /indúktiv/ *adj.* **1** (of reasoning, etc.) of or based on induction. **2** of electric or magnetic induction. ▫▫ **in·duc·tive·ly** *adv.* **in·duc·tive·ness** *n.*

in·dulge /indúlj/ *v.* **1** *intr.* (often foll. by *in*) take pleasure freely. **2** *tr.* yield freely to (a desire, etc.). **3** *tr.* gratify the wishes of; favor (*indulged them with money*). **4** *intr. colloq.* take alcoholic liquor. ▫▫ **in·dulg·er** *n.*

in·dul·gence /indúljəns/ *n.* **1 a** the act of indulging. **b** the state of being indulgent. **2** something indulged in. **3** *RC Ch.* the remission of temporal punishment in purgatory. **4** a privilege granted.

in·dul·gent /indúljənt/ *adj.* **1** ready or too ready to overlook faults, etc. **2** indulging or tending to indulge. ▫▫ **in·dul·gent·ly** *adv.*

in·dus·tri·al /indústreeəl/ *adj.* & *n.* • *adj.* **1** of or relating to industry or industries. **2** designed or suitable for industrial use. **3** characterized by highly developed industries (*the industrial nations*). • *n.* (in *pl.*) shares in industrial companies. ▫▫ **in·dus·tri·al·ly** *adv.*

in·dus·tri·al·ism /indústreeəlizəm/ *n.* a social or economic system in which manufacturing industries are prevalent.

in·dus·tri·al·ist /indústreeəlist/ *n.* a person engaged in the management or ownership of industry.

in·dus·tri·al·ize /indústreeəlīz/ *v.* **1** *tr.* introduce industries to (a country or region, etc.). **2** *intr.* become industrialized. ▫▫ **in·dus·tri·al·i·za·tion** *n.*

in·dus·tri·al park *n.* an area of land developed for a complex of factories and other businesses.

in·dus·tri·al rev·o·lu·tion *n.* the rapid development of a nation's industry (esp. the **Industrial Revolution**, in the late 18th and early 19th c.).

in·dus·tri·ous /indústreeəs/ *adj.* diligent; hardworking. ▫▫ **in·dus·tri·ous·ly** *adv.* **in·dus·tri·ous·ness** *n.*

in·dus·try /indəstree/ *n.* (*pl.* **-tries**) **1 a** a branch of trade or manufacture. **b** trade and manufacture collectively (*incentives to industry*). **2** concerted or copious activity (*the building was a hive of industry*). **3 a** diligence. **b** *colloq.* the diligent study or promotion of a particular topic or cause (*the Shakespeare industry*). **4** habitual employment in useful work.

in·e·bri·ate *v., adj.,* & *n.* • *v.tr.* /ineébreeayt/ **1** make drunk; intoxicate. **2** excite. • *adj.* /ineébreeət/ drunken. • *n.* /ineébreeət/ a drunken person, esp. a habitual drunkard. ▫▫ **in·e·bri·a·tion** /–áyshən/ *n.* **in·e·bri·e·ty** /inibríətee/ *n.*

in·ed·i·ble /inédibəl/ *adj.* not edible, esp. not suitable for eating (cf. UNEATABLE). ▫▫ **in·ed·i·bil·i·ty** *n.*

in·ed·u·ca·ble /inéjəkəbəl/ *adj.* incapable of being educated. ▫▫ **in·ed·u·ca·bil·i·ty** *n.*

in·ef·fa·ble /inéfəbəl/ *adj.* **1** unutterable; too great for description in words. **2** that must not be uttered. ▫▫ **in·ef·fa·bil·i·ty** *n.* **in·ef·fa·bly** *adv.*

in·ef·fec·tive /iniféktiv/ *adj.* **1** not producing the desired effect. **2** (of a person) inefficient; not achieving results. **3** lacking artistic effect. ▫▫ **in·ef·fec·tive·ly** *adv.* **in·ef·fec·tive·ness** *n.*

in·ef·fec·tu·al /inifékchōōəl/ *adj.* **1 a** without effect. **b** not producing the desired or expected effect. **2** (of a person) lacking the ability to achieve results (*an ineffectual leader*). ▫▫ **in·ef·fec·tu·al·i·ty** /–álitee/ *n.* **in·ef·fec·tu·al·ly** *adv.* **in·ef·fec·tu·al·ness** *n.*

in·ef·fi·cient /ínifishənt/ *adj.* **1** not efficient. **2** (of a person) not fully capable; not well qualified. ▫▫ **in·ef·fi·cien·cy** *n.* **in·ef·fi·cient·ly** *adv.*

in·e·las·tic /ínilástik/ *adj.* **1** not elastic. **2** not likely to change; inflexible; unyielding. ▫▫ **in·e·las·ti·cal·ly** *adv.* **in·e·las·tic·i·ty** /–lastísitee/ *n.*

in·el·e·gant /inéligənt/ *adj.* **1** ungraceful. **2 a** unrefined. **b** (of a style) unpolished. ▫▫ **in·el·e·gance** /–gəns/ *n.* **in·el·e·gant·ly** *adv.*

in·el·i·gi·ble /inélijibəl/ *adj.* **1** not eligible. **2** undesirable. ▫▫ **in·el·i·gi·bil·i·ty** *n.* **in·el·i·gi·bly** *adv.*

in·e·luc·ta·ble /ínilúktəbəl/ *adj.* **1** irresistible. **2** inescapable. ▫▫ **in·e·luc·ta·bil·i·ty** *n.* **in·e·luc·ta·bly** *adv.*

in·ept /inépt/ *adj.* **1** unskillful. **2** absurd; silly. **3** out of place. ▫▫ **in·ept·i·tude** *n.* **in·ept·ly** *adv.* **in·ept·ness** *n.*

in·e·qual·i·ty /ínikwólitee/ *n.* (*pl.* **-ties**) **1 a** lack of equality in any respect. **b** an instance of this. **2** the state of being variable.

in·eq·ui·ta·ble /inékwitəbəl/ *adj.* unfair; unjust. ▫▫ **in·eq·ui·ta·bly** *adv.*

in·eq·ui·ty /inékwitee/ *n.* (*pl.* **-ties**) unfairness; bias.

in·ert /inə́rt/ *adj.* **1** without inherent power of action, motion, or resistance. **2** without active chemical or other properties. **3** sluggish; slow. ▫▫ **in·ert·ly** *adv.* **in·ert·ness** *n.*

in·ert gas *n.* = NOBLE GAS.

in·er·tia /inə́rshə/ *n.* **1** *Physics* a property of matter by which it continues in its existing state of rest or uniform motion in a straight line, unless that state is changed by an external force. **2** inertness; sloth. ▫▫ **in·er·tial** *adj.* **in·er·tia·less** *adj.*

in·es·cap·a·ble /íniskáypəbəl/ *adj.* that cannot be escaped or avoided. ▫▫ **in·es·cap·a·bil·i·ty** *n.* **in·es·cap·a·bly** *adv.*

in·es·sen·tial /ínisénshəl/ *adj.* & *n.* • *adj.* **1** not necessary. **2** dispensable. • *n.* an inessential thing.

in·es·ti·ma·ble /inéstiməbəl/ *adj.* too great, intense, precious, etc., to be estimated. ▫▫ **in·es·ti·ma·bly** *adv.*

in·ev·i·ta·ble /inévitəbəl/ *adj.* **1 a** unavoidable; sure to happen. **b** that is bound to occur or appear. **2** *colloq.* that is tiresomely familiar. **3** (of character drawing, the development of a plot, etc.) so true to nature, etc., as to preclude alternative treatment or solution; convincing. ▫▫ **in·ev·i·ta·bil·i·ty** *n.* **in·ev·i·ta·bly** *adv.*

in·ex·act /inigzákt/ *adj.* not exact. ▫▫ **in·ex·act·i·tude** /–titood, –tyood/ *n.* **in·ex·act·ly** *adv.* **in·ex·act·ness** *n.*

in·ex·cus·a·ble /ínikskyóozəbəl/ *adj.* (of a person, action, etc.) that cannot be excused or justified. ▫▫ **in·ex·cus·a·bly** *adv.*

in·ex·haust·i·ble /inigzáwstibəl/ *adj.* **1** that cannot be exhausted or used up. **2** that cannot be worn out. ▫▫ **in·ex·haust·i·bil·i·ty** *n.* **in·ex·haust·i·bly** *adv.*

in·ex·o·ra·ble /inéksərəbəl/ *adj.* **1** relentless. **2** (of a person or attribute) that cannot be persuaded by request or entreaty. ▫▫ **in·ex·o·ra·bil·i·ty** /–bílitee/ *n.* **in·ex·o·ra·bly** *adv.*

in·ex·pen·sive /íníkspénsiv/ *adj.* **1** not expensive; cheap. **2** offering good value for the price. ▫▫ **in·ex·pen·sive·ly** *adv.*

in·ex·pe·ri·ence /íníkspeéreeəns/ *n.* lack of experience, or of the resulting knowledge or skill. ▫▫ **in·ex·pe·ri·enced** *adj.*

in·ex·pert /inékspərt/ *adj.* unskillful; lacking expertise. ▫▫ **in·ex·pert·ly** *adv.* **in·ex·pert·ness** *n.*

in·ex·pli·ca·ble /ínikspliкəbəl, inéks–/ *adj.* that cannot be explained or accounted for. ▫▫ **in·ex·pli·ca·bly** *adv.*

in·ex·press·i·ble /íníksprésibəl/ *adj.* that cannot be expressed in words. ▫▫ **in·ex·press·i·bly** *adv.*

in ex·tre·mis /in ekstreémis, –tré–/ *adj.* **1** at the point of death. **2** in great difficulties.

in·ex·tri·ca·ble /inékstrikəbəl, ínikstrík–/ *adj.* **1** (of a circumstance) that cannot be escaped from. **2** (of a knot, problem, etc.) that cannot be unraveled or solved. **3** intricately confused. ▫▫ **in·ex·tri·ca·bly** *adv.*

inf. *abbr.* **1** infantry. **2** inferior. **3** infinitive.

in·fal·li·ble /infálibəl/ *adj.* **1** incapable of error. **2** (of a method, test, proof, etc.) unfailing; sure to succeed. ▫▫ **in·fal·li·bil·i·ty** /–bílitee/ *n.* **in·fal·li·bly** *adv.*

in·fa·mous /ínfəməs/ *adj.* **1** notoriously bad; having a bad reputation. **2** abominable. ▫▫ **in·fa·mous·ly** *adv.* **in·fa·my** /ínfəmee/ *n.* (*pl.* **-mies**).

in·fan·cy /ínfənsee/ *n.* (*pl.* **-cies**) **1** early childhood; babyhood. **2** an early state in the development of an idea, undertaking, etc.

in·fant /ínfənt/ *n.* **1** a child during the earliest period of its life. **2** (esp. *attrib.*) a thing in an early stage of its development.

in·fan·ti·cide /infántisīd/ *n.* **1** the killing of an infant soon after birth. **2** the practice of killing newborn infants. **3** a person who kills an infant. ▫▫ **in·fan·ti·cid·al** /–sīd'l/ *adj.*

in·fan·tile /ínfəntīl/ *adj.* **1 a** like or characteristic of a child. **b** childish (*infantile humor*). **2** in its infancy.

in·fan·tile pa·ral·y·sis *n.* poliomyelitis.

in·fan·try /ínfəntree/ *n.* (*pl.* **-tries**) a body of soldiers who fight on foot; foot soldiers collectively.

in·fan·try·man /ínfəntreemən/ *n.* (*pl.* **-men**) a soldier of an infantry unit.

in·farct /ínfaarkt/ *n. Med.* a localized area of dead tissue caused by an inadequate blood supply. ▫▫ **in·farc·tion** /–fáarkshən/ *n.*

in·fat·u·ate /infáchoo-ayt/ *v.tr.* (usu. as **infatuated** *adj.*) **1** (often foll. by *with*) inspire with intense, usu. transitory fondness or admiration. **2** affect with extreme folly. ▫▫ **in·fat·u·a·tion** /–áyshən/ *n.*

in·fect /infékt/ *v.tr.* **1** contaminate (air, water, etc.) with harmful organisms or noxious matter. **2** affect (a person) with disease, etc. **3** instill bad feeling or opinion into (a person). ▫▫ **in·fec·tor** *n.*

in·fec·tion /infékshən/ *n.* **1** the process of infecting or state of being infected. **2** an instance of this; an infectious disease.

in·fec·tious /infékshəs/ *adj.* **1** infecting with disease. **2** (of a disease) liable to be transmitted by air, water, etc. **3** (of emotions, etc.) apt to spread; quickly affecting others. ▫▫ **in·fec·tious·ly** *adv.* **in·fec·tious·ness** *n.*

in·fe·lic·i·tous /infilísitəs/ *adj.* not felicitous; unfortunate. ▫▫ **in·fe·lic·i·tous·ly** *adv.*

in·fe·lic·i·ty /infilísitee/ *n.* (*pl.* **-ties**) **1** a thing that is inappropriate, esp. a remark or expression. **2** unhappiness; misfortune.

in·fer /infə́r/ *v.tr.* (**inferred, inferring**) (often foll. by *that* + clause) **1** deduce or conclude from facts and reasoning. **2** *disp.* imply; suggest. ▫▫ **in·fer·a·ble** *adj.*

▶**Infer** means 'to deduce or conclude,' as in *We can infer from the evidence that the car's brakes failed.* Its use in place of **imply,** to mean 'to hint or suggest,' is widely considered incorrect.

in·fer·ence /ínfərəns/ *n.* **1** the act or an instance of inferring. **2** *Logic* **a** the forming of a conclusion from premises. **b** a thing inferred. ▫▫ **in·fer·en·tial** /–rénshəl/ *adj.*

in·fe·ri·or /infeéreeər/ *adj.* & *n.* • *adj.* **1** (often foll. by *to*) **a** lower; in a lower position. **b** of lower rank, quality, etc. **2** poor in quality. **3** (of figures or letters) written or printed below the line. • *n.* **1** a person inferior to another, esp. in rank. **2** an inferior letter or figure. ▫▫ **in·fe·ri·or·ly** *adv.*

in·fe·ri·or·i·ty /infeéree-áwritee, –ór–/ *n.* the state of being inferior.

in·fe·ri·or·i·ty com·plex *n.* an unrealistic feeling of general inadequacy caused by actual or supposed inferiority in one sphere, sometimes marked by aggressive behavior in compensation.

in·fer·nal /infə́rnəl/ *adj.* **1 a** of hell or the underworld. **b** hellish; fiendish. **2** *colloq.* detestable; tiresome. ◻◻ **in·fer·nal·ly** *adv.*

infernal late Middle English: from Old French, from Christian Latin *infernalis*, from Latin *infernus* 'below, underground', used by Christians to mean 'hell', on the pattern of *inferni* (masculine plural) 'the shades' and *inferna* (neuter plural) 'the lower regions'.

in·fer·no /infə́rnō/ *n.* (*pl.* **-nos**) **1** a raging fire. **2** a scene of horror or distress.

in·fest /infést/ *v.tr.* (of harmful persons or things, esp. vermin or disease) overrun (a place) in large numbers. ◻◻ **in·fes·ta·tion** *n.*

in·fi·del /infid'l, –del/ *n. & adj.* • *n.* a person who does not believe in religion or in a particular religion; an unbeliever. • *adj.* **1** that is an infidel. **2** of unbelievers.

infidel late 15th cent.: from French *infidèle* or Latin *infidelis*, from *in-* 'not' + *fidelis* 'faithful' (from *fides* 'faith', related to *fidere* 'to trust'). The word originally denoted a person of a religion other than one's own, specifically a Muslim (to a Christian), a Christian (to a Muslim), or a Gentile (to a Jew).

in·fi·del·i·ty /infidélitee/ *n.* (*pl.* **-ties**) disloyalty or unfaithfulness, esp. to a husband or wife.

in·field /infeeld/ *n. Baseball* **1** the area enclosed by the four bases. **2** the four fielders stationed near the bases. ◻◻ **in·field·er** *n.*

in·fight·ing /infiting/ *n.* **1** hidden conflict or competitiveness within an organization. **2** boxing at closer quarters than arm's length. ◻◻ **in·fight·er** *n.*

in·fil·trate /infiltrayt/ *v.* **1** *tr.* **a** gain entrance or access to surreptitiously and by degrees (as spies, etc.). **b** cause to do this. **2** *tr.* permeate by filtration. **3** *tr.* (often foll. by *into, through*) introduce (fluid) by filtration. ◻◻ **in·fil·tra·tion** /–tráyshən/ *n.* **in·fil·tra·tor** *n.*

in·fi·nite /infinit/ *adj.* **1** boundless or endless. **2** very great in amount or degree. **3** *Math.* **a** greater than any assignable quantity or countable number. **b** (of a series) that may be continued indefinitely. ◻◻ **in·fi·nite·ly** *adv.* **in·fi·nite·ness** *n.*

in·fin·i·tes·i·mal /infinitésiməl/ *adj. & n.* • *adj.* infinitely or very small. • *n.* an infinitesimal amount. ◻◻ **in·fin·i·tes·i·mal·ly** *adv.*

▶Although it is widely assumed to refer to large numbers, **infinitesimal** describes only very small size. While there may be an *infinite* number of grains of sand on the beach, a single grain may be said to be *infinitesimal.*

in·fin·i·tive /infinitiv/ *n.* a form of a verb expressing the verbal notion without reference to a particular subject, tense, etc. (e.g., *see* in *we came to see, let him see*). ◻◻ **in·fin·i·ti·val** /–tívəl/ *adj.* **in·fin·i·ti·val·ly** /–tívəlee/ *adv.*

▶Writers who insisted that English could be modeled on Latin long ago created the "rule" that the English infinitive must not be split: *to clearly state* was wrong; one must say *to state clearly.* But the Latin infinitive is one word, and cannot be split, so the "rule" is not firmly grounded, and treating two English words as one can lead to awkward, stilted sentences.

in·fin·i·ty /infinitee/ *n.* (*pl.* **-ties**) **1** the state of being infinite. **2** an infinite number or extent. **3** infinite distance. **4** *Math.* infinite quantity. ¶ Symb.: ∞

in·firm /infə́rm/ *adj.* **1** physically weak, esp. through age. **2** (of a person, mind, judgment, etc.) weak; irresolute. ◻◻ **in·fir·mi·ty** *n.* (*pl.* **-ties**). **in·firm·ly** *adv.*

in·fir·ma·ry /infə́rməree/ *n.* (*pl.* **-ries**) **1** a hospital. **2** a place for those who are ill in a monastery, school, etc.

in fla·gran·te de·lic·to /in fləgrántee dilíktō/ *adv.* in the very act of committing an offense.

in·flame /infláym/ *v.* **1** *tr. & intr.* (often foll. by *with, by*) provoke or become provoked to strong feeling, esp. anger. **2** *Med.* **a** *intr.* become hot, reddened, and sore. **b** *tr.* (esp. as **inflamed** *adj.*) cause inflammation or fever in (a body, etc.); make hot. **3** *tr.* aggravate. **4** *intr. & tr.* catch or set on fire. **5** *tr.* light up with or as if with flames. ◻◻ **in·flam·er** *n.*

in·flam·ma·ble /inflámәbəl/ *adj. & n.* • *adj.* **1** easily set on fire; flammable. **2** easily excited. • *n.* (usu. in *pl.*) a flammable substance. ◻◻ **in·flam·ma·bil·i·ty** *n.* **in·flam·ma·ble·ness** *n.* **in·flam·ma·bly** *adv.*

▶Both **inflammable** and **flammable** mean 'easily set on fire or excited.' The opposite is **nonflammable.** Where there is a danger that **inflammable** could be understood to mean its opposite, i.e., 'not easily set on fire,' **flammable** should be used—and is used, as in the labeling of many products—to avoid confusion.

in·flam·ma·tion /ínfləmáyshən/ *n.* **1** the act or an instance of inflaming. **2** *Med.* a localized physical condition with heat, swelling, redness, and usu. pain, esp. as a reaction to injury or infection.

in·flam·ma·to·ry /inflámətáwree/ *adj.* **1** (esp. of speeches, leaflets, etc.) tending to cause anger, etc. **2** of or tending to inflammation of the body.

in·flat·a·ble /infláytəbəl/ *adj. & n.* • *adj.* that can be inflated. • *n.* an inflatable plastic or rubber object, esp. a small boat or raft.

in·flate /infláyt/ *v.tr.* **1** distend (a balloon, etc.) with air. **2** (usu. foll. by *with*; usu. in *passive*) puff up (a person with pride, etc.). **3 a** (often *absol.*) bring about inflation (of the currency). **b** raise (prices) artificially. **4** (as **inflated** *adj.*) (esp. of language, sentiments, etc.) bombastic. ◻◻ **in·flat·ed·ly** *adv.* **in·flat·ed·ness** *n.* **in·flat·er** *n.* **in·fla·tor** *n.*

in·fla·tion /infláyshən/ *n.* **1 a** the act or condition of inflating or being inflated. **b** an instance of this. **2** *Econ.* **a** a general increase in prices and fall in the purchasing value of money. **b** an increase in available currency regarded as causing this. ◻◻ **in·fla·tion·ar·y** *adj.* **in·fla·tion·ism** *n.* **in·fla·tion·ist** *n. & adj.*

in·flect /inflékt/ *v.* **1** *tr.* change the pitch of (the voice, a musical note, etc.). **2** *Gram.* **a** *tr.* change the form of (a word) to express tense, gender, number, mood, etc. **b** *intr.* (of a word, language, etc.) undergo such change. **3** *tr.* bend inward; curve. ◻◻ **in·flec·tive** *adj.*

in·flec·tion /inflékshən/ *n.* (also, esp. *Brit.* **inflexion**) **1 a** the act or condition of inflecting or being inflected. **b** an instance of this. **2** *Gram.* **a** the process or practice of inflecting words. **b** an inflected form of a word. **c** a suffix, etc., used to inflect, e.g., *-ed.* **3** a modulation of the voice. ◻◻ **in·flec·tion·al** *adj.* **in·flec·tion·al·ly** *adv.* **in·flec·tion·less** *adj.*

in·flex·i·ble /infléksibəl/ *adj.* **1** unbendable. **2** stiff; immovable; obstinate. **3** unchangeable; inexorable. ◻◻ **in·flex·i·bil·i·ty** *n.* **in·flex·i·bly** *adv.*

in·flict /inflíkt/ *v.tr.* (usu. foll. by *on, upon*) **1** administer; deal (a stroke, wound, defeat, etc.). **2** (also *refl.*) often *joc.* impose (suffering, a penalty, oneself, one's company, etc.) on (*shall not inflict myself on you any longer*).

in·flo·res·cence /inflərésəns/ *n.* **1** *Bot.* **a** the complete flower head of a plant including stems, stalks, bracts, and flowers. **b** the arrangement of this. **2** the process of flowering.

in·flu·ence /ínflōōəns/ *n. & v.* • *n.* **1** (usu. foll. by *on, upon*) the effect a person or thing has on another. **2** (usu. foll. by *over, with*) moral ascendancy or power. **3** a thing or person exercising such power (*is a good influence on them*). • *v.tr.* exert influence on; have an effect on. □ **under the influence** *colloq.* affected by alcoholic drink. □□ **in·flu·ence·a·ble** *adj.* **in·flu·enc·er** *n.*

influence late Middle English: from Old French, or from medieval Latin *influentia* 'inflow', from Latin *influere*, from *in-* 'into' + *fluere* 'to flow'. The word originally had the general sense 'an influx, flowing matter', also specifically (in astrology) 'the flowing in of ethereal fluid (affecting human destiny)'. The sense 'imperceptible or indirect action exerted to cause changes' was established in Scholastic Latin by the 13th cent., but not recorded in English until the late 16th cent.

in·flu·en·tial /inflōō-énshəl/ *adj.* having a great influence or power (*influential in the financial world*). □□ **in·flu·en·tial·ly** *adv.*

in·flu·en·za /inflōō-énzə/ *n.* a highly contagious viral infection causing fever, severe aching, and catarrh.

in·flux /ínfluks/ *n.* a continual stream of people or things.

in·fo /ínfō/ *n. colloq.* information.

in·fo·mer·cial /ínfōmərshəl/ *n.* a television program promoting a commercial product.

in·form /infáwrm/ *v.* **1** *tr.* (usu. foll. by *of, about, on,* or *that, how* + clause) tell (*informed them of their rights; informed us that the train was late*). **2** *intr.* (usu. foll. by *against, on*) give incriminating information about a person to the authorities. **3** *tr.* impart its quality to; permeate. □□ **in·form·ant** *n.*

in·for·mal /infáwrməl/ *adj.* **1** without ceremony or formality (*just an informal chat*). **2** (of language, clothing, etc.) everyday; normal. □□ **in·for·mal·i·ty** /–málitee/ *n.* (*pl.* **-ties**). **in·for·mal·ly** *adv.*

in·for·mat·ics /infərmátiks/ *n.pl.* (usu. treated as *sing.*) the science of processing data for storage and retrieval; information science.

in·for·ma·tion /infərmáyshən/ *n.* **1 a** something told; knowledge. **b** (usu. foll. by *on, about*) items of knowledge; news. **2** *Law* (usu. foll. by *against*) a charge or complaint lodged with a court or magistrate. **3 a** the act of informing or telling. **b** an instance of this. □□ **in·for·ma·tion·al** *adj.* **in·for·ma·tion·al·ly** *adv.*

in·for·ma·tion sci·ence *n.* computing the study of processes for storing and retrieving information, especially scientific or technical information.

in·for·ma·tion (su·per)high·way *n.* a putative worldwide computer network offering information, shopping, and other services.

in·for·ma·tive /infáwrmətiv/ *adj.* (also **in·for·ma·to·ry** /infáwrmətáwree/) giving information; instructive. □□ **in·for·ma·tive·ly** *adv.* **in·for·ma·tive·ness** *n.*

in·formed /infáwrmd/ *adj.* **1** knowing the facts; instructed (*his answers show that he is badly informed*). **2** educated; intelligent. □□ **in·form·ed·ly** /infáwrmidlee/ *adv.* **in·form·ed·ness** /infáwrmidnis/ *n.*

in·form·er /infáwrmər/ *n.* **1** a person who informs against another. **2** a person who informs or advises.

in·fo·tain·ment /infōtáynmənt/ *n.* **1** factual information presented in dramatized form on television. **2** a television program mixing news and entertainment.

in·fra /ínfrə/ *adv.* below, further on (in a book or writing).

infra- /ínfrə/ *comb. form* **1** below. **2** *Anat.* below or under a part of the body.

in·frac·tion /infrákshən/ *n.* esp. *Law* a violation or infringement. □□ **in·fract** *v.tr.* **in·frac·tor** *n.*

in·fra dig /ínfrə díg/ *predic.adj. colloq.* beneath one's dignity; unbecoming.

in·fra·red /ínfrəréd/ *adj.* **1** having a wavelength just greater than the red end of the visible light spectrum but shorter than that of radio waves. **2** of or using such radiation.

in·fra·struc·ture /ínfrəstrukchər/ *n.* **1 a** the basic structural foundations of a society or enterprise; a substructure or foundation. **b** roads, bridges, sewers, etc., regarded as a country's economic foundation. **2** permanent installations as a basis for military, etc., operations.

in·fre·quent /infréékwənt/ *adj.* not frequent. □□ **in·fre·quen·cy** *n.* **in·fre·quent·ly** *adv.*

in·fringe /infrínj/ *v.* **1** *tr.* **a** act contrary to; violate (a law, an oath, etc.). **b** act in defiance of (another's rights, etc.). **2** *intr.* (usu. foll. by *on, upon*) encroach; trespass. □□ **in·fringe·ment** *n.* **in·fring·er** *n.*

in·fu·ri·ate *v.tr.* /infyŏŏreeayt/ fill with fury; enrage. □□ **in·fu·ri·at·ing** *adj.* **in·fu·ri·at·ing·ly** *adv.*

in·fuse /infyŏŏz/ *v.* **1** *tr.* (usu. foll. by *with*) imbue; pervade (*anger infused with resentment*). **2** *tr.* steep (herbs, tea, etc.) in liquid to extract the content. **3** *tr.* (usu. foll. by *into*) instill (grace, spirit, life, etc.). **4** *intr.* undergo infusion (*let it infuse for five minutes*). □□ **in·fus·a·ble** *adj.* **in·fus·er** *n.* **in·fu·sive** /–fyŏŏsiv/ *adj.*

in·fu·sion /infyŏŏzhən/ *n.* **1** a liquid obtained by infusing. **2** an infused element; an admixture. **3** *Med.* a slow injection of a substance into a vein or tissue. **4 a** the act of infusing. **b** an instance of this.

in·gen·ious /injéényəs/ *adj.* **1** clever at inventing, constructing, organizing, etc.; skillful; resourceful. **2** (of a machine, theory, etc.) cleverly contrived. □□ **in·gen·ious·ly** *adv.* **in·gen·ious·ness** *n.*

▶**Ingenious** and **ingenuous** are sometimes confused. **Ingenious** means 'clever, skillful, or resourceful,' e.g., *an ingenious device,* while **ingenuous** means 'artless' or 'frank,', e.g., *charmed by the ingenuous honesty of the child.*

in·ge·nue /ánzhənŏŏ/ *n.* (also **ingénue**) **1** an innocent or unsophisticated young woman. **2** *Theatr.* **a** such a part in a play. **b** the actress who plays this part.

in·ge·nu·i·ty /injinŏŏitee, –nyŏŏ–/ *n.* skill in devising or contriving; ingeniousness.

in·gen·u·ous /injényōōəs/ *adj.* **1** innocent; artless. **2** open; frank. □□ **in·gen·u·ous·ly** *adv.* **in·gen·u·ous·ness** *n.*

in·gest /injést/ *v.tr.* **1** take in (food, etc.); eat. **2** absorb (facts, knowledge, etc.). □□ **in·ges·tion** /injés-chən/ *n.* **in·ges·tive** *adj.*

in·gle·nook /inggəlnŏŏk/ *n.* a space within the opening on either side of a large fireplace; chimney corner.

in·glo·ri·ous /in-gláwreeəs/ *adj.* **1** shameful; ignominious. **2** not famous. □□ **in·glo·ri·ous·ly** *adv.* **in·glo·ri·ous·ness** *n.*

in·got /inggət/ *n.* a usu. oblong piece of cast metal, esp. of gold, silver, or steel.

in·grain *adj. & v.* • *adj.* /in-grayn/ inherent; ingrained. • *v.tr.* /in-gráyn/ cause to become embedded.

in·grained /in-gráynd/ *attrib.adj.* **1** deeply rooted; inveterate. **2** thorough. **3** (of dirt, etc.) deeply embedded. □□ **in·grain·ed·ly** /–gráynidlee/ *adv.*

in·gra·ti·ate /in-gráysheeayt/ *v.refl.* (usu. foll. by *with*) bring oneself into favor. □□ **in·gra·ti·at·ing** *adj.* **in·gra·ti·at·ing·ly** *adv.* **in·gra·ti·a·tion** /–áyshən/ *n.*

in·grat·i·tude /in-grátitōōd, –tyōōd/ *n.* a lack of due gratitude.

in·gre·di·ent /in-gréedeeənt/ *n.* a component part or element in a recipe, mixture, or combination.

in·gress /ín-gres/ *n.* the act or right of going in or entering. □□ **in·gres·sion** /–gréshən/ *n.*

in-group /ín-grōōp/ *n.* a small exclusive group of people with a common interest.

in·grow·ing /in-grṓing/ *adj.* growing inward, esp. (of a toenail) growing into the flesh. ▫▫ **in·grown** *adj.*

in·gui·nal /ínggwinəl/ *adj.* of the groin.

in·hab·it /inhábit/ *v.tr.* (of a person or animal) dwell in; occupy (a region, town, house, etc.). ▫▫ **in·hab·it·a·bil·i·ty** /–təbílitee/ *n.* **in·hab·it·a·ble** *adj.* **in·hab·it·ant** *n.* **in·hab·i·ta·tion** /–táyshən/ *n.*

in·hal·ant /inháylənt/ *n.* a medicinal preparation for inhaling.

in·hale /inháyl/ *v.tr.* (often *absol.*) breathe in (air, gas, tobacco smoke, etc.). ▫▫ **in·ha·la·tion** /–həláyshən/ *n.*

in·hal·er /inháylər/ *n.* a portable device used for relieving esp. asthma by inhaling.

in·here /inhéer/ *v.intr.* be inherent.

in·her·ent /inhéerənt, inhér–/ *adj.* (often foll. by *in*) **1** existing in something, esp. as a permanent or characteristic attribute. **2** vested in (a person, etc.) as a right or privilege. ▫▫ **in·her·ence** /–rəns/ *n.* **in·her·ent·ly** *adv.*

in·her·it /inhérit/ *v.* **1** *tr.* receive (property, etc.) by legal succession. **2** *tr.* derive (a quality or characteristic) genetically from one's ancestors. **3** *absol.* succeed as an heir (*a younger son rarely inherited*). ▫▫ **in·her·i·tor** *n.*

in·her·it·a·ble /inhéritəbəl/ *adj.* **1** capable of being inherited. **2** capable of inheriting.

in·her·it·ance /inhérit'ns/ *n.* **1** something that is inherited. **2 a** the act of inheriting. **b** an instance of this.

in·hib·it /inhíbit/ *v.tr.* **1** hinder, restrain, or prevent (an action or progress). **2** (as **inhibited** *adj.*) subject to inhibition. **3** (usu. foll. by *from* + verbal noun) forbid or prohibit (a person, etc.). ▫▫ **in·hib·i·tive** *adj.* **in·hib·i·tor** *n.* **in·hib·i·to·ry** *adj.*

in·hi·bi·tion /ínhibíshən/ *n.* **1** *Psychol.* a restraint on the direct expression of an instinct. **2** *colloq.* an emotional resistance to a thought, an action, etc. (*has inhibitions about singing in public*). **3** *Law* an order forbidding alteration to property rights. **4 a** the act of inhibiting. **b** the process of being inhibited.

in·hos·pi·ta·ble /inhospítəbəl, inhóspi–/ *adj.* **1** not hospitable. **2** (of a region, coast, etc.) not affording shelter, etc. ▫▫ **in·hos·pi·ta·ble·ness** *n.* **in·hos·pi·ta·bly** *adv.*

in-house *adj.* & *adv.* • *adj.* /ínhóws/ done or existing within an institution, company, etc. (*an in-house project*). • *adv.* /inhóws/ internally, without outside assistance.

in·hu·man /inhyóomən/ *adj.* **1** (of a person, conduct, etc.) brutal; unfeeling; barbarous. **2** not of a human type. ▫▫ **in·hu·man·ly** *adv.*

in·hu·mane /ínhyoomáyn/ *adj.* not humane. ▫▫ **in·hu·mane·ly** *adv.*

in·hu·man·i·ty /ínhyoománitee/ *n.* (*pl.* **-ties**) **1** brutality; barbarousness; callousness. **2** an inhumane act.

in·im·i·cal /inímikəl/ *adj.* (usu. foll. by *to*) **1** hostile. **2** harmful. ▫▫ **in·im·i·cal·ly** *adv.*

in·im·i·ta·ble /inímitəbəl/ *adj.* impossible to imitate. ▫▫ **in·im·i·ta·bil·i·ty** *n.* **in·im·i·ta·ble·ness** *n.* **in·im·i·ta·bly** *adv.*

in·iq·ui·ty /iníkwitee/ *n.* (*pl.* **-ties**) **1** wickedness; unrighteousness. **2** a gross injustice. ▫▫ **in·iq·ui·tous** *adj.* **in·iq·ui·tous·ly** *adv.* **in·iq·ui·tous·ness** *n.*

in·i·tial /iníshəl/ *adj., n., & v.* • *adj.* of, existing, or occurring at the beginning (*initial stage*; *initial expenses*). • *n.* **1** the letter at the beginning of a word. **2** (usu. in *pl.*) the first letter or letters of the words of a (esp. a person's) name or names. • *v.tr.* (**initialed, initialing**) mark or sign with one's initials. ▫▫ **in·i·tial·ly** *adv.*

in·i·tial·ize /iníshəlīz/ *v.tr. Computing* set to the value or put in the condition appropriate to the start of an operation. ▫▫ **in·i·tial·i·za·tion** *n.*

in·i·ti·ate *v., n., & adj.* • *v.tr.* /inísheeayt/ **1** begin; set going; originate. **2 a** (usu. foll. by *into*) admit (a person) into a society, an office, a secret, etc., esp. with a ritual. **b** (usu. foll. by *in, into*) instruct (a person) in science, art, etc. • *n.* /iníshееət/ a person who has been newly initiated. • *adj.* /inísheeət/ (of a person) newly initiated (*an initiate member*). ▫▫ **in·i·ti·a·tion** /–sheeáyshən/ *n.* **in·i·ti·a·tor** *n.* **in·i·ti·a·to·ry** /inísheeətáwree/ *adj.*

in·i·ti·a·tive /iníshətiv, inísheeətiv/ *n.* & *adj.* • *n.* **1** the ability to initiate things; enterprise (*I'm afraid he lacks all initiative*). **2** a first step; origination or overture (*a peace initiative*). **3** the power or right to begin something. • *adj.* beginning; originating.

in·ject /injékt/ *v.tr.* **1** *Med.* **a** (usu. foll. by *into*) drive or force (a solution, medicine, etc.) by or as if by a syringe. **b** (usu. foll. by *with*) fill (a cavity, etc.) by injecting. **c** administer medicine, etc., to (a person) by injection. **2** place or insert (an object, a quality, etc.) into something (*may I inject a note of realism?*). ▫▫ **in·ject·a·ble** *adj.* & *n.* **in·jec·tor** *n.*

in·jec·tion /injékshən/ *n.* **1 a** the act of injecting. **b** an instance of this. **2** a liquid or solution (to be) injected.

in·junc·tion /injúngkshən/ *n.* **1** an authoritative warning or order. **2** *Law* a judicial order restraining a person from an act or compelling redress to an injured party. ▫▫ **in·junc·tive** *adj.*

in·jure /ínjər/ *v.tr.* **1** do physical harm or damage to; hurt. **2** harm or impair (*illness might injure her chances*). **3** do wrong to. ▫▫ **in·jur·er** *n.*

in·jured /ínjərd/ *adj.* **1** harmed or hurt (*the injured passengers*). **2** offended; wronged (*in an injured tone*).

in·ju·ri·ous /injóoreeəs/ *adj.* **1** hurtful. **2** (of language) insulting; libelous. **3** wrongful. ▫▫ **in·ju·ri·ous·ly** *adv.* **in·ju·ri·ous·ness** *n.*

in·ju·ry /ínjəree/ *n.* (*pl.* **-ries**) **1 a** a physical harm or damage. **b** an instance of this (*suffered head injuries*). **2** esp. *Law* **a** wrongful action or treatment. **b** an instance of this. **3** damage to one's good name, etc.

in·jus·tice /injústis/ *n.* **1** a lack of fairness or justice. **2** an unjust act. ▫ **do a person an injustice** judge a person unfairly.

ink /ingk/ *n.* & *v.* • *n.* **1 a** a colored fluid used for writing with a pen, marking with a rubber stamp, etc. **b** a thick paste used in printing, duplicating, in ballpoint pens, etc. **2** *Zool.* a black liquid ejected by a cuttlefish, octopus, etc., to confuse a predator. • *v.tr.* **1** (usu. foll. by *in, over,* etc.) mark with ink. **2** cover (type, etc.) with ink before printing. **3** apply ink to. **4** sign (a contract).

ink-jet print·er *n.* a computer-controlled printer in which minute droplets of ink are projected onto the paper.

ink·ling /íngkling/ *n.* (often foll. by *of*) a slight knowledge or suspicion; a hint.

ink pad *n.* an ink-soaked pad, usu. in a box, used for inking a rubber stamp, etc.

ink·well /íngkwel/ *n.* a pot for ink usu. housed in a hole in a desk.

ink·y /íngkee/ *adj.* (**inkier, inkiest**) of, as black as, or stained with ink. ▫▫ **ink·i·ness** *n.*

in·laid *past* and *past part.* of INLAY.

in·land /ínlənd, ínland/ *adj., n., & adv.* • *adj.* **1** situated in the interior of a country. **2** esp. *Brit.* carried on within the limits of a country; domestic (*inland trade*). • *n.* the parts of a country remote from the sea or frontiers; the interior. • *adv.* in or toward the interior of a country. ▫▫ **in·land·er** *n.* **in·land·ish** *adj.*

in-law /ínlaw/ *n.* (often in *pl.*) a relative by marriage.

in·lay *v.* & *n.* • *v.tr.* /inláy/ (*past* and *past part.* **inlaid** /inláyd/) **1 a** embed (a thing in another) so that the surfaces are even. **b** (usu. foll. by *with*) ornament (a thing with inlaid work). **2** (as **inlaid** *adj.*) (of a piece of furniture, etc.) ornamented by inlaying. •*n.* /ínlay/ **1** inlaid work. **2** material inlaid. ▫▫ **in·lay·er** *n.*

in·let /ínlet, –lit/ *n.* **1** a small arm of the sea, a lake, or a river. **2** a way of entry.

in-line /inlín/ *adj.* **1** having parts arranged in a line. **2** constituting an integral part of a continuous sequence of operations or machines.

in-line skate *n.* a roller skate in which usu. four hard rubber wheels are fixed in a single line along its sole.

in lo·co pa·ren·tis /in lṓkō pəréntis/ *adv.* in the place or position of a parent (used of a teacher, school, etc., responsible for children).

in·mate /ínmayt/ *n.* (usu. foll. by *of*) **1** an occupant of a hospital, prison, institution, etc. **2** an occupant of a house, etc., esp. one of several.

in me·mo·ri·am /in mimáwreeəm/ *prep. & n.* •*prep.* in memory of (a dead person). •*n.* a written article or notice, etc., in memory of a dead person; an obituary.

in·most /ínmōst/ *adj.* **1** most inward. **2** most intimate; deepest.

inn /in/ *n.* a public house providing alcoholic liquor for consumption on the premises, and sometimes accommodation, etc.

inn Old English (in the sense 'dwelling place, lodging'): of Germanic origin; related to IN. In Middle English the word was used to translate Latin *hospitium* (see HOSPICE), denoting a house of residence for students: this sense is preserved in the names of some buildings formerly used for this purpose, notably Gray's Inn and Lincoln's Inn, found in London's legal district. The current sense dates from late Middle English.

in·nards /ínərdz/ *n.pl. colloq.* **1** entrails. **2** works (of an engine, etc.).

in·nate /ináyt, ínayt/ *adj.* **1** inborn; natural. **2** *Philos.* originating in the mind. ▫▫ **in·nate·ly** *adv.* **in·nate·ness** *n.*

in·ner /ínər/ *adj.* (usu. *attrib.*) **1** farther in; inside; interior (*the inner compartment*). **2** (of thoughts, feelings, etc.) deeper; more secret. ▫▫ **in·ner·ly** *adv.* **in·ner·most** *adj.* **in·ner·ness** *n.*

in·ner cit·y *n.* the central, most densely populated area of a city (also (with hyphen) *attrib.*: *inner-city housing*).

in·ner ear *n.* the semicircular canals and cochlea, which form the organs of balance and hearing.

in·ner tube *n.* a separate inflatable tube inside the cover of a pneumatic tire.

in·ning /íning/ *n.* **1** *Baseball* **a** a division of a game in which the two teams alternate as offense and defense and during which each team is allowed three outs. **b** a single turn at bat for a team until they make three outs. **2** a similar division of play in other games, as horseshoes.

inn·keep·er /ínkeepər/ *n.* a person who keeps an inn.

in·no·cent /ínəsənt/ *adj. & n.* •*adj.* **1** free from moral wrong; sinless. **2** (usu. foll. by *of*) not guilty (of a crime, etc.). **3 a** simple; guileless; naive. **b** pretending to be guileless. **4** harmless. **5** (foll. by *of*) *colloq.* without; lacking (*appeared, innocent of shoes*). •*n.* an innocent person, esp. a young child. ▫▫ **in·no·cence** /–səns/ *n.* **in·no·cen·cy** *n.* **in·no·cent·ly** *adv.*

▶**Innocent** properly means 'harmless' but has long been extended in general language to mean 'not guilty.' The jury (or judge) in a criminal trial does not, strictly speaking, find a defendant 'innocent.' Rather, a defendant may be *guilty* or *not guilty* of the charges brought. In common use, however, owing perhaps to the concept of the *presumption of innocence*, which instructs a jury to consider a defendant free of wrongdoing until proven guilty on the basis of evidence, 'not guilty' and 'innocent' have come to be thought one and the same.

in·noc·u·ous /inókyōōəs/ *adj.* **1** not injurious; harmless. **2** inoffensive. ▫▫ **in·no·cu·i·ty** /inəkyṓō-itee/ *n.* **in·noc·u·ous·ly** *adv.* **in·noc·u·ous·ness** *n.*

in·no·vate /ínəvayt/ *v.intr.* **1** bring in new methods, ideas, etc. **2** (often foll. by *in*) make changes. ▫▫ **in·no·va·tion** /–váyshən/ *n.* **in·no·va·tion·al** /–váyshənəl/ *adj.* **in·no·va·tor** *n.* **in·no·va·tive** *adj.* **in·no·va·tive·ness** *n.*

in·nu·en·do /ínyōō-éndō/ *n.* (*pl.* **-dos** or **-does**) **1** an allusive or oblique remark or hint, usu. disparaging. **2** a remark with a double meaning, usu. suggestive.

in·nu·mer·a·ble /inṓōmərəbəl, inyṓō–/ *adj.* too many to be counted. ▫▫ **in·nu·mer·a·bly** *adv.*

in·nu·mer·ate /inṓōmərət, inyṓō–/ *adj.* having no knowledge of or feeling for mathematical operations; not numerate. ▫▫ **in·nu·mer·a·cy** /–rəsee/ *n.*

in·oc·u·late /inókyəlayt/ *v.tr.* treat (a person or animal) with a vaccine or serum, usu. by injection, to promote immunity against disease. ▫▫ **in·oc·u·la·ble** *adj.* **in·oc·u·la·tion** /–láyshən/ *n.* **in·oc·u·la·tor** *n.*

in·of·fen·sive /inəfénsiv/ *adj.* not objectionable; harmless. ▫▫ **in·of·fen·sive·ly** *adv.* **in·of·fen·sive·ness** *n.*

in·op·er·a·ble /inópərəbəl/ *adj.* **1** *Surgery* that cannot suitably be operated on (*inoperable cancer*). **2** that cannot be operated; inoperative. ▫▫ **in·op·er·a·bil·i·ty** *n.* **in·op·er·a·bly** *adv.*

in·op·er·a·tive /inópərətiv/ *adj.* not working.

in·op·por·tune /inópərtṓōn, –tyṓōn/ *adj.* not appropriate, esp. as regards time; unseasonable. ▫▫ **in·op·por·tune·ly** *adv.* **in·op·por·tune·ness** *n.*

in·or·di·nate /ináwrd'nət/ *adj.* **1** immoderate; excessive. **2** intemperate. **3** disorderly. ▫▫ **in·or·di·nate·ly** *adv.*

in·or·gan·ic /ínawrgánik/ *adj.* **1** *Chem.* (of a compound) not organic, usu. of mineral origin. **2** without organized physical structure. **3** not arising by natural growth; extraneous. **4** *Philol.* not explainable by normal etymology. ▫▫ **in·or·gan·i·cal·ly** *adv.*

in·pa·tient /ínpayshənt/ *n.* a patient who stays in the hospital while under treatment.

in·put /ínpōōt/ *n. & v.* •*n.* **1** what is put in or taken in, or operated on by any process or system. **2** *Electronics* **a** a place where, or a device through which, energy, information, etc., enters a system (*a tape recorder with inputs for microphone and radio*). **b** energy supplied to a device or system; an electrical signal. **3** the information fed into a computer. **4** the action or process of putting in or feeding in. **5** a contribution of information, etc. •*v.tr.* (**inputting**; *past* and *past part.* **input** or **inputted**) (often foll. by *into*) **1** put in. **2** *Computing* supply (data, programs, etc., to a computer, program, etc.). ▫ **input-**(or **input/**)**output** *Computing*, etc. of, relating to, or for input and output. ▫▫ **in·put·ter** *n.*

in·quest /ínkwest, íng–/ *n.* **1** *Law* **a** an inquiry by a coroner's court into the cause of a death. **b** a judicial inquiry to ascertain the facts relating to an incident, etc. **c** a coroner's jury. **2** *colloq.* a discussion analyzing the outcome of a game, an election, etc.

in·qui·e·tude /inkwí-itōōd, –tyōōd/ *n.* uneasiness.

in·quire /inkwír, ing–/ *v.* **1** *intr.* (often foll. by *of*) seek information formally; make a formal investigation. **2** *intr.* (foll. by *about, after, for*) ask about a person, a person's health, etc. **3** *intr.* (foll. by *for*) ask about the availability of. **4** *tr.* ask for information as to (*inquired whether we were coming*). **5** *tr.* (foll. by *into*) investigate; look into. ▫▫ **in·quir·er** *n.*

in·quir·y /inkwíree, ing–, ínkwəree, íng–/ *n.* (*pl.* **-ies**) **1** an investigation, esp. an official one. **2** the act or an instance of asking or seeking information.

in·qui·si·tion /ínkwizíshən, íng–/ *n.* **1** usu. *derog.* an intensive search or investigation. **2** a judicial or official inquiry. **3** (**the Inquisition**) *RC Ch. hist.* an ecclesiastical tribunal for the suppression of heresy, esp. in Spain, operating through torture and execution. ▫▫ **in·qui·si·tion·al** *adj.*

in·quis·i·tive /inkwízitiv, ing–/ *adj.* **1** unduly curious; prying. **2** seeking knowledge; inquiring. ▫▫ **in·quis·i·tive·ly** *adv.* **in·quis·i·tive·ness** *n.*

in·quis·i·tor /inkwízitər, ing–/ *n.* **1** an official investigator. **2** *hist.* an officer of the Inquisition.

in·quis·i·to·ri·al /inkwízitáwreeəl, ing–/ *adj.* **1** of or like an inquisitor. **2** offensively prying. **3** *Law* (of a trial, etc.) in which the judge has a prosecuting role (opp. ACCUSATORIAL). ▫▫ **in·quis·i·to·ri·al·ly** *adv.*

in re /in rée, ráy/ *prep.* = RE[1].

in·road /ínrōd/ *n.* **1** (often in *pl.*) **a** (usu. foll. by *on, into*) an encroachment; a using up of resources, etc. (*makes inroads on my time*). **b** (often foll. by *in, into*) progress; an advance (*making inroads into a difficult market*). **2** a hostile attack; a raid.

in·rush /ínrush/ *n.* a rushing in; an influx. ▫▫ **in·rush·ing** *adj. & n.*

INS *abbr.* (US) Immigration and Naturalization Service.

ins. *abbr.* **1** inches. **2** insurance.

in·sane /insáyn/ *adj.* **1** not of sound mind; mad. **2** *colloq.* extremely foolish; irrational. ▫▫ **in·sane·ly** *adv.* **in·sane·ness** *n.* **in·san·i·ty** /–sánitee/ *n.* (*pl.* **-ties**).

in·sa·tia·ble /insáyshəbəl/ *adj.* **1** unable to be satisfied. **2** (usu. foll. by *of*) extremely greedy. ▫▫ **in·sa·tia·bil·i·ty** *n.* **in·sa·tia·bly** *adv.*

in·scribe /inskríb/ *v.tr.* **1 a** (usu. foll. by *in, on*) write or carve (words, etc.) on stone, metal, paper, a book, etc. **b** (usu. foll. by *with*) mark (a sheet, tablet, etc.) with characters. **2** (usu. foll. by *to*) write an informal dedication (to a person) in or on (a book, etc.). **3** enter the name of (a person) on a list or in a book. ▫▫ **in·scrib·a·ble** *adj.* **in·scrib·er** *n.*

in·scrip·tion /inskrípshən/ *n.* **1** words inscribed. **2** the act of inscribing. ▫▫ **in·scrip·tion·al** *adj.* **in·scrip·tive** *adj.*

in·scru·ta·ble /inskróótəbəl/ *adj.* wholly mysterious; impenetrable. ▫▫ **in·scru·ta·bil·i·ty** *n.* **in·scru·ta·ble·ness** *n.* **in·scru·ta·bly** *adv.*

in·sect /insekt/ *n.* **1 a** any arthropod of the class Insecta, having a head, thorax, abdomen, two antennae, three pairs of thoracic legs, and usu. one or two pairs of thoracic wings. **b** (loosely) any other small segmented invertebrate animal. **2** an insignificant or contemptible person or creature. ▫▫ **in·sec·tile** /–séktəl, –tīl/ *adj.*

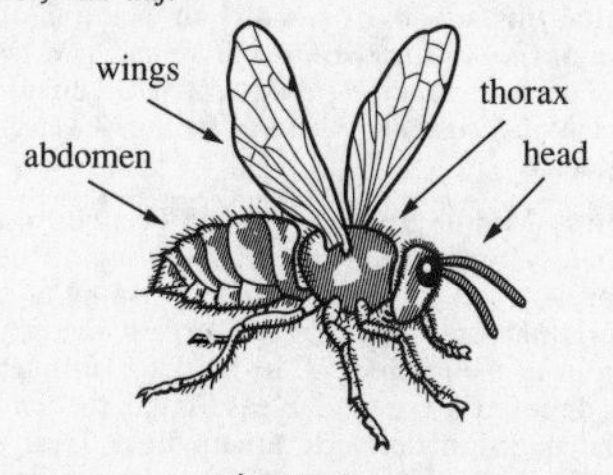

insect, 1a

in·sec·ti·cide /inséktisīd/ *n.* a substance used for killing insects. ▫▫ **in·sec·ti·cid·al** /–síd'l/ *adj.*

in·sec·ti·vore /inséktivawr/ *n.* **1** any mammal of the order Insectivora feeding on insects, etc., e.g., a hedgehog or mole. **2** any plant that captures and absorbs insects. ▫▫ **in·sec·tiv·o·rous** /–tívərəs/ *adj.*

in·se·cure /insikyóór/ *adj.* **1** uncertain; lacking confidence. **2 a** unsafe; not firm or fixed. **b** (of ice, ground, etc.) liable to give way. **c** lacking security; unprotected. ▫▫ **in·se·cure·ly** *adv.* **in·se·cu·ri·ty** *n.*

in·sem·i·nate /inséminayt/ *v.tr.* **1** introduce semen into (a female) by natural or artificial means. **2** sow. ▫▫ **in·sem·i·na·tion** /–náyshən/ *n.* **in·sem·i·na·tor** *n.*

in·sen·sate /insénsayt/ *adj.* **1** without physical sensation; unconscious. **2** without sensibility; unfeeling. **3** stupid. ▫▫ **in·sen·sate·ly** *adv.*

in·sen·si·ble /insénsibəl/ *adj.* **1 a** without one's mental faculties; unconscious. **b** (of the extremities, etc.) numb; without feeling. **2** (usu. foll. by *of, to*) unaware; indifferent (*insensible of her needs*). **3** without emotion; callous. **4** too small or gradual to be perceived; inappreciable. ▫▫ **in·sen·si·bil·i·ty** /insénsibílitee/ *n.* **in·sen·si·bly** *adv.*

in·sen·si·tive /insénsitiv/ *adj.* (often foll. by *to*) **1** unfeeling; boorish; crass. **2** not sensitive to physical stimuli. ▫▫ **in·sen·si·tive·ly** *adv.* **in·sen·si·tive·ness** *n.* **in·sen·si·tiv·i·ty** /–tívitee/ *n.*

in·sen·ti·ent /insénshənt/ *adj.* not sentient; inanimate. ▫▫ **in·sen·ti·ence** /–shəns/ *n.*

in·sep·a·ra·ble /insépərəbəl/ *adj.* **1** (esp. of friends) unable or unwilling to be separated. **2** *Gram.* (of a prefix, or a verb in respect of it) unable to be used as a separate word, e.g., *dis-, mis-, un-*. ▫▫ **in·sep·a·ra·bly** *adv.*

in·sert *v. & n.* • *v.tr.* /insə́rt/ **1** (usu. foll. by *in, into, between*, etc.) place, fit, or thrust (a thing) into another. **2** (usu. foll. by *in, into*) introduce (a letter, word, article, advertisement, etc.) into a newspaper, etc. • *n.* /insərt/ something inserted, e.g., a loose page in a magazine, a piece of cloth in a garment, a motion-picture cut-in. ▫▫ **in·sert·a·ble** *adj.* **in·sert·er** *n.*

in·ser·tion /insə́rshən/ *n.* **1** the act or an instance of inserting. **2** an amendment, etc., inserted in writing or printing. **3** each appearance of an advertisement in a newspaper, etc. **4** an ornamental section of needlework inserted into plain material (*lace insertions*).

in-ser·vice /ínsərvis/ *adj.* (of training) intended for those actively engaged in the profession or activity concerned.

in·set *n. & v.* • *n.* /inset/ **1 a** an extra page or pages inserted in a folded sheet or in a book; an insert. **b** a small map, photograph, etc., inserted within the border of a larger one. **2** a piece let into a dress, etc. • *v.tr.* /insét/ (**insetting**; *past* and *past part.* **inset** or **insetted**) **1** put in as an inset. **2** decorate with an inset. ▫▫ **in·set·ter** *n.*

in·shore /insháwr/ *adv. & adj.* at sea but close to the shore.

in·side *n., adj., adv., & prep.* • *n.* /insíd/ **1 a** the inner side or surface of a thing. **b** the inner part; the interior. **2** (of a roadway, etc.) the side or lane nearer the center. **3** (usu. in *pl.*) *colloq.* **a** the stomach and bowels (*something wrong with my insides*). **b** the operative part of a machine, etc. **4** *colloq.* a position affording inside information (*knows someone on the inside*). • *adj.* /insīd/ **1** situated on or in, or derived from, the inside; (of information, etc.) available only to those on the inside. **2** *Soccer* nearer to the center of the field (*inside forward*). • *adv.* /insíd/ **1** on, in, or to the inside. **2** *sl.* in prison. • *prep.* /insíd/ **1** on the inner side of; within (*inside the house*). **2** in less than (*inside an hour*). ▫ **inside of** *colloq.* in less than (a week, etc.).

in·side out *adj.* with the inner surface turned outward. ▫ **know a thing inside out** know a thing thoroughly.

in·sid·er /insídər/ *n.* **1** a person who is within a society, organization, etc. **2** a person privy to a secret, esp. when using it to gain advantage.

---

in·sid·er trad·ing *n. Stock Exch.* the illegal practice of trading to one's own advantage through having access to confidential information.

in·side track *n.* **1** the track (as an oval racecourse) that is shorter, because of the curve. **2** a position of advantage.

in·sid·i·ous /insídeeəs/ *adj.* **1** proceeding or progressing inconspicuously but harmfully (*an insidious disease*). **2** treacherous; crafty. ▫▫ **in·sid·i·ous·ly** *adv.* **in·sid·i·ous·ness** *n.*

in·sight /ínsīt/ *n.* (usu. foll. by *into*) **1** the capacity of understanding hidden truths, etc., esp. of character or situations. **2** an instance of this. ▫▫ **in·sight·ful** *adj.* **in·sight·ful·ly** *adv.*

in·sig·ni·a /insígneeə/ *n.* (treated as *sing.* or *pl.* formerly with *sing.* **insigne**); usu. foll. by *of*) **1** badges (*wore his insignia of office*). **2** distinguishing marks.

▶**Insignia** is the plural of the Latin word *insigne*, and some traditionalists insist on *insigne* as the singular. *Insignia* and its plural, **insignias**, have long been standard, however.

in·sig·nif·i·cant /ínsigníffikənt/ *adj.* **1** unimportant; trifling. **2** (of a person) undistinguished. **3** meaningless. ▫▫ **in·sig·nif·i·cance** /–kəns/ *n.* **in·sig·nif·i·can·cy** *n.* **in·sig·nif·i·cant·ly** *adv.*

in·sin·cere /ínsinseér/ *adj.* not sincere; not candid. ▫▫ **in·sin·cere·ly** *adv.* **in·sin·cer·i·ty** /–séritee/ *n.* (*pl.* **-ties**).

in·sin·u·ate /insínyoo-ayt/ *v.tr.* **1** (often foll. by *that* + clause) convey indirectly or obliquely; hint (*insinuated that she was lying*). **2** (often *refl.*; usu. foll. by *into*) **a** introduce (oneself, a person, etc.) into favor, office, etc., by subtle manipulation. **b** introduce (a thing, an idea, oneself, etc.) subtly or deviously into a place (*insinuated himself into their inner circle*). ▫▫ **in·sin·u·a·tion** /–áyshən/ *n.* **in·sin·u·a·tive** *adj.* **in·sin·u·a·tor** *n.* **in·sin·u·a·to·ry** /–sínyooətáwree/ *adj.*

in·sip·id /insípid/ *adj.* **1** lacking vigor or interest; dull. **2** lacking flavor; tasteless. ▫▫ **in·sip·id·i·ty** /–píditee/ *n.* **in·sip·id·ly** *adv.* **in·sip·id·ness** *n.*

in·sist /insíst/ *v.tr.* (usu. foll. by *that* + clause; also *absol.*) maintain or demand positively and assertively (*insisted that he was innocent*). ▫ **insist on** demand or maintain (*I insist on being present*). ▫▫ **in·sist·er** *n.* **in·sist·ing·ly** *adv.*

in·sist·ent /insístənt/ *adj.* **1** (often foll. by *on*) insisting; demanding positively or continually (*is insistent on taking me with him*). **2** obtruding itself on the attention (*the insistent rattle of the window frame*). ▫▫ **in·sist·ence** /–təns/ *n.* **in·sist·en·cy** *n.* **in·sist·ent·ly** *adv.*

in si·tu /in seetoo, sī–/ *adv.* **1** in its place. **2** in its original place.

in·so·far as /ínsōfaár az/ *conj.* to the extent that.

in·sole /ínsōl/ *n.* **1** a removable sole worn in a boot or shoe for warmth, etc. **2** the fixed inner sole of a boot or shoe.

in·so·lent /ínsələnt/ *adj.* offensively contemptuous or arrogant; insulting. ▫▫ **in·so·lence** /–ləns/ *n.* **in·so·lent·ly** *adv.*

in·sol·u·ble /insólyəbəl/ *adj.* **1** incapable of being solved. **2** incapable of being dissolved. ▫▫ **in·sol·u·bil·i·ty** *n.* **in·sol·u·bil·ize** /–bilīz/ *v.tr.* **in·sol·u·ble·ness** *n.* **in·sol·u·bly** *adv.*

in·sol·vent /insólvənt/ *adj.* & *n.* • *adj.* **1** unable to pay one's debts. **2** relating to insolvency (*insolvent laws*). • *n.* a debtor. ▫▫ **in·sol·ven·cy** *n.*

in·som·ni·a /insómneeə/ *n.* habitual sleeplessness; inability to sleep. ▫▫ **in·som·ni·ac** /–neeak/ *n.* & *adj.*

in·sou·ci·ant /insóoseeənt, aNsóosyaáN/ *adj.* carefree; unconcerned. ▫▫ **in·sou·ci·ance** /–seeəns/ *n.* **in·sou·ci·ant·ly** *adv.*

in·spect /inspékt/ *v.tr.* **1** look closely at or into. **2** examine (a document, etc.) officially. ▫▫ **in·spec·tion** /–spékshən/ *n.*

in·spec·tor /inspéktər/ *n.* **1** a person who inspects. **2** an official employed to supervise a service, a machine, etc., and make reports. **3** a police officer usu. ranking just below a superintendent. ▫▫ **in·spec·tor·ate** /–tərеeət/ *n.* **in·spec·to·ri·al** /–táwreeəl/ *adj.* **in·spec·tor·ship** *n.*

in·spi·ra·tion /ínspiráyshən/ *n.* **1 a** a supposed creative force or influence on poets, artists, musicians, etc., stimulating the production of works of art. **b** a person, principle, faith, etc., stimulating artistic or moral fervor and creativity. **2** a sudden brilliant, creative, or timely idea. **3** a drawing in of breath; inhalation. ▫▫ **in·spi·ra·tion·al** *adj.* **in·spi·ra·tion·ism** *n.* **in·spi·ra·tion·ist** *n.*

in·spire /inspír/ *v.tr.* **1** stimulate or arouse (a person) to do or feel something, esp. to do something creative (*these mountains have inspired artists for many centuries*). **2 a** (usu. foll. by *with*) animate (a person) with a feeling. **b** (usu. foll. by *into*) instill (a feeling) into a person, etc. **c** (usu. foll. by *in*) create (a feeling) in a person. **3** prompt; give rise to (*the poem was inspired by the autumn*). **4** (as **inspired** *adj.*) **a** (of a work of art, etc.) as if prompted by or emanating from a supernatural source; characterized by inspiration (*an inspired speech*). **b** (of a guess) intuitive but accurate. ▫▫ **in·spir·a·to·ry** /–rətáwree/ *adj.* **in·spir·ed·ly** /–ridlee/ *adv.* **in·spir·er** *n.* **in·spir·ing** *adj.* **in·spir·ing·ly** *adv.*

inst. *abbr.* **1** instance. **2** institute. **3** institution. **4** instrument.

in·sta·bil·i·ty /ínstəbílitee/ *n.* (*pl.* **-ties**) **1** a lack of stability. **2** *Psychol.* unpredictability in behavior, etc. **3** an instance of instability.

in·stall /instáwl/ *v.tr.* (**installed, installing**) **1** place (equipment, machinery, etc.) in position ready for use. **2** place (a person) in an office or rank with ceremony (*installed in the office of attorney general*). **3** establish (oneself, a person, etc.) in a place, condition, etc. (*installed herself at the head of the table*). ▫▫ **in·stall·er** *n.*

in·stal·la·tion /ínstəláyshən/ *n.* **1 a** the act or an instance of installing. **b** the process or an instance of being installed. **2** a piece of apparatus, a machine, etc., installed or the place where it is installed.

in·stall·ment /instáwlmənt/ *n.* **1** a sum of money due as one of several usu. equal payments for something, spread over an agreed period of time. **2** any of several parts, esp. of a television or radio serial or a magazine story, published or shown in sequence at intervals.

in·stance /ínstəns/ *n.* & *v.* • *n.* **1** an example or illustration of (*just another instance of his lack of determination*). **2** a particular case (*that's not true in this instance*). **3** *Law* a legal suit. • *v.tr.* cite (a fact, case, etc.) as an instance.

instance Middle English: via Old French from Latin *instantia* 'presence, urgency', from *instare* 'be present, press upon', from *in-* 'upon' + *stare* 'to stand'. The original sense was 'urgency, urgent entreaty', surviving in *at the instance of.* In the late 16th cent. the word denoted a particular case cited to disprove a general assertion, derived from medieval Latin *instantia* 'example to the contrary' (translating Greek *enstasis* 'objection'); hence the meaning 'single occurrence.'

in·stant /ínstənt/ *adj.* & *n.* • *adj.* **1** occurring immediately (*gives an instant result*). **2 a** (of food, etc.) ready for immediate use, with little or no preparation. **b** prepared hastily and with little effort (*I have no instant solution*). **3** urgent; pressing. • *n.* **1** a precise moment of time, esp. the present (*come here this instant; told you* *the instant I heard*). **2** a short space of time (*was there in an instant; not an instant too soon*).

in·stan·ta·ne·ous /ìnstəntáyneeəs/ *adj.* occurring or done in an instant or instantly. ▫▫ **in·stan·ta·ne·ous·ly** *adv.*

in·stant·ly /ínstəntlee/ *adv.* immediately; at once.

in·stant re·play *n.* the immediate repetition of part of a videotaped sports event, often in slow motion.

in·stead /instéd/ *adv.* **1** (foll. by *of*) as a substitute or alternative to; in place of (*instead of this one; stayed instead of going*). **2** as an alternative (*took me instead*).

in·step /ínstep/ *n.* **1** the inner arch of the foot between the toes and the ankle. **2** the part of a shoe, etc., fitting over or under this.

in·sti·gate /ínstigayt/ *v.tr.* **1** bring about by incitement or persuasion; provoke (*who instigated the inquiry?*). **2** (usu. foll. by *to*) urge on; incite (a person, etc.) to esp. an evil act. ▫▫ **in·sti·ga·tion** /–gáyshən/ *n.* **in·sti·ga·tive** *adj.* **in·sti·ga·tor** *n.*

in·still /instíl/ *v.tr.* (esp. *Brit.* **instil**) (**instilled, instilling**) (often foll. by *into*) **1** introduce (a feeling, idea, etc.) into a person's mind, etc., gradually. **2** put (a liquid) into something in drops. ▫▫ **in·stil·la·tion** *n.* **in·still·er** *n.* **in·still·ment** *n.*

in·stinct *n.* & *adj.* •*n.* /ínstingkt/ **1 a** an innate, usu. fixed, pattern of behavior in most animals in response to certain stimuli. **b** a similar propensity in human beings to act without conscious intention; innate impulsion. **2** (usu. foll. by *for*) unconscious skill; intuition. •*predic.adj.* /instíngkt/ (foll. by *with*) imbued; filled (with life, beauty, force, etc.). ▫▫ **in·stinc·tu·al** /–stíngkchōōəl/ *adj.* **in·stinc·tu·al·ly** *adv.*

in·stinc·tive /instíngktiv/ *adj.* **1** relating to or prompted by instinct. **2** apparently unconscious or automatic (*an instinctive reaction*). ▫▫ **in·stinc·tive·ly** *adv.*

in·sti·tute /ínstitōōt, –tyōōt/ *n.* & *v.* •*n.* **1** a society or organization for the promotion of science, education, etc. **2** a building or buildings used by an institute. •*v.tr.* **1** establish; found. **2 a** initiate (an inquiry, etc.). **b** begin (proceedings) in a court. **3** (usu. foll. by *to, into*) appoint (a person) as a cleric in a church, etc.

in·sti·tu·tion /ínstitōōshən, –tyōō–/ *n.* **1** the act or an instance of instituting. **2 a** a society or organization founded esp. for charitable, religious, educational, or social purposes. **b** a building or buildings used by an institution. **3** an established law, practice, or custom. **4** *colloq.* (of a person, a custom, etc.) a familiar object. **5** the establishment of a cleric, etc., in a church.

in·sti·tu·tion·al /ínstitōōshənəl, –tyōō–/ *adj.* **1** of or like an institution. **2** typical of institutions, esp. in being regimented or unimaginative (*the food was dreadfully institutional*). **3** (of religion) expressed or organized through institutions (churches, etc.). ▫▫ **in·sti·tu·tion·al·ism** *n.* **in·sti·tu·tion·al·ly** *adv.*

in·sti·tu·tion·al·ize /ínstitōōshənəlīz, –tyōō–/ *v.tr.* **1** (as **institutionalized** *adj.*) (of a prisoner, a long-term patient, etc.) made apathetic and dependent after a long period in an institution. **2** place or keep (a person) in an institution. **3** convert into an institution; make institutional. ▫▫ **in·sti·tu·tion·al·i·za·tion** *n.*

in·struct /instrúkt/ *v.tr.* **1** (often foll. by *in*) teach (a person) a subject, etc. (*instructed her in French*). **2** (usu. foll. by *to* + infin.) direct; command (*instructed him to fill in the hole*). **3** (often foll. by *of*, or *that*, etc. + clause) inform (a person) of a fact, etc. **4** *Law* (of a judge) give information (esp. clarification of legal principles) to (a jury).

in·struc·tion /instrúkshən/ *n.* **1** (often in *pl.*) a direction; an order (*gave him his instructions*). **2** teaching; education (*took a course of instruction*). **3** *Law* (in *pl.*) directions issued to a jury, etc. **4** *Computing* a direction in a computer program defining and effecting an operation. ▫▫ **in·struc·tion·al** *adj.*

in·struc·tive /instrúktiv/ *adj.* tending to instruct; conveying a lesson; enlightening (*found the experience instructive*). ▫▫ **in·struc·tive·ly** *adv.* **in·struc·tive·ness** *n.*

in·struc·tor /instrúktər/ *n.* **1** a person who instructs; a teacher, demonstrator, etc. **2** a university teacher ranking below assistant professor. ▫▫ **in·struc·tor·ship** *n.*

in·stru·ment /ínstrəmənt/ *n.* & *v.* •*n.* **1** a tool or implement, esp. for delicate or scientific work. **2** (in full **musical instrument**) a device for producing musical sounds by vibration, wind, percussion, etc. **3 a** a thing used in performing an action (*the meeting was an instrument in his success*). **b** a person made use of (*is merely their instrument*). **4** a measuring device, esp. in an airplane, serving to determine its position in darkness, etc. **5** a formal, esp. legal, document. •*v.tr.* **1** arrange (music) for instruments. **2** equip with instruments (for measuring, recording, controlling, etc.).

in·stru·men·tal /ínstrəmént'l/ *adj.* & *n.* •*adj.* **1** (usu. foll. by *to, in*, or *in* + verbal noun) serving as an instrument or means (*was instrumental in finding the money*). **2** (of music) performed on instruments, without singing (cf. VOCAL). **3** of, or arising from, an instrument (*instrumental error*). **4** *Gram.* of or in the instrumental. •*n.* **1** a piece of music performed by instruments, not by the voice. **2** *Gram.* the case of nouns and pronouns (and words in grammatical agreement with them) indicating a means or instrument. ▫▫ **in·stru·men·tal·ist** *n.* **in·stru·men·tal·i·ty** /–mentálitee/ *n.* **in·stru·men·tal·ly** *adv.*

in·stru·men·ta·tion /ínstrəmentáyshən/ *n.* **1 a** the arrangement or composition of music for a particular group of musical instruments. **b** the instruments used in any one piece of music. **2 a** the design, provision, or use of instruments in industry, science, etc. **b** such instruments collectively.

in·stru·ment pan·el *n.* (also **in·stru·ment board**) a surface, esp. in a car or airplane, containing the dials, etc., of measuring devices.

in·sub·or·di·nate /ínsəbáwrd'nət/ *adj.* disobedient; rebellious. ▫▫ **in·sub·or·di·nate·ly** *adv.* **in·sub·or·di·na·tion** /–náyshən/ *n.*

in·sub·stan·tial /ínsəbstánshəl/ *adj.* **1** lacking solidity or substance. **2** not real. ▫▫ **in·sub·stan·ti·al·i·ty** /–sheeálitee/ *n.* **in·sub·stan·tial·ly** *adv.*

in·suf·fer·a·ble /insúfərəbəl/ *adj.* **1** intolerable. **2** unbearably arrogant or conceited, etc. ▫▫ **in·suf·fer·a·ble·ness** *n.* **in·suf·fer·a·bly** *adv.*

in·suf·fi·cient /ínsəfíshənt/ *adj.* not sufficient; inadequate. ▫▫ **in·suf·fi·cien·cy** *n.* **in·suf·fi·cient·ly** *adv.*

in·su·lar /ínsələr, ínsyə–/ *adj.* **1 a** of or like an island. **b** separated or remote, like an island. **2** ignorant of or indifferent to cultures, peoples, etc., outside one's own experience; narrow-minded. ▫▫ **in·su·lar·ism** *n.* **in·su·lar·i·ty** /–láritee/ *n.* **in·su·lar·ly** *adv.*

in·su·late /ínsəlayt, ínsyə–/ *v.tr.* **1** prevent the passage of electricity, heat, or sound from (a thing, room, etc.) by interposing nonconductors. **2** detach (a person or thing) from its surroundings; isolate. ▫▫ **in·su·la·tion** /–láyshən/ *n.*

in·su·lin /ínsəlin/ *n. Biochem.* a hormone produced in the pancreas by the islets of Langerhans, regulating the amount of glucose in the blood and the insufficiency of which causes diabetes.

in·sult *v.* & *n.* •*v.tr.* /insúlt/ **1** speak to or treat with scornful abuse or indignity. **2** offend the self-respect or modesty of. •*n.* /ínsult/ **1** an insulting remark or action. **2** *colloq.* something so worthless or contemptible as to be offensive. ▫▫ **in·sult·er** *n.* **in·sult·ing·ly** *adv.*

See page xii for the *Key to Pronunciation*.

insult mid-16th cent. (as a verb in the sense 'exult, act arrogantly'): from Latin *insultare* 'jump or trample on', from *in-* 'on' + *saltare*, from *salire* 'to leap'. The noun (in the early 17th cent. denoting an attack) is from French *insulte* or ecclesiastical Latin *insultus*. The main current senses date from the 17th cent., the medical use dating from the early 20th cent.

in·su·per·a·ble /insóopərəbəl/ *adj.* **1** (of a barrier) impossible to surmount. **2** (of a difficulty, etc.) impossible to overcome. ▫▫ **in·su·per·a·bil·i·ty** *n.* **in·su·per·a·bly** *adv.*

in·sup·port·a·ble /insəpáwrtəbəl/ *adj.* **1** unable to be endured. **2** unjustifiable. ▫▫ **in·sup·port·a·ble·ness** *n.* **in·sup·port·a·bly** *adv.*

in·sur·ance /inshóorəns/ *n.* **1** the act or an instance of insuring. **2 a** a sum paid for this; a premium. **b** a sum paid out as compensation for theft, damage, loss, etc. **3** = INSURANCE POLICY. **4** a measure taken to provide for a possible contingency (*take an umbrella as insurance*).

in·sur·ance pol·i·cy *n.* **1** a contract of insurance. **2** a document detailing such a policy and constituting a contract.

in·sure /inshóor/ *v.tr.* **1** (often foll. by *against*; also *absol.*) secure the contractual payment of a sum of money in the event of loss or damage to (property, life, a person, etc.) by regular payments or premiums (*insured the house for $100,000; we have insured against flood damage*). **2** (of the owner of a property, an insurance company, etc.) secure the payment of (a sum of money) in this way. **3** (usu. foll. by *against*) provide for (a possible contingency) (*insured themselves against the rain by taking umbrellas*). **4** = ENSURE. ▫▫ **in·sur·a·ble** *adj.* **in·sur·a·bil·i·ty** /–shóorəbílitee/ *n.*

▶**Insure** is standard for the sense 'protect against loss' (**assure** was long also used for this). For the nontechnical sense 'make sure,' **insure** and **ensure** are interchangeable: *My telephone call will ensure* (or *insure*) you introduction to the director, not a formal interview.

in·sur·er /inshóorər/ *n.* **1** a person or company offering insurance policies for premiums; an underwriter. **2** a person that insures.

in·sur·gent /insə́rjənt/ *adj. & n.* • *adj.* **1** rising in active revolt. **2** (of the sea, etc.) rushing in. • *n.* a rebel; a revolutionary. ▫▫ **in·sur·gence** /–jəns/ *n.* **in·sur·gen·cy** *n.* (*pl.* **-cies**).

in·sur·mount·a·ble /insərmówntəbəl/ *adj.* unable to be surmounted or overcome. ▫▫ **in·sur·mount·a·bly** *adv.*

in·sur·rec·tion /insərékshən/ *n.* a rising in open resistance to established authority; a rebellion. ▫▫ **in·sur·rec·tion·ar·y** *adj.* **in·sur·rec·tion·ist** *n.*

int. *abbr.* **1** interior. **2** internal. **3** international.

in·tact /intákt/ *adj.* **1** entire; unimpaired. **2** untouched. ▫▫ **in·tact·ness** *n.*

in·tagl·io /intályō, –taal–/ *n.* (*pl.* **-os**) **1** a gem with an incised design (cf. CAMEO). **2** an engraved design. **3** a carving, esp. incised, in hard material. **4** a process of printing from an engraved design.

in·take /íntayk/ *n.* **1 a** the action of taking in. **b** an instance of this. **2** a number or the amount taken in or received. **3** a place where water is taken into a channel or pipe from a river, or fuel or air enters an engine, etc.

in·te·ger /íntijər/ *n.* **1** a whole number. **2** a thing complete in itself.

in·te·gral /íntigrəl, intégrəl/ *adj. & n.* • *adj.* **1 a** of a whole or necessary to the completeness of a whole. **b** forming a whole (*integral design*). **c** whole; complete. **2** *Math.* **a** of or denoted by an integer. **b** involving only integers, esp. as coefficients of a function. • *n.* /íntigrəl/ *Math.* **1** a quantity of which a given function is the derivative, either containing an indeterminate additive constant (**indefinite integral**), or calculated as the difference between its values at specified limits (**definite integral**). **2** a function satisfying a given differential equation. ▫▫ **in·te·gral·i·ty** /–grálitee/ *n.* **in·te·gral·ly** *adv.*

in·te·gral cal·cu·lus *n.* mathematics concerned with finding integrals, their properties and application, etc. (cf. DIFFERENTIAL CALCULUS).

in·te·grate /íntigrayt/ *v.* **1** *tr.* **a** combine (parts) into a whole. **b** complete (an imperfect thing) by the addition of parts. **2** *tr. & intr.* bring or come into equal participation in or membership of society, a school, etc. **3** *tr.* desegregate, esp. racially (a school, etc.). **4** *tr. Math.* find the integral of. ▫▫ **in·te·gra·ble** /íntigrəbəl/ *adj.* **in·te·gra·bil·i·ty** *n.* **in·te·gra·tive** /íntigraytiv/ *adj.* **in·te·gra·tor** *n.*

in·te·gra·ted cir·cuit *n. Electronics* a small chip, etc., of material replacing several separate components in a conventional electrical circuit.

in·te·gra·tion /intigráyshən/ *n.* **1** the act or an instance of integrating. **2** the intermixing of persons previously segregated. ▫▫ **in·te·gra·tion·ist** *n.*

in·teg·ri·ty /intégritee/ *n.* **1** moral uprightness; honesty. **2** wholeness; soundness.

in·teg·u·ment /intégyəmənt/ *n.* a natural outer covering, as a skin, husk, rind, etc. ▫▫ **in·teg·u·men·tal** /–mént'l/ *adj.* **in·teg·u·men·ta·ry** /–méntəree/ *adj.*

in·tel·lect /íntilekt/ *n.* **1 a** the faculty of reasoning, knowing, and thinking, as distinct from feeling. **b** the understanding or mental powers (of a particular person, etc.) (*his intellect is not great*). **2** a clever or knowledgeable person.

in·tel·lec·tu·al /intilékchōōəl/ *adj. & n.* • *adj.* **1** of or appealing to the intellect. **2** possessing a high level of understanding or intelligence; cultured. **3** requiring, or given to the exercise of, the intellect. • *n.* a person possessing a highly developed intellect. ▫▫ **in·tel·lec·tu·al·i·ty** /–chōōálitee/ *n.* **in·tel·lec·tu·al·ize** *v.tr. & intr.* **in·tel·lec·tu·al·ly** *adv.*

in·tel·lec·tu·al·ism /intilékchōōəlizəm/ *n.* **1** the exercise, esp. when excessive, of the intellect at the expense of the emotions. **2** *Philos.* the theory that knowledge is wholly or mainly derived from pure reason. ▫▫ **in·tel·lec·tu·al·ist** *n.*

in·tel·li·gence /intélijəns/ *n.* **1 a** the intellect; the understanding. **b** (of a person or an animal) quickness of understanding; wisdom. **2 a** the collection of information, esp. of military or political value. **b** people employed in this. **c** information; news. **3** an intelligent or rational being.

in·tel·li·gence quo·tient *n.* a number denoting the ratio of a person's intelligence to the normal or average. ¶ Abbr.: **IQ**.

in·tel·li·gent /intélijənt/ *adj.* **1** having or showing intelligence, esp. of a high level. **2** quick of mind; clever. **3 a** (of a device or machine) able to vary its behavior in response to varying situations and requirements and past experience. **b** (esp. of a computer terminal) having its own data-processing capability; incorporating a microprocessor (opp. DUMB). ▫▫ **in·tel·li·gent·ly** *adv.*

in·tel·li·gent·si·a /intélijéntseeə/ *n.* **1** the class of intellectuals regarded as possessing culture and political initiative. **2** people doing intellectual work; intellectuals.

in·tel·li·gi·ble /intélijibəl/ *adj.* able to be understood; comprehensible. ▫▫ **in·tel·li·gi·bil·i·ty** *n.* **in·tel·li·gi·bly** *adv.*

in·tem·per·ate /intémpərət/ *adj.* **1** (of a person, conduct, or speech) immoderate; unbridled; violent (*used intemperate language*). **2 a** given to excessive indulgence in alcohol. **b** excessively indulgent in one's appetites. ▫▫ **in·tem·per·ance** /–rəns/ *n.* **in·tem·per·ate·ly** *adv.* **in·tem·per·ate·ness** *n.*

in·tend /inténd/ *v.tr.* **1** have as one's purpose; propose (*we intend to go; we intend that it shall be done*). **2** (usu. foll. by *for, as*) design or destine (a person or a thing) (*I intend for him to go; I intend it as a warning*). **3** mean (*what does he intend by that?*). **4** (in *passive*; foll. by *for*) be meant for a person to have or use, etc. (*they are intended for the children*).

in·tend·ed /inténdid/ *adj.* & *n.* • *adj.* **1** done on purpose; intentional. **2** designed; meant. • *n. colloq.* the person one intends to marry; one's fiancé or fiancée (*is this your intended?*). ▫▫ **in·tend·ed·ly** *adv.*

in·tense /inténs/ *adj.* (**intenser, intensest**) **1** (of a quality, etc.) existing in a high degree; violent; forceful (*intense cold*). **2** (of a person) feeling, or apt to feel, strong emotion (*very intense about her music*). **3** (of a feeling or action, etc.) extreme (*intense joy; intense thought*). ▫▫ **in·tense·ly** *adv.* **in·tense·ness** *n.*

▶**Intense** is sometimes wrongly used instead of **intensive** to describe a course of study that covers a large amount of material in a short space of time.

in·ten·si·fi·er /inténsifīər/ *n.* **1** a person or thing that intensifies. **2** *Gram.* = INTENSIVE *n.*

in·ten·si·fy /inténsifī/ *v.* (**-fies, -fied**) *tr.* & *intr.* make or become more intense. ▫▫ **in·ten·si·fi·ca·tion** *n.*

in·ten·si·ty /inténsitee/ *n.* (*pl.* **-ties**) **1** the quality or an instance of being intense. **2** esp. *Physics* the measurable amount of some quality, e.g., force, brightness, a magnetic field, etc.

in·ten·sive /inténsiv/ *adj.* & *n.* • *adj.* **1** thorough; vigorous; directed to a single point, area, or subject (*intensive study; intensive bombardment*). **2** of or relating to intensity as opposed to extent; producing intensity. **3** serving to increase production in relation to costs (*intensive farming methods*). **4** (usu. in *comb.*) *Econ.* making much use of (*a labor-intensive industry*). **5** *Gram.* (of an adjective, adverb, etc.) expressing intensity; giving force, as *really* in *my feet are really cold.* • *n. Gram.* an intensive adjective, adverb, etc. ▫▫ **in·ten·sive·ly** *adv.* **in·ten·sive·ness** *n.*

in·ten·sive care *n.* medical treatment with constant monitoring, etc., of a dangerously ill patient (also (with hyphen) *attrib.*: *intensive-care unit* see ICU).

in·tent /intént/ *n.* & *adj.* • *n.* (usu. without article) intention; a purpose (*with intent to defraud; my intent to reach the top; with evil intent*). • *adj.* **1** (usu. foll. by *on*) **a** resolved; bent; determined (*was intent on succeeding*). **b** attentively occupied (*intent on his books*). **2** (esp. of a look) earnest; eager; meaningful. ▫ **to** (or for) all intents and purposes practically; virtually. ▫▫ **in·tent·ly** *adv.* **in·tent·ness** *n.*

in·ten·tion /inténshən/ *n.* **1** (often foll. by *to* + infin., or *of* + verbal noun) a thing intended; an aim or purpose (*it was not her intention to interfere; have no intention of staying*). **2** the act of intending (*done without intention*). **3** *colloq.* (usu. in *pl.*) a person's, esp. a man's, designs in respect to marriage (*are his intentions strictly honorable?*). ▫▫ **in·ten·tioned** *adj.* (usu. in *comb.*).

in·ten·tion·al /inténshənəl/ *adj.* done on purpose. ▫▫ **in·ten·tion·al·i·ty** /–álitee/ *n.* **in·ten·tion·al·ly** *adv.*

in·ter /intə́r/ *v.tr.* (**interred, interring**) deposit (a corpse, etc.) in the earth, a tomb, etc.; bury.

inter- /íntər/ *comb. form* **1** between; among (*intercontinental*). **2** mutually; reciprocally (*interbreed*).

in·ter·act /íntərákt/ *v.intr.* act reciprocally; act on each other. ▫▫ **in·ter·ac·tant** *adj.* & *n.* **in·ter·ac·tion** *n.*

in·ter·ac·tive /íntəráktiv/ *adj.* **1** reciprocally active; acting upon or influencing each other. **2** (of a computer or other electronic device) allowing a two-way flow of information between it and a user, responding to the user's input. ▫▫ **in·ter·ac·tive·ly** *adv.*

in·ter a·li·a /íntər áyleeə, áaleeə/ *adv.* among other things.

in·ter·breed /íntərbréed/ *v.* (*past* and *past part.* **-bred** /–bréd/) **1** *intr.* & *tr.* breed or cause to breed with members of a different race or species to produce a hybrid. **2** *tr.* breed within one family, etc., in order to produce desired characteristics.

in·ter·cede /íntərséed/ *v.intr.* (usu. foll. by *with*) interpose or intervene on behalf of another; plead (*they interceded with the governor for clemency*). ▫▫ **in·ter·ced·er** *n.*

in·ter·cept /íntərsépt/ *v.tr.* **1** seize, catch, or stop (a person, message, vehicle, ball, etc.) going from one place to another. **2** (usu. foll. by *from*) cut off (light, etc.). **3** check or stop (motion, etc.). ▫▫ **in·ter·cep·tion** /–sépshən/ *n.* **in·ter·cep·tive** /–séptiv/ *adj.* **in·ter·cep·tor** *n.*

in·ter·ces·sion /íntərséshən/ *n.* **1** the act of interceding, esp. by prayer. **2** an instance of this. **3** a prayer. ▫▫ **in·ter·ces·sion·al** *adj.* **in·ter·ces·sor** *n.* **in·ter·ces·so·ri·al** /–sesáwreeəl/ *adj.* **in·ter·ces·so·ry** *adj.*

in·ter·change *v.* & *n.* • *v.tr.* /íntərcháynj/ **1** (of two people) exchange (things) with each other. **2** put each of (two things) in the other's place; alternate. • *n.* /íntərchaynj/ **1** (often foll. by *of*) a reciprocal exchange between two people, etc. **2** alternation (*the interchange of woods and fields*). **3** a road junction designed so that traffic streams do not intersect. ▫▫ **in·ter·change·a·ble** *adj.* **in·ter·change·a·bil·i·ty** /–cháynjəbílitee/ *n.* **in·ter·change·a·ble·ness** *n.* **in·ter·change·a·bly** *adv.*

in·ter·cit·y /íntərsítee/ *adj.* existing or traveling between cities.

in·ter·com /íntərkom/ *n. colloq.* a system of intercommunication by radio or telephone between or within offices, aircraft, etc.

in·ter·com·mu·ni·cate /íntərkəmyóonikayt/ *v.intr.* **1** communicate reciprocally. **2** (of rooms, etc.) have free passage into each other; have a connecting door. ▫▫ **in·ter·com·mu·ni·ca·tion** /–káyshən/ *n.* **in·ter·com·mu·ni·ca·tive** /–kaytiv, –kətiv/ *adj.*

in·ter·con·nect /íntərkənékt/ *v.tr.* & *intr.* connect with each other. ▫▫ **in·ter·con·nec·tion** /–nékshən/ *n.*

in·ter·con·ti·nen·tal /íntərkóntinént'l/ *adj.* connecting or traveling between continents. ▫▫ **in·ter·con·ti·nen·tal·ly** *adv.*

in·ter·course /íntərkawrs/ *n.* **1** communication or dealings between individuals, nations, etc. **2** = SEXUAL INTERCOURSE.

---

intercourse late Middle English (denoting communication or dealings): from Old French *entrecours* 'exchange, commerce', from Latin *intercursus*, from *intercurrere* 'intervene', from *inter-* 'between' + *currere* 'run'. The specifically sexual use arose in the late 18th cent.

---

in·ter·de·nom·i·na·tion·al /íntərdinóminàyshənəl/ *adj.* concerning more than one (religious) denomination. ▫▫ **in·ter·de·nom·i·na·tion·al·ly** *adv.*

in·ter·de·part·men·tal /íntərdeépaartmént'l/ *adj.* concerning more than one department. ▫▫ **in·ter·de·part·men·tal·ly** *adv.*

in·ter·de·pend /íntərdipénd/ *v.intr.* depend on each other. ▫▫ **in·ter·de·pend·ence** *n.* **in·ter·de·pend·en·cy** *n.* **in·ter·de·pend·ent** *adj.*

in·ter·dict *n.* & *v.* • *n.* /íntərdikt/ **1** an authoritative prohibition. **2** *RC Ch.* decree debarring a person, or esp. a place, from ecclesiastical functions and privileges. • *v.tr.* /íntərdíkt/ **1** prohibit (an action). **2** forbid the use of. **3** (usu. foll. by *from* + verbal noun) restrain (a person). **4** (usu. foll. by *to*) forbid (a thing) to a person. ▫▫ **in·ter·dic·tion** /–díkshən/ *n.* **in·ter·dic·to·ry** /–díktəree/ *adj.*

interdict Middle English *entredite* (in the ecclesiastical sense), from Old French *entredit*, from Latin *interdictum*, past participle of *interdicere* 'interpose, forbid by decree', from *inter-* 'between' + *dicere* 'say'. The spelling change in the 16th cent. was due to association with the Latin form.

in·ter·dis·ci·pli·nar·y /intərdísiplinéree/ *adj.* of or between more than one branch of learning.

in·ter·est /íntərist, –trist/ *n.* & *v.* • *n.* **1 a** a feeling of curiosity or concern (*have no interest in mathematics*). **b** a quality exciting curiosity or holding the attention (*this magazine lacks interest*). **c** the power of an issue, action, etc., to hold the attention; noteworthiness; importance (*findings of no particular interest*). **2** a subject, hobby, etc., in which one is concerned (*his interests are gardening and sports*). **3** advantage or profit, esp. when financial (*it is in your interest to go; look after your own interests*). **4** money paid for the use of money lent, or for not requiring the repayment of a debt. **5** (usu. foll. by *in*) **a** a financial stake (in an undertaking, etc.). **b** a legal concern, title, or right (in property). **6 a** a party or group having a common interest (*the mining interest*). **b** a principle in which a party or group is concerned. **7** the selfish pursuit of one's own welfare; self-interest. • *v.tr.* **1** excite the curiosity or attention of (*your story interests me greatly*). **2** (usu. foll. by *in*) cause (a person) to take a personal interest or share (*can I interest you in a weekend cruise?*). **3** (as **interested** *adj.*) having a private interest; not impartial or disinterested (*an interested party*). □ **in the interest** (or **interests**) **of** as something that is advantageous to. **lose interest** become bored or boring. □□ **in·ter·est·ed·ly** *adv.* **in·ter·est·ed·ness** *n.*

in·ter·est·ing /intristing, –təresting/ *adj.* causing curiosity; holding the attention. □□ **in·ter·est·ing·ly** *adv.* **in·ter·est·ing·ness** *n.*

in·ter·face /íntərfays/ *n.* & *v.* • *n.* **1** esp. *Physics* a surface forming a common boundary between two regions. **2** a point where interaction occurs between two systems, processes, subjects, etc. (*the interface between psychology and education*). **3** esp. *Computing* **a** an apparatus for connecting two pieces of equipment so that they can be operated jointly. **b** a means by which a user interacts with a program or utilizes an application. • *v.tr.* & *intr.* (often foll. by *with*) connect with (another piece of equipment, etc.) by an interface.

in·ter·fere /intərféer/ *v.intr.* **1** (usu. foll. by *with*) **a** (of a person) meddle; obstruct a process, etc. **b** (of a thing) be a hindrance; get in the way. **2** (usu. foll. by *in*) take part or intervene, esp. without invitation or necessity. **3** *Sports* to illegally obstruct an opposing player according to game rules. **4** *Physics* (of light or other waves) combine so as to cause interference. □□ **in·ter·fer·er** *n.* **in·ter·fer·ing** *adj.* **in·ter·fer·ing·ly** *adv.*

in·ter·fer·ence /intərféerəns/ *n.* **1** (usu. foll. by *with*) **a** the act of interfering. **b** an instance of this. **2** the fading or disturbance of received radio signals by the interference of waves from different sources, or esp. by atmospherics or unwanted signals. **3** *Physics* the combination of two or more wave motions to form a resultant wave in which the displacement is reinforced or canceled. **4** *Football* illegally interfering with a receiver's ability to catch a passed or kicked ball. □□ **in·ter·fe·ren·tial** /–fərénshəl/ *adj.*

in·ter·fer·on /intərféeron/ *n. Biochem.* any of various proteins that can inhibit the development of a virus in a cell, etc.

in·ter·ga·lac·tic /intərgəláktik/ *adj.* of or situated between two or more galaxies. □□ **in·ter·ga·lac·ti·cal·ly** *adv.*

in·ter·gov·ern·men·tal /intərgúvərnmént'l/ *adj.* concerning or conducted between two or more governments. □□ **in·ter·gov·ern·men·tal·ly** *adv.*

in·ter·im /íntərim/ *n.* & *adj.* • *n.* the intervening time (*in the interim he had died*). • *adj.* intervening; provisional; temporary.

in·te·ri·or /intéereeər/ *adj.* & *n.* • *adj.* **1** inner (opp. EXTERIOR). **2** remote from the coast or frontier; inland. **3** internal; domestic (opp. FOREIGN). **4** (usu. foll. by *to*) situated farther in or within. **5** existing in the mind or soul; inward. **6** drawn, photographed, etc., within a building. **7** coming from inside. • *n.* **1** the interior part; the inside. **2** the interior part of a country or region. **3 a** the internal affairs of a country. **b** a department dealing with these (*Secretary of the Interior*). **4** a representation of the inside of a building or a room (*Dutch interior*). **5** the inner nature; the soul. □□ **in·te·ri·or·ize** *v.tr.* **in·te·ri·or·ly** *adv.*

interj. *abbr.* interjection.

in·ter·ject /intərjékt/ *v.tr.* **1** utter (words) abruptly or parenthetically. **2** interrupt with (words, etc.). □□ **in·ter·jec·to·ry** *adj.*

in·ter·jec·tion /intərjékshən/ *n.* an exclamation, esp. as a part of speech (e.g., *ah!, dear me!*). □□ **in·ter·jec·tion·al** *adj.*

in·ter·lace /intərláys/ *v.* **1** *tr.* bind intricately together; interweave. **2** *tr.* mingle; intersperse. **3** *intr.* cross each other intricately. □□ **in·ter·lace·ment** *n.*

in·ter·lard /intərlaárd/ *v.tr.* (usu. foll. by *with*) mix (writing or speech) with unusual words or phrases.

in·ter·leave /intərléev/ *v.tr.* insert (usu. blank) leaves between the leaves of (a book, etc.).

in·ter·li·brar·y /intərlíbreree/ *adj.* between libraries (esp. *interlibrary loan*).

in·ter·line /intərlín/ *v.tr.* put an extra lining between the ordinary lining and the fabric of (a garment).

in·ter·lock /intərlók/ *v., adj., & n.* • *v.* **1** *intr.* engage with each other by overlapping or by the fitting together of projections and recesses. **2** *tr.* (usu. in *passive*) lock or clasp within each other. *adj.* (of a fabric) knitted with closely interlocking stitches. *n.* a device or mechanism for connecting or coordinating the function of different components. □□ **in·ter·lock·er** *n.*

in·ter·loc·u·tor /intərlókyətər/ *n.* a person who takes part in a dialogue or conversation. □□ **in·ter·lo·cu·tion** /–ləkyóoshən/ *n.*

in·ter·loc·u·to·ry /intərlókyətawree/ *adj.* of dialogue or conversation.

in·ter·lop·er /intərlópər/ *n.* **1** an intruder. **2** a person who interferes in others' affairs, esp. for profit. □□ **in·ter·lope** *v.intr.*

in·ter·lude /intərlood/ *n.* **1 a** a pause between the acts of a play. **b** something performed or done during this pause. **2 a** an intervening time, space, or event that contrasts with what goes before or after. **b** a temporary amusement or entertaining episode. **3** a piece of music played between other pieces, the verses of a hymn, etc.

in·ter·mar·riage /intərmárij/ *n.* **1** marriage between people of different races, castes, families, etc. **2** (loosely) marriage between near relations.

in·ter·mar·ry /intərmáree/ *v.intr.* (**-ries, -ried**) (foll. by *with*) (of races, castes, families, etc.) become connected by marriage.

in·ter·me·di·ar·y /intərméedee-eree/ *n.* & *adj.* • *n.* (*pl.* **-ies**) an intermediate person or thing, esp. a mediator. • *adj.* acting as mediator; intermediate.

in·ter·me·di·ate *adj., n., & v.* • *adj.* /intərméedeeət/ coming between two things in time, place, order, character, etc. • *n.* /intərméedeeət/ **1** an intermediate thing. **2** a chemical compound formed by one reaction and then used in another, esp. during synthesis. • *v.intr.* /intərméedeeáyt/ (foll. by *between*) act as intermediary; mediate. □□ **in·ter·me·di·a·cy** /–deeəsee/ *n.* **in·ter·me·di·ate·ly** *adv.* **in·ter·me·di·ate·ness** *n.* **in·ter·me·di·a·tion** /–deeáyshən/ *n.* **in·ter·me·di·a·tor** /–deeaytər/ *n.*

in·ter·ment /intə́rmənt/ *n.* the burial of a corpse, esp. with ceremony.

▶**Interment,** which means 'burial,' should not be confused with *internment,* which means 'imprisonment.'

in·ter·mez·zo /intərmétsō/ *n.* (*pl.* **intermezzi** /–see/ or **-zos**) **1 a** a short connecting instrumental movement in an opera or other musical work. **b** a similar piece performed independently. **c** a short piece for a solo instrument. **2** a short, light dramatic or other performance inserted between the acts of a play.

in·ter·mi·na·ble /intə́rminəbəl/ *adj.* **1** endless. **2** tediously long or habitual. **3** with no prospect of an end. □□ **in·ter·mi·na·ble·ness** *n.* **in·ter·mi·na·bly** *adv.*

in·ter·min·gle /intərmínggəl/ *v.tr.* & *intr.* (often foll. by *with*) mix together; mingle.

in·ter·mis·sion /intərmíshən/ *n.* **1** a pause or cessation. **2** an interval between parts of a play, motion picture, concert, etc. **3** a period of inactivity.

in·ter·mit·tent /íntərmít'nt/ *adj.* occurring at intervals; not continuous or steady. □□ **in·ter·mit·tence** /–mít'ns/ *n.* **in·ter·mit·ten·cy** *n.* **in·ter·mit·tent·ly** *adv.*

in·tern *n.* & *v.* • *n.* /íntərn/ (also **in·terne**) a recent graduate of medical school who works in a hospital as an assistant physician or surgeon. • *v.* **1** *tr.* /intə́rn/ confine; oblige (a prisoner, alien, etc.) to reside within prescribed limits. **2** *intr.* /íntərn/ serve as an intern. □□ **in·tern·ment** /–tə́rn–/ *n.* **in·tern·ship** /íntərn–/ *n.*

▶See note at INTERMENT.

in·ter·nal /intə́rnəl/ *adj.* & *n.* • *adj.* **1** of or situated in the inside or invisible part. **2** relating or applied to the inside of the body (*internal injuries*). **3** of a nation's domestic affairs. **4** (of a student) attending a university, etc., as well as taking its examinations. **5** used or applying within an organization. **6 a** of the inner nature of a thing; intrinsic. **b** of the mind or soul. • *n.* (in *pl.*) intrinsic qualities. □□ **in·ter·nal·i·ty** /–nálitee/ *n.* **in·ter·nal·ize** *v.tr.* **in·ter·nal·i·za·tion** *n.* **in·ter·nal·ly** *adv.*

in·ter·nal com·bus·tion en·gine *n.* an engine with its motive power generated by the explosion of gases or vapor with air in a cylinder.

in·ter·nal med·i·cine *n.* a branch of medicine specializing in the diagnosis and nonsurgical treatment of diseases.

internat. *abbr.* international.

in·ter·na·tion·al /íntərnáshənəl/ *adj.* & *n.* • *adj.* **1** existing, involving, or carried on between two or more nations. **2** agreed on or used by all or many nations (*international date line; international driver's license*). • *n.* **1 a** a contest, esp. in sport, between teams representing different countries. **b** a member of such a team. **2 a** (**International**) any of four associations founded (1864–1936) to promote socialist or communist action. **b** a member of any of these. □□ **in·ter·na·tion·al·i·ty** /–nálitee/ *n.* **in·ter·na·tion·al·ly** *adv.*

in·ter·na·tion·al date line *n.* (also **International Date Line**) see DATELINE 1.

in·ter·na·tion·al·ism /íntərnáshənəlizəm/ *n.* **1** the advocacy of a community of interests among nations. **2** (**Internationalism**) the principles of any of the Internationals. □□ **in·ter·na·tion·al·ist** *n.*

in·ter·na·tion·al sys·tem of u·nits *n.* a system of physical units based on the meter, kilogram, second, ampere, kelvin, candela, and mole, with prefixes to indicate multiplication or division by a power of ten.

in·ter·ne·cine /intərnéeseen, –néseen/ *adj.* **1** mutually destructive. **2** of or relating to conflict within a group or organization

In·ter·net /íntərnét/ *n.* a communications network enabling the linking of computers worldwide for data interchange.

in·ter·nun·cial /intərnúnshəl/ *adj.* (of nerves) communicating between different parts of the system.

in·ter·o·ce·an·ic /íntərósheeánik/ *adj.* between or connecting two oceans.

in·ter·per·son·al /intərpə́rsənəl/ *adj.* (of relations) occurring between persons, esp. reciprocally. □□ **in·ter·per·son·al·ly** *adv.*

in·ter·plan·e·tar·y /intərplániteree/ *adj.* **1** between planets. **2** relating to travel between planets.

in·ter·play /íntərplay/ *n.* **1** reciprocal action. **2** the operation of two things on each other.

In·ter·pol /íntərpōl/ *n.* International Criminal Police Organization.

in·ter·po·late /intə́rpəlayt/ *v.tr.* **1 a** insert (words) in a book, etc., esp. to give false impressions as to its date, etc. **b** make such insertions in (a book, etc.). **2** interject (a remark) in a conversation. **3** estimate (values) from known ones in the same range. □□ **in·ter·po·la·tion** /–láyshən/ *n.* **in·ter·po·la·tive** /–lətiv/ *adj.* **in·ter·po·la·tor** *n.*

in·ter·pose /intərpṓz/ *v.* **1** *tr.* (often foll. by *between*) place or insert (a thing) between others. **2** *tr.* say (words) as an interruption. **3** *tr.* exercise or advance (a veto or objection) so as to interfere. **4** *intr.* (foll. by *between*) intervene (between parties). □□ **in·ter·po·si·tion** *n.*

in·ter·pret /intə́rprit/ *v.* (**interpreted, interpreting**) **1** *tr.* explain the meaning of (foreign or abstruse words, a dream, etc.). **2** *tr.* make out or bring out the meaning of (creative work). **3** *intr.* act as an interpreter, esp. of foreign languages. **4** *tr.* explain or understand (behavior, etc.) in a specified manner (*interpreted his gesture as mocking*). □□ **in·ter·pret·a·ble** *adj.* **in·ter·pret·a·bil·i·ty** *n.* **in·ter·pre·ta·tion** *n.* **in·ter·pre·ta·tion·al** *adj.* **in·ter·pre·ta·tive** /–táytiv/ *adj.* **in·ter·pre·tive** *adj.* **in·ter·pre·tive·ly** *adv.*

in·ter·pret·er /intə́rpritər/ *n.* a person who interprets, esp. one who translates speech orally.

in·ter·ra·cial /intəráyshəl/ *adj.* existing or occurring between or affecting different races. □□ **in·ter·ra·cial·ly** *adv.*

in·ter·reg·num /intərégnəm/ *n.* (*pl.* **interregnums** or **interregna** /–nə/) **1** an interval when the normal government is suspended, esp. between successive reigns or regimes. **2** an interval or pause.

in·ter·re·late /intəriláyt/ *v.tr.* relate (two or more things) to each other. □□ **in·ter·re·la·tion** /–láyshən/ *n.* **in·ter·re·la·tion·ship** *n.*

in·ter·ro·gate /intérəgayt/ *v.tr.* ask questions of (a person) esp. closely, thoroughly, or formally. □□ **in·ter·ro·ga·tor** *n.*

in·ter·ro·ga·tion /intérəgáyshən/ *n.* **1** the act or an instance of interrogating; the process of being interrogated. **2** a question or inquiry. □□ **in·ter·ro·ga·tion·al** *adj.*

in·ter·rog·a·tive /intərógətiv/ *adj.* & *n.* • *adj.* **1 a** of or like a question; used in questions. **b** *Gram.* (of an adjective or pronoun) asking a question (e.g., *who?, which?*). **2** having the form or force of a question. **3** suggesting inquiry (*an interrogative tone*). • *n.* an interrogative word (e.g., *what?, why?*). □□ **in·ter·rog·a·tive·ly** *adv.*

in·ter·rog·a·to·ry /intərógətáwree/ *adj.* & *n.* • *adj.* questioning; of or suggesting inquiry (*an interrogatory eyebrow*). • *n.* (*pl.* **-ries**) a formal set of questions, esp. *Law* one formally put to an accused person, etc.

in·ter·rupt /intərúpt/ *v.tr.* **1** act so as to break the continuous progress of (an action, speech, a person speaking, etc.). **2** obstruct (a person's view, etc.). **3** break or suspend the continuity of. ▫▫ **in·ter·rupt·i·ble** *adj.* **in·ter·rup·tion** /–rúpshən/ *n.* **in·ter·rup·tive** *adj.* **in·ter·rup·to·ry** *adj.*

in·ter·sect /intərsékt/ *v.* **1** *tr.* divide (a thing) by passing or lying across it. **2** *intr.* (of lines, roads, etc.) cross or cut each other.

in·ter·sec·tion /íntərsékshən/ *n.* **1** the act of intersecting. **2** a place where two roads intersect. **3** a point or line common to lines or planes that intersect. ▫▫ **in·ter·sec·tion·al** *adj.*

in·ter·sperse /intərspə́rs/ *v.tr.* **1** (often foll. by *between, among*) scatter; place here and there. **2** (foll. by *with*) diversify (a thing or things with others so scattered). ▫▫ **in·ter·sper·sion** /–pérzhən/ *n.*

in·ter·state *adj.* & *n.* • *adj.* /intərstáyt/ existing or carried on between states, esp. of the US. • *n.* /íntərstayt/ a limited access highway that is part of the US Interstate Highway System.

in·ter·stel·lar /intərstélər/ *adj.* occurring or situated between stars.

in·ter·stice /intə́rstis/ *n.* **1** an intervening space. **2** a chink or crevice.

in·ter·sti·tial /intərstíshəl/ *adj.* of, forming, or occupying interstices. ▫▫ **in·ter·sti·tial·ly** *adv.*

in·ter·twine /intərtwín/ *v.* **1** *tr.* (often foll. by *with*) entwine (together). **2** *intr.* become entwined. ▫▫ **in·ter·twine·ment** *n.*

in·ter·val /íntərvəl/ *n.* **1** an intervening time or space. **2** *Brit.* a pause or break, esp. between the parts of a theatrical or musical performance. **3** the difference in pitch between two sounds. **4** the distance between persons or things in respect of qualities. ▫ **at intervals** here and there; now and then. ▫▫ **in·ter·val·lic** /–válik/ *adj.*

in·ter·vene /intərvéen/ *v.intr.* (often foll. by *between, in*) **1** occur in time between events. **2** interfere; come between so as to prevent or modify the result or course of events. **3** be situated between things. **4** come in as an extraneous factor or thing. ▫▫ **in·ter·ven·er** *n.* **in·ter·ven·ient** *adj.* **in·ter·ve·nor** *n.*

in·ter·ven·tion /intərvénshən/ *n.* **1** the act or an instance of intervening. **2** interference, esp. by a state in another's affairs. **3** mediation.

in·ter·ven·tion·ist /íntərvénshənist/ *n.* a person who favors intervention. ▫▫ **in·ter·ven·tion·ism** *n.*

in·ter·view /íntərvyoo/ *n.* & *v.* • *n.* **1** an oral examination of an applicant for employment, a college place, etc. **2** a conversation between a reporter, etc., and a person of public interest, used as a basis of a broadcast or publication. **3** a meeting of persons face to face, esp. for consultation. • *v.tr.* **1** hold an interview with. **2** question to discover the opinions or experience of (a person). ▫▫ **in·ter·view·ee** /–vyoo-ée/ *n.* **in·ter·view·er** *n.*

in·ter·weave /intərwéev/ *v.tr.* (*past* **-wove** /–wṓv/; *past part.* **-woven** /–wṓvən/) **1** (often foll. by *with*) weave together. **2** blend intimately.

in·tes·tate /intéstayt, –tət/ *adj.* & *n.* • *adj.* (of a person) not having made a will before death. • *n.* a person who has died intestate. ▫▫ **in·tes·ta·cy** /–téstəsee/ *n.*

in·tes·tine /intéstin/ *n.* (in *sing.* or *pl.*) the lower part of the alimentary canal from the end of the stomach to the anus. ▫▫ **in·tes·ti·nal** *adj.*

in·ti·ma·cy /íntiməsee/ *n.* (*pl.* **-cies**) **1** the state of being intimate. **2** an intimate act, esp. sexual intercourse. **3** an intimate remark; an endearment.

in·ti·mate[1] /íntimət/ *adj.* & *n.* • *adj.* **1** closely acquainted; familiar; close (*an intimate friend*; *an intimate relationship*). **2** private and personal (*intimate thoughts*). **3** (usu. foll. by *with*) having sexual relations. **4** (of knowledge) detailed; thorough. **5** (of a relationship between things) close. **6** (of mixing, etc.) thorough. **7** essential; intrinsic. **8** (of a place, etc.) friendly; promoting close personal relationships. • *n.* a very close friend. ▫▫ **in·ti·mate·ly** *adv.*

in·ti·mate[2] /íntimayt/ *v.tr.* **1** (often foll. by *that* + clause) state or make known. **2** imply; hint. ▫▫ **in·ti·mat·er** *n.* **in·ti·ma·tion** /–máyshən/ *n.*

in·tim·i·date /intímidayt/ *v.tr.* frighten or overawe, esp. to subdue or influence. ▫▫ **in·tim·i·da·tion** /–dáyshən/ *n.* **in·tim·i·da·tor** *n.*

in·to /íntoo/ *prep.* **1** expressing motion or direction to a point on or within (*walked into a tree*; *ran into the house*). **2** expressing direction of attention or concern (*will look into it*). **3** expressing a change of state (*turned into a dragon*; *separated into groups*; *forced into cooperation*). **4** *colloq.* interested in; knowledgeable about (*is really into art*).

in·tol·er·a·ble /intólərəbəl/ *adj.* that cannot be endured. ▫▫ **in·tol·er·a·ble·ness** *n.* **in·tol·er·a·bly** *adv.*

in·tol·er·ant /intólərənt/ *adj.* not tolerant, esp. of views, beliefs, or behavior differing from one's own. ▫▫ **in·tol·er·ance** /–rəns/ *n.* **in·tol·er·ant·ly** *adv.*

in·to·na·tion /intənáyshən/ *n.* **1** modulation of the voice; accent. **2** the act of intoning. **3** accuracy of pitch in playing or singing (*has good intonation*).

in·tone /intṓn/ *v.tr.* **1** recite (prayers, etc.) with prolonged sounds, esp. in a monotone. **2** utter with a particular tone. ▫▫ **in·ton·er** *n.*

in to·to /in tṓtō/ *adv.* completely.

in·tox·i·cant /intóksikənt/ *adj.* & *n.* • *adj.* intoxicating. • *n.* an intoxicating substance.

in·tox·i·cate /intóksikayt/ *v.tr.* **1** make drunk. **2** excite or elate beyond self-control. ▫▫ **in·tox·i·ca·tion** /–káyshən/ *n.*

in·tox·i·cat·ing /intóksikayting/ *adj.* **1** liable to cause intoxication; alcoholic. **2** exhilarating; exciting. ▫▫ **in·tox·i·cat·ing·ly** *adv.*

intr. *abbr.* intransitive.

intra- /íntrə/ *prefix* forming adjectives usu. from adjectives, meaning 'on the inside, within' (*intramural*).

in·trac·ta·ble /intráktəbəl/ *adj.* **1** hard to control or deal with. **2** difficult; stubborn. ▫▫ **in·trac·ta·bil·i·ty** *n.* **in·trac·ta·ble·ness** *n.* **in·trac·ta·bly** *adv.*

in·tra·mu·ral /intrəmyoorəl/ *adj.* **1** situated or done within walls. **2** taking place among or involving students of one university or college, etc. ▫▫ **in·tra·mu·ral·ly** *adv.*

in·tran·si·gent /intránsijənt, –tránz–/ *adj.* & *n.* • *adj.* uncompromising; stubborn. • *n.* an intransigent person. ▫▫ **in·tran·si·gence** /–jəns/ *n.* **in·tran·si·gen·cy** *n.* **in·tran·si·gent·ly** *adv.*

in·tran·si·tive /intránsitiv, –tránz–/ *adj.* (of a verb or sense of a verb) that does not take or require a direct object (whether expressed or implied), e.g., *look* in *look at the sky* (opp. TRANSITIVE). ▫▫ **in·tran·si·tive·ly** *adv.* **in·tran·si·tiv·i·ty** /–tívitee/ *n.*

in·tra·u·ter·ine de·vice *n.* a device inserted into the uterus that provides birth control by preventing implantation. Abbr.: **IUD**.

in·tra·ve·nous /íntrəvéenəs/ *adj.* in or into a vein or veins. ▫▫ **in·tra·ve·nous·ly** *adv.*

in·trep·id /intrépid/ *adj.* fearless; very brave. ▫▫ **in·tre·pid·i·ty** /–tripíditee/ *n.* **in·trep·id·ly** *adv.*

in·tri·cate /íntrikit/ *adj.* very complicated; perplexingly detailed or obscure. ▫▫ **in·tri·ca·cy** /–kəsee/ *n.* (*pl.* **-cies**). **in·tri·cate·ly** *adv.*

in·trigue *v.* & *n.* • *v.* /intréeg/ (**intrigues, intrigued, intriguing**) **1** *intr.* (foll. by *with*) **a** carry on an underhand plot. **b** use secret influence. **2** *tr.* arouse the curiosity of; fascinate. • *n.* /intréeg, ín–/ **1** an underhand plot or plotting. **2** *archaic* a secret love affair. ▫▫ **in·tri·guer** /intréegər/ *n.* **in·tri·guing** /intréeging/ *adj.* (esp. in sense 2 of *v.*). **in·tri·guing·ly** *adv.*

in·trin·sic /intrínzik/ *adj.* inherent; essential; belonging naturally (opp. EXTRINSIC). ▫▫ **in·trin·si·cal·ly** *adv.*
intro- /intrō/ *comb. form* into (*introgression*).
intro. *abbr.* **1** introduction. **2** introductory.
in·tro·duce /intrədóos, –dyóos/ *v.tr.* **1** (foll. by *to*) make (a person or oneself) known by name to another, esp. formally. **2** announce or present to an audience. **3** bring (a custom, idea, etc.) into use. **4** bring (a piece of legislation) before a legislative assembly. **5** (foll. by *to*) draw the attention or extend the understanding of (a person) to a subject. **6** insert; place in. **7** bring in; usher in; bring forward. **8** begin; occur just before the start of. ▫▫ **in·tro·duc·er** *n.* **in·tro·duc·i·ble** *adj.*
in·tro·duc·tion /intrədúkshən/ *n.* **1** the act or an instance of introducing; the process of being introduced. **2** a formal presentation of one person to another. **3** an explanatory section at the beginning of a book, etc. **4** a preliminary section in a piece of music, often thematically different from the main section. **5** an introductory treatise on a subject. **6** a thing introduced.
in·tro·duc·to·ry /intrədúktəree/ *adj.* serving as an introduction; preliminary.
in·tro·spec·tion /intrəspékshən/ *n.* the examination or observation of one's own mental and emotional processes, etc. ▫▫ **in·tro·spec·tive** *adj.* **in·tro·spec·tive·ly** *adv.* **in·tro·spec·tive·ness** *n.*
in·tro·vert /intrəvərt/ *n. & adj.* • *n.* **1** *Psychol.* a person predominantly concerned with his or her own thoughts and feelings rather than with external things. **2** a shy, inwardly thoughtful person. • *adj.* (also **in·tro·vert·ed** /–tid/) typical or characteristic of an introvert. ▫▫ **in·tro·ver·sion** /–vérzhən, –shən/ *n.* **in·tro·ver·sive** /–vérsiv/ *adj.* **in·tro·vert·ed** *adj.* **in·tro·ver·tive** /–vərtiv/ *adj.*
in·trude /intróod/ *v.* (foll. by *on, upon, into*) **1** *intr.* come uninvited or unwanted; force oneself abruptly on others. **2** *tr.* thrust or force (something unwelcome) on a person. ▫▫ **in·trud·ing·ly** *adv.*
in·trud·er /intróodər/ *n.* a person who intrudes, esp. into a building with criminal intent.
in·tru·sion /intróozhən/ *n.* **1** the act or an instance of intruding. **2** an unwanted interruption, etc. **3** *Geol.* an influx of molten rock between or through strata, etc., but not reaching the surface.
in·tru·sive /intróosiv/ *adj.* **1** that intrudes or tends to intrude. **2** characterized by intrusion. ▫▫ **in·tru·sive·ly** *adv.* **in·tru·sive·ness** *n.*
in·tu·it /intóoit, –tyóo–/ *v.* **1** *tr.* know by intuition. **2** *intr.* receive knowledge by direct perception. ▫▫ **in·tu·it·a·ble** *adj.*
in·tu·i·tion /intoo-íshən, –tyoo–/ *n.* **1** immediate apprehension by the mind without reasoning. **2** immediate apprehension by a sense. **3** immediate insight. ▫▫ **in·tu·i·tion·al** *adj.*
in·tu·i·tive /intóoitiv, –tyóo–/ *adj.* **1** of, characterized by, or possessing intuition. **2** perceived by intuition. ▫▫ **in·tu·i·tive·ly** *adv.* **in·tu·i·tive·ness** *n.*
In·u·it /inyoo-it/ *n.* (also **In·nu·it**) (*pl.* same or **Inuits**) a N. American Eskimo.
in·un·date /inəndayt/ *v.tr.* (often foll. by *with*) **1** flood. **2** overwhelm (*inundated with inquiries*). ▫▫ **in·un·da·tion** /–dáyshən/ *n.*
in·ure /inyóor/ *v. tr.* (often in *passive*; foll. by *to*) accustom (a person) to something esp. unpleasant. ▫▫ **in·ure·ment** *n.*
in u·ter·o /in yóotərō/ *adv.* in the womb; before birth.
in vac·u·o /in vákyoo-ō/ *adv.* in a vacuum.
in·vade /inváyd/ *v.tr.* (often *absol.*) **1** enter (a country, etc.) under arms to control or subdue it. **2** swarm into. **3** (of a disease) attack (a body, etc.). **4** encroach upon (a person's rights, esp. privacy). ▫▫ **in·vad·er** *n.*
in·va·lid[1] /invəlid/ *n. & v.* • *n.* **1** a person enfeebled or disabled by illness or injury. **2** (*attrib.*) **a** of or for invalids (*invalid car; invalid diet*). **b** being an invalid (*caring for her invalid mother*). • *v.* **1** *tr.* (often foll. by *out*, etc.) remove from active service (one who has become an invalid). **2** *tr.* (usu. in *passive*) disable (a person) by illness. **3** *intr.* become an invalid. ▫▫ **in·va·lid·ism** *n.*
in·val·id[2] /inválid/ *adj.* not valid, esp. having no legal force. ▫▫ **in·val·id·ly** *adv.*
in·val·i·date /inválidayt/ *v.tr.* **1** make (esp. an argument, etc.) invalid. **2** remove the validity or force of (a treaty, contract, etc.). ▫▫ **in·val·i·da·tion** /–dáyshən/ *n.*
in·val·u·a·ble /inválydoobəl/ *adj.* above valuation; inestimable. ▫▫ **in·val·u·a·ble·ness** *n.* **in·val·u·a·bly** *adv.*
in·va·sion /inváyzhən/ *n.* **1** the act of invading or process of being invaded. **2** an entry of a hostile army into a country. ▫▫ **in·va·sive** /–váysiv/ *adj.*
in·vec·tive /invéktiv/ *n.* **1 a** strongly attacking words. **b** the use of these. **2** abusive rhetoric.
in·veigh /inváy/ *v.intr.* (foll. by *against*) speak or write with strong hostility.
in·vei·gle /inváygəl, –vée–/ *v.tr.* (foll. by *into*, or *to* + infin.) entice; persuade by guile. ▫▫ **in·vei·gle·ment** *n.*
in·vent /invént/ *v.tr.* **1** create by thought; devise; originate (a new method, an instrument, etc.). **2** concoct (a false story, etc.). ▫▫ **in·vent·a·ble** *adj.* **in·ven·tor** *n.*
in·ven·tion /invénshən/ *n.* **1** the process of inventing. **2** a thing invented; a contrivance, esp. one for which a patent is granted. **3** a fictitious story. **4** inventiveness.
in·ven·tive /invéntiv/ *adj.* **1** able or inclined to invent; original in devising. **2** showing ingenuity of devising. ▫▫ **in·ven·tive·ly** *adv.* **in·ven·tive·ness** *n.*
in·ven·to·ry /invəntáwree/ *n. & v.* • *n.* (*pl.* **-ries**) **1** a complete list of goods in stock, house contents, etc. **2** the goods listed in this. **3** the total of a firm's commercial assets. • *v.tr.* (**-ries, -ried**) **1** make an inventory of. **2** enter (goods) in an inventory.
in·verse /invərs, –vérs/ *adj. & n.* • *adj.* inverted in position, order, or relation. • *n.* **1** the state of being inverted. **2** (often foll. by *of*) a thing that is the opposite or reverse of another. ▫▫ **in·verse·ly** *adv.*
in·verse pro·por·tion *n.* (also **in·verse ra·tio**) a relation between two quantities such that one increases in proportion as the other decreases.
in·ver·sion /invérzhən, –shən/ *n.* **1** the act of turning upside down or inside out. **2** the reversal of a normal order, position, or relation. **3** the reversal of the order of words, for rhetorical effect. **4** the reversal of the normal variation of air temperature with altitude. **5** the process or result of inverting. ▫▫ **in·ver·sive** /–vérsiv/ *adj.*
in·vert /invért/ *v.tr.* **1** turn upside down. **2** reverse the position, order, or relation of. **3** *Mus.* change the relative position of the notes of (a chord or interval) by placing the lowest note higher, usu. by an octave. **4** subject to inversion. ▫▫ **in·vert·er** *n.* **in·vert·i·ble** *adj.* **in·vert·i·bil·i·ty** *n.*
in·ver·te·brate /invértibrət, –brayt/ *adj. & n.* • *adj.* **1** (of an animal) not having a backbone. **2** lacking firmness of character. • *n.* an invertebrate animal.
in·vest /invést/ *v.* **1** *tr.* (often foll. by *in*) apply or use (money), esp. for profit. **2** *intr.* (foll. by *in*) **a** put money for profit (into stocks, etc.). **b** *colloq.* buy (*invested in a new car*). **3** *tr.* **a** (foll. by *with*) provide *or* endue (a person with qualities, insignia, or rank). **b** (foll. by *in*) attribute or entrust (qualities or feelings to a person). ▫▫ **in·vest·a·ble** *adj.* **in·vest·i·ble** *adj.* **in·ves·tor** *n.*

---

invest mid-16th cent. (in the senses 'clothe', 'clothe with the insignia of a rank', and 'endow with author-

---

ity'): from French *investir* or Latin *investire*, from *in-* 'into, upon' + *vestire* 'clothe' (from *vestis* 'clothing'). Sense 1 (early 17th cent.) is influenced by Italian *investire.*

---

in·ves·ti·gate /invéstigayt/ *v.* **1** *tr.* **a** inquire into; examine; study carefully. **b** make an official inquiry into. **2** *intr.* make a systematic inquiry or search. □□ **in·ves·ti·ga·tor** *n.* **in·ves·ti·ga·to·ry** /–gətáwree/ *adj.*

in·ves·ti·ga·tion /invéstigáyshən/ *n.* **1** the process or an instance of investigating. **2** a formal examination or study.

in·ves·ti·ga·tive /invéstigaytiv/ *adj.* seeking or serving to investigate, esp. (of journalism) inquiring intensively into controversial issues.

in·ves·ti·ture /invéstichoor, –chər/ *n.* **1** the formal investing of a person with honors or rank, esp. a ceremony at which a sovereign confers honors. **2** (often foll. by *with*) the act of enduing (with attributes).

in·vest·ment /invéstmənt/ *n.* **1** the act or process of investing. **2** money invested. **3** property, etc., in which money is invested.

in·vet·er·ate /invétərət/ *adj.* **1** (of a person) confirmed in an (esp. undesirable) habit, etc. (*an inveterate gambler*). **2** (of a habit, etc.) long-established. □□ **in·vet·er·a·cy** /–rəsee/ *n.* **in·vet·er·ate·ly** *adv.*

in·vid·i·ous /invídeeəs/ *adj.* (of an action, conduct, attitude, etc.) likely to excite resentment or indignation against the person responsible, esp. by real or seeming injustice (*an invidious position*; *an invidious task*). □□ **in·vid·i·ous·ly** *adv.* **in·vid·i·ous·ness** *n.*

in·vig·or·ate /invígərayt/ *v.tr.* give vigor or strength to. □□ **in·vig·or·at·ing** *adj.* **in·vig·or·at·ing·ly** *adv.* **in·vig·or·a·tion** /–ráyshən/ *n.*

in·vin·ci·ble /invínsibəl/ *adj.* unconquerable; that cannot be defeated. □□ **in·vin·ci·bil·i·ty** *n.* **in·vin·ci·ble·ness** *n.* **in·vin·ci·bly** *adv.*

in·vi·o·la·ble /invíələbəl/ *adj.* not to be violated or profaned. □□ **in·vi·o·la·bil·i·ty** /–bílitee/ *n.* **in·vi·o·la·bly** *adv.*

in·vi·o·late /invíələt/ *adj.* not violated or profaned. □□ **in·vi·o·la·cy** /–ləsee/ *n.* **in·vi·o·late·ly** *adv.* **in·vi·o·late·ness** *n.*

in·vis·i·ble /invízibəl/ *adj.* **1** not visible to the eye, either characteristically or because hidden. **2** too small to be seen or noticed. **3** artfully concealed (*invisible mending*). □□ **in·vis·i·bil·i·ty** *n.* **in·vis·i·ble·ness** *n.* **in·vis·i·bly** *adv.*

in·vi·ta·tion /invitáyshən/ *n.* **1 a** the process of inviting or fact of being invited, esp. to a social occasion. **b** the spoken or written form in which a person is invited. **2** the action or an act of enticing; attraction; allurement.

in·vite *v.* & *n.* •*v.* /invít/ **1** *tr.* (often foll. by *to*, or *to* + infin.) ask (a person) courteously to come, or to do something (*were invited to lunch*; *invited them to reply*). **2** *tr.* make a formal courteous request for (*invited comments*). **3** *tr.* tend to call forth unintentionally (something unwanted). **4 a** *tr.* attract. **b** *intr.* be attractive. •*n.* /invīt *colloq.*/ an invitation. □□ **in·vi·tee** /–teé/ *n.* **in·vit·er** *n.*

in·vit·ing /invíting/ *adj.* **1** attractive. **2** enticing; tempting. □□ **in·vit·ing·ly** *adv.* **in·vit·ing·ness** *n.*

in vi·tro /in veétrō/ *adv. Biol.* (of processes or reactions) taking place in a test tube or other laboratory environment.

in·vo·ca·tion /invəkáyshən/ *n.* **1** the act or an instance of invoking, esp. in prayer. **2** an appeal to a supernatural being or beings, e.g., the Muses, for psychological or spiritual inspiration. □□ **in·voc·a·to·ry** /invókətáwree/ *adj.*

in·voice /invoys/ *n.* & *v.* •*n.* an itemized bill for goods or services. •*v.tr.* **1** make an invoice of (goods and services). **2** send an invoice to (a person).

in·voke /invṓk/ *v.tr.* **1** call on (a deity, etc.) in prayer or as a witness. **2** appeal to (the law, a person's authority, etc.). **3** summon (a spirit) by charms. **4** ask earnestly for (vengeance, help, etc.). □□ **in·vo·ca·ble** *adj.* **in·vok·er** *n.*

in·vol·un·tar·y /invóləntéree/ *adj.* **1** done without the exercise of the will; unintentional. **2** (of a limb, muscle, or movement) not under the control of the will. □□ **in·vol·un·tar·i·ly** /–térilee/ *adv.* **in·vol·un·tar·i·ness** *n.*

in·vo·lu·tion /invəloóshən/ *n.* **1** the process of involving. **2** an entanglement. **3** intricacy. **4** curling inward. **5** a part that curls upward.

in·volve /invólv/ *v.tr.* **1** (often foll. by *in*) cause (a person or thing) to participate, or share the experience or effect (in a situation, activity, etc.). **2** imply; entail; make necessary. **3** (foll. by *in*) implicate (a person in a charge, crime, etc.). **4** include or affect in its operations. **5** (as **involved** *adj.*) **a** (often foll. by *in*) concerned or interested. **b** complicated in thought or form. □□ **in·volve·ment** *n.*

in·vul·ner·a·ble /invúlnərəbəl/ *adj.* that cannot be wounded or hurt, physically or mentally. □□ **in·vul·ner·a·bil·i·ty** *n.* **in·vul·ner·a·bly** *adv.*

in·ward /inwərd/ *adj.* & *adv.* •*adj.* **1** directed toward the inside; going in. **2** situated within. **3** mental; spiritual. •*adv.* (also **in·wards**) **1** (of motion or position) toward the inside. **2** in the mind or soul. □□ **in·ward·ly** *adv.*

I/O *abbr. Computing* input/output.

IOC *abbr.* International Olympic Committee.

i·o·dine /íədīn, –din, –deen/ *n.* **1** *Chem.* a nonmetallic element of the halogen group, forming black crystals and a violet vapor, used in medicine and photography, and important as an essential element for living organisms. ¶ Symb.: **I**. **2** a solution of this in alcohol used as a mild antiseptic.

i·o·dize /íədīz/ *v.tr.* treat or impregnate with iodine. □□ **i·o·di·za·tion** *n.*

i·on /íən, íon/ *n.* an atom or group of atoms that has lost one or more electrons (= CATION), or gained one or more electrons (= ANION). □□ **i·on·ic** *adj.* **i·on·i·cal·ly** *adv.*

I·on·ic /íónik/ *adj.* & *n.* •*adj.* **1** of the order of Greek architecture characterized by a column with scroll shapes on either side of the capital. **2** of the ancient Greek dialect used in Ionia. •*n.* the Ionic dialect.

i·on·i·za·tion /íənizáyshən/ *n.* the process of producing ions as a result of solvation, heat, radiation, etc.

i·on·ize /íənīz/ *v.tr.* & *intr.* convert or be converted into an ion or ions. □□ **i·on·iz·a·ble** *adj.*

i·on·iz·er /íənīzər/ *n.* any thing that produces ionization, esp. a device used to improve the quality of the air in a room, etc.

i·on·o·sphere /íónəsfeer/ *n.* an ionized region of the atmosphere above the stratosphere, extending to about 600 miles (1,000 km) above the earth's surface and able to reflect radio waves, allowing long-distance transmission around the earth (cf. TROPOSPHERE □□ **i·on·o·spher·ic** /–sféerik, –sfér–/ *adj.*

i·o·ta /ī-ṓtə/ *n.* **1** the ninth letter of the Greek alphabet (Ι, ι). **2** (usu. with *neg.*) the smallest possible amount.

IOU /ī-ō-yoó/ *n.* a signed document acknowledging a debt.

IPA *abbr.* International Phonetic Alphabet (or Association).

ip·e·cac /ipikak/ *n. colloq.* ipecacuanha.

ip·e·cac·u·an·ha /ípikákyoo-áanə/ *n.* the root of a S. American shrub, *Cephaelis ipecacuanha*, used as an emetic and purgative.

ip·so fac·to /ípsō fáktō/ *adv.* **1** by that very fact or act. **2** thereby.

IQ *abbr.* intelligence quotient.

Ir *symb. Chem.* the element iridium.

IRA *abbr.* **1** individual retirement account. **2** Irish Republican Army.

I·ra·ni·an /iráyneeən/ *adj. & n.* • *adj.* **1** of or relating to Iran (formerly Persia) in the Middle East. **2** of the Indo-European group of languages including Persian, Pashto, Avestan, and Kurdish. • *n.* **1** a native or national of Iran. **2** a person of Iranian descent.

I·ra·qi /iraákee/ *adj. & n.* • *adj.* of or relating to Iraq in the Middle East. • *n.* (*pl.* **Iraqis**) **1 a** a native or national of Iraq. **b** a person of Iraqi descent. **2** the form of Arabic spoken in Iraq.

i·ras·ci·ble /irásibəl/ *adj.* irritable; hot-tempered. ▫▫ **i·ras·ci·bil·i·ty** *n.* **i·ras·ci·bly** *adv.*

i·rate /īráyt/ *adj.* angry, enraged. ▫▫ **i·rate·ly** *adv.* **i·rate·ness** *n.*

ire /īr/ *n. literary* anger. ▫▫ **ire·ful** *adj.*

ir·i·des·cent /iridésənt/ *adj.* **1** showing rainbowlike luminous or gleaming colors. **2** changing color with position. ▫▫ **ir·i·des·cence** /–səns/ *n.* **ir·i·des·cent·ly** *adv.*

i·rid·i·um /irídeeəm/ *n. Chem.* a hard, white metallic element of the transition series used esp. in alloys. ¶ Symb.: **Ir**.

i·ris /īris/ *n.* **1** the flat, circular colored membrane behind the cornea of the eye, with a circular opening (pupil) in the center. **2** any herbaceous plant of the genus *Iris*, usu. with tuberous roots, sword-shaped leaves, and showy flowers. **3** (in full **iris diaphragm**) an adjustable diaphragm of thin overlapping plates for regulating the size of a central hole esp. for the admission of light to a lens.

I·rish /īrish/ *adj. & n.* • *adj.* of or relating to Ireland; of or like its people. • *n.* **1** the Celtic language of Ireland. **2** (prec. by *the*; treated as *pl.*) the people of Ireland. **get one's Irish up** cause one to become angry

I·rish cof·fee *n.* coffee mixed with Irish whiskey and served with cream on top.

I·rish set·ter *n.* a silky-haired, dark red breed of setter.

I·rish Wolf·hound *n.* a large, often greyish hound of a rough-coated breed.

irk /ərk/ *v.tr.* (usu. *impers.*; often foll. by *that* + clause) irritate; bore; annoy.

irk·some /ə́rksəm/ *adj.* tedious; annoying; tiresome. ▫▫ **irk·some·ly** *adv.* **irk·some·ness** *n.*

i·ron /íərn/ *n., adj., & v.* • *n.* **1** *Chem.* a silver-white ductile metallic element occurring naturally as hematite, magnetite, etc., much used for tools and implements, and an essential element in all living organisms. ¶ Symb.: **Fe**. **2** this as a type of unyieldingness or a symbol of firmness (*man of iron*; *will of iron*). **3** a tool or implement made of iron (*branding iron*; *curling iron*). **4** a household implement, now usu. electrical, with a flat base that is heated to smooth clothes, etc. **5** a golf club with an iron or steel sloping face used for lofting the ball. **6** (usu. in *pl.*) a fetter (*clapped in irons*). **7** (usu. in *pl.*) a stirrup. **8** (often in *pl.*) an iron support for a malformed leg. **9** a preparation of iron as a tonic or dietary supplement (*iron pills*). • *adj.* **1** made of iron. **2** very robust. **3** unyielding; merciless (*iron determination*). • *v.tr.* **1** smooth (clothes, etc.) with an iron. **2** furnish or cover with iron. **3** shackle with irons. ▫ **in irons** handcuffed, chained, etc. **iron in the fire** an undertaking, opportunity, or commitment (usu. in *pl.*: *too many irons in the fire*). **iron out** remove or smooth over (difficulties, etc.). ▫▫ **i·ron·er** *n.* **i·ron·less** *adj.* **i·ron·like** *adj.*

I·ron Age *n. Archaeol.* the period following the Bronze Age when iron replaced bronze in the making of implements and weapons.

i·ron·clad *adj. & n.* • *adj.* /íərnklád/ **1** clad or protected with iron. **2** impregnable; rigorous. • *n.* /íərnklad *hist.*/ an early name for a 19th-c. warship built of iron or protected by iron plates.

I·ron Cur·tain *n. hist.* a notional barrier to the passage of people and information between the former Soviet bloc and the West.

i·ron hand *n.* firmness or inflexibility (cf. VELVET GLOVE).

i·ron·ic /irónik/ *adj.* (also **i·ron·i·cal**) **1** using or displaying irony. **2** in the nature of irony. ▫▫ **i·ron·i·cal·ly** *adv.*

i·ron·ing board *n.* a flat surface usu. on legs and of adjustable height on which clothes, etc., are ironed.

i·ron lung *n.* a rigid case fitted over a patient's body, used for administering prolonged artificial respiration by means of mechanical pumps.

i·ron·stone /íərnstōn/ *n.* **1** any rock containing a substantial proportion of an iron compound. **2** a kind of hard, white, opaque stoneware.

i·ron·ware /íərnwair/ *n.* articles made of iron, esp. domestic implements.

i·ron·wood /íərnwood/ *n.* **1** any of various tough-timbered trees and shrubs, esp. American hornbeam, *Carpinus caroliniana*. **2** the wood from these trees.

i·ron·works /íərnwərks/ *n.* (as *sing.* or *pl.*) a place where iron is smelted or iron goods are made.

i·ro·ny /írənee/ *n.* (*pl.* **-nies**) **1** an expression of meaning, often humorous or sarcastic, by the use of language of a different or opposite tendency. **2** an ill-timed or perverse arrival of an event or circumstance that is in itself desirable. **3** the use of language with one meaning for a privileged audience and another for those addressed or concerned.

Ir·o·quoi·an /írəkwóyən/ *n. & adj.* • *n.* **1** a language family of eastern N. America, including Cherokee and Mohawk. **2** a member of the Iroquois people. • *adj.* of or relating to the Iroquois or the Iroquoian language family or one of its members.

Ir·o·quois /írəkwoy/ *n. & adj.* • *n.* (*pl.* same) **1 a** a Native American confederacy of five (later six) peoples formerly inhabiting New York State. **b** a member of any of these peoples. **2** any of the languages of these peoples. • *adj.* of or relating to the Iroquois or their languages.

ir·ra·di·ate /iráydee-áyt/ *v.tr.* **1** subject to (any form of) radiation. **2** shine upon; light up. **3** throw light on (a subject). ▫▫ **ir·ra·di·a·tive** /–deeətiv/ *adj.*

ir·ra·di·a·tion /iráydee-áyshən/ *n.* **1** the process of irradiating. **2** shining; illumination. **3** the apparent extension of the edges of an illuminated object seen against a dark background.

ir·ra·tion·al /iráshənəl/ *adj.* **1** illogical; unreasonable. **2** not endowed with reason. **3** *Math.* (of a root, etc.) not rational; not able to be expressed as a ratio between two integers; not commensurate with the natural numbers (e.g., a nonterminating decimal). ▫▫ **ir·ra·tion·al·i·ty** /–álitee/ *n.* **ir·ra·tion·al·ize** *v.tr.* **ir·ra·tion·al·ly** *adv.*

ir·rec·on·cil·a·ble /irékənsīləbəl/ *adj. & n.* • *adj.* **1** implacably hostile. **2** (of ideas, etc.) incompatible. • *n.* **1** an uncompromising opponent of a political measure, etc. **2** (usu. in *pl.*) any of two or more items, ideas, etc., that cannot be made to agree. ▫▫ **ir·rec·on·cil·a·bil·i·ty** *n.* **ir·rec·on·cil·a·ble·ness** *n.* **ir·rec·on·cil·a·bly** *adv.*

ir·re·cov·er·a·ble /irikúvərəbəl/ *adj.* that cannot be recovered or remedied. ▫▫ **ir·re·cov·er·a·bly** *adv.*

ir·re·deem·a·ble /iridéeməbəl/ *adj.* **1** that cannot be redeemed. **2** hopeless; absolute. ▫▫ **ir·re·deem·a·bil·i·ty** *n.* **ir·re·deem·a·bly** *adv.*

ir·re·duc·i·ble /íridóosibəl, –dyóo–/ *adj.* **1** that cannot be reduced or simplified. **2** (often foll. by *to*) that cannot be brought to a desired condition. ▫▫ **ir·re·duc·i·bil·i·ty** *n.* **ir·re·duc·i·bly** *adv.*

ir·ref·u·ta·ble /iréfyətəbəl, írifyóo–/ *adj.* that cannot be refuted. ▫▫ **ir·ref·u·ta·bil·i·ty** *n.* **ir·ref·u·ta·bly** *adv.*

ir·reg·u·lar /irégyələr/ *adj. & n.* • *adj.* **1** not regular; unsymmetrical; uneven; varying in form. **2** (of a surface) uneven. **3** contrary to a rule, moral principle, or custom; abnormal. **4** uneven in duration, order, etc. **5** (of troops) not belonging to the regular army. **6** *Gram.* (of a verb, noun, etc.) not inflected according to the usual rules. **7** disorderly. • *n.* (in *pl.*) irregular troops. ▫▫ **ir·reg·u·lar·i·ty** /–láritee/ *n.* (*pl.* **-ties**). **ir·reg·u·lar·ly** *adv.*

ir·rel·e·vant /irélivənt/ *adj.* (often foll. by *to*) not relevant; not applicable (to a matter in hand). ▫▫ **ir·rel·e·vance** /–vəns/ *n.* **ir·rel·e·van·cy** *n.* **ir·rel·e·vant·ly** *adv.* ▶See note at IMMATERIAL.

ir·re·li·gious /irilíjəs/ *adj.* **1** indifferent or hostile to religion. **2** lacking a religion. ▫▫ **ir·re·li·gious·ly** *adv.* **ir·re·li·gious·ness** *n.*

ir·re·me·di·a·ble /irimeédeeəbəl/ *adj.* that cannot be remedied. ▫▫ **ir·re·me·di·a·bly** *adv.*

ir·rep·a·ra·ble /irépərəbəl/ *adj.* (of an injury, loss, etc.) that cannot be rectified or made good. ▫▫ **ir·rep·a·ra·bil·i·ty** *n.* **ir·rep·a·ra·ble·ness** *n.* **ir·rep·a·ra·bly** *adv.*

ir·re·place·a·ble /íripláysəbəl/ *adj.* **1** that cannot be replaced. **2** of which the loss cannot be made good. ▫▫ **ir·re·place·a·bly** *adv.*

ir·re·press·i·ble /iriprésibəl/ *adj.* that cannot be repressed or restrained. ▫▫ **ir·re·press·i·bil·i·ty** *n.* **ir·re·press·i·ble·ness** *n.* **ir·re·press·i·bly** *adv.*

ir·re·proach·a·ble /íriprṓchəbəl/ *adj.* faultless; blameless. ▫▫ **ir·re·proach·a·bil·i·ty** *n.* **ir·re·proach·a·ble·ness** *n.* **ir·re·proach·a·bly** *adv.*

ir·re·sist·i·ble /írizístibəl/ *adj.* **1** too strong or convincing to be resisted. **2** delightful; alluring. ▫▫ **ir·re·sist·i·bil·i·ty** *n.* **ir·re·sist·i·ble·ness** *n.* **ir·re·sist·i·bly** *adv.*

ir·res·o·lute /irézəloot/ *adj.* **1** hesitant; undecided. **2** lacking in resoluteness. ▫▫ **ir·res·o·lute·ly** *adv.* **ir·res·o·lute·ness** *n.* **ir·res·o·lu·tion** /–lóoshən/ *n.*

ir·re·spec·tive /írispéktiv/ *adj.* (foll. by *of*) not taking into account; regardless of. ▫▫ **ir·re·spec·tive·ly** *adv.*

ir·re·spon·si·ble /írispónsibəl/ *adj.* **1** acting or done without due sense of responsibility. **2** not responsible for one's conduct. ▫▫ **ir·re·spon·si·bil·i·ty** *n.* **ir·re·spon·si·bly** *adv.*

ir·re·triev·a·ble /íritreévəbəl/ *adj.* that cannot be retrieved or restored. ▫▫ **ir·re·triev·a·bil·i·ty** *n.* **ir·re·triev·a·bly** *adv.*

ir·rev·er·ent /irévərənt/ *adj.* lacking reverence. ▫▫ **ir·rev·er·ence** /–rəns/ *n.* **ir·rev·er·en·tial** /–rénshəl/ *adj.* **ir·rev·er·ent·ly** *adv.*

ir·re·vers·i·ble /írivə́rsibəl/ *adj.* not reversible or alterable. ▫▫ **ir·re·vers·i·bil·i·ty** *n.* **ir·re·vers·i·bly** *adv.*

ir·rev·o·ca·ble /irévəkəbəl, írivṓk–/ *adj.* **1** unalterable. **2** gone beyond recall. ▫▫ **ir·rev·o·ca·bil·i·ty** /–bílitee/ *n.* **ir·rev·o·ca·bly** *adv.*

ir·ri·gate /írigayt/ *v.tr.* **1 a** water (land) by means of channels. **b** (of a stream, etc.) supply (land) with water. **2** *Med.* supply (a wound, etc.) with a constant flow of liquid. ▫▫ **ir·ri·ga·ble** *adj.* **ir·ri·ga·tion** /–gáyshən/ *n.* **ir·ri·ga·tive** *adj.* **ir·ri·ga·tor** *n.*

ir·ri·ta·ble /íritəbəl/ *adj.* **1** easily annoyed or angered. **2** (of an organ, etc.) very sensitive to contact. ▫▫ **ir·ri·ta·bil·i·ty** *n.* **ir·ri·ta·bly** *adv.*

ir·ri·tant /írit'nt/ *adj. & n.* • *adj.* causing irritation. • *n.* an irritant substance. ▫▫ **ir·ri·tan·cy** *n.*

ir·ri·tate /íritayt/ *v.tr.* **1** excite to anger; annoy. **2** stimulate discomfort or pain in (a part of the body). **3** *Biol.* stimulate (an organ) to action. ▫▫ **ir·ri·tat·ed·ly** *adv.* **ir·ri·tat·ing** *adj.* **ir·ri·tat·ing·ly** *adv.* **ir·ri·ta·tion** /–táyshən/ *n.* **ir·ri·ta·tive** *adj.* **ir·ri·ta·tor** *n.*

ir·rupt /irúpt/ *v.intr.* (foll. by *into*) enter forcibly or violently. ▫▫ **ir·rup·tion** /irúpshən/ *n.*

IRS *abbr.* Internal Revenue Service.

Is. *abbr.* **1 a** Island(s). **b** Isle(s). **2** (also **Isa.**) Isaiah (Old Testament).

is *3rd sing. present* of BE.

ISBN *abbr.* international standard book number.

is·chi·um /iskeeəm/ *n.* (*pl.* **ischia** /–keeə/) the curved bone forming the base of each half of the pelvis. ▫▫ **is·chi·al** *adj.*

i·sin·glass /ízinglas/ *n.* **1** a kind of gelatin obtained from fish, esp. sturgeon, and used in making jellies, glue, etc. **2** mica.

isl. *abbr.* island.

Is·lam /islaam, íz–, isla̋am, iz–/ *n.* **1** a monotheistic religious faith regarded as revealed through Muhammad as the Prophet of Allah. **2** collectively, those countries in which Islam is the principal religion. ▫▫ **Is·lam·ic** *adj.* **Is·lam·ism** *n.* **Is·lam·ist** *n.* **Is·lam·ize** *v.tr.* **Is·lam·i·za·tion** /–mizáyshən/ *n.*

is·land /ílənd/ *n.* **1** a piece of land surrounded by water. **2** anything compared to an island, esp. in being surrounded in some way. **3 a** a detached or isolated thing. **b** *Physiol.* a detached portion of tissue or group of cells (cf. ISLET).

is·land·er /íləndər/ *n.* a native or inhabitant of an island.

isle /īl/ *n. poet.* (and in place-names) an island or peninsula, esp. a small one.

is·let /ílit/ *n.* **1** a small island. **2** *Anat.* a portion of tissue structurally distinct from surrounding tissues. **3** an isolated place.

is·lets of Lang·er·hans /la̋anggərha̋ans, –ha̋anz/ *n.pl. Physiol.* groups of pancreatic cells secreting insulin and glucagon.

ism /ízəm/ *n. colloq.* usu. *derog.* any distinctive but unspecified doctrine or practice of a kind with a name ending in *-ism.*

isn't /ízənt/ *contr.* is not.

iso- /ísō/ *comb. form* **1** equal (*isometric*). **2** *Chem.* isomeric, esp. of a hydrocarbon with a branched chain of carbon atoms (*isobutane*).

i·so·bar /ísəbaar/ *n.* a line on a map connecting positions having the same atmospheric pressure at a given time or on average over a given period. ▫▫ **i·so·bar·ic** /–bárik/ *adj.*

i·so·late /ísəláyt/ *v.tr.* **1 a** place apart or alone, cut off from society. **b** place (a patient thought to be contagious or infectious) in quarantine. **2 a** identify and separate for attention (*isolated the problem*). **b** *Chem.* separate (a substance) from a mixture. **3** insulate (electrical apparatus). ▫▫ **i·so·la·ble** /ísələbəl/ *adj.* **i·so·lat·a·ble** *adj.* **i·so·la·tor** *n.*

i·so·lat·ed /ísəlaytid/ *adj.* **1** lonely; cut off from society or contact; remote (*feeling isolated; an isolated farmhouse*). **2** untypical; unique (*an isolated example*).

i·so·la·tion /ísəláyshən/ *n.* **1** the act or an instance of isolating. **2** the state of being isolated or separated. ▫ **in isolation** considered singly and not relatively.

i·so·la·tion·ism /ísəláyshənizəm/ *n.* the policy of holding aloof from the affairs of other countries or groups esp. in politics. ▫▫ **i·so·la·tion·ist** *n.*

i·so·mer /ísəmər/ *n.* **1** *Chem.* one of two or more compounds with the same molecular formula but a different arrangement of atoms and different properties. **2** *Physics* one of two or more atomic nuclei that have the same atomic number and the same mass number but different energy states. ▫▫ **i·so·mer·ic** /–mérik/ *adj.* **i·som·er·ism** /īsómərizəm/ *n.* **i·som·er·ize** *v.*

i·so·met·ric /ísəmétrik/ *adj.* **1** of equal measure. **2** *Physiol.* (of muscle action) developing tension while the muscle is prevented from contracting. **3** (of a drawing, etc.) with the plane of projection at equal angles to the three principal axes of the object shown. **4** *Math.* (of a transformation) without change of shape or size. □□ **i·so·met·ri·cal·ly** *adv.* **i·som·e·try** /īsómitree/ *n.* (in sense 4).

i·so·met·rics /ísəmétriks/ *n.pl.* a system of physical exercises in which muscles are caused to act against each other or against a fixed object.

i·sos·ce·les /īsósileez/ *adj.* (of a triangle) having two sides equal.

i·so·ton·ic /ísətónik/ *adj.* **1** having the same osmotic pressure. **2** *Physiol.* (of muscle action) taking place with normal contraction. □□ **i·so·ton·i·cal·ly** *adv.* **i·so·to·nic·i·ty** /–tənísitee/ *n.*

i·so·tope /ísətōp/ *n. Chem.* one of two or more forms of an element differing from each other in relative atomic mass, and in nuclear but not chemical properties. □□ **i·so·top·ic** /–tópik/ *adj.* **i·so·top·i·cal·ly** *adv.* **i·sot·o·py** /īsótəpee, ísətōpee/ *n.*

Is·rae·li /izráylee/ *adj. & n.* • *adj.* of or relating to the modern state of Israel in the Middle East. • *n.* **1** a native or national of Israel. **2** a person of Israeli descent.

Is·ra·el·ite /ízreeəlīt, –rəlīt/ *n. hist.* a native of ancient Israel; a Jew.

is·sue /íshoo/ *n. & v.* • *n.* **1 a** a giving out or circulation of shares, notes, stamps, etc. **b** a quantity of coins, supplies, copies of a newspaper or book, etc., circulated or put on sale at one time. **c** an item or amount given out or distributed. **d** each of a regular series of a magazine, etc. (*the May issue*). **2 a** an outgoing; an outflow. **b** a way out; an outlet, esp. the place of the emergence of a stream, etc. **3** a point in question; an important subject of debate or litigation. **4** a result; an outcome; a decision. **5** *Law* children; progeny (*without male issue*). • *v.* (**issues, issued, issuing**) **1** *intr.* (often foll. by *out, forth*) *literary* go or come out. **2** *tr.* **a** send forth; publish; put into circulation. **b** supply, esp. officially or authoritatively (usu. foll. by *to*): *issued passports to them*; *issued orders to the staff*). **3** *intr.* **a** (often foll. by *from*) be derived or result. **b** (foll. by *in*) end; result. **4** *intr.* (foll. by *from*) emerge from a condition. □ **at issue 1** under discussion; in dispute. **2** at variance. **join issue** identify and submit an issue for formal argument (foll. by *with, on*). **make an issue of** make a fuss about; turn into a subject of contention. **take issue** disagree, esp. on a specific issue (foll. by *with, on*). □□ **is·su·a·ble** *adj.* **is·su·ance** *n.* **is·sue·less** *adj.* **is·su·er** *n.*

isth·mus /ísməs/ *n.* **1** a narrow piece of land connecting two larger bodies of land. **2** *Anat.* a narrow part connecting two larger parts. □□ **isth·mi·an** *adj.*

IT *abbr.* information technology.

It. *abbr.* Italian.

it /it/ *pron.* (*poss.* **its**; *pl.* **they**) **1** the thing (or occas. the animal or child) previously named or in question (*took a stone and threw it*). **2** the person in question (*Who is it? It is I; is it a boy or a girl?*). **3** as the subject of an impersonal verb (*it is raining*; *it is winter*; *it is Tuesday*; *it is twenty miles to Denver*). **4** as a substitute for a deferred subject or object (*it is intolerable, this delay*; *it is silly to talk like that*; *I take it that you agree*). **5** as a substitute for a vague object (*tough it out*; *run for it!*). **6** as the antecedent to a relative word (*it was an owl I heard*). **7** exactly what is needed (*absolutely it*). **8** the extreme limit of achievement. **9** *colloq.* **a** sexual intercourse **b** sex appeal. **10** (in children's games) a player who has to perform a required feat, esp. to catch the others. □ **that's it** *colloq.* that is: **1** what is required. **2** the difficulty. **3** the end; enough. **this is it** *colloq.* **1** the expected event is at hand. **2** this is the difficulty.

Ital. *abbr.* Italian.

ital. *abbr.* italic (type).

I·tal·ian /itályən/ *n. & adj.* • *n.* **1 a** a native or national of Italy. **b** a person of Italian descent. **2** the Romance language used in Italy and parts of Switzerland. • *adj.* of or relating to Italy or its people or language.

I·tal·ian·ate /itályənayt/ *adj.* of Italian style or appearance.

i·tal·ic /itálik/ *adj. & n.* • *adj.* **1 a** *Printing* of the sloping kind of letters now used esp. for emphasis or distinction and in foreign words. **b** (of handwriting) compact and pointed like early Italian handwriting. **2** (**Italic**) of ancient Italy. • *n.* **1** a letter in italic type. **2** this type.

i·tal·i·cize /itálisīz/ *v.tr.* print in italics. □□ **i·tal·i·ci·za·tion** *n.*

itch /ich/ *n. & v.* • *n.* **1** an irritation in the skin. **2** an impatient desire; a hankering. **3** (prec. by *the*) (in general use) scabies. • *v.intr.* **1** feel an irritation in the skin, causing a desire to scratch it. **2** (usu. foll. by *to* + infin.) (of a person) feel a desire to do something (*am itching to tell you the news*).

itch·y /íchee/ *adj.* (**itchier, itchiest**) having or causing an itch. □□ **itch·i·ness** *n.*

it'd /ítəd/ *contr. colloq.* **1** it had. **2** it would.

i·tem /ítəm/ *n.* **1 a** any of a number of enumerated or listed things. **b** an entry in an account. **2** an article, esp. one for sale (*household items*). **3** a separate or distinct piece of news, information, etc.

i·tem·ize /ítəmīz/ *v.tr.* state or list item by item. □□ **i·tem·i·za·tion** *n.* **i·tem·iz·er** *n.*

it·er·ate /ítərayt/ *v.tr.* repeat; state repeatedly. □□ **it·er·a·tion** /–áyshən/ *n.*

i·tin·er·ant /ītínərənt, itín–/ *adj. & n.* • *adj.* traveling from place to place. • *n.* an itinerant person; a tramp. □□ **i·tin·er·a·cy** *n.* **i·tin·er·an·cy** *n.*

i·tin·er·ar·y /ītínəreree, itín–/ *n. & adj.* • *n.* (*pl.* **-ies**) **1** a detailed route. **2** a record of travel. **3** a guidebook. • *adj.* of roads or traveling.

it'll /ít'l/ *contr. colloq.* it will; it shall.

its /its/ *poss.pron.* of it; of itself (*can see its advantages*). ▶Although formerly written with an apostrophe, note that **its** is an attributive adjective indicating possession, meaning 'of it, belonging to it'. **It's** is a contraction of 'it is': *It's going to be a good day to tour the city and see its attractions.*

it's /its/ *contr.* **1** it is. **2** it has.

it·self /itsélf/ *pron.* emphatic and refl. form of IT. □ **by itself** apart from its surroundings, automatically, spontaneously. **in itself** viewed in its essential qualities (*not in itself a bad thing*).

it·ty-bit·ty /íteebítee/ *adj.* (also **it·sy-bit·sy** /ítseebítsee/) *colloq.* usu. *derog.* tiny; insubstantial; slight.

IUD *abbr.* intrauterine (contraceptive) device.

IV *abbr.* intravenous(ly).

I've /īv/ *contr.* I have.

IVF *abbr.* in vitro fertilization.

i·vo·ry /ívəree, ívree/ *n.* (*pl.* **-ries**) **1** a hard, creamy-white substance composing the main part of the tusks of an elephant, hippopotamus, walrus, and narwhal. **2** the color of this. **3** (usu. in *pl.*) **a** an article made of ivory. **b** *sl.* anything made of or resembling ivory, esp. a piano key or a tooth. □□ **i·vo·ried** *adj.*

i·vo·ry tow·er *n.* a state of seclusion or separation from the ordinary world and the harsh realities of life.

i·vy /ívee/ *n.* (*pl.* **-vies**) **1** a climbing evergreen shrub, *Hedera helix*, with usu. dark-green, shining five-angled leaves. **2** any of various other climbing plants including ground ivy and poison ivy.

J

J[1] /jay/ *n.* (also **j**) (*pl.* **Js** or **J's**) the tenth letter of the alphabet.

J[2] *symb.* (also **J.**) joule(s).

jab /jab/ *v.* & *n.* • *v.tr.* (**jabbed, jabbing**) **1 a** poke roughly. **b** stab. **2** (foll. by *into*) thrust (a thing) hard or abruptly. • *n.* **1** an abrupt blow with one's fist or a pointed implement. **2** *colloq.* a hypodermic injection, esp. a vaccination. • *n.* a quick, sharp blow, especailly with the fist.

jab·ber /jábər/ *v.* & *n.* • *v.* **1** *intr.* chatter volubly and incoherently. **2** *tr.* utter (words) fast and indistinctly. *n.* meaningless jabbering; a gabble.

jab·ber·wock·y /jábərwokee/ *n.* (*pl.* **-ies**) a piece of nonsensical writing or speech, esp. for comic effect (for the title of an 1871 poem by Lewis Carroll).

ja·bot /zhabṓ, ja–/ *n.* an ornamental frill or ruffle of lace, etc., on the front of a shirt or blouse.

ja·cinth /jáysinth, jás–/ *n.* a reddish-orange variety of zircon used as a gem.

jack /jak/ *n.* & *v.* • *n.* **1** a device for lifting heavy objects, esp. the axle of a vehicle, off the ground while changing a wheel, etc. **2** a playing card with a picture of a man, esp. a soldier, page, or knave, etc. **3** a ship's flag, esp. one flown from the bow and showing nationality. **4** a device using a single plug to connect an electrical circuit. **5** a small white ball in lawn bowling, at which the players aim. **6 a** (also **jack·stone**) a small piece of metal, etc., used with others in tossing games. **b** (in *pl.*) a game with a ball and jacks. **7** (**Jack**) the familiar form of *John* esp. typifying the common man or the male of a species (*I'm all right, Jack*). **8** *sl.* money. **9** = LUMBERJACK. **10** = STEEPLEJACK. **11** any of various marine perchlike fish of the family Carangidae, including the amberjack. • *v.tr.* **1** (usu. foll. by *up*) raise with or as with a jack (in sense 1). **2** (usu. foll. by *up*) *colloq.* raise, e.g., prices. **3** (foll. by *off*) **a** go away; depart. **b** *coarse sl.* masturbate. □ **every man jack** each and every person.

jack late Middle English: from *Jack*, pet form of the given name *John*. The term was used originally to denote an ordinary man (sense 7), also a youth (mid-16th cent.), hence the 'knave' in cards and 'male animal'. The word also denoted various devices saving human labor, as though one had a helper (senses 1 and 4), and in compounds such as JACKHAMMER and JACKKNIFE); the general sense 'laborer' arose in the early 18th cent. and survives in LUMBERJACK, STEEPLEJACK, etc. Since the mid-16th cent. a notion of 'smallness' has arisen, hence senses 5 and 6.

jack·al /jákəl/ *n.* **1** any of various wild doglike mammals of the genus *Canis*, esp. *C. aureus*, found in Africa and S. Asia, usu. hunting or scavenging for food in packs. **2** *colloq.* **a** a person who does preliminary drudgery for another. **b** a person who assists another's immoral behavior.

jack·ass /jákas/ *n.* **1** a male ass. **2** a stupid person.

jack·boot /jákbōōt/ *n.* **1** a large boot reaching above the knee. **2** this as a symbol of fascism or military oppression. □□ **jack·boot·ed** *adj.*

jack·daw /jákdaw/ *n.* a small gray-headed crow, *Corvus monedula.*

jack·et /jákit/ *n.* & *v.* • *n.* **1 a** a sleeved, short outer garment. **b** a thing worn esp. around the torso for protection or support (*life jacket*). **2** a casing or covering, e.g., as insulation around a boiler. **3** = DUST JACKET. **4** the skin of a potato, esp. when baked whole. **5** an animal's coat. • *v.tr.* cover with a jacket.

jack·fish /jákfish/ *n.* (*pl.* same) = PIKE[1].

Jack Frost *n.* frost personified.

jack·ham·mer /ják-hamər/ *n.* a pneumatic hammer or drill.

jack-in-the-box *n.* a toy figure that springs out of a box when it is opened.

jack-in-the-pul·pit *n.* a N. American plant having an upright flower spike and an over-arching hoodlike spathe.

jack-in-the-pulpit

jack·knife /jáknīf/ *n.* & *v.* • *n.* (*pl.* **-knives**) **1** a large pocketknife. **2** a dive in which the body is first bent at the waist and then straightened. • *v.intr.* (**-knifed, -knifing**) (of an articulated vehicle) fold against itself in an accidental skidding movement.

jack-of-all-trades *n.* a person who can do many different kinds of work.

jack-o'-lan·tern *n.* **1** a will-o'-the wisp. **2** a lantern made from a hollowed-out pumpkin in which holes are cut to represent facial features, typically made at Halloween.

jack·pot /jákpot/ *n.* a large prize or amount of winnings, esp. accumulated in a game or lottery, etc. □ **hit the jackpot** *colloq.* **1** win a large prize. **2** have remarkable luck or success.

jack·rab·bit /jákrabit/ *n.* any of various large prairie hares of the genus *Lepus* with very long ears and hind legs.

jack·stone /jákstōn/ *n.* **1** = JACK[1] 6. **2** (in *pl.*) the game of jacks.

jack·straw /jákstraw/ *n.* **1** a splinter of wood, straw, etc., esp. one of a bundle, pile, etc. **2** (in *pl.*) a game in which a heap of jackstraws is to be removed one at a time without moving the others.

Ja·cob's lad·der /jáykəbz/ *n.* **1** a plant, *Polemonium caeruleum*, with corymbs of blue or white flowers, and leaves suggesting a ladder. **2** a rope ladder with wooden rungs.

Jac·quard /jákaard, jəkaárd/ *n.* **1** an apparatus using perforated cards that record a pattern and are fitted to a loom to mechanize the weaving of figured fabrics. **2** (in full **Jacquard loom**) a loom fitted with this. **3** a fabric or article made with this, with an intricate variegated pattern.

Ja·cuz·zi /jəkṓōzee/ *n.* (*pl.* **Jacuzzis**) *Trademark* a large bath with underwater jets of water to massage the body.

jade[1] /jayd/ *n.* **1** a hard, usu. green stone composed of silicates of calcium and magnesium, or of sodium and aluminum, used for ornaments and implements. **2** the green color of jade.

jade[2] /jayd/ *n.* **1** an inferior or worn-out horse. **2** *derog.* a disreputable woman.

jad·ed /jáydid/ *adj.* tired, bored, or lacking enthusiasm, usu. after having had too much of something. ▫▫ **jad·ed·ly** *adv.* **jad·ed·ness** *n.*

jag[1] /jag/ *n.* & *v.* • *n.* a sharp projection of rock, etc. • *v.tr.* (**jagged, jagging**) **1** cut or tear unevenly. **2** make indentations in. ▫▫ **jag·ger** *n.*

jag[2] /jag/ *n. sl.* **1** a drinking bout; a spree. **2** a period of indulgence in an activity, emotion, etc.

jag·ged /jágid/ *adj.* **1** with an unevenly cut or torn edge. **2** deeply indented; with sharp points. ▫▫ **jag·ged·ly** *adv.* **jag·ged·ness** *n.*

jag·gy /jágee/ *adj.* (**jaggier, jaggiest**) **1** = JAGGED. **2** (also **jag·gie**) *Sc.* prickly.

jag·uar /jágwaar/ *n.* a large, flesh-eating spotted feline, *Panthera onca*, of Central and S. America.

jai a·lai /hí lī, əlí/ *n.* an indoor court game somewhat resembling handball in which the ball is propelled with large curved wicker baskets.

jail /jayl/ *n.* & *v.* (also *Brit.* **gaol** • *pronunc.* same) • *n.* **1** a place to which persons are committed by a court for detention. **2** confinement in a jail. • *v.tr.* put in jail.

jail·bait /jáylbayt/ *n.* sl. a girl under the age of consent.

jail·bird /jáylbərd/ *n.* (also *Brit.* **gaolbird**) a prisoner or habitual criminal.

jail·break /jáylbrayk/ *n.* (also *Brit.* **gaolbreak**) an escape from jail.

jail·er /jáylər/ *n.* (also **jail·or**, *Brit.* **gaoler**) a person in charge of a jail or of the prisoners in it.

jake /jayk/ *adj. sl.* all right; satisfactory.

ja·la·pe·ño /halapáynyō, –péen–/ *n.* a variety of hot pepper commonly used in Mexican and other highly spiced cooking.

ja·lop·y /jəlópee/ *n.* (*pl.* **-ies**) *colloq.* a dilapidated old motor vehicle.

jal·ou·sie /jáləsee/ *n.* a blind or shutter made of a row of angled slats to keep out rain, etc., and control the influx of light.

jam[1] /jam/ *v.* & *n.* • *v.tr.* & *intr.* (**jammed, jamming**) **1 a** *tr.* (usu. foll. by *into*) squeeze or wedge into a space. **b** *intr.* become wedged. **2 a** *tr.* cause (machinery or a component) to become wedged or immovable so that it cannot work. **b** *intr.* become jammed in this way. **3** *tr.* push or cram together in a compact mass. **4** *intr.* (foll. by *in, onto*) push or crowd (*they jammed onto the bus*). **5** *tr.* **a** block (a passage, road, etc.) by crowding or obstructing. **b** (foll. by *in*) obstruct the exit of (*we were jammed in*). **6** *tr.* (usu. foll. by *on*) apply (brakes, etc.) forcefully or abruptly. **7** *tr.* make (a radio transmission) unintelligible by causing interference. **8** *intr. colloq.* (in jazz, etc.) improvise with other musicians. • *n.* **1** a squeeze or crush. **2** a crowded mass (*traffic jam*). **3** *colloq.* an awkward situation or predicament. **4** a stoppage (of a machine, etc.) due to jamming. **5** (in full **jam session**) *colloq.* improvised playing by a group of musicians. ▫▫ **jam·mer** *n.*

jam[2] /jam/ *n.* & *v.* • *n.* **1** a conserve of fruit and sugar boiled to a thick consistency. **2** *Brit. colloq.* something easy or pleasant (*money for jam*). • *v.tr.* (**jammed, jamming**) **1** spread jam on. **2** make (fruit, etc.) into jam.

jamb /jam/ *n. Archit.* a side post or surface of a doorway, window, or fireplace.

jam·ba·lay·a /júmbəlíə/ *n.* a dish of rice with shrimp, chicken, etc.

jam·bo·ree /jámbəreé/ *n.* **1** a celebration or merrymaking. **2** a large rally of Boy Scouts or Girl Scouts.

jam-packed *adj. colloq.* full to capacity.

Jan. *abbr.* January.

jane /jayn/ *n. sl.* a woman (*a plain jane*).

jan·gle /jánggəl/ *v.* & *n.* • *v.* **1** *intr.* & *tr.* make, or cause (a bell, etc.) to make, a harsh metallic sound. **2** *tr.* irritate (the nerves, etc.) by discordant sound or speech, etc. • *n.* a harsh metallic sound.

jan·i·tor /jánitər/ *n.* **1** a caretaker of a building. **2** *Brit.* a doorman. ▫▫ **jan·i·to·ri·al** /–táwreeəl/ *adj.*

Jan·u·ar·y /jányōōeree/ *n.* (*pl.* **-ies**) the first month of the year.

Jap /jap/ *n.* & *adj. colloq.* often *offens.* = JAPANESE.

ja·pan /jəpán/ *n.* & *v.* • *n.* **1** a hard, usu. black varnish, esp. of a kind brought orig. from Japan. **2** work in a Japanese style. • *v.tr.* (**japanned, japanning**) **1** varnish with japan. **2** make black and glossy as with japan.

Jap·a·nese /jápəneéz/ *n.* & *adj.* • *n.* (*pl.* same) **1 a** a native or national of Japan. **b** a person of Japanese descent. **2** the language of Japan. • *adj.* of or relating to Japan, its people, or its language.

Jap·a·nese bee·tle *n.* an iridescent green and brown beetle that is a garden and crop pest.

jape /jayp/ *n.* & *v.* • *n.* a practical joke. • *v.intr.* play a joke. ▫▫ **jap·er·y** *n.*

ja·pon·i·ca /jəpónikə/ *n.* a camellia, *Camellia japonica*, with variously colored waxy flowers.

jar[1] /jaar/ *n.* **1** a container of glass, earthenware, plastic, etc., usu. cylindrical. **2** the contents of this. ▫▫ **jar·ful** *n.* (*pl.* **-fuls**).

jar[2] /jaar/ *v.* & *n.* • *v.* (**jarred, jarring**) **1** *intr.* (often foll. by *on*) (of sound, words, manner, etc.) sound discordant or grating (on the nerves, etc.). **2 a** *tr.* (foll. by *against, on*) strike or cause to strike with vibration or a grating sound. **b** *intr.* (of a body affected) vibrate gratingly. **3** *tr.* send a shock through (a part of the body) (*the fall jarred his neck*). **4** *intr.* (often foll. by *with*) (of an opinion, fact, etc.) be at variance; be in conflict or in dispute. • *n.* **1** a jarring sound or sensation. **2** a physical shock or jolt. **3** lack of harmony; disagreement.

jar[3] /jaar/ *n.* ▫ **on the jar** ajar.

jar·di·niere /jaárd'neér, zhaárdinyáir/ *n.* (also **jar·di·nière**) **1** an ornamental pot or stand for the display of growing plants. **2** a dish of mixed vegetables.

jar·gon /jaárgən/ *n.* **1** words or expressions used by a particular group or profession (*medical jargon*). **2** barbarous or debased language. **3** gibberish. ▫▫ **jar·gon·ic** /–gónik/ *adj.* **jar·gon·is·tic** *adj.* **jar·gon·ize** *v.tr.* & *intr.*

jas·mine /jázmin/ *n.* (also **jes·sa·mine** /jésəmin/) any of various fragrant ornamental shrubs of the genus *Jasminum* usu. with white or yellow flowers.

jas·per /jáspər/ *n.* an opaque variety of quartz, usu. red, yellow, or brown in color.

jaun·dice /jáwndis/ *n.* & *v.* • *n.* **1** *Med.* a condition with yellowing of the skin or whites of the eyes, often caused by obstruction of the bile duct or by liver disease. **2** disordered (esp. mental) vision. **3** envy. • *v.tr.* **1** affect with jaundice. **2** (esp. as **jaundiced** *adj.*) affect (a person) with envy, resentment, or jealousy.

jaunt /jawnt/ *n.* & *v.* • *n.* a short excursion for enjoyment. • *v.intr.* take a jaunt.

jaun·ty /jáwntee/ *adj.* (**jauntier, jauntiest**) **1** cheerful and self-confident. **2** sprightly. ▫▫ **jaun·ti·ly** *adv.* **jaun·ti·ness** *n.*

Ja·van /jaávən/ *n.* & *adj.* = JAVANESE.

Jav·a·nese /jávəneéz, jaá–/ *n.* & *adj.* • *n.* (*pl.* same) **1 a** a native of Java in Indonesia. **b** a person of Javanese descent. **2** the language of Java. • *adj.* of or relating to Java, its people, or its language.

jave·lin /jávəlin, jávlin/ *n.* **1** a light spear thrown in a competitive sport or as a weapon. **2** the athletic event or sport of throwing the javelin.

jaw /jaw/ *n.* & *v.* • *n.* **1 a** each of the upper and lower bony structures in vertebrates forming the framework of the mouth and containing the teeth. **b** the parts of certain invertebrates used for the ingestion of food. **2 a** (in *pl.*) the mouth with its bones and teeth. **b** the narrow mouth of a valley, channel, etc. **c** the gripping parts of a tool or machine. **d** gripping power (*jaws of death*). **3** *colloq.* **a** talkativeness; tedious talk. **b** a sermonizing talk; a lecture. •*v. colloq.* **1** *intr.* speak, esp. at tedious length. **2** *tr.* **a** persuade by talking. **b** admonish or lecture.

jaw·bone /jáwbōn/ *n.&v.* •*n.* **1** each of the two bones forming the lower jaw in most mammals. **2** these two combined into one in other mammals. •*v.* attempt to persuade or pressure by the force of one's position of authority.

jaw·break·er /jáwbraykər/ *n.* **1** *colloq.* a word that is very long or hard to pronounce. **2** a round, very hard candy.

jay /jay/ *n.* **1 a** a noisy chattering European bird, *Garrulus glandarius*, with vivid pinkish-brown, blue, black, and white plumage. **b** any other bird of the subfamily Garrulinae. **2** a person who chatters impertinently.

jay·walk /jáywawk/ *v.intr.* cross or walk in the street or road without regard for traffic. ▫▫ **jay·walk·er** *n.*

jazz /jaz/ *n. & v.* •*n.* **1** music of American origin characterized by improvisation, syncopation, and usu. a regular or forceful rhythm. **2** *sl.* pretentious talk or behavior, nonsensical stuff (*all that jazz*). •*v.intr.* play or dance to jazz. ▫ **jazz up** brighten or enliven. ▫▫ **jazz·er** *n.*

jazz·y /jázee/ *adj.* (**jazzier, jazziest**) **1** of or like jazz. **2** vivid; unrestrained; showy. ▫▫ **jazz·i·ly** *adv.* **jazz·i·ness** *n.*

JCS *abbr.* (also **J.C.S.**) Joint Chiefs of Staff.

jct. *abbr.* junction.

jeal·ous /jéləs/ *adj.* **1** (often foll. by *of*) fiercely protective (of rights, etc.). **2** afraid, suspicious, or resentful of rivalry in love or affection. **3** (often foll. by *of*) envious or resentful (of a person or a person's advantages, etc.). **4** (of God) intolerant of disloyalty. **5** (of inquiry, supervision, etc.) vigilant. ▫▫ **jeal·ous·ly** *adv.*

jeal·ous·y /jéləsee/ *n.* (*pl.* **-ies**) **1** a jealous state or feeling. **2** an instance of this.

jean /jeen/ *n.* twilled cotton cloth.

jeans /jeenz/ *n.pl.* pants made of jean or (more usually) denim, for informal wear.

jeep /jeep/ *n.* (also *Trademark* **Jeep**) a small, sturdy, esp. military motor vehicle with four-wheel drive.

jee·pers /jeépərz/ *int. sl.* expressing surprise, etc.

jeer /jeer/ *v. & n.* •*v.* **1** *intr.* (usu. foll. by *at*) scoff derisively. **2** *tr.* scoff at; deride. *n.* a scoff or taunt. ▫▫ **jeer·ing·ly** *adv.*

jeez /jeez/ *int. sl.* a mild expression of surprise, discovery, etc. (cf. GEE[1]).

je·had var. of JIHAD.

Je·ho·vah /jəhṓvə/ *n.* the Hebrew name of God in the Old Testament.

je·june /jijoōn/ *adj.* **1** intellectually unsatisfying; shallow. **2** puerile. **3** (of ideas, writings, etc.) meager; scanty; dry and uninteresting. **4** (of the land) barren; poor. ▫▫ **je·june·ly** *adv.* **je·june·ness** *n.*

je·ju·num /jijoōnəm/ *n. Anat.* the part of the small intestine between the duodenum and ileum.

jell /jel/ *v.intr. colloq.* **1 a** set as a jelly. **b** (of ideas, etc.) take a definite form. **2** (of two different things) cohere.

jel·li·fy /jélifī/ *v.tr. & intr.* (**-fies, -fied**) turn into jelly; make or become like jelly. ▫▫ **jel·li·fi·ca·tion** *n.*

jel·ly /jélee/ *n. & v.* •*n.* (*pl.* **-lies**) **1 a** a gelatinous preparation of fruit juice, etc., for use as a jam or a condiment (*grape jelly*). **b** esp. *Brit.* a soft, stiffish, semitransparent preparation of boiled sugar and fruit juice or milk, etc., often cooled in a mold and eaten as a dessert. **c** a similar preparation derived from meat, bones, etc., and gelatin (*marrowbone jelly*). **2** any substance of a similar consistency. **3** an inexpensive sandal or shoe made of molded plastic. •*v.* (**-lies, -ied**) **1** *intr. & tr.* set or cause to set as a jelly; congeal. **2** *tr.* set (food) in a jelly (*jellied eels*). ▫▫ **jel·ly·like** *adj.*

jel·ly bean *n.* a chewy, gelatinous candy in the shape of a bean with a hard sugar coating.

jel·ly·fish /jéleefish/ *n.* (*pl.* usu. same) **1** a marine coelenterate of the class Scyphozoa having an umbrella-shaped jellylike body and stinging tentacles. **2** *colloq.* a feeble person.

jel·ly roll *n.* a rolled sponge cake with a jelly filling.

je ne sais quoi /zhə nə say kwaá/ *n.* an indefinable something.

jen·net /jénit/ *n.* a small Spanish horse.

jen·ny /jénee/ *n.* (*pl.* **-nies**) **1** *hist.* = SPINNING JENNY. **2** a female donkey or ass.

jeop·ard·ize /jépərdīz/ *v.tr.* endanger; put into jeopardy.

jeop·ard·y /jépərdee/ *n.* **1** danger, esp. of severe harm or loss. **2** *Law* danger resulting from being on trial for a criminal offense.

Jer. *abbr.* Jeremiah (Old Testament).

jerbil esp. *Brit.* var. of GERBIL.

jer·e·mi·ad /jérimíad/ *n.* a doleful complaint or lamentation; a list of woes.

Jer·e·mi·ah /jérimíə/ *n.* a dismal prophet; a denouncer of the times.

jerk[1] /jərk/ *n. & v.* •*n.* **1** a sharp sudden pull, twist, twitch, start, etc. **2** a spasmodic muscular twitch. **3** *sl.* a fool; a stupid or contemptible person. •*v.* **1** *intr.* move with a jerk. **2** *tr.* pull, thrust, twist, etc., with a jerk. **3** *tr.* throw with a suddenly arrested motion. **4** *tr. Weightlifting* raise (a weight) from shoulder level to above the head. ▫ **jerk off** *coarse sl.* masturbate.

▶Usually considered a taboo use. ▫▫ **jerk·er** *n.*

jerk[2] /jərk/ *v.tr.* cure (beef) by cutting it in long slices and drying it in the sun.

jer·kin /jə́rkin/ *n.* **1** a sleeveless jacket. **2** *hist.* a man's close-fitting jacket, often of leather.

jerk·y[1] /jə́rkee/ *adj.* (**jerkier, jerkiest**) **1** having sudden abrupt movements. **2** spasmodic. ▫▫ **jerk·i·ly** *adv.* **jerk·i·ness** *n.*

jerk·y[2] *n.* meat that has been cured by being cut into long, thin strips and dried.

jer·o·bo·am /jérəbṓəm/ *n.* a wine bottle of 4–12 times the ordinary size.

jer·ry-build·er /jéribildər/ *n.* a builder of unsubstantial houses, etc., with poor-quality materials. ▫▫ **jer·ry-build·ing** *n.* **jer·ry-built** *adj.*

jer·ry·man·der esp. *Brit.* var. of GERRYMANDER.

jer·sey /jə́rzee/ *n.* (*pl.* **-seys**) **1 a** a knitted, usu. woolen pullover or similar garment. **b** a plain-knitted (orig. woolen) fabric. **2** (**Jersey**) a light brown dairy cow from Jersey.

jess /jes/ *n. & v.* •*n.* a short strap of leather, silk, etc., put around the leg of a hawk in falconry. •*v.tr.* put jesses on (a hawk, etc.).

jes·sa·mine var. of JASMINE.

jest /jest/ *n. & v.* •*n.* **1 a** a joke. **b** fun. **2 a** raillery; banter. **b** an object of derision (*a standing jest*). •*v.intr.* **1** joke; make jests. **2** fool about; play or act triflingly. ▫ **in jest** in fun. ▫▫ **jest·ful** *adj.*

---

jest late Middle English: from earlier *gest*, from Old French *geste*, from Latin *gesta* 'actions, exploits', from *gerere* 'do'. The original sense was 'exploit, heroic deed', hence 'a narrative of such deeds' (originally in verse); later the term denoted an idle tale, hence a joke (mid-16th cent.).

---

jest·er /jéstər/ *n.* a professional joker or fool at a medieval court, etc., traditionally wearing a cap and bells and carrying a scepter.

Jes·u·it /jézhōōit, jézōō–, jézyōō–/ *n.* a member of the Society of Jesus, a Roman Catholic order founded by St. Ignatius Loyola and others in 1534.

Je·sus /jeézəs/ *n.* the name of the source of the Christian religion d. *c.* AD 30.

jet[1] /jet/ *n. & v.* •*n.* **1** a stream of water, steam, gas, flame, etc., shot out esp. from a small opening. **2** a spout or nozzle for emitting water, etc., in this way. **3 a** a jet engine. **b** an aircraft powered by one or more jet engines. •*v.* (**jetted, jetting**) **1** *intr.* spurt out in jets. **2** *tr. & intr. colloq.* send or travel by jet plane.

jet[2] /jet/ *n.* **1 a** a hard black variety of lignite capable of being carved and highly polished. **b** (*attrib.*) made of this. **2** (in full **jet-black**) a deep glossy black color.

jet·é /zhətáy/ *n. Ballet* a spring or leap with one leg forward and the other stretched backward.

jet en·gine *n.* an engine using jet propulsion for forward thrust, esp. of an aircraft.

jet lag *n.* extreme tiredness and other bodily effects felt after a long flight involving marked differences of local time.

jet-pro·pelled *adj.* **1** having jet propulsion. **2** (of a person, etc.) very fast.

jet pro·pul·sion *n.* propulsion by the backward ejection of a high-speed jet of gas, etc.

jet·sam /jétsəm/ *n.* discarded material washed ashore, esp. that thrown overboard to lighten a ship, etc. (cf. FLOTSAM).

jet set *n. colloq.* wealthy people frequently traveling by air, esp. for pleasure. ▫▫ **jet-set·ter** *n.*

jet stream *n.* **1** a narrow current of very strong winds encircling the globe several miles above the earth. **2** the stream of exhaust from a jet engine.

jet·ti·son /jétisən, –zən/ *v. & n.* •*v.tr.* **1 a** throw (esp. heavy material) overboard to lighten a ship, hot-air balloon, etc. **b** drop (goods) from an aircraft. **2** abandon; get rid of (something no longer wanted). •*n.* the act of jettisoning.

jet·ty /jétee/ *n.* (*pl.* **-ties**) **1** a pier or breakwater constructed to protect or defend a harbor, coast, etc. **2** a landing pier.

Jew /jōō/ *n.* a person of Hebrew descent or whose religion is Judaism.

jew·el /jōōəl/ *n. & v.* •*n.* **1 a** a precious stone. **b** this as used for its hardness as a bearing in watchmaking. **2** a personal ornament containing a jewel or jewels. **3** a precious person or thing. •*v.tr.* (**jeweled, jeweling**; esp. *Brit.* **jewelled, jewelling**) **1** (esp. as **jeweled** *adj.*) adorn or set with jewels. **2** (in watchmaking) set with jewels. ▫▫ **jew·el·like** *adj.*

jew·el box *n.* a plastic case for a compact disc or CD-ROM.

jew·el·er /jōōələr/ *n.* (esp. *Brit.* **jeweller**) a maker of or dealer in jewels or jewelry.

jew·el·ry /jōōəlree/ *n.* (esp. *Brit.* **jewellery** /jōōəlree/) jewels or other ornamental objects, esp. for personal adornment, regarded collectively.

▶Avoid pronouncing this word "joo-luh-ree"; many regard this as uneducated.

jew·el·ry box *n.* a box in which jewelry is kept.

Jew·ish /jōōish/ *adj.* **1** of or relating to Jews. **2** of Judaism. ▫▫ **Jew·ish·ly** *adv.* **Jew·ish·ness** *n.*

Jew's (or **Jews'**) **harp** *n.* a small lyre-shaped musical instrument held between the teeth and struck with the finger.

Jez·e·bel /jézəbel/ *n.* a shameless or immoral woman.

jg *abbr.* (also **J.G.**) *US Navy* junior grade.

jib[1] /jib/ *n. & v.* •*n.* **1** a triangular staysail from the outer end of a forward-extending boom (the jibboom) to the top of the foremast or from the bowsprit to the mast-head. **2** the projecting arm of a crane. •*v.tr. & intr.* (**jibbed, jibbing**) (of a sail, etc.) pull or swing around from one side of the ship to the other; jibe.

jib[2] /jib/ *v.intr.* (**jibbed, jibbing**) esp. *Brit.* **1 a** (of an animal, esp. a horse) stop and refuse to go on; move backward or sideways instead of going on. **b** (of a person) refuse to continue. **2** (foll. by *at*) show aversion to (a person or course of action). ▫▫ **jib·ber** *n.*

jibe[1] var. of GIBE.

jibe[2] /jīb/ *v. & n.* (*Brit.* **gybe**) •*v.* **1** *intr.* (of a fore-and-aft sail or boom) swing from side to side in running before the winds. **2** *tr.* cause (a sail) to do this. **3** *intr.* (of a ship or its crew) change course so that this happens. •*n.* a change of course causing jibing.

jibe[3] /jīb/ *v.intr.* (usu. foll. by *with*) *colloq.* agree; be in accord.

▶**Jibe** means 'agree; go together'; **gibe** means 'jeer; deride.' The two words are pronounced identically, but neither should be confused with **jive**, a jazz term applied to a style of music and dance, as well as having the sense 'misleading or pretentious talk.' **Jive** is sometimes informally substituted for **jibe.**

jiff /jif/ *n.* (also **jif·fy**, *pl.* **-ies**) *colloq.* a short time; a moment (*in a jiffy*; *half a jiff*).

jig /jig/ *n. & v.* •*n.* **1 a** a lively dance with leaping movements. **b** the music for this, usu. in triple time. **2** a device that holds a piece of work and guides the tools operating on it. •*v.* (**jigged, jigging**) **1** *intr.* dance a jig. **2** *tr. & intr.* move quickly and jerkily up and down. **3** *tr.* work on or equip with a jig or jigs. ▫ **jig about** (esp. *Brit.*) fidget. **the jig is up** sl. all hope is gone, esp. of committing a wrong without being caught.

jig·ger[1] /jígər/ *n.* **1** *Naut.* **a** a small tackle consisting of a double and single block with a rope. **b** a small sail at the stern. **c** a small smack having this. **2** *sl.* a gadget. **3** *Golf* an iron club with a narrow face. **4** *Billiards colloq.* a cue rest. **5 a** a measure of spirits, etc. **b** a small glass holding this. **6** a person or thing that jigs.

jig·ger[2] /jígər/ *n.* CHIGGER.

jig·gered /jígərd/ *adj. colloq.* (as a mild oath) confounded (*I'll be jiggered*).

jig·gle /jígəl/ *v.* (often foll. by *about*, etc.) **1** *tr.* shake lightly; rock jerkily. **2** *intr.* fidget. ▫▫ **jig·gly** *adj.*

jig·saw /jígsaw/ *n.* **1 a** (in full **jigsaw puzzle**) a puzzle consisting of a picture on board or wood, etc., cut into irregular interlocking pieces to be reassembled. **b** a mental puzzle resolvable by assembling various pieces of information. **2** a machine saw with a fine blade enabling it to cut curved lines in a sheet of wood, metal, etc.

jill /jil/ *n.* sl. (also **Jill**) a young woman.

jil·lion /jílyən/ *n. colloq.* a very large indefinite number.

jilt /jilt/ *v. & n.* •*v.tr.* abruptly reject or abandon (a lover, etc.). •*n.* a person (esp. a woman) who jilts a lover.

jim crow /jim krṓ/ *n.* (also **Jim Crow**) **1** the practice of segregating blacks. **2** *offens.* a black person. **3** an implement for straightening iron bars or bending rails by screw pressure. ▫▫ **jim crow·ism** *n.* (in sense 1).

jim·my /jímee/ *n. & v.* (*Brit.* **jemmy** /jémee/) •*n.* (*pl.* **-mies**) a burglar's short crowbar, usu. made in sections. •*v.tr.* (**-mies, -mied**) force open with a jimmy.

jim·son·weed /jímsənweed/ *n.* = THORN APPLE.

jin·gle /jinggəl/ *n. & v.* •*n.* **1** a mixed noise as of bells or light metal objects being shaken together. **2 a** a repetition of the same sound in words, esp. as an aid to memory or to attract attention. **b** a short verse of this kind used in advertising, etc. •*v. intr. & tr.* make or cause to make a jingling sound. ▫▫ **jin·gly** *adj.* (**jinglier, jingliest**).

jin·go /jínggō/ *n.* (*pl.* **-goes**) a supporter of policy favoring war; a blustering patriot. □□ **jin·go·ism** *n.* **jin·go·ist** *n.* **jin·go·is·tic** /–gō-ístik/ *adj.*

jin·ni /jínee, jinée/ *n.* (also **jinn, djinn** /jin/) (*pl.* **jinn** or **jinns, djinn** or **djinns**) (in Muslim mythology) an intelligent being lower than the angels, able to appear in human and animal forms, and having power over people.

jinx /jingks/ *n. & v. colloq.* •*n.* a person or thing that seems to cause bad luck. •*v.tr.* (often in *passive*) subject (a person) to an unlucky force.

jit·ter /jítər/ *n. & v. colloq.* •*n.* (**the jitters**) extreme nervousness. •*v.intr.* be nervous; act nervously. □□ **jit·ter·y** *adj.* **jit·ter·i·ness** *n.*

jit·ter·bug /jítərbug/ *n. & v.* •*n.* **1** a nervous person. **2** *hist.* **a** a fast popular dance. **b** a person fond of dancing this. •*v.intr.* (**-bugged, -bugging**) dance the jitterbug.

jive /jīv/ *n. & v.* •*n.* **1** a jerky lively style of dance esp. popular in the 1950s. **2** music for this. **3** *sl.* talk, conversation, esp. when misleading or pretentious. •*v.intr.* **1** dance the jive. **2** play jive music. □□ **jiv·er** *n.* ▶See note at JIBE.

job /job/ *n. & v.* •*n.* **1** a piece of work, esp. one done for hire or profit. **2** a paid position of employment. **3** *colloq.* anything one has to do. **4** *colloq.* a difficult task (*had a job to find them*). **5** a product of work, esp. if well done. **6** *Computing* an item of work regarded separately. **7** *sl.* a crime, esp. a robbery. **8** a transaction in which private advantage prevails over duty or public interest. **9** a state of affairs or set of circumstances (*is a bad job*). •*v.* (**jobbed, jobbing**) **1 a** *intr.* do jobs; do piecework. **b** *tr.* (usu. foll. by *out*) let or deal with for profit; subcontract. **2 a** *intr.* deal in stocks. **b** *tr.* buy and sell (stocks or goods) as a middleman. **3 a** *intr.* turn a position of trust to private advantage. **b** *tr.* deal corruptly with (a matter). **4** *tr. sl.* swindle. □ **make a job** (or **good job**) **of** do thoroughly or successfully. **on the job** *colloq.* at work; in the course of doing a piece of work. **out of a job** unemployed.

job·ber /jóbər/ *n.* **1 a** a wholesaler. **b** *derog.* a broker (see BROKER 2). **2** *Brit.* before 1986, a principal or wholesaler dealing on the stock exchange. **3** a person who jobs.

job·ber·y /jóbəree/ *n.* corrupt dealing.

job·less /jóblis/ *adj.* without a job; unemployed. □□ **job·less·ness** *n.*

job lot *n.* a miscellaneous group of articles, esp. bought together.

job-shar·ing *n.* an arrangement by which a full-time job is done jointly by several part-time employees who share the remuneration.

jock[1] /jok/ *n. colloq.* a jockey.

jock[2] /jok/ *n. sl.* **1** = JOCKSTRAP. **2** an athlete.

jock·ey /jókee/ *n. & v.* •*n.* (*pl.* **-eys**) a rider in horse races, esp. a professional one. •*v.* (**-eys, -eyed**) **1** *tr.* **a** trick or cheat (a person). **b** outwit. **2** *tr.* (foll. by *away, out, in*, etc.) draw (a person) by trickery. **3** *intr.* cheat. □ **jockey for position** try to gain an advantageous position, esp. by skillful maneuvering or unfair action. □□ **jock·ey·dom** *n.* **jock·ey·ship** *n.*

jockey late 16th cent.: diminutive of JOCK. Originally the name for an ordinary man, lad, or underling, the word came to mean 'mounted courier', hence the current sense (late 17th cent.). Another early use 'horse-dealer' (long a byword for dishonesty) probably gave rise to the verb sense 'manipulate', whereas the main verb sense probably relates to the behavior of jockeys maneuvering for an advantageous position during a race.

jock·strap /jókstrap/ *n.* a support or protection for the male genitals, worn esp. by athletes.

joc·u·lar /jókyələr/ *adj.* **1** merry; fond of joking. **2** of the nature of a joke; humorous. □□ **joc·u·lar·i·ty** /–láritee/ *n.* (*pl.* **-ties**). **joc·u·lar·ly** *adv.*

joc·und /jókənd, jṓ–/ *adj. literary* merry; cheerful; sprightly. □□ **jo·cun·di·ty** /jəkúnditee/ *n.* (*pl.* **-ties**).

Joe Blow /jō blṓ/ *n. colloq.* a hypothetical average man.

jo·ey /jṓee/ *n.* (*pl.* **-eys**) *Austral.* a young kangaroo.

jog /jog/ *v. & n.* •*v.* (**jogged, jogging**) **1** *intr.* run at a slow pace, esp. as physical exercise. **2** *intr.* (of a horse) move at a jog trot. **3** *intr.* (often foll. by *on, along*) proceed laboriously; trudge. **4** *intr.* go on one's way. **5** *intr.* proceed; get through the time (*we must jog on somehow*). **6** *intr.* move up and down with an unsteady motion. **7** *tr.* nudge (a person), esp. to arouse attention. **8** *tr.* shake with a push or jerk. **9** *tr.* stimulate (a person's or one's own memory). •*n.* **1** a shake, push, or nudge. **2** a slow walk or trot.

jog·ger /jógər/ *n.* a person who jogs, esp. one who runs for physical exercise.

jog·gle[1] /jógəl/ *v. & n.* •*v.tr. & intr.* shake or move by or as if by repeated jerks. •*n.* **1** a slight shake. **2** the act or action of joggling.

jog·gle[2] /jógəl/ *n. & v.* •*n.* **1** a joint of two pieces of stone or lumber, contrived to prevent their sliding on one another. **2** a notch in one of the two pieces, a projection in the other, or a small piece let in between the two, for this purpose. •*v.tr.* join with a joggle.

john /jon/ *n. sl.* a toilet or bathroom.

John Bull /jon bŏŏl/ *n.* a personification of England or the typical Englishman.

john·ny /jónee/ *n.* (*pl.* **-nies**) **1** *colloq.* (also **Johnny**) a fellow; a man. **2** *sl.* a short-sleeved, collarless gown worn by patients in hospitals, examining rooms, etc.

joie de vi·vre /zhwaá də veévrə/ *n.* a feeling of healthy and exuberant enjoyment of life.

join /joyn/ *v. & n.* •*v.* **1** *tr.* (often foll. by *to, together*) put together; fasten; unite (one thing or person to another or several together). **2** *tr.* connect (points) by a line, etc. **3** *tr.* become a member of (an association, society, organization, etc.). **4** *tr.* take one's place with or in (a company, group, procession, etc.). **5** *tr.* **a** come into the company of (a person). **b** (foll. by *in*) take part with (others) in an activity, etc. (*joined me in condemnation of the outrage*). **c** (foll. by *for*) share the company of for a specified occasion (*may I join you for lunch?*). **6** *intr.* (often foll. by *with, to*) come together; be united. **7** *intr.* (often foll. by *in*) take part with others in an activity, etc. **8** *tr.* be or become connected or continuous with (*the Gila River joins the Colorado at Yuma*). *n.* a point, line, or surface at which two or more things are joined. □ **join battle** begin fighting. **join forces** combine efforts. **join hands 1 a** clasp each other's hands. **b** clasp one's hands together. **2** combine in an action or enterprise. **join up 1** enlist for military service. **2** (often foll. by *with*) unite. □□ **join·a·ble** *adj.*

join·der /jóyndər/ *n. Law* the act of bringing together.

join·er /jóynər/ *n.* **1** a person who makes furniture and light woodwork. **2** *colloq.* a person who readily joins societies, etc. □□ **join·er·y** *n.* (in sense 1).

joint /joynt/ *n., adj., & v.* •*n.* **1 a** a place at which two things are joined together. **b** a point at which, or a contrivance by which, two parts of an artificial structure are joined. **2** a structure in an animal body by which two bones are fitted together. **3 a** any of the parts into which an animal carcass is divided for food. **b** any of the parts of which a body is made up. **4** *sl.* a place of meeting for drinking, etc. **5** *sl.* a marijuana cigarette. **6** the part of a stem from which a leaf or branch grows. **7** a piece of flexible material forming the hinge of a book cover. **8** *Geol.* a fissure in a mass of rock. •*adj.* **1** held or done by, or belonging to, two or more persons, etc., in conjunction (*a joint mortgage; joint action*). **2** sharing with another in some action, state, etc. (*joint author; joint favorite*). •*v.tr.* **1** connect by joints. **2** divide (a body or member) at a joint or into joints. **3** fill up the joints of (masonry, etc.) with mortar, etc.; trim the surface of (a mortar joint). **4** prepare (a board, etc.) for being joined to another by planing its edge. □ **out of joint 1** (of a bone) dislocated. **2 a** out of order. **b** inappropriate. □□ **joint·less** *adj.* **joint·ly** *adv.*

Joint Chiefs of Staff *n.pl. Mil.* a military advisory group made up of the Army Chief of Staff, the Air Force Chief of Staff, the Marine Corps commandant, and the Chief of Naval Operations.

joint stock *n.* capital held jointly; a common fund.

joist /joyst/ *n.* each of a series of parallel supporting beams of lumber, steel, etc., used in floors, ceilings, etc. □□ **joist·ed** *adj.*

jo·jo·ba /hōhṓbə/ *n.* a plant, *Simmondsia chinensis*, with seeds yielding an oily extract used in cosmetics, etc.

joke /jōk/ *n. & v.* •*n.* **1 a** a thing said or done to excite laughter. **b** a witticism or jest. **2** a ridiculous thing, person, or circumstance. •*v.* **1** *intr.* make jokes. **2** *tr.* poke fun at; banter. □ **no joke** *colloq.* a serious matter. □□ **jok·ing·ly** *adv.* **jok·ey** *adj.* (also **jok·y**). **jok·i·ly** *adv.* **jok·i·ness** *n.*

jok·er /jṓkər/ *n.* **1** a person who jokes. **2** *sl.* a fellow; a man. **3** a playing card usu. with a figure of a jester, used in some games esp. as a wild card. **4** an unexpected factor or resource.

jol·li·fy /jólifī/ *v.tr. & intr.* (**-fies, -fied**) make or be merry, esp. in drinking. □□ **jol·li·fi·ca·tion** *n.*

jol·li·ty /jólitee/ *n.* (*pl.* **-ties**) **1** merrymaking; festiveness. **2** (in *pl.*) festivities.

jol·ly[1] /jólee/ *adj., adv., v., & n.* •*adj.* (**jollier, jolliest**) **1** cheerful and good-humored; merry. **2** festive; jovial. **3** slightly drunk. •*adv.* esp. *Brit. colloq.* very (*they were jolly unlucky*). •*v.tr.* (**-lies, -lied**) **1** (usu. foll. by *along*) *colloq.* coax or humor (a person) in a friendly way. **2** chaff; banter. •*n.* (*pl.* **-lies**) *colloq.* a party or celebration; an outing. □□ **jol·li·ly** *adv.* □ **get one' jollies** *informal* have fun or find pleasure **jol·li·ness** *n.*

jol·ly[2] /jólee/ *n.* (*pl.* **-lies**) (in full **jolly boat**) a ship's boat smaller than a cutter.

jolt /jōlt/ *v. & n.* •*v.* **1** *tr.* disturb or shake from the normal position (esp. in a moving vehicle) with a jerk. **2** *tr.* give a mental shock to; perturb. **3** *intr.* (of a vehicle) move along with jerks, as on a rough road. *n.* **1** such a jerk. **2** a surprise or shock. □□ **jolt·y** *adj.* (**joltier, joltiest**).

jon·quil /jóngkwil/ *n.* a bulbous plant, *Narcissus jonquilla*, with clusters of small fragrant yellow flowers.

Jor·da·ni·an /jawrdáyneeən/ *adj. & n.* •*adj.* of or relating to the kingdom of Jordan in the Middle East. •*n.* **1** a native or national of Jordan. **2** a person of Jordanian descent.

josh /josh/ *n. & v. sl.* •*n.* a good-natured or teasing joke. •*v.* **1** *tr.* tease or banter. **2** *intr.* indulge in ridicule. □□ **josh·er** *n.*

jos·tle /jósəl/ *v. & n.* •*v.* **1** *tr.* push against; elbow. **2** *tr.* (often foll. by *away, from*, etc.) push (a person) abruptly or roughly. **3** *intr.* (foll. by *against*) knock or push, esp. in a crowd. **4** *intr.* (foll. by *with*) struggle; have a rough exchange. *n.* **1** the act or an instance of jostling. **2** a collision.

jot /jot/ *v. & n.* •*v.tr.* (**jotted, jotting**) (usu. foll. by *down*) write briefly or hastily. •*n.* (usu. with *neg.* expressed or implied) a very small amount (*not one jot*).

jot·ting /jóting/ *n.* (usu. in *pl.*) a note; something jotted down.

joule /jōōl/ *n.* the SI unit of work or energy equal to the work done by a force of one newton when its point of application moves one meter in the direction of action of the force, equivalent to a watt-second. ¶ Symb.: **J**.

jounce /jowns/ *v.tr. & intr.* bump; bounce; jolt.

jour·nal /jə́rnəl/ *n.* **1** a newspaper or periodical. **2** a daily record of events. **3** *Naut.* a logbook. **4** a book in which business transactions are entered, with a statement of the accounts to which each is to be debited and credited. **5** the part of a shaft or axle that rests on bearings.

jour·nal·ism /jə́rnəlizəm/ *n.* the business or practice of writing and producing newspapers.

jour·nal·ist /jə́rnəlist/ *n.* a person employed to report for or edit a newspaper, journal, or newscast. □□ **jour·nal·is·tic** *adj.* **jour·nal·is·ti·cal·ly** /–ístikəlee/ *adv.*

jour·ney /jə́rnee/ *n. & v.* •*n.* (*pl.* **-neys**) **1** an act of going from one place to another, esp. at a long distance. **2** the distance traveled in a specified time (*a day's journey*). **3** the traveling of a vehicle along a route at a stated time. •*v.intr.* (**-neys, -neyed**) make a journey. □□ **jour·ney·er** *n.*

jour·ney·man /jə́rneemən/ *n.* (*pl.* **-men**) **1** a qualified mechanic or artisan who works for another. **2** *derog.* a reliable but not outstanding worker.

joust /jowst/ *n. & v. hist.* •*n.* a combat between two knights on horseback with lances. •*v.intr.* engage in a joust. □□ **joust·er** *n.*

Jove /jōv/ *n.* (in Roman mythology) Jupiter. □ **by Jove!** an exclamation of surprise or approval.

jo·vi·al /jṓveeəl/ *adj.* **1** merry. **2** convivial. **3** hearty and good-humored. □□ **jo·vi·al·i·ty** /–álitee/ *n.* **jo·vi·al·ly** *adv.*

Jo·vi·an /jṓveeən/ *adj.* **1** (in Roman mythology) of or like Jupiter. **2** of the planet Jupiter.

jowl[1] /jowl/ *n.* **1** the jaw or jawbone. **2** the cheek (*cheek by jowl*). □□ **-jowled** *adj.* (in *comb.*).

jowl[2] /jowl/ *n.* **1** the external loose skin on the throat or neck when prominent. **2** the dewlap of oxen, wattle of a bird, etc. □□ **jowl·y** *adj.*

joy /joy/ *n. & v.* •*n.* **1** (often foll. by *at, in*) a vivid emotion of pleasure; extreme gladness. **2** a thing that causes joy. •*v.* esp. *poet.* **1** *intr.* rejoice. **2** *tr.* gladden. □□ **joy·less** *adj.* **joy·less·ly** *adv.*

joy·ful /jóyfōōl/ *adj.* full of, showing, or causing joy. □□ **joy·ful·ly** *adv.* **joy·ful·ness** *n.*

joy·ous /jóyəs/ *adj.* (of an occasion, circumstance, etc.) characterized by pleasure or joy; joyful. □□ **joy·ous·ly** *adv.* **joy·ous·ness** *n.*

joy·ride /jóyrīd/ *n. & v. colloq.* •*n.* a ride for pleasure in an automobile, esp. without the owner's permission. •*v.intr.* (*past* **-rode** /–rōd/; *past part.* **-ridden** /–rid'n/) go for a joyride. □□ **joy·rid·er** *n.*

joy·stick /jóystik/ *n.* **1** *colloq.* the control column of an aircraft. **2** a lever that can be moved in several directions to control the movement of an image on a computer monitor.

JP *abbr.* **1** justice of the peace. **2** jet propulsion.

Jr. *abbr.* junior.

jt. *abbr.* joint.

ju·bi·lant /jṓōbilənt/ *adj.* exultant; rejoicing; joyful. □□ **ju·bi·lance** /–ləns/ *n.* **ju·bi·lant·ly** *adv.*

ju·bi·lee /jṓōbilee/ *n.* **1** a time or season of rejoicing. **2** an anniversary, esp. the 25th or 50th.

Ju·da·ism /jṓōdeeizəm, –day–/ *n.* **1** the religion of the Jews, with a belief in one God and a basis in Mosaic and rabbinical teachings. **2** the Jews collectively. □□ **Ju·da·ist** *n.*

Ju·das /jṓōdəs/ *n.* a person who betrays a friend.

Judeo- /jōōdáy-ō, –dée-ō/ *comb. form* (*Brit.* **Judaeo-**) Jewish; Jewish and.

judge /juj/ *n. & v.* •*n.* **1** a public officer appointed to hear and try causes in a court of justice. **2** a person appointed to decide a dispute or contest. **3 a** a person who decides a question. **b** a person regarded in terms of capacity to decide on the merits of a thing or question (*am no judge of that; a good judge of art*). •*v.* **1** *tr.* **a** try (a cause) in a court of justice. **b** pronounce sentence on (a person). **2** *tr.* form an opinion about; estimate, appraise. **3** *tr.* act as a judge of (a dispute or contest). **4** *tr.* (often foll. by *to* + infin. or *that* + clause) conclude, consider, or suppose. **5** *intr.* **a** form a judgment. **b** act as judge. ▫▫ **judge•like** *adj.* **judge•ship** *n.*

judg•ment /júǰmənt/ *n.* (also **judge•ment**) **1** the critical faculty; discernment (*an error of judgment*). **2** good sense. **3** an opinion or estimate (*in my judgment*). **4** the sentence of a court of justice; a decision by a judge. **5** often *joc.* a misfortune viewed as a deserved recompense (*it is a judgment on you for getting up late*). **6** criticism. ▫ **against one's better judgment** contrary to what one really feels to be advisable.

Judg•ment Day *n.* the day on which the Last Judgment is believed to take place.

judg•men•tal /jujmént'l/ *adj.* (also **judge•men•tal**) **1** of or concerning or by way of judgment. **2** condemning; critical. ▫▫ **judg•men•tal•ly** *adv.*

ju•di•ca•ture /jóódikəchər/ *n.* **1** the administration of justice. **2** a judge's office or term of office. **3** judges collectively; judiciary. **4** a court of justice.

ju•di•cial /jōōdíshəl/ *adj.* **1** of, done by, or proper to a court of law. **2** having the function of judgment (*a judicial assembly*). **3** of or proper to a judge. **4** expressing a judgment; critical. **5** impartial. **6** regarded as a divine judgment. ▫▫ **ju•di•cial•ly** *adv.*

▶**Judicial** means 'relating to judgment and the administration of justice': *judicial robes, the judicial system.* Do not confuse it with **judicious**, which means 'prudent, reasonable': *Getting off the highway the minute you felt tired was a judicious choice.*

ju•di•ci•ar•y /jōōdíshee-eree, –díshəree/ *n.* (*pl.* **-ies**) the judges of a state or nation's judicial branch collectively.

ju•di•cious /jōōdíshəs/ *adj.* **1** sensible; prudent. **2** sound in discernment and judgment. ▫▫ **ju•di•cious•ly** *adv.* **ju•di•cious•ness** *n.*

ju•do /jóódō/ *n.* a sport of unarmed combat derived from jujitsu. ▫▫ **ju•do•ist** *n.*

jug /jug/ *n.* & *v.* •*n.* **1 a** a deep vessel for holding liquids, with a handle and often with a spout or lip shaped for pouring. **b** the contents of this; a jugful. **2** a large jar with a narrow mouth. **3** *sl.* prison. **4** (in *pl.*) *coarse sl.* a woman's breasts. •*v.tr.* (**jugged, jugging**) **1** (usu. as **jugged** *adj.*) stew or boil (a hare or rabbit) in a covered vessel. **2** *sl.* imprison. ▫▫ **jug•ful** *n.* (*pl.* **-fuls**).

jug•gle /júgəl/ *v.* & *n.* •*v.* **1 a** *intr.* (often foll. by *with*) perform feats of dexterity, esp. by tossing objects in the air and catching them, keeping several in the air at the same time. **b** *tr.* perform such feats with. **2** *tr.* continue to deal with (several activities) at once, esp. with ingenuity. **3** *intr.* (foll. by *with*) & *tr.* **a** deceive or cheat. **b** misrepresent (facts). **c** rearrange adroitly. •*n.* **1** a piece of juggling. **2** a fraud.

jug•gler /júglər/ *n.* **1** a person who juggles. **2** a trickster or impostor. ▫▫ **jug•gler•y** *n.*

jug•u•lar /júgyələr/ *adj.* **1** of the neck or throat. **2** (of fish) having ventral fins in front of the pectoral fins.

juice /jōōs/ *n.* **1** the liquid part of vegetables or fruits. **2** the fluid part of an animal body or substance, esp. a secretion (*gastric juice*). **3** the essence or spirit of anything. **4** *colloq.* electricity as a source of power. **5** *sl.* alcoholic liquor. ▫▫ **juice•less** *adj.*

juic•er /jóósər/ *n.* **1** a kitchen tool or appliance for extracting the juice from fruits and vegetables. **2** *sl.* an alcoholic.

juic•y /jóósee/ *adj.* (**juicier, juiciest**) **1** full of juice; succulent. **2** *colloq.* substantial or interesting; racy; scandalous. **3** *colloq.* profitable. ▫▫ **juic•i•ly** *adv.* **juic•i•ness** *n.*

ju•jit•su /jōōjítsōō/ *n.* (also **jiu•jit•su**) a Japanese system of unarmed combat and physical training.

ju•jube /jóójōōb/ *n.* **1 a** any plant of the genus *Zizyphus* bearing edible acidic berrylike fruits. **b** this fruit. **2** a small lozenge or candy of gelatin, etc., flavored with or imitating this.

juke•box /jóókboks/ *n.* a machine that automatically plays a selected musical recording when a coin is inserted.

Jul. *abbr.* July.

ju•lep /jóólip/ *n.* **1** iced and flavored spirits and water (*mint julep*). **2 a** a sweet drink, esp. as a vehicle for medicine. **b** a medicated drink as a mild stimulant, etc.

Jul•ian /jóólyən/ *adj.* of or associated with Julius Caesar.

Jul•ian cal•en•dar *n.* a calendar introduced by Julius Caesar, in which the year consisted of 365 days, every fourth year having 366 (cf. GREGORIAN CALENDAR).

ju•li•enne /jóólee-én/ *n.* & *adj.* •*n.* foodstuff, esp. vegetables, cut into short, thin strips. •*adj.* cut into thin strips.

Ju•ly /jōōlí/ *n.* (*pl.* **Julies** or **Julys**) the seventh month of the year.

jum•ble /júmbəl/ *v.* & *n.* •*v.* **1** *tr.* (often foll. by *up*) confuse; mix up. **2** *intr.* move about in disorder. •*n.* a confused state or heap; a muddle. ▫▫ **jum•bly** *adj.*

jum•bo /júmbō/ *n.* & *adj. colloq.* •*n.* (*pl.* **-bos**) **1** a large animal (esp. an elephant), person, or thing. **2** (in full **jumbo jet**) a large airliner with capacity for several hundred passengers. •*adj.* **1** very large of its kind. **2** extra large (*jumbo packet*).

jump /jump/ *v.* & *n.* •*v.* **1** *intr.* move off the ground or other surface (usu. upward, at least initially) by sudden muscular effort in the legs. **2** *intr.* (often foll. by *up, from, in, out,* etc.) move suddenly or hastily in a specified way (*we jumped into the car*). **3** *intr.* give a sudden bodily movement from shock or excitement, etc. **4** *intr.* undergo a rapid change, esp. an advance in status. **5** *intr.* (often foll. by *about*) change or move rapidly from one idea or subject to another. **6 a** *intr.* rise or increase suddenly (*prices jumped*). **b** *tr.* cause to do this. **7** *tr.* **a** pass over (an obstacle, barrier, etc.) by jumping. **b** move or pass over (an intervening thing) to a point beyond. **8** *tr.* skip or pass over (a passage in a book, etc.). **9** *tr.* cause (a thing, or an animal, esp. a horse) to jump. **10** *intr.* (foll. by *to, at*) reach a conclusion hastily. **11** *tr.* (of a train) leave (the rails) owing to a fault. **12** *tr.* esp. *Brit.* ignore and pass (a red traffic light, etc.). **13** *tr.* get on or off (a train, etc.) quickly, esp. illegally or dangerously. **14** *tr.* pounce on or attack (a person) unexpectedly. **15** *tr.* take summary possession of (a claim allegedly abandoned or forfeit by the former occupant). •*n.* **1** the act or an instance of jumping. **2 a** a sudden bodily movement caused by shock or excitement. **b** (**the jumps**) *colloq.* extreme nervousness or anxiety. **3** an abrupt rise in amount, price, value, status, etc. **4** an obstacle to be jumped, esp. by a horse. **5 a** a sudden transition. **b** a gap in a series, logical sequence, etc. ▫ **get** (or **have**) **the jump on** *colloq.* get (or have) an advantage over (a person) by prompt action. **jump at** accept eagerly. **jump bail** see BAIL[1]. **jump down a person's throat** *colloq.* reprimand or contradict a person fiercely. **jump the gun** see GUN. **jump on** *colloq.* attack or criticize severely and without warning. **jump ship** (of a seaman) desert. **jump to it** *colloq.* act promptly and energetically. **one jump ahead** one stage further on than a rival, etc. ▫▫ **jump•a•ble** *adj.*

jump•er[1] /júmpər/ *n.* **1** sleeveless one-piece dress usu. worn over a blouse or shirt. **2** a loose outer jacket of canvas, etc., worn esp. by sailors. **3** *Brit.* a pullover sweater.

jump·er² /júmpər/ *n.* **1** a person or animal that jumps. **2** *Electr.* a short wire used to make or break a circuit. **3** a rope made fast to keep a yard, mast, etc., from jumping. **4** a heavy chisel-ended iron bar for drilling blast holes.

jump·er ca·bles *n.pl.* a pair of electrical cables attached to a battery and used to start a motor vehicle with a weak or discharged battery.

jump·ing bean /júmping/ *n.* the seed of a Mexican plant that jumps with the movement of the larva inside.

jump rope *n.* a length of rope held at each end and swung over the head and under the feet of the jumper, who must skip over the rope each time it revolves under the feet, used for exercise or a children's game.

jump seat *n.* a folding extra seat in a motor vehicle.

jump-start *v. & n.* • *v.tr.* **1** start (a car with a dead battery) with jumper cables or by a sudden release of the clutch while it is being pushed. **2** give an added impetus to something that is proceeding slowly or at a standstill (*jump-start the sluggish educational system*). • *n.* **1** the act of jump-starting a car. **2** an added impetus.

jump·suit /júmpsoot/ *n.* a one-piece garment for the whole body, of a kind orig. worn by paratroopers.

jump·y /júmpee/ *adj.* (**jumpier, jumpiest**) **1** nervous; easily startled. **2** making sudden movements, esp. of nervous excitement. ▫▫ **jump·i·ly** *adv.* **jump·i·ness** *n.*

Jun. *abbr.* **1** June. **2** Junior.

jun·co /júngkō/ *n.* (*pl.* **-cos** or **-coes**) any small American finch of the genus *Junco.*

junc·tion /júngkshən/ *n.* **1** a point at which two or more things are joined. **2** a place where two or more railroad lines or roads meet, unite, or cross. **3** the act or an instance of joining. **4** *Electronics* a region of transition in a semiconductor between regions where conduction is mainly by electrons and regions where it is mainly by holes.

junc·tion box *n.* a box containing a junction of electric cables, etc.

junc·ture /júngkchər/ *n.* **1** a critical convergence of events; a critical point of time (*at this juncture*). **2** a place where things join. **3** an act of joining.

June /joon/ *n.* the sixth month of the year.

June bug *n.* any of several large brown scarab beetles, esp. *Phyllophaga fusca.*

jun·gle /júnggəl/ *n.* **1 a** land overgrown with underwood or tangled vegetation, esp. in the tropics. **b** an area of such land. **2** a wild tangled mass. **3** a place of bewildering complexity or confusion, or of a struggle for survival (*blackboard jungle*). ▫ **law of the jungle** a state of ruthless competition. ▫▫ **jun·gled** *adj.* **jun·gly** *adj.*

jun·gle gym *n.* a playground structure with bars, ladders, etc., for children to climb.

jun·ior /joonyər/ *adj. & n.* • *adj.* **1** less advanced in age. **2** (foll. by *to*) inferior in age, standing, or position. **3** the younger (esp. appended to a name for distinction from an older person of the same name). **4** of less or least standing; of the lower or lowest position (*junior partner*). **5** *Brit.* (of a school) having pupils in a younger age-range, usu. 7–11. **6** of the year before the final year at college, high school, etc. • *n.* **1** a junior person. **2** one's inferior in length of service, etc. **3** a junior student. **4** *colloq.* a young male child, esp. in relation to his family.

jun·ior col·lege *n.* a college offering a two-year course, esp. in preparation for completion at senior college.

jun·ior high school *n.* school attended between elementary and high school and usu. consisting of grades seven and eight and sometimes nine.

ju·ni·per /joonipər/ *n.* any evergreen shrub or tree of the genus *Juniperus*, esp. *J. communis* with prickly leaves and dark purple berrylike cones.

junk¹ /jungk/ *n. & v.* • *n.* **1** discarded articles; rubbish. **2** anything regarded as of little value. **3** *sl.* a narcotic drug, esp. heroin. • *v.tr.* discard as junk.

junk² /jungk/ *n.* a flat-bottomed sailing vessel used in the China seas, with a prominent stern.

jun·ket /júngkit/ *n. & v.* • *n.* **1** a dish of sweetened and flavored curds, often served with fruit or cream. **2** a feast. **3** a pleasure outing. **4** an official's tour at public expense. • *v.intr.* feast; picnic. ▫▫ **jun·ket·ing** *n.*

junk food *n.* food with low nutritional value.

junk·ie /júngkee/ *n. sl.* a drug addict.

junk mail *n.* unsolicited advertising matter sent through the mail.

junk·yard /júngkyard/ *n.* a yard in which junk is collected and sometimes resold.

jun·ta /hóontə, júntə/ *n.* a political or military clique or faction taking power after a revolution or coup d'état.

Ju·pi·ter /joopitər/ *n.* the largest planet of the solar system, orbiting about the sun between Mars and Saturn.

Ju·ras·sic /joorásik/ *adj. & n. Geol.* • *adj.* of or relating to the second period of the Mesozoic era with evidence of many large dinosaurs, the first birds (including Archaeopteryx), and mammals. • *n.* this era or system.

ju·rid·i·cal /joorídikəl/ *adj.* **1** of judicial proceedings. **2** relating to the law. ▫▫ **ju·rid·i·cal·ly** *adv.*

ju·ris·dic·tion /joorisdíkshən/ *n.* **1** (often foll. by *over, of*) the administration of justice. **2 a** legal or other authority. **b** the extent of this; the territory it extends over. ▫▫ **ju·ris·dic·tion·al** *adj.*

ju·ris·pru·dence /joorisprood'ns/ *n.* **1** the science or philosophy of law. **2** skill in law. ▫▫ **ju·ris·pru·dent** /–dənt/ *adj. & n.* **ju·ris·pru·den·tial** /–dénshəl/ *adj.*

ju·rist /joorist/ *n.* **1** an expert in law. **2** a legal writer. **3** a lawyer. ▫▫ **ju·ris·tic** /–rístik/ *adj.* **ju·ris·ti·cal** /–rístikəl/ *adj.*

ju·ror /joorər/ *n.* **1** a member of a jury. **2** a person who takes an oath.

ju·ry /jooree/ *n.* (*pl.* **-ries**) **1** (also **grand ju·ry**) a body of persons sworn to render a verdict on the basis of evidence submitted to them in a court of justice. **2** a body of persons selected to award prizes in a competition.

ju·ry·man /jooreemən/ *n.* (*pl.* **-men**) a member of a jury.

ju·ry-rigged /jooreerigd/ *adj.* having temporary makeshift rigging.

ju·ry·wom·an /jooreewoomən/ *n.* (*pl.* **-women**) a woman member of a jury.

just /just/ *adj. & adv.* • *adj.* **1** acting or done in accordance with what is morally right or fair. **2** (of treatment, etc.) deserved (*a just reward*). **3** (of feelings, opinions, etc.) well-grounded (*just resentment*). **4** right in amount, etc.; proper. • *adv.* **1** exactly (*just what I need*). **2** exactly or nearly at this or that moment; a little time ago (*I have just seen them*). **3** *colloq.* simply; merely (*we were just good friends; it just doesn't make sense*). **4** barely; no more than (*I just managed it; just a minute*). **5** *colloq.* positively (*it is just splendid*). **6** quite (*not just yet; it is just as well that I checked*). **7** *colloq.* really; indeed (*won't I just tell him!*). **8** in questions, seeking precise information (*just how did you manage?*). ▫ **just about** *colloq.* almost exactly; almost completely. **just in case** **1** lest. **2** as a precaution. **just now** **1** at this moment. **2** a little time ago. **just so** **1** exactly arranged (*they like everything just so*). **2** it is exactly as you say. ▫▫ **just·ly** *adv.* **just·ness** *n.*

jus·tice /jústis/ *n.* **1** just conduct. **2** fairness. **3** the exercise of authority in the maintenance of right. **4** judicial proceedings (*was duly brought to justice*). **5 a** a magistrate. **b** a judge, esp. of a supreme court. □ **do justice to** treat fairly or appropriately; show due appreciation of. **do oneself justice** perform in a manner worthy of one's abilities. □□ **jus•tice•ship** *n.* (in sense 5).

jus•tice of the peace *n.* a local magistrate appointed to hear minor cases, grant licenses, perform marriages, etc.

jus•ti•fi•a•ble /jústifīəbəl/ *adj.* that can be justified or defended. □□ **jus•ti•fi•a•bil•i•ty** *n.* **jus•ti•fi•a•ble•ness** *n.* **jus•ti•fi•a•bly** *adv.*

jus•ti•fy /jústifī/ *v.tr.* (**-fies, -fied**) **1** show the justice or rightness of (a person, act, etc.). **2** demonstrate the correctness of (an assertion, etc.). **3** adduce adequate grounds for (conduct, a claim, etc.). **4 a** (esp. in *passive*) (of circumstances) be such as to justify. **b** vindicate. **5** (as **justified** *adj.*) just; right (*am justified in assuming*). **6** *Printing* adjust (a line of type) to fill a space evenly. □□ **jus•ti•fi•ca•tion** /–fikáyshən/ *n.* **jus•tif•i•ca•to•ry** /–stífikətáwree/ *adj.* **jus•ti•fi•er** *n.*

jut /jut/ *v. & n.* •*v.intr.* (**jutted, jutting**) (often foll. by *out, forth*) protrude; project. •*n.* a projection; a protruding point.

jute /jōōt/ *n.* a rough fiber made from the bark of E. Indian plants of the genus *Corchorus*, used for making twine and rope, and woven into sacking, mats, etc.

ju•ve•nile /jōōvənīl/ *adj. & n.* •*adj.* **1 a** young; youthful. **b** of or for young persons. **2** suited to or characteristic of youth. **3** often *derog.* immature (*behaving in a very juvenile way*). •*n.* **1** a young person. **2** *Commerce* a book intended for young people. **3** an actor playing the part of a youthful person. □□ **ju•ve•nile•ly** *adv.* **ju•ve•nil•i•ty** /–nílitee/ *n.*

ju•ve•nile court *n.* a court for the trial of children usu. under 18.

ju•ve•nile de•lin•quen•cy *n.* offenses committed by a person or persons below the age of legal responsibility. □□ **ju•ve•nile de•lin•quent** *n.*

jux•ta•pose /júkstəpōz/ *v.tr.* **1** place (things) side by side. **2** (foll. by *to, with*) place (a thing) beside another. □□ **jux•ta•po•si•tion** /–pəzíshən/ *n.* **jux•ta•po•si•tion•al** /–pəzíshənəl/ *adj.*

JV *abbr.* junior varsity.

K

K[1] /kay/ *n.* (also **k**) (*pl.* **Ks** or **K's**) the eleventh letter of the alphabet.

K[2] *abbr.* (also **K.**) **1** kelvin(s). **2** King; King's. **3** (also **k**) (prec. by a numeral) **a** *Computing* a unit of 1,024 (i.e., 2^{10}) bytes or bits, or loosely 1,000. **b** 1,000. **4** *Baseball* strikeout.

K[3] *symb. Chem.* the element potassium.

k *abbr.* **1** kilo-. **2** knot(s).

kab·ba·la var. of CABALA.

ka·bob /kəbób/ *n.* (also **ke·bab, ke·bob**) (usu. in *pl.*) small pieces of meat, vegetables, etc., packed closely on a skewer and broiled.

ka·bu·ki /kəbóokee/ *n.* a form of popular traditional Japanese drama with highly stylized song, acted by males only.

Kad·dish /kaádish/ *n. Judaism* **1** a Jewish mourner's prayer. **2** a doxology in the synagogue service.

Kaf·fir /káfər/ *n.* **1** a member of the Xhosa-speaking peoples of South Africa. **2** the language of these peoples.

Kaf·ka·esque /kaáfkəésk/ *adj.* (of a situation, atmosphere, etc.) impenetrably oppressive, nightmarish, in a manner characteristic of the fictional world of Franz Kafka, German-speaking novelist (d. 1924).

kaf·tan var. of CAFTAN.

kai·ser /kízər/ *n. hist.* an emperor, esp. the German emperor, the emperor of Austria, or the head of the Holy Roman Empire. ▫▫ **kai·ser·ship** *n.*

kal·an·cho·e /kalənkóee/ *n.* a succulent plant of the mainly African genus *Kalanchoe*, which includes several house plants.

kale /kayl/ *n.* **1** a variety of cabbage, esp. one with wrinkled leaves and no compact head. **2** *sl.* money.

ka·lei·do·scope /kəlídəskōp/ *n.* **1** a tube containing mirrors and pieces of colored glass, paper, plastic, etc., whose reflections produce changing patterns when the tube is rotated. **2** a constantly changing group of bright or interesting objects. ▫▫ **ka·lei·do·scop·ic** /–skópik/ *adj.* **ka·lei·do·scop·i·cal** *adj.*

Ka·ma Su·tra /sóotrə/ *n.* an ancient Sanskrit treatise on the art of erotic love.

ka·mi·ka·ze /kámikaázee/ *n. & adj.* •*n. hist.* **1** a Japanese aircraft loaded with explosives and deliberately crashed by its pilot onto its target. **2** the pilot of such an aircraft. •*adj.* **1** of or relating to a kamikaze. **2** reckless; dangerous; potentially self-destructive.

Kam·pu·che·an /kámpoocheéən/ *n. & adj.* = CAMBODIAN.

Kan. *abbr.* Kansas.

kan·ga·roo /kánggəróo/ *n.* a plant-eating marsupial of the genus *Macropus*, native to Australia and New Guinea, with a long tail and strongly developed hindquarters enabling it to travel by jumping.

kan·ga·roo court *n.* an improperly constituted or illegal court held by a mob, etc.

kan·gar·oo rat *n.* any burrowing rodent of the genus*Dipodomys*, having elongated hind feet.

Kans. *abbr.* Kansas.

ka·o·lin /káyəlin/ *n.* a fine, soft, white clay produced by the decomposition of other clays or feldspar, used esp. for making porcelain and in medicines. Also called **china clay**. ▫▫ **ka·o·lin·ic** /–línik/ *adj.* **ka·o·lin·ize** *v.tr.*

ka·on /káyon/ *n. Physics* an unstable meson created from a high-energy particle collision.

ka·pok /káypok/ *n.* a fine, fibrous, cottonlike substance found surrounding the seeds of a tropical tree, *Ceiba pentandra*, used for stuffing cushions, soft toys, etc.

Ka·po·si's sar·co·ma /kápəseez, kapó–/ *n. Med.* a malignant neoplasm of connective tissue marked by bluish-red lesions on the skin; often associated with AIDS.

kap·pa /kápə/ *n.* the tenth letter of the Greek alphabet (Κ, κ).

ka·put /kaapóot/ *predic. adj. sl.* broken; ruined; done for.

kar·a·bi·ner /kárəbeénər/ *n.* a coupling link with safety closure, used by mountaineers.

kar·a·kul /kárəkool/ *n.* (also **Kar·a·kul, caracul**) **1** a variety of Asian sheep with a dark curled fleece when young. **2** fur made from or resembling this.

kar·a·o·ke /káreeókee, kárə–/ *n.* a form of entertainment in which people sing popular songs as soloists against a prerecorded backing.

kar·at /kárət/ *n.* (*Brit.* **carat**) a measure of purity of gold, pure gold being 24 karats.

ka·ra·te /kəraátee/ *n.* a Japanese system of unarmed combat using the hands and feet as weapons.

kar·ma /kaármə/ *n. Buddhism & Hinduism* **1** the sum of a person's actions in previous states of existence, viewed as deciding his or her fate in future existences. **2** destiny. ▫▫ **kar·mic** *adj.*

karst /kaarst/ *n.* a limestone region with underground drainage and many cavities and passages caused by the dissolution of the rock.

Kas·bah var. of CASBAH.

ka·ty·did /káyteedid/ *n.* any of various green grasshoppers of the family Tettigoniidae, native to the US.

kay·ak /kíak/ *n.* **1** an Eskimo canoe for one paddler, consisting of a light wooden frame covered with skins. **2** a small covered canoe resembling this.

kay·o /káyó, káyō/ *v. & n. colloq.* •*v.tr.* (**-oes, -oed**) knock out; stun by a blow. •*n.* (*pl.* **-os**) a knockout.

ka·zoo /kəzóo/ *n.* a toy musical instrument into which the player sings or hums.

KC *abbr.* **1** Kansas City. **2** Knights of Columbus.

kc *abbr.* kilocycle(s).

ke·a /keéə, káyə/ *n.* a parrot, *Nestor notabilis*, of New Zealand, with brownish-green and red plumage.

ke·bab var. of KABOB.

ke·bob var. of KABOB.

kedge /kej/ *v. & n.* •*v.* **1** *tr.* move (a ship) by means of a hawser attached to a small anchor that is dropped at some distance away. **2** *intr.* (of a ship) move in this way. *n.* (in full **kedge anchor**) a small anchor for this purpose.

keel /keel/ *n. & v.* •*n.* **1** the lengthwise timber or steel structure along the base of a ship, airship, or some aircraft, on which the framework of the whole is built up. **2** *poet.* a ship. **3** a ridge along the breastbone of many birds; a carina. **4** *Bot.* a prow-shaped pair of petals in a corolla, etc. •*v.* **1** (often foll. by *over*) **a** *intr.* turn over or fall down. **b** *tr.* cause to do this. **2** *tr. & intr.* turn keel upward. ▫▫ **keel·less** *adj.*

keel·haul /keélhawl/ *v.tr.* **1** *hist.* drag (a person) through the water under the keel of a ship as a punishment. **2** scold or rebuke severely.

keen[1] /keen/ *adj.* **1** (of a person, desire, or interest) eager; ardent (*a keen sportsman; keen to be involved*). **2** (foll. by *on*) much attracted by; fond of or enthusiastic about. **3 a** (of the senses) sharp; highly sensitive. **b** (of memory, etc.) clear; vivid. **4 a** (of a person) intellectually acute. **b** (of a remark, etc.) quick; sharp; biting. **5 a** having a sharp edge or point. **b** (of an edge, etc.) sharp. **6** (of a sound, light, etc.) penetrating; vivid; strong. **7** (of a wind, frost, etc.) piercingly cold. **8** (of a pain, etc.) acute; intense. □□ **keen·ly** *adv.* **keen·ness** *n.*

keen[2] /keen/ *n. & v.* • *n.* an Irish funeral song accompanied with wailing. • *v.* **1** *intr.* utter the keen. **2** *tr.* bewail (a person) in this way. **3** *tr.* utter in a wailing tone. □□ **keen·er** *n.*

keep /keep/ *v. & n.* • *v.* (*past* and *past part.* **kept** /kept/) **1** *tr.* have continuous charge of; retain possession of; save or hold on to. **2** *tr.* (foll. by *for*) retain or reserve for a future occasion or time (*will keep it for tomorrow*). **3** *tr. & intr.* retain or remain in a specified condition, position, course, etc. (*keep cool; keep off the grass; keep them happy*). **4** *tr.* put or store in a regular place (*knives are kept in this drawer*). **5** *tr.* (foll. by *from*) cause to avoid or abstain from something (*will keep you from going too fast*). **6** *tr.* detain; cause to be late (*what kept you?*). **7** *tr.* **a** observe or pay due regard to (a law, custom, etc.) (*keep one's word*). **b** honor or fulfill (a commitment, undertaking, etc.). **c** respect the commitment implied by (a secret, etc.). **d** act fittingly on the occasion of (*keep the Sabbath*). **8** *tr.* own and look after (animals) for amusement or profit (*keeps bees*). **9** *tr.* **a** provide for the sustenance of (a person, family, etc.). **b** (foll. by *in*) maintain (a person) with a supply of. **10** *tr.* manage (a shop, business, etc.). **11** *tr.* **a** maintain (accounts, a diary, etc.) by making the requisite entries. **b** maintain (a house) in proper order. **12** *tr.* have (a commodity) regularly on sale (*do you keep buttons?*). **13** *tr.* **a** confine or detain (a person, animal, etc.). **b** guard or protect (a person or place, a goal in soccer, etc.). **14** *tr.* preserve in being; continue to have (*keep order*). **15** *intr.* (foll. by verbal noun) continue or do repeatedly or habitually (*why do you keep saying that?*). **16** *tr.* continue to follow (a way or course). **17** *intr.* **a** (esp. of perishable commodities) remain in good condition. **b** (of news or information, etc.) admit of being withheld for a time. **18** *tr.* esp. *Brit.* remain in (one's bed, room, house, etc.). **19** *tr.* retain one's place in (a seat or saddle, one's ground, etc.) against opposition or difficulty. **20** *tr.* maintain (a person) in return for sexual favors (*a kept woman*). • *n.* **1** maintenance or the essentials for this (esp. food) (*hardly earn your keep*). **2** charge or control (*is in your keep*). **3** *hist.* a tower or stronghold. □ **for keeps** *colloq.* (esp. of something received or won) permanently; indefinitely. **keep at** persist or cause to persist with. **keep away** (often foll. by *from*) **1** avoid being near. **2** prevent from being near. **keep back 1** remain or keep at a distance. **2** retard the progress of. **3** conceal; decline to disclose. **4** retain; withhold (*kept back $50*). **keep down 1** hold in subjection. **2** keep low in amount. **3** lie low; stay hidden. **4** manage not to vomit (food eaten). **keep in mind** take into account having remembered. **keep off 1** stay or cause to stay away from. **2** ward off; avert. **3** abstain from. **4** avoid (a subject) (*let's keep off religion*). **keep on 1** continue to do something; do continually (*kept on laughing*). **2** continue to use or employ. **3** (foll. by *at*) pester or harass. **keep out 1** keep or remain outside. **2** exclude. **keep to 1** adhere to (a course, schedule, etc.). **2** observe (a promise). **3** confine oneself to. **keep to oneself 1** avoid contact with others. **2** refuse to disclose or share. **keep under** hold in subjection. **keep up 1** maintain (progress, etc.). **2** prevent (prices, one's spirits, etc.) from sinking. **3** keep in repair, in an efficient or proper state, etc. **4** carry on (a correspondence, etc.). **5** prevent (a person) from going to bed, esp. when late. **6** (often foll. by *with*) manage not to fall behind. **keep up with the Joneses** strive to compete socially with one's neighbors.

keep·er /keépər/ *n.* **1** a person who keeps or looks after something or someone. **2 a** = GAMEKEEPER. **b** a person in charge of animals in a zoo.

keep·ing /keéping/ *n.* **1** custody; charge (*in safe keeping*). **2** agreement; harmony (*not in keeping with good taste*).

keep·sake /keépsayk/ *n.* a thing kept for the sake of or in remembrance of the giver.

kef /kef, keef/ *n.* (also **kif** /kif/) **1** a drowsy state induced by marijuana, etc. **2** the enjoyment of idleness. **3** a substance smoked to produce kef.

keg /keg/ *n.* a small barrel of less than 30 gallons (usu. 5–10 gallons).

keg par·ty *n.* a party at which keg beer is served.

keis·ter /keéstər/ (also **keester**) *n. sl.* the buttocks.

kelp /kelp/ *n.* **1** any of several large, broad-fronded brown seaweeds, esp. of the genus *Laminaria*, suitable for use as manure. **2** the calcined ashes of seaweed formerly used in glassmaking and soap manufacture because of their high content of sodium, potassium, and magnesium salts.

Kelt var. of CELT.

kel·ter var. of KILTER.

kel·vin /kélvin/ *n.* the SI unit of thermodynamic temperature, equal in magnitude to the degree celsius. ¶ Abbr.: **K.**

Kel·vin scale *n.* a scale of temperature with absolute zero as zero.

kempt /kempt/ *adj.* combed; neatly kept.

ken /ken/ *n.* range of sight or knowledge.

ken·do /kéndō/ *n.* a Japanese form of fencing with bamboo swords.

ken·nel /kénəl/ *n. & v.* • *n.* **1** a small shelter for a dog. **2** (in *pl.*) a breeding or boarding establishment for dogs. **3** a mean dwelling. • *v.* (**kenneled, kenneling;** esp. *Brit.* **kennelled, kennelling**) **1** *tr.* put into or keep in a kennel. **2** *intr.* live in or go to a kennel.

Ken·yan /kényən, keén–/ *adj. & n.* • *adj.* of or relating to Kenya in E. Africa. • *n.* **1** a native or national of Kenya. **2** a person of Kenyan descent.

kep·i /képee, káypee/ *n.* (*pl.* **kepis**) a French military cap with a horizontal peak.

kepi

kept *past* and *past part.* of KEEP.

ker·a·tin /kérətin/ *n.* a fibrous protein that occurs in hair, feathers, hooves, claws, horns, etc.

kerb *Brit.* var. of CURB 2.

ker·chief /kə́rchif, –cheef/ *n.* **1** a cloth used to cover the head. **2** *poet.* a handkerchief. ◻◻ **ker·chiefed** *adj.*

kerf /kərf/ *n.* **1** a slit made by cutting, esp. with a saw. **2** the cut end of a felled tree.

ker·nel /kə́rnəl/ *n.* **1** a central, softer, usu. edible part within a hard shell of a nut, fruit stone, seed, etc. **2** the whole seed of a cereal. **3** the nucleus or essential part of anything.

ker·o·sene /kérəseen/ *n.* (also **ker·o·sine**) a liquid mixture obtained by distillation from petroleum or shale, used esp. as a fuel or solvent.

kes·trel /késtrəl/ *n.* any small falcon, esp. *Falco tinnunculus*, that hovers while searching for its prey.

ketch /kech/ *n.* a two-masted, fore-and-aft rigged sailing boat with a mizzenmast stepped forward of the rudder and smaller than its foremast.

ketch·up /kéchup, káchup/ *n.* (also **catsup** /kátsəp/) a spicy sauce made from tomatoes, mushrooms, vinegar, etc., used as a condiment.

ke·tone /kéetōn/ *n.* any of a class of organic compounds in which two hydrocarbon groups are linked by a carbonyl group, e.g., propanone (acetone). ◻◻ **ke·ton·ic** /kitónik/ *adj.*

ke·to·sis /keetṓsis/ *n.* a condition characterized by raised levels of ketone bodies in the body, associated with fat metabolism and diabetes. ◻◻ **ke·tot·ic** /–tótik/ *adj.*

ket·tle /két'l/ *n.* **1** a vessel, usu. of metal with a lid, spout, and handle, for boiling water in. **2** (in full **kettle hole**) a depression in the ground in a glaciated area. ◻ **a fine** (or **pretty**) **kettle of fish** an awkward state of affairs. ◻◻ **ket·tle·ful** *n.* (*pl.* **-fuls**).

ket·tle·drum /két'ldrum/ *n.* a large drum shaped like a bowl with a membrane adjustable for tension (and thus pitch) stretched across. ◻◻ **ket·tle·drum·mer** *n.*

kettledrum

keV *abbr.* kilo-electronvolt.

Kev·lar /kévlaar/ *n. Trademark* a synthetic fiber of high tensile strength used esp. as a reinforcing agent in the manufacture of tires and other rubber products and protective gear such as helmets and vests.

Kew·pie /kyṓōpee/ *n. Trademark* a small, chubby doll with a curl or topknot.

key[1] /kee/ *n., adj., & v.* • *n.* (*pl.* **keys**) **1** an instrument, usu. of metal, for moving the bolt of a lock forward or backward to lock or unlock. **2** a similar implement for operating a switch in the form of a lock. **3** an instrument for grasping screws, pegs, nuts, etc., esp. one for winding a clock, etc. **4** a lever depressed by the finger in playing the organ, piano, flute, saxophone, concertina, etc. **5** (often in *pl.*) each of several buttons for operating a typewriter, word processor, or computer terminal, etc. **6** what gives or precludes the opportunity for or access to something. **7** a place that by its position gives control of a sea, territory, etc. **8 a** a solution or explanation. **b** a word or system for solving a cipher or code. **c** an explanatory list of symbols used in a map, table, etc. **d** a book of solutions to mathematical problems, etc. **e** a literal translation of a book written in a foreign language. **f** the first move in a chess-problem solution. **9** *Mus.* a system of notes definitely related to each other, based on a particular note, and predominating in a piece of music; tone or pitch (*a study in the key of C major*). **10** a tone or style of thought or expression. **11** a piece of wood or metal inserted between others to secure them. **12** the part of a first coat of wall plaster that passes between the laths and so secures the rest. **13** the roughness of a surface, helping the adhesion of plaster, etc. **14** the samara of a sycamore, etc. **15** a mechanical device for making or breaking an electric circuit, e.g., in telegraphy. • *adj.* essential; of vital importance (*the key element in the problem*). • *v.tr.* (**keys, keyed**) **1** (foll. by *in, on,* etc.) fasten with a pin, wedge, bolt, etc. **2** (often foll. by *in*) enter (data) by means of a keyboard. **3** roughen (a surface) to help the adhesion of plaster, etc. **4** (foll. by *to*) align or link (one thing to another). **5** regulate the pitch of the strings of (a violin, etc.). **6** word (an advertisement in a particular periodical) so that answers to it can be identified (usu. by varying the form of address given). ◻ **key up** make (a person) nervous or tense; excite. ◻◻ **key·er** *n.*

key[2] /kee/ *n.* a low-lying island or reef, esp. off the Florida coast (cf. CAY).

key·board /kéebawrd/ *n. & v.* • *n.* **1 a** a set of keys on a typewriter, computer, piano, etc. **b** the keys of a computer terminal regarded as a person's place of work. **2** an electronic musical instrument with keys arranged as on a piano. • *v.tr. & intr.* enter (data) by means of a keyboard; work at a keyboard. ◻◻ **key·board·er** *n.* **key·board·ist** *n.*

key·hole /kéehōl/ *n.* a hole by which a key is put into a lock.

Keynes·i·an /káynzeeən/ *adj. & n.* • *adj.* of or relating to the economic theories of J. M. Keynes (d. 1946), esp. regarding government control of the economy through money and taxation. • *n.* an adherent of these theories. ◻◻ **Keynes·i·an·ism** *n.*

key·note /kéenōt/ *n.* **1** a prevailing tone or idea (*the keynote of the whole occasion*). **2** (*attrib.*) intended to set the prevailing tone at a meeting or conference (*keynote address*). **3** *Mus.* the note on which a key is based.

key·pad /kéepad/ *n.* a miniature keyboard or set of buttons for operating a portable electronic device, telephone, etc.

key·punch /kéepunch/ *n. & v.* • *n.* a device for transferring data by means of punched holes or notches on a series of cards or paper tape. • *v.tr.* transfer (data) by means of a keypunch. ◻◻ **key·punch·er** *n.*

key ring *n.* a ring for keeping keys on.

key sig·na·ture *n. Mus.* any of several combinations of sharps or flats after the clef at the beginning of each staff indicating the key of a composition.

key·stone /kéestōn/ *n.* **1** the central principle of a system, policy, etc., on which all the rest depends. **2** a central stone at the summit of an arch locking the whole together.

key·stroke /kéestrōk/ *n.* a single depression of a key on a keyboard, esp. as a measure of work.

key·word /kéewərd/ *n.* (also **key word**) **1** the key to a cipher, etc. **2 a** a word of great significance. **b** a significant word used in indexing.

kg *abbr.* kilogram(s).
KGB /káyjeebée/ *n.* the state security police of the former USSR from 1954.
khak·i /kákee, káa–/ *adj. & n.* •*adj.* dust-colored; dull brownish-yellow. •*n.* (*pl.* **khakis**) **1 a** khaki fabric of twilled cotton or wool, used esp. in military dress. **b** (in *pl.*) a garment, esp. pants or a military uniform, made of this fabric. **2** the dull brownish-yellow color of this.
khan /kaan, kan/ *n.* a title given to rulers and officials in Central Asia, Afghanistan, etc. ▫▫ **khan·ate** *n.*
khe·dive /kidéev/ *n. hist.* the title of the viceroy of Egypt under Turkish rule 1867–1914.
Khmer /kmair/ *n. & adj.* •*n.* **1** a native of the ancient Khmer kingdom in SE Asia, or of modern Cambodia. **2** the language of this people. •*adj.* of the Khmers or their language.
kHz *abbr.* kilohertz.
kib·ble /kíbəl/ *v. & n.* •*v.tr.* grind coarsely. •*n.* coarsely ground pellets of meal, etc., used as a dry pet food.
kib·butz /kibóots/ *n.* (*pl.* **kibbutzim** /–bootséem/) a communal, esp. farming, settlement in Israel.
kib·itz /kíbits/ *v.intr. colloq.* act as a kibitzer.
kib·itz·er /kíbitsər/ *n. colloq.* **1** an onlooker at cards, etc., esp. one who offers unwanted advice. **2** a busybody; a meddler.
ki·bosh /kíbosh/ *n. sl.* nonsense. ▫ **put the kibosh on** put an end to; finally dispose of.
kick /kik/ *v. & n.* •*v.* **1** *tr.* strike or propel forcibly with the foot or hoof, etc. **2** *intr.* (usu. foll. by *at, against*) **a** strike out with the foot. **b** express annoyance at or dislike of (treatment, a proposal, etc.); rebel against. **3** *tr. sl.* give up (a habit). **4** *tr.* (often foll. by *out*, etc.) expel or dismiss forcibly. **5** *refl.* be annoyed with oneself (*I'll kick myself if I'm wrong*). **6** *tr. Football* score (a goal) by a kick. •*n.* **1 a** a blow with the foot or hoof, etc. **b** the delivery of such a blow. **2** *colloq.* **a** a sharp stimulant effect, esp. of alcohol. **b** (often in *pl.*) a pleasurable thrill (*did it just for kicks; got a kick out of flying*). **3** strength; resilience (*have no kick left*). **4** *colloq.* a specified temporary interest or enthusiasm (*on a jogging kick*). **5** the recoil of a gun when discharged. ▫ **kick around** *colloq.* **1** drift idly from place to place. **2** treat roughly or scornfully. **3** discuss (an idea) unsystematically. **kick the bucket** *sl.* die. **kick in 1** knock down (a door, etc.) by kicking. **2** *sl.* contribute (esp. money); pay one's share. **kick in the teeth** *colloq.* a humiliating punishment or setback. **kick off 1 a** *Football*, etc. begin or resume play. **b** *colloq.* begin. **2** remove (shoes, etc.) by kicking. **kick up** (or **kick up a fuss**) create a disturbance; object or register strong disapproval. **kick up one's heels** frolic. **kick a person upstairs** shelve a person by giving him or her a promotion or a title. ▫▫ **kick·a·ble** *adj.* **kick·er** *n.*
Kick·a·poo /kíkəpoo/ *n.* **1 a** a N. American people native to the upper Midwest. **b** a member of this people. **2** the language of this people.
kick·back /kíkbak/ *n. colloq.* **1** the force of a recoil. **2** payment made to someone who has facilitated a transaction, esp. illicitly.
kick·off /kíkawf/ *n.* **1** *Football & Soccer* the start or resumption of play. **2** the start of something, esp. a campaign, drive, or project.
kick·stand /kíkstand/ *n.* a rod attached to a bicycle or motorcycle and kicked into a vertical position to support the vehicle when stationary.
kick-start *v.tr.* **1** start (a motorcycle, etc.) by the downward thrust of a pedal. **2** start or restart (a process, etc.) by providing some initial impetus. ▫▫ **kick start·er** *n.*
kid[1] /kid/ *n. & v.* •*n.* **1** a young goat. **2** the leather made from its skin. **3** *colloq.* a child or young person. •*v.intr.* (**kidded, kidding**) (of a goat) give birth. ▫ **handle with kid gloves** handle in a gentle, delicate, or gingerly manner.
▶**Kid**, meaning 'child,' although widely seen in advertising and other contexts, should be avoided in formal writing.
kid[2] /kid/ *v.* (**kidded, kidding**) *colloq.* **1** *tr.* & also refl. deceive; trick (*don't kid yourself; kidded his mother that he was ill*). **2** *tr. & intr.* tease (*only kidding*). ▫ **no kidding** *sl.* that is the truth. ▫▫ **kid·der** *n.* **kid·ding·ly** *adv.*
kid·die /kídee/ *n.* (also **kid·dy**) (*pl.* **-dies**) *sl.* = KID[1] *n.* 3.
kid·do /kídō/ *n.* (*pl.* **-dos**) *sl.* = KID[1] *n.* 3.
kid-glove *attrib.adj.* careful or delicate treatment of a person or situation.
kid·nap /kídnap/ *v.tr.* (**kidnapped, kidnapping** *or* **kidnaped, kidnaping**) **1** carry off (a person, etc.) by illegal force or fraud esp. to obtain a ransom. **2** steal (a child). ▫▫ **kid·nap·per** *n.*
kid·ney /kídnee/ *n.* (*pl.* **-neys**) **1** either of a pair of organs in the abdominal cavity of mammals, birds, and reptiles, which remove nitrogenous wastes from the blood and excrete urine. **2** the kidney of a sheep, ox, or pig as food.
kid·ney bean *n.* **1** a dwarf French bean. **2** a scarlet runner bean.
kid·ney ma·chine *n.* = ARTIFICIAL KIDNEY.
kiel·ba·sa /keelbaásə, kib–/ *n.* a variety of smoked, seasoned sausage.
kif var. of KEF.
kill[1] /kil/ *v. & n.* •*v.tr.* **1 a** deprive of life or vitality; put to death; cause the death of. **b** (*absol.*) cause or bring about death (*must kill to survive*). **2** destroy; put an end to (feelings, etc.) (*overwork killed my enthusiasm*). **3** *refl.* (often foll. by pres. part.) *colloq.* **a** overexert oneself (*don't kill yourself lifting them all at once*). **b** laugh heartily. **4** *colloq.* overwhelm (a person) with amusement, delight, etc. (*the things he says really kill me*). **5** switch off (a spotlight, engine, etc.). **6** *colloq.* delete (a line, paragraph, etc.) from a computer or newspaper file. **7** *colloq.* cause pain or discomfort to (*my feet are killing me*). **8** pass (time, or a specified amount of it) usu. while waiting for a specific event (*had an hour to kill before the interview*). **9** defeat (a bill in Congress, etc.). **10** *colloq.* consume the entire contents of (a bottle of wine, etc.). **11 a** *Tennis*, etc., hit (the ball) so skillfully that it cannot be returned. **b** stop (the ball) dead. **12** neutralize or render ineffective (taste, sound, color, etc.) (*thick carpet killed the sound of footsteps*). •*n.* **1** an act of killing (esp. an animal). **2** an animal or animals killed, esp. by a sportsman. **3** *colloq.* the destruction or disablement of an enemy aircraft, submarine, etc. ▫ **dressed to kill** dressed showily, alluringly, or impressively. **kill off 1** get rid of or destroy completely (esp. a number of persons or things). **2** (of an author) bring about the death of (a fictional character). **kill two birds with one stone** achieve two aims at once. **kill with kindness** spoil (a person) with overindulgence.
kill[2] /kil/ *n.* esp. *New York State dial.* a stream, creek, or tributary river.
kill·deer /kíldeer/ *n.* a large American plover, *Charadrius vociferus*, with a plaintive song.
kill·er /kílər/ *n.* **1 a** a person, animal, or thing that kills. **b** a murderer. **2** *colloq.* **a** an impressive, formidable, or excellent thing (*this one is quite difficult, but the next one is a real killer*). **b** a hilarious joke. **c** a decisive blow (*his home run proved to be the killer*).
kill·er bee *n.* a very aggressive honeybee, *Apis mellifera adansonii*, orig. from Africa.
kill·er cell *n. Immunology* a cell that attacks and destroys a cell (as a tumor cell) that bears a specific antigen on its surface.

kill·er in·stinct *n.* **1** an innate tendency to kill. **2** a ruthless streak.

kill·er whale *n.* a voracious cetacean, *Orcinus orca*, with a white belly and prominent dorsal fin.

kill·ing /kíling/ *n. & adj.* •*n.* **1 a** the causing of death. **b** an instance of this. **2** a great (esp. financial) success (*make a killing*). •*adj. colloq.* **1** overwhelmingly funny. **2** exhausting; very strenuous. ▫▫ **kill·ing·ly** *adv.*

kill·joy /kíljoy/ *n.* a person who throws gloom over or prevents other people's enjoyment.

kiln /kiln, kil/ *n.* a furnace or oven for burning, baking, or drying, esp. for calcining lime or firing pottery, etc.

ki·lo /kéelō/ *n.* (*pl.* **-los**) **1** a kilogram. **2** a kilometer.

kilo- /kílō/ *comb. form* denoting a factor of 1,000 (esp. in metric units). ¶ Abbr.: **k**, or **K** in *Computing.*

kil·o·byte /kíləbīt/ *n. Computing* 1,024 (i.e. 2^{10}) bytes as a measure of memory size.

kil·o·cal·o·rie /kíləkáləree/ *n.* = CALORIE 2.

kil·o·cy·cle /kíləsīkəl/ *n.* a former measure of frequency, equivalent to 1 kilohertz. ¶ Abbr.: **kc.**

kil·o·gram /kíləgram/ *n.* the SI unit of mass, equivalent to the international standard kept at Sèvres near Paris (approx. 2.205 lb.). ¶ Abbr.: **kg.**

kil·o·hertz /kíləhərts/ *n.* a measure of frequency equivalent to 1,000 cycles per second. ¶ Abbr.: **kHz.**

kil·o·li·ter /kíləleetər/ *n.* 1,000 liters (equivalent to 220 imperial gallons). ¶ Abbr.: **kl.**

kil·o·me·ter /kilómitər, kíləmeetər/ *n.* a metric unit of measurement equal to 1,000 meters (approx. 0.62 miles). ¶ Abbr.: **km.** ▫▫ **kil·o·met·ric** /kíləmétrik/ *adj.*

kil·o·ton /kílətun/ *n.* a unit of explosive power equivalent to 1,000 tons of TNT.

kil·o·volt /kíləvōlt/ *n.* 1,000 volts. ¶ Abbr.: **kV.**

kil·o·watt /kíləwot/ *n.* 1,000 watts. ¶ Abbr.: **kW.**

kil·o·watt-hour /kíləwot-ówr/ *n.* a measure of electrical energy equivalent to a power consumption of 1,000 watts for one hour. ¶ Abbr.: **kWh.**

kilt /kilt/ *n. & v.* •*n.* **1** a skirtlike garment, usu. of pleated tartan cloth and reaching to the knees, as traditionally worn in Scotland by Highland men. **2** a similar garment worn by women and children. •*v.tr.* **1** tuck up (skirts) around the body. **2** (esp. as **kilted** *adj.*) gather in vertical pleats. ▫▫ **kilt·ed** *adj.*

kilt

kil·ter /kíltər/ *n.* /kél–/) good working order (esp. *out of kilter*).

kim·ber·lite /kímbərlīt/ *n. Mineral.* a rare igneous bluetinged rock sometimes containing diamonds, found in South Africa and Siberia. Also called **blue ground.**

ki·mo·no /kimṓnō/ *n.* (*pl.* **-nos**) **1** a long, loose Japanese robe worn with a sash. **2** a dressing gown modeled on this. ▫▫ **ki·mo·noed** *adj.*

kimono

kin /kin/ *n. & adj.* •*n.* one's relatives or family. •*predic.adj. (of a person) related (*we are kin; *he is kin to me)* (see also AKIN). ▫ **kith and kin** see KITH. **near of kin** closely related by blood, or in character. ▫▫ **kin·less** *adj.*

-kin /kin/ *suffix* forming diminutive nouns (*catkin*; *manikin*).

kind[1] /kīnd/ *n.* **1 a** a race or species (*humankind*). **b** a natural group of animals, plants, etc. (*the wolf kind*). **2** class; type; sort; variety (*what kind of job are you looking for?*). **3** each of the elements of the Eucharist (*communion under* (or *in*) *both kinds*). **4** the manner or fashion natural to a person, etc. (*act after their kind*; *true to kind*). ▫ **kind of** *colloq.* to some extent (*felt kind of sorry*; *I kind of expected it*). **a kind of** used to imply looseness, vagueness, exaggeration, etc., in the term used (*a kind of Jane Austen of our times*; *I suppose he's a kind of doctor*). **in kind 1** in the same form; likewise (*was insulted and replied in kind*). **2** (of payment) in goods or labor as opposed to money (*received their wages in kind*). **3** in character or quality (*differ in degree but not in kind*). **nothing of the kind 1** not at all like the thing in question. **2** (expressing denial) not at all. **of its kind** within the limitations of its own class (*good of its kind*). **of a kind 1** *derog.* scarcely deserving the name (*a choir of a kind*). **2** similar in some important respect (*they're two of a kind*). **one's own kind** those with whom one has much in common.

▶**1. Kind of** is sometimes used to be deliberately vague: *It was kind of a big evening. I was kind of hoping you'd call.* More often, it reveals an inability to speak clearly: *He's kind of, like, awesome, you know?* Used precisely, it means 'sort, type': *A maple is a kind of tree.* **2.** The plural of **kind** often causes difficulty. With *this* or *that*, speaking of one kind, use a singular: *That kind of fabric doesn't need ironing;* with *these* or *those,* speaking of more than one kind, use the plural: *Those kinds of animals ought to be left in the wild.* The same recommendations apply to *sort* and *sorts.*

kind[2] /kīnd/ *adj.* **1** of a friendly, generous, benevolent, or gentle nature. **2** (usu. foll. by *to*) showing friendliness, affection, or consideration. **3** affectionate.

kind·a /kíndə/ *colloq.* = *kind of* (see KIND[1] 2).

kin·der·gar·ten /kíndərgaart'n/ *n.* an establishment or class for preschool learning.

kind·heart·ed /kíndhaártid/ *adj.* of a kind disposition. ▫▫ **kind·heart·ed·ly** *adv.* **kind·heart·ed·ness** *n.*

kin·dle /kínd'l/ *v.* **1** *tr.* light or set on fire (a flame, fire, substance, etc.). **2** *intr.* catch fire, burst into flame. **3** *tr.* arouse or inspire (*kindle enthusiasm for the project*; *kindle jealousy in a rival*). **4** *intr.* (usu. foll. by *to*) respond; react (to a person, an action, etc.). **5** *intr.* become animated, glow with passion, etc. (*her imagination kindled*). **6** *tr. & intr.* make or become bright (*kindle the embers to a glow*). ▫▫ **kin·dler** *n.*

kin·dling /kíndling/ *n.* small sticks, etc., for lighting fires.

kind·ly[1] /kíndlee/ *adv.* **1** in a kind manner (*spoke to the child kindly*). **2** often *iron.* used in a polite request or demand (*kindly leave me alone*). ▫ **take kindly to** be pleased by or endeared to (a person or thing).

kind·ly[2] /kíndlee/ *adj.* (**kindlier, kindliest**) **1** kind; kindhearted. **2** (of climate, etc.) pleasant; genial. ▫▫ **kind·li·ly** *adv.* **kind·li·ness** *n.*

kind·ness /kíndnis/ *n.* **1** the state or quality of being kind. **2** a kind act.

kin·dred /kíndrid/ *n. & adj.* •*n.* **1** one's relations, referred to collectively. **2** a relationship by blood. **3** a resemblance or affinity in character. •*adj.* **1** related by blood or marriage. **2** allied or similar in character (*other kindred symptoms*).

kin·dred spir·it *n.* a person whose character and outlook have much in common with one's own.

kin•e•mat•ics /kínimátiks/ *n.pl.* (usu. treated as *sing.*) the branch of mechanics concerned with the motion of objects without reference to the forces which cause the motion. ▫▫ **kin•e•mat•ic** *adj.* **kin•e•mat•i•cal•ly** *adv.*

ki•ne•sics /kinéesiks, –ziks/ *n.pl.* (usu. treated as *sing.*) **1** the study of body movements and gestures that contribute to communication. **2** these movements; body language.

ki•ne•si•ol•o•gy /kinéeseeóləjee, –zee–/ *n.* the study of the mechanics of body movements.

ki•net•ic /kinétik, kī–/ *adj.* of or due to motion. ▫▫ **ki•net•i•cal•ly** *adv.*

ki•net•ic en•er•gy *n.* the energy of motion.

ki•net•ics /kinétiks, kī–/ *n.pl.* **1** = DYNAMICS 1a. **2** (usu. treated as *sing.*) the branch of physical chemistry concerned with measuring and studying the rates of chemical reactions.

kin•folk /kínfōk/ *n.pl.* (also **kin•folks, kins•folk**) one's relations by blood.

king /king/ *n.* & *v.* •*n.* **1** (as a title usu. **King**) a male sovereign, esp. the hereditary ruler of an independent nation. **2** a person or thing preeminent in a specified field or class (*railroad king*). **3** a large (or the largest) kind of plant, animal, etc. (*king penguin*). **4** *Chess* the piece on each side that the opposing side has to checkmate to win. **5** a piece in checkers with extra capacity of moving, made by crowning an ordinary piece that has reached the opponent's baseline. **6** a playing card bearing a representation of a king and usu. ranking next below an ace. **7** (**Kings** or **Books of Kings**) two Old Testament books dealing with history, esp. of the kingdom of Judah. •*v.tr.* make (a person) king. ▫▫ **king•ly** *adj.* **king•li•ness** *n.* **king•ship** *n.*

king•bird /kíngbərd/ *n.* any flycatcher of the genus *Tyrannus*, with olive-gray plumage and long pointed wings.

king co•bra *n.* a large and venomous hooded Indian snake, *Ophiophagus hannah*.

king crab *n.* **1** = HORSESHOE CRAB. **2** any of various large edible spider crabs.

king•dom /kíngdəm/ *n.* **1** an organized community headed by a king. **2** the territory subject to a king. **3 a** the spiritual reign attributed to God (*Thy kingdom come*). **b** the sphere of this (*kingdom of heaven*). **4** a domain belonging to a person, animal, etc. **5** a province of nature (*the vegetable kingdom*). **6** a specified mental or emotional province (*kingdom of the heart*; *kingdom of fantasy*). **7** *Biol.* the highest category in taxonomic classification. ▫ **kingdom come** *colloq.* eternity; the next world. **till kingdom come** *colloq.* forever.

king•fish /kíngfish/ *n.* any of various large fish, esp. the opah or mulloway.

king•fish•er /kíngfishər/ *n.* any bird of the family Alcedinidae, esp. *Alcedo atthis*, with a long sharp beak and brightly colored plumage, which dives for fish in rivers, etc.

king•let /kínglit/ *n.* **1** a petty king. **2** any of various small birds of the family Regulidae, esp. the goldcrest.

king•mak•er /kíngmaykər/ *n.* a person with the political influence to make kings, leaders, etc.

king•pin /kíngpin/ *n.* **1 a** a main or large bolt in a central position. **b** a vertical bolt used as a pivot. **2** an essential person or thing, esp. in a complex system; the most important person in an organization.

king-size *adj.* (also **king-sized**) larger than normal; very large.

king's ran•som *n.* a fortune.

kink /kingk/ *n.* & *v.* •*n.* **1 a** a short backward twist in wire or tubing, etc., such as may cause an obstruction. **b** a tight wave in human or animal hair. **2** a mental twist or quirk. •*v.intr.* & *tr.* form or cause to form a kink.

kin•ka•jou /kíngkəjōō/ *n.* a Central and S. American nocturnal fruit-eating mammal, *Potos flavus*, with a prehensile tail and living in trees.

kink•y /kíngkee/ *adj.* (**kinkier, kinkiest**) **1** *colloq.* **a** given to or involving abnormal sexual behavior. **b** (of clothing, etc.) bizarre in a sexually provocative way. **2** strange; eccentric. **3** having kinks or twists. ▫▫ **kink•i•ly** *adv.* **kink•i•ness** *n.*

kins•folk var. of KINFOLK.

kin•ship /kínship/ *n.* **1** blood relationship. **2** the sharing of characteristics or origins.

kins•man /kínzmən/ *n.* (*pl.* **-men**; *fem.* **kinswoman**, *pl.* **-women**) **1** a blood relation or *disp.* a relation by marriage. **2** a member of one's own tribe or people.

ki•osk /kéeosk, –ósk/ *n.* **1** a light, open-fronted booth or cubicle from which food, newspapers, tickets, etc., are sold. **2** *Brit.* a telephone booth. **3** a building in which refreshments are served in a park, zoo, etc.

Ki•o•wa /kíəwə/ *n.* **1 a** a N. American people native to the southwest. **b** a member of this people. **2** the language of this people.

kip•per /kípər/ *n.* & *v.* •*n.* **1** a kippered fish, esp. herring. **2** a male salmon in the spawning season. •*v.tr.* cure (a herring, etc.) by splitting open, salting, and drying in the open air or smoke.

Kir /keer/ *n.* a drink made from dry white wine and crème de cassis.

kirk /kurk/ *n. Sc.* & *No. of Engl.* a church.

kirsch /keersh/ *n.* (also **kirsch•was•ser** /kéershvaasər/) a brandy distilled from the fermented juice of cherries.

kis•met /kízmet/ *n.* destiny; fate.

kiss /kis/ *v.* & *n.* •*v.* **1** *tr.* touch with the lips, esp. as a sign of love, affection, greeting, or reverence. **2** *tr.* express (greeting or farewell) in this way. **3** *absol.* (of two persons) touch each others' lips in this way. **4** *tr.* (also *absol.*) (of a billiard ball, etc., in motion) lightly touch (another ball). *n.* **1** a touch with the lips in kissing. **2** the slight impact when one billiard ball, etc., lightly touches another. **3** a usu. droplet-shaped piece of candy or small cookie. ▫ **kiss and tell** recount sexual exploits. **kiss a person's ass** (or **butt**) *coarse sl.* act obsequiously toward a person. **kiss the dust** submit abjectly; be overthrown. **kiss good-bye to** *colloq.* accept the loss of. **kiss the ground** prostrate oneself as a token of homage. **kiss off** *sl.* **1** dismiss; get rid of. **2** go away; die. ▫▫ **kiss•a•ble** *adj.*

kiss•er /kísər/ *n.* **1** a person who kisses. **2** (orig. *Boxing*) *sl.* the mouth; the face.

kiss•ing cous•in *n.* (also **kiss•ing kin**) a distant relative (given a formal kiss on occasional meetings).

kiss of death *n.* an apparently friendly act that causes ruin.

kiss of life *n.* mouth-to-mouth resuscitation.

kiss•y /kísee/ *adj. colloq.* given to kissing (*not the kissy type*).

kist var. of CIST.

kit[1] /kit/ *n.* **1** a set of articles, equipment, or clothing needed for a specific purpose (*first-aid kit*; *bicycle-repair kit*). **2** a set of all the parts needed to assemble an item, e.g., a piece of furniture, a model, etc. ▫ **the whole kit and caboodle** see CABOODLE.

kit[2] /kit/ *n.* **1** a kitten. **2** a young fox, badger, etc.

kit bag *n.* a large, usu. cylindrical bag used for carrying a soldier's, traveler's, or sportsman's equipment.

kitch•en /kíchin/ *n.* **1** the room or area where food is prepared and cooked. **2** (*attrib.*) of or belonging to the kitchen (*kitchen knife*; *kitchen table*). ▫ **everything but the kitchen sink** everything imaginable.

kitch•en cab•i•net *n.* a group of unofficial advisers thought to be unduly influential.

kitch·en·ette /kíchinét/ *n.* a small kitchen or part of a room fitted as a kitchen.

kitch·en·ware /kíchinwair/ *n.* the utensils used in the kitchen.

kite /kīt/ *n. & v.* •*n.* **1** a toy consisting of a light framework with thin material stretched over it, flown in the wind at the end of a long string. **2** any of various soaring birds of prey esp. of the genus *Milvus* with long wings and usu. a forked tail. **3** *Brit. sl.* an airplane. **4** *sl.* a fraudulent check, bill, or receipt. **5** *Geom.* a quadrilateral figure symmetrical about one diagonal. **6** *sl.* a letter or note, esp. one that is illicit or surreptitious. **7** (in *pl.*) the highest sail of a ship, set only in a light wind. •*v.* **1** *intr.* soar like a kite. **2** *tr.* (also *absol.*) originate or pass (fraudulent checks, bills, or receipts). **3** *tr.* (also *absol.*) raise (money by dishonest means) (*kite a loan*).

kith /kith/ *n.* □ **kith and kin** friends and relations.

kitsch /kich/ *n.* (often *attrib.*) garish, pretentious, or sentimental art, usu. vulgar and worthless (*kitsch plastic models of the Venus de Milo*). □□ **kitsch·y** *adj.* (**kitschier, kitschiest**). **kitsch·i·ness** *n.*

kit·ten /kít'n/ *n. & v.* •*n.* **1** a young cat. **2** a young ferret, etc. •*v.intr. & tr.* (of a cat, etc.) give birth or give birth to. □ **have kittens** *colloq.* be extremely upset, anxious, or nervous.

kit·ten·ish /kít'nish/ *adj.* **1** like a young cat; playful and lively. **2** flirtatious. □□ **kit·ten·ish·ly** *adv.* **kit·ten·ish·ness** *n.*

kit·ti·wake /kíteewayk/ *n.* either of two small gulls, *Rissa tridactyla* and *R. brevirostris*, nesting on sea cliffs.

kit·ty[1] /kítee/ *n.* (*pl.* **-ties**) **1** a fund of money for communal use. **2** the pool in some card games.

kit·ty[2] /kítee/ *n.* (*pl.* **-ties**) a pet name or a child's name for a kitten or cat.

kit·ty-cor·ner var. of CATERCORNERED.

Kit·ty Lit·ter *n. prop.* a granular clay used in boxes to absorb pet (esp. cat) waste.

ki·wi /kéewee/ *n.* (*pl.* **kiwis**) **1** a flightless New Zealand bird of the genus *Apteryx* with hairlike feathers and a long bill. Also called APTERYX. **2** (**Kiwi**) *colloq.* a New Zealander, esp. a soldier or member of a national sports team.

ki·wi fruit *n.* the fruit of a climbing plant, *Actinidia chinensis*, having a thin hairy skin, green flesh, and black seeds: also called **Chinese gooseberry**.

KKK *abbr.* Ku Klux Klan.

kl *abbr.* kiloliter(s).

klep·to·ma·ni·a /kléptəmáyneeə/ *n.* a recurrent urge to steal, usu. without regard for need or profit. □□ **klep·to·ma·ni·ac** *n. & adj.*

kludge /kloōj/ *n. sl.* **1** an ill-assorted collection of poorly matching parts. **2** *Computing* a machine, system, or program that has been badly put together.

klutz /kluts/ *n. sl.* **a** a clumsy awkward person. **b** a fool. □□ **klutz·y** *adj.*

klys·tron /klístron/ *n.* an electron tube that generates or amplifies microwaves by velocity modulation.

km *abbr.* kilometer(s).

K-me·son /kaymézon, –més–, –méezon, –son/ *n.* = KAON.

knack /nak/ *n.* **1** an acquired or intuitive faculty of doing a thing adroitly. **2** a trick or habit of action or speech, etc. (*has a knack of offending people*).

knack·wurst var. of KNOCKWURST.

knap·sack /nápsak/ *n.* a soldier's or hiker's bag with shoulder straps, carried on the back, and usu. made of canvas or weatherproof material.

knar /naar/ *n.* a knot or protuberance in a tree trunk, root, etc.

knave /nayv/ *n.* **1** a rogue; a scoundrel. **2** = JACK[1] *n.* 2. □□ **knav·er·y** *n.* (*pl.* **-ies**). **knav·ish** *adj.* **knav·ish·ly** *adv.* **knav·ish·ness** *n.*

knead /need/ *v.tr.* **1 a** work (a yeast mixture, clay, etc.) into dough, paste, etc., by pressing and folding. **b** make (bread, pottery, etc.) in this way. **2** blend or weld together (*kneaded them into a unified group*). **3** massage (muscles, etc.) as if kneading. □□ **knead·a·ble** *adj.* **knead·er** *n.*

knee /nee/ *n. & v.* •*n.* **1 a** (often *attrib.*) the joint between the thigh and the lower leg in humans. **b** the corresponding joint in other animals. **c** the area around this. **d** the upper surface of the thigh of a sitting person; the lap (*held her on his knee*). **2** the part of a garment covering the knee. **3** anything resembling a knee in shape or position, esp. a piece of wood or iron bent at an angle, a sharp turn in a graph, etc. •*v.tr.* (**knees, kneed, kneeing**) touch or strike with the knee (*kneed him in the groin*). □ **bring a person to his** or **her knees** reduce a person to submission. **on** (or **on one's**) **bended knee** (or **knees**) kneeling, esp. in supplication, submission, or worship.

knee·cap /néekap/ *n. & v.* •*n.* **1** the convex bone in front of the knee joint. **2** a protective covering for the knee. •*v.tr.* (**-capped, -capping**) *colloq.* shoot (a person) in the knee or leg as a punishment, esp. for betraying a terrorist group. □□ **knee·cap·ping** *n.*

knee-deep *adj.* **1** (usu. foll. by *in*) **a** immersed up to the knees. **b** deeply involved. **2** so deep as to reach the knees.

knee·hole /néehōl/ *n.* a space for the knees, esp. under a desk.

knee jerk *n.* a sudden involuntary kick caused by a blow on the tendon just below the knee.

knee-jerk *attrib.adj.* predictable; automatic; stereotyped.

kneel /neel/ *v.intr.* (*past* and *past part.* **knelt** /nelt/ or **kneeled**) fall or rest on the knees or a knee.

knell /nel/ *n. & v.* •*n.* **1** the sound of a bell, esp. when rung solemnly for a death or funeral. **2** an announcement, event, etc., regarded as a solemn warning of disaster. •*v.* **1** *intr.* **a** (of a bell) ring solemnly, esp. for a death or funeral. **b** make a doleful or ominous sound. **2** *tr.* proclaim by or as by a knell (*knelled the death of all their hopes*).

knelt *past* and *past part.* of KNEEL.

knew *past* of KNOW.

knick·ers /níkərz/ *n.pl.* **1** loose-fitting pants gathered at the knee or calf. **2** *Brit.* = PANTIES.

knick·knack /níknak/ *n.* **1** a useless and usu. worthless ornament; a trinket. **2** a small, dainty article of furniture, dress, etc. □□ **knick·knack·er·y** *n.*

knife /nīf/ *n. & v.* •*n.* (*pl.* **knives** /nīvz/) **1 a** a metal blade used as a cutting tool with usu. one long, sharp edge fixed rigidly in a handle or hinged (cf. PENKNIFE). **b** a similar tool used as a weapon. **2** a cutting blade forming part of a machine. •*v.tr.* **1** cut or stab with a knife. **2** *sl.* bring about the defeat of (a person) by underhand means. □ **that one could cut with a knife** *colloq.* (of an accent, atmosphere, etc.) very obvious, oppressive, etc. **under the knife** undergoing a surgical operation or operations. □□ **knife·like** *adj.* **knif·er** *n.*

knife pleat *n.* a narrow flat pleat on a skirt, etc., usu. overlapping another.

knife·point /nīfpoynt/ *n.* the point of a knife. □ **at knifepoint** threatened with a knife or an ultimatum, etc.

knight /nīt/ *n. & v.* •*n.* **1** a man awarded a non-hereditary title (*Sir*) by a sovereign in recognition of merit or service. **2** *hist.* **a** a man, usu. noble, raised esp. by a sovereign to honorable military rank after service as a page and squire. **b** a military follower or attendant, esp. of a lady as her champion in a war or tournament. **3** a man devoted to the service of a woman, cause, etc.

4 *Chess* a piece usu. shaped like a horse's head. •*v.tr.* confer a knighthood on. ▫▫ **knight·hood** *n.* **knight·like** *adj.* **knight·ly** *adj. & adv. poet.* **knight·li·ness** *n.*

knight-er·rant *n.* **1** a medieval knight wandering in search of chivalrous adventures. **2** a man of a chivalrous or quixotic nature. ▫▫ **knight-er·rant·ry** *n.*

knish /knish/ *n.* a dumpling of flaky dough filled with potato, meat, cheese, etc., and baked or fried.

knit /nit/ *v. & n.* •*v.* (**knitting**; *past* and *past part.* **knitted** or (esp. in senses 2–4) **knit**) **1** *tr.* (also *absol.*) **a** make (a garment, blanket, etc.) by interlocking loops of yarn with knitting needles. **b** make (a garment, etc.) with a knitting machine. **c** make (a plain stitch) in knitting (*knit one, purl one*). **2 a** *tr.* contract (the forehead) in vertical wrinkles. **b** *intr.* (of the forehead) contract; frown. **3** *tr. & intr.* (often foll. by *together*) make or become close or compact, esp. by common interests, etc. (*a close-knit group*). **4** *intr.* (often foll. by *together*) (of parts of a broken bone) become joined; heal. •*n.* knitted material or a knitted garment. ▫▫ **knit·ter** *n.*

knit Old English *cnyttan*, of West Germanic origin; related to German dialect *knütten*, also to KNOT[1]. The original sense was 'tie in or with a knot', hence 'join, unite' (sense 2); an obsolete Middle English sense 'knot string to make a net' gave rise to sense 1.

knit·ting /níting/ *n.* **1** a garment, etc., in the process of being knitted. **2 a** the act of knitting. **b** an instance of this.

knit·ting nee·dle *n.* a thin pointed rod of steel, wood, plastic, etc., used esp. in pairs for knitting.

knit·wear /nítwair/ *n.* knitted garments.

knives *pl.* of KNIFE.

knob /nob/ *n.* **1** a rounded protuberance, esp. at the end or on the surface of a thing. **2** a handle of a door, drawer, etc., shaped like a knob. ▫▫ **knob·by** *adj.* **knob·like** *adj.*

knob·bly *adj.* (**·ier, –iest**) having lumps that give a misshapen appearance.

knock /nok/ *v. & n.* •*v.* **1 a** *tr.* strike (a hard surface) with an audible sharp blow (*knocked the table three times*). **b** *intr.* strike, esp. a door, to gain admittance (*do you hear someone knocking?*; *knocked at the door*). **2** *tr.* make (a hole, a dent, etc.) by knocking (*knock a hole in the fence*). **3** *tr.* (usu. foll. by *in, out, off*, etc.) drive (a thing, a person, etc.) by striking (*knocked the ball into the hole*; *knocked those ideas out of his head*; *knocked her hand away*). **4** *tr. sl.* criticize. **5** *intr.* **a** (of a motor or other engine) make a thumping or rattling noise esp. as the result of a loose bearing. **b** (of a vehicle engine) emit a series of high-pitched explosive sounds caused by faulty combustion. •*n.* **1** an act of knocking. **2** a sharp rap, esp. at a door. **3** an audible sharp blow. **4** the sound of knocking, esp. in a motor engine. ▫ **knock around** (or **about**) **1** strike repeatedly; treat roughly. **2** lead a wandering adventurous life; wander aimlessly. **knock down 1** strike (esp. a person) to the ground with a blow. **2** demolish. **3** (usu. foll. by *to*) (at an auction) dispose of (an article) to a bidder by a knock with a hammer (*knocked the Picasso down to him for a million*). **4** *colloq.* lower the price of (an article). **5** take (machinery, furniture, etc.) to pieces for transportation. **6** *sl.* steal. **knock one's head against** come into collision with (unfavorable facts or conditions). **knock into the middle of next week** *colloq.* send (a person) flying, esp. with a blow. **knock off 1** strike off with a blow. **2** *colloq.* **a** finish work (*knocked off at 5:30*). **b** finish (work) (*knocked off work early*). **3** *colloq.* dispatch (business). **4** *colloq.* rapidly produce (a work of art, verses, etc.). **5** (often foll. by *from*) deduct (a sum) from a price, bill, etc. **6** *sl.* steal from (*knocked off a liquor store*). **7** *sl.* kill. **knock on** (or **knock**) **wood** knock something wooden with the knuckles to avert bad luck. **knock out 1** make (a person) unconscious by a blow on the head. **2** knock down (a boxer) for a count of 10, thereby winning the contest. **3** defeat, esp. in a knockout competition. **4** *sl.* astonish. **5** (*refl.*) *colloq.* exhaust (*knocked themselves out swimming*). **6** *colloq.* make or write (a plan, etc.) hastily. **7** empty (a tobacco pipe) by tapping. **knock sideways** *colloq.* disconcert; astonish. **knock together** put together or assemble hastily or roughly. **knock up 1** make or arrange hastily. **2** damage or mar. **3** *coarse sl.* make pregnant.

knock·a·bout /nókəbowt/ *attrib.adj.* **1** (of comedy) boisterous; slapstick. **2** (of clothes) suitable for rough use.

knock·down /nókdown/ *adj.* (of a blow, misfortune, argument, etc.) overwhelming.

knock·er /nókər/ *n.* **1** a metal or wooden instrument hinged to a door for knocking to call attention. **2** a person or thing that knocks. **3** (in *pl.*) *coarse sl.* a woman's breasts.

knock-knees *n.pl.* a condition in which the legs curve inward at the knee. ▫▫ **knock-kneed** *adj.*

knock·out /nókowt/ *n.* **1** the act of making unconscious by a blow. **2** *Boxing*, etc., a blow that knocks an opponent out. **3** a competition in which the loser in each round is eliminated (also *attrib.*: *a knockout round*). **4** *colloq.* an outstanding or irresistible person or thing.

knock·wurst /na͡akwərst/ *n.* a variety of thick, seasoned sausage.

knoll /nōl/ *n.* a small hill or mound.

knot /not/ *n. & v.* •*n.* **1 a** an intertwining of a rope, string, tress of hair, etc., with another, itself, or something else to join or fasten together. **b** a set method of tying a knot (*a reef knot*). **c** a ribbon, etc., tied as an ornament and worn on a dress, etc. **d** a tangle in hair, knitting, etc. **2 a** a unit of a ship's or aircraft's speed equivalent to one nautical mile per hour (see NAUTICAL MILE). **b** *colloq.* a nautical mile. **3** (usu. foll. by *of*) a group or cluster (*a small knot of journalists at the gate*). **4** something forming or maintaining a union; a bond or tie, esp. of wedlock. **5** a hard lump of tissue in an animal or human body. **6 a** a knob or protuberance in a stem, branch, or root. **b** a hard mass formed in a tree trunk at the intersection with a branch. **c** a round cross-grained piece in lumber where a branch has been cut through. **d** a node on the stem of a plant. **7** a difficulty; a problem. **8** a central point in a problem or the plot of a story, etc. •*v.* (**knotted, knotting**) **1** *tr.* tie (a string, etc.) in a knot. **2** *tr.* entangle. **3** *tr.* esp. *Brit.* knit (the brows). **4** *tr.* unite closely or intricately (*knotted together in intrigue*). **5 a** *intr.* make knots for fringing. **b** *tr.* make (a fringe) with knots. ▫ **tie in knots** *colloq.* baffle or confuse completely. **tie the knot** get married. ▫▫ **knot·less** *adj.* **knot·ter** *n.* **knot·ting** *n.* (esp. in sense 5 of *v.*).

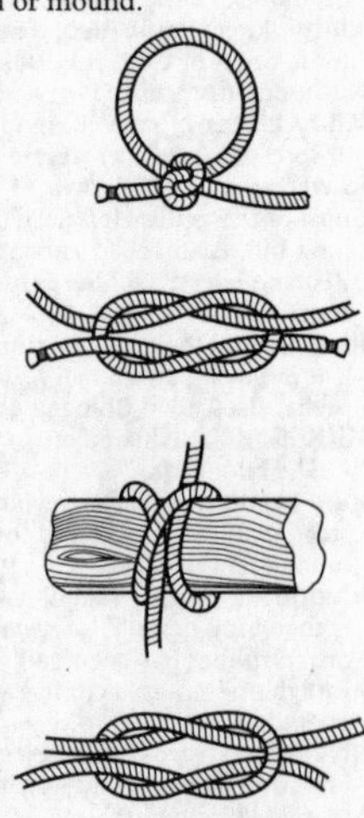

knot, 1a

knot·hole /nót-hōl/ *n.* a hole in a piece of lumber where a knot has fallen out.

knot·ty /nótee/ *adj.* (**knottier, knottiest**) **1** full of knots. **2** hard to explain; puzzling (*a knotty problem*). ▫▫ **knot·ti·ly** *adv.* **knot·ti·ness** *n.*

knot·work /nótwərk/ *n.* ornamental work representing or consisting of intertwined cords.

know /nō/ *v. & n.* • *v.* (*past* **knew** /noo, nyoo/; *past part.* **known** /nōn/) **1** *tr.* (often foll. by *that, how, what,* etc.) **a** have in the mind; have learned; be able to recall (*knows a lot about cars; knows what to do*). **b** (also *absol.*) be aware of (a fact) (*he knows I am waiting; I think she knows*). **c** have a good command of (a subject or language) (*knew German; knows his multiplication tables*). **2** *tr.* be acquainted or friendly with (a person or thing). **3** *tr.* **a** recognize; identify (*I knew him at once; knew him to be an Englishman*). **b** (foll. by *to* + infin.) be aware of (a person or thing) as being or doing what is specified (*knew them to be rogues*). **c** (foll. by *from*) be able to distinguish (one from another) (*did not know him from Adam*). **4** *tr.* be subject to (*her joy knew no bounds*). **5** *tr.* have personal experience of (fear, etc.). **6** *tr.* (as **known** *adj.*) **a** publicly acknowledged (*a known thief; a known fact*). **b** *Math.* (of a quantity, etc.) having a value that can be stated. **7** *intr.* have understanding or knowledge. **8** *tr. archaic* have sexual intercourse with. • *n.* (in phr. **in the know**) *colloq.* well-informed; having special knowledge. ▫ **don't I know it!** *colloq.* an expression of rueful assent. **don't you know** *colloq.* or *joc.* an expression used for emphasis (*such a bore, don't you know*). **for all I know** so far as my knowledge extends. **have been known to** be known to have done (*they have been known to not turn up*). **I knew it!** I was sure that this would happen. **know about** have information about. **know best** be or claim to be better informed, etc., than others. **know better than** (foll. by *that,* or *to* + infin.) be wise, well-informed, or well-mannered enough to avoid (specified behavior, etc.). **know by name 1** have heard the name of. **2** be able to give the name of. **know by sight** recognize the appearance (only) of. **know of** be aware of; have heard of (*not that I know of*). **know the ropes** (or **one's stuff**) be fully knowledgeable or experienced. **know a thing or two** be experienced or shrewd. **know what's what** have adequate knowledge of the world, life, etc. **know who's who** be aware of who or what each person is. **not know that ...** *colloq.* be fairly sure that something is not the case (*I don't know that I want to go*). **not know what hit one** be suddenly injured, killed, disconcerted, etc. **not want to know** refuse to take any notice of. **what do you know?** *colloq.* an expression of surprise. **you know** *colloq.* **1** an expression implying something generally known or known to the hearer (*you know, the store on the corner*). **2** an expression used as a gap-filler in conversation. **you know something** (or **what**)? I am going to tell you something. **you never know** nothing in the future is certain. ▫▫ **know·a·ble** *adj.* **know·er** *n.*

know-how *n.* **1** practical knowledge; technique; expertise. **2** natural skill or invention.

know·ing /nōing/ *n. & adj.* • *n.* the state of being aware or informed of any thing. • *adj.* **1** usu. *derog.* cunning; sly. **2** showing knowledge; shrewd. ▫ **there is no knowing** no one can tell. ▫▫ **know·ing·ness** *n.*

know·ing·ly /nōinglee/ *adv.* **1** consciously; intentionally (*had never knowingly injured him*). **2** in a knowing manner (*smiled knowingly*).

know-it-all *n. colloq.* a person who acts as if he or she knows everything.

knowl·edge /nólij/ *n.* **1 a** (usu. foll. by *of*) awareness or familiarity gained by experience (of a person, fact, or thing) (*have no knowledge of their character*). **b** a person's range of information (*is not within his knowledge*). **c** specific information; facts or intelligence about something (*received knowledge of their imminent departure*). **2 a** (usu. foll. by *of*) a theoretical or practical understanding of a subject, language, etc. (*has a good knowledge of Greek*). **b** the sum of what is known (*every branch of knowledge*). **c** learning; scholarship. **3** *Philos.* true, justified belief; certain understanding, as opp. to opinion. **4** = CARNAL KNOWLEDGE. ▫ **to my knowledge 1** so far as I know. **2** as I know for certain.

knowl·edge·a·ble /nólijəbəl/ *adj.* (also **knowl·edg·a·ble**) well-informed; intelligent. ▫▫ **knowl·edge·a·bil·i·ty** *n.* **knowl·edge·a·ble·ness** *n.* **knowl·edge·a·bly** *adv.*

know-noth·ing *n.* an ignorant person.

known *past part.* of KNOW.

knuck·le /núkəl/ *n. & v.* • *n.* **1** the bone at a finger joint, esp. that adjoining the hand. **2 a** a projection of the carpal or tarsal joint of a quadruped. **b** a joint of meat consisting of this with the adjoining parts, esp. of bacon or pork. • *v.tr.* strike, press, or rub with the knuckles. ▫ **knuckle down** (often foll. by *to*) **1** apply oneself seriously (to a task, etc.). **2** give in; submit. **knuckle under** give in; submit. ▫▫ **knuck·ly** *adj.*

---

knuckle Middle English *knokel* (originally denoting the rounded shape when a joint such as the elbow or knee is bent), from Middle Low German, Middle Dutch *knökel*, diminutive of *knoke* 'bone'. In the mid-18th cent. the verb *knuckle (down)* expressed setting the knuckles down to shoot the taw in a game of marbles, hence the notion of applying oneself with concentration.

---

knuck·le·ball /núkəlbawl/ *n. Baseball* a pitch delivered with the ball held by the knuckles or fingernails such that the thrown ball has minimal spin and moves erratically (also **knuck·ler**). ▫▫ **knuck·le·ball·er** *n.*

knuck·le·bone /núkəlbōn/ *n.* **1** bone forming a knuckle. **2** the bone of a sheep or other animal corresponding to or resembling a knuckle. **3** a knuckle of meat. **4** (in *pl.*) animal knucklebones used in the game of jacks. **5** (in *pl.*) the game of jacks.

knuck·le·head /núkəlhed/ *n. colloq.* a slow-witted or stupid person.

knuck·le sand·wich *n. sl.* a punch in the mouth

knur /nər/ *n.* **1** a hard excrescence on the trunk of a tree. **2** a hard concretion.

knurl /nərl/ *n.* a small projecting knob, ridge, etc. ▫▫ **knurled** /nərld/ *adj.*

KO *abbr.* **1** knockout. **2** kickoff.

ko·a /kṓə/ *n.* **1** a Hawaiian tree, *Acacia koa,* which produces dark red wood. **2** this wood.

ko·a·la /kō-aálə/ *n.* a bearlike Australian marsupial, *Phascolarctos cinereus,* having thick, gray fur and feeding on eucalyptus leaves.

▶The fuller form *koala bear* is now considered incorrect.

KO'd /kayṓd, káyōd/ *adj.* knocked out.

Ko·di·ak /kṓdeeak/ *n.* (in full **Kodiak bear**) a large Alaskan brown bear, *Ursus arctos middendorffi.*

kohl /kōl/ *n.* a black powder, usu. antimony sulfide or lead sulfide, used as eye makeup esp. in Eastern countries.

kohl·ra·bi /kōlraábee/ *n.* (*pl.* **kohlrabies**) a variety of cabbage with an edible turniplike swollen stem.

ko·la var. of COLA.

Ko·mo·do drag·on /kəmṓdō/ *n.* (also **Ko·mo·do liz·ard**) a large monitor lizard, *Varanus komodoensis,* native to the E. Indies.

kook /kook/ *n. & adj. sl.* • *n.* a crazy or eccentric person. • *adj.* crazy; eccentric.

---

kook·a·bur·ra /ko͝okəbərə, –burə/ *n.* any Australian kingfisher of the genus *Dacelo,* esp. *D. novaeguineae,* which makes a harsh cry that sounds like laughter. Also called **laughing jackass.**

kook·y /ko͝okee/ *adj.* (**kookier, kookiest**) *sl.* crazy or eccentric. ▫▫ **kook·i·ly** *adv.* **kook·i·ness** *n.*

ko·peck /kṓpek, kópek/ *n.* (also **ko·pek, copeck**) a Russian coin and monetary unit worth one-hundredth of a ruble.

Ko·ran /kərán, –ra̋an, kaw–/ *n.* (also **Qur'an** /kə–/) the Islamic sacred book, believed to be the word of God as dictated to Muhammad and written down in Arabic. ▫▫ **Ko·ran·ic** *adj.*

Ko·re·an /kəréeən, kaw–/ *n.* & *adj.* • *n.* **1** a native or national of N. or S. Korea in SE Asia. **2** the language of Korea. • *adj.* of or relating to Korea or its people or language.

ko·sher /kṓshər/ *adj.* & *n.* • *adj.* **1** (of food or premises in which food is sold, cooked, or eaten) fulfilling the requirements of Jewish law. **2** *colloq.* correct; genuine; legitimate. • *n.* kosher food. ▫ **keep kosher** adhere to kosher practices.

kow·tow /kowtów/ *n.* & *v.* (also **ko·tow** /kōtów/) • *n. hist.* the Chinese custom of kneeling and touching the ground with the forehead in worship or submission. • *v.intr.* **1** *hist.* perform the kowtow. **2** (usu. foll. by *to*) act obsequiously.

KP *n. Mil. colloq.* **1** enlisted person detailed to help the cooks. **2** kitchen duty.

k.p.h. *abbr.* kilometers per hour.

Kr *symb. Chem.* the element krypton.

kraal /kraal/ *n. S.Afr.* **1** a village of huts enclosed by a fence. **2** an enclosure for cattle or sheep.

kraft /kraft/ *n.* (in full **kraft paper**) a kind of strong smooth brown wrapping paper.

krait /krīt/ *n.* any venomous snake of the genus *Bungarus* of E. Asia.

kraut /krowt/ *n.* **1** *colloq.* sauerkraut. **2** (also **Kraut**) *sl. offens.* a German.

krem·lin /krémlin/ *n.* **1** a citadel within a Russian city or town. **2** (**the Kremlin**) **a** the citadel in Moscow. **b** the Russian or former USSR government housed within it.

krill /kril/ *n.* tiny planktonic crustaceans found in the seas around the Antarctic and eaten by baleen whales.

kro·na /krṓnə/ *n.* **1** (*pl.* **kronor** /krṓnər, –nawr/) the chief monetary unit of Sweden. **2** (*pl.* **kronur** /krṓnər/) the chief monetary unit of Iceland.

kro·ne /krṓnə/ *n.* (*pl.* **kroner** /krṓnər/) the chief monetary unit of Denmark and of Norway.

Kru·ger·rand /kro͞ogərand, –raant/ *n.* (also **kru·ger·rand**) a S. African gold coin depicting President Kruger.

krumm·horn /krúmhawrn/ *n.* (also **krum·horn, crumhorn**) a medieval wind instrument with a double reed and a curved end.

kryp·ton /krípton/ *n. Chem.* an inert gaseous element of the noble gas group, forming a small portion of the earth's atmosphere and used in fluorescent lamps, etc. ¶ Symb.: **Kr.**

KS *abbr.* Kansas (in official postal use).

kt. *abbr.* **1** karat(s). **2** kiloton(s). **3** knots.

ku·dos /ko͞odōz, –dōs, –dos, kyo͞o–/ *n. colloq.* glory; renown.

▶**Kudos** from Greek, is a singular noun meaning 'praise, honor.' However, because of its *-s* ending, it has come to be used as a plural noun meaning 'compliments, congratulations.' As a result the (etymologically incorrect) singular form *kudo,* also meaning 'praise, honor,' has come into existence.

Ku Klux Klan /ko͞o kluks klán, kyo͞o–/ *n.* a secret society founded in the southern US, orig. formed after the Civil War and dedicated to white supremacy. ▫▫ **Ku Klux Klans·man** *n.* (*pl.* **-men**).

kum·quat /kúmkwot/ *n.* (also **cumquat**) **1** an orange-like fruit with a sweet rind and acid pulp, used in preserves. **2** any shrub or small tree of the genus *Fortunella* yielding this.

kung fu /kung fo͞o, ko͝ong/ *n.* the Chinese form of karate.

Kurd /kərd/ *n.* a member of a mainly pastoral Aryan Islamic people living in Kurdistan (contiguous areas of Iraq, Iran, and Turkey).

Kurd·ish /kə́rdish/ *adj.* & *n.* • *adj.* of or relating to the Kurds or their language. • *n.* the Iranian language of the Kurds.

kV *abbr.* kilovolt(s).

kvass /kvaas/ *n.* a Russian fermented beverage, low in alcohol, made from rye flour or bread with malt.

kvetch /kvech/ *n.* & *v. sl.* • *n.* an objectionable person, esp. one who complains a great deal. • *v.intr.* complain; whine. ▫▫ **kvetch·er** *n.*

kW *abbr.* kilowatt(s).

kwan·za /kwanzə/ *n.* (*pl.* **·za,–zas**) the basic monetary unit of Angola.

kWh *abbr.* kilowatt-hour(s).

KY *abbr.* Kentucky (in official postal use).

Ky. *abbr.* Kentucky.

ky·a·nite /kíənīt/ *n.* a blue crystalline mineral of aluminum silicate. ▫▫ **ky·a·nit·ic** /–nítik/ *adj.*

L

L[1] /el/ *n.* (also **l**) (*pl.* **Ls** or **L's**) **1** the twelfth letter of the alphabet. **2** (as a Roman numeral) 50. **3** a thing shaped like an L, esp. a joint connecting two pipes at right angles.

L[2] *abbr.* (also **L.**) **1** Lake. **2** Latin. **3** Liberal. **4** large. **5** *Biol.* Linnaeus. **6** lire.

l *abbr.* (also **l.**) **1** left. **2** line. **3** liter(s). **4** length. **5** *archaic* pound(s) (money).

£ *abbr.* (preceding a numeral) pound or pounds (of money).

LA *abbr.* **1** Los Angeles. **2** Louisiana (in official postal use).

La *symb. Chem.* the element lanthanum.

La. *abbr.* Louisiana.

la /laa/ *n. Mus.* **1** (in tonic sol-fa) the sixth note of a major scale. **2** the note A in the fixed-do system.

Lab. *abbr.* **1** *Brit.* Labour Party. **2** Labrador.

lab /lab/ *n. colloq.* a laboratory.

lab·a·rum /lábərəm/ *n.* **1** a symbolic banner. **2** Constantine the Great's imperial standard, with Christian symbols added to Roman military symbols.

la·bel /láybəl/ *n. & v.* • *n.* **1** a usu. small piece of paper, card, linen, metal, etc., for attaching to an object and giving its name, information about it, instructions for use, etc. **2** esp. *derog.* a short classifying phrase or name applied to a person, a work of art, etc. **3 a** a small fabric label sewn into a garment bearing the maker's name. **b** the logo, title, or trademark of esp. a fashion or recording company (*brought it out under their own label*). **c** the piece of paper in the center of a phonograph record describing its contents, etc. **4** an adhesive stamp on a parcel, etc. **5** a word placed before, after, or in the course of a dictionary definition, etc., to specify its subject, register, nationality, etc. **6** *Heraldry* the mark of an eldest son, consisting of a superimposed horizontal bar with usu. three downward projections. • *v.tr.* (**labeled, labeling**; esp. *Brit.* **labelled, labelling**) **1** attach a label to. **2** (usu. foll. by *as*) assign to a category (*labeled them as irresponsible*). **3 a** replace (an atom) by an atom of a usu. radioactive isotope as a means of identification. **b** replace an atom in (a molecule) or atoms in the molecules of (a substance). **4** (as **labeled** *adj.*) made identifiable by the replacement of atoms. ▫▫ **la·bel·er** *n.*

la·bi·a *pl.* of LABIUM.

la·bi·al /láybeeəl/ *adj. & n.* • *adj.* **1 a** of the lips. **b** *Zool.* of, like, or serving as a lip, a liplike part, or a labium. **2** *Dentistry* designating the surface of a tooth adjacent to the lips. **3** *Phonet.* (of a sound) requiring partial or complete closure of the lips (e.g., *p, b, f, v, m, w*; and vowels in which lips are rounded, e.g., *oo* in *moon*). • *n. Phonet.* a labial sound. ▫▫ **la·bi·al·ism** *n.* **la·bi·al·ize** *v.tr.* **la·bi·al·ly** *adv.*

la·bi·ate /láybeeət, –ayt/ *n. & adj.* • *n.* any plant of the family Labiatae, including mint and rosemary, having square stems and a corolla or calyx divided into two parts suggesting lips. • *adj.* **1** *Bot.* of or relating to the Labiatae. **2** *Bot. & Zool.* like a lip or labium.

labio- /láybeeō/ *comb. form* of the lips.

la·bi·o·den·tal /láybeeōdént'l/ *adj.* (of a sound) made with the lips and teeth, e.g., *f* and *v*.

la·bi·um /láybeeəm/ *n.* (*pl.* **labia** /–beeə/) **1** (usu. in *pl.*) *Anat.* each of the two pairs of skin folds that enclose the vulva. **2** the lower lip in the mouthparts of an insect or crustacean. **3** a lip, esp. the lower one of a labiate plant's corolla.

la·bor /láybər/ *n. & v.* (*Brit.* **labour**) • *n.* **1 a** physical or mental work; exertion. **b** such work considered as supplying the needs of a community. **2** workers, esp. manual, considered as a class or political force. **3** the process of childbirth, esp. the period from the start of uterine contractions to delivery. **4** a particular task, esp. of a difficult nature. • *v.* **1** *intr.* work hard; exert oneself. **2** *intr.* (usu. foll. by *for*, or *to* + infin.) strive for a purpose. **3** *tr.* **a** elaborate needlessly (*I will not labor the point*). **b** (as **labored** *adj.*) not spontaneous or fluent. **4** *intr.* (often foll. by *under*) suffer under (a disadvantage or delusion) (*labored under universal disapproval*). **5** *intr.* proceed with trouble or difficulty (*labored slowly up the hill*). **6** *intr.* (of a ship) roll or pitch heavily.

lab·o·ra·to·ry /lábrətáwree/ *n.* (*pl.* **-ries**) a room or building fitted out for scientific experiments, research, or the manufacture of drugs and chemicals.

la·bor camp *n.* a prison camp enforcing a regime of hard labor.

La·bor Day *n.* in the US and Canada, the first Monday in September (or in most other countries May 1), celebrated in honor of working people.

la·bor·er /láybərər/ *n.* **1** a person doing unskilled, usu. manual, work for wages. **2** a person who labors.

la·bor-in·ten·sive *adj.* (of a form of work) needing a large workforce.

la·bo·ri·ous /ləbáwreeəs/ *adj.* **1** needing hard work or toil (*a laborious task*). **2** (esp. of literary style) pedestrian; not fluent. ▫▫ **la·bo·ri·ous·ly** *adv.* **la·bo·ri·ous·ness** *n.*

la·bor·sav·ing /láybərsáyving/ *adj.* (of an appliance, etc.) designed to reduce or eliminate human work.

la·bor un·ion *n.* an organized association of workers, often in a trade or profession, formed to protect and further their rights and interests.

la·bour *Brit.* var. of LABOR.

La·bour Par·ty *n.* **1** a British political party formed to represent the interests of ordinary working people. **2** (or **Labor Party**) any similar political party in other countries.

Lab·ra·dor /lábrədawr/ *n.* (in full **Labrador retriever**) **1** a retriever of a breed with a black or golden coat. **2** this breed.

lab·y·rinth /lábərinth/ *n.* **1** a complicated network of passages, etc.; a maze. **2** an intricate or tangled arrangement. ▫▫ **lab·y·rin·thi·an** /–ríntheeən/ *adj.* **lab·y·rin·thine** /–rínthin, –thīn/ *adj.*

lac /lak/ *n.* a resinous substance secreted as a protective covering by an Asian insect.

lace /lays/ *n. & v.* • *n.* **1** a fine open fabric made by weaving thread in patterns and used esp. to trim blouses, underwear, etc. **2** a cord or leather strip passed through eyelets or hooks on opposite sides of a shoe, corset, etc., pulled tight and fastened. **3** braid used for trimming esp. dress uniform (*gold lace*). • *v.* **1** *tr.* (usu. foll. by *up*) **a** fasten or tighten with a lace or laces. **b** compress the waist of (a person) with a laced corset. **2** *tr.*

flavor or fortify (coffee, beer, etc.) with a dash of liquor. **3** *tr.* (usu. foll. by *with*) **a** streak with color (*cheek laced with blood*). **b** interlace or embroider (fabric) with thread, etc. **4** *tr.* & (foll. by *into*) intr. *colloq.* lash; beat; defeat. **5** *tr.* (often foll. by *through*) pass (a shoelace, etc.) through. **6** *tr.* trim with lace.

lac•er•ate /lásərayt/ *v.tr.* **1** mangle or tear (esp. flesh or tissue). **2** cause pain to (the feelings, etc.). ▫▫ **lac•er•a•ble** *adj.* **lac•er•a•tion** /–ráyshən/ *n.*

lace-up *n.* & *adj.* •*n.* a shoe fastened with a lace. •*attrib.adj.* (of a shoe, etc.) fastened with a lace or laces.

lach•es /láchiz/ *n. Law* delay in asserting a right, claiming a privilege, etc.

lach•ry•mal /lákriməl/ *adj* (also **lac•ri•mal**) **1** *literary* of or for tears. **2** (usu. as **lacrimal**) *Anat.* concerned in the secretion of tears (*lacrimal canal*; *lacrimal duct*).

lach•ry•ma•tion /lákrimáyshən/ *n.* (also **lac•ri•ma•tion**) *formal* the flow of tears.

lach•ry•ma•to•ry /lákrimətáwree/ *adj. formal* of or causing tears.

lach•ry•mose /lákrimōs/ *adj. formal* given to weeping; tearful; inducing tears. ▫▫ **lach•ry•mose•ly** *adv.*

lac•ing /láysing/ *n.* **1** lace trimming, esp. on a uniform. **2** a laced fastening on a shoe or corsets. **3** *colloq.* a beating. **4** a dash of spirits in a beverage.

lack /lak/ *n.* & *v.* •*n.* (usu. foll. by *of*) an absence, want, or deficiency. •*v.tr.* be without or deficient in (*lacks courage*). ▫ **for lack of** owing to the absence of. **lack for** lack.

lack•a•dai•si•cal /lákədáyzikəl/ *adj.* **1** listless; idle. **2** feebly sentimental and affected. ▫▫ **lack•a•dai•si•cal•ly** *adv.*

lack•er var. of LACQUER.

lack•ey /lákee/ *n.* (also **lac•quey**) (*pl.* **-eys**) **1** *derog.* **a** a servile political follower. **b** an obsequious parasitical person. **2 a** a (usu. liveried) footman or manservant. **b** a servant.

lack•ing /láking/ *adj.* **1** absent or deficient. **2** *colloq.* deficient in intellect; mentally subnormal.

lack•lus•ter /láklustər/ *adj.* **1** lacking in vitality, force, or conviction. **2** (of the eye) dull.

la•con•ic /ləkónik/ *adj.* **1** (of a style of speech or writing) brief; concise; terse. **2** (of a person) laconic in speech, etc. ▫▫ **la•con•i•cal•ly** *adv.* **la•con•i•cism** /–sizəm/ *n.* **lac•o•nism** /lákənizəm/ *n.*

lac•quer /lákər/ *n.* & *v.* (also **lack•er**) •*n.* **1** a sometimes colored liquid made of shellac dissolved in alcohol, or of synthetic substances, that dries to form a hard protective coating for wood, brass, etc. **2** the sap of the lacquer tree, *Rhus verniciflua*, used to varnish wood, etc. •*v.tr.* coat with lacquer. ▫▫ **lac•quer•er** *n.*

lac•quey var. of LACKEY.

lac•ri•mal var. of LACHRYMAL.

lac•ri•ma•tion var. of LACHRYMATION.

la•crosse /ləkráws, –krós/ *n.* a game like field hockey, but with a ball driven by, caught, and carried in a crosse, a long-handled stick ending in a small basket.

lac•tate[1] /láktayt/ *v.intr.* (of mammals) secrete milk. ▫▫ **lac•ta•tion** /–táyshən/ *n.*

lac•tate[2] /láktayt/ *n. Chem.* any salt or ester of lactic acid.

lac•te•al /lákteeəl/ *adj.* & *n.* •*adj.* **1** of milk. **2** conveying chyle or other milky fluid. •*n.* (in *pl.*) the lymphatic vessels of the small intestine that absorb digested fats.

lac•tes•cent /laktésənt/ *adj.* **1** milky. **2** yielding a milky juice.

lac•tic /láktik/ *adj. Chem.* of, relating to, or obtained from milk.

lac•tic ac•id *n.* a carboxylic acid formed in sour milk, and produced in the muscle tissues during strenuous exercise.

lacto- /láktō/ *comb. form* milk.

lac•tose /láktōs/ *n. Chem.* a sugar that occurs in milk, and is less sweet than sucrose.

la•cu•na /ləkyóonə/ *n.* (*pl.* **lacunae** /–nee/or **lacunas**) **1** a hiatus, blank, or gap. **2** a missing portion or empty page, esp. in an ancient manuscript, etc. **3** *Anat.* a cavity or depression, esp. in bone. ▫▫ **la•cu•nar** *adj.* **la•cu•nar•y** /lákyoonéree, ləkyóonəree/ *adj.* **la•cu•nose** *adj.*

lac•y /láysee/ *adj.* (**lacier, laciest**) of or resembling lace fabric. ▫▫ **lac•i•ly** *adv.* **lac•i•ness** *n.*

lad /lad/ *n.* **1** a boy or youth. **2** a young son.

lad•der /ládər/ *n.* **1** a set of horizontal bars of wood, etc., fixed between two uprights and used for climbing up or down. **2 a** a hierarchical structure. **b** such a structure as a means of advancement, promotion, etc.

lad•der-back *n.* an upright chair with a back resembling a ladder.

lad•die /ládee/ *n. colloq.* a young boy or lad.

lade /layd/ *v.* (*past part.* **laden** /láyd'n/) **1** *tr.* **a** put cargo on board (a ship). **b** ship (goods) as cargo. **2** *intr.* (of a ship) take on cargo. **3** *tr.* (as **laden** *adj.*) (usu. foll. by *with*) **a** (of a vehicle, donkey, person, tree, table, etc.) heavily loaded. **b** (of the conscience, spirit, etc.) painfully burdened with sorrow, etc.

la-di-da /laádeedaá/ *adj.* & *n. colloq.* (also **la-de-da**) •*adj.* pretentious or snobbish, esp. in manner or speech. •*n.* **1** a la-di-da person. **2** la-di-da speech or manners.

la•dies *pl.* of LADY.

lad•ies' man *n.* (also **lad•y's man**) **1** a man fond of female company. **2** a seducer.

lad•ing /láyding/ *n.* **1** a cargo. **2** the act or process of lading.

la•dle /láyd'l/ *n.* & *v.* •*n.* **1** a large, long-handled spoon with a cup-shaped bowl used for serving esp. soups and gravy. **2** a vessel for transporting molten metal in a foundry. •*v.tr.* (often foll. by *out*) transfer (liquid) from one receptacle to another. ▫ **ladle out** distribute, esp. lavishly. ▫▫ **la•dle•ful** *n.* (*pl.* **-fuls**). **la•dler** *n.*

la•dy /láydee/ *n.* (*pl.* **-dies**) **1 a** a woman regarded as being of superior social status or as having the refined manners associated with this (cf. GENTLEMAN). **b** (**Lady**) a title used by peeresses, wives and widows of knights, etc. **2** (often *attrib.*) a female person or animal (*ask that lady over there*; *lady butcher*; *lady dog*). **3** *colloq.* **a** a wife. **b** a man's girlfriend. **4** a ruling woman (*lady of the house*). **5** (in *pl.* as a form of address) a female audience or the female part of an audience. ▫▫ **la•dy•hood** *n.*

lady Old English *hlǣfdīge* (denoting a woman to whom homage or obedience is due, such as the wife of a lord or the mistress of a household, also specifically the Virgin Mary), from *hlāf* 'loaf' + a Germanic base meaning 'knead', related to DOUGH; compare with LORD. In *Lady Day* and other compounds where it signifies possession, it represents the Old English genitive *hlǣfdīgan* '(Our) Lady's'.

la•dy•bug /láydeebug/ *n.* a coleopterous insect of the family Coccinellidae, with wing covers usu. of a reddish-brown color with black spots.

la•dy•fin•ger /láydeefinggər/ *n.* a finger-shaped sponge cake.

la•dy-in-wait•ing *n.* (*pl.* **ladies-in-waiting**) a lady attending a queen or princess.

la•dy-kill•er *n.* **1** a man very attractive to women. **2** a practiced and habitual seducer.

la•dy•like /láydeelīk/ *adj.* **1 a** with the modesty, manners, etc., of a lady. **b** befitting a lady. **2** (of a man) effeminate.

la•dy•ship /láydeeship/ *n.* ▫ **her** (or **your**) **ladyship** (*pl.*

their or **your ladyships**) **1** a respectful form of reference or address to a titled lady or ladies. **2** *iron.* a form of reference or address to a woman thought to be giving herself airs.

la·dy's man var. of LADIES' MAN.

la·dy's slip·per *n.* any orchidaceous plant of the genus *Cypripedium*, with a usu. yellow or pink slipper-shaped lip on its flowers.

lag[1] /lag/ *v. & n.* • *v.intr.* (**lagged, lagging**) (often foll. by *behind*) fall behind; not keep pace. • *n.* a delay.

lag[2] /lag/ *v. & n.* • *v.tr.* (**lagged, lagging**) enclose or cover in lagging. • *n.* **1** the non-heat-conducting cover of a boiler, etc. **2** a piece of this.

la·ger /la̋agər/ *n.* a kind of beer, effervescent and light in color and body.

lag·gard /lágərd/ *n. & adj.* • *n.* a dawdler. • *adj.* dawdling; slow. ▫▫ **lag·gard·ly** *adj. & adv.*

lag·ging /láging/ *n.* material providing heat insulation for a boiler, pipes, etc.

la·goon /ləgóon/ *n.* **1** a stretch of salt water separated from the sea by a low sandbank, coral reef, etc. **2** the enclosed water of an atoll. **3** a small freshwater lake near a larger lake or river. **4** an artificial pool for the treatment of effluent or to accommodate an overspill from surface drains during heavy rain.

la·ic /láyik/ *adj. & n.* • *adj.* nonclerical; lay; secular; temporal. • *n. formal* a lay person; a noncleric. ▫▫ **la·i·cal** *adj.* **la·i·cal·ly** *adv.*

laid *past* and *past part.* of LAY[1].

laid-back *adj. colloq.* relaxed; unbothered; easygoing.

laid up *adj.* confined to bed or the house.

lain *past part.* of LIE[1].

lair /lair/ *n. & v.* • *n.* **1 a** a wild animal's resting place. **b** a person's hiding place (*tracked him to his lair*). **2** a place where domestic animals lie down. • *v.* **1** *intr.* go to or rest in a lair. **2** *tr.* place (an animal) in a lair.

lais·sez-faire /lésayfáir/ *n.* (also **lais·ser-faire**) the theory or practice of governmental abstention from interference in the workings of the market, etc.

la·i·ty /láy-itee/ *n.* (usu. prec. by *the*; usu. treated as *pl.*) **1** lay people, as distinct from the clergy. **2** nonprofessionals.

lake[1] /layk/ *n.* a large body of water surrounded by land.

lake[2] /layk/ *n.* **1** a reddish coloring orig. made from lac (*crimson lake*). **2** a complex formed by the action of dye and mordants applied to fabric to fix color. **3** any insoluble product of a soluble dye and mordant.

lake·side /láyksīd/ *attrib.adj.* beside a lake.

lal·la·tion /laláyshən/ *n.* **1** the pronunciation of *r* as *l*. **2** imperfect speech, esp. that of young children.

lam /lam/ *v.* (**lammed, lamming**) *sl.* **1** *tr.* thrash; hit. **2** *intr.* (foll. by *into*) hit (a person, etc.) hard with a stick, etc.

lam /lam/ *n. sl.* ▫ **on the lam** fleeing, esp. from the police.

la·ma /la̋amə/ *n.* a Tibetan or Mongolian Buddhist monk.

la·ma·ser·y /la̋aməseree/ *n.* (*pl.* **-ies**) a monastery of lamas.

lamb /lam/ *n. & v.* • *n.* **1** a young sheep. **2** the flesh of a lamb as food. **3** a mild or gentle person, esp. a young child. • *v.* **1 a** *tr.* (in *passive*) (of a lamb) be born. **b** *intr.* (of a ewe) give birth to lambs. **2** *tr.* tend (lambing ewes). ▫ **The Lamb** (or **The Lamb of God**) a name for Christ (John 1:29) (cf. AGNUS DEI). **like a lamb** meekly; obediently. ▫▫ **lamb·kin** *n.* **lamb·like** *adj.*

lam·ba·da /ləmba̋adə/ *n.* a fast erotic Brazilian dance in which couples dance with their hips touching each other.

lam·baste /lambáyst/ *v.tr.* (also **lam·bast** /–bást/) *colloq.* **1** thrash; beat. **2** criticize severely.

lamb·da /lámdə/ *n.* **1** the eleventh letter of the Greek alphabet (Λ, λ). **2** (as λ) the symbol for wavelength.

lam·bent /lámbənt/ *adj.* **1** (of a flame or a light) playing on a surface with a soft radiance. **2** (of the eyes, sky, etc.) softly radiant. **3** (of wit, etc.) lightly brilliant. ▫▫ **lam·ben·cy** *n.*

lame /laym/ *adj. & v.* • *adj.* **1** disabled, esp. in the foot or leg; limping. **2 a** (of an argument, excuse, etc.) unconvincing; unsatisfactory. **b** (of verse, etc.) halting. • *v.tr.* **1** make lame; disable. **2** harm permanently. ▫▫ **lame·ly** *adv.* **lame·ness** *n.*

la·mé /lamáy/ *n. & adj.* • *n.* a fabric with gold or silver threads interwoven. • *adj.* (of fabric, etc.) having such threads.

lame·brain /láymbrayn/ *n. colloq.* a stupid person.

lame duck *n.* **1** a disabled or weak person. **2** a defaulter in the stock market. **3** an official (esp. the president) in the final period of office, after the election of a successor.

la·ment /ləmént/ *n. & v.* • *n.* **1** a passionate expression of grief. **2** a song or poem of mourning or sorrow. • *v.tr.* (also *absol.*) **1** express or feel grief for or about; regret (*lamented the loss of his ticket*). **2** (as **lamented** *adj.*) a conventional expression referring to a recently dead person (*your late lamented father*). ▫ **lament for** (or **over**) mourn or regret. ▫▫ **lam·en·ta·tion** /láməntáyshən/ *n.* **la·ment·er** *n.* **la·ment·ing·ly** *adv.*

lam·en·ta·ble /ləméntəbəl, lámənt–/ *adj.* deplorable; regrettable. ▫▫ **lam·en·ta·bly** *adv.*

lam·i·na /láminə/ *n.* (*pl.* **laminae** /–nee/or **laminas**) a thin plate or scale, e.g., of bone, stratified rock, or vegetable tissue. ▫▫ **lam·i·nar** /láminər/ *adj.*

lam·i·nate *v., n., & adj.* • *v.* /láminayt/ **1** *tr.* beat or roll (metal) into thin plates. **2** *tr.* overlay with metal plates, a plastic layer, etc. **3** *tr.* manufacture by placing layer on layer. **4** *tr. & intr.* split into layers or leaves. • *n.* /láminət/ a laminated structure or material. • *adj.* /láminət/ in the form of lamina or laminae. ▫▫ **lam·i·na·tion** /–náyshən/ *n.* **lam·i·na·tor** *n.*

Lam·mas /láməs/ *n.* (in full **Lammas Day**) the first day of August, formerly observed as harvest festival.

lamp /lamp/ *n. & v.* • *n.* **1** a device for producing a steady light, esp.: **a** an electric bulb, and usu. its holder (*bedside lamp*). **b** an oil lamp. **c** a usu. glass holder for a candle. **d** a gas jet and mantle. **2** a source of spiritual or intellectual inspiration. **3** a device producing esp. ultraviolet or infrared radiation as a treatment for various complaints. • *v.* **1** *intr. poet.* shine. **2** *tr.* supply with lamps; illuminate. **3** *tr. sl.* look at. ▫▫ **lamp·less** *adj.*

lamp·black /lámpblak/ *n.* a pigment made from soot.

lamp·light /lámplīt/ *n.* light given by a lamp or lamps.

lamp·light·er /lámplītər/ *n. hist.* **1** a person who lights street lamps. **2** a device for lighting lamps.

lam·poon /lampóon/ *n. & v.* • *n.* a satirical attack on a person, etc. • *v.tr.* satirize. ▫▫ **lam·poon·ist** *n.*

lamp·post /lámp-pōst/ *n.* a tall post supporting an outdoor light.

lam·prey /lámpree, –pray/ *n.* (*pl.* **-preys**) any eellike aquatic vertebrate of the family Petromyzonidae, without scales, paired fins, or jaws, but having a sucker mouth.

lamp·shade /lámpshayd/ *n.* a translucent cover for a lamp used to soften or direct its light.

LAN /lan/ *n. Computing* local area network.

lance /lans/ *n. & v.* • *n.* **1 a** a long weapon with a wooden shaft and a pointed steel head, used by a horseman in charging. **b** a similar weapon used for spearing a fish. **2** = LANCER. • *v.tr.* **1** *Surgery* prick or cut open with a lancet. **2** pierce with a lance.

lanc·er /lánsər/ *n.* **1** *hist.* a soldier of a cavalry regiment armed with lances. **2** (in *pl.*) **a** a quadrille for 8 or 16 pairs. **b** the music for this.

lan·cet /lánsit/ *n.* a small, broad, two-edged surgical knife with a sharp point.

land /land/ *n. & v.* •*n.* **1** the solid part of the earth's surface (opp. SEA, WATER, AIR). **2 a** an expanse of country; ground. **b** such land in relation to its use, etc., or (often prec. by *the*) as a basis for agriculture (*works on the land*). **3** a country, nation, or state (*land of hope and glory*). **4 a** landed property. **b** (in *pl.*) estates. **5** the space between the rifling grooves in a gun. **6** a strip of plow land or pastureland parted from others by drain furrows. •*v.* **1 a** *tr. & intr.* set or go ashore. **b** *intr.* (often foll. by *at*) disembark. **2** *tr.* bring (an aircraft, etc.) to the ground or the surface of water. **3** *intr.* (of an aircraft, parachutist, etc.) alight on the ground or water. **4** *tr.* bring (a fish) to land or to a boat. **5** *tr. & intr.* (also *refl.*; often foll. by *up*) *colloq.* bring to, reach, or find oneself in a certain situation, place, or state. **6** *tr. colloq.* **a** deal (a person, etc.) a blow, etc. (*landed him one in the eye*). **b** (foll. by *with*) present (a person) with (a problem, etc.). **7** *tr.* set down (a person, cargo, etc.) from a vehicle, ship, etc. **8** *tr. colloq.* win or obtain (a prize, job, etc.). □ **how the land lies** what is the state of affairs. **in the land of the living** *joc.* still alive. **land on one's feet** attain a good position, job, etc., by luck. □□ **land·less** *adj.* **land·ward** *adj. & adv.*

land bridge *n.* a neck of land joining two large landmasses.

land·ed /lándid/ *adj.* **1** owning land (*landed gentry*). **2** consisting of, including, or relating to land (*landed property*).

land·fall /lándfawl/ *n.* the approach to land, esp. for the first time on a sea or air journey.

land·fill /lándfil/ *n.* **1** waste material, etc., used to landscape or reclaim areas of ground. **2** the process of disposing of rubbish in this way. **3** landfill site; a place where rubbish is disposed of by burying it in the ground.

land·form /lándfawrm/ *n.* a natural feature of the earth's surface.

land·hold·er /lándhōldər/ *n.* the proprietor or, esp., the tenant of land.

land·ing /lánding/ *n.* **1 a** the act or process of coming to land. **b** an instance of this. **c** (also **land·ing place**) a place where ships, etc., land. **2 a** a platform between two flights of stairs. **b** a passage leading to upstairs rooms.

land·ing craft *n.* any of several types of craft esp. designed for putting troops and equipment ashore.

land·ing gear *n.* the undercarriage of an aircraft.

land·ing stage *n.* a platform, often floating, on which goods and passengers are disembarked.

land·la·dy /lándlaydee/ *n.* (*pl.* **-dies**) **1** a woman who rents land, a building, etc., to a tenant. **2** a woman who keeps a boardinghouse, an inn, etc.

land·locked /lándlokt/ *adj.* almost or entirely enclosed by land.

land·lord /lándlawrd/ *n.* **1** a man who rents land, a building, etc., to a tenant. **2** a man who keeps a boardinghouse, an inn, etc.

land·lub·ber /lándlubər/ *n.* a person unfamiliar with the sea or sailing.

land·mark /lándmaark/ *n.* **1 a** a conspicuous object in a district, etc. **b** an object marking the boundary of an estate, country, etc. **2** an event, change, etc., marking a stage or turning point in history, etc. **3** *attrib.* serving as a landmark; signifying an important change, development, etc.

land·mass /lándmas/ *n.* a large area of land.

land mine *n.* **1** an explosive mine laid in or on the ground. **2** *fig.* a hazard

land·own·er /lándōnər/ *n.* an owner of land. □□ **land·own·ing** *adj. & n.*

land·scape /lándskayp/ *n. & v.* •*n.* **1** natural or imaginary scenery, as seen in a broad view. **2** (often *attrib.*) a picture representing this; the genre of landscape painting. **3** (in graphic design, etc.) a format in which the width of an illustration, etc., is greater than the height (cf. PORTRAIT). •*v.tr.* (also *absol.*) improve (a piece of land) by landscape gardening. □□ **land·scap·ist** *n.*

land·scape gar·den·ing *n.* the laying out of esp. extensive grounds to resemble natural scenery. □□ **land·scape gar·den·er** *n.*

land·slide /lándslīd/ *n.* **1** the sliding down of a mass of land from a mountain, cliff, etc. **2** an overwhelming majority for one side in an election.

land·slip /lándslip/ *n. Brit.* = LANDSLIDE 1.

lands·man /lándzmən/ *n.* (*pl.* **-men**) a nonsailor.

lane /layn/ *n.* **1** a narrow, often rural, road, street, or path. **2** a division of a road for a stream of traffic. **3** a strip of track or water for a runner, rower, or swimmer in a race. **4** a path or course prescribed for or regularly followed by a ship, aircraft, etc. **5** *Bowling* a long, narrow strip of floor down which the ball is rolled.

lang·lauf /laánglowf/ *n.* cross-country skiing; a cross-country skiing race.

lan·guage /lánggwij/ *n.* **1** the method of human communication, gestured, spoken or written, consisting of the use of words in an agreed way. **2** the language of a particular community or country, etc. **3 a** the faculty of speech. **b** a style of expression; the use of words, etc. (*his language was poetic*). **c** (also **bad language**) coarse, crude, or abusive speech. **4** a system of symbols and rules for writing computer programs or algorithms. **5** any method of expression (*the language of flowers*; *sign language*). **6** a professional or specialized vocabulary. **7** literary style.

lan·guid /lánggwid/ *adj.* **1** lacking vigor; idle; inert. **2** (of ideas, etc.) lacking force; uninteresting. **3** (of trade, etc.) slow-moving; sluggish. **4** faint; weak. □□ **lan·guid·ly** *adv.* **lan·guid·ness** *n.*

lan·guish /lánggwish/ *v.intr.* **1** be or grow feeble; lose or lack vitality. **2** put on a sentimentally tender or languid look. □ **languish for** droop or pine for. **languish under** suffer under (esp. depression, confinement, etc.). □□ **lan·guish·ment** *n.*

lan·guor /lánggər/ *n.* **1** lack of energy or alertness; idleness. **2** faintness; fatigue. **3** a soft or tender mood or effect. **4** an oppressive stillness (of the air, etc.). □□ **lan·guor·ous** *adj.* **lan·guor·ous·ly** *adv.*

la·nif·er·ous /lənífərəs/ *adj.* wool-bearing.

lank /langk/ *adj.* **1** (of hair, grass, etc.) long, limp, and straight. **2** thin and tall. **3** shrunken; spare. □□ **lank·ly** *adv.* **lank·ness** *n.*

lank·y /lángkee/ *adj.* (**lankier, lankiest**) (of limbs, a person, etc.) ungracefully thin and long or tall. □□ **lank·i·ly** *adv.* **lank·i·ness** *n.*

lan·o·lin /lánəlin/ *n.* a fat found naturally on sheep's wool and used purified for cosmetics, etc.

lan·tern /lántərn/ *n.* **1 a** a lamp with a transparent usu. glass case protecting a candle flame, etc. **b** a similar electric, etc., lamp. **c** its case. **2** a raised structure on a dome, room, etc., glazed to admit light or ventilation. **3** the light chamber of a lighthouse. **4** = MAGIC LANTERN.

lan·tern fish *n.* any marine fish of the family Myctophidae, having small light organs on the head and body.

lan·tha·nide /lánthənīd/ *n. Chem.* an element of the lanthanide series.

lan·tha·nide se·ries *n.* a series of 15 metallic elements from lanthanum to lutetium in the periodic table, having similar chemical properties. Also called **rare earth.**

lan·tha·num /lánthənəm/ *n. Chem.* a silvery metallic element of the lanthanide series that occurs naturally and is used in the manufacture of alloys. ¶ Symb.: **La.**

la·nu·go /lənóogō, –nyóo–/ *n.* fine, soft hair, esp. that which covers the body and limbs of a human fetus.

lan·yard /lányərd/ *n.* **1** a cord hanging around the neck or looped around the shoulder, esp. of a scout or sailor, etc., to which a knife, etc., may be attached. **2** *Naut.* a short rope or line used for securing, tightening, etc. **3** a cord attached to a breech mechanism for firing a gun.

La·od·i·ce·an /layódiséeən/ *adj. & n.* • *adj.* lukewarm or halfhearted, esp. in religion or politics. • *n.* such a person.

lap[1] /lap/ *n.* **1 a** the front of the body from the waist to the knees of a sitting person. **b** the clothing, esp. a skirt, covering the lap. **c** the front of a skirt held up to catch or contain something. **2** a hollow among hills. **3** a hanging flap on a garment, a saddle, etc. □ **in** (or **on**) **a person's lap** as a person's responsibility. **in the lap of the gods** (of an event, etc.) open to chance; beyond human control. **in the lap of luxury** in extremely luxurious surroundings. □□ **lap·ful** *n.* (*pl.* **-fuls**).

lap Old English *læppa*, of Germanic origin; related to Dutch *lap*, German *Lappen* 'piece of cloth'. The word originally denoted a fold or flap of a garment (compare with LAPEL), later specifically one that could be used as a pocket or pouch, or the front of a skirt when held up to catch or carry something (Middle English), hence the area between the waist and knees as a place where a child could be nursed or an object held.

lap[2] /lap/ *n. & v.* • *n.* **1 a** one circuit of a racetrack, etc. **b** a section of a journey, etc. (*on the last lap*). **2 a** an amount of overlapping. **b** an overlapping or projecting part. **3 a** a layer or sheet (of cotton, etc., being made) wound on a roller. **b** a single turn of rope, thread, etc., around a drum or reel. **4** a rotating disk for polishing a gem or metal. • *v.* (**lapped, lapping**) **1** *tr.* lead or overtake (a competitor) by one or more laps. **2** *tr.* (often foll. by *about, around*) coil, fold, or wrap (a garment, etc.) around. **3** *tr.* (usu. foll. by *in*) enfold or wrap (a person) in clothing, etc. **4** *tr.* (as **lapped** *adj.*) (usu. foll. by *in*) enfolded caressingly. **5** *tr.* surround (a person) with an influence, etc. **6** *intr.* (usu. foll. by *over*) project; overlap. **7** *tr.* cause to overlap. **8** *tr.* polish (a gem, etc.) with a lap.

lap[3] /lap/ *v. & n.* • *v.* (**lapped, lapping**) **1** *tr.* **a** (also *absol.*) (usu. of an animal) drink (liquid) with the tongue. **b** (usu. foll. by *up, down*) consume greedily. **c** (usu. foll. by *up*) consume (gossip, praise, etc.) greedily. **2 a** *tr.* (of water) move or beat upon (a shore) with a rippling sound as of lapping. **b** *intr.* (of waves, etc.) move in ripples; make a lapping sound. • *n.* **1 a** the process or an act of lapping. **b** the amount of liquid taken up. **2** the sound of wavelets on a beach. **3** liquid food for dogs. **4** *sl.* **a** a weak beverage. **b** any liquor.

lap·a·ro·scope /lápərəskōp/ *n. Surgery* a fiber-optic instrument inserted through the abdominal wall to give a view of the organs in the abdomen. □□ **lap·a·ros·co·py** /–róskəpee/ *n.* (*pl.* **-pies**).

lap·a·rot·o·my /lápərótəmee/ *n.* (*pl.* **-mies**) a surgical incision into the abdominal cavity for exploration or diagnosis.

lap·dog /lápdawg/ *n.* **1** a small pet dog. **2** a person or organization that is influenced or controlled by another.

la·pel /ləpél/ *n.* the part of a coat, jacket, etc., folded back against the front around the neck opening. □□ **la·pelled** or **la·peled** *adj.*

lap·i·dar·y /lápideree/ *adj. & n.* • *adj.* **1** concerned with stone or stones. **2** engraved upon stone. **3** (of writing style) dignified and concise, suitable for inscriptions. • *n.* (*pl.* **-ies**) a cutter, polisher, or engraver of gems.

lap·is laz·u·li /lápis lázoolee, lázyə–, lázhə–/ *n.* **1** a blue mineral containing sodium aluminum silicate and sulfur, used as a gemstone. **2** a bright blue pigment formerly made from this. **3** its color.

lap joint *n.* a joint made with two pieces of metal, timber, etc., by halving the thickness of each at the joint and fitting them together.

lap·pet /lápit/ *n.* **1** a small flap or fold of a garment, etc. **2** a hanging or loose piece of flesh, such as a lobe or wattle.

lapse /laps/ *n. & v.* • *n.* **1** a slight error; a slip of memory, etc. **2** a weak or careless decline into an inferior state. **3** (foll. by *of*) an interval or passage of time (*after a lapse of three years*). **4** *Law* the termination of a right or privilege through disuse or failure to follow appropriate procedures. • *v.intr.* **1** fail to maintain a position or standard. **2** (foll. by *into*) fall back into an inferior or previous state. **3** (of a right or privilege, etc.) become invalid because it is not used or claimed or renewed. **4** (as **lapsed** *adj.*) (of a person or thing) that has lapsed.

lap·top /láptop/ *n.* (often *attrib.*) a microcomputer that is portable and suitable for use while traveling.

lap·wing /lápwing/ *n.* a plover, *Vanellus vanellus,* with black and white plumage, crested head, and a shrill cry.

lar·board /laárbərd/ *n. & adj. Naut. archaic* = PORT[3].

lar·ce·ny /laársənee/ *n.* (*pl.* **-nies**) the theft of personal property. □□ **lar·ce·nist** *n.* **lar·ce·nous** *adj.*

larch /laarch/ *n.* **1** a deciduous coniferous tree of the genus *Larix,* with bright foliage and producing tough wood. **2** (in full **larchwood**) its wood.

lard /laard/ *n. & v.* • *n.* the internal fat of the abdomen of pigs, esp. when rendered for use in cooking and pharmacy. • *v.tr.* **1** insert strips of fat or bacon in (meat, etc.) before cooking. **2** (foll. by *with*) embellish (talk or writing) with foreign or technical terms.

lard·er /laárdər/ *n.* **1** a room or cupboard for storing food. **2** a wild animal's store of food, esp. for winter.

large /laarj/ *adj. & n.* • *adj.* **1** of considerable or relatively great size or extent. **2** of the larger kind (*the large intestine*). **3** of wide range; comprehensive. **4** pursuing an activity on a large scale (*large farmer*). • *n.* (**at large**) **1** at liberty. **2** as a body or whole (*the people at large*). **3** (of a narration, etc.) at full length and with all details. **4** without a specific target (*scatters insults at large*). **5** representing a whole area and not merely a part of it (*councilwoman at large*). □ **in large** on a large scale. **large as life** see LIFE. **larger than life** see LIFE. □□ **large·ness** *n.* **larg·ish** *adj.*

large in·tes·tine *n.* the cecum, colon, and rectum collectively.

large·ly /laárjlee/ *adv.* to a great extent; principally (*is largely due to laziness*).

large-scale *adj.* made or occurring on a large scale or in large amounts.

lar·gesse /laarzhés/ *n.* (also **lar·gess**) **1** money or gifts freely given, esp. on an occasion of rejoicing, by a person in high position. **2** generosity; beneficence.

lar·go /laárgō/ *adv., adj., & n. Mus.* • *adv. & adj.* in a slow tempo and dignified in style. • *n.* (*pl.* **-gos**) a largo passage or movement.

lar·i·at /láreeət/ *n.* **1** a lasso. **2** a tethering rope, esp. used by cowboys.

lark[1] /laark/ *n.* **1** any small bird of the family Alaudidae with brown plumage, elongated hind claws and tuneful song. **2** any of various similar birds.

lark[2] /laark/ *n. & v. colloq.* • *n.* a frolic or spree; an amusing incident. • *v.intr.* (foll. by *about*) play tricks; frolic. ▫▫ **lark·y** *adj.* **lark·i·ness** *n.*

lark·spur /laárkspur/ *n.* any of various plants of the genus *Consolida*, with a spur-shaped calyx.

lar·va /laárvə/ *n.* (*pl.* **larvae** /–vee/) **1** the stage of development of an insect between egg and pupa, e.g., a caterpillar. **2** an immature form of other animals that undergo some metamorphosis, e.g. a tadpole. ▫▫ **lar·val** *adj.*

lar·yn·gi·tis /lárinjítis/ *n.* inflammation of the larynx.

lar·ynx /láringks/ *n.* (*pl.* **larynges** /lərínjeez/or **larynxes**) the hollow muscular organ forming an air passage to the lungs and holding the vocal cords.

la·sa·gna /ləzaányə/ *n.* (also **la·sa·gne**) pasta in the form of sheets or wide ribbons.

las·civ·i·ous /ləsíveeəs/ *adj.* **1** lustful. **2** inciting to or evoking lust. ▫▫ **las·civ·i·ous·ly** *adv.* **las·civ·i·ous·ness** *n.*

lase /layz/ *v.intr.* **1** function as or in a laser. **2** (of a substance) undergo the physical processes employed in a laser.

la·ser /láyzər/ *n.* a device that generates an intense beam of coherent monochromatic radiation in the infrared, visible, or ultraviolet region of the electromagnetic spectrum, by stimulated emission of photons from an excited source.

la·ser disc *n.* a disk on which signals and data are recorded to be reproduced by directing a laser beam on to the surface.

la·ser print·er *n.* a printer in which a laser is used to form a pattern of dots on a photosensitive drum corresponding to the pattern of print required.

La·ser·Vi·sion /láyzərvizhən/ *n. Trademark* a system for the reproduction of video signals recorded on a disk with a laser.

lash /lash/ *v. & n.* • *v.* **1** *intr.* make a sudden whiplike movement. **2** *tr.* beat with a whip, etc. **3** *intr.* pour or rush with great force. **4** *intr.* (foll. by *at, against*) strike violently. **5** *tr.* castigate in words. **6** *tr.* urge on as with a lash. **7** *tr.* (foll. by *down, together*, etc.) fasten with a cord, rope, etc. **8** *tr.* (of rain, wind, etc.) beat forcefully upon. • *n.* **1 a** a sharp blow made by a whip, rope, etc. **b** (prec. by *the*) punishment by beating with a whip, etc. **2** the flexible end of a whip. **3** (usu. in *pl.*) an eyelash. ▫ **lash out** (often foll. by *at*) speak or hit out angrily. ▫▫ **lash·less** *adj.*

lash·ing /láshing/ *n.* **1** a beating. **2** cord used for lashing.

lass /las/ *n.* a girl or young woman.

las·sie /lásee/ *n. colloq.* = LASS.

las·si·tude /lásitood, –tyood/ *n.* **1** languor; weariness. **2** disinclination to exert or interest oneself.

las·so /lásō, lasóo/ *n. & v.* • *n.* (*pl.* **-sos** or **-oes**) a rope with a noose at one end, used esp. in N. America for catching cattle, etc. • *v.tr.* (**-soes, -soed**) catch with a lasso. ▫▫ **las·so·er** *n.*

last[1] /last/ *adj., adv., & n.* • *adj.* **1** after all others; coming at or belonging to the end. **2 a** most recent; next before a specified time (*last Christmas*). **b** preceding (*got on at the last station*). **3** only remaining (*the last cookie*). **4** (prec. by *the*) least likely or suitable (*the last person I'd want*). **5** the lowest in rank (*last place*). • *adv.* **1** after all others (esp. in *comb.*: *last-mentioned*). **2** on the last occasion before the present (*when did you last see him?*). **3** (esp. in enumerating) lastly. • *n.* **1** a person or thing that is last, last-mentioned, etc. **2** (prec. by *the*) the last mention or sight, etc. (*shall never hear the last of it*). **3** the last performance of certain acts (*breathed his last*). **4** (prec. by *the*) **a** the end or last moment. **b** death. ▫ **at last** (or **long last**) in the end; after much delay. **on one's last legs** see LEG. **pay one's last respects** see RESPECT. **to** (or **till**) **the last** till the end; esp. till death.

▶In precise usage, **latest** means 'most recent' and **last** means 'final.' But **last** is commonly used in either case: *I read his last novel. The last time she called, she told me about her new job.* **Latest** should be used when it is important to distinguish between 'most recent' and 'final': *The last day of the school year will be June 18. My latest project is wallpapering my dining room.* See also note at FORMER.

last[2] /last/ *v.intr.* **1** remain unexhausted or adequate or alive for a specified or considerable time (*enough food to last us a week*). **2** continue for a specified time (*the journey lasts an hour*). ▫ **last out** remain adequate or in existence for the whole of a period previously stated or implied.

last[3] /last/ *n.* a shoemaker's model for shaping or repairing a shoe or boot.

last·ing /lásting/ *adj.* **1** continuing; permanent. **2** durable. ▫▫ **last·ing·ly** *adv.*

last·ly /lástlee/ *adv.* finally; in the last place.

last rites *n.pl.* sacred rites for a person about to die.

last straw *n.* (prec. by *the*) a slight addition to a burden or difficulty that makes it finally unbearable.

Last Sup·per *n.* that of Christ and his disciples on the eve of the Crucifixion, as recorded in the New Testament.

lat. *abbr.* latitude.

latch /lach/ *n. & v.* • *n.* **1** a bar with a catch and lever used as a fastening for a gate, etc. **2** a springlock preventing a door from being opened from the outside without a key after being shut. • *v.tr. & intr.* fasten or be fastened with a latch. ▫ **latch on** (often foll. by *to*) *colloq.* **1** attach oneself (to). **2** understand.

latch·key /láchkee/ *n.* (*pl.* **-keys**) a key of an outer door.

latch·key child *n.* (also **latchkey kid**) a child who is alone at home after school until a parent returns from work.

late /layt/ *adj. & adv.* • *adj.* **1** after the due or usual time; occurring or done after the proper time. **2 a** far on in the day or night or in a specified time or period. **b** far on in development. **3** flowering or ripening toward the end of the season. **4** (prec. by *the* or *my, his*, etc.) no longer alive or having the specified status (*the late president*). **5** of recent date (*the late storms*). **6** (as **latest**, prec. by *the*) fashionable, up to date. • *adv.* **1** after the due or usual time (*arrived late*). **2** far on in time (*this happened later on*). **3** at or till a late hour. **4** at a late stage of development. **5** formerly but not now (*a family late of New England*). ▫ **at the latest** as the latest time envisaged (*by six at the latest*). **late in the day** *colloq.* at a late stage in the proceedings, esp. too late to be useful. **the latest** the most recent news, fashion, etc. ▫▫ **late·ness** *n.*

▶See note at LAST [1].

late·com·er /láytkumər/ *n.* a person who arrives late.

la·teen /ləteén/ *adj.* (of a ship) rigged with a triangular sail on a long yard at an angle of 45° to the mast.

late·ly /láytlee/ *adv.* not long ago; recently; in recent times.

la·tent /láyt'nt/ *adj.* **1** concealed; dormant. **2** existing but not developed or manifest. ▫▫ **la·ten·cy** *n.* **la·tent·ly** *adv.*

lat·er·al /látərəl/ *adj. & n.* • *adj.* **1** of, at, toward, or from the side or sides. **2** descended from a brother or sister of a person in direct line. • *n.* a side part, etc., esp. a lateral shoot or branch. ▫▫ **lat·er·al·ly** *adv.*

lat·er·ite /látərīt/ *n.* a red or yellow iron-bearing clay, friable and hardening in air, used for making roads in the tropics. ▫▫ **lat·er·it·ic** /–rítik/ *adj.*

la·tex /láyteks/ *n.* (*pl.* **latices** /–tiseez/or **latexes**) **1** a milky fluid of mixed composition found in various plants and trees, esp. the rubber tree. **2** a synthetic product resembling this.

lath /lath/ *n.* & *v.* •*n.* (*pl.* **laths** /laths, lathz/) a thin flat strip of wood, esp. each of a series forming a framework or support for plaster, etc. •*v.tr.* attach laths to (a wall or ceiling).

lathe /layth/ *n.* a machine for shaping wood, metal, etc., by means of a rotating drive that turns the piece being worked on against changeable cutting tools.

lath·er /láthər/ *n.* & *v.* •*n.* **1** a froth produced by agitating soap, etc., and water. **2** frothy sweat, esp. of a horse. **3** a state of agitation. •*v.* **1** *intr.* (of soap, etc.) form a lather. **2** *tr.* cover with lather. **3** *intr.* (of a horse, etc.) develop or become covered with lather. **4** *tr. colloq.* thrash. □□ **lath·er·y** *adj.*

lat·i·ces *pl.* of LATEX.

Lat·in /lát'n/ *n.* & *adj.* •*n.* **1** the Italic language of ancient Rome and its empire, originating in Latium. **2** *Rom.Hist.* an inhabitant of ancient Latium in Central Italy. •*adj.* **1** of or in Latin. **2** of the countries or peoples using languages developed from Latin. **3** *Rom.Hist.* of or relating to ancient Latium or its inhabitants. **4** of the Roman Catholic Church. □□ **Lat·in·ism** *n.* **Lat·in·ist** *n.*

Lat·in A·mer·i·ca *n.* the parts of North, Central and S. America where Spanish or Portuguese is the main language. □□ **Lat·in A·mer·i·can** *n.* & *adj.*

La·ti·no /ləteénō/ *n.* (*pl.* **Latinos**; *fem.* **Latina** /–nə/, *pl.* **Latinas**) **1** a native or inhabitant of Latin America. **2** a person of Spanish-speaking or Latin-American descent.

lat·ish /láytish/ *adj.* & *adv.* fairly late.

lat·i·tude /látitōōd, –tyōōd/ *n.* **1** *Geog.* **a** the angular distance on a meridian north or south of the equator, expressed in degrees and minutes. **b** (usu. in *pl.*) regions or climes, esp. with reference to temperature (*warm latitudes*). **2** freedom from narrowness; liberality of interpretation. **3** tolerated variety of action or opinion. **4** *Astron.* the angular distance of a celestial body or point from the ecliptic. □□ **lat·i·tu·di·nal** /–tōōd'nəl, –tyōōd–/ *adj.* **lat·i·tu·di·nal·ly** *adv.*

latitude, 1a

la·trine /lətreén/ *n.* a communal toilet, esp. in a barracks, etc.

lat·ter /látər/ *adj.* **1 a** denoting the second-mentioned of two, or *disp.* the last-mentioned of three or more. **b** (prec. by *the*; usu. *absol.*) the second- or last-mentioned person or thing. **2** nearer to the end (*the latter part of the year*). **3** recent. **4** belonging to the end of a period, of the world, etc.

▶This word means 'the second-mentioned of two.' Its use to mean 'the last-mentioned of three or more' is common, but considered incorrect by some since *latter* means 'later' rather than 'latest.' *Last* or *last-mentioned* is preferred where three or more things are involved. See note at FORMER.

Lat·ter-day Saints *n.pl.* the Mormons' name for themselves.

lat·ter·ly /látərlee/ *adv.* **1** in the latter part of life or of a period. **2** recently.

lat·tice /látis/ *n.* **1** a structure of crossed laths or bars with spaces between, used as a fence, etc. **2** *Crystallog.* a regular periodic arrangement of atoms, ions, or molecules. □□ **lat·ticed** *adj.* **lat·tic·ing** *n.*

lat·tice win·dow *n.* a window with small panes set in diagonally crossing strips of lead.

Lat·vi·an /látveeən/ *n.* & *adj.* •*n.* **1 a** a native of Latvia, a Baltic republic. **b** a person of Latvian descent. **2** the language of Latvia. •*adj.* of or relating to Latvia or its people or language.

laud /lawd/ *v.* & *n.* •*v.tr.* praise or extol, esp. in hymns. •*n.* **1** *literary* praise; a hymn of praise. **2** (in *pl.*) the traditional morning prayer of the Roman Catholic Church.

laud·a·ble /láwdəbəl/ *adj.* commendable; praiseworthy. □□ **laud·a·bly** *adv.*

lau·da·num /láwd'nəm/ *n.* a solution containing morphine, prepared from opium and formerly used as a narcotic painkiller.

laud·a·to·ry /láwdətáwree/ *adj.* expressing praise.

laugh /laf/ *v.* & *n.* •*v.* **1** *intr.* make the spontaneous sounds and movements usual in expressing lively amusement, scorn, derision, etc. **2** *tr.* express by laughing. **3** *tr.* bring (a person) into a certain state by laughing (*laughed them into agreeing*). **4** *intr.* (foll. by *at*) ridicule; make fun of. **5** *intr.* (**be laughing**) *colloq.* be in a fortunate or successful position. •*n.* **1** the sound or act or manner of laughing. **2** *colloq.* a comical or ridiculous person or thing. □ **have the last laugh** be ultimately the winner. **laugh in a person's face** show open scorn for a person. **laugh off** get rid of (embarrassment or humiliation) with a jest. **laugh out of court** deprive of a hearing by ridicule. **laugh out of the other side of one's mouth (or on the other side of one's face)** change from enjoyment or amusement to displeasure, shame, apprehension, etc. **laugh up one's sleeve** be secretly or inwardly amused.

laugh·a·ble /láfəbəl/ *adj.* ludicrous; highly amusing. □□ **laugh·a·bly** *adv.*

laugh·ing /láfing/ *n.* & *adj.* •*n.* laughter. •*adj.* in senses of LAUGH *v.* □ **no laughing matter** something serious. □□ **laugh·ing·ly** *adv.*

laugh·ing gas *n.* nitrous oxide as an anesthetic.

laugh·ing hy·e·na *n.* the spotted hyena, *Crocuta crocuta*, with a loud laughing call.

laugh·ing·stock /láfingstok/ *n.* a person or thing open to general ridicule.

laugh·ter /láftər/ *n.* the act or sound of laughing.

laugh track *n.* recorded laughter added to a comedy show, esp. a television situation comedy.

launch[1] /lawnch/ *v.* & *n.* •*v.* **1** *tr.* set (a vessel) afloat. **2** *tr.* hurl or send forth (a weapon, rocket, etc.). **3** *tr.* start or set in motion (an enterprise, a person on a course of action, etc.). **4** *tr.* formally introduce (a new product) with publicity, etc. **5** *intr.* (often foll. by *out*, *into*, etc.) **a** make a start, esp. on an ambitious enterprise. **b** burst into strong language, etc. •*n.* the act or an instance of launching. tc. □ **launch into** begin (something or someone) energetically and enthusiastically.

launch[2] /lawnch/ *n.* **1** a motorboat, used esp. for pleasure. **2** a man-of-war's largest boat.

launch·pad /láwnchpad/ *n.* (also **launch·ing pad**) a platform from which rockets are launched.

See page xii for the *Key to Pronunciation*.

laun·der /láwndər, laán–/ *v.* & *n.* • *v.tr.* **1** wash and iron (clothes, linen, etc.). **2** *colloq.* transfer (funds) to conceal a dubious or illegal origin. • *n.* a channel for conveying liquids, esp. molten metal. □□ **laun·der·er** *n.*

laun·dress /láwndris, laán–/ *n.* a woman who launders clothes, linen, etc., esp. professionally.

Laun·dro·mat /láwndrəmat, laán–/ *n. Trademark* an establishment with coin-operated washing machines and dryers for public use.

laun·dry /láwndree, laán–/ *n.* (*pl.* **-dries**) **1** an establishment for washing clothes or linen. **2** clothes or linen for laundering or newly laundered.

laun·dry list *n. colloq.* a lengthy and often random list of items (*a laundry list of weekend projects*).

lau·re·ate /láwreeət, lór–/ *adj.* & *n.* • *adj.* **1** wreathed with laurel as a mark of honor. **2** consisting of laurel; laurellike. • *n.* **1** a person who is honored for outstanding achievement (*Nobel laureate*). **2** = POET LAUREATE. □□ **lau·re·ate·ship** *n.*

lau·rel /láwrəl, lór–/ *n.* & *v.* • *n.* **1** = BAY[2]. **2 a** (in *sing.* or *pl.*) the foliage of the bay tree used as an emblem of victory or distinction in poetry, usu. formed into a wreath or crown. **b** (in *pl.*) honor or distinction. **3** any plant with dark-green glossy leaves like a bay tree. • *v.tr.* wreathe with laurel. □ **look to one's laurels** beware of losing one's preeminence. **rest on one's laurels** be satisfied with what one has done and not seek further success.

lav /lav/ *n. colloq.* lavatory.

la·va /laávə, lávə/ *n.* **1** the molten rock that flows from a volcano. **2** the solid substance that it forms on cooling.

la·vage /ləvaázh, lávij/ *n. Med.* the washing out of a body cavity, such as the colon or stomach, with water or a medicated solution.

la·va·tion /ləváyshən/ *n. formal* washing.

lav·a·to·ry /lávətawree/ *n.* (*pl.* **-ries**) **1** a sink or wash basin in a bathroom. **2** a room or compartment with a toilet and wash basin. **3** *Brit.* a flush toilet.

lave /layv/ *v.tr. literary* **1** wash; bathe. **2** (of water) wash against; flow along.

lav·en·der /lávindər/ *n.* & *adj.* • *n.* **1 a** any small evergreen shrub of the genus *Lavandula*, with narrow leaves and blue, purple, or pink aromatic flowers. **b** its flowers and stalks dried and used to scent linen, clothes, etc. **2** a pale blue color with a trace of red. • *adj.* **1** pale blue with a trace of red. **2** having the fragrance of lavender flowers.

lav·ish /lávish/ *adj.* & *v.* • *adj.* **1** giving or producing in large quantities; profuse. **2** generous; unstinting. **3** excessive; overabundant. • *v.tr.* (often foll. by *on*) bestow or spend (money, praise, etc.) abundantly. □□ **lav·ish·ly** *adv.* **lav·ish·ness** *n.*

law /law/ *n.* **1 a** a rule enacted or customary in a community and recognized as enjoining or prohibiting certain actions and enforced by the imposition of penalties (*an environmental protection law*). **b** a body of such rules (*the law of the land; forbidden under state law*). **2** the controlling influence of laws; respect for laws (*law and order*). **3** laws collectively as a social system or subject of study (*was reading law*). **4** (with defining word) any of the specific branches or applications of law (*commercial law*). **5** binding force or effect (*their word is law*). **6** (prec. by *the*) **a** the legal profession. **b** *colloq.* the police. **7** the statute and common law (opp. EQUITY). **8** (in *pl.*) jurisprudence. **9 a** the judicial remedy; litigation. **b** courts of law as providing this (*go to law*). **10** a rule of action or procedure, e.g., in a game, form of art, etc. **11** a regularity in natural occurrences, esp. as formulated or propounded in particular instances (*the law of gravity*). **12 a** divine commandments. **b** (**Law of Moses**) the precepts of the Pentateuch. □ **at** (or **in**) **law** according to the laws. **be a law unto oneself** do what one feels is right; disregard custom. **lay down the law** be dogmatic or authoritarian. **take the law into one's own hands** redress a grievance by one's own means, esp. by force.

law·break·er /láwbraykər/ *n.* a person who breaks the law. □□ **law·break·ing** *n.* & *adj.*

law·ful /láwfŏŏl/ *adj.* conforming with, permitted by, or recognized by law. □□ **law·ful·ly** *adv.* **law·ful·ness** *n.*

law·giv·er /láwgivər/ *n.* a person who lays down laws.

law·less /láwlis/ *adj.* **1** having no laws or enforcement of them. **2** disregarding laws. **3** unbridled; uncontrolled. □□ **law·less·ly** *adv.* **law·less·ness** *n.*

law·mak·er /láwmaykər/ *n.* a legislator.

law·man /láwman/ *n.* (*pl.* **-men**) a law-enforcement officer, esp. a sheriff or policeman.

lawn[1] /lawn/ *n.* a piece of grass kept mown and smooth in a yard, garden, park, etc.

lawn[2] /lawn/ *n.* a fine linen or cotton fabric used for clothes. □□ **lawn·y** *adj.*

lawn mow·er *n.* a machine for cutting the grass on a lawn.

law of av·er·ag·es *n.* the supposed principle that future events are likely to balance any past deviation from a presumed average.

law·ren·ci·um /lərénseeəm, law–/ *n. Chem.* an artificially made transuranic radioactive metallic element. ¶ Symb.: **Lw.**

law·suit /láwsŏŏt/ *n.* the process or an instance of making a claim in a court of law.

law·yer /láwyər, lóyər/ *n.* a member of the legal profession. □□ **law·yer·ly** *adj.*

lax /laks/ *adj.* **1** lacking care, concern, or firmness. **2** loose, relaxed; not compact. □□ **lax·i·ty** *n.* **lax·ly** *adv.* **lax·ness** *n.*

lax·a·tive /láksətiv/ *adj.* & *n.* • *adj.* tending to stimulate or facilitate evacuation of the bowels. • *n.* a laxative medicine.

lay[1] /lay/ *v.* & *n.* • *v.* (*past* and *past part.* **laid** /layd/) **1** *tr.* place on a surface, esp. horizontally or in the proper or specified place. **2** *tr.* put or bring into a certain or the required position or state (*lay a carpet*). **3** *intr. dial.* or *erron.* lie. **4** *tr.* make by laying (*lay the foundations*). **5** *tr.* (often *absol.*) (of a bird) produce (an egg). **6** *tr.* **a** cause to subside or lie flat. **b** deal with to remove (a ghost, fear, etc.). **7** *tr.* place or present for consideration (a case, proposal, etc.). **8** *tr.* set down as a basis or starting point. **9** *tr.* (usu. foll. by *on*) attribute or impute (blame, etc.). **10** *tr.* locate (a scene, etc.) in a certain place. **11** *tr.* prepare or make ready (a plan or a trap). **12** *tr.* prepare (a table) for a meal. **13** *tr.* place or arrange the material for (a fire). **14** *tr.* put down as a wager; stake. **15** *tr.* (foll. by *with*) coat or strew (a surface). **16** *tr. sl. offens.* have sexual intercourse with (esp. a woman). • *n.* **1** the way, position, or direction in which something lies. **2** *sl. offens.* a partner (esp. female) in sexual intercourse. **3** the direction or amount of twist in rope strands. □ **in lay** (of a hen) laying eggs regularly. **lay about one 1** hit out on all sides. **2** criticize indiscriminately. **lay aside 1** put to one side. **2** cease to practice or consider. **3** save (money, etc.) for future needs. **lay at the door of** see DOOR. **lay bare** expose; reveal. **lay a charge** make an accusation. **lay claim to** claim as one's own. **lay down 1** put on the ground. **2** relinquish; give up (an office). **3** formulate or insist on (a rule or principle). **4** pay or wager (money). **5** store (wine) in a cellar. **6** set down on paper. **7** sacrifice (one's life). **8** convert (land) into pasture. **9** record (esp. popular music). **lay down the law** see LAW. **lay hands on 1** seize or attack. **2** place one's hands on or over, esp. in confirmation, ordination, or spiritual healing. **lay one's hands on** obtain; acquire;

locate. **lay hold of** seize or grasp. **lay in** provide oneself with a stock of. **lay into** *colloq.* punish or scold severely. **lay it on thick** (or **with a trowel**) *colloq.* flatter or exaggerate grossly. **lay low** overthrow, kill, or humble. **lay off 1** discharge (workers) temporarily because of a shortage of work. **2** *colloq.* desist. **lay on 1** spread on (paint, etc.). **2** inflict (blows). **3** impose (a penalty, obligation, etc.). **lay open 1** break the skin of. **2** (foll. by *to*) expose (to criticism, etc.). **lay out 1** spread out. **2** expose to view. **3** prepare (a corpse) for burial. **4** *colloq.* knock unconscious. **5** prepare a layout. **6** expend (money). **7** *refl.* (foll. by *to* + infin.) take pains (to do something) (*laid themselves out to help*). **lay store by** see STORE. **lay to rest** bury in a grave. **lay up 1** store; save. **2** put (a ship, etc.) out of service. **lay waste** see WASTE. ▶**Lay,** 'to put down on a surface,' is a transitive verb, and **lie,** 'to be horizontal,' is intransitive. Avoid the intransitive use of **lay,** as in *I'm going to lay on the grass at lunchtime.*. Similarly, avoid the transitive use of **lie,** as in *Lie it on the table.* These two verbs are often confused, especially because the past of *lie* is *lay: We lay on the grass for an hour.* The past of **lay** is *laid: I laid down my tools and lay on the grass.*

lay[2] /lay/ *adj.* **1 a** nonclerical. **b** not ordained into the clergy. **2 a** not professionally qualified, esp. in law or medicine. **b** of or done by such persons.

lay[3] /lay/ *n.* **1** a short lyric or narrative poem meant to be sung. **2** a song.

lay[4] *past* of LIE[1].

lay·a·bout /láyəbowt/ *n.* a habitual loafer or idler.

lay·a·way *n.* a system of paying a deposit to secure an item for later purchase.

lay·er /láyər/ *n.* & *v.* •*n.* **1** a thickness of matter, esp. one of several, covering a surface. **2** a person or thing that lays. **3** a hen that lays eggs. **4** a shoot fastened down to take root while attached to the parent plant. •*v.tr.* **1 a** arrange in layers. **b** cut (hair) in layers. **2** propagate (a plant) as a layer. □□ **lay·ered** *adj.*

lay·ette /layét/ *n.* a set of clothing, toilet articles, and bedclothes for a newborn child.

lay·man /láymən/ *n.* (*pl.* **-men**; *fem.* **laywoman**, *pl.* **-women**) **1** any nonordained member of a church. **2** a person without professional or specialized knowledge in a particular subject.

lay·off /láyawf/ *n. n.* **1** a usu. temporary discharge of workers. **2** a period when this is in force.

lay of the land *n.* (prec. by *the*) the current state of affairs.

lay·out /láyowt/ *n.* **1** the disposing or arrangement of a site, ground, etc. **2** the way in which plans, printed matter, etc., are arranged or set out. **3** something arranged or set out in a particular way. **4** the makeup of a book, newspaper, etc.

lay·o·ver /láyōvər/ *n.* a period of rest or waiting before a further stage in a journey, etc.; a stopover.

lay·wom·an see LAYMAN.

laze /layz/ *v.* & *n.* •*v.* **1** *intr.* spend time lazily or idly. **2** *tr.* (often foll. by *away*) pass (time) in this way. •*n.* a spell of lazing.

la·zy /láyzee/ *adj.* (**lazier, laziest**) **1** disinclined to work; doing little work. **2** of or inducing idleness. **3** (of a river, etc.) slow-moving. □□ **la·zi·ly** *adv.* **la·zi·ness** *n.*

la·zy·bones /láyzeebōnz/ *n.* (*pl.* same) *colloq.* a lazy person.

la·zy eye *n.* an eye with poor vision that is mainly caused by underuse, esp. the unused eye in strabismus.

lb. *abbr.* a pound or pounds (weight).

LC *abbr.* (also **L.C.** or **l.c.**) **1** landing craft. **2** left center. **3** letter of credit. **4** (**LC** or **L.C.**) Library of Congress. **5** lowercase. **6** in the passage, etc., cited.

LCD *abbr.* **1** liquid crystal display. **2** lowest (or least) common denominator.

LCM *abbr.* lowest (or least) common multiple.

Ld. *abbr.* Lord.

lea /lee, láy/ *n. poet.* (also **ley**) a piece of meadow or pasture or arable land.

leach /leech/ *v.* **1** *tr.* make (a liquid) percolate through some material. **2** *tr.* subject (bark, ore, ash, or soil) to the action of percolating fluid. **3** *tr.* & *intr.* (foll. by *away, out*) remove (soluble matter) or be removed in this way.

lead[1] /leed/ *v., n.,* & *adj.* •*v.* (*past* and *past part.* **led** /led/) **1** *tr.* cause to go with one, esp. by guiding or showing the way or by going in front. **2** *tr.* **a** direct the actions or opinions of. **b** (often foll. by *to*, or *to* + infin.) guide by persuasion or example or argument (*what led you to that conclusion?*; *was led to think you may be right*). **3** *tr.* (also *absol.*) provide access to; bring to a certain position or destination (*this door leads you into a small room*; *the road leads to Atlanta*; *the path leads uphill*). **4** *tr.* pass or go through (a life, etc., of a specified kind) (*led a miserable existence*). **5** *tr.* **a** have the first place in (*lead the dance*; *leads the world in sugar production*). **b** (*absol.*) go first; be ahead in a race or game. **c** (*absol.*) be preeminent in some field. **6** *tr.* be in charge of (*leads a team of researchers*). **7** *tr.* **a** direct by example. **b** set (a fashion). **c** be the principal player of (a group of musicians). **8** *tr.* (also *absol.*) begin a round of play at cards by playing (a card) or a card of (a particular suit). **9** *intr.* (foll. by *to*) have as an end or outcome; result in (*what does all this lead to?*). **10** *intr.* (foll. by *with*) *Boxing* make an attack (with a particular hand or blow). **11 a** *intr.* (foll. by *with*) (of a newspaper) use a particular item as the main story (*led with the stock-market crash*). **b** *tr.* (of a story) be the main feature of (a newspaper or part of it) (*the governor's wedding will lead the front page*). **12** *tr.* (foll. by *through*) make (a liquid, strip of material, etc.) pass through a pulley, channel, etc. •*n.* **1** guidance given by going in front; example. **2 a** a leading place; the leadership (*is in the lead*; *take the lead*). **b** the amount by which a competitor is ahead of the others (*a lead of ten yards*). **3** a clue, esp. an early indication of the resolution of a problem (*is the first real lead in the case*). **4** a strap or cord for leading a dog, etc. **5** a conductor (usu. a wire) conveying electric current from a source to an appliance. **6 a** the chief part in a play, etc. **b** the person playing this. **7** (in full **lead story**) the item of news given the greatest prominence in a newspaper or magazine. **8 a** the act or right of playing first in a game or round of cards. **b** the card led. **9** the distance advanced by a screw in one turn. **10 a** an artificial watercourse, esp. one leading to a mill. **b** a channel of water in an icefield. •*attrib.adj.* leading; principal; first. □ **lead astray** see ASTRAY. **lead by the nose** cajole (a person) into compliance. **lead off 1** begin; make a start. **2** *Baseball* be the first batter in the batting order or the inning. **lead on 1** entice into going further than was intended. **2** mislead or deceive. **lead up the garden path** *colloq.* give someone misleading clues or signals; deceive. **lead up to 1** form an introduction to; precede; prepare for. **2** direct one's talk gradually or cautiously to a particular topic, etc. **lead the way** see WAY. □□ **lead·a·ble** *adj.*

lead[2] /led/ *n.* & *v.* •*n.* **1** *Chem.* a heavy, bluish-gray soft ductile metallic element used in building and the manufacture of alloys. ¶ Symb.: **Pb**. **2 a** graphite. **b** a thin length of this for use in a pencil. **3** a lump of lead suspended on a line to determine the depth of water. **4** *Printing* a blank space between lines of print (orig. with ref. to the metal strip used to give this space). **5** (*attrib.*) made of lead. •*v.tr.* **1** cover, weight, or frame (a roof or window panes) with lead. **2** *Printing* separate lines of (printed matter) with leads. **3** add a lead compound to (gasoline, etc.). ▫▫ **lead·less** *adj.*

lead·en /léd'n/ *adj.* **1** of or like lead. **2** heavy; slow; burdensome (*leaden limbs*). **3** inert; depressing (*leaden rule*). **4** lead-colored (*leaden skies*). ▫▫ **lead·en·ly** *adv.* **lead·en·ness** *n.*

lead·er /léedər/ *n.* **1 a** a person or thing that leads. **b** a person followed by others. **2 a** the principal player in a music group or of the first violins in an orchestra. **b** a conductor of an orchestra. **3** a short strip of nonfunctioning material at each end of a reel of film or recording tape for connection to the spool. **4** a shoot of a plant at the apex of a stem or of the main branch. **5** (in *pl.*) *Printing* a series of dots or dashes across the page to guide the eye, esp. in tabulated material. **6** the horse placed at the front in a team or pair. ▫▫ **lead·er·less** *adj.* **lead·er·ship** *n.*

lead-in /léed in/ *n.* **1** an introduction, opening, etc. **2** a wire leading in from outside, esp. from an antenna to a receiver or transmitter.

lead·ing[1] /léeding/ *adj.* & *n.* •*adj.* chief; most important. •*n.* guidance; leadership.

lead·ing[2] /léding/ *n. Printing* = LEAD[2] *n.* 4.

lead·ing ques·tion *n.* a question that prompts the answer wanted.

▶The phrase **leading question**, originally a legal term, means 'a question that prompts the answer wanted,' that 'leads' the answerer to the answer. In common use it has come to mean 'a pointed or loaded question,' 'a question that is awkward to answer,' or even 'the most important question,' but these usages are avoided in precise usage.

lead-off /léedawf/ *adj.* **1** (of an action) beginning a process (the album's lead-off track). **2** *Baseball* denoting the first batter in the batting order or the inning.

lead sto·ry see LEAD[1] *n.* 6.

lead time *n.* the time between the initiation and completion of a production or other process.

leaf /leef/ *n.* & *v.* •*n.* (*pl.* **leaves** /leevz/) **1 a** each of several flattened usu. green structures of a plant, usu. on the side of a stem or branch and the main organ of photosynthesis. **b** other similar plant structures, e.g., bracts, sepals, and petals (*floral leaf*). **2 a** foliage regarded collectively. **b** the state of having leaves out (*a tree in leaf*). **3** the leaves of tobacco or tea. **4 a** single thickness of paper, esp. in a book with each side forming a page. **5** a very thin sheet of metal, esp. gold or silver. **6 a** the hinged part or flap of a door, shutter, table, etc. **b** an extra section inserted to extend a table. •*v.* **1** *intr.* put forth leaves. **2** *tr.* (foll. by *through*) turn over the pages of (a book, etc.). ▫▫ **leaf·age** *n.* **leafed** *adj.* (also in *comb.*). **leaf·less** *adj.* **leaf·like** *adj.*

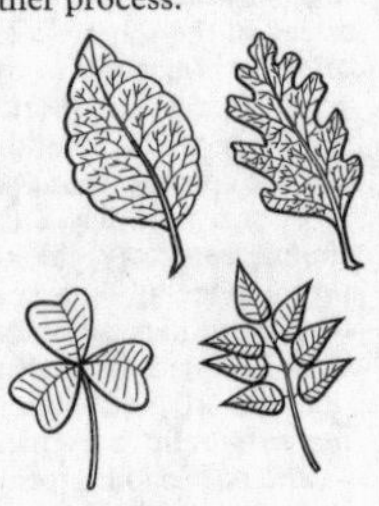

leaf, 1

leaf·let /léeflit/ *n.* & *v.* •*n.* **1** a young leaf. **2** *Bot.* any division of a compound leaf. **3** a sheet of (usu. printed) paper (sometimes folded) giving information, esp. for free distribution. •*v.tr.* (**leafleted, leafleting; leafletted, leafletting**) distribute leaflets to.

leaf·y /léefee/ *adj.* (**leafier, leafiest**) **1** having many leaves; (of a place) rich in foliage; verdant. **2** resembling a leaf. ▫▫ **leaf·i·ness** *n.*

league[1] /leeg/ *n.* & *v.* •*n.* **1** people, countries, groups, etc., combining for a particular purpose, esp. mutual protection or cooperation. **2** an agreement to combine in this way. **3** a group of sports organizations that compete over a period for a championship. **4** a class of contestants. **5** a class or category of quality or excellence (*he's not even in her league*). •*v.intr.* (**leagues, leagued, leaguing**) (often foll. by *together*) join in a league. ▫ **in league** allied; conspiring.

league[2] /leeg/ *n. archaic* a measure of traveling distance by land, usu. about three miles.

League of Na·tions *n.* an association of countries established in 1919 to promote international cooperation and peace; it was replaced by the United Nations in 1945.

leak /leek/ *n.* & *v.* •*n.* **1 a** a hole in a pipe, container, etc., caused by wear or damage, through which matter, esp. liquid or gas, passes accidentally in or out. **b** the matter passing in or out through this. **c** the act or an instance of leaking. **2 a** a similar escape of electrical charge. **b** the charge that escapes. **3** the intentional disclosure of secret information. •*v.* **1 a** *intr.* (of liquid, gas, etc.) pass in or out through a leak. **b** *tr.* lose or admit (liquid, gas, etc.) through a leak. **2** *tr.* intentionally disclose (secret information). **3** *intr.* (often foll. by *out*) (of a secret, secret information) become known. ▫ **take a leak** *sl.* urinate. ▫▫ **leak·er** *n.*

leak·age /léekij/ *n.* **1** the action or result of leaking. **2** what leaks in or out. **3** an intentional disclosure of secret information.

leak·y /léekee/ *adj.* (**leakier, leakiest**) **1** having a leak or leaks. **2** given to letting out secrets. ▫▫ **leak·i·ness** *n.*

lean[1] /leen/ *v.* & *n.* •*v.* (*past* and *past part.* **leaned** /leend, lent/or **leant** /lent/) **1** *intr.* & *tr.* (often foll. by *across, back, over*, etc.) be or place in a sloping position. **2** *intr.* & *tr.* (foll. by *against, on, upon*) rest or cause to rest for support against, etc. **3** *intr.* (foll. by *on, upon*) rely on. **4** *intr.* (foll. by *to, toward*) be inclined or partial to. •*n.* a deviation from the perpendicular; an inclination (*has a decided lean to the right*). ▫ **lean on** *colloq.* put pressure on (a person) to act in a certain way. **lean over backward** see BACKWARD.

lean[2] /leen/ *adj.* & *n.* •*adj.* **1** (of a person or animal) thin; having no superfluous fat. **2** (of meat) containing little fat. **3 a** meager (*lean crop*). **b** not nourishing (*lean diet*). **4** unremunerative. •*n.* the lean part of meat. ▫▫ **lean·ly** *adv.* **lean·ness** *n.*

lean·ing /léening/ *n.* a tendency or partiality.

lean-to *n.* (*pl.* **-tos**) **1** a building with its roof leaning against a larger building or a wall. **2** a shed with an inclined roof usu. leaning against trees, posts, etc.

leap /leep/ *v.* & *n.* •*v.* (*past* and *past part.* **leaped** /leept, lept/or **leapt** /lept/) **1** *intr.* jump or spring forcefully. **2** *tr.* jump across. **3** *intr.* (of prices, etc.) increase dramatically. **4** *intr.* hurry; rush; proceed without pausing for thought (*leaped to the wrong conclusion*; *leapt to their defense*). •*n.* a forceful jump. ▫ **by leaps and bounds** with startlingly rapid progress. **leap at 1** rush toward; pounce upon. **2** accept eagerly. **leap to the eye** be immediately apparent. ▫▫ **leap·er** *n.*

leap·frog /léepfrawg, –frog/ *n.* & *v.* •*n.* a game in which players in turn vault with parted legs over another who is bending down. •*v.* (**-frogged, -frogging**) **1** *intr.* (foll. by *over*) perform such a vault. **2** *tr.* vault over in this way. **3** *tr.* & *intr.* (of two or more people, vehicles, etc.) overtake alternately.

leap year *n.* a year, occurring once in four, with 366 days (including Feb. 29).

learn /lərn/ *v.* (*past* and *past part.* **learned** /lərnd, lərnt/) **1** *tr.* gain knowledge of or skill in by study, experience, or being taught. **2** *tr.* (foll. by *to* + infin.) acquire or develop a particular ability (*learn to swim*). **3** *tr.* commit to memory (*will try to learn your names*). **4** *intr.* (foll. by *of*) be informed about. **5** *tr.* (foll. by *that, how*, etc. + clause) become aware of by information or from observation. **6** *intr.* receive instruction; acquire knowledge or skill. □ **learn one's lesson** see LESSON. □□ **learn·a·ble** *adj.* **learn·a·bil·i·ty** /lárnəbílitee/ *n.*

▶**Learn** was once commonly used to mean 'teach, impart knowledge,' but today this is regarded as uneducated.

learn·ed /lárnid/ *adj.* **1** having much knowledge acquired by study. **2** showing or requiring learning (*a learned work*). **3** studied or pursued by learned persons. **4** scholarly (*a learned journal*). **5** as a courteous description of a lawyer or colleague in certain formal contexts (*my learned friend*). □□ **learn·ed·ly** *adv.* **learn·ed·ness** *n.*

learn·ing /lárning/ *n.* knowledge acquired by study.

learn·ing curve *n.* the rate of a person's progress in gaining experience or new skills (*the latest software packages have a steep learning curve.*

learn·ing dis·a·bil·i·ty *n.* a disorder (such as dyslexia) that interferes with the learning process in a child of usu. normal intelligence.

lease /lees/ *n.* & *v.* • *n.* an agreement by which the owner of a building or land allows another to use it for a specified time, usu. in return for payment. • *v.tr.* grant or take on lease. □ **a new lease on life** a substantially improved prospect of living or flourishing, or of use after repair. □□ **leas·a·ble** *adj.* **leas·er** *n.*

lease·hold /lées-hōld/ *n.* & *adj.* • *n.* **1** the holding of property by lease. **2** property held by lease. • *adj.* held by lease. □□ **lease·hold·er** *n.*

leash /leesh/ *n.* & *v.* • *n.* a rope, cord, strip of leather, etc., for restraining and guiding a dog or other domestic animal. • *v.tr.* **1** put a leash on. **2** restrain. □ **straining at the leash** eager to begin.

least /leest/ *adj.*, *n.*, & *adv.* • *adj.* **1** smallest; slightest; most insignificant. **2** (prec. by *the*; esp. with *neg.*) any at all (*it does not make the least difference*). **3** (of a species or variety) very small (*least tern*). • *n.* the least amount. • *adv.* in the least degree. □ **at least 1** at all events; anyway. **2** (also **at the least**) not less than. **in the least** (or **the least**) (usu. with *neg.*) in the smallest degree; at all (*not in the least offended*). **to say the least** (or **the least of it**) used to imply the moderation of a statement (*that is doubtful to say the least*).

least com·mon mul·ti·ple *n.* = LOWEST COMMON MULTIPLE.

leath·er /léthər/ *n.* & *v.* • *n.* **1 a** material made from the skin of an animal by tanning or a similar process. **b** (*attrib.*) made of leather. **2** a piece of leather for polishing with. **3** the leather part or parts of something. **4** *sl.* a football. **5** (in *pl.*) leather clothes. **6** a thong (*stirrup-leather*). • *v.tr.* **1** cover with leather. **2** polish or wipe with leather. **3** beat; thrash.

leath·er·back /léthərbak/ *n.* a large marine turtle, *Dermochelys coriacea*, having a thick leathery carapace.

leath·er·ette /léthərét/ *n.* imitation leather.

leath·er·neck /léthərnek/ *n.* sl. a US Marine (with reference to the leather collar formerly worn by them).

leave[1] /leev/ *v.* (*past* and *past part.* **left** /left/) **1 a** *tr.* go away from. **b** *intr.* (often foll. by *for*) depart. **2** *tr.* cause to or let remain; depart without taking (*has left his gloves*; *left a slimy trail*). **3** *tr.* (also *absol.*) cease to reside at or attend or belong to or work for (*has left the school*; *I am leaving for another firm*). **4** *tr.* abandon; forsake; desert. **5** *tr.* have remaining after one's death (*leaves a wife and two children*). **6** *tr.* bequeath. **7** *tr.* (foll. by *to* + infin.) allow (a person or thing) to do something without interference or assistance (*leave the future to take care of itself*). **8** *tr.* (foll. by *to*) commit or refer to another person (*leave that to me*; *nothing was left to chance*). **9** *tr.* **a** abstain from consuming or dealing with. **b** (in *passive*; often foll. by *over*) remain over. **10** *tr.* **a** deposit or entrust (a thing) to be attended to, collected, delivered, etc., in one's absence (*left a message with his assistant*). **b** depute (a person) to perform a function in one's absence. **11** *tr.* allow to remain or cause to be in a specified state or position (*left the door open*). **12** *tr.* pass (an object) so that it is in a specified relative direction (*leave the church on the left*). □ **be left with 1** retain (a feeling, etc.). **2** be burdened with (a responsibility, etc.). **be well left** be well provided for by a legacy, etc. **get left** *colloq.* be deserted. **have left** have remaining. **leave alone 1** refrain from disturbing; not interfere with. **2** not have dealings with. **leave be** *colloq.* refrain from disturbing; not interfere with. **leave behind 1** go away without. **2** leave as a consequence or a visible sign of passage. **3** pass. **leave a person cold** (or **cool**) not impress or excite a person. **leave go** *colloq.* relax one's hold. **leave hold of** cease holding. **leave it at that** *colloq.* abstain from comment or further action. **leave much** (or **a lot**, etc.) **to be desired** be highly unsatisfactory. **leave off 1** come to or make an end. **2** discontinue (*leave off work*; *leave off talking*). **3** not wear. **leave out** omit; not include. **leave a person to himself** (or **herself**) **1** not attempt to control a person. **2** leave a person solitary. **left at the gate (post)** beaten from the start of a race. **left for dead** abandoned as being beyond rescue. □□ **leav·er** *n.*

▶**Leave** means 'go away from': *We left town together.* The common expression, *Leave me alone*, literally means 'leave (me), so that I can be by myself.' **Let** means 'allow.' Thus *Let me be* and *Let me alone* literally mean 'don't bother me.'

leave[2] /leev/ *n.* **1** (often foll. by *to* + infin.) permission. **2 a** (in full **leave of absence**) permission to be absent from duty. **b** the period for which this lasts. □ **by** (or **with**) **your leave** often *iron.* an expression of apology for taking a liberty or making an unwelcome statement. **on leave** legitimately absent from duty. **take one's leave (of)** bid farewell (to).

leaved /leevd/ *adj.* **1** having leaves. **2** (in *comb.*) having a leaf or leaves of a specified kind or number (*red-leaved maple*).

leav·en /lévən/ *n.* & *v.* • *n.* **1** a substance added to dough to make it ferment and rise, esp. yeast, or fermenting dough reserved for the purpose. **2 a** a pervasive transforming influence. **b** (foll. by *of*) a tinge or admixture. • *v.tr.* **1** ferment (dough) with leaven. **2 a** permeate and transform. **b** (foll. by *with*) modify with a tempering element.

leaves *pl.* of LEAF.

leav·ings /léevingz/ *n.pl.* things left over, esp. as worthless.

lech /lech/ *v.* & *n.* *colloq.* • *v.intr.* feel lecherous; behave lustfully. • *n.* **1** a strong desire, esp. sexual. **2** a lecher.

lech·er /léchər/ *n.* a lecherous man.

lech·er·ous /léchərəs/ *adj.* lustful; having strong or excessive sexual desire. □□ **lech·er·ous·ly** *adv.* **lech·er·ous·ness** *n.*

lech·er·y /léchəree/ *n.* unrestrained indulgence of sexual desire.

lec·i·thin /lésithin/ *n.* **1** any of a group of phospholipids found naturally in animals, egg yolk, and some higher plants. **2** a preparation of this used to emulsify foods, etc.

lec·tern /léktərn/ *n.* **1** a stand for holding a book in a church or chapel. **2** a similar stand for a lecturer, etc.

lec·tion·ar·y /lékshənéree/ *n.* (*pl.* **-ies**) **1** a list of portions of Scripture appointed to be read at divine service. **2** a book containing such portions.

lec·ture /lékchər/ *n.* & *v.* • *n.* **1** a discourse giving information about a subject to a class or other audience. **2** a long, serious speech, esp. as a scolding or reprimand. • *v.* **1** *intr.* (often foll. by *on*) deliver a lecture or lectures. **2** *tr.* talk seriously or reprovingly to (a person). **3** *tr.* instruct or entertain (a class or other audience) by a lecture.

lec•ture•ship /lékchərship/ *n.* the office of lecturer.

LED *abbr.* light-emitting diode; a device used to display the time, meter readings, etc.

led *past* and *past part.* of LEAD[1].

ledge /lej/ *n.* **1** a narrow horizontal surface projecting from a wall, etc. **2** a shelflike projection on the side of a rock or mountain. **3** a ridge of rocks, esp. below water. **4** *Mining* a stratum of metal-bearing rock. ▫▫ **ledged** *adj.* **ledg•y** *adj.*

ledg•er /léjər/ *n.* **1** a traditionally tall, narrow book in which a firm's accounts are kept, esp. one which is the principal book of a set and contains debtor-and-creditor accounts. **2** a flat gravestone. **3** a horizontal timber in scaffolding, parallel to the face of the building.

led•ger line *n.* **1** a short line added for notes above or below the range of a musical staff. **2** a kind of fishing tackle in which a lead weight keeps the bait on the bottom.

lee /lee/ *n.* **1** shelter given by a neighboring object (*under the lee of*). **2** (in full **lee side**) the sheltered side; the side away from the wind (opp. WEATHER SIDE).

leech[1] /leech/ *n.* **1** any freshwater or terrestrial annelid worm of the class *Hirudinea* with suckers at both ends, esp. *Hirudo medicinalis*, a bloodsucking parasite of vertebrates formerly much used medically. **2** a person who extorts profit from or sponges on others. ▫ **like a leech** persistently or clingingly present.

leech[2] /leech/ *n. archaic* or *joc.* a physician; a healer.

leech[3] /leech/ *n.* **1** a perpendicular or sloping side of a square sail. **2** the side of a fore-and-aft sail away from the mast or stay.

leek /leek/ *n.* **1** an alliaceous plant, *Allium porrum*, with flat overlapping leaves forming a cylindrical bulb, used as food. **2** this as a Welsh national emblem.

leer /leer/ *v.* & *n.* • *v.intr.* look slyly or lasciviously or maliciously. • *n.* a leering look. ▫▫ **leer•ing•ly** *adv.*

leer•y /léeree/ *adj.* (**leerier, leeriest**) *sl.* **1** knowing; sly. **2** (foll. by *of*) wary. ▫▫ **leer•i•ness** *n.*

lees /leez/ *n.pl.* **1** the sediment of wine, etc. **2** dregs; refuse.

lee•ward /léeward, *Naut.* lóoərd/ *adj., adv.,* & *n.* • *adj.* & *adv.* on or toward the side sheltered from the wind (opp. WINDWARD). • *n.* the leeward region, side, or direction (*to leeward*).

lee•way /léeway/ *n.* **1** the sideways drift of a ship to leeward of the desired course. **2 a** allowable deviation or freedom of action. **b** margin of safety. ▫ **make up leeway** recover lost time, etc.

left[1] /left/ *adj., adv.,* & *n.* (opp. RIGHT). • *adj.* **1** on or toward the side of the human body that corresponds to the position of west if one regards oneself as facing north. **2** on or toward the part of an object that is analogous to a person's left side or (with opposite sense) that is nearer to an observer's left hand. **3** (also **Left**) *Polit.* of the Left. • *adv.* on or to the left side. • *n.* **1** the left-hand part or region or direction. **2** *Boxing* **a** the left hand. **b** a blow with this. **3 a** (often **Left**) *Polit.* a group or section favoring liberalism, social reform, etc. **b** the more advanced or innovative section of any group. **4** the side of a stage to the left of a person facing the audience. **5** (esp. in marching) the left foot. **6** the left wing of an army. ▫ **have two left feet** be clumsy. **left and right** = *right and left* (see RIGHT). ▫▫ **left•ish** *adj.*

left[2] *past* and *past part.* of LEAVE[1].

left field *n. Baseball* the part of the outfield to the left of the batter as he or she faces the pitcher. ▫ **out in left field** confused or in error; mistaken.

left-hand *adj.* **1** on or toward the left side of a person or thing (*left-hand drive*). **2** done with the left hand (*left-hand blow*). **3 a** (of rope) twisted counterclockwise. **b** (of a screw) = LEFT-HANDED 4c.

left-hand•ed /léft-hándid/ *adj.* **1** using the left hand by preference as more serviceable than the right. **2** (of a tool, etc.) made to be used with the left hand. **3** (of a blow) struck with the left hand. **4 a** turning to the left; toward the left. **b** (of a racecourse) turning counterclockwise. **c** (of a screw) advanced by turning to the left (counterclockwise). **5** awkward; clumsy. **6 a** (of a compliment) ambiguous. **b** of doubtful sincerity or validity. ▫▫ **left-hand•ed•ly** *adv.* **left-hand•ed•ness** *n.*

left•ie var. of LEFTY.

left•ism /léftizəm/ *n. Polit.* the principles or policy of the left. ▫▫ **left•ist** *n.* & *adj.*

left•most /léftmōst/ *adj.* farthest to the left.

left•o•ver /léftōvər/ *adj.* & *n.* • *adj.* remaining over; not used up or disposed of. • *n.* (in *pl.*) items (esp. of food) remaining after the rest has been used.

left wing *n.* **1** the liberal or socialist section of a political party. **2** the left side of a soccer, etc., team on the field. **3** the left side of an army. ▫▫ **left-wing** *adj.* **left-wing•er** *n.*

left•y /léftee/ *n.* (also **left•ie**) (*pl.* **-ies**) *colloq.* **1** *Polit.* a left-winger. **2** a left-handed person.

leg /leg/ *n.* **1 a** each of the limbs on which a person or animal walks and stands. **b** the part of this from the hip to the ankle. **2** a leg of an animal or bird as food. **3** an artificial leg (*wooden leg*). **4** a part of a garment covering a leg or part of a leg. **5 a** a support of a chair, table, bed, etc. **b** a long, thin support or prop, esp. a pole. **6** *Cricket* the half of the field (as divided lengthways through the pitch) in which the striker's feet are placed. **7 a** a section of a journey. **b** a section of a relay race. **c** a stage in a competition. **d** one of two or more games constituting a round. **8** one branch of a forked object. **9** *Naut.* a run made on a single tack. ▫ **feel** (or **find**) **one's legs** become able to stand or walk. **give a person a leg up** help a person to mount a horse, etc., or get over an obstacle or difficulty. **have no legs** *colloq.* (of a golf ball, etc.) have not enough momentum to reach the desired point. **keep one's legs** not fall. **leg it** *colloq.* walk or run fast. **not have a leg to stand on** be unable to support one's argument by facts or sound reasons. **on one's last legs** near death or the end of one's usefulness, etc. **on one's legs 1** (also **on one's hind legs**) standing, esp. to make a speech. **2** well enough to walk about. **take to one's legs** run away. ▫▫ **leg•ged** /legd, légid/ *adj.* (also in *comb.*).

leg•a•cy /légəsee/ *n.* (*pl.* **-cies**) **1** a gift left in a will. **2** something handed down by a predecessor (*legacy of corruption*).

le•gal /léegəl/ *adj.* **1** of or based on law; concerned with law; falling within the province of law. **2** appointed or required by law. **3** permitted by law; lawful. **4** recognized by law, as distinct from equity. ▫▫ **le•gal•ly** *adv.*

le•gal age *n.* age at which a person assumes adult rights and privileges by law.

le•gal•ese /léegəléez/ *n. colloq.* the technical language of legal documents.

le•gal•ism /léegəlizəm/ *n.* excessive adherence to law or formula. ▫▫ **le•gal•ist** *n.* **le•gal•is•tic** /–lístik/ *adj.* **le•gal•is•ti•cal•ly** /–lístikəlee/ *adv.*

le•gal•i•ty /ligálitee, leegál–/ *n.* (*pl.* **-ties**) **1** lawfulness. **2** legalism. **3** (in *pl.*) obligations imposed by law.

le•gal•ize /léegəlīz/ *v.tr.* **1** make lawful. **2** bring into harmony with the law. ▫▫ **le•gal•i•za•tion** *n.*

le•gal ten•der *n.* currency that cannot legally be refused in payment of a debt.

leg•ate /légət/ *n.* **1** a member of the clergy representing the Pope. **2** *Rom.Hist.* **a** a deputy of a general. **b** a governor or deputy governor of a province. ▫▫ **leg•ate•ship** *n.* **leg•a•tine** /–teen, –tīn/ *adj.*

leg•a•tee /légətée/ *n.* the recipient of a legacy.

le•ga•tion /ligáyshən/ *n.* **1** a body of deputies. **2 a** the office and staff of a diplomatic minister. **b** the official residence of a diplomatic minister. **3** a legateship. **4** the sending of a legate or deputy.

le•ga•to /ligaátō/ *adv., adj., & n. Mus.* • *adv. & adj.* in a smooth flowing manner. (cf. STACCATO). • *n.* (*pl.* **-tos**) **1** a legato passage. **2** legato playing.

le•ga•tor /ligáytər/ *n.* the giver of a legacy.

leg•end /léjənd/ *n.* **1 a** a traditional story sometimes popularly regarded as historical but unauthenticated. **b** such stories collectively. **c** a popular but unfounded belief. **d** *colloq.* a subject of such beliefs (*became a legend in his own lifetime*). **2 a** an inscription, esp. on a coin or medal. **b** *Printing* a caption. **c** wording on a map, etc., explaining the symbols used. **3** *hist.* **a** the story of a saint's life. **b** a collection of lives of saints or similar stories.

leg•end•ar•y /léjənderee/ *adj.* **1** of or connected with legends. **2** described in a legend. **3** *colloq.* remarkable. **4** based on a legend. ▫▫ **leg•end•ar•i•ly** *adv.*

leg•er•de•main /léjərdəmáyn/ *n.* **1** sleight of hand. **2** trickery; sophistry.

leg•er line *n.* = LEDGER LINE.

leg•ging /léging/ *n.* **1** (usu. in *pl.*) a stout protective outer covering for the leg from the knee to the ankle. **2** (pl.) a close-fitting stretch garment covering the legs and the lower part of the torso.

leg•gy /légee/ *adj.* (**leggier, leggiest**) **1 a** long-legged. **b** (of a woman) having attractively long legs. **2** long-stemmed. ▫▫ **leg•gi•ness** *n.*

leg•i•ble /léjibəl/ *adj.* (of handwriting, print, etc.) clear enough to read; readable. ▫▫ **leg•i•bil•i•ty** *n.* **leg•i•bly** *adv.*

le•gion /léejən/ *n. & adj.* • *n.* **1** a division of 3,000–6,000 men in the ancient Roman army. **2** a large organized body. **3** a vast host, multitude, or number. • *predic.adj.* great in number (*his good works have been legion*).

le•gion•ar•y /léejəneree/ *adj. & n.* • *adj.* of a legion or legions. • *n.* (*pl.* **-ies**) a member of a legion.

le•gioned /léejənd/ *adj. poet.* arrayed in legions.

le•gion•naires' dis•ease *n.* a form of bacterial pneumonia first identified after an outbreak at an American Legion meeting in 1976.

leg i•ron *n.* a shackle or fetter for the leg.

leg•is•late /léjislayt/ *v.intr.* **1** make laws. **2** (foll. by *for*) make provision by law.

leg•is•la•tion /léjisláyshən/ *n.* **1** the process of making laws. **2** laws collectively.

leg•is•la•tive /léjislaytiv/ *adj.* of or empowered to make laws. ▫▫ **leg•is•la•tive•ly** *adv.*

leg•is•la•tor /léjislaytər/ *n.* **1** a member of a legislative body. **2** a lawgiver.

leg•is•la•ture /léjislaychər/ *n.* the legislative body of a nation or state.

le•git /lijít/ *adj. & n. colloq.* • *adj.* legitimate. • *n.* legitimate drama.

le•git•i•mate *adj. & v.* • *adj.* /lijítimət/ **1 a** born of parents lawfully married to each other. **b** (of a parent, birth, descent, etc.) with, of, through, etc., a legitimate child. **2** lawful; proper; regular. **3** logically admissible. **4 a** (of a sovereign's title) based on strict hereditary right. **b** (of a sovereign) having a legitimate title. **5** constituting or relating to serious drama as distinct from musical comedy, revue, etc. • *v.tr.* /lijítimayt/ **1** make legitimate by decree, enactment, or proof. **2** justify. ▫▫ **le•git•i•ma•cy** /–məsee/ *n.* **le•git•i•mate•ly** /–mətlee/ *adv.* **le•git•i•ma•tion** /–máyshən/ *n.*

le•git•i•ma•tize /lijítimətīz/ *v.tr.* legitimize. ▫▫ **le•git•i•ma•ti•za•tion** *n.*

le•git•i•mize /lijítimīz/ *v.tr.* **1** make legitimate. **2** serve as a justification for. ▫▫ **le•git•i•mi•za•tion** *n.*

Le•go /légō/ *n. Trademark* a construction toy consisting of interlocking plastic building blocks.

leg•room /légroōm/ *n.* space for the legs of a seated person.

leg•ume /légyoōm/ *n.* **1** the seedpod of a leguminous plant. **2** any seed, pod, or other edible part of a leguminous plant used as food.

le•gu•mi•nous /ligyoóminəs/ *adj.* of or like the family Leguminosae, including peas and beans, having seeds in pods.

leg warm•er *n.* either of a pair of tubular knitted garments covering the leg from ankle to thigh.

leg•work /légwərk/ *n.* work which involves a lot of walking, traveling, or physical activity, esp. preliminary research.

lei /láy-ee, lay/ *n.* a garland of flowers usu. worn on the head or shoulders.

leish•man•i•a•sis /léeshmənīəsis/ *n.* any of several diseases caused by parasitic protozoans of the genus *Leishmania* transmitted by the bite of sandflies.

leis•ter /léestər/ *n. & v.* • *n.* a pronged spear, used to spear fish. • *v.tr.* pierce with a leister.

lei•sure /léezhər, lézh–/ *n.* **1** free time; time at one's own disposal. **2** enjoyment of free time. **3** (usu. foll. by *for*, or *to* + infin.) opportunity afforded by free time. ▫ **at leisure 1** not occupied. **2** in an unhurried manner. **at one's leisure** when one has time.

lei•sured /léezhərd, lézh–/ *adj.* having ample leisure.

lei•sure•ly /léezhərlee, lézh–/ *adj. & adv.* • *adj.* having leisure; acting or done at leisure; unhurried; relaxed. • *adv.* without hurry. ▫▫ **lei•sure•li•ness** *n.*

lei•sure•wear /léezhərwair, lézh–/ *n.* informal clothes, especially sportswear.

leit•mo•tiv /lītmōteéf/ *n.* (also **leit•mo•tif**) a recurrent theme associated throughout a musical, literary, etc., composition with a particular person, idea, or situation.

lek[1] /lek/ *n.* the chief monetary unit of Albania.

lek[2] /lek/ *n.* a patch of ground used by groups of certain birds during the breeding season as a setting for the males' display and their meeting with the females.

LEM /lem/ *abbr.* lunar excursion module.

lem•ming /léming/ *n.* any small arctic rodent of the genus *Lemmus*, esp. *L. lemmus* of Norway, which is reputed to rush headlong into the sea and drown during periods of mass migration.

lem•on /lémən/ *n.* **1 a** a pale-yellow, thick-skinned, oval citrus fruit with acidic juice. **b** a tree of the species *Citrus limon* that produces this fruit. **2** a pale-yellow color. **3** *colloq.* a thing, esp. a car, that is unsatisfactory or disappointing. ▫▫ **lem•on•y** *adj.*

lem•on•ade /lémənáyd/ *n.* **1** a beverage made from sweetened lemon juice. **2** a synthetic substitute for this.

le•mur /léemər/ *n.* any arboreal primate of the family Lemuridae, native to Madagascar, with a pointed snout and long tail.

lend /lend/ *v.tr.* (*past* and *past part.* **lent** /lent/) **1** (usu. foll. by *to*) grant (to a person) the use of (a thing) on the understanding that it or its equivalent shall be returned. **2** allow the use of (money) at interest. **3** bestow or contribute (something temporary) (*lend assistance; lends a certain charm*). ▫ **lend an ear** (or **one's ears**) listen. **lend a hand** see HAND. **lend itself to** (of a thing) be suitable for. **lend oneself to** accommodate oneself to (a policy or purpose). ▫▫ **lend•a•ble** *adj.* **lend•er** *n.* **lend•ing** *n.*

▶See note at LOAN.

lend·ing li·brar·y *n.* a library from which books may be temporarily taken away.

length /length, lengkth/ *n.* **1** measurement or extent from end to end; the greater of two or the greatest of three dimensions of a body. **2** extent in, of, or with regard to, time (*a stay of some length; the length of a speech*). **3** the distance a thing extends (*at arm's length; ships a cable's length apart*). **4** the length of a horse, boat, etc., as a measure of the lead in a race. **5** a long stretch or extent (*a length of hair*). **6** a degree of thoroughness in action (*went to great lengths; prepared to go to any length*). **7** a piece of material of a certain length (*a length of cloth*). **8** *Prosody* the quantity of a vowel or syllable. **9** the extent of a garment in a vertical direction when worn. **10** the full extent of one's body. □ **at length 1** (also **at full** or **great**, etc., **length**) in detail. **2** after a long time; at last.

length·en /léngthən, léngk–/ *v.tr. & intr.* make or become longer. □□ **length·en·er** *n.*

length·ways /léngthwayz, léngkth–/ *adv.* lengthwise.

length·wise /léngthwīz, léngkth–/ *adv. & adj.* • *adv.* in a direction parallel with a thing's length. • *adj.* lying or moving lengthways.

length·y /léngthee, léngkthee/ *adj.* (**lengthier, lengthiest**) **1** of unusual length. **2** (of speech, writing, style, a speaker, etc.) tedious; prolix. □□ **length·i·ly** *adv.* **length·i·ness** *n.*

le·ni·ent /léenyənt/ *adj.* **1** merciful; tolerant; not disposed to severity. **2** (of punishment, etc.) mild. □□ **le·ni·ence** /–yəns/ *n.* **le·ni·en·cy** *n.* **le·ni·ent·ly** *adv.*

Len·in·ism /léninizəm/ *n.* Marxism as interpreted and applied by Lenin.

len·i·tive /lénitiv/ *adj. & n.* • *adj. Med.* soothing. • *n.* **1** *Med.* a soothing drug or appliance. **2** a palliative.

len·i·ty /lénitee/ *n.* (*pl.* **-ties**) *literary* **1** mercifulness. **2** an act of mercy.

le·no /léenō/ *n.* (*pl.* **-nos**) an openwork fabric with the warp threads twisted in pairs before weaving.

lens /lenz/ *n.* **1** a piece of a transparent substance with one or (usu.) both sides curved for concentrating or dispersing light rays, esp. in optical instruments. **2** a combination of lenses used in photography. **3** *Physics* a device for focusing or otherwise modifying the direction of movement of light, sound, electrons, etc. □□ **lensed** *adj.* **lens·less** *adj.*

Lent /lent/ *n. Eccl.* the period from Ash Wednesday to Holy Saturday, devoted to fasting and penitence in commemoration of Christ's fasting in the wilderness.

lent *past* and *past part.* of LEND.

Lent·en /léntən/ *adj.* of, in, or appropriate to Lent.

len·ti·cel /léntisel/ *n. Bot.* any of the raised pores in the stems of woody plants that allow gas exchange between the atmosphere and the internal tissues.

len·tic·u·lar /lentíkyələr/ *adj.* **1** shaped like a lentil or a biconvex lens. **2** of the lens of the eye.

len·til /léntəl/ *n.* **1** a leguminous plant, *Lens culinaris*, yielding edible biconvex seeds. **2** this seed, esp. used as food with the husk removed.

len·to /léntō/ *adj. & adv. Mus.* • *adj.* slow. • *adv.* slowly.

Le·o /lée-ō/ *n.* (*pl.* **-os**) **1** a constellation, traditionally regarded as contained in the figure of a lion. **2 a** the fifth sign of the zodiac (the Lion). **b** a person born when the sun is in this sign.

le·o·nine /léeənīn/ *adj.* **1** like a lion. **2** of or relating to lions.

leop·ard /lépərd/ *n.* (*fem.* **leopardess** /–dis/) **1** a large African or Asian feline, *Panthera pardus*, with a black-spotted, yellowish-fawn, or all black coat. Also called PANTHER. **2** (*attrib.*) spotted like a leopard (*leopard moth*).

le·o·tard /léeətaard/ *n.* **1** a close-fitting one-piece garment worn by ballet dancers, acrobats, etc. **2** = TIGHTS.

lep·er /lépər/ *n.* **1** a person suffering from leprosy. **2** a person shunned on moral or other grounds.

lep·re·chaun /léprəkon, –kawn/ *n.* a small mischievous sprite in Irish folklore.

lep·ro·sy /léprəsee/ *n.* **1** a contagious bacterial disease that affects the skin, mucous membranes, and nerves, causing disfigurement. Also called HANSEN'S DISEASE. **2** moral corruption or contagion. □□ **lep·rous** /léprəs/ *adj.*

lep·to·dactyl /léptōdáktil/ *adj. & n.* • *adj.* having long, slender toes. • *n.* a bird having these.

les·bi·an /lézbeeən/ *n. & adj.* • *n.* a homosexual woman. • *adj.* **1** of homosexuality in women. **2** (**Lesbian**) of Lesbos. □□ **les·bi·an·ism** *n.*

lese-maj·es·ty /leez májistee/ *n.* (also **lèse-maj·es·té** /layz mázhestay/) **1** treason. **2** an insult to a sovereign or ruler. **3** presumptuous conduct.

le·sion /léezhən/ *n.* **1** damage. **2** injury. **3** *Med.* a morbid change in the functioning or texture of an organ, etc.

less /les/ *adj., adv., n., & prep.* • *adj.* **1** smaller in extent, degree, duration, number, etc. (*of less importance; in a less degree*). **2** of smaller quantity; not so much (opp. MORE) (*find less difficulty; eat less meat*). **3** *disp.* fewer (*eat less cookies*). **4** of lower rank, etc. (*no less a person than*). • *adv.* to a smaller extent; in a lower degree. • *n.* a smaller amount or quantity or number (*cannot take less; for less than $10*). *prep.* minus (*made $1,000 less tax*). □ **in less than no time** *joc.* very quickly or soon. **much less** with even greater force of denial (*do not suspect him of negligence, much less of dishonesty*).

▶See note at FEW.

les·see /lesée/ *n.* (often foll. by *of*) a person who holds a property by lease. □□ **les·see·ship** *n.*

less·en /lésən/ *v.tr. & intr.* make or become less; diminish.

less·er /lésər/ *adj.* (usu. *attrib.*) **1** not so great as the other or the rest (*the lesser evil*. **2** denoting names of animals and plants that are smaller than similar kinds (*lesser spotted woodpecker*).

les·son /lésən/ *n.* **1 a** an amount of teaching given at one time. **b** the time assigned to this. **2** (in *pl.*; foll. by *in*) systematic instruction (*gives lessons in dancing*). **3** a thing learned or to be learned by a pupil; an assignment. **4 a** an occurrence, example, rebuke, or punishment, that serves to warn or encourage (*let that be a lesson to you*). **b** a thing inculcated by experience or study. **5** a passage from the Bible read aloud during a church service. □ **learn one's lesson** profit from or bear in mind a particular (usu. unpleasant) experience. **teach a person a lesson** punish a person, esp. as a deterrent.

les·sor /lésawr/ *n.* a person who lets a property by lease.

lest /lest/ *conj.* **1** in order that not; for fear that (*lest we forget*). **2** that (*afraid lest we should be late*).

let[1] /let/ *v.* (**letting**; *past* and *past part.* **let**) **1** *tr.* **a** allow to; not prevent or forbid (*we let them go*). **b** cause to (*let me know; let it be known*). **2** *tr.* (foll. by *into*) **a** allow to enter. **b** make acquainted with (a secret, etc.). **c** inlay in. **3** *tr.* allow or cause (liquid or air) to escape (*let blood*). **4** *tr.* award (a contract for work). **5** *aux.* supplying the first and third persons of the imperative in exhortations (*let us pray*), commands (*let it be done at once; let there be light*), assumptions (*let AB be equal to CD*), and permission or challenge (*let him do his worst*). □ **let alone 1** not to mention (*hasn't got a television, let alone a VCR*). **2** = *let be*. **let be** not interfere with, attend to, or do. **let down 1** lower. **2** fail to support or satisfy; disappoint. **3** lengthen (a garment). **let down gently** avoid humiliating abruptly. **let drop** (or **fall**) drop (esp. a word or hint) intentionally or by accident. **let fly 1** (often foll. by *at*) attack physically or verbally. **2** discharge (a missile). **let go 1** release. **2 a** (often foll. by *of*) lose or relinquish one's hold. **b** lose hold of. **3** cease to think or talk about. **let oneself go 1** give way to enthusiasm, impulse, etc. **2** neglect one's appearance or habits. **let in 1** allow to enter (*let the dog in; let in a flood of light; this would let in all sorts of evils*). **2** (usu. foll. by *for*) involve (a person, often oneself) in loss or difficulty. **3** (foll. by *on*) allow (a person) to share privileges, information, etc. **4** inlay (a thing) in another. **let oneself in** unassistedly enter another person's home, office, etc., usu. with permission. **let loose** release or unchain (a dog, fury, a maniac, etc.). **let me see** see SEE[1]. **let off 1 a** fire (a gun). **b** explode (a bomb or firework). **2** allow or cause (steam, liquid, etc.) to escape. **3** allow to alight from a vehicle, etc. **4 a** not punish or compel. **b** (foll. by *with*) punish lightly. **let off steam** see STEAM. **let on** *colloq.* **1** reveal a secret. **2** pretend (*let on that he had succeeded*). **let out 1** allow to go out. **2** release from restraint. **3** (often foll. by *that* + clause) reveal (a secret, etc.). **4** make (a garment) looser. **5** exculpate. **6** give vent or expression to; emit (a sound, etc.) **let rip** see RIP[1]. **let slip** see SLIP[1]. **let through** allow to pass. **let up** *colloq.* **1** become less intense or severe. **2** relax one's efforts.

▶See note at LEAVE.

let[2] /let/ *n.* **1** (in tennis, squash, etc.) an obstruction of a ball or a player, requiring the ball to be served again. **2** *archaic* (except in **without let or hindrance**) obstruction; hindrance.

let·down /létdown/ *n.* **1** a disappointment. **2** the release of milk in a nursing mother as a reflex response to suckling or massage.

le·thal /leéthəl/ *adj.* causing or sufficient to cause death. ◻◻ **le·thal·i·ty** /–álitee/ *n.* **le·thal·ly** *adv.*

leth·ar·gy /léthərjee/ *n.* **1** lack of energy. **2** *Med.* morbid drowsiness. ◻◻ **le·thar·gic** /lithaárjik/ *adj.* **le·thar·gi·cal·ly** *adv.*

let's /lets/ *contr.* let us (*let's go now*).

let·ter /létər/ *n.* & *v.* • *n.* **1 a** a character representing one or more of the simple or compound sounds used in speech. **b** (in *pl.*) *colloq.* the initials of a degree, etc., after the holder's name. **c** a school or college initial as a mark of proficiency in sports, etc. **2 a** a written, typed, or printed communication, usu. sent by mail or messenger. **b** (in *pl.*) an addressed legal or formal document for any of various purposes. **3** the precise terms of a statement; the strict verbal interpretation (opp. SPIRIT *n.* 6) (*according to the letter of the law*). **4** (in *pl.*) **a** literature. **b** acquaintance with books; erudition. • *v.tr.* **1 a** inscribe letters on. **b** impress a title, etc., on (a book cover, etc.). **2** classify with letters. ◻ **to the letter** with adherence to every detail.

let·ter bomb *n.* an explosive device in the form of or enclosed in a posted envelope.

let·ter car·ri·er *n.* one who delivers mail, usu. as an employee of the postal service.

let·tered /létərd/ *adj.* well-read or educated.

let·ter·head /létərhed/ *n.* **1** a printed heading on stationery. **2** stationery with this.

let·ter·ing /létəring/ *n.* **1** the process of inscribing letters. **2** letters inscribed.

let·ter of cred·it *n.* a letter from a banker authorizing a person to draw money up to a specified amount, usu. from another bank.

let·ter-per·fect *adj.* **1** *Theatr.* knowing one's part perfectly. **2** precise; verbatim.

let·ter·press /létərpres/ *n.* printing from a hard, raised image under pressure, using viscous ink.

let·ter-qual·i·ty *adj.* of the quality of printing suitable for a business letter; producing print of this quality.

let·tuce /létis/ *n.* **1** a composite plant, *Lactuca sativa*, with crisp edible leaves used in salads. **2** any of various plants resembling this.

let·up /létup/ *n. colloq.* **1** a reduction in intensity. **2** a relaxation of effort.

leu·ke·mi·a /lookeémeeə/ *n. Med.* any of a group of malignant diseases in which the bone marrow and other blood-forming organs produce increased numbers of leukocytes. ◻◻ **leu·ke·mic** *adj.*

leuko- /lóokō/ *comb. form* white.

leu·ko·cyte /lóokəsīt/ *n.* **1** a white blood cell. **2** any blood cell that contains a nucleus.

Le·vant /livánt/ *n.* (prec. by *the*) the eastern part of the Mediterranean with its islands and neighboring countries. ◻◻ **Le·van·tine** /lévəntīn, –teen *adj.* & *n.*

le·va·tor /liváytər/ *n.* a muscle that lifts a body part.

lev·ee[1] /lévee, livée/ *n.* **1** an assembly of visitors or guests, esp. at a formal reception. **2** *hist.* a reception of visitors on rising from bed.

lev·ee[2] /lévee/ *n.* **1** an embankment against river floods. **2** a natural embankment built up by a river. **3** a landing place.

lev·el /lévəl/ *n., adj., & v.* • *n.* **1** a horizontal line or plane. **2** a height or value reached; a position on a scale (*eye level; sugar level in the blood; danger level*). **3** a social, moral, or intellectual standard (*at age six, he could read at a fifth-grade level*). **4** a plane of rank or authority (*discussions at cabinet level*). **5 a** an instrument giving a line parallel to the plane of the horizon. **b** *Surveying* an instrument for giving a horizontal line of sight. **6** a more or less level surface. **7** a flat tract of land. **8** a floor or story in a building, ship, etc. • *adj.* **1** having a flat and even surface; not bumpy (*a level road*). **2** horizontal; perpendicular to the plumb line. **3** (often foll. by *with*) **a** on the same horizontal plane as something else. **b** having equality with something else. **4** even, uniform, equable, or well-balanced in quality, style, temper, judgment, etc. • *v.* **1** *tr.* make level, even, or uniform. **2** *tr.* (often foll. by *to* (or *with*) *the ground*) raze or demolish. **3** *tr.* (also *absol.*) aim (a missile or gun). **4** *tr.* (also *absol.*; foll. by *at, against*) direct (an accusation, criticism, or satire). **5** *tr.* abolish (distinctions). **6** *intr.* (usu. foll. by *with*) *sl.* be frank or honest (*please level with me*). **7** *tr.* place on the same level. ◻ **do one's level best** *colloq.* do one's utmost. **find its** (or **its own**) **level** (of a liquid) reach the same height in receptacles or regions that communicate with each other. **level off** make or become level or smooth. **level out** make or become level; remove differences from. **on the level** *colloq. adv.* honestly; without deception. *adj.* honest; truthful. **on a level with 1** in the same horizontal plane as. **2** equal with.

lev·el·er /lévələr/ *n.* **1** a person who advocates the abolition of social distinctions. **2** a person or thing that levels.

lev·el·head·ed /lévəlhédid/ *adj.* having good judgment; sensible. ◻◻ **lev·el·head·ed·ly** *adv.* **lev·el·head·ed·ness** *n.*

lev·er /lévər, leév–/ *n.* & *v.* • *n.* **1** a bar resting on a pivot, used to help lift a heavy or firmly fixed object. **2** *Mech.* a simple machine consisting of a rigid bar pivoted about a fulcrum (fixed point) which can be acted upon by a force (effort) in order to move a load. **3** a projecting handle moved to operate a mechanism. **4** a means of exerting moral pressure. • *v.* **1** *intr.*

lever, 2

use a lever. **2** *tr.* (often foll. by *away*, *out*, *up*, etc.) lift, move, or act on with a lever.

lev·er·age /lévərij, leé–/ *n.* **1** the action of a lever; a way of applying a lever. **2** the power of a lever; the mechanical advantage gained by use of a lever. **3** a means of accomplishing a purpose; power; influence. **4** a set or system of levers. **5** *Commerce* the use of a relatively small investment or value in equity to acquire or control a much larger investment.

lev·er·aged buy·out *n.* the buyout of a company by its management using outside capital.

lev·i·a·ble /léveeəbəl/ *adj.* that which may be levied.

le·vi·a·than /livíəthən/ *n.* **1** *Bibl.* a sea monster. **2** anything very large or powerful, esp. a ship. **3** an autocratic monarch or state (in allusion to a book by Hobbes, 1651).

lev·i·gate /lévigayt/ *v.tr.* **1** reduce to a fine, smooth powder. **2** make a smooth paste of. □□ **lev·i·ga·tion** /–gáyshən/ *n.*

lev·i·tate /lévitayt/ *v.* **1** *intr.* rise and float in the air (esp. with reference to spiritualism). **2** *tr.* cause to do this. □□ **lev·i·ta·tion** /–táyshən/ *n.*

lev·i·ty /lévitee/ *n.* **1** lack of serious thought; frivolity. **2** inconstancy. **3** undignified behavior.

lev·u·lose /leévyəlōs/ *n.* = FRUCTOSE.

le·vy /lévee/ *v.* & *n.* •*v.tr.* (**-vies**, **-vied**) **1 a** impose (a rate or toll). **b** raise (contributions or taxes). **c** (also *absol.*) raise (a sum of money) by legal execution or process (*the debt was levied on the debtor's goods*). **d** seize (goods) in this way. **e** extort (*levy blackmail*). **2** enlist or enroll (troops, etc.). **3** (usu. foll. by *upon*, *against*) wage; proceed to make (war). •*n.* (*pl.* **-vies**) **1 a** the collecting of a contribution, tax, etc., or of property to satisfy a legal judgment. **b** a contribution, tax, etc., levied. **2 a** the act or an instance of enrolling troops, etc. **b** (in *pl.*) persons enrolled. **c** a body of persons enrolled. **d** the number of persons enrolled. □□ **le·vi·a·ble** *adj.*

lewd /lo͞od/ *adj.* **1** lascivious. **2** indecent; obscene. □□ **lewd·ly** *adv.* **lewd·ness** *n.*

lex·eme /lékseem/ *n.* *Linguistics* a basic lexical unit of a language comprising one or several words, the elements of which do not separately convey the meaning of the whole.

lex·i·cal /léksikəl/ *adj.* **1** of the words of a language. **2** of or as of a lexicon. □□ **lex·i·cal·ly** *adv.*

lex·i·cog·ra·phy /léksikógrəfee/ *n.* the compiling of dictionaries. □□ **lex·i·cog·ra·pher** *n.* **lex·i·co·graph·ic** /–kəgráfik/ *adj.* **lex·i·co·graph·i·cal** *adj.*

lex·i·col·o·gy /léksikóləjee/ *n.* the study of the form, history, and meaning of words. □□ **lex·i·co·log·i·cal** /–kəlójikəl/ *adj.* **lex·i·col·o·gist** /–kóləjist/ *n.*

lex·i·con /léksikon/ *n.* **1** a dictionary, esp. of Greek, Hebrew, Syriac, or Arabic. **2** the vocabulary of a person, language, branch of knowledge, etc.

lex·is /léksis/ *n.* **1** words; vocabulary. **2** the total stock of words in a language.

lex ta·li·o·nis /léks taleeṓnis/ *n.* the law of retaliation, whereby a punishment resembles the offense committed, in kind and degree.

ley /lay/ see LEA.

Ley·den jar /líd'n/ *n.* an early form of capacitor consisting of a glass jar with layers of metal foil on the outside and inside.

LF *abbr.* low frequency.

l.h. *abbr.* left hand.

Li *symb. Chem.* the element lithium.

li·a·bil·i·ty /líəbílitee/ *n.* (*pl.* **-ties**) **1** the state of being liable. **2** a person or thing that is troublesome as an unwelcome responsibility; a handicap. **3** what a person is liable for, esp. (in *pl.*) debts.

li·a·ble /líəbəl/ *predic.adj.* **1** legally bound. **2** (foll. by *to*) subject to (a tax or penalty). **3** (foll. by *to* + infin.) under an obligation. **4** (foll. by *to*) exposed or open to (something undesirable). **5** *disp.* (foll. by *to* + infin.) apt; likely (*it is liable to rain*). **6** (foll. by *for*) answerable.

li·aise /lee-áyz/ *v.intr.* (foll. by *with*, *between*) *colloq.* establish cooperation; act as a link.

li·ai·son /lee-áyzon, leé-ay–/ *n.* **1 a** communication or cooperation, esp. between military forces or units. **b** a person who initiates such. **2** an illicit sexual relationship. **3** the binding or thickening agent of a sauce. **4** the sounding of an ordinarily silent final consonant before a word beginning with a vowel (or a mute *h* in French).

li·ai·son of·fi·cer *n.* an officer acting as a link between allied forces or units of the same force.

li·ar /líər/ *n.* a person who tells a lie or lies, esp. habitually.

lib /lib/ *n. colloq.* liberation (*women's lib*).

li·ba·tion /lībáyshən/ *n.* **1 a** the pouring out of a drink offering to a god. **b** such a drink offering. **2** *joc.* a drink.

li·bel /líbəl/ *n.* & *v.* •*n.* **1** *Law* **a** a published false statement damaging to a person's reputation (cf. SLANDER). **b** the act of publishing this. **2 a** a false and defamatory written statement. **b** (foll. by *on*) a thing that brings discredit by misrepresentation, etc. (*the portrait is a libel on him*; *the book is a libel on human nature*). •*v.tr.* **1** defame by libelous statements. **2** accuse falsely and maliciously. **3** *Law* publish a libel against. □□ **li·bel·er** *n.*

li·bel·ous /líbələs/ *adj.* containing or constituting a libel. □□ **li·bel·ous·ly** *adv.*

lib·er·al /líbərəl, líbrəl/ *adj.* & *n.* •*adj.* **1** given freely; ample; abundant. **2** (often foll. by *with*) giving freely; generous; not sparing. **3** open-minded; not prejudiced. **4** not strict or rigorous; (of interpretation) not literal. **5** for general broadening of the mind; not professional or technical (*liberal studies*). **6 a** favoring individual liberty and political and social reform. **b** (**Liberal**) of or characteristic of Liberals or a Liberal party. **7** *Theol.* regarding many traditional beliefs as dispensable, invalidated by modern thought, or liable to change (*liberal Protestant*; *liberal Judaism*). •*n.* **1** a person of liberal views. **2** (**Liberal**) a supporter or member of a Liberal party. □□ **lib·er·al·ism** *n.* **lib·er·al·ly** *adv.*

---

liberal Middle English: via Old French from Latin *liberalis*, from *liber* 'free (man)'. The original sense was 'suitable for a free man', hence 'suitable for a gentleman' (one not tied to a trade), surviving in *liberal arts*. Another early sense 'generous' (compare with sense 5) gave rise to an obsolete meaning 'free from restraint', leading to sense 1 (late 18th cent.).

---

lib·er·al arts *n.pl.* the arts as distinct from science and technology.

lib·er·al·i·ty /líbərálitee/ *n.* **1** free giving; munificence. **2** freedom from prejudice; breadth of mind.

lib·er·al·ize /líbərəlīz, líbrə–/ *v.tr.* & *intr.* make or become more liberal or less strict. □□ **lib·er·al·i·za·tion** *n.*

lib·er·ate /líbərayt/ *v.tr.* **1** (often foll. by *from*) set at liberty; set free. **2** free (a country, etc.) from an oppressor or an enemy occupation. **3** (often as **liberated** *adj.*) free (a person) from rigid social conventions, esp. in sexual behavior. **4** *sl.* steal. □□ **lib·er·a·tion** *n.* **lib·er·a·tor** *n.*

lib·er·tar·i·an /líbərtáireeən/ *n.* an advocate of civil liberty. □□ **lib·er·tar·i·an·ism** *n.*

lib·er·tine /líbərteen, –tin/ *n.* & *adj.* •*n.* **1** a dissolute or licentious person. **2** a free thinker on religion. **3** a person who follows his or her own inclinations. •*adj.* **1** licentious; dissolute. **2** freethinking. **3** following one's own inclinations. □□ **lib·er·tin·ism** /–nízəm/ *n.*

lib·er·ty /líbərtee/ *n.* (*pl.* **-ties**) **1 a** freedom from captivity, imprisonment, slavery, or despotic control. **b** a personification of this. **2 a** the right or power to do as one pleases. **b** (foll. by *to* + infin.) right; power; opportunity; permission. **3 a** (usu. in *pl.*) a right, privilege, or immunity, enjoyed by prescription or grant. **b** (in *sing.* or *pl.*) *hist.* an area having such privileges, etc., esp. a distric controlled by a city though outside its boundary or an area outside a prison where some prisoners might reside. **4** setting aside of rules or convention. □ **at liberty 1** free; not imprisoned (*set at liberty*). **2** (foll. by *to* + infin.) entitled; permitted. **3** available; disengaged. **take liberties 1** (often foll. by *with*) behave in an unduly familiar manner. **2** (foll. by *with*) deal freely or superficially with rules or facts. **take the liberty** (foll. by *to* + infin., or *of* + verbal noun) presume; venture.

li·bid·i·nous /libídənəs/ *adj.* lustful.

li·bi·do /libeédō, –bí–/ *n.* (*pl.* **-dos**) *Psychol.* psychic drive or energy, esp. that associated with sexual desire. □□ **li·bid·i·nal** /libídənəl/ *adj.* **li·bid·i·nous** /libídənəs/ *adj.*

Li·bra /leébrə, lí–/ *n.* **1** a constellation, traditionally regarded as contained in the figure of scales. **2 a** the seventh sign of the zodiac (the Balance or Scales). **b** a person born when the sun is in this sign. □□ **Li·bran** *n.* *& adj.*

li·brar·i·an /lībráireeən/ *n.* a person in charge of, or an assistant in, a library. □□ **li·brar·i·an·ship** *n.*

li·brar·y /líbreree/ *n.* (*pl.* **-ies**) **1 a** a collection of books, etc., for use by the public or by members of a group. **b** a person's collection of books. **2** a room or building containing a collection of books (for reading or reference rather than for sale). **3 a** a similar collection of films, records, computer software, etc. **b** the place where these are kept. **4** a series of books issued by a publisher in similar bindings, etc., usu. as a set. **5** a public institution charged with the care of a collection of books, films, etc.

▶Avoid pronouncing **library** "lie-berry," which many regard as uneducated.

li·bret·to /librétō/ *n.* (*pl.* **-tos** or **libretti** /–tee/) the text of an opera or other musical vocal work. □□ **li·bret·tist** *n.*

Lib·y·an /líbeeən, líbyən/ *adj. & n.* •*adj.* **1** of or relating to modern Libya in N. Africa. **2** of ancient N. Africa west of Egypt. **3** of or relating to the Berber group of languages. •*n.* **1 a** a native or national of modern Libya. **b** a person of Libyan descent. **2** an ancient language of the Berber group.

lice *pl.* of LOUSE.

li·cense /lísəns/ *n. & v.* •*n.* **1** a permit from an authority to own or use something (esp. a dog, gun, television set, or vehicle), do something (esp. marry, print something, preach, or drive on a public road), or carry on a business (esp. in alcoholic liquor). **2** permission (*have I your license to remove the fence?*). **3 a** liberty of action, esp. when excessive; abuse of freedom. **b** licentiousness. **4** a writer's or artist's irregularity in grammar, meter, perspective, etc., or deviation from fact, esp. for effect (*poetic license*). •*v.tr.* **1** grant a license to (a person). **2** authorize the use of (premises) for a certain purpose, esp. the sale and consumption of alcoholic liquor. **3** authorize the publication of (a book, etc.) or the performance of (a play). □□ **li·cens·a·ble** *adj.*

li·cen·see /lísənseé/ *n.* the holder of a license, esp. to sell alcoholic liquor.

li·cense plate *n.* the usu. metal plate of a motor vehicle that attests to its registration.

li·cen·ti·ate /līsénsheeət/ *n.* a holder of a certificate of competence to practice a certain profession.

li·cen·tious /līsénshəs/ *adj.* immoral in sexual relations. □□ **li·cen·tious·ly** *adv.* **li·cen·tious·ness** *n.*

li·chee var. of LITCHI.

li·chen /líkən/ *n.* **1** any plant organism of the group Lichenes, composed of a fungus and an alga in symbiotic association, growing on and coloring rocks, tree trunks, roofs, walls, etc. **2** any of several types of skin disease in which small, round, hard lesions occur close together. □□ **li·chened** *adj.* (in sense 1). **li·chen·ol·o·gy** *n.* (in sense 1). **li·chen·ous** *adj.* (in sense 2).

lic·it /lísit/ *adj.* not forbidden; lawful. □□ **lic·it·ly** *adv.*

lick /lik/ *v. & n.* •*v.* **1** *tr.* pass the tongue over. **2** *tr.* bring into a specified condition or position by licking (*licked it all up*; *licked it clean*). **3 a** *tr.* (of a flame, waves, etc.) play lightly over. **b** *intr.* move gently or caressingly. **4** *tr.* *colloq.* **a** defeat; excel. **b** surpass the comprehension or competence of (*has got me licked*). **5** *tr.* *colloq.* thrash. •*n.* **1** an act of licking with the tongue. **2** = SALT LICK. **3** *colloq.* a fast pace (*at a lick*). **4** *colloq.* **a** a small amount; quick treatment with (foll. by *of*: *a lick of paint*). **b** a quick wash. **5** a smart blow with a stick, etc. □ **a lick and a promise** *colloq.* a hasty performance of a task, esp. of washing oneself. **lick one's lips** (or **chops**) **1** look forward with relish. **2** show one's satisfaction. **lick one's wounds** be in retirement after defeat. □□ **lick·er** *n.* (also in *comb.*).

lick·e·ty-split /líkəteesplít/ *adv. colloq.* at full speed; headlong.

lick·ing /líking/ *n. colloq.* **1** a thrashing. **2** a defeat.

lic·o·rice /líkərish, –ris/ *n.* **1** a black root extract used as a candy and in medicine. **2** the leguminous plant, *Glycyrrhiza glabra*, from which it is obtained.

lid /lid/ *n.* **1** a hinged or removable cover, esp. for the top of a container. **2** = EYELID. **3** the operculum of a shell or a plant. **4** *sl.* a hat. □ **put a lid on** be quiet about; keep secret. **take the lid off** *colloq.* expose (a scandal, etc.). □□ **lid·ded** *adj.* (also in *comb.*). **lid·less** *adj.*

lie[1] /lī/ *v. & n.* •*v.intr.* (**lying** /lí-ing/; *past* **lay** /lay/; *past part.* **lain** /layn/) **1** be in or assume a horizontal position on a supporting surface; be at rest on something. **2** (of a thing) rest flat on a surface (*snow lay on the ground*). **3** (of abstract things) remain undisturbed or undiscussed, etc. (*let matters lie*). **4 a** be kept or remain or be in a specified state or place (*lie hidden*; *lie in wait*; *malice lay behind those words*; *they lay dying*; *the books lay unread*; *the money is lying in the bank*). **b** (of abstract things) exist; reside; be in a certain position or relation (foll. by *in*, *with*, etc.: *the answer lies in education*; *my sympathies lie with the family*). **5 a** be situated or stationed (*the village lay to the east*; *the ships are lying off the coast*). **b** (of a road, route, etc.) lead (*the road lies over mountains*). **c** be spread out to view (*the desert lay before us*). **6** (of the dead) be buried in a grave. **7** (foll. by *with*) *archaic* have sexual intercourse. •*n.* **1 a** the way or direction or position in which a thing lies. **b** *Golf* the position of a golf ball when about to be struck. **2** the place of cover of an animal or a bird. □ **let lie** not raise (a controversial matter, etc.) for discussion, etc. **lie about** (or **around**) be left carelessly out of place. **lie ahead** be going to happen; be in store. **lie back** recline so as to rest. **lie in state** (of a deceased great personage) be laid in a public place of honor before burial. **lie low 1** keep quiet or unseen. **2** be discreet about one's intentions. **lie with** (often foll. by *to* + infin.) be the responsibility of (a person) (*it lies with you to answer*). **take lying down** (usu. with *neg.*) accept (defeat, rebuke, etc.) without resistance or protest, etc.

▶See note at LAY[1].

lie[2] /lī/ *n. & v.* •*n.* **1** an intentionally false statement (*tell a lie*; *pack of lies*). **2** imposture; false belief (*live a lie*).

•*v.* (**lies, lied, lying** /lī́-ing/) **1** *intr.* **a** tell a lie or lies (*they lied to me*). **b** (of a thing) be deceptive (*the camera cannot lie*). **2** *tr.* (usu. *refl.*; foll. by *into, out of*) get (oneself) into or out of a situation by lying (*lied themselves into trouble; lied my way out of danger*). □ **give the lie to** serve to show the falsity of (a supposition, etc.).

lied /leed, leet/ *n.* (*pl.* **lieder** /léedər/) a type of German song, esp. of the Romantic period.

lie de·tec·tor *n.* an instrument for determining whether a person is telling the truth by testing for physiological changes considered to be symptomatic of lying.

liege /leej, leezh/ *adj. & n.* usu. *hist.* •*adj.* (of a superior) entitled to receive or (of a vassal) bound to give feudal service or allegiance. •*n.* (in full **liege lord**) a feudal superior or sovereign.

lien /leen, léeən/ *n. Law* a right over another's property to protect a debt charged on that property.

lieu /lo͞o/ *n.* □ **in lieu 1** instead. **2** (foll. by *of*) in the place of.

lieut. *abbr.* lieutenant.

lieu·ten·ant /lo͞oténənt/ *n.* **1** a deputy. **2 a** an army officer next in rank below captain. **b** a naval officer next in rank below lieutenant commander. **3** a police officer next in rank below captain. □□ **lieu·ten·an·cy** *n.* (*pl.* **-cies**).

lieu·ten·ant colo·nel *n.* an army officer ranking below a colonel and above a major.

lieu·ten·ant com·man·der *n.* a naval officer ranking below a commander and above a lieutenant.

lieu·ten·ant gen·er·al *n.* an army officer ranking below a general and above a major general.

lieu·ten·ant gov·er·nor *n.* (in the US) the elected official next in rank to a state's governor.

life /līf/ *n.* (*pl.* **lives** /līvz/) **1** the condition that distinguishes active animals and plants from inorganic matter, including the capacity for growth, functional activity, and continual change preceding death. **2 a** living things and their activity (*insect life; is there life on Mars?*). **b** human presence or activity (*no sign of life*). **3 a** the period during which life lasts, or the period from birth to the present time or from the present time to death (*have done it all my life; will regret it all my life; life membership*). **b** the duration of a thing's existence or of its ability to function (*the battery has a life of two years*). **4 a** a person's state of existence as a living individual (*sacrificed their lives; took many lives*). **b** a living person (*many lives were lost*). **5 a** an individual's occupation, actions, or fortunes; the manner of one's existence (*that would make life easy; start a new life*). **b** a particular aspect of this (*love life; private life*). **6** the business and pleasures of the world (*travel is the best way to see life*). **7** a human's earthly or supposed future existence. **8 a** energy; liveliness (*full of life; put some life into it!*). **b** an animating influence (*was the life of the party*). **c** (of an inanimate object) power; force; ability to perform its intended function. **9** the living form or model (*drawn from life*). **10** a biography. **11** *colloq.* a sentence of imprisonment for life (*they were all serving life*). □ **come to life 1** emerge from unconsciousness or inactivity; begin operating. **2** (of an inanimate object) assume an imaginary animation. **for dear** (or **one's**) **life** as if or in order to escape death (*hanging on for dear life; run for your life*). **for the life of** (foll. by pers. pron.) even if (one's) life depended on it (*cannot for the life of me remember*). **get a life** start living a fuller or more interesting existence. **give one's life 1** (foll. by *for*) die; sacrifice oneself. **2** (foll. by *to*) dedicate oneself. **large as life** *colloq.* in person, esp. prominently (*stood there large as life*). **larger than life 1** exaggerated. **2** (of a person) having an exuberant personality. **a matter of life and death** a matter of vital importance. **not on your life** *colloq.* most certainly not. **take one's life in one's hands** take a crucial personal risk.

life-and-death *adj.* vitally important; desperate (*a life-and-death struggle*).

life·blood /lī́fblud/ *n.* **1** the blood, as being necessary to life. **2** the vital factor or influence.

life·boat /lī́fbōt/ *n.* **1** a specially constructed boat launched from land to rescue those in distress at sea. **2** a ship's small boat for use in emergency.

life bu·oy *n.* a buoyant support for keeping a person afloat.

life cy·cle *n.* the series of changes in the life of an organism including reproduction.

life ex·pec·tan·cy *n.* the average period that a person may expect to live.

life force *n.* inspiration or a driving force or influence.

life-giv·ing *adj.* that sustains life or uplifts and revitalizes.

life·guard /lī́fgaard/ *n.* an expert swimmer employed to rescue bathers from drowning.

life in·sur·ance *n.* insurance for a sum to be paid on the death of the insured person.

life jack·et *n.* a buoyant jacket for keeping a person afloat.

life·less /lī́flis/ *adj.* **1** lacking life; no longer living. **2** unconscious. **3** lacking activity or vitality. □□ **life·less·ly** *adv.* **life·less·ness** *n.*

life·like /lī́flīk/ *adj.* closely resembling the person or thing represented.

life·line /lī́flīn/ *n.* **1 a** a rope, etc., used for lifesaving. **b** a diver's signaling line. **2** a sole means of communication or transport. **3** a fold in the palm of the hand, regarded as significant in palmistry. **4** an emergency telephone counseling service.

life·long /lī́flawng, –long/ *adj.* lasting a lifetime.

life pre·serv·er *n.* a life jacket, etc.

lif·er /lī́fər/ *n. sl.* **1** a person serving a life sentence. **2** a person committed to a long career in a profession.

life raft *n.* an inflatable or log, etc., raft for use in an emergency instead of a boat.

life·sav·er /lī́fsayvər/ *n.* a person or thing that saves one from serious difficulty.

life sci·ences *n.pl.* biology and related subjects.

life sen·tence *n.* **1** a sentence of imprisonment for life. **2** an illness or commitment, etc., perceived as a continuing threat to one's freedom.

life-size *adj.* (also **life-sized**) of the same size as the person or thing represented.

life·style /lī́fstīl/ *n.* the particular way of life of a person or group.

life-sup·port *adj.* (of equipment) allowing vital functions to continue.

life·time /lī́ftīm/ *n.* **1** the duration of a person's life. **2** the duration of a thing or its usefulness. □ **of a lifetime** such as does not occur more than once in a person's life (*the chance of a lifetime; the journey of a lifetime*).

life·work /lī́fwə́rk/ *n.* a task, profession, etc., pursued throughout one's lifetime.

lift /lift/ *v. & n.* •*v.* **1** *tr.* (often foll. by *up, off, out,* etc.) raise or remove to a higher position. **2** *intr.* go up; be raised; yield to an upward force (*the window will not lift*). **3** *tr.* give an upward direction to (the eyes or face). **4** *tr.* **a** elevate to a higher plane of thought or feeling (*the news lifted their spirits*). **b** make less heavy or dull; add interest to. **c** enhance; improve (*lifted their game after halftime*). **5** *intr.* (of a cloud, fog, etc.) rise; disperse. **6** *tr.* remove (a barrier or restriction). **7** *tr.* transport (supplies, troops, etc.) by air. **8** *tr. colloq.* **a** steal. **b** plagiarize (a passage of writing, etc.). **9** *intr.* (of the voice) rise. **10** *intr.* (of a floor) swell upward, bulge. **11** *tr.* (usu. in *passive*) perform cosmetic surgery on to reduce sagging. •*n.* **1** the act of lifting or process of being lifted. **2** a free ride in another person's vehicle (*gave them a lift*). **3 a** *Brit.* = ELEVATOR 3a. **b** an apparatus for carrying persons up or down a mountain, etc. (see SKI LIFT). **4 a** transport by air (see AIRLIFT *n.*). **b** a quantity of goods transported by air. **5** the upward pressure that air exerts on an airfoil. **6** a supporting or elevating influence; a feeling of elation. **7** a layer of leather in the heel of a boot or shoe, esp. to correct shortening of a leg or increase height. □ **lift a finger** (or **hand,** etc.) (in *neg.*) make the slightest effort (*didn't lift a finger to help*). **lift up one's voice** sing out. □□ **lift·a·ble** *adj.* **lift·er** *n.*

lift·off /líftawf/ *n.* the vertical takeoff of a spacecraft or rocket.

lig·a·ment /lígəmənt/ *n.* **1** *Anat.* a short band of tough, flexible, fibrous connective tissue linking bones together. **2** any membranous fold keeping an organ in position. □□ **lig·a·men·tal** /–mént'l/ *adj.* **lig·a·men·ta·ry** /–méntəree/ *adj.* **lig·a·men·tous** /–méntəs/ *adj.*

li·gate /lígayt/ *v.tr. Surgery* tie up (a bleeding artery, etc.). □□ **li·ga·tion** /–gáyshən/ *n.*

li·ga·ture /lígəchər/ *n.* **1** a tie or bandage. **2** *Mus.* a slur; a tie. **3** *Printing* two or more letters joined, e.g., *æ*. **4** a bond; a thing that unites.

light[1] /līt/ *n., v., & adj.* • *n.* **1** the natural agent (electromagnetic radiation of wavelength between about 390 and 740 nm) that stimulates sight and makes things visible. **2** the medium or condition of the space in which this is present. **3** an appearance of brightness (*saw a distant light*). **4 a** a source of light. **b** (in *pl.*) illuminations. **5** (often in *pl.*) a traffic light (*went through a red light; stop at the lights*). **6 a** the amount or quality of illumination in a place (*bad light stopped play*). **b** one's fair or usual share of this (*you are standing in my light*). **7** a flame or spark serving to ignite (*struck a light*). **8** the aspect in which a thing is regarded (*appeared in a new light*). **9 a** mental illumination; enlightenment. **b** hope; happiness; a happy outcome. **c** spiritual illumination by divine truth. **10** vivacity, enthusiasm, or inspiration visible in a person's face, esp. in the eyes. **11** (in *pl.*) a person's mental powers or ability (*according to one's lights*). **12** an eminent person (*a leading light*). **13 a** the bright part of a thing; a highlight. **b** the bright parts of a picture, etc., esp. suggesting illumination (*light and shade*). • *v.* (*past* **lit** /lit/; *past part.* **lit** or (*attrib.*) **lighted**) **1** *tr. & intr.* set burning or begin to burn; ignite. **2** *tr.* provide with light or lighting. **3** *tr.* show (a person) the way or surroundings with a light. **4** *intr.* (usu. foll. by *up*) (of the face or eyes) brighten with animation. • *adj.* **1** well provided with light; not dark. **2** (of a color) pale (*light blue; a light-blue ribbon*). □ **bring** (or **come**) **to light** reveal or be revealed. **in a good** (or **bad**) **light** giving a favorable (or unfavorable) impression. **in (the) light of** having regard to; drawing information from. **light of one's life** usu. *joc.* a much-loved person. **light up 1** *colloq.* begin to smoke a cigarette, etc. **2** switch on lights or lighting; illuminate a scene. **out like a light** deeply asleep or unconscious. **throw** (or **shed**) **light on** help to explain. □□ **light·ish** *adj.* **light·less** *adj.* **light·ness** *n.*

light Old English *lēoht, līht* (noun and adjective), *līhtan* (verb), of Germanic origin; related to Dutch *licht* and German *Licht*, from an Indo-European root shared by Greek *leukos* 'white' and Latin *lux* 'light'.

light[2] /līt/ *adj., adv., & v.* • *adj.* **1** not heavy. **2** relatively low in weight, amount, density, intensity, etc. (*light arms; light traffic; light metal; light rain; a light breeze*). **3 a** carrying or suitable for small loads (*light aircraft*). **b** (of a ship) unladen. **c** carrying only light arms, armaments, etc. (*light brigade; light infantry*). **d** (of a locomotive) with no train attached. **4 a** (of food, a meal, etc.) small in amount; easy to digest (*had a light lunch*). **b** (of drink) not heavy on the stomach or strongly alcoholic. **5 a** (of entertainment, music, etc.) intended for amusement, rather than edification; not profound. **b** frivolous; thoughtless; trivial (*a light remark*). **6** (of sleep or a sleeper) easily disturbed. **7** easily borne or done (*light duties*). **8** nimble; quick-moving (*a light step; a light rhythm*). **9** (of a building, etc.) graceful; elegant. **10** (of type) not heavy or bold. **11 a** free from sorrow; cheerful (*a light heart*). **b** giddy (*light in the head*). **12** (of pastry, sponge cake, etc.) fluffy and well-aerated during cooking and with the fat fully absorbed. • *adv.* **1** in a light manner (*tread light; sleep light*). **2** with a minimum load or minimum luggage (*travel light*). • *v.intr.* (*past* and *past part.* **lit** /lit/or **lighted**) (foll. by *on, upon*) come upon or find by chance. □ **light into** *colloq.* attack. **light out** *colloq.* depart. **make light of** treat as unimportant. **make light work of** do a thing quickly and easily. □□ **light·ish** *adj.* **light·ness** *n.*

light·bulb /lītbulb/ *n.* a glass bulb inserted into a lamp that provides light by passing an electric current through a pocket of inert gas.

light-e·mit·ting di·ode see LED.

light·en[1] /lít'n/ *v.* **1 a** *tr. & intr.* make or become lighter in weight. **b** *tr.* reduce the weight or load of. **2** *tr.* bring relief to (the heart, mind, etc.). **3** *tr.* mitigate (a penalty).

light·en[2] /lít'n/ *v.* **1 a** *tr.* shed light on. **b** *tr. & intr.* make or grow lighter or brighter. **2** *intr.* **a** shine brightly; flash. **b** emit lightning (*it is lightening*).

light·er /lítər/ *n.* a device for lighting cigarettes, etc.

light·er-than-air *adj.* (of an aircraft) weighing less than the air it displaces.

light-fin·gered *adj.* given to stealing.

light-foot·ed *adj.* nimble. □□ **light-foot·ed·ly** *adv.*

light-head·ed *n.* giddy; delirious. □□ **light-head·ed·ly** *adj.* **light-head·ed·ness** *adv.*

light·heart·ed /līt-haartid/ *adj.* **1** cheerful. **2** (unduly) casual; thoughtless. □□ **light·heart·ed·ly** *adv.* **light·heart·ed·ness** *n.*

light·house /līt-hows/ *n.* a tower or other structure containing a beacon light to warn or guide ships at sea.

light in·dus·try *n.* the manufacture of small articles.

light·ing /líting/ *n.* **1** equipment in a room or street, etc., for producing light. **2** the arrangement or effect of lights.

light·ly /lítlee/ *adv.* in a light (esp. frivolous or unserious) manner. □ **get off lightly** escape with little or no punishment. **take lightly** not be serious about (a thing).

light me·ter *n.* an instrument for measuring the intensity of the light, esp. to indicate the correct photographic exposure.

light·ning /lítning/ *n. & adj.* • *n.* a flash of bright light produced by an electric discharge between clouds or between clouds and the ground. • *attrib.adj.* very quick (*with lightning speed*).

light·ning bug *n.* = FIREFLY.

light·ning rod *n.* (also **light·ning con·duc·tor**) a metal rod or wire fixed to an exposed part of a building or to a mast to divert lightning into the earth or sea.

light pen *n.* **1** a penlike photosensitive device held to the screen of a computer terminal for passing information on to it. **2** a light-emitting device used for reading bar codes.

light·proof /lītpro͞of/ *adj.* able to block out light completely (*a lightproof envelope*).

light·ship /lītship/ *n.* an anchored ship with a beacon light.

light·some /lītsəm/ *adj.* gracefully light; nimble; merry. □□ **lightsomely** *adv.* **lightsomeness** *n.*

light touch *n.* delicate or tactful treatment.

light·weight /lítwayt/ *adj.* & *n.* • *adj.* **1** of below average weight. **2** of little importance or influence. • *n.* **1** a lightweight person, animal, or thing. **2 a** a weight in certain sports intermediate between featherweight and welterweight. **b** an athlete of this weight.

light-year *n.* **1** *Astron.* the distance light travels in one year, nearly 6 trillion miles. **2** (in *pl.*) *colloq.* a long distance or great amount.

lig·ne·ous /ligneeəs/ *adj.* **1** (of a plant) woody (opp. HERBACEOUS). **2** of the nature of wood.

lig·nin /lígnin/ *n. Bot.* a complex organic polymer deposited in the cell walls of many plants, making them rigid and woody.

lig·nite /lígnīt/ *n.* a soft brown coal showing traces of plant structure, intermediate between bituminous coal and peat.

li·gus·trum /ligústrəm/ *n.* = PRIVET.

lik·a·ble /líkəbəl/ *adj.* (also **like·a·ble**) pleasant; easy to like. ▫▫ **lik·a·ble·ness** *n.* **lik·a·bly** /–blee/ *adv.*

like[1] /līk/ *adj., prep., adv., conj.,* & *n.* • *adj.* (often governing a noun as if a transitive participle such as *resembling*) (**more like, most like**) **1 a** having some or all of the qualities of another or each other or an original (*in like manner; as like as two peas; is very like her brother*). **b** resembling in some way, such as (*good writers like Poe*). **c** (usu. in pairs correlatively) as one is so will the other be (*like mother, like daughter*). **2** characteristic of (*it is not like them to be late*). **3** in a suitable state or mood for (*felt like working; felt like a cup of coffee*). • *prep.* in the manner of; to the same degree as (*drink like a fish; sell like hotcakes; acted like an idiot*). • *adv.* **1** *archaic* likely (*they will come, like enough*). **2** *sl.* so to speak (*did a quick getaway, like; as I said, like, I'm no Shakespeare*). • *conj. colloq. disp.* **1** as (*cannot do it like you do*). **2** as if (*ate like they were starving*). • *n.* **1** a counterpart; an equal; a similar person or thing (*shall not see its like again; compare like with like*). **2** (prec. by *the*) a thing or things of the same kind (*will never do the like again*). ▫ **and the like** and similar things (*music, painting, and the like*). **like** (or **as like**) **as not** *colloq.* probably. **like so** *colloq.* like this; in this manner. **the likes of** *colloq.* a person such as (*I wouldn't trust the likes of him*). **more like it** *colloq.* nearer what is required.

▶The use of **like** as a conjunction meaning 'as' or 'as if,' e.g., *I don't have a wealthy set of in-laws like you do; They sit up like they're begging for food,* is considered incorrect by many. In more precise use, **like** is a preposition, used before nouns and pronouns: *to fly like a bird, a town like ours.*

like[2] /līk/ *v.* & *n.* • *v.tr.* **1 a** find agreeable or enjoyable (*like reading; like the sea; like to dance*). **b** be fond of (a person). **2 a** choose to have; prefer (*like my coffee black; do not like such things discussed*). **b** wish for or be inclined to (*would like a cup of tea*). **3** (usu. in *interrog.*; prec. by *how*) feel about; regard (*how would you like it if it happened to you?*). • *n.* (in *pl.*) the things one likes or prefers. ▫ **like it or not** *colloq.* whether it is acceptable or not.

-like /līk/ *comb. form* forming adjectives from nouns, meaning 'similar to, characteristic of' (*doglike; tortoiselike*).

▶In (esp. polysyllabic) formations intended as nonce words, or not generally current, a hyphen is often used (*celebration-like*). Nouns ending in *-ll* always require it (*shell-like*).

like·a·ble var. of LIKABLE.

like·li·hood /líkleehŏŏd/ *n.* probability. ▫ **in all likelihood** very probably.

like·ly /líklee/ *adj.* & *adv.* • *adj.* (**likelier, likeliest**) **1** probable; such as well might happen or be true (*it is not likely that they will come; the most likely place is California; a likely story*). **2** (foll. by *to* + infin.) to be reasonably expected (*he is not likely to come now*). **3** promising; apparently suitable (*this is a likely spot; three likely candidates*). • *adv.* probably (*is very likely true*). ▫ **as likely as not** probably. **not likely!** *colloq.* certainly not; I refuse. ▫▫ **like·li·ness** *n.*

like-mind·ed *adj.* having the same tastes, opinions, etc. ▫▫ **like-mind·ed·ly** *adv.* **like-mind·ed·ness** *n.*

lik·en /líkən/ *v.tr.* (foll. by *to*) point out the resemblance of (a person or thing to another).

like·ness /líknis/ *n.* **1** (foll. by *between, to*) resemblance. **2** (foll. by *of*) a semblance or guise (*in the likeness of a ghost*). **3** a portrait or representation (*is a good likeness*).

like·wise /líkwīz/ *adv.* **1** also; moreover. **2** similarly (*do likewise*).

lik·ing /líking/ *n.* **1** what one likes; one's taste (*is it to your liking?*). **2** (foll. by *for*) regard or fondness; taste or fancy (*had a liking for chocolate*).

li·lac /lílək, –lok, –lak/ *n.* & *adj.* • *n.* **1** any shrub or small tree of the genus *Syringa*, esp. *S. vulgaris* with fragrant pale pinkish-violet or white blossoms. **2** a pale pinkish-violet color. • *adj.* of this color.

lil·i·a·ceous /lílee-áyshəs/ *adj.* **1** of or relating to the family Liliaceae of plants with elongated leaves growing from a corm, bulb, or rhizome. **2** lilylike.

lil·li·pu·tian /lílipyŏŏshən/ *n.* & *adj.* (also **Lil·li·pu·tian**) • *n.* a diminutive person or thing. • *adj.* diminutive.

lilt /lilt/ *n.* & *v.* • *n.* **1 a** a light springing rhythm or gait. **b** a song or tune marked by this. **2** (of the voice) a characteristic cadence or inflection. • *v.intr.* (esp. as **lilting** *adj.*) move or speak, etc., with a lilt.

lil·y /lílee/ *n.* (*pl.* **-ies**) **1 a** any bulbous plant of the genus *Lilium* with large, trumpet-shaped flowers on a tall, slender stem. **b** any of several other plants of the family Liliaceae with similar flowers. **c** the water lily. **2** a person or thing of special whiteness or purity. **3** a heraldic fleur-de-lis.

lil·y-liv·ered *adj.* cowardly.

lil·y of the val·ley *n.* any liliaceous plant of the genus *Convallaria*, with racemes of white, bell-shaped, fragrant flowers.

lil·y pad *n.* a floating leaf of a water lily.

lil·y-white *adj.* **1** as white as a lily. **2** faultless.

li·ma bean /līmə/ *n.* **1** a tropical American bean plant, *Phaseolus lunatus*, having large, flat, greenish-white edible seeds. **2** the seed of this plant.

limb[1] /lim/ *n.* **1** any of the projecting parts of a person's or animal's body used for contact or movement. **2** a large branch of a tree. **3** a branch of a cross. **4** a spur of a mountain. **5** a clause of a sentence. ▫ **out on a limb 1** isolated; stranded. **2** at a disadvantage. **tear limb from limb** violently dismember. ▫▫ **limbed** *adj.* (also in *comb.*). **limb·less** *adj.*

limb[2] /lim/ *n.* **1** *Astron.* **a** a specified edge of the sun, moon, etc. **b** the graduated edge of a quadrant, etc. **2** *Bot.* the broad part of a petal, sepal, or leaf.

lim·ber /límbər/ *adj.* & *v.* • *adj.* **1** lithe; agile; nimble. **2** flexible. • *v.* (usu. foll. by *up*) **1** *tr.* make (oneself or a part of the body, etc.) supple. **2** *intr.* warm up in preparation for athletic, etc., activity. ▫▫ **lim·ber·ness** *n.*

lim·bo[1] /límbō/ *n.* (*pl.* **-bos**) **1** (in some Christian beliefs) the supposed abode of the souls of unbaptized infants, and of the just who died before Christ. **2** an intermediate state or condition of awaiting a decision, etc.

lim·bo[2] /límbō/ *n.* (*pl.* **-bos**) a W. Indian dance in which the dancer bends backward to pass under a horizontal bar that is progressively lowered.

lime[1] /līm/ *n.* & *v.* • *n.* **1** (in full **quicklime**) a white caustic alkaline substance (calcium oxide) obtained by heating limestone. **2** = BIRDLIME. • *v.tr.* treat (wood, skins, land, etc.) with lime. ▫▫ **lime·less** *adj.* **lim·y** *adj.* (**lim·i·er, lim·i·est**).

lime[2] /līm/ *n.* **1 a** a round citrus fruit like a lemon but greener, smaller, and more acid. **b** the tree, *Citrus aurantifolia*, bearing this. **2** (in full **lime juice**) the juice of limes as a drink. **3** (in full **lime green**) a pale green color like a lime.

lime[3] /līm/ *n.* **1** (in full **lime tree**) any ornamental tree of the genus *Tilia*, esp. *T. europaea* with heart-shaped leaves and fragrant yellow blossoms. Also called LINDEN. **2** the wood of this.

lime·kiln /límkiln, –kil/ *n.* a kiln for heating limestone.

lime·light /límlīt/ *n.* **1** an intense white light used formerly in theaters. **2** (prec. by *the*) the full glare of publicity; the focus of attention.

lim·er·ick /límərik, límrik/ *n.* a humorous or comic form of five-line stanza with a rhyme scheme *aabba*.

lime·stone /límstōn/ *n. Geol.* a sedimentary rock composed mainly of calcium carbonate.

lim·it /límit/ *n. & v.* •*n.* **1** a point, line, or level beyond which something does not or may not extend or pass. **2** (often in *pl.*) the boundary of an area. **3** the greatest or smallest amount permissible or possible. **4** *Math.* a quantity that a function or sum of a series can be made to approach as closely as desired. •*v.tr.* **1** set or serve as a limit to. **2** (foll. by *to*) restrict. □ **within limits** moderately; with some degree of freedom. **without limit** with no restriction. □□ **lim·it·a·ble** *adj.* **lim·it·er** *n.*

lim·i·tar·y /límiteree/ *adj.* **1** subject to restriction. **2** of, on, or serving as a limit.

lim·i·ta·tion /límitáyshən/ *n.* **1** the act or an instance of limiting; the process of being limited. **2** a condition of limited ability (often in *pl.*: *know one's limitations*). **3** a limiting circumstance (often in *pl.*: *has its limitations*). **4** a legally specified period beyond which an action cannot be brought, or a property right is not to continue.

lim·it·ed /límitid/ *adj.* **1** confined within limits. **2** not great in scope or talents (*has limited experience*). **3 a** few; scanty; restricted (*limited accommodation*). **b** restricted to a few examples (*limited edition*). □□ **lim·it·ed·ness** *n.*

lim·it·less /límitlis/ *adj.* **1** extending or going on indefinitely (*a limitless expanse*). **2** unlimited (*limitless generosity*). □□ **lim·it·less·ly** *adv.* **lim·it·less·ness** *n.*

lim·nol·o·gy /limnóləjee/ *n.* the study of the physical phenomena of lakes and other fresh waters. □□ **lim·no·log·i·cal** /–nəlójikəl/ *adj.* **lim·nol·o·gist** /–nól–/ *n.*

lim·o /límō/ *n.* (*pl.* **-os**) *colloq.* a limousine.

lim·ou·sine /líməzéen/ *n.* a large, luxurious automobile.

limp[1] /limp/ *v. & n.* •*v.intr.* **1** walk lamely. **2** (of a damaged ship, aircraft, etc.) proceed with difficulty. **3** (of verse) be defective. •*n.* a lame walk. □□ **limp·ing·ly** *adv.*

limp[2] /limp/ *adj.* **1** not stiff or firm; easily bent. **2** without energy or will. **3** (of a book) having a soft cover. □□ **limp·ly** *adv.* **limp·ness** *n.*

lim·pet /límpit/ *n.* any of various marine gastropod mollusks with a shallow conical shell and a broad muscular foot that sticks tightly to rocks.

lim·pet mine *n.* a mine designed to be attached to a ship's hull and set to explode after a certain time.

lim·pid /límpid/ *adj.* **1** (of water, eyes, etc.) clear; transparent. **2** (of writing) easily comprehended. □□ **lim·pid·i·ty** /–píditee/ *n.* **lim·pid·ly** *adv.* **lim·pid·ness** *n.*

limp-wrist·ed *adj. sl. offens.* effeminate; weak; feeble.

linch·pin /línchpin/ *n.* **1** a pin passed through the end of an axle to keep a wheel in position. **2** a person or thing vital to an enterprise, organization, etc.

lin·den /líndən/ *n.* **1** any ornamental tree of the genus *Tilia*, with heart-shaped leaves and fragrant yellow blossoms. **2** the wood of this.

line[1] /līn/ *n. & v.* •*n.* **1** a continuous mark or band made on a surface (*drew a line*). **2** use of lines in art, esp. draftsmanship or engraving (*boldness of line*). **3** a thing resembling such a mark, esp. a furrow or wrinkle. **4** *Mus.* **a** each of (usu. five) horizontal marks forming a stave in musical notation. **b** a sequence of notes or tones forming a melody. **5 a** a straight or curved continuous extent of length without breadth. **b** the track of a moving point. **6** a contour or outline, esp. as a feature of design (*the sculpture's clean lines*). **7 a** (on a map or graph) a curve connecting all points having a specified common property. **b** (**the Line**) the Equator. **8 a** a limit or boundary. **b** a mark limiting the area of play, the starting or finishing point in a race, division of a playing field, etc. **9 a** a row of persons or things. **b** a direction as indicated by them (*line of march*). **10 a** a row of printed or written words. **b** a portion of verse written in one line. **11** (in *pl.*) **a** a piece of poetry. **b** the words of an actor's part. **12** a short letter or note (*drop me a line*). **13** a length of cord, etc., usu. serving a specified purpose, esp. a fishing line or clothesline. **14 a** a wire or cable for a telephone or telegraph. **b** a connection by means of this (*am trying to get a line*). **15 a** a single track of a railroad. **b** one branch or route of a railroad system. **16 a** a regular succession of buses, ships, etc., plying between certain places. **b** a company conducting this (*shipping line*). **17** a connected series of persons following one another in time (esp. several generations of a family) (*a long line of craftsmen*). **18 a** a course or manner of procedure, conduct, etc. (*along these lines*). **b** policy (*the party line*). **c** conformity (*bring them into line*). **19** a direction, course, or channel (*lines of communication*). **20** a department of activity; a branch of business (*not my line*). **21** a class of commercial goods (*a new line of hats*). **22** *colloq.* a false account (*gave me a line about missing the bus*). **23** a connected series of military defenses, etc. (*behind enemy lines*). •*v.* **1** *tr.* mark with lines. **2** *tr.* cover with lines (*a face lined with pain*). **3** *tr. & intr.* position or stand at intervals along. □ **all along the line** at every point. **bring into line** make conform. **come into line** conform. **end of the line** the point at which further effort is unproductive or one can go no further. **get a line on** *colloq.* learn something about. **in line for** likely to receive. **in the line of** in the course of (esp. duty). **in** (or **out of**) **line with** in (or not in) alignment or accordance with. **lay** (or **put**) **it on the line** speak frankly. **line up 1** arrange or be arranged in a line or lines. **2** organize (*had a job lined up*). **on the line 1** at risk (*put my reputation on the line*). **2** speaking on the telephone. **out of line 1** not in alignment; discordant. **2** inappropriate; (of behavior, etc.) improper. **step out of line** behave inappropriately.

line[2] /līn/ *v.tr.* **1 a** cover the inside surface of (a garment, box, etc.) with a layer of usu. different material. **b** serve as a lining for. **2** cover as if with a lining (*shelves lined with books*). **3** *colloq.* fill, esp. plentifully. □ **line one's pocket** (or **purse**) make money, usu. by corrupt means.

lin·e·age /línee-ij/ *n.* lineal descent; ancestry; pedigree.

lin·e·al /líneeəl/ *adj.* **1** in the direct line of descent or ancestry. **2** linear; of or in lines. □□ **lin·e·al·ly** *adv.*

lin·e·a·ment /líneeəmənt/ *n.* (usu. in *pl.*) a distinctive feature or characteristic, esp. of the face.

lin·e·ar /líneeər/ *adj.* **1 a** of or in lines. **b** of length (*linear extent*). **2** long and narrow and of uniform breadth. **3** involving one dimension only. □□ **lin·e·ar·i·ty** /–neeáritee/ *n.* **lin·e·ar·ize** *v.tr.* **lin·e·ar·ly** *adv.*

lin·e·ar e·qua·tion *n.* an equation between two variables that gives a straight line when plotted on a graph.

lin·e·a·tion /línee-áyshən/ *n.* **1** a marking with or drawing of lines. **2** a division into lines.

See page xii for the *Key to Pronunciation*.

line drive *n. Baseball* a hard-hit ball that travels nearly parallel to the ground.
line•man /línmən/ *n.* (*pl.* **-men**) **1 a** a person who repairs and maintains telephone or electrical, etc., lines. **b** a person who tests the safety of railroad lines. **2** *Football* a player positioned along the line of scrimmage.
lin•en /línin/ *n. & adj.* •*n.* **1 a** cloth woven from flax. **b** a particular kind of this. **2** (*collect.*) articles made or orig. made of linen, as sheets, cloths, etc. •*adj.* made of linen or flax. □ **wash one's dirty linen in public** be indiscreet about one's domestic quarrels, etc.
line of fire *n.* the expected path of gunfire, a missile, etc.
line print•er *n.* a machine that prints output from a computer a line at a time.
lin•er[1] /línər/ *n.* a ship or aircraft, etc., carrying passengers on a regular line.
lin•er[2] /línər/ *n.* a removable lining.
lin•er notes *n.pl.* printed information packaged with records, cassette tapes, and compact disks.
lines•man /línzmən/ *n.* (*pl.* **-men**) (in games played on a field or court) a referee's assistant who decides whether a ball falls within the playing area.
line•up /línup/ *n.* **1** a line of people for inspection. **2** an arrangement of persons on a team, or of nations, etc., in an alliance.
lin•ger /línggər/ *v.intr.* **1 a** be slow or reluctant to depart. **b** stay about. **c** (foll. by *over*, *on*, etc.) dally. **2** (esp. of an illness) be protracted. **3** (foll. by *on*) (of a dying person or custom) be slow in dying. □□ **lin•ger•er** *n.* **lin•ger•ing** *adj.* **lin•ger•ing•ly** *adv.*
lin•ge•rie /laáNzhəráy, láNzhəreé/ *n.* women's underwear and nightclothes.
lin•go /línggō/ *n.* (*pl.* **-goes**) *colloq.* **1** a foreign language. **2** the vocabulary of a special subject or group.
lin•gua fran•ca /línggwə frángkə/ *n.* (*pl.* **lingua francas** or **linguae francae** /–gwee frángkee/) a language adopted as a common language between speakers whose native languages are different.
lin•gual /línggwəl/ *adj.* **1** of or formed by the tongue. **2** of speech or languages. □□ **lin•gual•ly** *adv.*
lin•gui•form /línggwifawrm/ *adj. Bot.*, *Zool.*, & *Anat.* tongue-shaped.
lin•gui•ne /linggweénee/ *n.* (also **lin•gui•ni**) a variety of pasta made in slender flattened strips.
lin•guist /línggwist/ *n.* a person skilled in languages or linguistics.
lin•guis•tic /linggwístik/ *adj.* of or relating to language or the study of languages. □□ **lin•guis•ti•cal•ly** *adv.*
lin•guis•tics /linggwístiks/ *n.* the scientific study of language and its structure.
lin•i•ment /línimənt/ *n.* a soothing lotion rubbed on sore muscles, etc., to relieve pain.
lin•ing /líning/ *n.* **1** a layer of material used to line a surface, etc. **2** an inside layer or surface, etc.
link /lingk/ *n. & v.* •*n.* **1** one loop or ring of a chain, etc. **2 a** a connecting part; one in a series. **b** a state or means of connection. **3** a means of contact by radio or telephone between two points. **4** a means of travel or transport between two places. **5** = CUFF LINK. •*v.* **1** *tr.* (foll. by *together*, *to*, *with*) connect or join. **2** *tr.* clasp or intertwine (hands or arms). **3** *intr.* (foll. by *on*, *to*, *in to*) be joined; attach oneself to (a system, company, etc.). □ **link up** (foll. by *with*) connect or combine.
link•age /língkij/ *n.* **1** a connection. **2** a system of links; a linking or link.
links /lingks/ *n.pl.* (treated as *sing.* or *pl.*) a golf course, esp. one having undulating ground, coarse grass, etc.
link•up /língkup/ *n.* an act or result of linking up.
Lin•nae•an /lineéən, –náyən/ *adj. & n.* (also **Lin•ne•an**) •*adj.* of or relating to the Swedish naturalist Linnaeus or his system of classification of plants and animals. •*n.* a follower of Linnaeus.
li•no•cut /línōkut/ *n.* **1** a design carved in relief on a block of linoleum. **2** a print made from this. □□ **li•no•cut•ting** *n.*
li•no•le•um /linóleeəm/ *n.* a material consisting of a canvas backing thickly coated with a preparation of linseed oil and powdered cork, etc., used esp. as a floor covering. □□ **li•no•le•umed** *adj.*
lin•seed /línseed/ *n.* the seed of flax.
lin•seed oil *n.* oil extracted from linseed and used esp. in paint and varnish.
lint /lint/ *n.* **1** a fabric, orig. of linen, with a raised nap on one side, used for dressing wounds. **2** fluff. □□ **lint•y** *adj.*
lin•tel /línt'l/ *n. Archit.* a horizontal supporting piece of wood, stone, etc., across the top of a door or window. □□ **lin•teled** *adj.*
lint•er /líntər/ *n.* **1** a machine for removing the short fibers from cottonseed after ginning. **2** (in *pl.*) these fibers.
li•on /líən/ *n.* **1** (*fem.* **lioness** /–nis/) a large feline, *Panthera leo*, of Africa and S. Asia, with a tawny coat. **2** (**the Lion**) the zodiacal sign or constellation Leo. **3** a brave or celebrated person. □□ **li•on•like** *adj.*
li•on•heart /líənhaart/ *n.* a courageous person (esp. as a sobriquet of Richard I of England). □□ **li•on•heart•ed** *adj.*
li•on•ize /líənīz/ *v.tr.* treat as a celebrity. □□ **li•on•i•za•tion** *n.* **li•on•iz•er** *n.*
li•on's share *n.* (prec. by *the*) the largest or best part.
lip /lip/ *n. & v.* •*n.* **1 a** either of the two fleshy parts forming the edges of the mouth opening. **b** a thing resembling these. **c** = LABIUM. **2** the edge of a cup, vessel, etc., esp. the part shaped for pouring from. **3** *colloq.* impudent talk. •*v.tr.* (**lipped, lipping**) **1 a** touch with the lips; apply the lips to. **b** touch lightly. **2** *Golf* **a** hit a ball just to the edge of (the cup). **b** (of a ball) reach the edge of (the cup) but fail to drop in. □ **bite one's lip** repress an emotion; stifle laughter, a retort, etc. **curl one's lip** express scorn. **pass a person's lips** be eaten, drunk, spoken, etc. **smack one's lips** part the lips noisily in relish or anticipation, esp. of food. □□ **lip•less** *adj.* **lip•like** *adj.* **lipped** *adj.* (also in *comb.*).
lip•gloss /lípglos, –glaws/ *n.* a cosmetic preparation for adding shine or color to the lips.
lip•id /lípid/ *n. Chem.* any of a group of organic compounds that are insoluble in water but soluble in organic solvents, including fatty acids, oils, waxes, and steroids.
li•pog•ra•phy /lipógrəfee/ *n.* the omission of letters or words in writing.
lip•oid /lípoyd/ *adj.* resembling fat.
lip•o•pro•tein /lípōprōteen, lí–/ *n. Biochem.* any of a group of proteins that are combined with fats or other lipids.
lip•o•some /lípōsōm, lí–/ *n. Biochem.* a minute artificial spherical sac usu. of a phospholipid membrane enclosing an aqueous core.
lip•o•suc•tion /lípōsúkshən, lí–/ *n.* a technique in cosmetic surgery for removing excess fat from under the skin by suction.
lip•py /lípee/ *adj.* (**lippier, lippiest**) *colloq.* **1** insolent; impertinent. **2** talkative.
lip-read *v.intr.* (*past* and *past part.* **-read** /–red/) practice lipreading. □□ **lip-read•er** *n.*
lip•reading /lípreeding/ *n.* the practice of understanding (speech) entirely from observing a speaker's lip movements.
lip serv•ice *n.* an insincere expression of support, etc.
lip•stick /lípstik/ *n.* a small stick of cosmetic for coloring the lips.

lip-sync *v.intr.* synchronize lip movements to recorded sound to appear to be singing or talking.

liq·ue·fy /líkwifī/ *v.tr. & intr.* (also **liq·ui·fy**) (**-fies, -fied**) *Chem.* make or become liquid. ▫▫ **liq·ue·fa·cient** /–fáyshənt/ *adj. & n.* **liq·ue·fac·tion** /–fákshən/ *n.* **liq·ue·fi·a·ble** *adj.* **liq·ue·fi·er** *n.*

li·ques·cent /likwésənt/ *adj.* becoming or apt to become liquid.

li·queur /likə́r, –kyŏŏr/ *n.* any of several sweet alcoholic liquors, variously flavored, usu. drunk after a meal.

liq·uid /líkwid/ *adj. & n.* • *adj.* **1** having a consistency like that of water or oil, flowing freely but of constant volume. **2** having the qualities of water in appearance (*liquid blue; a liquid luster*). **3** (of a gas, e.g., air, hydrogen) reduced to a liquid state by intense cold. **4** (of sounds) clear and pure; harmonious; fluent. **5** (of assets) easily converted into cash; having ready cash or liquid assets. • *n.* **1** a liquid substance. **2** *Phonet.* the sound of *l* or *r*. ▫▫ **liq·uid·ly** *adv.* **liq·uid·ness** *n.*

liq·ui·date /líkwidayt/ *v.* **1 a** *tr.* wind up the affairs of (a company or firm) by ascertaining liabilities and apportioning assets. **b** *intr.* (of a company) be liquidated. **2** *intr.* convert assets into cash. **3** *tr.* clear or pay off (a debt). **4** *tr.* put an end to or get rid of (esp. by violent means). ▫▫ **liq·ui·da·tion** /–áyshən/ *n.* **liq·ui·da·tor** /–aytər/ *n.*

liq·uid crys·tal *n.* a crystallinelike liquid with order in its molecular arrangement.

liq·uid crys·tal dis·play *n.* a form of visual display in electronic devices, in which the reflectivity of a matrix of liquid crystals changes as a signal is applied.

liq·uid·i·ty /likwíditee/ *n.* (*pl.* **-ties**) **1** the state of being liquid. **2** availability of liquid assets.

liq·uid·ize /líkwidīz/ *v.tr.* reduce (esp. food) to a liquid or puréed state. ▫▫ **liq·uid·iz·er** *n.*

liq·uid meas·ure *n.* a unit for measuring the volume of liquids.

liq·ui·fy var. of LIQUEFY.

liq·uor /líkər/ *n.* **1** an alcoholic (esp. distilled) drink. **2** water used in brewing. **3** other liquid, esp. that produced in cooking.

liq·uor·ish /líkərish/ *adj.* **1** = LICKERISH. **2** fond of or indicating a fondness for liquor. ▫▫ **liq·uor·ish·ly** *adv.* **liq·uor·ish·ness** *n.*

li·ra /leérə/ *n.* (*pl.* **lire** /leére/or **liras**) **1** the chief monetary unit of Italy. **2** the chief monetary unit of Turkey.

lisle /līl/ *n.* (in full **lisle thread**) a fine, smooth cotton thread for stockings, etc.

lisp /lisp/ *n. & v.* • *n.* a speech defect in which *s* is pronounced like *th* in *thick* and *z* is pronounced like *th* in *this*. • *v.intr. & tr.* speak with a lisp. ▫▫ **lisp·er** *n.* **lisp·ing** *adj.*

lis·some /lísəm/ *adj.* (also **lis·som**) lithe; supple; agile. ▫▫ **lis·some·ly** *adv.* **lis·some·ness** *n.*

list[1] /list/ *n. & v.* • *n.* **1** a number of connected items, names, etc., written or printed together usu. consecutively to form a record or aid to memory. **2** (in *pl.*) **a** palisades enclosing an area for a tournament. **b** the scene of a contest. • *v.tr.* **1 a** make a list of. **b** enumerate; name one by one as if in a list. **2** enter in a list. ▫▫ **list·a·ble** *adj.*

list[2] /list/ *v. & n.* • *v.intr.* (of a ship, etc.) lean over to one side, esp. owing to a leak or shifting cargo (cf. HEEL[2]). • *n.* the process or an instance of listing.

lis·ten /lísən/ *v.intr.* **1 a** make an effort to hear something. **b** attentively hear a person speaking. **2** (foll. by *to*) **a** give attention with the ear (*listened to my story*). **b** respond to advice or a request or to the person expressing it. **3** (also **lis·ten out**) (often foll. by *for*) seek to hear by waiting alertly. ▫ **listen in 1** eavesdrop. **2** listen to a radio or television broadcast.

lis·ten·a·ble /lísənəbəl/ *adj.* easy or pleasant to listen to. ▫▫ **lis·ten·a·bil·i·ty** *n.*

lis·ten·er /lísənər, lísnər/ *n.* **1** a person who listens. **2** a person receiving broadcast radio programs.

lis·ten·ing post *n.* **1** a point near an enemy's lines for detecting movements by sound. **2** a station for intercepting electronic communications.

lis·te·ri·a /listeéreeə/ *n.* any motile rodlike bacterium of the genus *Listeria*, esp. *L. monocytogenes* infecting humans and animals eating contaminated food.

list·ing /lísting/ *n.* **1** a list or catalog (see LIST[1] 1). **2** the drawing up of a list. **3** an entry in a list or register.

list·less /lístlis/ *adj.* lacking energy or enthusiasm. ▫▫ **list·less·ly** *adv.* **list·less·ness** *n.*

list price *n.* the price of something as shown in a published list.

lit *past* and *past part.* of LIGHT[1], LIGHT[2].

lit·a·ny /lít'nee/ *n.* (*pl.* **-nies**) **1** a series of petitions for use in church services or processions. **2** a tedious recital (*a litany of woes*).

li·tchi /leéchee/ *n.* (also **li·chee, ly·chee**) **1** a sweet, fleshy fruit with a thin, spiny skin. **2** the tree, *Nephelium litchi*, orig. from China, bearing this.

li·ter /leétər/ *n.* a metric unit of capacity equal to 1 cubic decimeter (about 1.057 quarts).

lit·er·a·cy /lítərəsee/ *n.* **1** the ability to read and write. **2** knowledge in a particular area (*computer literacy*).

lit·er·al /lítərəl/ *adj.* **1** taking words in their usual or primary sense without metaphor or allegory. **2** following the letter, text, or exact or original words (*literal translation*). **3** (in full **literal-minded**) (of a person) prosaic; lacking irony. **4 a** not exaggerated (*the literal truth*). **b** so called without exaggeration (*a literal extermination*). ▫▫ **lit·er·al·ize** *v.tr.* **lit·er·al·ly** *adv.* **lit·er·al·ness** *n.* ▶**Literally** means 'in fact, not figuratively.' Out of exaggeration, though, some speakers (and writers) cannot resist saying things such as, *We were literally scared to death.*

lit·er·al·ism /lítərəlizəm/ *n.* insistence on a literal interpretation. ▫▫ **lit·er·al·ist** *n.*

lit·er·ar·y /lítəreree/ *adj.* **1** of, constituting, or occupied with books or written composition. **2** (of a word or idiom) used chiefly in literary works or other formal writing. ▫▫ **lit·er·ar·i·ly** /–áirilee/ *adv.* **lit·er·ar·i·ness** *n.*

lit·er·ate /lítərət/ *adj. & n.* • **1** *adj.* able to read and write. **2** having or showing knowledge in a specified area (*economically and politically literate; computer literate*. • *n.* a literate person. ▫▫ **lit·er·ate·ly** *adv.*

lit·e·ra·ti /lítəraátee/ *n.pl.* persons concerned with literature; intellectuals.

lit·er·a·ture /lítərəchər, –chŏŏr/ *n.* **1** written works, esp. those whose value lies in beauty of language or in emotional effect. **2** the realm of letters. **3** the writings of a country or period. **4** literary production. **5** *colloq.* printed matter, leaflets, etc. **6** material in print on a particular subject (*a considerable literature on geraniums*).

lithe /līth/ *adj.* flexible; supple. ▫▫ **lithe·ly** *adv.* **lithe·ness** *n.* **lithe·some** *adj.*

lith·ic /líthik/ *adj.* of, like, or made of stone.

lith·i·um /lítheeəm/ *n. Chem.* **1** a soft, silver-white metallic element. ¶ Symb.: **Li**. **2** lithium carbonate or another lithium salt, used as a mood-stabilizing drug.

lith·o /líthō/ *n. & v. colloq.* • *n.* = LITHOGRAPHY. • *v.tr.* (**-oes, -oed**) produce by lithography.

litho- /líthō/ *comb. form* stone.

lith·o·graph /líthəgraf/ *n. & v.* • *n.* a lithographic print. • *v.tr.* **1** print by lithography. **2** write or engrave on stone.

lith·og·ra·phy /lithógrəfee/ *n.* a process of obtaining prints from a specially treated stone or metal surface. ▫▫ **lith·og·ra·pher** *n.* **lith·o·graph·ic** /líthəgráfik/ *adj.* **lith·o·graph·i·cal·ly** *adv.*

li·thol·o·gy /lithóləjee/ *n.* the science of the nature and composition of rocks. ▫▫ **lith·o·log·i·cal** /líthəlójikəl/ *adj.*

lith·o·sphere /líthəsfeer/ *n.* **1** the layer including the earth's crust and upper mantle. **2** solid earth (opp. HYDROSPHERE, ATMOSPHERE). ▫▫ **lith·o·spher·ic** /–sféerik, –sfér–/ *adj.*

li·thot·o·my /lithótəmee/ *n.* (*pl.* **-mies**) the surgical removal of a stone from the urinary tract, esp. the bladder. ▫▫ **li·thot·o·mist** *n.* **li·thot·o·mize** *v.tr.*

Lith·u·a·ni·an /líthoo-áyneeən/ *n. & adj.* •*n.* **1 a** a native of Lithuania, a Baltic republic. **b** a person of Lithuanian descent. **2** the language of Lithuania. •*adj.* of or relating to Lithuania or its people or language.

lit·i·gant /lítigənt/ *n. & adj.* •*n.* a party to a lawsuit. •*adj.* engaged in a lawsuit.

lit·i·gate /lítigayt/ *v.* **1** *intr.* engage in a lawsuit. **2** *tr.* contest (a point) in a lawsuit. ▫▫ **lit·i·ga·ble** /–gəbəl/ *adj.* **lit·i·ga·tion** /–gáyshən/ *n.* **lit·i·ga·tor** *n.*

li·ti·gious /litíjəs/ *adj.* **1** given to litigation. **2** disputable in a court of law; offering matter for a lawsuit. **3** of lawsuits. ▫▫ **li·ti·gious·ly** *adv.* **li·ti·gious·ness** *n.*

lit·mus /lítməs/ *n.* a dye that is red under acid conditions and blue under alkaline conditions.

lit·mus pa·per *n.* a paper stained with litmus to be used as a test for acids or alkalis.

lit·mus test *n.* **1** a test for acids and alkalis using litmus paper. **2** a simple test to establish true character.

li·to·tes /lítəteez, lít–, lītṓteez/ *n.* the expressing of an affirmative by the negative of its contrary (e.g., *I won't be sorry* for *I will be glad*).

Litt.D. *abbr.* Doctor of Letters.

lit·ter /lítər/ *n. & v.* •*n.* **1 a** refuse, esp. paper, discarded in a public place. **b** odds and ends lying about. **2** disorderly accumulation of papers, etc. **3** the young animals brought forth at a birth. **4** a vehicle containing a couch shut in by curtains and carried on men's shoulders or by beasts of burden. **5** a framework with a couch for transporting the sick and wounded. •*v.tr.* **1** make (a place) untidy with litter. **2** scatter untidily and leave lying about. **3** give birth to (whelps, etc.).

litter, 4

lit·te·rae hu·ma·ni·o·res /lítərī hōōmáneeáwrez, litəree/ *n.* the formal study of the humanities.

lit·té·ra·teur /lítəraatṓr/ *n.* a literary person.

lit·ter·bug /lítərbug/ *n.* a person who carelessly leaves litter in a public place.

lit·tle /lít'l/ *adj., n., & adv.* •*adj.* (**littler, littlest; less** /les/ or **lesser** /lésər/; **least** /leest/) **1** small in size, amount, degree, etc.; often used to convey affectionate or emotional overtones (*a friendly little guy; a silly little fool*). **2 a** short in stature (*a little man*). **b** of short distance or duration (*wait a little while*). **3** (prec. by *a*) a certain though small amount of (*give me a little butter*). **4** trivial (*exaggerates every little difficulty*). **5** not much; inconsiderable (*gained little advantage from it*). **6** operating on a small scale (*the little storekeeper*). **7** as a distinctive epithet: **a** of a smaller or the smallest size, etc. (*little finger*). **b** that is the smaller or smallest of the name (*little auk*). **8** young or younger (*my little sister*). **9** as of a child, evoking tenderness, amusement, etc. (*we know their little ways*). **10** mean; contemptible (*you little sneak*). •*n.* **1** only a small amount (*did what little I could*). **2** (usu. prec. by *a*) **a** a certain but no great amount (*every little bit helps*). **b** a short time or distance (*after a little*). •*adv.* (**less, least**) **1** to a small extent only (*little-known authors*). **2** hardly (*they little thought*). **3** (prec. by *a*) somewhat (*is a little deaf*). ▫ **little by little** by degrees. **little or nothing** hardly anything. **no little** considerable. **not a little** *n.* much; a great deal. *adv.* extremely (*not a little concerned*). ▫▫ **lit·tle·ness** *n.*

Lit·tle Dip·per *n.* the constellation of seven bright stars in Ursa Minor in the shape of a dipper.

lit·tle fin·ger *n.* the smallest finger, at the outer end of the hand.

Lit·tle League *n.* an international organization that promotes youth baseball. ▫▫ **Lit·tle Lea·guer** *n.*

lit·tle peo·ple *n.pl.* **1** the ordinary people in a country, organization, etc., who do not have much power. **2** people of small physical stature; midgets. **3** supernatural creatures such as fairies and leprechauns.

lit·to·ral /lítərəl/ *adj. & n.* •*adj.* of or on the shore of the sea, a lake, etc. •*n.* a region lying along a shore.

li·tur·gi·cal /litə́rjikəl/ *adj.* of or related to liturgies. ▫▫ **li·tur·gi·cal·ly** *adv.* **lit·ur·gist** /lítərjist/ *n.*

lit·ur·gy /lítərjee/ *n.* (*pl.* **-gies**) **1** a form of public worship. **2** a set of formularies for this. **3** public worship in accordance with a prescribed form.

liv·a·ble /lívəbəl/ *adj.* (also **live·a·ble**) **1** (of a house, climate, etc.) fit to live in. **2** (of a life) worth living. **3** (of a person) easy to live with. ▫▫ **liv·a·bil·i·ty** *n.*

live[1] /liv/ *v.* **1** *intr.* have (esp. animal) life; be or remain alive. **2** *intr.* (foll. by *on*) subsist or feed. **3** *intr.* (foll. by *on, off*) depend for subsistence (*lives off the family*). **4** *intr.* (foll. by *on, by*) sustain one's position or repute (*lives by his wits*). **5** *tr.* **a** (with compl.) spend; experience (*lived a happy life*). **b** express in one's life (*was living a lie*). **6** *intr.* conduct oneself in a specified way (*live quietly*). **7** *intr.* arrange one's expenditure, etc. (*live modestly*). **8** *intr.* make or have one's abode. **9** *intr.* (foll. by *in*) spend the daytime (*the room does not seem to be lived in*). **10** *intr.* (of a person or thing) survive. **11** *intr.* enjoy life intensely or to the full (*you haven't lived till you've drunk champagne*). ▫ **live and let live** condone others' failings so as to be similarly tolerated. **live down** (usu. with *neg.*) cause (past guilt, etc.) to be forgotten. **live in** (of a domestic employee) reside on the premises of one's work. **live it up** *colloq.* live gaily and extravagantly. **live out 1** survive (a danger, difficulty, etc.). **2** (of a domestic employee) reside away from one's place of work. **live through** survive; remain alive at the end of. **live to oneself** live in isolation. **live together** share a home and have a sexual relationship. **live up to** honor or fulfill. **live with 1** share a home with. **2** tolerate. **long live ...!** an exclamation of loyalty (to a person, etc., specified).

live[2] /līv/ *adj.* **1** (*attrib.*) that is alive; living. **2** (of a broadcast, music, etc.) heard or seen at the time of its performance, not from a recording. **3** not obsolete or exhausted (*disarmament is still a live issue*). **4** expending or still able to expend energy, esp.: **a** (of coals) glowing; burning. **b** (of a shell) unexploded. **c** (of a wire, etc.) connected to a source of electrical power. **5** (of a wheel, etc., in machinery) moving or imparting motion.

live·a·ble var. of LIVABLE.

live-in *attrib.adj.* **1** (of a domestic employee) living in (*live-in maid*). **2** (of a sexual partner) cohabiting.

live·li·hood /lívleehŏŏd/ *n.* a means of living; sustenance.

live·long /lívlawng, –long/ *adj. poet.* or *rhet.* in its entire length or apparently so (*the livelong day*).

live·ly /lívlee/ *adj.* (**livelier, liveliest**) **1** full of life; vigorous; energetic. **2** brisk (*a lively pace*). **3** stimulating (*a lively discussion*). **4** vivacious; jolly; sociable. **5** *joc.* exciting; dangerous; difficult (*the press is making things lively for them*). **6** (of a color) bright and vivid. ▫▫ **live·li·ly** *adv.* **live·li·ness** *n.*

liv·en /lívən/ *v.tr. & intr.* (often foll. by *up*) *colloq.* brighten; cheer.

liv·er[1] /lívər/ *n.* **1 a** a large lobed glandular organ in the abdomen of vertebrates, functioning in many metabolic processes. **b** a similar organ in other animals. **2** the flesh of an animal's liver as food. **3** a dark reddish-brown color.

liv·er[2] /lívər/ *n.* a person who lives in a specified way (*a clean liver*).

Liv·er·pud·li·an /lívərpúdleeən/ *n. & adj.* • *n.* a native of Liverpool, England. • *adj.* of or relating to Liverpool.

liv·er spot(s) *n.(pl.)* brownish pigmentation of the skin, esp. of older people.

liv·er·wort /lívərwərt, –wawrt/ *n.* any small leafy or thalloid bryophyte of the class Hepaticae, of which some have liver-shaped parts.

liv·er·wurst /lívərwərst, –vərst/ *n.* a sausage containing cooked liver, etc.

liv·er·y /lívəree/ *n.* (*pl.* **-ies**) **1** distinctive clothing worn by a servant, official member of a guild, etc. **2** an establishment from which horses or vehicles can be hired. **3** a distinctive marking or outward appearance (*birds in their winter livery*). **4** a distinctive color scheme in which the vehicles, etc., of a particular company are painted. ▫▫ **liv·er·ied** *adj.* (esp. in senses 3, 4).

livery Middle English: from Old French *livree* 'delivered', feminine past participle of *livrer*, from Latin *liberare* 'liberate' (in medieval Latin 'hand over'). The original sense was 'the dispensing of food, provisions, or clothing to servants'; hence sense 4, also 'allowance of provender for horses', surviving in the phrase *at livery* and in LIVERY STABLE. SENSE 1 arose because medieval nobles provided matching clothes to distinguish their servants from others.

liv·er·y sta·ble *n.* a stable where horses are kept at livery or let out for hire.

lives *pl.* of LIFE.

live·stock /lívstok/ *n.* (usu. treated as *pl.*) animals, esp. on a farm, regarded as an asset.

live wire *n.* an energetic and forceful person.

liv·id /lívid/ *adj.* **1** *colloq.* furiously angry. **2 a** of a bluish leaden color. **b** discolored as by a bruise. ▫▫ **li·vid·i·ty** /–víditee/ *n.* **liv·id·ly** *adv.* **liv·id·ness** *n.*

liv·ing /líving/ *n. & adj.* • *n.* a livelihood or means of maintenance (*made my living as a journalist*; *what does she do for a living?*). • *adj.* **1** contemporary; now existent (*the greatest living poet*). **2** (of a likeness or image of a person) exact. **3** (of a language) still in vernacular use. **4** (of water) perennially flowing. ▫ **within living memory** within the memory of people still living.

liv·ing death *n.* a state of hopeless misery.

liv·ing room *n.* a room for general day use.

liv·ing wage *n.* a wage that affords the means of normal subsistence.

liv·ing will *n.* a written statement of a person's desire not to be kept alive by artificial means in the event of terminal illness or accident.

lix·iv·i·ate /liksívee-ayt/ *v.tr.* separate (a substance) into soluble and insoluble constituents by the percolation of liquid. ▫▫ **lix·iv·i·a·tion** /–áyshən/ *n.*

liz·ard /lízərd/ *n.* any reptile of the suborder Lacertilia, having usu. a long tail and a rough or scaly hide.

'll *v.* (usu. after pronouns) shall; will (*I'll*; *that'll*).

lla·ma /laámə, yáa–/ *n.* **1** a S. American ruminant, *Lama glama*, kept as a beast of burden and for its soft, woolly fleece. **2** the wool from this animal.

lla·no /laánō, yaá–/ *n.* (*pl.* **-nos**) a treeless grassy plain or steppe, esp. in S. America.

lo /lō/ *int. archaic* calling attention to an amazing sight. ▫ **lo and behold** *joc.* a formula introducing a surprising or unexpected fact.

load /lōd/ *n. & v.* • *n.* **1 a** what is carried or is to be carried; a burden. **b** an amount usu. or actually carried (often in *comb.*: *a busload of tourists*; *a truckload of bricks*). **2** a unit of measure or weight of certain substances. **3** a burden or commitment of work, responsibility, etc. **4** (in *pl.*; often foll. by *of*) *colloq.* plenty; a lot. **5 a** *Electr.* the amount of power supplied by a generating system at any given time. **b** *Electronics* an impedance or circuit that receives or develops the output of a transistor or other device. **6** the weight or force borne by the supporting part of a structure. **7** a material object or force acting as a weight or clog. **8** the resistance of machinery to motive power. • *v.* **1** *tr.* **a** put a load on or aboard (a person, ship, etc.). **b** place (a load or cargo) aboard a ship, etc. **2** *intr.* (often foll. by *up*) (of a ship, vehicle, or person) take a load aboard. **3** *tr.* (often foll. by *with*) **a** add weight to. **b** oppress. **4** *tr.* strain the bearing-capacity of (*a table loaded with food*). **5** *tr.* (also **load up**) (foll. by *with*) **a** supply overwhelmingly (*loaded us with work*). **b** assail overwhelmingly (*loaded us with abuse*). **6** *tr.* insert (the required operating medium) in a device, e.g., film in a camera, etc. **7** give a bias to (dice, a roulette wheel, etc.) with weights. ▫ **get a load of** *sl.* listen attentively to.

load·ed /lṓdid/ *adj.* **1** bearing or carrying a load. **2** *sl.* **a** wealthy. **b** drunk. **c** drugged. **3** (of dice, etc.) weighted or given a bias. **4** (of a question or statement) charged with some hidden or improper implication.

load·ing /lṓding/ *n.* **1** *Electr.* the maximum current or power taken by an appliance. **2** an increase in an insurance premium due to a factor increasing the risk involved (see LOAD *v.* 8).

load·star var. of LODESTAR.

load·stone var. of LODESTONE.

loaf[1] /lōf/ *n.* (*pl.* **loaves** /lōvz/) **1** a portion of baked bread, usu. of a standard size or shape. **2** (often in *comb.*) other food formed into a particular shape (*meat loaf*).

loaf[2] /lōf/ *v.* **1** *intr.* (often foll. by *around*) spend time idly. **2** *tr.* (foll. by *away*) waste (time) idly. **3** *intr.* saunter.

loaf·er /lṓfər/ *n.* **1** an idle person. **2** (**Loafer**) *Trademark* a leather shoe shaped like a moccasin with a flat heel.

loam /lōm/ *n.* **1** a fertile soil of clay and sand containing decayed vegetable matter. **2** a paste of clay and water with sand, chopped straw, etc., used in making bricks, plastering, etc. ▫▫ **loam·y** *adj.* **loam·i·ness** *n.*

loan /lōn/ *n. & v.* • *n.* **1** something lent, esp. a sum of money to be returned normally with interest. **2** the act of lending or state of being lent. **3** a word, custom, etc., adopted by one people from another. • *v.tr.* lend (esp. money). ▫▫ **loan·a·ble** *adj.* **loan·ee** /lōnée/ *n.* **loan·er** *n.*

▶Traditionally, **loan** was a noun and **lend** was a verb: *I went to ask for a loan. Can you lend me twenty dollars?* But **loan** is now widely used as a verb, especially in financial contexts.

loan shark *n. colloq.* a person who lends money at exorbitant rates of interest.

loan•word /lṓnwərd/ *n.* a word adopted, usu. with little modification, from a foreign language.

loath /lōth, lō<u>th</u>/ *predic.adj.* (also **loth**) (usu. foll. by *to* + infin.) disinclined; reluctant (*loath to admit it*). □ **nothing loath** *adj.* quite willing.

loathe /lō<u>th</u>/ *v.tr.* regard with disgust; detest. □□ **loath•ing** *n.*

loath•some /lṓ<u>th</u>səm, lṓth–/ *adj.* arousing hatred or disgust; offensive; repulsive. □□ **loath•some•ness** *n.*

loaves *pl.* of LOAF[1].

lob /lob/ *v. & n.* • *v.tr.* (**lobbed, lobbing**) **1** hit, throw, or fire slowly or in a high arc. **2** send (an opponent) a lobbed ball. • *n.* a ball traveling in a high arc.

lo•bar /lṓbər, –baar/ *adj.* **1** of the lungs (*lobar pneumonia*). **2** of, relating to, or affecting a lobe.

lo•bate /lṓbayt/ *adj. Biol.* having a lobe or lobes. □□ **lo•ba•tion** /–áyshən/ *n.*

lob•by /lóbee/ *n. & v.* • *n.* (*pl.* **-bies**) **1** a porch, anteroom, entrance hall, or corridor. **2** a body of persons seeking to influence legislators on behalf of a particular interest (*the tobacco lobby*). • *v.* (**-bies, -bied**) **1** *tr.* solicit the support of (an influential person). **2** *tr.* (of members of the public) seek to influence (the members of a legislature). □□ **lob•by•er** *n.* **lob•by•ism** *n.* **lob•by•ist** *n.*

lobe /lōb/ *n.* **1** a roundish and flattish projecting or pendulous part, often each of two or more such parts divided by a fissure (*lobes of the brain*). **2** = EARLOBE. □□ **lobed** *adj.* **lobe•less** *adj.*

lo•bec•to•my /lōbéktəmee/ *n.* (*pl.* **-mies**) *Surgery* the excision of a lobe of an organ such as the lung, etc.

lo•bel•ia /lōbéelyə/ *n.* any plant of the genus *Lobelia*, with blue, scarlet, white, or purple flowers having a deeply cleft corolla.

lo•bot•o•my /ləbótəmee/ *n.* (*pl.* **-mies**) *Surgery* see PREFRONTAL LOBOTOMY.

lob•ster /lóbstər/ *n. & v.* • *n.* **1** any large marine crustacean of the family Nephropidae, with two pincerlike claws as the first pair of ten limbs. **2** its flesh as food. • *v.intr.* catch lobsters.

lob•ster pot *n.* a basket in which lobsters are trapped.

lo•cal /lṓkəl/ *adj. & n.* • *adj.* **1** belonging to or existing in a particular place or places. **2** peculiar to or only encountered in a particular place or places. **3** of or belonging to the neighborhood (*the local doctor*). **4** of or affecting a part and not the whole (*local pain*). **5** in regard to place. • *n.* a local person or thing, esp.: **1** an inhabitant of a particular place regarded with reference to that place. **2** a local train, bus, etc. **3** a local anesthetic. **4** a local branch of a labor union. □□ **lo•cal•ize** /lṓkəlīz/ *v.tr.* **lo•cal•ly** *adv.* **lo•cal•ness** *n.*

lo•cal ar•e•a net•work *n. Computing* a system for linking telecommunications or computer equipment in several offices, a group of buildings, etc. ¶ Abbr.: **LAN**.

lo•cal col•or *n.* characteristics distinctive of a place, esp. as depicted in literature, film, etc.

lo•cale /lōkál/ *n.* a scene or locality, esp. with reference to an event or occurrence taking place there.

lo•cal•ism /lṓkəlizəm/ *n.* **1** preference for what is local. **2** a local idiom, custom, etc. **3 a** attachment to a place. **b** a limitation of ideas, etc., resulting from this.

lo•cal•i•ty /lōkálitee/ *n.* (*pl.* **-ties**) **1** a district or neighborhood. **2** the site or scene of something, esp. in relation to its surroundings. **3** the position of a thing; the place where it is.

lo•cal time *n.* **1** time measured from the sun's transit over the meridian of a place. **2** the time as reckoned in a particular place, esp. with reference to an event recorded there.

lo•cate /lṓkayt, lōkáyt/ *v.* **1** *tr.* discover the exact place or position of (*locate the enemy's camp*). **2** *tr.* establish or install in a place or in its proper place. **3** *tr.* state the locality of. **4** *tr.* (in *passive*) be situated. **5** *intr.* (often foll. by *in*) take up residence or business (in a place). □□ **lo•cat•a•ble** *adj.* **lo•cat•er** *n.* **lo•ca•tor** *n.*

▶In formal English one should avoid using **locate** to mean merely 'find,' e.g., *It drives him out of his mind when he can't locate something.* In precise usage **locate** means 'fix the position of, put in place,' e.g., *The studio should be located on a north-facing slope.*

locate early 16th cent.: from Latin *locat-* 'placed', from the verb *locare*, from *locus* 'place'. The original sense was as a legal term meaning 'let out on hire', later (late 16th cent.) 'assign to a particular place', then (particularly in North American usage) 'establish in a place'. The sense 'discover the exact position of' dates from the late 19th cent.

lo•ca•tion /lōkáyshən/ *n.* **1** a particular place. **2** the act of locating or process of being located. **3** an actual place or natural setting featured in a motion picture, etc.

loc•a•tive /lókətiv/ *n. & adj. Gram.* • *n.* the case of nouns, pronouns, and adjectives, expressing location. • *adj.* of or in the locative.

loc. cit. /lók sít/ *abbr.* in the passage already cited.

loch /lok, lo<u>kh</u>/ *n. Sc.* **1** a lake. **2** an arm of the sea, esp. when narrow or partially landlocked.

lo•ci *pl.* of LOCUS.

lock[1] /lok/ *n. & v.* • *n.* **1** a mechanism for fastening a door, lid, etc., with a bolt that requires a key or a combination of movements (see COMBINATION LOCK), to work it. **2** a confined section of a canal or river where the water level can be changed by the use of gates and sluices. **3** the turning of the front wheels of a vehicle. **4** an interlocked or jammed state. **5** *Wrestling* a hold that keeps an opponent's limb fixed. **6** an appliance to keep a wheel from revolving or slewing. **7** a mechanism for exploding the charge of a gun. • *v.* **1 a** *tr.* fasten with a lock. **b** *tr.* (foll. by *up*) shut and secure by locking. **c** *intr.* (of a door, window, etc.) have the means of being locked. **2** *tr.* (foll. by *up, in, into*) enclose by locking or as if by locking. **3** *tr.* (often foll. by *up, away*) allocate inaccessibly (*capital locked up in land*). **4** *tr.* (foll. by *in*) hold fast (in sleep or enchantment, etc.). **5** *tr.* (usu. in *passive*) (of land, hills, etc.) enclose. **6** *tr. & intr.* make or become rigidly fixed or immovable. **7** *intr. & tr.* become or cause to become caught. **8** *tr.* (often in *passive*; foll. by *in*) entangle in an embrace or struggle. □ **lock on to** locate or cause to locate by radar, etc., and then track. **lock out 1** keep (a person) out by locking the door. **2** (of an employer) submit (employees) to a lockout. □□ **lock•a•ble** *adj.* **lock•less** *adj.*

lock[2] /lok/ *n.* **1 a** a portion of hair that coils or hangs together. **b** (in *pl.*) the hair of the head. **2** a tuft of wool or cotton. □□ **-locked** *adj.* (in *comb.*).

lock•er /lókər/ *n.* **1** a small lockable cupboard or compartment, esp. each of several for public use. **2** *Naut.* a chest or compartment for clothes, ammunition, etc. **3** a person or thing that locks.

lock•et /lókit/ *n.* **1** a small ornamental case holding a portrait, lock of hair, etc., and usu. hung from the neck. **2** a metal plate or band on a scabbard.

lock•jaw /lókjaw/ *n.* = TRISMUS.

▶**Lockjaw** is not in technical use; the correct term is **trismus**.

lock•keep•er /lók-keépər/ *n.* a keeper of a lock on a river or canal.

lock•nut /lóknut/ *n. Mech.* a nut screwed down on another to keep it tight.

lock•out /lókowt/ *n.* the exclusion of employees by their employer from their place of work until certain terms are agreed to.

lock•smith /lóksmith/ *n.* a maker and repairer of locks.

lock•step /lókstep/ *n.* marching with each person as close as possible to the one in front.

lock•stitch /lókstich/ *n.* a stitch made by firmly locking together two threads or stitches.

lock, stock, and bar•rel *n. & adv.* • *n.* the whole of a thing. • *adv.* completely.

lock•up /lókup/ *n.* **1** a house or room for the temporary detention of prisoners. **2 a** the locking up of premises for the night. **b** the time of doing this. **3 a** the unrealizable state of invested capital. **b** an amount of capital locked up.

lo•co /lṓkō/ *adj. & n.* • *adj. sl.* crazy. • *n.* (*pl.* **-cos** or **-coes**) **1** *colloq.* = LOCOWEED. **2** *sl.* a crazy person; maniac.

lo•co•mo•tion /lṓkəmṓshən/ *n.* **1** motion or the power of motion from one place to another. **2** travel; a means of traveling, esp. an artificial one.

lo•co•mo•tive /lṓkəmṓtiv/ *n. & adj.* • *n.* (in full **locomotive engine**) an engine powered by steam, diesel fuel, or electricity, used for pulling trains. • *adj.* **1** of or relating to or effecting locomotion. **2** having the power of or given to locomotion; not stationary.

lo•co•mo•tor /lṓkəmṓtər/ *adj.* of or relating to locomotion.

lo•co•weed /lṓkōweed/ *n.* a poisonous leguminous plant of the southwestern US, causing brain disease in cattle eating it.

lo•cus /lṓkəs/ *n.* (*pl.* **loci** /lṓsī, –kee, –kī/) **1** a position or point, esp. in a text, treatise, etc. **2** *Math.* a curve, etc., formed by all the points satisfying a particular equation of the relation between coordinates, or by a point, line, or surface moving according to mathematically defined conditions.

lo•cust /lṓkəst/ *n.* **1** any of various African and Asian grasshoppers of the family Acrididae, migrating in swarms. **2** a cicada. **3** (in full **locust bean**) a carob. **4** (in full **locust tree**) **a** a carob tree. **b** = ACACIA 2.

lo•cu•tion /lōkyṓoshən/ *n.* **1** a word or phrase, esp. considered in regard to style or idiom. **2** style of speech.

lode /lōd/ *n.* a vein of metal ore.

lo•den /lṓd'n/ *n.* **1** a thick, waterproof woolen cloth. **2** the dark green color in which this is often made.

lode•star /lṓdstaar/ *n.* (also **load•star**) **1** a star that a ship, etc., is steered by, esp. the pole star. **2 a** a guiding principle. **b** an object of pursuit.

lode•stone /lṓdstōn/ *n.* (also **load•stone**) **1** magnetic oxide of iron; magnetite. **2 a** a piece of this used as a magnet. **b** a thing that attracts.

lodge /loj/ *n. & v.* • *n.* **1** a small house at the gates of a park or on the grounds of a large house, occupied by a gatekeeper, etc. **2** any large house or hotel, esp. in a resort. **3** a house occupied in the hunting or shooting season. **4** a porter's room or quarters at the gate of a college or other large building. **5** the members or the meeting place of a branch of a society such as the Freemasons. **6** a beaver's or otter's lair. **7** a type of Native American dwelling; a wigwam. • *v.* **1** *tr.* deposit in court or with an official a formal statement of (complaint or information). **2** *tr.* deposit (money, etc.) for security. **3** *tr.* bring forward (an objection, etc.). **4** *tr.* (foll. by *in, with*) place (power, etc.) in a person or group. **5** *tr. & intr.* make or become fixed without further movement (*the bullet lodged in his brain*). **6** *tr.* **a** provide with sleeping quarters. **b** receive as a guest or inmate. **c** establish as a resident in a house or room or rooms. **7** *intr.* reside or live, esp. as a guest paying for accommodations. **8** *tr.* serve as a habitation for; contain.

lodge•pole pine /lójpōl/ *n.* a straight-trunked pine tree (*Pinus contorta*) of western North America, widely grown for timber and traditionally used by some American Indians in the construction of lodges.

lodg•er /lójər/ *n.* a person receiving accommodations in another's house for payment.

lodg•ing /lójing/ *n.* **1** temporary accommodations. **2** a dwelling place.

lodg•ing house *n.* a house in which lodgings are rented.

lo•ess /lṓis, les, lus/ *n.* a deposit of fine, light-colored windblown dust found esp. in the basins of large rivers.

loft /lawft, loft/ *n. & v.* • *n.* **1** the space under the roof of a house, above the ceiling of the top floor; an attic. **2** a room over a stable, esp. for hay and straw. **3** a gallery in a church or hall (*organ loft*). **4** an upstairs room. **5** a pigeon house. **6** *Golf* **a** a backward slope in a club head. **b** a lofting stroke. • *v.tr.* **1 a** send (a ball, etc.) high up. **b** clear (an obstacle) in this way. **2** (esp. as **lofted** *adj.*) give a loft to (a golf club).

loft•y /láwftee, lóf–/ *adj.* (**loftier, loftiest**) **1** *literary* (of things) of imposing height; towering (*lofty heights*). **2** consciously haughty, aloof, or dignified (*lofty contempt*). **3** sublime (*lofty ideals*). □□ **loft•i•ly** *adv.* **loft•i•ness** *n.*

log[1] /lawg, log/ *n. & v.* • *n.* **1** an unhewn piece of a felled tree, or a similar rough mass of wood, esp. cut for firewood. **2 a** a float attached to a line wound on a reel for gauging the speed of a ship. **b** any other apparatus for the same purpose. **3** a record of events occurring during and affecting the voyage of a ship or aircraft (including the rate of a ship's progress shown by a log; see sense 2). **4** any systematic record of things done, experienced, etc. **5** = LOGBOOK. • *v.tr.* (**logged, logging**) **1 a** enter (the distance made or other details) in a logbook. **b** enter details about (a person or event) in a logbook. **c** (of a ship) achieve (a certain distance). **2 a** enter (information) in a regular record. **b** attain (a cumulative total of time, etc., recorded in this way) (*logged 50 hours on the computer*). **3** cut into logs. □ **like a log 1** in a helpless or stunned state (*the blow to the head made him fall like a log*). **2** without stirring (*slept like a log*). **log in** = *log on* **log on** (or **off**) go through the procedures to begin (or conclude) use of a computer system.

log[2] /lawg, log/ *n.* a logarithm (esp. prefixed to a number or algebraic symbol whose logarithm is to be indicated).

lo•gan•ber•ry /lṓgənberee/ *n.* (*pl.* **-ries**) **1** a hybrid, *Rubus loganobaccus*, between a blackberry and a raspberry with dull red acid fruits. **2** the fruit of this plant.

log•a•rithm /láwgərithəm, lóg–/ *n.* **1** one of a series of arithmetic exponents tabulated to simplify computation by making it possible to use addition and subtraction instead of multiplication and division. **2** the power to which a fixed number or base (see BASE[1] 7) must be raised to produce a given number (*the logarithm of 1,000 to base 10 is 3*). ¶ Abbr.: **log.** □□ **log•a•rith•mic** /–ríthmik/ *adj.* **log•a•rith•mi•cal•ly** *adv.*

log•book /láwgbook, lóg–/ *n.* a book containing a detailed record or log.

loge /lōzh/ *n.* (in a theater, etc.) **1** the front section of the first balcony. **2** a private box or enclosure.

log•ger /láwgər, lóg–/ *n.* a lumberjack.

log•ger•head /láwgərhed, lóg–/ *n.* **1** an iron instrument with a ball at the end heated for melting tar, etc. **2** any of various large-headed animals, esp. a turtle (*Caretta caretta*). □ **at loggerheads** (often foll. by *with*) disagreeing or disputing.

log•gia /lójeeə, láwj;n–/ *n.* **1** an open-sided gallery or arcade. **2** an open-sided extension of a house.

log•ging /láwging, lóg–/ *n.* the work of cutting and preparing forest timber.

log•ic /lójik/ *n.* **1 a** the science of reasoning, proof, thinking, or inference. **b** a particular scheme of or treatise on this. **2 a** a chain of reasoning (*I don't follow your logic*). **b** the correct or incorrect use of reasoning (*your logic is flawed*). **c** ability in reasoning (*argues with great learning and logic*). **d** arguments (*is not governed by logic*). **3 a** the inexorable force or compulsion of a thing (*the logic of events*). **b** the necessary consequence of (an argument, decision, etc.). **4 a** principles underlying the arrangements of elements in a computer or electronic device so as to perform a specified task. **b** logical operations collectively. □□ **lo•gi•cian** /ləjíshən/ *n.*

-logic /lójik/ *comb. form* (also **–logical** /lójikəl/) forming adjectives corresponding esp. to nouns in *–logy* (*analogic; theological*).

log•i•cal /lójikəl/ *adj.* **1** of logic or formal argument. **2** not contravening the laws of thought; correctly reasoned. **3** reasonably to be believed or done. **4** capable of or displaying correct reasoning. □□ **log•i•cal•i•ty** /–kálitee/ *n.* **log•i•cal•ly** *adv.*

log•i•cal ne•ces•si•ty the compulsion to believe that of which the opposite is inconceivable.

lo•gis•tics /ləjístiks/ *n.pl.* **1** the organization of moving, lodging, and supplying troops and equipment. **2** the detailed organization and implementation of a plan. □□ **lo•gis•tic** *adj.* **lo•gis•ti•cal** *adj.* **lo•gis•ti•cal•ly** *adv.*

log•jam /láwgjam, log–/ *n.* **1** a crowded mass of logs in a river. **2** a deadlock.

lo•go /lṓgō/ *n.* (*pl.* **-gos**) *colloq.* **1** = LOGOTYPE 2. **2** a motto, esp. of a commercial product, etc.

log•o•gram /láwgəgram, lóg;n–/ *n.* a sign or character representing a word, esp. in shorthand.

log•or•rhe•a /láwgərééə, lóg–/ *n.* an excessive flow of words, esp. in mental illness.

Lo•gos /lṓgōs, lógos/ *n. Theol.* the Word of God, associated with Jesus Christ.

lo•go•type /láwgətīp, lóg–/ *n.* **1** *Printing* a single piece of type that prints a word or group of separate letters. **2 a** an emblem or device used as the badge of an organization in display material. **b** *Printing* a single piece of type that prints this.

log•roll•ing /láwgrōling, lóg–/ *n.* **1** *colloq.* the practice of exchanging favors, esp. (in politics) of exchanging votes to mutual benefit. **2** a sport in which two contestants stand on a floating log and try to knock each other off. □□ **log•roll** *v.intr. & tr.* **log•roll•er** *n.*

log•wood /láwgwŏŏd, lóg;n–/ *n.* **1** a W. Indian tree, *Haematoxylon campechianum*. **2** the wood of this, producing a substance used in dyeing.

loin /loyn/ *n.* **1** (in *pl.*) the part of the body on both sides of the spine between the false ribs and the hipbones. **2** a cut of meat that includes the loin vertebrae.

loin•cloth /lóynklawth, –kloth/ *n.* a cloth worn around the loins, esp. as a sole garment.

loi•ter /lóytər/ *v.* **1** *intr.* hang around; linger idly. **2** *intr.* travel indolently and with long pauses. **3** *tr.* (foll. by *away*) pass (time, etc.) in loitering. □□ **loi•ter•er** *n.* **loi•ter•ing** *n.*

loll /lol/ *v.* **1** *intr.* stand, sit, or recline in a lazy attitude. **2** *intr.* (foll. by *out*) (of the tongue) hang out. **3** *tr.* (foll. by *out*) hang (one's tongue) out. **4** *tr.* let (one's head or limbs) rest lazily on something. □□ **loll•er** *n.*

lol•li•pop /lóleepop/ *n.* a large, usu. flat, round candy on a small stick.

lo•ment /lṓment/ *n. Bot.* a kind of pod that breaks up into one-seeded joints when mature. □□ **lo•men•ta•ceous** /–táyshəs/ *adj.*

lone /lōn/ *attrib.adj.* **1** (of a person) solitary; without a companion or supporter. **2** (of a place) unfrequented; uninhabited. **3** *literary* feeling or causing to feel lonely.

lone•ly /lṓnlee/ *adj.* (**lonelier, loneliest**) **1** solitary; companionless; isolated. **2** (of a place) unfrequented. **3** sad because without friends or company. □□ **lone•li•ness** *n.*

lone•ly heart *n.* a lonely (in sense 3) person.

lon•er /lṓnər/ *n.* a person or animal that prefers not to associate with others.

lone•some /lṓnsəm/ *adj.* **1** solitary; lonely. **2** feeling lonely or forlorn. **3** causing such a feeling. □ **by** (or **on**) **one's lonesome** all alone. □□ **lone•some•ness** *n.*

lone wolf *n.* a person who prefers to act alone.

long[1] /lawng, long/ *adj., n., & adv.* • *adj.* (**longer** /láwnggər, lóng–/; **longest** /láwnggist, lóng–/) **1** measuring much from end to end in space or time (*a long line; a long journey; a long time ago*). **2** (following a measurement) in length or duration (*three miles long*). **3** relatively great in extent or duration (*a long meeting*). **4 a** consisting of a large number of items (*a long list*). **b** seemingly more than the stated amount; tedious; lengthy (*ten long miles; tired after a long day*). **5** of elongated shape. **6 a** lasting or reaching far back or forward in time (*a long friendship*). **b** (of a person's memory) retaining things for a long time. **7** far-reaching; acting at a distance; involving a great interval or difference. **8** *Phonet. & Prosody* of a vowel or syllable: **a** having the greater of the two recognized durations. **b** stressed. **c** (of a vowel in English) having the pronunciation shown in the name of the letter (as in *pile* and *cute*, which have a long *i* and *u*, as distinct from *pill* and *cut*). **9** (of odds or a chance) reflecting or representing a low level of probability. **10** (of a cold drink) large and refreshing. **11** *colloq.* (of a person) tall. **12** (foll. by *on*) *colloq.* well supplied with. • *n.* **1** a long interval or period (*shall not be away for long; it will not take long*). **2** *Phonet.* **a** a long syllable or vowel. **b** a mark indicating that a vowel is long. **3 a** long-dated stock. **b** a person who buys this. • *adv.* (**longer** /lónggər/; **longest** /lónggist/) **1** by or for a long time (*long before; long ago; long live the king!*). **2** (following nouns of duration) throughout a specified time (*all day long*). **3** (in *compar.*; with *neg.*) after an implied point of time (*shall not wait any longer*). □ **as** (or **so**) **long as 1** during the whole time that. **2** provided that; only if. **before long** fairly soon (*shall see you before long*). **be long** (often foll. by *pres. part.* or *in* + verbal noun) take a long time; be slow (*I won't be long*). **in the long run 1** over a long period. **2** eventually; finally. **the long and the short of it 1** all that can or need be said. **2** the eventual outcome. □□ **long•ish** *adj.*

long[2] /lawng, long/ *v.intr.* (foll. by *for* or *to* + infin.) have a strong wish or desire for.

long. *abbr.* longitude.

long•board /láwngbawrd, lóng–/ *n.* a type of surfboard.

long•boat /láwngbōt, lóng–/ *n.* a sailing ship's largest boat.

long•bow /láwngbō, lóng–/ *n.* a bow drawn by hand and shooting a long feathered arrow.

long-dis•tance *adj.* **1** (of a telephone call, public transport, etc.) between distant places. **2** (of a weather forecast) long-range.

long di•vi•sion *n.* division of numbers with details of the calculations written down.

long-drawn *adj.* (also **long-drawn-out**) prolonged, esp. unduly.

longe /lonj/ *n. & v.* (also **lunge** /lunj/) • *n.* **1** a long rope on which a horse is held and made to move in a circle around its trainer. **2** a circular exercise ground for training horses. • *v.tr.* exercise (a horse) with or in a longe.

lon•ge•ron /lónjərən/ *n.* a longitudinal member of a plane's fuselage.

lon·gev·i·ty /lonjévitee, lawn–/ *n.* long life.

long face *n.* a dismal or disappointed expression. ▫▫ **long-faced** *adj.*

long·hand /láwnghand, lóng–/ *n.* ordinary handwriting (as opposed to shorthand or typing or printing).

long haul *adj.* **1** the transport of goods or passengers over a long distance. **2** a prolonged effort or task.

long·head·ed /láwnghedid, long–/ *adj.* shrewd; far-seeing. ▫▫ **long·head·ed·ness** *n.*

long·horn /láwnghawrn, lóng–/ *n.* **1** one of a breed of cattle with long horns. **2** any beetle of the family Cerambycidae with long antennae.

long·house /láwnghows, lóng–/ *n.* a tribal communal dwelling, esp. in N. America and the Far East.

long·ing /láwnging, lóng–/ *n. & adj.* •*n.* a feeling of intense desire. •*adj.* having or showing this feeling. ▫▫ **long·ing·ly** *adv.*

lon·gi·tude /lónjitood, –tyood, láwn–/ *n.* **1** *Geog.* the angular distance east or west from a standard meridian such as Greenwich to the meridian of any place. **2** *Astron.* the angular distance of a celestial body north or south of the ecliptic measured along a great circle through the body and the poles of the ecliptic.

longitude, 1

lon·gi·tu·di·nal /lónjitóod'nəl, –tyóod–, láwn–/ *adj.* **1** of or in length. **2** running lengthwise. **3** of longitude. ▫▫ **lon·gi·tu·di·nal·ly** *adv.*

long johns *n.pl. colloq.* = LONG UNDERWEAR.

long jump *n.* a track-and-field contest of jumping as far as possible along the ground in one leap.

long-lived *adj.* having a long life; durable.

long-range *adj.* **1** extending or designed to cover a long distance. **2** extending far into the future.

long-run·ning *adj.* continuing for a long time.

long·shore /láwngshawr, lóng–/ *adj.* **1** existing on or frequenting the shore. **2** directed along the shore.

long·shore·man /láwngshawrmən, lóng–/ *n.* (*pl.* **-men**) a person employed to load and unload ships.

long shot *n.* **1** a wild guess or venture. **2** a bet at long odds. **3** *Cinematog.* a shot including objects at a distance. ▫ **not by a long shot** by no means.

long·sight·ed /láwngsítid, lóng–/ *adj.* **1** able to see clearly only what is comparatively distant. **2** having imagination or foresight. ▫▫ **long·sight·ed·ness** *n.*

long-sleeved *adj.* with sleeves reaching to the wrist.

long-stand·ing *adj.* that has long existed; not recent.

long-suf·fer·ing *adj.* bearing provocation patiently. ▫▫ **long-suf·fer·ing·ly** *adv.*

long suit *n.* **1** many cards of one suit in a hand (esp. more than 3 or 4 in a hand of 13). **2** a thing at which one excels.

long-term *adj.* occurring in or relating to a long period of time (*long-term plans*).

long·time /láwngtīm, long–/ *adj.* that has been such for a long time.

long un·der·wear *n.* a warm, close-fitting undergarment with ankle-length legs and often a long-sleeved top.

long·ways /láwngwayz, lóng–/ *adv.* (also **long·wise** /–wīz/) = LENGTHWISE.

long-wind·ed /láwngwíndid, lóng–/ *adj.* **1** (of speech or writing) tediously lengthy. **2** able to run a long distance without rest. ▫▫ **long-wind·ed·ly** *adv.* **long-wind·ed·ness** *n.*

loo·fah /lóofə/ *n.* (also **luf·fa** /lúfə/) **1** a climbing gourdlike plant, *Luffa cylindrica*, native to Asia, producing edible marrowlike fruits. **2** the dried fibrous vascular system of this fruit used as a sponge.

look /look/ *v., n., & int.* •*v.* **1 a** *intr.* (often foll. by *at*) use one's sight; turn one's eyes in some direction. **b** *tr.* turn one's eyes on; contemplate or examine (*looked me in the eyes*). **2** *intr.* **a** make a visual or mental search (*I'll look in the morning*). **b** (foll. by *at*) consider; examine (*we must look at the facts*). **3** *intr.* (foll. by *for*) **a** search for. **b** hope or be on the watch for. **c** expect. **4** *intr.* inquire (*when one looks deeper*). **5** *intr.* have a specified appearance; seem (*look a fool*; *look foolish*). **6** *intr.* (foll. by *to*) **a** consider; take care of; be careful about (*look to the future*). **b** rely on (a person or thing) (*you can look to me for support*). **c** expect. **7** *intr.* (foll. by *into*) investigate or examine. **8** *tr.* (foll. by *what, where*, etc. + clause) ascertain or observe by sight (*look where we are*). **9** *intr.* (of a thing) face or be turned, or have or afford an outlook, in a specified direction. **10** *tr.* express, threaten, or show (an emotion, etc.) by one's looks. **11** *intr.* (foll. by *that* + clause) take care; make sure. **12** *intr.* (foll. by *to* + infin.) expect (*am looking to finish this today*). •*n.* **1** an act of looking; a glance (*a scornful look*). **2** (in *sing.* or *pl.*) the appearance of a face; a person's expression or personal aspect. **3** the (esp. characteristic) appearance of a thing (*the place has a European look*). *int.* (also **look here!**) calling attention, expressing a protest, etc. ▫ **look after 1** attend to; take care of. **2** follow with the eye. **3** seek for. **look alive** (or **lively**) *colloq.* be brisk and alert. **look around 1** look in every or another direction. **2** examine the objects of interest in a place. **3** examine the possibilities, etc., with a view to deciding on a course of action. **look as if** suggest by appearance the belief that (*it looks as if he's gone*). **look back 1** (foll. by *on, upon, to*) turn one's thoughts to (something past). **2** (usu. with *neg.*) cease to progress (*since then we have never looked back*). **look before you leap** avoid precipitate action. **look down on** (or **upon** or **look down one's nose at**) regard with contempt or a feeling of superiority. **look forward to** await (an expected event) eagerly or with specified feelings. **look in** make a short visit or call. **look a person in the eye** (or **eyes** or **face**) look directly and unashamedly at him or her. **look like** have the appearance of.. **look on 1** (often foll. by *as*) regard (*looks on you as a friend*). **2** be a spectator; avoid participation. **look oneself** appear in good health (esp. after illness, etc.). **look one's age** appear to be as old as one really is. **look out 1** direct one's sight out of a window, etc. **2** (often foll. by *for*) be vigilant or prepared. **3** (foll. by *on, over*, etc.) have or afford a specified outlook. **look over 1** inspect or survey (*looked over the house*). **2** examine (a document, etc.), esp. cursorily (*I'll look it over*). **look sharp** act promptly; make haste. **look through 1** examine the contents of, esp. cursorily. **2** penetrate (a pretense or pretender) with insight. **3** ignore by pretending not to see (*I waved, but you just looked through me*). **look up 1** search for (esp. information in a book). **2** *colloq.* go to visit (a person). **look up to** respect or venerate. **not like the look of** find alarming or suspicious. ▫▫ **-looking** *adj.* (in *comb.*).

look-a-like *n.* a person or thing closely resembling another (*an Elvis look-alike*).

look·er /lóókər/ *n.* **1** a person having a specified appearance (*a good-looker*). **2** *colloq.* an attractive person.

look·er-on *n.* a person who is a mere spectator.

look·ing glass /lóóking glas/ *n.* a mirror for looking at oneself.

look·out /lóókowt/ *n.* **1** a watch or looking out (*on the lookout for bargains*). **2 a** a post of observation. **b** a person or party or boat stationed to keep watch.

look-see *n. colloq.* a survey or inspection.

loom[1] /lōōm/ *n.* an apparatus for weaving yarn or thread into fabric.

loom[2] /lōōm/ *v.intr.* (often foll. by *up*) **1** come into sight dimly, esp. as a vague and often threatening shape. **2** (of an event or prospect) be ominously close.

loon /lōōn/ *n.* **1** any aquatic diving bird of the family Gaviidae, with a long, slender body and a sharp bill; a diver. **2** *colloq.* a crazy person (cf. LOONY).

loon·y /lóónee/ *n. & adj. sl.* • *n.* (*pl.* **-ies**) a mad or silly person; a lunatic. • *adj.* (**loonier, looniest**) crazy; silly. ▫▫ **loon·i·ness** *n.*

loon·y bin *n. sl.* a mental home or hospital.

loop /lōōp/ *n. & v.* • *n.* **1 a** a figure produced by a curve, or a doubled thread, etc., that crosses itself. **b** anything forming this figure. **2** a similarly shaped attachment or ornament formed of cord or thread, etc., and fastened at the crossing. **3** a ring or curved piece of material as a handle, etc. **4** a contraceptive coil. **5** a railroad or telegraph line that diverges from a main line and joins it again. **6** a maneuver in which an airplane describes a vertical loop. **7** *Skating* a maneuver describing a curve that crosses itself, made on a single edge. **8** *Electr.* a complete circuit for a current. **9** an endless strip of tape or film allowing continuous repetition. **10** *Computing* a programmed sequence of instructions that is repeated until or while a condition is satisfied. • *v.* **1** *tr.* form (thread, etc.) into a loop or loops. **2** *tr.* enclose with or as with a loop. **3** *tr.* (often foll. by *up, back, together*) fasten or join with a loop or loops. **4** *intr.* **a** form a loop. **b** move in looplike patterns.

loop·er /lóópər/ *n.* **1** a caterpillar of the geometer moth, which progresses by arching itself into loops. **2** a device for making loops.

loop·hole /lóóp-hōl/ *n.* **1** a means of evading a rule, etc., without infringing the letter of it. **2** a narrow vertical slit in a wall.

loop·y /lóópee/ *adj.* (**loopier, loopiest**) **1** *sl.* crazy. **2** having many loops.

loose /lōōs/ *adj., n., & v.* • *adj.* **1 a** not or no longer held by bonds or restraint. **b** (of an animal) not confined or tethered, etc. **2** detached or detachable from its place (*has come loose*). **3** not held together or contained or fixed. **4** not specially fastened or packaged (*loose papers; had her hair loose*). **5** hanging partly free (*a loose end*). **6** slack; relaxed; not tense or tight. **7** not compact or dense (*loose soil*). **8** (of language, concepts, etc.) inexact; conveying only the general sense. **9** (preceding an agent noun) doing the expressed action in a loose or careless manner (*a loose thinker*). **10** morally lax; dissolute (*loose living*). **11** (of the tongue) likely to speak indiscreetly. **12** (of the bowels) tending to diarrhea. • *n.* **1** a state of freedom or unrestrainedness. **2** loose play in soccer (*in the loose*). **3** free expression. • *v.tr.* **1** release; set free; free from constraint. **2** untie or undo (something that constrains). **3** detach from moorings. **4** relax (*loosed my hold on it*). **5** discharge (a bullet or arrow, etc.). ▫ **at loose ends** (of a person) unoccupied, esp. temporarily. **on the loose 1** escaped from captivity. **2** having a free enjoyable time. **play fast and loose** ignore one's obligations; be unreliable; trifle. ▫▫ **loose·ly** *adv.* **loose·ness** *n.*

▶The adjective **loose**, meaning 'not tight,' should not be confused with the verb **loose**, which means 'let go': *They loosed the reins and let the horse gallop.* This verb in turn should not be confused with the verb *lose*, which means 'be deprived of, fail to keep': *I will lose my keys if I don't mend the hole in my pocket. The neighbors will lose their house if the mortgage is not paid.*

loose change *n.* money as coins in the pocket, etc., for casual use.

loose-leaf *adj. & n.* • *adj.* (of a notebook, manual, etc.) with each leaf separate and removable. • *n.* a loose-leaf notebook, etc.

loose-limbed *adj.* having supple limbs.

loos·en /lóósən/ *v.* **1** *tr. & intr.* make or become less tight or compact or firm. **2** *tr.* make (a regime, etc.) less severe. **3** *tr.* release (the bowels) from constipation. ▫ **loosen a person's tongue** make a person talk freely. ▫▫ **loos·en·er** *n.*

loose·strife /lóós-strīf/ *n.* **1** any marsh plant of the genus *Lysimachia*, esp. the golden or yellow loosestrife, *L. vulgaris*. **2** any plant of the genus *Lythrum*, esp. the purple loosestrife, *L. salicaria*, with racemes of star-shaped purple flowers.

loot /lōōt/ *n. & v.* • *n.* **1** goods taken from an enemy; booty; spoils. **2** illicit gains made by an official. **3** *sl.* money. • *v.tr.* **1** plunder (premises) or steal (goods) left unprotected, esp. after riots. **2** plunder or sack (a city, building, etc.). **3** carry off as booty. ▫▫ **loot·er** *n.*

lop[1] /lop/ *v.* (**lopped, lopping**) **1** *tr.* **a** (often foll. by *off, away*) cut or remove (a part or parts) from a whole, esp. branches from a tree. **b** remove branches from (a tree). **2** *tr.* (often foll. by *off, away*) remove (items) as superfluous. **3** *intr.* (foll. by *at*) make lopping strokes on (a tree, etc.). ▫▫ **lop·per** *n.*

lop[2] /lop/ *v.* (**lopped, lopping**) **1** *intr. & tr.* hang limply. **2** *intr.* (foll. by *about*) slouch; dawdle. **3** *intr.* move with short bounds. **4** *tr.* (of an animal) let (the ears) hang.

lope /lōp/ *v. & n.* • *v.intr.* (esp. of animals) run with a long bounding stride. • *n.* a long bounding stride.

lop-eared *adj.* (of an animal) having drooping ears.

lop·sid·ed /lópsídid/ *adj.* **1** with one side lower or smaller than the other. **2** uneven or unbalanced (*a lopsided victory*). ▫▫ **lop·sid·ed·ly** *adv.* **lop·sid·ed·ness** *n.*

lo·qua·cious /lōkwáyshəs/ *adj.* **1** talkative. **2** (of birds or water) chattering; babbling. ▫▫ **lo·qua·cious·ly** *adv.* **lo·qua·cious·ness** *n.* **lo·quac·i·ty** /–kwásitee/ *n.*

lord /lawrd/ *n., int., & v.* • *n.* **1** a master or ruler. **2** *hist.* a feudal superior, esp. of a manor. **3** (in the UK) a peer of the realm or a person entitled to the title *Lord*. **4** (**Lord**) (often prec. by *the*) a name for God or Christ. **5** (**Lord**) prefixed as the designation of a marquess, earl, viscount, or baron. • *int.* (**Lord**) expressing surprise, dismay, etc. • *v.tr.* confer the title of Lord upon. ▫ **lord it over** domineer. **lord over** (usu. in *passive*) domineer; rule over. ▫▫ **lord·like** *adj.*

lord·ly /láwrdlee/ *adj.* (**lordlier, lordliest**) **1** haughty; imperious. **2** suitable for a lord. ▫▫ **lord·li·ness** *n.*

lord·ship /láwrdship/ *n.* **1** (usu. **Lordship**) a title used in addressing or referring to a man with the rank of Lord or (in the UK) a judge or a bishop (*Your Lordship; His Lordship*). **2** (foll. by *of, over*) dominion, rule, or ownership. **3** the condition of being a lord.

Lord's Prayer *n.* the prayer taught by Jesus to his disciples. Also called the **Our Father.**

lore /lawr/ *n.* a body of traditions and knowledge on a subject or of a particular group (*herbal lore; gypsy lore*).

lor·gnette /lawrnyét/ *n.* (in *sing.* or *pl.*) a pair of eyeglasses or opera glasses held by a long handle.

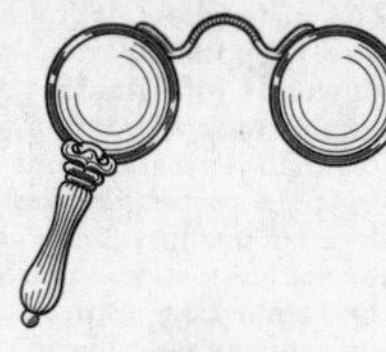
lorgnette

lor·i·cate /láwrikayt, –kit, lór;n–/ *adj.* & *n.* *Zool.*• *adj.* having a defensive armor of bone, plates, scales, etc.• *n.* an animal with this.

lo·ris /láwris/ *n.* (*pl.* same) either of two tailless nocturnal primates, *Loris tardigradus* of S. India (**slender loris**), and *Nycticebus coucang* of the E. Indies (**slow loris**).

lorn /lawrn/ *adj. literary* desolate; forlorn; abandoned.

lor·ry /láwree, lór–/ *n. Brit.* (*pl.* **-ries**) **1** a large strong motor vehicle for transporting goods, etc.; a truck. **2** a long flat low wagon. **3** a railway freight car.

lo·ry /láwree/ *n.* (*pl.* **-ries**) any of various brightly colored Australasian parrots of the subfamily Loriinae.

lose /lo͞oz/ *v.* (*past* and *past part.* **lost** /lawst, lost/) **1** *tr.* be deprived of or cease to have, esp. by negligence or misadventure. **2** *tr.* **a** be deprived of (a person, esp. a close relative) by death. **b** undergo the loss of (a baby) in childbirth. **3** *tr.* become unable to find; fail to keep in sight or follow or mentally grasp (*lose one's way*). **4** *tr.* let or have pass from one's control or reach (*lose one's chance*). **5** *tr.* be defeated in (a game, race, lawsuit, battle, etc.). **6** *tr.* evade; get rid of (*lost our pursuers*). **7** *tr.* fail to obtain, catch, or perceive (*lose a train; lose a word*). **8** *tr.* forfeit (a stake, deposit, right to a thing, etc.). **9** *tr.* spend (time, efforts, etc.) to no purpose (*lost no time in sounding the alarm*). **10** *intr.* **a** suffer loss or detriment. **b** be worse off, esp. financially. **11** *tr.* cause (a person) the loss of (*will lose you your job*). **12** *intr.* & *tr.* (of a timepiece) become slow; become slow by (a specified amount of time). **13** *tr.* (in *passive*) **a** disappear; perish; be dead (*was lost in the war*). **b** fall; be damned (*souls lost to drunkenness and greed*). **14** (as **lost** *adj.*) **a** gone; stray; mislaid; forgotten (*lost valuables; a lost art*). **b** dead; destroyed (*lost comrades*). **c** damned; fallen (*lost souls in hell*). □ **be lost on** be wasted on, or not noticed or appreciated by. **be lost to** be no longer affected by or accessible to. **be lost without** have great difficulty if deprived of (*am lost without my diary*). **get lost** *sl.* (usu. in *imper.*) go away. **lose face** be humiliated; lose one's credibility. **lose heart** be discouraged. **lose one's nerve** become timid or irresolute. **lose out** (often foll. by *on*) *colloq.* be unsuccessful; not get a fair chance or advantage (in). **lose sleep over a thing** lie awake worrying about a thing. **lose time** allow time to pass with something unachieved, etc. **lose touch** see TOUCH. **lose the** (or **one's**) **way** become lost; fail to reach one's destination.

▶See note at LOOSE.

los·er /lo͞ozər/ *n.* **1** a person or thing that loses or has lost (esp. a contest or game). **2** *colloq.* a person who regularly fails.

los·ing bat·tle *n.* a contest or effort in which failure seems certain.

loss /laws, los/ *n.* **1** the act or an instance of losing; the state of being lost. **2** a person, thing, or amount lost. **3** the detriment or disadvantage resulting from losing (*it's no great loss*). □ **at a loss** (sold, etc.) for less than was paid for it. **be at a loss** be puzzled or uncertain. **be at a loss for words** not know what to say.

loss lead·er *n.* an item sold at a loss to attract customers.

lost *past* and *past part.* of LOSE.

lost cause *n.* an enterprise, etc., with no chance of success.

lost gen·er·a·tion *n.* **1** a generation with many of its men killed in war, esp. (**the Lost Generation**) that of the World War I era. **2** an emotionally and culturally unstable generation coming to maturity.

lot /lot/ *n.* & *v.* •*n.* **1** *colloq.* (prec. by *a* or in *pl.*) **a** a large number or amount. **b** *colloq.* much (*took a lot of abuse; smiles a lot; we had lots of fun*). **2 a** each of a set of objects used in making a chance selection. **b** this method of deciding (*chosen by lot*). **3** a share, or the responsibility resulting from it. **4** a person's destiny, fortune, or condition. **5** a plot; an allotment of land (*parking lot*). **6** an article or set of articles for sale at an auction, etc. **7** a number or quantity of associated persons or things. •*v.tr.* (**lotted, lotting**) divide into lots. □ **cast** (or **draw**) **lots** decide by means of lots. **the** (or **the whole**) **lot** the whole number or quantity. **a whole lot** *colloq.* very much (*is a whole lot better*).

▶Avoid spelling two words as one: "alot," as in *I like skating alot.*

loth var. of LOATH.

lo·tion /lṓshən/ *n.* a medicinal or cosmetic liquid applied externally.

lot·ter·y /lótəree/ *n.* (*pl.* **-ies**) **1** a means of raising money by selling numbered tickets and giving prizes to the holders of numbers drawn at random. **2** an enterprise, process, etc., whose success is governed by chance.

lot·to /lótō/ *n.* a game of chance like bingo, but with numbers drawn instead of called.

lo·tus /lṓtəs/ *n.* **1** (in Greek mythology) a legendary plant inducing luxurious languor when eaten. **2 a** any water lily of the genus *Nelumbo*, esp. *N. nucifera* of India, with large pink flowers. **b** this flower used symbolically in Hinduism and Buddhism. **3** an Egyptian water lily, *Nymphaea lotus*, with white flowers. **4** any plant of the genus *Lotus*, e.g., bird's-foot trefoil.

lo·tus-eat·er *n.* a person given to indolent enjoyment.

lo·tus po·si·tion *n.* a cross-legged position of meditation with the feet resting on the thighs.

loud /lowd/ *adj.* & *adv.* •*adj.* **1 a** strongly audible, esp. noisily or oppressively so. **b** able or liable to produce loud sounds (*a loud engine*). **c** clamorous; insistent (*loud complaints*). **2** (of colors, design, etc.) gaudy; obtrusive. **3** (of behavior) aggressive and noisy. •*adv.* in a loud manner. □ **out loud 1** aloud. **2** loudly (*laughed out loud*). □□ **loud·en** *v.tr.* & *intr.* **loud·ish** *adj.* **loud·ly** *adv.* **loud·ness** *n.*

loud·mouth /lówdmowth/ *n. colloq.* a noisily self-assertive, vociferous person. □□ **loud·mouthed** *adj.*

loud·speak·er /lówdspeékər/ *n.* an apparatus that converts electrical impulses into sound.

lounge /lownj/ *v.* & *n.* •*v.intr.* **1** recline comfortably and casually; loll. **2** stand or move about idly. •*n.* **1** a place for lounging, esp.: **a** a bar or other public room (e.g., in a hotel). **b** a place in an airport, etc., with seats for waiting passengers. **2** a spell of lounging.

lounge liz·ard *n. colloq.* **1** a person, esp. a man, who frequents bars, etc. **2** an idler in fashionable society.

loung·er /lównjər/ *n.* **1** a person who lounges. **2** a piece of furniture for relaxing on. **3** a casual garment for wearing when relaxing.

loupe /lo͞op/ *n.* a small magnifying glass used by jewelers, etc.

lour var. of LOWER[3].

louse /lows/ *n.* & *v.* •*n.* **1** (*pl.* **lice** /līs/) **a** a parasitic insect, *Pediculus humanus*, infesting the human hair and skin and transmitting various diseases. **b** any insect of the order Anoplura or Mallophaga parasitic on mammals, birds, fish, or plants. **2** *sl.* (*pl.* **louses**) a contemptible or unpleasant person. •*v.tr.* remove lice from. □ **louse up** *sl.* make a mess of.

lous·y /lówzee/ *adj.* (**lousier, lousiest**) **1** infested with lice. **2** *colloq.* very bad; disgusting (also as a term of general disparagement). **3** *colloq.* (often foll. by *with*) well supplied; teeming (with). ▫▫ **lous·i·ly** *adv.* **lous·i·ness** *n.*

lout /lowt/ *n.* a crude or ill-mannered person (usu. a man). ▫▫ **lout·ish** *adj.* **lout·ish·ly** *adv.* **lout·ish·ness** *n.*

lou·ver /lóōvər/ *n.* **1** a set, or each of a set, of overlapping slats designed to admit air and some light and exclude rain. **2** a domed structure on a roof with side openings for ventilation, etc. ▫▫ **lou·vered** *adj.*

lov·a·ble /lúvəbəl/ *adj.* (also **love·a·ble**) inspiring or deserving love or affection. ▫▫ **lov·a·ble·ness** *n.* **lov·a·bly** *adv.*

lov·age /lúvij/ *n.* **1** a S. European herb, *Levisticum officinale*, used for flavoring, etc. **2** a white-flowered umbelliferous plant, *Ligusticum scoticum*.

love /luv/ *n. & v.* • *n.* **1** deep affection or fondness. **2** sexual passion. **3** sexual relations. **4** a beloved one; a sweetheart (often as a form of address). **5** *colloq.* a person of whom one is fond. **6** affectionate greetings (*give him my love*). **7** (often **Love**) a representation of Cupid. **8** (in some games) no score; nil. • *v.tr.* **1** (also *absol.*) feel love or deep fondness for. **2** delight in; admire; greatly cherish. **3** *colloq.* like very much (*loves books*). **4** (foll. by verbal noun, or *to* + infin.) be inclined, esp. as a habit; greatly enjoy (*children love dressing up*). ▫ **fall in love** (often foll. by *with*) develop a great (esp. sexual) love (for). **for love** for pleasure not profit. **for the love of** for the sake of. **in love** (often foll. by *with*) deeply enamored (of). **make love** (often foll. by *to*) **1** have sexual intercourse (with). **2** *archaic* pay amorous attention (to). **not for love or money** *colloq.* not in any circumstances. **out of love** no longer in love.

love·a·ble var. of LOVABLE.

love af·fair *n.* **1** a romantic or sexual relationship between two people in love. **2** a passion for something.

love·bird /lúvbərd/ *n.* **1** any of various African and Madagascan parrots, esp. *Agapornis personata*. **2** (in *pl.*) a pair of lovers who display much affection.

love child *n.* a child born out of wedlock.

love·less /lúvlis/ *adj.* without love; unloving or unloved or both. ▫▫ **love·less·ly** *adv.* **love·less·ness** *n.*

love·lock /lúvlok/ *n.* a curl or lock of hair worn on the temple or forehead.

love·lorn /lúvlawrn/ *adj.* pining from unrequited love.

love·ly /lúvlee/ *adj. & n.* • *adj.* (**lovelier, loveliest**) **1** exquisitely beautiful. **2** *colloq.* pleasing; delightful. • *n.* (*pl.* **-lies**) *colloq.* a pretty woman. ▫ **lovely and** *colloq.* delightfully (*lovely and warm*). ▫▫ **love·li·ness** *n.*

love·mak·ing /lúvmayking/ *n.* **1** amorous sexual activity, esp. sexual intercourse. **2** *archaic* courtship.

love nest *n.* a place of intimate lovemaking.

lov·er /lúvər/ *n.* **1** a person in love with another. **2** a person with whom another is having sexual relations. **3** (in *pl.*) a couple in love or having sexual relations. **4** a person who likes or enjoys something specified (*a music lover; a lover of words*).

love seat *n.* an armchair or small sofa for two.

love·sick /lúvsik/ *adj.* languishing with romantic love. ▫▫ **love·sick·ness** *n.*

love·y-dove·y /lúveedúvee/ *adj. colloq.* fondly affectionate, esp. unduly sentimental.

lov·ing /lúving/ *adj. & n.* • *adj.* feeling or showing love; affectionate. • *n.* affection; active love. ▫▫ **lov·ing·ly** *adv.* **lov·ing·ness** *n.*

lov·ing cup *n.* **1** a two-handled drinking cup passed around at banquets, etc. **2** a loving cup presented as a trophy.

low[1] /lō/ *adj., n., & adv.* • *adj.* **1** of less than average height; not high or tall or reaching far up (*a low wall*). **2 a** situated close to ground or sea level, etc.; not elevated in position (*low altitude*). **b** (of the sun) near the horizon. **c** (of latitude) near the equator. **3** of or in humble rank or position (*of low birth*). **4** of small or less than normal amount or extent or intensity (*low price; low temperature; low in calories*). **5** small or reduced in quantity (*stocks are low*). **6** coming below the normal level (*a dress with a low neck*). **7 a** dejected; lacking vigor (*feeling low; in low spirits*). **b** poorly nourished; indicative of poor nutrition. **8** (of a sound) not shrill or loud or high-pitched. **9** not exalted or sublime; commonplace. **10** unfavorable (*a low opinion*). **11** abject; mean; vulgar (*low cunning; low slang*). • *n.* **1** a low or the lowest level or number (*the dollar has reached a new low*). **2** an area of low pressure. • *adv.* **1** in or to a low position or state. **2** in a low tone (*speak low*). **3** (of a sound) at or to a low pitch. ▫▫ **low·ish** *adj.* **low·ness** *n.*

low[2] /lō/ *n. & v.* • *n.* a sound made by cattle; a moo. • *v.intr.* utter this sound.

low-ball *n. & v.* • *n. Cards* a type of poker. • *v.tr. & intr.* underestimate a price (usu. for a service) deliberately.

low beam *n.* an automobile headlight providing short-range illumination.

low·born /lṓbawrn/ *adj.* of humble birth.

low·boy /lṓboy/ *n.* a low chest or table with drawers and short legs.

low·brow /lṓbrow/ *adj. & n.* • *adj.* not intellectual or cultured. • *n.* a lowbrow person. ▫▫ **low·browed** *adj.*

low com·e·dy *n.* that in which the subject and the treatment border on farce.

Low Coun·tries *n.pl.* the Netherlands, Belgium, and Luxembourg.

low-cut *adj.* (of a dress, etc.) made with a low neckline.

low-down *adj. & n.* • *adj.* abject; mean; dishonorable. • *n. colloq.* (usu. foll. by *on*) the relevant information (about).

low·er[1] /lṓər/ *adj. & adv.* • *adj.* (*compar.* of LOW[1]). **1** less high in position or status. **2** situated below another part (*lower lip; lower atmosphere*). **3 a** situated on less high land (*Lower Egypt*). **b** situated to the south (*Lower California*). **4** (of a mammal, plant, etc.) evolved to a relatively small degree (*the lower primates*). • *adv.* in or to a lower position, status, etc. ▫▫ **low·er·most** *adj.*

low·er[2] /lṓər/ *v.* **1** *tr.* let or haul down. **2** *tr. & intr.* make or become lower. **3** *tr.* reduce the height or pitch or elevation of (*lower your voice; lower one's eyes*). **4** *tr.* degrade. **5** *tr. & intr.* diminish.

low·er[3] /lowər/ *v. & n.* (also **lour**) • *v.intr.* **1** frown; look sullen. **2** (of the sky, etc.) look dark and threatening. • *n.* **1** a scowl. **2** a gloomy look (of the sky, etc.). ▫▫ **low·er·y** *adj.*

low·er·case /lṓərkays/ *n., adj., & v.* • *n.* small letters as opposed to capital letters (uppercase). • *adj.* of or having small letters. • *v.tr.* print or write in lowercase.

low·er class *n.* working-class people and their families. ▫▫ **low·er-class** *adj.*

low·er court *n.* a court whose decisions may be overruled by another court on appeal.

low·er house *n.* the usu. larger body in a legislature, such as the House of Representatives.

low·est com·mon mul·ti·ple *n.* the least quantity that is a multiple of two or more given quantities.

low gear *n.* a gear such that the driven end of a transmission revolves slower than the driving end.

low-grade *adj.* of low quality or strength.

low-key *adj.* lacking intensity or prominence; restrained.

low·land /lṓlənd/ *n.* **1** (usu. in *pl.*) low-lying country. **2** (**Lowland**) (usu. in *pl.*) the region of Scotland lying south and east of the Highlands. ▫▫ **low·land·er** *n.*

low-lev·el *adj. Computing* (of a programming language) close in form to machine language.

low·light /lṓlīt/ *n.* **1** a monotonous or dull period; a feature of little prominence (*one of the lowlights of the evening*). **2** (usu. in *pl.*) a dark tint in the hair produced by dyeing.

low·ly /lṓlee/ *adj.* (**lowlier, lowliest**) **1** humble in feeling, behavior, or status. **2** modest; unpretentious. ▫▫ **low·li·ness** *n.*

low-ly·ing *adj.* at low altitude (above sea level, etc.).

low-mind·ed /lṓmíndid/ *adj.* vulgar or ignoble in mind or character. ▫▫ **low-mind·ed·ness** *n.*

low-pitched *adj.* **1** (of a sound) low. **2** (of a roof) having only a slight slope.

low pres·sure *n.* **1** little demand for activity or exertion. **2** an atmospheric condition with air pressure below average.

low pro·file *n.* avoidance of attention or publicity. ▫▫ **low-pro·file** *adj.*

low spir·its *n.pl.* dejection; depression. ▫▫ **low-spir·it·ed** *adj.* **low-spir·it·ed·ness** *n.*

low wa·ter *n.* the tide at its lowest.

low-wa·ter mark *n.* **1** the level reached at low water. **2** a minimum recorded level or value, etc.

lox /loks/ *n.* smoked salmon.

loy·al /lóyəl/ *adj.* **1** (often foll. by *to*) true or faithful (to duty, love, or obligation). **2** steadfast in allegiance; devoted to the legitimate sovereign or government of one's country. **3** showing loyalty. ▫▫ **loy·al·ly** *adv.*

loy·al·ist /lóyəlist/ *n.* **1** a person who remains loyal to the legitimate sovereign, etc. **2** (**Loyalist**) **a** *hist.* a resident of N. America who supported Great Britain during the American Revolution. **b** a supporter of the union between Great Britain and Northern Ireland. ▫▫ **loy·al·ism** *n.*

loy·al·ty /lóyəltee/ *n.* (*pl.* **-ties**) **1** the state of being loyal. **2** (often in *pl.*) a feeling or application of loyalty.

loz·enge /lózinj/ *n.* **1** a rhombus or diamond figure. **2** a small sweet or medicinal tablet for dissolving in the mouth. **3** a lozenge-shaped pane in a window.

LSD *abbr.* lysergic acid diethylamide.

Lt. *abbr.* **1** lieutenant. **2** light.

Ltd. *abbr.* limited.

Lu *symb. Chem.* the element lutetium.

lu·bri·cant /lóobrikənt/ *n.* & *adj.* • *n.* a substance used to reduce friction. • *adj.* lubricating.

lu·bri·cate /lóobrikayt/ *v.tr.* **1** reduce friction in (machinery, etc.) by applying oil or grease, etc. **2** make slippery or smooth with oil or grease. ▫▫ **lu·bri·ca·tion** /–káyshən/ *n.* **lu·bri·ca·tive** *adj.* **lu·bri·ca·tor** *n.*

lu·bri·cious /loobríshəs/ *adj.* (also **lu·bri·cous** /lóobrikəs/) **1** slippery; smooth; oily. **2** lewd; prurient. **3** evasive. ▫▫ **lu·bric·i·ty** /–brísitee/ *n.*

lu·cent /lóosənt/ *adj. literary* **1** shining; luminous. **2** translucent. ▫▫ **lu·cen·cy** *n.* **lu·cent·ly** *adv.*

lu·cid /lóosid/ *adj.* **1** expressing or expressed clearly; easy to understand. **2** of or denoting intervals of sanity between periods of insanity or dementia. ▫▫ **lu·cid·i·ty** /–síditee/ *n.* **lu·cid·ly** *adv.*

Lu·ci·fer /lóosifər/ *n.* Satan.

luck /luk/ *n.* **1** chance regarded as the bringer of good or bad fortune. **2** circumstances of life (beneficial or not) brought by this. **3** good fortune; success due to chance (*in luck*; *out of luck*). ▫ **for luck** to bring good fortune. **no such luck** *colloq.* unfortunately not. **try one's luck** make a venture.

luck·i·ly /lúkilee/ *adv.* **1** (qualifying a whole sentence or clause) fortunately (*luckily there was enough food*). **2** in a lucky or fortunate manner.

luck·less /lúklis/ *adj.* having no luck; unfortunate. ▫▫ **luck·less·ness** *n.*

luck·y /lúkee/ *adj.* (**luckier, luckiest**) **1** having or resulting from good luck, esp. as distinct from skill or design or merit. **2** bringing good luck (*a lucky mascot*). **3** fortunate; appropriate (*a lucky guess*).

lu·cra·tive /lóokrətiv/ *adj.* profitable; yielding financial gain. ▫▫ **lu·cra·tive·ly** *adv.* **lu·cra·tive·ness** *n.*

lu·cre /lóokər/ *n. derog.* financial profit or gain.

lu·cu·brate /lóokyoobráyt/ *v.intr. literary* **1** write or study, esp. by night. **2** express one's meditations in writing. ▫▫ **lu·cu·bra·tion** /–áyshən/ **lu·cu·bra·tor** *n.*

Lud·dite /lúdīt/ *n.* & *adj.* • *n.* **1** *hist.* a member of any of the bands of English artisans who rioted against mechanization and destroyed machinery (1811–16). **2** a person opposed to new technology. • *adj.* of the Luddites or their beliefs. ▫▫ **Lud·dism** *n.* **Lud·dit·ism** *n.*

lu·di·crous /lóodikrəs/ *adj.* absurd or ridiculous; laughable. ▫▫ **lu·di·crous·ly** *adv.* **lu·di·crous·ness** *n.*

luff /luf/ *n.* & *v.* (also **loof** /loof/) *Naut.* • *n.* the edge of the fore-and-aft sail next to the mast or stay. • *v.tr.* (also *absol.*) **1** steer (a ship) nearer the wind so that the sails shake. **2** turn (the helm) so as to achieve this. **3** obstruct (an opponent in yacht racing) by sailing closer to the wind. **4** raise or lower (the jib of a crane or derrick).

lug[1] /lug/ *v.* & *n.* • *v.* (**lugged, lugging**) **1** *tr.* **a** drag or tug (a heavy object) with effort or violence. **b** (usu. foll. by *around, about*) carry (something heavy) around with one. **2** *tr.* (usu. foll. by *in, into*) introduce (a subject, etc.) irrelevantly. **3** *tr.* (usu. foll. by *along, to*) force (a person) to join in an activity. **4** *intr.* (usu. foll. by *at*) pull hard. • *n.* **1** a hard or rough pull. **2** (in *pl.*) affectation (*put on lugs*).

lug[2] /lug/ *n.* **1** *colloq.* an ear. **2** a projection on an object by which it may be carried, fixed in place, etc. **3** *sl.* a lout; a sponger; a stupid person.

luge /loozh/ *n.* & *v.* • *n.* a light toboggan for one or two people. • *v.intr.* ride on a luge.

lug·gage /lúgij/ *n.* suitcases, bags, etc., to hold a traveler's belongings.

lug nut *n.* a nut that attaches to a heavy bolt, esp. as used to attach a wheel to a motor vehicle.

lu·gu·bri·ous /loogóobreeəs, –gyóo–/ *adj.* mournful; dismal. ▫▫ **lu·gu·bri·ous·ly** *adv.* **lu·gu·bri·ous·ness** *n.*

lug·worm /lúgwərm/ *n.* any worm of the genus *Arenicola*, living in muddy sand and often used as bait by fishermen.

luke·warm /lóokwáwrm/ *adj.* **1** moderately warm; tepid. **2** unenthusiastic; indifferent. ▫▫ **luke·warm·ly** *adv.* **luke·warm·ness** *n.*

lull /lul/ *v.* & *n.* • *v.* **1** *tr.* soothe or send to sleep gently. **2** *tr.* (usu. foll. by *into*) deceive (a person) into confidence (*lulled into a false sense of security*). **3** *tr.* allay (suspicions, etc.) usu. by deception. **4** *intr.* (of noise, a storm, etc.) abate or fall quiet. • *n.* a temporary quiet period in a storm or in any activity.

lull·a·by /lúləbī/ *n.* & *v.* • *n.* (*pl.* **-bies**) **1** a soothing song to send a child to sleep. **2** the music for this. • *v.tr.* (**-bies, -bied**) sing to sleep.

lum·ba·go /lumbáygō/ *n.* rheumatic pain in the muscles of the lower back.

lum·bar /lúmbər, –baar/ *adj. Anat.* relating to the loin, esp. the lower back area.

lum·ber[1] /lúmbər/ *v.intr.* (usu. foll. by *along, past, by,* etc.) move in a slow, clumsy, noisy way. ▫▫ **lum·ber·ing** *adj.*

lum·ber[2] /lúmbər/ *n.* & *v.* • *n.* logs or timber cut and prepared for use. • *v.* **1** *intr.* cut and prepare forest timber for transport. ▫▫ **lum·ber·er** *n.* **lum·ber·ing** *n.*

lum·ber·jack /lúmbərjak/ *n.* (also **lum·ber·man** /–mən/*pl.* **-men**) one who fells, prepares, or conveys lumber.

lum·ber jack·et *n.* a jacket, usu. of warm checked material, of the kind worn by lumberjacks.

lum·bri·cal mus·cle /lúmbrikəl/ *n.* any of the muscles flexing the fingers or toes.

lu·men /lóomən/ *n. Physics* the SI unit of luminous flux. ¶ Abbr.: **lm.**

lu·mi·nance /lóominəns/ *n. Physics* the intensity of light emitted from a surface per unit area in a given direction.

lu·mi·nar·y /lóomineree/ *n.* (*pl.* **-ies**) **1** *literary* a natural light-giving body, esp. the sun or moon. **2** a person as a source of intellectual light or moral inspiration. **3** a prominent member of a group or gathering (*a host of show-business luminaries*).

lu·mi·nes·cence /lóominésəns/ *n.* the emission of light by a substance other than as a result of incandescence. □□ **lu·mi·nes·cent** /–sənt/ *adj.*

lu·mi·nous /lóominəs/ *adj.* **1** full of or shedding light. **2** phosphorescent; visible in darkness (*luminous paint*). **3** (esp. of a writer or a writer's work) throwing light on a subject. **4** of visible radiation (*luminous intensity*). □□ **lu·mi·nos·i·ty** /–nósitee/ *n.* **lu·mi·nous·ly** *adj.*

lum·mox /lúməks/ *n. colloq.* a clumsy or stupid person.

lump[1] /lump/ *n. & v.* •*n.* **1** a compact shapeless or unshapely mass. **2** *sl.* a quantity or heap. **3** a tumor, swelling, or bruise. **4** a heavy, dull, or ungainly person. **5** a block or cube of granulated sugar. •*v.* **1** *tr.* (usu. foll. by *together, with, in with, under,* etc.) mass together or group indiscriminately. **2** *tr.* carry or throw carelessly (*lumping crates around the yard*). **3** *intr.* become lumpy (*the gravy is lumping*). **4** *intr.* □ **lump in the throat** a feeling of pressure in the throat, caused by emotion. □□ **lump·er** *n.* (in sense 2 of v.).

lump[2] /lump/ *v.tr. colloq.* endure or suffer (a situation) ungraciously. □ **like it or lump it** put up with something whether one likes it or not.

lump·ec·to·my /lumpéktəmee/ *n.* (*pl.* **-mies**) the surgical removal of a usu. cancerous lump from the breast.

lump·fish /lúmpfish/ *n.* (*pl.* **-fishes** or **-fish**) a spiny-finned fish, *Cyclopterus lumpus*, of the N. Atlantic, with modified pelvic fins for clinging to objects.

lump·ish /lúmpish/ *adj.* **1** heavy and clumsy. **2** stupid; lethargic. □□ **lump·ish·ly** *adv.* **lump·ish·ness** *n.*

lump sum *n.* **1** a sum covering a number of items. **2** money paid down at once (opp. INSTALLMENT).

lump·y /lúmpee/ *adj.* (**lumpier, lumpiest**) **1** full of or covered with lumps. **2** (of water) cut up by the wind into small waves. □□ **lump·i·ly** *adv.* **lump·i·ness** *n.*

lu·na·cy /lóonəsee/ *n.* (*pl.* **-cies**) **1** insanity. **2** *Law* such mental unsoundness as interferes with civil rights or transactions. **3** great folly or eccentricity; a foolish act.

luna moth /lóonə/ *n.* a N. American moth, *Actias luna*, with crescent-shaped spots on its pale green wings.

lu·nar /lóonər/ *adj.* **1** of, relating to, or determined by the moon. **2** concerned with travel to the moon and related research. **3** (of light, glory, etc.) pale; feeble. **4** crescent-shaped; lunate. **5** of or containing silver.

lu·nar mod·ule *n.* a small craft used for traveling between the moon's surface and a spacecraft in orbit around the moon.

lu·nar month *n.* **1** a month measured between successive new moons (about $29^1/_2$ days. **2** (in general use) a period of four weeks.

lu·nar year *n.* a period of 12 lunar months.

lu·nate /lóonayt/ *adj.* crescent-shaped.

lu·na·tic /lóonətik/ *n. & adj.* •*n.* **1** an insane person. **2** someone foolish or eccentric. •*adj.* mad; foolish.

lu·na·tic a·sy·lum *n. hist.* a mental home or hospital.

lu·na·tic fringe *n.* an extreme or eccentric minority group.

lu·na·tion /loonáyshən/ *n.* the interval between new moons, about 29 days.

lunch /lunch/ *n. & v.* •*n.* **1** the meal eaten in the middle of the day. **2** a light meal eaten at any time. •*v.* **1** *intr.* eat one's lunch. **2** *tr.* provide lunch for. □ **out to lunch** *sl.* unaware; incompetent. □□ **lunch·er** *n.*

lunch·box /lúnchboks/ *n.* a container for a packed lunch.

lunch·eon /lúnchən/ *n. formal* lunch.

lunch·eon·ette /lúnchənét/ *n.* a small restaurant or snack bar serving light lunches.

lunch·time /lúnchtīm/ *n.* the time (usu. around noon) at which lunch is eaten.

lu·nette /loonét/ *n.* **1** an arched aperture in a domed ceiling to admit light. **2** a crescent-shaped or semicircular space or alcove that contains a painting, statue, etc. **3** a watch crystal of flattened shape. **4** a ring through which a hook is placed to attach a vehicle to the vehicle towing it. **5** a temporary fortification with two faces forming a salient angle, and two flanks.

lung /lung/ *n.* either of the pair of respiratory organs that bring air into contact with the blood in humans and many other vertebrates. □□ **lunged** *adj.* **lung·ful** *n.* (*pl.* **-fuls**). **lung·less** *adj.*

lunge[1] /lunj/ *n. & v.* •*n.* **1** a sudden movement forward. **2** a thrust with a sword, etc., esp. the basic attacking move in fencing. **3** a movement forward by bending the front leg at the knee while keeping the back leg straight. •*v.* **1** *intr.* make a lunge. **2** *intr.* (usu. foll. by *at, out*) deliver a blow from the shoulder in boxing.

lunge[2] var. of LONGE.

lung·fish /lúngfish/ *n.* (*pl.* **fishes** or **-fish**) any freshwater fish of the order Dipnoi, having gills and a modified swim bladder used as lungs, and able to estivate to survive drought.

lung·wort /lúngwərt, –wawrt/ *n.* **1** any herbaceous plant of the genus *Pulmonaria*, esp. *P. officinalis* with white-spotted leaves likened to a diseased lung. **2** a lichen, *Lobaria pulmonaria*, formerly used as a remedy for lung disease.

lu·pine[1] /lóopin/ *n.* (also **lu·pin**) **1** any plant of the genus *Lupinus*, with long tapering spikes of blue, purple, pink, white, or yellow flowers. **2** (in *pl.*) seeds of the lupine.

lu·pine[2] /lóopīn/ *adj.* of or like a wolf or wolves.

lu·pus /lóopəs/ *n.* any of various ulcerous skin diseases, esp. lupus vulgaris and lupus erythematosus. □□ **lu·poid** *adj.* **lu·pous** *adj.*

lurch[1] /lərch/ *n. & v.* •*n.* a stagger; a sudden unsteady movement or leaning. •*v.intr.* stagger; move suddenly and unsteadily.

lurch[2] /lərch/ *n.* □ **leave in the lurch** desert (a friend, etc.) in difficulties.

lure /loor/ *v. & n.* •*v.tr.* **1** (usu. foll. by *away, into*) entice (a person, an animal, etc.) usu. with some form of bait. **2** attract back again or recall (a person, animal, etc.) with the promise of a reward. •*n.* **1** a thing used to entice, e.g., artificial bait for fishing. **2** (usu. foll. by *of*) the attractive or compelling qualities (of a pursuit, etc.). **3** a falconer's apparatus for recalling a hawk. □□ **lur·ing** *adj.* **lur·ing·ly** *adv.*

lu·rid /loorid/ *adj.* **1** vivid or glowing in color (*lurid orange*). **2** of an unnatural glare (*lurid nocturnal brilliance*). **3** sensational, horrifying, or terrible (*lurid details*). **4** showy; gaudy (*paperbacks with lurid covers*). **5** ghastly; wan (*lurid complexion*). □□ **lu·rid·ly** *adv.* **lu·rid·ness** *n.*

lurk /lərk/ *v.intr.* **1** linger furtively or unobtrusively. **2 a** lie in ambush. **b** (usu. foll. by *in, under, about,* etc.) hide, esp. for sinister purposes. **3** (as **lurking** *adj.*) latent; semiconscious (*a lurking suspicion*). □□ **lurk·er** *n.*

lus·cious /lúshəs/ *adj.* **1 a** richly sweet in taste or smell. **b** *colloq.* delicious. **2** (of literary style, music, etc.) overrich in sound, imagery, or voluptuous suggestion. **3** voluptuously attractive. □□ **lus·cious·ly** *adv.* **lus·cious·ness** *n.*

lush[1] /lush/ *adj.* **1** (of vegetation) luxuriant and succulent. **2** luxurious. ▫▫ **lush·ly** *adv.* **lush·ness** *n.*

lush[2] /lush/ *n. & v. sl.* •*n.* **1** alcohol; liquor. **2** an alcoholic; a drunkard. •*v.tr. & intr.* drink (alcohol).

lust /lust/ *n. & v.* •*n.* **1** strong sexual desire. **2 a** (usu. foll. by *for, of*) a passionate desire for (*a lust for power*). **b** (usu. foll. by *of*) a passionate enjoyment of (*the lust of battle*). **3** (usu. in *pl.*) a sensuous appetite regarded as sinful (*the lusts of the flesh*). •*v.intr.* (usu. foll. by *after, for*) have a strong or excessive (esp. sexual) desire. ▫▫ **lust·ful** *adj.* **lust·ful·ly** *adv.* **lust·ful·ness** *n.*

lus·ter /lústər/ *n. & v.* •*n.* **1** gloss; sheen. **2** a shining or reflective surface. **3 a** a thin metallic coating giving an iridescent glaze to ceramics. **b** = LUSTERWARE. **4** a radiance or attractiveness; splendor; glory; distinction (of achievements, etc.) (*add luster to*; *shed luster on*). **5 a** a prismatic glass pendant on a chandelier, etc. **b** a cut-glass chandelier or candelabra. •*v.tr.* put luster on (pottery, a cloth, etc.). ▫▫ **lus·ter·less** *adj.* **lus·trous** *adj.* **lus·trous·ly** *adv.* **lus·trous·ness** *n.*

lus·ter·ware /lústərwair/ *n.* ceramics with an iridescent glaze.

lus·tral /lústrəl/ *adj.* relating to or used in ceremonial purification.

lust·y /lústee/ *adj.* (**lustier, lustiest**) **1** healthy and strong. **2** vigorous or lively. ▫▫ **lust·i·ly** *adv.* **lust·i·ness** *n.*

lute[1] /loot/ *n.* a guitarlike instrument with a long neck and a pear-shaped body.

lute[2] /loot/ *n. & v.* •*n.* **1** clay or cement used to stop a hole, make a joint airtight, protect a graft, etc. **2** a rubber seal for a jar, etc. •*v.tr.* apply lute to.

lu·te·nist /lóot'nist/ *n.* (also **lu·ta·nist**) a lute player.

lu·te·ti·um /looteeshəm/ *n.* (also **lu·te·ci·um**) *Chem.* a silvery metallic element of the lanthanide series. ¶ Symb.: **Lu**.

Lu·ther·an /lóothərən/ *n. & adj.* •*n.* **1** a follower of Martin Luther, Ger. religious reformer d. 1546. **2** a member of the Lutheran Church with justification by faith alone as a cardinal doctrine. •*adj.* of or characterized by the theology. ▫▫ **Lu·ther·an·ism** *n.*

lutz /luts/ *n.* a jump in figure skating in which the skater takes off from the outside back edge of one skate and lands, after a complete rotation in the air, on the outside back edge of the opposite skate.

lux /luks/ *n.* (*pl.* same or **luxes**) *Physics* the SI unit of illumination, equivalent to one lumen per square meter.

luxe /looks, luks/ *n.* luxury (cf. DELUXE).

lux·u·ri·ant /lugzhóoreeənt, lukshóor–/ *adj.* **1** (of vegetation, etc.) lush; profuse in growth. **2** exuberant (*luxuriant imagination*). **3** (of artistic style) florid; richly ornate. ▫▫ **lux·u·ri·ance** /–eeəns/ *n.* **lux·u·ri·ant·ly** *adv.*

lux·u·ri·ate /lugzhóoreeayt, lukshóor–/ *v.intr.* **1** (foll. by *in*) take self-indulgent delight in; enjoy in a luxurious manner. **2** relax in comfort.

lux·u·ri·ous /lugzhóoreeəs, lukshóor–/ *adj.* **1** supplied with luxuries. **2** extremely comfortable. **3** self-indulgent; voluptuous. ▫▫ **lux·u·ri·ous·ly** *adv.* **lux·u·ri·ous·ness** *n.*

▶**Luxuriant** and **luxurious** are sometimes confused. **Luxuriant** means 'lush, profuse, or prolific,' e.g., *forests of dark luxuriant foliage; luxuriant black eyelashes.* **Luxurious**, a much commoner word, means 'supplied with luxuries, extremely comfortable,' e.g., *a luxurious mansion.*

lux·u·ry /lúgzhəree, lúkshəree/ *n.* (*pl.* **-ries**) **1** choice or costly surroundings, possessions, food, etc. (*a life of luxury*). **2** something desirable for comfort or enjoyment, but not indispensable. **3** (*attrib.*) providing great comfort; expensive (*a luxury apartment*; *a luxury vacation*).

Lw *symb. Chem.* the element lawrencium.

ly·can·thro·py /līkánthrəpee/ *n.* **1** the mythical transformation of a person into a wolf (see also WEREWOLF). **2** a form of madness involving the delusion of being a wolf, with changed appetites, voice, etc. ▫▫ **ly·can·thrope** /líkənthrōp, līkán–/ *n.*

ly·ce·um /līséeəm/ *n.* a literary institution, lecture hall, concert hall, etc.

ly·chee var. of LITCHI.

Ly·cra /líkrə/ *n. Trademark* an elastic polyurethane fiber or fabric used esp. for close-fitting sports clothing.

lye /lī/ *n.* **1** water that has been made alkaline by lixiviation of vegetable ashes. **2** any strong alkaline solution, esp. of potassium hydroxide used for washing or cleansing.

ly·ing[1] /lí-ing/ *pres. part.* of LIE[1].

ly·ing[2] /lí-ing/ *pres. part. & n.* •*adj. pres. part.* of LIE[2]. •*adj.* deceitful; false. ▫▫ **ly·ing·ly** *adv.*

Lyme dis·ease /līm/ *n.* a disease transmitted by ticks, usually characterized by rash, fatigue, and joint pain.

lymph /limf/ *n.* **1** *Physiol.* a colorless fluid containing white blood cells, drained from the tissues and conveyed through the body in the lymphatic system. **2** this fluid used as a vaccine. **3** exudation from a sore, etc. ▫▫ **lym·phoid** *adj.* **lym·phous** *adj.*

lym·phat·ic /limfátik/ *adj. & n.* •*adj.* **1** of or secreting or conveying lymph. **2** (of a person) pale, flabby, or sluggish. •*n.* a veinlike vessel conveying lymph.

lym·phat·ic sys·tem *n.* a network of vessels conveying lymph.

lymph node *n.* (also **lymph gland**) a small mass of tissue in the lymphatic system where lymph is purified and lymphocytes are formed.

lym·pho·cyte /límfəsīt/ *n.* a leukocyte occurring in the blood, in lymph, etc. ▫▫ **lym·pho·cyt·ic** /–sítik/ *adj.*

lym·pho·ma /limfṓmə/ *n.* (*pl.* **lymphomas** or **lymphomata** /–mətə/) any malignant tumor of the lymph nodes, excluding leukemia.

lynch /linch/ *v.tr.* (of a body of people) put (a person) to death for an alleged offense without a legal trial. ▫▫ **lynch·er** *n.* **lynch·ing** *n.*

lynch law *n.* the procedure of a self-constituted illegal court that punishes or executes.

lynch·pin var. of LINCHPIN.

lynx /lingks/ *n.* **1** a medium-sized feline, *Felis lynx*, with short tail, spotted fur, and tufted ear tips. **2** its fur. ▫▫ **lynx·like** *adj.*

lynx-eyed *adj.* keen-sighted.

lyre /līr/ *n. Gk Antiq.* an ancient stringed instrument like a small U-shaped harp, played usu. with a plectrum and accompanying the voice.

lyre

lyre·bird /líRbərd/ *n.* any Australian bird of the family Menuridae, the male of which has a lyre-shaped tail display.

lyr·ic /lírik/ *adj. & n.* •*adj.* **1** (of poetry) expressing the writer's emotions, usu. briefly and in stanzas. **2** (of a poet) writing in this manner. **3** of or for the lyre. **4** meant to be sung; fit to be expressed in song; songlike (*lyric drama; lyric opera*). •*n.* **1** a lyric poem. **2** (in *pl.*) lyric verses. **3** (usu. in *pl.*) the words of a song.

lyr·i·cal /lírikəl/ *adj.* **1** = LYRIC *adj.* 1, 2. **2** resembling, couched in, or using language appropriate to, lyric poetry. **3** *colloq.* highly enthusiastic (*wax lyrical about*). □□ **lyr·i·cal·ly** *adv.*

lyr·i·cism /lírisizəm/ *n.* **1** the character or quality of being lyric or lyrical. **2** a lyrical expression.

lyr·i·cist /lírisist/ *n.* a person who writes the words to a song.

ly·ser·gic ac·id di·eth·yl·am·ide /dī-éthilámīd/ *n.* a powerful hallucinogenic drug. ¶ Abbr.: **LSD**.

ly·sin /lísin/ *n. Biol.* a protein in the blood able to cause lysis.

ly·sine /líseen/ *n. Biochem.* an amino acid present in protein and essential in the diet of vertebrates.

ly·sis /lísis/ *n.* (*pl.* **lyses** /–seez/) *Biol.* the disintegration of a cell.

lyt·ic /lítik/ *adj.* of, relating to, or causing lysis.

M

M[1] /em/ *n.* (*pl.* **Ms** or **M's**) **1** the thirteenth letter of the alphabet. **2** (as a Roman numeral) 1,000.

M[2] *abbr.* (also **M.**) **1** Master. **2** *Monsieur.* **3** mega-.

m *abbr.* (also **m.**) **1 a** masculine. **b** male. **2** married. **3** mile(s). **4** meter(s). **5** million(s). **6** minute(s). **7** *Physics* mass. **8** *Currency* mark(s). **9** milli-.

'm *n. colloq.* madam (in *yes'm,* etc.).

MA *abbr.* **1** Master of Arts. **2** Massachusetts (in official postal use).

ma /maa/ *n. colloq.* mother.

ma'am /mam/ *n.* madam.

mac /mak/ *n.* (also **mack**) *colloq.* mackintosh.

ma·ca·bre /məkaábər/ *adj.* (also **ma·ca·ber**) grim, gruesome.

mac·ad·am /məkádəm/ *n.* **1** material for making roads with successive layers of compacted broken stone (named for J.L. *McAdam,* Brit. surveyor d. 1836). **2** a road made from such material. ▫▫ **mac·ad·am·ize** *v.tr.*

mac·a·da·mi·a /mákədáymeeə/ *n.* any Australian evergreen tree of the genus *Macadamia,* esp. *M. ternifolia,* bearing edible nutlike seeds.

ma·caque /məkák/ *n.* any monkey of the genus *Macaca,* including the rhesus monkey and Barbary ape.

mac·a·ro·ni /mákərṓnee/ *n.* **1** a tubular variety of pasta. **2** *hist.* an 18th-c. British dandy affecting Continental fashions.

mac·a·roon /mákəro͞on/ *n.* a small light cake or cookie made with egg white, sugar, and ground almonds or coconut.

ma·caw /məkáw/ *n.* any long-tailed brightly colored parrot of the genus *Ara* or *Anodorhynchus,* native to S. and Central America.

Mace /mays/ *n. Trademark* a chemical spray used to disable an attacker temporarily. ▫▫ **mace** *v.*

mace[1] /mays/ *n.* **1** a heavy club usu. having a metal head and spikes used esp. in the Middle Ages. **2** a ceremonial staff of office.

mace[2] /mays/ *n.* the fibrous layer between a nutmeg's shell and its husk, dried and ground as a spice.

mac·er·ate /másərayt/ *v.* **1** *tr. & intr.* make or become soft by soaking. **2** *intr.* waste away, as by fasting. ▫▫ **mac·er·a·tion** /–ráyshən/ *n.* **mac·er·a·tor** *n.*

Mach /maak, mak/ *n.* (in full **Mach number**) the ratio of the speed of a body to the speed of sound in the surrounding medium. ▫ **Mach one** (or **two,** etc.) the speed (or twice the speed) of sound.

ma·chet·e /məshétee, məchétee/ *n.* a broad heavy knife used as an implement and weapon.

Mach·i·a·vel·li·an /mákeeəvéleeən/ *adj.* elaborately cunning; scheming; unscrupulous (for N. dei *Machiavelli,* Florentine statesman d. 1527).

ma·chin·a·ble /məshe͞enəbəl/ *adj.* capable of being cut by machine tools. ▫▫ **ma·chin·a·bil·i·ty** *n.*

mach·i·nate /mákinayt, másh–/ *v.intr.* lay plots; intrigue. ▫▫ **mach·i·na·tion** *n.*

ma·chine /məshe͞en/ *n. & v.* • *n.* **1** an apparatus applying mechanical power, having several parts each with a definite function. **2** a particular kind of machine, esp. a vehicle, a piece of electrical or electronic apparatus, etc. **3** an instrument that transmits a force or directs its application. **4** the controlling system of an organization, etc. (*the party machine*). **5** a person who acts mechanically. • *v.tr.* make or operate on with a machine.

ma·chine code *n.* (also **ma·chine lan·guage**) a computer language to which a particular computer can respond directly.

ma·chine gun *n.* an automatic gun giving continuous fire.

ma·chine-read·a·ble *adj.* in a form that a computer can process.

ma·chin·er·y /məshe͞enəree/ *n.* (*pl.* **-ies**) **1** machines collectively. **2** the components of a machine; a mechanism. **3** (foll. by *of*) an organized system. **4** (foll. by *for*) the means devised or available (*the machinery for decision making*).

ma·chine tool *n.* a mechanically operated tool. ▫▫ **ma·chine-tooled** *adj.*

ma·chin·ist /məshe͞enist/ *n.* **1** a person who operates a machine, esp. a machine tool. **2** a person who makes machinery.

ma·chis·mo /məche͞ezmō, –chízmō/ *n.* exaggeratedly assertive manliness; a show of masculinity.

Mach num·ber see MACH.

ma·cho /maáchō/ *adj. & n.* • *adj.* showily manly or virile. • *n.* (*pl.* **-chos**) **1** a macho man. **2** = MACHISMO.

mac·in·tosh var. of MACKINTOSH.

mack var. of MAC.

mack·er·el /mákərəl, mákrəl/ *n.* (*pl.* same or **mackerels**) a N. Atlantic marine fish, *Scomber scombrus,* with a greenish-blue body, used for food.

mack·er·el sky *n.* a sky dappled with rows of small white fleecy clouds, like the pattern on a mackerel's back.

mack·in·tosh /mákintosh/ *n.* (also **mac·in·tosh**) **1** a waterproof, esp. rubberized, coat. **2** cloth waterproofed with rubber.

mack·le /mákəl/ *n.* a blurred impression in printing.

ma·cra·mé /mákrəmáy/ *n.* **1** the art of knotting cord or string in patterns to make decorative articles. **2** articles made in this way.

mac·ro /mákrō/ *n.* (also **mac·ro·in·struc·tion**) *Computing* a series of abbreviated instructions expanded automatically when required.

macro- /mákrō/ *comb. form* **1** long. **2** large; large-scale.

mac·ro·bi·ot·ic /mákrōbīótik/ *adj. & n.* • *adj.* relating to or following a diet intended to prolong life, comprising pure vegetable foods, brown rice, etc. • *n.* (in *pl.*; treated as *sing.*) the use or theory of such a dietary system.

mac·ro·cosm /mákrōkozəm/ *n.* **1** the universe. **2** the whole of a complex structure. ▫▫ **mac·ro·cos·mic** /–kózmik/ *adj.*

mac·ro·ec·o·nom·ics /mákrō-e͞ekənómiks, –ék–/ *n.* the study of large-scale or general economic factors. ▫▫ **mac·ro·ec·o·nom·ic** *adj.*

mac·ro·in·struc·tion /mákrō-instrúkshən/ *n.* = MACRO.

ma·cron /máykraan, mák–/ *n.* a diacritical mark (¯) over a long or stressed vowel.

mac·ro·pho·tog·ra·phy /mákrōfətógrəfee/ *n.* photography producing photographs larger than life.

mac·ro·scop·ic /mákrəskópik/ *adj.* **1** visible to the naked eye. **2** regarded in terms of large units. ▫▫ **mac·ro·scop·i·cal·ly** *adv.*

mad /mad/ *adj. & v.* • *adj.* (**madder, maddest**) **1** insane; having a disordered mind. **2** (of a person, conduct, or idea) wildly foolish. **3** (often foll. by *about*) wildly excited or infatuated (*mad about football; is chess-mad*). **4** *colloq.* angry. **5** (of an animal) rabid. **6** wildly lighthearted. • *v.* (**madded, madding**) **1** *intr. archaic* be mad; act madly (*the madding crowd*). □ **as mad as a hatter** wildly eccentric. **like mad** *colloq.* with great energy, intensity, or enthusiasm. □□ **mad·ness** *n.*

mad·am /mádəm/ *n.* **1** a polite or respectful form of address or mode of reference to a woman. **2** a woman brothel-keeper.

Mad·ame /mədaám, mádəm/ *n.* **1** (*pl.* **Mesdames** /maydaám, –dám/) a title or form of address used of or to a French-speaking woman, corresponding to Mrs. or madam. **2** (**madame**) = MADAM 1.

mad·cap /mádkap/ *adj. & n.* • *adj.* **1** wildly impulsive. **2** undertaken without forethought. • *n.* a wildly impulsive person.

mad·den /mád'n/ *v.* **1** *tr. & intr.* make or become mad. **2** *tr.* irritate intensely. □□ **mad·den·ing** *adj.* **mad·den·ing·ly** *adv.*

mad·der /mádər/ *n.* **1** a herbaceous plant, *Rubia tinctorum*, with yellowish flowers. **2** a red dye obtained from the root of the madder, or its synthetic substitute.

made /mayd/ **1** *past* and *past part.* of MAKE. **2** *adj.* (usu. in *comb.*) **a** (of a person or thing) built or formed (*well-made; strongly made*). **b** successful (*a self-made man*). □ **have it made** *colloq.* be sure of success. **made for** ideally suited to. **made of** consisting of. **made of money** *colloq.* very rich.

Ma·dei·ra /mədeérə/ *n.* an amber-colored fortified white wine from the island of Madeira off the coast of N. Africa.

Mad·e·moi·selle /mádəməzél, mádmwə–/ *n.* (*pl.* **-s** or **Mesdemoiselles** /máydmwə–/) **1** a title or form of address used of or to an unmarried French-speaking woman, corresponding to Miss. **2** (**mademoiselle**) **a** a young Frenchwoman. **b** a French governess.

mad·house /mádhows/ *n.* **1** *archaic* or *colloq.* a home or hospital for the mentally disturbed. **2** *colloq.* a scene of extreme confusion or uproar.

mad·ly /mádlee/ *adv.* **1** in a mad manner. **2** *colloq.* **a** passionately. **b** extremely.

mad·man /mádmən, –man/ *n.* (*pl.* **-men**) a man who is insane or who behaves insanely.

Ma·don·na /mədónə/ *n. Eccl.* **1** (prec. by *the*) a name for the Virgin Mary. **2** a picture or statue of the Madonna.

mad·ras /mádrəs, mədrás/ *n.* a strong, lightweight cotton fabric with colored or white stripes, checks, etc.

mad·ri·gal /mádrigəl/ *n.* **1** a usu. 16th-c. or 17th-c. part song for several voices, usu. arranged in elaborate counterpoint and without instrumental accompaniment. **2** a short love poem. □□ **mad·ri·gal·i·an** /–gáyleeən/ *adj.* **mad·ri·gal·ist** *n.*

mad·wom·an /mádwoomən/ *n.* (*pl.* **-women**) a woman who is insane or who behaves insanely.

mael·strom /máylstrəm/ *n.* **1** a great whirlpool. **2** a state of confusion.

maes·tro /místrō/ *n.* (*pl.* **maestri** /–stree/or **-tros**) **1** a distinguished musician, esp. a conductor. **2** a great performer in any sphere.

Ma·fi·a /maáfeeə, máf–/ *n.* **1** an organized body of criminals, orig. in Sicily, now also in Italy, the US, and elsewhere. **2** (**mafia**) a group regarded as exerting a hidden sinister influence.

Ma·fi·o·so /maafeeósō, máf–/ *n.* (*pl.* **Mafiosi** /–see/) a member of the Mafia.

mag·a·zine /mágəzeén/ *n.* **1** a periodical publication containing articles, stories, etc., usu. with illustrations. **2** a chamber for holding a supply of cartridges to be fed automatically to the breech of a gun. **3** a similar device feeding a camera, slide projector, etc. **4** a store for arms, ammunition, and provisions for use in war. **5** a store for explosives.

magazine late 16th century: from French *magasin*, from Italian *magazzino*, from Arabic *makzin*, *makzan* 'storehouse,' from *kazana* 'store up.' The original sense was 'store'; this was often used from the mid-17th century onward in the title of books providing information useful to particular groups of people, and from it arose sense 1 (mid-18th century). Sense 4, a contemporary specialization of the original meaning, gave rise to sense 2 in the mid-18th century.

ma·gen·ta /məjéntə/ *n. & adj.* • *n.* **1** a brilliant mauvish-crimson color. **2** an aniline dye of this color. • *adj.* of or colored with magenta.

mag·got /mágət/ *n.* the soft-bodied larva of a dipterous insect, esp. the housefly or bluebottle. □□ **mag·got·y** *adj.*

ma·gi *pl.* of MAGUS.

mag·ic /májik/ *n., adj., & v.* • *n.* **1 a** the supposed art of influencing the course of events by the occult control of nature or of the spirits. **b** witchcraft. **2** conjuring tricks. **3** an inexplicable or remarkable influence producing surprising results. **4** an enchanting quality or phenomenon. • *adj.* **1** of or resulting from magic. **2** producing surprising results. **3** *colloq.* wonderful; exciting. • *v.tr.* (**magicked, magicking**) change or create by magic, or apparently so. □ **like magic** very effectively or rapidly.

mag·i·cal /májikəl/ *adj.* **1** of or relating to magic. **2** resembling magic; produced as if by magic. **3** wonderful; enchanting. □□ **mag·i·cal·ly** *adv.*

ma·gi·cian /məjíshən/ *n.* **1** a person skilled in or practicing magic. **2** a person who performs magic tricks for entertainment. **3** a person with exceptional skill.

mag·is·te·ri·al /májisteéreeəl/ *adj.* **1** imperious. **2** invested with authority. **3** of or conducted by a magistrate. **4** highly authoritative. □□ **mag·is·te·ri·al·ly** *adv.*

mag·is·trate /májustrayt, –strət/ *n.* **1** a civil officer administering the law. **2** an official conducting a court for minor cases and preliminary hearings (*magistrates' court*).

mag·lev /máglev/ *n.* (usu. *attrib.*) magnetic levitation, a system in which trains glide above the track in a magnetic field.

mag·ma /mágmə/ *n.* (*pl.* **magmata** /–mətə/or **magmas**) **1** fluid or semifluid material from which igneous rock is formed by cooling. **2** a crude pasty mixture of mineral or organic matter. □□ **mag·mat·ic** /–mátik/ *adj.*

Mag·na Car·ta /mágnə kaártə/ *n.* (also **Mag·na Char·ta**) **1** a charter of liberty and political rights obtained from King John of England in 1215. **2** any similar document of rights.

mag·nan·i·mous /magnánimǝs/ *adj.* nobly generous; not petty in feelings or conduct. □□ **mag·na·nim·i·ty** /mágnənímitee/ *n.* **mag·nan·i·mous·ly** *adv.*

mag·nate /mágnayt, –nət/ *n.* a wealthy and influential person (*shipping magnate; financial magnate*).

mag·ne·sia /magneézhə, –shə, –zyə/ *n.* **1** *Chem.* magnesium oxide. **2** (in general use) hydrated magnesium carbonate, a white powder used as an antacid and laxative. □□ **mag·ne·sian** *adj.*

mag·ne·si·um /magneézeeəm/ *n. Chem.* a silvery metallic element used for making light alloys and important as an essential element in living organisms. ¶ Symb.: **Mg**.

mag·net /mágnit/ *n.* **1** a piece of iron, steel, alloy, ore, etc., having properties of attracting or repelling iron. **2** a lodestone. **3** a person or thing that attracts.

mag·net·ic /magnétik/ *adj.* **1 a** having the properties of a magnet. **b** producing, produced by, or acting by magnetism. **2** capable of being attracted by or acquiring the properties of a magnet. **3** very attractive or alluring (*a magnetic personality*). □□ **mag·net·i·cal·ly** *adv.*

mag·net·ic field *n.* a region of variable force around magnets, magnetic materials, or current-carrying conductors.

mag·net·ic north *n.* the point indicated by the north end of a compass needle.

mag·net·ic pole *n.* **1** each of the points near the extremities of the axis of rotation of the earth or another body where a magnetic needle dips vertically. **2** each of the regions of an artificial or natural magnet, from which the magnetic forces appear to originate.

mag·net·ic res·o·nance im·ag·ing *n.* a noninvasive diagnostic technique employing a scanner to obtain computerized images of internal body tissue. ¶ Abbr.: **MRI**.

mag·net·ic tape *n.* a tape coated with magnetic material for recording sound or pictures or for the storage of information.

mag·net·ism /mágnitizəm/ *n.* **1 a** magnetic phenomena and their study. **b** the property of producing these phenomena. **2** personal charm.

mag·net·ite /mágnitīt/ *n.* magnetic iron oxide.

mag·net·ize /mágnitīz/ *v.tr.* **1** give magnetic properties to. **2** make into a magnet. **3** attract as or like a magnet. □□ **mag·ne·ti·za·tion** *n.*

mag·ne·to /magneétō/ *n.* (*pl.* **-tos**) an electric generator using permanent magnets and producing high voltage, esp. for the ignition of an internal combustion engine.

mag·ne·to·e·lec·tric /magneétō-iléktrik/ *adj.* (of an electric generator) using permanent magnets. □□ **mag·ne·to·e·lec·tric·i·ty** /–trísitee/ *n.*

mag·net school *n.* a public school that draws students from throughout a district, offering superior facilities, specialized courses, etc.

mag·ni·fi·ca·tion /mágnifikáyshən/ *n.* **1** the act or an instance of magnifying; the process of being magnified. **2** the amount or degree of magnification. **3** the apparent enlargement of an object by a lens.

mag·nif·i·cent /magnífisənt/ *adj.* **1** splendid; stately. **2** sumptuously constructed or adorned. **3** *colloq.* fine; excellent. □□ **mag·nif·i·cence** /–səns/ *n.* **mag·nif·i·cent·ly** *adv.*

mag·nif·i·co /magnífikō/ *n.* (*pl.* **-coes**) a high ranking, eminent, or powerful person.

mag·ni·fy /mágnifī/ *v.tr.* (**-fies, -fied**) **1** make (a thing) appear larger than it is, as with a lens. **2** exaggerate. **3** intensify. □□ **mag·ni·fi·a·ble** *adj.* **mag·ni·fi·er** *n.*

mag·ni·fy·ing glass *n.* a lens used to produce an enlarged image.

mag·ni·tude /mágnitōōd, –tyōōd/ *n.* **1** largeness. **2** size. **3** importance. **4 a** the degree of brightness of a star. **b** a class of stars arranged according to this (*of the third magnitude*). □ **of the first magnitude** very important.

mag·no·lia /magnṓlyə/ *n.* **1** any tree or shrub of the genus *Magnolia*, cultivated for its dark-green foliage and large waxlike flowers in spring. **2** a pale creamy-pink color.

mag·num /mágnəm/ *n.* (*pl.* **magnums**) **1** a wine bottle of about twice the standard size. **2 a** a cartridge or shell that is especially powerful or large. **b** (often *attrib.*) a cartridge or gun adapted so as to be more powerful than its caliber suggests.

mag·num o·pus /mágnəm ṓpəs/ *n.* (*pl.* **magnum opuses** or **magna opera**) **1** a great work of art, literature, etc. **2** the most important work of an artist, writer, etc.

mag·pie /mágpī/ *n.* **1** a Eurasian crow (*Pica pica*) or a N. American crow (*P. nuttalli*) with a long pointed tail and black-and-white plumage. **2** any of various birds with plumage like a magpie, esp. *Gymnorhina tibicen* of Australia. **3** a chatterer. **4** a person who collects things indiscriminately. **5** *colloq.* a black-and-white cow or steer, esp. a Holstein.

ma·gus /máygəs/ *n.* (*pl.* **magi** /máyjī/) **1** a member of a priestly caste of ancient Persia. **2** a sorcerer. **3** (**the Magi**) the "wise men" from the East who brought gifts to the infant Christ (Matt. 2:1).

Mag·yar /mágyaar/ *n.* & *adj.* • *n.* **1** a member of a Ural-Altaic people now predominant in Hungary. **2** the language of this people. • *adj.* of or relating to this people or language.

ma·ha·ra·ja /maáhəraájə, –zhə/ *n.* (also **ma·ha·ra·jah**) *hist.* a title of some princes of India.

ma·ha·ra·ni /maáhəraánee/ *n.* (also **ma·ha·ra·nee**) *hist.* a maharaja's wife or widow.

ma·ha·ri·shi /maáhəreéshi/ *n.* a great Hindu sage or spiritual leader.

ma·hat·ma /məhaátmə, –hát–/ *n.* **1 a** (esp. in India) a person regarded with reverence. **b** a sage. **2** each of a class of persons in India and Tibet supposed by some to have preternatural powers.

Ma·hi·can /məheékən/ *n.* & *adj.* (also **Mo·hi·can** /mō–/) • *n.* **1** a N. American people native to the upper Hudson River Valley of New York state. **2** a member of this people. • *adj.* of or relating to this people.

mah-jongg /maajóng, –jáwng, –zhóng, -zháwng/ *n.* (also **mahjong**) a Chinese game for four resembling rummy and played with 136 or 144 pieces called tiles.

ma·hog·a·ny /məhógənee/ *n.* (*pl.* **-nies**) **1 a** a reddish-brown wood used for furniture. **b** the color of this. **2** any tropical tree of the genus *Swietenia*, esp. *S. mahagoni*, yielding this wood.

maid /mayd/ *n.* **1** a female domestic servant. **2** *archaic* or *poet.* a girl or young woman.

maid·en /máyd'n/ *n.* & *adj.* • *n.* **1** *archaic* or *poet.* a girl; a young unmarried woman. **2** (often *attrib.*) **a** a horse that has never won a race. **b** a race open only to such horses. • *adj.* **1** unmarried (*maiden aunt*). **2** being or involving the first attempt or occurrence (*maiden speech*; *maiden voyage*). **3** (of a female animal) unmated. □□ **maid·en·hood** *n.* **maid·en·ly** *adj.*

maid·en·hair /máyd'nhair/ *n.* (in full **maidenhair fern**) a fern of the genus *Adiantum*, esp. *A. capillus-veneris*, with delicate fronds.

maid·en·head /máyd'nhed/ *n.* **1** virginity. **2** the hymen.

maid·en name *n.* a wife's surname before marriage.

maid of hon·or *n.* **1** a principal bridesmaid. **2** an unmarried lady attending a queen or princess.

maid·serv·ant /máydservənt/ *n.* a female servant.

mail[1] /mayl/ *n.* & *v.* • *n.* **1 a** letters and parcels, etc., conveyed by the postal system. **b** the postal system. **c** one complete delivery or collection of mail. **d** one delivery of letters to one place, esp. to a business on one occasion. **2** (usu. **the mails**) the system that delivers the mail. **3** a vehicle carrying mail. • *v.tr.* send by mail.

mail[2] /mayl/ *n.* & *v.* • *n.* **1** armor made of rings, chains, or plates. **2** the protective shell, scales, etc., of an animal. • *v.tr.* clothe with or as if with mail. □□ **mailed** *adj.*

mail·box /máylboks/ *n.* **1** a public receptacle for depositing mail. **2** a private receptacle for at-home pickup and delivery of mail. **3** a computer file in which electronic mail is stored.

mail car·ri·er *n.* a person who delivers mail.

mail·ing list *n.* a list of people to whom advertising matter, information, etc., is to be mailed.

mail·man /máylmən/ *n.* (*pl.* **-men**) a mail carrier.

mail or·der *n.* an order for goods sent by mail.
mail·room /máylrōōm, –rōōm/ *n.* a room for sorting incoming and outgoing mail in a business or an organization.
maim /maym/ *v.tr.* **1** cripple, disable, mutilate. **2** harm; impair (*emotionally maimed by neglect*).
main /mayn/ *adj.* & *n.* • *adj.* **1** chief; principal (*the main part; the main point*). **2** exerted to the full (*by main force*). • *n.* **1** a principal channel, duct, etc., for water, sewage, etc. (*water main*). **2** *archaic* or *poet.* **a** the ocean or oceans (*the Spanish Main*). **b** the mainland. □ **in the main** for the most part. **with might and main** with all one's force.
main course *n.* **1** the chief course of a meal. **2** *Naut.* the mainsail.
main drag *n. US colloq.* = MAIN STREET.
main·frame /máynfraym/ *n.* **1** the central processing unit and primary memory of a computer. **2** (often *attrib.*) a large computer system.
main·land /máynlənd/ *n.* a large continuous extent of land, excluding neighboring islands, etc. □□ **main·land·er** *n.*
main·line /máynlīn/ *v. sl.* **1** *intr.* take drugs intravenously. **2** *tr.* inject (drugs) intravenously (*mainlining heroin*). □□ **main·lin·er** *n.*
main line *n.* **1** a chief railroad line. **2** *sl.* a principal vein (cf. MAINLINE). **3** a chief road or street.
main·ly /máynlee/ *adv.* for the most part; chiefly.
main·mast /máynmast, –məst/ *n. Naut.* the principal mast of a ship.
main·sail /máynsayl, –səl/ *n. Naut.* **1** (in a square-rigged vessel) the lowest sail on the mainmast. **2** (in a fore-and-aft-rigged vessel) a sail set on the after part of the mainmast.
main·spring /máynspring/ *n.* **1** the principal spring of a mechanical watch, clock, etc. **2** a chief motive power; an incentive.
main·stay /máynstay/ *n.* a chief support (*has been his mainstay since his trouble*).
main·stream /máynstreem/ *n.* **1** (often *attrib.*) the prevailing trend in opinion, fashion, etc. **2** a type of jazz based on the 1930s swing style and consisting esp. of solo improvisation on chord sequences. **3** the principal current of a river.
main street *n.* the principal street of a town.
main·tain /mayntáyn/ *v.tr.* **1** cause to continue; keep up, preserve (a state of affairs, an activity, etc.) (*maintained friendly relations*). **2** (often foll. by *in*; often *refl.*) support (life, a condition, etc.) by work, nourishment, expenditure, etc. (*maintained him in comfort; maintained themselves by fishing*). **3** (often foll. by *that* + clause) assert (an opinion, statement, etc.) as true (*maintained that she was the best; his story was true, he maintained*). **4** preserve (a building, machine, road, etc.) in good repair. **5** give aid to (a cause, party, etc.). **6** provide means for (a garrison, etc., to be equipped). □□ **main·tain·er** *n.* **main·tain·a·ble** *adj.* **main·tain·a·bil·i·ty** *n.*
main·te·nance /máyntənəns/ *n.* **1** the process of maintaining or being maintained. **2** the provision of the means to support life.
maî·tre d'hô·tel /métrə dōtél, máyt–/ *n.* (*pl.* **maîtres d'hôtel** *pronunc.* same) **1** (also **maitre d'**) a headwaiter. **2** the manager, head steward, etc., of a hotel.
maize /mayz/ *n.* **1** esp. *Brit.* = CORN[1] *n.* 1. **2** a pale golden-yellow color.
Maj. *abbr.* Major.
ma·jes·tic /məjéstik/ *adj.* stately and dignified; imposing. □□ **ma·jes·ti·cal·ly** *adv.*
maj·es·ty /májistee/ *n.* (*pl.* **-ties**) **1** impressive stateliness, dignity, or authority. **2 a** royal power. **b** (**Majesty**) part of several titles given to a sovereign or a sovereign's wife or widow or used in addressing them (*Your Majesty; Her Majesty the Queen Mother*).
ma·jor /máyjər/ *adj., n.,* & *v.* • *adj.* **1** important; large; serious; significant (*a major road; a major war; the major consideration must be their health*). **2** (of an operation) serious. **3** *Mus.* **a** (of a scale) having intervals of a semitone between the third and fourth, and seventh and eighth degrees. **b** (of an interval) greater by a semitone than a minor interval (*major third*). **c** (of a key) based on a major scale. **4** of full legal age. **5** *Brit.* (appended to a surname, esp. in public schools) the elder of two brothers (*Smith major*). • *n.* **1 a** an army officer next below lieutenant colonel and above captain. **b** a person in charge of a section of band instruments (*drum major*). **2** a person of full legal age. **3** *US* **a** a student's most emphasized subject or course. **b** a student specializing in a specified subject (*a philosophy major*). • *v.intr.* (foll. by *in*) study or qualify in as a special subject (*majored in theology*).
ma·jor·do·mo /máyjərdṓmō/ *n.* (*pl.* **-mos**) **1** the chief official of an Italian or Spanish princely household. **2** a house steward; a butler.
ma·jor gen·er·al *n.* an officer next below a lieutenant general.
ma·jor·i·ty /məjáwritee, –jór–/ *n.* (*pl.* **·ties**) **1** (usu. foll. by *of*) the greater number or part. ▶Strictly used only with countable nouns, e.g., *a majority of people*, and not with mass nouns, e.g., *a majority of the work*. **2** *Polit.* **a** the number by which the votes cast for one party, candidate, etc., exceed those of the next (*won by a majority of 151*). **b** a party, etc., receiving the greater number of votes. **3** full legal age (*attained his majority*). **4** the rank of major. □ **the great majority 1** much the greater number. **2** *euphem.* the dead (*has joined the great majority*). **in the majority** esp. *Polit.* belonging to or constituting a majority party, etc.
▶**Majority** means more than half: *Fifty-one out of 100 is a majority.*. A **plurality** is the largest number among three or more: *If Anne received 50 votes, Barry received 30, and Carlos received 20, then Anne received a plurality, and no candidate won a majority; if Anne got 35 votes, Barry 14, and Carlos 51, then Carlos won both the plurality and the majority.*
ma·jor league *n.* a professional league of highest classification in baseball, etc.
make /mayk/ *v.* & *n.* • *v.* (*past* and *past part.* **made** /mayd/) **1** *tr.* construct; create; form from parts or other substances. **2** *tr.* (often foll. by *to* + infin.) cause or compel (*make him repeat it*). **3** *tr.* **a** cause to exist; bring about (*made a noise*). **b** cause to become or seem (*made him angry*). **c** appoint; designate (*made him a cardinal*). **4** *tr.* prepare; draw up (*made her will*). **5** *tr.* amount to (*makes a difference; 2 and 2 make 4*). **6** *tr.* **a** undertake or agree to (an aim or purpose) (*made a promise*). **b** execute or perform (a bodily movement, a speech, etc.) (*made a face*). **7** *tr.* gain, acquire, procure (money, a profit, etc.). **8** *tr.* prepare (tea, coffee, a dish, etc.) for consumption. **9** *tr.* **a** arrange bedding neatly on (a bed). **b** arrange and ignite materials for (a fire). **10** *intr.* **a** proceed (*made toward the river*). **b** (foll. by *to* + infin.) begin an action (*he made to go*). **11** *tr. colloq.* **a** arrive at (a place) or in time for (a train, etc.) (*made the six o'clock train*). **b** manage to attend (*couldn't make the meeting last week; can make any day except Friday*). **c** achieve a place in (*made the first team*). **d** achieve the rank of (*made colonel in three years*). **12** *tr.* establish or enact (a distinction, rule, law, etc.). **13** *tr.* estimate as (*I'd make the time to be 7 o'clock*). **14** *tr.* secure the success or advancement of (*it made my day*). **15** *tr.* accomplish (a distance, score, etc.) (*made 60 m.p.h. on the freeway*). **16** *tr.* **a** become by development or training

(*made a great leader*). **b** serve as (*a log makes a useful seat*). **17** *tr.* (usu. foll. by *out*) cause to appear as (*makes him out a liar*). **18** *tr.* form in the mind (*I make no judgment*). **19** *tr.* (foll. by *it* + compl.) **a** determine, establish, or choose (*let's make it Tuesday*). **b** bring to (a chosen value, etc.) (*decided to make it a dozen*). **20** *tr. sl.* have sexual relations with. **21** *tr. Cards* **a** win (a trick). **b** play (a card) to advantage. **c** win the number of tricks that fulfills (a contract). **d** shuffle (a deck of cards) for dealing. **22** *tr. Electr.* complete or close (a circuit) (opp. BREAK[1] 10). • *n.* **1** (esp. of a product) a type, origin, brand, etc., of manufacture (*different make of car*). **2** a kind of mental, moral, or physical structure or composition. **3** an act of shuffling cards. □ **make as if** (or **though**) (foll. by *to* + infin. or conditional) act as if (*made as if to leave*). **make away with** = *make off with*. **make believe** pretend. **make a day** (or **night**, etc.) **of it** devote a whole day (or night, etc.) to an activity. **make do 1** manage with the means available. **2** (foll. by *with*) manage with (something) as an inferior substitute. **make an example of** punish as a warning to others. **make for 1** tend to result in (happiness, etc.). **2** proceed toward (a place). **3** assault; attack. **4** confirm (an opinion). **make friends** (often foll. by *with*) become friendly. **make headway** advance; progress. **make it 1** *colloq.* succeed in reaching, esp. in time. **2** *colloq.* be successful. **3** (usu. foll. by *with*) *sl.* have sexual intercourse (with). **make it up 1** be reconciled, esp. after a quarrel. **2** fill in a deficit. **make it up to** remedy negligence, an injury, etc., to (a person). **make much** (or **little** or **the best**) **of 1** derive much (or little, etc.) advantage from. **2** give much (or little, etc.) attention, importance, etc., to. **make nothing of 1** do without hesitation. **2** treat as a trifle. **3** be unable to understand, use, or deal with. **make of 1** construct from. **2** conclude to be the meaning or character of (*can you make anything of it?*). **make off** (or **away**) **with** carry away; steal. **make or break** cause the success or ruin of. **make out 1 a** distinguish by sight or hearing. **b** decipher (handwriting, etc.). **2** understand (*can't make him out*). **3** assert; pretend (*made out he liked it*). **4** *colloq.* make progress; fare (*how did you make out?*). **5** (usu. foll. by *to, in favor of*) draw up; write out (*made out a check to her*). **6** prove or try to prove (*how do you make that out?*). **7** (often foll. by *with*). *colloq.* **a** engage in sexual play or petting. **b** form a sexual relationship. **make over 1** transfer the possession of (a thing) to a person. **2** refashion; restyle. **make time 1** (usu. foll. by *for* or *to* + infin.) find an occasion when time is available. **2** (usu. foll. by *with*) *sl.* make sexual advances (to a person). **make up 1** serve or act to overcome (a deficiency). **2** complete (an amount, a party, etc.). **3** compensate. **4** be reconciled. **5** put together; compound; prepare (*made up the medicine*). **6** sew together. **7** get (a sum of money, a company, etc.) together. **8** concoct (a story). **9** (of parts) compose (a whole). **10** apply cosmetics. **11** settle (a dispute). **12** prepare (a bed) for use with fresh sheets, etc. **13** *Printing* arrange (type) in pages. **14** compile (a list, an account, etc.). **make up one's mind** decide; resolve. **make way 1** (often foll. by *for*) allow room for others to proceed. **2** achieve progress. **make one's way** proceed. **on the make** *colloq.* **1** intent on gain. **2** looking for sexual partners.

make-be·lieve *n. & adj.* • *n.* the action of pretending or imagining. • *adj.* imitating something real; pretend (*shooting a make-believe gun*).

make·o·ver /máykōvər/ *n.* a complete transformation or restyling.

mak·er /máykər/ *n.* **1** (often in *comb.*) a person or thing that makes. **2** (**our, the,** etc., **Maker**) God.

make·shift /máykshift/ *adj. & n.* • *adj.* temporary; serving for the time being. • *n.* a temporary substitute or device.

make·up /máykəp/ *n.* **1** cosmetics such as lipstick or powder for the face for enhancing or altering the appearance. **2** the appearance of the face, etc., when cosmetics have been applied (*his makeup was not convincing*). **3** *Printing* the making up of a type. **4** *Printing* the type made up. **5** a person's character, temperament, etc. **6** the composition or constitution of a thing.

mak·ing /máyking/ *n.* **1** in senses of MAKE *v.* **2** (in *pl.*) **a** earnings; profit. **b** (foll. by *of*) essential qualities or ingredients (*has the makings of a general*). **c** *colloq.* paper and tobacco for rolling a cigarette. □ **be the making of** ensure the success or favorable development of. **in the making** in the course of being made or formed.

ma·ko /máykō, maákō/ *n.* (*pl.* **-kos**) a blue shark, *Isurus oxyrinchus*.

mal- /mal/ *comb. form* **1** bad; badly (*malpractice*; *maltreat*). **2** faulty, faultily (*malfunction*). **3** not (*maladroit*).

mal·a·chite /máləkīt/ *n.* a bright-green mineral of hydrous copper carbonate, used for ornament.

mal·a·col·o·gy /máləkóləjee/ *n.* the study of mollusks.

mal·ad·just·ed /máləjústid/ *adj.* **1** not correctly adjusted. **2** (of a person) unable to adapt to or cope with the demands of a social environment. □□ **mal·ad·just·ment** *n.*

mal·a·droit /málədróyt/ *adj.* clumsy; bungling. □□ **mal·a·droit·ly** *adv.* **mal·a·droit·ness** *n.*

mal·a·dy /málədee/ *n.* (*pl.* **-dies**) **1** an ailment; a disease. **2** a morbid or depraved condition.

Mal·a·gas·y /máləgásee/ *adj. & n.* • *adj.* of or relating to Madagascar, an island in the Indian Ocean. • *n.* the language of Madagascar.

ma·laise /məláyz/ *n.* **1** a non-specific bodily discomfort not associated with the development of a disease. **2** a feeling of uneasiness.

mal·a·mute /máləmyōōt/ *n.* (also **malemute**) any of an Alaskan breed of large sled dogs.

mal·a·prop·ism /máləpropizəm/ *n.* (also **mal·a·prop** /mál əprop/) the use of a word in mistake for one sounding similar, to comic effect, e.g., *allegory* for *alligator*.

mal·ap·ro·pos /málaprəpṓ/ *adv., adj., & n.* • *adv.* inopportunely; inappropriately. • *adj.* inopportune; inappropriate. • *n.* something inappropriately said, done, etc.

ma·lar /máylər/ *adj. & n.* • *adj.* of the cheek. • *n.* (also **malar bone**) a bone of the cheek.

ma·lar·i·a /məláireeə/ *n.* a recurrent fever caused by a protozoan parasite of the genus *Plasmodium*, introduced by the bite of a mosquito. □□ **ma·lar·i·al** *adj.* **ma·lar·i·ous** *adj.*

ma·lar·key /məlaárkee/ *n. colloq.* humbug; nonsense.

Ma·lay /máylay, məláy/ *n. & adj.* • *n.* **1 a** a member of a people predominating in Malaysia and Indonesia. **b** a person of Malay descent. **2** the language of this people, the official language of Malaysia. • *adj.* of or relating to this people or language. □□ **Ma·lay·an** *n. & adj.*

mal·con·tent /málkəntent/ *n. & adj.* • *n.* a discontented person; a rebel. • *adj.* discontented or rebellious.

male /mayl/ *adj. & n.* • *adj.* **1** of the sex that can beget offspring by fertilization or insemination. **2** of men or male animals, plants, etc.; masculine. **3 a** (of plants or their parts) containing only fertilizing organs. **b** (of plants) thought of as male because of color, shape, etc. **4** (of parts of machinery, etc.) designed to enter or fill the corresponding female part (*a male plug*). • *n.* a male person or animal. □□ **male·ness** *n.*

male chau·vin·ist (**pig**) *n.* a man who is prejudiced against women or regards women as inferior.

---

mal·e·dic·tion /málidíkshən/ *n.* **1** a curse. **2** the utterance of a curse.

mal·e·fac·tor /málifaktər/ *n.* a criminal; an evildoer.

mal·e·fi·cent /məléfisənt/ *adj. literary* **1** (often foll. by *to*) hurtful. **2** criminal. ▫▫ **mal·e·fi·cence** /–səns/ *n.*

ma·lev·o·lent /məlévələnt/ *adj.* wishing evil to others. ▫▫ **ma·lev·o·lence** /–ləns/ *n.* **ma·lev·o·lent·ly** *adv.*

mal·fea·sance /malféezəns/ *n. Law* evildoing. ▫▫ **mal·fea·sant** /–zənt/ *n. & adj.*

mal·func·tion /málfúngkshən/ *n. & v.* • *n.* a failure to function in a normal or satisfactory manner. • *v.intr.* fail to function normally or satisfactorily.

mal·ice /mális/ *n.* **1 a** the intention to do evil. **b** a desire to tease, esp. cruelly. **2** *Law* wrongful intention, esp. as increasing guilt. ▫▫ **ma·li·cious** /məlíshəs/ *adj.* **ma·li·cious·ly** *adv.* **ma·li·cious·ness** *n.*

ma·lice a·fore·thought *n.* (also **mal·ice pre·pense**) *Law* the intention to commit a crime, esp. murder.

ma·lign /məlín/ *adj. & v.* • *adj.* **1** (of a thing) injurious. **2** (of a disease) malignant. **3** malevolent. • *v.tr.* speak ill of; slander. ▫▫ **ma·lig·ni·ty** /məlígnitee/ *n.* (*pl.* **-ties**). **ma·lign·ly** /–línlee/ *adv.*

ma·lig·nant /məlígnənt/ *adj.* **1 a** (of a disease) very virulent or infectious (*malignant cholera*). **b** (of a tumor) tending to invade normal tissue and recur after removal; cancerous. **2** harmful; feeling or showing intense ill will. ▫▫ **ma·lig·nan·cy** *n.* (*pl.* **-cies**). **ma·lig·nant·ly** *adv.*

ma·lin·ger /məlínggər/ *v.intr.* feign illness in order to escape work, etc. ▫▫ **ma·lin·ger·er** *n.*

mall /mawl/ *n.* **1** a sheltered walk or promenade. **2** an enclosed shopping center.

mal·lard /málərd/ *n.* (*pl.* same or **mallards**) **1** a wild duck or drake, *Anas platyrhynchos*, of the northern hemisphere. **2** the flesh of the mallard.

mal·le·a·ble /máleeəbəl/ *adj.* **1** (of metal, etc.) able to be hammered or pressed permanently out of shape without breaking or cracking. **2** adaptable; flexible. ▫▫ **mal·le·a·bil·i·ty** *n.* **mal·le·a·bly** *adv.*

mal·let /málit/ *n.* **1** a hammer, usu. of wood. **2** a long-handled wooden hammer for striking a croquet or polo ball.

mal·le·us /máleeəs/ (*pl.* **mallei** /–lee-ī/) *Anat.* a small bone in the middle ear transmitting the vibrations of the tympanum to the incus.

mal·low /málō/ *n.* **1** a herbaceous plant of the genus *Malva* with hairy stems and leaves and pink or purple flowers. **2** any of several other plants of the family Malvaceae, including marsh mallow.

mal·nour·ished /málnórisht, –núr–/ *adj.* suffering from malnutrition. ▫▫ **mal·nour·ish·ment** /–nórishmənt, –núr–/ *n.*

mal·nu·tri·tion /málnōōtríshən, –nyōō–/ *n.* a dietary condition resulting from the absence of foods necessary for health; insufficient nutrition.

mal·oc·clu·sion /maləklōōzhən/ *n. Dentistry* faulty contact of opposing teeth when the jaws are closed.

mal·o·dor·ous /malṓdərəs/ *adj.* having an unpleasant smell.

mal·prac·tice /malpráktis/ *n.* **1** improper or negligent professional treatment, as by a medical practitioner. **2 a** criminal wrongdoing. **b** an instance of this.

malt /mawlt/ *n. & v.* • *n.* barley or other grain that is steeped, germinated, and dried, esp. for brewing. • *v.* **1** *tr.* convert (grain) into malt. **2** *intr.* (of seeds) become malt when germination is checked by drought. ▫▫ **malt·y** /máwltee/ *adj.* (**maltier, maltiest**). **malt·i·ness** *n.*

Mal·tese /máwltéez, –tées/ *n. & adj.* • *n.* **1** (*pl.* same) **a** a native or national of Malta. **b** a person of Maltese descent. **2** the language of Malta. • *adj.* of or relating to Malta or its people or language.

Mal·tese cross *n.* a cross with arms of equal length broadening from the center, often indented at the ends.

malt liq·uor *n.* a kind of strong beer.

malt·ose /máwltōs, –tōz/ *n. Chem.* a sugar produced by the hydrolysis of starch under the action of the enzymes in malt, saliva, etc.

mal·treat /máltréet/ *v.tr.* ill-treat. ▫▫ **mal·treat·er** *n.* **mal·treat·ment** *n.*

ma·ma /maámə, məmaá/ *n. colloq.* (esp. as a child's term) mother.

mam·ba /maámbə/ *n.* any venomous African snake of the genus *Dendroaspis*, esp. the green mamba (*D. angusticeps*) or black mamba (*D. polylepis*).

mam·bo /maámbō/ *n. & v.* • *n.* (*pl.* **-bos**) **1** a Latin American dance like the rumba. **2** the music for this. • *v.intr.* (**-boes, -boed**) perform the mambo.

mam·ma[1] /maámə/ *n.* (also **mom·ma**) *colloq.* (esp. as a child's term) mother.

mam·ma[2] /maámə/ *n.* (*pl.* **mammae** /–mee/) **1** a milk-secreting organ of female mammals. **2** a corresponding nonsecretory structure in male mammals. ▫▫ **mam·mi·form** *adj.*

mam·mal /máməl/ *n.* any vertebrate of the class Mammalia, the females of which possess milk-secreting mammae for the nourishment of the young. ▫▫ **mam·ma·li·an** /–máyliən/ *adj. & n.*

mam·ma·ry /máməree/ *adj.* of the human female breasts or milk-secreting organs of other mammals.

mam·mog·ra·phy /mamógrəfee/ *n. Med.* an X-ray technique of diagnosing and locating abnormalities of the breasts.

mam·mon /mámən/ *n.* (also **Mammon**) **1** wealth regarded as a god or as an evil influence. **2** the worldly rich.

mam·moth /máməth/ *n. & adj.* • *n.* any large extinct elephant of the genus *Mammuthus*, with a hairy coat and curved tusks. • *adj.* huge.

mammoth

Man. *abbr.* Manitoba.

man /man/ *n. & v.* • *n.* (*pl.* **men** /men/) **1** an adult human male, esp. as distinct from a woman or boy. **2 a** a person (*no man is perfect*). **b** the human race (*man is mortal*). **3** a person showing characteristics associated with males (*she's more of a man than he is*). **4** a worker; an employee (*the manager spoke to the men*). **5 a** (usu. in *pl.*) soldiers, sailors, etc., esp. nonofficers. **b** an individual (*fought to the last man*). **c** (usu. prec. by *the*, or *poss. pron.*) a person fulfilling requirements (*I'm your man*). **6 a** a husband (*man and wife*). **b** *colloq.* a boyfriend or lover. **7 a** a human being of a specified historical period or character (*Renaissance man*). **b** a type of prehistoric man named after the place where the remains were found (*Peking man*). **8** any one of a set of pieces used in playing chess, etc. **9** (as second element in *comb.*) a man of a specified nationality, profession, etc. (*Dutchman*; *clergyman*). **10 a** an expression of impatience, etc., used in addressing a male (*nonsense, man!*). **b** *colloq.* a general mode of address (*blew my mind, man!*). **11** (prec. by *a*) one (*what can a man do?*). **12** a person pursued (*the police have so far not caught their man*). **13** (**the Man**) *sl.* **a** the police. **b** *sl.* a person with power or authority. **14** (in *comb.*) a ship of a specified type (*merchantman*; *Indiaman*). • *v.tr.* (**manned, manning**) **1** supply (a ship, factory, etc.) with a person or people for work or defense, etc. **2** work or service or defend (a specified piece of equipment, a fortification, etc.) (*man the pumps*). **3** *Naut.* place men at (a part of a ship). **4** fill (a post or office). **5** (usu. *refl.*) fortify the spirits or courage of (*manned herself for the task*). □ **be a man** be courageous. **be one's own man 1** be free to act; be independent. **2** be in full possession of one's faculties, etc. **separate** (or **sort out**) **the men from the boys** *colloq.* find those who are truly virile, competent, etc. **to a man** all without exception.

▶Many consider the use of **man** to mean 'human being' or 'the human race' offensive and sexist.

man a·bout town *n.* a fashionable man of leisure.

man·a·cle /mánəkəl/ *n. & v.* •*n.* (usu. in *pl.*) **1** a fetter or shackle for the hand. **2** a restraint. •*v.tr.* fetter with manacles.

man·age /mánij/ *v.* **1** *tr.* organize; regulate; be in charge of (a business, household, etc.). **2** *tr.* (often foll. by *to* + infin.) succeed in achieving (*managed a smile*). **3** *intr.* **a** (often foll. by *with*) succeed in one's aim, esp. against heavy odds (*managed with one assistant*). **b** meet one's needs with limited resources, etc. (*manages on a pension*). **4** *tr.* maintain control over (*cannot manage their teenage son*). **5** *tr.* (also *absol.*; often prec. by *can, be able to*) **a** cope with (*can you manage by yourself?*). **b** be free to attend on (a certain day) or at (a certain time) (*can you manage Thursday?*). **6** *tr.* handle or wield (a tool, weapon, etc.). **7** *tr.* take or have charge or control of (an animal or animals, esp. cattle).

man·age·a·ble /mánijəbəl/ *adj.* able to be managed, controlled, or accomplished, etc. □□ **man·age·a·bil·i·ty** *n.* **man·age·a·ble·ness** *n.* **man·age·a·bly** *adv.*

man·aged care *n.* health care administered by a health maintenance organization or similar system, intended to limit hospital and practioner fees.

man·age·ment /mánijmənt/ *n.* **1** the process or an instance of managing or being managed. **2 a** the professional administration of business concerns, etc. **b** the people engaged in this. **c** (prec. by *the*) a governing body. **3** (usu. foll. by *of*) *Med.* the technique of treating a disease, etc.

man·age·ment in·for·ma·tion sys·tem *n. Computing* a computer system used in business for processing data related to management activities.

man·ag·er /mánijər/ *n.* **1** a person controlling or administering a business or part of a business. **2** a person controlling the affairs, training, etc., of a person or team in sports, entertainment, etc. **3** a person regarded in terms of skill in management (*a good manager*). □□ **man·a·ge·ri·al** /mánijéereeəl/ *adj.* **man·a·ge·ri·al·ly** /–jéereeəlee/ *adv.* **man·a·ger·ship** *n.*

man·ag·ing /mánijing/ *adj.* **1** (in *comb.*) having executive authority (*managing partner*). **2** (*attrib.*) fond of controlling affairs, etc.

ma·ña·na /mənyáanə/ *adv. & n.* •*adv.* in the indefinite future (esp. to indicate procrastination). •*n.* an indefinite future time (from a Spanish word meaning 'tomorrow').

man·a·tee /mánətée/ *n.* any large aquatic plant-eating mammal.

man·da·la /mándələ, mún–/ *n.* a symbolic circular figure representing the universe in various religions.

man·da·mus /mandáyməs/ *n. Law* a judicial writ issued as a command to an inferior court, or ordering a person to perform a public or statutory duty.

man·da·rin[1] /mándərin/ *n.* **1** (**Mandarin**) the official language of China. **2** *hist.* a Chinese official. **3 a** a party leader; a bureaucrat. **b** a powerful member of the establishment. **4 a** a nodding Chinese figure, usu. of porcelain. **b** porcelain, etc., decorated with Chinese figures in mandarin dress.

man·da·rin[2] /mándərin/ *n.* (in full **mandarin orange**) **1** a small flattish deep-colored orange with a loose skin. **2** the tree, *Citrus reticulata*, yielding this. Also called TANGERINE.

man·date /mándayt/ *n. & v.* •*n.* **1** an official command or instruction. **2** support for a policy or course of action, regarded by a victorious party, etc., as derived from the wishes of the people in an election. **3** a commission to act for another. •*v.tr.* instruct (a delegate) to act or vote in a certain way.

man·da·to·ry /mándətáwree/ *adj.* **1** of or conveying a command. **2** compulsory. □□ **man·da·to·ri·ly** *adv.*

man·di·ble /mándibəl/ *n.* **1** the jaw, esp. the lower jaw in mammals and fishes. **2** the upper or lower part of a bird's beak. **3** either half of the crushing organ in an arthropod's mouthparts. □□ **man·dib·u·lar** /–díbyələr/ *adj.*

man·do·lin /mándəlín/ *n.* (also **man·do·line**) a musical instrument resembling a lute, having paired metal strings plucked with a plectrum. □□ **man·do·lin·ist** *n.*

mandolin

man·drake /mándrayk/ *n.* **1** a poisonous plant, *Mandragora officinarum*, having emetic and narcotic properties. **2** = MAYAPPLE.

man·drel /mándrəl/ *n.* **1** a shaft in a lathe to which work is fixed while being turned. **2** a cylindrical rod around which metal or other material is forged or shaped.

man·drill /mándril/ *n.* a large W. African baboon, *Papio* (or *Mandrillus*) *sphinx*.

mane /mayn/ *n.* **1** long hair growing in a line on the neck of a horse, lion, etc. **2** *colloq.* a person's long hair. □□ **maned** *adj.* (also in *comb.*). **mane·less** *adj.*

ma·nège /manézh/ *n.* (also **ma·nege**) **1** a riding school. **2** the movements of a trained horse. **3** horsemanship.

ma·nes /maánayz, máyneez/ *n.pl.* **1** the deified souls of dead ancestors. **2** (as *sing.*) the revered ghost of a dead person.

ma·neu·ver /mənóovər/ *n. & v.* •*n.* **1** a planned and controlled movement or series of moves. **2** (in *pl.*) a large-scale exercise of troops, warships, etc. **3 a** an often deceptive planned or controlled action designed to gain an objective. **b** a skillful plan. •*v.* **1** *intr. & tr.* perform or cause to perform a maneuver (*maneuvered the car into the space*). **2** *intr. & tr.* perform or cause (troops, etc.) to perform military maneuvers. **3 a** *tr.* (usu. foll. by *into, out, away*) force, drive, or manipulate (a person, thing, etc.) by scheming or adroitness. **b** *intr.* use artifice. □□ **ma·neu·ver·a·ble** *adj.* **ma·neu·ver·a·bil·i·ty** /–vrəbílitee, –vərə–/ *n.*

man Fri·day a helper or follower (after *Man Friday* in Defoe's *Robinson Crusoe*).

man·ga·nese /mánggənéez/ *n.* **1** *Chem.* a gray brittle metallic element used with steel to make alloys. ¶ Symb.: **Mn. 2** (in full **manganese oxide**) the black mineral oxide of this used in the manufacture of glass. □□ **man·ga·nous** /mánggənəs/ *adj.*

mange /maynj/ *n.* a skin disease in hairy and woolly animals, caused by an arachnid parasite.

man•ger /máynjər/ *n.* a long open box or trough for horses or cattle to eat from.

man•gle[1] /mánggəl/ *v.tr.* **1** hack, cut, or mutilate by blows, etc. **2** spoil (a quotation, text, etc.) by misquoting, mispronouncing, etc. **3** cut roughly so as to disfigure.

man•gle[2] /mánggəl/ *n. & v.* •*n.* a machine having two or more heated, revolving cylinders between which clothes, sheets, etc., are smoothed and pressed. •*v.tr.* press (clothes, etc.) in a mangle.

man•go /mánggō/ *n.* (*pl.* **-goes** or **-gos**) **1** a fleshy yellowish-red fruit, eaten ripe or used green for pickles, etc. **2** the E. Indian evergreen tree, *Mangifera indica*, bearing this.

man•go•steen /mánggəsteen/ *n.* **1** a white juicy-pulped fruit with a thick reddish-brown rind. **2** the E. Indian tree, *Garcinia mangostana*, bearing this.

man•grove /mánggrōv/ *n.* any tropical tree or shrub of the genus *Rhizophora*, growing in tidal-shore mud with many tangled roots above ground.

man•gy /máynjee/ *adj.* (**mangier, mangiest**) **1** (esp. of a domestic animal) having mange. **2** squalid; shabby. ▫▫ **man•gi•ly** *adv.* **man•gi•ness** *n.*

man•han•dle /mánhánd'l/ *v.tr.* **1** move (heavy objects) by hand with great effort. **2** *colloq.* handle (someone or something) roughly.

man•hole /mánhōl/ *n.* a covered opening in a floor, pavement, sewer, etc., for workers to gain access.

man•hood /mánhŏŏd/ *n.* **1** the state of being a man rather than a child or woman. **2 a** manliness; courage. **b** a man's sexual potency. **3** the men of a country, etc. **4** the state of being human.

man•hour *n.* (also **man-day**, etc.) an hour (or day, etc.) regarded in terms of the amount of work that could be done by one person within this period.

man•hunt /mánhunt/ *n.* an organized search for a person, esp. a criminal.

ma•ni•a /máyneeə/ *n.* **1** *Psychol.* mental illness marked by periods of great excitement and violence. **2** (often foll. by *for*) excessive enthusiasm.

-mania /máyneeə/ *comb. form* **1** *Psychol.* denoting a special type of mental abnormality or obsession (*megalomania*). **2** denoting extreme enthusiasm or admiration (*bibliomania*).

ma•ni•ac /máyneeak/ *n. & adj.* •*n.* **1** *colloq.* a person exhibiting extreme symptoms of wild behavior, etc.; a madman. **2** *colloq.* an obsessive enthusiast. •*adj.* of or behaving like a maniac. ▫▫ **ma•ni•a•cal** /məníəkəl/ *adj.* **ma•ni•a•cal•ly** /məníəklee/ *adv.*

-maniac /máyneeak/ *comb. form* forming adjectives and nouns meaning 'affected with -mania' or 'a person affected with -mania' (*kleptomaniac*).

man•ic /mánik/ *adj.* of or affected by mania. ▫▫ **man•i•cal•ly** *adv.*

man•ic-de•pres•sive *adj., & n. Psychol.* •*adj.* affected by or relating to a mental disorder with alternating periods of elation and depression. •*n.* a person having such a disorder.

man•i•cure /mánikyŏŏr/ *n. & v.* •*n.* a cosmetic treatment of the hands involving cutting, shaping, and often painting of the nails, removal of the cuticles, and softening of the skin. •*v.tr.* give a manicure to (the hands or a person). ▫▫ **man•i•cur•ist** *n.*

man•i•fest[1] /mánifest/ *adj. & v.* •*adj.* clear or obvious to the eye or mind. •*v.* **1** *tr.* display or show (a quality, feeling, etc.) by one's acts, etc. **2** *tr.* show plainly to the eye or mind. **3** *tr.* be evidence of. **4** *refl.* (of a thing) reveal itself. **5** *intr.* (of a ghost) appear. ▫▫ **man•i•fes•ta•tion** /–stáyshən/ *n.* **man•i•fest•ly** *adv.*

man•i•fest[2] /mánifest/ *n. & v.* •*n.* **1** a cargo list for the use of customs officers. **2** a list of passengers in an aircraft or of cars, etc., in a freight train. •*v.tr.* record (names, cargo, etc.) in a manifest.

Man•i•fest Des•ti•ny *n.* 19th-c. doctrine asserting that the United States was destined to expand westward to the Pacific and to exert economic and social control throughout N. America.

man•i•fes•to /mánifestō/ *n.* (*pl.* **-tos** or **-toes**) a public declaration of policy and aims, esp. political or social.

man•i•fold /mánifōld/ *adj. & n.* •*adj. literary* **1** many and various (*manifold vexations*). **2** having various forms, parts, applications, etc. **3** performing several functions at once. •*n.* **1** a thing with many different forms, parts, applications, etc. **2** *Mech.* a pipe or chamber branching into several openings. ▫▫ **man•i•fold•ly** *adv.* **man•i•fold•ness** *n.*

man•i•kin /mánikin/ *n.* (also **man•ni•kin**) **1** a little man. **2** an artist's lay figure. **3** an anatomical model of the body.

Ma•nil•a /mənílə/ *n.* (also **Ma•nil•la**) **1** (in full **Manila hemp**) the strong fiber of a Philippine tree, *Musa textilis*, used for rope, etc. **2** (also **manila**) a strong brown paper made from Manila hemp. **3** a cigar or cheroot made in Manila.

man•i•oc /máneeok/ *n.* **1** cassava. **2** the flour made from it.

ma•nip•u•late /mənípyəlayt/ *v.tr.* **1** handle, treat, or use, esp. skillfully. **2** manage (a person, situation, etc.) to one's own advantage, esp. unfairly or unscrupulously. **3** manually examine and treat (a part of the body). **4** *Computing* alter, edit, or move (text, data, etc.). ▫▫ **ma•nip•u•la•ble** /–ləbəl/ *adj.* **ma•nip•u•la•tion** /–láyshən/ *n.* **ma•nip•u•la•tor** *n.* **ma•nip•u•la•to•ry** /–lətáwree/ *adj.*

ma•nip•u•la•tive /mənípyələtiv/ *adj.* **1** characterized by unscrupulous exploitation for one's own ends. **2** of or concerning manipulation. ▫▫ **ma•nip•u•la•tive•ly** *adv.* **ma•nip•u•la•tive•ness** *n.*

man•i•tou /mánitŏŏ/ *n.* **1** a good or evil spirit as an object of reverence. **2** something regarded as having supernatural power.

man•kind *n.* **1** /mánkínd/ the human species. **2** /mánkīnd/ male people, as distinct from female.

man•ly /mánlee/ *adj.* (**manlier, manliest**) **1** having qualities regarded as admirable in a man, such as courage, frankness, etc. **2** (of a woman) mannish. **3** (of things, qualities, etc.) befitting a man. ▫▫ **man•li•ness** *n.*

man-made *adj.* (esp. of a textile fiber) artificial; synthetic.

man•na /mánə/ *n.* **1** the substance miraculously supplied as food to the Israelites in the wilderness (Exod. 16). **2** an unexpected benefit (esp. *manna from heaven*). **3** spiritual nourishment, esp. the Eucharist.

manned /mand/ *adj.* (of an aircraft, spacecraft, etc.) having a human crew.

man•ne•quin /mánikin/ *n.* **1** a model employed by a dressmaker, etc., to show clothes to customers. **2** a model of the human form, for fitting or displaying garments. **3** an artist's lay figure.

man•ner /mánər/ *n.* **1** a way a thing is done or happens. **2** (in *pl.*) **a** social behavior (*it is bad manners to stare*). **b** polite or well-bred behavior (*he has no manners*). **c** modes of life; conditions of society. **3** a person's outward bearing, etc. (*has an imperious manner*). **4 a** a style in literature, etc. (*in the manner of Rembrandt*). **b** = MANNERISM 2a. ▫ **all manner of** many different kinds of. **in a manner of speaking** in some sense; to some extent. **to the manner born 1** *colloq.* naturally at ease in a specified job, etc. **2** destined by birth to follow a custom or way of life (Shakesp. *Hamlet* I. iv. 17).

man•nered /mánərd/ *adj.* **1** (in *comb.*) behaving in a specified way (*ill-mannered*). **2** (of a style, artist, etc.)

showing idiosyncratic mannerisms. **3** (of a person) eccentrically affected in behavior.

man•ner•ism /mánərizəm/ *n.* **1** a habitual gesture or way of speaking, etc. **2 a** excessive addiction to a distinctive style in art or literature. **b** a stylistic trick. **3** a style of Italian art preceding the Baroque, characterized by lengthened figures. ▫▫ **man•ner•ist** *n.* **man•ner•is•tic** /–rístik/ *adj.*

man•ner•ly /mánərlee/ *adj. & adv.* • *adj.* well-mannered; polite. • *adv.* politely. ▫▫ **man•ner•li•ness** *n.*

man•ni•kin var. of MANIKIN.

man•nish /mánish/ *adj.* **1** (of a woman) masculine in appearance or manner. **2** characteristic of a man. ▫▫ **man•nish•ly** *adv.* **man•nish•ness** *n.*

man of let•ters *n.* a scholar; an author.

man-of-war *n.* (*pl.* **men-of-war**) an armed ship, esp. of a specified country.

ma•nom•e•ter /mənómitər/ *n.* a pressure gauge for gases and liquids. ▫▫ **man•o•met•ric** /mánəmétrik/ *adj.*

man•or /mánər/ *n.* (also **man•or house**) **1** a large country house with lands. **2** the house of the lord of the manor. ▫▫ **ma•no•ri•al** /mənáwreeəl/ *adj.*

man•pow•er /mánpowr/ *n.* **1** the power generated by a person working. **2** the number of people available or required for work, service, etc.

man•sard /mánsaard/ *n.* a roof that has four sloping sides, each of which becomes steeper halfway down.

manse /mans/ *n.* **1** the house of a minister, esp. a Presbyterian. **2** a mansion.

man•serv•ant /mánservənt/ *n.* (*pl.* **menservants**) a male servant.

man•sion /mánshən/ *n.* a large house.

man-size *adj.* (also **man•sized**) **1** of the size of a man; very large. **2** big enough for a man.

man•slaugh•ter /mánslawtər/ *n.* **1** the killing of one human being by another. **2** *Law* the unlawful killing of a human being without malice aforethought.

man•ta /mántə/ *n.* **1** esp. *SW US & Latin Amer.* a cloak or shawl made from a square cloth. **2** any large ray of the family Mobulidae, esp. *Manta birostris*, having winglike pectoral fins and a whiplike tail.

man•tel /mánt'l/ *n.* **1** = MANTELPIECE 1. **2** = MANTELSHELF.

man•tel•piece /mánt'lpees/ *n.* **1** a structure of wood, marble, etc., above and around a fireplace. **2** = MANTELSHELF.

man•tel•shelf /mánt'lshelf/ *n.* a shelf above a fireplace.

man•til•la /mantílə, –téeə/ *n.* a lace scarf worn by Spanish women over the hair and shoulders.

man•tis /mántis/ *n.* (*pl.* same or **mantises**) any insect of the family Mantidae, feeding on other insects, etc.

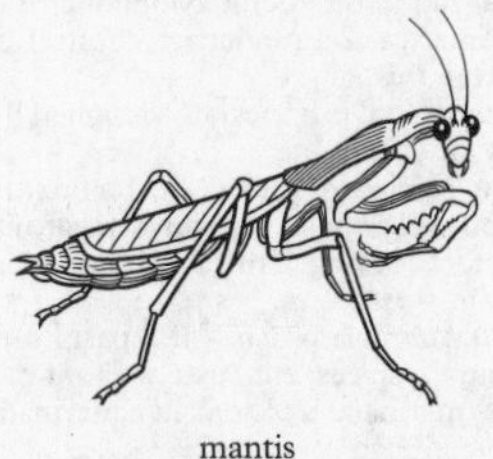

mantis

man•tle /mánt'l/ *n. & v.* • *n.* **1** a loose sleeveless cloak. **2** a covering of a specified sort (*a mantle of snow*). **3** a fragile lacelike tube fixed around a gas jet to give an incandescent light. **4** an outer fold of skin enclosing a mollusk's viscera. **5** a bird's back, scapulars, and wing coverts, esp. if of a distinctive color. **6** the region between the crust and the core of the earth. • *v.* **1** *tr.* clothe in or as if in a mantle; cover; envelop. **2** *intr.* **a** (of the blood) suffuse the cheeks. **b** (of the face) glow with a blush.

man-to-man *adv.* with candor; honestly.

man•tra /mántrə, máan–, mún–/ *n.* **1** a word or sound repeated to aid concentration in meditation, orig. in Hinduism and Buddhism. **2** a Vedic hymn.

man•u•al /mányooəl/ *adj. & n.* • *adj.* **1** of or done with the hands (*manual labor*). **2** (of a machine, etc.) worked by hand. • *n.* **1 a** a book of instructions; a handbook. **b** any small book. **2** a nonelectric typewriter. **3** an organ keyboard played only with the hands. ▫▫ **man•u•al•ly** *adv.*

man•u•fac•ture /mányəfákchər/ *n. & v.* • *n.* **1 a** the making of articles, esp. in a factory, etc. **b** a branch of an industry (*woolen manufacture*). **2** esp. *derog.* the merely mechanical production of literature, etc. • *v.tr.* **1** make (articles), esp. on an industrial scale. **2** invent or fabricate (evidence, etc.). **3** esp. *derog.* make or produce in a mechanical way. ▫▫ **man•u•fac•tur•a•bil•i•ty** /–chərəbílitee/ *n.* **man•u•fac•tur•a•ble** *adj.* **man•u•fac•tur•er** *n.*

man•u•mit /mányəmít/ *v.tr.* (**manumitted, manumitting**) *hist.* set (a slave) free. ▫▫ **man•u•mis•sion** /–míshən/ *n.*

ma•nure /mənóor, –nyóor/ *n. & v.* • *n.* **1** animal dung used for fertilizing land. **2** any compost or artificial fertilizer. • *v.tr.* (also *absol.*) apply manure to (land, etc.).

man•u•script /mányəskript/ *n. & adj.* • *n.* **1** a book, document, etc., written by hand. **2** an author's handwritten or typed text, submitted for publication. **3** handwritten form (*produced in manuscript*). • *adj.* written by hand.

Manx /mangks/ *adj. & n.* • *adj.* of or relating to the Isle of Man. • *n.* **1** the now extinct Celtic language formerly spoken in the Isle of Man. **2** (prec. by *the*; treated as *pl.*) the Manx people.

Manx cat *n.* a breed of tailless cat.

man•y /ménee/ *adj. & n.* • *adj.* (**more** /mawr/; **most** /mōst/) great in number; numerous (*many times*). • *n.* (as *pl.*) **1** a large number (*many went*). **2** (prec. by *the*) the multitude of esp. working people.

man•y-sid•ed *adj.* having many sides, aspects, interests, capabilities, etc. ▫▫ **man•y-sid•ed•ness** *n.*

Mao•ism /mówizəm/ *n.* the Communist doctrines of Mao Zedong (d. 1976), Chinese statesman. ▫▫ **Mao•ist** *n. & adj.*

Ma•o•ri /mówree/ *n. & adj.* • *n.* (*pl.* same or **Maoris**) **1** a member of the Polynesian aboriginal people of New Zealand. **2** the language of the Maori. • *adj.* of or concerning the Maori or their language.

map /map/ *n. & v.* • *n.* **1 a** a usu. flat representation of the earth's surface, or part of it, showing physical features, cities, etc. **b** a diagrammatic representation of a route, etc. (*drew a map of the journey*). **2** a two-dimensional representation of the stars, etc. **3** a diagram showing the arrangement or components of a thing. **4** *sl.* the face. • *v.tr.* (**mapped, mapping**) **1** represent (a country, etc.) on a map. **2** *Math.* associate each element of (a set) with one element of another set. ▫ **map out** arrange in detail; plan. **on the map** *colloq.* prominent; important. ▫▫ **map•per** *n.*

ma•ple /máypəl/ *n.* **1** any tree or shrub of the genus *Acer* grown for shade, ornament, wood, or its sugar. **2** the wood of the maple.

ma•ple sug•ar *n.* a sugar produced by evaporating the sap of the sugar maple, etc.

ma•ple syr•up *n.* a syrup produced from the sap of the sugar maple, etc.

Mar. *abbr.* March.

mar /maar/ *v.tr.* (**marred, marring**) **1** ruin. **2** impair the perfection of; spoil; disfigure.

mar·a·bou /márəbōō/ *n.* (also **mar·a·bout**) **1** a large W. African stork, *Leptoptilos crumeniferus*. **2** a tuft of down from the wing or tail of the marabou used as a trimming for hats, etc.

ma·rac·a /məraákə/ *n.* a hollow clublike gourd or gourd-shaped container filled with beans, etc., and usu. shaken in pairs as a percussion instrument in Latin American music.

mar·a·schi·no /máraskeénō, –shée–/ *n.* (*pl.* **-nos**) a strong, sweet liqueur made from a small black Dalmatian cherry.

mar·a·schi·no cher·ry *n.* a cherry preserved in or flavored with maraschino and used to decorate cocktails, etc.

mar·a·thon /márəthon/ *n.* **1** a long-distance running race, usu. of 26 miles 385 yards (42.195 km). **2** a long-lasting or difficult task, operation, etc.

ma·raud /məráwd/ *v.* **1** *intr.* **a** make a plundering raid. **b** pilfer systematically; plunder. **2** *tr.* plunder (a place). ▫▫ **ma·raud·er** *n.*

mar·ble /maárbəl/ *n. & v.* •*n.* **1** limestone in a metamorphic crystalline (or granular) state, and capable of taking a polish, used in sculpture and architecture. **2** (often *attrib.*) **a** anything made of marble (*a marble clock*). **b** anything resembling marble in hardness, coldness, durability, etc. (*her features were marble*). **3 a** a small ball of marble, glass, etc., used as a toy. **b** (in *pl.*; treated as *sing.*) a game using these. **4** (in *pl.*) *sl.* one's mental faculties (*he's lost his marbles*). **5** (in *pl.*) a collection of sculptures (*Roman marbles*). •*v.tr.* **1** (esp. as **marbled** *adj.*) stain or color to look like variegated marble. **2** (as **marbled** *adj.*) (of meat) streaked with alternating layers of lean and fat.

mar·ble cake *n.* a cake with a streaked appearance, made of light and dark batter.

mar·bling /maárbling/ *n.* **1** coloring or marking like marble. **2** streaks of fat in lean meat.

mar·ca·site /maárkəsīt/ *n.* **1** a yellowish crystalline iron sulfide mineral. **2** these bronze-yellow crystals used in jewelry.

mar·cat·o /maarkaátō/ *adv. & adj. Mus.* played with emphasis.

mar·cel /maarsél/ *n. & v.* •*n.* (in full **marcel wave**) a deep wave in the hair. •*v.tr.* (**marcelled, marcelling**) wave (hair) with a deep wave.

March /maarch/ *n.* the third month of the year.

march[1] /maarch/ *v. & n.* •*v.* **1** *intr.* (usu. foll. by *away*, *off*, *out*, etc.) walk in a military manner with a regular tread. **2** *tr.* (often foll. by *away*, *on*, *off*, etc.) cause to march or walk. **3** *intr.* **a** walk or proceed steadily, esp. across country. **b** continue unrelentingly (*time marches on*). **4** *intr.* take part in a protest march. •*n.* **1 a** the act or an instance of marching. **b** the uniform step of troops, etc. (*a slow march*). **2** a long difficult walk. **3** a procession as a demonstration. **4** (usu. foll. by *of*) progress or continuity (*the march of events*). **5 a** a piece of music composed to accompany a march. **b** a composition of similar character and form. ▫▫ **march·er** *n.*

march[2] /maarch/ *n. hist.* **1** (usu. in *pl.*) a boundary; a frontier (esp. of the borderland between England and Scotland or Wales). **2** a tract of often disputed land between two countries.

march·er /maárchər/ *n.* an inhabitant of a march or border district.

march·ing or·ders *n.pl.* **1** *Mil.* instructions from a superior officer for troops to depart for war, etc. **2** a dismissal.

Mar·di Gras /maárdee graá/ *n.* a carnival held in some countries on the last day before Lent (Shrove Tuesday), most famously in New Orleans (literally, 'Fat Tuesday').

mare[1] /mair/ *n.* the female of any equine animal, esp. the horse.

mare[2] /maáray/ *n.* (*pl.* **maria** /maáreeə/or **mares**) **1** any of a number of large dark flat areas on the surface of the moon, once thought to be seas. **2** a similar area on Mars.

mare's nest *n.* **1** an illusory discovery; a hoax. **2** a muddle.

mar·ga·rine /maárjərin/ *n.* a butter substitute made from vegetable oils or animal fats with milk, etc.

mar·ga·ri·ta /maargəreétə/ *n.* a cocktail made with tequila, lime or lemon juice, and orange-flavored liqueur, usu. served in a salt-rimmed glass.

mar·gay /maárgay/ *n.* a small wild S. American cat, *Felis wiedii*.

mar·gin /maárjin/ *n. & v.* •*n.* **1** an edge or border. **2 a** the blank border on each side of the print on a page, etc. **b** a line or rule, as on paper, marking off a margin. **3** an amount (of time, money, etc.) by which a thing exceeds, falls short, etc. **4** the lower limit (*his effort fell below the margin*). **5** an amount deposited with a stockbroker by the customer when borrowing from the broker to purchase securities. **6** in banking, the difference between the current market value of a loan's collateral and the face value of the loan. •*v.tr.* (**margined, margining**) provide with a margin or marginal notes.

mar·gin·al /maárjinəl/ *adj.* **1 a** of or written in a margin. **b** having marginal notes. **2 a** of or at the edge. **b** not significant or decisive (*of marginal interest*). **3** close to the limit, esp. of profitability. **4** (of the sea) adjacent to the shore of a state. **5** (of land) difficult to cultivate; unprofitable. **6** barely adequate; unprovided for. ▫▫ **mar·gin·al·i·ty** /–nálitee/ *n.* **mar·gin·al·ly** *adv.*

mar·gi·na·li·a /maárjináyleeə/ *n.pl.* marginal notes.

mar·gin·al·ize /maárjinəlīz/ *v.tr.* make or treat as insignificant. ▫▫ **mar·gin·al·i·za·tion** *n.*

mar·gin of er·ror *n.* a usu. small difference allowed for miscalculation.

ma·ri·a *pl.* of MARE[2].

mar·i·ach·i /maareeaáchee, mar–/ *n.* **1** a Mexican band of strolling street musicians. **2** the music played by such a band.

mar·i·gold /márigōld/ *n.* any plant of the genus *Tagetes* or *Calendula*, with bright yellow, orange, or maroon flowers.

ma·ri·jua·na /máriwaánə/ *n.* (also **ma·ri·hua·na**) **1** the dried leaves, flowering tops, and stems of the hemp, used as a drug, often smoked in cigarettes. **2** the plant yielding these (cf. HEMP).

ma·rim·ba /mərímbə/ *n.* **1** a xylophone of Africa and Central America. **2** a modern orchestral instrument derived from this.

ma·ri·na /məreénə/ *n.* a specially designed harbor with moorings for yachts, etc.

mar·i·nade /márináyd/ *n. & v.* •*n.* **1** a mixture of wine, vinegar, oil, spices, etc., in which meat, fish, etc., is soaked before cooking. **2** meat, fish, etc., soaked in this liquid. •*v.tr.* = MARINATE.

ma·ri·na·ra /marinaárə/ *adj.* (of a pasta sauce) made with tomatoes, spices, etc., usu. without meat.

mar·i·nate /márinayt/ *v.tr.* soak in a marinade. ▫▫ **mar·i·na·tion** /–náyshən/ *n.*

ma·rine /məreén/ *adj. & n.* •*adj.* **1** of, found in, or produced by the sea. **2 a** of or relating to shipping or naval matters. **b** for use at sea. •*n.* **1** a country's shipping, fleet, or navy. **2 a** a member of the US Marine Corps. **b** a member of a body of troops trained to serve on land or sea. **3** a picture of a scene at sea.

mar·i·ner /márinər/ *n.* a seaman.

mar·i·on·ette /máreeənét/ *n.* a puppet worked by strings.

mar·i·tal /márit'l/ *adj.* **1** of marriage or the relations between husband and wife. **2** of or relating to a husband. □□ **mar·i·tal·ly** *adv.*

mar·i·time /máritīm/ *adj.* **1** connected with the sea or seafaring. **2** living or found near the sea.

mar·jo·ram /maárjərəm/ *n.* an aromatic culinary herb of the genus *Origanum*, esp. *O. majorana* (**sweet marjoram**), used as a flavoring in cooking.

mark[1] /maark/ *n. & v.* • *n.* **1** a trace, sign, stain, scar, etc., on a face, page, etc. **2** (esp. in *comb.*) **a** a written or printed symbol (*question mark*). **b** a numerical or alphabetical award denoting excellence, conduct, etc. (*got a good mark for effort*). **3** (usu. foll. by *of*) a sign or indication of quality, character, etc. (*as a mark of respect*). **4 a** a sign, seal, etc., used for distinction or identification. **b** a cross, etc., made in place of a signature by an illiterate person. **5 a** a target, object, goal, etc. (*missed the mark*). **b** a standard for attainment (*his work falls below the mark*). **6** a marker. **7** a runner's starting point in a race. • *v.tr.* **1 a** make a mark on (a thing or person), esp. by writing, cutting, etc. **b** put a distinguishing or identifying mark, name, etc., on (*marked the tree with their initials*). **2 a** allot marks to (a student's work, etc.). **b** record (the points gained in games, etc.). **3** attach a price to (goods, etc.) (*marked the doll at $2*). **4** (often foll. by *by*) show or manifest (displeasure, etc.) (*marked his anger by leaving early*). **5** notice or observe (*she marked his agitation*). **6 a** characterize or be a feature of (*the day was marked by storms*). **b** celebrate (*marked the occasion with a toast*). **7** name or indicate by a sign or mark. **8** characterize (a person or a thing) as (*marked them as weak*). **9** (as **marked** *adj.*) having natural marks (*marked with silver spots*). **10** (of a graduated instrument) show, register (so many degrees, etc.). **11** castrate (a lamb). □ **beside** (or **off** or **wide of**) **the mark 1** irrelevant. **2** not accurate. **mark down 1** mark (goods, etc.) at a lower price. **2** make a written note of. **3** choose (a person) as one's victim. **mark my words** heed my warning or prediction. **mark time 1** *Mil.* march on the spot, without moving forward. **2** act routinely. **3** await an opportunity to advance. **mark up 1** mark (goods, etc.) at a higher price. **2** mark or correct (text, etc.) for typesetting or alteration. **off the mark 1** having made a start. **2** = *beside the mark*. **on your mark** (or **marks**) (as an instruction) get ready to start (esp. a race).

mark[2] /maark/ *n.* = DEUTSCHEMARK.

mark·down /máarkdown/ *n.* a reduction in price.

marked /maarkt/ *adj.* **1** having a visible mark. **2** clearly noticeable (*a marked difference*). **3** (of playing cards) having distinctive marks to assist cheating. □□ **mark·ed·ly** /–kidlee/ *adv.* **mark·ed·ness** /–kidnis/ *n.*

mark·er /maárkər/ *n.* **1** a stone, post, etc., used to mark a place reached, etc. **2** a person or thing that marks. **3** a felt-tipped pen with a broad tip. **4** a flare, etc., used to direct a pilot to a target. **5** a bookmark.

mar·ket /maárkit/ *n. & v.* • *n.* **1 a** the gathering of people for the purchase and sale of provisions, livestock, etc. **b** the time of this. **2** an open space or covered building used for this. **3** (often foll. by *for*) a demand for a commodity or service (*a ready market*). **4** a place or group providing such a demand. **5** conditions as regards, or opportunity for, buying or selling. **6** the rate of purchase and sale, market value (*the market fell*). **7** (prec. by *the*) the trade in a specified commodity (*the grain market*). • *v.* **1** *tr.* sell. **2** *tr.* offer for sale. **3** *intr.* buy or sell goods in a market. □ **be in the market for** wish to buy. **be on** (or **come into**) **the market** be offered for sale. **put on the market** offer for sale. □□ **mar·ket·er** *n.*

mar·ket·a·ble /maárkitəbəl/ *adj.* able or fit to be sold. □□ **mar·ket·a·bil·i·ty** /–bílitee/ *n.*

mar·ket·eer /maárkitéer/ *n.* a marketer.

mar·ket·ing /máarkiting/ *n.* the activity or process involving research, promotion, sales, and distribution of a product or service.

mar·ket·place /máarkitpláys/ *n.* **1** an open space where a market is held in a town. **2** the scene of actual dealings. **3** a forum or sphere for the exchange of ideas, etc.

mar·ket val·ue *n.* value as a salable thing (opp. BOOK VALUE).

mark·ing /maárking/ *n.* (usu. in *pl.*) **1** an identification mark, esp. a symbol on an aircraft. **2** the coloring of an animal's fur, feathers, skin, etc.

marks·man /maárksmən/ *n.* (*pl.* **-men**; *fem.* **-woman**, *pl.* **-women**) a person skilled in shooting, esp. with a pistol or rifle. □□ **marks·man·ship** *n.*

mark·up /maárkup/ *n.* **1** the amount added to the cost of goods to cover overhead charges, etc. **2** the corrections made in marking up text.

marl /maarl/ *n. & v.* • *n.* soil consisting of clay and lime, with fertilizing properties. • *v.tr.* apply marl to. □□ **marl·y** *adj.*

mar·lin /maárlin/ *n.* any of various large marine fish of the family Istophoridae, esp. the blue marlin *Makaira nigricans*.

mar·ma·lade /maármәlayd/ *n.* a preserve of citrus fruit, usu. bitter oranges, made like jam.

mar·mo·set /maármәset, –zet/ *n.* any of several small tropical American monkeys of the family Callithricidae, having a long bushy tail.

mar·mot /maármət/ *n.* any burrowing rodent of the genus *Marmota*, with a heavyset body and short bushy tail.

ma·roon[1] /məróon/ *adj. & n.* • *adj.* brownish-crimson. • *n.* this color.

ma·roon[2] /məróon/ *v.tr.* **1** leave (a person) isolated in a desolate place (esp. an island). **2** (of a person or a natural phenomenon) cause (a person) to be unable to leave a place.

marque /maark/ *n.* a make of a product, as a sports car (*the Porsche marque*).

mar·quee /maarkée/ *n.* a rooflike projection over the entrance to a theater, hotel, etc.

mar·quess /maárkwis/ *n.* a British nobleman ranking between a duke and an earl (cf. MARQUIS). □□ **mar·quess·ate** /–kwisət/ *n.*

mar·que·try /maárkitree/ *n.* (also **mar·que·te·rie**) inlaid work in wood, ivory, etc.

mar·quis /maárkwis, –kée/ *n.* a nobleman ranking between a duke and a count (cf. MARQUESS). □□ **mar·quis·ate** /–kwisət/ *n.*

mar·quise /maarkéez, –kée/ *n.* **1 a** the wife or widow of a marquis. **b** a woman holding the rank of marquis in her own right. **2 a** a finger ring set with a pointed oval cluster of gems. **b** (also **marquise cut**) an oval cut gem with many facets.

mar·riage /márij/ *n.* **1** the legal union of a man and a woman in order to live together and often to have children. **2** an act or ceremony establishing this union. **3** one particular union of this kind (*by a previous marriage*). **4** an intimate union (*the marriage of true minds*). **5** *Cards* the union of a king and queen of the same suit. □ **by marriage** as a result of a marriage (*related by marriage*). **in marriage** as husband or wife (*give in marriage; take in marriage*).

mar·riage·a·ble /márijəbəl/ *adj.* **1** fit for marriage, esp. old or rich enough to marry. **2** (of age) fit for marriage. □□ **mar·riage·a·bil·i·ty** /–bílitee/ *n.*

mar·riage of con·ven·ience *n.* a marriage concluded to achieve some practical purpose, esp. financial or political.

mar·ried /máreed/ *adj. & n.* • *adj.* **1** united in marriage. **2** of or relating to marriage (*married name*; *married life*). • *n.* (usu. in *pl.*) a married person (*young marrieds*).

mar·row /márō/ *n.* **1** a soft fatty substance in the cavities of bones, in which blood cells are produced. **2** the essential part of something. □ **to the marrow** to one's innermost being.

mar·ry[1] /máree/ *v.* (**-ries, -ried**) **1** *tr.* **a** take as one's wife or husband in marriage. **b** (often foll. by *to*) (of a priest, etc.) join (persons) in marriage. **c** (of a parent or guardian) give (a son, daughter, etc.) in marriage. **2** *intr.* **a** enter into marriage. **b** (foll. by *into*) become a member of (a family) by marriage. **3** *tr.* **a** *tr.* unite intimately. **b** correlate (things) as a pair. □ **marry off** find a wife or husband for.

mar·ry[2] /máree/ *int. archaic* expressing surprise, asseveration, indignation, etc.

mar·ry·ing /máree-ing/ *adj.* likely or inclined to marry (*not a marrying man*).

Mars /maarz/ *n.* a reddish planet, fourth in order of distance from the sun and next beyond the earth.

marsh /maarsh/ *n.* **1** low land flooded in wet weather and usu. watery at all times. **2** (*attrib.*) of or inhabiting marshland. □□ **marsh·y** *adj.* (**marshier, marshiest**). **marsh·i·ness** *n.*

mar·shal /maárshəl/ *n. & v.* • *n.* **1** *US* an officer of a judicial district, similar to a sheriff. **2** *US* the head of a fire department. **3** a high-ranking officer in the armed forces of certain countries (*air marshal*; *field marshal*). **4** an officer arranging ceremonies, controlling procedure at races, etc. **5** *US* a court officer who assists a judge. • *v.* **1** *tr.* arrange (soldiers, facts, one's thoughts, etc.) in due order. **2** *tr.* (often foll. by *into*, *to*) conduct (a person) ceremoniously. **3** *intr.* take up positions in due arrangement. □□ **mar·shal·er** *n.* **marshal·ship** *n.*

marshal Middle English (denoting a high-ranking officer of state): from Old French *mareschal* 'farrier, commander,' from late Latin *mariscalcus*, from Germanic elements meaning 'horse' (related to *mare*) and 'servant.'

marsh·land /maárshland/ *n.* land consisting of marshes.

marsh·mal·low /maárshmélō, –málō/ *n.* a spongy confection made of sugar, albumen, gelatin, etc.

marsh mar·i·gold *n.* a golden-flowered ranunculaceous plant, *Caltha palustris*, growing in moist meadows, etc.: also called COWSLIP; KINGCUP.

mar·su·pi·al /maarsóopeeəl/ *n. & adj.* • *n.* any mammal of the order Marsupialia, characterized by being carried and suckled in a pouch on the mother's belly. • *adj.* **1** of or belonging to this order. **2** of or like a pouch (*marsupial muscle*).

mart /maart/ *n.* **1** a trade center. **2** an auction room. **3** **a** a market. **b** a marketplace.

mar·ten /maárt'n/ *n.* any weasellike carnivore of the genus *Martes*, having valuable fur.

mar·tial /maárshəl/ *adj.* **1** of or appropriate to warfare. **2** warlike; brave; fond of fighting. □□ **mar·tial·ly** *adv.*

mar·tial arts *n.pl.* fighting sports such as judo and karate.

mar·tial law *n.* military government, involving the suspension of ordinary law.

Mar·tian /maárshən/ *adj. & n.* • *adj.* of the planet Mars. • *n.* a hypothetical inhabitant of Mars.

mar·tin /maárt'n/ *n.* any of several swallows of the family Hirundinidae, esp. the house martin and purple martin.

mar·ti·net /maárt'nét/ *n.* a strict (esp. military or naval) disciplinarian.

mar·ti·ni /maartéenee/ *n.* a cocktail made of gin and dry vermouth, often garnished with a green olive, lemon peel, etc.

mar·tyr /maártər/ *n. & v.* • *n.* **1** **a** a person who is put to death for refusing to renounce a faith or belief. **b** a person who suffers for adhering to a principle, cause, etc. **2** a person who feigns or complains of suffering to gain sympathy. **3** (foll. by *to*) a constant sufferer from (an ailment). • *v.tr.* **1** put to death as a martyr. **2** torment.

mar·tyr·dom /maártərdəm/ *n.* **1** the sufferings and death of a martyr. **2** torment.

mar·vel /maárvəl/ *n. & v.* • *n.* **1** a wonderful thing or person. **2** (often foll. by *of*) a wonderful example (*she's a marvel of patience*). • *v.intr. literary* **1** (foll. by *at*, or *that* + clause) feel surprise or wonder. **2** (foll. by *how*, *why*, etc. + clause) wonder.

mar·vel·ous /maárvələs/ *adj.* **1** astonishing. **2** excellent. **3** extremely improbable. □□ **mar·vel·ous·ly** *adv.*

Marx·ism /maárksizəm/ *n.* the political and economic theories of Karl Marx (d. 1883), predicting the overthrow of capitalism and the eventual attainment of a classless society with the state controlling the means of production. □□ **Marx·ist** *n. & adj.*

mar·zi·pan /maárzipan/ *n. & v.* • *n.* **1** a paste of ground almonds, sugar, etc., made up into small cakes, etc., or used to coat large cakes. **2** a piece of marzipan. • *v.tr.* (**marzipanned, marzipanning**) cover with marzipan.

mas·car·a /maskárə/ *n.* a cosmetic for darkening the eyelashes.

mas·car·po·ne /maskápōni/ *n.* a soft, mild Italian cream cheese.

mas·cot /máskot/ *n.* a person, animal, or thing that is supposed to bring good luck.

mas·cu·line /máskyəlin/ *adj. & n.* • *adj.* **1** of or characteristic of men. **2** manly; vigorous. **3** (of a woman) having qualities considered appropriate to a man. **4** *Gram.* of or denoting the gender proper to men's names. • *n. Gram.* the masculine gender; a masculine word. □□ **mas·cu·lin·i·ty** /–línitee/ *n.*

ma·ser /máyzər/ *n.* a device using the stimulated emission of radiation by excited atoms to amplify or generate coherent monochromatic electromagnetic radiation in the microwave range (cf. LASER).

MASH /mash/ *abbr.* Mobile Army Surgical Hospital.

mash /mash/ *n. & v.* • *n.* **1** a soft mixture. **2** a mixture of boiled grain, bran, etc., given warm to horses, etc. **3** a mixture of malt or other grain and hot water used in brewing, distilling, etc. **4** *Brit. colloq.* mashed potatoes. **5** a soft pulp made by crushing, mixing with water, etc. • *v.tr.* **1** reduce (potatoes, etc.) to a uniform mass by crushing. **2** crush or pound to a pulp. **3** mix (malt) with hot water to form wort. □□ **mash·er** *n.*

mash·ie /máshee/ *n. Golf* former name of an iron used for lofting or for medium distances; five iron.

mask /mask/ *n. & v.* • *n.* **1** a covering for all or part of the face worn as a disguise, for protection (e.g., by a fencer) or by a surgeon to prevent infection of a patient. **2** a respirator used to filter inhaled air or to supply gas for inhalation. **3** a likeness of a person's face, esp. one made by taking a mold from the face (*death mask*). **4** a disguise or pretense (*throw off the mask*). **5** the face or head of an animal, esp. a fox. **6** a cosmetic preparation spread on the face and left to dry before removal. • *v.tr.* **1** cover (the face, etc.) with a mask. **2** disguise or conceal (a taste, one's feelings, etc.). **3** protect from a process. □□ **masked** /maskt/ *adj.* **mask·er** *n.*

mask·ing tape *n.* adhesive tape used in painting to cover areas on which paint is not wanted.

mas·och·ism /másəkizəm/ *n.* **1** a form of (esp. sexual) perversion characterized by gratification derived from one's own pain or humiliation (cf. SADISM). **2** *colloq.* the enjoyment of what appears to be painful or tiresome. □□ **mas·och·ist** *n.* **mas·och·is·tic** *adj.* **mas·och·is·ti·cal·ly** *adv.*

ma·son /máysən/ *n. & v.* •*n.* **1** a person who builds with stone or brick. **2** (**Mason**) a Freemason. •*v.tr.* build or strengthen with masonry.

Mas·on–Dix·on line /máysən-díksən/ *n.* the boundary between Maryland and Pennsylvania, taken as the northern limit of the slave-owning states before the abolition of slavery.

Ma·son·ic /məsónik/ *adj.* of or relating to Freemasons.

ma·son jar /máysən/ *n.* (also **Mason jar**) a glass jar with a wide mouth and tight-sealing lid, used for canning.

ma·son·ry /máysənree/ *n.* **1 a** the work of a mason. **b** stonework; brickwork. **2** (**Masonry**) Freemasonry.

masque /mask/ *n.* a dramatic and musical entertainment esp. of the 16th and 17th c.

mas·quer·ade /máskəráyd/ *n. & v.* •*n.* **1** a false show or pretense. **2** a masked ball. •*v.intr.* (often foll. by *as*) appear in disguise; assume a false appearance. □□ **mas·quer·ad·er** *n.*

Mass. *abbr.* Massachusetts.

mass[1] /mas/ *n. & v.* •*n.* **1** a body of matter of indefinite shape. **2** a dense aggregation of objects (*a mass of fibers*). **3** (in *sing.* or *pl.*; foll. by *of*) a large number or amount. **4** (usu. foll. by *of*) an unbroken expanse (of color, etc.). **5** (prec. by *a*; foll. by *of*) covered or abounding in (*was a mass of cuts and bruises*). **6** a main portion (of a painting, etc.) as perceived by the eye. **7** (prec. by *the*) **a** the majority. **b** (in *pl.*) the ordinary people. **8** *Physics* the quantity of matter a body contains. **9** (*attrib.*) relating to, done by, or affecting large numbers of people or things; large-scale (*mass audience; mass action; mass murder*). •*v.tr. & intr.* **1** assemble into a mass or as one body (*the bands massed at dawn*). **2** *Mil.* (with ref. to troops) concentrate or be concentrated.

mass[2] /mas/ *n.* **1** (often **Mass**) the Eucharist, esp. in the Roman Catholic Church. **2** a celebration of this. **3** the liturgy used in the Mass. **4** a musical setting of parts of this.

mas·sa·cre /másəkər/ *n. & v.* •*n.* **1** a general slaughter (of persons, occasionally of animals). **2** an utter defeat or destruction. •*v.tr.* **1** make a massacre of. **2** murder (esp. a large number of people) cruelly or violently.

mas·sage /məsaázh, –saáj/ *n. & v.* •*n.* **1** the rubbing, kneading, etc., of muscles and joints with the hands for therapeutic benefit. **2** an instance of this. •*v.tr.* **1** apply massage to. **2** manipulate (statistics) to give an acceptable result. □□ **mas·sag·er** *n.*

mas·sé /masáy/ *n. Billiards* a stroke made with the cue held nearly vertical.

mas·seur /masőr/ *n.* (*fem.* **masseuse** /masőz/) a person who provides massage professionally.

mas·sive /másiv/ *adj.* **1** large and heavy or solid. **2** (of the features, head, etc.) relatively large; of solid build. **3** exceptionally large (*took a massive overdose*). **4** substantial; impressive (*a massive reputation*). □□ **mas·sive·ly** *adv.* **mas·sive·ness** *n.*

mass-mar·ket *adj.* intended to be widely distributed through a variety of retail outlets.

mass me·di·a *n.* = MEDIA[1] 2.

mass num·ber *n.* the total number of protons and neutrons in a nucleus.

mass pro·duc·tion *n.* the production of large quantities of a standardized article by a standardized mechanical process. □□ **mass-pro·duce** *v.tr.*

mast[1] /mast/ *n. & v.* •*n.* **1** a long upright post of timber, iron, etc., set up from a ship's keel or deck, esp. to support sails. **2** a post or latticework upright for supporting a radio or television antenna. **3** a flagpole (*half-mast*). •*v.tr.* furnish (a ship) with masts. □□ **mast·ed** *adj.* (also in *comb.*). **mas·ter** *n.* (also in *comb.*).

mast[2] /mast/ *n.* the fruit of the beech, oak, chestnut, and other forest trees, esp. as food for pigs.

mas·tec·to·my /mastéktəmee/ *n.* (*pl.* **-mies**) *Surgery* the removal of breast tissue.

mas·ter /mástər/ *n., adj., & v.* •*n.* **1 a** a person having control of persons or things. **b** an employer, esp. of a servant. **c** a male head of a household (*master of the house*). **d** the owner of a dog, horse, etc. **e** the owner of a slave. **f** *Naut.* the captain of a merchant ship. **g** *Hunting* the person in control of a pack of hounds, etc. **2** esp. *Brit.* a male teacher or tutor, esp. a schoolmaster. **3 a** the head of a private school, etc. **b** the presiding officer of a Masonic lodge, etc. **4** a person who has or gets the upper hand. **5** a person skilled in a particular trade and able to teach others (often *attrib.*: *master carpenter*). **6** a holder of a university degree orig. giving authority to teach in the university (*Master of Arts*). **7 a** a revered teacher in philosophy, etc. **b** (**the Master**) Christ. **8** a great artist. **9** *Chess, etc.*, a player of proven ability at international level. **10** an original version (e.g., of a film or audio recording) from which copies can be made. **11** (**Master**) a title prefixed to the name of a boy not old enough to be called *Mr.* (*Master T. Jones; Master Tom*). **12** a machine or device directly controlling another (cf. SLAVE 4). •*adj.* **1** commanding; superior (*a master spirit*). **2** main; principal (*master bedroom*). **3** controlling others (*master plan*). •*v.tr.* **1** overcome; defeat. **2** reduce to subjection. **3** acquire complete knowledge of (a subject) or facility in using (an instrument, etc.). **4** rule as a master. □□ **mas·ter·less** *adj.* **mas·ter·ship** /mástərship/ *n.*

mas·ter·ful /mástərfool/ *adj.* **1** imperious; domineering. **2** masterly. □□ **mas·ter·ful·ly** *adv.* **mas·ter·ful·ness** *n.*

▶**Masterful** and **masterly** overlap in meaning and are sometimes confused. Leaving aside **masterful**'s meaning of 'domineering,' it also means 'very skillful, masterly.' However, **masterful** used in this sense generally describes a person, e.g., *He has limited talent but he's masterful at exploiting it,* while **masterly** usually describes an achievement or action, e.g., *That was a masterly response to our opponents' arguments.*

mas·ter key *n.* a key that opens several locks, each of which also has its own key.

mas·ter·ly /mástərlee/ *adj.* worthy of a master; very skillful (*a masterly piece of work*). □□ **mas·ter·li·ness** *n.*
▶See note at MASTERFUL.

mas·ter·mind /mástərmīnd/ *n. & v.* •*n.* **1 a** a person with an outstanding intellect. **b** such an intellect. **2** the person directing an intricate operation. •*v.tr.* plan and direct (a scheme or enterprise).

mas·ter·piece /mástərpees/ *n.* **1** an outstanding piece of artistry or workmanship. **2** a person's best work.

mas·ter·stroke *n.* an outstandingly skillful act of policy, etc.

mas·ter switch *n.* a switch controlling the supply of electricity, etc., to an entire system.

mas·ter·work *n.* a masterpiece.

mas·ter·y /mástəree/ *n.* **1** comprehensive knowledge or skill in a subject or accomplishment (*she played with some mastery*). **2** the action or process of mastering a subject or accomplishment (*mastery of language*). **3** control over someone or something.

mast·head /mást-hed/ *n. & v.* •*n.* **1** the highest part of a ship's mast, esp. as a place of observation or punishment. **2 a** the title of a newspaper, etc., at the head of the front or editorial page. **b** the printed notice in a newspaper, magazine, etc., giving details of staff, ownership, etc. • *v.tr.* **1** send (a sailor) to the masthead. **2** raise (a sail) to its position on the mast.

mas·tic /mástik/ *n.* **1** a gum or resin exuded from the bark of the mastic tree, used in making varnish. **2** (in full **mastic tree**) the evergreen tree, *Pistacia lentiscus*, yielding this. **3** a waterproof filler and sealant used in building. **4** a liquor flavored with mastic gum.

mas·ti·cate /mástikayt/ *v.tr.* grind or chew (food) with one's teeth. ▫▫ **mas·ti·ca·tion** /–káyshən/ *n.* **mas·ti·ca·to·ry** /–kətáwree/ *adj.*

mas·tiff /mástif/ *n.* **1** a dog of a large strong breed with drooping ears and pendulous lips. **2** this breed of dog.

mas·to·don /mástədon/ *n.* a large extinct mammal of the genus *Mammut*, resembling the elephant. ▫▫ **mas·to·don·tic** /–dóntik/ *adj.*

mas·toid /mástoyd/ *n.* **1** a conical prominence on the temporal bone behind the ear, to which muscles are attached. **2** *colloq.* mastoiditis.

mas·tur·bate /mástərbayt/ *v.intr. & tr.* arouse oneself sexually or cause (another person) to be aroused by manual stimulation of the genitals. ▫▫ **mas·tur·ba·tion** /–báyshən/ *n.* **mas·tur·ba·tor** *n.* **mas·tur·ba·to·ry** /–tə́rbətáwree/ *adj.*

mat[1] /mat/ *n. & v.* • *n.* **1** a piece of coarse material for wiping shoes on, esp. a doormat. **2** a piece of cork, rubber, plastic, etc., to protect a surface from the heat or moisture of an object placed on it. **3** a piece of resilient material for landing on in gymnastics, wrestling, etc. **4** a piece of coarse fabric of plaited rushes, straw, etc., for lying on, packing furniture, etc. **5** a small rug. • *v.* (**matted, matting**) **1 a** *tr.* (esp. as **matted** *adj.*) entangle in a thick mass (*matted hair*). **b** *intr.* become matted. **2** *tr.* cover or furnish with mats.

mat[2] var. of MATTE[1].

mat[3] /mat/ *n.* = MATRIX 1.

mat·a·dor /mátədawr/ *n.* a bullfighter whose task is to kill the bull.

match[1] /mach/ *n. & v.* • *n.* **1** a contest or game in which persons or teams compete against each other. **2 a** a person able to contend with another as an equal (*meet one's match*). **b** a person equal to another in some quality (*we shall never see his match*). **c** a person or thing exactly like or corresponding to another. **3** a marriage. **4** a person viewed in regard to his or her eligibility for marriage (*an excellent match*). • *v.* **1 a** *tr.* be equal to or harmonious with (*the curtains match the wallpaper*). **b** *intr.* (often foll. by *with*) correspond; harmonize (*his socks do not match; does the ribbon match with your hat?*). **c** (as **matching** *adj.*) having correspondence in some essential respect (*matching curtains*). **2** *tr.* (foll. by *against, with*) place (a person, etc.) in conflict, contest, or competition with (another). **3** *tr.* find material, etc., that matches (another) (*can you match this silk?*). **4** *tr.* find a person or thing suitable for another (*matching unemployed workers to available jobs*). **5** *tr.* prove to be a match for. ▫ **to match** corresponding in some essential respect with what has been mentioned (*yellow dress with gloves to match*). ▫▫ **match·a·ble** *adj.*

match[2] /mach/ *n.* **1** a short thin piece of flammable material tipped with a composition that can be ignited by friction. **2** a piece of wick, cord, etc., designed to burn at a uniform rate, for firing a cannon, etc.

match·box /máchboks/ *n.* a box for holding matches.

match·less /máchlis/ *adj.* without an equal; incomparable. ▫▫ **match·less·ly** *adv.*

match·lock /máchlok/ *n. hist.* **1** an old type of gun with a lock in which a match was placed for igniting the powder. **2** such a lock.

match·mak·er /máchmaykər/ *n.* a person who tries to arrange an agreement or relationship between two parties, esp. a marriage partnership. ▫▫ **match·mak·ing** *n.*

match point *n. Tennis*, etc. **1** the state of a game when one side needs only one more point to win the match. **2** this point.

match·stick /máchstik/ *n.* the stem of a match.

mate[1] /mayt/ *n. & v.* • *n.* **1** a friend or fellow worker. **2 a** each of a pair, esp. of animals, birds, or socks. **b** *colloq.* a partner in marriage. **c** (in *comb.*) a fellow member or joint occupant of (*teammate; roommate*). **3** *Naut.* an officer on a merchant ship subordinate to the master. **4** an assistant to a skilled worker (*plumber's mate*). • *v.* (often foll. by *with*) **1 a** *tr.* bring (animals or birds) together for breeding. **b** *intr.* (of animals or birds) come together for breeding. **2 a** *tr.* join (persons) in marriage. **b** *intr.* (of persons) be joined in marriage. **3** *intr. Mech.* fit well. ▫▫ **mate·less** *adj.*

mate[2] /mayt/ *n. & v.tr. Chess* = CHECKMATE.

ma·té /maátay/ *n.* **1** an infusion of the leaves of a S. American shrub, *Ilex paraguayensis*. **2** this shrub, or its leaves. **3** a vessel in which these leaves are infused.

ma·te·ri·al /mətéereeəl/ *n. & adj.* • *n.* **1** the matter from which a thing is made. **2** cloth; fabric. **3** (in *pl.*) things needed for an activity (*building materials; cleaning materials; writing materials*). **4** a person or thing of a specified kind or suitable for a purpose (*officer material*). **5** (in *sing.* or *pl.*) information, etc., to be used in writing a book, etc. **6** (in *sing.* or *pl.*, often foll. by *of*) the elements or constituent parts of a substance. • *adj.* **1** of matter; corporeal. **2** concerned with bodily comfort, etc. (*material well-being*). **3** (of conduct, points of view, etc.) not spiritual. **4** (often foll. by *to*) important; essential; relevant (*at the material time*). **5** concerned with the matter, not the form, of reasoning. ▫▫ **ma·te·ri·al·i·ty** /–reeálitee/ *n.*

ma·te·ri·al·ism /mətéereeəlizəm/ *n.* **1** a tendency to prefer material possessions and physical comfort to spiritual values. **2** *Philos.* **a** the opinion that nothing exists but matter and its movements and modifications. **b** the doctrine that consciousness and will are wholly due to material agency. ▫▫ **ma·te·ri·al·ist** *n.* **ma·te·ri·al·is·tic** /–lístik/ *adj.* **ma·te·ri·al·is·ti·cal·ly** /–lístiklee/ *adv.*

ma·te·ri·al·ize /mətéereeəlīz/ *v.* **1** *intr.* become actual fact. **2 a** *tr.* cause (a spirit) to appear in bodily form. **b** *intr.* (of a spirit) appear in this way. **3** *intr. colloq.* appear or be present when expected. **4** *tr.* represent or express in material form. ▫▫ **ma·te·ri·al·i·za·tion** *n.*

ma·te·ri·al·ly /mətéereeəlee/ *adv.* **1** substantially; considerably. **2** in respect of matter.

ma·té·ri·el /mətéeree-él/ *n.* available means, esp. materials and equipment in warfare (opp. PERSONNEL).

ma·ter·nal /mətə́rnəl/ *adj.* **1** of or like a mother. **2** motherly. **3** related through the mother (*maternal uncle*). **4** of the mother in pregnancy and childbirth. ▫▫ **ma·ter·nal·ism** *n.* **ma·ter·nal·ly** *adv.*

ma·ter·ni·ty /mətə́rnitee/ *n.* **1** motherhood. **2** motherliness. **3** (*attrib.*) **a** for women during and just after childbirth (*maternity hospital; maternity leave*). **b** suitable for a pregnant woman (*maternity dress; maternity wear*).

math /math/ *n. US colloq.* mathematics.

math·e·mat·i·cal /máthimátikəl/ *adj.* **1** of or relating to mathematics. **2** (of a proof, etc.) rigorously precise. ▫▫ **math·e·mat·i·cal·ly** *adv.*

math·e·mat·ics /máthimátiks/ *n.pl.* **1** (also treated as *sing.*) the abstract science of number, quantity, and space studied in its own right (**pure mathematics**), or as applied to other disciplines such as physics, engineering, etc. (**applied mathematics**). **2** (as *pl.*) the use of mathematics in calculation, etc. ▫▫ **math·e·ma·ti·cian** /–mətíshən/ *n.*

ma·tin·ée /mat'náy/ *n.* (also **matinee**) an afternoon performance in a theater, etc.

ma·tin·ée i·dol *n.* a handsome actor admired esp. by women.

mat·ins /mát'nz/ *n.* (also **mat·tins**) (as *sing.* or *pl.*) **1** a set prayer recited at daybreak or in the evening. **2** a service of morning prayer in churches of the Anglican communion.

ma·tri·arch /máytreeaark/ *n.* a woman who is the head of a family or tribe. □□ **ma·tri·ar·chal** /–aárkəl/ *adj.*

ma·tri·ar·chy /máytreeaárkee/ *n.* (*pl.* **-chies**) a form of social organization in which the mother is the head of the family and descent is reckoned through the female line.

ma·tri·ces *pl.* of MATRIX.

mat·ri·cide /mátrisīd, máy–/ *n.* **1** the killing of one's mother. **2** a person who does this. □□ **mat·ri·cid·al** *adj.*

ma·tric·u·late /mətríkyəlayt/ *v.* **1** *intr.* be enrolled at a college or university. **2** *tr.* admit (a student) to membership of a college or university. □□ **ma·tric·u·la·tion** /–láyshən/ *n.*

mat·ri·lin·e·al /mátrilíneeəl/ *adj.* of or based on kinship with the mother or the female line. □□ **mat·ri·lin·e·al·ly** *adv.*

mat·ri·mo·ny /mátrimōnee/ *n.* (*pl.* **-nies**) **1** the rite of marriage. **2** the state of being married. □□ **mat·ri·mo·ni·al** /–mṓneeəl/ *adj.* **mat·ri·mo·ni·al·ly** /–mṓneeəlee/ *adv.*

ma·trix /máytriks/ *n.* (*pl.* **matrices** /–triseez/or **matrixes**) **1** a mold in which a thing is cast or shaped, such as a phonograph record, printing type, etc. **2** an environment or substance in which a thing is developed. **3** a rock in which gems, fossils, etc., are embedded. **4** *Math.* a rectangular array of elements in rows and columns that is treated as a single element. **5** *Biol.* the substance between cells or in which structures are embedded. **6** *Computing* a gridlike array of interconnected circuit elements.

ma·tron /máytrən/ *n.* **1** a married woman, esp. a dignified and sober one. **2** a woman managing the domestic arrangements of a school, prison, etc. □□ **ma·tron·hood** *n.*

ma·tron·ly /máytrənlee/ *adj.* like or characteristic of a matron, esp. in respect of staidness or portliness.

ma·tron of hon·or *n.* a married woman attending the bride at a wedding.

matte[1] /mat/ *adj., n., & v.* (also **matt** or **mat**) • *adj.* (of a color, surface, etc.) dull; without luster. • *n.* **1** a border of dull gold around a framed picture. **2** (in full **matte paint**) paint formulated to give a dull flat finish (cf. GLOSS[1]). **3** the appearance of unburnished gold. • *v.tr.* (**matted, matting**) **1** make (gilding, etc.) dull. **2** frost (glass).

matte[2] /mat/ *n. Cinematog.* a mask to obscure part of an image and allow another image to be superimposed, giving a combined effect.

mat·ter /mátər/ *n. & v.* • *n.* **1 a** physical substance in general, as distinct from mind and spirit. **b** that which has mass and occupies space. **2** a particular substance (*coloring matter*). **3** (prec. by *the*; often foll. by *with*) the thing that is amiss (*what is the matter?*). **4** material for thought or expression. **5 a** the substance of a book, speech, etc., as distinct from its manner or form. **b** *Logic* the particular content of a proposition, as distinct from its form. **6** a thing or things of a specified kind (*printed matter; reading matter*). **7** an affair or situation being considered, esp. in a specified way (*a serious matter; a matter for concern*). **8** *Physiol.* **a** any substance in or discharged from the body (*fecal matter; gray matter*). **b** pus. **9** (foll. by *of, for*) what is or may be a good reason for (complaint, regret, etc.). **10** *Printing* the body of a printed work, as type or as printed sheets. • *v.intr.* **1** (often foll. by *to*) be of importance; have significance (*it does not matter to me when it happened*). **2** secrete or discharge pus. □ **for that matter** (or **for the matter of that**) **1** as far as that is concerned. **2** and indeed also. **a matter of 1** approximately (*for a matter of 40 years*). **2** a thing that relates to, depends on, or is determined by (*only a matter of time before they agree*). **no matter 1** (foll. by *when, how,* etc.) regardless of (*will do it no matter what the consequences*). **2** it is of no importance. **what is the matter with** surely there is no objection to.

mat·ter of fact *n. & adj.* • *n.* **1** what belongs to the sphere of fact as distinct from opinion, etc. **2** *Law* the part of a judicial inquiry concerned with the truth of alleged facts. • *adj.* (**matter-of-fact**) /mátərəfákt/ **1** unimaginative; prosaic. **2** unemotional. □ **as a matter of fact** in reality (esp. to correct a falsehood or misunderstanding). □□ **mat·ter-of-fact·ly** *adv.* **mat·ter-of-fact·ness** *n.*

mat·ting /máting/ *n.* **1** fabric of hemp, bast, grass, etc., for mats (*coconut matting*). **2** in senses of MAT[1] *v.*

mat·tins var. of MATINS.

mat·tress /mátris/ *n.* a fabric case stuffed with soft, firm, or springy material, or a similar case filled with air or water, used on or as a bed.

ma·ture /məchŏŏr, –tyŏŏr, –tŏŏr/ *adj. & v.* • *adj.* (**maturer, maturest**) **1** with fully developed powers of body and mind; adult. **2** complete in natural development; ripe. **3** (of thought, intentions, etc.) duly careful and adequate. **4** (of a bond, etc.) due for payment. • *v.* **1 a** *tr. & intr.* develop fully. **b** *tr. & intr.* ripen. **c** *intr.* come to maturity. **2** *tr.* perfect (a plan, etc.). **3** *intr.* (of a bond, etc.) become due for payment. □□ **ma·ture·ly** *adv.* **ma·tu·ri·ty** *n.*

mat·zo /maátsə/ *n.* (also **matzoh**; *pl.* **-zos** or **-zohs** or **matzoth** /–sōt/) **1** a wafer of unleavened bread for the Passover. **2** such bread collectively.

maud·lin /máwdlin/ *adj.* weakly or tearfully sentimental, esp. in a tearful and effusive stage of drunkenness.

maul /mawl/ *v. & n.* • *v.tr.* **1** beat and bruise. **2** handle roughly or carelessly. **3** damage by criticism. • *n.* a heavy hammer, used esp. to drive stakes and wedges. □□ **maul·er** *n.*

maun·der /máwndər/ *v.intr.* **1** talk in a dreamy or rambling manner. **2** move or act listlessly or idly.

Maun·dy Thurs·day *n.* the Thursday before Easter.

mau·so·le·um /máwsəleéəm/ *n.* (*pl.* **mausoleums** or **mausolea**) a large and grand tomb.

mauve /mōv/ *adj. & n.* • *adj.* pale purple. • *n.* **1** this color. **2** a bright but delicate pale purple dye from coal-tar aniline. □□ **mauv·ish** *adj.*

ma·ven /máyvən/ *n.* (also **ma·vin**) *colloq.* an expert or connoisseur.

mav·er·ick /mávərik, mávrik/ *n.* **1** an unbranded calf or yearling. **2** an unorthodox or independent-minded person.

maw /maw/ *n.* **1 a** the stomach of an animal. **b** the jaws or throat of a voracious animal. **2** *colloq.* the stomach of a greedy person.

mawk·ish /máwkish/ *adj.* **1** sentimental in a feeble or sickly way. **2** having a faint sickly flavor. □□ **mawk·ish·ly** *adv.* **mawk·ish·ness** *n.*

max. *abbr.* maximum. □ **to the max** *sl.* to the utmost; to the fullest extent.

max·i /máksee/ *n.* (*pl.* **maxis**) *colloq.* a maxiskirt or other garment with a long skirt.

maxi- /máksee/ *comb. form* very large or long (*maxicoat, maxiskirt*).

max·il·la /maksílə/ *n.* (*pl.* **maxillae** /–lee/or **maxillas**) **1** the jaw or jawbone, esp. the upper jaw in most vertebrates. **2** the mouthpart of many arthropods used in chewing. □□ **max·il·lar·y** /máksəléree/ *adj.*

See page xii for the *Key to Pronunciation*.

max·im /máksim/ *n.* a general truth or rule of conduct expressed in a sentence.

max·i·mal /máksiməl/ *adj.* being or relating to a maximum; the greatest possible in size, duration, etc. □□ **max·i·mal·ly** *adv.*

max·i·mize /máksimīz/ *v.tr.* increase or enhance to the utmost. □□ **max·i·mi·za·tion** *n.* **max·i·miz·er** *n.*

max·i·mum /máksiməm/ *n. & adj.* • *n.* (*pl.* **maxima** /–mə/) the highest possible or attainable amount. • *adj.* that is a maximum.

May /may/ *n.* the fifth month of the year.

may /may/ *v.aux.* (*3rd sing. present* **may**; *past* **might** /mīt/) **1** (often foll. by *well* for emphasis) expressing possibility (*it may be true*; *you may well lose your way*). **2** expressing permission (*you may not go*; *may I come in?*). **3** expressing a wish (*may he live to regret it*). **4** expressing uncertainty or irony in questions (*who may you be?*; *who are you, may I ask?*). **5** in purpose clauses and after *wish*, *fear*, etc. (*hope he may succeed*). □ **be that as it may** (or **that is as may be**) that may or may not be so.

▶Traditionalists insist that one should distinguish between **may** (present tense) and **might** (past tense) in expressing possibility: *I may have some dessert after dinner if I'm still hungry. I might have known that the highway would be closed because of the storm.* In casual use, though, **may** and **might** are generally interchangeable: *They might take a vacation next month. He may have called earlier, but the answering machine was broken.* For **may** vs. **can**, see note at CAN[1].

Ma·ya /ma̋yə/ *n.* **1** (*pl.* same or **Mayas**) a member of an ancient native people of Central America. **2** the language of this people. □□ **Ma·yan** *adj. & n.*

may·ap·ple /máyapəl/ *n.* (also **man·drake**) an American herbaceous plant, *Podophyllum peltatum*, bearing a yellow egg-shaped fruit in May.

may·be /máybee/ *adv.* perhaps, possibly.

May Day *n.* May 1, esp. as a festival with dancing, or as an international holiday in honor of workers.

May·day /máyday/ *n.* an international radio-telephone distress signal used esp. by ships and aircraft.

may·flow·er /máyflowər/ *n.* **1** any of various flowers that bloom in May, esp. the trailing arbutus, *Epigaea repens*. **2** (**Mayflower**) the ship on which the Pilgrims traveled from England to N. America in 1620.

may·fly /máyflī/ *n.* (*pl.* **-flies**) **1** any insect of the order Ephemeroptera, living briefly in spring in the adult stage. **2** an imitation mayfly used by anglers.

may·hap /máyháp/ *adv. archaic* perhaps; possibly.

may·hem /máyhem/ *n.* **1** violent or damaging action. **2** rowdy confusion; chaos.

mayn't /máyənt/ *contr.* may not.

may·on·naise /máyənáyz/ *n.* a thick creamy dressing made of egg yolks, oil, vinegar, etc.

may·or /máyər, mair/ *n.* the chief executive of a city or town. □□ **may·or·al** *adj.* **may·or·ship** *n.*

may·or·al·ty /máyərəltee, máir–/ *n.* (*pl.* **-ties**) **1** the office of mayor. **2** a mayor's period of office.

may·or·ess /máyəris, máir–/ *n.* **1** a woman holding the office of mayor. **2** the wife of a mayor.

may·pole /máypōl/ *n.* (also **Maypole**) a pole painted and decked with flowers and ribbons, for dancing around on May Day.

mayst /mayst/ *archaic 2nd sing. present* of MAY.

maz·a·rine /mázəre̋en/ *n. & adj.* a rich deep blue.

maze /mayz/ *n.* **1** a network of paths and hedges designed as a puzzle for those who try to penetrate it. **2** a complex network of paths or passages; a labyrinth. **3** a confused mass, etc. □□ **ma·zy** *adj.* (**mazier, maziest**).

ma·zur·ka /məzə́rkə/ *n.* **1** a usu. lively Polish dance in triple time. **2** the music for this.

MB *abbr. Computing* megabyte(s).

MBA *abbr.* Master of Business Administration.

MC *abbr.* **1** master of ceremonies. **2** Marine Corps. **3** Medical Corps. **4** Member of Congress.

Mc·Car·thy·ism /məka̋arthee-izəm/ *n.* the policy of hunting out suspected subversives or esp. Communists.

Mc·Coy /məkóy/ *n. colloq.* □ **the** (or **the real**) **McCoy** the real thing; the genuine article.

MD *abbr.* **1** Doctor of Medicine. **2** Maryland (in official postal use). **3** Managing Director. **4** muscular dystrophy.

Md *symb. Chem.* the element mendelevium.

Md. *abbr.* Maryland.

MDA *abbr.* methylene dioxymethamphetamine, an amphetamine-based drug that causes euphoric and hallucinatory effects, originally produced as an appetite suppressant (see ECSTASY 2).

ME *abbr.* **1** Maine (in official postal use). **2** Middle East. **3** middle English.

Me. *abbr.* Maine.

me[1] /mee/ *pron.* **1** *objective case* of I[2] (*he saw me*). **2** *colloq.* = I[2] (*it's me all right*; *is taller than me*). **3** *colloq.* myself; to or for myself (*I got me a gun*). **4** *colloq.* used in exclamations (*ah me!*; *dear me!*; *silly me!*). □ **me and mine** me and my relatives.

me[2] var. of MI.

me·a cul·pa /máyə ko͝olpə, me̋eə kúlpə/ *n. & int.* • *n.* an acknowledgment of one's fault or error (from Latin 'by my fault'). • *int.* expressing such an acknowledgment.

mead /meed/ *n.* an alcoholic drink of fermented honey and water.

mead·ow /médō/ *n.* **1** a piece of grassland, esp. one used for hay. **2** a piece of low well-watered ground, esp. near a river. □□ **mead·ow·y** *adj.*

mea·ger /me̋egər/ *adj.* **1** lacking in amount or quality (*a meager salary*). **2** (of literary composition, ideas, etc.) lacking fullness; unsatisfying. **3** (of a person or animal) lean; thin. □□ **mea·ger·ly** *adv.* **mea·ger·ness** *n.*

meal[1] /meel/ *n.* **1** an occasion when food is eaten. **2** the food eaten on one occasion. □ **make a meal of 1** treat (a task, etc.) too laboriously or fussily. **2** consume as a meal.

---

meal Old English *mǣl* (also in the sense 'measure,' surviving in words such as *piecemeal* 'measure taken at one time'), of Germanic origin. The early sense of *meal* involved a notion of 'fixed time'; compare with Dutch *maal* 'meal, (portion of) time' and German *Mal* 'time,' *Mahl* 'meal,' from an Indo-European root meaning 'to measure.'

---

meal[2] /meel/ *n.* **1** the edible part of any grain or pulse (usu. other than wheat) ground to powder. **2** any powdery substance made by grinding.

meal tick·et *n.* **1** a ticket entitling one to a meal, esp. at a specified place with reduced cost. **2** a person or thing that is a source of food or income.

meal·time /me̋eltīm/ *n.* any of the usual times of eating.

meal·worm /me̋elwərm/ *n.* the larva of the meal beetle.

meal·y /me̋elee/ *adj.* (**mealier, mealiest**) **1 a** of or like meal; soft and powdery. **b** containing meal. **2** (of a complexion) pale. **3** (of a horse) spotty. **4** (in full **mealy-mouthed**) not outspoken; afraid to use plain expressions. □□ **meal·i·ness** *n.*

mean[1] /meen/ *v.tr.* (*past* and *past part.* **meant** /ment/) **1 a** (often foll. by *to* + infin.) have as one's purpose or intention; have in mind (*they really mean mischief*; *I didn't mean to break it*). **b** (foll. by *by*) have as a motive in explanation (*what do you mean by that?*). **2** (often in *passive*) design or destine for a purpose (*mean it to be used; is meant to be a gift*). **3** intend to convey or indicate or refer to (a particular thing or notion) (*I mean we cannot go; I mean Springfield in Ohio*). **4** entail; involve (*it means catching the early train*). **5** (often foll. by *that* + clause) portend; signify (*this means trouble; your refusal means that we must look elsewhere*). **6** (of a word) have as its explanation in the same language or its equivalent in another language. **7** (foll. by *to*) be of some specified importance to (a person) (*that means a lot to me*). □ **mean business** be in earnest. **mean it** not be joking or exaggerating. **mean to say** really admit (usu. in *interrog.*: *do you mean to say you have lost it?*). **mean well** (often foll. by *to, toward, by*) have good intentions.

mean² /meen/ *adj.* **1** miserly; not generous. **2** ignoble; small-minded. **3** (of a person's capacity, understanding, etc.) inferior; poor. **4** (of housing) not imposing in appearance; shabby. **5 a** malicious; ill-tempered. **b** vicious or aggressive. **6** *colloq.* skillful; formidable (*is a mean fighter*). **7** *colloq.* ashamed (*feel mean*). □ **no mean** a very good (*that is no mean achievement*). □□ **mean·ly** *adv.* **mean·ness** *n.*

mean Middle English, shortening of Old English *gemǣne*, of Germanic origin, from an Indo-European root shared by Latin *communis* 'common.' The original sense was 'common to two or more persons,' later 'inferior in rank,' leading to senses 3 and 4, from which senses 1 and 2 (which became common in the 19th century) arose.

mean³ /meen/ *n. & adj.* • *n.* **1** a condition, quality, virtue, or course of action equally removed from two opposite (usu. unsatisfactory) extremes. **2** *Math.* **a** the term midway between the first and last terms of an arithmetical or geometrical, etc., progression (*2 and 8 have the arithmetic mean 5 and the geometric mean 4*). **b** average. • *adj.* **1** (of a quantity) equally far from two extremes. **2** calculated as a mean.

▶The difference between **median** and **mean** is most clearly expressed in numbers: **Mean,** or *average,* refers to the result obtained by dividing the sum of a set of quantities by the number of quantities in the set: *The mean or average of 3, 11, 9, and 5 is 28 divided by 4, or 7.* The **median** is the middle number in a sequence or, if the sequence has an even number of quantities, the average between the two middle numbers: *The median of 3, 4, 5, 8, and 14 is 5. The median of 2, 9, 10, and 35 is 9.5, that is, the mean or the average of 9 and 10.*

me·an·der /meeándər/ *v. & n.* • *v.intr.* **1** wander at random. **2** (of a stream) wind about. • *n.* **1 a** a curve in a winding river, etc. **b** a crooked or winding path or passage. **2** a circuitous journey. **3** an ornamental pattern of lines winding in and out; a fret. □□ **me·an·der·ing** *adj. & n.*

mean·ie /meénee/ *n.* (also **mean·y**) (*pl.* **-ies**) *colloq.* a mean or small-minded person.

mean·ing /meéning/ *n. & adj.* • *n.* **1** what is meant by a word, action, idea, etc. **2** significance. **3** importance. • *adj.* expressive; significant (*a meaning glance*). □□ **mean·ing·ly** *adv.*

mean·ing·ful /meéningfo͝ol/ *adj.* **1** full of meaning; significant. **2** *Logic* able to be interpreted. □□ **mean·ing·ful·ly** *adv.* **mean·ing·ful·ness** *n.*

mean·ing·less /meéninglis/ *adj.* having no meaning or significance. □□ **mean·ing·less·ly** *adv.* **mean·ing·less·ness** *n.*

means /meenz/ *n.pl.* **1** (often treated as *sing.*) that by which a result is brought about (*a means of quick travel*). **2 a** money resources (*live beyond one's means*). **b** wealth (*a man of means*). □ **by all means** (or **all manner of means**) **1** certainly. **2** in every possible way. **3** at any cost. **by any means** in any way. **by means of** by the agency or instrumentality of (a thing or action). **by no means** (or **no manner of means**) not at all; certainly not.

meant *past* and *past part.* of MEAN¹.

mean·time /meéntīm/ *adv. & n.* • *adv.* = MEANWHILE. ▶Less usual than *meanwhile.* • *n.* the intervening period (esp. *in the meantime*).

mean·while /meénwīl, –hwīl/ *adv. & n.* • *adv.* **1** in the intervening period of time. **2** at the same time. • *n.* the intervening period (esp. *in the meanwhile*).

mean·y var. of MEANIE.

mea·sles /meézəlz/ *n.pl.* (also treated as *sing.*) **1** an acute infectious viral disease marked by red spots on the skin. **2** the spots of measles.

mea·sly /meézlee/ *adj.* (**measlier, measliest**) **1** *colloq.* contemptibly small or few.

meas·ur·a·ble /mézhərəbəl/ *adj.* that can be measured. □□ **meas·ur·a·bil·i·ty** /–bílitee/ *n.* **meas·ur·a·bly** *adv.*

meas·ure /mézhər/ *n. & v.* • *n.* **1** a size or quantity found by measuring. **2** a system of measuring (*liquid measure; linear measure*). **3** a rod or tape, etc., for measuring. **4** a vessel of standard capacity for transferring or determining fixed quantities of liquids, etc. (*a pint measure*). **5 a** the degree, extent, or amount of a thing. **b** (foll. by *of*) some degree of (*there was a measure of wit in her remark*). **6** a unit of capacity, e.g., a bushel (*20 measures of wheat*). **7** a factor by which a person or thing is reckoned or evaluated (*their success is a measure of their determination*). **8** (usu. in *pl.*) suitable action to achieve some end (*took measures to ensure a good profit*). **9** a legislative act. **10** a quantity contained in another an exact number of times. **11** a prescribed extent or quantity. **12 a** poetical rhythm; meter. **b** a metrical group of a dactyl or two iambs, trochees, spondees, etc. **13** *US Mus.* a bar or the time content of a bar. • *v.* **1** *tr.* ascertain the extent or quantity of (a thing) by comparison with a fixed unit or with an object of known size. **2** *intr.* be of a specified size (*it measures six inches*). **3** *tr.* ascertain the size and proportion of (a person) for clothes. **4** *tr.* estimate (a quality, person's character, etc.) by some standard or rule. **5** *tr.* (often foll. by *off*) mark (a line, etc., of a given length). **6** *tr.* (foll. by *out*) distribute (a thing) in measured quantities. **7** *tr.* (foll. by *with, against*) bring (oneself or one's strength, etc.) into competition with. □ **beyond measure** excessively. **for good measure** as something beyond the minimum; as a finishing touch. **in a** (or **some**) **measure** partly. **measure up 1 a** determine the size, etc., of by measurement. **b** take comprehensive measurements. **2** (often foll. by *to*) have the necessary qualifications (for).

meas·ured /mézhərd/ *adj.* **1** rhythmical; regular in movement (*a measured tread*). **2** (of language) carefully considered.

meas·ure·less /mézhərlis/ *adj.* not measurable; infinite.

meas·ure·ment /mézhərmənt/ *n.* **1** the act or an instance of measuring. **2** an amount determined by measuring. **3** (in *pl.*) detailed dimensions.

meas·ur·ing cup *n.* a cup marked to measure its contents.

meat /meet/ *n.* **1** the flesh of animals (esp. mammals) as food. **2** (foll. by *of*) the essence or chief part of. **3** the edible part of fruits, nuts, eggs, shellfish, etc. □□ **meat·less** *adj.*

meat-and-po·ta·toes *adj.* essential; fundamental; basic.

meat·ball /meétbawl/ *n.* seasoned ground meat formed into a small round ball.

meat loaf *n.* seasoned ground meat molded into the shape of a loaf and baked.
meat·pack·ing /meétpaking/ *n.* the business of slaughtering animals and processing the meat for sale as food.
meat·y /meétee/ *adj.* (**meatier, meatiest**) **1** full of meat; fleshy. **2** of or like meat. **3** full of substance. ▫▫ **meat·i·ly** *adv.* **meat·i·ness** *n.*
Mec·ca /mékə/ *n.* **1** a place one aspires to visit. **2** the birthplace of a faith, policy, pursuit, etc.
me·chan·ic /mikánik/ *n.* a skilled worker, esp. one who makes or uses or repairs machinery.
me·chan·i·cal /mikánikəl/ *adj.* **1** of or relating to machines or mechanisms. **2** working or produced by machinery. **3** (of a person or action) automatic; lacking originality. **4 a** (of an agency, principle, etc.) belonging to mechanics. **b** (of a theory, etc.) explaining phenomena by the assumption of mechanical action. **5** of or relating to mechanics as a science. ▫▫ **me·chan·i·cal·ism** *n.* (in sense 4). **me·chan·i·cal·ly** *adv.* **me·chan·i·cal·ness** *n.*
me·chan·ics /mikániks/ *n.pl.* (usu. treated as *sing.*) **1** the branch of applied mathematics dealing with motion and tendencies to motion. **2** the science of machinery. **3** the method of construction or routine operation of a thing.
mech·an·ism /mékənizəm/ *n.* **1** the structure or adaptation of parts of a machine. **2** a system of parts working together in or as in a machine. **3** the mode of operation of a process. **4** *Art* mechanical execution; technique. **5** *Philos.* the doctrine that all natural phenomena, including life, allow mechanical explanation by physics and chemistry.
mech·a·nis·tic /mékənistik/ *adj.* of or connected with mechanics. ▫▫ **mech·a·nis·ti·cal·ly** /–nístiklee/ *adv.*
mech·a·nize /mékənīz/ *v.tr.* **1** introduce machines or automatic devices into (a process, activity, or place. **2** *Mil.* equip with tanks, armored cars, etc. ▫▫ **mech·a·ni·za·tion** *n.* **mech·a·niz·er** *n.*
med /med/ *adj. colloq.* medical (*med school*).
med·al /méd'l/ *n.* a piece of metal, usu. in the form of a disk, awarded as a distinction to a soldier, scholar, athlete, etc., for services rendered, for proficiency, etc.
med·al·ist /méd'list/ *n.* **1** a recipient of a (specified) medal (*gold medalist*). **2** an engraver or designer of medals.
me·dal·lion /midályən/ *n.* **1** a large medal. **2** a thing shaped like this, e.g., a decorative panel, etc.
Med·al of Free·dom *n.* (also **Pres·i·den·tial Med·al of Free·dom**) medal awarded by the US president for achievement in various fields.
Med·al of Hon·or *n.* (also **Con·gres·sion·al Med·al of Hon·or**) the highest US military decoration, awarded by Congress for exceptional valor.
med·dle /méd'l/ *v.intr.* (often foll. by *with, in*) interfere in or busy oneself unduly with others' concerns. ▫▫ **med·dler** *n.*
med·dle·some /méd'lsəm/ *adj.* fond of meddling; interfering.
me·di·a[1] /meédeeə/ *n.pl.* **1** *pl.* of MEDIUM. **2** (usu. prec. by *the*) the main means of mass communication (esp. newspapers and broadcasting) regarded collectively. ▶See note at MEDIUM.
me·di·a[2] /meédeeə/ *n.* (*pl.* **mediae** /–dee-ee/) **1** *Phonet.* a voiced stop, e.g., *g, b, d*. **2** *Anat.* a middle layer of the wall of an artery or other vessel.
me·di·ae·val var. of MEDIEVAL.
me·di·al /meédeeəl/ *adj.* **1** situated in the middle. **2** of average size. ▫▫ **me·di·al·ly** *adv.*
me·di·an /meédeeən/ *adj. & n.* • *adj.* situated in the middle. • *n.* **1** *Anat.* a median artery, vein, nerve, etc. **2** *Geom.* a straight line drawn from any vertex of a triangle to the middle of the opposite side. **3** *Math.* the middle value of a series of values arranged in order of size. **4** (also **median strip**) center divider separating opposing lanes on a divided highway. ▶See note at MEAN.
me·di·ant /meédeeənt/ *n. Mus.* the third note of a diatonic scale of any key.
me·di·ate *v. & adj.* • *v.* /meédeeayt/ **1** *intr.* (often foll. by *between*) intervene (between parties in a dispute) to produce agreement or reconciliation. **2** *tr.* be the medium for bringing about (a result) or for conveying (a gift, etc.). **3** *tr.* form a connecting link between. • *adj.* /meédeeət/ **1** connected not directly but through some other person or thing. **2** involving an intermediate agency. ▫▫ **me·di·a·tion** /–áyshən/ *n.* **me·di·a·tor** /meédeeaytər/ *n.* **me·di·a·to·ry** /meédeeətáwree/ *adj.*
med·ic /médik/ *n. colloq.* a medical practitioner or student.
med·i·ca·ble /médikəbəl/ *adj.* able to benefit from medical treatment.
Med·i·caid /médikayd/ *n.* a federal system of health insurance for those requiring financial assistance.
med·i·cal /médikəl/ *adj. & n.* • *adj.* **1** of or relating to the science of medicine in general. **2** of or relating to conditions requiring medical and not surgical treatment (*medical ward*). • *n. colloq.* = MEDICAL EXAMINATION. ▫▫ **med·i·cal·ly** *adv.*
med·i·cal ex·am·in·er *n.* a person, usu. a physician, employed by a city, county, etc., to conduct autopsies and determine the cause of death.
me·dic·a·ment /médikəmənt, midíkə–/ *n.* a substance used for medical treatment.
Med·i·care /médikair/ *n.* US federal government program for health insurance for persons esp. over 65 years of age.
med·i·cate /médikayt/ *v.tr.* **1** treat medically. **2** impregnate with a medicinal substance.
med·i·ca·tion /médikáyshən/ *n.* **1** a substance used for medical treatment. **2** treatment using drugs.
me·dic·i·nal /mədísinəl/ *adj. & n.* • *adj.* (of a substance) having healing properties. • *n.* a medicinal substance. ▫▫ **me·dic·i·nal·ly** *adv.*
med·i·cine /médisin/ *n.* **1** the science or practice of the diagnosis, treatment, and prevention of disease, esp. as distinct from surgical methods. **2** any drug or preparation used for the treatment or prevention of disease, esp. one taken by mouth. **3** a spell, charm, or fetish which is thought to cure afflictions. ▫ **give someone a dose** (or **taste**) **of one's own medicine** give someone the same bad treatment that they have given to others. **take one's medicine** submit to something disagreeable.
med·i·cine ball *n.* a stuffed leather ball thrown and caught for exercise.
med·i·cine man *n.* a person believed to have magical powers of healing, esp. among Native Americans.
med·i·co /médikō/ *n.* (*pl.* **-cos**) *colloq.* a medical practitioner or student.
me·di·e·val /meédee-eévəl, méd–, míd–/ *adj.* (also **me·di·ae·val**) **1** of, or in the style of, the Middle Ages. **2** *colloq.* old-fashioned. ▫▫ **me·di·e·val·ism** *n.* **me·di·e·val·ist** *n.*
me·di·o·cre /meédeeókər/ *adj.* **1** of middling quality, neither good nor bad. **2** second-rate.
me·di·oc·ri·ty /meédeeókritee/ *n.* (*pl.* **-ties**) **1** the state of being mediocre. **2** a mediocre person or thing.
med·i·tate /méditayt/ *v.* **1** *intr.* **a** exercise the mind in (esp. religious) contemplation. **b** (usu. foll. by *on, upon*) focus on a subject in this manner. **2** *tr.* plan mentally. ▫▫ **med·i·ta·tion** /–táyshən/ *n.* **med·i·ta·tor** *n.*
med·i·ta·tive /méditaytiv/ *adj.* **1** inclined to meditate. **2** indicative of meditation. ▫▫ **med·i·ta·tive·ly** *adv.*
Med·i·ter·ra·ne·an /méditəráyneeən/ *n. & adj.* • *n.* **1** a

large landlocked sea bordered by S. Europe, SW Asia, and N. Africa. **2** a native of a country bordering on the Mediterranean Sea. • *adj.* **1** of or characteristic of the Mediterranean or its surrounding region (*Mediterranean climate; Mediterranean cooking*). **2** (of a person) dark-complexioned and not tall.

me•di•um /me͞edeeəm/ *n. & adj.* • *n.* (*pl.* **media** or **mediums**) **1** the middle quality, degree, etc., between extremes (*find a happy medium*). **2** the means by which something is communicated (*the medium of sound; the medium of television*). **3** the intervening substance through which impressions are conveyed to the senses, etc. (*light passing from one medium into another*). **4** *Biol.* the physical environment or conditions of growth, storage, or transport of a living organism (*the shape of a fish is ideal for its fluid medium; growing mold on the surface of a medium*). **5** a means of doing something (*the medium through which money is raised*). **6** the material or form used by an artist, composer, etc. **7** the liquid (e.g., oil or gel) with which pigments are mixed for use in painting. **8** (*pl.* **mediums**) a person claiming to communicate between the dead and the living. • *adj.* **1** between two qualities, degrees, etc. **2** average; moderate (*of medium height*).

▶The Latin-derived noun **medium**, 'means for distributing information,' is singular. Its plural is **media:** *The newspaper is a powerful advertising medium. The government used all media to reach voters. Some media are more influential than others.* Many speakers now use the plural as singular: *The media is only as good as the integrity of the people who report the stories.*

med•ley /médlee/ *n.* (*pl.* **-leys**) **1** a varied mixture. **2** a collection of songs, parts of songs, or other musical items from one work or various sources performed as a continuous piece (*a medley of Beatles songs*).

me•dul•la /midúlə/ *n.* **1** the inner region of certain organs or tissues. **2** the myelin layer of certain nerve fibers. **3** the soft internal tissue of plants. ▫▫ **med•ul•lar•y** /méd'léree, mejə–, mədúləree/ *adj.*

me•dul•la ob•long•a•ta /midúlə óblonggaátə/ *n.* the continuation of the spinal cord within the skull, forming the lowest part of the brain stem.

me•du•sa /mido͞osə, –zə, –dyo͞o–/ *n.* (*pl.* **medusae** /–see/or **medusas**) **1** a jellyfish. **2** a free-swimming form of any coelenterate, having tentacles around the edge of a jellylike body.

meek /meek/ *adj.* **1** humble and submissive. **2** piously gentle in nature. ▫▫ **meek•ly** *adv.* **meek•ness** *n.*

meer•kat /me͞erkat/ *n.* a small S. African mongoose, esp. the suricate.

meer•schaum /me͞ershəm, –shawm/ *n.* **1** a soft white form of hydrated magnesium silicate, which resembles clay. **2** a tobacco pipe with the bowl made from this.

meet[1] /meet/ *v. & n.* • *v.* (*past* and *past part.* **met** /met/) **1 a** *tr.* encounter (a person or persons) by accident or design; come face to face with. **b** *intr.* (of two or more people) come into each other's company by accident or design (*decided to meet on the bridge*). **2** *tr.* go to a place to be present at the arrival of (a person, train, etc.). **3 a** *tr.* come together or into contact with (*where the road meets the river*). **b** *intr.* come together or into contact (*where the sea and the sky meet*). **4 a** *tr.* make the acquaintance of (*delighted to meet you*). **b** *intr.* (of two or more people) make each other's acquaintance. **5** *intr. & tr.* come together or come into contact with for the purposes of conference, business, worship, etc. (*the committee meets every week; the union met management yesterday*). **6** *tr.* **a** deal with or answer (a demand, objection, etc.) (*met the original proposal with hostility*). **b** satisfy or conform with (proposals, deadlines, a person, etc.) (*agreed to meet the new terms*). **7** *tr.* pay (a bill, etc.); provide the funds required by (*meet the cost of the move*). **8** *tr. &* (foll. by *with*) *intr.* experience, encounter, or receive (success, disaster, a difficulty, etc.) (*met their death; met with many problems*). **9** *tr.* oppose in battle, contest, or confrontation. • *n.* **1** the assembly of competitors for various sporting activities, as track, swimming, etc. **2** the assembly of riders and hounds for a hunt. ▫ **meet the eye** (or **the ear**) be visible (or audible). **meet a person's eye** check if another person is watching and look into his or her eyes in return. **meet a person halfway** make a compromise. **meet up** *colloq.* happen to meet. **meet with** **1** see sense 8 of *v.* **2** receive (a reaction) (*met with the committee's approval*). **3** see sense 1a of *v.* **more than meets the eye** possessing hidden qualities or complications.

meet[2] /meet/ *adj. archaic* suitable; fit; proper.

meet•ing /me͞eting/ *n.* **1** in senses of MEET[1]. **2** an assembly of people, esp. the members of a society, committee, etc. **3** an assembly (esp. of Quakers) for worship. **4** the persons assembled (*address the meeting*).

meet•ing•house /méetinghows/ *n.* a place of worship, esp. of Quakers, etc.

meg•a /mégə/ *adj. & adv. sl.* • *adj.* **1** excellent. **2** enormous. • *adv.* extremely.

mega- /mégə/ *comb. form* **1** large. **2** denoting a factor of one million (10^6) in the metric system of measurement. ¶ Abbr.: **M.**

meg•a•byte /mégəbīt/ *n. Computing* 1,048,576 (i.e., 2^{20}) bytes as a measure of data capacity, or loosely 1,000,000 bytes. ¶ Abbr.: **MB.**

meg•a•hertz /mégəhərts/ *n.* one million hertz, esp. as a measure of frequency of radio transmissions. ¶ Abbr.: **MHz.**

meg•a•lith /mégəlith/ *n. Archaeol.* a large stone, esp. as a monument or part of one. ▫▫ **meg•a•lith•ic** /mégəlíthik/ *adj*

megalo- /mégəlō/ *comb. form* great (*megalomania*).

meg•a•lo•ma•ni•a /mégəlōmáyneeə/ *n.* **1** a mental disorder producing delusions of grandeur. **2** a passion for grandiose schemes. ▫▫ **meg•a•lo•ma•ni•ac** *adj. & n.* **meg•a•lo•ma•ni•a•cal** /–məníəkəl/ *adj.*

meg•a•lop•o•lis /mégəlópəlis/ *n.* **1** a great city or its way of life. **2** an urban complex consisting of a city and its environs.

meg•a•phone /mégəfōn/ *n.* a large funnel-shaped device for amplifying the voice.

meg•a•ton /mégətun/ *n.* a unit of explosive power equal to one million tons of TNT.

meg•a•volt /mégəvōlt/ *n.* one million volts, esp. as a unit of electromotive force. ¶ Abbr.: **MV.**

meg•a•watt /mégəwot/ *n.* one million watts, esp. as a measure of electrical power as generated by power stations. ¶ Abbr.: **MW.**

mei•o•sis /mīósis/ *n.* **1** *Biol.* a type of cell division in reproductive cells (e.g., eggs or sperm) that results in daughter cells with half the chromosome number of the parent cell (cf. MITOSIS). **2** = LITOTES. ▫▫ **mei•ot•ic** /mīótik/ *adj.*

mel•a•mine /méləmeen/ *n.* **1** a white crystalline compound that can be copolymerized with methanal to give thermosetting resins. **2** (in full **melamine resin**) a plastic made from melamine and used esp. for laminated coatings.

mel•an•cho•li•a /mélənkóleeə/ *n.* a mental condition marked by depression and ill-founded fears.

mel•an•chol•y /mélənkolee/ *n. & adj.* • *n.* (*pl.* **-ies**) **1** a pensive sadness. **2 a** mental depression. **b** a habitual or constitutional tendency to this. **3** *hist.* one of the four humors; black bile (see HUMOR *n.* 4). • *adj.* sad;

gloomy; saddening; depressing; expressing sadness. □□ **mel·an·chol·ic** /–kólik/ *adj.*

Mel·a·ne·sian /méləneézhən, –shən/ *n.* & *adj.* • *n.* **1** a member of the dominant Negroid people of Melanesia, an island group in the W. Pacific. **2** the language of this people. • *adj.* of or relating to this people or their language.

mé·lange /maylónzh/ *n.* a mixture; a medley.

mel·a·nin /mélənin/ *n.* a dark pigment occurring in the hair, skin, and iris of the eye that is responsible for tanning of the skin when exposed to sunlight.

mel·a·no·ma /mélənṓmə/ *n.* a malignant tumor of melanin-forming cells, usu. in the skin.

Mel·ba toast /mélbə/ *n.* very thin crisp toast.

meld[1] /meld/ *v.* & *n.* • *v.tr.* (also *absol.*) (in rummy, canasta, etc.) lay down or declare (one's cards) in order to score points. • *n.* a completed set or run of cards in any of these games.

meld[2] /meld/ *v.tr.* & *intr.* merge; blend; combine.

me·lee /máyláy/ *n.* (also **mêlée**) **1** a confused fight, skirmish, or scuffle. **2** a muddle.

mel·lif·lu·ous /məlíflooəs/ *adj.* (of a voice or words) pleasing; musical; flowing. □□ **mel·lif·lu·ous·ly** *adv.*

mel·low /mélō/ *adj.* & *v.* • *adj.* **1** (of sound, color, light) soft and rich, free from harshness. **2** (of character) softened or matured by age or experience. **3** genial; jovial. **4** partly intoxicated. **5** (of fruit) soft, sweet, and juicy. **6** (of wine) well-matured; smooth. **7** (of earth) rich; loamy. • *v.tr.* & *intr.* make or become mellow. □ **mellow out** *sl.* relax. □□ **mel·low·ness** *n.*

me·lo·de·on /məlṓdeeən/ *n.* (also **me·lo·di·on**) **1** a small organ popular in the 19th c., similar to the harmonium. **2** a small German accordion.

me·lod·ic /məlódik/ *adj.* **1** of or relating to melody. **2** having or producing melody. □□ **me·lod·i·cal·ly** *adv.*

me·lo·di·ous /məlṓdeeəs/ *adj.* **1** of, producing, or having melody. **2** sweet-sounding. □□ **me·lo·di·ous·ly** *adv.* **me·lo·di·ous·ness** *n.*

mel·o·dra·ma /mélədraámə, –dramə/ *n.* **1** a dramatic piece with exaggerated characters and exciting events intended to appeal to the emotions. **2** the genre of drama of this type. **3** language, behavior, or an occurrence suggestive of this. □□ **mel·o·dra·mat·ic** /–drəmátik/ *adj.* **me·lo·dra·mat·i·cal·ly** /–drəmátiklee/ *adv.* **mel·o·dram·a·tize** /–drámətīz/ *v.tr.*

mel·o·dy /mélədee/ *n.* (*pl.* **-dies**) **1** an arrangement of single notes in a musically expressive succession. **2** the principal part in harmonized music. **3** a musical arrangement of words. **4** sweet music; tunefulness.

mel·on /mélən/ *n.* **1** the sweet fruit of various gourds. **2** the gourd producing this (*honeydew melon*; *watermelon*). **3** *Zool.* a mass of waxy material in the head of some toothed whales, thought to focus acoustic signals.

melt /melt/ *v.* & *n.* • *v.* **1** *intr.* become liquefied by heat. **2** *tr.* change to a liquid condition by heat. **3** *tr.* (as **molten** *adj.*) (usu. of materials that require a great deal of heat to melt them) liquefied by heat (*molten lava*; *molten lead*). **4 a** *intr.* & *tr.* dissolve. **b** *intr.* (of food) be easily dissolved in the mouth. **5** *intr.* **a** (of a person, feelings, the heart, etc.) be softened as a result of pity, love, etc. **b** dissolve into tears. **6** *tr.* soften (a person, feelings, the heart, etc.) (*a look to melt a heart of stone*). **7** *intr.* (usu. foll. by *into*) change or merge imperceptibly into another form or state (*night melted into dawn*). **8** *intr.* (often foll. by *away*) (of a person) leave or disappear unobtrusively (*melted into the background*; *melted away into the crowd*). **9** *intr.* (usu. as **melting** *adj.*) (of sound) be soft and liquid (*melting chords*). • *n.* **1** liquid metal, etc. **2** an amount melted at any one time. **3** the process or an instance of melting. □ **melt away** disappear or make disappear by liquefaction. **melt down** **1** melt (esp. metal articles) in order to reuse the raw material. **2** become liquid and lose structure (cf. MELTDOWN). □□ **melt·er** *n.* **melt·ing·ly** *adv.*

melt·down /méltdown/ *n.* **1** the melting of a structure, esp. the overheated core of a nuclear reactor. **2** a disastrous event, as a rapid fall in stock prices.

melt·ing point *n.* the temperature at which a solid will melt.

melt·ing pot *n.* **1** a pot in which metals, etc., are melted and mixed. **2** a place where races, theories, etc., are mixed, or an imaginary pool where ideas are mixed together.

melt·wa·ter /méltwawtər/ *n.* water formed by the melting of snow and ice, esp. from a glacier.

mem·ber /mémbər/ *n.* **1** a person, animal, or plant, etc., belonging to a society, team, taxonomic group, etc. **2** a person formally elected to take part in the proceedings of certain organizations (*Member of Congress*). **3** (also *attrib.*) a part or branch of a political body (*member state*; *a member of the United Nations*). **4** a constituent portion of a complex structure. **5** a part of a sentence, equation, group of figures, mathematical set, etc. **6 a** any part or organ of the body, esp. a limb. **b** = PENIS. □□ **mem·bered** *adj.* (also in *comb.*).

mem·ber·ship /mémbərship/ *n.* **1** being a member. **2** the number of members. **3** the body of members.

mem·brane /mémbrayn/ *n.* **1** any pliable sheetlike structure acting as a boundary, lining, or partition in an organism. **2** a thin pliable sheet or skin. □□ **mem·bra·nous** /–brənəs/ *adj.*

me·men·to /miméntō/ *n.* (*pl.* **-tos** or **-toes**) an object kept as a reminder or a souvenir of a person or an event.

mem·o /mémō/ *n.* (*pl.* **-os**) *colloq.* a memorandum.

mem·oir /mémwaar/ *n.* **1** a historical account or biography written from personal knowledge or special sources. **2** (in *pl.*) an autobiography or a written account of one's memory of certain events or people. **3 a** an essay on a learned subject specially studied by the writer. **b** (in *pl.*) the proceedings or transactions of a learned society. □□ **mem·oir·ist** *n.*

mem·o·ra·bil·i·a /mémərəbileeə, –bílyə/ *n.pl.* souvenirs of memorable events.

mem·o·ra·ble /mémərəbəl/ *adj.* **1** worth remembering. **2** easily remembered. □□ **mem·o·ra·bil·i·ty** /–bílitee/ *n.* **mem·o·ra·bly** *adv.*

mem·o·ran·dum /mémərándəm/ *n.* (*pl.* **memoranda** /–də/ or **memorandums**) **1** a note or record made for future use. **2** an informal written message, esp. in business, diplomacy, etc. **3** *Law* a document recording the terms of a contract or other legal details.

me·mo·ri·al /məmáwreeəl/ *n.* & *adj.* • *n.* an object, institution, or custom established in memory of a person or event (*the Albert Memorial*). • *adj.* intending to commemorate a person or thing (*memorial service*). □□ **me·mo·ri·al·ist** *n.*

Me·mo·ri·al Day *n.* holiday on which those who died in war are remembered, usu. the last Monday in May.

me·mo·ri·al·ize /məmáwreeəlīz/ *v.tr.* **1** commemorate. **2** address a memorial to.

mem·o·rize /mémərīz/ *v.tr.* commit to memory. □□ **mem·o·ri·za·tion** *n.*

mem·o·ry /méməree/ *n.* (*pl.* **-ries**) **1** the faculty by which things are recalled to or kept in the mind. **2 a** this faculty in an individual (*my memory is beginning to fail*). **b** one's store of things remembered (*buried deep in my memory*). **3** a recollection or remembrance (*the memory of better times*). **4** the storage capacity of a computer or other electronic machinery. **5** the remembrance of a person or thing (*his mother's memory haunted him*). **6 a** the reputation of a dead person (*his memory lives on*). **b** in formulaic phrases used of a dead sovereign, etc. (*of blessed memory*). **7** the length of time over which the memory or memories of any given person or group extends (*within living memory; within the memory of anyone still working here*). **8** the act of remembering (*a deed worthy of memory*). □ **commit to memory** learn (a thing) so as to be able to recall it. **from memory** without verification in books, etc. **in memory of** to keep alive the remembrance of.

mem•o•ry lane *n.* (usu. prec. by *down, along*) an imaginary and sentimental journey into the past.

men *pl.* of MAN.

men•ace /ménis/ *n. & v.* •*n.* **1** a threat. **2** a dangerous or obnoxious thing or person. **3** *joc.* a pest, a nuisance. •*v.tr. & intr.* threaten. □□ **men•ac•ing** *adj.* **men•ac•ing•ly** *adv.*

mé•nage à trois /maynaázh aa trwaá/ *n.* (*pl.* **ménages à trois** *pronunc.* same) an arrangement in which three people live together, usu. a married couple and the lover of one of them.

me•nag•er•ie /mənájəree, –názh–/ *n.* **1** a collection of wild animals in captivity for exhibition, etc. **2** the place where these are housed.

mend /mend/ *v. & n.* •*v.* **1** *tr.* restore to a sound condition; repair. **2** *intr.* heal. **3** *tr.* improve (*mend matters*). •*n.* a darn or repair in material, etc. (*a mend in my shirt*). □ **mend one's fences** make peace with a person. **mend one's ways** reform, improve one's habits. **on the mend** improving in health or condition. □□ **mend•er** *n.*

men•da•cious /mendáyshəs/ *adj.* lying; untruthful. □□ **men•da•cious•ly** *adv.* **men•dac•i•ty** /–dásitee/ *n.* (*pl.* **-ties**).

men•de•le•vi•um /méndəleéveeəm/ *n. Chem.* an artificially made transuranic radioactive metallic element. ¶ Symb.: **Md.**

men•di•cant /méndikənt/ *adj. & n.* •*adj.* **1** begging. **2** (of a friar) living solely on alms. •*n.* **1** a beggar. **2** a mendicant friar.

mend•ing /ménding/ *n.* **1** the action of a person who mends. **2** things, esp. clothes, to be mended.

men•folk /ménfōk/ *n.pl.* **1** men in general. **2** the men of one's family.

men•ha•den /menháyd'n/ *n.* (*pl.* same) any large herringlike fish of the genus *Brevoortia*, of the E. coast of N. America, yielding valuable oil and used for manure.

me•ni•al /meéneeəl/ *adj. & n.* •*adj.* **1** (esp. of work) degrading; servile. **2** usu. *derog.* (of a servant) domestic. •*n.* **1** a menial servant. **2** a servile person.

men•in•gi•tis /méninjítis/ *n.* an inflammation of the meninges due to infection by viruses or bacteria.

me•ninx /meéningks/ *n.* (*pl.* **meninges** /mənínjeez/) (usu. in *pl.*) any of the three membranes that line the skull and vertebral canal and enclose the brain and spinal cord. □□ **me•nin•ge•al** /minínjeeəl/ *adj.*

me•nis•cus /mənískəs/ *n.* (*pl.* **menisci** /–nísī/or **meniscuses**) **1** *Physics* the curved upper surface of a liquid in a tube. **2** a lens that is convex on one side and concave on the other. **3** *Math.* a crescent-shaped figure. **4** *Anat.* a cartilaginous disk within a joint, esp. the knee.

men•o•pause /ménəpawz/ *n.* **1** the ceasing of menstruation. **2** the period in a woman's life (usu. between 45 and 50) when this occurs. □□ **men•o•pau•sal** /–páwzəl/ *adj.*

me•nor•ah /mənáwrə, –nōrə/ *n.* a candelabrum used in Jewish worship, originally one with seven branches, now often replicated as a nine-branched candelabrum used at Hanukkah.

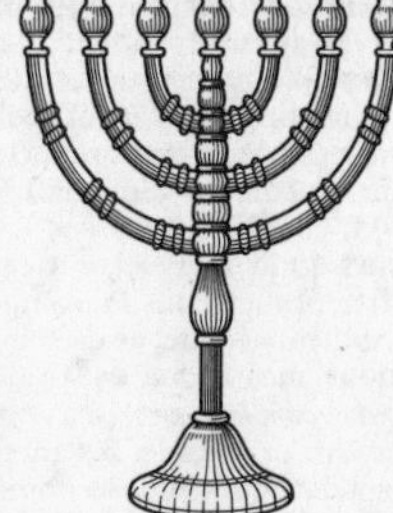

menorah

men•serv•ants see MANSERVANT.

men•ses /ménseez/ *n.pl.* **1** blood and other materials discharged from the uterus at menstruation. **2** the time of menstruation.

mens rea /menz reéə/ *n.* criminal intent; the knowledge of wrongdoing.

men's room *n.* a usu. public restroom for men.

men•stru•al /ménstrooəl/ *adj.* of or relating to the menses or menstruation.

men•stru•al cy•cle *n.* the process of ovulation and menstruation in female primates.

men•stru•ate /ménstroo-ayt/ *v.intr.* undergo menstruation.

men•stru•a•tion /ménstroo-áyshən/ *n.* the process of discharging blood and other materials from the uterus in sexually mature nonpregnant women at intervals of about one lunar month until the menopause.

men•su•ra•tion /ménshəráyshən, –sə–/ *n.* **1** measuring. **2** *Math.* the measuring of geometric magnitudes such as lengths, areas, and volumes.

mens•wear /ménzwair/ *n.* clothes for men.

men•tal / mént'l/ *adj.* **1** of or in the mind. **2** done by the mind. **3** *colloq.* **a** insane. **b** crazy; wild; eccentric (*is mental about pop music*). □□ **men•tal•ly** *adv.*

men•tal ill•ness *n.* a disorder of the mind.

men•tal•i•ty /mentálitee/ *n.* (*pl.* **-ties**) **1** mental character or disposition. **2** kind or degree of intelligence. **3** what is in or of the mind.

men•thol /ménthawl/ *n.* a mint-tasting organic alcohol found in oil of peppermint, etc., used as a flavoring and to relieve local pain.

men•tho•lat•ed /ménthəlaytid/ *adj.* treated with or containing menthol.

men•tion /ménshən/ *v. & n.* •*v.tr.* **1** refer to briefly. **2** specify by name. **3** reveal or disclose (*do not mention this to anyone*). •*n.* a reference, esp. by name, to a person or thing. □ **don't mention it** said in polite dismissal of an apology or thanks. **make mention** (or **no mention**) **of** refer (or not refer) to. **not to mention** introducing a fact or thing of secondary or (as a rhetorical device) of primary importance. □□ **men•tion•a•ble** *adj.*

men•tor /méntawr/ *n.* an experienced and trusted adviser.

men•u /ményoo/ *n.* **1 a** a list of dishes available in a restaurant, etc. **b** a list of items to be served at a meal. **2** *Computing* a list of options showing the commands or facilities available.

me•ow /mee-ów/ *n. & v.* •*n.* the characteristic cry of a cat. •*v.intr.* make this cry.

me•phit•ic /–fitik/ *adj.* **1** foul-smelling. **2** (of a vapor, etc.) noxious, poisonous.

mer•can•tile /márkəntīl/ *adj.* **1** of trade, trading. **2** commercial. **3** mercenary, fond of bargaining.

mer•can•til•ism /márkəntilizəm/ *n.* an old economic theory that money is the only form of wealth. □□ **mer•can•til•ist** *n.*

Mer•ca•tor pro•jec•tion /mərkáytər/ *n.* (also **Mercator's projection**) a projection of a map of the world onto a cylinder so that all the parallels of latitude have the same length as the equator.

mer•ce•nar•y /mársəneree/ *adj. & n.* •*adj.* primarily concerned with money or other reward (*mercenary motives*). •*n.* (*pl.* **-ies**) a hired soldier in foreign service.

mer•cer•ize /mársərīz/ *v.tr.* treat (cotton fabric or thread) under tension with caustic alkali to give greater strength and impart luster.

mer•chan•dise /márchəndīz/ *n. & v.* •*n.* goods for sale. •*v.* **1** *intr.* trade; traffic. **2** *tr.* trade or traffic in. **3** *tr.*

a promote the sale of (goods, etc.). **b** advertise; publicize (an idea or person). ▫▫ **mer•chan•dis•er** *n.*

mer•chant /mə́rchənt/ *n.* **1** a retail trader; dealer; storekeeper. **2** *colloq.* usu. *derog.* a person showing a partiality for a specified activity or practice (*speed merchant*).

mer•chant•man /mə́rchəntmən/ *n.* (*pl.* **-men**) a ship conveying merchandise.

mer•chant ma•rine *n.* a nation's commercial shipping.

mer•chant ship = MERCHANTMAN.

mer•ci•ful /mə́rsifŏŏl/ *adj.* having, showing, or feeling mercy.

mer•ci•ful•ly /mə́rsifŏŏlee/ *adv.* **1** in a merciful manner. **2** (qualifying a whole sentence) fortunately (*mercifully, the sun came out*).

mer•ci•less /mə́rsilis/ *adj.* **1** pitiless. **2** showing no mercy. ▫▫ **mer•ci•less•ly** *adv.*

mer•cu•ri•al /mərkyŏŏreeəl/ *adj.* **1** (of a person) ready-witted; volatile. **2** of or containing mercury. **3** (**Mercurial**) of the planet Mercury. ▫▫ **mer•cu•ri•al•ly** *adv.*

mer•cu•ry /mə́rkyəree/ *n.* **1** *Chem.* a silvery-white heavy liquid metallic element used in barometers, thermometers, and amalgams. ¶ Symb.: **Hg. 2** (**Mercury**) the planet nearest to the sun. **3** any plant of the genus *Mercurialis*, esp. *M. perenne*. ▫▫ **mer•cu•ric** /–kyŏŏrik/ *adj.*

mer•cy /mə́rsee/ *n. & int.* •*n.* (*pl.* **-cies**) **1** compassion or forbearance shown to enemies or offenders in one's power. **2** the quality of compassion. **3** an act of mercy. **4** (*attrib.*) administered or performed out of mercy or pity for a suffering person (*mercy killing*). **5** something to be thankful for (*small mercies*). •*int.* expressing surprise or fear. ▫ **at the mercy of 1** in the power of. **2** liable to danger or harm from. **have mercy on** (or **upon**) show mercy to.

mer•cy kill•ing *n.* = EUTHANASIA.

mere /meer/ *attrib.adj.* (**merest**) that is solely or no more or better than what is specified (*a mere boy; no mere theory*). ▫▫ **mere•ly** *adv.*

mer•e•tri•cious /méritríshəs/ *adj.* **1** showily but falsely attractive. **2** of or befitting a prostitute.

mer•gan•ser /mərgánsər/ *n.* any of various diving fish-eating northern ducks of the genus *Mergus*, with a serrated hooked bill.

merge /mərj/ *v.* **1** *tr. & intr.* (often foll. by *with*) **a** combine or be combined. **b** join or blend gradually. **2** *intr. & tr.* (foll. by *in*) lose or cause to lose character and identity in (something else). **3** *tr.* (foll. by *in*) embody (a title or estate) in (a larger one).

merg•er /mə́rjər/ *n.* **1** the combining of two commercial companies, etc., into one. **2** a merging.

me•rid•i•an /mərídeeən/ *n. & adj.* •*n.* **1** a circle passing through the celestial poles and zenith of any place on the earth's surface. **2 a** a circle of constant longitude, passing through a given place and the terrestrial poles. **b** the corresponding line on a map. **3** prime; full splendor. •*adj.* **1** of noon. **2** of the period of greatest splendor, vigor, etc.

me•ringue /məráng/ *n.* **1** a confection of sugar, egg whites, etc., browned by baking. **2** a small cake or shell of this, usu. decorated or filled with whipped cream, etc.

me•ri•no /məréenō/ *n.* (*pl.* **-nos**) **1** (in full **merino sheep**) a variety of sheep with long fine wool. **2** a soft woolen or wool-and-cotton material like cashmere, orig. of merino wool. **3** a fine woolen yarn.

mer•it /mérit/ *n. & v.* •*n.* **1** the quality of deserving well. **2** excellence; worth. **3** (usu. in *pl.*) **a** a thing that entitles one to reward or gratitude. **b** esp. *Law* intrinsic rights and wrongs (*the merits of a case*). •*v.tr.* deserve. ▫ **on its merits** with regard only to its intrinsic worth.

mer•i•toc•ra•cy /méritókrəsee/ *n.* (*pl.* **-cies**) **1** government by persons selected competitively according to merit. **2** a group of persons selected in this way. **3** a society governed by meritocracy.

mer•i•to•ri•ous /méritáwreeəs/ *adj.* **1** deserving reward, praise, or gratitude. **2** deserving commendation for thoroughness, etc.

mer•maid /mə́rmayd/ *n.* an imaginary sea creature, with the head and trunk of a woman and the tail of a fish.

mer•man /mə́rman/ *n.* (*pl.* **-men**) the male equivalent of a mermaid.

mer•ri•ment /mérimənt/ *n.* **1** exuberant enjoyment; being merry. **2** mirth; fun.

mer•ry /méree/ *adj.* (**merrier, merriest**) **1** joyous. **2** full of laughter or gaiety. ▫ **make merry 1** be festive; enjoy oneself. **2** (foll. by *over*) make fun of. ▫▫ **mer•ri•ly** *adv.*

mer•ry-go-round /méreegōrownd/ *n.* **1** a revolving machine with wooden horses or other animals, etc., for riding on at an amusement park, etc. **2** a cycle of bustling activities.

mer•ry•mak•ing /méreemayking/ *n.* festivity; fun. ▫▫ **mer•ry•mak•er** *n.*

me•sa /máysə/ *n.* an isolated flat-topped hill with steep sides.

mes•cal /méskal/ *n.* a peyote cactus.

mes•ca•line /méskəleen, –lin/ *n.* (also **mes•ca•lin** /–lin/) a hallucinogenic alkaloid present in mescal.

Mes•dames *pl.* of MADAME.

Mes•de•moi•selles *pl.* of MADEMOISELLE.

mesh /mesh/ *n. & v.* •*n.* **1** a network fabric or structure. **2** each of the open spaces between the strands of a net or sieve, etc. **3** (in *pl.*) **a** a network. **b** a snare. **4** (in *pl.*) *Physiol.* an interlaced structure. •*v.* **1** *intr.* (often foll. by *with*) (of the teeth of a wheel) be engaged. **2** *intr.* be harmonious. **3** *tr.* catch in or as in a net. ▫ **in mesh** (of the teeth of wheels) engaged.

mes•mer•ism /mézmərizəm/ *n.* **1** *Psychol.* **a** a hypnotic state produced in a person by another's influence. **b** a doctrine concerning this. **c** an influence producing this. **2** fascination. ▫▫ **mes•mer•ic** /mezmérik/ *adj.* **mes•mer•ist** *n.*

mes•mer•ize /mézməriz/ *v.tr.* **1** *Psychol.* hypnotize; exercise mesmerism on. **2** fascinate; spellbind (*mesmerized by the fireworks display*).

meso- /mésō, méz–/ *comb. form* middle; intermediate.

mes•o•lith•ic /mézəlíthik, més–/ *adj. Archaeol.* of or concerning the Stone Age between the Paleolithic and Neolithic periods.

mes•o•morph /mézəmawrf, més–/ *n.* a person with a compact and muscular build of body (cf. ECTOMORPH, ENDOMORPH). ▫▫ **mes•o•mor•phic** /–máwrfik/ *adj.*

me•son /mézon, més–, méezon, –son/ *n. Physics* any of a class of elementary particles believed to participate in the forces that hold nucleons together in the atomic nucleus.

mes•o•sphere /mésəsfeer, méz–/ *n.* the region of the atmosphere extending from the top of the stratosphere to an altitude of about 50 miles.

Mes•o•zo•ic /mésəzṓ-ik, méz–/ *adj. & n. Geol.* •*adj.* of or relating to an era of geological time marked by the development of dinosaurs, and with evidence of the first mammals, birds, and flowering plants. •*n.* this era (cf. CENOZOIC, PALEOZOIC).

mes•quite /meskéet/ *n.* **1** any N. American leguminous tree of the genus *Prosopis*, esp. *P. juliflora*. **2** the wood of the mesquite, as used in grilling food.

mess /mes/ *n. & v.* •*n.* **1** a dirty or untidy state of things (*the room is a mess*). **2** a state of confusion, embarrassment, or trouble. **3** something causing a mess, e.g., spilled liquid, etc. **4** a domestic animal's excreta. **5 a** a company of persons who take meals together, esp. in the armed forces. **b** a place where such meals or recreation take place communally. **c** a meal taken there. **6** *derog.* a disagreeable concoction. **7** a portion of liquid or pulpy food. • *v.* **1** *tr.* (often foll. by *up*) **a** make a mess of; dirty. **b** muddle; make into a state of confusion. **2** *intr.* (foll. by *with*) interfere with. **3** *intr.* take one's meals. **4** *intr. colloq.* defecate. □ **make a mess of** bungle. **mess around** (or **about**) **1** interfere with; make things awkward for; cause arbitrary inconvenience to. **2** philander.

mess Middle English: from Old French *mes* 'portion of food,' from late Latin *missum* 'something put on the table,' past participle of *mittere* 'send, put.' The original sense was 'a serving of food,' also 'a serving of liquid or partly liquid food,' and later 'liquid or mixed food for an animal'; this gave rise, in the early 19th century, to the senses 'unappetizing concoction' and 'predicament,' on which the present senses 1 and 2 are based. In late Middle English there was also a sense 'one of the small groups into which the company at a banquet was divided' (who were served from the same dishes); hence, 'a group who regularly eat together' (recorded in military use from the mid-16th century).

mes•sage /mésij/ *n. & v.* • *n.* **1** a communication sent by one person to another. **2 a** an inspired or significant communication from a prophet, writer, or preacher. **b** the central import or meaning of an artistic work, etc. **3** a mission or errand. • *v.tr.* **1** send as a message. **2** transmit (a plan, etc.) by signaling, etc. □ **get the message** *colloq.* understand what is meant.

Mes•sei•gneurs *pl.* of MONSEIGNEUR.

mes•sen•ger /mésinjər/ *n.* **1** a person who carries a message. **2** a person employed to carry messages.

mes•sen•ger RNA *n.* a form of RNA carrying genetic information from DNA to a ribosome. ¶ Abbr.: **mRNA**.

mess hall *n.* a communal, esp. military, dining area.

Mes•si•ah /misíə/ *n.* **1** (also **messiah**) a liberator or would-be liberator of an oppressed people or country. **2 a** the promised deliverer of the Jews. **b** (usu. prec. by *the*) Christ regarded as this. □□ **Mes•si•ah•ship** *n.*

Mes•si•an•ic /méseeánik/ *adj.* **1** of the Messiah. **2** inspired by hope or belief in a Messiah. □□ **Mes•si•a•nism** /mesíənizəm/ *n.*

Mes•sieurs *pl.* of MONSIEUR.

mess kit *n.* a soldier's cooking and eating utensils.

Messrs. /mésərz/ *pl.* of MR.

mess•y /mésee/ *adj.* (**messier, messiest**) **1** untidy or dirty. **2** causing or accompanied by a mess. **3** difficult to deal with; full of awkward complications. □□ **mess•i•ly** *adv.* **mess•i•ness** *n.*

mes•ti•zo /mesteézō/ *n.* (*pl.* **-zos**; *fem.* **mestiza** /–zə/, *pl.* **-as**) a Spaniard or Portuguese of mixed race, esp. the offspring of a Spaniard and a Native American.

Met /met/ *n.* (in full **the Met**) *colloq.* **1** the Metropolitan Opera House in New York. **2** the Metrolpolitan Museum of Art in New York.

met *past* and *past part.* of MEET[1].

met. /met/ *abbr.* **1** meteorology; meteorological. **2** metropolitan.

meta- /métə/ *comb. form* (usu. **met-** before a vowel or *h*) **1** denoting change of position or condition (*metabolism*). **2** denoting position: **a** behind. **b** after or beyond (*metaphysics*; *metacarpus*). **c** of a higher or second-order kind (*metalanguage*).

me•tab•o•lism /mətábəlizəm/ *n.* all the chemical processes that occur within a living organism, resulting in energy production (CATABOLISM) and growth (ANABOLISM). □□ **met•a•bol•ic** /métəbólik/ *adj.* **met•a•bol•i•cal•ly** /métəbóliklee/ *adv.*

me•tab•o•lite /mətábəlīt/ *n. Physiol.* a substance formed in or necessary for metabolism.

me•tab•o•lize /mətábəlīz/ *v.tr. & intr.* process or be processed by metabolism.

met•a•car•pus /métəkaárpəs/ *n.* (*pl.* **metacarpi** /–pī/) **1** the set of five bones of the hand that connects the wrist to the fingers. **2** this part of the hand. □□ **met•a•car•pal** *adj.*

met•a•cen•ter /métəsentər/ *n.* the point of intersection between a line (vertical in equilibrium) through the center of gravity of a floating body and a vertical line through the center of pressure after a slight angular displacement, which must be above the center of gravity to ensure stability. □□ **met•a•cen•tric** /–séntrik/ *adj.*

met•al /mét'l/ *n., adj., & v.* • *n.* **1 a** any of a class of chemical elements such as gold, silver, iron, and tin, usu. lustrous ductile solids and good conductors of heat and electricity. **b** an alloy of any of these. **2** material used for making glass, in a molten state. **3** (in *pl.*) the rails of a railroad line. • *adj.* made of metal. • *v.tr.* provide or fit with metal.

me•tal•lic /mətálik/ *adj.* **1** of, consisting of, or characteristic of metal or metals. **2** sounding sharp and ringing, like struck metal. **3** having the sheen or luster of metals. □□ **me•tal•li•cal•ly** *adv.*

met•al•log•ra•phy /mét'lógrəfee/ *n.* the descriptive science of the structure and properties of metals. □□ **met•al•lo•graph•ic** /metáləgráfik/ *adj.*

met•al•loid /mét'loyd/ *adj. & n.* • *adj.* having the form or appearance of a metal. • *n.* any element intermediate in properties between metals and nonmetals, e.g., boron, silicon, and germanium.

met•al•lur•gy /mét'lərjee/ *n.* the science concerned with the production, purification, and properties of metals and their application. □□ **met•al•lur•gic** /mét'lərjik/ *adj.* **met•al•lur•gi•cal** *adj.* **met•al•lur•gist** *n.*

met•al•work /mét'lwərk/ *n.* **1** the art of working in metal. **2** metal objects collectively. □□ **met•al•work•er** *n.*

met•a•mor•phic /métəmáwrfik/ *adj.* **1** of or marked by metamorphosis. **2** *Geol.* (of rock) that has undergone transformation by natural agencies such as heat and pressure. □□ **met•a•mor•phism** *n.*

met•a•mor•phose /métəmawrfōz/ *v.tr.* **1** change in form. **2** (foll. by *to, into*) **a** turn (into a new form). **b** change the nature of.

met•a•mor•pho•sis /métəmáwrfəsis / *n.* (*pl.* **metamorphoses** /–seez/) **1** a change of form. **2** a changed form. **3** a change of character, conditions, etc. **4** *Zool.* the transformation between an immature form and an adult form, e.g., from a pupa to an insect or from a tadpole to a frog.

met•a•phor /métəfawr/ *n.* **1** the application of a name or descriptive term or phrase to an object or action to which it is imaginatively but not literally applicable (e.g., *killing him with kindness*). **2** an instance of this. □□ **met•a•phor•ic** /–fáwrik, –fórik/ *adj.* **met•a•phor•i•cal** /–fáwrikəl, –fórikəl/ *adj.* **met•a•phor•i•cal•ly** /–fáwriklee, –fóriklee/ *adv.*

met•a•phys•i•cal /métəfízikəl/ *adj. & n.* • *adj.* **1** of or relating to metaphysics. **2** based on abstract general reasoning. **3** excessively subtle or theoretical. **4** incorporeal; supernatural. **5** visionary. **6** (of poetry, esp. in the 17th c. in England) characterized by subtlety of thought and complex imagery. • *n.* (**the Metaphysicals**) the metaphysical poets. □□ **met•a•phys•i•cal•ly** *adv.*

met•a•phys•ics /métəfíziks/ *n.pl.* (usu. treated as *sing.*) **1** the theoretical philosophy of being and knowing. **2** the philosophy of mind. **3** *colloq.* abstract talk; mere theory. □□ **met•a•phy•si•cian** /–zíshən/ *n.*

me•tas•ta•sis /metástəsis/ *n.* (*pl.* **metastases** /–seez/) *Physiol.* **1** the transference of a disease, etc., from one part or organ to another. **2** the transformation of chemical compounds into others in the process of assimilation by an organism. ▫▫ **me·tas·ta·size** *v.intr.* **met·a·stat·ic** /métəstátik/ *adj.*

met·a·tar·sus /métətaársəs/ *n.* (*pl.* **metatarsi** /–sī/) **1** the part of the foot between the ankle and the toes. **2** the set of bones in this. ▫▫ **met·a·tar·sal** *adj.*

me·tath·e·sis /mitáthisis/ *n.* (*pl.* **metatheses** /–seez/) **1** *Gram.* the transposition of sounds or letters in a word. **2** *Chem.* the interchange of atoms or groups of atoms between two molecules. **3** an instance of either of these. ▫▫ **met·a·thet·ic** /métəthétik/ *adj.* **met·a·thet·i·cal** /métəthétikəl/ *adj.*

mete /meet/ *v.tr.* **1** (usu. foll. by *out*) *literary* apportion or allot (a punishment or reward). **2** *poet.* or *Bibl.* measure.

me·te·or /meéteeər, –eeawr/ *n.* **1** a small body of matter from outer space that becomes incandescent as a result of friction with the earth's atmosphere. **2** a streak of light emanating from a meteor.

me·te·or·ic /meétee-áwrik, –ór–/ *adj.* **1 a** of or relating to the atmosphere. **b** dependent on atmospheric conditions. **2** of meteors. **3** dazzling; transient (*meteoric rise to fame*). ▫▫ **me·te·or·i·cal·ly** *adv.*

me·te·or·ite /meéteeərīt/ *n.* a fallen meteor, or fragment of natural rock or metal, that reaches the earth's surface from outer space. ▫▫ **me·te·or·it·ic** /–rítik/ *adj.*

me·te·or·oid /meéteeəróyd/ *n.* any small body, often the remnant of a comet, moving in the solar system that becomes visible as it passes through the earth's atmosphere as a meteor. ▫▫ **me·te·or·oid·al** /–róyd'l/ *adj.*

me·te·or·ol·o·gy /meéteeəróləjee/ *n.* **1** the study of the processes and phenomena of the atmosphere, esp. as a means of forecasting the weather. **2** the atmospheric character of a region. ▫▫ **me·te·or·o·log·i·cal** /–rəlójikəl/ *adj.* **me·te·or·o·log·i·cal·ly** *adv.* **me·te·or·ol·o·gist** *n.*

me·te·or show·er *n.* a group of meteors appearing to come from one point in the sky.

me·ter[1] /meétər/ *n.* a metric unit and the base SI unit of linear measure, equal to about 39.4 inches. ¶ Abbr.: **m.** ▫▫ **me·ter·age** /meétərij/ *n.*

me·ter[2] /meétər/ *n.* **1 a** any form of poetic rhythm, determined by the number and length of feet in a line. **b** a metrical group or measure. **2** the basic pulse and rhythm of a piece of music.

me·ter[3] /meétər/ *n.* & *v.* • *n.* **1** an instrument that measures, esp. one for recording a quantity of gas, electricity, etc. **2** = PARKING METER. • *v.tr.* measure by means of a meter.

-meter /mitər, meétər/ *comb. form* **1** forming nouns denoting measuring instruments (*barometer*). **2** *Prosody* forming nouns denoting lines of poetry with a specified number of measures (*pentameter*).

meth·a·done /méthədōn/ *n.* a powerful synthetic analgesic drug that is similar to morphine and is used as a substitute drug in the treatment of morphine and heroin addiction.

meth·am·phet·a·mine /méthamfétəmin, –meen/ *n.* an amphetamine derivative with quicker and longer action, used as a stimulant.

meth·ane /méthayn/ *n. Chem.* a colorless, odorless, flammable, gaseous hydrocarbon, the main constituent of natural gas. ¶ Chem. formula: CH_4.

meth·a·nol /méthənawl, –nol/ *n. Chem.* a colorless, volatile, flammable liquid, used as a solvent. ¶ Chem. formula: CH_3OH. Also called **methyl alcohol**.

me·thinks /mithíngks/ *v.intr.* (*past* **methought** /mitháwt/) *archaic* it seems to me.

meth·od /méthəd/ *n.* **1** a special form of procedure esp. in any branch of mental activity. **2** orderliness. **3** the orderly arrangement of ideas. **4** a scheme of classification. **5** *Theatr.* a technique of acting based on the actor's thorough emotional identification with the character. ▫ **method in** (or **to**) **one's madness** sense in what appears to be foolish or strange behavior.

me·thod·i·cal /mithódikəl/ *adj.* (also **me·thod·ic**) characterized by method or order. ▫▫ **me·thod·i·cal·ly** *adv.*

Meth·od·ist /méthədist/ *n.* **1** a member of any of several Protestant religious bodies (now united) originating in the 18th-c. evangelistic movement. **2** (**methodist**) a person who follows or advocates a particular method or system of procedure. ▫▫ **Meth·od·ism** *n.*

meth·od·ize /méthədīz/ *v.tr.* **1** reduce to order. **2** arrange in an orderly manner. ▫▫ **meth·od·iz·er** *n.*

meth·od·ol·o·gy /méthədóləjee/ *n.* (*pl.* **-gies**) **1** the science of method. **2** a body of methods used in a particular branch of activity. ▫▫ **meth·od·o·log·i·cal** /–dəlójikəl/ *adj.* **meth·od·o·log·i·cal·ly** *adv.* **meth·od·ol·o·gist** *n.*

me·thought *past* of METHINKS.

meth·yl /méthil/ *n. Chem.* the univalent hydrocarbon radical CH_3, present in many organic compounds. ▫▫ **me·thyl·ic** /methílik/ *adj.*

meth·yl al·co·hol *n.* = METHANOL.

meth·yl·ate /méthilayt/ *v.tr.* **1** mix or impregnate with methanol. **2** introduce a methyl group into (a molecule or compound). ▫▫ **meth·yl·a·tion** /–láyshən/ *n.*

meth·yl ben·zene *n.* = TOLUENE.

me·tic·u·lous /mətíkyələs/ *adj.* **1** giving great or excessive attention to details. **2** very careful and precise. ▫▫ **me·tic·u·lous·ly** *adv.* **me·tic·u·lous·ness** *n.*

mé·ti·er /métyáy/ *n.* (also **me·ti·er**) **1** one's trade, profession, or department of activity. **2** one's forte.

me·ton·y·my /mitónimee/ *n.* the substitution of the name of an attribute or adjunct for that of the thing meant (e.g., *White House* for *president*, *the turf* for *horse racing*). ▫▫ **met·o·nym** /métənim/ *n.* **met·o·nym·ic** /métənímik/ *adj.* **met·o·nym·i·cal** /métənímikəl/ *adj.*

met·ric /métrik/ *adj.* of or based on the meter.

met·ri·cal /métrikəl/ *adj.* **1** of, relating to, or composed in meter. **2** of or involving measurement. ▫▫ **met·ri·cal·ly** *adv.*

met·ric sys·tem *n.* the decimal measuring system with the meter, liter, and gram (or kilogram) as units of length, volume, and mass (see also SI).

met·ric ton *n.* (also **met·ric tonne**) 1,000 kilograms (2,205 lb.).

met·ro /métrō/ *n.* (*pl.* **-ros**) a subway system in a city, esp. Paris.

met·ro·nome /métrənōm/ *n. Mus.* an instrument marking time at a selected rate by giving a regular tick. ▫▫ **met·ro·nom·ic** /–nómik/ *adj.*

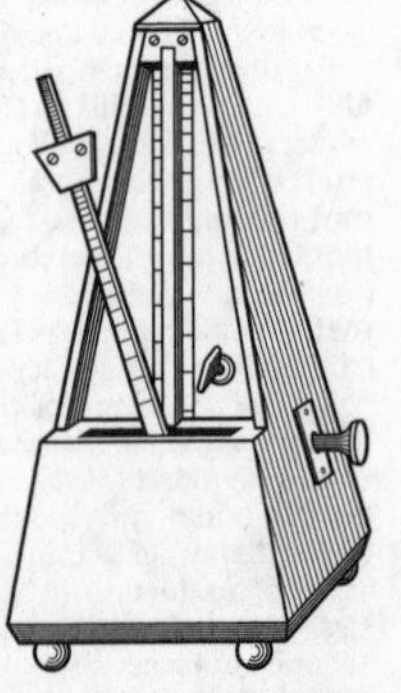

metronome

me·tro·nym·ic /métrənímik/ *adj.* & *n.* • *adj.* (of a name) derived from the name of a mother or female ancestor. • *n.* a metronymic name.

me·trop·o·lis /mitrópəlis/ *n.* **1** the chief city of a country. **2** a metropolitan bishop's see. **3** a center of activity.

met·ro·pol·i·tan /métrəpólit'n/ *adj.* & *n.* • *adj.* **1** of or relating to a metropolis, esp. as distinct from its environs (*metropolitan New York*). **2** belonging to, forming or forming part of, a mother country as distinct from its colonies, etc. (*metropolitan France*). **3** of an ecclesiastical metropolis. •*n.* **1** (in full **metropolitan bishop**) a bishop having authority over the bishops of a province. **2** an inhabitant of a metropolis. ▫▫ **met·ro·pol·i·tan·ate** *n.* (in sense 1 of *n.*). **met·ro·pol·i·tan·ism** *n.*

met·tle /mét'l/ *n.* **1** the quality of a person's disposition or temperament (*a chance to show your mettle*). **2** natural ardor. **3** spirit; courage. ▫ **on one's mettle** incited to do one's best. ▫▫ **met·tled** *adj.* (also in *comb.*). **met·tle·some** *adj.*

mew[1] /myōō/ *v. & n.* •*v.intr.* (of a cat, gull, etc.) utter its characteristic cry. •*n.* this sound, esp. of a cat.

mew[2] /myōō/ *n.* a gull.

mew[3] /myōō/ *n. & v.* •*n.* a cage for hawks, esp. while molting. •*v.tr.* **1** put (a hawk) in a cage. **2** (often foll. by *up*) shut up; confine.

mewl /myōōl/ *v.intr.* **1** cry feebly; whimper. **2** mew like a cat.

mews /myōōz/ *n.* esp. *Brit.* a set of stables around an open yard, now often converted into dwellings.

Mex·i·can /méksikən/ *n. & adj.* •*n.* **1 a** a native or national of Mexico, a country in southern N. America. **b** a person of Mexican descent. **2** a language spoken in Mexico, esp. Nahuatl. •*adj.* **1** of or relating to Mexico or its people. **2** of Mexican descent.

me·zu·zah /mezóózə, -zōōzaá/ *n.* (also **me·zu·za**; *pl.* **-s**; also **me·zu·zot** or **me·zu·zoth** /–zōōzót/) a parchment inscribed with religious texts and attached in a case to the doorpost of a Jewish house as a sign of faith.

mez·za·nine /mézəneén/ *n.* **1** a low story between two others (usu. between the first and second floors). **2 a** the lowest balcony in a theater. **b** the first several rows of this balcony.

mez·zo /métsō/ *adv. & n. Mus.* •*adv.* half; moderately. •*n.* (in full **mezzo-soprano**) (*pl.* **-zos**) **1 a** a female singing voice between soprano and contralto. **b** a singer with this voice. **2** a part written for mezzo-soprano.

mfg. *abbr.* manufacturing.

mfr. *abbr.* **1** manufacture. **2** manufacturer.

Mg *symb. Chem.* the element magnesium.

mg *abbr.* milligram(s).

Mgr. *abbr.* **1** Manager. **2** Monseigneur. **3** Monsignor.

mho /mō/ *n.* (*pl.* **·mhos**) *Electr.* the reciprocal of an ohm, a former unit of conductance.

MHz *abbr.* megahertz.

MI *abbr.* **1** Michigan (in official postal use). **2** myocardial infarction.

mi /mee/ *n.* (also **me**) *Mus.* **1** the third tone of the diatonic scale. **2** the note E in the fixed solmization system.

mi. *abbr.* mile(s).

MIA *abbr.* missing in action.

mi·as·ma /mī-ázmə, mee–/ *n.* (*pl.* **miasmata** /–mətə/ or **miasmas**) *archaic* an infectious or noxious vapor. ▫▫ **mi·as·mal** *adj.* **mi·as·mat·ic** /–mátik/ *adj.* **mi·as·mic** *adj.* **mi·as·mic·al·ly** *adv.*

Mic. *abbr.* Micah (Old Testament).

mi·ca /míkə/ *n.* any of a group of silicate minerals with a layered structure. ▫▫ **mi·ca·ceous** /–káyshəs/ *adj.*

mice *pl.* of MOUSE.

Mich. *abbr.* Michigan.

mi·cro /míkrō/ *n.* (*pl.* **-cros**) *colloq.* **1** = MICROCOMPUTER. **2** = MICROPROCESSOR.

micro- /míkrō/ *comb. form* **1** small (*microchip*). **2** denoting a factor of one millionth (10^{-6}) (*microgram*). ¶ Symb.: μ.

mi·cro·a·nal·y·sis /míkrōənálisis/ *n.* the quantitative analysis of chemical compounds using a sample of a few milligrams.

mi·crobe /míkrōb/ *n.* a microorganism (esp. a bacterium causing disease or fermentation). ▫▫ **mi·cro·bi·al** /–króbeeəl/ *adj.* **mi·cro·bic** /–króbik/ *adj.*

mi·cro·bi·ol·o·gy /míkrōbīóləjee/ *n.* the scientific study of microorganisms. ▫▫ **mi·cro·bi·o·log·i·cal** /–bīəlójikəl/ *adj.* **mi·cro·bi·o·log·i·cal·ly** /–bīəlójiklee/ *adv.* **mi·cro·bi·ol·o·gist** *n.*

mi·cro·brew·ery /mīkrōbróóəree/ *n.* a limited-production brewery, often selling only locally.

mic·ro·burst /míkrōbərst/ *n.* a particularly violent wind shear, esp. during a thunderstorm.

mi·cro·chip /míkrōchip/ *n.* a small piece of semiconductor (usu. silicon) used to carry electronic circuits.

mi·cro·com·pu·ter /míkrōkəmpyóótər/ *n.* a small computer that contains a microprocessor as its central processor.

mi·cro·cosm /míkrəkozəm/ *n.* **1** (often foll. by *of*) a miniature representation. **2** mankind viewed as the epitome of the universe. **3** any complex unity viewed in this way. ▫▫ **mi·cro·cos·mic** /–kózmik/ *adj.*

mi·cro·dot /míkrōdot/ *n.* a microphotograph, esp. of a printed or written document, reduced to the size of a period.

mi·cro·ec·o·nom·ics /míkrō-eékənómiks, –ék–/ *n.* the branch of economics dealing with individual commodities, producers, etc. ▫▫ **mi·cro·ec·o·nom·ic** *adj.*

mi·cro·e·lec·tron·ics /míkrō-ílektróniks/ *n.* the design, manufacture, and use of microchips and microcircuits. ▫▫ **mi·cro·e·lec·tron·ic** *adj.*

mi·cro·fiche /míkrōfeesh/ *n.* (*pl.* same or **microfiches**) a flat rectangular piece of film bearing microphotographs of the pages of a printed text or document.

mi·cro·film /míkrəfilm/ *n. & v.* •*n.* a length of film bearing microphotographs of documents, etc. •*v.tr.* photograph (a document, etc.) on microfilm.

mi·cro·in·struc·tion /míkrō-instrúkshən/ *n.* a machine-code instruction that effects a basic operation in a computer system.

mi·cro·light /míkrōlīt/ *n.* a kind of motorized hang glider.

mi·cro·man·age /míkrōmánij/ *v.tr.* control every part, no matter how detailed, of an enterprise or organization.

mi·crom·e·ter[1] /mīkrómitər/ *n.* a gauge for accurately measuring small distances, thicknesses, etc. ▫▫ **mi·crom·e·try** *n.*

mi·cro·me·ter[2] /míkrō-meétər/ *n.* = MICRON.

mi·cron /míkron/ *n.* one-millionth of a meter. Also called **micrometer**.

Mi·cro·ne·sian /míkrəneézhən/ *adj. & n.* •*adj.* of or relating to Micronesia, an island group in the W. Pacific. •*n.* a native of Micronesia.

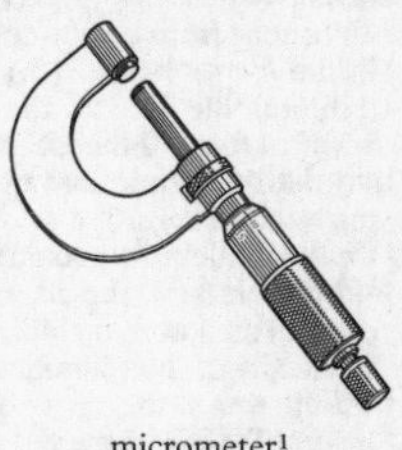

micrometer[1]

mi·cro·or·gan·ism /míkrō-áwrgənizəm/ *n.* any of various microscopic organisms, including algae, bacteria, fungi, protozoa, and viruses.

mi·cro·phone /míkrəfōn/ *n.* an instrument for converting sound waves into electrical energy variations that may be reconverted into sound after transmission or recording. ▫▫ **mi·cro·phon·ic** /–fónik/ *adj.*

mi·cro·proc·es·sor /míkrōprósesər/ *n.* an integrated circuit that contains all the functions of a central processing unit of a computer.

mi·cro·scope /míkrəskōp/ *n.* an instrument magnifying small objects by means of a lens or lenses so as to reveal details invisible to the naked eye.

mi·cro·scop·ic /míkrəskópik/ *adj.* **1** so small as to be visible only with a microscope. **2** extremely small. **3** regarded in terms of small units. **4** of the microscope. □□ **mi·cro·scop·i·cal** *adj.* (in sense 4). **mi·cro·scop·i·cal·ly** *adv.*

mi·cros·co·py /mīkróskəpee/ *n.* the use of the microscope. □□ **mi·cros·co·pist** *n.*

mi·cro·sec·ond /míkrōsekənd/ *n.* one-millionth of a second.

mi·cro·struc·ture /míkrōstrúkchər/ *n.* (in a metal or other material) the arrangement of crystals, etc., that can be made visible and examined with a microscope.

mi·cro·sur·ger·y /míkrōsúrjəree/ *n.* intricate surgery performed using microscopes. □□ **mi·cro·sur·gi·cal** /–súrjikəl/ *adj.*

mi·cro·wave /míkrəwayv/ *n.* & *v.* • *n.* **1** an electromagnetic wave with a wavelength in the range 0.001–0.3m. **2** (in full **microwave oven**) an oven that uses microwaves to cook or heat food. • *v.tr.* (**-ving**) cook in a microwave oven.

mid[1] /mid/ *attrib.adj.* **1** (usu. in *comb.*) that is the middle of (*in midair*). **2** that is in the middle; medium; half.

mid[2] /mid/ *prep. poet.* = AMID.

mid·air /midáir/ *n.* a place or point in the air far removed from the ground or other solid surface.

mid·brain /mídbrayn/ *n.* the part of the brain developing from the middle of the primitive or embryonic brain.

mid·day /míd-dáy/ *n.* the middle of the day; noon.

mid·den /míd'n/ *n.* **1** a dunghill. **2** a refuse heap.

mid·dle /míd'l/ *adj., n.,* & *v.* • *attrib.adj.* **1** at an equal distance from the extremities of a thing. **2** (of a member of a group) so placed as to have the same number of members on each side. **3** intermediate in rank, quality, etc. **4** average (*of middle height*). **5** (of a language) of the period between the old and modern forms. • *n.* **1** (often foll. by *of*) the middle point or position or part. **2** a person's waist. • *v.tr.* **1** place in the middle. **2** *Soccer* return (the ball) from the wing to the midfield. **3** *Naut.* fold in the middle. □ **in the middle of** (often foll. by *verbal noun*) in the process of; during.

mid·dle age *n.* the period between youth and old age, about 45 to 60. □□ **mid·dle-aged** *adj.*

Mid·dle Ag·es *n.pl.* (prec. by *the*) the period of European history from *c.*1000 to 1453.

Middle A·mer·i·ca *n.* **1** Mexico and Central America. **2** the middle class in the US, esp. as a conservative political force. **3** the US Middle West.

mid·dle·brow /míd'lbrow/ *adj.* & *n. colloq.* • *adj.* claiming to be or regarded as only moderately intellectual. • *n.* a middlebrow person.

mid·dle class *n.* the class of society between the upper and the lower, including professional and business workers and their families. □□ **mid·dle-class** *adj.*

mid·dle ear *n.* the cavity of the central part of the ear behind the eardrum.

Mid·dle Eng·lish *n.* the English language from *c.*1150 to 1500.

mid·dle ground *n.* a neutral position between two opposing extremes.

mid·dle-in·come *attrib.adj.* of the wages earned by the middle class.

mid·dle·man /míd'lman/ *n.* (*pl.* **-men**) **1** any of the traders who handle a commodity between its producer and its consumer. **2** an intermediary.

mid·dle man·age·ment *n.* in business and industry, the mid-level positions in administration.

mid·dle name *n.* **1** a person's name placed after the first name and before the surname. **2** a person's most characteristic quality (*sobriety is my middle name*).

mid·dle-of-the-road *adj.* (of a person, course of action, etc.) moderate; avoiding extremes.

mid·dle school *n.* a school for children from about 10 to 13 years old (grades 5–8).

mid·dle·weight /míd'lwayt/ *n.* **1** a weight in certain sports intermediate between welterweight and light heavyweight. **2** a sportsman of this weight.

Mid·dle West *n.* = MIDWEST.

mid·dling /mídling/ *adj.* & *adv.* • *adj.* **1 a** moderately good (esp. *fair to middling*). **b** second-rate. **2** (of goods) of the second of three grades. • *n.* (**mid·dlings**) bulk goods of medium grade, esp. flour of medium fineness. • *adv.* **1** fairly or moderately (*middling good*). **2** *colloq.* fairly well (esp. in health). □□ **mid·dling·ly** *adv.*

mid·field /mídfeeld/ *n.* in certain sports, esp. football and soccer, the area of the field midway between the two goals. □□ **mid·field·er** *n.*

midge /mij/ *n.* **1** *colloq.* **a** a gnatlike insect. **b** a small person. **2 a** any dipterous nonbiting insect of the family Chironomidae. **b** any similar insect of the family Ceratopogonidae with piercing mouthparts.

mid·get /míjit/ *n.* **1 a** *offens.* an extremely small person. **b** an extremely small thing. **2** (*attrib.*) very small.

MIDI /mídee/ *n.* a system for using combinations of electronic equipment, esp. audio and computer equipment (acronym of *m*usical *i*nstrument *d*igital *i*nterface).

mi·di /mídee/ *n.* (*pl.* **midis**) a garment of medium length, usu. reaching to mid-calf.

mid·land /mídlənd/ *n.* & *adj.* • *n.* **1** the middle part of a country. **2** the dialect of American English spoken in the east-central US, from southern New Jersey and northern Delaware west across the Appalachians and the Ohio and Mississippi river valleys. **3** (**the Midlands**) the inland counties of central England. • *adj.* (also **Mid·land**) of or in the midland or Midlands. □□ **mid·land·er** *n.*

mid·life /mídlíf/ *n.* middle age.

mid·life cri·sis *n.* an emotional crisis of self-confidence that can occur in early middle age.

mid·line /mídlīn/ *n.* a median line, or plane of bilateral symmetry.

mid·most /mídmōst/ *adj.* & *adv.* in the very middle.

mid·night /mídnīt/ *n.* **1** the middle of the night; 12 o'clock at night. **2** intense darkness.

mid·night blue *n.* a very dark blue.

mid·night sun *n.* the sun visible at midnight during the summer in polar regions.

mid·rib /mídrib/ *n.* the central rib of a leaf.

mid·riff /mídrif/ *n.* **1 a** the region of the front of the body between the thorax and abdomen. **b** the diaphragm. **2** a garment or part of a garment covering this area.

mid·ship /mídship/ *n.* the middle part of a ship or boat.

mid·ship·man /mídshipmən/ *n.* (*pl.* **-men**) **1** a cadet in the US Naval Academy. **2** *Brit.* a naval officer of rank between naval cadet and sublieutenant.

mid·ships /mídships/ *adv.* = AMIDSHIPS.

midst /midst/ *prep.* & *n.* • *prep. poet.* amidst. • *n.* middle (now only in phrases as below). □ **in the midst of** among; in the middle of. **in our** (or **your** or **their**) **midst** among us (or you or them).

mid·sum·mer /mídsúmər/ *n.* the period of or near the summer solstice.

mid·town /mídtown/ *n.* the central part of a city between the downtown and uptown areas.

mid·way /mídwáy/ *n.* & *adv.* • *n.* area for concessions and amusements at a carnival, fair, etc. • *adv.* in or toward the middle of the distance between two points.

Mid·west /mídwést/ *n.* region of northern US states

from Ohio west to the Rocky Mountains. □□ **Mid·west** *adj.* **Mid·western** *adj.*

mid·wife /mídwīf/ *n.* (*pl.* **-wives** /–wīvz/) **1** a person (usu. a woman) trained to assist women in childbirth. **2** a person who helps in producing or bringing something forth. □□ **mid·wife·ry** /–wífəree/ *n.*

mid·win·ter /mídwíntər/ *n.* the period of or near the winter solstice.

mien /meen/ *n. literary* a person's look or bearing.

miff /mif/ *v.* & *n. colloq.* • *v.tr.* (usu. in *passive*) put out of humor; offend. • *n.* **1** a petty quarrel. **2** a huff.

might[1] /mīt/ *past* of MAY, used esp.: **1** in reported speech, expressing possibility (*said he might come*) or permission (*asked if I might leave*) (cf. MAY 1, 2). **2** expressing a possibility based on a condition not fulfilled (*if you'd looked you might have found it*). **3** expressing complaint that an obligation or expectation is not or has not been fulfilled (*they might have asked*). **4** expressing a request (*you might call in at the butcher's*). **5** *colloq.* **a** = MAY 1 (*it might be true*). **b** (in tentative questions) = MAY 2 (*might I have the pleasure of this dance?*). **c** = MAY 4 (*who might you be?*). □ **might as well** expressing that it is probably at least as desirable to do a thing as not to do it (*won't win but might as well try*).
▶See note at MAY.

might[2] /mīt/ *n.* **1** great bodily or mental strength. **2** power to enforce one's will (usu. in contrast with *right*). □ **with all one's might** to the utmost of one's power. **with might and main** see MAIN.

mightn't /mít'nt/ *contr.* might not.

might·y /mítee/ *adj.* & *adv.* • *adj.* (**mightier, mightiest**) **1** powerful or strong, in body, mind, or influence. **2** massive; bulky. **3** *colloq.* great; considerable. • *adv. colloq.* very (*a mighty difficult task*). □□ **might·i·ly** *adv.* **might·i·ness** *n.*

mi·graine /mígrayn/ *n.* a recurrent throbbing headache that usually affects one side of the head, often accompanied by nausea and disturbance of vision.

mi·grant /mígrənt/ *adj.* & *n.* • *adj.* that migrates. • *n.* **1** a person who moves regularly, as for work. **2** an animal that changes habitats, as with the seasons.

mi·grate /mígráyt/ *v.intr.* **1** (of people) move from one place of abode to another, esp. in a different country. **2** (of a bird or fish) change its area of habitation with the seasons. **3** move under natural forces. □□ **mi·gra·tion** /–gráyshən/ *n.* **mi·gra·tion·al** /–gráyshənəl/ *adj.* **mi·gra·tor** *n.* **mi·gra·to·ry** /–grətáwree/ *adj.*

mi·ka·do /mikaádō/ *n.* (*pl.* **-dos**) *hist.* the emperor of Japan.

mike /mīk/ *n. colloq.* a microphone.

mil /mil/ *n.* one-thousandth of an inch, as a unit of measure for the diameter of wire, etc.

mi·la·dy /miláydee/ *n.* (*pl.* **-dies**) **1** an English noblewoman or great lady. **2** a form used in speaking of or to such a person.

mil·age var. of MILEAGE.

Mil·an·ese /mílənéez/ *adj.* & *n.* • *adj.* of or relating to Milan in N. Italy. • *n.* (*pl.* same) a native of Milan.

milch /milch/ *adj.* (of a domestic mammal) giving or kept for milk.

milch cow *n.* = MILK COW.

mild /mīld/ *adj.* **1** (esp. of a person) gentle and conciliatory. **2** (of a rule, illness, etc.) moderate; not severe. **3** (of the weather) moderately warm. **4** not sharp or strong in taste, etc. **5** (of medicine) operating gently. **6** lacking energy or vivacity. □□ **mild·ish** *adj.* **mild·ness** *n.*

mil·dew /míldoo, –dyoo/ *n.* & *v.* • *n.* **1** a destructive growth of minute fungi on plants. **2** a similar growth on paper, leather, etc., exposed to damp. • *v.tr.* & *intr.* taint or be tainted with mildew.

mild·ly /míldlee/ *adv.* in a mild fashion. □ **to put it mildly** as an understatement (implying the reality is more extreme).

mile /mīl/ *n.* **1** (also **stat·ute mile**) a unit of linear measure equal to 1,760 yards (approx. 1.609 kilometers). **2** (in *pl.*) *colloq.* a great distance or amount (*miles better*). **3** a race extending over a mile.

mile·age /mílij/ *n.* (also **milage**) **1 a** a number of miles traveled, used, etc. **b** the number of miles traveled by a vehicle per unit of fuel. **2** traveling expenses (per mile). **3** *colloq.* benefit; profit; advantage.

mile·post /mílpōst/ *n.* **1** a post or sign giving distance in miles, as along a highway. **2** a post one mile from the finish line of a race, etc.

mil·er /mílər/ *n. colloq.* a person or horse qualified or trained specially to run a mile.

mile·stone /mílstōn/ *n.* **1** a stone set up beside a road to mark a distance in miles. **2** a significant event or stage in a life, project, etc.

mi·lieu /milyố, meélyö/ *n.* (*pl.* **milieus** or **milieux** /–lyốz/) one's environment or social surroundings.

mil·i·tant /mílit'nt/ *adj.* & *n.* • *adj.* **1** aggressively active, esp. in support of a (usu. political) cause. **2** engaged in warfare. • *n.* **1** a militant person, esp. a political activist. **2** a person engaged in warfare. □□ **mil·i·tan·cy** *n.* **mil·i·tant·ly** *adv.*

mil·i·ta·rism /mílitərizəm/ *n.* **1** the spirit or tendencies of a professional soldier. **2** undue prevalence of the military spirit or ideals. □□ **mil·i·ta·rist** /–rist/ *n.* **mil·i·ta·ris·tic** /–rístik/ *adj.*

mil·i·ta·rist /mílitərist/ *n.* **1** a person dominated by militaristic ideas. **2** a student of military science.

mil·i·ta·rize /mílitərīz/ *v.tr.* **1** equip with military resources. **2** make military or warlike. **3** imbue with militarism. □□ **mil·i·ta·ri·za·tion** *n.*

mil·i·tar·y /míliteree/ *adj.* & *n.* • *adj.* of, relating to, or characteristic of soldiers or armed forces. • *n.* (as *sing.* or *pl.*; prec. by *the*) members of the armed forces. □□ **mil·i·tar·i·ly** /–táirəlee/ *adv.*

mil·i·tar·y po·lice *n.* a corps responsible for police and disciplinary duties in the army.

mil·i·tate /mílitayt/ *v.intr.* (usu. foll. by *against*) (of facts or evidence) have force or effect.
▶**Militate**, a word usually followed by *against*, means 'have a profound effect or force': *Overeagerness on our part would militate against success in negotiation.* Do not confuse it with **mitigate**, which means 'make less intense or severe': *Tension can lead to headaches unless mitigated by some form of regular relaxation.*

mi·li·tia /milíshə/ *n.* a military force, esp. one raised from the civil population and supplementing a regular army in an emergency. □□ **mi·li·tia·man** /–mən/ *n.* (*pl.* **-men**)

mi·li·tia·man /milíshəmən/ *n.* (*pl.* **·men**) a member of a militia.

milk /milk/ *n.* & *v.* • *n.* **1** an opaque white fluid secreted by female mammals for the nourishment of their young. **2** the milk of cows, goats, or sheep as food. **3** the milklike juice, e.g., in the coconut. **4** a milklike preparation of herbs, drugs, etc. • *v.tr.* **1** draw milk from (a cow, etc.). **2 a** exploit (a person) esp. financially. **b** get all possible advantage from (a situation). **3** extract sap, venom, etc., from. **4** *sl.* tap (telegraph or telephone wires, etc.). □ **cry over spilled milk** lament an irremediable loss or error. **in milk** secreting milk. □□ **milk·er** *n.*

milk cow *n.* a source of easy profit, esp. a person.

milk·maid /mílkmayd/ *n.* a girl or woman who milks cows or works in a dairy.

---

milk·man /mílkman/ *n.* (*pl.* **-men**) a person who sells or delivers milk.
milk of mag·ne·sia *n.* a white suspension of magnesium hydroxide usu. in water as an antacid or laxative.
milk run *n.* a routine expedition or service journey.
milk shake *n.* a drink of milk, flavoring, and usu. ice cream, mixed by shaking or blending.
milk·sop /mílksop/ *n.* a spiritless or meek person, esp. a man.
milk tooth *n.* a temporary tooth in young mammals.
milk·weed /mílkweed/ *n.* any of various wild plants with milky juice.
milk·wort /mílkwərt/ *n.* any plant of the genus *Polygala*, formerly supposed to increase women's milk.
milk·y /mílkee/ *adj.* (**milkier, milkiest**) **1** of, like, or mixed with milk. **2** (of a gem or liquid) cloudy; not clear. **3** effeminate; weakly amiable. □□ **milk·i·ness** *n.*
Milk·y Way *n.* a faint band of light emitted by countless stars encircling the heavens; the Galaxy.
mill[1] /mil/ *n.* & *v.* •*n.* **1 a** a building fitted with a mechanical apparatus for grinding grain. **b** such an apparatus. **2** an apparatus for grinding any solid substance to powder or pulp. **3 a** a building fitted with machinery for manufacturing processes, etc. (*cotton mill*). **b** such machinery. **4 a** a boxing match. **b** a fistfight. **5** a place that processes things or people in a mechanical way (*diploma mill*). •*v.* **1** *tr.* grind (grain), produce (flour), or hull (seeds) in a mill. **2** *tr.* produce regular ribbed markings on the edge of (a coin). **3** *tr.* cut or shape (metal) with a rotating tool. **4** *intr.* (often foll. by *about, around*) (of people or animals) move in an aimless manner, esp. in a confused mass. **5** *tr.* thicken (cloth, etc.) by fulling. **6** *tr.* beat (chocolate, etc.) to froth. **7** *tr. sl.* beat; strike; fight. □ **go** (or **put**) **through the mill** undergo (or cause to undergo) intensive work or training, etc. □□ **mill·a·ble** *adj.*
mill[2] /mil/ *n.* one-thousandth of a US dollar as money of account.
mil·le·nar·i·an /mílináireeən/ *adj.* & *n.* •*adj.* **1** of or related to the millennium. **2** believing in the millennium. •*n.* a person who believes in the millennium.
mil·le·nar·y /mílənéree/ *n.* & *adj.* •*n.* (*pl.* **-ies**) **1** a period of 1,000 years. **2** the festival of the 1,000th anniversary of a person or thing. **3** a person who believes in the millennium. •*adj.* of or relating to a millenary.
mil·len·ni·um /miléneeəm/ *n.* (*pl.* **millennia** /–neeə/ or **millenniums**) **1** a period of 1,000 years, esp. when calculated from the traditional date of the birth of Christ. **2** an anniversary of 1,000 years. **3** a period of happiness and prosperity. □□ **mil·len·ni·al** *adj.* **mil·len·ni·al·ist** *n.* & *adj.*

▶The spelling of **millennium** is less difficult if one remembers that it comes ultimately from two Latin words containing double letters: *mille*, 'thousand' and *annum*, 'year.'

mil·le·pede var. of MILLIPEDE.
mill·er /mílər/ *n.* **1** the proprietor or tenant of a mill. **2** a person who works or owns a mill.
mil·les·i·mal /milésiməl/ *adj.* & *n.* •*adj.* **1** thousandth. **2** of or belonging to a thousandth. **3** of or dealing with thousandths. •*n.* a thousandth part.
mil·let /mílit/ *n.* **1** any of various cereal plants, esp. *Panicum miliaceum*, bearing a large crop of small nutritious seeds. **2** the seed of this.
milli- /mílee, –i, –ə/ *comb. form* a thousand, esp. denoting a factor of one thousandth. ¶ Abbr.: **m**.
mil·liard /mílyərd, –yaard/ *n. Brit.* one thousand million.

▶Now largely superseded by *billion*.

mil·li·bar /míləbaar/ *n.* one-thousandth of a bar, the cgs unit of atmospheric pressure equivalent to 100 pascals.
mil·li·gram /míligram/ *n.* one-thousandth of a gram.
mil·li·li·ter /mílileetər/ *n.* one-thousandth of a liter (0.002 pint).
mil·li·me·ter /mílimeetər/ *n.* one-thousandth of a meter (0.039 in.).
mil·li·ner /mílinər/ *n.* a person who makes or sells women's hats. □□ **mil·li·ner·y** /–eree/ *n.*
mil·lion /mílyən/ *n.* & *adj.* •*n.* (*pl.* same or (in sense 2) **millions**) (in *sing.* prec. by *a* or *one*) **1** a thousand thousand. **2** (in *pl.*) *colloq.* a very large number (*millions of years*). **3** (prec. by *the*) the bulk of the population. **4** (prec. by *a*) a million dollars. •*adj.* that amount to a million. □□ **mil·lionth** *adj.* & *n.*
mil·lion·aire /mílyənáir/ *n.* (*fem.* **millionairess** /–ris/) **1** a person whose assets are worth at least one million dollars, pounds, etc. **2** a person of great wealth.
mil·li·pede /míləpeed/ *n.* (also **mil·le·pede**) any arthropod of the class Diplopoda, having a long segmented body with two pairs of legs on each segment.
mil·li·sec·ond /mílisekənd/ *n.* one-thousandth of a second.
mill·pond /mílpond/ *n.* a pool of water retained by a dam for the operation of a mill.
mill·race /mílrays/ *n.* a current of water that drives a mill wheel.
mill·stone /mílstōn/ *n.* **1** each of two circular stones used for grinding grain. **2** a heavy burden or responsibility.
mill·wright /mílrīt/ *n.* a person who designs, builds, or operates a mill or milling machinery.
milt /milt/ *n.* **1** a sperm-filled reproductive gland of a male fish. **2** the sperm-filled secretion of this gland.
mime /mīm/ *n.* & *v.* •*n.* **1** the theatrical technique of suggesting action, character, etc., by gesture and expression without using words. **2** a theatrical performance using this technique. **3** (also **mime art·ist**) a practitioner of mime. •*v. tr.* (also *absol.*) convey (an idea or emotion) by gesture without words. □□ **mim·er** *n.*
mim·e·o·graph /mímeeəgraf/ *n.* & *v.* •*n.* **1** (often *attrib.*) a duplicating machine that produces copies from a stencil. **2** a copy produced in this way. •*v.tr.* reproduce by this process.
mi·me·sis /mimeésis, mī–/ *n. Biol.* = MIMICRY 3.
mi·met·ic /mimétik/ *adj.* **1** relating to or habitually practicing imitation or mimicry. **2** *Biol.* of or exhibiting mimicry. □□ **mi·met·i·cal·ly** *adv.*
mim·ic /mímik/ *v.* & *n.* •*v.tr.* (**mimicked, mimicking**) **1** imitate (a person, gesture, etc.) esp. to entertain or ridicule. **2** copy minutely or servilely. **3** (of a thing) resemble closely. •*n.* a person skilled in imitation. □□ **mim·ick·er** *n.*
mim·i·cry /mímikree/ *n.* (*pl.* **·cries**) **1** the act or art of mimicking. **2** a thing that mimics another. **3** *Biol.* a close resemblance of an animal or plant (or part of one) to another animal, plant, or inanimate object.
mi·mo·sa /mimṓsə, –zə/ *n.* **1** any leguminous shrub of the genus *Mimosa*, esp. *M. pudica*, having globular usu. yellow flowers. **2** any of various acacia plants with showy yellow flowers. **3** a cocktail of champagne and orange juice.
min. *abbr.* **1** minute(s). **2** minimum. **3** minim (fluid measure).
mi·na var. of MYNAH.
min·a·ret /mínərét/ *n.* a slender turret connected to a mosque and having a

minaret

balcony from which the muezzin calls at hours of prayer. ▫▫ **min·a·ret·ed** *adj.*

min·a·to·ry /mínətáwree/ *adj.* threatening; menacing.

mince /mins/ *v.* **1** *tr.* cut up or grind into very small pieces. **2** *tr.* (usu. with *neg.*) restrain (one's words, etc.) within the bounds of politeness. **3** *intr.* (usu. as **mincing** *adj.*) speak or walk with an affected delicacy. ▫▫ **minc·er** *n.* **minc·ing·ly** *adv.* (in sense 3 of *v.*).

mince·meat /mínsmeet/ *n.* a mixture of currants, raisins, sugar, apples, candied peel, spices, often suet, and sometimes meat. ▫ **make mincemeat of** utterly defeat (a person, argument, etc.).

mind /mīnd/ *n. & v.* • *n.* **1 a** the seat of consciousness, thought, volition, and feeling. **b** attention; concentration (*my mind keeps wandering*). **2** the intellect; intellectual powers. **3** memory (*I can't call it to mind*). **4** one's opinion (*we're of the same mind*). **5** a way of thinking or feeling (*shocking to the Victorian mind*). **6** the focus of one's thoughts or desires (*put one's mind to it*). **7** the state of normal mental functioning (*lose one's mind*). **8** a person as embodying mental faculties (*a great mind*). • *v.tr.* **1** (usu. with *neg.* or *interrog.*) object to (*I don't mind your being late*). **2 a** take care to (*mind you come on time*). **b** take care; be careful. **3** have charge of temporarily (*mind the house while I'm away*). **4** concern oneself with (*I try to mind my own business*). **5** give heed to (*mind the step*). **6** be obedient to (*mind what your mother says*). ▫ **be of two minds** be undecided. **be of a mind** (often foll. by *to* + infin.) be prepared or disposed. **come into a person's mind** be remembered. **come to mind** (of a thought, idea, etc.) suggest itself. **cross one's mind** happen to occur to one. **don't mind me** *iron.* do as you please. **do you mind!** *iron.* an expression of annoyance. **give a person a piece of one's mind** scold or reproach a person. **have a good** (or **half a**) **mind to** (often as a threat, usu. unfulfilled) feel tempted to. **have (it) in mind** intend. **have a mind of one's own** be capable of independent opinion. **have on one's mind** be troubled by the thought of. **in one's mind's eye** in one's imagination. **mind one's Ps & Qs** be careful in one's behavior. **mind the store** have charge of affairs temporarily. **mind you** an expression used to qualify a previous statement (*I found it quite quickly—mind you, it wasn't easy*). **never mind 1** an expression used to comfort or console. **2** (also **never you mind**) an expression used to evade a question. **3** disregard (*never mind the cost*). **open** (or **close**) **one's mind to** be receptive (or unreceptive) to (changes, new ideas, etc.). **out of one's mind** crazy. **put** (or **set**) **a person's mind at rest** reassure a person. **put a person** (or **thing**) **out of one's mind** deliberately forget. **read a person's mind** discern a person's thoughts. **to my mind** in my opinion.

mind-bend·ing *adj. colloq.* (esp. of a psychedelic drug) influencing or altering one's state of mind.

mind-blow·ing *adj. sl.* **1** confusing; shattering. **2** (esp. of drugs, etc.) inducing hallucinations.

mind-bog·gling *adj. colloq.* overwhelming; startling.

mind·ed /míndid/ *adj.* **1** (in *comb.*) **a** inclined to think in some specified way (*fair-minded*). **b** having a specified kind of mind (*high-minded*). **c** interested in or enthusiastic about a specified thing (*car-minded*). **2** (usu. foll. by *to* + infin.) disposed or inclined (to an action).

mind·er /míndər/ *n.* a person whose job it is to attend to a person or thing.

mind·ful /míndfo͝ol/ *adj.* (often foll. by *of*) taking heed or care; being conscious. ▫▫ **mind·ful·ly** *adv.*

mind·less /míndlis/ *adj.* **1** lacking intelligence; stupid. **2** not requiring thought or skill (*totally mindless work*). **3** (usu. foll. by *of*) heedless of (advice, etc.). ▫▫ **mind·less·ly** *adv.* **mind·less·ness** *n.*

mind-read *v.tr.* (*past* and *past part.* **-read**) discern the thoughts of (another person). ▫▫ **mind read·er** *n.*

mind·set /míndset/ *n.* **1** a mental attitude that can influence one's interpretation of events or situations. **2** an inclination or a fixed way of thinking.

mine[1] /mīn/ *poss.pron.* **1** the one or ones belonging to or associated with me (*it is mine*). **2** (*attrib.* before a vowel) *archaic* = MY (*mine eyes have seen*). ▫ **of mine** of or belonging to me (*a friend of mine*).

mine[2] /mīn/ *n. & v.* • *n.* **1** an excavation in the earth for extracting metal, coal, etc. **2** an abundant source (of information, etc.). **3** a receptacle filled with explosive and placed in the ground or in the water for destroying enemy personnel, etc. **4** a subterranean gallery in which explosive is placed to blow up fortifications. • *v.tr.* **1** obtain (coal, etc.) from a mine. **2** (also *absol.*, often foll. by *for*) dig in (the earth, etc.) for ore, etc. **3 a** dig or burrow in (usu. the earth). **b** delve into (an abundant source) for information, etc. **c** make (a passage, etc.) underground. **4** lay explosive mines under or in. **5** = UNDERMINE. ▫▫ **min·ing** *n.*

mine·field /mínfeeld/ *n.* **1** an area planted with explosive mines. **2** a subject or situation presenting unseen hazards.

mine·lay·er /mínlayər/ *n.* a ship or aircraft for laying mines.

min·er /mínər/ *n.* **1** a person who works in a mine. **2** any burrowing insect or grub.

min·er·al /mínərəl/ *n. & adj.* • *n.* **1** any of the species into which inorganic substances are classified. **2** a substance obtained by mining. • *adj.* **1** of or containing a mineral or minerals. **2** obtained by mining.

min·er·al·o·gy /mínərolәjee/ *n.* the scientific study of minerals. ▫▫ **min·er·al·og·i·cal** /–rəlójikəl/ *adj.* **min·er·al·o·gist** *n.*

min·er·al oil *n. Pharm.* a colorless, odorless, oily liquid obtained from petroleum and used as a laxative, in manufacturing cosmetics, etc.

min·er·al wa·ter *n.* **1** water found in nature with some dissolved salts present. **2** an artificial imitation of this, esp. soda water.

min·e·stro·ne /mínistrṓnee,–strṓn/ *n.* a soup containing vegetables, pasta, and beans.

mine·sweep·er /mínsweepər/ *n.* a ship for clearing away floating and submarine mines.

mine·work·er /mínwərkər/ *n.* a person who works in a mine.

Ming /ming/ *n.* **1** the dynasty ruling China 1368–1644. **2** Chinese porcelain made during the rule of this dynasty.

min·gle /mínggəl/ *v.* **1** *tr. & intr.* mix; blend. **2** *intr.* (often foll. by *with*) (of a person) move about; associate.

min·i /mínee/ *n.* (*pl.* **minis**) *colloq.* a miniskirt, minidress, etc.

mini- /mínee/ *comb. form* miniature; very small or minor of its kind (*minibus*).

min·i·a·ture /míneeəchər, mínichər/ *adj., n., & v.* • *adj.* **1** much smaller than normal. **2** represented on a small scale. • *n.* **1** any object reduced in size. **2** a small-scale minutely finished portrait. **3** this branch of painting. **4** a picture or decorated letters in an illuminated manuscript. • *v.tr.* represent on a smaller scale. ▫ **in miniature** on a small scale. ▫▫ **min·i·a·tur·ist** *n.* (in senses 2 and 3 of *n.*). **min·i·a·tur·ize** /míneeəchərīz, mínichə–/ *v.tr.* **min·i·a·tur·i·za·tion** *n.*

min·i·a·tur·ize /míneeəchərīz, mínichə;n–/ *v.tr.* produce in a smaller version; make small. ▫▫ **min·i·a·tur·i·za·tion** *n.*

min·i·cam /míneekam/ *n.* a portable lightweight video camera.

min·i·com·pu·ter /míneekəmpyōōtər/ *n.* a computer of medium power, more than a microcomputer but less than a mainframe.

min·im /mínim/ *n.* **1** one-sixtieth of a fluid dram, about a drop. **2** an object or portion of the smallest size or importance. **3** a single downstroke of the pen.

min·i·ma *pl.* of MINIMUM.

min·i·mal /míniməl/ *adj.* **1** very minute or slight. **2** being or related to a minimum. **3** the least possible in size, duration, etc. **4** *Art* characterized by the use of simple or primary forms or structures, etc., often geometric or massive. ◻◻ **min·i·mal·ism** *n.* (in sense 4). **min·i·mal·ist** *n.* & *adj.* (in sense 4). **min·i·mal·ly** *adv.* (in senses 1–3).

min·i·max /míneemaks/ *n.* **1** *Math.* the lowest of a set of maximum values. **2** (usu. *attrib.*) **a** a strategy that minimizes the greatest risk to a participant in a game, etc. **b** the theory that in a game with two players, a player's smallest possible maximum loss is equal to the same player's greatest possible minimum gain.

min·i·mize /mínimīz/ *v.* **1** *tr.* reduce to, or estimate at, the smallest possible amount or degree. **2** *tr.* estimate or represent at less than the true value or importance. **3** *intr.* attain a minimum value. ◻◻ **min·i·mi·za·tion** *n.*

min·i·mum /míniməm/ *n.* & *adj.* (*pl.* **minima** /–mə/) • *n.* the least possible or attainable amount (*reduced to a minimum*). • *adj.* that is a minimum.

min·i·mum wage *n.* the lowest wage permitted by law.

min·ion /mínyən/ *n.* **1** *derog.* a servile agent; a slave. **2** a favorite servant, animal, etc. **3** a favorite of a sovereign, etc.

min·i·se·ries /míneeseereez/ *n.* a short series of television programs on a common theme.

min·i·skirt /míneeskərt/ *n.* a very short skirt.

min·is·ter /mínistər/ *n.* & *v.* • *n.* **1** a member of the clergy; a person authorized to officiate in religious worship. **2** a head of a government department (in some countries). **3** a diplomatic agent, usu. ranking below an ambassador. **4** (usu. foll. by *of*) a person employed in the execution of (a purpose, will, etc.) (*a minister of justice*). **5** (in full **minister general**) the superior of some religious orders. • *v. intr.* (usu. foll. by *to*) render aid or service (to a person, cause, etc.). ◻◻ **min·is·tra·ble** *adj.*

min·is·te·ri·al /ministéereeəl/ *adj.* **1** of a minister of religion or a minister's office. **2** instrumental or subsidiary in achieving a purpose. **3** of a government minister. ◻◻ **min·is·te·ri·al·ly** *adv.*

min·is·tra·tion /ministráyshən/ *n.* **1** (usu. in *pl.*) aid or service. **2** ministering, esp. in religious matters. **3** (usu. foll. by *of*) the supplying (of help, justice, etc.). ◻◻ **min·is·trant** /mínistrənt/ *adj.* & *n.* **min·is·tra·tive** /ministráytiv/ *adj.*

min·is·try /mínistree/ *n.* (*pl.* **-tries**) **1 a** (prec. by *the*) the vocation or profession of a religious minister. **b** the office of a religious minister, etc. **c** the period of tenure of this. **2** (prec. by *the*) the body of ministers of a government or of a religion. **3 a** a government department headed by a minister. **b** the building which it occupies. **4** a period of government under one Prime Minister. **5** ministering; ministration.

min·i·van /míneevan/ *n.* a vehicle, smaller than a full-sized van, for passengers, cargo, etc.

mink /mingk/ *n.* **1** either of two small semiaquatic stoatlike animals of the genus *Mustela*. **2** the thick brown fur of these. **3** a coat made of this.

Minn. *abbr.* Minnesota.

min·now /mínō/ *n.* any of various small freshwater fish of the carp family.

Mi·no·an /minṓən/ *adj.* & *n.* *Archaeol.* • *adj.* of or relating to the Bronze Age civilization centered on Crete (*c.*3000–1100 BC). • *n.* **1** an inhabitant of Minoan Crete or the Minoan world. **2** the language or scripts associated with the Minoans.

mi·nor /mínər/ *adj.*, *n.*, & *v.* • *adj.* **1** lesser or comparatively small in size or importance. **2** *Mus.* **a** (of a scale) having intervals of a semitone between the second and third, fifth and sixth, and seventh and eighth degrees. **b** (of an interval) less by a semitone than a major interval. **c** (of a key) based on a minor scale. **3** pertaining to a student's secondary field of study. • *n.* **1** a person under the legal age limit or majority. **2** *Mus.* a minor key, etc. **3** a student's subsidiary subject or course. • *v.intr.* (foll. by *in*) study in as a subsidiary to a main subject. ◻ **in a minor key** (of novels, events, people's lives, etc.) understated; uneventful.

mi·nor·i·ty /mīnáwritee, –nór–/ *n.* (*pl.* **-ties**) **1** (often foll. by *of*) a smaller number or part, esp. within a political party or structure. **2** the number of votes cast for this (*a minority of two*). **3** the state of being supported by less than half of the body of opinion (*in the minority*). **4** a relatively small group of people differing from others in race, religion, language, etc. **5** (*attrib.*) relating to or done by the minority (*minority interests*). **6 a** the state of being under full legal age. **b** the period of this.

mi·nor·i·ty lead·er *n.* the leader of the minority political party in a legislature.

mi·nor league *n.* (in baseball, etc.) a league of professional clubs other than a major league.

Min·o·taur /mínətawr/ *n.* (in Greek mythology) a man with a bull's head, kept in a Cretan labyrinth and fed with human flesh.

min·ox·i·dil /mənóksədil/ *n.* a vasodilator drug taken orally to treat hypertension or applied topically to stimulate hair growth in certain types of baldness.

min·strel /mínstrəl/ *n.* **1** a medieval singer or musician. **2** *hist.* a person who entertained patrons with singing, buffoonery, etc. **3** (usu. in *pl.*) a member of a band of public entertainers with blackened faces, etc., performing songs ostensibly of African-American origin. ◻◻ **min·strel·sy** /mínstrəlsee/ *n.* (*pl.* **-sies**)

mint[1] /mint/ *n.* **1** any aromatic plant of the genus *Mentha*. **2** a peppermint sweet or lozenge. ◻◻ **mint·y** *adj.* (**mintier, mintiest**).

mint[2] /mint/ *n.* & *v.* • *n.* **1** a place where money is coined, usu. under government authority. **2** a vast sum of money (*making a mint*). **3** a source of invention, etc. (*a mint of ideas*). • *v.tr.* **1** make (coin) by stamping metal. **2** invent; coin (a word, etc.). ◻ **in mint condition** as new.

mint ju·lep *n.* a sweet iced alcoholic drink of bourbon flavored with mint.

min·u·end /mínyōō-énd/ *n.* *Math.* a quantity or number from which another is to be subtracted.

min·u·et /mínyōō-ét/ *n.* & *v.* • *n.* **1** a slow stately dance for two in triple time. **2** *Mus.* the music for this, or music in the same rhythm and style. • *v.intr.* (**minueted, minueting**) dance a minuet.

mi·nus /mínəs/ *prep.*, *adj.*, & *n.* • *prep.* **1** with the subtraction of (*7 minus 4 equals 3*). ¶ Symb.: –. **2** (of temperature) below zero (*minus 2°*). **3** *colloq.* lacking (*returned minus their dog*). • *adj.* **1** *Math.* negative. **2** *Electronics* having a negative charge. • *n.* **1** = MINUS SIGN. **2** *Math.* a negative quantity. **3** a disadvantage.

mi·nus·cule /mínəskyōōl/ *n.* & *adj.* • *n.* a lowercase letter. • *adj.* **1** lowercase. **2** *colloq.* extremely small or unimportant.

▶Avoid the common misspelling of **minuscule** as "miniscule."

mi·nus sign *n.* the symbol (–) indicating subtraction or a negative value.

min·ute[1] /mínit/ *n.* & *v.* • *n.* **1** the sixtieth part of an hour. **2** a distance covered in one minute (*twenty min-*

utes from the station). **3 a** a moment (*expecting her any minute*). **b** (prec. by *this*) *colloq.* the present time (*what are you doing at this minute?*). **c** (foll. by clause) as soon as (*call me the minute you get back*). **4** the sixtieth part of an angular degree. **5** (in *pl.*) a brief summary of the proceedings at a meeting. **6** an official memorandum authorizing or recommending a course of action. • *v.tr.* **1** record in the minutes. **2** send the minutes to (a person). ▫ **just** (or **wait**) **a minute 1** a request to wait for a short time. **2** as a prelude to a query or objection.

minute late Middle English (in the singular in the sense 'note or memorandum'): from French *minute*, from the notion of a rough copy of a manuscript in 'small writing' (Latin *scriptura minuta*) as distinct from the finished copy in carefully formed book hand. The verb dates from the mid-16th century.

mi•nute[2] /mīnoōt, –yoōt/ *adj.* (**minutest**) **1** very small. **2** trifling; petty. **3** (of an inquiry, inquirer, etc.) accurate; detailed; precise. ▫▫ **mi•nute•ly** *adv.* **mi•nute•ness** *n.*

min•ute hand *n.* the hand on a watch or clock that indicates minutes.

min•ute•man /mínitman/ *n.* (*pl.* **-men**) **1** *US hist.* (also **Minuteman**) an American militiaman of the Revolutionary War period (ready to march at a minute's notice). **2** a type of three-stage intercontinental ballistic missile.

mi•nu•ti•a /minoōsheeə, –shə, –nyoō–/ *n.* (*pl.* **-iae** /–shee-ee/) (usu. in *pl.*) a precise, trivial, or minor detail.

minx /mingks/ *n.* a pert, sly, or playful girl.

Mi•o•cene /míəseen/ *adj.* & *n. Geol.* • *adj.* of or relating to the fourth epoch of the Tertiary period. • *n.* this epoch or system.

mi•o•sis /mīṓsis/ *n.* (also **myosis**) (*pl.* **-ses** /–seez/) excessive constriction of the pupil of the eye. ▫▫ **mi•ot•ic** /mīótik/ *adj.*

mir•a•cle /mírəkəl/ *n.* **1** an extraordinary event attributed to some supernatural agency. **2 a** any remarkable occurrence. **b** a remarkable development in some specified area (*an economic miracle*). **3** (usu. foll. by *of*) a remarkable specimen (*a miracle of ingenuity*).

mir•a•cle play *n.* a medieval play based on the Bible or the lives of the saints.

mi•rac•u•lous /mirákyələs/ *adj.* **1** of the nature of a miracle. **2** supernatural. **3** remarkable; surprising. ▫▫ **mi•rac•u•lous•ly** *adv.*

mi•rage /miraázh/ *n.* **1** an optical illusion caused by atmospheric conditions, esp. the appearance of a sheet of water in a desert or on a hot road from the reflection of light. **2** an illusory thing.

mire /mīr/ *n.* & *v.* • *n.* **1** a stretch of swampy ground. **2** mud; dirt. • *v.* **1** *tr.* & *intr.* plunge or sink in a mire. **2** *tr.* involve in difficulties. ▫ **in the mire** in difficulties.

mirk var. of MURK.

mirk•y var. of MURKY.

mir•ror /mírər/ *n.* & *v.* • *n.* **1** a polished surface, usu. of coated glass, which reflects an image. **2** anything regarded as giving an accurate reflection or description of something else. • *v.tr.* reflect as in a mirror.

mirth /mərth/ *n.* merriment; laughter. ▫▫ **mirth•ful** *adj.* **mirth•ful•ly** *adv.* **mirth•less** *adj.* **mirth•less•ly** *adv.* **mirth•less•ness** *n.*

MIRV /mərv/ *abbr.* multiple independently targeted reentry vehicle (a type of missile).

MIS *abbr. Computing* management information system.

mis•ad•ven•ture /mísədvénchər/ *n.* **1** *Law* an accident without concomitant crime or negligence (*death by misadventure*). **2** bad luck. **3** a misfortune.

mis•a•lign /mísəlín/ *v.tr.* give the wrong alignment to. ▫▫ **mis•a•lign•ment** *n.*

mis•al•li•ance /mísəlíəns/ *n.* an unsuitable alliance, esp. an unsuitable marriage.

mis•an•thrope /mísənthrōp, míz–/ *n.* (also **mis•an•thro•pist** /misánthrəpist/) **1** a person who hates mankind. **2** a person who avoids human society. ▫▫ **mis•an•throp•ic** /–thrópik/ *adj.* **mis•an•thro•py** /misánthrəpee/ *n.*

mis•ap•ply /mísəplí/ *v.tr.* (**-plies, -plied**) apply (esp. funds) wrongly. ▫▫ **mis•ap•pli•ca•tion** /mísaplikáyshən/ *n.*

mis•ap•pre•hend /mísaprihénd/ *v.tr.* misunderstand (words, a person). ▫▫ **mis•ap•pre•hen•sion** /–hénshən/ *n.* **mis•ap•pre•hen•sive** *adj.*

mis•ap•pro•pri•ate /mísəprṓpreeayt/ *v.tr.* apply (usu. another's money) to one's own use, or to a wrong use. ▫▫ **mis•ap•pro•pri•a•tion** /–áyshən/ *n.*

mis•be•got•ten /mísbigót'n/ *adj.* **1** illegitimate; bastard. **2** contemptible; disreputable.

mis•be•have /mísbiháyv/ *v.intr.* & *refl.* (of a person or machine) behave badly. ▫▫ **mis•be•hav•ior** *n.*

misc. *abbr.* MISCELLANEOUS.

mis•cal•cu•late /mískálkyəlayt/ *v.tr.* (also *absol.*) calculate (amounts, results, etc.) wrongly. ▫▫ **mis•cal•cu•la•tion** /–láyshən/ *n.*

mis•call /mískáwl/ *v.tr.* call by a wrong or inappropriate name.

mis•car•riage /mískárij/ *n.* **1** a spontaneous abortion, esp. before the 28th week of pregnancy. **2** the failure (of a plan, letter, etc.) to reach completion or its destination.

mis•car•riage of jus•tice *n.* any failure of the judicial system to attain the ends of justice.

mis•car•ry /mískáree/ *v.intr.* (**-ries, -ried**) **1** (of a woman) have a miscarriage. **2** (of a letter, etc.) fail to reach its destination. **3** (of a business, plan, etc.) fail; be unsuccessful.

mis•cast /mískást/ *v.tr.* (*past* and *past part.* **-cast**) allot an unsuitable part to (an actor).

mis•ceg•e•na•tion /miséjináyshən, mísəjə–/ *n.* the interbreeding of races, esp. of whites and nonwhites.

mis•cel•la•ne•ous /mísəláyneeəs/ *adj.* **1** of mixed composition or character. **2** (foll. by pl. noun) of various kinds. **3** (of a person) many-sided. ▫▫ **mis•cel•la•ne•ous•ly** *adv.*

mis•cel•la•ny /mísəláynee/ *n.* (*pl.* **-nies**) **1** a mixture; a medley. **2** a book containing various literary compositions.

mis•chance /míscháns/ *n.* **1** bad luck. **2** an instance of this.

mis•chief /míschif/ *n.* **1** conduct that is troublesome, but not malicious, esp. in children. **2** pranks; scrapes (*get into mischief*). **3** playful malice; archness; satire (*eyes full of mischief*). **4** harm or injury caused by a person or thing. **5** a person or thing responsible for harm or annoyance (*that loose connection is the mischief*). **6** (prec. by *the*) the annoying part or aspect (*the mischief of it is that*, etc.).

mis•chie•vous /míschivəs/ *adj.* **1** (of a person) disposed to mischief. **2** (of conduct) playfully malicious. **3** (of a thing) harmful. ▫▫ **mis•chie•vous•ly** *adv.* **mis•chie•vous•ness** *n.*

▶Do not pronounce this word with an extra syllable, "mis-chee-vee-uhs."

mischievous Middle English: from Anglo-Norman French *meschevous*, from Old French *meschever* 'come to an unfortunate end.' The early sense was 'unfortunate or calamitous,' later 'having harmful effects'; the sense of 'playfully malicious' dates from the late 17th century.

See page xii for the *Key to Pronunciation*.

mis·ci·ble /mísibəl/ *adj.* (often foll. by *with*) capable of being mixed. ▫▫ **mis·ci·bil·i·ty** /–bílitee/ *n.*
mis·con·ceive /mískənseév/ *v.* **1** *intr.* (often foll. by *of*) have a wrong idea or conception. **2** *tr.* (as **misconceived** *adj.*) badly planned, organized, etc. **3** *tr.* misunderstand (a word, person, etc.). ▫▫ **mis·con·cep·tion** /–sépshən/ *n.*
mis·con·duct *n.* & *v.* • *n.* /mískóndukt/ **1** improper or unprofessional behavior. **2** bad management. • *v.* /mískəndúkt/ **1** *refl.* misbehave. **2** *tr.* mismanage.
mis·con·strue /mískənstróō/ *v.tr.* (**-construes, -construed, -construing**) **1** interpret (a word, action, etc.) wrongly. **2** mistake the meaning of (a person). ▫▫ **mis·con·struc·tion** /–strúkshən/ *n.*
mis·count /mískównt/ *v.* & *n.* • *v.tr.* (also *absol.*) count wrongly. • *n.* a wrong count.
mis·cre·ant /mískreeənt/ *n.* & *adj.* • *n.* a wretch; a villain. • *adj.* depraved; villainous.
mis·cue /mískyóō/ *n.* & *v.* • *n.* (in billiards, etc.) the failure to strike the ball properly with the cue. • *v.intr.* (**-cues, -cued, -cueing** or **-cuing**) make a miscue.
mis·date /misdáyt/ *v.tr.* date (an event, a letter, etc.) wrongly.
mis·deal /mísdeél/ *v.* & *n.* • *v.tr.* (also *absol.*) (*past* and *past part.* –**dealt** /–délt/) make a mistake in dealing (cards). • *n.* **1** a mistake in dealing cards. **2** a misdealt hand.
mis·deed /misdeéd/ *n.* an evil deed, a wrongdoing; a crime.
mis·de·mean·or /mísdimeénər/ *n.* **1** an offense; a misdeed. **2** *Law* an indictable offense, less heinous than a felony.
mis·di·ag·nose /misdíəgnōs, –nōz/ *v.tr.* diagnose incorrectly. ▫▫ **mis·di·ag·no·sis** /–nṓsis/ *n.*
mis·di·rect /mísdirékt, –dī–/ *v.tr.* **1** direct (a person, letter, blow, etc.) wrongly. **2** (of a judge) instruct (the jury) wrongly. ▫▫ **mis·di·rec·tion** /–rékshən/ *n.*
mise-en-scène /meéz ON sén/ *n.* **1** *Theatr.* the scenery and properties of a play. **2** the setting or surroundings of an event.
mi·ser /mízər/ *n.* **1** a person who hoards wealth and lives miserably. **2** an avaricious person. ▫▫ **mi·ser·ly** *adj.*
mis·er·a·ble /mízərəbəl/ *adj.* **1** wretchedly unhappy or uncomfortable. **2** unworthy; inadequate (*a miserable hovel*); contemptible. **3** causing wretchedness or discomfort (*miserable weather*). **4** stingy; mean. ▫▫ **mis·er·a·ble·ness** *n.* **mis·er·a·bly** *adv.*
mis·er·y /mízəree/ *n.* (*pl.* **-ies**) **1** a wretched state of mind, or of outward circumstances. **2** a thing causing this. ▫ **put out of its**, etc., **misery 1** release (a person, animal, etc.) from suffering or suspense. **2** kill (an animal in pain).
mis·fire /mísfír/ *v.* & *n.* • *v.intr.* **1** (of a gun, motor engine, etc.) fail to go off or start or function regularly. **2** (of an action, etc.) fail to have the intended effect. • *n.* a failure of function or intention.
mis·fit /mísfit/ *n.* **1** a person unsuited to a particular kind of environment, occupation, etc. **2** a garment, etc., that does not fit.
mis·for·tune /misfáwrchən/ *n.* **1** bad luck. **2** an unfortunate condition or event.
mis·giv·ing /misgíving/ *n.* (usu. in *pl.*) a feeling of mistrust or apprehension.
mis·gov·ern /misgúvərn/ *v.tr.* govern (a state, etc.) badly. ▫▫ **mis·gov·ern·ment** *n.*
mis·guide /misgíd/ *v.tr.* **1** (as **misguided** *adj.*) mistaken in thought or action. **2** mislead; misdirect. ▫▫ **mis·guid·ed·ly** *adv.* **mis·guid·ed·ness** *n.*
mis·han·dle /mis-hánd'l/ *v.tr.* **1** deal with incorrectly or ineffectively. **2** handle (a person or thing) roughly or rudely; ill-treat.
mis·hap /mís-háp/ *n.* an unlucky accident.
mish·mash /míshmash, –maash/ *n.* a confused mixture.
mis·in·form /mísinfórm/ *v.tr.* give wrong information to; mislead. ▫▫ **mis·in·for·ma·tion** /–fərmáyshən/ *n.*
mis·in·ter·pret /mísintərprit/ *v.tr.* (**-interpreted, -interpreting**) **1** interpret wrongly. **2** draw a wrong inference from. ▫▫ **mis·in·ter·pre·ta·tion** /–táyshən/ *n.*
mis·judge /mísjúj/ *v.tr.* (also *absol.*) **1** judge wrongly. **2** have a wrong opinion of. ▫▫ **mis·judg·ment** *n.*
mis·key /mískeé/ *v.tr.* (**-keys, -keyed**) key (data) wrongly.
mis·lay /misláy/ *v.tr.* (*past* and *past part.* **-laid** /–láyd/) **1** unintentionally put (a thing) where it cannot readily be found. **2** *euphem.* lose.
mis·lead /misleéd/ *v.tr.* (*past* and *past part.* **-led** /–léd/) **1** cause (a person) to go wrong, in conduct, belief, etc. **2** lead astray or in the wrong direction. ▫▫ **mis·lead·ing** /misleéding/ *adj.* **mis·lead·ing·ly** *adv.*
mis·man·age /mismánij/ *v.tr.* manage badly or wrongly. ▫▫ **mis·man·age·ment** *n.*
mis·match *v.* & *n.* • *v.tr.* /mismách/ (usu. as **mismatched** *adj.*) match unsuitably or incorrectly, esp. in marriage. • *n.* /mísmach/ a bad match.
mis·no·mer /misnṓmər/ *n.* **1** a name or term used wrongly. **2** the wrong use of a name or term.
mi·so /meésō/ *n.* a paste made from fermented soy beans and barley or rice malt, used in Japanese cooking.
mi·sog·a·my /misógəmee/ *n.* the hatred of marriage. ▫▫ **mi·sog·a·mist** *n.*
mi·sog·y·ny /misójinee/ *n.* the hatred of women. ▫▫ **mi·sog·y·nist** *n.* **mi·sog·y·nous** *adj.*
mis·place /mispláys/ *v.tr.* **1** put in the wrong place. **2** bestow (affections, confidence, etc.) on an inappropriate object. **3** time (words, actions, etc.) badly. ▫▫ **mis·place·ment** *n.*
mis·print *n.* & *v.* • *n.* /mísprínt/ a mistake in printing. • *v.tr.* /misprínt/ print wrongly.
mis·pro·nounce /míspranówns/ *v.tr.* pronounce (a word, etc.) wrongly. ▫▫ **mis·pro·nun·ci·a·tion** /–nunseeáyshən/ *n.*
mis·quote /mískwṓt/ *v.tr.* quote wrongly. ▫▫ **mis·quo·ta·tion** /–táyshən/ *n.*
mis·read /mísreéd/ *v.tr.* (*past* and *past part.* **-read** /–réd/) read or interpret (text, a situation, etc.) wrongly.
mis·rep·re·sent /mísreprizént/ *v.tr.* represent wrongly; give a false or misleading account or idea of. ▫▫ **mis·rep·re·sen·ta·tion** /–táyshən/ *n.* **mis·rep·re·sen·ta·tive** *adj.*
Miss. *abbr.* Mississippi.
miss[1] /mis/ *v.* & *n.* • *v.* **1** *tr.* (also *absol.*) fail to hit, reach, find, catch, etc. (an object or goal). **2** *tr.* fail to catch (a bus, train, etc.). **3** *tr.* fail to experience, see, or attend (an occurrence or event). **4** *tr.* fail to meet (a person); fail to keep (an appointment). **5** *tr.* fail to seize (an opportunity, etc.) (*I missed my chance*). **6** *tr.* fail to hear or understand (*I missed what you said*). **7** *tr.* **a** regret the loss or absence of (a person or thing) (*did you miss me?*). **b** notice the loss or absence of (an object) (*bound to miss the key if it isn't there*). **8** *tr.* avoid (*go early to miss the traffic*). **9** *intr.* (of an engine, etc.) fail; misfire. • *n.* **1** a failure to hit, reach, etc. **2** *colloq.* = MISCARRIAGE 1. ▫ **miss the boat** (or **bus**) lose an opportunity. **miss out** (usu. foll. by *on*) *colloq.* fail to get or experience (*always misses out on the good times*). **not miss a trick** never fail to seize an opportunity, advantage, etc. ▫▫ **miss·a·ble** *adj.*
miss[2] /mis/ *n.* **1** a girl or unmarried woman. **2** (**Miss**) **a** respectful title of an unmarried woman or girl, or of a married woman retaining her maiden name for professional purposes (cf. **Ms.**). **b** the title of a beauty queen (*Miss World*). **3** usu. *derog.* or *joc.* a girl, esp. a

schoolgirl. **4** the title used to address a young woman or girl.

mis·sal /mísəl/ *n. RC Ch., Anglican Ch.* **1** a book containing the texts used in the service of the Mass throughout the year. **2** a book of prayers.

mis·shap·en /mís-sháypən/ *adj.* ill-shaped; deformed; distorted. ▫▫ **mis·shap·en·ness** *n.*

mis·sile /mísəl/ *n.* **1** an object or weapon for throwing at a target or for discharge from a machine. **2** a weapon directed by remote control or automatically. ▫▫ **mis·sile·ry** /–əlree/ *n.*

miss·ing /mísing/ *adj.* **1** not in its place; lost. **2** (of a person) not yet traced or confirmed as alive but not known to be dead. **3** not present.

miss·ing link *n.* **1** a thing lacking to complete a series. **2** a hypothetical intermediate type, esp. between humans and apes.

mis·sion /míshən/ *n.* **1 a** a particular task or goal assigned to a person or group. **b** a journey undertaken as part of this. **c** a person's vocation (*mission in life*). **2** a military or scientific operation or expedition for a particular purpose. **3** a body of persons sent, esp. to a foreign country, to conduct negotiations, etc. **4 a** a body sent to propagate a religious faith. **b** a field of missionary activity. **c** a missionary post or organization. **d** a place of worship attached to a mission. **5** a particular course or period of preaching, services, etc., undertaken by a parish or community.

mis·sion·ar·y /míshəneree/ *adj. & n.* • *adj.* of, concerned with, or characteristic of, religious missions. • *n.* (*pl.* **-ies**) a person doing missionary work.

mis·sion·er /míshənər/ *n.* **1** a missionary. **2** a person in charge of a religious mission.

mis·sis var. of MISSUS.

mis·sive /mísiv/ *n.* **1** *joc.* a letter. **2** an official letter.

Mis·sour·i /mizŏŏree, –zŏŏrə/ *n. & adj.* • *n.* **1** a N. American tribe native to the Missouri River valley. **2** a member of this people. • *adj.* of or relating to this people.

mis·spell /mís-spél/ *v.tr.* spell wrongly. ▫▫ **mis·spell·ing** *n.*

mis·state /mís-stáyt/ *v.tr.* state wrongly or inaccurately. ▫▫ **mis·state·ment** /–mənt/ *n.*

mis·sus /mísəz/ *n.* (also **mis·sis** /–siz/) *sl.* or *joc.* **1** a form of address to a woman. **2** a wife. ▫ **the missus** my or your wife.

miss·y /mísee/ *n.* (*pl.* **-ies**) an affectionate or derogatory form of address to a young girl.

mist /mist/ *n. & v.* • *n.* **1 a** water vapor near the ground in minute droplets limiting visibility. **b** condensed vapor settling on a surface and obscuring glass, etc. **2** dimness or blurring of the sight caused by tears, etc. **3** a cloud of particles resembling mist. • *v.tr. & intr.* (usu. foll. by *up, over*) cover or become covered with mist or as with mist.

mis·take /mistáyk/ *n. & v.* • *n.* **1** an incorrect idea or opinion; a thing incorrectly done or thought. **2** an error of judgment. • *v.tr.* (*past* **mistook** /–tŏŏk/; *past part.* **mistaken** /–táykən/) **1** misunderstand the meaning or intention of (a person, a statement, etc.). **2** (foll. by *for*) wrongly take or identify (*mistook me for you*). **3** choose wrongly (*mistake one's vocation*). ▫ **and** (or **make**) **no mistake** *colloq.* undoubtedly. **by mistake** accidentally; in error. **there is no mistaking** one is sure to recognize (a person or thing). ▫▫ **mis·tak·a·ble** *adj.*

mis·tak·en /mistáykən/ *adj.* **1** wrong in opinion or judgment. **2** based on or resulting from this (*mistaken loyalty; mistaken identity*). ▫▫ **mis·tak·en·ly** *adv.*

mis·ter /místər/ *n.* **1** (**Mister**) respectful title for a man, usu. abbr. (as **Mr.**). **2** *sl.* or *joc.* sir; a form of address to a man (*Hey, mister!*). **3** a husband.

mis·tle·toe /mísəltō/ *n.* **1** a parasitic plant, *Viscum album*, growing on apple and other trees and bearing white glutinous berries in winter. **2** a similar plant, genus *Phoradendron*, native to N. America.

mis·took *past* of MISTAKE.

mis·tral /místrəl, mistraál/ *n.* a cold northerly wind of southern France.

mis·treat /místreét/ *v.tr.* treat badly. ▫▫ **mis·treat·ment** *n.*

mis·tress /místris/ *n.* **1** a female head of a household. **2 a** a woman in authority over others. **b** the female owner of a pet. **3** a woman with power to control, etc. (often foll. by *of*: *mistress of the situation*). **4** a woman (other than his wife) with whom a married man has a sexual relationship.

mis·tri·al /mís-tríəl/ *n.* **1** a trial rendered invalid through some error in the proceedings. **2** a trial in which the jury cannot agree on a verdict.

mis·trust /mís-trúst/ *v. & n.* • *v.tr.* **1** be suspicious of. **2** feel no confidence in (a person, oneself, one's powers, etc.). • *n.* **1** suspicion. **2** lack of confidence.

mis·trust·ful /mís-trústfŏŏl/ *adj.* **1** (foll. by *of*) suspicious. **2** lacking confidence or trust. ▫▫ **mis·trust·ful·ly** *adv.*

mist·y /místee/ *adj.* (**mistier, mistiest**) **1** of or covered with mist. **2** indistinct or dim in outline. **3** obscure; vague (*a misty idea*). ▫▫ **mist·i·ly** *adv.* **mist·i·ness** *n.*

mis·un·der·stand /mísundərstánd/ *v.tr.* (*past* and *past part.* **-understood** /–stŏŏd/) **1** fail to understand correctly. **2** (usu. as **misunderstood** *adj.*) misinterpret the words or actions of (a person).

mis·un·der·stand·ing /mísundərstánding/ *n.* **1** a failure to understand correctly. **2** a slight disagreement or quarrel.

mis·use *v. & n.* • *v.tr.* /mísyŏŏz/ **1** use wrongly; apply to the wrong purpose. **2** ill-treat. • *n.* /mísyŏŏs/ wrong or improper use or application.

MIT *abbr.* Massachusetts Institute of Technology.

mite[1] /mīt/ *n.* any small arachnid of the order Acari.

mite[2] /mīt/ *n. & adv.* • *n.* **1** any small monetary unit. **2** a small object or person, esp. a child. **3** a modest contribution; the best one can do (*offered my mite of comfort*). • *adv.* (usu. prec. by *a*) *colloq.* somewhat (*is a mite shy*).

mi·ter /mítər/ *n. & v.* • *n.* **1** a tall deeply-cleft headdress worn by bishops and abbots, esp. as a symbol of office. **2** the joint of two pieces of wood or other material at an angle of 90°, such that the line of junction bisects this angle. **3** a diagonal join of two pieces of fabric that meet at a corner, made by folding. • *v.* **1** *tr.* bestow the miter on. **2** *tr. & intr.* join with a miter. ▫▫ **mi·tered** *adj.*

mi·ter box *n.* a frame with slits for guiding a saw in cutting miter joints.

mit·i·gate /mítigayt/ *v.tr.* make milder or less intense or severe. ▫▫ **mit·i·ga·tion** /–gáyshən/ *n.* **mit·i·ga·to·ry** /–gətáwree/ *adj.*

▶See note at MILITATE.

mit·i·gat·ing cir·cum·stances *n.pl. Law* circumstances permitting greater leniency.

mi·to·chon·drion /mítəkóndreeən/ *n.* (*pl.* **mitochondria** /–dreeə/) *Biol.* an organelle found in most eukaryotic cells, containing enzymes for respiration and energy production.

mi·to·sis /mītósis/ *n. Biol.* a type of cell division that results in two daughter cells each having the same number and kind of chromosomes as the parent nucleus (cf. MEIOSIS). ▫▫ **mi·tot·ic** /–tótik/ *adj.*

mi·tral /mítrəl/ *adj.* of or like a miter.

mi·tral valve *n.* a two-cusped valve between the left atrium and the left ventricle of the heart.

mitt /mit/ *n.* **1** a baseball glove for catching the ball. **2** = MITTEN. **3** *sl.* a hand or fist. **4** a glove leaving the fingers and thumb-tip exposed.
mit·ten /mít'n/ *n.* a glove with two sections, one for the thumb and the other for all four fingers.
mitz·vah /mítsvə/ *n.* (*pl.* **mitzvoth** /–vōt/ or **mitzvahs**) in Judaism: **1** a precept or commandment. **2** a good deed done from religious duty.
mix /miks/ *v.* & *n.* • *v.* **1** *tr.* combine or put together (two or more substances or things) so that they are diffused into each other. **2** *tr.* prepare (a compound, cocktail, etc.) by combining the ingredients. **3** *tr.* combine (an activity, etc.) with another simultaneously (*mix business and pleasure*). **4** *intr.* **a** join, be mixed, or combine, esp. readily (*oil and water will not mix*). **b** be compatible. **c** be sociable (*must learn to mix*). **5** *intr.* **a** (foll. by *with*) (of a person) be harmonious or sociable with; have regular dealings with. **b** (foll. by *in*) participate in. • *n.* **1 a** the act or an instance of mixing; a mixture. **b** the proportion of materials, etc., in a mixture. **2** *colloq.* a group of persons of different types (*social mix*). **3** the ingredients prepared commercially for making a cake, etc., or for a process such as making concrete. **4** the merging of film pictures or sound. □ **be mixed up in** (or **with**) be involved in or with (esp. something undesirable). **mix in** be harmonious or sociable. **mix up 1** mix thoroughly. **2** confuse; mistake the identity of.
mixed /mikst/ *adj.* **1** of diverse qualities or elements. **2** containing persons from various backgrounds, etc. **3** for or involving persons of both sexes (*a mixed school*).
mixed bag *n.* a diverse assortment of things or persons.
mixed bless·ing *n.* a thing having advantages and disadvantages.
mixed dou·bles *n.pl. Tennis* a doubles game with a man and a woman as partners on each side.
mixed feel·ings *n.pl.* a mixture of pleasure and dismay about something.
mixed mar·riage *n.* a marriage between persons of different races or religions.
mixed met·a·phor *n.* a combination of inconsistent metaphors (e.g., *this tower of strength will forge ahead*).
mixed-up *adj. colloq.* mentally or emotionally confused; socially ill-adjusted.
mix·er /míksər/ *n.* **1** a device for mixing foods, etc., or for processing other materials. **2** a person who manages socially in a specified way (*a good mixer*). **3** a (usu. soft) drink to be mixed with another. **4** *Broadcasting & Cinematog.* **a** a device for merging input signals to produce a combined output in the form of sound or pictures. **b** a person who operates this.
mix·ture /míks-chər/ *n.* **1** the process of mixing or being mixed. **2** the result of mixing; something mixed; a combination. **3** *Chem.* the product of the random distribution of one substance through another without any chemical reaction taking place between the components, as distinct from a chemical compound. **4** ingredients mixed together to produce a substance, esp. a medicine (*cough mixture*). **5** a person regarded as a combination of qualities and attributes.
mix-up *n.* a confusion, misunderstanding, or mistake.
miz·zen /mízən/ *n.* (also **miz·en**) *Naut.* (in full **mizzen sail**) the lowest fore-and-aft sail of a fully rigged ship's mizzenmast.
miz·zen·mast /mízənmast/ *n. Naut.* the mast next aft of a ship's mainmast.
ml *abbr.* milliliter(s).
M.Litt. *abbr.* Master of Letters.
Mlle. *abbr.* (*pl.* **Mlles.**) Mademoiselle.
MM *abbr.* (as **MM.**) Messieurs.
mm *abbr.* millimeter(s).
Mme. *abbr.* (*pl.* **Mmes.**) Madame.
MN *abbr.* Minnesota (in official postal use).
Mn *symb. Chem.* the element manganese.
mne·mon·ic /nimónik/ *adj.* & *n.* • *adj.* of or designed to aid the memory. • *n.* a mnemonic device. □□ **mne·mon·i·cal·ly** *adv.*
mne·mon·ics /nimóniks/ *n.pl.* (usu. treated as *sing.*) **1** the art of improving memory. **2** a system for this.
MO *abbr.* **1** Missouri (in official postal use). **2** money order.
Mo *symb. Chem.* the element molybdenum.
Mo. *abbr.* Missouri.
mo. *abbr.* month.
m.o. *abbr.* modus operandi.
mo·a /mṓə/ *n.* any extinct flightless New Zealand bird of the family Dinornithidae, resembling the ostrich.
moan /mōn/ *n.* & *v.* • *n.* **1** a long murmur expressing suffering or passion. **2** a low plaintive sound of wind, etc. **3** a complaint; a grievance. • *v.* **1** *intr.* make a moan or moans. **2** *intr. colloq.* complain or grumble. **3** *tr.* **a** utter with moans. **b** lament. □□ **moan·er** *n.*
moat /mōt/ *n.* & *v.* • *n.* a deep defensive ditch around a castle, town, etc., usu. filled with water. • *v.tr.* surround with or as with a moat.
mob /mob/ *n.* & *v.* • *n.* **1** a disorderly crowd; a rabble. **2** (prec. by *the*) usu. *derog.* the populace. **3** *colloq.* a gang; an associated group of persons. **4** = MAFIA. • *v.tr.* & *intr.* (**mobbed, mobbing**) **1** *tr.* **a** crowd around in order to attack or admire. **b** (of a mob) attack. **c** crowd into (a building). **2** *intr.* assemble in a mob.
mob·cap /móbkap/ *n. hist.* a woman's large indoor cap covering all the hair, worn in the 18th and early 19th c.
mo·bile /mṓbəl, –beel, –bīl/ *adj.* & *n.* • *adj.* **1** movable; not fixed; free or able to move or flow easily. **2** (of the face, etc.) readily changing its expression. **3** (of a business, library, etc.) accommodated in a vehicle so as to serve various places. **4** (of a person) able to change his or her social status. • *n.* /–beel/ a decorative structure hung so as to turn freely. □□ **mo·bil·i·ty** /mōbílitee/ *n.*
mo·bile home *n.* a transportable structure, usu. parked and used as a residence.
mo·bi·lize /mṓbilīz/ *v.* **1 a** *tr.* organize for service or action (esp. troops in time of war). **b** *intr.* be organized in this way. **2** *tr.* render movable; bring into circulation. □□ **mo·bi·li·za·tion** *n.*
Mö·bi·us strip /mṓbiəs, máy–, mṓ–/ *n. Math.* a one-sided surface formed by joining the ends of a rectangle after twisting one end through 180°.
mob rule *n.* rule imposed and enforced by a mob.
mob·ster /móbstər/ *n. sl.* a gangster.
moc·ca·sin /mókəsin/ *n.* **1** a type of soft leather shoe with combined sole and heel, as orig. worn by Native Americans. **2** (in full **water moccasin**) a poisonous American snake of the genus *Agkistrodon*, esp. the cottonmouth, *A. piscivorus*.
mo·cha /mṓkə/ *n.* **1** a coffee of fine quality. **2** a beverage or flavoring made with this. **3** a soft kind of sheepskin.
mock /mok/ *v.*, *adj.*, & *n.* • *v.* **1 a** *tr.* ridicule; scoff at. **b** *intr.* (foll. by *at*) act with scorn or contempt for. **2** *tr.* mimic contemptuously. **3** *tr.* jeer, defy, or delude contemptuously. • *attrib.adj.* sham; imitation (esp. without intention to deceive); pretended (*a mock battle*). • *n.* **1** a thing deserving scorn. **2** (in *pl.*) *colloq.* mock examinations. □□ **mock·er** *n.* **mock·ing·ly** *adv.*
mock·er·y /mókəree/ *n.* (*pl.* **-ies**) **1 a** derision; ridicule. **b** a subject or occasion of this. **2** (often foll. by *of*) a counterfeit or absurdly inadequate representation. **3** a ludicrously or insultingly futile action, etc.
mock·ing·bird /mókingbərd/ *n.* a bird, esp. the Amer-

ican songbird *Mimus polyglottos*, that mimics the notes of other birds.

mock or·ange *n.* a white-flowered heavy-scented shrub, *Philadelphus coronarius*.

mock tur·tle soup *n.* soup made from a calf's head, etc., to resemble turtle soup.

mock-up *n.* **1** an experimental model or replica of a proposed structure, etc. **2** an arrangement of text and pictures to be printed.

mod /mod/ *adj. colloq.* modern, esp. in style of dress.

mod·al /mṓd'l/ *adj.* **1** of or relating to mode or form as opposed to substance. **2** *Gram.* **a** of or denoting the mood of a verb. **b** (of an auxiliary verb, e.g., *would*) used to express the mood of another verb. **c** (of a particle) denoting manner. ▫▫ **mod·al·ly** *adv.*

mo·dal·i·ty /mōdálitee/ *n.* (*pl.* **-ties**) (in *sing.* or *pl.*) a prescribed method of procedure.

mode /mōd/ *n.* **1** a way or manner in which a thing is done. **2** a prevailing fashion or custom. **3** *Computing* a way of operating or using a system (*print mode*). **4** *Statistics* the value that occurs most frequently in a given set of data. **5** *Mus.* **a** each of the scale systems that result when the white notes of the piano are played consecutively over an octave (*Lydian mode*). **b** each of the two main modern scale systems, the major and minor (*minor mode*).

mod·el /mód'l/ *n.* & *v.* •*n.* **1** a representation in three dimensions of an existing person or thing or of a proposed structure, esp. on a smaller scale (often *attrib.*: *a model train*). **2** a simplified (often mathematical) description of a system, etc., to assist calculations and predictions. **3** a figure in clay, wax, etc., to be reproduced in another material. **4** a particular design or style, esp. of a car. **5 a** an exemplary person or thing (*a model of self-discipline*). **b** (*attrib.*) ideal; exemplary (*a model student*). **6** a person employed to pose for an artist or photographer or to display clothes, etc., by wearing them. **7** a garment, etc., by a well-known designer, or a copy of this. •*v.* **1** *tr.* **a** fashion or shape (a figure) in clay, wax, etc. **b** (foll. by *after*, *on*, etc.) form (a thing in imitation of). **2 a** *intr.* act or pose as a model. **b** *tr.* (of a person acting as a model) display (a garment). **3** *tr.* devise a (usu. mathematical) model of (a phenomenon, system, etc.). ▫▫ **mod·el·er** *n.*

mo·dem /mṓdem/ *n.* a device for modulation and demodulation, e.g., between a computer and a telephone line.

mod·er·ate *adj.*, *n.*, & *v.* •*adj.* /módərət/ **1** avoiding extremes; temperate in conduct or expression. **2** fairly or tolerably large or good. **3** (of the wind) of medium strength. **4** (of prices) fairly low. •*n.* /módərət/ a person who holds moderate views, esp. in politics. •*v.* /módərayt/ **1** *tr.* & *intr.* make or become less violent, intense, rigorous, etc. **2** *tr.* (also *absol.*) act as a moderator of or to. ▫▫ **mod·er·ate·ly** /–rətlee/ *adv.*

mod·er·a·tion /módəráyshən/ *n.* **1** the process or an instance of moderating. **2** the quality of being moderate. ▫ **in moderation** in a moderate manner or degree.

mod·e·ra·to /módəraátō/ *adj.*, *adv.*, & *n. Mus.* •*adj.* & *adv.* performed at a moderate pace. •*n.* (*pl.* **-tos**) a piece of music to be performed in this way.

mod·er·a·tor /módəraytər/ *n.* **1** an arbitrator or mediator. **2** a presiding officer. **3** *Eccl.* a Presbyterian minister presiding over an ecclesiastical body.

mod·ern /módərn/ *adj.* & *n.* •*adj.* **1** of the present and recent times. **2** in current fashion; not antiquated. •*n.* (usu. in *pl.*) a person living in modern times. ▫▫ **mo·der·ni·ty** /–dérnitee/ *n.*

mod·ern Eng·lish *n.* English from about 1500 onward.

mod·ern·ism /módərnizəm/ *n.* **1 a** modern ideas or methods. **b** the tendency of religious belief to harmonize with modern ideas. **2** a modern term or expression. ▫▫ **mod·ern·ist** *n.* **mod·ern·is·tic** /–nístik/ *adj.*

mod·ern·ize /módərnīz/ *v.* **1** *tr.* make modern; adapt to modern needs or habits. **2** *intr.* adopt modern ways or views. ▫▫ **mod·ern·i·za·tion** /–záyshən/ *n.* **mod·ern·iz·er** *n.*

mod·est /módist/ *adj.* **1** having or expressing a humble or moderate estimate of one's own merits or achievements. **2** diffident; bashful; retiring. **3** decorous. **4** moderate or restrained in amount, extent, severity, etc. (*a modest sum*). **5** (of a thing) unpretentious in appearance, etc. ▫▫ **mod·est·ly** *adv.*

mod·es·ty /módistee/ *n.* the quality of being modest.

mod·i·cum /módikəm/ *n.* (foll. by *of*) a small quantity.

mod·i·fi·ca·tion /módifikáyshən/ *n.* **1** the act or an instance of modifying or being modified. **2** a change made.

mod·i·fi·er /módifīər/ *n.* **1** a person or thing that modifies. **2** *Gram.* a word, esp. an adjective or noun used attributively, that qualifies the sense of another word (e.g., *good* and *family* in *a good family house*).

▶A modifier is said to be *misplaced* if it has no clear grammatical connection to another part of the sentence. Thus, in the sentence *Having seen the movie, my views were offered*, the meaning may be clear, but the first phrase appears to modify *views*. The sentence would be better worded as: *Having seen the movie, I offered my views.* Careful writers avoid such lapses in syntax, which can cause ludicrous images, especially in the case of **dangling participles** such as the one in the sentence *Filled with wine, the fireworks delighted us.*

mod·i·fy /módifī/ *v.tr.* (**-fies**, **-fied**) **1** make less severe or extreme (*modify one's demands*). **2** make partial changes in; make different. **3** *Gram.* qualify or expand the sense of (a word, etc.). ▫▫ **mod·i·fi·ca·tion** /–fikáyshən/ *n.* **mod·i·fi·ca·to·ry** /–fikətáwree/ *adj.*

mod·ish /mṓdish/ *adj.* fashionable. ▫▫ **mod·ish·ly** *adv.* **mod·ish·ness** *n.*

mod·u·lar /mójələr/ *adj.* of or consisting of modules or moduli. ▫▫ **mod·u·lar·i·ty** /–láritee/ *n.*

mod·u·late /mójəlayt/ *v.* **1** *tr.* **a** regulate or adjust. **b** moderate. **2** *tr.* adjust or vary the tone or pitch of (the speaking voice). **3** *tr.* alter the amplitude or frequency of (a wave) by a wave of a lower frequency to convey a signal. **4** *intr.* & *tr. Mus.* (often foll. by *from*, *to*) change or cause to change from one key to another. ▫▫ **mod·u·la·tion** /–láyshən/ *n.* **mod·u·la·tor** *n.*

mod·ule /mójōōl/ *n.* **1** a standardized part or independent unit used in construction, esp. of furniture, a building, or an electronic system. **2** an independent unit of a spacecraft (*lunar module*). **3** a unit or period of training or education. **4** a standard or unit of measurement.

mod·u·lus /mójələs/ *n.* (*pl.* **moduli** /–lī/) *Math.* **1 a** the magnitude of a real number without regard to its sign. **b** the positive square root of the sum of the squares of the real and imaginary parts of a complex number. **2** a constant factor or ratio.

mo·dus op·e·ran·di /mṓdəs ópərándee, –dī/ *n.* (*pl.* **modi operandi** /mṓdee, –dī/) **1** the particular way in which a person performs a task or action. **2** the way a thing operates.

mo·dus vi·ven·di /mṓdəs vivéndee, –dī/ *n.* (*pl.* **modi vivendi** /mṓdee, –dī/) **1** a way of living or coping. **2 a** an arrangement whereby those in dispute can carry on pending a settlement. **b** an arrangement between people who agree to differ.

mo·gul /mṓgəl/ *n.* **1** *colloq.* an important or influential person. **2** (**Mogul**) *hist.* (often **the Great Mogul**) any of the emperors of Delhi in the 16th–19th c.

mo·hair /mṓhair/ *n.* **1** the hair of the angora goat. **2** a yarn or fabric from this.

Mo·ham·med·an var. of MUHAMMADAN.
Mo·ha·ve var. of MOJAVE.
Mo·hawk /mṓhawk/ *n.* **1 a** a member of a Native American people of New York State. **b** the language of this people. **2** (of a hairstyle) with the head shaved except for a strip of hair from the middle of the forehead to the back of the neck, often worn in tall spikes.
Mo·he·gan /mōhéegən/ *n. & adj.* • *n.* a member of a Native American people of Connecticut. • *adj.* of or relating to this people.
Mo·hi·can var. of MAHICAN.
moi·e·ty /móyətee/ *n.* (*pl.* **-ties**) *Law* or *literary* **1** a half. **2** each of the two parts into which a thing is divided.
moire /mwaar, mawr/ *n.* (in full **moire antique**) watered fabric, now usu. silk.
moir·é /mwaaráy, máwray/ *adj. & n.* • *adj.* **1** (of silk) watered. **2** (of metal) having a patterned appearance like watered silk. • *n.* **1** this patterned appearance. **2** = MOIRE.
moist /moyst/ *adj.* **1 a** slightly wet; damp. **b** (of the season, etc.) rainy. **2** (of a disease) marked by a discharge of matter, etc. **3** (of the eyes) wet with tears. □□ **moist·ness** *n.*
mois·ten /móysən/ *v.tr. & intr.* make or become moist.
mois·ture /móys-chər/ *n.* water or other liquid diffused in a small quantity as vapor, or within a solid, or condensed on a surface.
mois·tur·ize /móys-chərīz/ *v.tr.* make less dry (esp. the skin by use of a cosmetic). □□ **mois·tur·iz·er** *n.*
Mo·ja·ve /mōhaávee/ *n. & adj.* (also **Mo·ha·ve**) • *n.* **1** a N. American people native to Arizona and California. **2** a member of this people. • *adj.* of or relating to this people.
mol /mōl/ *abbr.* = MOLE⁴.
mo·lar[1] /mṓlər/ *adj. & n.* • *adj.* (usu. of a mammal's back teeth) serving to grind. • *n.* a molar tooth.
mo·lar[2] /mṓlər/ *adj. Chem.* **1** of a mass of substance usu. per mole (*molar latent heat*). **2** (of a solution) containing one mole of solute per liter of solvent. □□ **mol·ar·i·ty** /məláritee/ *n.*
mo·las·ses /məlásiz/ *n.pl.* (treated as *sing.*) uncrystallized syrup extracted from raw sugar during refining.
mold[1] /mōld/ *n. & v.* • *n.* **1** a hollow container into which molten metal, etc., is poured or soft material is pressed to harden into a required shape. **2 a** a metal or earthenware vessel used to give shape to cakes, gelatins, etc. **b** a dessert, etc., made in this way. **3** *Archit.* a molding or group of moldings. **4** a frame or template for producing moldings. **5** character or disposition (*in heroic mold*). • *v.tr.* **1** make in a required shape or from certain ingredients (*was molded out of clay*). **2** give a shape to. **3** influence the formation or development of (*consultation helps to mold policies*). **4** (esp. of clothing) fit closely to (*the gloves molded his hands*). □□ **mold·er** *n.*
mold[2] /mōld/ *n.* a furry growth of minute fungi occurring esp. in moist warm conditions.
mold[3] /mōld/ *n.* **1** loose earth. **2** the upper soil of cultivated land, esp. when rich in organic matter.
mold·er /mṓldər/ *v.intr.* **1** decay to dust. **2** (foll. by *away*) rot or crumble. **3** deteriorate.
mold·ing /mṓlding/ *n.* **1 a** an ornamentally shaped outline as an architectural feature. **b** a strip of material in wood or stone, etc., for use as molding. **2** similar material in wood or plastic, etc., used for other decorative purposes.
mold·y /mṓldee/ *adj.* (**-ier, -iest**) **1** covered with mold. **2** stale; out of date. **3** *colloq.* dull; miserable; boring.
mole[1] /mōl/ *n.* **1** any small burrowing insect-eating mammal of the family Talpidae, esp. *Talpa europaea*, with dark velvety fur and very small eyes. **2** *colloq.* **a** a spy, within an organization, usu. dormant for a long period while attaining a position of trust. **b** a betrayer of confidential information.
mole[2] /mōl/ *n.* a small often slightly raised dark blemish on the skin caused by a high concentration of melanin.
mole[3] /mōl/ *n.* **1** a structure serving as a pier, breakwater, or causeway. **2** an artificial harbor.
mole[4] /mōl/ *n. Chem.* the SI unit of amount of substance equal to the quantity containing as many elementary units as there are atoms in 0.012 kg of carbon 12.
mo·lec·u·lar /məlékyələr/ *adj.* of, relating to, or consisting of molecules. □□ **mo·lec·u·lar·i·ty** /–láritee/ *n.*
mol·e·cule /mólikyōōl/ *n.* **1** *Chem.* the smallest fundamental unit (usu. a group of atoms) of a chemical compound that can take part in a chemical reaction. **2** (in general use) a small particle.
mole·hill /mṓlhil/ *n.* a small mound thrown up by a mole in burrowing. □ **make a mountain out of a molehill** exaggerate the importance of a minor difficulty.
mole·skin /mṓlskin/ *n.* **1** the skin of a mole used as fur. **2 a** a kind of cotton fustian with its surface shaved before dyeing. **b** (in *pl.*) clothes, esp. trousers, made of this.
mo·lest /məlést/ *v.tr.* **1** annoy or pester (a person) in a hostile or injurious way. **2** attack or interfere with (a person), esp. sexually. □□ **mo·les·ta·tion** /mṓlestáyshən, mól–/ *n.* **mo·lest·er** *n.*
moll /mol/ *n. sl.* **1** a gangster's female companion. **2** a prostitute.
mol·li·fy /mólifī/ *v.tr.* (**-fies, -fied**) **1** appease; pacify. **2** reduce the severity of; soften. □□ **mol·li·fi·ca·tion** /–fikáyshən/ *n.*
mol·lusk /móləsk/ *n.* (also **mollusc**) any invertebrate of the phylum Mollusca, with a soft body and usu. a hard shell, including snails, cuttlefish, mussels, etc. □□ **mol·lus·kan** or **mol·lus·can** /məlúskən/ *n. & adj.*
mol·ly·cod·dle /móleekodəl/ *v. & n.* • *v.tr.* coddle; pamper. • *n.* an effeminate man or boy; a milksop.
Mo·lo·tov cock·tail /mólətawf/ *n.* a crude incendiary device usu. consisting of a bottle filled with flammable liquid.
molt /mōlt/ *v. & n.* • *v.* **1** *intr.* shed feathers, hair, a shell, etc., in the process of renewing plumage, a coat, etc. **2** *tr.* shed (feathers, hair, etc.). • *n.* the act or an instance of molting (*is in molt once a year*).
mol·ten /mṓltən/ *adj.* melted, esp. made liquid by heat (*molten lava*).
mol·to /mṓltō/ *adv. Mus.* very (*molto sostenuto*; *allegro molto*).
mo·lyb·de·num /məlíbdinəm/ *n. Chem.* a silver-white brittle metallic transition element occurring naturally in molybdenite and used in steel to give strength and resistance to corrosion. ¶ Symb.: **Mo**.
mom /mom/ *n. colloq.* mother.
mom-and-pop *adj.* of or pertaining to a small retail business, as a grocery store, owned and operated by members of a family.
mo·ment /mṓmənt/ *n.* **1** a very brief portion of time; an instant. **2** a short period of time (*wait a moment*) (see also MINUTE¹ 3). **3** an exact or particular point of time (*at last the moment arrived*). **4** importance (*of no great moment*). **5** *Physics & Mech.*, etc. **a** the turning effect produced by a force acting at a distance on an object. **b** this effect expressed as the product of the force and the distance from its line of action to a point. □ **at the moment** at this time; now. **in a moment 1** very soon. **2** instantly. **man** (or **woman**, etc.) **of the moment** the one of importance at the time in question. **not for a** (or **one**) **moment** never; not at all.
mo·men·ta *pl.* of MOMENTUM.
mo·men·tar·i·ly /mṓməntairilee/ *adv.* **1** for a moment. **2 a** at any moment. **b** instantly.

mo•men•tar•y /mṓmənteree/ *adj.* **1** lasting only a moment. **2** short-lived; transitory.
mo•ment of truth *n.* a time of crisis or test (orig. the final sword thrust in a bullfight).
mo•men•tous /mōméntəs/ *adj.* having great importance. ▫▫ **mo•men•tous•ly** *adv.* **mo•men•tous•ness** *n.*
mo•men•tum /mōméntəm/ *n.* (*pl.* **momenta** /–tə/) **1** *Physics* the quantity of motion of a moving body, measured as a product of its mass and velocity. **2** the impetus gained by movement. **3** strength or continuity derived from an initial effort.
mom•ma /mómə/ *n.* var. of MAMMA[1].
mom•my /mómee/ *n.* (*pl.* **-mies**) *colloq.* mother.
Mon. *abbr.* Monday.
mon•ad /mónad, mṓ–/ *n.* **1** the number one; a unit. **2** *Philos.* any ultimate unit of being (e.g., a soul, an atom, a person, God). **3** *Biol.* a simple organism, e.g., one assumed as the first in the genealogy of living beings. ▫▫ **mo•nad•ic** /mənádik/ *adj.*
mon•arch /mónərk, –aark/ *n.* **1** a sovereign with the title of king, queen, emperor, empress, or the equivalent. **2** a supreme ruler. **3** a powerful or preeminent person. **4** a large orange and black butterfly, *Danaus plexippus*. ▫▫ **mo•nar•chic** /mənaárkik/ *adj.* **mo•nar•chi•cal** /mənaárkikəl/ *adj.*
mon•ar•chism /mónərkizəm/ *n.* the advocacy of or the principles of monarchy. ▫▫ **mon•ar•chist** *n.*
mon•ar•chy /mónərkee/ *n.* (*pl.* **-chies**) **1** a form of government with a monarch at the head. **2** a nation with this. ▫▫ **mo•nar•chi•al** /monaárkeeəl/ *adj.*
mon•as•ter•y /mónəstéree/ *n.* (*pl.* **-ies**) the residence of a religious community, esp. of monks living in seclusion.
mo•nas•tic /mənástik/ *adj.* & *n.* • *adj.* **1** of or relating to monasteries or the religious communities living in them. **2** resembling these or their way of life; solitary and celibate. • *n.* a monk or other follower of a monastic rule. ▫▫ **mo•nas•ti•cal•ly** *adv.* **mo•nas•ti•cism** /–tisizəm/ *n.*
mon•a•tom•ic /mónətómik/ *adj. Chem.* **1** (esp. of a molecule) consisting of one atom. **2** having one replaceable atom or radical.
Mon•day /múnday, –dee/ *n.* & *adv.* • *n.* the second day of the week, following Sunday. • *adv. colloq.* **1** on Monday. **2** (**Mondays**) on Mondays; each Monday.
mon•e•ta•rism /mónitərizəm, mún–/ *n.* the theory or practice of controlling the supply of money as the chief method of stabilizing the economy. ▫▫ **mon•e•ta•rist** /mónitərist, mún–/ *n.* & *adj.*
mon•e•tar•y /móniteree, –mún/ *adj.* **1** of the currency in use. **2** of or consisting of money.
mon•ey /múnee/ *n.* **1 a** a current medium of exchange in the form of coins and paper currency. **b** a particular form of this (*silver money*). **2** (*pl.* **-eys** or **-ies**) (in *pl.*) sums of money. **3 a** wealth. **b** a rich person or family (*has married into money*). **4 a** money as a resource (*time is money*). **b** profit; remuneration (*in it for the money*). ▫ **for my money** in my opinion or judgment; for my preference (*is too aggressive for my money*). ▫▫ **mon•ey•less** *adj.*
mon•ey•bags /múneebagz/ *n.pl.* (treated as *sing.*) *colloq.* usu. *derog.* a wealthy person.
mon•eyed /múneed/ *adj.* **1** having much money; wealthy. **2** consisting of money (*moneyed assistance*).
mon•ey-grub•ber *n. colloq.* a person greedily intent on amassing money. ▫▫ **mon•ey-grub•bing** *n.* & *adj.*
mon•ey•lend•er /múneelendər/ *n.* a person who lends money, esp. as a business, at interest. ▫▫ **mon•ey•lend•ing** *n.* & *adj.*
mon•ey•mak•er /múneemaykər/ *n.* **1** a person who earns much money. **2** a thing, idea, etc., that produces much money. ▫▫ **mon•ey•mak•ing** *n.* & *adj.*
mon•ey mar•ket *n. Stock Exch.* trade in short-term stocks, loans, etc.
mon•ger /múnggər, móng–/ *n.* (usu. in *comb.*) usu. *derog.* a person who promotes or deals in something specified (*warmonger; scaremonger*).
Mon•gol /mónggəl, –gōl/ *adj.* & *n.* • *adj.* **1** of or relating to the Asian people now inhabiting Mongolia in Central Asia. **2** resembling this people, esp. in appearance. • *n.* a Mongolian.
Mon•go•li•an /monggṓleeən/ *n.* & *adj.* • *n.* **1** a native or inhabitant of Mongolia. **2** the language of Mongolia. • *adj.* of or relating to Mongolia or its people or language.
mon•gol•ism /mónggəlizəm/ *n.* often *offens.* = DOWN'S SYNDROME.
▶The term *Down's syndrome* is now preferred.
Mon•gol•oid /mónggəloyd/ *adj.* & *n.* • *adj.* **1** characteristic of the Mongolians, esp. in having a broad flat yellowish face. **2** (**mongoloid**) often *offens.* having the characteristic symptoms of Down's syndrome. • *n.* a Mongoloid or mongoloid person.
mon•goose /mónggōōs/ *n.* (*pl.* **mongooses** or **mongeese**) any of various African or Asian carnivorous civetlike mammals of the genus *Herpestes* and related genera, with a long body and tail and a grizzled or banded coat.
mon•grel /múnggrəl, móng–/ *n.* & *adj.* • *n.* **1** a dog of no definable type or breed. **2** any other animal or plant resulting from the crossing of different breeds or types. **3** *derog.* a person of mixed race. • *adj.* of mixed origin, nature, or character.
'mongst *poet.* var. of AMONG.
mon•ick•er var. of MONIKER.
mon•ies see MONEY 2.
mon•i•ker /mónikər/ *n.* (also **mon•ick•er**) *sl.* a name.
mon•i•tor /mónitər/ *n.* & *v.* • *n.* **1** any of various persons or devices for checking or warning about a situation, operation, etc. **2** a school pupil with disciplinary or other special duties. **3** a cathode-ray tube used as a television receiver or computer display device. **4** a person who listens to and reports on foreign broadcasts, etc. **5** a detector of radioactive contamination. **6** *Zool.* any tropical lizard of the genus *Varanus*, supposed to give warning of the approach of crocodiles. • *v.tr.* **1** act as a monitor of. **2** maintain regular surveillance over. **3** regulate the strength of (a recorded or transmitted signal). ▫▫ **mon•i•to•ri•al** /–táwreeəl/ *adj.*
monk /mungk/ *n.* a member of a religious community of men living under certain vows, esp. of poverty, chastity, and obedience. ▫▫ **monk•ish** *adj.*
mon•key /múngkee/ *n.* & *v.* • *n.* (*pl.* **-keys**) **1** any of various New World and Old World primates esp. of the families Cebidae, Callithricidae, and Cercopithecidae. **2** a mischievous person, esp. a child (*little monkey*). **3** (in full **monkey engine**) a machine hammer for pile driving, etc. • *v.* (**-keys, -keyed**) **1** *tr.* mimic or mock. **2** *intr.* (often foll. by *with*) tamper or play mischievous tricks. **3** *intr.* (foll. by *around, about*) fool around. ▫ **have a monkey on one's back 1** *sl.* have a drug addiction. **2** have a persistent problem or hindrance. **make a monkey of** humiliate by making appear ridiculous.
mon•key busi•ness *n. colloq.* mischief.
mon•key•shine /múngkeeshīn/ *n.* (usu. in *pl.*) *US colloq.* = MONKEY BUSINESS.
mon•key suit *n. colloq.* formal attire, esp. a tuxedo.
mon•key wrench *n.* a wrench with an adjustable jaw.
monk•fish /múnkfish/ *n.* (*pl.* same) **1** an anglerfish, esp.

Lophius piscatorius, often used as food. **2** a large cartilaginous fish, *Squatina squatina*, with a flattened body and large pectoral fins. Also called **angel shark**.

monks•hood /múngks-ho͝od/ *n. Bot.* a poisonous garden plant *Aconitum napellus*, with hood-shaped blue or purple flowers.

mon•o /mónō/ *n. colloq.* infectious mononucleosis.

mono- /mónō/ *comb. form* (usu. **mon-** before a vowel) **1** one; alone, single. **2** *Chem.* (forming names of compounds) containing one atom or group of a specified kind.

mon•o•chro•mat•ic /mónəkrəmátik/ *adj.* **1** *Physics* (of light or other radiation) of a single wavelength or frequency. **2** containing only one color. ▫▫ **mon•o•chro•mat•i•cal•ly** *adv.*

mon•o•chrome /mónəkrōm/ *n. & adj.* • *n.* a photograph or picture done in one color or different tones of this, or in black and white only. • *adj.* having or using only one color or in black and white only.

mon•o•cle /mónəkəl/ *n.* a single eyeglass. ▫▫ **mon•o•cled** *adj.*

mon•o•cline /mónōklīn/ *n. Geol.* a bend in rock strata that are otherwise uniformly dipping or horizontal. ▫▫ **mon•o•cli•nal** /–klīn'l/ *adj.*

mon•o•clin•ic /mónōklínik/ *adj.* (of a crystal) having one axial intersection oblique.

mo•no•clo•nal /mónōklṓnəl/ *adj.* forming a single clone; derived from a single individual or cell.

mon•o•cot /mónōkot, –kōt/ *n.* = MONOCOTYLEDON.

mon•o•cot•y•le•don /mónəkót'lḗd'n/ *n. Bot.* any flowering plant with a single cotyledon. ▫▫ **mon•o•cot•y•le•don•ous** *adj.*

mo•noc•u•lar /mənókyələr/ *adj.* with or for one eye. ▫▫ **mo•noc•u•lar•ly** *adv.*

mo•nog•a•my /mənógəmee/ *n.* **1** the practice or state of being married to one person at a time. **2** *Zool.* the habit of having only one mate at a time. ▫▫ **mo•nog•a•mist** *n.* **mo•nog•a•mous** *adj.* **mo•nog•a•mous•ly** *adv.*

mon•o•gen•e•sis /mónōjénisis/ *n.* (also **mon•og•en•y** /mənójinee/) **1** the theory of the development of all beings from a single cell. **2** the theory that mankind descended from one pair of ancestors. ▫▫ **mon•o•gen•e•tic** /–jinétik/ *adj.*

mon•o•glot /mónəglot/ *adj. & n.* • *adj.* using only one language. • *n.* a monoglot person.

mon•o•gram /mónəgram/ *n.* two or more letters, esp. a person's initials, interwoven as a device. ▫▫ **mon•o•grammed** *adj.*

mon•o•graph /mónəgraf/ *n. & v.* • *n.* a separate treatise on a single subject. • *v.tr.* write a monograph on. ▫▫ **mon•o•graph•ic** /mónəgráfik/ *adj.*

mon•o•hull /mónōhul/ *n.* a boat with a single hull.

mon•o•lin•gual /mónōlínggwəl/ *adj.* speaking or using only one language.

mon•o•lith /mónəlith/ *n.* **1** a single block of stone, esp. shaped into a pillar or monument. **2** a person or thing like a monolith in being massive, immovable, or solidly uniform. **3** a large block of concrete. ▫▫ **mon•o•lith•ic** /–líthik/ *adj.*

mon•o•logue /mónəlawg, –log/ *n.* **1 a** a scene in a drama in which a person speaks alone. **b** a dramatic or comedic composition for one performer. **2** a long speech by one person in a conversation, etc. ▫▫ **mon•o•log•ic** /–lójik/ *adj.* **mon•o•log•i•cal** /–lójikəl/ *adj.* **mon•o•log•ist** /mənóləjist/ *n.* (also **-loguist**).

mon•o•ma•ni•a /mónəmáyneeə/ *n.* obsession of the mind by one idea or interest. ▫▫ **mon•o•ma•ni•ac** *n. & adj.*

mon•o•mer /mónəmər/ *n. Chem.* **1** a molecule that can be bonded to other identical molecules to form a polymer. **2** a molecule or compound that can be polymerized. ▫▫ **mon•o•mer•ic** /–mérik/ *adj.*

mo•no•nu•cle•o•sis /mónōnṓokleeṓsis, -nyṓo–/ *n.* an abnormally high proportion of monocytes in the blood, esp. = *infectious mononucleosis.*

mo•nop•o•lize /mənópəlīz/ *v.tr.* **1** obtain exclusive possession or control of (a trade or commodity, etc.). **2** dominate or prevent others from sharing in (a conversation, person's attention, etc.). ▫▫ **mo•nop•o•li•za•tion** *n.*

mo•nop•o•ly /mənópəlee/ *n.* (*pl.* **-lies**) **1 a** the exclusive possession or control of the trade in a commodity or service. **b** this conferred as a privilege by the government. **2 a** a commodity or service that is subject to a monopoly. **b** a company, etc., that possesses a monopoly. **3** (foll. by *on*) exclusive possession, control, or exercise.

mon•o•rail /mónōrayl/ *n.* a railway in which the track consists of a single rail, usu. elevated with the cars suspended from it.

mon•o•sac•cha•ride /mónōsákərīd/ *n. Chem.* a sugar that cannot be hydrolyzed to give a simpler sugar, e.g., glucose.

mon•o•so•di•um glu•ta•mate /mónəsṓdiəm glṓotəmayt/ *n. Chem.* white crystalline powder used to flavor food ¶ Abbr.: **MSG**.

mon•o•syl•lab•ic /mónəsilábik/ *adj.* **1** (of a word) having one syllable. **2** (of a person or statement) using or expressed in monosyllables. ▫▫ **mon•o•syl•lab•i•cal•ly** *adv.*

mon•o•syl•la•ble /mónəsiləbəl/ *n.* a word of one syllable. ▫ **in monosyllables** in simple direct words.

mon•o•the•ism /mónəthēeizəm/ *n.* the doctrine that there is only one God. ▫▫ **mon•o•the•ist** *n.* **mon•o•the•is•tic** /–ístik/ *adj.*

mon•o•tone /mónətōn/ *n. & adj.* • *n.* **1** a sound or utterance continuing or repeated on one note without change of pitch. **2** sameness of style in writing. • *adj.* without change of pitch.

mo•not•o•nous /mənót'nəs/ *adj.* **1** lacking in variety; tedious through sameness. **2** (of a sound or utterance) without variation in tone or pitch. ▫▫ **mo•not•o•nous•ly** *adv.*

mo•not•o•ny /mənót'nee/ *n.* **1** the state of being monotonous. **2** dull or tedious routine.

mon•ox•ide /mənóksīd/ *n. Chem.* an oxide containing one oxygen atom (*carbon monoxide*).

Mon•roe doc•trine /munrṓ/ *n.* the US policy of objecting to intervention by European powers in the affairs of the Western Hemisphere.

Mon•sei•gneur /máwnsenyṓr/ *n.* (*pl.* **Messeigneurs** /mésenyṓr/) a title given to an eminent French person, esp. a prince, cardinal, archbishop, or bishop.

Mon•sieur /məsyṓ/ *n.* (*pl.* **Messieurs** /mesyṓ/) **1** the title or form of address used of or to a French-speaking man, corresponding to Mr. or sir. **2** a Frenchman.

Mon•si•gnor /monsēenyər/ *n.* (*pl.* **Monsignors** or **Monsignori** /–nyáwree/) the title of various Roman Catholic prelates, officers of the papal court, etc.

mon•soon /monsṓon, món–/ *n.* **1** a wind in S. Asia, esp. in the Indian Ocean, blowing from the southwest in summer (**wet monsoon**) and the northeast in winter (**dry monsoon**). **2** a rainy season accompanying a wet monsoon. **3** any other wind with periodic alternations.

mons pubis /monz pyṓobis/ *n.* a rounded mass of fatty tissue lying over the joint of the pubic bones.

mon•ster /mónstər/ *n.* **1** an imaginary creature, usu. large or frightening, combining both human and animal features. **2** an inhumanly cruel or wicked person. **3** a misshapen animal or plant. **4** a large hideous animal or thing (e.g., a building). **5** (*attrib.*) huge; extremely large of its kind.

mon·strance /mónstrəns/ *n. RC Ch.* a vessel in which the consecrated Host is displayed for veneration.

mon·stros·i·ty /monstrósitee/ *n.* (*pl.* **-ties**) **1** a huge or outrageous thing. **2** monstrousness. **3** = MONSTER 3.

mon·strous /mónstrəs/ *adj.* **1** like a monster; abnormally formed. **2** huge. **3 a** outrageously wrong or absurd. **b** atrocious. ▫▫ **mon·strous·ly** *adv.* **mon·strous·ness** *n.*

Mont. *abbr.* Montana.

mon·tage /montaázh, mawN–/ *n.* **1 a** a process of selecting, editing, and piecing together separate sections of movie or television film to form a continuous whole. **b** a sequence of such film as a section of a longer film. **2 a** the technique of producing a new composite whole from fragments of pictures, words, music, etc. **b** a composition produced in this way.

mon·tane /móntayn/ *adj.* of or inhabiting mountainous country.

month /munth/ *n.* **1** (in full **calendar month**) **a** each of usu. twelve periods into which a year is divided. **b** a period of time between the same dates in successive calendar months. **2** a period of 28 days or of four weeks. **3** = LUNAR MONTH.

month·ly /múnthlee/ *adj., adv., & n.* • *adj.* done, produced, or occurring once a month. • *adv.* once a month; from month to month. • *n.* (*pl.* **-lies**) **1** a monthly periodical. **2** (in *pl.*) *colloq.* a menstrual period.

mon·u·ment /mónyəmənt/ *n.* **1** anything enduring that serves to commemorate or make celebrated, esp. a structure or building. **2** a stone or other structure placed over a grave or in a church, etc., in memory of the dead. **3** an ancient building or site, etc., that has been preserved. **4** (foll. by *of, to*) a typical or outstanding example (*a monument of indiscretion*). **5** a written record.

mon·u·men·tal /mónyəmént'l/ *adj.* **1 a** extremely great; stupendous (*a monumental achievement*). **b** (of a literary work) massive and permanent. **2** of or serving as a monument. **3** *colloq.* (as an intensifier) very great; calamitous (*a monumental blunder*). ▫▫ **mon·u·men·tal·i·ty** /–tálitee/ *n.* **mon·u·men·tal·ly** *adv.*

-mony /mōnee/ *suffix* forming nouns, esp. denoting an abstract state or quality (*acrimony*; *testimony*).

moo /moo/ *v. & n.* • *v.intr.* (**moos, mooed**) make the characteristic vocal sound of cattle. • *n.* (*pl.* **moos**) this sound.

mooch /mooch/ *v. colloq.* **1** borrow (an item, service, etc.) with no intention of making repayment. **2** beg. **3** steal. **4** sneak around; skulk. **5** *intr.* loiter or saunter desultorily. ▫▫ **mooch·er** *n.*

mood[1] /mood/ *n.* **1** a state of mind or feeling. **2** (in *pl.*) fits of melancholy or bad temper. **3** (*attrib.*) inducing a particular mood (*mood music*). ▫ **in the** (or **no**) **mood** (foll. by *for*, or *to* + infin.) inclined (or disinclined) (*was in no mood to agree*).

mood[2] /mood/ *n.* **1** *Gram.* a form or set of forms of a verb serving to indicate whether it is to express fact, command, wish, etc. (*subjunctive mood*). **2** the distinction of meaning expressed by different moods.

mood·swing /moódswing/ *n.* a marked change in temperament, as from euphoria to depression.

mood·y /moódee/ *adj. & n.* • *adj.* (**moodier, moodiest**) given to changes of mood; gloomy, sullen. • *n. colloq.* a bad mood; a tantrum. ▫▫ **mood·i·ly** *adv.* **mood·i·ness** *n.*

moon /moon/ *n. & v.* • *n.* **1 a** the natural satellite of the earth, orbiting it monthly, illuminated by the sun and reflecting some light to the earth. **b** this regarded in terms of its waxing and waning in a particular month (*new moon*). **c** the moon when visible (*there is no moon tonight*). **2** a satellite of any planet. **3** (prec. by *the*) something desirable but unattainable (*promised them the moon*). **4** *poet.* a month. • *v.* **1** *intr.* (often foll. by *about, around,* etc.) move or look listlessly. **2** *tr.* (foll. by *away*) spend (time) in a listless manner. **3** *intr.* (foll. by *over*) act aimlessly or inattentively from infatuation for (a person). **4** *tr. sl.* expose one's naked buttocks publicly as a joke, sign of disrespect, etc. ▫▫ **moon·less** *adj.*

moon Old English *mōna*, of Germanic origin; related to Dutch *maan* and German *Mond*, also to *month*, from an Indo-European root shared by Latin *mensis* and Greek *mēn* 'month,' and also Latin *metiri* 'to measure' (the moon being used since prehistory to measure time).

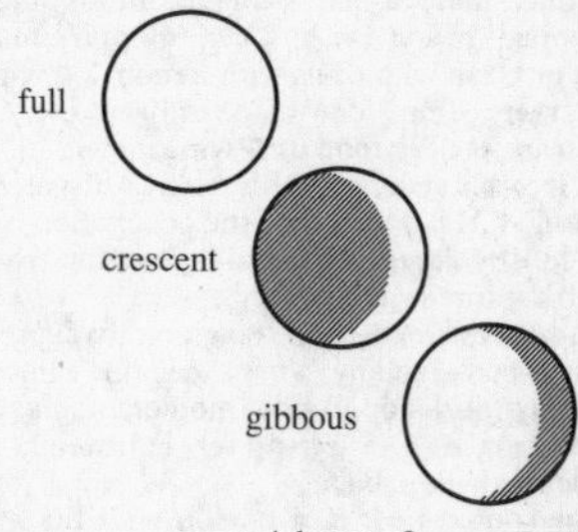

moon (phases of)

moon·beam /moónbeem/ *n.* a ray of moonlight.

moon-faced *adj.* having a round face.

moon·light /moónlīt/ *n. & v.* • *n.* **1** the light of the moon. **2** (*attrib.*) lighted by the moon. • *v.intr.* (**-lighted**) *colloq.* have two paid occupations, esp. one by day and one by night. ▫▫ **moon·light·er** *n.*

moon·lit /moónlit/ *adj.* lighted by the moon.

moon·scape /moónskayp/ *n.* **1** the surface or landscape of the moon. **2** an area resembling this; a wasteland.

moon·set /moónset/ *n.* **1** the setting of the moon. **2** the time of this.

moon·shine /moónshīn/ *n.* **1** foolish or unrealistic talk or ideas. **2** *sl.* illicitly distilled or smuggled alcoholic liquor. **3** moonlight.

moon·shin·er /moónshīnər/ *n. sl.* an illicit distiller or smuggler of alcoholic liquor.

moon·shot /moónshot/ *n.* the launching of a spacecraft to the moon.

moon·stone /moónstōn/ *n.* feldspar of pearly appearance.

moon·struck /moónstruk/ *adj.* **1** mentally deranged. **2** romantically distracted.

moon·y /moónee/ *adj.* (**moonier, mooniest**) **1** listless; stupidly dreamy. **2** of or like the moon.

Moor /moor/ *n.* a member of a Muslim people of mixed Berber and Arab descent, inhabiting NW Africa. ▫▫ **Moor·ish** *adj.*

moor[1] /moor/ *n.* **1** a tract of open uncultivated upland, esp. when covered with heather. **2** a tract of ground preserved for shooting. **3** a marsh.

moor[2] /moor/ *v.* **1** *tr.* make fast (a boat, buoy, etc.) by attaching a cable, etc., to a fixed object. **2** *intr.* (of a boat) be moored.

moor·ing /mooring/ *n.* **1 a** a fixed object to which a boat, buoy, etc., is moored. **b** (often in *pl.*) a place where a boat, etc., is moored. **2** (in *pl.*) a set of permanent anchors and chains laid down for ships to be moored to.

Moor·ish /mŏŏrish/ *adj.* of or relating to the Moors.

moor·land /mŏŏrlənd/ *n.* an extensive area of moor.

moose /mōōs/ *n.* (*pl.* same) largest variety of N. American deer.

moot /mōōt/ *adj., v., & n.* • *adj.* (orig. the noun used *attrib.*) **1** debatable; undecided (*a moot point*). **2** *Law* having no practical significance. • *v.tr.* raise (a question) for discussion. • *n.* **1** *hist.* an assembly. **2** *Law* a discussion of a hypothetical case as an academic exercise.

mop /mop/ *n. & v.* • *n.* **1** a wad or bundle of cotton or synthetic material fastened to the end of a stick, for cleaning floors, etc. **2** a similarly shaped implement for various purposes. **3** anything resembling a mop, esp. a thick mass of hair. **4** an act of mopping or being mopped (*gave it a mop*). • *v.tr.* (**mopped, mopping**) **1** wipe or clean with or as with a mop. **2 a** wipe tears or sweat, etc., from (one's face or brow, etc.). **b** wipe away (tears, etc.). □ **mop up 1** wipe up with or as with a mop. **2** *colloq.* absorb (profits, etc.). **3** dispatch; make an end of. **4** *Mil.* **a** complete the occupation of (a district, etc.) by capturing or killing enemy troops left there. **b** capture or kill (stragglers).

mope /mōp/ *v. & n.* • *v.intr.* be gloomily depressed or listless; behave sulkily. • *n.* a person who mopes. □□ **mop·ey** (also **mop·y**) *adj.* (**mopier, mopiest**)

mo·ped /mṓped/ *n.* a low-power, lightweight motorized bicycle with pedals.

mop·head /móp-hed/ *n.* a person with thick matted hair.

mop·pet /mópit/ *n. colloq.* (esp. as a term of endearment) a baby or small child.

mo·raine /məráyn/ *n.* an area covered by rocks and debris carried down and deposited by a glacier. □□ **mo·rain·ic** *adj.*

mor·al /máwrəl, mór–/ *adj. & n.* • *adj.* **1 a** concerned with goodness or badness of human character or behavior, or with the distinction between right and wrong. **b** concerned with accepted rules and standards of human behavior. **2 a** conforming to accepted standards of general conduct. **b** capable of moral action (*man is a moral agent*). **3** (of rights or duties, etc.) founded on moral law. **4 a** concerned with morals or ethics (*moral philosophy*). **b** (of a literary work, etc.) dealing with moral conduct. **5** concerned with or leading to a psychological effect associated with confidence in a right action (*moral support*; *moral victory*). • *n.* **1 a** a moral lesson of a fable, story, event, etc. **b** a moral maxim or principle. **2** (in *pl.*) moral behavior. □□ **mor·al·ly** *adv.*

moral late Middle English: from Latin *moralis*, from *mos, mor-* 'custom,' (plural) *mores* 'morals.' As a noun the word was first used to translate Latin *Moralia*, the title of St. Gregory the Great's moral exposition of the biblical Book of Job, and was subsequently applied to the works of various classical writers.

mo·rale /mərál/ *n.* the mental attitude or bearing of a person or group, esp. as regards confidence, discipline, etc.

mor·al·ism /máwrəlizəm, mór–/ *n.* **1** a natural system of morality. **2** religion regarded as moral practice.

mor·al·ist /máwrəlist, mór–/ *n.* **1** a person who practices or teaches morality. **2** a person who follows a natural system of ethics. □□ **mor·al·is·tic** /–lístik/ *adj.*

mo·ral·i·ty /mərálitee/ *n.* (*pl.* **-ties**) **1** the degree of conformity of an idea, practice, etc., to moral principles. **2** right moral conduct. **3** a lesson in morals. **4** the science of morals. **5** a particular system of morals *commercial morality*). **6** (in *pl.*) moral principles; points of ethics.

mo·ral·i·ty play *n. hist.* a kind of drama with personified abstract qualities as the main characters and inculcating a lesson about good conduct and moral character, popular in the 15th and 16th centuries.

mor·al·ize /máwrəlīz, mór–/ *v.* **1** *intr.* (often foll. by *on*) indulge in moral reflection or talk. **2** *tr.* interpret morally; point the moral of. **3** *tr.* make moral or more moral. □□ **mor·al·i·za·tion** *n.* **mor·al·iz·er** *n.*

mo·rass /mərás/ *n.* **1** an entanglement; a disordered situation, esp. one impeding progress. **2** *literary* a bog or marsh.

mor·a·to·ri·um /máwrətáwreeəm, mór–/ *n.* (*pl.* **moratoriums** or **moratoria** /–reeə/) **1** (often foll. by *on*) a temporary prohibition or suspension (of an activity). **2 a** a legal authorization to debtors to postpone payment. **b** the period of this postponement.

Mo·ra·vi·an /məráyveeən/ *n. & adj.* • *n.* **1** a native of Moravia, a region that is now part of the Czech Republic. **2** a member of a Protestant sect founded in Saxony by emigrants from Moravia, holding views derived from the Hussites and accepting the Bible as the only source of faith. • *adj.* of or relating to Moravia or its people.

mo·ray /máwray/ *n.* any tropical eellike fish of the family Muraenidae, esp. *Muraena helena* found in Mediterranean waters.

mor·bid /máwrbid/ *adj.* **1 a** (of the mind, ideas, etc.) unwholesome. **b** given to morbid feelings. **2** *colloq.* melancholy. **3** *Med.* of the nature of or indicative of disease. □□ **mor·bid·i·ty** /–bíditee/ *n.* **mor·bid·ly** *adv.*

mor·dant /máwrd'nt/ *adj. & n.* • *adj.* **1** (of sarcasm, etc.) caustic; biting. **2** pungent; smarting. **3** corrosive; cleansing. **4** (of a substance) serving to fix coloring matter or gold leaf on another substance. • *n.* a mordant substance (in senses 3 and 4 of *adj.*). □□ **mor·dant·ly** *adv.*

mor·dent /máwrd'nt/ *n. Mus.* an ornament consisting of one rapid alternation of a written note with the note immediately below or above it.

more /mawr/ *adj., n., & adv.* • *adj.* **1** existing in a greater or additional quantity, amount, or degree (*more problems than last time*; *bring some more water*). **2** greater in degree (*more's the pity*; *the more fool you*). • *n.* a greater quantity, number, or amount (*more than three people*; *more to it than meets the eye*). • *adv.* **1** in a greater degree (*do it more carefully*). **2** to a greater extent (*people like to walk more these days*). **3** forming the comparative of adjectives and adverbs, esp. those of more than one syllable (*more absurd*; *more easily*). **4** again (*once more*; *never more*). **5** moreover. □ **more and more** in an increasing degree. **more of** to a greater extent (*more of a poet than a musician*). **more or less 1** in a greater or less degree. **2** approximately; as an estimate. **more so** of the same kind to a greater degree.

mo·rel /mərél/ *n.* an edible fungus of the genus *Morchella*, esp. *M. esculenta*, with ridged mushroom caps.

more·o·ver /máwrṓvər/ *adv.* (introducing or accompanying a new statement) further; besides.

mo·res /máwrayz, –reez/ *n.pl.* customs or conventions regarded as characteristic of a community.

morgue /mawrg/ *n.* **1** a mortuary. **2** (in a newspaper office) a room or file of miscellaneous information, esp. for future obituaries.

mor·i·bund /máwribund, mór–/ *adj.* **1** at the point of death. **2** lacking vitality. **3** on the decline; stagnant.

Mor·mon /máwrmən/ *n.* a member of the Church of Jesus Christ of Latter-day Saints, a religion founded in 1830 by Joseph Smith on the basis of revelations in the Book of Mormon. □□ **Mor·mon·ism** *n.*

morn /mawrn/ *n. poet.* morning.

mor·nay /mawrnáy/ *n.* a cheese-flavored white sauce.

morn·ing /mawrning/ *n.* & *int.* • *n.* **1** the early part of the day, esp. from sunrise to noon (*this morning*; *during the morning*; *morning coffee*). **2** this time spent in a particular way (*had a busy morning*). **3** sunrise; daybreak. **4** a time compared with the morning, esp. the early part of one's life, etc. • *int.* = *good morning* (see GOOD *adj.* 14). □ **in the morning 1** during or in the course of the morning. **2** *colloq.* tomorrow.

morn·ing glo·ry *n.* any of various twining plants of the genus *Ipomoea*, with trumpet-shaped flowers.

morn·ing sick·ness *n.* nausea felt in the morning in pregnancy.

morn·ing star *n.* a planet or bright star, usu. Venus, seen in the east before sunrise.

Mo·roc·can /mərókən/ *n.* & *adj.* • *n.* **1** a native or national of Morocco in N. Africa. **2** a person of Moroccan descent. • *adj.* of or relating to Morocco.

mo·roc·co /mərókō/ *n.* (*pl.* **-cos**) **1** a fine flexible leather made from goatskins tanned with sumac. **2** an imitation of this in grained calf, etc.

mo·ron /máwron/ *n.* **1** *colloq.* a very stupid person. **2** an adult with a mental age of about 8–12. □□ **mo·ron·ic** /mərónik/ *adj.* **mo·ron·i·cal·ly** /məróniklee/ *adv.*

mo·rose /mərṓs/ *adj.* sullen and ill-tempered. □□ **mo·rose·ly** *adv.* **mo·rose·ness** *n.*

mor·pheme /máwrfeem/ *n.* *Linguistics* **1** a morphological element considered in respect of its functional relations in a linguistic system. **2** a meaningful morphological unit of a language that cannot be further divided (e.g., *in*, *come*, *-ing*, forming *incoming*). □□ **mor·phe·mic** /–féemik/ *adj.*

mor·phine /máwrfeen/ *n.* a narcotic drug obtained from opium and used to relieve pain.

mor·phol·o·gy /mawrfóləjee/ *n.* the study of the forms of things, esp.: **1** *Biol.* the study of the forms of organisms. **2** *Philol.* **a** the study of the forms of words. **b** the system of forms in a language. □□ **mor·pho·log·i·cal** /mawrfəlójikəl/ *adj.* **mor·pho·log·i·cal·ly** /–fəlójiklee/ *adv.* **mor·phol·o·gist** *n.*

mor·row /máwrō, mór–/ *n.* (usu. prec. by *the*) *literary* **1** the following day. **2** the time following an event.

Morse /mawrs/ *n.* & *v.* • *n.* (in full **Morse code**) a code in which letters are represented by combinations of long and short light or sound signals. • *v.tr.* & *intr.* signal by Morse code.

mor·sel /máwrsəl/ *n.* a mouthful; a small piece (esp. of food).

mor·tal /mawrt'l/ *adj.* & *n.* • *adj.* **1 a** subject to death. **b** (of material or earthly existence) temporal; ephemeral. **2** (often foll. by *to*) causing death; fatal. **3** (of a battle) fought to the death. **4** associated with death (*mortal agony*). **5** (of an enemy) implacable. **6** (of pain, fear, an affront, etc.) intense; very serious. **7** *colloq.* **a** very great (*in a mortal hurry*). **b** long and tedious (*for two mortal hours*). **8** *colloq.* conceivable; imaginable (*every mortal thing*; *of no mortal use*). • *n.* **1** a mortal being, esp. a human. **2** *joc.* a person described in some specified way (*a thirsty mortal*). □□ **mor·tal·ly** *adv.*

mor·tal·i·ty /mawrtálitee/ *n.* (*pl.* **-ties**) **1** the state of being subject to death. **2** loss of life on a large scale. **3 a** the number of deaths in a given period, etc. **b** (in full **mortality rate**) a death rate.

mor·tal sin *n.* *Theol.* a sin that is regarded as depriving the soul of divine grace.

mor·tar /máwrtər/ *n.* & *v.* • *n.* **1** a mixture of lime with cement, sand, and water, used in building to bond bricks or stones. **2** a short large-bore cannon for firing shells at high angles. **3** a contrivance for firing a lifeline or firework. **4** a vessel made of hard material, in which ingredients are pounded with a pestle. • *v.tr.* **1** plaster or join with mortar. **2** attack or bombard with mortar shells.

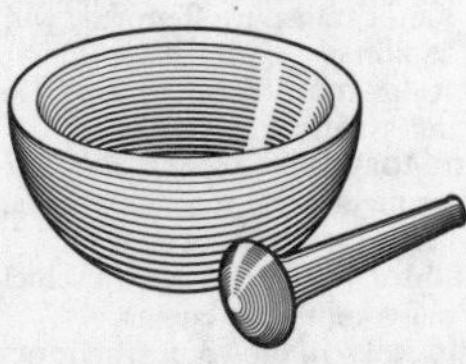
mortar, 4 with pestle

mor·tar·board /máwrtərbawrd/ *n.* **1** an academic cap with a stiff, flat square top. **2** a flat board with a handle on the undersurface, for holding mortar in bricklaying, etc.

mort·gage /máwrgij/ *n.* & *v.* • *n.* **1 a** a conveyance of property by a debtor to a creditor as security for a debt (esp. one incurred by the purchase of the property). **b** a deed effecting this. **2 a** a debt secured by a mortgage. **b** a loan resulting in such a debt. • *v.tr.* **1** convey (a property) by mortgage. **2** (often foll. by *to*) pledge (oneself, one's powers, etc.).

mort·ga·gee /máwrgijée/ *n.* the creditor in a mortgage.

mort·ga·gor /máwrgijər/ *n.* (also **mort·ga·ger** /–jər/) the debtor in a mortgage.

mor·tice var. of MORTISE.

mor·ti·cian /mawrtíshən/ *n.* an undertaker.

mor·ti·fy /máwrtifī/ *v.* (**-fies, -fied**) **1** *tr.* **a** cause (a person) to feel shamed or humiliated. **b** wound (a person's feelings). **2** *tr.* bring (the body, the flesh, the passions, etc.) into subjection by self-denial or discipline. **3** *intr.* (of flesh) be affected by gangrene or necrosis. □□ **mor·ti·fi·ca·tion** /–fikáyshən/ *n.* **mor·ti·fy·ing** *adj.* **mor·ti·fy·ing·ly** *adv.*

mor·tise /máwrtis/ *n.* & *v.* (also **mor·tice**) • *n.* a hole in a framework designed to receive the end of another part, esp. a tenon. • *v.tr.* **1** join securely, esp. by mortise and tenon. **2** cut a mortise in.

mor·tise lock *n.* a lock recessed into the frame of a door or window, etc.

mor·tu·ar·y /máwrchōō-eree/ *n.* & *adj.* • *n.* (*pl.* **-ies**) a room or building in which dead bodies may be kept until burial or cremation. • *adj.* of or concerning death or burial.

mo·sa·ic /mōzáyik/ *n.* & *v.* • *n.* **1 a** a picture or pattern produced by an arrangement of small variously colored pieces of glass or stone, etc. **b** work of this kind as an art form. **2** a diversified thing. **3** an arrangement of photosensitive elements in a television camera. **4** (in full **mosaic disease**) a virus disease causing leaf-mottling in plants. **5** (*attrib.*) **a** of or like a mosaic. **b** diversified. • *v.tr.* (**mosaicked, mosaicking**) **1** adorn with mosaics. **2** combine into or as into a mosaic. □□ **mo·sa·i·cist** /–záyisist/ *n.*

mo·sey /mṓzee/ *v.intr.* (**-seys, -seyed**) (often foll. by *along*) *sl.* walk in a leisurely manner.

Mos·lem var. of MUSLIM.
▶See note at MUSLIM.

mosque /mosk/ *n.* a Muslim place of worship.

mos·qui·to /məskéetō/ *n.* (*pl.* **-toes** or **-tos**) any of various slender biting insects, esp. of the genus *Culex*, *Anopheles*, or *Aedes*, the female of which punctures the skin of humans and other animals with a long proboscis to suck their blood and transmits diseases such as filariasis and malaria.

moss /maws/ *n.* & *v.* • *n.* any small cryptogamous plant of the class Musci, growing in dense clusters on the surface of the ground, in bogs, on trees, stones, etc. • *v.tr.* cover with moss. Also **von mot**.

moss·y /máwsee/ *adj.* (**mossier, mossiest**) **1** covered in or resembling moss. **2** *sl.* antiquated; old-fashioned.

most /mōst/ *adj.*, *n.*, & *adv.* • *adj.* **1** existing in the greatest quantity or degree (*see who can make the most noise*). **2** the majority of; nearly all of (*most people think so*).

•*n.* **1** the greatest quantity or number (*this is the most I can do*). **2** (**the most**) *sl.* the best of all. **3** the majority (*most of them are missing*). • *adv.* **1** in the highest degree (*this is most interesting; what most annoys me*). **2** forming the superlative of adjectives and adverbs, esp. those of more than one syllable (*most certain; most easily*). **3** *colloq.* almost. □ **at most** no more or better than (*this is at most a makeshift*). **at the most 1** as the greatest amount. **2** not more than. **for the most part 1** as regards the greater part. **2** usually. **make the most of 1** employ to the best advantage. **2** represent at its best or worst.

-most /mōst/ *suffix* forming superlative adjectives and adverbs from prepositions and other words indicating relative position (*foremost; uttermost*).

most·ly /mṓstlee/ *adv.* **1** as regards the greater part. **2** usually.

mot /mō/ *n.* (*pl.* **mots** *pronunc.* same) a witty saying.

mote /mōt/ *n.* a speck of dust.

mo·tel /mōtél/ *n.* a roadside hotel for motorists.

mo·tet /mōtét/ *n. Mus.* a short sacred choral composition.

moth /mawth, moth–/ *n.* **1** any usu. nocturnal insect of the order Lepidoptera excluding butterflies, having a stout body and without clubbed antennae. **2** any small lepidopterous insect of the family Tineidae breeding in cloth, etc., on which its larva feeds.

moth·ball /máwthbawl, móth–/ *n. & v.* •*n.* a ball of naphthalene, etc. placed in stored clothes to keep away moths. • *v.tr.* **1** place in mothballs. **2** leave unused. □ **in mothballs** stored unused for a considerable time.

moth-eat·en *adj.* **1** damaged by moths. **2** timeworn.

moth·er /mú<u>th</u>ər/ *n. & v.* •*n.* **1 a** a woman in relation to a child to whom she has given birth. **b** (in full **adoptive mother**) a woman who has continuous care of a child, esp. by adoption. **2** any female animal in relation to its offspring. **3** a quality or condition, etc., that gives rise to another (*necessity is the mother of invention*). **4** (in full **Mother Superior**) the head of a female religious community. **5** (*attrib.*) **a** designating an institution, etc., regarded as having maternal authority (*Mother Church; mother earth*). **b** designating the main ship, spacecraft, etc., in a convoy or mission (*the mother craft*). • *v.tr.* **1** give birth to; be the mother of. **2** protect as a mother. **3** give rise to; be the source of. **4** acknowledge or profess oneself the mother of. □□ **moth·er·hood** /–hood/ *n.* **moth·er·less** *adj.*

moth·er·board /mú<u>th</u>ərbawrd/ *n.* a computer's main circuit board, into which other boards can be plugged or wired.

moth·er coun·try *n.* a country in relation to its colonies.

Moth·er Goose *n.* the fictitious author of a collection of nursery rhymes published in 1781.

moth·er-in-law *n.* (*pl.* **mothers-in-law**) the mother of one's husband or wife.

moth·er·land /mú<u>th</u>ərland/ *n.* one's native country.

moth·er lode *n. Mining* the main vein of a system.

moth·er·ly /mú<u>th</u>ərlee/ *adj.* **1** like or characteristic of a mother in affection, care, etc. **2** of or relating to a mother. □□ **moth·er·li·ness** *n.*

moth·er-of-pearl *n.* a smooth iridescent substance forming the inner layer of the shell of some mollusks.

Moth·er's Day *n.* the second Sunday in May, traditionally a day for honoring mothers.

Moth·er Su·pe·ri·or see MOTHER *n.* 4.

moth·er tongue *n.* **1** one's native language. **2** a language from which others have evolved.

moth·proof /máwthproof, móth–/ *adj. & v.* • *adj.* (of clothes) treated so as to repel moths. •*v.tr.* treat (clothes) in this way.

mo·tif /mōtéef/ *n.* **1** a distinctive feature or dominant idea in artistic or literary composition. **2** *Mus.* = FIGURE *n.* 10. **3** an ornament of lace, etc., sewn separately on a garment.

mo·tile /mōt'l, –tīl, –til/ *adj. Zool. & Bot.* capable of motion. □□ **mo·til·i·ty** /–tílitee/ *n.*

mo·tion /mṓshən/ *n. & v.* •*n.* **1** the act or process of moving or of changing position. **2** a particular manner of moving the body in walking, etc. **3** a change of posture. **4** a gesture. **5** a formal proposal put to a committee, legislature, etc. **6** *Law* an application for a rule or order of court. **7** a piece of moving mechanism. • *v.* (often foll. by *to* + infin.) **1** *tr.* direct (a person) by a sign or gesture. **2** *intr.* (often foll. by *to* + a person) make a gesture directing (*motioned to me to leave*). □ **go through the motions 1** do something perfunctorily or superficially. **2** simulate an action by gestures. **in motion** moving; not at rest. **put** (or **set**) **in motion** set going or working. □□ **mo·tion·less** *adj.*

mo·tion pic·ture *n.* (often (with hyphen) *attrib.*) a film or movie with the illusion of movement (see FILM *n.* 3).

mo·ti·vate /mṓtivayt/ *v.tr.* **1** supply a motive to; be the motive of. **2** cause (a person) to act in a particular way. **3** stimulate the interest of (a person in an activity). □□ **mo·ti·va·tion** /–váyshən/ *n.* **mo·ti·va·tion·al** /–váyshənəl/ *adj.*

mo·tive /mṓtiv/ *n., adj., & v.* •*n.* **1** a factor or circumstance that induces a person to act in a particular way. **2** = MOTIF. • *adj.* **1** tending to initiate movement. **2** concerned with movement. • *v.tr.* = MOTIVATE. □□ **mo·tive·less** *adj.*

mot·ley /mótlee/ *adj. & n.* • *adj.* (**motlier, motliest**) **1** diversified in color. **2** of varied character (*a motley crew*). •*n.* **1** an incongruous mixture. **2** *hist.* the parti-colored costume of a jester. □ **wear motley** play the fool.

mo·to·cross /mṓtōkraws, –kros/ *n.* cross-country racing on motorcycles.

mo·tor /mṓtər/ *n. & adj.* •*n.* **1** a thing that imparts motion. **2** a machine supplying motive power for a vehicle, etc., or for some other device with moving parts. • *adj.* **1** giving, imparting, or producing motion. **2** driven by a motor. **3** of or for motor vehicles. **4** *Anat.* relating to muscular movement or the nerves activating it.

▶See note at ENGINE.

mo·tor·bike /mṓtərbīk/ *n.* **1** lightweight motorcyle. **2** motorized bicycle.

mo·tor·boat /mṓtərbōt/ *n. & v.* •*n.* a motor-driven boat. • *v.intr.* travel by motorboat.

mo·tor·bus /mṓtərbus/ *n.* = BUS 1.

mo·tor·cade /mṓtərkayd/ *n.* a procession of motor vehicles.

mo·tor·car /mṓtərkaar/ *n.* esp. *Brit.* see CAR 1.

mo·tor·cy·cle /mṓtərsīkəl/ *n.* two-wheeled motor-driven road vehicle without pedal propulsion. □□ **mo·tor·cy·clist** *n.*

mo·tor home *n.* a vehicle built on a truck frame that includes kitchen facilities, beds, etc. (see also TRAILER, MOBILE HOME).

mo·tor·ist /mṓtərist/ *n.* the driver or passenger of an automobile.

mo·tor·ize /mṓtərīz/ *v.tr.* **1** equip (troops, etc.) with motor transport. **2** provide with a motor. □□ **mo·tor·i·za·tion** *n.*

mo·tor·mouth /mṓtərmówth/ *n. sl.* a person who talks incessantly and trivially.

mo·tor pool *n.* a group of vehicles maintained by a government agency, military installation, etc., for use by personnel as needed.

mo·tor ve·hi·cle *n.* a road vehicle powered by an internal-combustion engine.

Mo·town /mṓtown/ *n.* a style of rhythm and blues music, popularized by Motown Records Corp.

mot·tle /mót'l/ *v. & n.* • *v.tr.* (esp. as **mottled** *adj.*) mark with spots or smears of color. • *n.* **1** an irregular arrangement of spots or patches of color. **2** any of these spots or patches.

mot·to /mótō/ *n.* (*pl.* **-toes** or **-tos**) **1** a maxim adopted as a rule of conduct. **2** a phrase or sentence accompanying a coat of arms. **3** a sentence inscribed on some object and expressing an appropriate sentiment. **4** quotation prefixed to a book or chapter.

moue /mōō/ *n.* = POUT *n.*

mould *Brit.* var. of MOLD[1], MOLD[2], MOLD[3].

mound /mownd/ *n. & v.* • *n.* **1** a raised mass of earth, stones, or other compacted material. **2** a heap or pile. **3** a hillock. • *v.tr.* **1** heap up in a mound or mounds. **2** enclose with mounds.

mount[1] /mownt/ *v. & n.* • *v.* **1** *tr.* ascend or climb. **2** *tr.* **a** get up on (an animal) to ride it. **b** set (a person) on horseback. **c** provide (a person) with a horse. **d** (as **mounted** *adj.*) serving on horseback (*mounted police*). **3** *tr.* go up or climb on to (a raised surface). **4** *intr.* **a** move upward. **b** (often foll. by *up*) increase; accumulate. **c** (of a feeling) become stronger or more intense (*excitement was mounting*). **d** (of the blood) rise into the cheeks. **5** *tr.* (esp. of a male animal) get on to (a female) to copulate. **6** *tr.* (often foll. by *on*) place (an object) on an elevated support. **7** *tr.* **a** set in or attach to a backing, setting, or other support. **b** attach (a picture, etc.) to a mount or frame. **c** fix (an object for viewing) on a microscope slide. **8** *tr.* **a** arrange (a play, exhibition, etc.) or present for public view or display. **b** take action to initiate (a program, campaign, etc.). **9** *tr.* prepare (specimens) for preservation. **10** *tr.* **a** bring into readiness for operation. **b** raise (guns) into position on a fixed mounting. **11** *intr.* rise to a higher level of rank, power, etc. • *n.* **1** a backing or setting on which a picture, etc., is set for display. **2** the margin surrounding a picture or photograph. **3 a** a horse available for riding. **b** an opportunity to ride a horse, esp. as a jockey. ▫▫ **mount·a·ble** *adj.*

mount[2] /mownt/ *n. archaic* (except before a name) mountain; hill (*Mount Everest*; *Mount of Olives*).

moun·tain /mównt'n/ *n.* **1** a large natural elevation of the earth's surface rising abruptly from the surrounding level; a large or high and steep hill. **2** a large heap or pile; a huge quantity (*a mountain of work*). **3** a large surplus stock (*butter mountain*). ▫ **move mountains 1** achieve spectacular results. **2** make every possible effort.

moun·tain ash *n.* **1** a tree, *Sorbus aucuparia*, with delicate pinnate leaves and scarlet berries. **2** any of several Australian eucalypti.

moun·tain bike *n.* a bicycle with a light sturdy frame, broad deep-treaded tires, and multiple gears, originally designed for riding on mountainous terrain.

moun·tain·eer /mównt'néer/ *n. & v.* • *n.* **1** a person skilled in mountain climbing. **2** a person living in an area of high mountains. • *v.intr.* climb mountains as a sport. ▫▫ **moun·tain·eer·ing** *n.*

moun·tain goat *n.* a white goatlike animal, *Oreamnos americanus*, of the Rocky Mountains, etc.

moun·tain li·on *n.* a puma.

moun·tain·ous /mównt'nəs/ *adj.* **1** having many mountains. **2** huge.

moun·tain range *n.* a line of mountains connected by high ground.

moun·tain·side /mównt'nsīd/ *n.* the slope of a mountain below the summit.

moun·tain time *n.* (also **Moun·tain Stand·ard Time**) the standard time of parts of Canada and the US in or near the Rocky Mountains.

moun·te·bank /mówntibángk/ *n.* **1** a swindler; a charlatan. **2** a clown. **3** *hist.* an itinerant quack appealing to an audience from a platform.

Moun·tie /mówntee/ *n. colloq.* a member of the Royal Canadian Mounted Police.

mount·ing /mównting/ *n.* **1** = MOUNT[1] *n.* 1. **2** in senses of MOUNT[1] *v.*

mourn /mawrn/ *v.* **1** *tr. &* (foll. by *for*) *intr.* feel or show deep sorrow or regret for (a dead person, a past event, etc.) **2** *intr.* show conventional signs of grief after a person's death.

mourn·er /mawrnər/ *n.* a person who mourns, esp. at a funeral.

mourn·ful /máwrnfōōl/ *adj.* **1** doleful; sad; sorrowing. **2** expressing or suggestive of mourning. ▫▫ **mourn·ful·ly** *adv.* **mourn·ful·ness** *n.*

mourn·ing /mawrning/ *n.* **1** the expression of deep sorrow, esp. for a dead person, by the wearing of solemn dress. **2** the clothes worn in mourning. ▫ **in mourning** assuming the signs of mourning, esp. in dress.

mourn·ing dove *n.* an American dove with a plaintive note, *Zenaida macroura*.

mou·sa·ka var. of MOUSSAKA.

mouse /mows/ *n. & v.* • *n.* (*pl.* **mice** /mīs/) **1 a** any of various small rodents of the family Muridae, usu. having a pointed snout and relatively large ears and eyes. **b** any of several similar rodents such as a small shrew or vole. **2** a timid or feeble person. **3** *Computing* a small hand-held device that controls the cursor on a computer monitor. **4** *sl.* a black eye. • *v.intr.* (also /mowz/) **1** (esp. of a cat, owl, etc.) hunt for or catch mice. **2** (foll. by *about*) search industriously; prowl about as if searching. ▫▫ **mouse·like** *adj. & adv.* **mous·er** *n.*

mouse·trap /mówstrap/ *n.* a spring trap with bait for catching and usu. killing mice.

mous·sa·ka /mōōsaáka, –saakaá/ *n.* (also **mou·sa·ka**) a Greek dish of ground meat, eggplant, etc., with a cheese sauce.

mousse /mōōs/ *n.* **1 a** a dessert of whipped cream, eggs, etc., usu. flavored with fruit or chocolate. **b** a meat or fish purée made with whipped cream, etc. **2** a preparation applied to the hair enabling it to be styled more easily. **3** a mixture of oil and seawater which forms a froth on the surface of the water after an oil spill.

mous·tache var. of MUSTACHE.

mous·y /mówsee/ *adj.* (**mousier, mousiest**) **1** of or like a mouse. **2** (of a person) shy or timid; ineffectual. **3** of a nondescript shade of light brown, mid brown, or gray. ▫▫ **mous·i·ly** *adv.* **mous·i·ness** *n.*

mouth *n. & v.* • *n.* /mowth/ (*pl.* **mouths** /mowthz/) **1 a** an external opening in the head, through which most animals admit food and emit communicative sounds. **b** (in humans and some animals) the cavity behind it containing the means of biting and chewing and the vocal organs. **2 a** the opening of a container such as a bag or sack. **b** the opening of a cave, volcano, etc. **c** the open end of a woodwind or brass instrument. **d** the muzzle of a gun. **3** the place where a river enters the sea. **4** *colloq.* **a** talkativeness. **b** impudent talk; cheek. **5** an individual regarded as needing sustenance (*an extra mouth to feed*). • *v.* /mowth/ **1** *tr. & intr.* utter or speak solemnly or with affectations. (*mouthing platitudes*). **2** *tr.* utter very distinctly. **3** *intr.* **a** move the lips silently. **b** grimace. **4** *tr.* take (food) in the mouth. **5** *tr.* touch with the mouth. **6** *tr.* train the mouth of (a horse). ▫ **keep one's mouth shut** *colloq.* not reveal a secret. **put words into a person's mouth** represent a person as having said something in a particular way. **take the words out of a person's mouth** say what another was about to say. ▫▫ **mouthed** /mowthd/ *adj.* (also in *comb.*).

mouth•breeder *n.* a fish which protects its eggs (and sometimes its young) by carrying them in its mouth.

mouth•ful /mówthfŏŏl/ *n.* (*pl.* **-fuls**) **1** a quantity, esp. of food, that fills the mouth. **2** a small quantity. **3** a long or complicated word or phrase. **4** *colloq.* something important said.

mouth•guard /mówthgaard/ *n.* a pad protecting an athlete's teeth and gums.

mouth or•gan *n.* = HARMONICA.

mouth•piece /mówthpees/ *n.* **1 a** the part of a musical instrument placed between or against the lips. **b** the part of a telephone for speaking into. **c** the part of a tobacco pipe placed between the lips. **2** a person who speaks for another or others.

mouth-to-mouth *adj.* (of resuscitation) in which a person breathes into a subject's lungs through the mouth.

mouth•wash /mówthwosh, –wawsh/ *n.* a liquid antiseptic, etc., for rinsing the mouth or gargling.

mouth•wa•ter•ing /mówthwawtəring/ *adj.* **1** (of food, etc.) having a delicious smell or appearance. **2** tempting; alluring.

mov•a•ble /mo͞ovəbəl/ *adj.* *&* *n.* (also **move•a•ble**) • *adj.* **1** that can be moved. **2** *Law* (of property) of the nature of a chattel, as distinct from land or buildings. **3** (of a feast or festival) variable in date from year to year. • *n.* **1** an article of furniture that may be removed from a house, as distinct from a fixture. **2** (in *pl.*) personal property. ▫▫ **mov•a•bil•i•ty** /–bílitee/ *n.* **mov•a•bly** *adv.*

move /mo͞ov/ *v.* *&* *n.* • *v.* **1** *intr.* *&* *tr.* change one's position or posture, or cause to do this. **2** *tr.* *&* *intr.* put or keep in motion. **3 a** *intr.* make a move in a board game. **b** *tr.* change the position of (a piece) in a board game. **4** *intr.* (often foll. by *about*, *away*, etc.) go from place to place. **5** *intr.* take action (*moved to reduce unemployment*). **6** *intr.* make progress (*the project is moving fast*). **7** *intr.* **a** change one's place of residence. **b** (of a business, etc.) change to new premises (also *tr.*: *move offices*). **8** *intr.* (foll. by *in*) be socially active in (*moves in the best circles*). **9** *tr.* affect (a person) with emotion. **10** *tr.* **a** (foll. by *in*) stimulate (laughter, anger, etc., in a person). **b** (foll. by *to*) provoke (a person to laughter, etc.). **11** *tr.* (foll. by *to*, or *to* + infin.) prompt or incline (a person to a feeling or action). **12 a** *tr.* cause (the bowels) to be evacuated. **b** *intr.* (of the bowels) be evacuated. **13** *tr.* (often foll. by *that* + clause) propose in a meeting, etc. **14** *intr.* (foll. by *for*) make a formal request or application. **15** *intr.* (of merchandise) be sold. • *n.* **1** the act or an instance of moving. **2** a change of house, business premises, etc. **3** an initiative. **4 a** the changing of the position of a piece in a board game. **b** a player's turn to do this. ▫ **get a move on** *colloq.* **1** hurry up. **2** make a start. **make a move** take action. **move along** (or **on**) change to a new position, esp. to avoid crowding, etc. **move in 1** take possession of a new house. **2** get into a position of influence, etc. **3** get into a position of readiness or proximity (for an offensive action, etc.). **move out 1** change one's place of residence. **2** leave a position, job, etc. **move over** (or **up**) adjust one's position to make room for another. **on the move 1** progressing. **2** moving about. ▫▫ **mov•er** *n.*

move•a•ble var. of MOVABLE.

move•ment /mo͞ovmənt/ *n.* **1** the act or an instance of moving or being moved. **2 a** the moving parts of a mechanism (esp. a clock or watch). **b** a particular group of these. **3 a** a body of persons with a common object (*the peace movement*). **b** a campaign undertaken by such a body. **4** (usu. in *pl.*) a person's activities and whereabouts. **5** *Mus.* a principal division of a longer musical work. **6** the progressive development of a poem, story, etc. **7** motion of the bowels. **8 a** an activity in a market for some commodity. **b** a rise or fall in price. **9** a mental impulse. **10** a development of position by a military force or unit. **11** a prevailing tendency in the course of events or conditions; trend.

mov•er /mo͞ovər/ *n.* **1** a person or thing that moves. **2** a person or company that moves household goods, etc., from one location to another as a business. **3** the author of a fruitful idea.

mov•ie /mo͞ovee/ *n.* esp. *colloq.* **1** a motion picture. **2** (**the movies**) **a** the motion-picture industry or medium. **b** the showing of a movie (*going to the movies*).

mov•ie•dom /mo͞oveedəm/ *n.* the movie industry and its associated businesses, personnel, etc.

mov•ie house *n.* a theater that shows movies.

mov•ing /mo͞oving/ *adj.* **1** that moves or causes to move. **2** affecting with emotion. ▫▫ **mov•ing•ly** *adv.* (in sense 2).

mov•ing van *n.* a large van used to move furniture, household goods, etc., from one house to another.

mow /mō/ *v.tr.* (*past part.* **mowed** or **mown**) **1** cut down (grass, hay, etc.) with a scythe or machine. **2** cut down the produce of (a field) or the grass, etc., of (a lawn) by mowing. ▫ **mow down** kill or destroy randomly or in great numbers. ▫▫ **mow•er** *n.*

mox•ie /móksee/ *n.* *sl.* energy; courage; daring.

moz•za•rel•la /mótsərélə/ *n.* an Italian semisoft cheese.

MP *abbr.* **1 a** military police. **b** military policeman. **2** Member of Parliament.

m.p. *abbr.* melting point.

m.p.g. *abbr.* miles per gallon.

m.p.h. *abbr.* miles per hour.

Mr. /místər/ *n.* (*pl.* **Messrs.**) **1** the title of a man without a higher title (*Mr. Jones*). **2** a title prefixed to a designation of office, etc. (*Mr. President*).

MRI *abbr.* magnetic resonance imaging.

mRNA *abbr.* *Biol.* messenger RNA.

Mrs. /mísiz/ *n.* (*pl.* same or **Mesdames** /mayddaám, -dám/) the title of a married woman without a higher title (*Mrs. Jones*).

MS *abbr.* **1** Mississippi (in official postal use). **2** Master of Science. **3** multiple sclerosis. **4** (also **ms.**) manuscript.

Ms. /miz/ *n.* form of address for a woman, used regardless of marital status.

MS-DOS /émesdáws, –dós/ *abbr.* *Trademark* a computer disk operating system developed by Microsoft Corp. for personal computers.

MSG *abbr.* MONOSODIUM GLUTAMATE.

Msgr. *abbr.* **1** Monseigneur. **2** Monsignor.

MSS *abbr.* (also **mss.**) manuscripts.

MST *abbr.* Mountain Standard Time.

MT *abbr.* **1** Montana (in official postal use). **2** Mountain Time.

Mt *abbr.* MEITNERIUM.

Mt. *abbr.* **1** mount. **2** mountain

mu /myo͞o, mo͞o/ *n.* **1** the twelfth Greek letter (Μ, μ). **2** (μ, as a symbol) = MICRO- 2.

much /much/ *adj.*, *n.*, *&* *adv.* • *adj.* **1** existing or occurring in a great quantity (*not much rain*). **2** (prec. by *as*, *how*, *that*, etc.) with relative rather than distinctive sense (*I don't know how much money you want*). • *n.* **1** a great quantity (*much of that is true*). **2** (prec. by *as*, *how*, *that*, etc.) with relative rather than distinctive sense (*we do not need that much*). **3** (usu. in *neg.*) a noteworthy or outstanding example (*not much of a party*). • *adv.* **1 a** in a great degree (*is much the same*). **b** greatly (*they much regret the mistake*). **c** qualifying a comparative or superlative adjective (*much better*). **2** for a large part of one's time (*is much away from home*). ▫ **as much** the extent or quantity just specified. (*I thought as much*). **a bit much** *colloq.* somewhat excessive or immoderate. **much as** even though (*much as I would like to*). **not much** *colloq.* **1** *iron.* very much. **2** certainly not. **too**

much *colloq.* an intolerable situation, etc. (*that really is too much*). **too much for 1** more than a match for. **2** beyond what is endurable by. ▫▫ **much·ly** *adv. joc.*

mu·ci·lage /myóosilij/ *n.* **1** a viscous substance obtained from plant seeds, etc., by maceration. **2** a solution of gum, glue, etc. ▫▫ **mu·ci·lag·i·nous** /–lájinəs/ *adj.*

muck /muk/ *n. & v.* • *n.* **1** farmyard manure. **2** *colloq.* dirt or filth; anything disgusting. **3** *colloq.* a mess. • *v.tr.* **1** (usu. foll. by *up*) *colloq.* bungle (a job). **2** (often foll. by *out*) remove muck from. **3** make dirty or untidy. **4** manure with muck.

muck·rake /múkrayk/ *v.intr.* search out and reveal scandal, esp. among famous people. ▫▫ **muck·rak·ing** *n.*

muck·y /múkee/ *adj.* (**muckier, muckiest**) **1** covered with muck. **2** dirty.

mu·cous /myóokəs/ *adj.* pertaining to or covered with mucus.

mu·cus /myóokəs/ *n.* **1** a slimy substance secreted by a mucous membrane. **2** a gummy substance found in all plants. **3** a slimy substance exuded by some animals, esp. fishes.

mud /mud/ *n.* **1** wet, soft, earthy matter. **2** hard ground from the drying of an area of this. **3** what is worthless or polluting. ▫ **as clear as mud** *colloq.* not at all clear. **fling** (or **sling** or **throw**) **mud** speak disparagingly or slanderously. **here's mud in your eye!** *colloq.* a drinking toast. **one's name is mud** one is unpopular or in disgrace.

mud·dle /múd'l/ *v. & n.* • *v.* **1** *tr.* (often foll. by *up, together*) bring into disorder. **2** *tr.* bewilder, confuse. **3** *tr.* mismanage (an affair). **4** *tr.* crush and mix (the ingredients for a drink). **5** *intr.* (often foll. by *with*) busy oneself in a confused and ineffective way. • *n.* **1** disorder. **2** a muddled condition. ▫ **make a muddle of 1** bring into disorder. **2** bungle. **muddle along** (or **on**) progress in a haphazard way. **muddle through** succeed by perseverance rather than skill or efficiency. **muddle up** confuse (two or more things). ▫▫ **mud·dler** *n.*

muddle late Middle English (in the sense 'wallow in mud'): perhaps from Middle Dutch *moddelen*, derived from *modden* 'dabble in mud' (related to *mud*). The sense 'confuse' was initially associated with alcoholic drink (late 17th century), giving rise to 'busy oneself in a confused way' and 'jumble up' (mid-19th century).

mud·dle-head·ed *adj.* stupid; confused. ▫▫ **mud·dle-head·ed·ness** *n.*

mud·dy /múdee/ *adj. & v.* • *adj.* (**muddier, muddiest**) **1** like mud. **2** covered in or full of mud. **3** (of liquid) turbid. **4** mentally confused. **5** obscure. **6** (of light) dull. **7** (of color) impure. • *v.tr.* (**-dies, -died**) make muddy. ▫▫ **mud·di·ly** *adv.*

mud·flap /múdflap/ *n.* a flap hanging behind the wheel of a vehicle, to catch mud and stones, etc., thrown up from the road.

mud·guard /múdgaard/ *n.* a curved strip or cover over a wheel of a bicycle or motorcycle to reduce the amount of mud, etc., thrown up from the road.

mud·pup·py *n.* a large nocturnal salamander, *Necturus maculosus*, of eastern US.

mues·li /móoslee, myóoz–/ *n.* a breakfast food of crushed cereals, dried fruits, nuts, etc., eaten with milk.

mu·ez·zin /myoo-ézin, moo–/ *n.* a Muslim crier who proclaims the hours of prayer.

muff[1] /muf/ *n.* a fur or other covering, usu. in the form of a tube with an opening at each end for the hands to be inserted for warmth.

muff[2] /muf/ *v. & n.* • *v.tr.* **1** bungle. **2** fail to catch or receive (a ball, etc.). **3** blunder in (a theatrical part, etc.). • *n.* a failure, esp. to catch a ball in baseball, etc.

muf·fin /múfin/ *n.* a small cake or quick bread made from batter or dough and baked in a muffin pan.

muf·fle /múfəl/ *v. & n.* • *v.tr.* **1** (often foll. by *up*) wrap or cover for warmth. **2** cover or wrap up (a source of sound) to reduce its loudness. **3** (usu. as **muffled** *adj.*) stifle (an utterance). **4** prevent from speaking. • *n.* **1** a receptacle in a furnace where substances may be heated without contact with combustion products. **2** a similar chamber in a kiln for baking painted pottery.

muf·fler /múflər/ *n.* **1** a wrap or scarf worn for warmth. **2** a noise-reducing device on a motor vehicle's exhaust system. **3** a mute.

muf·ti /múftee/ *n.* plain clothes worn by a person who also wears (esp. military) uniform (*in mufti*).

mug /mug/ *n. & v.* • *n.* **1 a** a drinking vessel, usu. cylindrical and with a handle and used without a saucer. **b** its contents. **2** *sl.* the face or mouth of a person. **3** *sl.* a hoodlum or thug. • *v.* (**mugged, mugging**) **1** *tr.* rob (a person) with violence, esp. in a public place. **2** *tr.* fight; thrash. **3** *tr.* strangle. **4** *intr. sl.* make faces, esp. before an audience, a camera, etc. ▫▫ **mug·ger** *n.* (esp. in sense 1 of *v.*). **mug·ging** *n.* (in sense 1 of *v.*).

mug·gy /múgee/ *adj.* (**muggier, muggiest**) (of the weather, a day, etc.) oppressively damp and warm; humid. ▫▫ **mug·gi·ness** *n.*

mug shot *n. sl.* a photograph of a face, esp. one taken when a person is arrested.

mug·wort /múgwərt, –wawrt/ *n.* any of various plants of the genus *Artemisia*, esp. *A. vulgaris*, with silver-gray aromatic foliage.

mug·wump /múgwump/ *n.* **1** a great man; a boss. **2** a person who remains aloof, esp. from party politics.

mu·lat·to /moolátō, –laá–, myoo–/ *n. & adj.* • *n.* (*pl.* **-toes** or **-tos**) a person of mixed white and black parentage. • *adj.* of the color of mulattoes; tawny.

mul·ber·ry /múlberee, –bəree/ *n.* (*pl.* **-ries**) **1** any deciduous tree of the genus *Morus*, grown, esp. for feeding silkworms or its fruit. **2** its dark-red or white berry. **3** a dark-red or purple color.

mulch /mulch/ *n. & v.* • *n.* a mixture of straw, leaves, etc., spread around or over a plant to enrich or insulate the soil. • *v.tr.* treat with mulch.

mulct /mulkt/ *v. & n.* • *v.tr.* **1** extract money from by fine or taxation. **2 a** (often foll. by *of*) swindle. **b** obtain by swindling. • *n.* a fine.

mule[1] /myool/ *n.* **1** the offspring of a male donkey and a female horse, or (in general use) of a female donkey and a male horse (cf. HINNY[1]). **2** a stupid or obstinate person. **3** (often *attrib.*) a hybrid and usu. sterile plant or animal (*mule canary*). **4** (in full **spinning mule**) a kind of spinning machine producing yarn on spindles.

mule[2] /myool/ *n.* a light shoe or slipper without a back.

mul·ish /myóolish/ *adj.* **1** like a mule. **2** stubborn. ▫▫ **mul·ish·ly** *adv.* **mul·ish·ness** *n.*

mull[1] /mul/ *v.tr. & intr.* (often foll. by *over*) ponder or consider.

mull[2] /mul/ *v.tr.* warm (wine or beer) with added spices, etc.

mul·lah /múlə, mool–/ *n.* a Muslim learned in Islamic theology and sacred law.

mul·lein /múlin/ *n.* any herbaceous plant of the genus *Verbascum*, with woolly leaves and yellow flowers.

mul·let /múlit/ *n.* any fish of the family Mullidae (**red mullet**) or Mugilidae (**gray mullet**), commonly used as food.

mul·li·ga·taw·ny /múligətáwnee/ *n.* a highly seasoned soup orig. from India.

mul·lion /múlyən/ *n.* (also **mun·nion** /mún–/) a vertical bar dividing the panes in a window (cf. TRANSOM). ▫▫ **mul·lioned** *adj.*

multi- /múltee, –tī/ *comb. form* many; more than one.

mul·ti·ac·cess /múlteeákses, –tī–/ *n.* (often *attrib.*) the simultaneous connection to a computer of a number of terminals.

mul·ti·col·or /múltikúlər/ *adj.* (also **mul·ti·col·ored**) of many colors.

mul·ti·cul·tur·al /múlteekúlchərəl/ *adj.* of or relating to or constituting several cultural or ethnic groups within a society. ▫▫ **mul·ti·cul·tur·al·ism** *n.* **mul·ti·cul·tur·al·ly** *adv.*

mul·ti·di·men·sion·al /múlteediménshənəl, –dī–/ *adj.* of or involving more than three dimensions. ▫▫ **mul·ti·di·men·sion·al·i·ty** /–nálitee/ *n.* **mul·ti·di·men·sion·al·ly** *adv.*

mul·ti·far·i·ous /múltifáireeəs/ *adj.* **1** (foll. by pl. noun) many and various. **2** having great variety. ▫▫ **mul·ti·far·i·ous·ness** *n.*

mul·ti·lat·er·al /múltilátərəl/ *adj.* **1 a** (of an agreement, treaty, conference, etc.) in which three or more parties participate. **b** performed by more than two parties (*multilateral disarmament*). **2** having many sides. ▫▫ **mul·ti·lat·er·al·ly** *adv.*

mul·ti·lin·gual /múlteelínggwəl, –tī–/ *adj.* in or using several languages. ▫▫ **mul·ti·lin·gual·ly** *adv.*

mul·ti·me·di·a /múltimeédeeə/ *adj.* & *n.* • *attrib.adj.* involving several media. • *n.* the combined use of several media, such as film, print, sound, etc.

mul·ti·mil·lion /múlteemílyən, –tī–/ *attrib.adj.* costing or involving several million (dollars, pounds, etc.).

mul·ti·mil·lion·aire /múlteemílyənáir, –tī–/ *n.* a person with a fortune of several millions.

mul·ti·na·tion·al /múlteenáshənəl, –tī–/ *adj.* & *n.* • *adj.* **1** (of a business organization) operating in several countries. **2** relating to or including several nationalities. • *n.* a multinational company. ▫▫ **mul·ti·na·tion·al·ly** *adv.*

mul·tip·a·rous /multípərəs/ *adj.* **1** bringing forth many young at a birth. **2** having borne more than one child.

mul·ti·ple /múltipəl/ *adj.* & *n.* • *adj.* **1** having several or many parts, elements, or individual components. **2** (foll. by pl. noun) many and various. **3** *Bot.* (of fruit) collective. • *n.* a number that may be divided by another a certain number of times without a remainder (*56 is a multiple of 7*). ▫▫ **mul·ti·ply** *adv.*

mul·ti·ple-choice *n.* (of a question in an examination) accompanied by several possible answers from which the correct one has to be chosen.

mul·ti·plex /múltipleks/ *adj.*, *v.*, & *n.* • *adj.* **1** manifold; of many elements. **2** involving simultaneous transmission of several messages along a single channel of communication. • *v.tr.* incorporate into a multiplex signal or system. • *n.* a building that houses several movie theaters. ▫▫ **mul·ti·plex·er** *n.* (also **mul·ti·plex·or**).

mul·ti·pli·cand /múltiplikánd/ *n.* a quantity to be multiplied by a multiplier.

mul·ti·pli·ca·tion /múltiplikáyshən/ *n.* **1** the arithmetical process of multiplying. **2** the act or an instance of multiplying. ▫▫ **mul·ti·pli·ca·tive** /–plíkətiv/ *adj.*

mul·ti·pli·ca·tion sign *n.* the sign (×) to indicate that one quantity is to be multiplied by another.

mul·ti·pli·ca·tion ta·ble *n.* a list of multiples of a particular number, usu. from 1 to 12.

mul·ti·plic·i·ty /múltiplísitee/ *n.* (*pl.* **-ties**) **1** manifold variety. **2** (foll. by *of*) a great number.

mul·ti·pli·er /múltiplīər/ *n.* a quantity by which a given number is multiplied.

mul·ti·ply /múltiplī/ *v.* (**-plies, -plied**) **1** *tr.* (also *absol.*) obtain from (a number) another that is a specified number of times its value (*multiply 6 by 4 and you get 24*). **2** *intr.* increase in number esp. by procreation. **3** *tr.* produce a large number of (instances, etc.). **4** *tr.* **a** breed (animals). **b** propagate (plants).

mul·ti·po·lar /múltipṓlər/ *adj.* having many poles (see POLE[2]).

mul·ti·proc·ess·ing /múlteeprósesing/ *n.* *Computing* processing by a number of processors sharing a common memory and common peripherals.

mul·ti·pro·gram·ming /múlteeprṓgraming/ *n.* *Computing* the execution of two or more independent programs concurrently.

mul·ti·pur·pose /múlteepárpəs, –tī–/ *n.* (*attrib.*) having several purposes.

mul·ti·ra·cial /múlteeráyshəl, –tī–/ *adj.* relating to or made up of many human races. ▫▫ **mul·ti·ra·cial·ly** *adv.*

mul·ti·sto·ry /múltistáwree/ *n.* (*attrib.*) (of a building) having several stories.

mul·ti·tude /múltitood, –tyood/ *n.* **1** (often foll. by *of*) a great number. **2** a large gathering of people; a crowd. **3** (**the multitude**) the common people. **4** the state of being numerous.

mul·ti·tu·di·nous /múltitóód'nəs, –tyood–/ *adj.* **1** very numerous. **2** consisting of many individuals or elements. **3** (of an ocean, etc.) vast. ▫▫ **mul·ti·tu·di·nous·ly** *adv.*

mul·ti·us·er /múltiyóózər/ *n.* (*attrib.*) (of a computer system) having a number of simultaneous users (cf. MULTI-ACCESS).

mum[1] /mum/ *adj. colloq.* silent (*keep mum*). ▫ **mum's the word** say nothing.

mum[2] /mum/ *v.intr.* (**mummed, mumming**) act in a traditional masked mime.

mum[3] /mum/ *n.* = CHRYSANTHEMUM.

mum[4] /mum/ *n.* esp. *Brit.* = MOM.

mum·ble /múmbəl/ *v.* & *n.* • *v.* **1** *intr.* & *tr.* speak or utter indistinctly. **2** *tr.* bite or chew with or as with toothless gums. • *n.* an indistinct utterance. ▫▫ **mum·bler** *n.*

mum·bo jum·bo /múmbōjúmbō/ *n.* (*pl.* **jumbos**) **1** meaningless or ignorant ritual. **2** language or action intended to mystify or confuse. **3** an object of senseless veneration.

mum·mer /múmər/ *n.* an actor in a traditional masked mime.

mum·mer·y /múməree/ *n.* (*pl.* **-ies**) **1** ridiculous (esp. religious) ceremonial. **2** a performance by mummers.

mum·mi·fy /múmifī/ *v.tr.* (**-fies, -fied**) **1** embalm and preserve (a body) in the form of a mummy (see MUMMY[2]). **2** (usu. as **mummified** *adj.*) shrivel or dry up (tissues, etc.). ▫▫ **mum·mi·fi·ca·tion** /–fikáyshən/ *n.*

mum·my[1] /múmee/ *n.* (*pl.* **-mies**) esp. *Brit.* = MOMMY.

mum·my[2] /múmee/ *n.* (*pl.* **-mies**) **1** a body of a human being or animal embalmed for burial, esp. in ancient Egypt. **2** a dried-up body. **3** a rich brown pigment.

mumps /mumps/ *n.pl.* (treated as *sing.*) a contagious and infectious viral disease with swelling of the salivary glands in the face.

munch /munch/ *v.tr.* eat steadily with a marked action of the jaws.

munch·ies /múncheez/ *n.pl. colloq.* **1** snack foods. **2** the urge to snack.

mun·dane /múndáyn/ *adj.* **1** dull; routine. **2** of this world; worldly. ▫▫ **mun·dane·ly** *adv.* **mun·dan·i·ty** /–dánitee/ *n.* (*pl.* **-ties**).

mung /mung/ *n.* (in full **mung bean**) a leguminous plant, *Phaseolus aureus*, native to India and used as food.

mu·nic·i·pal /myoonísipəl/ *adj.* of or concerning a municipality or its government. ▫▫ **mu·nic·i·pal·ize** *v.tr.* **mu·nic·i·pal·ly** *adv.*

mu·nic·i·pal·i·ty /myoonísipálitee/ *n.* (*pl.* **-ties**) **1** a town or district having local government. **2** the governing body of this area.

mu·nif·i·cent /myoonífisənt/ *adj.* (of a giver or a gift) splendidly generous; bountiful. ▫▫ **mu·nif·i·cence** *n.* /–səns/ **mu·nif·i·cent·ly** *adv.*

mu·ni·tion /myoonishən/ *n.* & *v.* • *n.* (usu. in *pl.*) military weapons, ammunition, equipment, and stores. • *v.tr.* supply with munitions.

mun·nion var. of MULLION.

mu·on /myo͞o-on/ *n. Physics* an unstable elementary particle like an electron, but with a much greater mass.

mu·ral /myo͝orəl/ *n. & adj.* • *n.* a painting executed directly on a wall. • *adj.* **1** of or like a wall. **2** on a wall.

mur·der /mə́rdər/ *n. & v.* • *n.* **1** the unlawful premeditated killing of a human being by another (cf. MANSLAUGHTER). **2** *colloq.* an unpleasant state of affairs (*it was murder here on Saturday*). • *v.tr.* **1** kill (a human being) unlawfully. **2** *Law* kill (a human being) with a premeditated motive. **3** *colloq.* utterly defeat or spoil by a bad performance, mispronunciation, etc. (*murdered the soliloquy in the second act*). □ **cry bloody murder** *sl.* make an extravagant outcry. **get away with murder** *colloq.* do whatever one wishes and escape punishment. □□ **mur·der·er** *n.* **mur·der·ess** *n.*

mur·der·ous /mə́rdərəs/ *adj.* **1** capable of, intending, or involving murder or great harm. **2** *colloq.* extremely troublesome, unpleasant, or dangerous.

murk /mərk/ *n.* (also **mirk**) **1** darkness; poor visibility. **2** air obscured by fog, etc.

murk·y /mə́rkee/ *adj.* (also **mirk·y**) (**-ier, -iest**) **1** dark; gloomy. **2** (of darkness) thick; dirty. **3** suspiciously obscure (*murky past*). □□ **murk·i·ly** *adv.* **murk·i·ness** *n.*

mur·mur /mə́rmər/ *n. & v.* • *n.* **1** a subdued continuous sound, as made by waves, a brook, etc. **2** a softly spoken or nearly inarticulate utterance. **3** *Med.* a recurring sound heard in the auscultation of the heart and usu. indicating abnormality. **4** a subdued expression of discontent. • *v.* **1** *intr.* make a subdued continuous sound. **2** *tr.* utter (words) in a low voice. **3** *intr.* (usu. foll. by *at, against*) complain in low tones; grumble. □□ **mur·mur·ing·ly** *adv.*

Mur·phy's Law /mə́rfeez/ *n. joc.* any of various maxims about the perverseness of things.

mus·cat /múskat, –kət/ *n.* = MUSCATEL.

mus·ca·tel /múskətél/ *n.* (also **mus·ca·del** /–dél/) a sweet fortified white wine made from a musk-flavored variety of grape.

mus·cle /músəl/ *n. & v.* • *n.* **1** a fibrous tissue with the ability to contract, producing movement in or maintaining the position of an animal body. **2** the part of an animal body that is composed of muscles. **3** physical power or strength. • *v.intr.* (usu. foll. by *in*) *colloq.* force oneself on others; intrude by forceful means. □ **not move a muscle** be completely motionless. □□ **mus·cly** *adj.*

mus·cle-bound *adj.* with muscles stiff and inelastic through excessive exercise or training.

mus·cle man *n.* a man with highly developed muscles, esp. one employed as an intimidator.

Mus·co·vite /múskəvīt/ *n. & adj.* • *n.* a native or citizen of Moscow. • *adj.* of or relating to Moscow.

Mus·co·vy duck *n.* a tropical American duck, *Cairina moschata*, having a small crest and red markings on its head.

mus·cu·lar /múskyələr/ *adj.* **1** of or affecting the muscles. **2** having well-developed muscles. □□ **mus·cu·lar·i·ty** /–láritee/ *n.* **mus·cu·lar·ly** *adv.*

mus·cu·lar dys·tro·phy *n.* a hereditary condition marked by progressive weakening and wasting of the muscles, sometimes also affecting the heart.

mus·cu·la·ture /múskyələchər/ *n.* the muscular system of a body or organ.

mus·cu·lo·skel·e·tal /məskyəlōskélət'l/ *adj.* of or involving both the muscles and the skeleton.

muse[1] /myo͞oz/ *n.* **1** (as **the Muses**) (in Greek and Roman mythology) nine goddesses who inspire poetry, music, drama, etc. **2** (usu. prec. by *the*) **a** a poet's inspiring goddess. **b** a poet's genius.

muse[2] /myo͞oz/ *v. literary* **1** *intr.* **a** (usu. foll. by *on, upon*) ponder; reflect. **b** (usu. foll. by *on*) gaze meditatively (on a scene, etc.). **2** *tr.* say meditatively.

mu·se·um /myo͞ozéeəm/ *n.* a building used for storing and exhibiting objects of historical, scientific, or cultural interest.

mush[1] /mush/ *n.* **1** soft pulp. **2** feeble sentimentality. **3** a boiled cornmeal dish. **4** *sl.* the mouth; the face. □□ **mush·y** *adj.* (**mushier, mushiest**). **mush·i·ly** *adv.* **mush·i·ness** *n.*

mush[2] *v. & n.* • *v.intr.* **1** (in *imper.*) used as a command to dogs pulling a sled to urge them forward. **2** go on a journey across snow with a dogsled. • *n.* a journey across snow with a dogsled.

mush·room /múshro͞om, –ro͝om/ *n. & v.* • *n.* **1** the usu. edible, spore-producing body of various fungi, esp. *Agaricus campestris*, with a stem and domed cap. **2** the pinkish-brown color of this. **3** any item resembling a mushroom in shape (*darning mushroom*). **4** (usu. *attrib.*) something that appears or develops suddenly or is ephemeral. • *v.intr.* **1** appear or develop rapidly. **2** expand and flatten like a mushroom cap. **3** gather mushrooms.

mush·room cloud *n.* a cloud suggesting the shape of a mushroom, esp. from a nuclear explosion.

mu·sic /myo͞ozik/ *n.* **1** the art of combining vocal or instrumental sounds (or both) to produce beauty of form, harmony, and expression of emotion. **2** the sounds so produced. **3** musical compositions. **4** the written or printed score of a musical composition. **5** certain pleasant sounds, e.g., birdsong, etc. □ **music to one's ears** something very pleasant to hear.

mu·si·cal /myo͞ozikəl/ *adj. & n.* • *adj.* **1** of or relating to music. **2** (of sounds, a voice, etc.) melodious; harmonious. **3** fond of or skilled in music (*the musical one of the family*). **4** set to or accompanied by music. • *n.* a movie or drama that features songs. □□ **mu·si·cal·i·ty** /–kálitee/ *n.* **mu·si·cal·ly** *adv.*

mu·si·cal chairs *n.pl.* **1** a party game in which the players compete in successive rounds for a decreasing number of chairs. **2** a series of changes or political maneuvering, etc., after the manner of the game.

mu·sic box *n.* a mechanical instrument playing a tune by causing a toothed cylinder to strike a comblike metal plate within a box.

mu·si·cian /myo͞ozíshən/ *n.* a person who plays a musical instrument, esp. professionally, or is otherwise musically gifted. □□ **mu·si·cian·ship** *n.*

mu·si·col·o·gy /myo͞ozikóləjee/ *n.* the study of music other than that directed to proficiency in performance or composition. □□ **mu·si·col·o·gist** *n.* **mu·si·co·log·i·cal** /–kəlójikəl/ *adj.*

mu·sic stand *n.* a rest or frame on which sheet music or a score is supported.

musk /musk/ *n.* **1** a strong-smelling reddish-brown substance produced by a gland in the male musk deer and used in perfumes. **2** the plant, *Mimulus moschatus*, with pale-green ovate leaves and yellow flowers. □□ **musk·y** *adj.* (**muskier, muskiest**). **musk·i·ness** *n.*

musk deer *n.* any small Asian deer of the genus *Moschus*, having no antlers.

mus·kel·lunge /múskəlunj/ *n.* (also **mas·ki·nonge**) a large N. American pike, *Esox masquinongy*, found esp. in the Great Lakes.

mus·ket /múskit/ *n. hist.* an infantryman's (esp. smooth-bored) light gun, often supported on the shoulder.

mus·ket·eer /múskitéer/ *n. hist.* a soldier armed with a musket.

musk·mel·on /múskmelən/ *n.* the common yellow or

green melon, *Cucumis melo*, usu. with a raised network of markings on the skin.

musk ox *n.* a large goat-antelope, *Ovibos moschatus*, native to N. America, with a thick shaggy coat and small curved horns.

musk•rat /múskrat/ *n.* **1** a large aquatic rodent, *Ondatra zibethica*, native to N. America, having a musky smell. **2** the fur of this.

Mus•lim /múzlim, mŏŏz–, mŏŏs–/ *n. & adj.* (also **Moslem** /mózləm/) •*n.* a follower of the Islamic religion. •*adj.* of or relating to the Muslims or their religion. ▶**Muslim** is the preferred term for 'follower of Islam,' although *Moslem* is also widely used. Avoid 'Mohammedan.'

mus•lin /múzlin/ *n.* **1** a fine delicately woven cotton fabric. **2** a cotton cloth in plain weave.

muss /mus/ *v. & n. colloq.* •*v.tr.* (often foll. by *up*) disarrange; throw into disorder. •*n.* a state of confusion; untidiness; mess. ▫▫ **muss•y** *adj.*

mus•sel /músəl/ *n.* **1** any bivalve mollusk of the genus *Mytilus*, living in seawater and often used for food. **2** any similar freshwater mollusk of the genus *Margaritifer* or *Anodonta*, forming pearls.

must[1] /must/ *v. & n.* •*v.aux.* (*3rd sing. present* **must**; *past* **had to** or in indirect speech **must**) (foll. by infin., or *absol.*) **1 a** be obliged to (*must we leave now?*). ▶The negative (i.e., lack of obligation) is expressed by *not have to* or *need not*; *must not* denotes positive forbidding, as in *you must not smoke*. **b** in ironic questions (*must you slam the door?*). **2** be certain to (*they must have left by now*). **3** ought to (*it must be said that*). **4** expressing insistence (*I must ask you to leave*). **5** (foll. by *not* + infin.) **a** be forbidden to (*you must not smoke*). **b** ought not; need not (*you must not worry*). **c** expressing insistence that something should not be done (*they must not be told*). **6** (as past or historic present) expressing the perversity of destiny (*what must I do but break my leg*). •*n. colloq.* a thing that cannot or should not be missed (*if you go to London, St. Paul's is a must*). ▫ **I must say** *often iron.* I cannot refrain from saying (*a fine way to behave, I must say*).

must[2] /must/ *n.* grape juice before fermentation is complete.

must[3] /must/ *n.* mustiness; mold.

mus•tache /mústash, məstásh/ *n.* (also **mous•tache**) **1** hair left to grow on a man's upper lip. **2** a similar growth around the mouth of some animals. ▫▫ **mus•tached** *adj.*

mus•tang /mústang/ *n.* a small wild horse native to Mexico and California.

mus•tard /mústərd/ *n.* **1 a** any of various plants of the genus *Brassica*, with slender pods and yellow flowers. **b** any of various plants of the genus *Sinapis*, eaten at the seedling stage. **2** the seeds of these which are crushed, made into a paste, and used as a spicy condiment. **3** the brownish-yellow color of this condiment. ▫ **cut the mustard** *sl.* be able to reach an expected level of performance.

mus•tard gas *n.* a colorless oily liquid whose vapor is a powerful irritant and causes blisters.

mus•te•lid /mústəlid/ *n. & adj.* •*n.* a mammal of the family Mustelidae, including weasels, stoats, badgers, skunks, otters, martens, etc. •*adj.* of or relating to this family.

mus•ter /mústər/ *v. & n.* •*v.* **1** *tr.* collect (orig. soldiers) for inspection, to check numbers, etc. **2** *tr. & intr.* gather together. •*n.* **1** the assembly of persons for inspection. **2** an assembly. ▫ **muster in** enroll (recruits). **muster out** discharge (soldiers, etc.). **muster up** collect or summon (courage, strength, etc.). **pass muster** be accepted as adequate.

mustn't /músənt/ *contr.* must not.

mus•ty /mústee/ *adj.* (**mustier, mustiest**) **1** moldy. **2** of a moldy or stale smell or taste. **3** stale; antiquated (*musty old books*). ▫▫ **mus•ti•ly** *adv.* **mus•ti•ness** *n.*

mu•ta•ble /myŏŏtəbəl/ *adj. literary* **1** liable to change. **2** fickle. ▫▫ **mu•ta•bil•i•ty** /–bílitee/ *n.*

mu•ta•gen /myŏŏtəjən/ *n.* an agent promoting mutation, e.g., radiation. ▫▫ **mu•ta•gen•ic** /–jénik/ *adj.* **mu•ta•gen•e•sis** /–jénisis/ *n.*

mu•tant /myŏŏt'nt/ *adj. & n.* •*adj.* resulting from mutation. •*n.* a mutant form.

mu•tate /myŏŏtáyt/ *v.intr. & tr.* undergo or cause to undergo mutation.

mu•ta•tion /myŏŏtáyshən/ *n.* **1** the process or an instance of change or alteration. **2** a genetic change which, when transmitted to offspring, gives rise to heritable variations. **3** a mutant. ▫▫ **mu•tate** /myŏŏtáyt/ *v.intr. & tr.* **mu•ta•tion•al** *adj.* **mu•ta•tion•al•ly** *adv.*

mute /myŏŏt/ *adj., n., & v.* •*adj.* **1** silent, refraining from or temporarily bereft of speech. **2** not emitting articulate sound. **3** (of a person or animal) dumb. **4** not expressed in speech (*mute protest*). **5 a** (of a letter) not pronounced. **b** (of a consonant) plosive. •*n.* **1** a dumb person (*a deaf mute*). **2** *Mus.* **a** a clamp for damping the resonance of the strings of a violin, etc. **b** a pad or cone for damping the sound of a wind instrument. **3** an unsounded consonant. **4** an actor whose part is in a dumb show. **5** a hired mourner. •*v.tr.* **1** deaden, muffle, or soften the sound of (a thing, esp. a musical instrument). **2 a** tone down; make less intense. **b** (as **muted** *adj.*) (of colors, etc.) subdued (*a muted green*). ▫▫ **mute•ly** *adv.* **mute•ness** *n.*

mute swan *n.* the common white swan, *Cygnus olor*.

mu•ti•late /myŏŏt'layt/ *v.tr.* **1 a** deprive of a limb or organ. **b** destroy the use of (a limb or organ). **2** render (a book, etc.) imperfect by excision or some act of destruction. ▫▫ **mu•ti•la•tion** /–láyshən/ *n.* **mu•ti•la•tor** *n.*

mu•ti•neer /myŏŏt'néer/ *n.* a person who mutinies.

mu•ti•nous /myŏŏt'nəs/ *adj.* rebellious; tending to mutiny. ▫▫ **mu•tin•ous•ly** *adv.*

mu•ti•ny /myŏŏt'nee/ *n. & v.* •*n.* (*pl.* **-nies**) an open revolt against constituted authority, esp. by soldiers or sailors against their officers. •*v.intr.* (**-nies, -nied**) (often foll. by *against*) revolt; engage in mutiny. ▫▫ **mu•ti•nous** /myŏŏt'nəs/ *adj.*

mutt /mut/ *n.* **1** a dog. **2** *sl.* an ignorant, stupid, or blundering person.

mut•ter /mútər/ *v. & n.* •*v.* **1** *intr.* speak low in a barely audible manner. **2** *intr.* (often foll. by *against*, *at*) murmur or grumble about. **3** *tr.* utter (words, etc.) in a low tone. **4** *tr.* say in secret. •*n.* **1** muttered words or sounds. **2** muttering. ▫▫ **mut•ter•er** *n.*

mut•ton /mút'n/ *n.* **1** the flesh of sheep used for food. **2** *joc.* a sheep.

mut•ton•chops /mút'nchops/ *n.* side whiskers trimmed narrow at the temples and broad along the cheeks.

mu•tu•al /myŏŏchŏŏəl/ *adj.* **1** (of feelings, actions, etc.) experienced or done by each of two or more parties with reference to the other or others (*mutual affection*). **2** *colloq. disp.* common to two or more persons (*a mutual friend*). **3** standing in (a specified) relation to each other (*mutual beneficiaries*). ▫▫ **mu•tu•al•ly** *adv.*

▶Traditionalists consider using **mutual** to mean 'common to two or more people,' as in *a mutual friend; a mutual interest*, to be incorrect, holding that the sense of reciprocity is necessary: *mutual respect; mutual need.* However, both senses are well established and acceptable in standard English.

mu•tu•al fund *n.* an investment program funded by shareholders that trades in diversified holdings and is professionally managed.

mu•tu•al•ism /myŏŏchŏŏəlizəm/ *n.* **1** the doctrine that mutual dependence is necessary to social well-being. **2** mutually beneficial symbiosis. ◻◻ **mu·tu·al·ist** *n. & adj.* **mu·tu·al·ist·ic** /–lístik/ *adj.* **mu·tu·al·ist·ic·al·ly** /–lístiklee/ *adv.*

muu·muu /mo͞omo͞o/ *n.* a woman's loose brightly colored dress, as originally worn in Hawaii.

Mu·zak /myo͞ozak/ *n.* **1** *Trademark* a system of music transmission for playing in public places. **2** (**muzak**) recorded light background music.

muz·zle /múzəl/ *n. & v.* • *n.* **1** the projecting part of an animal's face, including the nose and mouth. **2** a guard, usu. made of straps or wire, fitted over an animal's nose and mouth to stop it biting or feeding. **3** the open end of a firearm. • *v.tr.* **1** put a muzzle on (an animal, etc.). **2** impose silence upon.

muz·zy /múzee/ *adj.* (**muzzier, muzziest**) **1** mentally hazy. **2** blurred. ◻◻ **muz·zi·ly** *adv.* **muz·zi·ness** *n.*

MVP *abbr. Sports* most valuable player.

MW *abbr.* **1** megawatt(s). **2** medium wave.

mW *abbr.* milliwatt(s).

my /mī/ *poss.pron.* (*attrib.*) **1** of or belonging to me or myself (*my house*). **2** as a form of address in affectionate, sympathetic, contexts (*my dear boy*). **3** in various expressions of surprise (*my God!*; *oh my!*). **4** *colloq.* indicating the speaker's husband, wife, child, etc. (*my Johnny's ill again*).

my- *comb. form* var. of MYO-.

my·al·gi·a /mīáljə/ *n.* a pain in a muscle or group of muscles. ◻◻ **my·al·gic** *adj.*

my·as·the·ni·a gra·vis *n.* a disease characterized by fatigue and muscle weakness, caused by an autoimmune attack on acetylcholine receptors.

my·ce·li·um /mīséeleeəm/ *n.* (*pl.* **mycelia** /–leeə/) the vegetative part of a fungus.

-mycin /mísin/ *comb. form* used to form the names of antibiotic compounds derived from fungi.

my·col·o·gy /mīkóləjee/ *n.* **1** the study of fungi. **2** the fungi of a particular region. ◻◻ **my·co·log·i·cal** /–kəlójikəl/ *adj.* **my·col·o·gist** *n.*

my·co·sis /mīkṓsis/ *n.* any disease caused by a fungus, e.g., ringworm. ◻◻ **my·cot·ic** /–kótik/ *adj.*

my·e·lin /mí-ilin/ *n.* a white substance which forms a sheath around certain nerve fibers. ◻◻ **my·e·li·na·tion** *n.*

my·e·li·tis /mī-ilítis/ *n.* inflammation of the spinal cord.

my·e·lo·ma /mí-ilṓmə/ *n.* (*pl.* **myelomas** or **myelomata** /–mətə/) a malignant tumor of the bone marrow.

My·lar /mílaar/ *n. Trademark* an extremely strong polyester film made in thin sheets and used for recording tapes, insulation, etc.

my·nah /mínə/ *n.* (also **my·na, mi·na**) any of various SE Asian starlings, able to mimic the human voice.

myo- /míō/ *comb. form* (also **my-** before a vowel) muscle.

my·o·car·di·al in·farc·tion *n.* a heart attack.

my·o·car·di·um /míōkaárdeeəm/ *n.* (*pl.* **myocardia** /–deeə/) the muscular tissue of the heart. ◻◻ **my·o·car·di·al** *adj.*

my·ol·o·gy /mīóləjee/ *n.* the study of the structure and function of muscles.

my·o·pi·a /mīṓpeeə/ *n.* **1** nearsightedness. **2** lack of imagination or intellectual insight. ◻◻ **my·op·ic** /mīópik/ *adj.* **my·op·i·cal·ly** /mīópiklee/ *adv.*

my·o·sis var. of MIOSIS.

myr·i·ad /míreeəd/ *n. & adj. literary* • *n.* **1** an indefinitely great number. **2** ten thousand. • *adj.* of an indefinitely great number.

myrrh /mər/ *n.* a gum resin from several trees of the genus *Commiphora* used in perfumery, incense, etc. ◻◻ **myrrh·ic** *adj.* **myrrh·y** *adj.*

myr·tle /mə́rtəl/ *n.* **1** an evergreen shrub of the genus *Myrtus*, with aromatic foliage and white flowers. **2** = PERIWINKLE[1].

my·self /mīsélf/ *pron.* **1** *emphat. form* of I[2] or ME[1] (*I saw it myself*). **2** *refl. form* of ME[1] (*able to dress myself*). **3** in my normal state of body and mind (*I'm not myself today*). **4** *poet.* = I[2]. ◻ **by myself** see *by oneself* (BY). **I myself** I for my part (*I myself am doubtful*).

mys·te·ri·ous /mistéereeəs/ *adj.* **1** full of or wrapped in mystery. **2** (of a person) delighting in mystery. ◻◻ **mys·te·ri·ous·ly** *adv.* **mys·te·ri·ous·ness** *n.*

mys·ter·y /místəree/ *n.* (*pl.* **-ies**) **1** a secret, hidden, or inexplicable matter. **2** secrecy or obscurity (*wrapped in mystery*). **3** (*attrib.*) secret; undisclosed (*mystery guest*). **4** the practice of making a secret of (esp. unimportant) things (*engaged in mystery and intrigue*). **5** (in full **mystery story**) a fictional work dealing with a puzzling event, esp. a crime. **6 a** a religious truth divinely revealed. **b** *RC Ch.* a decade of the rosary. **7** (in *pl.*) the secret religious rites of the ancient Greeks, Romans, etc.

mys·tic /místik/ *n. & adj.* • *n.* a person who seeks by contemplation and self-surrender to obtain unity with or absorption into the Deity or the ultimate reality, or who believes in the spiritual apprehension of truths that are beyond understanding. • *adj.* **1** mysterious and awe-inspiring. **2** spiritually allegorical or symbolic. **3** occult; esoteric. **4** of hidden meaning. ◻◻ **mys·ti·cism** /–tisizəm/ *n.*

mystic Middle English (in the sense 'mystical meaning'): from Old French *mystique*, or via Latin from Greek *mustikos*, from *mustēs* 'initiated person' from *muein* 'close the eyes or lips,' also used to mean 'initiate,' as of initiations into ancient mystery religious. The current sense of the noun dates from the late 17th century.

mys·ti·cal /místikəl/ *adj.* of mystics or mysticism. ◻◻ **mys·ti·cal·ly** *adv.*

mys·ti·fy /místifī/ *v.tr.* (**-fies, -fied**) **1** bewilder; confuse. **2** hoax; take advantage of the credulity of. **3** wrap up in mystery. ◻◻ **mys·ti·fi·ca·tion** /–fikáyshən/ *n.*

mys·tique /mistéek/ *n.* **1** an atmosphere of mystery and veneration attending some activity or person. **2** an air of secrecy surrounding a particular activity or subject that makes it impressive or baffling to those without specialized knowledge.

myth /mith/ *n.* **1** a traditional narrative usu. involving supernatural or imaginary persons and embodying popular ideas on natural or social phenomena, etc. **2** such narratives collectively. **3** a widely held but false notion. **4** a fictitious person, thing, or idea. **5** an allegory (*the Platonic myth*). ◻◻ **myth·ic** *adj.* **myth·i·cal** *adj.* **myth·i·cal·ly** *adv.*

my·thol·o·gy /mithóləjee/ *n.* (*pl.* **-gies**) **1** a body of myths (*Greek mythology*). **2** the study of myths. ◻◻ **my·thol·o·ger** *n.* **myth·o·log·i·cal** /–thəlójikəl/ *adj.* **myth·o·log·i·cal·ly** /–thəlójiklee/ *adv.* **my·thol·o·gist** *n.*

N

N[1] /en/ *n.* (also **n**) (*pl.* **Ns** or **N's**) **1** the fourteenth letter of the alphabet. **2** *Math.* (**n**) an indefinite number. □ **to the nth degree 1** *Math.* to any required power. **2** to the utmost.

N[2] *abbr.* (also **N.**) north; northern.

N[3] *symb. Chem.* the element nitrogen.

n *abbr.* (also **n.**) **1** noun. **2** neuter. **3** northern.

'n *conj.* (also **'n'**) *colloq.* and.

Na *symb. Chem.* the element sodium.

N.A. *abbr.* North America.

n/a *abbr.* **1** not applicable. **2** not available.

NAACP /endəbəláyseepee/ *abbr.* National Association for the Advancement of Colored People.

nab /nab/ *v.tr.* (**nabbed, nabbing**) *sl.* **1** arrest; catch in wrongdoing. **2** seize; grab.

na·bob /náybob/ *n.* (formerly) a conspicuously wealthy person.

na·cho /naáchō/ *n.* (*pl.* **-chos**) (usu. in *pl.*) a tortilla chip, usu. topped with melted cheese and spices, etc.

na·cre /náykər/ *n.* mother-of-pearl from any shelled mollusk. □□ **na·cre·ous** /náykreeəs/ *adj.*

na·dir /náydər, –deer/ *n.* **1** the part of the celestial sphere directly below an observer (opp. ZENITH). **2** the lowest point in one's fortunes.

NAFTA /náftə/ *abbr.* North American Free Trade Agreement.

nag[1] /nag/ *v. & n.* • *v.* (**nagged, nagging**) **1 a** *tr.* annoy or irritate (a person) with persistent faultfinding. **b** *intr.* (often foll. by *at*) find fault persistently. **2** *intr.* (of a pain) ache dully but persistently. **3** *tr.* worry or preoccupy (a person, the mind, etc.) (*his mistake nagged him*). • *n.* a persistently nagging person. □□ **nag·ger** *n.* **nag·ging·ly** *adv.*

nag[2] /nag/ *n. colloq.* a horse.

Na·hua·tl /naáwaát'l/ *n. & adj.* • *n.* **1** a member of a group of peoples native to S. Mexico and Central America, including the Aztecs. **2** the language of these people. • *adj.* of or concerning the Nahuatl peoples or language. □□ **Na·hua·tlan** *adj.*

nai·ad /nī́ad/ *n.* (*pl.* **naiads** or **-des** /nī́ədeez/) *Mythol.* a water nymph.

nail /nayl/ *n. & v.* • *n.* **1** a small metal spike with a broadened flat head, driven in with a hammer to join things together or to serve as a peg, protection (cf. HOBNAIL), or decoration. **2** a horny covering on the upper surface of the tip of the finger or toe. • *v.tr.* **1** fasten with a nail. **2 a** secure or get hold of (a person or thing). **b** expose (a lie or a liar). □ **nail down 1** bind (a person) to a promise, etc. **2** define precisely. **3** fasten (a thing) with nails. **nail in a person's coffin** something thought to increase the risk of death. □□ **nailed** *adj.* (also in *comb.*).

na·ïve /naa-eév/ *adj.* (also **na·ive**) **1** artless; innocent. **2** foolishly credulous. □□ **na·ïve·ly** *adv.*

na·ïve·té /naa-eevtáy, –eévtáy/ *n.* (also **naiveté**) **1** the state or quality of being naïve. **2** a naïve action.

na·ked /náykid/ *adj.* **1** without clothes; nude. **2** plain; exposed (*the naked truth; his naked soul*). **3** (of a light, flame, etc.) unprotected from the wind, etc. **4** defenseless. **5 a** (of landscape) barren; treeless. **b** (of rock) exposed; without soil, etc. **6** (usu. foll. by *of*) devoid; without. **7** without leaves, hair, scales, shell, etc. **8** (of a room, wall, etc.) without decoration, furnishings, etc.; empty; plain. □□ **na·ked·ly** *adv.* **na·ked·ness** *n.*

na·ked eye *n.* (prec. by *the*) unassisted vision, e.g., without a telescope, microscope, etc.

nam·by-pam·by /námbeepámbee/ *adj. & n.* • *adj.* **1** lacking vigor or drive. **2** insipidly pretty or sentimental. • *n.* (*pl.* **-bies**) a namby-pamby person.

name /naym/ *n. & v.* • *n.* **1** the word by which an individual person, animal, place, or thing is known. **2 a** a usu. abusive term used of a person, etc. (*called him names*). **b** a word denoting an object or class of objects, ideas, etc. (*what is the name of that kind of vase?*). **3** a famous person. **4** a reputation, esp. a good one (*has a name for honesty*). • *v.tr.* **1** give a specified name to (*named the dog Spot*). **2** call (a person or thing) by the right name (*named the man in the photograph*). **3** mention; specify (*named her requirements*). **4** nominate, appoint, etc. (*was named the new chairman*). **5** specify as something desired (*named it as her dearest wish*). □ **by name** called (*Tom by name*). **have to one's name** possess. **in all but name** virtually. **in name** (or **name only**) as a mere formality (*is the leader in name only*). **in a person's name** = *in the name of*. **in the name of** calling to witness (*in the name of goodness*). **in one's own name** independently. **make a name for oneself** become famous. **name after** (also **for**) call (a person) by the name of (a specified person) (*named him after his uncle Roger*). **name the day** arrange a date (esp. for a wedding). **name names** mention specific names, esp. in accusation. **name of the game** *colloq.* the purpose or essence of an action, etc. **of** (or **by**) **the name of** called. **put one's name down for 1** apply for. **2** promise to subscribe (a sum). **you name it** *colloq.* whatever you like. □□ **name·a·ble** *adj.*

name-call·ing *n.* abusive language.

name-drop·ping *n.* the familiar mention of famous people as a form of boasting. □□ **name-drop** *v.intr.* (**-dropped, -dropping**). **name-drop·per** *n.*

name·less /náymlis/ *adj.* **1** having no name or name inscription. **2** unnamed; anonymous (*our informant, who shall be nameless*). **3** too horrific to be named (*nameless vices*). □□ **name·less·ly** *adv.* **name·less·ness** *n.*

name·ly /náymlee/ *adv.* that is to say; in other words.

name·sake /náymsayk/ *n.* a person having the same name as another (*was her aunt's namesake*).

nan·a /nánə/ *n. colloq.* grandmother.

nan·ny /nánee/ *n.* (*pl.* **-nies**) **1** a child's nursemaid. **2** (in full **nanny goat**) a female goat.

nano- /nánō, náynō/ *comb.form* denoting a factor of 10^{-9} (*nanosecond*).

nan·o·me·ter /nánōmeetər/ *n.* one billionth of a meter. ¶ Abbr.: **nm.**

nan·o·sec·ond /nánōsekənd/ *n.* one billionth of a second. ¶ abbr.: **ns.**

nap[1] /nap/ *v. & n.* • *v.intr.* (**napped, napping**) sleep briefly. • *n.* a short sleep (*took a nap*). □ **catch a person napping 1** find a person off guard. **2** detect in negligence.

nap[2] /nap/ *n.* the raised pile on textiles, esp. velvet.

na·palm /náypaam/ *n. & v.* • *n.* a jellied substance used in incendiary bombs. • *v.tr.* attack with napalm bombs.

nape /nayp/ *n.* the back of the neck.

naph·tha /náf-thə, náp–/ *n.* a flammable oil obtained by the dry distillation of organic substances such as coal, shale, or petroleum.

naph·tha·lene /náf-thəleen, náp–/ *n.* a white crystalline aromatic substance produced by the distillation of coal tar and used in mothballs and the manufacture of dyes, etc. ▫▫ **naph·thal·ic** /–thálik/ *adj.*

nap·kin /nápkin/ *n.* (in full **table napkin**) a square piece of linen, paper, etc., used for wiping the lips, fingers, etc., at meals.

nap·kin ring *n.* a ring used to hold (and distinguish) a person's table napkin when not in use.

narc /nark/ *n.* (also **nark**) *sl.* a federal agent or police officer who enforces the laws regarding illicit sale or use of drugs and narcotics.

nar·cis·sism /naársisizəm/ *n. Psychol.* excessive or erotic interest in oneself, one's physical features, etc. ▫▫ **nar·cis·sist** *n.* **nar·cis·sis·tic** *adj.* **nar·cis·sis·ti·cal·ly** *adv.*

nar·cis·sus /naarsísəs/ *n.* (*pl.* **narcissi** /–sī/or **narcissuses**) any bulbous plant of the genus *Narcissus,* esp. *N. poeticus* bearing a heavily scented single flower.

nar·co·lep·sy /naárkəlepsee/ *n. Med.* a disease with fits of sleepiness and drowsiness. ▫▫ **nar·co·lep·tic** /–léptik/ *adj. & n.*

nar·co·sis /naarkṓsis/ *n.* **1** *Med.* the working or effects of soporific narcotics. **2** a state of insensibility.

nar·cot·ic /naarkótik/ *adj. & n.* • *adj.* **1** (of a substance) inducing drowsiness, sleep, insensibility. **2** (of a drug) affecting the mind. • *n.* a narcotic substance, drug, or influence. ▫▫ **nar·cot·i·cal·ly** *adv.*

nar·es /náireez/ *n.pl. Anat.* the nostrils. ▫▫ **na·ri·al** *adj.*

Nar·ra·gan·sett /narəgánsət, –gánt–/ *n.* **1 a** a N. American people native to Rhode Island. **b** a member of this people. **2** the language of this people.

nar·rate /nárayt, naráyt/ *v.tr.* (also *absol.*) **1** give a continuous story or account of. **2** provide a spoken commentary or accompaniment for (a film, etc.). ▫▫ **nar·rat·a·ble** *adj.* **nar·ra·tion** /–ráyshən/ *n.*

nar·ra·tive /nárətiv/ *n. & adj.* • *n.* **1** a spoken or written account of connected events in order of happening. **2** the practice or art of narration. • *adj.* in the form of, or concerned with, narration (*narrative verse*). ▫▫ **nar·ra·tive·ly** *adv.*

nar·ra·tor /náraytər/ *n.* **1** an actor, announcer, etc., who delivers a commentary in a film, broadcast, etc. **2** a person who narrates.

nar·row /nárō/ *adj., n., & v.* • *adj.* (**narrower, narrowest**) **1 a** of small width in proportion to length. **b** confined or confining (*within narrow bounds*). **2** of limited scope (*in the narrowest sense*). **3** with little margin (*a narrow escape*). • *n.* **1** (usu. in *pl.*) the narrow part of a strait, river, etc. **2** a narrow pass. • *v.* **1** *intr.* become narrow; diminish. **2** *tr.* make narrow; constrict. ▫▫ **narrow·ly** *adv.* **nar·row·ness** *n.*

nar·row-mind·ed /nárōmíndid/ *adj.* rigid or restricted in one's views; intolerant. ▫▫ **nar·row-mind·ed·ly** *adv.* **nar·row-mind·ed·ness** *n.*

nar·thex /naártheks/ *n.* an antechamber in a church.

nar·whal /naárwəl/ *n.* an Arctic whale, *Monodon monoceros,* the male of which has a long spirally fluted tusk. Also called BELUGA.

nar·y /náiree/ *adj. colloq.* or *dial.* not any; no (*nary a one*).

NASA /násə/ *abbr.* National Aeronautics and Space Administration.

na·sal /náyzəl/ *adj. & n.* • *adj.* **1** of, for, or relating to the nose. **2** *Phonet.* (of a sound) pronounced with the breath passing through the nose, e.g., *m, n, ng,* or French *en.* **3** (of the voice or speech) having an intonation caused by breathing through the nose. • *n. Phonet.* a nasal sound. ▫▫ **na·sal·i·ty** /–zálitee/ *n.* **na·sal·ize** *v.intr. & tr.* **na·sal·i·za·tion** *n.* **na·sal·ly** *adv.*

nas·cent /násənt, náy–/ *adj.* **1** in the act of being born. **2** just beginning to be; not yet mature. **3** *Chem.* just being formed and therefore unusually reactive (*nascent hydrogen*). ▫▫ **nas·cen·cy** /násənsee, náy–/ *n.*

NASDAQ /názdak, nás–/ *abbr.* National Association of Securities Dealers Automated Quotations.

nas·tur·tium /nəstə́rshəm/ *n.* **1** (in general use) a trailing plant, *Tropaeolum majus,* with rounded edible leaves and bright orange, yellow, or red flowers. **2** any cruciferous plant of the genus *Nasturtium,* including watercress.

nas·ty /nástee/ *adj.* (**nastier, nastiest**) **1 a** highly unpleasant. **b** annoying; objectionable (*the car has a nasty habit of breaking down*). **2** difficult to negotiate; dangerous; serious (*a nasty fence; a nasty question; a nasty illness*). **3** (of a person or animal) ill-natured; spiteful; violent. **4** (of the weather) wet, stormy. ▫▫ **nas·ti·ly** *adv.* **nas·ti·ness** *n.*

nat. *abbr.* **1** national. **2** natural.

na·tal /náytəl/ *adj.* of or from one's birth.

na·tal·i·ty /naytálitee, nə–/ *n.* (*pl.* **-ties**) birth rate.

Natch·ez /náchiz/ *n.* **1 a** a N. American people native to Mississippi. **b** a member of this people. **2** the language of this people.

na·tion /náyshən/ *n.* **1** a community of people of mainly common descent, history, language, etc., forming a unified government or inhabiting a territory. **2** a tribe or confederation of tribes of Native Americans. ▫ **law of nations** *Law* international law. ▫▫ **na·tion·hood** *n.*

na·tion·al /náshənəl/ *adj. & n.* • *adj.* **1** of or common to a nation or the nation. **2** peculiar to or characteristic of a particular nation. • *n.* a citizen of a specified country, usu. entitled to hold that country's passport (*French nationals*). ▫▫ **na·tion·al·ly** *adv.*

na·tion·al an·them *n.* a song adopted by a nation, expressive of its identity, etc., and intended to inspire patriotism.

na·tion·al debt *n.* the money owed by a country because of loans to it.

Na·tion·al Guard *n.* the primary reserve force partly maintained by the states of the United States but available for federal use.

na·tion·al·ism /náshənəlizəm/ *n.* **1 a** patriotic feeling, principles, etc. **b** an extreme form of this. **2** a policy of national independence. ▫▫ **na·tion·al·ist** *n. & adj.* **na·tion·al·is·tic** *adj.* **na·tion·al·is·ti·cal·ly** *adv.*

na·tion·al·i·ty /náshənálitee/ *n.* (*pl.* **-ties**) **1 a** the status of belonging to a particular nation (*what is your nationality?; has Austrian nationality*). **b** a nation (*people of all nationalities*). **2** the condition of being national; distinctive national qualities. **3** an ethnic group forming a part of one or more political nations.

na·tion·al·ize /náshənəlīz/ *v.tr.* **1** take over (industry, land, etc.) from private ownership on behalf of the government. **2** make national. ▫▫ **na·tion·al·i·za·tion** *n.*

na·tion·al park *n.* an area of natural beauty protected by the government for the use of the general public.

na·tion·wide /náyshənwíd/ *adj.* extending over the whole nation.

na·tive /náytiv/ *n. & adj.* • *n.* **1 a** (usu. foll. by *of*) a person born in a specified place, or whose parents are domiciled in that place at the time of the birth (*a native of Chicago*). **b** a local inhabitant. **2** *offens.* a member of a nonwhite indigenous people, as regarded by the colonial settlers. **3** (usu. foll. by *of*) an indigenous animal or plant. • *adj.* **1** (usu. foll. by *to*) belonging to a person or thing by nature; inherent; innate (*spoke with the facility native to him*). **2** of one's birth or birthplace (*native dress; native country*). **3** (usu. foll. by *to*) belonging to a specified place (*the anteater is native to S. America*). **4 a** (esp. of a non-European) born in a place. **b** of the natives of a place (*native customs*). □□ **na•tive•ly** *adv.* **na•tive•ness** *n.*

Na•tive A•mer•i•can *n.* a member of the aboriginal peoples of America or their descendants.

na•tiv•i•ty /nətívitee, nay–/ *n.* (*pl.* **-ties**) **1** (esp. **the Nativity**) **a** the birth of Christ. **b** the festival of Christ's birth; Christmas. **2** a picture of the Nativity. **3** birth.

NATO /náytō/ *abbr.* North Atlantic Treaty Organization.

nat•ty /nátee/ *adj.* (**nattier, nattiest**) *colloq.* **1 a** smartly or neatly dressed. **b** spruce; smart (*a natty blouse*). **2** deft. □□ **nat•ti•ly** *adv.* **nat•ti•ness** *n.*

nat•u•ral /náchərəl/ *adj.* & *n.* • *adj.* **1 a** existing in or caused by nature (*natural landscape*). **b** uncultivated (*existing in its natural state*). **2** in the course of nature (*died of natural causes*). **3** (of human nature, etc.) to be expected (*natural for her to be upset*). **4 a** (of a person or a person's behavior) unaffected; spontaneous. **b** (foll. by *to*) spontaneous; easy (*friendliness is natural to him*). **5 a** (of qualities, etc.) inherent (*a natural talent for music*). **b** (of a person) having such qualities (*a natural linguist*). **6** not disguised or altered (by makeup, etc.). **7** lifelike (*the portrait looked very natural*). **8** likely by its or their nature to be such (*natural enemies; the natural antithesis*). **9 a** related by nature (*her natural son*). **b** illegitimate (*a natural child*). **10** *Mus.* (of a note) not sharpened or flattened (*B natural*). • *n.* **1** *colloq.* (usu. foll. by *for*) a person or thing naturally suitable, adept, etc. (*a natural for the championship*). **2** *Mus.* **a** a sign (♮) denoting a return to natural pitch after a sharp or a flat. **b** a natural note. □□ **nat•u•ral•ness** *n.*

nat•u•ral-born *adj.* having a character or position by birth.

nat•u•ral child•birth *n. Med.* childbirth with minimal medical or technological intervention.

nat•u•ral gas *n.* a flammable mainly methane gas found in the earth's crust, not manufactured.

nat•u•ral his•to•ry *n.* **1** the study of animals or plants. **2** the facts concerning the flora and fauna, etc., of a particular place or class (*a natural history of Florida*).

nat•u•ral•ism /náchərəlizəm/ *n.* the theory or practice in art and literature of representing nature, character, etc., realistically and in great detail.

nat•u•ral•ist /náchərəlist/ *n.* **1** an expert in natural history. **2** a person who believes in or practices naturalism.

nat•u•ral•is•tic /náchərəlístik/ *adj.* **1** lifelike. **2** of or according to naturalism. **3** of natural history. □□ **nat•u•ral•is•ti•cal•ly** *adv.*

nat•ur•al•ize /náchərəlīz/ *v. tr.* **1** admit (a foreigner) to the citizenship of a country. **2** introduce (an animal, plant, etc.) into another region so that it flourishes in the wild. **3** adopt (a foreign word, custom, etc.). □□ **nat•ur•al•i•za•tion** *n.*

nat•u•ral law *n. Philos.* unchanging moral principles common to all human beings.

nat•u•ral•ly /náchərəlee, náchrə–/ *adv.* **1** in a natural manner. **2** as a natural result. **3** (qualifying a whole sentence) as might be expected; of course.

nat•u•ral num•bers *n.pl.* the integers 1, 2, 3, etc.

nat•u•ral re•sources *n.pl.* materials or conditions occurring in nature and capable of economic exploitation.

nat•u•ral sci•ence *n.* the sciences used in the study of the physical world, e.g., physics, chemistry, geology, biology, botany.

nat•u•ral se•lec•tion *n.* the Darwinian theory of the survival and propagation of organisms best adapted to their environment.

na•ture /náychər/ *n.* **1** a thing's or person's innate or essential qualities or character (*not in their nature to be cruel; the nature of iron to rust*). **2** (often **Nature**) **a** the physical power causing all the phenomena of the material world. **b** these phenomena, including plants, animals, landscape, etc. **3** a kind, sort, or class (*things of this nature*). **4** = HUMAN NATURE. **5 a** a specified element of human character (*the rational nature; our animal nature*). **b** a person of specified character (*even strong natures quail*). **6 a** an uncultivated or wild area, condition, community, etc. **b** the countryside, esp. when picturesque. **7** inherent impulses determining character. **8** heredity as an influence on or determinant of personality. □ **by nature** innately. **from nature** *Art* using natural objects as models. **in** (or **of**) **the nature of** characteristically resembling or belonging to the class of (*the answer was in the nature of an excuse*).

na•tured /náychərd/ *adj.* (in *comb.*) having a specified disposition (*good-natured; ill-natured*).

na•tur•ism /náychərizəm/ *n.* **1** nudism. **2** naturalism in regard to religion. **3** the worship of natural objects. □□ **na•tur•ist** *n.*

naught /nawt/ *n.* & *adj.* • *n.* **1** *archaic* or *literary* nothing; nothingness. **2** zero; cipher. • *adj.* (usu. *predic.*) *archaic* or *literary* worthless; useless.

naugh•ty /náwtee/ *adj.* (**naughtier, naughtiest**) **1** (esp. of children) disobedient; badly behaved. **2** *colloq. joc.* indecent. □□ **naugh•ti•ly** *adv.* **naugh•ti•ness** *n.*

nau•se•a /náwzeeə, –zhə, –seeə, –shə/ *n.* **1** a feeling of sickness with an inclination to vomit. **2** loathing; revulsion.

nau•se•ate /náwzeeayt, –zhee, –see, –shee/ *v. tr.* **1** affect with nausea; disgust (*was nauseated by the smell*). **2** *intr.* (usu. foll. by *at*) loathe food, an occupation, etc.; feel sick. □□ **nau•se•at•ing** *adj.* **nau•se•at•ing•ly** *adv.*

▶A distinction has traditionally been drawn between **nauseated**, meaning 'affected with nausea,' and **nauseous**, meaning 'causing nausea.' Today, however, the use of **nauseous** to mean 'affected with nausea' is so common that it is generally considered to be standard.

nau•seous /náwshəs, –zeeəs/ *adj.* **1** affected with nausea; sick. **2** causing nausea; offensive to the taste or smell. **3** disgusting; loathsome. □□ **nau•seous•ly** *adv.*
▶See note at NAUSEATE.

nau•ti•cal /náwtikəl/ *adj.* of or concerning sailors or navigation; naval; maritime. □□ **nau•ti•cal•ly** *adv.*

nau•ti•cal mile *n.* a unit of approx. 2,025 yards (1,852 meters): also called **sea mile**.

nau•ti•lus /náwt'ləs/ *n.* (*pl.* **nautiluses** or **nautili** /–lī/) any cephalopod of the genus *Nautilus* with a light brittle spiral shell, esp. (**pearly nautilus**) one having a chambered shell with nacreous septa.

nautilus

Nav•a•jo /návəhō, náa–/ *n.* (also **Nav•a•ho**) (*pl.* **-jos**) **1** a member of a N. American people native to New Mexico and Arizona. **2** the language of this people.

na•val /náyvəl/ *adj.* **1** of, in, for, etc., the navy or a navy. **2** of or concerning ships (*a naval battle*).

nave /nayv/ *n.* the central part of a church, usu. from the west door to the chancel and excluding the side aisles.

na•vel /náyvəl/ *n.* a depression in the center of the belly caused by the detachment of the umbilical cord.

---

navel Old English *nafela*, of Germanic origin; related to Dutch *navel* and German *Nabel*, from an Indo-European root shared by Latin *umbo* 'boss (round knob in the middle) of a shield,' *umbilicus* 'navel,' and Greek *omphalos* 'boss, navel.'

nav·el or·ange *n.* a seedless orange with a navellike formation at the top.

nav·i·ga·ble /návigəbəl/ *adj.* (of a river, the sea, etc.) affording a passage for ships. ▫▫ **nav·i·ga·bil·i·ty** *n.*

nav·i·gate /návigayt/ *v.* **1** *tr.* manage or direct the course of (a ship, aircraft, etc.). **2** *tr.* **a** sail on (a sea, river, etc.). **b** travel or fly through (the air). **3** *intr.* (of a passenger in a vehicle) assist the driver by map-reading, etc. **4** *intr.* sail a ship; sail in a ship.

nav·i·ga·tion /návigáyshən/ *n.* **1** the act of navigating. **2** any of several methods of determining a ship's or aircraft's position and course. ▫▫ **nav·i·ga·tion·al** *adj.*

nav·i·ga·tor /návigaytər/ *n.* **1** a person skilled or engaged in navigation. **2** an explorer by sea.

na·vy /náyvee/ *n.* (*pl.* **-vies**) **1** (often **the Navy**) **a** the whole body of a nation's ships of war, including crews, maintenance systems, etc. **b** the officers, men, and women of a navy. **2** (in full **navy blue**) a dark-blue color.

na·vy bean *n.* a small white kidney bean, usu. dried for storage.

na·vy yard *n.* a government shipyard where naval vessels are built, maintained, etc., and where naval supplies are stored.

nay /nay/ *adv.* & *n.* • *adv.* **1** or rather; and more than that (*impressive, nay, magnificent*). **2** *archaic* = NO[2] *adv.* 1. • *n.* **1** the word 'nay.' **2** a negative vote.

nay·say /náysay/ *v.* (*3rd sing. present* **-says**; *past* and *past part.* **-said**) **1** *intr.* utter a denial or refusal. **2** *tr.* refuse or contradict. ▫▫ **nay·say·er** *n.*

Naz·a·rene /názəréen/ *n.* & *adj.* • *n.* **1 a** (prec. by *the*) Christ. **b** (esp. in Jewish or Muslim use) a Christian. **2** a native or inhabitant of Nazareth. **3** a member of an early Jewish-Christian sect. • *adj.* of or concerning Nazareth, Nazarenes, etc.

Na·zi /naátsee, nát–/ *n.* & *adj.* • *n.* (*pl.* **Nazis**) **1** *hist.* a member of the German National Socialist party. **2** *derog.* a person holding extreme racist or authoritarian views or behaving brutally. • *adj.* of or concerning the Nazis, Nazism, etc. ▫▫ **Na·zi·ism** /–see-izəm/ *n.* **Na·zism** /naátsizəm, nát–/ *n.*

NB *abbr.* **1** New Brunswick. **2** nota bene. **3** Scotland (North Britain).

Nb *symb. Chem.* the element niobium.

NBC *abbr.* National Broadcasting Company.

NC *abbr.* North Carolina (also in official postal use).

NCO *abbr.* noncommissioned officer.

ND *abbr.* North Dakota (in official postal use).

Nd *symb. Chem.* the element neodymium.

N.Dak. *abbr.* North Dakota.

NE *abbr.* **1** Nebraska (in official postal use). **2** northeast. **3** northeastern.

Ne *symb. Chem.* the element neon.

NEA *abbr.* National Education Association.

Ne·an·der·thal /neeándərthawl, –tawl, –taal/ *adj.* of or belonging to the type of human widely distributed in Paleolithic Europe, with a retreating forehead and massive brow ridges.

neap /neep/ *n.* (in full **neap tide**) a tide just after the first and third quarters of the moon when there is least difference between high and low water.

Ne·a·pol·i·tan /néeəpólitən/ *n.* & *adj.* • *n.* a native or citizen of Naples in Italy. • *adj.* of or relating to Naples.

Ne·a·pol·i·tan ice cream *n.* ice cream made in layers of different colors and flavors, esp. vanilla, chocolate, and strawberry.

near /neer/ *adv., prep., adj.,* & *v.* • *adv.* **1** (often foll. by *to*) to or at a short distance in space or time; close by (*the time drew near*). **2** closely (*as near as one can guess*). • *prep.* (*compar.* & *superl. also used*) **1** to or at a short distance (in space, time, condition, or resemblance) from (*stood near the back*). **2** (in *comb.*) that is almost (*near-hysterical; a near-Communist*). • *adj.* **1** close to, in place or time (*in the near future*). **2** closely related (*a near relation*). **3** (of a part of a vehicle, animal, or road) left (*the near foreleg*). **4** close; narrow (*a near escape*). **5** (of a road or way) direct. • *v.* **1** *tr.* approach; draw near to (*neared the harbor*). **2** *intr.* draw near (*could distinguish them as they neared*). ▫ **come** (or **go**) **near** (foll. by verbal noun, or *to* + verbal noun) almost succeed in (*came near to falling*). **go near** (foll. by *to* + infin.) narrowly fail. **near at hand 1** within easy reach. **2** in the immediate future. ▫▫ **near·ish** *adj.* **near·ness** *n.*

near·by /néerbí/ *adj.* & *adv.* • *adj.* situated in a near position (*a nearby hotel*). • *adv.* close; not far away.

Near East *n.* the region comprising the countries of the eastern Mediterranean. ▫▫ **Near East·ern** *adj.*

near·ly /néerlee/ *adv.* almost. ▫ **not nearly** nothing like (*not nearly enough*).

near miss *n.* **1** a bomb, etc., that is close to the target. **2** a situation in which a collision is narrowly avoided.

near·sight·ed /néersítid/ *adj.* having the inability to focus the eyes except on comparatively near objects. ▫▫ **near·sight·ed·ly** *adv.* **near·sight·ed·ness** *n.*

neat /neet/ *adj.* **1** tidy and methodical. **2** elegantly simple in form. **3** (of language, style, etc.) brief, clear, and pointed. **4 a** cleverly executed (*a neat piece of work*). **b** deft; dexterous. **5** (of alcoholic liquor) undiluted. **6** *sl.* (as a general term of approval) pleasing; excellent. ▫▫ **neat·ly** *adv.* **neat·ness** *n.*

neat·en /néet'n/ *v.tr.* make neat.

neath /neeth/ *prep. poet.* beneath.

Neb. *abbr.* Nebraska.

Nebr. *abbr.* Nebraska.

neb·u·la /nébyələ/ *n.* (*pl.* **nebulae** /–lee/or **nebulas**) *Astron.* **1** a cloud of gas and dust, sometimes glowing and sometimes appearing as a dark silhouette against other glowing matter. **2** a bright area caused by a galaxy, or a large cloud of distant stars. ▫▫ **neb·u·lar** *adj.*

neb·u·lous /nébyələs/ *adj.* **1** cloudlike. **2 a** formless; clouded. **b** hazy, indistinct; vague (*put forward a few nebulous ideas*). ▫▫ **neb·u·los·i·ty** /–lósitee/ *n.* **neb·u·lous·ly** *adv.* **neb·u·lous·ness** *n.*

nec·es·sar·i·ly /nésəsérilee/ *adv.* as a necessary result; inevitably.

nec·es·sar·y /nésəseree/ *adj.* & *n.* • *adj.* **1** requiring to be done, achieved, etc.; requisite; essential (*it is necessary to work; lacks the necessary documents*). **2** determined, existing, or happening by natural laws, predestination, etc., not by free will; inevitable (*a necessary evil*). • *n.* (*pl.* **-ies**) (usu. in *pl.*) any of the basic requirements of life, such as food, warmth, etc.

ne·ces·si·tate /nisésitayt/ *v.tr.* make necessary (esp. as a result) (*will necessitate some sacrifice*).

ne·ces·si·ty /nisésitee/ *n.* (*pl.* **-ties**) **1 a** an indispensable thing. **b** (usu. foll. by *of*) indispensability. **2** a state of things or circumstances enforcing a certain course (*there was a necessity to hurry*). **3** imperative need (*necessity is the mother of invention*). **4** want; poverty. ▫ **of necessity** unavoidably.

neck /nek/ *n.* & *v.* • *n.* **1 a** the part of the body connecting the head to the shoulders. **b** the part of a shirt, dress, etc., around the neck. **2** something resembling a neck, such as the narrow part of a cavity or vessel, a channel, isthmus, etc. **3** the part of a violin, etc., bearing the fingerboard. **4** the length of a horse's head and neck as a measure of its lead in a race. • *v. intr.* & *tr. colloq.* kiss and caress amorously. ▫ **neck and neck** running even in a race, etc. **up to one's neck** (often foll. by *in*) *colloq.* very deeply involved; very busy. □□ **necked** *adj.* (also in *comb.*). **neck·er** *n.* **neck·less** *adj.*

neck·band /nékband/ *n.* a strip of material around the neck of a garment.

neck·er·chief /nékərchif, –cheef/ *n.* a square of cloth worn around the neck.

neck·lace /nékləs/ *n.* a chain or string of beads, precious stones, links, etc., worn as an ornament around the neck.

neck·line /néklīn/ *n.* the edge or shape of the opening of a garment at the neck.

neck of the woods *n. colloq.* region; neighborhood.

neck·tie /néktī/ *n.* = TIE *n.* 2.

neck·wear /nékwair/ *n.* collars, ties, etc.

necro- /nékrō/ *comb. form* corpse.

nec·ro·man·cy /nékrōmansee/ *n.* **1** the prediction of the future by supposed communication with the dead. **2** witchcraft. □□ **nec·ro·man·cer** *n.* **nec·ro·man·tic** /–mántik/ *adj.*

nec·ro·phil·i·a /nékrəfileeə/ *n.* (also **nec·ro·phil·y** /nikrófilee/) a morbid and esp. erotic attraction to corpses. □□ **nec·ro·phile** /nékrəfīl/ *n.* **nec·ro·phil·i·ac** /–fileeak/ *n.* **nec·ro·phil·ic** *adj.* **ne·croph·i·lism** /–krófilizəm/ *n.*

ne·crop·o·lis /nekrópəlis/ *n.* an ancient cemetery or burial place.

ne·cro·sis /nekrṓsis/ *n. Med. & Physiol.* the death of tissue caused by disease or injury, esp. gangrene or pulmonary tuberculosis. □□ **ne·crot·ic** /–krótik/ *adj.* **nec·ro·tize** /nékrətīz/ *v.intr.*

nec·tar /néktər/ *n.* **1** a sugary substance produced by plants and made into honey by bees. **2** (in Greek and Roman mythology) the drink of the gods. **3** a drink compared to this. □□ **nec·tar·ous** *adj.*

nec·tar·ine /nektəréen/ *n.* a variety of peach with a smooth skin.

née /nay/ *adj.* (also **nee**) (used in adding a married woman's maiden name after her surname) born (*Mrs. Ann Smith, née Jones*).

need /need/ *v. & n.* • *v.tr.* **1** stand in want of; require. **2** (foll. by *to* + infin.; *3rd sing. present neg. or interrog.* **need** without *to*) be under the necessity or obligation (*it needs to be done carefully; need you ask?*). • *n.* **1** a want or requirement (*my needs are few*). **2** circumstances requiring some course of action (*there is no need to worry*). **3** destitution; poverty. □ **have need of** require; want. **in need** requiring help. **in need of** requiring. **need not have** did not need to (but did).

need·ful /néedfŏŏl/ *adj.* requisite; necessary. □□ **need·ful·ly** *adv.* **need·ful·ness** *n.*

nee·dle /néed'l/ *n. & v.* • *n.* **1 a** a very thin small piece of smooth steel, etc., pointed at one end and with a slit (eye) for thread at the other, used in sewing. **b** a larger plastic, wooden, etc., slender stick without an eye, used in knitting. **2** a pointer on a dial. **3** any of several small thin pointed instruments, esp.: **a** a surgical instrument for stitching. **b** the end of a hypodermic syringe. **c** = STYLUS. **4 a** an obelisk (*Cleopatra's Needle*). **b** a pointed rock or peak. **5** the leaf of a fir or pine tree. • *v.tr. colloq.* irritate; provoke (*the silence needled him*).

nee·dle·point /néed'lpoynt/ *n.* decorative needlework made with a needle.

need·less /néedlis/ *adj.* **1** unnecessary. **2** uncalled-for; gratuitous. □ **needless to say** of course; it goes without saying. □□ **need·less·ly** *adv.* **need·less·ness** *n.*

nee·dle·work /néed'lwərk/ *n.* sewing or embroidery.

needs /needz/ *adv. archaic* (usu. prec. or foll. by *must*) of necessity.

need·y /néedee/ *adj.* (**needier, neediest**) **1** (of a person) poor; destitute. **2** (of circumstances) characterized by poverty. □□ **need·i·ness** *n.*

ne'er /nair/ *adv. poet.* = NEVER.

ne'er-do-well *n. & adj.* • *n.* a good-for-nothing person. • *adj.* good-for-nothing.

ne·far·i·ous /nifáireeəs/ *adj.* wicked. □□ **ne·far·i·ous·ly** *adv.* **ne·far·i·ous·ness** *n.*

neg. *abbr.* negative.

ne·gate /nigáyt/ *v.tr.* **1** nullify; invalidate. **2** assert the nonexistence of. **3** be the negation of. □□ **ne·ga·tor** *n.*

ne·ga·tion /nigáyshən/ *n.* **1** the absence or opposite of something actual or positive. **2 a** the act of denying. **b** an instance of this. **3** a contradiction, or denial. **4** a negative statement. **5** a negative or unreal thing. □□ **neg·a·tory** /négətáwree/ *adj.*

neg·a·tive /négətiv/ *adj. & n.* • *adj.* **1** expressing or implying denial or refusal (*a negative vote; a negative answer*). **2** (of a person or attitude): lacking positive attributes; apathetic; pessimistic. **3** marked by the absence of qualities (*a negative reaction; a negative result from the test*). **4** of the opposite nature to a thing regarded as positive (*debt is negative capital*). **5** *Algebra* (of a quantity) less than zero. **6** *Electr.* **a** of the kind of charge carried by electrons. **b** containing or producing such a charge. • *n.* **1** a negative statement, reply, or word. **2** *Photog.* **a** an image with black and white reversed or colors replaced by complementary ones, from which positive pictures are obtained. **b** a developed film or plate bearing such an image. **3** (prec. by *the*) a position opposing the affirmative. □ **in the negative** so as to reject a proposal, etc.; no (*the answer was in the negative*). □□ **neg·a·tive·ly** *adv.* **neg·a·tive·ness** *n.* **neg·a·tiv·i·ty** /–tívitee/ *n.*

neg·a·tive pole *n.* the south-seeking pole of a magnet.

neg·a·tiv·ism /négətivizəm/ *n.* **1** a negative attitude; extreme skepticism, criticism, etc. **2** denial of accepted beliefs. □□ **neg·a·tiv·ist** *n.* **neg·a·tiv·is·tic** /–vístik/ *adj.*

ne·glect /niglékt/ *v. & n.* • *v.tr.* **1** fail to care for or to do (*neglected their duty; neglected his children*). **2** (foll. by verbal noun, or *to* + infin.) overlook or forget the need to (*neglected to inform them.* **3** not pay attention to (*neglected the obvious warning*). • *n.* **1** lack of caring; negligence (*the house suffered from neglect*). **2 a** the act of neglecting. **b** the state of being neglected (*the house fell into neglect*). **3** (usu. foll. by *of*) disregard. □□ **ne·glect·ful** *adj.* **ne·glect·ful·ly** *adv.*

neg·li·gee /néglizháy/ *n.* (also **negligée, néglige**) a woman's dressing gown made of sheer fabric.

neg·li·gence /néglijəns/ *n.* **1** a lack of proper care and attention. **2** an act of carelessness. □□ **neg·li·gent** /–jənt/ *adj.* **neg·li·gent·ly** *adv.*

neg·li·gi·ble /néglijibəl/ *adj.* not worth considering; trifling; insignificant. □□ **neg·li·gi·bil·i·ty** *n.* **neg·li·gi·bly** *adv.*

ne·go·ti·a·ble /nigṓshəbəl, –sheeə–/ *adj.* **1** open to discussion. **2** able to be negotiated.

ne·go·ti·ate /nigṓsheeayt, –seeayt/ *v.* **1** *intr.* (usu. foll. by *with*) confer with others in order to reach a compromise or agreement. **2** *tr.* arrange (an affair) or bring about (a result) by negotiating (*negotiated a settlement*). **3** *tr.* find a way over, through, etc. (an obstacle, difficulty, etc.). **4** *tr.* **a** transfer (a check, etc.) to another for a consideration. **b** convert (a check, etc.) into cash. □□ **ne·go·ti·a·tion** /–áyshən/ *n.* **ne·go·ti·a·tor** *n.*

neg·ri·tude /néegritōōd, –tyōōd, nég–/ (also **Neg·ri·tude**) *n.* the affirmation or consciousness of the value of Negro black culture.

Ne·gro /néegrō/ *n. & adj.* • *n.* (*pl.* **-groes**) a member of a dark-skinned race orig. native to Africa. • *adj.* of or concerning Negroes (black people).

▶The term *black* or *African American* is usually preferred.

Ne·groid /néegroyd/ *adj. & n.* • *adj.* **1** (of features, etc.)

characterizing a member of the Negro (black) race, esp. in having dark skin, tightly curled hair, and a broad flattish nose. **2** of or concerning Negroes (black people). • *n.* a Negro (black person).

neigh /nay/ *n.* & *v.* • *n.* the high whinnying sound of a horse. • *v.intr.* make such a sound.

neigh·bor /náybər/ *n.* & *v.* • *n.* **1** a person living next door to or near or nearest another. **2** a fellow human being. **3** a person or thing near or next to another. **4** (*attrib.*) neighboring. • *v.* **1** *tr.* border on; adjoin. **2** *intr.* (often foll. by *on, upon*) border; adjoin. ▫▫ **neigh·bor·ing** *adj.* **neigh·bor·less** *adj.* **neigh·bor·ship** *n.*

neigh·bor·hood /náybərhood/ *n.* **1** a district, esp. one forming a community within a town or city. **2** the people of a district. ▫ **in the neighborhood of** roughly; about (*paid in the neighborhood of $100*).

neigh·bor·ly /náybərlee/ *adj.* friendly; kind. ▫▫ **neigh·bor·li·ness** *n.*

nei·ther /neéthər, níth–/ *adj., pron., & adv.* • *adj. & pron.* (foll. by sing. verb) not the one nor the other (of two things); not either (*neither of them knows; neither wish was granted*). • *adv.* **1** not either; not on the one hand (foll. by *nor*; introducing the first of two or more things in the negative: *neither knowing nor caring; would neither come in nor go out*). **2** not either; also not (*if you do not, neither shall I*).

nel·lie /nélee/ *n.* a silly or effeminate person.

nel·son /nélsən/ *n.* a wrestling hold in which one arm is passed under the opponent's arm from behind and the hand is applied to the neck (**half nelson**), or both arms and hands are applied (**full nelson**).

nem·a·tode /némətōd/ *n.* any worm of the phylum Nematoda, with a slender unsegmented cylindrical shape. Also called ROUNDWORM.

nem·e·sis /némisis/ *n.* (*pl.* **nemeses** /–seez/) **1** retributive justice. **2 a** a downfall caused by this. **b** an agent of such a downfall.

neo- /neé-ō/ *comb. form* **1** new; modern. **2** a new or revived form of.

ne·o·clas·si·cal /neé-ōklásikəl/ *adj.* (also **ne·o·clas·sic** /–ik/) of or relating to a revival of a classical style in art. ▫▫ **ne·o·clas·si·cism** /–sisizəm/ *n.* **ne·o·clas·si·cist** *n.*

ne·o·co·lo·ni·al·ism /neé-ōkəlṓneeəlizəm/ *n.* the use of economic, political, or other pressures to influence other countries, esp. former dependencies. ▫▫ **ne·o·co·lo·ni·al·ist** *n.* & *adj.*

ne·o·dym·i·um /neéədímeeəm/ *n. Chem.* a silver-gray naturally occurring metallic element of the lanthanide series used in coloring glass, etc.

ne·o·lith·ic /neéəlíthik/ *adj.* of or relating to the later Stone Age.

ne·ol·o·gism /nee-óləjizəm/ *n.* **1** a new word or expression. **2** the coining or use of new words. ▫▫ **ne·ol·o·gist** *n.* **ne·ol·o·gize** /–jīz/ *v.intr.*

ne·on /neé-on/ *n. Chem.* an inert gaseous element giving an orange glow when electricity is passed through it (*neon sign*).

ne·o·nate /neéənayt/ *n.* a newborn child. ▫▫ **ne·o·na·tal** /–náyt'l/ *adj.*

ne·o·phyte /neéəfīt/ *n.* **1** a new convert, esp. to a religious faith. **2** *RC Ch.* **a** a novice of a religious order. **b** a newly ordained priest. **3** a beginner; a novice.

ne·o·plasm /neé-əplazəm/ *n.* a new and abnormal growth of tissue in some part of the body, esp. a tumor. ▫▫ **ne·o·plas·tic** /–plástik/ *adj.*

ne·o·prene /neé-əpreen/ *n.* a synthetic rubberlike polymer.

Nep·a·lese /népəleéz, –leés/ *adj.* & *n.* (*pl.* same) = NEPALI.

Ne·pal·i /nipáwlee/ *n.* & *adj.* • *n.* (*pl.* same or **Nepalis**) **1 a** a native or national of Nepal in Central Asia. **b** a person of Nepali descent. **2** the language of Nepal. • *adj.* of or relating to Nepal or its language or people.

neph·ew /néfyoo/ *n.* a son of one's brother or sister, or of one's brother-in-law or sister-in-law.

ne·phrit·ic /nəfrítik/ *adj.* **1** of or in the kidneys. **2** of or relating to nephritis.

ne·phri·tis /nefrítis/ *n.* inflammation of the kidneys. Also called **Bright's disease**.

ne plus ul·tra /náy ploos óoltraa, nee plus últrə/ *n.* **1** the furthest attainable point. **2** the culmination, acme, or perfection.

nep·o·tism /népətizəm/ *n.* favoritism shown to relatives in conferring offices or privileges. ▫▫ **nep·o·tist** *n.* **nep·o·tis·tic** *adj.*

Nep·tune /néptoon, –tyoon/ *n.* a distant planet of the solar system, eighth from the sun, discovered in 1846 from mathematical computations.

nep·tu·ni·um /neptóoneeəm, –tyóo–/ *n. Chem.* a radioactive transuranic metallic element produced when uranium atoms absorb bombarding neutrons.

nerd /nərd/ *n. sl.* **1** a foolish, feeble, or uninteresting person. **2** a person intellectually talented but socially unskilled. ▫▫ **nerd·y** *adj.*

nerve /nərv/ *n.* & *v.* • *n.* **1 a** a fiber or bundle of fibers that transmits impulses of sensation or motion between the brain or spinal cord and other parts of the body. **b** the material constituting these. **2 a** coolness in danger; bravery; assurance. **b** *colloq.* impudence; audacity (*they've got a nerve*). **3** (in *pl.*) nervousness; a condition of mental or physical stress (*need to calm my nerves*). • *v.tr.* **1** (usu. *refl.*) brace (oneself) to face danger, suffering, etc. **2** give strength, vigor, or courage to. ▫ **get on a person's nerves** irritate or annoy a person. **have nerves of iron** (or **steel**) (of a person, etc.) be not easily upset or frightened.

nerve cell *n.* an elongated branched cell transmitting impulses in nerve tissue.

nerve cen·ter *n.* **1** a group of closely connected nerve cells associated in performing some function. **2** the center of control of an organization, etc.

nerve gas *n.* a poisonous gas affecting the nervous system.

nerve·less /nərvlis/ *adj.* **1** lacking vigor or spirit. **2** confident; not nervous. **3** *Anat. & Zool.* without nerves. ▫▫ **nerve·less·ly** *adv.* **nerve·less·ness** *n.*

nerve-rack·ing *adj.* (also **nerve-wrack·ing**) stressful; frightening.

nerv·ous /nərvəs/ *adj.* **1** having delicate or disordered nerves. **2** timid or anxious. **3 a** excitable; highly strung; easily agitated. **b** resulting from this temperament (*nervous tension; a nervous headache*). **4** affecting or acting on the nerves. **5** (foll. by *about* + verbal noun) reluctant; afraid (*am nervous about meeting them*). ▫▫ **nerv·ous·ly** *adv.* **nerv·ous·ness** *n.*

nerv·ous break·down *n.* a period of mental illness, usu. resulting from severe depression or anxiety.

nerv·ous sys·tem *n.* the body's network of specialized cells that transmit nerve impulses.

nerv·ous wreck *n. colloq.* a person suffering from mental stress, exhaustion, etc.

nerv·y /nərvee/ *adj.* (**nervier, nerviest**) bold; impudent; pushy. ▫▫ **nerv·i·ly** *adv.* **nerv·i·ness** *n.*

ness /nes/ *n.* a headland or promontory.

nest /nest/ *n.* & *v.* • *n.* **1** a structure or place where a bird lays eggs and shelters its young. **2** an animal's or insect's breeding place or lair. **3** a snug retreat or shelter. **4** (often foll. by *of*) a place fostering something undesirable (*a nest of vice*). **5** a brood or swarm. **6** a group or set of similar objects, often of different sizes and fitting together for storage (*a nest of tables*). • *v.intr.* **1** use or build a nest. **2** collect wild birds' nests. **3** (of objects) fit together or one inside another. ◻◻ **nest·ful** *n.* (*pl.* **-fuls**). **nest·ing** *n.* (in sense 2 of *v.*).

nest egg *n.* a sum of money saved for the future.

nes·tle /nésəl/ *v.* **1** *intr.* (often foll. by *down, in,* etc.) settle oneself comfortably. **2** *intr.* press oneself against another in affection, etc. **3** *tr.* (foll. by *in, into,* etc.) push (a head or shoulder, etc.) affectionately or snugly. **4** *intr.* lie half hidden.

nest·ling /nésling, nést–/ *n.* a bird that is too young to leave its nest.

net[1] /net/ *n. & v.* • *n.* **1** an open-meshed fabric of cord, rope, etc.; a structure resembling this. **2** a piece of net used esp. to restrain, contain, or delimit, or to catch fish or other animals. **3** a structure with net used in various games, esp. forming the goal in soccer, hockey, etc., and dividing the court in tennis, etc. **4** a system or procedure for catching or entrapping a person or persons. **5** = NETWORK. • *v.tr.* (**netted, netting**) **1 a** cover, confine, or catch with a net. **b** procure as with a net. **2** hit (a ball) into the net, esp. of a goal. **3** (usu. as **netted** *adj.*) mark with a netlike pattern. ◻◻ **net·ful** *n.* (*pl.* **-fuls**).

net[2] /net/ *adj. & v.* • *adj.* **1** (esp. of money) remaining after all necessary deductions, or free from deductions. **2** (of a price) to be paid in full; not reducible. **3** (of a weight) excluding that of the packaging, etc. **4** (of an effect, etc.) ultimate; effective. • *v.tr.* (**netted, netting**) gain or yield (a sum) as net profit.

neth·er /néthər/ *adj. archaic* = LOWER[1]. ◻◻ **neth·er·most** *adj.*

neth·er re·gions *n.pl.* (also **world**) hell; the underworld.

net·ting /néting/ *n.* **1** netted fabric. **2** a piece of this.

net·tle /nét'l/ *n. & v.* • *n.* **1** any plant of the genus *Urtica,* esp. *U. dioica,* with jagged leaves covered with stinging hairs. **2** a plant resembling this. • *v.tr.* **1** irritate; annoy. **2** sting with nettles.

net·work /nétwərk/ *n. & v.* • *n.* **1** an arrangement of intersecting horizontal and vertical lines, like the structure of a net. **2** a complex system of railways, roads, canals, etc. **3** a group of people who exchange information, contacts, and experience for professional or social purposes. **4** a chain of interconnected computers, machines, or operations. **5** a system of connected electrical conductors. **6** a group of broadcasting stations connected for a simultaneous broadcast of a program. • *v.* **1** *tr.* link (machines, esp. computers) to operate interactively. **2** *intr.* establish a network. **3** *intr.* be a member of a network (see sense 3 of *n.*).

neu·ral /nŏŏrəl, nyŏŏr–/ *adj.* of or relating to a nerve or the central nervous system. ◻◻ **neu·ral·ly** *adv.*

neu·ral·gia /nŏŏráljə, nyōō–/ *n.* an intense intermittent pain along the course of a nerve, esp. in the head or face. ◻◻ **neu·ral·gic** *adj.*

neu·ral net·work *n.* (also **neu·ral net**) *Computing* a computer system modeled on the human brain and nervous system.

neur·as·the·ni·a /nŏŏrəsthéeneeə, nyŏŏr–/ *n.* a general term for fatigue, anxiety, listlessness, etc. (not in medical use). ◻◻ **neur·as·then·ic** /–thénik/ *adj. & n.*

neu·ri·tis /nōōrítis, nyōō–/ *n.* inflammation of a nerve. ◻◻ **neu·rit·ic** /–rítik/ *adj.*

neuro- /nŏŏrō, nyŏŏrō/ *comb. form* a nerve or the nerves.

neu·rol·o·gy /nōōróləjee, nyōō–/ *n.* the scientific study of the nervous system. ◻◻ **neu·ro·log·i·cal** /–rəlójikəl/ *adj.* **neu·ro·log·i·cal·ly** *adv.* **neu·rol·o·gist** *n.*

neu·ro·mus·cu·lar /nŏŏrōmúskyələr, nyŏŏr–/ *adj.* of or relating to nerves and muscles.

neu·ron /nŏŏron, nyŏŏr–/ *n.* (also **neu·rone** /–ōn/) a specialized cell transmitting nerve impulses. ◻◻ **neu·ron·al** *adj.*

neu·ro·path /nŏŏrōpath, nyŏŏr–/ *n.* a person affected by nervous disease, or with an abnormally sensitive nervous system. ◻◻ **neu·ro·path·ic** *adj.* **neu·rop·a·thy** /–rópəthee/ *n.*

neu·ro·pa·thol·o·gy /nŏŏrōpəthóləjee, nyŏŏr–/ *n.* the pathology of the nervous system. ◻◻ **neu·ro·pa·thol·o·gist** *n.*

neu·ro·phys·i·ol·o·gy /nŏŏrōfizeeóləjee, nyŏŏr–/ *n.* the physiology of the nervous system. ◻◻ **neu·ro·phys·i·o·log·i·cal** /–zeeəlójikəl/ *adj.* **neu·ro·phys·i·ol·o·gist** *n.*

neu·ro·sis /nōōrṓsis, nyōō–/ *n.* (*pl.* **neuroses** /–seez/) a mental illness characterized by irrational or depressive thought or behavior, caused by a disorder of the nervous system usu. without organic change.

neu·ro·sur·ger·y /nŏŏrōsə́rjəree, nyŏŏr–/ *n.* surgery performed on the nervous system, esp. the brain and spinal cord. ◻◻ **neu·ro·sur·geon** *n.* **neu·ro·sur·gi·cal** *adj.*

neu·rot·ic /nōōrótik, nyōō–/ *adj. & n.* • *adj.* **1** caused by or relating to neurosis. **2** (of a person) suffering from neurosis. **3** *colloq.* abnormally sensitive or obsessive. • *n.* a neurotic person. ◻◻ **neu·rot·ic·al·ly** *adv.*

neu·ro·trans·mit·ter /nŏŏrōtránsmitər, –tránz–, nyŏŏr–/ *n. Biochem.* a chemical substance released from a nerve fiber that effects the transfer of an impulse to another nerve or muscle.

neu·ter /nṓōtər, nyṓō–/ *adj., n., & v.* • *adj.* **1** *Gram.* (of a noun, etc.) neither masculine nor feminine. **2** (of a plant) having neither pistils nor stamen. **3** (of an insect, animal, etc.) sexually undeveloped; castrated or spayed. • *n.* **1** *Gram.* a neuter word. **2 a** a nonfertile insect, esp. a worker bee or ant. **b** a castrated animal. • *v.tr.* castrate or spay.

neu·tral /nṓōtrəl, nyṓō–/ *adj. & n.* • *adj.* **1** not helping nor supporting either of two opposing sides; impartial. **2** belonging to a neutral party, nation, etc. (*neutral ships*). **3** indistinct; indeterminate. **4** (of a gear) in which the engine is disconnected from the driven parts. **5** (of colors) not strong nor positive; gray or beige. **6** *Chem.* neither acid nor alkaline. **7** *Electr.* neither positive nor negative. • *n.* **1 a** a neutral nation, person, etc. **b** a subject of a neutral nation. **2** a neutral gear. ◻◻ **neu·tral·i·ty** /–trálitee/ *n.* **neu·tral·ly** *adv.*

neu·tral·ism /nṓōtrəlizəm, nyṓō–/ *n.* a policy of political neutrality. ◻◻ **neu·tral·ist** *n.*

neu·tral·ize /nṓōtrəlīz, nyṓō–/ *v.tr.* **1** make neutral. **2** counterbalance. **3** exempt or exclude (a place) from the sphere of hostilities. ◻◻ **neu·tral·i·za·tion** *n.* **neu·tral·iz·er** *n.*

neu·tri·no /nōōtréenō, nyōō–/ *n.* (*pl.* **-nos**) any of a group of stable elementary particles with zero electric charge and probably zero mass, which travel at the speed of light.

neu·tron /nṓōtron, nyṓō–/ *n.* an elementary particle of about the same mass as a proton but without an electric charge.

neu·tron bomb *n.* a bomb producing neutrons and little blast, causing damage to life but little destruction to property.

Nev. *abbr.* Nevada.

nev·er /névər/ *adv.* **1 a** at no time; on no occasion. **b** *colloq.* as an emphatic negative (*I never heard you come in*). **2** not at all (*never fear*). ◻ **never say die** see DIE[1]. **well I never!** expressing great surprise.

nev·er·more /névərmáwr/ *adv.* at no future time.

nev·er-nev·er land *n.* an imaginary utopian place.

nev·er·the·less /névərthəlés/ *adv.* in spite of that; notwithstanding.

ne·vus /néevəs/ *n.* (*pl.* **nevi** /–vī/) **1** a birthmark in the form of a raised red patch on the skin. **2** = MOLE[2].

new /nōō, nyōō/ *adj. & adv.* • *adj.* **1 a** of recent origin or arrival. **b** made, discovered, acquired, or experienced recently or now for the first time. **2** in original condition; not worn or used. **3 a** renewed or reformed (*the new order*). **b** reinvigorated (*felt like a new person*). **4** different from a recent previous one (*has a new job*). **5** (often foll. by *to*) unfamiliar or strange (*a new sensation*). **6** (often foll. by *at*) (of a person) inexperienced (*am new at this business*). **7** (usu. prec. by *the*) often *derog.* **a** later; modern. **b** newfangled. **c** recently affected by social change (*the new rich*). **8** (often prec. by *the*) advanced in method or theory (*the new formula*). **9** (in place names) discovered or founded later than and named after (*New York*). • *adv.* (usu. in *comb.*) **1** newly; recently (*new-baked*). **2** anew; afresh. □□ **new·ish** *adj.* **new·ness** *n.*

new Old English *nīwe, nēowe*, of Germanic origin; related to Dutch *nieuw* and German *neu*, from an Indo-European root shared by Sanskrit *nava*, Latin *novus*, and Greek *neos* 'new.'

New Age *n.* a set of beliefs intended to replace traditional Western Culture, with alternative approaches to religion, medicine, the environment, music, etc.

new·born /nóobawrn, nyóo–/ *adj.* (of a child, etc.) recently born.

new·com·er /nóokumər, nyóo–/ *n.* **1** a person who has recently arrived. **2** a beginner in some activity.

new·el /nóoəl, nyóo–/ *n.* **1** the supporting central post of winding stairs. **2** the top or bottom supporting post of a stair rail.

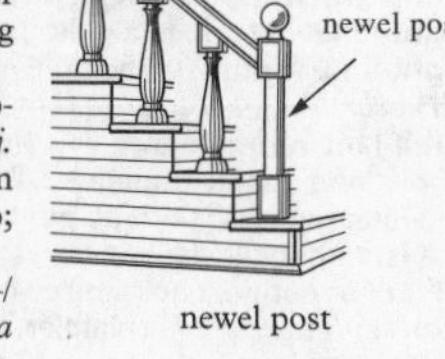

newel post

new·fan·gled /nóo-fánggəld, nyóo–/ *adj. derog.* different from what one is used to; objectionably new.

new·ly /nóolee, nyóo–/ *adv.* **1** recently (*a newly discovered country*). **2** afresh (*newly painted*). **3** in a different manner (*newly arranged*).

new·ly·wed /nóoleewed, nyóo–/ *n.* a recently married person.

new moon *n.* **1** the moon when first seen as a crescent after conjunction with the sun. **2** the time of its appearance.

news /nooz, nyooz/ *n.pl.* (usu. treated as *sing.*) **1** information about important or interesting recent events, esp. when published or broadcast. **2** (prec. by *the*) a broadcast report of news. **3** newly received or noteworthy information. **4** (foll. by *to*) *colloq.* information not previously known (to a person) (*that's news to me*).

news·cast /nóozkast, nyóoz–/ *n.* a broadcast of news reports. □□ **news·cast·er** /nóozkastər, nyóoz–/ *n.*

news flash /nóozflash, nyóoz–/ *n.* a single item of important news, broadcast separately and often interrupting other programs.

news·let·ter /nóozletər, nyóoz–/ *n.* an informal printed report issued periodically to the members of a society, business, organization, etc.

news·man /nóozman, –mən, nyóoz–/ *n.* (*pl.* **-men**) a journalist.

news·pa·per /nóozpaypər, nyóoz–, nóos–, nyóos–/ *n.* **1** a printed publication (usu. daily or weekly) containing news, advertisements, correspondence, etc. **2** the sheets of paper forming this (*wrapped in newspaper*).

news·pa·per·man /nóozpaypərman, –mən, nyóoz–, nóos–, nyóos–/ *n.* (*pl.* **-men**) a journalist.

new·speak /nóospeek, nyóo–/ *n.* (also **New·speak**) ambiguous euphemistic language used esp. in political propaganda.

news·print /nóozprint, nyóoz–/ *n.* a type of low-quality paper on which newspapers are printed.

news·reel /nóozreel, nyóoz–/ *n.* a short movie of recent events.

news·room /nóozroom, nyóoz–/ *n.* a room in a newspaper or broadcasting office where news stories are prepared.

news·stand /nóozstand, nyóoz–/ *n.* a stall for the sale of newspapers, etc.

news·wor·thy /nóozwərthee, nyóoz–/ *adj.* topical. □□ **news·wor·thi·ness** *n.*

news·y /nóozee, nyóo–/ *adj.* (**newsier, newsiest**) *colloq.* full of news.

newt /noot, nyoot/ *n.* any of various small amphibians, esp. of the genus *Triturus*, having a well-developed tail.

New Tes·ta·ment *n.* the part of the Bible concerned with the life and teachings of Christ and his earliest followers.

new·ton /nóot'n, nyóo–/ *n. Physics* the SI unit of force.

New·to·ni·an /nootóneeən, nyóo–/ *adj.* of or devised by Isaac Newton.

new wave *n.* **1** a non-traditional trend or movement. **2** a style of rock music popular in the 1970s.

New World *n.* N. and S. America regarded collectively in relation to Europe.

New Year's Day *n.* January 1.

New Year's Eve *n.* December 31.

New Zea·land·er /nóozéeləndər, nyóo–/ *n.* **1** a native or national of New Zealand, an island group in the Pacific. **2** a person of New Zealand descent.

next /nekst/ *adj. & adv.* • *adj.* **1** (often foll. by *to*) being or positioned or living nearest. **2** the nearest in order of time; the soonest encountered (*next Friday*; *ask the next person you see*). • *adv.* **1** (often foll. by *to*) in the nearest place or degree (*came next to last*). **2** on the first or soonest occasion (*when we next meet*). □ **next to** almost (*next to nothing*).

next-best *adj. & n.* the next in order of preference.

next door *adv. & adj.* (as *adj.* often hyphenated) in or to the next house or room.

next of kin *n.* the closest living relative or relatives.

nex·us /néksəs/ *n.* (*pl.* same) **1** a connected group or series. **2** a connection.

Nez Per·cé /náy persáy/ *n.* (also **Nez Perce** /néz pərs, nés pérs/) **1 a** a N. American people native to the northwestern US. **b** a member of this people. **2** the language of this people.

NH *abbr.* New Hampshire (also in official postal use).

Ni *symb. Chem.* the element nickel.

ni·a·cin /níəsin/ *n.* = NICOTINIC ACID.

nib /nib/ *n.* **1** the point of a pen, which touches the writing surface. **2** (in *pl.*) shelled and crushed coffee or cocoa beans. **3** the point of a tool, etc.

nib·ble /níbəl/ *v. & n.* • *v.* **1** *tr.* & (foll. by *at*) *intr.* **a** take small bites at. **b** eat in small amounts. **c** bite at gently. **2** *intr.* (foll. by *at*) show cautious interest in. • *n.* **1** an instance of nibbling. **2** a very small amount of food. **3** *Computing* half a byte, i.e., 4 bits. □□ **nib·bler** *n.*

ni·cad /nícad/ *adj. & n.* • *adj.* nickel and cadmium. • *n.* a nickel and cadmium battery.

nice /nīs/ *adj.* **1** pleasant; satisfactory. **2** (of a person) kind; good-natured. **3** *iron.* bad or awkward (*a nice mess you've made*). **4** fine or subtle (*a nice distinction*). **5** fastidious; delicately sensitive. **6** scrupulous (*were not too nice about their methods*). **7** (foll. by an adj., often with *and*) satisfactory in terms of the quality described (*nice and warm*). □ **nice work** a task well done. □□ **nice·ly** *adv.* **nice·ness** *n.*

▶**Nice** originally had a number of meanings, including 'fine, subtle, discriminating'; 'refined in taste, fastidious'; and 'precise, strict': *They are not very nice in regard to the company they keep. She has a nice sense of decorum.* The popular overuse of **nice** to mean 'pleasant, agreeable, satisfactory,' etc., has rendered the word trite: *We had a very nice time. This is a nice room. He's a nice boy.*

nice Middle English (in the sense 'stupid'): from Old French, from Latin *nescius* 'ignorant,' from *nescire* 'not know.' Other early senses included 'coy, reserved,' giving rise to 'fastidious, precise, scrupulous': this led both to the sense 'fine, subtle' (regarded by some as the 'correct' sense), and to the main current senses.

ni•ce•ty /nísitee/ *n.* (*pl.* **-ties**) **1** a subtle detail. **2** precision; accuracy. **3** subtle quality (*a point of great nicety*). **4** (in *pl.*) refinements. □ **to a nicety** with exactness.

niche /nich, neesh/ *n.* **1** a shallow recess, esp. in a wall to contain a statue, etc. **2** a comfortable or suitable position in life or employment.

nick /nik/ *n.* & *v.* • *n.* a small cut. • *v.tr.* make a nick or nicks in. □ **in the nick of time** only just in time.

nick•el /níkəl/ *n.* & *v.* • *n.* **1** *Chem.* a malleable ductile silver-white metallic element, used in magnetic alloys. **2** a five-cent coin. • *v.tr.* (**nickeled, nickeling**) coat with nickel.

nick•el-and-dime *adj.* & *v.* • *adj.* involving a small amount of money; trivial. • *v.tr.* weaken (one's financial position) by continued small expenses, etc.

nick•el•o•de•on /nikəlṓdeeən/ *n. colloq.* **1** an early movie theater, esp. one with admission priced at 5 cents. **2** a jukebox.

nick•nack var. of KNICKKNACK.

nick•name /níknaym/ *n.* & *v.* • *n.* a familiar name given to a person instead of or as well as the real name. • *v.tr.* **1** give a nickname to. **2** call by a nickname.

nic•o•tine /níkəteén/ *n.* a colorless poisonous alkaloid present in tobacco.

nic•o•tin•ic ac•id /níkətínik/ *n.* a vitamin of the B complex. Also called NIACIN.

nic•ti•tate /níktitayt/ *v.intr.* blink or wink. □□ **nic•ti•ta•tion** /–táyshən/ *n.*

nic•ti•tat•ing mem•brane *n.* a clear membrane forming a third eyelid in amphibians, birds, and some other animals.

niece /nees/ *n.* a daughter of one's brother or sister, or of one's brother-in-law or sister-in-law.

nif•ty /níftee/ *adj.* (**niftier, niftiest**) *colloq.* **1** clever. **2** stylish. □□ **nif•ti•ly** *adv.*

nig•gard /nígərd/ *n.* a mean or stingy person. □□ **nig•gard•ly** *adj.* & *adv.* **nig•gard•li•ness** *n.*

nig•ger /nígər/ *n.* **1** *offens.* a contemptuous term used of a black or dark-skinned person. **2** (in black English) a fellow person.

▶In sense 1, this term is considered a highly inflammatory expression of racial bigotry.

nig•gle /nígəl/ *v.* & *n.* • *v.* **1** *intr.* be overattentive to details. **2** *intr.* find fault in a petty way. **3** *tr. colloq.* irritate. • *n.* a trifling complaint. □□ **nig•gling** /nígling/ *adj.*

nigh /nī/ *adv., prep.,* & *adj. archaic* or *dial.* near.

night /nīt/ *n.* **1** the period of darkness between one day and the next; the time from sunset to sunrise. **2** nightfall. **3** the darkness of night. **4** a night or evening appointed for some activity (*last night of the performance*).

night blind•ness *n.* = NYCTALOPIA.

night•cap /nítkap/ *n.* **1** *hist.* a cap worn in bed. **2** a hot or alcoholic drink taken at bedtime.

night•club /nítklub/ *n.* a club that is open at night and provides refreshment and entertainment.

night•fall /nítfawl/ *n.* the onset of night; the end of daylight.

night•gown /nítgown/ *n.* **1** a woman's or child's loose garment worn in bed. **2** *hist.* a dressing gown.

night•ie /nítee/ *n. colloq.* a nightgown.

night•in•gale /nít'ngayl/ *n.* any small reddish-brown bird of the genus *Luscinia*, esp. *L. megarhynchos*, of which the male sings melodiously, esp. at night.

night•jar /nítjaar/ *n.* any nocturnal bird of the family Caprimulgidae, having a characteristic harsh cry.

night•life /nítlīf/ *n.* entertainment available at night in a town.

night•ly /nítlee/ *adj.* & *adv.* • *adj.* **1** happening, done, or existing in the night. **2** recurring every night. • *adv.* every night.

night•mare /nítmair/ *n.* **1** a frightening dream. **2** *colloq.* a very unpleasant experience. **3** a haunting fear. □□ **night•mar•ish** *adj.* **night•mar•ish•ly** *adv.*

night owl *n. colloq.* a person active at night.

night school *n.* an institution providing evening classes for those working by day.

night•shade /nítshayd/ *n.* any of various poisonous plants, esp. of the genus *Solanum*, including *S. nigrum* (**black nightshade**) with black berries, and *S. dulcamara* (**woody nightshade**) with red berries.

night shift *n.* a shift of workers employed during the night.

night•shirt /nítshərt/ *n.* a long shirt worn in bed.

night•spot /nítspot/ *n.* a nightclub.

night•stick /nítstik/ *n.* a policeman's club.

night•time /níttīm/ *n.* the time of darkness.

NIH *abbr.* National Institutes of Health.

ni•hil•ism /ní-ilizəm, neé–/ *n.* **1** the rejection of all religious and moral principles. **2** a form of skepticism maintaining that nothing has a real existence. □□ **ni•hil•ist** *n.* **ni•hil•is•tic** *adj.*

nil /nil/ *n.* nothing; no number or amount.

nim•ble /nímbəl/ *adj.* (**nimbler, nimblest**) **1** quick and light in movement or action. **2** (of the mind) quick to comprehend. □□ **nim•ble•ness** *n.* **nim•bly** *adv.*

nim•bo•stra•tus /nímbōstráytəs, –strátəs/ *n.* (*pl.* **nimbostrati** /–tī/) *Meteorol.* a low dark-gray layer of cloud.

nim•bus /nímbəs/ *n.* (*pl.* **nimbi** /–bī/or **nimbuses**) **1** a halo. **2** *Meteorol.* a rain cloud. □□ **nim•bused** *adj.*

NIMBY /nímbee/ *abbr. colloq.* not in my backyard.

nin•com•poop /nínkəmpoop/ *n.* a simpleton; a fool.

nine /nīn/ *n.* & *adj.* • *n.* **1** one more than eight. **2** a symbol for this (9, ix, IX). **3** a size, etc., denoted by nine. **4** a set or team of nine. **5** nine o'clock. • *adj.* that amount to nine. □ **dressed to the nines** dressed very elaborately. **nine times out of ten** nearly always. **nine to five** a designation of typical office hours.

nine•fold /nínfōld/ *adj.* & *adv.* **1** nine times as much or as many. **2** consisting of nine parts.

nine•teen /nínteén/ *n.* & *adj.* • *n.* **1** one more than eighteen, nine more than ten. **2** the symbol for this (19, xix, XIX). **3** a size, etc., denoted by nineteen. • *adj.* that amount to nineteen. □□ **nine•teenth** *adj.* & *n.*

nine•ty /níntee/ *n.* & *adj.* • *n.* (*pl.* **-ties**) **1** the product of nine and ten. **2** a symbol for this (90, xc, XC). **3** (in *pl.*) the numbers from 90 to 99. • *adj.* that amount to ninety. □□ **nine•ti•eth** *adj.* & *n.*

nin•ja /nínjə/ *n.* a person skilled in ninjutsu.

nin•jut•su /ninjóōtsōō/ *n.* one of the Japanese martial arts, characterized by stealthy movement and camouflage.

nin•ny /nínee/ *n.* (*pl.* **-nies**) a foolish or simpleminded person.

ninth /nīnth/ *n.* & *adj.* • *n.* **1** the position in a sequence corresponding to the number 9 in the sequence 1–9. **2** something occupying this position. **3** each of nine equal parts of a thing. • *adj.* that is the ninth.

ni•o•bi•um /nīṓbeeəm/ *n. Chem.* a rare gray-blue metallic element occurring naturally in several minerals and used in alloys for superconductors. Also called COLUMBIUM. ▫▫ **ni·o·bic** *adj.* **ni·o·bous** *adj.*

nip[1] /nip/ *v. & n.* • *v.* (**nipped, nipping**) **1** *tr.* pinch, squeeze, or bite sharply. **2** *tr.* (often foll. by *off*) remove by pinching, etc. **3** *tr.* (of the frost, etc.) cause pain or harm to. • *n.* **1 a** a pinch; a sharp squeeze. **b** a bite. **2** biting cold. ▫ **nip and tuck** neck and neck. **nip in the bud** suppress or destroy (esp. an idea) at an early stage. ▫▫ **nip·ping** *adj.*

nip[2] /nip/ *n.* a small quantity of liquor.

nip·per /nípər/ *n.* **1** a person or thing that nips. **2** the claw of a crab, lobster, etc. **3** (in *pl.*) any tool for gripping or cutting, e.g., forceps or pincers.

nip·ple /nípəl/ *n.* **1** a small projection in which the mammary ducts of either sex of mammals terminate and from which in females milk is secreted for the young. **2** the mouthpiece of a feeding bottle or pacifier. **3** a device like a nipple in function, e.g., the tip of a grease gun. **4** a nipplelike protuberance.

nip·py /nípee/ *adj.* (**nippier, nippiest**) *colloq.* **1** esp. *Brit.* quick; nimble; active. **2** chilly; cold. ▫▫ **nip·pi·ly** *adv.*

nir·va·na /nərvaánə, neer–/ *n.* (in Buddhism) perfect bliss and release from karma, attained by the extinction of individuality.

ni·sei /néesay, neesáy/ (also **Ni·sei**) *n.* an American whose parents were immigrants from Japan.

nit /nit/ *n.* the egg or young form of a louse or other parasitic insect, esp. of human head lice or body lice.

ni·ter /nítər/ *n.* saltpeter; potassium nitrate.

nit·pick /nítpik/ *v.intr. colloq.* find fault in a petty manner; criticize. ▫▫ **nit·pick·er** *n.* **nit·pick·ing** *n.*

ni·trate /nítrayt/ *n. & v.* • *n.* **1** any salt or ester of nitric acid. **2** potassium or sodium nitrate when used as a fertilizer. • *v.tr. Chem.* treat, combine, or impregnate with nitric acid. ▫▫ **ni·tra·tion** /–áyshən/ *n.*

ni·tric /nítrik/ *adj.* of or containing nitrogen, esp. in the quinquevalent state.

ni·tric ac·id *n.* a colorless corrosive poisonous liquid.

ni·tri·fy /nítrifi/ *v.tr.* (**-fies, -fied**) **1** impregnate with nitrogen. **2** convert (nitrogen, usu. in the form of ammonia) into nitrites or nitrates. ▫▫ **ni·tri·fi·ca·tion** /–fikayshən/ *n.*

ni·trite /nítrīt/ *n.* any salt or ester of nitrous acid.

nitro- /nítrō/ *comb. form* **1** of or containing nitric acid, niter, or nitrogen. **2** made with any of these. **3** of or containing the monovalent -NO_2 group.

ni·tro·ben·zene /nítrōbénzeen/ *n.* a yellow oily liquid made by the nitration of benzene and used to make aniline, etc.

ni·tro·cel·lu·lose /nítrōsélyəlōs/ *n.* a highly flammable material made by treating cellulose with concentrated nitric acid.

ni·tro·gen /nítrəjən/ *n. Chem.* a colorless, odorless gaseous element that forms four-fifths of the atmosphere and is an essential constituent of proteins and nucleic acids. ▫▫ **ni·trog·e·nous** /–trójinəs/ *adj.*

ni·tro·glyc·er·in /nítrōglísərin/ *n.* (also **ni·tro·glyc·er·ine**) an explosive yellow liquid made by reacting glycerol with concentrated sulfuric and nitric acids.

ni·trous /nítrəs/ *adj.* of, like, or impregnated with nitrogen.

ni·trous ox·ide *n.* a colorless gas used as an anesthetic (= LAUGHING GAS) and as an aerosol propellant.

nit·ty-grit·ty /níteegrítee/ *n. sl.* the realities or practical details of a matter.

nit·wit /nítwit/ *n. colloq.* a stupid person.

nix /niks/ *n. & v. sl.* • *n.* **1** nothing. **2** a denial. • *v.tr.* **1** cancel. **2** reject.

NJ *abbr.* New Jersey (also in official postal use).

NM *abbr.* New Mexico (in official postal use).

N.Mex. *abbr.* New Mexico.

NMR *abbr.* (also **nmr**) nuclear magnetic resonance.

No[1] *symb. Chem.* the element nobelium.

No[2] /nō/ *n.* (also **Noh**) traditional Japanese drama with dance and song.

No. *abbr.* **1** number. **2** North.

no[1] /nō/ *adj.* **1** not any (*there is no excuse*). **2** not a; quite other than (*is no fool*). **3** hardly any (*did it in no time*). **4** used elliptically as a notice, etc., to forbid, reject, or deplore the thing specified (*no parking; no surrender*). ▫ **no entry** (of a notice) prohibiting vehicles or persons from entering a road or place. **no joy** no satisfaction or success. **no man** no person; nobody. **no sweat** *colloq.* no bother; no trouble. **no trumps** (or **trump**) *Bridge* a declaration or bid involving playing without a trump suit. **no way** *colloq.* **1** it is impossible. **2** I will not agree, etc. **... or no ...** regardless of the ... (*rain or no rain, I shall go out*). **there is no ...ing** it is impossible to ... (*there is no accounting for taste*).

no[2] /nō/ *adv. & n.* • *adv.* **1** equivalent to a negative sentence: the answer to your question is negative; your request will not be complied with; the statement made or conclusion arrived at is not correct or satisfactory; the negative statement made is correct. **2** (foll. by *compar.*) by no amount (*no better than before*). • *n.* (*pl.* **noes**) **1** an utterance of the word *no*. **2** a denial or refusal. **3** a negative vote. ▫ **is no more** has died or ceased to exist. **no can do** *colloq.* I am unable to do it. **no less** (often foll. by *than*) **1** as much (*gave me $50, no less*). **2** as important (*no less a person than the president*). **3** *disp.* no fewer (*no less than ten people*). **no longer** not now or henceforth as formerly. **no more** • *n.* nothing further (*have no more to say*). • *adj.* not any more (*no more wine?*). • *adv.* **1** no longer. **2** never again. **3** to no greater extent (*is no more an authority than I am*). **4** neither (*you did not come, and no more did he*). **no sooner ... than** see SOON. **not take no for an answer** persist in spite of refusals. **or no** or not (*pleasant or no, it is true*). **whether or no 1** in either case. **2** (as an indirect question) which of a case and its negative (*tell me whether or no*).

no-ac·count *adj.* unimportant; worthless.

No·ah's ark /nṓəz/ *n.* **1 a** the ship in which (according to the Bible) Noah, his family, and the animals were saved. **b** an imitation of this as a child's toy. **2** a large or cumbrous or old-fashioned trunk or vehicle. **3** a bivalve mollusk, *Arca noae*, with a boat-shaped shell.

No·bel·ist /nōbélist/ *n.* a winner of a Nobel prize.

no·bel·i·um /nōbéeleeəm/ *n. Chem.* a radioactive transuranic metallic element.

No·bel prize /nṓbél/ *n.* any of six international prizes awarded annually for physics, chemistry, physiology or medicine, literature, economics, and the promotion of peace.

no·bil·i·ty /nōbílitee/ *n.* (*pl.* **-ties**) **1** nobleness of character, mind, birth, or rank. **2** (prec. by *a, the*) a class of nobles, an aristocracy.

no·ble /nṓbəl/ *adj. & n.* • *adj.* (**nobler, noblest**) **1** belonging by rank, title, or birth to the aristocracy. **2** having lofty ideals; free from pettiness and meanness. **3** of imposing appearance. **4** excellent; admirable (*noble horse; noble cellar*). • *n.* a nobleman or noblewoman. ▫▫ **no·ble·ness** *n.* **no·bly** *adv.*

no·ble gas *n.* any one of a group of gaseous elements that almost never combine with other elements.

no·ble·man /nṓbəlmən/ *n.* (*pl.* **-men**) a man of noble rank or birth; a peer.

no·blesse /nōblés/ *n.* the class of nobles (as of France, etc.). ▫ **noblesse oblige** /ōbléezh/ privilege entails responsibility.

---

no·ble·wom·an /nṓbəlwŏŏmən/ *n.* (*pl.* **-women**) a woman of noble rank or birth.

no·bod·y /nṓbodee, –budee, –bədee/ *pron. & n.* •*pron.* no person. •*n.* (*pl.* **-ies**) a person of no importance.

no-brain·er *n.* a problem, question, examination, etc., that requires very little thought.

nock /nok/ *n. & v.* •*n.* **1** a notch at either end of a bow for holding the string. **2** a notch at the butt end of an arrow for receiving the bowstring. •*v.tr.* set (an arrow) on the string.

noc·tam·bu·list /noktámbyəlist/ *n.* a sleepwalker. ▫▫ **noc·tam·bu·lism** *n.*

noc·tur·nal /noktə́rnəl/ *adj.* of or in the night; active by night. ▫▫ **noc·tur·nal·ly** *adv.*

noc·turne /nóktərn/ *n.* **1** *Mus.* a short composition of a romantic nature, usu. for piano. **2** a picture of a night scene.

nod /nod/ *v. & n.* •*v.* (**nodded, nodding**) **1** *intr.* incline one's head slightly and briefly in greeting, assent, or command. **2** *intr.* let one's head fall forward in drowsiness. **3** *tr.* incline (one's head). **4** *tr.* signify (assent, etc.) by a nod. **5** *intr.* (of flowers, plumes, etc.) bend downward and sway. **6** *intr.* make a mistake due to a momentary lack of alertness or attention. •*n.* a nodding of the head. ▫ **get the nod** be chosen or approved. **nod off** *colloq.* fall asleep. **on the nod** *colloq.* with merely formal assent and no discussion.

node /nōd/ *n.* **1** *Bot.* **a** the part of a plant stem from which leaves emerge. **b** a knob on a root or branch. **2** *Anat.* a natural swelling in a part of the body. **3** *Astron.* either of two points at which a planet's orbit intersects the plane of the ecliptic or the celestial equator. **4** *Physics* a point of minimum disturbance in a standing wave system. **5** *Electr.* a point of zero current or voltage. **6** *Math.* a point at which a curve intersects itself. **7** a component in a computer network. ▫▫ **nod·al** *adj.* **nod·i·cal** *adj.* (in sense 3).

nod·ule /nójōōl/ *n.* **1** a small, rounded lump of anything. **2** a small tumor, node, or ganglion. ▫▫ **nod·u·lar** /–jələr/ *adj.* **nod·u·lat·ed** /–jəlaytid/ *adj.* **nod·u·la·tion** /–jəláyshən/ *n.* **nod·u·lose** /–jolōs/ *adj.*

No·el /nō-él/ *n.* Christmas (esp. as a refrain in carols).

no-fault *adj.* (of insurance) valid regardless of the allocation of blame for an accident, etc.

no-frills *adj.* lacking ornament or embellishment.

nog·gin /nógin/ *n.* **1** a small mug. **2** a small measure, usu. 1/4 pint, of liquor. **3** *sl.* the head.

no-go *adj.* impossible; hopeless.

no-good *adj.* useless.

Noh var. of No[2].

no-hit·ter *n. Baseball* a game in which a pitcher allows no hits.

no·how /nṓhow/ *adv.* in no way; by no means.

noise /noyz/ *n. & v.* •*n.* **1** a sound, esp. a loud or unpleasant one. **2** a series of loud sounds; a confused sound of voices. **3** irregular fluctuations accompanying a transmitted signal but not relevant to it. **4** (in *pl.*) conventional remarks, or speechlike sounds without actual words (*made sympathetic noises*). •*v.tr.* (usu. in *passive*) make public. ▫ **make a noise 1** (usu. foll. by *about*) talk or complain much. **2** attain notoriety.

noise·less /nóyzlis/ *adj.* **1** silent. **2** making no avoidable noise. ▫▫ **noise·less·ly** *adv.* **noise·less·ness** *n.*

noise pol·lu·tion *n.* harmful or annoying noise.

noi·some /nóysəm/ *adj. literary* **1** harmful; noxious. **2** evil-smelling. **3** objectionable; offensive. ▫▫ **noi·some·ness** *n.*

▶**Noisome** means 'bad-smelling.' It has no relation to the word **noise**.

nois·y /nóyzee/ *adj.* (**noisier, noisiest**) **1** full of noise. **2** making much noise. **3** clamorous; turbulent. **4** (of a color, etc.) conspicuous. ▫▫ **nois·i·ly** *adv.* **nois·i·ness** *n.*

no·mad /nṓmad/ *n.* **1** a member of a tribe roaming from place to place for pasture. **2** a wanderer. ▫▫ **no·mad·ic** /–mádik/ *adj.* **no·mad·i·cal·ly** *adv.* **no·mad·ism** *n.*

no man's land *n.* **1** *Mil.* the space between two opposing armies. **2** an area not assigned to any owner. **3** an area not clearly belonging to any one subject, etc.

nom de guerre /nóm də gáir/ *n.* (*pl.* **noms de guerre** *pronunc.* same) an assumed name under which a person fights, plays, writes, etc.

nom de plume /nóm də plŏŏm/ *n.* (*pl.* **noms de plume** *pronunc.* same) an assumed name under which a person writes.

no·men·cla·ture /nṓmənklaychər, nōménklə̄chər/ *n.* **1** a person's or community's system of names for things. **2** the terminology of a science, etc. **3** systematic naming. **4** a catalog. ▫▫ **no·men·cla·tur·al** /–kláchərəl/ *adj.*

nom·i·nal /nóminəl/ *adj.* **1** existing in name only (*nominal ruler*). **2** (of a sum of money, etc.) virtually nothing. **3** of or in names (*nominal and essential distinctions*). **4** consisting of or giving the names (*nominal list of officers*). **5** of or like a noun. ▫▫ **nom·i·nal·ly** *adv.*

nom·i·nal val·ue *n.* the face value (of a coin, shares, etc.).

nom·i·nate /nóminayt/ *v.tr.* **1** propose (a candidate) for election. **2** appoint to an office (*a board of six nominated and six elected members*). **3** appoint (a date or place). ▫▫ **nom·i·na·tor** *n.*

nom·i·na·tion /nómináyshən/ *n.* **1** the act of nominating. **2** the right of nominating for an appointment (*have a nomination at your disposal*).

nom·i·na·tive /nóminətiv/ *n. & adj.* •*n. Gram.* **1** the case of nouns, pronouns, and adjectives, expressing the subject of a verb. **2** a word in this case. •*adj.* **1** *Gram.* of or in this case. **2** /–naytiv/ of nomination (as distinct from election).

nom·i·nee /nóminée/ *n.* **1** a person who is nominated for an office or as the recipient of a grant, etc. **2** *Commerce* a person in whose name a stock, etc., is registered.

non- /non/ *prefix* giving the negative sense of words with which it is combined, esp.: **1** not doing or having or involved with (*nonattendance*). **2 a** not of the kind described (*nonalcoholic*). **b** forming terms used adjectivally (*nonunion*). **3** a lack of (*nonaccess*). **4** (with adverbs) not in the way described (*nonaggressively*). **5** forming adjectives from verbs, meaning "that does not" or "that is not meant to (or to be)" (*nonskid*). **6** used to form a neutral negative sense when a form in *in-* or *un-* has a special sense or (usu. unfavorable) connotation (*noncontroversial*). ▶The number of words that can be formed with this prefix is unlimited; consequently only a selection, considered the most current or semantically noteworthy, can be given here.

nona- /nónə/ *comb. form* nine.

non·ad·dic·tive /nónədíktiv/ *adj.* (of a drug, habit, etc.) not causing addiction.

non·a·ge·nar·i·an /nónəjináireeən, nṓ–/ *n. & adj.* •*n.* a person from 90 to 99 years old. •*adj.* of this age.

non·ag·gres·sion /nónəgréshən/ *n.* restraint from aggression (often *attrib.*: *nonaggression pact*).

non·a·gon /nónəgon/ *n.* a plane figure with nine sides and angles.

non·al·co·hol·ic /nónalkəhólik/ *adj.* (of a drink, etc.) not containing alcohol.

non·a·ligned /nónəlínd/ *adj.* (of nations, etc.) not aligned with another (esp. major) power. ▫▫ **non·a·lign·ment** *n.*

non·al·ler·gic /nónələ́rjik/ *adj.* not causing allergy; not allergic.

non·at·tached /nónətácht/ *adj.* that is not attached.

▶Neutral in sense: see NON- 6, UNATTACHED.

non·at·trib·ut·a·ble /nónətríbyōōtəbəl/ *adj.* that cannot or may not be attributed to a particular source, etc. ▫▫ **non·at·trib·ut·a·bly** *adv.*

non·be·liev·er /nónbiléevər/ *n.* a person who has no (esp. religious) faith.

non·bel·lig·er·ent /nónbəlíjərənt/ *adj. & n.* • *adj.* not engaged in hostilities. • *n.* a nonbelligerent nation, etc.

non·bi·o·log·i·cal /nónbīəlójikəl/ *adj.* not concerned with biology or living organisms.

non·black /nónblák/ *adj. & n.* • *adj.* **1** (of a person) not black. **2** of or relating to nonblack people. • *n.* a nonblack person.

non·cap·i·tal /nónkápit'l/ *adj.* (of an offense) not punishable by death.

non-Cath·o·lic /nónkáthəlik, –káthlik/ *adj. & n.* • *adj.* not Roman Catholic. • *n.* a non-Catholic person.

nonce /nons/ *n.* ▫ **for the nonce** for the time being; for the present occasion.

nonce word *n.* a word coined for one occasion.

non·cha·lant /nónshəlaánt/ *adj.* calm and casual. ▫▫ **non·cha·lance** /–aáns/ *n.* **non·cha·lant·ly** *adv.*

non-Chris·tian /nónkrís-chən/ *adj. & n.* • *adj.* not Christian. • *n.* a non-Christian person.

non·com /nónkom/ *n. colloq.* a noncommissioned officer.

non·com·bat·ant /nónkəmbát'nt, –kómbət'nt/ *n.* a person not fighting in a war, esp. a civilian, army chaplain, etc.

non·com·mis·sioned /nónkəmíshənd/ *adj. Mil.* (of an officer) not holding a commission.

non·com·mit·tal /nónkəmít'l/ *adj.* avoiding commitment to a definite opinion or course of action. ▫▫ **non·com·mit·tal·ly** *adv.*

non·com·mu·nist /nónkómyənist/ *adj. & n.* (also **non-Com·mu·nist** with ref. to a particular party) • *adj.* not advocating or practicing communism. • *n.* a noncommunist person.

non·com·pli·ance /nónkəmplíəns/ *n.* failure to comply; a lack of compliance.

non com·pos men·tis /nón kompəs méntis/ *adj.* (also **non com·pos**) not in one's right mind.

non·con·duc·tor /nónkəndúktər/ *n.* a substance that does not conduct heat or electricity. ▫▫ **non·con·duct·ing** *adj.*

non·con·form·ist /nónkənfáwrmist/ *n.* **1** a person who does not conform to the doctrine or discipline of an established Church, esp. (**Nonconformist**) a member of a (usu. Protestant) sect dissenting from the Anglican Church. **2** a person who does not conform to a prevailing principle. ▫▫ **non·con·form·ism** *n.* **Non·con·form·ism** *n.*

non·con·form·i·ty /nónkənfáwrmitee/ *n.* **1 a** nonconformists as a body, esp. (**Nonconformity**) Protestants dissenting from the Anglican Church. **b** the principles or practice of nonconformists, esp. (**Nonconformity**) Protestant dissent. **2** (usu. foll. by *to*) failure to conform. **3** lack of correspondence between things.

non·con·trib·u·to·ry /nónkəntríbyətawree/ *adj.* not contributing or (esp. of a pension plan) involving contributions.

non·con·tro·ver·sial /nónkóntrəvə́rshəl/ *adj.* not controversial.

▶Neutral in sense: see NON- 6, UNCONTROVERSIAL.

non·de·nom·i·na·tion·al /nóndinóminάyshənəl/ *adj.* not restricted as regards religious denomination.

non·de·script /nóndiskript/ *adj. & n.* • *adj.* lacking distinctive characteristics; not easily classified. • *n.* a nondescript person or thing.

non·drink·er /nóndríngkər/ *n.* a person who does not drink alcoholic liquor.

none /nun/ *pron., adj., & adv.* • *pron.* **1** (foll. by *of*) **a** not any of (*none of this concerns me*; *none of your impudence!*). **b** not any one of (*none of them has come*). **2 a** no persons (*none but fools have ever believed it*). **b** no person (*none can tell*). • *adj.* (usu. with a preceding noun implied) **1** no; not any (*you have money and I have none*). **2** not to be counted in a specified class (*his understanding is none of the clearest*). • *adv.* (foll. by *the* + compar., or *so*, *too*) not at all (*none the wiser*). ▫ **none other** (usu. foll. by *than*) no other person.

▶The verb following *none* in the sense of "not any one of" can be singular or plural according to the sense.

non·ef·fec·tive /nóniféktiv/ *adj.* that does not have an effect.

▶Neutral in sense: see NON- 6, INEFFECTIVE.

non·en·ti·ty /nonéntitee/ *n.* (*pl.* **-ties**) **1** a person of no importance. **2 a** nonexistence. **b** a nonexistent thing.

nones /nōnz/ *n.pl.* in the ancient Roman calendar, the ninth day before the ides by inclusive reckoning, i.e., the 7th day of March, May, July, and October, and the 5th of other months.

non·es·sen·tial /nónisénshəl/ *adj.* not essential.

▶Neutral in sense: see NON- 6, INESSENTIAL.

none·such /núnsuch/ *n.* (also **non·such**) **1** a person or thing that is unrivaled; a paragon. **2** a leguminous plant, *Medicago lupulina*, with black pods.

none·the·less /núnthəlés/ *adv.* nevertheless.

non-Eu·clid·e·an /nónyōōklídeeən/ *adj.* denying or going beyond Euclidean principles in geometry.

non·e·vent /nónivént/ *n.* an unimportant or anticlimactic occurrence.

non·fat·ten·ing /nónfát'ning/ *adj.* (of food) that does not fatten.

non·fer·rous /nónférəs/ *adj.* (of a metal) other than iron or steel.

non·fic·tion /nónfíkshən/ *n.* literary work other than fiction. ▫▫ **non·fic·tion·al** *adj.*

non·flam·ma·ble /nónflάməbəl/ *adj.* not flammable.

▶See note at INFLAMMABLE.

non·gov·ern·men·tal /nón-guvərnmént'l/ *adj.* not belonging to or associated with a government.

non·hu·man /nónhyōōmən/ *adj. & n.* • *adj.* (of a being) not human. • *n.* a nonhuman being.

▶Neutral in sense: see NON- 6, INHUMAN, UNHUMAN.

non·in·ter·ven·tion /nónintərvénshən/ *n.* the principle or practice of not becoming involved in others' affairs, esp. by one nation in regard to another.

non·lin·e·ar /nónlíneeər/ *adj.* not linear, esp. with regard to dimension.

non·lit·er·ar·y /nónlítəreree/ *adj.* (of writing, etc.) not literary in character.

non·mem·ber /nónmémbər/ *n.* a person who is not a member (of a particular association, club, etc.).

non·mil·i·tar·y /nónmíliteree/ *adj.* not military; not involving armed forces.

non·nat·u·ral /nón-náchərəl/ *adj.* not involving natural means nor processes.

▶Neutral in sense: see NON- 6, UNNATURAL.

non·ne·go·ti·a·ble /nón-nigṓshəbəl, –sheeə–/ *adj.* that cannot be negotiated (esp. in financial senses).

non·nu·cle·ar /nón-nōōkleeər, –nyōō–/ *adj.* **1** not involving nuclei nor nuclear energy. **2** (of a nation, etc.) not having nuclear weapons.

no-no *n. colloq.* a thing not possible or acceptable.

non·ob·serv·ance /nónəbzə́rvəns/ *n.* failure to observe (an agreement, etc.).

no-non·sense *adj.* serious; without flippancy.

non·op·er·a·tion·al /nónopəráyshənəl/ *adj.* **1** that does not operate. **2** out of order.

non·or·gan·ic /nóawrgánik/ *adj.* not organic.

▶Neutral in sense: see NON- 6, INORGANIC.

non·pa·reil /nónpərél/ *adj. & n.* • *adj.* unrivaled or unique. • *n.* **1** such a person or thing. **2** a chocolate candy disk, decorated with sugar pellets.
non·par·ty /nónpaártee/ *adj.* independent of political parties.
non·pay·ment /nónpáymənt/ *n.* failure to pay; a lack of payment.
non·per·son /nónpə́rsən/ *n.* a person regarded as nonexistent or insignificant (cf. UNPERSON).
non·per·son·al /nónpə́rsənəl/ *adj.* not personal.
▶Neutral in sense: see NON- 6, IMPERSONAL.
non·plus /nonplús/ *v.tr.* (**nonplussed** or **nonplused**, **nonplussing** or **nonplusing**) completely perplex.
non·po·lit·i·cal /nónpəlítikəl/ *adj.* not political; not involved in politics.
non·pro·duc·tive /nónprədúktiv/ *adj.* not productive. ▫▫ **non·pro·duc·tive·ly** *adv.*
▶Neutral in sense: see NON- 6, UNPRODUCTIVE.
non·pro·fes·sion·al /nónprəféshənəl/ *adj.* not professional (esp. in status).
▶Neutral in sense: see NON- 6, UNPROFESSIONAL.
non·prof·it /nónprófit/ *adj.* not involving nor making a profit.
non·pro·lif·er·a·tion /nónprəlífəráyshən/ *n.* the prevention of an increase in something, esp. possession of nuclear weapons.
non·ra·cial /nónráyshəl/ *adj.* not involving race or racial factors.
non·res·i·dent /nónrézidənt/ *adj.* **1** not residing in a particular place. **2** (of a post) not requiring the holder to reside at the place of work. ▫▫ **non·res·i·dence** /–dəns/ *n.* **non·res·i·den·tial** /–dénshəl/ *adj.*
non·re·sis·tance /nónrizístəns/ *n.* failure to resist; a lack of resistance.
non·re·turn·a·ble /nónritə́rnəbəl/ *adj.* that may or need or will not be returned.
non·sci·en·tif·ic /nónsīəntífik/ *adj.* not involving science or scientific methods. ▫▫ **non·sci·en·tist** /–síəntist/ *n.*
▶Neutral in sense: see NON- 6, UNSCIENTIFIC.
non·sense /nónsens, -səns/ *n.* **1 a** (often as *int.*) absurd or meaningless words or ideas; foolish conduct. **b** an instance of this. **2** a scheme, etc., that one disapproves of. **3** (often *attrib.*) a form of literature meant to amuse by absurdity (*nonsense verse*). ▫▫ **non·sen·si·cal** /–sénsikəl/ *adj.* **non·sen·si·cal·i·ty** /nónsensikálitee/ *n.* (*pl.* **-ties**). **non·sen·si·cal·ly** /–sénsiklee/ *adv.*
non se·qui·tur /non sékwitər/ *n.* a conclusion that does not logically follow from the premises.
non·sex·u·al /nónsékshooəl/ *adj.* not involving sex. ▫▫ **non·sex·u·al·ly** *adv.*
non·skid /nónskíd/ *adj.* **1** that does not skid. **2** that inhibits skidding.
non·slip /nónslíp/ *adj.* **1** that does not slip. **2** that inhibits slipping.
non·smok·er /nónsmṓkər/ *n.* **1** a person who does not smoke. **2** a train compartment, etc., in which smoking is forbidden. ▫▫ **non·smok·ing** *adj. & n.*
non·start·er /nónstaártər/ *n.* **1** a person or animal that does not start in a race. **2** *colloq.* a person or thing that is unlikely to succeed or be effective.
non·stick /nónstík/ *adj.* **1** that does not stick. **2** that does not allow things to stick to it.
non·stop /nónstóp/ *adj. & adv.* • *adj.* **1** (of a train, etc.) not stopping at intermediate places. **2** done without a stop or intermission. • *adv.* without stopping or pausing.
non·such var. of NONESUCH.
non·swim·mer /nónswímər/ *n.* a person who cannot swim.
non·tech·ni·cal /nóntéknikəl/ *adj.* **1** not technical. **2** without technical knowledge.
non·un·ion /nónyoonyən/ *adj.* **1** not belonging to a labor union. **2** not done or produced by members of a labor union.
non·ver·bal /nónvə́rbəl/ *adj.* not involving words. ▫▫ **non·ver·bal·ly** *adv.*
non·vi·o·lence /nónvíələns/ *n.* the avoidance of violence, esp. as a principle. ▫▫ **non·vi·o·lent** /–lənt/ *adj.*
non·vot·ing /nónvṓting/ *adj.* not having or using a vote. ▫▫ **non·vot·er** *n.*
non·white /nónhwīt, -wīt/ *adj. & n.* • *adj.* **1** (of a person) not white. **2** of or relating to nonwhite people. • *n.* a nonwhite person.
noo·dle[1] /nood'l/ *n.* a strip or ring of pasta.
noo·dle[2] /nood'l/ *n.* **1** a simpleton. **2** *sl.* the head.
nook /nook/ *n.* a corner or recess; a secluded place.
nook·y /nookee/ *n.* (also **nook·ie**) *coarse sl.* sexual intercourse.
noon /noon/ *n.* **1** twelve o'clock in the day; midday. **2** the culminating point.
noon·day /noonday/ *n.* midday.
no one /nṓ wun/ *n.* no person; nobody.
noon·time /noontīm/ *n.* (also **noon·tide** /–tīd/) midday.
noose /noos/ *n. & v.* • *n.* **1** a loop with a running knot, tightening as the rope or wire is pulled. **2** a snare or bond. • *v.tr.* catch with or enclose in a noose; ensnare. ▫ **put one's head in a noose** bring about one's own downfall.
nope /nōp/ *adv. colloq.* = NO[2] *adv.* 1.
nor /nawr, nər/ *conj.* **1** and not; and not either (*neither one thing nor the other*; *can neither read nor write*). **2** and no more; neither (*"I cannot go" – "Nor can I"*).
nor' /nawr/ *n., adj., & adv.* (esp. in compounds) = NORTH (*nor'ward*).
Nor·dic /náwrdik/ *adj. & n.* • *adj.* **1** of or relating to the tall blond Germanic people found in N. Europe, esp. in Scandinavia. **2** of or relating to Scandinavia or Finland. • *n.* a Nordic person.
nor'·easter /noreéstər/ *n.* a northeaster.
norm /nawrm/ *n.* **1** a standard or pattern or type. **2** a standard quantity to be produced or amount of work to be done. **3** customary behavior, etc.
nor·mal /náwrməl/ *adj. & n.* • *adj.* **1** conforming to a standard; regular; usual. **2** free from mental or emotional disorder. **3** *Geom.* (of a line) at right angles. • *n.* **1 a** the normal value of a temperature, etc. **b** the usual state, level, etc. **2** *Geom.* a line at right angles. ▫▫ **nor·mal·cy** *n.* **nor·mal·i·ty** /–málitee/ *n.*
▶**Normalcy** has been criticized as an uneducated alternative to **normality**, but actually is a common American usage and can be taken as standard.
nor·mal·ize /náwrməlīz/ *v.* **1** *tr.* make normal. **2** *intr.* become normal. **3** *tr.* cause to conform. ▫▫ **nor·mal·i·za·tion** *n.* **nor·mal·iz·er** *n.*
nor·mal·ly /náwrməlee/ *adv.* **1** in a normal manner. **2** usually.
Nor·man /náwrmən/ *n. & adj.* • *n.* **1** a native or inhabitant of medieval Normandy (now part of France). **2** a descendant of the people of mixed Scandinavian and Frankish origin established there in the 10th c., who conquered England in 1066. **3** Norman French. • *adj.* **1** of or relating to the Normans. **2** of or relating to the Norman style of architecture. ▫▫ **Nor·man·esque** /–nésk/ *adj.* **Nor·man·ism** *n.* **Nor·man·ize** *v.tr. & intr.*
nor·ma·tive /náwrmətiv/ *adj.* of or establishing a norm. ▫▫ **nor·ma·tive·ly** *adv.* **nor·ma·tive·ness** *n.*
Norse /nawrs/ *n. & adj.* • *n.* **1** the Norwegian language. **2** the Scandinavian language group. • *adj.* of ancient Scandinavia, esp. Norway. ▫▫ **Norse·man** *n.* (*pl.* **-men**).
north /nawrth/ *n., adj., & adv.* • *n.* **1 a** the point of the horizon 90° counterclockwise from east. **b** the compass point corresponding to this. **c** the direction in

which this lies. **2** (usu. **the North**) **a** the part of the world or a country or a town lying to the north. **b** the arctic. • *adj.* **1** toward, at, near, or facing north. **2** coming from the north (*north wind*). • *adv.* **1** toward, at, or near the north. **2** (foll. by *of*) further north than.

North A·mer·i·can *adj. & n.* • *adj.* of North America. • *n.* a native or inhabitant of North America, esp. a citizen of the US or Canada.

north·bound /náwrthbownd/ *adj.* traveling or leading northward.

North Coun·try *n.* the geographical region including Alaska and the Canadian Yukon.

north·east /nawrthe̍est/ *n., adj., & adv.* • *n.* **1** the point of the horizon midway between north and east. **2** the compass point corresponding to this. **3** the direction in which this lies. • *adj.* of, toward, or coming from the northeast. • *adv.* toward, at, or near the northeast.

north·east·er /náwrthe̍estər, náwréestər/ *n.* (also **nor'easter**) **1** a northeast wind. **2** a strong storm from the northeast, esp. in New England.

north·er·ly /náwrthərlee/ *adj., adv., & n.* • *adj. & adv.* **1** in a northern position or direction. **2** (of wind) blowing from the north. • *n.* (*pl.* **-lies**) (usu. in *pl.*) a wind blowing from the north.

north·ern /náwrthərn/ *adj.* **1** of or in the north. **2** toward the north. □□ **north·ern·most** *adj.*

north·ern·er /náwrthərnər/ *n.* a native or inhabitant of the north.

north·ern hem·i·sphere *n.* (also **North·ern Hem·i·sphere**) the half of the earth north of the equator.

north·ern lights *n.pl.* the aurora borealis.

north-north·east *n.* the point or direction midway between north and northeast.

north-north·west *n.* the point or direction midway between north and northwest.

north pole *n.* (also **North Pole**) the northernmost point of the earth's axis of rotation.

North Star *n.* the polestar.

north·ward /náwrthwərd/ *adj., adv., & n.* • *adj. & adv.* (also **north·wards**) toward the north. • *n.* a northward direction or region.

north·west /náwrthwést/ *n., adj., & adv.* • *n.* **1** the point of the horizon midway between north and west. **2** the compass point corresponding to this. **3** the direction in which this lies. • *adj.* of, toward, or coming from the northwest. • *adv.* toward, at, or near the northwest.

north·west·er /náwrthwéstər, náwrwés–/ *n.* (also **nor'wester**) a northwest wind.

Nor·we·gian /nawrwe̍ejən/ *n. & adj.* • *n.* **1 a** a native or national of Norway. **b** a person of Norwegian descent. **2** the language of Norway. • *adj.* of or relating to Norway or its people or language.

Nos. *abbr.* (also **nos.**) numbers.

nose /nōz/ *n. & v.* • *n.* **1** an organ above the mouth of a human or animal, used for smelling and breathing. **2 a** the sense of smell (*dogs have a good nose*). **b** the ability to detect a particular thing (*a nose for scandal*). **3** the odor or perfume of wine, tea, etc. **4** the open end or nozzle of a tube, pipe, etc. **5** the front end or projecting part of a thing, e.g., of a car or aircraft. • *v.* **1** *tr.* (often foll. by *out*) **a** perceive the smell of, discover by smell. **b** detect. **2** *tr.* thrust or rub one's nose against or into. **3** *intr.* (usu. foll. by *about, around,* etc.) pry or search. **4 a** *intr.* make one's way cautiously forward. **b** *tr.* make (one's or its way). □ **as plain as the nose on your face** easily seen. **by a nose** by a very narrow margin (*won the race by a nose*). **keep one's nose clean** *sl.* stay out of trouble. **on the nose** *sl.* precisely. **put a person's nose out of joint** *colloq.* disconcert or supplant a person. **turn up one's nose** (usu. foll. by *at*) *colloq.* show disdain. **under a person's nose** *colloq.* right before a person. **with one's nose in the air** haughtily. □□ **nosed** *adj.* (also in *comb.*).

nose·bag /nṓzbag/ *n.* a bag containing fodder, hung on a horse's head.

nose·band /nṓzband/ *n.* the lower band of a bridle, passing over the horse's nose.

nose·bleed /nṓzbleed/ *n.* an instance of bleeding from the nose.

nose cone *n.* the cone-shaped nose of a rocket, etc.

nose·dive /nṓzdīv/ *n. & v.* • *n.* **1** a steep downward plunge by an airplane. **2** a sudden plunge or drop. • *v.intr.* make a nosedive.

no-see-um *n.* (also **no-see-em**) a small bloodsucking insect, esp. a midge of the family *Ceratopogonidae.*

nose·gay /nṓzgay/ *n.* a bunch of flowers, esp. a sweet-scented posy.

nose job *n. sl.* surgery on the nose, esp. for cosmetic reasons.

nose·piece /nṓzpees/ *n.* **1** = NOSEBAND. **2** the part of a helmet, etc., protecting the nose. **3** the part of a microscope to which the objective is attached. **4** the bridge on the frame of eyeglasses.

nos·ey var. of NOSY.

nosh /nosh/ *v. & n. sl.* • *v.tr. & intr.* **1** eat or drink. **2** eat between meals. • *n.* **1** food or drink. **2** a snack.

no-show *n.* a person who has reserved a seat, etc., but neither uses it nor cancels the reservation.

nos·tal·gia /nostáljə, –jeeə, nə–/ *n.* **1** (often foll. by *for*) sentimental yearning for a period of the past. **2** regretful or wistful memory of an earlier time. **3** severe homesickness. □□ **nos·tal·gic** *adj.* **nos·tal·gi·cal·ly** *adv.*

nos·tril /nóstrəl/ *n.* either of two external openings of the nasal cavity in vertebrates that admit air to the lungs and smells to the olfactory nerves.

nos·trum /nóstrəm/ *n.* **1** a quack remedy, a patent medicine, esp. one prepared by the person recommending it. **2** a panacean scheme, esp. for political or social reform.

nos·y /nṓzee/ *adj.* (also **nos·ey**) (**nosier, nosiest**) *colloq.* inquisitive, prying. □□ **nos·i·ly** *adv.* **nos·i·ness** *n.*

not /not/ *adv.* expressing negation, esp.: **1** (also **n't** joined to a preceding verb) following an auxiliary verb or *be* or (in a question) the subject of such a verb (*she isn't there; didn't you tell me?*). **2** used elliptically for a negative sentence or verb or phrase (*Is she coming? — I hope not; Do you want it? — Certainly not!*). **3** used to express the negative of other words (*not a single one was left; Are they pleased? — Not they*). □ **not at all** (in polite reply to thanks) there is no need for thanks. **not least** notably. **not quite 1** almost (*not quite there*). **2** noticeably not (*not quite proper*). **not that** (foll. by clause) it is not to be inferred that (*if he said so — not that he ever did — he lied*). **not a thing** nothing at all.
▶Use with verbs other than auxiliary verbs or *be* is now *archaic* (*fear not*), except with participles and infinities (*not knowing, I cannot say; we asked them not to come*).

no·ta be·ne /nṓtə bénay/ *v.tr.* (as *imper.*) observe what follows, take notice (usu. drawing attention to a following qualification of what has preceded).

no·ta·bil·i·ty /nṓtəbílitee/ *n.* (*pl.* **-ties**) **1** the state of being notable (*names of no historical notability*). **2** a prominent person.

no·ta·ble /nṓtəbəl/ *adj. & n.* • *adj.* worthy of note; remarkable. • *n.* an eminent person. □□ **no·ta·bly** *adv.*

no·ta·rize /nṓtərīz/ *v.tr.* certify (a document) as a notary.

no·ta·ry /nṓtəree/ *n.* (*pl.* **-ries**) (in full **notary public**) a person authorized to perform certain legal formalities, esp. to draw up or certify contracts, deeds, etc. □□ **no·tar·i·al** /nōtáireeəl/ *adj.*

no·tate /nṓtayt/ *v.tr.* write in notation.

no·ta·tion /nōtáyshən/ *n.* **1 a** the representation of numbers, quantities, pitch and duration, etc., of musical notes, etc., by symbols. **b** any set of such symbols. **2** a set of symbols used to represent chess moves, dance steps, etc. **3 a** a note or annotation. **b** a record. ▫▫ **no·ta·tion·al** *adj.*

notch /noch/ *n. & v.* •*n.* **1** a V-shaped indentation on an edge or surface. **2** a nick made on a stick, etc., in order to keep count. **3** *colloq.* a step or degree (*move up a notch*). **4** a deep, narrow mountain pass. •*v.tr.* **1** make notches in. **2** (foll. by *up*) record or score with or as with notches. **3** secure or insert by notches. ▫▫ **notched** *adj.* **notch·er** *n.* **notch·y** *adj.* (**notchier, notchiest**).

note /nōt/ *n. & v.* •*n.* **1** a brief record as an aid to memory (often in *pl.*: *make notes; spoke without notes*). **2** an observation, usu. unwritten, of experiences, etc. (*compare notes*). **3** a short letter. **4** a formal diplomatic or parliamentary communication. **5** a short annotation in a book, etc. **6 a** notice; attention (*worthy of note*). **b** eminence (*a person of note*). **7 a** a written sign representing the pitch and duration of a musical sound. **b** a single tone of definite pitch made by a musical instrument, the human voice, etc. **c** a key of a piano, etc. **8 a** a bird's song or call. **b** a single tone in this. **9** a quality or tone of speaking, expressing mood or attitude, etc. (*sound a note of warning*). •*v.tr.* **1** give or draw attention to. **2** record as a thing to be remembered. **3** (in *passive*; often foll. by *for*) be famous or well known (for a quality, activity, etc.) (*were noted for their generosity*). ▫ **hit** (or **strike**) **the right note** act in exactly the right manner. **of note** distinguished (*a person of note*). **take note** (often foll. by *of*) pay attention (to). ▫▫ **not·ed** *adj.* (in sense 3 of *v.*). **note·less** *adj.*

note·book com·pu·ter *n.* a lightweight computer that closes to notebook size for portability.

note·wor·thy /nṓtwər<u>th</u>ee/ *adj.* worthy of attention. ▫▫ **note·wor·thi·ness** *n.*

noth·ing /núthing/ *n. & adv.* •*n.* **1** not anything (*nothing has been done; have nothing to do*). **2** no thing (often foll. by compl.: *I see nothing that I want*). **3** a person or thing of no importance (*was nothing to me*). **4** nonexistence; what does not exist. **5** (in calculations) no amount; naught (*a third of nothing is nothing*). •*adv.* not at all, in no way (*is nothing like what we expected*). ▫ **be nothing to 1** not concern. **2** not compare with. **be** (or **have**) **nothing to do with 1** have no connection with. **2** not be associated with. **for nothing 1** at no cost; without payment. **2** to no purpose. **have nothing on 1** be naked. **2** have no engagements. **nothing doing** *colloq.* **1 a** there is no prospect of success. **b** I refuse. **2** nothing is happening. **nothing** (or **not much**) **in it** (or **to it**) **1** unimportant. **2** simple to do. **3** no (or little) advantage to be seen in one possibility over another. **think nothing of it** do not apologize or feel bound to show gratitude.

noth·ing·ness /núthingnis/ *n.* **1** nonexistence; the nonexistent. **2** worthlessness; triviality.

no·tice /nṓtis/ *n. & v.* •*n.* **1** attention; observation (*it escaped my notice*). **2** a displayed sheet, etc., bearing an announcement. **3 a** an intimation or warning, esp. a formal one (*give notice; at a moment's notice*). **b** (often foll. by *to* + infin.) a formal announcement or declaration of intention to end an agreement or leave employment at a specified time (*hand in one's notice*). **4** a short published review or comment about a new play, book, etc. •*v.tr.* **1** (often foll. by *that, how*, etc., + clause) observe; take notice of. **2** remark upon. ▫ **at short** (or **a moment's**) **notice** with little warning. **take notice** (or **no notice**) show signs (or no signs) of interest. **take notice of 1** pay attention to. **2** act upon.

no·tice·a·ble /nṓtisəbəl/ *adj.* **1** easily seen or noticed; perceptible. **2** noteworthy. ▫▫ **no·tice·a·bly** *adv.*

no·ti·fy /nṓtifī/ *v.tr.* (**-fies, -fied**) **1** (often foll. by *of* or *that* + clause) inform or give notice to (a person). **2** make known; announce or report (a thing). ▫▫ **no·ti·fi·ca·tion** /–fikáyshən/ *n.*

no·tion /nṓshən/ *n.* **1 a** a concept or idea (*it was an absurd notion*). **b** an opinion (*has the notion that people are honest*). **c** a vague view or understanding (*have no notion what you mean*). **2** an inclination or intention (*has no notion of conforming*). **3** (in *pl.*) small, useful articles.

no·tion·al /nṓshənəl/ *adj.* hypothetical; imaginary. ▫▫ **no·tion·al·ly** *adv.*

no·to·chord /nṓtəkawrd/ *n.* a cartilaginous skeletal rod supporting the body in all embryo and some adult chordate animals.

no·to·ri·ous /nōtáwreeəs/ *adj.* well-known, esp. unfavorably (*a notorious criminal*). ▫▫ **no·to·ri·e·ty** /–tərī́ətee/ *n.* **no·to·ri·ous·ly** *adv.*

not·with·stand·ing /nótwithstánding, –wi<u>th</u>–/ *prep., adv., & conj.* •*prep.* in spite of (*notwithstanding your objections; this fact notwithstanding*). •*adv.* nevertheless. •*conj.* (usu. foll. by *that* + clause) although.

nou·gat /nóogət/ *n.* a chewy candy made from sugar or honey, nuts, egg white, and often fruit pieces.

nought var. of NAUGHT.

noun /nown/ *n. Gram.* a word (other than a pronoun) or group of words used to name or identify any of a class of persons, places, or things (**common noun**), or a particular one of these (**proper noun**).

nour·ish /nə́rish, núr–/ *v.tr.* **1 a** sustain with food. **b** promote the development of (the soil, etc.). **c** provide with intellectual or emotional sustenance. **2** cherish (a feeling, etc.).

nour·ish·ing /nə́rishing, núr–/ *adj.* (esp. of food) containing much nourishment. ▫▫ **nour·ish·ing·ly** *adv.*

nour·ish·ment /nə́rishmənt, núr–/ *n.* sustenance; food.

nou·veau riche /nóovō réesh/ *n.* (*pl.* **nouveaux riches** *pronunc.* same) a person who has recently acquired (usu. ostentatious) wealth.

nou·velle cui·sine /noovél kwizéen/ *n.* a modern style of cooking avoiding heaviness and emphasizing presentation.

Nov. *abbr.* November.

no·va /nṓvə/ *n.* (*pl.* **novas** or **novae** /–vee/) a star showing a sudden large increase of brightness that then subsides.

nov·el[1] /nóvəl/ *n.* **1** a fictitious prose story of book length. **2** (prec. by *the*) this type of literature.

> **novel** mid-16th century: from Italian *novella* (*storia*) 'new (story),' feminine of *novello* 'new,' from Latin *novellus*, from *novus* 'new.' The word is also found from late Middle English until the 18th century in the sense 'a novelty, a piece of news,' from Old French *novelle*, also from Latin *novellus* and the source of NOVEL[2].

nov·el[2] /nóvəl/ *adj.* of a new kind or nature; strange; previously unknown.

nov·el·ette /nóvəlét/ *n.* a short novel.

nov·el·ist /nóvəlist/ *n.* a writer of novels. ▫▫ **nov·el·is·tic** *adj.*

no·vel·la /nəvélə/ *n.* (*pl.* **novellas** or **novelle**) a short novel or narrative story; a tale.

nov·el·ty /nóvəltee/ *n.* (*pl.* **-ties**) **1 a** newness; new character. **b** originality. **2** a new or unusual thing or occurrence. **3** a small toy or decoration, etc., of novel design. **4** (*attrib.*) having novelty (*novelty toys*).

No·vem·ber /nōvémbər/ *n.* the eleventh month of the year.

no·ve·na /nōvéenə, nə–/ *n. RC Ch.* a devotion consisting of special prayers or services on nine successive days.

nov·ice /nóvis/ *n.* **1 a** a probationary member of a religious order, before the taking of vows. **b** a new convert. **2** a beginner; an inexperienced person.

no•vi•ti•ate /nōvísheeət, –ayt/ *n.* (also **no•vi•ci•ate**) **1** the period of being a novice. **2** a religious novice. **3** novices' quarters.

No•vo•caine /nṓvəkayn/ *n.* (also **novocaine**) *Trademark* a local anesthetic derived from benzoic acid.

now /now/ *adv., conj., & n.* • *adv.* **1** at the present or mentioned time. **2** immediately (*I must go now*). **3** by this or that time (*it was now clear*). **4** under the present circumstances (*I cannot now agree*). **5** on this further occasion (*what do you want now?*). **6** in the immediate past (*just now*). **7** (esp. in a narrative or discourse) then; next (*the police now arrived; now to consider the next point*). **8** (without reference to time, giving various tones to a sentence) surely, I insist, I wonder, etc. (*now what do you mean by that?; oh come now!*). • *conj.* (often foll. by *that* + clause) as a consequence of the fact (*now that I am older; now you mention it*). • *n.* this time; the present (*should be there by now; has happened before now*). □ **as of now** from or at this time. **for now** until a later time (*goodbye for now*). **now and again** (or **then**) from time to time; intermittently. **now or never** an expression of urgency.

now•a•days /nówədayz/ *adv. & n.* • *adv.* at the present time or age. • *n.* the present time.

no•where /nṓhwair, –wair/ *adv. & pron.* • *adv.* in or to no place. • *pron.* no place. □ **come from nowhere** be suddenly evident or successful. **get nowhere** make or cause to make no progress. **in the middle of nowhere** *colloq.* remote from urban life. **nowhere near** not nearly.

no-win *adj.* of or designating a situation in which success is impossible.

nox•ious /nókshəs/ *adj.* harmful; unwholesome. □□ **nox•ious•ly** *adv.* **nox•ious•ness** *n.*

noz•zle /nózəl/ *n.* a spout on a hose, etc., from which a jet issues.

Np *symb. Chem.* the element neptunium.

NRC *abbr.* Nuclear Regulatory Commission.

NS *abbr.* **1** new style. **2** new series. **3** Nova Scotia.

-n't /ənt/ *adv.* (in *comb.*) = NOT (usu. with *is, are, have, must,* and the auxiliary verbs *can, do, should, would*).

nth see N[1].

nu /nōō, nyōō/ *n.* the thirteenth letter of the Greek alphabet (Ν, ν).

nu•ance /nṓō-aans, nyṓō–/ *n. & v.* • *n.* a subtle difference in or shade of meaning, feeling, color, etc. • *v.tr.* give a nuance or nuances to.

nub /nub/ *n.* **1** the point or gist (of a matter or story). **2** a small lump, esp. of coal. **3** a stub; a small residue. □□ **nub•by** *adj.*

nu•bile /nṓōbil, –bil, nyṓō–/ *adj.* (of a woman) marriageable or sexually attractive. □□ **nu•bil•i•ty** /–bílitee/ *n.*

nu•cle•ar /nṓōkleeər, nyṓō–/ *adj.* **1** of, relating to, or constituting a nucleus. **2** using nuclear energy (*nuclear reactor*). **3** having nuclear weapons.

▶Although the pronunciation "noo-kyoo-luhr" has been used by many, including presidents, it is still widely regarded as uneducated.

nu•cle•ar bomb *n.* a bomb involving the release of energy by nuclear fission or fusion or both.

nu•cle•ar dis•ar•ma•ment *n.* the gradual or total reduction by a nation of its nuclear weapons.

nu•cle•ar en•er•gy *n.* energy obtained by nuclear fission or fusion.

nu•cle•ar fam•i•ly *n.* a couple and their children, regarded as a basic social unit.

nu•cle•ar fis•sion *n.* a nuclear reaction in which a heavy nucleus splits spontaneously or on impact with another particle, with the release of energy.

nu•cle•ar fu•sion *n.* a nuclear reaction in which atomic nuclei of low atomic number fuse to form a heavier nucleus with the release of energy.

nu•cle•ar mag•net•ic res•o•nance *n.* the absorption of electromagnetic radiation by a nucleus having a magnetic moment when in an external magnetic field, used mainly as an analytical technique and in body imaging for diagnosis.

nu•cle•ar med•i•cine *n. Med.* a specialty that uses radioactive materials for diagnosis and treatment.

nu•cle•ar phys•ics *n.* the physics of atomic nuclei and their interactions.

nu•cle•ar pow•er *n.* **1** power generated by a nuclear reactor. **2** a country that has nuclear weapons.

nu•cle•ar re•ac•tor *n.* a device in which a nuclear fission chain reaction is sustained and controlled in order to produce energy.

nu•cle•ar war•fare *n.* warfare in which nuclear weapons are used.

nu•cle•ar waste *n.* any radioactive waste material.

nu•cle•ate /nṓōkleeayt, nyṓō–/ *adj. & v.* • *adj.* having a nucleus. • *v.intr. & tr.* form or form into a nucleus. □□ **nu•cle•a•tion** /–áyshən/ *n.*

nu•cle•i *pl.* of NUCLEUS.

nu•cle•ic acid /nōōkléeik, –kláyik, nyṓō–/ *n.* either of two complex organic molecules (DNA and RNA), consisting of many nucleotides linked in a long chain, and present in all living cells.

nucleo- /nṓōkleeō, nyṓō–/ *comb. form* nucleus; nucleic acid (*nucleoprotein*).

nu•cle•o•lus /nṓōkléeələs, nyṓō–/ *n.* (*pl.* **nucleoli** /–lī/) a small dense spherical structure within a nondividing nucleus. □□ **nu•cle•o•lar** *adj.*

nu•cle•on /nṓōkleeon, nyṓō–/ *n. Physics* a proton or neutron.

nu•cle•o•tide /nṓōkleeətīd, nyṓō–/ *n. Biochem.* an organic compound that forms the basic constituent of DNA and RNA.

nu•cle•us /nṓōkleeəs/ *n.* (*pl.* **nuclei** /–lee-ī/) **1 a** the central part or thing around which others are collected. **b** the kernel of an aggregate or mass. **2** an initial part meant to receive additions. **3** *Astron.* the solid part of a comet's head. **4** *Physics* the central core of an atom. **5** *Biol.* a large dense organelle of eukaryotic cells, containing the genetic material.

nude /nōōd, nyōōd/ *adj. & n.* • *adj.* naked; unclothed. • *n.* **1** a painting, sculpture, photograph, etc., of a nude human figure. **2** a nude person. **3** (prec. by *the*) **a** an unclothed state. **b** the representation of an undraped human figure as a genre in art.

nudge /nuj/ *v. & n.* • *v.tr.* **1** prod gently with the elbow to attract attention. **2** push gently or gradually. **3** give a gentle reminder or encouragement to (a person). • *n.* the act or an instance of nudging; a gentle push.

nud•ist /nṓōdist, nyṓō–/ *n.* a person who advocates or practices going unclothed. □□ **nud•ism** *n.*

nu•di•ty /nṓōditee, nyṓō–/ *n.* the state of being nude; nakedness.

nu•ga•to•ry /nṓōgətáwree, nyṓō–/ *adj.* **1** futile; trifling; worthless. **2** inoperative.

nug•get /núgit/ *n.* **1 a** a lump of gold, platinum, etc., as found in the earth. **b** a lump of anything compared to this. **2** something valuable for its size.

nui•sance /nṓōsəns, nyṓō–/ *n.* **1** a person, thing, or circumstance causing trouble or annoyance. **2** anything harmful to the community for which a legal remedy exists.

nuke /nōōk, nyōōk/ *n. & v. colloq.* • *n.* a nuclear weapon. • *v.tr. colloq.* bomb or destroy with nuclear weapons.

null /nul/ *adj.* **1** (esp. **null and void**) invalid. **2** nonexistent. **3** having the value zero. **4** *Computing* **a** empty (*null list*). **b** all the elements of which are zeros (*null matrix*). **5** without character or expression.

nul·li·fy /núlifī/ *v.tr.* (**-fies, -fied**) make null; neutralize; invalidate; cancel. ▫▫ **nul·li·fi·ca·tion** /–fikáyshən/ *n.* **nul·li·fi·er** *n.*

numb /num/ *adj. & v.* • *adj.* (often foll. by *with*) deprived of feeling (*numb with cold*). • *v.tr.* **1** make numb. **2** paralyze. ▫▫ **numb·ly** *adv.* **numb·ness** *n.*

num·ber /númbər/ *n. & v.* • *n.* **1 a** an arithmetical value representing a particular quantity. **b** a word, symbol, or figure representing this. **c** an arithmetical value showing position in a series (*registration number*). **2** (often foll. by *of*) the total count or aggregate (*the number of accidents has decreased*). **3 a** numerical reckoning (*the laws of number*). **b** (in *pl.*) arithmetic (*not good at numbers*). **4 a** (in *sing.* or *pl.*) a quantity or amount (*a large number of people*). **b** (in *pl.*) numerical preponderance (*force of numbers*). **5 a** a person or thing having a place in a series, esp. a single issue of a magazine, etc. **b** a song, dance, etc. **6** company; group (*among our number*). **7** *Gram.* **a** the classification of words by their singular or plural forms. **b** a particular such form. **8** *colloq.* a person or thing regarded familiarly (usu. qualified in some way: *an attractive little number*). • *v.tr.* **1** include (*I number you among my friends*). **2** assign a number to. **3** amount to (a specified number). **4 a** count. **b** comprise (*numbering forty thousand men*). ▫ **one's days are numbered** one does not have long to live. **have a person's number** *colloq.* understand a person's real motives, character, etc. **one's number is up** *colloq.* one is finished or doomed to die.

num·ber crunch·er *n. Computing & Math. sl.* a machine capable of complex calculations, etc. ▫▫ **num·ber crunch·ing** *n.*

num·ber one *n. & adj.* • *n. colloq.* oneself (*take care of number one*). • *adj.* most important (*the number-one priority*).

numb·skull var. of NUMSKULL.

nu·mer·al /nóōmərəl, nyóō–/ *n. & adj.* • *n.* a word, figure, or group of figures denoting a number. • *adj.* of or denoting a number.

nu·mer·ate /nóōmərət, nyóō–/ *adj.* acquainted with the basic principles of mathematics. ▫▫ **nu·mer·a·cy** /–əsee/ *n.*

nu·mer·a·tion /nóōməráyshən, nyóō–/ *n.* **1** a method or process of numbering or computing. **2** the expression in words of a number written in figures.

nu·mer·a·tor /nóōməraytər, nyóō–/ *n.* the number above the line in a common fraction showing how many of the parts indicated by the denominator are taken (e.g., 2 in $^2/_3$).

nu·mer·i·cal /nōōmérikəl, nyóō–/ *adj.* (also **nu·mer·ic**) of or relating to a number or numbers. ▫▫ **nu·mer·i·cal·ly** *adv.*

nu·mer·ol·o·gy /nóōməróləjee, nyóō–/ *n.* (*pl.* **-gies**) the study of the supposed occult significance of numbers. ▫▫ **nu·mer·o·log·i·cal** /–rəlójikəl/ *adj.* **nu·mer·ol·o·gist** *n.*

nu·mer·ous /nóōmərəs, nyóō–/ *adj.* **1** (with *pl.*) great in number. **2** consisting of many. ▫▫ **nu·mer·ous·ly** *adv.*

nu·mi·nous /nóōminəs, nyóō–/ *adj.* **1** indicating the presence of a divinity. **2** spiritual. **3** awe-inspiring.

nu·mis·mat·ic /nóōmizmátik, nyóō–/ *adj.* of or relating to coins or medals. ▫▫ **nu·mis·mat·i·cal·ly** *adv.*

nu·mis·mat·ics /nóōmizmátiks, nyóō–/ *n.pl.* (usu. treated as *sing.*) the study of coins or medals. ▫▫ **nu·mis·ma·tist** /nōōmízmətist, nyōō–/ *n.*

num·skull /númskul/ *n.* (also **numb·skull**) a stupid or foolish person.

nun /nun/ *n.* a member of a community of women living apart under religious vows.

nun·ner·y /núnəree/ *n.* (*pl.* **-ies**) a religious house of nuns; a convent.

nup·tial /núpshəl/ *adj. & n.* • *adj.* of or relating to marriage or weddings. • *n.* (usu. in *pl.*) a wedding.

nurse /nərs/ *n. & v.* • *n.* **1** a person trained to care for the sick. **2** (formerly) a person employed to take charge of young children. • *v.* **1 a** *intr.* work as a nurse. **b** *tr.* attend to (a sick person). **c** *tr.* give medical attention to (an illness or injury). **2** *tr. & intr.* feed or be fed at the breast. **3** *tr.* **a** foster; promote the development of (the arts, plants, etc.). **b** harbor (a grievance, etc.).

---

nurse late Middle English: contraction of Middle English *nourice*, from Old French, from late Latin *nutricia*, feminine of Latin *nutricius* '(person) who nourishes,' from *nutrix* 'nurse,' from *nutrire* 'nourish.' The verb was originally a contraction of *nourish*, altered in form under the influence of the noun.

---

nurse·maid /nársmayd/ *n.* **1** a woman in charge of a child or children. **2** a person who watches over or guides another carefully.

nurse-prac·ti·tion·er *n.* a registered nurse who has received training in diagnosing and treating illness.

nurs·er·y /nársəree/ *n.* (*pl.* **-ies**) **1 a** a room or place equipped for young children. **b** a nursery where children are looked after during the working day. **2** a place where plants, etc., are reared for sale or transplantation.

nurs·er·y·man /nársəreemən/ *n.* (*pl.* **-men**) an owner of or worker in a plant nursery.

nurs·er·y rhyme *n.* a simple traditional song or story in rhyme for children.

nurs·er·y school *n.* a school for children from the age of about three to five.

nurs·ing /nársing/ *n.* **1** the practice or profession of caring for the sick as a nurse. **2** (*attrib.*) concerned with or suitable for nursing the sick or elderly, etc.

nur·ture /nárchər/ *n. & v.* • *n.* **1** the process of bringing up; fostering care. **2** nourishment. **3** sociological factors as a determinant of personality. • *v.tr.* **1** bring up; rear. **2** nourish. ▫▫ **nur·tur·er** *n.*

nut /nut/ *n.* **1 a** a fruit consisting of a hard or tough shell around an edible kernel. **b** this kernel. **2 a** pod containing hard seeds. **3** a small usu. hexagonal flat piece of metal or other material with a threaded hole through it for screwing on the end of a bolt to secure it. **4** *sl.* a person's head. **5** *sl.* **a** a crazy or eccentric person. **b** an obsessive enthusiast (*a health-food nut*). **6** (in *pl.*) *coarse sl.* the testicles. ▫ **off one's nut** *sl.* crazy. ▫▫ **nut·like** *adj.*

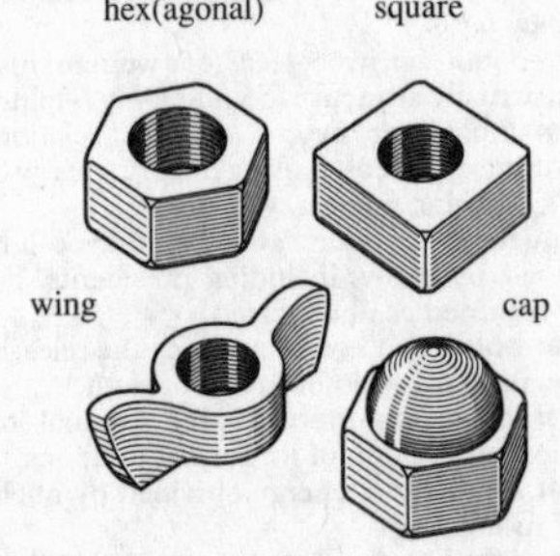

nut, 3

nut·case /nútkays/ *n. sl.* a crazy or foolish person.

nut·crack·er /nútkrakər/ *n.* a device for cracking nuts.

nut·hatch /nút-hach/ *n.* any small bird of the family Sittidae, climbing up and down tree trunks and feeding on nuts, insects, etc., esp. the Eurasian *Sitta europaea*.

nut·house /núthows/ *n. sl.* a mental home or hospital.

nut·meg /nútmeg/ *n.* **1** an evergreen E. Indian tree, *Myristica fragrans*, yielding a hard aromatic spheroidal seed. **2** the seed of this used as a spice.

nu·tri·a /nóotreeə, nyóo–/ *n.* **1** an aquatic beaverlike rodent, *Myocastor Coypus*, native to S. America. **2** its skin or fur.

nu·tri·ent /nóotreeənt, nyóo–/ *n. & adj.* •*n.* any substance that provides nourishment for the maintenance of life. •*adj.* providing nourishment.

nu·tri·ment /nóotrimənt, nyóo–/ *n.* **1** nourishing food. **2** an intellectual or artistic, etc., nourishment or stimulus. □□ **nu·tri·men·tal** /–mént'l/ *adj.*

nu·tri·tion /nootríshən, nyoo–/ *n.* **1 a** the process of providing or receiving nourishing substances. **b** food; nourishment. **2** the study of nutrients and nutrition. □□ **nu·tri·tion·al** *adj.*

nu·tri·tion·ist /nootríshənist, nyoo–/ *n.* a person who studies or is an expert on the processes of human nourishment.

nu·tri·tious /nootríshəs, nyoo–/ *adj.* efficient as food. □□ **nu·tri·tious·ly** *adv.*

nu·tri·tive /nóotritiv, nyóo–/ *adj.* **1** of or concerned in nutrition. **2** serving as nutritious food.

nuts /nuts/ *adj. & int.* •*adj. sl.* mad; eccentric. •*int. sl.* an expression of contempt (*nuts to you*). □ **be nuts about** *colloq.* be enthusiastic about or very fond of.

nuts and bolts *n.pl. colloq.* the practical details.

nut·shell /nútshel/ *n.* the hard exterior covering of a nut. □ **in a nutshell** in a few words.

nut·ty /nútee/ *adj.* (**nuttier, nuttiest**) **1 a** full of nuts. **b** tasting like nuts. **2** *sl.* = NUTS *adj.* □□ **nut·ti·ness** *n.*

nuz·zle /núzəl/ *v.* **1** *tr.* prod or rub gently with the nose. **2** *intr.* (foll. by *against*, *up to*) press the nose gently. **3** *tr.* (also *refl.*) nestle; lie snug.

NV *abbr.* Nevada (in official postal use).

NW *abbr.* **1** northwest. **2** northwestern.

NY *abbr.* New York (also in official postal use).

NYC *abbr.* New York City.

nyc·ta·lo·pi·a /níktəlópeeə/ *n.* inability to see in dim light. Also called **night blindness.**

ny·lon /nílon/ *n.* **1** any of various synthetic fibers having a proteinlike structure, with tough, lightweight, elastic properties, used in industry and for textiles, etc. **2** a nylon fabric. **3** (in *pl.*) stockings made of nylon.

nymph /nimf/ *n.* **1** any of various mythological semidivine spirits regarded as maidens and associated with aspects of nature. **2** *poet.* a beautiful young woman. **3** an immature form of some insects. □□ **nymph·al** *adj.*

nym·pho /nímfō/ *n.* (*pl.* **-phos**) *colloq.* a nymphomaniac.

nym·pho·ma·ni·a /nímfəmáyneeə/ *n.* excessive sexual desire in women. □□ **nym·pho·ma·ni·ac** *n. & adj.*

NYSE *abbr.* New York Stock Exchange.

NZ *abbr.* New Zealand.

O

O[1] /ō/ *n.* (also **o**) (*pl.* **Os** or **O's**) **1** the fifteenth letter of the alphabet. **2** (**0**) naught; zero (in a sequence of numerals, esp. when spoken). **3** a human blood type.

O[2] *symb. Chem.* the element oxygen.

O[3] /ō/ *int.* **1** var. of OH[1]. **2** prefixed to a name in the vocative (*O God*).

O' /ō, ə/ *prefix* of Irish patronymic names (*O'Connor*).

o' /ə/ *prep.* of, on (esp. in phrases: o'clock; *will-o'-the-wisp*).

-o /ō/ *suffix* forming usu. *sl.* or *colloq.* variants or derivatives (*weirdo*; *wino*).

oaf /ōf/ *n.* (*pl.* **oafs**) **1** an awkward lout. **2** a stupid person. ▫▫ **oaf·ish** *adj.* **oaf·ish·ly** *adv.* **oaf·ish·ness** *n.*

oak /ōk/ *n.* **1** any tree of the genus *Quercus* usu. having lobed leaves and bearing acorns. **2** the durable wood of this tree. **3** (*attrib.*) made of oak (*oak table*). ▫▫ **oak·en** *adj.*

oa·kum /ṓkəm/ *n.* a loose fiber obtained by picking old rope to pieces and used esp. in caulking.

oar /awr/ *n.* **1** a pole with a blade used for rowing or steering a boat by leverage against the water. **2** a rower. ▫ **put** (or **stick**) **one's oar in** interfere; meddle. ▫▫ **oared** *adj.* (also in *comb.*).

oar·lock /áwrlok/ *n.* a device on a boat's gunwale, esp. a pair of tholepins, serving as a fulcrum for an oar and keeping it in place.

oars·man /áwrzmən/ *n.* (*pl.* **-men**; *fem.* **oarswoman**, *pl.* **-women**) a rower. ▫▫ **oars·man·ship** *n.*

OAS *abbr.* Organization of American States.

o·a·sis /ō-áysis/ *n.* (*pl.* **oases** /–seez/) **1** a fertile spot in a desert, where water is found. **2** an area or period of calm in the midst of turbulence.

oat /ōt/ *n.* **1 a** a cereal plant, *Avena sativa*, cultivated in cool climates. **b** (in *pl.*) the grain yielded by this, used as food. **2** any other cereal of the genus *Avena*, esp. the wild oat, *A. fatua*. ▫ **off one's oats** *colloq.* not hungry.

oath /ōth/ *n.* (*pl.* **oaths** /ōthz, ōths/) **1** a solemn declaration or undertaking (often naming God). **2** a statement or promise contained in an oath (*oath of allegiance*). **3** a profane utterance. ▫ **under oath** having sworn a solemn oath.

oat·meal /ṓtmeel/ *n.* **1** meal made from ground oats used esp. in breakfast cereal, cookies, etc. **2** a grayish-fawn color flecked with brown.

OB *abbr.* **1 a** obstetric. **b** obstetrician. **c** obstetrics. **2** off Broadway.

ob. *abbr.* he or she died.

ob·bli·ga·to /óbligaátō/ *n.* (*pl.* **-tos**) *Mus.* an accompaniment, usu. special and unusual in effect, forming an integral part of a composition.

ob·du·rate /óbdŏŏrit, –dyŏŏr–/ *adj.* **1** stubborn. **2** hardened against influence. ▫▫ **ob·du·ra·cy** /–dŏŏrəsee, –dyŏŏr–/ *n.* **ob·du·rate·ly** *adv.*

o·be·di·ence /ōbeédeeəns/ *n.* **1** obeying as an act or quality. **2** submission to another's rule or authority.

o·be·di·ent /ōbeédeeənt/ *adj.* **1** obeying or ready to obey. **2** (often foll. by *to*) submissive to another's will. ▫▫ **o·be·di·ent·ly** *adv.*

o·bei·sance /ōbáysəns, ōbée–/ *n.* **1** a bow, curtsy, or other respectful or submissive gesture (*make an obeisance*). **2** homage.

ob·e·lisk /óbəlisk/ *n.* **1** a tapering, usu. four-sided stone pillar set up as a monument or landmark, etc. **2** = OBELUS.

ob·e·lus /óbələs/ *n.* (*pl.* **obeli** /–lī/) **1** a dagger-shaped reference mark in printed matter. **2** a mark (– or ÷) used in ancient manuscripts to mark a word.

o·bese /ōbeés/ *adj.* very fat; corpulent. ▫▫ **o·be·si·ty** *n.*

o·bey /ōbáy/ *v.* **1** *tr.* **a** carry out the command of. **b** carry out (a command). **2** *intr.* do what one is told to do. **3** *tr.* be actuated by (a force or impulse).

ob·fus·cate /óbfuskayt/ *v.tr.* **1** obscure or confuse (a mind, topic, etc.). **2** stupefy; bewilder. ▫▫ **ob·fus·ca·tion** /–káyshən/ *n.* **ob·fus·ca·to·ry** /obfúskətawree/ *adj.*

o·bit /óbit, ṓbit/ *n. colloq.* an obituary.

o·bit·u·ar·y /ōbíchōō-eree/ *n.* (*pl.* **-ies**) **1** a notice of a death or deaths. **2** an account of the life of a deceased person. **3** (*attrib.*) of an obituary. ▫▫ **o·bit·u·ar·i·al** /–áireeəl/ *adj.*

ob·ject *n.* & *v.* • *n.* /óbjikt, –jekt/ **1** a material thing that can be seen or touched. **2** (foll. by *of*) a person or thing to which action or feeling is directed (*the object of attention*). **3** a thing sought or aimed at. **4** *Gram.* a noun or its equivalent governed by an active transitive verb or by a preposition. **5** *Philos.* a thing external to the thinking mind or subject. • *v.* /əbjékt/ **1** *intr.* (often foll. by *to*) express or feel opposition, disapproval, or reluctance. **2** *tr.* (foll. by *that* + clause) state as an objection. **3** *tr.* (foll. by *to* or *that* + clause) adduce (a quality or fact) as contrary or damaging (to a case). ▫ **no object** not forming an important or restricting factor (*money no object*). ▫▫ **ob·ject·less** /óbjiktlis/ *adj.* **ob·jec·tor** /əbjéktər/ *n.*

ob·jec·ti·fy /əbjéktifī/ *v.tr.* (**-fies, -fied**) **1** make objective. **2** present as an object of perception. ▫▫ **ob·jec·ti·fi·ca·tion** /–fikáyshən/ *n.*

ob·jec·tion /əbjékshən/ *n.* **1** an expression of opposition or disapproval. **2** the act of objecting. **3** an adverse reason or statement.

ob·jec·tion·a·ble /əbjékshənəbəl/ *adj.* **1** open to objection. **2** unpleasant; offensive. ▫▫ **ob·jec·tion·a·ble·ness** *n.* **ob·jec·tion·a·bly** *adv.*

ob·jec·tive /əbjéktiv/ *adj.* & *n.* • *adj.* **1** external to the mind; real. **2** dealing with outward things or exhibiting facts uncolored by feelings or opinions. **3** *Gram.* (of a case or word) constructed as or appropriate to the object of a transitive verb or preposition. **4** aimed at (*objective point*). • *n.* **1** something sought or aimed at. **2** *Gram.* the objective case. ▫▫ **ob·jec·tive·ly** *adv.* **ob·jec·tiv·i·ty** /–tívitee/ *n.* **ob·jec·tiv·ize** *v.tr.*

ob·ject les·son *n.* a striking practical example of some principle.

ob·jet d'art /áwbzhay daár/ *n.* (*pl.* **objets d'art** *pronunc.* same) a small decorative object.

ob·la·tion /əbláyshən, ob–/ *n. Relig.* **1** a thing offered to a divine being. **2** the presentation of bread and wine to God in the Eucharist. ▫▫ **ob·la·tion·al** *adj.* **ob·la·to·ry** /óblətawree/ *adj.*

ob·li·gate /óbligayt/ *v.tr.* **1** (usu. in *passive*; foll. by *to* + infin.) bind (a person) legally or morally. **2** commit (assets) as security. ▫▫ **ob·li·ga·tor** *n.*

ob·li·ga·tion /óbligáyshən/ *n.* **1** the constraining power of a law, precept, duty, contract, etc. **2** a duty; a burdensome task. **3** a binding agreement. **4 a** a kindness done or received (*repay an obligation*). **b** indebtedness for this (*be under an obligation*).

ob·li·ga·to·ry /əblígətáwree/ *adj.* **1** legally or morally binding. **2** compulsory. **3** constituting an obligation. ▫▫ **ob·li·ga·to·ri·ly** *adv.*

o·blige /əblíj/ *v.tr.* **1** (foll. by *to* + infin.) constrain; compel. **2** be binding on. **3 a** make indebted by conferring a favor. **b** (foll. by *with*, or *by* + verbal noun) gratify (*oblige me by leaving*). **4** (in *passive*; foll. by *to*) be indebted. ▫ **much obliged** an expression of thanks.

o·blig·ing /əblíjing/ *adj.* courteous; accommodating; ready to do (someone) a service or kindness. ▫▫ **o·blig·ing·ly** *adv.*

o·blique /əbléek/ *adj.* **1 a** declining from the vertical or horizontal. **b** diverging from a straight line or course. **2** not going straight to the point; indirect. **3** *Geom.* inclined at other than a right angle. **4** *Bot.* (of a leaf) with unequal sides. **5** *Gram.* denoting any case other than the nominative or vocative. ▫▫ **o·blique·ly** *adv.* **o·blique·ness** *n.* **o·bliq·ui·ty** /əblíkwitee/ *n.*

ob·lit·er·ate /əblítərayt/ *v.tr.* **1 a** blot out; efface; erase; destroy. **b** leave no clear traces of. **2** deface (a postage stamp, etc.) to prevent further use. ▫▫ **ob·lit·er·a·tion** /–ráyshən/ *n.* **ob·lit·er·a·tive** /–rətiv/ *adj.* **ob·lit·er·a·tor** *n.*

ob·liv·i·on /əblíveeən/ *n.* the state of having or being forgotten.

ob·liv·i·ous /əblíveeəs/ *adj.* **1** (often foll. by *of*) forgetful; unmindful. **2** (foll. by *to*, *of*) unaware or unconscious of. ▫▫ **ob·liv·i·ous·ly** *adv.* **ob·liv·i·ous·ness** *n.*

ob·long /óblawng/ *adj.* & *n.* • *adj.* **1** rectangular with adjacent sides unequal. **2** greater in breadth than in height. • *n.* an oblong figure or object.

ob·lo·quy /óbləkwee/ *n.* **1** the state of being generally ill spoken of. **2** abuse.

ob·nox·ious /əbnókshəs/ *adj.* offensive; objectionable; disliked. ▫▫ **ob·nox·ious·ly** *adv.* **ob·nox·ious·ness** *n.*

o·boe /óbō/ *n.* a woodwind double-reed instrument of treble pitch and plaintive incisive tone. ▫▫ **o·bo·ist** /óbōist/ *n.*

oboe

ob·scene /əbséen/ *adj.* **1** offensively or repulsively indecent. **2** *colloq.* highly repugnant (*obscene wealth*). ▫▫ **ob·scene·ly** *adv.*

ob·scen·i·ty /əbsénitee/ *n.* (*pl.* **-ties**) **1** the quality of being obscene. **2** an obscene action, word, etc.

ob·scu·rant·ism /əbskyőőrəntizəm, óbskyőőrán–/ *n.* opposition to knowledge and enlightenment. ▫▫ **ob·scu·rant·ist** *n.*

ob·scure /əbskyőőr/ *adj.* & *v.* • *adj.* **1** not clearly expressed nor easily understood. **2** unexplained. **3** dark; dim. **4** not clear. **5** remote from observation. **6 a** unnoticed. **b** (of a person) undistinguished. • *v.tr.* **1** make obscure. **2** dim the glory of. **3** conceal from sight. ▫▫ **ob·scu·ra·tion** *n.* **ob·scure·ly** *adv.*

ob·scu·ri·ty /əbskyőőritee/ *n.* (*pl.* **-ties**) **1** the state of being obscure. **2** an obscure person or thing.

ob·se·quies /óbsikweez/ *n.pl.* **1** funeral rites. **2** a funeral.

ob·se·qui·ous /əbséekweeəs/ *adj.* servilely obedient or attentive. ▫▫ **ob·se·qui·ous·ly** *adv.* **ob·se·qui·ous·ness** *n.*

ob·serv·ance /əbzérvəns/ *n.* **1** the act or process of keeping or performing a law, duty, etc. **2** a customary rite.

ob·serv·ant /əbzérvənt/ *adj.* **1** acute or diligent in taking notice. **2** attentive in esp. religious observances (*an observant Jew*). ▫▫ **ob·serv·ant·ly** *adv.*

ob·ser·va·tion /óbzərváyshən/ *n.* **1** the act or an instance of noticing. **2** the faculty of taking notice. **3** a remark or statement. **4 a** the accurate watching and noting of phenomena with regard to cause and effect or mutual relations. **b** the noting of the symptoms of a patient, the behavior of a suspect, etc. ▫ **under observation** being watched. ▫▫ **ob·ser·va·tion·al** *adj.* **ob·ser·va·tion·al·ly** *adv.*

ob·serv·a·to·ry /əbzérvətawree/ *n.* (*pl.* **-ries**) a room or building equipped for the observation of natural, esp. astronomical or meteorological, phenomena.

ob·serve /əbzérv/ *v.tr.* **1** (often foll. by *that* or *how* + clause) perceive; note. **2** watch carefully. **3 a** follow or adhere to (a law, principle, etc.). **b** keep or adhere to (an appointed time). **c** maintain (silence). **d** duly perform (a rite). **e** celebrate (an anniversary). **4** examine and note (phenomena). **5** (often foll. by *that* + clause) say, esp. by way of comment. ▫▫ **ob·serv·a·ble** *adj.* **ob·serv·a·bly** *adv.*

ob·serv·er /əbzérvər/ *n.* **1** a person who observes. **2** an interested spectator. **3** a person who attends a conference, etc., to note the proceedings but does not participate.

ob·sess /əbsés/ *v.tr.* & *intr.* (often in *passive*) preoccupy; fill the mind of (a person) continually. ▫▫ **ob·ses·sive** *adj.* & *n.* **ob·ses·sive·ly** *adv.* **ob·ses·sive·ness** *n.*

ob·ses·sion /əbséshən/ *n.* **1** the state of being obsessed. **2** a persistent idea or thought dominating a person's mind. **3** a condition in which such ideas are present. ▫▫ **ob·ses·sion·al** *adj.* **ob·ses·sion·al·ly** *adv.*

ob·sid·i·an /əbsídeeən/ *n.* a dark volcanic rock formed from hardened lava.

ob·so·les·cent /óbsəlésənt/ *adj.* becoming obsolete. ▫▫ **ob·so·les·cence** /–səns/ *n.*

ob·so·lete /óbsəléet/ *adj.* **1** disused; antiquated. **2** *Biol.* rudimentary.

ob·sta·cle /óbstəkəl/ *n.* a person or thing that obstructs progress.

ob·stet·rics /əbstétriks, ob–/ *n.pl.* (usu. treated as *sing.*) the branch of medicine and surgery concerned with childbirth and midwifery. ▫▫ **ob·stet·ric** *adj.* **ob·ste·tri·cian** /–stətríshən/ *n.*

ob·sti·nate /óbstinət/ *adj.* **1** stubborn; intractable. **2** firmly adhering to one's chosen course of action or opinion despite dissuasion. **3** not readily responding to treatment, etc. ▫▫ **ob·sti·na·cy** *n.* **ob·sti·nate·ly** *adv.*

ob·strep·er·ous /əbstrépərəs/ *adj.* **1** turbulent; unruly. **2** noisy; vociferous. ▫▫ **ob·strep·er·ous·ly** *adv.* **ob·strep·er·ous·ness** *n.*

ob·struct /əbstrúkt/ *v.tr.* **1** block up; make hard to pass. **2** impede.

ob·struc·tion /əbstrúkshən/ *n.* **1** the act of blocking. **2** an obstacle or blockage. **3** the retarding of progress by deliberate delays, esp. within a legislative assembly. **4** *Sports* the act of unlawfully obstructing another player. ▫▫ **ob·struc·tion·ism** *n.* (in sense 3). **ob·struc·tion·ist** *n.* (in sense 3).

ob·tain /əbtáyn/ *v.* **1** *tr.* acquire; secure. **2** *intr.* be prevalent or in vogue. ▫▫ **ob·tain·a·ble** *adj.*

ob·trude /əbtrőőd/ *v.* **1** *intr.* be or become obtrusive. **2** *tr.* (often foll. by *on*, *upon*) thrust forward (oneself, one's opinion, etc.) importunately.

ob·tru·sive /əbtrőősiv/ *adj.* **1** unpleasantly or unduly noticeable. **2** obtruding oneself. ◻◻ **ob·tru·sive·ly** *adv.* **ob·tru·sive·ness** *n.*

ob·tuse /əbtóos, –tyóos/ *adj.* **1** slow to understand. **2** of blunt form. **3** (of an angle) more than 90° and less than 180°. ◻◻ **ob·tuse·ly** *adv.* **ob·tuse·ness** *n.*

ob·verse /óbvərs/ *n.* **1 a** the side of a coin or medal bearing the head or principal design. **b** this design. **2** the front or top side of a thing. **3** the counterpart of a fact or truth. ◻◻ **ob·verse·ly** *adv.*

ob·vi·ate /óbveeayt/ *v.tr.* get around or do away with (a need, inconvenience, etc.). ◻◻ **ob·vi·a·tion** /–áyshən/ *n.*

ob·vi·ous /óbveeəs/ *adj.* easily seen or understood. ◻◻ **ob·vi·ous·ly** *adv.* **ob·vi·ous·ness** *n.*

oc·a·ri·na /ókəréenə/ *n.* a small egg-shaped ceramic or metal wind instrument.

oc·ca·sion /əkáyzhən/ *n. & v.* • *n.* **1 a** a special or noteworthy event. **b** the time or occurrence of this. **2** (often foll. by *for*, or *to* + infin.) a reason or justification (*there is no occasion to be angry*). **3** a juncture suitable for doing something. **4** an immediate but subordinate cause (*the assassination was the occasion of the war*). • *v.tr.* **1** be the occasion or cause of. **2** (foll. by *to* + infin.) cause (a person or thing to do something). ◻ **on occasion** now and then. **rise to the occasion** produce the necessary will, energy, etc., in unusually demanding circumstances.

oc·ca·sion·al /əkáyzhənəl/ *adj.* **1** happening irregularly and infrequently. **2 a** meant for or associated with a special occasion. **b** (of furniture, etc.) made for infrequent and varied use. ◻◻ **oc·ca·sion·al·ly** *adv.*

Oc·ci·dent /óksidənt, –dent/ *n. poet.* or *rhet.* **1** (prec. by *the*) the West. **2** western Europe. **3** Europe, America, or both, as distinct from the Orient. **4** European, in contrast to Oriental, civilization. ◻◻ **oc·ci·den·tal** /óksidént'l/ *adj. & n.*

oc·ci·put /óksiput/ *n.* the back of the head. ◻◻ **oc·cip·i·tal** /–sípit'l/ *adj.*

oc·clude /əklóod/ *v.tr.* **1** stop up or close. **2** *Chem.* absorb and retain (gases or impurities).

oc·clu·sion /əklóozhən/ *n.* **1** the act or process of occluding. **2** *Meteorol.* a phenomenon in which the cold front of a depression overtakes the warm front. ◻◻ **oc·clu·sive** *adj.*

oc·cult /əkúlt, ókult/ *adj. & v.* • *adj.* **1** involving the supernatural. **2** kept secret. **3** beyond the range of ordinary knowledge. • *v.tr. Astron.* (of a concealing body) hide from view by passing in front; conceal by being in front. ◻ **the occult** occult phenomena generally. ◻◻ **oc·cult·ism** *n.* **oc·cult·ist** *n.*

oc·cu·pant /ókyəpənt/ *n.* **1** a person who occupies, resides in, or is in a place. **2** a person holding property, esp. land, in actual possession. ◻◻ **oc·cu·pan·cy** /–pənsee/ *n.* (*pl.* **-cies**).

oc·cu·pa·tion /ókyəpáyshən/ *n.* **1** what occupies one; a means of passing one's time. **2** a person's temporary or regular employment. **3** the act of occupying. **4 a** the act of taking possession of (a country, etc.) by military force. **b** the state or time of this. **5** tenure; occupancy.

oc·cu·pa·tion·al /ókyəpáyshənəl/ *adj.* **1** of or in the nature of an occupation. **2** (of a disease, hazard, etc.) rendered more likely by one's occupation.

oc·cu·pa·tion·al ther·a·py *n.* mental or physical activity designed to assist recovery from disease or injury.

oc·cu·py /ókyəpī/ *v.tr.* (**-pies, -pied**) **1** reside in. **2** take up or fill (space or time or a place). **3** hold (a position or office). **4** take military possession of. **5** place oneself in (a building, etc.) forcibly or without authority. **6** (usu. in *passive*; often foll. by *in*, *with*) keep busy or engaged.

oc·cur /əkə́r/ *v.intr.* (**occurred, occurring**) **1** come into being as an event or process at some time; happen. **2** exist or be encountered in some place or conditions. **3** (foll. by *to*; usu. foll. by *that* + clause) come into the mind of.

oc·cur·rence /əkə́rəns, əkúr–/ *n.* **1** an instance of occurring. **2** an event.

o·cean /óshən/ *n.* **1** a large expanse of sea, esp. each of the main areas called the Atlantic, Pacific, Indian, Arctic, and Antarctic Oceans. **2** (usu. prec. by *the*) the sea. **3** (often in *pl.*) a very large expanse or quantity of anything (*oceans of time*).

o·cea·nar·i·um /óshənáireeəm/ *n.* (*pl.* **oceanariums** or **-ria** /–reeə/) a large seawater aquarium for keeping sea animals.

o·cea·nog·ra·phy /óshənógrəfee/ *n.* the study of the oceans. ◻◻ **o·cea·nog·ra·pher** *n.* **o·cea·no·graph·ic** /–nəgráfik/ *adj.*

oc·e·lot /ósilot, ósi–/ *n.* **1** a medium-sized feline, *Felis pardalis*, having a deep yellow or orange coat with black striped and spotted markings. **2** its fur.

o·cher /ókər/ *n.* **1** a mineral of clay and ferric oxide, used as a pigment varying from light yellow to brown or red. **2** a pale brownish yellow. ◻◻ **o·cher·ous** *adj.* **o·cher·y** *adj.*

o'·clock /əklók/ *adv.* of the clock (used to specify the hour) (*6 o'clock*).

Oct. *abbr.* October.

oct- /okt/ *comb. form* assim. form of OCTA-, OCTO- before a vowel.

octa- /óktə/ *comb. form* (also **oct-** before a vowel) eight.

oc·ta·gon /óktəgon, –gən/ *n.* **1** a plane figure with eight sides and angles. **2** an object or building with this cross section. ◻◻ **oc·tag·o·nal** /–tágənəl/ *adj.* **oc·tag·o·nal·ly** *adv.*

oc·ta·he·dron /óktəhéedrən/ *n.* (*pl.* **octahedrons** or **octahedra** /–drə/) a solid figure contained by eight (esp. triangular) plane faces. ◻◻ **oc·ta·he·dral** *adj.*

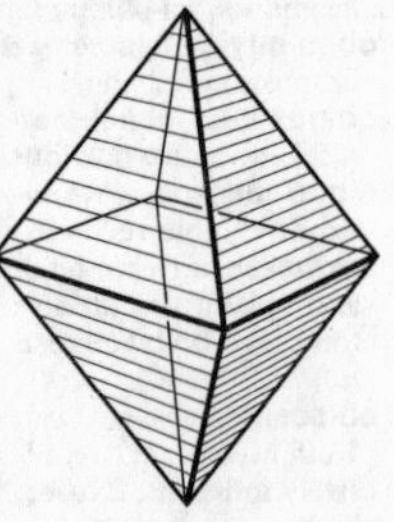
octahedron

oc·tane /óktayn/ *n.* a colorless flammable hydrocarbon of the alkane series.

oc·tave /óktiv, –tayv/ *n.* **1** *Mus.* **a** a series of eight notes occupying the interval between (and including) two notes, one having twice or half the frequency of vibration of the other. **b** this interval. **c** each of the two notes at the extremes of this interval. **d** these two notes sounding together. **2** a group or stanza of eight lines.

oc·ta·vo /oktáyvō, oktáavō/ *n.* (*pl.* **-vos**) **1** a size of book or page given by folding a standard sheet three times to form eight leaves. **2** a book or sheet of this size.

oc·tet /oktét/ *n.* (also **oc·tette**) **1** *Mus.* **a** a composition for eight voices or instruments. **b** the performers of such a piece. **2** a group of eight. **3** the first eight lines of a sonnet.

octo- /óktō/ *comb. form* (also **oct-** before a vowel) eight.

Oc·to·ber /októbər/ *n.* the tenth month of the year.

oc·to·cen·ten·ar·y /óktōsenténəree, –sént'neree/ *n. & adj.* • *n.* (*pl.* **-ies**) **1** an eight-hundredth anniversary. **2** a celebration of this. • *adj.* of or relating to an octocentenary.

oc·to·ge·nar·i·an /óktəjináireeən/ *n.* a person from 80 to 89 years old.

oc·to·pod /óktəpod/ *n.* any cephalopod of the order Octopoda, with eight arms.

oc·to·pus /óktəpəs/ *n.* (*pl.* **octopuses**) any cephalopod mollusk of the genus *Octopus* having eight suckered arms, a soft saclike body, and beaklike jaws.

oc·tu·ple /óktəpəl, októó–, –tyóó–/ *adj., n., & v.* • *adj.* eightfold. • *n.* an eightfold amount. • *v.tr. & intr.* multiply by eight.

oc·u·lar /ókyoolər/ *adj.* of or connected with the eyes or sight; visual.

oc·u·list /ókyəlist/ *n. formerly* **1** an ophthalmologist. **2** an optometrist. ▫▫ **oc·u·lis·tic** /–lístik/ *adj.*

OD[1] *abbr.* doctor of optometry.

OD[2] /ōdée/ *n. & v. sl.* • *n.* an overdose, esp. of a narcotic drug. • *v.intr.* (**OD's, OD'd, OD'ing**) take an overdose.

odd /od/ *adj.* **1** strange; queer; remarkable. **2** casual; occasional (*odd jobs; odd moments*). **3** not normally noticed or considered (*in some odd corner*). **4 a** (of numbers) not integrally divisible by two. **b** bearing such a number (*no parking on odd dates*). **5** left over when the rest have been distributed or divided into pairs (*have got an odd sock*). **6** detached from a set or series (*a few odd volumes*). **7** somewhat more than (*forty odd*). **8** by which a round number, given sum, etc., is exceeded (*we have 102—what shall we do with the odd 2?*). ▫▫ **odd·ly** *adv.* **odd·ness** *n.*

odd·ball /ódbawl/ *n. colloq.* **1** an odd person. **2** (*attrib.*) strange; bizarre.

odd·i·ty /óditee/ *n.* (*pl.* **-ties**) **1** a strange person, thing, or occurrence. **2** a peculiar trait. **3** the state of being odd.

odd·ment /ódmənt/ *n.* **1** something left over. **2** (in *pl.*) miscellaneous articles. **3** *Printing* matter other than the main text.

odds /odz/ *n.pl.* **1** the ratio between the amounts staked by the parties to a bet, based on the expected probability either way. **2** the chances or balance of probability (*the odds are against it*). **3** the balance of advantage (*the odds are in your favor*). **4** a difference giving an advantage (*makes no odds*). ▫ **at odds** (often foll. by *with*) in conflict. **take odds** offer a bet with odds unfavorable to the other bettor. **what's the odds?** *colloq.* what are the chances? (implying a slim likelihood).

odds and ends *n.pl.* miscellaneous articles or remnants.

odds-on *n.* a state when success is more likely than failure, esp. as indicated by the betting odds.

ode /ōd/ *n.* a lyric poem, usu. rhymed and in the form of an address, in varied or irregular meter.

o·di·ous /ṓdeeəs/ *adj.* hateful; repulsive. ▫▫ **o·di·ous·ly** *adv.* **o·di·ous·ness** *n.*

o·di·um /ṓdeeəm/ *n.* a general or widespread dislike or reprobation.

o·dom·e·ter /ōdómitər/ *n.* an instrument for measuring the distance traveled by a wheeled vehicle. ▫▫ **o·dom·e·try** *n.*

o·dor /ṓdər/ *n.* **1** the property of a substance that has an effect on the nasal sense of smell. **2** a lasting quality or trace (*an odor of intolerance*). **3** regard; repute (*in bad odor*). ▫▫ **o·dor·less** *adj.* (in sense 1).

o·dor·if·er·ous /ṓdəríf ərəs/ *adj.* diffusing a scent, esp. an agreeable one. ▫▫ **o·dor·if·er·ous·ly** *adv.*

o·dor·ous /ṓdərəs/ *adj.* **1** having a scent. **2** = ODORIFEROUS. ▫▫ **o·dor·ous·ly** *adv.*

od·ys·sey /ódisee/ *n.* (*pl.* **-seys**) a long adventurous journey. ▫▫ **Od·ys·se·an** *adj.*

OED *abbr.* Oxford English Dictionary.

Oed·i·pus com·plex /édipəs, éedi–/ *n. Psychol.* (according to Freud, etc.) the complex of emotions aroused in a young (esp. male) child by a subconscious sexual desire for the parent of the opposite sex. ▫▫ **Oed·i·pal** *adj.*

o'er /ṓər/ *adv. & prep. poet.* = OVER.

oeu·vre /ṓvrə/ *n.* the works of an author, painter, composer, etc.

of /uv, ov, əv/ *prep.* connecting a noun (often a verbal noun) or pronoun with a preceding noun, adjective, adverb, or verb, expressing a wide range of relations broadly describable as follows: **1** origin, cause, or authorship (*paintings of Turner; people of Rome*). **2** the material or substance constituting a thing (*a house of cards*). **3** belonging, connection, or possession (*articles of clothing; the tip of the iceberg*). **4** identity or close relation (*the city of Rome; a fool of a man*). **5** removal, separation, or privation (*north of the city; got rid of them*). **6** reference, direction, or respect (*beware of the dog; very good of you; the selling of goods*). **7** objective relation (*love of music*). **8** partition, classification, or inclusion (*no more of that; part of the story*). **9** description, quality, or condition (*the hour of prayer; a girl of ten*). **10** time in relation to the following hour (*a quarter of three*). ▫ **be of** possess intrinsically (*is of great interest*). **of all** designating the (nominally) least likely example (*you of all people!*). **of all the nerve** an exclamation of indignation at a person's impudence, etc. **of an evening** (or **morning**, etc.) *colloq.* **1** on most evenings (or mornings, etc.). **2** at some time in the evenings (or mornings, etc.). **of late** recently. **of old** formerly; long ago.

off. *abbr.* **1** office. **2** officer.

off /awf, of/ *adv., prep., & adj.* • *adv.* **1** at or to a distance (*drove off; is three miles off*). **2** out of position; not on or touching or attached (*has come off; take your coat off*). **3** so as to be rid of (*sleep it off*). **4** so as to break continuity; discontinued (*take a day off*). **5** to the end; entirely (*finish off; pay off*). **6** situated as regards money, etc. (*is badly off*). • *prep.* **1 a** from; away or down or up from (*fell off the chair*). **b** not on (*was already off the pitch*). **2 a** (temporarily) relieved of or abstaining from (*off duty*). **b** not attracted by for the time being (*off their food*). **c** not achieving or doing one's best in (*off one's game*). **3** using as a source or means of support (*live off the land*). **4** leading from (*a street off 1st Avenue*). **5** at a short distance to sea from (*sank off Cape Horn*). • *adj.* **1** far; further (*the off side of the wall*). **2** (of a part of a vehicle, animal, or road) right (*the off front wheel*). ▫ **off and on** intermittently; now and then. **off guard** see GUARD. **off of** *sl. disp.* = OFF *prep.* (*picked it off of the floor*). **off the point** *adj.* irrelevant. *adv.* irrelevantly. **off the record** see RECORD.

▶The use of **off of** to mean **off**, e.g., *He took the cup off of the table,* is nonstandard and to be avoided.

of·fal /áwfəl, óf–/ *n.* **1** the less valuable edible parts of a carcass, esp. the entrails and internal organs. **2** refuse or waste stuff.

off·beat *adj. & n.* • *adj.* /áwfbéet, óf–/ **1** not coinciding with the beat. **2** eccentric; unconventional. • *n.* /ófbeet/ any of the unaccented beats in a bar.

off-col·or *adj.* somewhat indecent.

of·fend /əfénd/ *v.* **1** *tr.* cause offense to. **2** *tr.* displease or anger. **3** *intr.* (often foll. by *against*) do wrong. ▫▫ **of·fend·ed·ly** *adv.* **of·fend·er** *n.* **of·fend·ing** *adj.*

of·fense /əféns/ *n.* **1** an illegal act; a misdemeanor. **2** a wounding of the feelings (*no offense was meant*). **3** /áwfens, óf–/ the act of attacking or taking the offensive. **4** /áwfens, óf–/ *Sports* the team in possession of the ball, puck, etc.

---

offense late Middle English: from Old French *offens* 'misdeed,' from Latin *offensus* 'annoyance,' reinforced by French *offense*, from Latin *offensa* 'a striking against, a hurt, or displeasure'; based on Latin *offendere* 'strike against.'

---

of·fen·sive /əfénsiv/ *adj. & n.* • *adj.* **1** giving or likely to give offense; insulting. **2** disgusting; repulsive. **3 a** aggressive; attacking. **b** (of a weapon) meant for use in attack. • *n.* **1** an aggressive action or attitude. **2** an attack. 3 aggressive action in pursuit of a cause. ▫▫ **of·fen·sive·ly** *adv.* **of·fen·sive·ness** *n.*

of·fer /áwfər, óf–/ *v.* & *n.* • *v.* **1** *tr.* present for acceptance or refusal. **2** *intr.* (foll. by *to* + infin.) express readiness or show intention (*offered to take the children*). **3** *tr.* give an opportunity for. **4** *tr.* make available for sale. **5** *tr.* (of a thing) present to one's attention (*each day offers new opportunities*). **6** *tr.* present (a sacrifice, etc.) to a deity. **7** *intr.* occur (*as opportunity offers*). **8** *tr.* attempt, or try to show (violence, resistance, etc.). • *n.* **1** an expression of readiness to do or give if desired, or to buy or sell (for a certain amount). **2** an amount offered. **3** a proposal (esp. of marriage). **4** a bid.

of·fer·ing /áwfəring, óf–/ *n.* **1** a contribution, esp. of money, to a church. **2** a thing offered as a sacrifice. **3** anything contributed or offered.

of·fer·to·ry /áwfərtáwree, óf–/ *n.* (*pl.* **-ries**) **1** *Eccl.* **a** the offering of the bread and wine at the Eucharist. **b** an anthem accompanying this. **2 a** the collection of money at a religious service. **b** the money collected.

off·hand /áwfhánd, óf–/ *adj.* & *adv.* • *adj.* curt or casual in manner. • *adv.* **1** in an offhand manner. **2** without preparation or premeditation. ▫▫ **off·hand·ed** *adj.* **off·hand·ed·ly** *adv.* **off·hand·ed·ness** *n.*

of·fice /áwfis, óf–/ *n.* **1** a room or building used as a place of business, esp. for clerical or administrative work. **2** a room or department or building for a particular kind of business (*post office*). **3** the local center of a large business (*our Honolulu office*). **4** a position with duties attached to it. **5** tenure of an official position, esp. that of government (*hold office*). **6** a duty attaching to one's position; a task or function. **7** (usu. in *pl.*) a piece of kindness (esp. **through the good offices of**). **8** *Eccl.* **a** an authorized form of worship (*Office for the Dead*). **b** (in full **divine office**) the daily service of the Roman Catholic breviary (*say the office*).

of·fi·cer /áwfisər, óf–/ *n.* **1** a person holding a position of authority or trust, esp. one with a commission in the armed services. **2** a policeman or policewoman. **3** a holder of a post in a society (e.g., the president or secretary). **4** a holder of a public, civil, or ecclesiastical office.

of·fi·cial /əfíshəl/ *adj.* & *n.* • *adj.* **1** of or relating to an office or its tenure or duties. **2** characteristic of officials and bureaucracy. **3** properly authorized. **4** employed in a public capacity. • *n.* a person holding office or engaged in official duties. ▫▫ **of·fi·cial·dom** *n.* **of·fi·cial·ism** *n.* **of·fi·cial·ly** *adv.*

of·fi·ci·ate /əfísheeáyt/ *v.intr.* **1** act in an official capacity, esp. on a particular occasion. **2** perform a divine service. ▫▫ **of·fi·ci·a·tion** /–áyshən/ *n.* **of·fi·ci·a·tor** *n.*

of·fi·cious /əfíshəs/ *adj.* **1** domineering. **2** intrusive in offering help, etc. **3** *Diplomacy* informal; unofficial. ▫▫ **of·fi·cious·ly** *adv.* **of·fi·cious·ness** *n.*

off·ing /áwfing, óf–/ *n.* the more distant part of the sea in view. ▫ **in the offing** not far away; likely to appear or happen soon.

off-key *adj.* **1** out of tune. **2** not quite suitable or fitting.

off lim·its *adj.* out of bounds.

off-line *adj. Computing* (of a computer terminal or process) not directly controlled by or connected to a central processor.

off-load *v.tr.* = UNLOAD.

off-peak *adj.* used or for use at times other than those of greatest demand.

off·print /áwfprint, óf–/ *n.* a printed copy of an article, etc., originally forming part of a larger publication.

off-put·ting *adj.* disconcerting; repellent.

off-road *attrib.adj.* **1** away from the road; on rough terrain. **2** (of a vehicle, etc.) designed for rough terrain or for cross-country driving.

off·screen /áwfskréen, óf–/ *adj.* & *adv.* • *adj.* not appearing on a movie, television, or computer screen. • *adv.* **1** without use of a screen. **2** outside the view presented by a filmed scene.

off-sea·son *n.* a time when business, etc., is slack.

off·set *n.* & *v.* • *n.* /áwfset, óf–/ **1** a side shoot from a plant serving for propagation. **2** an offshoot or scion. **3** a compensation. **4** *Archit.* a sloping ledge in a wall, etc. **5** a bend in a pipe, etc., to carry it past an obstacle. **6** (often *attrib.*) a method of printing in which ink is transferred from a plate or stone to a uniform rubber surface and from there to paper, etc. • *v.tr.* /áwfsét, óf–/ (**-setting**; *past* and *past part.* **-set**) **1** counterbalance; compensate. **2** place out of line. **3** print by the offset process.

off·shoot /áwfshōōt, óf–/ *n.* **1** a side shoot or branch. **2** something derivative.

off·shore /áwfsháwr, óf–/ *adj.* **1** at sea some distance from the shore. **2** (of the wind) blowing seaward. **3** made or registered abroad.

off·side /áwfsíd, óf–/ *adj. Sports* (of a player in a field game) in a position that is not allowed if it affects play.

off·spring /áwfspring, óf–/ *n.* (*pl.* same) **1** a person's child or children or descendant(s). **2** an animal's young or descendant(s). **3** a result.

off·stage /áwfstayj, óf–/ *adj.* & *adv. Theatr.* not on the stage and so not visible to the audience.

off-the-cuff *adj. colloq.* without preparation; extempore.

off-white *adj.* white with a gray or yellowish tinge.

oft /awft, oft/ *adv. archaic* or *literary* often (usu. in *comb.*: *oft-recurring*).

of·ten /áwfən, áwftən, óf–/ *adv.* (**oftener, oftenest**) **1 a** frequently. **b** at short intervals. **2** in many instances. ▫ **as often as not** in roughly half the instances.

▶Some speakers sound the *t*, saying "off-ten"; for others, it is silent, as in *soften*. Either pronunciation is acceptable.

o·gee /ōjée, ṓjee/ *adj.* & *n. Archit.* • *adj.* showing in section a double continuous S-shaped curve. • *n.* an S-shaped line or molding.

o·gle /ṓgəl/ *v.* & *n.* • *v.* **1** *tr.* eye amorously or lecherously. **2** *intr.* look amorously. • *n.* an amorous or lecherous look.

o·gre /ṓgər/ *n.* (*fem.* **ogress** /ṓgris/) **1** a human-eating giant in folklore, etc. **2** a terrifying person. ▫▫ **o·gre·ish** *adj.* (also **o·grish**) .

OH *abbr.* Ohio (in official postal use).

oh /ō/ *int.* (also **O**) expressing surprise, pain, etc. (*oh, what a mess*). ▫ **oh boy** expressing surprise, excitement, etc. **oh well** expressing resignation.

ohm /ōm/ *n. Electr.* the SI unit of resistance.

oho /ōhṓ/ *int.* expressing surprise or exultation.

oil /oyl/ *n.* & *v.* • *n.* **1** any of various thick, viscous, usu. flammable liquids insoluble in water but soluble in organic solvents **2** petroleum. **3** using oil as fuel (*oil heater*). **4 a** (usu. in *pl.*) = OIL PAINT. **b** *colloq.* a picture painted in oil paints. **5** (in *pl.*) = OILSKIN. • *v.* **1** *tr.* apply oil to; lubricate. **2** *tr.* impregnate or treat with oil (*oiled silk*). **3** *tr.* & *intr.* supply with or take on oil as fuel.

oil·cloth /óylklawth, –kloth/ *n.* **1** a fabric waterproofed with oil. **2** an oilskin. **3** a canvas coated with linseed or other oil and used to cover a table or floor.

oil·er /óylər/ *n.* **1** an oilcan. **2** an oil tanker. **3 a** an oil well. **b** (in *pl.*) oilskin.

oil paint *n.* (also **oil·col·or**) a mix of ground color pigment and oil.

oil paint·ing *n.* **1** the art of painting in oil paints. **2** a picture painted in oil paints.

oil plat·form *n.* a structure designed to stand on the seabed to provide a stable base above water for the drilling and regulation of oil wells.
oil rig *n.* a structure for drilling an oil well.
oil·skin /óylskin/ *n.* **1** cloth waterproofed with oil. **2 a** a garment made of this. **b** (in *pl.*) a suit made of this.
oil slick *n.* a smooth patch of oil, esp. one on the sea.
oil·stone /óylstōn/ *n.* a fine-grained flat stone used with oil for sharpening flat tools, e.g., chisels, planes, etc. (cf. WHETSTONE).
oil well *n.* a well from which petroleum is drawn.
oil·y /óylee/ *adj.* (**oilier, oiliest**) **1** of, like, or containing much oil. **2** covered or soaked with oil. **3** fawning; insinuating; unctuous. ▫▫ **oil·i·ness** *n.*
oink /oyngk/ *v.intr.* (of a pig) make its characteristic grunt.
oint·ment /óyntmənt/ *n.* a smooth greasy preparation for the skin.
O·jib·wa /ōjíbway/ *n.* & *adj.* • *n.* **1 a** a N. American people native to Canada and the eastern and central northern United States. **b** a member of this people. **2** the language of this people. • *adj.* of or relating to this people or their language. Also called CHIPPEWA.
OK[1] /ṓkáy/ *adj., adv., n.,* & *v.* (also **o·kay**) *colloq.* • *adj.* (often as *int.*) all right; satisfactory. • *adv.* well; satisfactorily (*that worked out OK*). • *n.* (*pl.* **OKs**) approval. • *v.tr.* (**OK's, OK'd, OK'ing**) approve.

OK mid-19th century (originally US): probably an abbreviation of *orl korrect,* humorous form of *all correct,* popularized as a slogan during President Van Buren's re-election campaign of 1840; his nickname *Old Kinderhook* (derived from his New York birthplace) provided the initials.

OK[2] *abbr.* Oklahoma (in official postal use).
okay var. of OK[1].
o·key·doke /ṓkeedṓk/ *adj.* & *adv.* (also **o·key·do·key** /–dṓkee/) *sl.* = OK[1].
Okla. *abbr.* Oklahoma.
o·kra /ṓkrə/ *n.* **1** a malvaceous African plant, *Abelmoschus esculentus*, yielding long ridged seedpods. **2** the seedpods eaten as a vegetable and used to thicken soups and stews. Also called GUMBO.
old /ōld/ *adj.* (**older, oldest**) (cf. ELDER, ELDEST). **1 a** advanced in age. **b** not young or near its beginning. **2** made long ago. **3** long in use. **4** worn or shabby from the passage of time. **5** having the characteristics of age (*the child has an old face*). **6** practiced; inveterate (*an old offender*). **7** belonging to the past; lingering on (*old times*). **8** dating from far back; long established or known (*old as the hills; old friends*). **9** (appended to a period of time) of age (*is four years old; a four-year-old boy*). **10** (of language) as used in former or earliest times. **11** *colloq.* as a term of affection or casual reference (*good old Charlie*). **12** the former or first of two or more similar things (*our old house*)). ▫▫ **old·ish** *adj.* **old·ness** *n.* ▶Where two, and no more, are involved, they may be **older** and **younger**: *The older of the twins, by ten minutes, is Sam; the younger is Pamela.* Where there are more than two, one may be the *oldest* or *youngest:* I have four siblings, of whom Jane is the oldest.
old age *n.* the later part of normal life.
old-boy net·work *n.* preferment in employment of those from a similar social background, esp. fellow alumni.
old·en /ṓldən/ *adj. archaic* of old; of a former age (esp. in olden times).
Old Eng·lish *n.* the English language up to *c.*1150.
old-fash·ioned *n.* in a fashion or tastes no longer current.
Old Glo·ry *n.* the US national flag.
old guard *n.* the original or conservative members of a group.
old hat *n. adj. colloq.* tediously familiar or out-of-date.
old·ie /ṓldee/ *n. colloq.* an old person or thing.
old la·dy *n. colloq.* **1** a mother. **2** a wife or girlfriend.
old maid *n.* **1** *derog.* an elderly unmarried woman. **2** a prim and fussy person. **3** a card game in which players try not to be left with an unpaired queen. ▫▫ **old-maid·ish** *adj.*
old man *n. colloq.* **1** one's husband or father. **2** one's employer or other person in authority over one.
old mas·ter *n.* **1** a great artist of former times, esp. of the 13th–17th c. in Europe. **2** a painting by such a painter.
old school *n.* **1** traditional attitudes. **2** people having such attitudes.
old·ster /ṓldstər/ *n.* an old person.
Old Tes·ta·ment *n.* the part of the Christian Bible containing the scriptures of the Hebrews.
old-time *adj.* belonging to former times.
old-tim·er *n.* a person with long experience or standing.
old wives' tale *n.* a foolish or unscientific belief.
Old World *n.* Europe, Asia, and Africa.
o·le·ag·i·nous /ṓleeájinəs/ *adj.* **1** having the properties of or producing oil. **2** oily; greasy. **3** obsequious; ingratiating.
o·le·an·der /ṓleeándər/ *n.* an evergreen poisonous shrub, *Nerium oleander*, native to the Mediterranean and bearing clusters of white, pink, or red flowers.
oleo- /ṓleeō/ *comb. form* oil.
o·le·o·mar·ga·rine /ṓleeōmaárjərin/ *n.* **1** a margarine made from vegetable oils. **2** a fatty substance extracted from beef fat and used in margarine.
ol·fac·to·ry /olfáktəree, ōl–/ *adj.* of or relating to the sense of smell. ▫▫ **ol·fac·tion** *n.*
ol·i·garch /óligaark, ṓli–/ *n.* a member of an oligarchy.
ol·i·gar·chy /óligaarkee, ṓli–/ *n.* (*pl.* **-chies**) **1** government by a small group of people. **2** a nation governed in this way. **3** the members of such a government. ▫▫ **ol·i·gar·chic** /–gaárkik/ *adj.* **ol·i·gar·chi·cal** *adj.*
Ol·i·go·cene /óligəseen, ṓli–/ *adj.* & *n. Geol.* • *adj.* of or relating to the third epoch of the Tertiary period, with evidence of the first primates. • *n.* this epoch or system.
ol·ive /óliv/ *n.* & *adj.* • *n.* **1** (in full **olive tree**) any evergreen tree of the genus *Olea*, having dark-green, lance-shaped leathery leaves with silvery undersides, esp. *O. europaea* of the Mediterranean, and *O. africana* native to S. Africa. **2** the small oval fruit of this, having a hard stone and bitter flesh, green when unripe and bluish-black when ripe. **3** (in full **olive-green**) the grayish-green color of an unripe olive. **4** the wood of the olive tree. • *adj.* **1** colored like an unripe olive. **2** (of the complexion) yellowish-brown.
ol·ive branch *n.* **1** the branch of an olive tree as a symbol of peace. **2** a gesture of reconciliation or friendship.
ol·ive drab *n.* the dull olive color of US Army uniforms.
ol·ive oil *n.* an oil extracted from olives used esp. in cooking.
ol·i·vine /óliveén/ *n. Mineral.* a naturally occurring form of magnesium-iron silicate, usu. olive-green.
O·lym·pi·ad /ōlímpeead/ *n.* **1 a** a period of four years between Olympic games, used by the ancient Greeks in dating events. **b** a four-yearly celebration of the ancient Olympic Games. **2** a celebration of the modern Olympic Games. **3** a regular international contest in chess, etc.
O·lym·pi·an /əlímpeeən, ōlím–/ *adj.* & *n.* • *adj.* **1 a** of or associated with Mount Olympus in NE Greece, tra-

ditionally the home of the Greek gods. **b** celestial. **2** (of manners, etc.) magnificent; condescending. **3 a** of or relating to ancient Olympia in S. Greece. **b** = OLYMPIC. •*n.* **1** any of the gods regarded as living on Olympus. **2** a person of great attainments or of superhuman calm and detachment.

O•lym•pic /əlímpik, ōlím–/ *adj. & n.* •*adj.* of ancient Olympia or the Olympic games. •*n.pl.* (**the Olympics**) the Olympic games.

O•lym•pic games *n.pl.* **1** an ancient Greek festival held at Olympia every four years, with athletic, literary, and musical competitions. **2** a modern international revival of this as a sports festival usu. held every four years since 1896 in different venues.

O•ma•ha /óməhaw, –haa/ *n. & adj.* •*n.* **1 a** a N. American people native to Nebraska. **b** a member of this people. **2** the language of this people. •*adj.* of or relating to this people or their language.

OMB *abbr.* Office of Management and Budget.

om•buds•man /ómbōōdzmən/ *n.* (*pl.* **-men**) an official appointed by a government to investigate individuals' complaints against public authorities, etc.

o•me•ga /ōmáygə, ṓmeegə, ōmégə/ *n.* **1** the last (24th) letter of the Greek alphabet (Ω, ω). **2** the last of a series; the final development.

om•e•lette /ómlit/ *n.* (also **om•e•let**) a dish of beaten eggs cooked in a frying pan and served plain or with a savory or sweet filling.

o•men /ṓmən/ *n.* **1** an occurrence or object regarded as portending good or evil. **2** prophetic significance (*of good omen*).

o•mer•tà /ṓmairtaá/ *n.* a code of silence, esp. as practiced by the Mafia.

om•i•cron /ómikron, ṓmi–/ *n.* the fifteenth letter of the Greek alphabet (Ο, ο).

om•i•nous /óminəs/ *adj.* **1** threatening; indicating disaster or difficulty. **2** of evil omen; inauspicious. **3** giving or being an omen. ▫▫ **om•i•nous•ly** *adv.*

o•mis•sion /ōmíshən/ *n.* **1** the act or an instance of omitting. **2** something omitted.

o•mit /ōmít/ *v.tr.* (**omitted, omitting**) **1** leave out. **2** leave undone. **3** (foll. by verbal noun or *to* + infin.) fail or neglect (*omitted to say*). ▫▫ **o•mis•si•ble** /–mísəbəl/ *adj.*

omni- /ómnee/ *comb. form* **1** all; of all things. **2** in all ways or places.

om•ni•bus /ómnibəs/ *n. & adj.* •*n. formal* = BUS. •*adj.* **1** serving several purposes at once. **2** comprising several items.

om•nip•o•tent /omnípət'nt/ *adj.* having absolute power. ▫▫ **om•nip•o•tence** /–t'ns/ *n.*

om•ni•pres•ent /ómniprézənt/ *adj.* present everywhere at the same time. ▫▫ **om•ni•pres•ence** /–zəns/ *n.*

om•nis•cient /omníshənt/ *adj.* knowing everything. ▫▫ **om•nis•cience** /–shəns/ *n.*

om•niv•o•rous /omnívərəs/ *adj.* **1** feeding on many kinds of food, esp. on both plants and flesh. **2** making use of everything available. ▫▫ **om•ni•vore** /ómnivawr/ *n.*

on /on, awn/ *prep., adv., & adj.* •*prep.* **1** (so as to be) supported by or attached to or covering or enclosing (*sat on a chair; stuck on the wall; rings on her fingers; leaned on his elbow*). **2** carried with; about the person (*do you have a pen on you?*). **3** (of time) exactly at; during; contemporaneously with (*on May 29; on schedule; on Tuesday*). **4** immediately after or before (*I saw them on my return*). **5** as a result of (*on further examination I found this*). **6** (so as to be) having membership, etc., of or residence at or in (*on the board of directors; lives on the waterfront*). **7** supported financially by (*lives on $200 a week; on his wits*). **8** close to; just by (*a house on the sea; lives on the main road*). **9** in the direction of. **10** so as to threaten (*advanced on him; a punch on the nose*). **11** having as an axis or pivot (*turned on his heels*). **12** having as a basis or motive (*arrested on suspicion*). **13** having as a standard, confirmation, or guarantee (*had it on good authority; did it on purpose*). **14** concerning or about (*writes on finance*). **15** using or engaged with (*is on the pill; here on business*). **16** so as to affect (*walked out on her*). **17** at the expense of (*the drinks are on me*). **18** added to (*disaster on disaster*). **19** in a specified manner or style (*on the cheap; on the run*). •*adv.* **1** (so as to be) covering or in contact (*put your boots on*). **2** in the appropriate direction (*look on*). **3** further forward (*getting on in years; it happened later on*). **4** with continued movement (*went plodding on; keeps on complaining*). **5** in operation or activity (*the light is on; the chase was on*). **6** due to take place as planned (*is the party still on?*). **7** *colloq.* willing to participate or approve, or make a bet. **8** being shown or performed (*a good movie on tonight*). **9** on stage. **10** on duty. **11** forward (*head on*). •*adj. Baseball* positioned at a base as a runner. ▫ **be on to 1** realize the significance or intentions of. **2** get in touch with. **on and off** intermittently; now and then. **on and on** continually. **on time** punctual; punctually.

on•a•ger /ónəgər/ *n.* a wild ass, esp. *Equus hemionus* of Central Asia.

o•nan•ism /ṓnənizəm/ *n.* **1** masturbation. **2** coitus interruptus. ▫▫ **o•nan•ist** *n.* **o•nan•is•tic** /–nístik/ *adj.*

once /wuns/ *adv., conj., & n.* •*adv.* **1** on one occasion or for one time only (*have read it once*). **2** at some point in the past (*could once play chess*). **3** ever or at all (*if you once forget it*). **4** multiplied by one. •*conj.* as soon as (*once they have gone we can relax*). •*n.* one time or occasion (*just the once*). ▫ **all at once 1** suddenly. **2** all together. **at once 1** immediately. **2** simultaneously. **for once** on this (or that) occasion. **once again** (or **more**) another time. **once and for all** (or **once for all**) (done) in a final or conclusive manner. **once** (or **every once**) **in a while** from time to time. **once or twice** a few times. **once upon a time** at some vague time in the past.

once-o•ver *n. colloq.* a rapid preliminary inspection.

onco- /óngkō/ *comb. form Med.* tumor.

on•co•gene /óngkəjeen/ *n.* a gene that can transform a cell into a tumor cell. ▫▫ **on•co•gen•ic** /–jénik/ *adj.*

on•col•o•gy /ongkóləjee/ *n. Med.* the study of tumors.

on•com•ing /ónkuming, áwn–/ *adj.* approaching from the front.

one /wun/ *adj., n., & pron.* •*adj.* **1** single and integral in number. **2** (with a noun implied) a single person or thing of the kind expressed or implied (*one of the best*). **3 a** particular but undefined, esp. as contrasted with another (*that is one view*). **b** *colloq.* a noteworthy example of (*that is one difficult question*). **4** only such (*the one man who can do it*). **5** forming a unity (*one and undivided*). **6** the same (*of one opinion*). •*n.* **1** the lowest cardinal number. **2** unity; a unit (*one is half of two; came in ones and twos*). **3** a single thing or person or example (often referring to a noun previously expressed or implied: *the big dog and the small one*). **4** *colloq.* an alcoholic drink (*have a quick one; have one on me*). **5** a story or joke (*the one about the frog*). •*pron.* **1** a person of a specified kind (*loved ones; like one possessed*). **2** any person, as representing people in general (*one is bound to lose in the end*). **3** I; me (*one would like to help*). ▶Often regarded as an affectation. ▫ **at one** in agreement. **for one** being one, even if the only one (*I for one do not believe it*). **for one thing** as a single consideration, ignoring others. **one another** each the other or others (as a formula of reciprocity: *love one another*). **one by one** singly; successively. **one day 1** on an unspecified day. **2** at some unspecified future date. **one or two** see OR[1]. **one up** (often foll. by *on*) *colloq.* having a particular advantage.

O·nei·da /ōnídə/ *n.* & *adj.* • *n.* **1 a** a N. American people native to New York state. **b** a member of this people. **2** the language of this people. • *adj.* of or relating to this people or their language.

one-armed ban·dit *n. colloq.* a slot machine worked by a long handle.

one-horse *adj.* **1** using a single horse. **2** *colloq.* small; poorly equipped.

one·ness /wún-nis/ *n.* **1** the fact or state of being one. **2** uniqueness. **3** agreement. **4** sameness.

one-lin·er *n. colloq.* a single brief sentence, often witty or apposite.

one-night stand *n.* **1** a single performance of a play, etc., in a place. **2** *colloq.* a sexual liaison lasting only one night.

one-on-one *adj.* **1** of a direct confrontation between two persons. **2** *Sports* playing directly against one opposing player.

one-piece *adj.* made as a single garment.

on·er·ous /ónərəs, ṓn–/ *adj.* **1** burdensome. **2** *Law* involving heavy obligations.

one·self /wunsélf/ *pron.* the reflexive and emphatic form of *one.*

one-sid·ed *adj.* **1** favoring one side in a dispute. **2** having or occurring on one side only. **3** larger or more developed on one side. □□ **one-sid·ed·ly** *adv.* **one-sid·ed·ness** *n.*

one·time /wúntím/ *adj.* & *adv.* former.

one-to-one *n.* with one member of one group corresponding to one of another.

one-track mind *n.* a mind preoccupied with one subject.

one-two *n. colloq. Boxing* the delivery of two punches in quick succession.

one-up·man·ship *n. colloq.* the art of maintaining a psychological advantage.

one-way *adj.* allowing movement or travel in one direction only.

on·go·ing /ón-gṓing, áwn–/ *adj.* **1** continuing. **2** in progress (*ongoing discussions*).

on·ion /únyən/ *n.* **1** a liliaceous plant, *Allium cepa*, having a short stem and bearing greenish-white flowers. **2** the bulb of this used in cooking, pickling, etc. □ **know one's onions** *colloq.* be fully knowledgeable. □□ **on·ion·y** *adj.*

on-line *adj. Computing* (of equipment or a process) directly controlled by or connected to a central processor.

on·look·er /ónlŏŏkər, áwn–/ *n.* a spectator. □□ **on·look·ing** *adj.*

on·ly /ṓnlee/ *adv., adj.,* & *conj.* • *adv.* **1** solely; merely; exclusively. (*I only want to sit down; is only a child*). **2** no longer ago than (*saw them only yesterday*). **3** not until (*arrives only on Tuesday*). **4** with no better result than (*hurried home only to find her gone*).

▶In informal English *only* is usually placed between the subject and verb regardless of what it refers to (e.g., *I only want to talk to you*); in more formal English it is often placed more exactly, esp. to avoid ambiguity (e.g., *I want to talk only to you*). In speech, intonation usually serves to clarify the sense. • *attrib.adj.* **1** existing alone of its or their kind (*their only son*). **2** best or alone worth knowing (*the only place to eat*). • *conj. colloq.* **1** except that (*I would go, only I feel ill*). **2** but then (as an extra consideration) (*he always makes promises, only he never keeps them*). □ **only too** extremely (*only too willing*).

on·o·mas·tics /ónəmástiks/ *n.pl.* (treated as *sing.*) the study of the origin and formation of (esp. personal) proper names.

on·o·mat·o·poe·ia /ónəmátəpéeə, –maátə–/ *n.* **1** the formation of a word from a sound associated with what is named (e.g., *cuckoo, sizzle*). **2** the use of such words. □□ **on·o·mat·o·poe·ic** *adj.*

On·on·da·ga /aanəndáwgə, –day–, –daa–/ *n.* & *adj.* • *n.* **1 a** a N. American people native to New York state. **b** a member of these people. **2** the language of these people. • *adj.* of or relating to these people or their language.

on·rush /ónrush, áwn–/ *n.* an onward rush.

on-screen *adj.* & *adv.* • *adj.* appearing in a movie or on television. • *adv.* **1** on or by means of a screen. **2** within the view presented by a filmed scene.

on·set /ónset, áwn–/ *n.* **1** an attack. **2** a beginning, esp. an energetic one.

on·shore /ónsháwr, áwn–/ *adj.* & *adv.* • *adj.* **1** on the shore. **2** (of the wind) blowing from the sea toward the land. • *adv.* ashore.

on·side /ónsíd, áwn–/ *adj.* (of a player in a field game) not offside.

on·slaught /ónslawt, áwn–/ *n.* a fierce attack.

on·stage /ónstáyj/ *Theatr. adj.* & *adv.* on the stage; visible to the audience.

Ont. *abbr.* Ontario.

on·to /óntoo, áwn–/ *prep. disp.* to a position or state on or in contact with (cf. *on to*).

▶The form *onto* is still not fully accepted in the way that *into* is, although it is in wide use. It is, however, useful in distinguishing sense as between *we drove on to the beach* (i.e., in that direction) and *we drove onto the beach* (i.e., in contact with it).

on·to·gen·e·sis /óntəjénisis/ *n.* the origin and development of an individual. □□ **on·to·ge·net·ic** /–jinétik/ *adj.*

on·tog·e·ny /ontójənee/ *n.* = ONTOGENESIS.

on·tol·o·gy /ontóləjee/ *n.* the branch of metaphysics dealing with the nature of being. □□ **on·to·log·i·cal** /–təlójikəl/ *adj.* **on·to·log·i·cal·ly** *adv.*

o·nus /ṓnəs/ *n.* (*pl.* **onuses**) a burden, duty, or responsibility.

on·ward /ónwərd, áwn–/ *adv.* & *adj.* • *adv.* (also **on·wards**) **1** further on. **2** toward the front. **3** with advancing motion. • *adj.* directed onward.

on·yx /óniks/ *n.* a semiprecious variety of agate with colors in layers.

oo·dles /ṓōd'lz/ *n.pl. colloq.* a very great amount.

oom·pah /ṓōmpaa/ *n. colloq.* the rhythmical sound of deep-toned brass instruments in a band.

oomph /ŏŏmf/ *n. sl.* **1** energy; enthusiasm. **2** attractiveness; esp. sexual appeal.

oops /ōōps, ŏŏps/ *int. colloq.* expressing surprise or apology.

ooze[1] /ōōz/ *v.* & *n.* • *v.* **1** *intr.* pass slowly through the pores of a body. **2** *intr.* trickle or leak slowly out. **3** *intr.* (of a substance) exude moisture. **4** *tr.* exude (a feeling) liberally (*oozed sympathy*). • *n.* a sluggish flow. □□ **ooz·y** *adj.*

ooze[2] /ōōz/ *n.* **1** a deposit of wet mud or slime. **2** a bog or marsh. □□ **ooz·y** *adj.*

op. /op/ *abbr.* **1** *Mus.* opus. **2** operator.

o·pac·i·ty /ōpásitee/ *n.* **1 a** the state of being opaque. **b** degree to which something is opaque. **2** obscurity of meaning. **3** obtuseness of understanding.

o·pal /ṓpəl/ *n.* a quartzlike form of hydrated silica, usu. white or colorless and sometimes showing changing colors, often used as a gemstone.

o·pal·es·cent /ṓpəlésənt/ *adj.* showing changing colors like an opal. □□ **o·pal·es·cence** /–səns/ *n.*

o·paque /ōpáyk/ *adj.* (**opaquer, opaquest**) **1** not transmitting light. **2** impenetrable to sight. **3** not lucid. **4** dull-witted. ◻◻ **o·paque·ly** *adv.* **o·paque·ness** *n.*

op art /op/ *n. colloq.* = OPTICAL ART.

op. cit. *abbr.* in the work already quoted.

OPEC /ṓpek/ *abbr.* Organization of Petroleum Exporting Countries.

o·pen /ṓpən/ *adj., v., & n.* • *adj.* **1** not closed nor locked nor blocked up. **2 a** (of a room, field, or other area) having its door or gate in a position allowing access, or part of its confining boundary removed. **b** (of a container) not fastened nor sealed. **3** unenclosed; unconfined (*the open road*; *open views*). **4 a** uncovered; bare; exposed (*open drain*; *open wound*). **b** *Sports* (of a goal or other object of attack) unprotected; vulnerable. **5** undisguised; public; manifest (*open scandal*; *open hostilities*). **6** expanded, unfolded, or spread out (*had the map open on the table*). **7** (of a fabric) with gaps. **8 a** frank and communicative. **b** accessible to new ideas. **9 a** (of a race, competition, etc.) unrestricted as to who may compete. **b** (of a champion, scholar, etc.) having won such a contest. **10** (of government) conducted in an informative manner receptive to inquiry, criticism, etc., from the public. **11** (foll. by *to*) **a** willing to receive (*is open to offers*). **b** (of a choice, or opportunity) still available (*there are three courses open to us*). **c** likely to suffer from (*open to abuse*). **12 a** (of the mouth) with lips apart. **b** (of the ears or eyes) eagerly attentive. **13** *Mus.* **a** (of a string) allowed to vibrate along its whole length. **b** (of a pipe) unstopped at each end. **c** (of a note) sounded from an open string or pipe. **14** (of an electrical circuit) having a break in the conducting path. **15** (of the bowels) not constipated. **16** (of a return ticket) not restricted as to day of travel. **17** (of a boat) without a deck. • *v.* **1** *tr. & intr.* make or become open or more open. **2 a** *tr.* change from a closed or fastened position so as to allow access (*opened the door*; *opened the box*). **b** *intr.* (of a door, lid, etc.) have its position changed to allow access (*the door opened slowly*). **3** *tr.* remove the fastening element of (a container) to get access to the contents (*opened the envelope*). **4** *intr.* (foll. by *into*, *on to*, etc.) (of a door, room, etc.) afford access as specified (*opened on to a large garden*). **5 a** *tr.* start or establish (a business, activity, etc.). **b** *intr.* start (*the session opens tomorrow*; *the story opens with a murder*). **c** *tr.* (of a counsel in a court of law) make a preliminary statement in (a case) before calling witnesses. **6** *tr.* **a** spread out or unfold (a map, newspaper, etc.). **b** (often *absol.*) refer to the contents of (a book). **7** *intr.* begin speaking, writing, etc. (*he opened with a warning*). **8** *intr.* (of a prospect) come into view. **9** *tr.* reveal (one's feelings, intentions, etc.). **10** *tr.* make (one's mind, heart, etc.) more sympathetic. **11** *tr.* ceremonially declare (a building, etc.) to be completed and in use. **12** *tr.* break up (ground) with a plow, etc. **13** *tr.* cause evacuation of (the bowels). • *n.* **1** (prec. by *the*) **a** open space or country or air. **b** public notice; general attention (esp. *into the open*). **2** an open championship, competition, or scholarship. ◻ **be open with** speak frankly to. **open the door to** see DOOR. **open a person's eyes** see EYE. **open out 1** unfold. **2** develop; expand. **3** *Brit.* become communicative. **4** *Brit.* accelerate. **open up 1** unlock (premises). **2** make accessible. **3** reveal; bring to notice. **4** accelerate. **5** begin shooting or sounding. **6** become communicative. ◻◻ **o·pen·ness** *n.*

o·pen air *n.* (usu. prec. by *the*) a free or unenclosed space outdoors. ◻◻ **o·pen-air** *adj.* (*attrib.*)

o·pen-and-shut *adj.* straightforward and conclusive.

o·pen book *n.* a person who is easily understood.

o·pen-end·ed *adj.* having no predetermined limit or boundary.

o·pen·er /ṓpənər/ *n.* **1** a device for opening cans, bottles, etc. **2** *colloq.* the first item on a program, etc.

o·pen-heart·ed *adj.* frank and kindly. ◻◻ **o·pen-heart·ed·ness** *n.*

o·pen-heart sur·ger·y *n.* surgery with the heart exposed and the blood made to bypass it.

o·pen house *n.* **1** hospitality for all visitors. **2** time when real estate offered for sale is open to prospective buyers.

o·pen·ing /ṓpəning/ *n. & adj.* • *n.* **1** an aperture or gap. **2** a favorable opportunity. **3** a beginning. **4** *Chess* a recognized sequence of moves at the beginning of a game. **5** a counsel's preliminary statement of a case in a court of law. • *adj.* initial; first.

o·pen·ly /ṓpənlee/ *adv.* **1** frankly; honestly. **2** publicly; without concealment.

o·pen-mind·ed *adj.* accessible to new ideas; unprejudiced. ◻◻ **o·pen-mind·ed·ly** *adv* **o·pen-mind·ed·ness** *n.*

o·pen ques·tion *n.* a matter on which differences of opinion are legitimate.

o·pen sea·son *n.* the season when restrictions on the hunting of game, etc., are lifted.

o·pen·work /ṓpənwərk/ *n.* a pattern with intervening spaces in metal, lace, etc.

op·er·a[1] /ópərə, óprə/ *n.* **1 a** a dramatic work set to music for singers and instrumentalists. **b** this as a genre. **2** a building for the performance of opera.

o·pe·ra[2] *pl.* of OPUS.

op·er·a·ble /ópərəbəl/ *adj.* **1** that can be operated. **2** suitable for treatment by surgical operation. ◻◻ **op·er·a·bil·i·ty** /–bílitee/ *n.*

op·er·a glass·es *n.pl.* small binoculars for use at the opera or theater.

op·er·and /ópərand/ *n. Math.* the quantity, etc., on which an operation is to be done.

op·er·ate /ópərayt/ *v.* **1** *tr.* manage; work; control; put or keep in a functional state. **2** *intr.* be in action; function. **3** *intr.* (often foll. by *on*) **a** perform a surgical operation. **b** conduct a military or naval action. **c** be active in business, etc., esp. dealing in stocks and shares. **4** *intr.* (foll. by *on*) influence or affect (feelings, etc.). **5** *tr.* bring about; accomplish.

op·er·at·ic /ópərátik/ *adj.* **1** of or relating to opera. **2** resembling or characteristic of opera. ◻◻ **op·er·at·i·cal·ly** *adv.*

op·er·at·ing room *n.* a room equipped for surgical operations.

op·er·at·ing sys·tem *n.* the basic software that enables the running of a computer program.

op·er·a·tion /ópəráyshən/ *n.* **1 a** the action or process or method of working or operating. **b** the scope or range of effectiveness of a thing's activity. **2** an active process (*the operation of breathing*). **3** a piece of work, esp. one in a series (often in *pl.*: *begin operations*). **4** an act of surgery performed on a patient. **5** a strategic movement of troops, ships, etc., for military action. **6** a financial transaction. **7** *Math.* the subjection of a number or quantity or function to a process affecting its value or form, e.g., multiplication, differentiation.

op·er·a·tion·al /ópəráyshənəl/ *adj.* **1 a** of or used for operations. **b** engaged or involved in operations. **2** able or ready to function. ◻◻ **op·er·a·tion·al·ly** *adv.*

op·er·a·tive /ópərətiv, óprə–/ *adj. & n.* • *adj.* **1** in operation; having effect. **2** having the principal relevance (*"may" is the operative word*). **3** of or by surgery. • *n.* **1** a worker, esp. a skilled one. **2** an agent employed by a detective agency or secret service. ◻◻ **op·er·a·tive·ly** *adv.* **op·er·a·tive·ness** *n.*

op·er·a·tor /ópəraytər/ *n.* **1** a person operating a machine, etc., esp. making connections of lines in a telephone exchange. **2** a person operating or engaging in business. **3** *colloq.* a person acting in a specified way (*a* *smooth operator*). **4** *Math.* a symbol or function denoting an operation (e.g., x, +).

op·er·et·ta /ópərétə/ *n.* **1** a one-act or short opera. **2** a light opera.

oph·thal·mic /of-thálmik, op–/ *adj.* of or relating to the eye and its diseases.

ophthalmo- /of-thálmō, op–/ *comb. form Optics* denoting the eye.

oph·thal·mol·o·gist /óf-thalmóləjist, –thə–, op–/ *n.* a medical doctor who specializes in ophthalmology.

oph·thal·mol·o·gy /óf-thalmóləjee, –thə–, op–/ *n.* the scientific study of the eye. ▫▫ **oph·thal·mo·log·i·cal** /–məlójikəl/ *adj.*

oph·thal·mo·scope /of-thálməskōp, op–/ *n.* an instrument for inspecting the retina and other parts of the eye.

o·pi·ate /ópeeət/ *adj. & n.* • *adj.* **1** containing opium. **2** narcotic; soporific. • *n.* **1** a drug containing opium, usu. to ease pain or induce sleep. **2** a thing which soothes or stupefies.

o·pine /ōpín/ *v.tr.* (often foll. by *that* + clause) hold or express as an opinion.

o·pin·ion /əpínyən/ *n.* **1** a belief or assessment based on grounds short of proof. **2** a view held as probable. **3** (often foll. by *on*) what one thinks about a particular topic (*my opinion on capital punishment*). **4** a formal statement of professional advice (*get a second opinion*). **5** an estimation (*had a low opinion of it*). ▫ **a matter of opinion** a disputable point.

o·pin·ion·at·ed /əpínyənaytid/ *adj.* conceitedly assertive in one's opinions.

o·pi·um /ópeeəm/ *n.* **1** a reddish-brown heavy-scented addictive drug prepared from the juice of the opium poppy, used in medicine as an analgesic and narcotic. **2** anything regarded as soothing or stupefying.

o·pos·sum /əpósəm/ *n.* any mainly tree-living marsupial of the family Didelphidae, native to America, having a prehensile tail.

opp. *abbr.* opposite.

op·po·nent /əpṓnənt/ *n.* a person who opposes or belongs to an opposing side.

op·por·tune /ópərtóon, –tyóon/ *adj.* **1** (of a time) especially favorable or appropriate (*an opportune moment*). **2** (of an action or event) done or occurring at a favorable or useful time. ▫▫ **op·por·tune·ly** *adv.* **op·por·tune·ness** *n.*

op·por·tun·ism /ópərtóonizəm, –tyóo–/ *n.* the adaptation of policy or judgment to circumstances or opportunity, esp. regardless of principle. ▫▫ **op·por·tun·ist** *n. & adj.* **op·por·tun·is·tic** *adj.* **op·por·tun·is·ti·cal·ly** *adv.*

op·por·tu·ni·ty /ópərtóonitee, –tyóo–/ *n.* (*pl.* **-ties**) a good chance; a favorable occasion. ▫ **opportunity knocks** an opportunity occurs.

op·pos·a·ble /əpṓzəbəl/ *adj. Zool.* (of the thumb in primates) capable of facing and touching the other digits on the same hand.

op·pose /əpṓz/ *v.tr.* (often *absol.*) **1** set oneself against. **2** take part in a game, sport, etc., against (another competitor or team). **3** (foll. by *to*) place in opposition or contrast. ▫ **as opposed to** in contrast with.

op·po·site /ópəzit/ *adj., n., adv., & prep.* • *adj.* **1** (often foll. by *to*) on the other or further side, facing or back to back. **2** (often foll. by *to, from*) **a** diametrically different. **b** being the other of a contrasted pair. **3** (of angles) between opposite sides of the intersection of two lines. • *n.* an opposite thing or person or term. • *adv.* in an opposite position (*the tree stands opposite*). • *prep.* in a position opposite to (*opposite the house is a tree*). ▫▫ **op·po·site·ly** *adv.* **op·po·site·ness** *n.*

op·po·site num·ber *n.* a person holding an equivalent position in another group or organization.

op·po·site sex *n.* women in relation to men or vice versa.

op·po·si·tion /ópəzíshən/ *n.* **1** resistance; antagonism. **2** the state of being hostile or in conflict. **3** contrast or antithesis. **4 a** a group of opponents. **b** (**the Opposition**) the principal political party opposed to that in office. **5** the act of opposing or placing opposite. ▫▫ **op·po·si·tion·al** *adj.*

op·press /əprés/ *v.tr.* **1** keep in subservience by coercion. **2** govern or treat harshly or with cruel injustice. **3** weigh down (with cares). ▫▫ **op·pres·sor** *n.*

op·pres·sion /əpréshən/ *n.* **1** the state of being oppressed. **2** prolonged harsh or cruel treatment. **3** mental distress.

op·pres·sive /əprésiv/ *adj.* **1** harsh or cruel. **2** (of weather) close and sultry. ▫▫ **op·pres·sive·ly** *adv.* **op·pres·sive·ness** *n.*

op·pro·bri·ous /əprṓbreeəs/ *adj.* (of language) severely scornful; abusive. ▫▫ **op·pro·bri·ous·ly** *adv.*

op·pro·bri·um /əprṓbreeəm/ *n.* **1** disgrace. **2** a cause of this.

opt /opt/ *v.intr.* (usu. foll. by *for, between*) exercise an option; make a choice. ▫ **opt out** (often foll. by *of*) choose not to participate (*opted out of the race*).

op·tic /óptik/ *adj. & n.* • *adj.* of or relating to the eye or vision (*optic nerve*). • *n.* a lens, etc., in an optical instrument.

op·ti·cal /óptikəl/ *adj.* **1** of sight; visual. **2 a** of sight or light in relation to each other. **b** belonging to optics. **3** (esp. of a lens) constructed to assist sight. ▫▫ **op·ti·cal·ly** *adv.*

op·ti·cal art *n.* a style of painting that gives the illusion of movement by the precise use of pattern and color.

op·ti·cal char·ac·ter rec·og·ni·tion *n.* the identification of printed characters using photoelectric devices.

op·ti·cal fi·ber *n.* thin glass fiber through which light can be transmitted.

op·ti·cal il·lu·sion *n.* **1** a thing having an appearance so resembling something else as to deceive the eye. **2** a mental misapprehension caused by this.

op·ti·cian /optíshən/ *n.* **1** a maker or seller of optical instruments. **2** a person trained in the detection and correction of poor eyesight (see OPHTHALMOLOGIST, OPTOMETRIST).

op·tic nerve *n.* each of the second pair of cranial nerves, transmitting impulses to the brain from the retina at the back of the eye.

op·tics /óptiks/ *n.pl.* (treated as *sing.*) the scientific study of sight and the behavior of light, or of other radiation or particles (*electron optics*).

op·ti·mal /óptiməl/ *adj.* best or most favorable. ▫▫ **op·ti·mal·ly** *adv.*

op·ti·mism /óptimizəm/ *n.* **1** an inclination to hopefulness and confidence. **2** *Philos.* **a** the doctrine that this world is the best of all possible worlds. **b** the theory that good must ultimately prevail over evil. ▫▫ **op·ti·mist** *n.* **op·ti·mis·tic** *adj.* **op·ti·mis·ti·cal·ly** *adv.*

op·ti·mize /óptimīz/ *v.* **1** *tr.* make the best or most effective use of (a situation, an opportunity, etc.). **2** *intr.* be an optimist. ▫▫ **op·ti·mi·za·tion** *n.*

op·ti·mum /óptiməm/ *n. & adj.* • *n.* (*pl.* **optima** /–mə/or **optimums**) **1** the most favorable conditions (for growth, reproduction, etc.). **2** the best possible compromise between opposing tendencies. • *adj.* = OPTIMAL.

op·tion /ópshən/ *n.* **1 a** the act or an instance of choosing. **b** a thing that is or may be chosen. **2** freedom of choice. **3** *Stock Exch.*, etc. the right to buy, sell, etc., specified stocks, etc., at a specified price within a set time.

op·tion·al /ópshənəl/ *adj.* not obligatory. ▫▫ **op·tion·al·i·ty** /–álitee/ *n.* **op·tion·al·ly** *adv.*

op·tom·e·try /optómitree/ *n.* the practice or profession of testing the eyes for defects in vision and prescribing corrective lenses or exercises. ▫▫ **op·tom·e·trist** *n.*

op·u·lent /ópyələnt/ *adj.* **1** ostentatiously rich. **2** luxurious. **3** abundant; profuse. ▫▫ **op·u·lence** /–ləns/ *n.* **op·u·lent·ly** *adv.*

o·pus /ṓpəs/ *n.* (*pl.* **opera** /ópərə/or **opuses**) **1** *Mus.* **a** a separate musical composition or set of compositions of any kind. **b** (also **op.**) used before a number given to a composer's work, usu. indicating the order of publication (*Beethoven, op. 15*). **2** any artistic work.

OR *abbr.* **1** Oregon (in official postal use). **2** operating room.

or /awr, ər/ *conj.* **1 a** introducing the second of two alternatives (*white or black*). **b** introducing all but the first, or only the last, of any number of alternatives (*white or gray or black*; *white, gray, or black*). **2** introducing a synonym or explanation of a preceding word, etc. (*suffered from vertigo or dizziness*). **3** introducing a significant afterthought (*he must know—or is he bluffing?*). **4** otherwise (*run or you'll be late*). ▫ **one or two** (or **two or three**, etc.) *colloq.* a few. **or else 1** otherwise (*do it now, or else you will have to do it tomorrow*). **2** *colloq.* expressing a warning or threat (*hand over the money or else*). **or rather** introducing a rephrasing or qualification of a preceding statement, etc. (*he was there, or rather I heard that he was*). **or so** (after a quantity or a number) or thereabouts (*send me ten or so*).

or·a·cle /áwrəkəl, ór–/ *n.* **1 a** a place at which advice or prophecy was sought from the gods in classical antiquity. **b** the usu. ambiguous or obscure response given at an oracle. **c** a prophet or prophetess at an oracle. **2 a** a person or thing regarded as an infallible guide to future action, etc. **b** a saying, etc., regarded as infallible guidance. ▫▫ **o·rac·u·lar** /awrákyələr/ *adj.*

o·ral /áwrəl/ *adj.* & *n.* • *adj.* **1** spoken; not written (*the oral tradition*). **2** done or taken by the mouth (*oral contraceptive*). **3** of the mouth. • *n. colloq.* a spoken examination, test, etc. ▫▫ **o·ral·ly** *adv.*

or·ange /áwrinj, ór–/ *n.* & *adj.* • *n.* **1 a** a large roundish juicy citrus fruit with a bright reddish-yellow tough rind. **b** any of various trees or shrubs of the genus *Citrus*, esp. *C. sinensis* or *C. aurantium*, bearing fragrant white flowers and yielding this fruit. **2** the reddish-yellow color of an orange. • *adj.* orange-colored.

or·ange·ade /áwrinjáyd, ór–/ *n.* a usu. carbonated nonalcoholic drink flavored with orange.

or·ange·ry /áwrinjree, ór–/ *n.* (*pl.* **-ries**) a place, esp. a special structure, where orange trees are cultivated.

o·rang·u·tan /awrángətán, əráng–/ *n.* (also **o·rang-ou·tang** /–táng/) a large red long-haired tree-living ape, *Pongo pygmaeus*, native to Borneo and Sumatra.

o·rate /awráyt, áwrayt/ *v.intr.* esp. *joc.* or *derog.* make a speech or speak, esp. pompously or at length.

o·ra·tion /awráyshən, ōráy–/ *n.* a formal speech, etc., esp. when ceremonial.

or·a·tor /áwrətər, ór–/ *n.* **1** a person making a speech. **2** an eloquent public speaker.

or·a·to·ri·o /áwrətáwreeō, ór–/ *n.* (*pl.* **-os**) a semidramatic work for orchestra and voices, esp. on a sacred theme.

or·a·to·ry /áwrətawree, ór–/ *n.* (*pl.* **-ries**) **1** the art or practice of formal speaking, esp. in public. **2** a small chapel, esp. for private worship. ▫▫ **or·a·tor·i·cal** /–táwrikəl/ *adj.*

orb /awrb/ *n.* **1** a globe surmounted by a cross, esp. carried by a sovereign at a coronation. **2** a sphere; a globe.

or·bit /áwrbit/ *n.* & *v.* • *n.* **1 a** the curved course of a planet, satellite, etc. **b** (prec. by *in, into, out of*, etc.) the state of motion in an orbit. **c** one complete passage around an orbited body. **2** the path of an electron around an atomic nucleus. **3** a range or sphere of action. • *v.* (**orbited, orbiting**) **1** *intr.* (of a satellite, etc.) go around in orbit. **2** *tr.* move in orbit around.

or·bit·al /áwrbitəl/ *adj. Astron.* & *Physics* of an orbit.

or·bit·al sand·er *n.* a sander having a circular and not oscillating motion.

or·ca /áwrkə/ *n.* the killer whale.

or·chard /áwrchərd/ *n.* a piece of land with fruit trees. ▫▫ **or·char·dist** *n.*

or·ches·tra /áwrkəstrə/ *n.* **1** a usu. large group of instrumentalists, esp. combining strings, woodwinds, brass, and percussion (*symphony orchestra*). **2 a** (in full **orchestra pit**) the part of a theater, etc., where the orchestra plays, usu. in front of the stage and on a lower level. **b** the main-floor seating area in a theater. **3** the semicircular space in front of an ancient Greek theater stage where the chorus danced and sang. ▫▫ **or·ches·tral** /–késtrəl/ *adj.* **or·ches·tral·ly** *adv.*

or·ches·trate /áwrkəstrayt/ *v.tr.* **1** arrange, score, or compose for orchestral performance. **2** combine, arrange, or build up (elements of a situation, etc.) for maximum effect. ▫▫ **or·ches·tra·tion** /–tráyshən/ *n.* **or·ches·tra·tor** *n.*

or·chid /áwrkid/ *n.* **1** any usu. epiphytic plant of the family Orchidaceae, bearing flowers in fantastic shapes and brilliant colors. **2** a flower of any of these plants. ▫▫ **or·chi·da·ceous** /–dáyshəs/ *adj.*

or·dain /awrdáyn/ *v.tr.* **1** appoint to the Christian ministry. **2 a** (often foll. by *that* + clause) decree (*ordained that he should go*). **b** (of God, fate, etc.) destine; appoint (*has ordained us to die*). ▫▫ **or·dain·er** *n.*

or·deal /awrdéel/ *n.* a painful or horrific experience; a severe trial.

or·der /áwrdər/ *n.* & *v.* • *n.* **1 a** the condition in which every part, unit, etc., is in its right place. **b** a usu. specified sequence, succession, etc. (*alphabetical order*). **2** (in *sing.* or *pl.*) an authoritative command, instruction, etc. **3** a state of peaceful harmony under a constituted authority (*order was restored*). **4** a kind (*talents of a high order*). **5 a** a direction to a manufacturer, waiter, etc., to supply something. **b** the goods, etc., supplied. **6** the constitution or nature of the world, society, etc. (*the moral order*; *the order of things*). **7** *Biol.* a taxonomic rank below a class and above a family. **8** (esp. **Order**) a fraternity of monks and friars bound by a common rule of life (*the Franciscan order*). **9 a** any of the grades of the Christian ministry. **b** (in *pl.*) the status of a member of the clergy (*Anglican orders*). **10** any of the five classical styles of architecture (Doric, Ionic, Corinthian, Tuscan, and Composite) based on the proportions of columns, amount of decoration, etc. **11** *Eccl.* the stated form of divine service (*the order of confirmation*). **12** the principles of procedure, decorum, etc., accepted by a meeting, legislative assembly, etc. **13** any of the nine grades of angelic beings (seraphim, cherubim, thrones, dominations, principalities, powers, virtues, archangels, angels). • *v.tr.* **1** (usu. foll. by *to* + infin., or *that* + clause) command; prescribe (*ordered him to go*). **2** command or direct (a person) to a specified destination (*was ordered to Singapore*). **3** direct a manufacturer, waiter, etc., to supply something (*ordered a new suit*). **4** put in order; regulate (*ordered her affairs*). **5** (of God, fate, etc.) ordain (*fate ordered it otherwise*). **6** command (a thing) done or (a person) dealt with (*ordered him expelled*). ▫ **by order** according to the proper authority. **in bad** (or **good**, etc.) **order** not working (or working properly, etc.). **in order 1** one after another according to some principle. **2** ready for use. **3** according to the rules (of procedure at a meeting, etc.). **in order that** so that. **in order to** with a view to. **keep order** enforce orderly behavior. **of** (or **in** or

on) the order of 1 approximately. **2** having the order of magnitude specified by (*of the order of one in a million*). **on order** (of goods, etc.) ordered but not yet received. **order about 1** command officiously. **2** send here and there. **out of order 1** not working properly. **2** not according to the rules (of a meeting, organization, etc.). **3** not in proper sequence. **take orders 1** accept commissions. **2** accept and carry out commands.

or·der·ly /áwrd'rlee/ *adj. & n.* • *adj.* **1** methodically arranged. **2** obedient to discipline; well-behaved. • *n.* (*pl.* **-lies**) **1** a hospital attendant with nonmedical duties, esp. cleaning. **2** a soldier who carries orders for an officer, etc. ▫▫ **or·der·li·ness** *n.*

or·di·nal /áwrd'nəl/ *n. & adj.* • *n.* (in full **ordinal number**) a number defining a thing's position in a series, e.g., "first," "second," etc. • *adj.* **1** of or relating to an ordinal number. **2** defining a thing's position in a series.

or·di·nance /áwrd'nəns/ *n.* **1** a decree. **2** an enactment by a local authority. **3** a religious rite.

or·di·nar·y /áwrd'neree/ *adj. & n.* • *adj.* **1** regular; normal; usual (*in the ordinary course of events*). **2** boring; commonplace (*an ordinary man*). • *n.* (*pl.* **-ies**) **1** *RC Ch.* (usu. **Ordinary**) those parts of a service, esp. the mass, that do not vary from day to day. **2** a rule or book laying down the order of divine service. ▫ **in the ordinary way** if the circumstances are or were not exceptional. **out of the ordinary** unusual. ▫▫ **or·di·nar·i·ly** /–áirəlee/ *adv.* **or·di·nar·i·ness** *n.*

or·di·nate /áwrd'nit/ *n. Math.* a straight line from any point drawn parallel to one coordinate axis and meeting the other, usually a coordinate measured parallel to the vertical.

or·di·na·tion /áwrd'náyshən/ *n.* the act of conferring holy orders, esp. on a priest or deacon.

ord·nance /áwrdnəns/ *n.* **1** mounted guns; cannon. **2** a branch of the armed forces dealing esp. with military stores and materials.

or·dure /áwrjər, –dyo͝or/ *n.* **1** excrement; dung. **2** obscenity; filth; foul language.

Ore. *abbr.* Oregon.

ore /awr/ *n.* a naturally occurring solid material from which metal or other valuable minerals may be extracted.

Oreg. *abbr.* Oregon.

o·reg·a·no /ərégənō, awrég–/ *n.* an aromatic herb, *Origanum vulgare*, the leaves of which are used as a flavoring in cooking. Also called **wild marjoram**.

or·gan /áwrgən/ *n.* **1 a** a usu. large musical instrument having pipes supplied with air from bellows, sounded by keys (*pedal organ*). **b** a smaller instrument without pipes, producing similar sounds electronically. **c** a smaller keyboard wind instrument with metal reeds. **d** = BARREL ORGAN. **2 a** a usu. self-contained part of an organism having a special vital function (*vocal organs*). **b** esp. *joc.* the penis. **3** a medium of communication, esp. a newspaper, etc.

or·gan·dy /áwrgəndee/ *n.* (also **or·gan·die**) (*pl.* **-dies**) a fine translucent cotton muslin, usu. stiffened.

or·gan·elle /áwrgənél/ *n. Biol.* any of various organized or specialized structures that form part of a cell.

or·gan-grind·er *n.* the player of a barrel organ.

or·gan·ic /awrgánik/ *adj.* **1 a** *Physiol.* of or relating to a bodily organ or organs. **b** *Med.* (of a disease) affecting the structure of an organ. **2** (of a plant or animal) having organs or an organized physical structure. **3** produced or involving production without chemical fertilizers, pesticides, etc. **4** *Chem.* (of a compound, etc.) containing carbon (opp. INORGANIC). **5 a** structural; inherent. **b** constitutional; fundamental. **6** organized; systematic (*an organic whole*). ▫▫ **or·gan·i·cal·ly** *adv.*

or·gan·ic chem·is·try *n.* the chemistry of carbon compounds.

or·gan·ism /áwrgənizəm/ *n.* **1** a living individual consisting of a single cell or of a group of interdependent parts. **2** an individual live plant or animal. **3** a whole with interdependent parts compared to a living being.

or·gan·ist /áwrgənist/ *n.* the player of an organ.

or·gan·i·za·tion /áwrgənizáyshən/ *n.* **1** the act of organizing. **2** an organized body, esp. a business, charity, etc. **3** systematic arrangement. ▫▫ **or·gan·i·za·tion·al** *adj.* **or·gan·i·za·tion·al·ly** *adv.*

or·gan·ize /áwrgənīz/ *v.tr.* **1 a** give an orderly structure to. **b** make arrangements for (a person). **2** (often *absol.*) **a** enroll (new members) in a labor union, political party, etc. **b** form (a labor union or other political group). **3** (esp. as **organized** *adj.*) make organic; make into a living being or tissue.

or·gan·ized crime *n.* **1** an organization of people who carry out illegal activities for profit. **2** the people involved in this.

or·gan·za /awrgánzə/ *n.* a thin stiff transparent silk or synthetic dress fabric.

or·gasm /áwrgazəm/ *n. & v.* • *n.* the climax of sexual excitement. • *v.intr.* experience a sexual orgasm. ▫▫ **or·gas·mic** /–gázmik/ *adj.* **or·gas·mic·al·ly** *adv.*

or·gi·as·tic /áwrjeeástik/ *adj.* of or resembling an orgy. ▫▫ **or·gi·as·ti·cal·ly** *adv.*

or·gy /áwrjee/ *n.* (*pl.* **-gies**) **1** a wild drunken festivity, esp. one at which indiscriminate sexual activity takes place. **2** excessive indulgence in an activity.

o·ri·el /áwreeəl/ *n.* (in full **oriel window**) the projecting window of an upper story.

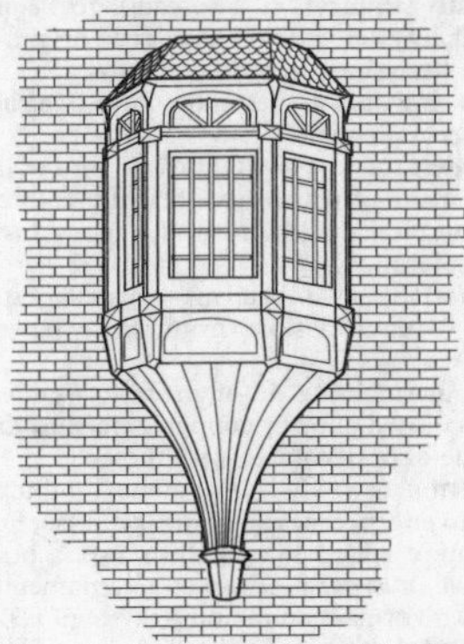

oriel

o·ri·ent *n. & v.* • *n.* /áwreeənt/ (**the Orient**) **1** *poet.* the east. **2** the countries E. of the Mediterranean, esp. E. Asia. • *v.* /áwree-ent/ **1** *tr.* **a** place or exactly determine the position of with the aid of a compass. **b** (often foll. by *toward*) direct. **2** *tr.* place or build (a church, etc.) facing toward the East. **3** *intr.* turn eastward or in a specified direction. ▫ **orient oneself** determine how one stands in relation to one's surroundings.

o·ri·en·tal /áwree-éntəl/ *adj. & n.* • *adj.* (often **Oriental**) **1** of or characteristic of Eastern civilization, etc. **2** of or concerning the East, esp. E. Asia. • *n.* (esp. **Oriental**) a native of the Orient. ▫▫ **o·ri·en·tal·ism** *n.* **o·ri·en·tal·ist** *n.* **o·ri·en·tal·ize** *v.intr. & tr.*

▶The term **Oriental**, which has many associations with European empire in Asia, is regarded as offensive by

See page xii for the *Key to Pronunciation*.

many Asians, especially Asian Americans. **Asian** or, if appropriate, **East Asian** is preferred.

o·ri·en·ta·tion /áwree-entáyshən/ *n.* **1** the act of orienting. **2 a** a relative position. **b** a person's attitude or adjustment in relation to circumstances, esp. psychologically. **3** an introduction to a subject or situation; a briefing. ▫▫ **o·ri·en·ta·tion·al** *adj.*

o·ri·en·teer·ing /áwree-enteéring/ *n.* a competitive sport in which runners cross open country with a map, compass, etc. ▫▫ **o·ri·en·teer** *n. & v.intr.*

or·i·fice /áwrifis, ór–/ *n.* an opening, esp. a bodily aperture, etc.

o·ri·ga·mi /áwrigaámee/ *n.* the Japanese art of folding paper into decorative shapes and figures.

or·i·gin /áwrijin, ór–/ *n.* **1** a beginning or starting point; a derivation (*a word of Latin origin*). **2** (often in *pl.*) a person's ancestry (*what are his origins?*). **3** *Math.* a fixed point from which coordinates are measured.

o·rig·i·nal /ərijinəl/ *adj. & n.* • *adj.* **1** existing from the beginning; innate. **2** novel; inventive; creative (*has an original mind*). **3** serving as a pattern; not derivative or imitative; firsthand (*in the original Greek*; *has an original Rembrandt*). • *n.* **1** an original model, picture, etc., from which another is copied or translated (*kept the copy and destroyed the original*). **2** an eccentric or unusual person. ▫▫ **o·rig·i·nal·ly** *adv.*

o·rig·i·nal·i·ty /ərijinálitee/ *n.* (*pl.* **-ties**) **1** the power of creating or thinking creatively. **2** newness or freshness (*this vase has originality*).

o·rig·i·nal sin *n.* the innate depravity of all humankind held to be a consequence of the Fall of Adam.

o·rig·i·nate /ərijinayt/ *v.* **1** *tr.* cause to begin. **2** *intr.* (usu. foll. by *from, in, with*) have as an origin. ▫▫ **o·rig·i·na·tion** /–náyshən/ *n.* **o·rig·i·na·tor** *n.*

O-ring /ṓ-ring/ *n.* a gasket in the form of a ring with a circular cross section.

o·ri·ole /áwreeōl/ *n.* **1** any Old World bird of the genus *Oriolus*, many of which have brightly colored plumage. **2** any New World bird of the genus *Icterus*, with similar coloration.

O·ri·on /əríən/ *n.* a brilliant constellation on the celestial equator visible from most parts of the earth.

or·mo·lu /áwrməlōō/ *n.* **1** (often *attrib.*) a gilded bronze or gold-colored alloy of copper, zinc, and tin. **2** articles made of or decorated with these.

or·na·ment *n. & v.* • *n.* /áwrnəmənt/ **1** a thing used or serving to adorn, esp. a small trinket, vase, figure, etc. **2** decoration added to embellish, esp. a building (*a tower rich in ornament*). • *v.tr.* /áwrnəment/ adorn; beautify. ▫▫ **or·na·men·ta·tion** /–táyshən/ *n.*

or·na·men·tal /áwrnəmént'l/ *adj. & n.* • *adj.* serving as an ornament. • *n.* a thing considered to be ornamental, esp. a cultivated plant. ▫▫ **or·na·men·tal·ism** *n.*

or·nate /awrnáyt/ *adj.* **1** elaborately adorned. **2** (of literary style) convoluted; flowery. ▫▫ **or·nate·ly** *adv.* **or·nate·ness** *n.*

or·ner·y /áwrnəree/ *adj. colloq.* **1** unpleasant. **2** of poor quality. ▫▫ **or·ner·i·ness** *n.*

ornitho- /áwrnithō/ *comb. form* bird.

or·ni·thol·o·gy /áwrnithóləjee/ *n.* the scientific study of birds. ▫▫ **or·ni·tho·log·i·cal** /–thəlójikəl/ *adj.* **or·ni·tho·log·i·cal·ly** *adv.* **or·ni·thol·o·gist** *n.*

o·ro·tund /áwrətund/ *adj.* **1** (of the voice or phrasing) full and round; imposing. **2** (of writing, style, expression, etc.) pompous; pretentious.

or·phan /áwrfən/ *n. & v.* • *n.* (often *attrib.*) a child bereaved of both parents. • *v.tr.* bereave (a child) of its parents. ▫▫ **or·phan·hood** *n.*

or·phan·age /áwrfənij/ *n.* a residential institution for the care and education of orphans.

or·rer·y /áwrəree, ór–/ *n.* (*pl.* **-ies**) a clockwork model of the solar system.

ortho- /áwrthō/ *comb. form* **1** straight; rectangular; upright. **2** right; correct.

or·tho·don·tics /áwrthədóntiks/ *n.pl.* (treated as *sing.*) (also **or·tho·don·tia** /–dónshə/) the treatment of irregularities in the teeth and jaws. ▫▫ **or·tho·don·tic** *adj.* **or·tho·don·tist** *n.*

or·tho·dox /áwrthədoks/ *adj.* **1** holding currently accepted opinions, esp. on religious doctrine, morals, etc. **2** (of religious doctrine, standards of morality, etc.) generally accepted as right or true; conventional. **3** (also **Orthodox**) (of Judaism) strictly keeping to traditional doctrine and ritual. ▫▫ **or·tho·dox·ly** *adv.*

Or·tho·dox Church *n.* the Eastern Christian Church having the Patriarch of Constantinople as its head, and including the national churches of Russia, Romania, Greece, etc.

or·tho·dox·y /áwrthədoksee/ *n.* (*pl.* **-ies**) **1** the state of being orthodox. **2 a** the orthodox practice of Judaism. **b** the body of orthodox Jews. **3** esp. *Relig.* an authorized or generally accepted theory, doctrine, etc.

or·thog·ra·phy /awrthógrəfee/ *n.* (*pl.* **-phies**) **1** correct spelling. **2** spelling with reference to its correctness (*dreadful orthography*). **3** the study or science of spelling. ▫▫ **or·tho·graph·ic** /awrthəgráfik/ *adj.* **or·tho·graph·i·cal** *adj.* **or·tho·graph·i·cal·ly** *adv.*

or·tho·pe·dics /áwrthəpeédiks/ *n.pl.* (treated as *sing.*) the branch of medicine dealing with the correction of deformities. ▫▫ **or·tho·pe·dic** *adj.* **or·tho·pe·dist** *n.*

OS *abbr.* **1** old style. **2** ordinary seaman. **3** *oculus sinister* (left eye). **4** outsize. **5** out of stock.

Os *symb. Chem.* the element osmium.

O·sage /ōsáyj, ṓ–/ *n. & adj.* • *n.* **1 a** a N. American people native to Missouri. **b** a member of this people. **2** the language of this people. • *adj.* of or relating to this people or their language.

Os·car /óskər/ *n.* any of the statuettes awarded by the Academy of Motion Picture Arts and Sciences for excellence in motion-picture acting, directing, etc.

os·cil·late /ósilayt/ *v.* **1** *intr. & tr.* **a** swing back and forth like a pendulum. **b** move back and forth between points. **2** *intr.* vary between extremes of opinion, action, etc. **3** *intr. Physics* move with periodic regularity. **4** *intr. Electr.* (of a current) undergo high-frequency alternations as across a spark gap. ▫▫ **os·cil·la·tion** /–áyshən/ *n.* **os·cil·la·tor** *n.* **os·cil·la·to·ry** /–ətáwree/ *adj.*

os·cil·lo·graph /əsíləgraf/ *n.* a device for recording oscillations.

os·cil·lo·scope /əsíləskōp/ *n.* a device for viewing oscillations by a display on the screen of a cathode-ray tube.

os·cu·lar /óskyələr/ *adj.* of or relating to the mouth.

os·cu·late /óskyəlayt/ *v.intr. & tr. joc.* kiss. ▫▫ **os·cu·la·tion** /–láyshən/ *n.*

OSHA /ṓshə/ *abbr.* Occupational Safety and Health Administration.

o·sier /ṓzhər/ *n.* **1** any of various willows, esp. *Salix viminalis*, with long flexible shoots used in basketwork. **2** a shoot of a willow.

os·mi·um /ózmeeəm/ *n. Chem.* a hard, bluish-white transition element, the heaviest known metal, used in certain alloys. ¶ Symb.: **Os**.

os·mo·sis /ozmṓsis, os–/ *n.* **1** *Biochem.* the passage of a solvent through a semipermeable partition into a more concentrated solution. **2** any process by which something is acquired by absorption. ▫▫ **os·mot·ic** /–mótik/ *adj.* **os·mot·i·cal·ly** /–mótikəlee/ *adv.*

os·prey /óspray, –pree/ *n.* (*pl.* **-preys**) a large bird of prey, *Pandion haliaetus*, with a brown back and white markings, feeding on fish. Also called **fish hawk**.

OSS *abbr.* Office of Strategic Services.

os•se•ous /óseeəs/ *adj.* **1** consisting of bone. **2** having a bony skeleton. **3** ossified.

os•si•fy /ósifī/ *v.tr. & intr.* (**-fies, -fied**) **1** turn into bone. **2** make or become rigid or unprogressive. ▫▫ **os•si•fi•ca•tion** /–fikáyshən/ *n.*

os•so bu•co /áwsō bóōkō/ *n.* (also **os•so buc•co**) veal stewed in wine with vegetables.

os•su•ar•y /óshōōeree, ósyōō–/ *n.* (*pl.* **-ies**) **1** a receptacle for the bones of the dead; a charnel house; a bone urn. **2** a cave in which ancient bones are found.

os•ten•si•ble /osténsibəl/ *adj.* apparent but not necessarily real; professed (*his ostensible function was that of interpreter*). ▫▫ **os•ten•si•bly** *adv.*

os•ten•sive /osténsiv/ *adj.* **1** directly demonstrative. **2** (of a definition) indicating by direct demonstration that which is signified by a term. ▫▫ **os•ten•sive•ly** *adv.* **os•ten•sive•ness** *n.*

os•ten•ta•tion /óstentáyshən/ *n.* **1** a vulgar display of wealth. **2** showing off. ▫▫ **os•ten•ta•tious** *adj.* **os•ten•ta•tious•ly** *adv.*

osteo- /ósteeō/ *comb. form* bone.

os•te•o•ar•thri•tis /ósteeōaarthrītis/ *n.* a degenerative disease of joint cartilage, esp. in the elderly. ▫▫ **os•te•o•ar•thrit•ic** /–thrítik/ *adj.*

os•te•ol•o•gy /ósteeóləjee/ *n.* the study of the structure and function of the skeleton. ▫▫ **os•te•o•log•i•cal** /–teeəlójikəl/ *adj.* **os•te•ol•o•gist** *n.*

os•te•o•my•e•li•tis /ósteeōmī-ilītis/ *n.* inflammation of the bone or of bone marrow, usu. due to infection.

os•te•op•a•thy /ósteeópəthee/ *n.* the treatment of disease through the manipulation of bones, esp. the spine. ▫▫ **os•te•o•path** /ósteeəpath/ *n.* **os•te•o•path•ic** *adj.*

os•te•o•po•ro•sis /ósteeōpərṓsis/ *n.* a condition of brittle bones caused by loss of bony tissue, esp. as a result of hormonal changes, or deficiency of calcium or vitamin D.

os•ti•na•to /óstinaátō/ *n.* (*pl.* **-tos**) (often *attrib.*) *Mus.* a persistent phrase or rhythm repeated through all or part of a piece.

os•tra•cize /óstrəsīz/ *v.tr.* exclude (a person) from a society, favor, common privileges, etc.; refuse to associate with. ▫▫ **os•tra•cism** /–sizəm/ *n.*

os•trich /óstrich, áw–/ *n.* **1** a large African swift-running flightless bird, *Struthio camelus*, with long legs and two toes on each foot. **2** a person who refuses to accept facts.

OT *abbr.* Old Testament.

OTB *abbr.* off-track betting.

oth•er /úthər/ *adj., n.* or *pron., & adv.* • *adj.* **1** not the same as one or some already mentioned or implied (*other people; use other means*). **2 a** additional (*a few other examples*). **b** alternative of two (*open your other eye*). **3** (prec. by *the*) that remains after all except the one in question have been considered, etc. (*must be in the other pocket; where are the other two?*). **4** (foll. by *than*) apart from (*any person other than you*). • *n.* or *pron.* **1** an additional, different, or extra person, thing, example, etc. (*some others have come*) (see also ANOTHER, EACH OTHER). **2** (in *pl.*; prec. by *the*) the ones remaining (*where are the others?*). • *adv.* (usu. foll. by *than*) *disp.* otherwise (*cannot react other than angrily*).

▶In this sense *otherwise* is standard except in less formal use. ▫ **on the other hand** see HAND. **the other day** (or **night** or **week**, etc.) a few days, etc., ago (*heard from him the other day*). **someone** (or **something** or **somehow**, etc.) **or other** some unspecified person, thing, manner, etc.

oth•er•ness /úthərnis/ *n.* **1** the state of being different. **2** a thing or existence other than the thing mentioned and the thinking subject.

oth•er•wise /úthərwīz/ *adv. & adj.* • *adv.* **1** else; or else (*bring your umbrella, otherwise you will get wet*). **2** in other respects (*he is somewhat unkempt, but otherwise very suitable*). **3** (often foll. by *than*) in a different way (*could not have acted otherwise*). **4** as an alternative (*otherwise known as Jack*). • *adj.* (*predic.*) in a different state (*the matter is quite otherwise*). ▫ **and** (or **or**) **otherwise** the negation or opposite (of a specified thing) (*the merits or otherwise of the proposal; experiences pleasant and otherwise*).

oth•er•world•ly /úthərwə́rldlee/ *adj.* **1** unworldly; impractical. **2** concerned with life after death, etc. ▫▫ **oth•er•world•li•ness** *n.*

o•ti•ose /ósheeōs, ṓtee–/ *adj.* serving no practical purpose; not required; functionless. ▫▫ **o•ti•ose•ly** *adv.* **o•ti•ose•ness** *n.*

o•ti•tis /ōtītis/ *n.* inflammation of the ear.

oto- /ṓtō/ *comb. form* ear.

o•to•scope /ṓtəskōp/ *n.* an apparatus for examining the eardrum and the passage leading to it from the ear. ▫▫ **o•to•scop•ic** /–skópik/ *adj.*

Ot•ta•wa /aátəwə, –waa, –waw/ *n. & adj.* • *n.* **1 a** a N. American people native to Canada and the Great Lakes region. **b** a member of this people. **2** the language of this people. • *adj.* of or relating to this people or their language.

ot•ter /ótər/ *n.* **1** any of several aquatic fish-eating mammals of the family Mustelidae, esp. of the genus *Lutra*, having strong claws and webbed feet. **2** its fur or pelt.

Ot•to•man /ótəmən/ *adj. & n.* • *adj. hist.* **1** of or concerning the dynasty of Osman or Othman I, the branch of the Turks to which he belonged, or the empire ruled by his descendants. **2** Turkish. • *n.* (*pl.* **Ottomans**) an Ottoman person; a Turk.

ot•to•man /ótəmən/ *n.* (*pl.* **ottomans**) **1** an upholstered seat, usu. square and without a back or arms, sometimes a box with a padded top. **2** a footstool of similar design.

ouch /owch/ *int.* expressing pain or annoyance.

ought /awt/ *v.aux.* (usu. foll. by *to* + infin.; present and past indicated by the following infin.) **1** expressing rightness (*we ought to love our neighbors*). **2** expressing shortcoming (*it ought to have been done long ago*). **3** expressing advisability (*you ought to go for your own good*). **4** expressing esp. strong probability (*he ought to be there by now*). ▫ **ought not** the negative form of *ought* (*he ought not to have stolen it*).

oughtn't /áwt'nt/ *contr.* ought not.

Oui•ja /wéejə, –jee/ *n.* (in full **Ouija board**) *Trademark* a board that purports to answer questions from attenders at a seance, etc.

ounce /owns/ *n.* **1** a unit of weight of one-sixteenth of a pound avoirdupois (approx. 28 grams). **2** a small quantity.

our /owr, aar/ *poss.pron.* (*attrib.*) **1** of or belonging to us or ourselves (*our house*). **2** of or belonging to all people (*our children's future*). **3** (esp. as **Our**) of Us the king or queen, emperor or empress, etc. (*given under Our seal*). **4** of us, the editorial staff of a newspaper, etc. (*a foolish adventure in our view*).

Our La•dy *n.* the Virgin Mary.

ours /owrz, aars/ *poss.pron.* the one or ones belonging to or associated with us (*it is ours*).

our•selves /owrsélvz, aar–/ *pron.* **1 a** *emphat. form* of WE or US (*we ourselves did it*). **b** *refl. form* of US (*are pleased with ourselves*). **2** in our normal state of body or mind (*not quite ourselves today*). ▫ **be ourselves** act in our normal unconstrained manner.

oust /owst/ *v.tr.* (usu. foll. by *from*) drive out or expel, esp. by forcing oneself into the place of.

oust•er /ówstər/ *n.* **1** ejection as a result of physical action, judicial process, or political upheaval. **2** dismissal; expulsion.

out /owt/ *adv., prep., n., adj., int., & v.* • *adv.* **1** away from or not in or at a place, etc. (*keep him out*). **2** (forming part of phrasal verbs) **a** indicating dispersal away from a center, etc. (*hire out*). **b** indicating coming or bringing into the open (*send out; shine out*). **c** indicating a need for attentiveness (*watch out; listen out*). **3 a** not in one's house, office, etc. (*went out for a walk*). **b** no longer in prison. **4** completely (*tired out*). **5** (of a fire, candle, etc.) not burning. **6** in error (*was 3% out in my calculations*). **7** *colloq.* unconscious (*she was out for five minutes*). **8 a** (of a tooth) extracted. **b** (of a joint, etc.) dislocated. **9** (of a party, politician, etc.) not in office. **10** (of a jury) considering its verdict in secrecy. **11** (of workers) on strike. **12** (of a secret) revealed. **13** (of a flower) blooming; open. **14** (of a book) published. **15** (of a star) visible after dark. **16** unfashionable (*wide lapels are out*). **17** *Sports* (of a batter, baserunner, etc.) no longer taking part, having been tagged, struck out, etc. **18** not worth considering (*that idea is out*). **19** *colloq.* (prec. by *superl.*) known to exist (*the best game out*). **20** (of a stain, etc.) removed (*painted out the sign*). **21** (of time) not spent working (*took five minutes out*). **22** (of a rash, bruise, etc.) visible. **23** (of the tide) at the lowest point. **24** *Boxing* unable to rise from the floor. **25** (in a radio conversation, etc.) transmission ends (*over and out*). • *prep.* out of (*looked out the window*). • *n.* **1** *colloq.* a way of escape; an excuse. **2** *Baseball* play in which a batter or baserunner is retired from an inning. • *adj.* (of an island) away from the mainland. • *int.* a peremptory dismissal, reproach, etc. (*out, you scoundrel!*). • *v.* **1** *tr.* **a** put out. **b** *colloq.* eject forcibly. **2** *intr.* come or go out (*murder will out*). **3** *tr. Boxing* knock out. **4** *tr. colloq.* expose the homosexuality of (a prominent person). □ **out and about** (of a person, esp. after an illness) engaging in normal activity. **out and away** by far. **out for** having one's interest or effort directed to. **out of 1** from within (*came out of the house*). **2** not within (*I was never out of the city*). **3** from among (*nine people out of ten*). **4** beyond the range of (*is out of reach*). **5** without or so as to be without. **6** from (*get money out of him*). **7** owing to (*out of curiosity*). **8** by the use of (material) (*what did you make it out of?*). **9** at a specified distance from (*seven miles out of Topeka*). **10** beyond (*something out of the ordinary*). **11** *Racing* (of an animal, esp. a horse) born of. **come out of the closet** see CLOSET. **out of doors** see DOOR. **out of hand** see HAND. **out of it 1** not included. **2** *sl.* extremely drunk or otherwise disoriented. **out of order** see ORDER. **out of pocket** see POCKET. **out of the question** see QUESTION. **out of sorts** see SORT. **out of temper** see TEMPER. **out of this world** see WORLD. **out of the way** see WAY. **out to** keenly striving to do. **out to lunch** *colloq.* crazy; mad. **out with it** say what you are thinking.

out·age /ówtij/ *n.* a period of time during which a power supply, etc., is not operating.

out-and-out *adj. & adv.* • *adj.* thorough; surpassing. • *adv.* thoroughly; surpassingly.

out·back /ówtbak/ *n.* esp. *Austral.* the remote and usu. uninhabited inland districts. □□ **out·back·er** *n.*

out·bal·ance /ówtbáləns/ *v.tr.* **1** count as more important than. **2** outweigh.

out·bid /ówtbíd/ *v.tr.* (**-bidding**; *past* and *past part.* **-bid**) bid higher than (another person) at an auction.

out·board /ówtbawrd/ *adj., adv., & n.* • *adj.* **1** (of a motor) portable and attachable to the outside of the stern of a boat. **2** (of a boat) having an outboard motor. • *adj. & adv.* on, toward, or near the outside of esp. a ship, an aircraft, etc. • *n.* **1** an outboard engine. **2** a boat with an outboard engine.

out·bound /ówtbownd/ *adj.* outward bound.

out·break /ówtbrayk/ *n.* **1** a sudden eruption of war, disease, etc. **2** an outcrop.

out·build·ing /ówtbilding/ *n.* a detached shed, barn, garage, etc., within the grounds of a main building.

out·burst /ówtbərst/ *n.* **1** an explosion of anger, etc., expressed in words. **2** an act or instance of bursting out. **3** an outcrop.

out·cast /ówtkast/ *n. & adj.* • *n.* **1** a person cast out from or rejected by his or her home, country, society, etc. **2** a tramp or vagabond. • *adj.* rejected; homeless.

out·class /ówtklás/ *v.tr.* **1** belong to a higher class than. **2** defeat easily.

out·come /ówtkum/ *n.* a result; a visible effect.

out·crop /ówtkrop/ *n. & v.* • *n.* **1 a** the emergence of a stratum, vein, or rock, at the surface. **b** a stratum, etc., emerging. **2** a noticeable manifestation or occurrence. • *v.intr.* (**-cropped, -cropping**) appear as an outcrop; crop out.

out·cry /ówtkrī/ *n.* (*pl.* **-cries**) **1** the act or an instance of crying out. **2** an uproar. **3** a noisy or prolonged public protest.

out·dat·ed /ówtdáytid/ *adj.* out of date; obsolete.

out·dis·tance /ówtdístəns/ *v.tr.* leave (a competitor) behind completely.

out·do /ówtdo͞o/ *v.tr.* (*3rd sing. present* **-does**; *past* **-did**; *past part.* **-done**) exceed or excel in doing or performance; surpass.

out·door /ówtdawr/ *adj.* done, existing, or used out of doors.

out·doors /owtdáwrz/ *adv. & n.* • *adv.* out of doors. • *n.* the open air.

out·doors·man /owtdórzmən, -dáwrz–/ *n.* a person who spends much time in outdoor activities, as fishing, camping, etc.

out·er /ówtər/ *adj.* **1** outside; external (*pierced the outer layer*). **2** farther from the center or inside. **3** objective or physical, not subjective nor psychical.

out·er·most /ówtərmōst/ *adj.* furthest from the inside; the most far out.

out·er space *n.* the universe beyond the earth's atmosphere.

out·er·wear /ówtərwair/ *n.* clothes worn over other clothes, esp. for warmth, protection, etc.

out·field /ówtfeeld/ *n.* the outer part of a baseball field. □□ **out·field·er** *n.*

out·fight /ówtfít/ *v.tr.* fight better than; beat in a fight.

out·fit /ówtfit/ *n. & v.* • *n.* **1** a set of clothes worn or esp. designed to be worn together. **2** a complete set of equipment, etc., for a specific purpose. **3** *colloq.* a group of people regarded as a unit, etc. • *v.tr.* (also *refl.*) (**-fitted, -fitting**) provide with an outfit, esp. of clothes.

out·fit·ter /ówtfitər/ *n.* **1** a business that supplies outdoor equipment, arranges tours, etc. **2** a supplier of men's clothing; a haberdasher.

out·flank /ówtflángk/ *v.tr.* **1 a** extend one's flank beyond that of (an enemy). **b** outmaneuver (an enemy) in this way. **2** get the better of (an opponent).

out·flow /ówtflō/ *n.* **1** an outward flow. **2** the amount that flows out.

out·fox /ówtfóks/ *v.tr. colloq.* outwit.

out·go·ing *adj.* /ówtgṓing/ **1** friendly; sociable; extrovert. **2** retiring from office. **3** going out or away.

out·grow /ówtgrṓ/ *v.tr.* (*past* **-grew**; *past part.* **-grown**) **1** grow too big for (one's clothes). **2** leave behind (a childish habit, ailment, etc.) as one matures. **3** grow faster or taller than.

out·growth /ówtgrōth/ *n.* **1** something that grows out. **2** an offshoot; a natural product. **3** the process of growing out.

out·gun /ówtgún/ *v.tr.* (**-gunned, -gunning**) **1** surpass in military or other power or strength. **2** shoot better than.

out·house /ówt-hows/ *n.* **1** a building, esp. a shed, barn, etc., built next to or in the grounds of a house. **2** an outbuilding used as a toilet.

out·ing /ówting/ *n.* **1** a short holiday away from home, esp. of one day or part of a day. **2** any brief journey from home. **3** an appearance in an athletic contest, race, etc. **4** *colloq.* the practice or policy of exposing the homosexuality of a prominent person.

out·land·ish /owtlándish/ *adj.* **1** looking or sounding foreign. **2** bizarre; strange; unfamiliar. ▫▫ **out·land·ish·ly** *adv.* **out·land·ish·ness** *n.*

out·last /owtlást/ *v.tr.* last longer than (a person, thing, or duration).

out·law /ówtlaw/ *n. & v.* • *n.* **1** a fugitive from the law. **2** *hist.* a person deprived of the protection of the law. • *v.tr.* **1** declare an outlaw. **2** make illegal. ▫▫ **out·law·ry** *n.*

out·lay /ówtlay/ *n.* what is spent on something.

out·let /ówtlet, –lit/ *n.* **1** a means of exit or escape. **2** (usu. foll. by *for*) a means of expression (*find an outlet for tension*). **3** an agency, distributor, or market for goods (*a new retail outlet*). **4** an electrical power receptacle.

out·line /ówtlīn/ *n. & v.* • *n.* **1** a rough draft of a diagram, plan, etc. **2 a** a précis of a proposed novel, article, etc. **b** a verbal description of essential parts only. **3** a sketch containing only contour lines. **4** (in *sing.* or *pl.*) **a** lines enclosing or indicating an object (*the outline of a shape under the blankets*). **b** a contour. **c** an external boundary. **5** (in *pl.*) the main features or general principles. • *v.tr.* **1** draw or describe in outline. **2** mark the outline of. ▫ **in outline** sketched or represented as an outline.

out·live /owtlív/ *v.tr.* **1** live longer than (another person). **2** live beyond (a specified date or time). **3** live through (an experience).

out·look /ówtlŏŏk/ *n.* **1** the prospect for the future (*the outlook is bleak*). **2** one's mental attitude (*narrow in their outlook*). **3** what is seen on looking out.

out·ly·ing /ówtlī-ing/ *adj.* situated far from a center; remote.

out·ma·neu·ver /ówtmənṓovər/ *v.tr.* **1** use skill and cunning to secure an advantage over (a person). **2** outdo in maneuvering.

out·mod·ed /owtmṓdid/ *adj.* **1** no longer in fashion. **2** obsolete.

out·num·ber /owtnúmbər/ *v.tr.* exceed in number.

out of date *adj.* (*attrib.* **out-of-date**) old fashioned; obsolete.

out·pace /owtpáys/ *v.tr.* **1** go faster than. **2** outdo in a contest.

out·pa·tient /ówtpayshənt/ *n.* a hospital patient whose treatment does not require overnight hospitalization.

out·per·form /owtpərfáwrm/ *v.tr.* **1** perform better than. **2** surpass in a specified field or activity. ▫▫ **out·per·for·mance** *n.*

out·place·ment /ówtplaysmənt/ *n.* the act or process of finding new employment for workers who have been dismissed.

out·post /ówtpōst/ *n.* **1** a detachment set at a distance from the main body of an army, esp. to prevent surprise. **2** a distant branch or settlement.

out·pour·ing /ówtpawring/ *n.* **1** (usu. in *pl.*) a copious spoken or written expression of emotion. **2** what is poured out.

out·put /ówtpŏŏt/ *n. & v.* • *n.* **1** the product of a process, esp. of manufacture, or of mental or artistic work. **2** the quantity or amount of this. **3** the printout, etc., supplied by a computer. **4** the power, etc., delivered by an apparatus. **5** a place where energy, etc., leaves a system. • *v.tr.* (**-putting**; *past* and *past part.* **-put** or **-putted**) **1** put or send out. **2** (of a computer) supply (results, etc.).

out·rage /ówt-rayj/ *n. & v.* • *n.* **1** an extreme violation of others' rights, sentiments, etc. **2** a gross offense. **3** fierce anger or resentment (*a feeling of outrage*). • *v.tr.* **1** subject to outrage. **2** injure, insult, etc., flagrantly. **3** shock and anger.

out·ra·geous /owt-ráyjəs/ *adj.* **1** immoderate. **2** shocking. **3** grossly cruel. **4** immoral; offensive. ▫▫ **out·ra·geous·ly** *adv.* **out·ra·geous·ness** *n.*

out·rank /owt-rángk/ *v.tr.* **1** be superior in rank to. **2** take priority over.

ou·tré /ōōtráy/ *adj.* **1** outside the bounds of what is usual. **2** eccentric.

out·reach /ówtreech/ *n. & v.* • *n.* any organization's involvement with or influence in the community, esp. in the context of social welfare. • *v.tr.* **1** reach further than. **2** surpass.

out·rid·er /ówt-rīdər/ *n.* **1** a mounted attendant riding ahead of a carriage, etc. **2** a motorcyclist acting as a guard in a similar manner. **3** a cowhand, etc., keeping cattle, etc., within bounds. ▫▫ **out·rid·ing** *n.*

out·rig·ger /ówt-rigər/ *n.* **1** a beam, spar, or framework, rigged out and projecting from or over a ship's side. **2** a similar projecting beam, etc., in a building. **3** a log, etc., fixed parallel to a canoe to stabilize it. **4 a** an iron bracket bearing an oarlock attached horizontally to a boat's side to increase the leverage of the oar. **b** a boat fitted with these.

out·right *adv. & adj.* • *adv.* /owt-rít/ **1** altogether; entirely (*proved outright*). **2** not gradually, nor by degrees, nor by installments (*bought it outright*). **3** without reservation (*denied the charge outright*). • *adj.* /ówt-rīt/ **1** downright; complete (*resentment turned to outright anger*). **2** undisputed; clear (*the outright winner*).

out·run /owt-rún/ *v.tr.* (**-running**; *past* **-ran**; *past part.* **-run**) **1 a** run faster or farther than. **b** escape from. **2** go beyond (a specified point or limit).

out·sell /owtsél/ *v.tr.* (*past* and *past part.* **-sold**) **1** sell more than. **2** be sold in greater quantities than.

out·set /ówtset/ *n.* the start; the beginning. ▫ **at** (or **from**) **the outset** at or from the beginning.

out·shine /owtshín/ *v.tr.* (*past* and *past part.* **-shone**) shine brighter than; surpass in ability, excellence, etc.

out·shoot /owtshṓot/ *v.tr.* (*past* and *past part.* **-shot**) **1** shoot better or further than (another person). **2** attempt or score more goals, points, etc., than.

out·side *n., adj., adv., & prep.* • *n.* /owtsíd/ **1** the external side or surface (*painted blue on the outside*). **2** the outward aspect of a building, etc. **3** (also *attrib.*) all that is without (*learn about the outside world*). **4** a position on the outer side (*the gate opens from the outside*). **5** *colloq.* the highest computation (*it is a mile at the outside*). • *adj.* /ówtsīd/ **1** of or on or nearer the outside. **2** not of or belonging to some circle or institution (*outside help*). **3** (of a chance, etc.) remote. **4** (of an estimate, etc.) the greatest or highest possible (*the outside price*). **5** *Baseball* (of a pitched ball) missing the strike zone by passing home plate on the side away from the batter. • *adv.* /owtsíd/ **1** on or to the outside. **2** not within or enclosed or included. **3** *sl.* not in prison. • *prep.* /owtsíd/ (also *disp.* foll. by *of*) **1** to or at the exterior of (*meet me outside the post office*). **2** beyond the limits of (*outside the law*). ▫ **at the outside** (of an estimate, etc.) at the most. **get outside of** *sl.* eat or drink. **outside and in** outside and inside. **outside in** = INSIDE OUT.

out·sid·er /owtsídər/ *n.* **1 a** a nonmember of some circle, party, etc. **b** an uninitiated person; a layman. **2** a competitor, applicant, etc., thought to have little chance of success.

out·size /ówtsīz/ *adj.* unusually large.
out·skirts /ówtskərts/ *n.pl.* the outer border or fringe of a town, etc.
out·smart /ówtsmaart/ *v.tr. colloq.* outwit; be cleverer than.
out·spend /ówtspénd/ *v.tr.* (*past* and *past part.* **-spent**) spend more than (one's resources or another person).
out·spo·ken /ówtspṓkən/ *adj.* frank in stating one's opinions. ▫▫ **out·spo·ken·ly** *adv.* **out·spo·ken·ness** *n.*
out·spread /ówtspréd/ *adj.* & *v.* • *adj.* spread out; fully extended or expanded. • *v.tr.* & *intr.* (*past* and *past part.* **-spread**) spread out; expand.
out·stand·ing /ówtstánding/ *adj.* **1 a** conspicuous; eminent, esp. because of excellence. **b** (usu. foll. by *at*, *in*) remarkable in (a specified field). **2** (esp. of a debt) not yet settled (*$200 still outstanding*). ▫▫ **out·stand·ing·ly** *adv.*
out·sta·tion /ówtstayshən/ *n.* a branch of a business in a remote area.
out·stay /ówtstáy/ *v.tr.* **1** stay beyond the limit of (one's welcome). **2** stay or endure longer than (another person, etc.).
out·step /ówtstép/ *v.tr.* (**-stepped, -stepping**) step outside or beyond.
out·stretch /ówtstréch/ *v.tr.* **1** (usu. as **outstretched** *adj.*) reach out or stretch out (esp. one's hands or arms). **2** reach or stretch further than.
out·strip /ówtstríp/ *v.tr.* (**-stripped, -stripping**) **1** pass in running, etc. **2** surpass in competition or relative progress or ability.
out·take /ówt-tayk/ *n.* a length of film or tape rejected in editing.
out·vote /ówtvṓt/ *v.tr.* defeat by a majority of votes.
out·ward /ówt-wərd/ *adj., adv.,* & *n.* • *adj.* **1** situated on or directed toward the outside. **2** going out (*on the outward voyage*). **3** external; apparent; superficial (*in all outward respects*). • *adv.* (also **out·wards**) in an outward direction. • *n.* the outward appearance of something. ▫▫ **out·ward·ly** *adv.*
out·wash /ówt-wosh, –wawsh/ *n.* the material carried from a glacier by meltwater and deposited beyond the moraine.
out·weigh /ówt-wáy/ *v.tr.* exceed in weight, value, importance, or influence.
out·wit /ówt-wít/ *v.tr.* (**-witted, -witting**) be too clever or crafty for.
ou·zo /óozō/ *n.* (*pl.* **-zos**) a Greek anise-flavored liqueur.
o·va *pl.* of OVUM.
o·val /ṓvəl/ *adj.* & *n.* • *adj.* **1** egg-shaped; ellipsoidal. **2** having the outline of an egg. • *n.* **1** an egg-shaped or elliptical closed curve. **2** any object with an oval outline.
O·val Of·fice *n.* the office of the US president in the White House.
o·va·ry /ṓvəree/ *n.* (*pl.* **-ries**) **1** each of the female reproductive organs in which ova are produced. **2** the hollow base of the carpel of a flower, containing one or more ovules. ▫▫ **o·var·i·an** /ōváireeən/ *adj.* **o·var·i·ec·to·my** /–ree-éktəmee/ *n.* (*pl.* **-mies**) (in sense 1). **o·var·i·ot·o·my** /–reeótəmee/ *n.* (*pl.* **-mies**) (in sense 1). **o·va·ri·tis** /–rítis/ *n.* (in sense 1).
o·vate /ṓvayt/ *adj. Biol.* egg-shaped as a solid or in outline; oval.
o·va·tion /ōváyshən/ *n.* an enthusiastic reception, esp. spontaneous and sustained applause. ▫▫ **o·va·tion·al** *adj.*
ov·en /úvən/ *n.* **1** an enclosed compartment of brick, stone, or metal for cooking food. **2** a chamber for heating or drying.
ov·en·proof /úvənproof/ *adj.* suitable for use in an oven; heat-resistant.
ov·en·ware /úvənwair/ *n.* dishes that can be used for cooking food in the oven.
o·ver /ṓvər/ *adv., prep.,* & *adj.* • *adv.* expressing movement or position or state above or beyond something stated or implied: **1** outward and downward from a brink or from any erect position (*knocked the man over*). **2** so as to cover or touch a whole surface (*paint it over*). **3** so as to produce a fold, or reverse a position. **4 a** across a street or other space (*decided to cross over*). **b** for a visit, etc. (*invited them over last night*). **5** with transference or change from one hand or part to another (*handed them over*). **6** with motion above something (*climb over*). **7** from beginning to end with repetition or detailed concentration (*think it over*). **8** in excess (*left over*). **9** for a later time (*hold it over*). **10** at an end (*the crisis is over*). **11** (in full **over to you**) (as *int.*) (in radio conversations, etc.) said to indicate that it is the other person's turn to speak. • *prep.* **1** above, in, or to a position higher than. **2** out and down from (*fell over the cliff*). **3** so as to cover (*a hat over his eyes*). **4** above and across (*a bridge over the Hudson*). **5** concerning; as a result of; while occupied with (*laughed over a good joke*). **6 a** in superiority of; in charge of (*a victory over the enemy*). **b** in preference to. **7** divided by. **8 a** throughout; covering (*a blush spread over his face*). **b** so as to deal with completely (*went over the plans*). **9 a** for the duration of (*stay over Saturday night*). **b** at any point during the course of (*I'll do it over the weekend*). **10** more than (*bids of over $50*). **11** transmitted by (*heard it over the radio*). **12** in comparison with (*gained 20% over last year*). **13** having recovered from (*am now over my cold*). • *adj.* **1** upper; outer. **2** superior. **3** extra. ▫ **begin** (or **start**, etc.) **over** begin again. **get it over with** do or undergo something unpleasant, etc., so as to be rid of it. **over and above** in addition to (*$100 over and above the asking price*). **over and over** so that the same thing comes up again and again.

---

over Old English *ofer*, of Germanic origin; related to Dutch *over* and German *über*, from an Indo-European word (originally a comparative of the word element represented by *-ove* in *above*) that is also the base of Latin *super* and Greek *huper*.

---

o·ver·a·bun·dant /ṓvərəbúndənt/ *adj.* in excessive quantity. ▫▫ **o·ver·a·bun·dance** *n.* **o·ver·a·bun·dant·ly** *adv.*
o·ver·a·chieve /ṓvərəchéev/ *v.* **1** *intr.* do more than might be expected (esp. scholastically). **2** *tr.* achieve more than (an expected goal or objective, etc.). ▫▫ **o·ver·a·chieve·ment** *n.* **o·ver·a·chiev·er** *n.*
o·ver·act /ṓvərákt/ *v.tr.* & *intr.* act in an exaggerated manner.
o·ver·ac·tive /ṓvəráktiv/ *adj.* excessively active. ▫▫ **o·ver·ac·tiv·i·ty** /–tívitee/ *n.*
o·ver·all *adj., adv.,* & *n.* • *adj.* /ṓvərawl/ **1** from end to end (*overall length*). **2** inclusive of all (*overall cost*). • *adv.* /ṓvəráwl/ taken as a whole (*overall, the performance was excellent*). • *n.* /ṓvərawl/ (in *pl.*) protective trousers, dungarees, usually with a bib, worn by workmen, etc. ▫▫ **o·ver·alled** /ṓvərawld/ *adj.*
o·ver·arch /ṓvəraarch/ *v.tr.* form an arch over.
o·ver·arch·ing /ṓvəraarching/ *adj.* **1** forming an arch. **2** dominating.
o·ver·arm /ṓvəraarm/ *adj.* & *adv.* **1** thrown with the hand above the shoulder (*an overarm tennis serve*). **2** *Swimming* with one or both arms lifted out of the water during a stroke.
o·ver·awe /ṓvər-áw/ *v.tr.* **1** restrain by awe. **2** keep in awe.
o·ver·bal·ance /ṓvərbáləns/ *v.* **1** *tr.* outweigh. **2** *intr.* fall over; capsize.
o·ver·bear /ṓvərbáir/ *v.tr.* (*past* **-bore**; *past part.* **-borne**)

1 upset by force or emotional pressure. **2** put down or repress by power or authority.

o·ver·bear·ing /ṓvərbéring/ *adj.* **1** domineering; masterful. **2** overpowerful. ▫▫ **o·ver·bear·ing·ly** *adv.* **o·ver·bear·ing·ness** *n.*

o·ver·bid *v. & n.* •*v.tr.* /ṓvərbíd/ (**-bidding**; *past* and *past part.* **-bid**) **1** make a higher bid than. **2** (also *absol.*) *Bridge* **a** bid more on (one's hand) than warranted. **b** overcall. •*n.* /ṓvərbid/ a bid that is higher than another, or higher than is justified. ▫▫ **o·ver·bid·der** *n.*

o·ver·bite /ṓvərbīt/ *n.* a condition in which the teeth of the upper jaw project forward over those of the lower jaw.

o·ver·blouse /ṓvərblows, –blowz/ *n.* a garment like a blouse, but worn without tucking it into a skirt or slacks.

o·ver·blown /ṓvərblṓn/ *adj.* **1** excessively inflated or pretentious. **2** (of a flower or a woman's beauty, etc.) past its prime.

o·ver·board /ṓvərbáwrd/ *adv.* from a ship into the water (*fall overboard*). ▫ **go overboard 1** be highly enthusiastic. **2** behave immoderately. **throw overboard** discard.

o·ver·bur·den /ṓvərbə́rd'n/ *v.tr.* burden (a person, thing, etc.) to excess. ▫▫ **o·ver·bur·den·some** *adj.*

o·ver·came *past* of OVERCOME.

o·ver·care·ful /ṓvərkáirfŏŏl/ *adj.* excessively careful. ▫▫ **o·ver·care·ful·ly** *adv.*

o·ver·cast /ṓvərkást/ *adj. & v.* •*adj.* **1** covered with cloud. **2** (in sewing) edged with stitching to prevent fraying. •*v.tr.* (*past* and *past part.* **-cast**) **1** cover (the sky, etc.) with clouds or darkness. **2** stitch over to prevent fraying.

o·ver·cau·tious /ṓvərkáwshəs/ *adj.* excessively cautious. ▫▫ **o·ver·cau·tion** *n.* **o·ver·cau·tious·ly** *adv.* **o·ver·cau·tious·ness** *n.*

o·ver·charge /ṓvərchaárj/ *v.tr.* **1 a** charge too high a price to (a person) for (a thing). **b** charge (a specified sum) beyond the right price. **2** put too much charge into (a battery, etc.).

o·ver·coat /ṓvərkōt/ *n.* a heavy coat, esp. one worn over indoor clothes.

o·ver·come /ṓvərkúm/ *v.* (*past* **-came**; *past part.* **-come**) **1** *tr.* prevail over; conquer. **2** *tr.* (as **overcome** *adj.*) **a** exhausted; made helpless. **b** (usu. foll. by *with, by*) affected by (emotion, etc.). **3** *intr.* be victorious.

o·ver·com·pen·sate /ṓvərkómpensayt/ *v.* **1** *tr.* (usu. foll. by *for*) compensate excessively for (something). **2** *intr. Psychol.* strive for power, etc., in an exaggerated way, esp. to make amends for a grievance, handicap, etc. ▫▫ **o·ver·com·pen·sa·tion** /–áyshən/ *n.* **o·ver·com·pen·sa·to·ry** /–kəmpénsitawree/ *adj.*

o·ver·con·fi·dent /ṓvərkónfidənt/ *adj.* excessively confident. ▫▫ **o·ver·con·fi·dence** *n.* **o·ver·con·fi·dent·ly** *adv.*

o·ver·cook /ṓvərkŏŏk/ *v.tr.* cook too much or for too long. ▫▫ **o·ver·cooked** *adj.*

o·ver·crowd /ṓvərkrówd/ *v.tr.* fill (a space, object, etc.) beyond what is usual or comfortable. ▫▫ **o·ver·crowd·ing** *n.*

o·ver·do /ṓvərdṓō/ *v.tr.* (*3rd sing. present* **-does**; *past* **-did**; *past part.* **-done**) **1** carry to excess (*I think you overdid the sarcasm*). **2** (esp. as **overdone** *adj.*) overcook. ▫ **overdo it** (or **things**) exhaust oneself.

o·ver·dose /ṓvərdōs/ *n. & v.* •*n.* an excessive dose (of a drug, etc.). •*v.* **1** *tr.* give an excessive dose of (a drug, etc.) to (a person). **2** *intr.* take an excessive dose of a drug. ▫▫ **o·ver·dos·age** /ṓvərdṓsij/ *n.*

o·ver·draft /ṓvərdraft/ *n.* **1** a deficit in a bank account caused by drawing more money than is credited to it. **2** the amount of this.

o·ver·draw /ṓvərdráw/ *v.* (*past* **-drew**; *past part.* **-drawn**) **1** *tr.* **a** draw a sum of money in excess of the amount credited to (one's bank account). **b** (as **overdrawn** *adj.*) having overdrawn one's account. **2** *intr.* overdraw one's account.

o·ver·drive /ṓvərdrīv/ *n.* **1 a** a mechanism in a motor vehicle providing a gear ratio higher than that of the usual gear. **b** an additional speed-increasing gear. **2** (usu. prec. by *in, into*) a state of high or excessive activity.

o·ver·due /ṓvərdṓō, –dyṓō/ *adj.* **1** past the time when due or ready. **2** not yet paid, arrived, born, etc., although after the expected time.

o·ver·ea·ger /ṓvərēégər/ *adj.* excessively eager. ▫▫ **o·ver·ea·ger·ly** *adv.* **o·ver·ea·ger·ness** *n.*

o·ver·eat /ṓvərēét/ *v.intr. & refl.* (*past* **-ate**; *past part.* **-eaten**) eat too much.

o·ver·es·ti·mate *v. & n.* •*v.tr.* (also *absol.*) /ṓvəréstimayt/ form too high an estimate of (a person, ability, cost, etc.). •*n.* /ṓvəréstimit/ too high an estimate. ▫▫ **o·ver·es·ti·ma·tion** /–áyshən/ *n.*

o·ver·ex·cite /ṓvəriksít/ *v.tr.* excite excessively. ▫▫ **o·ver·ex·cite·ment** *n.*

o·ver·ex·ert /ṓvərigzə́rt/ *v.tr. & refl.* exert too much. ▫▫ **o·ver·ex·er·tion** /–zə́rshən/ *n.*

o·ver·ex·pose /ṓvərikspṓz/ *v.tr.* (also *absol.*) **1** expose too much, esp. to the public eye. **2** *Photog.* expose (film) for too long a time. ▫▫ **o·ver·ex·po·sure** /–spṓzhər/ *n.*

o·ver·ex·tend /ṓvərikstend/ *v.tr.* **1** extend (a thing) too far. **2** (also *refl.*) take on (oneself) or impose on (another person) an excessive burden of work.

o·ver·fill /ṓvərfíl/ *v.tr. & intr.* fill to excess or to overflowing.

o·ver·flow *v. & n.* •*v.* /ṓvərflṓ/ **1** *tr.* **a** flow over (the brim, etc.). **b** flow over the brim or limits of. **2** *intr.* **a** (of a receptacle, etc.) be so full that the contents overflow it. **b** (of contents) overflow a container. **3** *tr.* (of a crowd, etc.) extend beyond the limits of (a room, etc.). **4** *tr.* flood (a surface or area). **5** *intr.* (foll. by *with*) be full of. **6** *intr.* (of kindness, a harvest, etc.) be very abundant. •*n.* /ṓvərflō/ (also *attrib.*) **1** what overflows or is superfluous (*mop up the overflow*). **2** an instance of overflowing. **3** (esp. in a bath or sink) an outlet for excess water, etc. **4** *Computing* the generation of a number having more digits than the assigned location.

o·ver·fly /ṓvərflí/ *v.tr.* (**-flies**; *past* **-flew**; *past part.* **-flown**) fly over or beyond (a place or territory). ▫▫ **o·ver·flight** /ṓvərflīt/ *n.*

o·ver·fond /ṓvərfónd/ *adj.* (often foll. by *of*) having too great an affection or liking (for a person or thing). ▫▫ **o·ver·fond·ly** *adv.* **o·ver·fond·ness** *n.*

o·ver·full /ṓvərfŏŏl/ *adj.* filled excessively or to overflowing.

o·ver·gen·er·al·ize /ṓvərjénərəlīz/ *v.* **1** *intr.* draw general conclusions from inadequate data, etc. **2** *intr.* argue more widely than is justified by the available evidence, etc. **3** *tr.* draw an overgeneral conclusion from (data, etc.). ▫▫ **o·ver·gen·er·al·i·za·tion** *n.*

o·ver·ground /ṓvərgrownd/ *adj.* **1** raised above the ground. **2** not underground.

o·ver·grow /ṓvərgrṓ/ *v.tr.* (*past* **-grew**; *past part.* **-grown**) **1** (as **overgrown** *adj.* /ṓvərgrṓn/) **a** abnormally large (*an overgrown eggplant*). **b** grown over with vegetation (*an overgrown pond*). **2** grow over, esp. so as to choke (*brambles have overgrown the pathway*). ▫▫ **o·ver·growth** *n.*

o·ver·hand /ṓvərhand/ *adj. & adv.* (in tennis, baseball, etc.) thrown or played with the hand above the shoulder; overarm.

o•ver•hang *v. & n.* •*v.* /ṓvərháng/ (*past* and *past part.* **-hung**) **1** *tr. & intr.* hang over. **2** *tr.* menace; threaten. •*n.* /ṓvərhang/ **1** the overhanging part of a structure or rock formation. **2** the amount by which this projects.

o•ver•haul *v. & n.* •*v.tr.* /ṓvərháwl/ **1 a** take to pieces in order to examine. **b** examine the condition of (and repair if necessary). **2** overtake. •*n.* /ṓvərhawl/ a thorough examination, with repairs if necessary.

o•ver•head *adv., adj., & n.* •*adv.* /ṓvərhéd/ **1** above one's head. **2** in the sky or on the floor above. •*adj.* /ṓvərhed/ **1** (of a driving mechanism, etc.) above the object driven. **2** (of expenses) arising from general operating costs, as distinct from particular business transactions. •*n.* /ṓvərhed/ overhead expenses.

o•ver•head pro•jec•tor *n.* a device that projects an enlarged image of a transparency onto a surface above and behind the user.

o•ver•hear /ṓvərhéer/ *v.tr.* (*past* and *past part.* **-heard**) (also *absol.*) hear as an eavesdropper or as an unperceived or unintentional listener.

o•ver•heat /ṓvərhéet/ *v.* **1** *tr. & intr.* make or become too hot. **2** *tr.* (as **overheated** *adj.*) too passionate about a matter.

o•ver•in•dulge /ṓvərindúlj/ *v.tr. & intr.* indulge to excess. □□ **o•ver•in•dul•gence** *n.* **o•ver•in•dul•gent** *adj.*

o•ver•in•sure /ṓvərinshóor/ *v.tr.* insure (property, etc.) for more than its real value; insure excessively. □□ **o•ver•in•sur•ance** *n.*

o•ver•joyed /ṓvərjóyd/ *adj.* (often foll. by *at, to hear,* etc.) filled with great joy.

o•ver•kill /ṓvərkil/ *n.* **1** the amount by which capacity for destruction exceeds what is necessary for victory or annihilation. **2** excess; excessive behavior.

o•ver•land /ṓvərland, –lənd/ *adj. & adv.* (also /ṓvərlánd/) **1** by land. **2** not by sea.

o•ver•lap *v. & n.* •*v.* /ṓvərláp/ (**-lapped, -lapping**) **1** *tr.* (of part of an object) partly cover (another object). **2** *tr.* cover and extend beyond. **3** *intr.* (of two things) partly coincide. •*n.* /ṓvərlap/ **1** an instance of overlapping. **2** the amount of this.

o•ver•lay *v. & n.* •*v.tr.* /ṓvərláy/ (*past* and *past part.* **-laid**) **1** lay over. **2** (foll. by *with*) cover the surface of (a thing) with (a coating, etc.). **3** overlie. •*n.* /ṓvərlay/ a thing laid over another.

o•ver•leaf /ṓvərléef/ *adv.* on the other side of the leaf (of a book).

o•ver•lie /ṓvərlī́/ *v.tr.* (**-lying**; *past* **-lay**; *past part.* **-lain**) **1** lie on top of. **2** smother (a child, etc.) by lying on top.

o•ver•load *v. & n.* •*v.tr.* /ṓvərlṓd/ force (a person, thing, etc.) beyond normal or reasonable capacity. •*n.* /ṓvərlōd/ an excessive quantity.

o•ver•look *v.tr.* /ṓvərlóok/ **1** ignore or condone (an offense, etc.). **2** be higher than. **3** supervise; oversee. **4** bewitch with the evil eye. □□ **o•ver•look•er** *n.*

o•ver•lord /ṓvərlawrd/ *n.* a supreme lord. □□ **o•ver•lord•ship** *n.*

o•ver•ly /ṓvərlee/ *adv.* excessively; too.

o•ver•much /ṓvərmúch/ *adv. & adj.* •*adv.* excessively. •*adj.* excessive.

o•ver•night *adv. & adj.* •*adv.* /ṓvərnī́t/ **1** for the duration of a night (*stay overnight*). **2** during the course of a night. **3** suddenly (*the situation changed overnight*). •*adj.* /ṓvərnīt/ **1** for use overnight (*an overnight bag*). **2** done, etc., overnight (*an overnight stop*).

o•ver•night•er /ṓvərnī́tər/ *n.* **1** a person who stops at a place overnight. **2** an overnight bag.

o•ver•paid *past* and *past part.* of OVERPAY.

o•ver•par•tic•u•lar /ṓvərpərtíkyələr, –pətík–/ *adj.* excessively particular or fussy.

o•ver•pass /ṓvərpas/ *n.* a road or railroad line that passes over another by means of a bridge.

o•ver•pay /ṓvərpáy/ *v.tr.* (*past* and *past part.* **-paid**) recompense (a person, service, etc.) too highly. □□ **o•ver•pay•ment** *n.*

o•ver•play /ṓvərpláy/ *v.tr.* give undue importance to. □ **overplay one's hand 1** be unduly optimistic about one's capabilities. **2** spoil a good case by exaggerating its value.

o•ver•pop•u•lat•ed /ṓvərpópyəlaytid/ *adj.* having too large a population. □□ **o•ver•pop•u•la•tion** /–láyshən/ *n.*

o•ver•pow•er /ṓvərpówr/ *v.tr.* **1** reduce to submission. **2** make (a thing) ineffective by greater intensity. **3** (of heat, emotion, etc.) overwhelm. □□ **o•ver•pow•er•ing** *adj.* **o•ver•pow•er•ing•ly** *adv.*

o•ver•price /ṓvərprī́s/ *v.tr.* price (a thing) too highly.

o•ver•print *v. & n.* •*v.tr.* /ṓvərprínt/ **1** print further matter on (a surface already printed, esp. a postage stamp). **2** print (further matter) in this way. •*n.* /ṓvərprint/ the words, etc., overprinted.

o•ver•pro•duce /ṓvərprədóos, –dyóos/ *v.tr.* (usu. *absol.*) **1** produce more of (a commodity) than is wanted. **2** produce to an excessive degree. □□ **o•ver•pro•duc•tion** /–dúkshən/ *n.*

o•ver•pro•tec•tive /ṓvərprətéktiv/ *adj.* excessively protective.

o•ver•qual•i•fied /ṓvərkwólifīd/ *adj.* too highly qualified for a particular job.

o•ver•rate /ṓvəráyt/ *v.tr.* assess too highly.

o•ver•reach /ṓvəréech/ *v.tr.* circumvent; outwit. □ **overreach oneself 1** strain oneself by reaching too far. **2** defeat one's object by going too far.

o•ver•re•act /ṓvəreeákt/ *v.intr.* respond more forcibly, etc., than is justified. □□ **o•ver•re•ac•tion** /–ákshən/ *n.*

o•ver•re•fine /ṓvərifī́n/ *v.tr.* (also *absol.*) **1** refine too much. **2** make too subtle distinctions in (an argument, etc.).

o•ver•ride *v. & n.* •*v.tr.* /ṓvərī́d/ (*past* **-rode**; *past part.* **-ridden**) **1** (often as **overriding** *adj.*) have or claim precedence over (*an overriding consideration*). **2 a** intervene and make ineffective. **b** interrupt the action of (an automatic device), esp. to take manual control. **3 a** trample down or underfoot. **b** supersede arrogantly. •*n.* /ṓvərīd/ **1** the action of suspending an automatic function. **2** a device for this.

o•ver•ripe /ṓvərī́p/ *adj.* (esp. of fruit, etc.) past its best; excessively ripe.

o•ver•rule /ṓvəróol/ *v.tr.* **1** set aside (a decision, etc.) by exercising a superior authority. **2** annul a decision by or reject a proposal of (a person) in this way.

o•ver•run *v. & n.* •*v.tr.* /ṓvərún/ (**-running**; *past* **-ran**; *past part.* **-run**) **1** (of pests, weeds, etc.) swarm or spread over. **2** conquer or ravage (territory) by force. **3** (of time, expenditure, etc.) exceed (a fixed limit). **4** *Printing* carry over (a word, etc.) to the next line or page. •*n.* /ṓvərun/ **1** an instance of overrunning. **2** the amount of this.

o•ver•scru•pu•lous /ṓvərskróopyələs/ *adj.* excessively particular.

o•ver•seas *adv. & adj.* •*adv.* /ṓvərséez/ abroad. •*adj.* /ṓvərseez/ foreign; across or beyond the sea.

o•ver•see /ṓvərsée/ *v.tr.* (**-sees**; *past* **-saw**; *past part.* **-seen**) officially supervise. □□ **o•ver•seer** *n.*

o•ver•sexed /ṓvərsékst/ *adj.* having unusually strong sexual desires.

o•ver•shad•ow /ṓvərshádō/ *v.tr.* **1** appear much more prominent or important than. **2** cast into the shade.

o•ver•shoe /ṓvərshoo/ *n.* a shoe of rubber, etc., worn over another as protection from wet, cold, etc.

o•ver•shoot *v. & n.* •*v.tr.* /ṓvərshóot/ (*past* and *past part.* **-shot**) **1** pass or send beyond (a target or limit). **2** (of an aircraft) fly beyond (the runway) when landing or taking off. •*n.* /ṓvərshoot/ **1** the act of overshooting. **2** the amount of this. □ **overshoot the mark** go beyond what is intended or proper.

o·ver·sight /óvərsīt/ *n.* **1** a failure to notice something. **2** an inadvertent mistake. **3** supervision.

o·ver·sim·pli·fy /óvərsímplifī/ *v.tr.* (**-fies, -fied**) (also *absol.*) distort (a problem, etc.) by stating it in too simple terms. □□ **o·ver·sim·pli·fi·ca·tion** *n.*

o·ver·size /óvərsīz/ *adj.* (also **-sized** /–sīzd/) of more than the usual size.

o·ver·sleep /óvərsleép/ *v.intr. & refl.* (*past* and *past part.* **-slept**) continue sleeping beyond the intended time of waking.

o·ver·spe·cial·ize /óvərspéshəlīz/ *v.intr.* concentrate too much on one aspect or area. □□ **o·ver·spe·cial·i·za·tion** *n.*

o·ver·spend /óvərspénd/ *v.* (*past* and *past part.* **-spent**) **1** *intr. & refl.* spend too much. **2** *tr.* spend more than (a specified amount).

o·ver·spill /óvərspil/ *n.* what is spilled over or overflows.

o·ver·state /óvərstáyt/ *v.tr.* **1** state (esp. a case or argument) too strongly. **2** exaggerate. □□ **o·ver·state·ment** *n.*

o·ver·stay /óvərstáy/ *v.tr.* stay longer than (one's welcome, a time limit, etc.).

o·ver·steer /óvərsteér/ *v. & n.* • *v.intr.* (of a motor vehicle) have a tendency to turn more sharply than was intended. • *n.* this tendency.

o·ver·step /óvərstép/ *v.tr.* (**-stepped, -stepping**) **1** pass beyond (a boundary or mark). **2** violate (certain standards of behavior, etc.).

o·ver·stock /óvərstók/ *v. & n.* • *v.tr.* stock excessively. • *n.* stock that is in excess of need or demand.

o·ver·stretch /óvərstréch/ *v.tr.* **1** stretch too much. **2** (esp. as **overstretched** *adj.*) make excessive demands on (resources, a person, etc.).

o·ver·strung /óvərstrúng/ *adj.* (of a person, disposition, etc.) intensely strained; highly strung.

o·ver·stuff /óvərstúf/ *v.tr.* **1** stuff more than is necessary. **2** (as **overstuffed** *adj.*) (of furniture) made soft and comfortable by thick upholstery.

o·ver·sub·scribe /óvərsəbskríb/ *v.tr.* (usu. as **oversubscribed** *adj.*) subscribe for more than the amount available of (*the offer was oversubscribed*).

o·ver·sup·ply /óvərsəplī/ *v. & n.* • *v.tr.* (**-plies, -plied**) supply with too much. • *n.* an excessive supply.

o·vert /ōvórt, óvərt/ *adj.* done openly. □□ **o·vert·ly** *adv.* **o·vert·ness** *n.*

o·ver·take /óvərtáyk/ *v.tr.* (*past* **-took**; *past part.* **-taken**) (of a misfortune, etc.) come suddenly upon.

o·ver·tax /óvərtáks/ *v.tr.* **1** make excessive demands on (a person's strength, etc.). **2** tax too heavily.

o·ver-the-coun·ter *adj.* (of medicine) sold without a prescription.

o·ver-the-top *adj. Brit. colloq.* (esp. of behavior, etc.) outrageous; excessive.

o·ver·throw *v. & n.* • *v.tr.* /óvərthró/ (*past* **-threw**; *past part.* **-thrown**) **1** remove forcibly from power. **2** put an end to (an institution, etc.). **3** conquer; overcome. **4** knock down; upset. **5** *Baseball* **a** (of a fielder) throw beyond the intended place. **b** (of a pitcher) throw too vigorously. • *n.* /óvərthrō/ a defeat or downfall.

o·ver·time /óvərtīm/ *n. & adv.* • *n.* **1** the time during which a person works at a job in addition to the regular hours. **2** payment for this. • *adv.* in addition to regular hours.

o·ver·tire /óvərtír/ *v.tr. & refl.* exhaust or wear out (esp. an invalid, etc.).

o·ver·tone /óvərtōn/ *n.* **1** *Mus.* any of the tones above the lowest in a harmonic series. **2** a subtle or elusive quality or implication (*sinister overtones*).

o·ver·train /óvərtráyn/ *v.tr. & intr.* subject to or undergo too much (esp. athletic) training with a consequent loss of proficiency.

o·ver·ture /óvərchər, –chŏŏr/ *n.* **1** an orchestral piece opening an opera, etc. **2** a one-movement composition in this style. **3** (usu. in *pl.*) **a** an opening of negotiations. **b** a formal proposal or offer.

o·ver·turn *v. & n.* • *v.* /óvərtórn/ **1** *tr.* cause to turn over. **2** *tr.* reverse; invalidate. **3** *intr.* turn over. • *n.* /óvərtərn/ a subversion; an act of upsetting.

o·ver·use *v. & n.* • *v.tr.* /óvəryóoz/ use too much. • *n.* /óvəryóos/ excessive use.

o·ver·val·ue /óvərvályōō/ *v.tr.* (**-values, -valued, -valuing**) value too highly.

o·ver·view /óvərvyōō/ *n.* a general survey.

o·ver·ween·ing /óvərweéning/ *adj.* arrogant; presumptuous; conceited; self-confident. □□ **o·ver·ween·ing·ly** *adv.*

o·ver·weight *adj., n., & v.* • *adj.* /óvərwáyt/ beyond an allowed or suitable weight. • *n.* /óvərwayt/ excessive or extra weight; preponderance. • *v.tr.* /óvərwáyt/ (usu. foll. by *with*) load unduly.

o·ver·whelm /óvərhwélm, –wélm/ *v.tr.* **1** overpower with emotion. **2** (usu. foll. by *with*) overpower with an excess of business, etc. **3** bring to sudden ruin or destruction. **4** submerge utterly.

o·ver·whelm·ing /óvərhwélming, –wél–/ *adj.* irresistible by force of numbers, influence, amount, etc. □□ **o·ver·whelm·ing·ly** *adv.*

o·ver·wind /óvərwínd/ *v.tr.* (*past* and *past part.* **-wound**) wind (a mechanism, esp. a watch) beyond the proper stopping point.

o·ver·win·ter /óvərwíntər/ *v.* **1** *intr.* (usu. foll. by *at, in*) spend the winter. **2** *intr.* (of insects, fungi, etc.) live through the winter. **3** *tr.* keep (animals, plants, etc.) alive through the winter.

o·ver·work /óvərwórk/ *v. & n.* • *v.* **1** *intr.* work too hard. **2** *tr.* cause (another person) to work too hard. **3** *tr.* weary or exhaust with too much work. **4** *tr.* make excessive use of. • *n.* excessive work.

o·ver·write /óvərít/ *v.* (*past* **-wrote**; *past part.* **-written**) **1** *tr.* write on top of (other writing). **2** *tr. Computing* destroy (data) in (a file, etc.) by entering new data. **3** *intr.* (esp. as **overwritten** *adj.*) write too elaborately.

o·ver·wrought /óvəráwt/ *adj.* **1** overexcited; nervous; distraught. **2** overdone.

ovi- /óvee/ *comb. form* egg; ovum.

o·vi·duct /óvidukt/ *n.* the tube through which an ovum passes from the ovary. □□ **o·vi·duc·tal** /–dúktəl/ *adj.*

o·vi·form /óvifawrm/ *adj.* egg-shaped.

o·vine /óvīn/ *adj.* of or like sheep.

o·vip·a·rous /ōvípərəs/ *adj. Zool.* producing young by means of eggs expelled from the body before they are hatched. □□ **o·vi·par·i·ty** /–páritee/ *n.* **o·vip·a·rous·ly** *adv.*

o·void /óvoyd/ *adj. & n.* • *adj.* **1** (of a solid or of a surface) egg-shaped. **2** oval, with one end more pointed than the other. • *n.* an ovoid body or surface.

ov·u·late /óvyəlayt, óvyə–/ *v.intr.* produce ova or ovules, or discharge them from the ovary. □□ **ov·u·la·tion** /–láyshən/ *n.* **ov·u·la·to·ry** /–lətáwree/ *adj.*

ov·ule /áavyōōl, óvyōōl/ *n.* the part of the ovary of seed plants that contains the germ cell; an unfertilized seed. □□ **ov·u·lar** *adj.*

o·vum /óvəm/ *n.* (*pl.* **ova** /óvə/) **1** a mature reproductive cell of female animals, produced by the ovary. **2** the egg cell of plants.

ow /ow/ *int.* expressing sudden pain.

owe /ō/ *v.tr.* **1 a** be under obligation (to a person, etc.) to pay or repay (money, etc.). **b** (*absol.*, usu. foll. by *for*) be in debt (*still owe for my car*). **2** (often foll. by *to*) be under obligation to render (*owe grateful thanks to*).

3 (usu. foll. by *to*) be indebted to a person or thing for (*we owe to Newton the principle of gravitation*). ▫ **owe it to oneself** (often foll. by *to* + infin.) need (to do) something to protect one's own interests.

ow·ing /ṓ-ing/ *predic.adj.* **1** yet to be paid (*the balance owing*). **2** (foll. by *to*) **a** caused by. **b** (as *prep.*) because of (*owing to bad weather*).

owl /owl/ *n.* **1** any nocturnal bird of prey of the order Strigiformes, with large eyes and a hooked beak. **2** *colloq.* a person compared to an owl, esp. in looking wise. ▫▫ **owl·ish** *adj.* **owl·ish·ly** *adv.* **owl·like** *adj.*

owl·et /ówlit/ *n.* a small or young owl.

own /ōn/ *adj. & v.* • *adj.* (prec. by possessive) **1 a** belonging to oneself or itself (*saw it with my own eyes*). **b** individual; particular (*a charm all of its own*). **2** used to emphasize identity rather than possession (*cooks his own meals*). **3** (*absol.*) **a** private property (*is it your own?*). **b** kindred (*among my own*). • *v.* **1** *tr.* have as property. **2 a** *tr.* confess (*own their faults*). **b** *intr.* (foll. by *to*) confess to (*owned to a prejudice*). **3** *tr.* acknowledge paternity, authorship, or possession of. ▫ **come into one's own 1** receive one's due. **2** achieve recognition. **get one's own back** (often foll. by *on*) *colloq.* get revenge. **hold one's own** maintain one's position. **of one's own** belonging to oneself alone. **on one's own 1** alone. **2** independently; without help. **own up** (often foll. by *to*) confess frankly. ▫▫ **-owned** *adj.* (in *comb.*).

own·er /ṓnər/ *n.* **1** a person who owns something. **2** *sl.* the captain of a ship. ▫▫ **own·er·ship** *n.*

ox /oks/ *n.* (*pl.* **oxen** /óksən/) **1** any bovine animal, esp. a large horned ruminant used for draft, milk, and meat. **2** a castrated male of a domesticated species of cattle, *Bos taurus*.

ox- var. of OXY-.

ox·bow /óksbō/ *n.* **1** a U-shaped collar of an ox yoke. **2 a** a loop formed by a horseshoe bend in a river. **b** a lake formed when the river cuts across the narrow end of the loop.

ox·en *pl.* of ox.

ox·eye /óksī/ *n.* any plant of the genus *Heliopsis*, with dark-centered, daisylike flowers.

ox·ford /óksfərd/ *n.* **1** a low-heeled shoe that laces over the instep. **2** a fabric of cotton or a cotton blend made in a basket weave, used for shirts and sportswear.

ox·i·dant /óksidənt/ *n.* an oxidizing agent. ▫▫ **ox·i·da·tion** /–dáyshən/ *n.*

ox·ide /óksīd/ *n.* a binary compound of oxygen.

ox·i·dize /óksidīz/ *v.tr. & intr.* **1** combine or cause to combine with oxygen. **2** cover (metal) or (of metal) become covered with a coating of oxide; make or become rusty. ▫▫ **ox·i·diz·a·ble** *adj.* **ox·i·di·za·tion** *n.* **ox·i·diz·er** *n.*

ox·tail /ókstayl/ *n.* the tail of an ox, often used in making soup.

oxy- /óksee/ *comb. form* (also **ox-** /oks/) *Chem.* oxygen (*oxyacetylene*).

ox·y·a·cet·y·lene /ókseeəsét'leen/ *adj.* of or using a mixture of oxygen and acetylene, esp. in cutting or welding metals (*oxyacetylene burner*).

ox·y·gen /óksijən/ *n. Chem.* a colorless, tasteless, odorless gaseous element essential to plant and animal life. ¶ Symb.: **O**. ▫▫ **ox·yg·e·nous** /oksíjinəs/ *adj.*

ox·y·gen·ate /óksijənayt/ *v.tr.* supply, treat, or mix with oxygen. ▫▫ **ox·y·gen·a·tion** /–náyshən/ *n.*

ox·y·gen mask *n.* a mask placed over the nose and mouth to supply oxygen for breathing.

ox·y·gen tent *n.* a tentlike enclosure supplying a patient with air rich in oxygen.

ox·y·mo·ron /ókseemáwron/ *n. rhet.* a figure of speech in which apparently contradictory terms appear in conjunction (e.g., *faith unfaithful kept him falsely true*).

ox·y·to·cin /óksitósin/ *n.* **1** a hormone released by the pituitary gland that causes increased contraction of the womb during labor and stimulates the ejection of milk into the ducts of the breasts. **2** a synthetic form of this used to induce labor, etc.

oys·ter /óystər/ *n.* **1** any of various bivalve mollusks of the family Ostreidae or Aviculidae. **2** an oyster-shaped morsel of meat in a fowl's back. **3** something regarded as containing all that one desires (*the world is my oyster*).

oz. *abbr.* ounce(s).

o·zone /ṓzōn/ *n.* **1** *Chem.* a colorless unstable gas with a pungent odor and powerful oxidizing properties. **2** *colloq.* invigorating air at the seaside, etc. ▫▫ **o·zon·ic** /ōzónik/ *adj.* **o·zon·ize** *v.tr.* **o·zon·i·za·tion** *n.* **o·zon·iz·er** *n.*

o·zone hole *n.* an area of the ozone layer in which depletion has occurred.

o·zone lay·er *n.* a layer in the stratosphere that absorbs most of the sun's ultraviolet radiation.

P

P[1] /pee/ *n.* (also **p**) (*pl.* **Ps** or **P's**) the sixteenth letter of the alphabet.

P[2] *abbr.* (also **P.**) (on road signs) parking.

P[3] *symb. Chem.* the element phosphorus.

p *abbr.* (also **p.**) **1** page. **2** piano (softly). **3** *Brit.* penny; pence.

PA *abbr.* **1** Pennsylvania (in official postal use). **2** public address (esp. **PA system**). **3** Press Association.

Pa *symb. Chem.* the element protactinium.

pa /paa/ *n. colloq.* father.

Pab·lum /pábləm/ *n.* **1** *Trademark* a bland cereal food for infants. **2** (**pablum**) simplistic or unimaginative writing, speech, or ideas.

pab·u·lum /pábyələm/ *n.* **1** food; a nourishing substance. **2** insipid or bland ideas, writings, etc.

PAC /pak/ *abbr.* = POLITICAL ACTION COMMITTEE.

pace /pays/ *n. & v.* •*n.* **1 a** a single step in walking or running. **b** the distance covered in this (about 30 in. or 75 cm). **c** the distance between two successive stationary positions of the same foot in walking. **2** speed in walking or running. **3** *Theatr. & Mus.* speed or tempo in theatrical or musical performance (*played with great pace*). **4** a rate of progression. **5 a** a manner of walking or running; a gait. **b** any of various gaits, esp. of a trained horse, etc. (*rode at an ambling pace*). •*v.* **1** *intr.* **a** walk (esp. repeatedly or methodically) with a slow or regular pace (*pacing up and down*). **b** (of a horse) = AMBLE. **2** *tr.* traverse by pacing. **3** *tr.* set the pace for (a rider, runner, etc.). **4** *tr.* (often foll. by *out*) measure (a distance) by pacing. □ **keep pace** (often foll. by *with*) advance at an equal rate (as). **put a person through his** (or **her**) **paces** test a person's qualities in action, etc. **set the pace** determine the speed, esp. by leading. **stand** (or **stay**) **the pace** be able to keep up with others. □□ **paced** *adj.* **pac·er** *n.*

pace·mak·er /páysmaykər/ *n.* **1** a natural or artificial device for stimulating the heart muscle and determining the rate of its contractions. **2** a competitor who sets the pace in a race.

pace·set·ter /páys-setər/ *n.* a leader.

pach·y·derm /pákidərm/ *n.* any thick-skinned mammal, esp. an elephant or rhinoceros. □□ **pach·y·der·ma·tous** /-dérmətəs/ *adj.*

pa·cif·ic /pəsífik/ *adj. & n.* •*adj.* **1** characterized by or tending to peace; tranquil. **2** (**Pacific**) of or adjoining the Pacific. •*n.* (**the Pacific**) the expanse of ocean between N. and S. America to the east and Asia to the west. □□ **pa·cif·i·cal·ly** *adv.*

Pa·cif·ic Time *n.* the standard time used in the Pacific region of Canada and the US.

pac·i·fi·er /pásifīər/ *n.* **1** a person or thing that pacifies. **2** a rubber or plastic nipple for a baby to suck on.

pac·i·fism /pásifizəm/ *n.* the belief that war and violence are morally unjustified and that all disputes can be settled by peaceful means. □□ **pac·i·fist** *n. & adj.*

pac·i·fy /pásifī/ *v.tr.* (**-fies, -fied**) **1** appease (a person, anger, etc.). **2** bring (a country, etc.) to a state of peace. □□ **pa·cif·i·ca·to·ry** *adj.* **pac·i·fi·ca·tion** *n.*

pack[1] /pak/ *n. & v.* •*n.* **1 a** a collection of things wrapped up or tied together for carrying. **b** = BACKPACK. **2** a set of items packaged for use or disposal together. **3** usu. *derog.* a lot or set (of similar things or persons) (*a pack of lies; a pack of thieves*). **4** a set of playing cards. **5 a** a group of hounds esp. for foxhunting. **b** a group of wild animals, esp. wolves, hunting together. **6** an organized group of Cub Scouts or Brownies. •*v.* **1** *tr.* (often foll. by *up*) **a** fill (a suitcase, bag, etc.) with clothes and other items. **b** put (things) together in a bag or suitcase, esp. for traveling. **2** *intr. & tr.* come or put closely together; crowd or cram (*packed a lot into a few hours; passengers packed like sardines*). **3** *tr.* (in *passive*; often foll. by *with*) be filled (with); contain extensively (*the restaurant was packed; the book is packed with information*). **4** *tr.* fill (a hall, theater, etc.) with an audience, etc. **5** *tr.* cover (a thing) with something pressed tightly around. **6** *intr.* be suitable for packing. **7** *tr. colloq.* **a** carry (a gun, etc.). **b** be capable of delivering (a punch) with skill or force. **8** *intr.* (of animals, etc.) form a pack. □ **pack it in** *colloq.* end or stop it. **pack off** send (a person) away, esp. abruptly or promptly. **send packing** *colloq.* dismiss (a person) summarily. □□ **pack·a·ble** *adj.*

pack[2] /pak/ *v.tr.* select (a jury, etc.) or fill (a meeting) so as to secure a decision in one's favor.

pack·age /pákij/ *n. & v.* •*n.* **1 a** a bundle of things packed. **b** a box, parcel, etc., in which things are packed. **2** (in full **package deal**) a set of proposals or items offered or agreed to as a whole. **3** *Computing* a piece of software suitable for various applications rather than one which is custom-built. **4** *colloq.* = PACKAGE TOUR. •*v.tr.* make up into or enclose in a package. □□ **pack·ag·er** *n.*

pack·age store *n.* a retail store selling alcoholic beverages in sealed containers.

pack·ag·ing /pákijing/ *n.* **1** a wrapping or container for goods. **2** the process of packing goods.

pack an·i·mal *n.* an animal used for carrying packs.

pack·er /pákər/ *n.* a person or thing that packs, esp. a dealer who processes and packs food for transportation and sale.

pack·et /pákit/ *n.* a small package.

pack·horse /pák-hawrs/ *n.* a horse for carrying loads.

pack ice *n.* an area of large crowded pieces of floating ice in the sea.

pack·ing /páking/ *n.* **1** the act or process of packing. **2** material used as padding to pack esp. fragile articles.

pack rat *n.* **1** a busy-tailed N. American wood rat that hoards various items in its nest. **2** a person who hoards unneeded things.

pact /pakt/ *n.* an agreement or a treaty.

pad[1] /pad/ *n. & v.* •*n.* **1** a piece of soft material used to reduce friction or jarring, fill out hollows, hold or absorb liquid, etc. **2** a number of sheets of blank paper fastened together at one edge, for writing or drawing on. **3** the fleshy underpart of an animal's foot or of a human finger. **4** a soft guard for the limbs or joints protecting them from injury, esp. in sports. **5** a flat surface for helicopter takeoff or rocket launching. **6** *colloq.* an apartment or bedroom. **7** the floating leaf of a water lily. •*v.tr.* (**padded, padding**) **1** provide with a pad or padding; stuff. **2 a** (foll. by *out*) lengthen or fill out (a book, etc.) with unnecessary material. **b** to increase fraudulently, as an expense account.

pad[2] /pad/ *v. & n.* •*v.* (**padded, padding**) **1** *intr.* walk with a soft dull steady step. **2 a** *tr.* hike along (a road, etc.) on foot. **b** *intr.* travel on foot. •*n.* the sound of soft steady steps.

pad•ded cell *n.* a room with padded walls in a mental hospital.

pad•ding /páding/ *n.* **1** soft material used to pad or stuff with. **2** material laid under a carpet as protection or support.

pad•dle[1] /pád'l/ *n. & v.* •*n.* **1** a short broad-bladed oar used without an oarlock. **2** a paddle-shaped instrument. **3** *Zool.* a fin or flipper. **4** each of the boards fitted around the circumference of a paddle wheel or mill wheel. **5** esp. *Brit.* the action or a period of paddling. •*v.* **1** *intr. & tr.* move on water or propel a boat by means of paddles. **2** *intr. & tr.* row gently. **3** *tr. colloq.* spank. ▫▫ **pad•dler** *n.*

pad•dle[2] /pád'l/ *v. & n.* esp. *Brit.* •*v.intr.* walk barefoot or dabble the feet or hands in shallow water. •*n.* the action or a period of paddling. ▫▫ **pad•dler** *n.*

pad•dle•boat /pád'lbōt/ *n.* a boat propelled by a paddle wheel.

pad•dle wheel *n.* a wheel for propelling a ship, with boards around the circumference so as to press backward against the water.

paddle wheel

pad•dock /pádək/ *n.* **1** a small field, esp. for keeping horses in. **2** an enclosure adjoining a racecourse where horses or cars are assembled before a race. **3** *Austral. & NZ* a field; a plot of land.

pad•dy /pádee/ *n.* (*pl.* **-dies**) **1** a field where rice is grown. **2** rice before threshing or in the husk.

pad•dy wag•on *n. colloq.* a police van for transporting those under arrest.

pad•lock /pádlok/ *n. & v.* •*n.* a detachable lock hanging by a pivoted hook on the object fastened. •*v.tr.* secure with a padlock.

pa•dre /paádray, -dree/ *n.* **1** a clergyman, esp. a priest. **2** a chaplain in any of the armed services.

pae•an /peéən/ *n.* a song of praise or triumph.

pa•el•la /pī-élə, paa-áyaa/ *n.* a Spanish dish of rice, saffron, chicken, seafood, etc., cooked and served in a large shallow pan.

pae•on /peéən/ *n.* a metrical foot of one long syllable and three short syllables in any order. ▫▫ **pae•on•ic** /pee-ónik/ *adj.*

pa•gan /páygən/ *n. & adj.* •*n.* **1** a person not subscribing to any of the main religions of the world. **2** a person following a polytheistic or pantheistic religion. **3** a hedonist. •*adj.* **1 a** of or relating to or associated with pagans. **b** irreligious. **2** identifying divinity or spirituality in nature; pantheistic. ▫▫ **pa•gan•ish** *adj.* **pa•gan•ism** *n.* **pa•gan•ize** *v.tr. & intr.*

page[1] /payj/ *n. & v.* •*n.* **1 a** a leaf of a book, periodical, etc. **b** each side of this. **c** what is written or printed on this. **2 a** an episode that might fill a page in written history, etc.; a record. **b** a memorable event. **3** *Computing* a section of computer memory of specified size, esp. one that can be readily transferred between main and auxiliary memories. •*v.tr.* paginate.

page[2] /payj/ *n. & v.* •*n.* **1** a person employed to run errands, attend to a door, etc. **2** a boy employed as a personal attendant of a bride, etc. **3** *hist.* a boy in training for knighthood and attached to a knight's service. •*v.tr.* **1** (in hotels, airports, etc.) summon by making an announcement or by sending a messenger. **2** summon by means of a pager.

---

page[2] Middle English (in the sense 'youth, male of uncouth manners'): from Old French, perhaps from Italian *paggio*, from Greek *paidion*, diminutive of *pais, paid-* 'boy.' Early use of the verb (mid-16th century) was in the sense 'follow as or like a page'; its current sense 1 dates from the early 20th century.

---

pag•eant /pájənt/ *n.* **1 a** an elaborate parade or spectacle. **b** a spectacular procession, or play performed in the open, illustrating historical events. **c** a tableau, etc., on a fixed stage or moving vehicle. **2** an empty or specious show.

pag•eant•ry /pájəntree/ *n.* (*pl.* **-ries**) **1** elaborate or sumptuous show or display. **2** an instance of this.

page boy *n.* **1** = PAGE[2] *n.* 2. **2** a hairstyle with the hair reaching to the shoulder and rolled under at the ends.

pag•er /páyjər/ *n.* a radio device with a beeper, activated from a central point to alert the person wearing it.

pag•i•nate /pájinayt/ *v.tr.* assign numbers to the pages of a book, etc. ▫▫ **pag•i•na•tion** /-náyshən/ *n.*

pa•go•da /pəgṓdə/ *n.* **1** a Hindu or Buddhist temple or sacred building, esp. a many-tiered tower, in India and the Far East. **2** an ornamental imitation of this.

paid *past* and *past part.* of PAY[1].

pail /payl/ *n.* **1** a bucket. **2** an amount contained in this. ▫▫ **pail•ful** *n.* (*pl.* **-fuls**).

pain /payn/ *n. & v.* •*n.* **1 a** the range of unpleasant bodily sensations produced by illness or by harmful physical contact, etc. **b** a particular kind or instance of this (often in *pl.*: *suffering from stomach pains*). **2** mental suffering or distress. **3** (in *pl.*) careful effort; trouble taken (*take pains; got nothing for my pains*). **4** (also **pain in the neck**, etc.) *colloq.* a troublesome person or thing; a nuisance. •*v.tr.* **1** cause pain to. **2** (as **pained** *adj.*) expressing pain (*a pained expression*). ▫ **in pain** suffering pain. **on** (or **under**) **pain of** with (death, etc.) as the penalty.

pain•ful /páynfōōl/ *adj.* **1** causing bodily or mental pain or distress. **2** (esp. of part of the body) suffering pain. **3** causing trouble or difficulty; laborious (*a painful climb*). ▫▫ **pain•ful•ly** *adv.* **pain•ful•ness** *n.*

pain•kil•ler /páynkilər/ *n.* a medicine or drug for alleviating pain. ▫▫ **pain•kil•ling** *adj.*

pain•less /páynlis/ *adj.* not causing suffering or pain. ▫▫ **pain•less•ly** *adv.* **pain•less•ness** *n.*

pain•stak•ing /páynztayking/ *adj.* careful, industrious, thorough. ▫▫ **pain•stak•ing•ly** *adv.* **pain•stak•ing•ness** *n.*

paint /paynt/ *n. & v.* •*n.* **1 a** coloring matter, esp. in liquid form for imparting color to a surface. **b** this as a dried film or coating (*the paint peeled off*). **2** cosmetic makeup, esp. rouge or nail polish. **3** = PINTO. •*v.tr.* **1 a** cover the surface of (a wall, object, etc.) with paint. **b** apply paint of a specified color to (*paint the door green*). **2** depict (an object, scene, etc.) with paint; produce (a picture) by painting. **3** describe vividly as if by painting (*painted a gloomy picture of the future*). **4 a** apply liquid or cosmetic to (the face, skin, etc.). **b** apply (a liquid to the skin, etc.). ▫ **paint out** efface with paint. **paint the town red** *colloq.* enjoy oneself flamboyantly; celebrate. ▫▫ **paint•a•ble** *adj.*

paint•box /páyntboks/ *n.* a box holding dry paints for painting pictures.

paint•brush /páyntbrush/ *n.* a brush for applying paint.

paint·ed la·dy *n.* **1** an orange-red butterfly, esp. *Vanessa cardui*, with black and brown markings. **2** (also **painted woman**) PROSTITUTE.

paint·er[1] /páyntər/ *n.* a person who paints, esp. an artist or decorator.

paint·er[2] /páyntər/ *n.* a rope attached to the bow of a boat for tying it to a pier, dock, etc.

paint·ing /páynting/ *n.* **1** the process or art of using paint. **2** a painted picture.

paint·work /páyntwərk/ *n.* **1** a painted surface or area in a building, etc. **2** the work of painting.

pair /pair/ *n. & v.* •*n.* **1** a set of two persons or things used together or regarded as a unit (*a pair of gloves*; *a pair of eyes*). **2** an article (e.g., scissors, pants, or pajamas) consisting of two joined or corresponding parts not used separately. **3 a** a romantically involved couple. **b** a mated couple of animals. **4** two horses harnessed side by side (*a coach and pair*). **5** the second member of a pair in relation to the first (*cannot find its pair*). **6** two playing cards of the same denomination. **7** either or both of two members of a legislative assembly on opposite sides absenting themselves from voting by mutual arrangement. •*v.tr. & intr.* **1** (often foll. by *off* or *up*) arrange or be arranged in couples. **2 a** join or be joined in marriage. **b** (of animals) mate. **3** form a legislative pair. □ **in pairs** in twos.

Pais·ley /páyzlee/ *n.* (also **pais·ley**) (often *attrib.*) **1** a distinctive detailed pattern of curved feather-shaped figures. **2** a soft woolen garment or fabric having this pattern.

Pai·ute /píyōōt/ *n.* (also **Pi·ute**) **1 a** a N. American people native to the southwestern US. **b** a member of this people. **2** the language of this people.

pa·ja·mas /pəjaáməz, -jám-/ *n.pl.* **1** a suit of loose pants and jacket for sleeping in. **2** loose pants tied at the waist, worn by both sexes in some Asian countries. **3** (**pajama**) (*attrib.*) designating parts of a suit of pajamas (*pajama top; pajama pants; pajama bottoms*).

Pak·i·sta·ni /pákistánee, paákistaánee/ *n. & adj.* •*n.* **1** a native or national of Pakistan. **2** a person of Pakistani descent. •*adj.* of or relating to Pakistan.

pal /pal/ *n. & v.* •*n. colloq.* a friend or comrade. •*v.intr.* (**palled, palling**) (usu. foll. by *up*) associate; form a friendship.

pal·ace /pális/ *n.* **1 a** the official residence of a president or sovereign. **b** esp. *Brit.* the official residence of an archbishop or bishop. **2** a mansion; a spacious building.

palaeo- *comb.form Brit.* var. of PALEO-.

Pa·lae·o·zo·ic *Brit.* var. of PALEOZOIC.

pal·at·a·ble /pálətəbəl/ *adj.* **1** pleasant to taste. **2** (of an idea, suggestion, etc.) acceptable, satisfactory. □□ **pal·at·a·bil·i·ty** *n.* **pal·at·a·ble·ness** *n.* **pal·at·a·bly** *adv.*

pal·ate /pálət/ *n.* **1** a structure closing the upper part of the mouth cavity in vertebrates. **2** the sense of taste. **3** a mental taste or inclination; liking.

pa·la·tial /pəláyshəl/ *adj.* (of a building) like a palace, esp. spacious and magnificent. □□ **pa·la·tial·ly** *adv.*

pal·a·tine /pálətīn/ *adj.* (also **Palatine**) *hist.* **1** (of an official or feudal lord) having local authority that elsewhere belongs only to a sovereign (*Count Palatine*). **2** (of a territory) subject to this authority.

pa·lav·er /pəlávər, -laávər/ *n. & v.* •*n.* **1** fuss and bother, esp. prolonged. **2** profuse or idle talk. **3** cajolery. **4** *colloq.* a prolonged or tiresome business. **5** esp. *hist.* a parley between European traders and Africans or other indigenous peoples. •*v.* **1** *intr.* talk profusely. **2** *tr.* flatter, wheedle.

pale[1] /payl/ *adj. & v.* •*adj.* **1** (of a person or complexion) diminished in coloration; of a whitish or ashen appearance. **2 a** (of a color) faint; not dark or deep. **b** faintly colored. **3** of faint luster; dim. **4** lacking intensity, vigor, or strength (*pale imitation*). •*v.* **1** *intr. & tr.* grow or make pale. **2** *intr.* (often foll. by *before, beside*) become feeble in comparison (with). □□ **pale·ly** *adv.* **pale·ness** *n.* **pal·ish** *adj.*

pale[2] /payl/ *n.* **1** a pointed piece of wood for fencing, etc.; a stake. **2** a boundary or enclosed area. **3** *Heraldry* a vertical stripe in the middle of a shield. □ **beyond the pale** outside the bounds of acceptable behavior.

pale·face /páylfays/ *n.* a white person.

paleo- /páyleeō/ *comb.form* ancient; old; of ancient (esp. prehistoric) times.

pa·le·o·gra·phy /páyleeógrəfee/ *n.* (*Brit.* **palaeography**) the study of writing and documents from the past. □□ **pa·le·og·ra·pher** *n.* **pa·le·o·graph·ic** /-leeəgráfik/ *adj.* **pa·le·o·graph·i·cal** *adj.* **pa·le·o·graph·i·cal·ly** *adv.*

pa·le·o·lith·ic /páyleeəlíthik/ *adj.* (*Brit.* **palaeolithic**) *Archaeol.* of or relating to the early part of the Stone Age.

pa·le·on·tol·o·gy /páyleeontóləjee/ *n.* (*Brit.* **palaeontology**) the study of life in the geological past. □□ **pa·le·on·to·log·i·cal** *adj.* **pa·le·on·tol·o·gist** *n.*

Pa·le·o·zo·ic /páyleeəzṓik/ *adj. & n. Geol.* •*adj.* of or relating to an era of geological time marked by the appearance of marine and terrestrial plants and animals, esp. invertebrates. •*n.* this era (cf. CENOZOIC, MESOZOIC).

Pal·es·tin·i·an /pálistíneeən/ *adj. & n.* •*adj.* of or relating to Palestine, a region (in ancient and modern times) and former British territory on the E. Mediterranean coast. •*n.* **1** a native of Palestine in ancient or modern times. **2** an Arab, or a descendant of one, born or living in the area called Palestine.

pal·ette /pálit/ *n.* **1** a thin board or slab or other surface, usu. with a hole for the thumb, on which an artist holds and mixes colors. **2** the range of colors, etc., used by an artist.

pal·i·mo·ny /pálimōnee/ *n. colloq.* usu. court-ordered allowance made by one member of an unmarried couple to the other after separation.

pal·imp·sest /pálimpsest/ *n.* **1** a piece of writing material or manuscript on which the original writing has been erased to make room for other writing. **2** a place, etc., showing layers of history, etc. **3** a monumental brass turned and re-engraved on the reverse side.

pal·in·drome /pálindrōm/ *n.* a word or phrase that reads the same backward as forward (e.g., *rotator, nurses run*). □□ **pal·in·drom·ic** /-drómik, -drṓ-/ *adj.* **pa·lin·dro·mist** *n.*

pal·ing /páyling/ *n.* **1** a fence of pales. **2** a pale.

pal·i·sade /pálisáyd/ *n. & v.* •*n.* **1 a** a fence of pales or iron railings. **b** a strong pointed wooden stake used in a close row for defense. **2** (in *pl.*) a line of high cliffs. •*v.tr.* enclose or provide (a building or place) with a palisade.

pall[1] /pawl/ *n.* **1** a cloth spread over a coffin, hearse, or tomb. **2** a shoulder band with pendants, worn as an ecclesiastical vestment and sign of authority. **3** a dark covering (*a pall of darkness*; *a pall of smoke*).

pall[2] /pawl/ *v.* **1** *intr.* (often foll. by *on*) become uninteresting (to). **2** *tr.* satiate; cloy.

pal·la·di·um /pəláydeeəm/ *n. Chem.* a white ductile metallic element occurring naturally in various ores and used in chemistry as a catalyst and for making jewelry. ¶ Symb.: **Pd**.

pall·bear·er /páwlbairər/ *n.* a person helping to carry or officially escorting a coffin at a funeral.

pal·let[1] /pálit/ *n.* **1** a straw mattress. **2** a mean or makeshift bed.

pal·let[2] /pálit/ *n.* **1** a flat wooden blade with a handle, used in ceramics to shape clay. **2** = PALETTE. **3** a portable platform for transporting and storing loads. □□ **pal·let·ize** *v.tr.* (in sense 3).

pal·liasse /palyás/ *n.* a straw mattress.

pal·li·ate /páleeayt/ *v.tr.* **1** alleviate (disease) without curing it. **2** excuse; extenuate. □□ **pal·li·a·tion** /-áyshən/ *n.* **pal·li·a·tor** *n.*

pal·li·a·tive /páleeətiv/ *n. & adj.* •*n.* anything used to alleviate pain, anxiety, etc. •*adj.* serving to alleviate. □□ **pal·li·a·tive·ly** *adv.*

pal·lid /pálid/ *adj.* pale, esp. from illness. □□ **pal·lid·i·ty** /-líditee/ *n.* **pal·lid·ly** *adv.* **pal·lid·ness** *n.*

pal·lor /pálər/ *n.* pallidness; paleness.

palm[1] /paam, paw(l)m/ *n.* **1** any usu. tropical tree of the family Palmae, with no branches and a mass of large pinnate or fan-shaped leaves at the top. **2 a** the leaf of this tree as a symbol of victory. **b** a military decoration shaped like a palm leaf. **3 a** supreme excellence. **b** a prize for this. **4** a branch of various trees used instead of a palm in non-tropical countries, esp. in celebrating Palm Sunday. □□ **pal·ma·ceous** /palmáyshəs, paa(l)-/ *adj.*

palm[2] /paam, paw(l)m/ *n. & v.* •*n.* **1** the inner surface of the hand between the wrist and fingers. **2** the part of a glove, etc., that covers this. **3** the palmate part of an antler. •*v.tr.* **1** conceal in the hand. **2** *Basketball* to hold (the ball) in one hand. □ **in the palm of one's hand** under one's control or influence. **palm off 1** (often foll. by *on*) **a** impose or thrust fraudulently (on a person). **b** cause a person to accept unwillingly or unknowingly (*palmed my old typewriter off on him*). **2** (often foll. by *with*) cause (a person) to accept unwillingly or unknowingly (*palmed him off with my old typewriter*). □□ **pal·mar** /pálmər, paá(l)-/ *adj.* **palmed** *adj.* **palm·ful** *n.* (*pl.* **-fuls**).

pal·mate /pálmayt, paál-, paámayt/ *adj.* **1** shaped like an open hand. **2** having lobes, etc., like spread fingers.

pal·met·to /palmétō/ *n.* (*pl.* **-tos**) **1** a small palm tree, e.g., any of various fan palms of the genus *Sabal*. **2** palm fronds used in weaving.

palm·is·try /paámistree/ *n.* supposed divination from lines and other features on the palm of the hand. □□ **palm·ist** *n.*

Palm Sun·day *n.* the Sunday before Easter, celebrating Christ's entry into Jerusalem.

pal·o·mi·no /páləmeénō/ *n.* (*pl.* **-nos**) a golden or tan-colored horse with a light-colored mane and tail, orig. bred in the southwestern US.

pal·pa·ble /pálpəbəl/ *adj.* **1** that can be touched or felt. **2** readily perceived by the senses or mind. □□ **pal·pa·bil·i·ty** *n.* **pal·pa·bly** *adv.*

pal·pate /pálpáyt/ *v.tr.* examine (esp. medically) by touch. □□ **pal·pa·tion** /-páyshən/ *n.*

pal·pi·tate /pálpitayt/ *v.intr.* **1** pulsate; throb. **2** tremble. □□ **pal·pi·tant** *adj.*

pal·pi·ta·tion /pálpitáyshən/ *n.* **1** throbbing; trembling. **2** (often in *pl.*) increased activity of the heart due to exertion, agitation, or disease.

pal·sy /páwlzee/ *n. & v.* •*n.* (*pl.* **-sies**) **1** paralysis, esp. with involuntary tremors. **2 a** a condition of utter helplessness. **b** a cause of this. •*v.tr.* (**-sies, -sied**) **1** affect with palsy. **2** render helpless.

pal·try /páwltree/ *adj.* (**paltrier, paltriest**) worthless; contemptible; trifling. □□ **pal·tri·ness** *n.*

pam·pas /pámpəs/ *n.pl.* large treeless plains in S. America.

pam·pas grass *n.* a tall grass, *Cortaderia selloana*, from S. America, with silky flowering plumes.

pam·per /pámpər/ *v.tr.* **1** overindulge (a person, taste, etc.). **2** spoil (a person) with luxury. □□ **pam·per·er** *n.*

pam·phlet /pámflit/ *n. & v.* •*n.* a small, usu. unbound booklet or leaflet containing information or a short treatise. •*v.tr.* (**pamphleted, pamphleting**) distribute pamphlets to.

pam·phlet·eer /pámfliteér/ *n. & v.* •*n.* a writer of (esp. political) pamphlets. •*v.intr.* write pamphlets.

pan[1] /pan/ *n. & v.* •*n.* **1 a** a vessel of metal, earthenware, etc., usu. broad and shallow, used for cooking and other domestic purposes. **b** the contents of this. **2** a panlike vessel in which substances are heated, etc. **3** any similar shallow container such as the bowl of a pair of scales or that used for washing gravel, etc., to separate gold. **4** *Brit.* toilet bowl. **5** part of the lock that held the priming in old guns. **6** a hollow in the ground (*salt pan*). **7** a hard substratum of soil. **8** *sl.* the face. **9** a negative or unfavorable review. •*v.* (**panned, panning**) **1** *tr. colloq.* criticize severely. **2 a** *tr.* (often foll. by *off, out*) wash (gold-bearing gravel) in a pan. **b** *intr.* search for gold by panning gravel. **c** *intr.* (foll. by *out*) (of gravel) yield gold. □ **pan out** (of an action, etc.) turn out well or in a specified way. □□ **pan·ful** *n.* (*pl.* **-fuls**).

pan[2] /pan/ *v. & n.* •*v.* (**panned, panning**) **1** *tr.* swing (a video or movie camera) horizontally to give a panoramic effect or to follow a moving object. **2** *intr.* (of a video or movie camera) be moved in this way. •*n.* a panning movement.

pan- /pan/ *comb.form* **1** all; the whole of. **2** relating to the whole or all the parts of a continent, racial group, religion, etc. (*pan-American*; *pan-African*; *pan-Hellenic*; *pan-Anglican*).

pan·a·ce·a /pánəseéə/ *n.* a universal remedy. □□ **pan·a·ce·an** *adj.*

pa·nache /pənásh, -naásh/ *n.* assertiveness or flamboyant confidence of style or manner.

pan·a·ma /pánəmaa/ *n.* a hat of strawlike material made from the leaves of a palmlike tropical plant.

Pan·a·ma·ni·an /pánəmáyneeən/ *n. & adj.* •*n.* **1** a native or national of the Republic of Panama in Central America. **2** a person of Panamanian descent. •*adj.* of or relating to Panama.

pan·a·tel·la /pánətélə/ *n.* a long thin cigar.

pan·cake /pánkayk/ *n. & v.* •*n.* **1** a thin flat cake of batter usu. fried and turned in a pan or on a griddle. **2** a flat cake of makeup, etc. •*v.* **1** *intr.* make a pancake landing. **2** *tr.* cause (an aircraft) to pancake. □ **flat as a pancake** completely flat.

pan·chro·mat·ic /pánkrōmátik/ *adj. Photog.* (of film, etc.) sensitive to all visible colors of the spectrum.

pan·cre·as /pángkreeəs/ *n.* a gland near the stomach supplying the duodenum with digestive fluid and secreting insulin into the blood. □□ **pan·cre·at·ic** /-kreeátik/ *adj.* **pan·cre·a·ti·tis** /-kreeətítis/ *n.*

pan·da /pándə/ *n.* **1** (also **giant panda**) a large bearlike mammal, *Ailuropoda melanoleuca*, native to China and Tibet, having characteristic black and white markings. **2** (also **red panda**) a Himalayan raccoonlike mammal, *Ailurus fulgens*, with reddish-brown fur and a long bushy tail.

pan·dem·ic /pandémik/ *adj. & n.* •*adj.* **1** (of a disease) prevalent over a whole country or the world. **2** universal; widespread (*a pandemic fear of nuclear weapons*). •*n.* a pandemic disease.

pan·de·mo·ni·um /pándimṓneeəm/ *n.* **1** uproar; utter confusion. **2** a scene of this.

pan·der /pándər/ *v. & n.* •*v.intr.* (foll. by *to*) gratify or indulge a person, a desire or weakness, etc. •*n.* (also **panderer**) **1** a go-between in illicit love affairs; a procurer. **2** a person who encourages licentiousness.

pan·dit var. of PUNDIT 1.

Pan·do·ra's box /pandáwrəz/ *n.* a process that once activated will generate many unmanageable problems.

pane /payn/ *n.* **1** a single sheet of glass in a window or door. **2** a rectangular division of a checkered pattern, etc. **3** a sheet of postage stamps.

pan·e·gyr·ic /pánijírik, -jīrik/ *n.* a laudatory discourse; a eulogy. ▫▫ **pan·e·gyr·i·cal** *adj.*

pan·el /pánəl/ *n.* & *v.* •*n.* **1 a** a distinct, usu. rectangular, section of a surface (e.g., of a wall or door). **b** a control panel (see CONTROL *n.* 5). **c** = INSTRUMENT PANEL. **2** a strip of material as part of a garment. **3** a group of people gathered to form a team in a broadcast game, for a discussion, etc. **4** a list of available jurors; a jury. •*v.tr.* (**paneled** or **panelled, paneling** or **panelling**) **1** fit or provide with panels. **2** cover or decorate with panels.

panel Middle English: from Old French, literally 'piece of cloth', based on Latin *pannus* '(piece of) cloth.' An early sense, 'piece of parchment,' was extended to mean 'list,' whence the notion 'advisory group.' Sense 1 derives from the late Middle English sense 'distinct (usually framed) section of a surface.'

pan·el·ing /pánəling/ *n.* (also **pan·el·ling**) **1** paneled work. **2** wood for making panels.

pan·el·ist /pánəlist/ *n.* (also **pan·el·list**) a member of a panel (esp. in broadcasting).

pan·el truck *n.* a small enclosed delivery truck.

pang /pang/ *n.* (often in *pl.*) a sudden sharp pain or painful emotion.

pan·go·lin /pánggəlin, panggṓ-/ *n.* any scaly anteater of the genus *Manis,* native to Asia and Africa, having a small head with elongated snout and tongue, and a tapering tail.

pan·han·dle /pánhand'l/ *n.* & *v.* •*n.* a narrow strip of territory extending from one state into another. •*v.tr.* & *intr. colloq.* beg for money in the street. ▫▫ **pan·han·dler** *n.*

pan·ic /pánik/ *n.* & *v.* •*n.* **1 a** a sudden uncontrollable fear or alarm. **b** (*attrib.*) characterized or caused by panic (*panic buying*). **2** infectious apprehension or fright esp. in commercial dealings. •*v.tr.* & *intr.* (**panicked, panicking**) (often foll. by *into*) affect or be affected with panic (*was panicked into buying*). ▫▫ **pan·ick·y** *adj.*

pan·ic but·ton *n.* a button for summoning help in an emergency.

pan·i·cle /pánikəl/ *n. Bot.* a loose branching cluster of flowers, as in oats. ▫▫ **pan·i·cled** *adj.*

pan·ic-strick·en *adj.* (also **pan·ic-struck**) affected with panic; very apprehensive.

pan·nier /pányər/ *n.* **1** a basket, esp. one of a pair carried by a beast of burden. **2** each of a pair of bags or boxes on either side of the rear wheel of a bicycle or motorcycle.

pan·o·ply /pánəplee/ *n.* (*pl.* **-plies**) **1** a complete or magnificent array. **2** a complete suit of armor. ▫▫ **pan·o·plied** *adj.*

pan·o·ram·a /pánərámə, -ráa-/ *n.* **1** an unbroken view of a surrounding region. **2** a complete survey or presentation of a subject, sequence of events, etc. **3** a picture or photograph containing a wide view. **4** a continuous passing scene. ▫▫ **pan·o·ram·ic** *adj.* **pan·o·ram·i·cal·ly** *adv.*

pan·pipes /pánpīps/ *n.pl.* a musical instrument orig. associated with the Greek rural god Pan, made of a series of short pipes graduated in length and fixed together with the mouthpieces in line.

pan·sy /pánzee/ *n.* (*pl.* **-sies**) **1** any garden plant of the genus *Viola,* with flowers of various rich colors. **2** *colloq. derog.* **a** an effeminate man. **b** a male homosexual.

pant /pant/ *v.* & *n.* •*v.* **1** *intr.* breathe with short quick breaths. **2** *tr.* (often foll. by *out*) utter breathlessly. **3** *intr.* (often foll. by *for*) yearn or crave. **4** *intr.* (of the heart, etc.) throb violently. •*n.* **1** a panting breath. **2** a throb.

pan·ta·loon /pántəlóonz/ *n.* **1** (in *pl.*) *hist.* men's close-fitting breeches fastened below the calf or at the foot. **2** (**Pantaloon**) a character in Italian comedy wearing pantaloons.

pan·the·ism /pántheeizəm/ *n.* **1** the belief that God is identifiable with the forces of nature and with natural substances. **2** worship that admits or tolerates all gods. ▫▫ **pan·the·ist** *n.* **pan·the·is·tic** *adj.* **pan·the·is·ti·cal** *adj.* **pan·the·is·ti·cal·ly** *adv.*

pan·the·on /pántheeon, -ən/ *n.* **1** a building in which illustrious dead are buried or have memorials. **2** the deities of a people collectively. **3** a temple dedicated to all the gods, esp. the circular one at Rome. **4** a group of esteemed persons.

pan·ther /pánthər/ *n.* **1** a leopard, esp. with black fur. **2** a cougar.

pant·ies /pánteez/ *n.pl. colloq.* short-legged or legless underpants worn by women and girls.

pan·tile /pántīl/ *n.* a roofing tile curved to form an S-shaped section, fitted to overlap.

pan·to·graph /pántəgraf/ *n.* **1** *Art & Painting* an instrument for copying a plan or drawing, etc., on a different scale by a system of jointed rods. **2** a jointed framework conveying a current to an electric vehicle from overhead wires. ▫▫ **pan·to·graph·ic** *adj.*

pan·to·mime /pántəmīm/ *n.* **1** the use of gestures and facial expression to convey meaning without speech, esp. in drama and dance. **2** *Brit.* a theatrical entertainment based on a fairy tale, with music, topical jokes, etc., usu. produced around Christmas. **3** *colloq.* an absurd or outrageous piece of behavior. ▫▫ **pan·to·mim·ic** /-mímik/ *adj.*

pan·to·then·ic ac·id /pántəthénik/ *n.* a vitamin of the B complex, found in rice, bran, and many other foods, and essential for the oxidation of fats and carbohydrates.

pan·try /pántree/ *n.* (*pl.* **-tries**) **1** a small room or cupboard in which dishes, silverware, table linen, etc., are kept. **2** a small room or cupboard in which groceries, etc., are kept.

pants /pants/ *n.pl.* **1** an outer garment reaching from the waist usu. to the ankles, divided into two parts to cover the legs. **2** *Brit.* underpants. ▫ **bore** (or **scare,** etc.) **the pants off** *colloq.* bore, scare, etc., to an intolerable degree. **wear the pants** be the dominant partner in a marriage.

pant·suit /pántsōōt/ *n.* (also **pants suit**) a woman's suit with pants and a jacket.

pan·ty hose /pánteehōz/ *n.* (usu. treated as *pl.*) usu. sheer one-piece garment combining panties and stockings.

pan·zer /pánzər, paánts-/ *n.* **1** (in *pl.*) armored troops. **2** (*attrib.*) heavily armored (*panzer division*).

pap /pap/ *n.* **1 a** soft or semiliquid food for infants or invalids. **b** a mash or pulp. **2** light or trivial reading matter; nonsense. ▫▫ **pap·py** *adj.*

pa·pa /paápə, pəpaá/ *n.* father (esp. as a child's word).

pa·pa·cy /páypəsee/ *n.* (*pl.* **-cies**) **1** a pope's office or tenure. **2** the papal system.

Pap·a·go /paápəgō, pá-/ *n.* **1 a** a N. American people native to southwestern Arizona and adjoining parts of Mexico. **b** a member of this people. **2** the language of this people.

pa·pa·in /pəpáyin, -pī-in/ *n.* an enzyme obtained from unripe papaya, used to tenderize meat and as a food supplement to aid digestion.

pa·pal /páypəl/ *adj.* of or relating to a pope or to the papacy. ▫▫ **pa·pal·ly** *adv.*

pa·pa·raz·zo /paápəraátsō/ *n.* (*pl.* **paparazzi** /-see/) a freelance photographer who pursues celebrities to get photographs of them.

pa·paw var. of PAWPAW.

pa·pa·ya /pəpíə/ *n.* **1** an elongated melon-shaped fruit with edible orange flesh and small black seeds. **2** a tropical tree, *Carica papaya*, bearing this and producing a milky sap from which papain is obtained.

pa·per /páypər/ *n. & v.* •*n.* **1** a material manufactured in thin sheets from the pulp of wood or other fibrous substances, used for writing or drawing or printing on, or as wrapping material, etc. **2** (*attrib.*) **a** made of or using paper. **b** flimsy like paper. **3** = NEWSPAPER. **4 a** a document printed on paper. **b** (in *pl.*) documents attesting identity or credentials. **c** (in *pl.*) documents belonging to a person or relating to a matter. **5** *Commerce* **a** negotiable documents, e.g., bills of exchange. **b** (*attrib.*) recorded on paper though not existing (*paper profits*). **6 a** a set of questions to be answered at one session in an examination. **b** the written answers to these. **7** = WALLPAPER. **8** an essay or dissertation, esp. one read to a learned society or published in a learned journal. **9** a piece of paper, esp. as a wrapper, etc. •*v.tr.* **1** apply paper to, esp. decorate (a wall, etc.) with wallpaper. **2** (foll. by *over*) **a** cover (a hole or blemish) with paper. **b** disguise or try to hide (a fault, etc.). **3** distribute flyers, pamphlets, etc., as in a neighborhood. □ **on paper 1** in writing. **2** in theory; to judge from written or printed evidence. □□ **pa·per·er** *n.* **pa·per·less** *adj.*

pa·per·back /páypərbak/ (*US* also **paperbound**) *adj. & n.* •*adj.* (of a book) bound in stiff paper. •*n.* a paperback book.

pa·per·boy /páypərboy/ *n.* (*fem.* **pa·per·girl** /-gərl/) a boy or girl who delivers or sells newspapers.

pa·per clip *n.* a clip of bent wire or of plastic for holding several sheets of paper together.

pa·per mon·ey *n.* money in the form of bills.

pa·per route *n.* **1** a job of regularly delivering newspapers. **2** a route taken doing this.

pa·per ti·ger *n.* an apparently threatening, but ineffectual, person or thing.

pa·per trail *n.* documentation of transactions, etc.

pa·per·weight /páypərwayt/ *n.* a small heavy object for keeping loose papers in place.

pa·per·work /páypərwərk/ *n.* **1** routine clerical or administrative work. **2** documents, esp. for a particular purpose.

pa·pier mâ·ché /páypər məsháy, papyáy/ *n.* paper pulp used for molding into boxes, trays, etc.

pa·pil·la /pəpílə/ *n.* (*pl.* **papillae** /-pílee/) **1** a small nipplelike protuberance in a part or organ of the body. **2** *Bot.* a small fleshy projection on a plant. □□ **pap·il·la·ry** *adj.* **pa·pil·late** /pápilayt/ *adj.* **pap·il·lose** /pápilōs/ *adj.*

pap·il·lon /paapeeyóɴ, pá-/ *n.* **1** a toy dog of a breed with ears suggesting the form of a butterfly. **2** this breed.

pa·pist /páypist/ *n. & adj.* often *derog.* •*n.* **1** a Roman Catholic. **2** *hist.* an advocate of papal supremacy. •*adj.* of or relating to Roman Catholics. □□ **pa·pis·tic** *adj.* **pa·pis·ti·cal** *adj.* **pa·pist·ry** *n.*

pa·poose /papóōs, pə-/ *n.* a young Native American child.

pap·ri·ka /pəpréekə, páprikə/ *n.* **1** *Bot.* a red pepper. **2** a condiment made from it.

Pap smear /pap/ *n.* (also **Pap test**) a test for cervical cancer, etc., done by a cervical smear.

pa·py·rus /pəpírəs/ *n.* (*pl.* **papyri** /-rī/) **1** an aquatic plant, *Cyperus papyrus*, with dark green stems topped with fluffy inflorescences. **2 a** a writing material prepared in ancient Egypt from the pithy stem of this. **b** a document written on this.

par /paar/ *n. & v.* •*n.* **1** the average or normal amount, degree, condition, etc. (*be up to par*). **2** equality; an equal status or footing (*on a par with*). **3** *Golf* the number of strokes a skilled player should normally require for a hole or course. **4** *Stock Exch.* the face value of stocks and shares, etc. (*at par*). **5** (in full **par of exchange**) the recognized value of one country's currency in terms of another's. •*v.intr. Golf* to score par. □ **below par** less good than usual in health or other quality. **par for the course** *colloq.* what is normal or expected in any given circumstances.

par. *abbr.* (also **para.**) paragraph.

par·a /párə/ *n. colloq.* **1** a paratrooper. **2** a paraprofessional. **3** *Brit.* a paragraph.

par·a-a·min·o·ben·zo·ic ac·id /parə-əméenōbenzóik/ *n. Biochem.* a yellow crystalline compound, often used in suntan lotions and sunscreens to absorb ultraviolet light. ¶ Abbr.: **PABA**.

par·a·ble /párəbəl/ *n.* **1** a narrative of imagined events used to illustrate a moral or spiritual lesson. **2** an allegory.

pa·rab·o·la /pərábələ/ *n.* an open plane curve formed by the intersection of a cone with a plane parallel to its side, resembling the path of a projectile under the action of gravity.

par·a·bol·ic /párəbólik/ *adj.* **1** of or expressed in a parable. **2** of or like a parabola. □□ **par·a·bol·i·cal·ly** *adv.*

par·a·chute /párəshōōt/ *n. & v.* •*n.* **1** a rectangular or umbrella-shaped canopy allowing a person or heavy object attached to it to descend slowly from a height, esp. from an aircraft, or to retard motion in other ways. **2** (*attrib.*) dropped or to be dropped by parachute (*parachute drop*). •*v.tr. & intr.* convey or descend by parachute.

par·a·chut·ist /párəshōōtist/ *n.* **1** a person who uses a parachute. **2** (in *pl.*) parachute troops.

pa·rade /pəráyd/ *n. & v.* •*n.* **1 a** a formal or ceremonial muster of troops for inspection. **b** = PARADE GROUND. **2** a public procession. **3** ostentatious display (*made a parade of their wealth*). **4** *Brit.* a public square, promenade, or row of shops. •*v.* **1** *intr.* assemble for parade. **2 a** *tr.* march through (streets, etc.) in procession. **b** *intr.* march ceremonially. **3** *tr.* display ostentatiously. □ **on parade 1** taking part in a parade. **2** on display. □□ **pa·rad·er** *n.*

par·a·digm /párədīm/ *n.* **1** an example or pattern. **2** *Gram.* a representative set of the inflections of a noun, verb, etc. □□ **par·a·dig·mat·ic** /-digmátik/ *adj.* **par·a·dig·mat·i·cal·ly** *adv.*

par·a·dise /párədīs/ *n.* **1** (in some religions) heaven as the ultimate abode of the just. **2** a place or state of complete happiness. **3** (in full **earthly paradise**) the abode of Adam and Eve in the biblical account of the Creation; the garden of Eden. □□ **par·a·di·sa·i·cal** /-disáyikəl/ *adj.* **par·a·dis·al** /párədīsəl/ *adj.* **par·a·di·si·a·cal** /-disíəkəl/ *adj.* **par·a·di·si·cal** /-dísikəl/ *adj.*

par·a·dox /párədoks/ *n.* **1 a** a seemingly absurd or contradictory statement, even if actually well-founded. **b** a self-contradictory or essentially absurd statement. **2** a person or thing conflicting with a preconceived notion of what is reasonable or possible. **3** a paradoxical quality or character.

par·a·dox·i·cal /párədóksikəl/ *adj.* **1** of or like or involving paradox. **2** fond of paradox. □□ **par·a·dox·i·cal·ly** *adv.*

par·af·fin /párəfin/ *n.* **1** (also **paraffin wax**) a waxy mixture of hydrocarbons used in candles, waterproofing, etc. **2** *Brit.* = KEROSENE. **3** *Chem.* = ALKANE.

par·a·go·ge /páragójee/ *n.* the addition of a letter or syllable to a word in some contexts or as a language develops (e.g., *t* in *peasant*).

par·a·gon /párəgon, -gən/ *n.* **1 a** a model of excellence. **b** a supremely excellent person or thing. **2** (foll. by *of*) a model (of virtue, etc.). **3** a perfect diamond of 100 carats or more.

par·a·graph /párəgraf/ *n.* & *v.* • *n.* **1** a distinct section of a piece of writing, beginning on a new usu. indented line. **2** a symbol (usu. ¶) used to mark a new paragraph, and also as a reference mark. **3** a short item in a newspaper, usu. of only one paragraph. • *v.tr.* arrange (a piece of writing) in paragraphs. ▫▫ **par·a·graph·ic** /-gráfik/ *adj.*

par·a·keet /párəkeét/ *n.* any of various small usu. long-tailed parrots.

par·a·le·gal /párəleégəl/ *adj.* & *n.* • *adj.* of or relating to auxiliary aspects of the law. • *n.* a person trained in subsidiary legal matters.

par·al·lax /párəlaks/ *n.* **1** the apparent difference in the position or direction of an object caused when the observer's position is changed. **2** the angular amount of this. ▫▫ **par·al·lac·tic** /-láktik/ *adj.*

par·al·lel /párəlel/ *adj.*, *n.*, & *v.* • *adj.* **1 a** (of lines or planes) side by side and having the same distance continuously between them. **b** (foll. by *to*, *with*) (of a line or plane) having this relation (to another). **2** (of circumstances, etc.) precisely similar, analogous, or corresponding. **3 a** (of processes, etc.) occurring or performed simultaneously. **b** *Computing* involving the simultaneous performance of operations. • *n.* **1** a person or thing precisely analogous or equal to another. **2** a comparison (*drew a parallel between the two situations*). **3** (in full **parallel of latitude**) *Geog.* **a** each of the imaginary parallel circles of constant latitude on the earth's surface. **b** a corresponding line on a map (*the 49th parallel*). **4** *Printing* two parallel lines (| |) as a reference mark. • *v.tr.* (**paralleled, paralleling**) **1** be parallel to; correspond to. **2** represent as similar; compare. **3** adduce as a parallel instance. ▫▫ **par·al·lel·ism** *n.*

par·al·lel bars *n.pl.* a pair of parallel rails on posts for gymnastics.

par·al·lel·o·gram /párəléləgram/ *n. Geom.* a four-sided plane rectilinear figure with opposite sides parallel.

pa·ral·y·sis /pərálisis/ *n.* (*pl.* **paralyses** /-seez/) **1** impairment or loss of esp. the motor function of the nerves. **2** a state of utter powerlessness.

par·a·lyt·ic /párəlítik/ *adj.* & *n.* • *adj.* affected by paralysis. • *n.* a person affected by paralysis.

par·a·lyze /párəlīz/ *v.tr.* (also *Brit.* **paralyse**) **1** affect with paralysis. **2** render powerless; cripple. ▫▫ **par·a·ly·za·tion** *n.* **par·a·lyz·ing·ly** *adv.*

par·a·me·ci·um /párəméeseeəm/ *n.* any freshwater protozoan of the genus *Paramecium*, of a characteristic slipper-like shape covered with eilia.

par·a·med·ic /párəmédik/ *n.* **1** a paramedical worker. **2** a person trained in emergency medical procedures.

par·a·med·i·cal /párəmédikəl/ *adj.* (of services, etc.) supplementing and supporting medical work.

pa·ram·e·ter /pərámitər/ *n.* **1** *Math.* a quantity constant in the case considered but varying in different cases. **2 a** an (esp. measurable or quantifiable) characteristic or feature. **b** (loosely) a constant element or factor, esp. serving as a limit or boundary. ▫▫ **par·a·met·ric** /párəmétrik/ *adj.* **pa·ram·e·trize** *v.tr.*

par·a·mil·i·tar·y /párəmíliteree/ *adj.* (of forces) ancillary to and similarly organized to military forces.

par·a·mount /párəmownt/ *adj.* **1** supreme; requiring first consideration; preeminent (*of paramount importance*). **2** in supreme authority. ▫▫ **par·a·mount·cy** *n.* **par·a·mount·ly** *adv.*

par·a·mour /párəmŏŏr/ *n.* an illicit lover, esp. of a married person.

par·a·noi·a /párənóyə/ *n.* **1** a personality disorder esp. characterized by delusions of persecution and self-importance. **2** an abnormal tendency to suspect and mistrust others. ▫▫ **par·a·noi·ac** *adj.* & *n.* **par·a·noi·a·cal·ly** *adv.* **par·a·no·ic** /-nóyik, -nṓ-ik/ *adj.* **par·a·no·i·cal·ly** *adv.* **par·a·noid** /-noyd/ *adj.* & *n.*

par·a·nor·mal /párənórməl/ *adj.* beyond the scope of normal objective investigation or explanation. ▫▫ **par·a·nor·mal·ly** *adv.*

par·a·pet /párəpit/ *n.* **1** a low wall at the edge of a roof, balcony, etc., or along the sides of a bridge. **2** a defense of earth or stone to conceal and protect troops. ▫▫ **par·a·pet·ed** *adj.*

par·a·pher·na·lia /párəfərnáylyə/ *n.pl.* (also treated as *sing.*) miscellaneous belongings, items of equipment, accessories, etc.

par·a·phrase /párəfrayz/ *n.* & *v.* • *n.* a free rendering or rewording of a passage. • *v.tr.* express the meaning of (a passage) in other words. ▫▫ **par·a·phras·tic** /-frástik/ *adj.*

par·a·ple·gi·a /párəpleéjə/ *n.* paralysis of the legs and part or the whole of the trunk. ▫▫ **par·a·ple·gic** *adj.* & *n.*

par·a·psy·chol·o·gy /párəsīkóləjee/ *n.* the study of mental phenomena outside the sphere of ordinary psychology (hypnosis, telepathy, etc.). ▫▫ **par·a·psy·cho·log·i·cal** /-sīkəlójikəl/ *adj.* **par·a·psy·chol·o·gist** *n.*

par·a·quat /párəkwot/ *n.* a quick-acting herbicide, becoming inactive on contact with the soil.

par·a·site /párəsīt/ *n.* **1** an organism living in or on another and benefiting at the expense of the other. **2** a person who lives off or exploits another or others. **3** *Philol.* an inorganic sound or letter developing from an adjacent one. ▫▫ **par·a·sit·ic** /-sítik/ *adj.* **par·a·sit·i·cal** /-sítikəl/ *adj.* **par·a·sit·i·cal·ly** *adv.* **par·a·sit·i·cide** /-sítisīd/ *n.* **par·a·sit·ism** /-sitízəm/ *n.* **par·a·si·tol·o·gy** /-tóləjee/ *n.* **par·a·si·tol·o·gist** /-tóləjist/ *n.*

par·a·sol /párəsawl, -sol/ *n.* **1** a light umbrella used to give shade from the sun. **2** (in full **parasol mushroom**) any of several fungi of the genus *Lepiota*, typically with a broad, scaly, shaggy domed cap.

par·a·sym·pa·thet·ic /párəsímpəthétik/ *adj. Anat.* relating to the part of the nervous system that consists of nerves leaving the lower end of the spinal cord and connecting with those in or near the viscera.

par·a·thy·roid /párəthíroyd/ *n.* & *adj. Anat.* • *n.* a gland next to the thyroid, secreting a hormone that regulates calcium levels in the body. • *adj.* of or associated with this gland.

par·a·troop /párətrōōp/ *n.* (*attrib.*) of or consisting of paratroops (*paratroop regiment*).

par·a·troop·er /párətrōōpər/ *n.* a member of a body of paratroops.

par·a·troops /párətrōōps/ *n.pl.* troops equipped to be dropped by parachute from aircraft.

par·boil /paárboyl/ *v.tr.* partly cook by boiling.

par·cel /paársəl/ *n.* & *v.* • *n.* **1 a** goods, etc., wrapped up in a single package. **b** a bundle of things wrapped up, usu. in paper. **2** a piece of land, esp. as part of a larger lot. **3** a quantity dealt with in one commercial transaction. **4** a group or collection of things, people, etc. **5** part. • *v.tr.* (**parceled, parceling** or **parcelled, parcelling**) **1** (foll. by *out*) divide into portions **2** (foll. by *up*) wrap as a parcel. **3** cover (rope) with strips of canvas.

par·cel post *n.* **1** a mail service dealing with parcels. **2** a postage rate for parcels.

parch /paarch/ *v.* **1** *tr.* & *intr.* make or become hot and dry. **2** *tr.* roast (peas, grain, etc.) slightly.

parched /paarcht/ *adj.* **1** hot and dry; dried out with heat. **2** *colloq.* thirsty.

parch·ment /paárchmənt/ *n.* **1** an animal skin, esp. that of a sheep or goat, prepared as a writing or painting surface. **2** a manuscript written on this.

pard·ner /paárdnər/ *n. US dial. colloq.* a partner or comrade.

par·don /paárd'n/ *n., v., & int.* • *n.* **1** the act of excusing or forgiving an offense, error, etc. **2** (in full **full pardon,** *Brit.* **free pardon**) a remission of the legal consequences of a crime or conviction. **3** *RC Ch.* an indulgence. • *v.tr.* **1** release from the consequences of an offense, error, etc. **2** forgive or excuse a person for (an offense, etc.). **3** make (esp. courteous) allowances for; excuse. • *int.* (also **pardon me** or **I beg your pardon**) **1** a formula of apology or disagreement. **2** a request to repeat something said. ▫▫ **par·don·a·ble** *adj.* **par·don·a·bly** *adv.*

pare /pair/ *v.tr.* **1 a** trim (esp. fruit and vegetables) by cutting away the surface or edge. **b** (often foll. by *off, away*) cut off (the surface or edge). **2** (often foll. by *away, down*) diminish little by little. ▫▫ **par·er** *n.*

par·e·gor·ic /párigáwrik, -gór-/ *n.* a camphorated tincture of opium used to reduce pain or relieve diarrhea.

par·ent /páirənt, pár-/ *n. & v.* • *n.* **1** a person who has begotten or borne offspring; a father or mother. **2** a person who holds the position or exercises the functions of such a parent. **3** an ancestor. **4** an animal or plant from which others are derived. **5** a source or origin. **6** an initiating organization or enterprise. • *v.tr.* (also *absol.*) be a parent of. ▫▫ **pa·ren·tal** /pərént'l/ *adj.* **pa·ren·tal·ly** /pəréntəlee/ *adv.* **par·ent·hood** *n.*

par·ent·age /páirəntij, pár-/ *n.* lineage; descent from or through parents (*their parentage is unknown*).

pa·ren·the·sis /pərénthəsis/ *n.* (*pl.* **parentheses** /-seez/) **1 a** a word, clause, or sentence inserted as an explanation or afterthought into a passage which is grammatically complete without it, and usu. marked off by brackets or dashes or commas. **b** (in *pl.*) a pair of rounded brackets () used for this. **2** an interlude or interval. ▫ **in parenthesis** as a parenthesis or afterthought.

par·en·thet·ic /párənthétik/ *adj.* **1** of or by way of a parenthesis. **2** interposed. ▫▫ **par·en·thet·i·cal** *adj.* **par·en·thet·i·cal·ly** *adv.*

pa·re·ve /paárəvə, paárvə/ *adj.* made without milk or meat and thus suitable for kosher use.

par ex·cel·lence /paár eksəlóns/ *adv.* as having special excellence; being the supreme example of its kind (*the short story par excellence*).

par·fait /paarfáy/ *n.* **1** a rich frozen custard of whipped cream, eggs, etc. **2** layers of ice cream, meringue, etc., served in a tall glass.

pa·ri·ah /pəríə/ *n.* **1** a social outcast. **2** *hist.* a member of a low caste or of no caste in S. India.

pa·ri·e·tal /pəríətəl/ *adj.* **1** *Anat.* of the wall of the body or any of its cavities. **2** *Bot.* of the wall of a hollow structure, etc. **3** relating to residence and visitation rules in a college dormitory.

par·i·mu·tu·el /párimyóochooəl/ *n.* **1** a form of betting in which those backing the first three places divide the losers' stakes (less the operator's commission). **2 a** a device showing the number and amount of bets staked on a race, to facilitate the division of the total among those backing the winner. **b** a system of betting based on this.

par·ing /páiring/ *n.* a strip or piece cut off.

par·ish /párish/ *n.* **1** an area having its own church and clergy. **2** a county in Louisiana. **3** *Brit.* (in full **civil parish**) a district constituted for purposes of local government. **4** the inhabitants of a parish.

par·ish·ion·er /pərishənər/ *n.* an inhabitant or member of a parish.

Pa·ri·sian /pəreézhən, -rízhən, -rízeeən/ *adj. & n.* • *adj.* of or relating to Paris in France. • *n.* **1** a native or inhabitant of Paris. **2** the kind of French spoken in Paris.

par·i·ty[1] /páritee/ *n.* **1** equality or equal status, esp. as regards status or pay. **2** parallelism or analogy (*parity of reasoning*). **3** equivalence of one currency with another; being at par. **4 a** (of a number) the fact of being even or odd. **b** *Computing* mathematical parity used for error detection. **5** *Physics* (of a quantity) the fact of changing its sign or remaining unaltered under a given transformation of coordinates, etc.

par·i·ty[2] /páritee/ *n. Med.* **1** the fact or condition of having borne children. **2** the number of children previously borne.

park /paark/ *n. & v.* • *n.* **1** a large public area in a town, used for recreation. **2** a large enclosed piece of ground, usu. with woodland and pasture, attached to a country house, etc. **3 a** a large area of land kept in its natural state for public recreational use. **b** esp. *Brit.* a large enclosed area of land used to accommodate wild animals in captivity (*wildlife park*). **4** esp. *Brit.* an area for motor vehicles, etc., to be left in (*car park*). **5** the gear position or function in an automatic transmission in which the gears are locked, preventing the vehicle's movement. **6** an area devoted to a specified purpose (*industrial park*). **7** a sports arena or stadium. • *v.* **1** *tr.* (also *absol.*) leave (a vehicle) usu. temporarily, in a parking lot, by the side of the road, etc. **2** *tr. colloq.* deposit and leave, usu. temporarily. **3** *intr. sl.* engage in petting or kissing in a parked car. ▫ **park oneself** *colloq.* sit down.

---

park Middle English: from Old French *parc*, from medieval Latin *parricus*, of Germanic origin; related to German *Pferch* 'pen, fold,' also to *paddock*. The word was originally a legal term designating land held by royal grant for keeping game animals: this was enclosed and therefore distinct from a *forest* or *chase*, and (also unlike a *forest*) had no special laws or officers. A military sense 'space occupied by artillery, wagons, stores, etc., in an encampment' (late 17th century) is the origin of the verb sense (mid-19th century) and of sense 3 (early 20th century).

---

par·ka /paárkə/ *n.* **1** a skin jacket with hood, worn by Eskimos. **2** a similar windproof fabric garment worn in cold weather.

park·ing me·ter *n.* a coin-operated meter that receives payment for vehicles parked in the street and indicates the time available.

Par·kin·son's dis·ease /paárkinsənz/ *n.* a progressive disease of the nervous system with tremor, muscular rigidity, and emaciation. Also called **Parkinsonism.**

Par·kin·son's law /paárkinsənz/ *n.* the notion that work expands so as to fill the time available for its completion.

park·land /paárkland/ *n.* open grassland with clumps of trees, etc.

park·way /paárkway/ *n.* an open landscaped highway.

par·lance /paárləns/ *n.* a particular way of speaking, esp. as regards choice of words, idiom, etc.

par·lay /paárlay/ *v. & n.* • *v.tr.* **1** use (money won on a bet) as a further stake. **2** increase in value by or as if by parlaying. • *n.* **1** an act of parlaying. **2** a bet made by parlaying.

par·ley /paárlee/ *n. & v.* • *n.* (*pl.* **-leys**) a conference for debating points in a dispute, esp. a discussion of terms for an armistice, etc. • *v.intr.* (**-leys, -leyed**) (often foll. by *with*) hold a parley.

par·lia·ment /paárləmənt/ *n.* **1** (**Parliament**) **a** (in the UK) the highest legislature, consisting of the Sovereign, the House of Lords, and the House of Commons. **b** the members of this legislature for a particular period, esp. between one dissolution and the next. **2** a similar legislature in other nations.

par·lia·men·tar·i·an /paárləmentáireeən/ *n. & adj.* • *n.* **1** a member of a parliament. **2** a person who is well-versed in parliamentary procedures. **3** *hist.* an adherent of Parliament in the English Civil War of the 17th c. • *adj.* = PARLIAMENTARY.

par·lia·men·ta·ry /paárləméntəree, -tree/ *adj.* **1** of or relating to a parliament. **2** enacted or established by a parliament. **3** (of language) admissible in a parliament; polite.

par·lor /paárlər/ *n.* **1** a sitting room in a private house. **2** a room in a hotel, club, etc., for the private use of residents. **3** a store providing specified goods or services (*beauty parlor; ice cream parlor*). **4** a room or building equipped for milking cows. **5** (*attrib.*) *derog.* denoting support for esp. political views by those who do not try to practice them (*parlor socialist*).

Par·me·san /paármizaán, -zán, -zən/ *n.* a kind of hard dry cheese made orig. at Parma and used esp. in grated form.

pa·ro·chi·al /pərṓkeeəl/ *adj.* **1** of or concerning a parish. **2** (of affairs, views, etc.) merely local, narrow or restricted in scope. ▫▫ **pa·ro·chi·al·ism** *n.* **pa·ro·chi·al·i·ty** /-álitee/ *n.* **pa·ro·chi·al·ly** *adv.*

pa·ro·chi·al school *n.* a private elementary or high school maintained by a religious organization, esp. the Roman Catholic Church.

par·o·dy /párədee/ *n.* & *v.* • *n.* (*pl.* **-dies**) **1** a humorous exaggerated imitation of an author, literary work, style, etc. **2** a feeble imitation; a travesty. • *v.tr.* (**-dies, -died**) **1** compose a parody of. **2** mimic humorously. ▫▫ **par·o·dic** /pəródik/ *adj.* **par·o·dist** *n.*

pa·role /pərṓl/ *n.* & *v.* • *n.* **1 a** the release of a prisoner temporarily for a special purpose or completely before the fulfillment of a sentence, on the promise of good behavior. **b** such a promise. **2** a word of honor. • *v.tr.* put (a prisoner) on parole. ▫ **on parole** released on the terms of parole. ▫▫ **pa·rol·ee** /-leé/ *n.*

par·ox·ysm /párəksizəm/ *n.* **1** (often foll. by *of*) a sudden attack or outburst (of rage, laughter, etc.). **2** a fit of disease. ▫▫ **par·ox·ys·mal** /-sízməl/ *adj.*

par·quet /paárkáy/ *n.* **1** a flooring of wooden blocks arranged in a pattern. **2** the main-floor seating area of a theater.

par·quet·ry /paárkitree/ *n.* the use of wooden blocks to make floors or inlay for furniture.

parr /paar/ *n.* a young salmon with blue-gray fingerlike markings on its sides, younger than a smolt.

par·ri·cide /párisīd/ *n.* **1** the killing of a near relative, esp. of a parent. **2** an act of parricide. **3** a person who commits parricide. ▫▫ **par·ri·cid·al** /-síd'l/ *adj.*

par·rot /párət/ *n.* & *v.* • *n.* **1** any of various mainly tropical birds of the order Psittaciformes, with a short hooked bill, often having vivid plumage and able to mimic the human voice. **2** a person who mechanically repeats the words or actions of another. • *v.tr.* (**parroted, parroting**) repeat mechanically.

par·rot·fish *n.* any fish of the family Scaridae, with a mouth like a parrot's bill and forming a protective mucous cocoon against predators.

par·ry /páree/ *v.* & *n.* • *v.tr.* (**-ries, -ried**) **1** avert or ward off (a weapon or attack), esp. with a countermove. **2** deal skillfully with (an awkward question, etc.). • *n.* (*pl.* **-ries**) an act of parrying.

parse /paars/ *v.tr.* **1** describe (a word in context) grammatically, stating its inflection, relation to the sentence, etc. **2** resolve (a sentence) into its component parts and describe them grammatically. ▫▫ **pars·er** *n.* esp. *Computing.*

par·sec /paársek/ *n.* a unit of stellar distance, equal to about 3.25 light years (3.08 x 10^{16} meters), the distance at which the mean radius of the earth's orbit subtends an angle of one second of arc.

par·si·mo·ny /paársimōnee/ *n.* **1** carefulness in the use of money or other resources. **2** stinginess. ▫▫ **par·si·mo·ni·ous** /-mṓneeəs/ *adj.* **par·si·mo·ni·ous·ly** *adv.* **par·si·mo·ni·ous·ness** *n.*

pars·ley /paárslee/ *n.* a biennial herb, *Petroselinum crispum*, with white flowers and crinkly aromatic leaves, used for seasoning and garnishing food.

pars·nip /paársnip/ *n.* **1** a biennial umbelliferous plant, *Pastinaca sativa*, with yellow flowers and a large pale yellow tapering root. **2** this root eaten as a vegetable.

par·son /paársən/ *n.* **1** a rector. **2** any (esp. Protestant) member of the clergy. ▫▫ **par·son·i·cal** /-sónikəl/ *adj.*

par·son·age /paársənij/ *n.* a church house provided for a parson.

part /paart/ *n., v.,* & *adv.* • *n.* **1** some but not all of a thing or number of things. **2** an essential member or constituent of anything (*part of the family; a large part of the job*). **3** a component of a machine, etc. (*spare parts; needs a new part*). **4 a** a portion of a human or animal body. **b** (in *pl.*) *colloq.* = PRIVATE PARTS. **5** a division of a book, broadcast serial, etc., esp. as much as is issued or broadcast at one time. **6** each of several equal portions of a whole (*the recipe has 3 parts sugar to 2 parts flour*). **7 a** a portion allotted; a share. **b** a person's share in an action or enterprise (*will have no part in it*). **c** one's duty (*was not my part to interfere*). **8 a** a character assigned to an actor on stage. **b** the words spoken by an actor on stage. **c** a copy of these. **9** *Mus.* a melody or other constituent of harmony assigned to a particular voice or instrument. **10** each of the sides in an agreement or dispute. **11** (in *pl.*) a region or district (*am not from these parts*). **12** (in *pl.*) abilities (*a man of many parts*). **13** a dividing line in combed hair. • *v.* **1** *tr.* & *intr.* divide or separate into parts (*the crowd parted to let them through*). **2** *intr.* **a** leave one another's company (*they parted the best of friends*). **b** (foll. by *from*) say goodbye to. **3** *tr.* cause to separate (*they fought hard and had to be parted*). **4** *intr.* (foll. by *with*) give up possession of; hand over. **5** *tr.* separate (the hair of the head on either side of the part) with a comb. • *adv.* to some extent; partly (*is part iron and part wood; a lie that is part truth*). ▫ **for one's part** as far as one is concerned. **in part** (or **parts**) to some extent; partly. **look the part** appear suitable for a role. **on the part of** on the behalf or initiative of (*no objection on my part*). **part and parcel** (usu. foll. by *of*) an essential part. **play a part 1** be significant or contributory. **2** act deceitfully. **3** perform a theatrical role. **take part** (often foll. by *in*) assist or have a share (in). **take the part of 1** support; back up. **2** perform the role of.

par·take /paartáyk/ *v.intr.* (*past* **partook** /-tŏŏk/; *past part.* **partaken** /-táykən/) **1** (foll. by *of, in*) take a share or part. **2** (foll. by *of*) eat or drink some or *colloq.* all (of a thing). **3** (foll. by *of*) have some (of a quality, etc.) (*their manner partook of insolence*). ▫▫ **par·tak·a·ble** *adj.* **par·tak·er** *n.*

par·the·no·gen·e·sis /paárthinōjénisis/ *n. Biol.* reproduction by a female gamete without fertilization, esp. as a normal process in invertebrates and lower plants. ▫▫ **par·the·no·ge·net·ic** /-jinétik/ *adj.* **par·the·no·ge·net·i·cal·ly** *adv.*

par·tial /paárshəl/ *adj.* & *n.* • *adj.* **1** not complete; forming only part (*a partial success*). **2** biased; unfair. **3** (foll. by *to*) having a liking for. • *n.* **1** *Mus.* any of the component tones of a complex tone. **2** a denture for replacing one or several, but not all, of the teeth. ▫ **partial to** having a liking for; fond of. ▫▫ **par·tial·ly** *adv.* **par·tial·ness** *n.*

▶In the sense 'to some extent, not entirely' traditionalists prefer **partly** to **partially**: *The piece was written partly in poetry. What we decide will depend partly on the amount of the contract.* The form **partial**, however, appears in many phrases as the adjectival form of **part:**

partial blindness, partial denture, partial paralysis, partial payment, partial shade, partial vacuum, etc. **Partially** is therefore widely used, with the same sense as **partly:** *partially blind in one eye.*

par·ti·al·i·ty /paársheeálitee/ *n.* **1** bias; favoritism. **2** (foll. by *for*) fondness.

par·tic·i·pant /paartísipənt/ *n.* someone who or something that participates.

par·tic·i·pate /paartísipayt/ *v.intr.* **1** (often foll. by *in*) take a part or share (in). **2** *literary* or *formal* (foll. by *of*) have a certain quality (*the speech participated of wit*). □□ **par·tic·i·pa·tion** /-páyshən/ *n.* **par·tic·i·pa·tor** *n.* **par·tic·i·pa·to·ry** /-tísəpətáwree/ *adj.*

par·ti·ci·ple /paártisipəl/ *n. Gram.* a word formed from a verb (e.g., *going, gone, being, been*) and used in compound verb forms (e.g., *is going, has been*) or as an adjective (e.g., *working woman, burned toast*). □□ **par·ti·cip·i·al** /-sípeeəl/ *adj.* **par·ti·cip·i·al·ly** /-sípeeəlee/ *adv.*

par·ti·cle /paártikəl/ *n.* **1** a minute portion of matter. **2** the least possible amount (*not a particle of sense*). **3** *Gram.* **a** a minor part of speech, esp. a short indeclinable one. **b** a common prefix or suffix such as *in-*, *-ness*.

par·ti·cle·board /paártikəlbōrd, -bawrd/ *n.* a building material made in flat sheets from scrap wood bonded with adhesive.

par·ti·col·ored /paárteekúlərd/ *adj.* partly of one color, partly of another or others.

par·tic·u·lar /pərtíkyələr, pətík-/ *adj. & n.* •*adj.* **1** relating to or considered as one thing or person as distinct from others; individual (*in this particular instance*). **2** more than is usual; special; noteworthy (*took particular trouble*). **3** scrupulously exact; fastidious. **4** detailed (*a full and particular account*). **5** *Logic* (of a proposition) in which something is asserted of some but not all of a class (opp. UNIVERSAL *adj.* 2). •*n.* **1** a detail; an item. **2** (in *pl.*) points of information; a detailed account. □ **in particular** especially; specifically.

par·tic·u·lar·ism /pərtíkyələrízəm, pətík-/ *n.* **1** exclusive devotion to one party, sect, etc. **2** the principle of leaving political independence to each state in an empire or federation. **3** the theological doctrine of individual election or redemption. □□ **par·tic·u·lar·ist** *n.*

par·tic·u·lar·i·ty /pərtíkyəláritee, pətík-/ *n.* **1** the quality of being individual or particular. **2** fullness or minuteness of detail in a description.

par·tic·u·lar·ize /pərtíkyələrīz, pətík-/ *v.tr.* (also *absol.*) **1** name specifically or one by one. **2** specify (items). □□ **par·tic·u·lar·i·za·tion** *n.*

par·tic·u·lar·ly /pərtíkyələrlee, pətík-/ *adv.* **1** especially; very. **2** specifically (*they particularly asked for you*). **3** in a particular or fastidious manner.

par·tic·u·late /pərtíkyəlayt, -lət, paar-/ *adj. & n.* •*adj.* in the form of separate particles. •*n.* matter in this form.

part·ing /paárting/ *n.* **1** a leave-taking or departure (often *attrib.*: *parting words*). **2** a division; an act of separating.

par·ti·san /paártizən/ *n. & adj.* •*n.* **1** a strong, esp. unreasoning, supporter of a party, cause, etc. **2** *Mil.* a guerrilla in wartime. •*adj.* **1** of or characteristic of partisans. **2** loyal to a particular cause; biased. □□ **par·ti·san·ship** *n.*

par·tite /paártīt/ *adj.* **1** divided (esp. in *comb.*: *tripartite*). **2** *Bot. & Zool.* divided to or nearly to the base.

par·ti·tion /paartíshən/ *n. & v.* •*n.* **1** division into parts, esp. *Polit.* of a country with separate areas of government. **2** a structure dividing a space into two parts, esp. a light interior wall. •*v.tr.* **1** divide into parts. **2** (foll. by *off*) separate (part of a room, etc.) with a partition. □□ **par·ti·tioned** *adj.* **par·ti·tion·er** *n.* **par·ti·tion·ist** *n.*

part·ly /paártlee/ *adv.* **1** with respect to a part or parts. **2** to some extent.

▶See note at PARTIAL.

part·ner /paártnər/ *n. & v.* •*n.* **1** a person who shares or takes part with another or others, esp. in a business firm with shared risks and profits. **2** a companion in dancing. **3** a player (esp. one of two) on the same side in a game. **4** either member of a married couple, or of an unmarried couple living together. •*v.tr.* **1** be the partner of. **2** associate as partners. □□ **part·ner·less** *adj.*

part·ner·ship /paártnərship/ *n.* **1** the state of being a partner or partners. **2** a joint business. **3** a pair or group of partners.

part of speech *n.* each of the categories to which words are assigned in accordance with their grammatical and semantic functions (in English esp. noun, pronoun, adjective, adverb, verb, preposition, conjunction, and interjection).

par·took *past* of PARTAKE.

par·tridge /paártrij/ *n.* (*pl.* same or **partridges**) **1** any game bird of the genus *Perdix*, esp. *P. perdix* of Europe and Asia. **2** any other of various similar birds of Europe or N. America, including the snow partridge, ruffed grouse, and bobwhite.

part-song *n.* a song with three or more voice parts, often without accompaniment, and harmonic rather than contrapuntal in character.

part-time *adj.* occupying or using only part of one's working time. □□ **part-tim·er** *n.*

par·tu·ri·tion /paártoorishən, -tyoo-, -choo-/ *n. Med.* the act of bringing forth young; childbirth.

par·ty /paártee/ *n. & v.* •*n.* (*pl.* **-ties**) **1** a social gathering, usu. of invited guests. **2** a body of persons engaged in an activity or traveling together (*fishing party; search party*). **3** a group of people united in a cause, opinion, etc., esp. an organized political group. **4** a person or persons forming one side in an agreement or dispute. **5** (foll. by *to*) *Law* an accessory (to an action). **6** *colloq.* a person. •*v.tr. & intr.* (**-ties, -tied**) entertain at or attend a party.

par·ty line *n.* **1** the policy adopted by a political party. **2** a telephone line shared by two or more subscribers.

par·ty poop·er *n. sl.* a person whose manner or behavior inhibits other people's enjoyment; a killjoy.

par·ve·nu /paárvənoo/ *n. & adj.* •*n.* (*fem.* **parvenue**) **1** a person who has recently gained wealth or position. **2** an upstart. •*adj.* **1** associated with or characteristic of such a person. **2** upstart.

pas /paa/ *n.* (*pl.* same) a step in dancing, esp. in classical ballet.

pas·cal /paskál, paaskaál/ *n.* **1** a standard unit of pressure, equal to one newton per square meter. **2** (**Pascal** or **PASCAL**) *Computing* a programming language esp. used in education.

pas·chal /páskəl/ *adj.* **1** of or relating to the Jewish Passover. **2** of or relating to Easter.

pas de deux /də dő/ *n.* a dance for two persons.

pa·sha /paáshə/ *n. hist.* the title (placed after the name) of a Turkish officer of high rank, e.g., a military commander, the governor of a province, etc.

Pash·to /páshtō/ *n. & adj.* •*n.* the official language of Afghanistan, also spoken in areas of Pakistan. •*adj.* of or in this language.

pasque·flow·er /páskflowər/ *n.* a ranunculaceous plant, genus *Anemone*, with bell-shaped purple flowers and fernlike foliage. Also called ANEMONE.

pass[1] /pas/ *v. & n.* •*v.* (*past part.* **passed**) (see also PAST). **1** *intr.* (often foll. by *along, by, down, on*, etc.) move onward; proceed, esp. past some point of reference. **2** *tr.* **a** go past; leave (a thing, etc.) on one side or behind in proceeding. **b** overtake, esp. in a vehicle.

c go across (a frontier, mountain range, etc.). **3** *intr. & tr.* be transferred or cause to be transferred from one person or place to another (*pass the butter; the estate passes to his son*). **4** *tr.* surpass; be too great for (*it passes my comprehension*). **5** *intr.* get through; effect a passage. **6** *intr.* **a** be accepted as adequate; go uncensured (*let the matter pass*). **b** (foll. by *as, for*) be accepted or currently known as. **7** *tr.* move; cause to go (*passed her hand over her face; passed a rope round it*). **8 a** *intr.* (of a candidate in an examination) be successful. **b** *tr.* be successful in (an examination). **c** *tr.* (of an examiner) judge the performance of (a candidate) to be satisfactory. **9 a** *tr.* (of a bill) be approved by (a parliamentary body or process). **b** *tr.* cause or allow (a bill) to proceed to further legislative processes. **c** *intr.* (of a bill or proposal) be approved. **10** *intr.* **a** occur; elapse (*the remark passed unnoticed; time passes slowly*). **b** happen; be done or said (*heard what passed between them*). **11 a** *intr.* circulate; be current. **b** *tr.* put into circulation (*was passing forged checks*). **12** *tr.* spend or use up (a certain time or period). **13** *tr.* (also *absol.*) *Sports* send (the ball) to another player of one's own team. **14** *intr.* forgo one's turn or chance in a game, etc. **15** *intr.* (foll. by *to, into*) change from one form (to another). **16** *intr.* come to an end. **17** *tr.* discharge from the body as or with excreta. **18** *tr.* (foll. by *on, upon*) **a** utter (criticism) about. **b** pronounce (a judicial sentence) on. **19** *intr.* (often foll. by *on, upon*) adjudicate. **20** *tr.* not declare or pay (a dividend). **21** *tr.* cause (troops, etc.) to go by, esp. ceremonially. • *n.* **1** an act or instance of passing. **2** *Brit.* **a** success in an examination. **b** the status of a university degree without honors. **3** written permission to pass into or out of a place, or to be absent from quarters. **4** a ticket or permit giving free entry or access, etc. **5** *Sports* a transference of the ball to another player on the same side. **6** *Baseball* a base on balls. **7** a thrust in fencing. **8** an act of passing the hands over anything, as in conjuring or hypnotism. **9** a critical position (*has come to a fine pass*). □ **make a pass at** *colloq.* make amorous or sexual advances to. **pass around 1** distribute. **2** send or give to each of a number in turn. **pass away 1** *euphem.* die. **2** cease to exist; come to an end. **pass the buck** *US colloq.* deny or shift responsibility. **pass by 1** go past. **2** disregard; omit. **pass off 1** (of feelings, etc.) disappear gradually. **2** (of proceedings) be carried through (in a specified way). **3** (foll. by *as*) misrepresent (a person or thing) as something else. **pass on 1** proceed on one's way. **2** *euphem.* die. **3** transmit to the next person in a series. **pass out 1** become unconscious. **2** distribute. **pass over 1** omit, ignore, or disregard. **2** ignore the claims of (a person) to promotion or advancement. **3** *euphem.* die. **pass up** *colloq.* refuse or neglect (an opportunity, etc.). **pass water** urinate. □□ **pass·er** *n.*

pass[2] /pas/ *n.* **1** a narrow passage through mountains. **2** a navigable channel, esp. at the mouth of a river.

pass·a·ble /pásəbəl/ *adj.* **1** barely satisfactory; just adequate. **2** (of a road, pass, etc.) that can be passed. □□ **pass·a·ble·ness** *n.* **pass·a·bly** *adv.*

pas·sage /pásij/ *n.* **1** the process or means of passing; transit. **2** = PASSAGEWAY. **3** the liberty or right to pass through. **4 a** the right of conveyance as a passenger by sea or air. **b** a journey by sea or air. **5** a transition from one state to another. **6 a** a short extract from a book, etc. **b** a section of a piece of music. **c** a detail or section of a painting. **7** the passing of a bill, etc., into law. **8** (in *pl.*) an interchange of words, etc. **9** *Anat.* a duct, etc., in the body. □ **work one's passage** earn a right (orig. of passage) by working for it.

pas·sage·way /pásijway/ *n.* a narrow way for passing along, esp. with walls on either side; a corridor.

pass·book /pásbŏŏk/ *n.* a book issued by a bank, etc., to an account holder for recording amounts deposited and withdrawn.

pass·é /pasáy/ *adj.* **1** behind the times; out-of-date. **2** past its prime.

pas·sen·ger /pásinjər/ *n.* **1** a traveler in or on a public or private conveyance (other than the driver, pilot, crew, etc.). **2** *colloq.* a member of a team, crew, etc., who does no effective work. **3** (*attrib.*) for the use of passengers (*passenger seat*).

pas·sen·ger pi·geon *n.* an extinct wild migratory pigeon of N. America.

pass·er·by /pásərbī́/ *n.* (*pl.* **passersby**) a person who goes past, esp. by chance.

pas·ser·ine /pásərīn, -reen/ *n. & adj.* • *n.* any perching bird of the order Passeriformes, having feet with three toes pointing forward and one pointing backward, including sparrows and most land birds. • *adj.* **1** of or relating to this order. **2** of the size of a sparrow.

pas·si·ble /pásibəl/ *adj.* capable of feeling or suffering. □□ **pas·si·bil·i·ty** *n.*

pas·sim /pásim/ *adv.* (of allusions or references in a published work) to be found at various places throughout the text.

pass·ing /pásing/ *adj., adv., & n.* • *adj.* **1** in senses of PASS *v.* **2** transient; fleeting (*a passing glance*). **3** cursory; incidental (*a passing reference*). • *adv.* exceedingly; very. • *n.* **1** in senses of PASS *v.* **2** *euphem.* the death of a person (*mourned his passing*). □ **in passing 1** by the way. **2** in the course of speech, conversation, etc. □□ **pass·ing·ly** *adv.*

pas·sion /páshən/ *n.* **1** strong barely controllable emotion. **2** an outburst of anger (*flew into a passion*). **3 a** intense sexual love. **b** a person arousing this. **4 a** strong enthusiasm (*has a passion for football*). **b** an object arousing this. **5** (**the Passion**) **a** *Relig.* the suffering of Christ during his last days. **b** a narrative of this from the Gospels. **c** a musical setting of any of these narratives. □□ **pas·sion·less** *adj.*

pas·sion·ate /páshənət/ *adj.* **1** dominated by or easily moved to strong feeling, esp. love or anger. **2** showing or caused by passion. □□ **pas·sion·ate·ly** *adv.* **pas·sion·ate·ness** *n.*

pas·sion·flow·er /páshənflowr, -flowər/ *n.* any climbing plant of the genus *Passiflora*, with a flower that was supposed to suggest the instruments of the Crucifixion.

pas·sion play *n.* a miracle play representing Christ's Passion.

pas·sive /pásiv/ *adj.* **1** suffering action; acted upon. **2** offering no opposition; submissive. **3** not active; inert. **4** *Gram.* designating the voice in which the subject undergoes the action of the verb (e.g., in *they were killed*). **5** (of a debt) incurring no interest payment. **6** collecting or distributing the sun's energy without use of machinery (*passive solar heating*). □□ **pas·sive·ly** *adv.* **pas·sive·ness** *n.* **pas·siv·i·ty** /-sívətee/ *n.*

pas·sive re·sist·ance *n.* a nonviolent refusal to cooperate.

pas·sive smok·ing *n.* the involuntary inhaling, esp. by a nonsmoker, of smoke from others' cigarettes, etc.

pass·key /páskee/ *n.* **1** a private key to a gate, etc., for special purposes. **2** a skeleton key or master key.

Pass·o·ver /pásōvər/ *n.* the Jewish spring festival commemorating the liberation of the Israelites from Egyptian bondage, held from the 14th to the 21st day of the seventh month of the Jewish year.

pass·port /páspawrt/ *n.* **1** an official document issued by a government certifying the holder's identity and citizenship, and entitling the holder to travel under its protection to and from foreign countries. **2** (foll. by *to*) a thing that ensures admission or attainment (*a passport to success*).

pass•word /páswərd/ *n.* **1** a selected word or phrase securing recognition, admission, etc., when used by those to whom it is disclosed. **2** *Computing* a word or string of characters securing access to an account or file for those authorized.

past /past/ *adj., n., prep., & adv.* • *adj.* **1** gone by in time and no longer existing (*in past years; the time is past*). **2** recently completed or gone by (*the past month; for some time past*). **3** relating to a former time (*past president*). **4** *Gram.* expressing a past action or state. • *n.* **1** (prec. by *the*) **a** a past time. **b** what has happened in past time (*cannot undo the past*). **2** a person's past life or career, esp. if discreditable (*a man with a past*). **3** a past tense or form. • *prep.* **1** beyond in time or place (*is past two o'clock; ran past the house*). **2** beyond the range, duration, or compass of (*past belief; past endurance*). • *adv.* so as to pass by (*hurried past*). □ **not put it past a person** believe it possible of a person.

pas•ta /paástə/ *n.* **1** a dried flour paste used in various shapes in cooking (e.g., lasagna, spaghetti). **2** a cooked dish made from this.

paste /payst/ *n. & v.* • *n.* **1** any moist fairly stiff mixture, esp. of powder and liquid. **2** a dough of flour with fat, water, etc., used in baking. **3** an adhesive of flour, water, etc., esp. for sticking paper and other light materials. **4** an easily spread preparation of ground meat, fish, etc. **5** a hard vitreous composition used in making imitation gems. **6** a mixture of clay, water, etc., used in making ceramic ware, esp. porcelain. • *v.tr.* **1** fasten or coat with paste. **2** *sl.* **a** beat soundly. **b** bomb or bombard heavily. □□ **past•ing** *n.* (esp. in sense 2 of *v.*).

paste•board /páystbawrd/ *n.* **1** a sheet of stiff material made by pasting together sheets of paper. **2** (*attrib.*) **a** flimsy; unsubstantial. **b** fake.

pas•tel /pastél/ *n.* **1** a crayon consisting of powdered pigments bound with a gum solution. **2** a work of art in pastel. **3** a light and subdued shade of a color. □□ **pas•tel•ist** or **pas•tel•list** *n.*

pas•tern /pástərn/ *n.* **1** the part of a horse's foot between the fetlock and the hoof. **2** a corresponding part in other animals.

pas•teur•ize /páschərīz, pástyə-/ *v.tr.* subject (milk, etc.) to the process of partial sterilization by heating. □□ **pas•teur•i•za•tion** /-záyshən/ *n.* **pas•teur•iz•er** *n.*

pas•tiche /pasteésh/ *n.* **1** a medley, esp. a picture or a musical composition, made up from or imitating various sources. **2** a literary or other work of art composed in the style of a well-known author.

pas•tille /pasteél, -tíl/ *n.* a small candy or medicated lozenge.

pas•time /pástīm/ *n.* **1** a pleasant recreation or hobby. **2** a sport or game.

past mas•ter *n.* **1** a person who is especially adept or expert in an activity, subject, etc. **2** a person who has been a master in a guild, lodge, etc.

pas•tor /pástər/ *n.* **1** a priest or minister in charge of a church or a congregation. **2** a person exercising spiritual guidance. □□ **pas•tor•ship** *n.*

pas•to•ral /pástərəl/ *adj. & n.* • *adj.* **1** of, relating to, or associated with shepherds or flocks and herds. **2** (of land) used for pasture. **3** (of a poem, picture, etc.) portraying country life, usu. in a romantic or idealized form. **4** of or appropriate to a pastor. • *n.* **1** a pastoral poem, play, picture, etc. **2** a letter from a pastor (esp. a bishop) to the clergy or people. □□ **pas•to•ral•ism** *n.* **pas•to•ral•i•ty** /-álitee/ *n.* **pas•to•ral•ly** *adv.*

pas•to•rale /pástəraál, -rál, -raálee/ *n.* (*pl.* **pastorales** or **pastorali** /-lee/) **1** a slow instrumental composition in compound time, usu. with drone notes in the bass. **2** a simple musical play with a rural subject.

past per•fect *n. Gram.* = PLUPERFECT.

pas•tra•mi /pəstraámee/ *n.* seasoned smoked beef.

pas•try /páystree/ *n.* (*pl.* **-tries**) **1** a dough of flour, fat, and water baked and used as a base and covering for pies, etc. **2 a** food, made wholly or partly of this. **b** a piece or item of this food.

pas•tur•age /páschərij/ *n.* **1** land for pasture. **2** the process of pasturing cattle, etc.

pas•ture /páschər/ *n. & v.* • *n.* **1** land covered with grass, etc., suitable for grazing animals, esp. cattle or sheep. **2** herbage for animals. • *v.* **1** *tr.* put (animals) to graze in a pasture. **2** *intr. & tr.* (of animals) graze.

past•y[1] /pástee/ *n.* esp. *Brit.* (*pl.* **-ies**) a pastry case with a sweet or savory filling, baked without a dish to shape it.

pas•ty[2] /páystee/ *adj.* (**pastier, pastiest**) **1** of or like or covered with paste. **2** unhealthily pale (esp. in complexion) (*pasty-faced*). □□ **past•i•ly** *adv.* **past•i•ness** *n.*

pat[1] /pat/ *v. & n.* • *v.* (**patted, patting**) **1** *tr.* strike gently with the hand or a flat surface. **2** *tr.* flatten or mold by patting. **3** *tr.* strike gently with the inner surface of the hand, esp. as a sign of affection, sympathy, or congratulation. **4** *intr.* beat lightly. • *n.* **1** a light stroke or tap, esp. with the hand in affection, etc. **2** the sound made by this. **3** a small mass (esp. of butter) formed by patting. □ **pat on the back** a gesture of approval or congratulation. **pat a person on the back** congratulate a person.

pat[2] /pat/ *adj. & adv.* • *adj.* **1** known thoroughly and ready for any occasion. **2** apposite or opportune, esp. unconvincingly so (*gave a pat answer*). • *adv.* **1** in a pat manner. **2** appositely; opportunely. □ **have** (or **know**) down pat know or have memorized perfectly. **stand pat 1** stick stubbornly to one's opinion or decision. **2** *Poker* retain one's hand as dealt; not draw other cards. □□ **pat•ly** *adv.* **pat•ness** *n.*

patch /pach/ *n. & v.* • *n.* **1** a piece of material or metal, etc., used to mend a hole or as reinforcement. **2** a pad worn to protect an injured eye. **3** a dressing, etc., put over a wound. **4** a large or irregular distinguishable area on a surface. **5** *Brit. colloq.* a period of time in terms of its characteristic quality (*went through a bad patch*). **6** a piece of ground. **7** a number of plants growing in one place (*brier patch*). **8** a scrap or remnant. **9** a temporary electrical connection. **10** a temporary correction in a computer program. **11** *hist.* a small disk, etc., of black silk attached to the face, worn esp. by women in the 17th–18th c. for adornment. **12** *Mil.* a piece of cloth on a uniform as the badge of a unit. • *v.tr.* **1** (often foll. by *up*) repair with a patch or patches; put a patch or patches on. **2** (of material) serve as a patch to. **3** (often foll. by *up*) put together, esp. hastily or in a makeshift way. **4** (foll. by *up*) settle (a quarrel, etc.) esp. hastily or temporarily. □□ **patch•er** *n.*

patch•ou•li /pəchoolee, páchoolee/ *n.* **1** a strongly scented E. Indian plant, *Pogostemon cablin*. **2** the perfume obtained from this.

patch•work /páchwərk/ *n.* **1** sewn work using small pieces of cloth with different designs, forming a pattern. **2** a thing composed of various small pieces or fragments.

patch•y /pachee/ *adj.* (**patchier, patchiest**) **1** uneven in quality. **2** having or existing in patches. □□ **patch•i•ly** *adv.* **patch•i•ness** *n.*

pate /payt/ *n. colloq.* or joc. **1** the top of the head **2** the head, esp. representing the seat of intellect.

pâ•té /paatáy, pa-/ *n.* a rich paste or spread of finely chopped and spiced meat or fish, etc.

pa•tel•la /pətélə/ *n.* (*pl.* **patellae** /-lee/) the kneecap. □□ **pa•tel•lar** *adj.* **pa•tel•late** /-lət/ *adj.*

pat·ent /pát'nt/ *n., adj., & v.* •*n.* **1** a government authority to an individual or organization conferring a right or title, esp. the sole right to make or use or sell some invention. **2** a document granting this authority. **3** an invention or process protected by it. •*adj.* **1** /páyt'nt/ obvious; plain. **2** conferred or protected by patent. **3 a** made and marketed under a patent; proprietary. **b** to which one has a proprietary claim. **4** such as might be patented; ingenious; well-contrived. **5** (of an opening, etc.) allowing free passage. •*v.tr.* obtain a patent for (an invention). ▫▫ **pa·ten·cy** *n.* **pat·ent·a·ble** *adj.* **pat·ent·ee** *n.* **pat·ent·ly** /páytəntlee, pát-/ *adv.* (in sense 1 of *adj.*).

pat·ent leath·er *n.* leather with a glossy varnished surface.

pat·ent med·i·cine *n.* medicine made and marketed under a patent and available without prescription.

pa·ter·nal /pətárnəl/ *adj.* **1** of or like or appropriate to a father. **2** fatherly. **3** related through the father. **4** (of a government, etc.) limiting freedom and responsibility by well-meaning regulations. ▫▫ **pa·ter·nal·ly** *adv.*

pa·ter·nal·ism /pətárnəlizəm/ *n.* the policy of governing in a paternal way, or behaving paternally to one's associates or subordinates. ▫▫ **pa·ter·nal·ist** *n.* **pa·ter·nal·is·tic** *adj.* **pa·ter·nal·is·ti·cal·ly** *adv.*

pa·ter·ni·ty /pətárnitee/ *n.* **1** fatherhood. **2** one's paternal origin. **3** the source or authorship of a thing.

path /path/ *n.* (*pl.* **paths** /paathz/) **1** a way or track laid or trodden down for walking. **2** the line along which a person or thing moves (*flight path*). **3** a course of action or conduct. **4** a sequence of movements or operations taken by a system. ▫▫ **path·less** *adj.*

-path /path/ *comb.form* forming nouns denoting: **1** a practitioner of curative treatment (*homeopath*; *osteopath*). **2** a person who suffers from a disease (*psychopath*).

pa·thet·ic /pəthétik/ *adj.* **1** arousing pity or sadness or contempt. **2** *colloq.* miserably inadequate. **3** *archaic* of the emotions. ▫▫ **pa·thet·i·cal·ly** *adv.*

path·find·er /páthfīndər/ *n.* **1** a person who explores new territory, investigates a new subject, etc. **2** an aircraft or its pilot sent ahead to locate and mark the target area for bombing.

patho- /páthō/ *comb.form* disease.

path·o·gen /páthəjən/ *n.* an agent causing disease. ▫▫ **path·o·gen·ic** /-jenik/ *adj.* **pa·thog·e·nous** /-thójənəs/ *adj.*

path·o·log·i·cal /páthəlójikəl/ *adj.* **1** of pathology. **2** of or caused by a physical or mental disorder (*a pathological fear of spiders*). ▫▫ **path·o·log·i·cal·ly** *adv.*

pa·thol·o·gy /pəthóləjee/ *n.* **1** the science of bodily diseases. **2** the symptoms of a disease. ▫▫ **pa·thol·o·gist** *n.*

pa·thos /páythos, -thaws, -thōs/ *n.* a quality in speech, writing, events, etc., that evokes pity or sadness.

path·way /páthway/ *n.* **1** a path or its course. **2** *Biochem.*, etc., a sequence of reactions undergone in a living organism.

-pathy /pəthee/ *comb.form* forming nouns denoting: **1** curative treatment (*allopathy*; *homeopathy*). **2** feeling (*telepathy*).

pa·tience /páyshəns/ *n.* **1** calm endurance of hardship, provocation, pain, delay, etc. **2** tolerant perseverance or forbearance. **3** the capacity for calm self-possessed waiting. **4** esp. *Brit.* = SOLITAIRE 4.

pa·tient /páyshənt/ *adj. & n.* •*adj.* having or showing patience. •*n.* a person receiving or registered to receive medical treatment. ▫▫ **pa·tient·ly** *adv.*

pat·i·na /pətéenə, pát'nə/ *n.* (*pl.* **patinas**) **1** a film, usu. green, formed on the surface of old bronze. **2** a similar film on other surfaces. **3** a gloss produced by age on woodwork. ▫▫ **pat·i·nat·ed** /pát'naytid/ *adj.* **pat·i·na·tion** *n.*

pat·i·o /páteeō/ *n.* (*pl.* **-os**) **1** a paved usu. roofless area adjoining and belonging to a house. **2** an inner court open to the sky esp. in a Spanish or Spanish-American house.

pa·tis·se·rie /pətísəree, paateesrée/ *n.* **1** a shop where pastries are made and sold. **2** pastries collectively.

pat·ois /patwaá, pátwaa/ *n.* (*pl.* same, *pronunc.* /-waaz/) the dialect of the common people in a region, differing fundamentally from the literary language.

pa·tri·arch /páytreeaark/ *n.* **1** the male head of a family or tribe. **2** (often in *pl.*) *Bibl.* any of those regarded as fathers of the human race, esp. Adam and his descendants, including Noah; Abraham, Isaac, and Jacob; or the sons of Jacob, founders of the tribes of Israel. **3** *Eccl.* **a** the title of a chief bishop, esp. those presiding over the Churches of Antioch, Alexandria, Constantinople, and (formerly) Rome; now also the title of the heads of certain autocephalous Orthodox Churches. **b** (in the Roman Catholic Church) a bishop ranking next above primates and metropolitans, and immediately below the pope. **c** the head of a Uniate community. **d** a high dignitary of the Mormon church. **4 a** the founder of an order, science, etc. **b** a venerable old man. **c** the oldest member of a group. ▫▫ **pa·tri·ar·chal** /-aárkəl/ *adj.* **pa·tri·ar·chal·ly** /-aárkəlee/ *adv.*

pa·tri·arch·ate /páytreeaarkət, -kayt/ *n.* **1** the office, see, or residence of an ecclesiastical patriarch. **2** the rank of a tribal patriarch.

pa·tri·arch·y /páytreeaarkee/ *n.* (*pl.* **-ies**) a system of society, government, etc., ruled by a man or men and with descent through the male line. ▫▫ **pa·tri·arch·ism** *n.*

pa·tri·cian /pətríshən/ *n. & adj.* •*n.* **1** *hist.* a member of the ancient Roman nobility (cf. PLEBEIAN). **2** *hist.* a nobleman in some Italian republics. **3** an aristocrat. **4** a person of educated or refined tastes and upbringing. •*adj.* **1** noble; aristocratic; well-bred. **2** *hist.* of the ancient Roman nobility.

pat·ri·cide /pátrisīd/ *n.* = PARRICIDE (esp. with reference to the killing of one's father). ▫▫ **pat·ri·cid·al** /-síd'l/ *adj.*

pat·ri·lin·e·al /pátrilineeəl/ *adj.* of or relating to, or based on kinship with, the father or descent through the male line.

pat·ri·mo·ny /pátrimōnee/ *n.* (*pl.* **-nies**) **1** property inherited from one's father or ancestor. **2** a heritage. **3** the endowment of a church, etc. ▫▫ **pat·ri·mo·ni·al** *adj.*

pa·tri·ot /páytreeət, -ot/ *n.* a person who is devoted to and ready to support or defend his or her country. ▫▫ **pa·tri·ot·ic** /-reeótik/ *adj.* **pa·tri·ot·i·cal·ly** *adv.* **pa·tri·ot·ism** *n.*

pa·trol /pətrṓl/ *n. & v.* •*n.* **1** the act of walking or traveling around an area, esp. at regular intervals, in order to protect or supervise it. **2** one or more persons or vehicles assigned or sent out on patrol, esp. a detachment of guards, police, etc. **3 a** a detachment of troops sent out to reconnoiter. **b** such reconnaissance. **4** a routine operational voyage of a ship or aircraft. **5** a unit of Boy or Girl Scouts. •*v.* (**patrolled, patrolling**) **1** *tr.* carry out a patrol of. **2** *intr.* act as a patrol. ▫▫ **pa·trol·ler** *n.*

pa·trol car *n.* a police car used in patrolling roads and streets.

pa·trol·man /pətrṓlmən/ *n.* (*pl.* **-men**) a police officer assigned to or patrolling a specific route.

pa·tron /páytrən/ *n.* (*fem.* **patroness**) **1** a person who gives financial or other support to a person, cause, work of art, etc., esp. one who buys works of art. **2** a usu. regular customer of a store, etc.

pa·tron·age /pátrənij/ *n.* **1** the support, promotion, or encouragement given by a patron. **2** a patronizing or condescending manner. **3 a** the power to appoint others to government jobs. **b** the distribution of such jobs. **4** a customer's support for a store, etc.

pa·tron·ize /páytrənīz, pát-/ *v.tr.* **1** treat condescendingly. **2** act as a patron toward (a person, cause, artist, etc.); support; encourage. **3** frequent (a store, etc.) as a customer. □□ **pa·tron·i·za·tion** *n.* **pa·tron·iz·er** *n.* **pa·tron·iz·ing** *adj.* **pa·tron·iz·ing·ly** *adv.*

pa·tron saint *n.* the protecting or guiding saint of a person, place, etc.

pat·ro·nym·ic /pátrənímik/ *n. & adj.* •*n.* a name derived from the name of a father or ancestor, e.g., *Johnson, O'Brien, Ivanovich.* •*adj.* (of a name) so derived.

pa·troon /pətrōōn/ *n. hist.* a landowner with manorial privileges under the Dutch governments of New York and New Jersey.

pat·sy /pátsee/ *n.* (*pl.* **-sies**) *sl.* a person who is deceived, ridiculed, tricked, etc.

pat·ter[1] /pátər/ *v. & n.* •*v.* **1** *intr.* make a rapid succession of taps, as of rain on a windowpane. **2** *intr.* run with quick short steps. **3** *tr.* cause (water, etc.) to patter. •*n.* a rapid succession of taps, short light steps, etc.

pat·ter[2] /pátər/ *n.* **1 a** the rapid speech used by a comedian or introduced into a song. **b** the words of a comic song. **2** the words used by a person selling or promoting a product; a sales pitch. **3** the special language or jargon of a profession, class, etc. **4** *colloq.* mere talk; chatter.

pat·tern /pátərn/ *n. & v.* •*n.* **1** a repeated decorative design on wallpaper, cloth, a carpet, etc. **2** a regular or logical form, order, or arrangement of parts (*behavior pattern; the pattern of one's daily life*). **3** a model or design, e.g., of a garment, from which copies can be made. **4** an example of excellence; an ideal; a model (*a pattern of elegance*). **5** the prescribed flight path for an airplane taking off or esp. landing at an airport. **6** a wooden or metal figure from which a mold is made for a casting. **7** a sample (of cloth, wallpaper, etc.). **8** the marks made by shots, bombs, etc. on a target or target area. •*v.tr.* **1** (usu. foll. by *after, on*) model (a thing) on a design, etc. **2** decorate with a pattern.

pat·ty /pátee/ *n.* (*pl.* **-ties**) **1** a small flat cake of ground meat, etc., sometimes breaded and fried. **2** esp. *Brit.* a little pie or pastry.

pat·ty·pan /páteepan/ *n.* **1** a flattish summer squash having a scalloped edge. **2** a pan for baking a patty.

pau·ci·ty /páwsitee/ *n.* smallness of number or quantity.

paunch /pawnch/ *n.* **1** the belly or stomach, esp. when protruding. **2** a ruminant's first stomach; the rumen. □□ **paunch·y** *adj.* (**paunchier, paunchiest**). **paunch·i·ness** *n.*

pau·per /páwpər/ *n.* **1** a person without means; a beggar. **2** a person dependent on private or government charity. □□ **pau·per·dom** /-pərdəm/ *n.* **pau·per·ism** /-rizəm/ *n.* **pau·per·ize** *v.tr.* **pau·per·i·za·tion** /-rīzáysh'n/ *n.*

pause /pawz/ *n. & v.* •*n.* **1** an interval of inaction, esp. when due to hesitation; a temporary stop. **2** a break in speaking or reading; a silence. **3** *Mus.* a fermata. •*v.* **1** *intr.* make a pause; wait. **2** *intr.* (usu. foll. by *upon*) linger over (a word, etc.). **3** *tr.* cause to hesitate or pause.

pave /payv/ *v.tr.* **1** cover (a street, floor, etc.) with paving, etc. **2** cover or strew (a floor, etc.) with anything (*paved with flowers*). □ **pave the way for** prepare for; facilitate. □□ **pav·er** *n.* **pav·ing** *n.*

pave·ment /páyvmənt/ *n.* **1** the hard, durable covering of a street, driveway, etc., as of asphalt or concrete. **2** esp. *Brit.* = SIDEWALK. **3** a roadway.

pa·vil·ion /pəvílyən/ *n.* **1** a usu. open building at a fairground, park, etc., used for exhibits, refreshments, etc. **2** a decorative building in a garden. **3** a tent, esp. a large one at a show, fair, etc. **4** a building used for entertainments. **5** a temporary stand at an exhibition. **6** a detached building that is part of a connected set of buildings, as at a hospital. **7** the part of a cut gemstone below the girdle.

Pav·lov·i·an /pavlṓviən/ *adj.* of or relating to I. P. Pavlov, Russian physiologist d. 1936, or his work, esp. on conditioned reflexes.

paw /paw/ *n. & v.* •*n.* **1** a foot of an animal having claws or nails. **2** *colloq.* a person's hand. •*v.* **1** *tr.* strike or scrape with a paw or foot. **2** *intr.* scrape the ground with a paw or hoof. **3** *tr. colloq.* fondle awkwardly or indecently.

pawl /pawl/ *n. & v.* •*n.* **1** a lever with a catch for the teeth of a wheel or bar. **2** *Naut.* a short bar used to lock a capstan, windlass, etc., to prevent it from recoiling. •*v.tr.* secure (a capstan, etc.) with a pawl.

pawn[1] /pawn/ *n.* **1** *Chess* a piece of the smallest size and value. **2** a person used by others for their own purposes.

pawn[2] /pawn/ *v.tr.* **1** deposit an object, esp. with a pawnbroker, as security for money lent. **2** pledge or wager (one's life, honor, word, etc.).

pawn·brok·er /páwnbrōkər/ *n.* a person who lends money at interest on the security of personal property pawned. □□ **pawn·brok·ing** *n.*

Paw·nee /pawnée, paa-/ *n.* **1 a** a N. American people native to Kansas and Nebraska. **b** a member of this people. **2** the language of this people.

pawn·shop /páwnshop/ *n.* a shop where pawnbroking is conducted.

paw·paw /páwpaw/ *n.* (also **pa·paw**) a N. American tree, *Asimina triloba,* with purple flowers and edible fruit.

pay /pay/ *v., n., & adj.* •*v.tr.* (*past* and *past part.* **paid** /payd/) **1** (also *absol.*) give (a person, etc.) what is due for services done, goods received, debts incurred, etc. (*paid him in full; I assure you I have paid*). **2 a** give (a usu. specified amount) for work done, a debt, a ransom, etc. (*they pay $6 an hour*). **b** (foll. by *to*) hand over the amount of (a debt, wages, recompense, etc.) to (*paid the money to the assistant*). **3 a** give, bestow, or express (attention, respect, a compliment, etc.) (*paid them no heed*). **b** make (a visit, a call, etc.) (*paid a visit to their uncle*). **4** (also *absol.*) (of a business, undertaking, attitude, etc.) be profitable or advantageous to (a person, etc.). **5** reward or punish (*can never pay you for what you have done for us; I shall pay you for that*). **6** (usu. as **paid** *adj.*) recompense (work, time, etc.) (*paid holiday*). **7** (usu. foll. by *out, away*) let out (a rope) by slackening it. •*n.* wages; payment. •*adj.* **1** requiring payment for (a service, etc.). **2** requiring payment of a coin for use (*pay phone*) □ **pay back 1** repay. **2** punish or be revenged on. **pay for 1** hand over the price of. **2** bear the cost of. **3** suffer or be punished for (a fault, etc.). **pay in** pay (money) into a bank account. **pay off 1** dismiss (workers) with a final payment. **2** *colloq.* yield good results; succeed. **3** pay (a debt) in full. **4** (of a ship) turn to leeward through the movement of the helm. **pay out 1** spend; hand out (money). **2** let out (a rope). **pay up** pay the full amount, or the full amount of. □□ **pay·ee** /payée/ *n.* **pay·er** *n.*

pay Middle English (in the sense 'pacify'): from Old French *paie* (noun), *payer* (verb), from Latin *pacare* 'appease,' from *pax, pac-* 'peace.' The notion of 'payment' arose from the sense of 'pacifying' a creditor.

pay·a·ble /páyəbəl/ *adj.* **1** that must be paid; due (*payable in April*). **2** that may be paid. **3** (of a mine, etc.) profitable.

pay·back /páybak/ *n.* **1** a financial return; a reward. **2** the profit from an investment, etc., esp. one equal to the initial outlay.

pay·day /páyday/ *n.* a day on which salary or wages are paid.

pay dirt *n.* **1** *Mineral.* ground worth working for ore. **2** a financially promising situation.

pay·load /páylōd/ *n.* **1** the part of an aircraft's load from which revenue is derived, as paying passengers. **2 a** the explosive warhead carried by an aircraft or rocket. **b** the instruments, etc., carried by a spaceship.

pay·mas·ter /páymastər/ *n.* **1** an official who pays troops, workers, etc. **2** a person, organization, etc., to whom another owes duty or loyalty because of payment given.

pay·ment /páymənt/ *n.* **1** the act or an instance of paying. **2** an amount paid. **3** reward; recompense.

pay·off /páyawf/ *n. sl.* **1** an act of payment. **2** a climax. **3** a final reckoning. **4** *colloq.* a bribe; bribery.

pay·o·la /payṓlə/ *n.* **1** a bribe offered in return for unofficial promotion of a product, etc., in the media. **2** the practice of such bribery.

pay·roll /páyrōl/ *n.* a list of employees receiving regular pay.

Pb *symb. Chem.* the element lead.

PBS *abbr.* Public Broadcasting Service.

PC *abbr.* **1** personal computer. **2** political correctness; politically correct. **3** Peace Corps.

PCB *abbr.* **1** *Computing* printed circuit board. **2** *Chem.* polychlorinated biphenyl, any of several toxic compounds containing two benzene molecules in which hydrogens have been replaced by chlorine atoms, formed as waste in industrial processes.

PCP *n.* **1** *sl.* an illicit hallucinogenic drug, phencyclidine hydrochloride (*p*henyl *c*yclohexyl *p*iperidine). **2** primary care physician.

pct. *abbr.* percent.

PD *abbr.* Police Department.

Pd *symb. Chem.* the element palladium.

pd. *abbr.* paid.

p.d.q. *abbr. colloq.* pretty damn quick.

PDT *abbr.* Pacific Daylight Time.

PE *abbr.* physical education.

pea /pee/ *n.* **1 a** a hardy climbing plant, *Pisum sativum*, with seeds growing in pods and used for food. **b** its seed. **2** any of several similar plants (*sweet pea*; *chick-pea*).

peace /pees/ *n.* **1 a** quiet; tranquillity (*needs peace to work well*). **b** mental calm; serenity (*peace of mind*). **2 a** (often *attrib.*) freedom from or the cessation of war (*peace talks*). **b** (esp. **Peace**) a treaty of peace between two nations, etc., at war. **3** freedom from civil disorder. □ **keep the peace** prevent, or refrain from, strife. **make one's peace** (often foll. by *with*) reestablish friendly relations.

peace·a·ble /péesəbəl/ *adj.* **1** disposed to peace; unwarlike. **2** free from disturbance; peaceful. □□ **peace·a·ble·ness** *n.* **peace·a·bly** *adv.*

Peace Corps *n.* a federal governmental organization sending people to work as volunteers in developing countries.

peace·ful /péesfŏŏl/ *adj.* **1** characterized by peace; tranquil. **2** not violating or infringing peace (*peaceful coexistence*). **3** belonging to a state of peace. □□ **peace·ful·ly** *adv.* **peace·ful·ness** *n.*

peace·mak·er /péesmaykər/ *n.* a person who brings about peace. □□ **peace·mak·ing** *n. & adj.*

peace of·fer·ing *n.* **1** a propitiatory or conciliatory gift. **2** *Bibl.* an offering presented as a thanksgiving to God.

peace pipe *n.* a tobacco pipe smoked as a token of peace among some Native Americans.

peace·time /péestīm/ *n.* a period when a country is not at war.

peach[1] /peech/ *n.* **1 a** a round juicy fruit with downy cream or yellow skin flushed with red. **b** the tree, *Prunus persica*, bearing it. **2** the yellowish pink color of a peach. **3** *colloq.* a person or thing of superlative quality. □□ **peach·y** *adj.* (**peachier, peachiest**). **peach·i·ness** *n.*

peach[2] /peech/ *v.* **1** *intr.* (usu. foll. by *against, on*) *colloq.* turn informer; inform. **2** *tr.* inform against.

pea·cock /péekok/ *n.* **1** a male peafowl, having brilliant plumage and a tail (with eyelike markings) that can be expanded erect in display like a fan. **2** an ostentatious strutting person.

pea·fowl /péefowl/ *n.* **1** a peacock or peahen. **2** a pheasant of the genus *Pavo*.

pea·hen /péehen/ *n.* a female peafowl.

peak[1] /peek/ *n. & v.* • *n.* **1** a projecting usu. pointed part, esp.: **a** the pointed top of a mountain. **b** a mountain with a peak. **c** a stiff brim at the front of a cap. **d** a pointed beard. **e** the narrow part of a ship's hold at the bow or stern. **f** *Naut.* the upper outer corner of a sail extended by a gaff. **2 a** the highest point in a curve (*on the peak of the wave*). **b** the time of greatest success (in a career, etc.). **c** the highest point on a graph, etc. • *v.intr.* reach the highest value, quality, etc. (*output peaked in September*). □□ **peaked** *adj.* **peak·i·ness** *n.*

peak[2] /peek/ *v.intr.* **1** waste away. **2** (as **peaked** /péekid/ *adj.*) pale; sickly.

peal /peel/ *n. & v.* • *n.* **1 a** the loud ringing of a bell or bells, esp. a series of changes. **b** a set of bells. **2** a loud repeated sound, esp. of thunder, laughter, etc. • *v.* **1** *intr.* sound forth in a peal. **2** *tr.* utter sonorously. **3** *tr.* ring (bells) in peals.

pea·nut /péenut/ *n.* **1** a leguminous plant, *Arachis hypogaea*, bearing pods that ripen underground and contain seeds used as food and yielding oil. **2** the seed of this plant. **3** (in *pl.*) *colloq.* a paltry or trivial thing or amount, esp. of money.

pea·nut but·ter *n.* a paste of ground roasted peanuts.

pear /pair/ *n.* **1** a yellowish or brownish green fleshy fruit, tapering toward the stalk. **2** any of various trees of the genus *Pyrus* bearing it, esp. *P. communis*.

pearl /pərl/ *n.* **1 a** (often *attrib.*) a usu. white or bluish gray hard mass formed within the shell of a pearl oyster or other bivalve mollusk, highly prized as a gem for its luster (*pearl necklace*). **b** an imitation of this. **c** (in *pl.*) a necklace of pearls. **d** = MOTHER-OF-PEARL (cf. SEED PEARL). **2** a precious thing; the finest example. **3** anything resembling a pearl, e.g., a dewdrop, tear, etc. □ **cast pearls before swine** offer a treasure to a person unable to appreciate it. □□ **pearl·er** *n.*

pearl bar·ley *n.* barley reduced to small round grains by grinding.

pearl·es·cent /pərlésənt/ *adj.* having or producing the appearance of mother-of-pearl.

pearl·ite /pərlīt/ *n.* a ferrite and cementite mixture occurring in iron and carbon steel.

pearl on·ion *n.* a very small onion, often pickled.

pearl oys·ter *n.* any of various marine bivalve mollusks of the genus *Pinctada*, bearing pearls.

pearl·y /pə́rlee/ *adj.* (**pearlier, pearliest**) **1** resembling a pearl; lustrous. **2** containing pearls or mother-of-pearl. **3** adorned with pearls. □□ **pearl·i·ness** *n.*

peas·ant /pézənt/ *n.* **1** esp. *colloq.* a rural person; a rustic. **2 a** a worker on the land, esp. a laborer or farmer. **b** *hist.* a member of an agricultural class dependent on subsistence farming. **3** *derog.* a boorish or unsophisticated person. □□ **peas·ant·ry** *n.* (*pl.* **-ries**). **peas·ant·y** *adj.*

pease /peez/ *n.pl. archaic* peas.

pea·shoot·er /péeshootər/ *n.* a small tube for blowing dried peas through as a toy.

peat /peet/ *n.* **1** vegetable matter decomposed in water and partly carbonized, used for fuel, in horticulture, etc. **2** a cut piece of this. □□ **peat·y** *adj.*

peat·bog /péetbawg, -bog/ *n.* a bog composed of peat.

peat·moss /péetmaws, -mos/ *n.* **1** a peatbog. **2** any of various mosses of the genus *Sphagnum,* which grow in damp conditions and form peat as they decay.

peb·ble /pébəl/ *n.* **1** a small smooth stone worn by the action of water. **2 a** a type of colorless transparent rock crystal used for eyeglasses. **b** a lens of this. **c** (*attrib.*) *colloq.* (of a lens) very thick and convex. **3** an agate or other gem, esp. when found as a pebble in a stream, etc. **4** an irregular or grainy surface, as on paper, leather, etc. □□ **peb·bly** *adj.*

pec /pek/ *abbr.* pectoral (muscle).

pe·can /pikaán, -kán, péekan/ *n.* **1** a pinkish brown smooth nut with an edible kernel. **2** a hickory, *Carya illinoensis,* of the southern US, producing this.

pec·ca·dil·lo /pékədílō/ *n.* (*pl.* **-loes** or **-los**) a trifling offense; a venial sin.

pec·ca·ry /pékəree/ *n.* (*pl.* **-ries**) any American wild pig of the family Tayassuidae, esp. *Tayassu tajacu* and *T. pecari.*

peck[1] /pek/ *v.* & *n.* •*v.tr.* **1** strike or bite (something) with a beak. **2** kiss (esp. a person's cheek) hastily or perfunctorily. **3 a** make (a hole) by pecking. **b** (foll. by *out, off*) remove or pluck out by pecking. **4** *colloq.* (also *absol.*) eat (food) listlessly; nibble at. **5** mark with short strokes. •*n.* **1 a** a stroke or bite with a beak. **b** a mark made by this. **2** a hasty or perfunctory kiss. □ **peck at 1** eat (food) listlessly; nibble. **2** carp at; nag. **3** strike (a thing) repeatedly with a beak.

peck[2] /pek/ *n.* **1** a measure of capacity for dry goods, equal to 2 gallons or 8 quarts. **2** a vessel used to contain this amount. □ **a peck of** a large number or amount of (troubles, dirt, etc.).

peck·er /pékər/ *n.* **1** a bird that pecks (*woodpecker*). **2** *coarse sl.* the penis.

peck·ing or·der *n.* a social hierarchy, orig. as observed among hens.

peck·ish /pékish/ *adj. colloq.* **1** esp. *Brit.* hungry. **2** irritable.

pec·o·ri·no /pékəréenō/ *n.* (*pl.* **-nos**) an Italian cheese made from sheep's milk.

pec·tin /péktin/ *n. Biochem.* any of various soluble gelatinous polysaccharides found in ripe fruits, etc., and used as a gelling agent in jams and jellies. □□ **pec·tic** *adj.*

pec·to·ral /péktərəl/ *adj.* & *n.* •*adj.* **1** of or relating to the breast or chest; thoracic (*pectoral fin; pectoral muscle*). **2** worn on the chest (*pectoral cross*). •*n.* **1** (esp. in *pl.*) a pectoral muscle. **2** a pectoral fin. **3** an ornamental breastplate esp. of a Jewish high priest.

pec·u·late /pékyəlayt/ *v.tr.* & *intr.* embezzle (money). □□ **pec·u·la·tion** /-láyshən/ *n.* **pec·u·la·tor** *n.*

pe·cu·liar /pikyóolyər/ *adj.* **1** strange; odd; unusual (*a peculiar flavor; is a little peculiar*). **2 a** (usu. foll. by *to*) belonging exclusively (*a fashion peculiar to the time*). **b** belonging to the individual (*in their own peculiar way*). **3** particular; special (*a point of peculiar interest*).

peculiar late Middle English (in the sense 'particular, special'): from Latin *peculiaris* 'of private property,' from *peculium* 'property,' from *pecu* 'cattle' (cattle being private property). The sense 'odd' dates from the early 17th century.

pe·cu·li·ar·i·ty /pikyóoleeáritee/ *n.* (*pl.* **-ties**) **1 a** idiosyncrasy; oddity. **b** an instance of this. **2** a characteristic or habit (*meanness is his peculiarity*). **3** the state of being peculiar.

pe·cu·liar·ly /pikyóolyərlee/ *adv.* **1** more than usually; especially (*peculiarly annoying*). **2** oddly. **3** as regards oneself alone; individually (*does not affect him peculiarly*).

pe·cu·ni·ar·y /pikyóonee-eree/ *adj.* **1** of, concerning, or consisting of, money (*pecuniary aid; pecuniary considerations*). **2** (of an offense) entailing a money penalty or fine. □□ **pe·cu·ni·ar·i·ly** *adv.*

ped·a·gogue /pédəgog, -gawg/ *n.* a schoolmaster or teacher, esp. a pedantic one. □□ **ped·a·gog·ic** /-gójik, -gójik/ *adj.* **ped·a·gog·i·cal** *adj.* **ped·a·gog·i·cal·ly** *adv.* **ped·a·gog·ism** *n.* (also **ped·a·gogu·ism**).

ped·a·go·gy /pédəgōjee, -gojee/ *n.* the science of teaching. □□ **ped·a·gog·ics** /-gójiks, -gójiks/ *n.*

ped·al /péd'l/ *n.* & *v.* •*n.* any of several types of foot-operated levers or controls for mechanisms, esp.: **a** either of a pair of levers for transmitting power to a bicycle or tricycle wheel, etc. **b** any of the foot-operated controls in a motor vehicle. **c** any of the foot-operated keys of an organ used for playing notes, or for drawing out several stops at once, etc. **d** each of the foot-levers on a piano, etc., for making the tone fuller or softer. **e** each of the foot-levers on a harp for altering the pitch of the strings. •*v.* (**pedaled** or **pedalled, pedaling** or **pedalling**) **1** *intr.* operate a cycle, organ, etc., by using the pedals. **2** *tr.* work (a bicycle, etc.) with the pedals.

ped·ant /péd'nt/ *n.* **1** a person who insists on strict adherence to formal rules or literal meaning at the expense of a wider view. **2** a person who rates academic learning or technical knowledge above everything. **3** a person who is obsessed by a theory; a doctrinaire. □□ **pe·dan·tic** /pidántik/ *adj.* **pe·dan·ti·cal·ly** *adv.* **ped·ant·ize** *v.intr.* & *tr.* **ped·ant·ry** *n.* (*pl.* **-ries**).

ped·dle /péd'l/ *v.* **1** *tr.* **a** sell (goods), esp. in small quantities, as a peddler. **b** advocate or promote (ideas, a philosophy, a way of life, etc.). **2** *tr.* sell (drugs) illegally. **3** *intr.* engage in selling, esp. as a peddler.

ped·dler /pédlər/ *n.* **1** a traveling seller of small items esp. carried in a pack, etc. **2** (usu. foll. by *of*) a dealer in gossip, influence, etc. **3** a person who sells drugs illegally. □□ **ped·dler·y** *n.*

ped·er·as·ty /pédərastee/ *n.* anal intercourse esp. between a man and a boy. □□ **ped·er·ast** *n.*

ped·es·tal /pédistəl/ *n.* & *v.* •*n.* **1** a base supporting a column or pillar. **2** the stone, etc., base of a statue, etc. **3** either of the two supports of a desk or table, usu. containing drawers. •*v.tr.* (**pedestaled, pedestaling** or **pedestalled, pedestalling**) set or support on a pedestal. □ **put** (or **set**) **on a pedestal** regard as highly admirable, important, etc.; venerate.

pe·des·tri·an /pidéstreeən/ *n.* & *adj.* •*n.* (often *attrib.*) a person who is walking, esp. in a town (*pedestrian crossing*). •*adj.* prosaic; dull; uninspired. □□ **pe·des·tri·an·ism** *n.* **pe·des·tri·an·ize** *v.tr.* & *intr.* **pe·des·tri·an·i·za·tion** *n.*

pe·di·at·rics /péedeeátriks/ *n.pl.* (treated as *sing.*) the branch of medicine dealing with children and their diseases. □□ **pe·di·at·ric** *adj.* **pe·di·a·tri·cian** /-deeətríshən/ *n.*

ped·i·cure /pédikyoor/ *n.* & *v.* •*n.* **1** the care or treatment of the feet, esp. of the toenails. **2** a person practicing this, esp. professionally. •*v.tr.* treat (the feet) by removing corns, etc.

ped·i·gree /pédigree/ *n.* **1** (often *attrib.*) a recorded line of descent of a person or esp. a pure-bred domestic or pet animal. **2** the derivation of a word. **3** a genealogical table. □□ **ped·i·greed** *adj.*

ped·i·ment /pédimənt/ *n.* **1 a** the triangular front part of a building in Grecian style, surmounting esp. a portico of columns. **b** a similar part of a building in Roman or Renaissance style. **2** *Geol.* a broad flattish rock surface at the foot of a mountain slope. □□ **ped·i·men·tal** /-mént'l/ *adj.* **ped·i·ment·ed** *adj.*

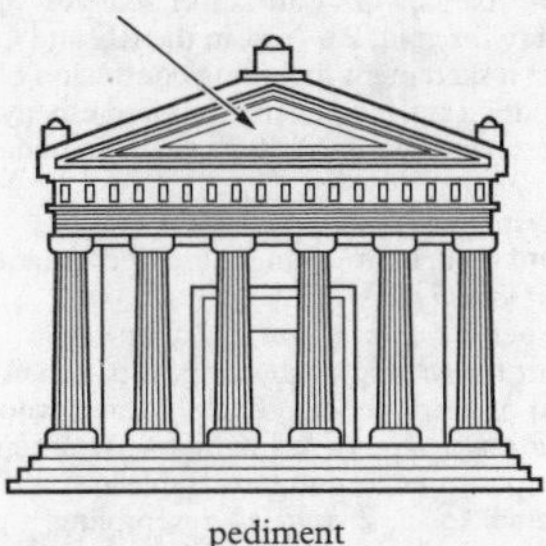

pediment

pe·dom·e·ter /pidómitər/ *n.* an instrument for estimating the distance traveled on foot by recording the number of steps taken.

ped·o·phile /péedəfīl, péd–/ *n.* a person who displays pedophilia.

pe·do·phil·i·a /péedəfíleeə, pédə-/ *n.* sexual desire directed toward children. □□ **pe·do·phile** *n.*

pe·dun·cle /pedúngkəl, péedung-/ *n.* **1** *Bot.* the stalk of a flower, fruit, or cluster, esp. a main stalk bearing a solitary flower or subordinate stalks. **2** *Zool.* a stalklike projection in an animal body. □□ **pe·dun·cu·lar** /-kyələr/ *adj.* **pe·dun·cu·late** /-kyələt/ *adj.*

pee /pee/ *v. & n. colloq.* or *coarse* • *v.* (**pees, peed**) **1** *intr.* urinate. **2** *tr.* pass (urine, blood, etc.) from the bladder. • *n.* **1** urination. **2** urine.

peek /peek/ *v. & n.* • *v.intr.* (usu. foll. by *in, out, at*) look quickly or slyly; peep. • *n.* a quick or sly look.

peek·a·boo /péekəboo/ *adj. & n.* • *adj.* **1** (of a garment, etc.) transparent or having a pattern of small holes. **2** (of a hairstyle) concealing one eye with the bangs or a wave. • *n.* game of hiding and suddenly reappearing, played with a young child.

peel[1] /peel/ *v. & n.* • *v.* **1** *tr.* **a** strip the skin, rind, bark, wrapping, etc., from (a fruit, vegetable, tree, etc.). **b** (usu. foll. by *off*) strip (skin, peel, wrapping, etc.) from a fruit, etc. **2** *intr.* **a** (of a tree, an animal's or person's body, a painted surface, etc.) become bare of bark, skin, paint, etc. **b** (often foll. by *off*) (of bark, a person's skin, paint, etc.) flake off. **3** *intr.* (often foll. by *off*) *colloq.* (of a person) strip for exercise, etc. • *n.* the outer covering of a fruit, vegetable, shrimp, etc.; rind. □ **peel off 1** veer away and detach oneself from a group of marchers, a formation of aircraft, etc. **2** *colloq.* strip off one's clothes. □□ **peel·er** *n.* (in sense 1 of *v.*).

peel[2] /peel/ *n.* a shovel, esp. a baker's shovel for bringing loaves, etc., into or out of an oven.

peel·ing /péeling/ *n.* a strip of the outer skin of a vegetable, fruit, etc. (*potato peelings*).

peen /peen/ *n.* the wedge-shaped or thin or curved end of a hammer head (opp. FACE *n.* 5a).

peep[1] /peep/ *v. & n.* • *v.intr.* **1** (usu. foll. by *at, in, out, into*) look through a narrow opening; look furtively. **2** (usu. foll. by *out*) **a** (of daylight, a flower beginning to bloom, etc.) come slowly into view; emerge. **b** (of a quality, etc.) show itself unconsciously. • *n.* **1** a furtive or peering glance. **2** the first appearance (*at peep of day*).

peep[2] /peep/ *v. & n.* • *v.intr.* make a shrill feeble sound as of young birds, mice, etc.; squeak; chirp. • *n.* **1** such a sound; a cheep. **2** the slightest sound or utterance, esp. of protest, etc.

peep·er /péepər/ *n.* **1** a person who peeps. **2** *colloq.* an eye. **3** *NE US* any of several species of frogs with a high peeping cry.

peep·hole /péephōl/ *n.* a tiny hole in a solid door, fence, etc., to look through.

peep·ing Tom *n.* a furtive voyeur.

peep show *n.* **1** a small exhibition of pictures, etc., viewed through a lens or hole set into a box, etc. **2** an erotic movie or picture viewed through a usu. coin-operated machine.

peer[1] /peer/ *v.intr.* **1** (usu. foll. by *into, at,* etc.) look keenly or with difficulty (*peered into the fog*). **2** appear; peep out.

peer[2] /peer/ *n.* **1** a person who is equal in ability, standing, rank, or value; a contemporary (*tried by a jury of his peers*). **2 a** (*fem.* **peeress**) a member of one of the degrees of the nobility in Britain, i.e. a duke, marquis, earl, viscount, or baron. **b** a noble of any country. □□ **peer·less** *adj.*

peer·age /péerij/ *n.* **1** peers as a class; the nobility. **2** the rank of peer or peeress (*was given a life peerage*). **3** a book containing a list of peers with their genealogy, etc.

peer group *n.* a group of people of the same age, status, interests, etc.

peeve /peev/ *v. & n. colloq.* • *v.tr.* (usu. as **peeved** *adj.*) annoy; vex; irritate. • *n.* **1** a cause of annoyance. **2** vexation.

peev·ish /péevish/ *adj.* querulous; irritable. □□ **peev·ish·ly** *adv.* **peev·ish·ness** *n.*

peg /peg/ *n. & v.* • *n.* **1 a** a usu. cylindrical pin or bolt of wood or metal, often tapered at one end, and used for holding esp. two things together. **b** such a peg attached to a wall, etc., and used for hanging garments, etc., on. **c** a peg driven into the ground and attached to a rope for holding up a tent. **d** a bung for stoppering a cask, etc. **e** each of several pegs used to tighten or loosen the strings of a violin, etc. **f** a small peg, matchstick, etc., stuck into holes in a board for calculating the scores at cribbage. **2** *Brit.* = CLOTHESPIN. • *v.tr.* (**pegged, pegging**) **1** (usu. foll. by *down, in, out,* etc.) fix (a thing) with a peg. **2** *Econ.* **a** stabilize (prices, wages, exchange rates, etc.). **b** prevent the price of (stock, etc.) from falling or rising by freely buying or selling at a given price. □ **a round** (or **square**) **peg in a square** (or **round**) **hole** a misfit. **take a person down a peg or two** humble a person.

peg·board /pégbawrd/ *n.* a board having a regular pattern of small holes for pegs, used for commercial displays, games, etc.

peg leg *n.* **1** an artificial leg. **2** a person with an artificial leg.

PEI *abbr.* Prince Edward Island.

peign·oir /paynwaár, pen–, páynwaar, pén-/ *n.* a woman's loose dressing gown.

pe·jo·ra·tive /pijáwrətiv, -jór-, péjəra-, pée-/ *adj. & n.* • *adj.* (of a word, an expression, etc.) depreciatory. • *n.* a depreciatory word. □□ **pe·jo·ra·tive·ly** *adv.*

pek·an /pékən/ = FISHER 1.

peke /peek/ *n. colloq.* a Pekingese dog.

Pe·king·ese /péekinéez, -ées/ (also **Pe·kin·ese**) *n.* (*pl.* same) **1** a lapdog of a short-legged breed with long hair and a snub nose. **2** this breed.

pe·koe /péekō/ *n.* a superior kind of black tea.

pe·la·gi·an /piláyjeeən/ *adj. & n.* • *adj.* inhabiting the open sea. • *n.* an inhabitant of the open sea.

pe·lag·ic /pilájik/ *adj.* **1** of or performed on the open sea (*pelagic whaling*). **2** (of marine life) belonging to the upper layers of the open sea.

pelf /pelf/ *n. derog.* or *joc.* money; wealth.

pel·i·can /pélikən/ *n.* any large gregarious waterfowl of the family Pelecanidae with a large bill and a pouch in the throat for storing fish.

pel·la·gra /pilágrə, -láygrə, -láa-/ *n.* a disease caused by deficiency of nicotinic acid, characterized by cracking of the skin and often resulting in insanity. ▫▫ **pel·la·grous** *adj.*

pel·let /pélit/ *n.* & *v.* •*n.* **1** a small compressed ball of paper, bread, etc. **2** a pill. **3 a** a small mass of bones, feathers, etc., regurgitated by a bird of prey. **b** a small hard piece of animal, usu. rodent, excreta. **4 a** a piece of small shot. **b** an imitation bullet for a toy gun. •*v.tr.* (**pelleted, pelleting**) **1** make into a pellet or pellets. **2** hit with (esp. paper) pellets. ▫▫ **pel·let·ize** *v.tr.*

pell-mell /pélmél/ *adv.* **1** headlong; recklessly (*rushed pell-mell out of the room*). **2** in disorder or confusion (*stuffed the papers together pell-mell*).

pel·lu·cid /pilóosid/ *adj.* **1** (of water, light, etc.) transparent; clear. **2** (of style, speech, etc.) not confused; clear. **3** mentally clear. ▫▫ **pel·lu·cid·i·ty** /-síditee/ *n.* **pel·lu·cid·ly** *adv.*

pe·lo·ta /pilótə/ *n.* **1** a Basque or Spanish game similar to jai alai played in a walled court with a ball and basket-like rackets attached to the hand. **2** the ball used in jai alai.

pelt[1] /pelt/ *v.* & *n.* •*v.* **1** *tr.* (usu. foll. by *with*) **a** hurl many small missiles at. **b** strike repeatedly with missiles. **c** assail (a person, etc.) with insults, abuse, etc. **2** *intr.* (usu. foll. by *down*) (of rain, etc.) fall quickly and torrentially. **3** *intr.* run fast. **4** *intr.* (often foll. by *at*) fire repeatedly. •*n.* the act or an instance of pelting.

pelt[2] /pelt/ *n.* **1** the undressed skin of a fur-bearing mammal. **2** the skin of a sheep, goat, etc., with short wool, or stripped ready for tanning. ▫▫ **pelt·ry** *n.*

pel·vic /pélvik/ *adj.* of or relating to the pelvis.

pel·vis /pélvis/ *n.* (*pl.* **pelvises** or **pelves** /-veez/) **1** a basin-shaped cavity at the lower end of the torso of most vertebrates, formed from the innominate bones with the sacrum and other vertebrae. **2** the basin-like cavity of the kidney.

pen[1] /pen/ *n.* & *v.* •*n.* **1** an instrument for writing or drawing with ink, orig. consisting of a shaft with a sharpened quill or metal nib, now more widely applied. **2 a** (usu. prec. by *the*) the occupation of writing. **b** a style of writing. **3** *Zool.* the internal feather-shaped cartilaginous shell of certain cuttlefish, esp. squid. •*v.tr.* (**penned, penning**) **1** write. **2** compose and write. ▫ **put pen to paper** begin writing.

pen[2] /pen/ *n.* & *v.* •*n.* **1** a small enclosure for cows, sheep, poultry, etc. **2** a place of confinement. **3** an enclosure for sheltering submarines. •*v.tr.* (**penned, penning**) (often foll. by *in, up*) enclose or shut in a pen.

pen[3] /pen/ *n.* a female swan.

pen[4] /pen/ *n. sl.* = PENITENTIARY *n.* 1.

pe·nal /péenəl/ *adj.* **1 a** of or concerning punishment or its infliction (*penal laws*; *a penal sentence*; *a penal colony*). **b** (of an offense) punishable, esp. by law. **2** extremely severe (*penal taxation*). ▫▫ **pe·nal·ly** *adv.*

pe·nal·ize /péenəlīz/ *v.tr.* **1** subject (a person) to a penalty or comparative disadvantage. **2** make or declare (an action) penal. ▫▫ **pe·nal·i·za·tion** *n.*

pen·al·ty /pénəltee/ *n.* (*pl.* **-ties**) **1 a** a punishment, esp. a fine, for a breach of law, contract, etc. **b** a fine paid. **2** a disadvantage, loss, etc., esp. as a result of one's own actions. **3 a** a disadvantage imposed on a competitor or team in a game, etc., for a breach of the rules, etc. **b** (*attrib.*) awarded against a side incurring a penalty (*clipping penalty*; *penalty kick*). **4** *Bridge*, etc., points gained by opponents when a contract is not fulfilled. ▫ **under** (or **on**) **penalty of** under the threat of (dismissal, etc.).

pen·al·ty box *n. Ice Hockey* an area reserved for penalized players and some officials.

pen·ance /pénəns/ *n.* **1** an act of self-punishment as reparation for guilt. **2 a** (esp. in the RC and Orthodox Church) a sacrament including confession of and absolution for a sin. **b** a penalty imposed esp. by a priest, or undertaken voluntarily, for a sin. ▫ **do penance** perform a penance.

pence *Brit. pl.* of PENNY.

pen·chant /pénchənt/ *n.* an inclination or liking (*has a penchant for old films*).

pen·cil /pénsil/ *n.* & *v.* •*n.* **1** (often *attrib.*) **a** an instrument for writing or drawing, usu. consisting of a thin rod of graphite, etc., enclosed in a wooden cylinder (*a pencil sketch*). **b** a similar instrument with a metal or plastic cover and retractable lead. **c** a cosmetic in pencil form. **2** (*attrib.*) resembling a pencil in shape (*pencil skirt*). •*v.tr.* (**penciled, penciling** or **pencilled, pencilling**) **1** tint or mark with or as if with a pencil. **2** (usu. foll. by *in*) **a** write, esp. tentatively or provisionally (*have penciled in the 29th for our meeting*). **b** (esp. as **penciled** *adj.*) fill (an area) with soft pencil strokes (*penciled in her eyebrows*). ▫▫ **pen·cil·er** *or Brit.* **pen·cil·ler** *n.*

pen·cil push·er *n. colloq. derog.* a clerical worker or one who does considerable paperwork.

pend·ant /péndənt/ *n.* (also **pend·ent**) **1** a hanging jewel, etc., esp. one attached to a necklace, bracelet, etc. **2** a light fitting, ornament, etc., hanging from a ceiling.

pend·ent /péndənt/ *adj.* (also **pend·ant**) **1 a** hanging. **b** overhanging. **2** undecided; pending. **3** *Gram.* (esp. of a sentence) incomplete; not having a finite verb (*pendent nominative*). ▫▫ **pen·den·cy** *n.*

pend·ing /pénding/ *adj.* & *prep.* •*predic. adj.* **1** awaiting decision or settlement; undecided (*a settlement was pending*). **2** about to come into existence (*patent pending*). •*prep.* **1** during (*pending these negotiations*). **2** until (*pending his return*).

pen·du·lous /pénjələs, péndə-, -dyə-/ *adj.* **1** (of ears, breasts, flowers, bird's nests, etc.) hanging down; drooping and esp. swinging. **2** oscillating. ▫▫ **pen·du·lous·ly** *adv.*

pen·du·lum /pénjələm, péndə-, -dyə-/ *n.* a weight suspended so as to swing freely, esp. a rod with a weighted end regulating the movement of a clock's works.

pendulum

pen·e·trate /pénitrayt/ *v.* **1** *tr.* **a** find access into or through, esp. forcibly. **b** (usu. foll. by *with*) imbue (a person or thing) with; permeate. **2** *tr.* see into, find out, or discern (a person's mind, the truth, a meaning, etc.). **3** *tr.* see through (darkness, fog, etc.) (*could not penetrate the gloom*). **4** *intr.* be absorbed by the mind (*my hint did not penetrate*). **5** *tr.* (as **penetrating** *adj.*) **a** having or suggesting sensitivity or insight (*a penetrating remark*). **b** (of a voice, etc.) easily heard through or above other sounds; piercing. **c** (of a smell) sharp; pungent. **6** *tr.* (of a man) put the penis into the vagina of (a woman). **7** *intr.* (usu. foll. by *into, through, to*) make a way. □□ **pen·e·tra·ble** *adj.* **pen·e·tra·bil·i·ty** *n.* **pen·e·trant** *adj.* & *n.* **pen·e·trat·ing·ly** *adv.* **pen·e·tra·tion** *n.* **pen·e·tra·tive** /-trətiv/ *adj.* **pen·e·tra·tor** *n.*

pen·guin /pénggwin/ *n.* any flightless sea bird of the family Spheniscidae of the southern hemisphere, with black upperparts and white underparts, and wings developed into scaly flippers for swimming underwater.

pen·i·cil·lin /pénisílin/ *n.* any of various antibiotics produced naturally by molds of the genus *Penicillium*, or synthetically, and able to prevent the growth of certain disease-causing bacteria.

pe·nile /péenil, -nəl/ *adj.* of or concerning the penis.

pen·in·su·la /pənínsələ, -syələ/ *n.* a piece of land almost surrounded by water or projecting far into a sea or lake, etc. □□ **pen·in·su·lar** *adj.*

pe·nis /péenis/ *n.* (*pl.* **penises** or **penes** /-neez/) **1** the male organ of copulation and (in mammals) urination. **2** the male copulatory organ in lower vertebrates.

pen·i·tent /pénitənt/ *adj.* & *n.* • *adj.* regretting and wishing to atone for sins, etc.; repentant. • *n.* **1** a person who repents their sins and (in the Christian church) seeks forgiveness from God. **2** (in the Roman Catholic Church) a person who confesses their sins to a priest and submits to the penance he imposes. □□ **pen·i·tence** *n.* **pen·i·tent·ly** *adv.*

pen·i·ten·tial /pénitén shəl/ *adj.* of or concerning penitence or penance. □□ **pen·i·ten·tial·ly** *adv.*

pen·i·ten·tia·ry /pénitén shəree/ *n.* & *adj.* • *n.* (*pl.* **-ries**) **1** a reformatory prison, esp. a state or federal prison. **2** an office in the papal court deciding questions of penance, dispensations, etc. • *adj.* **1** of or concerning penance. **2** of or concerning reformatory treatment. **3** (of an offense) making a culprit liable to a prison sentence.

pen·knife /pén-nīf/ *n.* a small folding knife, esp. for carrying in a pocket.

pen·light /pénlīt/ *n.* a pen-sized flashlight.

Penn. *abbr.* (also **Penna.**) Pennsylvania.

pen name *n.* a literary pseudonym.

pen·nant /pénənt/ *n.* **1** *Naut.* a tapering flag, esp. that flown at the masthead of a vessel in commission. **2** = PENNON. **3 a** a flag denoting a sports championship, etc. **b** (by extension) a sports championship.

pen·ni·less /pénilis/ *adj.* having no money; destitute. □□ **pen·ni·less·ly** *adv.* **pen·ni·less·ness** *n.*

pen·non /pénən/ *n.* a long narrow flag, triangular or swallow-tailed, esp. as the military ensign of lancer regiments. □□ **pen·noned** *adj.*

Penn·syl·va·ni·a Dutch /pénsilváynyə/ *n.* **1** a dialect of High German spoken by descendants of 17th–18th-c. German and Swiss immigrants to Pennsylvania, etc. **2** (as *pl.*) these settlers or their descendants.

Penn·syl·va·nian /pénsilváynyən/ *n.* & *adj.* • *n.* **1** a native or inhabitant of Pennsylvania. **2** (prec. by *the*) *Geol.* the upper Carboniferous period or system in N. America. • *adj.* **1** of or relating to Pennsylvania. **2** *Geol.* of or relating to the upper Carboniferous period or system in N. America.

pen·ny /pénee/ *n.* (*pl.* for separate coins **-nies**, *Brit.* for a sum of money **pence** /pens/) **1** (in the US, Canada, etc.) a one-cent coin. **2** a British coin and monetary unit equal to one hundredth of a pound. ¶ Abbr.: **p.** **3** *hist.* a former British bronze coin and monetary unit equal to one two-hundred-and-fortieth of a pound. ¶ Abbr.: **d.** **4** *Bibl.* a denarius. □ **like a bad penny** continually returning when unwanted. **pennies from heaven** unexpected benefits. **penny wise and pound foolish** frugal in small expenditures but wasteful of large amounts. **a pretty penny** a large sum of money.

pen·ny-pinch·ing *n.* & *adj.* • *n.* frugality; cheapness. • *adj.* frugal. □□ **pen·ny-pinch·er** *n.*

pen·ny·roy·al /péneeróyəl/ *n.* **1** a European creeping mint, *Mentha pulegium*, cultivated for its supposed medicinal properties. **2** an aromatic N. American plant, *Hedeoma pulegioides*.

pen·ny·weight /péneewayt/ *n.* a unit of weight, 24 grains or one twentieth of an ounce troy.

pen·ny whis·tle *n.* a tin pipe with six holes giving different notes.

pen·ny·wort /péneewərt, -wawrt/ *n.* any of several wild plants with rounded leaves, esp.: **1** (**wall pennywort**) *Umbilicus rupestris*, growing in crevices. **2** (**marsh** or **water pennywort**) *Hydrocotyle vulgaris*, growing in marshy places.

Pe·nob·scot /pənóbskot, -skət/ *n.* **1 a** a N. American people native to Maine. **b** a member of this people. **2** the language of this people.

pe·nol·o·gy /peenóləjee/ *n.* the study of the punishment of crime and of prison management. □□ **pe·no·log·i·cal** /-nəlójikəl/ *adj.* **pe·nol·o·gist** *n.*

pen pal *n. colloq.* a friend communicated with by letter only.

pen·sile /pénsīl/ *adj.* **1** hanging down; pendulous. **2** (of a bird, etc.) building a pensile nest.

pen·sion /pénshən/ *n.* & *v.* • *n.* **1** a regular payment made by an employer, etc., after the retirement of an employee. **2** a similar payment made by a government to people above a specified age, to the disabled, etc. • *v.tr.* grant a pension to. □ **pension off** dismiss with a pension. □□ **pen·sion·less** *adj.*

pen·sive /pénsiv/ *adj.* **1** deep in thought. **2** sorrowfully thoughtful. □□ **pen·sive·ly** *adv.* **pen·sive·ness** *n.*

pent /pent/ *adj.* (often foll. by *in, up*) closely confined; shut in (*pent-up feelings*).

penta- /péntə/ *comb.form* **1** five. **2** *Chem.* (forming the names of compounds) containing five atoms or groups of a specified kind (*pentachloride*; *pentoxide*).

pen·ta·cle /péntəkəl/ *n.* a figure used as a symbol, esp. in magic, e.g., a pentagram.

pen·ta·gon /péntəgon/ *n.* **1** a plane figure with five sides and angles. **2** (**the Pentagon**) **a** the pentagonal headquarters building of the US armed forces, located near Washington, D.C. **b** the US Department of Defense; the leaders of the US armed forces. □□ **pen·tag·o·nal** /-tágənəl/ *adj.*

pen·ta·gram /péntəgram/ *n.* a five-pointed star formed by extending the sides of a pentagon both ways until they intersect, formerly used as a mystic symbol.

pen·tam·e·ter /pentámitər/ *n.* **1** a verse of five feet, e.g., English iambic verse of ten syllables. **2** a form of Gk or Latin dactylic verse composed of two halves each of two feet and a long syllable, used in elegiac verse.

pen·tan·gle /péntanggəl/ *n.* = PENTAGRAM.

Pen·ta·teuch /péntətōōk, -tyōōk/ *n.* the first five books of the Old Testament, traditionally ascribed to Moses. □□ **pen·ta·teuch·al** *adj.*

pen·tath·lon /pentáthlən, -laan/ *n.* an athletic event comprising five different events for each competitor. □□ **pen·tath·lete** /-táthleet/ *n.*

Pen·te·cost /péntikawst, -kost/ *n.* **1** a Christian holiday commemorating the descent of the Holy Spirit, fifty days after Easter. **2 a** the Jewish harvest festival, on the fiftieth day after the second day of Passover (Lev. 23:15–16). **b** a synagogue ceremony on the anniversary of the giving of the Law on Mount Sinai.

Pen·te·cos·tal /péntikóst'l, -káwst'l/ *adj.* & *n.* • *adj.* (also **pentecostal**) **1** of or relating to Pentecost. **2** of or designating Christian sects and individuals who emphasize the gifts of the Holy Spirit, are often fundamentalist in outlook, and express religious feelings by clapping, shouting, dancing, etc. • *n.* a Pentecostalist. ▫▫ **Pen·te·cos·tal·ism** *n.* **Pen·te·cos·tal·ist** *adj. & n.*

pent·house /pént-hows/ *n.* **1** a house or apartment on the roof or the top floor of a tall building. **2** a sloping roof, esp. of an outhouse built on to another building. **3** an awning; a canopy.

Pen·to·thal /péntəthawl/ *n. Trademark* an intravenous anesthetic, thiopental sodium.

pe·nul·ti·mate /pinúltimət/ *adj. & n.* • *adj.* next to the last. • *n.* **1** the next to the last. **2** the next to the last syllable.

pe·num·bra /pinúmbrə/ *n.* (*pl.* **penumbrae** /-bree/ or **penumbras**) **1 a** the partly shaded region around the shadow of an opaque body, esp. that around the total shadow of the moon or earth in an eclipse. **b** the less dark outer part of a sunspot. **2** a partial shadow. ▫▫ **pe·num·bral** *adj.*

pe·nu·ri·ous /pinóoreeəs, pinyóor-/ *adj.* **1** poor; destitute. **2** stingy; grudging. **3** scanty. ▫▫ **pe·nu·ri·ous·ly** *adv.* **pe·nu·ri·ous·ness** *n.*

pen·u·ry /pényəree/ *n.* (*pl.* **-ries**) **1** destitution; poverty. **2** a lack; scarcity.

pe·on /péeon, péeən/ *n.* **1** a Spanish American day laborer or farmworker. **2** an unskilled worker; drudge. **3** *hist.* a worker held in servitude in the southwestern US. ▫▫ **pe·on·age** *n.*

pe·o·ny /péeənee/ *n.* (*pl.* **-nies**) any herbaceous plant of the genus *Paeonia*, with large globular red, pink, or white flowers, often double in cultivated varieties.

peo·ple /péepəl/ *n. & v.* • *n.* **1** (usu. as *pl.*) **a** persons composing a community, tribe, race, nation, etc. (*the American people*; *a warlike people*). **b** a group of persons of a usu. specified kind (*the chosen people*; *these people here*; *right-thinking people*). **2** (prec. by *the*; treated as *pl.*) **a** the mass of people in a country, etc., not having special rank or position. **b** these considered as an electorate (*the people will reject it*). **3** parents or other relatives. **4 a** subjects, armed followers, a retinue, etc. **b** a congregation of a parish priest, etc. **5** persons in general (*people do not like rudeness*). • *v.tr.* (usu. foll. by *with*) **1** fill with people, animals, etc.; populate. **2** (esp. as **peopled** *adj.*) inhabit; occupy; fill (*thickly peopled*).

▶See note at PERSON.

pep /pep/ *n. & v. colloq.* • *n.* vigor; go; spirit. • *v.tr.* (**pepped, pepping**) (usu. foll. by *up*) fill with vigor.

pe·per·o·ni var. of PEPPERONI.

pep·lum /pépləm/ *n.* **1** a short flounce, ruffle, etc., at waist level, esp. of a blouse or jacket over a skirt. **2** *Gk Antiq.* a woman's outer garment.

pep·per /pépər/ *n. & v.* • *n.* **1 a** a hot aromatic condiment from the dried berries of certain plants used whole or ground. **b** any climbing vine of the genus *Piper*, esp. *P. nigrum*, yielding these berries. **2** anything hot or pungent. **3 a** any plant of the genus *Capsicum*, esp. *C. annuum*. **b** the fruit of this used esp. as a vegetable or salad ingredient. **4** = CAYENNE. • *v.tr.* **1** sprinkle or treat with or as if with pepper. **2 a** pelt with missiles. **b** hurl abuse, etc., at. **3** punish severely.

pep·per·corn /pépərkawrn/ *n.* **1** the dried berry of *Piper nigrum* as a condiment. **2** *Brit.* (in full **peppercorn rent**) a nominal rent.

pep·per mill *n.* a device for grinding pepper by hand.

pep·per·mint /pépərmint/ *n.* **1 a** a mint plant, *Mentha piperita*, grown for the strong-flavored oil obtained from its leaves. **b** the oil from this. **2** a candy flavored with peppermint. ▫▫ **pep·per·mint·y** *adj.*

pep·per·o·ni /pépərónee/ *n.* (also **pep·er·o·ni**) beef and pork sausage seasoned with pepper.

pep·per·y /pépəree/ *adj.* **1** of, like, or containing much pepper. **2** hot-tempered. **3** pungent; stinging. ▫▫ **pep·per·i·ness** *n.*

pep pill *n.* a pill containing a stimulant drug.

pep·py /pépee/ *adj.* (**peppier, peppiest**) *colloq.* vigorous; energetic; bouncy. ▫▫ **pep·pi·ly** *adv.* **pep·pi·ness** *n.*

pep·sin /pépsin/ *n.* an enzyme contained in the gastric juice that hydrolyzes proteins.

pep talk *n.* a usu. short talk intended to enthuse, encourage, etc.

pep·tic /péptik/ *adj.* concerning or promoting digestion.

pep·tic ul·cer *n.* an ulcer in the stomach or duodenum.

pep·tide /péptīd/ *n. Biochem.* any of a group of organic compounds consisting of two or more amino acids bonded in sequence.

Pe·quot /péekwot/ *n.* **1 a** a N. American people native to eastern Connecticut. **b** a member of this people. **2** the language of this people.

per /pər/ *prep. & adv.* • *prep.* **1** for each; for every (*two cupcakes per child*; *five miles per hour*). **2** by means of; by; through (*per rail*). **3** (in full **as per**) in accordance with (*as per instructions*). • *adv. colloq.* each; apiece. ▫ **as per usual** *colloq.* as usual.

per- /pər/ *prefix* **1** forming verbs, nouns, and adjectives meaning: **a** through; all over (*perforate*; *perforation*; *pervade*). **b** completely; very (*perfervid*; *perturb*). **c** to destruction; to the bad (*pervert*; *perdition*). **2** *Chem.* having the maximum of some element in combination, esp.: **a** in the names of binary compounds in *-ide* (*peroxide*). **b** in the names of oxides, acids, etc., in *-ic* (*perchloric*; *permanganic*). **c** in the names of salts of these acids (*perchlorate*; *permanganate*).

per·ad·ven·ture /pərədvénchər, pér-/ *adv. & n. archaic* or *joc.* • *adv.* perhaps. • *n.* uncertainty; chance; conjecture; doubt (esp. beyond or without peradventure).

per·am·bu·late /pərámbyəlayt/ *v.* **1** *tr.* walk through, over, or about (streets, the country, etc.). **2** *intr.* walk from place to place. **3** *tr.* **a** travel through and inspect (territory). **b** formally establish the boundaries of (a parish, etc.) by walking round them. ▫▫ **per·am·bu·la·tion** /-láyshən/ *n.* **per·am·bu·la·to·ry** /-lətáwree/ *adj.*

per·am·bu·la·tor /pərámbyəláytər/ *n. Brit. formal* = PRAM.

per an·num /pər ánəm/ *adv.* for each year.

per·cale /pərkáyl/ *n.* a closely woven cotton fabric like calico.

per cap·i·ta /pər kápitə/ *adv. & adj.* (also **per ca·put** /kápoot/) for each person.

per·ceive /pərséev/ *v.tr.* **1** apprehend, esp. through the sight; observe. **2** (usu. foll. by *that, how*, etc., + clause) apprehend with the mind; understand. **3** regard mentally in a specified manner (*perceives the universe as infinite*). ▫▫ **per·ceiv·a·ble** *adj.* **per·ceiv·er** *n.*

per·cent /pərsént/ *adv. & n.* (also **per cent**) • *adv.* in every hundred. • *n.* **1** percentage. **2** one part in every hundred (*half a percent*). **3** (in *pl.*) *Brit.* public securities yielding interest of so much percent (*three percents*).

▶Both spellings, **percent** and **per cent**, are acceptable, but one should be consistent. **Percent** is more common in US usage, and **per cent** is more common in British usage.

per·cent·age /pərséntij/ *n.* **1** a rate or proportion percent. **2** a proportion. **3** *colloq.* personal benefit or advantage.

per·cen·tile /pərséntīl/ *n. Statistics* one of 99 values of a variable dividing a population into 100 equal groups as regards the value of that variable.

per·cept /pérsept/ *n. Philos.* **1** an object of perception. **2** a mental concept resulting from perceiving, esp. by sight.

per·cep·ti·ble /pərséptibəl/ *adj.* capable of being perceived by the senses or intellect. ▫▫ **per·cep·ti·bil·i·ty** /-bílitee/ *n.* **per·cep·ti·bly** *adv.*

per·cep·tion /pərsépshən/ *n.* **1 a** the faculty of perceiving. **b** an instance of this. **2** (often foll. by *of*) **a** the intuitive recognition of a truth, aesthetic quality, etc. **b** an instance of this (*a sudden perception of the true position*). **3** *Philos.* the ability of the mind to refer sensory information to an external object as its cause. ▫▫ **per·cep·tion·al** *adj.* **per·cep·tu·al** /-chōōəl/ *adj.* **per·cep·tu·al·ly** *adv.*

per·cep·tive /pərséptiv/ *adj.* **1** capable of perceiving. **2** sensitive; discerning; observant (*a perceptive remark*). ▫▫ **per·cep·tive·ly** *adv.* **per·cep·tive·ness** *n.* **per·cep·tiv·i·ty** /-septívitee/ *n.*

perch[1] /pərch/ *n.* & *v.* • *n.* **1** a usu. horizontal bar, branch, etc., used by a bird to rest on. **2** a usu. high or precarious place for a person or thing to rest on. • *v.intr.* & *tr.* (usu. foll. by *on*) settle or rest, or cause to settle or rest on or as if on a perch, etc. (*the bird perched on a branch; a town perched on a hill*).

perch[2] /pərch/ *n.* (*pl.* same or **perches**) **1** any spiny-finned freshwater edible fish of the genus *Perca*, esp. *P. flavescens* of N. America or *P. fluviatilis* of Europe. **2** any fish of several similar or related species.

per·chance /pərcháns/ *adv.* **1** by chance. **2** possibly; maybe.

per·co·late /pérkəlayt/ *v.* **1** *intr.* (often foll. by *through*) **a** (of liquid, etc.) filter or ooze gradually (esp. through a porous surface). **b** (of an idea, etc.) permeate gradually. **2** *tr.* prepare (coffee) by repeatedly passing boiling water through ground beans. **3** *tr.* ooze through; permeate. **4** *tr.* strain (a liquid, powder, etc.) through a fine mesh, etc. **5** *intr. colloq.* become livelier, more active, etc. ▫▫ **per·co·la·tion** /-láyshən/ *n.*

per·co·la·tor /pérkəlaytər/ *n.* a machine for making coffee by circulating boiling water through ground beans.

per·cus·sion /pərkúshən/ *n.* **1** *Mus.* **a** (often *attrib.*) the playing of music by striking instruments with sticks, etc. (*a percussion band*). **b** the section of such instruments in an orchestra or band (*asked the percussion to stay behind*). **2** *Med.* the act or an instance of percussing. **3** the forcible striking of one esp. solid body against another. ▫▫ **per·cus·sion·ist** *n.* **per·cus·sive** *adj.* **per·cus·sive·ly** *adv.* **per·cus·sive·ness** *n.*

per·cus·sion cap *n.* a small amount of explosive powder contained in metal or paper and exploded by striking, used esp. in toy guns and formerly in some firearms.

per di·em /pər dée-em, díem/ *adv.*, *adj.*, & *n.* • *adv.* & *adj.* for each day. • *n.* an allowance or payment for each day.

per·di·tion /pərdíshən/ *n.* eternal death; damnation.

per·e·gri·nate /périgrinayt/ *v.intr.* travel; journey, esp. extensively or at leisure. ▫▫ **per·e·gri·na·tion** /-náyshən/ *n.* **per·e·gri·na·tor** *n.*

per·e·grine /périgrin, -green/ *n.* (in full **peregrine falcon**) a widely distributed falcon, *Falco peregrinus*, much used for falconry.

per·emp·to·ry /pərémptəree/ *adj.* **1** (of a statement or command) admitting no denial or refusal. **2** (of a person, a person's manner, etc.) dogmatic; imperious; dictatorial. **3** *Law* not open to appeal or challenge; final. ▫▫ **per·emp·to·ri·ly** *adv.* **per·emp·to·ri·ness** *n.*

per·en·ni·al /pəréneeəl/ *adj.* & *n.* • *adj.* **1** lasting through a year or several years. **2** (of a plant) lasting several years. **3** lasting a long time or forever. **4** (of a stream) flowing through all seasons of the year. • *n.* a perennial plant (*a herbaceous perennial*). ▫▫ **per·en·ni·al·i·ty** /-neeálitee/ *n.* **per·en·ni·al·ly** *adv.*

pe·re·stroi·ka /pérestróykə/ *n. hist.* (in the former Soviet Union) the policy or practice of restructuring or reforming the economic and political system.

per·fect *adj.*, *v.*, & *n.* • *adj.* /pə́rfikt/ **1** complete; not deficient. **2 a** faultless (*a perfect diamond*). **b** blameless in morals or behavior. **3 a** very satisfactory (*a perfect evening*). **b** (often foll. by *for*) most appropriate; suitable. **4** exact; precise (*a perfect circle*). **5** entire; unqualified (*a perfect stranger*). **6** *Math.* (of a number) equal to the sum of its divisors. **7** *Gram.* (of a tense) denoting a completed action or event in the past, formed in English with *have* or *has* and the past participle, as in *they have eaten*. **8** *Mus.* (of pitch) absolute. **9** (often foll. by *in*) thoroughly trained or skilled (*is perfect in geometry*). • *v.tr.* /pərfékt/ **1** make perfect; improve. **2** carry through; complete. **3** complete (a sheet) by printing the other side. • *n.* /pə́rfikt/ *Gram.* the perfect tense. ▫▫ **per·fect·er** *n.* **per·fect·i·ble** *adj.* **per·fect·i·bil·i·ty** *n.* **per·fect·ness** *n.*

▶Literally, **perfect, unique**, etc., are absolute words and should not be modified, as they often are in such phrases as "most perfect, quite unique," etc.

per·fec·ta /pərféktə/ *n.* a bet in which the first two places must be predicted in the correct order.

per·fec·tion /pərfékshən/ *n.* **1** the act or process of making perfect. **2** the state of being perfect; faultlessness; excellence. **3** a perfect person, thing, or example. **4** an accomplishment. **5** full development; completion.

per·fec·tion·ism /pərfékshənizəm/ *n.* **1** the uncompromising pursuit of excellence. **2** *Philos.* the belief that religious or moral perfection is attainable. ▫▫ **per·fec·tion·ist** *n.* & *adj.*

per·fec·tive /pərféktiv/ *adj.* & *n. Gram.* • *adj.* (of an aspect of a verb, etc.) expressing the completion of an action. • *n.* the perfective aspect or form of a verb.

per·fect·ly /pérfiktlee/ *adv.* **1** completely; absolutely (*I understand you perfectly*). **2** quite; completely (*is perfectly capable of doing it*). **3** in a perfect way. **4** very (*you know perfectly well*).

per·fec·to /pərféktō/ *n.* (*pl.* **-tos**) a large thick cigar pointed at each end.

per·fect pitch *n.* the ability to recognize and reproduce correct musical tones by ear.

per·fi·dy /pə́rfidee/ *n.* breach of faith; treachery. ▫▫ **per·fid·i·ous** /-fídeeəs/ *adj.* **per·fid·i·ous·ly** *adv.*

per·fo·rate *v.* & *adj.* • *v.* /pə́rfərayt/ **1** *tr.* make a hole or holes through; pierce. **2** *tr.* make a row of small holes in (paper, etc.) so that a part may be torn off easily. **3** *tr.* make an opening into; pass into or extend through. **4** *intr.* (usu. foll. by *into*, *through*, etc.) penetrate. • *adj.* /pə́rfərət/ perforated. ▫▫ **per·fo·ra·tion** /-ráyshən/ *n.* **per·fo·ra·tive** /pə́rfərətiv/ *adj.* **per·fo·ra·tor** /pə́rfəraytər/ *n.*

per·force /pərfáwrs/ *adv. archaic* unavoidably; necessarily.

per·form /pərfawrm/ *v.* **1** *tr.* (also *absol.*) carry into effect; be the agent of; do (a command, promise, task, etc.). **2** *tr.* (also *absol.*) go through; execute (a public function, play, piece of music, etc.). **3** *intr.* act in a play; play an instrument or sing, etc. (*likes performing*). **4** *intr.* operate; function. ▫▫ **per·form·a·ble** *adj.* **per·form·a·bil·i·ty** *n.* **per·form·er** *n.* **per·form·ing** *adj.*

per·for·mance /pərfáwrməns/ *n.* **1** (usu. foll. by *of*) **a** the act or process of performing or carrying out. **b** the execution or fulfillment (of a duty, etc.). **2** a staging or production (of a drama, piece of music, etc.) (*the afternoon performance*). **3** a person's achievement under test conditions, etc. (*put up a good performance*). **4** *colloq.* a fuss; a scene; a public exhibition (*made such a performance about leaving*). **5 a** the capabilities of a machine, esp. a car or aircraft. **b** (*attrib.*) of high capability (*a performance car*).

per·for·ma·tive /pərfáwrmətiv/ *adj. & n.* • *adj.* **1** of or relating to performance. **2** denoting an utterance that effects an action by being spoken or written (e.g., *I bet, I apologize*). • *n.* a performative utterance.

per·form·ing arts /pərfáwrming/ *n.pl.* the arts, such as drama, music, and dance, that require performance for their realization.

per·fume /pə́rfyoom/ *n. & v.* • *n.* **1** a sweet smell. **2** fluid containing the essence of flowers, etc.; scent. • *v.tr.* (also /pərfyóom/) (usu. as **perfumed** *adj.*) impart a sweet scent to; impregnate with a sweet smell. ▫▫ **per·fum·y** *adj.*

per·fum·er /pərfyóomər/ *n.* a maker or seller of perfumes. ▫▫ **per·fum·er·y** *n.* (*pl.* **-ies**).

per·func·to·ry /pərfúngktəree/ *adj.* **1 a** done merely for the sake of getting through a duty. **b** done in a cursory or careless manner. **2** superficial; mechanical. ▫▫ **per·func·to·ri·ly** *adv.* **per·func·to·ri·ness** *n.*

per·go·la /pə́rgələ/ *n.* an arbor or covered walk, formed of growing plants trained over a trellis.

per·haps /pərháps/ *adv.* **1** it may be; possibly (*perhaps it is lost*). **2** introducing a polite request (*perhaps you would open the window?*).

peri- /péree/ *prefix* **1** around; about. **2** *Astron.* the point nearest to (*perigee; perihelion*).

per·i·anth /péreeánth/ *n.* the outer part of a flower.

per·i·car·di·um /périkaárdeeəm/ *n.* (*pl.* **pericardia** /-deeə/) the membranous sac enclosing the heart. ▫▫ **per·i·car·di·ac** /-deeak/ *adj.* **per·i·car·di·al** *adj.* **per·i·car·di·tis** /-dítis/ *n.*

per·i·carp /périkaarp/ *n.* the part of a fruit formed from the wall of the ripened ovary.

per·i·dot /péridō; -dot/ *n.* a green variety of olivine, used esp. as a semiprecious stone.

per·i·gee /périjee/ *n.* the point in an orbit where the orbiting body is nearest the center of the body it is orbiting. (opp. APOGEE). ▫▫ **per·i·ge·an** /périjéeən/ *adj.*

per·i·he·li·on /périhéelyən/ *n.* (*pl.* **perihelia** /-lyə/) the point of a planet's or comet's orbit nearest to the sun's center.

per·il /péril/ *n. & v.* • *n.* serious and immediate danger. • *v.tr.* (**periled, periling** or **perilled, perilling**) threaten; endanger. ▫ **at one's peril** at one's own risk. **in peril of** with great risk to (*in peril of your life*).

per·il·ous /périləs/ *adj.* **1** full of risk; dangerous; hazardous. **2** exposed to imminent risk of destruction, etc. ▫▫ **per·il·ous·ly** *adv.* **per·il·ous·ness** *n.*

pe·rim·e·ter /pərímitər/ *n.* **1 a** the circumference or outline of a closed figure. **b** the length of this. **2 a** the outer boundary of an enclosed area. **b** a defended boundary. **3** an instrument for measuring a field of vision. ▫▫ **per·i·met·ric** /périmétrik/ *adj.*

per·i·ne·um /périnéeəm/ *n.* the region of the body between the anus and the scrotum or vulva. ▫▫ **per·i·ne·al** *adj.*

pe·ri·od /péereeəd/ *n. & adj.* • *n.* **1** a length or portion of time (*periods of rain*). **2** a distinct portion of history, a person's life, etc. (*the Federal period; Picasso's Blue Period*). **3** *Geol.* a time forming part of a geological era (*the Quaternary period*). **4 a** an interval between recurrences of an astronomical or other phenomenon. **b** the time taken by a planet to rotate about its axis. **5** the time allowed for a lesson in school. **6** an occurrence of menstruation. **7 a** a complete sentence, esp. one consisting of several clauses. **b** (in *pl.*) rhetorical language. **8 a** a punctuation mark (.) used at the end of a sentence or an abbreviation. **b** used at the end of a sentence, etc., to indicate finality, absoluteness, etc. (*we want the best, period*). **9 a** a set of figures repeated in a recurring decimal. **b** the smallest interval over which a function takes the same value. **10** *Chem.* a sequence of elements between two noble gases forming a row in the periodic table. **11** *Music* a discrete division of a musical composition, containing two or more phrases and ending in a cadence. • *adj.* belonging to or characteristic of some past period (*period furniture*). ▫ **of the period** of the era under discussion (*the custom of the period*).

period late Middle English (denoting the time during which something, especially a disease, runs its course): from Old French *periode,* via Latin from Greek *periodos* 'orbit, recurrence, course,' from *peri-* 'around' + *hodos* 'way, course.' The sense 'portion of time' dates from the early 17th century.

pe·ri·od·ic /péereeódik/ *adj.* **1** appearing or occurring at regular intervals. **2** of or concerning the period of a celestial body (*periodic motion*). **3** (of diction, etc.) expressed in periods (see PERIOD *n.* 7a). ▫▫ **pe·ri·o·dic·i·ty** /-reeədísitee/ *n.*

pe·ri·od·i·cal /péereeódikəl/ *n. & adj.* • *n.* a newspaper, magazine, etc., issued at regular intervals, usu. monthly or weekly. • *adj.* **1** published at regular intervals. **2** periodic; occasional. ▫▫ **pe·ri·od·i·cal·ly** *adv.*

pe·ri·od·ic ta·ble *n.* an arrangement of elements in order of increasing atomic number and in which elements of similar chemical properties appear at regular intervals.

per·i·o·don·tics /péreeədóntiks/ *n.pl.* (treated as *sing.*) the branch of dentistry concerned with the structures surrounding and supporting the teeth. ▫▫ **per·i·o·don·tal** *adj.* **per·i·o·don·tist** *n.*

pe·ri·od piece *n.* an object or work whose main interest lies in its historical, etc., associations.

per·i·pa·tet·ic /péripətétik/ *adj.* **1** (of a teacher) working in more than one school or college, etc. **2** going from place to place; itinerant. ▫▫ **per·i·pa·tet·i·cal·ly** *adv.* **per·i·pa·tet·i·cism** *n.*

pe·riph·er·al /pərífərəl/ *adj. & n.* • *adj.* **1** of minor importance; marginal. **2** of the periphery; on the fringe. **3** *Anat.* near the surface of the body, with special reference to the circulation and nervous system. **4** (of equipment) used with a computer, etc., but not an integral part of it. • *n.* a peripheral device or piece of equipment. ▫▫ **pe·riph·er·al·ly** *adv.*

pe·riph·er·al ner·vous sys·tem *n. Anat.* the nervous system outside the brain and spinal cord.

pe·riph·er·al vi·sion *n.* **1** area seen around the outside of one's field of vision. **2** ability to perceive in this area.

pe·riph·er·y /pərífəree/ *n.* (*pl.* **-ies**) **1** the boundary of an area or surface. **2** an outer or surrounding region (*built on the periphery of the old town*).

pe·riph·ra·sis /pərífrəsis/ *n.* (*pl.* **periphrases** /-seez/) **1** a roundabout way of speaking; circumlocution. **2** a roundabout phrase. ▫▫ **per·i·phras·tic** *adj.*

per·i·scope /périskōp/ *n.* an apparatus with a tube and mirrors or prisms, by which an observer in a trench, submerged submarine, or at the rear of a crowd, etc., can see things otherwise out of sight. ▫▫ **per·i·scop·ic** *adj.* **per·i·scop·i·cal·ly** *adv.*

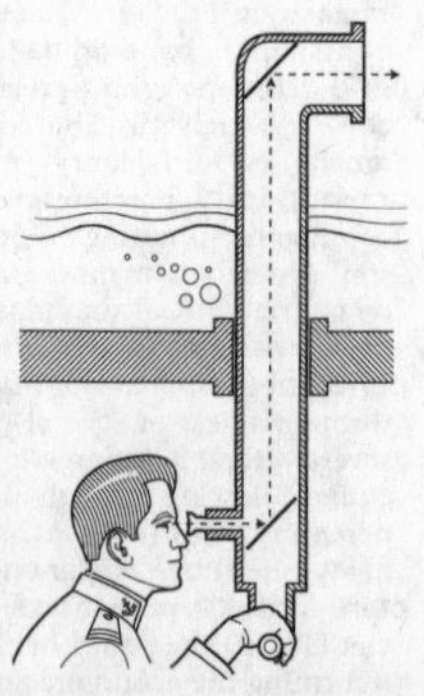
periscope

per·ish /pérish/ *v.* **1** *intr.* be destroyed; suffer death or ruin (*a great part of his army perished* *of hunger and disease*). **2** *Brit.* **a** *intr.* (esp. of rubber, a rubber object, etc.) lose its normal qualities; deteriorate; rot. **b** *tr.* cause to rot or deteriorate. **3** *Brit. tr.* (in *passive*) suffer from cold or exposure (*we were perished standing outside*). □ **perish the thought** an exclamation of horror against an unwelcome idea. □□ **per·ish·less** *adj.*

per·ish·a·ble /périshəbəl/ *adj. & n.* • *adj.* liable to perish; subject to decay. • *n.* a thing, esp. a foodstuff, subject to speedy decay. □□ **per·ish·a·bil·i·ty** /-bílitee/ *n.* **per·ish·a·ble·ness** *n.*

per·i·to·ne·um /périt'nééəm/ *n.* (*pl.* **peritoneums** or **peritonea** /-nééə/) the serous membrane lining the cavity of the abdomen. □□ **per·i·to·ne·al** *adj.*

per·i·to·ni·tis /périt'nítis/ *n.* an inflammatory disease of the peritoneum.

per·i·wig /périwig/ *n.* esp. *hist.* a highly-styled wig worn formerly as a fashionable headdress by both men and women and retained by judges and barristers in the UK as part of their professional dress. □□ **per·i·wigged** *adj.*

per·i·win·kle[1] /périwingkəl/ *n.* **1** any plant of the genus *Vinca*, esp. an evergreen trailing plant with blue or white flowers. **2** a tropical shrub, *Catharanthus roseus*, native to Madagascar.

per·i·win·kle[2] /périwingkəl/ *n.* any edible marine gastropod mollusk of the genus *Littorina*; a winkle.

per·jure /pə́rjər/ *v.refl. Law* **1** willfully tell an untruth when under oath. **2** (as **perjured** *adj.*) guilty of or involving perjury. □□ **per·jur·er** *n.*

per·ju·ry /pə́rjəree/ *n.* (*pl.* **-ries**) *Law* **1** a breach of an oath, esp. the act of willfully telling an untruth when under oath. **2** the practice of this. □□ **per·ju·ri·ous** /-jŏóreeəs/ *adj.*

perk[1] /pərk/ *v. & adj.* • *v.tr.* raise (one's head, etc.) briskly. • *adj.* perky; pert. □ **perk up 1** recover confidence, courage, life, or zest. **2** restore confidence or courage or liveliness in (esp. another person). **3** freshen up.

perk[2] /pərk/ *n. colloq.* a perquisite.

perk[3] /pərk/ *v. colloq.* **1** *intr.* (of coffee) percolate; make a bubbling sound in the percolator. **2** *tr.* percolate (coffee).

perk·y /pə́rkee/ *adj.* (**perkier, perkiest**) **1** self-assertive; cocky; pert. **2** lively; cheerful. □□ **perk·i·ly** *adv.* **perk·i·ness** *n.*

per·lite /pə́rlīt/ *n.* (also **pear·lite**) a glassy type of vermiculite, expandable to a solid form by heating, used for insulation, etc.

perm /perm/ *n. & v.* • *n.* a permanent wave. • *v.tr.* give a permanent wave to (a person or a person's hair).

per·ma·frost /pə́rməfrawst, -frost/ *n.* subsoil that remains frozen throughout the year, as in polar regions.

per·ma·nent /pə́rmənənt/ *adj. & n.* • *adj.* lasting, or intended to last or function, indefinitely (opp. TEMPORARY). • *n.* = PERMANENT WAVE. □□ **per·ma·nence** *n.* **per·ma·nen·cy** *n.* **per·ma·nent·ize** *v.tr.* **per·ma·nent·ly** *adv.*

per·ma·nent press *n.* a process applied to a fabric to make it wrinkle-free.

per·ma·nent wave *n.* an artificial wave in the hair, intended to last for some time.

per·me·a·bil·i·ty /pérmeeəbílitee/ *n.* **1** the state or quality of being permeable. **2** a quantity measuring the influence of a substance on the magnetic flux in the region it occupies.

per·me·a·ble /pə́rmeeəbəl/ *adj.* capable of being permeated.

per·me·ate /pə́rmeeayt/ *v.* **1** *tr.* penetrate throughout; pervade; saturate. **2** *intr.* (usu. foll. by *through, among,* etc.) diffuse itself. □□ **per·me·ance** *n.* **per·me·ant** *adj.* **per·me·a·tion** /-áyshən/ *n.* **per·me·a·tor** *n.*

per·mis·si·ble /pərmísibəl/ *adj.* allowable. □□ **per·mis·si·bil·i·ty** *n.* **per·mis·si·bly** *adv.*

per·mis·sion /pərmíshən/ *n.* (often foll. by *to* + infin.) consent; authorization.

per·mis·sive /pərmísiv/ *adj.* **1** tolerant; liberal, esp. in sexual matters (*the permissive society*). **2** giving permission. □□ **per·mis·sive·ly** *adv.* **per·mis·sive·ness** *n.*

per·mit *v. & n.* • *v.* /pərmít/ (**permitted, permitting**) **1** *tr.* give permission or consent to; authorize (*permit me to say*). **2 a** *tr.* allow as possible; give an opportunity to (*permit the traffic to flow again*). **b** *intr.* give an opportunity (*circumstances permitting*). **3** *intr.* (foll. by *of*) admit; allow for. • *n.* /pə́rmit/ **1 a** a document giving permission to act in a specified way (*was granted a work permit*). **b** a document, etc., that allows entry into a specified zone. **2** permission. □□ **per·mit·tee** /pə́rmitée/ *n.* **per·mit·ter** *n.*

per·mu·tate /pə́rmyootayt/ *v.tr.* change the order or arrangement of.

per·mu·ta·tion /pə́rmyootáyshən/ *n.* **1 a** an ordered arrangement or grouping of a set of numbers, items, etc. **b** any one of the range of possible groupings. **2** any combination or selection of a specified number of things from a larger group. □□ **per·mu·ta·tion·al** *adj.*

per·mute /pərmyóót/ *v.tr.* alter the sequence or arrangement of.

per·ni·cious /pərníshəs/ *adj.* destructive; ruinous; fatal. □□ **per·ni·cious·ly** *adv.* **per·ni·cious·ness** *n.*

per·ni·cious a·ne·mi·a *n.* a defective formation of red blood cells through a lack of vitamin B_{12} or folic acid.

per·o·ra·tion /pérəráyshən/ *n.* **1** the concluding part of a speech, forcefully summing up what has been said. **2** a long or overly rhetorical speech.

per·ox·ide /pəróksīd/ *n. & v.* • *n. Chem.* **1 a** = HYDROGEN PEROXIDE. **b** (often *attrib.*) a solution of hydrogen peroxide used to bleach the hair or as an antiseptic. **2** a compound of oxygen with another element containing the greatest possible proportion of oxygen. **3** any salt or ester of hydrogen peroxide. • *v.tr.* bleach (the hair) with peroxide.

per·pen·dic·u·lar /pə́rpəndíkyələr/ *adj. & n.* • *adj.* **1 a** at right angles to the plane of the horizon. **b** (usu. foll. by *to*) *Geom.* at right angles (to a given line, plane, or surface). **2** upright; vertical. **3** (of a slope, etc.) very steep. **4** (**Perpendicular**) *Archit.* of the third stage of English Gothic (15th–16th c.) with vertical tracery in large windows. **5** in a standing position. • *n.* **1** a perpendicular line. **2** a plumb rule or a similar instrument. **3** (prec. by *the*) a perpendicular line or direction (*is out of the perpendicular*). □□ **per·pen·dic·u·lar·i·ty** /-dikyooláritee/ *n.* **per·pen·dic·u·lar·ly** *adv.*

per·pe·trate /pə́rpitrayt/ *v.tr.* commit or perform (a crime, blunder, or anything outrageous). □□ **per·pe·tra·tion** /-tráyshən/ *n.* **per·pe·tra·tor** *n.*

▶To **perpetrate** something is to commit it: *The gang perpetrated outrages against several citizens.* To **perpetuate** something is to cause it to continue or to keep happening: *The stories only serve to perpetuate the myth that the house is haunted.*

---

perpetrate mid-16th century: from Latin *perpetrat-* 'performed,' from the verb *perpetrare*, from *per-* 'to completion' + *patrare* 'bring about.' In Latin the act perpetrated might be good or bad; in English the verb was first used in statutes referring to crime, hence it acquired a negative association.

---

per·pet·u·al /pərpéchooəl/ *adj.* **1** eternal; lasting forever or indefinitely. **2** continuous; uninterrupted. **3** *colloq.* frequent; much repeated (*perpetual interruptions*). **4** (of an office, etc.) held for life (*perpetual secretary*). □□ **per·pet·u·al·ism** *n.* **per·pet·u·al·ly** *adv.*

per·pet·u·al mo·tion *n.* the motion of a hypothetical machine which once set in motion would run forever unless subject to an external force or to wear.

per·pet·u·ate /pərpéchōō-ayt/ *v.tr.* **1** make perpetual. **2** preserve from oblivion. □□ **per·pet·u·ance** *n.* **per·pet·u·a·tion** /-áyshən/ *n.* **per·pet·u·a·tor** *n.*

▶See note at PERPETRATE.

per·pe·tu·i·ty /pə́rpitóō-itee, -tyóō-/ *n.* (*pl.* **-ties**) **1** the state or quality of being perpetual. **2** a perpetual annuity. **3** a perpetual possession or position. □ **in** (or **to** or **for**) **perpetuity** forever.

per·plex /pərpléks/ *v.tr.* **1** puzzle, bewilder, or disconcert (a person, a person's mind, etc.). **2** complicate or confuse (a matter). □□ **per·plex·ed·ly** /-pléksidlee/ *adv.* **per·plex·ing** *adj.* **per·plex·ing·ly** *adv.*

per·plex·i·ty /pərpléksitee/ *n.* (*pl.* **-ties**) **1** bewilderment; the state of being perplexed. **2** a thing which perplexes. **3** the state of being complicated.

per·qui·site /pə́rkwizit/ *n.* **1** an extra profit or allowance additional to a main income, etc. **2** a customary extra right or privilege. **3** an incidental benefit attached to employment, etc.

▶**Perquisite** and **prerequisite** are sometimes confused. **Perquisite** usually means 'an extra allowance or privilege,' e.g., *He had all the perquisites of a movie star, including a stand-in.* **Prerequisite** means 'something required as a precondition,' e.g., *Passing the examination was one of the prerequisites for a teaching position.*

per se /pər sáy/ *adv.* by or in itself; intrinsically.

per·se·cute /pə́rsikyōōt/ *v.tr.* **1** subject (a person, etc.) to hostility or ill-treatment, esp. on the grounds of political or religious belief. **2** harass; worry. **3** (often foll. by *with*) bombard (a person) with questions, etc. □□ **per·se·cu·tor** *n.* **per·se·cu·to·ry** *adj.*

per·se·cu·tion /pérsikyóōshən/ *n.* the act or an instance of persecuting; the state of being persecuted.

per·se·ver·ance /pə́rsivéerəns/ *n.* **1** the steadfast pursuit of an objective. **2** (often foll. by *in*) constant persistence (in a belief, etc.).

per·se·vere /pə́rsivéer/ *v.intr.* (often foll. by *in, at, with*) continue steadfastly or determinedly; persist.

Per·sian /pérzhən, -shən/ *n.* & *adj.* •*n.* **1 a** a native or inhabitant of ancient or modern Persia (now Iran). **b** a person of Persian descent. **2** the language of ancient Persia or modern Iran. ▶With modern reference the preferred terms are *Iranian* and *Farsi.* **3** (in full **Persian cat**) **a** a cat of a breed with long silky hair and a thick tail. **b** this breed. •*adj.* of or relating to Persia or its people or language.

per·si·flage /pə́rsiflaazh/ *n.* light raillery; banter.

per·sim·mon /pərsímən/ *n.* **1** any usu. tropical evergreen tree of the genus *Diospyros,* bearing edible tomatolike fruits. **2** the fruit of this.

per·sist /pərsíst/ *v.intr.* **1** (often foll. by *in*) continue firmly or obstinately (in an opinion or a course of action), esp. despite obstacles, remonstrance, etc. **2** (of an institution, custom, phenomenon, etc.) continue in existence; survive.

per·sist·ent /pərsístənt/ *adj.* **1** continuing obstinately; persisting. **2** enduring. **3** constantly repeated (*persistent nagging*). □□ **per·sist·ence** *n.* **per·sist·en·cy** *n.* **per·sist·ent·ly** *adv.*

per·snick·et·y /pərsníkitee/ *adj. colloq.* **1** fastidious. **2** precise or overprecise. **3** requiring tact or careful handling.

per·son /pə́rsən/ *n.* **1** an individual human being (*a cheerful and forthright person*). **2** the living body of a human being (*hidden about your person*). **3** *Gram.* any of three classes of personal pronouns, verb forms, etc.: the person speaking (**first person**); the person spoken to (**second person**); the person spoken of (**third person**). **4** (in *comb.*) used to replace *-man* in words referring to either sex (*salesperson*). **5** (in Christianity) God as Father, Son, or Holy Ghost (*three persons in one God*). □ **in person** physically present.

▶Some prefer the plural **persons** to **people,** considering the former more formal and specific, and holding **people** to be more general and indefinite. General usage, however, does not support this distinction. In some contexts, **persons,** by pointing to the individual, may sound less friendly than **people**: *The number should not be disclosed to any unauthorized persons.*

per·so·na /pərsṓnə/ *n.* (*pl.* **personae** /-nee/) **1** an aspect of the personality as shown to or perceived by others (opp. ANIMA). **2** *Literary criticism* an author's assumed character in his or her writing.

per·son·a·ble /pə́rsənəbəl/ *adj.* pleasing in appearance and behavior. □□ **per·son·a·ble·ness** *n.* **per·son·a·bly** *adv.*

per·son·age /pə́rsənij/ *n.* **1** a person, esp. of rank or importance. **2** a character in a play, etc.

per·son·al /pə́rsənəl/ *adj.* **1** one's own; individual; private. **2** done or made in person (*made a personal appearance; my personal attention*). **3** directed to or concerning an individual (*a personal letter*). **4 a** referring (esp. in a hostile way) to an individual's private life or concerns (*making personal remarks; no need to be personal*). **b** close; intimate (*a personal friend*). **5** of the body and clothing (*personal hygiene; personal appearance*). **6** existing as a person, not as an abstraction or thing (*a personal God*). **7** *Gram.* of or denoting one of the three persons (*personal pronoun*).

per·son·al col·umn *n.* (also **per·son·als**) the part of a newspaper devoted to private advertisements or messages.

per·son·al com·pu·ter *n.* a computer designed for use by a single individual.

per·son·al i·den·ti·fi·ca·tion num·ber *n.* a number allocated to an individual, serving as a password esp. for an ATM, computer, etc. ¶ Abbr.: **PIN**.

per·son·al·i·ty /pə́rsənálitee/ *n.* (*pl.* **-ties**) **1** the distinctive character or qualities of a person, often as distinct from others (*an attractive personality*). **2** a famous person; a celebrity (*a TV personality*). **3** a person who stands out from others by virtue of his or her character (*is a real personality*).

per·son·al·ize /pə́rsənəlīz/ *v.tr.* **1** make personal, esp. by marking with one's name, etc. **2** personify. □□ **per·son·al·i·za·tion** *n.*

per·son·al·ly /pə́rsənəlee/ *adv.* **1** in person (*see to it personally*). **2** for one's own part (*speaking personally*). **3** in the form of a person (*a god existing personally*). **4** in a personal manner (*took the criticism personally*). **5** as a person; on a personal level.

per·son·al pro·noun *n.* a pronoun replacing the subject, object, etc., of a clause, etc., e.g., *I, we, you, them, us.*

per·so·na non gra·ta /non graátə, grátə/ *n.* a person not acceptable.

per·son·i·fi·ca·tion /pərsónifikáyshən/ *n.* **1** the act of personifying. **2** (foll. by *of*) a person or thing viewed as a striking example of (a quality, etc.) (*the personification of ugliness*).

per·son·i·fy /pərsónifī/ *v.tr.* (**-fies, -fied**) **1** attribute a personal nature to (an abstraction or thing). **2** symbolize (a quality, etc.) by a figure in human form. **3** (usu. as **personified** *adj.*) embody (a quality) in one's own person; exemplify typically (*has always been kindness personified*). □□ **per·son·i·fi·er** *n.*

per·son·nel /pə́rsənél/ *n.* a body of employees, persons involved in a public undertaking, armed forces, etc.

per·spec·tive /pərspéktiv/ *n.* & *adj.* •*n.* **1 a** the art of drawing solid objects on a two-dimensional surface so as to give the right impression of relative positions, size, etc. **b** a picture drawn in this way. **2** the apparent relation between visible objects as to position, distance, etc. **3** a mental view of the relative importance of things (*keep the right perspective*). **4** a geographical or imaginary prospect. • *adj.* of or in perspective. □ **in perspective 1** drawn or viewed according to the rules of perspective. **2** correctly regarded in terms of relative importance. □□ **per·spec·tiv·al** *adj.* **per·spec·tive·ly** *adv.*

per·spi·ca·cious /pə́rspikáyshəs/ *adj.* having mental penetration or discernment. □□ **per·spi·ca·cious·ly** *adv.* **per·spi·ca·cious·ness** *n.* **per·spi·cac·i·ty** /-kásitee/ *n.*

per·spic·u·ous /pərspíkyōōəs/ *adj.* **1** easily understood; clearly expressed. **2** (of a person) expressing things clearly. □□ **per·spi·cu·i·ty** /pə́rspikyṓō-itee/ *n.* **per·spic·u·ous·ly** *adv.* **per·spic·u·ous·ness** *n.*

per·spi·ra·tion /pə́rspiráyshən/ *n.* **1** = SWEAT. **2** sweating. □□ **per·spir·a·to·ry** /pərspīrətawree, pə́rspirə-/ *adj.*

per·spire /pərspír/ *v.* **1** *intr.* sweat or exude perspiration, esp. as the result of heat, exercise, anxiety, etc. **2** *tr.* sweat or exude (fluid, etc.).

per·suade /pərswáyd/ *v.tr. & refl.* **1** (often foll. by *of*, or *that* + clause) cause (another person or oneself) to believe; convince (*persuaded them that it would be helpful*). **2 a** (often foll. by *to* + infin.) induce (another person or oneself) (*managed to persuade them at last*). **b** (foll. by *away from*, *down to*, etc.) lure, attract, entice, etc. (*persuaded them away from the pub*). □□ **per·suad·a·ble** *adj.* **per·suad·a·bil·i·ty** *n.* **per·sua·si·ble** *adj.*

per·sua·sion /pərswáyzhən/ *n.* **1** persuading (*yielded to persuasion*). **2** persuasiveness (*use all your persuasion*). **3** a belief or conviction (*my private persuasion*). **4** a religious belief, or the group or sect holding it (*of a different persuasion*). **5** *colloq.* any group or party (*the male persuasion*).

per·sua·sive /pərswáysiv, -ziv/ *adj.* able to persuade. □□ **per·sua·sive·ly** *adv.* **per·sua·sive·ness** *n.*

pert /pərt/ *adj.* **1** saucy or impudent, esp. in speech or conduct. **2** (of clothes, etc.) neat and jaunty. □□ **pert·ly** *adv.* **pert·ness** *n.*

pert. *abbr.* pertaining.

per·tain /pərtáyn/ *v.intr.* **1** (foll. by *to*) **a** relate or have reference to. **b** belong to as a part or appendage or accessory. **2** (usu. foll. by *to*) be appropriate to.

per·ti·na·cious /pə́rt'náyshəs/ *adj.* stubborn; persistent; obstinate (in a course of action, etc.). □□ **per·ti·na·cious·ly** *adv.* **per·ti·na·cious·ness** *n.* **per·ti·nac·i·ty** /-násitee/ *n.*

per·ti·nent /pə́rt'nənt/ *adj.* **1** (often foll. by *to*) relevant to the matter in hand; apposite. **2** to the point. □□ **per·ti·nence** *n.* **per·ti·nen·cy** *n.* **per·ti·nent·ly** *adv.*

per·turb /pərtə́rb/ *v.tr.* **1** throw into confusion or disorder. **2** disturb mentally; agitate. □□ **per·turb·a·ble** *adj.* **per·tur·ba·tion** *n.* **per·tur·ba·tive** /pərtúrbətiv, pə́rtərbáytiv/ *adj.* **per·turb·ing·ly** *adv.*

per·tus·sis /pərtúsis/ *n.* whooping cough.

pe·ruse /pərṓōz/ *v.tr.* **1** (also *absol.*) read or study, esp. thoroughly or carefully. **2** examine (a person's face, etc.) carefully. □□ **pe·rus·al** *n.* **pe·rus·er** *n.*

Per·u·vi·an /pərṓōveeən/ *n. & adj.* • *n.* **1** a native or national of Peru. **2** a person of Peruvian descent. • *adj.* of or relating to Peru.

per·vade /pərváyd/ *v.tr.* **1** spread throughout; permeate. **2** (of influences, etc.) become widespread among or in. **3** be rife among or through. □□ **per·va·sion** /-váyzhən/ *n.*

per·va·sive /pərváysiv, -ziv/ *adj.* **1** pervading. **2** able to pervade. □□ **per·va·sive·ly** *adv.* **per·va·sive·ness** *n.*

per·verse /pərvə́rs/ *adj.* **1** (of a person or action) deliberately or stubbornly departing from what is reasonable or required. **2** persistent in error. **3** wayward; intractable; peevish. **4** perverted; wicked. **5** (of a verdict, etc.) against the weight of evidence or the judge's direction. □□ **per·verse·ly** *adv.* **per·verse·ness** *n.* **per·ver·si·ty** *n.* (*pl.* **-ties**).

per·ver·sion /pərvə́rzhən, -shən/ *n.* **1** an act of perverting; the state of being perverted. **2** a perverted form of an act or thing. **3 a** preference for an abnormal form of sexual activity. **b** such an activity.

per·vert *v. & n.* • *v.tr.* /pərvə́rt/ **1** turn (a person or thing) aside from its proper use or nature. **2** misapply or misconstrue (words, etc.). **3** lead astray (a person, a person's mind, etc.) from right opinion or conduct, or esp. religious belief. **4** (as **perverted** *adj.*) showing perversion. • *n.* /pə́rvərt/ **1** a perverted person. **2** a person showing sexual perversion. □□ **per·ver·sive** /-və́rsiv/ *adj.* **per·vert·ed·ly** /-və́rtidlee/ *adv.* **per·vert·er** /-və́rtər/ *n.*

per·vi·ous /pə́rveeəs/ *adj.* **1** permeable. **2** (usu. foll. by *to*) **a** affording passage. **b** accessible (to reason, etc.). □□ **per·vi·ous·ness** *n.*

pe·se·ta /pəsáytə/ *n.* the chief monetary unit of Spain, orig. a silver coin.

pes·ky /péskee/ *adj.* (**peskier, peskiest**) *colloq.* troublesome; annoying. □□ **pesk·i·ly** *adv.* **pesk·i·ness** *n.*

pe·so /páysō/ *n.* (*pl.* **-sos**) **1** the chief monetary unit of several Latin American countries and of the Philippines. **2** a note or coin worth one peso.

pes·sa·ry /pésəree/ *n.* (*pl.* **-ries**) *Med.* **1** a device worn in the vagina to support the uterus or as a contraceptive. **2** a vaginal suppository.

pes·si·mism /pésimizəm/ *n.* a tendency to take the worst view or expect the worst outcome. □□ **pes·si·mist** *n.* **pes·si·mis·tic** *adj.* **pes·si·mis·ti·cal·ly** *adv.*

pest /pest/ *n.* **1** a troublesome or annoying person or thing; a nuisance. **2** a destructive animal, esp. an insect which attacks crops, livestock, etc.

pes·ter /péstər/ *v.tr.* trouble or annoy, esp. with frequent or persistent requests. □□ **pes·ter·er** *n.*

pes·ti·cide /péstisīd/ *n.* a substance used for destroying insects or other organisms harmful to cultivated plants or to animals. □□ **pes·ti·cid·al** /-síd'l/ *adj.*

pes·ti·lence /péstələns/ *n.* **1** a fatal epidemic disease, esp. bubonic plague. **2** something evil or destructive.

pes·ti·lent /péstələnt/ *adj.* **1** destructive to life; deadly. **2** harmful or morally destructive. **3** *colloq.* troublesome; annoying. □□ **pes·ti·lent·ly** *adv.*

pes·ti·len·tial /péstəlénshəl/ *adj.* **1** of or relating to pestilence. **2** dangerous; troublesome; pestilent. □□ **pes·ti·len·tial·ly** *adv.*

pes·tle /pésəl/ *n.* **1** a club-shaped instrument for pounding substances in a mortar. **2** an appliance for pounding, etc.

pes·to /péstō/ *n.* a sauce made of fresh chopped basil, garlic, olive oil, and Parmesan cheese, used for pasta, fish, etc.

pet[1] /pet/ *n., adj., & v.* • *n.* **1** a domestic or tamed animal kept for pleasure or companionship. **2** a darling; a favorite (often as a term of endearment). • *attrib.adj.* **1** kept as a pet (*pet lamb*). **2** of or for pet animals (*pet food*). **3** often *joc.* favorite or particular (*pet aversion*). **4** expressing fondness or familiarity (*pet name*). • *v.tr.* (**petted, petting**) **1** treat as a pet. **2** (also *absol.*) fondle, esp. erotically. □□ **pet·ter** *n.*

pet[2] /pet/ *n.* a feeling of petty resentment or ill-humor (esp. *be in a pet*).

peta- /pétə/ *comb.form* denoting a factor of 10^{15}.

pet·al /pét'l/ *n.* each of the parts of the corolla of a flower. □□ **pet·al·ine** /-līn, -lin/ *adj.* **pet·alled** *adj.* (also in *comb.*). **pet·al·like** *adj.* **pet·al·oid** *adj.*

See page xii for the *Key to Pronunciation*.

pe·tard /pitaard/ *n. hist.* **1** a small bomb used to blast down a door, etc. **2** a kind of firework. □ **hoist with** (or **by**) **one's own petard** affected oneself by one's schemes against others.

pe·ter /peetər/ *v.intr.* (foll. by *out*) (orig. of a vein of ore, etc.) diminish; come to an end.

Pe·ter Prin·ci·ple /peetər/ *n. joc.* the principle that members of a hierarchy are promoted until they reach the level at which they are no longer competent.

pet·i·ole /péteeōl/ *n.* the slender stalk joining a leaf to a stem. □□ **pet·i·o·lar** *adj.* **pet·i·o·late** /pétiəláyt/ *adj.*

pet·it /pétee/ *adj.* esp. *Law* petty; small; of lesser importance.

pe·tit bour·geois /pétee bóorzhwaa, boorzhwaa, pətée/ *n.* (*pl.* **petits bourgeois** *pronunc.* same) a member of the lower middle classes.

pe·tite /pəteet/ *adj.* & *n.* • *adj.* (of a woman) of small and dainty build. • *n.* a clothing size for petite women.

pe·tite bour·geoi·sie *n.* the lower middle classes.

pe·tit four /pétee fáwr/ *n.* (*pl.* **petits fours** /fórz/) a very small fancy frosted cake.

pe·ti·tion /pətíshən/ *n.* & *v.* • *n.* **1** a supplication or request. **2** a formal written request, esp. one signed by many people, appealing to authority in some cause. **3** *Law* an application to a court for a writ, etc. • *v.* **1** *tr.* make or address a petition to (*petition the court*). **2** *intr.* (often foll. by *for, to*) appeal earnestly or humbly. □□ **pe·ti·tion·a·ble** *adj.* **pe·ti·tion·ar·y** *adj.* **pe·ti·tion·er** *n.*

pe·tit ju·ry *n.* a jury of 12 persons who try the final issue of fact in civil or criminal cases and pronounce a verdict.

pe·tit mal /pétee maal, mál/ *n.* a mild form of epilepsy with only momentary loss of consciousness (cf. GRAND MAL).

pe·tit point /pétee póynt, pətee pwáN/ *n.* **1** embroidery on canvas using small stitches. **2** tent stitch.

pet peeve *n. colloq.* something especially annoying to an individual.

pet·rel /pétrəl/ *n.* any of various seabirds of the family Procellariidae or Hydrobatidae, usu. flying far from land.

Pe·tri dish /peetree/ *n.* a shallow covered dish used for the culture of bacteria, etc.

pet·ri·fy /pétrifī/ *v.* (**-fies, -fied**) **1** *tr.* (also as **petrified** *adj.*) paralyze with fear, astonishment, etc. **2** *tr.* change (organic matter) into a stony substance. **3** *intr.* become like stone. □□ **pet·ri·fac·tion** *n.*

petro- /pétrō/ *comb.form* **1** rock. **2** petroleum (*petrochemistry*).

pet·ro·chem·i·cal /pétrōkémikəl/ *n.* & *adj.* • *n.* a substance industrially obtained from petroleum or natural gas. • *adj.* of or relating to petrochemistry or petrochemicals.

pet·ro·dol·lar /pétrōdolər/ *n.* a notional unit of currency earned by a petroleum-exporting country.

pet·ro·glyph /pétrəglif/ *n.* a rock carving, esp. a prehistoric one.

pet·rol /pétrəl/ *n. Brit.* **1** refined petroleum used as a fuel in motor vehicles, aircraft, etc.; gasoline. **2** (*attrib.*) concerned with the supply of petrol (*petrol pump*; *petrol station*).

pe·tro·le·um /pətróleeəm/ *n.* a hydrocarbon oil found in the upper strata of the earth, refined for use as a fuel for heating and in internal combustion engines, for lighting, dry cleaning, etc.

pe·tro·le·um jel·ly *n.* a translucent solid mixture of hydrocarbons used as a lubricant, ointment, etc.

pe·trol·o·gy /petróləjee/ *n.* the study of the origin, structure, composition, etc., of rocks. □□ **pet·ro·log·ic** /pétrəlójik/ *adj.* **pet·ro·log·i·cal** *adj.* **pe·trol·o·gist** *n.*

pet·ti·coat /péteekōt/ *n.* **1** a woman's or girl's skirted undergarment hanging from the waist or shoulders. **2** often *derog. sl.* **a** a woman or girl. **b** (in *pl.*) the female sex. **3** (*attrib.*) often *derog.* feminine; associated with women (*petticoat pedantry*). □□ **pet·ti·coat·ed** *adj.* **pet·ti·coat·less** *adj.*

pet·ti·fog /péteefawg, -fog/ *v.intr.* (**pettifogged, pettifogging**) **1** practice legal deception or trickery. **2** quibble or wrangle about petty points.

pet·ti·fog·ger /péteefáwgər, -fóg-/ *n.* **1** a rascally lawyer; an inferior legal practitioner. **2** a petty practitioner in any activity. □□ **pet·ti·fog·ger·y** *n.* **pet·ti·fog·ging** *adj.*

pet·tish /pétish/ *adj.* peevish, petulant; easily put out. □□ **pet·tish·ly** *adv.* **pet·tish·ness** *n.*

pet·ty /pétee/ *adj.* (**pettier, pettiest**) **1** unimportant; trivial. **2** mean; small-minded; contemptible. **3** minor; inferior; on a small scale (*petty princes*). **4** *Law* (of a crime) of lesser importance (*a shoplifter convicted of petty theft*). □□ **pet·ti·ly** *adv.* **pet·ti·ness** *n.*

pet·ty bour·geois = PETIT BOURGEOIS.

pet·ty bour·geoi·sie = PETITE BOURGEOISIE.

pet·ty cash *n.* money from or for small items of receipt or expenditure.

pet·ty of·fi·cer *n.* a naval NCO.

pet·u·lant /péchələnt/ *adj.* peevishly impatient or irritable (*a petulant child*). □□ **pet·u·lance** *n.* **pet·u·lant·ly** *adv.*

pe·tu·nia /pitóonyə, -tyóon-/ *n.* **1** any plant of the genus *Petunia* with white, purple, red, etc., funnel-shaped flowers. **2** a dark violet or purple color.

pew /pyoo/ *n.* & *v.* • *n.* **1** (in a church) a long bench with a back; an enclosed compartment. **2** *Brit. colloq.* a seat (esp. *take a pew*). • *v.tr.* furnish with pews. □□ **pew·age** *n.* **pew·less** *adj.*

pew·ter /pyóotər/ *n.* **1** a gray alloy of tin with lead, copper, antimony, or various other metals. **2** utensils made of this. □□ **pew·ter·er** *n.*

pe·yo·te /payṓtee/ *n.* **1** any Mexican cactus of the genus *Lophophora*, esp. *L. williamsii* having no spines and button-like tops when dried. **2** a hallucinogenic drug containing mescaline prepared from this.

Pfc. *abbr.* (also **PFC**) Private First Class.

PG *abbr.* (of movies) classified as suitable for children subject to parental guidance.

pg. *abbr.* page.

PGA *abbr.* Professional Golfers' Association.

PG-13 *abbr.* (of a film) classified as suitable for children under age 13 subject to parental guidance.

pH /pee-áych/ *n. Chem.* a logarithm of the reciprocal of the hydrogen-ion concentration in moles per liter of a solution, giving a measure of its acidity or alkalinity.

pha·e·ton /fáyit'n, fáyt'n/ *n.* **1** a light open four-wheeled carriage, usu. drawn by a pair of horses. **2** a vintage touring car.

phag·o·cyte /fágəsīt/ *n.* a type of cell capable of engulfing and absorbing foreign matter, esp. a leukocyte ingesting bacteria in the body. □□ **phag·o·cyt·ic** /-sítik/ *adj.*

-phagous /fəgəs/ *comb.form* that eats (as specified) (*ichthyophagous*).

-phagy /fəjee/ *comb.form* the eating of (specified food) (*ichthyophagy*).

pha·lanx /fálangks/ *n.* (*pl.* **phalanxes** or **phalanges** /fəlánjeez/) **1** *Gk Antiq.* a line of battle, esp. a body of Macedonian infantry drawn up in close order. **2** a set of people, etc., forming a compact mass, or banded for a common purpose. **3** a bone of the finger or toe.

phal·li *pl.* of PHALLUS.

phal·lic /fálik/ *adj.* **1** of, relating to, or resembling a phallus. **2** *Psychol.* denoting the stage of male sexual development characterized by preoccupation with the genitals. □□ **phal·li·cal·ly** *adv.*

phal·lus /fáləs/ *n.* (*pl.* **phalli** /-lī/ or **phalluses**) **1** the (esp.

erect) penis. **2** an image of this as a symbol of generative power in nature. □□ **phal·li·cism** /-lisízəm/ *n.* **phal·lism** *n.*

phan·tasm /fántazəm/ *n.* **1** an illusion; a phantom. **2** (usu. foll. by *of*) an illusory likeness. **3** a supposed vision of an absent (living or dead) person. □□ **phan·tas·mal** /-tázm'l/ *adj.* **phan·tas·mic** /-tázmik/ *adj.*

phan·tas·ma·go·ri·a /fántazməgáwreeə/ *n.* **1** a shifting series of real or imaginary figures as seen in a dream. **2** an optical device for rapidly varying the size of images on a screen. □□ **phan·tas·ma·gor·ic** /-gáwrik, -gór-/ *adj.* **phan·tas·ma·gor·i·cal** *adj.*

phan·tom /fántəm/ *n. & adj.* •*n.* **1** a ghost; an apparition; a specter. **2** a form without substance or reality; a mental illusion. **3** *Med.* a model of the whole or part of the body used to practice or demonstrate operative or therapeutic methods. •*adj.* merely apparent; illusory.

Phar·aoh /fáirō, fárō, fáyrō/ *n.* **1** the ruler of ancient Egypt. **2** the title of this ruler. □□ **Phar·a·on·ic** /fáirayónik/ *adj.*

Phar·i·see /fárisee/ (also **phar·i·see**) *n.* **1** a member of an ancient Jewish sect, distinguished by strict observance of the traditional and written law. **2** a self-righteous person; a hypocrite. □□ **Phar·i·sa·ic** /fárisáyik/ *adj.* **Phar·i·sa·i·cal** /fárisáyikəl/ *adj.* **Phar·i·sa·ism** /fárisayizəm/ *n.*

phar·ma·ceu·ti·cal /faármasóōtikəl/ *adj. & n.* •*adj.* **1** of or engaged in pharmacy. **2** of the use or sale of medicinal drugs. •*n.* a medicinal drug. □□ **phar·ma·ceu·ti·cal·ly** *adv.* **phar·ma·ceu·tics** *n.*

phar·ma·cist /faármasist/ *n.* a person qualified to prepare and dispense drugs.

phar·ma·col·o·gy /faármakóləjee/ *n.* the science of the action of drugs on the body. □□ **phar·ma·co·log·i·cal** *adj.* **phar·ma·co·log·i·cal·ly** *adv.* **phar·ma·col·o·gist** *n.*

phar·ma·co·poe·ia /faármakəpeéə/ *n.* **1** a book, esp. one officially published, containing a list of drugs with directions for use. **2** a stock of drugs. □□ **phar·ma·co·poe·ial** *adj.*

phar·ma·cy /faárməsee/ *n.* (*pl.* **-cies**) **1** the preparation and the (esp. medicinal) dispensing of drugs. **2** a drugstore; a dispensary.

pharyngo- /fəringgō/ *comb.form* denoting the pharynx.

phar·ynx /fáringks/ *n.* (*pl.* **pharynges** /fərínjeez/) a cavity behind the nose and mouth, connecting them to the esophagus. □□ **pha·ryn·gal** /-ríngəl/ *adj.* **pha·ryn·ge·al** /fərínjeeəl, -jəl, fárinjeéəl/ *adj.*

phase /fayz/ *n. & v.* •*n.* **1** a distinct period or stage in a process of change or development. **2** each of the aspects of the moon or a planet, according to the amount of its illumination, esp. the new moon, the first quarter, the last quarter, and the full moon. **3** *Physics* a stage in a periodically recurring sequence, esp. of alternating electric currents or light vibrations. **4** a difficult or unhappy period, esp. in adolescence. **5** a genetic or seasonal variety of an animal's coloration, etc. **6** *Chem.* a distinct and homogeneous form of matter separated by its surface from other forms. •*v.tr.* carry out (a program, etc.) in phases or stages. □ **phase in** (or **out**) bring gradually into (or out of) use. □□ **pha·sic** *adj.*

Ph.D. *abbr.* Doctor of Philosophy.

pheas·ant /fézənt/ *n.* any of several long-tailed game birds of the family Phasianidae, orig. from Asia. □□ **pheas·ant·ry** *n.* (*pl.* **-ries**).

pheno- /feénō/ *comb.form* **1** *Chem.* derived from benzene (*phenol*; *phenyl*). **2** showing (*phenocryst*).

phe·no·bar·bi·tal /feénōbaárbitawl, -tal/ *n.* a narcotic and sedative barbiturate drug used esp. to treat epilepsy.

phenol /feénawl, -nol/ *n. Chem.* **1** the monohydroxyl derivative of benzene used in dilute form as an antiseptic and disinfectant. Also called CARBOLIC. ¶ Chem. formula: C_6H_5OH. **2** any hydroxyl derivative of an aromatic hydrocarbon. □□ **phe·no·lic** /finólik/ *adj.*

phe·nom·e·na *pl.* of PHENOMENON.

phe·nom·e·nal /finóminəl/ *adj.* **1** of the nature of a phenomenon. **2** extraordinary; remarkable; prodigious. **3** perceptible by, or perceptible only to, the senses. □□ **phe·nom·e·nal·ize** *v.tr.* **phe·nom·e·nal·ly** *adv.*

▶The singular of this Greek word is **phenomenon**, the plural **phenomena**: *Halley's Comet is a rare phenomenon, one of the most spectacular of celestial phenomena.*

phe·nom·e·non /finóminən/ *n.* (*pl.* **phenomena** /-nə/) **1** a fact or occurrence that appears or is perceived, esp. one of which the cause is in question. **2** a remarkable person or thing.

phen·yl /fénil, feé-/ *n. Chem.* the univalent radical formed from benzene by the removal of a hydrogen atom.

phen·yl·al·a·nine /fénilaləneen/ *n. Biochem.* an amino acid widely distributed in plant proteins, essential in the diet of vertebrates.

phen·yl·ke·to·nu·ri·a /fénilkeétōnóōreeə, -yóōr-, feé-/ *n.* an inherited inability to metabolize phenylalanine, ultimately leading to brain and nerve damage if untreated. ¶ Abbr.: **PKU**.

pher·o·mone /férəmōn/ *n.* a chemical substance secreted and released by an animal for detection and response by another usu. of the same species. □□ **pher·o·mo·nal** /-mṓn'l/ *adj.*

phew /fyōō/ *int.* an expression of impatience, discomfort, relief, astonishment, or disgust.

phi /fī/ *n.* the twenty-first letter of the Greek alphabet (Φ, ϕ).

phi·al /fīəl/ *n.* a small glass bottle, esp. for liquid medicine; vial.

Phil. *abbr.* **1** Philharmonic. **2** Philippines. **3** Philosophy.

phil- *comb.form* var. of PHILO-.

-phil *comb.form* var. of -PHILE.

phi·lan·der /filándər/ *v.intr.* (often foll. by *with*) flirt or have casual affairs with women; womanize. □□ **phi·lan·der·er** *n.*

phil·an·thrope /filənthrōp/ *n. dated* a philanthropist.

phil·an·throp·ic /filənthrópik/ *adj.* loving one's fellow people; benevolent. □□ **phil·an·throp·i·cal·ly** *adv.*

phi·lan·thro·pist /filánthrəpist/ *n.* a person who seeks to promote the welfare of others, esp. by the generous donation of money to good causes.

phi·lan·thro·py /filánthrəpee/ *n.* **1** a love of humankind. **2** practical benevolence, esp. charity on a large scale. □□ **phi·lan·thro·pism** *n.* **phi·lan·thro·pize** *v.tr. & intr.*

phi·lat·e·ly /filát'lee/ *n.* the collection and study of postage stamps. □□ **phil·a·tel·ic** /filətélik/ *adj.* **phil·a·tel·i·cal·ly** *adv.* **phi·lat·e·list** *n.*

-phile /fīl/ *comb.form* (also **-phil** /fil/) forming nouns and adjectives denoting fondness for what is specified (*bibliophile*; *Francophile*).

phil·har·mon·ic /filhaarmónik/ *adj.* **1** fond of music. **2** used characteristically in the names of orchestras, choirs, etc. (*New York Philharmonic Orchestra*).

-philia /fileeə/ *comb.form* **1** denoting (esp. abnormal) fondness or love for what is specified (*necrophilia*). **2** denoting undue inclination (*hemophilia*). □□ **-philiac** /-leeak/ *comb.form* forming nouns and adjectives. **-philic** /-ik/ *comb.form*> forming adjectives. **-philous** /-əs/ *comb.form* forming adjectives.

phi·lip·pic /filípik/ *n.* a bitter verbal attack or denunciation.

Phil·ip·pine /filipeen/ *adj.* of or relating to the Philippine Islands or their people; Filipino.

Phil·is·tine /filisteen, -stīn, filístin, -teen/ *n. & adj.* • *n.* **1** a member of a people opposing the Israelites in ancient Palestine. **2** (usu. **philistine**) a person who is hostile or indifferent to culture, or one whose interests or tastes are commonplace or material. • *adj.* hostile or indifferent to culture; commonplace; prosaic. ▫▫ **phil·is·tin·ism** /filistinízəm/ *n.*

Phil·lips /filips/ *n.* (usu. *attrib.*) *Trademark* denoting a screw with a cross-shaped slot for turning, or a corresponding screwdriver.

philo- /filō/ *comb.form* (also **phil-** before a vowel or *h*) denoting a liking for what is specified.

phil·o·den·dron /filədéndrən/ *n.* (*pl.* **philodendrons** or **philodendra** /-drə/) any tropical American climbing plant of the genus *Philodendron*, with bright foliage.

phi·lol·o·gy /filóləjee/ *n.* **1** the science of language, esp. in its historical and comparative aspects. **2** the love of learning and literature. ▫▫ **phil·o·lo·gi·an** /-ləlṓjeeən/ *n.* **phi·lol·o·gist** *n.* **phil·o·log·i·cal** /-ləlójikəl/ *adj.* **phil·o·log·i·cal·ly** /-ləlójiklee/ *adv.* **phi·lol·o·gize** *v.intr.*

phi·los·o·pher /filósəfər/ *n.* **1** a person engaged or learned in philosophy or a branch of it. **2** a person who lives by philosophy. **3** a person who shows philosophic calmness in trying circumstances.

phil·o·soph·i·cal /filəsófikəl/ *adj.* (also **phil·o·soph·ic**) **1** of or according to philosophy. **2** skilled in or devoted to philosophy or learning; learned (*philosophical society*). **3** wise; serene; temperate. **4** calm in adverse circumstances. ▫▫ **phil·o·soph·i·cal·ly** *adv.*

phi·los·o·phize /filósəfīz/ *v.* **1** *intr.* reason like a philosopher. **2** *intr.* moralize. **3** *intr.* speculate; theorize. **4** *tr.* render philosophic. ▫▫ **phi·los·o·phiz·er** *n.*

phi·los·o·phy /filósəfee/ *n.* (*pl.* **-phies**) **1** the use of reason and argument in seeking truth and knowledge of reality, esp. of the causes and nature of things and of the principles governing existence, the material universe, perception of physical phenomena, and human behavior. **2 a** a particular system or set of beliefs reached by this. **b** a personal rule of life. **3** advanced learning in general (*doctor of philosophy*).

phil·ter /filtər/ *n.* (also **phil·tre**) a drink supposed to excite sexual love in the drinker.

-phily /filee/ *comb.form* = -PHILIA.

phiz /fiz/ *n. colloq.* **1** a person's face or expression (abbreviation of *physiognomy*).

phle·bi·tis /flibítis/ *n.* inflammation of the walls of a vein. ▫▫ **phle·bit·ic** /-bítik/ *adj.*

phle·bot·o·my /flibótəmee/ *n.* the surgical opening or puncture of a vein. ▫▫ **phle·bot·o·mist** *n.* **phle·bot·o·mize** *v.tr.*

phlegm /flem/ *n.* **1** the thick viscous substance secreted by the mucous membranes of the respiratory passages, discharged by coughing. **2 a** coolness and calmness of disposition. **b** sluggishness or apathy (supposed to result from too much phlegm in the constitution). ▫▫ **phlegm·y** *adj.*

---

phlegm Middle English *fleem*, *fleume*, from Old French *fleume*, from late Latin *phlegma* 'clammy moisture (of the body),' from Greek *phlegma* 'inflammation,' from *phlegein* 'to burn.' The spelling change in the 16th century was due to association with the Latin and Greek forms.

---

phleg·mat·ic /flegmátik/ *adj.* stolidly calm; unexcitable; unemotional. ▫▫ **phleg·mat·i·cal·ly** *adv.*

phlo·em /flṓem/ *n. Bot.* the tissue conducting food material in plants (cf. XYLEM).

phlo·gis·ton /flōjístən/ *n.* a substance formerly supposed to exist in all combustible bodies, and to be released in combustion.

phlox /floks/ *n.* any cultivated plant of the genus *Phlox*, with scented clusters of esp. white, blue, and red flowers.

-phobe /fōb/ *comb.form* forming nouns and adjectives denoting a person having a fear or dislike of what is specified (*xenophobe*).

pho·bi·a /fṓbeeə/ *n.* an abnormal or morbid fear or aversion. ▫▫ **pho·bic** *adj. & n.*

-phobia /fṓbeeə/ *comb.form* forming abstract nouns denoting a fear or dislike of what is specified (*agoraphobia*; *xenophobia*). ▫▫ **-phobic** *comb.form* forming adjectives.

phoe·be /féebee/ *n.* any American flycatcher of the genus *Sayornis*.

Phoe·ni·cian /fənéeshən, fəní-/ *n. & adj.* • *n.* a member of a Semitic people of ancient Phoenicia in S. Syria or of its colonies. • *adj.* f or relating to Phoenicia.

phoe·nix /féeniks/ *n.* **1** a mythical bird, the only one of its kind, that after living for five or six centuries in the Arabian desert, burned itself on a funeral pyre and rose from the ashes with renewed youth to live through another cycle. **2 a** a unique person or thing. **b** a person or thing having recovered, esp. seemingly miraculously, from a disaster.

phone[1] /fōn/ *n. & v.tr. & intr. colloq.* = TELEPHONE.

phone[2] /fōn/ *n.* a simple vowel or consonant sound.

-phone /fōn/ *comb.form* forming nouns and adjectives meaning: **1** an instrument using or connected with sound (*telephone*; *xylophone*). **2** a person who uses a specified language (*anglophone*).

phone book *n.* = TELEPHONE BOOK.

pho·neme /fṓneem/ *n.* any of the units of sound in a specified language that distinguish one word from another (e.g., *p*, *b*, *d*, *t* as in pad, pat, bad, bat, in English). ▫▫ **pho·ne·mic** /-néemik/ *adj.* **pho·ne·mics** /-néemiks/ *n.*

pho·net·ic /fənétik/ *adj.* **1** representing vocal sounds. **2** (of a system of spelling, etc.) having a direct correspondence between symbols and sounds. **3** of or relating to phonetics. ▫▫ **pho·net·i·cal·ly** *adv.* **pho·net·i·cism** /-nétəsizəm/ *n.* **pho·net·i·cist** /-nétəsist/ *n.* **pho·net·i·cize** /-nétəsīz/ *v.tr.*

pho·net·ics /fənétiks/ *n.pl.* (usu. treated as *sing.*) **1** vocal sounds and their classification. **2** the study of these. ▫▫ **pho·ne·ti·cian** /fṓnitíshən/ *n.*

pho·ne·tist /fṓnitist/ *n.* an advocate of phonetic spelling.

phon·ic /fónik/ *adj. & n.* • *adj.* of sound; acoustic; of vocal sounds. • *n.* (in *pl.*) a method of teaching reading based on sounds. ▫▫ **phon·i·cal·ly** *adv.*

phono- /fṓnō/ *comb.form* denoting sound.

pho·no·gram /fṓnəgram/ *n.* a symbol representing a spoken sound.

pho·no·graph /fṓnəgraf/ *n.* **1** an instrument that reproduces recorded sound by a stylus that is in contact with a rotating grooved disk. ▶Now more usually called a RECORD PLAYER. **2** *Brit.* an early form of phonograph, usually called a gramophone, using cylinders and able to record as well as reproduce sound.

pho·nog·ra·phy /fənógrəfee/ *n.* **1** writing in esp. shorthand symbols, corresponding to the sounds of speech. **2** the recording of sounds by phonograph. ▫▫ **pho·no·graph·ic** /fṓnəgráfik/ *adj.*

pho·nol·o·gy /fənóləjee/ *n.* the study of sounds in a language. ▫▫ **pho·no·log·i·cal** /fṓnəlójikəl/ *adj.* **pho·no·log·i·cal·ly** *adv.* **pho·nol·o·gist** /fənóləjist/ *n.*

pho·ny /fṓnee/ *adj. & n.* (also **pho·ney**) *colloq.* • *adj.* (**phonier, phoniest**) **1** sham; counterfeit. **2** fictitious; fraudulent. • *n.* (*pl.* **-nies** or **-neys**) a phony person or thing. ▫▫ **pho·ni·ly** *adv.* **pho·ni·ness** *n.*

phoo·ey /fṓō-ee/ *int.* an expression of disgust or disbelief.

-phore /fawr/ *comb.form* forming nouns meaning 'bearer' (*ctenophore*; *semaphore*). ▫▫ **-phorous** /fərəs/ *comb.form* forming adjectives.

phos·gene /fósjeen, fóz-/ *n.* a colorless poisonous gas (carbonyl chloride), formerly used in warfare. ¶ Chem. formula: $COCl_2$.

phos·phate /fósfayt/ *n.* **1** any salt or ester of phosphoric acid, esp. used as a fertilizer. **2** a flavored effervescent drink containing a small amount of phosphate. ▫▫ **phos·phat·ic** /-fátik/ *adj.*

phos·phor /fósfər/ *n.* **1** = PHOSPHORUS. **2** a synthetic fluorescent or phosphorescent substance esp. used in cathode-ray tubes.

phos·pho·rate /fósfərayt/ *v.tr.* combine or impregnate with phosphorus.

phos·pho·res·cence /fósfərésəns/ *n.* **1** radiation similar to fluorescence but detectable after excitation ceases. **2** the emission of light without combustion or perceptible heat. ▫▫ **phos·pho·resce** *v.intr.* **phos·pho·res·cent** *adj.*

phos·pho·rus /fósfərəs/ *n. Chem.* a nonmetallic element occurring naturally in various phosphate rocks and existing in allotropic forms, esp. as a poisonous whitish waxy substance burning slowly at ordinary temperatures and so appearing luminous in the dark, and a reddish form used in matches, fertilizers, etc. ¶ Symb.: **P.** ▫▫ **phos·phor·ic** /-fórik/ *adj.* **phos·pho·rous** *adj.*

pho·to /fṓtō/ *n. & v.* •*n.* (*pl.* **-tos**) = PHOTOGRAPH *n.* •*v.tr.* (**-toes, -toed**) = PHOTOGRAPH *v.*

photo- /fṓtō/ *comb.form* denoting: **1** light (*photosensitive*). **2** photography (*photocomposition*).

pho·to·cell /fṓtōsel/ *n.* = PHOTOELECTRIC CELL.

pho·to·chem·is·try /fṓtōkémistree/ *n.* the study of the chemical effects of light. ▫▫ **pho·to·chem·ic·al** *adj.*

pho·to·com·po·si·tion /fṓtōkómpəzíshən/ *n. Printing* a typesetting process in which characters, etc., are projected onto a light-sensitive material such as photographic film.

pho·to·con·duc·tiv·i·ty /fṓtōkónduktívitee/ *n.* conductivity due to the action of light. ▫▫ **pho·to·con·duc·tive** /-dúktiv/ *adj.* **pho·to·con·duc·tor** /-dúktər/ *n.*

pho·to·cop·i·er /fṓtōkópeeər/ *n.* a machine for producing photocopies.

pho·to·cop·y /fṓtōkópee/ *n. & v.* •*n.* (*pl.* **-ies**) a photographic copy of printed or written material produced by a process involving the action of light on a specially prepared surface. •*v.tr.* (**-ies, -ied**) make a photocopy of. ▫▫ **pho·to·cop·i·a·ble** *adj.*

pho·to·e·lec·tric /fṓtōiléktrik/ *adj.* marked by or using emissions of electrons from substances exposed to light. ▫▫ **pho·to·e·lec·tric·i·ty** /-trísitee/ *n.*

pho·to·e·lec·tric cell *n.* a device using this effect to generate current.

pho·to fin·ish *n.* a close finish of a race or contest, esp. one where the winner is only distinguishable on a photograph.

pho·to·fin·ish·ing /fōtōfínishing/ *n.* the process of developing and printing photographic film.

pho·to·gen·ic /fṓtəjénik/ *adj.* **1** (esp. of a person) having an appearance that looks pleasing in photographs. **2** *Biol.* producing or emitting light. ▫▫ **pho·to·gen·i·cal·ly** *adv.*

pho·to·graph /fṓtəgraf/ *n. & v.* •*n.* a picture taken by means of the chemical action of light or other radiation on sensitive film. •*v.tr.* (also *absol.*) take a photograph of (a person, etc.). ▫▫ **pho·to·graph·a·ble** *adj.* **pho·tog·ra·pher** /fətógrəfər/ *n.*

pho·to·graph·ic /fṓtəgráfik/ *adj.* **1** of, used in, or produced by photography. **2** having the accuracy of a photograph (*photographic likeness*). ▫▫ **pho·to·graph·i·cal·ly** *adv.*

pho·tog·ra·phy /fətógrəfee/ *n.* the taking and processing of photographs.

pho·to·gra·vure /fṓtōgrəvyŏŏr/ *n.* **1** an image produced from a photographic negative transferred to a metal plate and etched in. **2** this process.

pho·to·jour·nal·ism /fṓtōjə́rnəlizəm/ *n.* the art or practice of relating news by photographs, with or without an accompanying text, esp. in magazines, etc. ▫▫ **pho·to·jour·nal·ist** *n.*

pho·ton /fṓton/ *n.* **1** a quantum of electromagnetic radiation energy, proportional to the frequency of radiation. **2** a unit of luminous intensity as measured at the retina.

pho·to·sen·si·tive /fṓtōsénsitiv/ *adj.* reacting chemically, electrically, etc., to light. ▫▫ **pho·to·sen·si·tiv·i·ty** /-tívitee/ *n.*

Pho·to·stat /fṓtəstat/ *n. & v.* •*n. Trademark* **1** a type of machine for making photocopies. **2** a copy made by this means. •*v.tr.* (**photostat**) (**-statted, -statting**) make a Photostat of. ▫▫ **pho·to·stat·ic** /-státik/ *adj.*

pho·to·syn·the·sis /fṓtōsínthisis/ *n.* the process in which the energy of sunlight is used by organisms, esp. green plants, to synthesize carbohydrates from carbon dioxide and water. ▫▫ **pho·to·syn·the·size** *v.tr. & intr.* **pho·to·syn·thet·ic** /-thétik/ *adj.* **pho·to·syn·thet·i·cal·ly** *adv.*

pho·to·vol·ta·ic /fṓtōvoltáyik, –vōl–/ *adj.* relating to the production of electric current at the junction of two substances exposed to light.

phras·al /fráyzəl/ *adj. Gram.* consisting of a phrase.

phras·al verb *n.* an idiomatic phrase consisting of a verb and an adverb (e.g., *break down*), a verb and a preposition (e.g., *see to*), or a combination of both (e.g., *look down on*).

phrase /frayz/ *n. & v.* •*n.* **1** a group of words forming a conceptual unit, but not a sentence. **2** an idiomatic or short pithy expression. **3** a manner or mode of expression (*a nice turn of phrase*). **4** *Mus.* a group of notes forming a distinct unit within a larger piece. •*v.tr.* **1** express in words (*phrased the reply badly*). **2** (esp. when reading aloud or speaking) divide (sentences, etc.) into units so as to convey the meaning of the whole. **3** *Mus.* divide (music) into phrases, etc., in performance. ▫▫ **phras·ing** *n.*

phra·se·ol·o·gy /fráyzeeóləjee/ *n.* (*pl.* **-gies**) **1** a choice or arrangement of words. **2** a mode of expression. ▫▫ **phra·se·o·log·i·cal** /-əlójikəl/ *adj.*

phre·net·ic /frənétik/ *adj.* (also **fre·net·ic**) **1** frantic. **2** fanatic. ▫▫ **phre·net·i·cal·ly** *adv.*

phre·nol·o·gy /frinóləjee/ *n. hist.* the study of the shape and size of the cranium as a supposed indication of character and mental faculties. ▫▫ **phren·o·log·i·cal** /-nəlójikəl/ *adj.* **phre·nol·o·gist** *n.*

phy·la *pl.* of PHYLUM.

phy·lac·ter·y /filáktəree/ *n.* (*pl.* **-ies**) **1** a small leather box containing Hebrew texts on vellum, worn by Jewish men at morning prayer as a reminder to keep the law. **2** an amulet; a charm.

phy·lum /fíləm/ *n.* (*pl.* **phyla** /-lə/) *Biol.* a taxonomic rank below kingdom comprising a class or classes and subordinate taxa.

phys·ic /fízik/ *n. & v.* esp. *archaic* •*n.* **1 a** a medicine or drug. **b** a laxative; cathartic (*a dose of physic*). **2** the art of healing. **3** the medical profession. •*v.tr.* (**physicked, physicking**) dose with physic.

phys·i·cal /fízikəl/ *adj. & n.* •*adj.* **1** of or concerning the body (*physical exercise; physical education*). **2** of matter; material (*both mental and physical force*). **3 a** of, or according to, the laws of nature (*a physical impossibility*). **b** belonging to physics (*physical science*). **4** rough; violent. •*n.* (in full **physical examination**) a medical examination to determine physical fitness. □□ **phys·i·cal·i·ty** /-kálitee/ *n.* **phys·i·cal·ly** *adv.* **phys·i·cal·ness** *n.*

phys·i·cal ed·u·ca·tion *n.* instruction in physical exercise, sports and games, esp. in schools. ¶ Abbr.: **PE** or **Phys. Ed.**

phys·i·cal sci·ence *n.* the sciences used in the study of inanimate natural objects, e.g., physics, chemistry, astronomy, etc.

phys·i·cal ther·a·py *n.* the treatment of disease, injury, deformity, etc., by physical methods including manipulation, massage, infrared heat treatment, remedial exercise, etc., not by drugs. □□ **phys·i·cal ther·a·pist** *n.*

phy·si·cian /fizíshən/ *n.* **1 a** a person legally qualified to practice medicine and surgery. **b** a specialist in medical diagnosis and treatment. **c** any medical practitioner. **2** a healer (*work is the best physician*).

phys·i·cist /fízisist/ *n.* a person skilled or qualified in physics.

physico- /fízikō/ *comb.form* **1** physical (and). **2** of physics (and).

phys·i·co·chem·i·cal /fízikōkémikəl/ *adj.* relating to physics and chemistry or to physical chemistry.

phys·ics /fíziks/ *n.* the science dealing with the properties and interactions of matter and energy.

physio- /fízeeō/ *comb.form* nature; what is natural.

phys·i·og·no·my /fízeeógnəmee, -ónəmee/ *n.* (*pl.* **-mies**) **1 a** the cast or form of a person's features, expression, body, etc. **b** the art of supposedly judging character from facial characteristics, etc. **2** the external features of a landscape, etc. **3** a characteristic, esp. moral, aspect. □□ **phys·i·og·nom·ic** /-ognómik, -ənómik/ *adj.* **phys·i·og·nom·i·cal** *adj.* **phys·i·og·nom·i·cal·ly** *adv.* **phys·i·og·no·mist** *n.*

phys·i·o·log·i·cal /fízeeəlójikəl/ *adj.* (also **phys·i·o·log·ic**) of or concerning physiology. □□ **phys·i·o·log·i·cal·ly** *adv.*

phys·i·ol·o·gy /fízeeóləjee/ *n.* **1** the science of the functions of living organisms and their parts. **2** these functions. □□ **phys·i·ol·o·gist** *n.*

phys·i·o·ther·a·py /fízeeōthérəpee/ = PHYSICAL THERAPY.

phy·sique /fizéek/ *n.* the bodily structure, development, and organization of an individual (*an athletic physique*).

-phyte /fīt/ *comb.form* forming nouns denoting a vegetable or plantlike organism (*saprophyte*; *zoophyte*). □□ **-phytic** /fítik/ *comb.form* forming adjectives.

phy·to·plank·ton /fītōplángktən/ *n.* plankton consisting of plants.

pi /pī/ *n.* **1** the sixteenth letter of the Greek alphabet (Π, π). **2** (as π) the symbol of the ratio of the circumference of a circle to its diameter (approx. 3.14159).

pi·a ma·ter /píə máytər, péeə/ *n. Anat.* the delicate innermost membrane enveloping the brain and spinal cord (see MENINX).

pi·a·nis·si·mo /péeənísimō/ *adj., adv., & n. Mus.* • *adj.* performed very softly. • *adv.* very softly. • *n.* (*pl.* **-mos** or **pianissimi** /-mee/) a passage to be performed very softly.

pi·an·ist /péeənist, pee-án-/ *n.* the player of a piano.

pi·an·o[1] /peeánō, pyánō/ *n.* (*pl.* **-os**) a large musical instrument played by pressing down keys on a keyboard and causing hammers to strike metal strings, the vibration from which is stopped by dampers when the keys are released.

pi·a·no[2] /pyaánō/ *adj., adv., & n.* • *adj.* **1** *Mus.* performed softly. **2** subdued. • *adv.* **1** *Mus.* softly. **2** in a subdued manner. • *n.* (*pl.* **-nos** or **piani** /-nee/) *Mus.* a piano passage.

pi·an·o·forte /pyánōfáwrt, -fáwrtee/ *n. Mus.* a piano.

pi·as·tre /peeástər/ *n.* (also **pi·as·ter**) a small coin and monetary unit of several Middle Eastern countries.

pi·az·za /pee-aátsə, -saa/ *n.* **1** a public square or marketplace, esp. in an Italian town. **2** /peeázə, -aázə/ *dial.* the veranda of a house.

pic /pik/ *n. colloq.* a picture, esp. a movie.

pi·ca /píkə/ *n. Printing* **1** a unit of type size ($^1/_6$ inch). **2** a size of letters in typewriting (10 per inch).

pi·ca·dor /píkədawr/ *n.* a mounted man with a lance who goads the bull in a bullfight.

pic·a·resque /píkərésk/ *adj.* (of a style of fiction) dealing with the episodic adventures of rogues, etc.

pic·a·yune /píkəyóon/ *n. & adj.* • *n.* **1** *colloq.* a small coin of little value, esp. a 5-cent piece. **2** an insignificant person or thing. • *adj.* **1** of little value; trivial. **2** mean; contemptible; petty (*the picayune squabbling of party politicians*).

pic·ca·lil·li /píkəlílee/ *n.* (*pl.* **piccalillis**) a pickle of chopped vegetables, mustard, and hot spices.

pic·co·lo /píkəlō/ *n. & adj.* • *n.* (*pl.* **-los**) **1** a small flute sounding an octave higher than the ordinary one. **2** its player. • *adj.* (esp. of a musical instrument) smaller or having a higher range than usual (*piccolo trumpet*).

pick[1] /pik/ *v. & n.* • *v.tr.* **1** (also *absol.*) choose carefully from a number of alternatives. **2** detach or pluck (a flower, fruit, etc.) from a stem, tree, etc. **3 a** probe (the teeth, nose, ears, a pimple, etc.) with the finger, an instrument, etc., to remove unwanted matter. **b** clear (a bone, carcass, etc.) of scraps of meat, etc. **4** (also *absol.*) (of a person) eat (food, a meal, etc.) in small bits; nibble without appetite. **5** (also *absol.*) pluck the strings of (a banjo, etc.). **6** remove stalks, etc., from (esp. soft fruit) before cooking. **7 a** select (a route or path) carefully over difficult terrain by foot. **b** place (one's steps, etc.) carefully. **8** pull apart. **9** (of a bird) take up (grains, etc.) in the beak. **10** open (a lock) with an instrument other than the proper key. • *n.* **1** the act or an instance of picking. **2 a** a selection or choice. **b** the right to select (*had first pick of the prizes*). **3** (usu. foll. by *of*) the best (*the pick of the bunch*). □ **pick and choose** select carefully or fastidiously. **pick at 1** eat (food) without interest; nibble. **2** = *pick on* 1 (PICK[1]). **pick a person's brains** extract ideas, information, etc., from a person for one's own use. **pick off 1** pluck (leaves, etc.) off. **2** shoot (people, etc.) one by one without haste. **3** eliminate (opposition, etc.) singly. **4** *Baseball* put out a base runner caught off base. **pick on 1** find fault with; nag at. **2** select, as for special attention. **pick out 1** take from a larger number (*picked him out from the others*). **2** distinguish from surrounding objects or at a distance (*can just pick out the church spire*). **3** play (a tune) by ear on the piano, etc. **pick over** select the best from. **pick a quarrel** (or **fight**) start an argument or a fight deliberately. **pick up 1 a** grasp and raise (from the ground, etc.) (*picked up his hat*). **b** clean up; straighten up. **2** gain or acquire by chance or without effort (*picked up a cold*). **3 a** fetch (a person, animal, or thing) left in another person's charge. **b** stop for and take along with one, esp. in a vehicle (*pick me up on the corner*). **4** make the acquaintance of (a person) casually, esp. as a sexual overture. **5** (of one's health, the weather, stock prices, etc.) recover; prosper; improve. **6** (of an engine, etc.) recover speed; accelerate. **7** (of the police, etc.) take into custody; arrest. **8** detect by scrutiny or with a telescope, searchlight, radio, etc. (*picked up most of the mistakes*; *picked up a distress signal*). **9** (often foll. by *with*) form or renew a friendship. **10** accept the responsibility of paying (a bill, etc.). **11** (*refl.*) raise (oneself, etc.) after a fall, etc. **12** raise (the feet, etc.) clear of the ground. **take one's pick** make a choice. □□ **pick·a·ble** *adj.*

pick[2] /pik/ *n. & v.* • *n.* **1** a long-handled tool having a usu. curved iron bar pointed at one or both ends, used for breaking up hard ground, masonry, etc. **2** *colloq.* a plectrum. **3** any instrument for picking, such as a toothpick. • *v.tr.* **1** break the surface of (the ground, etc.) with or as if with a pick. **2** make (holes, etc.) in this way.

pick·ax /píkaks/ *n.* & *v.* (also **pick·axe**) • *n.* = PICK² *n.* 1. • *v.* **1** *tr.* break (the ground, etc.) with a pickaxe. **2** *intr.* work with a pickax.

pick·er /píkər/ *n.* **1** a person or thing that picks. **2** (often in *comb.*) a person who gathers or collects (*grape-picker; rag-picker*).

pick·er·el /píkərəl/ *n.* (*pl.* same or **pickerels**) **1** any of various species of N. American pike of the genus *Esox.* **2** = WALLEYE.

pick·et /píkit/ *n.* & *v.* • *n.* **1** a person or group of people outside a place of work, intending to persuade esp. workers not to enter during a strike, etc. **2** a pointed stake or peg driven into the ground to form a fence or palisade, to tether a horse, etc. **3** (also **pic·quet, pi·quet**) *Mil.* **a** a small body of troops or a single soldier sent out to watch for the enemy, held in readiness, etc. **b** a party of sentries. **c** an outpost. **d** a camp guard on police duty in a garrison town, etc. • *v.* (**picketed, pick·eting**) **1 a** *tr.* & *intr.* station or act as a picket. **b** *tr.* beset or guard (a factory, workers, etc.) with a picket or pickets. **2** *tr.* secure with stakes. **3** *tr.* tether (an animal). ▫▫ **pick·et·er** *n.*

pick·et line *n.* a boundary established by workers on strike, esp. at the entrance to the place of work, which others are asked not to cross.

pick·ings /píkingz/ *n.pl.* **1** perquisites; pilferings (*rich pickings*). **2** remaining scraps; gleanings.

pick·le /píkəl/ *n.* & *v.* • *n.* **1 a** (often in *pl.*) vegetables, esp. cucumbers, preserved in brine, vinegar, mustard, etc., and used as a relish. **b** the brine, vinegar, etc., in which food is preserved. **2** *colloq.* a plight (*a fine pickle we are in!*). **3** *Brit. colloq.* a mischievous child. **4** an acid solution for cleaning metal, etc. • *v.tr.* **1** preserve in pickle. **2** treat with pickle. **3** (as **pickled** *adj.*) *sl.* drunk.

pick·lock /píklok/ *n.* **1** a person who picks locks. **2** an instrument for this.

pick-me-up *n.* **1** a restorative tonic, as for the nerves, etc. **2** a good experience, good news, etc., that cheers.

pick·pock·et /píkpókit/ *n.* a person who steals from the pockets of others.

pick·up /píkəp/ *n.* **1** *sl.* a person met casually, esp. for sexual purposes. **2** a small truck with an enclosed cab and open back. **3 a** the part of a record player carrying the stylus. **b** a detector of vibrations, etc. **4 a** the act of picking up. **b** something picked up. **5** the capacity for acceleration. **6** = PICK-ME-UP.

pick·y /píkee/ *adj.* (**pickier, pickiest**) *colloq.* excessively fastidious; choosy. ▫▫ **pick·i·ness** *n.*

pic·nic /píknik/ *n.* & *v.* • *n.* **1** an outing or excursion including a packed meal eaten out of doors. **2** any meal eaten out of doors or without preparation, tables, chairs, etc. **3** (usu. with *neg.*) *colloq.* something agreeable or easily accomplished, etc. (*it was no picnic organizing the meeting*). • *v.intr.* (**picnicked, picnicking**) take part in a picnic. ▫▫ **pic·nick·er** *n.* **pic·nick·y** *adj. colloq.*

pico- /péekō, píkō/ *comb. form* denoting a factor of 10^{-12} (*picometer*).

pi·cot /péekō, peekó/ *n.* a small loop of twisted thread in a lace edging, etc.

pic·quet var. of PICKET 3.

pic·to·graph /píktəgraf/ *n.* (also **pic·to·gram** /píktəgram/) **1 a** a pictorial symbol for a word or phrase. **b** an ancient record consisting of these. **2** a pictorial representation of statistics, etc., on a chart, graph, etc. ▫▫ **pic·to·graph·ic** *adj.* **pic·tog·ra·phy** /-tógrəfee/ *n.*

pic·to·ri·al /piktáwreeəl/ *adj.* & *n.* • *adj.* **1** of or expressed in a picture or pictures. **2** illustrated. **3** picturesque. • *n.* a journal, postage stamp, etc., with a picture or pictures as the main feature. ▫▫ **pic·to·ri·al·ly** *adv.*

pic·ture /píkchər/ *n.* & *v.* • *n.* **1 a** (often *attrib.*) a painting, drawing, photograph, etc., esp. as a work of art (*picture frame*). **b** a portrait, esp. a photograph, of a person. **c** a beautiful object (*her hat is a picture*). **2 a** a total visual or mental impression produced; a scene (*the picture looks bleak*). **b** a written or spoken description (*drew a vivid picture of moral decay*). **3 a** a movie. **b** (in *pl.*) a showing of movies at a movie theater (*went to the pictures*). **c** (in *pl.*) movies in general. **4** an image on a television screen. **5** *colloq.* **a** esp. *iron.* a person or thing exemplifying something (*he was the picture of innocence*). **b** a person or thing resembling another closely (*the picture of her aunt*). • *v.tr.* **1** represent in a picture. **2** (also *refl.*; often foll. by *to*) imagine, esp. visually or vividly (*pictured it to herself*). **3** describe graphically. ▫ **get the picture** *colloq.* grasp the tendency or drift of circumstances, information, etc.

pic·tur·esque /píkchərésk/ *adj.* **1** (of landscape, etc.) beautiful or striking, as in a picture. **2** (of language, etc.) strikingly graphic; vivid. ▫▫ **pic·tur·esque·ly** *adv.* **pic·tur·esque·ness** *n.*

pic·ture tube *n.* the cathode-ray tube of a television set.

pic·ture win·dow *n.* a very large window consisting of one pane of glass.

pid·dle /píd'l/ *v.* & *n.* • *v.intr.* **1** *colloq.* urinate (used esp. to or by children). **2** work or act in a trifling way. **3** (as **piddling** *adj.*) *colloq.* trivial; trifling. • *n. colloq.* **1** urination. **2** urine (used esp. to or by children). ▫▫ **pid·dler** *n.*

pidg·in /píjin/ *n.* a simplified language containing vocabulary from two or more languages, used for communication between people not having a common language.

pidg·in Eng·lish *n.* a pidgin in which the chief language is English, used orig. between Chinese and Europeans.

pie /pī/ *n.* **1** a baked dish of fruit, meat, custard, etc., usu. with a top and base of pastry. **2** anything resembling a pie in form (*a mud pie*).

pie·bald /píbawld/ *adj.* & *n.* • *adj.* **1** (usu. of an animal, esp. a horse) having irregular patches of two colors, esp. black and white. **2** motley; mongrel. • *n.* a piebald animal, esp. a horse.

piece /pees/ *n.* & *v.* • *n.* **1 a** (often foll. by *of*) one of the distinct portions forming part of or broken off from a larger object; a bit; a part (*a piece of string*). **b** each of the parts of which a set or category is composed (*a five-piece band; a piece of furniture*). **2** a coin of specified value (*50-cent piece*). **3 a** a usu. short literary or musical composition or a picture. **b** a theatrical play. **4** an item, instance, or example (*a piece of news*). **5 a** any of the objects used to make moves in board games. **b** a chessman (strictly, other than a pawn). **6** a definite quantity in which a thing is sold. **7** (often foll. by *of*) an enclosed portion (of land, etc.). **8** *sl. derog.* a woman. **9** (foll. by *of*) *sl.* a financial share or investment in (*has a piece of the new production*). **10** *colloq.* a short distance. **11** *sl.* = PISTOL. • *v.tr.* **1** (usu. foll. by *together*) form into a whole; put together; join (*finally pieced his story together*). **2** (usu. foll. by *out*) **a** eke out. **b** form (a theory, etc.) by combining parts, etc. **3** (usu. foll. by *up*) patch. **4** join (threads) in spinning. ▫ **break to pieces** break into fragments. **go to pieces** collapse emotionally; suffer a breakdown. **in one piece 1** unbroken. **2** unharmed. **in pieces** broken. **a piece of the action** *sl.* a share of the profits; a share in the excitement. **a piece of one's mind** a sharp rebuke or lecture. **say one's piece** give one's opinion or make a prepared statement. **take to pieces 1** break up or dismantle. **2** criticize harshly. □□ **piec·er** *n.* (in sense 4 of *v.*).

pi·èce de ré·sis·tance /pyés də rayzéestoNs/ *n.* (*pl.* **pièces de résistance** *pronunc.* same) **1** the most important or remarkable item. **2** the most substantial dish at a meal.

piece·meal /péesmeel/ *adv. & adj.* • *adv.* piece by piece; gradually. • *adj.* partial; gradual; unsystematic.

piece of eight *n. hist.* a Spanish dollar, equivalent to 8 reals.

piece work *n.* work paid for by the amount produced.

pie chart *n.* a circle divided into sections to represent relative quantities.

pied /pīd/ *adj.* particolored.

pied-à-terre /pyáydaatáir/ *n.* (*pl.* **pieds-à-terre** *pronunc.* same) a usu. small apartment, house, etc., kept for occasional use.

pied·mont /péedmont/ *n.* a gentle slope leading from the foot of mountains to a region of flat land.

Pied Pip·er *n.* a person enticing followers, esp. to their doom.

pier /peer/ *n.* **1 a** a structure of iron or wood raised on piles and leading out to sea, a lake, etc., used as a promenade and landing place. **b** a breakwater; a mole. **2 a** a support of an arch or of the span of a bridge; a pillar. **b** solid masonry between windows, etc.

pierce /peers/ *v.* **1** *tr.* **a** (of a sharp instrument, etc.) penetrate the surface of. **b** (often foll. by *with*) prick with a sharp instrument, esp. to make a hole in. **c** make (a hole, etc.) (*pierced a hole in the belt*). **d** (of cold, grief, etc.) affect keenly or sharply. **e** (of a light, glance, sound, etc.) penetrate keenly or sharply. **2** (as **piercing** *adj.*) (of a glance, intuition, high noise, bright light, etc.) keen, sharp, or unpleasantly penetrating. **3** *tr.* force (a way, etc.) through or into (something) (*pierced their way through the jungle*). **4** *intr.* (usu. foll. by *through*, *into*) penetrate. □□ **pierc·er** *n.* **pierc·ing·ly** *adv.*

pie·ro·gi /pərṓgee, pee-/ *n.* (also **pirogi**) (*pl.* **-gi** or **-gies**) small pastry envelopes filled with mashed potatoes, cabbage, or chopped meat.

pi·et·à /pyetaá/ *n.* a picture or sculpture of the Virgin Mary holding the dead body of Christ on her lap or in her arms.

pi·e·tism /píətizəm/ *n.* **1** pious sentiment. **2** an exaggerated or affected piety. □□ **pi·e·tist** *n.* **pi·e·tis·tic** *adj.* **pi·e·tis·ti·cal** *adj.*

pi·e·ty /pí-itee/ *n.* (*pl.* **-ties**) **1** the quality of being pious. **2** a pious act.

pif·fle /pífəl/ *n. & v. colloq.* • *n.* nonsense; empty speech. • *v.intr.* talk or act feebly; trifle. □□ **pif·fler** *n.*

pif·fling /pífling/ *adj. colloq.* trivial; worthless.

pig /pig/ *n. & v.* • *n.* **1 a** any omnivorous hoofed bristly mammal of the family Suidae, esp. a domesticated kind, *Sus scrofa.* **b** a young pig; a piglet. **c** (often in *comb.*) any similar animal (*guinea pig*). **2** the flesh of esp. a young or suckling pig as food (*roast pig*). **3** *colloq.* **a** a greedy, dirty, obstinate, sulky, or annoying person. **b** a person who eats too much or too fast. **c** an unpleasant, awkward, or difficult thing, task, etc. **4** an oblong mass of metal (esp. iron or lead) from a smelting furnace. **5** *sl. derog.* a policeman. **6** *sl. derog.* a sexist or racist person. • *v.* (**pigged, pigging**) *tr.* **1** (also *absol.*) (of a sow) bring forth (piglets). **2** *colloq.* eat (food) greedily. □ **buy a pig in a poke** buy, accept, etc., something without knowing its value or esp. seeing it. **in a pig's eye** *colloq.* certainly not. **make a pig of oneself** overeat. **pig out** (often foll. by *on*) *sl.* eat gluttonously. □□ **pig·gish** *adj.* **pig·gish·ly** *adv.* **pig·gish·ness** *n.* **pig·let** *n.* **pig·like** *adj.* **pig·ling** *n.*

pi·geon /píjin/ *n.* **1** any of several large usu. gray and white birds of the family Columbidae, esp. *Columba livia*, often domesticated and bred and trained to carry messages, etc.; a dove (cf. ROCK PIGEON). **2** a person easily swindled; a simpleton. □□ **pi·geon·ry** *n.* (*pl.* **-ries**).

pi·geon·hole /píjinhōl/ *n. & v.* • *n.* **1** each of a set of compartments in a cabinet or on a wall for papers, letters, etc. **2** a small recess for a pigeon to nest in. • *v.tr.* **1** deposit (a document) in a pigeonhole. **2** put (a matter) aside for future consideration or to forget it. **3** assign (a person or thing) to a preconceived category.

pi·geon-toed *adj.* (of a person) having the toes turned inward.

pig·ger·y /pígəree/ *n.* (*pl.* **-ies**) **1** a pig-breeding farm, etc. **2** = PIGSTY. **3** piggishness.

pig·gy /pígee/ *n. & adj.* • *n.* (also **pig·gie**) *colloq.* **1** a little pig. **2 a** a child's word for a pig. **b** a child's word for a toe. • *adj.* (**piggier, piggiest**) **1** like a pig. **2** (of features, etc.) like those of a pig (*little piggy eyes*).

pig·gy·back /pígeebak/ *n. & adv.* /píkəbak/) • *n.* a ride on the back and shoulders of another person. • *adv.* **1** on the back and shoulders of another person. **2 a** on the back or top of a larger object. **b** in addition to; along with.

pig·gy bank *n.* a pig-shaped box for coins.

pig·head·ed /píghédid/ *adj.* obstinate. □□ **pig·head·ed·ly** *adv.* **pig·head·ed·ness** *n.*

pig i·ron *n.* crude iron from a smelting furnace.

pig Lat·in *n.* a jargon formed from English sounds by transferring the initial consonant or consonant cluster of each word to the end of the word and adding the sound *ay* (e.g., "igpay atinlay" for *pig Latin*).

pig·ment /pígmənt/ *n. & v.* • *n.* **1** coloring matter used as paint or dye, usu. as an insoluble suspension. **2** the natural coloring matter of animal or plant tissue, e.g., chlorophyll, hemoglobin. • *v.tr.* color with or as if with pigment. □□ **pig·men·tal** /-mént'l/ *adj.* **pig·men·tar·y** /-məntéree/ *adj.*

pig·men·ta·tion /pígməntáyshən/ *n.* **1** the natural coloring of plants, animals, etc. **2** the excessive coloring of tissue by the deposition of pigment.

pig·my var. of PYGMY.

pig·pen /pígpen/ *n.* = PIGSTY.

pig·skin /pígskin/ *n.* **1** the hide of a pig. **2** leather made from this. **3** a football.

pig·sty /pígstī/ *n.* (*pl.* **-sties**) **1** a pen or enclosure for a pig or pigs. **2** an untidy house, room, etc.

pig·tail /pígtayl/ *n.* **1** a braid or gathered hank of hair hanging from the back of the head, or either of a pair at the sides. **2** a thin twist of tobacco. □□ **pig·tailed** *adj.*

pike[1] /pīk/ *n.* (*pl.* same) **1** a large voracious freshwater fish, *Esox lucius*, with a long narrow snout and sharp teeth. **2** any other fish of the family Esocidae.

pike[2] /pīk/ *n. hist.* an infantry weapon with a pointed steel or iron head on a long wooden shaft.

pike[3] /pīk/ *n.* a turnpike. □ **come down the pike** *colloq.* appear; occur.

pike[4] /pīk/ *n.* a jackknife position in diving or gymnastics.

pik·er /píkər/ *n.* a cautious, timid, or cheap person.

pi·laf /pilaáf, péelaaf/ *n.* (also **pi·laff; pi·law, pi·lau** /-láw, -lów/) a dish of spiced rice or wheat with meat, fish, vegetables, etc.

pi·las·ter /pilástər/ *n.* a rectangular column, esp. one projecting from a wall. □□ **pi·las·tered** *adj.*

pil·chard /pílchərd/ *n.* a small marine fish, *Sardinia pilchardus*, of the herring family (see SARDINE).

pile[1] /pīl/ *n. & v.* • *n.* **1** a heap of things laid or gathered upon one another (*a pile of leaves*). **2 a** a large imposing building (*a stately pile*). **b** a large group of tall buildings. **3** *colloq.* **a** a large quantity. **b** a large amount of money; a fortune (*made his pile*). **4 a** a series of plates of dissimilar metals laid one on another alternately to produce an electric current. **b** a nuclear reactor. Also called **atomic pile**. **5** a funeral pyre. • *v.* **1** *tr.* **a** (often foll. by *up*, *on*) heap up (*piled the plates on the table*). **b** (foll. by *with*) load (*piled the bed with coats*). **2** *intr.* (usu. foll. by *in*, *into*, *on*, *out of*, etc.) crowd hurriedly or tightly. □ **pile it on** *colloq.* exaggerate. **pile up 1** accumulate; heap up. **2** *colloq.* run (a ship) aground or cause (a vehicle, etc.) to crash.

pile[2] /pīl/ *n.* & *v.* • *n.* **1** a heavy beam driven vertically into the bed of a river, soft ground, etc., to support the foundations of a superstructure. **2** a pointed stake or post. • *v.tr.* **1** provide with piles. **2** drive (piles) into the ground, etc.

pile[3] /pīl/ *n.* the soft projecting surface on velvet, plush, etc., or esp. on a carpet; nap.

pi·le·at·ed wood·peck·er /píleeaytid/ *n.* a black-and-white N. American woodpecker, *Dryocopus pileatus*, with a red crest.

pile driv·er *n.* a machine for driving piles into the ground.

piles /pīlz/ *n.pl. colloq.* hemorrhoids.

pile·up /pīlup/ *n.* **1** a collision of (esp. several) motor vehicles. **2** any mass or pile resulting from accumulation.

pil·fer /pílfər/ *v.tr.* (also *absol.*) steal (objects) esp. in small quantities. □□ **pil·fer·age** /-fərij/ *n.* **pil·fer·er** *n.*

pil·grim /pílgrim/ *n.* **1** a person who journeys to a sacred place for religious reasons. **2** a person regarded as journeying through life, etc. **3** a traveler.

pil·grim·age /pílgrimij/ *n.* & *v.* • *n.* **1** a pilgrim's journey (*go on a pilgrimage*). **2** life viewed as a journey. **3** any journey taken for nostalgic or sentimental reasons. • *v.intr.* go on a pilgrimage.

Pil·i·pi·no /pílipeénō/ *n.* the national language of the Philippines.

pill /pil/ *n.* **1 a** solid medicine formed into a ball or a flat disk for swallowing whole. **b** (usu. prec. by *the*) *colloq.* a contraceptive pill. **2** an unpleasant or painful necessity; a humiliation (*a bitter pill*; *must swallow the pill*). **3** *colloq.* or *joc.* a ball. **4** *sl.* a difficult or unpleasant person. □ **sweeten** (or **sugar**) **the pill** make an unpleasant necessity acceptable.

pil·lage /pílij/ *v.* & *n.* • *v.tr.* (also *absol.*) plunder; sack (a place or a person). • *n.* the act or an instance of pillaging, esp. in war. □□ **pil·lag·er** *n.*

pil·lar /pílər/ *n.* **1 a** a usu. slender vertical structure of wood, metal, or esp. stone used as a support for a roof, etc. **b** a similar structure used for ornament. **c** a post supporting a structure. **2** a person regarded as a mainstay or support (*a pillar of the faith*). **3** an upright mass of air, water, rock, etc. □ **from pillar to post** (driven, etc.) from one place to another; back and forth. □□ **pillared** *adj.* **pil·lar·et** *n.*

pill·box /pílboks/ *n.* **1** a small shallow cylindrical box for holding pills. **2** a hat of a similar shape. **3** *Mil.* a small partly underground enclosed concrete fort used as an outpost.

pil·lo·ry /píləree/ *n.* & *v.* • *n.* (*pl.* **-ries**) *hist.* a wooden framework with holes for the head and hands, enabling the public to assault or ridicule a person so imprisoned. • *v.tr.* (**-ries, -ried**) **1** expose (a person) to ridicule or public contempt. **2** *hist.* put in the pillory.

pil·low /pílō/ *n.* & *v.* • *n.* **1** a usu. oblong support for the head, esp. in bed, with a cloth cover stuffed with feathers, down, foam rubber, etc. **2** any pillow-shaped block or support. • *v.tr.* **1** rest (the head, etc.) on or as if on a pillow (*pillowed his head on his arms*). **2** serve as a pillow for (*moss pillowed her head*). □□ **pil·low·y** *adj.*

pil·low·case /pílōkays/ *n.* a washable cotton, etc., cover for a pillow.

pil·low talk *n.* romantic or intimate conversation in bed.

pi·lot /pílət/ *n.* & *v.* • *n.* **1** a person who operates the flying controls of an aircraft. **2** a person qualified to take charge of a ship entering or leaving a harbor. **3** (usu. *attrib.*) an experimental undertaking or test, esp. in advance of a larger one (*a pilot project*). **4** a guide; a leader. **5** = PILOT LIGHT. • *v.tr.* (**piloted, piloting**) **1** act as a pilot on (a ship) or of (an aircraft). **2** conduct, lead, or initiate as a pilot (*piloted the new scheme*). □□ **pi·lot·age** *n.* **pi·lot·less** *adj.*

pi·lot fish *n.* a small fish, *Naucrates ductor*, said to act as a pilot leading a shark to food.

pi·lot·house /pílət-hows/ *n.* an enclosed area on a vessel for the helmsman, etc.

pi·lot light *n.* **1** a small gas burner kept alight to light another. **2** an electric indicator light or control light.

Pil·sner /pílznər, píls-/ *n.* (also **Pil·sen·er**) **1** a lager beer brewed or like that brewed at Pilsen (Plzeň) in the Czech Republic. **2** (usu. **pil·sner**) a tall tapered glass used for serving beer, etc.

Pi·ma /peémə/ *n.* **1 a** a N. American people native to southern Arizona and adjoining parts of Mexico. **b** a member of this people. **2** the language of this people. □□ **Pi·man** *adj.*

pi·men·to /piméntō/ *n.* (*pl.* **-tos**) **1** a small tropical tree, *Pimenta dioica*, native to Jamaica. **2** the unripe dried berries of this, usu. crushed for culinary use. Also called ALLSPICE. **3** = PIMIENTO.

pi·mien·to /piméntō, pímyéntō/ *n.* (*pl.* **-tos**) **1** = SWEET PEPPER. **2** a sweet red pepper used as a garnish, esp. in olives.

pimp /pimp/ *n.* & *v.* • *n.* a man who lives off the earnings of a prostitute or a brothel; a pander. • *v.intr.* act as a pimp.

pim·per·nel /pímpərnel/ *n.* any plant of the genus *Anagallis*.

pim·ple /pímpəl/ *n.* **1** a small hard inflamed spot on the skin. **2** anything resembling a pimple, esp. in relative size. □□ **pim·pled** *adj.* **pim·ply** *adj.*

PIN /pin/ *n.* personal identification number (as issued by a bank, etc., to validate electronic transactions).

pin /pin/ *n.* & *v.* • *n.* **1 a** a small thin pointed piece of esp. steel wire with a round or flattened head used (esp. in sewing) for holding things in place, attaching one thing to another, etc. **b** any of several types of pin (*safety pin*; *hairpin*). **c** a small brooch (*diamond pin*). **d** a badge fastened with a pin. **2** a peg of wood or metal for various purposes, e.g., one of the slender rods making up part of an electrical connector. **3** something of small value (*don't care a pin*). **4** (in *pl.*) *colloq.* legs (*quick on his pins*). **5** *Med.* a steel rod used to join the ends of fractured bones while they heal. **6** *Chess* a position in which a piece is pinned to another. **7** *Golf* a stick with a flag placed in a hole to mark its position. • *v.tr.* (**pinned, pinning**) **1 a** (often foll. by *to*, *up*, *together*) fasten with a pin or pins. **b** transfix with a pin, lance, etc. **2** (usu. foll. by *on*) fix (blame, responsibility, etc.) on a person, etc. **3** (often foll. by *against*, *on*, etc.) seize and hold fast. **4** *US* show affection for a woman by giving her a fraternity pin. □ **on pins and needles** in an agitated state of suspense. **pin down 1** (often foll. by *to*) bind (a person, etc.) to a promise, arrangement, etc. **2** force (a person) to declare his or her intentions. **3** restrict the actions or movement of (an enemy, etc.). **4** specify (a thing) precisely (*could not pin down his reason for leaving*). **5** hold (a person, etc.) down by force. **pin one's faith** (or **hopes**, etc.) **on** rely implicitly on.

pi·na co·la·da /peénə kəlaádə/ *n.* (also **piña colada** /peényə/) a drink made from pineapple juice, rum, and cream of coconut.

pin·a·fore /pínəfawr/ *n.* **1 a** *Brit.* an apron, esp. with a bib. **b** a woman's sleeveless, wraparound, washable covering for the clothes, tied at the back. **2** (in full **pinafore dress**) a collarless sleeveless dress worn over a blouse or sweater.

pi·ña·ta /peenyaátə/ *n.* a decorated container, often of papier mâché, filled with toys, candy, etc., that is used in a game in which it is suspended at a height and attempts are made to break it open with a stick while blindfolded.

pin·ball /pínbawl/ *n.* a game in which small metal balls are shot across a board and score points by striking pins with lights, etc.

pince-nez /pánsnáy, píns-/ *n.* (*pl.* same) a pair of eyeglasses with a nose-clip instead of earpieces.

pin·cers /pínsərz/ *n.pl.* **1** (also **pair of pincers**) a gripping tool resembling scissors but with blunt usu. concave jaws to hold a nail, etc., for extraction. **2** the front claws of lobsters and some other crustaceans.

pince-nez

pinch /pinch/ *v.* & *n.* •*v.* **1** *tr.* **a** grip (esp. the skin of part of the body or of another person) tightly, esp. between finger and thumb. **b** (often *absol.*) (of a shoe, garment, etc.) constrict (the flesh) painfully. **2** *tr.* (of cold, hunger, etc.) grip (a person) painfully (*her face was pinched with cold*). **3** *tr. sl.* **a** steal; take without permission. **b** arrest (a person). **4** (as **pinched** *adj.*) (of the features) drawn, as with cold, hunger, worry, etc. **5 a** *tr.* (usu. foll. by *in, of, for,* etc.) stint (a person). **b** *intr.* be stingy with money, food, etc. **6** *tr.* (usu. foll. by *out, back, down*) *Hort.* remove (leaves, buds, etc.) to encourage bushy growth. •*n.* **1** the act or an instance of pinching, etc., the flesh. **2** an amount that can be taken up with fingers and thumb (*a pinch of snuff*). **3** the stress or pain caused by poverty, cold, hunger, etc. **4** *sl.* **a** an arrest. **b** a theft. □ **feel the pinch** experience the effects of poverty. **in a pinch** in an emergency; if necessary.

pinch-hit *v.intr.* **1** *Baseball* bat instead of another player. **2** fill in as a substitute, esp. at the last minute. □□ **pinch hit·ter** *n.*

pinch·pen·ny /pínchpenee/ *n.* (*pl.* **-nies**) (also *attrib.*) a miserly person.

pin·cush·ion /pínkŏŏshən/ *n.* a small cushion for holding pins.

pine[1] /pīn/ *n.* **1** any evergreen tree of the genus *Pinus* native to northern temperate regions, with needle-shaped leaves growing in clusters. **2** the soft timber of this. **3** (*attrib.*) made of pine. □□ **pin·er·y** *n.* (*pl.* **-ies**).

pine[2] /pīn/ *v.intr.* **1** (often foll. by *away*) decline or waste away, esp. from grief, disease, etc. **2** (usu. foll. by *for, after,* or *to* + infin.) long eagerly; yearn.

pin·e·al gland *n.* (also **pineal body**) a pea-sized conical mass of tissue behind the third ventricle of the brain, secreting a hormonelike substance in some mammals.

pine·ap·ple /pínapəl/ *n.* **1** a tropical plant, *Ananas comosus*, with a spiral of sword-shaped leaves and a thick stem bearing a large fruit developed from many flowers. **2** the fruit of this, consisting of yellow flesh surrounded by a tough segmented skin and topped with a tuft of stiff leaves.

pine cone *n.* the cone-shaped fruit of the pine tree.

pine mar·ten *n.* a weasellike mammal, *Martes martes*, native to Europe and America, with a dark brown coat and white throat and stomach.

pine nut *n.* the edible seed of various pine trees.

pine·y var. of PINY.

ping /ping/ *n.* a single short high ringing sound.

Ping-Pong /píngpong/ *n. Trademark* = TABLE TENNIS.

pin·head /pínhed/ *n.* **1** the flattened head of a pin. **2** a very small thing. **3** *colloq.* a stupid or foolish person.

pin·head·ed /pínhédid/ *adj. colloq.* stupid; foolish. □□ **pin·head·ed·ness** *n.*

pin·hole /pínhōl/ *n.* **1** a hole made by a pin. **2** a hole into which a peg fits.

pin·hole cam·era *n.* a camera with a pinhole aperture and no lens.

pin·ion[1] /pínyən/ *n.* & *v.* •*n.* **1** the outer part of a bird's wing, usu. including the flight feathers. **2** *poet.* a wing; a flight feather. •*v.tr.* **1** cut off the pinion of (a wing or bird) to prevent flight. **2 a** bind the arms of (a person). **b** (often foll. by *to*) bind (the arms, a person, etc.) esp. to a thing.

pin·ion[2] /pínyən/ *n.* **1** a small toothed gear engaging with a larger one. **2** a toothed spindle engaging with a wheel.

pink[1] /pingk/ *n.* & *adj.* •*n.* **1** a pale red color (*decorated in pink*). **2 a** any cultivated plant of the genus *Dianthus*, with sweet-smelling white, pink, crimson, etc., flowers. **b** the flower of this plant. **3** (prec. by *the*) the most perfect condition, etc. (*the pink of health*). **4** (also **hunting pink**) **a** a foxhunter's red coat. **b** the cloth for this. **c** a foxhunter. •*adj.* **1** (often in *comb.*) of a pale red color of any of various shades (*rose pink*; *salmon pink*). **2** esp. *derog.* tending to socialism. □ **in the pink** *colloq.* in very good health. □□ **pink·ish** *adj.* **pink·ly** *adv.* **pink·ness** *n.* **pink·y** *adj.*

pink[2] /pingk/ *v.tr.* **1** pierce slightly with a sword, etc. **2** cut a scalloped or zigzag edge on.

pink·eye /píngkī/ *n.* acute conjunctivitis.

pink·ie /píngkee/ *n.* (also **pink·y**) esp. *US & Sc.* the little finger.

pink·ing shears /píngking/ *n.pl.* (also **pinking scissors**) a dressmaker's serrated shears for cutting a zigzag edge.

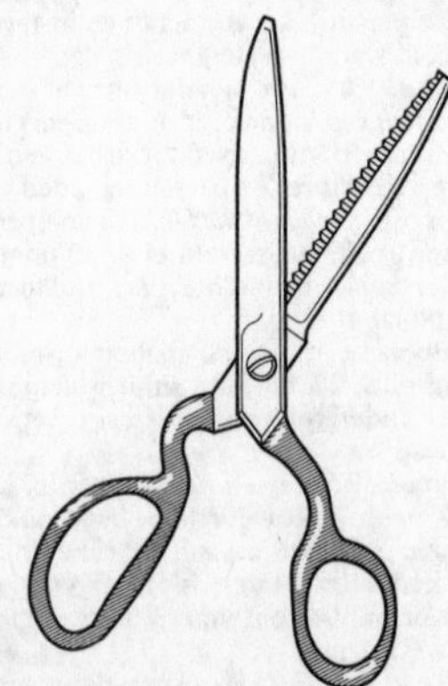
pinking shears

pink slip *n.* a notice of layoff or termination from one's job.

pink·y var. of PINKIE.

pin mon·ey *n.* **1** *hist.* an allowance to a woman for clothing, etc., from her husband. **2** a very small sum of money, esp. for spending on inessentials (*only works for pin money*).

pin·na /pínə/ *n.* (*pl.* **pinnae** /–nee/or **pinnas**) **2** the auricle; the external part of the ear. **2** a pirmary division of a pinnate leaf. **3** a fin or finlike structure, feather, wing, etc.

pin·na·cle /pínəkəl/ *n. & v.* •*n.* **1** the culmination or climax (of endeavor, success, etc.). **2** a natural peak. **3** a small ornamental turret usu. ending in a pyramid or cone, crowning a buttress, roof, etc. •*v.tr.* **1** set on or as if on a pinnacle. **2** form the pinnacle of. **3** provide with pinnacles.

pin·nae *pl.* of PINNA.

pin·nate /pínayt/ *adj.* **1** (of a compound leaf) having leaflets arranged on either side of the stem, usu. in pairs opposite each other. **2** having branches, tentacles, etc., on each side of an axis. □□ **pin·nat·ed** *adj.* **pin·nate·ly** *adv.* **pin·na·tion** /–náyshən/ *n.*

pin·ni·ped /píniped/ *adj. & n.* •*adj.* denoting any aquatic mammal with limbs ending in fins. •*n.* a pinniped mammal.

pin·nule /pínyoo͞l/ *n.* **1** the secondary division of a pinnate leaf. **2** a part or organ like a small wing or fin. □□ **pin·nu·lar** *adj.*

pi·noch·le /péenokəl/ *n.* **1** a card game with a double pack of 48 cards (nine to ace only). **2** the combination of queen of spades and jack of diamonds in this game.

pi·ñon /peenyṓn, pínyən/ *n.* **1** a pine, *Pinus cembra*, bearing edible seeds. **2** the seed of this, a type of pine nut.

pin·point /pínpoynt/ *n. & v.* •*n.* **1** the point of a pin. **2** something very small or sharp. **3** (*attrib.*) **a** very small. **b** precise; accurate. •*v.tr.* locate with precision (*pinpointed the target*).

pin·prick /pínprik/ *n.* **1** a prick caused by a pin. **2** a trifling irritation.

pins and nee·dles *n.pl.* a tingling sensation in a limb recovering from numbness.

pin·stripe /pínstrīp/ *n.* **1** a very narrow stripe in cloth. **2** a fabric or garment with this.

pint /pīnt/ *n.* **1** a measure of capacity for liquids, etc., one eighth of a gallon or 16 fluid oz. (0.47 liter). **2** esp. *Brit.* **a** *colloq.* a pint of beer. **b** a pint of a liquid, esp. milk. **3** *Brit.* a measure of shellfish, being the amount containable in a pint mug (*bought a pint of whelks*).

pin·tail /píntayl/ *n.* a duck, esp. *Anas acuta*, or a grouse with a pointed tail.

pin·to /píntō/ *adj. & n.* •*adj.* piebald. •*n.* (*pl.* **-tos**) a piebald horse.

pin·to bean *n.* a variety of bean with a mottled or spotted appearance, grown mainly in the southwestern US.

pint-sized *adj.* (also **pint-size**) *colloq.* very small, esp. of a person.

pin·up /pínup/ *n.* **1** a photograph of a movie star, etc., for display. **2** a person in such a photograph.

pin·wheel /pínhweel/ *n.* **1** a fireworks device that whirls and emits colored fire. **2** a child's toy consisting of a stick with vanes that twirl in the wind.

pin·worm /pínwərm/ *n.* a small parasitic nematode worm, *Enterobius vermicularis*, of which the female has a pointed tail.

pin·y /pínee/ *adj.* (also **pine·y**) of, like, or full of pines.

Pin·yin /pínyín/ *n.* a system of romanized spelling for transliterating Chinese.

pi·o·neer /píəneér/ *n. & v.* •*n.* **1** an initiator of a new enterprise, an inventor, etc. **2** an explorer or settler; a colonist. **3** *Mil.* a member of an infantry group preparing roads, terrain, etc., for the main body of troops. •*v.* **1 a** *tr.* initiate or originate (an enterprise, etc.). **b** *intr.* act or prepare the way as a pioneer. **2** *tr. Mil.* open up (a road, etc.) as a pioneer. **3** *tr.* go before, lead, or conduct (another person or persons).

pi·ous /píəs/ *adj.* **1** devout; religious. **2** hypocritically virtuous; sanctimonious. **3** dutiful. □□ **pi·ous·ly** *adv.* **pi·ous·ness** *n.*

pip[1] /pip/ *n.* **1** the seed of an apple, pear, orange, grape, etc. **2** an extraordinary person or thing.

pip[2] /pip/ *n.* any of the spots on playing cards, dice, or dominos.

pipe /pīp/ *n. & v.* •*n.* **1** a tube of metal, plastic, wood, etc., used to convey water, gas, etc. **2 a** (also **tobacco pipe**) a narrow wooden or clay, etc., tube with a bowl at one end containing burning tobacco, etc., the smoke from which is drawn into the mouth. **b** the quantity of tobacco held by this (*smoked a pipe*). **3** *Mus.* **a** a wind instrument consisting of a single tube. **b** any of the tubes by which sound is produced in an organ. **c** (in *pl.*) = BAGPIPE(S). **d** (in *pl.*) a set of pipes joined together, e.g., panpipes. **4** a tubal organ, vessel, etc., in an animal's body. **5** a high note or song, esp. of a bird. **6** a cylindrical vein of ore. **7** a cavity in cast metal. **8 a** a boatswain's whistle. **b** the sounding of this. **9** a cask for wine, esp. as a measure of two hogsheads, usu. equivalent to 105 gallons (about 477 liters). **10** *colloq.* (also in *pl.*) the voice, esp. in singing. •*v.tr.* **1** (also *absol.*) play (a tune, etc.) on a pipe or pipes. **2 a** convey (oil, water, gas, etc.) by pipes. **b** provide with pipes. **3** transmit (music, a radio program, etc.) by wire or cable. **4** (usu. foll. by *up, on, to*, etc.) *Naut.* **a** summon (a crew) to a meal, work, etc. **b** signal the arrival of (an officer, etc.) on board. **5** utter in a shrill voice; whistle. **6 a** arrange (icing, etc.) in decorative lines or twists on a cake, etc. **b** ornament (a cake, etc.) with piping. **7** trim (a dress, etc.) with piping. **8** lead or bring (a person, etc.) by the sound of a pipe. **9** propagate (pinks, etc.) by taking cuttings at the joint of a stem. □ **pipe away** give a signal for (a boat) to start. **pipe down 1** *colloq.* be quiet or less insistent. **2** *Naut.* dismiss from duty. **pipe up** begin to play, sing, speak, etc. **put that in your pipe and smoke it** *colloq.* a challenge to another to accept something frank or unwelcome. □□ **pipe·ful** *n.* (*pl.* **-fuls**). **pipe·less** *adj.* **pip·y** *adj.*

pipe bomb *n.* a homemade bomb made by sealing explosives inside a metal pipe.

pipe clean·er *n.* a piece of flexible wire covered with tufts or bristles, used for cleaning a tobacco pipe and in handicrafts.

pipe dream /píp dreem/ *n.* an unattainable or fanciful hope or scheme.

pipe·fish /pípfish/ *n.* (*pl.* usu. same) any of various long slender fish of the family Syngnathidae, with an elongated snout.

pipe·fit·ter /pípfitər/ *n.* a person who installs and repairs pipes.

pipe·fit·ting /pípfiting/ *n.* **1** a coupling, elbow, etc., used as a connector in a pipe system. **2** the work of a pipefitter.

pipe·line /píplīn/ *n.* **1** a long, usu. underground, pipe for conveying esp. oil. **2** a channel supplying goods, information, etc. □ **in the pipeline** awaiting imminent completion or processing.

pipe or·gan *n. Mus.* an organ using pipes instead of or as well as reeds.

pip·er /pípər/ *n.* **1** a bagpipe player. **2** a person who plays a pipe, esp. an itinerant musician.

pipe·stem /pípstem/ *n.* **1** the stem of a tobacco pipe. **2** something very thin or slender, as an arm or leg.

pi·pette /pīpét/ *n. & v.* •*n.* a slender tube for transferring or measuring small quantities of liquids esp. in chemistry. • *v.tr.* transfer or measure (a liquid) using a pipette.

pip·ing /píping/ *n. & adj.* • *n.* **1** the act or an instance of piping, esp. whistling or singing. **2** a thin pipelike fold used to edge hems or frills on clothing, seams on upholstery, etc. **3** ornamental lines of icing, potato, etc., on a cake or other dish. **4** lengths of pipe, or a system of pipes, esp. in domestic use. • *adj.* (of a noise) high; whistling.

pip·ing hot *adj.* very or suitably hot (esp. as required of food, water, etc.).

pip·i·strelle /pípistrél/ *n.* any bat of the genus *Pipistrellus*, native to temperate regions and feeding on insects.

pip·it /pípit/ *n.* any of various birds of the family Motacillidae, esp. of the genus *Anthus*, found worldwide and having brown plumage often heavily streaked with a lighter color.

pip·pin /pípin/ *n.* **1 a** an apple grown from seed. **b** a red and yellow dessert apple. **2** *colloq.* an excellent person or thing; a beauty.

pip·squeak /pípskweek/ *n. colloq.* an insignificant or contemptible person or thing.

pi·quant /péekənt, –kaant, peekáant/ *adj.* **1** agreeably pungent, sharp, or appetizing. **2** pleasantly stimulating, or disquieting, to the mind. ▫▫ **pi·quan·cy** *n.* **pi·quant·ly** *adv.*

pique /peek/ *v. & n.* • *v.tr.* (**piques, piqued, piquing**) **1** wound the pride of; irritate. **2** arouse (curiosity, interest, etc.). **3** (*refl.*; usu. foll. by *on*) pride or congratulate oneself. • *n.* ill-feeling; enmity; resentment (*in a fit of pique*).

pi·qué /peekáy/ *n.* a stiff ribbed cotton or other fabric.

pi·quet[1] /pikáy, –két/ *n.* a game for two players with a pack of 32 cards (seven to ace only).

pi·quet[2] var. of PICKET *n.* 3.

pi·ra·cy /pírəsee/ *n.* (*pl.* **-cies**) **1** the practice or an act of robbery of ships at sea. **2** a similar practice or act in other forms, esp. hijacking. **3** the infringement of copyright.

pi·ra·nha /piraánə, –ránə, –raányə, –rányə/ *n.* any of various freshwater predatory fish of the genera *Pygocentrus*, *Rooseveltiella*, or *Serrasalmus*, native to S. America and having sharp cutting teeth.

pi·rate /pírət/ *n. & v.* • *n.* **1 a** a person who commits piracy. **b** a ship used by pirates. **2** a person who infringes another's copyright or other business rights; a plagiarist. **3** (often *attrib.*) a person, organization, etc., that broadcasts without official authorization. • *v.tr.* **1** appropriate or reproduce (the work or ideas, etc., of another) without permission, for one's own benefit. **2** plunder. ▫▫ **pi·rat·ic** /–rátik/ *adj.* **pi·rat·i·cal** *adj.* **pi·rat·i·cal·ly** *adv.*

pi·ro·gi /pərṓgee/ *n.* var. of PIEROGI.

pir·ou·ette /píroo-ét/ *n. & v.* • *n.* a dancer's spin on one foot or the point of the toe. • *v.intr.* perform a pirouette.

pis·ca·to·ri·al /pískətáwreeəl/ *adj.* = PISCATORY 1. ▫▫ **pis·ca·to·ri·al·ly** *adv.*

pis·ca·to·ry /pískətawree/ *adj.* **1** of or concerning fishermen or fishing. **2** addicted to fishing.

Pis·ces /píseez/ *n.* (*pl.* same) **1** a constellation, traditionally regarded as contained in the figure of fishes. **2 a** the twelfth sign of the zodiac (the Fishes). **b** a person born when the sun is in this sign. ▫▫ **Pis·cean** /píseeən/ *n. & adj.*

pis·cine /píseen, písīn/ *adj.* of or concerning fish.

pish /pish/ *int. & n.* • *int.* an expression of contempt, impatience, or disgust. • *n.* nonsense; rubbish.

piss /pis/ *v. & n. coarse sl.* • *v.* **1** *intr.* urinate. ▶Usually considered a taboo word. **2** *tr.* **a** discharge (blood, etc.) when urinating. **b** wet with urine. **3** *tr.* (as **pissed** *adj.*) **a** esp. *Brit.* drunk. **b** angry; annoyed. • *n.* **1** urine. **2** an act of urinating.

pis·tach·i·o /pistásheeō, –staásheeō/ *n.* (*pl.* **-os**) **1** an evergreen tree, *Pistacia vera*, bearing small brownish green flowers and ovoid reddish fruit. **2** (in full **pistachio nut**) the edible pale green seed of this. **3** a pale green color.

piste /peest/ *n.* a ski run of compacted snow.

pis·til /pístil/ *n.* the female organs of a flower, comprising the stigma, style, and ovary.

pis·tol /pístəl/ *n. & v.* • *n.* **1** a small hand-held firearm. **2** anything of a similar shape. • *v.tr.* (**pistoled, pistoling** or **pistolled, pistolling**) shoot with a pistol.

---

pistol mid-16th century: from obsolete French *pistole*, from German *Pistole*, from Czech *pišt'ala*, of which the original meaning was 'whistle, fife,' hence 'a firearm' because of the resemblance in shape of the barrel to a fife or pipe.

---

pis·tol-whip *v.tr.* (**-whipped, -whipping**) beat with a pistol.

pis·ton /pístən/ *n.* **1** a disk or short cylinder fitting closely within a tube in which it moves up and down against a liquid or gas, used in an internal combustion engine to impart motion, or in a pump to receive motion. **2** a sliding valve in a trumpet, etc.

pis·ton ring *n.* a ring on a piston sealing the gap between the piston and the cylinder wall.

pis·ton rod *n.* a rod or crankshaft attached to a piston to drive a wheel or to impart motion.

pit[1] /pit/ *n. & v.* • *n.* **1 a** a usu. large deep hole in the ground. **b** a hole made in digging for industrial purposes, esp. for coal (*chalk pit*; *gravel pit*). **c** a covered hole as a trap for esp. wild animals. **2 a** an indentation left after smallpox, acne, etc. **b** a hollow in a plant or animal body or on any surface. **3** the part of a theater in which the orchestra is situated. **4 a** (**the pit** or **bottomless pit**) hell. **b** (**the pits**) *sl.* a wretched or the worst imaginable place, situation, person, etc. **5 a** an area at the side of a track where racing cars are serviced and refueled. **b** a sunken area in a workshop floor for access to a car's underside. **6** the part of the floor of an exchange allotted to special trading (*wheat pit*). **7** = COCKPIT. **8** *Brit. sl.* a bed. • *v.tr.* (**pitted, pitting**) **1** (usu. foll. by *against*) **a** set (one's wits, strength, etc.) in opposition or rivalry. **b** set (a cock, dog, etc.) to fight, orig. in a pit, against another. **2** (usu. as **pitted** *adj.*) make pits, esp. scars, in. ▫ **dig a pit for** try to ensnare.

pit[2] /pit/ *n. & v.* • *n.* the stone of a fruit. • *v.tr.* (**pitted, pitting**) remove pits from (fruit).

pi·ta /péetə/ *n.* (also **pit·ta**) a flat, hollow, unleavened bread that can be split and filled with salad, etc.

pit-a-pat /pítəpát/ *adv. & n.* (also **pit·ter-pat·ter** /pítərpátər/) • *adv.* **1** with a sound like quick light steps. **2** with a faltering sound (*heart went pit-a-pat*). • *n.* such a sound.

pit bull ter·ri·er *n.* a strong, compact breed of American dog, usu. the American Staffordshire terrier.

pitch[1] /pich/ *v. & n.* • *v.* **1** *tr.* (also *absol.*) erect and fix (a tent, camp, etc.). **2** *tr.* **a** throw; fling. **b** (in games) throw (an object) toward a mark. **3** *tr.* fix or plant (a thing) in a definite position. **4** *tr.* express in a particular style or at a particular level (*pitched his argument at the most basic level*). **5** *intr.* (often foll. by *against*, *into*, etc.) fall heavily, esp. headlong. **6** *intr.* (of a ship, aircraft, etc.) plunge in a longitudinal direction (cf. ROLL *v.* 8a). **7** *tr. Mus.* set at a particular pitch. **8** *intr.* (of a roof, etc.) slope downwards. **9** *intr.* (often foll. by *about*) move with a vigorous jogging motion, as in a train, carriage, etc. **10** *Baseball* **a** *tr.* deliver (the ball) to the batter. **b** *intr.* play at the position of pitcher. • *n.*

1 *Brit.* the area of play in a field game. **2** height, degree, intensity, etc. (*the pitch of despair*). **3 a** the steepness of a slope, esp. of a roof, stratum, etc. **b** the degree of such a pitch. **4** *Mus.* **a** that quality of a sound which is governed by the rate of vibrations producing it; the degree of highness or lowness of a tone. **b** = CONCERT PITCH 1. **5** the pitching motion of a ship, etc. **6** the delivery of a baseball by a pitcher. **7** *colloq.* a salesman's advertising or selling approach. □ **pitch in** *colloq.* **1** set to work vigorously. **2** assist; cooperate.

pitch[2] /pich/ *n. & v.* •*n.* **1** a sticky resinous black or dark brown substance obtained by distilling tar or turpentine, semiliquid when hot, hard when cold, and used for caulking the seams of ships, etc. **2** any of various bituminous substances including asphalt. •*v.tr.* cover, coat, or smear with pitch.

pitch-black *adj.* (also **pitch-dark**) very or completely dark.

pitch·blende /píchblend/ *n.* a mineral form of uranium oxide occurring in pitchlike masses and yielding radium.

pitched bat·tle *n.* **1** a vigorous argument, etc. **2** *Mil.* a battle planned beforehand and fought on chosen ground.

pitch·er[1] /píchər/ *n.* **1** a large usu. earthenware or glass jug with a lip and a handle, for holding liquids. **2** a modified leaf in pitcher form. □□ **pitch·er·ful** *n.* (*pl.* **-fuls**).

pitch·er[2] /píchər/ *n.* **1** a person or thing that pitches. **2** *Baseball* a player who delivers the ball to the batter.

pitch·er plant *n.* any of various plants, esp. of the family Nepenthaceae or Sarraceniaceae, with pitcher leaves that can hold liquids, trap insects, etc.

pitch·fork /píchfawrk/ *n. & v.* •*n.* a long-handled two-pronged fork for pitching hay, etc. •*v.tr.* **1** throw with or as if with a pitchfork. **2** (usu. foll. by *into*) thrust (a person) forcibly into a position, office, etc.

pitch·man /píchmən/ *n.* **1** a salesperson who uses overly aggressive selling tactics. **2** a person who delivers commercial messages on radio or television.

pitch pine *n.* any of various pine trees, esp. *Pinus rigida* or *P. palustris*, yielding much resin.

pitch pipe *n. Mus.* a small pipe blown to set the pitch for singing or tuning.

pit·e·ous /píteeəs/ *adj.* deserving or causing pity; wretched. □□ **pit·e·ous·ly** *adv.* **pit·e·ous·ness** *n.*

pit·fall /pítfawl/ *n.* **1** an unsuspected snare, danger, or drawback. **2** a covered pit for trapping animals, etc.

pith /pith/ *n.* **1** spongy white tissue lining the rind of an orange, lemon, etc. **2** the essential part; the quintessence (*came to the pith of his argument*). **3** *Bot.* the spongy cellular tissue in the stems and branches of dicotyledonous plants. **4 a** physical strength; vigor. **b** force; energy. □□ **pith·less** *adj.*

pith·y /píthee/ *adj.* (**pithier, pithiest**) **1** (of style, speech, etc.) condensed, terse, and forceful. **2** of, like, or containing much pith. □□ **pith·i·ly** *adv.* **pith·i·ness** *n.*

pit·i·a·ble /píteeəbəl/ *adj.* **1** deserving or causing pity. **2** contemptible. □□ **pit·i·a·ble·ness** *n.* **pit·i·a·bly** *adv.*

pit·i·ful /pítifōōl/ *adj.* **1** causing pity. **2** contemptible. **3** *archaic* compassionate. □□ **pit·i·ful·ly** *adv.* **pit·i·ful·ness** *n.*

pit·i·less /pítilis/ *adj.* showing no pity. □□ **pit·i·less·ly** *adv.* **pit·i·less·ness** *n.*

pit·man /pítmən/ *n.* **1** (*pl.* **-men**) a person who works in a pit, as a miner. **2** (*pl.* **-mans**) a connecting rod in machinery.

pi·ton /péeton/ *n.* a peg or spike driven into a rock or crack to support a climber or a rope.

pit stop *n.* **1** a brief stop at the pit by a racing car for servicing or refueling. **2** *colloq.* **a** a stop, as during a long journey, for food, rest, etc. **b** the place where such a stop is made.

pit·ta var. of PITA.

pit·tance /pít'ns/ *n.* **1** a scanty or meager allowance, remuneration, etc. (*paid him a mere pittance*). **2** a small number or amount.

pit·ter-pat·ter var. of PIT-A-PAT.

pi·tu·i·tar·y /pitōō-iteree, –tyōō–/ *n. & adj.* •*n.* (*pl.* **-ies**) (also **pituitary gland** or **body**) a small ductless gland at the base of the brain secreting various hormones essential for growth and other bodily functions. •*adj.* of or relating to this gland.

pit·y /pítee/ *n. & v.* •*n.* (*pl.* **-ies**) **1** sorrow and compassion aroused by another's condition (*felt pity for the child*). **2** something to be regretted; grounds for regret (*what a pity!*). •*v.tr.* (**-ies, -ied**) feel (often contemptuous) pity for. □ **for pity's sake** an exclamation of urgent supplication, anger, etc. **more's the pity** so much the worse. **take pity on** feel or act compassionately toward. □□ **pit·y·ing** *adj.* **pit·y·ing·ly** *adv.*

Pi·ute /píoot, pīōōt/ *n.* = PAIUTE.

piv·ot /pívət/ *n. & v.* •*n.* **1** a short shaft or pin on which something turns or oscillates. **2** a crucial or essential person, point, etc., in a scheme or enterprise. **3** *Mil.* the man or men about whom a body of troops wheels. •*v.* (**pivoted, pivoting**) **1** *intr.* turn on or as if on a pivot. **2** *intr.* (foll. by *on, upon*) hinge on; depend on. **3** *tr.* provide with or attach by a pivot. □□ **piv·ot·a·ble** *adj.* **piv·ot·a·bil·i·ty** *n.* **piv·ot·al** *adj.*

pix[1] /piks/ *n.pl. colloq.* pictures, esp. photographs.

pix[2] var. of PYX.

pix·el /píksəl/ *n. Electronics* any of the minute areas of uniform illumination of which an image on a display screen is composed.

pix·ie /píksee/ *n.* (also **pix·y**) (*pl.* **-ies**) a being like a fairy; an elf.

pix·i·lat·ed /píksilaytid/ *adj.* (also **pix·il·lat·ed**) **1** bewildered; crazy. **2** drunk.

piz·za /péetsə/ *n.* a flat round base of dough baked with a topping of tomatoes, cheese, onions, etc.

piz·zazz /pizáz/ *n.* (also **pi·zazz**) *sl.* verve; energy; liveliness; sparkle.

piz·ze·ri·a /péetsəréeə/ *n.* a place where pizzas are made or sold.

piz·zi·ca·to /pítsikaátō/ *adv., adj., & n. Mus.* •*adv.* plucking the strings of a violin, etc., with the finger. •*adj.* (of a note, passage, etc.) performed pizzicato. •*n.* (*pl.* **pizzicatos** or **pizzicati** /–tee/) a note, passage, etc., played pizzicato.

pk. *abbr.* **1** park. **2** peak. **3** peck(s). **4** pack.

pkg. *abbr.* (also **pkge.**) package.

PKU *abbr.* phenylketonuria.

pl. *abbr.* **1** plural. **2** place. **3** plate. **4** esp. *Mil.* platoon.

plac·a·ble /plákəbəl, pláy–/ *adj.* easily placated; mild; forgiving. □□ **plac·a·bil·i·ty** *n.* **plac·a·bly** *adv.*

plac·ard /plákaard, –kərd/ *n. & v.* •*n.* a printed or handwritten poster, esp. for advertising. •*v.tr.* **1** set up placards on (a wall, etc.). **2** advertise by placards. **3** display (a poster, etc.) as a placard.

pla·cate /pláykayt, plák–/ *v.tr.* pacify; conciliate. □□ **pla·cat·ing·ly** *adv.* **pla·ca·tion** /–áyshən/ *n.* **pla·ca·to·ry** /–kətawree/ *adj.*

place /plays/ *n. & v.* •*n.* **1 a** a particular portion of space. **b** a portion of space occupied by a person or thing. **c** a proper or natural position (*he is out of his place; take your places*). **d** situation; circumstances (*put yourself in my place*). **2** a city, town, village, etc. (*was born in this place*). **3** a residence; a dwelling (*has a place in the country; come around to my place*). **4 a** a group of houses in a town, etc., esp. a square. **b** a country house with its surroundings. **5** a person's rank or status (*know* *their place; a place in history*). **6** a space, esp. a seat, for a person (*two places in the coach*). **7** a building or area for a specific purpose (*place of worship; fireplace*). **8 a** a point reached in a book, etc. (*lost my place*). **b** a passage in a book. **9** a particular spot on a surface, esp. of the skin (*a sore place on his wrist*). **10 a** employment or office (*lost his place at the university*). **b** the duties or entitlements of office, etc. (*is his place to hire staff*). **11** a position as a member of a team, a student in a college, etc. **12** the second finishing position, esp. in a horse race. **13** the position of a number in a series indicated in decimal or similar notation (*calculated to 5 decimal places*). • *v.tr.* **1** put (a thing, etc.) in a particular place or state; arrange. **2** identify, classify, or remember correctly (*cannot place him*). **3** assign to a particular place; locate. **4 a** appoint (a person, esp. a member of the clergy) to a post. **b** find a job, clerical post, etc., for. **c** (usu. foll. by *with*) consign to a person's care, etc. (*placed her with her aunt*). **5** assign rank, importance, or worth to (*place him among the best teachers*). **6 a** dispose of (goods) to a customer. **b** make (an order for goods, etc.). **7** (often foll. by *in*, *on*, etc.) have (confidence, etc.). **8** invest (money). **9** *tr.* (as **placed** *adj.*) second in a race. □ **all over the place** in disorder; chaotic. **go places** *colloq.* be successful. **in place** in the right position; suitable. **in place of** in exchange for; instead of. **in places** at some places or in some parts, but not others. **keep a person in his** (or **her**) **place** suppress a person's esp. social pretensions. **out of place 1** in the wrong position. **2** unsuitable. **put oneself in another's place** imagine oneself in another's position. **put a person in his** (or **her**) **place** deflate or humiliate a person. **take place** occur. **take one's place** go to one's correct position, be seated, etc. **take the place of** replace. □□ **place·less** *adj.* **place·ment** *n.*

pla·ce·bo /pləséebō/ *n.* (*pl.* **-bos**) **1** a medicine, etc., prescribed more for psychological reasons than for any physiological effect. **2** an inactive substance used as a control in testing new drugs, etc.

place card *n.* a card marking a person's place at a table, etc.

place·kick /pláyskik/ *n. Football* a kick made with the ball held on the ground or on a tee.

place mat *n.* a small mat on a table underneath a person's plate.

place-name *n.* the name of a geographic location, as a city, town, hill, lake, etc.

pla·cen·ta /pləséntə/ *n.* (*pl.* **placentae** /–tee/or **placentas**) a flattened circular organ in the uterus of pregnant mammals nourishing and maintaining the fetus through the umbilical cord and expelled after birth. □□ **pla·cen·tal** *adj.*

plac·er /plásər/ *n.* a deposit of sand, gravel, etc., in the bed of a stream, etc., containing valuable minerals in particles.

place set·ting *n.* a set of plates, silverware, etc., for one person at a meal.

plac·id /plásid/ *adj.* **1** (of a person) not easily aroused or disturbed; peaceful. **2** mild; calm; serene. □□ **pla·cid·i·ty** /pləsíditee/ *n.* **plac·id·ly** *adv.* **plac·id·ness** *n.*

pla·gia·rism /pláyjərizəm/ *n.* **1** the act or an instance of plagiarizing. **2** something plagiarized. □□ **pla·gia·rist** *n.* **pla·gia·ris·tic** *adj.*

pla·gia·rize /pláyjərīz/ *v.tr.* (also *absol.*) **1** take and use (the thoughts, writings, inventions, etc., of another person) as one's own. **2** pass off the thoughts, etc., of (another person) as one's own. □□ **pla·gia·riz·er** *n.*

plague /playg/ *n.* & *v.* • *n.* **1** a deadly contagious disease spreading rapidly over a wide area. **2** (foll. by *of*) an unusual infestation of a pest, etc. (*a plague of frogs*). **3 a** great trouble. **b** an affliction, esp. as regarded as divine punishment. **4** *colloq.* a nuisance. • *v.tr.* (**plagues, plagued, plaguing**) **1** affect with plague. **2** *colloq.* pester or harass continually. □□ **plague·some** *adj.*

plaice /plays/ *n.* (*pl.* same) **1** a European flatfish, *Pleuronectes platessa,* having a brown back with orange spots and a white underside, much used for food. **2** (in full **American plaice**) a N. Atlantic fish, *Hippoglossoides platessoides.*

plaid /plad/ *n.* **1 a** (often *attrib.*) tartan usu. woolen twilled cloth (*a plaid skirt*). **b** any cloth with a tartan pattern. **2** a long piece of plaid worn over the shoulder as part of Highland Scottish costume. □□ **plaid·ed** *adj.*

plain /playn/ *adj., adv.,* & *n.* • *adj.* **1** clear; evident (*is plain to see*). **2** readily understood; simple (*in plain words*). **3 a** (of food, sewing, decoration, etc.) uncomplicated; not elaborate; unembellished; simple. **b** without a decorative pattern. **4** (esp. of a woman or girl) not good-looking; homely. **5** outspoken; straightforward. **6** (of manners, dress, etc.) unsophisticated; homely (*a plain man*). **7** (of drawings, etc.) not colored. **8** not in code. • *adv.* **1** clearly; unequivocally (*to speak plain, I don't approve*). **2** simply (*that is plain stupid*). • *n.* **1** a level tract of esp. treeless country. **2** a basic knitting stitch made by putting the needle through the back of the stitch and passing the wool round the front of the needle (opp. PURL[1]). □□ **plain·ly** *adv.* **plain·ness** /pláyn-nis/ *n.*

plain·clothes·man /playnklṓzmən, klṓthz–, –man/ *n.* a police officer who wears civilian clothes while on duty.

plains·man /pláynzmən/ *n.* (*pl.* **-men**) a person who lives on a plain, esp. in N. America.

plain·song /pláynsawng, –song/ *n.* unaccompanied church music sung in unison in medieval modes and in free rhythm corresponding to the accentuation of the words (cf. GREGORIAN CHANT).

plain-speak·ing *n.* blunt or candid expression of one's opinions etc.

plain-spo·ken *adj.* outspoken; blunt.

plaint /playnt/ *n.* **1** *Brit. Law* an accusation; a charge. **2** *literary* or *archaic* a complaint; a lamentation.

plain·tiff /pláyntif/ *n. Law* a person who brings a case against another into court (opp. DEFENDANT).

plain·tive /pláyntiv/ *adj.* **1** expressing sorrow; mournful. **2** mournful-sounding. □□ **plain·tive·ly** *adv.* **plain·tive·ness** *n.*

plait /playt, plat/ *n.* & *v.* • *n.* **1** = BRAID 2. **2** = PLEAT. • *v.tr.* = BRAID 1.

plan /plan/ *n.* & *v.* • *n.* **1 a** a formulated and esp. detailed method by which a thing is to be done; a design or scheme. **b** an intention or proposed proceeding (*my plan was to distract them; plan of campaign*). **2** a drawing or diagram made by projection on a horizontal plane, esp. showing a building or one floor of a building (cf. ELEVATION). **3** a large-scale detailed map of a town or district. **4 a** a table, etc., indicating times, places, etc., of intended proceedings. **b** a scheme or arrangement (*prepared the seating plan*). **5** an imaginary plane perpendicular to the line of vision and containing the objects shown in a picture. • *v.* (**planned, planning**) **1** *tr.* (often foll. by *that* + clause or *to* + infin.) arrange (a procedure, etc.) beforehand; form a plan (*planned to catch the evening ferry*). **2** *tr.* **a** design (a building, new town, etc.). **b** make a plan of (an existing building, an area, etc.). **3** *tr.* (as **planned** *adj.*) in accordance with a plan (*his planned arrival*). **4** *intr.* make plans. □ **plan on** *colloq.* aim at doing; intend. □□ **plan·ning** *n.*

plan·chette /planshét/ *n.* a small usu. heart-shaped board on casters with a pencil that is supposedly caused to write spirit messages when a person's fingers rest lightly on it.

plane[1] /playn/ *n., adj., & v.* •*n.* **1 a** a flat surface on which a straight line joining any two points on it would wholly lie. **b** an imaginary flat surface through or joining, etc., material objects. **2** a level surface. **3** *colloq.* = AIRPLANE. **4** a flat surface producing lift by the action of air or water over and under it (usu. in *comb.*: *hydroplane*). **5** (often foll. by *of*) a level of attainment, thought, knowledge, etc. **6** a flat thin object such as a tabletop. •*adj.* **1** (of a surface, etc.) perfectly level. **2** (of an angle, figure, etc.) lying in a plane. •*v.intr.* **1** (often foll. by *down*) travel or glide in an airplane. **2** (of a speedboat, etc.) skim over water. **3** soar.

plane[2] /playn/ *n. & v.* •*n.* **1** a tool consisting of a wooden or metal block with a projecting steel blade, used to smooth a wooden surface by paring shavings from it. **2** a similar tool for smoothing metal. •*v.tr.* **1** smooth (wood, metal, etc.) with a plane. **2** (often foll. by *away, down*) pare (irregularities) with a plane.

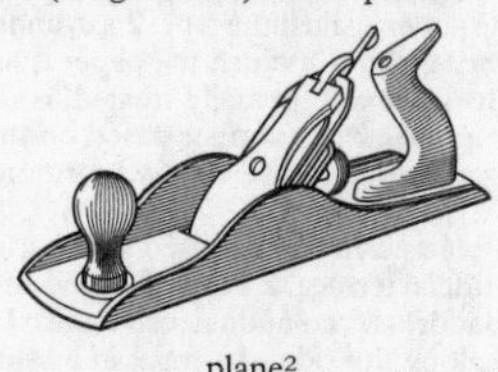

plane[2]

plane[3] /playn/ *n.* (in full **plane tree**) any tree of the genus *Platanus*, often growing to great heights, with maple-like leaves and bark which peels in uneven patches.

plan·et /plánit/ *n.* **1 a** a celestial body moving in an elliptical orbit around a star. **b** the earth. **2** esp. *Astrol. hist.* a celestial body distinguished from the fixed stars by having an apparent motion of its own (including the moon and sun), esp. with reference to its supposed influence on people and events. ▫▫ **plan·e·tol·o·gy** /–tóləjee/ *n.*

plan·e·tar·i·um /plánitáireeəm/ *n.* (*pl.* **planetariums** or **planetaria** /–reeə/) **1** a domed building in which images of stars, planets, constellations, etc., are projected for public entertainment or education. **2** the device used for such projection. **3** = ORRERY.

plan·e·tar·y /plániteree/ *adj.* **1** of or like planets (*planetary influence*). **2** terrestrial; mundane. **3** wandering; erratic.

plan·et·oid /plánitoyd/ *n.* = ASTEROID 1.

plan·gent /plánjənt/ *adj.* **1** (of a sound) loud and reverberating. **2** (of a sound) plaintive; sad. ▫▫ **plan·gen·cy** *n.*

plank /plangk/ *n. & v.* •*n.* **1** a long flat piece of timber used esp. in building, flooring, etc. **2** an item of a political or other program (cf. PLATFORM). •*v.tr.* **1** provide, cover, or floor with planks. **2** cook and serve (fish, steak, etc.) on a plank. **3** (usu. foll. by *down*; also *absol.*) *colloq.* **a** put (a thing, person, etc.) down roughly or violently. **b** pay (money) on the spot or abruptly (*planked down $5*). ▫ **walk the plank** *hist.* (of a pirate's captive, etc.) be made to walk blindfold along a plank over the side of a ship to one's death in the sea.

plank·ing /plángking/ *n.* planks as flooring, etc.

plank·ton /plángktən/ *n.* the chiefly microscopic organisms drifting or floating in the sea or fresh water. ▫▫ **plank·ton·ic** /–tónik/ *adj.*

plan·ner /plánər/ *n.* **1** a person who controls or plans the development of towns, designs buildings, etc. **2** a person who makes plans. **3** a list, table, booklet, etc., with information helpful in planning.

plant /plant/ *n. & v.* •*n.* **1 a** any living organism of the kingdom Plantae, usu. containing chlorophyll enabling it to live wholly on inorganic substances and lacking specialized sense organs and the power of voluntary movement. **b** a small organism of this kind, as distinguished from a shrub or tree. **2 a** machinery, fixtures, etc., used in industrial processes. **b** a factory. **c** buildings, fixtures, equipment, etc., of an institution. **3 a** *colloq.* something, esp. incriminating or compromising, positioned or concealed so as to be discovered later. **b** *sl.* a spy or detective; hidden police officers. •*v.tr.* **1** place (a seed, bulb, or growing thing) in the ground so that it may take root and flourish. **2** (often foll. by *in, on*, etc.) put or fix in position. **3** deposit (young fish, spawn, oysters, etc.) in a river or lake. **4** station (a person, etc.), esp. as a spy or source of information. **5** *refl.* take up a position (*planted myself by the door*). **6** cause (an idea, etc.) to be established esp. in another person's mind. **7** deliver (a blow, kiss, etc.) with a deliberate aim. **8 a** *colloq.* position or conceal (something incriminating or compromising) for later discovery. **b** *sl.* post or infiltrate (a person) as a spy. **9 a** settle or people (a colony, etc.). **b** found or establish (a city, community, etc.). **10** bury. ▫ **plant out** transfer (a plant) from a pot or frame to the open ground; set out (seedlings) at intervals. ▫▫ **plant·a·ble** *adj.* **plant·let** *n.* **plant·like** *adj.*

plan·tain[1] /plántin/ *n.* any shrub of the genus *Plantago*, with broad flat leaves spread out close to the ground and seeds used as food for birds and as a mild laxative.

plan·tain[2] /plántin/ *n.* **1** a banana plant, *Musa paradisiaca*, widely grown for its fruit. **2** the starchy fruit of this containing less sugar than a banana and chiefly used in cooking.

plan·tar /plántər/ *adj.* of or relating to the sole of the foot.

plan·ta·tion /plantáyshən/ *n.* **1** an estate on which cotton, tobacco, etc., is cultivated esp. by resident (formerly slave) labor. **2** an area planted with trees, etc., for cultivation. **3** *hist.* a colony; colonization.

plant·er /plántər/ *n.* **1** a person who cultivates the soil. **2** the manager or occupier of a coffee, cotton, tobacco, etc., plantation. **3** a large container for decorative plants. **4** a machine for planting seeds, etc.

plan·ti·grade /plántigrayd/ *adj. & n.* •*adj.* (of an animal) walking on the soles of its feet. •*n.* a plantigrade animal, e.g., humans or bears.

plaque /plak/ *n.* **1** an ornamental tablet of metal, porcelain, etc., esp. affixed to a building in commemoration. **2** a deposit on teeth where bacteria proliferate. ▫▫ **pla·quette** /plakét/ *n.*

plas·ma /plázmə/ *n.* (also **plasm** /plázəm/) **1** the colorless fluid part of blood, lymph, or milk, in which corpuscles or fat globules are suspended. **2** = PROTOPLASM. **3** a gas of positive ions and free electrons with an approximately equal positive and negative charge. ▫▫ **plas·mic** *adj.*

plas·mo·di·um /plazmṓdeeəm/ *n.* (*pl.* **plasmodia** /–deeə/) **1** any parasitic protozoan of the genus *Plasmodium*, including those causing malaria in humans. **2** a form within the life cycle of various microorganisms, including slime molds, usu. consisting of a mass of naked protoplasm containing many nuclei. ▫▫ **plas·mo·di·al** *adj.*

plas·ter /plástər/ *n. & v.* •*n.* **1** a soft pliable mixture, esp. of lime putty with sand or cement, etc., for spreading on walls, ceilings, etc., to form a smooth hard surface when dried. **2** *hist.* a curative or protective substance spread on a bandage, etc., and applied to the body (*mustard plaster*). •*v.tr.* **1** cover (a wall, etc.) with plaster or a similar substance. **2** (often foll. by *with*) coat thickly or to excess; bedaub (*plastered the bread with jam; the wall was plastered with slogans*). **3** stick or apply (a thing) thickly like plaster (*plastered glue all over it*). **4** (often foll. by *down*) make (esp. hair) smooth with water, gel, etc.; fix flat. **5** (as **plastered** *adj.*) *sl.* drunk. **6** apply a medical plaster or plaster cast to. □□ **plas·ter·er** *n.* **plas·ter·y** *adj.*

plas·ter·board /plástərbawrd/ *n.* a type of board with a center filling of plaster, used to form or line the inner walls of houses, etc.

plas·ter of Par·is *n.* fine white plaster made of gypsum and used for making plaster casts, etc.

plas·tic /plástik/ *n.* & *adj.* • *n.* **1** any of a number of synthetic polymeric substances that can be given any required shape. **2** (*attrib.*) made of plastic (*plastic bag*); made of cheap materials. **3** = PLASTIC MONEY. • *adj.* **1 a** capable of being molded; pliant; supple. **b** susceptible; impressionable. **c** artificial; unsincere. **2** molding or giving form to clay, wax, etc. **3** *Biol.* exhibiting an adaptability to environmental changes. **4** (esp. in philosophy) formative; creative. □□ **plas·ti·cal·ly** *adv.* **plas·tic·i·ty** /–tísitee/ *n.* **plas·ti·cize** /–tisīz/ *v.tr.* **plas·ti·ci·za·tion** /–tisīzáyshən/ *n.* **plas·ti·ciz·er** *n.* **plas·tick·y** *adj.*

plas·tic mon·ey *n. colloq.* a credit card, charge card, or other plastic card that can be used in place of money.

plas·tic sur·ge·ry *n.* the process of reconstructing parts of the body, esp. by the transfer of tissue, either in the treatment of injury or for cosmetic reasons. □□ **plas·tic sur·geon** *n.*

plas·tid /plástid/ *n.* any small organelle in the cytoplasm of a plant cell, containing pigment or food.

plat du jour /plaá də zhŏŏr/ *n.* a dish specially featured on a day's menu.

plate /playt/ *n.* & *v.* • *n.* **1 a** a shallow vessel, usu. circular and of earthenware or china, from which food is eaten or served. **b** the contents of this (*ate a plate of sandwiches*). **2** a similar vessel usu. of metal or wood, used esp. for making a collection in a church, etc. **3** a main course of a meal, served on one plate. **4** food and service for one person (*a fundraiser with a $30 per plate dinner*). **5 a** (*collect.*) utensils of silver, gold, or other metal. **b** (*collect.*) objects of plated metal. **c** = PLATING. **6 a** a piece of metal with a name or inscription for affixing to a door, container, etc. **b** = LICENSE PLATE. **7** an illustration on special paper in a book. **8** a thin sheet of metal, glass, etc., coated with a sensitive film for photography. **9** a flat thin usu. rigid sheet of metal, etc., with an even surface and uniform thickness, often as part of a mechanism. **10 a** a smooth piece of metal, etc., for engraving. **b** an impression made from this. **11 a** a thin piece of plastic material, molded to the shape of the mouth and gums, to which artificial teeth or another orthodontic appliance are attached. **b** *colloq.* a complete denture or orthodontic appliance. **12** *Geol.* each of several rigid sheets of rock thought to form the earth's outer crust. **13** *Biol.* a thin flat organic structure or formation. **14** a light shoe for a racehorse. **15** a stereotype, electrotype, or plastic cast of a page of composed movable types, or a metal or plastic copy of filmset matter, from which sheets are printed. **16** *Baseball* a flat five-sided piece of whitened rubber at which the batter stands and by stepping on which a runner scores. **17** the anode of a vacuum tube. **18** a horizontal timber laid along the top of a wall to support the ends of joists or rafters. • *v.tr.* **1** apply a thin coat esp. of silver, gold, or tin to (another metal). **2** cover (esp. a ship) with plates of metal, esp. for protection. **3** make a plate of (type, etc.) for printing. □ **on one's plate** for one to deal with or consider. □□ **plate·ful** *n.* (*pl.* **-fuls**). **plate·less** *adj.* **plat·er** *n.*

---

plate Middle English (denoting a flat, thin sheet (usually of metal)): from Old French, from medieval Latin *plata* 'plate armor,' based on Greek *platus* 'flat.' Sense 1 represents Old French *plat* 'platter, large dish,' also 'dish of meat,' a noun use of Old French *plat* 'flat.'

---

plate ar·mor *n.* armor of metal plates, for a man, ship, etc.

pla·teau /plató/ *n.* & *v.* • *n.* (*pl.* **plateaux** /–tóz/ or **plateaus**) **1** an area of fairly level high ground. **2** a state of little variation after an increase. • *v.intr.* (**plateaus, plateaued**) (often foll. by *out*) reach a level or stable state after an increase.

plate glass *n.* thick fine-quality glass for storefront windows, etc., orig. cast in plates.

plate·let /pláytlit/ *n.* a small colorless disk of protoplasm found in blood and involved in clotting.

plat·en /plát'n/ *n.* **1** a plate in a printing press which presses the paper against the type. **2** a cylindrical roller in a typewriter against which the paper is held.

plate tec·ton·ics *n.pl.* (usually treated as *sing.*) *Geol.* the study of the earth's surface based on the concept of moving plates (see sense 13 of *n.*) forming its structure.

plat·form /plátfawrm/ *n.* **1** a raised level surface; a natural or artificial terrace. **2** a raised surface from which a speaker addresses an audience. **3** a raised elongated structure along the side of a track in a railroad, subway station, etc. **4** the floor area at the entrance to a bus. **5** a thick sole of a shoe. **6** the declared policy of a political party.

plat·ing /pláyting/ *n.* **1** a coating of gold, silver, etc. **2** an act of plating.

plat·i·num /plát'nəm/ *n. Chem.* a ductile malleable silvery-white metallic element occurring naturally in nickel and copper ores, unaffected by simple acids and fusible only at a very high temperature, used in making jewelry and laboratory apparatus. ¶ Symb.: **Pt**.

plat·i·num black *n.* platinum in powder form like lampblack.

plat·i·num blonde *adj.* & *n.* • *adj.* (also **platinum blond**) silvery-blond. • *n.* a person with esp. bleached or dyed silvery-blond hair.

plat·i·tude /plátitōōd, –tyōōd/ *n.* **1** a trite or commonplace remark, esp. one solemnly delivered. **2** the use of platitudes; dullness; insipidity. □□ **plat·i·tu·di·nize** /–tōōd'nīz, –tyōō–/ *v.intr.* **plat·i·tu·di·nous** /–tōōdənəs/ *adj.*

Pla·ton·ic /plətónik/ *adj.* **1** of or associated with the Greek philosopher Plato (d. 347 BC) or his ideas. **2** (**platonic**) (of love or friendship) purely spiritual; not sexual. **3** (**platonic**) confined to words or theory; not leading to action; harmless. □□ **Pla·ton·i·cal·ly** *adv.*

Pla·to·nism /pláyt'nizəm/ *n.* the philosophy of Plato or his followers. □□ **Pla·to·nist** *n.*

pla·toon /plətóōn/ *n.* **1** *Mil.* a subdivision of a company, a tactical unit commanded by a lieutenant and usu. divided into three sections. **2** a group of persons acting together.

plat·ter /plátər/ *n.* **1** a large flat dish or plate, esp. for food. **2** *colloq.* a phonograph record. □ **on a platter** = *on a plate* (see PLATE).

plat·y·pus /plátipəs/ *n.* an Australian aquatic egg-laying mammal, *Ornithorhynchus anatinus*, having a pliable ducklike bill, webbed feet, and sleek gray fur. Also called DUCKBILL.

plau·dit /pláwdit/ *n.* (usu. in *pl.*) **1** a round of applause. **2** an emphatic expression of approval.

plau·si·ble /pláwzibəl/ *adj.* **1** (of an argument, statement, etc.) seeming reasonable or probable. **2** (of a person) persuasive but deceptive. □□ **plau·si·bil·i·ty** /–bílitee/ *n.* **plau·si·bly** *adv.*

play /play/ *v.* & *n.* •*v.* **1** *intr.* (often foll. by *with*) occupy or amuse oneself pleasantly with some recreation, game, exercise, etc. **2** *intr.* (foll. by *with*) act lightheartedly or flippantly (with feelings, etc.). **3** *tr.* **a** perform on or be able to perform on (a musical instrument). **b** perform (a piece of music, etc.). **c** cause (a record, record player, etc.) to produce sounds. **4 a** *intr.* (foll. by *in*) perform a role in (a drama, etc.). **b** *tr.* perform (a drama or role) on stage, or in a movie or broadcast. **c** *tr.* give a dramatic performance at (a particular theater or place). **5** *tr.* act in real life the part of (*play truant; play the fool*). **6** *tr.* (foll. by *on*) perform (a trick or joke, etc.) on (a person). **7** *tr.* (foll. by *for*) regard (a person) as (something specified) (*played me for a fool*). **8** *intr. colloq.* participate; cooperate; do what is wanted (*they won't play*). **9** *intr.* gamble. **10** *tr.* gamble on. **11** *tr.* **a** take part in (a game or recreation). **b** compete with (another player or team) in a game. **c** occupy (a specified position) in a team for a game. **d** (foll. by *in, on, at*, etc.) assign (a player) to a position. **12** *tr.* move (a piece) or display (a playing card) in one's turn in a game. **13** *tr.* (also *absol.*) strike or catch (a ball, etc.) or execute (a stroke) in a game. **14** *intr.* move about in a lively or unrestrained manner. **15** *intr.* (often foll. by *on*) touch gently. **16** *intr.* (often foll. by *at*) **a** engage in a half-hearted way (in an activity). **b** pretend to be. **17** *intr.* (of a court, field, etc.) be conducive to play as specified (*the greens are playing fast*). **18** *intr. colloq.* act or behave (as specified) (*play fair*). **19** *tr.* (foll. by *in, out*, etc.) accompany (a person) with music (*were played out with bagpipes*). •*n.* **1** recreation, amusement, esp. as the spontaneous activity of children and young animals. **2 a** the playing of a game. **b** the action or manner of this. **c** the status of the ball, etc., in a game as being available to be played according to the rules (*in play; out of play*). **3** a dramatic piece for the stage, etc. **4** activity or operation (*are in full play; brought into play*). **5 a** freedom of movement. **b** space or scope for this. **6** brisk, light, or fitful movement. **7** gambling. **8** an action or maneuver, esp. in or as in a game. □ **at play** engaged in recreation. **in play** for amusement; not seriously. **make a play for** *colloq.* make a conspicuous attempt to acquire or attract. **play along** pretend to cooperate. **play around 1** behave irresponsibly. **2** philander. **play back** play (sounds recently recorded), esp. to monitor recording quality, etc. **play by ear 1** perform (music) previously heard without having or having seen a score. **2** (also **play it by ear**) proceed instinctively or step by step according to results and circumstances. **play one's cards right)** make good use of opportunities; act shrewdly. **play down** minimize the importance of. **played out** exhausted of energy or usefulness. **play fast and loose** act unreliably; ignore one's obligations. **play for time** seek to gain time by delaying. **play into a person's hands** act so as unwittingly to give a person an advantage. **play it cool** *colloq.* **1** affect indifference. **2** be relaxed or unemotional. **play the market** speculate in stocks, etc. **play off** (usu. foll. by *against*) **1** oppose (one person against another), esp. for one's own advantage. **2** play an extra match to decide a draw or tie. **play on 1** continue to play. **2** take advantage of (a person's feelings, etc.). **play on words** a pun. **play safe** avoid risks. **play up** make the most of; emphasize. **play up to** flatter, esp. to win favor. **play with fire** take foolish risks. □□ **play·a·ble** *adj.* **play·a·bil·i·ty** /pláyabílitee/ *n.*

play·act /pláyakt/ *v.* **1** *intr.* act in a play. **2** *intr.* behave affectedly or insincerely. **3** *tr.* act (a scene, part, etc.). □□ **play·act·ing** *n.* **play·ac·tor** *n.*

play·back /pláybak/ *n.* an act or instance of replaying recorded audio or video from a tape, etc.

play·bill /pláybil/ *n.* **1** a poster announcing a theatrical performance. **2** a theater program.

play·boy /pláyboy/ *n.* an irresponsible pleasure-seeking man, esp. a wealthy one.

play-by-play *adj.* & *n.* •*adj.* pertaining to a description, esp. of a sports event, with continuous commentary. •*n.* such a description (*he called the play-by-play for the big game*).

play·er /pláyər/ *n.* **1 a** a person taking part in a sport or game. **b** a gambler. **2** a person playing a musical instrument. **3** a person who plays a part on the stage; an actor. **4** = RECORD PLAYER.

play·er pi·an·o *n.* a piano fitted with an apparatus enabling it to be played automatically.

play·ful /pláyfool/ *adj.* **1** fond of or inclined to play. **2** done in fun; humorous; jocular. □□ **play·ful·ly** *adv.* **play·ful·ness** *n.*

play·go·er /pláygōər/ *n.* a person who goes often to the theater.

play·ground /pláygrownd/ *n.* an outdoor area set aside for children to play.

play·house /pláyhows/ *n.* **1** a theater. **2** a toy house for children to play in.

play·ing card /pláying/ *n.* each of a set of usu. 52 rectangular pieces of card or other material with an identical pattern on one side and different values represented by numbers and symbols on the other, used to play various games.

play·mate /pláymayt/ *n.* a child's companion in play.

play-off *n. Sports* **1** a game played to break a tie. **2** a series of games or matches, usu. between the leading teams of different leagues or divisions, played to determine a championship.

play·pen /pláypen/ *n.* a portable enclosure for young children to play in.

play·thing /pláything/ *n.* **1** a toy or other thing to play with. **2** a person treated as a toy.

play·wright /pláyrīt/ *n.* a person who writes plays.

pla·za /plaázə/ *n.* **1** a marketplace or open square (esp. in a town). **2** a public area beside an expressway with facilities such as restaurants or service stations.

plea /plee/ *n.* **1** an earnest appeal or entreaty. **2** *Law* a formal statement by or on behalf of a defendant. **3** an argument or excuse.

plea bar·gain *n.* (also **plea bargaining**) an arrangement between prosecutor and defendant whereby the defendant pleads guilty to a lesser charge in the expectation of leniency. □□ **plea-bar·gain** *v.intr.*

plead /pleed/ *v.* (*past* and *past part.* **pleaded** or **pled** /pled/) **1** *intr.* (foll. by *with*) make an earnest appeal to. **2** *intr. Law* address a court of law as an advocate on behalf of a party. **3** *tr.* maintain (a cause) esp. in a court of law. **4** *tr. Law* declare to be one's state as regards guilt in or responsibility for a crime (*plead guilty; plead insanity*). **5** *tr.* offer or allege as an excuse (*pleaded forgetfulness*). **6** *intr.* make an appeal or entreaty. □ **plead** (or **take**) **the Fifth** refuse to incriminate oneself legally, in accordance with the Fifth Amendment to the Constitution. □□ **plead·a·ble** *adj.* **plead·er** *n.* **plead·ing·ly** *adv.*

plead·ing /pleéding/ *n.* (usu. in *pl.*) a formal statement of the cause of an action or defense.

pleas·ant /plézənt/ *adj.* (**pleasanter, pleasantest**) pleasing to the mind, feelings, or senses. □□ **pleas·ant·ly** *adv.* **pleas·ant·ness** *n.*

pleas·ant·ry /plézəntree/ *n.* (*pl.* **-ries**) **1** a pleasant or amusing remark, esp. made in casual conversation. **2** a humorous manner of speech. **3** jocularity.

please /pleez/ *v.* **1** *tr.* (also *absol.*) be agreeable to; make glad; give pleasure to. **2** *tr.* (in *passive*) **a** (foll. by *to* + infin.) be glad or willing to. **b** (often foll. by *about, at,* *with*) derive pleasure or satisfaction (from). **3** *tr.* (with *it* as subject; usu. foll. by *to* + infin.) be the inclination or wish of. **4** *intr.* think fit; have the will or desire (*take as many as you please*). **5** *tr.* used in polite requests (*come in, please*). □ **if you please** if you are willing, esp. *iron.* to indicate unreasonableness (*then, if you please, we had to pay*). **please oneself** do as one likes. □□ **pleased** *adj.* **pleas·ing** *adj.* **pleas·ing·ly** *adv.*

pleas·ur·a·ble /plézhərəbəl/ *adj.* causing pleasure; agreeable. □□ **pleas·ur·a·ble·ness** *n.* **pleas·ur·a·bly** *adv.*

pleas·ure /plézhər/ *n.* & *v.* • *n.* **1** a feeling of satisfaction or joy. **2** enjoyment. **3** a source of pleasure or gratification. **4** *formal* a person's will or desire (*what is your pleasure?*). **5** sensual gratification or enjoyment. **6** (*attrib.*) done or used for pleasure (*pleasure ground*). • *v.* **1** *tr.* give (esp. sexual) pleasure to. **2** *intr.* (often foll. by *in*) take pleasure. □ **take pleasure in** like doing. **with pleasure** gladly.

pleat /pleet/ *n.* & *v.* • *n.* a fold or crease, esp. a flattened fold in cloth doubled upon itself. • *v.tr.* make a pleat or pleats in.

pleb /pleb/ *n. colloq.* usu. *derog.* an ordinary insignificant person. □□ **pleb·by** *adj.*

plebe /pleeb/ *n.* a first-year student at a military academy.

ple·be·ian /plibeéən/ *n.* & *adj.* • *n.* a commoner, esp. in ancient Rome. (cf. PATRICIAN). • *adj.* **1** of low birth; of the common people. **2** uncultured. **3** coarse; ignoble. □□ **ple·be·ian·ism** *n.*

pleb·i·scite /plébisīt, –sit/ *n.* **1** the direct vote of all the electors of a nation, etc., on an important public question, e.g., a change in the constitution. **2** the public expression of a community's opinion, with or without binding force. **3** *Rom.Hist.* a law enacted by the plebeians' assembly. □□ **ple·bi·sci·ta·ry** /pləbísiteree, plebisít–/ *adj.*

---

plebiscite mid-16th century (referring to Roman history): from French *plébiscite*, from Latin *plebiscitum*, from *plebs, pleb-* 'the common people' + *scitum* 'decree' (from *sciscere* 'vote for'). The sense 'direct vote of the whole electorate' dates from the mid-19th century.

---

plec·trum /pléktrəm/ *n.* (*pl.* **plectrums** or **plectra** /–trə/) a thin flat piece of plastic or horn, etc., held in the hand and used to pluck a string, esp. of a guitar.

pled *past* of PLEAD.

pledge /plej/ *n.* & *v.* • *n.* **1** a solemn promise or undertaking. **2** a thing given as security for the fulfillment of a contract, the payment of a debt, etc., and liable to forfeiture in the event of failure. **3** a thing put in pawn. **4** a thing given as a token of love, favor, or something to come. **5** the drinking of a person's health; a toast. **6** a solemn undertaking to abstain from alcohol (*sign the pledge*). **7** a person who has promised to join a fraternity or sorority. • *v.tr.* **1 a** deposit as security. **b** pawn. **2** promise solemnly by the pledge of (one's honor, word, etc.). **3** (often *refl.*) bind by a solemn promise. **4** drink to the health of. □ **pledge one's troth** see TROTH. □□ **pledg·er** *n.* **pledg·or** *n.*

Ple·ia·des /pleéədeez, pláy–/ *n.pl.* a cluster of six visible stars in the constellation Taurus, usu. known as the Seven Sisters after seven sisters in Greek mythology.

Pleis·to·cene /plístəseen/ *adj.* & *n. Geol.* • *adj.* of or relating to the first epoch of the Quaternary period marked by great fluctuations in temperature with glacial periods followed by interglacial periods. • *n.* this epoch or system. Also called **Ice Age**.

ple·na·ry /pleénəree, plén–/ *adj.* **1** entire; unqualified; absolute (*plenary indulgence*). **2** (of an assembly) to be attended by all members.

plen·i·po·ten·ti·ar·y /plénipəténsharee, –shee-eree/ *n.* & *adj.* • *n.* (*pl.* **-ies**) a person (esp. a diplomat) invested with the full power of independent action. • *adj.* **1** having this power. **2** (of power) absolute.

plen·i·tude /plénitōōd, –tyōōd/ *n.* **1** fullness; completeness. **2** abundance.

plen·te·ous /plénteeəs/ *adj.* plentiful. □□ **plen·te·ous·ly** *adv.* **plen·te·ous·ness** *n.*

plen·ti·ful /pléntifōōl/ *adj.* abundant; copious. □□ **plen·ti·ful·ly** *adv.* **plen·ti·ful·ness** *n.*

plen·ty /pléntee/ *n., adj.,* & *adv.* • *n.* **1** (often foll. by *of*) a great or sufficient quantity or number (*we have plenty; plenty of time*). **2** abundance (*in great plenty*). • *adj. colloq.* existing in an ample quantity. • *adv. colloq.* fully; entirely (*it is plenty large enough*).

ple·num /pleénəm, plénəm/ *n.* **1** a full assembly of people or a committee, etc. **2** *Physics* space filled with matter.

ple·o·nasm /pleéənazəm/ *n.* the use of more words than are needed to give the sense (e.g., *see with one's eyes*). □□ **ple·o·nas·tic** /–nástik/ *adj.* **ple·o·nas·ti·cal·ly** *adv.*

pleth·o·ra /pléthərə/ *n.* **1** an oversupply, glut, or excess. **2** *Med.* **a** an abnormal excess of red corpuscles in the blood. **b** an excess of any body fluid. □□ **ple·thor·ic** /pləthάwrik, –thór–/ *adj.* **ple·thor·i·cal·ly** *adv.*

pleu·ra /plŏŏrə/ *n.* (*pl.* **pleurae** /–ree/) each of a pair of serous membranes lining the thorax and enveloping the lungs in mammals. □□ **pleu·ral** *adj.*

pleu·ri·sy /plŏŏrisee/ *n.* inflammation of the pleura, marked by pain in the chest or side, fever, etc. □□ **pleu·rit·ic** /–ritik/ *adj.*

pleuro- /plŏŏrō/ *comb. form* **1** denoting the pleura. **2** denoting the side.

Plex·i·glas /pléksiglas/ *n. Trademark* tough, clear thermoplastic used instead of glass.

plex·us /pléksəs/ *n.* (*pl.* same or **plexuses**) **1** *Anat.* a network of nerves or vessels in an animal body (*gastric plexus*). **2** any network or weblike formation. □□ **plex·i·form** *adj.*

pli·a·ble /plíəbəl/ *adj.* **1** bending easily; supple. **2** yielding; compliant. □□ **pli·a·bil·i·ty** *n.* **pli·a·ble·ness** *n.* **pli·a·bly** *adv.*

pli·ant /plíənt/ *adj.* = PLIABLE 1. □□ **pli·an·cy** *n.* **pli·ant·ly** *adv.*

plié /plee-áy/ *n. Ballet* a bending of the knees with the feet on the ground.

pli·ers /plíərz/ *n.pl.* pincers with parallel flat usu. serrated surfaces for holding small objects, bending wire, etc.

plight[1] /plīt/ *n.* a condition or state, esp. an unfortunate one.

plight[2] /plīt/ *v.tr. archaic* **1** pledge or promise solemnly (one's faith, loyalty, etc.). **2** (foll. by *to*) engage, esp. in marriage. □ **plight one's troth** see TROTH.

plim·soll /plímsəl, –sōl/ *n.* (also **plim·sole**) *Brit.* a kind of sneaker with a canvas upper.

plinth /plinth/ *n.* **1** the lower square slab at the base of a column. **2** a base supporting a vase or statue, etc.

Pli·o·cene /plíəseen/ *adj.* & *n. Geol.* • *adj.* of or relating to the last epoch of the Tertiary period with evidence of the extinction of many mammals, and the development of hominids. • *n.* this epoch or system.

PLO *abbr.* Palestine Liberation Organization.

plod /plod/ *v.* & *n.* • *v.* (**plodded, plodding**) **1** *intr.* (often foll. by *along, on*, etc.) walk doggedly or laboriously; trudge. **2** *intr.* (often foll. by *at*) work slowly and steadily. **3** *tr.* tread or make (one's way) laboriously. • *n.* the act or a spell of plodding. □□ **plod·der** *n.* **plod·ding·ly** *adv.*

plop /plop/ *n., v.,* & *adv.* • *n.* **1** a sound as of a smooth object dropping into water without a splash. **2** an act of falling with this sound. • *v.* (**plopped, plopping**) *intr.* & *tr.* fall or drop with a plop. *adv.* with a plop.

plo·sive /plṓsiv/ *adj.* & *n. Phonet.* • *adj.* pronounced with a sudden release of breath. • *n.* a plosive sound.

plot /plot/ *n.* & *v.* • *n.* **1** a defined and usu. small piece of ground. **2** the interrelationship of the main events in a play, novel, movie, etc. **3** a conspiracy or secret plan, esp. to achieve an unlawful end. **4** a graph or diagram. **5** a graph showing the relation between two variables. • *v.* (**plotted, plotting**) *tr.* **1** make a plan or map of (an existing object, a place or thing to be laid out, constructed, etc.). **2** (also *absol.*) plan or contrive secretly (a crime, conspiracy, etc.). **3** mark (a point or course, etc.) on a chart or diagram. **4 a** mark out or allocate (points) on a graph. **b** make (a curve, etc.) by marking out a number of points. ▫▫ **plot·less** *adj.* **plot·less·ness** *n.* **plot·ter** *n.*

plough esp. *Brit.* var. of PLOW. ▫ **the Plough** *Brit.* = BIG DIPPER.

plov·er /plúvər, plṓ–/ *n.* any plump-breasted shorebird of the family Charadriidae, including the lapwing, sandpiper, etc.

plow /plow/ *n.* & *v.* (also *Brit.* **plough**) • *n.* **1** an implement with a cutting blade fixed in a frame drawn by a tractor or by horses, for cutting furrows in the soil and turning it up. **2** an implement resembling this and having a comparable function (*snowplow*). **3** plowed land. • *v.* **1** *tr.* (also *absol.*) turn up (the earth) with a plow, esp. before sowing. **2** *tr.* (foll. by *out, up, down,* etc.) turn or extract (roots, weeds, etc.) with a plow. **3 a** *tr.* furrow, or scratch (a surface) as if with a plow. **b** move through or break the surface of (water). **4** *tr.* produce (a furrow, line, or wake) in this way. **5** *intr.* (foll. by *through*) advance laboriously, esp. through work, a book, etc. **6** *intr.* (foll. by *through, into*) move like a plow steadily or violently. ▫▫ **plow·a·ble** *adj.* **plow·er** *n.*

plow·share /plówshair/ *n.* the cutting blade of a plow.

ploy /ploy/ *n. colloq.* a stratagem; a cunning maneuver to gain an advantage.

pluck /pluk/ *v.* & *n.* • *v.* **1** *tr.* (often foll. by *out, off,* etc.) remove by picking or pulling out or away. **2** *tr.* strip (a bird) of feathers. **3** *tr.* pull at; twitch. **4** *intr.* (foll. by *at*) tug or snatch at. **5** *tr.* sound (the string of a musical instrument) with the finger or plectrum, etc. **6** *tr.* plunder. **7** *tr.* swindle. • *n.* **1** courage; spirit. **2** an act of plucking; a twitch. ▫ **pluck up** summon up (one's courage, spirits, etc.). ▫▫ **pluck·er** *n.* **pluck·less** *adj.*

pluck·y /plúkee/ *adj.* (**pluckier, pluckiest**) brave; spirited. ▫▫ **pluck·i·ly** *adv.* **pluck·i·ness** *n.*

plug /plug/ *n.* & *v.* • *n.* **1** a piece of solid material fitting tightly into a hole, used to fill a gap or cavity or act as a wedge or stopper. **2 a** a device of metal pins in an insulated casing fitting into holes in a socket for making an electrical connection, esp. between an appliance and a power supply. **b** *colloq.* an electric socket. **3** = SPARK PLUG. **4** *colloq.* a piece of (often free) publicity for an idea, product, etc. **5** a mass of solidified lava filling the neck of a volcano. **6** a cake or stick of tobacco; a piece of this for chewing. **7** = FIREPLUG. • *v.* (**plugged, plugging**) **1** *tr.* (often foll. by *up*) stop up (a hole, etc.) with a plug. **2** *tr. sl.* shoot or hit (a person, etc.). **3** *tr. colloq.* seek to popularize (an idea, product, etc.) by constant recommendation. **4** *intr. colloq.* (often foll. by *at*) work steadily away (at). ▫ **plug away (at)** work steadily (at). **plug in** connect electrically by inserting a plug in a socket. **plug into** connect with, as by means of a plug. ▫▫ **plug·ger** *n.*

plum /plum/ *n.* **1 a** an oval fleshy fruit, usu. purple or yellow when ripe, with sweet pulp and a flattish pointed stone. **b** any deciduous tree of the genus *Prunus,* bearing this. **2** a reddish-purple color. **3** a dried grape or raisin used in cooking. **4** *colloq.* the best of a collection; something especially prized (often *attrib.*: *a plum job*).

plum·age /plṓōmij/ *n.* a bird's feathers. ▫▫ **plum·aged** *adj.* (usu. in *comb.*).

plumb[1] /plum/ *n., adv., adj.,* & *v.* • *n.* a ball of lead or other heavy material, esp. one attached to the end of a line for finding the depth of water or determining the vertical on an upright surface. • *adv.* **1** exactly (*plumb in the center*). **2** vertically. **3** *sl.* quite; utterly (*plumb crazy*). • *adj.* **1** vertical. **2** downright; sheer (*plumb nonsense*). • *v.tr.* **1 a** measure the depth of (water) with a plumb. **b** determine (a depth). **2** test (an upright surface) to determine the vertical. **3** reach or experience in extremes (*plumb the depths of fear*). **4** learn in detail the facts about (a matter). ▫ **out of plumb** not vertical.

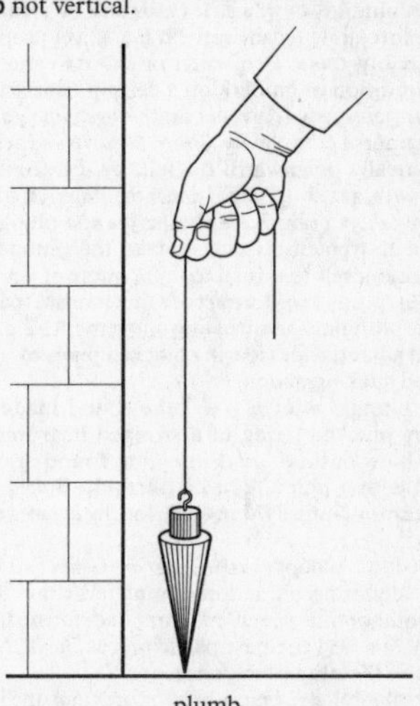
plumb

plumb[2] /plum/ *v.* **1** *tr.* provide (a building or room, etc.) with plumbing. **2** *tr.* (often foll. by *in*) fit as part of a plumbing system. **3** *intr.* work as a plumber.

plumb·er /plúmər/ *n.* a person who fits and repairs the apparatus of a water supply system.

plumb·ing /plúming/ *n.* **1** the system or apparatus of water supply, heating, etc., in a building. **2** the work of a plumber. **3** *colloq.* any system of tubes, vessels, etc., that carry fluids.

plume /plōōm/ *n.* & *v.* • *n.* **1** a feather, esp. a large one used for ornament. **2** an ornament of feathers, etc., attached to a helmet or hat or worn in the hair. **3** something resembling this (*a plume of smoke*). **4** *Zool.* a feather-like part or formation. • *v.* **1** *tr.* decorate or provide with a plume or plumes. **2** *refl.* (foll. by *on, upon*) pride (oneself on esp. something trivial). ▫▫ **plume·less** *adj.* **plume·like** *adj.* **plum·er·y** *n.*

plum·met /plúmit/ *n.* & *v.* • *n.* **1** a plumb or plumb line. **2** a sounding line. **3** a weight attached to a fishing line to keep the float upright. • *v.intr.* (**plummeted, plummeting**) fall or plunge rapidly.

plu·mose /plṓōmōs/ *adj.* **1** feathered. **2** feather-like.

plump[1] /plump/ *adj.* & *v.* • *adj.* (esp. of a person or animal or part of the body) having a full rounded shape; fleshy; filled out. • *v.tr.* & *intr.* (often foll. by *up, out*) make or become plump; fatten. □□ **plump·ish** *adj.* **plump·ly** *adv.* **plump·ness** *n.* **plump·y** *adj.*

plump[2] /plump/ *v., n., adv., & adj.* •*v.* **1** *intr. & tr.* (often foll. by *down*) drop or fall abruptly (*plumped down on the chair*). **2** *intr.* (foll. by *for*) decide definitely in favor of (one of two or more possibilities). **3** *tr.* (often foll. by *out*) utter abruptly; blurt out. •*n.* an abrupt plunge; a heavy fall. •*adv. colloq.* **1** with a sudden or heavy fall. **2** directly; bluntly (*I told him plump*). •*adj. colloq.* direct; unqualified (*answered with a plump 'no'*).

plun·der /plúndər/ *v. & n.* •*v.tr.* **1** rob (a place or person) forcibly of goods, e.g., as in war. **2** rob systematically. **3** (also *absol.*) steal or embezzle (goods). •*n.* **1** the violent or dishonest acquisition of property. **2** property acquired by plundering. **3** *colloq.* profit; gain. □□ **plun·der·er** *n.*

plunge /plunj/ *v. & n.* •*v.* **1** (usu. foll. by *in, into*) **a** *tr.* thrust forcefully or abruptly. **b** *intr.* dive; propel oneself forcibly. **c** *intr. & tr.* enter or cause to enter a certain condition or embark on a certain course abruptly or impetuously (*the room was plunged into darkness*). **2** *tr.* immerse completely. **3** *intr.* **a** move suddenly and dramatically downward. **b** (foll. by *down, into,* etc.) move with a rush (*plunged down the stairs*). **c** diminish rapidly (*share prices have plunged*). •*n.* a plunging action or movement; a dive. □ **take the plunge** *colloq.* commit oneself to a (usu. risky) course of action.

plung·er /plúnjər/ *n.* **1** a part of a mechanism that works with a plunging or thrusting movement. **2** a rubber cup on a handle for clearing blocked pipes by a plunging and sucking action.

plunk /plungk/ *n. & v.* •*n.* **1** the sound made by the sharply plucked string of a stringed instrument. **2** a heavy blow or thud. •*v.* **1** *intr. & tr.* sound or cause to sound with a plunk. **2** *tr.* hit abruptly. **3** *tr.* set down hurriedly or clumsily. **4** *tr.* (usu. foll. by *down*) set down firmly.

plu·per·fect /plōōpə́rfikt/ *adj. & n. Gram.* •*adj.* (of a tense) denoting an action completed prior to some past point of time specified or implied, formed in English by *had* and the past participle, as: *he had gone by then.* •*n.* the pluperfect tense.

plu·ral /plŏŏrəl/ *adj. & n.* •*adj.* **1** more than one in number. **2** *Gram.* (of a word or form) denoting more than one, or (in languages with dual number) more than two. •*n. Gram.* **1** a plural word or form. **2** the plural number. □□ **plu·ral·ly** *adv.*

▶**1.** The apostrophe is often, but not always, used to form the plural of letters (*r's*) and numbers (*7's*), as well as single words referred to themselves (*four the's in one sentence*). **2.** The regular plurals of abbreviations and acronyms may be spelled by simply adding an *-s: CDs, MiGs.* They may also, especially if periods are involved, employ an apostrophe: *D.D.S.'s.* **3.** The plurals of all proper names should end in *-s* or *-es,* with no apostrophe: *the Smiths, the Joneses, the Rosses.* Exceptions include a few names that would have an *-es* but that would not be pronounced that way: *all the Kings Louis of France.*

plu·ral·ism /plŏŏrəlizəm/ *n.* **1** holding more than one office, esp. an ecclesiastical office or benefice, at a time. **2** a form of society in which the members of minority groups maintain their independent cultural traditions. □□ **plu·ral·ist** *n.* **plu·ral·is·tic** *adj.* **plu·ral·is·ti·cal·ly** *adv.*

plu·ral·i·ty /plōōrálitee/ *n.* (*pl.* **-ties**) **1** the state of being plural. **2** = PLURALISM 1. **3** a large or the greater number. **4** a majority that is not absolute.

▶See note at MAJORITY.

plu·ral·ize /plŏŏrəlīz/ *v.* **1** *tr. & intr.* make or become plural. **2** *tr.* express in the plural. **3** *intr.* hold more than one ecclesiastical office or benefice.

plus /plus/ *prep., adj., n., & conj.* •*prep.* **1** *Math.* with the addition of (*3 plus 4 equals 7*). ¶ Symbol: +. **2** (of temperature) above zero (*plus 2° C*). **3** *colloq.* with; having gained; newly possessing (*returned plus a new car*). •*adj.* **1** (after a number) at least (*fifteen plus*). **2** (after a grade, etc.) somewhat better than (*C plus*). **3** *Math.* positive. **4** having a positive electrical charge. **5** (*attrib.*) additional; extra (*plus business*). •*n.* **1** = PLUS SIGN. **2** *Math.* an additional or positive quantity. **3** an advantage (*experience is a definite plus*). •*conj. colloq. disp.* also; and furthermore (*they arrived late, plus they were hungry*).

▶The use of **plus** as a conjunction meaning 'and furthermore,' e.g., *plus we will be pleased to give you personal financial advice,* is considered incorrect by many people.

plus fours *n.* long baggy men's knickers formerly worn for golf, etc.

plush /plush/ *n. & adj.* •*n.* cloth of silk, cotton, etc., with a long soft nap. •*adj.* **1** made of plush. **2** richly luxurious and expensive. □□ **plush·ly** *adv.* **plush·ness** *n.* **plush·y** *adj.*

plus sign *n.* the symbol +, indicating addition or a positive value.

plu·tarch·y /plŏŏtaarkee/ *n.* (*pl.* **-ies**) plutocracy.

Plu·to /plŏŏtō/ *n.* the outermost known planet of the solar system.

plu·toc·ra·cy /plōōtókrəsee/ *n.* (*pl.* **-cies**) **1 a** government by the wealthy. **b** a nation governed in this way. **2** a wealthy élite or ruling class. □□ **plu·to·crat·ic** /plŏŏtəkrátik/ *adj.* **plu·to·crat·i·cal·ly** *adv.*

plu·to·crat /plŏŏtəkrat/ *n.* **1** a member of a plutocracy or wealthy élite. **2** a wealthy and influential person.

plu·to·ni·um /plōōtóneeəm/ *n. Chem.* a dense silvery radioactive metallic transuranic element of the actinide series, used in some nuclear reactors and weapons. ¶ Symb.: **Pu.**

plu·vi·al /plŏŏveeəl/ *adj. & n.* •*adj.* **1** of rain; rainy. **2** *Geol.* caused by rain. •*n.* a period of prolonged rainfall. □□ **plu·vi·ous** *adj.* (in sense 1).

ply[1] /plī/ *n.* (*pl.* **plies**) **1** a thickness or layer of certain materials, esp. wood or cloth (*three-ply*). **2** a strand of yarn or rope, etc.

ply[2] /plī/ *v.* (**plies, plied**) **1** *tr.* use or wield vigorously (a tool, weapon, etc.). **2** *tr.* work steadily at (one's business or trade). **3** *tr.* (foll. by *with*) **a** supply (a person) continuously (with food, drink, etc.). **b** approach repeatedly (with questions, demands, etc.). **4 a** *intr.* (often foll. by *between*) (of a vehicle, etc.) travel regularly (back and forth between two points). **b** *tr.* work (a route) in this way. **5** *intr.* (of a taxi driver, boatman, etc.) attend regularly for custom (*ply for trade*).

ply·wood /plíwŏŏd/ *n.* a strong thin board consisting of two or more layers glued and pressed together with the direction of the grain alternating.

PM *abbr.* **1** Postmaster. **2** postmortem. **3** Prime Minister.

Pm *symb. Chem.* the element promethium.

p.m. *abbr.* between noon and midnight.

PMS *abbr.* premenstrual syndrome.

pneu·mat·ic /nōōmátik, nyōō–/ *adj.* **1** of or relating to air or wind. **2** containing or operated by compressed air. **3** connected with or containing air cavities esp. in the bones of birds or in fish. □□ **pneu·mat·i·cal·ly** *adv.* **pneu·ma·tic·i·ty** /nōōmətisitee, nyōō–/ *n.*

pneu·mat·ic drill *n.* a drill driven by compressed air, for breaking up a hard surface.

pneu·mat·ics /nōōmátiks, nyōō–/ *n.pl.* (treated as *sing.*) the science of the mechanical properties of gases.

pneumo- /nōōmō, nyōō–/ *comb. form* denoting the lungs.

pneu·mo·nia /nōōmṓnyə, nyōō–/ *n.* a bacterial inflammation of one lung (**single pneumonia**) or both lungs (**double pneumonia**) causing the air sacs to fill with pus and become solid. ◻◻ **pneu·mon·ic** /–mónik/ *adj.*

PO *abbr.* **1** Post Office. **2** postal order. **3** Petty Officer.

Po *symb. Chem.* the element polonium.

poach[1] /pōch/ *v.tr.* **1** cook (an egg) without its shell in or over boiling water. **2** cook (fish, etc.) by simmering in a small amount of liquid. ◻◻ **poach·er** *n.*

poach[2] /pōch/ *v.* **1** *tr.* (also *absol.*) catch (game or fish) illegally. **2** *intr.* (often foll. by *on*) trespass or encroach (on another's property, ideas, etc.). **3** *tr.* appropriate illicitly or unfairly (a person, thing, idea, etc.). ◻◻ **poach·er** *n.*

pock /pok/ *n.* (also **pock·mark**) **1** a small pus-filled spot on the skin, esp. caused by chickenpox or smallpox. **2** a mark resembling this. ◻◻ **pock·y** *adj.*

pock·et /pókit/ *n.* & *v.* • *n.* **1** a small bag sewn into or on clothing, for carrying small articles. **2** a pouchlike compartment in a suitcase, car door, etc. **3** one's financial resources (*it is beyond my pocket*). **4** an isolated group or area (*a few pockets of resistance remain*). **5 a** a cavity in the earth containing ore, esp. gold. **b** a cavity in rock, esp. filled with foreign matter. **6** a pouch at the corner or on the side of a billiard table into which balls are driven. **7** = AIR POCKET. **8** (*attrib.*) **a** of a suitable size and shape for carrying in a pocket. **b** smaller than the usual size. **9** the area of a baseball mitt or glove around the center of the palm. • *v.tr.* (**pocketed, pocketing**) **1** put into one's pocket. **2** appropriate, esp. dishonestly. **3** confine as in a pocket. **4** submit to (an injury or affront). **5** conceal or suppress (one's feelings). **6** *Billiards*, etc. drive (a ball) into a pocket. ◻ **in a person's pocket 1** under a person's control. **2** close to or intimate with a person. **out of pocket** (of an expense) paid for with one's own money, rather than from a particular fund or account. ◻◻ **pock·et·a·ble** *adj.* **pock·et·less** *adj.* **pock·et·y** *adj.* (in sense 5 of *n.*).

pock·et·book /pókitbŏŏk/ *n.* **1** a notebook. **2** a booklike case for papers or money carried in a pocket. **3** a purse or handbag. **4** a paperback or other small book. **5** economic resources.

pock·et·ful /pókitfŏŏl/ *n.* (*pl.* **-fuls**) as much as a pocket will hold.

pock·et knife *n.* a knife with a folding blade or blades, for carrying in the pocket.

pock·et ve·to *n.* executive veto of a legislative bill by allowing it to go unsigned.

pock·marked *adj.* bearing marks resembling or left by such spots.

pod /pod/ *n.* & *v.* • *n.* **1** a long seed vessel esp. of a leguminous plant, e.g., a pea. **2** the cocoon of a silkworm. **3** the case surrounding grasshopper eggs. **4** a narrow-necked eel net. **5** a compartment suspended under an aircraft for equipment, etc. • *v.* (**podded, podding**) **1** *intr.* bear or form pods. **2** *tr.* remove (peas, etc.) from pods.

po·di·a·try /pədíətree/ *n. Med.* care and treatment of the foot. ◻◻ **po·di·a·trist** *n.*

po·di·um /pṓdeeəm/ *n.* (*pl.* **podiums** or **podia** /–deeə/) **1** a continuous projecting base or pedestal around a room or house, etc. **2** a raised platform around the arena of an amphitheater. **3** a platform or rostrum.

po·em /pṓəm/ *n.* **1** a metrical composition, usu. concerned with feeling or imaginative description. **2** an elevated composition in verse or prose. **3** something with poetic qualities (*a poem in stone*).

po·e·sy /pṓəzee, –see/ *n. archaic* **1** poetry. **2** the art or composition of poetry.

po·et /pṓit/ *n.* (*fem.* **poetess** /pṓətis/) **1** a writer of poems. **2** a person possessing high powers of imagination or expression, etc.

po·et·ic /pō-étik/ *adj.* (also **po·et·i·cal** /–tikəl/) **1 a** of or like poetry or poets. **b** written in verse. **2** elevated or sublime in expression. ◻◻ **po·et·i·cal·ly** *adv.*

po·et·ic jus·tice *n.* well-deserved unforeseen retribution or reward.

po·et·ic li·cense *n.* a writer's or artist's transgression of established rules for effect.

po·et·ics /pō-étiks/ *n.* **1** the art of writing poetry. **2** the study of poetry and its techniques.

po·et lau·re·ate *n.* a poet appointed to write poems for official state occasions.

po·et·ry /pṓətree/ *n.* **1** the art or work of a poet. **2** poems collectively. **3** a poetic or tenderly pleasing quality. **4** anything compared to poetry.

po·go stick /pṓgō/ *n.* a toy consisting of a spring-loaded stick with rests for the feet, for jumping around on.

po·grom /pṓgrəm, pəgrúm, –gróm/ *n.* an organized massacre (orig. of Jews in Russia).

poign·ant /póynyənt/ *adj.* **1** painfully sharp to the emotions or senses; deeply moving. **2** arousing sympathy. **3** sharp or pungent in taste or smell. **4** pleasantly piquant. ◻◻ **poign·ance** *n.* **poign·an·cy** *n.* **poign·ant·ly** *adv.*

poi·ki·lo·therm /poykíləthərm, póykilə;n–/ *n.* an organism that regulates its body temperature by behavioral means, such as basking or burrowing; a cold-blooded organism (cf. HOMEOTHERM). ◻◻ **poi·kil·o·ther·mal** *adj.* **poi·kil·o·ther·mi·a** /–thə́rmeeə/ *n.* **poi·kil·o·ther·mic** *adj.* **poi·kil·o·ther·my** *n.*

poin·set·ti·a /poynséteeə, –sétə/ *n.* a shrub, *Euphorbia pulcherrima*, with large showy scarlet or cream-colored bracts surrounding small yellow flowers.

point /poynt/ *n.* & *v.* • *n.* **1** the sharp or tapered end of a tool, weapon, pencil, etc. **2** a tip or extreme end. **3** that which in geometry has position but not magnitude, e.g., the intersection of two lines. **4** a particular place or position (*Bombay and points east*; *point of contact*). **5 a** a precise or particular moment (*at the point of death*). **b** the critical or decisive moment (*when it came to the point, he refused*). **6** a very small mark on a surface. **7** a dot or other punctuation mark, esp. = PERIOD 8a. **8** = DECIMAL POINT. **9** a stage or degree in progress or increase (*abrupt to the point of rudeness*; *at that point we gave up*). **10** a level of temperature at which a change of state occurs (*freezing point*). **11** a single item; a detail or particular (*we differ on these points*; *it is a point of principle*). **12 a** a unit of scoring in games or of measuring value, etc. **b** an advantage or success in less quantifiable contexts such as an argument or discussion. **c** a unit of weight (2 mg) for diamonds. **d** a unit (of varying value) in quoting the price of stocks, etc. **e** a percentage point. **13 a** (usu. prec. by *the*) the significant or essential thing; what is actually intended or under discussion (*that was the point of the question*). **b** (usu. with *neg.* or *interrog.*; often foll. by *in*) sense or purpose; advantage or value (*saw no point in staying*). **c** (usu. prec. by *the*) a salient feature of a story, joke, remark, etc. (*don't see the point*). **14** a distinctive feature or characteristic (*it has its points*; *tact is not his good point*). **15 a** each of 32 directions marked at equal distances round a compass. **b** the corresponding direction toward the horizon. **16** (usu. in *pl.*) each of a set of electrical contacts in the distributor of a motor vehicle. **17** the tip of the toe in ballet. **18** a promontory. **19** the prong of a deer's antler. **20** *Printing* a unit of measurement for type bodies (in the US and UK 0.351 mm, in Europe 0.376 mm). **21** *Mil.* a small leading party of an advanced guard, or the lead soldier's position in a patrol unit. • *v.* **1** (usu. foll. by *to*, *at*) **a** *tr.* direct or aim (a finger, weapon, etc.). **b** *intr.* direct attention in a certain direction (*pointed to the house across the road*). **2** *intr.* (foll. by *at*, *toward*) **a** aim or be directed to. **b** tend toward. **3** *intr.* (foll. by *to*) indicate; be evidence of (*it all points to murder*). **4** *tr.* give point or force to (words or actions). **5** *tr.* fill in or repair the joints of (brickwork) with smoothly finished mortar or cement. **6** *tr.* **a** punctuate. **b** insert points in (written Hebrew, etc.). **7** *tr.* (also *absol.*) (of a dog) indicate the presence of (game) by acting as pointer. □ **at all points** in every part or respect. **at the point of** (often foll. by verbal noun) on the verge of; about to do (the action specified). **beside the point** irrelevant or irrelevantly. **have a point** be correct or effective in one's contention. **in point** apposite; relevant. **in point of fact** see FACT. **make** (or **prove**) **a** (or **one's**) **point** establish a proposition; prove one's contention. **make a point of** (often foll. by verbal noun) insist on; treat or regard as essential. **on** (or **upon**) **the point of** (foll. by verbal noun) about to do (the action specified). **point out** (often foll. by *that* + clause) indicate; show; draw attention to. **score points off** get the better of in an argument, etc. **to the point** relevant or relevantly. **up to a point** to some extent but not completely. **win on points** *Boxing* win by scoring more points, not by a knockout.

point Middle English: the noun partly from Old French *point*, from Latin *punctum* 'something that is pricked,' giving rise to the senses 'unit, mark, point in space or time'; partly from Old French *pointe*, from Latin *puncta* 'pricking,' giving rise to the senses 'sharp tip, promontory.' The verb derives partly from Old French *pointer* 'sharpen,' but some senses derive from the English noun.

point-blank *adj. & adv.* • *adj.* **1 a** (of a shot) aimed or fired horizontally at a range very close to the target. **b** (of a distance or range) very close. **2** (of a remark, question, etc.) blunt; direct. • *adv.* **1** at very close range. **2** directly, bluntly.

point·ed /póyntid/ *adj.* **1** sharpened or tapering to a point. **2** (of a remark, etc.) having point; penetrating; cutting. **3** emphasized; made evident. □□ **point·ed·ly** *adv.* **point·ed·ness** *n.*

point·er /póyntər/ *n.* **1** a thing that points, e.g., the index hand of a gauge, etc. **2** a rod for pointing to features on a map, chart, etc. **3** *colloq.* a hint, clue, or indication. **4 a** a dog of a breed that on scenting game stands rigid looking toward it. **b** this breed.

poin·til·lism /pwántilizəm, póyn–/ *n. Art* a technique of impressionist painting using tiny dots of various pure colors, which become blended in the viewer's eye. □□ **poin·til·list** *n. & adj.* **poin·til·lis·tic** /–lístik/ *adj.*

point·ing /póynting/ *n.* **1** cement or mortar filling the joints of brickwork. **2** facing produced by this. **3** the process of producing this.

point·less /póyntlis/ *adj.* **1** without a point. **2** lacking force, purpose, or meaning. **3** (in games) without a point scored. □□ **point·less·ly** *adv.* **point·less·ness** *n.*

point of no re·turn *n.* a point in a journey or enterprise at which it becomes essential or more practical to continue to the end.

point of or·der *n.* a query in a debate, etc., as to whether correct procedure is being followed.

point of view *n.* **1** a position from which a thing is viewed. **2** a particular way of considering a matter.

point·y /póyntee/ *adj.* (**pointier, pointiest**) having a noticeably sharp end; pointed.

poise /poyz/ *n. & v.* • *n.* **1** composure or self-possession of manner. **2** equilibrium; a stable state. **3** carriage (of the head, etc.). • *v.* **1** *tr.* balance; hold suspended or supported. **2** *tr.* carry (one's head, etc., in a specified way). **3** *intr.* be balanced; hover in the air, etc.

poise late Middle English (in the sense 'weight'): from Old French *pois* (noun), *peser* (verb), from an alteration of Latin *pensum* 'weight,' from the verb *pendere* 'weigh.' From the early senses of 'weight' and 'measure of weight' arose the notion of 'equal weight, balance,' leading to the extended senses 'composure' and 'elegant deportment.'

poised /poyzd/ *adj.* **1** composed; self-assured. **2** (often foll. by *for*, or *to* + infin.) ready for action.

poi·son /póyzən/ *n. & v.* • *n.* **1** a substance that when introduced into or absorbed by a living organism causes death or injury, esp. one that kills by rapid action even in a small quantity. **2** *colloq.* a harmful influence or principle, etc. • *v.tr.* **1** administer poison to (a person or animal). **2** kill or injure or infect with poison. **3** infect (air, water, etc.) with poison. **4** (esp. as **poisoned** *adj.*) treat (a weapon) with poison. **5** corrupt or pervert (a person or mind). **6** spoil or destroy (a person's pleasure, etc.). **7** render (land, etc.) foul and unfit for its purpose by a noxious application, etc. □□ **poi·son·er** *n.* **poi·son·ous** *adj.* **poi·son·ous·ly** *adv.*

poi·son i·vy *n.* a N. American climbing plant, *Rhus toxicodendron*, secreting an irritant oil from its leaves.

poke[1] /pōk/ *v. & n.* • *v.* **1** (foll. by *in*, *up*, *down*, etc.) **a** *tr.* thrust or push with the hand, point of a stick, etc. **b** *intr.* be thrust forward. **2** *intr.* (foll. by *at*, etc.) make thrusts with a stick, etc. **3** *tr.* thrust the end of a finger, etc., against. **4** *tr.* (foll. by *in*) produce (a hole, etc., in a thing) by poking. **5** *tr.* thrust forward, esp. obtrusively. **6** *tr.* stir (a fire) with a poker. **7** *intr.* **a** (often foll. by *about*, *along*, *around*) move or act desultorily; putter. **b** (foll. by *about*, *into*) pry; search casually. • *n.* **1** the act or an instance of poking. **2** a thrust or nudge. **3** a punch; a jab. □ **poke fun at** ridicule; tease. **poke** (or **stick**) **one's nose into** *colloq.* pry or intrude into (esp. a person's affairs).

poke[2] /pōk/ *n. dial.* a bag or sack. □ **buy a pig in a poke** see PIG.

pok·er[1] /pṓkər/ *n.* a stiff metal rod with a handle for stirring an open fire.

pok·er[2] /pṓkər/ *n.* a card game in which bluff is used as players bet on the value of their hands.

pok·er face *n.* **1** the impassive countenance appropriate to a poker player. **2** a person with this. □□ **pok·er-faced** *adj.*

poke·weed /pṓkweed/ *n.* a tall hardy American plant, *Phytolacca americana*, with spikes of cream flowers and purple berries that yield emetics and purgatives.

pok·ey /pṓkee/ *n. sl.* prison.

pok·y /pṓkee/ *adj.* (**pokier, pokiest**) **1** (of a room, etc.) small and cramped. **2** slow. □□ **pok·i·ly** *adv.* **pok·i·ness** *n.*

po·lar /pṓlər/ *adj.* **1 a** of or near a pole of the earth or a celestial body, or of the celestial sphere. **b** (of a species or variety) living in the north polar region. **2** having magnetic polarity. **3 a** (of a molecule) having a positive charge at one end and a negative charge at the other. **b** (of a compound) having electric charges. **4** *Geom.* of or relating to a pole. **5** directly opposite in character or tendency. **6** *colloq.* (esp. of weather) very cold. □□ **po·lar·ly** *adv.*

po·lar bear *n.* a white bear, *Ursus maritimus*, of the Arctic regions.

po·lar·im·e·ter /pṓlərímitər/ *n.* an instrument used to measure the polarization of light or the effect of a substance on the rotation of the plane of polarized light. □□ **po·lar·i·met·ric** /–métrik/ *adj.* **po·lar·im·e·try** *n.*

po·lar·i·ty /pəláritee/ *n.* (*pl.* **-ties**) **1** the tendency of a lodestone, magnetized bar, etc., to point with its extremities to the magnetic poles of the earth. **2** the condition of having two poles with contrary qualities. **3** the state of having two opposite tendencies, opinions, etc.

4 the electrical condition of a body (positive or negative). 5 a magnetic attraction toward an object or person.

po·lar·ize /pṓlərīz/ *v.* **1** *tr.* restrict the vibrations of (a transverse wave, esp. light) to one direction. **2** *tr.* give magnetic or electric polarity to (a substance or body). **3** *tr.* reduce the voltage of (an electric cell) by the action of electrolysis products. **4** *tr. & intr.* divide into two groups of opposing opinion, etc. ▫▫ **po·lar·iz·a·ble** *adj.* **po·lar·i·za·tion** *n.* **po·lar·iz·er** *n.*

Po·lar·oid /pṓləroyd/ *n. Trademark* **1** material in thin plastic sheets that produces a high degree of plane polarization in light passing through it. **2 a** a type of camera with internal processing that produces a finished print rapidly after each exposure. **b** a print made with such a camera. **3** (in *pl.*) sunglasses with lenses made from Polaroid.

Pole /pōl/ *n.* **1** a native or national of Poland. **2** a person of Polish descent.

pole[1] /pōl/ *n. & v.* • *n.* **1** a long slender rounded piece of wood or metal, esp. with the end placed in the ground as a support, etc. **2** a wooden shaft fitted to the front of a vehicle and attached to the yokes or collars of the draft animals. • *v.tr.* **1** provide with poles. **2** push or propel (a small boat) with a pole.

pole[2] /pōl/ *n.* **1** (in full **north pole, south pole**) **a** each of the two points in the celestial sphere about which the stars appear to revolve. **b** each of the extremities of the axis of rotation of the earth or another body. **c** see MAGNETIC POLE.

▶The spelling is *North Pole* and *South Pole* when used as geographical designations. **2** each of the two opposite points on the surface of a magnet at which magnetic forces are strongest. **3** each of two terminals (positive and negative) of an electric cell or battery, etc. **4** each of two opposed principles or ideas. **5** *Geom.* each of two points in which the axis of a circle cuts the surface of a sphere. ▫ **be poles apart** differ greatly, esp. in nature or opinion. ▫▫ **pole·ward** *adj.* **pole·wards** *adj. & adv.*

pole·ax /pṓlaks/ *n. & v.* • *n.* **1** a battleax. **2** a butcher's ax. • *v.tr.* hit or kill with or as if with a poleax.

pole·cat /pṓlkat/ *n.* **1** *US* a skunk. **2** *Brit.* a small European brownish black flesh-eating mammal, *Mustela putorius*, of the weasel family.

po·lem·ic /pəlémik/ *n. & adj.* • *n.* **1** a controversial discussion. **2** *Polit.* a verbal or written attack, esp. on a political opponent. • *adj.* (also **po·lem·i·cal**) involving dispute; controversial. ▫▫ **po·lem·i·cal·ly** *adv.* **po·lem·i·cist** /–misist/ *n.* **po·lem·i·cize** *v.tr.* **pol·e·mize** /pólimīz/ *v.tr.*

po·lem·ics /pəlémiks/ *n.pl.* the art or practice of controversial discussion.

po·len·ta /pəléntə, pō–/ *n.* mush made of cornmeal, etc.

pole·star /pṓlstar/ *n.* **1** *Astron.* a star in Ursa Minor now about 1° distant from the celestial north pole. **2 a** a thing or principle serving as a guide. **b** a center of attraction.

pole vault *n. & v.* • *n.* the sport of vaulting over a high bar with the aid of a long flexible pole held in the hands and giving extra spring. • *v.intr.* (**pole-vault**) take part in this sport. ▫▫ **pole-vault·er** *n.*

po·lice /pəlḗes/ *n. & v.* • *n.* **1** (usu. prec. by *the*) the civil force of a government, responsible for maintaining public order. **2** (as *pl.*) the members of a police force (*several hundred police*). **3** a force with similar functions of enforcing regulations (*military police; transit police*). • *v.tr.* **1** control (a country or area) by means of police. **2** provide with police. **3** keep order in; control; monitor.

po·lice·man /pəlḗesmən/ *n.* (*pl.* **-men**; *fem.* **policewoman**, *pl.* **-women**) a member of a police force.

po·lice of·fi·cer *n.* a policeman or policewoman.

po·lice state *n.* a totalitarian country controlled by political police supervising the citizens' activities.

po·lice sta·tion *n.* the office of a local police force.

pol·i·cy[1] /pólisee/ *n.* (*pl.* **-cies**) **1** a course or principle of action adopted or proposed by a government, party, business, or individual, etc. **2** prudent conduct; sagacity.

pol·i·cy[2] /pólisee/ *n.* (*pl.* **-cies**) **1** a contract of insurance. **2** a document containing this.

pol·i·cy·hold·er /póliseehṓldər/ *n.* a person or body holding an insurance policy.

po·li·o /pṓleeō/ *n.* = POLIOMYELITIS.

po·li·o·my·e·li·tis /pṓleeōmī́-ilī́tis/ *n. Med.* an infectious viral disease that affects the central nervous system and that can cause temporary or permanent paralysis.

Po·lish /pṓlish/ *adj. & n.* • *adj.* **1** of or relating to Poland. **2** of the Poles or their language. • *n.* the language of Poland.

pol·ish /pólish/ *v. & n.* • *v.* **1** *tr. & intr.* make or become smooth or glossy, esp. by rubbing. **2** (esp. as **polished** *adj.*) refine or improve; add finishing touches to. • *n.* **1** a substance used for polishing. **2** smoothness or glossiness produced by friction. **3** the act or an instance of polishing. **4** refinement or elegance of manner, conduct, etc. ▫ **polish off 1** finish (esp. food) quickly. **2** *colloq.* kill; murder. **polish up** revise or improve (a skill, etc.). ▫▫ **pol·ish·a·ble** *adj.* **pol·ish·er** *n.*

po·lit·bu·ro /pólitbyŏŏrō, pəlít–/ *n.* (*pl.* **-ros**) the principal policy-making committee of a Communist party, esp. in the former USSR.

po·lite /pəlī́t/ *adj.* (**politer, politest**) **1** having good manners; courteous. **2** cultivated; cultured. **3** refined; elegant (*polite letters*). ▫▫ **po·lite·ly** *adv.* **po·lite·ness** *n.*

pol·i·tic /pólitik/ *adj. & v.* • *adj.* **1** (of an action) judicious; expedient. **2** (of a person:) **a** prudent; sagacious. **b** scheming; sly. **3** political (now only in *body politic*). • *v.intr.* (**politicked, politicking**) engage in politics. ▫▫ **pol·i·tic·ly** *adv.*

po·lit·i·cal /pəlítikəl/ *adj.* **1 a** of or concerning government, or public affairs generally. **b** of, relating to, or engaged in politics. **c** belonging to or forming part of a civil administration. **2** having an organized form of society or government. **3** taking or belonging to a side in politics or in controversial matters. **4** relating to or affecting interests of status or authority in an organization rather than matters of principle (*a political decision*). ▫▫ **po·lit·i·cal·ly** *adv.*

po·lit·i·cal ac·tion com·mit·tee *n.* a permanent organization that collects and distributes funds for political purposes. ¶ Abbr.: **PAC**.

po·lit·i·cal a·sy·lum *n.* protection given by a government to a political refugee.

po·lit·i·cal cor·rect·ness *n.* avoidance of forms of expression and action that exclude or marginalize sexual, racial, and cultural minorities; advocacy of this.

po·lit·i·cal·ly cor·rect *adj.* in conformance with political correctness.

po·lit·i·cal pris·on·er *n.* a person imprisoned for political beliefs or actions.

po·lit·i·cal sci·ence *n.* the study of systems of government. ▫▫ **po·lit·i·cal sci·en·tist** *n.*

pol·i·ti·cian /pólitíshən/ *n.* **1** a person engaged in or concerned with politics, esp. as a practitioner. **2** a person skilled in politics. **3** *derog.* a person with self-interested political concerns.

po·lit·i·cize /pəlítisīz/ *v.* **1** *tr.* **a** give a political character to. **b** make politically aware. **2** *intr.* engage in or talk politics. ▫▫ **po·lit·i·ci·za·tion** *n.*

---

po•lit•i•co /pəlítikō/ *n.* (*pl.* **-cos**) *colloq.* a politician or political enthusiast.

pol•i•tics /pólitiks/ *n.pl.* **1** (treated as *sing.* or *pl.*) **a** the art and science of government. **b** public life and affairs as involving authority and government. **2** (usu. treated as *pl.*) **a** a particular set of ideas, principles, or commitments in politics (*what are their politics?*). **b** activities concerned with the acquisition or exercise of authority or government. **c** an organizational process or principle affecting authority, status, etc. (*the politics of the decision*).

pol•i•ty /pólitee/ *n.* (*pl.* **-ties**) **1** a form or process of civil government or constitution. **2** an organized society; a nation as a political entity.

pol•ka /pṓlkə, pṓkə/ *n.* & *v.* • *n.* **1** a lively dance of Bohemian origin in duple time. **2** the music for this. • *v.intr.* (**polkas, polkaed** /–kəd/or **polka'd, polkaing** /–kəing/) dance the polka.

pol•ka dot *n.* a round dot as one of many forming a regular pattern on a textile fabric, etc.

poll /pōl/ *n.* & *v.* • *n.* **1 a** the process of voting at an election. **b** the counting of votes at an election. **c** the result of voting. **d** the number of votes recorded (*a heavy poll*). **e** (also **polls**) place for voting. **2** an assessment of public opinion by questioning a representative sample, as for forecasting the results of voting, etc. **3 a** a human head. **b** the part of this on which hair grows (*flaxen poll*). **4** a hornless animal, esp. one of a breed of hornless cattle. • *v.* **1** *tr.* **a** take the vote or votes of. **b** (in *passive*) have one's vote taken. **c** (of a candidate) receive (so many votes). **d** give (a vote). **2** *tr.* record the opinion of (a person or group) in an opinion poll. **3** *intr.* give one's vote. **4** *tr.* cut off the top of (a tree or plant), esp. make a pollard of. **5** *tr.* (esp. as **polled** *adj.*) cut the horns off (cattle). **6** *tr.* *Computing* check the status of (a computer system) at intervals. □□ **poll•ee** /pōlée/ *n.* (in sense 2 of *n.*). **poll•ster** *n.*

pol•lack /pólək/ *n.* (also **pol•lock**) a European marine fish, *Pollachius pollachius*, with a characteristic protruding lower jaw, used for food.

pol•lard /pólərd/ *n.* & *v.* • *n.* **1** an animal that has lost or cast its horns; an ox, sheep, or goat of a hornless breed. **2** a tree whose branches have been cut off to encourage the growth of new young branches, esp. a riverside willow. **3 a** the bran sifted from flour. **b** a fine bran containing some flour. • *v.tr.* make (a tree) a pollard.

pol•len /pólən/ *n.* the fine dustlike grains discharged from the male part of a flower containing the gamete that fertilizes the female ovule.

pol•li•nate /pólinayt/ *v.tr.* (also *absol.*) sprinkle (a stigma) with pollen. □□ **pol•li•na•tion** /–náyshən/ *n.* **pol•li•na•tor** *n.*

poll•ing booth *n.* a compartment in which a voter stands to mark a paper ballot or use a voting machine.

pol•li•wog /póleewog/ *n.* (also **pollywog**) *dial.* a tadpole.

pol•lute /pəlóot/ *v.tr.* **1** contaminate or defile (the environment). **2** make foul or filthy. **3** destroy the purity or sanctity of. □□ **pol•lu•tant** *adj.* & *n.* **pol•lut•er** *n.* **pol•lu•tion** *n.*

Pol•ly•an•na /póleeánə/ *n.* a cheerful optimist; an excessively cheerful person. □□ **Pol•ly•an•na•ish** *adj.* **Pol•ly•an•na•ism** *n.*

po•lo /pṓlō/ *n.* a game of Asian origin played on horseback with a long-handled mallet.

pol•o•naise /pólənáyz, pṓ–/ *n.* & *adj.* • *n.* **1** a dance of Polish origin in triple time. **2** the music for this. **3** *hist.* a woman's dress consisting of a bodice and a draped skirt open from the waist downward to show an underskirt. • *adj.* cooked in a Polish style.

po•lo•ni•um /pəlṓneeəm/ *n.* *Chem.* a rare radioactive metallic element, occurring naturally in uranium ores. ¶ Symb.: **Po**.

po•lo shirt *n.* a pullover shirt, usu. of knit fabric, with a rounded neckband or a turnover collar.

pol•ter•geist /pṓltərgīst/ *n.* a noisy mischievous ghost, esp. one manifesting itself by physical damage.

pol•troon /poltróon/ *n.* a spiritless coward. □□ **pol•troon•er•y** *n.*

poly-[1] /pólee/ *comb. form* denoting many or much.

poly-[2] /pólee/ *comb. form Chem.* polymerized (*polyunsaturated*).

pol•y•an•dry /póleeandree/ *n.* polygamy in which a woman has more than one husband. □□ **pol•y•an•drous** /–ándrəs/ *adj.*

▶See note at POLYGAMY.

pol•y•chro•mat•ic /póleekrōmátik/ *adj.* **1** many-colored. **2** (of radiation) containing more than one wavelength. □□ **pol•y•chro•ma•tism** /–krṓmətizəm/ *n.*

pol•y•chrome /póleekrōm/ *adj.* & *n.* • *adj.* painted, printed, or decorated in many colors. • *n.* **1** a work of art in several colors, esp. a colored statue. **2** varied coloring. □□ **pol•y•chro•mic** /–krṓmik/ *adj.* **pol•y•chro•mous** /–krṓməs/ *adj.* **pol•y•chro•my** *n.*

pol•y•dac•tyl /póleedáktil/ *adj.* & *n.* • *adj.* (of an animal) having more than five fingers or toes. • *n.* a polydactyl animal.

pol•y•es•ter /pólee-éstər/ *n.* any of a group of condensation polymers used to form synthetic fibers or to make resins.

pol•y•eth•yl•ene /pólee-éthileen/ *n.* *Chem.* a tough light thermoplastic polymer of ethylene, usu. translucent and flexible or opaque and rigid, used for packaging and insulating materials. Also called POLYETHENE, POLYTHENE.

po•lyg•a•mous /pəlígəməs/ *adj.* **1** having more than one wife or husband at the same time. **2** having more than one mate. **3** bearing some flowers with stamens only, some with pistils only, and some with both on the same or different plants. □□ **pol•y•gam•ic** /póligámik/ *adj.* **po•lyg•a•mist** /–gəmist/ *n.* **po•lyg•a•mous•ly** *adv.*

po•lyg•a•my /pəlígəmee/ *n.* the practice of having more than one husband or wife at the same time. □□ **pol•y•gam•ic** /póligámik/ *adj.* **po•lyg•a•mist** /–gəmist/ *n.* **po•lyg•a•mous** /pəlígəməs/ *adj.* **po•lyg•a•mous•ly** *adv.*

▶**Polygamy** is having more than one spouse. It may apply to men or women; **polygyny** is specifically the practice of having more than one wife. **Polyandry** is the term for having more than one husband.

pol•y•glot /póleeglot/ *adj.* & *n.* • *adj.* **1** of many languages. **2** (of a person) speaking or writing several languages. **3** (of a book, esp. the Bible) with the text translated into several languages. • *n.* **1** a polyglot person. **2** a polyglot book, esp. a Bible. □□ **pol•y•glot•tal** *adj.* **pol•y•glot•tic** *adj.* **pol•y•glot•ism** *n.* **pol•y•glot•tism** *n.*

pol•y•gon /póleegon/ *n.* a plane figure with many (usu. a minimum of three) sides and angles. □□ **po•lyg•o•nal** /pəlígənəl/ *adj.*

pol•y•graph /póleegraf/ *n.* a machine designed to detect and record changes in physiological characteristics (e.g., rates of pulse and breathing), used esp. as a lie-detector.

pol•y•he•dron /póleehéedrən/ *n.* (*pl.* **polyhedra** /–drə/or **polyhedrous**) a solid figure with many (usu. more than six) faces. □□ **pol•y•he•dral** *adj.* **pol•y•he•dric** *adj.*

pol•y•math /póleemath/ *n.* **1** a person of much or varied learning. **2** a great scholar. □□ **pol•y•math•ic** /–máthik/ *adj.* **po•lym•a•thy** /pəlíməthee/ *n.*

pol•y•mer /pólimər/ *n.* a compound composed of one or more large molecules that are formed from repeated units of smaller molecules. □□ **pol•y•mer•ic** /–mérik/

adj. **po·lym·er·ism** *n.* **po·lym·er·ize** *v.intr. & tr.* **po·lym·er·i·za·tion** *n.*

Pol·y·ne·sian /pólinée̱zhən/ *adj. & n.* • *adj.* of or relating to Polynesia, a group of Pacific islands including New Zealand, Hawaii, Samoa, etc. • *n.* **1 a** a native of Polynesia. **b** a person of Polynesian descent. **2** the family of languages including Maori, Hawaiian, and Samoan.

pol·y·no·mi·al /pólinṓmeeəl/ *n. & adj. Math.* • *n.* an expression of more than two algebraic terms, esp. the sum of several terms that contain different powers of the same variable(s). • *adj.* of or being a polynomial.

pol·yp /pólip/ *n.* **1** *Zool.* an individual coelenterate. **2** *Med.* a small usu. benign growth protruding from a mucous membrane. ▫▫ **pol·yp·oid** /póleepoyd/ *adj.* **pol·yp·ous** /–pəs/ *adj.*

pol·y·phon·ic /póleefónik/ *adj.* **1** *Mus.* (of vocal music, etc.) in two or more relatively independent parts; contrapuntal. **2** *Phonet.* (of a letter, etc.) representing more than one sound. ▫▫ **pol·y·phon·i·cal·ly** *adv.*

po·lyph·o·ny /pəlífənee/ *n.* (*pl.* **-nies**) **1** *Mus.* **a** polyphonic style in musical composition; counterpoint. **b** a composition written in this style. **2** *Philol.* the symbolization of different vocal sounds by the same letter or character. ▫▫ **po·lyph·o·nous** *adj.*

pol·y·pro·pyl·ene /póleeprṓpileen/ *n. Chem.* any of various polymers of propylene including thermoplastic materials used for films, fibers, or molding materials. Also called POLYPROPENE.

pol·y·sac·cha·ride /póleesákərīd/ *n.* any of a group of carbohydrates whose molecules consist of long chains of monosaccharides.

pol·y·sty·rene /póleestíreen/ *n.* a thermoplastic polymer of styrene, usu. hard and colorless or expanded with a gas to produce a lightweight rigid white substance, used for insulation and in packaging.

pol·y·syl·lab·ic /póleesilábik/ *adj.* **1** (of a word) having many syllables. **2** characterized by the use of words of many syllables. ▫▫ **pol·y·syl·lab·i·cal·ly** *adv.*

pol·y·tech·nic /póleetéknik/ *n. & adj.* • *n.* an institution of higher education offering courses in many esp. vocational or technical subjects. • *adj.* dealing with or devoted to various vocational or technical subjects.

pol·y·the·ism /póleethée̱izəm/ *n.* the belief in or worship of more than one god. ▫▫ **pol·y·the·ist** *n.* **pol·y·the·is·tic** *adj.*

pol·y·un·sat·u·rat·ed /póleeunsáchəraytid/ *adj. Chem.* (of a compound, esp. a fat or oil molecule) containing several double or triple bonds and therefore capable of further reaction.

pol·y·u·re·thane /póleeyŏŏrəthayn/ *n.* any polymer containing the urethane group, used in adhesives, paints, plastics, foams, etc.

pol·y·vi·nyl chlo·ride /póleevínil/ *n.* a tough transparent solid polymer of vinyl chloride, easily colored and used for a wide variety of products including pipes, flooring, etc. ¶ Abbr.: **PVC.**

po·made /pomáyd, –maád/ *n. & v.* • *n.* scented dressing for the hair and the skin of the head. • *v.tr.* anoint with pomade.

po·man·der /pṓmandər, pōmán–/ *n.* **1** a ball of mixed aromatic substances placed in a cupboard, etc., or *hist.* carried in a box, bag, etc., as a protection against infection. **2** a (usu. spherical) container for this. **3** a spiced orange, etc., similarly used.

pome·gran·ate /pómigranit, pómgranit, púm–/ *n.* **1** an orange-sized fruit with a tough reddish outer skin and containing many seeds in a red pulp. **2** the tree bearing this fruit, *Punica granatum,* native to N. Africa and W. Asia.

Pom·er·a·ni·an /pómərǽyneeən/ *n.* a small dog with long silky hair, a pointed muzzle, and pricked ears.

pom·mel /púməl, póm–/ *n. & v.* • *n.* **1** a knob, esp. at the end of a sword hilt. **2** the upward projecting front part of a saddle. • *v.tr.* (**pommeled, pommeling** or **pommelled, pommelling**) = PUMMEL.

pom·mel horse *n.* a vaulting horse fitted with a pair of curved handgrips.

pomp /pomp/ *n.* **1** a splendid display; splendor. **2** (often in *pl.*) vainglory (*the pomps and vanities of this wicked world*).

pom·pom /pómpom/ *n.* (also **pom·pon** /–pon/) **1** an ornamental ball or tuft of wool, silk, or ribbons, often worn on hats or clothing. **2** (often *attrib.*) (usu. **pompon**) a dahlia or chrysanthemum with small tightly-clustered petals.

pomp·ous /pómpəs/ *adj.* **1** self-important, affectedly grand or solemn. **2** (of language) pretentious; unduly grand in style. ▫▫ **pom·pos·i·ty** /pompósitee/ *n.* (*pl.* **-ties**). **pomp·ous·ly** *adv.* **pomp·ous·ness** *n.*

pon·cho /pónchō/ *n.* (*pl.* **-chos**) **1** a S. American cloak made of a blanket-like piece of cloth with a slit in the middle for the head. **2** a garment in this style, esp. one waterproof and worn as a raincoat. ▫▫ **pon·choed** *adj.*

pond /pond/ *n. & v.* • *n.* **1** a fairly small body of still water formed naturally or by hollowing or embanking. **2** *joc.* the sea. • *v.* **1** *tr.* hold back; dam up (a stream, etc.) **2** *intr.* form a pond.

pon·der /póndər/ *v.* **1** *tr.* weigh mentally; think over; consider. **2** *intr.* (usu. foll. by *on, over*) think; muse.

pon·der·o·sa /póndərṓsə/ *n.* **1** a N. American pine tree, *Pinus ponderosa.* **2** the timber of this tree.

pon·der·ous /póndərəs/ *adj.* **1** heavy; unwieldy. **2** laborious. **3** (of style, etc.) dull; tedious. ▫▫ **pon·der·os·i·ty** /–rósitee/ *n.* **pon·der·ous·ly** *adv.* **pon·der·ous·ness** *n.*

pone /pōn/ *n. US dial.* **1** unleavened cornbread, esp. as made by Native Americans. **2** a fine light bread made with milk, eggs, etc. **3** a cake or loaf of this.

pon·tiff /póntif/ *n. RC Ch.* (in full **sovereign** or **supreme pontiff**) the pope.

pon·tif·i·cal /pontífikəl/ *adj. & n.* • *adj.* **1** *RC Ch.* of or befitting a pontiff; papal. **2** pompously dogmatic; with an attitude of infallibility. • *n.* **1** an office book containing rites to be performed by bishops. **2** (in *pl.*) the vestments and insignia of a bishop, cardinal, or abbot. ▫▫ **pon·tif·i·cal·ly** *adv.*

pon·tif·i·cate *v. & n.* • *v.intr.* /pontífikayt/ **1 a** play the pontiff; pretend to be infallible. **b** be pompously dogmatic. **2** *RC Ch.* officiate as bishop, esp. at mass. • *n.* /pontífikət/ **1** the office of pontifex, bishop, or pope. **2** the period of this.

pon·toon /pontŏŏn/ *n.* **1** a flat-bottomed boat. **2 a** each of several boats, hollow metal cylinders, etc., used to support a temporary bridge. **b** a bridge so formed; a floating platform. **3** = CAISSON 1, 2. **4** a float for a seaplane.

pontoon, 3

po·ny /pṓnee/ *n.* (*pl.* **-nies**) **1** a horse of any small breed. **2** a small drinking glass. **3** (in *pl.*) *sl.* racehorses. **4** a literal translation of a foreign-language text, used by students.

po·ny ex·press *n.* (also **Pony Express**) *US Hist.* an express delivery system of the early 1860s that carried mail, etc., by relays of pony riders.

po·ny·tail /pṓneetayl/ *n.* a person's hair drawn back, tied, and hanging down like a pony's tail.

pooch /po͞och/ *n. sl.* a dog.

poo·dle /po͞od'l/ *n.* **1 a** a dog of a breed with a curly coat that is usually clipped. **b** this breed. **2** *Brit.* a lackey or servile follower.

pooh /po͞o/ *int. & n.* (also **poo**) • *int.* expressing impatience or contempt. • *n. sl.* **1** excrement. **2** an act of defecation.

pooh-pooh /po͞opo͞o/ *v.tr.* express contempt for; ridicule; dismiss (an idea, etc.) scornfully.

pool[1] /po͞ol/ *n. & v.* • *n.* **1** a small body of still water, usu. of natural formation. **2** a small shallow body of any liquid. **3** = SWIMMING POOL. **4** a deep place in a river. • *v.* **1** *tr.* form into a pool. **2** *intr.* (of blood) become static.

pool[2] /po͞ol/ *n. & v.* • *n.* **1 a** (often *attrib.*) a common supply of persons, vehicles, commodities, etc., for sharing by a group of people (*a typing pool*; *a car pool*). **b** a group of persons sharing duties, etc. **2 a** the collective amount of players' stakes in gambling, etc. **b** a receptacle for this. **3 a** a joint commercial venture, esp. an arrangement between competing parties to fix prices and share business to eliminate competition. **b** the common funding for this. **4** any of several games similar to billiards played on a pool table with usu. 16 balls. **5** a group of contestants who compete against each other in a tournament for the right to advance to the next round. • *v.tr.* **1** put (resources, etc.) into a common fund. **2** share (things) in common. **3** (of transport or organizations, etc.) share (traffic, receipts).

pool·room /po͞olro͞om, –ro͝om/ *n.* **1** a place for playing pool; pool hall. **2** a bookmaking establishment.

poop[1] /po͞op/ *n.* the stern of a ship; the aftermost and highest deck.

poop[2] /po͞op/ *v.tr.* (esp. as **pooped** *adj.*) *colloq.* exhaust; tire out.

poop[3] /po͞op/ *n. sl.* up to date or inside information; the lowdown.

poop[4] /po͞op/ *n. & v. sl.* • *n.* excrement. • *v.intr.* defecate.

poor /po͝or/ *adj.* **1** lacking adequate money or means to live comfortably. **2 a** (foll. by *in*) deficient in (a possession or quality) (*the poor in spirit*). **b** (of soil, ore, etc.) unproductive. **3 a** scanty; inadequate (*a poor crop*). **b** less good than is usual or expected (*poor visibility*; *is a poor driver*; *in poor health*). **c** paltry; inferior (*poor condition*; *came a poor third*). **4 a** deserving pity or sympathy; unfortunate (*you poor thing*). **b** with reference to a dead person (*as my poor father used to say*). **5** spiritless; despicable (*is a poor creature*). **6** often *iron.* or *joc.* humble; insignificant (*in my poor opinion*). □ **take a poor view of** regard with disfavor or pessimism.

poor·house /po͝orhows/ *n. hist.* = WORKHOUSE 2.

poor·ly /po͝orlee/ *adv. & adj.* • *adv.* **1** scantily; defectively. **2** with no great success. **3** meanly; contemptibly. • *predic. adj. unwell.*

poor·ness /po͝ornis/ *n.* **1** defectiveness. **2** the lack of some good quality or constituent.

pop[1] /pop/ *n., v., & adv.* • *n.* **1** a sudden sharp explosive sound as of a cork when drawn. **2** *colloq.* an effervescent soft drink. • *v.* (**popped, popping**) **1** *intr. & tr.* make or cause to make a pop. **2** *intr. & tr.* (foll. by *in*, *out*, *up*, *down*, etc.) go, move, come, or put unexpectedly or in a quick or hasty manner (*pop out to the store*; *pop in for a visit*; *pop it on your head*). **3 a** *intr. & tr.* burst, making a popping sound. **b** *tr.* heat (popcorn, etc.) until it pops. **4** *intr.* (often foll. by *at*) *colloq.* fire a gun (at birds, etc.). • *adv.* with the sound of a pop (*heard it go pop*). □ **pop the question** *colloq.* propose marriage.

pop[2] /pop/ *adj. & n. colloq.* • *adj.* **1** in a popular or modern style. **2** performing popular music, etc. (*pop group*; *pop star*). • *n.* **1** pop music. **2** a pop record or song (*top of the pops*).

pop[3] /pop/ *n.* esp. *colloq.* father.

pop. *abbr.* population.

pop art *n.* art based on modern popular culture and the mass media, esp. as a critical comment on traditional fine art values.

pop·corn /pópkawrn/ *n.* **1** corn which bursts open when heated. **2** these kernels when popped.

pop cul·ture *n.* commercial culture based on popular taste.

pope /pōp/ *n.* **1** (as title usu. **Pope**) the head of the Roman Catholic Church (also called the **Bishop of Rome**). **2** the head of the Coptic Church and Orthodox patriarch of Alexandria. □□ **pope·dom** *n.* **pope·less** *adj.*

pop·in·jay /pópinjay/ *n.* **1** a fop; a conceited person; a coxcomb. **2 a** *archaic* a parrot. **b** *hist.* a figure of a parrot on a pole as a mark to shoot at.

pop·lar /póplər/ *n.* **1** any tree of the genus *Populus*, with a usu. rapidly growing trunk and tremulous leaves. **2** = TULIP TREE.

pop·lin /póplin/ *n.* a plain woven fabric usu. of cotton, with a corded surface.

pop·o·ver /pópōvər/ *n.* a light puffy hollow muffin made from an egg-rich batter.

pop·pa /pópə/ *n. colloq.* father (esp. as a child's word).

pop·py /pópee/ *n.* (*pl.* **-pies**) any plant of the genus *Papaver*, with showy often red flowers and a milky sap with narcotic properties.

pop·py·cock /pópeekok/ *n. sl.* nonsense.

Pop·si·cle /pópsikəl/ *n. Trademark* a flavored ice confection on a stick.

pop·u·lace /pópyələs/ *n.* **1** the common people. **2** *derog.* the rabble.

pop·u·lar /pópyələr/ *adj.* **1** liked or admired by many people or by a specified group (*popular teachers*; *a popular hero*). **2 a** of or carried on by the general public (*popular meetings*). **b** prevalent among the general public (*popular discontent*). **3** adapted to the understanding, taste, or means of the people (*popular science*; *popular medicine*). □□ **pop·u·lar·ism** *n.* **pop·u·lar·i·ty** /–láritee/ *n.* **pop·u·lar·ly** *adv.*

pop·u·lar front *n.* a party or coalition representing left-wing elements.

pop·u·lar·ize /pópyələrīz/ *v.tr.* **1** make popular. **2** cause (a person, principle, etc.) to be generally known or liked. **3** present (a technical subject, specialized vocabulary, etc.) in a popular or readily understandable form. □□ **pop·u·lar·i·za·tion** /–rəzáyshən/ *n.* **pop·u·lar·iz·er** *n.*

pop·u·lar mu·sic *n.* music appealing to the popular taste, including rock, soul, country, reggae, rap and dance music.

pop·u·late /pópyəlayt/ *v.tr.* **1** inhabit; form the population of (a town, country, etc.). **2** supply with inhabitants; people (*a densely populated district*).

pop·u·la·tion /pópyəláyshən/ *n.* **1 a** the inhabitants of a place, country, etc., referred to collectively. **b** any specified group within this (*the Polish population of Chicago*). **2** the total number of any of these (*a population of eight million*; *the seal population*). **3** the act or process of supplying with inhabitants (*the population of forest areas*). **4** *Statistics* any finite or infinite collection of items under consideration.

pop·u·list /pópyəlist/ *n. & adj.* • *n.* a member or adherent of a political party seeking support mainly from the ordinary people. • *adj.* of or relating to such a political party. □□ **pop·u·lism** *n.* **pop·u·lis·tic** /–lístik/ *adj.*

Pop·u·list Par·ty *n.* a US political party formed in 1891 that advocated the interests of labor and farmers, free coinage of silver, a graduated income tax, and government control of monopolies.

pop·u·lous /pópyələs/ *adj.* thickly inhabited. ▫▫ **pop·u·lous·ly** *adv.* **pop·u·lous·ness** *n.*

pop-up *adj.* **1** (of a toaster, etc.) operating so as to move the object (toast when ready, etc.) quickly upward. **2** (of a book, greeting card, etc.) containing three-dimensional figures, illustrations, etc., that rise up when the page is turned. **3** *Computing* (of a menu) able to be superimposed on the screen being worked on and suppressed rapidly.

por·ce·lain /páwrsəlin, páwrslin/ *n.* **1** a hard vitrified translucent ceramic. **2** objects made of this.

porch /pawrch/ *n.* **1** a covered shelter for the entrance of a building. **2** a veranda. ▫▫ **porched** *adj.*

por·cine /páwrsīn, –sin/ *adj.* of or like pigs.

por·cu·pine /páwrkyəpīn/ *n.* any rodent of the family Hystricidae native to Africa, Asia, and SE Europe, or the family Erethizontidae native to America, having defensive spines or quills. ▫▫ **por·cu·pin·ish** *adj.* **por·cu·pin·y** *adj.*

pore[1] /pawr/ *n.* esp. *Biol.* a minute opening in a surface through which gases, liquids, or fine solids may pass.

pore[2] /pawr/ *v.intr.* (foll. by *over*) **1** be absorbed in studying (a book, etc.). **2** meditate on, think intently about (a subject).

por·gy /páwrgee/ *n.* (*pl.* **-gies**) any usu. marine fish of the family Sparidae, used as food. Also called **sea bream.**

pork /pawrk/ *n.* **1** the (esp. unsalted) flesh of a pig, used as food. **2** = PORK BARREL.

pork bar·rel *n. US colloq.* government funds as a source of political benefit.

pork·er /páwrkər/ *n.* **1** a pig raised for food. **2** a young fattened pig.

pork·pie hat /páwrkpī/ *n.* a hat with a flat crown and a brim turned up all around.

pork·y /páwrkee/ *adj.* (**porkier, porkiest**) **1** *colloq.* fleshy; fat. **2** of or like pork.

porn /pawrn/ *n. colloq.* pornography.

por·no /páwrnō/ *n.* & *adj. colloq.* •*n.* pornography. •*adj.* pornographic.

por·nog·ra·phy /pawrnógrəfee/ *n.* **1** the explicit description or exhibition of sexual activity in literature, films, etc., intended to stimulate erotic rather than aesthetic or emotional feelings. **2** literature, etc., characterized by this. ▫▫ **por·nog·ra·pher** *n.* **por·no·graph·ic** /–nəgráfik/ *adj.* **por·no·graph·i·cal·ly** *adv.*

po·rous /páwrəs/ *adj.* **1** full of pores. **2** letting through air, water, etc. **3** (of an argument, security system, etc.) leaky; admitting infiltration. ▫▫ **po·ros·i·ty** /porósitee/ *n.* **po·rous·ly** *adv.* **po·rous·ness** *n.*

por·phy·ry /páwrfiree/ *n.* (*pl.* **-ries**) **1** a hard rock quarried in ancient Egypt, composed of crystals of white or red feldspar in a red matrix. **2** *Geol.* an igneous rock with large crystals scattered in a matrix of much smaller crystals. ▫▫ **por·phy·rit·ic** /–rítik/ *adj.*

por·poise /páwrpəs/ *n.* any of various small toothed whales of the family Phocaenidae, esp. of the genus *Phocaena,* with a low triangular dorsal fin and a blunt rounded snout.

por·ridge /páwrij, pór–/ *n.* a dish consisting of oatmeal or another cereal boiled in water or milk.

por·rin·ger /páwrinjər, pór–/ *n.* a small bowl, often with a handle, for soup, stew, etc.

port[1] /pawrt/ *n.* **1** a harbor. **2** a place of refuge. **3** a town or place possessing a harbor, esp. one where customs officers are stationed.

port[2] /pawrt/ *n.* (in full **port wine**) a strong, sweet, dark red (occas. brown or white) fortified wine of Portugal.

port[3] /pawrt/ *n.* the left side (looking forward) of a ship, boat, or aircraft (cf. STARBOARD).

port[4] /pawrt/ *n.* **1 a** an opening in the side of a ship for entrance, loading, etc. **b** a porthole. **2** an aperture for the passage of steam, water, etc. **3** *Electr.* a socket or aperture in an electronic circuit, esp. in a computer network, where connections can be made with peripheral equipment. **4** an aperture in a wall, etc., for a gun to be fired through. **5** esp. *Sc.* a gate or gateway, esp. of a walled town.

port[5] /pawrt/ *v.tr.* & *n.* •*v.tr. Mil.* carry (a rifle, or other weapon) diagonally across and close to the body with the barrel, etc., near the left shoulder (esp. *port arms!*). •*n.* **1** *Mil.* this position. **2** external deportment; carriage; bearing.

port·a·ble /páwrtəbəl/ *adj.* & *n.* •*adj.* easily movable; convenient for carrying (*portable TV; portable computer*). •*n.* a portable object, e.g., a radio, typewriter, etc. (*decided to buy a portable*). ▫▫ **port·a·bil·i·ty** *n.* **port·a·ble·ness** *n.* **port·a·bly** *adv.*

por·tage /páwrtij, –taázh/ *n.* & *v.* •*n.* **1** the carrying of boats or goods between two navigable waters. **2** a place at which this is necessary. **3 a** the act or an instance of carrying or transporting. **b** the cost of this. •*v.tr.* convey (a boat or goods) between navigable waters.

por·tal[1] /páwrt'l/ *n.* a doorway or gate, etc., esp. a large and elaborate one.

por·tal[2] /páwrt'l/ *adj.* of or relating to an aperture in an organ through which its associated vessels pass.

por·ta·men·to /páwrtəméntō/ *n.* (*pl.* **portamenti** /–tee/) *Mus.* **1** the act or an instance of gliding from one note to another in singing, playing the violin, etc. **2** piano playing in a manner intermediate between legato and staccato.

port·cul·lis /pawrtkúlis/ *n.* a strong heavy grating sliding up and down in vertical grooves, lowered to block a gateway in a fortress, etc. ▫▫ **port·cul·lised** *adj.*

porticullis

por·tend /pawrténd/ *v.tr.* **1** foreshadow as an omen. **2** give warning of.

por·tent /páwrtent/ *n.* **1** an omen, a sign of something to come, esp. something of a momentous or calamitous nature. **2** a prodigy; a marvelous thing.

por·ten·tous /pawrténtəs/ *adj.* **1** like or serving as a portent. **2** pompously solemn. ▫▫ **por·ten·tous·ly** *adv.*

por·ter /páwrtər/ *n.* **1 a** a person employed to carry luggage, etc., at an airport, hotel, etc. **b** a hospital employee who moves equipment, trolleys, etc. **2** a dark brown bitter beer brewed from charred or browned malt. **3** a sleeping-car attendant. **4** a cleaning person or maintenance worker, as in a hospital, etc. ▫▫ **por·ter·age** *n.*

por·ter·house steak /páwrtərhows/ *n.* a thick steak cut from the thick end of a sirloin.

port·fo·li·o /pawrtfṓleeō/ *n.* (*pl.* **-os**) **1** a case for keeping loose sheets of paper, drawings, etc. **2** a range of investments held by a person, a company, etc. **3** the office of a minister of state. **4** samples of an artist's work.

port·hole /páwrt-hōl/ *n.* an (esp. glassed-in) aperture in a ship's or aircraft's side for the admission of light.

por·ti·co /páwrtikō/ *n.* (*pl.* **-coes** or **-cos**) a colonnade; a roof supported by columns at regular intervals usu. attached as a porch to a building.

portico

por·tion /páwrshən/ *n. & v.* •*n.* **1** a part or share. **2** the amount of food allotted to one person. **3** a specified or limited quantity. **4** one's destiny or lot. **5** a dowry. •*v.tr.* **1** divide (a thing) into portions. **2** (foll. by *out*) distribute. **3** give a dowry to. **4** (foll. by *to*) assign (a thing) to (a person). □□ **por·tion·less** *adj.* (in sense 5 of *n.*).

port·ly /páwrtlee/ *adj.* (**portlier, portliest**) **1** corpulent; stout. **2** *archaic* of a stately appearance. □□ **port·li·ness** *n.*

port·man·teau /pawrtmántō, páwrtmantṓ/ *n.* (*pl.* **portmanteaus** or **portmanteaux** /–tōz, –tṓz/) a leather trunk for clothes, etc., opening into two equal parts.

port·man·teau word *n.* a word blending the sounds and combining the meanings of two others, e.g., *motel* from *motor* and *hotel.*

port of call *n.* a place where a ship or a person stops on a journey.

por·trait /páwrtrit, –trayt/ *n.* **1** a representation of a person or animal, esp. of the face, made by drawing, painting, photography, etc. **2** a verbal picture; a graphic description. **3** (in graphic design, etc.) a format in which the height of an illustration, etc., is greater than the width (cf. LANDSCAPE).

por·trait·ist /páwrtritist/ *n.* a person who takes or paints portraits.

por·trai·ture /páwrtrichər/ *n.* **1** the art of painting or taking portraits. **2** graphic description. **3** a portrait.

por·tray /pawrtráy/ *v.tr.* **1** represent (an object) by a painting, carving, etc; make a likeness of. **2** describe graphically. **3** represent dramatically. □□ **por·tray·a·ble** *adj.* **por·tray·al** *n.* **por·tray·er** *n.*

Por·tu·guese /páwrchəgéez, –gées/ *n. & adj.* •*n.* (*pl.* same) **1 a** a native or national of Portugal. **b** a person of Portuguese descent. **2** the language of Portugal. •*adj.* of or relating to Portugal or its people or language.

Por·tu·guese man-of-war *n.* a dangerous tropical or subtropical marine hydrozoan of the genus *Physalia* with a large crest and a poisonous sting.

pose[1] /pōz/ *v. & n.* •*v.* **1** *intr.* assume a certain attitude of body, esp. when being photographed or being painted for a portrait. **2** *intr.* (foll. by *as*) set oneself up as or pretend to be (another person, etc.) (*posing as a celebrity*). **3** *intr.* behave affectedly in order to impress others. **4** *tr.* put forward or present (a question, etc.). **5** *tr.* place (an artist's model, etc.) in a certain attitude or position. •*n.* **1** an attitude of body or mind. **2** an attitude or pretense, esp. one assumed for effect (*his generosity is a mere pose*).

pose[2] /pōz/ *v.tr.* puzzle (a person) with a question or problem.

pos·er /pṓzər/ *n.* **1** a person who poses (see POSE[1] *v.* 3). **2** a puzzling question or problem.

po·seur /pōzṓr/ *n.* (*fem.* **poseuse** /pōzṓz/) a person who poses for effect or behaves affectedly.

posh /posh/ *adj. colloq.* elegant; stylish. □□ **posh·ly** *adv.* **posh·ness** *n.*

posh early 20th century: perhaps from slang *posh*, denoting a dandy. There is no evidence to support the popular etymology that *posh* is formed from the initials of *port out starboard home* (referring to the more comfortable staterooms out of the heat of the sun, on ships between England and India).

pos·it /pózit/ *v.tr.* (**posited, positing**) **1** assume as a fact; postulate. **2** put in place or position.

po·si·tion /pəzíshən/ *n. & v.* •*n.* **1** a place occupied by a person or thing. **2** the way in which a thing or its parts are placed or arranged (*sitting in an uncomfortable position*). **3** the proper place (*in position*). **4** the state of being advantageously placed (*jockeying for position*). **5** a person's mental attitude; a way of looking at a question (*changed their position on nuclear disarmament*). **6** a person's situation in relation to others (*puts one in an awkward position*). **7** rank or status; high social standing. **8** paid employment. **9** a place where troops, etc., are posted for strategical purposes (*the position was stormed*). **10** a specific pose in ballet, etc. (*hold first position*). •*v.tr.* place in position. □ **in a position to** enabled by circumstances, resources, information, etc., to (do, state, etc.). □□ **po·si·tion·al** *adj.* **po·si·tion·al·ly** *adv.* **po·si·tion·er** *n.*

pos·i·tive /pózitiv/ *adj. & n.* •*adj.* **1** formally or explicitly stated; definite; unquestionable (*positive proof*). **2** (of a person) convinced, confident, or overconfident in his or her opinion (*positive that I was not there*). **3 a** absolute; not relative. **b** *Gram.* (of an adjective or adverb) expressing a simple quality without comparison (cf. COMPARATIVE, SUPERLATIVE). **4** *colloq.* downright; complete (*it would be a positive miracle*). **5 a** constructive; directional (*positive criticism; positive thinking*). **b** favorable; optimistic (*positive reaction; positive outlook*). **6** marked by the presence rather than absence of qualities or *Med.* symptoms (*the test was positive*). **7** esp. *Philos.* dealing only with matters of fact; practical (cf. POSITIVISM 1). **8** tending in a direction naturally or arbitrarily taken as that of increase or progress (*clockwise rotation is positive*). **9** greater than zero (*positive and negative integers*). **10** *Electr.* of, containing, or producing the kind of electrical charge produced by rubbing glass with silk; an absence of electrons. **11** (of a photographic image) showing lights and shades or colors true to the original (opp. NEGATIVE). •*n.* a positive adjective, photograph, quantity, etc. □□ **pos·i·tive·ly** *adv.* **pos·i·tive·ness** *n.* **pos·i·tiv·i·ty** /pózitívitee/ *n.*

positive late Middle English: from Old French *positif, -ive* or Latin *positivus*, from *posit-* 'placed,' from the verb *ponere*. The original sense referred to laws as being formally 'laid down,' which gave rise to the sense 'explicitly laid down and admitting no question,' hence 'very sure, convinced.'

pos·i·tive feed·back *n.* **1** a constructive response to an experiment, questionnaire, etc. **2** *Electronics* the return of part of an output signal to the input, tending to increase the amplification, etc.

pos·i·tiv·ism /pózitivizəm/ *n.* **1** *Philos.* the philosophical system of Auguste Comte, recognizing only nonmetaphysical facts and observable phenomena, and rejecting metaphysics and theism. **2** a religious system founded on this. **3** = LOGICAL POSITIVISM. □□ **pos·i·tiv·ist** *n.* **pos·i·tiv·is·tic** *adj.* **pos·i·tiv·is·ti·cal·ly** /–vístiklee/ *adv.*

pos·i·tron /pózitron/ *n. Physics* an elementary particle with a positive charge equal to the negative charge of an electron and having the same mass as an electron.

poss. *abbr.* **1** possession. **2** possessive. **3** possible. **4** possibly.

pos·se /pósee/ *n.* **1** a strong force or company or assemblage. **2** (in full **posse comitatus** /kómitáytəs)/ **a** a body of constables, enforcers of the law, etc. **b** a body of men summoned by a sheriff, etc., to enforce the law.

pos·sess /pəzés/ *v.tr.* **1** hold as property; own. **2** have a faculty, quality, etc. (*they possess a special value for us*). **3** (also *refl.*; foll. by *in*) maintain (oneself, one's soul, etc.) in a specified state (*possess oneself in patience*). **4 a** (of a demon, etc.) occupy; have power over (a person, etc.) (*possessed by the devil*). **b** (of an emotion, infatuation, etc.) dominate; be an obsession of (*possessed by fear*). **5** have sexual intercourse with (esp. a woman). □ **be possessed of** own; have. **possess oneself of** take or get for one's own. **what possessed you?** an expression of incredulity. □□ **pos·ses·sor** *n.* **pos·ses·so·ry** *adj.*

pos·ses·sion /pəzéshən/ *n.* **1** the act or state of possessing or being possessed. **2 a** the thing possessed. **b** a foreign territory subject to a state or ruler. **3** the act or state of actual holding or occupancy. **4** *Law* power or control similar to lawful ownership but which may exist separately from it (*prosecuted for possession of narcotic drugs*). **5** (in *pl.*) property, wealth, subject territory, etc. **6** *Sports* temporary control, in team sports, of the ball, puck, etc., by a particular player. □ **in possession 1** (of a person) possessing. **2** (of a thing) possessed. **in possession of 1** having in one's possession. **2** maintaining control over (*in possession of one's wits*). **in the possession of** held or owned by. **take possession** (often foll. by *of*) become the owner or possessor (of a thing). □□ **pos·ses·sion·less** *adj.*

pos·ses·sive /pəzésiv/ *adj.* & *n.* • *adj.* **1** showing a desire to possess or retain what one already owns. **2** showing jealous and domineering tendencies toward another person. **3** *Gram.* indicating possession. • *n.* (in full **possessive case**) *Gram.* the case of nouns and pronouns expressing possession. □□ **pos·ses·sive·ly** *adv.* **pos·ses·sive·ness** *n.*

▶**1.** Form the possessive of all singulars by adding *-'s: Ross's, Fox's, Reese's.* A few classical and other foreign names are traditional exceptions to this rule, e.g., *Jesus', Euripides',* which take an apostrophe only. **2.** Form the possessive of plurals by adding an apostrophe to the plural form: *the Rosses' house, the Perezes' car.* See also note at ITS.

pos·ses·sive pro·noun *n.* each of the pronouns indicating possession (*my, your, his, their,* etc.) or the corresponding absolute forms (*mine, yours, his, theirs,* etc.).

pos·si·bil·i·ty /pósibilitee/ *n.* (*pl.* **-ties**) **1** the state or fact of being possible, or an occurrence of this. **2** a thing that may exist or happen (*there are three possibilities*). **3** (usu. in *pl.*) the capability of being used, improved, etc.; the potential of an object or situation (esp. *have possibilities*).

pos·si·ble /pósibəl/ *adj.* & *n.* • *adj.* **1** capable of existing or happening; that may be managed, achieved, etc. (*came as early as possible; did as much as possible*). **2** that is likely to happen, etc. (*few thought their victory possible*). **3** acceptable; potential (*a possible way of doing it*). • *n.* **1** a possible candidate, member of a team, etc. **2** (prec. by *the*) whatever is likely, manageable, etc.

pos·si·bly /pósiblee/ *adv.* **1** perhaps. **2** in accordance with possibility (*cannot possibly refuse*).

pos·sum /pósəm/ *n. colloq.* = OPOSSUM. □ **play possum 1** pretend to be asleep or unconscious when threatened. **2** feign ignorance.

post- /pōst/ *prefix* after in time or order.

post[1] /pōst/ *n.* & *v.* • *n.* **1** a long stout piece of timber or metal set upright in the ground, etc.: **a** to support something, esp. in building. **b** to mark a position, boundary, etc. **c** to carry notices. **2** a pole, etc., marking the start or finish of a race. **3** a metal pin, as on a pierced earring. • *v.tr.* **1** (often foll. by *up*) **a** attach (a paper, etc.) in a prominent place; stick up (*post no bills*). **b** announce or advertise by placard or in a published text. **2** publish the name of (a ship, etc.) as overdue or missing. **3** placard (a wall, etc.) with handbills, etc. **4** achieve (a score in a game, etc.).

post[2] /pōst/ *n., v.,* & *adv.* • *n.* **1** esp. *Brit.* the official conveyance of packages, letters, etc.; the mail (*send it by post*). **2** esp. *Brit.* a single collection, dispatch, or delivery of the mail; the letters, etc., dispatched (*has the post arrived yet?*). **3** esp. *Brit.* a place where letters, etc., are dealt with; a post office or mailbox (*take it to the post*). **4** *hist.* **a** one of a series of couriers who carried mail on horseback between fixed stages. **b** a letter carrier; a mail cart. • *v.* **1** *tr.* esp. *Brit.* put (a letter, etc.) in the mail. **2** *tr.* (esp. as **posted** *adj.*) supply a person with information (*keep me posted*). **3** *tr.* **a** enter (an item) in a ledger. **b** (often foll. by *up*) complete (a ledger) in this way. **c** carry (an entry) from an auxiliary book to a more formal one, or from one account to another. **4** *intr.* **a** travel with haste; hurry. **b** *hist.* travel with relays of horses. • *adv.* express; with haste.

post[3] /pōst/ *n.* & *v.* • *n.* **1** a place where a soldier is stationed or which he patrols. **2** a place of duty. **3 a** a position taken up by a body of soldiers. **b** a force occupying this. **c** a fort. **4** a situation; paid employment. **5** = TRADING POST. • *v.tr.* **1** place or station (soldiers, an employee, etc.). **2** esp. *Brit.* appoint to a post or command.

post·age /póstij/ *n.* the amount charged for sending a letter, etc., by mail, usu. prepaid in the form of a stamp (*$5 for postage*).

pos·tage me·ter *n.* a machine for printing prepaid postage and a postmark.

pos·tage stamp *n.* an official stamp affixed to or imprinted on a letter, etc., indicating the amount of postage paid.

post·al /póst'l/ *adj.* **1** of the post office or mail. **2** by mail. □□ **post·al·ly** *adv.*

pos·tal code *n.* **1** = POSTCODE. **2** a Canadian system equivalent to a postcode postage meter or ZIP code.

post·card /póstkaard/ *n.* a card, often with a photograph on one side, for sending a short message by mail without an envelope.

post·date *v.* & *n.* • *v.tr.* /póstdáyt/ affix or assign a date later than the actual one to (a document, event, etc.). • *n.* /póstdayt/ such a date.

post·er /póstər/ *n.* **1** a placard in a public place. **2** a large printed picture. **3** *Brit.* a billposter.

pos·te·ri·or /posteéreeər, pō–/ *adj.* & *n.* • *adj.* **1** later; coming after in series, order, or time. **2** situated at the back. • *n.* (in *sing.* or *pl.*) the buttocks. □□ **pos·te·ri·or·i·ty** /–áwritee, –ór–/ *n.* **pos·te·ri·or·ly** *adv.*

pos·ter·i·ty /postéritee/ *n.* **1** all succeeding generations. **2** the descendants of a person.

post·grad·u·ate /pōstgrájōōət/ *adj.* & *n.* • *adj.* **1** (of a course of study) carried on after taking a high school or college degree. **2** of or relating to students following this course of study (*postgraduate fees*). • *n.* a postgraduate student.

post-haste *adv.* with great speed.

post·hu·mous /póschəməs/ *adj.* **1** occurring after death. **2** (of a child) born after the death of its father. **3** (of a book, etc.) published after the author's death. □□ **post·hu·mous·ly** *adv.*

Post·im·pres·sion·ism /póstimpréshənizəm/ *n.* artistic aims and methods developed as a reaction against impressionism and intending to express the individual artist's conception of the objects represented rather than the ordinary observer's view. □□ **Post·im·pres·sion·ist** *n.* & *adj.* **Post·im·pres·sion·is·tic** *adj.*

post·in·dus·tri·al /póstindústreeəl/ *adj.* relating to or characteristic of a society or economy that no longer relies on heavy industry.

post·man /póstmən/ *n.* (*pl.* **-men**; *fem.* **postwoman**, *pl.* **-women**) a person who is employed to deliver and collect letters, etc.

post·mark /póstmaark/ *n.* & *v.* • *n.* an official mark stamped on a letter, esp. one giving the place, date, etc., of sending or arrival, and serving to cancel the stamp. • *v.tr.* mark (an envelope, etc.) with this.

post·mas·ter /póstmastər/ *n.* the person in charge of a post office.

post·mod·ern /pṓstmódərn/ *adj.* (in literature, architecture, the arts, etc.) denoting a movement reacting against modern tendencies, esp. by drawing attention to former conventions. ▫▫ **post·mod·ern·ism** *n.* **post·mod·ern·ist** *n.* & *adj.*

post·mor·tem /pōstmáwrtəm/ *n., adv., & adj.* •*n.* **1** (in full **postmortem examination**) an examination made after death, esp. to determine its cause. **2** *colloq.* a discussion analysing the course and result of a game, election, etc. •*adv.* & adj. after death.

post·na·tal /pṓstnáyt'l/ *adj.* characteristic of or relating to the period after childbirth.

post·nup·tial /pṓstnúpshəl/ *adj.* after marriage.

Post Of·fice *n.* **1** the public department or corporation responsible for postal services and (in some countries) telecommunication. **2** (**post office**) a room or building where postal business is carried on.

post·paid /pōstpáyd/ *adj.* on which postage has been paid.

post·pone /pōstpṓn, pəspṓn/ *v.tr.* cause or arrange (an event, etc.) to take place at a later time. ▫▫ **post·pon·a·ble** *adj.* **post·pone·ment** *n.* **post·pon·er** *n.*

post·script /pṓstskript, pṓskript/ *n.* **1** an additional paragraph or remark, usu. at the end of a letter after the signature and introduced by 'PS.' **2** any additional information, action, etc.

pos·tu·lant /póschələnt/ *n.* a candidate, esp. for admission into a religious order.

pos·tu·late *v.* & *n.* •*v.tr.* /póschəlayt/ **1** (often foll. by *that* + clause) assume as a necessary condition, esp. as a basis for reasoning; take for granted. **2** claim. **3** (in ecclesiastical law) nominate or elect to a higher rank. •*n.* /póschələt/ **1** a thing postulated. **2** a fundamental prerequisite or condition. **3** *Math.* an assumption used as a basis for mathematical reasoning. ▫▫ **pos·tu·la·tion** /–láyshən/ *n.* **pos·tu·la·tor** *n.*

pos·ture /póschər/ *n.* & *v.* •*n.* **1** the relative position of parts, esp. of the body (*in a reclining posture*). **2** carriage or bearing (*improved by good posture and balance*). **3** a mental or spiritual attitude or condition. **4** the condition or state (of affairs, etc.) (*in more diplomatic postures*). •*v.* **1** *intr.* assume a mental or physical attitude, esp. for effect (*inclined to strut and posture*). **2** *tr.* pose (a person). ▫▫ **pos·tur·al** *adj.* **pos·tur·er** *n.*

post·war /pṓstwáwr/ *adj.* occurring or existing after a war (esp. the most recent major war).

po·sy /pṓzee/ *n.* (*pl.* **-sies**) a small bunch of flowers.

pot[1] /pot/ *n.* & *v.* •*n.* **1** a vessel, usu. rounded, of ceramic ware or metal or glass for holding liquids or solids or for cooking in. **2** a coffeepot, flowerpot, teapot, etc. **3** a drinking vessel of pewter, etc. **4** the contents of a pot (*ate a whole pot of jam*). **5** the total amount of the bet in a game, etc. **6** *colloq.* a large sum (*pots of money*). **7** *Brit. sl.* a vessel given as a prize in an athletic contest, esp. a silver cup. **8** = POTBELLY 1. •*v.tr.* (**potted, potting**) **1** place in a pot. **2** (usu. as **potted** *adj.*) preserve in a sealed pot (*potted shrimps*). **3** *Brit.* sit (a young child) on a chamber pot. **4** *Brit.* pocket (a ball) in billiards, etc. **5** shoot at, hit, or kill (an animal) with a potshot. **6** seize or secure. ▫ **go to pot** *colloq.* deteriorate; be ruined. ▫▫ **pot·ful** *n.* (*pl.* **-fuls**).

pot[2] /pot/ *n. sl.* marijuana.

po·ta·ble /pṓtəbəl/ *adj.* drinkable. ▫▫ **po·ta·bil·i·ty** /–bílitee/ *n.*

po·tage /pōtaázh/ *n.* thick soup.

pot·ash /pótash/ *n.* an alkaline potassium compound, usu. potassium carbonate or hydroxide.

po·tas·si·um /pətáseeəm/ *n. Chem.* a soft silvery white metallic element occurring naturally in seawater and various minerals, an essential element for living organisms, and forming many useful compounds used industrially. ¶ Symb.: **K.** ▫▫ **po·tas·sic** *adj.*

po·ta·tion /pōtáyshən/ *n.* **1** a drink. **2** the act or an instance of drinking. **3** (usu. in *pl.*) the act or an instance of tippling. ▫▫ **po·ta·to·ry** /pṓtətawree/ *adj.*

po·ta·to /pətáytō/ *n.* (*pl.* **-toes**) **1** a starchy plant tuber that is cooked and used for food. **2** the plant, *Solanum tuberosum*, bearing this. **3** = SWEET POTATO.

pot·bel·ly /pótbelee/ *n.* (*pl.* **-lies**) **1** a protruding stomach. **2** a person with this. **3** a small bulbous stove. ▫▫ **pot·bel·lied** *adj.*

pot·boil·er /pótboylər/ *n.* **1** a work of literature or art done merely to make the writer or artist a living. **2** a writer or artist who does this.

po·tent /pṓt'nt/ *adj.* **1** powerful; strong. **2** (of a reason) cogent; forceful. **3** (of a male) capable of sexual erection or orgasm. **4** *literary* mighty. ▫▫ **po·tence** *n.* **po·ten·cy** *n.* **po·tent·ly** *adv.*

po·ten·tate /pṓt'ntayt/ *n.* a monarch or ruler.

po·ten·tial /pəténshəl/ *adj.* & *n.* •*adj.* capable of coming into being or action; latent. •*n.* **1** the capacity for use or development; possibility (*achieved its highest potential*). **2** usable resources. **3** *Physics* the quantity determining the energy of mass in a gravitational field or of charge in an electric field. ▫▫ **po·ten·ti·al·i·ty** /–sheeálitee/ *n.* **po·ten·tial·ize** *v.tr.* **po·ten·tial·ly** *adv.*

po·ten·tial dif·fer·ence *n.* the difference of electric potential between two points.

po·ten·ti·ate /pəténsheeayt/ *v.tr.* **1** make more powerful, esp. increase the effectiveness of (a drug). **2** make possible.

pot·head /pót-hed/ *n. sl.* a person who smokes marijuana frequently.

poth·er /póthər/ *n.* & *v.* •*n.* a noise; commotion; fuss. •*v.* **1** *tr.* fluster; worry. **2** *intr.* make a fuss.

pot·hole /pót-hōl/ *n.* & *v.* •*n.* **1** *Geol.* a deep hole or system of caves and underground riverbeds formed by the erosion of rock esp. by the action of water. **2** a deep hole in the ground or a riverbed. **3** a hole in a road surface caused by wear, weather, or subsidence. •*v.intr. Brit.* explore potholes. ▫▫ **pot·holed** *adj.* **pot·hol·er** *n.* **pot·hol·ing** *n.*

po·tion /pṓshən/ *n.* a liquid medicine, drug, poison, etc.

pot·luck /pótluk/ *n.* **1** whatever (hospitality, food, etc.) is available. **2** a meal to which each guest brings a dish to share.

pot·pie /pótpī/ *n.* a pie of meat, vegetables, etc., with a crust baked in a pot or deep-dish pie plate.

pot·pour·ri /pṓpŏŏrée/ *n.* **1** a mixture of dried petals and spices used to perfume a room, etc. **2** a musical or literary medley.

pot roast *n.* a piece of meat cooked slowly in a covered dish. ▫▫ **pot-roast** *v.tr.*

pot·sherd /pótshərd/ *n.* a broken piece of pottery, esp. one found on an archaeological site.

pot·shot /pótshot/ *n.* **1** a random shot aimed at someone or something with no chance of self-defense. **2** a shot at a bird or other animal to kill it for food, without regard to the rules of the sport. **3** a criticism, esp. a random or unfounded one.

pot·ter /pótər/ *n.* a maker of ceramic vessels.

pot·ter's field *n.* a burial place for paupers, strangers, etc.

pot·ter's wheel *n.* a horizontal revolving disk to carry clay for making pots.

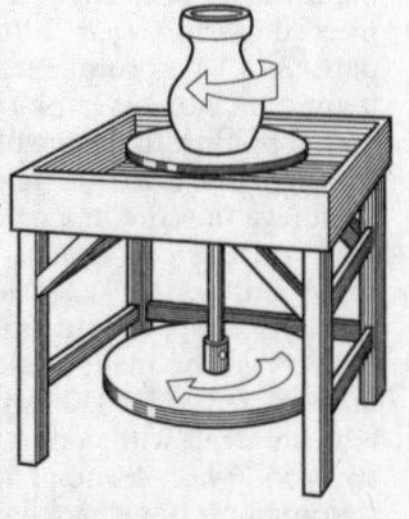

potter's wheel

pot·ter·y /pótəree/ *n.* (*pl.* **-ies**) **1** vessels, etc., made of fired clay. **2** a potter's work. **3** a potter's workshop.

pot·ting shed /póting/ *n.* a building in which plants are potted and tools, etc., are stored.

pot·ty /pótee/ *n.* (*pl.* **-ties**) *colloq.* a small pot for toilet-training a child.

pouch /powch/ *n.* & *v.* • *n.* **1** a small bag or detachable outside pocket. **2** a baggy area of skin underneath the eyes, etc. **3 a** a pocketlike receptacle in which marsupials carry their young during lactation. **b** any of several similar structures in various animals, e.g., in the cheeks of rodents. **4** a soldier's ammunition bag. **5** a lockable bag for mail or dispatches. **6** *Bot.* a baglike cavity, esp. the seed vessel, in a plant. • *v.tr.* put or make into a pouch. ▫▫ **pouched** *adj.* **pouch·y** *adj.*

poul·tice /pṓltis/ *n.* & *v.* • *n.* a soft medicated and usu. heated mass applied to the body and kept in place with muslin, etc., for relieving soreness and inflammation. • *v.tr.* apply a poultice to.

poul·try /pṓltree/ *n.* domestic fowls (ducks, geese, turkeys, chickens, etc.), esp. as a source of food.

pounce /powns/ *v.* & *n.* • *v.intr.* **1** spring or swoop, esp. as in capturing prey. **2** (often foll. by *on, upon*) **a** make a sudden attack. **b** seize eagerly upon an object, remark, etc. • *n.* **1** the act or an instance of pouncing. **2** the claw or talon of a bird of prey. ▫▫ **pounc·er** *n.*

pound[1] /pownd/ *n.* **1** a unit of weight equal to 16 oz. avoirdupois (0.4536 kg), or 12 oz. troy (0.3732 kg). **2** (in full **pound sterling**) (*pl.* same or **pounds**) the chief monetary unit of the UK and several other countries.

pound[2] /pownd/ *v.* & *n.* • *v.* **1** *tr.* **a** crush or beat with repeated heavy blows. **b** pummel, esp. with the fists. **c** grind to a powder or pulp. **2** *intr.* (foll. by *at, on*) deliver heavy blows or gunfire. **3** *intr.* (foll. by *along*, etc.) make one's way heavily or clumsily. **4** *intr.* (of the heart) beat heavily. • *n.* a heavy blow or thump; the sound of this. ▫ **pound out** produce with or as if with heavy blows. ▫▫ **pound·er** *n.*

pound[3] /pownd/ *n.* **1** an enclosure where stray animals or officially removed vehicles are kept until redeemed. **2** a place of confinement.

pound·age /pówndij/ *n.* **1 a** weight in pounds. **b** a person's weight, esp. that which is regarded as excess. **2** *Brit.* a commission or fee of so much per pound sterling or weight. **3** *Brit.* a percentage of the total earnings of a business, paid as wages.

pound cake *n.* a rich cake orig. containing a pound (or equal weights) of each chief ingredient.

pound·er /pówndər/ *n.* (usu. in *comb.*) **1** a thing or person weighing a specified number of pounds (*a five-pounder*). **2** a gun carrying a shell of a specified number of pounds. **3** a thing worth, or a person possessing, so many pounds sterling.

pound of flesh *n.* any legitimate but crippling demand.

pound sign *n.* **1** the sign #. **2** the sign £, representing a pound sterling.

pour /pawr/ *v.* **1** *intr.* & *tr.* (usu. foll. by *down, out, over*, etc.) flow or cause to flow esp. downwards in a stream or shower. **2** *tr.* dispense (a drink) by pouring. **3** *intr.* (of rain, or with *it* as subject) fall heavily. **4** *intr.* (usu. foll. by *in, out*, etc.) come or go in profusion or rapid succession (*the crowd poured out; letters poured in*). **5** *tr.* discharge or send freely (*poured forth arrows*). **6** *tr.* (often foll. by *out*) utter at length or in a rush (*poured out their story; poured scorn on my attempts*). ▫ **it never rains but it pours** misfortunes rarely come singly. **pour oil on the waters** (or **on troubled waters**) calm a disagreement or disturbance, esp. with conciliatory words. ▫▫ **pour·a·ble** *adj.* **pour·er** *n.*

pout /powt/ *v.* & *n.* • *v.* **1** *intr.* **a** push the lips forward as an expression of displeasure or sulking. **b** (of the lips) be pushed forward. **2** *tr.* push (the lips) forward in pouting. • *n.* **1** such an action or expression. **2** (**the pouts**) a fit of sulking. ▫▫ **pout·er** *n.* **pout·ing·ly** *adv.* **pout·y** *adj.*

pov·er·ty /póvərtee/ *n.* **1** the state of being poor; want of the necessities of life. **2** (often foll. by *of, in*) scarcity or lack. **3** inferiority; poorness; meanness. **4** *Eccl.* renunciation of the right to individual ownership of property esp. by a member of a religious order.

pov·er·ty-strick·en *adj.* extremely poor.

POW *abbr.* prisoner of war.

pow /pow/ *int.* expressing the sound of a blow or explosion.

pow·der /pówdər/ *n.* & *v.* • *n.* **1** a substance in the form of fine dry particles. **2** a medicine or cosmetic in this form. **3** = GUNPOWDER. • *v.tr.* **1 a** apply powder to. **b** sprinkle or decorate with or as with powder. **2** (esp. as **powdered** *adj.*) reduce to a fine powder (*powdered milk*). ▫ **keep one's powder dry** be cautious and alert. **take a powder** *sl.* depart quickly. ▫▫ **pow·der·y** *adj.*

pow·der blue *n.* pale blue.

pow·der keg *n.* **1** a barrel of gunpowder. **2** a dangerous or volatile situation.

pow·der puff *n.* a soft pad for applying powder to the skin, esp. the face.

pow·der room *n.* a women's toilet in a public building.

pow·er /powər/ *n.* & *v.* • *n.* **1** the ability to do or act (*has the power to change color*). **2** a particular faculty of body or mind (*lost the power of speech*). **3 a** government, influence, or authority. **b** political or social ascendancy or control. **4** authorization; delegated authority (*power of attorney; police powers*). **5** (often foll. by *over*) personal ascendancy. **6** an influential person, group, or organization (*the press is a power in the land*). **7 a** military strength. **b** a nation having international influence, esp. based on military strength (*the leading powers*). **8** vigor; energy. **9** an active property or function (*has a high heating power*). **10** *colloq.* a large number or amount (*has done me a power of good*). **11** the capacity for exerting mechanical force or doing work (*horsepower*). **12** mechanical or electrical energy as distinct from hand labor (often *attrib.*: *power tools; power steering*). **13 a** a public supply of (esp. electrical) energy. **b** a particular source or form of energy (*hydroelectric power*). **14** a mechanical force applied, e.g., by means of a lever. **15** *Physics* the rate of energy output. **16** the product obtained when a number is multiplied by itself a certain number of times (*2 to the power of 3 = 8*). **17** the magnifying capacity of a lens. **18 a** a deity. **b** (in *pl.*) the sixth order of the ninefold celestial hierarchy. • *v.tr.* **1** supply with mechanical or electrical energy. **2** (foll. by *up, down*) increase or decrease the power supplied to (a device); switch on or off. ▫ **the powers that be** those in authority. ▫▫ **pow·ered** *adj.* (also in *comb.*).

pow·er·boat /pówərbōt/ *n.* a powerful motorboat.

pow·er·ful /pówərfo͝ol/ *adj.* **1** having much power or strength. **2** politically or socially influential. ▫▫ **pow·er·ful·ly** *adv.* **pow·er·ful·ness** *n.*

pow·er·house /pówərhows/ *n.* **1** = POWER PLANT. **2** a person or thing of great energy.

pow·er·less /pówərlis/ *adj.* **1** without power or strength. **2** (often foll. by *to* + infin.) wholly unable (*powerless to help*). ▫▫ **pow·er·less·ly** *adv.* **pow·er·less·ness** *n.*

pow·er of at·tor·ney *n.* the authority to act for another person in legal or financial matters.

pow·er plant *n.* **1** (also **power station**) a facility producing esp. electrical power. **2** a source of power, as an engine.

pow•er play *n.* **1** tactics involving the concentration of players at a particular point. **2** similar tactics in business, politics, etc., involving a concentration of resources, effort, etc. **3** *Ice Hockey* situation in which one team has an extra skater owing to a penalty on the opposing team.

pow•er-shar•ing *n.* a policy agreed between parties or within a coalition to share responsibility for decision making and political action.

pow•wow /pów-wow/ *n. & v.* • *n.* a conference or meeting for discussion (orig. among Native Americans). • *v.tr.* hold a powwow.

pox /poks/ *n.* **1** any virus disease producing a rash of pimples that become pus-filled and leave pockmarks on healing. **2** *colloq.* = SYPHILIS.

pp *abbr.* pianissimo.

pp. *abbr.* pages.

p.p.b. *abbr.* parts per billion.

ppd. *abbr.* **1** postpaid. **2** prepaid.

p.p.m. *abbr.* parts per million.

PPS *abbr.* additional postscript.

PR *abbr.* **1** public relations. **2** Puerto Rico. **3** proportional representation.

Pr *symb. Chem.* the element praseodymium.

pr. *abbr.* pair.

prac•ti•ca•ble /práktikəbəl/ *adj.* **1** that can be done or used. **2** possible in practice. □□ **prac•ti•ca•bil•i•ty** /–bílitee/ *n.* **prac•ti•ca•ble•ness** *n.* **prac•ti•ca•bly** *adv.*

▶See note at PRACTICAL.

prac•ti•cal /práktikəl/ *adj. & n.* • *adj.* **1** of or concerned with practice or use rather than theory. **2** suited to use or action; designed mainly to fulfill a function (*practical shoes*). **3** (of a person) inclined to action rather than speculation; able to make things function well. **4 a** that is such in effect though not nominally (*for all practical purposes*). **b** virtual (*in practical control*). **5** feasible; concerned with what is actually possible (*practical politics*). • *n. Brit.* a practical examination or lesson. □□ **prac•ti•cal•i•ty** /–kálitee/ *n.* (*pl.* **-ties**). **prac•ti•cal•ness** *n.*

▶**Practical** and **practicable** are sometimes confused. **Practical** means 'concerning practice,' that is, 'useful; functional.' **Practicable** comes from *practice*, meaning 'able to be practiced,' or 'able to be done; possible.' Some things—especially ideas—can be both: Nuclear rockets may be both practical (that is, there is something to be gained from developing them) and practicable (that is, they may be possible).

prac•ti•cal joke *n.* a humorous trick played on a person.

prac•ti•cal•ly /práktiklee/ *adv.* **1** virtually; almost (*practically nothing*). **2** in a practical way.

prac•tice /práktis/ *n. & v.* • *n.* **1** habitual action or performance (*the practice of teaching*; *makes a practice of saving*). **2** a habit or custom (*has been my regular practice*). **3 a** repeated exercise in an activity requiring the development of skill (*to sing well needs much practice*). **b** a session of this (*time for target practice*). **4** action or execution as opposed to theory. **5** the professional work or business of a doctor, lawyer, etc. (*has a practice in town*). **6** an established method of legal procedure. **7** procedure generally, esp. of a specified kind (*bad practice*). • *v.tr. & intr.* (also *Brit.* **practise**) **1** *tr.* perform habitually; carry out in action (*practice the same method*; *practice what you preach*). **2** *tr. &* (foll. by *in, on*) *intr.* do repeatedly as an exercise to improve a skill; exercise oneself in or on (an activity requiring skill) (*practice your reading*). **3** *tr.* (as **practiced** *adj.*) experienced, expert (*a practiced liar*). **4** *tr.* **a** pursue or be engaged in (a profession, religion, etc.). **b** (as **practicing** *adj.*) currently active or engaged in (a profession or activity) (*a practicing Christian*; *a practicing lawyer*). **5** *intr.* (foll. by *on, upon*) take advantage of; impose upon. **6** *intr. archaic* scheme; contrive (*when first we practice to deceive*). □ **in practice 1** when actually applied; in reality. **2** skillfull because of recent exercise in a particular pursuit. **out of practice** lacking a former skill from lack of recent practice. **put into practice** actually apply (an idea, method, etc.).

prac•ti•tion•er /praktíshənər/ *n.* a person practicing a profession, esp. medicine (*general practitioner*).

prae- /pree/ *prefix* = PRE- (esp. in words regarded as Latin or relating to Roman antiquity).

prae•ci•pe /préesipee, prés;n–/ *n.* **1** a writ demanding action or an explanation of inaction. **2** an order requesting a writ.

prae•sid•i•um var. of PRESIDIUM.

prae•tor /préetər/ *n.* (also **pre•tor**) *Rom.Hist.* each of two ancient Roman magistrates ranking below consul. □□ **prae•to•ri•al** /–tóreeəl/ *adj.* **prae•tor•ship** *n.*

prae•to•ri•an /preetáwreeən/ *adj. & n.* (also **pre•to•ri•an**) *Rom.Hist.* • *adj.* of or having the powers of a praetor. • *n.* a man of praetorian rank.

prae•to•ri•an guard *n.* the bodyguard of the Roman emperor.

prag•mat•ic /pragmátik/ *adj.* **1** dealing with matters with regard to their practical requirements or consequences. **2** treating the facts of history with reference to their practical lessons. **3** *hist.* of or relating to the affairs of a state. **4** (also **prag•mat•i•cal**) **a** concerning pragmatism. **b** meddlesome. **c** dogmatic. □□ **prag•mat•i•cal•i•ty** /–tikálitee/ *n.* **prag•mat•i•cal•ly** *adv.*

prag•mat•ics /pragmátiks/ *n.pl.* (usu. treated as *sing.*) the branch of linguistics dealing with language in use.

prag•ma•tism /prágmətizəm/ *n.* **1** a pragmatic attitude or procedure. **2** a philosophy that evaluates assertions solely by their practical consequences and bearing on human interests. □□ **prag•ma•tist** *n.* **prag•ma•tis•tic** /–tístik/ *adj.*

prag•ma•tize /prágmətīz/ *v.tr.* **1** represent as real. **2** rationalize (a myth).

prai•rie /práiree/ *n.* a large area of usu. treeless grassland esp. in central N. America.

prai•rie dog *n.* any central or western N. American rodent of the genus *Cynomys*, living in burrows and making a barking sound.

prai•rie schoon•er *n.* a covered wagon used by the 19th-c. pioneers in crossing the prairies.

praise /prayz/ *v. & n.* • *v.tr.* **1** express warm approval or admiration of. **2** glorify (God) in words. • *n.* the act or an instance of praising; commendation (*won high praise*; *were loud in their praises*). □ **praise be!** an exclamation of pious gratitude. **sing the praises of** commend (a person) highly. □□ **praise•ful** *adj.* **prais•er** *n.*

praise•wor•thy /práyzwərthee/ *adj.* worthy of praise; commendable. □□ **praise•wor•thi•ly** *adv.* **praise•wor•thi•ness** *n.*

pra•line /práaleen, práy–/ *n.* any of several candies made with almonds, pecans, or other nuts and sugar.

pram /pram/ *n. Brit.* a baby carriage.

prance /prans/ *v. & n.* • *v.intr.* **1** (of a horse) move with high springy steps. **2** (of a person) walk around with arrogant or exaggerated movements. • *n.* an act or instance of prancing. □□ **pranc•er** *n.*

pran•di•al /prándeeəl/ *adj.* of a meal, usu. dinner.

prang /prang/ *v. & n. Brit. sl.* • *v.tr.* **1** crash or damage (an aircraft or vehicle). **2** bomb (a target) successfully. • *n.* the act or an instance of pranging.

prank /prangk/ *n.* a practical joke; a piece of mischief. □□ **prank•ful** *adj.* **prank•ish** *adj.* **prank•some** *adj.*

prank•ster /prángkstər/ *n.* a person fond of playing pranks.

prate /prayt/ *v. & n.* • *v.* **1** *intr.* chatter; talk too much. **2** *intr.* talk foolishly or irrelevantly. **3** *tr.* tell or say in a prating manner. •*n.* prating; idle talk. ▫▫ **prat·er** *n.* **prat·ing** *adj.*

prat·fall /prátfawl/ *n. sl.* **1** a fall on the buttocks. **2** a humiliating failure.

prat·tle /prát'l/ *v. & n.* •*v.intr. & tr.* chatter or say in a childish or inconsequential way. •*n.* **1** childish chatter. **2** inconsequential talk. ▫▫ **prat·tler** *n.* **prat·tling** *adj.*

prawn /prawn/ *n. & v.* •*n.* any of various marine crustaceans, resembling a shrimp but usu. larger. •*v.intr.* fish for prawns.

pray /pray/ *v.* (often foll. by *for* or *to* + infin. or *that* + clause) **1** *intr.* (often foll. by *to*) say prayers (to God, etc.); make devout supplication. **2 a** *tr.* entreat; beseech. **b** *tr. & intr.* ask earnestly (*prayed to be released*). **3** *tr.* (as *imper.*) *old-fashioned* please (*pray tell me*).

prayer /prair/ *n.* **1 a** a solemn request or thanksgiving to God or an object of worship (*say a prayer*). **b** a formula or form of words used in praying (*the Lord's prayer*). **c** the act of praying (*be at prayer*). **d** a religious service consisting largely of prayers (*morning prayers*). **2 a** an entreaty to a person. **b** a thing entreated or prayed for. ▫ **not have a prayer** *colloq.* have no chance (of success, etc.).

prayer·ful /práirfo͝ol/ *adj.* **1** (of a person) given to praying; devout. **2** (of speech, actions, etc.) characterized by or expressive of prayer. ▫▫ **prayer·ful·ly** *adv.* **prayer·ful·ness** *n.*

pray·ing man·tis *n.* a mantis, *Mantis religiosa*, that holds its forelegs in a position suggestive of hands folded in prayer, while waiting to pounce on its prey.

preach /preech/ *v.* **1 a** *intr.* deliver a sermon or religious address. **b** *tr.* deliver (a sermon); proclaim or expound. **2** *intr.* give moral advice in an obtrusive way. **3** *tr.* advocate or inculcate (a quality or practice, etc.).

preach·er /préechər/ *n.* a person who preaches, esp. a minister of religion.

preach·i·fy /préechifī/ *v.intr.* (**-fies, -fied**) *colloq.* preach or moralize tediously.

preach·y /préechee/ *adj.* (**preachier, preachiest**) *colloq.* inclined to preach or moralize. ▫▫ **preach·i·ness** *n.*

pre·am·ble /prée-ámbəl/ *n.* **1** a preliminary statement or introduction. **2** the introductory part of a constitution, statute, or deed, etc. ▫▫ **pre·am·bu·lar** /–ámbyo͞olər/ *adj.*

pre·amp /prée-ámp/ *n.* = PREAMPLIFIER.

pre·am·pli·fi·er /prée-ámplifiər/ *n.* an electronic device that amplifies a very weak signal (e.g., from a microphone or pickup) and transmits it to a main amplifier. ▫▫ **pre·am·pli·fied** *adj.*

pre·ar·range /préeəráynj/ *v.tr.* arrange beforehand. ▫▫ **pre·ar·range·ment** *n.*

pre·a·tom·ic /préeətómik/ *adj.* existing or occurring before the use of atomic weapons or energy.

Pre·cam·bri·an /préekámbreeən/ *adj. & n. Geol.* •*adj.* of or relating to the earliest era of geological time from the formation of the earth to the first forms of life. •*n.* this era.

pre·can·cer·ous /preekánsrəs, –kántsər–/ *adj.* having the tendency to develop into a cancer. ▫▫ **pre·can·cer·ous·ly** *adv.*

pre·car·i·ous /prikáireeəs/ *adj.* **1** uncertain; dependent on chance (*makes a precarious living*). **2** insecure; perilous (*precarious health*). ▫▫ **pre·car·i·ous·ly** *adv.* **pre·car·i·ous·ness** *n.*

pre·cast /préekást/ *adj.* (of concrete) cast in its final shape before positioning.

prec·a·tive /prékətiv/ *adj.* (also **precatory** /–tawree/) (of a word or form) expressing a wish or request.

pre·cau·tion /prikáwshən/ *n.* **1** an action taken beforehand to avoid risk or ensure a good result. **2** (in *pl.*) *colloq.* the use of contraceptives. **3** caution exercised beforehand; prudent foresight. ▫▫ **pre·cau·tion·ar·y** *adj.*

pre·cede /priséed/ *v.tr.* **1 a** (often as **preceding** *adj.*) come or go before in time, order, importance, etc. (*preceding generations*). **b** walk, etc., in front of (*preceded by our guide*). **2** (foll. by *by*) cause to be preceded (*must precede this measure by milder ones*).

prec·e·dence /présidəns, priséed'ns/ *n.* (also **prec·e·den·cy**) **1** priority in time, order, or importance, etc. **2** the right to precede others on formal occasions. ▫ **take precedence** (often foll. by *over, of*) have priority (over).

prec·e·dent *n. & adj.* •*n.* /président/ a previous case or legal decision, etc., taken as a guide for subsequent cases or as a justification. •*adj.* /priséed'nt, présidənt/ preceding in time, order, importance, etc. ▫▫ **prec·e·dent·ly** /présidəntlee/ *adv.*

pre·cept /préesept/ *n.* **1** a command; a rule of conduct. **2 a** moral instruction (*example is better than precept*). **b** a general or proverbial rule; a maxim. **3** *Law* a writ, order, or warrant. ▫▫ **pre·cep·tive** /–séptiv/ *adj.*

pre·cep·tor /priséptər/ *n.* a teacher or instructor. ▫▫ **pre·cep·to·ri·al** /préeseptawreeəl/ *adj.* **pre·cep·tor·ship** *n.* **pre·cep·tress** /–tris/ *n.*

pre·ces·sion /priséshən/ *n.* the slow movement of the axis of a spinning body around another axis. ▫▫ **pre·ces·sion·al** *adj.*

pre·cinct /préesingkt/ *n.* **1** an enclosed or specially designated area. **2** (in *pl.*) **a** the surrounding area or environs. **b** the boundaries. **3 a** a subdivision of a county, city, etc., for police or electoral purposes. **b** a police station in such a subdivision. **c** (in *pl.*) a neighborhood.

pre·cious /préshəs/ *adj. & adv.* •*adj.* **1** of great value or worth. **2** beloved; much prized (*precious memories*). **3** affectedly refined, esp. in language or manner. **4** *colloq.* often *iron.* **a** considerable (*a precious lot you know about it*). **b** expressing contempt or disdain (*you can keep your precious flowers*). •*adv. colloq.* extremely; very (*had precious little left*). ▫▫ **pre·cious·ly** *adv.* **pre·cious·ness** *n.*

pre·cious met·als *n.pl.* gold, silver, and platinum.

prec·i·pice /présipis/ *n.* **1** a vertical or steep face of a rock, cliff, mountain, etc. **2** a dangerous situation.

pre·cip·i·tant /prisípit'nt/ *adj. & n.* •*adj.* = PRECIPITATE *adj.* •*n. Chem.* a substance that causes another substance to precipitate. ▫▫ **pre·cip·i·tance** *n.* **pre·cip·i·tan·cy** *n.*

pre·cip·i·tate *v., adj., & n.* •*v.tr.* /prisípitayt/ **1** hasten the occurrence of; cause to occur prematurely. **2** (foll. by *into*) send rapidly into a certain state or condition (*were precipitated into war*). **3** throw down headlong. **4** *Chem.* cause (a substance) to be deposited in solid form from a solution. **5** *Physics* **a** cause (dust, etc.) to be deposited from the air on a surface. **b** condense (vapor) into drops and so deposit it. •*adj.* /prisípitət/ **1** headlong; violently hurried (*precipitate departure*). **2** (of a person or act) hasty; rash; inconsiderate. •*n.* /prisípitət/ **1** *Chem.* a substance precipitated from a solution. **2** *Physics* moisture condensed from vapor by cooling and depositing, e.g., rain or dew. ▫▫ **pre·cip·i·ta·ble** /–sípitəbəl/ *adj.* **pre·cip·i·ta·bil·i·ty** *n.* **pre·cip·i·tate·ly** /–sípitətlee/ *adv.* **pre·cip·i·tate·ness** /–sípitətnəs/ *n.* **pre·cip·i·ta·tor** *n.*

▶The adjective **precipitate** means 'sudden, hasty'; *a precipitate decision, precipitate flight by the fugitive.* **Precipitous** means 'steep': *precipitous slope of the moutain, precipitous decline in stock prices.*

pre·cip·i·ta·tion /prisípitáyshən/ *n.* **1** the act of precipitating or the process of being precipitated. **2** rash haste. **3 a** rain or snow, etc., falling to the ground. **b** a quantity of this.

pre·cip·i·tous /prisípitəs/ *adj.* **1 a** of or like a precipice. **b** dangerously steep. **2** = PRECIPITATE *adj.* ▫▫ **pre·cip·i·tous·ly** *adv.* **pre·cip·i·tous·ness** *n.*

▶See note at PRECIPITATE.

pré·cis /práysee/ *n.* & *v.* •*n.* (*pl.* same /–seez/) a summary or abstract, esp. of a text or speech. •*v.tr.* (**pré·cises** /–seez/; **précised** /–seed/; **précising** /–seeing/) make a précis of.

pre·cise /prisís/ *adj.* **1 a** accurately expressed. **b** definite; exact. **2 a** punctilious; scrupulous in being exact, observing rules, etc. **b** often *derog.* rigid; fastidious. **3** identical; exact (*at that precise moment*). ▫▫ **pre·cise·ness** *n.*

pre·cise·ly /prisíslee/ *adv.* **1** in a precise manner; exactly. **2** (as a reply) quite so; as you say.

pre·ci·sion /prisízhən/ *n.* **1** the condition of being precise; accuracy. **2** the degree of refinement in measurement, etc. **3** (*attrib.*) marked by or adapted for precision (*precision instruments*). ▫▫ **pre·ci·sion·ism** *n.* **pre·ci·sion·ist** *n.*

pre·clin·i·cal /preéklínikəl/ *adj.* **1** of or relating to the first, chiefly theoretical, stage of a medical or dental education. **2** (of a stage in a disease) before symptoms can be identified.

pre·clude /priklóod/ *v.tr.* **1** (foll. by *from*) prevent; exclude (*precluded from taking part*). **2** make impossible; remove (*so as to preclude all doubt*). ▫▫ **pre·clu·sion** /–klóozhən/ *n.* **pre·clu·sive** /–klóosiv/ *adj.*

pre·co·cious /prikóshəs/ *adj.* **1** (of a person, esp. a child) prematurely developed in some faculty or characteristic. **2** (of an action, etc.) indicating such development. **3** (of a plant) flowering or fruiting early. ▫▫ **pre·co·cious·ly** *adv.* **pre·co·cious·ness** *n.* **pre·coc·i·ty** /–kósitee/ *n.*

pre·cog·ni·tion /preékogníshən/ *n.* (supposed) foreknowledge, esp. of a supernatural kind. ▫▫ **pre·cog·ni·tive** /–kógnitiv/ *adj.*

pre-Co·lum·bi·an /preékəlúmbeeən/ *adj.* before the arrival in America of Columbus.

pre·con·ceive /preékənseév/ *v.tr.* (esp. as **preconceived** *adj.*) form (an idea or opinion, etc.) beforehand; anticipate in thought.

pre·con·cep·tion /preékənsépshən/ *n.* **1** a preconceived idea. **2** a prejudice.

pre·con·di·tion /preékəndíshən/ *n.* & *v.* •*n.* a prior condition, that must be fulfilled before other things can be done. •*v.tr.* bring into a required condition beforehand.

pre·cur·sor /prikárser, preékar–/ *n.* **1 a** a forerunner. **b** a person who precedes in office, etc. **2** a harbinger. **3** a substance from which another is formed by decay or chemical reaction, etc.

pre·cur·so·ry /prikársəree/ *adj.* (also **pre·cur·sive** /–siv/) **1** preliminary; introductory. **2** (foll. by *of*) serving as a harbinger of.

pre·da·cious /pridáyshəs/ *adj.* (also **pre·da·ceous**) **1** (of an animal) predatory. **2** relating to such animals (*predacious instincts*). ▫▫ **pre·da·cious·ness** *n.* **pre·dac·i·ty** /–dásitee/ *n.*

pre·date /preédáyt/ *v.tr.* exist or occur at a date earlier than.

pre·da·tion /pridáyshən/ *n.* **1** (usu. in *pl.*) = DEPREDATION. **2** *Zool.* the natural preying of one animal on others.

pred·a·tor /prédətər/ *n.* **1** an animal naturally preying on others. **2** a predatory person, institution, etc.

pred·a·to·ry /prédətawree/ *adj.* **1** (of an animal) preying naturally upon others. **2** (of a nation, state, or individual) plundering or exploiting others. ▫▫ **pred·a·to·ri·ly** *adv.* **pred·a·to·ri·ness** *n.*

pre·de·cease /preédisees/ *v.* & *n.* •*v.tr.* die earlier than (another person). •*n.* a death preceding that of another.

pred·e·ces·sor /prédisesər, preé–/ *n.* **1** a former holder of an office or position with respect to a later holder (*my immediate predecessor*). **2** an ancestor. **3** a thing to which another has succeeded (*the new plan will share the fate of its predecessor*).

pre·des·ti·na·tion /preédestináyshən/ *n. Theol.* (as a belief or doctrine) the divine foreordaining of all that will happen, esp. with regard to the salvation of some and not others.

pre·des·tine /preédéstin/ *v.tr.* **1** determine beforehand. **2** ordain in advance by divine will or as if by fate.

pre·de·ter·mine /preéditármin/ *v.tr.* **1** determine or decree beforehand. **2** predestine. ▫▫ **pre·de·ter·min·a·ble** *adj.* **pre·de·ter·mi·nate** /–nət/ *adj.* **pre·de·ter·mi·na·tion** *n.*

pred·i·ca·ble /prédikəbəl/ *adj.* & *n.* •*adj.* that may be predicated or affirmed. •*n.* **1** a predicable thing. **2** (in *pl.*) *Logic* the five classes to which predicates belong: genus, species, difference, property, and accident. ▫▫ **pred·i·ca·bil·i·ty** *n.*

pre·dic·a·ment /pridíkəmənt/ *n.* **1** a difficult, unpleasant, or embarrassing situation. **2** *Philos.* a category in (esp. Aristotelian) logic.

pred·i·cant /prédikənt/ *adj.* & *n.* •*adj. hist.* (of a religious order) engaged in preaching. •*n. hist.* a predicant person, esp. a Dominican friar.

pred·i·cate *v.* & *n.* •*v.tr.* /prédikayt/ **1** assert or affirm as true or existent. **2** (foll. by *on*) found or base (a statement, etc.) on. •*n.* /–kət/ **1** *Gram.* what is said about the subject of a sentence, etc. (e.g., *went home* in *John went home*). **2** *Logic* **a** what is predicated. **b** what is affirmed or denied of the subject by means of the copula (e.g., *mortal* in *all men are mortal*). ▫▫ **pred·i·ca·tion** /–káyshən/ *n.*

pred·i·ca·tive /prédikaytiv/ *adj.* **1** *Gram.* (of an adjective or noun) forming or contained in the predicate, as *old* in *the dog is old* (but not in *the old dog*) and *house* in *there is a large house* (opp. ATTRIBUTIVE). **2** that predicates. ▫▫ **pred·i·ca·tive·ly** *adv.*

pre·dict /pridíkt/ *v.tr.* (often foll. by *that* + clause) make a statement about the future; foretell; prophesy. ▫▫ **pre·dic·tive** *adj.* **pre·dic·tive·ly** *adv.* **pre·dic·tor** *n.*

pre·dict·a·ble /pridíktəbəl/ *adj.* that can be predicted or is to be expected. ▫▫ **pre·dict·a·bil·i·ty** *n.* **pre·dict·a·bly** *adv.*

pre·dic·tion /pridíkshən/ *n.* **1** the art of predicting or the process of being predicted. **2** a thing predicted; a forecast.

pre·di·lec·tion /préd'lékshən, preé–/ *n.* (often foll. by *for*) a preference or special liking.

pre·dis·pose /preédispóz/ *v.tr.* **1** influence favorably in advance. **2** (foll. by *to*, or *to* + infin.) render liable or inclined beforehand. ▫▫ **pre·dis·po·si·tion** /–pəzíshən/ *n.*

pre·dom·i·nant /pridóminənt/ *adj.* **1** predominating. **2** being the strongest or main element. ▫▫ **pre·dom·i·nance** *n.* **pre·dom·i·nant·ly** *adv.*

pre·dom·i·nate /pridóminayt/ *v.intr.* **1** (foll. by *over*) have or exert control. **2** be superior. **3** be the strongest or main element; preponderate (*a garden in which dahlias predominate*).

pre·dom·i·nate·ly /pridóminətlee/ *adv.* = *predominantly* (see PREDOMINANT).

pree·mie /preémee/ *n. colloq.* an infant born prematurely.

pre·em·i·nent /preé-éminənt/ *adj.* **1** surpassing others. **2** outstanding; distinguished in some quality. **3** principal; leading; predominant. □□ **pre·em·i·nence** *n.* **pre·em·i·nent·ly** *adv.*

pre·empt /préé-émpt/ *v.* **1** *tr.* **a** forestall. **b** acquire or appropriate in advance. **2** *tr.* prevent (an attack) by disabling the enemy. **3** *tr.* obtain by preemption. □□ **pre·emp·tor** *n.* **pre·emp·to·ry** *adj.*

▶**Peremptory** and **preemptive** can be confused, as both involve stopping something. A **peremptory** act or statement is absolute; it cannot be denied: *Peremptory challenges kept two potential jurors from joining the panel.* A **preemptive** action is one taken before an adversary can act: *Preemptive air strikes stopped the enemy from launching the new warship.*

pre·emp·tion /préé-émpshən/ *n.* **1 a** the purchase or appropriation by one person or party before the opportunity is offered to others. **b** the right to purchase (esp. public land) in this way. **2** prior appropriation or acquisition.

pre·emp·tive /préé-émptiv/ *adj.* **1** preempting; serving to preempt. **2** (of military action) intended to prevent attack by disabling the enemy (*a preemptive strike*). **3** *Bridge* (of a bid) intended to be high enough to discourage further bidding.

▶See note at PEREMPTORY.

preen /preen/ *v.tr. & refl.* **1** (of a bird) straighten (the feathers or itself) with its beak. **2** (of a person) primp or admire (oneself, one's hair, clothes, etc.). **3** (often foll. by *on*) congratulate or pride (oneself). □□ **preen·er** *n.*

pre·ex·ist /préeigzíst/ *v.intr.* exist at an earlier time. □□ **pre·ex·ist·ence** *n.* **pre·ex·ist·ent** *adj.*

pre·fab /préefáb/ *n. colloq.* a prefabricated building, esp. a small house.

pre·fab·ri·cate /préefábrikayt/ *v.tr.* **1** manufacture sections of (a building, etc.) prior to their assembly on a site. **2** produce in an artificially standardized way. □□ **pre·fab·ri·ca·tion** /–brikáyshən/ *n.*

pref·ace /préfəs/ *n. & v.* • *n.* **1** an introduction to a book stating its subject, scope, etc. **2** the preliminary part of a speech. **3** *Eccl.* the introduction to the central part of a Eucharistic service. • *v.tr.* **1** (foll. by *with*) introduce or begin (a speech or event) (*prefaced my remarks with a warning*). **2** provide (a book, etc.) with a preface. **3** (of an event, etc.) lead up to (another). □□ **pref·a·to·ri·al** /–fətáwreeəl/ *adj.* **pref·a·to·ry** /–fətawree/ *adj.*

pre·fect /préefekt/ *n.* **1** *Rom. Antiq.* a senior magistrate or military commander. **2** a student monitor, as in a private school. **3** the chief administrative officer of certain government departments, esp. in France. □□ **pre·fec·tor·al** /–féktərəl/ *adj.* **pre·fec·to·ri·al** /–táwreeəl/ *adj.*

pre·fec·ture /préefekchər/ *n.* **1** a district under the government of a prefect. **2** a prefect's office, tenure, or official residence. □□ **pre·fec·tur·al** /prifékchərəl/ *adj.*

pre·fer /prifə́r/ *v.tr.* (**preferred, preferring**) **1** (often foll. by *to*, or *to* + infin.) choose; like better (*would prefer to stay*; *prefers coffee to tea*). **2** submit (information, an accusation, etc.) for consideration. **3** promote or advance (a person).

pref·er·a·ble /préfərəbəl, *disp.* prifér–/ *adj.* **1** to be preferred. **2** more desirable. □□ **pref·er·a·bly** *adv.*

pref·er·ence /préfərəns, préfrəns/ *n.* **1** the act or an instance of preferring or being preferred. **2** a thing preferred. **3** the favoring of one person, etc., before others. **4** *Law* a prior right, esp. to the payment of debts. □ **in preference to** as a thing preferred over (another).

pref·er·en·tial /préfərénshəl/ *adj.* **1** of or involving preference (*preferential treatment*). **2** giving or receiving a favor. **3** (of voting) in which the voter puts candidates in order of preference. □□ **pref·er·en·tial·ly** *adv.*

pre·fer·ment /prifə́rmənt/ *n.* **1** act or state of being preferred. **2** promotion to office.

pre·ferred stock *n.* stock whose entitlement to dividend takes priority over that of common stock.

pre·fig·ure /préefígyər/ *v.tr.* **1** represent beforehand by a figure or type. **2** imagine beforehand. □□ **pre·fig·u·ra·tion** *n.* **pre·fig·ur·a·tive** /–rətiv/ *adj.* **pre·fig·ure·ment** *n.*

pre·fix /préefiks/ *n. & v.* • *n.* **1** a verbal element placed at the beginning of a word to adjust or qualify its meaning (e.g., *ex-*, *non-*, *re-*) or (in some languages) as an inflectional formative. **2** a title placed before a name (e.g., *Mr.*). • *v.tr.* (often foll. by *to*) **1** add as an introduction. **2** join (a word or element) as a prefix. □□ **pre·fix·a·tion** *n.* **pre·fix·ion** /–fikshən/ *n.*

pre·front·al lo·bot·o·my *n.* the surgical cutting of the nerve fibers that connect the frontal lobes with the rest of the brain, formerly used in psychosurgery.

preg·nan·cy /prégnənsee/ *n.* (*pl.* **-cies**) the condition or an instance of being pregnant.

preg·nant /prégnənt/ *adj.* **1** (of a woman or female animal) having a child or young developing in the uterus. **2** full of meaning; significant or suggestive (*a pregnant pause*). **3** (esp. of a person's mind) imaginative; inventive. **4** (foll. by *with*) full of; abundant in (*pregnant with danger*). □□ **preg·nant·ly** *adv.* (in sense 2).

pre·hen·sile /préehénsəl, –sil/ *adj. Zool.* (of a tail or limb) capable of grasping. □□ **pre·hen·sil·i·ty** /–sílitee/ *n.*

pre·his·tor·ic /préehistáwrik, –stór–/ *adj.* **1** of or relating to the period before written records. **2** *colloq.* utterly out of date. □□ **pre·his·to·ri·an** /–stáwreeən, –stór–/ *n.* **pre·his·tor·i·cal·ly** *adv.* **pre·his·to·ry** /–hístəree/ *n.*

pre·judge /préejúj/ *v.tr.* **1** form a premature judgment on (a person, issue, etc.). **2** pass judgment on (a person) before a trial or proper inquiry. □□ **pre·judg·ment** *n.* **pre·ju·di·ca·tion** /–jo͞odikáyshən/ *n.*

prej·u·dice /préjədis/ *n. & v.* • *n.* **1 a** a preconceived opinion. **b** (usu. foll. by *against, in favor of*) bias or partiality. **c** intolerance of or discrimination against a person or group, esp. on account of race, religion, or gender; bigotry (*racial prejudice*). **2** harm or injury that results or may result from some action or judgment (*to the prejudice of*). • *v.tr.* **1** impair the validity or force of (a right, claim, statement, etc.). **2** (esp. as **prejudiced** *adj.*) cause (a person) to have a prejudice. □ **without prejudice** (often foll. by *to*) without detriment (to any existing right or claim).

prej·u·di·cial /préjədíshəl/ *adj.* causing prejudice; detrimental. □□ **prej·u·di·cial·ly** *adv.*

prel·ate /prélət/ *n.* a high ecclesiastical dignitary, e.g., a bishop, abbot, etc. □□ **pre·lat·ic** /prilátik/ *adj.* **pre·lat·i·cal** *adj.*

pre·lim·i·nar·y /prilíminəree/ *adj., n., & adv.* • *adj.* introductory; preparatory. • *n.* (*pl.* **-ies**) (usu. in *pl.*) **1** a preliminary action or arrangement (*dispense with the preliminaries*). **2 a** a preliminary trial or contest. **b** a preliminary examination. • *adv.* (foll. by *to*) preparatory to; in advance of (*was completed preliminary to the main event*). □□ **pre·lim·i·nar·i·ly** *adv.*

prel·ude /prélyo͞od, práylo͞od, prée–/ *n. & v.* • *n.* (often foll. by *to*) **1** an action, event, or situation serving as an introduction. **2** the introductory part of a poem, etc. **3 a** an introductory piece of music, often preceding a fugue or forming the first piece of a suite or beginning an act of an opera. **b** a short piece of music of a similar type, esp. for the piano. • *v.tr.* **1** serve as a prelude to. **2** introduce with a prelude. □□ **pre·lu·di·al** /prilo͞odeeəl/ *adj.*

pre·mar·i·tal /préemárit'l/ *adj.* existing or (esp. of sexual relations) occurring before marriage. □□ **pre·mar·i·tal·ly** *adv.*

pre·ma·ture /preemәchŏŏr, –tyŏŏr, –tŏŏr/ *adj.* **1 a** occurring or done before the usual or proper time; too early (*a premature decision*). **b** too hasty (*must not be premature*). **2** (of a baby, esp. a viable one) born (esp. three or more weeks) before the end of the full term of gestation. ▫▫ **pre·ma·ture·ly** *adv.* **pre·ma·ture·ness** *n.* **pre·ma·tu·ri·ty** /–chŏŏrәtee/ *n.*

pre·med /preeméd/ *n. colloq.* a premedical course of study or student.

pre·med·i·cal /préemédikәl/ *adj.* of or relating to preparation for a course of study in medicine.

pre·med·i·tate /préeméditayt/ *v.tr.* (often as **premeditated** *adj.*) think out or plan (an action) beforehand (*premeditated murder*). ▫▫ **pre·med·i·ta·tion** *n.*

pre·men·stru·al /préeménstrōōәl/ *adj.* of, occurring, or experienced before menstruation (*premenstrual tension*). ▫▫ **pre·men·stru·al·ly** *adv.*

pre·men·stru·al syn·drome *n.* any of a complex of symptoms (including tension, fluid retention, etc.) experienced by some women in the days immediately preceding menstruation. ¶ Abbr.: **PMS**.

pre·mier /prәméer, –myéer, préemeer/ *n. & adj.* •*n.* a prime minister or other head of government in certain countries. •*adj.* **1** first in importance, order, or time. **2** of earliest creation; oldest. ▫▫ **pre·mier·ship** *n.*

pre·miere /prәméer, –myáir/ *n., adj., & v.* (also **première**) •*n.* the first performance or showing of a play or movie. •*adj.* = PREMIER *adj.* 1. •*v.tr.* give a premiere of.

prem·ise /prémis/ *n. & v.* •*n.* **1** *Logic* (also esp. *Brit.* **premiss**) a previous statement from which another is inferred. **2** (in *pl.*) **a** a house or building with its grounds and appurtenances. **b** *Law* houses, land, etc., previously specified in a document, etc. •*v.* **1** *tr.* say or write by way of introduction. **2** *tr. & intr.* assert or assume as a premise. ▫ **on the premises** in the building, etc., concerned.

pre·mi·um /préemeeәm/ *n.* **1** an amount to be paid for a contract of insurance. **2 a** a sum added to interest, wages, etc.; a bonus. **b** a sum added to ordinary charges. **3** a reward or prize. **4** (*attrib.*) (of a commodity) of best quality and therefore more expensive. **5** an item offered free or cheaply as an incentive to buy, sample, or subscribe to something. ▫ **at a premium 1** highly valued; above the usual or nominal price. **2** scarce and in demand. **put a premium on 1** provide or act as an incentive to. **2** attach special value to.

pre·mo·lar /preemṓlәr/ *adj. & n.* •*adj.* in front of a molar tooth. •*n.* (in an adult human) each of eight teeth situated in pairs between each of the four canine teeth and each first molar.

pre·mo·ni·tion /prémәníshәn, prée–/ *n.* a forewarning; a presentiment. ▫▫ **pre·mon·i·tor** /primónitәr/ *n.* **pre·mon·i·to·ry** /primónitawree/ *adj.*

pre·na·tal /préenáyt'l/ *adj.* of or concerning the period before birth. ▫▫ **pre·na·tal·ly** *adv.*

pren·tice /préntis/ *n. & v. archaic* •*n.* = APPRENTICE. •*v.tr.* (as **prenticed** *adj.*) apprenticed. ▫▫ **pren·tice·ship** *n.*

pre·nup·tial /preenúpshәl, –chәl/ *adj.* existing or occurring before marriage.

pre·nup·tial a·gree·ment *n.* an agreement made by a couple before they marry concerning the ownership of their respective assets should the marriage fail.

pre·oc·cu·pa·tion /prée-ókyәpáyshәn/ *n.* **1** the state of being preoccupied. **2** a thing that engrosses or dominates the mind.

pre·oc·cu·py /prée-ókyәpī/ *v.tr.* (**-pies, -pied**) **1** (of a thought, etc.) dominate or engross the mind of (a person) to the exclusion of other thoughts. **2** (as **preoccupied** *adj.*) otherwise engrossed; mentally distracted. **3** occupy beforehand.

pre·or·dain /préeawrdáyn/ *v.tr.* ordain or determine beforehand.

prep /prep/ *n. colloq.* **1 a** a student in a preparatory school. **b** a preparatory school. **2** *Brit.* **a** the preparation of school work by a pupil. **b** the period when this is done.

prep. *abbr.* preposition.

pre·pack·age /préepákij/ *v.tr.* (also **pre·pack** /–pák/) package (goods) on the site of production or before retail.

pre·paid *past* and *past part.* of PREPAY.

prep·a·ra·tion /prépәráyshәn/ *n.* **1** the act or an instance of preparing; the process of being prepared. **2** (often in *pl.*) something done to make ready. **3** a specially prepared substance, esp. a food or medicine. **4** work done by students to prepare for a lesson. **5** *Mus.* the sounding of the discordant note in a chord in the preceding chord where it is not discordant, lessening the effect of the discord.

pre·par·a·tive /pripárәtiv, –páir–/ *adj. & n.* •*adj.* preparatory. •*n.* a preparatory act. ▫▫ **pre·par·a·tive·ly** *adv.*

pre·par·a·to·ry /pripárәtawree, –páir–, prépәrә–/ *adj. & adv.* •*adj.* (often foll. by *to*) serving to prepare; introductory. •*adv.* (often foll. by *to*) in a preparatory manner (*was packing preparatory to departure*). ▫▫ **pre·par·a·to·ri·ly** *adv.*

pre·par·a·to·ry school *n.* a usu. private school preparing pupils for college.

pre·pare /pripáir/ *v.* **1** *tr.* make or get ready for use, consideration, etc. **2** *tr.* make ready or assemble (food, a meal, etc.) for eating. **3 a** *tr.* make (a person or oneself) ready or disposed in some way (*prepares students for university; prepared them for a shock*). **b** *intr.* put oneself or things in readiness; get ready (*prepare to jump*). **4** *tr.* make (a chemical product, etc.) by a regular process; manufacture. ▫ **be prepared** (often foll. by *for*, or *to* + infin.) be disposed or willing to. ▫▫ **pre·par·er** *n.*

pre·par·ed·ness /pripáiridnis/ *n.* a state of readiness, esp. for war.

pre·pay /préepáy/ *v.tr.* (*past* and *past part.* **prepaid**) **1** pay (a charge) in advance. **2** pay postage on (a letter or package, etc.) before mailing. ▫▫ **pre·pay·a·ble** *adj.* **pre·pay·ment** *n.*

pre·pon·der·ant /pripóndәrәnt/ *adj.* surpassing in influence, power, number, or importance; predominant; preponderating. ▫▫ **pre·pon·der·ance** *n.* **pre·pon·der·ant·ly** *adv.*

pre·pon·der·ate /pripóndәrayt/ *v.intr.* (often foll. by *over*) **1 a** be greater in influence, quantity, or number. **b** predominate. **2 a** be of greater importance. **b** weigh more.

prep·o·si·tion /prépәzíshәn/ *n. Gram.* a word governing (and usu. preceding) a noun or pronoun and expressing a relation to another word or element, as in: "the man *on* the platform," "came *after* dinner," "what did you do it *for*?". ▫▫ **prep·o·si·tion·al** *adj.* **prep·o·si·tion·al·ly** *adv.*

▶Many sentences and clauses in English end with prepositions, and this has been true through the language's history. The "rule" that forbids placing a preposition at the end of a clause or sentence should be disregarded.

pre·pos·sess /préepәzés/ *v.tr.* **1** (usu. in *passive*) (of an idea, feeling, etc.) take possession of (a person); imbue. **2 a** prejudice (usu. favorably and spontaneously). **b** (as **prepossessing** *adj.*) attractive; appealing. ▫▫ **pre·pos·ses·sion** /–zéshәn/ *n.*

pre·pos·ter·ous /pripóstәrәs/ *adj.* **1** utterly absurd; outrageous. **2** contrary to nature, reason, or common sense. ▫▫ **pre·pos·ter·ous·ly** *adv.* **pre·pos·ter·ous·ness** *n.*

prep·py /prépee/ *n. & adj.* (also **prep·pie**) *US colloq.* • *n.* (*pl.* **-pies**) a person attending an expensive private school or who strives to look like such a person. • *adj.* (**preppier, preppiest**) **1** like a preppy. **2** neat and fashionable.

pre·proc·es·sor /preeprósesər/ *n.* a computer program that modifies data to conform with the input requirements of another program.

prep school /prep/ *n.* = PREPARATORY SCHOOL.

pre·pu·bes·cence /préepyoobésəns/ *n.* the time, esp. the last two or three years, before puberty. ▫▫ **pre·pu·bes·cent** *adj.*

pre·puce /préepyoos/ *n.* **1** = FORESKIN. **2** the fold of skin surrounding the clitoris. ▫▫ **pre·pu·tial** /preepyóoshəl/ *adj.*

pre·quel /préekwəl/ *n.* a story, movie, etc., whose events or concerns precede those of an existing work.

pre·req·ui·site /preerékwizit/ *adj. & n.* • *adj.* required as a precondition. • *n.* a prerequisite thing.
▶See note at PERQUISITE.

pre·rog·a·tive /prirógətiv/ *n.* **1** a right or privilege exclusive to an individual or class. **2** (in full **royal prerogative**) *Brit.* the right of the sovereign, theoretically subject to no restriction.

Pres. *abbr.* President.

pres·age /présij/ *n. & v.* • *n.* **1** an omen or portent. **2** a presentiment or foreboding. • *v.tr.* (also /prisáyj/) **1** portend; foreshadow. **2** give warning of (an event, etc.) by natural means. **3** (of a person) predict or have a presentiment of. ▫▫ **pres·age·ful** *adj.* **pres·ag·er** *n.*

pres·by·ter /prézbitər/ *n.* **1** an elder in the early Christian Church. **2** (in episcopal churches) a minister of the second order; a priest. **3** (in the Presbyterian Church) an elder. ▫▫ **pres·byt·er·al** /–bítərəl/ *adj.* **pres·byt·er·ate** /–bítərət/ *n.* **pres·by·te·ri·al** /–téereeəl/ *adj.* **pres·byt·er·ship** *n.*

Pres·by·te·ri·an /prézbitéereeən/ *adj. & n.* • *adj.* (of a church) governed by elders all of equal rank. • *n.* **1** a member of a Presbyterian Church. **2** an adherent of the Presbyterian system. ▫▫ **Pres·by·te·ri·an·ism** *n.*

pres·by·ter·y /prézbiteree/ *n.* (*pl.* **-ies**) **1** the eastern part of a chancel beyond the choir; the sanctuary. **2 a** a body of presbyters. **b** a district represented by this. **3** the house of a Roman Catholic priest.

pre·school /préeskóol/ *adj. & n.* • *adj.* of or relating to the time before a child is old enough to go to school. • *n.* a nursery school. ▫▫ **pre·school·er** *n.*

pre·scient /préshənt, –eeənt, pré–/ *adj.* having foreknowledge or foresight. ▫▫ **pre·science** *n.* **pre·scient·ly** *adv.*

pre·scind /prisínd/ *v.* **1** *tr.* (foll. by *from*) cut off (a part from a whole), esp. prematurely or abruptly. **2** *intr.* (foll. by *from*) leave out of consideration. **3** withdraw or turn away in thought.

pre·scribe /priskríb/ *v.* **1** *tr.* **a** advise the use of (a medicine, etc.), esp. by an authorized prescription. **b** recommend, esp. as a benefit (*prescribed a change of scenery*). **2** *tr.* lay down or impose authoritatively. **3** *intr.* (foll. by *to, for*) assert a prescriptive right or claim. ▫▫ **pre·scrib·er** *n.*
▶**Prescribe** and **proscribe** are sometimes confused, but they are nearly opposite in meaning. **Prescribe** means 'to advise the use of' or 'impose authoritatively,' whereas **proscribe** means 'to denounce or ban.' Examples of each are as follows: *Our teacher prescribed topics to be covered. The doctor prescribed a painkiller. The principal proscribed tabloid newspapers from the school library. A totalitarian regime may prescribe some books and proscribe others.*

pre·scrip·tion /priskrípshən/ *n.* **1** the act or an instance of prescribing. **2 a** a doctor's (usu. written) instruction for the preparation and use of a medicine. **b** a medicine prescribed.

pre·scrip·tive /priskríptiv/ *adj.* **1** prescribing. **2** *Linguistics* concerned with or laying down rules of usage. **3** based on prescription (*prescriptive right*). **4** prescribed by custom. ▫▫ **pre·scrip·tive·ly** *adv.* **pre·scrip·tive·ness** *n.* **pre·scrip·tiv·ism** *n.* **pre·scrip·tiv·ist** *n. & adj.*

pres·ence /prézəns/ *n.* **1 a** the state or condition of being present (*your presence is requested*). **b** existence; location (*the presence of a hospital nearby*). **2** a place where a person is (*was admitted to their presence*). **3 a** a person's appearance or bearing, esp. when imposing (*an august presence*). **b** a person's force of personality (esp. *have presence*). **4** a person or thing that is present (*there was a presence in the room*). ▫ **in the presence of** in front of; observed by.

pres·ence of mind *n.* ability to think, act constructively, etc., during a crisis.

pres·ent[1] /prézənt/ *adj. & n.* • *adj.* **1** (usu. *predic.*) being in the place in question (*was present at the trial*). **2 a** now existing, occurring, or being such (*during the present season*). **b** now being considered or discussed, etc. (*in the present case*). **3** *Gram.* expressing an action, etc., now going on or habitually performed (*present participle*; *present tense*). • *n.* (prec. by *the*) **1** the time now passing (*no time like the present*). **2** *Gram.* the present tense. ▫ **at present** now. **for the present 1** just now. **2** as far as the present is concerned. **present company excepted** excluding those who are here now.

pre·sent[2] /prizént/ *v. & n.* • *v.tr.* **1** introduce, offer, or exhibit, esp. for public attention or consideration. **2 a** (with a thing as object, usu. foll. by *to*) offer, give, or award as a gift (to a person), esp. formally or ceremonially. **b** (with a person as object, foll. by *with*) make available to; cause to have (*presented them with a new car; that presents us with a problem*). **3 a** (of a company, producer, etc.) put (a form of entertainment) before the public. **b** (of a performer, etc.) introduce or put before an audience. **4** introduce (a person) formally (*may I present my fiancé?*). **5** offer; give (compliments, etc.) (*may I present my card; present my regards to your family*). **6 a** (of a circumstance) reveal (some quality, etc.) (*this presents some difficulty*). **b** exhibit (an appearance, etc.) (*presented a tough exterior*). **7** (of an idea, etc.) offer or suggest itself. **8** deliver (a check, bill, etc.) for acceptance or payment. **9 a** (usu. foll. by *at*) aim (a weapon). **b** hold out (a weapon) in a position for aiming. **10** (*refl.* or *absol.*) *Med.* (of a patient or illness, etc.) come forward for or undergo initial medical examination. **11** (*absol.*) *Med.* (of a part of a fetus) be directed toward the cervix at the time of delivery. **12** (foll. by *to*) *Law* bring formally under notice; submit (an offense, complaint, etc.). • *n.* the position of presenting arms in salute. ▫ **present arms** hold a rifle, etc., vertically in front of the body as a salute. **present oneself 1** appear. **2** come forward for examination, etc. ▫▫ **pre·sent·er** *n.* (in sense 3 of *v.*).

pres·ent[3] /prézənt/ *n.* a gift; a thing given or presented. ▫ **make a present of** give as a gift.

pre·sent·a·ble /prizéntəbəl/ *adj.* **1** of good appearance; fit to be presented to other people. **2** fit for presentation. ▫▫ **pre·sent·a·bil·i·ty** /–bílitee/ *n.* **pre·sent·a·ble·ness** *n.* **pre·sent·a·bly** *adv.*

pres·en·ta·tion /prézəntáyshən, préezen–/ *n.* **1 a** the act or an instance of presenting; the process of being presented. **b** a thing presented. **2** the manner or quality of presenting. **3** a demonstration or display of materials, information, etc.; a lecture. **4** an exhibition or theatrical performance. **5** a formal introduction. **6** the position of the fetus in relation to the cervix at the time of delivery. □□ **pres·en·ta·tion·al** *adj.* **pres·en·ta·tion·al·ly** *adv.*

pres·ent-day *adj.* of this time; modern.

pre·sen·tient /preesénshənt, –sheeənt/ *adj.* (often foll. by *of*) having a presentiment.

pre·sen·ti·ment /prizéntimənt, –séntimənt/ *n.* a vague expectation; a foreboding (esp. of misfortune).

pres·ent·ly /prézəntlee/ *adv.* **1** soon; after a short time. **2** at the present time; now.

▶In *The pain will lessen presently,* the meaning of **presently** is 'soon'; in *Limited resources are presently available,* the meaning is 'at this moment.' Both senses are widely used.

pre·sent·ment /prizéntmənt/ *n.* **1** an act or a manner of presenting. **2** the presenting of a bill, note, etc., esp. for payment. **3** the act of presenting information, esp. a statement on oath by a jury of a fact known to them.

pres·er·va·tion /prézərváyshən/ *n.* **1** the act of preserving or process of being preserved. **2** a state of being well or badly preserved (*in an excellent state of preservation*).

pres·er·va·tion·ist /prézərváyshənist/ *n.* a supporter or advocate of preservation, esp. of wildlife or historic buildings.

pre·serv·a·tive /prizə́rvətiv/ *n. & adj.* •*n.* a substance for preserving perishable foods, wood, etc. •*adj.* tending to preserve.

pre·serve /prizə́rv/ *v. & n.* •*v.tr.* **1 a** keep safe or free from harm, decay, etc. **b** keep alive (a name, memory, etc.). **2** maintain (a thing) in its existing state. **3** retain (a quality or condition). **4 a** treat or refrigerate (food) to prevent decomposition or fermentation. **b** prepare (fruit or vegetables) by boiling with sugar, canning, etc., for long-term storage. **5** keep (wildlife, a river, etc.) undisturbed for private use. •*n.* (in *sing.* or *pl.*) **1** preserved fruit; jam. **2** a place where game or fish, etc., are preserved. **3** a sphere or area of activity regarded as a person's own. □□ **pre·serv·a·ble** *adj.* **pre·serv·er** *n.*

pre·set /préesét/ *v.tr.* (**-setting;** *past* and *past part.* **-set**) **1** set or fix (a device) in advance of its operation. **2** settle or decide beforehand.

pre·shrunk /préeshrúngk/ *adj.* (of a fabric or garment) treated so that it shrinks during manufacture and not in use.

pre·side /prizī́d/ *v.intr.* **1** (often foll. by *at, over*) be in a position of authority, esp. as the chairperson or president. **2 a** exercise control or authority. **b** (foll. by *at*) play a featured instrument (*presided at the piano*).

pres·i·den·cy /prézidənsee/ *n.* (*pl.* **-cies**) **1** the office, term, or function of president. **2** the office of the President of the United States. **3** a Mormon administrative or governing body.

pres·i·dent /prézidənt/ *n.* **1** the elected head of a republican government. **2** the head of a college, university, company, society, etc. **3** a person in charge of a meeting, council, etc. □□ **pres·i·den·tial** /–dénshəl/ *adj.* **pres·i·den·tial·ly** *adv.* **pres·i·dent·ship** *n.*

pre·sid·i·um /prisídeeəm, –zídeeəm/ *n.* (also **prae·sid·i·um**) a standing executive committee in a Communist country, esp. *hist.* in the former USSR.

press[1] /pres/ *v. & n.* •*v.* **1** *tr.* apply steady force to (a thing in contact) (*pressed the two surfaces together*). **2** *tr.* **a** compress or apply pressure to a thing to flatten, shape, or smooth it, as by ironing (*got the curtains pressed*). **b** squeeze (a fruit, etc.) to extract its juice. **c** manufacture (a record, etc.) by molding under pressure. **3** *tr.* (foll. by *out of, from,* etc.) squeeze (juice, etc.). **4** *tr.* embrace or caress by squeezing (*pressed my hand*). **5** *intr.* (foll. by *on, against,* etc.) exert pressure. **6** *intr.* be urgent; demand immediate action (*time was pressing*). **7** *intr.* (foll. by *for*) make an insistent demand. **8** *intr.* (foll. by *up, round,* etc.) form a crowd. **9** *intr.* (foll. by *on, forward,* etc.) hasten insistently. **10** *tr.* (often in *passive*) (of an enemy, etc.) bear heavily on. **11** *tr.* (often foll. by *for,* or *to* + infin.) urge or entreat (*pressed me for an answer*). **12** *tr.* (foll. by *on, upon*) **a** put forward or urge (an opinion, claim, or course of action). **b** insist on the acceptance of (an offer, a gift, etc.). **13** *tr.* insist on (*did not press the point*). **14** *intr.* (foll. by *on*) produce a strong mental or moral impression; oppress; weigh heavily. •*n.* **1** the act or an instance of pressing. **2 a** a device for compressing, flattening, shaping, extracting juice, etc. (*wine press*). **b** a machine that applies pressure to a workpiece by means of a tool, in order to punch shapes, bend it, etc. **3** = PRINTING PRESS. **4** (prec. by *the*) **a** the art or practice of printing. **b** newspapers, journalists, etc., generally or collectively (*read it in the press; pursued by the press*). **5** a notice or piece of publicity in newspapers, etc. (*got a good press*). **6** (**Press**) **a** a printing house or establishment. **b** a publishing company (*Yale University Press*). **7 a** crowding. **b** a crowd (of people, etc.). **8** the pressure of affairs. **9** a large usu. shelved cupboard for clothes, books, etc. □ **be pressed for** have barely enough (time, etc.). **go** (or **send**) **to press** go or send to be printed.

press[2] /pres/ *v.tr.* **1** *hist.* force to serve in the army or navy; impress. **2** bring into use as a makeshift (*was pressed into service*).

press a·gent *n.* a person employed to attend to advertising and press publicity.

press box *n.* a reporters' enclosure esp. at a sports event.

press con·fer·ence *n.* an interview given to journalists to make an announcement or answer questions.

press-gang /présgang/ *n. & v.* •*n.* **1** *hist.* a body of men employed to press men into service in the army or navy. **2** any group using similar coercive methods. •*v.tr.* force into service.

press·ing /présing/ *adj. & n.* •*adj.* **1** urgent (*pressing business*). **2 a** urging strongly (*a pressing invitation*). **b** persistent; importunate (*since you are so pressing*). •*n.* **1** a thing made by pressing, esp. a record, compact disc, etc. **2** a series of these made at one time. **3** the act or an instance of pressing a thing, esp. a record or grapes, etc. (*all at one pressing*). □□ **press·ing·ly** *adv.*

pres·sure /préshər/ *n. & v.* •*n.* **1 a** the exertion of continuous force on or against a body by another in contact with it. **b** the force exerted. **c** the amount of this (expressed by the force on a unit area) (*atmospheric pressure*). **2** urgency; the need to meet a deadline, etc. (*work under pressure*). **3** affliction or difficulty (*under financial pressure*). **4** constraining influence (*if pressure is brought to bear*). •*v.tr.* **1** apply pressure to. **2 a** coerce. **b** (often foll. by *into*) persuade (*was pressured into attending*).

pres·sure cook·er *n.* an airtight pot for cooking quickly under steam pressure. □□ **pres·sure-cook** *v.tr.*

pres·sure gauge *n.* a gauge showing the pressure of steam, etc.

pres·sure group *n.* a group or association formed to promote a particular interest or cause by influencing public policy.

pres·sure point *n.* **1** a point where an artery can be pressed against a bone to inhibit bleeding. **2** a point on the skin sensitive to pressure. **3** a target for political pressure or influence.

pres·sur·ize /préshərīz/ *v.tr.* **1** (esp. as **pressurized** *adj.*) maintain normal atmospheric pressure in (an aircraft cabin, etc.) at a high altitude. **2** raise to a high pressure. **3** pressure (a person). ▫▫ **pres·sur·i·za·tion** *n.*

pres·ti·dig·i·ta·tor /préstidíjitaytər/ *n. formal* a magician. ▫▫ **pres·ti·dig·i·ta·tion** /–táyshən/ *n.*

pres·tige /presteézh/ *n.* **1** respect, reputation, or influence derived from achievements, power, associations, etc. **2** (*attrib.*) having or conferring prestige. ▫▫ **pres·tige·ful** *adj.*

---

prestige mid-17th century (in the sense 'illusion, magic trick'): from French, literally 'illusion, glamor', from late Latin *praestigium* 'illusion', from Latin *praestigiae* (plural) 'magic tricks.' The transference of meaning occurred by way of the sense 'dazzling influence, glamor,' used with negative intent.

---

pres·tig·ious /presteéjəs, –stíj–/ *adj.* having or showing prestige. ▫▫ **pres·tig·ious·ly** *adv.* **pres·tig·ious·ness** *n.*

pres·tis·si·mo /prestísimō/ *adv. & n. Mus.* • *adv.* in a very quick tempo. • *n.* (*pl.* **-mos**) a movement or passage played in this way.

pres·to /préstō/ *adv. & n.* • *adv.* **1** *Mus.* in quick tempo. **2** (in a magician's formula in performing a trick) quickly. • *n.* (*pl.* **-tos**) *Mus.* a movement to be played in a quick tempo.

pre·sum·a·bly /prizóoməblee/ *adv.* as may reasonably be presumed.

pre·sume /prizóom/ *v.* **1** *tr.* (often foll. by *that* + clause) suppose to be true; take for granted. **2** *tr.* (often foll. by *to* + infin.) **a** take the liberty; be impudent enough (*presumed to question their authority*). **b** dare; venture (*may I presume to ask?*). **3** *intr.* be presumptuous; take liberties. **4** *intr.* (foll. by *on, upon*) take advantage of or make unscrupulous use of (a person's good nature, etc.). ▫▫ **pre·sum·a·ble** *adj.* **pre·sum·ed·ly** /–zóomidlee/ *adv.*

pre·sum·ing /prizóoming/ *adj.* presumptuous. ▫▫ **pre·sum·ing·ly** *adv.* **pre·sum·ing·ness** *n.*

pre·sump·tion /prizúmpshən/ *n.* **1** arrogance; presumptuous behavior. **2 a** the act of presuming a thing to be true. **b** a thing that is or may be presumed to be true; a belief based on reasonable evidence. **3** a ground for presuming (*a strong presumption against their being guilty*). **4** *Law* an inference from known facts.

pre·sump·tive /prizúmptiv/ *adj.* **1** based on presumption or inference. **2** giving reasonable grounds for presumption (*presumptive evidence*). ▫▫ **pre·sump·tive·ly** *adv.*

pre·sump·tu·ous /prizúmpchooəs/ *adj.* unduly or overbearingly confident and presuming. ▫▫ **pre·sump·tu·ous·ly** *adv.* **pre·sump·tu·ous·ness** *n.*

pre·sup·pose /preésəpóz/ *v.tr.* (often foll. by *that* + clause) **1** assume beforehand. **2** require as a precondition; imply. ▫▫ **pre·sup·po·si·tion** /preésupəzishən/ *n.*

pre·tax /preétáks/ *adj.* (of income or profits) before the deduction of taxes.

pre·teen /preéteén/ *adj.* of or relating to a child just under the age of thirteen.

pre·tend /priténd/ *v. & adj.* • *v.* **1** *tr.* claim or assert falsely so as to deceive (*pretended that they were foreigners*). **2 a** *tr.* imagine to oneself in play (*pretended to be monsters*). **b** *absol.* make pretense, esp. in imagination or play; make believe (*they're just pretending*). **3** *tr.* **a** profess, esp. falsely or extravagantly (*does not pretend to be a scholar*). **b** (as **pretended** *adj.*) falsely claim to be such (*a pretended friend*). **4** *intr.* (foll. by *to*) **a** lay claim to (a right or title, etc.). **b** profess to have (a quality, etc.). **5** *tr.* (foll. by *to*) aspire or presume; venture (*I cannot pretend to guess*). • *adj. colloq.* pretended; in pretense (*pretend money*).

pre·tend·er /priténdər/ *n.* **1** a person who claims a throne or title, etc. **2** a person who pretends.

pre·tense /preétens, priténs/ *n.* **1** pretending; make-believe. **2 a** a pretext or excuse (*on the slightest pretense*). **b** a false show of intentions or motives (*under the pretense of friendship; under false pretenses*). **3** (foll. by *to*) a claim, esp. a false or ambitious one (*has no pretense to any great talent*). **4 a** affectation; display. **b** pretentiousness; ostentation (*stripped of all pretense*).

pre·ten·sion /priténshən/ *n.* **1** (often foll. by *to*) **a** an assertion of a claim. **b** a justifiable claim (*has no pretensions to the name; has some pretensions to be included*). **2** pretentiousness.

pre·ten·tious /priténshəs/ *adj.* **1** making an excessive claim to great merit or importance. **2** ostentatious. ▫▫ **pre·ten·tious·ly** *adv.* **pre·ten·tious·ness** *n.*

pre·term /preétərm/ *adj.* born or occurring prematurely.

pre·ter·nat·u·ral /preétərnáchərəl/ *adj.* outside the ordinary course of nature; supernatural. ▫▫ **pre·ter·nat·u·ral·ism** *n.* **pre·ter·nat·u·ral·ly** *adv.*

pre·text /preétekst/ *n.* **1** an ostensible or alleged reason or intention. **2** an excuse offered. ▫ **on** (or **under**) **the pretext** (foll. by *of*, or *that* + clause) professing as one's object or intention.

pretor var. of PRAETOR.

pre·tor·i·an var. of PRAETORIAN.

pret·ti·fy /prítifī/ *v.tr.* (**-fies, -fied**) make (a thing or person) pretty esp. in an affected way. ▫▫ **pret·ti·fi·ca·tion** *n.* **pret·ti·fi·er** *n.*

pret·ty /prítee/ *adj., n., v., & adv.* • *adj.* (**prettier, prettiest**) **1** attractive in a delicate way without being truly beautiful or handsome (*a pretty child; a pretty dress; a pretty tune*). **2** fine or good of its kind (*a pretty wit*). **3** *iron.* considerable; fine (*a pretty penny; a pretty mess you have made*). • *adv. colloq.* fairly; moderately; considerably (*am pretty well; find it pretty difficult*). • *n.* (*pl.* **-ties**) a pretty person (esp. as a form of address to a child). *v.tr.* (**-ties, -tied**) (often foll. by *up*) make pretty or attractive. ▫ **pretty much** (or **nearly** or **well**) *colloq.* almost; very nearly. **sitting pretty** *colloq.* in a favorable or advantageous position. ▫▫ **pret·ti·ly** *adv.* **pret·ti·ness** *n.* **pret·ty·ish** *adj.*

---

pretty Old English *prættig*; related to Middle Dutch *pertich* 'brisk, clever,' obsolete Dutch *prettig* 'humorous, sporty,' from a West Germanic base meaning 'trick.' The sense development 'deceitful, cunning, clever, skillful, admirable, pleasing' has parallels in adjectives such as *fine, nice*, etc.

---

pret·zel /prétsəl/ *n.* a crisp or chewy knot-shaped or stick-shaped bread, usu. salted.

pre·vail /priváyl/ *v.intr.* **1** (often foll. by *against, over*) be victorious or gain mastery. **2** be the more usual or predominant. **3** exist or occur in general use or experience; be current. **4** (foll. by *on, upon*) persuade. **5** (as **prevailing** *adj.*) predominant; generally current or accepted (*prevailing opinion*). ▫▫ **pre·vail·ing·ly** *adv.*

pre·vail·ing wind *n.* the wind that most frequently occurs at a place.

prev·a·lent /prévələnt/ *adj.* **1** generally existing or occurring. **2** predominant. ▫▫ **prev·a·lence** *n.* **prev·a·lent·ly** *adv.*

pre·var·i·cate /privárikayt/ *v.intr.* **1** speak or act evasively or misleadingly. **2** quibble; equivocate. ▫▫ **pre·var·i·ca·tion** /–rikáyshən/ *n.* **pre·var·i·ca·tor** *n.*

▶**Prevaricate** means 'to act or speak evasively,' e.g., *When the teacher asked what I was reading, I knew I would have to prevaricate or risk a detention.* It is sometimes confused with **procrastinate**, which means 'to postpone or put off an action,' e.g., *He procrastinated until it was too late.*

See page xii for the *Key to Pronunciation.*

pre•vent /privént/ *v.tr.* (often foll. by *from* + verbal noun) stop from happening or doing something; hinder; make impossible (*the weather prevented me from going*). ▫▫ **pre•vent•a•ble** *adj.* (also **pre•vent•i•ble**). **pre•vent•a•bil•i•ty** *n.* **pre•vent•er** *n.* **pre•ven•tion** /–vénshən/ *n.*

pre•ven•ta•tive /privéntətiv/ *adj. & n.* = PREVENTIVE. ▫▫ **pre•ven•ta•tive•ly** *adv.*

pre•ven•tive /privéntiv/ *adj. & n.* • *adj.* serving to prevent, esp. preventing disease, breakdown, etc. (*preventive medicine; preventive maintenance*). • *n.* a preventive agent, measure, drug, etc. ▫▫ **pre•ven•tive•ly** *adv.* ▶Avoid adding an unnecessary syllable to **preventive**. The variant "preventative" is considered uneducated by many.

pre•view /préevyoo/ *n. & v.* • *n.* **1** the act of seeing in advance. **2 a** the showing of a movie, play, exhibition, etc., before it is seen by the general public. **b** (also **pre•vue**) an advance promotional sample of a movie; trailer. • *v.tr.* see or show in advance.

pre•vi•ous /préeveeəs/ *adj. & adv.* • *adj.* **1** (often foll. by *to*) coming before in time or order. **2** done or acting hastily. • *adv.* (foll. by *to*) before (*had called previous to writing*). ▫▫ **pre•vi•ous•ly** *adv.* **pre•vi•ous•ness** *n.*

pre•vue var. of PREVIEW *n.* 2b.

pre•war /préewáwr/ *adj.* existing or occurring before a war (esp. the most recent major war).

prey /pray/ *n. & v.* • *n.* **1** an animal that is hunted or killed by another for food. **2** (often foll. by *to*) a person or thing that is influenced by or vulnerable to (something undesirable) (*became a prey to morbid fears*). • *v.intr.* (foll. by *on, upon*) **1** seek or take as prey. **2** make a victim of. **3** (of a disease, emotion, etc.) exert a harmful influence (*fear preyed on his mind*). ▫▫ **prey•er** *n.*

price /prīs/ *n. & v.* • *n.* **1 a** the amount of money or goods for which a thing is bought or sold. **b** value or worth (*a pearl of great price; beyond price*). **2** what is or must be given, done, sacrificed, etc., to obtain or achieve something. **3** the odds in betting (*starting price*). **4** a sum of money offered or given as a reward, esp. for the capture or killing of a person. • *v.tr.* **1** fix or find the price of (a thing for sale). **2** estimate the value of. ▫ **above** (or **beyond** or **without**) **price** so valuable that no price can be stated. **at any price** no matter what the cost, sacrifice, etc. (*peace at any price*). **at a price** at a high cost. **price oneself out of the market** lose to one's competitors by charging more than customers are willing to pay. **set a price on** declare the price of. ▫▫ **priced** *adj.* (also in *comb.*). **pric•er** *n.*

price-fix•ing *n.* (also **price fixing**) the maintaining of prices at a certain level by agreement between competing sellers.

price•less /príslis/ *adj.* **1** invaluable; beyond price. **2** *colloq.* very amusing or absurd. ▫▫ **price•less•ly** *adv.* **price•less•ness** *n.*

price tag *n.* **1** the label on an item showing its price. **2** the cost of an enterprise or undertaking.

price war *n.* fierce competition among traders cutting prices.

pric•ey /prísee/ *adj.* (also **pric•y**) (**pricier, priciest**) *colloq.* expensive. ▫▫ **pric•i•ness** *n.*

prick /prik/ *v. & n.* • *v.* **1** *tr.* pierce slightly; make a small hole in. **2** *tr.* (foll. by *off, out*) mark (esp. a pattern) with small holes or dots. **3** *tr.* trouble mentally (*my conscience is pricking me*). **4** *intr.* feel a pricking sensation. **5** *intr.* (foll. by *at, into,* etc.) make a thrust as if to prick. **6** *tr.* (foll. by *in, off, out*) plant (seedlings, etc.) in small holes pricked in the earth. • *n.* **1** the act or an instance of pricking. **2** a small hole or mark made by pricking. **3** a pain caused as by pricking. **4** a mental pain (*felt the pricks of conscience*). **5** *coarse sl.* **a** the penis. **b** *derog.* (as a term of contempt) a contemptible or mean-spirited person. ▶Usually considered a taboo use. ▫ **prick up one's ears 1** (of a dog, etc.) make the ears erect when on the alert. **2** (of a person) become suddenly attentive.

prick•er /príkər/ *n.* **1** one that pricks, as an animal or plant. **2** a small thorn or other sharp pointed outgrowth.

prick•le /príkəl/ *n. & v.* • *n.* **1 a** a small thorn. **b** *Bot.* a thornlike process developed from the epidermis of a plant. **2** a hard pointed spine of a hedgehog, etc. **3** a prickling sensation. • *v.tr. & intr.* affect or be affected with a sensation as of pricking.

prick•ly /príklee/ *adj.* (**pricklier, prickliest**) **1** (esp. in the names of plants and animals) having prickles. **2 a** (of a person) ready to take offense. **b** (of a topic, argument, etc.) full of contentious or complicated points; thorny. **3** tingling. ▫▫ **prick•li•ness** *n.*

prick•ly heat *n.* an itchy inflammation of the skin, causing a tingling sensation and common in hot countries.

prick•ly pear *n.* **1** any cactus of the genus *Opuntia*, native to arid regions of America, bearing barbed bristles and large pear-shaped prickly fruits. **2** its fruit.

pricy var. of PRICEY.

pride /prīd/ *n. & v.* • *n.* **1 a** a feeling of elation or satisfaction at achievements, qualities, or possessions, etc., that do one credit. **b** an object of this feeling. **2** a high or overbearing opinion of one's worth or importance. **3** a proper sense of what befits one's position; self-respect. **4** a group or company (of animals, esp. lions). **5** the best condition; the prime. • *v.refl.* (foll. by *on, upon*) be proud of. ▫ **pride and joy** a thing of which one is very proud. **take pride in 1** be proud of. **2** maintain in good condition or appearance. ▫▫ **pride•ful** *adj.* **pride•ful•ly** *adv.* **pride•less** *adj.*

prie-dieu /preedyṓ/ *n.* (*pl.* **prie-dieux** *pronunc.* same) a kneeling desk for prayer.

priest /preest/ *n.* **1** an ordained minister of the Roman Catholic or Orthodox Church, or of the Anglican Church (above a deacon and below a bishop), authorized to perform certain rites and administer certain sacraments. **2** an official minister of a non-Christian religion. ▫▫ **priest•less** *adj.* **priest•like** *adj.*

priest•ess /préestis/ *n.* a female priest of a non-Christian religion.

priest•hood /préest-hood/ *n.* (usu. prec. by *the*) **1** the office or position of a priest. **2** priests in general.

priest•ly /préestlee/ *adj.* of or associated with priests. ▫▫ **priest•li•ness** *n.*

prig /prig/ *n.* a self-righteously correct or moralistic person. ▫▫ **prig•ger•y** *n.* **prig•gish** *adj.* **prig•gish•ly** *adv.* **prig•gish•ness** *n.*

prim /prim/ *adj. & v.* • *adj.* (**primmer, primmest**) **1** (of a person or manner) stiffly formal and precise. **2** (of a woman or girl) demure. **3** prudish. • *v.tr.* (**primmed, primming**) **1** form (the face, lips, etc.) into a prim expression. **2** make prim. ▫▫ **prim•ly** *adv.* **prim•ness** *n.*

pri•ma bal•ler•i•na /préemə/ *n.* the chief female dancer in a ballet or ballet company.

pri•ma•cy /príməsee/ *n.* (*pl.* **-cies**) **1** preeminence. **2** the office of an ecclesiastical primate.

pri•ma don•na /préemə/ *n.* (*pl.* **prima donnas**) **1** the chief female singer in an opera or opera company. **2** a temperamentally self-important person. ▫▫ **pri•ma don•na•ish** *adj.*

pri•ma fa•cie /prímə fáyshee, –shee-ee, shə, préemə/ *adv. & adj.* • *adv.* at first sight; from a first impression (*seems prima facie to be guilty*). • *adj.* (of evidence) based on the first impression (*can see a prima facie reason for it*).

pri•mal /príməl/ *adj.* **1** primitive; primeval. **2** chief; fundamental. ▫▫ **pri•mal•ly** *adv.*

pri•ma•ry /prímeree, –məree/ *adj. & n.* • *adj.* **1 a** of the first importance; chief (*that is our primary concern*). **b** fundamental; basic. **2** earliest; original; first in a series. **3** of the first rank in a series; not derived (*the primary meaning of a word*). **4** designating any of the colors red, green, and blue, or for pigments red, blue, and yellow, from which all other colors can be obtained by mixing. **5** (of a battery or cell) generating electricity by irreversible chemical reaction. **6** (of education) for young children, esp. below the age of 11. **7** (**Primary**) *Geol.* of the lowest series of strata. **8** *Biol.* belonging to the first stage of development. **9** (of an industry or source of production) concerned with obtaining or using raw materials. •*n.* (*pl.* **-ries**) **1** a thing that is primary. **2** (in full **primary election**) a preliminary election to appoint delegates to a party convention or to select the candidates for a principal election. **3** (**Primary**) *Geol.* the Primary period. ▫▫ **pri•ma•ri•ly** /prīmérilee/ *adv.*

pri•ma•ry school *n.* a school where young children are taught, esp. the first three elementary grades and kindergarten.

pri•mate /prímayt/ *n.* **1** any animal of the order Primates, the highest order of mammals, including tarsiers, lemurs, apes, monkeys, and human beings. **2** an archbishop. ▫▫ **pri•ma•tial** /–máyshəl/ *adj.* **pri•ma•tol•o•gy** /–mətóləjee/ *n.* (in sense 1).

pri•ma•ve•ra /preémәvairә/ *adj.* (of pasta, seafood, etc.) made with or containing an assortment of sliced vegetables.

prime[1] /prīm/ *adj. & n.* •*adj.* **1** chief; most important (*the prime agent; the prime motive*). **2** (esp. of beef) first-rate; excellent. **3** primary; fundamental. **4** *Math.* **a** (of a number) divisible only by itself and 1 (e.g., 2, 3, 5, 7, 11). **b** (of numbers) having no common factor but 1. •*n.* **1** the state of the highest perfection of something (*in the prime of life*). **2** (prec. by *the*; foll. by *of*) the best part. **3** the beginning or first age of anything. **4** a prime number. ▫▫ **prime•ness** *n.*

prime[2] /prīm/ *v.tr.* **1** prepare (a thing) for use or action. **2** prepare (a gun) for firing or (an explosive) for detonation. **3 a** pour (liquid) into a pump to prepare it for working. **b** inject fuel into (the cylinder or carburetor of an internal-combustion engine). **4** prepare (wood, etc.) for painting by applying a substance that prevents paint from being absorbed. **5** equip (a person) with information, etc.

prime min•is•ter *n.* the head of an elected parliamentary government; the principal minister of a nation or sovereign.

prime mov•er *n.* **1** an initial natural or mechanical source of motive power. **2** the author of a fruitful idea.

prim•er[1] /prímər/ *n.* **1** a substance used to prime wood, etc. **2** a cap, cylinder, etc., used to ignite the powder of a cartridge, etc.

prim•er[2] /prímər, prīmər/ *n.* **1** an elementary textbook for teaching children to read. **2** an introductory book.

prime rate *n.* the lowest rate at which money can be borrowed commercially.

prime time *n.* the time at which a radio or television audience is expected to consist of the greatest number of people.

pri•me•val /prīmeévəl/ *adj.* **1** of or relating to the earliest age of the world. **2** ancient; primitive. ▫▫ **pri•me•val•ly** *adv.*

prim•i•tive /prímitiv/ *adj. & n.* •*adj.* **1** early; ancient; at an early stage of civilization (*primitive humans*). **2** undeveloped; crude; simple (*primitive methods*). **3** original; primary. **4** *Gram. & Philol.* (of words or language) radical; not derivative. **5** (of a color) primary. •*n.* **1 a** a painter of the period before the Renaissance. **b** a modern imitator of such. **2 a** an untutored painter with a direct naïve style. **b** a picture by such a painter. ▫▫ **prim•i•tive•ly** *adv.* **prim•i•tive•ness** *n.*

prim•i•tiv•ism /prímitivizəm/ *n.* **1** primitive behavior. **2** belief in the superiority of what is primitive. **3** the practice of primitive art. ▫▫ **prim•i•tiv•ist** *n. & adj.*

pri•mo /preémō/ *n.* (*pl.* **-mos**) **1** *Mus.* the leading or upper part in a duet, etc. **2** *colloq.* first-rate; excellent.

pri•mo•gen•i•tor /prímōjénitər/ *n.* **1** the earliest ancestor of a people, etc. **2** an ancestor.

pri•mo•gen•i•ture /prímōjénichər/ *n.* **1** the fact or condition of being the firstborn child. **2** (in full **right of primogeniture**) the right of succession belonging to the firstborn, esp. the feudal rule by which the whole real estate of an intestate passes to the eldest son.

pri•mor•di•al /prīmáwrdeeəl/ *adj.* **1** existing at or from the beginning; primeval. **2** original; fundamental. ▫▫ **pri•mor•di•al•i•ty** /–mawrdeeálitee/ *n.* **pri•mor•di•al•ly** *adv.*

primp /primp/ *v.tr.* **1** make (the hair, one's clothes, etc.) neat or overly tidy. **2** *refl.* groom (oneself) painstakingly.

prim•rose /prímrōz/ *n.* **1 a** any plant of the genus *Primula*, esp. *P. vulgaris*, bearing pale yellow flowers. **b** the flower of this. **2** a pale yellow color.

prim•rose path *n.* the pursuit of pleasure, esp. with disastrous consequences.

prim•u•la /prímyələ/ *n.* any plant of the genus *Primula*, bearing primrose-like flowers in a wide variety of colors during the spring, including primroses and cowslips.

prince /prins/ *n.* (as a title usu. **Prince**) **1** a male member of a royal family other than a reigning king. **2** (in full **prince of the blood**) a son or grandson of a British monarch. **3** a ruler of a small nation, actually or nominally subject to a king or emperor. **4** (as an English rendering of foreign titles) a noble usu. ranking next below a duke. **5** (as a courtesy title in some connections) a duke, marquess, or earl. **6** (often foll. by *of*) the chief or greatest (*the prince of novelists*). ▫▫ **prince•dom** *n.* **prince•like** *adj.* **prince•ship** *n.*

Prince Charm•ing *n.* an idealized young hero or lover.

prince•ly /prínslee/ *adj.* (**princelier, princeliest**) **1 a** of or worthy of a prince. **b** held by a prince. **2 a** sumptuous; generous; splendid. **b** (of a sum of money) substantial. ▫▫ **prince•li•ness** *n.*

Prince of Wales *n.* the heir apparent to the British throne, as a title conferred by the monarch.

prin•cess /prínses/ *n.* (as a title usu. **Princess**) **1** the wife of a prince. **2** a female member of a royal family other than a reigning queen. **3** (in full **princess of the blood**) a daughter or granddaughter of a British monarch. **4** a preeminent woman or thing personified as a woman.

prin•ci•pal /prínsipəl/ *adj. & n.* •*adj.* **1** (usu. *attrib.*) first in rank or importance; chief (*the principal town of the district*). **2** main; leading (*a principal cause of my success*). **3** (of money) constituting the original sum invested or lent. •*n.* **1** a head, ruler, or superior. **2** the head of an elementary, middle, or high school. **3** the leading performer in a concert, play, etc. **4** a capital sum as distinguished from interest or income. **5** a person for whom another acts as agent, etc. **6** (in the UK) a civil servant of the grade below Secretary. **7** the person actually responsible for a crime. **8** a person for whom another is surety. **9** *Mus.* the leading player in each section of an orchestra. ▫▫ **prin•ci•pal•ship** *n.*

▶**Principal** means 'important; person in charge': *the high school principal.* It also means 'a capital sum': *the principal would be repaid in five years.* **Principle** means 'rule, basis for conduct': *Her principles kept her from stealing despite her poverty.*

---

prin·ci·pal·i·ty /prínsipálitee/ *n.* (*pl.* **-ties**) **1** a nation ruled by a prince. **2** the government of a prince. **3** (in *pl.*) the fifth order of the ninefold celestial hierarchy.

prin·ci·pal·ly /prínsiplee/ *adv.* for the most part; chiefly.

prin·ci·ple /prínsipəl/ *n.* **1** a fundamental truth or law as the basis of reasoning or action (*arguing from first principles; moral principles*). **2 a** a personal code of conduct (*a person of high principle*). **b** (in *pl.*) such rules of conduct (*has no principles*). **3** a general law in physics, etc. (*the uncertainty principle*). **4** a law of nature forming the basis for the construction or working of a machine, etc. **5** a fundamental source; a primary element (*held water to be the first principle of all things*). **6** *Chem.* a constituent of a substance, esp. one giving rise to some quality, etc. □ **in principle** as regards fundamentals but not necessarily in detail. **on principle** on the basis of a moral attitude (*I refuse on principle*). ▶See note at PRINCIPAL.

prin·ci·pled /prínsipəld/ *adj.* based on or having (esp. praiseworthy) principles of behavior.

print /print/ *n., v., & adj.* • *n.* **1** an indentation or mark on a surface left by the pressure of a thing in contact with it (*fingerprint; footprint*). **2 a** printed lettering or writing (*large print*). **b** words in printed form. **c** a printed publication, esp. a newspaper. **d** the quantity of a book, etc., printed at one time. **e** the state of being printed. **3** a picture or design printed from a block or plate. **4 a** *Photog.* a picture produced on paper from a negative. **b** a copy of a motion picture suitable for showing. **5** a printed cotton fabric. • *v.tr.* **1 a** produce or reproduce (a book, picture, etc.) by applying inked types, blocks, or plates, to paper, vellum, etc. **b** (of an author, publisher, or editor) cause (a book or manuscript, etc.) to be produced or reproduced in this way. **2** express or publish in print. **3 a** (often foll. by *on, in*) impress or stamp (a mark or figure on a surface). **b** (often foll. by *with*) impress or stamp (a soft surface, e.g., of butter or wax, with a seal, die, etc.). **4** (often *absol.*) write (words or letters) without joining, in imitation of typography. **5** (often foll. by *off, out*) *Photog.* produce (a picture) by the transmission of light through a negative. **6** (usu. foll. by *out*) (of a computer, etc.) produce output in printed form. **7** mark (a textile fabric) with a decorative design in colors. **8** (foll. by *on*) impress (an idea, scene, etc., on the mind or memory). **9** transfer (a colored or plain design) from paper, etc., to the unglazed or glazed surface of ceramic ware. • *adj.* of, for, or concerning printed publications. □ **in print 1** (of a book, etc.) available from the publisher. **2** in printed form. **out of print** no longer available from the publisher. □□ **print·a·ble** *adj.* **print·a·bil·i·ty** /príntəbílitee/ *n.* **print·less** *adj.* (in sense 1 of *n.*).

print·er /príntər/ *n.* **1** a person who prints books, magazines, advertising matter, etc. **2** the owner of a printing business. **3** a device that prints, esp. as part of a computer system.

print·ing /prínting/ *n.* **1** the production of printed books, etc. **2** a single impression of a book. **3** printed letters or writing imitating them.

print·ing press *n.* a machine for printing from types or plates, etc.

print·mak·er /príntmaykər/ *n.* a person who makes a print. □□ **print·mak·ing** *n.*

print·out /príntowt/ *n.* computer output in printed form.

print·works /príntwərks/ *n.* a factory where fabrics are printed.

pri·or /príər/ *adj., adv., & n.* • *adj.* **1** earlier. **2** (often foll. by *to*) coming before in time, order, or importance. • *adv.* (foll. by *to*) before (*decided prior to their arrival*). • *n.* **1** the superior officer of a religious house or order. **2** (in an abbey) the officer next under the abbot. □□ **pri·or·ate** /–rət/ *n.* **pri·or·ess** /príəris/ *n.* **pri·or·ship** *n.*

pri·or·i·ty /priáwritee, –ór–/ *n.* (*pl.* **-ties**) **1** the fact or condition of being earlier or antecedent. **2** precedence in rank, etc. **3** an interest having prior claim to consideration. □□ **pri·or·i·tize** *v.tr.* **pri·or·i·ti·za·tion** *n.*

pri·o·ry /príəree/ *n.* (*pl.* **-ries**) a monastery governed by a prior or a convent governed by a prioress.

prism /prízəm/ *n.* **1** a solid geometric figure whose two ends are similar, equal, and parallel rectilinear figures, and whose sides are parallelograms. **2** a transparent body in this form, usu. triangular with refracting surfaces at an acute angle with each other, which separates white light into a spectrum of colors. □□ **pris·mal** /prízməl/ *adj.*

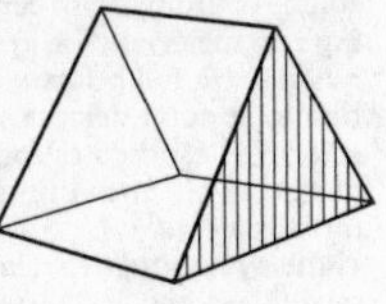
prism, 1

pris·mat·ic /prizmátik/ *adj.* **1** of, like, or using a prism. **2 a** (of colors) distributed by or as if by a transparent prism. **b** (of light) displayed in the form of a spectrum. □□ **pris·mat·i·cal·ly** *adv.*

pris·on /prízən/ *v.tr. & n.* • *n.* **1** a place in which a person is kept in captivity, esp. a building to which persons are legally committed while awaiting trial or for punishment; a jail. **2** custody; confinement (*in prison*). • *v.tr. poet.* (**prisoned, prisoning**) put in prison.

pris·on camp *n.* **1** a camp for prisoners of war or political prisoners. **2** a minimum-security prison.

pris·on·er /príznər/ *n.* **1** a person kept in prison. **2** *Brit.* (in full **prisoner at the bar**) a person in custody on a criminal charge and on trial. **3** a person or thing confined by illness, another's grasp, etc. **4** (in full **prisoner of war**) a person who has been captured in war. □ **take prisoner** seize and hold as a prisoner.

pris·on·er of con·science *n.* a person imprisoned by a government for holding political or religious views it does not tolerate.

pris·sy /prísee/ *adj.* (**prissier, prissiest**) prim; prudish. □□ **pris·si·ly** *adv.* **pris·si·ness** *n.*

pris·tine /prísteen, pristéen/ *adj.* **1** in its original condition; unspoiled. **2** *disp.* spotless; fresh as if new. **3** ancient; primitive.

prith·ee /príthee/ *int. archaic* pray; please.

pri·va·cy /prívəsee/ *n.* **1 a** the state of being private and undisturbed. **b** a person's right to this. **2** freedom from intrusion or public attention. **3** avoidance of publicity.

pri·vate /prívət/ *adj. & n.* • *adj.* **1** belonging to an individual; one's own; personal (*private property*). **2** confidential; not to be disclosed to others (*private talks*). **3** kept or removed from public knowledge or observation. **4 a** not open to the public. **b** for an individual's exclusive use (*private room*). **5** (of a place) secluded; affording privacy. **6** (of a person) not holding public office or an official position. **7** (of education) conducted outside the government system. **8** (of a person) retiring; reserved; unsociable. **9** (of a company) not having publicly traded shares. • *n.* **1** a soldier with a rank below corporal. **2** (in *pl.*) *colloq.* the genitals. □ **in private** privately; in private company or life. □□ **pri·vate·ly** *adv.*

pri·vate de·tec·tive *n.* a usu. freelance detective employed privately, outside an official police force.

pri·vate en·ter·prise *n.* **1** a business or businesses not under government control. **2** individual initiative.

pri·va·teer /prívətéer/ *n.* **1** an armed vessel owned and officered by private individuals holding a government commission and authorized for war service. **2 a** a commander of such a vessel. **b** (in *pl.*) its crew. ▫▫ **pri·va·teer·ing** *n.*

pri·vate eye *n. colloq.* a private detective.

pri·vate in·ves·ti·ga·tor *n.* private detective. ¶ Abbr.: **PI.**

pri·vate parts *n.pl.* the genitals.

pri·vate prac·tice *n.* **1** *US* an independent practice, esp. of law, medicine, or counseling services. **2** *Brit.* medical practice that is not part of the National Health Service.

pri·vate school *n.* **1** *US* a school not supported mainly by the government. **2** *Brit.* a school supported wholly by the payment of fees.

pri·vate sec·tor *n.* the part of the economy free of direct government control.

pri·va·tion /prīváyshən/ *n.* **1** lack of the comforts or necessities of life (*suffered many privations*). **2** (often foll. by *of*) loss or absence (of a quality).

pri·va·tize /prívətīz/ *v.tr.* make private, esp. transfer (a business, etc.) to private as distinct from government control or ownership. ▫▫ **pri·va·ti·za·tion** *n.*

priv·et /prívit/ *n.* any deciduous or evergreen shrub of the genus *Ligustrum*, esp. *L. vulgare* bearing small white flowers and black berries, and much used for hedges.

priv·i·lege /prívilij, prívlij/ *n.* & *v.* • *n.* **1 a** a right, advantage, or immunity, belonging to a person, class, or office. **b** the freedom of members of a legislative assembly when speaking at its meetings. **2** a special benefit or honor (*it is a privilege to meet you*). **3** a monopoly or patent granted to an individual, corporation, etc. **4** *Stock Exch.* an option to buy or sell. • *v.tr.* **1** invest with a privilege. **2** (foll. by *to* + infin.) allow (a person) as a privilege (to do something). **3** (often foll. by *from*) exempt (a person from a liability, etc.).

priv·i·leged /prívilijd, prívlijd/ *adj.* **1 a** invested with or enjoying a certain privilege or privileges; honored; favored. **b** exempt from standard regulations or procedures. **c** powerful; affluent. **2** (of information, etc.) confidential; restricted.

priv·y /prívee/ *adj.* & *n.* • *adj.* **1** (foll. by *to*) sharing in the secret of (a person's plans, etc.). **2** *archaic* hidden; secret. • *n.* (*pl.* **-ies**) **1** a toilet, esp. an outhouse. **2** *Law* a person having a part or interest in any action, matter, or thing. ▫▫ **priv·i·ly** *adv.*

prize[1] /prīz/ *n.* & *v.* • *n.* **1** something that can be won in a competition, lottery, etc. **2** a reward given as a symbol of victory or superiority. **3** something striven for or worth striving for (*missed all the great prizes of life*). **4** (*attrib.*) **a** to which a prize is awarded (*a prize bull*). **b** supremely excellent or outstanding of its kind. • *v.tr.* value highly (*a much prized possession*).

prize[2] /prīz/ *v.* & *n.* (also **prise**) • *v.tr.* force open or out by leverage (*prized up the lid*; *prized the box open*). • *n.* leverage; purchase.

prize·fight /prízfīt/ *n.* a boxing match fought for prize money. ▫▫ **prize·fight·er** *n.*

pro[1] /prō/ *n.* & *adj. colloq.* • *n.* (*pl.* **pros**) a professional. • *adj.* professional.

pro[2] /prō/ *adj.*, *n.*, & *prep.* • *adj.* (of an argument or reason) for; in favor. • *n.* (*pl.* **pros**) a reason or argument for or in favor. • *prep.* in favor of.

pro·a /prṓə/ *n.* (also **prau, prah·u** /praá-ōō/) a Malay boat, esp. with a large triangular sail and a canoe-like outrigger.

pro·ac·tive /prō-áktiv/ *adj.* **1** (of a person, policy, etc.) creating or controlling a situation by taking the initiative. **2** of or relating to mental conditioning or a habit, etc., which has been learned. ▫▫ **pro·ac·tive·ly** *adv.*

pro-am *adj.* involving professionals and amateurs.

prob. *abbr.* **1** probable. **2** probably. **3** problem.

prob·a·bi·lis·tic /probəbəlístik/ *adj.* based on or subject to probability.

prob·a·bil·i·ty /próbəbílitee/ *n.* (*pl.* **-ties**) **1** the state or condition of being probable. **2** the likelihood of something happening. **3** a probable or most probable event (*the probability is that they will come*). **4** *Math.* the extent to which an event is likely to occur, measured by the ratio of the favorable cases to the whole number of cases possible. ▫ **in all probability** most probably.

prob·a·ble /próbəbəl/ *adj.* & *n.* • *adj.* **1** (often foll. by *that* + clause) that may be expected to happen or prove true; likely (*the probable explanation*; *it is probable that they forgot*). **2** statistically likely but not proven. • *n.* a probable candidate, member of a team, etc. ▫▫ **prob·a·bly** *adv.*

pro·bate /prṓbayt/ *n.* & *v.* • *n.* **1** the official proving of a will. **2** a verified copy of a will. • *v.tr.* **1** establish the validity of (a will). **2** to put (a criminal offender) on probation.

pro·ba·tion /prəbáyshən/ *n.* **1** *Law* a system of suspending the sentence of a criminal offender subject to a period of good behavior under supervision. **2** a process or period of testing the character or abilities of a person in a certain role, esp. of a new employee. ▫ **on probation** undergoing probation, esp. legal supervision. ▫▫ **pro·ba·tion·al** *adj.* **pro·ba·tion·ar·y** *adj.*

pro·ba·tion·er /prōbáyshənər/ *n.* **1** a person on probation, e.g., a newly appointed nurse, teacher, etc. **2** a criminal offender on probation. ▫▫ **pro·ba·tion·er·ship** *n.*

pro·ba·tion of·fi·cer *n.* an official supervising offenders on probation.

probe /prōb/ *n.* & *v.* • *n.* **1** a penetrating investigation. **2** any small device, esp. an electrode, for measuring, testing, etc. **3** a blunt surgical instrument usu. of metal for exploring a wound, etc. **4** (in full **space probe**) an unmanned exploratory spacecraft transmitting information about its environment. • *v.* **1** *tr.* examine or inquire into closely. **2** *tr.* explore (a wound or part of the body) with a probe. **3** *tr.* penetrate with or as with a sharp instrument, esp. in order to explore. **4** *intr.* make an investigation with or as with a probe (*the detective probed into her past life*). ▫▫ **probe·a·ble** *adj.* **prob·er** *n.* **prob·ing·ly** *adv.*

pro·bi·ty /prṓbitee, prób–/ *n.* uprightness; honesty.

prob·lem /próbləm/ *n.* **1** a doubtful or difficult matter requiring a solution (*how to prevent it is a problem*; *the problem of ventilation*). **2** something hard to understand, accomplish, or deal with. **3** (*attrib.*) **a** causing problems; difficult to deal with (*problem child*). **b** (of a play, novel, etc.) in which a social or other problem is treated. **4 a** *Physics & Math.* an inquiry starting from given conditions to investigate or demonstrate a fact, result, or law. **b** *Geom.* a proposition in which something has to be constructed (cf. THEOREM).

prob·lem·at·ic /próbləmátik/ *adj.* (also **prob·lem·at·i·cal**) **1** difficult; posing a problem. **2** doubtful or questionable. ▫▫ **prob·lem·at·i·cal·ly** *adv.*

pro bo·no *adj.* pertaining to a service, esp. legal work, for which no fee is charged.

pro·bos·cis /prōbósis/ *n.* **1** the long flexible trunk or snout of some mammals, e.g., an elephant or tapir. **2** the elongated mouth parts of some insects. **3** the sucking organ in some worms. ▫▫ **pro·bos·cid·if·er·ous** /–sidífərəs/ *adj.* **pro·bos·cid·i·form** /–sídifawrm/ *adj.*

pro·car·y·ote var. of PROKARYOTE.

pro·ce·dure /prəseéjər/ *n.* **1** a way of proceeding, esp. a mode of conducting business or a legal action. **2** a mode of performing a task. **3** a series of actions conducted in a certain order or manner. **4** a proceeding.

See page xii for the *Key to Pronunciation.*

5 *Computing* = SUBROUTINE. □□ **pro·ce·dur·al** *adj.* **pro·ce·dur·al·ly** *adv.*

pro·ceed /prōseéd, prə–/ *v.intr.* **1** (often foll. by *to*) go forward or on further; make one's way. **2** (often foll. by *with*, or *to* + infin.) continue; go on with an activity (*proceeded with their work*; *proceeded to tell the whole story*). **3** (of an action) be carried on or continued (*the case will now proceed*). **4** adopt a course of action (*how shall we proceed?*). **5** go on to say. **6** (foll. by *against*) start a lawsuit (against a person). **7** (often foll. by *from*) come forth or originate (*shouts proceeded from the bedroom*).

pro·ceed·ing /prōseéding, prə–/ *n.* **1** an action or piece of conduct. **2** (in *pl.*) (in full **legal proceedings**) a legal action; a lawsuit. **3** (in *pl.*) a published report of discussions or a conference. **4** (in *pl.*) business, actions, or events in progress (*the proceedings were enlivened by a dog running onto the field*).

pro·ceeds /prṓseedz/ *n.pl.* money produced by a transaction or other undertaking.

proc·ess[1] /próses, prṓ–/ *n.* & *v.* •*n.* **1** a course of action or proceeding, esp. a series of stages in manufacture or some other operation. **2** the progress or course of something (*in process of construction*). **3** a natural or involuntary operation or series of changes (*the process of growing old*). **4** a legal action; a summons or writ. **5** *Anat.*, *Zool.*, & Bot. a natural appendage or outgrowth on an organism. •*v.tr.* **1** handle or deal with by a particular process. **2** treat (food, esp. to prevent decay) (*processed cheese*). **3** *Computing* operate on (data) by means of a program. □□ **proc·ess·a·ble** *adj.*

proc·ess[2] /prəsés/ *v.intr.* walk in procession.

pro·ces·sion /prəséshən/ *n.* **1** a number of people or vehicles, etc., moving forward in orderly succession, esp. at a ceremony, demonstration, or festivity. **2** the movement of such a group (*go in procession*). **3** a regular succession of things; a sequence. **4** *Theol.* the emanation of the Holy Spirit. □□ **pro·ces·sion·ist** *n.*

pro·ces·sion·al /prəséshənəl/ *adj.* & *n.* •*adj.* **1** of processions. **2** used, carried, or sung in processions. •*n.* *Eccl.* a book of processional hymns, etc.

proc·es·sor /prósesər, prṓ–/ *n.* a machine that processes things, esp.: **1** = CENTRAL PROCESSOR. **2** = FOOD PROCESSOR.

pro-choice *adj.* in favor of the right to legal abortion.

pro·claim /prōkláym, prə–/ *v.tr.* **1** (often foll. by *that* + clause) announce or declare publicly or officially. **2** declare (a person) to be (a king, traitor, etc.). **3** reveal as being (*an accent that proclaims you a Southerner*). □□ **pro·claim·er** *n.* **proc·la·ma·tion** /prókləmáyshən/ *n.* **pro·clam·a·to·ry** /–klámətawree/ *adj.*

pro·cliv·i·ty /prōklívitee/ *n.* (*pl.* **-ties**) a tendency or inclination.

pro·con·sul /prōkónsəl/ *n.* **1** *Rom.Hist.* a governor of a province, in the later republic usu. an ex-consul. **2** a governor of a modern colony, etc. **3** a deputy consul. □□ **pro·con·su·lar** /–kónsələr/ *adj.* **pro·con·su·late** /–kónsələt/ *n.* **pro·con·sul·ship** *n.*

pro·cras·ti·nate /prōkrástinayt/ *v.* **1** *intr.* defer action; delay, esp. intentionally. **2** *tr.* defer or delay, esp. intentionally or habitually. □□ **pro·cras·ti·na·tion** /–náyshən/ *n.* **pro·cras·ti·na·tive** /–nətiv/ *adj.* **pro·cras·ti·na·tor** *n.* **pro·cras·ti·na·to·ry** /–nətawree/ *adj.*

pro·cre·ate /prṓkreeayt/ *v.tr.* (often *absol.*) bring (offspring) into existence by the natural process of reproduction. □□ **pro·cre·ant** /prṓkreeənt/ *adj.* **pro·cre·a·tive** *adj.* **pro·cre·a·tion** *n.* **pro·cre·a·tor** *n.*

proc·tol·o·gy /proktóləjee/ *n.* the branch of medicine concerned with the anus and rectum. □□ **proc·to·log·i·cal** /–təlójikəl/ *adj.* **proc·tol·o·gist** *n.*

proc·tor /próktər/ *n.* **1** a supervisor of students in an examination, etc. **2** *Brit.* an officer (usu. one of two) at certain universities. **3** *Brit. Law* a person managing causes in a court (now chiefly ecclesiastical) that administers civil or canon law. □□ **proc·to·ri·al** /–táwreeəl/ *adj.* **proc·tor·ship** *n.*

pro·cum·bent /prōkúmbənt/ *adj.* **1** lying on the face; prostrate. **2** *Bot.* growing along the ground.

proc·u·ra·tion /prókyŏoráyshən/ *n.* **1** the action of procuring, obtaining, or bringing about. **2** the function or an authorized action of an attorney.

proc·u·ra·tor /prókyŏoraytər/ *n.* **1** an agent or proxy, esp. one who has power of attorney. **2** *Rom.Hist.* a treasury officer in an imperial province. □□ **proc·u·ra·to·ri·al** /–rətáwreeəl/ *adj.* **proc·u·ra·tor·ship** *n.*

pro·cure /prōkyŏor, prə–/ *v.tr.* **1** obtain, esp. by care or effort; acquire (*managed to procure a copy*). **2** bring about (*procured their dismissal*). **3** (also *absol.*) obtain (people) for prostitution. □□ **pro·cur·a·ble** *adj.* **pro·cu·ral** *n.* **pro·cure·ment** *n.*

pro·cur·er /prōkyŏ́rər, prə–/ *n.* a person who obtains people for prostitution.

prod /prod/ *v.* & *n.* •*v.* (**prodded, prodding**) **1** *tr.* poke with the finger or a pointed object. **2** *tr.* stimulate or goad to action. **3** *intr.* (foll. by *at*) make a prodding motion. •*n.* **1** a poke or thrust. **2** a stimulus to action. **3** a pointed instrument. □□ **prod·der** *n.*

prod·i·gal /pródigəl/ *adj.* & *n.* •*adj.* **1** recklessly wasteful. **2** (foll. by *of*) lavish. •*n.* **1** a prodigal person. **2** (in full **prodigal son**) a repentant wastrel, returned wanderer, etc. □□ **prod·i·gal·i·ty** /–gálitee/ *n.* **prod·i·gal·ly** *adv.*

pro·di·gious /prədíjəs/ *adj.* **1** marvelous or amazing. **2** enormous. **3** abnormal. □□ **pro·di·gious·ly** *adv.* **pro·di·gious·ness** *n.*

prod·i·gy /pródijee/ *n.* (*pl.* **-gies**) **1** a person endowed with exceptional qualities or abilities, esp. a precocious child. **2** a marvelous thing, esp. one out of the ordinary course of nature. **3** (foll. by *of*) a wonderful example (of a quality).

pro·duce *v.* & *n.* •*v.tr.* /prədŏŏs, –dyŏŏs/ **1** bring forward for consideration, inspection, or use (*will produce evidence*). **2** manufacture (goods) from raw materials, etc. **3** bear or yield (offspring, fruit, a harvest, etc.). **4** bring into existence. **5** cause or bring about (a reaction, sensation, etc.). **6** *Geom.* extend or continue (a line). **7 a** bring (a play, performer, book, etc.) before the public. **b** supervise the production of (a movie, broadcast, etc.). •*n.* /pródŏŏs, –dyŏŏs, prṓ–/ **1 a** what is produced, esp. agricultural products. **b** fruits and vegetables collectively. **2** (often foll. by *of*) a result (of labor, efforts, etc.). **3** a yield, esp. in the assay of ore. □□ **pro·duc·i·ble** /–sib'l/ *adj.* **pro·duc·i·bil·i·ty** *n.*

pro·duc·er /prədŏŏsər, –dyŏŏ–/ *n.* **1 a** *Econ.* a person who produces goods or commodities. **b** a person who or thing which produces something or someone. **2 a** a person generally responsible for the production of a movie, play, or radio or television program (apart from the direction of the acting). **b** *Brit.* the director of a play or broadcast program.

prod·uct /pródukt/ *n.* **1** a thing or substance produced by natural process or manufacture. **2** a result (*the product of their labors*). **3** *Math.* a quantity obtained by multiplying quantities together.

pro·duc·tion /prədúkshən/ *n.* **1** the act or an instance of producing; the process of being produced. **2** the process of being manufactured, esp. in large quantities (*go into production*). **3** a total yield. **4** a thing produced, esp. a literary or artistic work, a movie, broadcast, play, etc. □□ **pro·duc·tion·al** *adj.*

pro·duc·tive /prədúktiv/ *adj.* **1** of or engaged in the production of goods. **2 a** producing much (*productive soil*; *a productive writer*). **b** (of the mind) inventive; creative. **3** *Econ.* producing commodities of exchangeable value (*productive labor*). **4** (foll. by *of*) producing or giving rise to (*productive of great annoyance*). ▫▫ **pro·duc·tive·ly** *adv.* **pro·duc·tive·ness** *n.*

pro·duc·tiv·i·ty /próduktívitee, prṓ–/ *n.* **1** the capacity to produce. **2** the quality or state of being productive. **3** the effectiveness of productive effort, esp. in industry. **4** production per unit of effort.

pro·em /prṓim/ *n.* **1** a preface or preamble to a book or speech. **2** a beginning or prelude. ▫▫ **pro·e·mi·al** /prōéemeeəl/ *adj.*

Prof. *abbr.* Professor.

prof /prof/ *n. colloq.* a professor.

pro·fane /prōfáyn, prə–/ *adj.* **1** not belonging to what is sacred or biblical; secular. **2 a** irreverent; blasphemous. **b** vulgar; obscene. **3** (of a rite, etc.) heathen; pagan. **4** not initiated into religious rites or any esoteric knowledge. ▫▫ **pro·fane·ly** *adv.* **pro·fane·ness** *n.*

pro·fan·i·ty /prōfánitee, prə–/ *n.* (*pl.* **-ties**) **1** a profane act. **2** profane language; blasphemy.

pro·fess /prəfés, prō–/ *v.* **1** *tr.* claim openly to have (a quality or feeling). **2** *tr.* (foll. by *to* + infin.) pretend. **3** *tr.* (often foll. by *that* + clause; also *refl.*) declare (*profess ignorance; professed herself satisfied*). **4** *tr.* affirm one's faith in or allegiance to.

pro·fessed /prəfést, prō–/ *adj.* **1** self-acknowledged (*a professed Christian*). **2** alleged; ostensible. **3** claiming to be duly qualified. **4** (of a monk or nun) having taken the vows of a religious order. ▫▫ **pro·fess·ed·ly** /–fésidlee/ *adv.* (in senses 1, 2).

pro·fes·sion /prəféshən/ *n.* **1** a vocation or calling, esp. one that involves some branch of advanced learning or science (*the medical profession*). **2** a body of people engaged in a profession. **3** a declaration or avowal. **4** a declaration of belief in a religion. ▫ **the oldest profession** prostitution. ▫▫ **pro·fes·sion·less** *adj.*

---

profession Middle English (denoting the vow made on entering a religious order): via Old French from Latin *professio(n-)*, from *profiteri* 'declare publicly' (source of *profess*). Sense 1 derives from the notion of an occupation that one 'professes' to be skilled in.

---

pro·fes·sion·al /prəféshənəl/ *adj.* & *n.* • *adj.* **1** of or belonging to or connected with a profession. **2 a** having or showing the skill of a professional; competent. **b** worthy of a professional (*professional conduct*). **3** engaged in a specified activity as one's main paid occupation (cf. AMATEUR) (*a professional boxer*). **4** *derog.* engaged in a specified activity regarded with disfavor (*a professional agitator*). • *n.* a professional person. ▫▫ **pro·fes·sion·al·ly** *adv.*

pro·fes·sion·al·ism /prəféshənəlizəm/ *n.* the qualities or typical features of a profession or of professionals, esp. competence, skill, etc. ▫▫ **pro·fes·sion·al·ize** *v.tr.*

pro·fes·sor /prəfésər/ *n.* **1 a** (often as a title) a university academic of the highest rank. **b** a university teacher. **c** a teacher of some specific art, sport, or skill. **2** a person who professes a religion. ▫▫ **pro·fes·sor·ate** /–rət/ *n.* **pro·fes·so·ri·al** /prófisáwreeəl/ *adj.* **pro·fes·so·ri·al·ly** *adv.* **pro·fes·so·ri·ate** /–fisáwreeət/ *n.* **pro·fes·sor·ship** *n.*

prof·fer /prófər/ *v.* & *n.* • *v.tr.* (esp. as **proffered** *adj.*) offer (a gift, services, a hand, etc.). • *n.* an offer or proposal.

pro·fi·cient /prəfishənt/ *adj.* & *n.* • *adj.* (often foll. by *in, at*) adept; expert. • *n.* a person who is proficient. ▫▫ **pro·fi·cien·cy** /–shənsee/ *n.* **pro·fi·cient·ly** *adv.*

pro·file /prṓfil/ *n.* & *v.* • *n.* **1 a** an outline (esp. of a human face) as seen from one side. **b** a representation of this. **2 a** a short biographical or character sketch. **b** a report, esp. one written by a teacher on a pupil's academic and social progress. **3** *Statistics* a representation by a graph or chart of information (esp. on certain characteristics) recorded in a quantified form. **4** a characteristic personal manner or attitude. **5** a vertical cross section of a structure. **6** a flat outline piece of scenery on stage. • *v.tr.* **1** represent in profile. **2** give a profile to. **3** write a profile about. ▫ **in profile** as seen from one side. **keep a low profile** remain inconspicuous. ▫▫ **pro·fil·er** *n.* **pro·fil·ist** *n.*

prof·it /prófit/ *n.* & *v.* • *n.* **1** an advantage or benefit. **2** financial gain; excess of returns over expenditures. • *v.* (**profited, profiting**) **1** *tr.* (also *absol.*) be beneficial to. **2** *intr.* obtain an advantage or benefit (*profited by the experience*). **3** *intr.* make a profit. ▫ **at a profit** with financial gain. ▫▫ **prof·it·less** *adj.*

prof·it·a·ble /prófitəbəl/ *adj.* **1** yielding profit; lucrative. **2** beneficial; useful. ▫▫ **prof·it·a·bil·i·ty** /–bílitee/ *n.* **prof·it·a·ble·ness** *n.* **prof·it·a·bly** *adv.*

prof·it·eer /prófitéer/ *v.* & *n.* • *v.intr.* make or seek to make excessive profits, esp. illegally or in black market conditions. • *n.* a person who profiteers.

pro·fit·er·ole /prəfitərōl/ *n.* a small hollow pastry usu. filled with cream and covered with chocolate sauce.

prof·it mar·gin *n.* the profit remaining in a business after costs have been deducted.

prof·li·gate /prófligət/ *adj.* & *n.* • *adj.* **1** licentious; dissolute. **2** recklessly extravagant. • *n.* a profligate person. ▫▫ **prof·li·ga·cy** /–gəsee/ *n.* **prof·li·gate·ly** *adv.*

pro for·ma /prō fáwrmə/ *adv., adj.,* & *n.* • *adv.* & *adj.* as or being a matter of form; for the sake of form. • *n.* (in full **pro-forma invoice**) an invoice sent in advance of goods supplied.

pro·found /prəfównd, prō–/ *adj.* (**profounder, profoundest**) **1 a** having or showing great knowledge or insight (*a profound treatise*). **b** demanding deep study or thought (*profound doctrines*). **2** (of a state or quality) deep; intense; unqualified (*a profound sleep; profound indifference*). **3** at or extending to a great depth (*profound crevasses*). **4** coming from a great depth (*a profound sigh*). **5** (of a disease) deep-seated. ▫▫ **pro·found·ly** *adv.* **pro·found·ness** *n.* **pro·fun·di·ty** /–fúnditee/ *n.* (*pl.* **-ties**).

pro·fuse /prəfyṓos, prō–/ *adj.* **1** (often foll. by *in, of*) lavish; extravagant (*was profuse in her generosity*). **2** (of a thing) exuberantly plentiful; abundant (*profuse bleeding*). ▫▫ **pro·fuse·ly** *adv.* **pro·fuse·ness** *n.* **pro·fu·sion** /–fyṓozhən/ *n.*

pro·gen·i·tive /prōjénitiv/ *adj.* capable of or connected with the production of offspring.

pro·gen·i·tor /prōjénitər/ *n.* **1** the ancestor of a person, animal, or plant. **2** a political or intellectual predecessor. **3** the origin of a copy. ▫▫ **pro·gen·i·to·ri·al** /–táwreeəl/ *adj.* **pro·gen·i·tor·ship** *n.*

prog·e·ny /prójinee/ *n.* **1** the offspring of a person or other organism. **2** a descendant or descendants. **3** an outcome or issue.

pro·ges·ter·one /prōjéstərōn/ *n.* a steroid hormone that stimulates the preparation of the uterus for pregnancy.

pro·ges·to·gen /prōjéstəjin/ *n.* **1** any of a group of steroid hormones (including progesterone) that maintain pregnancy and prevent further ovulation during it. **2** a similar hormone produced synthetically.

prog·na·thous /prognáythəs, prógnəthəs/ *adj.* **1** having a projecting jaw. **2** (of a jaw) projecting. ▫▫ **prog·nath·ic** /prognáthik/ *adj.* **prog·na·thism** *n.*

prog·no·sis /prognṓsis/ *n.* (*pl.* **prognoses** /–seez/) **1** a forecast; a prognostication. **2** a forecast of the course of a disease.

prog·nos·tic /prognóstik/ *n.* & *adj.* • *n.* **1** (often foll. by *of*) an advance indication or omen, esp. of the course of a disease, etc. **2** a prediction; a forecast. • *adj.* foretelling; predictive (*prognostic of a good result*). □□ **prog·nos·ti·cal·ly** *adv.*

prog·nos·ti·cate /prognóstikayt/ *v.tr.* **1** (often foll. by *that* + clause) foretell; foresee; prophesy. **2** (of a thing) betoken; indicate (future events, etc.). □□ **prog·nos·ti·ca·ble** /–kəbəl/ *adj.* **prog·nos·ti·ca·tion** *n.* **prog·nos·ti·ca·tive** /–kətiv/ *adj.* **prog·nos·ti·ca·tor** *n.* **prog·nos·ti·ca·to·ry** /–kətawree/ *adj.*

pro·gram /prṓgram, –grəm/ *n.* & *v.* (*Brit.* **programme**) •*n.* **1** a usu. printed list of a series of events, performers, etc., at a public function, etc. **2** a radio or television broadcast. **3** a plan of future events (*the program is dinner and an early night*). **4** a course or series of studies, lectures, etc.; a syllabus. **5** a series of coded instructions to control the operation of a computer or other machine. •*v.tr.* (**programmed, programming**; also **programed, programing**) **1** make a program or definite plan of. **2** express (a problem) or instruct (a computer) by means of a program. □□ **pro·gram·mable** *adj.* **pro·gram·ma·bil·i·ty** /–gramәbílitee/ *n.* **pro·gram·mat·ic** /–grəmátik/ *adj.* **pro·gram·mat·i·cal·ly** /–grəmátiklee/ *adv.* **pro·gram·mer** *n.* **pro·gram·er** *n.*

pro·gress *n.* & *v.* •*n.* /prógres/ **1** forward or onward movement toward a destination. **2** advance or development toward completion, betterment, etc.; improvement (*has made little progress this term*; *the progress of civilization*). **3** *Brit. archaic* a state journey or official tour, esp. by royalty. •*v.* /prəgrés/ **1** *intr.* move or be moved forward or onward; continue (*the argument is progressing*). **2** /prəgrés/ *intr.* advance or develop toward completion, improvement, etc. (*science progresses*). **3** *tr.* cause (work, etc.) to make regular progress. □ **in progress** in the course of developing; going on.

pro·gres·sion /prəgréshən/ *n.* **1** the act or an instance of progressing (*a mode of progression*). **2** a succession; a series. **3** *Math.* a sequence of numbers related by some rule (see ARITHMETIC PROGRESSION, GEOMETRIC PROGRESSION). **4** *Mus.* passing from one note or chord to another. □□ **pro·gres·sion·al** *adj.*

pro·gres·sive /prəgrésiv/ *adj.* & *n.* •*adj.* **1** moving forward (*progressive motion*). **2** proceeding step-by-step; cumulative (*progressive drug use*). **3 a** (of a political party, government, etc.) favoring or implementing rapid progress or social reform. **b** modern; efficient (*this is a progressive company*). **4** (of disease, violence, etc.) increasing in severity or extent. **5** (of taxation) at rates increasing with the sum taxed. **6** (of a card game, dance, etc.) with periodic changes of partners. **7** *Gram.* (of an aspect) expressing an action in progress, e.g., *am writing, was writing.* **8** (of education) informal and without strict discipline, stressing individual needs. •*n.* (also **Progressive**) an advocate of progressive political policies. □□ **pro·gres·sive·ly** *adv.* **pro·gres·sive·ness** *n.* **pro·gres·siv·ism** *n.* **pro·gres·siv·ist** *n.* & *adj.*

pro·hib·it /prōhíbit/ *v.tr.* (**prohibited, prohibiting**) (often foll. by *from* + verbal noun) **1** formally forbid, esp. by authority. **2** prevent; make impossible (*his accident prohibits him from playing football*). □□ **pro·hib·it·er** *n.* **pro·hib·i·tor** *n.*

pro·hi·bi·tion /próhibíshən, próibíshən/ *n.* **1** the act or an instance of forbidding; a state of being forbidden. **2** *Law* an edict or order that forbids. **3** (usu. **Prohibition**) the period (1920–33) in the US when the manufacture and sale of alcoholic beverages was prohibited by law. □□ **pro·hi·bi·tion·ar·y** *adj.* **pro·hi·bi·tion·ist** *n.*

pro·hib·i·tive /prōhíbitiv/ *adj.* **1** prohibiting. **2** (of prices, taxes, etc.) so high as to prevent purchase, use, abuse, etc. (*published at a prohibitive price*). □□ **pro·hib·i·tive·ly** *adv.* **pro·hib·i·tive·ness** *n.* **pro·hib·i·to·ry** *adj.*

pro·ject *n.* & *v.* •*n.* /prójekt/ **1** a plan; a scheme. **2** a planned undertaking. **3** a usu. long-term task undertaken by a student or group of students to be submitted for grading. **4** (often *pl.*) a housing development, esp. for low-income residents. •*v.* /prəjékt/ **1** *tr.* plan or contrive (a course of action, scheme, etc.). **2** *intr.* protrude; jut out. **3** *tr.* throw; cast; impel. **4** *tr.* extrapolate (results, etc.) to a future time; forecast (*I project that we will produce two million next year*). **5** *tr.* cause (light, shadow, images, etc.) to fall on a surface, screen, etc. **6** *tr.* cause (a sound, esp. the voice) to be heard at a distance. **7** *tr.* (often *refl.* or *absol.*) express or promote (oneself or an image) forcefully or effectively. **8** *tr. Geom.* **a** draw straight lines from a center or parallel lines through every point of (a given figure) to produce a corresponding figure on a surface or a line by intersecting it. **b** draw (such lines). **c** produce (such a corresponding figure). **9** *tr.* make a projection of (the earth, sky, etc.). **10** *tr. Psychol.* **a** (also *absol.*) attribute (an emotion, etc.) to an external object or person, esp. unconsciously. **b** (*refl.*) project (oneself) into another's feelings, the future, etc.

---

project late Middle English (in the sense 'preliminary design, tabulated statement'): from Latin *projectum* 'something prominent,' neuter past participle of *projicere* 'throw forth,' from *pro-* 'forth' + *jacere* 'to throw.' Early senses of the verb were 'plan, devise' and 'cause to move forward.'

---

pro·jec·tile /prəjéktəl, –tīl/ *n.* & *adj.* •*n.* **1** a missile, esp. fired by a rocket. **2** a bullet, shell, etc., fired from a gun. **3** any object thrown as a weapon. •*adj.* **1** capable of being projected by force, esp. from a gun. **2** projecting or impelling.

pro·jec·tion /prəjékshən/ *n.* **1** the act or an instance of projecting; the process of being projected. **2** a thing that projects or obtrudes. **3** the presentation of an image, etc., on a surface or screen. **4 a** a forecast or estimate based on present trends. **b** this process. **5 a** a mental image or preoccupation viewed as an objective reality. **b** the unconscious transfer of one's own impressions or feelings to external objects or persons. **6** *Geom.* the act or an instance of projecting a figure. **7** the representation on a plane surface of any part of the surface of the earth or a celestial sphere (*Mercator projection*). □□ **pro·jec·tion·ist** *n.* (in sense 3).

pro·jec·tive /prəjéktiv/ *adj.* **1** *Geom.* **a** relating to or derived by projection. **b** (of a property of a figure) unchanged by projection. **2** *Psychol.* mentally projecting or projected (*a projective imagination*). □□ **pro·jec·tive·ly** *adv.*

pro·jec·tor /prəjéktər/ *n.* **1 a** an apparatus containing a source of light and a system of lenses for projecting slides or movies onto a screen. **b** an apparatus for projecting rays of light. **2** a person who forms or promotes a project. **3** *archaic* a promoter of speculative companies.

pro·kar·y·ote /prōkáreeōt/ *n.* (also **procaryote**) an organism in which the chromosomes are not separated from the cytoplasm by a membrane; a bacterium (cf. EUKARYOTE). □□ **pro·kar·y·o·tic** /–reeótik/ *adj.*

pro·lapse /prṓlaps/ *n.* & *v.* •*n.* (also **pro·lap·sus** /–lápsəs/) **1** the forward or downward displacement of a part or organ. **2** the prolapsed part or organ, esp. the womb or rectum. •*v.intr.* undergo prolapse.

prole /prōl/ *adj.* & *n. derog. colloq.* •*adj.* proletarian. •*n.* a proletarian.

pro·le·tar·i·an /prṓlitáireeən/ *adj.* & *n.* •*adj.* of or concerning the proletariat. •*n.* a member of the proletariat. □□ **pro·le·tar·i·an·ism** *n.* **pro·le·tar·i·an·ize** *v.tr.*

pro·le·tar·i·at /prṓlitáireeət/ *n.* (also **pro·le·tar·i·ate**) **1 a** *Econ.* wage earners collectively, esp. those without capital and dependent on selling their labor. **b** esp.

derog. the lowest class of the community, esp. when considered as uncultured. **2** *Rom.Hist.* the lowest class of citizens.

pro-life /prṓlīf/ *adj.* opposing abortion. ▫▫ **pro-lif·er** *n.*

pro·lif·er·ate /prəlífərayt/ *v.* **1** *intr.* reproduce; increase rapidly in numbers; grow by multiplication. **2** *tr.* produce (cells, etc.) rapidly. ▫▫ **pro·lif·er·a·tion** /–fəráyshən/ *n.* **pro·lif·er·a·tive** /–rətiv/ *adj.*

pro·lif·er·ous /prəlífərəs/ *adj.* **1** (of a plant) producing many leaf or flower buds; growing luxuriantly. **2** growing or multiplying by budding. **3** spreading by proliferation.

pro·lif·ic /prəlífik/ *adj.* **1** producing many offspring or much output. **2** (often foll. by *of*) abundantly productive. **3** (often foll. by *in*) abounding; copious. ▫▫ **pro·lif·i·ca·cy** *n.* **pro·lif·i·cal·ly** *adv.* **pro·lif·ic·ness** *n.*

pro·lix /prōlíks, prṓliks/ *adj.* (of speech, writing, etc.) lengthy; tedious. ▫▫ **pro·lix·i·ty** /–líksitee/ *n.* **pro·lix·ly** *adv.*

pro·logue /prṓlawg, –log/ *n.* & *v.* (also **pro·log**) • *n.* **1 a** a preliminary speech, poem, etc., esp. introducing a play (cf. EPILOGUE). **b** the actor speaking the prologue. **2** (usu. foll. by *to*) any act or event serving as an introduction. • *v.tr.* (**prologues, prologued, prologuing**) introduce with or provide with a prologue.

pro·long /prəláwng, –lóng/ *v.tr.* **1** extend (an action, condition, etc.) in time or space. **2** lengthen the pronunciation of (a syllable, etc.). **3** (as **prolonged** *adj.*) lengthy, esp. tediously so. ▫▫ **pro·lon·ga·tion** *n.* **pro·long·ed·ly** /–idli/ *adv.* **pro·long·er** *n.*

prom /prom/ *n. colloq.* **1** a school or college formal dance. **2** *Brit.* = PROMENADE *n.* 4a.

prom·e·nade /prómənáyd, –naád/ *n.* & *v.* • *n.* **1** a walk, or sometimes a ride or drive, taken esp. for display, social intercourse, etc. **2** a school or university ball or dance. **3** a march of dancers in country dancing, etc. **4 a** *Brit.* a paved public walk along the sea front at a resort. **b** any paved public walk. • *v.* **1** *intr.* make a promenade. **2** *tr.* lead (a person, etc.) about a place esp. for display. **3** *tr.* make a promenade through (a place).

prom·e·nade deck *n.* an upper deck on a passenger ship where passengers may promenade.

Pro·me·the·an /prəmeétheeən/ *adj.* daring or inventive like Prometheus, who in Greek myth was punished for stealing fire from the gods and giving it to the human race.

pro·me·thi·um /prəmeétheeəm/ *n. Chem.* a radioactive metallic element of the lanthanide series occurring in nuclear waste material. ¶ Symb.: **Pm**.

prom·i·nence /próminəns/ *n.* **1** the state of being prominent. **2** a prominent thing, esp. a jutting outcrop, mountain, etc.

prom·i·nent /próminənt/ *adj.* **1** jutting out; projecting. **2** conspicuous. **3** distinguished; important. ▫▫ **prom·i·nen·cy** *n.* **prom·i·nent·ly** *adv.*

pro·mis·cu·ous /prəmískyoōəs/ *adj.* **1 a** (of a person) having frequent and diverse sexual relationships, esp. transient ones. **b** (of sexual relationships) of this kind. **2** *colloq.* carelessly irregular; casual. ▫▫ **prom·is·cu·i·ty** /prómiskyoṓitee/ *n.* **pro·mis·cu·ous·ly** *adv.* **pro·mis·cu·ous·ness** *n.*

prom·ise /prómis/ *n.* & *v.* • *n.* **1** an assurance that one will or will not undertake a certain action, behavior, etc. (*a promise of help; gave a promise to be generous*). **2** a sign or signs of future achievements, good results, etc. (*a writer of great promise*). • *v.tr.* **1** (usu. foll. by *to* + infin., or *that* + clause; also *absol.*) make (a person) a promise, esp. to do, give, or procure (a thing) (*I promise you a fair hearing; cannot positively promise*) **2 a** afford expectations of (*the discussions promise future problems; promises to be a good cook*). **b** (foll. by *to* + infin.) seem likely to (*is promising to rain*). **3** *colloq.* assure; confirm (*I promise you, it will not be easy*). **4** (usu. in *passive*) *esp. archaic* betroth (*she is promised to another*). ▫▫ **prom·is·ee** /–seé/ *n.* esp. *Law* **prom·is·er** *n.* **prom·i·sor** *n.* esp. *Law.*

prom·is·ing /prómising/ *adj.* likely to turn out well; hopeful; full of promise (*a promising start*). ▫▫ **prom·is·ing·ly** *adv.*

prom·is·so·ry note *n.* a signed document containing a written promise to pay a stated sum to a specified person or the bearer at a specified date or on demand.

pro·mo /prṓmō/ *n.* & *adj. colloq.* • *n.* (*pl.* **-mos**) **1** publicity blurb or advertisement. **2** a trailer for a television program. • *adj.* promotional.

prom·on·to·ry /prómantawree/ *n.* (*pl.* **-ries**) a point of high land jutting out into the sea, etc.; a headland.

pro·mote /prəmṓt/ *v.tr.* **1** (often foll. by *to*) advance or raise (a person) to a higher office, rank, grade, etc. (*was promoted to captain*). **2** help forward; encourage; support actively (a cause, process, desired result, etc.) (*promoted women's suffrage*). **3** publicize and sell (a product). **4** attempt to ensure the passing of (a legislative act). **5** *Chess* raise (a pawn) to the rank of queen, etc., when it reaches the opponent's end of the board. ▫▫ **pro·mot·a·ble** *adj.* **pro·mot·a·bil·i·ty** *n.* **pro·mo·tion** /–mṓshən/ *n.* **pro·mo·tion·al** *adj.* **pro·mo·tive** *adj.*

pro·mot·er /prəmṓtər/ *n.* **1** a person who promotes. **2** a person who finances, organizes, etc., a sporting event, theatrical production, etc. **3** a person who promotes the formation of a company, project, etc. **4** *Chem.* an additive that increases the activity of a catalyst.

prompt /prompt/ *adj., adv., v.,* & *n.* • *adj.* **1 a** acting with alacrity; ready. **b** made, done, etc., readily or at once (*a prompt reply*). **2 a** (of a payment) made quickly or immediately. **b** (of goods) for immediate delivery and payment. • *adv.* punctually. • *v.tr.* **1** (usu. foll. by *to*, or *to* + infin.) incite; urge (*prompted them to action*). **2 a** (also *absol.*) supply a forgotten word, sentence, etc., to (an actor, reciter, etc.). **b** assist (a hesitating speaker) with a suggestion. **3** give rise to; inspire (a feeling, thought, action, etc.). • *n.* **1 a** an act of prompting. **b** a thing said to help the memory of an actor, etc. **c** = PROMPTER 2. **d** *Computing* an indication or sign on a computer screen to show that the system is waiting for input. **2** the time limit for the payment of an account, stated on a prompt note. ▫▫ **prompt·ing** *n.* **promp·ti·tude** *n.* **prompt·ly** *adv.* **prompt·ness** *n.*

prompt·er /prómptər/ *n.* **1** a person who prompts. **2** *Theatr.* a person seated out of sight of the audience who prompts the actors.

prom·ul·gate /próməlgayt/ *v.tr.* **1** make known to the public; disseminate; promote (a cause, etc.). **2** proclaim (a decree, news, etc.). ▫▫ **prom·ul·ga·tion** /–gáyshən/ *n.* **prom·ul·ga·tor** *n.*

prone /prōn/ *adj.* **1 a** lying face downward (cf. SUPINE). **b** lying flat; prostrate. **c** having the front part downwards, esp. the palm of the hand. **2** (usu. foll. by *to*, or *to* + infin.) disposed or liable, esp. to a bad action, condition, etc. (*is prone to bite his nails*). **3** (usu. in *comb.*) more than usually likely to suffer (*accident-prone*). ▫▫ **prone·ly** *adv.* **prone·ness** /prṓn-nis/ *n.*

prong /prong/ *n.* & *v.* • *n.* each of two or more projecting pointed parts at the end of a fork, etc. • *v.tr.* **1** pierce or stab with a fork. **2** turn up (soil) with a fork. ▫▫ **pronged** *adj.* (also in *comb.*).

prong·horn /prónghawrn/ *n.* a N. American deerlike ruminant, *Antilocapra americana*, the male of which has horns with forward-pointing prongs.

pro·noun /prṓnown/ *n.* a word used instead of and to

indicate a noun already mentioned or known, esp. to avoid repetition (e.g., *we, their, this, ourselves*).

pro•nounce /prənówns/ *v.* **1** *tr.* (also *absol.*) utter or speak (words, sounds, etc.) in a certain way. **2** *tr.* **a** utter or deliver (a judgment, sentence, curse, etc.) formally or solemnly. **b** proclaim or announce officially (*I pronounce you husband and wife*). **3** *tr.* state or declare, as being one's opinion (*the apples were pronounced excellent*). **4** *intr.* (usu. foll. by *on, for, against, in favor of*) pass judgment; give one's opinion (*pronounced for the defendant*). ▫▫ **pro•nounce•a•ble** /–nównsəbəl/ *adj.* **pro•nounce•ment** *n.* **pro•nounc•er** *n.*

pro•nounced /prənównst/ *adj.* **1** (of a word, sound, etc.) uttered. **2** strongly marked; decided (*a pronounced flavor; a pronounced limp*). ▫▫ **pro•nounc•ed•ly** /–nównsidlee/ *adv.*

pron•to /próntō/ *adv. colloq.* promptly; quickly.

pro•nun•ci•a•tion /prənúnseeáyshən/ *n.* **1** the way in which a word is pronounced, esp. with reference to a standard. **2** the act or an instance of pronouncing. **3** a person's way of pronouncing words, etc.

proof /proōf/ *n., adj., & v.* • *n.* **1** facts, evidence, argument, etc., establishing or helping to establish a fact (*proof of their honesty*). **2** *Law* the spoken or written evidence in a trial. **3** a demonstration or act of proving (*not capable of proof; in proof of my assertion*). **4** a test or trial (*the proof of the pudding is in the eating*). **5** the standard of strength of distilled alcoholic spirits. **6** *Printing* a trial impression taken from type or film, used for making corrections before final printing. **7** the stages in the resolution of a mathematical or philosophical problem. **8** each of a limited number of impressions from an engraved plate. **9** a photographic print made for selection, etc. **10** a newly issued coin struck from a polished die esp. for collectors, etc. • *adj.* **1** impervious to penetration, ill effects, etc. (*proof against the harshest weather*). **2** (in *comb.*) able to withstand damage or destruction by a specified agent (*soundproof; childproof*). **3** being of proof alcoholic strength. **4** (of armor) of tried strength. • *v.tr.* **1** proofread **2** make (something) proof, esp. make (fabric) waterproof. **3** make a proof of (a printed work, engraving, etc.). ▫▫ **proof•less** *adj.*

proof•read /proōfreed/ *v.tr.* (*past* and *past part.* **-read** /–red/) read (esp. printer's proofs) and mark any errors. ▫▫ **proof•read•er** *n.* **proof•read•ing** *n.*

prop[1] /prop/ *n. & v.* • *n.* **1** a rigid support, esp. one not an integral part of the thing supported. **2** a person who supplies support, assistance, comfort, etc. • *v.tr.* (**propped, propping**) (often foll. by *against, up*, etc.) support with or as if with a prop (*propped him against the wall; propped it up with a brick*).

prop[2] /prop/ *n. Theatr. colloq.* **1** = PROPERTY 3. **2** (in *pl.*) a property man or mistress.

prop[3] /prop/ *n. colloq.* an aircraft propeller.

prop. *abbr.* **1** proper; properly. **2** property. **3** proprietary. **4** proprietor. **5** proposition.

prop•a•gan•da /própəgándə/ *n.* **1** an organized program of publicity, selected information, etc., used to propagate a doctrine, practice, etc. **2** usu. *derog.* the information, doctrines, etc., propagated in this way.

prop•a•gan•dist /própəgándist/ *n.* a member or agent of a propaganda organization; a person who spreads propaganda. ▫▫ **prop•a•gan•dism** *n.* **prop•a•gan•dis•tic** *adj.* **prop•a•gan•dis•ti•cal•ly** *adv.* **prop•a•gan•dize** *v.intr. & tr.*

prop•a•gate /própəgayt/ **1** *tr.* **a** breed specimens of (a plant, animal, etc.) by natural processes from the parent stock. **b** (*refl.* or *absol.*) (of a plant, animal, etc.) reproduce itself. **2 a** *tr.* disseminate; spread (a statement, belief, theory, etc.). **b** *intr.* grow more widespread or numerous; spread. **3** *tr.* hand down (a quality, etc.) from one generation to another. **4** *tr.* extend the operation of; transmit (a vibration, earthquake, etc.). ▫▫ **prop•a•ga•tion** /–gáyshən/ *n.* **prop•a•ga•tive** *adj.*

pro•pane /própayn/ *n.* a gaseous hydrocarbon of the alkane series used as bottled fuel. ¶ Chem. formula: C_3H_8.

pro•pel /prəpél/ *v.tr.* (**propelled, propelling**) **1** drive or push forward. **2** urge on; encourage.

pro•pel•lant /prəpélənt/ *n. & adj.* (also **pro•pel•lent**) • *n.* **1** a thing that propels. **2** an explosive that fires bullets, etc., from a firearm. **3** a substance used as a reagent in a rocket engine, etc., to provide thrust. • *adj.* propelling; capable of driving or pushing forward.

pro•pel•ler /prəpélər/ *n.* **1** a person or thing that propels. **2** a revolving shaft with blades, esp. for propelling a ship or aircraft (cf. SCREW PROPELLER *n.* 6).

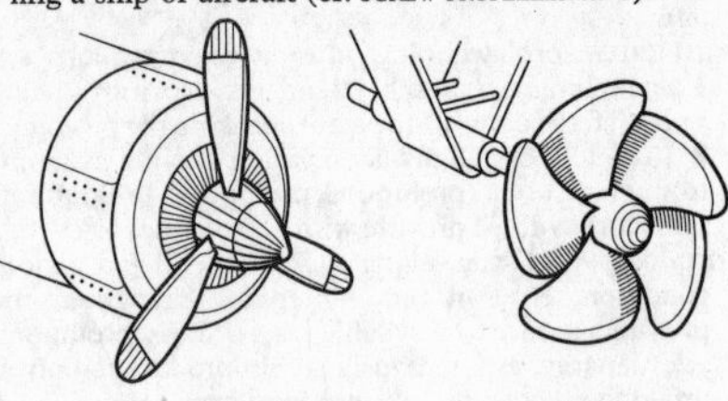

propeller, 2

pro•pen•si•ty /prəpénsitee/ *n.* (*pl.* **-ties**) an inclination or tendency (*has a propensity for wandering*).

prop•er /própər/ *adj. & adv.* • *adj.* **1 a** accurate; correct (*in the proper sense of the word; gave him the proper amount*). **b** fit; suitable; right (*at the proper time; do it the proper way*). **2** decent; respectable, esp. excessively so (*not quite proper*). **3** (usu. foll. by *to*) belonging or relating exclusively or distinctively; particular; special (*with the respect proper to them*). **4** (usu. placed after noun) strictly so called; real; genuine (*this is the crypt, not the cathedral proper*). **5** esp. *Brit. colloq.* thorough; complete (*had a proper row about it*). **6** (usu. placed after noun) *Heraldry* in the natural, not conventional, colors (*a peacock proper*). • *adv. Brit. dial.* or *colloq.* (with reference to speech) in a genteel manner (*learn to talk proper*). ▫▫ **prop•er•ness** *n.*

prop•er frac•tion *n.* a fraction that is less than unity, with the numerator less than the denominator.

prop•er•ly /própərlee/ *adv.* **1** fittingly; suitably (*do it properly*). **2** accurately; correctly (*properly speaking*). **3** rightly (*he very properly refused*). **4** with decency; respectably (*behave properly*). **5** esp. *Brit. colloq.* thoroughly (*they were properly ashamed*).

prop•er noun *n.* (also **proper name**) *Gram.* a name used for an individual person, place, animal, country, title, etc., and spelled with a capital letter, e.g., Jane, London, Everest.

prop•er•ty /própərtee/ *n.* (*pl.* **-ties**) **1 a** something owned; a possession, esp. a house, land, etc. **b** *Law* the right to possession, use, etc. **c** possessions collectively, esp. real estate (*has money in property*). **2** an attribute, quality, or characteristic (*has the property of dissolving grease*). **3** a movable object used on a theater stage, in a movie, etc.

proph•e•cy /prófisee/ *n.* (*pl.* **-cies**) **1 a** a prophetic utterance, esp. Biblical. **b** a prediction of future events (*a prophecy of massive inflation*). **2** the faculty, function, or practice of prophesying (*the gift of prophecy*).

▶Note that **prophesy** is the verb, **prophecy** the noun.

proph•e•sy /prófisī/ *v.* (**-sies, -sied**) **1** *tr.* (usu. foll. by *that, who,* etc.) foretell (an event, etc.). **2** *intr.* speak as a prophet; foretell future events. ▫▫ **proph·e·si·er** /–sīər/ *n.*

proph·et /prófit/ *n.* (*fem.* **prophetess** /–tis/) **1** a teacher or interpreter of the supposed will of God, esp. any of the Old Testament or Hebrew prophets. **2 a** a person who foretells events. **b** a person who advocates and speaks innovatively for a cause (*a prophet of the new order*). **3** (**the Prophet**) **a** Muhammad. **b** Joseph Smith, founder of the Mormons, or one of his successors. **c** (in *pl.*) the prophetic writings of the Old Testament. ▫▫ **proph·et·hood** *n.* **proph·et·ism** *n.* **proph·et·ship** *n.*

pro·phet·ic /prəfétik/ *adj.* **1** (often foll. by *of*) containing a prediction; predicting. **2** of or concerning a prophet. ▫▫ **pro·phet·i·cal** *adj.* **pro·phet·i·cal·ly** *adv.* **pro·phet·i·cism** /–sizəm/ *n.*

pro·phy·lac·tic /prṓfiláktik, próf–/ *adj.* & *n.* • *adj.* tending to prevent disease. • *n.* **1** a preventive medicine or course of action. **2** a condom.

pro·phy·lax·is /prṓfiláksis, próf–/ *n.* (*pl.* **prophylaxes** /–seez/) preventive treatment against disease.

pro·pin·qui·ty /prəpíngkwitee/ *n.* **1** nearness in space; proximity. **2** close kinship. **3** similarity.

pro·pi·ti·ate /prōpísheeayt/ *v.tr.* appease (an offended person, etc.). ▫▫ **pro·pi·ti·a·tion** *n.* **pro·pi·ti·a·tor** *n.*

pro·pi·ti·a·to·ry /prōpísheeətawree, –píshə–/ *adj.* serving or intended to propitiate (*a propitiatory smile*). ▫▫ **pro·pi·ti·a·to·ri·ly** *adv.*

pro·pi·tious /prəpíshəs/ *adj.* **1** (of an omen, etc.) favorable. **2** (often foll. by *for, to*) (of the weather, an occasion, etc.) suitable. **3** well-disposed (*the fates were propitious*). ▫▫ **pro·pi·tious·ly** *adv.* **pro·pi·tious·ness** *n.*

prop·jet /própjet/ *n.* a jet airplane powered by turboprops.

pro·po·nent /prəpṓnənt/ *n.* & *adj.* • *n.* a person advocating a motion, theory, or proposal. • *adj.* proposing or advocating a theory, etc.

pro·por·tion /prəpáwrshən/ *n.* & *v.* • *n.* **1 a** a comparative part or share (*a large proportion of the profits*). **b** a comparative ratio (*the proportion of births to deaths*). **2** the correct or pleasing relation of things or parts of a thing (*the house has fine proportions; exaggerated out of all proportion*). **3** (in *pl.*) dimensions; size (*large proportions*). **4** *Math.* **a** an equality of ratios between two pairs of quantities, e.g., 3:5 and 9:15. **b** a set of such quantities. • *v.tr.* (usu. foll. by *to*) make (a thing, etc.) proportionate (*must proportion the punishment to the crime*). ▫ **in proportion 1** by the same factor. **2** without exaggerating (importance, etc.) (*must get the facts in proportion*). ▫▫ **pro·por·tioned** *adj.* (also in *comb.*). **pro·por·tion·less** *adj.* **pro·por·tion·ment** *n.*
▶Except in certain long-established phrases, such as *proportional representation, proportional* and *proportionate* may be used interchangeably.

pro·por·tion·al /prəpáwrshənəl/ *adj.* in due proportion; comparable (*a proportional increase in the expense; resentment proportional to his injuries*). ▫▫ **pro·por·tion·al·i·ty** /–nálitee/ *n.* **pro·por·tion·al·ly** *adv.*

pro·por·tion·ate /prəpáwrshənət/ *adj.* = PROPORTIONAL. ▫▫ **pro·por·tion·ate·ly** *adv.*

pro·pos·al /prəpṓzəl/ *n.* **1 a** the act or an instance of proposing something. **b** a course of action, etc., so proposed (*the proposal was never carried out*). **2** an offer of marriage.

pro·pose /prəpṓz/ *v.* **1** *tr.* (also *absol.*) put forward for consideration or as a plan. **2** *tr.* (usu. foll. by *to* + infin., or verbal noun) intend; purpose (*propose to open a restaurant*). **3** *intr.* (usu. foll. by *to*) make an offer of marriage. **4** *tr.* nominate (a person) as a member of a society, for an office, etc. **5** *tr.* offer (a person's health, a person, etc.) as a subject for a toast. ▫▫ **pro·pos·er** *n.*

prop·o·si·tion /própəzíshən/ *n.* & *v.* • *n.* **1** a statement or assertion. **2** a scheme proposed; a proposal. **3** *Logic* a statement consisting of subject and predicate that is subject to proof or disproof. **4** *colloq.* a problem, opponent, prospect, etc., that is to be dealt with (*a difficult proposition*). **5** *Math.* a formal statement of a theorem or problem, often including the demonstration. **6 a** an enterprise, etc., with regard to its likelihood of commercial, etc., success. **b** a person regarded similarly. **7** *colloq.* a sexual proposal. • *v.tr. colloq.* make a proposal (esp. of sexual intercourse) to. ▫ **not a proposition** unlikely to succeed. ▫▫ **prop·o·si·tion·al** *adj.*

pro·pound /prəpównd/ *v.tr.* offer for consideration; propose. ▫▫ **pro·pound·er** *n.*

pro·pri·e·tar·y /prəpríəteree/ *adj.* **1 a** of, holding, or concerning property (*the proprietary classes*). **b** of or relating to a proprietor (*proprietary rights*). **2** held in private ownership.

pro·pri·e·tar·y name *n.* a name of a product, etc., registered by its owner as a trademark and not usable by another without permission.

pro·pri·e·tor /prəpríətər/ *n.* (*fem.* **proprietress**) **1** a holder of property. **2** the owner of a business, etc., esp. of a hotel. ▫▫ **pro·pri·e·to·ri·al** /–táwreeəl/ *adj.* **pro·pri·e·to·ri·al·ly** /–táwreeəlee/ *adv.* **pro·pri·e·tor·ship** *n.*

pro·pri·e·ty /prəprí-itee/ *n.* (*pl.* **-ties**) **1** fitness; rightness (*doubt the propriety of refusing him*). **2** correctness of behavior or morals (*highest standards of propriety*). **3** (in *pl.*) the details or rules of correct conduct (*must observe the proprieties*).

pro·pul·sion /prəpúlshən/ *n.* **1** the act or an instance of driving or pushing forward. **2** an impelling influence. ▫▫ **pro·pul·sive** /–púlsiv/ *adj.*

pro·pyl /prṓpil/ *n. Chem.* the univalent radical of propane. ¶ Chem. formula: C_3H_7.

pro·pyl·ene /prṓpəleen/ *n. Chem.* a gaseous hydrocarbon of the alkene series used in the manufacture of chemicals. ¶ Chem. formula: C_3H_6.

pro ra·ta /prō ráytə, raátə/ *adj.* & *adv.* • *adj.* proportional. • *adv.* proportionally.

pro·rate /prōráyt/ *v.tr.* allocate or distribute pro rata. ▫▫ **pro·ra·tion** *n.*

pro·rogue /prōrṓg/ *v.* (**prorogues, prorogued, proroguing**) **1** *tr.* discontinue the meetings of (a parliament, etc.) without dissolving it. **2** *intr.* (of a parliament, etc.) be prorogued. ▫▫ **pro·ro·ga·tion** /prṓrəgáyshən/ *n.*

pro·sa·ic /prōzáyik/ *adj.* **1** like prose; lacking poetic beauty. **2** unromantic; dull; commonplace (*took a prosaic view of life*). ▫▫ **pro·sa·i·cal·ly** *adv.* **pro·sa·ic·ness** *n.*

pros and cons *n.pl.* reasons or considerations for and against a proposition, etc.

pro·sce·ni·um /prəseéneeəm/ *n.* (*pl.* **prosceniums** or **proscenia** /–neeə/) **1** the part of the stage in front of the drop or curtain, usu. with the enclosing arch. **2** the stage of an ancient theater.

pro·sciut·to /prōshṓōtō/ *n.* (*pl.* **-tos**) specially cured ham, usu. sliced thin and used as an hors d'oeuvre.

pro·scribe /prəskríb/ *v.tr.* **1** banish; exile (*proscribed from the club*). **2** put (a person) outside the protection of the law. **3** reject or denounce (a practice, etc.) as dangerous, etc. ▫▫ **pro·scrip·tion** /–skrípshən/ *n.* **pro·scrip·tive** /–skríptiv/ *adj.*
▶See note at PRESCRIBE.

prose /prōz/ *n.* & *v.* • *n.* **1** the ordinary form of the written or spoken language (cf. POETRY, VERSE 1) (*Milton's prose works*). **2** a passage of prose, esp. for translation into a foreign language. **3** a tedious speech or conversation. • *v.* **1** *intr.* (usu. foll. by *about, away,* etc.) talk tediously (*was prosing away about his dog*). **2** *tr.* turn (a poem, etc.) into prose. **3** *tr.* write prose. ▫▫ **pros·er** *n.*

pros·e·cute /prósikyoot/ *v.tr.* **1** (also *absol.*) **a** institute legal proceedings against (a person). **b** institute a prosecution with reference to (a claim, crime, etc.) (*decided not to prosecute*). **2** follow up; pursue (an inquiry, studies, etc.). **3** carry on (a trade, pursuit, etc.). ▫▫ **pros·e·cut·a·ble** *adj.*

pros·e·cu·tion /prósikyóoshən/ *n.* **1 a** the institution and carrying on of a criminal charge in a court. **b** the carrying on of legal proceedings against a person. **c** the prosecuting party in a court case (*the prosecution denied this*). **2** the act or an instance of prosecuting (*met her in the prosecution of his hobby*).

pros·e·cu·tor /prósikyootər/ *n.* (also **pros·e·cut·ing at·tor·ney**) a person who prosecutes, esp. in a criminal court. ▫▫ **pros·e·cu·to·ri·al** /–táwreeəl/ *adj.*

pros·e·lyte /prósilīt/ *n.* & *v.* • *n.* **1** a person converted, esp. recently, from one opinion, creed, party, etc., to another. **2** a convert to Judaism. • *v.tr.* = PROSELYTIZE. ▫▫ **pros·e·lyt·ism** /–səlitízəm/ *n.*

pros·e·lyt·ize /prósilitīz/ *v.tr.* (also *absol.*) convert (a person or people) from one belief, etc., to another, esp. habitually. ▫▫ **pros·e·lyt·iz·er** *n.*

pro·sim·i·an /prōsímeeən/ *Zool. n.* & *adj.* • *n.* a primitive primate of the suborder Prosimii, which includes lemurs, lorises, galagos, and tarsiers. • *adj.* of or relating to this suborder.

pros·o·dy /prósədee/ *n.* **1** the theory and practice of versification; the laws of meter. **2** the study of speech rhythms. ▫▫ **pro·sod·ic** /prəsódik/ *adj.* **pros·o·dist** *n.*

pros·pect /próspekt/ *n.* & *v.* • *n.* **1 a** (often in *pl.*) an expectation, esp. of success in a career, etc. (*his prospects were brilliant*; *offers a gloomy prospect*; *no prospect of success*). **b** something one has to look forward to (*don't relish the prospect of meeting him*). **2** an extensive view of landscape, etc. (*a striking prospect*). **3** a mental picture (*a new prospect in his mind*). **4 a** a place likely to yield mineral deposits. **b** a sample of ore for testing. **c** the resulting yield. **5** a possible or probable customer, subscriber, etc. • *v.* **1** *intr.* (usu. foll. by *for*) **a** explore a region for gold, etc. **b** look out for or search for something. **2** *tr.* **a** explore (a region) for gold, etc. **b** work (a mine) experimentally. **c** (of a mine) promise (a specified yield). ▫ **in prospect 1** in sight; within view. **2** within the range of expectation, likely. ▫▫ **pros·pect·less** *adj.* **pros·pec·tor** *n.*

prospect late Middle English (as a noun denoting the action of looking toward a distant object): from Latin *prospectus* 'view,' from *prospicere* 'look forward,' from *pro-* 'forward' + *specere* 'to look.' Early use, referring to a view or landscape, gave rise to the meaning 'mental picture' (mid-16th century), whence 'anticipated event.'

pro·spec·tive /prəspéktiv/ *adj.* **1** concerned with or applying to the future (*implies a prospective obligation*) (cf. RETROSPECTIVE). **2** some day to be; expected; future (*prospective bridegroom*). ▫▫ **pro·spec·tive·ly** *adv.* **pro·spec·tive·ness** *n.*

pro·spec·tus /prəspéktəs/ *n.* a printed document advertising or describing a school, commercial enterprise, forthcoming book, etc.

pros·per /próspər/ *v.* **1** *intr.* succeed; thrive (*nothing he touches prospers*). **2** *tr.* make successful (*Heaven prosper him*).

pros·per·i·ty /prospéritee/ *n.* a state of being prosperous; wealth or success.

pros·per·ous /próspərəs/ *adj.* **1** successful; rich (*a prosperous merchant*). **2** flourishing; thriving (*a prosperous enterprise*). **3** auspicious (*a prosperous wind*). ▫▫ **pros·per·ous·ly** *adv.* **pros·per·ous·ness** *n.*

pros·tate /próstayt/ *n.* (in full **prostate gland**) a gland surrounding the neck of the bladder in male mammals and releasing a fluid forming part of the semen. ▫▫ **pros·tat·ic** /–státik/ *adj.*

pros·the·sis /prósthéesis/ *n.* (*pl.* **prostheses** /–seez/) an artificial part supplied to replace a missing body part, e.g., a false breast, leg, tooth, etc. ▫▫ **pros·thet·ic** /–thétik/ *adj.* **pros·thet·i·cal·ly** *adv.*

pros·thet·ics /prosthétiks/ *n.pl.* (usu. treated as *sing.*) the branch of medicine or dentistry supplying and fitting prostheses.

pros·ti·tute /próstitoot, -tyoot/ *n.* & *v.* • *n.* **1 a** a woman who engages in sexual activity for payment. **b** (usu. **male prostitute**) a man or boy who engages in sexual activity, esp. with homosexual men, for payment. **2** a person who debases himself or herself for personal gain. • *v.tr.* **1** (esp. *refl.*) make a prostitute of (esp. oneself). **2 a** misuse (one's talents, skills, etc.) for money. **b** offer (oneself, one's honor, etc.) for unworthy ends, esp. for money. ▫▫ **pros·ti·tu·tion** /–tóoshən/ *n.* **pros·ti·tu·tor** *n.*

pros·trate /próstrayt/ *adj.* & *v.* • *adj.* **1 a** lying face downwards, esp. in submission. **b** lying horizontally. **2** overcome, esp. by grief, exhaustion, etc. (*prostrate with self-pity*). **3** *Bot.* growing along the ground. • *v.tr.* **1** lay (a person, etc.) flat on the ground. **2** (*refl.*) throw (oneself) down in submission, etc. **3** (of fatigue, illness, etc.) overcome; reduce to extreme physical weakness. ▫▫ **pros·tra·tion** /prostráyshən/ *n.*

pros·y /prózee/ *adj.* (**prosier, prosiest**) tedious; commonplace; dull. ▫▫ **pros·i·ly** *adv.* **pros·i·ness** *n.*

Prot. *abbr.* Protestant.

pro·tag·o·nist /prōtágənist/ *n.* **1** the chief person in a drama, story, etc. **2** the leading person in a contest, etc.; a principal performer. **3** (usu. foll. by *of, for*) *disp.* an advocate or champion of a cause, course of action, etc. (*a protagonist of women's rights*).

▶The correct meaning of this word is 'chief or leading person,' e.g., *The novelist's first challenge is to create a protagonist the reader can identify with.* However, it is also used, usually with *of* or *for,* to mean 'a supporter or champion of a cause, etc.,' e.g., *Protagonists of peace rallied at the Capitol.*

pro·te·an /próteeən, -téeən/ *adj.* **1** variable; taking many forms. **2** (of an artist, writer, etc.) versatile.

pro·te·ase /próteeays/ *n.* any enzyme able to hydrolyze proteins and peptides.

pro·tect /prətékt/ *v.tr.* **1** (often foll. by *from, against*) keep (a person, thing, etc.) safe; defend; guard (*goggles protected her eyes from dust*; *guards protected the military base*). **2** *Econ.* shield (domestic industry) from competition by imposing import duties on foreign goods. **3** cover; provide funds to meet (a bill, bank draft, etc.).

pro·tec·tion /prətékshən/ *n.* **1 a** the act or an instance of protecting. **b** the state of being protected; defense (*affords protection against the weather*). **c** a thing, person, or animal that provides protection (*bought a dog as protection*). **2** (also **pro·tec·tion·ism**) *Econ.* the theory or practice of protecting domestic industries. **3** *colloq.* **a** immunity from molestation obtained by payment to organized criminals, etc., under threat of violence. **b** (in full **protection money**) payment, as bribes, made to police, etc., for overlooking criminal activities. **c** (in full **protection money**) the money so paid, esp. on a regular basis. **4** = SAFE-CONDUCT. ▫▫ **pro·tec·tion·ist** *n.*

pro·tec·tive /prətéktiv/ *adj.* **1** protecting; intended or intending to protect. **2** (of a person) tending to protect in a possessive way. ▫▫ **pro·tec·tive·ly** *adv.* **pro·tec·tive·ness** *n.*

pro·tec·tor /prətéktər/ *n.* (*fem.* **protectress** /–tris/) **1 a** a person who protects. **b** a guardian or patron. **2** *hist.* a regent in charge of a kingdom during the minority, absence, etc., of the sovereign. **3** (often in *comb.*) a thing or device that protects. ▫▫ **pro·tec·tor·al** *adj.*

pro·tec·tor·ate /prətéktərət/ *n.* **1** a nation that is controlled and protected by another. **2** such a relation of one nation to another.

pro·té·gé /prṓtizhay, prōtizháy/ *n.* (*fem.* **protégée** *pronunc.* same) a person under the protection, patronage, tutelage, etc., of another.

pro·tein /prṓteen/ *n.* any of a group of organic compounds composed of one or more chains of amino acids and forming an essential part of all living organisms. ▫▫ **pro·tein·a·ceous** /–teenáyshəs/ *adj.* **pro·tein·ic** /–teénik/ *adj.* **pro·tei·nous** /–teénəs/ *adj.*

pro tem /prō tém/ *adj.* & *adv. colloq.* = PRO TEMPORE.

pro tem·po·re /prō témpəree/ *adj.* & *adv.* for the time being.

pro·test *n.* & *v.* • *n.* /prṓtest/ **1** a statement of dissent or disapproval; a remonstrance (*made a protest*). **2** (often *attrib.*) a usu. public demonstration of objection to government, etc., policy (*marched in protest; protest demonstration*). **3** a solemn declaration. • *v.* /prətést, prō–/ **1** *intr.* (usu. foll. by *against, at, about,* etc.) make a protest against an action, proposal, etc. **2** *tr.* (often foll. by *that* + clause; also *absol.*) affirm (one's innocence, etc.) solemnly, esp. in reply to an accusation, etc. **3** *tr.* object to (a decision, etc.). ▫ **under protest** unwillingly. ▫▫ **pro·test·er** *n.* **pro·test·ing·ly** *adv.* **pro·tes·tor** *n.*

Prot·es·tant /prótistənt/ *n.* & *adj.* • *n.* a member or follower of any of the western Christian Churches that are separate from the Roman Catholic Church in accordance with the principles of the Reformation. • *adj.* of or relating to any of the Protestant Churches or their members, etc. ▫▫ **Prot·es·tant·ism** *n.* **Prot·es·tant·ize** *v.tr.* & *intr.*

prot·es·ta·tion /prótistáyshən, prṓte–/ *n.* **1** a strong affirmation. **2** a protest.

pro·to·col /prṓtəkawl, –kol/ *n.* & *v.* • *n.* **1 a** official, esp. diplomatic, formality and etiquette observed on governmental or military occasions, etc. **b** the rules, formalities, etc., of any procedure, group, etc. **2** the original draft of a diplomatic document, esp. of the terms of a treaty agreed to in conference and signed by the parties. **3** a formal statement of a transaction. **4** the official formulae at the beginning and end of a charter, papal bull, etc. **5** a plan or record of experimental observation, medical treatment, etc. **6** *Computing* a set of rules governing the electronic transmission of data between computers. • *v.* (**protocolled, protocolling**) **1** *intr.* draw up a protocol or protocols. **2** *tr.* record in a protocol.

protocol late Middle English (denoting the original notation of an agreement, forming the legal authority for future dealings relating to it): from Old French *prothocole,* via medieval Latin from Greek *prōtokollon* 'first page, flyleaf,' from *prōtos* 'first' + *kolla* 'glue.' Sense 1 derives from French *protocole,* the collection of set forms of etiquette to be observed by the French head of state, and the name of the government department responsible for this (in the 19th century).

pro·to·lan·guage /prṓtōlanggwij/ *n.* a language from which other languages are believed to have been derived.

pro·ton /prṓton/ *n. Physics* a stable elementary particle with a positive electric charge, equal in magnitude to that of an electron, and occurring in all atomic nuclei. ▫▫ **pro·ton·ic** /prətónik/ *adj.*

pro·to·plasm /prṓtəplazəm/ *n.* the material comprising the living part of a cell, consisting of a nucleus embedded in membrane-enclosed cytoplasm. ▫▫ **pro·to·plas·mal** /–plazməl/ *adj.* **pro·to·plas·mat·ic** /–mátik/ *adj.* **pro·to·plas·mic** *adj.*

pro·to·plast /prṓtəplast/ *n.* the protoplasm of one cell. ▫▫ **pro·to·plas·tic** *adj.*

pro·to·type /prṓtətīp/ *n.* **1** an original thing or person of which or whom copies, imitations, improved forms, representations, etc., are made. **2** a trial model or preliminary version of a vehicle, machine, etc. **3** a thing or person representative of a type; an exemplar. ▫▫ **pro·to·typ·al** *adj.* **pro·to·typ·ic** /–típik/ *adj.* **pro·to·typ·i·cal** *adj.* **pro·to·typ·i·cal·ly** *adv.*

pro·to·zo·an /prṓtəzṓən/ *n.* & *adj.* • *n.* (also **pro·to·zo·on** /–zṓ–on/) (*pl.* **protozoa** /–zṓə/or **protozoans**) any usu. unicellular and microscopic organism of the subkingdom Protozoa, including amoebas and ciliates. • *adj.* (also **pro·to·zo·ic** /–zṓ–ik/) of or relating to this phylum. ▫▫ **pro·to·zo·al** *adj.*

pro·tract /prōtrákt, prə–/ *v.tr.* **1 a** prolong or lengthen in space or esp. time (*protracted their stay for some weeks*). **b** (as **protracted** *adj.*) of excessive length or duration (*a protracted illness*). **2** draw (a plan, etc.) to scale. ▫▫ **pro·tract·ed·ly** *adv.* **pro·tract·ed·ness** *n.*

pro·trac·tion /prōtrákshən, prə–/ *n.* **1** the act or an instance of protracting; the state of being protracted. **2** a drawing to scale.

pro·trac·tor /prōtráktər, prə–/ *n.* an instrument for measuring angles, usu. in the form of a graduated semicircle.

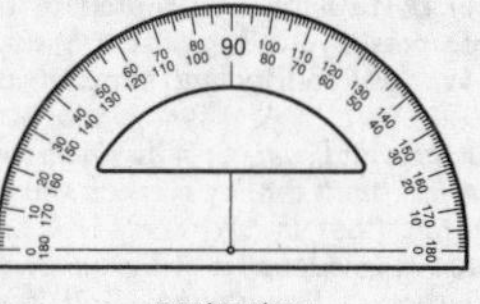

protractor

pro·trude /prōtróod/ *v.* **1** *intr.* extend beyond or above a surface; project. **2** *tr.* thrust or cause to thrust forth. ▫▫ **pro·trud·ent** *adj.* **pro·tru·si·ble** /–səbəl, –zə–/ *adj.* **pro·tru·sion** /–tróozhən/ *n.* **pro·tru·sive** *adj.*

pro·tu·ber·ant /prōtóobərənt, –tyóo–, prə–/ *adj.* bulging out; prominent (*protuberant eyes*). ▫▫ **pro·tu·ber·ance** *n.*

proud /prowd/ *adj.* **1** feeling greatly honored or pleased (*am proud to know him; proud of his friendship*). **2 a** (often foll. by *of*) valuing oneself, one's possessions, etc., highly, or esp. too highly; haughty; arrogant (*proud of his ancient name*). **b** (often in *comb.*) having a proper pride; satisfied (*proud of a job well done*). **3 a** (of an occasion, etc.) justly arousing pride (*a proud day for us; a proud sight*). **b** (of an action, etc.) showing pride (*a proud wave of the hand*). **4** (of a thing) imposing; splendid. **5** *Brit.* slightly projecting from a surface, etc. (*the nail stood proud of the plank*). **6** (of flesh) overgrown around a healing wound. ▫ **do proud** *colloq.* **1** treat (a person) with lavish generosity or honor (*they did us proud on our anniversary*). **2** (*refl.*) act honorably or worthily. ▫▫ **proud·ly** *adv.* **proud·ness** *n.*

Prov. *abbr.* **1** Proverbs (Old Testament). **2** Province. **3** Provençal.

prove /proov/ *v.* (*past part.* **proved** or **proven**) **1** *tr.* (often foll. by *that* + clause) demonstrate the truth of by evidence or argument. **2** *intr.* **a** (usu. foll. by *to* + infin.) be found (*it proved to be untrue*). **b** emerge incontrovertibly as (*will prove the winner*). **3** *tr. Math.* test the accuracy of (a calculation). **4** *tr.* establish the genuineness and validity of (a will). **5** *intr.* (of dough) rise in breadmaking. **6** *tr.* = PROOF 3. **7** *tr.* subject (a gun, etc.) to a testing process. □ **prove oneself** show one's abilities, courage, etc. □□ **prov·a·ble** *adj.* **prov·a·bil·i·ty** /pro͞ovəbílitee/ *n.* **prov·a·bly** *adv.*

prov·e·nance /próvinəns/ *n.* **1** the place of origin or history, esp. of a work of art, etc. **2** origin.

Pro·ven·çal /prṓvonsaál, próv–/ *adj.* & *n.* • *adj.* **1** of or concerning the language, inhabitants, landscape, etc., of Provence, a former province of SE France. **2** (also **Pro·ven·çale**) cooked with garlic and tomato and usu. onions, olive oil, and herbs. • *n.* **1** a native of Provence. **2** the language of Provence.

prov·en·der /próvindər/ *n.* **1** animal fodder. **2** *joc.* food for human beings.

pro·verb /próvərb/ *n.* **1** a short pithy saying in general use, held to embody a general truth. **2** a person or thing that is notorious (*he is a proverb for inaccuracy*). **3** (**Proverbs** or **Book of Proverbs**) a didactic poetic Old Testament book of maxims attributed to Solomon and others.

pro·ver·bi·al /prəvə́rbeeəl/ *adj.* **1** (esp. of a specific characteristic, etc.) as well-known as a proverb; notorious (*his proverbial honesty*). **2** of or referred to in a proverb (*the proverbial ill wind*). □□ **pro·ver·bi·al·i·ty** /–beeálitee/ *n.* **pro·ver·bi·al·ly** *adv.*

pro·vide /prəvíd/ *v.* **1** *tr.* supply; furnish (*provided them with food; provided food for them*). **2** *intr.* **a** (usu. foll. by *for, against*) make due preparation (*provided for any eventuality*). **b** (usu. foll. by *for*) prepare for the maintenance of a person, etc. **3** *tr.* (also *refl.*) equip with necessities. **4** *tr.* (usu. foll. by *that*) stipulate in a will, statute, etc.

pro·vid·ed /prəvídid/ *adj.* & *conj.* • *adj.* supplied; furnished. • *conj.* (often foll. by *that*) on the condition or understanding (that).

prov·i·dence /próvidəns/ *n.* **1** the protective care of God or nature. **2** (**Providence**) God in this aspect. **3** timely care or preparation; foresight; thrift.

prov·i·dent /próvidənt, –dent/ *adj.* having or showing foresight; thrifty. □□ **prov·i·dent·ly** *adv.*

prov·i·den·tial /próvidénshəl/ *adj.* **1** of or by divine foresight or interposition. **2** opportune; lucky. □□ **prov·i·den·tial·ly** *adv.*

pro·vid·er /prəvídər/ *n.* **1** a person or thing that provides. **2** the breadwinner of a family, etc.

pro·vid·ing /prəvíding/ *conj.* = PROVIDED *conj.*

prov·ince /próvins/ *n.* **1** a principal administrative division of some countries. **2** (**the provinces**) the whole of a country outside major cities, esp. regarded as uncultured, unsophisticated, etc. **3** a sphere of action; business (*outside my province as a teacher*). **4** a branch of learning, etc. (*in the province of aesthetics*). **5** *Eccl.* a district under an archbishop or a metropolitan. **6** *Rom.Hist.* a territory outside Italy under a Roman governor.

pro·vin·cial /prəvínshəl/ *adj.* & *n.* • *adj.* **1 a** of or concerning a province. **b** of or concerning the provinces. **2** unsophisticated or uncultured in manner, speech, opinion, etc. • *n.* **1** an inhabitant of a province or the provinces. **2** an unsophisticated or uncultured person. **3** *Eccl.* the head or chief of a province or of a religious order in a province. □□ **pro·vin·ci·al·i·ty** /–sheeálitee/ *n.* **pro·vin·cial·ize** *v.tr.* **pro·vin·cial·ly** *adv.*

pro·vin·cial·ism /prəvínshəlizəm/ *n.* **1** provincial manners, fashion, mode of thought, etc., esp. regarded as restricting or narrow. **2** a word or phrase peculiar to a provincial region. **3** concern for one's local area rather than one's country. □□ **pro·vin·cial·ist** *n.*

pro·vi·sion /prəví<u>zh</u>ən/ *n.* & *v.* • *n.* **1 a** the act or an instance of providing (*made no provision for his future*). **b** something provided (*a provision of bread*). **2** (in *pl.*) food, drink, etc., esp. for an expedition. **3 a** a legal or formal statement providing for something. **b** a clause of this. • *v.tr.* supply (an expedition, etc.) with provisions. □□ **pro·vi·sion·er** *n.* **pro·vi·sion·less** *adj.* **pro·vi·sion·ment** *n.*

pro·vi·sion·al /prəví<u>zh</u>ənəl/ *adj.* & *n.* • *adj.* **1** providing for immediate needs only; temporary. **2** (**Provisional**) designating the unofficial wing of the Irish Republican Army (IRA), advocating terrorism. • *n.* (**Provisional**) a member of the Provisional wing of the IRA. □□ **pro·vi·sion·al·i·ty** /–álitee/ *n.* **pro·vi·sion·al·ly** *adv.* **pro·vi·sion·al·ness** *n.*

pro·vi·so /prəvízō/ *n.* (*pl.* **-sos**) **1** a stipulation. **2** a clause of stipulation or limitation in a document.

pro·vi·so·ry /prəvízəree/ *adj.* conditional; having a proviso. □□ **pro·vi·so·ri·ly** *adv.*

prov·o·ca·tion /próvəkáyshən/ *n.* **1** the act or an instance of provoking; a state of being provoked (*did it under severe provocation*). **2** a cause of annoyance.

pro·voc·a·tive /prəvókətiv/ *adj.* & *n.* • *adj.* **1** (usu. foll. by *of*) tending to provoke, esp. anger or sexual desire. **2** intentionally annoying. • *n.* a provocative thing. □□ **pro·voc·a·tive·ly** *adv.* **pro·voc·a·tive·ness** *n.*

pro·voke /prəvṓk/ *v.tr.* **1 a** (often foll. by *to*, or *to* + infin.) rouse or incite (*provoked him to fury*). **b** (often as **provoking** *adj.*) annoy; irritate; exasperate. **2** call forth; instigate (indignation, an inquiry, a storm, etc.). **3** (usu. foll. by *into* + verbal noun) irritate or stimulate (a person) (*the itch provoked him into scratching*). **4** tempt; allure. **5** cause; give rise to (*will provoke discussion*). □□ **pro·vok·a·ble** *adj.* **pro·vok·ing·ly** *adv.*

pro·vo·lo·ne /prōvəlṓnee/ *n.* a medium hard Italian cheese, often with a mild smoked flavor.

pro·vost /prṓvōst, próvəst/ *n.* **1** a high administrative officer in a university. **2** *Brit.* the head of some colleges, esp. at Oxford or Cambridge. **3** *Eccl.* **a** the head of a chapter in a cathedral. **b** *hist.* the head of a religious community. **4** *Sc.* the head of a municipal corporation or burgh. **5** = PROVOST MARSHAL. □□ **pro·vost·ship** *n.*

pro·vost mar·shal /prṓvō/ *n.* **1** the head of military police within a military command, as on a military base. **2** the master-at-arms of a ship in which a court-martial is to be held.

prow /prow/ *n.* **1** the bow of a ship adjoining the stem. **2** a pointed or projecting front part.

prow·ess /prówis/ *n.* **1** skill; expertise. **2** valor; gallantry.

prowl /prowl/ *v.* & *n.* • *v.* **1** *tr.* roam (a place) in search or as if in search of prey, plunder, etc. **2** *intr.* (often foll. by *about, around*) move about like a hunter. • *n.* the act or an instance of prowling. □ **on the prowl** in search of something, esp. sexual contact, etc. □□ **prowl·er** *n.*

prox·i·mal /próksiməl/ *adj.* situated toward the center of the body or point of attachment. □□ **prox·i·mal·ly** *adv.*

prox·im·i·ty /proksímitee/ *n.* nearness in space, time, etc. (*sat in close proximity to them*).

prox·y /próksee/ *n.* (*pl.* **-ies**) (also *attrib.*) **1** the authorization given to a substitute or deputy (*a proxy vote; was married by proxy*). **2** a person authorized to act as a substitute, etc. **3 a** a document giving the power to act as a proxy, esp. in voting. **b** a vote given by this.

prude /pro͞od/ *n.* a person having or affecting an attitude of extreme propriety or modesty, esp. in sexual matters. □□ **prud·er·y** /pro͞odəree/ *n.* (*pl.* **-ies**). **prud·ish** *adj.* **prud·ish·ly** *adv.* **prud·ish·ness** *n.*

pru·dent /pro͞od'nt/ *adj.* **1** (of a person or conduct) careful to avoid undesired consequences; circumspect. **2** discreet. □□ **pru·dence** *n.* **pru·dent·ly** *adv.*

pru·den·tial /pro͞odénshəl/ *adj.* & *n.* • *adj.* of, involving, or marked by prudence (*prudential motives*). •*n.* (in *pl.*) **1** prudential considerations or matters. **2** minor administrative or financial matters. ▫▫ **pru·den·tial·ism** *n.* **pru·den·tial·ist** *n.* **pru·den·tial·ly** *adv.*

prune[1] /proōn/ *n.* **1** a dried plum. **2** *colloq.* a stupid or disliked person.

prune[2] /proōn/ *v.tr.* **1 a** (often foll. by *down*) trim (a tree, etc.) by cutting away dead or overgrown branches, etc. **b** (usu. foll. by *off, away*) lop (branches, etc.) from a tree. **2** reduce (costs, etc.) (*must try to prune expenses*). ▫▫ **prun·er** *n.*

pru·ri·ent /proŏreeənt/ *adj.* **1** having an unhealthy obsession with sexual matters. **2** encouraging such an obsession. ▫▫ **pru·ri·ence** *n.* **pru·ri·en·cy** *n.* **pru·ri·ent·ly** *adv.*

Prus·sian /prúshən/ *adj.* & *n.* •*adj.* of or relating to Prussia, a former German kingdom, or relating to its rigidly militaristic tradition. •*n.* a native of Prussia.

pry[1] /prī/ *v.intr.* (**pries, pried**) **1** (usu. foll. by *into*) inquire presumptuously (into a person's private affairs, etc.). **2** (usu. foll. by *into, about,* etc.) look or peer inquisitively. ▫▫ **pry·ing** *adj.* **pry·ing·ly** *adv.*

pry[2] /prī/ *v.tr.* (**pries, pried**) (often foll. by *out of, open,* etc.) = PRIZE[2].

PS *abbr.* **1** postscript. **2** private secretary.

Ps. *abbr.* (*pl.* **Pss.**) Psalm, Psalms (Old Testament).

psalm /saam/ *n.* **1 a** (also **Psalm**) any of the sacred songs contained in the Book of Psalms. **b** (**the Psalms** or **the Book of Psalms**) the book of the Old Testament containing the Psalms. **2** a sacred song or hymn. ▫▫ **psalm·ic** *adj.*

psalm·ist /saámist/ *n.* **1** the author or composer of a psalm. **2** (**the Psalmist**) David or the author of any of the Psalms.

psal·ter /sáwltər/ *n.* **1 a** the Book of Psalms. **b** a version of this (*the English Psalter*). **2** a copy of the Psalms, esp. for liturgical use.

psal·ter·y /sáwltəree/ *n.* (*pl.* **-ies**) an ancient and medieval instrument like a dulcimer but played by plucking the strings with the fingers or a plectrum.

p's and q's *n.pl.* ▫ **mind one's p's and q's 1** attend to one's own conduct and manners. **2** attend to one's own accuracy in work.

PSAT *abbr.* Preliminary Scholastic Assessment Test.

pseud- var. of PSEUDO-.

pseud. *abbr.* pseudonym.

pseu·do /soŏdō/ *adj.* & *n.* •*adj.* **1** sham; spurious. **2** insincere. •*n. Brit.* (*pl.* **-dos**) a pretentious or insincere person.

pseudo- /soŏdō/ *comb. form* (also **pseud-** before a vowel) **1** supposed or purporting to be but not really so; false; not genuine (*pseudointellectual*). **2** resembling or imitating (often in technical applications) (*pseudomalaria*).

pseu·do·nym /soŏdənim/ *n.* a fictitious name, esp. one assumed by an author.

pseu·don·y·mous /soōdónimәs/ *adj.* writing or written under a false name. ▫▫ **pseu·do·nym·i·ty** /soŏdənímitee/ *n.* **pseu·don·y·mous·ly** *adv.*

psf. *abbr.* (also **p.s.f.**) pounds per square foot.

p.s.i. *abbr.* pounds per square inch.

psi /sī, psī/ *n.* **1** the twenty-third letter of the Greek alphabet (Ψ, ψ). **2** supposed parapsychological faculties, phenomena, etc., regarded collectively.

pso·ri·a·sis /səríəsis/ *n.* a skin disease marked by red scaly patches. ▫▫ **pso·ri·at·ic** /sáwreeátik/ *adj.*

PST *abbr.* Pacific Standard Time.

psych /sīk/ *v.tr. colloq.* (also **psyche**) **1** (usu. foll. by *up*; often *refl.*) prepare (oneself or another person) mentally for an ordeal, etc. **2 a** (usu. foll. by *out*) analyze (a person's motivation, etc.) for one's own advantage (*can't psych him out*). **b** subject to psychoanalysis. **3** (often foll. by *out*) influence a person psychologically, esp. negatively; intimidate; frighten.

psy·che /síkee/ *n.* & *v.* •*n.* **1** the soul; the spirit. **2** the mind. •*v.* var. of PSYCH.

psych·e·de·lia /síkideéleeə, –deélyə/ *n.pl.* **1** psychedelic articles, esp. posters, paintings, etc. **2** psychedelic drugs.

psych·e·del·ic /síkidélik/ *adj.* & *n.* •*adj.* **1 a** expanding the mind's awareness, etc., esp. through the use of hallucinogenic drugs. **b** (of an experience) hallucinatory; bizarre. **c** (of a drug) producing hallucinations. **2** *colloq.* **a** producing an effect resembling that of a psychedelic drug; having vivid colors or designs, etc. **b** (of colors, patterns, etc.) bright, bold and often abstract. •*n.* a hallucinogenic drug. ▫▫ **psych·e·del·i·cal·ly** *adv.*

psy·chi·a·try /sīkíətree/ *n.* the study and treatment of mental disease. ▫▫ **psy·chi·at·ric** /–keeátrik/ *adj.* **psy·chi·at·ri·cal** *adj.* **psy·chi·at·ri·cal·ly** *adv.* **psy·chi·a·trist** /–kīətrist/ *n.*

psy·chic /síkik/ *adj.* & *n.* •*adj.* **1 a** (of a person) considered to have occult powers, such as telepathy, clairvoyance, etc. **b** (of a faculty, phenomenon, etc.) inexplicable by natural laws. **2** of the soul or mind. •*n.* a person considered to have psychic powers; a medium.

psy·chi·cal /síkikəl/ *adj.* **1** concerning psychic phenomena or faculties (*psychical research*). **2** of the soul or mind. ▫▫ **psy·chi·cal·ly** *adv.* **psy·chi·cism** /–kisizəm/ *n.* **psy·chi·cist** /–kisist/ *n.*

psy·cho /síkō/ *n.* & *adj. colloq.* •*n.* (*pl.* **-chos**) a psychopath. •*adj.* psychopathic.

psycho- /síkō/ *comb. form* relating to the mind or psychology.

psy·cho·ac·tive /síkō-áktiv/ *adj.* affecting the mind (*psychoactive drugs*).

psy·cho·a·nal·y·sis /síkōənálisis/ *n.* a therapeutic method of treating mental disorders by investigating the interaction of conscious and unconscious elements in the mind and bringing repressed fears and conflicts into the conscious mind. ▫▫ **psy·cho·an·a·lyze** /–ánəlīz/ *v.tr.* **psy·cho·an·a·lyst** /–ánəlist/ *n.* **psy·cho·an·a·lyt·ic** /–anəlítik/ *adj.* **psy·cho·an·a·lyt·i·cal** *adj.* **psy·cho·an·a·lyt·i·cal·ly** *adv.*

psy·cho·bab·ble /síkōbabəl/ *n. colloq. derog.* jargon used in popular psychology. ▫▫ **psy·cho·bab·bler** *n.*

psy·cho·dra·ma /síkōdraamə, –drámə/ *n.* **1** a form of psychotherapy in which patients act out events from their past. **2** a play or movie, etc., in which psychological elements are the main interest.

psy·cho·ki·ne·sis /síkōkineésis/ *n.* the movement of objects supposedly by mental effort without the action of natural forces.

psy·cho·log·i·cal /síkəlójikəl/ *adj.* **1** of, relating to, or arising in the mind. **2** of or relating to psychology. **3** *colloq.* (of an ailment, etc.) having a basis in the mind; imaginary (*her cold is psychological*). ▫▫ **psy·cho·log·i·cal·ly** *adv.*

psy·cho·log·i·cal war·fare *n.* a campaign directed at reducing an opponent's morale.

psy·chol·o·gy /sīkóləjee/ *n.* (*pl.* **-gies**) **1** the scientific study of the human mind and its functions, esp. those affecting behavior in a given context. **2** a treatise on or theory of this. **3 a** the mental characteristics or attitude of a person or group. **b** the mental factors governing a situation or activity (*the psychology of crime*). ▫▫ **psy·chol·o·gist** *n.* **psy·chol·o·gize** *v.tr.* & *intr.*

psy·cho·met·rics /síkōmétriks/ *n.pl.* (treated as *sing.*) the science of measuring mental capacities and processes.

psy·chom·e·try /sīkómitree/ *n.* **1** the supposed divination of facts about events, people, etc., from inanimate objects associated with them. **2** the measurement of mental **psy·cho·met·ri·cal·ly** *adv.* **psy·chom·e·trist** *n.*

psy·cho·path /sīkəpath/ *n.* **1** a person suffering from chronic mental disorder, esp. with abnormal or violent social behavior. **2** a mentally or emotionally unstable person. ▫▫ **psy·cho·path·ic** /–páthik/ *adj.* **psy·cho·path·i·cal·ly** *adv.*

psy·cho·pa·thol·o·gy /síkōpəthóləjee/ *n.* **1** the scientific study of mental disorders. **2** a mentally or behaviorally disordered state. ▫▫ **psy·cho·path·o·log·i·cal** /–pathəlójikəl/ *adj.*

psy·chop·a·thy /sīkópəthee/ *n.* psychopathic or psychologically abnormal behavior.

psy·cho·sis /sīkṓsis/ *n.* (*pl.* **psychoses** /–seez/) a severe mental derangement, esp. when resulting in delusions and loss of or defective contact with external reality.

psy·cho·so·mat·ic /síkōsəmátik/ *adj.* **1** (of an illness, etc.) caused or aggravated by mental conflict, stress, etc. **2** of the mind and body together. ▫▫ **psy·cho·so·mat·i·cal·ly** *adv.*

psy·cho·ther·a·py /síkōthérəpee/ *n.* the treatment of mental disorder by psychological means. ▫▫ **psy·cho·ther·a·peu·tic** /–pyṓōtik/ *adj.* **psy·cho·ther·a·pist** *n.*

psy·chot·ic /sīkótik/ *adj.* & *n.* • *adj.* of or characterized by a psychosis. • *n.* a person suffering from a psychosis. ▫▫ **psy·chot·i·cal·ly** *adv.*

psy·cho·tro·pic /síkōtrṓpik, –tróp–/ *n.* (of a drug) acting on the mind.

PT *abbr.* **1** physical therapy. **2** physical training.

Pt *symb. Chem.* the element platinum.

pt. *abbr.* **1** part. **2** pint. **3** point. **4** port.

PTA *abbr.* Parent-Teacher Association.

ptar·mi·gan /taármigən/ *n.* any of various grouses of the genus *Lagopus*, esp. *L. mutus*, with black or gray plumage in the summer and white in the winter.

PT boat *n.* a military patrol boat armed with torpedoes, etc.

pter·o·dac·tyl /térədáktil/ *n.* a large extinct flying birdlike reptile with a long slender head and neck.

PTO *abbr.* **1** Parent-Teacher Organization. **2** please turn over.

Ptol·e·ma·ic /tólimáyik/ *adj. hist.* **1** of or relating to Ptolemy, a 2nd-c. Alexandrian astronomer, or his theories. **2** of or relating to the Ptolemies, Macedonian rulers of Egypt from the death of Alexander the Great (323 BC) to the death of Cleopatra (30 BC).

Ptol·e·ma·ic sys·tem *n.* the theory that the earth is the stationary center of the universe (cf. COPERNICAN SYSTEM).

pto·maine /tṓmayn/ *n.* any of various amine compounds, some toxic, in putrefying animal and vegetable matter.

Pu *symb. Chem.* the element plutonium.

pub /pub/ *n. colloq.* **1** a tavern or bar. **2** *Brit.* a public house.

pub. *abbr.* (also **publ.**) **1** public. **2** publication. **3** published. **4** publisher. **5** publishing.

pu·ber·ty /pyṓōbərtee/ *n.* the period during which adolescents reach sexual maturity and become capable of reproduction. ▫▫ **pu·ber·tal** *adj.*

pu·bes[1] /pyṓōbeez/ *n.* (*pl.* same) **1** the lower part of the abdomen at the front of the pelvis, covered with hair from puberty. **2** the hair appearing on the pubic region.

pubes[2] *pl.* of PUBIS.

pu·bes·cence /pyōōbésəns/ *n.* the time when puberty begins. ▫▫ **pu·bes·cent** *adj.*

pu·bic /pyṓōbik/ *adj.* of or relating to the pubes or pubis.

pu·bis /pyṓōbis/ *n.* (*pl.* **pubes** /–beez/) either of a pair of bones forming the two sides of the pelvis.

pub·lic /públik/ *adj.* & *n.* • *adj.* **1** of or concerning the people as a whole (*a public holiday*; *the public interest*). **2** open to or shared by all the people (*public library*; *public meeting*). **3** done or existing openly (*made his views public*; *a public protest*). **4 a** (of a service, funds, etc.) provided by or concerning local or central government (*public money*; *public records*; *public expenditure*). **b** (of a person) in government (*had a distinguished public career*). **5** well-known; famous (*a public figure*). **6** *Brit.* of, for, or acting for, a university (*public examination*). • *n.* **1** (as *sing.* or *pl.*) the community in general, or members of the community. **2** a section of the community having a particular interest or some special connection (*the reading public*; *my public demands my loyalty*). ▫ **go public** become a public company or corporation. **in public** openly; publicly. **in the public domain** belonging to the public as a whole, esp. not subject to copyright. **in the public eye** famous or notorious. **make public** publicize; make known; publish. ▫▫ **pub·lic·ly** *adv.*

pub·lic-ad·dress sys·tem *n.* loudspeakers, microphones, amplifiers, etc., used in addressing large audiences. ¶ Abbr.: **PA system**.

pub·li·can /públikən/ *n.* **1 a** *Brit.* the keeper of a public house. **b** *Austral.* the keeper of a hotel. **2** *Rom.Hist.* & *Bibl.* a tax collector.

pub·li·ca·tion /públikáyshən/ *n.* **1 a** the preparation and issuing of a book, newspaper, engraving, music, etc., to the public. **b** a book, etc., so issued. **2** the act or an instance of making something publicly known.

pub·lic de·fen·der *n.* an attorney who provides legal representation at public expense for defendants who cannot afford their own attorney.

pub·lic en·e·my *n.* a notorious wanted criminal.

pub·li·cist /públisist/ *n.* **1** a publicity agent or public relations manager. **2** a journalist, esp. concerned with current affairs. ▫▫ **pub·li·cism** *n.* **pub·li·cis·tic** /–sístik/ *adj.*

pub·lic·i·ty /publísitee/ *n.* **1 a** the professional exploitation of a product, company, person, etc., by advertising or popularizing. **b** material or information used for this. **2** public exposure; notoriety.

pub·lic·i·ty a·gent *n.* a person employed to produce or heighten public exposure.

pub·li·cize /públisīz/ *v.tr.* advertise; make publicly known.

pu·blic o·pin·ion *n.* views generally prevalent, esp. on moral questions.

pub·lic re·la·tions *n.pl.* the professional maintenance of a favorable public image, esp. by a company, famous person, etc.

pub·lic school *n.* **1** *US*, *Austral.*, & *Sc.*, etc. a free, government-supported school. **2** *Brit.* a private tuition-paying secondary school, esp. for boarders.

pub·lic sec·tor *n.* that part of an economy, industry, etc., that is controlled by the government.

pub·lic serv·ant *n.* a government official.

pub·lic tel·e·vi·sion *n.* television funded by government appropriation and private donations rather than by advertising.

pub·lic u·til·i·ty *n.* an organization supplying water, gas, etc., to the community.

pub·lish /públish/ *v.tr.* **1** (also *absol.*) (of an author, publisher, etc.) prepare and issue (a book, newspaper, etc.) for public sale. **2** make generally known. **3** announce (an edict, etc.) formally; read (marriage banns). ▫▫ **pub·lish·a·ble** *adj.*

pub·lish·er /públishər/ *n.* **1** a person or esp. a company that produces and distributes copies of a book, newspaper, etc., for sale. **2** the owner or chief executive of a publishing company. **3** a person or thing that publishes.

puce /pyo͞os/ *adj. & n.* dark red or purplish brown.

puck[1] /puk/ *n.* a rubber disk used in ice hockey.

puck[2] /puk/ *n.* **1** a mischievous or evil sprite. **2** a mischievous child. ▫▫ **puck·ish** *adj.* **puck·ish·ly** *adv.* **puck·ish·ness** *n.* **puck·like** *adj.*

puck·er /púkər/ *v. & n.* • *v.tr. & intr.* (often foll. by *up*) gather or cause to gather into wrinkles, folds, or bulges (*puckered her eyebrows; this seam is puckered up*). • *n.* such a wrinkle, bulge, fold, etc. ▫ **pucker up** *colloq.* get ready for a kiss. ▫▫ **puck·er·y** *adj.*

pud·ding /po͝oding/ *n.* **1 a** any of various dessert dishes, usu. containing flavoring, sugar, milk, etc. (*chocolate pudding; rice pudding*). **b** *Brit.* a savory dish containing flour, suet, etc. (*steak and kidney pudding*). **c** *Brit.* the dessert course of a meal. **d** the intestines of a pig, etc., stuffed with oatmeal, spices, blood, etc. **2** *colloq.* a person or thing resembling a pudding. ▫▫ **pud·ding·like** *adj.*

pud·dle /púd'l/ *n. & v.* • *n.* **1** a small pool, esp. of rainwater on a road, etc. **2** clay and sand mixed with water and used as a watertight covering for embankments, etc. **3** a circular patch of disturbed water made by the blade of an oar at each stroke. • *v.* **1** *tr.* **a** knead (clay and sand) into puddle. **b** line (a canal, etc.) with puddle. **c** to coat the roots of (a plant) with mud to reduce water loss during transplantation. **2** *intr.* make puddle from clay, etc. **3** *tr.* stir (molten iron) to produce wrought iron by expelling carbon. **4** *intr.* **a** wade or wallow in mud or shallow water. **b** busy oneself in an untidy way. **5** *tr.* make (water, etc.) muddy. ▫▫ **pud·dler** *n.* **pud·dly** *adj.*

pu·den·dum /pyo͞odéndəm/ *n.* (*pl.* **pudenda** /–də/) (usu. in *pl.*) the genitals, esp. of a woman. ▫▫ **pu·den·dal** *adj.* **pu·dic** /pyo͞odik/ *adj.*

pudg·y /pújee/ *adj.* (**pudgier, pudgiest**) *colloq.* (esp. of a person) plump; slightly overweight. ▫▫ **pudge** *n.* **pudg·i·ly** *adv.* **pudg·i·ness** *n.*

pueb·lo /pwéblō/ *n.* (*pl.* **-los**) **1** (**Pueblo**) a member of a Native American people of the southwestern US. **2** a Native American settlement of the southwestern US, esp. one consisting of multistoried adobe houses built by the Pueblo people.

pu·er·ile /pyo͞oəril, pyo͝oril, –rīl/ *adj.* **1** trivial; childish; immature. **2** of or like a child. ▫▫ **pu·er·ile·ly** *adv.* **pu·er·il·i·ty** /–rílitee/ *n.* (*pl.* **-ties**).

Pu·er·to Ri·can /pwértō réekən, páwrtə/ *n. & adj.* • *n.* **1** a native of Puerto Rico, an island of the West Indies. **2** a person of Puerto Rican descent. • *adj.* of or relating to Puerto Rico or its inhabitants.

puff /puf/ *n. & v.* • *n.* **1 a** a short quick blast of breath or wind. **b** the sound of this; a similar sound. **c** a small quantity of vapor, smoke, etc., emitted in one blast; an inhalation or exhalation from a cigarette, pipe, etc. (*went up in a puff of smoke; took a puff from his cigarette*). **2** a light pastry containing jam, cream, etc. **3** a gathered mass of material in a dress, etc. (*puff sleeve*). **4** a protuberant roll of hair. **5 a** an extravagantly enthusiastic review of a book, etc., esp. in a newspaper. **b** *Brit.* an advertisement for goods, etc., esp. in a newspaper. **6** = POWDER PUFF. **7** an eiderdown. **8** *Brit. colloq.* one's life (*in all my puff*). • *v.* **1** *intr.* emit a puff of air or breath; blow with short blasts. **2** *intr.* (usu. foll. by *away, out,* etc.) (of a person smoking, a steam engine, etc.) emit or move with puffs (*puffing away at his cigar; a train puffed out of the station*). **3** *tr.* esp. *Brit.* (usu. in *passive*; often foll. by *out*) put out of breath (*arrived somewhat puffed; completely puffed him out*). **4** *intr.* breathe hard; pant. **5** *tr.* utter pantingly (*"No more," he puffed*). **6** *intr. & tr.* (usu. foll. by *up, out*) become or cause to become inflated; swell (*his eye was inflamed and puffed up*). **7** *tr.* (usu. foll. by *out, up, away*) blow or emit (dust, smoke, a light object, etc.) with a puff. **8** *tr.* smoke (a pipe, etc.) in puffs. **9** *tr.* (usu. as **puffed up** *adj.*) elate; make proud or boastful. **10** *tr.* advertise or promote (goods, a book, etc.) with exaggerated or false praise. ▫ **puff up** = sense 9 of *v.*

puff add·er *n.* a large venomous African viper, *Bitis arietans*, which inflates the upper part of its body and hisses when excited.

puff·ball /púfbawl/ *n.* any fungus of the genus *Lycoperdon* and related genera producing a ball-shaped spore-bearing structure that releases its contents in a powdery cloud when broken.

puff·er /púfər/ *n.* **1** a person or thing that puffs. **2** any tropical fish of the family *Tetraodontidae*, able to inflate itself into a spherical form. Also called **globe fish**. ▫▫ **puff·er·y** *n.*

puf·fin /púfin/ *n.* any of various seabirds of the family Alcidae native to the N. Atlantic and N. Pacific, esp. *Fratercula arctica*, having a large head with a brightly colored triangular bill and black and white plumage.

puff·y /púfee/ *adj.* (**puffier, puffiest**) **1** swollen, esp. of the face, etc. **2** fat. **3** gusty. **4** short-winded. ▫▫ **puff·i·ly** *adv.* **puff·i·ness** *n.*

pug[1] /pug/ *n.* (in full **pugdog**) **1** a dwarf breed of dog like a bulldog with a broad flat nose and deeply wrinkled face. **2** a dog of this breed. ▫▫ **pug·gish** *adj.* **pug·gy** *adj.*

pug[2] /pug/ *n.* the footprint of an animal.

pu·gi·list /pyo͞ojilist/ *n.* a boxer, esp. a professional. ▫▫ **pu·gi·lism** *n.* **pu·gi·lis·tic** *adj.*

pug·na·cious /pugnáyshəs/ *adj.* quarrelsome; disposed to fight. ▫▫ **pug·na·cious·ly** *adv.* **pug·na·cious·ness** *n.* **pug·nac·i·ty** /–násitee/ *n.*

pug nose *n.* a short squat or snub nose. ▫▫ **pug-nosed** *adj.*

puis·sant /pwísənt, pyo͞oisənt/ *adj. literary* or *archaic* having great power or influence; mighty. ▫▫ **pu·is·sance** *n.* **puis·sant·ly** *adv.*

puke /pyo͞ok/ *v.tr. & intr. sl.* vomit. ▫▫ **puk·ey** *adj.*

pul·chri·tude /púlkritood, –tyo͞od/ *n. literary* beauty. ▫▫ **pul·chri·tu·di·nous** /–to͞odinəs, –tyo͞od–/ *adj.*

pule /pyo͞ol/ *v.intr.* cry querulously or weakly; whine; whimper.

Pu·litz·er prize /po͝olitsər, pyo͞o–/ *n.* each of a group of annual awards for achievements in American journalism, literature, and music.

pull /po͝ol/ *v. & n.* • *v.* **1** *tr.* exert force upon (a thing) tending to move it to oneself or the origin of the force (*stop pulling my hair*). **2** *tr.* cause to move in this way (*pulled it nearer; pulled me into the room*). **3** *intr.* exert a pulling force (*the horse pulls well; the engine will not pull*). **4** *tr.* extract (a cork or tooth) by pulling. **5** *tr.* damage (a muscle, etc.) by abnormal strain. **6 a** *tr.* move (a boat) by pulling on the oars. **b** *intr.* (of a boat, etc.) be caused to move, esp. in a specified direction. **7** *intr.* (often foll. by *up*) proceed with effort (up a hill, etc.). **8** *tr.* (foll. by *on*) bring out (a weapon) for use against (a person). **9 a** *tr.* check the speed of (a horse), esp. so as to make it lose the race. **b** *intr.* (of a horse) strain against the bit. **10** *tr.* attract or secure (custom or support). **11** *tr.* draw (liquor) from a barrel, etc. **12** *intr.* (foll. by *at*) tear or pluck at. **13** *intr.* (often foll. by *on, at*) inhale deeply; draw or suck (on a pipe, etc.). **14** *tr.* (often foll. by *up*) remove (a plant) by the root. **15** *tr.* **a** *Baseball* hit (a ball) to the left (for a right-handed batter) or to the right (for a left-handed batter). **b** *Golf* strike (the ball) widely to the left (or right for a left-handed swing). **16** *tr.* print (a proof, etc.). **17** *tr. colloq.*

achieve or accomplish (esp. something illicit). **18** *tr.* to stretch repeatedly, as candy. • *n.* **1** the act of pulling. **2** the force exerted by this. **3** a means of exerting influence; an advantage. **4** something that attracts or draws attention. **5** a deep draft of esp. liquor. **6** a prolonged effort, e.g., in going up a hill. **7** a handle, etc., for applying a pull. **8** a spell of rowing. **9** a printer's rough proof. **10** *Golf* a pulling stroke. **11** a suck at a cigarette. □ **pull away** withdraw; move away; move ahead. **pull back** retreat or cause to retreat. **pull down** **1** demolish (esp. a building). **2** humiliate. **3** *colloq.* earn (a sum of money) as income, etc. **pull a fast one** see FAST[1]. **pull in 1 a** arrive, esp. at a destination. **b** to restrain; tighten. **2** (of a bus, train, etc.) arrive to take passengers. **3** earn or acquire. **4** *colloq.* arrest. **pull a person's leg** deceive a person playfully. **pull off 1** remove by pulling. **2** succeed in achieving or winning. **pull oneself together** recover control of oneself. **pull out 1** take out by pulling. **2** depart. **3** withdraw from an undertaking. **4** (of a bus, train, etc.) leave with its passengers. **5 a** (of a vehicle) move out from the side of the road, or from its normal position to overtake. **b** (of an airplane) resume level flight from a dive. **pull over** (of a vehicle) move to the side of or off the road. **pull the plug on** *colloq.* withdraw support. **pull one's punches** avoid using one's full force. **pull rank** take unfair advantage of one's seniority. **pull strings** exert (esp. clandestine) influence. **pull the strings** be the real actuator of what another does. **pull through** recover or cause to recover from an illness. **pull together** work in harmony. **pull up 1** stop or cause to stop moving. **2** pull out of the ground. **3** draw closer to or even with, as in a race. **4** check oneself. **pull one's weight** do one's fair share of work. □□ **pull·er** *n.*

pull-down *adj. Computing* (of a menu) appearing below a menu title when selected.

pul·let /pŏŏlit/ *n.* a young hen, esp. one less than one year old.

pul·ley /pŏŏlee/ *n.* (*pl.* **-leys**) **1** a grooved wheel or set of wheels for a rope, etc., to pass over, set in a block and used for changing the direction of a force. **2** a wheel or drum fixed on a shaft and turned by a belt, used esp. to increase speed or power.

Pull·man /pŏŏlmən/ *n.* a railroad car affording special comfort, esp. one with sleeping berths.

pull·o·ver /pŏŏlōvər/ *n.* a knitted garment put on over the head and covering the top half of the body.

pul·mo·nar·y /pŏŏlməneree, púl–/ *adj.* **1** of or relating to the lungs. **2** having lungs or lunglike organs. **3** affected with or susceptible to lung disease. □□ **pul·mo·nate** /–nayt, –nət/ *adj.*

pul·mon·ic /pŏŏlmónik, pul–/ *adj.* = PULMONARY 1.

pulp /pulp/ *n.* & *v.* • *n.* **1** the soft fleshy part of fruit, etc. **2** any soft thick wet mass. **3** a soft shapeless mass derived from rags, wood, etc., used in papermaking. **4** (often *attrib.*) poor quality (often sensational) writing orig. printed on rough paper (*pulp fiction*). **5** vascular tissue filling the interior cavity and root canals of a tooth. **6** *Mining* pulverized ore mixed with water. • *v.* **1** *tr.* reduce to pulp. **2** *tr.* withdraw (a publication) from the market, usu. recycling the paper. **3** *tr.* remove pulp from. **4** *intr.* become pulp. □□ **pulp·er** *n.* **pulp·less** *adj.* **pulp·y** *adj.* **pulp·i·ness** *n.*

pul·pit /pŏŏlpit, púl–/ *n.* a raised enclosed platform in a church, etc., from which the preacher delivers a sermon.

pulp·wood /púlpwŏŏd/ *n.* timber suitable for making pulp.

pul·que /pŏŏlkay, pŏŏlkee, pŏŏl–/ *n.* a Mexican fermented drink made from the sap of an agave plant.

pul·sar /púlsaar/ *n. Astron.* a cosmic source of regular and rapid pulses of radiation usu. at radio frequencies, e.g., a rotating neutron star.

pul·sate /púlsayt/ *v.intr.* **1** expand and contract rhythmically; throb. **2** vibrate; quiver; thrill. □□ **pul·sa·tion** /–sáyshən/ *n.* **pul·sa·tor** *n.* **pul·sa·to·ry** /púlsətawree/ *adj.*

pulse[1] /puls/ *n.* & *v.* • *n.* **1 a** a rhythmical throbbing of the arteries as blood is propelled through them, esp. as felt in the wrists, temples, etc. **b** each successive beat of the arteries or heart. **c** (in full **pulse rate**) the number of such beats in a specified period of time, esp. one minute. **2** a throb or thrill of life or emotion. **3** a latent feeling. **4** a single vibration of sound, electric current, light, etc., esp. as a signal. **5** a musical beat. **6** any regular or recurrent rhythm, e.g., of the stroke of oars. • *v.intr.* **1** pulsate. **2** (foll. by *out, in,* etc.) transmit, etc., by rhythmical beats. □□ **pulse·less** *adj.*

pulse[2] /puls/ *n.* (as *sing.* or *pl.*) **1** the edible seeds of various leguminous plants, e.g., chickpeas, lentils, beans, etc. **2** the plant or plants producing this.

pul·ver·ize /púlvərīz/ *v.* **1** *tr.* reduce to fine particles. **2** *intr.* be reduced to dust. **3** *tr. colloq.* **a** demolish. **b** defeat utterly. □□ **pul·ver·iz·a·ble** *adj.* **pul·ver·i·za·tion** *n.* **pul·ver·iz·er** *n.*

pu·ma /pyŏŏmə, pŏŏ–/ *n.* a large American wild cat, *Felis concolor*, usu. with a plain tawny coat. Also called COUGAR, PANTHER, MOUNTAIN LION.

pum·ice /púmis/ *n.* & *v.* • *n.* (in full **pumice stone**) **1** a light porous volcanic rock often used as an abrasive in cleaning or polishing substances. **2** a piece of this used for removing callused skin, etc. • *v.tr.* rub or clean with a pumice. □□ **pu·mi·ceous** /pyŏŏmíshəs/ *adj.*

pum·mel /púməl/ *v.tr.* (**pummeled** or **pummelled, pummeling** or **pummelling**) strike repeatedly, esp. with the fist.

pump[1] /pump/ *n.* & *v.* • *n.* **1** a machine, usu. with rotary action or the reciprocal action of a piston, for raising or moving liquids, compressing gases, inflating tires, etc. **2** a physiological or electromagnetic process or mechanism having a similar purpose. **3** an instance of pumping; a stroke of a pump. • *v.* **1** *tr.* (often foll. by *in, out, into, up,* etc.) raise or remove (liquid, gas, etc.) with a pump. **2** *tr.* (often foll. by *up*) fill (a tire, etc.) with air. **3** *tr.* **a** remove (water, etc.) with a pump. **b** (foll. by *out*) remove liquid from (a place, well, etc.) with a pump. **4** *intr.* work a pump. **5** *tr.* (often foll. by *out*) cause to move, pour forth, etc., as if by pumping. **6** *tr.* question (a person) persistently to obtain information. **7** *tr.* **a** move vigorously up and down. **b** shake (a person's hand) effusively. **8** *tr.* (usu. foll. by *up*) arouse; excite. □ **pump iron** (also **pump up**) *colloq.* exercise with weights.

pump[2] /pump/ *n.* **1** a usu. medium-heeled slip-on women's dress shoe. **2** a slip-on men's patent leather shoe for formal wear.

pum·per·nick·el /púmpərnikəl/ *n.* German-style dark, coarse rye bread.

pump·kin /púmpkin, púng–/ *n.* **1** any of various plants of the genus *Cucurbita*, with large lobed leaves and tendrils. **2** the large rounded edible orange or yellow fruit of this.

pun /pun/ *n.* & *v.* • *n.* the humorous use of a word to suggest different meanings, or of words of the same sound and different meanings. • *v.intr.* (**punned, punning**) (foll. by *on*) make a pun or puns with (words). □□ **pun·ning·ly** *adv.*

punch[1] /punch/ *v.* & *n.* • *v.tr.* **1** strike bluntly, esp. with a closed fist. **2** prod or poke with a blunt object. **3 a** pierce a hole in (metal, paper, a ticket, etc.) as or with a punch. **b** pierce (a hole) by punching. **4** drive (cattle) by prodding with a stick, etc. • *n.* **1** a blow with a fist. **2** the ability to deliver this. **3** *colloq.* vigor; momentum; effective force. □ **punch in** (or **out**) record the time of one's arrival at (or departure from) work by punching a time clock. ▫▫ **punch·er** *n.*

punch[2] /punch/ *n.* **1** any of various devices or machines for punching holes in materials (e.g., paper, leather, metal, plaster). **2** a tool or machine for impressing a design or stamping a die on a material.

punch[3] /punch/ *n.* a drink of fruit juices, sometimes mixed with wine or liquor, served cold or hot.

punch-drunk *adj.* stupefied from or as though from a series of heavy blows.

pun·cheon[1] /púnchən/ *n.* **1** a short post, esp. one supporting a roof in a coal mine. **2** = PUNCH[2]. **3** a heavy timber finished on one side only, used in flooring, etc.

pun·cheon[2] /púnchən/ *n.* a large cask for liquids, etc., holding from 72 to 120 gallons.

punch·ing bag *n.* **1** a stuffed or inflated bag, usu. cylindrical or pear-shaped, suspended so it can be punched for exercise or training, usu. by boxers. **2** a person on whom another person vents their anger.

punch line *n.* words giving the point of a joke or story.

punch·y /púnchee/ *adj.* (**punchier, punchiest**) **1** having punch or vigor; forceful. **2** = PUNCH-DRUNK. ▫▫ **punch·i·ly** *adv.* **punch·i·ness** *n.*

punc·til·i·ous /pungktíleeəs/ *adj.* **1** attentive to formality or etiquette. **2** precise in behavior. ▫▫ **punc·til·i·ous·ly** *adv.* **punc·til·i·ous·ness** *n.*

punc·tu·al /púngkchōōəl/ *adj.* **1** observant of the appointed time. **2** neither early nor late. **3** *Geom.* of a point. ▫▫ **punc·tu·al·i·ty** /–álitee/ *n.* **punc·tu·al·ly** *adv.*

punc·tu·ate /púngkchōō-ayt/ *v.tr.* **1** insert punctuation marks in. **2** interrupt at intervals (*punctuated his tale with heavy sighs*). **3** emphasize.

punc·tu·a·tion /púngkchōō-áyshən/ *n.* **1** the system or arrangement of marks used to punctuate a written passage. **2** the practice or skill of punctuating.

punc·tu·a·tion mark *n.* any of the marks (e.g., period and comma) used in writing to separate sentences and phrases, etc., and to clarify meaning.

punc·ture /púngkchər/ *n.* & *v.* •*n.* **1** a pierced hole, esp. the accidental piercing of a pneumatic tire. **2** a hole made in this way. •*v.* **1** *tr.* make a puncture in. **2** *intr.* become punctured. **3** *tr.* prick or pierce. **4** *tr.* cause (hopes, confidence, etc.) to collapse; dash; deflate.

pun·dit /púndit/ *n.* **1** (also **pan·dit**) a Hindu learned in Sanskrit and in the philosophy, religion, and jurisprudence of India. **2** often *iron.* **a** a learned expert or teacher. **b** a critic. ▫▫ **pun·dit·ry** *n.*

pun·gent /púnjənt/ *adj.* **1** having a sharp or strong taste or smell. **2** (of remarks) penetrating; biting; caustic. ▫▫ **pun·gen·cy** *n.* **pun·gent·ly** *adv.*

pun·ish /púnish/ *v.tr.* **1** cause (an offender) to suffer for an offense. **2** inflict a penalty for (an offense). **3** *colloq.* inflict severe blows on (an opponent). **4 a** tax severely; subject to severe treatment. **b** abuse or treat improperly. ▫▫ **pun·ish·a·ble** *adj.* **pun·ish·er** *n.* **pun·ish·ing** *adj.* (in sense 4a). **pun·ish·ing·ly** *adv.*

pun·ish·ment /púnishmənt/ *n.* **1** the act or an instance of punishing; the condition of being punished. **2** the loss or suffering inflicted in this. **3** *colloq.* severe treatment or suffering.

pu·ni·tive /pyōōnitiv/ *adj.* (also **pu·ni·to·ry** /–tawree/) **1** inflicting or intended to inflict punishment. **2** (of taxation, etc.) extremely severe. ▫▫ **pu·ni·tive·ly** *adv.*

punk /pungk/ *n.* & *adj.* •*n.* **1 a** a worthless person or thing (often as a general term of abuse). **b** nonsense. **2 a** (in full **punk rock**) a loud fast-moving form of rock music with crude and aggressive effects. **b** (in full **punk rocker**) a devotee of this. **3** a hoodlum or ruffian. **4** a young male homosexual partner. **5** an inexperienced person; a novice. **6** soft crumbly wood used as tinder. **7** a spongy fungal substance, esp. as used as a fuse. •*adj.* **1** worthless; poor in quality. **2** denoting punk rock and its associations. **3** (of wood) rotten; decayed. ▫▫ **punk·y** *adj.*

pun·ster /púnstər/ *n.* a person who makes puns, esp. habitually.

punt[1] /punt/ *n.* & *v.* •*n.* a long narrow flat-bottomed boat, square at both ends, used mainly on rivers and propelled by a long pole. •*v.* **1** *tr.* propel (a punt) with a pole. **2** *intr.* & *tr.* travel or convey in a punt. ▫▫ **punt·er** *n.*

punt[2] /punt/ *v.* & *n.* •*v.tr.* kick (a ball, as in football or rugby) after it has dropped from the hands and before it reaches the ground. •*n.* such a kick. ▫▫ **punt·er** *n.*

pu·ny /pyōōnee/ *adj.* (**punier, puniest**) **1** undersized. **2** weak; feeble. **3** petty. ▫▫ **pu·ni·ly** *adv.* **pu·ni·ness** *n.*

pup /pup/ *n.* **1** a young dog. **2** a young wolf, rat, seal, etc.

pu·pa /pyōōpə/ *n.* (*pl.* **pupae** /–pee/) an insect in the stage of development between larva and imago. ▫▫ **pu·pal** *adj.*

pu·pate /pyōōpayt/ *v.intr.* become a pupa. ▫▫ **pu·pa·tion** *n.*

pu·pil[1] /pyōōpəl/ *n.* a person who is taught by another, esp. a student in relation to a teacher. ▫▫ **pu·pil·age** *n.* (also **pu·pil·lage**). **pu·pil·lar·y** *adj.*

pu·pil[2] /pyōōpəl/ *n.* the dark circular opening in the center of the iris of the eye, varying in size to regulate the passage of light to the retina. ▫▫ **pu·pil·lar** *adj.* (also **pu·pil·ar**). **pu·pil·lar·y** *adj.* (also **pu·pi·lar·y**).

pup·pet /púpit/ *n.* **1** a small figure representing a human being or animal and moved by various means as entertainment. **2** a person whose actions are controlled by another. ▫▫ **pup·pet·ry** *n.*

pup·pet·eer /púpiteér/ *n.* a person who works puppets.

pup·pet state *n.* a country that is nominally independent but actually under the control of another power.

pup·py /púpee/ *n.* (*pl.* **-pies**) **1** a young dog. **2** a conceited or arrogant young man. ▫▫ **pup·py·hood** *n.* **pup·py·ish** *adj.*

pup·py love *n.* romantic attachment or affection between adolescents.

pup tent *n.* a small two-person tent, usu. made of two pieces fastened together.

pur·blind /pə́rblīnd/ *adj.* **1** partly blind. **2** obtuse; dim-witted. ▫▫ **pur·blind·ness** *n.*

pur·chase /pə́rchis/ *v.* & *n.* •*v.tr.* **1** acquire by payment; buy. **2** obtain or achieve at some cost. •*n.* **1** the act or an instance of buying. **2** something bought. **3** *Law* the acquisition of property by one's personal action and not by inheritance. **4** a firm hold on a thing to move it or to prevent it from slipping; leverage. ▫▫ **pur·chas·a·ble** *adj.* **pur·chas·er** *n.*

pure /pyōōr/ *adj.* **1** unmixed; unadulterated (*pure white*; *pure alcohol*). **2** of unmixed origin or descent (*pure-blooded*). **3** chaste. **4** morally or sexually undefiled; not corrupt. **5** conforming absolutely to a standard of quality; faultless. **6** guiltless. **7** sincere. **8** mere; simple; nothing but; sheer (*it was pure malice*). **9** (of a sound) not discordant; perfectly in tune. **10** (of a subject of study) dealing with abstract concepts and not practical application. ▫▫ **pure·ness** *n.*

pure·bred /pyōōrbred/ *adj.* & *n.* •*adj.* belonging to a recognized breed of unmixed lineage. •*n.* a purebred animal.

pu·rée /pyōōráy, pyōōrée/ *n.* & *v.* •*n.* a pulp of vegetables or fruit, etc., reduced to a smooth, creamy substance. •*v.tr.* (**purées, puréed**) make a purée of.

pure·ly /pyōōrlee/ *adv.* **1** in a pure manner. **2** merely; solely; exclusively.

pur·ga·tive /pɔ́rgətiv/ *adj. & n.* • *adj.* **1** serving to purify. **2** strongly laxative. • *n.* **1** a purgative thing. **2** a laxative.

pur·ga·to·ry /pɔ́rgətawree/ *n. & adj.* • *n.* (*pl.* **-ries**) **1** the condition or supposed place of spiritual cleansing, esp. (*RC Ch.*) of those dying in the grace of God but having to expiate venial sins, etc. **2** a place or state of temporary suffering or expiation. • *adj.* purifying. ▫▫ **pur·ga·to·ri·al** /–táwreeəl/ *adj.*

purge /pərj/ *v. & n.* • *v.tr.* **1** (often foll. by *of, from*) make physically or spiritually clean. **2** remove by a cleansing or erasing (as of computer files) process. **3 a** rid (an organization, party, etc.) of persons regarded as undesirable. **b** remove (a person regarded as undesirable) from an organization, party, etc., often violently or by force. **4 a** empty (the bowels). **b** empty the bowels of. • *n.* **1 a** the act or an instance of purging. **b** the removal, often in a forcible or violent manner, of people regarded as undesirable from an organization, party, etc. **2** a purgative. ▫▫ **purg·er** *n.*

pu·ri·fy /pyŏŏrifī/ *v.tr.* (**-fies, -fied**) **1** (often foll. by *of, from*) cleanse or make pure. **2** make ceremonially clean. **3** clear of extraneous elements. ▫▫ **pu·ri·fi·ca·tion** /–fikáshən/ *n.* **pu·rif·i·ca·to·ry** /–rífəkətáwree/ *adj.* **pu·ri·fi·er** *n.*

Pu·rim /pŏŏrim, pŏŏréem/ *n.* a Jewish spring festival commemorating the defeat of Haman's plot to massacre the Jews (Esth. 9).

pur·ist /pyŏŏrist/ *n.* a stickler for or advocate of scrupulous purity, esp. in language or art. ▫▫ **pur·ism** *n.* **pu·ris·tic** *adj.*

pu·ri·tan /pyŏŏrit'n/ *n. & adj.* • *n.* **1** (**Puritan**) *hist.* a member of a group of English Protestants who regarded the Reformation of the Church under Elizabeth as incomplete and sought to simplify and regulate forms of worship. **2** a purist member of any party. **3** a person practicing or affecting extreme strictness in religion or morals. • *adj.* **1** *hist.* of or relating to the Puritans. **2** scrupulous and austere in religion or morals. ▫▫ **pu·ri·tan·ism** *n.*

pu·ri·tan·i·cal /pyŏŏritánikəl/ *adj.* often *derog.* practicing or affecting strict religious or moral behavior. ▫▫ **pu·ri·tan·i·cal·ly** *adv.*

pu·ri·ty /pyŏŏritee/ *n.* **1** pureness; cleanness. **2** freedom from physical or moral pollution.

purl /pərl/ *n. & v.* • *n.* a knitting stitch made by putting the needle through the front of the previous stitch and passing the yarn around the back of the needle. • *v.tr.* (also *absol.*) knit with a purl stitch.

pur·lieu /pɔ́rlyōō/ *n.* (*pl.* **purlieus**) **1** a person's bounds or limits. **2** a person's usual haunts. **3** (in *pl.*) the outskirts; an outlying region.

pur·loin /pərlóyn/ *v.tr.* literary steal; pilfer. ▫▫ **pur·loin·er** *n.*

pur·ple /pɔ́rpəl/ *n., adj., & v.* • *n.* **1** a color intermediate between red and blue. **2** a purple robe, esp. as the dress of an emperor or senior magistrate. **3** the scarlet official dress of a cardinal. **4** (prec. by *the*) a position of rank, authority, or privilege. • *adj.* of a purple color. • *v.tr. & intr.* make or become purple. ▫▫ **pur·plish** *adj.*

Pur·ple Heart *n.* a US military decoration for those wounded in action.

pur·ple pas·sage *n.* (also **purple prose** or **purple patch**) an overly ornate or elaborate passage, esp. in a literary composition.

pur·port *v. & n.* • *v.tr.* /pərpáwrt/ **1** profess; be intended to seem (*purports to be the royal seal*). **2** (often foll. by *that* + clause) (of a document or speech) have as its meaning; state. • *n.* /pɔ́rpawrt/ the ostensible meaning; sense or tenor. ▫▫ **pur·port·ed·ly** /–páwrtidlee/ *adv.*

pur·pose /pɔ́rpəs/ *n. & v.* • *n.* **1** an object to be attained; a thing intended. **2** the intention to act. **3** resolution; determination. **4** the reason for which something is done or made. • *v.tr.* have as one's purpose; intend. ▫ **on purpose** intentionally.

pur·pose·ful /pɔ́rpəsfŏŏl/ *adj.* **1** having or indicating purpose. **2** intentional. **3** resolute. ▫▫ **pur·pose·ful·ly** *adv.* **pur·pose·ful·ness** *n.*

pur·pose·less /pɔ́rpəslis/ *adj.* having no aim or plan. ▫▫ **pur·pose·less·ly** *adv.* **pur·pose·less·ness** *n.*

pur·pose·ly /pɔ́rpəslee/ *adv.* intentionally.

pur·pos·ive /pɔ́rpəsiv, pərpṓ–/ *adj.* **1** having, serving, or done with a purpose. **2** resolute; purposeful. ▫▫ **pur·pos·ive·ly** *adv.* **pur·pos·ive·ness** *n.*

pur·pu·ra /pɔ́rpyŏŏrə/ *n.* a disease characterized by purple or livid spots on the skin, due to internal bleeding from small blood vessels. ▫▫ **pur·pur·ic** /–pyŏŏrik/ *adj.*

purr /pɔ́r/ *v. & n.* • *v.* **1** *intr.* (of a cat) make a low vibratory sound expressing contentment. **2** *intr.* (of machinery, etc.) make a similar sound. **3** *intr.* (of a person) express pleasure. **4** *tr.* utter or express (words or contentment) in this way. • *n.* a purring sound.

purse /pɔ́rs/ *n. & v.* • *n.* **1** a small pouch of leather, etc., for carrying money on the person. **2** a small bag for carrying personal effects, esp. one carried by a woman. **3** a receptacle resembling a purse in form or purpose. **4** money; funds. **5** a sum collected as a present or given as a prize in a contest. • *v.* **1** *tr.* (often foll. by *up*) pucker or contract (the lips). **2** *intr.* become contracted and wrinkled. ▫ **hold the purse strings** have control of expenditure.

purs·er /pɔ́rsər/ *n.* an officer on a ship who keeps the accounts, esp. the head steward in a passenger vessel. ▫▫ **purs·er·ship** *n.*

purs·lane /pɔ́rslayn/ *n.* any of various plants of the genus *Portulaca*, esp. *P. oleracea*, with green or golden leaves, used as a salad vegetable and herb.

pur·su·ance /pərsṓōəns/ *n.* (foll. by *of*) the carrying out or observance (of a plan, idea, etc.).

pur·su·ant /pərsṓōənt/ *adj. & adv.* • *adj.* pursuing. • *adv.* (foll. by *to*) conforming to or in accordance with. ▫▫ **pur·su·ant·ly** *adv.*

pur·sue /pərsṓō/ *v.* (**pursues, pursued, pursuing**) **1** *tr.* follow with intent to overtake or capture or do harm to. **2** *tr.* continue or proceed along (a route or course of action). **3** *tr.* follow or engage in (study or other activity). **4** *tr.* proceed in compliance with (a plan, etc.). **5** *tr.* seek after; aim at. **6** *tr.* continue to investigate or discuss (a topic). **7** *tr.* seek the attention or acquaintance of (a person) persistently. **8** *tr.* (of misfortune, etc.) persistently assail. **9** *tr.* persistently attend; stick to. **10** *intr.* go in pursuit. ▫▫ **pur·su·a·ble** *adj.* **pur·su·er** *n.*

pur·suit /pərsṓōt/ *n.* **1** the act or an instance of pursuing. **2** an occupation or activity pursued. ▫ **in pursuit of** pursuing.

pu·ru·lent /pyŏŏrələnt, pyŏŏryə–/ *adj.* **1** consisting of or containing pus. **2** discharging pus. ▫▫ **pu·ru·lence** *n.* **pu·ru·len·cy** *n.* **pu·ru·lent·ly** *adv.*

pur·vey /pərváy/ *v.* **1** *tr.* provide or supply (articles of food) as one's business. **2** *intr.* (often foll. by *for*) **a** make provision. **b** act as supplier. ▫▫ **pur·vey·ance** *n.* **pur·vey·or** *n.*

pur·view /pɔ́rvyōō/ *n.* **1** the scope or range of a document, scheme, etc. **2** the range of physical or mental vision.

pus /pus/ *n.* a thick yellowish or greenish liquid produced from infected tissue.

push /pŏŏsh/ *v. & n.* • *v.* **1** *tr.* exert a force on (a thing) to move it away from oneself or from the origin of the force. **2** *tr.* cause to move in this direction. **3** *intr.* exert such a force (*do not push against the door*). **4** *tr.* press; depress (*push the button for service*). **5** *intr. & tr.* **a** thrust forward or upward. **b** project or cause to project (*push-*

es out new roots). **6** *intr.* move forward by force or persistence. **7** *tr.* make (one's way) by pushing. **8** *intr.* exert oneself, esp. to surpass others. **9** *tr.* (often foll. by *to*, *into*, or *to* + infin.) urge or impel. **10** *tr.* tax the abilities or tolerance of; press (a person) hard. **11** *tr.* pursue (a claim, etc.). **12** *tr.* promote the use or sale or adoption of, e.g., by advertising. **13** *intr.* (foll. by *for*) demand persistently (*pushed hard for reform*). **14** *tr. colloq.* sell (a drug) illegally. **15** *tr. colloq.* to approach, esp. in age (*pushing thirty*). • *n.* **1** the act or an instance of pushing; a shove or thrust. **2** the force exerted in this. **3** a vigorous effort. **4** a military attack in force. **5** enterprise; determination to succeed. **6** the use of influence to advance a person. **7** the pressure of affairs. **8** a crisis. □ **be pushed for** *colloq.* have very little of (esp. time). **if** (or **when**) **push comes to shove** when a problem must be faced; in a crisis. **push around** *colloq.* bully. **push one's luck 1** take undue risks. **2** act presumptuously. **push off 1 a** set off; depart. **b** push with an oar, etc., to get a boat out into a river, etc. **2** esp. *Brit.* (often in *imper.*) *colloq.* go away. **push through** get (a scheme, proposal, etc.) completed or accepted quickly.

push but·ton *n.* **1** a button to be pushed, esp. to operate an electrical device. **2** (*attrib.*) operated in this way.

push·cart /po͝oshkaart/ *n.* a handcart or barrow, esp. one used by a street vendor.

push·er /po͝oshər/ *n.* **1** *colloq.* an illegal seller of drugs. **2** *colloq.* a pushing or pushy person.

push·ing /po͝oshing/ *adj.* **1** pushy; aggressively ambitious. **2** *colloq.* having nearly reached (a specified age). □□ **push·ing·ly** *adv.*

push·o·ver /po͝oshōvər/ *n. colloq.* **1** something that is easily done. **2** a person who can easily be overcome, persuaded, etc.

push start *n. & v.* • *n.* the starting of a motor vehicle by pushing it to turn the engine. • *v.tr.* start (a vehicle) in this way.

push-up *n.* an exercise in which the body, extended and prone, is raised upwards by pushing down with the hands until the arms are straight.

push·y /po͝oshee/ *adj.* (**pushier, pushiest**) *colloq.* **1** excessively self-assertive. **2** selfishly determined to succeed. □□ **push·i·ly** *adv.* **push·i·ness** *n.*

pu·sil·lan·i·mous /pyo͞osilánimәs/ *adj.* lacking courage; timid. □□ **pu·sil·la·nim·i·ty** /–lənímitee/ *n.* **pu·sil·lan·i·mous·ly** *adv.*

puss /po͝os/ *n. colloq.* **1** a cat (esp. as a form of address). **2** a girl. **3** *Brit.* a hare.

pus·sy /po͝osee/ *n.* (*pl.* **-sies**) **1** (also **pus·sy·cat**) *colloq.* a cat. **2** *coarse sl.* the vulva. ▶Usually considered a taboo use. **3** *coarse sl.* a weak, cowardly or effeminate man.

pus·sy·foot /po͝oseefo͝ot/ *v.intr.* **1** move stealthily or warily. **2** act cautiously or noncommittally. □□ **pus·sy·foot·er** *n.*

pus·sy wil·low *n.* any of various willows, esp. *Salix discolor*, with furry catkins.

pus·tule /púschoo͞l/ *n.* a pimple containing pus. □□ **pus·tu·lar** *adj.* **pus·tu·lous** *adj.*

put[1] /po͝ot/ *v., n., & adj.* • *v.* (**putting**; *past* and *past part.* **put**) **1** *tr.* move to or cause to be in a specified place or position (*put it in your pocket*; *put the children to bed*). **2** *tr.* bring into a specified condition, relation, or state (*an accident put the car out of action*). **3** *tr.* **a** (often foll. by *on*) impose or assign (*where do you put the blame?*). **b** (foll. by *on, to*) impose or enforce the existence of (*put a stop to it*). **4** *tr.* **a** cause (a person) to go or be, habitually or temporarily (*put them at their ease*; *put them on the right track*). **b** *refl.* imagine (oneself) in a specified situation (*put yourself in my shoes*). **5** *tr.* (foll. by *for*) substitute (one thing for another). **6** *tr.* express (a thought or idea) in a specified way (*to put it mildly*). **7** *tr.* (foll. by *at*) estimate (an amount, etc., at a specified amount) (*put the cost at $50*). **8** *tr.* (foll. by *into*) express or translate in (words, or another language). **9** *tr.* (foll. by *into*) invest (money in an asset, e.g., land). **10** *tr.* (foll. by *on*) stake (money) on (a horse, etc.). **11** *tr.* (foll. by *to*) apply or devote to a use or purpose (*put it to good use*). **12** *tr.* (foll. by *to*) submit for consideration or attention (*let me put it to you another way*; *shall now put it to a vote*). **13** *tr.* (foll. by *to*) subject (a person) to (death, suffering, etc.). **14** *tr.* throw (esp. a shot or weight) as an athletic sport or exercise. **15** *tr.* (foll. by *to*) couple (an animal) with (another of the opposite sex) for breeding. **16** *intr.* (foll. by *back, off, out*, etc.) (of a ship, etc.) proceed or follow a course in a specified direction. • *n.* **1** a throw of the shot or weight. **2** *Stock Exch.* the option of selling stock or a commodity at a fixed price at a given date. • *adj.* stationary; fixed (*stay put*). □ **put across 1** make acceptable or effective. **2** express in an understandable way. **3** (often in **put it** (or **one**) **across**) achieve by deceit. **put away 1** put (a thing) back in the place where it is normally kept. **2** set (money, etc.) aside for future use. **3 a** confine or imprison. **b** commit to a mental institution. **4** consume (food and drink), esp. in large quantities. **5** put (an old or sick animal) to death. **put by** lay (money, etc.) aside for future use. **put down 1** suppress by force or authority. **2** *colloq.* snub or humiliate. **3** record or enter in writing. **4** enter the name of (a person) on a list, esp. as a member or subscriber. **5** (foll. by *as, for*) account, reckon, or categorize. **6** (foll. by *to*) attribute (*put it down to bad planning*). **7** put (an old or sick animal) to death. **8** preserve or store (eggs, etc.) for future use. **9** pay (a specified sum) as a deposit. **10** put (a baby) to bed. **11** land (an aircraft). **12** stop to let (passengers) get off. **put forth 1** (of a plant) send out (buds or leaves). **2** *formal* submit or put into circulation. **put forward** suggest or propose. **put in 1 a** enter or submit (a claim, etc.). **b** (foll. by *for*) submit a claim for (a specified thing). **2** (foll. by *for*) be a candidate for (an appointment, election, etc.). **3** spend (time). **4** perform (a spell of work) as part of a whole. **5** interpose (a remark, blow, etc.). **6** insert as an addition. **put it to a person** (often foll. by *that* + clause) challenge a person to deny. **put off 1 a** postpone. **b** postpone an engagement with (a person). **2** (often foll. by *with*) evade (a person) with an excuse, etc. **3** hinder or dissuade. **put on 1** clothe oneself with. **2** cause (an electrical device, light, etc.) to function. **3** cause (esp. transport) to be available; provide. **4** stage (a play, show, etc.). **5 a** pretend to be affected by (an emotion). **b** assume; take on (a character or appearance). **c** (**put it on**) exaggerate one's feelings, etc. **6** increase one's weight by (a specified amount). **7** (foll. by *to*) make aware of or put in touch with (*put us on to their new accountant*). **8** *colloq.* tease; play a trick on. **put out 1 a** (often as **put out** *adj.*) disconcert or annoy. **b** (often *refl.*) inconvenience (*don't put yourself out*). **2** extinguish (a fire or light). **3** *Baseball* cause (a batter or runner) to be out. **4** dislocate (a joint). **5** exert (strength, etc.). **6** allocate (work) to be done off the premises. **7** issue; publish. **put one over** (usu. foll. by *on*) get the better of; outsmart; trick. **put through 1** carry out or complete (a task or transaction). **2** (often foll. by *to*) connect (a person) by telephone to another. **put together 1** assemble (a whole) from parts. **2** combine (parts) to form a whole. **put under** render unconscious by anesthetic, etc. **put up 1** build or erect. **2** to can; preserve (food) for later use. **3** take or provide accommodation for (*friends put me up for the night*).

4 engage in (a fight, struggle, etc.) as a form of resistance. **5** present (a proposal). **6 a** present oneself for election. **b** propose for election. **7** provide (money) as a backer in an enterprise. **8** display (a notice). **9** publish (banns). **10** offer for sale or competition. **11** esp. *Brit.* raise (a price, etc.). **put upon** *colloq.* make unfair or excessive demands on; take advantage of (a person). **put a person up to** (usu. foll. by verbal noun) instigate a person in (*put them up to stealing the money*). **put up with** endure; tolerate; submit to. □□ **put·ter** *n.*

put[2] var. of PUTT.

pu·ta·tive /pyo͞otətiv/ *adj.* reputed; supposed (*his putative father*). □□ **pu·ta·tive·ly** *adv.*

put-down *n.* colloq. an act or instance of snubbing or humiliating (someone).

put-on *n. colloq.* a deception or hoax.

put-put /pútpút/ *n. & v.* • *n.* **1** the rapid intermittent sound of a small gasoline engine. **2** *colloq.* a small boat using such an engine. • *v.intr.* (**put-putted, put-putting**) make this sound.

pu·tre·fy /pyo͞otrifī/ *v.* (**-fies, -fied**) **1** *intr. & tr.* become or make putrid; go bad. **2** *intr.* fester; suppurate. **3** *intr.* become morally corrupt. □□ **pu·tre·fa·cient** /–fáyshənt/ *adj.* **pu·tre·fac·tion** /–fákshən/ *n.* **pu·tre·fac·tive** /–fáktiv/ *adj.*

pu·tres·cent /pyo͞otrésənt/ *adj.* **1** in the process of rotting. **2** of or accompanying this process. □□ **pu·tres·cence** *n.*

pu·trid /pyo͞otrid/ *adj.* **1** decomposed; rotten. **2** foul; noxious. **3** corrupt. **4** *sl.* of poor quality; contemptible; very unpleasant. □□ **pu·trid·i·ty** /–tríditee/ *n.* **pu·trid·ly** *adv.* **pu·trid·ness** *n.*

putsch /po͝och/ *n.* an attempt at political revolution; a violent uprising.

putt /put/ *v. & n.* (also *Brit.* **put**) • *v.tr.* (**putted, putting**) strike (a golf ball) gently to get it into or nearer to a hole on a putting green. • *n.* a putting stroke.

put·tee /putée, pútee/ *n.* **1** a long strip of cloth wound spirally around the leg from ankle to knee for protection and support. **2** *US* a leather legging.

put·ter[1] /pútər/ *n.* **1** a golf club used in putting. **2** a golfer who putts.

put·ter[2] /pútər/ *v.* (also *Brit.* **potter**) **1** *intr.* **a** (often foll. by *about, around*) work or occupy oneself in a desultory but pleasant manner (*likes puttering around in the garden*). **b** (often foll. by *at, in*) dabble in a subject or occupation. **2** *intr.* go slowly; dawdle; loiter. **3** *tr.* (foll. by *away*) fritter away (one's time, etc.). □□ **put·ter·er** *n.*

put·ty /pútee/ *n. & v.* • *n.* (*pl.* **-ties**) **1** a cement made from whiting and raw linseed oil, used for fixing panes of glass, filling holes in woodwork, etc. **2** a fine white mortar of lime and water, used in pointing brickwork, etc. **3** a polishing powder usu. made from tin oxide, used in jewelry work. • *v.tr.* (**-ties, -tied**) cover, fix, join, or fill up with putty. □ **putty in a person's hands** someone who is overcompliant, or easily influenced.

putz /puts/ *n. & v.* • *n. sl.* a simple-minded foolish person. • *v.intr. sl.* (usu. foll. by *around*) move (about) or occupy oneself in an aimless or idle manner.

puz·zle /púzəl/ *n. & v.* • *n.* **1** a difficult or confusing problem; an enigma. **2** a problem or toy designed to test knowledge or ingenuity. • *v.* **1** *tr.* confound or disconcert mentally. **2** *intr.* (usu. foll. by *over*, etc.) be perplexed (about). **3** *tr.* (usu. as **puzzling** *adj.*) require much thought to comprehend (*a puzzling situation*). **4** *tr.* (foll. by *out*) solve or understand by hard thought. □□ **puz·zle·ment** *n.* **puz·zling·ly** *adv.*

puz·zler /púzlər/ *n.* a difficult question or problem.

PVC *abbr.* polyvinyl chloride.

Pvt. *abbr.* private.

PX *abbr.* post exchange.

pyg·my /pígmee/ *n.* (also **pig·my**) (*pl.* **-mies**) **1** a member of a small people of equatorial Africa and parts of SE Asia. **2** a very small person, animal, or thing. **3** an insignificant person. **4** (*attrib.*) **a** of or relating to pygmies. **b** (of a person, animal, etc.) dwarf. □□ **pyg·mae·an** /pigmeéən, pígmee–/ *adj.* (also **pyg·me·an**)

py·lon /pílon/ *n.* **1** a tall structure erected as a support (esp. for electric power cables) or boundary or decoration. **2** a gateway, esp. of an ancient Egyptian temple. **3** a structure marking a path for aircraft. **4** a structure supporting an aircraft engine.

py·or·rhe·a /píəreéə/ *n.* **1** a disease of periodontal tissue causing shrinkage of the gums and loosening of the teeth. **2** any discharge of pus.

pyr·a·mid /pírəmid/ *n.* **1 a** a monumental structure, usu. of stone, with a square base and sloping sides meeting centrally at an apex, esp. an ancient Egyptian royal tomb. **b** a similar structure, esp. a Mayan temple of this type. **2** a solid of this type with a base of three or more sides. **3** a pyramid-shaped thing or pile of things. □□ **py·ram·i·dal** /–rámid'l/ *adj.* **py·ram·i·dal·ly** *adv.* **pyr·a·mid·ic** /–mídik/ *adj.* (also **pyr·a·mid·i·cal**). **pyr·a·mid·i·cal·ly** *adv.*

pyre /pīr/ *n.* a heap of combustible material, esp. a funeral pile for burning a corpse.

py·re·thrum /pīreéthrəm, –réth–/ *n.* **1** any of several aromatic chrysanthemums of the genus *Chrysanthemum.* **2** an insecticide made from the dried flowers of these plants.

py·ret·ic /pīrétik/ *adj.* of, for, or producing fever.

Py·rex /píreks/ *n. Trademark* a hard heat-resistant type of glass, often used for cookware.

py·rex·i·a /pīrékseeə/ *n. Med.* = FEVER 1. □□ **py·rex·i·al** *adj.* **py·rex·ic** *adj.* **py·rex·i·cal** *adj.*

pyr·i·dox·ine /píridókseen, –sin/ *n.* a vitamin of the B complex found in yeast, and important in the body's use of unsaturated fatty acids. Also called **vitamin B_6**.

py·rite /pírīt/ *n.* = PYRITES.

py·ri·tes /pīríteez, pírīts/ *n.* (in full **iron pyrites**) a yellow lustrous form of iron disulfide. □□ **py·rit·ic** /–rítik/ *adj.* **py·ri·tif·er·ous** /–ritífərəs/ *adj.* **py·ri·tize** /pírītīz/ *v.tr.* **py·ri·tous** /píritəs/ *adj.*

py·ro·gen·ic /pīrōjénik/ *adj.* (also **py·rog·e·nous** /pīrójinəs/) **1 a** producing heat, esp. in the body. **b** producing fever. **2** produced by combustion or volcanic processes.

py·ro·ma·ni·a /pīrōmáyneeə/ *n.* an obsessive desire to set fire to things. □□ **py·ro·ma·ni·ac** *n.*

py·rom·e·ter /pīrómitər/ *n.* an instrument for measuring high temperatures, esp. in furnaces and kilns. □□ **py·ro·met·ric** /–rəmétrik/ *adj.* **py·ro·met·ri·cal·ly** *adv.* **py·rom·e·try** /–rómitree/ *n.*

py·ro·tech·nic /pīrōtéknik/ *adj.* **1** of or relating to fireworks. **2** (of wit, etc.) brilliant or sensational. □□ **py·ro·tech·ni·cal** *adj.* **py·ro·tech·nist** *n.* **py·ro·tech·ny** *n.*

py·ro·tech·nics /pīrōtékniks/ *n.pl.* **1** the art of making fireworks. **2** a display of fireworks. **3** any brilliant display.

py·rox·ene /pīrókseen/ *n.* any of a group of minerals commonly found as components of igneous rocks, composed of silicates of calcium, magnesium, and iron.

pyr·rhic[1] /pírik/ *adj.* (of a victory) won at too great a cost to be of use to the victor.

pyr·rhic[2] /pírik/ *n. & adj.* • *n.* a metrical foot of two short or unaccented syllables. • *adj.* written in or based on pyrrhics.

Py·thag·o·re·an /pīthágəreéən/ *adj. & n.* • *adj.* of or relating to the Greek philosopher Pythagoras (6th c. BC) or his philosophy, esp. regarding the transmigration of souls. • *n.* a follower of Pythagoras.

Py·thag·o·re·an the·o·rem /pīthágəreéən/ *n.* the theorem attributed to Pythagoras (see PYTHAGOREAN) that the square of the hypotenuse of a right triangle is equal to the sum of the squares of the other two sides.

py·thon /píthon, –thən/ *n.* any constricting snake of the family Pythonidae, esp. of the genus *Python*, found throughout the tropics in the Old World. ▫▫ **py·thon·ic** /–thónik/ *adj.*

pyx /piks/ *n.* (also **pix**) **1** *Eccl.* the vessel in which the consecrated bread of the Eucharist is kept. **2** (also **pyx chest**) a box at a mint in which specimen gold and silver coins are deposited to be tested by weight and assayed.

Q

Q /kyoo/ *n.* (also **q**) (*pl.* **Qs** or **Q's**) the seventeenth letter of the alphabet.
qb *abbr.* quarterback.
QED *abbr.* QUOD ERAT DEMONSTRANDUM.
qt. *abbr.* quart(s).
q.t. *n. colloq.* quiet (esp. *on the q.t.*).
qty. *abbr.* quantity.
quack[1] /kwak/ *n. & v.* • *n.* the harsh sound made by ducks. • *v.intr.* **1** utter this sound. **2** *colloq.* talk loudly and foolishly.
quack[2] /kwak/ *n.* **1 a** an unqualified practitioner of medicine. **b** (*attrib.*) of or characteristic of unskilled medical practice (*quack cure*). **2 a** a charlatan. **b** (*attrib.*) of or characteristic of a charlatan; fraudulent; sham. **3** *sl.* any doctor or medical officer. ▫▫ **quack·er·y** *n.* **quack·ish** *adj.*
quad[1] /kwod/ *n. colloq.* a quadrangle.
quad[2] /kwod/ *n. colloq.* = QUADRUPLET 1.
quad[3] /kwod/ *n. Printing* a piece of blank metal type used in spacing.
quad[4] /kwod/ *n. & adj.* • *n.* quadraphony. • *adj.* quadraphonic.
quad·ran·gle /kwódranggəl/ *n.* **1** a four-sided plane figure, esp. a square or rectangle. **2 a** a four-sided yard or courtyard, esp. enclosed by buildings, as in some colleges. **b** such a courtyard with the buildings around it. **3** the land area represented on one map sheet as published by the U.S. Geological Survey. ▫▫ **quad·ran·gu·lar** /-ránggyələr/ *adj.*
quad·rant /kwódrənt/ *n.* **1** a quarter of a circle's circumference. **2** a plane figure enclosed by two radii of a circle at right angles and the arc cut off by them. **3** a quarter of a sphere, etc. **4 a** a thing, esp. a graduated strip of metal, shaped like a quarter circle. **b** an instrument graduated (esp. through an arc of 90°) for taking angular measurements. ▫▫ **quad·ran·tal** /-drán-t'l/ *adj.*
quad·ra·phon·ic /kwódrəfónik/ *adj.* (also **quad·ro·phon·ic** or **quad·ri·phon·ic**) (of sound reproduction) using four transmission channels. ▫▫ **quad·ra·phon·i·cal·ly** *adv.* **quad·ra·phon·ics** *n.pl.* **qua·draph·o·ny** /-rófənee/ *n.*
quad·rat·ic /kwodrátik/ *adj. & n. Math.* • *adj.* **1** involving the second and no higher power of an unknown quantity or variable (*quadratic equation*). **2** square. • *n.* **1** a quadratic equation. **2** (in *pl.*) the branch of algebra dealing with these.
quad·ren·ni·al /kwodréneeəl/ *adj.* **1** lasting four years. **2** recurring every four years. ▫▫ **quad·ren·ni·al·ly** *adv.*
quadri- /kwódree/ (also **quadr-** or **quadru-**) *comb.form* denoting four.
quad·ri·ceps /kwódriseps/ *n. Anat.* a four-part muscle at the front of the thigh.
quad·ri·lat·er·al /kwódrilátərəl/ *adj. & n.* • *adj.* having four sides. • *n.* a four-sided figure.
quad·rille[1] /kwodríl/ *n.* **1** a square dance typically performed by four couples. **2** the music for this.
quad·rille[2] /kwodríl/ *n.* a card game for four players with forty cards, fashionable in the 18th c.
quad·ril·lion /kwodrílyən/ *n.* (*pl.* same or **quad·ril·lions**) a thousand raised to the fifth (or esp. *Brit.* the eighth) power (10^{15} and 10^{24} respectively).
quad·ri·ple·gi·a /kwódripléejeeə, -jə/ *n. Med.* paralysis of all four limbs. ▫▫ **quad·ri·ple·gic** *adj. & n.*
quad·roon /kwodróon/ *n.* a person of one-quarter black by descent.
quad·ro·phon·ic var. of QUADRAPHONIC.
quadru- var. of QUADRI-.
quad·ru·ped /kwódrəped/ *n. & adj.* • *n.* a four-footed animal, esp. a four-footed mammal. • *adj.* four-footed. ▫▫ **quad·ru·pe·dal** /-róopid'l/ *adj.*
quad·ru·ple /kwodróopəl, -drúp-, kwódroopəl/ *adj., n., & v.* • *adj.* **1** fourfold. **2 a** having four parts. **b** involving four participants (*quadruple alliance*). **3** being four times as many or as much. **4** (of time in music) having four beats in a bar. • *n.* a fourfold number or amount. • *v.tr. & intr.* multiply by four; increase fourfold. ▫▫ **quad·ru·ply** *adv.*
quad·ru·plet /kwodróoplit, -drúp-, kwódrooplit/ *n.* **1** each of four children born at one birth. **2** a set of four things working together. **3** *Mus.* a group of four notes to be performed in the time of three.
quad·ru·pli·cate *adj. & v.* • *adj.* /kwodróoplikət/ **1** fourfold. **2** of which four copies are made. • *v.tr.* /-kayt/ **1** multiply by four. **2** make four identical copies of. ▫ **in quadruplicate** in four identical copies. ▫▫ **quad·ru·pli·ca·tion** /-káyshən/ *n.*
quaff /kwof, kwaf, kwawf/ *v. literary* **1** *tr. & intr.* drink deeply. **2** *tr.* drain (a cup, etc.) in long drafts. ▫▫ **quaff·a·ble** *adj.* **quaff·er** *n.*
quag·ga /kwágə/ *n.* an extinct zebralike mammal, *Equus quagga*, formerly native to S. Africa, with yellowish-brown stripes on the head, neck, and forebody.
quag·mire /kwágmīr, kwóg-/ *n.* **1** a soft boggy or marshy area that gives way underfoot. **2** a hazardous or awkward situation.
qua·hog /kwáwhawg, -hog, kwó-, kó-/ *n.* (also **qua·haug**) an edible clam, *Marcenaria* (formerly *Venus*) *mercinaria*, of the Atlantic coast of N. America.
quail[1] /kwayl/ *n.* (*pl.* same or **quails**) **1** any small migratory Old World bird of the genus *Coturnix*, with a short tail and related to the partridge. **2** any small migratory New World bird of the genus *Colinus*, esp. the bobwhite.
quail[2] /kwayl/ *v.intr.* flinch; be apprehensive with fear.
quaint /kwaynt/ *adj.* **1** piquantly or attractively unfamiliar or old-fashioned. **2** unusual; odd. ▫▫ **quaint·ly** *adv.* **quaint·ness** *n.*

quadrilaterals

quaint Middle English: from Old French *cointe*, from Latin *cognitus* 'ascertained,' past participle of *cognoscere* 'to know, understand.' The original sense was 'wise, clever,' also 'marked by ingenuity or cunning; intricate,' hence 'out of the ordinary,' giving rise to the current sense (late 18th century)

quake /kwayk/ *v. & n.* • *v.intr.* **1** shake; tremble. **2** (of a person) shake or shudder (*was quaking with fear*). • *n.* **1** *colloq.* an earthquake. **2** an act of quaking. ▫▫ **quak·y** *adj.* (**quak·i·er, quak·i·est**).

Quak·er /kwáykər/ *n.* a member of the Society of Friends, a Christian movement devoted to peaceful principles and eschewing formal doctrine, sacraments, and ordained ministers. ▫▫ **Quak·er·ish** *adj.* **Quak·er·ism** *n.*

quak·ing grass *n.* any grass of the genus *Briza*, having slender stalks that tremble in the wind. Also called **dodder-grass**.

qual·i·fi·ca·tion /kwólifikáyshən/ *n.* **1** the act or an instance of qualifying. **2** (often in *pl.*) a quality, skill, or accomplishment fitting a person for a position or purpose. **3 a** a circumstance, condition, etc., that modifies or limits (*the statement had many qualifications*). **b** a thing that detracts from completeness or absoluteness (*their relief had one qualification*). **4** a condition that must be fulfilled before a right can be acquired, etc. **5** an attribution of a quality (*the qualification of our policy as opportunist is unfair*). ▫▫ **qual·i·fi·ca·to·ry** /-lífikətawree/ *adj.*

qual·i·fy /kwólifī/ *v.* (**-fies, -fied**) **1** *tr.* make competent or fit for a position or purpose. **2** *tr.* make legally entitled. **3** *intr.* (foll. by *for* or *as*) (of a person) satisfy the conditions or requirements for (a position, award, competition, etc.). **4** *tr.* add reservations to; modify or make less absolute (a statement or assertion). **5** *tr. Gram.* (of a word, esp. an adjective) attribute a quality to another word, esp. a noun. **6** *tr.* moderate; mitigate; make less severe or extreme. **7** *tr.* alter the strength or flavor of. **8** *tr.* (foll. by *as*) attribute a specified quality to; describe as (*the idea was qualified as absurd*). **9** *tr.* (as **qualifying** *adj.*) serving to determine those that qualify (*qualifying examination*). **10** (as **qualified** *adj.*) **a** having the qualifications necessary for a particular office or function. **b** dependent on other factors; not definite (*a qualified "yes"*). ▫▫ **qual·i·fi·a·ble** *adj.* **qual·i·fi·er** *n.*

qual·i·ta·tive /kwólitaytiv/ *adj.* concerned with or depending on quality (*led to a qualitative change in society*). ▫▫ **qual·i·ta·tive·ly** *adv.*

qual·i·ty /kwólitee/ *n.* (*pl.* **-ties**) **1** the degree of excellence of a thing (*of good quality; poor in quality*). **2 a** general excellence (*their work has quality*). **b** (*attrib.*) of high quality (*a quality product*). **3** a distinctive attribute or faculty; a characteristic trait. **4** the relative nature or kind or character of a thing. **5** the distinctive timbre of a voice or sound. **6** *archaic* high social standing (*people of quality*).

qual·i·ty con·trol *n.* a system of maintaining standards in manufactured products by testing a sample of the output against the specification.

qualm /kwaam, kwawm/ *n.* **1** a misgiving; an uneasy doubt esp. about one's own conduct. **2** a scruple of conscience. **3** a momentary faint or sick feeling. ▫▫ **qualm·ish** *adj.*

quan·da·ry /kwóndəree, -dree/ *n.* (*pl.* **-ries**) **1** a state of perplexity. **2** a difficult situation; a practical dilemma.

quan·tal /kwónt'l/ *adj.* **1** composed of discrete units; varying in steps, not continuously. **2** of or relating to a quantum or quantum theory. ▫▫ **quan·tal·ly** *adv.*

quan·ti·fy /kwóntifī/ *v.tr.* (**-fies, -fied**) **1** determine the quantity of. **2** measure or express as a quantity. ▫▫ **quan·ti·fi·a·ble** *adj.* **quan·ti·fi·a·bil·i·ty** *n.* **quan·ti·fi·ca·tion** /-fikáyshən/ *n.* **quan·ti·fi·er** *n.*

quan·ti·ta·tive /kwóntitaytiv/ *adj.* **1 a** concerned with quantity. **b** measured or measurable by quantity. **2** of or based on the quantity of syllables. ▫▫ **quan·ti·ta·tive·ly** *adv.*

quan·ti·tive /kwóntitiv/ *adj.* = QUANTITATIVE. ▫▫ **quan·ti·tive·ly** *adv.*

quan·ti·ty /kwóntitee/ *n.* (*pl.* **-ties**) **1** the property of things that is measurable. **2** the size, extent, weight, amount, or number. **3** a specified or considerable portion or number or amount (*buys in quantity; the quantity of heat in a body*). **4** (in *pl.*) large amounts or numbers; an abundance (*quantities of food*). **5** *Math.* **a** a value, component, etc., that may be expressed in numbers. **b** the figure or symbol representing this.

quan·tum /kwóntəm/ *n.* (*pl.* **quan·ta** /-tə/) **1** *Physics* **a** a discrete quantity of energy proportional in magnitude to the frequency of radiation it represents. **b** an analogous discrete amount of any other physical quantity. **2 a** a required or allowed amount. **b** a share or portion.

quan·tum jump *n.* (also **quan·tum leap**) **1** a sudden large increase or advance. **2** *Physics* an abrupt transition in an atom or molecule from one quantum state to another.

quan·tum me·chan·ics *n.pl.* (*treated as* sing.) *Physics* a system or theory using the assumption that energy exists in discrete units. Also called **quantum theory**.

quar·an·tine /kwáwrənteen, kwór-/ *n. & v.* • *n.* **1** isolation imposed on persons or animals that have arrived from elsewhere or been exposed to, and might spread, infectious or contagious disease. **2** the period of this isolation. • *v.tr.* impose such isolation on; put in quarantine.

quark /kwawrk, kwaark/ *n. Physics* any of several postulated components of elementary particles.

quar·rel /kwáwrəl, kwór-/ *n. & v.* • *n.* **1** a usu. verbal contention or altercation between individuals or with others. **2** a rupture of friendly relations. **3** an occasion of complaint against a person, a person's actions, etc. • *v.intr.* (**quarreled** or **quarrelled, quarreling** or **quarrelling**) **1** (often foll. by *with*) take exception; find fault. **2** fall out; have a dispute; break off friendly relations. ▫▫ **quar·rel·er** *n.* **quar·rel·ler** *n.*

quar·rel·some /kwáwrəlsəm, kwór-/ *adj.* given to or characterized by quarreling. ▫▫ **quar·rel·some·ly** *adv.* **quar·rel·some·ness** *n.*

quar·ry[1] /kwáwree, kwór-/ *n. & v.* • *n.* (*pl.* **-ries**) **1** an excavation made by taking stone, etc., for building, etc. **2** a place from which stone, etc., may be extracted. **3** a source of information, knowledge, etc. • *v.tr.* (**-ries, -ried**) extract (stone) from a quarry.

quar·ry[2] /kwáwree, kwór-/ *n.* (*pl.* **-ries**) **1** the object of pursuit by a bird of prey, hounds, hunters, etc. **2** an intended victim or prey.

quarry[2] Middle English: from Old French *cuiree*, an alteration, influenced by *cuir* 'leather' and *curer* 'clean, disembowel,' of *couree*, which is based on Latin *cor* 'heart.' Originally the term denoted the parts of a deer that, after a hunt, were placed on the hide and given as a reward to the hounds.

quart /kwawrt/ *n.* **1** a liquid measure equal to a quarter of a gallon; two pints (.95 liter). **2** a vessel containing this amount. **3** a unit of dry measure, equivalent to one-thirty-second of a bushel (1.1 liter).

quar·ter /kwáwrtər/ *n. & v.* • *n.* **1** each of four equal parts into which a thing is or might be divided. **2** a period of three months. **3** a point of time 15 minutes before or after any hour. **4** a school term, usu. 10–12 weeks. **5 a** 25 cents. **b** a coin of this denomination. **6** a part of a town, esp. as occupied by a particular class or group (*residential quarter*). **7 a** a point of the compass. **b** a region at such a point. **8** the direction, district, or source of supply, etc. (*help from any quarter; came from all quarters*). **9** (in *pl.*) **a** lodgings; an abode. **b** *Mil.* the living accommodation of troops, etc. **10 a** one fourth of a lunar month. **b** the moon's position between the first and second (**first quarter**) or third and fourth (**last quarter**) of these. **11 a** each of the four parts into which an animal's or bird's carcass is divided, each including a leg or wing. **b** (in *pl.*) *hist.* the four parts into which a traitor, etc., was cut after execution. **c** (in *pl.*) *Brit.* = HINDQUARTERS. **12** mercy offered or granted to an enemy in battle, etc., on condition of surrender. **13 a** *Brit.* a grain measure equivalent to 8 bushels. **b** one-fourth of a hundredweight (25 lb. or *Brit.* 28 lb.). **14** *Heraldry* **a** each of four divisions on a shield. **b** a charge occupying this, placed in chief. **15** either side of a ship abaft the beam. **16** *Sports* each of four equal periods into which a game is divided, as in football or basketball. • *v.tr.* **1** divide into quarters. **2** *hist.* divide (the body of an executed person) in this way. **3 a** put (troops, etc.) into quarters. **b** station or lodge in a specified place. **4** (foll. by *on*) impose (a person) on another as a lodger. **5** cut (a log) into quarters, and these into planks so as to show the grain well. **6** range or traverse (the ground) in every direction. **7** *Heraldry* **a** place or bear (charges or coats of arms) on the four quarters of a shield's surface. **b** add (another's coat) to one's hereditary arms. **c** (foll. by *with*) place in alternate quarters with. **d** divide (a shield) into four or more parts by vertical and horizontal lines.

quar·ter·back /kwáwrtərbak/ *n.* & *v. Football* • *n.* a player who directs offensive play. • *v.* **1** *intr.* play at this position. **2** *tr.* direct the action of, as a quarterback.

quar·ter·deck /kwáwrtərdek/ *n.* **1** part of a ship's upper deck near the stern, usu. reserved for officers. **2** the officers of a ship or the navy.

quar·ter·fi·nal /kwáwrtərfín'l/ *adj.* & *n. Sports* • *adj.* relating to a match or round immediately preceding a semifinal. • *n.* a quarterfinal match, round, or contest.

quar·ter·ing /kwáwrtəring/ *n.* **1** (in *pl.*) the coats of arms marshaled on a shield to denote the alliances of a family with others. **2** the provision of quarters for soldiers. **3** the act or an instance of dividing, esp. into four equal parts. **4** timber sawn into lengths, used for high-quality floorboards, etc.

quar·ter·ly /kwáwrtərlee/ *adj., adv.,* & *n.* • *adj.* **1** produced, payable, or occurring once every quarter of a year. **2** (of a shield) quartered. • *adv.* **1** once every quarter of a year. **2** in the four, or in two diagonally opposite, quarters of a shield. • *n.* (*pl.* **-lies**) a quarterly review or magazine.

quar·ter·mas·ter /kwáwrtərmastər/ *n.* **1** an army officer in charge of quartering, rations, etc. **2** a naval petty officer in charge of steering, signals, etc.

quar·ter note *n. Mus.* a note with a duration of one quarter of a whole note.

quar·tet /kwawrtét/ *n.* (also **quar·tette**) **1** *Mus.* **a** a composition for four voices or instruments. **b** the performers of such a piece. **2** any group of four.

quar·to /kwáwrtō/ *n.* (*pl.* **-tos**) *Printing* **1** the size given by folding a (usu. specified) sheet of paper twice. **2** a book consisting of sheets folded in this way. ¶ Abbr.: **4to.**

quartz /kwawrts/ *n.* a mineral form of silica that crystallizes as hexagonal prisms.

qua·sar /kwáyzaar, -zər, -saar, -sər/ *n. Astron.* any of a class of starlike celestial objects having a spectrum with a large red shift.

quash /kwosh/ *v.tr.* **1** annul; reject as not valid, esp. by a legal procedure. **2** suppress; crush (a rebellion, etc.).

quasi- /kwáyzī, kwaázee/ *comb.form* **1** seemingly; apparently but not really (*quasi-scientific*). **2** being partly or almost (*quasi-independent*).

quat·er·cen·ten·ar·y /kwótərsenténəree, -sént'neree/ *n.* & *adj.* • *n.* (*pl.* **-ies**) **1** a four-hundredth anniversary. **2** a festival marking this. • *adj.* of this anniversary.

quat·er·nar·y /kwótərneree, kwətárnəree/ *adj.* & *n.* • *adj.* **1** having four parts. **2** (**Quaternary**) *Geol.* of or relating to the most recent period in the Cenozoic era with evidence of many species of present-day plants and animals (cf. PLEISTOCENE, HOLOCENE). ¶ Cf. Appendix VII. • *n.* (*pl.* **-ies**) **1** a set of four things. **2** (**Quaternary**) *Geol.* the Quaternary period or system.

quat·rain /kwótrayn/ *n.* a stanza of four lines, usu. with alternate rhymes.

quat·re·foil /kátərfoyl, kátrə-/ *n.* a four-pointed or four-leafed figure, esp. as an ornament in architectural tracery, resembling a flower or clover leaf.

quat·tro·cen·to /kwátrōchéntō/ *n.* the style of Italian art of the 15th c. ▫▫ **quat·tro·cen·tist** *n.*

qua·ver /kwáyvər/ *v.* & *n.* • *v.* **1** *intr.* **a** (esp. of a voice or musical sound) vibrate; shake; tremble. **b** use trills or shakes in singing. **2** *tr.* **a** sing (a note or song) with quavering. **b** (often foll. by *out*) say in a trembling voice. • *n.* **1** *Mus.* = EIGHTH NOTE. **2** a trill in singing. **3** a tremble in speech. ▫▫ **qua·ver·ing·ly** *adv.*

qua·ver·y /kwáyvəree/ *adj.* (of a voice, etc.) tremulous. ▫▫ **qua·ver·i·ness** *n.*

quay /kee, kay/ *n.* a solid, stationary, artificial landing place lying alongside or projecting into water for loading and unloading ships. ▫▫ **quay·age** *n.*

quay·side /keésīd, káy-/ *n.* the land forming or near a quay.

quea·sy /kweézee/ *adj.* (**-ier, -iest**) **1 a** (of a person) feeling nausea. **b** (of a person's stomach) easily upset; weak of digestion. **2** (of the conscience, etc.) overscrupulous; tender. **3** (of a feeling, thought, etc.) uncomfortable; uneasy. ▫▫ **quea·si·ly** *adv.* **quea·si·ness** *n.*

Quech·ua /kéchwə, -waa/ *n.* **1** a member of a central Peruvian native people. **2** a S. American native language widely spoken in Peru and neighboring countries. ▫▫ **Quech·uan** *adj.*

queen /kween/ *n.* & *v.* • *n.* **1** (as a title usu. **Queen**) a female sovereign, etc., esp. the hereditary ruler of an independent nation. **2** (in full **queen consort**) a king's wife. **3** a woman, country, or thing preeminent or supreme in a specified area or of its kind (*tennis queen; the queen of roses*). **4** the fertile female among ants, bees, etc. **5** the most powerful piece in chess. **6** a playing card with a picture of a queen. **7** *sl.* a male homosexual, esp. an effeminate one. **8** an ancient goddess (*Venus, queen of love*). **9** a woman or girl chosen to hold the most important position in a festival or event (*beauty queen; homecoming queen*). • *v.* **1** *tr.* make (a woman) queen. **2** *tr. Chess* convert (a pawn) into a queen when it reaches the opponent's side of the board. **3** *intr.* to act like a queen, esp. to act imperiously or flamboyantly. ▫▫ **queen·dom** *n.* **queen·hood** *n.* **queen·less** *adj.* **queen·like** *adj.* **queen·ship** *n.*

Queen Anne's lace *n.* a widely cultivated orig. Eurasian herb, *Dancus carota*, with a whitish taproot; wild carrot.

queen bee *n.* **1** the fertile female in a hive. **2** the chief or controlling woman in an organization or social group.

queen·ly /kweénlee/ *adj.* (**queenlier, queenliest**) **1** fit for or appropriate to a queen. **2** majestic; queenlike. ▫▫ **queen·li·ness** *n.*

queen-size *adj.* (also **queen-sized**) of an extra-large size, between full-size and king-size.

queer /kweer/ *adj., n., & v.* • *adj.* **1** strange; odd; eccentric. **2** shady; suspect; of questionable character. **3 a** esp. *Brit.* slightly ill; giddy; faint. **b** *Brit. sl.* drunk. **4** *derog. sl.* homosexual. **5** *colloq.* (of a person or behavior) crazy; unbalanced; slightly mad. **6** *sl.* counterfeit. • *n. derog. sl.* a homosexual. • *v.tr. sl.* spoil; put out of order. ▫▫ **queer·ish** *adj.* **queer·ly** *adv.* **queer·ness** *n.*

quell /kwel/ *v.tr.* **1 a** crush or put down (a rebellion, etc.). **b** reduce (rebels, etc.) to submission. **2** suppress or alleviate (fear, anger, etc.). ▫▫ **quell·er** *n.* (also in *comb.*).

quench /kwench/ *v.tr.* **1** satisfy (thirst) by drinking. **2** extinguish (a fire or light, etc.). **3** cool, esp. with water (heat, a heated thing). **4** esp. *Metallurgy* cool (a hot substance) in cold water, air, oil, etc. **5 a** stifle or suppress (desire, etc.). **b** *Physics & Electronics* inhibit or prevent (oscillation, luminescence, etc.) by counteractive means. ▫▫ **quench·a·ble** *adj.* **quench·er** *n.* **quench·less** *adj.*

quer·u·lous /kwérələs, kwéryə-/ *adj.* complaining; peevish. ▫▫ **quer·u·lous·ly** *adv.* **quer·u·lous·ness** *n.*

que·ry /kweéree/ *n. & v.* • *n.* (*pl.* **-ries**) **1** a question, esp. expressing doubt or objection. **2** a question mark, or the word *query* spoken or written to question accuracy or as a mark of interrogation. • *v.tr.* (**-ries, -ried**) **1** (often foll. by *whether, if,* etc. + clause) ask or inquire. **2** call (a thing) in question in speech or writing. **3** dispute the accuracy of.

quest /kwest/ *n.* **1** a search or the act of seeking. **2** the thing sought, esp. the object of a medieval knight's pursuit. ▫▫ **quest·er** *n.* **quest·ing·ly** *adv.*

ques·tion /kwéschən/ *n. & v.* • *n.* **1** a sentence worded or expressed so as to seek information. **2 a** doubt about or objection to a thing's truth, credibility, advisability, etc. (*allowed it without question*). **b** the raising of such doubt, etc. **3** a matter to be discussed or decided or voted on. **4** a problem requiring an answer or solution. **5** (foll. by *of*) a matter or concern depending on conditions (*it's a question of money*). • *v.tr.* **1** ask questions of; interrogate. **2** subject (a person) to examination. **3** throw doubt upon; raise objections to. **4** seek information from the study of (phenomena, facts). ▫ **be a question of time** be certain to happen sooner or later. **beyond all question** undoubtedly. **call in** (or **into**) **question** make a matter of dispute; query. **come into question** be discussed; become of practical importance. **in question 1** that is being discussed or referred to (*the person in question*). **2** in dispute (*that was never in question*). **is not the question** is irrelevant. **out of the question** too impracticable, etc., to be worth discussing; impossible. **put the question** require supporters and opponents of a proposal to record their votes, divide a meeting. **without question** see *beyond all question* above. ▫▫ **ques·tion·er** *n.* **ques·tion·ing·ly** *adv.* **ques·tion·less** *adj.*

ques·tion·a·ble /kwéschənəbəl/ *adj.* **1** doubtful as regards truth or quality. **2** not clearly in accordance with honesty, honor, wisdom, etc. ▫▫ **ques·tion·a·bil·i·ty** /-əbílitee/ *n.* **ques·tion·a·ble·ness** *n.* **ques·tion·a·bly** *adv.*

ques·tion mark *n.* a punctuation mark (?) indicating a question.

ques·tion·naire /kwéschənáir/ *n.* **1** a formulated series of questions, esp. for statistical study. **2** a document containing these.

quet·zal /ketsaál, -sál/ *n.* **1** any of various brightly colored birds of the family Trogonidae, esp. the Central and S. American *Pharomachrus mocinno*, the male of which has long green tail coverts. **2** the chief monetary unit of Guatemala.

queue /kyoo/ *n. & v.* • *n.* **1** esp. *Brit.* a line or sequence of persons, vehicles, etc., awaiting their turn to be attended to or to proceed. **2** a pigtail or braid of hair. **3** *Computing* a sequence of jobs or processes waiting to be acted upon. • *v.intr.* (**queues, queued, queuing** or **queueing**) esp. *Brit.* (often foll. by *up*) (of persons, etc.) form a line; take one's place in a line.

quib·ble /kwíbəl/ *n. & v.* • *n.* **1** a petty objection; a trivial point of criticism. **2** a play on words; a pun. **3** an evasion; an insubstantial argument which relies on an ambiguity, etc. • *v.intr.* use quibbles. ▫▫ **quib·bler** *n.* **quib·bling** *adj.* **quib·bling·ly** *adv.*

quiche /keesh/ *n.* an unsweetened custard pie with a savory filling.

quick /kwik/ *adj., adv., & n.* • *adj.* **1** taking only a short time (*a quick worker; a quick visit*). **2 a** arriving after a short time; prompt (*quick action; quick results*). **b** (of an action, occurrence, etc.) sudden; hasty; abrupt. **3** with only a short interval (*in quick succession*). **4** lively; intelligent. **5 a** acute; alert (*has a quick ear*). **b** agile; nimble; energetic. **6** (of a temper) easily roused. **7** *archaic* living; alive (*the quick and the dead*). • *adv.* **1** quickly; at a rapid rate. **2** (as *int.*) come, go, etc., quickly. • *n.* **1** the soft flesh below the nails, or the skin, or a sore. **2** the seat of feeling or emotion (*cut to the quick*). ▫▫ **quick·ly** *adv.* **quick·ness** *n.*

---

quick Old English *cwic, cwicu* 'alive, animated, alert' (hence the sense in the biblical phrase "the quick and the dead"), of Germanic origin; related to Dutch *kwiek* 'sprightly' and German *keck* 'saucy,' from an Indo-European root shared by Latin *vivus* 'alive' and Greek *bios* 'life.'

---

quick·en /kwíkən/ *v.* **1** *tr. & intr.* make or become quicker; accelerate. **2** *tr.* give life or vigor to; rouse; animate; stimulate. **3** *intr.* **a** (of a woman) reach a stage in pregnancy when movements of the fetus can be felt. **b** (of a fetus) begin to show signs of life. **4** *tr. archaic* kindle; make (a fire) burn brighter. **5** *intr.* come to life.

quick·ie /kwíkee/ *n. colloq.* **1** a thing done or made quickly or hastily. **2** a drink taken quickly. **3** hasty act of sexual intercourse.

quick·lime /kwíklīm/ *n.* = LIME[1] *n.* 1.

quick·sand /kwíksand/ *n.* **1** loose wet sand that sucks in anything placed or falling into it. **2** a bed of this.

quick·sil·ver /kwíksilvər/ *n.* **1** mercury. **2** mobility of temperament or mood.

quick·step /kwíkstep/ *n. & v.* • *n.* a fast foxtrot (cf. QUICK STEP). • *v.intr.* (**-stepped, -stepping**) dance the quickstep.

quick step *n. Mil.* a step used in quick time (cf. QUICKSTEP).

quick stud·y *n.* one who learns rapidly.

quick-tem·pered *adj.* quick to lose one's temper; irascible.

quick-wit·ted /kwíkwítid/ *adj.* quick to grasp a situation, make repartee, etc. ▫▫ **quick-wit·ted·ness** *n.*

quid[1] /kwid/ *n.* (*pl.* same) *Brit. sl.* one pound sterling.

quid[2] /kwid/ *n.* a lump of tobacco for chewing.

quid pro quo /kwíd prō kwṓ/ *n.* **1** a thing given as compensation. **2** return made (for a gift, favor, etc.).

qui·es·cent /kwīésənt, kwee-/ *adj.* **1** motionless; inert. **2** silent; dormant. ▫▫ **qui·es·cence** *n.* **qui·es·cen·cy** *n.* **qui·es·cent·ly** *adv.*

qui·et /kwíət/ *adj., n., & v.* • *adj.* (**quieter, quietest**) **1** with little or no sound or motion. **2 a** of gentle or peaceful disposition. **b** shy; reticent; reserved. **3** (of a color, piece of clothing, etc.) unobtrusive; not showy. **4** not overt; private; disguised (*quiet resentment*). **5** undisturbed; uninterrupted; free or far from vigorous ac-

---

tion (*a quiet time for prayer*). **6** informal; simple (*just a quiet wedding*). **7** enjoyed in quiet (*a quiet smoke*). **8** tranquil; not anxious or remorseful. • *n.* **1** silence; stillness. **2** an undisturbed state; tranquillity. **3** a state of being free from urgent tasks or agitation (*a period of quiet*). **4** a peaceful state of affairs (*could do with some quiet*). • *v.* **1** *tr.* soothe; make quiet. **2** *intr.* (often foll. by *down*) become quiet or calm. □ **be quiet** (esp. in *imper.*) cease talking, etc. **keep quiet 1** refrain from making a noise. **2** (often foll. by *about*) suppress or refrain from disclosing information, etc. **on the quiet** unobtrusively; secretly. □□ **qui·et·ly** *adv.* **qui·et·ness** *n.*

qui·e·tude /kwī́-itōōd, -tyōōd/ *n.* a state of quiet.

qui·e·tus /kwī-éetəs/ *n.* **1** something which quiets or represses. **2** discharge or release from life; death; final riddance.

quill /kwil/ *n.* **1** a large feather in a wing or tail. **2** the hollow stem of this. **3** (in full **quill pen**) a pen made of a quill. **4** (usu. in *pl.*) the spines of a porcupine. **5** a musical pipe made of a hollow stem.

quilt /kwilt/ *n.* & *v.* • *n.* **1** a bedcovering made of padding enclosed between layers of cloth, etc., and kept in place by patterned stitching. **2** a bedspread of similar design (*patchwork quilt*). • *v.tr.* **1** cover or line with padded material. **2** make or join together (pieces of cloth with padding between) after the manner of a quilt. □□ **quilt·er** *n.* **quilt·ing** *n.*

qui·na·ry /kwī́nəree/ *adj.* **1** of the number five. **2** having five parts.

quince /kwins/ *n.* **1** a hard acidic pear-shaped fruit used chiefly in preserves. **2** any shrub or small tree of the genus *Cydonia*, esp. *C. oblonga*, bearing this fruit.

quin·cen·ten·ar·y /kwínsenténəree, -sént'neree/ *n.* & *adj.* • *n.* (*pl.* **-ies**) **1** a five-hundredth anniversary. **2** a festival marking this. • *adj.* of this anniversary. □□ **quin·cen·ten·ni·al** /-téneeəl/ *adj.* & *n.*

quin·ella /kwinélə/ *n.* a form of betting in which the bettor must select the first two place winners in a race, not necessarily in the correct order.

qui·nine /kwī́nīn, kwín-/ *n.* **1** an alkaloid found esp. in cinchona bark. **2** a bitter drug containing this, used as a tonic and to reduce fever.

quin·qua·ge·nar·i·an /kwíngkwəjináireeən/ *n.* & *adj.* • *n.* a person from 50 to 59 years old. • *adj.* of or relating to this age.

quinque- /kwíngkwee/ *comb.form* five.

quin·que·va·lent /kwíngkwəváylənt/ *adj.* having a valence of five.

quin·sy /kwínzee/ *n.* an inflammation of the throat, esp. an abscess in the region around the tonsils. □□ **quin·sied** *adj.*

quint /kwint/ *n. colloq.* **1** a sequence of five cards in the same suit in piquet, etc. **2** a quintuplet.

quin·tal /kwínt'l/ *n.* **1** a weight of about 100 lb. **2** (in the UK) a weight of 112 lb. (a hundredweight). **3** a weight of 100 kg.

quin·tes·sence /kwintésəns/ *n.* **1** the most essential part of any substance; a refined extract. **2** (usu. foll. by *of*) the purest and most perfect, or most typical, form, manifestation, or embodiment of some quality or class. □□ **quin·tes·sen·tial** /kwíntisénshəl/ *adj.* **quin·tes·sen·tial·ly** *adv.*

quin·tet /kwintét/ *n.* (also **quin·tette**) **1** *Mus.* **a** a composition for five voices or instruments. **b** the performers of such a piece. **2** any group of five.

quin·til·lion /kwintílyən/ *n.* (*pl.* same or **quintillions**) a thousand raised to the sixth (or esp. *Brit.* the tenth) power (10^{18} and 10^{30} respectively). □□ **quin·til·lionth** *adj.* & *n.*

quin·tu·ple /kwintóopəl, -tyóo-, -túpəl, kwíntəpəl/ *adj.*, *n.*, & *v.* • *adj.* **1** fivefold; consisting of five parts. **2** involving five parties. **3** (of time in music) having five beats in a bar. • *n.* a fivefold number or amount. • *v.tr.* & *intr.* multiply by five; increase fivefold. □□ **quin·tu·ply** *adv.*

quin·tu·plet /kwintúplit, -tóo-, -tyóo-, kwíntə-/ *n.* **1** each of five children born at one birth. **2** a set of five things working together.

quip /kwip/ *n.* & *v.* • *n.* **1** a clever saying; an epigram; a sarcastic remark, etc. **2** a quibble; an equivocation. • *v.intr.* (**quipped, quipping**) make quips. □□ **quip·ster** *n.*

quire /kwīr/ *n.* **1** four sheets of paper, etc., folded to form eight leaves, as often in medieval manuscripts. **2** any collection of leaves one within another in a manuscript or book. **3** 25 (also 24) sheets of paper.

quirk /kwərk/ *n.* **1** a peculiarity of behavior. **2** a trick of fate; a freak. □□ **quirk·ish** *adj.* **quirk·y** *adj.* (**quirkier, quirkiest**). **quirk·i·ly** *adv.* **quirk·i·ness** *n.*

quirt /kwərt/ *n.* a short-handled riding whip with a braided leather lash.

quis·ling /kwízling/ *n.* **1** a person cooperating with an occupying enemy; a collaborator or fifth columnist. **2** a traitor. □□ **quis·ling·ite** *adj.* & *n.*

quit /kwit/ *v.* & *adj.* • *v.tr.* (**quitting**; *past* and *past part.* **quit** or **quitted**) **1** (also *absol.*) give up; let go; abandon (a task, etc.). **2** cease; stop (*quit grumbling*). **3 a** leave or depart from (a place, person, employment, etc.). **b** (*absol.*) (of a tenant) leave occupied premises (esp. notice to quit). **4** (*refl.*) acquit; behave (*quit oneself well*). • *predic.adj.* (foll. by *of*) rid (*glad to be quit of the problem*). □ **quit hold of** loose. □□ **quit·ter** *n.*

quite /kwīt/ *adv.* **1** completely; entirely; wholly; to the utmost extent; in the fullest sense. **2** somewhat; rather; to some extent. **3** (often foll. by *so*) said to indicate agreement. **4** absolutely; definitely; very much. □ **quite another** (or **other**) very different (*that's quite another matter*). **quite a few** *colloq.* a fairly large number of. **quite something** a remarkable thing.

quits /kwits/ *predic.adj.* on even terms by retaliation or repayment (*then we'll be quits*). □ **call it** (or *Brit.* **cry**) **quits** acknowledge that things are now even; agree not to proceed further in a quarrel, etc.

quit·ter /kwítər/ *n.* **1** a person who gives up easily. **2** a shirker.

quiv·er[1] /kwívər/ *v.* & *n.* • *v.* **1** *intr.* tremble or vibrate with a slight rapid motion, esp.: **a** (usu. foll. by *with*) as the result of emotion (*quiver with anger*). **b** (usu. foll. by *in*) as the result of air currents, etc. (*quiver in the breeze*). **2** *tr.* (of a bird) make (its wings) quiver. • *n.* a quivering motion or sound. □□ **quiv·er·ing·ly** *adv.* **quiv·er·y** *adj.*

quiv·er[2] /kwívər/ *n.* a case for holding arrows.

quix·ot·ic /kwiksótik/ *adj.* **1** extravagantly and romantically chivalrous; regardless of material interests in comparison with honor or devotion. **2** visionary; pursuing lofty but unattainable ideals. **3** *derog.* ridiculously impractical; preposterous; foolhardy. □□ **quix·ot·i·cal·ly** *adv.* **quix·o·tism** /kwíksətizəm/ *n.* **quix·o·try** /kwíksətree/ *n.*

quiz /kwiz/ *n.* & *v.* • *n.* (*pl.* **quizzes**) **1 a** a quick or informal test. **b** an interrogation, examination, or questionnaire. **2** (also **quiz show**) a test of knowledge, esp. between individuals or teams as a form of entertainment. • *v.tr.* (**quizzed, quizzing**) examine by questioning.

quiz·zi·cal /kwízikəl/ *adj.* **1** expressing or done with mild or amused perplexity. **2** strange; comical. □□ **quiz·zi·cal·i·ty** /-kálitee/ *n.* **quiz·zi·cal·ly** *adv.* **quiz·zi·cal·ness** *n.*

quod e·rat de·mon·stran·dum /kwod érat démənstrándəm, éraat démōnstraándōōm/ (esp. at the conclusion of a proof, etc.) which was the thing to be proved. ¶ Abbr.: **QED**.

quod vi·de /kwod véeday, vídee/ which see (in cross-references, etc.). ¶ Abbr.: **q.v.**

quoin /koyn, kwoin/ *n.* **1** an external angle of a building. **2** a stone or brick forming an angle; a cornerstone. **3** *Printing* a wedge used for securing composed type. **4** a wedge for raising the level of a gun barrel or for keeping it from rolling. □□ **quoin·ing** *n.*

quoit /koyt, kwoit/ *n.* **1** a heavy flattish sharp-edged iron ring thrown to encircle an iron peg or to land as near as possible to the peg. **2** (in *pl.*) a game consisting of aiming and throwing these. **3** a ring of rope, rubber, etc., for use in a similar game.

quon·dam /kwóndəm, -dam/ *predic.adj.* that once was; sometime; former.

Quon·set hut /kwónsit/ *n. Trademark* a prefabricated metal building with a semicylindrical corrugated roof.

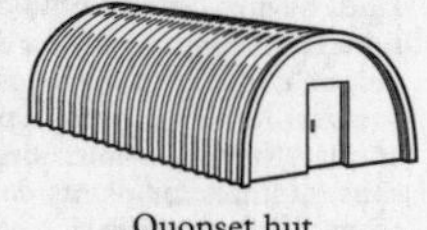

Quonset hut

quo·rum /kwáwrəm/ *n.* the fixed minimum number of members that must be present to make the proceedings of an assembly or society legally valid.

quo·ta /kwṓtə/ *n.* **1** the share that an individual person, group, or company is bound to contribute to or entitled to receive from a total. **2** a quantity of goods, etc., which under official controls must be manufactured, exported, imported, etc. **3** the number of immigrants allowed to enter a country annually, students allowed to enroll in a course, etc.

quot·a·ble /kwṓtəbəl/ *adj.* worth, or suitable for, quoting. □□ **quot·a·bil·i·ty** *n.*

quo·ta·tion /kwōtáyshən/ *n.* **1** the act or an instance of quoting or being quoted. **2** a passage or remark quoted. **3** *Mus.* a short passage or tune taken from one piece of music to another. **4** *Stock Exch.* an amount stated as the current price of stocks or commodities. **5** a contractor's estimate.

quo·ta·tion mark *n.* each of a set of punctuation marks, single (' ') or double (" "), used to mark the beginning and end of a quoted passage, a book title, etc., or words regarded as slang or jargon.

quote /kwōt/ *v. & n.* • *v.tr.* **1** cite or appeal to (an author, book, etc.) in confirmation of some view. **2** repeat a statement by (another person) or copy out a passage from (*don't quote me*). **3** (often *absol.*) **a** repeat or copy out (a passage) usu. with an indication that it is borrowed. **b** (foll. by *from*) cite (an author, book, etc.). **4** (foll. by *as*) cite (an author, etc.) as proof, evidence, etc. **5 a** enclose (words) in quotation marks. **b** (as *int.*) (in dictation, reading aloud, etc.) indicate the presence of opening quotation marks (*he said, quote, "I shall stay"*). **6** (often foll. by *at*) state the price of (a commodity, bet, etc.) (*quoted at 200 to 1*). **7** *Stock Exch.* regularly list the price of. • *n. colloq.* **1** a passage quoted. **2 a** a price quoted. **b** a contractor's estimate. **3** (usu. in *pl.*) quotation marks.

quoth /kwōth/ *v.tr.* (only in 1st and 3rd person) *archaic* said.

quo·tid·i·an /kwotídeeən/ *adj. & n.* • *adj.* **1** daily; of every day. **2** commonplace; trivial. • *n.* (in full **quotidian fever**) a fever recurring every day.

quo·tient /kwṓshənt/ *n.* a result obtained by dividing one quantity by another.

q.v. *abbr.* quod vide.

qwerty /kwártee/ *attrib.adj.* denoting the standard keyboard on English-language typewriters, word processors, etc., with *q, w, e, r, t,* and *y* as the first keys on the top row of letters.

R

R[1] /aar/ *n.* (also **r**) (*pl.* **Rs** or **R's**) the eighteenth letter of the alphabet.

R[2] *abbr.* (also **R.**) **1** river. **2** *Brit. Regina* (*Elizabeth R*). **3** *Brit. Rex.* **4** (also ®) registered as a trademark. **5** *Chess* rook. **6** rand. **7** *Electr.* resistance. **8** radius. **9** roentgen. **10** (of movies) classified as restricted to people under a certain age (as 17) unless accompanied by a parent or guardian.

r. *abbr.* (also **r**) **1** right. **2** recto. **3** run(s). **4** radius.

Ra *symb. Chem.* the element radium.

rab·bet /rábit/ *n. & v.* •*n.* a step-shaped channel, etc., cut along the edge or face or projecting angle of a length of wood, etc. •*v.tr.* **1** join or fix with a rabbet. **2** make a rabbet in.

rab·bi /rábī/ *n.* (*pl.* **rabbis**) **1** a Jewish scholar or teacher, esp. of the law. **2** a person appointed as a Jewish religious leader. ▫▫ **rab·bin·ate** /rábinət/ *n.* **rab·bin·i·cal** /rəbínikəl/ *adj.*

rab·bit /rábit/ *n. & v.* •*n.* **1** any of various burrowing gregarious plant-eating mammals of the family Leporidae, with long ears and a short tail. **2** a hare. **3** the fur of the rabbit. •*v.intr.* hunt rabbits. ▫▫ **rab·bit·y** *adj.*

rab·bit ears *n.pl.* a television antenna consisting of two movable rods, usu. on top of the set.

rab·bit punch *n.* a short chop with the edge of the hand to the nape of the neck.

rab·ble[1] /rábəl/ *n.* **1** a disorderly crowd; a mob. **2** a contemptible or inferior set of people. **3** (prec. by *the*) the lower or disorderly classes of the populace.

rab·ble[2] /rábəl/ *n.* an iron bar with a bent end for stirring molten metal, etc.

rab·ble-rous·er *n.* a person who stirs up a crowd of people in agitation for social or political change. ▫▫ **rab·ble-rous·ing** *adj. & n.*

Rab·e·lai·si·an /rábəláyzeeən, –zhən/ *adj.* **1** of or like Rabelais or his writings. **2** marked by exuberant imagination and language, coarse humor, and satire.

rab·id /rábid/ *adj.* **1** furious; violent (*rabid hatred*). **2** unreasoning; headstrong; fanatical (*a rabid anarchist*). **3** affected with rabies; mad. **4** of or connected with rabies. ▫▫ **rab·id·ly** *adv.* **rab·id·ness** *n.*

ra·bies /ráybeez/ *n.* a contagious and fatal viral disease, esp. of dogs, cats, raccoons, etc., transmissible to humans, etc., and causing madness and convulsions.

rac·coon /rakōōn/ *n.* (also **ra·coon**) **1** any furry N. American nocturnal mammal of the genus *Procyon*, with a bushy tail and masklike band across the eyes. **2** the fur of the raccoon.

race[1] /rays/ *n. & v.* •*n.* **1** a contest of speed between runners, vehicles, etc. **2** (in *pl.*) a series of these for horses, dogs, etc., at a fixed time on a regular course. **3** a contest between persons to be first to achieve something. **4 a** a strong or rapid current flowing through a narrow channel in the sea or a river. **b** the channel of a stream, etc. (*a millrace*). **5** each of two grooved rings in a ball bearing or roller bearing. •*v.* **1** *intr.* take part in a race. **2** *tr.* have a race with. **3** *tr.* try to surpass in speed. **4** *intr.* (foll. by *with*) compete in speed with. **5** *tr.* cause (a horse, car, etc.) to race. **6 a** *intr.* go at full or (of an engine, etc.) excessive speed. **b** *tr.* cause (a person or thing) to do this (*raced the bill through*).

race[2] /rays/ *n.* **1** each of the major divisions of humankind, having distinct physical characteristics. **2** a nation, etc., regarded as of a distinct ethnic stock. **3** the fact or concept of division into races (*discrimination based on race*). **4** a genus, species, breed, or variety of animals, plants, or microorganisms. **5** a group of persons, animals, or plants connected by common descent. **6** any great division of living creatures (*the feathered race; the four-footed race*). **7** descent; kindred (*of noble race*). **8** a class of persons, etc., with some common feature (*the race of poets*).

race·course /ráyskawrs/ *n.* **1** = RACETRACK. **2** any path laid out for racing, esp. skiing, cross-country running, etc.

race·horse /ráys-hors/ *n.* a horse bred or kept for racing.

ra·ceme /rayseem, rə–/ *n. Bot.* a flower cluster with the separate flowers attached by short equal stalks at equal distances along a central stem.

rac·er /ráysər/ *n.* **1** a horse, yacht, bicycle, etc., of a kind used for racing. **2** a circular horizontal rail along which the traversing platform of a heavy gun moves. **3** a person or thing that races.

race re·la·tions *n.pl.* relations between members of different races, usu. in the same country.

race ri·ot *n.* an outbreak of violence due to racial antagonism.

race·track /ráystrak/ *n.* a usu. oval track for horse, dog, or automobile racing.

race·way /ráysway/ *n.* **1** a track or channel along which something runs, esp. a groove in which ball bearings run. **2 a** a track for trotting, pacing, or harness racing. **b** = RACETRACK.

ra·cial /ráyshəl/ *adj.* **1** of or concerning race. **2** on the grounds of or connected with difference in race. ▫▫ **ra·cial·ly** *adv.*

ra·cial·ism /ráyshəlizəm/ *n.* = RACISM 1. ▫▫ **ra·cial·ist** *n. & adj.*

rac·ism /ráysizəm/ *n.* **1 a** a belief in the superiority of a particular race; prejudice based on this. **b** antagonism toward other races, esp. as a result of this. **2** the theory that human abilities, etc., are determined by race. ▫▫ **rac·ist** *n. & adj.*

rack[1] /rak/ *n. & v.* •*n.* **1 a** a framework usu. with rails, hooks, etc., for holding or storing things. **b** a frame for holding animal fodder. **2** a cogged or toothed bar or rail engaging with a wheel or pinion, etc. **3 a** *hist.* an instrument of torture stretching the victim's joints by the turning of rollers to which the wrists and ankles were tied. **b** a cause of suffering or anguish. •*v.tr.* **1** (of disease or pain) inflict suffering on. **2** *hist.* torture (a person) on the rack. **3** place in or on a rack. **4** shake violently. **5** injure by straining. **6** exhaust (the land) by excessive use. ▫ **rack one's brains** make a great mental effort. **rack up** accumulate or achieve (a score, etc.).

rack[2] /rak/ *n.* destruction (esp. rack and ruin).

rack[3] /rak/ *n.* a joint of lamb, etc., including the front ribs.

rack[4] /rak/ *v.tr.* (often foll. by *off*) draw off (wine, etc.) from the lees.

rack[5] /rak/ *n. & v.* • *n.* driving clouds. • *v.intr.* (of clouds) be driven before the wind.

rack[6] /rak/ *n. & v.* • *n.* a horse's gait between a trot and a canter. • *v.intr.* progress in this way.

rack·et[1] /rákit/ *n.* (also **rac·quet**) **1** a hand-held implement with a round or oval frame strung with catgut, nylon, etc., used in tennis, squash, etc. **2** (in *pl.*) a ball game for two or four persons played with rackets in a plain four-walled court. **3** a snowshoe resembling a tennis racket.

rack·et[2] /rákit/ *n.* **1 a** a disturbance; a din. **b** social excitement; gaiety. **2** *sl.* **a** a scheme for obtaining money or attaining other ends by fraudulent and often violent means. **b** a dodge; a sly game. **3** *colloq.* an activity; a way of life; a line of business. ▫▫ **rack·et·y** *adj.*

rack·et·eer /rákitéer/ *n.* a person who operates a dishonest business. ▫▫ **rack·et·eer·ing** *n.*

ra·con /ráykon/ *n.* a radar beacon that can be identified and located by its response to a radar signal from a ship, etc.

rac·on·teur /rákontőr/ *n.* (*fem.* **raconteuse** /–tőz/) a teller of anecdotes.

ra·coon var. of RACCOON.

rac·quet var. of RACKET[1].

rac·quet·ball /rákətbawl/ *n.* a game played with rackets and a rubber ball on an enclosed, four-walled court.

rac·y /ráysee/ *adj.* (**racier, raciest**) **1** lively and vigorous in style. **2** risqué, suggestive. **3** having characteristic qualities in a high degree. ▫▫ **rac·i·ly** *adv.* **rac·i·ness** *n.*

rad[1] /rad/ *n.* (*pl.* same) radian.

rad[2] /rad/ *n. & adj.* • *n. sl.* a political radical. • *adj. sl.* wonderful; terrific.

rad[3] /rad/ *n. Physics* a unit of absorbed dose of ionizing radiation.

ra·dar /ráydaar/ *n.* **1** a system for detecting the direction, range, or presence of objects by sending out pulses of high-frequency electromagnetic waves (acronym of *ra*dio *d*etecting *a*nd *r*anging).

rad·dle /rád'l/ *n. & v.* (also **rud·dle**) • *n.* red ocher (often used to mark sheep). • *v.tr.* **1** color with raddle or too much rouge. **2** (as **raddled** *adj.*) worn out; untidy, unkempt.

ra·di·al /ráydeeəl/ *adj. & n.* • *adj.* **1** of, concerning, or in rays. **2 a** arranged like rays or radii; having the position or direction of a radius. **b** having spokes or radiating lines. **c** acting or moving along lines diverging from a center. **3** *Anat.* relating to the radius (*radial artery*). **4** (of a vehicle tire) having the core fabric layers arranged radially and the tread strengthened. • *n.* **1** *Anat.* the radial nerve or artery. **2** a radial tire.

ra·di·an /ráydeeən/ *n. Geom.* a unit of angle, equal to an angle at the center of a circle, the arc of which is equal in length to the radius.

ra·di·ant /ráydeeənt/ *adj. & n.* • *adj.* **1** emitting rays of light. **2** (of eyes or looks) beaming with joy or hope or love. **3** (of beauty) splendid or dazzling. **4** (of light) issuing in rays. **5** operating radially. **6** extending radially; radiating. • *n.* **1** the point or object from which light or heat radiates. **2** *Astron.* a radiant point. ▫▫ **ra·di·ance** *n.* **ra·di·ant·ly** *adv.*

ra·di·ant heat *n.* heat transmitted by radiation.

ra·di·ate *v. & adj.* • *v.* /ráydeeayt/ **1** *intr.* **a** emit rays of light, heat, etc. **b** (of light or heat) be emitted in rays. **2** *tr.* emit (light, heat, or sound) from a center. **3** *tr.* transmit or demonstrate (life, love, joy, etc.) (*radiates happiness*). **4** *intr. & tr.* diverge or cause to diverge or spread from a center. **5** *tr.* (as **radiated** *adj.*) with parts arranged in rays. • *adj.* /ráydeeət/ having divergent rays or parts radially arranged. ▫▫ **ra·di·a·tive** /–ətiv/ *adj.*

ra·di·a·tion /ráydeeáyshən/ *n.* **1** the act or an instance of radiating; the process of being radiated. **2** *Physics* **a** the emission of energy as electromagnetic waves or as moving particles. **b** the energy transmitted in this way, esp. invisibly. **3** (in full **radiation therapy**) treatment of cancer and other diseases using radiation, such as X rays or ultraviolet light.

ra·di·a·tion sick·ness *n.* sickness caused by exposure to radiation, such as X rays or gamma rays.

ra·di·a·tor /ráydeeaytər/ *n.* **1** a person or thing that radiates. **2 a** a device for heating a room, etc., consisting of a metal case through which hot water or steam circulates. **b** a usu. portable oil or electric heater resembling this. **3** an engine-cooling device in a motor vehicle or aircraft.

rad·i·cal /rádikəl/ *adj. & n.* • *adj.* **1** of the root or roots; fundamental. **2** far-reaching; thorough (*radical change*). **3 a** advocating thorough reform; holding extreme political views. **b** (of a measure, etc.) advanced by or according to principles of this kind. **4** forming the basis; primary (*the radical idea*). **5** *Math.* of the root of a number or quantity. **6** (of surgery, etc.) seeking to ensure the removal of all diseased tissue. **7** of the roots of words. • *n.* **1** a person holding radical views or belonging to a radical party. **2** *Chem.* **a** a free radical. **b** an element or atom or a group of these normally forming part of a compound and remaining unaltered during the compound's ordinary chemical changes. **3** the root of a word. **4** a fundamental principle; a basis. **5** *Math.* a quantity forming or expressed as the root of another. ▫▫ **rad·i·cal·ism** *n.* **rad·i·cal·ize** *v.tr. & intr.* **rad·i·cal·ly** *adv.* **rad·i·cal·ness** *n.*

ra·dic·chi·o /rədeékeeō/ *n.* (*pl.* **-os**) a variety of chicory with dark red leaves.

ra·di·ces *pl.* of RADIX.

rad·i·cle /rádikəl/ *n.* **1** the part of a plant embryo that develops into the primary root. **2** a rootlike subdivision of a nerve or vein.

ra·di·i *pl.* of RADIUS.

ra·di·o /ráydeeō/ *n. & v.* • *n.* (*pl.* **-os**) **1** (often *attrib.*) **a** the transmission and reception of sound messages, etc., by electromagnetic waves of radio frequency. **b** an apparatus for receiving, broadcasting, or transmitting radio signals. **c** a message sent or received by radio. **2 a** sound broadcasting in general (*prefers the radio*). **b** a broadcasting station, channel, or organization (*Armed Forces Radio*). • *v.* (**-oed**) **1** *tr.* **a** send (a message) by radio. **b** send a message to (a person) by radio. **2** *intr.* communicate or broadcast by radio.

radio- /ráydeeō/ *comb. form* **1** denoting radio or broadcasting. **2 a** connected with radioactivity. **b** denoting artificially prepared radioisotopes of elements (*radiocesium*). **3** connected with rays or radiation.

ra·di·o·ac·tive /ráydeeō-áktiv/ *adj.* of or exhibiting radioactivity. ▫▫ **ra·di·o·ac·tive·ly** *adv.*

ra·di·o·ac·tiv·i·ty /ráydeeō-aktívitee/ *n.* the spontaneous disintegration of atomic nucleii, with the emission of usu. penetrating radiation or particles.

ra·di·o as·tron·o·my *n.* the branch of astronomy concerned with the radio-frequency range of the electromagnetic spectrum.

ra·di·o·car·bon /ráydeeōkaárbən/ *n.* a radioactive isotope of carbon.

ra·di·o·car·bon dat·ing *n.* = CARBON DATING.

ra·di·o·el·e·ment /ráydeeō-élimənt/ *n.* a natural or artificial radioactive element or isotope.

ra·di·o·gen·ic /ráydeeōjénik/ *adj.* **1** produced by radioactivity. **2** suitable for broadcasting by radio. ▫▫ **ra·di·o·gen·i·cal·ly** *adv.*

ra·di·o·gram /ráydeeōgram/ *n.* **1** a picture obtained by X rays, gamma rays, etc. **2** a radiotelegram.

ra·di·o·graph /ráydeeōgráf/ *n. & v.* • *n.* **1** an instrument recording the intensity of radiation. **2** = RADIOGRAM 1.

• *v.tr.* obtain a picture of by X ray, gamma ray, etc. ▫▫ **ra·di·og·ra·pher** /–deeógrəfər/ *n.* **ra·di·o·graph·ic** *adj.* **ra·di·o·graph·i·cal·ly** *adv.* **ra·di·og·ra·phy** /–deeógrəfee/ *n.*

ra·di·o·i·so·tope /ráydeeō-ísətōp/ *n.* a radioactive isotope. ▫▫ **ra·di·o·i·so·top·ic** /–tópik/ *adj.*

ra·di·ol·o·gy /ráydeeóləjee/ *n.* the scientific study of X rays and other high-energy radiation, esp. as used in medicine. ▫▫ **ra·di·o·log·ic** /–deeəlójik/ *adj.* **ra·di·o·log·i·cal** /–deeəlójikəl/ *adj.* **ra·di·ol·o·gist** *n.*

ra·di·om·e·ter /ráydeeómitər/ *n.* an instrument for measuring the intensity or force of radiation. ▫▫ **ra·di·o·met·ric** /–deeōmétrik/ *adj.* **ra·di·om·e·try** *n.*

radiometer

ra·di·on·ics /ráydeeóniks/ *n.pl.* (usu. treated as *sing.*) the study and interpretation of radiation believed to be emitted from substances, esp. as a form of diagnosis.

ra·di·o·phon·ic /ráydeeōfónik/ *adj.* of or relating to synthetic sound, esp. music, produced electronically.

ra·di·os·co·py /ráydeeóskəpee/ *n.* the examination by X rays, etc., of objects opaque to light. ▫▫ **ra·di·o·scop·ic** /–deeəskópik/ *adj.*

ra·di·o·tel·e·gram /ráydeeōtéligram/ *n.* a telegram sent by radio, usu. from a ship to land.

ra·di·o·te·leg·ra·phy /ráydeeōtilégrəfee/ *n.* telegraphy using radio transmission. ▫▫ **ra·di·o·tel·e·graph** /–téligraaf/ *n.*

ra·di·o·te·leph·o·ny /ráydeeōtiléfənee/ *n.* telephony using radio transmission. ▫▫ **ra·di·o·tel·e·phone** /–télifōn/ *n.*

ra·di·o tel·e·scope *n.* a directional aerial system for collecting and analyzing radiation in the radio-frequency range from stars, etc.

ra·di·o·tel·ex /ráydeeōtéleks/ *n.* a telex sent usu. from a ship to land.

ra·di·o·ther·a·py /ráydeeōthérəpee/ *n.* radiation therapy (see RADIATION 3). ▫▫ **ra·di·o·ther·a·peu·tic** /–pyóótik/ *adj.* **ra·di·o·ther·a·pist** *n.*

rad·ish /rádish/ *n.* **1** a cruciferous plant, *Raphanus sativus*, with a fleshy pungent root. **2** this root, eaten esp. raw in salads, etc.

ra·di·um /ráydeeəm/ *n. Chem.* a radioactive metallic element orig. obtained from pitchblende, etc., used esp. in radiotherapy. ¶ Symb.: **Ra.**

ra·di·us /ráydeeəs/ *n.* (*pl.* **radii** /–dee-ī/ or **radiuses**) **1** *Math.* **a** a straight line from the center to the circumference of a circle or sphere. **b** a radial line from the focus to any point of a curve. **c** the length of the radius of a circle, etc. **2** a usu. specified distance from a center in all directions. **3 a** the thicker and shorter of the two bones in the human forearm (cf. ULNA). **b** the corresponding bone in a vertebrate's foreleg or a bird's wing. **4** any of the five armlike structures of a starfish. **5 a** any of a set of lines diverging from a point like the radii of a circle. **b** an object of this kind, e.g., a spoke.

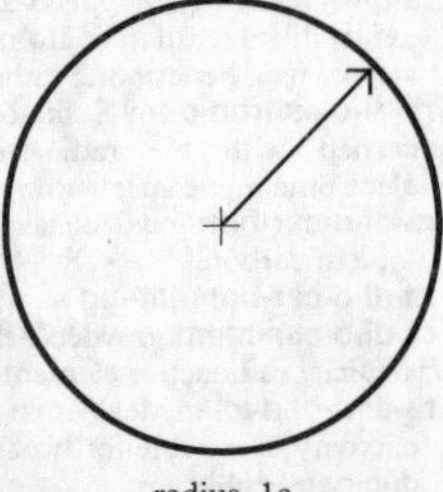

radius, 1a

ra·dix /ráydiks/ *n.* (*pl.* **radices** /–diseez/ or **radixes**) **1** *Math.* a number or symbol used as the basis of a numeration scale (e.g., ten in the decimal system). **2** (usu. foll. by *of*) a source or origin.

ra·dome /ráydōm/ *n.* a dome or other structure, transparent to radio waves, protecting radar equipment, esp. on the outer surface of an aircraft.

ra·don /ráydon/ *n. Chem.* a gaseous radioactive inert element arising from the disintegration of radium. ¶ Symb.: **Rn.**

RAF *abbr.* (in the UK) Royal Air Force.

raf·fi·a /ráfeeə/ *n.* (also **ra·phi·a**) **1** a palm tree, *Raphia ruffia*, native to Madagascar, having very long leaves. **2** the fiber from its leaves used for making hats, baskets, etc., and for tying plants, etc.

raff·ish /ráfish/ *adj.* **1** disreputable; rakish. **2** tawdry. ▫▫ **raff·ish·ly** *adv.* **raff·ish·ness** *n.*

raf·fle /ráfəl/ *n. & v.* • *n.* a fund-raising lottery with goods as prizes. • *v.tr.* (often foll. by *off*) dispose of by means of a raffle.

raft[1] /raft/ *n. & v.* • *n.* **1** a flat floating structure of logs or other materials for conveying persons or things. **2** a lifeboat or small (often inflatable) boat, esp. for use in emergencies. **3** a floating accumulation of trees, ice, etc. • *v.* **1** *tr.* transport as or on a raft. **2** *tr.* cross (water) on a raft. **3** *tr.* form into a raft. **4** *intr.* (often foll. by *across*) work a raft (across water, etc.).

raft[2] /raft/ *n. colloq.* **1** a large collection. **2** (foll. by *of*) a crowd.

raft·er[1] /ráftər/ *n.* each of the sloping beams forming the framework of a roof. ▫▫ **raft·ered** *adj.*

raft·er[2] /ráftər/ *n.* **1** a person who builds rafts. **2** a person who travels by raft.

rag[1] /rag/ *n.* **1 a** a torn, frayed, or worn piece of woven material. **b** one of the irregular scraps to which cloth, etc., is reduced by wear and tear. **2 a** (in *pl.*) old or worn clothes. **b** (usu. in *pl.*) *colloq.* a garment of any kind. **3** (*collect.*) scraps of cloth used as material for paper, stuffing, etc. **4** *derog.* **a** a newspaper. **b** a flag, handkerchief, curtain, etc. ▫ **in rags 1** much torn. **2** in old torn clothes. **rags to riches** poverty to affluence.

rag[2] /rag/ *n. & v.* • *n. Brit.* a fund-raising program of stunts, parades, and entertainment organized by students. • *v.* (**ragged, ragging**) **1** *tr.* scold. **2** *tr.* tease; torment.

rag[3] /rag/ *n.* **1** a large, coarse roofing slate. **2** any of various kinds of hard, coarse, sedimentary stone that break into thick slabs.

rag[4] /rag/ *n. Mus.* a ragtime composition or tune.

ra·ga /ráagə/ *n.* (also **rag** /raag/) *Ind. Mus.* **1** a pattern of notes used as a basis for improvisation. **2** a piece using a particular raga.

rag·a·muf·fin /rágəmufin/ *n.* a person in ragged dirty clothes, esp. a child.

rag·bag /rágbag/ *n.* **1** a bag in which scraps of fabric, etc., are kept for use. **2** a miscellaneous collection.

rag doll *n.* a stuffed doll made of cloth.

rage /rayj/ *n. & v.* • *n.* **1** fierce or violent anger. **2** a fit of this. **3** the violent action of a natural force. **4** (foll. by *for*) **a** a vehement desire or passion. **b** a widespread temporary enthusiasm or fashion. • *v.tr.* **1** be full of anger. **2** (often foll. by *at, against*) speak furiously or madly; rave. **3** (of wind, fever, etc.) be violent; be at its height. ▫ **all the rage** popular; fashionable.

rag·ged /rágid/ *adj.* **1 a** (of clothes, etc.) torn; frayed. **b** (of a place) dilapidated. **2** rough; shaggy. **3** (of a person) in ragged clothes. **4** with a broken or jagged outline or surface. **5** faulty; imperfect. **6 a** lacking finish, smoothness, or uniformity. **b** (of a sound) harsh, discordant. **7** exhausted (esp. *be run ragged*). ▫▫ **rag·ged·ly** *adv.* **rag·ged·ness** *n.* **rag·ged·y** *adj.*

rag·lan /ráglən/ *n.* (often *attrib.*) an overcoat without shoulder seams, the sleeves running up to the neck.

rag·lan sleeve *n.* a sleeve that continues in one piece up to the neck of a garment, without a shoulder seam.
ra·gout /ragóō/ *n. & v.* • *n.* meat in small pieces stewed with vegetables and highly seasoned. • *v.tr.* cook (food) in this way.
rag·stone /rágstōn/ *n.* = RAG[3] 2.
rag·tag /rágtag/ *adj.* **1** disheveled; shabby. **2** motley; diverse.
rag·time /rágtīm/ *n. & adj.* • *n.* music characterized by a syncopated melodic line and regularly accented accompaniment, played esp. on the piano. • *adj. sl.* disorderly, disreputable, inferior (*a ragtime army*).
rag trade *n. colloq.* the business of designing, making, and selling clothes.
rag·weed /rágweed/ *n.* any plant of the genus *Ambrosia*, esp. *A. trifida*, with allergenic pollen.
rag·worm /rágwərm/ *n.* a carnivorous marine worm of the family Nereidae, esp. *Nereis diversicolor*, often used for bait.
rag·wort /rágwərt, –wawrt/ *n.* any yellow-flowered ragged-leaved plant of the genus *Senecio*.
rah /raa/ *int. colloq.* an expression of encouragement, approval, etc., esp. to a team or a player.
raid /rayd/ *n. & v.* • *n.* **1** a rapid surprise attack, esp.: **a** in warfare. **b** to commit a crime or do harm. **2** a surprise attack by police, etc., to arrest suspected persons or seize illicit goods. **3** *Stock Exch.* an attempt to lower prices by the concerted selling of shares. **4** (foll. by *on, upon*) a forceful or insistent attempt to make a person or thing provide something. • *v.tr.* **1** make a raid on. **2** plunder; deplete. □□ **raid·er** *n.*
rail[1] /rayl/ *n. & v.* • *n.* **1** a level or sloping bar or series of bars: **a** used to hang things on. **b** running along the top of a set of banisters. **c** forming part of a barrier. **2** a steel bar or continuous line of bars laid on the ground, usu. as one of a pair forming a railroad track. **3** (often *attrib.*) a railroad (*by rail*). **4** (in *pl.*) the inside boundary fence of a racecourse. **5** a horizontal piece in the frame of a paneled door, etc. • *v.tr.* **1** furnish with a rail or rails. **2** (usu. foll. by *in, off*) enclose with rails. **3** convey (goods) by rail. □□ **rail·less** *adj.*
rail[2] /rayl/ *v.intr.* (often foll. by *at, against*) complain using abusive language. □□ **rail·er** *n.* **rail·ing** *n. & adj.*
rail[3] /rayl/ *n.* any bird of the family Rallidae, often inhabiting marshes.
rail·car /ráylkaar/ *n.* **1** any railroad car. **2** a railroad vehicle consisting of a single powered car.
rail·head /ráylhed/ *n.* **1** the furthest point reached by a railroad under construction. **2** the point on a railroad at which road transport of goods begins.
rail·ing /ráyling/ *n.* **1** (usu. in *pl.*) a fence or barrier made of rails. **2** the material for these.
rail·ler·y /ráyləree/ *n.* (*pl.* **-ies**) **1** good-humored ridicule; rallying. **2** an instance of this.
rail·road /ráylrōd/ *n. & v.* • *n.* **1** a track or set of tracks made of steel rails upon which goods trucks and passenger trains run. **2** such a system worked by a single company (*B & O Railroad*). **3** the organization and personnel required for its working. **4** a similar set of tracks for other vehicles, etc. • *v.tr.* **1** (often foll. by *to, into, through*, etc.) rush or coerce (a person or thing) (*railroaded me into going too*). **2** send (a person) to prison by means of false evidence. **3** transport by railroad.
rail·way /ráylway/ *n.* esp. *Brit.* = RAILROAD.
rai·ment /ráymənt/ *n. archaic* clothing.
rain /rayn/ *n. & v.* • *n.* **1 a** the condensed moisture of the atmosphere falling visibly in separate drops. **b** the fall of such drops. **2** (in *pl.*) **a** rainfalls. **b** (prec. by *the*) the rainy season in tropical countries. **3 a** falling liquid or solid particles or objects. **b** the rainlike descent of these. **c** a large or overwhelming quantity (*a rain of congratulations*). • *v.* **1** *intr.* (prec. by *it* as subject) rain falls (*if it rains*). **2 a** *intr.* fall in showers or like rain. **b** *tr.* (prec. by *it* as subject) send in large quantities (*it rained blood*). **3** *tr.* send down like rain; lavishly bestow (*rained blows upon him*). **4** *intr.* (of the sky, etc.) send down rain. □ **rain out** (esp. in *passive*) cause (an event, etc.) to be terminated or canceled because of rain. **rain or shine** whether it rains or not. □□ **rain·less** *adj.*
rain·bow /ráynbō/ *n. & adj.* • *n.* **1** an arch of colors formed in the sky by reflection, twofold refraction, and dispersion of the sun's rays in falling rain or in spray or mist. **2** a similar effect formed by the moon's rays. • *adj.* many-colored.
rain·bow trout *n.* a large trout, *Salmo gairdneri*, orig. of the Pacific coast of N. America.
rain check *n.* **1** a ticket given for later use when an outdoor event is interrupted or postponed by rain. **2** a promise that an offer will be maintained though deferred.
rain·coat /ráynkōt/ *n.* a waterproof or water-resistant coat.
rain date *n.* a date on which an event postponed by rain is held.
rain·drop /ráyndrop/ *n.* a single drop of rain.
rain·fall /ráynfawl/ *n.* **1** a fall of rain. **2** the quantity of rain falling within a given area in a given time.
rain for·est *n.* luxuriant tropical forest with heavy rainfall.
rain gauge *n.* an instrument measuring rainfall.
rain·mak·er *n.* a person who is highly successful, esp. in business.
rain·mak·ing /ráynmayking/ *n.* the action of attempting to increase rainfall by artificial means.
rain·proof /ráynprōōf/ *adj.* (esp. of a building, garment, etc.) resistant to rainwater.
rain·storm /ráynstawrm/ *n.* a storm with heavy rain.
rain·wa·ter /ráynwawtər, –wotər/ *n.* water obtained from collected rain, as distinct from a well, etc.
rain·y /ráynee/ *adj.* (**rainier, rainiest**) **1** (of weather, a climate, day, region, etc.) in or on which rain is falling or much rain usually falls. **2** (of cloud, wind, etc.) laden with or bringing rain. □□ **rain·i·ly** *adv.* **rain·i·ness** *n.*
rain·y day *n.* a time of special need in the future.
raise /rayz/ *v. & n.* • *v.tr.* **1** put or take into a higher position. **2** (often foll. by *up*) cause to rise or be vertical. **3** increase the amount or value or strength of. **4** (often foll. by *up*) construct or build up. **5** levy or collect or bring together. **6** cause to be heard or considered (*raise an objection*). **7** bring into being; arouse (*raise hopes*). **8** bring up; educate. **9** breed or grow (*raise one's own vegetables*). **10** promote to a higher rank. **11** (foll. by *to*) *Math.* multiply a quantity to a specified power. **12** cause (bread) to rise with yeast. **13** *Cards* **a** bet more than (another player). **b** increase (a stake). **c** *Bridge* make a bid contracting for more tricks in the same suit as (one's partner); increase (a bid) in this way. **14** abandon or force an enemy to abandon (a siege or blockade). **15** remove (a barrier or embargo). **16** cause (a ghost, etc.) to appear (opp. LAY[1] *v.* 6b). **17** *colloq.* find (a person, etc., wanted). **18** establish contact with (a person, etc.) by radio or telephone. • *n.* **1** *Cards* an increase in a stake or bid (cf. sense 13 of *v.*). **2** an increase in salary. □ **raise from the dead** restore to life. **raise one's glass to** drink the health or good fortune of. **raise one's hand to** make as if to strike (a person). **raise hell** *colloq.* make a disturbance. □□ **rais·a·ble** *adj.*
rai·sin /ráyzən/ *n.* a partially dried grape. □□ **rai·sin·y** *adj.*
rai·son d'êt·re /ráyzoN détrə/ *n.* (*pl.* **raisons d'être** *pro-*

nunc. same) a purpose or reason that accounts for or justifies or originally caused a thing's existence.

raj /raaj/ *n.* (prec. by *the*) *hist.* British sovereignty in India.

ra·ja /ra͞ajə/ *n.* (also **ra·jah**) *hist.* **1** an Indian king or prince. **2** a petty dignitary or noble in India.

rake[1] /rayk/ *n. & v.* •*n.* **1 a** an implement consisting of a pole with a crossbar toothed like a comb at the end, or with several tines held together by a crosspiece, for drawing together hay, etc., or smoothing loose soil or gravel. **b** a wheeled implement for the same purpose. **2** a similar implement used for other purposes, e.g., by a croupier. •*v.* **1** *tr.* (usu. foll. by *out*, *together*, *up*, etc.) collect or gather or remove with or as with a rake. **2** *tr.* make tidy or smooth with a rake. **3** *intr.* use a rake. **4** *tr. & intr.* search thoroughly; ransack. **5** *tr.* **a** direct gunfire along (a line) from end to end. **b** sweep with the eyes. **c** (of a window, etc.) have a commanding view of. **6** *tr.* scratch or scrape. □ **rake in** *colloq.* amass (profits, etc.). **rake up** (or **over**) revive the memory of (past quarrels, etc.). □□ **rak·er** *n.*

rake[2] /rayk/ *n.* a dissolute man of fashion.

rake[3] /rayk/ *v. & n.* •*v.* **1** *tr. & intr.* set or be set at a sloping angle. **2** *intr.* **a** (of a mast or funnel) incline from the perpendicular toward the stern. **b** (of a ship or its bow or stern) project at the upper part of the bow or stern beyond the keel. •*n.* **1** a raking position or build. **2** the amount by which a thing rakes.

rak·ish[1] /ráykish/ *adj.* of or like a rake (see RAKE[2]); dashing; jaunty. □□ **rak·ish·ly** *adv.* **rak·ish·ness** *n.*

rak·ish[2] /ráykish/ *adj.* (of a ship) smart and fast looking, and therefore open to suspicion of piracy.

rale /raal/ *n.* an abnormal rattling sound heard in the auscultation of unhealthy lungs.

ral·len·tan·do /rálǝntándō, ra͞alǝnta͞andō/ *adv., adj., & n. Mus.* •*adv. & adj.* with a gradual decrease of speed. •*n.* (*pl.* **-dos** or **rallentandi** /–dee/) a passage to be performed in this way.

ral·ly /rálee/ *v. & n.* •*v.* (**-lies, -lied**) **1** *tr. & intr.* (often foll. by *round*, *behind*, *to*) bring or come together as support or for concentrated action. **2** *tr. & intr.* bring or come together again after a rout or dispersion. **3 a** *intr.* renew a conflict. **b** *tr.* cause to do this. **4 a** *tr.* revive (courage, etc.) by an effort of will. **b** *tr.* rouse (a person or animal) to fresh energy. **c** *intr.* pull oneself together. **5** *intr.* recover after illness or prostration or fear. **6** *intr.* (of share prices, etc.) increase after a fall. •*n.* (*pl.* **-lies**) **1** an act of reassembling forces or renewing conflict. **2** a recovery of energy after or in the middle of exhaustion or illness. **3** a mass meeting of supporters or persons having a common interest. **4** a competition for motor vehicles, usu. over public roads. **5** (in tennis, etc.) an extended exchange of strokes between players. □□ **ral·li·er** *n.*

RAM /ram/ *abbr. Computing* random-access memory; internally stored software or data that is directly accessible, not requiring sequential search or reading.

ram /ram/ *n. & v.* •*n.* **1** an uncastrated male sheep. **2** (**the Ram**) the zodiacal sign or constellation Aries. **3** *hist.* **a** = BATTERING RAM. **b** a beak projecting from the bow of a battleship, for piercing the sides of other ships. **c** a battleship with such a beak. **4** the falling weight of a pile-driving machine. •*v.tr.* (**rammed, ramming**) **1** force or squeeze into place by pressure. **2** (usu. foll. by *down*, *in*, *into*) beat down or in by heavy blows. **3** (of a ship, etc.) strike violently; crash against. **4** (foll. by *against*, *at*, *on*, *into*) violently impel. □ **ram home** stress forcefully (a lesson, etc.). □□ **ram·mer** *n.*

Ram·a·dan /rámǝdan, ramǝda͞an/ *n.* (also **Ram·a·dhan**) the ninth month of the Muslim year, during which strict fasting is observed from sunrise to sunset.

ram·ble /rámbǝl/ *v. & n.* •*v.intr.* **1** walk for pleasure, with or without a definite route. **2** wander in discourse; talk or write disconnectedly. •*n.* a walk taken for pleasure.

ram·bler /rámblǝr/ *n.* **1** a person who rambles. **2** a straggling or climbing rose.

ram·bling /rámbling/ *adj.* **1** peripatetic; wandering. **2** desultory; incoherent. **3** (of a house, etc.) irregularly arranged. **4** (of a plant) straggling. □□ **ram·bling·ly** *adv.*

ram·bunc·tious /rambúngkshǝs/ *adj. colloq.* **1** uncontrollably exuberant. **2** unruly. □□ **ram·bunc·tious·ly** *adv.* **ram·bunc·tious·ness** *n.*

ram·e·kin /rámikin/ *n.* (also **ram·e·quin**) **1** a small dish for baking and serving an individual portion of food. **2** food served in such a dish.

ram·i·fi·ca·tion /rámifikáyshǝn/ *n.* **1** the act or an instance of ramifying; the state of being ramified. **2** a subdivision of a complex structure or process comparable to a tree's branches. **3** a consequence, esp. when complex or unwelcome.

ram·i·fy /rámifī/ *v.* (**-fies, -fied**) **1** *intr.* form branches or subdivisions or offshoots. **2** *tr.* (usu. in *passive*) cause to branch out; arrange in a branching manner.

ram·jet /rámjet/ *n.* a type of jet engine in which air is drawn in and compressed by the forward motion of the engine.

ram·mer see RAM.

ra·mose /rámōs, ráy;n–/ *adj.* branched; branching.

ramp /ramp/ *n. & v.* •*n.* **1** a slope or inclined plane, esp. for joining two levels of ground, etc. **2** (in full **boarding ramp**) movable stairs for entering or leaving an aircraft. **3** an upward bend in a staircase railing. •*v.* **1** *tr.* furnish or build with a ramp. **2** *intr. Archit.* (of a wall) ascend or descend to a different level.

ram·page *v. & n.* •*v.intr.* /rámpáyj/ **1** (often foll. by *about*) rush wildly or violently about. **2** rage; storm. •*n.* /rámpayj/ wild or violent behavior. □ **on the rampage** rampaging. □□ **ram·pa·geous** *adj.* **ram·pag·er** *n.*

ramp·ant /rámpǝnt/ *adj.* **1** flourishing excessively (*rampant violence*). **2** violent or extravagant in action or opinion (*rampant theorists*). **3** rank; luxuriant. □□ **ramp·an·cy** *n.* **ramp·ant·ly** *adv.*

ram·part /rámpaart/ *n.* **1 a** a defensive wall with a broad top and usu. a stone parapet. **b** a walkway on top of such a wall. **2** a defense or protection.

ram·rod /rámrod/ *n.* **1** a rod for ramming down the charge of a muzzleloading firearm. **2** a thing that is very straight or rigid.

ram·shack·le /rámshakǝl/ *adj.* (usu. of a house or vehicle) tumbledown; rickety.

ran *past* of RUN.

ranch /ranch/ *n. & v.* •*n.* **1 a** a cattle-breeding establishment, esp. in the western US and Canada. **b** a farm where other animals are bred (*mink ranch*). **2** (in full **ranch house**) a single-story or split-level house. •*v.intr.* farm on a ranch.

ranch·er /ránchǝr/ *n.* a person who farms on a ranch.

ran·che·ro /rancháirō/ *n.* (*pl.* **·ros**) a person who farms or works on a ranch, esp. in Mexico.

ran·cid /ránsid/ *adj.* smelling or tasting like rank stale fat. □□ **ran·cid·i·ty** /–síditee/ *n.*

ran·cor /rángkǝr/ *n.* inveterate bitterness; malignant hate. □□ **ran·cor·ous** *adj.* **ran·cor·ous·ly** *adv.*

rand /rand, raant/ *n.* the chief monetary unit of South Africa.

R & B *abbr.* (also **R. & B.**) rhythm and blues.

R & D *abbr.* (also **R. & D.**) research and development.

ran·dom /rándǝm/ *adj.* **1** made, done, etc., without method or conscious choice. **2** *Statistics* **a** with equal chances for each item. **b** given by a random process. **3** (of masonry) with stones of irregular size and shape.

□ **at random** without aim or purpose or principle. □□ **ran•dom•ly** *adv.* **ran•dom•ness** *n.*

ran•dom-ac•cess *adj. Computing* (of a memory or file) having all parts directly accessible, so that it need not be read sequentially.

R and R *abbr.* (also **R. and R.**) **1** rescue and resuscitation. **2** rest and recreation (or recuperation or relaxation). **3** rock and roll.

ra•nee var. of RANI.

rang *past* of RING[2].

range /raynj/ *n. & v.* •*n.* **1 a** the region between limits of variation, esp. a scope of effective operation. **b** such limits. **c** a limited scale or series (*the range is about 10 degrees*). **d** a series representing variety or choice; a selection. **2** the area included in or concerned with something. **3 a** the distance attainable by a gun or projectile. **b** the distance between a gun or projectile and its objective. **4** a row, series, line, or tier, esp. of mountains or buildings. **5 a** an open or enclosed area with targets for shooting. **b** a testing ground for military equipment. **6** a cooking stove with one or more ovens and a set of burners on the top surface. **7** the area over which a thing, esp. a plant or animal, is distributed. **8** the distance that can be covered by a vehicle or aircraft without refueling. **9** the distance between a camera and the subject to be photographed. **10** the extent of time covered by a forecast, etc. **11 a** a large area of open land for grazing or hunting. **b** a tract over which one wanders. •*v.* **1** *intr.* **a** reach; lie spread out; extend; vary between limits. **b** run in a line (*ranges north and south*). **2** *tr.* (usu. in *passive* or *refl.*) place or arrange in ranks or in a specified situation or order or company. **3** *intr.* rove; wander (*ranged through the woods*). **4** *tr.* traverse in all directions (*ranging the woods*).

range find•er *n.* an instrument for estimating the distance of an object, esp. one to be shot at or photographed.

rang•er /ráynjər/ *n.* **1** a keeper of a national or royal park or forest. **2** a member of a body of armed men, esp.: **a** a mounted soldier. **b** a commando. **3** a wanderer.

rang•y /ráynjee/ *adj.* (**rangier, rangiest**) **1** (of a person) tall and slim. **2** hilly; mountainous.

ra•ni /raʹanee/ *n.* (also **ra•nee**) *hist.* a raja's wife or widow; a Hindu queen.

rank[1] /rangk/ *n. & v.* •*n.* **1 a** a position in a hierarchy; a grade of advancement. **b** a grade of dignity or achievement (*in the top rank of performers*). **c** high social position (*persons of rank*). **d** a place in a scale. **2** a row or line. **3** a single line of soldiers drawn up abreast. **4** order; array. **5** *Chess* a row of squares across the board (cf. FILE[2]). •*v.* **1** *intr.* have rank or place (*ranks next to the chief of staff*). **2** *tr.* classify. **3** *tr.* arrange (esp. soldiers) in a rank or ranks. **4 a** *tr.* take precedence of (a person) in respect to rank. **b** *intr.* have the senior position among the members of a hierarchy, etc. □ **break rank** fail to remain in line. **close ranks** maintain solidarity. **pull rank** use one's superior rank to gain advantage.

rank[2] /rangk/ *adj.* **1** too luxuriant; choked with or apt to produce weeds or excessive foliage. **2 a** foul-smelling; offensive. **b** loathsome; corrupt. **3** flagrant; virulent; gross; complete (*rank outsider*). □□ **rank•ness** *n.*

rank and file *n.* (usu. treated as *pl.*) ordinary undistinguished people.

rank•ing /rángking/ *n. & adj.* •*n.* ordering by rank; classification. •*adj.* having a high rank or position.

ran•kle /rángkəl/ *v.intr.* (of envy, disappointment, etc.) cause persistent annoyance or resentment.

ran•sack /ránsak/ *v.tr.* **1** pillage or plunder. **2** thoroughly search (a place, a receptacle, a person's pockets, etc.). □□ **ran•sack•er** *n.*

ran•som /ránsəm/ *n. & v.* •*n.* **1** a sum of money or other payment demanded or paid for the release of a prisoner. **2** the liberation of a prisoner in return for this. •*v.tr.* **1** buy the freedom or restoration of; redeem. **2** hold to ransom. **3** release for a ransom.

rant /rant/ *v. & n.* •*v.* **1** *intr.* use bombastic language. **2** *tr. & intr.* declaim; recite theatrically. **3** *tr. & intr.* preach noisily. **4** *intr.* (often foll. by *about, on*) speak vehemently or intemperately. •*n.* **1** a piece of ranting; a tirade. **2** empty turgid talk. □□ **rant•er** *n.* **rant•ing•ly** *adv.*

ra•nun•cu•la•ceous /rənúngkyəláyshəs/ *adj.* of or relating to the family Ranunculaceae of flowering plants, including clematis and delphiniums.

rap[1] /rap/ *n. & v.* •*n.* **1** a smart, slight blow. **2** a knock; a sharp tapping sound. **3** *sl.* blame; censure; punishment. **4** *sl.* a conversation. **5 a** a rhyming monologue recited rhythmically to prerecorded music. **b** (in full **rap music**) a style of pop music with a pronounced beat and words recited rather than sung. •*v.* (**rapped, rapping**) **1** *tr.* strike smartly. **2** *intr.* make a sharp tapping sound. **3** *tr.* criticize adversely. **4** *intr. sl.* talk. □ **beat the rap** escape punishment. **take the rap** suffer the consequences. □□ **rap•per** *n.*

rap[2] /rap/ *n.* a small amount, the least bit.

ra•pa•cious /rəpáyshəs/ *adj.* grasping; extortionate; predatory. □□ **ra•pa•cious•ly** *adv.* **ra•pa•cious•ness** *n.* **ra•pac•i•ty** /rəpásitee/ *n.*

rape[1] /rayp/ *n. & v.* •*n.* **1 a** the act of forcing another person to have sexual intercourse. **b** forcible sodomy. **2** (often foll. by *of*) violent assault; forcible interference; violation. **3** an instance of rape. •*v.tr.* **1** commit rape on (a person, usu. a woman). **2** violate; assault.

rape[2] /rayp/ *n.* a plant, *Brassica napus*, grown as food for livestock and for its seed (rapeseed), from which oil is made. Also called COLE.

rape[3] /rayp/ *n.* **1** the refuse of grapes after wine making, used in making vinegar. **2** a vessel used in vinegar making.

ra•phia var. of RAFFIA.

rap•id /rápid/ *adj. & n.* •*adj.* **1** quick; swift. **2** acting or completed in a short time. **3** (of a slope) descending steeply. **4** *Photog.* fast. •*n.* (usu. in *pl.*) a steep descent in a riverbed, with a swift current. □□ **ra•pid•i•ty** /rəpíditee/ *n.* **rap•id•ly** *adv.* **rap•id•ness** *n.*

rap•id eye move•ment *n.* a type of jerky movement of the eyes during periods of dreaming.

rap•id-fire *adj. attrib.* fired, asked, etc., in quick succession.

ra•pi•er /ráypeeər, ráypyər/ *n.* a light slender sword used for thrusting.

rap•ine /rápin, –īn/ *n. rhet.* plundering; robbery.

rap•ist /ráypist/ *n.* a person who commits rape.

rap•pel /rapél/ *n. & v.* (**rappelled, rappelling**; or **rappeled, rappeling**) •*n.* technique or act of controlled descent from a height, as a steep rockface, by using a doubled rope coiled around the body and fixed at a higher point, with which one slides downward gradually. •*v.intr.* make a descent in this way.

rap•port /rapáwr/ *n.* relationship or communication, esp. when useful and harmonious (*in rapport with*; *establish a rapport*).

rap•proche•ment /raprōshmóɴ/ *n.* the resumption of harmonious relations, esp. between nations.

rap•scal•lion /rapskályən/ *n. archaic* or *joc.* rascal; scamp; rogue.

rapt /rapt/ *adj.* **1** fully absorbed or intent. **2** carried away with joyous feeling or lofty thought. **3** carried away bodily. □□ **rapt•ly** *adv.* **rapt•ness** *n.*

rap·tor /ráptər/ *n.* a bird of prey, e.g., an owl, falcon, or eagle. □□ **rap·to·ri·al** /raptáwreeəl/ *adj. & n.*

rap·ture /rápchər/ *n.* **1 a** ecstatic delight; mental transport. **b** (in *pl.*) great pleasure or enthusiasm or the expression of it. **2** a mystical experience in which the soul gains a knowledge of divine things. □ **go into** (or **be in**) **raptures** be enthusiastic; talk enthusiastically. □□ **rap·tur·ous** *adj.* **rap·tur·ous·ly** *adv.*

rare[1] /rair/ *adj.* (**rarer, rarest**) **1** seldom done or found or occurring; uncommon. **2** of less than the usual density. □□ **rare·ness** *n.*

rare[2] /rair/ *adj.* (**rarer, rarest**) (of meat) cooked lightly, so as to be still red inside.

rare·bit /ráirbit/ *n.* = WELSH RABBIT.

rare earth *n.* **1** a lanthanide element. **2** an oxide of such an element.

rar·e·fy /ráirifī/ *v.* (**-fies, -fied**) (esp. as **rarefied** *adj.*) **1** *tr. & intr.* make or become less dense (*rarefied air*). **2** *tr.* refine (a person's nature, etc.). **3** *tr.* **a** make (an idea, etc.) subtle. **b** (as **rarefied** *adj.*) refined; subtle; elevated; exalted; select. □□ **rar·e·fac·tion** /–fákshən/ *n.* **rar·e·fac·tive** *adj.* **rar·e·fi·ca·tion** /–fikáyshən/ *n.*

rare·ly /ráirlee/ *adv.* **1** seldom; not often. **2** in an unusual degree; exceptionally. **3** exceptionally well.

rar·ing /ráiring/ *adj.* (foll. by *to* + infin.) *colloq.* enthusiastic, eager (*raring to go*).

rar·i·ty /ráiritee/ *n.* (*pl.* **-ties**) **1** rareness. **2** an uncommon thing, esp. one valued for being rare.

ras·cal /ráskəl/ *n.* often *joc.* a dishonest or mischievous person, esp. a child. □□ **ras·cal·ly** *adj.*

rash[1] /rash/ *adj.* reckless; impetuous; hasty. □□ **rash·ly** *adv.* **rash·ness** *n.*

rash[2] /rash/ *n.* **1** an eruption of the skin in spots or patches. **2** (usu. foll. by *of*) a sudden widespread phenomenon (*a rash of strikes*).

rash·er /ráshər/ *n.* a thin slice of bacon or ham.

rasp /rasp/ *n. & v.* •*n.* **1** a coarse kind of file having separate teeth. **2** a rough grating sound. •*v.* **1** *tr.* **a** scrape with a rasp. **b** scrape roughly. **c** (foll. by *off*, *away*) remove by scraping. **2 a** *intr.* make a grating sound. **b** *tr.* say gratingly or hoarsely. **3** *tr.* grate upon (a person or a person's feelings). □□ **rasp·ing·ly** *adv.* **rasp·y** *adj.*

rasp·ber·ry /rázberee/ *n.* (*pl.* **-ries**) **1 a** a bramble, *Rubus idaeus*, having usu. red berries. **b** this berry. **2** any of various red colors. **3** *colloq.* **a** a sound made with the lips expressing derision or disapproval (orig. *raspberry tart*, rhyming sl. = *fart*). **b** a show of strong disapproval (*got a raspberry from the audience*).

Ras·ta /raástə, rást–/ *n. & adj. colloq.* = RASTAFARIAN.

Ras·ta·far·i·an /raástəfaáreeən, rástəfáir–/ *n. & adj.* •*n.* a member of a sect of Jamaican origin regarding the former Emperor Haile Selassie of Ethiopia (d. 1975, entitled *Ras Tafari*) as God. •*adj.* of or relating to this sect. □□ **Ras·ta·far·i·an·ism** *n.*

rat /rat/ *n. & v.* •*n.* **1 a** any of several rodents of the genus *Rattus*. **b** any similar rodent (*muskrat*). **2** a deserter from a party, cause, etc. **3** *colloq.* an unpleasant person. **4** a worker who refuses to join a strike, or a strikebreaker. **5** (in *pl.*) *sl.* an exclamation of contempt, annoyance, etc. •*v.intr.* (**ratted, ratting**) **1** (of a person or dog) hunt or kill rats. **2** *colloq.* desert a cause, party, etc. **3** *colloq.* (foll. by *on*) betray; let down.

rat·a·ble /ráytəbəl/ *adj.* (also **rate·a·ble**) able to be rated or estimated.

ra·tan var. of RATTAN.

rat-a-tat /rátətát/ *n.* (also **rat-a-tat-tat**) a rapping or knocking sound.

ra·ta·touille /rátətoō-ee, raátaa–/ *n.* a vegetable dish made of stewed eggplant, onions, tomatoes, zucchini, and peppers.

ratch /rach/ *n.* **1** a ratchet. **2** a ratchet wheel.

ratch·et /ráchit/ *n. & v.* •*n.* **1** a set of teeth on the edge of a bar or wheel in which a device engages to ensure motion in one direction only. **2** (in full **ratchet wheel**) a wheel with a rim so toothed. •*v.* **1** *tr.* **a** provide with a ratchet. **b** make into a ratchet. **2** *tr. & intr.* move as under the control of a ratchet. □ **ratchet up** (or **down**) move steadily or by degrees (*health costs continue to ratchet up*).

rate[1] /rayt/ *n. & v.* •*n.* **1** a stated numerical proportion between two sets of things (*at a rate of 50 miles per hour*) or as the basis of calculating an amount or value (*rate of taxation*). **2** a fixed or appropriate charge or cost or value; a measure of this (*postal rates*). **3** rapidity of movement or change (*a great rate*). **4** class or rank (*first-rate*). •*v.* **1** *tr.* **a** estimate the worth or value of. **b** assign a fixed value to (a coin or metal) in relation to a monetary standard. **c** assign a value to (work, the power of a machine, etc.). **2** *tr.* consider; regard as. **3** *intr.* (foll. by *as*) rank or be rated. **4** *tr.* be worthy of, deserve. □ **at any rate** in any case; whatever happens. **at this** (or **that**) **rate** if this example is typical or this assumption is true.

rate[2] /rayt/ *v.tr.* scold angrily.

rate·a·ble var. of RATABLE.

rat·fink /rátfingk/ *n. sl.* = FINK.

rath·er /ráthər/ *adv.* **1** (often foll. by *than*) by preference (*would rather not go*). **2** (usu. foll. by *than*) as a more likely alternative (*is stupid rather than honest*). **3** more precisely (*a book, or rather, a pamphlet*). **4** slightly; somewhat (*rather drunk*). □ **had** (or **would**) **rather** prefer to.

rat·i·fy /rátifī/ *v.tr.* (**-fies, -fied**) confirm or accept (an agreement made in one's name) by formal consent, signature, etc. □□ **rat·i·fi·a·ble** *adj.* **rat·i·fi·ca·tion** /–fikáyshən/ *n.* **rat·i·fi·er** *n.*

rat·ing[1] /ráyting/ *n.* **1** the act or an instance of placing in a rank or class or assigning a value to. **2** the estimated standing of a person as regards credit, etc. **3** *Naut.* a person's position or class on a ship's books. **4** the relative popularity of a broadcast program as determined by the estimated size of the audience.

rat·ing[2] /ráyting/ *n.* an angry reprimand.

ra·tio /ráysheeō, ráyshō/ *n.* (*pl.* **-os**) the quantitative relation between two similar magnitudes determined by the number of times one contains the other integrally or fractionally (*the ratios 1:5 and 20:100 are the same*).

ra·ti·oc·i·nate /rásheeósinayt/ *v.intr. literary* go through logical processes of reasoning, esp. using syllogisms. □□ **ra·ti·oc·i·na·tion** /–ōsináyshən, –ósináyshən/ *n.*

ra·tion /ráshən, ráy–/ *n. & v.* •*n.* **1** a fixed official allowance of food, clothing, etc., in a time of shortage. **2** (foll. by *of*) a single portion of provisions, etc. **3** (usu. in *pl.*) a fixed daily allowance of food, esp. in the armed forces. **4** (in *pl.*) provisions. •*v.tr.* **1** limit (persons or provisions) to a fixed ration. **2** (usu. foll. by *out*) distribute (food, etc.) in fixed quantities.

ra·tion·al /ráshənəl/ *adj.* **1** of or based on reasoning or reason. **2** sensible, sane, moderate; not foolish, absurd, or extreme. **3** endowed with reason or reasoning. **4** rejecting what is unreasonable or cannot be tested by reason in religion or custom. **5** *Math.* (of a quantity or ratio) expressible as a ratio of whole numbers. □□ **ra·tion·al·i·ty** /–nálitee/ *n.* **ra·tion·al·ly** *adv.*

ra·tion·ale /ráshənál/ *n.* **1** (often foll. by *for*) the fundamental reason or logical basis of anything. **2** a reasoned exposition.

ra·tion·al·ism /ráshənəlizəm/ *n.* **1** *Philos.* the theory that reason is the foundation of certainty in knowledge (opp. *empiricism* (see EMPIRIC)), sensationalism. **2** *Theol.* the practice of treating reason as the ultimate authority in religion. **3** a belief in reason rather than religion as a guiding principle in life. ▫▫ **ra·tion·al·ist** *n.* **ra·tion·al·is·tic** *adj.* **ra·tion·al·is·ti·cal·ly** *adv.*

ra·tion·al·ize /ráshənəlīz/ *v.* **1 a** *tr.* offer a rational but specious explanation of (one's behavior or attitude). **b** *intr.* explain one's behavior or attitude in this way. **2** *tr.* make logical and consistent. **3** *tr.* make (a business, etc.) more efficient by reorganizing it to reduce or eliminate waste. **4** *tr.* (often foll. by *away*) explain or explain away rationally. **5** *tr. Math.* eliminate irrational quantities from (an equation, etc.) **6** *intr.* be or act as a rationalist. ▫▫ **ra·tion·al·i·za·tion** *n.* **ra·tion·al·iz·er** *n.*

rat race *n.* a fiercely competitive struggle for position, power, etc.

rat·tan /rətán/ *n.* (also **ra·tan**) **1** any East Indian climbing palm of the genus *Calamus*, etc., with long, thin, jointed pliable stems. **2** a piece of rattan stem used as a walking stick, etc.

rat·ter /rátər/ *n.* a dog or other animal that hunts rats.

rat·tle /rát'l/ *v.* & *n.* • *v.* **1 a** *intr.* give out a rapid succession of short, sharp, hard sounds. **b** *tr.* make (a cup and saucer, window, etc.) do this. **c** *intr.* cause such sounds by shaking something. **2 a** *intr.* move with a rattling noise. **b** *intr.* ride or run briskly. **3 a** *tr.* (usu. foll. by *off*) say or recite rapidly. **b** *intr.* (usu. foll. by *on*) talk in a lively thoughtless way. **4** *tr. colloq.* disconcert; alarm. • *n.* **1** a rattling sound. **2** an instrument or plaything made to rattle. **3** the set of horny rings in a rattlesnake's tail. **4** a plant with seeds that rattle in their cases when ripe. **5** uproar; bustle; noisy gaiety; racket. **6 a** a noisy flow of words. **b** empty chatter; trivial talk. ▫▫ **rat·tly** *adj.*

rat·tler /rátlər/ *n.* **1** a thing that rattles, esp. an old or rickety vehicle. **2** *colloq.* a rattlesnake.

rat·tle·snake /rát'lsnayk/ *n.* any of various poisonous American snakes of the family Viperidae, esp. of the genus *Crotalus* or *Sistrurus*, with a rattling structure of horny rings in its tail.

rat·tle·trap /rát'ltrap/ *n.* & *adj. colloq.* • *n.* a rickety old vehicle, etc. • *adj.* rickety.

rat·tling /rátling/ *adj.* **1** that rattles. **2** brisk; vigorous (*a rattling pace*).

rat·ty /rátee/ *adj.* (**rattier, rattiest**) **1** relating to or infested with rats. **2** *colloq.* **a** shabby; wretched; nasty. **b** unkempt; seedy; dirty. ▫▫ **rat·ti·ly** *adv.* **rat·ti·ness** *n.*

rau·cous /ráwkəs/ *adj.* harsh sounding; loud and hoarse. ▫▫ **rau·cous·ly** *adv.* **rau·cous·ness** *n.*

raun·chy /ráwnchee/ *adj.* (**raunchier, raunchiest**) *colloq.* **1** coarse; boisterous; sexually provocative. **2** slovenly; grubby. ▫▫ **raun·chi·ly** *adv.* **raun·chi·ness** *n.*

rav·age /rávij/ *v.* & *n.* • *v.tr.* & *intr.* devastate; plunder. • *n.* **1** the act or an instance of ravaging; devastation; damage. **2** (usu. in *pl.*; foll. by *of*) destructive effect (*survived the ravages of winter*). ▫▫ **rav·ag·er** *n.*

rave /rayv/ *v.* & *n.* • *v.* **1** *intr.* talk wildly or furiously in or as in delirium. **2** *intr.* (usu. foll. by *about, of, over*) speak with rapturous admiration; go into raptures. **3** *tr.* bring into a specified state by raving. **4** *tr.* utter with ravings. **5** *intr.* (of the sea, wind, etc.) howl; roar. • *n.* **1** (usu. *attrib.*) *colloq.* a highly enthusiastic review (*a rave review*). **2** a dance party, often involving drug use.

rav·el /rávəl/ *v.* & *n.* • *v.* **1** *tr.* & *intr.* entangle or become entangled. **2** *tr.* confuse or complicate (a question or problem). **3** *intr.* fray out. **4** *tr.* (often foll. by *out*) disentangle; unravel; distinguish the separate threads or subdivisions of. • *n.* **1** a tangle or knot. **2** a complication. **3** a frayed or loose end.

ra·ven[1] /ráyvən/ *n.* & *adj.* • *n.* a large glossy blue-black crow, *Corvus corax*, having a hoarse cry. • *adj.* glossy black (*raven tresses*).

rav·en[2] /rávən/ *v.* **1** *intr.* **a** plunder. **b** (foll. by *after*) seek prey or booty. **c** (foll. by *about*) go plundering. **d** prowl for prey (*ravening beast*). **2 a** *tr.* devour voraciously. **b** *intr.* (usu. foll. by *for*) have a ravenous appetite. **c** *intr.* (often foll. by *on*) feed voraciously.

rav·en·ous /rávənəs/ *adj.* **1** very hungry. **2** voracious. **3** rapacious. ▫▫ **rav·en·ous·ly** *adv.*

rav·in /rávin/ *n. poet.* or *rhet.* **1** robbery; plundering. **2** the seizing and devouring of prey. **3** prey.

ra·vine /rəvéen/ *n.* a deep narrow gorge or cleft.

rav·ing /ráyving/ *n., adj.,* & *adv.* • *n.* (usu. in *pl.*) wild or delirious talk. • *adj.* **1** delirious; frenzied. **2** remarkable; intensive. • *adv.* intensively; wildly.

ra·vi·o·li /ráveeṓlee/ *n.* small pasta envelopes containing ground meat, etc.

rav·ish /rávish/ *v.tr.* **1** commit rape on (a person). **2** enrapture. ▫▫ **rav·ish·er** *n.* **rav·ish·ment** *n.*

rav·ish·ing /rávishing/ *adj.* entrancing; delightful. ▫▫ **rav·ish·ing·ly** *adv.*

raw /raw/ *adj.* & *n.* • *adj.* **1** uncooked. **2** in the natural state; not processed or manufactured (*raw sewage*). **3** (of alcoholic spirit) undiluted. **4** (of statistics, etc.) not analyzed or processed. **5** inexperienced; untrained (*raw recruits*). **6 a** stripped of skin; having the flesh exposed. **b** sensitive to the touch from having the flesh exposed. **c** sensitive to emotional pain, etc. **7** (of the atmosphere, day, etc.) chilly and damp. **8 a** crude in artistic quality; lacking finish. **b** unmitigated; brutal. **9** (of the edge of cloth) without hem or selvage. **10** (of silk) as reeled from cocoons. **11** (of grain) unmalted. • *n.* a raw place on a person's or horse's body. ▫ **in the raw 1** in its natural state without mitigation (*life in the raw*). **2** naked. ▫▫ **raw·ly** *adv.* **raw·ness** *n.*

raw·boned /ráwbōnd/ *adj.* gaunt.

raw deal *n.* harsh or unfair treatment.

raw·hide /ráwhīd/ *n.* **1** untanned hide. **2** a rope or whip of this.

raw ma·te·ri·al *n.* that from which the process of manufacture makes products.

raw si·en·na *n.* a brownish-yellow ferrous earth used as a pigment.

raw um·ber *n.* umber in its natural state, dark yellow in color.

ray[1] /ray/ *n.* & *v.* • *n.* **1** a single line or narrow beam of light from a small or distant source. **2** a straight line in which radiation travels to a given point. **3** (in *pl.*) radiation of a specified type (*gamma rays; X rays*). **4** a trace or beginning of an enlightening or cheering influence (*a ray of hope*). **5 a** any of a set of radiating lines or parts or things. **b** any of a set of straight lines passing through one point. • *v.* **1** *intr.* (foll. by *forth, out*) (of light, thought, emotion, etc.) issue in or as if in rays. **2** *intr.* & *tr.* radiate. ▫▫ **rayed** *adj.* **ray·less** *adj.*

ray[2] /ray/ *n.* a cartilaginous fish of the order Batoidea, with a broad flat body, winglike pectoral fins, and a long slender tail.

Ray·naud's dis·ease /raynoz/ *n.* a disease characterized by spasm of the arteries in the extremities, esp. the fingers.

ray·on /ráyon/ *n.* any of various textile fibers or fabrics made from cellulose.

raze /rayz/ *v.tr.* **1** completely destroy; tear down (esp. *raze to the ground*). **2** erase; scratch out (esp. in abstract senses).

ra·zor /ráyzər/ *n.* & *v.* • *n.* an instrument with a sharp blade used in cutting hair, esp. from the skin. • *v.tr.* **1** use a razor on. **2** shave; cut down close.

ra·zor·back /ráyzərbak/ *n.* an animal with a sharp ridged back, esp. a wild hog of the southern US.

ra·zor·bill /ráyzərbil/ *n.* a black and white auk, *Alca torda*, with a sharp-edged bill.

ra•zor clam *n.* any of various bivalve mollusks of the family Solenidae, with a thin, elongated shell.

ra•zor's edge *n.* **1** a keen edge. **2** a sharp mountain ridge. **3** a critical situation (*found themselves on the razor's edge*). **4** a sharp line of division.

ra•zor wire *n.* wire with sharpened projections, often coiled atop walls for security.

raz•zle-daz•zle /rázəldázəl/ *n.* (also **raz•zle**) *sl.* **1 a** excitement; bustle. **b** a spree. **2** extravagant publicity.

razz•ma•tazz /rázmətáz/ *n.* (also **raz•za•ma•tazz** /rázəmə–/) *colloq.* **1** = RAZZLE-DAZZLE. **2** insincere actions.

Rb *symb. Chem.* the element rubidium.

RC *abbr.* **1** Roman Catholic. **2** reinforced concrete.

Rd. *abbr.* Road (in names).

RDA *abbr.* **1** recommended daily allowance. **2** recommended dietary allowance.

Re *symb. Chem.* the element rhenium.

re[1] /ray, ree/ *prep.* **1** in the matter of (as the first word in a heading). **2** *colloq.* about; concerning.

re[2] /ray/ *n. Mus.* **1** (in tonic sol-fa) the second note of a major scale. **2** the note D in the fixed-do system.

re- /ree, ri, re/ *prefix* **1** attachable to almost any verb or its derivative; meaning: **a** once more; afresh; anew (*readjust*; *renumber*). **b** back; with return to a previous state (*reassemble*; *reverse*). **2** (also **red-** before a vowel, as in *redolent*) in verbs and verbal derivatives denoting: **a** in return; mutually (*react*; *resemble*). **b** opposition (*repel*; *resist*). **c** behind or after (*relic*; *remain*). **d** retirement or secrecy (*recluse*; *reticence*). **e** off; away; down (*recede*; *relegate*; *repress*). **f** frequentative or intensive force (*redouble*; *refine*; *resplendent*). **g** negative force (*recant*; *reveal*).

▶A hyphen is sometimes used when the word begins with *e* (*re-enact*), or to distinguish the compound from a more familiar one-word form (*re-form* = form again).

re•ab•sorb /réeəbsáwrb, –záwrb/ *v.tr.* absorb again. ▫▫ **re•ab•sorp•tion** /–absáwrpshən, –zawrp–/ *n.*

re•ac•cus•tom /réeəkústəm/ *v.tr.* accustom again.

reach /reech/ *v. & n.* • *v.* **1** *intr. & tr.* (often foll. by *out*) stretch out; extend. **2** *intr.* stretch out a limb, the hand, etc.; make a reaching motion or effort. **3** *intr.* (often foll. by *for*) make a motion or effort to touch or get hold of, or to attain (*reached for his pipe*). **4** *tr.* get as far as (*reached Lincoln at lunchtime*; *your letter reached me today*). **5** *tr.* get to or attain (a specified point) on a scale (*the temperature reached 90°*). **6** *intr.* (foll. by *to*) attain to; be adequate for (*my income will not reach to it*). **7** *tr.* succeed in achieving; attain (*have reached an agreement*). **8** *tr.* make contact with the hand, etc., or by telephone, etc. (*was out all day and could not be reached*). **9** *tr.* succeed in influencing or having the required effect on (*could not manage to reach their audience*). **10** *tr.* take with an outstretched hand. **11** *intr. Naut.* sail with the wind abeam or abaft the beam. • *n.* **1** the extent to which a hand, etc., can be reached out, influence exerted, motion carried out, or mental powers used. **2** an act of reaching out. **3** a continuous extent, esp. a stretch of river between two bends, or the part of a canal between locks. ▫ **out of reach** not able to be reached or attained. ▫▫ **reach•a•ble** *adj.*

re•ac•quaint /réeəkwáynt/ *v.tr. & refl.* (usu. foll. by *with*) make acquainted again. ▫▫ **re•ac•quaint•ance** *n.*

re•act /reeákt/ *v.* **1** *intr.* (foll. by *to*) respond to a stimulus; undergo a change or show behavior due to some influence (*how did they react to the news?*). **2** *intr.* (often foll. by *against*) be actuated by repulsion to; tend in a reverse or contrary direction. **3** *intr.* (often foll. by *upon*) produce a reciprocal or responsive effect; act upon the agent. **4** *intr.* (foll. by *with*) *Chem. & Physics* (of a substance or particle) be the cause of activity or interaction with another (*nitrous oxide reacts with the metal*). **5** *tr.* (foll. by *with*) *Chem.* cause (a substance) to react with another.

re•act•ant /reeáktənt/ *n. Chem.* a substance that takes part in, and undergoes change during, a reaction.

re•ac•tion /reeákshən/ *n.* **1** the act or an instance of reacting; a responsive or reciprocal action. **2 a** a responsive feeling (*what was your reaction to the news?*). **b** an immediate or first impression. **3** the occurrence of a condition after a period of its opposite. **4** a bodily response to an external stimulus. **5** a tendency to oppose change or to advocate return to a former system. **6** the interaction of substances undergoing chemical change. **7** propulsion by emitting a jet of particles, etc., in the direction opposite to that of the intended motion.

re•ac•tion•ar•y /reeákshəneree/ *adj. & n.* • *adj.* tending to oppose change and advocate return to a former system. • *n.* (*pl.* **-ies**) a reactionary person.

re•ac•ti•vate /reeáktivayt/ *v.tr.* restore to a state of activity. ▫▫ **re•ac•ti•va•tion** /–váyshən/ *n.*

re•ac•tive /reeáktiv/ *adj.* **1** showing reaction. **2** of or relating to reactance. ▫▫ **re•ac•tiv•i•ty** /–tívitee/ *n.*

re•ac•tor /reeáktər/ *n.* **1** a person or thing that reacts. **2** (in full **nuclear reactor**) an apparatus or structure in which a controlled nuclear chain reaction releases energy.

read /reed/ *v. & n.* • *v.* (*past* and *past part.* **read** /red/) **1** *tr.* (also *absol.*) reproduce mentally or (often foll. by *aloud*, *out*, *off*, etc.) vocally the written or printed words of (a book, author, etc.). **2** *tr.* convert or be able to convert into the intended words or meaning (written or other symbols or the things expressed in this way). **3** *tr.* interpret mentally. **4** *tr.* deduce or declare an interpretation of (*read the expression on my face*). **5** *tr.* (often foll. by *that* + clause) find (a thing) recorded or stated in print, etc. (*I read somewhere that you are leaving*). **6** *tr.* interpret (a statement or action) in a certain sense (*my silence is not to be read as consent*). **7** *tr.* (often foll. by *into*) assume as intended or deducible (*you read too much into my letter*). **8** *tr.* bring into a specified state by reading (*read myself to sleep*). **9** *tr.* (of a meter or other recording instrument) show (a specified figure, etc.). **10** *intr.* convey meaning in a specified manner when read (*it reads persuasively*). **11** *intr.* sound or affect a hearer or reader as specified when read (*the book reads like a parody*). **12** *intr.* carry out a course of study by reading (*is reading for the bar*). **13** *tr.* (as **read** /red/ *adj.*) versed in a subject by reading (*a well-read person*). **14** *tr.* **a** (of a computer) copy or transfer (data). **b** (foll. by *in*, *out*) enter or extract (data) in an electronic storage device. **15** *tr.* **a** understand or interpret (a person) by hearing words or seeing signs, gestures, etc. **b** interpret (cards, a person's hand, etc.) as a fortune teller. **c** interpret (the sky) as an astrologer or meteorologist. **16** *tr. Printing* check the correctness of and emend (a proof). **17** *tr.* (of a text) give as the word or words probably used or intended by an author. • *n. colloq.* a book, etc., as regards its readability (*is a really good read*). ▫ **read a person like a book** understand a person's motives, etc. **read between the lines** look for or find hidden meaning. **read lips** determine what is being said by a person who cannot be heard by studying the movements of the speaker's lips.

read•a•ble /réedəbəl/ *adj.* **1** able to be read; legible. **2** interesting or pleasant to read. ▫▫ **read•a•bil•i•ty** /–bílitee/ *n.* **read•a•bly** *adv.*

re•a•dapt /réeədápt/ *v.intr. & tr.* become or cause to become adapted anew. ▫▫ **re•ad•ap•ta•tion** /rée-adaptáyshən/ *n.*

re•ad•dress /réeədrés/ *v.tr.* **1** change the address of (a letter or parcel). **2** address (a problem, etc.) anew. **3** speak or write to anew.

read·er /réedər/ *n.* **1** a person who reads or is reading. **2** a book of extracts for learning. **3** a device for producing an image that can be read from microfilm, etc. **4** a publisher's employee who reports on submitted manuscripts. **5** a printer's proof-corrector. **6** a person appointed to read aloud, esp. parts of a service in a church.

read·er·ship /réedərship/ *n.* **1** the readers of a newspaper, etc. **2** the number or extent of these.

read·i·ly /réd'lee/ *adv.* **1** without showing reluctance; willingly. **2 a** without difficulty. **b** without delay.

read·ing /réeding/ *n.* **1 a** the act or an instance of reading (*the reading of the will*) . **b** matter to be read (*have plenty of reading with me*). **c** the specified quality of this (*it made exciting reading*). **2** (in *comb.*) used for reading (*reading lamp* ; *reading room*). **3** literary knowledge (*a person of wide reading*). **4** an entertainment at which a play, poems, etc., are read (*poetry reading*). **5** a figure, etc., shown by a recording instrument. **6** an interpretation or view taken. **7** an interpretation made (of drama, music, etc.).

re·ad·just /réeəjúst/ *v.tr.* adjust again or to a former state. □□ **re·ad·just·ment** *n.*

re·ad·mit /réeədmít/ *v.tr.* (**readmitted, readmitting**) admit again. □□ **re·ad·mis·sion** /–admíshən/ *n.*

read-on·ly *adj. Computing* (of a memory) able to be read at high speed but not capable of being changed by program instructions (cf. READ-WRITE).

re·a·dopt /réeədópt/ *v.tr.* adopt again. □□ **re·a·dop·tion** *n.*

read·out /réedowt/ *n.* **1** display of information, as on a gauge, etc. **2** the information displayed.

read-write *adj. Computing* capable of reading existing data and accepting alterations or further input (cf. READ-ONLY).

read·y /rédee/ *adj. & v.* • *adj.* (**readier, readiest**) (usu. *predic.*) **1** with preparations complete (*dinner is ready*). **2** in a fit state (*are you ready to go?*). **3** willing, inclined, or resolved (*he is always ready to complain*; *I am ready for anything*). **4** within reach; easily secured (*a ready source of income*). **5** fit for immediate use (*was ready to hand*). **6** immediate; unqualified (*found ready acceptance*). **7** prompt (*is always ready with excuses*). **8** (foll. by *to* + infin.) about to do something (*a bud just ready to burst*). **9** provided beforehand. • *v.tr.* (**-ies, -ied**) make ready; prepare. □ **at the ready** ready for action. **make ready** prepare. **ready, steady** (or **get set**), **go** the usual formula for starting a race. □□ **read·i·ness** *n.*

read·y-made *adj.* **1** made in a standard size, not to measure. **2** already available; convenient (*a ready-made excuse*).

read·y mon·ey *n.* **1** available cash. **2** payment on the spot.

read·y-to-wear *adj.* made in a standard size, not to measure.

re·af·firm /réeəfórm/ *v.tr.* affirm again. □□ **re·af·fir·ma·tion** /–afərmáyshən/ *n.*

re·a·gent /ree-áyjənt/ *n. Chem.* **1** a substance used to cause a reaction, esp. to detect another substance. **2** a reactive substance or force.

re·al[1] /reel/ *adj. & adv.* • *adj.* **1** actually existing or occurring. **2** genuine; rightly so called; not artificial. **3** *Law* consisting of or relating to immovable property such as land or houses (*real estate*) (cf. PERSONAL PROPERTY). **4** appraised by purchasing power; adjusted for changes in the value of money (*real value*). **5** *Philos.* having an absolute and necessary and not merely contingent existence. **6** *Math.* (of a quantity) having no imaginary part (see IMAGINARY 2). • *adv. colloq.* really, very.

re·al[2] /rayaál/ *n.* **1** the chief monetary unit of Brazil since 1994. **2** *hist.* a former coin and monetary unit of various Spanish-speaking countries.

re·al es·tate *n.* property, esp. land and buildings.

re·a·lign /réeəlín/ *v.tr.* **1** align again. **2** regroup in politics, etc. □□ **re·a·lign·ment** *n.*

re·al·ism /réeəlizəm/ *n.* **1** the practice of regarding things in their true nature and dealing with them as they are. **2** fidelity to nature in representation; the showing of life, etc., as it is in fact. **3** *Philos.* **a** the doctrine that universals or abstract concepts have an objective existence. **b** the belief that matter as an object of perception has real existence. □□ **re·al·ist** *n.*

re·al·is·tic /réeəlístik/ *adj.* **1** regarding things as they are; following a policy of realism. **2** based on facts rather than ideals. □□ **re·al·is·ti·cal·ly** *adv.*

re·al·i·ty /reeálitee/ *n.* (*pl.* **-ties**) **1** what is real or existent or underlies appearances. **2** (foll. by *of*) the real nature of. **3** real existence; the state of being real. **4** resemblance to an original. □ **in reality** in fact.

re·al·ize /réeəlīz/ *v.tr.* **1** (often foll. by *that* + clause) (also *absol.*) be fully aware of; conceive as real. **2** (also *absol.*) understand clearly. **3** present as real (*the story was powerfully realized on stage*). **4** convert into actuality; achieve (*realized a childhood dream*). **5 a** convert into money. **b** acquire (profit). **c** be sold for (a specified price). □□ **re·al·i·za·ble** *adj.* **re·al·i·za·tion** *n.* **re·al·iz·er** *n.*

re·al life *n.* that lived by actual people, as distinct from fiction, drama, etc.

re·al live *(attrib.)* often as **joc.** actual; not pretended or simulated (*a real live burglar*).

re·al·lo·cate /rée-áləkayt/ *v.tr.* allocate again or differently. □□ **re·al·lo·ca·tion** /–káyshən/ *n.*

re·al·ly /réeəlee, réelee/ *adv.* **1** in reality. **2** positively; assuredly (*really useful*). **3** indeed; I assure you. **4** an expression of mild protest or surprise. **5** (in *interrog.*) is that so? (*They're musicians. — Really?*).

realm /relm/ *n.* **1** *formal* esp. *Law* a kingdom. **2** a sphere or domain (*the realm of imagination*).

re·al mon·ey *n.* **1** current coin or notes; cash. **2** large amount of money.

re·al·po·li·tik /rayaálpōliteék/ *n.* politics based on realities and material needs, rather than on morals or ideals.

re·al time *n.* the actual time during which a process or event occurs. □□ **re·al-time** (*attrib. adj.*)

re·al-time *adj. Computing* (of a system) in which the response time is of the order of milliseconds, e.g., in an airline booking system.

re·al·tor /réeəltər/ *n.* a real estate agent, esp. (**Realtor**) a member of the National Association of Realtors.

re·al·ty /réeəltee/ *n. Law* real estate (opp. PERSONALTY).

ream[1] /reem/ *n.* **1** twenty quires of paper. **2** (in *pl.*) a large quantity of paper or writing (*wrote reams about it*).

ream[2] /reem/ *v.tr.* **1** widen (a hole in metal, etc.) with a borer. **2** turn over the edge of (a cartridge case, etc.). **3** squeeze the juice from (fruit). □□ **ream·er** *n.*

re·an·i·mate /rée-ánimayt/ *v.tr.* **1** restore to life. **2** restore to activity or liveliness. □□ **re·an·i·ma·tion** /–máyshən/ *n.*

reap /reep/ *v.tr.* **1** cut or gather (a crop, esp. grain) as a harvest. **2** harvest the crop of (a field, etc.). **3** receive as the consequence of one's own or others' actions.

reap·er /réepər/ *n.* **1** a person who reaps. **2** a machine for reaping. □ **the reaper** (or **grim reaper**) death personified.

re·ap·pear /réeəpéer/ *v.intr.* appear again or as previously. □□ **re·ap·pear·ance** *n.*

re·ap·ply /réeəplí/ *v.tr. & intr.* (**-plies, -plied**) apply again, esp. submit a further application (for a position, etc.). □□ **re·ap·pli·ca·tion** /rée-aplikáyshən/ *n.*

---

re·ap·point /réeəpóynt/ *v.tr.* appoint again to a position previously held. □□ **re·ap·point·ment** *n.*

re·ap·por·tion /réeəpáwrshən/ *v.tr.* apportion again or differently. □□ **re·ap·por·tion·ment** *n.*

re·ap·praise /réeəpráyz/ *v.tr.* appraise or assess again. □□ **re·ap·prais·al** *n.*

rear[1] /reer/ *n. & adj.* •*n.* **1** the back part of anything. **2** the space behind, or position at the back of, anything (*a large house with a terrace at the rear*). **3** the hindmost part of an army or fleet. **4** *colloq.* the buttocks. •*adj.* at the back. □ **bring up the rear** come last.

rear[2] /reer/ *v.* **1** *tr.* **a** bring up and educate (children). **b** breed and care for (animals). **c** cultivate (crops). **2** *intr.* (of a horse, etc.) raise itself on its hind legs. **3** *tr.* **a** set upright. **b** build. **c** hold upward (*rear one's head*). **4** *intr.* extend to a great height. □□ **rear·er** *n.*

rear ad·mi·ral *n.* a naval officer ranking below vice admiral.

rear guard *n.* **1** a body of troops detached to protect the rear, esp. in retreats. **2** a defensive or conservative element in an organization, etc.

rear·guard ac·tion *n.* **1** *Mil.* an engagement undertaken by a rear guard. **2** a defensive stand in argument, etc., esp. when losing.

re·arm /rée-áarm/ *v.tr.* (also *absol.*) arm again, esp. with improved weapons. □□ **re·ar·ma·ment** *n.*

rear·most /réermōst/ *adj.* furthest back.

re·ar·range /réeəráynj/ *v.tr.* arrange again in a different way. □□ **re·ar·range·ment** *n.*

re·ar·rest /réeərést/ *v. & n.* •*v.tr.* arrest again. •*n.* an instance of rearresting or being rearrested.

rear·ward /réerwərd/ *n., adj., & adv.* •*n.* rear, esp. in prepositional phrases (*to the rearward of; in the rearward*). •*adj.* to the rear. •*adv.* (also **rear·wards**) toward the rear.

rea·son /réezən/ *n. & v.* •*n.* **1** a motive, cause, or justification (*there is no reason to be angry*). **2** a fact adduced or serving as this (*I can give you my reasons*). **3** the intellectual faculty by which conclusions are drawn from premises. **4** sanity (*has lost his reason*). **5** *Logic* a premise of a syllogism, esp. a minor premise when given after the conclusion. **6** a faculty transcending the understanding and providing a priori principles; intuition. **7** sense; sensible conduct; what is right or practical or practicable; moderation. •*v.* **1** *intr.* form or try to reach conclusions by connected thought. **2** *intr.* (foll. by *with*) use an argument (with a person) by way of persuasion. **3** *tr.* (foll. by *that* + clause) conclude or assert in argument. **4** *tr.* (foll. by *why, whether, what* + clause) discuss; ask oneself. **5** *tr.* (foll. by *into, out of*) persuade or move by argument. **6** *tr.* (foll. by *out*) think or work out (consequences, etc.). **7** *tr.* (often as **reasoned** *adj.*) express in logical or argumentative form. **8** *tr.* embody reason in (an amendment, etc.). □ **by reason of** owing to. **in** (or **within**) **reason** within the bounds of moderation. **it stands to reason** (often foll. by *that* + clause) it is evident or logical. **listen to reason** be persuaded to act sensibly. □□ **rea·son·er** *n.* **rea·son·ing** *n.*

▶**Reason** means 'cause or basis,' and it is redundant to say "the reason is because"; the preferred usage is *the reason is that*: *The reason the car won't start is that* (not *because*) *the battery cable came loose.*

rea·son·a·ble /réezənəbəl/ *adj.* **1** having sound judgment; moderate; ready to listen to reason. **2** not absurd. **3 a** not greatly less or more than might be expected. **b** inexpensive. **c** tolerable; fair. □□ **rea·son·a·ble·ness** *n.* **rea·son·a·bly** *adv.*

re·as·sem·ble /réeəsémbəl/ *v.intr. & tr.* assemble again or into a former state. □□ **re·as·sem·bly** *n.*

re·as·sert /réeəsə́rt/ *v.tr.* assert again. □□ **re·as·ser·tion** /–sə́rshən/ *n.*

re·as·sess /réeəsés/ *v.tr.* assess again, esp. differently. □□ **re·as·sess·ment** *n.*

re·as·sign /réeəsín/ *v.tr.* assign again or differently. □□ **re·as·sign·ment** *n.*

re·as·sure /réeəshŏŏr/ *v.tr.* **1** restore confidence to; dispel the apprehensions of. **2** confirm in an opinion or impression. □□ **re·as·sur·ance** *n.* **re·as·sur·ing** *adj.* **re·as·sur·ing·ly** *adv.*

re·at·tach /réeətách/ *v.tr.* attach again or in a former position. □□ **re·at·tach·ment** *n.*

re·at·tempt /réeətémpt/ *v.tr.* attempt again, esp. after failure.

Ré·au·mur /ráyōmyŏŏr/ *adj.* expressed in or related to the scale of temperature at which water freezes at 0 and boils 80 under standard conditions.

reave /reev/ *v.* (*past* and *past part.* **reaved** or **reft** /reft/) *archaic* **1** *tr.* **a** (foll. by *of*) forcibly deprive of. **b** (foll. by *away, from*) take by force or carry off. **2** *intr.* make raids; plunder.

re·a·wak·en /réeəwáykən/ *v.tr. & intr.* awaken again.

re·bar·ba·tive /reebaárbətiv/ *adj. literary* repellent; unattractive.

re·bate[1] /réebayt/ *n. & v.* •*n.* **1** a partial refund. **2** a deduction from a sum to be paid; a discount. •*v.tr.* pay back as a rebate.

re·bate[2] /réebayt/ *n. & v.tr.* = RABBET.

re·bec /réebek/ *n.* (also **re·beck**) *Mus.* a medieval usu. three-stringed instrument played with a bow.

reb·el *n., adj., & v.* •*n.* /rébəl/ **1** a person who fights against, resists, or refuses allegiance to, the established government. **2** a person or thing that resists authority or control. •*adj.* /rébəl/ (*attrib.*) **1** rebellious. **2** of or concerning rebels. **3** in rebellion. •*v.intr.* /ribél/ (**re·belled, re·bel·ling**) (usu. foll. by *against*) **1** act as a rebel; revolt. **2** feel or display repugnance.

re·bel·lion /ribélyən/ *n.* open resistance to authority, esp. organized armed resistance to an established government.

re·bel·lious /ribélyəs/ *adj.* **1** tending to rebel. **2** in rebellion. **3** defying authority. **4** (of a thing) unmanageable; refractory. □□ **re·bel·lious·ly** *adv.* **re·bel·lious·ness** *n.*

re·bind /réebínd/ *v.tr.* (*past* and *past part.* **rebound**) bind (esp. a book) again or differently.

re·birth /réebə́rth/ *n.* **1** a new incarnation. **2** spiritual enlightenment. **3** a revival (*the rebirth of learning*). □□ **re·born** /réebáwrn/ *adj.*

re·boot /réebŏŏt/ *v.tr.* (often *absol.*) *Computing* start (a system) again.

re·bore *v. & n.* •*v.tr.* /réebáwr/ make a new boring in, esp. widen the bore of (the cylinder in an internal combustion engine).•*n.* /réebawr/ **1** the process of doing this. **2** a rebored engine.

re·bound[1] *v. & n.* •*v.intr.* /ribównd/ **1** spring back after action or impact. **2** (foll. by *upon*) (of an action) have an adverse effect upon (the doer). •*n.* /réebownd/ **1** the act or an instance of rebounding; recoil. **2** a reaction after a strong emotion. □ **on the rebound** while still recovering from an emotional shock, esp. rejection by a lover.

re·bound[2] /réebównd/ *past* and *past part.* of REBIND.

re·broad·cast /réebráwdkast/ *v. & n.* •*v.tr.* (*past* **rebroadcast** or **rebroadcasted**; *past part.* **rebroadcast**) broadcast again. •*n.* a repeat broadcast.

re·buff /ribúf/ *n. & v.* •*n.* **1** a rejection of one who makes advances, proffers help or sympathy, shows interest, makes a request, etc. **2** a repulse; a snub. •*v.tr.* give a rebuff to.

re·build /réebíld/ *v.tr.* (*past* and *past part.* **rebuilt**) build again or differently.

re·buke /ribyŏŏk/ *v. & n.* •*v.tr.* reprove sharply; subject to protest or censure. • *n.* **1** the act of rebuking. **2** the process of being rebuked. **3** a reproof.

re·bus /réebəs/ *n.* an enigmatic representation of a word (esp. a name), by pictures, etc., suggesting its parts.

re·but /ribút/ *v.tr.* (**rebutted, rebutting**) **1** refute or disprove (evidence or a charge). **2** force or turn back; check. ▫▫ **re·but·ta·ble** *adj.* **re·but·tal** *n.*

re·cal·ci·trant /rikálsitrənt/ *adj.* & *n.* • *adj.* **1** obstinately disobedient. **2** objecting to restraint. • *n.* a recalcitrant person. ▫▫ **re·cal·ci·trance** *n.* **re·cal·ci·trant·ly** *adv.*

re·cal·cu·late /reékálkyəlayt/ *v.tr.* calculate again. ▫▫ **re·cal·cu·la·tion** /–láyshən/ *n.*

re·call /rikáwl/ *v.* & *n.* • *v.tr.* **1** summon to return from a place, a different occupation, inattention, etc. **2** recollect; remember. **3** bring back to memory; serve as a reminder of. **4** revoke or annul (an action or decision). **5** cancel or suspend the appointment of (an official sent overseas, etc.). **6** revive; resuscitate. **7** take back (a gift). • *n.* (also /réekawl/) **1** the act or an instance of recalling, esp. a summons to come back. **2** the act of remembering. **3** the ability to remember. **4** the possibility of recalling, esp. in the sense of revoking (*beyond recall*). **5** removal of an elected official from office. **6** a request from a manufacturer that consumers return a product for repair, replacement, etc. ▫▫ **re·call·a·ble** *adj.*

re·cant /rikánt/ *v.* **1** *tr.* withdraw and renounce (a former belief or statement) as erroneous or heretical. **2** *intr.* disavow a former opinion, esp. wtih a public confession on error. ▫▫ **re·can·ta·tion** /réekantáyshən/ *n.*

re·cap /réekap/ *v.* & *n. colloq.* • *v.tr.* & *intr.* (**recapped, recapping**) recapitulate. • *n.* recapitulation.

re·cap·i·tal·ize /reekápitəlīz/ *v.tr.* capitalize (shares, etc.) again. ▫▫ **re·cap·i·tal·i·za·tion** *n.*

re·ca·pit·u·late /réekəpíchəlayt/ *v.tr.* **1** go briefly through again; summarize. **2** go over the main points or headings of. ▫▫ **re·ca·pit·u·la·to·ry** /–lətáwree/ *adj.*

re·ca·pit·u·la·tion /réekəpíchəláyshən/ *n.* **1** the act or an instance of recapitulating. **2** *Biol.* the reappearance in embryos of successive type-forms in the evolutionary line of development. **3** *Mus.* part of a movement in which themes are restated.

re·cap·ture /réekápchər/ *v.* & *n.* • *v.tr.* **1** capture again; recover by capture. **2** reexperience (a past emotion, etc.). • *n.* the act or an instance of recapturing.

re·cast /réekást/ *v.* & *n.* • *v.tr.* (*past* and *past part.* **recast**) **1** put into a new form. **2** improve the arrangement of. **3** change the cast of (a play, etc.). • *n.* **1** the act or an instance of recasting. **2** a recast form.

re·cede /riseéd/ *v.intr.* **1** go or shrink back or further off. **2** be left at an increasing distance by an observer's motion. **3** slope backward (*a receding chin*). **4** decline in force or value. **5** (foll. by *from*) withdraw from (an engagement, opinion, etc.). **6** (of a man's hair) cease to grow at the front, sides, etc.

re·ceipt /riseét/ *n.* & *v.* • *n.* **1** the act or an instance of receiving or being received into one's possession. **2** a written acknowledgment of this, esp. of the payment of money. **3** (usu. in *pl.*) an amount of money, etc., received. • *v.tr.* place a written or printed receipt on (a bill).

re·ceive /riseév/ *v.tr.* **1** take or accept (something offered or given) into one's hands or possession. **2** acquire; be provided with or given (*have received no news; will receive a small fee*). **3** accept delivery of (something sent). **4** have conferred or inflicted on one (*received a heavy blow to the head*). **5 a** stand the force or weight of. **b** bear up against; encounter with opposition. **6** consent to hear (a confession or oath) or consider (a petition). **7** (also *absol.*) accept stolen property (knowing of the theft). **8** admit; consent or prove able to hold; provide accommodation for (*received many visitors*). **9** (of a receptacle) be able to hold (a specified amount or contents). **10** greet or welcome, esp. in a specified manner (*how did they receive your offer?*). **11** entertain as a guest, etc. **12** admit to membership of a society, organization, etc. **13** be marked with (an impression, etc.). **14** convert (broadcast signals) into sound or pictures. **15 a** *Tennis* be the player to whom the server serves (the ball). **b** *Football* be the player or team to whom the ball is kicked or thrown. **16** (often as **received** *adj.*) give credit to; accept as authoritative or true (*received opinion*). ▫▫ **re·ceiv·a·ble** *adj.*

re·ceiv·er /riseévər/ *n.* **1** a person or thing that receives. **2** the part of a machine or instrument that receives sound, signals, etc. (esp. the part of a telephone that contains the earpiece). **3** a radio or television receiving apparatus. **4** a person who receives stolen goods. **5** *Football* an offensive player eligible to catch a forward pass.

re·ceiv·er·ship /riseévərship/ *n.* the state of being dealt with by a receiver (esp. *in receivership*).

re·cen·sion /risénshən/ *n.* **1** the revision of a text. **2** a particular form or version of a text resulting from such revision.

re·cent /réesənt/ *adj.* & *n.* • *adj.* **1** not long past; that happened, appeared, began to exist, or existed lately. **2** not long established; lately begun; modern. **3** (**Recent**) *Geol.* = HOLOCENE. • *n.* (**Recent**) *Geol.* = HOLOCENE. ▫▫ **re·cen·cy** *n.* **re·cent·ly** *adv.* **re·cent·ness** *n.*

re·cep·ta·cle /riséptəkəl/ *n.* **1** a containing vessel, place, or space. **2** *Bot.* **a** the common base of floral organs. **b** the part of a leaf or thallus in some algae where the reproductive organs are situated.

re·cep·tion /risépshən/ *n.* **1** the act of receiving or the process of being received, esp. of a person into a place or group. **2** the manner in which a person or thing is received. **3** a social occasion for receiving guests, esp. after a wedding. **4** a formal or ceremonious welcome. **5** (also **reception desk**) a place where guests or clients, etc., report on arrival at a hotel, office, etc. **6 a** the receiving of broadcast signals. **b** the quality of this.

re·cep·tion·ist /risépshənist/ *n.* a person employed in a hotel, office, etc., to receive guests, clients, etc.

re·cep·tive /riséptiv/ *adj.* **1** able or quick to receive impressions or ideas. **2** concerned with receiving stimuli, etc. ▫▫ **re·cep·tive·ly** *adv.* **re·cep·tive·ness** *n.* **re·cep·tiv·i·ty** /réeseptívitee/ *n.*

re·cep·tor /riséptər/ *n.* (often *attrib.*) *Biol.* **1** an organ able to respond to an external stimulus such as light, heat, or a drug, and transmit a signal to a sensory nerve. **2** a region of a cell, tissue, etc., that responds to a molecule or other substance.

re·cess /réeses, risés/ *n.* & *v.* • *n.* **1** a space set back in a wall; a niche. **2** (often in *pl.*) a remote or secret place (*the innermost recesses*). **3** a temporary cessation from work, esp. of Congress, a court of law, or during a school day. • *v.* **1** *tr.* make a recess in. **2** *tr.* place in a recess. **3 a** *intr.* take a recess; adjourn. **b** *tr.* order a temporary cessation from the work of (a court, etc.).

re·ces·sion /riséshən/ *n.* **1** a temporary decline in economic activity or prosperity. **2** a receding or withdrawal from a place or point. **3** a receding part of an object; a recess. ▫▫ **re·ces·sion·ar·y** *adj.*

re·ces·sion·al /riséshənəl/ *adj.* & *n.* • *adj.* sung while the clergy and choir withdraw after a service. • *n.* a recessional hymn.

re·ces·sive /risésiv/ *adj.* **1** tending to recede. **2** *Phonet.* (of an accent) falling near the beginning of a word.

3 *Genetics* (of an inherited characteristic) appearing in offspring only when not masked by a dominant characteristic. ▫▫ **re·ces·sive·ly** *adv.* **re·ces·sive·ness** *n.*

re·charge *v.* & *n.* • *v.tr.* /réechaárj/ **1** charge again. **2** reload. • *n.* /réechaarj/ **1** a renewed charge. **2** material, etc., used for this. ▫▫ **re·charge·a·ble** *adj.*

re·check *v.* & *n.* • *v.tr.* & *intr.* /réechék/ check again. • *n.* /réechek/ a further check or inspection.

re·cher·ché /rəsháirsháy/ *adj.* **1** carefully sought out; rare or exotic. **2** far-fetched.

re·chris·ten /réekrísən/ *v.tr.* **1** christen again. **2** give a new name to.

re·cid·i·vist /risídivist/ *n.* a person who relapses into crime. ▫▫ **re·cid·i·vism** *n.*

rec·i·pe /résipee/ *n.* **1** a statement of the ingredients and procedure required for preparing cooked food. **2** an expedient; a device for achieving something. **3** a medical prescription.

re·cip·i·ent /risípeeənt/ *n.* & *adj.* • *n.* a person who receives something. • *adj.* **1** receiving. **2** receptive.

re·cip·ro·cal /risíprəkəl/ *adj.* & *n.* • *adj.* **1** in return (*offered a reciprocal greeting*). **2** mutual (*their feelings are reciprocal*). **3** *Gram.* (of a pronoun) expressing mutual action or relation (as in *each other*). **4** inversely correspondent; complementary. • *n.* *Math.* an expression or function so related to another that their product is one ($^1/_2$ is the reciprocal of 2). ▫▫ **re·cip·ro·cal·ly** *adv.*

re·cip·ro·cate /risíprəkayt/ *v.* **1** *tr.* return or requite (affection, etc.). **2** *intr.* (foll. by *with*) offer or give something in return (*reciprocated with an invitation to lunch*). **3** *tr.* give and receive mutually; interchange. **4 a** *intr.* (of a part of a machine) move backward and forward. **b** *tr.* cause to do this. ▫▫ **re·cip·ro·ca·tion** /–káyshən/ *n.*

rec·i·proc·i·ty /résiprósitee/ *n.* **1** the condition of being reciprocal. **2** mutual action. **3** give and take, esp. the interchange of privileges.

re·cir·cu·late /réesórkyəlayt/ *v.tr.* & *intr.* circulate again, esp. make available for reuse. ▫▫ **re·cir·cu·la·tion** /–láyshən/ *n.*

re·cit·al /rısít'l/ *n.* **1** the act or an instance of reciting or being recited. **2** the performance of a program of music by a solo instrumentalist or singer or by a small group. **3** (foll. by *of*) a detailed account of (connected things or facts); a narrative. ▫▫ **re·cit·al·ist** *n.*

rec·i·ta·tion /résitáyshən/ *n.* **1** the act or an instance of reciting. **2** a thing recited.

rec·i·ta·tive /résitəteév/ *n.* **1** musical declamation of the kind usual in the narrative and dialogue parts of opera and oratorio. **2** the words or part given in this form.

re·cite /risít/ *v.* **1** *tr.* repeat aloud or declaim (a poem or passage) from memory. **2** *intr.* give a recitation. **3** *tr.* enumerate. ▫▫ **re·cit·er** *n.*

reck·less /réklis/ *adj.* disregarding the consequences or danger, etc.; rash. ▫▫ **reck·less·ly** *adv.* **reck·less·ness** *n.*

reck·on /rékən/ *v.* **1** *tr.* count or compute by calculation. **2** *tr.* (foll. by *in*) count in or include in computation. **3** *tr.* (often foll. by *as* or *to be*) consider or regard. **4** *tr.* **a** (foll. by *that* + clause) be of the considered opinion. **b** *colloq.* (foll. by *to* + infin.) expect (*reckons to finish by Friday*). **5** *intr.* make calculations; add up an account or sum. **6** *intr.* (foll. by *on*, *upon*) rely on, count on, or base plans on. **7** *intr.* (foll. by *with*) **a** take into account. **b** settle accounts with. **8** *US dial.* think; suppose (*I reckon I'll just stay home tonight*). ▫ **reckon up 1** count up; find the total of. **2** settle accounts. **to be reckoned with** of considerable importance; not to be ignored.

reckon Old English *(ge)recenian* 'recount, relate,' of West Germanic origin; related to Dutch *rekenen* and German *rechnen* 'to count (up).' Early senses included 'give an account of items received' and 'mention things in order,' which gave rise to the notion of 'calculation' and hence of 'coming to a conclusion.'

reck·on·ing /rékəning/ *n.* **1** the act or an instance of counting or calculating. **2** a consideration or opinion. **3 a** the settlement of an account. **b** an account.

re·claim /rikláym/ *v.* & *n.* • *v.tr.* **1** seek the return of (one's property). **2** claim in return or as a rebate, etc. **3** bring under cultivation, esp. from a state of being under water. **4 a** win back or away from vice or error or a waste condition. **b** tame; civilize. • *n.* the act or an instance of reclaiming; the process of being reclaimed. ▫▫ **re·claim·a·ble** *adj.* **rec·la·ma·tion** /rékləmáyshən/ *n.*

re·clas·si·fy /réeklásifī/ *v.tr.* (**-fies, -fied**) classify again or differently. ▫▫ **re·clas·si·fi·ca·tion** /–fikáyshən/ *n.*

rec·li·nate /réklinayt/ *adj.* *Bot.* bending downward.

re·cline /riklín/ *v.* **1** *intr.* assume or be in a horizontal or leaning position, esp. in resting. **2** *tr.* cause to recline or move from the vertical.

re·clin·er /riklínər/ *n.* **1** a comfortable chair for reclining in. **2** a person who reclines.

re·clothe /réeklóth/ *v.tr.* clothe again or differently.

rec·luse /réklōōs, riklóōs/ *n.* & *adj.* • *n.* a person given to or living in seclusion or isolation, esp. as a religious discipline. • *adj.* favoring seclusion; solitary. ▫▫ **re·clu·sion** /riklóōzhən/ *n.* **re·clu·sive** *adj.*

rec·og·ni·tion /rékəgníshən/ *n.* the act or an instance of recognizing or being recognized.

re·cog·ni·zance /rikógnizəns/ *n.* **1** a bond by which a person undertakes before a court, etc., to observe some condition, e.g., to appear when summoned. **2** a sum pledged as surety for this.

re·cog·ni·zant /rikógnizənt/ *adj.* (usu. foll. by *of*) **1** showing recognition (of a favor, etc.). **2** conscious or showing consciousness (of something).

rec·og·nize /rékəgnīz/ *v.tr.* **1** identify as already known. **2** realize or discover the nature of. **3** (foll. by *that*) realize or admit. **4** acknowledge the existence, validity, character, or claims of. **5** show appreciation of; reward. **6** (foll. by *as*, *for*) treat or acknowledge. **7** (of a chairperson, etc.) allow (a person) to speak in a debate, etc. ▫▫ **rec·og·niz·a·ble** *adj.* **rec·og·niz·a·bly** *adv.*

re·coil /rikóyl/ *v.* & *n.* • *v.intr.* **1** suddenly move or spring back in fear, horror, or disgust. **2** shrink mentally in this way. **3** rebound after an impact. **4** (foll. by *on*, *upon*) have an adverse reactive effect on (the originator). **5** (of a gun) be driven backward by its discharge. **6** retreat under an enemy's attack. • *n.* (also /rée koyl/) **1** the act or an instance of recoiling. **2** the sensation of recoiling.

rec·ol·lect /rékəlékt/ *v.tr.* **1** remember. **2** succeed in remembering; call to mind.

re·col·lect /réekəlékt/ *v.tr.* **1** collect again. **2** (*refl.*) recover control of (oneself).

rec·ol·lec·tion /rékəlékshən/ *n.* **1** the act or power of recollecting. **2** a thing recollected. **3 a** a person's memory (*to the best of my recollection*). **b** the time over which memory extends (*happened within my recollection*). ▫▫ **rec·ol·lec·tive** *adj.*

re·col·o·nize /réekólənīz/ *v.tr.* colonize again. ▫▫ **re·co·lo·ni·za·tion** *n.*

re·com·bi·na·tion /réekombináyshən/ *n.* *Biol.* the rearrangement, esp. by crossing over in chromosomes, of nucleic acid molecules forming a new sequence of the constituent nucleotides.

re·com·bine /réekəmbín/ *v.tr.* & *intr.* combine again or differently.

re·com·mence /réekəméns/ *v.tr.* & *intr.* begin again. ▫▫ **re·com·mence·ment** *n.*

rec·om·mend /rékəménd/ *v.tr.* **1 a** suggest as fit for some purpose or use. **b** suggest (a person) as suitable for a particular position. **2** (often foll. by *that* + clause or *to* + infin.) advise as a course of action, etc. **3** (of qualities, conduct, etc.) make acceptable or desirable. ◻◻ **rec·om·mend·a·ble** *adj.* **rec·om·men·da·tion** *n.*

rec·om·pense /rékəmpens/ *v. & n.* •*v.tr.* **1** make amends to (a person) or for (a loss, etc.). **2** requite; reward or punish (a person or action). •*n.* **1** a reward; requital. **2** retribution.

rec·on·cile /rékənsīl/ *v.tr.* **1** make friendly again after an estrangement. **2** (usu. in *refl.* or *passive*; foll. by *to*) make acquiescent or contentedly submissive to (something disagreeable) (*was reconciled to failure*). **3** settle (a quarrel, etc.). **4** harmonize; make compatible. ◻◻ **rec·on·cil·a·ble** *adj.* **rec·on·cil·i·a·tion** /–sileeáyshən/ *n.*

rec·on·dite /rékəndīt, rikón–/ *adj.* **1** (of a subject or knowledge) abstruse; out of the way; little known. **2** (of an author or style) dealing in abstruse knowledge or allusions; obscure.

re·con·di·tion /réekəndíshən/ *v.tr.* **1** overhaul; refit; renovate. **2** make usable again.

re·con·fig·ure /réekənfigyər/ *v.tr.* configure again or differently. ◻◻ **re·con·fig·u·ra·tion** *n.*

re·con·firm /réekənfə́rm/ *v.tr.* confirm, establish, or ratify anew. ◻◻ **re·con·fir·ma·tion** /–konfərmáyshən/ *n.*

re·con·nais·sance /rikónisəns/ *n.* **1** a survey of a region, esp. to locate an enemy or ascertain strategic features. **2** a preliminary survey.

re·con·nect /réekənékt/ *v.tr.* connect again. ◻◻ **re·con·nec·tion** /–nékshən/ *n.*

re·con·noi·ter /réekənóytər, rékə–/ *v. & n.* •*v.* **1** *tr.* make a reconnaissance of. **2** *intr.* make a reconnaissance. •*n.* a reconnaissance.

re·con·quer /réekóngkər/ *v.tr.* conquer again. ◻◻ **re·con·quest** *n.*

re·con·sid·er /réekənsídər/ *v.tr. & intr.* consider again, esp. for a possible change of decision. ◻◻ **re·con·sid·er·a·tion** *n.*

re·con·sti·tute /réekónstitōōt, –tyōōt/ *v.tr.* **1** reconstruct. **2** reorganize. **3** restore the previous constitution of (dried food, etc.) by adding water. ◻◻ **re·con·sti·tu·tion** / –tōōshən/ *n.*

re·con·struct /réekənstrúkt/ *v.tr.* **1** build or form again. **2 a** form a mental or visual impression of (past events) by assembling the evidence for them. **b** reenact (a crime). **3** reorganize. ◻◻ **re·con·struc·tion** /–strúkshən/ *n.* **re·con·struc·tive** *adj.*

re·con·vene /réekənvéen/ *v.tr. & intr.* convene again, esp. after a pause in proceedings.

re·con·vert /réekənvə́rt/ *v.tr.* convert back to a former state. ◻◻ **re·con·ver·sion** /–və́rzhən/ *n.*

re·cord *n. & v.* •*n.* /rékərd/ **1 a** a piece of evidence or information constituting an account of something that has occurred, been said, etc. **b** a document preserving this. **2** the state of being set down or preserved in writing or some other permanent form (*is a matter of record*). **3 a** (in full **phonograph record**) a thin plastic disk carrying recorded sound in grooves on each surface, for reproduction by a record player. **b** a trace made on this or some other medium, e.g., magnetic tape. **4 a** an official report of the proceedings and judgment in a court of justice. **b** a copy of the pleadings, etc., constituting a case to be decided by a court. **5 a** the facts known about a person's past (*has an honorable record of service*). **b** a list of a person's previous criminal convictions. **6** the best performance (esp. in sport) or most remarkable event of its kind on record (often *attrib.*: *a record attempt*). **7** an object serving as a memorial; a portrait. **8** *Computing* a number of related items of information which are handled as a unit. •*v.tr.* /rikáwrd/ **1** set down in writing or some other permanent form for later reference. **2** convert (sound, a broadcast, etc.) into permanent form for later reproduction. **3** establish or constitute a historical or other record of. ◻ **for the record** as an official statement, etc. **go on record** state one's opinion openly, so that it is recorded. **a matter of record** a thing established as a fact by being recorded. **off the record** as an unofficial or confidential statement, etc. **put** (or **get** or **set**, etc.) **the record straight** correct a misapprehension. ◻◻ **re·cord·a·ble** *adj.*

---

record Middle English: from Old French *record* 'remembrance,' from *recorder* 'bring to remembrance,' from Latin *recordari* 'remember,' based on *cor*, *cord*- 'heart.' The noun was earliest used in law to denote the fact of something being written down as evidence. The verb originally meant 'narrate orally or in writing,' also 'repeat so as to commit to memory.'

---

re·cord·er /rikáwrdər/ *n.* **1** an apparatus for recording, esp. a tape recorder. **2 a** a keeper of records. **b** a person who makes an official record. **3** *Mus.* a woodwind instrument like a flute but blown through the end and having a more hollow tone.

re·cord·ing /rikáwrding/ *n.* **1** the process by which audio or video signals are recorded for later reproduction. **2** material or a program recorded.

re·cord·ist /rikáwrdist/ *n.* a person who records sound.

rec·ord play·er *n.* an apparatus for reproducing sound from phonograph records.

re·count[1] /rikównt/ *v.tr.* **1** narrate. **2** tell in detail.

re·count[2] /réekównt/ *v. & n.* •*v. tr.* count again. •*n.* /réekownt/ a recounting, esp. of votes in an election.

re·coup /rikōōp/ *v.tr.* **1** recover or regain (a loss). **2** compensate or reimburse for a loss. **3** *Law* deduct or keep back (part of a sum due). ◻ **recoup oneself** recover a loss. ◻◻ **re·coup·a·ble** *adj.* **re·coup·ment** *n.*

re·course /réekawrs, rikáwrs/ *n.* **1** resorting to a possible source of help. **2** a person or thing resorted to. ◻ **have recourse to** turn to (a person or thing) for help.

re·cov·er /rikúvər/ *v.* **1** *tr.* regain possession or use or control of; reclaim. **2** *intr.* return to health or consciousness or to a normal state or position. **3** *tr.* obtain or secure (compensation, etc.) by legal process. **4** *tr.* retrieve or make up for (a loss, setback, etc.). **5** *refl.* regain composure or consciousness or control of one's limbs. **6** *tr.* retrieve (reusable substances) from industrial waste. ◻◻ **re·cov·er·a·ble** *adj.*

re-cov·er /réekúvər/ *v.tr.* **1** cover again. **2** provide (a chair, etc.) with a new cover.

re·cov·er·y /rikúvəree/ *n.* (*pl.* **-ies**) **1** the act or an instance of recovering; the process of being recovered. **2** *Golf* a stroke bringing the ball out of a bunker, etc.

rec·re·ant /rékreeənt/ *adj. & n. literary*• *adj.* **1** craven; cowardly. **2** apostate. •*n.* **1** a coward. **2** an apostate. ◻◻ **rec·re·an·cy** *n.* **rec·re·ant·ly** *adv.*

re-cre·ate /réekree-áyt/ *v.tr.* create over again. ◻◻ **re-cre·a·tion** *n.*

rec·re·a·tion /rékree-áyshən/ *n.* **1** the process or means of refreshing or entertaining oneself. **2** a pleasurable activity. ◻◻ **rec·re·a·tion·al** *adj.* **rec·re·a·tion·al·ly** *adv.* **rec·re·a·tive** /rekreeáytiv/ *adj.*

re·crim·i·nate /rikríminayt/ *v.intr.* make mutual or counter accusations. ◻◻ **re·crim·i·na·tion** /–náyshən/ *n.* **re·crim·i·na·to·ry** /–nətawree/ *adj.*

re·cross /réekráws, –krós/ *v.tr. & intr.* cross or pass over again.

re·cru·desce /réekrōōdés/ *v.intr.* (of a disease or difficulty, etc.) break out again. ◻◻ **re·cru·des·cence** *n.* **re·cru·des·cent** *adj.*

---

re·cruit /rikrṓot/ *n. & v.* • *n.* **1** a serviceman or servicewoman newly enlisted and not yet fully trained. **2** a new member of a society or organization. **3** a beginner. • *v.* **1** *tr.* enlist (a person) as a recruit. **2** *tr.* form (an army, etc.) by enlisting recruits. **3** *intr.* get or seek recruits. **4** *tr.* replenish or reinvigorate (numbers, strength, etc.). □□ **re·cruit·er** *n.* **re·cruit·ment** *n.*

re·crys·tal·lize /re͞ekrístəlīz/ *v.tr. & intr.* crystallize again. □□ **re·crys·tal·li·za·tion** *n.*

rec·ta *pl.* of RECTUM.

rec·tal /réktəl/ *adj.* of or by means of the rectum. □□ **rec·tal·ly** *adv.*

rec·tan·gle /réktanggəl/ *n.* a plane figure with four straight sides and four right angles, esp. one with the adjacent sides unequal. □□ **rec·tan·gu·lar** /rektánggyələr/ *adj.* **rec·tan·gu·lar·i·ty** /–láritee/ *n.*

rec·ti·fy /réktifī/ *v.tr.* (**-fies, -fied**) **1** adjust or make right; correct; amend. **2** purify or refine, esp. by repeated distillation. **3** find a straight line equal in length to (a curve). **4** convert (alternating current) to direct current. □□ **rec·ti·fi·a·ble** *adj.*

rec·ti·lin·e·ar /réktilíneeər/ *adj.* (also **rec·ti·lin·e·al** /–eeəl/) **1** bounded or characterized by straight lines. **2** in or forming a straight line. □□ **rec·ti·lin·e·ar·i·ty** /–neeáritee/ *n.* **rec·ti·lin·e·ar·ly** *adv.*

rec·ti·tude /réktitōōd, –tyōōd/ *n.* **1** moral uprightness. **2** righteousness. **3** correctness.

rec·to /réktō/ *n.* (*pl.* **-tos**) **1** the right-hand page of an open book. **2** the front of a printed leaf of paper or manuscript (opp. VERSO).

rec·tor /réktər/ *n.* **1** (in the Church of England) the clergy member in charge of a parish or religious institution. **2** the head of some schools, universities, and colleges. □□ **rec·to·ri·al** /–táwreeəl / *adj.* **rec·tor·ship** *n.*

rec·to·ry /réktəree/ *n.* (*pl.* **-ries**) a rector's house.

rec·tum /réktəm/ *n.* (*pl.* **rectums** or **recta** /–tə/) the final section of the large intestine, terminating at the anus.

rec·tus /réktəs/ *n.* (*pl.* **recti** /–tī/) *Anat.* a straight muscle.

re·cum·bent /rikúmbənt/ *adj.* lying down; reclining. □□ **re·cum·ben·cy** *n.* **re·cum·bent·ly** *adv.*

re·cu·per·ate /rikṓopərayt/ *v.* **1** *intr.* recover from illness, exhaustion, loss, etc. **2** *tr.* regain (health, something lost, etc.). □□ **re·cu·per·a·tion** /–ráyshən/ *n.* **re·cu·per·a·tive** /–rətiv/ *adj.*

re·cur /rikə́r/ *v.intr.* (**recurred, recurring**) **1** occur again; be repeated. **2** (of a thought, etc.) come back to one's mind. **3** (foll. by *to*) go back in thought or speech.
▶**Recur** and **recurrence** are generally regarded as better style than *reoccur* and *reoccurrence*.

re·cur·rent /rikə́rənt, –kúr–/ *adj.* recurring; happening repeatedly. □□ **re·cur·rence** *n.* **re·cur·rent·ly** *adv.*

re·cur·sion /rikə́rzhən/ *n.* the act or an instance of returning. □□ **re·cur·sive** *adj.*

re·curve /rikə́rv/ *v.tr. & intr.* bend backward. □□ **re·curv·ate** /–vayt, –vət/ *adj.* **re·cur·va·ture** *n.*

rec·u·sant /rékyəzənt, rikyṓo–/ *n. & adj.* • *n.* a person who refuses submission to an authority or compliance with a regulation. • *adj.* of or being a recusant. □□ **rec·u·sance** *n.*

re·cy·cle /re͞esíkəl/ *v.tr.* convert (waste) to reusable material. □□ **re·cy·cla·ble** *adj.*

red /red/ *adj. & n.* • *adj.* (**redder, reddest**) **1** of or near the color seen at the least-refracted end of the visible spectrum, of shades ranging from that of blood to pink or deep orange. **2** flushed in the face with shame, anger, etc. **3** (of the eyes) bloodshot or red-rimmed with weeping. **4** (of the hair) reddish-brown; tawny. **5** having to do with bloodshed, burning, violence, or revolution. **6** *colloq.* communist or socialist. **7** (**Red**) (formerly) Soviet, Russian (*the Red Army*). • *n.* **1** a red color or pigment. **2** red clothes or material. **3** *colloq.* a communist or socialist. **4** the debit side of an account. □□ **red·dish** *adj.* **red·dy** *adj.* **red·ly** *adv.* **red·ness** *n.*

red Old English *rēad*, of Germanic origin; related to Dutch *rood* and German *rot*, from an Indo-European root shared by Latin *rufus*, *ruber*, Greek *eruthros*, and Sanskrit *rudhira* 'red.'

re·dact /ridákt/ *v.tr.* put into literary form; edit for publication. □□ **re·dac·tor** *n.* **re·dac·tion** /ridákshən/ *n.*

red a·lert *n.* **1** *Mil.* an alert sounded or given when an enemy attack appears imminent. **2** the signal for this.

red-blood·ed *adj.* virile; vigorous.

red car·pet *n.* privileged treatment of an eminent visitor.

red cell *n.* (also **red cor·pus·cle**) an erythrocyte.

red cent *n.* the lowest-value (orig. copper) coin; a trivial sum (*not worth a red cent*).

red·coat /rédkōt/ *n. hist.* a British soldier (so called from the scarlet uniform of most regiments).

Red Cross *n.* **1** an international organization (originally medical) bringing relief to victims of war or natural disaster. **2** the emblem of this organization.

red·den /réd'n/ *v.tr. & intr.* make or become red.

re·dec·o·rate /re͞edékərayt/ *v.tr.* decorate again or differently. □□ **re·dec·o·ra·tion** /–ráyshən/ *n.*

re·deem /ride͞em/ *v.tr.* **1** recover by expenditure of effort or by a stipulated payment. **2** make a single payment to discharge (a regular charge or obligation). **3** convert (tokens or bonds, etc.) into goods or cash. **4** deliver from sin and damnation. **5** be a compensating factor in. **6** (foll. by *from*) save from (a defect). **7** *refl.* save (oneself) from blame. □□ **re·deem·a·ble** *adj.*

re·deem·er /ride͞emər/ *n.* **1** a person who redeems. **2** (**the Redeemer**) Christ.

re·de·fine /re͞edifín/ *v.tr.* define again or differently. □□ **re·def·i·ni·tion** /–definíshən/ *n.*

re·demp·tion /ridémpshən/ *n.* **1** the act or an instance of redeeming; the process of being redeemed. **2** man's deliverance from sin and damnation. **3** a thing that redeems. □□ **re·demp·tive** *adj.*

re·de·ploy /re͞ediplóy/ *v.tr.* send (troops, workers, etc.) to a new place or task. □□ **re·de·ploy·ment** *n.*

re·de·sign /re͞edizín/ *v.tr.* design again or differently.

re·de·vel·op /re͞edivéləp/ *v.tr.* develop anew (esp. an urban area). □□ **re·de·vel·op·er** *n.* **re·de·vel·op·ment** *n.*

red-eye *n.* **1** = RUDD. **2** late-night or overnight airline flight. **3** *sl.* cheap whiskey.

red-faced *adj.* embarrassed, ashamed.

red flag *n.* **1** the symbol of socialist revolution. **2** a warning of danger.

red gi·ant *n.* a relatively cool giant star.

red-hand·ed *adv.* in or just after the act of committing a crime, doing wrong, etc.

red·head /rédhed/ *n.* a person with red hair.

red-head·ed *adj.* **1** (of a person) having red hair. **2** (of birds, etc.) having a red head.

red her·ring *n.* **1** dried smoked herring. **2** a misleading clue or distraction (so called from the practice of using the scent of red herring in training hounds).

red hot *n. & adj.* • *n.* **1** a small, red candy with a strong cinnamon flavor. **2** *colloq.* a hot dog. • *adj.* (**red-hot**) **1** heated until red. **2** (of news) fresh. **3** intensely excited or angry.

re·di·al /re͞edíəl, –díl/ *v.tr. & intr.* **1** dial again. **2** a telephone feature that allows the number just previously dialed to be automatically redialed by pressing a single button.

re·did *past* of REDO.

red·in·te·grate /ridíntigrayt/ *v.tr.* **1** restore to wholeness or unity. **2** renew or reestablish in a united or perfect state. ▫▫ **red·in·te·gra·tion** /–gráyshən/ *n.* **red·in·te·gra·tive** /–grətiv/ *adj.*

re·di·rect /réedirékt, –dī–/ *v.tr.* direct again, esp. change the address of (a letter). ▫▫ **re·di·rec·tion** *n.*

re·dis·cov·er /réediskúvər/ *v.tr.* discover again. ▫▫ **re·dis·cov·er·y** *n.* (*pl.* **-ies**).

re·dis·tri·bute /réedistríbyoot/ *v.tr.* distribute again or differently. ▫▫ **re·dis·tri·bu·tion** /–byóoshən/ *n.*

re·di·vide /réedivíd/ *v.tr.* divide again or differently. ▫▫ **re·di·vi·sion** /–vízhən/ *n.*

red·i·vi·vus /rédivívəs, –véevəs/ *adj.* (placed after noun) come back to life.

red lead *n.* a red form of lead oxide used as a pigment.

red-let·ter day *n.* a day that is pleasantly noteworthy or memorable.

red light *n.* **1** a signal to stop on a road, railroad, etc. **2** a warning or refusal.

red-light dis·trict *n.* a district containing brothels.

red·neck /rédnek/ *n.* often *derog.* a working-class, politically conservative or reactionary white person, esp. in the rural southern US.

re·do /réedóo/ *v.tr.* (*3rd sing. present* **redoes**; *past* **redid**; *past part.* **redone**) **1** do again or differently. **2** redecorate.

red·o·lent /réd'lənt/ *adj.* **1** (foll. by *of*, *with*) strongly reminiscent or suggestive or mentally associated. **2** fragrant. **3** having a strong smell. ▫▫ **red·o·lence** *n.*

re·dou·ble /réedúbəl/ *v. tr. & intr.* make or grow greater or more intense; intensify.

re·doubt /ridówt/ *n. Mil.* an outwork or fieldwork usu. square or polygonal and without flanking defenses.

re·doubt·a·ble /ridówtəbəl/ *adj.* formidable, esp. as an opponent. ▫▫ **re·doubt·a·bly** *adv.*

re·dound /ridównd/ *v.intr.* **1** (foll. by *to*) (of an action, etc.) make a great contribution to (one's credit or advantage, etc.). **2** (foll. by *upon*, *on*) come as the final result to; come back or recoil upon.

red pep·per *n.* **1** cayenne pepper. **2** the ripe fruit of the capsicum plant, *Capsicum annuum*.

re·draft /réedráft/ *v.tr.* draft (a document) again.

re·draw /réedráw/ *v.tr.* (*past* **redrew**; *past part.* **redrawn**) draw again or differently.

re·dress /ridrés/ *v. & n.* • *v.tr.* **1** remedy or rectify (a wrong, etc.). **2** readjust; set straight again. • *n.* (also /réedres/) **1** reparation for a wrong. **2** (foll. by *of*) the act or process of redressing (a grievance, etc.). ▫▫ **re·dress·a·ble** *adj.* **re·dress·al** *n.* **re·dress·er** *n.* (also **re·dres·sor**) .

red·skin /rédskin/ *n. colloq. offens.* a Native American.

red squir·rel *n.* **1** a N. American squirrel, *Tamiasciurus hudsonicus*, with reddish fur. **2** a common Eurasian red squirrel, *Sciurus vulgaris*, with reddish fur.

red·start /rédstaart/ *n.* **1** any European red-tailed songbird of the genus *Phoenicurus*. **2** any of various similar American warblers of the family Parulidae.

red tape *n.* excessive bureaucracy or adherence to formalities.

re·duce /ridóos, –dyóos/ *v.* **1** *tr. & intr.* make or become smaller or less. **2** *tr.* (foll. by *to*) bring by force or necessity (to some undesirable state or action). **3** *tr.* convert to another (esp. simpler) form. **4** *tr.* convert (a fraction) to the form with the lowest terms. **5** *tr.* (foll. by *to*) simplify or adapt by classification or analysis (*reduced to three issues*). **6** *tr.* make lower in status or rank. **7** *tr.* lower the price of. **8** *intr.* lessen one's weight or size. **9** *tr.* weaken (*is in a very reduced state*). **10** *tr.* impoverish. **11** *tr.* subdue; bring back to obedience. **12** *tr. Cooking* boil off excess liquid from. ▫▫ **re·duc·er** *n.* **re·duc·i·ble** *adj.* **re·duc·i·bil·i·ty** *n.*

---

reduce late Middle English: from Latin *reducere*, from *re-* 'back, again' + *ducere* 'bring, lead.' The original sense was 'bring back' (hence 'restore'); from this developed the senses 'bring to a different state' and then 'bring to a simpler or lower state' (hence sense 3); and finally 'diminish in size or amount' (sense 1, dating from the late 18th century).

---

re·duced cir·cum·stanc·es *n.pl.* poverty after relative prosperity.

re·duc·ti·o ad ab·surd·um /ridúkteeō ad absárdəm/ *n.* a method of proving the falsity of a premise by showing that the logical consequence is absurd.

re·duc·tion /ridúkshən/ *n.* **1** the act or an instance of reducing; the process of being reduced. **2** an amount by which prices, etc., are reduced. **3** a reduced copy of a picture, etc. **4** an arrangement of an orchestral score for piano, etc. ▫▫ **re·duc·tive** *adj.*

re·duc·tion·ism /ridúkshənizəm/ *n.* **1** the tendency to or principle of analyzing complex things into simple constituents. **2** often *derog.* the doctrine that a system can be fully understood in terms of its isolated parts. ▫▫ **re·duc·tion·ist** *n.* **re·duc·tion·is·tic** /–nístik/ *adj.*

re·dun·dant /ridúndənt/ *adj.* **1** superfluous; not needed. **2** that can be omitted without any loss of significance. ▫▫ **re·dun·dan·cy** *n.* (*pl.* **-cies**). **re·dun·dant·ly** *adv.*

re·du·pli·cate /ridóoplikayt, –dyóo–/ *v.tr.* **1** make double. **2** repeat. **3** repeat (a letter or syllable or word) exactly or with a slight change (e.g., hurly-burly, go-go). ▫▫ **re·du·pli·ca·tion** /–káyshən/ *n.* **re·du·pli·ca·tive** /–kətiv/ *adj.*

red·wing /rédwing/ *n.* a thrush, *Turdus iliacus*, with red underwings showing in flight.

red·wood /rédwood/ *n.* **1** an exceptionally large Californian conifer, *Sequoia sempervirens*, yielding red wood. **2** any tree yielding red wood.

ree·bok var of RHEBOK.

re·ech·o /rée-ékō/ *v.intr. & tr.* (**-oes**, **-oed**) **1** echo. **2** echo repeatedly; resound.

reed /reed/ *n. & v.* • *n.* **1 a** any of various water or marsh plants with a firm stem. **b** a tall straight stalk of this. **2** (*collect.*) reeds growing in a mass or used as material esp. for thatching. **3** a pipe of reed or straw. **4 a** the vibrating part of the mouthpiece of some wind instruments, made of reed or other material and producing the sound. **b** (esp. in *pl.*) a reed instrument. • *v.tr.* **1** thatch with reed. **2** make (straw) into reed. **3** fit (a musical instrument) with a reed.

reed·ing /réeding/ *n. Archit.* a small semicylindrical molding or ornamentation.

reed in·stru·ment *n.* a wind instrument with a single reed (e.g., clarinet) or double reed (e.g., oboe).

re·ed·u·cate /rée-édjəkayt/ *v.tr.* educate again, esp. to change a person's views or beliefs. ▫▫ **re·ed·u·ca·tion** /–káyshən/ *n.*

reed·y /réedee/ *adj.* (**reedier**, **reediest**) **1** full of reeds. **2** like a reed, esp. in weakness or slenderness. **3** (of a voice) not full. ▫▫ **reed·i·ness** *n.*

reef[1] /reef/ *n.* **1** a ridge of rock or coral, etc., at or near the surface of the sea. **2 a** a lode of ore. **b** the bedrock surrounding this.

reef[2] /reef/ *n. & v. Naut.* • *n.* each of several strips across a sail, for taking it in or rolling it up to reduce the surface area in a high wind. • *v.tr.* **1** take in a reef or reefs of (a sail). **2** shorten (a topmast or a bowsprit).

reef·er /réefər/ *n.* **1** *sl.* a marijuana cigarette. **2** a thick close-fitting double-breasted jacket.

reef knot *n.* a double knot made symmetrically to hold securely and cast off easily.

reek /reek/ *v. & n.* • *v.intr.* (often foll. by *of*) **1** smell strongly and unpleasantly. **2** have unpleasant or

---

suspicious associations. **3** give off smoke or fumes. • *n.* **1** a foul or stale smell. **2** vapor; a visible exhalation.

reel /reel/ *n. & v.* • *n.* **1** a cylindrical device on which thread, film, etc., are wound. **2** a quantity of thread, etc., wound on a reel. **3** a device for winding a line as required, esp. in fishing. **4** a revolving part in various machines. **5 a** a lively folk or Scottish dance. **b** a piece of music for this. • *v.* **1** *tr.* wind on a reel. **2** *tr.* (foll. by *in, up*) draw (fish, etc.) in or up by the use of a reel. **3** *intr.* stand or walk or run unsteadily. **4** *intr.* be shaken mentally or physically. **5** *intr.* rock from side to side, or swing violently. **6** *intr.* dance a reel.

re•el•ect /re͞eilékt/ *v.tr.* elect again, esp. to a further term of office. ▫▫ **re•e•lec•tion** /–ilékshən/ *n.*

re•em•bark /re͞eimbaárk/ *v.intr. & tr.* go or put on board ship again. ▫▫ **re•em•bar•ka•tion** *n.*

re•e•merge /re͞eimə́rj/ *v.intr.* emerge again. ▫▫ **re•e•mer•gence** *n.* **re•e•mer•gent** *adj.*

re•em•pha•size /rée-émfəsīz/ *v.tr.* place renewed emphasis on. ▫▫ **re•em•pha•sis** /–émfəsis/ *n.*

re•em•ploy /re͞eimplóy/ *v.tr.* employ again. ▫▫ **re•em•ploy•ment** *n.*

re•en•act /re͞einákt/ *v.tr.* act out (a past event). ▫▫ **re•en•act•ment** *n.*

re•en•list /re͞einlíst/ *v.intr.* enlist again, esp. in the armed services.

re•en•ter /rée-éntər/ *v.tr. & intr.* go back in. ▫▫ **re•en•trance** /–éntrəns/ *n.*

re•en•try /rée-éntree/ *n.* (*pl.* **-tries**) **1** the act of entering again, esp. (of a spacecraft, etc.) reentering the earth's atmosphere. **2** *Law* an act of retaking or repossession.

re•e•quip /re͞eikwíp/ *v.tr. & intr.* (**-equipped, -equipping**) provide or be provided with new equipment.

re•e•rect /re͞eirékt/ *v.tr.* erect again.

re•es•tab•lish /re͞eistáblish/ *v.tr.* establish again or anew. ▫▫ **re•es•tab•lish•ment** *n.*

re•e•val•u•ate /re͞eiványoo-ayt/ *v.tr.* evaluate again or differently. ▫▫ **re•e•val•u•a•tion** /–áyshən/ *n.*

reeve /reev/ *v.tr.* (*past* **rove** /rōv/ or **reeved**) *Naut.* **1** (usu. foll. by *through*) thread (a rope or rod, etc.) through a ring or other aperture. **2** pass a rope through (a block, etc.). **3** fasten (a rope or block) in this way.

re•ex•am•ine /re͞eigzámin/ *v.tr.* examine again or further (esp. a witness). ▫▫ **re•ex•am•i•na•tion** /–náyshən/ *n.*

re•ex•port /re͞eikspáwrt/ *v. & n.* • *v.tr.* export again (esp. imported goods after further processing or manufacture). • *n.* /rée-ékspawrt/ **1** the process of reexporting. **2** something reexported. ▫▫ **re•ex•por•ta•tion** *n.* **re•ex•port•er** *n.*

ref /ref/ *n. colloq.* a referee in sports.

re•face /re͞efáys/ *v.tr.* put a new facing on (a building).

re•fash•ion /re͞efáshən/ *v.tr.* fashion again or differently.

re•fec•to•ry /riféktəree/ *n.* (*pl.* **-ries**) a room used for communal meals, esp. in a monastery or college.

re•fer /rifə́r/ *v.* (**referred, referring**) (usu. foll. by *to*) **1** *tr.* trace or ascribe (to a person or thing as a cause or source) (*referred their success to their popularity*). **2** *tr.* consider as belonging (to a certain date or place or class). **3** *tr.* send on or direct (a person, or a question for decision). **4** *intr.* make an appeal or have recourse to (*referred to his notes*). **5** *tr.* send (a person) to a medical specialist, etc. **6** *tr.* (foll. by *back to*) send (a proposal, etc.) back to (a lower body, court, etc.). **7** *intr.* (foll. by *to*) (of a person speaking) make an allusion or direct the hearer's attention. **8** *intr.* (foll. by *to*) (of a statement, etc.) have a particular relation; be directed (*this refers to last year*). **9** *tr.* (foll. by *to*) interpret (a statement) as being directed to (a particular context, etc.). ▫▫ **re•fer•a•ble** /rif érəbəl, réfər–/ *adj.*

ref•er•ee /réfəre͞e/ *n. & v.* • *n.* **1** an umpire, esp. in sports, such as football, boxing, etc. **2** a person whose opinion or judgment is sought in a dispute, etc. • *v.* (**referees, refereed**) **1** *intr.* act as referee. **2** *tr.* be the referee of (a game, etc.).

ref•er•ence /réfərəns, réfrəns/ *n. & v.* • *n.* **1** the referring of a matter for decision or settlement or consideration to some authority. **2** the scope given to this authority. **3** (foll. by *to*) **a** a relation or respect or correspondence (*success has little reference to merit*). **b** an allusion (*made no reference to it*). **c** a direction to a book, etc., (or a passage in it) where information may be found. **d** a book or passage so cited. **4 a** the act of looking up a passage, etc., or looking in a book for information. **b** the act of referring to a person, etc., for information. **5 a** a written testimonial supporting an applicant for employment, etc. **b** a person giving this. • *v.tr.* provide (a book, etc.) with references to authorities. ▫ **with** (or **in**) **reference to** regarding; as regards. **without reference to** not taking account of. ▫▫ **ref•er•en•tial** /réfərénshəl/ *adj.*

ref•er•ence book *n.* a book intended to be consulted for information rather than read continuously.

ref•er•en•dum /réfəréndəm/ *n.* (*pl.* **referendums** or **referenda** /–də/) **1** the process of referring a political question to the electorate for a direct decision by general vote. **2** a vote taken by referendum.

ref•er•ent /réfərənt/ *n.* the idea or thing that a word, etc., symbolizes.

re•fer•ral /rifə́rəl/ *n.* the referring of an individual to an expert or specialist for advice, esp. the directing of a patient by a GP to a medical specialist.

re•fill *v. & n.* • *v.tr.* /re͞efíl/ **1** fill again. **2** provide a new filling for. • *n.* /re͞efil/ **1** a new filling. **2** the material for this. ▫▫ **re•fill•a•ble** *adj.*

re•fine /rifīn/ *v.* **1** *tr.* free from impurities or defects. **2** *tr. & intr.* make or become more polished or elegant or cultured. **3** *tr. & intr.* make or become more subtle or delicate in feelings, etc. ▫▫ **re•fin•a•ble** *adj.*

re•fined /rifīnd/ *adj.* **1** characterized by polish or elegance or subtlety. **2** purified; clarified.

re•fine•ment /rifīnmənt/ *n.* **1** the act of refining or the process of being refined. **2** fineness of feeling or taste. **3** polish or elegance in manner. **4** an added development or improvement (*a car with several refinements*). **5** a piece of subtle reasoning. **6** a fine distinction. **7** a subtle or ingenious example or display.

re•fin•er /rifīnər/ *n.* a person or firm whose business is to refine crude oil, metal, sugar, etc.

re•fin•er•y /rifīnəree/ *n.* (*pl.* **-ies**) a place where oil, etc., is refined.

re•fit *v. & n.* • *v.tr. & intr.* /re͞efit/ (**refitted, refitting**) make or become fit or serviceable again (esp. of a ship undergoing renewal and repairs). • *n.* /re͞efit/ the act or an instance of refitting; the process of being refitted.

re•flect /riflékt/ *v.* **1** *tr.* **a** (of a surface or body) throw back (heat, light, etc.). **b** cause to rebound (*reflected light*). **2** *tr.* (of a mirror) show an image of; reproduce to the eye or mind. **3** *tr.* correspond in appearance or effect to (*their behavior reflects a wish to succeed*). **4** *tr.* **a** (of an action, result, etc.) show or bring (credit, discredit, etc.). **b** (*absol.*; usu. foll. by *on, upon*) bring discredit on. **5 a** *intr.* (often foll. by *on, upon*) meditate on. **b** *tr.* (foll. by *that, how*, etc., + clause) consider; remind oneself.

re•flec•tion /riflékshən/ *n.* **1** the act or an instance of reflecting; the process of being reflected. **2 a** reflected light, heat, or color. **b** a reflected image. **3** reconsideration (*on reflection*). **4** (often foll. by *on*) discredit or a thing bringing discredit. **5** (often foll. by *on, upon*) an idea arising in the mind; a comment or apothegm. **6** (usu. foll. by *of*) a consequence; evidence.

re•flec•tive /rifléktiv/ *adj.* **1** (of a surface, etc.) giving a reflection or image. **2** (of mental faculties) concerned in reflection or thought. **3** (of a person or mood, etc.) thoughtful; given to meditation. □□ **re·flec·tive·ly** *adv.* **re·flec·tive·ness** *n.*

re·flec·tor /rifléktər/ *n.* **1** a piece of glass or metal, etc., for reflecting light in a required direction, e.g., on the back of a bicycle. **2 a** a telescope, etc., using a mirror to produce images. **b** the mirror itself.

re·flet /rəfláy/ *n.* luster or iridescence, esp. on pottery.

re·flex /réefleks/ *adj.* & *n.* • *adj.* **1** (of an action) independent of the will, as an automatic response to the stimulation of a nerve (e.g., a sneeze). **2** (of an angle) exceeding 180°. **3** bent backward. **4** (of light) reflected. **5** (of a thought, etc.) introspective; directed back upon itself or its own operations. **6** (of an effect or influence) reactive; coming back upon its author or source. • *n.* **1** a reflex action. **2** a sign or secondary manifestation (*law is a reflex of public opinion*). **3** reflected light or a reflected image.

re·flex cam·er·a *n.* a camera with a ground-glass focusing screen on which the image is formed by a combination of lens and mirror.

re·flex·i·ble /rifléksibəl/ *adj.* capable of being reflected. □□ **re·flex·i·bil·i·ty** /–bílitee/ *n.*

re·flex·ive /rifléksiv/ *adj.* & *n. Gram.* • *adj.* **1** (of a word or form) referring back to the subject of a sentence (e.g., *myself*). **2** (of a verb) having a reflexive pronoun as its object (as in *to wash oneself*). • *n.* a reflexive word or form, esp. a pronoun. □□ **re·flex·ive·ly** *adv.*

re·flex·ol·o·gy /réefleksóləjee/ *n.* **1** a system of massage through reflex points on the feet, hands, and head, used to relieve tension and treat illness. **2** *Psychol.* the scientific study of reflexes. □□ **re·flex·ol·o·gist** *n.*

ref·lu·ent /réflōōənt/ *adj.* flowing back (*refluent tide*). □□ **ref·lu·ence** *n.*

re·flux /réefluks/ *n.* **1** a backward flow. **2** *Chem.* a method of boiling a liquid so that any vapor is liquefied and returned to the boiler.

re·fo·cus /réefṓkəs/ *v.tr.* (**refocused, refocusing** or **refocussed, refocussing**) adjust the focus of.

re·for·est /réefáwrist, fór–/ *v.tr.* replant (former forest land) with trees. □□ **re·for·est·a·tion** /–stáyshən/ *n.*

re·form /rifáwrm/ *v.* & *n.* • *v.* **1** *tr.* & *intr.* make or become better by the removal of faults and errors. **2** *tr.* abolish or cure (an abuse or malpractice). **3** *tr.* correct (a legal document). • *n.* **1** the removal of faults or abuses, esp. of a moral or political or social kind. **2** an improvement made or suggested. □□ **re·form·a·ble** *adj.*

re-form /réefáwrm/ *v.tr.* & *intr.* form again. □□ **re-for·ma·tion** /réefawrmáyshən/ *n.*

re·for·mat /réefáwrmat/ *v.tr.* (**reformatted, reformatting**) format anew.

ref·or·ma·tion /réfərmáyshən / *n.* **1** the act of reforming or process of being reformed, esp. a radical change for the better in political or religious or social affairs. **2** (**the Reformation**) *hist.* a 16th-c. movement for the reform of abuses in the Roman Church ending in the establishment of the Reformed and Protestant churches.

re·form·a·tive /rifáwrmətiv/ *adj.* tending or intended to produce reform.

re·form·a·to·ry /rifáwrmətawree/ *n.* & *adj.* • *n.* (*pl.* **-ries**) = REFORM SCHOOL. • *adj.* reformative.

re·form·er /rifáwrmər/ *n.* a person who advocates or brings about (esp. political or social) reform.

re·form·ism /rifáwrmizəm/ *n.* a policy of reform rather than abolition or revolution. □□ **re·form·ist** *n.*

re·form school *n.* an institution to which young offenders are sent to be reformed.

re·for·mu·late /réefáwrmyəlayt/ *v.tr.* formulate again or differently. □□ **re·for·mu·la·tion** /–láyshən/ *n.*

re·fract /rifrákt/ *v.tr.* **1** (of water, air, glass, etc.) deflect (a ray of light, etc.) at a certain angle when it enters obliquely from another medium. **2** determine the refractive condition of (the eye). □□ **re·frac·tion** /rifrákshən/ *n.* **re·frac·tive** /rifráktiv/ *adj.*

re·frac·tom·e·ter /reefraktómitər/ *n.* an instrument for measuring refraction. □□ **re·frac·to·met·ric** /–təmétrik/ *adj.* **re·frac·tom·e·try** *n.*

re·frac·tor /rifráktər/ *n.* **1** a refracting medium or lens. **2** a telescope using a lens to produce an image.

re·frac·to·ry /rifráktəree/ *adj.* & *n.* • *adj.* **1** stubborn; unmanageable, rebellious. **2 a** (of a wound, disease, etc.) not yielding to treatment. **b** (of a person, etc.) resistant to infection. **3** (of a substance) hard to fuse or work. • *n.* (*pl.* **-ries**) a substance especially resistant to heat, corrosion, etc. □□ **re·frac·to·ri·ly** *adv.*

re·frain[1] /rifráyn/ *v.intr.* (foll. by *from*) avoid doing (an action); forbear; desist.

re·frain[2] /rifráyn/ *n.* **1** a recurring phrase or number of lines, esp. at the ends of stanzas. **2** the music accompanying this.

re·fran·gi·ble /rifránjibəl/ *adj.* that can be refracted. □□ **re·fran·gi·bil·i·ty** *n.*

re·freeze /réefréez/ *v.tr.* & *intr.* (*past* **refroze**; *past part.* **refrozen**) freeze again.

re·fresh /rifrésh/ *v.tr.* **1 a** give fresh spirit or vigor to. **b** (esp. *refl.*) revive with food, rest, etc. (*refreshed myself with a short sleep*). **2** revive or stimulate (the memory), esp. by consulting the source of one's information. **3** make cool. **4** restore to a certain condition, esp. by provision of fresh supplies, equipment, etc.; replenish. **5** *Computing* **a** restore an image to the screen. **b** replace an image with one that displays more recent information.

re·fresh·er /rifréshər/ *n.* something that refreshes, esp. a drink.

re·fresh·er course *n.* a course reviewing or updating previous studies.

re·fresh·ing /rifréshing/ *adj.* **1** serving to refresh. **2** welcome or stimulating. □□ **re·fresh·ing·ly** *adv.*

re·fresh·ment /rifréshmənt/ *n.* **1** the act of refreshing or the process of being refreshed in mind or body. **2** (usu. in *pl.*) food or drink that refreshes. **3** something that refreshes or stimulates the mind.

re·frig·er·ant /rifríjərənt/ *n.* & *adj.* • *n.* **1** a substance used for refrigeration. **2** *Med.* a substance that cools or allays fever. • *adj.* cooling.

re·frig·er·ate /rifríjərayt/ *v.* **1** *tr.* & *intr.* make or become cool or cold. **2** *tr.* subject (food, etc.) to cold in order to freeze or preserve it. □□ **re·frig·er·a·tion** /–ráyshən/ *n.*

re·frig·er·a·tor /rifríjəraytər/ *n.* a cabinet or room in which food, etc., is kept cold.

re·froze *past* of REFREEZE.

re·froz·en *past part.* of REFREEZE.

reft *past part.* of REAVE.

re·fu·el /réefyṓōəl/ *v.* **1** *intr.* replenish a fuel supply. **2** *tr.* supply with more fuel.

ref·uge /réfyōōj/ *n.* **1** a shelter from pursuit or danger or trouble. **2** a person or place, etc., offering this. **3** a person, thing, or course resorted to in difficulties.

ref·u·gee /réfyōōjée/ *n.* a person taking refuge, esp. in a foreign country.

re·ful·gent /rifúljənt/ *adj. literary* shining; gloriously bright. □□ **re·ful·gence** *n.* **re·ful·gent·ly** *adv.*

re·fund[1] *v.* & *n.* • *v.* /rifúnd/ *tr.* (also *absol.*) **1** pay back (money or expenses). **2** reimburse (a person). • *n.* /réefund/ **1** an act of refunding. **2** a sum refunded; a repayment. □□ **re·fund·a·ble** *adj.*

re·fund[2] /réefúnd/ *v.tr.* fund (a debt, etc.) again.

re·fur·bish /rifə́rbish/ *v.tr.* **1** brighten up. **2** restore and redecorate. ▫▫ **re·fur·bish·ment** *n.*

re·fur·nish /reéfə́rnish/ *v.tr.* furnish again or differently.

re·fus·al /rifyóozəl/ *n.* **1** the act or an instance of refusing; the state of being refused. **2** (in full **first refusal**) the right or privilege of deciding to take or leave a thing before it is offered to others.

re·fuse[1] /rifyóoz/ *v.* **1** *tr.* withhold acceptance of or consent to. **2** *tr.* (often foll. by *to* + infin.) indicate unwillingness. **3** *tr.* (often with double object) not grant (a request) made by (a person). **4** *tr.* (also *absol.*) (of a horse) be unwilling to jump (a fence, etc.). ▫▫ **re·fus·er** *n.*

ref·use[2] /réfyoos/ *n.* items rejected as worthless; waste.

re·fuse·nik /rifyóoznik/ *n. hist.* a Jew refused permission to emigrate to Israel from the former Soviet Union.

re·fute /rifyóot/ *v.tr.* **1** prove the falsity or error of (a statement, etc., or the person advancing it). **2** rebut or repel by argument. **3** *disp.* deny or contradict (without argument). ▫▫ **re·fut·a·ble** *adj.* **ref·u·ta·tion** /réfyootáyshən/ *n.*

▶Strictly speaking, **refute** means 'to prove (a person or statement) to be wrong,' e.g., *No amount of research can either confirm or refute the story.* However, it is sometimes used to mean simply 'to deny or repudiate.' This usage is considered incorrect by some.

reg /reg/ *n. colloq.* regulation.

re·gain /rigáyn/ *v.tr.* obtain possession or use of after loss.

re·gal /reégəl/ *adj.* **1** royal; of or by a monarch or monarchs. **2** fit for a monarch; magnificent. ▫▫ **re·gal·i·ty** /rigálitee/ *n.* **re·gal·ly** *adv.*

re·gale /rigáyl/ *v.tr.* **1** entertain lavishly with feasting. **2** (foll. by *with*) entertain with (talk, etc.).

re·ga·li·a /rigáylyə/ *n.pl.* **1** the insignia of royalty used at coronations. **2** the insignia of an order or of civic dignity. **3** any distinctive or elaborate clothes, accoutrements, etc.; trappings; finery.

re·gal·ism /reégəlizəm/ *n.* the doctrine of a sovereign's ecclesiastical supremacy.

re·gard /rigaárd/ *v. & n.* • *v.tr.* **1** gaze on steadily (usu. in a specified way) (*regarded them suspiciously*). **2** give heed to; take into account. **3** look upon or contemplate mentally in a specified way (*I regard it as an insult*). **4** (of a thing) have relation to; have some connection with. • *n.* **1** a gaze; a steady or significant look. **2** (foll. by *to, for*) attention or care. **3** (foll. by *for*) esteem; kindly feeling; respectful opinion. **4 a** a point attended to (*in this regard*). **b** (usu. foll. by *to*) reference; connection, relevance. **5** (in *pl.*) an expression of friendliness in a letter, etc. (*sent my best regards*).

re·gard·ful /rigaárdfool/ *adj.* (foll. by *of*) mindful of; paying attention to.

re·gard·ing /rigaárding/ *prep.* concerning; in respect of.

re·gard·less /rigaárdlis/ *adj. & adv.* • *adj.* (foll. by *of*) without regard or consideration for. • *adv.* without paying attention (*carried on regardless*).

▶See note at IRREGARDLESS.

re·gat·ta /rigaátə, –gátə/ *n.* a sporting event consisting of a series of boat or yacht races.

re·gen·cy /reéjənsee/ *n.* (*pl.* **-cies**) **1** the office of regent. **2** a commission acting as regent. **3 a** the period of office of a regent or regency commission. **b** (**Regency**) a particular period of a regency, esp. (in Britain) from 1811 to 1820, and (in France) from 1715 to 1723.

re·gen·er·ate *v. & adj.* • *v.* /rijénərayt/ **1** *tr. & intr.* bring or come into renewed existence; generate again. **2** *tr.* improve the moral condition of. **3** *tr.* impart new, more vigorous, and spiritually greater life to (a person or institution, etc.). **4** *intr.* reform oneself. **5** *tr.* invest with a new and higher spiritual nature. **6** *intr. & tr. Biol.* regrow or cause (new tissue) to regrow. • *adj.* /rijénərət/ **1** spiritually born again. **2** reformed. ▫▫ **re·gen·er·a·tion** /–jenəráyshən/ *n.* **re·gen·er·a·tive** /–rətiv/ *adj.*

re·gent /reéjənt/ *n. & adj.* • *n.* **1** a person appointed to administer a kingdom because the monarch is a minor or is absent or incapacitated. **2** a member of the governing body of a state university. • *adj.* (placed after noun) acting as regent (*prince regent*).

reg·gae /régay/ *n.* a W. Indian style of music with a strongly accented subsidiary beat.

reg·i·cide /réjisīd/ *n.* **1** a person who kills or takes part in killing a king. **2** the act of killing a king. ▫▫ **reg·i·cid·al** *adj.*

re·gild /reegíld/ *v.tr.* gild again, esp. to renew faded or worn gilding.

re·gime /rayzheém/ *n.* (also **ré·gime**) **1 a** a method or system of government. **b** *derog.* a particular government. **2** a prevailing order or system of things.

reg·i·men /réjimen/ *n.* esp. *Med.* a prescribed course of exercise, way of life, and diet.

reg·i·ment *n. & v.* • *n.* /réjimənt/ **1 a** a permanent unit of an army usu. commanded by a colonel and divided into several companies or troops. **b** an operational unit of artillery, etc. **2** (usu. foll. by *of*) a large array or number. • *v.tr.* /réjiment/ **1** organize (esp. oppressively) in groups or according to a system. **2** form into a regiment or regiments. ▫▫ **reg·i·men·ta·tion** *n.*

reg·i·men·tal /réjimént'l/ *adj. & n.* • *adj.* of or relating to a regiment. • *n.* (in *pl.*) military uniform, esp. of a particular regiment. ▫▫ **reg·i·men·tal·ly** *adv.*

re·gion /reéjən/ *n.* **1** an area of land, or division of the earth's surface, having definable boundaries or characteristics (*a mountainous region*). **2** an administrative district, esp. in Scotland. **3** a part of the body around or near some organ, etc. (*the lumbar region*). **4** a sphere or realm (*the region of metaphysics*). **5 a** a separate part of the world or universe. **b** a layer of the atmosphere or the sea according to its height or depth. ▫▫ **re·gion·al** *adj.* **re·gion·al·ly** *adv.*

reg·is·ter /réjistər/ *n. & v.* • *n.* **1** an official list, e.g., of births, marriages, and deaths; of shipping; of professionally qualified persons; or of qualified voters in a constituency. **2** a book in which items are recorded for reference. **3** a device recording speed, force, etc. **4** (in electronic devices) a location in a store of data. **5 a** the range of a voice or instrument. **b** a part of this range (*lower register*) . **6** an adjustable plate for widening or narrowing an opening and regulating a draft, esp. in a fire grate. **7 a** a set of organ pipes. **b** a sliding device controlling this. **8** = CASH REGISTER. • *v.* **1** *tr.* set down (a name, fact, etc.) formally. **2** *tr.* make a mental note of; notice. **3** *tr.* enter or cause to be entered in a particular register. **4** *tr.* entrust (a letter, etc.) to registered mail. **5** *intr. & refl.* put one's name on a register, esp. as an eligible voter or as a guest in a register kept by a hotel, etc. **6** *tr.* (of an instrument) record automatically; indicate. **7 a** *tr.* express (an emotion) facially or by gesture (*registered surprise*). **b** *intr.* (of an emotion) show in a person's face or gestures. **8** *intr.* make an impression on a person 's mind (*did not register at all*).

reg·is·tered mail *n.* mail recorded at the post office and guaranteed against loss, damage, etc., during transmission.

reg·is·tered nurse *n.* a nurse with graduate training who has passed a state certification exam and is licensed to practice nursing.

reg·is·trar /réjistraar/ *n.* **1** an official responsible for keeping a register or official records. **2** the chief administrative officer in a university. ▫▫ **reg·is·trar·ship** *n.*

reg·is·tra·tion /réjistráyshən/ *n.* **1** the act or an instance of registering; the process of being registered. **2** a certificate, etc., that attests to the registering (of a person, vehicle, etc.).

reg·is·try /réjistree/ *n.* (*pl.* **-tries**) **1** a place or office where registers or records are kept. **2** registration.

reg·nant /régnənt/ *adj.* **1** reigning (*queen regnant*). **2** (of things, qualities, etc.) predominant, prevalent.

re·gorge /rigáwrj/ *v.* **1** *tr.* bring up or expel again after swallowing. **2** *intr.* gush or flow back from a pit, channel, etc.

re·grade /réegráyd/ *v.tr.* grade again or differently.

re·gress *v.* & *n.* • *v.* /rigrés/ **1** *intr.* move backward, esp. (in abstract senses) return to a former state. **2** *intr.* & *tr. Psychol.* return or cause to return mentally to a former stage of life. • *n.* /réegres/ **1** the act or an instance of going back. **2** reasoning from effect to cause.

re·gres·sion /rigréshən/ *n.* **1** a backward movement, esp. a return to a former state. **2** a relapse or reversion. **3** *Psychol.* a return to an earlier stage of development.

re·gres·sive /rigrésiv/ *adj.* **1** regressing; characterized by regression. **2** (of a tax) proportionally greater on lower incomes. ▫▫ **re·gres·sive·ly** *adv.* **re·gres·sive·ness** *n.*

re·gret /rigrét/ *v.* & *n.* • *v.tr.* (**regretted, regretting**) **1** (often foll. by *that* + clause) feel or express sorrow or repentance or distress over (an action or loss, etc.). **2** (often foll. by *to* + infin. or *that* + clause) acknowledge with sorrow or remorse (*I regret to say*). • *n.* **1** a feeling of sorrow, repentance, etc., over an action or loss, etc. **2** (often in *pl.*) an (esp. polite or formal) expression of disappointment or sorrow at an occurrence, inability to comply, etc. ▫ **give** (or **send**) **one's regrets** formally decline an invitation.

re·gret·ful /rigrétfool/ *adj.* feeling or showing regret. ▫▫ **re·gret·ful·ly** *adv.* **re·gret·ful·ness** *n.*

re·gret·ta·ble /rigrétəbəl/ *adj.* (of events or conduct) undesirable; unwelcome; deserving censure. ▫▫ **re·gret·ta·bly** *adv.*

re·group /réegróop/ *v.tr.* & *intr.* group or arrange again or differently. ▫▫ **re·group·ment** *n.*

re·grow /réegró/ *v.intr.* & *tr.* (*past* **regrew**; *past part.* **regrown**) grow again, esp. after an interval. ▫▫ **re·growth** *n.*

reg·u·la·ble /régyələbəl/ *adj.* able to be regulated.

reg·u·lar /régyələr/ *adj.* & *n.* • *adj.* **1** conforming to a rule or principle; systematic. **2 a** harmonious; symmetrical. **b** (of a surface, line, etc.) smooth; level; uniform. **3** acting or done or recurring uniformly or calculably in time or manner. **4** conforming to a standard of etiquette or procedure. **5** properly constituted or qualified; pursuing an occupation as one's main pursuit (*has no regular profession*). **6** *Gram.* (of a noun, verb, etc.) following the normal type of inflection. **7** *colloq.* complete; thorough; absolute (*a regular hero*). **8** *Geom.* **a** (of a figure) having all sides and all angles equal. **b** (of a solid) bounded by a number of equal figures. **9** relating to or constituting a permanent professional body (*regular soldiers*). **10** (of a person) defecating or menstruating at predictable times. **11** *colloq.* likable; normal; reliable (esp. as *regular guy*). • *n.* **1** a regular soldier. **2** *colloq.* a regular customer, visitor, etc. ▫ **keep regular hours** do the same thing, esp. going to bed and getting up, at the same time each day. ▫▫ **reg·u·lar·i·ty** /–láritee/ *n.* **reg·u·lar·ize** *v.tr.* **reg·u·lar·i·za·tion** *n.* **reg·u·lar·ly** *adv.*

reg·u·late /régyəlayt/ *v.tr.* **1** control by rule. **2** subject to restrictions. **3** adapt to requirements. **4** alter the speed of (a machine or clock) so that it may work accurately. ▫▫ **reg·u·la·tor** *n.* **reg·u·la·to·ry** /–lətáwree/ *adj.*

reg·u·la·tion /régyəláyshən/ *n.* **1** the act or an instance of regulating; the process of being regulated. **2** a prescribed rule. **3** (*attrib.*) **a** in accordance with regulations; of the correct type, etc. (*the regulation tie*). **b** *colloq.* usual (*the regulation soup*).

re·gur·gi·tate /rigə́rjitayt/ *v.* **1** *tr.* bring (swallowed food) up again to the mouth. **2** *tr.* cast or pour out again (*regurgitate facts*). **3** *intr.* be brought up again; gush back. ▫▫ **re·gur·gi·ta·tion** /–táyshən/ *n.*

re·hab /réehab/ *n. colloq.* rehabilitation.

re·ha·bil·i·tate /réehəbílitayt/ *v.tr.* **1** restore to effectiveness or normal life by training, etc., esp. after imprisonment or illness. **2** restore to former privileges or reputation or a proper condition. ▫▫ **re·ha·bil·i·ta·tion** /–táyshən/ *n.* **re·ha·bil·i·ta·tive** *adj.*

re·hang /réeháng/ *v.tr.* (*past* and *past part.* **rehung**) hang (esp. a picture or a curtain) again or differently.

re·hash *v.* & *n.* • *v.tr.* /réehásh/ put (old material) into a new form without significant change or improvement. • *n.* /réehash/ **1** material rehashed. **2** the act or an instance of rehashing.

re·hear /réeheer/ *v.tr.* (*past* and *past part.* **reheard** /réehérd/) hear again.

re·hears·al /rihə́rsəl/ *n.* **1** the act or an instance of rehearsing. **2** a trial performance or practice of a play, recital, etc.

re·hearse /rihə́rs/ *v.* **1** *tr.* practice (a play, recital, etc.) for later public performance. **2** *intr.* hold a rehearsal. **3** *tr.* train (a person) by rehearsal. **4** *tr.* recite or say over. **5** *tr.* give a list of; enumerate. ▫▫ **re·hears·er** *n.*

re·heat /réeheet/ *v.tr.* heat again.

re·heel /réeheel/ *v.tr.* fit (a shoe, etc.) with a new heel.

re·ho·bo·am /réehəbóəm/ *n.* a wine bottle of about six times the standard size.

re·house /réehówz/ *v.tr.* provide with new housing.

re·hung *past* and *past part.* of REHANG.

re·hy·drate /réehīdráyt/ *v.* **1** *intr.* absorb water again after dehydration. **2** *tr.* add water to (esp. food) again to restore to a palatable state. ▫▫ **re·hy·dra·tion** /–dráyshən/ *n.*

Reich /rīkh/ *n.* the former German state, esp. the Third Reich.

re·i·fy /réeifī/ *v.tr.* (**·fies, ·fied**) convert (a concept, abstraction, etc.) into a thing; materialize. ▫▫ **re·i·fi·ca·tion** /–fikáyshən/ *n.* **re·if·i·ca·to·ry** /–ífikətáwree/ *adj.*

reign /rayn/ *v.* & *n.* • *v.intr.* **1** hold royal office; be king or queen. **2** have power or predominance; prevail (*confusion reigns*). **3** (as **reigning** *adj.*) (of a champion, etc.) currently holding the title, etc. • *n.* **1** sovereignty, rule. **2** the period during which a sovereign rules.

re·ig·nite /réeignít/ *v.tr.* & *intr.* ignite again.

reign of ter·ror *n.* a period of remorseless repression or bloodshed, esp. a period of the French Revolution 1793–94.

re·im·burse /réeimbə́rs/ *v.tr.* **1** repay (a person who has expended money). **2** repay (a person's expenses). ▫▫ **re·im·burs·a·ble** *adj.* **re·im·burse·ment** *n.*

re·im·port /réeimpáwrt/ *v.* & *n.* • *v.tr.* import (goods processed from exported materials). • *n.* /rée-ímpawrt/ **1** the act or an instance of reimporting. **2** a reimported item. ▫▫ **re·im·por·ta·tion** *n.*

re·im·pose /réeimpóz/ *v.tr.* impose again, esp. after a lapse. ▫▫ **re·im·po·si·tion** /–pəzíshən/ *n.*

rein /rayn/ *n.* & *v.* • *n.* (in *sing.* or *pl.*) **1** a long narrow strap with each end attached to the bit, used to guide or check a horse, etc. **2** a similar device used to restrain a young child. **3** (a means of) control. • *v.tr.* **1** check or manage with reins. **2** (foll. by *up*, *back*) pull up or back with reins. **3** (foll. by *in*) hold in as with reins. **4** govern; restrain; control. ▫ **give free rein to** remove constraints from; allow full scope to.

---

re·in·car·na·tion /réeinkaarnáyshən/ *n.* (in some beliefs) the rebirth of a soul in a new body. □□ **re·in·car·nate** /–kaárnayt/ *v.tr.* **re·in·car·nate** /–kaárnət/ *adj.*
re·in·cor·po·rate /réeinkáwrpərayt/ *v.tr.* incorporate afresh. □□ **re·in·cor·po·ra·tion** /–ráyshən/ *n.*
rein·deer /rāyndeer/ *n.* (*pl.* same or **reindeers**) a subarctic deer, *Rangifer tarandus*, of which both sexes have large antlers.
re·in·fect /réeinfékt/ *v.tr.* infect again. □□ **re·in·fec·tion** /réeinfékshən/ *n.*
re·in·force /réeinfáwrs/ *v.tr.* strengthen or support, esp. with additional personnel or material or by an increase of quantity, size, etc. □□ **re·in·forc·er** *n.*
re·in·forced con·crete *n.* concrete with metal bars or wire, etc., embedded to increase its tensile strength.
re·in·force·ment /réeinfáwrsmənt/ *n.* **1** the act or an instance of reinforcing; the process of being reinforced. **2** a thing that reinforces. **3** (in *pl.*) reinforcing personnel, etc.
re·in·sert /réeinsə́rt/ *v.tr.* insert again. □□ **re·in·ser·tion** /–sérshən/ *n.*
re·in·state /réeinstáyt/ *v.tr.* **1** replace in a former position. **2** restore (a person, etc.) to former privileges. □□ **re·in·state·ment** *n.*
re·in·sure /réeinshŏŏr/ *v.tr.* & *intr.* insure again (esp. by transferring some or all of it to another insurer). □□ **re·in·sur·ance** *n.* **re·in·sur·er** *n.*
re·in·te·grate /rée-íntigrayt/ *v.tr.* integrate back into society. □□ **re·in·te·gra·tion** /–gráyshən/ *n.*
re·in·ter /réeintə́r/ *v.tr.* inter (a corpse) again. □□ **re·in·ter·ment** *n.*
re·in·ter·pret /réeintə́rprit/ *v.tr.* interpret again or differently. □□ **re·in·ter·pre·ta·tion** *n.*
re·in·tro·duce /réeintrədŏŏs, –dyŏŏs/ *v.tr.* introduce again. □□ **re·in·tro·duc·tion** /–dúkshən/ *n.*
re·in·vest /réeinvést/ *v.tr.* invest again (esp. money in other property, etc.). □□ **re·in·vest·ment** *n.*
re·in·vig·or·ate /réeinvígərayt/ *v.tr.* impart fresh vigor to.
re·is·sue *v.* & *n.* • *v.tr.* /rée-íshoo/ (**reissues, reissued, reissuing**) issue again or in a different form. • *n.* /reeíshoo/ a new issue, esp. of a previously published book.
re·it·er·ate /rée-ítərayt/ *v.tr.* say or do again or repeatedly. □□ **re·it·er·a·tion** /–ráyshən/ *n.* **re·it·er·a·tive** /–raytiv, –rətiv/ *adj.*
re·ject *v.* & *n.* • *v.tr.* /rijékt/ **1** put aside or send back as not to be used or done or complied with, etc. **2** refuse to accept or believe in. **3** rebuff or snub (a person). **4** (of a body or digestive system) cast up again; vomit; evacuate. **5** *Med.* show an immune response to (a transplanted organ or tissue) so that it fails to survive. • *n.* /réejekt/ a thing or person rejected as unfit or below standard. □□ **re·ject·a·ble** /rijéktəbəl/ *adj.* **re·ject·er** /rijéktər/ *n.* (also **re·jec·tor**) **re·jec·tion** /–jékshən/ *n.*
re·jig·ger /réejígər/ *v.tr.* rearrange or alter, esp. in an unethical way.
re·joice /rijóys/ *v.* **1** *intr.* feel great joy. **2** *intr.* (foll. by *that* + clause or *to* + infin.) be glad. **3** *intr.* (foll. by *in*, *at*) take delight. **4** *intr.* celebrate some event. **5** *tr.* cause joy to. □□ **re·joic·er** *n.* **re·joic·ing·ly** *adv.*
re·join[1] /réejóyn/ *v.* **1** *tr.* & *intr.* join together again; reunite. **2** *tr.* join (a companion, etc.) again.
re·join[2] /rijóyn/ *v.* **1** *tr.* say in answer; retort. **2** *intr. Law* reply to a charge or pleading in a lawsuit.
re·join·der /rijóyndər/ *n.* **1** what is said in reply. **2** a retort. **3** *Law* a reply by rejoining.
re·ju·ve·nate /rijŏŏvinayt/ *v.tr.* make young or as if young again. □□ **re·ju·ve·na·tion** /–náyshən/ *n.*
re·ju·ve·nesce /rijŏŏvinés/ *v.* **1** *intr.* become young again. **2** *Biol.* **a** *intr.* (of cells) gain fresh vitality. **b** *tr.* impart fresh vitality to (cells). □□ **re·ju·ve·nes·cent** *adj.* **re·ju·ve·nes·cence** *n.*
re·kin·dle /réekínd'l/ *v.tr.* & *intr.* kindle again.
-rel /rəl/ *suffix* with diminutive or derogatory force (*cockerel*; *scoundrel*).
rel. *abbr.* **1** relating. **2** relative. **3** released. **4** religion. **5** religious.
re·la·bel /réeláybəl/ *v.tr.* label (esp. a commodity) again or differently.
re·laid *past* and *past part.* of RELAY[2].
re·lapse /riláps/ *v.* & *n.* • *v.intr.* (usu. foll. by *into*) fall back or sink again (into a worse state after an improvement). • *n.* (also /réelaps/) the act or an instance of relapsing, esp. a deterioration in a patient's condition after a partial recovery. □□ **re·laps·er** *n.*
re·late /riláyt/ *v.* **1** *tr.* narrate or recount. **2** *tr.* (in *passive*; often foll. by *to*) be connected by blood or marriage. **3** *tr.* (usu. foll. by *to*, *with*) bring into relation (with one another); establish a connection between. **4** *intr.* (foll. by *to*) have reference to. **5** *intr.* (foll. by *to*) **a** bring oneself into relation to. **b** feel emotionally or sympathetically involved or connected. □□ **re·lat·a·ble** *adj.*
re·lat·ed /riláytid/ *adj.* **1** connected by blood or marriage. **2** having (mutual) relation; associated; connected. □□ **re·lat·ed·ness** *n.*
re·la·ter /riláytər/ *n.* (also **re·la·tor**) a person who relates something, esp. a story; a narrator.
re·la·tion /riláyshən/ *n.* **1 a** what one person or thing has to do with another. **b** the way in which one person stands or is related to another. **c** a connection, correspondence, or feeling prevailing between persons or things, esp. when qualified in some way (*bears no relation to the facts*). **2** a relative. **3** (in *pl.*) **a** (foll. by *with*) dealings (with others). **b** sexual intercourse. **4** = RELATIONSHIP. **5 a** narration (*his relation of the events*). **b** a narrative.
re·la·tion·al /riláyshənəl/ *adj.* **1** of, belonging to, or characterized by relation. **2** having relation.
re·la·tion·ship /riláyshənship/ *n.* **1** the fact or state of being related. **2** *colloq.* a connection or association (esp. sexual) between two people. **3** a condition or character due to being related. **4** kinship.
rel·a·tive /rélətiv/ *adj.* & *n.* • *adj.* **1** considered or having significance in relation to something else (*relative velocity*). **2** (also foll. by *to*) existing or quantifiable only in terms of individual perception or consideration; not absolute nor independent. **3** (foll. by *to*) proportioned to (something else) (*growth is relative to input*). **4** implying comparison or contextual relation. **5** compared one with another (*their relative advantages*). **6** having mutual relations; corresponding in some way; related to each other. **7** (foll. by *to*) having reference (*the facts relative to the issue*). **8** involving a different but corresponding idea. **9** *Gram.* **a** (of a word, esp. a pronoun) referring to an expressed or implied antecedent and attaching a subordinate clause to it, e.g., *which*, *who*. **b** (of a clause) attached to an antecedent by a relative word. **10** pertinent; relevant; related to the subject. • *n.* **1** a person connected by blood or marriage. **2** a species related to another by common origin. □□ **rel·a·tive·ly** *adv.*
rel·a·tive hu·mid·i·ty *n.* the proportion of moisture to the value for saturation at the same temperature.
rel·a·tiv·ism /rélətivizəm/ *n.* the doctrine that knowledge is relative, not absolute. □□ **rel·a·tiv·ist** *n.*
rel·a·tiv·is·tic /rélətivístik/ *adj. Physics* (of phenomena, etc.) accurately described only by the theory of relativity. □□ **rel·a·tiv·is·ti·cal·ly** *adv.*
rel·a·tiv·i·ty /rélətívitee/ *n.* **1** the fact or state of being relative. **2** *Physics* **a** (**special theory of relativity** or **special relativity**) a theory based on the principle that all motion is relative and that light has constant veloc-

ity. **b** (**general theory of relativity** or **general relativity**) a theory extending this to gravitation and accelerated motion.

re·lax /riláks/ *v.* **1 a** *tr. & intr.* make or become less stiff or rigid. **b** *tr. & intr.* make or become loose or slack; diminish in force or tension (*relaxed my grip*). **c** *tr. & intr.* (also as *int.*) make or become less tense or anxious. **2** *tr. & intr.* make or become less formal or strict (*rules were relaxed*). **3** *tr.* reduce or abate (one's attention, efforts, etc.). **4** *intr.* cease work or effort. **5** *tr.* (as **relaxed** *adj.*) at ease; unperturbed.

re·lax·ant /riláksənt/ *n. & adj.* •*n.* a drug, etc., that relaxes and reduces tension. •*adj.* causing relaxation.

re·lax·a·tion /réelaksáyshən/ *n.* **1** the act of relaxing or state of being relaxed. **2** recreation. **3** a partial remission or relaxing of a penalty, duty, etc. **4** a lessening of severity, precision, etc.

re·lay[1] /réelay/ *n. & v.* •*n.* **1** a fresh set of people or horses substituted for tired ones. **2** a gang of workers, supply of material, etc., deployed on the same basis. **3** = RELAY RACE. **4** a device activating changes in an electric circuit, etc., in response to other changes affecting itself. **5 a** a device to receive, reinforce, and transmit a message, broadcast, etc. **b** a relayed message or transmission. •*v.tr.* (also /riláy/) receive (a message, broadcast, etc.) and transmit it to others.

re·lay[2] /réeláy/ *v.tr.* (*past* and *past part.* **relaid**) lay again or differently.

re·lay race *n.* a race between teams of which each member in turn covers part of the distance.

re·learn /réelərn/ *v.tr.* learn again.

re·lease /riléés/ *v. & n.* •*v.tr.* **1** (often foll. by *from*) set free; liberate; unfasten. **2** allow to move from a fixed position. **3** make (information, a film, etc.) publicly or generally available. **4** *Law* **a** remit (a debt). **b** surrender (a right). •*n.* **1** deliverance or liberation from a restriction, duty, or difficulty. **2** a handle or catch that releases part of a mechanism. **3** a document or item of information made available for publication (*press release*). **4 a** a film or record, etc., that is released. **b** the act or an instance of releasing or the process of being released in this way. **5** *Law* **a** the act of releasing (property, money, or a right) to another. **b** a document effecting this.

rel·e·gate /réligayt/ *v.tr.* **1** consign or dismiss to an inferior or less important position; demote. **2** banish. **3** (foll. by *to*) transfer (a matter) for decision or implementation. ▫▫ **rel·e·ga·tion** /–gáyshən/ *n.*

re·lent /rilént/ *v.intr.* **1** abandon a harsh intention. **2** yield to compassion. **3** relax one's severity; become less stern.

re·lent·less /riléntlis/ *adj.* **1** unrelenting. **2** oppressively constant. ▫▫ **re·lent·less·ly** *adv.* **re·lent·less·ness** *n.*

rel·e·vant /rélivənt/ *adj.* (often foll. by *to*) bearing on or having reference to the matter in hand. ▫▫ **rel·e·vance** *n.* **rel·e·van·cy** *n.* **rel·e·vant·ly** *adv.*

re·li·a·ble /rilíəbəl/ *adj.* **1** that may be relied on. **2** of sound and consistent character or quality. ▫▫ **re·li·a·bil·i·ty** /–bílitee/ *n.* **re·li·a·bly** *adv.*

re·li·ance /rilíəns/ *n.* **1** (foll. by *in, on*) trust, confidence. **2** a thing relied upon. ▫▫ **re·li·ant** *adj.*

rel·ic /rélik/ *n.* an object interesting because of its age or association. **2** a part of a deceased holy person's body or belongings kept as an object of reverence. **3** a surviving custom or belief, etc., from a past age. **4** a memento or souvenir. **5** (in *pl.*) what has survived destruction or wasting or use.

rel·ict /rélikt/ *n.* **1** an object surviving in its primitive form. **2** an animal or plant known to have existed in the same form in previous geological ages.

re·lief /riléef/ *n.* **1 a** the alleviation of or deliverance from pain, distress, anxiety, etc. **b** the feeling accompanying such deliverance. **2** a feature, etc., that diversifies monotony or relaxes tension. **3** assistance given to those in special need. **4 a** the replacing of a person or persons on duty by another or others. **b** a person or persons replacing others in this way. **5** a method of molding or carving or stamping in which the design stands out from the surface. **6** vividness; distinctness (*brings the facts out in sharp relief*).

re·lief map *n.* **1** a map indicating hills and valleys by shading, etc., rather than by contour lines alone. **2** a map model showing elevations and depressions, usu. on an exaggerated relative scale.

re·lieve /riléev/ *v.tr.* **1** bring or provide aid or assistance to. **2** alleviate or reduce (pain, suffering, etc.). **3** mitigate the tedium or monotony of. **4** bring military support for (a besieged place). **5** release (a person) from a duty by acting as or providing a substitute. **6** (foll. by *of*) take (a burden or responsibility) away from (a person). **7** bring into relief; cause to appear solid or detached. ▫ **relieve oneself** urinate or defecate.

re·lieved /riléevd/ *predic.adj.* freed from anxiety or distress (*am very relieved to hear it*). ▫▫ **re·liev·ed·ly** *adv.*

re·light /réelít/ *v.tr.* (*past* and *past part.* **relighted** or **relit**) light (a fire, etc.) again.

re·li·gion /rilíjən/ *n.* **1** the belief in a superhuman controlling power, esp. in a personal God or gods entitled to obedience and worship. **2** the expression of this in worship. **3** a particular system of faith and worship. **4** life under monastic vows (*the way of religion*). **5** a thing that one is devoted to (*football is their religion*).

re·li·gi·ose /rilíjeeōs/ *adj.* excessively religious. ▫▫ **re·li·gi·os·i·ty** /rilíjeeósitee/ *n.*

re·li·gious /rilíjəs/ *adj.* **1** devoted to religion; pious; devout. **2** of or concerned with religion. **3** of or belonging to a monastic order. **4** scrupulous; conscientious (*a religious attention to detail*). ▫▫ **re·li·gious·ly** *adv.* **re·li·gious·ness** *n.*

re·line /réelín/ *v.tr.* renew the lining of (a garment, etc.).

re·lin·quish /rilíngkwish/ *v.tr.* **1** surrender or resign (a right or possession). **2** give up or cease from (a habit, plan, belief, etc.). **3** relax hold of (an object held). ▫▫ **re·lin·quish·ment** *n.*

rel·i·quar·y /rélikweree/ *n.* (*pl.* **-ies**) esp. *Relig.* a receptacle for relics.

rel·ish /rélish/ *n. & v.* •*n.* **1** (often foll. by *for*) **a** great liking or enjoyment. **b** keen or pleasurable longing (*had no relish for traveling*). **2 a** an appetizing flavor. **b** an attractive quality. **3** a condiment eaten with plainer food to add flavor. **4** (foll. by *of*) a distinctive taste or tinge. •*v.tr.* **1** get pleasure out of; enjoy greatly. **2** anticipate with pleasure (*did not relish what lay before her*).

---

relish Middle English : alteration of obsolete *reles*, from Old French *reles* 'remainder,' from *relaisser* 'to release.' The early noun sense was 'odor, taste' giving rise to 'appetizing flavor, piquant taste' (mid-17th century), and hence sense 3 (late 18th century).

---

re·live /réelív/ *v.tr.* live (an experience, etc.) over again, esp. in the imagination.

re·load /réelṓd/ *v.tr.* (also *absol.*) load again.

re·lo·cate /reelṓkayt/ *v.* **1** *tr.* locate in a new place. **2** *tr. & intr.* move to a new place. ▫▫ **re·lo·ca·tion** /–káyshən/ *n.*

re·luc·tant /rilúktənt/ *adj.* (often foll. by *to* + infin.) unwilling or disinclined (*most reluctant to agree*). ▫▫ **re·luc·tance** *n.* **re·luc·tant·ly** *adv.*

re·ly /rilí/ *v.intr.* (**-lies, -lied**) (foll. by *on, upon*) **1** depend on with confidence or assurance. **2** be dependent on.

REM /rem/ *abbr.* rapid eye movement.

rem /rem/ *n.* (*pl.* same) a unit of effective absorbed dose of ionizing radiation in human tissue.

re•made *past* and *past part.* of REMAKE.

re•main /rimáyn/ *v.intr.* **1 a** be left over after others or other parts have been removed or used or dealt with. **b** (of a period of time) be still to elapse. **2** be in the same place or condition during further time (*remained at home*). **3** continue to be. **4** (as **remaining** *adj.*) left behind; not having been used or dealt with (*remaining supplies*).

re•main•der /rimáyndər/ *n.* & *v.* •*n.* **1** a part remaining or left over. **2** remaining persons or things. **3** a number left after division or subtraction. **4** the copies of a book left unsold when demand has fallen. •*v.tr.* dispose of (a remainder of books) at a reduced price.

re•mains /rimáynz/ *n.pl.* **1** what remains after other parts have been removed or used, etc. **2 a** traces of former animal or plant life (*fossil remains*). **b** relics of antiquity (*Roman remains*). **3** a person's body after death.

re•make *v.* & *n.* •*v.tr.* /réemáyk/ (*past* and *past part.* **remade**) make again or differently. •*n.* /réemayk/ a thing that has been remade, esp. a movie.

re•man /réemán/ *v.tr.* (**remanned, remanning**) **1** equip (troops, etc.) with new personnel. **2** make courageous again.

re•mand /rimánd/ *v.* & *n.* •*v.tr.* **1** return (a prisoner) to custody, esp. to allow further inquiries. **2** return (a case) to a lower court for reconsideration. •*n.* a recommittal to custody. □ **on remand** in custody pending trial.

rem•a•nent /rémənənt/ *adj.* **1** remaining; residual. **2** (of magnetism) remaining after the magnetizing field has been removed. □□ **rem•a•nence** *n.*

re•mark /rimaárk/ *v.* & *n.* •*v.* **1** *tr.* (often foll. by *that* + clause) **a** say by way of comment. **b** take notice of; regard with attention. **2** *intr.* (usu. foll. by *on, upon*) make a comment. •*n.* **1** a written or spoken comment; anything said. **2 a** the act of noticing or observing. **b** the act of commenting (*let it pass without remark*).

re•mark•a•ble /rimaárkəbəl/ *adj.* **1** worth notice; exceptional. **2** striking; conspicuous. □□ **re•mark•a•bly** *adv.*

re•mar•ry /réemáree/ *v.intr.* & *tr.* (**-ries, -ried**) marry again. □□ **re•mar•riage** *n.*

re•mas•ter /réemástər/ *v.tr.* make a new master of (a recording).

re•match /réemach/ *n.* a return match or game.

re•me•di•al /riméedeeəl/ *adj.* **1** affording or intended as a remedy (*remedial therapy*). **2** (of teaching) for those in need of improvement in a particular discipline.

rem•e•dy /rémidee/ *n.* & *v.* •*n.* (*pl.* **-dies**) (often foll. by *for, against*) **1** a medicine or treatment (for a disease, etc.). **2** a means of counteracting or removing anything undesirable. **3** redress; legal or other reparation. •*v.tr.* (**-dies, -died**) **1** rectify; make good. **2** heal; cure (a person, diseased part, etc.) □□ **re•me•di•a•ble** /riméedeeəbəl/ *adj.*

re•mem•ber /rimémbər/ *v.tr.* **1** keep in the memory; not forget. **2 a** (also *absol.*) bring back into one's thoughts. **b** (often foll. by *to* + infin. or *that* + clause) have in mind (a duty, commitment, etc.) (*will you remember to lock the door?*). **3** think of or acknowledge (a person), esp. in making a gift, etc. **4** (foll. by *to*) convey greetings from (one person) to (another).

re•mem•brance /rimémbrəns/ *n.* **1** the act of remembering or process of being remembered. **2** a memory or recollection. **3** a keepsake or souvenir. **4** (in *pl.*) greetings conveyed through a third person.

re•mind /rimínd/ *v.tr.* **1** (foll. by *of*) cause (a person) to think of. **2** (foll. by *to* + infin. or *that* + clause) cause (a person) to remember a commitment, etc.

re•mind•er /rimíndər/ *n.* **1** a thing that reminds, esp. a letter or bill. **2** (often foll. by *of*) a memento or souvenir.

rem•i•nisce /réminís/ *v.intr.* (often foll. by *about*) indulge in reminiscence. □□ **rem•i•nis•cer** *n.*

rem•i•nis•cence /réminísəns/ *n.* **1** the act of remembering things past. **2 a** a past fact or experience that is remembered. **b** the process of narrating this. **3** (in *pl.*) a collection in literary form of incidents and experiences that a person remembers. **4** a characteristic of one thing reminding or suggestive of another.

rem•i•nis•cent /réminísənt/ *adj.* **1** (foll. by *of*) tending to remind one of or suggest. **2** concerned with reminiscence. **3** (of a person) given to reminiscing.

re•miss /rimís/ *adj.* careless of duty; lax; negligent. □□ **re•miss•ness** *n.*

re•mis•si•ble /rimísibəl/ *adj.* that may be remitted.

re•mis•sion /rimíshən/ *n.* **1** (often foll. by *of*) forgiveness (of sins, etc.). **2** the remitting of a debt or penalty, etc. **3** a diminution of force, effect, or degree (esp. of disease or pain).

re•mit *v.* & *n.* •*v.* /rimít/ (**remitted, remitting**) **1** *tr.* cancel or refrain from exacting or inflicting (a debt or punishment, etc.). **2** *intr.* & *tr.* abate or slacken; cease or cease from partly or entirely. **3** *tr.* send (money, etc.) in payment. **4** *tr.* cause to be conveyed by mail. **5** *tr.* **a** (foll. by *to*) refer (a matter for decision, etc.) to some authority. **b** *Law* send back (a case) to a lower court. **6** *tr.* **a** (often foll. by *to*) postpone or defer. **b** (foll. by *in, into*) send or put back into a previous state. **7** *tr.* *Theol.* pardon (sins, etc.). •*n.* /réemit, rimít/ **1** the terms of reference of a committee, etc. **2** an item remitted for consideration. □□ **re•mit•ta•ble** /–mítəbəl/ *adj.*

re•mit•tance /rimít'ns/ *n.* **1** money sent, esp. by mail. **2** the act of sending money.

re•mit•tent /rimít'nt/ *adj.* (of a fever) that abates at intervals.

re•mix *v.* & *n.* •*v.tr.* /réemíks/ mix again. •*n.* /réemiks/ a sound recording that has been remixed.

rem•nant /rémnənt/ *n.* **1** a small remaining quantity. **2** a piece of cloth, etc., left when the greater part has been used or sold. **3** (foll. by *of*) a surviving trace.

re•mod•el /réemód'l/ *v.tr.* **1** model again or differently. **2** reconstruct.

re•mold /réemṓld/ *v.tr.* mold again; refashion.

re•mon•strance /rimónstrəns/ *n.* **1** the act or an instance of remonstrating. **2** an expostulation or protest.

re•mon•strate /rémonstráyt, rimón–/ *v.* **1** *intr.* (foll. by *with*) make a protest; argue forcibly. **2** *tr.* (often foll. by *that* + clause) urge protestingly. □□ **re•mon•stra•tion** /rémənstráyshən/ *n.*

re•mon•tant /rimóntənt/ *adj.* & *n.* •*adj.* blooming more than once a year. •*n.* a remontant rose.

re•morse /rimáwrs/ *n.* **1** deep regret for a wrong committed. **2** compunction; a compassionate reluctance to inflict pain (esp. in *without remorse*).

re•morse•ful /rimáwrsfool/ *adj.* filled with repentance. □□ **re•morse•ful•ly** *adv.*

re•morse•less /rimáwrslis/ *adj.* **1** without compassion or compunction. **2** relentless; unabating. □□ **re•morse•less•ly** *adv.* **re•morse•less•ness** *n.*

re•mort•gage /réemáwrgij/ *v.* & *n.* •*v.tr.* (also *absol.*) mortgage again; revise the terms of an existing mortgage on (a property). •*n.* a different or altered mortgage.

re•mote /rimṓt/ *adj.* (**remoter, remotest**) **1** far away in place or time. **2** situated away from the main centers of population, society, etc. **3** distantly related (*a remote ancestor*). **4** slight; faint (esp. in *not the remotest chance, idea*, etc.). **5** (of a person) aloof; not friendly. **6** (foll. by *from*) widely different; separate by nature. □□ **re•mote•ly** *adv.* **re•mote•ness** *n.*

re•mote con•trol *n.* control of a machine or apparatus

from a distance by means of signals transmitted from a radio or electronic device. ▫▫ **re·mote-con·trolled** *adj.*

re·mount *v. & n.* •*v.* /reémównt/ **1 a** *tr.* mount (a horse, etc.) again. **b** *intr.* get on horseback again. **2** *tr.* get on to or ascend (a ladder, hill, etc.) again. **3** *tr.* provide (a person) with a fresh horse, etc. **4** *tr.* put (a picture) on a fresh mount. •*n.* /reémownt/ **1** a fresh horse for a rider. **2** a supply of fresh horses for a regiment.

re·mov·al /rimóóvəl/ *n.* **1** the act or an instance of removing; the process of being removed. **2 a** dismissal from an office or post; deposition. **b** (an act of) murder.

re·move /rimóóv/ *v. & n.* •*v.* **1** *tr.* take off or away from the place or position occupied; detach. **2** *tr.* **a** move or take to another place; change the situation of. **b** get rid of; eliminate. **3** *tr.* cause to be no longer present or available; take away. **4** *tr.* (often foll. by *from*) dismiss (from office). **5** *tr. colloq.* kill; assassinate. **6** *tr.* (in *passive*; foll. by *from*) distant or remote in condition (*the country is not far removed from anarchy*). **7** *tr.* (as **removed** *adj.*) (esp. of cousins) separated by a specified number of steps of descent (*a first cousin twice removed* = a grandchild of a first cousin). **8** *formal* **a** *intr.* (usu. foll. by *from, to*) change one's home or place of residence. **b** *tr.* conduct the removal of. •*n.* a stage in a gradation; a degree (*is several removes from what I expected*). ▫▫ **re·mov·a·ble** *adj.* **re·mov·a·bil·i·ty** /–móóvəbílitee/ *n.*

re·mu·ner·ate /rimyóónərayt/ *v.tr.* **1** reward; pay for services rendered. **2** serve as or provide recompense for (toil, etc.) or to (a person). ▫▫ **re·mu·ner·a·tion** /–ráyshən/ *n.* **re·mu·ner·a·tive** /–rətiv, –raytiv/ *adj.*

Ren·ais·sance /rénəsaáns, –zaáns, esp. *Brit.* rináysəns/ *n.* **1** the revival of art and literature in the 14th–16th c. **2** the period of this. **3** the culture and style of art, architecture, etc., developed during this era. **4** (**renaissance**) any similar revival.

re·nal /reénəl/ *adj.* of or concerning the kidneys.

re·name /reénáym/ *v.tr.* name again; give a new name to.

re·nas·cence /rinásəns, rináy–/ *n.* **1** rebirth; renewal. **2** = RENAISSANCE.

re·nas·cent /rinásənt, rináy–/ *adj.* springing up anew; being reborn.

ren·coun·ter /renkówntər/ *n. & v.* •*n.* **1** an encounter; a chance meeting. **2** a battle, skirmish, or duel.•*v.tr.* encounter; meet by chance.

rend /rend/ *v.* (*past* and *past part.* **rent** /rent/) *archaic* or *rhet.* **1** *tr.* (foll. by *off, from, away*, etc.; also *absol.*) tear or wrench forcibly. **2** *tr. & intr.* divide in pieces or into factions (*a country rent by civil war*). **3** *tr.* cause emotional pain to (the heart, etc.). ▫ **rend one's garments** (or **hair**) display extreme grief or rage.

rend·er /réndər/ *v.tr.* **1** cause to be or become (*rendered us helpless*). **2** give or pay (money, service, etc.), esp. in return or as a thing due (*render thanks*). **3** (often foll. by *to*) **a** give (assistance) (*rendered aid to the injured man*). **b** show (obedience, etc.). **c** do (a service, etc.). **4 a** submit; send in; present (an account, reason, etc.). **b** *Law* (of a judge or jury) deliver formally (a judgment or verdict). **5 a** represent or portray artistically, musically, etc. **b** act (a role); represent (a character, idea, etc.). **c** *Mus.* perform; execute. **6** translate (*rendered the poem into French*). **7** (often foll. by *down*) melt down (fat, etc.) esp. to clarify; extract by melting. **8** cover (stone or brick) with a coat of plaster. **9** *archaic* give back; hand over; deliver; give up; surrender.

rend·er·ing /réndəring/ *n.* **1 a** the act or an instance of performing music, drama, etc.; an interpretation or performance (*an excellent rendering of the part*). **b** a translation. **c** a work of visual art, esp. a detailed drawing. **2** an act of giving, yielding, or surrendering.

ren·dez·vous /róndayvoo, –də–/ *n. & v.* •*n.* (*pl.* same /–vooz/) **1** an agreed or regular meeting place. **2** a meeting by arrangement. **3** a place appointed for assembling troops, ships, etc. •*v.intr.* (**rendezvouses** /–vooz/; **rendezvoused** /–vood/; **rendezvousing** /–vooing/) meet at a rendezvous.

ren·di·tion /rendíshən/ *n.* (often foll. by *of*) **1** an interpretation or rendering of a dramatic role, piece of music, etc. **2** a visual representation.

ren·e·gade /rénigayd/ *n., adj., & v.* •*n.* **1** a person who deserts a party or principles. **2** an apostate; a person who abandons one religion for another. •*adj.* traitorous, heretical. •*v.intr.* be a renegade.

re·nege /riníg, –nég, –neég/ *v.* **1** *intr.* **a** go back on one's word; change one's mind; recant. **b** (foll. by *on*) go back on (a promise or undertaking or contract). **2** *tr.* deny; renounce; abandon (a person, faith, etc.).

re·ne·go·ti·ate /reénigósheeayt/ *v.tr.* (also *absol.*) negotiate again or on different terms. ▫▫ **re·ne·go·ti·a·ble** /–sheeəbəl, –shəbəl/ *adj.* **re·ne·go·ti·a·tion** /–sheeáyshən/ *n.*

re·new /rinóó, –nyóó/ *v.tr.* **1** revive; make new again; restore to the original state. **2** reinforce; resupply; replace. **3** repeat or reestablish; resume after an interruption. **4** get, begin, make, say, give, etc., anew. **5** (also *absol.*) grant or be granted a continuation of (a license, subscription, lease, etc.). **6** recover (one's youth, strength, etc.). ▫▫ **re·new·a·ble** *adj.* **re·new·al** *n.*

ren·net /rénit/ *n.* **1** curdled milk found in the stomach of an unweaned calf, used in curdling milk for cheese, junket, etc. **2** a preparation made from the stomach membrane of a calf or from certain fungi.

ren·nin /rénin/ *n. Biochem.* an enzyme secreted into the stomach of unweaned mammals causing the clotting of milk.

re·nom·i·nate /reénóminayt/ *v.tr.* nominate for a further term of office. ▫▫ **re·nom·i·na·tion** /–náyshən/ *n.*

re·nounce /rinówns/ *v.* **1** *tr.* consent formally to abandon (a claim, right, possession, etc.). **2** *tr.* repudiate; refuse to recognize any longer (*renouncing their father's authority*). **3** *tr.* **a** decline further association or disclaim relationship with. **b** withdraw from; discontinue; forsake. **4** *intr. Law* refuse or resign a right or position esp. as an heir or trustee.

ren·o·vate /rénəvayt/ *v.tr.* **1** restore to good condition; repair. **2** make new again. ▫▫ **ren·o·va·tion** /–váyshən/ *n.* **ren·o·va·tor** *n.*

re·nown /rinówn/ *n.* fame; high distinction (*a city of great renown*).

re·nowned /rinównd/ *adj.* famous; celebrated.

rent[1] /rent/ *n. & v.* •*n.* **1** a tenant's periodical payment to an owner for the use of land or premises. **2** payment for the use of a service, equipment, etc. •*v.* **1** *tr.* (often foll. by *from*) take, occupy, or use at a rent (*rented a boat from the marina*) . **2** *tr.* (often foll. by *out*) let or hire (a thing) for rent. **3** *intr.* (foll. by *for, at*) be let or hired out at a specified rate (*the room rents for $300 per month*).

rent[2] /rent/ *n.* **1** a large tear in a garment, etc. **2** an opening in clouds, etc. **3** a cleft, fissure, or gorge.

rent[3] *past* and *past part.* of REND.

rent-a- *comb. form* often *joc.* denoting availability for hire (*rent-a-car*).

rent·a·ble /réntəbəl/ *adj.* **1** available or suitable for renting. **2** giving an adequate ratio of profit to capital. ▫▫ **rent·a·bil·i·ty** /–bílitee/ *n.*

rent·al /rént'l/ *n.* **1** the amount paid or received as rent. **2** the act of renting. **3** an income from rents. **4** a rented house, car, etc.

rent·er /réntər/ *n.* a person who rents.

re•num•ber /reénúmbər/ *v.tr.* change the number or numbers given.

re•nun•ci•a•tion /rinúnseeáyshən/ *n.* **1** the act or an instance of renouncing. **2** self-denial. **3** a document expressing renunciation. ▫▫ **re•nun•ci•ant** /rinúnseeənt/ *n.* & *adj.* **re•nun•ci•a•to•ry** /–seeətáwree, –shətáwree/ *adj.*

re•oc•cu•py /reé-ókyəpī/ *v.tr.* (**-pies, -pied**) occupy again. ▫▫ **re•oc•cu•pa•tion** /–páyshən/ *n.*

re•oc•cur /reéəkə́r/ *v.intr.* (**reoccurred, reoccurring**) occur again or habitually. ▫▫ **re•oc•cur•rence** /–kúrəns/ *n.*

re•o•pen /reé-ṓpən/ *v.tr.* & *intr.* open again.

re•or•der /reé-áwrdər/ *v.* & *n.* • *v.tr.* order again. • *n.* a renewed or repeated order for goods.

re•or•gan•ize /reé-áwrgənīz/ *v.tr.* organize differently. ▫▫ **re•or•gan•i•za•tion** /–záyshən/ *n.*

re•or•i•ent /reé-áwree-ent, –óree-ent/ *v.tr.* **1** give a new direction to (ideas, etc.); redirect (a thing). **2** help (a person) find his or her bearings again. **3** change the outlook of (a person). **4** (*refl.*, often foll. by *to*) adjust oneself to or come to terms with something.

re•or•i•en•tate /reé-áwreeəntayt, –óreeən–/ *v.tr.* = REORIENT. ▫▫ **re•or•i•en•ta•tion** /–táyshən/ *n.*

Rep. *abbr.* **1** Representative (in Congress, state legislature, etc.). **2** Republican. **3** Republic.

rep[1] /rep/ *n. colloq.* a representative, esp. a salesperson.

rep[2] /rep/ *n. colloq.* **1** repertory. **2** a repertory theater or company.

re•pack /reépák/ *v.tr.* pack again.

re•pack•age /reépákij/ *v.tr.* **1** package again or differently. **2** present in a new form. ▫▫ **re•pack•ag•ing** *n.*

re•pag•i•nate /reépájinayt/ *v.tr.* paginate again; renumber the pages of.

re•paid *past* and *past part.* of REPAY.

re•paint *v.* & *n.* • *v.tr.* /reépáynt/ **1** paint again or differently. **2** restore the paint or coloring of. • *n.* /reépaynt/ the act of repainting.

re•pair[1] /ripáir/ *v.* & *n.* • *v.tr.* **1** restore to good condition after damage or wear. **2** renovate or mend by replacing or fixing parts or by compensating for loss or exhaustion. **3** set right or make amends for (loss, wrong, error, etc.). • *n.* **1** the act or an instance of restoring to sound condition. **2** the result of this. **3** good or relative condition for working or using. ▫▫ **re•pair•a•ble** *adj.* **re•pair•er** *n.*

re•pair[2] /ripáir/ *v.intr.* (foll. by *to*) resort; have recourse; go often or in great numbers or for a specific purpose.

re•pand /ripánd/ *adj. Bot.* with an undulating margin; wavy.

re•pap•er /reépáypər/ *v.tr.* paper (a wall, etc.) again.

rep•a•ra•ble /répərəbəl, ripáirəbəl/ *adj.* (of a loss, etc.) that can be made good.

rep•a•ra•tion /répəráyshən/ *n.* **1** the act or an instance of making amends. **2 a** compensation. **b** (esp. in *pl.*) compensation for war damage paid by the defeated nation, etc. **3** the act or an instance of repairing or being repaired.

rep•ar•tee /répaarteé, –táy/ *n.* **1** the practice or faculty of making witty retorts. **2** witty banter.

re•pass /reépás/ *v.tr.* & *intr.* pass again, esp. on the way back.

re•past /ripást/ *n.* **1** a meal. **2** food and drink supplied for or eaten at a meal.

re•pa•tri•ate /reépáytreeayt/ *v.* & *n.* • *v.* **1** *tr.* restore (a person) to his or her native land. **2** *intr.* return to one's own native land. • *n.* a person who has been repatriated. ▫▫ **re•pa•tri•a•tion** /–áyshən/ *n.*

re•pay /reépáy/ *v.* (*past* and *past part.* **repaid**) **1** *tr.* pay back (money). **2** *tr.* return (a blow, visit, etc.). **3** *tr.* make repayment to. **4** *tr.* requite (a service, action, etc.). **5** *tr.* (often foll. by *for*) give in recompense. **6** *intr.* make repayment. ▫▫ **re•pay•a•ble** *adj.* **re•pay•ment** *n.*

re•peal /ripeél/ *v.* & *n.* • *v.tr.* revoke or annul (a law, act of Congress, etc.). • *n.* the act or an instance of repealing.

re•peat /ripeét/ *v.* & *n.* • *v.* **1** *tr.* say or do over again. **2** *tr.* recite, rehearse, report, or reproduce (something from memory) (*repeated a poem*). **3** *tr.* imitate (an action, etc.). **4 a** *intr.* recur; appear again. **b** *refl.* recur in the same or a similar form. **5** *tr.* used for emphasis (*I am not, repeat not, going*). **6** *intr.* (of food) be tasted intermittently for some time after being swallowed as a result of belching or indigestion. **7** *intr.* (of a watch, etc.) strike the last quarter, etc., over again when required. **8** *intr.* (of a firearm) fire several shots without reloading. **9** *intr.* illegally vote more than once in an election. • *n.* **1 a** the act or an instance of repeating. **b** a thing repeated (often *attrib.*: *repeat performance*). **2** a repeated broadcast. **3** *Mus.* **a** a passage intended to be repeated. **b** a mark indicating this. **4** a pattern repeated in wallpaper, etc. ▫ **repeat oneself** say or do the same thing over again. ▫▫ **re•peat•a•ble** *adj.* **re•peat•ed•ly** *adv.*

re•peat•ing dec•i•mal *n.* a decimal fraction in which the same figures repeat indefinitely.

re•pel /ripél/ *v.tr.* (**repelled, repelling**) **1** drive back; ward off. **2** refuse admission or approach or acceptance to. **3** be repulsive or distasteful to. ▫▫ **re•pel•ler** *n.*

re•pel•lent /ripélənt/ *adj.* & *n.* • *adj.* **1** that which repels. **2** disgusting; repulsive. • *n.* a substance that repels esp. insects, etc. ▫▫ **re•pel•lence** *n.* **re•pel•lent•ly** *adv.*

▶**Repellent** and **repulsive** are very close in meaning, but the latter, perhaps because of its sound, is felt to express stronger feeling.

re•pent /ripént/ *v.* **1** *intr.* (often foll. by *of*) feel deep sorrow about one's actions, etc. **2** *tr.* (also *absol.*) wish one had not done; regret (one's wrong, omission, etc.); resolve not to continue (a wrongdoing, etc.). ▫▫ **re•pent•ance** *n.* **re•pent•ant** *adj.* **re•pent•er** *n.*

re•peo•ple /reépeépəl/ *v.tr.* people again; increase the population of.

re•per•cus•sion /reépərkúshən, répər–/ *n.* **1** (often foll. by *of*) an indirect effect or reaction following an event or action (*consider the repercussions of moving*). **2** the recoil after impact. **3** an echo.

rep•er•toire /répərtwaar/ *n.* **1** a stock of pieces, etc., that a company or a performer knows or is prepared to give. **2** a stock of regularly performed pieces, regularly used techniques, etc. (*went through his repertoire of excuses*).

rep•er•to•ry /répərtawree/ *n.* (*pl.* **-ries**) **1** = REPERTOIRE. **2** the theatrical performance of various plays for short periods by one company. **3 a** a repertory company. **b** repertory theaters regarded collectively. **4** a store or collection, esp. of information, instances, etc.

rep•e•tend /répitend/ *n.* **1** the recurring figures of a decimal. **2** a recurring word or phrase; a refrain.

rep•e•ti•tion /répitíshən/ *n.* **1 a** the act or an instance of repeating or being repeated. **b** the thing repeated. **2** a copy. **3** a piece to be learned by heart.

rep•e•ti•tious /répitíshəs/ *adj.* characterized by repetition, esp. when unnecessary or tiresome. ▫▫ **rep•e•ti•tious•ly** *adv.* **rep•e•ti•tious•ness** *n.*

re•pet•i•tive /ripétitiv/ *adj.* characterized by, or consisting of, repetition; monotonous. ▫▫ **re•pet•i•tive•ly** *adv.* **re•pet•i•tive•ness** *n.*

re•phrase /reéfráyz/ *v.tr.* express in an alternative way.

re•pine /ripín/ *v.intr.* (often foll. by *at, against, for*) fret; be discontented.

re•place /ripláys/ *v.tr.* **1** put back in place. **2** take the place of; be substituted for. **3** find or provide a substitute for. **4** (often foll. by *with, by*) fill up the place of. **5** (in *passive*, often foll. by *by*) be succeeded or have one's place filled by another; be superseded. ◻◻ **re·place·a·ble** *adj.*

re·place·ment /ripláysmənt/ *n.* **1** the act or an instance of replacing or being replaced. **2** a person or thing that takes the place of another.

re·plan /réeplán/ *v.tr.* (**replanned, replanning**) plan again or differently.

re·plant /réeplánt/ *v.tr.* **1** transfer (a plant, etc.) to a larger pot, a new site, etc. **2** plant (ground) again.

re·play *v.* & *n.* • *v.tr.* /réepláy/ play (a match, recording, etc.) again. • *n.* /réeplay/ the act or an instance of replaying a match, a recording, etc.

re·plen·ish /riplénish/ *v.tr.* **1** (often foll. by *with*) fill up again. **2** renew (a supply, etc.). **3** (as **replenished** *adj.*) filled; fully stocked; full. ◻◻ **re·plen·ish·ment** *n.*

re·plete /ripléet/ *adj.* (often foll. by *with*) **1** filled or well-supplied. **2** stuffed; gorged; sated. ◻◻ **re·ple·tion** *n.*

rep·li·ca /réplikə/ *n.* **1** a duplicate of a work made by the original artist. **2 a** a facsimile; an exact copy. **b** (of a person) an exact likeness; a double. **3** a copy or model, esp. on a smaller scale.

rep·li·cate /réplikayt/ *v.tr.* **1** repeat (an experiment, etc.). **2** make a replica of. **3** fold back. ◻◻ **rep·li·ca·ble** /–kəbəl/ *adj.* (in sense 1). **rep·li·ca·bil·i·ty** /–bílitee/ *n.* (in sense 1). **rep·li·ca·tive** /–kətiv/ *adj.*

rep·li·ca·tion /réplikáyshən/ *n.* **1** a reply or response, esp. a reply to an answer. **2** *Law* the plaintiff's reply to the defendant's plea. **3 a** the act or an instance of copying. **b** a copy. **c** the process by which genetic material or a living organism gives rise to a copy of itself.

re·ply /riplí/ *v.* & *n.* • *v.* (**-plies, -plied**) **1** *intr.* (often foll. by *to*) make an answer; respond in word or action. **2** *tr.* say in answer (*he replied, "Suit yourself"*). • *n.* (*pl.* **-plies**) **1** the act of replying (*what did they say in reply?*). **2** what is replied; a response. **3** *Law* = REPLICATION.

re·pop·u·late /réepópyəlayt/ *v.tr.* populate again or increase the population of. ◻◻ **re·pop·u·la·tion** /–láyshən/ *n.*

re·port /ripáwrt/ *v.* & *n.* • *v.* **1** *tr.* **a** bring back or give an account of. **b** state as fact or news; narrate or describe or repeat, esp. as an eyewitness or hearer, etc. **c** relate as spoken by another. **2** *tr.* make an official or formal statement about. **3** *tr.* (often foll. by *to*) name or specify (an offender or offense). **4** *intr.* (often foll. by *to*) present oneself as having returned or arrived. **5** *tr.* (also *absol.*) take down word for word or summarize or write a description of for publication. **6** *intr.* make or draw up or send in a report. **7** *intr.* (often foll. by *to*) be responsible to (a superior, supervisor, etc.). **8** *tr.* (often foll. by *out*) (of a committee, etc.) send back (a bill, etc.), with comments and recommendations, to a legislature, etc. **9** *intr.* (often foll. by *of*) give a report to convey that one is well, badly, etc., impressed. **10** *intr.* (usu. foll. by *on*) investigate or scrutinize for a journalistic report; act as a reporter. • *n.* **1** an account given or opinion formally expressed after investigation or consideration. **2** a description, summary, or reproduction of an event, speech or legal case, esp. for newspaper publication or broadcast. **3** common talk; rumor. **4** the way a person or thing is spoken of. **5** a periodical statement on (esp. a student's) work, conduct, etc. **6** the sound of an explosion. ◻◻ **re·port·a·ble** *adj.* **re·port·ed·ly** *adv.*

report late Middle English: from Old French *reporter* (verb), *report* (noun), from Latin *reportare* 'bring back,' from *re-* 'back' + *portare* 'carry.' The sense 'give an account' gave rise to 'submit a formal report' and hence 'inform an authority of one's presence' (sense 4, mid-19th century) and 'be accountable for one's activities (to a superior)' (sense 6, late 19th century).

re·port·age /ripáwrtij, répawrtáazh/ *n.* **1** the reporting of news, etc., for the press and for broadcasting. **2** the typical style of this. **3** factual presentation in a book, etc.

re·port card *n.* an official report issued by a school showing a student's grades, progress, etc.

re·port·ed speech *n.* a speaker's words reported by another with the changes of person, tense, etc., e.g., *he said that he would go*, based on *I will go*.

re·port·er /ripáwrtər/ *n.* **1** a person employed to report news, etc., for newspapers or broadcasts. **2** a person who reports.

rep·or·to·ri·al /rípawrtáwreeəl/ *adj.* **1** of newspaper reporters. **2** relating to or characteristic of a report.

re·pose[1] /ripṓz/ *n.* & *v.* • *n.* **1** the cessation of activity or excitement or toil. **2** sleep. **3** a peaceful or quiescent state; stillness; tranquillity. • *v.* **1** *intr.* & *refl.* lie down in rest. **2** *tr.* (often foll. by *on*) lay (one's head, etc.) to rest. **3** *intr.* (often foll. by *in, on*) lie, be lying or laid, esp. in sleep or death. **4** *tr.* give rest to; refresh with rest. ◻◻ **re·pose·ful** *adj.* **re·pose·ful·ly** *adv.*

re·pose[2] /ripṓz/ *v.tr.* (foll. by *in*) place (trust, etc.) in.

re·po·si·tion /réepəzíshən/ *v.* **1** *tr.* move or place in a different position. **2** *intr.* alter one's position.

re·pos·i·to·ry /ripózitawree/ *n.* (*pl.* **-ries**) **1** a place where things are stored or may be found, esp. a warehouse or museum. **2** a receptacle. **3** (often foll. by *of*) **a** a book, person, etc., regarded as a store of information, etc. **b** the recipient of confidences or secrets.

re·pos·sess /réepəzés/ *v.tr.* regain possession of (esp. property or goods on which repayment of a debt is in arrears). ◻◻ **re·pos·ses·sion** *n.*

re·pous·sé /rəpōōsáy/ *adj.* & *n.* • *adj.* hammered into relief from the reverse side. • *n.* ornamental metalwork fashioned in this way.

rep·re·hend /réprihénd/ *v.tr.* rebuke; find fault with. ◻◻ **rep·re·hen·sion** *n.*

rep·re·hen·si·ble /réprihénsibəl/ *adj.* deserving censure or rebuke; blameworthy. ◻◻ **rep·re·hen·si·bil·i·ty** *n.* **rep·re·hen·si·bly** *adv.*

rep·re·sent /réprizént/ *v.tr.* **1** stand for or correspond to. **2** (often in *passive*) be a specimen or example of. **3** act as an embodiment of; symbolize. **4** place a likeness of before the mind or senses. **5** serve or be meant as a likeness of. **6 a** state by way of expostulation or persuasion (*represented the rashness of it*). **b** (foll. by *to*) try to make (the facts influencing conduct) clear to (*represented the risks to his client*). **7 a** (often foll. by *as, to be*) describe or depict as; declare or make out (*represented them as martyrs*). **b** (often *refl.*; usu. foll by *as*) portray; assume the guise of; pose as (*represents himself as an honest broker*). **8** (foll. by *that* + clause) allege. **9** show, or play the part of, on stage. **10** be a substitute or deputy for; be entitled to act or speak for (*the president was represented by the secretary of state*). **11** be elected as a member of Congress, a legislature, etc., by. ◻◻ **rep·re·sent·a·ble** *adj.*

rep·re·sen·ta·tion /réprizentáyshən/ *n.* **1** the act or an instance of representing or being represented. **2** a thing (esp. a painting, etc.) that represents another. **3** (esp. in *pl.*) a statement made by way of allegation or to convey opinion. ◻◻ **rep·re·sen·ta·tion·al** /–shənəl/ *adj.*

rep·re·sen·ta·tion·ism /réprizentáyshənizəm/ *n.* the doctrine that perceived objects are only a representation of real external objects. ◻◻ **rep·re·sen·ta·tion·ist** *n.*

rep·re·sen·ta·tive /réprizéntətiv/ *adj.* & *n.* • *adj.* **1** typical of a class. **2** containing typical specimens of all or many classes (*a representative sample*). **3 a** consisting of elected deputies, etc. **b** based on representation by such deputies. **4** (foll. by *of*) serving as a portrayal or symbol of. **5** that presents or can present ideas to the mind (*imagination is a representative faculty*). •*n.* **1** (foll. by *of*) a sample, specimen, or typical embodiment of. **2 a** the agent of a person or society. **b** a salesperson. **3** a delegate; a substitute. **4** a deputy in a representative assembly.

re•press /riprés/ *v.tr.* **1 a** keep under; quell. **b** suppress; prevent from sounding, rioting, or bursting out. **2** *Psychol.* actively exclude (an unwelcome thought) from conscious awareness. **3** (usu. as **repressed** *adj.*) subject (a person) to the suppression of his or her thoughts or impulses. ▫▫ **re•press•i•ble** *adj.* **re•pres•sion** /–préshən/ *n.* **re•pres•sive** *adj.* **re•pres•sive•ly** *adv.*

re•prieve /ripréev/ *v.* & *n.* •*v.tr.* **1** remit, commute, or postpone the execution of (a condemned person). **2** give respite to. •*n.* **1 a** the act or an instance of reprieving or being reprieved. **b** a warrant for this. **2** respite; a respite or temporary escape.

reprieve late 15th century (as the past participle *repryed*): from Anglo-Norman French *repris* (source of *reprise*), past participle of *reprendre*, from Latin *re-* 'back' + *prehendere* 'seize.' The insertion of *-v-* (16th century) remains unexplained. Sense development has undergone a reversal, from the early meaning 'send back to prison,' via 'postpone (a legal process),' to the current sense 'rescue from impending punishment.'

rep•ri•mand /réprimand/ *n.* & *v.* •*n.* (often foll. by *for*) an official or sharp rebuke. •*v.tr.* administer this to.

re•print *v.* & *n.* •*v.tr.* /reéprínt/ print again. •*n.* /reéprint/ **1** the act or an instance of reprinting a book, etc. **2** the book, etc., reprinted. **3** the quantity reprinted.

re•pris•al /riprízəl/ *n.* (an act of) retaliation.

re•prise /ripréez/ *n.* **1** a repeated passage in music. **2** a repeated item in a musical program.

re•pro /reéprō/ *n.* (*pl.* **-pros**) (often *attrib.*) **1** a reproduction or copy. **2** (also **reproduction proof**) a proof, usu. on glossy paper, that can be used as photographic copy for a printing plate.

re•proach /riprṓch/ *v.* & *n.* •*v.tr.* **1** express disapproval to (a person) for a fault, etc. **2** scold; rebuke; censure. •*n.* **1** a rebuke or censure. **2** (often foll. by *to*) a thing that brings disgrace or discredit (*their behavior is a reproach to us all*). **3** a disgraced or discredited state. ▫ **above** (or **beyond**) **reproach** perfect.

re•proach•ful /riprṓchfŏŏl/ *adj.* full of or expressing reproach. ▫▫ **re•proach•ful•ly** *adv.*

rep•ro•bate /réprəbayt/ *n.*, *adj.*, & *v.* •*n.* **1** an unprincipled person; a person of highly immoral character. **2** a person who is condemned by God. •*adj.* **1** immoral. **2** hardened in sin. •*v.tr.* **1** express or feel disapproval of; censure. **2** (of God) condemn; exclude from salvation. ▫▫ **rep•ro•ba•tion** /–báyshən/ *n.*

re•proc•ess /reéprόses, –prṓ–/ *v.tr.* process again or differently.

re•pro•duce /reéprədŏŏs, –dyŏŏs/ *v.* **1** *tr.* produce a copy or representation of. **2** *tr.* cause to be seen or heard, etc., again. **3** *intr.* produce further members of the same species by natural means. **4** *refl.* produce offspring. **5** *intr.* give a specified quality or result when copied. ▫▫ **re•pro•duc•er** *n.* **re•pro•duc•i•ble** *adj.* **re•pro•duc•i•bil•i•ty** /–əbílitee/ *n.*

re•pro•duc•tion /reéprədúkshən/ *n.* **1** the act or an instance of reproducing. **2** a copy of a work of art. **3** (*attrib.*) (of furniture, etc.) made in imitation of a certain style or of an earlier period. ▫▫ **re•pro•duc•tive** *adj.* **re•pro•duc•tive•ly** *adv.*

re•pro•duc•tive or•gans *n.pl.* the internal and external structures of a person, animal, or plant which are concerned with reproduction, especially sexual reproduction.

re•pro•gram /reéprṓgram/ *v.tr.* (**reprogrammed, reprogramming**) program (esp. a computer) again or differently. ▫▫ **re•pro•gram•ma•ble** /–prṓgraməbəl, –prōgrám–/ *adj.*

re•prog•ra•phy /riprógrəfee/ *n.* the science and practice of copying documents by photography, xerography, etc. ▫▫ **re•pro•graph•ic** /reéprəgráfik/ *adj.*

re•proof /riprŏŏf/ *n.* **1** blame (*a glance of reproof*). **2** a rebuke.

re•prove /riprŏŏv/ *v.tr.* rebuke. ▫▫ **re•prov•ing•ly** *adv.*

rep•tile /réptīl/ *n.* & *adj.* •*n.* **1** any cold-blooded scaly animal of the class Reptilia, including snakes, lizards, crocodiles, turtles, etc. **2** a mean, groveling, or repulsive person. •*adj.* **1** (of an animal) creeping. **2** mean; groveling. ▫▫ **rep•til•i•an** /–tíleeən, –tílyən/ *adj.* & *n.*

re•pub•lic /ripúblik/ *n.* **1** a nation in which supreme power is held by the people or their elected representatives or by an elected or nominated president, not by a monarch, etc. **2** a society with equality between its members (*the literary republic*).

re•pub•li•can /ripúblikən/ *adj.* & *n.* •*adj.* **1** of or constituted as a republic. **2** characteristic of a republic. **3** advocating or supporting republican government. •*n.* **1** a person advocating or supporting republican government. **2** (**Republican**) a member or supporter of the Republican party. **3** an advocate of a united Ireland. ▫▫ **re•pub•li•can•ism** *n.*

Re•pub•li•can par•ty *n.* one of the two main US political parties, favoring a lesser degree of central power (cf. DEMOCRATIC PARTY).

re•pub•lish /reépúblish/ *v.tr.* (also *absol.*) publish again or in a new edition. ▫▫ **re•pub•li•ca•tion** /–likáyshən/ *n.*

re•pu•di•ate /ripyŏŏdeeayt/ *v.tr.* **1 a** disown; disavow; reject. **b** refuse dealings with. **c** deny. **2** refuse to recognize or obey (authority or a treaty). **3** refuse to discharge (an obligation or debt). ▫▫ **re•pu•di•a•tion** /–áyshən/ *n.*

re•pug•nance /ripúgnəns/ *n.* (also **re•pug•nan•cy**) **1** (usu. foll. by *to*, *against*) antipathy; aversion. **2** (usu. foll. by *of*, *between*, *to*, *with*) inconsistency or incompatibility of ideas, statements, etc. ▫▫ **re•pug•nant** /ripúgnənt/ *adj.*

re•pulse /ripúls/ *v.* & *n.* •*v.tr.* **1** drive back by force of arms. **2 a** rebuff. **b** refuse. **3** be repulsive to; repel. **4** foil in controversy. •*n.* **1** the act or an instance of repulsing or being repulsed. **2** a rebuff.

re•pul•sion /ripúlshən/ *n.* **1** aversion; disgust. **2** esp. *Physics* the force by which bodies tend to repel each other or increase their mutual distance (opp. ATTRACTION).

re•pul•sive /ripúlsiv/ *adj.* **1** causing aversion or loathing; disgusting. **2** *Physics* exerting repulsion. ▫▫ **re•pul•sive•ly** *adv.* **re•pul•sive•ness** *n.*

re•pur•chase /reépə́rchis/ *v.* & *n.* •*v.tr.* purchase again. •*n.* the act or an instance of purchasing again.

rep•u•ta•ble /répyətəbəl/ *adj.* of good repute; respectable. ▫▫ **rep•u•ta•bly** *adv.*

rep•u•ta•tion /répyətáyshən/ *n.* **1** what is generally said or believed about a person's or thing's character (*has a reputation for dishonesty*). **2** the state of being well thought of; distinction; respectability. **3** (foll. by *of*, *for* + verbal noun) credit or discredit (*has the reputation of driving hard bargains*).

re•pute /ripyŏŏt/ *n.* & *v.* •*n.* reputation (*known by repute*). •*v.tr.* **1** (as **reputed** *adj.*) (often foll. by *to* + infin.) be generally considered or reckoned. **2** (as **reputed** *adj.*) passing as, but probably not. ▫▫ **re•put•ed•ly** *adv.*

re•quest /rikwést/ *n.* & *v.* •*n.* **1** the act or an instance of asking for something. **2** a thing asked for. **3** the state of being sought after; demand (*in great request*). **4** a letter, etc., asking for a particular recording, etc., to be played on a radio program, often with a personal message. • *v.tr.* **1** ask to be given or allowed or favored with. **2** (foll. by *to* + infin.) ask a person to do something. **3** (foll. by *that* + clause) ask that. □ **by** (or **on**) **request** in response to an expressed wish. □□ **re·quest·er** *n.*

req·ui·em /rékweeəm, réekwee–/ *n.* **1** (**Requiem**) (also *attrib.*) *RC Ch., Anglican Ch.* a Mass for the repose of the souls of the dead. **2** *Mus.* the musical setting for this.

re·quire /rikwír/ *v.tr.* **1** need; depend on for success or fulfillment. **2** lay down as an imperative (*did all that was required by law*). **3** command; instruct (a person, etc.). **4** order; insist on (an action or measure). **5** (often foll. by *of*, *from*, or *that* + clause) demand (of or from a person) as a right. **6** wish to have (*is there anything else you require?*). □□ **re·quire·ment** *n.*

req·ui·site /rékwizit/ *adj.* & *n.* • *adj.* required by circumstances; necessary to success, etc. • *n.* (often foll. by *for*) a thing needed.

req·ui·si·tion /rékwizíshən/ *n.* & *v.* • *n.* **1** an official order laying claim to the use of property or materials. **2** a formal written demand that some duty should be performed. **3** being called or put into service. • *v.tr.* demand the use or supply of, esp. by requisition order. □□ **req·ui·si·tion·er** *n.*

re·quite /rikwít/ *v.tr.* **1** make return for (a service). **2** (often foll. by *with*) reward or avenge (a favor or injury). **3** (often foll. by *for*) make return to (a person). **4** (often foll. by *for*, *with*) repay with good or evil. □□ **re·quit·al** *n.*

re·read /rée-réed/ *v.* & *n.* • *v.tr.* (*past* and *past part.* **re·read** /–réd/) read again. • *n.* an instance of reading again. □□ **re·read·a·ble** *adj.*

rere·dos /rérədos, rírə–/ *n. Eccl.* an ornamental screen covering the wall at the back of an altar.

re·re·lease /rée-rilées/ *v.* & *n.* • *v.tr.* release (a recording, motion picture, etc.) again. • *n.* a rereleased recording, motion picture, etc.

re·route /rée-rŏŏt, –rówt/ *v.tr.* send or carry by a different route.

re·run *v.* & *n.* • *v.tr.* /rée-rún/ (**rerunning**; *past* **reran**; *past part.* **rerun**) run (a race, television program, etc.) again. • *n.* /rée-run/ **1** the act or an instance of rerunning. **2** a television program, etc., shown again.

re·sale /réesáyl/ *n.* the sale of a thing previously bought. □□ **re·sal·a·ble** *adj.*

re·sched·ule /réeskéjōōl/ *v.tr.* alter the schedule of; replan.

re·scind /risínd/ *v.tr.* abrogate; revoke; cancel. □□ **re·scis·sion** /–sízhən/ *n.*

res·cue /réskyōō/ *v.* & *n.* • *v.tr.* (**rescues, rescued, rescuing**) **1** (often foll. by *from*) save or set free from danger or harm. **2** *Law* **a** unlawfully liberate (a person). **b** forcibly recover (property). • *n.* the act or an instance of rescuing or being rescued; deliverance. □□ **res·cu·er** *n.*

re·seal /réeséel/ *v.tr.* seal again. □□ **re·seal·a·ble** *adj.*

re·search /risə́rch, réesərch/ *n.* & *v.* • *n.* **1** the systematic investigation into and study of materials, sources, etc., in order to establish facts and reach new conclusions. **2** (*attrib.*) engaged in or intended for research. • *v. tr.* do research into or for. □□ **re·search·er** *n.*

re·search and de·vel·op·ment *n.* (in industry, etc.) work directed toward the innovation, introduction, and improvement of products and processes.

re·seat /réeséet/ *v.tr.* **1** (also *refl.*) seat (oneself, a person, etc.) again. **2** provide with a fresh seat or seats.

re·se·lect /réesilékt/ *v.tr.* select again or differently. □□ **re·se·lec·tion** *n.*

re·sell /réesél/ *v.tr.* (*past* and *past part.* **resold**) sell (an object, etc.) after buying it.

re·sem·blance /rizémbləns/ *n.* (often foll. by *to*, *between*, *of*) a likeness or similarity. □□ **re·sem·blant** *adj.*

re·sem·ble /rizémbəl/ *v.tr.* be like; have a similarity to, or the same appearance as.

re·sent /rizént/ *v.tr.* show or feel indignation at; be aggrieved by. □□ **re·sent·ful** /rizéntfōōl/ *adj.* **re·sent·ful·ly** *adv.*

re·sent·ment /rizéntmənt/ *n.* (often foll. by *at*, *of*) indignant or bitter feelings; anger.

res·er·va·tion /rézərváyshən/ *n.* **1** the act or an instance of reserving or being reserved. **2** a booking (of a room, etc.). **3** the thing booked, e.g., a room in a hotel. **4** an express or tacit limitation or exception to an agreement, etc. **5** an area of land reserved for a particular group, as a tract designated by the federal government for use by Native Americans.

re·serve /rizə́rv/ *v.* & *n.* • *v.tr.* **1** postpone; put aside; keep back for a later occasion or special use. **2** order to be specially retained or allocated for a particular person or at a particular time. **3** retain or secure (*reserve the right to*). **4** postpone delivery of (judgment, etc.). • *n.* **1** a thing reserved for future use; an extra amount (*energy reserves*). **2** a limitation, qualification, or exception attached to something. **3 a** self-restraint; reticence. **b** (in artistic or literary expression) absence from exaggeration or ill-proportioned effects. **4** a company's profit added to capital. **5** (in *sing.* or *pl.*) assets kept readily available as cash or at a central bank, or as gold or foreign exchange. **6** (in *sing.* or *pl.*) **a** troops withheld from action to reinforce or protect others. **b** forces in addition to the regular army, navy, air force, etc., but available in an emergency. **7** a member of the military reserve. **8** an extra player chosen to be a possible substitute on a team. **9** a place reserved for special use, esp. as a habitat for a native tribe or for wildlife. **10** the intentional suppression of the truth. □ **in reserve** unused and available if required. □□ **re·serv·a·ble** *adj.*

re-serve /réesə́rv/ *v.tr.* & *intr.* serve again.

re·served /rizə́rvd/ *adj.* **1** reticent; slow to reveal emotion or opinions. **2 a** set apart; destined for some use or fate. **b** (often foll. by *for*, *to*) left by fate for; falling first or only to. □□ **re·serv·ed·ly** /–vidlee/ *adv.* **re·serv·ed·ness** *n.*

re·serv·ist /rizə́rvist/ *n.* a member of the reserve forces.

res·er·voir /rézərvwaar/ *n.* **1** a large natural or artificial lake used as a source of water supply. **2 a** any natural or artificial receptacle esp. for or of fluid. **b** a place where fluid, etc., collects. **3** a part of a machine, etc., holding fluid.

re·set /réesét/ *v.tr.* (**resetting**; *past* and *past part.* **reset**) set again or differently. □□ **re·set·ta·ble** *adj.*

re·set·tle /réesét'l/ *v.tr.* & *intr.* settle again. □□ **re·set·tle·ment** *n.*

re·shape /réesháyp/ *v.tr.* shape or form again or differently.

re·shuf·fle /réeshúfəl/ *v.* & *n.* • *v.tr.* **1** shuffle (cards) again. **2** interchange the posts of (government ministers, etc.). • *n.* the act or an instance of reshuffling.

re·side /rizíd/ *v.intr.* **1** (often foll. by *at*, *in*, *abroad*, etc.) (of a person) have one's home; dwell permanently. **2** (of power, a right, etc.) rest or be vested in. **3** (of an incumbent official) be in residence. **4** (foll. by *in*) (of a quality) be present or inherent in.

res·i·dence /rézidəns/ *n.* **1** the act or an instance of residing. **2** the place where a person resides. □ **in residence** dwelling at a specified place, esp. for the performance of duties or work (*writer-in-residence*).

res·i·den·cy /rézidənsee/ *n.* (*pl.* **-cies**) **1** = RESIDENCE 1, 2a. **2** a period of specialized medical training; the position of a resident. **3** *attrib.* based on or related to residence (*residency requirement for in-state tuition*).

res·i·dent /rézidənt/ *n.* & *adj.* • *n.* **1** (often foll. by *of*) a permanent inhabitant. **2** a medical graduate engaged in specialized practice under supervision in a hospital. • *adj.* **1** residing; in residence. **2 a** having quarters on the premises of one's work, etc. **b** working regularly in a particular place. **3** located in; inherent.

res·i·den·tial /rézidénshəl/ *adj.* **1** suitable for or occupied by private houses (*residential area*). **2** used as a residence (*residential hotel*). **3** based on or connected with residence. ▫▫ **res·i·den·tial·ly** *adv.*

res·i·den·ti·ar·y /rézidénshee-eree, –shəree/ *adj.* of, subject to, or requiring official residence.

re·sid·u·a *pl.* of RESIDUUM.

re·sid·u·al /rizíjo͞oəl/ *adj.* & *n.* • *adj.* **1** remaining; left as a residue or residuum. **2** *Math.* resulting from subtraction. • *n.* **1** a quantity left over or *Math.* resulting from subtraction. **2** (usu. in *pl.*) a royalty paid to a writer, performer, etc. ▫▫ **re·sid·u·al·ly** *adv.*

res·i·due /rézido͞o, –dyo͞o/ *n.* **1** what is left over or remains; a remainder; the rest. **2** *Law* what remains of an estate after the payment of charges, debts, and bequests. **3** esp. *Chem.* a residuum.

re·sid·u·um /rizíjo͞oəm/ *n.* (*pl.* **residua** /–jo͞oə/) **1** *Chem.* a substance left after combustion or evaporation. **2** a remainder or residue.

re·sign /rizín/ *v.* **1** *intr.* **a** (often foll. by *from*) give up office, one's employment, etc. **b** (often foll. by *as*) retire. **2** *tr.* surrender; hand over (a right, charge, task, etc.). **3** *tr.* give up (hope, etc.). **4** *refl.* (usu. foll. by *to*) **a** reconcile (oneself, one's mind, etc.) to the inevitable. **b** surrender (oneself to another's guidance).

res·ig·na·tion /rézignáyshən/ *n.* **1** the act or an instance of resigning, esp. from one's job or office. **2** the document, etc., conveying this intention. **3** the state of being resigned; the uncomplaining endurance of a sorrow or difficulty.

re·signed /rizínd/ *adj.* (often foll. by *to*) having resigned oneself; submissive, acquiescent. ▫▫ **re·sign·ed·ly** /–zínidlee/ *adv.* **re·sign·ed·ness** *n.*

re·sil·ient /rizílyənt/ *adj.* **1** (of a substance, etc.) springing back; resuming its original shape after bending, compression, etc. **2** (of a person) readily recovering from shock, depression, etc. ▫▫ **re·sil·ience** *n.* **re·sil·ien·cy** *n.* **re·sil·ient·ly** *adv.*

res·in /rézin/ *n.* **1** an adhesive flammable substance insoluble in water, secreted by some plants (cf. GUM [1]). **2** (in full **synthetic resin**) a solid or liquid organic compound made by polymerization, etc., and used in plastics, etc. ▫▫ **res·in·ate** /–nayt / *v.tr.* **res·in·ous** *adj.*

re·sist /rizíst/ *v.* **1** *tr.* withstand the action or effect of; repel. **2** *tr.* stop the course or progress of; prevent from reaching, penetrating, etc. **3** *tr.* abstain from (pleasure, temptation, etc.). **4** *tr.* try to impede; refuse to comply with (*resist arrest*). **5** *intr.* offer opposition; refuse to comply. ▫ **cannot resist 1** (foll. by verbal noun) feel strongly inclined to. **2** is certain to be attracted, etc., by. ▫▫ **re·sist·ant** *adj.* **re·sist·i·ble** *adj.*

re·sist·ance /rizístəns/ *n.* **1** the act or an instance of resisting; refusal to comply. **2** the power of resisting. **3** *Biol.* the ability to withstand adverse conditions. **4** the impeding or stopping effect exerted by one material thing on another. **5** *Physics* **a** the property of hindering the conduction of electricity, heat, etc. **b** the measure of this in a body. ¶ Symb.: **R.** **6** a resistor. **7** (in full **resistance movement**) a secret organization resisting authority, esp. in an occupied country.

re·sis·tiv·i·ty /reézistívitee/ *n.* *Electr.* a measure of the resisting power of a specified material to the flow of an electric current.

re·sis·tor /rizístər/ *n.* *Electr.* a device having resistance to the passage of an electrical current.

re·sold *past* and *past part.* of RESELL.

res·o·lute /rézəlo͞ot/ *adj.* (of a person or a person's mind or action) determined; decided; firm of purpose. ▫▫ **res·o·lute·ly** *adv.* **res·o·lute·ness** *n.*

res·o·lu·tion /rézəlo͞oshən/ *n.* **1** a resolute temper or character; boldness and firmness of purpose. **2** a thing resolved on; an intention. **3 a** a formal expression of opinion or intention by a legislative body or public meeting. **b** the formulation of this. **4** (usu. foll. by *of*) the act or an instance of solving doubt or a problem or question. **5 a** separation into components; decomposition. **b** the replacing of a single force, etc., by two or more jointly equivalent to it. **6** (foll. by *into*) analysis; conversion into another form. **7** *Mus.* causing discord to pass into concord.

re·solve /rizólv/ *v.* & *n.* • *v.* **1** *intr.* make up one's mind; decide firmly. **2** *tr.* (of circumstances, etc.) cause (a person) to do this. **3** *tr.* (foll. by *that* + clause) (of an assembly or meeting) pass a resolution by vote. **4** *intr.* & *tr.* (often foll. by *into*) separate or cause to separate into constituent parts; analyze. **5** *tr.* (of optical or photographic equipment) separate or distinguish between closely adjacent objects. **6** *tr.* & *intr.* (foll. by *into*) convert or be converted. **7** *tr.* & *intr.* (foll. by *into*) reduce by mental analysis into. **8** *tr.* solve; clear up; settle (doubt, argument, etc.). **9** *tr.* & *intr.* *Mus.* convert or be converted into concord. • *n.* **1 a** a firm mental decision or intention; a resolution. **b** a formal resolution by a legislative body or public meeting. **2** resoluteness; steadfastness. ▫▫ **re·solved** /rizólvd/ *adj.* **re·solv·ed·ly** /–zólvidlee/ *adv.* **re·solv·ed·ness** *n.*

res·o·nant /rézənənt/ *adj.* **1** (of sound) echoing; resounding; continuing to sound; reinforced or prolonged by reflection or synchronous vibration. **2** (of a body, room, etc.) tending to reinforce or prolong sounds esp. by synchronous vibration. **3** (often foll. by *with*) (of a place) resounding. **4** of or relating to resonance. ▫▫ **res·o·nance** /rézənəns/ *n.* **res·o·nant·ly** *adv.*

res·o·nate /rézənayt/ *v.intr.* produce or show resonance; resound. ▫▫ **res·o·na·tor** /rézənaytər/ *n.*

re·sorb /risáwrb, –záwrb/ *v.tr.* absorb again. ▫▫ **re·sorb·ence** *n.* **re·sorb·ent** *adj.*

re·sort /rizáwrt/ *n.* & *v.* • *n.* **1** a place frequented esp. for vacations or for a specified purpose or quality. **2** a thing to which one has recourse; an expedient or measure (*a taxi was our best resort*). **3** a tendency to frequent or be frequented (*places of great resort*). • *v.intr.* **1** (foll. by *to*) recourse to; use of (*to resort to violence*). **2** (foll. by *to*) turn to as an expedient. **3** (foll. by *to*) go often or in large numbers to. ▫ **as a last resort** when all else has failed.

re-sort /reé-sáwrt/ *v.tr.* sort again or differently.

re·sound /rizównd/ *v.* **1** *intr.* (often foll. by *with*) (of a place) ring or echo. **2** *intr.* (of a voice, sound, etc.) produce echoes; go on sounding. **3** *intr.* **a** (of fame, etc.) be much talked of. **b** (foll. by *through*) produce a sensation. **4** *tr.* (often foll. by *of*) proclaim or repeat loudly (the praises) of a person or thing. **5** *tr.* (of a place) reecho (a sound).

re·sound·ing /rizównding/ *adj.* **1** in senses of RESOUND. **2** unmistakable; emphatic (*was a resounding success*).

re·source /reésawrs, –zawrs, risáwrs, –záwrs/ *n.* **1** an expedient or device. **2** (usu. in *pl.*) **a** the means available to achieve an end, fulfill a function, etc. **b** a stock or supply that can be drawn on. **c** available assets. **3** (in *pl.*) a country's collective wealth or means of defense. **4 a** (often in *pl.*) skill in devising expedients (*a person of great resource*). **b** practical ingenuity; quick wit (*full of resource*). ▫ **one's own resources** one's own abilities, ingenuity, etc. ▫▫ **re·source·ful** *adj.* **re·source·ful·ly** *adv.* **re·source·ful·ness** *n.*

re·spect /rispékt/ *n. & v.* •*n.* **1** deferential esteem felt or shown toward a person or quality. **2 a** (foll. by *of, for*) heed or regard. **b** (foll. by *to*) attention to or consideration of (*without respect to the results*). **3** an aspect, detail, etc. **4** relation (*a morality that has no respect to religion*). **5** (in *pl.*) a person's polite messages or attentions (*give my respects to your mother*). •*v.tr.* **1** regard with deference, esteem, or honor. **2 a** avoid interfering with, harming, degrading, insulting, injuring, or interrupting. **b** treat with consideration. **c** refrain from offending (a person, a person's feelings, etc.). □ **with all due respect** a mollifying formula preceding an expression of disagreement with another's views. **with respect to** in reference to. □□ **re·spect·er** *n.*

re·spect·a·ble /rispéktəbəl/ *adj.* **1** deserving respect. **2 a** of good social standing. **b** characteristic of or associated with people of such status or character. **3 a** honest and decent in conduct. **b** characterized by (a sense of) convention or propriety; socially acceptable. **c** *derog.* highly conventional; prim. **4 a** commendable; meritorious (*an entirely respectable ambition*). **b** comparatively good or competent (*a respectable effort*). **5** reasonably good in condition or appearance. **6** appreciable in number, size, etc. **7** accepted or tolerated on account of prevalence (*materialism has become respectable again*). □□ **re·spect·a·bil·i·ty** /rispéktəbílitee/ *n.* **re·spect·a·bly** *adv.*

re·spect·ful /rispéktfŏŏl/ *adj.* showing deference. □□ **re·spect·ful·ly** *adv.* **re·spect·ful·ness** *n.*

re·spect·ing /rispékting/ *prep.* with reference or regard to; concerning.

re·spec·tive /rispéktiv/ *adj.* concerning or appropriate to each of several individually. □□ **re·spec·tive·ly** /rispéktivlee/ *adv.*

res·pir·ate /réspirayt/ *v.tr.* subject to artificial respiration.

res·pi·ra·tion /réspiráyshən/ *n.* **1 a** the act or an instance of breathing. **b** a breath. **2** *Biol.* in living organisms, the process involving the release of energy and carbon dioxide from the oxidation of complex organic substances.

res·pi·ra·tor /réspiraytər/ *n.* **1** an apparatus worn over the face to prevent poison gas, cold air, dust particles, etc., from being inhaled. **2** *Med.* an apparatus for maintaining artificial respiration.

re·spire /rispír/ *v.* **1** *intr.* breathe air. **2** *intr.* inhale and exhale air. **3** *intr.* (of a plant) carry out respiration. **4** *tr.* breathe (air, etc.). **5** *intr.* breathe again; take a breath. **6** *intr.* get rest or respite; recover hope or spirit. □□ **res·pi·ra·to·ry** /réspərətawree, rispírə–/ *adj.*

res·pite /réspit/ *n. & v.* •*n.* **1** an interval of rest or relief. **2** a delay permitted before the discharge of an obligation or the suffering of a penalty. •*v.tr.* **1** grant respite to; reprieve. **2** postpone the execution or exaction of (a sentence, obligation, etc.). **3** give temporary relief from (pain or care) or to (a sufferer).

re·splend·ent /rispléndənt/ *adj.* brilliant; dazzlingly or gloriously bright. □□ **re·splend·ence** *n.*

re·spond /rispónd/ *v.* **1** *intr.* answer; give a reply. **2** *intr.* act or behave in an answering or corresponding manner. **3** *intr.* (usu. foll. by *to*) show sensitivity to by behavior or change. **4** *intr.* (of a congregation) make answers to a priest, etc. □□ **re·spond·er** *n.*

re·spond·ent /rispóndənt/ *n. & adj.* •*n.* **1** a defendant, esp. in an appeal or divorce case. **2** a person who makes an answer or defends an argument, etc. •*adj.* **1** giving answers. **2** (foll. by *to*) responsive. **3** in the position of defendant.

re·sponse /rispóns/ *n.* **1** an answer given in word or act; a reply. **2** a feeling, movement, change, etc., caused by a stimulus or influence. **3** (often in *pl.*) *Eccl.* any part of the liturgy said or sung in answer to the priest.

re·spon·si·bil·i·ty /rispónsibílitee/ *n.* (*pl.* **-ties**) **1 a** (often foll. by *for, of*) the state or fact of being responsible. **b** the ability to act independently and make decisions (*a job with more responsibility*). **2** the person or thing for which one is responsible.

re·spon·si·ble /rispónsibəl/ *adj.* **1** (often foll. by *to, for*) liable to be called to account (to a person or for a thing). **2** morally accountable for one's actions; capable of rational conduct. **3** of good credit, position, or repute; respectable; evidently trustworthy. **4** (often foll. by *for*) being the primary cause (*a short circuit was responsible*). **5** (of a ruler or government) not autocratic. **6** involving responsibility. □□ **re·spon·si·bly** *adv.*

re·spon·sive /rispónsiv/ *adj.* **1** (often foll. by *to*) responding readily (to some influence). **2** sympathetic; impressionable. **3 a** answering. **b** by way of answer. **4** (of a liturgy, etc.) using responses. □□ **re·spon·sive·ly** *adv.* **re·spon·sive·ness** *n.*

rest[1] /rest/ *v. & n.* •*v.* **1** *intr.* cease, abstain, or be relieved from exertion, action, etc. **2** *intr.* be still or asleep, esp. to refresh oneself. **3** *tr.* give relief or repose to (*a chair to rest my legs*). **4** *intr.* (foll. by *on, upon, against*) lie on; be supported by; be spread out on; be propped against. **5** *intr.* (foll. by *on, upon*) depend; be based; rely. **6** *intr.* (foll. by *on, upon*) (of a look) light upon or be steadily directed on. **7** *tr.* (foll. by *on, upon*) place for support or foundation. **8** *intr.* (of a problem or subject) be left without further investigation or discussion (*let the matter rest*). **9** *intr.* **a** lie in death. **b** (foll. by *in*) lie buried in (a churchyard, etc.). **10** *tr.* (as **rested** *adj.*) refreshed or reinvigorated by resting. **11** *intr.* conclude the calling of witnesses in a court case (*the prosecution rests*). **12** *intr.* (of land) lie fallow. **13** *intr.* (foll. by *in*) repose trust in (*am content to rest in God*). •*n.* **1** repose or sleep, esp. in bed at night. **2** the cessation of exertion, worry, activity, etc. **3** a period of resting. **4** a support or prop for holding or steadying something. **5** *Mus.* **a** an interval of silence of a specified duration. **b** the sign denoting this. □ **at rest** not moving; not agitated or troubled; dead. **lay to rest** inter (a corpse). **rest one's case** conclude one's argument, etc. **rest up** rest oneself thoroughly. **set (or put) to (or at) rest** settle or relieve (a question, a person's mind, etc.).

rest[2] /rest/ *n. & v.* •*n.* (prec. by *the*) the remaining part or parts; the others; the remainder of some quantity or number. •*v.intr.* **1** remain in a specified state (*rest assured*). **2** (foll. by *with*) be left in the charge of.

rest ar·e·a *n.* = REST STOP.

re·start *v. & n.* •*v.tr. & intr.* /reéstaárt/ begin again. •*n.* /reéstaart/ a new beginning.

re·state /reéstáyt/ *v.tr.* express again or differently, esp. more clearly or convincingly. □□ **re·state·ment** *n.*

res·tau·rant /réstərənt, –raant, réstraant/ *n.* public premises where meals or refreshments may be had.

res·tau·ra·teur /réstərətőr/ *n.* a restaurant owner or manager.

▶Despite its close relation to *restaurant,* there is no *n* in **restaurateur**, either in its spelling or in its pronunciation.

rest·ful /réstfŏŏl/ *adj.* **1** favorable to quiet or repose. **2** free from disturbing influences. **3** soothing. □□ **rest·ful·ly** *adv.* **rest·ful·ness** *n.*

rest home *n.* a place where old or frail people can be cared for.

res·ti·tu·tion /réstitőőshən, –työő–/ *n.* **1** (often foll. by *of*) the act or an instance of restoring a thing to its proper owner. **2** reparation for an injury (esp. *make restitution*).

res·tive /réstiv/ *adj.* **1** fidgety; restless. **2** unmanageable. ▫▫ **res·tive·ly** *adv.* **res·tive·ness** *n.*
rest·less /réstlis/ *adj.* **1** finding or affording no rest. **2** uneasy; agitated. **3** constantly in motion, fidgeting, etc. ▫▫ **rest·less·ly** *adv.* **rest·less·ness** *n.*
re·stock /reéstók/ *v.tr.* (also *absol.*) stock again or differently.
res·to·ra·tion /réstəráyshən/ *n.* **1 a** the act or an instance of restoring or of being restored. **b** = RESTITUTION 1. **2** a model or drawing representing the supposed original form of an extinct animal, ruined building, etc. **3 a** the reestablishment of a monarch, etc. **b** the period of this. **4** (**Restoration**) *hist.* (prec. by *the*) the reestablishment of Charles II as king of England in 1660.
re·stor·a·tive /ristáwrətiv, –stór–/ *adj. & n.* • *adj.* tending to restore health or strength. • *n.* a restorative medicine, food, etc.
re·store /ristáwr/ *v.tr.* **1** bring back or attempt to bring back to the original state by rebuilding, repairing, etc. **2** bring back to health, etc.; cure. **3** give back to the original owner, etc. **4** reinstate; bring back to dignity or right. **5** replace; put back; bring back to a former condition. **6** make a representation of the supposed original state of (a ruin, extinct animal, etc.). **7** reinstate by conjecture (missing words in a text, missing pieces, etc.). ▫▫ **re·stor·a·ble** *adj.* **re·stor·er** *n.*
re·strain /ristráyn/ *v.tr.* **1** (often *refl.*, usu. foll. by *from*) check or hold in; keep in check or under control or within bounds. **2** repress; keep down. **3** confine; imprison. ▫▫ **re·strain·a·ble** *adj.* **re·strain·er** *n.*
re·strain·ed·ly /ristráynidlee/ *adv.* with self-restraint.
re·straint /ristráynt/ *n.* **1** the act or an instance of restraining or being restrained. **2** a controlling agency or influence. **3** self-control; avoidance of excess or exaggeration. **4** reserve of manner. **5** confinement, esp. because of insanity. **6** something that restrains or holds in check.
re·strict /ristríkt/ *v.tr.* (often foll. by *to*, *within*) **1** confine; bound; limit. **2** subject to limitation. **3** withhold from general circulation or disclosure. ▫▫ **re·strict·ed·ly** *adv.* **re·strict·ed·ness** *n.*
re·stric·tion /ristríkshən/ *n.* **1** the act or an instance of restricting; the state of being restricted. **2** a thing that restricts. **3** a limitation placed on action.
re·stric·tive /ristríktiv/ *adj.* imposing restrictions. ▫▫ **re·stric·tive·ly** *adv.* **re·stric·tive·ness** *n.*
re·string /reéstríng/ *v.tr.* (*past* and *past part.* **restrung**) **1** fit (a musical instrument) with new strings. **2** thread (beads, etc.) on a new string.
rest room *n.* a public toilet in a restaurant, store, office building, etc.
re·struc·ture /reéstrúkchər/ *v.tr.* give a new structure to; rebuild; rearrange.
rest stop *n.* an area along a highway for travelers to stop for rest, refreshment, etc.
re·style /reéstíl/ *v.tr.* **1** reshape; remake in a new style. **2** give a new designation to (a person or thing).
re·sult /rizúlt/ *n. & v.* • *n.* **1** a consequence, issue, or outcome of something. **2** a satisfactory outcome (*gets results*). **3** a quantity, formula, etc., obtained by calculation. **4** (in *pl.*) a list of scores or winners, etc. • *v.intr.* **1** (often foll. by *from*) arise as the actual consequence or follow as a logical consequence. **2** (often foll. by *in*) have a specified end or outcome. ▫▫ **re·sult·less** *adj.*
re·sult·ant /rizúlt'nt/ *adj.* resulting, esp. as the total outcome of more or less opposed forces.
re·sume /rizóom/ *v. & n.* • *v.* **1** *tr. & intr.* begin again or continue after an interruption. **2** *tr. & intr.* begin to speak, work, or use again; recommence. **3** *tr.* recover; reoccupy. • *n.* = RÉSUMÉ. ▫▫ **re·sum·a·ble** *adj.*
ré·su·mé /rézoomay/ *n.* (also **re·su·mé, re·su·me**) **1** a summary. **2** a curriculum vitae.
re·sump·tion /rizúmpshən/ *n.* the act or an instance of resuming. ▫▫ **re·sump·tive** *adj.*
re·sur·face /reésə́rfis/ *v.* **1** *tr.* lay a new surface on (a road, etc.). **2** *intr.* rise or arise again; turn up again.
re·sur·gent /risə́rjənt/ *adj.* **1** rising or arising again. **2** tending to rise again. ▫▫ **re·sur·gence** *n.*
res·ur·rect /rézərékt/ *v.* **1** *tr. colloq.* revive the practice, use, or memory of. **2** *tr.* take from the grave; exhume. **3** *tr.* dig up. **4** *tr. & intr.* raise or rise from the dead.
res·ur·rec·tion /rézərékshən/ *n.* **1** the act or an instance of rising from the dead. **2** (**Resurrection**) **a** Christ's rising from the dead. **b** the rising of the dead at the Last Judgment. **3** a revival after disuse, inactivity, or decay. **4** exhumation. **5** restoration to vogue or memory.
re·sus·ci·tate /risúsitayt/ *v.tr. & intr.* **1** revive from unconsciousness or apparent death. **2** return or restore to vogue, vigor, or vividness. ▫▫ **re·sus·ci·ta·tion** /–táyshən/ *n.* **re·sus·ci·ta·tive** *adj.* **re·sus·ci·ta·tor** *n.*
re·tail /reétayl/ *n., adj., adv., & v.* • *n.* the sale of goods in relatively small quantities to the public, and usu. not for resale (cf. WHOLESALE). • *adj. & adv.* by retail; at a retail price. • *v.* (also /ritáyl/) **1** *tr.* sell (goods) in retail trade. **2** *intr.* (often foll. by *at*, *for*) (of goods) be sold in this way (esp. for a specified price). ▫▫ **re·tail·er** *n.*
re·tain /ritáyn/ *v.tr.* **1 a** keep possession of; not lose; continue to have. **b** not abolish, discard, nor alter. **2** keep in one's memory. **3 a** keep in place; hold fixed. **b** hold (water, etc.). **4** secure the services of (a person) with a preliminary payment. ▫▫ **re·tain·a·ble** *adj.* **re·tain·a·bil·i·ty** /–taynəbílitee/ *n.* **re·tain·ment** *n.*
re·tain·er /ritáynər/ *n.* **1** a person or thing that retains. **2** *Law* a fee for retaining an attorney, etc. **3 a** *hist.* a dependent of a person of rank. **b** *joc.* a faithful friend or servant (esp. *old retainer*).
re·take *v. & n.* • *v.tr.* /reétáyk/ (*past* **retook**; *past part.* **retaken**) **1** take again. **2** recapture. • *n.* /reétayk/ **1 a** the act or an instance of retaking. **b** a thing retaken, e.g., an examination. **2 a** the act or an instance of filming a scene or recording music, etc., again. **b** the scene or recording obtained in this way.
re·tal·i·ate /ritáleeayt/ *v.* **1** *intr.* repay an injury, insult, etc., in kind; attack in return; make reprisals. **2** *tr.* **a** (usu. foll. by *upon*) cast (an accusation) back upon a person. **b** repay (an injury or insult) in kind. ▫▫ **re·tal·i·a·tion** /–áyshən/ *n.* **re·tal·i·a·tor** *n.* **re·tal·i·a·to·ry** /–táleeətáwree/ *adj.*
re·tard /ritaárd/ *v.tr.* **1** make slow or late. **2** delay the progress, development, arrival, or accomplishment of. ▫▫ **re·tar·dant** *adj. & n.* **re·tar·da·tion** /reétaardáyshən/ *n.*
re·tard·ed /ritaárdid/ *adj.* less advanced in mental, physical, or social development than usual for one's age.
retch /rech/ *v. & n.* • *v.intr.* make a motion of vomiting esp. involuntarily and without effect. • *n.* such a motion or the sound of it.
re·tell /reétél/ *v.tr.* (*past* and *past part.* **retold**) tell again or in a different version.
re·ten·tion /riténshən/ *n.* **1 a** the act or an instance of retaining; the state of being retained. **b** the ability to retain things experienced or learned; memory. **2** *Med.* the failure to evacuate urine or another secretion.
re·ten·tive /riténtiv/ *adj.* **1** (often foll. by *of*) tending to retain (moisture, etc.). **2** not forgetful. ▫▫ **re·ten·tive·ly** *adv.* **re·ten·tive·ness** *n.*
re·think *v. & n.* • *v.tr.* /reéthíngk/ (*past* and *past part.* **rethought**) think about (something) again, esp. with a

view to making changes. •*n.* /reéthingk/ a reassessment.

ret•i•cence /rétisəns/ *n.* **1** the avoidance of saying all one knows or feels, or of saying more than is necessary. **2** a disposition to silence. **3** the act or an instance of holding back some fact. **4** abstinence from overemphasis in art. ▫▫ **ret•i•cent** *adj.* **ret•i•cent•ly** *adv.*

ret•i•cle /rétikəl/ *n.* a network of fine threads or lines in the focal plane of an optical instrument to help accurate observation.

re•ti•cu•la *pl.* of RETICULUM.

re•tic•u•late *v.* & *adj.* •*v.tr.* & *intr.* /ritíkyəlayt/ **1** divide or be divided in fact or appearance into a network. **2** arrange or be arranged in small squares or with intersecting lines. •*adj.* /–yələt, –layt/ reticulated. ▫▫ **re•tic•u•la•tion** /–láyshən/ *n.*

ret•i•cule /rétikyoōl/ *n. hist.* a woman's netted or other bag, esp. with a drawstring, carried or worn to serve the purpose of a pocket.

re•tic•u•lum /ritíkyələm/ *n.* (*pl.* **reticula** /–lə/) **1** a netlike structure; a fine network, esp. of membranes, etc., in living organisms. **2** a ruminant's second stomach. ▫▫ **re•tic•u•lar** *adj.* **re•tic•u•lose** *adj.*

re•tie /reétí/ *v.tr.* (**retying**) tie again.

re•ti•form /reétifawrm, réti;n–/ *adj.* netlike; reticulated.

ret•i•na /rét'nə/ *n.* (*pl.* **retinas, retinae** /–nee/) a layer at the back of the eyeball sensitive to light. ▫▫ **ret•i•nal** *adj.*

ret•i•nol /rét'nawl, –nol/ *n.* a vitamin found in green and yellow vegetables, egg yolk, and fish-liver oil, essential for growth and vision in dim light. Also called **vitamin A.**

ret•i•nue /rét'noō, –yoō/ *n.* a body of attendants accompanying an important person.

re•tire /ritír/ *v.* **1 a** *intr.* leave office or employment, esp. because of age. **b** *tr.* cause (a person) to retire from work. **2** *intr.* withdraw; go away; retreat. **3** *intr.* seek seclusion or shelter. **4** *intr.* go to bed. **5** *tr. Baseball* put out (a batter or side).

re•tired /ritírd/ *adj.* **1** having retired from employment. **2** withdrawn from society or observation.

re•tire•ment /ritírmənt/ *n.* **1 a** the act or an instance of retiring. **b** the condition of having retired. **2 a** seclusion or privacy. **b** a secluded place. **3** income, esp. pension, on which a retired person lives.

re•tir•ing /ritíring/ *adj.* shy; fond of seclusion.

re•told *past* and *past part.* of RETELL.

re•took *past* of RETAKE.

re•tool /reétoōl/ *v.tr.* equip (a factory, etc.) with new tools.

re•tort[1] /ritáwrt/ *n.* & *v.* •*n.* **1** an incisive or witty or angry reply. **2** the turning of a charge or argument against its originator. **3** a retaliation. •*v.* **1 a** *tr.* say by way of a retort. **b** *intr.* make a retort. **2** *tr.* repay (an insult or attack) in kind. **3** *tr.* (often foll. by *on, upon*) return (mischief, a charge, sarcasm, etc.) to its originator. **4** *tr.* (often foll. by *against*) make (an argument) tell against its user.

re•tort[2] /ritáwrt, reétawrt/ *n.* & *v.* •*n.* **1** a vessel usu. of glass with a long curved neck used in distilling liquids. **2** a vessel for heating mercury for purification, coal to generate gas, or iron and carbon to make steel. •*v.tr.* purify (mercury) by heating in a retort.

re•touch /reétúch/ *v.* & *n.* •*v.tr.* improve or repair (a composition, picture, etc.) by fresh touches or alterations. •*n.* the act or an instance of retouching.

re•trace /reetráys/ *v.tr.* **1** go back over (one's steps, etc.). **2** trace back to a source or beginning. **3** recall the course of in one's memory.

re•tract /ritrákt/ *v.* **1** *tr.* (also *absol.*) withdraw (a statement or undertaking). **2 a** *tr.* & *intr.* (esp. with ref. to part of the body) draw or be drawn back or in. **b** *tr.* draw (an undercarriage, etc.) into the body of an aircraft. ▫▫ **re•tract•a•ble** *adj.* **re•trac•tion** *n.*

re•trac•tile /ritráktil, –tīl/ *adj.* capable of being retracted. ▫▫ **re•trac•til•i•ty** /–tílitee/ *n.*

re•trac•tor /ritráktər/ *n.* **1** a muscle used for retracting. **2** a device for retracting.

re•train /reétráyn/ *v.tr.* & *intr.* train again or further, esp. for new work.

re•trans•late /reétranzláyt, –trans–, reetránzlayt, –tráns–/ *v.tr.* translate again, esp. back into the original language. ▫▫ **re•trans•la•tion** *n.*

re•trans•mit /reétranzmít, –trans–/ *v.tr.* (**retransmitted, retransmitting**) transmit (esp. radio signals or broadcast programs) back again or to a further distance. ▫▫ **re•trans•mis•sion** /–míshən/ *n.*

re•tread *v.* & *n.* •*v.tr.* /reétréd/ (*past* **retrod**; *past part.* **retrodden**) **1** tread (a path, etc.) again. **2** put a fresh tread on (a tire). •*n.* /reétred/ a retreaded tire.

re•treat /ritreét/ *v.* & *n.* •*v.* **1 a** *intr.* (esp. of military forces) go back, retire; relinquish a position. **b** *tr.* cause to retreat; move back. **2** *intr.* (esp. of features) recede. •*n.* **1 a** the act or an instance of retreating. **b** *Mil.* a signal for this. **2** withdrawal into privacy or security. **3** a place of shelter or seclusion. **4** a period of seclusion for prayer and meditation. **5** *Mil.* a bugle call at sunset. **6** a place for the reception of the elderly or others in need of care.

re•trench /ritrénch/ *v.* **1 a** *tr.* reduce the amount of (costs). **b** *intr.* cut down expenses. **2** *tr.* shorten or abridge. ▫▫ **re•trench•ment** *n.*

re•tri•al /reétríəl/ *n.* a second or further (judicial) trial.

ret•ri•bu•tion /rétribyoōshən/ *n.* requital usu. for evil done; vengeance. ▫▫ **re•trib•u•tive** /ritríbyətiv/ *adj.* **re•trib•u•to•ry** /ritríbyətawree/ *adj.*

re•trieve /ritreév/ *v.tr.* **1 a** regain possession of. **b** recover by investigation or effort of memory. **2 a** recall to mind. **b** obtain (information stored in a computer, etc.). **3** (of a dog) find and bring in (killed or wounded game, etc.). **4** (foll. by *from*) rescue (esp. from a bad state). ▫▫ **re•triev•a•ble** *adj.* **re•triev•al** *n.*

re•triev•er /ritreévər/ *n.* **1 a** a dog of a breed used for retrieving game. **b** this breed. **2** a person who retrieves something.

ret•ro /rétrō/ *sl. adj.* **1** reviving or harking back to the past. **2** retroactive.

retro- /rétrō/ *comb. form* **1** denoting action back or in return (*retroact; retroflex*). **2** *Anat. & Med.* denoting location behind.

ret•ro•act /rétrō-ákt/ *v.intr.* **1** operate in a backward direction. **2** have a retrospective effect. **3** react. ▫▫ **ret•ro•ac•tion** *n.*

ret•ro•ac•tive /rétrō-áktiv/ *adj.* (esp. of legislation) having retrospective effect. ▫▫ **ret•ro•ac•tive•ly** *adv.*

ret•ro•cede /rétrōseéd/ *v.* **1** *intr.* move back; recede. **2** *tr.* cede back again. ▫▫ **ret•ro•ced•ence** *n.* **ret•ro•ced•ent** *adj.* **ret•ro•ces•sion** /–séshən/ *n.*

ret•ro•choir /rétrōkwīr/ *n.* the part of a cathedral or large church behind the high altar.

re•trod *past* of RETREAD.

re•trod•den *past part.* of RETREAD.

ret•ro•fit /rétrōfit/ *v.tr.* (**-fitted, -fitting**) modify (machinery, vehicles, etc.) to incorporate changes and developments introduced after manufacture.

ret•ro•flex /rétrəfleks/ *adj.* (also **ret•ro•flexed**) **1** *Anat., Med., & Bot.* turned backward. **2** *Phonet.* pronounced with the tip of the tongue curled up toward the hard palate. ▫▫ **ret•ro•flex•ion** /–flékshən/ *n.*

ret•ro•gra•da•tion /rétrōgrədáyshən/ *n. Astron.* **1** the apparent backward motion of a planet in the zodiac. **2** the apparent motion of a celestial body from east to west. **3** backward movement of the lunar nodes on the ecliptic.

ret·ro·grade /rétrəgrayd/ *adj., n., & v.* • *adj.* **1** directed backward; retreating. **2** reverting esp. to an inferior state; declining. **3** inverse; reversed (*in retrograde order*). • *n.* a degenerate person. • *v.intr.* **1** move backward; recede; retire. **2** decline; revert. ▫▫ **ret·ro·grade·ly** *adv.*

ret·ro·gress /rétrəgrés/ *v.intr.* **1** go back; move backward. **2** deteriorate. ▫▫ **ret·ro·gres·sion** /–gréshən/ *n.* **ret·ro·gres·sive** /–grésiv/ *adj.*

ret·ro·ject /rétrōjekt/ *v.tr.* throw back (usu. opp. PROJECT).

ret·ro-rock·et /rétrō-rokit/ *n.* an auxiliary rocket for slowing down a spacecraft, etc.

ret·ro·spect /rétrəspekt/ *n.* **1** (foll. by *to*) regard or reference to precedent or authority, or to previous conditions. **2** a survey of past time or events. ▫ **in retrospect** when looked back on.

ret·ro·spec·tion /rétrəspékshən/ *n.* **1** the action of looking back esp. into the past. **2** an indulgence or engagement in retrospect.

ret·ro·spec·tive /rétrəspéktiv/ *adj. & n.* • *adj.* **1** looking back on or dealing with the past. **2** (of an exhibition, recital, etc.) showing an artist's development over his or her lifetime. **3** (of a view) lying to the rear. • *n.* a retrospective exhibition, etc. ▫▫ **ret·ro·spec·tive·ly** *adv.*

re·trous·sé /retrōōsáy/ *adj.* (of the nose) turned up at the tip.

ret·ro·vert /rétrōvərt/ *v.tr.* **1** turn backward. **2** *Med.* (as **retroverted** *adj.*) (of the womb) having a backward inclination. ▫▫ **ret·ro·ver·sion** /–vərzhən, -shən/ *n.*

ret·ro·vi·rus /rétrōvīrəs/ *n. Biol.* any of a group of RNA viruses that form DNA during the replication of their RNA.

re·try /réétrí/ *v.tr.* (**-tries, -tried**) try (a defendant or lawsuit) a second or further time.

ret·si·na /retséénə/ *n.* a Greek wine flavored with resin.

re·tune /réétóón, –tyóón/ *v.tr.* **1** tune (a musical instrument) again or differently. **2** tune (a radio, etc.) to a different frequency.

re·turn /ritə́rn/ *v. & n.* • *v.* **1** *intr.* come or go back. **2** *tr.* bring or put or send back. **3** *tr.* pay back or reciprocate; give in response. **4** *tr.* yield (a profit). **5** *tr.* say in reply; retort. **6** *tr.* (in tennis, etc.) hit or send (the ball) back after receiving it. **7** *tr.* state or mention or describe officially, esp. in answer to a writ or formal demand. **8** *tr.* elect, esp. reelect, to political office, etc. **9** *tr. Cards* **a** lead (a suit) previously led or bid by a partner. **b** lead (a suit or card) after taking a trick. **10** *tr. Archit.* continue (a wall, etc.) in a changed direction, esp. at right angles. • *n.* **1** the act or an instance of coming or going back. **2 a** the act or an instance of giving or sending or putting or paying back. **b** a thing given or sent back. **3** a key on a computer or typewriter to start a new line. **4** (in *sing.* or *pl.*) **a** the proceeds or profit of an undertaking. **b** the acquisition of these. **5** a formal report or statement compiled or submitted by order (*an income-tax return*). **6** (in full **return match** or **game**) a second match, etc., between the same opponents. **7** a response or reply. **8** (in *pl.*) a report on votes counted in an election (*early returns from the third district*). **9** *Archit.* a part receding from the line of the front, e.g., the side of a house or of a window opening.

re·turn·a·ble /ritə́rnəbəl/ *adj. & n.* • *adj.* intended to be returned, as an empty beverage container. • *n.* an empty beverage container, especially a bottle or can, that can be returned for a refund of the deposit paid at purchase.

re·turn·ee /ritərnéé/ *n.* a person who returns home from abroad, esp. after war service.

re·ty·ing *pres. part.* of RETIE.

re·type /réétíp/ *v.tr.* type again, esp. to correct errors.

re·u·ni·fy /rééyóónifī/ *v.tr.* (**-fies, -fied**) restore (esp. separated territories) to a political unity. ▫▫ **re·u·ni·fi·ca·tion** /–fikáyshən/ *n.*

re·un·ion /reeyóónyən/ *n.* **1 a** the act or an instance of reuniting. **b** the condition of being reunited. **2** a social gathering esp. of people formerly associated.

re·u·nite /rééyōōnít/ *v.tr. & intr.* bring or come back together.

re·up·hol·ster /rééəphṓlstər, –əpṓl–/ *v.tr.* upholster anew. ▫▫ **re·up·hol·ster·y** *n.*

re·use *v. & n.* • *v.tr.* /rééyóóz/ use again or more than once. • *n.* /rééyóós/ a second or further use. ▫▫ **re·us·a·ble** /–yóózəbəl/ *adj.*

re·u·ti·lize /rééyóót'līz/ *v.tr.* utilize again or for a different purpose. ▫▫ **re·u·ti·li·za·tion** /–záyshən/ *n.*

Rev. *abbr.* **1** Reverend. **2** Revelation (New Testament).

rev /rev/ *n. & v. colloq.* • *n.* (in *pl.*) the number of revolutions of an engine per minute. • *v.* (**revved, revving**) **1** *intr.* (of an engine) revolve; turn over. **2** *tr.* (also *absol.*; often foll. by *up*) cause (an engine) to run quickly.

re·val·ue /réévályōō/ *v.tr.* (**revalues, revalued, revaluing**) *Econ.* give a different value to, esp. give a higher value to, (a currency) in relation to other currencies or gold (opp. DEVALUE). ▫▫ **re·val·u·a·tion** /–vályōōáyshən/ *n.*

re·vamp /réévámp/ *v.tr.* **1** renovate; revise; improve. **2** patch up.

re·veal[1] /rivéél/ *v.tr.* **1** display or show; allow to appear. **2** (often as **revealing** *adj.*) disclose; divulge; betray. **3** *tr.* (in *refl.* or *passive*) come to sight or knowledge. **4** *Relig.* (esp. of God) make known by inspiration or supernatural means. ▫▫ **re·veal·a·ble** *adj.* **re·veal·er** *n.* **re·veal·ing·ly** *adv.*

re·veal[2] /rivéél/ *n.* an internal side surface of an opening or recess, esp. of a doorway or a window aperture.

rev·eil·le /révəlee/ *n.* a military wake-up signal.

rev·el /révəl/ *v. & n.* • *v.* (**reveled, reveling** or **revelled, revelling**) **1** *intr.* have a good time; be extravagantly festive. **2** *intr.* (foll. by *in*) take keen delight in. **3** *tr.* (foll. by *away*) throw away (money or time) in revelry. • *n.* (in *sing.* or *pl.*) the act or an instance of reveling. ▫▫ **rev·el·er** *n.* **rev·el·ry** *n.* (*pl.* **-ries**).

rev·e·la·tion /révəláyshən/ *n.* **1 a** the act or an instance of revealing, esp. the supposed disclosure of knowledge to humankind by a divine or supernatural agency. **b** knowledge disclosed in this way. **2** a striking disclosure. **3** (**Revelation** or *colloq.* **Revelations**) (in full **the Revelation of St. John the Divine**) the last book of the New Testament. ▫▫ **rev·e·la·tion·al** *adj.*

rev·e·la·tion·ist /revəláyshənist/ *n.* a believer in divine revelation.

re·vel·a·to·ry /révələtawree, rəvélə–/ *adj.* serving to reveal, esp. something significant.

rev·e·nant /révənənt/ *n.* a person who has returned, esp. supposedly from the dead.

re·venge /rivénj/ *n. & v.* • *n.* **1** retaliation for an offense or injury. **2** an act of retaliation. **3** the desire for this; a vindictive feeling. **4** (in games) a chance to win after an earlier defeat. • *v.* **1** *tr.* (in *refl.* or *passive*; often foll. by *on, upon*) inflict retaliation for an offense. **2** *tr.* take revenge for (an offense). **3** *tr.* avenge (a person). **4** *intr.* take revenge. ▫▫ **re·veng·er** *n.*

re·venge·ful /rivénjfōōl/ *adj.* eager for revenge. ▫▫ **re·venge·ful·ly** *adv.*

rev·e·nue /révənōō, –nyōō/ *n.* **1 a** income, esp. of a large amount, from any source. **b** (in *pl.*) items constituting this. **2** a government's annual income from which public expenses are met.

re·verb /rivə́rb, réevərb/ *v. & n.* • *v.tr. & intr.* reverberate. • *n. Mus. colloq.* **1** reverberation. **2** a device to produce this.

re·ver·ber·ate /rivə́rbərayt/ *v.* **1 a** *intr.* (of sound, light, or heat) be returned or echoed repeatedly. **b** *tr.* return (a sound, etc.) in this way. **2** *intr.* (of a rumor, etc.) be heard much or repeatedly. ▫▫ **re·ver·ber·ant** *adj.* **re·ver·ber·a·tion** /–ráyshən/ *n.* **re·ver·ber·a·tive** /–rətiv/ *adj.*

re·vere /riveér/ *v.tr.* hold in deep and usu. affectionate or religious respect; venerate.

rev·er·ence /révərəns, révrəns/ *n. & v.* • *n.* **1 a** the act of revering or the state of being revered. **b** the capacity for revering. **2** (**Reverence**) a title used of or to some members of the clergy. • *v.tr.* regard or treat with reverence.

rev·er·end /révərənd, révrənd/ *adj. & n.* • *adj.* (esp. as the title of a clergyman) deserving reverence. • *n. colloq.* a clergyman.

rev·er·ent /révərənt, révrənt/ *adj.* feeling or showing reverence. ▫▫ **rev·er·ent·ly** *adv.*

rev·er·en·tial /révərénshəl/ *adj.* of the nature of, due to, or characterized by reverence. ▫▫ **rev·er·en·tial·ly** *adv.*

rev·er·ie /révəree/ *n.* **1** a state of being pleasantly lost in one's thoughts; a daydream. **2** *Mus.* an instrumental piece suggesting a dreamy or musing state.

re·vers /riveér/ *n.* (*pl.* same /–veérz/) **1** the turned-back edge of a garment revealing the undersurface. **2** the material on this surface.

re·verse /rivə́rs/ *v., adj., & n.* • *v.* **1** *tr.* turn the other way around or up or inside out. **2** *tr.* change to the opposite character or effect. **3** *intr. & tr.* travel or cause to travel backward. **4** *tr.* make (an engine, etc.) work in a contrary direction. **5** *tr.* revoke or annul (a decree, act, etc.). **6** *intr.* (of a dancer, esp. in a waltz) revolve in the opposite direction. • *adj.* **1** placed or turned in an opposite direction or position. **2** opposite or contrary in character or order; inverted. • *n.* **1** the opposite or contrary. **2** the contrary of the usual manner. **3** an occurrence of misfortune; a disaster, esp. a defeat. **4** reverse gear or motion. **5** the reverse side of something. **6 a** the side of a coin or medal, etc., bearing the secondary design. **b** this design (cf. OBVERSE). ▫▫ **re·ver·sal** *n.* **re·verse·ly** *adv.* **re·vers·er** *n.* **re·vers·i·ble** *adj.*

re·ver·sion /rivə́rzhən/ *n.* **1 a** the legal right (esp. of the original owner, or his or her heirs) to possess or succeed to property on the death of the present possessor. **b** property to which a person has such a right. **2** *Biol.* a return to ancestral type. **3** a return to a previous state, habit, etc. **4** a sum payable on a person's death, esp. by way of life insurance. ▫▫ **re·ver·sion·al** *adj.* **re·ver·sion·ar·y** *adj.*

re·vert /rivə́rt/ *v.* **1** *intr.* (foll. by *to*) return to a former state, practice, opinion, etc. **2** *intr.* (of property, an office, etc.) return by reversion. **3** *intr.* fall back into a wild state. **4** *tr.* turn (one's eyes or steps) back.

re·vert·i·ble /rivə́rtibəl/ *adj.* (of property) subject to reversion.

re·vet·ment /rivétmənt/ *n.* a retaining wall or facing.

re·view /rivyóo/ *n. & v.* • *n.* **1** a general survey or assessment of a subject or thing. **2** a retrospect or survey of the past. **3** revision or reconsideration. **4** a display and formal inspection of troops, etc. **5** a published account or criticism of a book, play, etc. **6** a periodical publication with critical articles on current events, the arts, etc. • *v.tr.* **1** survey or look back on. **2** reconsider or revise. **3** hold a review of (troops, etc.). **4** write a review of (a book, play, etc.). **5** view again. ▫▫ **re·view·er** *n.*

re·vile /rivíl/ *v.* **1** *tr.* abuse; criticize abusively. **2** *intr.* talk abusively; rail. ▫▫ **re·vile·ment** *n.* **re·vil·er** *n.*

re·vise /rivíz/ *v. & n.* • *v.tr.* **1** examine or reexamine and improve or amend (esp. written or printed matter). **2** consider and alter (an opinion, etc.). • *n. Printing* a proof sheet including corrections made in an earlier proof. ▫▫ **re·vis·a·ble** *adj.* **re·vis·al** *n.* **re·vis·er** *n.*

re·vi·sion /rivízhən/ *n.* **1** the act or an instance of revising; the process of being revised. **2** a revised edition or form. ▫▫ **re·vi·sion·ar·y** *adj.*

re·vi·sion·ism /rivízhənizəm/ *n.* often *derog.* **1** a policy of revision or modification, esp. of Marxism. **2** any departure from or modification of accepted doctrine, theory, view of history, etc. ▫▫ **re·vi·sion·ist** *n. & adj.*

re·vis·it /reévízit/ *v.tr.* visit again.

re·vi·tal·ize /reévít'līz/ *v.tr.* imbue with new life and vitality. ▫▫ **re·vi·tal·i·za·tion** /–záyshən/ *n.*

re·viv·al /rivívəl/ *n.* **1** the act or an instance of reviving; the process of being revived. **2** a new production of an old play, etc. **3** a revived use of an old practice, custom, etc. **4 a** a reawakening of religious fervor. **b** one or a series of evangelistic meetings to promote this. **5** restoration to bodily or mental vigor or to life or consciousness.

re·viv·al·ism /rivívəlizəm/ *n.* belief in or the promotion of a revival, esp. of religious fervor. ▫▫ **re·viv·al·ist** *n.*

re·vive /rivív/ *v.intr. & tr.* **1** come or bring back to consciousness or life or strength. **2** come or bring back to existence, use, notice, etc. ▫▫ **re·viv·a·ble** *adj.* **re·viv·er** /rivívər/ *n.*

re·viv·i·fy /rivívifī/ *v.tr.* (**-fies, -fied**) restore to animation, activity, vigor, or life. ▫▫ **re·viv·i·fi·ca·tion** /–fikáyshən/ *n.*

re·voke /rivók/ *v.tr.* rescind, withdraw, or cancel. ▫▫ **rev·o·ca·ble** /révəkəbəl/ *adj.* **rev·o·ca·tion** /révəkáyshən/ *n.*

re·volt /rivólt/ *v. & n.* • *v.* **1** *intr.* **a** rise in rebellion. **b** (as **revolted** *adj.*) having revolted. **2 a** *tr.* (often in *passive*) affect with strong disgust; nauseate. **b** *intr.* (often foll. by *at, against*) feel strong disgust. • *n.* **1** an act of rebelling. **2** a state of insurrection. **3** a sense of loathing. **4** a mood of protest or defiance. ▫▫ **re·volt·ing** /rivólting/ *adj.*

rev·o·lu·tion /révəlóoshən/ *n.* **1 a** the forcible overthrow of a government or social order. **b** (in Marxism) the replacement of one ruling class by another; the class struggle that is expected to lead to political change and the triumph of communism. **2** any fundamental change or reversal of conditions. **3** the act or an instance of revolving. **4 a** motion in orbit or a circular course or around an axis or center; rotation. **b** the single completion of an orbit or rotation. **c** the time taken for this. **5** a cyclic recurrence. ▫▫ **rev·o·lu·tion·ism** *n.* **rev·o·lu·tion·ist** *n.*

rev·o·lu·tion·ar·y /révəlóoshəneree/ *adj. & n.* • *adj.* **1** involving great and often violent change or innovation. **2** of or causing political revolution. **3** (**Revolutionary**) of or relating to a particular revolution, esp. the American Revolution. • *n.* (*pl.* **-ies**) an instigator or supporter of political revolution.

rev·o·lu·tion·ize /révəlóoshənīz/ *v.tr.* introduce fundamental change to.

re·volve /rivólv/ *v.* **1** *intr. & tr.* turn or cause to turn around, esp. on an axis; rotate. **2** *intr.* move in a circular orbit. **3** *tr.* ponder (a problem, etc.) in the mind.

re·volv·er /rivólvər/ *n.* a pistol with revolving chambers enabling several shots to be fired without reloading.

re·volv·ing door *n.* a door with usu. four partitions turning around a central axis.

re·vue /rivyóo/ *n.* a theatrical entertainment of a series of short usu. satirical sketches and songs.

re·vul·sion /rivúlshən/ *n.* **1** abhorrence; a sense of disgust and loathing. **2** a sudden violent change of feeling.

re·ward /riwáwrd/ *n. & v.* •*n.* **1 a** a return or recompense for service or merit. **b** requital for good or evil; retribution. **2** a sum offered for the detection of a criminal, the restoration of lost property, etc. •*v.tr.* give a reward to (a person) or for (a service, etc.).

re·ward·ing /riwáwrding/ *adj.* (of an activity, etc.) well worth doing; providing satisfaction.

re·wash /réewáwsh, –wósh/ *v.tr.* wash again.

re·weigh /réewáy/ *v.tr.* weigh again.

re·wind /réewínd/ *v. & n.* •*v.tr.* (*past* and *past part.* **rewound**) wind (a film or tape, etc.) back to the beginning. •*n.* **1** function on a tape deck, camera, etc., to rewind (tape, film, etc.). **2** the button that activates this function. ▫▫ **re·wind·er** *n.*

re·wire /réewír/ *v.tr.* provide (a building, etc.) with new wiring. ▫▫ **re·wir·a·ble** *adj.*

re·word /réewə́rd/ *v.tr.* change the wording of.

re·work /réewə́rk/ *v.tr.* revise; refashion; remake.

re·wound *past* and *past part.* of REWIND.

re·write *v. & n.* •*v.tr.* /réerít/ (*past* **rewrote**; *past part.* **rewritten**) write again or differently. •*n.* /réerit/ **1** the act or an instance of rewriting. **2** a thing rewritten.

Reye's syn·drome /ríz, ráz/ *n. Med.* an acute, often fatal brain disease of children that usually follows a viral infection such as influenza or chicken pox and that is associated with the use of aspirin.

Rf *symb. Chem.* the element rutherfordium.

r.f. *abbr.* (also **RF**) radio frequency.

RFD *abbr.* rural free delivery.

Rh[1] *symb. Chem.* the element rhodium.

Rh[2] see RH FACTOR.

r.h. *abbr.* right hand.

rhab·do·man·cy /rábdəmansee/ *n.* the use of a divining rod, esp. for discovering subterranean water or mineral ore.

Rhad·a·man·thine /rádəmánthin, –thīn/ *adj.* stern and incorruptible in judgment.

rhap·so·dize /rápsədīz/ *v.intr.* talk or write rhapsodies.

rhap·so·dy /rápsədee/ *n.* (*pl.* **-dies**) **1** speak or write about someone or something with great enthusiasm and delight. **2** *Mus.* a piece of music in one extended movement, usu. emotional in character. ▫▫ **rhap·sod·ic** /rapsódik/ *adj.* **rhap·sod·i·cal** *adj.* **rhap·so·dist** /rápsədist/ *n.*

rhe·a /réeə/ *n.* any of several S. American flightless birds of the family Rheidae, like but smaller than an ostrich.

rhe·bok /réebok/ *n.* (also **ree·bok**) a small S. African antelope, *Pelea capreolus*, with sharp horns.

rhe·ni·um /réeneeəm/ *n. Chem.* a rare metallic element of the manganese group, occurring naturally in molybdenum ores and used in the manufacture of superconducting alloys. ¶ Symb.: **Re**.

rhe·ol·o·gy /reeóləjee/ *n.* the science dealing with the flow and deformation of matter. ▫▫ **rhe·o·log·i·cal** /–əlójikəl/ *adj.* **rhe·ol·o·gist** *n.*

rhe·o·stat /réeəstat/ *n. Electr.* an instrument used to control a current by varying the resistance. ▫▫ **rhe·o·stat·ic** /–státik/ *adj.*

rhe·sus /réesəs/ *n.* (in full **rhesus monkey**) a small monkey, *Macaca mulatta*, common in N. India.

rhe·sus fac·tor *n.* = RH FACTOR.

rhet·o·ric /rétərik/ *n.* **1** the art of effective or persuasive speaking or writing. **2** language designed to persuade or impress (often with an implication of exaggeration, etc.).

rhe·tor·i·cal /ritáwrikəl, –tór–/ *adj.* **1 a** expressed in terms intended to persuade or impress. **b** (of a question) asked in order to produce an effect or to make a statement rather than to elicit information. **2** of the nature of rhetoric. **3 a** of or relating to the art of rhetoric. **b** given to rhetoric; oratorical. ▫▫ **rhe·tor·i·cal·ly** *adv.*

rhe·tor·i·cal ques·tion *n.* a question asked not for information but to produce an effect, e.g., *who cares?* for *nobody cares.*

rhet·o·ri·cian /rétərishən/ *n.* **1** an orator. **2** a teacher of or expert in rhetoric. **3** a rhetorical speaker or writer.

rheum /rōōm/ *n.* a watery discharge from a mucous membrane, esp. of the eyes or nose. ▫▫ **rheum·y** *adj.*

rheu·mat·ic /roomátik/ *adj. & n.* •*adj.* **1** of, relating to, or suffering from rheumatism. **2** producing or produced by rheumatism. •*n.* a person suffering from rheumatism.

rheu·mat·ic fe·ver *n.* a noninfectious fever with inflammation and pain in the joints.

rheu·ma·tism /rṓōmətizəm/ *n.* any disease marked by inflammation and pain in the joints, muscles, or fibrous tissue, esp. rheumatoid arthritis.

rheu·ma·toid /rṓōmətoyd/ *adj.* having the character of rheumatism.

rheu·ma·toid ar·thri·tis *n.* a chronic progressive disease causing inflammation and stiffening of the joints.

rheu·ma·tol·o·gy /rṓōmətóləjee/ *n.* the study of rheumatic diseases. ▫▫ **rheu·ma·tol·o·gist** *n.*

Rh factor *Physiol.* an antigen occurring on the red blood cells of most humans and some other primates.

rhi·nal /rínəl/ *adj. Anat.* of a nostril or the nose.

rhine·stone /rínstōn/ *n.* an imitation diamond.

rhi·ni·tis /rinítis/ *n.* inflammation of the mucous membrane of the nose.

rhi·no /rínō/ *n.* (*pl.* same or **-nos**) *colloq.* a rhinoceros.

rhino- /rínō/ *comb. form Anat.* the nose.

rhi·noc·er·os /rīnósərəs/ *n.* (*pl.* same or **rhinoceroses**) any of various large thick-skinned plant-eating ungulates of the family Rhinocerotidae, with usu. one horn.

rhi·no·plas·ty /rínōplastee/ *n.* plastic surgery of the nose. ▫▫ **rhi·no·plas·tic** *adj.*

rhi·zoid /rízoyd/ *adj. & n. Bot.* •*adj.* rootlike. •*n.* a root hair or filament in mosses, ferns, etc.

rhi·zome /rízōm/ *n.* an underground rootlike stem bearing both roots and shoots.

rho /rō/ *n.* the seventeenth letter of the Greek alphabet (Ρ, ρ).

rho·di·um /rṓdeeəm/ *n. Chem.* a hard white metallic element of the platinum group, used in making alloys and plating jewelry. ¶ Symb.: **Rh**.

rho·do·den·dron /rṓdədéndrən/ *n.* any evergreen shrub of the genus *Rhododendron*, with large clusters of trumpet-shaped flowers.

rho·dop·sin /rōdópsin/ *n.* a light-sensitive pigment in the retina. Also called **visual purple**.

rhomb /rom/ *n.* = RHOMBUS. ▫▫ **rhom·bic** *adj.*

rhom·bi *pl.* of RHOMBUS.

rhom·bo·he·dron /rómbəhéedrən/ *n.* (*pl.* **-hedrons** or **-hedra** /–drə/) **1** a solid bounded by six equal rhombuses. **2** a crystal in this form. ▫▫ **rhom·bo·he·dral** *adj.*

rhom·boid /rómboyd/ *adj. & n.* •*adj.* (also **rhom·boi·dal** /–bóyd'l/) having or nearly having the shape of a rhombus. •*n.* a quadrilateral of which only the opposite sides and angles are equal.

rhom·bus /rómbəs/ *n.* (*pl.* **rhombuses** or **rhombi** /–bī/) *Geom.* a parallelogram with oblique angles and equal sides.

rhu·barb /rṓōbaarb/ *n.* **1 a** any of various plants of the genus *Rheum*, producing long fleshy dark-red leafstalks that are cooked and used as food. **b** the leafstalks of this. **2 a** a root of a Chinese and Tibetan plant of the genus *Rheum*. **b** a purgative made from this. **3** *sl.* nonsense. **4** *sl.* a heated dispute.

---

rhubarb late Middle English (denoting the rootstock of other plants of this genus used medicinally): from Old French *reubarbe*, from a shortening of medieval

Latin *rheubarbarum*, an alteration (by association with *rheum* 'rhubarb') of *rhabarbarum* 'foreign rhubarb,' from Greek *rha* (also meaning 'rhubarb') + *barbaros* 'foreign.'

rhumb /rum/ *n. Naut.* **1** any of the 32 points of the compass. **2** the angle between two successive compass points. **3** (in full **rhumb line**) **a** a line cutting all meridians at the same angle. **b** the line followed by a ship sailing in a fixed direction.

rhum·ba var. of RUMBA.

rhyme /rīm/ *n. & v.* •*n.* **1** identity of sound between words or the endings of words, esp. in verse. **2** (in *sing.* or *pl.*) verse having rhymes. **3 a** the use of rhyme. **b** a poem having rhymes. **4** a word providing a rhyme. •*v.* **1** *intr.* **a** (of words or lines) produce a rhyme. **b** (foll. by *with*) act as a rhyme (with another). **2** *intr.* make or write rhymes. **3** *tr.* put or make (a story, etc.) into rhyme. **4** *tr.* (foll. by *with*) treat (a word) as rhyming with another.

rhythm /rí*th*əm/ *n.* **1** a measured flow of words and phrases in verse or prose determined by various relations of long and short or accented and unaccented syllables. **2** the aspect of musical composition concerned with periodical accent and the duration of notes. **3** *Physiol.* movement with a regular succession of strong and weak elements. **4** a regularly recurring sequence of events. ▫▫ **rhythm·less** *adj.*

rhythm and blues (*abbrev.* **R&B**) *n.* popular music with a blues theme and a strong rhythm.

rhyth·mic /rí*th*mik/ *adj.* (also **rhyth·mic·al**) **1** relating to or characterized by rhythm. **2** regularly occurring. ▫▫ **rhyth·mi·cal·ly** *adv.* **rhyth·mic·i·ty** /ri*th*mísitee/ *n.*

rhythm meth·od *n.* method of birth control by which sexual intercourse is restricted to the times when ovulation is least likely to occur during a woman's menstrual cycle.

RI *abbr.* Rhode Island (also in official postal use).

ri·a /réeə/ *n. Geog.* a long narrow inlet formed by the partial submergence of a river valley.

rib /rib/ *n. & v.* •*n.* **1** each of the curved bones articulated in pairs to the spine and protecting the thoracic cavity and its organs. **2** a joint of meat from this part of an animal. **3** a ridge or long, raised piece often of stronger or thicker material across a surface or through a structure serving to support or strengthen it. **4** any of a ship's transverse curved timbers forming the framework of the hull. **5** *Knitting* a combination of plain and purl stitches producing a ribbed somewhat elastic fabric. •*v.tr.* (**ribbed, ribbing**) **1** provide with ribs; act as the ribs of. **2** *colloq.* make fun of; tease. **3** mark with ridges. ▫▫ **rib·less** *adj.*

rib Old English *rib, ribb* (in sense 1), of Germanic origin; related to Dutch *rib(be)* and German *Rippe*. Sense 1 of the *verb* dates from the mid-16th century; the sense 'make fun of' arises from a US slang usage in the sense 'to fool, dupe' (1930s).

rib·ald /ríbəld/ *adj.* (of language or its user) coarsely or disrespectfully humorous.

rib·ald·ry /ríbəldree/ *n.* ribald talk or behavior.

rib·and /ríbənd/ *n.* a ribbon.

ribbed /ribd/ *adj.* having ribs or riblike markings.

rib·bing /ríbing/ *n.* **1** ribs or a riblike structure. **2** *colloq.* the act or an instance of teasing.

rib·bon /ríbən/ *n.* **1 a** a narrow strip or band of fabric, used esp. for trimming or decoration. **b** material in this form. **2** a ribbon of a special color, etc., worn to indicate some honor or membership of a sports team, etc. **3** a long, narrow strip of anything, e.g., a band of inked material forming the printing agent in a typewriter. **4** (in *pl.*) ragged strips (*torn to ribbons*). ▫▫ **rib·boned** *adj.*

rib cage *n.* the wall of bones formed by the ribs around the chest.

ri·bo·fla·vin /ríbōfláyvin/ *n.* a vitamin of the B complex, found in liver, milk, and eggs, essential for energy production. Also called **vitamin B_2**.

ri·bo·nu·cle·ic ac·id /ríbənóokléeik, –kláyik, –nyóo–/ *n.* a nucleic acid present in living cells, esp. in ribosomes where it is involved in protein synthesis. ¶ Abbr.: **RNA**.

ri·bose /ríbōs/ *n.* a sugar found in many nucleosides and in several vitamins and enzymes.

ri·bo·some /ríbəsōm/ *n. Biochem.* each of the minute particles consisting of RNA and associated proteins found in the cytoplasm of living cells, concerned with the synthesis of proteins. ▫▫ **ri·bo·so·mal** *adj.*

rice /rīs/ *n. & v.* •*n.* **1** a swamp grass, *Oryza sativa*, cultivated in marshes, esp. in Asia. **2** the grains of this, used as cereal food. •*v.tr.* sieve (cooked potatoes, etc.) into thin strings. ▫▫ **ric·er** *n.*

rich /rich/ *adj. & n.* •*adj.* **1** having much wealth. **2** (often foll. by *in, with*) splendid; costly; elaborate. **3** valuable (*rich offerings*). **4** copious; abundant; ample. **5** (often foll. by *in, with*) (of soil or a region, etc.) abounding in natural resources or means of production; fertile (*rich in nutrients*). **6** (of food or diet) containing much fat or spice, etc. **7** (of the mixture in an internal-combustion engine) containing a high proportion of fuel. **8** (of color or sound or smell) mellow and deep; strong and full. **9 a** (of an incident or assertion, etc.) ludicrous. **b** (of humor) earthy. •*n.* (**the rich**) (used with a *pl. v.*) wealthy persons, collectively. ▫▫ **rich·ly** *adv.* **rich·ness** *n.*

rich·es /ríchiz/ *n.pl.* abundant means; valuable possessions.

Rich·ter scale /ríktər/ *n.* a scale of 0 to 10 for representing the strength of an earthquake.

rick /rik/ *n. & v.* •*n.* (also **hay·rick**) a stack of hay, wheat, etc., built into a regular shape and usu. thatched. •*v.tr.* form into a rick or ricks.

rick·ets /ríkits/ *n.* (treated as *sing.* or *pl.*) a disease of children caused by a deficiency of vitamin D, with softening of the bones often resulting in bowlegs.

rick·et·y /ríkitee/ *adj.* **1 a** insecure or shaky in construction. **b** feeble. **2 a** suffering from rickets. **b** resembling or of the nature of rickets. ▫▫ **rick·et·i·ness** *n.*

rick·rack /ríkrak/ *n.* a zigzag braided trimming for garments.

rick·sha /ríkshaw/ *n.* (also **rick·shaw**) a light two-wheeled hooded vehicle drawn by one or more persons.

ricksha

ric·o·chet /ríkəshay, rikəsháy/ *n. & v.* •*n.* **1** the action of esp. a shell or bullet in rebounding off a surface. **2** a hit made after this. •*v.intr.* (**ricocheted** /–shayd/; **ricocheting** /–shaying/) (of a projectile) rebound one or more times from a surface.

ri·cot·ta /rikótə, –káwtaa/ *n.* a soft Italian cheese.

ric·tus /ríktəs/ *n. Anat. & Zool.* the expanse or gape of a mouth or beak. □□ **ric·tal** *adj.*

rid /rid/ *v.tr.* (**ridding;** *past* and *past part.* **rid** or *archaic* **ridded**) (foll. by *of*) make (a person or place) free of something unwanted. □ **be** (or **get**) **rid of** be freed or relieved of (something unwanted); dispose of.

rid·dance /rídəns/ *n.* the act of getting rid of something. □ **good riddance** welcome relief from an unwanted person or thing.

rid·den *past part.* of RIDE.

rid·dle[1] /ríd'l/ *n. & v.* •*n.* **1** a question or statement testing ingenuity in divining its answer or meaning. **2** a puzzling fact or thing or person. •*v.* **1** *intr.* speak in or propound riddles. **2** *tr.* solve or explain (a riddle).

rid·dle[2] /ríd'l/ *v. & n.* •*v.tr.* (usu. foll. by *with*) **1** make many holes in, esp. with gunshot. **2** (in *passive*) permeate (*riddled with errors*). **3** pass through a riddle. •*n.* a coarse sieve.

rid·dling /rídling/ *adj.* expressed in riddles; puzzling.

ride /rīd/ *v. & n.* •*v.* (*past* **rode** /rōd/; *past part.* **ridden** /ríd'n/) **1** *tr.* travel or be carried on (a bicycle, etc.) or in (a vehicle). **2** *intr.* (often foll. by *on, in*) travel or be conveyed (on a bicycle or in a vehicle). **3** *tr.* sit on and control or be carried by (a horse, etc.). **4** *intr.* (often foll. by *on*) be carried (on a horse, etc.). **5** *tr.* be carried or supported by. **6** *tr.* **a** traverse on horseback, etc.. **b** compete or take part in on horseback, etc. **7** *intr.* lie at anchor; float buoyantly. **8** *intr.* (foll. by *in, on*) rest in or on while moving. **9** *tr.* yield to (a blow) so as to reduce its impact. **10** *tr.* give a ride to; cause to ride (*rode the child on his back*). **11** *tr.* (of a rider) cause (a horse, etc.) to move forward. **12** *tr.* **a** (in *passive*; foll. by *by, with*) be dominated by; be infested with (*was ridden with guilt*). **b** (as **ridden** *adj.*) infested or afflicted (usu. in *comb.*: *a rat-ridden cellar*). **13** *intr.* (of a thing normally level or even) project or overlap. **14** *tr. colloq.* mount (a sexual partner) in copulation. **15** *tr.* annoy or seek to annoy. •*n.* **1** an act or period of travel in a vehicle. **2** a spell of riding on a horse, bicycle, etc. **3** the quality of sensations when riding (*gives a bumpy ride*). □ **let a thing ride** leave it alone; let it take its natural course. **ride high** be elated or successful. **ride out** come safely through (a storm, etc., or a danger or difficulty). **ride roughshod over** see ROUGHSHOD. **ride shotgun 1** *hist.* carry a shotgun while riding on top of a stage coach as a guard. **2** guard or keep watch (over someone or something), esp. in transit. **3** ride in the front passenger seat of a vehicle. **4** a means or arrangement of transportation by motor vehicle. **5** the motor vehicle used for transportation (*my ride is here*). **ride up** (of a garment, carpet, etc.) work or move out of its proper position. **take for a ride 1** *colloq.* hoax or deceive. **2** *sl.* abduct in order to murder. □□ **rid·a·ble** *adj.*

rid·er /rídər/ *n.* **1** a person who rides (esp. a horse). **2 a** an additional clause amending or supplementing a document. **b** an addition or amendment to a legislative bill. **c** a corollary. □□ **rid·er·less** *adj.*

ridge /rij/ *n. & v.* •*n.* **1** the line of the junction of two surfaces sloping upward toward each other (*the ridge of a roof*). **2** a long, narrow hilltop, mountain range, or watershed. **3** any narrow elevation across a surface. **4** *Meteorol.* an elongated region of high barometric pressure. **5** *Agriculture* a raised strip of arable land, usu. one of a set separated by furrows. •*v.* **1** *tr.* mark with ridges. **2** *tr. Agriculture* break up (land) into ridges. **3** *tr. & intr.* gather into ridges. □□ **ridg·y** *adj.*

ridge·pole /ríjpōl/ *n.* **1** the horizontal pole of a long tent. **2** a beam along the ridge of a roof.

rid·i·cule /rídikyōōl/ *n. & v.* •*n.* subjection to derision or mockery. •*v.tr.* make fun of; subject to ridicule.

ri·dic·u·lous /ridíkyələs/ *adj.* **1** deserving or inviting ridicule. **2** unreasonable; absurd. □□ **ri·dic·u·lous·ly** *adv.* **ri·dic·u·lous·ness** *n.*

rid·ing /ríding/ *n.* **1** in senses of RIDE *v.* **2** the practice or skill of riders of horses.

rife /rīf/ *predic.adj.* **1** of common occurrence; widespread. **2** (foll. by *with*) abounding in; teeming with.

riff /rif/ *n. & v.* •*n.* a short repeated phrase in jazz, etc. •*v.intr.* play riffs.

rif·fle /rífəl/ *v. & n.* •*v.* **1** *tr.* **a** turn (pages) in quick succession. **b** shuffle (playing cards), esp. by flexing and combining the two halves of a pack. **2** *intr.* (often foll. by *through*) leaf quickly (through pages). •*n.* **1** the act or an instance of riffling. **2 a** a shallow part of a stream where the water flows brokenly. **b** a patch of waves or ripples on water.

riff-raff /rífraf/ *n.* (often prec. by *the*) rabble; disreputable or undesirable persons.

ri·fle[1] /rífəl/ *n. & v.* •*n.* **1** a gun with a long, rifled barrel, esp. one fired from shoulder level. **2** (in *pl.*) riflemen. •*v.tr.* make spiral grooves in (a gun or its barrel or bore) to make a bullet spin.

ri·fle[2] /rífəl/ *v.tr. &* (foll. by *through*) intr. **1** search and rob, esp. of all that can be found. **2** carry off as booty.

ri·fle range *n.* a place for rifle practice.

ri·fling /rífling/ *n.* the arrangement of grooves on the inside of a gun's barrel.

rift /rift/ *n. & v.* •*n.* **1 a** a crack or split in an object. **b** an opening in a cloud, etc. **2** a cleft or fissure in earth or rock. **3** a breach in friendly relations. •*v.tr.* tear or burst apart. □□ **rift·less** *adj.*

rift val·ley *n.* a steep-sided valley formed by subsidence of the earth's crust between nearly parallel faults.

rig[1] /rig/ *v. & n.* •*v.tr.* (**rigged, rigging**) **1 a** provide (a sailing ship) with sails, rigging, etc. **b** prepare ready for sailing. **2** (often foll. by *out, up*) fit with clothes or other equipment. **3** (foll. by *up*) set up hastily or as a makeshift. **4** assemble and adjust the parts of (an aircraft). •*n.* **1** the arrangement of masts, sails, rigging, etc., of a sailing ship. **2** equipment for a special purpose, e.g., a radio transmitter. **3** a truck, esp. a tractor-trailer. □□ **rigged** *adj.* (also in *comb.*).

rig[2] /rig/ *v. & n.* •*v.tr.* (**rigged, rigging**) manage or conduct fraudulently. •*n.* **1** a trick or dodge. **2** a way of swindling.

rig·ger /rígər/ *n.* **1** a person who rigs or who arranges rigging. **2** (of a rowboat) = OUTRIGGER 5a. **3** a ship rigged in a specified way. **4** a worker on an oil rig.

rig·ging /ríging/ *n.* **1** a ship's ropes, etc., supporting and controlling the sails. **2** the ropes and wires supporting the structure of an airship or biplane.

right /rīt/ *adj., n., v., adv., & int.* •*adj.* **1** (of conduct, etc.) just; morally or socially correct (*do the right thing*). **2** true; correct (*the right time*). **3** less wrong or not wrong (*which is the right way?*). **4** more or most suitable or preferable (*the right person for the job*). **5** in a sound or normal condition (*the engine doesn't sound right*). **6 a** on or toward the side of the human body that corresponds to the position of east if one regards oneself as facing north. **b** on or toward that part of an object that is analogous to a person's right side or (with opposite sense) that is nearer to a spectator's right hand. **7** (of a side of fabric, etc.) meant for display or use (*turn it right side up*). •*n.* **1** that which is morally or socially correct or just; fair treatment (often in *pl.*: *the rights and wrongs of the case*). **2** (often foll. by *to*, or *to* + infin.) a justification or fair claim (*has no right to speak like that*). **3** a thing one may legally or morally claim; authority to act. **4** the right-hand part or region or direction. **5** *Boxing* **a** the right hand. **b** a blow with this. **6** (often **Right**) *Polit.* **a** a group or section favoring conservatism. **b** such conservatives collectively. •*v.tr.* **1** (often *refl.*) restore to a proper or straight or vertical position. **2 a** correct (mistakes, etc.); set in order. **b** avenge (a wrong or a wronged person); make reparation for or to. **c** vindicate; justify; rehabilitate. •*adv.* **1** straight (*go right on*). **2** *colloq.* immediately; without delay (*do it right now*). **3** (foll. by *to, around, through,* etc.) all the way (*right to the bottom*). **4** exactly; quite (*right in the middle*). **5** justly; properly; correctly; truly; satisfactorily (*not holding it right; if I remember right*). **6** on or to the right side. •*int. colloq.* expressing agreement or assent. □ **as right as rain** perfectly sound and healthy. **at right angles** placed to form a right angle. **by right** (or **rights**) if right were done. **do right by** act dutifully toward (a person). **in one's own right** through one's own position or effort, etc. **in the right** having justice or truth on one's side. **in one's right mind** sane; competent to think and act. **on the right side of 1** in the favor of (a person, etc.). **2** somewhat less than (a specified age). **put** (or **set**) **right 1** restore to order, health, etc. **2** correct the mistaken impression, etc., of (a person). **put** (or **set**) **to rights** make correct or well ordered. **right and left** (or **right, left, and center**) on all sides. **right away** (or **off**) immediately. **right on!** *colloq.* an expression of strong approval or encouragement. **right you are!** *colloq.* an exclamation of assent. **within one's rights** not exceeding one's authority or entitlement. □□ **right•ness** *n.*

right an•gle *n.* an angle of 90°, made by lines meeting with equal angles on either side. □□ **right-an•gled** *adj.*

right arm *n.* one's most reliable helper.

right•eous /ríchəs/ *adj.* (of a person or conduct) morally right; virtuous; law-abiding. □□ **right•eous•ly** *adv.* **right•eous•ness** *n.*

right•ful /rítfŏŏl/ *adj.* **1 a** (of a person) legitimately entitled to (a position, etc.). **b** (of status or property, etc.) that one is entitled to. **2** (of an action, etc.) equitable; fair. □□ **right•ful•ly** *adv.* **right•ful•ness** *n.*

right-hand *adj.* **1** on or toward the right side of a person or thing. **2** done with the right hand.

right-hand•ed *adj.* **1** using the right hand by preference as more serviceable than the left. **2** (of a tool, etc.) made to be used with the right hand. **3** (of a blow) struck with the right hand. **4** turning to the right; toward the right.

right-hand man *n.* (*pl.* **men**) an indispensable or chief assistant.

right•ism /rítizəm/ *n. Polit.* the principles or policy of the right. □□ **right•ist** *n. & adj.*

right•ly /rítlee/ *adv.* justly; properly; correctly; justifiably.

right-mind•ed *adj.* having sound views and principles.

right•most /rítmōst/ *adj.* furthest to the right.

right of way *n.* **1** a right established by usage to pass over another's ground. **2** a path subject to such a right. **3** the right of one vehicle to proceed before another.

right-think•ing *adj.* = RIGHT-MINDED.

right-to-die *adj.* pertaining to the avoidance of using artificial life support in case of severe illness or injury.

right-to-life *adj.* pertaining to the movement opposing abortion.

right•ward /rítwərd/ *adv. & adj.* •*adv.* (also **right•wards** /–wərdz/) toward the right. •*adj.* going toward or facing the right.

right whale *n.* any large-headed whale of the family Balaenidae, rich in whalebone and easily captured.

right wing *n.* **1** the right side of a soccer, etc., team on the field. **2** the conservative section of a political party or system. □□ **right-wing** *adj.* **right-wing•er** *n.*

rig•id /rijid/ *adj.* **1** not flexible; that cannot be bent. **2** (of a person, conduct, etc.) **a** inflexible (*a rigid disciplinarian*). **b** strict; punctilious. □□ **ri•gid•i•ty** /rəjíditee/ *n.* **rig•id•ly** *adv.* **rig•id•ness** *n.*

ri•gid•i•fy /rijídifī/ *v.tr. & intr.* (**-fies, -fied**) make or become rigid.

rig•ma•role /rígmərōl/ (also **rig•a•mo•role** /rígə–/) *n.* **1** a lengthy and complicated procedure. **2 a** a rambling or meaningless account or tale. **b** such talk.

rig•or[1] /rígər/ *n. Med.* **1** a sudden feeling of cold with shivering accompanied by a rise in temperature. **2** rigidity of the body caused by shock or poisoning, etc.

rig•or[2] /rígər/ *n.* **1 a** severity; strictness; harshness. **b** (often in *pl.*) severity of weather or climate; extremity of cold. **c** (in *pl.*) harsh measures or conditions. **2** logical exactitude. **3** strict enforcement of rules, etc. (*the utmost rigor of the law*).

rig•or mor•tis /rígər máwrtis/ *n.* stiffening of the body after death.

rig•or•ous /rígərəs/ *adj.* **1** characterized by or showing rigor; strict, severe. **2** strictly exact or accurate. **3** (of the weather) cold, severe. □□ **rig•or•ous•ly** *adv.* **rig•or•ous•ness** *n.*

rile /rīl/ *v.tr.* **1** *colloq.* anger; irritate. **2** make (water) turbulent or muddy.

Ri•ley /rílee/ *n.* □ **the life of Riley** *colloq.* a carefree existence.

rill /ril/ *n.* **1** a small stream. **2** a shallow channel cut in the surface of soil or rocks by running water.

rim /rim/ *n. & v.* •*n.* **1 a** a raised edge or border. **b** a margin or verge, esp. of something circular. **2** the part of a pair of spectacles surrounding the lenses. **3** the outer edge of a wheel, on which the tire is fitted. **4** a boundary line (*the rim of the horizon*). •*v.tr.* (**rimmed, rimming**) **1 a** provide with a rim. **b** be a rim for or to. **2** edge; border. □□ **rim•less** *adj.* **rimmed** *adj.* (also in *comb.*).

rime[1] /rīm/ *n. & v.* •*n.* **1** frost, esp. formed from cloud or fog. **2** *poet.* hoarfrost. •*v.tr.* cover with rime. □□ **rim•y** /rímee/ *adj.* (**rimier, rimiest**)

rime[2] *archaic* var. of RHYME.

rind /rīnd/ *n. & v.* •*n.* **1** the tough outer layer or covering of fruit, cheese, bacon, etc. **2** the bark of a tree or plant. •*v.tr.* strip the bark from. □□ **rind•less** *adj.*

ring[1] /ring/ *n. & v.* •*n.* **1** a circular band, usu. of precious metal, worn on a finger. **2** a circular band of any material. **3** the rim of a cylindrical or circular object, or a line or band around it. **4** a mark or part having the form of a circular band (*smoke rings*). **5 a** an enclosure for a circus performance, betting at races, the showing of cattle, etc. **b** (prec. by *the*) bookmakers collectively. **c** a roped enclosure for boxing or wrestling. **6 a** a group of people or things arranged in a circle. **b** such an arrangement. **7** a combination of traders, bookmakers, spies, politicians, etc., acting together usu. illicitly for profit, etc. **8** a circular or spiral course. **9** *Astron.* a thin band or disk of particles, etc., around a planet. **10** *Archaeol.* a circular prehistoric earthwork usu. of a bank and ditch. •*v.tr.* **1** make or draw a circle around. **2** (often foll. by *around, about, in*) encircle or hem in (game or cattle). **3** put a ring through the nose of (a pig, bull, etc.). **4** cut (fruit, vegetables, etc.) into rings. □ **run** (or **make**) **rings around** *colloq.* outclass or outwit (another person). □□ **ringed** *adj.* (also in *comb.*). **ring•less** *adj.*

ring[2] /ring/ *v. & n.* •*v.* (*past* **rang** /rang/; *past part.* **rung** /rung/) **1** *intr.* (often foll. by *out,* etc.) give a clear resonant or vibrating sound of or as of a bell (*a shot rang out*). **2** *tr.* **a** make (esp. a bell) ring. **b** (*absol.*) call for service or attention by ringing a bell. **3** *intr.* (usu. foll. by *with, to*) (of a place) resound or be permeated with a sound, or an attribute (*the theater rang with applause*). **4** *intr.* (of the ears) be filled with a sensation of ringing. **5** *tr.* **a** sound (a peal, etc.) on bells. **b** (of a bell) sound (the hour, etc.). **6** *tr.* (foll. by *in, out*) usher in or out with bell-ringing (*rang out the Old Year*). **7** *intr.* (of sentiments, etc.) convey a specified impression (*words rang hollow*). •*n.* **1** a ringing sound or tone. **2 a** the act of ringing a bell. **b** the sound caused by this. **3** *colloq.* a telephone call. **4** a specified feeling conveyed by an utterance (*had a melancholy ring*). **5** a set of, esp. church, bells. ▫ **ring in one's ears** (or **heart,** etc.) linger in the memory. **ring true** (or **false**) convey an impression of truth or falsehood. **ring up** record (an amount, etc.) on a cash register. ▫▫ **ringed** *adj.* (also in *comb.*). **ring·er** *n.* **ring·ing** *adj.*

ring bind·er *n.* a loose-leaf binder with ring-shaped clasps that can be opened to pass through holes in the paper.

ring·er /ríngər/ *n. sl.* **1 a** an athlete or horse entered in a competition by fraudulent means, esp. as a substitute. **b** a person's double, esp. an impostor. **2** a person who rings, esp. a bell ringer. ▫ **be a ringer** (or **dead ringer**) **for** resemble (a person) exactly.

ring fin·ger *n.* the finger next to the little finger, esp. of the left hand, on which the wedding ring is usu. worn.

ring·lead·er /ríngleedər/ *n.* a leading instigator in an illicit or illegal activity.

ring·let /rínglit/ *n.* **1** a curly lock of hair, esp. a long one. **2** a butterfly, *Aphantopus hyperantus*, with spots on its wings. ▫▫ **ring·let·ed** *adj.*

ring·mas·ter /ríngmastər/ *n.* the person directing a circus performance.

ring·side /ríngsīd/ *n.* (often *attrib.*) **1** the area immediately beside a boxing ring or circus ring, etc. **2** an advantageous position from which to observe or monitor something. ▫▫ **ring·sid·er** *n.*

ring·ster /ríngstər/ *n.* a person who participates in a political or commercial ring (see RING[1] *n.* 8).

ring·worm /ríngwərm/ *n.* any of various fungous infections of the skin causing circular inflamed patches, esp. on the scalp.

rink /ringk/ *n.* **1** an area of natural or artificial ice for skating or playing ice hockey, etc. **2** an enclosed area for roller-skating. **3** a building containing either of these.

rinse /rins/ *v. & n.* •*v.tr.* (often foll. by *through, out*) **1** wash with clean water. **2** apply liquid to. **3** wash lightly. **4** put (clothes, etc.) through clean water to remove soap or detergent. **5** (foll. by *out, away*) clear (impurities) by rinsing. **6** treat (hair) with a rinse. •*n.* **1** the act or an instance of rinsing. **2** a solution for cleansing the mouth. **3** a dye for the temporary tinting of hair.

ri·ot /ríət/ *n. & v.* •*n.* **1 a** a disturbance of the peace by a crowd; an occurrence of public disorder. **b** (*attrib.*) involved in suppressing riots (*riot police*). **2** uncontrolled revelry; noisy behavior. **3** (foll. by *of*) a lavish display or enjoyment (*a riot of color and sound*). **4** *colloq.* a very amusing thing or person (*everyone thought she was a riot*). •*v.intr.* **1** make or engage in a riot. **2** behave in an unrestrained way. ▫ **read the Riot Act** put a firm stop to insubordination, etc.; give a severe warning. **run riot 1** throw off all restraint. **2** (of plants) grow or spread uncontrolled. ▫▫ **ri·ot·er** *n.*

ri·ot·ous /ríətəs/ *adj.* **1** marked by or involving rioting. **2** characterized by wanton conduct. **3** wildly profuse. ▫▫ **ri·ot·ous·ly** *adv.* **ri·ot·ous·ness** *n.*

RIP *abbr.* rest in peace (used on gravestones).

rip /rip/ *v. & n.* •*v.tr. & intr.* (**ripped, ripping**) **1** *tr.* tear or cut (a thing) quickly or forcibly away or apart. **2** *tr.* **a** make (a hole, etc.) by ripping. **b** make a long tear or cut in. **3** *intr.* come violently apart. **4** *intr.* rush along. •*n.* **1** a long tear or cut. **2** an act of ripping. ▫ **let rip** *colloq.* **1** act or proceed without restraint. **2** speak violently. **3** not check the speed of or interfere with (a person or thing). **rip into** attack (a person) verbally.

ri·par·i·an /rīpáireeən/ *adj. & n.* esp. *Law* •*adj.* of or on a riverbank. •*n.* an owner of property on a riverbank.

rip cord *n.* a cord for releasing a parachute from its pack.

ripe /rīp/ *adj.* **1** (of grain, cheese, etc.) ready to be reaped or picked or eaten. **2** mature; fully developed. **3** (of a person's age) advanced. **4** (often foll. by *for*) fit or ready (*when the time is ripe*). **5** (of the complexion, etc.) red and full like ripe fruit. ▫▫ **ripe·ly** *adv.* **ripe·ness** *n.*

rip·en /rípən/ *v.tr. & intr.* make or become ripe.

rip-off *n. & v. colloq.* •*n.* **1** a fraud or swindle. **2** financial exploitation. •*v.tr.* (**rip off**) defraud; steal.

ri·poste /ripóst/ *n. & v.* •*n.* **1** a quick sharp reply or retort. **2** a quick return thrust in fencing. •*v.intr.* deliver a riposte.

rip·per /rípər/ *n.* **1** a person or thing that rips. **2** a murderer who rips the victims' bodies.

rip·ple /rípəl/ *n. & v.* •*n.* **1** a ruffling of the water's surface; a small wave or series of waves. **2 a** a gentle lively sound that rises and falls, e.g., of applause. **b** a brief wave of emotion, excitement, etc. (*the new recruit caused a ripple of interest in the company*). **3** a wavy appearance in hair, material, etc. **4** *Electr.* a slight variation in the strength of a current, etc. **5** ice cream with added syrup giving a colored ripple effect (*raspberry ripple*). **6** a riffle in a stream. •*v.* **1 a** *intr.* form ripples; flow in ripples. **b** *tr.* cause to do this. **2** *intr.* show or sound like ripples. ▫▫ **rip·ply** *adj.*

rip·rap /ríprap/ *n.* a collection of loose stone as a foundation for a structure.

rip-roar·ing /ríprawring/ *adj.* **1** wildly noisy or boisterous. **2** excellent, first-rate. ▫▫ **rip-roar·ing·ly** *adv.*

rip·saw /rípsaw/ *n.* a coarse saw for sawing wood along the grain.

rip·snort·er /rípsnawrtər/ *n. colloq.* an energetic, remarkable, or excellent person or thing. ▫▫ **rip·snort·ing** *adj.* **rip·snort·ing·ly** *adv.*

rise /rīz/ *v. & n.* •*v.intr.* (*past* **rose** /rōz/; *past part.* **ris·en** /rízən/) **1** come or go up. **2** grow, project, expand, or incline upward; become higher. **3** appear above the horizon. **4 a** get up from lying or sitting or kneeling. **b** get out of bed, esp. in the morning. **5** become erect. **6** reach a higher position or level or amount. **7** develop greater intensity, strength, volume, or pitch (*their voices rose*). **8** make progress; reach a higher social position (*rose from the ranks*). **9 a** come to the surface of liquid. **b** (of a person) react to provocation (*rise to the bait*). **10** become or be visible above the surroundings, etc. **11 a** (of buildings, etc.) undergo construction from the foundations. **b** (of a tree, etc.) grow to a (usu. specified) height. **12** come to life again (*rise from the ashes*). **13** (of dough) swell by the action of yeast, etc. **14** (often foll. by *up*) rebel (*rise in arms*). **15** originate (*the river rises in the mountains*). **16** (of wind) start to blow. **17** (of a person's spirits) become cheerful. **18** (of a barometer) show a higher atmospheric pressure. **19** (of a horse) rear (*rose on its hind legs*). **20** (of a bump, blister, etc.) form. •*n.* **1** an act or manner or amount of rising. **2** an upward slope or hill or movement (*the house stood on a rise*). **3** an increase in sound or pitch. **4** an increase in amount, extent, etc. (*a rise in unemployment*). **5** an increase in status or power. **6** social, commercial, or political advancement. **7 a** the vertical height of a step, arch, etc. **b** = RISER 2. ▫ **get a rise out of** *colloq.* provoke an emotional reaction from (a person), esp. by teasing. **on the rise** on the increase. **rise above 1** be superior to (petty feelings, etc.). **2** show dignity or strength in the face of (difficulty, poor conditions, etc.). **rise and shine** (usu. as *imper.*) *colloq.* get out of bed; wake up.

ris·er /rízər/ *n.* **1** a person who rises, esp. from bed (*an* *early riser*). **2** a vertical section between the treads of a staircase. **3** a vertical pipe for the flow of liquid or gas. **4** a low platform on a stage or in an auditorium, used to give greater prominence to a speaker, performer, spectator, etc.

rish·i /ríshee/ *n.* (*pl.* **rishis**) a Hindu sage or saint.

ris·i·ble /rízibəl/ *adj.* **1** laughable; ludicrous. **2** inclined to laugh. ▫▫ **ris·i·bil·i·ty** *n.* **ris·i·bly** *adv.*

ris·ing /rízing/ *adj. & n.* • *adj.* **1** going up; getting higher. **2** increasing (*rising costs*). **3** advancing to maturity or high standing (*a rising young lawyer*). **4** approaching a higher level, grade, etc. (*rising seniors*) or a specified age (*the rising fives*). **5** (of ground) sloping upward. • *n.* a revolt or insurrection.

risk /risk/ *n. & v.* • *n.* **1** a chance or possibility of danger, loss, injury, etc. (*a health risk*). **2** a person or thing causing a risk or regarded in relation to risk (*is a poor risk*). • *v.tr.* **1** expose to risk. **2** accept the chance of (*risk getting wet*). **3** venture on. ▫ **at risk** exposed to danger. **at one's (own) risk** accepting responsibility or liability. **at the risk of** with the possibility of (an adverse consequence). **put at risk** expose to danger. **risk one's neck** put one's own life in danger. **run a** (or **the**) **risk** (often foll. by *of*) expose oneself to danger or loss, etc.

risk·y /ráskee/ *adj.* (**riskier, riskiest**) involving risk. ▫▫ **risk·i·ly** *adv.* **risk·i·ness** *n.*

ri·sot·to /risáwtō, –sótō, –záwtō/ *n.* (*pl.* **-tos**) an Italian dish of rice cooked in stock with meat, onions, etc.

ris·qué /riskáy/ *adj.* (of a story, etc.) slightly indecent.

rite /rīt/ *n.* **1** a religious or solemn observance or act. **2** an action or procedure required or usual in this. **3** a body of customary observances characteristic of a church or a part of it (*the Latin rite*).

rite of pas·sage *n.* (often in *pl.*) a ritual or event marking a stage of a person's advance through life, e.g., marriage.

rit·u·al /ríchōōəl/ *n. & adj.* • *n.* **1** a prescribed order of performing rites. **2** a procedure regularly followed. • *adj.* of or done as a ritual or rites. ▫▫ **rit·u·al·ize** *v.tr. & intr.* **rit·u·al·i·za·tion** *n.* **rit·u·al·ly** *adv.*

rit·u·al·ism /ríchōōəlizəm/ *n.* the regular or excessive practice of ritual. ▫▫ **rit·u·al·ist** *n.* **rit·u·al·is·tic** *adj.* **rit·u·al·is·ti·cal·ly** *adv.*

ritz·y /rítsee/ *adj.* (**ritzier, ritziest**) *colloq.* **1** high-class; luxurious. **2** ostentatiously smart. ▫▫ **ritz·i·ly** *adv.* **ritz·i·ness** *n.*

ri·val /rívəl/ *n. & v.* • *n.* **1** a person competing with another for the same objective. **2** a person or thing that equals another in quality. **3** (*attrib.*) being a rival or rivals (*a rival firm*). • *v.tr.* **1** be the rival of or comparable to. **2** seem or claim to be as good as.

ri·val·ry /rívəlree/ *n.* (*pl.* **-ries**) the state or an instance of being rivals; competition.

rive /rīv/ *v.* (*past* **rived**; *past part.* **riven** /rívən/) *archaic* or *poet.* **1** *tr.* split or tear apart violently. **2 a** *tr.* split (wood or stone). **b** *intr.* be split.

riv·er /rívər/ *n.* **1** a copious natural stream of water flowing in a channel to the sea or a lake, etc. **2** a copious flow (*rivers of blood*). **3** (*attrib.*) (in the names of animals, plants, etc.) living in or associated with the river. ▫▫ **riv·ered** *adj.* (also in *comb.*). **riv·er·less** *adj.*

riv·er·ine /rívərīn, –reen/ *adj.* of or on a river or riverbank; riparian.

riv·er·side /rívərsīd/ *n.* the ground along a riverbank.

riv·et /rívit/ *n. & v.* • *n.* a nail or bolt for holding together metal plates, etc., its headless end being beaten out or pressed down when in place. • *v.tr.* **1 a** join or fasten with rivets. **b** beat out or press down the end of (a nail or bolt). **c** fix; make immovable. **2 a** (foll. by *on, upon*) direct intently (one's eyes or attention, etc.). **b** (esp. as **riveting** *adj.*) engross (a person or the attention). ▫▫ **riv·et·er** *n.*

ri·vi·er·a /ríveeáirə/ *n.* (often **Riv·i·er·a**) a coastal region with a subtropical climate, vegetation, etc., esp. that of SE France and NW Italy.

ri·vi·ère /reevyáir/ *n.* a gem necklace, esp. of more than one string.

riv·u·let /rívyəlit/ *n.* a small stream.

Rn *symb. Chem.* the element radon.

RNA *abbr.* ribonucleic acid.

roach /rōch/ *n.* **1** *colloq.* a cockroach. **2** *sl.* the butt of a marijuana cigarette.

road /rōd/ *n.* **1 a** a path or way with a specially prepared surface, used by vehicles, pedestrians, etc. **b** the part of this used by vehicles (*don't step in the road*). **2 a** one's way or route. **b** a method or means of accomplishing something. ▫ **by road** using transport along roads. **one for the road** *colloq.* a final (esp. alcoholic) drink before departure. **on the road** traveling, esp. as a firm's representative, itinerant performer, or vagrant. **the road to** the way of getting to or achieving (*the road to Miami; the road to ruin*). ▫▫ **road·less** *adj.*

road·bed /rṓdbed/ *n.* **1** the foundation structure of a railroad. **2** the material laid down to form a road. **3** the part of a road on which vehicles travel.

road·block /rṓdblok/ *n.* a barrier on a road set up to stop and examine traffic.

road hog *n. colloq.* a reckless or inconsiderate motorist.

road·house /rṓdhows/ *n.* an inn or club on a country road.

road·ie /rṓdee/ *n. colloq.* an assistant employed by a touring band of musicians to erect and maintain equipment.

road man·ag·er *n.* the organizer and supervisor of a musicians' tour.

road·run·ner /rṓdrunər/ *n.* a bird of Mexican and US deserts, *Geococcyx californianus*, related to the cuckoo, known as a poor flier but a fast runner.

road show *n.* **1 a** a performance given by a touring company, esp. a group of pop musicians. **b** a company giving such performances. **2** a radio or television program done on location.

road·side /rṓdsīd/ *n.* the strip of land beside a road.

road·ster /rṓdstər/ *n.* **1** an open car without rear seats. **2** a horse or bicycle for use on the road.

road test *n.* a test of the performance of a vehicle on the road.

road·way /rṓdway/ *n.* **1** a road. **2** = ROAD 1b. **3** the part of a bridge or railroad used for traffic.

road·work /rṓdwərk/ *n.* **1** the construction or repair of roads, or other work involving digging up a road surface. **2** athletic exercise or training involving running on roads.

roam /rōm/ *v. & n.* • *v.* **1** *intr.* ramble; wander. **2** *tr.* travel unsystematically over, through, or about. • *n.* an act of roaming; a ramble. ▫▫ **roam·er** *n.*

roan /rōn/ *adj. & n.* • *adj.* (of esp. a horse) having a coat of which the prevailing color is thickly interspersed with hairs of another color, esp. bay, chestnut, or black mixed with white or gray. • *n.* a roan animal.

roar /rawr/ *n. & v.* • *n.* **1** a loud, deep, hoarse sound, as made by a lion, thunder, a loud engine, or a person in pain, rage, or excitement. **2** a loud laugh. • *v.* **1** *intr.* **a** utter or make a roar. **b** utter loud laughter. **2** *intr.* travel in a vehicle at high speed, esp. with the engine roaring. **3** *tr.* (often foll. by *out*) say, sing, or utter (words, an oath, etc.) in a loud tone. ▫▫ **roar·er** *n.*

roar·ing /ráwring/ *adj.* in senses of ROAR *v.* ▫ **roaring drunk** very drunk and noisy. ▫▫ **roar·ing·ly** *adv.*

See page xii for the *Key to Pronunciation*.

roar·ing for·ties *n.pl.* (prec. by *the*) stormy ocean tracts between lat. 40° and 50° S.

roar·ing twen·ties *n.pl.* the decade of the 1920s (with ref. to its postwar buoyancy).

roast /rōst/ *v., adj., & n.* •*v.* **1** *tr.* **a** cook (food, esp. meat) in an oven or by exposure to open heat. **b** heat (coffee beans) before grinding. **2** *tr.* heat (the ore of metal) in a furnace. **3** *tr.* **a** expose (a torture victim) to fire or great heat. **b** *tr. & refl.* expose (oneself or part of oneself) to warmth. **4** *tr.* criticize severely; denounce. **5** *intr.* undergo roasting. •*attrib.adj.* (of meat or a potato, chestnut, etc.) roasted. •*n.* **1 a** roast meat. **b** a dish of this. **c** a piece of meat for roasting. **2** the process of roasting. **3** a party where roasted food is eaten. **4** a banquet to honor a person at which the honoree is subjected to good-natured ridicule.

roast·er /rṓstər/ *n.* **1** a person or thing that roasts. **2 a** an oven or dish for roasting food in. **b** an ore-roasting furnace. **c** a coffee-roasting apparatus. **3** something fit for roasting, e.g., a fowl, a potato, etc.

roast·ing /rṓsting/ *adj. & n.* •*adj.* very hot. •*n.* **1** in senses of ROAST *v.* **2** a severe criticism or denunciation.

rob /rob/ *v.tr.* (**robbed, robbing**) (often foll. by *of*) **1** take unlawfully from, esp. by force or threat of force. **2** deprive of what is due or normal (*was robbed of my sleep*). **3** (*absol.*) commit robbery. **4** *colloq.* cheat; swindle. ▫▫ **rob·ber** /róbər/ *n.*

▶In law, to **rob** is to take something from someone by causing fear of harm, whether or not actual harm occurs. The term is widely, but incorrectly, used to mean simple *theft,*, e.g.: *Our house was robbed while we were away.*

rob·ber /róbər/ *n.* a person who commits robbery.

rob·ber bar·on *n.* **1** a plundering feudal lord. **2** an unscrupulous plutocrat.

rob·ber·y /róbəree/ *n.* (*pl.* **-ies**) **1 a** the act or process of robbing, esp. with force or threat of force. **b** an instance of this. **2** excessive financial demand or cost; swindling or overcharging (*it set us back $50—it was sheer robbery*).

robe /rōb/ *n. & v.* •*n.* **1** a long, loose outer garment. **2** a loose, usu. belted garment worn over nightwear, while resting, or after bathing. **3** a baby's outer garment, esp. at a christening. **4** (often in *pl.*) a long outer garment worn as an indication of the wearer's rank, office, profession, etc. **5** a blanket or wrap of fur. •*v.* **1** *tr.* clothe (a person) in a robe; dress. **2** *intr.* put on one's robes or vestments.

rob·in /róbin/ *n.* **1** a red-breasted thrush, *Turdus migratorius*. **2** (also **robin red·breast**) a small brown European bird, *Erithacus rubecula*, the adult of which has a red throat and breast. **3** a bird similar in appearance, etc., to either of these.

Rob·in Hood *n.* (with ref. to the legend of the medieval forest outlaw) a person who acts illegally or unfavorably toward the rich for the benefit of the poor.

ro·bot /rṓbot/ *n.* **1** a machine capable of carrying out a complex series of actions automatically, esp. one programmable by a computer. **2** (esp. in science fiction) a machine resembling a human being and able to replicate certain human functions automatically. **3** a person who behaves in a mechanical or unemotional manner. ▫▫ **ro·bot·ic** /–bótik/ *adj.* **ro·bot·ize** *v.tr.*

ro·bot·ics /rōbótiks/ *n.pl.* (usu. treated as *sing.*) the study of robots; the art or science of their design and operation.

ro·bust /rōbúst/ *adj.* (**robuster, robustest**) **1** (of a person, animal, or thing) strong and sturdy, esp. in physique or construction. **2** (of exercise, discipline, etc.) vigorous; requiring strength. **3** (of intellect or mental attitude) straightforward. **4** (of a statement, reply, etc.) bold; firm; unyielding. **5** (of wine, etc.) full-bodied. ▫▫ **ro·bust·ly** *adv.* **ro·bust·ness** *n.*

ro·caille /rōkí/ *n.* **1** an 18th-c. style of ornamentation based on rock and shell motifs. **2** a rococo style.

rock[1] /rok/ *n.* **1 a** the hard material of the earth's crust, exposed on the surface or underlying the soil. **b** a similar material on other planets. **2** *Geol.* any natural material, hard or soft (e.g., clay), consisting of one or more minerals. **3 a** a mass of rock projecting and forming a hill, cliff, reef, etc. **b** (**the Rock**) Gibraltar. **4** a large detached stone. **5** a stone of any size. **6** a firm and dependable support or protection. **7** (in *pl.*) *sl.* money. **8** *sl.* a precious stone, esp. a diamond. **9** *sl.* a solid form of cocaine. ▫ **between a rock and a hard place** forced to choose between two unpleasant or difficult alternatives. **get one's rocks off** *coarse sl.* **1** achieve sexual satisfaction. **2** obtain enjoyment. **on the rocks** *colloq.* **1** short of money. **2** broken down. **3** (of a drink) served over ice cubes. ▫▫ **rock·less** *adj.* **rock·like** *adj.*

rock[2] /rok/ *v. & n.* •*v.* **1** *tr.* move gently back and forth in or as if in a cradle; set or maintain such motion (*rock him to sleep*; *the ship was rocked by the waves*). **2** *intr.* be or continue in such motion (*sat rocking in his chair*). **3 a** *intr.* sway from side to side; shake; oscillate; reel. **b** *tr.* cause to do this (*an earthquake rocked the house*). **4** *tr.* distress; perturb. **5** *intr.* dance to or play rock music. •*n.* **1** a rocking movement. **2** a spell of rocking. **3 a** = ROCK AND ROLL. **b** any of a variety of types of modern popular music with a rocking or swinging beat, derived from rock and roll. ▫ **rock the boat** *colloq.* disturb the equilibrium of a situation.

rock·a·bil·ly /rókəbilee/ *n.* a type of popular music combining elements of rock and roll and hillbilly music.

rock and roll *n.* (also **rock 'n' roll**) a type of popular dance music originating in the 1950s, characterized by a heavy beat and simple melodies, often with a blues element. ▫▫ **rock and rol·ler** *n.* (also **rock 'n' roller**)

rock-bot·tom *adj.* (of prices, etc.) the very lowest. ▫▫ **rock bot·tom** *n.*

rock·bound /rókbównd/ *adj.* (of a coast) rocky and inaccessible.

rock climb·ing *n.* the sport of climbing rock faces, esp. with the aid of ropes, etc.

rock crys·tal *n.* transparent colorless quartz usu. in hexagonal prisms.

rock·er /rókər/ *n.* **1** a person or thing that rocks. **2** a curved bar or similar support, on which something can rock. **3** a rocking chair. **4 a** a young devotee of rock music, characteristically associated with leather clothing and motorcycles. **b** a performer of rock music. **5** an ice skate with a highly curved blade. **6** a switch constructed on a pivot mechanism operating between the "on" and "off" positions. **7** any rocking device forming part of a mechanism. ▫ **off one's rocker** *sl.* crazy.

rock·et /rókit/ *n. & v.* •*n.* **1** a cylindrical projectile that can be propelled to a great height or distance by combustion of its contents. **2** an engine using a similar principle but not dependent on air intake for its operation. **3** a rocket-propelled missile, spacecraft, etc. •*v.* **1** *tr.* bombard with rockets. **2** *intr.* **a** move rapidly upward or away. **b** increase rapidly (*prices rocketed*).

rock·et·ry /rókitree/ *n.* the science or practice of rocket propulsion.

rock·fall /rókfawl/ *n.* **1** a descent of loose rocks. **2** a mass of fallen rock.

rock gar·den *n.* a garden in which interesting stones and rocks are a chief feature.

rock·ing chair *n.* a chair mounted on rockers or springs for gently rocking in.

rock·ing horse *n.* a model of a horse on rockers or springs for a child to rock on.

rock 'n' roll var. of ROCK AND ROLL.
rock pool *n.* a pool of water among rocks
rock·rose /rókrōz/ *n.* any plant of the genus *Cistus, Helianthum,* etc., with roselike flowers.
rock salt *n.* common salt as a solid mineral.
rock·shaft /rókshaft/ *n.* a shaft that oscillates about an axis without making complete revolutions.
rock·y[1] /rókee/ *adj. & n.* • *adj.* (**rockier, rockiest**) **1** of or like rock. **2** full of or abounding in rock or rocks (*a rocky shore*). **3 a** firm as a rock; determined; steadfast. **b** unfeeling; cold; hard. • *n.* (**the Rockies**) the Rocky Mountains in western N. America. ▫▫ **rock·i·ness** *n.*
rock·y[2] /rókee/ *adj.* (**rockier, rockiest**) *colloq.* unsteady; tottering. ▫▫ **rock·i·ly** *adv.* **rock·i·ness** *n.*
ro·co·co /rəkṓkō/ *adj. & n.* • *adj.* **1** of a late baroque style of decoration prevalent in 18th-c. continental Europe, with asymmetrical patterns. **2** (of literature, music, architecture, and the decorative arts) highly ornamented; florid. • *n.* the rococo style.
rod /rod/ *n.* **1** a slender straight bar, esp. of wood or metal. **2** this as a symbol of office. **3 a** a stick or bundle of twigs used in caning or flogging. **b** (prec. by *the*) the use of this; punishment; chastisement. **4 a** = FISHING ROD. **b** an angler using a rod. **5 a** a slender straight round stick growing as a shoot on a tree. **b** this when cut. **6** *sl.* a pistol or revolver. **7** *Anat.* any of numerous rod-shaped structures in the eye, detecting dim light. ▫▫ **rod·like** *adj.*
rode *past* of RIDE.
ro·dent /rṓd'nt/ *n. & adj.* • *n.* any mammal of the order Rodentia with strong incisors and no canine teeth, e.g., rat, mouse, squirrel, beaver, porcupine. • *adj.* of the order Rodentia. ▫▫ **ro·den·tial** /–dénshəl/ *adj.*
ro·de·o /rṓdiō, rōdáyō/ *n.* (*pl.* **-os**) **1** an exhibition or entertainment involving cowboys' skills in handling animals. **2** an exhibition of other skills, e.g., in motorcycling. **3 a** a roundup of cattle on a ranch for branding, etc. **b** an enclosure for this.
rod·o·mon·tade /ródəmontáyd, –taád, rṓdə–/ *n., adj., & v.* • *n.* **1** boastful or bragging talk or behavior. **2** an instance of this. • *adj.* boastful or bragging. • *v.intr.* brag; talk boastfully.
roe[1] /rō/ *n.* **1** (also **hard roe**) the mass of eggs in a female fish's ovary. **2** (also **soft roe**) the milt of a male fish. ▫▫ **roed** *adj.* (also in *comb.*).
roe[2] /rō/ *n.* (*pl.* same or **roes**) (also **roe deer**) a small European and Asian deer, *Capreolus capreolus.*
roe·buck /rṓbuk/ *n.* (*pl.* same or **roebucks**) a male roe deer.
roent·gen /réntgən, –jən, rúnt–/ *n.* (also **rönt·gen**) a unit of ionizing radiation.
roent·gen·og·ra·phy /réntgənógrəfee, –jə–, rúnt–/ *n.* photography using X rays.
roent·gen·ol·o·gy /réntgənóləjee, –jə–, rúnt–/ *n.* = RADIOLOGY.
rog·er /rójər/ *int.* **1** your message has been received and understood (used in radio communication, etc.). **2** *sl.* I agree.
rogue /rōg/ *n.* **1** a dishonest or unprincipled person. **2** *joc.* a mischievous person, esp. a child. **3** (usu. *attrib.*) **a** a wild animal driven away or living apart from the herd and of fierce temper (*rogue elephant*). **b** a stray, irresponsible, or undisciplined person or thing (*rogue trader*). **4** an inferior or defective specimen among many acceptable ones.
ro·guer·y /rṓgəree/ *n.* (*pl.* **-ies**) conduct or an action characteristic of rogues.
rogues' gal·ler·y *n.* a collection of photographs of known criminals, etc., used for identification of suspects.
ro·guish /rṓgish/ *adj.* **1** playfully mischievous. **2** characteristic of rogues. ▫▫ **ro·guish·ly** *adv.* **ro·guish·ness** *n.*
roist·er /róystər/ *v.intr.* (esp. as **roistering** *adj.*) revel noisily; be uproarious. ▫▫ **roist·er·er** *n.* **roist·er·ous** *adj.*
role /rōl/ *n.* (also **rôle**) **1** an actor's part in a play, motion picture, etc. **2** a person's or thing's characteristic or expected function.
role mod·el *n.* a person looked to by others as an example in a particular role.
role-play·ing *n.* an exercise in which participants act the part of another character, used in psychotherapy, language teaching, etc.
roll /rōl/ *v. & n.* • *v.* **1 a** *intr.* move or go in some direction by turning over and over on an axis. **b** *tr.* cause to do this. **2** *tr.* make revolve between two surfaces (*rolled the clay between his palms*). **3 a** *intr.* (foll. by *along, by,* etc.) move or advance on or (of time, etc.) as if on wheels, etc. (*the years rolled by*). **b** *tr.* cause to do this. **c** *intr.* (of a person) be conveyed in a vehicle (*rolled by on his tractor*). **4 a** *tr.* turn over and over on itself to form a more or less cylindrical or spherical shape (*rolled a newspaper*). **b** *tr.* make by forming material into a cylinder or ball (*rolled a cigarette*). **c** *tr.* accumulate into a mass (*rolled the dough into a ball*). **d** *intr.* (foll. by *into*) make a specified shape of itself (*the caterpillar rolled into a ball*). **5** *tr.* flatten or form by passing a roller, etc., over or by passing between rollers. **6** *intr. & tr.* change or cause to change direction by rotatory movement (*his eyes rolled*). **7** *intr.* **a** wallow, turn about in a fluid or a loose medium (*the dog rolled in the dust*). **b** (of a horse, etc.) lie on its back and kick about, esp. in an attempt to dislodge its rider. **8** *intr.* **a** (of a moving ship, aircraft, or vehicle) sway back and forth on an axis parallel to the direction of motion. **b** walk with an unsteady swaying gait. **9 a** *intr.* undulate; show or go with an undulating surface or motion (*rolling hills*). **b** *tr.* carry or propel with such motion. **10 a** *intr.* (of machinery) start functioning or moving (*the cameras rolled*). **b** *tr.* cause (machinery) to do this. **11** *intr. & tr.* sound or utter with a vibratory or trilling effect (*he rolls his rrrs*). **12** *sl.* **a** *tr.* overturn (a car, etc.). **b** *intr.* (of a car, etc.) overturn. **13** *tr.* throw (dice). **14** *tr. sl.* rob (esp. a helpless victim). • *n.* **1** a rolling motion or gait; undulation. **2 a** a spell of rolling (*a roll in the mud*). **b** a gymnastic exercise in which the body is rolled into a tucked position and turned in a forward or backward circle. **c** (esp. **a roll in the hay**) *colloq.* an act of sexual intercourse or erotic fondling. **3** the continuous rhythmic sound of thunder or a drum. **4** *Aeron.* a complete revolution of an aircraft about its longitudinal axis. **5** a cylinder formed by turning flexible material over and over on itself without folding (*a roll of carpet*). **6 a** a small portion of bread individually baked. **b** this with a specified filling (*ham roll*). **7** a more or less cylindrical or semicylindrical straight or curved mass of something (*rolls of fat*). **8 a** an official list or register. **b** the total numbers on this (*the schools' rolls have fallen*). **c** a document, esp. an official record, in scroll form. **9** a cylinder or roller, esp. to shape metal in a rolling mill. **10** *colloq.* money, esp. as bills rolled together. ▫ **be rolling in** *colloq.* have plenty of (esp. money). **on a roll** *sl.* experiencing a bout of success or progress; engaged in a period of intense activity. **roll back** cause (esp. prices) to decrease. **roll in 1** arrive in great numbers or quantity. **2** wallow; luxuriate in. **roll out** unroll; spread out. **roll over 1** *Econ.* finance the repayment of (maturing stock, etc.) by an issue of new stock. **2** reinvest funds in a similar financial instrument (*we decided to roll over the CDs*). **roll up 1** *colloq.* arrive in a vehicle; appear on the scene. **2** make into or form a

roll. **roll with the punches** withstand adversity, difficulties, etc. **roll up one's sleeves** see SLEEVE. ▫▫ **roll·a·ble** *adj.*

roll bar *n.* an overhead metal bar strengthening the frame of a vehicle (esp. in racing) and protecting the occupants if the vehicle overturns.

roll call *n.* a process of calling out a list of names to establish who is present.

rol·led gold *n.* gold in the form of a thin coating applied to a baser metal by rolling.

roll·er /rṓlər/ *n.* **1 a** a hard revolving cylinder for smoothing the ground, spreading ink or paint, crushing or stamping, rolling up cloth on, etc., used alone or as a rotating part of a machine. **b** a cylinder for diminishing friction when moving a heavy object. **2** a small cylinder on which hair is rolled for setting. **3** a long, swelling wave. **4** (also **roller bandage**) a long surgical bandage rolled up for convenient application.

roll·er bear·ing *n.* a bearing like a ball bearing but with small cylinders instead of balls.

Roll·er·blade /rṓlərblayd/ *n.* & *v.* • *n. Trademark* an inline skate. • *v.intr.* (**roll·er·blade**) skate using Rollerblades.

roll·er coast·er *n.* an amusement ride consisting of an elevated track with open-car trains that rise and plunge steeply.

rol·lick /rólik/ *v.intr.* (esp. as **rollicking** *adj.*) be jovial or exuberant.

roll·ing pin *n.* a cylinder for rolling out pastry, dough, etc.

roll·ing stone *n.* a person who is unwilling to settle for long in one place.

roll-on *attrib.adj.* (of a deodorant, etc.) applied by means of a rotating ball in the neck of the container.

roll·o·ver /rṓlōvər/ *n.* **1** *Econ.* the extension or transfer of a debt or other financial relationship. **2** *colloq.* the overturning of a vehicle, etc.

roll-top desk *n.* a desk with a flexible cover sliding in curved grooves.

ro·ly-po·ly /rṓleepṓlee/ *adj.* pudgy; plump.

ROM /rom/ *abbr. Computing* read-only memory.

ro·maine /rōmáyn/ *n.* a cos lettuce.

Ro·man /rṓmən/ *adj.* & *n.* • *adj.* **1** of ancient Rome or its territory or people. **2** of medieval or modern Rome. **3** = ROMAN CATHOLIC. **4** of a kind ascribed to the early Romans. **5** surviving from a period of Roman rule. **6** (**roman**) (of type) of a plain upright kind used in ordinary print. **7** (of the alphabet, etc.) based on the ancient Roman system with letters A–Z. • *n.* **1 a** a citizen of Rome. **b** a soldier of the Roman Empire. **2** a citizen of modern Rome. **3** = ROMAN CATHOLIC. **4** (**roman**) roman type. **5** (in *pl.*) the Christians of ancient Rome.

ro·man à clef /rōmaánaakláy/ *n.* (*pl.* **romans à clef** *pronunc.* same) a novel in which real persons or events appear with invented names.

Ro·man can·dle *n.* a firework discharging a series of flaming colored balls.

Ro·man Cath·o·lic /rṓmən/ *adj.* & *n.* • *adj.* of the part of the Christian Church acknowledging the pope as its head. • *n.* a member of this Church. ▫▫ **Ro·man Cath·ol·i·cism** *n.*

ro·mance /rōmáns/ *n.*, *adj.*, & *v.* • *n.* (also *disp.* /rṓmans/) **1** an atmosphere or tendency characterized by a sense of remoteness from or idealization of everyday life. **2 a** a prevailing sense of wonder or mystery surrounding the mutual attraction in a love affair. **b** sentimental or idealized love. **c** a love affair. **3 a** a literary genre with romantic love or highly imaginative unrealistic episodes forming the central theme. **b** a work of this genre. **4** a medieval tale of some hero of chivalry. **5 a** exaggeration or picturesque falsehood. **b** an instance of this. **6** (**Romance**) the languages descended from Latin. **7** *Mus.* a short informal piece. • *adj.* (**Romance**) of any of the languages descended from Latin. • *v.* **1** *intr.* exaggerate or distort the truth. **2** *tr.* court; woo.

ro·manc·er /rōmánsər/ *n.* **1** a writer of romances. **2** a liar who resorts to fantasy.

Ro·man Em·pire *n. hist.* that established by Augustus in 27 BC and divided by Theodosius in AD 395 into the Western or Latin and Eastern or Greek Empire.

Ro·man·esque /rṓmənésk/ *n.* & *adj.* • *n.* a style of architecture prevalent in Europe *c.* 900–1200, with massive vaulting and round arches. • *adj.* of the Romanesque style of architecture.

ro·man-fleuve /rṓmoɴflṓv/ *n.* (*pl.* **romans-fleuves** *pronunc.* same) **1** a novel featuring the leisurely description of the lives of members of a family, etc. **2** a sequence of self-contained novels.

Ro·ma·ni·an /rōmáyneeən/ *n.* & *adj.* (also **Ru·ma·ni·an** /roo–/) • *n.* **1 a** a native or national of Romania in E. Europe. **b** a person of Romanian descent. **2** the language of Romania. • *adj.* of or relating to Romania or its people or language.

Ro·man·ic /rōmánik/ *n.* & *adj.* • *n.* = ROMANCE *n.* 6. • *adj.* **1 a** of or relating to Romance. **b** Romance-speaking. **2** descended from the ancient Romans or inheriting aspects of their social or political life.

Ro·man·ist /rṓmənist/ *n.* **1** a student of Roman history or law or of the Romance languages. **2 a** a supporter of Roman Catholicism. **b** a Roman Catholic.

ro·man·ize /rṓmənīz/ *v.tr.* **1** make Roman or Roman Catholic in character. **2** put into the Roman alphabet or into roman type. ▫▫ **ro·man·i·za·tion** *n.*

Ro·man nu·mer·al *n.* any of the Roman letters representing numbers: I = 1, V = 5, X = 10, L = 50, C = 100, D = 500, M = 1000.

Romano- /rōmaánō/ *comb. form* Roman; Roman and (*Romano-British*).

ro·man·tic /rōmántik/ *adj.* & *n.* • *adj.* **1** of, characterized by, or suggestive of an idealized, sentimental, or fantastic view of reality (*a romantic picture*; *a romantic setting*). **2** inclined toward or suggestive of romance in love (*a romantic woman*; *a romantic evening*). **3** (of a person) imaginative; visionary; idealistic. **4 a** (of style in art, music, etc.) concerned more with feeling and emotion than with form and aesthetic qualities. **b** (also **Romantic**) of or relating to the 18th–19th-c. romantic movement or style in the European arts. **5** (of a project, etc.) unpractical; fantastic. • *n.* **1** a romantic person. **2** a romanticist. ▫▫ **ro·man·ti·cal·ly** *adv.*

ro·man·ti·cism /rōmántisizəm/ *n.* (also **Romanticism**) adherence to a romantic style in art, music, etc.

ro·man·ti·cist /rōmántisist/ *n.* (also **Romanticist**) a writer or artist of the romantic school.

ro·man·ti·cize /rōmántisīz/ *v.* **1** *tr.* **a** make romantic. **b** describe or portray in a romantic fashion. **2** *intr.* indulge in romantic thoughts or actions. ▫▫ **ro·man·ti·ci·za·tion** *n.*

Rom·a·ny /rómənee, rṓ–/ *n.* & *adj.* • *n.* (*pl.* **-nies**) **1** a Gypsy. **2** the language of the Gypsies. • *adj.* **1** of or concerning Gypsies. **2** of the Romany language.

romp /romp/ *v.* & *n.* • *v.intr.* **1** play about roughly and energetically. **2** (foll. by *along*, *past*, etc.) *colloq.* proceed without effort. • *n.* a spell of romping.

romp·er /rómpər/ *n.* (usu. in *pl.*) a one-piece garment, esp. for a child, that covers the trunk and has short pants.

ronde /rond/ *n.* **1** a dance in which the dancers move in a circle. **2** a course of talk, activity, etc.

ron·deau /róndō, rondṓ/ *n.* (*pl.* **rondeaux** *pronunc.* same or /–dōz/) a poem of ten or thirteen lines with only two rhymes throughout and with the opening words used twice as a refrain.

ron·del /róndʼl, rondél/ *n.* a rondeau, esp. one of special form.
ron·do /róndō/ *n.* (*pl.* **-dos**) *Mus.* a form with a recurring leading theme.
rönt·gen var. of ROENTGEN.
rood /rōōd/ *n.* **1** a crucifix, esp. one raised on a screen or beam at the entrance to the chancel. **2** a quarter of an acre.
rood screen *n.* a wooden or stone carved screen separating nave and chancel.
roof /rōōf, rŏŏf/ *n.* & *v.* •*n.* (*pl.* **roofs** or *disp.* **rooves** /rōōvz, rŏŏvz/) **1 a** the upper covering of a building. **b** the top of a covered vehicle. **c** the top inner surface of an oven, refrigerator, etc. **2** the overhead rock in a cave or mine, etc. **3** the branches or the sky, etc., overhead. **4** (of prices, etc.) the upper limit or ceiling. •*v.tr.* **1** (often foll. by *in, over*) cover with or as with a roof. **2** be the roof of. □ **go through the roof** *colloq.* (of prices, etc.) reach extreme or unexpected heights. **hit** (or **go through** or **raise**) **the roof** *colloq.* become very angry. **raise the roof 1** create a noisy racket. **2** protest noisily. □□ **roofed** *adj.* (also in *comb.*). **roof·less** *adj.*

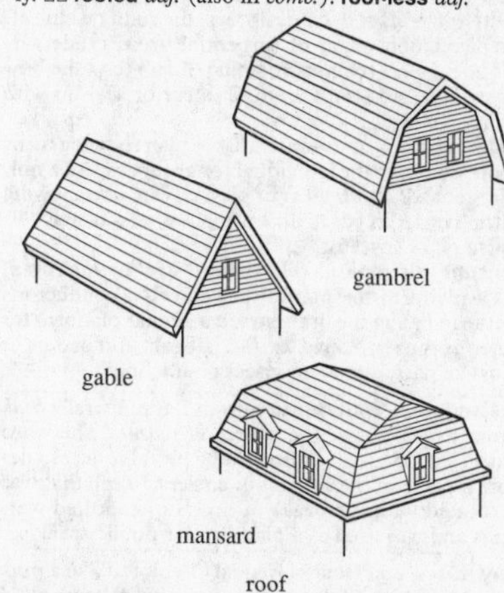

roof

roof·er /rōōfər, rŏŏf–/ *n.* a person who constructs or repairs roofs.
roof·ing /rōōfing, rŏŏf–/ *n.* **1** material for constructing a roof. **2** the process of constructing a roof or roofs.
roof of the mouth *n.* the palate.
roof rack *n.* a framework for luggage, etc. on the roof of a vehicle.
roof·top /rōōftop, rŏŏf–/ *n.* **1** the outer surface of a roof. **2** (esp. in *pl.*) the level of a roof.
rook[1] /rŏŏk/ *n.* & *v.* •*n.* **1** a black European and Asiatic bird, *Corvus frugilegus*, of the crow family, nesting in colonies. **2** a sharper, esp. at dice or cards; a person who lives off inexperienced gamblers, etc. •*v.tr.* **1** charge (a customer) extortionately. **2** win money from (a person) at cards, etc., esp. by swindling.
rook[2] /rŏŏk/ *n.* a chess piece with its top in the shape of a battlement; castle.
rook·er·y /rŏŏkəree/ *n.* (*pl.* **-ies**) **1 a** a colony of rooks. **b** a clump of trees having rooks' nests. **2** a colony of seabirds (esp. penguins) or seals.
rook·ie /rŏŏkee/ *n. sl.* **1** a new recruit. **2** a member of a sports team in his or her first season.
room /rōōm, rŏŏm/ *n.* & *v.* •*n.* **1 a** space that is or might be occupied by something; capaciousness or ability to accommodate contents (*we have no room here for idlers*). **b** space in or on (*shelf room*). **2 a** a part of a building enclosed by walls, floor, and ceiling. **b** (in *pl.*) apartments, etc. **c** persons present in a room (*the room fell silent*). **3** (in *comb.*) a room or area for a specified purpose (*reading room*). **4** (foll. by *for*, or *to* + infin.) opportunity or scope (*no room for dispute*). •*v.intr.* have a room or rooms; lodge; board. □ **make room** (often foll. by *for*) clear a space (for a person or thing) by removal of others; make way; yield place. □□ **-roomed** *adj.* (in *comb.*). **room·ful** *n.* (*pl.* **-fuls**).
room·er /rōōmər, rŏŏ–/ *n.* a renter of a room in another's house.
room·ie /rōōmee, rŏŏ–/ *n. colloq.* a roommate.
room·ing house *n.* a house with rented rooms for lodging.
room·mate /rōōm-mayt, rŏŏm–/ *n.* a person occupying the same room, apartment, etc., as another.
room serv·ice *n.* (in a hotel, etc.) service of food or drink taken to a guest's room.
room·y /rōōmee, rŏŏ–/ *adj.* (**roomier, roomiest**) having much room; spacious. □□ **room·i·ness** *n.*
roost /rōōst/ *n.* & *v.* •*n.* **1** a support on which a bird perches, esp. a place where birds regularly settle to sleep. **2** a place offering temporary sleeping accommodation. •*v.* **1** *intr.* **a** (of a bird) settle for rest or sleep. **b** (of a person) stay for the night. **2** *tr.* provide with a sleeping place. □ **come home to roost** (of a scheme, etc.) recoil unfavorably upon the originator. **rule the roost** hold a position of control; be in charge.
roost·er /rōōstər/ *n.* esp. a male domestic fowl; cock.
root[1] /rōōt, rŏŏt/ *n.* & *v.* •*n.* **1 a** the part of a plant normally below the ground, conveying nourishment to it from the soil. **b** (in *pl.*) such a part divided into branches or fibers. **c** the corresponding organ of an epiphyte; the part attaching ivy to its support. **d** the permanent underground stock of a plant. **e** any small plant with a root for transplanting. **2 a** any plant with an edible root. **b** such a root. **3** (in *pl.*) the sources of or reasons for one's long-standing emotional attachment to a place, community, etc. **4 a** the embedded part of a bodily organ or structure, e.g., hair, tooth, nail, etc. **b** the part of a thing attaching it to a greater whole. **c** (in *pl.*) the base of a mountain, etc. **5 a** the basic cause, source, or origin. **b** (*attrib.*) (of an idea, etc.) from which the rest originated. **6** the basis of something, its means of continuance or growth. **7** the essential substance or nature of something (*get to the root of things*). **8** *Math.* **a** a number or quantity that when multiplied by itself a usu. specified number of times gives a specified number or quantity (*the cube root of eight is two*). **b** a square root. **c** a value of an unknown quantity satisfying a given equation. **9** *Philol.* a basis on which words are made by the addition of prefixes or suffixes or by other modification. **10** *Mus.* the fundamental note of a chord. •*v.* **1 a** *intr.* take root or grow roots. **b** *tr.* cause to do this. **2** *tr.* **a** fix firmly; establish. **b** (as **rooted** *adj.*) firmly established (*her affection was deeply rooted*; *rooted objection to*). **3** *tr.* (usu. foll. by *out, up*) drag or dig up by the roots. □ **pull up by the roots 1** uproot. **2** eradicate; destroy. **put down roots 1** begin to draw nourishment from the soil. **2** become settled or established. **root out** find and get rid of. **strike at the root** (or **roots**) **of** set about destroying. **take root 1** begin to grow and draw nourishment from the soil. **2** become fixed or established. □□ **root·ed·ness** *n.* **root·less** *adj.*
root[2] /rōōt, rŏŏt/ *v.* **1 a** *intr.* turn up the ground with the snout, beak, etc., in search of food. **b** *tr.* (foll. by *up*) turn up (the ground) by rooting. **2 a** *intr.* (foll. by *around, in*, etc.) rummage. **b** *tr.* (foll. by *out* or *up*) find

or extract by rummaging. **3** *intr.* (foll. by *for*) *sl.* encourage by applause or support. ◻◻ **root·er** *n.* (in sense 3).

root beer *n.* a carbonated drink made from an extract of roots of certain plants.

root ca·nal *n. Dentistry* surgery to remove the diseased nerve of a tooth.

root·stock /rṓotstok, rṓot–/ *n.* **1** a rhizome. **2** a plant into which a graft is inserted. **3** a primary form from which offshoots have arisen.

rooves see ROOF.

rope /rōp/ *n. & v.* •*n.* **1 a** stout cord made by twisting together strands of hemp, sisal, flax, cotton, nylon, wire, or similar material. **b** a piece of this. **c** a lasso. **2** (foll. by *of*) a quantity of onions, garlic bulbs, pearls, etc., strung together. **3** (in *pl.*, prec. by *the*) **a** the conditions in some sphere of action (*show a person the ropes*). **b** the ropes enclosing a boxing or wrestling ring, etc. **4** (prec. by *the*) **a** a noose or halter for hanging a person. **b** execution by hanging. •*v.* **1** *tr.* fasten, secure, or catch with rope. **2** *tr.* (usu. foll. by *off, in*) enclose (a space) with rope. **3** *Mountaineering* **a** *tr.* connect (a party) with a rope; attach (a person) to a rope. **b** (*absol.*) put on a rope. **c** *intr.* (foll. by *down, up*) climb down or up using a rope. ◻ **give a person plenty of rope** (or **enough rope to hang himself** or **herself**) give a person enough freedom of action to bring about his or her own downfall. **rope in** persuade to take part.

rop·ing /rṓping/ *n.* a set or arrangement of ropes.

rop·y /rṓpee/ *adj.* (also **rop·ey**) (**ropier, ropiest**) **1** (of wine, bread, etc.) forming viscous or gelatinous threads. **2** like a rope.

Roque·fort /rṓkfərt/ *n. Trademark* **1** a soft blue cheese made from sheep's milk. **2** a salad dressing made of this.

ror·qual /ráwrkwəl/ *n.* any of various whales of the family Balaenopteridae, having a dorsal fin. Also called **finback.**

Ror·schach test /ráwrshaak/ *n. Psychol.* a type of personality test in which a standard set of inkblot designs is presented one by one to the subject, who is asked to describe what they suggest or resemble.

ro·sa·ceous /rōzáyshəs/ *adj. Bot.* of the large plant family Rosaceae, which includes the rose.

ro·sar·i·an /rəzáireeən/ *n.* a person who cultivates roses, esp. professionally.

ro·sa·ry /rṓzəree/ *n.* (*pl.* **-ies**) **1** *RC Ch.* **a** a form of devotion in which prayers are said while counting them on a special string of beads. **b** a string of 55 (or 165) beads for keeping count in this. **c** a book containing this devotion. **2** a similar string of beads used in other religions. **3** a rose garden or rose bed.

rose[1] /rōz/ *n. & adj.* •*n.* **1** any prickly bush or shrub of the genus *Rosa*, bearing usu. fragrant flowers generally of a red, pink, yellow, or white color. **2** this flower. **3** any flowering plant resembling this (*rose of Sharon*; *rockrose*). **4 a** a light crimson color; pink. **b** (usu. in *pl.*) a rosy complexion (*roses in her cheeks*). **5** (in *pl.*) used in various phrases to express favorable circumstances, ease, success, etc. (*roses all the way*; *everything's roses*). **6** an excellent person or thing, esp. a beautiful woman (*English rose*; *rose between two thorns*). •*adj.* = ROSE-COLORED 1. ◻ **see** (or **look**) **through rose-colored** (or **-tinted**) **glasses** regard (circumstances, etc.) with unfounded favor or optimism. ◻◻ **rose·like** *adj.*

rose[2] *past* of RISE.

rosé /rōzáy/ *n.* any light pink wine.

ro·se·ate /rṓzeeət, –ayt/ *adj.* **1** = ROSE-COLORED. **2** having a partly pink plumage.

rose·bud /rṓzbud/ *n.* a bud of a rose.

rose-col·ored *adj.* **1** of a light crimson color; pink. **2** optimistic; cheerful (*takes rose-colored views*).

rose·mar·y /rṓzmairee, –məree/ *n.* an evergreen fragrant shrub, *Rosmarinus officinalis*, with leaves used as a culinary herb, in perfumery, etc.

ro·se·o·la /rōzeeólə, rōzéeələ/ *n.* **1** a rosy rash in measles and similar diseases. **2** a mild febrile disease of infants. ◻◻ **ro·se·o·lar** *adj.* **ro·se·o·lous** *adj.*

ro·sette /rōzét/ *n.* **1** a rose-shaped ornament made usu. of ribbon and worn esp. as the badge of a contest official, etc., or as an award or the symbol of an award in a competition. **2** *Archit.* **a** a carved or molded ornament resembling or representing a rose. **b** a rose window. **3** an object or symbol or arrangement of parts resembling a rose. **4** *Biol.* **a** a roselike cluster of parts. **b** markings resembling a rose. ◻◻ **ro·set·ted** *adj.*

rose wa·ter *n.* perfume made from roses.

rose win·dow *n.* a circular window with roselike or spokelike tracery.

rose·wood /rṓzwood/ *n.* any of several fragrant close-grained woods used in making furniture.

Rosh Ha·sha·nah /ráwsh həsháwnə, –sháa–, haashaanaá, rṓsh/ *n.* (also **Rosh Hashana**) the Jewish New Year.

ros·in /rózin/ *n. & v.* •*n.* resin, esp. the solid residue after distillation of oil of turpentine from crude turpentine. •*v.tr.* (**rosined, rosining**) **1** rub (esp. the bow of a violin, etc.) with rosin. **2** smear or seal up with rosin.

ros·ter /róstər/ *n. & v.* •*n.* **1** a list or plan showing turns of duty or leave for individuals or group, esp. of a military force. **2** *Sports* a list of players, esp. one showing batting order in baseball. •*v.tr.* place on a roster.

ros·tra *pl.* of ROSTRUM.

ros·trum /róstrəm/ *n.* (*pl.* **rostra** /–strə/ or **rostrums**) **1 a** a platform for public speaking. **b** a conductor's platform facing the orchestra. **c** a similar platform for other purposes. **2** *Zool. & Bot.* a beak, stiff snout, or beaklike part, esp. of an insect or arachnid.

---

rostrum mid-16th century: from Latin, literally *beak* (from *rodere* 'gnaw,' the source of *rodent*). The word was originally used (at first in the plural *rostra*) to denote a place in the Forum in ancient Rome that was decorated with the beaks or prows of captured warships and was used as a platform for public speakers.

---

ros·y /rṓzee/ *adj.* (**rosier, rosiest**) **1** colored like a pink or red rose (esp. of the complexion as indicating good health, of a blush, wine, the sky, etc.). **2** optimistic; hopeful (*a rosy future*). ◻◻ **ros·i·ly** *adv.* **ros·i·ness** *n.*

rot /rot/ *v., n., & int.* •*v.* (**rotted, rotting**) **1** *intr.* **a** (of animal or vegetable matter) lose its original form by the chemical action of bacteria, fungi, etc.; decay. **b** (foll. by *off, away*) crumble or drop from a stem, etc., through decomposition. **2** *intr.* **a** (of society, institutions, etc.) gradually perish from lack of activity or use. **b** (of a prisoner, etc.) waste away (*left to rot in prison*); (of a person) languish. **3** *tr.* cause to rot; make rotten. •*n.* **1** the process or state of rotting. **2** *sl.* nonsense. •*int.* expressing incredulity or ridicule.

Ro·tar·i·an /rōtáireeən/ *n. & adj.* •*n.* a member of a Rotary club. •*adj.* of Rotarians or Rotary club.

ro·ta·ry /rṓtəree/ *adj. & n.* •*adj.* acting by rotation (*rotary drill*; *rotary pump*). •*n.* (*pl.* **-ries**) **1** a rotary machine. **2** a traffic circle. **3** (**Rotary**) (in full **Rotary International**) a worldwide charitable society of business people, orig. named from members entertaining in rotation.

Ro·ta·ry Club *n.* a local branch of Rotary.

ro·tate[1] /rṓtayt/ *v.* **1** *intr. & tr.* move around an axis or center, revolve. **2 a** *tr.* take or arrange in rotation. **b** *intr.* act or take place in rotation (*the chairmanship will rotate*). ◻◻ **ro·tat·a·ble** *adj.* **ro·ta·tive** /rṓtaytiv/ *adj.* **ro·ta·to·ry** /rṓtətawree/ *adj.*

ro·tate[2] /rṓtayt/ *adj. Bot.* wheel-shaped.

ro·ta·tion /rōtáyshən/ *n.* **1** the act or an instance of rotating or being rotated. **2** a recurrence; a recurrent series or period; a regular succession. **3** a system of growing different crops in regular order to avoid exhausting the soil. ▫▫ **ro·ta·tion·al** *adj.* **ro·ta·tion·al·ly** *adv.*

ro·ta·tor /rṓtaytər/ *n.* **1** a machine or device for causing something to rotate. **2** *Anat.* a muscle that rotates a limb, etc. **3** a revolving apparatus or part.

ROTC /rótsee/ *abbr.* Reserve Officers Training Corps.

rote /rōt/ *n.* (usu. prec. by *by*) mechanical or habitual repetition.

rot·gut /rótgut/ *n.* inferior whiskey.

ro·ti·fer /rṓtifər/ *n.* any minute aquatic animal of the phylum Rotifera, with rotatory organs used in swimming and feeding.

ro·tis·ser·ie /rōtísəree/ *n.* a cooking appliance with a rotating spit for roasting and barbecuing meat.

ro·to·gra·vure /rṓtəgrəvyŏŏr/ *n.* **1** a printing system using a rotary press with intaglio cylinders, usu. running at high speed. **2** a sheet, etc., printed with this system.

ro·tor /rṓtər/ *n.* **1** a rotary part of a machine, esp. in the distributor of an internal combustion engine. **2** a set of radiating airfoils around a hub on a helicopter, providing lift when rotated.

ro·to·till·er /rṓtətilər/ *n.* a machine with a rotating blade for breaking up or tilling the soil. ▫▫ **ro·to·till** *v.tr.*

rot·ten /rót'n/ *adj.* (**rottener, rottenest**) **1** rotting or rotted; falling to pieces or liable to break or tear. **2 a** morally or politically corrupt. **b** despicable; contemptible. **3** *sl.* **a** disagreeable; unpleasant (*had a rotten time*). **b** (of a plan, etc.) ill-advised, unsatisfactory (*a rotten idea*). **c** disagreeably ill. ▫▫ **rot·ten·ness** *n.*

rot·ten·stone /rot'nstōn/ *n.* decomposed siliceous limestone used as a powder for polishing metals.

Rott·wei·ler /rótwīlər/ *n.* **1** a dog of a tall black-and-tan breed. **2** this breed.

ro·tund /rōtúnd/ *adj.* **1 a** circular; round. **b** (of a person) plump, pudgy. **2** (of speech, literary style, etc.) sonorous, grandiloquent. ▫▫ **ro·tun·di·ty** *n.*

ro·tun·da /rōtúndə/ *n.* **1** a building with a circular ground plan, esp. one with a dome. **2** a circular hall or room.

rou·ble var. of RUBLE.

rou·é /rōō-áy/ *n.* a debauchee, esp. an elderly one.

rouge /rōōzh/ *n.* & *v.* • *n.* **1** a red powder or cream used for coloring the cheeks. **2** powdered ferric oxide, etc., as a polishing agent. • *v.* **1** *tr.* color with rouge. **2** *intr.* **a** apply rouge to one's cheeks. **b** become red; blush.

rough /ruf/ *adj., adv., n.,* & *v.* • *adj.* **1 a** having an uneven or irregular surface, not smooth or level or polished. **b** *Tennis* applied to the side of a racket from which the twisted gut projects. **2** (of ground, country, etc.) having many bumps, obstacles, etc. **3 a** hairy; shaggy. **b** (of cloth) coarse in texture. **4 a** (of a person or behavior) not mild nor quiet nor gentle; boisterous; unrestrained (*rough play*). **b** (of language, etc.) coarse; indelicate. **c** (of wine, etc.) sharp or harsh in taste. **d** (of a sound, the voice, etc.) harsh; discordant; gruff; hoarse. **5** (of the sea, weather, etc.) violent; stormy. **6** disorderly; riotous (*a rough part of town*). **7** harsh; insensitive (*rough words*). **8 a** unpleasant; severe; demanding (*had a rough time*). **b** (foll. by *on*) hard or unfair toward. **9** lacking finish, elaboration, comfort, etc. (*rough accommodations*). **10** incomplete; rudimentary. **11** inexact; approximate; preliminary (*a rough estimate; a rough sketch*). • *adv.* in a rough manner. • *n.* **1** (usu. prec. by *the*) a hard part or aspect of life; hardship (*take the rough with the smooth*). **2** rough ground. **3** *Golf* rough ground off the fairway between tee and green. **4** an unfinished or provisional or natural state. • *v.tr.* **1** (foll. by *up*) ruffle (feathers, hair, etc.) by rubbing against the grain. **2 a** (foll. by *out*) shape or plan roughly. **b** (foll. by *in*) sketch roughly. **3** give the first shaping to (a gun, lens, etc.). ▫ **rough it** do without basic comforts. **rough up** *sl.* attack violently. ▫▫ **rough·ness** *n.*

rough·age /rúfij/ *n.* **1** coarse material with a high fiber content, the part of food that stimulates digestion. **2** coarse fodder.

rough-and-read·y *adj.* crude but effective; not elaborate or over-particular.

rough-and-tum·ble *adj.* & *n.* • *adj.* irregular; scrambling; disorderly. • *n.* a haphazard fight; a scuffle.

rough·cast /rúfkast/ *n., adj.,* & *v.* • *n.* plaster of lime and gravel, used on outside walls. • *adj.* **1** (of a wall, etc.) coated with roughcast. **2** (of a plan, etc.) roughly formed; preliminary. • *v.tr.* (*past* and *past part.* **-cast**) **1** coat (a wall) with roughcast. **2** prepare (a plan, essay, etc.) in outline.

rough draft *n.* a first or original draft (of a story, report, document, etc.).

rough·en /rúfən/ *v.tr.* & *intr.* make or become rough.

rough-hewn *adj.* uncouth; unrefined.

rough·house /rúfhows/ *n.* & *v. sl.* • *n.* a disturbance or row; boisterous play. • *v.* **1** *tr.* handle (a person) roughly. **2** *intr.* make a disturbance; act violently.

rough·ly /rúflee/ *adv.* **1** in a rough manner. **2** approximately (*roughly 20 people attended*). ▫ **roughly speaking** in an approximate sense (*it is, roughly speaking, a square*).

rough·neck /rúfnek/ *n. colloq.* **1** a rough or rowdy person. **2** a worker on a drill rig.

rough pas·sage *n.* **1** a crossing over rough sea. **2** a difficult time or experience.

rough·rid·er /rúfrīdər/ *n.* **1** a person who breaks in or can ride unbroken horses. **2** (**Rough Rider**) a member of the cavalry unit in which Theodore Roosevelt fought during the Spanish-American War.

rough·shod /rúfshod/ *adj.* (of a horse) having shoes with nail heads projecting to prevent slipping. ▫ **ride roughshod over** treat inconsiderately or arrogantly.

rou·lade /rōōlaád/ *n.* **1** a dish cooked or served in the shape of a roll, esp. a rolled piece of meat with a filling. **2** *Mus.* a florid passage of runs in classical music for a solo virtuoso, esp. one sung to one syllable.

rou·lette /rōōlét/ *n.* a gambling game using a table in which a ball is dropped on to a revolving wheel with numbered compartments.

round /rownd/ *adj., n., adv., prep.,* & *v.* • *adj.* **1** shaped like a circle, sphere, or cylinder; having a convex or circular outline or surface; curved; not angular. **2** done with or involving circular motion. **3 a** entire; continuous; complete. **b** (of a sum of money) considerable. **4** candid; outspoken; (of a statement, etc.) categorical; unmistakable. **5** (usu. *attrib.*) (of a number) expressed for convenience or as an estimate in fewer significant numerals or with a fraction removed (*spent $297.32, or in round figures $300*). • *n.* **1** a round object or form. **2 a** a revolving motion; a circular or recurring course (*the earth in its yearly round*). **b** a regular recurring series of activities or functions (*one's daily round*). **c** a recurring succession or series of meetings for discussion, etc. (*a new round of talks on disarmament*). **3** a route or sequence by which people or things are regularly supervised or inspected (*a doctor's rounds*). **4** an allowance of something distributed or measured out, esp.: **a** a single provision of drinks, etc., to each member of a group. **b** ammunition to fire one shot; the act of firing this. **5** a thick disk of beef cut from the haunch as a joint. **6** each of a set or series, a sequence of actions by each member of a group in turn, esp. **a** one spell of play in a game, etc. **b** one stage in a competition. **7** *Golf* the playing of all the holes in a course once. **8** *Archery* a fixed number of arrows shot from a fixed distance. **9** (**the round**) a form of sculpture in which the figure stands clear of any ground (cf. RELIEF 5a). **10** *Mus.* a canon for three or more unaccompanied voices singing at the same pitch or in octaves. •*adv.* = AROUND *adv.* 5-12. •*prep.* = AROUND *prep.* 5-12. •*v.* **1 a** *tr.* give a round shape to. **b** *intr.* assume a round shape. **2** *tr.* pass around (a corner, cape, etc.). **3** *tr.* express (a number) in a less exact but more convenient form (also foll. by *down* when the number is decreased and *up* when it is increased). **4** *tr.* pronounce (a vowel) with rounded lips. ▫ **in the round 1** with all features shown; all things considered. **2** *Theatr.* with the audience around at least three sides of the stage. **3** (of sculpture) with all sides shown. **make one's rounds** take a customary route for inspection, etc. **make the rounds** (of news, etc.) be passed on from person to person, etc. **round about 1** all around; on all sides (of). **2** with a change to an opposite position. **3** approximately (*cost round about $50*). **round and round** several times around. **round down** see sense 3 of *v.* **round off** (or **out**) **1** bring to a complete or symmetrical or well-ordered state. **2** blunt the corners or angles of. **round out** = *round off* 1. **round peg in a square hole** = *square peg in a round hole* (see PEG). **round up** collect or bring together (see also sense 3 of *v.*). ▫▫ **round·ish** *adj.* **round·ness** *n.*

round·a·bout /równdəbowt/ *adj.* circuitous.

roun·del /równd'l/ *n.* **1** a small disk, esp. a decorative medallion. **2** a poem, esp. a modified rondeau, of eleven lines in three stanzas.

roun·de·lay /równdilay/ *n.* a short simple song with a refrain.

round·house /równdhows/ *n.* **1** a repair shed for railroad locomotives, built around a turntable. **2** *sl.* **a** a blow given with a wide sweep of the arm. **b** *Baseball* a pitch made with a sweeping sidearm motion.

round·ly /równdlee/ *adv.* **1** bluntly; severely (*was roundly criticized*). **2** in a thoroughgoing manner. **3** in a circular way (*swells out roundly*).

round rob·in *n.* **1** a petition, esp. with signatures written in a circle to conceal the order of writing. **2** a tournament in which each competitor plays in turn against every other.

round-shoul·dered *adj.* with shoulders bent forward so that the back is rounded.

Round Ta·ble *n.* (in allusion to that at which King Arthur and his knights sat so that none should have precedence) **1** an international charitable association that holds discussions, debates, etc., and undertakes community service. **2** (**round table**) an assembly for discussion, esp. at a conference (often *attrib.*: *round-table talks*).

round trip *n.* a trip to one or more places and back again.

round·up /równdup/ *n.* **1** a systematic gathering together of people or things. **2** a summary; a résumé of facts or events.

round·worm /równdwərm/ *n.* a nematode worm, esp. a parasitic one found in the intestines of mammals.

rouse /rowz/ *v.* **1** *tr.* (often foll. by *from*, *out of*) bring out of sleep; wake. **2** (often foll. by *up*) **a** *tr.* stir up; make active or excited (*roused them from their complacency*). **b** *intr.* become active. **3** *tr.* provoke to anger. **4** *tr.* evoke (feelings). **5** *tr.* startle (game) from a lair or cover. ▫▫ **rous·er** *n.*

rous·ing /rówzing/ *adj.* **1** exciting; stirring (*a rousing cheer*; *a rousing song*). **2** (of a fire) blazing strongly.

roust /rowst/ *v.tr.* **1** (often foll. by *up*, *out*) **a** rouse; stir up. **b** root out. **2** *sl.* jostle; harass; rough up.

roust·a·bout /rówstəbowt/ *n.* **1** a laborer in an oil field. **2** an unskilled or casual laborer. **3** a dock laborer or deckhand. **4** a circus laborer.

rout[1] /rowt/ *n.* & *v.* •*n.* **1 a** a disorderly retreat of defeated troops. **b** a heavy defeat. **2 a** an assemblage or company, esp. of revelers or rioters. **b** *Law* an assemblage of three or more persons who have made a move toward committing an illegal act. **3** riot; tumult; disturbance; clamor; fuss. •*v.tr.* cause to retreat in disorder; defeat.

rout[2] /rowt/ *v.* **1** *intr.* & *tr.* = ROOT[2]. **2** *tr.* cut a groove, or any pattern not extending to the edges, in (a wooden or metal surface). ▫ **rout out** force or fetch out of bed or from a house or a hiding place.

route /ro͞ot, rowt/ *n.* & *v.* •*n.* **1** a way or course taken in getting from a starting point to a destination. **2** a round traveled in delivering, selling, or collecting goods. •*v.tr.* send or forward or direct to be sent by a particular route.

▶Rhyming this word with *out* is now standard pronunciation, but older and more conservative speakers still rhyme it with *root.*

rout·er /rówtər/ *n.* any of various tools used in routing, including a two-handled plane used in carpentry, esp. a power machine for routing, etc.

rou·tine /ro͞oteén/ *n.* & *adj.* •*n.* **1** a regular course or procedure, an unvarying performance of certain acts. **2** a set sequence in a dance, comedy act, etc. **3** *Computing* a sequence of instructions for performing a task. •*adj.* **1** performed as part of a routine (*routine duties*). **2** of a customary or standard kind. ▫▫ **rou·tine·ly** *adv.*

rou·tin·ize /ro͞oteéniz, ró͞ot'nīz/ *v.tr.* subject to a routine; make into a matter of routine. ▫▫ **rou·tin·i·za·tion** *n.*

roux /ro͞o/ *n.* (*pl.* same) a cooked mixture of fat and flour used in making sauces, etc.

rove[1] /rōv/ *v.* **1** *intr.* wander without a settled destination; roam; ramble. **2** *intr.* (of eyes) look in changing directions. **3** *tr.* wander over or through.

rove[2] *past* of REEVE[2].

rove[3] /rōv/ *n.* & *v.* •*n.* a sliver of cotton, wool, etc., drawn out and slightly twisted. •*v.tr.* form into roves.

rove[4] /rōv/ *n.* a small metal plate or ring for a rivet to pass through and be clenched over, esp. in boat building.

rov·er[1] /rṓvər/ *n.* a wanderer.

rov·er[2] /rṓvər/ *n.* a pirate.

rov·ing eye *n.* a tendency to ogle or toward infidelity.

row[1] /rō/ *n.* **1** a number of persons or things in a more or less straight line. **2** a line of seats across a theater, etc. (*in the front row*). **3** a street with a continuous line of houses along one or each side. **4** a line of plants in a field or garden. **5** a horizontal line of entries in a table, etc. ▫ **a hard** (or **tough**) **row to hoe** a difficult task. **in a row 1** forming a row. **2** *colloq.* in succession (*two Sundays in a row*).

row[2] /rō/ *v.* & *n.* •*v.* **1** *tr.* propel (a boat) with oars. **2** *tr.* convey (a passenger) in a boat in this way. **3** *intr.* propel a boat in this way. **4** *tr.* make (a stroke) or achieve (a rate of striking) in rowing. **5** *tr.* compete in (a race) by rowing. **6** *tr.* row a race with. •*n.* **1** a spell of rowing. **2** an excursion in a rowboat. ▫▫ **row·er** *n.*

row[3] /row/ *n.* & *v. colloq.* •*n.* **1** a loud noise or commotion. **2** a fierce quarrel or dispute. **3 a** a severe reprimand. **b** the condition of being reprimanded (*shall get into a row*). •*v.* **1** *intr.* make or engage in a row. **2** *tr.* reprimand. ▫ **make** (or **kick up**) **a row 1** raise a noise. **2** make a vigorous protest.

row·an /rṓən, rów–/ *n.* **1** the mountain ash. **2** a similar tree, *Sorbus americana*, native to N. America. **3** (also **row·an·ber·ry**) the scarlet berry of either of these trees.

row·boat /rṓbōt/ *n.* a small boat propelled by oars.

row·dy /rówdee/ *adj. & n.* • *adj.* (**rowdier, rowdiest**) noisy and disorderly. • *n.* (*pl.* **-dies**) a rowdy person. ▫▫ **row·di·ly** *adv.* **row·di·ness** *n.* **row·dy·ism** *n.*

row·el /rówəl/ *n. & v.* • *n.* a spiked revolving disk at the end of a spur. • *v.tr.* urge with a rowel.

row·en /rówən/ *n.* (in *sing.* or *pl.*) a season's second growth of hay or grass; an aftermath.

row·ing ma·chine *n.* a device for exercising the muscles used in rowing.

roy·al /róyəl/ *adj. & n.* • *adj.* **1** of or suited to or worthy of a king or queen. **2** in the service or under the patronage of a king or queen. **3** belonging to the king or queen (*the royal hands; the royal anger*). **4** of the family of a king or queen. **5** majestic; splendid. **6** of exceptional size or quality; first-rate (*gave us royal entertainment*). • *n. colloq.* a member of the royal family. ▫▫ **roy·al·ly** *adv.*

roy·al blue *n.* a deep vivid blue.

roy·al fam·i·ly *n.* (*pl.* **-lies**) the family to which a sovereign belongs.

roy·al·ist /róyəlist/ *n.* **1 a** a supporter of monarchy. **b** *hist.* a supporter of the royal side in the English Civil War. **2** *hist.* a loyalist in the American Revolution. ▫▫ **roy·al·ism** *n.*

roy·al·ty /róyəltee/ *n.* (*pl.* **-ties**) **1** the office or dignity or power of a king or queen. **2 a** royal persons. **b** a member of a royal family. **3** a sum paid to a patentee for the use of a patent or to an author, etc., for each copy of a book, etc., sold or for each public performance of a work. **4 a** a royal right (now esp. over minerals) granted by the sovereign. **b** a payment made by a producer of minerals, oil, or natural gas to the owner of the site or of the mineral rights over it.

royalty late Middle English: from Old French *roialte*, from *roial* (as in *royal*). The sense 'royal right (especially over minerals)' (late 15th century) developed into the sense 'payment made by a mining company to the site owner' (mid-19th century), which was then transferred to payments for the permission to hold patents and issue published materials; this permission was originally granted by a monarch.

r.p.m. *abbr.* revolutions per minute.

RR *abbr.* **1** railroad. **2** rural route.

RSVP *abbr.* (in an invitation, etc.) please reply [*répondez s'il vous plaît*].

rt. *abbr.* right.

rte. *abbr.* route.

Rt. Hon. *abbr.* Right Honorable.

Rt. Revd. *abbr.* (also **Rt. Rev.**) Right Reverend.

Ru *symb. Chem.* the element ruthenium.

rub /rub/ *v. & n.* • *v.* (**rubbed, rubbing**) **1** *tr.* move one's hand or another object with firm pressure over the surface of. **2** *tr.* (usu. foll. by *against, in, on, over*) apply (one's hand, etc.) in this way. **3** *tr.* clean or polish or make dry or bare by rubbing. **4** *tr.* (often foll. by *over*) apply (polish, ointment, etc.) by rubbing. **5** *tr.* (foll. by *in, into, through*) use rubbing to make (a substance) go into or through something. **6** *tr.* (often foll. by *together*) move or slide (objects) against each other. **7** *intr.* (foll. by *against, on*) move with contact or friction. **8** *tr.* chafe or make sore by rubbing. **9** *intr.* (of cloth, skin, etc.) become frayed or worn or sore or bare with friction. **10** *tr.* reproduce the design of (a sepulchral brass or stone, etc.) by rubbing paper laid on it with colored chalk, etc. **11** *tr.* (foll. by *to*) reduce to powder, etc., by rubbing. • *n.* **1** a spell or an instance of rubbing (*give it a rub*). **2** an impediment or difficulty (*there's the rub*). ▫ **rub away** remove by rubbing. **rub elbows with** associate or come into contact with. **rub it in** (or **rub a person's nose in it**) emphasize or repeat an embarrassing fact, etc. **rub off 1** (usu. foll. by *on*) be transferred by contact; be transmitted (*some of his attitudes have rubbed off on me*). **2** remove by rubbing. **rub out 1** erase with an eraser. **2** *sl.* kill; eliminate. **rub shoulders with** = *rub elbows with.* **rub the wrong way** irritate or repel as by stroking a cat against the lie of its fur.

rub·ber /rúbər/ *n.* **1** a tough elastic substance made from the latex of plants or synthetically. **2** *colloq.* a condom. **3** (in *pl.*) galoshes. ▫▫ **rub·ber·y** *adj.* **rub·ber·i·ness** *n.*

rubber mid-16th century: from the verb RUB + -ER[1]. The original sense was 'an implement (such as a hard brush) used for rubbing and cleaning.' Because an early use of the elastic substance (previously known as *caoutchouc*) was to rub out pencil marks, *rubber* gained the sense 'eraser' in the late 18th century. The sense was subsequently (mid-19th century) generalized to refer to the substance in any form or use, at first often differentiated as *India rubber.*

rub·ber band *n.* a loop of rubber for holding papers, etc., together.

rub·ber·ize /rúbərīz/ *v.tr.* treat or coat with rubber.

rub·ber·neck /rúbərnek/ *n. & v. colloq.* • *n.* a person who stares inquisitively or stupidly, esp. by craning or turning the neck. • *v.intr.* act in this way.

rub·ber plant *n.* **1** an evergreen plant, *Ficus elastica*, often cultivated as a houseplant. **2** (also **rubber tree**) any of various tropical trees yielding latex.

rub·ber stamp *n.* **1** a device for inking and imprinting on a surface. **2 a** a person who mechanically agrees to others' actions. **b** an indication of such agreement. ▫▫ **rub·ber-stamp** *v.tr.*

rub·bing /rúbing/ *n.* **1** in senses of RUB *v.* **2** an impression or copy made by rubbing (see RUB *v.* 10).

rub·bing al·co·hol *n.* an isopropyl alcohol solution for external application.

rub·bish /rúbish/ *n.* esp. *Brit.* **1** waste material; refuse; litter. **2** worthless material or articles; junk. **3** (often as *int.*) nonsense. ▫▫ **rub·bish·y** *adj.*

rub·ble /rúbəl/ *n.* **1** rough fragments of stone or brick, etc., esp. as the debris from the demolition of buildings. **2** pieces of undressed stone used, esp. as fill, for walls. **3** *Geol.* loose angular stones, etc., as the covering of some rocks. **4** water-worn stones. ▫▫ **rub·bly** *adj.*

rube /rōōb/ *n. colloq.* a country bumpkin.

Rube Gold·berg /rōōb góldbərg/ *adj.* unnecessarily or comically complex in design. Also **Rube Goldbergian**

ru·bel·la /rōōbélə/ *n. Med.* an acute infectious viral disease with a red rash; German measles.

ru·be·o·la /rōōbeeólə, –béeələ/ *n. Med.* measles.

Ru·bi·con /rōōbikon/ *n.* a boundary which once crossed signifies irrevocable commitment; a point of no return.

ru·bi·cund /rōōbikund/ *adj.* (of a face, complexion, or person) ruddy; high-colored.

ru·bid·i·um /rōōbídeeəm/ *n. Chem.* a soft silvery element occurring naturally in various minerals and as the radioactive isotope rubidium-87. ¶ Symb.: **Rb**.

ru·bi·fy /rōōbifī/ *v.tr.* (**·fies, ·fied**) **1** make red. **2** *Med.* (of a counterirritant) stimulate (the skin, etc.) to redness. ▫▫ **ru·be·fa·cient** /–fáyshənt/ *adj. & n.* **ru·be·fac·tion** /–fákshən/ *n.*

ru·big·i·nous /rōōbíjinəs/ *adj. formal* rust-colored.

ru·ble /rōōbəl/ *n.* (also **rou·ble**) the chief monetary unit of Russia, the USSR (*hist.*), and some other former republics of the USSR.

ru·bric /rōōbrik/ *n.* **1** a direction for the conduct of divine service in a liturgical book. **2** a heading or passage in red or special lettering. **3** explanatory words. **4** an established custom.

rubric late Middle English *rubrish* (originally referring to a heading, section of text, etc., written in red for distinctiveness), from Old French *rubriche,* from Latin *rubrica* (*terra*) 'red (earth or ocher as writing material),' from the base of *rubeus* 'red'; the later spelling is influenced by the Latin form.

ru·bri·cate /róobrikayt/ *v.tr.* **1** mark with red; print or write in red. **2** provide with rubrics. ▫▫ **ru·bri·ca·tion** /–káyshən/ *n.* **ru·bri·ca·tor** *n.*

ru·by /róobee/ *n. & adj.* • *n.* (*pl.* **-ies**) **1** a rare precious stone consisting of corundum with a color varying from deep crimson or purple to pale rose. **2** a glowing, purple-tinged red color. • *adj.* of this color.

ruche /róosh/ *n.* a frill or gathering of lace, etc., as a trimming. ▫▫ **ruched** *adj.* **ruch·ing** *n.*

ruck /ruk/ *v. & n.* • *v.tr. & intr.* (often foll. by *up*) make or become creased or wrinkled. • *n.* a crease or wrinkle.

ruck·sack /rúksak, róok–/ *n.* = BACKPACK *n.*

ruck·us /rúkəs/ *n.* a fracas or commotion.

ruc·tion /rúkshən/ *n. colloq.* **1** a disturbance or tumult. **2** (in *pl.*) unpleasant arguments or reactions.

rud·der /rúdər/ *n.* **1 a** a flat piece hinged vertically to the stern of a ship for steering. **b** a vertical airfoil pivoted from the horizontal stabilizer of an aircraft, for controlling its horizontal movement. **2** a guiding principle, etc. ▫▫ **rud·der·less** *adj.*

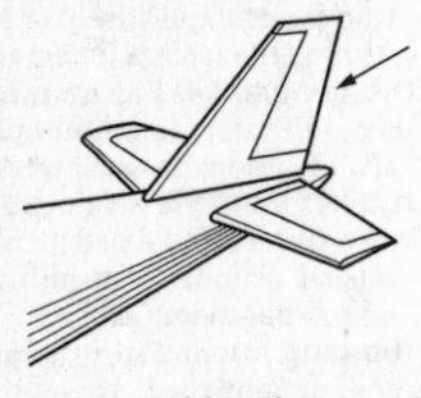
rudder, 1b

rud·dle var. of RADDLE.

rud·dy /rúdee/ *adj. & v.* • *adj.* (**ruddier, ruddiest**) **1 a** (of a person or complexion) freshly or healthily red. **b** (of health, youth, etc.) marked by this. **2** reddish. • *v.tr. & intr.* (**-dies, -died**) make or grow ruddy. ▫▫ **rud·di·ness** *n.*

rude /róod/ *adj.* **1** impolite or offensive. **2** roughly made or done (*a rude shelter*). **3** primitive or uneducated. **4** abrupt; sudden; startling (*a rude awakening*) **5** *colloq.* indecent; lewd (*a rude joke*). ▫ **be rude to** speak impolitely to; insult. ▫▫ **rude·ly** *adv.* **rude·ness** *n.*

ru·der·al /róodərəl/ *adj. & n.* • *adj.* (of a plant) growing on or in rubbish or rubble. • *n.* a ruderal plant.

ru·di·ment /róodimənt/ *n.* **1** (in *pl.*) the elements or first principles of a subject. **2** (in *pl.*) an imperfect beginning of something undeveloped or yet to develop. **3** a part or organ imperfectly developed as being vestigial or having no function (e.g., the breast in males).

ru·di·men·ta·ry /róodiméntəree/ *adj.* **1** involving basic principles; fundamental. **2** incompletely developed; vestigial.

rue[1] /róo/ *v.tr.* (**rues, rued, ruing**) repent of; wish to be undone or nonexistent (esp. *rue the day*).

rue[2] /róo/ *n.* a perennial evergreen shrub, *Ruta graveolens,* with bitter strong-scented leaves.

rue·ful /róofool/ *adj.* expressing sorrow, genuine or humorously affected. ▫▫ **rue·ful·ly** *adv.* **rue·ful·ness** *n.*

ru·fes·cent /róofésənt/ *adj.* reddish. ▫▫ **ru·fes·cence** *n.*

ruff /ruf/ *n.* **1** a projecting starched frill worn around the neck, esp. in the 16th c. **2** a projecting or conspicuously colored ring of feathers or hair around a bird's or animal's neck. **3** a domestic pigeon.

ruf·fi·an /rúfeeən/ *n.* a violent, lawless person. ▫▫ **ruf·fi·an·ism** *n.* **ruf·fi·an·ly** *adv.*

ruf·fle /rúfəl/ *v. & n.* • *v.* **1** *tr.* disturb the smoothness or tranquillity of. **2** *tr.* upset the calmness of (a person). **3** *tr.* gather (lace, etc.) into a ruffle. **4** *tr.* (often foll. by *up*) (of a bird) erect (its feathers) in anger, display, etc. **5** *intr.* undergo ruffling. **6** *intr.* lose smoothness or calmness. • *n.* **1** an ornamental frill of lace, etc., worn at the opening of a garment esp. around the wrist, breast, or neck. **2** perturbation; bustle. **3** a rippling effect on water. **4** the ruff of a bird, etc. (see RUFF[1] 2).

ru·fous /róofəs/ *adj.* (esp. of animals) reddish-brown.

rug /rug/ *n.* **1** a floor covering of shaggy material or thick pile. **2** a toupee or wig. ▫ **pull the rug (out) from under** deprive of support; weaken; unsettle.

rug·by /rúgbee/ *n.* (also **Rugby football**) a team game played with an oval ball that may be kicked, carried, and passed from hand to hand.

rug·ged /rúgid/ *adj.* **1** (of ground or terrain) having a rough uneven surface. **2** (of features) strongly marked; irregular in outline. **3 a** unpolished; lacking refinement. **b** harsh in sound. **c** austere; unbending (*rugged honesty*). **d** involving hardship (*a rugged life*). **4** (esp. of a machine) robust; sturdy. ▫▫ **rug·ged·ly** *adv.* **rug·ged·ness** *n.*

ru·gose /róogōs/ *adj.* esp. *Biol.* wrinkled; corrugated. ▫▫ **ru·gose·ly** *adv.* **ru·gos·i·ty** /–gósitee/ *n.*

ru·in /róoin/ *n. & v.* • *n.* **1** a destroyed or wrecked state. **2** a person's or thing's downfall or elimination (*the ruin of my hopes*). **3 a** the complete loss of one's property or position (*bring to ruin*). **b** a person who has suffered ruin. **4** (in *sing.* or *pl.*) the remains of a building, etc., that has suffered ruin. **5** a cause of ruin (*will be the ruin of us*). • *v.* **1** *tr.* **a** bring to ruin. **b** utterly impair or wreck (*the rain ruined my hat*). **2** *tr.* (esp. as **ruined** *adj.*) reduce to ruins. ▫ **in ruins 1** in a state of ruin. **2** completely wrecked (*their hopes were in ruins*).

ru·in·a·tion /róoináyshən/ *n.* **1** the act of bringing to ruin. **2** the act of ruining or the state of being ruined.

ru·in·ous /róoinəs/ *adj.* **1** bringing ruin; disastrous (*at ruinous expense*). **2** dilapidated. ▫▫ **ru·in·ous·ly** *adv.*

rule /róol/ *n. & v.* • *n.* **1** a principle to which an action conforms or is required to conform. **2** a prevailing custom or standard; the normal state of things. **3** government or dominion (*under British rule; the rule of law*). **4** a graduated straight measure used in carpentry, etc.; a ruler. **5** *Printing* **a** a thin strip of metal for separating headings, columns, etc. **b** a thin line or dash. **6** a code of discipline of a religious order. **7** *Law* an order made by a judge or court with reference to a particular case only. • *v.* **1** *tr.* keep under control. **2** *tr.* & (often foll. by *over*) *intr.* have sovereign control of (*rules over a vast kingdom*). **3** *tr.* (often foll. by *that* + clause) pronounce authoritatively (*was ruled out of order*). **4** *tr.* **a** make parallel lines across (paper). **b** make (a straight line) with a ruler, etc. **5** *tr.* (in *passive*; foll. by *by*) consent to follow (advice, etc.); be guided by. ▫ **as a rule** usually. **rule out** exclude; pronounce irrelevant or ineligible. **rule the roost** be in control.

rule of thumb *n.* a rule for general guidance, based on experience or practice rather than theory.

rul·er /róolər/ *n.* **1** a person exercising government or dominion. **2** a straight usu. graduated strip or cylinder of wood, metal, etc., used to draw lines or measure distance. ▫▫ **rul·er·ship** *n.*

rul·ing /róoling/ *n. & adj.* • *n.* an authoritative decision or announcement. • *adj.* dominant; prevailing; currently in force (*ruling prices*).

rum /rum/ *n.* **1** a spirit distilled from sugarcane residues or molasses. **2** *colloq.* intoxicating liquor.

Ru·ma·ni·an var. of ROMANIAN.

rum·ba /rúmbə, róom–/ *n. & v.* (also **rhum·ba**) • *n.* **1** Cuban dance. **2 a** a ballroom dance imitative of this. **b** the music for it. • *v.tr.* (**rumbas, rumbaed** /–bəd/, **rumbaing** /–bə-ing/) dance the rumba.

rum·ble /rúmbəl/ *v. & n.* • *v.* **1** *intr.* make a continuous deep resonant sound as of distant thunder. **2** *intr.* (foll. by *along, by, past,* etc.) move with a rumbling noise.

3 *intr.* engage in a street fight, esp. as part of a gang. **4** *tr.* (often foll. by *out*) utter or say with a rumbling sound. • *n.* **1** a rumbling sound. **2** *sl.* a street fight between gangs.

ru•men /ro͞omen/ *n.* (*pl.* **rumina** /–minə/ or **rumens**) the first stomach of a ruminant, in which food, esp. cellulose, is partly digested by bacteria.

ru•mi•nant /ro͞ominənt/ *n.* & *adj.* • *n.* an animal that chews the cud. • *adj.* **1** of or belonging to ruminants. **2** contemplative; given to or engaged in meditation.

ru•mi•nate /ro͞ominayt/ *v.* **1** *tr.* & (foll. by *over, on,* etc.) *intr.* meditate, ponder. **2** *intr.* (of ruminants) chew the cud. □□ **ru•mi•na•tion** /–náyshən/ *n.* **ru•mi•na•tive** /–nətiv/ *adj.* **ru•mi•na•tive•ly** *adv.*

rum•mage /rúmij/ *v.* & *n.* • *v.* **1** *tr.* & (foll. by *in, through, among*) *intr.* search, esp. unsystematically. **2** *tr.* (foll. by *out, up*) find among other things. **3** *tr.* (foll. by *about*) disarrange; make untidy in searching. • *n.* **1** an instance of rummaging. **2** things found by rummaging; a miscellaneous accumulation.

rummage late 15th century: from Old French *arrumage*, from *arrumer* 'stow (in a hold),' from Middle Dutch *ruim* 'room.' In early use the word referred to the arranging of items such as casks in the hold of a ship, giving rise (early 17th century) to the verb sense 'make a search of (a vessel).'

rum•mage sale *n.* a sale of miscellaneous usu. secondhand articles, esp. for charity.

rummy[1] /rúmee/ *n.* any of various card games in which the players try to form sets and sequences of cards.

rummy[2] /rúmee/ *n. sl.* a drunkard or sot.

ru•mor /ro͞omər/ *n.* & *v.* • *n.* **1** general talk or hearsay of doubtful accuracy. **2** (often foll. by *of,* or *that* + clause) a current but unverified statement (*heard a rumor that you are leaving*). • *v.tr.* (usu. in *passive*) report by way of rumor (*it is rumored that you are leaving*).

rump /rump/ *n.* **1** the hind part of a mammal, esp. the buttocks. **2** a small or contemptible remnant.

rum•ple /rúmpəl/ *v.tr.* & *intr.* make or become creased or ruffled.

rum•pus /rúmpəs/ *n. colloq.* a disturbance, brawl, row, or uproar.

rum•pus room *n.* a room, usu. in the basement of a house, for games and play.

run /run/ *v.* & *n.* • *v.* (**running**; *past* **ran** /ran/; *past part.* **run**) **1** *intr.* go with quick steps on alternate feet, never having both or all feet on the ground at the same time. **2** *intr.* flee; abscond. **3** *intr.* go or travel hurriedly, briefly, etc. **4** *intr.* **a** advance by or as by rolling or on wheels, or smoothly or easily. **b** be in action or operation (*left the engine running*). **5** *intr.* be current or operative (*the lease runs for 99 years*). **6** *intr.* travel or be traveling on its route (*the train is running late*). **7** *intr.* (of a play, exhibition, etc.) be staged or presented. **8** *intr.* extend; have a course or order or tendency (*the road runs by the coast*). **9 a** *intr.* compete in a race. **b** *intr.* finish a race in a specified position. **c** *tr.* compete in (a race). **10** *intr.* (often foll. by *for*) seek election (*ran for president*). **11 a** *intr.* (of a liquid, etc.) flow; drip. **b** *tr.* flow with. **12** *tr.* **a** cause (water, etc.) to flow. **b** fill (a bath) with water. **13** *intr.* spread rapidly or beyond the proper place (*ink ran over the table*; *a shiver ran down my spine*). **14** *tr.* traverse (a course, race, or distance). **15** *tr.* perform (an errand). **16** *tr.* publish (an article, etc.) in a newspaper or magazine. **17 a** *tr.* cause to operate. **b** *intr.* (of a mechanism or component, etc.) move or work freely. **18** *tr.* direct or manage (a business, etc.). **19** *tr.* take (a person) for a journey in a vehicle. **20** *tr.* cause to run or go in a specified way (*ran the car into a tree*). **21** *tr.* enter (a horse, etc.) for a race. **22** *tr.* smuggle (guns, etc.). **23** *tr.* chase or hunt. **24** *tr.* allow (an account) to accumulate for a time before paying. **25** *intr.* (of a color in a fabric) spread from the dyed parts. **26 a** *intr.* (of a thought, the eye, the memory, etc.) pass in a transitory or cursory way (*ideas ran through my mind*). **b** *tr.* cause (one's eye) to look cursorily (*ran my eye down the page*). **c** *tr.* pass (a hand, etc.) rapidly over (*ran his fingers through her hair*). **27** *intr.* (of hosiery) unravel along a line from the point of a snag. **28** *intr.* (of a candle) gutter. **29** *intr.* (of the eyes or nose) exude liquid matter. • *n.* **1** an act or spell of running. **2** a short excursion. **3** a distance traveled. **4** a general tendency. **5** a rapid motion. **6** a regular route. **7 a** a continuous or long stretch or spell or course (*a 50-foot run of wiring; had a run of bad luck*). **b** a series or sequence, esp. of cards in a specified suit. **8** (often foll. by *on*) **a** a high general demand (for a commodity, currency, etc.) (*a run on the dollar*). **b** a sudden demand for repayment by a large number of customers (of a bank). **9** a quantity produced in one period of production (*a print run*). **10** a general or average type or class (*not typical of the general run*). **11** *Baseball* a point scored by a base runner upon touching home plate safely. **12** (foll. by *of*) free use of or access to (*had the run of the house*). **13 a** an animal's regular track. **b** an enclosure for domestic animals or fowls. **c** a range of pasture. **14** a line of unraveled stitches, esp. from the point of a snag (in hosiery). **15** *Mus.* a rapid scale passage. **16** a class or line of goods. **17** a batch or drove of animals born or reared together. **18** a shoal of fish in motion. **19 a** a single journey, esp. by an aircraft. **b** (of an aircraft) a flight on a straight and even course at a constant speed before or while dropping bombs. **c** an offensive military operation. **20** a slope used for skiing or tobogganing, etc. **21** (**the runs**) *colloq.* an attack of diarrhea. □ **at a** (or **the**) **run** running. **on the run 1** escaping; running away. **2** hurrying about. **run about 1** bustle; hurry from one person or place to another. **2** (esp. of children) play without restraint. **run across 1** happen to meet. **2** (foll. by *to*) make a brief journey or a flying visit (to a place). **run afoul of** collide or become entangled with (another vessel, etc.). **run after 1** pursue with attentions; seek the society of. **2** give much time to (a pursuit, etc.). **3** pursue at a run. **run against** oppose, as in an election. **run along** *colloq.* depart. **run around 1** deceive or evade repeatedly. **2** (often foll. by *with*) *sl.* engage in sexual relations. **run at** attack by charging or rushing. **run a temperature** be feverish. **run away 1** flee; abscond. **2** elope. **3** (of a horse) bolt. **run away with 1** carry off. **2** win easily. **3** accept (a notion) hastily. **4** (of expense, etc.) consume (money, etc.). **5** (of a horse) bolt with (a rider, a carriage or its occupants). **run down 1** knock down. **2** reduce the strength or numbers of. **3** (of an unwound clock, etc.) stop. **4** (of a person or a person's health) become feeble from overwork or underfeeding. **5** discover after a search. **6** disparage. **run dry** cease to flow. **run for it** seek safety by fleeing. **a run** (or **a good run**) **for one's money 1** vigorous competition. **2** pleasure derived from an activity. **run high 1** (of the sea) have a strong current with a high tide. **2** (of feelings) be strong. **run in 1** *colloq.* arrest. **2** (of a combatant) rush to close quarters. **3** incur (a debt). **run in the family** (of a trait) be common in a family. **run into 1** collide with. **2** encounter. **3** reach as many as (a specified figure). **4** fall into (a practice, absurdity, etc.). **5** be continuous or coalesce with. **run into the ground** *colloq.* bring (a person, etc.) to exhaustion, etc. **run its course** follow its natural progress. **run low** (or **short**) become depleted; have too little (*our money ran short*). **run off 1** flee. **2** produce (copies, etc.) on a machine. **3** decide (a race or other contest) after a series of heats or in the event of a tie. **4** flow or cause to flow away. **5** write or recite fluently. **6** digress suddenly. **run off at the mouth** *sl.* talk incessantly. **run on 1** (of written characters) be joined together. **2** continue in operation. **3** elapse. **4** speak volubly. **5** talk incessantly. **6** *Printing* continue on the same line as the preceding matter. **run out 1** come to an end. **2** (foll. by *of*) exhaust one's stock of. **3** escape from a containing vessel. **4** expel; drive out (*they ran him out of town*). **run out on** *colloq.* desert (a person). **run over 1** overflow. **2** study or repeat quickly. **3** (of a vehicle or its driver) pass over; knock down or crush. **4** touch (the notes of a piano, etc.) in quick succession. **5** (often foll. by *to*) go quickly by a brief journey or for a quick visit. **run ragged** exhaust (a person). **run through 1** examine or rehearse briefly. **2** peruse. **3** deal successively with. **4** consume (an estate, etc.) by reckless or quick spending. **5** traverse. **6** pervade. **7** pierce with a sword, etc. **8** draw a line through (written words). **run to 1** have the money or ability for. **2** reach (an amount or number). **3** (of a person) show a tendency to (*runs to fat*). **4 a** be enough for (some expense or undertaking). **b** have the resources or capacity for. **5** fall into (ruin). **run up 1** accumulate (a debt, etc.) quickly. **2** build or make hurriedly. **3** raise (a flag). **4** grow quickly. **5** rise in price. **6** (foll. by *to*) amount to. **7** force (a rival bidder) to bid higher. **8** add up (a column of figures). **9** (foll. by *to*) go quickly by a brief journey or for a quick visit. **run up against** meet with (a difficulty or difficulties). **run wild** grow or stray unchecked or undisciplined or untrained.

run·a·bout /rúnəbowt/ *n.* a light car, boat, or aircraft.

run·a·round /rúnərownd/ *n.* (esp. in phr. *give a person the runaround*) deceit or evasion.

run·a·way /rúnəway/ *n.* **1** a fugitive. **2** an animal or vehicle that is running out of control. **3** (*attrib.*) **a** that is running away or out of control (*runaway inflation*; *had a runaway success*). **b** done or performed after running away (*a runaway wedding*).

run·ci·ble spoon /rúnsibəl/ *n.* a fork curved like a spoon, with three broad prongs.

run·down /rúndown/ *n.* **1** *Baseball* a play in which a base runner is caught between two bases and is chased by fielders who try to tag the runner out. **2** a summary or brief analysis.

run-down *adj.* **1** decayed after prosperity. **2** enfeebled through overwork, etc.

rune /ro͞on/ *n.* **1** any of the letters of the earliest Germanic alphabet used by Scandinavians and Anglo-Saxons from about the 3rd c. **2** a similar mark of mysterious or magic significance. **3** a Finnish poem or a division of it. □□ **ru·nic** *adj.*

rung[1] /rung/ *n.* **1** each of the horizontal supports of a ladder. **2** a strengthening crosspiece in a chair, etc.

rung[2] *past part.* of RING[2].

run-in *n.* **1** the approach to an action or event. **2** a quarrel.

run·nel /rúnəl/ *n.* **1** a brook. **2** a gutter.

run·ner /rúnər/ *n.* **1** a person, horse, etc. that runs, esp. in a race. **2 a** a creeping plant stem that can take root. **b** a twining plant. **3** a rod or groove or blade on which a thing slides. **4** a sliding ring on a rod, etc. **5** a messenger, scout, collector, or agent for a bank, etc. **6** a running bird. **7** a smuggler. **8** a revolving millstone. **9** each of the long pieces on the underside of a sled, etc., that forms the contact in sliding. **10** a roller for moving a heavy article. **11** a long, narrow ornamental cloth or rug.

run·ner-up *n.* (*pl.* **runners-up** or **runner-ups**) the competitor or team taking second place.

run·ning /rúning/ *n.* & *adj.* • *n.* **1** the action of runners in a race, etc. **2** the way a race, etc., proceeds. **3** management; control; operation • *adj.* **1** continuing on an essentially continuous basis though changing in detail (*a running battle*). **2** consecutive (*three days running*). **3** done with a run (*a running jump*). □ **in** (or **out of**) **the running** (of a competitor) with a good (or poor) chance of winning.

run·ning board *n.* a footboard on either side of a vehicle.

run·ning com·men·ta·ry *n.* an oral description of events as they occur.

run·ning light *n.* any of the navigational lights displayed by a ship, aircraft, etc., during hours of darkness.

run·ning mate *n.* **1** a candidate for a secondary position in an election. **2** a horse entered in a race in order to set the pace for another horse from the same stable which is intended to win.

run·ning stitch *n.* **1** a line of small nonoverlapping stitches for gathering, etc. **2** one of these stitches.

run·ny /rúnee/ *adj.* (**runnier, runniest**) **1** tending to run or flow. **2** excessively fluid.

run·off /rúnawf/ *n.* **1** an additional competition, election, race, etc., after a tie. **2** an amount of rainfall that is carried off an area by streams and rivers.

run-of-the-mill *adj.* ordinary; undistinguished.

runt /runt/ *n.* **1** a small piglet, puppy, etc., esp. the smallest in a litter. **2** a weakling; an undersized person. □□ **runt·y** *adj.*

run-through *n.* **1** a rehearsal. **2** a brief survey.

run·way /rúnway/ *n.* **1** a specially prepared surface along which aircraft take off and land. **2** a trail to an animals' watering place. **3** an incline down which logs are slid. **4** a narrow walkway extending out from a stage into an auditorium. **5** a passageway along which football players, etc., run to enter the field.

ru·pee /ro͞opée, ro͞opee/ *n.* the chief monetary unit of India, Pakistan, Sri Lanka, Nepal, Mauritius, and the Seychelles.

rup·ture /rúpchər/ *n.* & *v.* • *n.* **1** the act or an instance of breaking; a breach. **2** a breach of harmonious relations; a disagreement and parting. **3** *Med.* an abdominal hernia. • *v.* **1** *tr.* break or burst (a cell or membrane, etc.). **2** *tr.* sever (a connection). **3** *intr.* undergo a rupture. **4** *tr.* & *intr.* affect with or suffer a hernia.

ru·ral /ro͝orəl/ *adj.* **1** in, of, or suggesting the country (opp. URBAN) (*in rural seclusion*; *a rural constituency*). **2** often *derog.* characteristic of country people; rustic; plain; simple. □□ **ru·ral·ism** *n.* **ru·ral·ize** *v.* **ru·ral·ly** *adv.*

ru·ral free de·liv·er·y *n.* (also **rural delivery service**) postal delivery to mailboxes in rural areas.

ruse /ro͞oz/ *n.* a stratagem or trick.

rush[1] /rush/ *v.* & *n.* • *v.* **1** *intr.* go, move, or act precipitately or with great speed. **2** *tr.* move or transport with great haste (*was rushed to the hospital*). **3** *intr.* (foll. by *at*) **a** move suddenly toward. **b** begin impetuously. **4** *tr.* perform or deal with hurriedly (*don't rush your dinner*). **5** *tr.* force (a person) to act hastily. **6** *tr.* attack or capture by sudden assault. **7** *tr.* pay attentions to (a person) with a view to securing acceptance of a proposal. **8** *tr.* pass (an obstacle) with a rapid dash. **9** *intr.* flow, fall, spread, or roll impetuously or fast (*felt the blood rush to my face*). **10** *tr.* & *intr. Football* advance the ball in a running play or plays. • *n.* **1** an act of rushing; a violent advance or attack. **2** a period of great activity. **3** (*attrib.*) done with great haste or speed (*a rush job*). **4** a sudden migration of large numbers. **5** a surge of emotion, excitement, etc. **6** (foll. by *on, for*) a sudden, strong demand for a commodity. **7** (in *pl.*) *colloq.* the first prints of a film. **8** *Football* **a** the act of carrying the ball. **b** an attempt by a defensive player or players to reach the passer or kicker.

rush[2] /rush/ *n.* **1** any marsh or waterside plant of the family Juncaceae, with naked slender tapering pith-filled stems used for making chair bottoms and baskets, etc. **2** a stem of this. **3** (*collect.*) rushes as a material. □□ **rush·y** *adj.*

rush hour *n.* a time each day when traffic is at its heaviest.

rusk /rusk/ *n.* a slice of bread rebaked usu. as a light biscuit, esp. as food for babies.

rus·set /rúsit/ *adj. & n.* •*adj.* reddish-brown. •*n.* **1** a reddish-brown color. **2** a kind of rough-skinned, russet-colored apple. **3** a baking potato, esp. one from Idaho.

Rus·sian /rúshən/ *n. & adj.* •*n.* **1 a** a native or national of Russia or the former Soviet Union. **b** a person of Russian descent. **2** the language of Russia and the official language of the former Soviet Union. •*adj.* **1** of or relating to Russia. **2** of or in Russian.

Rus·sian rou·lette *n.* **1** an act of daring in which one squeezes the trigger of a revolver held to one's head with one chamber loaded, having first spun the chamber. **2** a potentially dangerous enterprise.

Rus·si·fy /rúsifī/ *v.tr.* (**-fies, -fied**) make Russian in character. □□ **Rus·si·fi·ca·tion** *n.*

Russo- /rúsō/ *comb. form* Russian; Russian and (*Russo-Japanese*).

rust /rust/ *n. & v.* •*n.* **1 a** a reddish or yellowish-brown coating formed on iron or steel by oxidation, esp. as a result of moisture. **b** a similar coating on other metals. **2 a** any of various plant diseases with rust-colored spots caused by fungi of the order Uredinales. **b** the fungus causing this. **3** an impaired state due to disuse or inactivity. •*v.* **1** *tr. & intr.* affect or be affected with rust; undergo oxidation. **2** *intr.* (of bracken, etc.) become rust-colored. **3** *intr.* (of a plant) be attacked by rust. **4** *intr.* lose quality or efficiency by disuse or inactivity.

rus·tic /rústik/ *adj. & n.* •*adj.* **1** having the characteristics of or associations with the country or country life. **2** unsophisticated. **3** of rude workmanship. **4** made of untrimmed branches or rough lumber (*a rustic bench*). **5** (of lettering) freely formed. **6** *Archit.* with rough-hewn or roughened surface or with sunken joints. •*n.* a person from or living in the country, esp. a simple, unsophisticated one. □□ **rus·tic·i·ty** /–tísitee/ *n.*

rus·tle /rúsəl/ *v. & n.* •*v.* **1** *intr. & tr.* make or cause to make a gentle sound as of dry leaves blown in a breeze. **2** *intr.* (often foll. by *along*, etc.) move with a rustling sound. **3** *tr.* (also *absol.*) steal (cattle or horses). **4** *intr. colloq.* hustle. •*n.* a rustling sound or movement. □ **rustle up** *colloq.* produce quickly when needed. □□ **rus·tler** *n.* (esp. in sense 3 of *v.*).

rust·proof /rústproōf/ *adj. & v.* •*adj.* (of a metal) not susceptible to corrosion by rust. •*v.tr.* make rustproof.

rust·y /rústee/ *adj.* (**rustier, rustiest**) **1** rusted or affected by rust. **2** stiff with age or disuse. **3** (of knowledge, etc.) impaired by neglect. **4** rust-colored. **5** (of black clothes) discolored by age. **6 a** of antiquated appearance. **b** antiquated or behind the times. **7** (of a voice) croaking or creaking. □□ **rust·i·ly** *adv.* **rust·i·ness** *n.*

rut[1] /rut/ *n. & v.* •*n.* **1** a deep track made by the passage of wheels. **2** an established mode of practice or procedure. •*v.tr.* (**rutted, rutting**) mark with ruts. □ **in a rut** following a fixed pattern of behavior that is difficult to change. □□ **rut·ty** *adj.*

rut[2] /rut/ *n. & v.* •*n.* the periodic sexual excitement of a male deer, goat, sheep, etc. •*v.intr.* (**rutted, rutting**) be affected with rut. □□ **rut·tish** *adj.*

ru·ta·ba·ga /róotəbáygə/ *n.* a large yellow-fleshed turnip, *Brassica napus*, orig. from Sweden. Also called **swede**.

ru·the·ni·um /roōtheéneeəm/ *n. Chem.* a rare hard white metallic transition element, occurring naturally in platinum ores, and used as a chemical catalyst and in certain alloys. ¶ Symb.: **Ru**.

ruth·er·for·di·um /rúthərfáwrdeeəm/ *n. Chem.* an artificially made, unstable metallic element produced by bombarding an isotope of Californium. ¶ Symb.: **Rf**.

ruth·less /róothlis/ *adj.* having no pity nor compassion. □□ **ruth·less·ly** *adv.* **ruth·less·ness** *n.*

RV *abbr.* **1** Revised Version (of the Bible). **2** recreational vehicle.

rye /rī/ *n.* **1 a** a cereal plant, *Secale cereale*, with spikes bearing florets which yield wheatlike grains. **b** the grain of this used for bread and fodder. **2** (in full **rye whiskey**) whiskey distilled from fermented rye.

rye·grass /rígras/ *n.* any forage or lawn grass of the genus *Lolium*, esp. *L. perenne*.

S

S[1] /es/ *n.* (also **s**) (*pl.* **Ss** or **S's** /ésiz/) **1** the nineteenth letter of the alphabet. **2** an S-shaped object or curve.

S[2] *abbr.* (also **S.**) **1** Saint. **2** siemens. **3** south, southern.

S[3] *symb. Chem.* the element sulfur.

s. *abbr.* **1** second(s). **2** shilling(s). **3** singular. **4** son.

-s' /s; z after a vowel sound or voiced consonant/ *suffix* denoting the possessive case of plural nouns and sometimes of singular nouns ending in *s* (*the boys' shoes*; *Charles' book*).

's /s; z after a vowel sound or voiced consonant/ *abbr.* **1** is; has (*he's*; *it's*; *John's*). **2** us (*let's*). **3** *colloq.* does (*what's he say?*).

-s[1] /s; z after a vowel sound or voiced consonant, e.g., *ways*, *bags*/ *suffix* denoting the plurals of nouns.

-s[2] /s; z after a vowel sound or voiced consonant, e.g., *ties*, *begs*/ *suffix* forming the 3rd person sing. present of verbs.

-s[3] /s; z after a vowel sound or voiced consonant, e.g., *besides*/ *suffix* **1** forming adverbs (*afterwards*; *besides*; *mornings*). **2** forming possessive pronouns (*hers*; *ours*).

SA *abbr.* **1** Salvation Army. **2 a** South Africa. **b** South America. **c** South Australia.

Sab·bath /sábəth/ *n.* (in full **Sabbath day**) a day of rest and religious observance kept by Christians on Sunday, Jews on Saturday, and Muslims on Friday.

sab·bat·i·cal /səbátikəl/ *adj.* & *n.* • *adj.* **1** of or appropriate to the Sabbath. **2** (of leave) granted at intervals to a university teacher for study or travel. • *n.* a period of sabbatical leave.

sa·ber /sáybər/ *n.* & *v.* • *n.* **1** a cavalry sword with a curved blade. **2** a cavalry soldier and horse. **3** a light fencing sword with a tapering blade. • *v.tr.* cut down or wound with a saber.

sa·ber rat·tling *n.* a display or threat of military force.

sa·ber-toothed ti·ger *n.* (also **saber-toothed cat**) an extinct mammal of the cat family with long curved upper canine teeth.

Sa·bi·an /sáybeeən/ *adj.* & *n.* • *adj.* of a sect classed in the Koran with Muslims, Jews, and Christians, as believers in the true God. • *n.* a member of this sect.

Sa·bine /sáybīn/ *adj.* & *n.* • *adj.* of or relating to a people of the central Apennines in ancient Italy. • *n.* a member of this people.

sa·ble[1] /sáybəl/ *n.* **1 a** a small, brown-furred, flesh-eating mammal, *Martes zibellina*, of N. Europe and parts of N. Asia, related to the marten. **b** its skin or fur. **2** a fine paintbrush made of sable fur.

sa·ble[2] /sáybəl/ *n.* & *adj.* • *n.* **1** esp. *poet.* black. **2** (in *pl.*) mourning garments. **3** (in full **sable antelope**) a large stout-horned African antelope, *Hippotragus niger*, the males of which are mostly black in old age. • *adj.* esp. *poet.* dark, gloomy.

sab·ot /sabṓ, sábō/ *n.* **1** a kind of simple shoe hollowed out from a block of wood. **2** a wooden-soled shoe.

sab·o·tage /sábətaazh/ *n.* & *v.* • *n.* deliberate damage to productive capacity. • *v.tr.* **1** commit sabotage on. **2** destroy; spoil (*sabotaged my plans*).

sab·o·teur /sábətṓr/ *n.* a person who commits sabotage.

sa·bra /sa͞abrə/ *n.* a Jew born in Israel.

SAC /sak/ Strategic Air Command.

Sac /sak, sawk/ *n.* SAUK.

sac /sak/ *n.* a baglike cavity, enclosed by a membrane, in an animal or plant.

sac·cha·rin /sákərin/ *n.* a substance used as a substitute for sugar.

sac·cha·rine /sákərin, -reen, -rīn/ *adj.* **1** sugary. **2** of, containing, or like sugar. **3** unpleasantly overpolite, sentimental, etc.

sac·cha·rom·e·ter /sákərómitər/ *n.* any instrument, esp. a hydrometer, for measuring the sugar content of a solution.

sac·er·do·tal /sásərdṓtəl, sák-/ *adj.* of priests or the priestly office; priestly. ▫▫ **sac·er·do·tal·ism** *n.*

sa·chem /sáychəm/ *n.* the supreme leader of some Native American tribes.

sa·chet /sasháy/ *n.* **1** a small bag or packet containing a small portion of a substance, esp. shampoo. **2** a small perfumed bag. **3 a** dry perfume for laying among clothes, etc. **b** a packet of this.

sack[1] /sak/ *n.* & *v.* • *n.* **1 a** a large, strong bag, for storing or conveying goods. **b** (usu. foll. by *of*) this with its contents (*a sack of potatoes*). **c** a quantity contained in a sack. **2** (prec. by *the*) *colloq.* dismissal from employment. **3** (prec. by *the*) *sl.* bed. **4** a woman's short, loose dress with a sacklike appearance. **5** a man's or woman's loose-hanging coat not shaped to the back. • *v.tr.* **1** put into a sack or sacks. **2** *colloq.* dismiss from employment. ▫▫ **sack·ful** *n.* (*pl.* **-fuls**). **sack·like** *adj.*

sack[2] /sak/ *v.* & *n.* • *v.tr.* **1** plunder and destroy (a captured town, etc.). **2** steal valuables from (a place). • *n.* the sacking of a captured place.

sack·but /sákbut/ *n.* an early form of trombone.

sack·cloth /sák-klawth, -kloth/ *n.* **1** a coarse fabric of flax or hemp. **2** clothing made of this, formerly worn as a penance (esp. *sackcloth and ashes*).

sack·ing /sáking/ *n.* material for making sacks; sackcloth.

sack race *n.* a race between competitors in sacks up to the waist or neck.

sa·cra *pl.* of SACRUM.

sa·cral /sáykrəl, sa-/ *adj.* **1** *Anat.* of or relating to the sacrum. **2** *Anthropol.* of or for sacred rites.

sac·ra·ment /sákrəmənt/ *n.* **1** a religious ceremony or act of the Christian churches regarded as an outward and visible sign of inward and spiritual grace, baptism, and the Eucharist. **2** a thing of mysterious and sacred significance; a sacred influence, symbol, etc. **3** (also **Blessed** or **Holy Sacrament**) (prec. by *the*) **a** the Eucharist. **b** the consecrated elements, esp. the bread or Host. ▫▫ **sac·ra·men·tal** *adj.*

---

sacrament Middle English: from Old French *sacrement*, from Latin *sacramentum* 'solemn oath' (from *sacrare* 'to hallow,' from *sacer* 'sacred'), used in Christian Latin as a translation of Greek *mustērion* 'mystery.'

---

sa·cred /sáykrid/ *adj.* **1 a** (often foll. by *to*) exclusively dedicated or appropriated (to a god or to some religious purpose). **b** made holy by religious association. **c** connected with religion (*sacred music*). **2 a** safeguarded or required by religion, reverence, or tradition. **b** sacrosanct. **3** (of writings, etc.) embodying the laws or doctrines of a religion. ▫▫ **sa·cred·ly** *adv.* **sa·cred·ness** *n.*

sa•cred cow *n. colloq.* an idea or institution unreasonably held to be above criticism (with ref. to the Hindus' respect for the cow as a holy animal).

sac•ri•fice /sákrifīs/ *n. & v.* •*n.* **1 a** the act of giving up something valued for the sake of something else more important or worthy. **b** a thing given up in this way. **c** the loss entailed in this. **2 a** the slaughter of an animal or person or the surrender of a possession as an offering to a deity. **b** an animal, person, or thing offered in this way. **3** an act of prayer, thanksgiving, or penitence as propitiation. **4** (in games) a loss incurred deliberately to avoid a greater loss or to obtain a compensating advantage. •*v.tr.* **1** give up (a thing) as a sacrifice. **2** (foll. by *to*) devote or give over to. **3** (also *absol.*) offer or kill as a sacrifice. ▫▫ **sac•ri•fi•cial** /–físhəl/ *adj.* **sac•ri•fi•cial•ly** /–físhəlee/ *adv.*

sac•ri•lege /sákrilij/ *n.* the violation or misuse of what is regarded as sacred. ▫▫ **sac•ri•le•gious** /–líjəs/ *adj.* **sac•ri•le•gious•ly** *adv.*

sac•ris•ty /sákristee/ *n.* (*pl.* **-ties**) a room in a church where the vestments, sacred vessels, etc., are kept and the celebrant can prepare for a service.

sacro- /sákrō, sáy;n–/ *comb. form* denoting the sacrum (*sacroiliac*).

sac•ro•il•i•ac /sákrōíleeak, sáykrō–/ *adj.* relating to the juncture of the sacrum and the ilium bones of the pelvis

sac•ro•sanct /sákrōsangkt/ *adj.* (of a person, place, law, etc.) most sacred; inviolable. ▫▫ **sac•ro•sanc•ti•ty** /–sángktitee/ *n.*

sac•rum /sáykrəm, sák–/ *n.* (*pl.* **sacra** /–krə/ or **sacrums**) *Anat.* a triangular bone formed from fused vertebrae and situated between the two hipbones of the pelvis.

sad /sad/ *adj.* (**sadder, saddest**) **1** unhappy. **2** causing or suggesting sorrow (*a sad story*). **3** regrettable. **4** shameful; deplorable (*a sad state*). ▫▫ **sad•ly** *adv.* **sad•ness** *n.*

sad Old English *sæd* 'sated, weary,' also 'weighty, dense,' of Germanic origin; related to Dutch *zat* and German *satt*, from an Indo-European root shared by Latin *satis* 'enough.' The original meaning was replaced in Middle English by the senses 'steadfast, firm' and 'serious, sober,' and later 'sorrowful.'

sad•den /sád'n/ *v.tr. & intr.* make or become sad.

sad•dle /sád'l/ *n. & v.* •*n.* **1** a seat of leather, etc., fastened on a horse, etc., for riding. **2** a seat for the rider of a bicycle, etc. **3** a cut of meat consisting of the two loins. **4** a ridge rising to a summit at each end. **5** the part of a draft horse's harness to which the shafts are attached. **6** a part of an animal's back resembling a saddle in shape or marking. •*v.tr.* **1** put a saddle on (a horse, etc.). **2 a** (foll. by *with*) burden (a person) with a task, responsibility, etc. **b** (foll. by *on, upon*) impose (a burden) on a person. ▫ **in the saddle 1** mounted. **2** in office or control. ▫▫ **sad•dle•less** *adj.*

saddle, 1

sad•dle•back /sád'lbak/ *n.* **1** *Archit.* a tower-roof with two opposite gables. **2** a hill with a concave upper outline. **3** a black pig with a white stripe across the back. **4** any of various birds with a saddlelike marking. ▫▫ **sad•dle•backed** *adj.*

sad•dle•bag /sád'lbag/ *n.* **1** each of a pair of bags laid across a horse, etc., behind the saddle. **2** a bag attached behind the saddle of a bicycle.

sad•dle•cloth /sád'lklawth/ *n.* a cloth laid on a horse's back under the saddle.

sad•dler /sádlər/ *n.* a dealer in saddles and other equipment for horses.

sad•dle shoes *n.pl.* laced shoes with yokes that contrast in color with the rest of the upper.

sad•dle sore *n.&adj.* > •*n.* a bruise or sore on a horse or rider caused by the pressure of a saddle. •*adj.* (**sad•dle-sore**) chafed or sore from riding on a saddle

Sad•du•cee /sájəsee, sádyə–/ *n.* a member of a Jewish sect or party of the time of Christ that denied the resurrection of the dead, the existence of spirits, and the obligation of the traditional oral law. ▫▫ **Sad•du•ce•an** /–seéən/ *adj.*

sa•dism /sáydizəm, sád–/ *n.* **1** a form of sexual perversion characterized by the enjoyment of inflicting pain or suffering on others (cf. MASOCHISM). **2** *colloq.* the enjoyment of cruelty to others. ▫▫ **sa•dist** *n.* **sa•dis•tic** /sədístik/ *adj.* **sa•dis•ti•cal•ly** *adv.*

sa•do•mas•o•chism /sáydōmásəkizəm, sádō–/ *n.* the combination of sadism and masochism in one person. ▫▫ **sa•do•mas•o•chist** *n.* **sa•do•mas•o•chis•tic** /–kístik/ *adj.*

sad sack *n. colloq.* a very inept person, esp. an inept soldier.

sa•fa•ri /səfaáree/ *n.* (*pl.* **safaris**) **1** a hunting or scientific expedition, esp. in E. Africa (*go on safari*). **2** a sightseeing trip to see African animals in their natural habitat.

safe /sayf/ *adj. & n.* •*adj.* **1 a** free of danger or injury. **b** (often foll. by *from*) out of or not exposed to danger (*safe from their enemies*). **2** affording security or not involving danger or risk (*put it in a safe place*). **3** reliable; certain (*a safe catch; a safe method; is safe to win*). **4** prevented from escaping or doing harm (*have got him safe*). **5** (also **safe and sound**) uninjured; with no harm done. **6** cautious and unenterprising. •*n.* a strong, lockable cabinet, etc., for valuables. ▫ **on the safe side** with a margin of security against risks. ▫▫ **safe•ly** *adv.* **safe•ness** *n.*

safe-con•duct *n.* **1** a privilege of immunity from arrest or harm, esp. on a particular occasion. **2** a document securing this.

safe-de•pos•it box *n.* a secured box (esp. in a bank vault) for storing valuables.

safe•guard /sáyfgaard/ *n. & v.* •*n.* **1** a proviso, stipulation, quality, or circumstance that tends to prevent something undesirable. **2** a safe conduct. •*v.tr.* guard or protect (rights, etc.) by a precaution or stipulation.

safe house *n.* a place of refuge or rendezvous for spies or criminals.

safe•keep•ing /sáyfkeeping/ *n.* preservation in a safe place.

safe sex *n.* sexual activity in which precautions are taken to reduce the risk of spreading sexually transmitted diseases.

safe•ty /sáyftee/ *n.* (*pl.* **-ties**) **1** the condition of being safe; freedom from danger or risks. **2** (*attrib.*) **a** designating any of various devices for preventing injury from machinery (*safety bar; safety lock*). **b** designating items of protective clothing (*safety helmet*).

safe•ty belt *n.* **1** = SEAT BELT. **2** a belt or strap securing a person to prevent injury.

safe•ty-de•pos•it box *n.* = SAFE-DEPOSIT BOX.

safe•ty glass *n.* glass that will not splinter when broken.

safe·ty har·ness *n.* a system of belts or restraints to hold a person to prevent falling or injury.
safe·ty match *n.* a match igniting only on a specially prepared surface.
safe·ty net *n.* **1** a net placed to catch an acrobat, etc., in case of a fall. **2** a safeguard against hazard or adversity.
safe·ty pin *n.* a pin for fastening with a point that is held in a guard when closed.
safe·ty ra·zor *n.* a razor with a guard to reduce the risk of cutting the skin.
safe·ty valve *n.* **1** (in a steam boiler) a valve opening automatically to relieve excessive pressure. **2** a means of giving harmless vent to excitement, etc.
saf·flow·er /sáflowr/ *n.* **1 a** a thistlelike plant, *Carthamus tinctorius*, yielding a red dye. **b** its dried petals. **2** a dye made from these.
saf·fron /sáfrən/ *n. & adj.* • *n.* **1** a bright yellow-orange food coloring and flavoring made from the dried stigmas of the crocus, *Crocus sativus*. **2** the color of this. • *adj.* saffron-colored.
sag /sag/ *v. & n.* • *v.intr.* (**sagged, sagging**) **1** sink or subside, esp. unevenly. **2** have a downward bulge or curve in the middle. **3** fall in price. • *n.* **1 a** the amount that a rope, etc., sags. **b** the distance from the middle of its curve to a straight line between its supports. **2** a sinking condition; subsidence. **3** a fall in price. ▫▫ **sag·gy** *adj.*
sa·ga /saágə/ *n.* **1** a long story of heroic achievement, esp. a medieval Icelandic or Norwegian prose narrative. **2** a series of connected books giving the history of a family, etc. **3** a long, involved story.
sa·ga·cious /səgáyshəs/ *adj.* **1** mentally penetrating; having practical wisdom. **2** acute-minded; shrewd. **3** (of a saying, plan, etc.) showing wisdom. ▫▫ **sa·ga·cious·ly** *adv.* **sa·gac·i·ty** /səgásitee/ *n.*
sag·a·more /ságəmawr/ *n.* = SACHEM.
sage[1] /sayj/ *n.* **1** an aromatic herb, *Salvia officinalis*, with dull grayish-green leaves. **2** its leaves used in cooking.
sage[2] /sayj/ *n. & adj.* • *n.* **1** often *iron.* a wise person. **2** any of the ancients traditionally regarded as the wisest of their time. • *adj.* **1** wise, esp. from experience. **2** of or indicating wisdom. **3** often *iron.* wise-looking. ▫▫ **sage·ly** *adv.*
sage·brush /sáyjbrush/ *n.* **1** a growth of shrubby aromatic plants of the genus *Artemisia*, found in some semiarid regions of western N. America. **2** this plant.
Sag·it·tar·i·us /sájitáireeəs/ *n.* **1** a constellation, traditionally regarded as contained in the figure of an archer. **2 a** the ninth sign of the zodiac (the Archer). **b** a person born when the sun is in this sign. ▫▫ **Sag·it·tar·i·an** *adj. & n.*
sa·go /sáygō/ *n.* (*pl.* **-gos**) **1** a kind of starch, made from the powdered pith of the sago palm and used in puddings, etc. **2** (in full **sago palm**) any of several tropical palms and cycads, esp. *Cycas circinalis* and *Metroxylon sagu*, from which sago is made.
sa·gua·ro /səgwarō, səwarō/ *n.* (*pl.* **-ros**) a giant cactus, *Carnegiea gigantea*, of the SW United States and Mexico.
sa·hib /saab, saáhib/ *n.* **1** *hist.* (in India) a form of address, often placed after the name, to European men. **2** *colloq.* a gentleman (*pukka sahib*).
said *past* and *past part.* of SAY.
sail /sayl/ *n. & v.* • *n.* **1** a piece of material extended on rigging to catch the wind and propel a boat or ship. **2** a ship's sails collectively. **3 a** a voyage or excursion in a sailing ship. **b** a voyage of specified duration. **4** a ship, esp. as discerned from its sails. **5** a wind-catching apparatus attached to the arm of a windmill. • *v.* **1** *intr.* travel on water by the use of sails or engine power. **2** *tr.* **a** navigate (a ship, etc.). **b** travel on (a sea). **3** *tr.* set (a toy boat) afloat. **4** *intr.* glide or move smoothly or in a stately manner. **5** *intr. colloq.* succeed easily (*sailed through the exams*). ▫ **sail close to** (or **near**) **the wind 1** sail as nearly against the wind as possible. **2** come close to indecency or dishonesty. **take in sail** furl the sail or sails of a vessel. **under sail** with sails set. ▫▫ **sail·a·ble** *adj.* **sailed** *adj.* (also in *comb.*). **sail·less** *adj.*
sail·board /sáylbawrd/ *n.* a board with a mast and sail, used in windsurfing. ▫▫ **sail·board·er** *n.* **sail·board·ing** *n.*
sail·boat /sáylbōt/ *n.* a boat driven by sails.
sail·cloth /sáylklawth, –kloth/ *n.* **1** canvas for sails, upholstery, tents, etc. **2** a canvaslike dress material.
sail·fish /sáylfish/ *n.* any fish of the genus *Istiophorus*, with a large dorsal fin.
sail·or /sáylər/ *n.* **1** a seaman or mariner, esp. one below the rank of officer. **2** a person who goes sailing as a sport or recreation. ▫▫ **sail·or·less** *adj.* **sail·or·ly** *adj.*
sail·plane /sáylplayn/ *n.* a glider designed for sustained flight.
saint /saynt/ *n. & v.* • *n.* (*abbr.* **St.** or **S.**; *pl.* **Sts.** or **SS.**) **1** a holy or (in some churches) a canonized person regarded as having a place in heaven. **2** (**Saint** or **St.**) the title of a saint or archangel, hence the name of a church, etc. (*St. Paul's*) or (often with the loss of the apostrophe) the name of a town, etc. (*St. Andrews*). **3** a very virtuous person. (*would try the patience of a saint*). • *v.tr.* **1** canonize; admit to the calendar of saints. **2** call or regard as a saint. **3** (as **sainted** *adj.*) sacred; of a saintly life. ▫▫ **saint·hood** *n.* **saint·like** *adj.*
St. Ber·nard /bərnaárd/ *n.* (in full **St. Bernard dog**) **1** a very large dog of a breed orig. kept to rescue travelers by the monks of the Hospice on the Great St. Bernard pass in the Alps. **2** this breed.
St. El·mo's fire /élmōz/ *n.* a luminous electrical discharge sometimes seen on a ship or aircraft during a storm.
St. John's-wort /jónzwərt/ *n.* any yellow-flowered plant of the genus *Hypericum*, esp. *H. androsaemum*.
saint·ly /sáyntlee/ *adj.* (**saintlier, saintliest**) very virtuous. ▫▫ **saint·li·ness** *n.*
St. Vi·tus's dance /vítəsiz, vítəs/ *n.* = SYDENHAM'S CHOREA.
saith /seth, sáyith/ *archaic 3rd sing. present* of SAY.
sake[1] /sayk/ *n.* ▫ **for Christ's** (or **God's** or **goodness'** or **Heaven's** or **Pete's**) **sake** an expression of urgency, impatience, etc. **for old times' sake** in memory of former times. **for the sake of** (or **for a person's sake**) **1** out of consideration for; in the interest of (*for my own sake as well as yours*). **2** in order to please, get, or keep (*for the sake of uniformity*).
sake[2] /saákee, –ke/ *n.* a Japanese alcoholic drink made from rice.
sa·laam /səlaám/ *n. & v.* • *n.* **1** the esp. Islamic salutation denoting 'peace.' **2** (in India) an obeisance consisting of a low bow of the head and body with the right palm on the forehead. **3** (in *pl.*) respectful compliments. • *v.* **1** *tr.* make a salaam to (a person). **2** *intr.* make a salaam.
sal·a·ble /sáyləbəl/ *adj.* (also **sale·a·ble**) fit to be sold. ▫▫ **sal·a·bil·i·ty** /–bílitee/ *n.*
sa·la·cious /səláyshəs/ *adj.* **1** lustful; lecherous. **2** (of writings, pictures, talk, etc.) tending to cause sexual desire. ▫▫ **sa·la·cious·ly** *adv.* **sa·la·cious·ness** *n.*
sal·ad /sáləd/ *n.* **1** a cold dish of various mixtures of raw or cooked vegetables, usu. seasoned with oil, vinegar, etc. **2** a vegetable or herb suitable for eating raw.
sal·ad days *n.pl.* a period of youthful inexperience.
sal·ad dress·ing *n.* a mixture of oil, vinegar, etc., used in a salad.
sal·a·man·der /sáləmandər/ *n.* **1** *Zool.* any tailed newt-

like amphibian of the order Urodela, esp. the genus *Salamandra*, once thought able to endure fire. **2** a mythical lizardlike creature credited with this property. **3** a metal plate heated and placed over food to brown it. ▫▫ **sal·a·man·drine** /-mándrin/ *adj.*

sa·la·mi /səlaámee/ *n.* (*pl.* **salamis**) a highly seasoned orig. Italian sausage.

sal·a·ry /sáləree/ *n.* & *v.* • *n.* (*pl.* **-ries**) a fixed regular payment, usu. monthly or quarterly, made by an employer to an employee, esp. a white-collar worker (cf. WAGE *n.* 1). • *v.tr.* (**-ies, -ried**) (usu. as **salaried** *adj.*) pay a salary to.

sale /sayl/ *n.* **1** the exchange of a commodity for money, etc.; an act of selling. **2** the amount sold (*the sales were enormous*). **3** the rapid disposal of goods at reduced prices for a period. **4 a** an event at which goods are sold. **b** a public auction. ▫ **for** (or **up for**) **sale** offered for purchase. **on sale** available for purchase, esp. at a reduced price.

sale·a·ble var. of SALABLE.

sales·clerk /sáylzklərk/ *n.* a salesperson in a retail store.

sales·girl /sáylzgərl/ *n.* a saleswoman.

Sa·le·sian /səleézhən, -shən/ *n.* & *adj.* • *n.* a member of an educational religious order within the RC Church. • *adj.* of or relating to this order.

sales·la·dy /sáylzlaydee/ *n.* (*pl.* **-dies**) a saleswoman.

sales·man /sáylzmən/ *n.* (*pl.* **-men**; *fem.* **sales·wom·an**, *pl.* **-women**) a person employed to sell goods or services in a store or on a route, etc.

sales·man·ship /sáylzmənship/ *n.* **1** skill in selling. **2** the techniques used in selling.

sales·per·son /sáylzpərsən/ *n.* a salesman or saleswoman.

sales·room /sáylzroōm, -rŏŏm/ *n.* a room for the display and purchase of items, esp. at an auction.

sales talk *n.* persuasive talk to promote the sale of goods or the acceptance of an idea, etc.

sales tax *n.* a tax on sales or on the receipts from sales.

sal·i·cyl·ic ac·id /sálisílik/ *n.* a bitter chemical used as a fungicide and in the manufacture of aspirin and dyestuffs. ▫▫ **sa·lic·y·late** /səlísilayt/ *n.*

sa·li·ent /sáylyənt/ *adj.* & *n.* • *adj.* **1** prominent; conspicuous. **2** (of an angle, esp. in fortification) pointing outward. • *n.* a salient angle or part of a work in fortification; an outward bulge in a line of military attack or defense. ▫▫ **sa·li·ence** *n.* **sa·li·en·cy** *n.* **sa·li·ent·ly** *adv.*

sa·lif·er·ous /səlífərəs/ *adj. Geol.* (of rock, etc.) containing much salt.

sa·line /sáyleen, -līn/ *adj.* & *n.* • *adj.* **1** (of natural waters, springs, etc.) impregnated with or containing salt or salts. **2** tasting of salt. **3** of chemical salts. **4** of the nature of a salt. **5** (of medicine) containing a salt or salts of alkaline metal or magnesium. • *n.* **1** a saline substance. **2** a solution of salt in water. ▫▫ **sa·lin·i·ty** /səlínitee/ *n.* **sal·i·ni·za·tion** /sálinizáyshən/ *n.* **sal·i·nom·e·ter** /sálinómitər/ *n.*

sa·li·va /səlívə/ *n.* liquid secreted into the mouth by glands to provide moisture and facilitate chewing and swallowing. ▫▫ **sal·i·var·y** /sáliveree/ *adj.*

sal·i·vate /sálivayt/ *v. intr.* secrete or discharge saliva esp. in excess or in greedy anticipation. ▫▫ **sal·i·va·tion** /-váyshən/ *n.*

Salk vac·cine /sawlk/ *n.* a vaccine developed against polio (after J.E. Salk, d. 1995).

sal·low /sálō/ *adj.* (**sallower, sallowest**) (of the skin or complexion, or of a person) of a sickly yellow or pale brown. ▫▫ **sal·low·ness** *n.*

sal·ly /sálee/ *n.* & *v.* (*pl.* **-lies**) • *n.* **1** a sudden charge from a fortification upon its besiegers. **2** an excursion. **3** a witticism; a piece of banter; a lively remark. **4** a sudden start into activity; an outburst. • *v.intr.* (**-lies, -lied**) **1** (usu. foll. by *out, forth*) go for a walk, set out on a journey, etc. **2** (usu. foll. by *out*) make a military sally.

sal·ma·gun·di /sálməgúndee/ *n.* (*pl.* **salmagundis**) **1** a dish of chopped meat, anchovies, eggs, onions, etc., and seasoning, usu. served as a salad. **2** a general mixture; a miscellaneous collection of articles, subjects, qualities, etc.

salm·on /sámən/ *n.* & *adj.* • *n.* (*pl.* same or (esp. of types) **salmons**) **1** any anadromous fish of the family Salmonidae, esp. of the genus *Salmo*, much prized for its (often smoked) pink flesh. **2** *Austral.* & *NZ* the barramundi or a similar fish. • *adj.* salmon pink. ▫▫ **sal·mo·noid** *adj.* & *n.* (in sense 1). **sal·mon·y** *adj.*

sal·mo·nel·la /sálmənélə/ *n.* (*pl.* **salmonellae** /-lee/) **1** any bacterium of the genus *Salmonella*, esp. any of various types causing food poisoning. **2** food poisoning caused by infection with salmonellae. ▫▫ **sal·mo·nel·lo·sis** /-lṓsis/ *n.*

sa·lon /səlón, saláwN/ *n.* **1** the reception room of a large or fashionable house. **2** a room or establishment where a hairdresser, beautician, etc., conducts business. **3** *hist.* a meeting of eminent people in the reception room of a lady of fashion.

sa·loon /səlóōn/ *n.* **1** a drinking establishment; bar. **2** a public room on a ship. **3** esp. *Brit.* **a** a large room or hall, esp. in a hotel or public building. **b** a public room or gallery for a specified purpose (*billiard saloon*; *shooting saloon*).

sal·sa /saálsə/ *n.* **1** a kind of dance music of Latin American origin, incorporating jazz and rock elements. **2** a dance performed to this music. **3** a spicy sauce made from tomatoes, chilies, onions, etc., often served as a dip.

SALT /sawlt/ *abbr.* Strategic Arms Limitation Talks (or Treaty).

salt /sawlt/ *n., adj.,* & *v.* • *n.* **1** (also **common salt**) sodium chloride; the substance that gives seawater its characteristic taste, got in crystalline form by mining or by the evaporation of seawater, and used for seasoning or preserving food, or for other purposes. **2** a chemical compound formed from the reaction of an acid with a base, with all or part of the hydrogen of the acid replaced by a metal or metallike radical. **3** piquancy; wit (*added salt to the conversation*). **4** (in *sing.* or *pl.*) **a** a substance resembling salt in taste, form, etc. (*bath salts*; *smelling salts*). **b** (esp. in *pl.*) this type of substance used as a laxative. **5** (also **old salt**) an experienced sailor. • *adj.* **1** impregnated with, containing, or tasting of salt; cured or preserved or seasoned with salt. **2** (of a plant) growing in the sea or in salt marshes. **3** (of tears, etc.) bitter. **4** (of wit) pungent. • *v.tr.* **1** cure or preserve with salt or brine. **2** season with salt. **3** make (a narrative, etc.) piquant. **4** sprinkle (the ground, etc.) with salt. **5** treat with a solution of salt or mixture of salts. ▫ **salt away** (or **down**) *sl.* lay away money, etc.; save. **salt a mine** *sl.* introduce extraneous ore, material, etc., to make the source seem rich. **the salt of the earth** a person or people of great worthiness, reliability, honesty, etc. (Matt. 5:13). **take with a grain of salt** regard as exaggerated; be skeptical about. **worth one's salt** efficient; capable. ▫▫ **salt·ish** *adj.* **salt·less** *adj.* **salt·ness** *n.*

salt-and-pep·per *adj.* with light and dark colors mixed together.

sal·ta·rel·lo /sáltərélō, sáwl;n-/ *n.* (*pl.* **-los** or **saltarelli** /-lee/) an Italian and Spanish dance for one or two persons, with sudden skips.

salt·cel·lar /sáwltselər/ *n.* a vessel holding salt for table use.

sal·ti·grade /sáltigrayd, sáwl;n–/ *adj. & n. Zool.* • *adj.* (of arthropods) moving by leaping or jumping. • *n.* a saltigrade arthropod, e.g., a jumping spider, beach flea, etc.

sal·tine /sawltéen/ *n.* a lightly salted, square, flat cracker.

salt lake *n.* a lake of salt water.

salt lick *n.* **1** a place where animals go to lick salt from the ground. **2** this salt.

salt marsh *n.* a marsh, esp. one flooded by the tide, often used as a pasture or for collecting water for salt making.

salt mine *n.* a mine yielding rock salt.

salt pan *n.* a vessel, or a depression near the sea, used for getting salt by evaporation.

salt·pe·ter /sáwltpéetər/ *n.* potassium nitrate, a white crystalline salty substance used in preserving meat and as a constituent of gunpowder.

salt·shak·er /sáwltshaykər/ *n.* a container of salt for sprinkling on food.

salt·wa·ter /sáwltwawtər/ *adj.* of or living in the sea.

salt wa·ter *n.* **1** sea water. **2** *sl.* tears.

salt·works /sáwltwərks/ *n.* a place where salt is produced.

salt·wort /sáwltwərt, –wawrt/ *n.* any plant of the genus *Salsola*; glasswort.

salt·y /sáwltee/ *adj.* (**saltier, saltiest**) **1** tasting of, containing, or preserved with salt. **2** racy, risqué. ▫▫ **salt·i·ness** *n.*

sa·lu·bri·ous /səlóobreeəs/ *adj.* **1** health-giving; healthy. **2** (of surroundings, etc.) pleasant; agreeable. ▫▫ **sa·lu·bri·ous·ly** *adv.* **sa·lu·bri·ous·ness** *n.* **sa·lu·bri·ty** *n.*

sa·lu·ki /səlóokee/ *n.* (*pl.* **salukis**) a tall, slender dog of a silky-coated breed.

sal·u·tar·y /sályəteree/ *adj.* producing good effects; beneficial.

sal·u·ta·tion /sályətáyshən/ *n.* **1** a sign or expression of greeting or recognition of another's arrival or departure. **2** (usu. in *pl.*) words spoken or written to inquire about another's health or well-being.

sa·lu·ta·to·ry /səlóotətawree/ *adj.* of salutation.

sa·lute /səlóot/ *n. & v.* • *n.* **1** a gesture of respect, homage, or courteous recognition. **2 a** *Mil. & Naut.* a prescribed or specified movement of the hand or of weapons or flags as a sign of respect or recognition. **b** (prec. by *the*) the attitude taken by an individual soldier, sailor, policeman, etc., in saluting. **3** the discharge of a gun or guns as a ceremonial sign of respect or celebration. • *v.* **1 a** *tr.* make a salute to. **b** *intr.* perform a salute. **2** *tr.* greet; make a salutation to. **3** *tr.* (foll. by *with*) receive or greet with (a smile, etc.). ▫ **take the salute 1** (of the highest officer present) acknowledge it by gesture as meant for him. **2** receive ceremonial salutes by members of a procession.

sal·vage /sálvij/ *n. & v.* • *n.* **1** the rescue of a ship, its cargo, or other property, from loss at sea, destruction by fire, etc. **2** the property, etc., saved in this way. **3 a** the saving and utilization of waste paper, scrap material, etc. **b** the materials salvaged. • *v.tr.* **1** save from a wreck, fire, etc. **2** retrieve or preserve in adverse circumstances (*tried to salvage some dignity*). ▫▫ **sal·vage·a·ble** *adj.* **sal·vag·er** *n.*

sal·va·tion /salváyshən/ *n.* **1** the act of saving or being saved. **2** deliverance from sin and its consequences and admission to heaven. **3** a religious conversion. **4** a person or thing that saves (*was the salvation of*). ▫▫ **sal·va·tion·ism** *n.* **sal·va·tion·ist** *n.* (both nouns esp. with ref. to the Salvation Army).

salve /sav, saav/ *n. & v.* • *n.* **1** a healing ointment. **2** a thing that is soothing or consoling for wounded feelings, an uneasy conscience, etc. • *v.tr.* soothe (pride, self-love, conscience, etc.).

sal·ver /sálvər/ *n.* a tray usu. of gold, silver, brass, or electroplate, on which drinks, letters, etc., are offered.

sal·vo /sálvō/ *n.* (*pl.* **-voes** or **-vos**) **1** the simultaneous firing of artillery or other guns. **2** a number of bombs released from aircraft at the same moment. **3** a round of applause.

sal vo·la·ti·le /sál vōlát'lee/ *n.* ammonium carbonate, esp. in the form of a flavored solution in alcohol used as smelling salts.

SAM *abbr.* surface-to-air missile.

sa·ma·dhi /səmáadee/ *n. Buddhism & Hinduism* **1** a state of concentration induced by meditation. **2** a state into which a perfected holy man is said to pass at his apparent death.

sam·a·ra /sámərə, səmáirə, səmáa–/ *n. Bot.* a winged seed from the sycamore, ash, etc.

Sa·mar·i·tan /səmárit'n/ *n. & adj.* • *n.* **1** (in full **good Samaritan**) a charitable or helpful person (with ref. to Luke 10:33, etc.). **2** a native of Samaria in West Jordan. • *adj.* of Samaria or the Samaritans. ▫▫ **Sa·mar·i·tan·ism** *n.*

sa·mar·i·um /səmáireeəm/ *n. Chem.* a soft, silvery metallic element of the lanthanide series, used in making ferromagnetic alloys.

sam·ba /sámbə, sáam–/ *n. & v.* • *n.* **1** a Brazilian dance of African origin. **2** a ballroom dance imitative of this. **3** the music for this. • *v.intr.* (**sambas, sambaed** /–bəd/, **sambaing** /–bə-ing/) dance the samba.

Sam Browne /sam brówn/ *n.* (in full **Sam Browne belt**) an army officer's belt and the shoulder strap supporting it.

same /saym/ *adj., pron., & adv.* • *adj.* **1** identical; not different; unchanged (*everyone was looking in the same direction*; *the same car was used in another crime*; *saying the same thing over and over*). **2** unvarying; uniform; monotonous (*the same old story*). **3** (usu. prec. by *this, these, that, those*) previously alluded to; just mentioned (*this same man was later my husband*). • *pron.* (prec. by *the*) **1** the same person or thing (*the others asked for the same*). **2** *Law* or *archaic* the person or thing just mentioned (*detected the youth breaking in and apprehended the same*). • *adv.* (usu. prec. by *the*) similarly; in the same way (*we all feel the same*; *I want to go, the same as you do*). ▫ **all** (or **just**) **the same 1** emphatically the same. **2** in spite of changed conditions, adverse circumstances, etc. (*but you should offer, all the same*). **at the same time 1** simultaneously. **2** notwithstanding. **be all** (or **just**) **the same to** an expression of indifference or impartiality (*it's all the same to me what we do*). **by the same token** see TOKEN. **same here** *colloq.* the same applies to me. **the same to you!** may you do, have, find, etc., the same thing. **the very same** emphatically the same. ▫▫ **same·ness** *n.*

▶Do not use **same** in place of *identical.* You and your friend may have bought *identical* sweaters, but if you bought the *same* sweater, you will be sharing one clothing item between the two of you.

Sa·mo·an /səmóən/ *n. & adj.* • *n.* **1** a native of Samoa, a group of islands in the Pacific. **2** the language of this people. • *adj.* of or relating to Samoa or its people or language.

sam·o·var /sáməvaar/ *n.* a Russian urn for making tea, with an internal heating tube to keep water at boiling point.

samovar

Sam·o·yed /sáməyed, səmóyed/ *n.* **1** a member of a people of northern Siberia. **2** the language of this people. **3** (also **samoyed**) **a** a dog of a white Arctic breed. **b** this breed.
sam·pan /sámpan/ *n.* a small boat used in the Far East.
sam·phire /sámfīr/ *n.* **1** an umbelliferous maritime rock plant, *Crithmum maritimum*, with aromatic fleshy leaves used in pickles. **2** the glasswort.
sam·ple /sámpəl/ *n.* & *v.* •*n.* **1** (also *attrib.*) a small part intended to show what the whole is like. **2** a small amount of fabric, food, or other commodity, given to a prospective customer. **3** a specimen, esp. one taken for scientific testing. **4** an illustrative or typical example. •*v.tr.* **1** take or give samples of. **2** try the qualities of. **3** get a representative experience of.
sam·pler[1] /sámplər/ *n.* a piece of embroidery worked in various stitches as a specimen of proficiency (often displayed on a wall, etc.).
sam·pler[2] /sámplər/ *n.* **1** a person who samples. **2** a collection of representative items, etc.
sam·pling /sámpling/ *n.* **1** the action of selecting a sample for testing. **2** a technique in electronic music involving digitally encoding a piece of sound and reusing it as part of a composition or recording.
sam·sa·ra /səmsaárə/ *n. Ind. Philos.* the endless cycle of death and rebirth to which life in the material world is bound. ▫▫ **sam·sa·ric** *adj.*
sam·ska·ra /səmskaárə/ *n. Ind. Philos.* **1** a purificatory ceremony or rite marking an event in one's life. **2** a mental impression, instinct, or memory.
Sam·son /sámsən/ *n.* a person of great strength.
sam·u·rai /sámoorī, saá–/ *n.* (*pl.* same) **1** a Japanese army officer. **2** *hist.* a military retainer; a member of a military caste in Japan.
san·a·tive /sánətiv/ *adj.* **1** healing; curative. **2** of or tending to physical or moral health.
san·a·to·ri·um /sánətáwreeəm/ *n.* (*pl.* **sanatoriums** or **sanatoria** /–reeə/) an establishment for the treatment of invalids, esp. of convalescents and the chronically sick.
sanc·ti·fy /sángktifī/ *v.tr.* (**-fies, -fied**) **1** consecrate; set apart as holy. **2** free from sin. **3** make legitimate or binding by religious sanction; justify. **4** make productive of or conducive to holiness. ▫▫ **sanc·ti·fi·ca·tion** /–fikáyshən/ *n.* **sanc·ti·fi·er** *n.*
sanc·ti·mo·ni·ous /sángktimóneeəs/ *adj.* making a show of sanctity or piety. ▫▫ **sanc·ti·mo·ni·ous·ly** *adv.* **sanc·ti·mo·ni·ous·ness** *n.* **sanc·ti·mo·ny** /sángktimōnee/ *n.*
sanc·tion /sángkshən/ *n.* & *v.* •*n.* **1** approval by custom or tradition; express permission. **2** confirmation of a law, etc. **3 a** a penalty for disobeying a law or rule, or a reward for obeying it. **b** a clause containing this. **4** *Ethics* a consideration operating to enforce obedience to any rule of conduct. **5** (esp. in *pl.*) esp. economic action by a nation to coerce another to conform to an international agreement or norms of conduct. •*v.tr.* **1** authorize or agree to (an action, etc.). **2** ratify; make binding. ▫▫ **sanc·tion·a·ble** *adj.*
▶**Sanction** is confusing because it has two meanings that are almost opposite, depending on whether you are discussing domestic or foreign relations. In domestic terms, **sanction** means 'approval; permission': *Voters gave the measure their sanction.* In foreign affairs, **sanction** means 'penalty; deterrent': *International sanctions against the republic go into effect in January.*
sanc·ti·ty /sángktitee/ *n.* (*pl.* **-ties**) **1** holiness of life; saintliness. **2** sacredness. **3** inviolability. **4** (in *pl.*) sacred obligations, feelings, etc.
sanc·tu·ar·y /sángkchooeree/ *n.* (*pl.* **-ies**) **1** a holy place. **2 a** the holiest part of a temple, etc. **b** the part of the chancel containing the high altar. **3** a place of refuge for birds, wild animals, etc. **4** a place of refuge. **5 a** immunity from arrest. **b** the right to offer this. **6** *hist.* a sacred place where a fugitive from the law or a debtor was secured by medieval church law against arrest or violence. ▫ **take sanctuary** resort to a place of refuge.

---

sanctuary Middle English (in sense 1): from Old French *sanctuaire*, from Latin *sanctuarium*, from *sanctus* 'holy.' The early sense 'a church or other sacred place where a fugitive was immune, by the law of the medieval church, from arrest' gave rise to senses 2 and 3.

---

sanc·tum /sángktəm/ *n.* (*pl.* **sanctums**) **1** a holy place. **2** *colloq.* a person's private room, study, or den.
Sanc·tus /sángktəs, saángktoos/ *n.* (also **sanctus**) **1** the prayer or hymn beginning "Holy, holy, holy" said or sung at the end of the Eucharistic preface. **2** the music for this.
sand /sand/ *n.* & *v.* •*n.* **1** a loose granular substance resulting from the wearing down of esp. siliceous rocks and found on the seashore, riverbeds, deserts, etc. **2** (in *pl.*) grains of sand. **3** (in *pl.*) an expanse or tracts of sand. **4** a light yellow-brown color like that of sand. **5** (in *pl.*) a sandbank. •*v.tr.* **1** smooth with sandpaper or sand. **2** sprinkle or overlay with sand. ▫ **the sands are running out** the allotted time is nearly at an end. ▫▫ **sand·er** *n.* **sand·like** *adj.*
san·dal /sánd'l/ *n.* a light shoe with an openwork upper or no upper, attached to the foot usu. by straps.
san·dal tree *n.* any tree yielding sandalwood, esp. the white sandalwood.
san·dal·wood /sánd'lwood/ *n.* **1** the scented wood of a sandal tree. **2** a perfume derived from this.
sand·bag /sándbag/ *n.* & *v.* •*n.* a bag filled with sand for use: **1** for making temporary defenses or for the protection of a building, etc., against blast and splinters or floodwaters. **2** as ballast esp. for a boat or balloon. **3** as a weapon to inflict a heavy blow without leaving a mark. **4** to stop a draft from a window or door. •*v.tr.* (**-bagged, -bagging**) **1** barricade or defend. **2** place sandbags against (a window, chink, etc.). **3** fell with a blow from a sandbag. **4** coerce by harsh means. ▫▫ **sand·bag·ger** *n.*
sand·bank /sándbangk/ *n.* a deposit of sand forming a shallow place in the sea.
sand·bar /sándbaar/ *n.* a sandbank at the mouth of a river or on the coast.
sand·blast /sándblast/ *v.* & *n.* •*v.tr.* roughen, treat, or clean with a jet of sand driven by compressed steam or air. •*n.* this jet. ▫▫ **sand·blast·er** *n.*
sand·box /sándboks/ *n.* a box of sand, esp. one for children to play in.
sand·cas·tle /sándkasəl/ *n.* a shape like a castle made in sand, usu. by a child.
sand dol·lar *n.* any of various round, flat sea urchins, esp. of the order Clypeasteroida.
sand dune *n.* (also **sand hill**) a mound of sand formed by the wind.
sand·hog /sándhawg, –hog/ *n.* a person who works underwater laying foundations, constructing tunnels, etc.
sand·lot /sándlot/ *n.* a piece of unoccupied sandy land used for children's games.
sand·man /sándman/ *n.* a fictional man supposed to make children sleep by sprinkling sand in their eyes.
sand·pa·per /sándpaypər/ *n.* & *v.* •*n.* paper with sand or another abrasive stuck to it for smoothing or polishing. •*v.tr.* smooth with sandpaper.
sand·pi·per /sándpīpər/ *n.* any of various wading shore birds of the family Scolopacidae.

See page xii for the *Key to Pronunciation*.

sand·pit /sándpit/ *n.* a pit from which sand is excavated.
sand·stone /sándstōn/ *n.* a sedimentary rock of consolidated sand.
sand·storm /sándstawrm/ *n.* a desert storm of wind with clouds of sand.
sand·wich /sándwich, sán–/ *n.* & *v.* •*n.* two or more slices of bread with a filling of meat, cheese, etc., between them. •*v.tr.* **1** put (a thing, statement, etc.) between two of another character. **2** squeeze in between others (*sat sandwiched in the middle*).
sand·wich board *n.* two hinged advertisement boards made to hang from the shoulders.
sand·y /sándee/ *adj.* (**sandier, sandiest**) **1** having the texture of sand. **2** having much sand. **3 a** (of hair) yellowish-red. **b** (of a person) having sandy hair. ▫▫ **sand·i·ness** *n.* **sand·y·ish** *adj.*
sane /sayn/ *adj.* **1** of sound mind; not mad. **2** (of views, etc.) moderate; sensible. ▫▫ **sane·ly** *adv.* **sane·ness** *n.*
sang *past* of SING.
sang-froid /saaNfrwáa/ *n.* composure, coolness, etc., in danger or under agitating circumstances.
san·gri·a /sanggréeə/ *n.* a sweet Spanish drink of iced red wine with lemonade, fruit, spices, etc.
san·gui·nar·y /sánggwəneree/ *adj.* **1** accompanied by or delighting in bloodshed. **2** bloody; bloodthirsty.
san·guine /sánggwin/ *adj.* **1** optimistic; confident. **2** (of the complexion) florid; ruddy. ▫▫ **san·guine·ly** *adv.* **san·guine·ness** *n.* (both in sense 1).
san·guin·e·ous /sanggwíneeəs/ *adj.* **1** sanguinary. **2** *Med.* of or relating to blood. **3** blood-red. **4** full-blooded; plethoric.
San·hed·rin /sanhédrin, –hée–, saan–/ *n.* (also **San·hed·rim** /–drim/) the highest court of justice and the supreme council in ancient Jerusalem.
san·i·tar·i·um /sánitáireeəm/ *n.* (*pl.* **sanitariums** or **sanitaria** /–reeə/) **1** an establishment for the restoration of health; sanatorium. **2** a health resort.
san·i·tar·y /sániteree/ *adj.* **1** of the conditions that affect health. **2** hygienic. ▫▫ **san·i·tar·i·an** /–áireeən/ *n.* & *adj.* **san·i·tar·i·ly** *adv.*
san·i·tar·y en·gi·neer *n.* a person dealing with systems needed to maintain public health.
san·i·tar·y nap·kin *n.* an absorbent pad used during menstruation.
san·i·ta·tion /sánitáyshən/ *n.* **1** sanitary conditions. **2** the maintenance or improving of these. **3** the disposal of sewage and refuse from houses, etc.
san·i·tize /sánitīz/ *v.tr.* **1** make sanitary. **2** render (information, etc.) more acceptable by removing improper or disturbing material. ▫▫ **san·i·tiz·er** *n.*
san·i·ty /sánitee/ *n.* **1 a** the state of being sane. **b** mental health. **2** the tendency to avoid extreme views.
sans /sanz, SON/ *prep.* without.
San·skrit /sánskrit/ *n.* & *adj.* •*n.* the ancient and sacred language of the Hindus in India. •*adj.* of or in this language. ▫▫ **San·skrit·ic** /–skrítik/ *adj.* **San·skrit·ist** *n.*
sans ser·if /sansérif/ *n.* & *adj.* (also **san·ser·if**) *Printing* •*n.* a form of type without serifs, the slight projections which finish off each stroke of a letter. (Cf. SERIF.) •*adj.* without serifs.
San·ta Claus /sántə klawz/ *n.* (also *colloq.* **Santa**) a legendary person said to bring children presents on the night before Christmas.
sap[1] /sap/ *n.* & *v.* •*n.* **1** the vital juice circulating in plants. **2** vigor; vitality. **3** = SAPWOOD. •*v.tr.* (**sapped, sapping**) drain or dry (wood) of sap. ▫▫ **sap·ful** *adj.* **sap·less** *adj.*
sap[2] /sap/ *n.* & *v.* •*n.* a tunnel or trench to conceal assailants' approach to a fortified place. •*v.* (**sapped, sapping**) **1** *intr.* **a** dig a sap or saps. **b** approach by a sap. **2** *tr.* undermine; make insecure by removing the foundations. **3** *tr.* weaken or destroy insidiously.
sap[3] /sap/ *n. sl.* a foolish person.
sap·id /sápid/ *adj. literary* **1** having flavor; palatable; not insipid. **2** (of talk, writing, etc.) not vapid or uninteresting.
sa·pi·ent /sáypeeənt/ *adj. literary* **1** wise. **2** aping wisdom. ▫▫ **sa·pi·ence** *n.* **sa·pi·ent·ly** *adv.*
sap·ling /sápling/ *n.* **1** a young tree. **2** a youth. **3** a greyhound in its first year.
sap·o·dil·la /sápədílə, –déeyə/ *n.* a large evergreen tropical American tree, *Manilkara zapota*, with sap from which chicle is obtained.
sap·o·nin /sápənin/ *n.* any of a group of plant glycosides, esp. those derived from the bark of the tree *Quillaja saponaria*, that foam when shaken with water and are used in detergents and fire extinguishers.
sa·por /sáypər, –pawr/ *n.* **1** a quality perceptible by taste, e.g., sweetness. **2** the distinctive taste of a substance. **3** the sensation of taste.
sap·per /sápər/ *n.* **1** a person who digs saps. **2** a military demolitions expert.
Sap·phic /sáfik/ *adj.* & *n.* •*adj.* **1** of or relating to Sappho, poetess of Lesbos *c.*600 BC, or her poetry. **2** lesbian. •*n.* (in *pl.*) (**sapphics**) verse in a meter associated with Sappho.
sap·phire /sáfīr/ *n.* & *adj.* •*n.* **1** a transparent blue precious stone consisting of corundum. **2** precious transparent corundum of any color. **3** the bright blue of a sapphire. •*adj.* of sapphire blue. ▫▫ **sap·phir·ine** /sáfirīn, –rín, –reen/ *adj.*
sap·py /sápee/ *adj.* (**sappier, sappiest**) **1** full of sap. **2** young and vigorous. **3** overly emotional or sentimental. ▫▫ **sap·pi·ly** *adv.* **sap·pi·ness** *n.*
sapro- /sáprō/ *comb. form Biol.* rotten, putrefying.
sap·ro·gen·ic /sáprəjénik/ *adj.* causing or produced by putrefaction.
sap·ro·phyte /sáprəfīt/ *n.* any plant or microorganism living on dead or decayed organic matter. ▫▫ **sap·ro·phyt·ic** /–fítik/ *adj.*
sap·wood /sápwŏŏd/ *n.* the soft outer layers of recently formed wood between the heartwood and the bark.
sar·a·band /sárəband/ *n.* **1** a stately Spanish dance. **2** music for this or in its rhythm, usu. in triple time often with a long note on the second beat of the bar.
Sar·a·cen /sárəsən/ *n.* & *adj. hist.* •*n.* **1** an Arab or Muslim at the time of the Crusades. **2** a nomad of the Syrian and Arabian desert. •*adj.* of the Saracens. ▫▫ **Sar·a·cen·ic** /sárəsénik/ *adj.*
sar·casm /sáarkazəm/ *n.* **1** a bitter or wounding remark. **2** language consisting of such remarks. **3** the use of this. ▫▫ **sar·cas·tic** /–kástik/ *adj.* **sar·cas·ti·cal·ly** *adv.*
sar·co·ma /saarkṓmə/ *n.* (*pl.* **sarcomas** or **sarcomata** /–mətə/) a malignant tumor of connective tissue. ▫▫ **sar·co·ma·to·sis** /–mətṓsis/ *n.* **sar·co·ma·tous** *adj.*
sar·coph·a·gus /saarkófəgəs/ *n.* (*pl.* **sarcophagi** /–gī, –jī/) a stone coffin.
sar·dine /saardéen/ *n.* a young pilchard or similar young or small herringlike marine fish. ▫ **like sardines** crowded close together (as sardines are in cans).
sar·don·ic /saardónik/ *adj.* **1** grimly jocular. **2** (of laughter, etc.) bitterly mocking or cynical. ▫▫ **sar·don·i·cal·ly** *adv.* **sar·don·i·cism** /–nisizəm/ *n.*
sar·gas·so /saargásō/ *n.* (also **sar·gas·sum**) (*pl.* **-sos** or **-soes** or **sargassa**) any seaweed of the genus *Sargassum*, with berrylike air vessels, found floating in islandlike masses.
sarge /saarj/ *n. sl.* sergeant.
sa·ri /sáaree/ *n.* (also **sa·ree**) (*pl.* **saris** or **sarees**) a length of cotton or silk draped around the body, traditionally worn as a main garment by women of India.
sar·men·tose /sáarməntōs/ *adj.* (also **sar·men·tous** /–méntəs/) *Bot.* having long, thin trailing shoots.

sa·rong /səráwng, –róng/ *n.* **1** a Malay and Javanese garment consisting of a long strip of cloth worn by both sexes tucked around the waist or under the armpits. **2** a woman's garment resembling this.

sar·sa·pa·ril·la /sáspərílə, saárs–/ *n.* **1** a preparation of the dried roots of various plants, used to flavor some drinks and medicines and formerly as a tonic. **2** any of the plants yielding this.

sar·sen /saársən/ *n. Geol.* a sandstone boulder carried by ice during a glacial period.

sar·to·ri·al /saartáwreeəl/ *adj.* **1** of a tailor or tailoring. **2** of men's clothes. ▫▫ **sar·to·ri·al·ly** *adv.*

sar·to·ri·us /saartáwreeəs/ *n. Anat.* the long, narrow muscle running across the front of each thigh.

SASE *abbr.* self-addressed stamped envelope.

sash[1] /sash/ *n.* a strip or loop of cloth worn over one shoulder or around the waist. ▫▫ **sashed** *adj.*

sash[2] /sash/ *n.* a frame holding the glass in a window and usu. made to slide up and down in the grooves of a window aperture. ▫▫ **sashed** *adj.*

sa·shay /sasháy/ *v.intr. colloq.* walk in an ostentatious yet casual manner, with exaggerated movements of the hips and shoulders.

sa·shi·mi /saasheémee/ *n.* a Japanese dish of garnished raw fish in thin slices.

sash win·dow *n.* a window with one or two sashes of which one or each can be slid vertically over the other to make an opening.

Sask. *abbr.* Saskatchewan.

Sas·quatch /sáskwoch, –kwach/ *n.* a supposed yetilike animal of NW America. Also called *Bigfoot.*

sass /sas/ *n.* & *v. colloq.* • *n.* impudence; disrespectful mannerism or speech. • *v.tr.* be impudent to.

sas·sa·fras /sásəfras/ *n.* **1** a small tree, *Sassafras albidum*, native to N. America, with aromatic leaves and bark. **2** a preparation of oil extracted from the leaves or bark of this tree, used medicinally or in perfumery.

sas·sy /sásee/ *adj.* (**sassier, sassiest**) *colloq.* = SAUCY. ▫▫ **sas·si·ly** *adv.* **sas·si·ness** *n.*

sas·tru·gi /sastroógee/ *n.pl.* wavelike irregularities on the surface of hard polar snow, caused by winds.

SAT *abbr. Trademark* Scholastic Aptitude Test.

Sat. *abbr.* Saturday.

sat *past* and *past part.* of SIT.

Sa·tan /sáyt'n/ *n.* the Devil; Lucifer.

sa·tan·ic /sətánik, say–/ *adj.* **1** of, like, or befitting Satan. **2** diabolical; hellish. ▫▫ **sa·tan·i·cal·ly** *adv.*

Sa·tan·ism /sáyt'nizəm/ *n.* **1** the worship of Satan. **2** the pursuit of evil for its own sake. ▫▫ **Sa·tan·ist** *n.* **Sa·tan·ize** *v.tr.*

sa·tay /saátay/ *n.* (also **sa·tai, saté**) an Indonesian and Malaysian dish consisting of small pieces of meat grilled on a skewer and usu. served with spiced peanut sauce.

satch·el /sáchəl/ *n.* a small bag usu. of leather and hung from the shoulder with a strap, for carrying books, etc., esp. to and from school.

sate /sayt/ *v.tr.* **1** gratify to the full. **2** cloy; surfeit (*sated with pleasure*).

sa·teen /sateén/ *n.* cotton fabric woven like satin with a glossy surface.

sat·el·lite /sát'līt/ *n.* & *adj.* • *n.* **1** a celestial body orbiting the earth or another planet. **2** an artificial body placed in orbit around the earth or another planet. **3** a follower; a hanger-on. **4** an underling; a member of an important person's staff or retinue. • *adj.* transmitted by satellite (*satellite communications; satellite television*).

sat·el·lite dish *n.* a dish-shaped antenna for receiving broadcasting signals transmitted by satellite.

sa·ti var. of SUTTEE.

sa·ti·ate /sáysheeayt/ *adj.* & *v.* • *adj. archaic* satiated. • *v.tr.* = SATE. ▫▫ **sa·tia·ble** /–shəbəl/ *adj. archaic* **sa·ti·a·tion** /–áyshən/ *n.*

sa·ti·e·ty /sətī́-itee/ *n.* **1** the state of being glutted or satiated. **2** the feeling of having too much of something. **3** (foll. by *of*) a cloyed dislike of. ▫ **to satiety** to an extent beyond what is desired.

sat·in /sát'n/ *n.* & *adj.* • *n.* a fabric of silk or various synthetic fibers, with a glossy surface on one side. • *adj.* smooth as satin. ▫▫ **sat·in·ized** *adj.* **sat·in·y** *adj.*

sat·in fin·ish *n.* **1** a polish given to silver, etc., with a metallic brush. **2** any effect resembling satin in texture produced on materials in various ways.

sat·in stitch *n.* a long, straight embroidery stitch, giving the appearance of satin.

sat·in·wood /sát'nwŏŏd/ *n.* **1 a** (in full **Ceylon satinwood**) a tree, *Chloroxylon swietenia*, native to central and southern India and Sri Lanka. **b** (in full **West Indian satinwood**) a tree, *Fagara flava*, native to the West Indies, Bermuda, and southern Florida. **2** the yellow, glossy wood of either of these trees.

sat·ire /sátīr/ *n.* **1** the use of ridicule, irony, sarcasm, etc., to expose folly or vice or to lampoon an individual. **2** a work using satire. **3** this branch of literature.

sa·tir·ic /sətírik/ *adj.* **1** of satire or satires. **2** containing satire (*wrote a satiric review*). **3** writing satire (*a satiric poet*).

sa·tir·i·cal /sətírikəl/ *adj.* **1** = SATIRIC. **2** given to the use of satire in speech or writing or to cynical observation of others; sarcastic; humorously critical. ▫▫ **sa·tir·i·cal·ly** *adv.*

sat·i·rist /sátərist/ *n.* **1** a writer of satires. **2** a satirical person.

sat·i·rize /sátirīz/ *v.tr.* **1** assail or ridicule with satire. **2** write a satire upon. **3** describe satirically. ▫▫ **sat·i·ri·za·tion** *n.*

sat·is·fac·tion /sátisfákshən/ *n.* **1** the act or an instance of satisfying; the state of being satisfied (*heard this with great satisfaction*). **2** a thing that satisfies desire or gratifies feeling (*is a great satisfaction to me*). **3** a thing that settles an obligation or pays a debt. **4** (foll. by *for*) atonement; compensation (*demanded satisfaction*). ▫ **to one's satisfaction** so that one is satisfied.

sat·is·fac·to·ry /sátisfáktəree/ *adj.* **1** adequate; giving satisfaction (*was a satisfactory pupil*). **2** satisfying expectations or needs; leaving no room for complaint (*a satisfactory result*). ▫▫ **sat·is·fac·to·ri·ly** *adv.* **sat·is·fac·to·ri·ness** *n.*

sat·is·fy /sátisfī/ *v.* (**-ies, -fied**) **1** *tr.* **a** meet the expectations or desires of; comply with (a demand). **b** be accepted by (a person, his or her taste) as adequate; be equal to (a preconception, etc.). **2** *tr.* put an end to (an appetite or want) by supplying what was required. **3** *tr.* rid (a person) of an appetite or want in a similar way. **4** *intr.* give satisfaction; leave nothing to be desired. **5** *tr.* pay (a debt or creditor). **6** *tr.* adequately meet, fulfill, or comply with (conditions, obligations, etc.) (*has satisfied all the legal conditions*). **7** *tr.* provide with adequate information or proof; convince (*satisfied the others that they were right; satisfy the court of their innocence*). **8** *tr. Math.* (of a quantity) make (an equation) true. **9** *tr.* (in *passive*) **a** (foll. by *with*) contented or pleased with. **b** (foll. by *to*) demand no more than or consider it enough to do. ▫▫ **sat·is·fy·ing** *adj.* **sat·is·fy·ing·ly** *adv.*

sa·to·ri /sətáwree/ *n. Buddhism* sudden enlightenment.

sa·trap /sátrap, sáy;n–/ *n.* **1** a provincial governor in the ancient Persian empire. **2** a subordinate ruler, colonial governor, etc.

sat·u·rate /sáchərayt/ *v.tr.* **1** fill with moisture; soak thoroughly. **2** fill to capacity. **3** cause (a substance) to absorb, hold, or combine with the greatest possible amount of another substance, or of moisture, magnetism, electricity, etc. **4** supply (a market) beyond the point at which the demand for a product is satisfied. **5** (foll. by *with, in*) imbue with or steep in (learning, tradition, prejudice, etc.). **6** overwhelm by concentrated bombing. **7** (as **saturated** *adj.*) **a** (of color) full; rich; free from an admixture of white. **b** (of fat molecules) containing the greatest number of hydrogen atoms. ▫▫ **sat·u·ra·ble** /–rəbəl/ *adj.*

sat·u·ra·tion /sáchəráyshən/ *n.* the act or an instance of saturating; the state of being saturated.

sat·u·ra·tion point *n.* the stage beyond which no more can be absorbed or accepted.

Sat·ur·day /sátərday, –dee/ *n. & adv.* • *n.* the seventh day of the week, following Friday. • *adv. colloq.* **1** on Saturday. **2** (**Saturdays**) on Saturdays; each Saturday.

Sat·ur·day-night spe·cial *n. sl.* any inexpensive handgun that is easy to obtain and conceal.

Sat·urn /sátərn/ *n.* **1 a** the sixth planet from the sun, with a system of broad flat rings circling it, and the most distant of the five planets known in the ancient world. **b** *Astrol.* Saturn as a supposed astrological influence on those born under its sign, characterized by coldness and gloominess. **2** *Alchemy* the metal lead. ▫▫ **Sat·ur·ni·an** /satərneeən/ *adj.*

sat·ur·na·li·a /sátərnáyleeə/ *n.* (*pl.* same or **saturnalias**) **1** (usu. **Saturnalia**) *Rom.Hist.* the festival of Saturn in December, characterized by unrestrained merrymaking. **2** (as *sing.* or *pl.*) a scene of wild revelry. ▫▫ **sat·ur·na·li·an** *adj.*

sat·ur·nine /sátərnīn/ *adj.* **1** of a sluggish gloomy temperament. **2** (of looks, etc.) dark and brooding.

sat·ya·gra·ha /sutyaágrəhə/ *n. Ind.* **1** *hist.* a policy of passive resistance to British rule advocated by Gandhi. **2** passive resistance as a policy.

sa·tyr /sáytər, sát–/ *n.* **1** (in Greek mythology) one of a class of Greek woodland gods with a horse's ears and tail, or (in Roman representations) with a goat's ears, tail, legs, and budding horns. **2** a lustful or sensual man.

sauce /saws/ *n. & v.* • *n.* **1** any of various liquid or semisolid preparations taken as a relish with food; the liquid constituent of a dish (*mint sauce; tomato sauce; chicken in a lemon sauce*). **2** something adding piquancy or excitement. **3** esp. *Brit. colloq.* impudence; impertinence. **4** stewed fruit, etc., eaten as dessert or used as a garnish. • *v.tr.* **1** *colloq.* be impudent to. **2** *archaic* **a** season with sauce or condiments. **b** add excitement to. ▫▫ **sauce·less** *adj.*

sauce·pan /sáwspan/ *n.* a cooking pan, usu. round with a lid and a long handle at the side, used for boiling, stewing, etc., on top of a stove. ▫▫ **sauce·pan·ful** *n.* (*pl.* **-fuls**).

sau·cer /sáwsər/ *n.* **1** a shallow circular dish used for standing a cup on. **2** any similar dish used to stand a plant pot, etc., on. ▫▫ **sau·cer·ful** *n.* (*pl.* **-fuls**). **sau·cer·less** *adj.*

sau·cy /sáwsee/ *adj.* (**saucier, sauciest**) **1** impudent. **2** *colloq.* smart-looking (*a saucy hat*). **3** *colloq.* smutty; suggestive. ▫▫ **sau·ci·ly** *adv.* **sau·ci·ness** *n.*

Sau·di /sówdee, sáw–/ *n. & adj.* (also **Sau·di A·ra·bi·an**) • *n.* (*pl.* **Saudis**) **1 a** a native or national of Saudi Arabia. **b** a person of Saudi descent. **2** a member of the dynasty founded by King Saud. • *adj.* of or relating to Saudi Arabia or the Saudi dynasty.

sau·er·kraut /sówərkrowt/ *n.* a German dish of chopped pickled cabbage.

Sauk /sawk/ *n.* (also **Sac**) **1 a** a N. American people native to Wisconsin. **b** a member of this people. **2** the language of this people.

sau·na /sáwnə, sow–/ *n.* **1** a Finnish-style steam bath. **2** a building used for this.

saun·ter /sáwntər/ *v. & n.* • *v.intr.* **1** walk slowly; stroll. **2** proceed without hurry or effort. • *n.* **1** a leisurely ramble. **2** a slow gait. ▫▫ **saun·ter·er** *n.*

sau·ri·an /sáwreeən/ *adj.* of or like a lizard.

sau·ro·pod /sáwrōpod/ *n.* any of a group of plant-eating dinosaurs with a long neck and tail, and four thick limbs.

sau·sage /sáwsij/ *n.* **1 a** ground pork, beef, or other meat seasoned and often mixed with other ingredients, encased in cylindrical form in a skin, for cooking and eating hot or cold. **b** a length of this. **2** a sausage-shaped object.

sauté /sōtáy, saw–/ *adj., n., & v.* • *adj.* quickly browned in a little hot fat. • *n.* food cooked in this way. • *v.tr.* (**sautéed** or **sautéd**) cook in this way.

sav·age /sávij/ *adj., n., & v.* • *adj.* **1** fierce; cruel (*savage persecution; a savage blow*). **2** wild; primitive (*savage tribes; a savage animal*). **3** *colloq.* angry; bad-tempered (*in a savage mood*). • *n.* **1** *Anthropol. derog.* a member of a primitive tribe. **2** a cruel or barbarous person. • *v.tr.* **1** (esp. of a dog, wolf, etc.) attack and bite or trample. **2** (of a critic, etc.) attack fiercely. ▫▫ **sav·age·ly** *adv.* **sav·age·ness** *n.* **sav·age·ry** *n.* (*pl.* **-ries**).

sa·van·na /səvánə/ *n.* (also **sa·van·nah**) a grassy plain in tropical and subtropical regions, with few or no trees.

sa·vant /savaánt, sávənt/ *n.* (*fem.* **savante**) a learned person.

save[1] /sayv/ *v. & n.* • *v.* **1** *tr.* rescue, preserve, protect, or deliver from danger, harm, discredit, etc. (*saved my life; saved me from drowning*). **2** *tr.* keep for future use (*saved up $150 for a new bike; likes to save plastic bags*). **3** *tr.* (often *refl.*) **a** relieve (another person or oneself) from spending (money, time, trouble, etc.) (*saved myself $50; a word processor saves time*). **b** obviate the need or likelihood of (*soaking saves scrubbing*). **4** *tr.* preserve from damnation; convert (*saved her soul*). **5** *tr. & refl.* husband or preserve (one's strength, health, etc.) (*saving himself for the last lap; save your energy*). **6** *intr.* save money for future use. **7** *tr.* **a** avoid losing (a game, match, etc.). **b** prevent an opponent from scoring (a goal, etc.). **c** stop (a ball, etc.) from entering the goal. • *n. Ice hockey, soccer,* etc. the act of preventing an opponent's scoring, etc. ▫ **save appearances** present a prosperous, respectable, etc., appearance. **save face** see FACE. **save one's breath** not waste time speaking to no effect. **save the day** find or provide a solution to difficulty or disaster. **save one's skin** (or **neck** or **bacon**) avoid loss, injury, or death; escape from danger. ▫▫ **sav·a·ble** *adj.* (also **save·a·ble**) .

save[2] /sayv/ *prep. & conj. archaic* or *poet.* • *prep.* except; but (*all save him*). • *conj.* (often foll. by *for*) unless; but; except (*happy save for one want; is well save that he has a cold*).

sav·er /sáyvər/ *n.* **1** a person who saves, esp. money. **2** (often in *comb.*) a device for economical use (of time, etc.) (*found the shortcut a time-saver*).

sav·in /sávin/ *n.* (also **sav·ine**) **1** a bushy juniper, *Juniperus sabina*, usu. spreading horizontally, and yielding oil formerly used in the treatment of amenorrhea. **2** = RED CEDAR.

sav·ing /sáyving/ *adj., n., & prep.* • *adj.* (often in *comb.*) making economical use of (*labor-saving*). • *n.* **1** anything that is saved. **2** an economy (*a saving in expenses*). **3** (usu. in *pl.*) money saved. • *prep.* **1** except (*all saving that one*). **2** without offense to (*saving your presence*).

▶Use **savings** in the modifying position *(savings bank,*

savings bond) and when referring to money saved in a bank: *Your savings are fully insured.* When speaking of an act of saving, as when one obtains a discount on a purchase, the preferred form is **saving**: *This coupon entitles you to a saving* (not *savings*) *of $3.*

sav·ing grace *n.* **1** the redeeming grace of God. **2** a redeeming quality.

sav·ings ac·count *n.* a bank account that earns interest and from which withdrawals are usu. made in person.

sav·ings and loan as·so·ci·a·tion *n.* an institution, usu. owned by depositors and regulated by state or federal government, that accepts funds for savings accounts and lends funds for mortgages. ¶ Abbr.: **S&L.**

sav·ings bank *n.* a bank receiving deposits at interest and returning the profits to the depositors.

sav·ior /sáyvyər/ *n.* (esp. *Brit.* **saviour**) **1** a person who saves from danger, destruction, etc. (*the savior of the nation*). **2** (**Savior**) (prec. by *the*, *our*) Christ.

sav·oir faire /sávwaar fáir/ *n.* the ability to act suitably in any situation; tact.

sa·vor /sáyvər/ *n.* & *v.* • *n.* **1** a characteristic taste, flavor, etc. **2** a quality suggestive of or containing a small amount of another. **3** *archaic* a characteristic smell. • *v.* **1** *tr.* **a** appreciate and enjoy the taste of (food). **b** enjoy or appreciate (an experience, etc.). **2** *intr.* (foll. by *of*) **a** suggest by taste, smell, etc. (*savors of mushrooms*). **b** imply or suggest a specified quality (*savors of impertinence*). ▫▫ **sa·vor·less** *adj.*

sa·vor·y[1] /sáyvəree/ *n.* (*pl.* **-ies**) any herb of the genus *Satureia*, esp. *S. hortensis* and *S. montana*, used in cooking.

sa·vor·y[2] /sáyvəree/ *adj.* **1** having an appetizing taste or smell. **2** (of food) salty or piquant, not sweet (*a savory omelette*). **3** pleasant; acceptable. ▫▫ **sa·vor·i·ly** *adv.* **sa·vor·i·ness** *n.*

sa·voy /səvóy/ *n.* a hardy variety of cabbage with wrinkled leaves.

sav·vy /sávee/ *v.*, *n.*, & *adj. sl.* • *v.intr.* & *tr.* (**-vies, -vied**) know. • *n.* knowingness; shrewdness; understanding. • *adj.* (**savvier, savviest**) knowing; wise.

saw[1] /saw/ *n.* & *v.* • *n.* **1** a hand tool having a toothed blade used to cut esp. wood with a to-and-fro movement. **2** any of several power-driven devices with a toothed rotating disk or moving band, for cutting. **3** *Zool.* etc., a serrated organ or part. • *v.* (*past part.* **sawed** or **sawn** /sawn/) **1** *tr.* **a** cut (wood, etc.) with a saw. **b** make (boards, etc.) with a saw. **2** *intr.* use a saw. **3 a** *intr.* move back and forth with a motion as of a saw or person sawing (*sawing away on his violin*). **b** *tr.* divide (the air, etc.) with gesticulations. ▫▫ **saw·like** *adj.*

saw[2] *past* of SEE[1].

saw[3] /saw/ *n.* a proverb; a maxim (*that's just an old saw*).

saw·buck /sáwbuk/ *n. sl.* a $10 bill.

saw·dust /sáwdust/ *n.* powdery particles of wood produced in sawing.

saw-edged *adj.* with a jagged edge like a saw.

sawed-off *adj.* (also **sawn-off**) **1** (of a gun) having part of the barrel sawed off to make it easier to handle and give a wider field of fire. **2** *colloq.* (of a person) short.

saw·fish /sáwfish/ *n.* any large marine fish of the family Pristidae, with a toothed flat snout used as a weapon.

saw·horse /sáwhawrs/ *n.* a rack supporting wood for sawing.

saw·mill /sáwmil/ *n.* a factory in which wood is sawed mechanically into planks or boards.

sawn *past part.* of SAW[1].

saw·tooth /sáwtōōth/ *adj.* (also **saw·toothed** /–tōōtht/) shaped like the teeth of a saw with one steep and one slanting side.

saw-whet owl *n.* a small N. American owl, *Aegolius acadicus*, noted for its harsh cry.

saw·yer /sáwyər/ *n.* a person who saws lumber professionally.

sax /saks/ *n. colloq.* **1** a saxophone. **2** esp. *Brit.* a saxophone player. ▫▫ **sax·ist** *n.*

sax·horn /sáks-hawrn/ *n.* any of a series of different-sized brass wind instruments with valves and a funnel-shaped mouthpiece, used mainly in military and brass bands.

Sax·on /sáksən/ *n.* & *adj.* • *n.* **1** *hist.* **a** a member of the Germanic people that conquered parts of England in 5th–6th c. **b** (usu. **Old Saxon**) the language of the Saxons. **2** = ANGLO-SAXON. • *adj.* **1** *hist.* of or concerning the Saxons. **2** belonging to or originating from the Saxon language or Old English. ▫▫ **Sax·on·ize** /–nīz/ *v.tr.* & *intr.*

sax·o·phone /sáksəfōn/ *n.* a keyed brass reed instrument in several sizes and registers, used esp. in jazz and dance music. ▫▫ **sax·o·phon·ic** /–fónik/ *adj.* **sax·o·phon·ist** /–sófənist, –səfōnist/ *n.*

say /say/ *v.* & *n.* • *v.* (*3rd sing. present* **says** /sez/; *past* and *past part.* **said** /sed/) **1** *tr.* **a** utter (specified words) in a speaking voice; remark (*said "Damn!"*; *said that he was satisfied*). **b** express (*that was well said*; *cannot say what I feel*). **2** *tr.* **a** state; promise or prophesy (*says that there will be war*). **b** have specified wording; indicate (*says here that he was killed*; *the clock says ten to six*). **3** *tr.* (in *passive*; usu. foll. by *to* + infin.) be asserted or described (*is said to be 93 years old*). **4** *tr.* (foll. by *to* + infin.) *colloq.* tell a person to do something (*he said to bring the car*). **5** *tr.* convey (information) (*spoke for an hour but said little*). **6** *tr.* put forward as an argument or excuse (*much to be said in favor of it*; *what have you to say for yourself?*). **7** *tr.* (often *absol.*) form and give an opinion or decision as to (*who did it I cannot say*; *please say which you prefer*). **8** *tr.* select, assume, or take as an example or as near enough (*shall we say this one?*; *paid, say, $20*). **9** *tr.* **a** speak the words of (prayers, Mass, a grace, etc.). **b** repeat (a lesson, etc.); recite (*can't say his tables*). **10** *tr.* *Art*, etc. convey (inner meaning or intention) (*what is the director saying in this film?*). **11** *tr.* (**the said**) *Law* or *joc.* the previously mentioned (*the said witness*). **12** *intr.* (as *int.*) an exclamation of surprise, to attract attention, etc. • *n.* **1 a** an opportunity for stating one's opinion, etc. (*let him have his say*). **b** a stated opinion. **2** a share in a decision (*had no say in the matter*). ▫ **how say you?** *Law* how do you find? (addressed to the jury requesting its verdict). **I, etc., cannot** (or **could not**) **say** I, etc., do not know. **I'll say** *colloq.* yes indeed. **it is said** the rumor is that. **not to say** or possibly even (*his language was rude, not to say offensive*). **said he** (or **I**, etc.) *colloq.* or *poet.* he, etc., said. **say for oneself** say by way of conversation, etc. **say much** (or **something**) **for** indicate the high quality of. **say no** refuse or disagree. **says you!** *colloq.* I disagree. **say when** *colloq.* indicate when enough drink or food has been given. **say the word 1** indicate that you agree or give permission. **2** give the order, etc. **that is to say 1** in other words, more explicitly. **2** or at least. **they say** it is rumored. **to say nothing of** = *not to mention* (see MENTION). **when all is said and done** after all; in the long run. **you can say that again!** (or **you said it!**) *colloq.* I agree emphatically. **you don't say so** *colloq.* an expression of amazement or disbelief. ▫▫ **say·a·ble** *adj.* **say·er** *n.*

say·ing /sáying/ *n.* **1** the act or an instance of saying. **2** a maxim, proverb, etc. ▫ **as the saying goes** (or **is**) an expression used in introducing a proverb, cliché, etc. **go without saying** be too well known or obvious to need mention. **there is no saying** it is impossible to know.

say-so *n.* **1** the power of decision. **2** mere assertion (*cannot proceed merely on his say-so*).
Sb *symb. Chem.* the element antimony.
SBA *abbr.* Small Business Administration.
SC *abbr.* South Carolina (also in official postal use).
Sc *symb. Chem.* the element scandium.
s.c. *abbr.* small capitals.
scab /skab/ *n.* & *v.* • *n.* **1** a dry rough crust formed over a cut, sore, etc., in healing. **2** (often *attrib.*) *colloq. derog.* a person who refuses to strike or join a trade union, or who tries to break a strike by working. **3** a skin disease, esp. in animals. **4** a fungus plant disease causing scablike roughness. **5** a dislikeable person. • *v.intr.* (**scabbed, scabbing**) **1** act as a scab. **2** (of a wound, etc.) form a scab; heal over. ▫▫ **scabbed** *adj.* **scab·by** *adj.* (**scabbier, scabbiest**). **scab·bi·ness** *n.* **scab·like** *adj.*
scab·bard /skábərd/ *n.* **1** *hist.* a sheath for a sword, bayonet, etc. **2** a sheath for a revolver, etc.
sca·bies /skáybeez/ *n.* a contagious skin disease causing severe itching.
scab·rous /skábrəs, skáy–/ *adj.* **1** having a rough surface; bearing short stiff hairs, scales, etc. **2** (of a subject, situation, etc.) requiring tactful treatment. **3 a** indecent; salacious. **b** behaving licentiously. ▫▫ **scab·rous·ly** *adv.* **scab·rous·ness** *n.*
scad /skad/ *n.* any fish of the family Carangidae native to tropical and subtropical seas, usu. having an elongated body and very large spiky scales.
scads /skadz/ *n.pl. colloq.* large quantities.
scaf·fold /skáfəld, –fōld/ *n.* & *v.* • *n.* **1** *hist.* a platform used for the execution of criminals. **2** = SCAFFOLDING. **3** (prec. by *the*) death by execution. • *v.tr.* attach scaffolding to (a building). ▫▫ **scaf·fold·er** *n.*
scaf·fold·ing /skáfəlding, –fōlding/ *n.* **1** a temporary structure formed of poles, planks, etc., erected by workers and used by them while building or repairing a house, etc. **2** materials used for this.
scal·a·ble /skáyləbəl/ *adj.* **1** capable of being scaled or climbed. **2** *Computing* capable of being used in a range of sizes. ▫▫ **scal·a·bil·i·ty** /–bílitee/ *n.*
sca·lar /skáylər/ *adj.* & *n. Math.* & *Physics* • *adj.* (of a quantity) having only magnitude, not direction. • *n.* a scalar quantity (cf. VECTOR).
scal·a·wag /skáləwag/ *n.* (also **scal·ly·wag**) **1** a scamp; a rascal. **2** *US hist.* a white Southerner who supported Reconstructionists usu. for personal profit.
scald[1] /skawld/ *v.* & *n.* • *v.tr.* **1** burn (the skin, etc.) with hot liquid or steam. **2** heat (esp. milk) to near boiling point. **3** (usu. foll. by *out*) clean (a pan, etc.) by rinsing with boiling water. • *n.* a burn, etc., caused by scalding.
scald[2] var. of SKALD.
scale[1] /skayl/ *n.* & *v.* • *n.* **1** each of the small, thin, overlapping plates protecting the skin of fish and reptiles. **2** something resembling a fish scale, esp. a flake of skin. **3** a thick, white deposit formed in a kettle, boiler, etc., by the action of heat on water. **4** plaque formed on teeth. • *v.* **1** *tr.* remove scale or scales from (fish, etc.). **2** *tr.* remove plaque from (teeth) by scraping. **3** *intr.* (of skin, etc.) form, come off in, or drop, scales. ▫ **scales fall from a person's eyes** a person is no longer deceived (cf. Acts 9:18). ▫▫ **scaled** *adj.* (also in *comb.*). **scale·less** *adj.* **scal·er** *n.*
scale[2] /skayl/ *n.* **1 a** (often in *pl.*) a weighing machine or device (*bathroom scales*). **b** (also **scale·pan**) each of the dishes on a simple scale balance. **2** (**the Scales**) the zodiacal sign or constellation Libra. ▫ **throw into the scale** cause to be a factor in a contest, debate, etc. **tip** (or **turn**) **the scales 1** (usu. foll. by *at*) outweigh the opposite scalepan (at a specified weight); weigh. **2** (of a motive, circumstance, etc.) be decisive.
scale[3] /skayl/ *n.* & *v.* • *n.* **1** a series of degrees; a graded classification system (*high on the social scale*; *seven points on the Richter scale*). **2 a** (often *attrib.*) *Geog.* & *Archit.* a ratio of size in a map, model, picture, etc. (*on a scale of one inch to the mile*; *a scale model*). **b** relative dimensions or degree (*generosity on a grand scale*). **3** *Mus.* an arrangement of all the notes in any system of music in ascending or descending order. **4 a** a set of marks on a line used in measuring, reducing, enlarging, etc. **b** a rule determining the distances between these. **c** a piece of metal, apparatus, etc., on which these are marked. **5** (in full **scale of notation**) *Math.* the ratio between units in a numerical system (*decimal scale*). • *v.* **1** *tr.* **a** climb (a wall, height, etc.) esp. with a ladder. **b** climb (the social scale, heights of ambition, etc.). **2** *tr.* represent in proportional dimensions; reduce to a common scale. **3** *intr.* (of quantities, etc.) have a common scale; be commensurable. ▫ **in scale** (of drawing, etc.) in proportion to the surroundings, etc. **scale down** make smaller in proportion; reduce in size. **scale up** make larger in proportion; increase in size. **to scale** with a uniform reduction or enlargement. ▫▫ **scal·er** *n.*

scale late Middle English (in the senses 'ladder' and 'climb with a scaling ladder'): from Latin *scala* 'ladder' (the verb via Old French *escaler* or medieval Latin *scalare*), from the base of Latin *scandere* 'to climb.'

scale in·sect *n.* any of various insects, esp. of the family Coccidae, clinging to plants and secreting a shieldlike scale as covering.
sca·lene /skáyleen/ *adj.* (esp. of a triangle) having sides unequal in length.
sca·le·nus /skəleénəs/ *n.* (*pl.* **scaleni** /–nī/) any of several muscles extending from the neck to the first and second ribs.
scal·lion /skályən/ *n.* a shallot or spring onion; any long-necked onion with a small bulb.
scal·lop /skáləp, skól–/ *n.* & *v.* (also **scol·lop** /skól–/) • *n.* **1** any of various bivalve mollusks of the family Pectinidae, esp. of the genus *Chlamys* or *Pecten*, much prized as food. **2** (in full **scallop shell**) a single valve from the shell of a scallop, often used for cooking or serving food. **3** (in *pl.*) an ornamental edging cut in material in imitation of a scallop edge. • *v.tr.* (**scalloped, scalloping**) **1** cook in a scallop. **2** ornament (an edge or material) with scallops or scalloping. ▫▫ **scal·lop·er** *n.* **scal·lop·ing** *n.* (in sense 3 of *n.*).

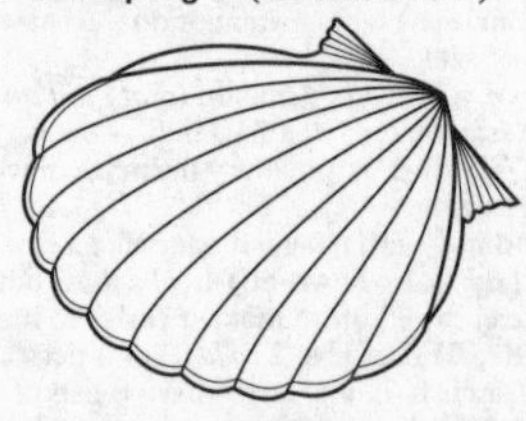
scallop, 2

scal·ly·wag var. of SCALAWAG.
scalp /skalp/ *n.* & *v.* • *n.* **1** the skin covering the top of the head, with the hair, etc., attached. **2** *hist.* the scalp of an enemy cut or torn away as a trophy by a Native American. • *v.tr.* **1** *hist.* take the scalp of (an enemy). **2** defeat; humiliate. **3** *colloq.* resell (shares, tickets, etc.) at a high or quick profit. ▫▫ **scalp·er** *n.* **scalp·less** *adj.*
scal·pel /skálpəl/ *n.* a surgeon's small sharp knife.
scal·y /skáylee/ *adj.* (**scalier, scaliest**) covered in scales. ▫▫ **scal·i·ness** *n.*

scam /skam/ *n. sl.* a trick or swindle; a fraud.

scamp /skamp/ *n. colloq.* a rascal; a rogue. ▫▫ **scamp·ish** *adj.*

scamp·er /skámpər/ *v. & n.* • *v.intr.* (usu. foll. by *about, through*) run and skip impulsively or playfully. • *n.* the act or an instance of scampering.

scam·pi /skámpee/ *n.pl.* **1** large shrimp. **2** (often treated as *sing.*) a dish of these sautéed in garlic butter.

scan /skan/ *v. & n.* • *v.* (**scanned, scanning**) **1** *tr.* look at intently or quickly (*scanned the horizon; scanned the speech for errors*). **2** *intr.* (of a verse, etc.) be metrically correct (*this line doesn't scan*). **3** *tr.* **a** examine all parts of (a surface, etc.) to detect radioactivity, etc. **b** cause (a particular region) to be traversed by a radar, etc., beam. **4** *tr.* resolve (a picture) into its elements of light and shade in a prearranged pattern for the purposes, esp. of television transmission. **5** *tr.* test the meter of (a line of verse, etc.) by reading with the emphasis on its rhythm, or by examining the number of feet, etc. **6** *tr.* make a scan of (the body or part of it). • *n.* **1** the act or an instance of scanning. **2** an image obtained by scanning or with a scanner. ▫▫ **scan·na·ble** *adj.*

scan·dal /skánd'l/ *n.* **1** a thing or a person causing public outrage or indignation. **2** the outrage, etc., so caused. **3** malicious gossip or backbiting. ▫▫ **scan·dal·ous** *adj.* **scan·dal·ous·ly** *adv.* **scan·dal·ous·ness** *n.*

---

scandal Middle English (in the sense 'one who discredits religion (by reprehensible behavior)'): from Old French *scandale,* from ecclesiastical Latin *scandalum* 'cause of offense,' from Greek *skandalon* 'snare, stumbling block.'

---

scan·dal·ize /skándəlīz/ *v.tr.* offend the moral feelings, sensibilities, etc., of.

scan·dal·mon·ger /skánd'lmənggər, –monggər/ *n.* a person who spreads malicious scandal.

scan·dal sheet *n. derog.* a newspaper, etc., giving prominence to esp. malicious gossip.

Scan·di·na·vi·an /skándináyveeən/ *n. & adj.* • *n.* **1 a** a native or inhabitant of Scandinavia (Denmark, Norway, Sweden, and sometimes Finland and Iceland). **b** a person of Scandinavian descent. **2** the family of languages of Scandinavia. • *adj.* of or relating to Scandinavia or its people or languages.

scan·di·um /skándeeəm/ *n. Chem.* a rare, soft, silver-white metallic element occurring naturally in lanthanide ores.

scan·ner /skánər/ *n.* **1 a** a device for scanning or systematically examining something. **b** a device for monitoring several radio frequencies, esp. police or emergency frequencies. **2** a machine for measuring the intensity of radiation, ultrasound reflections, etc., from the body as a diagnostic aid.

scan·sion /skánshən/ *n.* **1** the metrical scanning of verse. **2** the way a verse, etc., scans.

scant /skant/ *adj.* barely sufficient; deficient (*scant regard for the truth*). ▫▫ **scant·ly** *adv.* **scant·ness** *n.*

scant·y /skántee/ *adj.* (**scantier, scantiest**) **1** of small extent or amount. **2** barely sufficient. ▫▫ **scant·i·ly** *adv.* **scant·i·ness** *n.*

-scape /skayp/ *comb. form* forming nouns denoting a view or a representation of a view (*seascape*).

scape·goat /skáypgōt/ *n. & v.* • *n.* a person bearing the blame for the sins, shortcomings, etc., of others. • *v.tr.* make a scapegoat of. ▫▫ **scape·goat·er** *n.*

scape·grace /skáypgrays/ *n.* a rascal; a scamp, esp. a young person or child.

scap·u·la /skápyələ/ *n.* (*pl.* **scapulae** /–lee/ or **scapulas**) the shoulder blade.

scap·u·lar /skápyələr/ *adj. & n.* • *adj.* of or relating to the shoulder or shoulder blade. • *n.* a monastic short cloak.

scar[1] /skaar/ *n. & v.* • *n.* **1** a usu. permanent mark on the skin left after the healing of a wound, burn, or sore. **2** the lasting effect of grief, etc., on a person. **3** a mark left by damage, etc. (*the table bore many scars*). **4** a mark left on the stem, etc., of a plant by the fall of a leaf, etc. • *v.* (**scarred, scarring**) **1** *tr.* (esp. as **scarred** *adj.*) mark with a scar or scars (*scarred for life*). **2** *intr.* heal over; form a scar. **3** *tr.* form a scar on. ▫▫ **scar·less** *adj.*

scar[2] /skaar/ *n.* a steep craggy outcrop of a mountain or cliff.

scar·ab /skárəb/ *n.* **1** the sacred dung beetle of ancient Egypt. **2** an ancient Egyptian gem cut in the form of a beetle and engraved with symbols on its flat side.

scarce /skairs/ *adj. & adv.* • *adj.* **1** (usu. *predic.*) (esp. of food, money, etc.) insufficient for the demand. **2** hard to find; rare. • *adv. archaic* or *literary* scarcely. ▫ **make oneself scarce** *colloq.* keep out of the way; surreptitiously disappear. ▫▫ **scarce·ness** *n.*

scarce·ly /skáirslee/ *adv.* **1** hardly; only just (*I scarcely know her*). **2** surely not (*he can scarcely have said so*). **3** a mild or apologetic or ironical substitute for "not" (*I scarcely expected to be insulted*).

scar·ci·ty /skáirsitee/ *n.* (*pl.* **-ties**) (often foll. by *of*) a lack or inadequacy.

scare /skair/ *v. & n.* • *v.* **1** *tr.* frighten, esp. suddenly (*his expression scared us*). **2** *tr.* (as **scared** *adj.*) (usu. foll. by *of,* or *to* + infin.) frightened; terrified (*scared of his own shadow*). **3** *tr.* (usu. foll. by *away, off, up,* etc.) drive away by frightening. **4** *intr.* become scared (*they don't scare easily*). • *n.* **1** a sudden attack of fright (*gave me a scare*). **2** a general, esp. baseless, fear of war, invasion, epidemic, etc. (*a measles scare*). ▫ **scare up** (or **out**) **1** frighten (game, etc.) out of cover. **2** *colloq.* manage to find (*see if we can scare up a meal*). ▫▫ **scar·er** *n.*

scare·crow /skáirkrō/ *n.* **1** a human figure dressed in old clothes and set up in a field to scare birds away. **2** *colloq.* a badly dressed, grotesque-looking, or very thin person.

scared·y-cat /skáirdeekat/ *n. colloq.* a timid person.

scare·mon·ger /skáirmunggər, –monggər/ *n.* a person who spreads frightening reports or rumors. ▫▫ **scare·mon·ger·ing** *n.*

scarf[1] /skaarf/ *n.* (*pl.* **scarfs** or **scarves** /skaarvz/) a square, triangular, or esp. long narrow strip of material worn around the neck, over the shoulders, or tied around the head for warmth or ornament. ▫▫ **scarfed** *adj.*

scarf[2] /skaarf/ *v. & n.* • *v.tr.* join the ends of (pieces of esp. lumber, metal, or leather) by beveling or notching them to fit and then bolting, brazing, or sewing them together. • *n.* a joint made by scarfing.

scarf[3] /skaarf/ *v.tr. & intr.* (often foll. by *up* or *down*) eat, esp. quickly, voraciously, greedily, etc.

scar·i·fy[1] /skárifī, skáir–/ *v.tr.* (**-fies, -fied**) **1 a** make superficial incisions in. **b** cut off skin from. **2** hurt by severe criticism, etc. **3** loosen (soil) with a scarifier. ▫▫ **scar·i·fi·ca·tion** /–fikáyshən/ *n.*

scar·i·fy[2] /skáirifī/ *v.tr. & intr.* (**-fies, -fied**) *colloq.* scare; terrify.

scar·i·ous /skáireeəs/ *adj.* (of a part of a plant, etc.) having a dry membranous appearance; thin and brittle.

scar·la·ti·na /skaárlətéenə/ *n.* = SCARLET FEVER.

scar·let /skaárlit/ *n. & adj.* • *n.* **1** a brilliant red color tinged with orange. **2** clothes or material of this color (*dressed in scarlet*). • *adj.* of a scarlet color.

scar·let fe·ver *n.* an infectious bacterial fever, affecting esp. children, with a scarlet rash.

scar·let pim·per·nel *n.* a small annual wild plant, *Anagallis arvensis,* with small, esp. scarlet, flowers closing in rainy or cloudy weather: also called *poor man's weather-glass*.

scar·let wom·an *n. derog.* a notoriously promiscuous woman; a prostitute.

scarp /skaarp/ *n. & v.* •*n.* **1** the inner wall or slope of a ditch in a fortification. **2** a steep slope. •*v.tr.* make (a slope) perpendicular or steep.

scar·us /skáirəs/ *n.* any fish of the genus *Scarus*, with brightly colored scales, and teeth fused to form a parrotlike beak used for eating coral. Also called PARROT FISH.

scarves *pl.* of SCARF[1].

scar·y /skáiree/ *adj.* (**scarier, scariest**) *colloq.* frightening. ▫▫ **scar·i·ly** *adv.*

scat[1] /skat/ *v. & int. colloq.* •*v.intr.* (**scatted, scatting**) depart quickly. •*int.* go!

scat[2] /skat/ *n. & v.* •*n.* improvised jazz singing using sounds imitating instruments, instead of words. •*v.intr.* (**scatted, scatting**) sing scat.

scathe /skayth/ *v. & n.* •*v.tr.* **1** *poet.* injure esp. by blasting or withering. **2** (as **scathing** *adj.*) witheringly scornful (*scathing sarcasm*). •*n.* (usu. with *neg.*) *archaic* harm; injury (*without scathe*). ▫▫ **scathe·less** *predic. adj.* **scath·ing·ly** *adv.*

sca·tol·o·gy /skatóləjee, skə–/ *n.* **1** a morbid interest in excrement. **2** a preoccupation with obscene literature, esp. that concerned with the excretory functions. **3** such literature. ▫▫ **scat·o·log·i·cal** /–təlójikəl/ *adj.*

sca·toph·a·gous /skatófəgəs/ *adj.* feeding on dung.

scat·ter /skátər/ *v. & n.* •*v.* **1** *tr.* **a** throw here and there (*scattered gravel on the road*). **b** cover by scattering (*scattered the road with gravel*). **2** *tr. & intr.* **a** move or cause to move in flight, etc. (*scattered to safety at the sound*). **b** disperse or cause (hopes, clouds, etc.) to disperse. **3** *tr.* (as **scattered** *adj.*) not clustered together; wide apart (*scattered villages*). **4** *tr. Physics* deflect or diffuse (light, particles, etc.). **5 a** *intr.* (of esp. a shotgun) fire a charge of shot diffusely. **b** *tr.* fire (a charge) in this way. •*n.* **1** the act or an instance of scattering. **2** a small amount scattered. **3** the extent of distribution of esp. shot. ▫▫ **scat·ter·er** *n.*

scat·ter·brain /skátərbrayn/ *n.* a person given to silly or disorganized thought with lack of concentration. ▫▫ **scat·ter·brained** *adj.*

scat·ter·shot /skátərshot/ *n. & adj.* firing at random.

scav·enge /skávinj/ *v.* **1** *tr. & intr.* (usu. foll. by *for*) search for and collect (discarded items). **2** *tr.* remove unwanted products from (an internal-combustion engine cylinder, etc.). **3** *intr.* feed on carrion.

scav·en·ger /skávinjər/ *n.* **1** a person who seeks and collects discarded items. **2** an animal feeding on carrion. ▫▫ **sca·ven·ger·y** *n.*

sce·nar·i·o /sináreeō, –naáreeō/ *n.* (*pl.* **-os**) **1** an outline of the plot of a play, film, opera, etc., with details of the scenes, situations, etc. **2** a postulated sequence of future events. ▫▫ **sce·nar·ist** *n.* (in sense 1).

▶The proper meaning of this word is 'an outline of a plot' or 'a postulated sequence of events.' It should not be used loosely to mean 'situation,' e.g., *a nightmare scenario*.

scene /seen/ *n.* **1** a place in which events in real life, drama, or fiction occur; the locality of an event, etc. (*the scene was set in India*; *the scene of the disaster*). **2 a** an incident in real life, fiction, etc. (*distressing scenes occurred*). **b** a description or representation of an incident, etc. (*scenes of clerical life*). **3** a public incident displaying emotion, temper, etc. (*made a scene in the restaurant*). **4 a** a continuous portion of a play in a fixed setting and usu. without a change of personnel; a subdivision of an act. **b** a similar section of a film, book, etc. **5 a** any of the pieces of scenery used in a play. **b** these collectively. **6** a landscape or a view (*a desolate scene*). **7** *colloq.* **a** an area of action or interest (*not my scene*). **b** a way of life; a milieu (*well-known on the jazz scene*). ▫ **behind the scenes 1** *Theatr.* among the actors, scenery, etc., offstage. **2** unknown to the public; secret(ly). **come on the scene** arrive. **quit the scene** die; leave. **set the scene 1** describe the location of events. **2** give preliminary information.

scen·er·y /séenəree/ *n.* **1** the general appearance of the natural features of a landscape, esp. when picturesque. **2** *Theatr.* the painted representations of landscape, rooms, etc., used as the background in a play, etc.

sce·nic /séenik/ *adj.* **1 a** picturesque; impressive or beautiful (*took the scenic route*). **b** of or concerning natural scenery (*hills are the main scenic feature*). **2** (of a picture, etc.) representing an incident. ▫▫ **sce·ni·cal·ly** *adv.*

scent /sent/ *n. & v.* •*n.* **1** a distinctive, esp. pleasant, smell. **2 a** a scent trail left by an animal perceptible to hounds, etc. **b** clues, etc., that can be followed like a scent trail (*lost the scent in Paris*). **c** the power of detecting or distinguishing smells, etc., or of discovering things (*some dogs have little scent*; *the scent for talent*). •*v.* **1** *tr.* **a** discern by scent (*the dog scented game*). **b** sense the presence of (*scent treachery*). **2** *tr.* make fragrant or foul-smelling. **3** *tr.* (as **scented** *adj.*) having esp. a pleasant smell (*scented soap*). ▫ **on the scent** having a clue. **put** (or **throw**) **off the scent** deceive by false clues, etc. **scent out** discover by smelling or searching. ▫▫ **scent·less** *adj.*

scent gland *n.* (also **scent or·gan**) a gland in some musk-secreting animals such as civets or skunks.

scep·ter /séptər/ *n.* a staff borne esp. at a coronation as a symbol of sovereignty. ▫▫ **scep·tered** *adj.*

scha·den·freu·de /shaád'nfroydə/ *n.* the malicious enjoyment of another's misfortunes.

sched·ule /skéjōōl, –ōōəl/ *n. & v.* •*n.* **1 a** a list or plan of intended events, times, etc. **b** a plan of work. **2** a list of rates or prices. **3** a timetable. **4** a tabulated inventory. •*v.tr.* **1** include in a schedule. **2** make a schedule of. ▫▫ **sched·ul·er** *n.*

---

schedule late Middle English (in the sense 'scroll, explanatory note, appendix'): from Old French *cedule*, from late Latin *schedula* 'slip of paper,' diminutive of *scheda*, from Greek *skhedē* 'papyrus leaf.' The verb dates from the mid-19th century.

---

sche·ma /skéemə/ *n.* (*pl.* **schemata** /–mətə/ or **schemas**) **1** a synopsis, outline, or diagram. **2** a proposed arrangement.

sche·mat·ic /skimátik, skee–/ *adj. & n.* •*adj.* **1** of or concerning a scheme or schema. **2** representing objects by symbols, etc. •*n.* a schematic diagram, esp. of an electronic circuit. ▫▫ **sche·mat·i·cal·ly** *adv.*

scheme /skeem/ *n. & v.* •*n.* **1 a** a systematic plan or arrangement. **b** a proposed or operational systematic arrangement (*a color scheme*). **2** an artful or deceitful plot. **3** a timetable, outline, syllabus, etc. •*v.* **1** *intr.* (often foll. by *for*, or *to* + infin.) plan esp. secretly or deceitfully. **2** *tr.* plan to bring about, esp. artfully or deceitfully (*schemed their downfall*). ▫▫ **schem·er** *n.*

---

scheme mid-16th century (denoting a figure of speech): from Latin *schema*, from Greek. An early sense included 'horoscope, representation of the position of celestial objects,' giving rise to 'diagram, design,' whence the current senses. The unfavorable notion 'plot' arose in the early 18th century.

---

schem·ing /skéeming/ *adj. & n.* •*adj.* artful, cunning, or deceitful. •*n.* plots; intrigues. ▫▫ **schem·ing·ly** *adv.*

scher·zan·do /skairtsaándō/ *adv., adj., & n. Mus.* •*adv. & adj.* in a playful manner. •*n.* (*pl.* **scherzandos** or **scherzandi** /–dee/) a passage played in this way.

scher·zo /skáirtsō/ *n.* (*pl.* **-zos**) *Mus.* a vigorous, light, or playful composition, usu. as a movement in a symphony, sonata, etc.
schil·ling /shíling/ *n.* **1** the chief monetary unit of Austria. **2** a coin equal to the value of one schilling.
schism /sízəm, skíz–/ *n.* **1** the division of a group into opposing sections or parties. **2** any of the sections so formed.
schis·mat·ic /sizmátik, skiz–/ *adj. & n.* (also **schis·mat·i·cal**) • *adj.* inclining to, concerning, or guilty of, schism. • *n.* **1** a holder of schismatic opinions. **2** a member of a schismatic faction or a seceded branch of a church. ▫▫ **schis·mat·i·cal·ly** *adv.*
schist /shist/ *n.* a foliated metamorphic rock composed of layers of different minerals and splitting into thin irregular plates. ▫▫ **schis·tose** *adj.*
schi·zan·thus /skizánthəs/ *n.* any plant of the genus *Schizanthus*, with showy flowers in various colors, and finely divided leaves.
schiz·o /skítsō/ *adj. & n. colloq.* • *adj.* schizophrenic. • *n.* (*pl.* **-os**) a schizophrenic.
schiz·o·carp /skízəkaarp, skítsə;n–/ *n. Bot.* any of a group of dry fruits that split into single-seeded parts when ripe. ▫▫ **schiz·o·car·pic** /–kaárpik/ *adj.* **schiz·o·car·pous** /–kaárpəs/ *adj.*
schiz·oid /skítsoyd/ *adj. & n.* • *adj.* (of a person or personality, etc.) tending to schizophrenia, but usu. without delusions. • *n.* a schizoid person.
schiz·o·phre·ni·a /skítsəfreéneeə, –fréneeə/ *n.* a mental disease marked by a breakdown in the relation between thoughts, feelings, and actions, frequently accompanied by delusions and retreat from social life. ▫▫ **schiz·o·phren·ic** /–frénik/ *adj. & n.*
schle·miel /shləmeél/ *n. colloq.* a foolish or unlucky person.
schlep /shlep/ *v. & n.* (also **schlepp**) *colloq.* • *v.* (**schlepped, schlepping**) **1** *tr.* carry; drag. **2** *intr.* go or work tediously or effortfully. • *n.* a person or thing that is tedious, awkward, or slow.
schlock /shlok/ *n. colloq.* inferior goods; trash.
schmaltz /shmaalts/ *n. colloq.* sentimentality, esp. in music, drama, etc. ▫▫ **schmaltz·y** *adj.* (**schmaltzier, schmaltziest**).
schmuck /shmuk/ *n. sl.* a foolish or contemptible person.
schnapps /shnaaps, shnaps/ *n.* any of various spirits drunk in N. Europe.
schnau·zer /shnówzər, shnówtsər/ *n.* **1** a dog of a German breed with a close wiry coat and heavy whiskers around the muzzle. **2** this breed.
schnit·zel /shnítsəl/ *n.* a cutlet of veal.
schol·ar /skólər/ *n.* **1** a learned person, esp. in language, literature, etc.; an academic. **2** the holder of a scholarship. **3** a person with specified academic ability (*a poor scholar*). ▫▫ **schol·ar·ly** *adj.* **schol·ar·li·ness** *n.*
schol·ar·ship /skólərship/ *n.* **1 a** academic achievement; learning of a high level. **b** the methods and standards characteristic of a good scholar (*shows great scholarship*). **2** payment from the funds of a school, university, local government, etc., to maintain a student in full-time education, awarded on the basis of scholarly achievement.
scho·las·tic /skəlástik/ *adj.* of or concerning universities, schools, education, teachers, etc. ▫▫ **scho·las·ti·cal·ly** *adv.* **scho·las·ti·cism** /–tisizəm/ *n.*
school[1] /skool/ *n. & v.* • *n.* **1 a** an institution for educating or giving instruction at any level including college or university. **b** (*attrib.*) associated with or for use in school (*a school bag; school dinners*). **2 a** the buildings used by such an institution. **b** the pupils, staff, etc., of a school. **c** the time during which teaching is done, or the teaching itself (*no school today*). **3** a university department or faculty (*the history school*). **4 a** the disciples, imitators, or followers of a philosopher, artist, etc. **b** a group of artists, etc., whose works share distinctive characteristics. **c** a group of people sharing a cause, principle, method, etc. (*school of thought*). **5** *colloq.* instructive or disciplinary circumstances, occupation, etc. (*the school of adversity; learned in a hard school*). • *v.tr.* **1** send to school; provide for the education of. **2** (often foll. by *to*) discipline; train. **3** (as **schooled** *adj.*) (foll. by *in*) educated or trained (*schooled in humility*). **of the old school** according to former and esp. better tradition.
school[2] /skool/ *n. & v.* • *n.* (often foll. by *of*) a shoal of fish, porpoises, whales, etc. • *v.intr.* form schools.
school·a·ble /skóoləbəl/ *adj.* liable by age, etc., to compulsory education.
school age *n.* the age range in which children normally attend school.
school board *n.* a board or authority for local education.
school·boy /skóolboy/ *n.* a boy attending school.
school·child /skóolchīld/ *n.* a child attending school.
school days *n.pl.* the time of being at school, esp. in retrospect.
school·girl /skóolgərl/ *n.* a girl attending school.
school·house /skóolhows/ *n.* a building used as a school.
school·ing /skóoling/ *n.* **1** education, esp. at school. **2** training or discipline, esp. of an animal.
school·marm /skóolmaarm/ *n. colloq.* (also **school·ma'am** /–maam/) a female schoolteacher. ▫▫ **school·marm·ish** *adj.*
school·mas·ter /skóolmastər/ *n.* a male teacher. ▫▫ **school·mas·ter·ly** *adj.*
school·mate /skóolmayt/ *n.* a past or esp. present member of the same school.
school·mis·tress /skóolmistris/ *n.* a head or assistant female teacher.
school of hard knocks *n.* experience gained from hard work, tough circumstances, etc.
school·room /skóolrōom, –rōom/ *n.* a room used for lessons in a school.
school·teach·er /skóolteechər/ *n.* a person who teaches in a school. ▫▫ **school·teach·ing** *n.*
school year *n.* = ACADEMIC YEAR.
schoon·er /skóonər/ *n.* **1** a fore-and-aft rigged ship with two or more masts, the foremast being smaller than the other masts. **2** a tall beer glass. **3** *US hist.* = PRAIRIE SCHOONER.
schot·tische /shótish, shoteésh/ *n.* **1** a kind of slow polka. **2** the music for this.
Schott·ky effect /shótkee/ *n. Electronics* the increase in thermionic emission from a solid surface due to the presence of an external electric field.
schuss /shoos/ *n. & v.* • *n.* a straight downhill run on skis. • *v.intr.* make a schuss.
schwa /schwaa/ *n.* (also **sheva** /shəva/) *Phonet.* **1** the indistinct unstressed vowel sound as in *a* moment *a*go. **2** the symbol /ə/ representing this in the International Phonetic Alphabet.
sci·at·ic /sīátik/ *adj.* **1** of the hip. **2** of or affecting the sciatic nerve. **3** suffering from or liable to sciatica. ▫▫ **sci·at·i·cal·ly** *adv.*
sci·at·i·ca /sīátikə/ *n.* neuralgia of the hip and thigh; a pain in the sciatic nerve.
sci·at·ic nerve *n.* the largest nerve in the body, running from the pelvis to the thigh.
sci·ence /sīəns/ *n.* **1** a branch of knowledge involving the systematized observation of and experiment with

phenomena (see also NATURAL SCIENCE). **2 a** systematic and formulated knowledge, esp. of a specified type or on a specified subject (*political science*). **b** the pursuit or principles of this.

sci•ence fic•tion *n.* fiction based on imagined future scientific discoveries or environmental changes, frequently dealing with space travel, life on other planets, etc.

sci•ence park *n.* an area devoted to scientific research or the development of science-based industries.

sci•en•tif•ic /sīəntífik/ *adj.* **1 a** (of an investigation, etc.) according to rules laid down in exact science for performing observations and testing the soundness of conclusions. **b** systematic; accurate. **2** used in, engaged in, or relating to (esp. natural) science (*scientific discoveries*). ▫▫ **sci•en•tif•i•cal•ly** *adv.*

sci•en•tism /síəntizəm/ *n.* **1 a** a method or doctrine regarded as characteristic of scientists. **b** the use or practice of this. **2** often *derog.* an excessive belief in or application of scientific method. ▫▫ **sci•en•tis•tic** /–tístik/ *adj.*

sci•en•tist /sīəntist/ *n.* a person with expert knowledge of a (usu. physical or natural) science.

Sci•en•tol•o•gy /sīəntólajee/ *n.* a religious system based on self-improvement and promotion through grades of esp. self-knowledge. ▫▫ **Sci•en•tol•o•gist** *n.*

sci-fi /sīfī/ *n.* (often *attrib.*) *colloq.* science fiction.

scil•i•cet /skeéliket, sīliset/ *adv.* that is to say; namely (introducing a word to be supplied or an explanation of an ambiguity).

scil•la /sílə/ *n.* any liliaceous plant of the genus *Scilla*, related to the bluebell, usu. bearing small blue star-shaped or bell-shaped flowers and having long, glossy, straplike leaves.

scim•i•tar /símitər, –taar/ *n.* an Oriental curved sword usu. broadening toward the point.

scin•ti•gram /síntigram/ *n.* an image of an internal part of the body, produced by scintigraphy.

scin•tig•ra•phy /sintígrəfee/ *n.* the use of a radioisotope and a scintillation counter to get an image or record of a bodily organ, etc.

scin•til•la /sintílə/ *n.* **1** a trace. **2** a spark.

scin•til•late /síntilayt/ *v.intr.* **1** (esp. as **scintillating** *adj.*) talk cleverly or wittily; be brilliant. **2** sparkle; twinkle. ▫▫ **scin•til•lant** *adj.* **scin•til•lat•ing•ly** *adv.*

scin•til•la•tion /síntiláyshən/ *n.* **1** the process of scintillating. **2** the twinkling of a star. **3** a flash produced in a material by an ionizing particle, etc.

sci•on /sīən/ *n.* **1** (also **cion**) a shoot of a plant, etc., esp. one cut for grafting or planting. **2** a descendant; a younger member of (esp. a noble) family.

sci•roc•co var. of SIROCCO.

scis•sile /sísil, –īl/ *adj.* able to be cut or divided.

scis•sion /sízhən, síshən–/ *n.* **1** the act or an instance of cutting; the state of being cut. **2** a division or split.

scis•sor /sízər/ *v.tr.* **1** (usu. foll. by *off, up, into*, etc.) cut with scissors. **2** (usu. foll. by *out*) clip out (a newspaper cutting, etc.).

scis•sors /sízərz/ *n.pl.* **1** (also **pair of scissors** *sing.*) an instrument for cutting fabric, paper, hair, etc., having two pivoted blades with finger and thumb holes in the handles, operating by closing on the material to be cut. **2** (treated as *sing.*) a hold in wrestling in which the opponent's body or esp. head is gripped between the legs. ▫▫ **scis•sor•wise** *adv.*

scle•ra /skleérə/ *n.* the white of the eye; a white membrane coating the eyeball. ▫▫ **scle•ral** *adj.* **scle•ri•tis** /skleerītis/ *n.* **scle•rot•o•my** /–rótəmee/ *n.* (*pl.* **-mies**).

scle•ro•ma /sklərṓmə/ *n.* (*pl.* **scleromata** /–mətə/) an abnormal patch of hardened skin or mucous membrane.

scle•rom•e•ter /sklərómitər/ *n.* an instrument for determining the hardness of materials.

scle•ro•sis /sklərṓsis/ *n.* **1** an abnormal hardening of body tissue. **2** (in full **multiple** or **disseminated sclerosis**) a chronic and progressive disease of the nervous system resulting in symptoms including paralysis and speech defects.

scle•rot•ic /sklərótik/ *adj. & n.* •*adj.* **1** of or having sclerosis. **2** of or relating to the sclera. •*n.* = SCLERA. ▫▫ **scle•ro•ti•tis** /–rətītis/ *n.*

scoff[1] /skof/ *v. & n.* •*v.intr.* (usu. foll. by *at*) speak derisively, esp. of serious subjects; mock. •*n.* mocking words; a taunt. ▫▫ **scoff•er** *n.* **scoff•ing•ly** *adv.*

scoff[2] /skof/ *v. & n. colloq.* •*v.tr. & intr.* eat greedily. •*n.* food; a meal.

scold /skōld/ *v. & n.* •*v.* **1** *tr.* rebuke (esp. a child). **2** *intr.* find fault noisily; complain. •*n. archaic* a nagging or grumbling woman. ▫▫ **scold•er** *n.* **scold•ing** *n.*

sco•li•o•sis /skōlee+sis, skól–/ *n.* an abnormal lateral curvature of the spine.

scol•lop var. of SCALLOP.

sconce[1] /skons/ *n.* **1** a flat candlestick with a handle. **2** a bracket candlestick to hang on a wall.

---

sconce late Middle English (originally denoting a portable lantern with a screen to protect the flame): shortening of Old French *esconse* 'lantern,' or from medieval Latin *sconsa*, from Latin *absconsa* (*laterna*) 'dark (lantern),' from *abscondere* 'to hide.'

---

sconce[2] /skons/ *n.* **1** a small fort or earthwork usu. defending a ford, pass, etc. **2** *archaic* a shelter or screen.

scone /skon, skōn/ *n.* a small sweet or savory cake of flour, shortening, and milk, baked quickly in an oven.

scoop /sko͞op/ *n. & v.* •*n.* **1** any of various objects resembling a spoon, esp.: **a** a short-handled deep shovel used for transferring grain, sugar, coal, coins, etc. **b** the excavating part of a digging machine, etc. **c** an instrument used for serving portions of mashed potato, ice cream, etc. **2** a quantity taken up by a scoop. **3** a movement of or resembling scooping. **4** a piece of news published by a newspaper, etc., in advance of its rivals. **5** a large profit made quickly or by anticipating one's competitors. •*v.tr.* **1** (usu. foll. by *out*) hollow out with or as if with a scoop. **2** (usu. foll. by *up*) lift with or as if with a scoop. **3** forestall (a rival newspaper, reporter, etc.) with a scoop. **4** secure (a large profit, etc.), esp. suddenly. ▫▫ **scoop•er** *n.* **scoop•ful** *n.* (*pl.* **-fuls**).

scoop neck *n.* the rounded low-cut neck of a garment.

scoot /sko͞ot/ *v. & n. colloq.* •*v.intr.* run or dart away, esp. quickly. •*n.* the act or an instance of scooting.

scoot•er /sko͞otər/ *n. & v.* •*n.* **1** a child's toy consisting of a footboard mounted on two wheels and a long steering handle. **2** (in full **motor scooter**) a light two-wheeled open motor vehicle with a shieldlike protective front. •*v.intr.* travel or ride on a scooter. ▫▫ **scoot•er•ist** *n.*

scope[1] /skōp/ *n.* **1** the extent to which it is possible to range; the opportunity for action, etc. (*this is beyond the scope of our research*). **2** the sweep or reach of mental activity, observation, or outlook (*an intellect limited in its scope*).

scope[2] /skōp/ *n. colloq.* a telescope, microscope, or other device ending in *-scope*.

-scope /skōp/ *comb. form* forming nouns denoting: **1** a device looked at or through (*telescope*). **2** an instrument for observing or showing (*gyroscope*). ▫▫ **-scopic** /skópik/ *comb. form* forming adjectives.

sco•pol•a•mine /skəpóləmeen, –min/ *n.* = HYOSCINE.

-scopy /skəpee/ *comb. form* indicating viewing or observation, usu. with an instrument ending in *-scope* (*microscopy*).

scor•bu•tic /skawrbyo͞otik/ *adj. & n.* •*adj.* relating to, resembling, or affected with scurvy. • *n.* a person affected with scurvy.

scorch /skawrch/ *v. & n.* • *v.* **1** *tr.* **a** burn the surface of with flame or heat so as to discolor, parch, injure, or hurt. **b** affect with the sensation of burning. **2** *intr.* become discolored, etc., with heat. **3** *tr.* (as **scorching** *adj.*) *colloq.* **a** (of the weather) very hot. **b** (of criticism, etc.) stringent; harsh. • *n.* a mark made by scorching. ▫▫ **scorch·ing·ly** *adv.*

scorched earth pol·i·cy *n.* the burning of crops, etc., and the removing or destroying of anything that might be of use to an occupying enemy force.

scorch·er /skáwrchər/ *n.* a very hot day.

score /skawr/ *n. & v.* • *n.* **1 a** the number of points, goals, runs, etc., made by a player, side, etc., in some games. **b** the total number of points, etc., at the end of a game (*the score was five to one*). **c** the act of gaining, esp. a goal. **2** (*pl.* same or **scores**) twenty or a set of twenty. **3** (in *pl.*) a great many (*scores of people arrived*). **4 a** a reason or motive (*rejected on the score of absurdity*). **b** topic; subject (*no worries on that score*). **5** *Mus.* **a** a usu. printed copy of a composition. **b** the music composed for a film or play, esp. for a musical. **6** *colloq.* the state of affairs (*asked what the score was*). **7** a notch, line, etc., cut or scratched into a surface. • *v.* **1** *tr.* **a** win or gain (a goal, run, points, or success, etc.). **b** count for a score of (points in a game, etc.) (*a bull's-eye scores the most points*). **c** make a record of (a point, etc.). **2** *intr.* **a** make a score in a game. **b** keep the tally of points, runs, etc., in a game. **3** *tr.* mark with notches, incisions, lines, etc.; slash (*scored his name on the desk*). **4** *intr.* secure an advantage (*that is where he scores*). **5** *tr. Mus.* **a** orchestrate (a piece of music). **b** (usu. foll. by *for*) arrange for an instrument or instruments. **6** *intr. sl.* **a** obtain drugs illegally. **b** make a sexual conquest. ▫ **keep score** register the score as it is made. **know the score** *colloq.* be aware of the essential facts. **on that score** so far as that is concerned. **score out** draw a line through (words, etc.). **score points with** make a favorable impression on. ▫▫ **scor·er** *n.* **scor·ing** *n. Mus.*

score·board /skáwrbawrd/ *n.* a large board for publicly displaying the score in a game or match.

score·card /skáwrkaard/ *n.* a card prepared for entering scores on and usu. for indicating players by name, number, etc.

scorn /skawrn/ *n. & v.* • *n.* **1** disdain; contempt. **2** an object of contempt, etc. • *v.tr.* **1** hold in contempt. **2** (often foll. by *to* + infin.) abstain from or refuse to do as unworthy. ▫▫ **scorn·er** *n.*

scorn·ful /skáwrnfo͝ol/ *adj.* (often foll. by *of*) full of scorn; contemptuous. ▫▫ **scorn·ful·ly** *adv.* **scorn·ful·ness** *n.*

Scor·pi·o /skáwrpeeō/ *n.* (*pl.* **-os**) **1** a constellation, traditionally regarded as contained in the figure of a scorpion. **2 a** the eighth sign of the zodiac (the Scorpion). **b** a person born when the sun is in this sign. ▫▫ **Scor·pi·an** *adj. & n.*

scor·pi·oid /skáwrpeeoyd/ *adj. & n.* • *adj.* **1** *Zool.* of, relating to, or resembling a scorpion; of the scorpion order. **2** *Bot.* (of an inflorescence) curled up at the end, and uncurling as the flowers develop. • *n.* this type of inflorescence.

scor·pi·on /skáwrpeeən/ *n.* **1** an arachnid of the order Scorpionida, with lobsterlike pincers and a jointed tail that can be bent over to inflict a poisoned sting. **2** (**the Scorpion**) the zodiacal sign or constellation Scorpio.

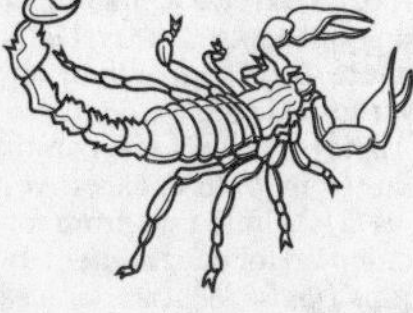
scorpion

Scot /skot/ *n.* **1 a** a native of Scotland. **b** a person of Scottish descent. **2** *hist.* a member of a Gaelic people that migrated from Ireland to Scotland around the 6th c.

Scotch /skoch/ *adj. & n.* • *adj.* var. of SCOTTISH or SCOTS. • *n.* **1** var. of SCOTTISH or SCOTS. **2** Scotch whiskey.
▶In Scotland the terms **Scots** and **Scottish** are preferred to **Scotch**, and they mean the same (e.g., *a Scots/Scottish accent, miner, farmer,* etc.) **Scotch** is used in various compound nouns such as *Scotch broth, egg, fir, mist, terrier,* and *whisky.* Similarly, **Scotsman** and **Scotswoman** are preferred to **Scotchman** and **Scotchwoman.**

scotch /skoch/ *v.tr.* **1** put an end to; frustrate. **2** *archaic* wound without killing.

Scotch broth *n.* a soup made from beef or mutton with pearl barley, etc.

Scotch·man /skóchmən/ *n.* (*pl.* **-men**; *fem.* **Scotch·wom·an**, *pl.* **-women**) = SCOTS·MAN.
▶*Scotsman, Scotswoman,* etc., are generally preferred in Scotland.

Scotch whis·key *n.* whiskey distilled in Scotland, esp. from malted barley.

scot-free *adj.* unharmed; unpunished; safe.

Scot·land Yard /skótlənd/ *n.* **1** the headquarters of the London Metropolitan Police. **2** its Criminal Investigation Department.

sco·to·ma /skətṓmə/ *n.* (*pl.* **scotomata** /–mətə/) a partial loss of vision or blind spot in an otherwise normal visual field.

Scots /skots/ *adj. & n.* esp. *Sc.* • *adj.* **1** = SCOTTISH *adj.* **2** in the dialect, accent, etc., of (esp. Lowlands) Scotland. • *n.* **1** = SCOTTISH *n.* **2** the form of English spoken in (esp. Lowlands) Scotland.

Scots·man /skótsmən/ *n.* (*pl.* **-men**; *fem.* **Scots·wom·an**, *pl.* **-women**) **1** a native of Scotland. **2** a person of Scottish descent.

Scots pine *n.* a pine tree, *Pinus sylvestris,* native to Europe and much planted for its wood.

Scot·tie /skótee/ *n. colloq.* **1** (also **Scottie dog**) a Scottish terrier. **2** a Scot.

Scot·tish /skótish/ *adj. & n.* • *adj.* of or relating to Scotland or its inhabitants. • *n.* (prec. by *the*; treated as *pl.*) the people of Scotland (see also SCOTS). ▫▫ **Scot·tish·ness** *n.*

Scot·tish ter·ri·er *n.* a small terrier of a rough-haired short-legged breed.

scoun·drel /skówndrəl/ *n.* an unscrupulous villain; a rogue. ▫▫ **scoun·drel·ism** *n.* **scoun·drel·ly** *adj.*

scour[1] /skowr/ *v. & n.* • *v.tr.* **1 a** cleanse or brighten by rubbing, esp. with soap, chemicals, sand, etc. **b** (usu. foll. by *away, off,* etc.) clear (rust, stains, reputation, etc.) by rubbing, hard work, etc. (*scoured the slur from his name*). **2** clear out (a pipe, channel, etc.) by flushing through. • *n.* the act or an instance of scouring. ▫▫ **scour·er** *n.*

scour[2] /skowr/ *v. tr.* hasten over (an area, etc.) searching thoroughly (*scoured the streets for him; scoured the newspaper*).

scourge /skərj/ *n. & v.* • *n.* **1** a whip used for punishment, esp. of people. **2** a person or thing seen as punishing, esp. on a large scale (*Genghis Khan, the scourge of Asia*). • *v.tr.* **1** whip. **2** punish; oppress. ▫▫ **scourg·er** *n.*

scout /skowt/ *n. & v.* • *n.* **1** a person, esp. a soldier, sent out to get information about the enemy's position, strength, etc. **2** the act of seeking (esp. military) information (*on the scout*). **3** = TALENT SCOUT. **4** (**Scout**) a Boy Scout or Girl Scout. **5** a ship or aircraft designed for reconnoitering, esp. a small fast aircraft. • *v.* **1** *intr.* act as a scout. **2** *intr.* (foll. by *about, around*) make a search. **3** *tr.* (often foll. by *out*) *colloq.* explore to get information about (territory, etc.). ▫▫ **scout·er** *n.* **scout·ing** *n.*

scout·mas·ter /skówtmastər/ *n.* a person in charge of a group of Scouts.

scow /skow/ *n.* a flat-bottomed boat used as a lighter, etc.

scowl /skowl/ *n. & v.* • *n.* a severe frown producing a sullen, bad-tempered, or threatening look on a person's face. • *v.intr.* make a scowl. ▫▫ **scowl·er** *n.*

scrab·ble /skrábəl/ *v. & n.* • *v.intr.* (often foll. by *about, at*) scratch or grope to find or hold on to something. • *n.* **1** an act of scrabbling. **2** (**Scrabble**) *Trademark* a game in which players build up words from letter blocks on a board.

scrag·gly /skráglee/ *adj.* sparse and irregular.

scrag·gy /skrágee/ *adj.* (**scraggier, scraggiest**) thin and bony. ▫▫ **scrag·gi·ly** *adv.* **scrag·gi·ness** *n.*

scram /skram/ *v.intr.* (**scrammed, scramming**) (esp. in *imper.*) *colloq.* go away.

scram·ble /skrámbəl/ *v. & n.* • *v.* **1** *intr.* make one's way over rough ground, rocks, etc., by clambering, crawling, etc. **2** *intr.* (foll. by *for, at*) struggle with competitors (for a thing or share of it). **3** *intr.* move with difficulty or awkwardly. **4** *tr.* **a** mix together indiscriminately. **b** jumble or muddle. **5** *tr.* cook (eggs) by heating them when broken and well mixed, often with butter, milk, etc. **6** *tr.* change the speech frequency of (a broadcast transmission or telephone conversation) so as to make it unintelligible without a corresponding decoding device. **7** *intr.* (of fighter aircraft or their pilots) take off quickly in an emergency or for action. • *n.* **1** an act of scrambling. **2** a difficult climb or walk. **3** (foll. by *for*) an eager struggle or competition. **4** an emergency takeoff by fighter aircraft.

scram·bler /skrámblər/ *n.* a device for scrambling telephone conversations.

scrap[1] /skrap/ *n. & v.* • *n.* **1** a small detached piece; a fragment or remnant. **2** rubbish or waste material. **3** discarded metal for reprocessing (often *attrib.*: *scrap metal*). **4** (with *neg.*) the smallest piece or amount (*not a scrap of food left*). **5** (in *pl.*) **a** odds and ends. **b** bits of uneaten food. • *v.tr.* (**scrapped, scrapping**) discard as useless.

scrap[2] /skrap/ *n. & v. colloq.* • *n.* a fight or rough quarrel. • *v.tr.* (**scrapped, scrapping**) (often foll. by *with*) have a scrap. ▫▫ **scrap·per** *n.*

scrap·book /skrápbŏŏk/ *n.* a book of blank pages for sticking cuttings, drawings, etc., in.

scrape /skrayp/ *v. & n.* • *v.* **1** *tr.* **a** move a hard or sharp edge across (a surface), esp. to make something smooth. **b** apply (a hard or sharp edge) in this way. **2** *tr.* (foll. by *away, off,* etc.) remove (a stain, projection, etc.) by scraping. **3** *tr.* **a** rub (a surface) harshly against another. **b** scratch or damage by scraping. **4** *tr.* make (a hollow) by scraping. **5** **a** *tr.* draw or move with a sound of, or resembling, scraping. **b** *intr.* emit or produce such a sound. **c** *tr.* produce such a sound from. **6** *intr.* (often foll. by *along, by, through,* etc.) move or pass along while almost touching close or surrounding features, obstacles, etc. (*the car scraped through the narrow lane*). **7** *tr.* just manage to achieve (a living, an examination pass, etc.). **8** *intr.* (often foll. by *by, through*) **a** barely manage. **b** pass an examination, etc., with difficulty. **9** *tr.* (foll. by *together, up*) contrive to bring or provide; amass with difficulty. **10** *intr.* be economical. **11** *intr.* draw back a foot in making a clumsy bow. • *n.* **1** the act or sound of scraping. **2** a scraped place (on the skin, etc.). **3** the scraping of a foot in bowing. **4** *colloq.* an awkward predicament, esp. resulting from an escapade. **scrape the barrel** *colloq.* be reduced to one's last resources.

scrap·er /skráypər/ *n.* a device used for scraping, esp. for removing dirt, etc., from a surface.

scrap heap *n.* **1** a pile of scrap materials. **2** a state of uselessness.

scrap·py /skrápee/ *adj.* (**scrappier, scrappiest**) **1** consisting of scraps. **2** incomplete; carelessly arranged or put together. **3** fond of fighting; not easily intimidated. ▫▫ **scrap·pi·ly** *adv.* **scrap·pi·ness** *n.*

scrap·yard /skrápyaard/ *n.* a place where (esp. metal) scrap is collected.

scratch /skrach/ *v., n., & adj.* • *v.* **1** *tr.* score or mark the surface of with a sharp or pointed object. **2** *tr.* make a long, narrow superficial wound in (the skin). **3** *tr.* (also *absol.*) scrape without marking, esp. with the hand to relieve itching. **4** *tr.* make or form by scratching. **5** *tr.* (foll. by *together, up,* etc.) obtain (a thing) by scratching or with difficulty. **6** *tr.* (foll. by *out, off, through*) cancel or strike (out) with a pencil, etc. **7** *tr.* (also *absol.*) withdraw (a competitor, candidate, etc.) from a race or competition. **8** *intr.* (often foll. by *about, around,* etc.) **a** scratch the ground, etc., in search. **b** look around haphazardly (*they were scratching about for evidence*). • *n.* **1** a mark or wound made by scratching. **2** a sound of scratching. **3** a spell of scratching oneself. • *attrib.adj.* **1** collected by chance. **2** collected or made from whatever is available (*a scratch crew*). **3** with no handicap given (*a scratch race*). ▫ **from scratch** **1** from the beginning. **2** without help or advantage. **scratch along** make a living, etc., with difficulty. **scratch one's head** be perplexed. **scratch the surface** deal with a matter only superficially. **up to scratch** up to the required standard. ▫▫ **scratch·er** *n.*

scratch pad *n.* **1** a pad of paper for scribbling. **2** *Computing* a small fast memory for the temporary storage of data.

scratch·y /skráchee/ *adj.* (**scratchier, scratchiest**) **1** tending to make scratches or a scratching noise. **2** (esp. of a garment) tending to cause itchiness. **3** (of a drawing, etc.) done carelessly. ▫▫ **scratch·i·ly** *adv.* **scratch·i·ness** *n.*

scrawl /skrawl/ *v. & n.* • *v.* **1** *tr. & intr.* write in a hurried untidy way. **2** *tr.* (foll. by *out*) cross out by scrawling over. • *n.* **1** a piece of hurried writing. **2** a scrawled note. ▫▫ **scrawl·y** *adj.*

scrawn·y /skráwnee/ *adj.* (**scrawnier, scrawniest**) lean; scraggy. ▫▫ **scrawn·i·ness** *n.*

scream /skreem/ *n. & v.* • *n.* **1** a loud, high-pitched, piercing cry expressing fear, pain, extreme fright, etc. **2** *colloq.* an irresistibly funny occurrence or person. • *v.* **1** *intr.* emit a scream. **2** *tr.* speak or sing (words, etc.) in a screaming tone. **3** *intr.* make or move with a shrill sound like a scream. **4** *intr.* laugh uncontrollably. **5** *intr.* be blatantly obvious or conspicuous.

scree /skree/ *n.* small loose stones.

screech /skreech/ *n. & v.* • *n.* a harsh, high-pitched scream. • *v.tr. & intr.* utter with or make a screech. ▫▫ **screech·er** *n.* **screech·y** *adj.* (**screechier, screechiest**).

screech owl *n.* any owl that screeches instead of hooting.

screed /skreed/ *n.* **1** a long usu. tiresome piece of writing or speech. **2** a leveled layer of material (e.g., concrete) applied to a floor or other surface.

screen /skreen/ *n. & v.* • *n.* **1** a fixed or movable upright partition for separating, concealing, or sheltering from drafts or excessive heat or light. **2** a thing used as a shelter, esp. from observation. **3** **a** a measure adopted for concealment. **b** the protection afforded by this (*under the screen of night*). **4** **a** a blank usu. white or silver surface on which a photographic image is projected. **b** (prec. by *the*) the motion-picture industry *the silver screen.* **5** the surface of a cathode-ray tube or similar electronic device, esp. of a television, computer monitor, etc., on which images appear. **6** = WINDSCREEN. **7** a frame with fine wire netting to keep out flies, mosquitoes, etc. **8** a large sieve or riddle, esp. for sorting grain, coal, etc., into sizes. **9** a system of checking for the presence or absence of a disease, ability, attribute, etc. **10** *Printing* a transparent, finely ruled plate or film used in halftone reproduction. • *v.tr.* **1** (often foll. by *from*) **a** afford shelter to; hide. **b** protect from detection, censure, etc. **2** (foll. by *off*) hide behind a screen. **3 a** show (a film, etc.). **b** broadcast (a television program). **4** prevent from causing, or protect from, electrical interference. **5 a** test (a person or group) for the presence or absence of a disease. **b** check on (a person) for the presence or absence of a quality, esp. reliability or loyalty. **6** pass (grain, coal, etc.) through a screen. ◻◻ **screen·a·ble** *adj.* **screen·er** *n.*

screen·ing /skréening/ *n.* the showing of a motion picture.

screen·play /skréenplay/ *n.* the script of a motion picture etc., with acting instructions, scene directions, etc.

screen print·ing *n.* a process like stenciling with ink forced through a prepared sheet of fine material (orig. silk).

screen test *n.* an audition for a part in a motion picture.

screen·writ·er /skréenrītər/ *n.* a person who writes a screenplay.

screw /skroo/ *n.* & *v.* • *n.* **1** a thin cylinder or cone with a spiral ridge or thread running around the outside (**male screw**) or the inside (**female screw**). **2** (in full **wood screw**) a metal male screw with a slotted head and a sharp point. **3** (in full **screw bolt**) a metal male screw with a blunt end on which a nut is threaded to bolt things together. **4** a wooden or metal straight screw used to exert pressure. **5** (in *sing.* or *pl.*) an instrument of torture acting in this way. **6** (in full **screw propeller**) a form of propeller with twisted blades acting like a screw on the water or air. **7** one turn of a screw. **8** *sl.* a prison warden or guard. **9** *coarse sl.* **a** an act of sexual intercourse. **b** a partner in this. ▶Usually considered a taboo use. • *v.* **1** *tr.* fasten or tighten with a screw or screws. **2** *tr.* turn (a screw). **3** *intr.* twist or turn around like a screw. **4** *tr.* **a** put psychological, etc., pressure on to achieve an end. **b** oppress. **5** *tr.* (foll. by *out of*) extort (consent, money, etc.) from (a person). **6** *tr.* (also *absol.*) *coarse sl.* have sexual intercourse with. ▶Usually considered a taboo use. **7** *intr.* (of a rolling ball, or of a person, etc.) take a curling course. ◻ **have one's head screwed on the right way** *colloq.* have common sense. **have a screw loose** *colloq.* be slightly crazy. **put the screws on** *colloq.* exert pressure on, esp. to extort or intimidate. **screw up 1** contract or contort (one's face, etc.). **2** contract and crush into a tight mass (a piece of paper, etc.). **3** summon up (one's courage, etc.). **4** *sl.* **a** bungle or mismanage. **b** spoil (an event, opportunity, etc.). ◻◻ **screw·a·ble** *adj.* **screw·er** *n.*

screw·ball /skróobawl/ *n.* & *adj.* *sl.* • *n.* **1** *Baseball* a pitch thrown with spin opposite that of a curveball. **2** a crazy or eccentric person. • *adj.* crazy.

screw·driv·er /skróodrīvər/ *n.* a tool with a shaped tip to fit into the head of a screw to turn it.

screwed /skrood/ *adj.* **1** twisted. **2** *sl.* ruined; rendered ineffective.

screw·y /skróo-ee/ *adj.* (**screwier, screwiest**) *sl.* **1** crazy or eccentric. **2** absurd. ◻◻ **screw·i·ness** *n.*

scrib·ble /skríbəl/ *v.* & *n.* • *v.* **1** *tr.* & *intr.* write carelessly or hurriedly. **2** *intr.* often *derog.* be an author or writer. **3** *intr.* & *tr.* draw carelessly or meaninglessly. • *n.* **1** a scrawl. **2** a hasty note, etc. **3** careless handwriting. ◻◻ **scrib·bler** *n.* **scrib·bly** *adj.*

scribe /skrīb/ *n.* & *v.* • *n.* **1** a person who writes out documents, esp. an ancient or medieval copyist of manuscripts. **2** *Bibl.* an ancient Jewish record keeper or professional theologian and jurist. **3** (in full **scribe awl**) a pointed instrument for making marks on wood, bricks, etc. **4** *colloq.* a writer, esp. a journalist. • *v.tr.* mark (wood, etc.) with a scribe (see sense 3 of *n.*). ◻◻ **scrib·al** *adj.* **scrib·er** *n.*

scrim /skrim/ *n.* open-weave fabric for lining or upholstery, etc.

scrim·mage /skrímij/ *n.* & *v.* • *n.* **1** a struggle; a brawl. **2** *Football* a single play from the snap of the ball till the ball is dead. • *v. intr.* engage in a scrimmage. ◻◻ **scrim·mag·er** *n.*

scrimp /skrimp/ *v.* **1** *intr.* be thrifty or parsimonious; economize (*I have scrimped and saved to give you a good education*). **2** *tr.* use sparingly; limit (*scrimp provisions*). ◻◻ **scrimp·y** *adj.*

scrim·shaw /skrímshaw/ *v.* & *n.* • *v.tr.* (also *absol.*) adorn (shells, ivory, etc.) with carved or colored designs (as sailors' pastime at sea). • *n.* work or a piece of work of this kind.

scrip /skrip/ *n.* **1** a provisional certificate of money subscribed to a bank, etc., entitling the holder to dividends. **2** (*collect.*) such certificates. **3** an extra share or shares instead of a dividend.

script /skript/ *n.* & *v.* • *n.* **1** handwriting as distinct from print; written characters. **2** type imitating handwriting. **3** an alphabet or system of writing. **4** the text of a play, film, or broadcast. **5** an examinee's set of written answers. • *v.tr.* write a script for (a motion picture, etc.).

scrip·tur·al /skrípchərəl/ *adj.* **1** of or relating to a scripture, esp. the Bible. **2** having the authority of a scripture. ◻◻ **scrip·tur·al·ly** *adv.*

scrip·ture /skrípchər/ *n.* **1** sacred writings. **2** (**Scripture** or **the Scriptures**) the Bible as a collection of sacred writings in Christianity. ◻◻ **scrip·tur·al** *adj.*

script·writ·er /skríptrītər/ *n.* a person who writes a script for a motion picture, broadcast, etc. ◻◻ **script·writ·ing** *n.*

scrive·ner /skrívənər, skrívnər/ *n.* *hist.* **1** a drafter of documents. **2** a notary.

scrod /skrod/ *n.* a young cod or haddock, esp. as food.

scrof·u·la /skrófyələ/ *n.* *archaic* a disease with glandular swellings, prob. a form of tuberculosis. ◻◻ **scrof·u·lous** *adj.*

scroll /skrōl/ *n.* & *v.* • *n.* **1** a roll of parchment or paper esp. with writing on it. **2** a book in the ancient roll form. **3** an ornamental design or carving imitating a roll of parchment. • *v.* **1** *tr.* (often foll. by *down, up*) move (a display on a computer screen) in order to view new material. **2** *tr.* inscribe in or like a scroll. **3** *intr.* curl up like paper.

scroll·work /skrólwərk/ *n.* decoration of spiral lines, esp. as cut by a scroll saw.

Scrooge /skrooj/ *n.* a mean or miserly person (from a character in the 1843 Charles Dickens novel *A Christmas Carol*).

scro·tum /skrótəm/ *n.* (*pl.* **scrota** /–tə/ or **scrotums**) a pouch of skin containing the testicles. ◻◻ **scro·tal** *adj.*

scrounge /skrownj/ *v.* & *n.* *colloq.* • *v.* **1** *tr.* (also *absol.*) obtain (things) illicitly or by cadging. **2** *intr.* search about to find something at no cost. • *n.* an act of scrounging. ◻ **on the scrounge** engaged in scrounging. ◻◻ **scroung·er** *n.*

scrub[1] /skrub/ *v.* & *n.* • *v.* (**scrubbed, scrubbing**) **1** *tr.* rub hard so as to clean, esp. with a hard brush. **2** *intr.*

use a brush in this way. **3** *intr.* (often foll. by *up*) (of a surgeon, etc.) thoroughly clean the hands and arms by scrubbing, before operating. **4** *tr. colloq.* scrap or cancel. •*n.* the act or an instance of scrubbing; the process of being scrubbed.

scrub[2] /skrub/ *n.* **1 a** vegetation consisting mainly of brushwood or stunted forest growth. **b** an area of land covered with this. **2** an animal of inferior breed or physique (often *attrib.*: *scrub horse*). **3** a small or dwarf variety (often *attrib.*: *scrub pine*). ▫▫ **scrub·by** *adj.*

scruff /skruf/ *n.* the back of the neck (esp. *scruff of the neck*).

scruff·y /skrúfee/ *adj.* (**scruffier, scruffiest**) *colloq.* shabby; slovenly; untidy. ▫▫ **scruff·i·ly** *adv.* **scruff·i·ness** *n.*

scrum /skrum/ *n.* **1** *Rugby* an arrangement of the forwards of each team in two opposing groups, each with arms interlocked and heads down, with the ball thrown in between them to restart play. **2** *Brit. colloq.* a milling crowd.

scrump·tious /skrúmpshəs/ *adj. colloq.* **1** delicious. **2** pleasing; delightful. ▫▫ **scrump·tious·ly** *adv.* **scrump·tious·ness** *n.*

scrunch /skrunch/ *v.* & *n.* •*v.tr.* & *intr.* **1** (usu. foll. by *up*) make or become crushed or crumpled. **2** make or cause to make a crunching sound. •*n.* the act or an instance of scrunching.

scrunch·ie /skrúnchee/ *n.* a hair band of elastic enclosed by crumpled fabric, used for ponytails, etc.

scru·ple /skróopəl/ *n.* & *v.* •*n.* **1** (in *sing.* or *pl.*) regard to the morality or propriety of an action. **2** a feeling of doubt or hesitation caused by this. •*v.intr.* **1** (foll. by *to* + infin.; usu. with *neg.*) be reluctant because of scruples (*did not scruple to stop their allowance*). **2** feel or be influenced by scruples.

scru·pu·lous /skróopyələs/ *adj.* **1** conscientious or thorough. **2** careful to avoid doing wrong. **3** punctilious; overattentive to details. ▫▫ **scru·pu·los·i·ty** /–lósitee/ *n.* **scru·pu·lous·ly** *adv.* **scru·pu·lous·ness** *n.*

scru·ti·nize /skróot'nīz/ *v.tr.* look closely at; examine with close scrutiny. ▫▫ **scru·ti·niz·er** *n.*

scru·ti·ny /skróot'nee/ *n.* (*pl.* **-nies**) **1** a critical gaze. **2** a close investigation or examination of details. **3** an official examination of ballot papers to check their validity or accuracy of counting.

scry /skrī/ *v.intr.* (**scries, scried**) divine by crystal gazing. ▫▫ **scry·er** *n.*

scu·ba /skóobə/ *n.* (*pl.* **scubas**) gear that provides an air supply from a portable tank for swimming underwater (acronym for *s*elf-*c*ontained *u*nderwater *b*reathing *a*pparatus).

scu·ba div·ing *n.* swimming underwater using a scuba, esp. as a sport. ▫▫ **scu·ba dive** *v.intr.* **scu·ba div·er** *n.*

scud /skud/ *v.* & *n.* •*v.intr.* (**scudded, scudding**) **1** fly or run straight, fast, and lightly. **2** *Naut.* run before the wind. •*n.* **1** a spell of scudding. **2** a scudding motion. **3** vapory driving clouds. **4** a driving shower; a gust. **5** wind-blown spray. **6** (**Scud**) a type of long-range surface-to-surface guided missile originally developed in the former Soviet Union.

scuff /skuf/ *v.* & *n.* •*v.* **1** *tr.* graze or brush against. **2** *tr.* mark or wear down (shoes) in this way. **3** *intr.* walk with dragging feet. •*n.* a mark of scuffing.

scuf·fle /skúfəl/ *n.* & *v.* •*n.* a confused struggle or disorderly fight at close quarters. •*v.intr.* engage in a scuffle.

scull /skul/ *n.* & *v.* •*n.* **1** either of a pair of small oars used by a single rower. **2** an oar placed over the stern of a boat to propel it, usu. by a twisting motion. **3** a small boat propelled with a scull or a pair of sculls. **4** (in *pl.*) a race between boats with single pairs of oars. •*v.tr.* propel (a boat) with sculls.

scul·ler·y /skúləree/ *n.* (*pl.* **-ies**) a small kitchen or room at the back of a house for washing dishes, etc.

scul·lion /skúlyən/ *n. archaic* **1** a cook's boy. **2** a person who washes dishes.

scul·pin /skúlpin/ *n.* any of numerous fish of the family Cottidae, native to nontropical regions, having large spiny heads.

sculpt /skulpt/ *v.tr.* & *intr.* (also **sculp**) sculpture.

sculp·tor /skúlptər/ *n.* (*fem.* **sculptress** /–tris/) an artist who makes sculptures.

sculp·ture /skúlpchər/ *n.* & *v.* •*n.* **1** the art of making forms, often representational, in the round or in relief by chiseling, carving, modeling, casting, etc. **2** a work or works of sculpture. •*v.* **1** *tr.* represent in or adorn with sculpture. **2** *intr.* practice sculpture. ▫▫ **sculp·tur·al** *adj.* **sculp·tur·al·ly** *adv.* **sculp·tur·esque** *adj.*

scum /skum/ *n.* & *v.* •*n.* **1** a layer of dirt, froth, etc., forming at the top of liquid. **2** (foll. by *of*) the most worthless part of something. **3** *colloq.* a worthless person or group. •*v.* (**scummed, scumming**) **1** *tr.* remove scum from. **2** *tr.* be or form a scum on. ▫▫ **scum·my** *adj.* (**scummier, scummiest**)

scum·bag /skúmbag/ *n. sl.* a worthless despicable person.

scum·ble /skúmbəl/ *v.* & *n.* •*v.tr.* **1** modify (a painting) by applying a thin opaque coat of paint to give a softer or duller effect. **2** modify (a drawing) similarly with light penciling, etc. •*n.* **1** material used in scumbling. **2** the effect produced by scumbling.

scup /skup/ *n.* an E. American fish, *Stenostomus chrysops*, a kind of porgy.

scup·per /skúpər/ *n.* a hole at the edge of a boat's deck to allow water to run off.

scurf /skərf/ *n.* **1** flakes on the surface of the skin, cast off as fresh skin develops below; dandruff. **2** any scaly matter on a surface. ▫▫ **scurf·y** *adj.*

scur·ril·ous /skəriləs, skúr–/ *adj.* **1** (of a person or language) grossly or indecently abusive. **2** given to or expressed with low humor. ▫▫ **scur·ril·i·ty** /–rílitee/ *n.* (*pl.* **-ties**). **scur·ril·ous·ly** *adv.* **scur·ril·ous·ness** *n.*

scur·ry /skəree, skúree/ *v.* & *n.* •*v.intr.* (**-ries, -ried**) run or move hurriedly, esp. with short quick steps; scamper. •*n.* (*pl.* **-ries**) **1** the act or sound of scurrying. **2** a flurry of rain or snow.

scur·vy /skúrvee/ *n.* & *adj.* •*n.* a disease caused by a deficiency of vitamin C. •*adj.* (**scurvier, scurviest**) dishonorable; contemptible. ▫▫ **scur·vied** *adj.* **scur·vi·ly** *adv.*

scut /skut/ *n.* a short tail, esp. of a hare, rabbit, or deer.

scu·ta *pl.* of SCUTUM.

scutch·eon /skúchən/ *n.* **1** = ESCUTCHEON. **2** an ornamented brass, etc., plate around or over a keyhole. **3** a plate for a name or inscription.

scute /skyoot/ *n. Zool.* = SCUTUM.

scu·tel·lum /skyootéləm/ *n.* (*pl.* **scutella** /–lə/) *Bot.* & *Zool.* a scale, plate, or any shieldlike formation on a plant, insect, bird, etc., esp. one of the horny scales on a bird's foot. ▫▫ **scu·tel·late** /skyootélit, skyóotəlayt/ *adj.* **scu·tel·la·tion** /skyóotəláyshən/ *n.*

scut·tle[1] /skút'l/ *n.* a receptacle for carrying and holding a small supply of coal.

scut·tle[2] /skút'l/ *v.* & *n.* •*v.intr.* **1** scurry; hurry along. **2** run away. •*n.* **1** a hurried gait. **2** a precipitate flight.

scut·tle[3] /skút'l/ *n.* & *v.* •*n.* a hole with a lid in a ship's deck or side. •*v.tr.* let water into (a ship) to sink it.

scut·tle·butt /skút'lbut/ *n. colloq.* **1** a water cask on the deck of a ship, for drinking from. **2** rumor; gossip.

scu·tum /skyóotəm/ *n.* (*pl.* **scuta** /–tə/) each of the shieldlike plates or scales forming the bony covering of a crocodile, sturgeon, turtle, armadillo, etc. ▫▫ **scu·tal** *adj.* **scu·tate** *adj.*

scuzz·y /skúzee/ *adj. sl.* abhorrent or disgusting.
scy·phus /sífəs/ *n.* (*pl.* **scyphi** /–fī/) **1** *Gk Antiq.* a footless drinking cup with two handles below the level of the rim. **2** *Bot.* a cup-shaped part as in a narcissus flower or in lichens. ▫▫ **scy·phose** *adj.*
scythe /sīth/ *n.* & *v.* • *n.* a mowing and reaping implement with a long curved blade swung over the ground by a long pole with two short handles projecting from it. • *v.tr.* cut with a scythe.

scythe

Scyth·i·an /sítheeən, –theeən/ *adj.* & *n.* • *adj.* of or relating to ancient Scythia, a region north of the Black Sea. • *n.* **1** an inhabitant of Scythia. **2** the language of this region.
SD *abbr.* South Dakota (in official postal use).
S.Dak. *abbr.* South Dakota.
SDI *abbr.* Strategic Defense Initiative.
SE *abbr.* **1** southeast. **2** southeastern. **3** Standard English.
Se *symb. Chem.* the element selenium.
sea /see/ *n.* **1** the expanse of salt water that covers most of the earth's surface. **2** any part of this. **3** a particular (usu. named) tract of salt water partly or wholly enclosed by land (*the North Sea*). **4** a large inland lake (*the Sea of Galilee*). **5** the waves of the sea, esp. with reference to their local motion or state (*a choppy sea*). **6** (foll. by *of*) a vast quantity or expanse (*a sea of faces*). **7** (*attrib.*) living or used in, on, or near the sea (often prefixed to the name of a marine animal, plant, etc., having a superficial resemblance to what it is named after) (*sea lettuce*). ▫ **at sea 1** in a ship on the sea. **2** (also **all at sea**) perplexed; confused. **by sea** in a ship or ships. **go to sea** become a sailor. **on the sea 1** in a ship at sea. **2** situated on the coast. **put** (or **put out**) **to sea** leave land or port.
sea a·nem·o·ne *n.* any of various coelenterates of the order Actiniaria bearing a ring of tentacles around the mouth.
sea bass *n.* any of various marine fishes like the bass, esp. *Centropristis striatus.*
sea·bed /seébed/ *n.* the ground under the sea; the ocean floor.
sea·bird /seébərd/ *n.* a bird frequenting the sea or the land near the sea.
sea·board /seébawrd/ *n.* **1** the seashore or coastal region. **2** the line of a coast.
sea·bor·gi·um /seebáwrgeeəm/ *n.* an artificially produced chemical element, atomic number 106. ¶ Symb.: **Sg.**
sea·borne /seébawrn/ *adj.* transported by sea.
sea bream *n.* = PORGY.
sea change *n.* a notable or unexpected transformation.
sea·coast /seékōst/ *n.* the land adjacent to the sea.
sea·cock /seékok/ *n.* a valve below a ship's waterline for letting water in or out.
sea cu·cum·ber *n.* a holothurian, esp. a bêche-de-mer.
sea dog *n.* an old or experienced sailor.
sea·far·er /seéfairər/ *n.* **1** a sailor. **2** a traveler by sea.
sea·far·ing /seéfairing/ *adj.* & *n.* traveling by sea, esp. regularly.
sea·food /seéfood/ *n.* edible sea fish or shellfish.
sea·go·ing /seégōing/ *adj.* **1** (of ships) fit for crossing the sea. **2** (of a person) seafaring.
sea green *adj.* bluish green (as of the sea).
sea·gull /seégul/ *n.* = GULL[1].
sea hare *n.* any of various marine mollusks of the order Anaspidea, having an internal shell and long extensions from its foot.
sea hol·ly *n.* a spiny-leaved blue-flowered evergreen plant, *Eryngium maritimum.*
sea horse *n.* **1** any of various small upright marine fish of the family Syngnathidae, having a body suggestive of the head and neck of a horse. **2** a mythical creature with a horse's head and fish's tail.
seal[1] /seel/ *n.* & *v.* • *n.* **1** a piece of wax, lead, paper, etc., with a stamped design, attached to a document as a guarantee of authenticity. **2** a similar material attached to a receptacle, envelope, etc., affording security by having to be broken to allow access to the contents. **3** an engraved piece of metal, gemstone, etc., for stamping a design on a seal. **4 a** a substance or device used to close an aperture. **b** an amount of water standing in the trap of a drain to prevent foul air from rising. **5** an act or gesture or event regarded as a confirmation or guarantee (*seal of approval*). **6** a decorative adhesive stamp. • *v.tr.* **1** close securely or hermetically. **2** stamp or fasten with a seal. **3** fix a seal to. **4** certify as correct with a seal or stamp. **5** (often foll. by *up*) confine or fasten securely. **6** settle or decide (*their fate is sealed*). **7** (foll. by *off*) put barriers around (an area) to prevent entry and exit. **8** apply a nonporous coating to (a surface) to make it impervious. ▫ **one's lips are sealed** one is obliged to keep a secret. **set one's seal to** (or **on**) authorize or confirm. ▫▫ **seal·a·ble** *adj.*
seal[2] /seel/ *n.* & *v.* • *n.* any fish-eating amphibious sea mammal of the family Phocidae or Otariidae, with flippers and webbed feet. • *v.intr.* hunt for seals.
seal·ant /seélənt/ *n.* material for sealing, esp. to make something airtight or watertight.
sea legs *n.pl.* the ability to keep one's balance and avoid seasickness when at sea.
sea lev·el *n.* the mean level of the sea's surface, used in reckoning the height of hills, etc., and as a barometric standard.
sea lil·y *n.* any of various sessile echinoderms, esp. of the class Crinoidea, with long jointed stalks and featherlike arms for trapping food.
seal·ing wax *n.* a mixture of shellac and rosin with turpentine and pigment, softened by heating and used to make seals.
sea li·on *n.* any large, eared seal of the Pacific, esp. of the genus *Zalophus* or *Otaria.*
seal·skin /seélskin/ *n.* **1** the skin or prepared fur of a seal. **2** (often *attrib.*) a garment made from this.
seam /seem/ *n.* & *v.* • *n.* **1** a line where two edges join, esp. of two pieces of cloth, etc., turned back and stitched together, or of boards fitted edge to edge. **2** a fissure between parallel edges. **3** a wrinkle or scar. **4** a stratum of coal, etc. • *v.tr.* **1** join with a seam. **2** (esp. as **seamed** *adj.*) mark or score with or as with a seam. ▫▫ **seam·er** *n.* **seam·less** *adj.*
sea·man /seémən/ *n.* (*pl.* **-men**) **1** a sailor, esp. one below the rank of officer. **2** a person regarded in terms of skill in navigation (*a poor seaman*). ▫▫ **sea·man·like** *adj.* **sea·man·ly** *adj.*
sea·man·ship /seémənship/ *n.* skill in managing a ship or boat.
sea mile *n.* = NAUTICAL MILE.

See page xii for the *Key to Pronunciation.*

seam·stress /séemstris/ *n.* (also **semp·stress** /semp–/) a woman who sews, esp. professionally.

seam·y /séemee/ *adj.* (**seamier, seamiest**) **1** marked with or showing seams. **2** unpleasant; disreputable (esp. *the seamy side*). ▫▫ **seam·i·ness** *n.*

se·ance /sáyoNs/ *n.* (also **séance**) a meeting at which spiritualists attempt to make contact with the dead.

sea ot·ter *n.* a Pacific otter, *Enhydra lutris*.

sea·plane /séeplayn/ *n.* an aircraft designed to take off from and land and float on water.

sea·port /séepawrt/ *n.* a town with a harbor for seagoing ships.

sear /seer/ *v. & adj.* •*v.tr.* **1 a** scorch, esp. with a hot iron; cauterize. **b** (as **searing** *adj.*) burning (*searing pain*). **2** cause pain or great anguish to. **3** brown (meat) quickly at a high temperature so that it will retain its juices in cooking. •*adj.* var. of SERE[1].

search /sərch/ *v. & n.* •*v.* **1** *tr.* look through or go over thoroughly to find something. **2** *tr.* examine or feel over (a person) to find anything concealed. **3** *tr.* **a** probe or penetrate into. **b** examine (one's mind, etc.) thoroughly. **4** *intr.* (often foll. by *for*) make a search or investigation. **5** *intr.* (as **searching** *adj.*) (of an examination) thorough. **6** *tr.* (foll. by *out*) look probingly for. •*n.* **1** an act of searching. **2** an investigation. ▫ **in search of** trying to find. **search me!** *colloq.* I do not know. ▫▫ **search·a·ble** *adj.* **search·er** *n.* **search·ing·ly** *adv.*

search en·gine *n. Computing* software for the retrieval of data from a database or network.

search·light /sérchlīt/ *n.* **1** a powerful outdoor electric light with a concentrated beam that can be turned in any direction. **2** the light or beam from this.

search par·ty *n.* a group of people organized to look for a lost person or thing.

search war·rant *n.* an official authorization to enter and search a building.

sea salt *n.* salt produced by evaporating seawater.

sea·scape /séeskayp/ *n.* a picture or view of the sea.

sea ser·pent *n.* (also **sea snake**) **1** a snake of the family Hydrophidae, living in the sea. **2** an enormous legendary serpentlike sea monster.

sea·shell /séeshel/ *n.* the shell of a saltwater mollusk.

sea·shore /séeshawr/ *n.* land close to or bordering on the sea.

sea·sick /séesik/ *adj.* suffering from sickness or nausea from the motion of a ship at sea. ▫▫ **sea·sick·ness** *n.*

sea·side /séesīd/ *n.* the seacoast, esp. as a holiday resort.

sea·son /séezən/ *n. & v.* •*n.* **1** each of the four divisions of the year (spring, summer, autumn, and winter). **2** a time of year characterized by climatic or other features (*the dry season*). **3 a** the time of year when a plant is flowering, etc. **b** the time of year when an animal breeds or is hunted. **4** a proper or suitable time. **5** a time when something is plentiful or active or in vogue. **6** the time of year regularly devoted to an activity (*the football season*). •*v.* **1** *tr.* flavor (food) with salt, herbs, etc. **2** *tr.* enhance with wit, etc. **3** *tr.* temper or moderate. **4** *tr. & intr.* **a** make or become suitable, esp. by exposure to the air or weather. **b** make or become experienced or accustomed (*seasoned soldiers*). ▫ **in season 1** (of foodstuff) available in plenty and in good condition. **2** (of an animal) in heat.

sea·son·a·ble /séezənəbəl/ *adj.* **1** suitable to or usual in the season. **2** opportune. **3** meeting the needs of the occasion. ▫▫ **sea·son·a·ble·ness** *n.* **sea·son·a·bly** *adv.*

▶**Seasonable** means 'usual or suitable for the season' or 'opportune,' e.g., *Although seasonable, the weather was not warm enough for a picnic.* **Seasonal** means 'of, depending on, or varying with the season,' e.g., *Seasonal changes in labor requirements draw migrant workers to the area in spring and fall.*

sea·son·al /séezənəl/ *adj.* of, depending on, or varying with the season. ▫▫ **sea·son·al·i·ty** /–nálitee/ *n.* **sea·son·al·ly** *adv.*

sea·son·ing /séezəning/ *n.* condiments added to food.

seat /seet/ *n. & v.* •*n.* **1** a thing made or used for sitting on. **2** the buttocks. **3** the part of a garment covering the buttocks. **4** the part of a chair, etc., on which the sitter's weight directly rests. **5** a place for one person in a theater, etc. **6** *Polit.* the right to occupy a seat, esp. as a member of Congress, etc. **7** the part of a machine that supports or guides another part. **8** a site or location of something specified (*a seat of learning*). **9** a country mansion. **10** the manner of sitting on a horse, etc. •*v.tr.* **1** cause to sit. **2 a** provide sitting accommodation for (*the theater seats 500*). **b** provide with seats. **3** (as **seated** *adj.*) sitting. **4** put or fit in position. ▫ **be seated** sit down. **by the seat of one's pants** *colloq.* by instinct rather than logic or knowledge. **take a** (or **one's**) **seat** sit down. ▫▫ **seat·less** *adj.*

seat belt *n.* a belt securing a person in the seat of a car, aircraft, etc.

seat·ing /séeting/ *n.* **1** seats collectively. **2** sitting accommodation.

SEATO /séetō/ *abbr.* Southeast Asia Treaty Organization.

sea ur·chin *n.* a small marine echinoderm of the class Echinoidea, with a spherical or flattened spiny shell.

sea·wall /séewawl/ *n.* a wall erected to prevent encroachment by the sea.

sea·ward /séeward/ *adv., adj., & n.* •*adv.* (also **seawards** /–wərdz/) toward the sea. •*adj.* going or facing toward the sea. •*n.* such a direction or position.

sea·wa·ter /séewawtər/ *n.* water in or taken from the sea.

sea·way /séeway/ *n.* **1** an inland waterway open to seagoing ships. **2** a ship's progress. **3** a ship's path across the sea.

sea·weed /séeweed/ *n.* any of various algae growing in the sea or on the rocks on a shore.

sea·wor·thy /séewərthee/ *adj.* (of a ship) fit to put to sea. ▫▫ **sea·wor·thi·ness** *n.*

se·ba·ceous /sibáyshəs/ *adj.* fatty; of or relating to tallow or fat.

seb·or·rhe·a /sébəréeə/ *n.* excessive discharge of sebum from the sebaceous glands. ▫▫ **seb·or·rhe·ic** *adj.*

se·bum /séebəm/ *n.* the oily secretion of the sebaceous glands.

Sec. *abbr.* secretary.

sec[1] *abbr.* secant.

sec[2] /sek/ *n. colloq.* (in phrases) a second (of time).

sec[3] /sek/ *adj.* (of wine) dry.

sec. *abbr.* second(s).

se·cant /séekant, –kənt/ *adj. & n. Math.* •*adj.* cutting (*secant line*). •*n.* **1** a line cutting a curve at one or more points. **2** the ratio of the hypotenuse to the shorter side adjacent to an acute angle (in a right triangle).

se·cede /siséed/ *v.intr.* (usu. foll. by *from*) withdraw formally from membership of a political federation or a religious body. ▫▫ **se·ced·er** *n.*

se·ces·sion /siséshən/ *n.* **1** the act or an instance of seceding. **2** (**Secession**) *hist.* the withdrawal of eleven southern states from the US Union in 1860–61, leading to the Civil War. ▫▫ **se·ces·sion·al** *adj.* **se·ces·sion·ism** *n.* **se·ces·sion·ist** *n.*

se·clude /siklóōd/ *v.tr.* (also *refl.*) **1** keep (a person or place) retired or away from company. **2** (esp. as **secluded** *adj.*) hide or screen from view.

se·clu·sion /siklóōzhən/ *n.* **1** a secluded state; retirement; privacy. **2** a secluded place. ▫▫ **se·clu·sion·ist** *n.* **se·clu·sive** /–klóōsiv/ *adj.*

sec·ond[1] /sékənd/ *n., adj., & v.* •*n.* **1** the position in a sequence corresponding to that of the number 2 in the sequence 1–2. **2** something occupying this position. **3** the second person, etc., in a race or competition. **4** another person or thing in addition to one previously mentioned (*the officer was then joined by a second*). **5** (in *pl.*) goods of a second or inferior quality. **6** (in *pl.*) *colloq.* **a** a second helping of food at a meal. **b** the second course of a meal. **7** an attendant assisting a combatant in a duel, etc. **8** esp. *Brit.* **a** a place in the second class of an examination. **b** a person having this. • *adj.* **1** that is the second; next after first. **2** additional; further (*ate a second cupcake*). **3** subordinate; inferior. **4** *Mus.* performing a lower or subordinate part (*second violins*). **5** such as to be comparable to (*a second Callas*). • *v.tr.* **1** supplement; support. **2** formally support or endorse (a nomination or resolution, etc., or its proposer). □ **in the second place** as a second consideration, etc. **second to none** surpassed by no other. ▶See notes at FIRST and FORMER.

sec·ond[2] /sékənd/ *n.* **1** a sixtieth of a minute of time or angular distance. **2** *colloq.* a very short time (*wait a second*).

sec·ond·ar·y /sékənderee/ *adj. & n.* • *adj.* **1** coming after or next below what is primary. **2** derived from or depending on or supplementing what is primary. **3** (of education, a school, etc.) for those who have had primary education, usu. from 11 to 18 years. • *n.* (*pl.* **-ies**) a secondary thing. □□ **sec·ond·ar·i·ly** *adv.* **sec·ond·ar·i·ness** *n.*

sec·ond·ar·y col·or *n.* the result of mixing two primary colors.

sec·ond class *n.* the second-best group or category, esp. of hotel or train accommodation or of postal services. □□ **sec·ond-class** *adj. & adv.*

sec·ond cous·in *n.* a child of one's parent's first cousin.

sec·ond-de·gree *adj. Med.* denoting burns that cause blistering but not permanent scars.

sec·ond-gen·er·a·tion *adj.* denoting the offspring of a first generation, esp. of immigrants.

sec·ond-guess *v.tr. colloq.* **1** anticipate or predict by guesswork. **2** judge or criticize with hindsight.

sec·ond·hand /sékəndhánd/ *adj. & adv.* • *adj.* **1 a** (of goods) having had a previous owner. **b** (of a store, etc.) where such goods can be bought. **2** (of information, etc.) accepted on another's authority and not from original investigation. • *adv.* **1** on a secondhand basis. **2** at second hand; not directly.

sec·ond hand *n.* a hand in some watches and clocks, recording seconds.

sec·ond lieu·ten·ant *n.* in the US, the lowest-ranked commissioned officer of the army, air force, or marines.

sec·ond·ly /sékəndlee/ *adv.* **1** furthermore. **2** as a second item.

sec·ond na·ture *n.* (often foll. by *to*) an acquired tendency that has become instinctive (*is second nature to him*).

sec·ond-rate *adj.* of mediocre quality; inferior.

sec·ond sight *n.* the supposed power of being able to perceive future or distant events.

sec·ond string *n.* an alternative available in case of need.

sec·ond thoughts *n.pl.* a new opinion or resolution reached after further consideration.

sec·ond wind *n.* **1** recovery of the power of normal breathing during exercise after initial breathlessness. **2** renewed energy to continue an effort.

se·cre·cy /séekrisee/ *n.* **1** the keeping of secrets as a fact, habit, or faculty. **2** a state in which all information is withheld (*was done in great secrecy*). □ **sworn to secrecy** having promised to keep a secret.

se·cret /séekrit/ *adj. & n.* • *adj.* **1** kept or meant to be kept private, unknown, or hidden. **2** acting or operating secretly. **3** fond of, prone to, or able to preserve secrecy. **4** (of a place) completely secluded. • *n.* **1** a thing kept or meant to be kept secret. **2** a thing known only to a few. **3** a mystery. **4** a valid but not commonly known method (*what's their secret?*). □ **in secret** secretly. **in** (or **in on**) **the secret** among the number of those who know it. **keep a secret** not reveal it. □□ **se·cret·ly** *adv.*

se·cret a·gent *n.* a spy acting for a country.

sec·re·taire /sékritáir/ *n.* an escritoire.

sec·re·tar·i·at /sékritáireeət/ *n.* **1** a permanent administrative office or department, esp. a governmental one. **2** its members or premises.

sec·re·tar·y /sékriteree/ *n.* (*pl.* **-ies**) **1** a person employed to assist with correspondence, keep records, make appointments, etc. **2** an official appointed by a society, etc., to conduct its correspondence, keep its records, etc. **3** (in the UK) the principal assistant of a government minister, ambassador, etc. □□ **sec·re·tar·i·al** /–táireeəl/ *adj.* **sec·re·tar·y·ship** *n.*

sec·re·tar·y bird *n.* a long-legged, snake-eating African bird, *Sagittarius sepentarius*, with a crest likened to a quill pen stuck over a writer's ear.

sec·re·tar·y-gen·er·al *n.* the principal administrator of certain organizations, as the United Nations.

sec·re·tar·y of state *n.* **1** (in the US) the chief government official responsible for foreign affairs. **2** (in the UK) the head of a major government department.

se·cret bal·lot *n.* a ballot in which votes are cast in secret.

se·crete[1] /sikréet/ *v.tr. Biol.* (of a cell, organ, etc.) produce and discharge (a substance). □□ **se·cre·tor** *n.* **se·cre·to·ry** /séekrətáwree/ *adj.*

se·crete[2] /sikréet/ *v.tr.* conceal; put into hiding.

se·cre·tion /sikréeshən/ *n.* **1** *Biol.* **a** a process by which substances are produced and discharged from a cell for a function in the organism or for excretion. **b** the secreted substance. **2** the act or an instance of concealing.

se·cre·tive /séekritiv, səkrée–/ *adj.* inclined to make or keep secrets; uncommunicative. □□ **se·cre·tive·ly** *adv.* **se·cre·tive·ness** *n.*

se·cret po·lice *n.* a police force operating in secret for political purposes.

se·cret serv·ice *n.* **1** a government department concerned with espionage. **2** (**Secret Service**) a branch of the US Treasury Department charged with apprehending counterfeiters and protecting the president and certain other officials and their families.

sect /sekt/ *n.* **1 a** a body of people subscribing to religious doctrines usu. different from those of an established church from which they have separated. **b** a religious denomination. **2** the followers of a particular philosopher or philosophy, or school of thought in politics, etc.

sec·tar·i·an /sektáireeən/ *adj. & n.* • *adj.* **1** of or concerning a sect. **2** bigoted or narrow-minded in following the doctrines of one's sect. • *n.* **1** a member of a sect. **2** a bigot. □□ **sec·tar·i·an·ism** *n.* **sec·tar·i·an·ize** *v.tr.*

sec·tion /sékshən/ *n. & v.* • *n.* **1** a part cut off or separated from something. **2** each of the parts into which a thing is divided (actually or conceptually) or divisible or out of which a structure can be fitted together. **3** a group or subdivision of a larger body of people (*the wind section*). **4** a subdivision of a book, document, etc. **5 a** one square mile of land. **b** a particular district of a town (*residential section*). **6** a subdivision of an army platoon. **7** esp. *Surgery* a separation by cutting. **8** *Biol.* a thin slice of tissue, etc., cut off for microscopic examination. **9 a** the cutting of a solid by or along a plane. **b** the resulting figure or the area of this. • *v.tr.* **1** arrange in or divide into sections. **2** *Biol.* cut into thin slices for microscopic examination.

sec·tion·al /sékshənəl/ *adj.* **1 a** relating to a section, esp. of a community. **b** partisan. **2** made in sections. **3** local rather than general. ▫▫ **sec·tion·al·ism** *n.* **sec·tion·al·ist** *n. & adj.* **sec·tion·al·ize** *v.tr.* **sec·tion·al·ly** *adv.*

sec·tor /séktər/ *n.* **1** a distinct part or branch of an enterprise, or of society, the economy, etc. **2** *Mil.* a subdivision of an area for military operations, controlled by one commander or headquarters. **3** the plane figure enclosed by two radii of a circle, ellipse, etc., and the arc between them. ▫▫ **sec·tor·al** *adj.*

sec·u·lar /sékyələr/ *adj. & n.* • *adj.* **1** concerned with the affairs of this world; not spiritual nor sacred. **2** (of education, etc.) not concerned with religion or religious belief. **3 a** not ecclesiastical or monastic. **b** (of clergy) not bound by a religious rule. **4** occurring once in an age or century. • *n.* a secular priest. ▫▫ **sec·u·lar·ism** *n.* **sec·u·lar·ist** *n.* **sec·u·lar·i·ty** /–láirətee/ *n.* **sec·u·lar·ize** *v.tr.* **sec·u·lar·i·za·tion** *n.* **sec·u·lar·ly** *adv.*

se·cure /sikyŏŏr/ *adj. & v.* • *adj.* **1** untroubled by danger or fear. **2** safe against attack. **3** certain not to fail (*the plan is secure*). **4** fixed or fastened so as not to give way or get loose or be lost (*made the door secure*). **5 a** (foll. by *of*) certain to achieve (*secure of victory*). **b** (foll. by *against, from*) protected (*secure against attack*). • *v.tr.* **1** make secure or safe; fortify. **2** fasten, close, or confine securely. **3** succeed in obtaining (*secured front seats*). **4** guarantee against loss (*a loan secured by property*). ▫▫ **se·cur·a·ble** *adj.* **se·cure·ly** *adv.* **se·cure·ment** *n.*

se·cu·ri·ty /sikyŏŏritee/ *n.* (*pl.* **-ties**) **1** a secure condition or feeling. **2** a thing that guards or guarantees. **3 a** the safety of a nation, company, etc., against espionage, theft, or other danger. **b** an organization for ensuring this. **4** a thing deposited or pledged as a guarantee of an undertaking or a loan, to be forfeited in case of default. **5** (often in *pl.*) a certificate attesting credit or the ownership of stock, bonds, etc. ▫ **on security of** using as a guarantee.

se·cu·ri·ty blan·ket *n.* **1** an official sanction on information in the interest of security. **2** a blanket or other familiar object given as a comfort to a child.

Se·cu·ri·ty Coun·cil *n.* a permanent body of the United Nations seeking to maintain peace and security.

se·cu·ri·ty guard *n.* a person employed to protect the security of buildings, vehicles, etc.

se·dan /sidán/ *n.* **1** (in full **sedan chair**) an enclosed chair for conveying one person, carried between horizontal poles by two porters. **2** an enclosed automobile for four or more people.

se·date[1] /sidáyt/ *adj.* tranquil and dignified; equable; serious. ▫▫ **se·date·ly** *adv.* **se·date·ness** *n.*

se·date[2] /sidáyt/ *v.tr.* put under sedation.

se·da·tion /sidáyshən/ *n.* a state of rest or sleep, esp. produced by a sedative drug.

sed·a·tive /sédətiv/ *n. & adj.* • *n.* a drug, influence, etc., that tends to calm or soothe. • *adj.* calming; soothing; inducing sleep.

sed·en·tar·y /séd'nteree/ *adj.* **1** sitting (*a sedentary posture*). **2** (of work, etc.) characterized by much sitting and little physical exercise. **3** (of a person) spending much time seated. ▫▫ **sed·en·tar·i·ly** /–táirəlee/ *adv.* **sed·en·tar·i·ness** *n.*

sedge /sej/ *n.* **1** any grasslike plant of the genus *Carex* with triangular stems, usu. growing in wet areas. **2** an expanse of this plant. ▫▫ **sedg·y** *adj.*

sed·i·ment /sédimənt/ *n.* **1** matter that settles to the bottom of a liquid. **2** *Geol.* matter that is carried by water or wind and deposited on the surface of the land. ▫▫ **sed·i·men·ta·ry** /–méntəree/ *adj.* **sed·i·men·ta·tion** /–táyshən/ *n.*

se·di·tion /sidíshən/ *n.* **1** conduct or speech inciting to rebellion. **2** agitation against the authority of a government. ▫▫ **se·di·tious** *adj.* **se·di·tious·ly** *adv.*

se·duce /sidŏŏs, –dyŏŏs/ *v.tr.* **1** tempt or entice into sexual activity. **2** lead astray; tempt. ▫▫ **se·duc·er** *n.* **se·duc·i·ble** *adj.*

se·duc·tion /sidúkshən/ *n.* **1** the act or an instance of seducing; the process of being seduced. **2** something that tempts or allures.

se·duc·tive /sidúktiv/ *adj.* tending to seduce; alluring; enticing. ▫▫ **se·duc·tive·ly** *adv.* **se·duc·tive·ness** *n.*

se·duc·tress /sidúktris/ *n.* a female seducer.

sed·u·lous /séjələs/ *adj.* **1** persevering; diligent; assiduous. **2** (of an action, etc.) deliberately and consciously continued. ▫▫ **se·du·li·ty** /sidŏŏlitee, –dyŏŏ–/ *n.* **sed·u·lous·ly** *adv.* **sed·u·lous·ness** *n.*

se·dum /seédəm/ *n.* any plant of the genus *Sedum*, with fleshy leaves and star-shaped yellow, pink, or white flowers, e.g., stonecrop.

see[1] /see/ *v.* (*past* **saw** /saw/; *past part.* **seen** /seen/) **1** *tr.* discern by use of the eyes; observe. **2** *intr.* have or use the power of discerning objects with the eyes (*sees best at night*). **3** *tr.* discern mentally; understand (*I see what you mean*). **4** *tr.* watch; be a spectator of (a game, etc.). **5** *tr.* ascertain or establish by inquiry or research or reflection (*see if the door is open*). **6** *tr.* consider; deduce from observation (*I see you are a brave man*). **7** *tr.* contemplate; foresee mentally (*we saw that no good would come of it*). **8** *tr.* look at for information (usu. in *imper.*: *see page 15*). **9** *tr.* meet or be near and recognize (*I saw your mother in town*). **10** *tr.* **a** meet socially (*sees her sister most weeks*). **b** meet regularly as a boyfriend or girlfriend (*is still seeing that tall man*). **11** *tr.* give an interview to (*the doctor will see you now*). **12** *tr.* visit to consult (*went to see the doctor*). **13** *tr.* find, esp. from a visual source (*I see the match has been canceled*). **14** *intr.* reflect; wait until one knows more (*we shall have to see*). **15** *tr.* interpret (*I see things differently now*). **16** *tr.* experience (*I never thought I would see this day*). **17** *tr.* recognize as acceptable; foresee (*do you see your daughter marrying this man?*). **18** *tr.* observe without interfering (*stood by and saw them squander my money*). **19** *tr.* find attractive (*can't think what she sees in him*). **20** *intr.* (usu. foll. by *to*, or *that* + infin.) ensure; attend to (*shall see to your request*) (cf. *see to it*). **21** *tr.* escort or conduct (to a place, etc.) (*saw them home*). **22** *tr.* be a witness of (an event, etc.) (*see the New Year in*). **23** *tr.* supervise (an action, etc.) (*stay and see the doors locked*). **24** *tr.* **a** (in gambling, esp. poker) equal (a bet). **b** equal the bet of (a player), esp. to see the player's cards. ▫ **as far as I can see** to the best of my understanding or belief. **as I see it** in my opinion. **do you see?** do you understand? **has seen better days** has declined from former prosperity, good condition, etc. **I see** I understand (referring to an explanation, etc.). **let me see** an appeal for time to think before speaking, etc. **see about** attend to. **see after 1** take care of. **2** = *see about*. **see eye to eye** see EYE. **see fit** see FIT[1]. **see into** investigate. **see life** gain experience of the world, often by enjoying oneself. **see the light 1** realize one's mistakes, etc. **2** suddenly see the way to proceed. **3** undergo religious conversion. **see the light of day** (usu. with *neg.*) come into existence. **see off** be present at the departure of (a person). **see out 1** accompany out of a building, etc. **2** finish (a project, etc.) completely. **see reason** see REASON. **see red** become suddenly enraged. **see serv-**

ice see SERVICE. **see stars** *colloq.* see lights before one's eyes as a result of a blow on the head. **see things** have hallucinations or false imaginings. **see through 1** not be deceived by; detect the true nature of. **2** penetrate visually. **see a person through** support a person during a difficult time. **see a thing through** persist with it until it is completed. **see to it** (foll. by *that* + clause) ensure (*see to it that I am not disturbed*) (cf. sense 20 of *v.*). **see one's way clear to** feel able or entitled to. **see you** (or **see you later**) *colloq.* an expression on parting. **we shall see 1** let us await the outcome. **2** a formula for declining to act at once. **will see about it** attend to; deal with at once. **you see 1** you understand. **2** you will understand when I explain. ▫▫ **see·a·ble** *adj.*

see[2] /see/ *n.* **1** the area under the authority of a bishop or archbishop; a diocese. **2** the office or jurisdiction of a bishop or archbishop.

seed /seed/ *n.* & *v.* • *n.* **1 a** a flowering plant's unit of reproduction (esp. in the form of grain) capable of developing into another such plant. **b** seeds collectively, esp. as collected for sowing (*kept for seed*). **2 a** semen. **b** milt. **3** (foll. by *of*) prime cause; beginning (*seeds of doubt*). **4** *archaic* offspring; descendants (*the seed of Abraham*). **5** *Sports* a seeded player. • *v.* **1** *tr.* **a** place seeds in. **b** sprinkle with or as with seed. **2** *intr.* sow seeds. **3** *intr.* produce or drop seed. **4** *tr.* remove seeds from (fruit, etc.). **5** *tr.* place a crystal or crystalline substance in (a solution, etc.) to cause crystallization or condensation. **6** *tr. Sports* **a** assign to (a strong competitor in a knockout competition) a position in an ordered list so that strong competitors do not meet each other in early rounds. **b** arrange (the order of play) in this way. **7** *intr.* go to seed. ▫ **go** (or **run**) **to seed 1** cease flowering as seed develops. **2** become degenerate, unkempt, ineffective, etc. ▫▫ **seed·less** *adj.*

seed·bed /seédbed/ *n.* **1** a bed of fine soil in which to sow seeds. **2** a place of development.

seed·cake /seédkayk/ *n.* cake containing whole seeds of sesame or caraway.

seed·er /seédər/ *n.* **1** a person or thing that seeds. **2** a machine for sowing seed.

seed·ling /seédling/ *n.* a young plant, esp. one raised from seed and not from a cutting, etc.

seed mon·ey *n.* money allocated to initiate a project.

seed pearl *n.* a very small pearl.

seed·y /seédee/ *adj.* (**seedier, seediest**) **1** full of seed. **2** going to seed. **3** shabby looking; in worn clothes. **4** *colloq.* unwell. ▫▫ **seed·i·ly** *adv.* **seed·i·ness** *n.*

see·ing /seéing/ *conj.* (usu. foll. by *that* + clause) considering that; inasmuch as; because (*seeing that you do not know it yourself*).

seek /seek/ *v.* (*past* and *past part.* **sought** /sawt/) **1 a** *tr.* make a search or inquiry for. **b** *intr.* (foll. by *for, after*) make a search or inquiry. **2** *tr.* **a** try or want to find or get. **b** ask for; request (*seeks my aid*). **3** *tr.* (foll. by *to* + infin.) endeavor or try. **4** *tr.* make for or resort to (*sought his bed; sought a fortune-teller*). **5** *tr. archaic* aim at; attempt. ▫ **seek out 1** search for and find. **2** single out for companionship, etc. ▫▫ **seek·er** *n.* (also in *comb.*).

seem /seem/ *v.intr.* **1** give the impression or sensation of being. **2** (foll. by *to* + infin.) appear or be perceived or ascertained (*they seem to have left*). ▫ **can't seem to** *colloq.* seem unable to. **do not seem to** *colloq.* somehow do not (*I do not seem to like him*). **it seems** (or **would seem**) (often foll. by *that* + clause) it appears to be true or the fact (in a hesitant, guarded, or ironical statement).

seem·ing /seéming/ *adj.* **1** apparent but perhaps not real. **2** apparent only; ostensible. ▫▫ **seem·ing·ly** *adv.*

seem·ly /seémlee/ *adj.* (**seemlier, seemliest**) conforming to propriety or good taste; decorous; suitable. ▫▫ **seem·li·ness** *n.*

seen *past part.* of SEE[1].

seep /seep/ *v.intr.* ooze out; percolate slowly.

seep·age /seépij/ *n.* **1** the act of seeping. **2** the quantity that seeps out.

seer /seéər, seer/ *n.* **1** a person who sees. **2** a prophet.

seer·suck·er /seérsukər/ *n.* material of cotton, etc., with a puckered surface, typically in a striped pattern.

see·saw /seésaw/ *n., v., adj.,* & *adv.* • *n.* **1 a** a device consisting of a long plank balanced on a central support for children to sit on at each end and move up and down by pushing the ground with their feet. **b** a game played on this. **2** an up-and-down or to-and-fro motion. **3** a contest in which the advantage repeatedly changes from one side to the other. • *v.intr.* **1** play on a seesaw. **2** move up and down as on a seesaw. **3** vacillate in policy, emotion, etc. • *adj.* & *adv.* with up-and-down or backward-and-forward motion (*seesaw motion*).

seethe /seeth/ *v.* **1** *intr.* boil; bubble over. **2** *intr.* be very agitated, esp. with anger. ▫▫ **seeth·ing·ly** *adv.*

see-through *adj.* (esp. of clothing) translucent.

seg·ment /ségmənt/ *n.* & *v.* • *n.* **1** each of several parts into which a thing is or can be divided or marked off. **2** *Geom.* a part of a figure cut off by a line or plane intersecting it. **3** *Zool.* each of the longitudinal sections of the body of certain animals (e.g., worms). • *v.* (usu. /–mént/) *intr.* & *tr.* divide into segments. ▫▫ **seg·men·tal** /–mént'l/ *adj.* **seg·men·tal·ly** /–mént'lee/ *adv.* **seg·men·ta·ry** /ségməntairee/ *adj.* **seg·men·ta·tion** /–táyshən/ *n.*

se·go /seégō/ *n.* (*pl.* **-gos**) (in full **sego lily**) a N. American plant, *Calochortus nuttallii*, with green and white bell-shaped flowers.

seg·re·gate /ségrigayt/ *v.* **1** *tr.* put apart from the rest; isolate. **2** *tr.* enforce racial segregation on (persons) or in (a community, etc.). **3** *intr.* separate from a mass and collect together.

seg·re·ga·tion /ségrigáyshən/ *n.* **1** enforced separation of racial groups in a community, etc. **2** the act or an instance of segregating; the state of being segregated. ▫▫ **seg·re·ga·tion·al** *adj.* **seg·re·ga·tion·ist** *n.* & *adj.*

se·gue /ségway/ *v.* & *n.* esp. *Mus.* • *v.intr.* (**segues, segued, segueing**) (usu. foll. by *into*) go on without a pause. • *n.* an uninterrupted transition from one song or melody to another.

sei·cen·to /saychéntō/ *n.* the style of Italian art and literature of the 17th c. ▫▫ **sei·cen·tist** *n.* **sei·cen·to·ist** *n.*

seiche /saysh/ *n.* a fluctuation in the water level of a lake, etc., usu. caused by changes in barometric pressure.

seif /seef, sayf/ *n.* (in full **seif dune**) a sand dune in the form of a long narrow ridge.

sei·gneur /saynyőr/ *n.* (also **seign·ior** /sáynyáwr/) a feudal lord; the lord of a manor. ▫▫ **sei·gneu·ri·al** *adj.* **seign·ior·i·al** /–nyáwreeəl/ *adj.*

seine /sayn/ *n.* & *v.* • *n.* a fishing net for encircling fish, with floats at the top and weights at the bottom edge, and usu. hauled ashore. • *v.intr.* & *tr.* fish or catch with a seine. ▫▫ **sein·er** *n.*

seis·mic /sízmik/ *adj.* of or relating to an earthquake or earthquakes. ▫▫ **seis·mal** *adj.* **seis·mi·cal** *adj.* **seis·mi·cal·ly** *adv.*

seismo- /sízmō/ *comb. form* earthquake.

seis·mo·gram /sízməgram/ *n.* a record given by a seismograph.

seis·mo·graph /sízməgraf/ *n.* an instrument that records the force, direction, etc., of earthquakes. ▫▫ **seis·mo·graph·ic** *adj.* **seis·mo·graph·i·cal** *adj.*

seis·mol·o·gy /sízmóləjee/ *n.* the scientific study and recording of earthquakes and related phenomena.

□□ **seis·mo·log·i·cal** /–məlójikəl/ *adj.* **seis·mo·log·i·cal·ly** /–lójiklee/ *adv.* **seis·mol·o·gist** *n.*

seize /seez/ *v.* **1** *tr.* take hold of forcibly or suddenly. **2** *tr.* take possession of forcibly (*seized power*). **3** *tr.* take possession of by warrant or legal right. **4** *tr.* affect suddenly (*panic seized us*). **5** *tr.* take advantage of (an opportunity). **6** *tr.* comprehend quickly or clearly. **7** *intr.* (usu. foll. by *on, upon*) **a** take hold forcibly or suddenly. **b** take advantage eagerly (*seized on a pretext*). **8** *intr.* (usu. foll. by *up*) (of a moving part in a machine) become jammed. **9** *tr.* (also **seise**) (usu. foll. by *of*) *Law* put in possession of. **10** *tr. Naut.* fasten or attach by binding with turns of yarn, etc. □ **seized** (or **seised**) **of 1** possessing legally. **2** aware or informed of. □□ **seiz·a·ble** *adj.* **seiz·er** *n.*

sei·zure /séezhər/ *n.* **1** the act or an instance of seizing; the state of being seized. **2** a sudden attack of apoplexy, etc.; a stroke.

sel·dom /séldəm/ *adv. & adj.* • *adv.* rarely; not often. • *adj.* rare; uncommon.

se·lect /silékt/ *v. & adj.* • *v.tr.* choose, esp. as the best or most suitable. • *adj.* **1** chosen for excellence or suitability; choice. **2** (of a society, etc.) exclusive; cautious in admitting members. □□ **se·lect·a·ble** *adj.* **se·lect·ness** *n.*

se·lec·tion /silékshən/ *n.* **1** the act or an instance of selecting. **2** a selected person or thing. **3** things from which a choice may be made. **4** *Biol.* the process in which environmental and genetic influences determine which types of organism thrive better than others, regarded as a factor in evolution. □□ **se·lec·tion·al** *adj.* **se·lec·tion·al·ly** *adv.*

se·lec·tive /siléktiv/ *adj.* **1** using or characterized by selection. **2** able to select. □□ **se·lec·tive·ly** *adv.* **se·lec·tive·ness** *n.* **se·lec·tiv·i·ty** /silektívitee, sél–, séel–/ *n.*

se·lec·tive serv·ice *n.* service in the armed forces under conscription.

se·lec·tor /siléktər/ *n.* **1** a person who selects, esp. a representative team in a sport. **2** a device that selects, esp. a device in a vehicle that selects the required gear.

se·le·ni·um /siléeneeəm/ *n. Chem.* a nonmetallic element occurring naturally in various metallic sulfide ores.

sel·e·nol·o·gy /sélinóləjee/ *n.* the scientific study of the moon. □□ **sel·e·nol·o·gist** *n.*

self /self/ *n. & adj.* • *n.* (*pl.* **selves** /selvz/) **1** a person's or thing's own individuality or essence (*his true self*). **2** a person or thing as the object of introspection or reflexive action (*the consciousness of self*). **3 a** one's own interests or pleasure. **b** concentration on these. **4** *Commerce* or *colloq.* myself, yourself, himself, etc. (*check drawn to self*). **5** used in phrases equivalent to *myself, yourself, himself*, etc. (*your good selves*). • *adj.* **1** of the same color as the rest or throughout. **2** (of a flower) of the natural wild color. **3** (of color) uniform, the same throughout. □ **one's better self** one's nobler impulses. **one's former** (or **old**) **self** oneself as one formerly was.

self- /self/ *comb. form* expressing reflexive action: **1** of or directed toward oneself or itself (*self-respect*; *self-cleaning*). **2** by oneself or itself, esp. without external agency (*self-evident*). **3** on, in, for, or relating to oneself or itself (*self-confident*).

self-a·base·ment /sélfəbáysmənt/ *n.* the abasement of oneself; self-humiliation.

self-ab·hor·rence /sélfəbháwrəns, –hór–/ *n.* self-hatred.

self-ab·ne·ga·tion /sélfábnigáyshən/ *n.* self-sacrifice.

self-a·buse /sélfəbyóos/ *n.* **1** the reviling or abuse of oneself. **2** masturbation.

self-act·ing /sélfákting/ *adj.* acting without external influence or control.

self-ad·dressed /sélfədrést/ *adj.* (of an envelope, etc.) having one's own address on for return communication.

self-ad·he·sive /sélfədhéesiv/ *adj.* (of an envelope, label, etc.) adhesive, esp. without being moistened.

self-ad·just·ing /sélfəjústing/ *adj.* (of machinery, etc.) adjusting itself. □□ **self-ad·just·ment** *n.*

self-ad·mi·ra·tion /sélfádməráyshən/ *n.* the admiration of oneself; pride; conceit.

self-ag·gran·dize·ment /sélfəgrándizmənt/ *n.* the act or process of enriching oneself or making oneself powerful. □□ **self-ag·gran·diz·ing** /–grándīzing/ *adj.*

self-a·nal·y·sis /sélfənálisis/ *n. Psychol.* the analysis of oneself, one's motives, character, etc. □□ **self-an·a·lyz·ing** /–ánəlīzing/ *adj.*

self-ap·point·ed /sélfəpóyntid/ *adj.* designated so by oneself; not authorized by another (*a self-appointed guardian*).

self-as·sem·bly /sélfəsémblee/ *n.* (often *attrib.*) construction (of furniture, etc.) from materials sold in kit form.

self-as·ser·tion /sélfəsórshən/ *n.* the aggressive promotion of oneself, one's views, etc. □□ **self-as·ser·tive** *adj.* **self-as·ser·tive·ness** *n.*

self-as·sur·ance /sélfəshóorəns/ *n.* confidence in one's own abilities, etc. □□ **self-as·sured** *adj.* **self-as·sur·ed·ly** *adv.*

self-a·ware /sélfəwáir/ *adj.* conscious of one's character, feelings, motives, etc. □□ **self-a·ware·ness** *n.*

self-be·tray·al /sélfbitráyəl/ *n.* **1** the betrayal of oneself. **2** the inadvertent revelation of one's true thoughts, etc.

self-cen·tered /sélfséntərd/ *adj.* preoccupied with one's own personality or affairs. □□ **self-cen·tered·ly** *adv.* **self-cen·tered·ness** *n.*

self-clean·ing /sélfkléening/ *adj.* (esp. of an oven) cleaning itself when heated, etc.

self-col·lect·ed /sélfkəléktid/ *adj.* composed; serene; self-assured.

self-col·ored /sélfkúlərd/ *adj.* **1 a** having the same color throughout (*buttons and belt are self-colored*). **b** (of material) natural; undyed. **2** (of a flower) **a** of uniform color. **b** having its color unchanged by cultivation or hybridization.

self-con·ceit /sélfkənséet/ *n.* = SELF-SATISFACTION. □□ **self-con·ceit·ed** *adj.*

self-con·dem·na·tion /sélfkóndemnáyshən/ *n.* **1** the blaming of oneself. **2** the inadvertent revelation of one's own sin, crime, etc.

self-con·fessed /sélfkənfést/ *adj.* openly admitting oneself to be (*a self-confessed thief*).

self-con·fi·dence /sélfkónfidəns/ *n.* = SELF-ASSURANCE. □□ **self-con·fi·dent** *adj.* **self-con·fi·dent·ly** *adv.*

self-con·scious /sélfkónshəs/ *adj.* **1** feeling undue awareness of oneself, one's appearance, or one's actions. **2** *Philos.* having knowledge of one's own existence; self-contemplating. □□ **self-con·scious·ly** *adv.* **self-con·scious·ness** *n.*

self-con·sti·tut·ed /sélfkónstitootid –tyoo–/ *adj.* (of a person, group, etc.) assuming a function without authorization or right; self-appointed.

self-con·tained /sélfkəntáynd/ *adj.* (of a person) uncommunicative; independent. □□ **self-con·tain·ment** *n.*

self-con·tent /sélfkəntént/ *n.* satisfaction with oneself, one's life, achievements, etc. □□ **self-con·tent·ed** *adj.*

self-con·tra·dic·tion /sélfkóntrədíkshən/ *n.* internal inconsistency. □□ **self-con·tra·dic·to·ry** *adj.*

self-con·trol /sélfkəntrṓl/ *n.* the power of controlling one's external reactions, emotions, etc.; equanimity. □□ **self-con·trolled** *adj.*

self-cor·rect·ing /sélfkərékting/ *adj.* correcting itself without external help.

self-de•cep•tion /sélfdisépshən/ *n.* deceiving oneself esp. concerning one's true feelings, etc. ▫▫ **self-de•ceit** /–diséet/ *n.* **self-de•ceiv•er** /–diséevər/ *n.* **self-de•ceiv•ing** /–diséeving/ *adj.* **self-de•cep•tive** *adj.*

self-de•feat•ing /sélfdiféeting/ *adj.* (of an attempt, action, etc.) doomed to failure because of internal inconsistencies, etc.

self-de•fense /sélfdiféns/ *n.* **1** an aggressive act, speech, etc., intended as defense (*had to hit him in self-defense*). **2** (usu. **the noble art of self-defense**) boxing. ▫▫ **self-de•fen•sive** *adj.*

self-de•ni•al /sélfdiníəl/ *n.* the negation of one's interests, needs, or wishes; self-control. ▫▫ **self-de•ny•ing** *adj.*

self-dep•re•ca•tion /sélfdéprikáyshən/ *n.* the act of disparaging or belittling oneself. ▫▫ **self-dep•re•cat•ing** /–kayting/ *adj.* **self-dep•re•cat•ing•ly** *adv.*

self-de•struct /sélfdistrúkt/ *v.* & *adj.* • *v.intr.* (of a spacecraft, bomb, etc.) explode or disintegrate automatically, esp. when preset to do so. • *attrib.adj. enabling a thing to self-destruct (*a self-destruct device).

self-de•ter•mi•na•tion /sélfditə́rmináyshən/ *n.* **1** a nation's right to determine its own allegiance, government, etc. **2** the ability to act with free will, as opposed to fatalism. ▫▫ **self-de•ter•mined** /–tə́rmind/ *adj.* **self-de•ter•min•ing** /–tə́rmining/ *adj.*

self-de•vel•op•ment /sélfdivéləpmənt/ *n.* the development of one's abilities, etc.

self-dis•ci•pline /sélfdísiplin/ *n.* the act of or ability to apply oneself, control one's feelings, etc.; self-control. ▫▫ **self-dis•ci•plined** *adj.*

self-dis•cov•er•y /sélfdiskúvəree/ *n.* the process of acquiring insight into oneself, one's character, desires, etc.

self-doubt /sélfdówt/ *n.* lack of confidence in oneself, one's abilities, etc.

self-ed•u•cat•ed /sélféjəkaytid/ *adj.* educated by oneself by reading, etc., without formal instruction. ▫▫ **self-ed•u•ca•tion** /–káyshən/ *n.*

self-ef•fac•ing /sélfifáysing/ *adj.* retiring; modest; timid. ▫▫ **self-ef•face•ment** *n.* **self-ef•fac•ing•ly** *adv.*

self-em•ployed /sélfimplóyd/ *adj.* working for oneself, as a freelance or owner of a business, etc.; not employed by an employer. ▫▫ **self-em•ploy•ment** *n.*

self-es•teem /sélfistéem/ *n.* **1** a good opinion of oneself; self-confidence. **2** an unduly high regard for oneself; conceit.

self-ev•i•dent /sélfévidənt/ *adj.* obvious; without the need of evidence or further explanation. ▫▫ **self-ev•i•dence** *n.* **self-ev•i•dent•ly** *adv.*

self-ex•am•i•na•tion /sélfigzámináyshən/ *n.* **1** the study of one's own conduct, reasons, etc. **2** the examining of one's body for signs of illness, etc.

self-ex•e•cut•ing /sélféksikyooting/ *adj. Law* (of a law, legal clause, etc.) not needing legislation, etc., to be enforced; automatic.

self-ex•ist•ent /sélfigzístənt/ *adj.* existing without prior cause; independent.

self-ex•plan•a•to•ry /sélfiksplánətawree/ *adj.* not needing explanation.

self-ex•pres•sion /sélfikspréshən/ *n.* the expression of one's feelings, thoughts, etc., esp. in writing, painting, music, etc. ▫▫ **self-ex•pres•sive** *adj.*

self-feed•er /sélf-féedər/ *n.* **1** a furnace, machine, etc., that renews its own fuel or material automatically. **2** a device for supplying food to farm animals automatically. ▫▫ **self-feed•ing** *adj.*

self-fer•ti•li•za•tion /sélf-fə́rt'lizáyshən/ *n.* the fertilization of plants by their own pollen, not from others. ▫▫ **self-fer•ti•lized** /–fə́rt'līzd/ *adj.* **self-fer•ti•liz•ing** /–fə́rt'līzing/ *adj.*

self-fi•nanc•ing /sélf-fínansing, –fənán–/ *adj.* that finances itself, esp. (of a project or undertaking) that pays for its own implementation or continuation. ▫▫ **self-fi•nance** *v.tr.*

self-ful•fill•ing /sélf-foolfíling/ *adj.* (of a prophecy, forecast, etc.) bound to come true as a result of actions brought about by its being made.

self-ful•fill•ment /sélf-foolfílmənt/ *n.* the fulfillment of one's own hopes and ambitions.

self-gen•er•at•ing /sélfjénəraytíng/ *adj.* generated by itself or oneself.

self-gov•ern•ment /sélfgúvərnmənt/ *n.* **1** (esp. of a former colony, etc.) government by its own people. **2** = SELF-CONTROL. ▫▫ **self-gov•erned** *adj.*

self-grat•i•fi•ca•tion /sélfgrátifikáyshən/ *n.* **1** gratification or pleasing of oneself. **2** self-indulgence; dissipation. **3** masturbation. ▫▫ **self-grat•i•fy•ing** *adj.*

self-ha•tred /sélfháytrid/ *n.* hatred of oneself, esp. of one's actual self when contrasted with one's imagined self.

self-heal /sélfhéel/ *n.* any of several plants, esp. *Prunella vulgaris*, believed to have healing properties.

self-help /sélfhélp/ *n.* **1** the theory that individuals should provide for their own support and improvement in society. **2** the act or faculty of providing for or improving oneself.

self•hood /sélfhood/ *n.* personality; separate and conscious existence.

self-im•age /sélfímij/ *n.* one's own idea or picture of oneself.

self-im•por•tance /sélfimpáwrt'ns/ *n.* a high opinion of oneself; pompousness. ▫▫ **self-im•por•tant** *adj.* **self-im•por•tant•ly** *adv.*

self-im•posed /sélfimpṓzd/ *adj.* (of a task or condition, etc.) imposed on and by oneself, not externally (*self-imposed exile*).

self-im•prove•ment /sélfimpróovmənt/ *n.* the improvement of one's own position or disposition by one's own efforts.

self-in•duced /sélfindóost, –dyóost/ *adj.* induced by oneself or itself.

self-in•dul•gent /sélfindúljənt/ *adj.* indulging oneself in pleasure, idleness, etc. ▫▫ **self-in•dul•gence** *n.* **self-in•dul•gent•ly** *adv.*

self-in•flict•ed /sélfinflíktid/ *adj.* inflicted by and on oneself.

self-in•ter•est /sélfintrist, –tərist/ *n.* one's personal interest or advantage. ▫▫ **self-in•ter•est•ed** *adj.*

self•ish /sélfish/ *adj.* **1** concerned chiefly with one's own personal profit or pleasure; actuated by self-interest. **2** (of a motive, etc.) appealing to self-interest. ▫▫ **self•ish•ly** *adv.* **self•ish•ness** *n.*

self-jus•ti•fi•ca•tion /sélfjústifikáyshən/ *n.* the justification of one's actions.

self-knowl•edge /sélfnólij/ *n.* the understanding of oneself or one's own motives or character.

self•less /sélflis/ *adj.* disregarding oneself or one's own interests; unselfish. ▫▫ **self•less•ly** *adv.* **self•less•ness** *n.*

self-love /sélflúv/ *n.* **1** selfishness; self-indulgence. **2** *Philos.* regard for one's own well-being and happiness.

self-made /sélfmáyd/ *adj.* **1** rich by one's own effort. **2** made by oneself.

self-mo•tion /sélfmṓshən/ *n.* motion caused by oneself or itself, not externally. ▫▫ **self-mov•ing** /–móoving/ *adj.*

self-mo•ti•vat•ed /sélfmṓtivaytid/ *adj.* acting on one's own initiative without external pressure. ▫▫ **self-mo•ti•va•tion** /–váyshən/ *n.*

self-mur·der /sélfmə́rdər/ *n.* = SUICIDE. ▫▫ **self-mur·der·er** *n.*

self·ness /sélfnis/ *n.* **1** individuality; personality; essence. **2** selfishness or self-regard.

self-o·pin·ion·at·ed /sélfəpínyənaytid/ *adj.* **1** stubbornly adhering to one's own opinions. **2** arrogant. ▫▫ **self-o·pin·ion** *n.*

self-per·pet·u·at·ing /sélfpərpéchōō-ayting/ *adj.* perpetuating itself or oneself without external agency. ▫▫ **self-per·pet·u·a·tion** /–áyshən/ *n.*

self-pit·y /sélfpítee/ *n.* excessive, self-absorbed sorrow for one's own troubles, etc. ▫▫ **self-pit·y·ing** *adj.* **self-pit·y·ing·ly** *adv.*

self-pol·li·na·tion /sélfpólináyshən/ *n.* the pollination of a flower by pollen from the same plant. ▫▫ **self-pol·li·nat·ed** *adj.* **self-pol·li·nat·ing** *adj.* **self-pol·li·na·tor** *n.*

self-por·trait /sélfpáwrtrit/ *n.* a portrait or description of an artist, writer, etc., by himself or herself.

self-pos·sessed /sélfpəzést/ *adj.* habitually exercising self-control; composed. ▫▫ **self-pos·ses·sion** /–zéshən/ *n.*

self-praise /sélfpráyz/ *n.* boasting; self-glorification.

self-pres·er·va·tion /sélfprézərváyshən/ *n.* **1** the preservation of one's own life, safety, etc. **2** this as a basic instinct of human beings and animals.

self-pro·claimed /sélfprəkláymd/ *adj.* proclaimed by oneself or itself to be such.

self-pro·pelled /sélfprəpéld/ *adj.* (esp. of a motor vehicle, etc.) moving or able to move without external propulsion. ▫▫ **self-pro·pel·ling** *adj.*

self-re·al·i·za·tion /sélfréeəlizáyshən/ *n.* **1** the development of one's faculties, abilities, etc. **2** this as an ethical principle.

self-re·cord·ing /sélfrikáwrding/ *adj.* (of a scientific instrument, etc.) automatically recording its measurements.

self-re·gard /sélfrigaárd/ *n.* **1** a proper regard for oneself. **2 a** selfishness. **b** conceit.

self-reg·u·lat·ing /sélfrégyəlayting/ *adj.* regulating oneself or itself without intervention. ▫▫ **self-reg·u·la·tion** /–láyshən/ *n.* **self-reg·u·la·to·ry** /–lətawree/ *adj.*

self-re·li·ance /sélfrilíəns/ *n.* reliance on one's own resources, etc.; independence. ▫▫ **self-re·li·ant** *adj.* **self-re·li·ant·ly** *adv.*

self-re·proach /sélfripróch/ *n.* reproach or blame directed at oneself. ▫▫ **self-re·proach·ful** *adj.*

self-re·spect /sélfrispékt/ *n.* respect for oneself. ▫▫ **self-re·spect·ing** *adj.*

self-re·straint /sélfristráynt/ *n.* = SELF-CONTROL. ▫▫ **self-re·strained** *adj.*

self-re·veal·ing /sélfrivéeling/ *adj.* revealing one's character, motives, etc., esp. inadvertently. ▫▫ **self-rev·e·la·tion** /–révəláyshən/ *n.*

self-right·eous /sélfríchəs/ *adj.* excessively conscious of or insistent on one's rectitude, correctness, etc. ▫▫ **self-right·eous·ly** *adv.* **self-right·eous·ness** *n.*

self-right·ing /sélfríting/ *adj.* (of a boat) righting itself when capsized.

self-ris·ing /sélfrízing/ *adj.* (of flour) having a raising agent already added.

self-rule /sélfrool/ *n.* = SELF-GOVERNMENT 1.

self-sac·ri·fice /sélfsákrifis/ *n.* the negation of one's own interests, wishes, etc., in favor of those of others. ▫▫ **self-sac·ri·fic·ing** *adj.*

self·same /sélfsaym/ *attrib.adj.* (prec. by *the*) the very same.

self-sat·is·fac·tion /sélfsátisfákshən/ *n.* excessive and unwarranted satisfaction with oneself; complacency. ▫▫ **self-sat·is·fied** /–sátisfīd/ *adj.*

self-seal·ing /sélfséeling/ *adj.* **1** (of a tire, fuel tank, etc.) automatically able to seal small punctures. **2** (of an envelope) self-adhesive.

self-seek·ing /sélfséeking/ *adj.* & *n.* seeking one's own welfare before that of others. ▫▫ **self-seek·er** *n.*

self-se·lec·tion /sélfsilékshən/ *n.* the act of selecting oneself or itself. ▫▫ **self-se·lect·ing** *adj.*

self-serv·ice /sélfsə́rvis/ *adj.* & *n.* • *adj.* (often *attrib.*) **1** (of a store, restaurant, gas station, etc.) where customers serve themselves and pay at a checkout, etc. **2** (of a machine) serving goods after the insertion of coins. • *n. colloq.* a self-service store, gas station, etc.

self-serv·ing /sélfsə́rving/ *adj.* = SELF-SEEKING.

self-start·er /sélfstaártər/ *n.* **1** an electric appliance for starting a motor vehicle engine without the use of a crank. **2** an ambitious person who needs no external motivation.

self-styled /sélfstíld/ *adj.* called so by oneself (*a self-styled artist*).

self-suf·fi·cient /sélfsəfíshənt/ *adj.* **1 a** needing nothing; independent. **b** able to supply one's needs from one's own resources. **2** content with one's own opinion; arrogant. ▫▫ **self-suf·fi·cien·cy** *n.* **self-suf·fi·cient·ly** *adv.*

self-sup·port·ing /sélfsəpáwrting/ *adj.* **1** capable of maintaining oneself or itself financially. **2** staying up without external aid. ▫▫ **self-sup·port** *n.*

self-sur·ren·der /sélfsəréndər/ *n.* the surrender of oneself or one's will, etc., to an influence, emotion, or other person.

self-sus·tain·ing /sélfsəstáyning/ *adj.* sustaining oneself or itself. ▫▫ **self-sus·tained** *adj.*

self-tap·ping *adj.* (of a screw) able to cut its own thread.

self-taught /sélftáwt/ *adj.* educated or trained by oneself, not externally.

self-tor·ture /sélftáwrchər/ *n.* the inflicting of pain, esp. mental, on oneself.

self-willed /sélfwíld/ *adj.* obstinately pursuing one's own wishes. ▫▫ **self-will** *n.*

self-wind·ing /sélfwínding/ *adj.* (of a watch, etc.) having an automatic winding apparatus.

self-worth /sélfwə́rth/ *n.* = SELF-ESTEEM.

sell /sel/ *v.* & *n.* • *v.* (*past* and *past part.* **sold** /sōld/) **1** *tr.* make over or dispose of in exchange for money. **2** *tr.* keep a stock of for sale or be a dealer in (*do you sell candles?*). **3** *intr.* (of goods) be purchased (*these are selling well*). **4** *intr.* (foll. by *at*, *for*) have a specified price (*sells at $5*). **5** *tr.* betray for money or other reward (*sell one's country*). **6** *tr.* offer dishonorably for money or other consideration; make a matter of corrupt bargaining (*sell justice; sell one's honor*). **7** *tr.* **a** advertise or publish the merits of. **b** inspire with a desire to buy or acquire or agree to something. **8** *tr.* cause to be sold (*the author's name alone will sell many copies*). • *n. colloq.* **1** a manner of selling (*soft sell*). **2** a deception or disappointment. ▫ **sell off** sell the remainder of (goods) at reduced prices. **sell out 1** sell (all or some of one's stock, shares, etc.). **2** betray. **sell short** disparage; underestimate. **sold on** *colloq.* enthusiastic about. ▫▫ **sell·a·ble** *adj.* **sell·er** *n.*

sell-by date *n.* the latest recommended date of sale.

sel·ler's mar·ket *n.* (also **sellers' market**) an economic position in which goods are scarce and expensive.

sell·ing point *n.* an advantageous feature.

sell·out /sélowt/ *n.* **1** a commercial success, esp. the selling of all tickets for a show. **2** a betrayal.

selt·zer /séltsər/ *n.* (in full **seltzer water**) **1** medicinal mineral water from Nieder-Selters in Germany. **2** an artificial substitute for this; soda water.

sel·vage /sélvij/ *n.* (also **sel·vedge**) **1** an edging that prevents cloth from unraveling. **2** a border of different material or finish intended to be removed or hidden.

selves *pl.* of SELF.

se•man•tic /simántik/ *adj.* relating to meaning in language. ▫▫ **se•man•ti•cal•ly** *adv.*

se•man•tics /simántiks/ *n.pl.* (usu. treated as *sing.*) the branch of linguistics concerned with meaning. ▫▫ **se•man•ti•cist** /–tisist/ *n.*

sem•a•phore /séməfawr/ *n. & v.* • *n.* **1** *Mil.*, etc. a system of sending messages by holding the arms or two flags in certain positions according to an alphabetic code. **2** a signaling apparatus consisting of a post with a movable arm or arms, lanterns, etc. • *v.intr. & tr.* signal or send by semaphore. ▫▫ **sem•a•phor•ic** *adj.* **sem•a•phor•i•cal•ly** /–fáwriklee/ *adv.*

se•mat•ic /simátik/ *adj. Zool.* (of coloring, markings, etc.) significant; serving to warn off enemies or attract attention.

sem•blance /sémbləns/ *n.* **1** the outward or superficial appearance of something (*put on a semblance of anger*). **2** resemblance.

se•men /seémən/ *n.* the reproductive fluid of male animals.

se•mes•ter /siméstər/ *n.* **1** half of the academic year in an educational institution, usu. an 18-week period. **2** a half-year course or term in (esp. German) universities.

sem•i /sémī, sémee/ *n.* (*pl.* **semis**) *colloq.* **1** a semitrailer. **2** a semifinal.

semi- /sémee, sémī/ *prefix* **1** half (*semicircle*). **2** partly (*semiofficial; semidetached*). **3** almost (*a semismile*). **4** occurring or appearing twice in a specified period (*semiannual*).

sem•i•an•nu•al /sémeeányōōəl, sémī;n–/ *adj.* occurring, published, etc., twice a year. ▫▫ **sem•i•an•nu•al•ly** *adv.*

sem•i•au•to•mat•ic /sémeeáwtəmátik, sémī–/ *adj.* **1** partially automatic. **2** (of a firearm) having a mechanism for continuous loading but not for continuous firing.

sem•i•breve /sémeebrev, –breev, sémī–/ *n.* esp. *Brit. Mus.* = WHOLE NOTE.

sem•i•cir•cle /sémeesərkəl, sémī–/ *n.* **1** half of a circle or of its circumference. **2** an object, or arrangement of objects, forming a semicircle. ▫▫ **sem•i•cir•cu•lar** /sémeesə́rkyələr, sémī–/ *adj.*

sem•i•co•lon /sémikṓlən/ *n.* a punctuation mark (;) of intermediate value between a comma and a period.

sem•i•con•duct•ing /sémeekəndúkting, sémī–/ *adj.* having the properties of a semiconductor.

sem•i•con•duc•tor /sémeekəndúktər, sémī–/ *n.* a solid substance that is a nonconductor when pure or at a low temperature but has a conductivity between that of insulators and that of most metals when containing a suitable impurity or at a higher temperature.

sem•i•con•scious /sémeekónshəs, sémī–/ *adj.* partly or imperfectly conscious.

sem•i•cyl•in•der /sémeesílindər, sémī;n–/ *n.* half of a cylinder cut longitudinally. ▫▫ **sem•i•cy•lin•dri•cal** /–líndrikəl/ *adj.*

sem•i•de•tached /sémeeditácht, sémī–/ *adj. & n.* • *adj.* (of a house) joined to another by a common wall on one side only. • *n.* a semidetached house.

sem•i•di•am•e•ter /sémeedīámitər, sémī;n–/ *n.* half of a diameter; radius.

sem•i•fi•nal /sémeefīnəl, sémī–/ *n.* a match or round immediately preceding the final.

sem•i•fi•nal•ist /sémeefīnəlist, sémī–/ *n.* a competitor in a semifinal.

sem•i•flu•id /sémeeflṓōid, sémī–/ *adj. & n.* • *adj.* of a consistency between solid and liquid. • *n.* a semifluid substance.

sem•i•in•va•lid /sémee-ínvəlid, sémī–/ *n.* a person somewhat enfeebled or partially disabled.

sem•i•liq•uid /sémeelíkwid, sémī–/ *adj. & n.* = SEMIFLUID.

sem•i•lu•nar /sémeelṓōnər, sémī–/ *adj.* shaped like a half moon or crescent.

sem•i•me•tal /sémeemét'l, sémī;n–/ *n.* a substance with some of the properties of metals.

sem•i•month•ly /sémeemúnthlee, sémī;n–/ *adj. & adv.* • *adj.* occurring, published, etc., twice a month. • *adv.* twice a month.

sem•i•nal /sémin əl/ *adj.* **1** of or relating to seed, semen, or reproduction. **2** (of ideas, etc.) providing the basis for future development. ▫▫ **sem•i•nal•ly** *adv.*

sem•i•nar /séminaar/ *n.* **1** a small class at a university, etc., for discussion and research. **2** a short intensive course of study. **3** a conference of specialists.

sem•i•nar•y /sémineree/ *n.* (*pl.* **-ies**) **1** a training college for priests, rabbis, etc. **2** a place of education. ▫▫ **sem•i•nar•i•an** /–náireeən/ *n.* **sem•i•na•rist** *n.*

sem•i•nif•er•ous /sémeenífərəs, sémī;n–/ *adj.* **1** bearing seed. **2** conveying semen.

Sem•i•nole /sémənōl/ *n.* **1 a** a N. American people native to Florida. **b** a member of this people. **2** the language of this people.

sem•i•of•fi•cial /sémeeəfishəl, sémī–/ *adj.* **1** partly official. **2** (of communications) made by an official with the stipulation that the source should not be revealed. ▫▫ **sem•i•of•fi•cial•ly** *adv.*

se•mi•ol•o•gy /seémeeóləjee, sémee–/ *n.* (also **se•mei•ol•o•gy**) = SEMIOTICS. ▫▫ **se•mi•o•log•i•cal** /–meeəlójikəl/ *adj.* **se•mi•ol•o•gist** *n.*

se•mi•ot•ics /seémeeótiks, sém–/ *n.* (also **se•mei•ot•ics**) the study of signs and symbols in various fields, esp. language. ▫▫ **se•mi•ot•ic** *adj.* **se•mi•ot•i•cal** *adj.* **se•mi•ot•i•cal•ly** *adv.* **se•mi•o•ti•cian** /–tíshən/ *n.*

sem•i•per•me•a•ble /sémeepə́rmeeəbəl, sémī–/ *adj.* (of a membrane, etc.) allowing small molecules, but not large ones, to pass through.

sem•i•pre•cious /sémeepréshəs, sémī–/ *adj.* less valuable than a precious stone.

sem•i•pro /sémeeprō, sémī–/ *adj. & n.* (*pl.* **-pros**) *colloq.* = SEMIPROFESSIONAL.

sem•i•pro•fes•sion•al /sémeeprəféshənəl, sémī–/ *adj. & n.* • *adj.* **1** receiving payment for an activity but not relying on it for a living. **2** involving semiprofessionals. • *n.* a semiprofessional musician, sportsman, etc.

sem•i•skilled /sémeeskíld, sémī–/ *adj.* (of work or a worker) having or needing some training but less than for a skilled worker.

sem•i•sol•id /sémeesólid, sémī–/ *adj.* viscous; semifluid.

sem•i•sweet /sémeesweét, sémī–/ *adj.* slightly sweetened.

sem•i•syn•thet•ic /sémeesinthétik, sémī;n–/ *adj. Chem.* (of a substance) that is prepared synthetically but derives from a naturally occurring material.

Sem•ite /sémīt/ *n.* a member of any of the peoples supposed to be descended from Shem, son of Noah (Gen. 10:21 ff.), including the Jews, Arabs, Assyrians, and Phoenicians. ▫▫ **Sem•i•tism** /sémitizəm/ *n.* **Sem•i•tize** /–tīz/ *v.tr.* **Sem•i•ti•za•tion** *n.*

Se•mit•ic /simítik/ *adj.* **1** of or relating to the Semites, esp. the Jews. **2** of or relating to the languages of the family including Hebrew and Arabic.

sem•i•tone /sémeetōn, sémī–/ *n. Mus.* the smallest interval used in classical European music; a half step.

sem•i•trail•er /sémeetráylər, sémī–/ *n.* a trailer having wheels at the back but supported at the front by a towing vehicle.

sem•i•vow•el /sémeevowəl/ *n.* **1** a sound intermediate between a vowel and a consonant (e.g., *w*, *y*). **2** a letter representing this.

See page xii for the *Key to Pronunciation*.

sem·i·week·ly /sémeeweéklee, sémī;n–/ *adj.* & *adv.* • *adj.* occurring, published, etc., twice a week. • *adv.* twice a week.

sem·o·li·na /séməleénə/ *n.* **1** the hard grains left after the milling of flour, used in puddings, etc., and in pasta. **2** a pudding, etc., made of this.

sem·pi·ter·nal /sémpitə́rnəl/ *adj. rhet.* eternal; everlasting. ▫▫ **sem·pi·ter·nal·ly** *adv.* **sem·pi·ter·ni·ty** *n.*

sem·pli·ce /sémplichay/ *adv. Mus.* in a simple style of performance.

sem·pre /sémpray/ *adv. Mus.* throughout; always (*sempre forte*).

sen. *abbr.* **1 a** senator. **b** senate. **2** senior.

sen·ate /sénit/ *n.* **1** a legislative body, esp. the upper and smaller assembly in the US, France, and other countries, in the states of the US, etc. **2** the governing body of a university or college. **3** *Rom.Hist.* the state council of the republic and empire.

sen·a·tor /sénətər/ *n.* **1** a member of a senate. **2** (in Scotland) a Lord of Session. ▫▫ **sen·a·to·ri·al** /–táwreeəl/ *adj.* **sen·a·tor·ship** *n.*

send /send/ *v.* (*past* and *past part.* **sent** /sent/) **1** *tr.* **a** order or cause to go or be conveyed (*send a message to headquarters*; *sent me a book*). **b** propel; cause to move (*send a bullet*; *sent him flying*). **c** cause to go or become (*send into raptures*; *send to sleep*). **d** dismiss with or without force (*sent her away*; *sent him about his business*). **2** *intr.* send a message or letter (*he sent to warn me*). **3** *tr.* (of God, providence, etc.) grant or bestow or inflict; bring about (*send rain*; *send a judgment*). **4** *tr. sl.* put into ecstasy. ▫ **send away for** send an order to a dealer for (goods). **send for 1** summon. **2** order by mail. **send in 1** cause to go in. **2** submit (an entry, etc.) for a competition, etc. **send off 1** get (a letter, parcel, etc.) dispatched. **2** attend the departure of (a person) as a sign of respect, etc. **3** *Sports* (of a referee) order (a player) to leave the field. **send on** transmit to a further destination or in advance of one's own arrival. **send up 1** cause to go up. **2** transmit to a higher authority. **3** *colloq.* satirize or ridicule, esp. by mimicking. **4** sentence to imprisonment. **send word** send information. ▫▫ **send·er** *n.*

send-off *n.* a demonstration of goodwill, etc., at the departure of a person, the start of a project, etc.

send-up *n. colloq.* a satire or parody.

Sen·e·ca /sénikə/ *n.* **1 a** a N. American people native to western New York. **b** a member of this people. **2** the language of this people. ▫▫ **Sen·e·can** *adj.*

se·nesce /sinés/ *v.intr.* grow old. ▫▫ **se·nes·cence** *n.* **se·nes·cent** *adj.*

se·nile /seénīl/ *adj.* **1** of or characteristic of old age (*senile decay*). **2** having the weaknesses or diseases of old age. ▫▫ **se·nil·i·ty** /sinílitee/ *n.*

se·nile de·men·tia *n.* a severe form of mental deterioration in old age, characterized by loss of memory and disorientation.

sen·ior /seényər/ *adj.* & *n.* • *adj.* **1** more or most advanced in age or standing. **2** of high or highest position. **3** (placed after a person's name) senior to another of the same name. **4** of the final year at a university, high school, etc. • *n.* **1** a person of advanced age or long service, etc. **2** one's elder, or one's superior in length of service, membership, etc. (*is my senior*). **3** a senior student. ▫▫ **sen·ior·i·ty** /seényáwritee, –yor–/ *n.*

sen·ior cit·i·zen *n.* an elderly person, esp. a retiree.

sen·na /sénə/ *n.* **1** a cassia tree. **2** a laxative prepared from the dried pod of this.

sen·night /sénīt/ *n. archaic* a week.

sen·nit /sénit/ *n.* **1** *hist.* plaited straw, palm leaves, etc., used for making hats. **2** *Naut.* braided cordage made in flat or round or square form from 3 to 9 cords.

se·ñor /senyáwr/ *n.* (*pl.* **señores** /–rez/) a title used of or to a Spanish-speaking man.

se·ño·ra /senyáwrə/ *n.* a title used of or to a Spanish-speaking married woman.

se·ño·ri·ta /sényəreétə/ *n.* a title used of or to a Spanish-speaking unmarried woman.

sen·sate /sénsayt/ *adj.* perceived by the senses.

sen·sa·tion /sensáyshən/ *n.* **1** the consciousness of perceiving or seeming to perceive some state or condition of one's body or its parts or senses; an instance of such consciousness (*lost all sensation in my left arm*; *had a sensation of giddiness*). **2 a** a stirring of emotions or intense interest esp. among a large group of people (*the news caused a sensation*). **b** a person, event, etc., causing such interest.

sen·sa·tion·al /sensáyshənəl/ *adj.* **1** causing great public excitement, etc. **2** of or causing sensation. ▫▫ **sen·sa·tion·al·ize** *v.tr.* **sen·sa·tion·al·ly** *adv.*

sen·sa·tion·al·ism /sensáyshənəlizəm/ *n.* the use of or interest in the sensational. ▫▫ **sen·sa·tion·al·ist** *n.* & *adj.* **sen·sa·tion·al·is·tic** /–lístik/ *adj.*

sense /sens/ *n.* & *v.* • *n.* **1 a** any of the special bodily faculties by which sensation is roused (*has keen senses*; *has a dull sense of smell*). **b** sensitiveness of all or any of these. **2** the ability to perceive or feel. **3** (foll. by *of*) consciousness (*sense of having done well*; *sense of one's own importance*). **4 a** quick or accurate appreciation, understanding, or instinct regarding a specified matter (*sense of the ridiculous*; *road sense*). **b** the habit of basing one's conduct on such instinct. **5** practical wisdom or judgment; common sense (*has plenty of sense*; *what is the sense of talking like that?*). **6 a** a meaning; the way in which a word, etc., is to be understood (*the sense of the word is clear*; *I mean that in the literal sense*). **b** intelligibility or coherence. **7** the prevailing opinion among a number of people. **8** (in *pl.*) a person's sanity or normal state of mind. • *v.tr.* **1** perceive by a sense or senses. **2** be vaguely aware of. **3** realize. **4** (of a machine, etc.) detect. **5** understand. ▫ **bring a person to his** (or **her) senses 1** cure a person of folly. **2** restore a person to consciousness. **come to one's senses 1** regain consciousness. **2** become sensible after acting foolishly. **in a** (or **one**) **sense** if the statement is understood in a particular way (*what you say is true in a sense*). **in one's senses** sane. **make sense** be intelligible or practicable.

sense·less /sénslis/ *adj.* **1** unconscious. **2** wildly foolish. **3** without meaning or purpose. **4** incapable of sensation. ▫▫ **sense·less·ly** *adv.* **sense·less·ness** *n.*

sen·si·bil·i·ty /sénsibílitee/ *n.* (*pl.* **-ties**) **1 a** openness to emotional impressions; susceptibility (*sensibility to kindness*). **b** an exceptional degree of this (*sense and sensibility*). **2** (in *pl.*) emotional capacities or feelings.

sen·si·ble /sénsibəl/ *adj.* **1** having or showing wisdom or common sense. **2 a** perceptible by the senses (*sensible phenomena*). **b** great enough to be perceived (*a sensible difference*). **3** (of clothing, etc.) practical. **4** (foll. by *of*) aware; not unmindful (*was sensible of his peril*). ▫▫ **sen·si·ble·ness** *n.* **sen·si·bly** *adv.*

sen·si·tive /sénsitiv/ *adj.* & *n.* • *adj.* **1** very open to or acutely affected by external stimuli or mental impressions. **2** easily offended or emotionally hurt. **3** (of an instrument, etc.) responsive to or recording slight changes. **4 a** (of photographic materials) prepared so as to respond rapidly to the action of light. **b** (of any material) responsive to external action. **5** (of a topic, etc.) subject to restriction of discussion to prevent embarrassment, ensure security, etc. ▫▫ **sen·si·tive·ly** *adv.* **sen·si·tive·ness** *n.*

sen·si·tive plant *n.* **1** a plant whose leaves curve downward and leaflets fold together when touched, esp. mimosa. **2** a sensitive person.

sen·si·tiv·i·ty /sénsitívitee/ *n.* the quality or degree of being sensitive.

sen·si·tize /sénsitīz/ *v.tr.* **1** make sensitive. **2** *Photog.* make sensitive to light. **3** make (an organism, etc.) abnormally sensitive to a foreign substance. □□ **sen·si·ti·za·tion** *n.* **sen·si·tiz·er** *n.*

sen·sor /sénsər/ *n.* a device giving a signal for the detection or measurement of a physical property to which it responds.

sen·so·ri·um /sensáwreeəm/ *n.* (*pl.* **sensoria** /–reeə/ or **sensoriums**) **1** the seat of sensation; the brain, brain and spinal cord, or gray matter of these. **2** *Biol.* the whole sensory apparatus including the nerve system. □□ **sen·so·ri·al** *adj.* **sen·so·ri·al·ly** *adv.*

sen·so·ry /sénsəree/ *adj.* of sensation or the senses. □□ **sen·so·ri·ly** *adv.*

sen·su·al /sénshōōəl/ *adj.* **1 a** of or depending on the senses only and not on the intellect or spirit (*sensual pleasures*). **b** given to the pursuit of sensual pleasures or the gratification of the appetites; self-indulgent sexually or in regard to food and drink. **c** indicative of a sensual nature (*sensual lips*). **2** of sense or sensation; sensory. □□ **sen·su·al·ism** *n.* **sen·su·al·ist** *n.* **sen·su·al·ize** *v.tr.* **sen·su·al·ly** *adv.*

sen·su·al·i·ty /sénshōō-álitee/ *n.* gratification of the senses, self-indulgence.

sen·su·ous /sénshōōəs/ *adj.* **1** of or derived from or affecting the senses, esp. aesthetically rather than sensually; aesthetically pleasing. **2** readily affected by the senses. □□ **sen·su·ous·ly** *adv.* **sen·su·ous·ness** *n.*

sent *past* and *past part.* of SEND.

sen·tence /séntəns/ *n.* & *v.* • *n.* **1 a** a set of words complete in itself as the expression of a thought, containing or implying a subject and predicate, and conveying a statement, question, exclamation, or command. **b** a piece of writing or speech between two periods or equivalent pauses, often including several grammatical sentences (e.g., *I went*; *he came*). **2 a** a decision of a court of law, esp. the punishment allotted to a person convicted in a criminal trial. **b** the declaration of this. • *v.tr.* **1** declare the sentence of (a convicted criminal, etc.). **2** (foll. by *to*) declare (such a person) to be condemned to a specified punishment. □ **under sentence of** having been condemned to (*under sentence of death*).

sen·ten·tious /senténshəs/ *adj.* **1** fond of pompous moralizing. **2** affectedly formal. **3** aphoristic; pithy; given to the use of maxims. □□ **sen·ten·tious·ly** *adv.* **sen·ten·tious·ness** *n.*

sen·tient /sénshənt/ *adj.* having the power of perception by the senses. □□ **sen·tience** *n.* **sen·tient·ly** *adv.*

sen·ti·ment /séntimənt/ *n.* **1** a mental feeling (*the sentiment of pity*). **2** the sum of what one feels on some subject. **3** an opinion as distinguished from the words meant to convey it (*the sentiment is good though the words are injudicious*). **4** the tendency to be swayed by feeling rather than by reason. **5 a** mawkish tenderness. **b** the display of this. **6** an emotional feeling conveyed in literature or art.

sen·ti·men·tal /séntimént'l/ *adj.* **1** of or characterized by sentiment. **2** showing or affected by emotion rather than reason. **3** appealing to sentiment. □□ **sen·ti·men·tal·ism** *n.* **sen·ti·men·tal·ist** *n.* **sen·ti·men·tal·i·ty** /–tálitee/ *n.* **sen·ti·men·tal·ize** *v.intr.* & *tr.* **sen·ti·men·tal·i·za·tion** *n.* **sen·ti·men·tal·ly** *adv.*

sen·ti·nel /séntinəl/ *n.* a sentry or lookout.

sen·try /séntree/ *n.* (*pl.* **-tries**) a soldier, etc., stationed to keep guard.

sen·try box *n.* a wooden cabin intended to shelter a standing sentry.

se·pal /séepəl/ *n.* *Bot.* each of the divisions or leaves of the calyx.

sep·a·ra·ble /sépərəbəl/ *adj.* able to be separated. □□ **sep·a·ra·bil·i·ty** *n.* **sep·a·ra·bly** *adv.*

sep·a·rate *adj.*, *n.*, & *v.* • *adj.* /sépərət, séprət/ forming a unit that is apart or by itself; physically disconnected, distinct, or individual (*living in separate rooms*; *the two questions are essentially separate*). • *n.* /sépərət, séprət/ **1** (in *pl.*) separate articles of clothing suitable for wearing together in various combinations. **2** an offprint. • *v.* /sépərayt/ **1** *tr.* make separate; sever. **2** *tr.* prevent union or contact of. **3** *intr.* go different ways. **4** *intr.* cease to live together as a married couple. **5** *intr.* (foll. by *from*) secede. **6** *tr.* **a** divide or sort (milk, ore, fruit, light, etc.) into constituent parts or sizes. **b** extract or remove (an ingredient, waste product, etc.) by such a process for use or rejection. □□ **sep·a·rate·ly** *adv.* **sep·a·rate·ness** *n.*

sep·a·ra·tion /sépəráyshən/ *n.* **1** the act or an instance of separating; the state of being separated. **2** (in full **judicial separation** or **legal separation**) an arrangement by which a husband and wife remain married but live apart.

sep·a·ra·tist /sépərətist, séprə–/ *n.* a person who favors separation, esp. for political or ecclesiastical independence. □□ **sep·a·ra·tism** *n.*

sep·a·ra·tor /sépəraytər/ *n.* a machine for separating, e.g., cream from milk.

Se·phar·di /sifaárdee/ *n.* (*pl.* **Sephardim** /–dim/) a Jew of Spanish or Portuguese descent (cf. ASHKENAZI). □□ **Se·phar·dic** *adj.*

se·pi·a /séepeeə/ *n.* **1** a dark reddish-brown color. **2 a** a brown pigment prepared from a black fluid secreted by cuttlefish, used in monochrome drawing and in watercolors. **b** a brown tint used in photography. **3** a drawing done in sepia. **4** the fluid secreted by cuttlefish.

sep·sis /sépsis/ *n.* **1** the state of being septic. **2** blood poisoning.

Sept. *abbr.* **1** September. **2** Septuagint.

sept- var. of SEPTI-.

sep·ta *pl.* of SEPTUM.

sep·tate /séptayt/ *adj.* *Bot.*, *Zool.*, & *Anat.* having a septum or septa; partitioned. □□ **sep·ta·tion** /–táyshən/ *n.*

sept·cen·ten·ar·y /séptsenténəree/ *n.* & *adj.* • *n.* (*pl.* • **ies**) **1** a seven-hundredth anniversary. **2** a festival marking this. • *adj.* of or concerning a septcentenary.

Sep·tem·ber /septémbər/ *n.* the ninth month of the year.

sep·ten·ni·al /septéneeəl/ *adj.* **1** lasting for seven years. **2** recurring every seven years.

sep·ten·ni·um /septéneeəm/ *n.* (*pl.* **septenniums** or **septennia** /–neeə/) a period of seven years.

sep·tet /septét/ *n.* (also **sep·tette**) **1** *Mus.* **a** a composition for seven performers. **b** the performers of such a composition. **2** any group of seven.

sept·foil /sétfoyl/ *n.* a seven-lobed ornamental figure.

septi- /séptee/ *comb. form* (also **sept-** before a vowel) seven.

sep·tic /séptik/ *adj.* contaminated; putrefying. □□ **sep·ti·cal·ly** *adv.* **sep·tic·i·ty** /–tísitee/ *n.*

sep·ti·ce·mi·a /séptiséemeeə/ *n.* blood poisoning. □□ **sep·ti·ce·mic** *adj.*

sep·tic tank *n.* a tank in which the organic matter in sewage is disintegrated through bacterial activity.

sep·tu·a·ge·nar·i·an /sépchōōəjináireeən, –tōō–, –tyōō–/ *n.* & *adj.* • *n.* a person from 70 to 79 years old. • *adj.* of this age.

Sep·tu·a·gint /séptōōəjint, –tyōō–/ *n.* a Greek version of the Old Testament including the Apocrypha.

sep·tum /séptəm/ *n.* (*pl.* **septa** /–tə/) *Anat.*, *Bot.*, & *Zool.*

a partition such as that between the nostrils or the chambers of a poppy fruit or of a shell.

sep·tu·ple /septóopəl, –tyóo–, –túpəl, séptoopəl/ *adj., n., & v.* • *adj.* **1** sevenfold; having seven parts. **2** being seven times as many or as much. • *n.* a sevenfold number or amount. • *v.tr. & intr.* multiply by seven.

sep·tup·let /septúplit, -tóo-, -tyóo–/ *n.* **1** one of seven children born at one birth. **2** *Mus.* a group of seven notes to be played in the time of four or six.

se·pul·chral /sipúlkrəl/ *adj.* **1** of a tomb or interment (*sepulchral mound*). **2** suggestive of the tomb; gloomy (*sepulchral look*). ▫▫ **se·pul·chral·ly** *adv.*

sep·ul·cher /sépəlkər/ *n. & v.* (also **sep·ul·chre**) • *n.* a tomb esp. cut in rock or built of stone or brick. • *v.tr.* **1** lay in a sepulcher. **2** serve as a sepulcher for.

seq. *abbr.* (*pl.* **seqq.**) the following.

se·quel /seékwəl/ *n.* **1** what follows (esp. as a result). **2** a novel, motion picture, etc., that continues the story of an earlier one.

se·que·la /sikwélə/ *n.* (*pl.* **sequelae** /–ee/) *Med.* (esp. in *pl.*) a morbid condition or symptom following a disease.

se·quence /seékwəns/ *n. & v.* • *n.* **1** succession; coming after or next. **2** order of succession (*in historical sequence*). **3** a set of things belonging next to one another on some principle of order. **4** a part of a motion picture dealing with one scene or topic. • *v.tr.* arrange in a definite order.

se·quenc·er /seékwənsər/ *n.* a programmable device for storing sequences of musical notes, chords, etc., and transmitting them when required to an electronic musical instrument.

se·quent /seékwənt/ *adj.* **1** following as a sequence or consequence. 2 consecutive. ▫▫ **se·quent·ly** *adv.*

se·quen·tial /sikwénshəl/ *adj.* forming a sequence or consequence. ▫▫ **se·quen·ti·al·i·ty** /–sheeálitee/ *n.* **se·quen·tial·ly** *adv.*

se·ques·ter /sikwéstər/ *v.tr.* **1** (esp. as **sequestered** *adj.*) seclude; isolate; set apart (*a sequestered jury*). **2** = SEQUESTRATE.

se·ques·trate /sikwéstrayt/ *v.tr.* **1** confiscate; appropriate. **2** *Law* take temporary possession of (a debtor's estate, etc.). ▫▫ **se·ques·tra·ble** /–trəbəl/ *adj.* **se·ques·tra·tion** /seékwistráyshən/ *n.* **se·ques·tra·tor** /seékwistraytər/ *n.*

se·quin /seékwin/ *n.* a circular spangle for attaching to clothing as an ornament. ▫▫ **se·quined** *adj.* (also **se·quinned**).

se·quoi·a /sikwóyə/ *n.* one of two Californian evergreen coniferous trees with reddish bark and of very great height.

se·ra *pl.* of SERUM.

se·ragl·io /sərályō, raál–/ *n.* (*pl.* **-os**) **1** a harem. **2** *hist.* a Turkish palace.

se·ra·pe /səraápee/ *n.* a shawl or blanket worn (esp. in Mexico) as a cloak.

ser·aph /sérəf/ *n.* (*pl.* **seraphim** /–fim/ or **seraphs**) an angelic being, one of the highest order of the ninefold celestial hierarchy.

se·raph·ic /səráfik/ *adj.* **1** of or like the seraphim. **2** ecstatically adoring, fervent, or serene. ▫▫ **se·raph·i·cal·ly** *adv.*

Serb /sərb/ *n. & adj.* • *n.* **1** a native of Serbia in the former Yugoslavia. **2** a person of Serbian descent. • *adj.* = SERBIAN.

Ser·bi·an /sə́rbeeən/ *n. & adj.* • *n.* **1** the dialect of the Serbs. **2** = SERB. • *adj.* of or relating to the Serbs or their dialect.

Serbo- /sə́rbō/ *comb. form* Serbian.

Ser·bo-Cro·at /sə́rbōkrṓat/ *n. & adj.* (also **Ser·bo-Cro·a·tian** /–krō-áyshən/) • *n.* the main official language of the former Yugoslavia, combining Serbian and Croatian dialects. • *adj.* of or relating to this language.

sere[1] /seer/ *adj.* (also **sear**) *literary* (esp. of a plant, etc.) withered; dried up.

sere[2] /seer/ *n. Ecol.* a sequence of animal or plant communities.

se·rein /sərán/ *n.* a fine rain falling in tropical climates from a cloudless sky.

ser·e·nade /sérənáyd/ *n. & v.* • *n.* a piece of music sung or played at night, esp. by a lover under his lady's window. • *v.tr.* sing or play a serenade to. ▫▫ **ser·e·nad·er** *n.*

ser·en·dip·i·ty /sérəndípitee/ *n.* the faculty of making happy and unexpected discoveries by accident. ▫▫ **ser·en·dip·i·tous** *adj.* **ser·en·dip·i·tous·ly** *adv.*

se·rene /sireén/ *adj. & n.* • *adj.* (**serener, serenest**) **1 a** (of the sky, etc.) clear and calm. **b** (of the sea, etc.) unruffled. **2** placid; tranquil. ▫▫ **se·rene·ly** *adv.* **se·rene·ness** *n.*

se·ren·i·ty /sirénitee/ *n.* (*pl.* **-ties**) tranquillity; being serene.

serf /sərf/ *n.* **1** *hist.* a laborer not allowed to leave the land on which he worked; a villein. **2** an oppressed person; a drudge. ▫▫ **serf·dom** *n.*

serge /sərj/ *n.* a durable twilled worsted, etc., fabric.

ser·geant /saárjənt/ *n.* **1** a noncommissioned army, marine, or air force officer next below warrant officer. **2** a police officer ranking below captain.

ser·geant ma·jor *n. Mil.* the highest-ranking noncommissioned officer.

se·ri·al /seéreeəl/ *n. & adj.* • *n.* **1** a story, play, etc., that is published, broadcast, or shown in regular installments. **2** a periodical. • *adj.* **1** of or in or forming a series. **2** (of a story, etc.) in the form of a serial. **3** *Mus.* using transformations of a fixed series of notes. ▫▫ **se·ri·al·i·ty** /–reeálitee/ *n.* **se·ri·al·ly** *adv.*

se·ri·al·ist /seéreeəlist/ *n.* a composer or advocate of serial music. ▫▫ **se·ri·al·ism** *n.*

se·ri·al·ize /seéreeəlīz/ *v.tr.* **1** publish or produce in installments. **2** arrange in a series. **3** *Mus.* compose according to a serial technique. ▫▫ **se·ri·al·i·za·tion** *n.*

se·ri·al kill·er *n.* a person who murders continually with no apparent motive.

se·ri·al num·ber *n.* a number showing the position of an item in a series, esp. one printed on paper currency or on a manufactured article for the the purposes of identification.

se·ri·ate *adj. & v.* • *adj.* /seéreeət/ in the form of a series; in orderly sequence. • *v.tr.* /seéreeayt/ arrange in a seriate manner. ▫▫ **se·ri·a·tion** /–reeáyshən/ *n.*

ser·i·cul·ture /sérikulchər/ *n.* **1** silkworm breeding. **2** the production of raw silk. ▫▫ **ser·i·cul·tur·al** *adj.* **ser·i·cul·tur·ist** *n.*

se·ries /seéreez/ *n.* (*pl.* same) **1** a number of things of which each is similar to the preceding or in which each successive pair are similarly related; a succession, row, or set. **2** a set of successive games between the same teams. **3** a set of programs with the same actors, etc., or on related subjects but each complete in itself. **4** a set of lectures by the same speaker or on the same subject. **5 a** a set of successive issues of a periodical, of articles on one subject or by one writer, etc., esp. when numbered separately from a preceding or following set (*second series*). **b** a set of independent books in a common format or under a common title or supervised by a common general editor. **6** *Geol.* a set of strata with a common characteristic. **7** *Mus.* = TONE ROW. **8** *Electr.* **a** a set of circuits or components arranged so that the current passes through each successively. **b** a set of batteries, etc., having the positive electrode of each connected with the negative electrode of the next. ▫ **in series 1** in ordered succession. **2** *Electr.* (of a set of circuits or components) arranged so that the current passes through each successively.

ser•if /sérif/ *n.* a slight projection finishing off a stroke of a letter as in T contrasted with T (cf. SANS SERIF). □□ **ser•iffed** *adj.*

se•rig•ra•phy /sərígrəfee/ *n.* the art or process of printing designs by means of a silk screen. □□ **ser•i•graph** /sérigraf/ *n.* **se•rig•ra•pher** /sərígrəfər/ *n.*

se•ri•o•com•ic /séeree-ōkómik/ *adj.* combining the serious and the comic; jocular in intention but simulating seriousness or vice versa. □□ **se•ri•o•com•i•cal•ly** *adv.*

se•ri•ous /séereeəs/ *adj.* **1** thoughtful; earnest; not reckless nor given to trifling (*a serious young person*). **2** important (*a serious matter*). **3** not slight or negligible (*a serious injury*). **4** sincere; not ironic or joking (*are you serious?*). **5** (of music and literature) not merely for amusement. **6** not perfunctory (*serious thought*). **7** not to be trifled with (*a serious opponent*). □□ **se•ri•ous•ness** *n.*

se•ri•ous•ly /séereeəslee/ *adv.* **1** in a serious manner (esp. introducing a sentence, implying that irony, etc., is now to cease). **2** to a serious extent. **3** *colloq.* (as an intensifier) very; really; substantially (*seriously rich*).

ser•mon /sə́rmən/ *n.* **1** a spoken or written discourse on a religious or moral subject, esp. a discourse based on a text or passage of Scripture and delivered in a service by way of religious instruction or exhortation. **2** a piece of admonition; a lecture. **3** a moral reflection suggested by natural objects, etc. (*sermons in stones*).

ser•mon•ette /sə́rmənét/ *n.* a short sermon.

ser•mon•ize /sə́rmənīz/ *v.* **1** *tr.* deliver a moral lecture to. **2** *intr.* deliver a moral lecture. □□ **ser•mon•iz•er** *n.*

se•rol•o•gy /seeróləjee/ *n.* the scientific study of blood sera and their effects. □□ **se•ro•log•i•cal** /–rəlójikəl/ *adj.* **se•rol•o•gist** *n.*

ser•o•tine /sérətin, –tīn/ *n.* a chestnut-colored European bat, *Eptesicus serotinus*.

ser•o•to•nin /sérətṓnin/ *n. Biol.* a compound present in blood serum, which constricts the blood vessels and acts as a neurotransmitter.

se•rous /séerəs/ *adj.* of or like or producing serum; watery. □□ **se•ros•i•ty** /–rósitee/ *n.*

ser•pent /sə́rpənt/ *n.* **1** usu. *literary* **a** a snake, esp. of a large kind. **b** a scaly limbless reptile. **2** a sly or treacherous person, esp. one who exploits a position of trust to betray it. **3** *Mus.* an old bass wind instrument made from leather-covered wood, roughly in the form of an S. **4** (**the Serpent**) *Bibl.* Satan.

ser•pen•tine /sə́rpəntīn/ *adj. & n.* • *adj.* **1** of or like a serpent. **2** coiling; sinuous; meandering. **3** cunning; subtle; treacherous. • *n.* a soft rock mainly of hydrated magnesium silicate, usu. dark green and sometimes mottled or spotted like a serpent's skin.

ser•pig•i•nous /sərpíjinəs/ *adj.* (of a skin disease, etc.) creeping from one part to another.

ser•ra /sérə/ *n.* (*pl.* **serrae** /–ree/) a serrated organ, structure, or edge.

ser•ra•dil•la /sérədílə/ *n.* (*pl.* **serradillae** /–lee/) a clover, *Ornithopus sativus*, grown as fodder.

ser•rate *v. & adj.* • *v.tr.* /seráyt/ (usu. as **serrated** *adj.*) provide with a sawlike edge. • *adj.* /sérayt/ esp. *Anat., Bot., & Zool.* notched like a saw. □□ **ser•ra•tion** /–ráyshən/ *n.*

ser•ried /séreed/ *adj.* (of ranks of soldiers, etc.) pressed together; without gaps.

se•rum /séerəm/ *n.* (*pl.* **sera** /–rə/ or **serums**) **1 a** an amber-colored liquid that separates from a clot when blood coagulates. **b** whey. **2** *Med.* blood serum (usu. from a nonhuman mammal) as an antitoxin or therapeutic agent, esp. in inoculation. **3** a watery fluid in animal bodies.

serv•ant /sə́rvənt/ *n.* **1** a person who has undertaken to carry out the orders of an individual or corporate employer, esp. a person employed in a house on domestic duties. **2** a devoted follower (*a servant of Jesus Christ*).

serve /sərv/ *v. & n.* • *v.* **1** *tr.* do a service for (a person, community, etc.). **2** *tr.* (also *absol.*) be a servant to. **3** *intr.* carry out duties (*served on six committees*). **4** *intr.* **a** (foll. by *in*) be employed in (an organization, esp. the armed forces, or a place, esp. a foreign country). **b** be a member of the armed forces. **5 a** *tr.* be useful to or serviceable for; meet the needs of; do what is required for (*serve a purpose*). **b** *intr.* perform a function (*a sofa serving as a bed*). **c** *intr.* (foll. by *to* + infin.) avail; suffice (*served only to postpone the inevitable*). **6** *tr.* go through a due period of (office, apprenticeship, a prison sentence, etc.). **7** *tr.* set out or present (food) for those about to eat it (*dinner was then served*). **8** *intr.* act as a waiter. **9** *tr.* **a** attend to (a customer in a store). **b** (foll. by *with*) supply with (goods) (*served the town with gas*). **10** *tr.* treat or act toward (a person) in a specified way (*has served me shamefully*). **11** *tr.* **a** (often foll. by *on*) deliver (a writ, etc.) to the person concerned in a legally formal manner. **b** (foll. by *with*) deliver a writ, etc., to (a person) in this way (*served her with a summons*). **12** *tr. Tennis,* etc. **a** (also *absol.*) deliver (a ball, etc.) to begin or resume play. **b** produce (a fault, etc.) by doing this. **13** *tr. Mil.* keep (a gun, battery, etc.) firing. **14** *tr.* (of an animal, esp. a stallion, etc., hired for the purpose) copulate with (a female). **15** *tr.* distribute (*served out the ammunition*). **16** *tr.* render obedience to (a deity, etc.). • *n.* **1** *Tennis,* etc. the act or an instance of serving. **2** a manner of serving. **3** a person's turn to serve. □ **it will serve** it will be adequate. **serve one's needs** (or **need**) be adequate. **serve the purpose of** take the place of; be used as. **serve a person right** be a person's deserved punishment or misfortune. **serve one's time 1** esp. *Brit.* hold office for the normal period. **2** (also **serve time**) undergo imprisonment, apprenticeship, etc. **serve up** offer for acceptance.

serv•er /sə́rvər/ *n.* **1** a person who serves. **2** *Eccl.* a person assisting the celebrant at a service, esp. the Eucharist.

serv•ice /sə́rvis/ *n. & v.* • *n.* **1** the act of helping or doing work for another or for a community, etc. **2** work done in this way. **3** assistance or benefit given to someone. **4** the provision or system of supplying a public need, e.g., transport. **5 a** the fact or status of being a servant. **b** employment or a position as a servant. **6** a state or period of employment doing work for an individual or organization (*resigned after 15 years' service*). **7 a** a public department or organization (*civil service*). **b** employment in this. **8** (in *pl.*) the armed forces. **9** (*attrib.*) of the kind issued to the armed forces (*a service revolver*). **10 a** a ceremony of worship according to prescribed forms. **b** a form of liturgy for this. **11 a** the provision of what is necessary for the installation and maintenance of a machine, etc., or operation. **b** a periodic routine maintenance of a motor vehicle, etc. **12** assistance or advice given to customers after the sale of goods. **13 a** the act or process of serving food, drinks, etc. **b** an extra charge nominally made for this. **14** a set of dishes, etc., used for serving meals (*a dinner service*). **15** *Tennis,* etc. **a** the act or an instance of serving. **b** a person's turn to serve. • *v.tr.* **1** provide service or services for, esp. maintain. **2** maintain or repair (a car, machine, etc.). **3** pay interest on (a debt). **4** supply with a service. □ **at a person's service** ready to serve or assist a person. **be of**

service be available to assist. **in service 1** employed as a servant. **2** available for use. **on active service** serving in the armed forces in wartime. **out of service** not available for use. **see service 1** have experience of service, esp. in the armed forces. **2** (of a thing) be much used.

serv•ice•a•ble /sə́rvisəbəl/ *adj.* **1** useful or usable. **2** able to render service. **3** durable. **4** suited for ordinary use rather than ornamental. □□ **serv•ice•a•bil•i•ty** *n.* **serv•ice•a•ble•ness** *n.* **serv•ice•a•bly** *adv.*

serv•ice ar•e•a *n.* **1** an area beside a major road for the supply of gasoline, refreshments, etc. **2** the area served by a broadcasting station.

serv•ice charge *n.* an additional charge for service in a restaurant, hotel, etc.

serv•ice in•dus•try *n.* one providing services not goods.

serv•ice•man /sə́rvismən/ *n.* (*pl.* **-men**) **1** a man serving in the armed forces. **2** a man providing service or maintenance.

serv•ice road *n.* a road parallel to a main road, serving houses, stores, etc.

serv•ice sta•tion *n.* an establishment beside a road selling gasoline and oil, etc., to motorists and often able to carry out maintenance.

serv•ice•wom•an /sə́rviswŏŏmən/ *n.* (*pl.* **-women**) a woman serving in the armed forces.

ser•vi•ette /sə́rvee-ét/ *n.* esp. *Brit.* a napkin for use at table.

ser•vile /sə́rvīl/ *adj.* **1** of or being or like a slave or slaves. **2** slavish; fawning; completely dependent. □□ **ser•vile•ly** *adv.* **ser•vil•i•ty** /–vílitee/ *n.*

serv•ing /sə́rving/ *n.* a quantity of food served to one person.

ser•vi•tude /sə́rvitōōd, –tyōōd/ *n.* **1** slavery. **2** subjection (esp. involuntary).

ser•vo /sə́rvō/ *n.* (*pl.* **-vos**) **1** (in full **servomechanism**) a powered mechanism producing motion or forces at a higher level of energy than the input level. **2** (in full **servomotor**) the motive element in a servomechanism. **3** (in *comb.*) of or involving a servomechanism (*servo-assisted*).

ses•a•me /sésəmee/ *n. Bot.* **1** an E. Indian herbaceous plant, *Sesamum indicum*, whose seeds yield an edible oil. **2** its seeds. □ **open sesame** a means of acquiring or achieving what is normally unattainable.

sesqui- /séskwee/ *comb. form* denoting one and a half.

ses•qui•cen•ten•ar•y /séskwisenténəree/ *n.* (*pl.* **-ies**) = SESQUICENTENNIAL.

ses•qui•cen•ten•n•ial /séskwisenténeeəl/ *n. & adj.* • *n.* a one-hundred-and-fiftieth anniversary. • *adj.* of or relating to a sesquicentennial.

ses•sile /sésīl, –əl/ *adj.* **1** *Bot. & Zool.* (of a flower, eye, etc.) attached directly by its base without a stalk or peduncle. **2** fixed in one position; immobile.

ses•sion /séshən/ *n.* **1** the process of assembly of a deliberative or judicial body to conduct its business. **2** a single meeting for this purpose. **3** a period during which such meetings are regularly held. **4 a** an academic year. **b** the period during which a school, etc., has classes. **5** a period devoted to an activity (*poker session*). **6** the governing body of a Presbyterian church. □ **in session** assembled for business; not on vacation. □□ **ses•sion•al** *adj.*

ses•tet /sestét/ *n.* **1** the last six lines of a sonnet. **2** a sextet.

ses•ti•na /sesteénə/ *n.* a form of rhymed or unrhymed poem with six stanzas of six lines and a final triplet, all stanzas having the same six words at the line ends in six different sequences.

set[1] /set/ *v.* (**setting**; *past* and *past part.* **set**) **1** *tr.* put, lay, or stand (a thing) in a certain position or location (*set it upright*). **2** *tr.* (foll. by *to*) apply (one thing) to (another) (*set pen to paper*). **3** *tr.* **a** fix ready or in position. **b** dispose suitably for use, action, or display. **4** *tr.* **a** adjust the hands of (a clock or watch) to show the right time. **b** adjust (an alarm clock) to sound at the required time. **5** *tr.* **a** fix, arrange, or mount. **b** insert (a jewel) in a ring, etc. **6** *tr.* make (a device) ready to operate. **7** *tr.* lay (a table) for a meal. **8** *tr.* arrange (the hair) while damp. **9** *tr.* (foll. by *with*) ornament or provide (a surface, esp. a precious item) (*gold set with gems*). **10** *tr.* cause to be (*set things in motion*). **11** *intr. & tr.* harden or solidify (*the jelly is set*). **12** *intr.* (of the sun, moon, etc.) appear to move toward and below the earth's horizon (as the earth rotates). **13** *tr.* represent (a scene, etc.) as happening in a certain time or place. **14** *tr.* **a** (foll. by *to* + infin.) cause or instruct (a person) to perform a specified activity (*set them to work*). **b** (foll. by pres. part.) start (a person or thing) doing something (*set the ball rolling*). **15** *tr.* present or impose as work to be done or a matter to be dealt with (*set them an essay*). **16** *tr.* exhibit as a type or model (*set a good example*). **17** *tr.* initiate; take the lead in (*set the pace*). **18** *tr.* establish (a record, etc.). **19** *tr.* determine or decide (*the itinerary is set*). **20** *tr.* appoint or establish (*set them in authority*). **21** *tr.* join, attach, or fasten. **22** *tr.* **a** put parts of (a broken bone, etc.) into the correct position for healing. **b** deal with (a fracture or dislocation) in this way. **23** *tr.* (in full **set to music**) provide (words, etc.) with music for singing. **24** *tr.* (often foll. by *up*) *Printing* **a** arrange or produce (type or film, etc.) as required. **b** arrange the type or film, etc., for (a book, etc.). **25** *intr.* (of a tide, etc.) have a certain motion or direction. **26** *intr.* (of a face) assume a hard expression. **27** *tr.* **a** cause (a hen) to sit on eggs. **b** place (eggs) for a hen to sit on. **28** *tr.* put (a seed, etc.) in the ground to grow. **29** *tr.* give the teeth of (a saw) an alternate outward inclination. **30** *tr.* start (a fire). **31** *intr.* (of eyes, etc.) become motionless. **32** *intr.* feel or show a certain tendency (*opinion is setting against it*). **33** *intr.* **a** (of a blossom) form into fruit. **b** (of fruit) develop from a blossom. **c** (of a tree) develop fruit. **34** *intr.* (of a hunting dog) take a rigid attitude indicating the presence of game. □ **set about** begin or take steps toward. **set a person** (or **thing**) **against** (**another**) **1** consider or reckon (a person or thing) as a compensation for. **2** cause to oppose. **set apart** separate; reserve; differentiate. **set aside** see ASIDE. **set back 1** place further back in place or time. **2** impede or reverse the progress of. **3** *colloq.* cost (a person) a specified amount. **set by** save for future use. **set down 1** record in writing. **2** land an aircraft. **3** (foll. by *to*) attribute to. **4** (foll. by *as*) explain or describe to oneself as. **set eyes on** see EYE. **set one's face against** see FACE. **set foot on** (or **in**) see FOOT. **set forth 1** begin a journey. **2** make known; expound. **set forward** begin to advance. **set free** release. **set one's hand to** see HAND. **set one's heart** (or **hopes**) **on** want or hope for eagerly. **set in 1** (of weather, etc.) begin; become established. **2** insert (esp. a sleeve, etc., into a garment). **set a person's mind at rest** see MIND. **set much by** consider to be of much value. **set off 1** begin a journey. **2** detonate (a bomb, etc.). **3** initiate; stimulate. **4** cause (a person) to start laughing, talking, etc. **5** serve as an adornment to; enhance. **6** (foll. by *against*) use as a compensating item. **set on** (or **upon**) **1** attack violently. **2** cause or urge to attack. **set out 1** begin a journey. **2** (foll. by *to* + infin.) aim or intend. **3** demonstrate, arrange, or exhibit. **4** mark out. **5** declare. **set the pace** determine the rate of speed, proficiency, etc. for others to follow. **set sail 1** hoist the sails. **2** begin a voyage. **set the scene** see SCENE. **set the stage** see STAGE. **set store by** (or **on**) see STORE. **set one's teeth 1** clench them. **2** summon one's resolve. **set to** begin vigorously, esp. fighting, arguing, or eating. **set up 1** place in position or view. **2** organize or start (a business, etc.). **3** establish in some capacity. **4** supply the needs of. **5** begin making (a loud sound). **6** cause or make arrangements for (a condition or situation). **7** prepare (a task, etc., for another). **8** restore or enhance the health of (a person). **9** establish (a record). **10** propound (a theory). **11** *colloq.* put (a person) in a dangerous position. **set oneself up as** make pretensions to being.

▶**Set** means 'to place or put': *Set the flowers on top of the piano.* **Sit** means 'to be seated': *Sit in this chair while I check the light meter.*

set[2] /set/ *n.* **1** a number of things or persons that belong together or resemble one another or are usually found together. **2** a collection or group. **3** a section of society consorting together or having similar interests, etc. **4** a collection of implements, etc., needed for a specified purpose (*croquet set; tea set*). **5** a radio or television receiver. **6** (in tennis, etc.) a group of games counting as a unit toward a match for the player or side that wins a defined number or proportion of the games. **7** *Math. & Logic* a collection of distinct entities forming a unit. **8** a group of pupils or students having the same average ability. **9 a** a slip, shoot, bulb, etc., for planting. **b** a young fruit just set. **10 a** a habitual posture or conformation; the way the head, etc., is carried or a dress, etc., flows. **b** (also **dead set**) a setter's pointing in the presence of game. **11** the way, drift, or tendency (of public opinion, etc.) (*the set of public feeling is against it*). **12** the way in which a machine, device, etc., is set or adjusted. **13** a setting, stage furniture, etc., for a play or motion picture, etc. **14** a sequence of songs or pieces performed in jazz or popular music. **15** the setting of the hair when damp. **16** (also **sett**) a badger's burrow. **17** (also **sett**) a granite paving block. **18** a number of people making up a square dance.

set[3] /set/ *adj.* **1** in senses of SET[1]. **2** prescribed or determined in advance. **3** fixed; unchanging; unmoving. **4** (of a phrase or speech, etc.) having invariable or predetermined wording. **5** prepared for action. **6** (foll. by *on, upon*) determined to acquire or achieve, etc. **7** (of a book, etc.) specified for reading in preparation for an examination.

se•ta /séetə/ *n.* (*pl.* **setae** /–tee/) *Bot.* & *Zool.* stiff hair; bristle. ▫▫ **se•ta•ceous** /–táyshəs/ *adj.*

set•back /sétbak/ *n.* **1** a reversal or arrest of progress. **2** a relapse.

set point *n. Tennis*, etc. **1** the state of a game when one side needs only one more point to win the set. **2** this point.

set screw *n.* a screw for adjusting or clamping parts of a machine.

set square *n.* a right-angled triangular plate for drawing lines, esp at 90°, 45°, 60°, or 30°.

sett var. of SET[2] 16, 17.

set•tee /setée/ *n.* a seat (usu. upholstered), with a back and usu. arms, for more than one person.

set•ter /sétər/ *n.* **1** a dog of a large, long-haired breed trained to stand rigid when scenting game. **2** a person or thing that sets.

set the•o•ry *n.* the branch of mathematics concerned with the manipulation of sets.

set•ting /séting/ *n.* **1** the position or manner in which a thing is set. **2** the immediate surroundings (of a house, etc.). **3** the surroundings of any object regarded as its framework. **4** the place and time, etc., of a drama, etc. **5** a frame in which a jewel is set. **6** the music to which words are set. **7** a set of cutlery and other accessories for one person at a table. **8** the way in which or level at which a machine is set to operate.

set•tle /sét'l/ *v.* **1** *tr. & intr.* (often foll. by *down*) establish or become established in a more or less permanent abode or way of life. **2** *intr. & tr.* (often foll. by *down*) **a** cease or cause to cease from wandering, disturbance, movement, etc. **b** adopt a regular or secure style of life. **c** (foll. by *to*) apply oneself (*settled down to writing letters*). **3 a** *intr.* sit or come down to stay for some time. **b** *tr.* cause to do this. **4** *tr. & intr.* bring to or attain fixity, certainty, composure, or quietness. **5** *tr.* determine or decide or agree upon. **6** *tr.* **a** resolve (a dispute, etc.). **b** deal with (a matter) finally. **7** *tr.* terminate (a lawsuit) by mutual agreement. **8** *intr.* **a** (foll. by *for*) accept or agree to (esp. an alternative not one's first choice). **b** (foll. by *on*) decide on. **9** *tr.* (also *absol.*) pay (a debt, an account, etc.). **10** *intr.* (as **settled** *adj.*) not likely to change for a time (*settled weather*). **11** *tr.* **a** aid the digestion of (food). **b** remedy the disordered state of (nerves, etc.). **12** *tr.* **a** colonize. **b** establish colonists in. **13** *intr.* subside; fall to the bottom or on to a surface (*the dust will settle*). ▫ **settle one's affairs** make any necessary arrangements (e.g., write a will) when death is near. **settle in** become established in a place. **settle up 1** (also *absol.*) pay (an account, etc.). **2** finally arrange (a matter). **settle with 1** pay all or part of an amount due to (a creditor). **2** get revenge on. ▫▫ **set•tle•a•ble** *adj.*

set•tle•ment /sét'lmənt/ *n.* **1** the act of settling. **2 a** the colonization of a region. **b** a place or area occupied by settlers. **c** a small village. **3 a** a political or financial, etc., agreement. **b** an arrangement ending a dispute. **4 a** the terms on which property is given to a person. **b** a deed stating these. **c** the amount or property given. **5** subsidence of a wall, house, soil, etc.

set•tler /sétlər/ *n.* a person who goes to settle in a new country or place.

set•tlor /sétlər/ *n. Law* a person who makes a settlement, esp. of a property.

set-to *n.* (*pl.* **-tos**) *colloq.* a fight or argument.

set•up /setup/ *n.* **1** an arrangement or organization. **2** the manner of this. **3** *colloq.* a trick or conspiracy, esp. to make an innocent person appear guilty.

sev•en /sévən/ *n. & adj.* •*n.* **1** one more than six. **2** a symbol for this (7, vii, VII). **3** a size, etc., denoted by seven. **4** a set or team of seven individuals. **5** the time of seven o'clock. **6** a card with seven pips. •*adj.* that amount to seven.

sev•en•fold /sévənfōld/ *adj. & adv.* **1** seven times as much or as many. **2** consisting of seven parts.

sev•en•teen /sévəntéen/ *n. & adj.* •*n.* **1** one more than sixteen. **2** a symbol for this (17, xvii, XVII). **3** a size, etc., denoted by seventeen. •*adj.* that amount to seventeen. ▫▫ **sev•en•teenth** *adj. & n.*

sev•enth /sévənth/ *n. & adj.* •*n.* **1** the position in a sequence corresponding to the number 7 in the sequence 1–7. **2** something occupying this position. **3** one of seven equal parts of a thing. **4** *Mus.* **a** an interval or chord spanning seven consecutive notes in the diatonic scale. **b** a note separated from another by this interval. •*adj.* that is the seventh. ▫▫ **sev•enth•ly** *adv.*

sev•en•ty /sévəntee/ *n. & adj.* •*n.* (*pl.* **-ties**) **1** the product of seven and ten. **2** a symbol for this (70, lxx, LXX). **3** (in *pl.*) the numbers from 70 to 79, esp. the years of a century or of a person's life. •*adj.* that amount to seventy. ▫▫ **sev•en•ti•eth** *adj. & n.* **sev•en•ty•fold** *adj. & adv.*

sev•en-year itch *n.* a supposed tendency to infidelity after seven years of marriage.

sev•er /sévər/ *v.* **1** *tr. & intr.* (often foll. by *from*) divide, break, or make separate, esp. by cutting. **2** *tr. & intr.* break off or away (*severed our friendship*). **3** *tr.* end the employment contract of (a person). ▫▫ **sev·er·a·ble** *adj.*

sev·er·al /sévrəl/ *adj. & n.* • *adj. & n.* more than two but not many. • *adj.* separate or respective; distinct (*all went their several ways*). ▫▫ **sev·er·al·ly** *adv.*

sev·er·al·ty /sévrəltee/ *n.* **1** separateness. **2** the individual or unshared tenure of an estate, etc. (esp. *in severalty*).

sev·er·ance /sévərəns, sévrəns/ *n.* **1** the act or an instance of severing. **2** a severed state.

sev·er·ance pay *n.* an amount paid to an employee on dismissal or discharge from employment.

se·vere /sivéer/ *adj.* **1** rigorous, strict, and harsh in attitude or treatment (*a severe critic*). **2** serious; critical (*a severe shortage*). **3** vehement or forceful (*a severe storm*). **4** extreme (in an unpleasant quality) (*a severe winter*). **5** exacting (*severe competition*). **6** plain in style (*severe dress*). ▫▫ **se·vere·ly** *adv.* **se·ver·i·ty** /–véritee/ *n.*

sew /sō/ *v.tr.* (*past part.* **sewn** /sōn/ or **sewed**) **1** (also *absol.*) fasten, join, etc., by making stitches with a needle and thread or a sewing machine. **2** make (a garment, etc.) by sewing. **3** (often foll. by *on*, *in*, etc.) attach by sewing. ▫ **sew up 1** join or enclose by sewing. **2** *colloq.* (esp. in *passive*) satisfactorily arrange or finish dealing with (a project, etc.). ▫▫ **sew·er** *n.*

sew·age /sóōij/ (also **sew·er·age** /sóōwərij/) *n.* waste matter conveyed in sewers.

sew·er /sóōər/ *n.* a conduit, usu. underground, for carrying off sewage.

sew·er·age /sóōərij/ *n.* **1** a system of or drainage by sewers. **2** = SEWAGE.

sew·ing /sóing/ *n.* a piece of material or work to be sewn.

sew·ing ma·chine /sóing/ *n.* a machine for sewing or stitching.

sewn *past part.* of SEW.

sex /seks/ *n., adj., & v.* • *n.* **1** either of the main divisions (male and female) into which living things are placed on the basis of their reproductive functions. **2** the fact of belonging to one of these. **3** males or females collectively. **4** sexual desires, etc., or their manifestation. **5** *colloq.* sexual intercourse. • *adj.* **1** of or relating to sex (*sex education*). **2** arising from a difference or consciousness of sex (*sex urge*). • *v.tr.* **1** determine the sex of. **2** (as **sexed** *adj.*) **a** having a sexual appetite (*highly sexed*). **b** having sexual characteristics.

sex·a·ge·nar·i·an /séksəjináireeən/ *n. & adj.* • *n.* a person from 60 to 69 years old. • *adj.* of this age.

sex·a·ges·i·mal /séksəjésiməl/ *adj. & n.* • *adj.* **1** of sixtieths. **2** of sixty. **3** reckoning or reckoned by sixtieths. • *n.* (in full **sexagesimal fraction**) a fraction with a denominator equal to a power of 60 as in the divisions of the degree and hour. ▫▫ **sex·a·ges·i·mal·ly** *adv.*

sex ap·peal *n.* sexual attractiveness.

sex·cen·ten·ar·y /séksenténəree/ *n. & adj.* • *n.* (*pl.* **·ies**) **1** a six-hundredth anniversary. **2** a celebration of this. • *adj.* **1** of or relating to a sexcentenary. **2** occurring every six hundred years.

sex chro·mo·some *n.* a chromosome concerned in determining the sex of an organism.

sex hor·mone *n.* a hormone affecting sexual development or behavior.

sex·ism /séksizəm/ *n.* prejudice or discrimination, esp. against women, on the grounds of sex. ▫▫ **sex·ist** *adj. & n.*

sex·less /séksl is/ *adj.* **1** *Biol.* neither male nor female. **2** lacking in sexual desire or attractiveness. ▫▫ **sex·less·ly** *adv.* **sex·less·ness** *n.*

sex ob·ject *n.* a person regarded mainly in terms of sexual attractiveness.

sex·ol·o·gy /seksóləjee/ *n.* the study of sexual life or relationships, esp. in human beings. ▫▫ **sex·o·log·i·cal** /séksəlójikəl/ *adj.* **sex·ol·o·gist** *n.*

sex·ploi·ta·tion /séksploytáyshən/ *n. colloq.* the exploitation of sex, esp. commercially.

sex·pot /sékspot/ *n. colloq.* a sexy person (esp. a woman).

sex sym·bol *n.* a person widely noted for sex appeal.

sext /sekst/ *n. Eccl.* **1** the canonical hour of prayer appointed for the sixth daytime hour (i.e., noon). **2** the office of sext.

sex·tant /sékstənt/ *n.* an instrument with a graduated arc of 60° used in navigation and surveying for measuring the angular distance of objects by means of mirrors.

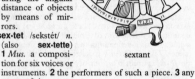

sextant

sex·tet /sekstét/ *n.* (also **sex·tette**) **1** *Mus.* a composition for six voices or instruments. **2** the performers of such a piece. **3** any group of six.

sex·til·lion /sekstílyən/ *n.* (*pl.* same or **sextillions**) a thousand raised to the seventh (or formerly, esp. *Brit.*, the twelfth) power (10^{21} and 10^{36}, respectively). ▫▫ **sex·til·lionth.**

sex·to /séksto/ *n.* (*pl.* **-tos**) **1** a size of book or page in which each leaf is one-sixth that of a printing sheet. **2** a book or sheet of this size.

sex·ton /sékstən/ *n.* a person who looks after a church and churchyard, often acting as bell ringer and gravedigger.

sex·tu·ple /sekstóōpəl, –tyóō–, –túpəl, sékstōōpəl/ *adj., n., & v.* • *adj.* **1** sixfold. **2** having six parts. **3** being six times as many or much. • *n.* a sixfold number or amount. • *v.tr. & intr.* multiply by six; increase sixfold. ▫▫ **sex·tu·ply** *adv.*

sex·tu·plet /sekstúplit, –tóō–, –tyóō–, sékstōō–, tyōō–/ *n.* each of six children born at one birth.

sex·u·al /sékshōōəl/ *adj.* **1** of or relating to sex, or to the sexes or the relations between them. **2** *Biol.* having a sex. ▫▫ **sex·u·al·i·ty** /–álitee/ *n.* **sex·u·al·ly** *adv.*

sex·u·al in·ter·course *n.* the insertion of a man's erect penis into a woman's vagina, usu. followed by the ejaculation of semen.

sex·y /séksee/ *adj.* (**sexier, sexiest**) **1** sexually attractive or stimulating. **2** sexually aroused. **3** concerned with sex. **4** *sl.* exciting; appealing. ▫▫ **sex·i·ly** *adv.* **sex·i·ness** *n.*

sfor·zan·do /sfawrtsaándō/ *adj., adv., & n.* (also **sfor·za·to** /–saátō/) • *adj. & adv. Mus.* with sudden emphasis. • *n.* (*pl.* **-dos** or **sforzandi** /–dee/) **1** a note or group of notes especially emphasized. **2** an increase in emphasis and loudness.

sfu·ma·to /sfōōmaátō/ *adj. & n. Painting* • *adj.* with indistinct outlines. • *n.* the technique of allowing tones and colors to shade gradually into one another.

sfz *abbr. Mus.* sforzando.

SG *abbr.* **1** senior grade. **2** *Law* solicitor general. **3** specific gravity.

Sgt. (also **SGT**) *abbr.* Sergeant.

shab·by /shábee/ *adj.* (**shabbier, shabbiest**) **1** in bad repair or condition; faded and worn. **2** dressed in old or worn clothes. **3** of poor quality. **4** dishonorable (*a shabby trick*). ▫▫ **shab·bi·ly** *adv.* **shab·bi·ness** *n.*

shack /shak/ *n. & v.* • *n.* a roughly built hut. • *v.intr.* (foll. by *up*) *sl.* cohabit, esp. as lovers.

shack·le /shákəl/ *n. & v.* • *n.* **1** a metal loop or link, closed by a bolt, to connect chains, etc. **2** a fetter enclosing the ankle or wrist. **3** (usu. in *pl.*) a restraint or impediment. • *v.tr.* fetter; impede; restrain.

shad /shad/ *n.* (*pl.* same or **shads**) *Zool.* any deep-bodied edible marine fish of the genus *Alosa*, spawning in fresh water.

shad•dock /shádək/ *n. Bot.* **1** the largest citrus fruit, with a thick yellow skin and bitter pulp. Also called POMELO. **2** the tree, *Citrus grandis*, bearing these.

shade /shayd/ *n. & v.* • *n.* **1** comparative darkness (and usu. coolness) caused by shelter from direct light and heat. **2** a place or area sheltered from the sun. **3** a darker part of a picture, etc. **4** a color, esp. as distinguished from one nearly like it. **5** a slight amount (*a shade better*). **6** a screen excluding or moderating light. **7** an eye shield. **8** (in *pl.*) *colloq.* sunglasses. **9** a slightly differing variety (*all shades of opinion*). **10** *literary* **a** a ghost. **b** (in *pl.*) Hades. **11** (in *pl.*; foll. by *of*) suggesting reminiscence (*shades of Dr. Johnson!*). • *v.* **1** *tr.* screen from light. **2** *tr.* cover, moderate, or exclude the light of. **3** *tr.* darken, esp. with parallel pencil lines to represent shadow, etc. **4** *intr. & tr.* (often foll. by *away, off, into*) pass or change by degrees. □ **put in the shade** appear superior to. □□ **shade•less** *adj.*

shad•ing /sháyding/ *n.* **1** the representation of light and shade, e.g., by penciled lines, on a map or drawing. **2** the graduation of tones from light to dark to create a sense of depth.

shad•ow /shádō/ *n. & v.* • *n.* **1** shade or a patch of shade. **2** a dark figure projected by a body intercepting rays of light. **3** an inseparable companion. **4** a person secretly following another. **5** the slightest trace (*not the shadow of a doubt*). **6** a weak or insubstantial remnant (*a shadow of his former self*). **7** the shaded part of a picture. **8** a substance used to color the eyelids. **9** gloom or sadness. • *v.tr.* **1** cast a shadow over. **2** secretly follow and watch the movements of. □□ **shad•ow•er** *n.* **shad•ow•less** *adj.*

shad•ow•box /shádōboks/ *v.intr.* box against an imaginary opponent as a form of training.

shad•ow•graph /shádōgraf/ *n.* **1** an image or photograph made by means of X rays; = RADIOGRAM 2. **2** a picture formed by a shadow cast on a lighted surface. **3** an image formed by light refracted differently by different densities of a fluid.

shad•ow•y /shádōee/ *adj.* **1** like or having a shadow. **2** full of shadows. **3** vague; indistinct. □□ **shad•ow•i•ness** *n.*

shad•y /sháydee/ *adj.* (**shadier, shadiest**) **1** giving shade. **2** situated in shade. **3** (of a person or behavior) disreputable. □□ **shad•i•ly** *adv.* **shad•i•ness** *n.*

shaft /shaft/ *n. & v.* • *n.* **1 a** an arrow or spear. **b** the long slender stem of these. **2** a remark intended to hurt or provoke (*shafts of wit*). **3** (foll. by *of*) **a** a ray (of light). **b** a bolt (of lightning). **4** the stem or handle of a tool, etc. **5** a column, esp. between the base and capital. **6** a long narrow space, usu. vertical, for an elevator, ventilation, etc. **7** a long and narrow part supporting or connecting or driving a part or parts of greater thickness, etc. **8** each of the pair of poles between which a horse is harnessed to a vehicle. **9** *Mech.* a large axle or revolving bar transferring force by belts or cogs. **10** *colloq.* harsh or unfair treatment. • *v.tr. colloq.* treat unfairly.

shag[1] /shag/ *n.* **1** a rough growth or mass of hair, etc. **2** a coarse kind of cut tobacco. **3** a cormorant, esp. the crested cormorant, *Phalacrocorax aristotelis*. **4 a** a thick, shaggy carpet pile. **b** the carpet itself.

shag[2] /shag/ *v.tr.* (**shagged, shagging**) *Baseball* catch and return (fly balls) during practice.

shag•gy /shágee/ *adj.* (**shaggier, shaggiest**) **1** hairy; rough-haired. **2** unkempt. **3** (of the hair) coarse and abundant. □□ **shag•gi•ly** *adv.* **shag•gi•ness** *n.*

shag•gy-dog sto•ry *n.* a long rambling story amusing only by its being inconsequential.

shah /shaa/ *n. hist.* a title of the former monarch of Iran. □□ **shah•dom** *n.*

shake /shayk/ *v. & n.* • *v.* (*past* **shook** /shŏŏk/; *past part.* **shaken** /sháykən/) **1** *tr. & intr.* move (an object) forcefully or quickly up and down or back and forth. **2 a** *intr.* tremble or vibrate markedly. **b** *tr.* cause to do this. **3** *tr.* **a** agitate or shock. **b** *colloq.* upset the composure of. **4** *tr.* weaken or impair (*shook his confidence*). **5** *intr.* make tremulous sounds (*his voice shook with emotion*). **6** *tr.* make a threatening gesture with (one's fist, etc.). **7** *intr. colloq.* shake hands. **8** *tr. colloq.* = *shake off.* • *n.* **1** the act of shaking. **2** a jerk or shock. **3** (in *pl.*; prec. by *the*) a fit of or tendency to trembling. **4** = MILK SHAKE. □ **in two shakes (of a lamb's** or **dog's tail)** very quickly. **no great shakes** *colloq.* not very good or significant. **shake a person by the hand** = *shake hands.* **shake down 1** settle or cause to fall by shaking. **2** settle down. **3** get into harmony with circumstances, surroundings, etc. **4** *sl.* extort money from. **shake the dust off one's feet** depart indignantly or disdainfully. **shake hands** (often foll. by *with*) clasp right hands at meeting or parting, in reconciliation or congratulation, or over a concluded bargain. **shake one's head** move one's head from side to side in refusal, denial, disapproval, or concern. **shake in one's shoes** tremble with apprehension. **shake a leg 1** begin dancing. **2** make a start. **shake off 1** get rid of (something unwanted). **2** manage to evade (a person). **shake out 1** empty by shaking. **2** spread or open by shaking. **shake up 1** mix (ingredients) by shaking. **2** restore to shape by shaking. **3** disturb or make uncomfortable. **4** rouse from lethargy. □□ **shak•a•ble** *adj.* (also **shake•a•ble**).

shake•down /sháykdown/ *n.* **1** a makeshift bed. **2** *sl.* a swindle; a piece of extortion.

shake•out /sháykowt/ *n.* **1** a rapid devaluation of securities, etc., sold in a stock exchange, etc. **2** a decline in the number of companies, services, products, etc., esp. as a result of competitive pressures.

shak•er /sháykər/ *n. & adj.* • *n.* **1** a person or thing that shakes. **2** a container for shaking together the ingredients of cocktails, etc. **3** (**Shaker**) a member of an American religious sect living in celibate mixed communities. • *adj.* used to describe a simple, wholesome style of furniture made by Shakers.

Shake•spear•e•an /shaykspéereeən/ *adj. & n.* (also **Shake•spear•i•an**) • *adj.* **1** of or relating to William Shakespeare, English dramatist d. 1616. **2** in the style of Shakespeare. • *n.* a student of Shakespeare's works, etc.

shake-up *n.* an upheaval or drastic reorganization.

shak•o /sháykō/ *n.* (*pl.* **-os**) a cylindrical peaked military hat with a plume.

shak•y /sháykee/ *adj.* (**shakier, shakiest**) **1** unsteady; apt to shake; trembling. **2** unsound; infirm (*a shaky hand*). **3** unreliable; wavering (*a shaky promise; get off to a shaky start*). □□ **shak•i•ly** *adv.* **shak•i•ness** *n.*

shale /shayl/ *n.* soft, finely stratified rock that splits easily, consisting of consolidated mud or clay. □□ **shal•y** *adj.*

shale oil *n.* oil obtained from bituminous shale.

shall /shal, shəl/ *v.aux.* (*3rd sing. present* **shall**; *archaic 2nd sing. present* **shalt** as below; *past* **should** /shŏŏd, shəd/) (foll. by infin. without *to*, or *absol.*; present and past only in use) **1** (in the 1st person) expressing the future tense (*I shall return soon*) or (with *shall* stressed) emphatic intention (*I shall have a party*). **2** (in the 2nd and 3rd persons) expressing a strong assertion or command rather than a wish (cf. WILL[1]) (*you shall not catch me again*; *they shall go to the party*). ▶For the other persons in senses 1 and 2, see WILL[1]. **3** expressing a command or duty (*thou shalt not steal*; *they shall obey*). **4** (in 2nd-person questions) expressing an inquiry, esp. to avoid the form of a request (cf. WILL[1]) (*shall you go to France?*). □ **shall I?** do you want me to?

▶**Shall** and **should** were traditionally used after *I* or *we*, and **will** and **would** after other pronouns, to express the ordinary future. **Shall** was sometimes also used to indicate an order: *You shall disperse or be arrested.* **Should** is still heard, especially in British English, in first-person conditional sentences: *I should like to visit America.* However, these distinctions are all but lost in today's speech and writing.

shal·lot /shálət, shəlót/ *n.* an onionlike plant, *Allium ascalonicum*, with a cluster of small bulbs.

shal·low /shálō/ *adj. & n.* •*adj.* **1** of little depth. **2** superficial; trivial (*a shallow mind*). •*n.* (often in *pl.*) a shallow place. □□ **shal·low·ly** *adv.* **shal·low·ness** *n.*

sha·lom /shaalṓm/ *n. & int.* a Jewish salutation at meeting or parting.

shalt /shalt/ *archaic 2nd person sing.* of SHALL.

sham /sham/ *v., n., & adj.* •*v.* (**shammed, shamming**) **1** *intr.* feign; pretend. **2** *tr.* **a** pretend to be. **b** simulate. •*n.* **1** imposture; pretense. **2** a person or thing pretending to be what he or she or it is not. •*adj.* pretended; counterfeit. □□ **sham·mer** *n.*

sha·man /sha'amən, sháy–/ *n.* a witch doctor or priest claiming to communicate with and receive healing powers from gods, etc. □□ **sha·man·ism** *n.* **sha·man·ist** *n. & adj.* **sha·man·is·tic** /–nístik/ *adj.*

sham·ble /shámbəl/ *v. & n.* •*v.intr.* walk or run with a shuffling or awkward gait. •*n.* a shambling gait.

sham·bles /shámbəlz/ *n.pl.* (usu. treated as *sing.*) **1** *colloq.* a mess or muddle (*the room was a shambles*). **2** a butcher's slaughterhouse. **3** a scene of carnage.

shame /shaym/ *n. & v.* •*n.* **1** a feeling of distress or humiliation caused by consciousness of the guilt or folly of oneself or an associate. **2** a capacity for experiencing this feeling (*has no shame*). **3** a state of disgrace, discredit, or intense regret. **4 a** a person or thing that brings disgrace, etc. **b** a thing or action that is wrong or regrettable. •*v.tr.* **1** bring shame on; make ashamed. **2** (foll. by *into*, *out of*) force by shame. □ **for shame!** a reproof to a person for not showing shame. **put to shame** humiliate by revealing superior qualities, etc. **shame on you!** you should be ashamed. **what a shame!** how unfortunate!

shame·faced /sháymfáyst/ *adj.* **1** showing shame. **2** bashful; diffident. □□ **shame·fac·ed·ly** /–fáystlee, ;nfáysidlee/ *adv.* **shame·fac·ed·ness** *n.*

shame·ful /sháymfool/ *adj.* **1** that causes or is worthy of shame. **2** disgraceful; scandalous. □□ **shame·ful·ly** *adv.* **shame·ful·ness** *n.*

shame·less /sháymlis/ *adj.* **1** having or showing no sense of shame. **2** impudent. □□ **shame·less·ly** *adv.* **shame·less·ness** *n.*

sham·my /shámee/ *n.* (*pl.* **-mies**) (in full **shammy leather**) *colloq.* = CHAMOIS 2.

sham·poo /shampoo/ *n. & v.* •*n.* **1** liquid or cream used to lather and wash the hair. **2** a similar substance for washing a car or carpet, etc. **3** an act or instance of cleaning with shampoo. •*v.tr.* (**shampoos, shampooed**) wash with shampoo.

sham·rock /shámrok/ *n.* any of various plants with trifoliate leaves, esp. *Trifolium repens* or *Medicago lupulina*, used as the national emblem of Ireland.

shang·hai /shanghí/ *v.tr.* (**shanghais, shanghaied, shanghaiing**) **1** force (a person) to be a sailor on a ship by using drugs or other trickery. **2** *colloq.* put into detention or an awkward situation by trickery.

Shan·gri-la /shánggrilaa/ *n.* an imaginary paradise on earth.

shank /shangk/ *n.* **1 a** the leg. **b** the lower part of the leg; the leg from knee to ankle. **c** the shinbone. **2** the lower part of an animal's foreleg, esp. as a cut of meat. **3** a shaft or stem. **4 a** the long narrow part of a tool, etc., joining the handle of it to the working end. **b** the stem of a key, spoon, anchor, etc. **c** the straight part of a nail or fishhook. **5** the narrow middle of the sole of a shoe. □□ **shanked** *adj.* (also in *comb.*).

shan't /shant/ *contr.* shall not.

shan·ty[1] /shántee/ *n.* (*pl.* **-ties**) **1** a hut or cabin. **2** a crudely built shack.

shan·ty[2] /shántee/ *n.* (*pl.* **-ties**) var. of CHANTEY.

shan·ty·town *n.* a poor or depressed area of a town, consisting of shanties.

shape /shayp/ lis>n. & v. •*n.* **1** the total effect produced by the outlines of a thing. **2** the external form or appearance of a person or thing. **3** a specific form or guise. **4** a description or sort or way (*not in any shape or form*). **5** a definite or proper arrangement (*get our ideas into shape*). **6 a** condition, as qualified in some way (*in good shape*). **b** (when unqualified) good condition (*back in shape*). **7** a person or thing seen indistinctly or in the imagination (*a shape emerged from the mist*). **8** a mold or pattern. **9** a piece of material, paper, etc., made or cut in a particular form. •*v.* **1** *tr.* give a certain shape or form to; fashion. **2** *tr.* (foll. by *to*) adapt or make conform. **3** *intr.* give signs of a future shape or development. **4** *tr.* frame mentally. **5** *intr.* assume or develop into a shape. **6** *tr.* direct (one's life, etc.). □ **shape up 1** take a (specified) form. **2** show promise; make good progress. **shape up well** be promising. **whip** (or **knock**) **into shape** make presentable or efficient. □□ **shap·a·ble** *adj.* (also **shape·a·ble**). **shaped** *adj.* (also in *comb.*). **shap·er** *n.*

shape·less /sháyplis/ *adj.* lacking definite or attractive shape. □□ **shape·less·ly** *adv.* **shape·less·ness** *n.*

shape·ly /sháyplee/ *adj.* (**shapelier, shapeliest**) **1** well formed or proportioned. **2** of elegant or pleasing shape or appearance. □□ **shape·li·ness** *n.*

shard /shaard/ *n.* **1** a broken piece of pottery or glass, etc. **2** = POTSHERD. **3** a fragment of volcanic rock.

share[1] /shair/ *n. & v.* •*n.* **1** a portion that a person receives from or gives to a common amount. **2 a** a part contributed by an individual to an enterprise or commitment. **b** a part received by an individual from this (*got a large share of the credit*). **3** any of the equal parts into which a company's capital is divided entitling its owner to a proportion of the profits. •*v.* **1** *tr.* get or have or give a share of. **2** *tr.* use or benefit from jointly with others. **3** *intr.* have a share; be a sharer (*shall I share with you?*). **4** *intr.* (foll. by *in*) participate. □ **share and share alike** make an equal division. □□ **share·a·ble** *adj.* (also **shar·a·ble**). **shar·er** *n.*

share[2] /shair/ *n.* = PLOWSHARE.

share·crop·per /sháirkropər/ *n.* a tenant farmer who gives a part of each crop as rent. □□ **share·crop** *v.tr. & intr.* (**-cropped, -cropping**).

share·hold·er /sháirhōldər/ *n.* an owner of shares in a company.

share·ware /sháirwair/ *n. Computing* software that is developed for sharing free of charge with other computer users rather than for sale.

sha·ri'·ah /shaareé-aa/ *n.* the Muslim code of religious law.

sha·rif /shəreéf/ *n.* (also **she·reef, she·rif**) **1** a descendant of Muhammad through his daughter Fatima, entitled to wear a green turban or veil. **2** a Muslim leader.

shark[1] /shaark/ *n.* any of various large, usu. voracious marine fish with a long body and prominent dorsal fin.

shark[2] /shaark/ *n. colloq.* a person who unscrupulously exploits others.

shark·skin /shaárkskin/ *n.* **1** the skin of a shark. **2** a smooth, dull-surfaced fabric.

sharp /shaarp/ *adj., n., & adv.* • *adj.* **1** having an edge or point able to cut or pierce. **2** tapering to a point or edge. **3** abrupt; steep; angular (*a sharp turn*). **4** well-defined. **5 a** intense (*has a sharp temper*). **b** (of food, etc.) pungent; keen (*a sharp appetite*). **c** (of a frost) severe; hard. **6** (of a voice or sound) shrill and piercing. **7** (of sand, etc.) composed of angular grains. **8** (of words, etc.) harsh or acrimonious. **9** (of a person) acute; quick to perceive or comprehend. **10** quick to take advantage; unscrupulous; dishonest. **11** vigorous or brisk. **12** *Mus.* **a** above the normal pitch. **b** (of a key) having a sharp or sharps in the signature. **c** (**C**, **F**, etc., **sharp**) a half step higher than C, F, etc. **13** *colloq.* stylish or flashy with regard to dress. • *n.* **1** *Mus.* **a** a note raised a semitone above natural pitch. **b** the sign (♯) indicating this. **2** *colloq.* a swindler or cheat. **3** a fine sewing needle. • *adv.* **1** punctually (*at nine o'clock sharp*). **2** suddenly (*pulled up sharp*). **3** at a sharp angle. **4** *Mus.* above the true pitch (*sings sharp*). □□ **sharp·ly** *adv.* **sharp·ness** *n.*

sharp·en /shaárpən/ *v.tr. & intr.* make or become sharp. □□ **sharp·en·er** *n.*

sharp·er /shaárpər/ *n.* a swindler, esp. at cards.

sharp-shinned hawk /shaárpshind/ *n.* a N. American hawk, *Accipiter striatus*, with slender legs and a barred breast.

sharp·shoot·er /shaárpshōōtər/ *n.* a skilled marksman. □□ **sharp·shoot·ing** *n. & adj.*

sharp-wit·ted *adj.* keenly perceptive or intelligent.

Shas·ta /shástə/ *n.* (in full **Shasta daisy**) any of several plants of the genus *Chrysanthemum* with large daisylike flowers.

shat·ter /shátər/ *v.* **1** *tr. & intr.* break suddenly in pieces. **2** *tr.* severely damage or utterly destroy. **3** *tr.* greatly upset or discompose. **4** *tr.* (usu. as **shattered** *adj.*) exhaust. □□ **shat·ter·er** *n.* **shat·ter·ing** *adj.* **shat·ter·ing·ly** *adv.* **shat·ter-proof** *adj.*

shave /shayv/ *v. & n.* • *v.tr.* (*past part.* **shaved** or (as *adj.*) **shaven**) **1** remove (bristles or hair) from the face, etc., with a razor. **2** (also *absol.*) remove bristles or hair with a razor from (a part of the body). **3 a** reduce by a small amount. **b** take (a small amount) away from. **4** cut thin slices from the surface of (wood, etc.) to shape it. **5** pass close to without touching. • *n.* **1** an act of shaving or the process of being shaved. **2** a close approach without contact. **3** a narrow miss or escape. **4** a tool for shaving wood, etc.

shav·er /sháyvər/ *n.* **1** a person or thing that shaves. **2** an electric razor. **3** *colloq.* a young lad.

shav·ing /sháyving/ *n.* **1** a thin strip cut off the surface of wood, etc. **2** (*attrib.*) used in shaving the face (*shaving cream*).

shawl /shawl/ *n.* a piece of fabric, usu. rectangular and folded into a triangle, worn over the shoulders or head or wrapped around a baby. □□ **shawled** *adj.*

shawm /shawm/ *n. Mus.* a medieval double-reed wind instrument with a sharp penetrating tone.

Shaw·nee /shawneé, shaa–/ *n.* **1 a** a N. American people native to the central Ohio valley. **b** a member of this people. **2** the language of this people.

she /shee/ *pron. & n.* • *pron.* (*obj.* **her**; *poss.* **her**; *pl.* **they**) **1** the woman or girl or female animal previously named or in question. **2** a thing regarded as female, e.g., a vehicle or ship. • *n.* **1** a female; a woman. **2** (in *comb.*) female (*she-goat*).
▶See note at EVERYBODY.

s/he *pron.* a written representation of "he or she" used to indicate both sexes.

sheaf /sheef/ *n. & v.* • *n.* (*pl.* **sheaves** /sheevz/) a group of things laid lengthways together, esp. a bundle of grain stalks or papers. • *v.tr.* make into sheaves.

shear /sheer/ *v. & n.* • *v.* (*past* **sheared**, *archaic* **shore** /shor/; *past part.* **shorn** /shorn/ or **sheared**) **1** *tr.* cut with scissors or shears, etc. **2** *tr.* remove or take off by cutting. **3** *tr.* clip the wool off (a sheep, etc.). **4** *tr.* (foll. by *of*) **a** strip bare. **b** deprive. **5** *tr. & intr.* (often foll. by *off*) distort or be distorted, or break, from a structural strain. • *n.* **1** *Mech. & Geol.* a strain produced by pressure in the structure of a substance. **2** (in *pl.*) (also **pair of shears** *sing.*) a large clipping or cutting instrument shaped like scissors for use in gardens, etc. □□ **shear·er** *n.*

shear·wa·ter /sheérwawtər, –wotər/ *n.* any long-winged seabird of the genus *Puffinus*, usu. flying near the surface of the water.

sheath /sheeth/ *n.* (*pl.* **sheaths** /shee<u>th</u>z, sheeths/) **1** a close-fitting cover, esp. for the blade of a knife or sword. **2** a condom. **3** *Bot., Anat., & Zool.* an enclosing case or tissue. **4** the protective covering around an electric cable. **5** a woman's close-fitting dress. □□ **sheath·less** *adj.*

sheathe /shee<u>th</u>/ *v.tr.* **1** put into a sheath. **2** encase; protect with a sheath.

sheath·ing /sheé<u>th</u>ing/ *n.* a protective casing or covering.

sheaves *pl.* of SHEAF.

she·bang /shibáng/ *n. sl.* a matter or affair (esp. *the whole shebang*).

shed[1] /shed/ *n.* **1** a one-story structure usu. of wood for storage or shelter for animals, etc., or as a workshop. **2** a large roofed structure with one side open, for storing or maintaining machinery, etc.

shed[2] /shed/ *v.tr.* (**shedding**; *past* and *past part.* **shed**) **1** let or cause to fall off (*trees shed their leaves*). **2** take off (clothes). **3** reduce (an electrical power load) by disconnection, etc. **4** cause to fall or flow (*shed blood*; *shed tears*). **5** disperse; diffuse; radiate (*shed light*). □ **shed light on** see LIGHT[1].

she'd /sheed/ *contr.* **1** she had. **2** she would.

she-dev·il *n.* a malicious or spiteful woman.

sheen /sheen/ *n.* **1** a gloss or luster. **2** radiance; brightness. □□ **sheen·y** *adj.*

sheep /sheep/ *n.* (*pl.* same) **1** any ruminant mammal of the genus *Ovis* with a thick woolly coat, esp. kept in flocks for its wool or meat, and noted for its timidity. **2** a bashful, timid, or silly person. **3** (usu. in *pl.*) **a** a member of a minister's congregation. **b** a parishioner. □□ **sheep·like** *adj.*

sheep·dog /sheépdawg, –dog/ *n.* **1** a dog trained to guard and herd sheep. **2** a dog of various breeds suitable for this.

sheep·fold /sheépfōld/ *n.* an enclosure for penning sheep.

sheep·ish /sheépish/ *adj.* **1** bashful; shy; reticent. **2** embarrassed through shame or lack of self-confidence. □□ **sheep·ish·ly** *adv.* **sheep·ish·ness** *n.*

sheep·shank /sheépshangk/ *n.* a knot used to shorten a rope temporarily.

sheep·skin /sheépskin/ *n.* **1** a garment or rug of sheep's skin with the wool on. **2** leather from a sheep's skin used in bookbinding.

sheer[1] /sheer/ *adj. & adv.* • *adj.* **1** no more or less than; mere (*sheer luck*; *sheer determination*). **2** (of a cliff or ascent, etc.) perpendicular; very steep. **3** (of a textile) diaphanous. • *adv.* **1** directly; outright. **2** perpendicularly. □□ **sheer·ly** *adv.* **sheer·ness** *n.*

sheer[2] /sheer/ *v.intr.* **1** esp. *Naut.* swerve or change course. **2** (foll. by *away, off*) go away, esp. from a person or topic one dislikes or fears.

sheer[3] /sheer/ *n.* the upward slope of a ship's lines toward the bow and stern.

sheer·legs /sheérlegz/ *n.pl.* (treated as *sing.*) a hoisting apparatus made from poles joined at or near the top and separated at the bottom for masting ships, installing engines, etc.

sheet[1] /sheet/ *n. & v.* •*n.* **1** a large rectangular piece of cotton or other fabric, used esp. in pairs as inner bedclothes. **2 a** a broad usu. thin flat piece of material (e.g., paper or metal). **b** (*attrib.*) made in sheets (*sheet iron*). **3** a wide continuous surface or expanse of water, ice, flame, falling rain, etc. **4** a set of unseparated postage stamps. **5** *derog.* a newspaper. **6** a complete piece of paper of the size in which it was made, for printing and folding as part of a book. •*v.* **1** *tr.* provide or cover with sheets. **2** *tr.* form into sheets. **3** *intr.* (of rain, etc.) fall in sheets.

sheet[2] /sheet/ *n.* a rope or chain attached to the lower corner of a sail for securing or controlling it.

sheet·ing /sheéting/ *n.* fabric for making bed linen.

sheet light·ning *n.* lightning with its brightness diffused by reflection.

sheet met·al *n.* metal formed into thin sheets by rolling, hammering, etc.

sheet mu·sic *n.* music published in cut or folded sheets, not bound.

sheikh /sheek, shayk/ *n.* (also **sheik, shaikh**) **1** a chief or head of an Arab tribe, family, or village. **2** a Muslim leader. □□ **sheikh·dom** *n.*

shei·la /sheélə/ *n. Austral.* & *NZ sl.* a girl or young woman.

shek·el /shékəl/ *n.* **1** the chief monetary unit of modern Israel. **2** *hist.* a silver coin and unit of weight used in ancient Israel and the Middle East. **3** (in *pl.*) *colloq.* money; riches.

shel·duck /shélduk/ *n.* (*pl.* same or **shelducks**; *masc.* **sheldrake,** *pl.* same or **sheldrakes**) any bright-plumaged coastal wild duck of the genus *Tadorna*, esp. *T. tadorna*.

shelf /shelf/ *n.* (*pl.* **shelves** /shelvz/) **1 a** a thin flat piece of wood or metal, etc., projecting from a wall, or as part of a unit, used to support books, etc. **b** a flat-topped recess in a wall, etc., used for supporting objects. **2 a** a projecting horizontal ledge in a cliff face, etc. **b** a reef or sandbank. □ **on the shelf 1** (of a woman) past the age when she might expect to be married. **2** (esp. of a retired person) no longer active or of use. □□ **shelved** /shelvd/ *adj.* **shelf·ful** *n.* (*pl.* **-fuls**). **shelf·like** *adj.*

shelf life *n.* the amount of time for which a stored item remains usable.

shell /shel/ *n. & v.* •*n.* **1 a** the hard outer case of many marine mollusks. **b** the hard but fragile outer covering of an egg. **c** the usu. hard outer case of a nut kernel, seed, etc. **d** the carapace of a tortoise, turtle, etc. **e** the elytron or cocoon, etc., of many insects, etc. **2 a** an explosive projectile or bomb for use in a big gun or mortar. **b** a hollow container for fireworks, explosives, cartridges, etc. **c** a cartridge. **3** a mere semblance or outer form without substance. **4** any of several things resembling a shell in being an outer case, esp.: **a** a light racing boat. **b** a hollow pastry case. **c** the metal framework of a vehicle body, etc. **d** the walls of an unfinished or gutted building, ship, etc. •*v.tr.* **1** remove the shell or pod from. **2** bombard with shells. □ **come out of one's shell** cease to be shy. **shell out** *colloq.* **1** pay (money). **2** hand over (a required sum). □□ **shelled** *adj.* **shell-less** *adj.* **shell-like** *adj.* **shell·proof** *adj.* (in sense 2a of *n.*). **shell·y** *adj.*

she'll /sheel, shil/ *contr.* she will; she shall.

shel·lac /shəlák/ *n. & v.* •*n.* lac resin melted into thin flakes and used for making varnish (cf. LAC). •*v.tr.* (**shellacked, shellacking**) **1** varnish with shellac. **2** *sl.* defeat or thrash soundly.

shell·fish /shélfish/ *n.* **1** an aquatic shelled mollusk, e.g., an oyster, mussel, etc. **2** a crustacean, e.g., a crab, shrimp, etc.

shell shock *n.* a nervous breakdown resulting from exposure to battle (also called **battle fatigue**). □□ **shell-shocked** *adj.*

shel·ter /shéltər/ *n. & v.* •*n.* **1** anything serving as a shield or protection from danger, bad weather, etc. **2 a** a place of refuge provided esp. for the homeless. **b** an animal sanctuary. **3** a shielded condition; protection (*took shelter under a tree*). •*v.* **1** *tr.* act or serve as shelter to; protect; conceal; defend (*sheltered them from the storm*; *a sheltered upbringing*). **2** *intr. & refl.* find refuge; take cover (*sheltered under a tree*; *sheltered themselves behind the wall*). □□ **shel·ter·er** *n.* **shel·ter·less** *adj.*

shelve[1] /shelv/ *v.tr.* **1** put (books, etc.) on a shelf. **2 a** abandon or defer (a plan, etc.). **b** remove (a person) from active work, etc. **3** fit (a cupboard, etc.) with shelves. □□ **shelv·er** *n.* **shelv·ing** *n.*

shelve[2] /shelv/ *v.intr.* (of ground, etc.) slope (*land shelved away to the horizon*).

shelves *pl.* of SHELF.

she·nan·i·gan /shinánigən/ *n.* (esp. in *pl.*) *colloq.* **1** high-spirited behavior; nonsense. **2** trickery; dubious maneuvers.

She·ol /sheé-ōl/ *n.* the Hebrew underworld abode of the dead.

shep·herd /shépərd/ *n. & v.* •*n.* **1** (*fem.* **shepherdess** /shépərdis/) a person employed to tend sheep. **2** a member of the clergy, etc., who cares for and guides a congregation. •*v.tr.* **1 a** tend (sheep, etc.). **b** guide (followers, etc.). **2** marshal or drive (a crowd, etc.).

sher·ard·ize /shérərdīz/ *v.tr.* coat (iron or steel) with zinc by heating in contact with zinc dust.

sher·bet /shə́rbət/ *n.* **1** a fruit-flavored ice confection. **2** a cooling drink of sweet, diluted fruit juices, used esp. in the Middle East.

▶Avoid the pronunciation "sher-bert." **Sherbet** has only one *r*, in the first syllable.

sherd /shərd/ *n.* = POTSHERD.

sher·iff /shérif/ *n.* an elected officer in a county, responsible for keeping the peace.

Sher·pa /shə́rpə/ *n.* (*pl.* same or **Sherpas**) **1** a Himalayan people living on the borders of Nepal and Tibet. **2** a member of this people.

sher·ry /shéree/ *n.* (*pl.* **-ries**) **1** a fortified wine orig. from S. Spain. **2** a glass of this.

she's /sheez/ *contr.* **1** she is. **2** she has.

Shet·land po·ny *n.* a pony of a small, hardy, rough-coated breed.

Shet·land sheep·dog *n.* a small dog of a collielike breed.

Shet·land wool *n.* a fine, loosely twisted wool from Shetland sheep.

shew *archaic* var. of SHOW.

shew·bread /shṓbred/ *n.* twelve loaves that were displayed in a Jewish temple and renewed each Sabbath.

Shi·a /sheéə/ *n.* one of the two main branches of Islam, esp. in Iran, that rejects the first three Sunni caliphs and regards Ali as Muhammad's first successor (cf. SUNNI).

shi·at·su /shiátsoo/ *n.* a kind of therapy of Japanese origin, in which pressure is applied with the fingers to certain points of the body.

shib·bo·leth /shíbəleth/ *n.* a doctrine, phrase, etc., held to be true by a party or sect.

shield /sheeld/ *n. & v.* •*n.* **1 a** esp. *hist.* a piece of armor carried on the arm or in the hand to deflect blows from the head or body. **b** a thing serving to protect (*insurance is a shield against disaster*). **2** a thing resembling a shield, esp.: **a** a trophy in the form of a shield. **b** a protective plate or screen in machinery, etc. **c** a shieldlike part of an animal, esp. a shell. **d** a similar part of a plant. • *v.tr.* protect or screen.

shier *compar.* of SHY[1].

shiest *superl.* of SHY[1].

shift /shift/ *v. & n.* • *v.* **1** *intr. & tr.* change or move or cause to change or move from one position to another. **2** *intr.* contrive or manage as best one can. **3 a** *tr.* change (gear) in a vehicle. **b** *intr.* change gear. **4** *intr.* (of cargo) get shaken out of place. • *n.* **1 a** the act of shifting. **b** the substitution of one thing for another. **2 a** a relay of workers (*the night shift*). **b** the time for which they work (*an eight-hour shift*). **3 a** a device, stratagem, or expedient. **b** a trick or evasion. **4 a** a woman's straight unwaisted dress. **b** *archaic* a loose-fitting undergarment. **5** a displacement of spectral lines (*red shift*). **6** a key on a keyboard used to switch between lowercase and uppercase, etc. **7 a** a gear lever in a motor vehicle. **b** a mechanism for this. □ **shift for oneself** rely on one's own efforts. **shift one's ground** take up a new position in an argument, etc. □□ **shift·a·ble** *adj.* **shift·er** *n.*

shift·less /shíftlis/ *adj.* lacking resourcefulness. □□ **shift·less·ly** *adv.* **shift·less·ness** *n.*

shift·y /shíftee/ *adj. colloq.* (**shiftier, shiftiest**) evasive; deceitful. □□ **shift·i·ly** *adv.* **shift·i·ness** *n.*

Shi·ite /shée-īt/ *n. & adj.* • *n.* an adherent of the Shia branch of Islam. • *adj.* of or relating to Shia. □□ **Shi·ism** /shée-izəm/ *n.*

shill /shil/ *n.* a person employed to decoy or entice others into buying, gambling, etc.

shil·le·lagh /shiláylee, –lə/ *n.* a thick stick of blackthorn or oak used in Ireland esp. as a weapon.

shil·ling /shíling/ *n.* **1** *hist.* a former British coin and monetary unit worth one-twentieth of a pound. **2** a monetary unit in Kenya, Tanzania, and Uganda.

shil·ly-shal·ly /shíleeshálee/ *v., adj., & n.* • *v.intr.* (**-lies, -lied**) be undecided; vacillate. • *adj.* vacillating. • *n.* indecision; vacillation. □□ **shil·ly-shal·ly·er** *n.* (also **-shallier**).

shim /shim/ *n. & v.* • *n.* a thin strip of material used in machinery, etc., to make parts fit. • *v.tr.* (**shimmed, shimming**) fit or fill up with a shim.

shim·mer /shímər/ *v. & n.* • *v.intr.* shine with a tremulous or faint diffused light. • *n.* such a light. □□ **shim·mer·ing·ly** *adv.* **shim·mer·y** *adj.*

shim·my /shímee/ *n. & v.* • *n.* (*pl.* **-mies**) *hist.* a kind of ragtime dance in which the whole body is shaken. • *v.intr.* (**-mies, -mied**) **1** *hist.* dance a shimmy. **2** move in a similar manner.

shin /shin/ *n. & v.* • *n.* **1** the front of the leg below the knee. **2** a cut of beef from the lower foreleg. • *v.tr. &* (usu. foll. by *up, down*) *intr.* (**shinned, shinning**) climb quickly by clinging with the arms and legs.

shin·bone /shínbōn/ = TIBIA.

shin·dig /shíndig/ *n. colloq.* **1** a festive, esp. noisy, party. **2** = SHINDY 1.

shine /shīn/ *v. & n.* • *v.* (*past* and *past part.* **shone** /shon/ or **shined**) **1** *intr.* emit or reflect light; be bright (*the lamp was shining; his face shone with gratitude*). **2** *intr.* (of the sun, a star, etc.) be visible. **3** *tr.* cause (a lamp, etc.) to shine. **4** *tr.* (*past* and *past part.* **shined**) polish (*shined his shoes*). **5** *intr.* be brilliant; excel (*does not shine in conversation*). • *n.* **1** brightness, esp. reflected. **2** a high polish. **3** the act of shining, esp. shoes. □ **shine up to** seek to ingratiate oneself with. **take the shine out of 1** spoil the brilliance or newness of. **2** throw into the shade by surpassing. **take a shine to** *colloq.* take a fancy to. □□ **shin·ing·ly** *adv.*

shin·er /shínər/ *n.* **1** a thing that shines. **2** *colloq.* a black eye.

shin·gle[1] /shínggəl/ *n.* (in *sing.* or *pl.*) small rounded pebbles, esp. on a seashore. □□ **shin·gly** *adj.*

shin·gle[2] /shínggəl/ *n. & v.* • *n.* **1** a rectangular wooden tile used on roofs, spires, or esp. walls. **2** *archaic* **a** shingled hair. **b** the act of shingling hair. **3** a small signboard, esp. of a doctor, lawyer, etc. • *v.tr.* **1** roof or clad with shingles. **2** *archaic* **a** cut (a woman's hair) very short. **b** cut the hair of (a person or head) in this way.

shin·gles /shínggəlz/ *n.pl.* (usu. treated as *sing.*) an acute painful viral inflammation of the nerve ganglia, with a skin eruption often forming a girdle around the middle of the body.

shin·ny /shínee/ *v.intr.* (**-nies, -nied**) (usu. foll. by *up, down*) *colloq.* shin (up or down a tree, etc.).

Shin·to /shíntō/ *n.* the official religion of Japan incorporating the worship of ancestors and nature spirits. □□ **Shin·to·ism** *n.* **Shin·to·ist** *n.*

shin·y /shínee/ *adj.* (**shinier, shiniest**) **1** having a shine; glistening; polished; bright. **2** (of clothing) having the nap worn off. □□ **shin·i·ly** *adv.* **shin·i·ness** *n.*

ship /ship/ *n. & v.* • *n.* **1 a** any large seagoing vessel. **b** a sailing vessel with a bowsprit and three, four, or five square-rigged masts. **2** an aircraft. **3** a spaceship. **4** *colloq.* a boat, esp. a racing boat. • *v.* (**shipped, shipping**) **1** *tr.* put, take, or send away on board ship. **2** *tr.* **a** take in (water) over the side of a ship, boat, etc. **b** take (oars) from the oarlocks and lay them inside a boat. **c** fix (a rudder, etc.) in its place. **d** step (a mast). **3** *intr.* **a** embark. **b** (of a sailor) take service on a ship (*shipped for Africa*). **4** *tr.* deliver (goods) to a forwarding agent for conveyance. □ **ship off 1** send or transport by ship. **2** *colloq.* send (a person) away. **take ship** embark. **when a person's ship comes in** when a person's fortune is made. □□ **ship·less** *adj.*

-ship /ship/ *suffix* forming nouns denoting: **1** a quality or condition (*friendship; hardship*). **2** status, office, or honor (*authorship; lordship*). **3** a tenure of office (*chairmanship*). **4** a skill in a certain capacity (*workmanship*). **5** the collective individuals of a group (*membership*).

ship·board /shípbawrd/ *n.* (usu. *attrib.*) used or occurring on board a ship (*a shipboard romance*). □ **on shipboard** on board ship.

ship·build·er /shípbildər/ *n.* a person, company, etc., that constructs ships. □□ **ship·build·ing** *n.*

ship·load /shíplōd/ *n.* a quantity of goods forming a cargo.

ship·mate /shípmayt/ *n.* a fellow member of a ship's crew.

ship·ment /shípmənt/ *n.* **1** an amount of goods shipped. **2** the act of shipping goods, etc.

ship·per /shípər/ *n.* a person or company that sends or receives goods by ship, or by land or air.

ship·ping /shíping/ *n.* **1** the act or an instance of shipping goods, etc. **2** ships.

ship·shape /shípshayp/ *adv. & predic.adj.* in good order; trim and neat.

ship·wreck /shíprek/ *n. & v.* • *n.* **1 a** the destruction of a ship by a storm, foundering, etc. **b** a ship so destroyed. **2** (often foll. by *of*) the destruction of hopes, dreams, etc. • *v.* **1** *tr.* inflict shipwreck on. **2** *intr.* suffer shipwreck.

ship·wright /shíprīt/ *n.* **1** a shipbuilder. **2** a ship's carpenter.

ship·yard /shípyaard/ *n.* a place where ships are built, repaired, etc.

---

shirk /shərk/ *v.tr.* (also *absol.*) avoid; get out of (duty, work, responsibility, fighting, etc.). ▫▫ **shirk·er** *n.*

shirr /shər/ *n. & v.* • *n.* **1** two or more rows of esp. elastic gathered threads in a garment, etc., forming smocking. **2** elastic webbing. • *v.tr.* **1** gather (material) with parallel threads. **2** bake (eggs) without shells. ▫▫ **shirr·ing** *n.*

shirt /shərt/ *n.* **1** an upper-body garment of cotton, etc., having a collar, sleeves, and buttons down the front. **2 a** an undershirt. **b** a T-shirt. ▫ **keep one's shirt on** *colloq.* keep one's temper. **lose one's shirt** lose all that one has. **the shirt off one's back** *colloq.* one's last remaining possessions. ▫▫ **shirt·ed** *adj.* **shirt·ing** *n.* **shirt·less** *adj.*

---

shirt Old English *scyrte,* of Germanic origin; related to Old Norse *skyrta* (source of *skirt*), Dutch *schort,* German *Schürze* 'apron,' also to *short*; probably from a base meaning 'short garment.'

---

shirt·dress /shə́rtdress/ *n.* = SHIRTWAIST.

shirt·front /shə́rtfrunt/ *n.* the breast of a shirt, esp. of a stiffened evening shirt.

shirt·sleeve /shə́rtsleev/ *n.* (usu. in *pl.*) the sleeve of a shirt. ▫ **in shirtsleeves** wearing a shirt with no jacket, etc., over it.

shirt·tail /shə́rttayl/ *n.* the lower curved part of a shirt below the waist.

shirt·waist /shə́rtwayst/ *n.* a woman's blouse resembling a shirt.

shish ke·bab /shísh kibób/ *n.* a dish of pieces of marinated meat and vegetables cooked and served on skewers.

shit /shit/ *v., n., & int. coarse sl.*
▶Usually considered a taboo word. • *v.* (**shitting;** *past* and *past part.* **shit** or **shat**) *intr. & tr.* expel feces from the body or cause (feces, etc.) to be expelled. • *n.* **1** feces. **2** an act of defecating. **3** a contemptible or worthless person or thing. **4** nonsense. **5** an intoxicating drug, esp. cannabis. • *int.* an exclamation of disgust, anger, etc.

shit·ty /shítee/ *adj.* (**shittier, shittiest**) *coarse sl.* **1** disgusting; contemptible. **2** covered with excrement.

shiv·er[1] /shívər/ *v. & n.* • *v.intr.* **1** tremble with cold, fear, etc. **2** suffer a quick trembling movement of the body. • *n.* **1** a momentary shivering movement. **2** (in *pl.*) an attack of shivering, esp. from fear or horror (*got the shivers in the dark*). ▫▫ **shiv·er·ing·ly** *adv.* **shiv·er·y** *adj.*

shiv·er[2] /shívər/ *n. & v.* • *n.* (esp. in *pl.*) each of the small pieces into which esp. glass is shattered when broken; a splinter. • *v.tr. & intr.* break into shivers. ▫ **shiver my** (or **me**) **timbers** a reputed pirate's curse.

shoal[1] /shōl/ *n. & v.* • *n.* **1** a great number of fish swimming together. **2** a multitude; a crowd (*shoals of letters*). • *v.intr.* (of fish) form shoals.

shoal[2] /shōl/ *n., v., & adj.* • *n.* **1 a** an area of shallow water. **b** a submerged sandbank visible at low water. **2** (esp. in *pl.*) hidden danger. • *v.intr.* (of water) get shallower. *adj. archaic* (of water) shallow. ▫▫ **shoal·y** *adj.*

shoat /shōt/ *n.* a young pig, esp. newly weaned.

shock[1] /shok/ *n. & v.* • *n.* **1** a violent collision, impact, tremor, etc. **2** a sudden and disturbing effect on the emotions, physical reactions, etc. (*the news was a great shock*). **3** an acute state of prostration following a wound, pain, etc. (*died of shock*). **4** the effect of a sudden discharge of electricity on a person or animal, usually with stimulation of the nerves and contraction of the muscles. • *v.* **1** *tr.* **a** affect with shock; horrify; outrage. **b** (*absol.*) cause shock. **2** *tr.* (esp. in *passive*) affect with an electric or pathological shock. **3** *intr.* experience shock (*I don't shock easily*). ▫▫ **shock·a·ble** *adj.* **shock·a·bil·i·ty** *n.*

shock[2] /shok/ *n. & v.* • *n.* a group of sheaves of grain stood up with their heads together in a field. • *v.tr.* arrange (grain) in shocks.

shock[3] /shok/ *n.* an unkempt or shaggy mass of hair.

shock ab·sorb·er *n.* a device on a vehicle, etc., for absorbing shocks, vibrations, etc.

shock·er /shókər/ *n. colloq.* **1** a shocking person or thing. **2** *hist.* a sordid or sensational novel, etc.

shock·ing /shóking/ *adj. & adv.* • *adj.* causing indignation or disgust. • *adv. colloq.* shockingly (*shocking bad manners*). ▫▫ **shock·ing·ly** *adv.* **shock·ing·ness** *n.*

shock·ing pink *n.* a vibrant shade of pink.

shock·proof /shókproof/ *adj.* resistant to the effects of (esp. physical) shock.

shock ther·a·py *n.* (also **shock treat·ment**) *Psychol.* a method of treating depressive patients by means of electric shock or drugs inducing coma and convulsions.

shock troops *n.pl.* troops specially trained for assault.

shock wave *n.* a sharp change of pressure in a narrow region traveling through air, etc., caused by explosion or by a body moving faster than sound.

shod *past* and *past part.* of SHOE.

shod·dy /shódee/ *adj. & n.* • *adj.* (**shoddier, shoddiest**) **1** poorly made. **2** counterfeit. • *n.* (*pl.* **-dies**) **1 a** an inferior cloth made partly from the shredded fiber of old woolen cloth. **b** such fiber. **2** any thing of shoddy quality. ▫▫ **shod·di·ly** *adv.* **shod·di·ness** *n.*

shoe /shoo/ *n. & v.* • *n.* **1** either of a pair of protective foot coverings of leather, plastic, etc., having a sturdy sole and not reaching above the ankle. **2** a metal rim nailed to the hoof of a horse, etc. **3** anything resembling a shoe in shape or use, esp.: **a** a drag for a wheel. **b** = BRAKE SHOE. **c** a socket. • *v.tr.* (**shoes, shoeing;** *past* and *past part.* **shod** /shod/) **1** fit (esp. a horse, etc.) with a shoe or shoes. **2** (as **shod** *adj.*) (in *comb.*) having shoes, etc., of a specified kind (*dry-shod*; *roughshod*). ▫ **be in a person's shoes** be in his or her situation, difficulty, etc. ▫▫ **shoe·less** *adj.*

shoe·bill /shóobil/ *n.* an African storklike bird, *Balaeniceps rex,* with a large flattened bill for catching aquatic prey.

shoe·box /shóoboks/ *n.* **1** a box for packing shoes. **2** a very small space.

shoe·horn /shóohawrn/ *n.* a curved piece of horn, metal, etc., for easing the heel into a shoe.

shoe·lace /shóolays/ *n.* a cord for lacing up shoes.

shoe·mak·er /shóomaykər/ *n.* a maker of boots and shoes. ▫▫ **shoe·mak·ing** *n.*

shoe·shine /shóoshīn/ *n.* a polish given to shoes.

shoe·string /shóostring/ *n.* **1** a shoelace. **2** *colloq.* a small esp. inadequate amount of money (*living on a shoestring*). **3** (*attrib.*) barely adequate.

shoe tree *n.* a shaped block for keeping a shoe in shape.

sho·far /shōfər, shawfar/ *n.* (*pl.* **shofroth** /sh+frōt/) a ram's-horn trumpet used by Jews in religious ceremonies and as an ancient battle signal.

sho·gun /shógən, –gun/ *n. hist.* any of a succession of Japanese hereditary commanders in chief and virtual rulers before 1868. ▫▫ **sho·gun·ate** /–nət, –nayt/ *n.*

shone *past* and *past part.* of SHINE.

shoo /shoo/ *int. & v.* • *int.* an exclamation used to frighten away birds, children, etc. • *v.* (**shoos, shooed**) **1** *intr.* utter the word "shoo!" **2** *tr.* (usu. foll. by *away*) drive (birds, etc.) away by shooing.

shoo-in *n.* something easy or certain to succeed (*she's a shoo-in to win the election*).

shook /shook/ *past* of SHAKE. *predic.adj. colloq.* (foll. by *up*) emotionally or physically disturbed.

shoot /shoot/ *v., n., & int.* • *v.* (*past* and *past part.* **shot** /shot/) **1** *tr.* **a** cause (a gun, bow, etc.) to fire. **b** discharge (a bullet, arrow, etc.) from a gun, bow, etc. **c** kill or wound with a bullet, arrow, etc., from a gun, bow, etc. **2** *intr.* discharge a gun, etc. (*shoots well*). **3** *tr.* send out, discharge, propel, etc., esp. swiftly (*shot out the contents; shot a glance at his neighbor*). **4** *intr.* come or go swiftly or vigorously. **5** *intr.* **a** (of a plant, etc.) put forth buds, etc. **b** (of a bud, etc.) appear. **6** *intr.* hunt game, etc., with a gun. **7** *tr.* film or photograph. **8** *tr.* (also *absol.*) *Basketball,* etc. **a** score (a goal). **b** take a shot at (the goal). **9** *tr.* (of a boat) sweep swiftly down or under (a bridge, rapids, falls, etc.). **10** *tr.* move (a door bolt) to fasten or unfasten a door, etc. **11** *tr.* (often foll. by *up*) *sl.* inject esp. oneself with (a drug). **12** *tr. colloq.* **a** play a game of (craps, pool, etc.). **b** throw (a die or dice). **13** *tr. Golf colloq.* make (a specified score) for a round or hole. **14** *tr. colloq.* pass (traffic lights at red). •*n.* **1** the act of shooting. **2 a** a young branch or sucker. **b** the new growth of a plant. **3** = CHUTE[1]. •*int. colloq. euphem.* an exclamation of disgust, anger, etc. (see SHIT). □ **shoot ahead** come quickly to the front of competitors, etc. **shoot down 1** kill by shooting. **2** cause (an aircraft, its pilot, etc.) to crash by shooting. **3** argue effectively against. **shoot it out** *sl.* engage in a decisive gun battle. **shoot one's mouth off** *sl.* talk too much or indiscreetly. **shoot up 1** grow rapidly. **2** rise suddenly. **3** terrorize (a district) by indiscriminate shooting.

shoot·er /shoōtər/ *n.* **1** a person or thing that shoots. **2 a** (in *comb.*) a gun or other device for shooting (*peashooter; six-shooter*). **b** *sl.* a pistol, etc. **3** a player who shoots or is able to shoot a goal in basketball, etc.

shoot·ing /shoōting/ *n. & adj.* •*n.* **1** the act of shooting (*two of the suspects in the shooting*). **2 a** the right of shooting over an area of land. **b** an estate, etc., rented to shoot over. •*adj.* moving, growing, etc., quickly (*a shooting pain in the arm*).

shoot·ing gal·ler·y *n.* a place used for shooting at targets with rifles, etc.

shoot·ing range *n.* a controlled area provided with targets for shooting practice.

shoot·ing star *n.* a small meteor moving rapidly and burning up on entering the earth's atmosphere.

shoot-out *n. colloq.* a decisive gun battle.

shop /shop/ *n. & v.* •*n.* **1** a building, room, etc., for the retail sale of goods or services (*dress shop; beauty shop*). **2** a place in which manufacture or repairing is done (*metal shop*). **3** a profession, trade, business, etc., esp. as a subject of conversation (*talk shop*). **4** *colloq.* an institution, establishment, place of business, etc. •*v.* (**shopped, shopping**) *intr.* go to a shop or shops to buy goods. □ **set up shop** establish oneself in business, etc. **shop around** look for the best bargain.

shop·keep·er /shópkeepər/ *n.* the owner and manager of a store. □□ **shop·keep·ing** *n.*

shop·lift·er /shópliftər/ *n.* a person who steals goods while appearing to shop. □□ **shop·lift** *v.tr. & intr.* **shop·lift·ing** *n.*

shop·per /shópər/ *n.* a person who makes purchases in a store.

shop·ping /shóping/ *n.* **1** (often *attrib.*) the purchase of goods, etc. (*shopping expedition*). **2** goods purchased (*put the shopping on the table*).

shop·ping cen·ter *n.* an area or complex of stores.

shop stew·ard *n.* a person elected by workers in a factory, etc., to represent them in dealings with management.

shop·worn /shópwawrn/ *adj.* **1** faded by display in a shop. **2** (of a person, idea, etc.) no longer fresh or new.

shor·an /sháwran/ *n.* a system of aircraft navigation using the return of two radar signals by two ground stations (acronym of *short-range navigation*).

shore[1] /shawr/ *n.* **1** the land that adjoins the sea or a large body of water. **2** (usu. in *pl.*) a country; a seacoast (*often visits these shores*). □□ **shore·less** *adj.* **shore·ward** *adj. & adv.* **shore·wards** *adv.*

shore[2] /shawr/ *v. & n.* •*v.tr.* support with or as if with a shore or shores. •*n.* a prop or beam set against a ship, wall, tree, etc., as a support. □□ **shor·ing** *n.*

shore[3] see SHEAR.

shore leave *n Naut.* **1** permission to go ashore. **2** a period of time ashore.

shore·line /sháwrlīn/ *n.* the line along which a stretch of water meets the shore.

shorn *past part.* of SHEAR.

short /shawrt/ *adj., adv., n., & v.* •*adj.* **1 a** measuring little; not long from end to end (*a short distance*). **b** not long in duration (*a short time ago*). **c** seeming less than the stated amount (*a few short years of happiness*). **2** not tall (*a short square tower*). **3 a** (usu. foll. by *of, on*) having a partial or total lack; deficient (*short of spoons; short on sense*). **b** not far-reaching; acting or being near at hand (*within short range*). **4 a** concise; brief (*kept his speech short*). **b** curt; uncivil (*was short with her*). **5** (of the memory) unable to remember distant events. **6** *Phonet. & Prosody* of a vowel or syllable: **a** having the lesser of the two recognized durations. **b** (of a vowel) having a sound other than that called long (cf. LONG[1] *adj.* 8). **7** (of pastry) crumbling. **8** esp. *Stock Exch.* (of stocks, a stockbroker, crops, etc.) sold or selling when the amount is not in hand, with reliance on getting the deficit in time for delivery. •*adv.* **1** before the natural or expected time or place (*pulled up short; cut short the celebrations*). **2** rudely (*spoke to him short*). •*n.* **1** a short circuit. **2** a short movie. **3** *Stock Exch.* **a** a person who sells short. **b** (in *pl.*) short-dated stocks. •*v.tr. & intr.* short-circuit. □ **be caught short** be put at a disadvantage. **bring up** (or **pull up**) **short** check or pause abruptly. **come short of** fail to reach or amount to. **for short** as a short name (*Tom for short*). **get** (or **have**) **by the short hairs** *colloq.* be in complete control of (a person). **in short order** immediately. **in the short run** over a short period of time. **in short supply** scarce. **in the short term** = *in the short run.* **make short work of** accomplish, dispose of, destroy, etc., quickly. **short and sweet** esp. *iron.* brief and pleasant. **short for** an abbreviation for (*"Bob" is short for "Robert"*). **short of 1** see sense 3a of *adj.* **2** less than (*nothing short of a miracle*). **3** distant from (*two miles short of home*). **4** except (*did everything short of destroying it*). **short of breath** panting, short-winded. **short on** *colloq.* see sense 3a of *adj.* □□ **short·ish** *adj.* **short·ness** *n.*

short·age /sháwrtij/ *n.* (often foll. by *of*) a deficiency; an amount lacking.

short·bread /sháwrtbred/ *n.* a crisp, rich, crumbly type of cookie made with butter, flour, and sugar.

short·cake /sháwrtkayk/ *n.* **1** = SHORTBREAD. **2** a cake made of short pastry and filled with fruit and cream.

short·change /sháwrtcháynj/ *v.tr.* **1** cheat by giving insufficient money as change. **2** treat unfairly by witholding something of value.

short cir·cuit *n.* an electric circuit through small resistance, esp. instead of the resistance of a normal circuit. □□ **short-cir·cuit** *v.*

short·com·ing /sháwrtkuming/ *n.* failure to come up to a standard; a defect.

short·cut *n.* **1** a route shortening the distance traveled. **2** a quick way of accomplishing something.

short·en /sháwrt'n/ *v.* **1** *intr. & tr.* become or make shorter or short. **2** *tr. Naut.* reduce the amount of (sail spread).

short•en•ing /sháwrt'ning, sháwrtning/ *n.* fat used for making pastry, etc.

short•fall /sháwrtfawl/ *n.* a deficit below what was expected.

short•hand /sháwrt-hand/ *n.* **1** (often *attrib.*) a method of rapid writing in abbreviations and symbols. **2** an abbreviated or symbolic mode of expression.

short•hand•ed /shawrt-hánded/ *adj.* undermanned or understaffed.

short haul *n.* **1** the transport of goods over a short distance. **2** a short-term effort.

short•horn /sháwrt-horn/ *n.* an animal of a breed of cattle with short horns.

short•list /sháwrtlist/ *n.* a selective list of candidates from which a final choice is made. ▫▫ **short-list** *v.tr.*

short-lived *adj.* ephemeral.

short•ly /sháwrtlee/ *adv.* **1** (often foll. by *before, after*) before long; soon (*will arrive shortly; arrived shortly after him*). **2** in a few words; briefly. **3** curtly.

short or•der *n.&adj.* •*n.* an order or dish of food that can be quickly prepared and served. •*adj.* (**short-or•der**) **1** prepared quickly, esp. simple restaurant fare. **2** pertaining to one who provides such fare (*a short-order cook*).

short-range *adj.* **1** having a short range. **2** relating to a fairly immediate future time (*short-range possibilities*).

shorts /shawrts/ *n.pl.* **1** pants reaching to the knees or higher. **2** underpants.

short shrift *n.* curt treatment.

short•sight•ed /sháwrtsítid/ *adj.* **1** esp. *Brit.* = NEARSIGHTED. **2** lacking foresight or imagination. ▫▫ **short•sight•ed•ly** *adv.* **short•sight•ed•ness** *n.*

short-sleeved *adj.* with sleeves not reaching below the elbow.

short-staffed *adj.* having insufficient staff.

short•stop /sháwrtstop/ *n.* a baseball fielder between second and third base.

short sto•ry *n.* a story with a fully developed theme but shorter than a novel.

short tem•per *n.* self-control soon or easily lost. ▫▫ **short-tem•pered** *adj.*

short-term *adj.* occurring in or relating to a short period of time.

short•wave /sháwrtwáyv/ *n.* a radio wave of frequency greater than 3 MHz.

short-wind•ed *adj.* **1** quickly exhausted of breath. **2** incapable of sustained effort.

short•y /sháwrtee/ *n.* (also **short•ie**) (*pl.* **-ies**) *colloq.* **1** a person shorter than average. **2** a short garment.

Sho•sho•ne /shəshṓn, –shṓnee/ *n.* (also **Sho•sho•ni**) **1 a** a N. American people native to the western US. **b** a member of this people. **2** the language of this people. ▫▫ **Sho•sho•ne•an** *adj.*

shot[1] /shot/ *n.* **1** the act of firing a gun, etc. (*several shots were heard*). **2** an attempt to hit by shooting or throwing, etc. (*took a shot at him*). **3 a** a single nonexplosive missile for a gun, etc. **b** (*pl.* same or **shots**) a small lead pellet used in quantity in a single charge or cartridge in a shotgun. **c** (as *pl.*) these collectively. **4 a** a photograph. **b** a film sequence photographed continuously by one camera. **5 a** a stroke or kick in a ball game. **b** *colloq.* an attempt to guess or do something (*let her have a shot at it*). **6** *colloq.* a person having a specified skill with a gun, etc. (*is not a good shot*). **7** a heavy ball thrown by a shot-putter. **8** the launch of a space rocket. **9** the range, reach, or distance to or at which a thing will carry or act. **10** a remark aimed at a person. **11** *colloq.* **a** a drink of esp. liquor. **b** an injection of a drug, vaccine, etc. ▫ **like a shot** *colloq.* without hesitation; willingly. **shot in the arm** *colloq.* stimulus or encouragement. **shot in the dark** a mere guess.

shot[2] /shot/ *past* and *past part.* of SHOOT. *adj.* **1** (of colored material) woven so as to show different colors at different angles. **2** *colloq.* **a** exhausted; finished. **b** drunk. ▫ **shot through** permeated or suffused.

shot•gun /shótgun/ *n.* a smoothbore gun for firing small shot at short range.

shot put *n.* an athletic contest in which a shot is thrown. ▫▫ **shot-put•ter** *n.*

should /shŏŏd/ *v.aux.* (*3rd sing.* **should**) *past* of SHALL, used esp.: **1** in reported speech, esp. with the reported element in the 1st person (*I said I should be home by evening*). ▶Cf. WOULD. **2 a** to express a duty, obligation, or likelihood (*I should tell you; you should have been more careful*). **b** (in the 1st person) to express a tentative suggestion (*I should like to say something*). **3 a** expressing the conditional mood in the 1st person (cf. WOULD) (*I should have been killed if I had gone*). **b** forming a conditional clause (*if you should see him; should they arrive, tell them where to go*). **4** expressing purpose (*in order that we should not worry*).

▶See note at SHALL.

shoul•der /shṓldər/ *n. & v.* •*n.* **1 a** the part of the body at which the arm, foreleg, or wing is attached. **b** (in full **shoulder joint**) the end of the upper arm joining with the clavicle and scapula. **c** either of the two projections below the neck from which the arms hang. **2** the upper foreleg and shoulder blade of a pig, lamb, etc., when butchered. **3** (often in *pl.*) **a** the upper part of the back and arms. **b** this part of the body regarded as capable of bearing a burden or blame, providing comfort, etc. (*needs a shoulder to cry on*). **4** a strip of land next to a paved road. **5** a part of a garment covering the shoulder. **6** a part of anything resembling a shoulder in form or function, as in a bottle, mountain, tool, etc. •*v.* **1 a** *tr.* push with the shoulder; jostle. **b** *intr.* make one's way by jostling (*shouldered through the crowd*). **2** *tr.* take (a burden, etc.) on one's shoulders (*shouldered the family's problems*). ▫ **put** (or **set**) **one's shoulder to the wheel** make an effort. **shoulder arms** hold a rifle with the barrel against the shoulder and the butt in the hand. **shoulder to shoulder 1** side by side. **2** with closed ranks or united effort. ▫▫ **shoul•dered** *adj.* (also in *comb.*).

shoul•der blade *n. Anat.* either of the large flat bones of the upper back.

should•n't /shŏŏd'nt/ *contr.* should not.

shout /showt/ *v. & n.* •*v.* **1** *intr.* make a loud cry or vocal sound (*shouted for attention*). **2** *tr.* say or express loudly (*shouted that the coast was clear*). •*n.* a loud cry expressing joy, etc., or calling attention. ▫ **all over but the shouting** *colloq.* the contest is virtually decided. **shout at** speak loudly to, etc. **shout down** reduce to silence by shouting. **shout for** call for by shouting. ▫▫ **shout•er** *n.*

shove /shuv/ *v. & n.* •*v.* **1** *tr.* (also *absol.*) push vigorously (*shoved him out of the way*). **2** *intr.* (usu. foll. by *along, past, through,* etc.) make one's way by pushing (*shoved through the crowd*). **3** *tr. colloq.* put somewhere (*shoved it in the drawer*). •*n.* an act of shoving or of prompting a person into action. ▫ **shove off 1** start from the shore in a boat. **2** *sl.* depart; go away.

shov•el /shúvəl/ *n. & v.* •*n.* **1 a** a spadelike tool for shifting quantities of coal, earth, etc., esp. having the sides curved upward. **b** the amount contained in a shovel. **2** a machine or part of a machine having a similar form or function. •*v.tr.* **1** shift or clear (coal, etc.) with or as if with a shovel. **2** *colloq.* move in large quantities or roughly (*shoveled peas into his mouth*). ▫▫ **shov•el•ful** *n.* (*pl.* **-fuls**).

show /shō/ *v. & n.* •*v.* (*past part.* **shown** /shōn/ or **showed**) **1** *intr. & tr.* be, or allow or cause to be, visible (*the buds are beginning to show; white shows the dirt*).

2 *tr.* offer, exhibit, or produce (a thing) for scrutiny, etc. (*show your tickets please*). **3** *tr.* indicate (one's feelings) by one's behavior, etc. (*showed mercy to him*). **4** *intr.* (of feelings, etc.) be manifest (*his dislike shows*). **5** *tr.* **a** point out; prove (*has shown it to be false*; *showed that he knew the answer*). **b** (usu. foll. by *how to* + infin.) cause (a person) to understand or be capable of doing (*showed them how to knit*). **6** *tr.* (*refl.*) exhibit oneself as being (*showed herself to be fair*). **7** *tr. & intr.* (with ref. to a movie) be presented or cause to be presented. **8** *tr.* exhibit in a show. **9** *tr.* conduct or lead (*showed them to their rooms*). **10** *intr.* = SHOW UP 3 (*waited but he didn't show*). •*n.* **1** the act of showing. **2 a** a spectacle, display, exhibition, etc. (*a fine show of blossom*). **b** a collection of things, etc., shown for public entertainment or in competition (*dog show*; *flower show*). **3 a** a play, etc., esp. a musical. **b** an entertainment program on television, etc. **c** any public entertainment or performance. **4 a** an outward appearance or display (*a show of strength*). **b** empty appearance; mere display (*did it for show*; *that's all show*). **5** esp. *Brit. colloq.* an opportunity of acting, defending oneself, etc. (*made a good show of it*). **6** *Med.* a discharge of blood, etc., from the vagina at the onset of childbirth. □ **give the show** (or **whole show**) **away** demonstrate the inadequacies or reveal the truth. **good** (or **bad** or **poor**) **show!** esp. *Brit. colloq.* **1** that was well (or badly) done. **2** that was lucky (or unlucky). **nothing to show for** no visible result of (effort, etc.). **on show** being exhibited. **show oneself** be seen in public. **show one's cards** = *show one's hand.* **show one's colors** make one's opinion clear. **show a person the door** dismiss or eject a person. **show one's face** make an appearance. **show fight** be persistent or belligerent. **show forth** *archaic* exhibit; expound. **show one's hand 1** disclose one's plans. **2** reveal one's cards. **show off 1** display to advantage. **2** *colloq.* act pretentiously; display one's wealth, knowledge, etc. **show around** take (a person) to places of interest. **show through 1** be visible although supposedly concealed. **2** (of real feelings, etc.) be revealed inadvertently. **show up 1** make or be conspicuous or clearly visible. **2** expose (a fraud, impostor, inferiority, etc.). **3** *colloq.* appear; arrive. **4** *colloq.* embarrass or humiliate (*don't show me up by wearing jeans*). **show the way 1** indicate what has to be done, etc., by attempting it first. **2** show others which way to go, etc.

show•boat /shṓbōt/ *n.* a river steamer on which theatrical performances are given.

show busi•ness *n. colloq.* the theatrical profession; the business of entertainment.

show•case /shṓkays/ *n. & v.* •*n.* **1** a glass case used for exhibiting goods, etc. **2** a place or medium for presenting to general attention. •*v.tr.* display in or as if in a showcase.

show•down /shṓdown/ *n.* **1** a final test or confrontation; a decisive situation. **2** the laying down face up of the players' cards in poker.

show•er /showr/ *n. & v.* •*n.* **1** a brief fall of rain, hail, sleet, or snow. **2 a** a brisk flurry of arrows, bullets, dust, sparks, etc. **b** a flurry of gifts, praise, etc. **3** (in full **shower bath**) **a** a cubicle, bath, etc. in which one stands under a spray of water. **b** the apparatus, etc., used for this. **c** the act of bathing in a shower. **4** a party for giving presents to a prospective bride, etc. •*v.* **1** *tr.* discharge (water, missiles, etc.) in a shower. **2** *intr.* use a shower bath. **3** *tr.* (usu. foll. by *on, upon*) lavishly bestow (gifts, etc.). **4** *intr.* descend in a shower (*it showered on and off all day*). □□ **show•er•y** *adj.*

show•er•proof /shówrpro͞of/ *adj. & v.* •*adj.* resistant to light rain. •*v.tr.* render showerproof.

show•girl /shṓgərl/ *n.* an actress who sings and dances in musicals, etc.

show jump•ing *n.* the sport of riding horses over a course of fences and other obstacles, with penalty points for errors.

show•man /shṓmən/ *n.* (*pl.* **-men**) **1** the proprietor or manager of a circus, etc. **2** a person skilled in self-advertisement or publicity. □□ **show•man•ship** *n.*

shown *past part.* of SHOW.

show-off *n. colloq.* a person who shows off.

show•piece /shṓpees/ *n.* **1** an item of work presented for exhibition or display. **2** an outstanding example or specimen.

show•place /shṓplays/ *n.* a house, etc., that tourists go to see.

show•room /shṓro͞om, –ro͝om/ *n.* a room in a factory, office building, etc., used to display goods for sale.

show•stop•per /shṓstopər/ *n. colloq.* an act receiving prolonged applause.

show•y /shṓee/ *adj.* (**showier, showiest**) **1** brilliant; gaudy, esp. vulgarly so. **2** striking. □□ **show•i•ly** *adv.* **show•i•ness** *n.*

shrank *past* of SHRINK.

shrap•nel /shrápnəl/ *n.* **1** fragments of a bomb, etc., thrown out by an explosion. **2** a shell containing pieces of metal timed to burst short of impact.

shred /shred/ *n. & v.* •*n.* **1** a scrap, fragment, or strip. **2** the least amount; remnant (*not a shred of evidence*). •*v.tr.* (**shredded, shredding**) tear or cut into shreds. □ **tear to shreds** completely refute (an argument, etc.).

shred•der /shrédər/ *n.* **1** a machine used to tear documents to shreds. **2** any device used for shredding.

shrew /shro͞o/ *n.* **1** any small, usu. insect-eating, mouse-like mammal of the family Soricidae, with a long pointed snout. **2** a bad-tempered or scolding woman. □□ **shrew•ish** *adj.* (in sense 2). **shrew•ish•ly** *adv.* **shrew•ish•ness** *n.*

shrewd /shro͞od/ *adj.* **1** showing astute powers of judgment; clever and judicious. **2** (of a face, etc.) shrewd-looking. □□ **shrewd•ly** *adv.* **shrewd•ness** *n.*

shrewd Middle English (in the sense 'evil in nature or character'): from *shrew* in the sense 'evil person or thing,' or as the past participle of obsolete *shrew* 'to curse.' The word developed the sense 'cunning,' and gradually a favorable connotation during the 16th century.

shriek /shreek/ *v. & n.* •*v.* **1** *intr.* **a** utter a shrill screeching sound or words. **b** (foll. by *of*) provide a clear or blatant indication of. **2** *tr.* **a** utter by shrieking (*shrieked his name*). **b** indicate clearly or blatantly. •*n.* a high-pitched piercing cry or sound. □ **shriek out** say in shrill tones. **shriek with laughter** laugh uncontrollably. □□ **shriek•er** *n.*

shrift /shrift/ *n. archaic* **1** confession to a priest. **2** confession and absolution. □ **short shrift 1** curt treatment. **2** *archaic* little time between condemnation and execution or punishment.

shrike /shrīk/ *n.* any bird of the family Laniidae that impales its prey of small birds and insects on thorns.

shrill /shril/ *adj. & v.* •*adj.* **1** piercing and high-pitched in sound. **2** *derog.* (esp. of a protester) sharp; unrestrained. •*v.* **1** *intr.* (of a cry, etc.) sound shrilly. **2** *tr.* (of a person, etc.) utter (a song, complaint, etc.) shrilly. □□ **shril•ly** *adv.* **shrill•ness** *n.*

shrimp /shrimp/ *n. & v.* •*n.* **1** (*pl.* same or **shrimps**) any of various small (esp. marine) edible crustaceans, with ten legs, gray-green when alive and pink when cooked. **2** *colloq.* a very small slight person. •*v.intr.* go catching shrimps. □□ **shrimp•er** *n.*

shrine /shrīn/ *n. & v.* •*n.* **1** esp. *RC Ch.* **a** a chapel, altar, etc., sacred to a saint, relic, etc. **b** the tomb of a saint, etc. **c** a casket, esp. containing sacred relics; a reliquary. **d** a niche containing a holy statue, etc. **2** a place associated with or containing memorabilia of a particular person, event, etc. **3** a Shinto place of worship. • *v.tr. poet.* enshrine.

shrink /shringk/ *v. & n.* • *v.* (*past* **shrank** /shrangk/; *past part.* **shrunk** /shrungk/ or (esp. as *adj.*) **shrunken** /shrúngkən/) **1** *tr. & intr.* make or become smaller; contract, esp. by the action of moisture, heat, or cold. **2** *intr.* (usu. foll. by *from*) **a** retire; recoil; flinch; cower (*shrank from her touch*). **b** be averse from doing (*shrinks from meeting them*). **3** (as **shrunken** *adj.*) (esp. of a person, etc.) having grown smaller esp. because of age, illness, etc. • *n.* **1** the act of shrinking. **2** *sl.* a psychiatrist. □ **shrink into oneself** become withdrawn. □□ **shrink•a•ble** *adj.* **shrink•er** *n.* **shrink•ing•ly** *adv.* **shrink•proof** *adj.*

shrink•age /shríngkij/ *n.* **1 a** the process of shrinking. **b** the degree of shrinking. **2** an allowance made for the reduction in takings due to wastage, etc.

shrink•ing vi•o•let *n.* an exaggeratedly shy person.

shrink-wrap *v. & n.* • *v.tr.* (**-wrapped, -wrapping**) enclose (an article) in (esp. transparent) film that shrinks tightly on to it. • *n.* plastic film used to shrink-wrap.

shrive /shrīv/ *v.tr.* (*past* **shrove** /shrōv/; *past part.* **shriven** /shrívən/) *Eccl. archaic* **1** (of a priest) hear the confession of, assign penance to, and absolve. **2** (*refl.*) (of a penitent) submit oneself to a priest for confession, etc.

shriv•el /shrívəl/ *v.tr. & intr.* wither into a wrinkled or dried-up state.

shriv•en *past part.* of SHRIVE.

shroud /showd/ *n. & v.* • *n.* **1** a sheetlike garment for wrapping a corpse for burial. **2** anything that conceals like a shroud (*a shroud of mystery*). **3** (in *pl.*) *Naut.* a set of ropes supporting the mast or topmast. • *v.tr.* **1** clothe (a body) for burial. **2** cover, conceal, or disguise (*shrouded in mist*). □□ **shroud•less** *adj.*

Shrove Tues•day /shrōv/ *n.* the day before Ash Wednesday.

shrub /shrub/ *n.* a woody plant smaller than a tree and having a very short stem with branches near the ground. □□ **shrub•by** *adj.*

shrub•ber•y /shrúbəree/ *n.* (*pl.* **-ies**) shrubs collectively. (*pl.* **·ies**) an area planted with shrubs.

shrug /shrug/ *v. & n.* • *v.* (**shrugged, shrugging**) **1** *tr.* raise (one's shoulders) slightly and momentarily to express doubt, ignorance, or indifference. slightly and momentarily raise the shoulders to express indifference, etc. **2** *intr.* **a** raise (the shoulders) in this way. **b** shrug the shoulders to express (indifference, etc.). • *n.* the act of shrugging. □ **shrug off** dismiss as unimportant, etc., by or as if by shrugging.

shrunk (also **shrunk•en**) *past part.* of SHRINK.

shtick /shtik/ *n. sl.* a theatrical routine, gimmick, etc.

shuck /shuk/ *n. & v.* • *n.* **1** a husk or pod. **2** the shell of an oyster or clam. **3** (in *pl.*) *colloq.* an expression of contempt or self-deprecation in response to praise. • *v.tr.* **1** remove the shucks of. **2** remove (*shucked his coat*). □□ **shuck•er** *n.*

shud•der /shúdər/ *v. & n.* • *v.intr.* **1** shiver esp. convulsively from fear, cold, repugnance, etc. **2** feel strong repugnance, etc. (*shudder to think*). **3** (of a machine, etc.) vibrate or quiver. • *n.* **1** the act or an instance of shuddering. **2** (in *pl.*; prec. by *the*) *colloq.* a state of shuddering. □□ **shud•der•ing•ly** *adv.* **shud•der•y** *adj.*

shuf•fle /shúfəl/ *v. & n.* • *v.* **1** *tr. & intr.* move with a scraping, sliding, or dragging motion. **2** *tr.* **a** (also *absol.*) rearrange (a deck of cards) by sliding them over each other quickly. **b** rearrange; intermingle (*shuffled the documents*). **3** *tr.* (usu. foll. by *on, off, into*) assume or remove esp. clumsily or evasively (*shuffled on his clothes; shuffled off responsibility*). **4** *intr.* **a** equivocate; prevaricate. **b** continually shift one's position. • *n.* **1** a shuffling movement. **2** the act of shuffling cards. **3** a change of relative positions. **4** a quick alternation of the position of the feet in dancing. □□ **shuf•fler** *n.*

shuf•fle•board /shúfəlbawrd/ *n.* a game played by pushing disks with the hand or esp. with a long-handled cue over a marked surface.

shun /shun/ *v.tr.* (**shunned, shunning**) avoid (*shuns human company*).

shunt /shunt/ *v. & n.* • *v.* **1** *intr. & tr.* diverge or cause (a train) to be diverted esp. onto a siding. **2** divert (a decision, etc.) on to another person, etc. • *n.* **1** the act of shunting on to a siding. **2** *Electr.* a conductor joining two points of a circuit, through which more or less of a current may be diverted. **3** an alternative path for the passage of blood or other body fluid (*a shunt was put in to drain the fluid*). □□ **shunt•er** *n.*

shush /shoosh, shush/ *int. & v.* • *int.* = HUSH *int.* • *v.* **1** *intr.* **a** call for silence by saying *shush*. **b** be silent (*they shushed at once*). **2** *tr.* make or attempt to make silent.

shut /shut/ *v.* (**shutting**; *past* and *past part.* **shut**) **1** *tr.* **a** move (a door, lid, lips, etc.) into position so as to block an aperture. **b** close or seal (a room, window, box, etc.) by moving a door, etc. (*shut the box*). **2** *intr.* become or be capable of being closed or sealed (*the door shut with a bang*). **3** *intr. & tr.* esp. *Brit.* become or make (a store, etc.) closed for trade. **4** *tr.* bring (a book, hand, etc.) into a folded-up or contracted state. **5** *tr.* (usu. foll. by *in, out*) keep (a person, sound, etc.) in or out of a room, etc., by shutting a door, etc. (*shut out the noise*). **6** *tr.* (usu. foll. by *in*) catch (a finger, dress, etc.) by shutting something on it (*shut her finger in the door*). □ **be** (or **get**) **shut of** *sl.* be (or get) rid of. **shut the door on** refuse to consider; make impossible. **shut down 1** stop (a factory, etc.) from operating. **2** (of a factory, etc.) stop operating. **shut one's eyes** (or **ears** or **heart** or **mind**) **to** pretend not, or refuse, to see (or hear or feel sympathy for or think about). **shut in** (of hills, houses, etc.) encircle, prevent access, etc., to or escape from (*shut in on three sides*). **shut off 1** stop the flow of (water, gas, etc.) by shutting a valve. **2** separate from society, etc. **shut out 1** exclude. **2** screen from view. **3** prevent (a possibility, etc.). **4** block from the mind. **shut up 1** close all doors and windows of; bolt and bar. **2** imprison (a person). **3** close (a box, etc.) securely. **4** *colloq.* reduce to silence by rebuke, etc. **5** put (a thing) away in a box, etc. **6** (esp. in *imper.*) *colloq.* stop talking.

shut•down /shútdown/ *n.* the closure of a factory, etc.

shut-eye *n. colloq.* sleep.

shut-in *n.* a person confined to home, bed, etc., due to infirmity, etc.

shut•ter /shútər/ *n. & v.* • *n.* **1** a person or thing that shuts. **2 a** each of a pair or set of panels fixed inside or outside a window for security or privacy or to keep the light in or out. **b** a structure of slats on rollers used for the same purpose. **3** a device that exposes the film in a photographic camera. • *v.tr.* **1** put up the shutters of. **2** provide with shutters. □ **put up the shutters 1** cease business for the day. **2** cease business, etc., permanently. □□ **shut•ter•less** *adj.*

shut•ter•bug /shútərbəg/ *n. colloq.* an amateur photographer who takes many pictures.

shut•tle /shút'l/ *n. & v.* • *n.* **1 a** a bobbin used for carrying the weft thread across between the warp threads in weaving. **b** a bobbin carrying the lower thread in a sewing machine. **2** a train, bus, etc., going back and forth over a short route continuously. **3** = SHUTTLECOCK. **4** = SPACE SHUTTLE. • *v.* **1** *intr. & tr.* move or cause to move back and forth like a shuttle. **2** *intr.* travel in a shuttle.

shut·tle·cock /shútʼlkok/ *n.* **1** a cork with a ring of feathers, or a similar device of plastic, used instead of a ball in badminton. **2** a thing passed repeatedly back and forth.
shut·tle di·plo·ma·cy *n.* negotiations conducted by a mediator who travels successively to several countries.
shy[1] /shī/ *adj., v., & n.* • *adj.* (**shyer, shyest**) **1 a** diffident or uneasy in company. **b** (of an animal, bird, etc.) easily startled. **2** (foll. by *of*) avoiding; wary of (*shy of his aunt*). **3** (in *comb.*) showing fear of or distaste for (*work-shy*). • *v.intr.* (**shies, shied**) **1** (usu. foll. by *at*) (esp. of a horse) start suddenly aside in fright. **2** (usu. foll. by *away from, at*) avoid accepting or becoming involved in (a proposal, etc.) in alarm. • *n.* a sudden startled movement. ▫▫ **shy·ly** *adv.* **shy·ness** *n.*
shy[2] /shī/ *v. & n.* • *v.tr.* (**shies, shied**) (also *absol.*) fling or throw (a stone, etc.). • *n.* (*pl.* **shies**) the act or an instance of shying. ▫▫ **shy·er** *n.*
shy·ster /shístər/ *n. colloq.* a lawyer who uses unscrupulous methods.
SI *abbr.* the international system of units of measurement (F *Système International*).
Si *symb. Chem.* the element silicon.
si /see/ *n. Mus.* = TI.
si·a·mang /seéəmang/ *n.* a large black gibbon, *Hylobates syndactylus*, native to Sumatra and the Malay peninsula.
Si·a·mese /síəméez/ *n. & adj.* • *n.* (*pl.* same) **1 a** a native of Siam (now Thailand) in SE Asia. **b** the language of Siam. **2** (in full **Siamese cat**) a cat of a cream-colored short-haired breed with blue eyes. • *adj.* of or concerning Siam, its people, or language.
Si·a·mese twins *n.pl.* **1** twins joined at any part of the body. **2** any closely associated pair.
sib /sib/ *n.* **1** a brother or sister. **2** a relative. **3** a group of people one recognizes as relatives.
Si·be·ri·an /sībeéreeən/ *n. & adj.* • *n.* **1** a native of Siberia in the northeastern part of the Russian Federation. **2** a person of Siberian descent. • *adj.* of or relating to Siberia.
sib·i·lant /síbilənt/ *adj. & n.* • *adj.* **1** (of a letter or set of letters, as *s, sh*) sounded with a hiss. **2** hissing. • *n.* a sibilant letter or letters. ▫▫ **sib·i·lance** *n.*
sib·ling /síbling/ *n.* each of two or more children having one or both parents in common.
sib·ship /síbship/ *n.* **1** the state of belonging to a sib or the same sib. **2** a group of children having the same two parents.
sib·yl /síbil/ *n.* a prophetess, fortune-teller, or witch.
sib·yl·line /síbilīn, –leen/ *adj.* **1** of or from a sibyl. **2** oracular; prophetic.
sic[1] /sik/ *v.tr.* (**sicced, siccing**; also **sicked** /sikt/, **sicking**) (usu. in *imper.*) (esp. to a dog) set upon (a rat, etc.).
sic[2] /sik, seek/ *adv.* (usu. in brackets) used, spelled, etc., as written (confirming, or calling attention to, the form of quoted or copied words).
sic·ca·tive /síkətiv/ *n. & adj.* • *n.* a substance causing drying, esp. mixed with oil paint, etc., for quick drying. • *adj.* having such properties.
Si·cil·ian /sisílyən/ *n. & adj.* • *n.* **1** a native of Sicily, an island off the S. coast of Italy. **2** a person of Sicilian descent. **3** the Italian dialect of Sicily. • *adj.* of or relating to Sicily.
sick /sik/ *adj.* **1** (often in *comb.*) vomiting or tending to vomit (*I think I'm going to be sick; seasick*). **2** ill; affected by illness (*has been sick for a week; a sick man; sick with measles*). **3 a** (often foll. by *at*) esp. mentally perturbed (*the product of a sick mind*). **b** (often foll. by *for*, or in *comb.*) pining; longing (*lovesick*). **4** (often foll. by *of*) *colloq.* **a** disgusted; surfeited (*sick of chocolates*). **b** angry, esp. because of surfeit (*sick of being teased*). **5** *colloq.* (of humor, etc.) jeering at misfortune, illness, etc. (*sick joke*). ▫ **look sick** *colloq.* be unimpressive or embarrassed. **sick to one's stomach** vomiting or tending to vomit. **take sick** *colloq.* be taken ill. ▫▫ **sick·ish** *adj.*
sick·bay /síkbay/ *n.* **1** part of a ship used as a hospital. **2** any room for sick people.
sick·bed /síkbed/ *n.* **1** an invalid's bed. **2** the state of being an invalid.
sick·en /síkən/ *v.* **1** *tr.* affect with disgust. **2** *intr.* (often foll. by *at*, or *to* + infin.) feel nausea or disgust (*he sickened at the sight*). **3** (as **sickening** *adj.*) **a** loathsome; disgusting. **b** *colloq.* very annoying. ▫▫ **sick·en·ing·ly** *adv.*
sick·le /síkəl/ *n.* a short-handled farming tool with a semicircular blade, used for cutting grain, lopping, or trimming.

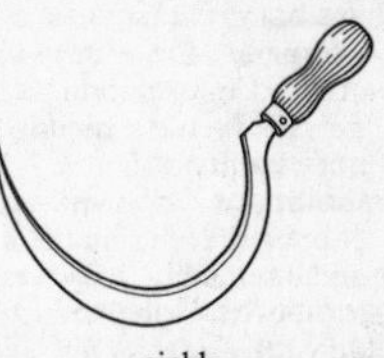
sickle

sick leave *n.* leave of absence granted because of illness.
sick·le cell *n.* a sickle-shaped blood cell, esp. as found in a type of severe hereditary anemia.
sick·ly /síklee/ *adj.* (**sicklier, sickliest**) **1 a** of weak health. **b** (of a person's complexion, etc.) languid, faint, or pale. **c** (of light or color) faint; feeble. **2** causing ill health (*a sickly climate*). **3** (of a book, etc.) sentimental or mawkish. **4** inducing or connected with nausea (*a sickly taste*). ▫▫ **sick·li·ness** *n.*
sick·ness /síknis/ *n.* **1** the state of being ill; disease. **2** a specified disease (*sleeping sickness*). **3** vomiting or a tendency to vomit.
sick·o /síkō/ *n.* a person who is mentally deranged or morally debased.
sick pay *n.* pay given to an employee, etc., on sick leave.
sick·room /síkrōōm, –rōōm/ *n.* **1** a room occupied by a sick person. **2** a room adapted for sick people.
side /sīd/ *n. & v.* • *n.* **1 a** each of the more or less flat surfaces bounding an object (*this side up*). **b** a more or less vertical inner or outer plane or surface (*a mountainside*). **c** such a vertical lateral surface or plane as distinct from the top or bottom, front or back, or ends (*at the side of the house*). **2 a** the half of a person or animal that is on the right or the left, esp. of the torso (*pain in his right side*). **b** the left or right half or a specified part of a thing, area, etc. (*put the box on that side*). **c** (often in *comb.*) a position next to a person or thing (*graveside*). **d** a specified direction relating to a person or thing (*came from all sides*). **e** half of a butchered carcass (*a side of beef*). **3 a** either surface of a thing regarded as having two surfaces. **b** the amount of writing needed to fill one side of a sheet of paper (*write three sides*). **4** any of several aspects of a question, character, etc. (*look on the bright side*). **5 a** each of two sets of opponents in war, politics, games, etc. (*the side that bats first*). **b** a cause or philosophical position, etc., regarded as being in conflict with another (*on the side of right*). **6 a** a part or region near the edge and remote from the center. **b** (*attrib.*) a subordinate, peripheral, or detached part (*a side road*). **7 a** each of the bounding lines of a plane rectilinear figure (*a hexagon has six sides*). **b** each of two quantities stated to be equal in an equation. **8** a position nearer or farther than, or right or left of, a dividing line (*on this side of the Mississippi*). **9** a line of hereditary descent through the father or the mother. • *v.intr.* (usu. foll. by *with*) take part or be on the same side as a disputant, etc. (*sided with his father*). ▫ **by the side of 1** close to. **2** compared with. **from side**

to side 1 right across. 2 alternately each way from a central line. **on one side 1** not in the main or central position. **on the . . . side** fairly; somewhat (qualifying an adjective: *on the high side*). **on the side 1** as a sideline; in addition to one's regular work, etc. **2** secretly or illicitly. **3** as a side dish. **side by side** standing close together, esp. for mutual support. **take sides** support one or other cause, etc. ▫▫ **side·less** *adj.*

side arms *n.pl.* swords, bayonets, or pistols.

side·band /sídband/ *n.* a range of frequencies near the carrier frequency of a radio wave, concerned in modulation.

side·bar /sídbaar/ *n.* **1** a short news article, printed alongside a major news story, that contains related incidental information. **2** *Law* discussion or consultation between a trial judge and counsel that the jury is not permitted to hear.

side·board /sídbawrd/ *n.* a table or esp. a flat-topped cupboard at the side of a dining room for supporting and containing dishes, table linen, etc.

side·burns /sídbərnz/ *n.pl. colloq.* hair grown by a man down the sides of his face; side-whiskers.

side·car /sídkaar/ *n.* a small car for a passenger or passengers attached to the side of a motorcycle.

sid·ed /sídid/ *adj.* **1** having sides. **2** (in *comb.*) having a specified side or sides (*one-sided*). ▫▫ **-sidedly** *adv.* **sid·ed·ness** *n.* (also in *comb.*).

side dish *n.* an extra dish subsidiary to the main course.

side drum *n.* (see SNARE *n.* 5).

side ef·fect *n.* a secondary, usu. undesirable, effect.

side·kick /sídkik/ *n. colloq.* a close associate.

side·light /sídlīt/ *n.* **1** a light from the side. **2** incidental information, etc.

side·line /sídlīn/ *n. & v.* •*n.* **1** work, etc., done in addition to one's main activity. **2** (usu. in *pl.*) **a** a line bounding the side of a football field, etc. **b** the space next to these where spectators, etc., sit. •*v.tr.* remove (a player) from a team through injury, suspension, etc. ▫ **on** (or **from**) **the sidelines** in (or from) a position removed from the main action.

side·long /sídlawng, –long/ *adj. & adv.* •*adj.* inclining to one side; oblique (*a sidelong glance*). •*adv.* obliquely (*moved sidelong*).

si·de·re·al /sīdéereeəl/ *adj.* of or concerning the constellations or fixed stars.

si·de·re·al day *n.* the time between successive meridional transits of a star or esp. of the first point of Aries, about four minutes shorter than the solar day.

sid·er·ite /sídərīt/ *n.* **1** a mineral form of ferrous carbonate. **2** a meteorite consisting mainly of nickel and iron.

side·sad·dle /sídsad'l/ *n. & adv.* •*n.* a saddle for a woman rider having supports for both feet on the same side of the horse. •*adv.* sitting in this position on a horse.

side·show /sídshō/ *n.* **1** a minor show or attraction in an exhibition or entertainment. **2** a minor incident or issue.

side·slip /sídslip/ *n. & v.* •*n.* **1** a skid. **2** *Aeron.* a sideways movement instead of forward. •*v.intr.* **1** skid. **2** *Aeron.* move sideways instead of forward.

side·split·ting /sídspliting/ *adj.* causing violent laughter.

side·step /sídstep/ *n. & v.* •*n.* a step taken sideways. •*v.tr.* (**-stepped, -stepping**) **1** esp. *Football* avoid (esp. a tackle) by stepping sideways. **2** evade. ▫▫ **side·step·per** *n.*

side·stroke /sídstrōk/ *n.* **1** a stroke toward or from a side. **2** an incidental action. **3** a swimming stroke in which the swimmer lies on his or her side.

side·swipe /sídswīp/ *n. & v.* •*n.* **1** a glancing blow along the side. **2** incidental criticism, etc. •*v.tr.* hit with or as if with a sideswipe.

side·track /sídtrak/ *n. & v.* •*n.* a railroad siding. •*v.tr.* **1** turn into a siding. **2 a** postpone, evade, or divert treatment or consideration of. **b** divert (a person) from considering, etc.

side·walk /sídwawk/ *n.* a usu. paved pedestrian path at the side of a road.

side·wall /sídwawl/ *n.* **1** the part of a tire between the tread and the wheel rim. **2** a wall that forms the side of a structure.

side·ward /sídwərd/ *adj. & adv.* •*adj.* = SIDEWAYS. •*adv.* (also **side·wards** /–wərdz/) = SIDEWAYS.

side·ways /sídwayz/ *adv. & adj.* •*adv.* **1** to or from a side (*moved sideways*). **2** with one side facing forward (*sat sideways*). •*adj.* to or from a side (*a sideways movement*). ▫▫ **side·wise** *adv. & adj.*

side·wind·er /sídwīndər/ *n.* a desert rattlesnake, *Crotalus cerastes*, native to N. America, moving with a lateral motion.

sid·ing /síding/ *n.* **1** a short track at the side of and opening on to a railroad line, used for switching trains. **2** material for the outside of a building, e.g., shingles, etc.

si·dle /síd'l/ *v. & n.* •*v.intr.* (usu. foll. by *along, up*) walk in a timid, furtive, stealthy, or cringing manner. •*n.* the act of sidling.

SIDS /sids/ *abbr.* sudden infant death syndrome; crib death.

siege /seej/ *n.* **1 a** a military operation to compel the surrender of a fortified place by surrounding it and cutting off supplies, etc. **b** a similar operation by police, etc., to force the surrender of an armed person. **c** the period during which a siege lasts. **2** a persistent attack or campaign of persuasion. ▫ **lay siege to** esp. *Mil.* conduct the siege of. **raise the siege of** abandon or cause the abandonment of an attempt to take (a place) by siege.

si·er·ra /seeérə/ *n.* a long jagged mountain chain, esp. in Spain.

si·es·ta /seeéstə/ *n.* an afternoon sleep or rest esp. in hot countries.

sieve /siv/ *n. & v.* •*n.* a utensil having a perforated or meshed bottom for separating solids or coarse material from liquids or fine particles, or for reducing a soft solid to a fine pulp. •*v.tr.* **1** put through or sift with a sieve. **2** examine (evidence, etc.) to select or separate. ▫▫ **sieve·like** *adj.*

sift /sift/ *v.* **1** *tr.* sieve (material) into finer and coarser parts. **2** *tr.* (usu. foll. by *from, out*) separate (finer or coarser parts) from material. **3** *tr.* sprinkle (esp. sugar) from a perforated container. **4** *tr.* examine (evidence, facts, etc.). ▫ **sift through** examine by sifting. ▫▫ **sift·er** *n.* (also in *comb.*).

sigh /sī/ *v. & n.* •*v.* **1** *intr.* emit a long, deep, audible breath expressive of sadness, weariness, relief, etc. **2** *intr.* (foll. by *for*) yearn for (a lost person or thing). **3** *intr.* (of the wind, etc.) make a sound like sighing. •*n.* **1** the act or an instance of sighing. **2** a sound made in sighing (*a sigh of relief*).

sight /sīt/ *n. & v.* •*n.* **1 a** the faculty of seeing with the eyes (*lost his sight*). **b** the act or an instance of seeing; the state of being seen. **2** a thing seen; a display, show, or spectacle (*not a pretty sight; a beautiful sight*). **3** a way of considering a thing (*in my sight he can do no wrong*). **4** a range of space within which a person, etc., can see or an object be seen (*he's out of sight; they are just coming into sight*). **5** (usu. in *pl.*) noteworthy features of a town, area, etc. (*went to see the sights*). **6 a** a device on a gun or optical instrument used for assisting the precise aim or observation. **b** the aim or observation so gained (*got a sight of him*). **7** *colloq.* a person or thing having a ridiculous, repulsive, or disheveled appearance (*looked a perfect sight*). **8** *colloq.* a great quantity (*a sight better than he was*). • *v.tr.* **1** get sight of, esp. by approaching (*they sighted land*). **2** observe the presence of (esp. aircraft, animals, etc.) (*sighted buffalo*). **3** take observations of (a star, etc.) with an instrument. **4** aim (a gun, etc.) with sights. □ **at first sight** on first glimpse or impression. **at** (or **on**) **sight** as soon as a person or a thing has been seen. **catch** (or **lose**) **sight of** begin (or cease) to see or be aware of. **get a sight of** glimpse. **have lost sight of** no longer know the whereabouts of. **in sight 1** visible. **2** near at hand (*salvation is in sight*). **in** (or **within**) **sight of** so as to see or be seen from. **lower one's sights** become less ambitious; reduce one's expectations. **out of my sight!** go at once! **out of sight 1** not visible. **2** *colloq.* excellent; delightful. **set one's sights on** aim at (*set her sights on a directorship*). **sight unseen** without previous inspection. □□ **sight·er** *n.*

sight·ed /sítid/ *adj.* **1** capable of seeing; not blind. **2** (in *comb.*) having a specified kind of sight (*farsighted*).

sight·less /sítlis/ *adj.* **1** blind. **2** *poet.* invisible. □□ **sight·less·ly** *adv.* **sight·less·ness** *n.*

sight·ly /sítlee/ *adj.* attractive to the sight; not unsightly. □□ **sight·li·ness** *n.*

sight·se·er /sítseeər/ *n.* a person who visits places of interest; a tourist. □□ **sight·see** *v.intr.* & *tr.* **sight·see·ing** *n.*

sig·ma /sígmə/ *n.* the eighteenth letter of the Greek alphabet (Σ, σ, or, when final, ς).

sig·mate /sígmət, –mayt/ *adj.* **1** sigma-shaped. **2** S-shaped.

sign /sīn/ *n.* & *v.* • *n.* **1 a** a thing indicating or suggesting a quality or state, etc.; a thing perceived as indicating a future state or occurrence (*violence is a sign of weakness*; *shows all the signs of decay*). **b** a miracle evidencing supernatural power; a portent (*signs and wonders*). **2 a** a mark, symbol, or device used to represent something or to distinguish the thing on which it is put (*marked the jar with a sign*). **b** a technical symbol used in algebra, music, etc. (*a minus sign*). **3** a gesture or action used to convey information, an order, request, etc. (*conversed by signs*). **4** a publicly displayed board, etc., giving information; a signboard or signpost. **5** a password (*advanced and gave the sign*). **6** any of the twelve divisions of the zodiac, named from constellations formerly situated in them (*the sign of Cancer*). • *v.* **1** *tr.* **a** (also *absol.*) write (one's name, initials, etc.) on a document, etc., indicating that one has authorized it. **b** write one's name, etc., on (a document) as authorization. **2** *intr.* & *tr.* communicate by gesture (*signed to me to come*). **3** *tr.* & *intr.* engage or be engaged by signing a contract, etc. (see also *sign on*, *sign up*). **4** *tr.* mark with a sign (esp. with the sign of the cross in baptism). □ **sign away** convey (one's right, property, etc.) by signing a deed, etc. **sign for** acknowledge receipt of by signing. **sign off** end work, broadcasting, a letter, etc., esp. by writing or speaking one's name. **sign on 1** agree to a contract, employment, etc. **2** begin work, broadcasting, etc., esp. by writing or announcing one's name. **3** employ (a person). **sign up 1** engage or employ (a person). **2** enlist in the armed forces. **3 a** commit (another person or oneself) by signing, etc. (*signed you up for dinner*). **b** enroll (*signed up for evening classes*). □□ **sign·a·ble** *adj.* **sign·er** *n.*

sig·nal[1] /sígnəl/ *n.* & *v.* • *n.* **1 a** a usu. prearranged sign conveying information, guidance, etc., esp. at a distance (*waved as a signal to begin*). **b** a message made up of such signs (*signals made with flags*). **2** an immediate occasion for or cause of movement, action, etc. (*the uprising was a signal for repression*). **3** *Electr.* **a** an electrical impulse or impulses or radio waves transmitted. **b** a sequence of these. **4** a light, semaphore, etc., on a railroad giving instructions or warnings to train engineers, etc. • *v.* **1** *intr.* make signals. **2** *tr.* **a** (often foll. by *to* + infin.) make signals to; direct. **b** transmit (an order, information, etc.) by signal; announce (*signaled her agreement*; *signaled that the town had been taken*). □□ **sig·nal·er** *or* **sig·nal·ler** *n.*

sig·nal[2] /sígnəl/ *adj.* remarkably good or bad (*a signal victory*). □□ **sig·nal·ly** *adv.*

sig·nal·ize /sígnəlīz/ *v.tr.* **1** make noteworthy or remarkable. **2** indicate.

sig·na·ry /sígnəree/ *n.* (*pl.* **-ries**) a list of signs constituting the syllabic or alphabetic symbols of a language.

sig·na·to·ry /sígnətawree/ *n.* & *adj.* • *n.* (*pl.* **-ries**) a party or esp. a nation that has signed an agreement or esp. a treaty. • *adj.* having signed such an agreement, etc.

sig·na·ture /sígnəchər/ *n.* **1 a** a person's name, initials, or mark used in signing a letter, document, etc. **b** the act of signing a document, etc. **2** *archaic* a distinctive action, characteristic, etc. **3** *Mus.* **a** = KEY SIGNATURE. **b** = TIME SIGNATURE. **4** *Printing* **a** a letter or figure placed at the foot of one or more pages of each sheet of a book as a guide for binding. **b** such a sheet after folding. **5** written directions given to a patient as part of a medical prescription.

sign·board /sínbawrd/ *n.* a board with a name or symbol, etc., displayed outside a store or hotel, etc.

sig·net /sígnit/ *n.* **1** a seal used instead of or with a signature as authentication. **2** (prec. by *the*) the royal seal formerly used for special purposes in England and Scotland, and in Scotland later as the seal of the Court of Session.

sig·nif·i·cance /signífikəns/ *n.* **1** importance, meaning (*of no significance*). **2** a basic, simple, or real meaning (*what is the significance*). **3** the state of being significant. **4** *Statistics* the extent to which a result deviates from a hypothesis such that the difference is due to more than errors in sampling.

sig·nif·i·cant /signífikənt/ *adj.* **1** having a meaning. **2** having an unstated or secret meaning; (*refused it with a significant gesture*). **3** noteworthy; important (*a significant figure in history*). □□ **sig·nif·i·cant·ly** *adv.*

sig·nif·i·cant oth·er *n.* a person who is very important in one's life, esp. a spouse or lover.

sig·nif·i·ca·tive /signífikaytiv/ *adj.* **1** (esp. of a symbol, etc.) signifying. **2** having a meaning. **3** (usu. foll. by *of*) serving as a sign or evidence.

sig·ni·fy /sígnifī/ *v.* (**-fies**, **-fied**) **1** *tr.* be a sign of (*a yawn signifies boredom*). **2** *tr.* mean (*"Dr." signifies "doctor"*). **3** *tr.* make known (*signified their agreement*). **4** *intr.* matter (*it signifies little*). □□ **sig·ni·fi·er** *n.*

sign lan·guage *n.* a system of communication by hand gestures, used esp. by the hearing impaired.

sign of the cross *n.* a Christian sign made in blessing or prayer, by tracing a cross from the forehead to the chest and to each shoulder, or in the air.

sign of the times *n.* a portent, etc., showing a likely trend.

si·gnor /seenyáwr/ *n.* (*pl.* **signori** /-nyóree/) a title used of or to an Italian man.

si·gno·ra /seenyáwrə/ *n.* a title used of or to an Italian married woman.

si·gno·ri·na /séenyəréenə/ *n.* a title used of or to an Italian unmarried woman.

sign·post /sínpōst/ *n.* & *v.* • *n.* **1** a post erected at a crossroads with arms indicating the direction to various places. **2** a means of guidance. • *v.tr.* provide with a signpost or signposts.

Sikh /seek/ *n.* a member of an Indian monotheistic faith founded in the 16th c.

Sikh·ism /séekizəm/ *n.* the religious tenets of the Sikhs.
si·lage /sílij/ *n. & v.* •*n.* **1** storage in a silo. **2** green fodder that has been stored in a silo. •*v.tr.* put into a silo.
si·lence /síləns/ *n. & v.* •*n.* **1** absence of sound. **2** abstinence from speech or noise. **3** the avoidance of mentioning a thing, betraying a secret, etc. **4** oblivion; the state of not being mentioned. •*v.tr.* make silent, esp. by coercion or superior argument. □ **in silence** without speech or other sound. **reduce** (or **put**) **to silence** refute in argument.
si·lenc·er /sílənsər/ *n.* any of various devices for reducing the noise emitted by a gun, etc.
si·lent /sílənt/ *adj.* **1** not speaking; not making or accompanied by any sound. **2** (of a letter) written but not pronounced, e.g., *b* in *doubt*. **3** (of a person) speaking little. **4** saying or recording nothing on some subject (*the records are silent on the incident*). □□ **si·lent·ly** *adv.*
si·lent part·ner *n.* a partner not sharing in the actual work of a firm.
sil·hou·ette /síloo-ét/ *n. & v.* •*n.* **1** a representation of a person or thing showing the outline only, usu. done in solid black on white or cut from paper. **2** the dark shadow or outline of a person or thing against a lighter background. •*v.tr.* represent or (usu. in *passive*) show in silhouette.

silhouette

sil·i·ca /sílikə/ *n.* silicon dioxide, occurring as quartz, etc., and as a principal constituent of sandstone and other rocks. □□ **si·li·ceous** /-líshəs/ *adj.* (also **si·li·cious**) **si·lic·ic** /-lísik/ *adj.* **si·lic·i·fy** /-lísifī/ *v.tr. & intr.* (**-fies, -fied**). **si·lic·i·fi·ca·tion** /-fikáyshən/ *n.*
sil·i·ca gel *n.* hydrated silica in a hard granular form used as a desiccant.
sil·i·cate /sílikayt, -kət/ *n.* any of the many insoluble compounds of a metal combined with silicon and oxygen.
sil·i·con /sílikən, -kon/ *n. Chem.* a nonmetallic element occurring widely in silica and silicates.
sil·i·con chip *n.* a silicon microchip.
sil·i·cone /sílikōn/ *n.* any of the many polymeric organic compounds of silicon and oxygen with high resistance to cold, heat, water, and electricity.
Sil·i·con Val·ley *n.* an area in California with a high concentration of electronics industries.
sil·i·co·sis /silikṓsis/ *n.* lung fibrosis caused by the inhalation of dust containing silica.
silk /silk/ *n.* **1** a fine, strong, soft lustrous fiber produced by silkworms. **2** a similar fiber spun by some spiders, etc. **3 a** thread or cloth made from silk fiber. **b** a thread or fabric resembling silk. **4** (in *pl.*) kinds of silk cloth or garments made from it, esp. as worn by a jockey. **5** (*attrib.*) made of silk (*silk blouse*). □□ **silk·like** *adj.*
silk·en /sílkən/ *adj.* **1** made of silk. **2** wearing silk. **3** soft or lustrous as silk. **4** (of a person's manner, etc.) suave or insinuating.
silk-screen print·ing *n.* = SCREEN PRINTING.
silk·worm /sílkwərm/ *n.* the caterpillar of the moth *Bombyx mori*, which spins its cocoon of silk.
silk·y /sílkee/ *adj.* (**silkier, silkiest**) **1** like silk in smoothness, softness, or luster. **2** (of a person's manner, etc.) suave; insinuating. □□ **silk·i·ly** *adv.* **silk·i·ness** *n.*
sill /sil/ *n.* **1** a shelf or slab of stone, wood, or metal at the foot of a window or doorway. **2** a horizontal timber at the bottom of a dock or lock entrance, against which the gates close.
sil·la·bub var. of SYLLABUB.
sil·ly /sílee/ *adj. & n.* •*adj.* (**sillier, silliest**) **1** lacking sense; foolish. **2** weak-minded. **3>** ridiculously trivial or frivolous. **4** dazed; confused (*She slapped me silly*). **5** (esp. of a woman, child, or animal) helpless; defenseless. •*n.* (*pl.* **-lies**) *colloq.* a foolish person. □□ **sil·li·ly** *adv.* **sil·li·ness** *n.*
si·lo /sílō/ *n. & v.* •*n.* (*pl.* **-los**) **1** a pit or airtight structure in which green crops are pressed and kept for fodder. **2** a tower for the storage of grain, etc. **3** an underground chamber in which a guided missile is kept. •*v.tr.* (**-loes, -loed**) make silage of.
silt /silt/ *n. & v.* •*n.* sediment in a channel, harbor, etc. •*v.tr. & intr.* (often foll. by *up*) choke with silt. □□ **sil·ta·tion** /-táyshən/ *n.* **silt·y** *adj.*
sil·va /silvəl/ *n.* (also **syl·va**) (*pl.* **sylvae** /–vee/ or **sylvas**) **1** the trees of a region, epoch, or environment. **2** a treatise on or a list of such trees.
sil·van var. of SYLVAN.
sil·ver /sílvər/ *n., adj., & v.* •*n. Chem.* **1** a grayish-white, lustrous, malleable, ductile, precious metallic element. **2** the color of silver. **3** silver or cupronickel coins. **4** silver vessels or implements, esp. cutlery. **5** = SILVER MEDAL. •*adj.* **1** made wholly or chiefly of silver. **2** colored like silver. •*v.* **1** *tr.* coat or plate with silver. **2** *tr.* provide (mirror glass) with a backing of tin amalgam, etc. **3** *tr.* (of the moon or a white light) give a silvery appearance to. **4 a** *tr.* turn (the hair) gray or white. **b** *intr.* (of the hair) turn gray or white.
sil·ver birch *n.* a common European birch, *Betula pendula*, with silver-colored bark.
sil·ver·fish /sílvərfish/ *n.* (*pl.* same) any small silvery wingless insect of the order Thysanura, esp. *Lepisma saccharina* in houses and other buildings.
sil·ver lin·ing *n.* a consolation or hopeful feature in misfortune.
sil·ver plate *n.* vessels, spoons, etc., of copper, etc., plated with silver.
sil·ver screen *n.* (usu. prec. by *the*) motion pictures collectively.
sil·ver·smith /sílvərsmith/ *n.* a worker in silver. □□ **sil·ver·smith·ing** *n.*
sil·ver spoon *n.* a sign of future prosperity.
Sil·ver Star *n. US Mil.* a decoration awarded for gallantry in action.
sil·ver tongue *n.* eloquence.
sil·ver·ware /sílvərwair/ *n.* articles made of or coated with silver.
sil·ver·weed /sílvərweed/ *n.* a plant with silvery leaves, esp. a potentilla, *Potentilla anserina*, with silver-colored leaves.
sil·ver·y /sílvəree/ *adj.* **1** like silver in color or appearance. **2** having a clear, gentle, ringing sound. **3** (of the hair) white and lustrous. □□ **sil·ver·i·ness** *n.*
sil·vi·cul·ture /sílvikulchər/ *n.* (also **syl·vi·cul·ture**) the growing and tending of trees as a branch of forestry. □□ **sil·vi·cul·tur·al** /-kúlchərəl/ *adj.* **sil·vi·cul·tur·ist** /-kúlchərist/
sim·i·an /símeeən/ *adj. & n.* •*adj.* **1** of or concerning the anthropoid apes. **2** like an ape or monkey (*a simian walk*). •*n.* an ape or monkey.
sim·i·lar /símilər/ *adj.* **1** like; alike. **2** (often foll. by *to*) having a resemblance. **3** of the same kind, nature, or amount. **4** *Geom.* shaped alike. □□ **sim·i·lar·i·ty** /-láritee/ *n.* (*pl.* **-ties**). **sim·i·lar·ly** *adv.*
sim·i·le /símilee/ *n.* **1** a figure of speech involving the comparison of one thing with another of a different

kind (e.g., *as brave as a lion*). **2** the use of such comparison.

si·mil·i·tude /simílitōōd, -tyōōd/ *n.* **1** the likeness, guise, or outward appearance of a thing or person. **2** a comparison or the expression of a comparison.

sim·mer /símər/ *v. & n.* • *v.* **1** *intr. & tr.* be or keep bubbling or boiling gently. **2** *intr.* be in a state of suppressed anger or excitement. • *n.* a simmering condition. □ **simmer down** become calm or less agitated.

si·mo·ny /símənee, sím-/ *n.* the buying or selling of ecclesiastical privileges. □□ **si·mo·ni·ac** /-mṓneeak/ *adj. & n.* **si·mo·ni·a·cal** /-níəkəl/ *adj.*

simp /simp/ *n. colloq.* a simpleton.

sim·pa·ti·co /simpátikō/ *adj.* congenial; likable.

sim·per /símpər/ *v. & n.* • *v. intr.* smile in a silly or affected way. • *n.* such a smile. □□ **sim·per·ing·ly** *adv.*

sim·ple /símpəl/ *adj.* **1** easily understood or done; presenting no difficulty (*a simple explanation; a simple task*). **2** not complicated or elaborate; without luxury or sophistication. **3** not compound; consisting of or involving only one element or operation, etc. **4** absolute; unqualified (*the simple truth; a simple majority*). **5** foolish or ignorant; gullible (*am not so simple as to agree to that*). **6** plain in appearance or manner; unsophisticated; ingenuous; artless. □□ **sim·ple·ness** *n.*

sim·ple eye *n.* an eye of an insect, having only one lens.

sim·ple frac·ture *n.* a fracture of the bone only, without a skin wound.

sim·ple in·ter·est *n.* interest payable on a capital sum only.

sim·ple·mind·ed /símpəlmíndid/ *adj.* **1** natural; unsophisticated. **2** feeble-minded. □□ **sim·ple·mind·ed·ly** *adv.* **sim·ple·mind·ed·ness** *n.*

sim·ple·ton /símpəltən/ *n.* a foolish, gullible, or halfwitted person.

sim·plex /símpleks/ *adj.* **1** simple; not compounded. **2** *Computing* (of a circuit) allowing transmission of signals in one direction only.

sim·plic·i·ty /simplísitee/ *n.* the fact or condition of being simple.

sim·pli·fy /símplifī/ *v.tr.* (**-fies, -fied**) make easy or easier to do or understand. □□ **sim·pli·fi·ca·tion** /-fikáyshən/ *n.*

sim·plism /símplizəm/ *n.* **1** affected simplicity. **2** the unjustifiable simplification of a problem, etc.

sim·plis·tic /simplístik/ *adj.* **1** excessively or affectedly simple. **2** oversimplified so as to conceal or distort difficulties. □□ **sim·plis·ti·cal·ly** *adv.*

sim·ply /símplee/ *adv.* **1** in a simple manner. **2** absolutely; without doubt (*simply astonishing*). **3** merely (*was simply trying to please*).

sim·u·late /símyəlayt/ *v.tr.* **1 a** pretend to have or feel. **b** pretend to be. **2** imitate or counterfeit. **3 a** imitate the conditions of (a situation, etc.), e.g., for training. **b** produce a computer model of (a process). **4** (as **simulated** *adj.*) made to resemble the real thing (*simulated fur*). □□ **sim·u·la·tion** /-láyshən/ *n.*

sim·u·la·tor /símyəlaytər/ *n.* **1** a person or thing that simulates. **2** a device designed to simulate the operations of a complex system, used esp. in training.

si·mul·cast /síməlkast, sím-/ *n.* simultaneous transmission of the same program, as on radio and television.

si·mul·ta·ne·ous /síməltáyneeəs, sím-/ *adj.* (often foll. by *with*) occurring or operating at the same time. □□ **si·mul·ta·ne·i·ty** /-tənáyitee/ *n.* **si·mul·ta·ne·ous·ly** *adv.*

sin[1] /sin/ *n. & v.* • *n.* **1 a** the breaking of divine or moral law, esp. by a conscious act. **b** such an act. **2** an offense against good taste or propriety, etc. • *v.* (**sinned, sinning**) **1** *intr.* commit a sin. **2** *intr.* (foll. by *against*) offend. **3** *tr. archaic* commit (a sin). □ **as sin** *colloq.* extremely (*ugly as sin*). **for one's sins** *joc.* as a judgment on one for something done. **live in sin** *colloq.* live together without being married. □□ **sin·less** *adj.* **sin·less·ly** *adv.* **sin·less·ness** *n.*

sin[2] /sīn/ *abbr.* sine.

since /sins/ *prep., conj., & adv.* • *prep.* throughout, or at a point in, the period between (a specified time, event, etc.) and the time present or being considered (*going on since June; the greatest since Beethoven*). • *conj.* **1** during or in the time after (*what have you been doing since we met?*). **2** for the reason that; inasmuch as (*since you are drunk I will drive*). **3** (*ellipt.*) as being (*more useful, since better designed*). • *adv.* **1** from that time or event until now or the time being considered (*have not seen them since*). **2** ago (*happened many years since*).

sin·cere /sinseér/ *adj.* (**sincerer, sincerest**) **1** free from pretense or deceit. **2** genuine; honest; frank. □□ **sin·cere·ness** *n.* **sin·cer·i·ty** /-séritee/ *n.*

sin·cere·ly /sinseérlee/ *adv.* in a sincere manner. □ **sincerely yours** a formula for ending an informal letter.

sin·ci·put /sínsipōōt/ *n. Anat.* the front of the skull from the forehead to the crown. □□ **sin·cip·i·tal** /-sípitəl/ *adj.*

sine /sīn/ *n. Math.* the trigonometric function that is equal to the ratio of the side opposite a given angle (in a right triangle) to the hypotenuse.

si·ne qua non /sínay kwaa nṓn/ *n.* an indispensable condition or qualification.

sin·ew /sínyōō/ *n.* **1** tough fibrous tissue attaching muscle to bone. **2** (in *pl.*) muscles; bodily strength; wiriness. **3** (in *pl.*) the strength or framework of a plan, city, organization, etc. □□ **sin·ew·less** *adj.* **sin·ew·y** *adj.*

sin·fo·ni·a /sinfəneéə/ *n. Mus.* **1** a symphony. **2** (in Baroque music) an orchestral piece used as an introduction to an opera, cantata, or suite. **3** (**Sinfonia**; usu. in names) a symphony orchestra.

sin·fo·niet·ta /sínfənyétə/ *n. Mus.* **1** a short or simple symphony. **2** (**Sinfonietta**; usu. in names) a small symphony orchestra.

sin·ful /sínfōōl/ *adj.* **1** (of a person) committing sin, esp. habitually. **2** (of an act) involving or characterized by sin. □□ **sin·ful·ly** *adv.* **sin·ful·ness** *n.*

sing /sing/ *v. & n.* • *v.* (*past* **sang** /sang/; *past part.* **sung** /sung/) **1** *intr.* utter musical sounds with the voice, esp. words with a set tune. **2** *tr.* utter or produce by singing. **3** *intr.* (of the wind, a kettle, etc.) make melodious or humming, or whistling sounds. **4** *intr.* (of the ears) be affected as with a buzzing sound. **5** *intr. sl.* turn informer; confess. • *n.* **1** an act or spell of singing. **2** a meeting for amateur singing. □ **sing out** call out loudly. **sing the praises of** see PRAISE. **sing up** sing more loudly. □□ **sing·a·ble** *adj.* **sing·er** *n.* **sing·ing·ly** *adv.*

sing. *abbr.* singular.

singe /sinj/ *v. & n.* • *v.* (**singeing**) **1** *tr. & intr.* burn superficially or lightly. **2** *tr.* burn the bristles or down off (the carcass of a pig or fowl) to prepare it for cooking. • *n.* a superficial burn.

Singh /sing/ *n.* **1** a title adopted by the warrior castes of N. India. **2** a surname adopted by male Sikhs.

Sin·gha·lese var. of SINHALESE.

sin·gle /sínggəl/ *adj., n., & v.* • *adj.* **1** one only; not double or multiple. **2** united or undivided. **3 a** designed or suitable for one person (*single room*). **b** used or done by one person, etc. **4** one by itself (*a single tree*). **5** regarded separately (*every single thing*). **6** not married. **7** (with *neg.* or *interrog.*) even one (*did not see a single person*). **8** (of a flower) having only one circle of petals. • *n.* **1** a single thing, or item in a series. **2** a recording with one piece of music, etc., on each side. **3** *Baseball* a hit that allows the batter to reach first base safely. **4** (usu. *in pl.*) a game, esp. tennis, with one player on each side. **5** an unmarried person (*young singles*). **6** *sl.* a one-dollar note. • *v.* **1** *tr.* (foll. by *out*) choose as an example or as distinguishable or to serve some purpose. **2** *intr. Baseball* hit a single. ◻◻ **sin·gle·ness** *n.* **sin·gly** *adv.*

sin·gle-breast·ed *adj.* (of a coat, etc.) having only one set of buttons and buttonholes, not overlapping.

sin·gle file *n.* a line of people or things arranged one behind another.

sin·gle-hand·ed *adv. & adj.* • *adv.* **1** without help from another. **2** with one hand. • *adj.* **1** done, etc., single-handed. **2** for one hand. ◻◻ **sin·gle-hand·ed·ly** *adv.*

sin·gle-lens re·flex *adj.* denoting a reflex camera in which a single lens serves the film and the viewfinder.

sin·gle-mind·ed *adj.* having or intent on only one purpose.

sin·gle par·ent *n.* a person bringing up a child or children without a partner.

sin·glet /sínglit/ *n.* a sleeveless athletic shirt.

sin·gle·ton /sínggəltən/ *n.* **1** *Cards* one card only of a suit, esp. as dealt to a player. **2 a** a single person or thing. **b** an only child.

sin·gle·tree /sínggəltree/ *n.* = WHIFFLETREE.

sing·song /síngsawng, -song/ *adj., n., & v.* • *adj.* uttered with a monotonous rhythm or cadence. • *n.* a singsong manner. • *v.intr. & tr.* (*past* and *past part.* **singsonged**) speak or recite in a singsong manner.

sin·gu·lar /síngyələr/ *adj. & n.* • *adj.* **1** unique; much beyond the average. **2** eccentric or strange. **3** *Gram.* (of a word or form) denoting or referring to a single person or thing. **4** single; individual. • *n. Gram.* **1** a singular word or form. **2** the singular number. ◻◻ **sin·gu·lar·ly** *adv.*

sin·gu·lar·i·ty /síngyəláritee/ *n.* (*pl.* **-ties**) **1** the state or condition of being singular. **2** an odd trait or peculiarity.

sin·gu·lar·ize /síngyələrīz/ *v.tr.* **1** distinguish; individualize. **2** make singular. ◻◻ **sin·gu·lar·i·za·tion** *n.*

Sin·ha·lese /sínhəleéz, sínə-/ *n. & adj.* (also **Sin·gha·lese** /sínggə-/) • *n.* (*pl.* same) **1** a member of a people originally from N. India and now forming the majority of the population of Sri Lanka. **2** an Indic language spoken by this people. • *adj.* of or relating to this people or language.

sin·is·ter /sínistər/ *adj.* **1** suggestive of evil; looking villainous. **2** wicked or criminal (*a sinister motive*). **3** of evil omen. **4** *Heraldry* on the left-hand side of a shield, etc. (i.e., to the observer's right). ◻◻ **sin·is·ter·ly** *adv.* **sin·is·ter·ness** *n.*

sink /singk/ *v. & n.* • *v.* (*past* **sank** /sangk/ or **sunk** /sungk/; *past part.* **sunk** or **sunken**) **1** *intr.* fall or come slowly downward. **2** *intr.* disappear below the horizon (*the sun is sinking*). **3** *intr.* **a** go or penetrate below the surface esp. of a liquid. **b** (of a ship) go to the bottom of the sea. **4** *intr.* settle comfortably (*sank into a chair*). **5** *intr.* **a** gradually lose strength or value or quality, etc. (*my heart sank*). **b** (of the voice) descend in pitch or volume. **c** (of a sick person) approach death. **6** *tr.* send (a ship) to the bottom of the sea, etc. **7** *tr.* cause or allow to sink or penetrate (*sank its teeth into my leg*). **8** *tr.* cause the failure of (a plan, etc.), or the discomfiture of (a person). **9** *tr.* dig (a well) or bore (a shaft). **10** *tr.* engrave (a die) or inlay (a design). **11** *tr.* **a** invest (money) (*sunk a large sum into the business*). **b** lose (money) by investment. **12 a** *tr.* cause (a ball) to enter a pocket in billiards, a hole at golf, etc. **b** achieve this by (a stroke). **13** *intr.* (of a price, etc.) become lower. **14** *intr.* (of a storm or river) subside. **15** *intr.* (of ground) slope down, or reach a lower level by subsidence. **16** *intr.* (foll. by *on, upon*) (of darkness) descend (on a place). **17** *tr.* lower the level of. **18** *tr.* (usu. in *passive*; foll. by *in*) absorb; hold the attention of (*sunk in thought*). • *n.* **1** a fixed basin with a water supply and outflow pipe. **2** a place where foul liquid collects. **3** a place of vice or corruption. **4** a pool or marsh in which a river's water disappears by evaporation or percolation. **5** *Physics* a body or process used to absorb or dissipate heat. ◻ **sink in 1** penetrate or make its way in. **2** become gradually comprehended (*paused to let the words sink in*). **sink or swim** even at the risk of complete failure. ◻◻ **sink·a·ble** *adj.* **sink·age** *n.*

sink·er /síngkər/ *n.* **1** a weight used to sink a fishing line or sounding line. **2** *Baseball* (in full **sinkerball**) a pitch thrown so that it curves sharply downward.

sink·hole /singkhōl/ *n. Geol.* a cavity in limestone, etc., into which a stream, etc., disappears.

sink·ing fund *n.* money set aside for the gradual repayment of a debt.

sin·ner /sínər/ *n.* a person who sins, esp. habitually.

sin·net var. of SENNIT.

Sinn Fein /shin fáyn/ *n.* a political movement and party seeking a united republican Ireland, often linked to the IRA. ◻◻ **Sinn Fein·er** *n.*

Sino- /sínō/ *comb.form* Chinese; Chinese and (*Sino-American*).

si·nol·o·gy /sīnóləjee, sin-/ *n.* the study of Chinese language, history, customs, etc. ◻◻ **si·no·log·i·cal** /-nəlójikəl/ *adj.* **si·nol·o·gist** *n.*

sin·u·ate /sínyōōət, –ayt/ *adj.* esp. Bot. wavy-edged; with distinct inward and outward bends along the edge.

sin·u·os·i·ty /sínyōō-ósitee/ *n.* (*pl.* **-ties**) the state of being sinuous.

sin·u·ous /sínyōōəs/ *adj.* with many curves; undulating. ◻◻ **sin·u·ous·ly** *adv.* **sin·u·ous·ness** *n.*

si·nus /sínəs/ *n.* a cavity of bone or tissue, esp. in the skull connecting with the nostrils.

si·nus·i·tis /sínəsítis/ *n.* inflammation of a nasal sinus.

si·nus·oid /sínəsoyd/ *n.* **1** a curve having the form of a sine wave. **2** a small irregular-shaped blood vessel, esp. found in the liver. ◻◻ **si·nus·oi·dal** /–sóyd'l/ *adj.*

-sion /shən, zhən/ *suffix* forming nouns (see –ION) from Latin participial stems in *–s-* (*mansion*; *mission*; *persuasion*).

Si·on var. of ZION.

Sioux /sōō/ *n. & adj.* • *n.* (*pl.* same) **1** a member of a group of native N. American peoples. **2** the language of this group. • *adj.* of or relating to this people or language.

sip /sip/ *v. & n.* • *v.tr. & intr.* (**sipped, sipping**) drink in one or more small amounts or by spoonfuls. • *n.* **1** a small mouthful of liquid (*a sip of brandy*). **2** the act of taking this. ◻◻ **sip·per** *n.*

si·phon /sífən/ *n. & v.* (also **sy·phon**) • *n.* **1** a pipe or tube shaped like an inverted V or U with unequal legs to convey a liquid from a container to a lower level by atmospheric pressure. **2** (in full **siphon bottle**) an aerated-water bottle from which liquid is forced out through a tube by the pressure of gas. • *v.tr. & intr.* (often foll. by *off*) **1** conduct or flow through a siphon. **2** divert or set aside (funds, etc.).

sir /sər/ *n.* **1** a polite form of address or mode of reference to a man. **2** (**Sir**) a titular prefix to the forename of a knight or baronet.

sire /sīr/ *n. & v.* • *n.* **1** the male parent of an animal, esp. a stallion. **2** *archaic* a respectful form of address, esp. to a king. **3** *archaic poet.* a father or male ancestor. • *v.tr.* (esp. of a stallion) beget.

si·ren /sírən/ *n.* **1 a** a device for making a loud prolonged signal or warning sound, esp. by revolving a perforated disk over a jet of compressed air or steam. **b** the sound made by this. **2** (in Greek mythology) each of a number of women or winged creatures whose singing lured unwary sailors onto rocks. **3 a** a temptress. **b** a tempting pursuit, etc.

sir•loin /sərloyn/ *n.* the upper and choicer part of a loin of beef.

si•roc•co /siróko/ *n.* (also **sci•roc•co**) (*pl.* **-cos**) **1** a Saharan simoom reaching the northern shores of the Mediterranean. **2** a warm rainy wind in S. Europe.

sir•rah /sírə/ *n. archaic* = SIR (as a form of address).

sir•ree /sirée/ *int. colloq.* as an emphatic, esp. after *yes* or *no.*

sir•up var. of SYRUP.

sis /sis/ *n. colloq.* a sister.

si•sal /sísəl/ *n.* **1** a Mexican plant, *Agave sisalana,* with large fleshy leaves. **2** the fiber made from this plant, used for cordage, ropes, etc.

sis•sy /sísee/ *n. & adj. colloq.* •*n.* (*pl.* **-sies**) an effeminate or cowardly person. •*adj.* (**sissier, sissiest**) effeminate; cowardly. ▫▫ **sis•si•fied** *adj.* **sis•si•ness** *n.* **sis•sy•ish** *adj.*

sis•ter /sístər/ *n.* **1** a woman or girl in relation to sons and other daughters of her parents. **2 a** a close female friend or associate. **b** a female fellow member of a trade union, class, sect, or the human race. **3** a member of a female religious order. **4** (*attrib.*) of the same type or design or origin, etc. (*sister ship*). ▫▫ **sis•ter•less** *adj.* **sis•ter•ly** *adj.* **sis•ter•li•ness** *n.*

sis•ter•hood /sístərhood/ *n.* **1 a** the relationship between sisters. **b** sisterly friendliness; mutual support. **2 a** a society or association of women, esp. when bound by monastic vows or devoting themselves to religious or charitable work or the feminist cause. **b** its members collectively.

sis•ter-in-law *n.* (*pl.* **sisters-in-law**) **1** the sister of one's wife or husband. **2** the wife of one's brother. **3** the wife of one's brother-in-law.

Sis•tine /sísteen, sistéen/ *adj.* of any of the Popes called Sixtus, esp. Sixtus IV. ▫ **Sistine Chapel** a chapel in the Vatican, with frescoes by Michelangelo and other painters.

Sis•y•phe•an /sísiféeən/ *adj.* (of toil) endless and fruitless, like that of Sisyphus in Greek mythology (whose task in the underworld was to push uphill a boulder that at once rolled down again).

sit /sit/ *v.* (**sitting**; *past* and *past part.* **sat** /sat/) **1** *intr.* adopt or be in a position in which the body is supported more or less upright by the buttocks resting on the ground or a raised seat, etc., with the thighs usu. horizontal. **2** *tr.* cause to sit; place in a sitting position. **3** *intr.* **a** (of a bird) perch. **b** (of an animal) rest with the hind legs bent and the body close to the ground. **4** *intr.* (of a bird) remain on its nest to hatch its eggs. **5** *intr.* **a** be engaged in an occupation in which the sitting position is usual. **b** (of a committee, legislative body, etc.) be engaged in business. **c** (of an individual) be entitled to hold some office or position (*sat as a magistrate*). **6** *intr.* (usu. foll. by *for*) pose in a sitting position (for a portrait). **7** *intr.* (followed by *for*) be a member of Parliament for (a constituency). **8** *intr.* be in a more or less permanent position or condition (esp. of inactivity or being out of use or out of place). **9** *intr.* (of clothes, etc.) fit or hang in a certain way. **10** *tr.* keep or have one's seat on (a horse, etc.). **11** *intr.* act as a babysitter. **12** *intr.* (often foll. by *before*) (of an army) take a position outside a city, etc., to besiege it. ▫ **make a person sit up** *colloq.* surprise or interest a person. **sit at a person's feet** be a person's pupil. **sit back** relax one's efforts. **sit by** look on without interfering. **sit down 1** sit after standing. **2** cause to sit. **sit in 1** occupy a place as a protest. **2** (foll. by *for*) take the place of. **3** (foll. by *on*) be present as a guest or observer at (a meeting, etc.). **sit in judgment** assume the right of judging others; be censorious. **sit on 1** be a member of (a committee, etc.). **2** hold a session or inquiry concerning. **3** *colloq.* delay action about (*the government has been sitting on the report*). **4** *colloq.* repress or rebuke or snub (*felt rather sat on*). **sit on the fence** see FENCE. **sit on one's hands 1** take no action. **2** refuse to applaud. **sit out 1** take no part in (a dance, etc.). **2** stay till the end of (esp. an ordeal). **sit tight** *colloq.* **1** remain firmly in one's place. **2** not be shaken off or move away or yield to distractions. **sitting pretty** be comfortably or advantageously placed. **sit up 1** rise from a lying to a sitting position. **2** sit firmly upright. **3** go to bed later. **4** *colloq.* become interested or aroused, etc.

▶See note at SET.

si•tar /sitáar, sítaar/ *n.* a long-necked E. Indian lute with movable frets. ▫▫ **si•tar•ist** /sitáarist/ *n.*

sit•com /sítkom/ *n. colloq.* a situation comedy.

sit-down *adj.* (of a meal) eaten sitting at a table.

site /sīt/ *n. & v.* •*n.* **1** the ground chosen or used for a town or building. **2** a place where some activity is or has been conducted (*camping site; launching site*). •*v.tr.* **1** locate or place. **2** provide with a site.

sit-in *n.* a protest involving sitting in.

sit•ter /sítər/ *n.* **1** baby-sitter or nanny. **2** a sitting hen. **3** a person who sits, esp. for a portrait.

sit•ting /síting/ *n. & adj.* •*n.* **1** a continuous period of being seated, esp. engaged in an activity (*finished the book in one sitting*). **2** a time during which an assembly is engaged in business. **3** a session in which a meal is served (*dinner will be served in two sittings*). **4** a clutch of eggs. •*adj.* **1** having sat down. **2** (of an animal or bird) not running or flying. **3** (of a hen) engaged in hatching. ▫ **sitting pretty** see SIT.

sit•ting duck *n.* (also **sit•ting tar•get**) *colloq.* a vulnerable person or thing.

sit•ting room *n.* esp. *Brit.* a room in a house for relaxed sitting in.

sit•u•ate *v. & adj.* •*v.tr.* /síchoo-ayt/ (usu. in *passive*) **1** put in a certain position or circumstances (*is situated at the top of a hill; how are you situated at the moment?*). **2** establish or indicate the place of; put in a context. •*adj.* /síchooət/ *Law* or *archaic* situated.

▶See note at LOCATE.

sit•u•a•tion /síchoo-áyshən/ *n.* **1** a place and its surroundings (*the house stands in a fine situation*). **2** a set of circumstances; a position in which one finds oneself; a state of affairs (*came out of a difficult situation with credit*). **3** an employee's position or job. **4** a critical point or complication in a drama. ▫▫ **sit•u•a•tion•al** *adj.*

sit•u•a•tion com•e•dy *n.* a comedy in which the humor derives from the situations the characters are placed in.

sit-up *n.* a physical exercise in which a person sits up without raising the legs from the ground.

Si•va /séevə, shéevə/ *n.* (also **Shi•va** /shéevə/) "the Destroyer," a Hindu deity associated with the powers of reproduction and dissolution, regarded by some as the supreme being and by others as a member of the triad along with Brahma and Vishnu. ▫▫ **Si•va•ism** *n.* **Si•va•ite** *n. & adj.*

six /siks/ *n. & adj.* •*n.* **1** one more than five. **2** a symbol for this (6, vi, VI). **3** a size, etc., denoted by six. **4** a set or team of six individuals. **5** the time of six o'clock. **6** a card, etc., with six pips. •*adj.* that amount to six. ▫ **at sixes and sevens** in confusion or disagreement. **six of one and half a dozen of another** a situation of little real difference between the alternatives.

six-gun *n.* = SIX-SHOOTER.

six-pack *n.* six cans or bottles, as of beer, a soft drink, etc., packaged and sold as a unit.

six·shoot·er *n.* a revolver with six chambers.

six·teen /síksteen/ *n.* & *adj.* • *n.* **1** one more than fifteen. **2** a symbol for this (16, xvi, XVI). **3** a size, etc., denoted by sixteen. • *adj.* that amount to sixteen. ▫▫ **six·teenth** *adj.* & *n.*

six·teenth note *n. Mus.* a note having the time value of one-sixteenth of a whole note and represented by a large dot with a two-hooked stem.

sixth /siksth/ *n.* & *adj.* • *n.* **1** the position in a sequence corresponding to that of the number 6 in the sequence 1–6. **2** something occupying this position. **3** any of six equal parts of a thing. **4** *Mus.* **a** an interval or chord spanning six consecutive notes in the diatonic scale (e.g., C to A). **b** a note separated from another by this interval. • *adj.* that is the sixth. ▫▫ **sixth·ly** *adv.*

sixth sense *n.* **1** a supposed faculty giving intuitive or extrasensory knowledge. **2** such knowledge.

six·ty /síkstee/ *n.* & *adj.* • *n.* (*pl.* **-ties**) **1** the product of six and ten. **2** a symbol for this (60, lx, LX). **3** (in *pl.*) the numbers from 60 to 69, esp. the years of a century or of a person's life. **4** a set of sixty persons or things. • *adj.* that amount to sixty. ▫▫ **six·ti·eth** *adj.* & *n.* **six·ty·fold** *adj.* & *adv.*

six·ty-nine *n. sl.* sexual activity between two people involving mutual oral stimulation of the genitals.

siz·a·ble /sízəbəl/ *adj.* (also **size·a·ble**) large or fairly large. ▫▫ **siz·a·bly** *adv.*

size[1] /sīz/ *n.* & *v.* • *n.* **1** the relative bigness or extent of a thing; dimensions (*is of vast size; size matters less than quality*). **2** each of the classes into which things otherwise similar are divided according to size (*is made in several sizes; is three sizes too big*). • *v.tr.* sort in sizes or according to size. ▫ **of a size** having the same size. **of some size** fairly large. **the size of** as big as. **the size of it** *colloq.* a true account of the matter (*that's the size of it*). **size up 1** estimate the size of. **2** *colloq.* form a judgment of. **what size?** how big? ▫▫ **sized** *adj.* (also in *comb.*). **siz·er** *n.*

size[2] /sīz/ *n.* & *v.* • *n.* a gelatinous solution used in stiffening textiles, preparing plastered walls for decoration, etc. • *v.tr.* glaze or stiffen or treat with size.

size·a·ble var. of SIZABLE.

siz·zle /sízəl/ *v.* & *n.* • *v.intr.* **1** make a sputtering or hissing sound as of frying. **2** *colloq.* be in a state of great heat or excitement or marked effectiveness. • *n.* **1** a sizzling sound. **2** *colloq.* a state of great heat or excitement. ▫▫ **siz·zler** *n.* **siz·zling** *adj.* & *adv.* (*sizzling hot*).

SJ *abbr.* Society of Jesus.

skald /skawld/ *n.* (also **scald**) (in ancient Scandinavia) a composer and reciter of poems honoring heroes and their deeds. ▫▫ **skald·ic** *adj.*

skate[1] /skayt/ *n.* & *v.* • *n.* **1** each of a pair of steel blades (or of boots with blades attached) for gliding on ice. **2** (in full **roller skate**) each of a pair of metal frames with small wheels, fitted to shoes for riding on a hard surface. **3** a device on which a heavy object moves. • *v.* **1 a** *intr.* move on skates. **b** *tr.* perform (a specified figure) on skates. **2** *intr.* (foll. by *over*) refer fleetingly to; disregard. ▫ **skate on thin ice** *colloq.* behave rashly; risk danger, esp. by dealing with a subject needing tactful treatment. ▫▫ **skat·er** *n.*

skate[2] /skayt/ *n.* (*pl.* same or **skates**) any ray of the family Rajidae, esp. *Raja batis*, a large, flat, rhomboidal fish used as food.

skate[3] /skayt/ *n. sl.* a contemptible or dishonest person (esp. *cheapskate*).

skate·board /skáytbawrd/ *n.* & *v.* • *n.* a short narrow board on roller-skate wheels for riding on while standing. • *v.intr.* ride on a skateboard. ▫▫ **skate·board·er** *n.*

skat·ing rink *n.* a piece of ice artificially made, or a floor used, for skating.

ske·dad·dle /skidád'l/ *v.* & *n.* • *v.intr. colloq.* run away; depart quickly; flee. • *n.* a hurried departure or flight.

skeet /skeet/ *n.* a shooting sport in which a clay target is thrown from a trap to simulate the flight of a bird.

skee·ter[1] /skeétər/ *n. US dial., Austral. sl.* a mosquito.

skee·ter[2] var. of SKITTER.

skeg /skeg/ *n.* **1** a fin underneath the rear of a surfboard. **2** the after part of a vessel's keel or a projection from it.

skein /skayn/ *n.* **1** a loosely coiled bundle of yarn or thread. **2** a flock of wild geese, etc., in flight. **3** a tangle or confusion.

skel·e·ton /skélit'n/ *n.* **1 a** a hard framework of bones, cartilage, shell, woody fiber, etc., supporting or containing the body of an animal or plant. **b** the dried bones of a human being or other animal fastened together in the same relative positions as in life. **2** the supporting framework or structure of a thing. **3** a very thin person or animal. **4** the remaining part of anything after its life or usefulness is gone. **5** an outline sketch. **6** (*attrib.*) having only the essential or minimum number of persons, parts, etc. (*skeleton staff*). ▫▫ **skel·e·tal** *adj.* **skel·e·tal·ly** *adv.* **skel·e·ton·ize** *v.tr.*

skel·e·ton in the clos·et *n.* a discreditable or embarrassing fact kept secret.

skel·e·ton key *n.* a key designed to fit many locks.

skep·tic /sképtik/ *n.* & *adj.* • *n.* **1** a person inclined to doubt all accepted opinions. **2** a person who doubts the truth of religions. • *adj.* = SKEPTICAL. ▫▫ **skep·ti·cism** /-tisizəm/ *n.*

skep·sis /sképsis/ *n.* (*Brit.* **scep·sis**) **1** philosophic doubt. **2** skeptical philosophy.

skep·ti·cal /sképtikəl/ *adj.* inclined to question the truth or soundness of accepted ideas, facts, etc. ▫▫ **skep·ti·cal·ly** *adv.*

sketch /skech/ *n.* & *v.* • *n.* **1** a rough, slight, merely outlined, or unfinished drawing or painting, often made to assist in making a more finished picture. **2** a brief account; a rough draft or general outline. **3** a very short play, usu. humorous and limited to one scene. **4** a short descriptive piece of writing. • *v.* **1** *tr.* make or give a sketch of. **2** *intr.* draw sketches (*went out sketching*). **3** *tr.* (often foll. by *in, out*) indicate briefly or in outline. ▫▫ **sketch·er** *n.*

sketch·book /skéchbŏŏk/ *n.* a book or pad of drawing paper for doing sketches on.

sketch·y /skéchee/ *adj.* (**sketchier, sketchiest**) **1** giving only a rough outline, like a sketch. **2** *colloq.* unsubstantial or imperfect esp. through haste. ▫▫ **sketch·i·ly** *adv.* **sketch·i·ness** *n.*

skew /skyōō/ *adj., n.,* & *v.* • *adj.* oblique; slanting; set askew. • *v.* **1** *tr.* make skew. **2** *tr.* distort. **3** *intr.* move obliquely. **4** *intr.* twist. ▫ **on the skew** askew. ▫▫ **skew·ness** *n.*

skew·er /skyōōər/ *n.* & *v.* • *n.* a long pin designed for holding meat compactly together while cooking. • *v.tr.* **1** fasten together or pierce with or as with a skewer. **2** criticize sharply.

ski /skee/ *n.* & *v.* • *n.* (*pl.* **skis** or **ski**) **1** each of a pair of long narrow pieces of wood, etc., usu. pointed and turned up at the front, fastened under the feet for traveling over snow. **2** a similar device under a vehicle or aircraft. **3** = WATER SKI. **4** (*attrib.*) for wear when skiing (*ski boots*). • *v.* (**skis, skied** /skeed/; **skiing**) **1** *intr.* travel on skis. **2** *tr.* ski at (a place). ▫▫ **ski·a·ble** *adj.*

ski·ag·ra·phy /skīágrəfee/ *n.* (also *Brit.* **sci·ag·ra·phy**) the art of shading in drawing, etc. ▫▫ **ski·a·gram** /skíəgram/ *n.* **ski·a·graph** /skíəgraf/ *n.* & *v.tr.* **ski·a·graph·ic** /-gráfik/ *adj.*

skid /skid/ *v.* & *n.* • *v.* (**skidded, skidding**) **1** *intr.* (of a vehicle, a wheel, or a driver) slide on slippery ground, esp. sideways or obliquely. **2** *tr.* cause (a vehicle, etc.) to skid. **3** *intr.* slip; slide. • *n.* **1** the act or an instance of skidding. **2** a piece of wood, etc., serving as a support, ship's fender, inclined plane, etc. **3** a braking device, esp. a wooden or metal shoe preventing a wheel from revolving or used as a drag. **4** a runner beneath an aircraft for use when landing. □ **hit the skids** *colloq.* enter a rapid decline or deterioration. **on the skids** *colloq.* about to be discarded or defeated. **put the skids under** *colloq.* **1** hasten the downfall or failure of. **2** cause to hasten.

skid row *n. colloq.* a part of a town frequented by vagrants, alcoholics, etc.

ski·er /skéeər/ *n.* a person who skis.

skiff /skif/ *n.* a light rowboat or scull.

ski lift *n.* a device for carrying skiers up a slope, usu. on seats hung from an overhead cable.

skill /skil/ *n.* expertness; practiced ability; facility in an action.

skilled /skild/ *adj.* **1** skillful. **2** (of a worker) highly trained or experienced. **3** (of work) requiring skill or special training.

skil·let /skílit/ *n.* a frying pan.

skill·ful /skílfŏŏl/ *adj.* having or showing skill. □□ **skill·ful·ly** *adv.* **skill·ful·ness** *n.*

skim /skim/ *v. & n.* •*v.* (**skimmed, skimming**) **1** *tr.* **a** take scum or cream or a floating layer from the surface of (a liquid). **b** take (cream, etc.) from the surface of a liquid. **2** *tr.* **a** keep touching lightly or nearly touching (a surface) in passing over. **b** deal with or treat (a subject) superficially. **3** *intr.* **a** go lightly over a surface, glide along in the air. **b** (foll. by *over*) = sense 2b of *v.* **4 a** *tr.* read superficially; look over cursorily. **b** *intr.* (usu. foll. by *through*) read or look over cursorily. •*n.* **1** the act of skimming. **2** a thin covering on a liquid (*skim of ice*).

skim·mer /skímər/ *n.* **1** a device for skimming liquids. **2** a person who skims. **3** a flat hat, esp. a broad-brimmed straw hat.

skim milk *n.* milk from which the cream has been skimmed.

ski·mo·bile /skéemōbeel/ *n.* = SNOWMOBILE.

skimp /skimp/ *v., adj., & n.* •*v.* **1** *tr.* supply (a person, etc.) meagerly with food, money, etc. **2** *tr.* use a meager or insufficient amount of; stint (material, expenses, etc.). **3** *intr.* be parsimonious.

skimp·y /skímpee/ *adj.* (**skimpier, skimpiest**) meager; not ample or sufficient. □□ **skimp·i·ly** *adv.* **skimp·i·ness** *n.*

skin /skin/ *n. & v.* •*n.* **1** the flexible covering of a body. **2 a** the skin of a flayed animal with or without the hair, etc. **b** a material prepared from skins, esp. of smaller animals. **3** a person's skin with reference to its color or complexion (*has fair skin*). **4** an outer layer or covering, esp. the coating of a plant, fruit, or sausage. **5** a filmlike skin on the surface of a liquid, etc. **6** a container for liquid, made of an animal's skin. **7 a** the planking or plating of a ship or boat, inside or outside the ribs. **b** the outer covering of any craft or vehicle, esp. an aircraft or spacecraft. •*v.* (**skinned, skinning**) **1** *tr.* remove the skin from. **2 a** *tr.* cover (a sore, etc.) with or as with skin. **b** *intr.* (of a wound, etc.) become covered with new skin. **3** *tr. sl.* swindle. □ **by** (or **with**) **the skin of one's teeth** by a very narrow margin. **get under a person's skin** *colloq.* interest or annoy a person intensely. **have a thick** (or **thin**) **skin** be insensitive (or sensitive) to criticism, etc. **no skin off one's nose** *colloq.* a matter of indifference or even benefit to one. **to the skin** through all one's clothing (*soaked to the skin*). □□ **skin·less** *adj.* **skinned** *adj.* (also in *comb.*).

skin-deep *adj.* (of a wound, or of an emotion, an impression, beauty, etc.) superficial; not deep or lasting.

skin div·er *n.* a person who swims underwater without a diving suit, usu. with a mask, snorkel, flippers, etc. □□ **skin div·ing** *n.*

skin·flint /skínflint/ *n.* a miserly person.

skin fric·tion *n.* friction at the surface of a solid and a fluid in relative motion.

skin graft *n.* **1** the surgical transplanting of skin. **2** a piece of skin transferred in this way.

skin·head /skínhed/ *n.* **1** a youth with close-cropped hair, esp. one of an aggressive gang. **2** a U.S. Marine recruit.

skin·ner /skínər/ *n.* **1** a person who skins animals or prepares skins. **2** a dealer in skins; a furrier. **3** *Austral. Racing sl.* a result very profitable to bookmakers.

skin·ny /skínee/ *adj.* (**skinnier, skinniest**) **1** thin or emaciated. **2** (of clothing) tight-fitting. **3** made of or like skin. □□ **skin·ni·ness** *n.*

skin·ny-dip·ping *n. colloq.* swimming in the nude.

skin·tight /skíntít/ *adj.* (of a garment) very close-fitting.

skip[1] /skip/ *v. & n.* •*v.* (**skipped, skipping**) **1** *intr.* **a** move along lightly, esp. by taking two steps with each foot in turn. **b** jump lightly from the ground, esp. so as to clear a jump rope. **c** gambol; caper; frisk. **2** *intr.* move quickly from one point, subject, or occupation to another. **3** *tr.* (also *absol.*) omit in dealing with a series or in reading (*skip every tenth row; always skips the small print*). **4** *tr. colloq.* not participate in. **5** *tr. colloq.* depart quickly from; leave hurriedly. •*n.* **1** a skipping movement or action. **2** *Computing* the action of passing over part of a sequence of data or instructions. □ **skip it** *sl.* **1** abandon a topic, etc. **2** make off; disappear. **skip rope** play or exercise with a jump rope.

skip[2] /skip/ *n.* **1** a cage, bucket, etc., in which workers or materials are lowered and raised in mines and quarries. **2** = SKEP.

skip·per /skípər/ *n. & v.* •*n.* **1** a sea captain, esp. the master of a small trading or fishing vessel. **2** the captain of an aircraft. **3** the captain of a side in games. •*v.tr.* act as captain of.

skip·pet /skípit/ *n.* a small, round wooden box to enclose and protect a seal attached to a document.

skirl /skərl/ *n. & v.*•*n.* the shrill sound characteristic of bagpipes.•*v.intr.* make a skirl.

skir·mish /skə́rmish/ *n. & v.* •*n.* **1** a piece of irregular or unpremeditated fighting, esp. between small or outlying parts of armies or fleets; a slight engagement. **2** a short argument, etc. •*v.intr.* engage in a skirmish. □□ **skir·mish·er** *n.*

skirt /skərt/ *n. & v.* •*n.* **1** a woman's outer garment hanging from the waist. **2** the part of a coat, etc., that hangs below the waist. **3** a hanging part around the base of a hovercraft. **4** (in *sing.* or *pl.*) an edge, border, or extreme part. **5** (in full **skirt of beef**, etc.) the diaphragm and other membranes as food. •*v.tr.* **1** go along or around or past the edge of. **2** be situated along. **3** avoid dealing with (an issue, etc.). □□ **skirt·ed** *adj.* (also in *comb.*).

skirt·ing /skə́rting/ *n.* **1** fabric suitable for skirt making. **2** a border or edge.

ski run *n.* a slope prepared for skiing.

skit /skit/ *n.* (often foll. by *on*) a light, usu. short, piece of satire or burlesque.

skit·ter /skítər/ *v.intr.* (also **skee·ter** /skéetər/) **1** (usu. foll. by *along, across*) move lightly or hastily. **2** (usu. foll. by *about, off*) hurry about; dart off. **3** fish by drawing bait jerkily across the surface of the water.

skit·ter·y /skítəree/ *adj.* skittish; restless.

skit·tish /skítish/ *adj.* **1** lively; playful. **2** (of a horse, etc.) nervous; inclined to shy; fidgety. □□ **skit·tish·ly** *adv.* **skit·tish·ness** *n.*

skit·tle /skít'l/ *n.* a pin used in the game of skittles.

skiv·vy /skívee/ *n.* (*pl.* **-vies**) **1** (in *pl.*) underwear of T-shirt and shorts. **2** a thin high-necked long-sleeved garment.

skoal /skōl/ *n.* used as a toast in drinking.

skul·dug·ger·y /skuldúgəree/ *n.* (also **scul·dug·ger·y**, **skull·dug·ger·y**) trickery; unscrupulous behavior.

skulk /skulk/ *v.intr.* **1** move stealthily, lurk, or keep oneself concealed. **2** stay or sneak away in time of danger. ▫▫ **skulk·er** *n.*

skull /skul/ *n.* **1** the bony case of the brain of a vertebrate. **2 a** the part of the skeleton corresponding to the head. **b** this with the skin and soft internal parts removed. **3** the head as the seat of intelligence. ▫▫ **skulled** *adj.* (also in *comb.*).

skull·cap /skúlkap/ *n.* **1** a small, close-fitting, peakless cap. **2** the top part of the skull.

skunk /skungk/ *n.* **1** any of various cat-sized flesh-eating mammals of the family Mustelidae, esp. *Mephitis mephitis* having a distinctive black and white striped fur and able to emit a powerful stench from a liquid secreted by its anal glands as a defense. **2** *colloq.* a contemptible person.

skunk cab·bage *n.* one of two N. American herbaceous plants, esp. *Symplocarpus foetidus*, with an offensive-smelling spathe.

sky /skī/ *n.* & *v.* • *n.* (*pl.* **skies**) (in *sing.* or *pl.*) **1** the region of the atmosphere and outer space seen from the earth. **2** the weather or climate evidenced by this. • *v.tr.* (**skies, skied**) **1** *Baseball*, etc. hit (a ball) high into the air. **2** hang (a picture) high on a wall. ▫ **to the skies** without reserve (*praised to the skies*). **under the open sky** out of doors. ▫▫ **sky·ey** *adj.* **sky·less** *adj.*

sky·box /skíboks/ *n.* an elevated enclosure in a sports stadium containing plush seating, food services, and other amenities.

sky·cap /skíkap/ *n.* a person who carries baggage for passengers at airports.

sky·div·ing /skídīving/ *n.* the sport of performing acrobatic maneuvers under free fall with a parachute. ▫▫ **sky·div·er** *n.*

Skye ter·ri·er /skī/ *n.* a small, long-bodied, short-legged, long-haired, slate- or fawn-colored variety of Scottish terrier.

sky-high *adv.* & *adj.* very high.

sky·jack /skíjak/ *v.tr.* hijack (an aircraft). ▫▫ **sky·jack·er** *n.*

sky·lark /skílaark/ *n.* & *v.* • *n.* a lark, *Alauda arvensis*, of Eurasia and N. Africa, that sings while hovering in flight. • *v.intr.* play tricks; frolic.

sky·light /skílīt/ *n.* a window set in the plane of a roof or ceiling.

sky·line /skílīn/ *n.* the outline of hills, buildings, etc., defined against the sky.

sky pi·lot *n. sl.* a clergyman.

sky·rock·et /skírokkit/ *n.* & *v.* • *n.* a rocket exploding high in the air. • *v.intr.* (esp. of prices, etc.) rise very rapidly.

sky·scape /skískayp/ *n.* **1** a picture chiefly representing the sky. **2** a view of the sky.

sky·scrap·er /skískraypər/ *n.* a very tall building of many stories.

sky·ward /skíwərd/ *adv.* & *adj.* • *adv.* (also **sky·wards** /-wərdz/) toward the sky. • *adj.* moving skyward.

sky·way /skíway/ *n.* **1** a route used by aircraft. **2** a covered overhead walkway between buildings.

sky·writ·ing /skírīting/ *n.* legible smoke trails made by an airplane, esp. for advertising.

slab /slab/ *n.* **1** a flat, broad, fairly thick, usu. square or rectangular piece of solid material, esp. stone. **2** a large flat piece of cake, chocolate, etc. **3** (of lumber) an outer piece sawn from a log.

slack[1] /slak/ *adj.*, *n.*, *v.*, & *adv.* • *adj.* **1** not taut. **2** inactive or sluggish. **3** negligent or remiss (*discipline was slack*). **4** (of tide, etc.) neither ebbing nor flowing. **5** (of trade or business or a market) with little happening. **6** loose. • *n.* **1** the slack part of a rope (*haul in the slack*). **2** a slack time in trade, etc. **3** *colloq.* a spell of inactivity or laziness. **4** (in *pl.*) full-length loosely cut trousers for informal wear. • *v.* **1** *tr.* & *intr.* slacken. **2** *tr.* loosen (rope, etc.). ▫ **give** or **cut** (someone) **some slack** *colloq.* ease off; relax one's demands, etc. **slack off 1** loosen. **2** lose or cause to lose vigor. **slack up** reduce the speed of a train, etc., before stopping. **take up the slack** use up a surplus or make up a deficiency. ▫▫ **slack·ly** *adv.* **slack·ness** *n.*

slack[2] /slak/ *n.* coal dust or small pieces of coal.

slack·en /slákən/ *v.tr.* & *intr.* make or become slack. ▫ **slacken off = slack off** (see SLACK[1]).

slack·er /slákər/ *n.* a shirker; an indolent person.

slag /slag/ *n.* & *v.* • *n.* vitreous refuse left after ore has been smelted. • *v.* (**slagged, slagging**) **1** *intr.* form slag. **2** cohere into a mass like slag.

slain *past part.* of SLAY[1].

slake /slayk/ *v.tr.* **1** assuage or satisfy (thirst, revenge, etc.). **2** disintegrate (quicklime) by chemical combination with water.

sla·lom /slaáləm/ *n.* **1** a ski race down a zigzag course defined by artificial obstacles. **2** an obstacle race in canoes or cars or on skateboards or water skis.

slam[1] /slam/ *v.* & *n.* • *v.* (**slammed, slamming**) **1** *tr.* & *intr.* shut forcefully and loudly. **2** *tr.* put down (an object) with a similar sound. **3** *intr.* move violently (*he slammed out of the room*). **4** *tr.* & *intr.* put or come into sudden action (*slam the brakes on*). **5** *tr. sl.* criticize severely. **6** *tr. sl.* hit. **7** *tr. sl.* gain an easy victory over. • *n.* **1** a sound of or as of a slammed door. **2** the shutting of a door, etc., with a loud bang. **3** (usu. prec. by *the*) *sl.* prison.

slam[2] /slam/ *n. Cards* the winning of every trick in a game.

slam dunk *n. Basketball* a shot in which a player thrusts the ball down through the basket. ▫▫ **slam-dunk** *v.tr.*

slam·mer /slámər/ *n.* (usu. prec. by *the*) *sl.* prison.

slan·der /slándər/ *n.* & *v.* • *n.* **1** a malicious, false, and injurious statement spoken about a person. **2** the uttering of such statements. **3** *Law* false oral defamation. • *v.tr.* utter slander about. ▫▫ **slan·der·er** *n.* **slan·der·ous** *adj.*

slang /slang/ *n.* & *v.* • *n.* words, phrases, and uses that are regarded as very informal and are often restricted to special contexts or are peculiar to a specified profession, class, etc. (*racing slang*; *schoolboy slang*). • *v.* **1** *tr.* use abusive language to. **2** *intr.* use such language.

slant /slant/ *v.*, *n.*, & *adj.* • *v.* **1** *intr.* slope; lie or go obliquely. **2** *tr.* cause to do this. **3** *tr.* (often as **slanted** *adj.*) present (information) from a particular angle, esp. in a biased or unfair way. • *n.* **1** a slope. **2** a point of view, esp. a biased one. • *adj.* sloping; oblique. ▫ **on a** (or **the**) **slant** aslant.

slap /slap/ *v.*, *n.*, & *adv.* • *v.* (**slapped, slapping**) **1** *tr.* & *intr.* strike with the palm of the hand or a flat object, or so as to make a similar noise. **2** *tr.* lay forcefully (*slapped the money on the table*). **3** *tr.* put hastily or carelessly (*slap some paint on the walls*). **4** *tr.* (often foll. by *down*) *colloq.* reprimand or snub. • *n.* **1** a blow with the palm of the hand or a flat object. **2** a slapping sound. • *adv.* suddenly; fully; directly (*ran slap into him*). ▫ **slap in the face** a rebuff or affront. **slap on the back** *n.* congratulations. *v.tr.* congratulate. **slap on the wrist** *n. colloq.* a mild reprimand or rebuke. *v.tr. colloq.* reprimand.

slap·dash /slápdash/ *adj.* & *adv.* • *adj.* hasty and careless. • *adv.* in a slapdash manner.

slap·hap·py /sláp-hápee/ *adj. colloq.* **1** cheerfully casual. **2** punch-drunk.

slap·jack /slápjak/ *n.* **1** a card game in which face-up jacks are slapped by the players' open hands. **2** a kind of pancake cooked on a griddle.

slap shot *n. Ice Hockey* a powerful shot made with a full swing of the stick.

slap·stick /slápstik/ *n.* boisterous knockabout comedy.

slash /slash/ *v. & n.* • *v.* **1** *intr.* make a sweeping or random cut or cuts with a knife, sword, whip, etc. **2** *tr.* make such a cut or cuts at. **3** *tr.* make a long narrow gash or gashes in. **4** *tr.* reduce (prices, etc.) drastically. **5** *tr.* censure vigorously. **6** *tr.* make (one's way) by slashing. **7** *tr.* **a** lash (a person, etc.) with a whip. **b** crack (a whip). • *n.* **1 a** a slashing cut or stroke. **b** a wound or slit made by this. **2** an oblique stroke. **3** debris resulting from the felling or destruction of trees. ◻◻ **slash·er** *n.*

slashed /slasht/ *adj.* (of a sleeve, etc.) having slits to show a lining or puffing of other material.

slat /slat/ *n.* a thin narrow piece of wood or plastic or metal, esp. used in an overlapping series as in a fence or Venetian blind.

slate /slayt/ *n., v., & adj.* • *n.* **1** a fine-grained, gray, green, or bluish-purple metamorphic rock easily split into flat smooth plates. **2** a piece of such a plate used as roofing material. **3** a piece of such a plate used for writing on, usu. framed in wood. **4** the color of slate. **5** a list of nominees for office, etc. • *v.tr.* **1** cover with slates esp. as roofing. **2** make arrangements for; schedule (an event, etc.). **3** nominate for office, etc. • *adj.* made of slate. ◻ **wipe the slate clean** forgive or cancel the record of past offenses. ◻◻ **slat·ing** *n.* **slat·y** *adj.*

slath·er /sláthər/ *n. & v.* • *n.* (usu. in *pl.*) *colloq.* a large amount. • *v.tr. colloq.* **1** spread thickly. **2** squander.

slat·tern /slátərn/ *n.* a slovenly woman. ◻◻ **slat·tern·ly** *adj.*

slaugh·ter /sláwtər/ *n. & v.* • *n.* **1** the killing of an animal or animals for food. **2** the killing of many persons or animals at once or continuously; carnage; massacre. • *v.tr.* **1** kill (people) in a ruthless manner or on a great scale. **2** kill for food; butcher. **3** *colloq.* defeat utterly. ◻◻ **slaugh·ter·er** *n.*

slaugh·ter·house /sláwtərhows/ *n.* **1** a place for the slaughter of animals as food. **2** a place of carnage.

Slav /slaav/ *n. & adj.* • *n.* a member of a group of peoples in Central and Eastern Europe speaking Slavic languages. • *adj.* **1** of or relating to the Slavs. **2** Slavic.

slave /slayv/ *n. & v.* • *n.* **1** a person who is the legal property of another or others and is bound to absolute obedience; a human chattel. **2** a drudge; a person working very hard. **3** (foll. by *of, to*) a helpless victim of some dominating influence (*slave of fashion*; *slave to duty*). **4** a machine, or part of one, directly controlled by another. • *v.* **1** *intr.* (often foll. by *at, over*) work very hard. **2** *tr.* (foll. by *to*) subject (a device) to control by another.

slave driv·er *n.* **1** an overseer of slaves. **2** a person who works others hard. ◻◻ **slave-drive** *v.tr.*

slav·er[1] /sláyvər/ *n. hist.* a ship or person engaged in the slave trade.

slav·er[2] /slávər/ *n. & v.* • *n.* **1** saliva running from the mouth. **2 a** fulsome flattery. **b** drivel; nonsense. • *v.intr.* **1** let saliva run from the mouth; dribble. **2** (foll. by *over*) show excessive sentimentality over, or desire for.

slav·er·y /sláyvəree, sláyvree/ *n.* **1** the condition of a slave. **2** exhausting labor; drudgery. **3** the custom of having slaves.

slave ship *n. hist.* a ship transporting slaves, esp. from Africa.

slave trade *n. hist.* the procuring, transporting, and selling of human beings, esp. African blacks, as slaves. ◻◻ **slave trad·er** *n.*

Slav·ic /slaavik/ *adj. & n.* • *adj.* **1** of or relating to the group of Indo-European languages including Russian, Polish, and Czech. **2** of or relating to the Slavs. • *n.* the Slavic language group.

slav·ish /sláyvish/ *adj.* **1** of, like, or as of slaves. **2** showing no attempt at originality or development. **3** abject; servile; base. ◻◻ **slav·ish·ly** *adv.*

Sla·von·ic /sləvónik/ *adj. & n.* = Slavic.

slay /slay/ *v.tr.* (*past* **slew** /sloo/; *past part.* **slain** /slayn/) **1** *literary* or *joc.* kill. **2** *sl.* overwhelm with delight; convulse with laughter. ◻◻ **slay·er** *n.*

sleaze /sleez/ *n. & v. colloq.* • *n.* **1** sleaziness. **2** a person of low moral standards. • *v.intr.* move in a sleazy fashion.

slea·zy /sleezee/ *adj.* (**sleazier, sleaziest**) **1** squalid; tawdry. **2** slatternly. **3** (of textiles, etc.) flimsy. ◻◻ **slea·zi·ly** *adv.* **slea·zi·ness** *n.*

sled /sled/ *n. & v.* • *n.* **1** a vehicle on runners for conveying loads or passengers esp. over snow, drawn by horses, dogs, or reindeer or pulled by one or more persons. **2** a toboggan. • *v.intr.* (**sledded, sledding**) ride on a sled.

sledge[1] /slej/ *n. & v.* • *n.* a heavy sled, esp. one drawn by draft animals. • *v.intr. & tr.* travel or convey by sledge.

sledge[2] /slej/ *n.* = SLEDGEHAMMER.

sledge·ham·mer /sléjhamər/ *n.* **1** a large heavy hammer used to break stone, etc. **2** (*attrib.*) heavy or powerful (*a sledgehammer blow*).

sleek /sleek/ *adj. & v.* • *adj.* **1** (of hair, fur, or skin, or an animal or person with such hair, etc.) smooth and glossy. **2** looking well-fed and comfortable. **3** ingratiating. **4** (of a thing) smooth and polished. • *v.tr.* make sleek. ◻◻ **sleek·ly** *adv.* **sleek·ness** *n.* **sleek·y** *adj.*

sleep /sleep/ *n. & v.* • *n.* **1** a condition of body and mind that normally recurs for several hours every night, in which the nervous system is inactive, the eyes closed, the postural muscles relaxed, and consciousness practically suspended. **2** a period of sleep (*shall try to get a sleep*). **3** a state like sleep, such as rest, quiet, or death. **4** the prolonged inert condition of hibernating animals. **5** a substance found in the corners of the eyes after sleep. • *v.* (*past* and *past part.* **slept** /slept/) **1** *intr.* **a** be in a state of sleep. **b** fall asleep. **2** *intr.* (foll. by *at, in,* etc.) spend the night. **3** *tr.* provide sleeping accommodation for (*the house sleeps six*). **4** *intr.* (foll. by *with, together*) have sexual intercourse, esp. in bed. **5** *intr.* (foll. by *on, over*) not decide (a question) until the next day. **6** *intr.* (foll. by *through*) fail to be woken by. **7** *intr.* be inactive or dormant. **8** *intr.* be dead; lie in the grave. ◻ **go to sleep 1** enter a state of sleep. **2** (of a limb) become numbed by pressure. **in one's sleep** while asleep. **put to sleep 1** anesthetize. **2** kill (an animal) painlessly. **sleep around** *colloq.* be sexually promiscuous. **sleep in 1** remain asleep later than usual in the morning. **2** sleep by night at one's place of work. **sleep out** sleep by night out of doors, or not at one's place of work.

sleep·er /sleepər/ *n.* **1** a person or animal that sleeps. **2** a wooden or concrete beam laid horizontally as a support, esp. for railroad track. **3 a** a sleeping car. **b** a berth in this. **4** a ring worn in a pierced ear to keep the hole from closing. **5** a thing that is suddenly successful after being undistinguished. **6** a spy who remains inactive while establishing a secure position.

sleep·ing bag *n.* a lined or padded bag to sleep in.

sleep·ing car *n.* a railroad car provided with beds or berths.

sleep·ing pill *n.* a pill to induce sleep.

sleep·ing sick·ness *n.* any of several tropical diseases with extreme lethargy.

sleep·less /sleéplis/ *adj.* **1** characterized by lack of sleep. **2** unable to sleep. **3** continually active or moving. □□ **sleep·less·ly** *adv.* **sleep·less·ness** *n.*

sleep·walk /sleépwawk/ *v.intr.* walk or perform other actions while asleep. □□ **sleep·walk·er** *n.*

sleep·y /sleépee/ *adj.* (**sleepier, sleepiest**) **1** drowsy; about to fall asleep. **2** lacking activity (*a sleepy little town*). **3** habitually indolent, unobservant, etc. □□ **sleep·i·ly** *adv.* **sleep·i·ness** *n.*

sleet /sleet/ *n. & v.* •*n.* **1** a mixture of snow and rain falling together. **2** hail or snow melting as it falls. **3** a thin coating of ice. •*v.intr.* (prec. by *it* as subject) sleet falls (*if it sleets*). □□ **sleet·y** *adj.*

sleeve /sleev/ *n.* **1** the part of a garment that wholly or partly covers an arm. **2** the cover of a phonograph record. **3** a tube enclosing a rod or smaller tube. **4** a wind sock. □ **roll up one's sleeves** prepare to fight or work. **up one's sleeve** in reserve. □□ **sleeved** *adj.* (also in *comb.*). **sleeve·less** *adj.*

sleigh /slay/ *n. & v.* •*n.* a sled, esp. one for riding on. •*v.intr.* travel on a sleigh.

sleigh bell *n.* any of a number of tinkling bells attached to the harness of a sleigh-horse, etc.

sleight /slīt/ *n. archaic* **1** a deceptive trick or device or movement. **2** dexterity. **3** cunning.

sleight of hand *n.* **1** dexterity, esp. in conjuring or fencing. **2** a display of dexterity, esp. a conjuring trick.

slen·der /sléndər/ *adj.* (**slenderer, slenderest**) **1 a** of small girth or breadth (*a slender pillar*). **b** gracefully thin (*a slender waist*). **2** slight; meager; inadequate (*slender hopes; slender resources*). □□ **slen·der·ly** *adv.* **slen·der·ness** *n.*

slen·der·ize /sléndərīz/ *v.* **1** *tr.* make slender. **2** *intr.* make oneself slender; slim.

slept *past* and *past part.* of SLEEP.

sleuth /slooth/ *n. & v. colloq.* •*n.* a detective. •*v.* **1** *intr.* act as a detective. **2** *tr.* investigate.

sleuth·hound /slóothhownd/ *n.* **1** a bloodhound. **2** *colloq.* a detective.

slew[1] /sloo/ *v. & n.* (also **slue**) •*v.tr. & intr.* (often foll. by *around*) turn or swing forcibly or with effort out of the forward or ordinary position. •*n.* such a change of position.

slew[2] *past* of SLAY[1].

slew[3] /sloo/ *n. colloq.* a large number or quantity.

slice /slīs/ *n. & v.* •*n.* **1** a thin, broad piece or wedge cut off or out esp. from meat or bread or a cake, pie, or large fruit. **2** a share; a part taken or allotted or gained (*a slice of the profits*). **3** an implement with a broad flat blade for serving fish, etc. **4** *Golf & Tennis* a slicing stroke. •*v.* **1** *tr.* (often foll. by *up*) cut into slices. **2** *tr.* (foll. by *off*) cut (a piece) off. **3** *intr.* (foll. by *into, through*) cut with or like a knife. **4** *tr.* (also *absol.*) **a** *Golf* strike (the ball) so that it deviates away from the striker. **b** (in other sports) propel (the ball) forward at an angle. **5** *tr.* go through (air, etc.) with a cutting motion. □□ **slice·a·ble** *adj.* **slic·er** *n.* (also in *comb.*).

slick /slik/ *adj., n., & v.* •*adj. colloq.* **1 a** (of a person or action) skillful or efficient (*a slick performance*). **b** superficially or pretentiously smooth and dexterous. **c** glib. **2 a** sleek; smooth. **b** slippery. •*n.* **1** a smooth patch of oil, etc., esp. on the sea. **2** *Motor Racing* a smooth tire. **3** *colloq.* a glossy magazine. **4** *sl.* a slick person. •*v.tr. colloq.* **1** make sleek or smart. **2** (usu. foll. by *down*) flatten (one's hair, etc.). □□ **slick·ly** *adv.* **slick·ness** *n.*

slick·er /slíkər/ *n.* **1** *colloq.* **a** a plausible rogue. **b** a smart and sophisticated city dweller (cf. CITY SLICKER). **2** a raincoat of smooth material.

slide /slīd/ *v. & n.* •*v.* (*past* and *past part.* **slid** /slid/) **1 a** *intr.* move along a smooth surface with continuous contact on the same part of the thing moving. **b** *tr.* cause to do this (*slide the drawer into place*). **2** *intr.* move quietly; glide; go smoothly along. **3** *intr.* pass gradually or imperceptibly. **4** *intr.* glide over ice on one or both feet without skates (under gravity or with momentum gotten by running). **5** *intr.* (foll. by *over*) barely touch upon (a delicate subject, etc.). **6** *intr. & tr.* (often foll. by *into*) move or cause to move quietly or unobtrusively (*slid his hand into mine*). **7** *intr.* take its own course (*let it slide*). **8** *intr.* decline (*shares slid to a new low*). •*n.* **1 a** the act of sliding. **b** a rapid decline. **2** an inclined plane down which children, goods, etc., slide; a chute. **3 a** a track made by or for sliding, esp. on ice. **b** a slope prepared with snow or ice for tobogganing. **4** a part of a machine or instrument that slides, esp. a slide valve. **5 a** a thing slid into place, esp. a piece of glass holding an object for a microscope. **b** a mounted transparency usu. placed in a projector for viewing on a screen. **6** a part or parts of a machine on or between which a sliding part works. □□ **slid·a·ble** *adj.* **slid·er** *n.*

slide rule *n.* a ruler with a sliding central strip, graduated logarithmically for making rapid calculations, esp. multiplication and division.

slid·ing door *n.* a door drawn across an aperture on a slide, not turning on hinges.

slid·ing scale *n.* a scale of fees, taxes, wages, etc., that varies as a whole in accordance with variation of some standard, as of income or the ability of individuals to pay.

slight /slīt/ *adj., v., & n.* •*adj.* **1 a** of little significance (*a slight cold*). **b** barely perceptible (*a slight smell of gas*). **c** not much or great or thorough; inadequate (*paid him slight attention*). **2** slender; frail-looking. **3** (in *superl.*, with *neg.* or *interrog.*) any whatever (*paid not the slightest attention*). •*v.tr.* treat or speak of (a person, etc.) as not worth attention, fail in courtesy or respect toward. •*n.* a marked piece of neglect. □□ **slight·ing·ly** *adv.* **slight·ish** *adj.* **slight·ly** *adv.* **slight·ness** *n.*

sli·ly var. of SLYLY (see SLY).

slim /slim/ *adj. & v.* •*adj.* (**slimmer, slimmest**) **1 a** of small girth or thickness. **b** gracefully thin. **c** not fat nor overweight. **2** small, insufficient (*a slim chance of success*). •*v.* (**slimmed, slimming**) **1** *intr.* esp. *Brit.* make oneself slimmer by dieting, exercise, etc. **2** *tr.* make slim or slimmer. □□ **slim·ly** *adv.* **slim·mer** *n.* **slim·ming** *n. & adj.* **slim·ness** *n.*

slime /slīm/ *n. & v.* •*n.* thick slippery mud or a substance of similar consistency. •*v.tr.* cover with slime.

slim·y /slímee/ *adj.* (**slimier, slimiest**) **1** of the consistency of slime. **2** covered, smeared with, or full of slime. **3** disgustingly dishonest, meek, or flattering. **4** slippery; hard to hold. □□ **slim·i·ly** *adv.* **slim·i·ness** *n.*

sling[1] /sling/ *n. & v.* •*n.* **1** a strap, belt, etc., used to support or raise a hanging weight, e.g., a rifle, a ship's boat, or goods being transferred. **2** a bandage looped around the neck to support an injured arm. **3** a strap or string used with the hand to give impetus to a small missile, esp. a stone. •*v.tr.* (*past* and *past part.* **slung** /slung/) **1** (also *absol.*) hurl (a stone, etc.) from a sling. **2** *colloq.* throw. **3** suspend with a sling; allow to swing suspended; arrange so as to be supported from above; hoist or transfer with a sling.

sling[2] /sling/ *n.* a sweetened drink of liquor (esp. gin) and water.

sling·shot /slíngshot/ *n.* a forked stick, etc., with elastic for shooting stones.

slink /slingk/ *v.intr.* (*past* and *past part.* **slunk** /slungk/) (often foll. by *off, away, by*) move in a stealthy or guilty or sneaking manner.

slink·y /slíngkee/ *adj.* (**slinkier, slinkiest**) **1** stealthy. **2** (of a garment) close-fitting and flowing; sinuous. **3** gracefully slender. □□ **slink·i·ly** *adv.* **slink·i·ness** *n.*

slip[1] /slip/ *v. & n.* •*v.* (**slipped, slipping**) **1** *intr.* slide unintentionally esp. for a short distance; lose one's footing or balance or place by unintended sliding. **2** *intr.* go or move with a sliding motion (*slipped into her nightgown*). **3** *intr.* escape restraint or capture by being slippery or hard to hold or by not being grasped (*the eel slipped through his fingers*). **4** *intr.* make one's or its way unobserved or quietly or quickly. **5** *intr.* **a** make a careless or casual mistake. **b** fall below the normal standard. **6** *tr.* insert or transfer stealthily or casually or with a sliding motion (*slipped a coin into his hand*). **7** *tr.* **a** release from restraint (*slipped the greyhounds from the leash*). **b** release (the clutch of a motor vehicle) for a moment. **8** *tr.* move (a stitch) to the other needle without knitting it. **9** *tr.* (foll. by *on, off*) pull (a garment) hastily on or off. **10** *tr.* escape from (*the dog slipped its collar*). •*n.* **1** the act or an instance of slipping. **2** an accidental or slight error. **3** a loose covering or garment, esp. pillowcase. **4 a** a reduction in the movement of a pulley, etc., due to slipping of the belt. **b** a reduction in the distance traveled by a ship or aircraft arising from the nature of the medium in which its propeller revolves. **5** (in *sing.* or *pl.*) an inclined structure on which ships are built or repaired. □ **give a person the slip** escape from or evade him or her. **let slip 1** release accidentally or deliberately. **2** miss (an opportunity). **3** utter inadvertently. **slip away** depart without leave-taking, etc. **slip off** depart without leave-taking, etc. **slip up** *colloq.* make a mistake.

slip[2] /slip/ *n.* **1** a small piece of paper esp. for writing on. **2** a cutting taken from a plant for grafting or planting.

slip[3] /slip/ *n.* clay in a creamy mixture with water, used mainly for decorating earthenware.

slip·case /slípcays/ *n.* a close-fitting case for a book.

slip·cov·er /slípkəvər/ *n.* **1** a removable covering for usu. upholstered furniture. **2** a jacket or slipcase for a book.

slip·knot /slípnot/ *n.* **1** a knot that can be undone by a pull. **2** a running knot.

slip of the tongue *n.* a small mistake in which something is written (or said) unintentionally.

slip-on *adj.* & *n.* •*adj.* (of shoes or clothes) that can be easily slipped on and off. •*n.* a slip-on shoe or garment.

slip·page /slípij/ *n.* **1** the act or an instance of slipping. **2 a** a decline, esp. in popularity or value. **b** failure to meet a deadline or fulfill a promise; delay.

slipped disk *n.* a disk between vertebrae that has become displaced and causes lumbar pain.

slip·per /slípər/ *n.* **1** a light, loose, comfortable indoor shoe. **2** a light slip-on shoe for dancing, etc. □□ **slip·pered** *adj.*

slip·per·y /slípəree/ *adj.* **1** difficult to hold firmly because of smoothness, wetness, or elusive motion. **2** (of a surface) difficult to stand on, causing slips by its smoothness or muddiness. **3** unreliable; shifty. **4** (of a subject) requiring tactful handling. □□ **slip·per·i·ly** *adv.* **slip·per·i·ness** *n.*

slip·py /slípee/ *adj.* (**slippier, slippiest**) *colloq.* slippery. □□ **slip·pi·ness** *n.*

slip·shod /slípshod/ *adj.* **1** careless; unsystematic; loose in arrangement. **2** slovenly. **3** having shoes down at the heel.

slip stitch *n.* **1** a loose stitch joining layers of fabric and not visible externally. **2** a stitch moved to the other needle without being knitted. □□ **slip-stitch** *v.tr.*

slip·up /slípəp/ *n.* a mistake; a blunder.

slip·way /slípway/ *n.* a slip for building ships or landing boats.

slit /slit/ *n.* & *v.* •*n.* **1** a long, straight, narrow incision. **2** a long, narrow opening comparable to a cut. •*v.tr.* (**slitting**; *past* and *past part.* **slit**) **1** make a slit in; cut or tear lengthwise. **2** cut into strips.

slith·er /slíthər/ *v.* & *n.* •*v.intr.* slide unsteadily; go with an irregular slipping motion. •*n.* an instance of slithering. □□ **slith·er·y** *adj.*

slit·ty /slítee/ *adj.* (**slittier, slittiest**) (of the eyes) long and narrow.

sliv·er /slívər/ *n.* & *v.* •*n.* **1** a long, thin piece cut or split off. **2** a piece of wood torn from a tree or from lumber. **3** a splinter, esp. from an exploded shell. •*v.tr.* & *intr.* **1** break off as a sliver. **2** break up into slivers. **3** form into slivers.

sliv·o·vitz /slívəvits/ *n.* a plum brandy made esp. in Romania and the former Yugoslavia.

slob /slob/ *n. colloq.* a stupid, coarse, or fat person. □□ **slob·bish** *adj.*

slob·ber /slóbər/ *v.* & *n.* •*v.intr.* **1** slaver. **2** (foll. by *over*) show excessive sentiment. •*n.* saliva running from the mouth; slaver. □□ **slob·ber·y** *adj.*

sloe /slō/ *n.* **1** = BLACKTHORN 1. **2** its small bluish-black fruit with a sour taste.

sloe-eyed *adj.* **1** having bluish-black eyes. **2** slant-eyed.

sloe gin *n.* a liqueur of sloes steeped in gin.

slog /slog/ *v.* & *n.* •*v.* (**slogged, slogging**) **1** *intr.* & *tr.* hit hard and usu. wildly, esp. in boxing or at cricket. **2** *intr.* (often foll. by *away, on*) walk or work doggedly. •*n.* **1** a hard random hit. **2 a** hard steady work or walking. **b** a spell of this. □□ **slog·ger** *n.*

slo·gan /slṓgən/ *n.* **1** a short catch phrase used in advertising, etc. **2** a party cry; a catchword or motto identified with a particular product, party, etc. **3** a war cry used among Scottish clans.

sloop /sloop/ *n.* a small, one-masted, fore-and-aft-rigged vessel with mainsail and jib.

slop[1] /slop/ *v.* & *n.* •*v.* (**slopped, slopping**) **1** (often foll. by *over*) **a** *intr.* spill or flow over the edge of a vessel. **b** *tr.* allow to do this. **2** *tr.* make (the floor, clothes, etc.) wet or messy by slopping. **3** *intr.* (usu. foll. by *over*) gush; be effusive or maudlin. •*n.* **1** a quantity of liquid spilled or splashed. **2** weakly sentimental language. **3** (in *pl.*) waste liquid. **4** (in *sing.* or *pl.*) unappetizing weak liquid food.

slop[2] /slop/ *n.* **1** a worker's loose outer garment. **2** (in *pl.*) esp. *Brit.* ready-made or cheap clothing. **3** (in *pl.*) clothes and bedding supplied to sailors in the navy. **4** (in *pl.*) *archaic* wide baggy trousers esp. as worn by sailors.

slope /slōp/ *n.* & *v.* •*n.* **1** an inclined position or direction. **2** a piece of rising or falling ground. **3 a** a difference in level between the two ends or sides of a thing (*a slope of 5 yards*). **b** the rate at which this increases with distance, etc. **4** a place for skiing on the side of a hill or mountain. **5** (prec. by *the*) the position of a rifle when sloped. •*v.* **1** *intr.* have or take a slope; slant esp. up or down. **2** *tr.* place or arrange or make in or at a slope. □ **slope arms** place one's rifle in a sloping position against one's shoulder.

slop·py /slópee/ *adj.* (**sloppier, sloppiest**) **1 a** (of the ground) wet with rain; full of puddles. **b** (of food, etc.) watery and disagreeable. **c** (of a floor, table, etc.) wet with slops, having water, etc., spilled on it. **2** careless; not thorough. **3** (of a garment) ill-fitting or untidy. **4** (of sentiment or talk) weakly emotional. □□ **slop·pi·ly** *adv.* **slop·pi·ness** *n.*

slosh /slosh/ *v.* & *n.* •*v.* **1** *intr.* (often foll. by *about*) splash or flounder about; move with a splashing sound. **2** *tr. colloq.* **a** pour (liquid) clumsily. **b** pour liquid on. •*n.* **1** slush. **2 a** an instance of splashing. **b** the sound of this. **3** a quantity of liquid.

sloshed /slosht/ *adj. sl.* drunk.

slot[1] /slot/ *n.* & *v.* •*n.* **1** a slit or other aperture in a machine, etc., for something (esp. a coin) to be inserted. **2** a slit, groove, channel, or long aperture into which something fits. **3** an allotted place in a scheme or schedule. •*v.* (**slotted, slotting**) **1** *tr. & intr.* place or be placed into or as if into a slot. **2** *tr.* provide with a slot or slots.

slot[2] /slot/ *n.* **1** the track of a deer, etc., esp. as shown by footprints. **2** a deer's foot.

sloth /slawth, slōth/ *n.* **1** laziness or indolence. **2** any slow-moving nocturnal mammal of the family Bradypodidae or Megalonychidae of S. America, having long limbs and hooked claws for hanging upside down from branches of trees.

slot ma·chine *n.* a machine worked by the insertion of a coin, esp. a gambling machine operated by a pulled handle.

slouch /slowch/ *v. & n.* •*v.* **1** *intr.* stand or move or sit in a drooping, ungainly fashion. **2** *tr.* bend one side of the brim of (a hat) downward. **3** *intr.* hang down loosely. •*n.* **1** a slouching posture or movement. **2** a downward bend of a hat brim. **3** *sl.* an incompetent or slovenly worker or operator or performance (*he's no slouch*). ▫▫ **slouch·y** *adj.* (**slouchier, slouchiest**).

slough[1] /slow/ *n.* **1** a swamp; a miry place; a quagmire. **2** a marshy pond, backwater. ▫▫ **slough·y** *adj.*

slough[2] /sluf/ *n. & v.* •*n.* **1** a part that an animal casts or molts, esp. a snake's cast skin. **2** dead tissue that drops off from living flesh, etc. •*v.* **1** *tr.* cast off as a slough. **2** *intr.* (often foll. by *off*) drop off as a slough. **3** *intr.* cast off a slough. **4** *intr.* (often foll. by *away, down*) (of soil, rock, etc.) slide into a hole or depression. ▫▫ **slough·y** *adj.*

Slo·vak /slṓvaak, -vak/ *n. & adj.* •*n.* **1** a member of a Slavic people inhabiting Slovakia in central Europe. **2** the West Slavic language of this people. •*adj.* of or relating to this people or language.

slov·en /slúvən/ *n.* a person who is habitually untidy or careless.

Slo·vene /slṓveen, sləvéen/ (also **Slo·ve·ni·an** /-véeneeən/) *n. & adj.* •*n.* **1** a member of a Slavic people in Slovenia in the formerYugoslavia. **2** the language of this people. •*adj.* of or relating to Slovenia or its people or language.

slov·en·ly /slúvənlee/ *adj. & adv.* •*adj.* careless and untidy; unmethodical. •*adv.* in a slovenly manner. ▫▫ **slov·en·li·ness** *n.*

slow /slō/ *adj., adv., & v.* •*adj.* **1 a** taking a relatively long time to do a thing or cover a distance (also foll. by *of*: *slow of speech*). **b** acting or moving or done without speed. **2** gradual (*slow growth*). **3** not producing, allowing, or conducive to speed (*in the slow lane*). **4** (of a clock, etc.) showing a time earlier than is the case. **5** (of a person) not understanding readily; not learning easily. **6** dull; uninteresting; tedious. **7** sluggish (*business is slow*). **8** (of a fire or oven) giving little heat. **9** *Photog.* **a** (of a film) needing long exposure. **b** (of a lens) having a small aperture. **10 a** reluctant; tardy (*not slow to defend himself*). **b** not hasty or easily moved (*slow to take offense*). •*adv.* **1** at a slow pace; slowly. **2** (in *comb.*) (*slow-moving traffic*). •*v.* (usu. foll. by *down, up*) **1** *intr. & tr.* reduce one's speed or the speed of (a vehicle, etc.). **2** *intr.* reduce one's pace of life; live or work less intensely. ▫▫ **slow·ish** *adj.* **slow·ly** *adv.* **slow·ness** *n.*

slow·down /slṓdown/ *n.* the action of slowing down, as in productivity.

slow mo·tion *n.* **1** the operation or speed of a film using slower projection or more rapid exposure so that actions, etc., appear much slower than usual. **2** the simulation of this in real action.

slow·worm /slṓwərm/ *n.* a small European legless lizard, *Anguis fragilis*, giving birth to live young. Also called **blindworm**.

SLR *abbr.* **1** *Photog.* single-lens reflex. **2** self-loading rifle.

sludge /sluj/ *n.* **1** thick, greasy mud. **2** muddy or slushy sediment. **3** sewage. **4** *Mech.* an accumulation of dirty oil, esp. in the sump of an internal-combustion engine. ▫▫ **sludg·y** *adj.*

slue var. of SLEW[1].

slug[1] /slug/ *n.* **1** a small shell-less mollusk of the class Gastropoda, usu. destructive to plants. **2 a** a bullet esp. of irregular shape. **b** a missile for an airgun. **3** a shot of liquor.

slug[2] /slug/ *v. & n.* •*v.tr.* (**slugged, slugging**) strike with a hard blow. •*n.* a hard blow. ▫ **slug it out 1** fight it out. **2** endure; stick it out. ▫▫ **slug·ger** *n.*

slug·gard /slúgərd/ *n.* a lazy, sluggish person. ▫▫ **slug·gard·ly** *adj.*

slug·gish /slúgish/ *adj.* inert; inactive. ▫▫ **slug·gish·ly** *adv.* **slug·gish·ness** *n.*

sluice /sloos/ *n. & v.* •*n.* **1** (also **sluice gate, sluice valve**) a sliding gate or other contrivance for controlling the volume or flow of water. **2** an artificial channel, esp. one for washing ore. **3** a place for rinsing. **4** the act or an instance of rinsing. **5** the water above or below or issuing through a floodgate. •*v.* **1** *tr.* provide or wash with a sluice or sluices. **2** *tr.* rinse, throw water freely upon. **3** *tr.* (foll. by *out, away*) wash out or away with a flow of water. **4** *tr.* flood with water from a sluice. **5** *intr.* (of water) rush out from a sluice, or as if from a sluice.

slum /slum/ *n. & v.* •*n.* **1** an overcrowded and squalid back street, district, etc., usu. in a city. **2** a house or building unfit for human habitation. •*v.intr.* (**slummed, slumming**) **1** live in slumlike conditions. **2** go about the slums through curiosity or for charitable purposes. ▫ **slum it** *colloq.* put up with conditions less comfortable than usual. ▫▫ **slum·my** *adj.* (**slummier, slummiest**). **slum·mi·ness** *n.*

slum·ber /slúmbər/ *v. & n. poet. rhet.* •*v.intr.* **1** sleep, esp. in a specified manner. **2** be idle, drowsy, or inactive. •*n.* a sleep, esp. of a specified kind (*fell into a fitful slumber*). ▫▫ **slum·ber·er** *n.* **slum·ber·ous** *adj.* **slum·brous** *adj.*

slump /slump/ *n. & v.* •*n.* **1** a sudden severe or prolonged fall in prices or values of commodities or securities. **2** a sharp or sudden decline in trade business. **3** a lessening of interest in a subject or undertaking. •*v.intr.* **1** undergo a slump; fail; fall in price. **2** sit or fall heavily or limply. **3** lean or subside.

slung *past* and *past part.* of SLING[1].

slunk *past* and *past part.* of SLINK[1].

slur /slər/ *v. & n.* •*v.* (**slurred, slurring**) **1** *tr. & intr.* pronounce or write indistinctly so that the sounds or letters run into one another. **2** *tr. Mus.* **a** perform (notes) legato. **b** mark (notes) with a slur. **3** *tr.* put a slur on (a person or a person's character). **4** *tr.* (usu. foll. by *over*) pass over (a fact, fault, etc.) lightly. •*n.* **1** an imputation of wrongdoing; stigma (*a slur on my reputation*). **2** a disparaging remark. **3** the act or an instance of slurring. **4** *Mus.* a curved line to show that two or more notes are to be sung to one syllable or played or sung legato.

slurp /slərp/ *v. & n.* •*v.tr.* eat or drink noisily. •*n.* the sound of this; a slurping gulp.

slur·ry /slúree/ *n.* (*pl.* **-ries**) **1** a semiliquid mixture of fine particles and water. **2** thin liquid cement. **3** a fluid form of manure.

slush /slush/ *n.* **1** watery mud or thawing snow. **2** silly sentiment.

slush·y /slúshee/ *adj.* (**slushier, slushiest**) like slush; watery. ▫▫ **slush·i·ness** *n.*

slut /slut/ *n. derog.* **1** a slovenly woman. **2** a prostitute. ▫▫ **slut·tish** *adj.* **slut·tish·ness** *n.*

sly /slī/ *adj.* (**slier, sliest** or **slyer, slyest**) **1** cunning; wily. **2 a** (of a person) practicing secrecy or stealth. **b** (of an action, etc.) done, etc., in secret. **3** hypocritical; ironic. **4** knowing; arch; insinuating. □ **on the sly** privately; covertly. □□ **sly·ly** *adv.* (also **sli·ly**). **sly·ness** *n.*

Sm *symb. Chem.* the element samarium.

SM *abbr.* **1** stage manager; service mark. **2** sergeant major.

S-M *abbr.* sadomasochism. (Also **S and M**).

smack[1] /smak/ *n., v., & adv.* • *n.* **1** a sharp slap or blow esp. with the palm of the hand or a flat object. **2** a hard hit in baseball, etc. **3** a loud kiss. **4** a loud, sharp sound. • *v.* **1** *tr.* strike with the open hand, etc. **2** *tr.* part (one's lips) noisily in eager anticipation or enjoyment of food. **3** *tr.* crack (a whip). **4** *tr. & intr.* move, hit, etc., with a smack. • *adv. colloq.* **1** with a smack. **2** suddenly; violently (*landed smack on my desk*). **3** exactly (*hit it smack in the center*). □ **a smack in the face** (or **eye**) *colloq.* a rebuff.

smack[2] /smak/ *v. & n.* (foll. by *of*) • *v.intr.* **1** have a flavor of (*smacked of garlic*). **2** suggest the effects of (*it smacks of nepotism*). • *n.* **1** a taste that suggests the presence of something. **2** (in a person's character, etc.) a barely discernible quality (*just a smack of superciliousness*).

smack[3] /smak/ *n.* a single-masted sailboat for coasting or fishing.

smack[4] /smak/ *n. sl.* a hard drug, esp. heroin.

smack·er /smákər/ *n. sl.* **1** a loud kiss. **2** a resounding blow. **3** (usu. in *pl.*) *sl.* a dollar.

small /smawl/ *adj., n., & adv.* • *adj.* **1** not large or big. **2** slender; thin. **3** not great in importance, amount, number, strength, or power. **4** trifling (*a small token*). **5** insignificant; unimportant (*a small matter*). **6** consisting of small particles (*small gravel*). **7** doing something on a small scale (*a small farmer*). **8** socially undistinguished. **9** petty; paltry (*a small spiteful nature*). **10** young; not fully developed (*a small child*). • *n.* the slenderest part of something (esp. **small of the back**). • *adv.* into small pieces (*chop it small*). □ **in a small way** unambitiously; on a small scale. **no small** considerable (*no small excitement*). **small potatoes** an insignificant person or thing. **small wonder** not very surprising. □□ **small·ish** *adj.* **small·ness** *n.*

small arms *n.pl.* portable firearms, esp. rifles, pistols, light machine guns, etc.

small-claims court *n.* a local court in which claims for small amounts can be heard and decided quickly without legal representation.

small fry *n.pl.* **1** young children or the young of various species. **2** small or insignificant things or people.

small in·tes·tine *n.* the duodenum, jejunum, and ileum collectively.

small-mind·ed /smáwlmíndid/ *adj.* petty; of rigid opinions or narrow outlook. □□ **small-mind·ed·ly** *adv.* **small-mind·ed·ness** *n.*

small·pox /smáwlpoks/ *n. hist.* an acute contagious viral disease, with fever and pustules, usu. leaving permanent scars.

small print *n.* **1** printed matter in small type. **2** inconspicuous and usu. unfavorable limitations, etc., in a contract.

small-scale *adj.* made or occurring in small amounts or to a lesser degree.

small talk *n.* light social conversation.

small-time *adj. colloq.* unimportant or petty.

smart /smaart/ *adj., v., n., & adv.* • *adj.* **1 a** clever; ingenious; quickwitted (*a smart answer*). **b** keen in bargaining. **c** (of transactions, etc.) unscrupulous to the point of dishonesty. **2** well-groomed; bright and fresh in appearance (*a smart suit*). **3** in good repair; showing bright colors, etc. (*a smart red bicycle*). **4** stylish; fashionable; prominent in society (*the smart set*). **5** brisk (*set a smart pace*). **6** painfully severe; sharp; vigorous (*a smart blow*). • *v.intr.* **1** feel or give acute pain or distress (*my eye smarts*). **2** (of an insult, grievance, etc.) rankle. **3** (foll. by *for*) suffer the consequences of (*you will smart for this*). • *n.* a bodily or mental sharp pain; a stinging sensation. *adv.* smartly; in a smart manner. □□ **smart·ing·ly** *adv.* **smart·ly** *adv.* **smart·ness** *n.*

smart al·eck /álik/ *n.* (also **alec**) *colloq.* a person displaying ostentatious or smug cleverness. □□ **smart-al·eck·y** *adj.*

smart-ass *n. sl.* = SMART ALECK.

smart bomb *n.* a bomb that can be guided directly to its target by use of radio waves, television, or lasers.

smart·en /smaárt'n/ *v.tr. & intr.* (usu. foll. by *up*) make or become smart.

smart·y /smaártee/ *n.* (*pl.* **-ies**) *colloq.* a know-it-all; a smart aleck.

smart·y-pants *n.* = SMARTY.

smash /smash/ *v., n., & adv.* • *v.* **1** *tr. & intr.* (often foll. by *up*) **a** break into pieces. **b** bring or come to sudden or complete destruction, defeat, or disaster. **2** *tr.* (foll. by *into*, *through*) move with great force and impact. **3** *tr. & intr.* (foll. by *in*) break in with a crushing blow (*smashed in the window*). **4** *tr.* (in tennis, squash, etc.) hit (a ball, etc.) with great force, esp. downward. **5** *tr.* (as **smashed** *adj.*) *sl.* intoxicated. • *n.* **1** the act of smashing; a violent fall, collision, or disaster. **2** the sound of this. **3** (in full **smash hit**) a very successful play, song, performer, etc. **4** a stroke in tennis, squash, etc., in which the ball is hit, esp. downward with great force. **5** a violent blow with a fist, etc. • *adv.* with a smash (*fell smash on the floor*).

smash·ing /smáshing/ *adj. colloq.* excellent; wonderful. □□ **smash·ing·ly** *adv.*

smash·up /smáshəp/ *n. colloq.* a violent collision, esp. of motor vehicles.

smat·ter /smátər/ *n.* (also **smat·ter·ing**) a slight superficial knowledge.

smear /smeer/ *v. & n.* • *v.tr.* **1** daub or mark with a greasy or sticky substance or with something that stains. **2** blot; smudge (writing, artwork, etc.). **3** defame the character of; slander publicly. • *n.* **1** the act or an instance of smearing. **2** *Med.* **a** material smeared on a microscopic slide, etc., for examination. **b** a specimen of this. □□ **smear·er** *n.* **smear·y** *adj.*

smeg·ma /smégmə/ *n.* a sebaceous secretion in the folds of the skin, esp. of the foreskin. □□ **smegmatic** /–mátik/ *adj.*

smell /smel/ *n. & v.* • *n.* **1** the faculty of perceiving odors or scents (*has a fine sense of smell*). **2** the quality in substances that is perceived by this (*the smell of thyme*). **3** an unpleasant odor. **4** the act of inhaling to ascertain smell. • *v.* (*past* and *past part.* **smelled** or **smelt** /smelt/) **1** *tr.* perceive the smell of; examine by smell. **2** *intr.* emit odor. **3** *intr.* seem by smell to be (*smells sour*). **4** *intr.* (foll. by *of*) **a** be redolent of (*smells of fish*). **b** be suggestive of (*smells of dishonesty*). **5** *intr.* stink; be rank. **6** *tr.* perceive as if by smell; detect (*smell a bargain*; *smell blood*). **7** *intr.* have or use a sense of smell. **8** *intr.* (foll. by *about*) sniff or search about. **9** *intr.* (foll. by *at*) inhale the smell of. □ **smell out** detect by smell; find out by investigation. **smell a rat** begin to suspect trickery, etc. □□ **smell·a·ble** *adj.* **smell·er** *n.* **smell-less** *adj.*

smell·ing salts *n.pl.* ammonium carbonate mixed with scent to be sniffed as a restorative in faintness, etc.

smell·y /smélee/ *adj.* (**smellier, smelliest**) having a strong smell. □□ **smell·i·ness** *n.*

smelt[1] /smelt/ *v.tr.* **1** separate metal from (ore) by melting. **2** extract or refine (metal) in this way. ◻◻ **smelt·er** *n.* **smelt·er·y** *n.* (*pl.* **-ies**).

smelt[2] *past* and *past part.* of SMELL.

smelt[3] /smelt/ *n.* (*pl.* same or **smelts**) any small green and silver fish of the genus *Osmerus*, etc., allied to salmon and used as food.

smid·gen /smíjən/ *n.* (also **smid·gin**) *colloq.* a small bit or amount.

smile /smīl/ *v.* & *n.* •*v.* **1** *intr.* relax the features into a pleased or kind or gently skeptical expression, usu. with the corners of the mouth turned up. **2** *tr.* express by smiling (*smiled their consent*). **3** *tr.* give (a smile) of a specified kind (*smiled a sardonic smile*). **4** *intr.* (foll. by *on, upon*) adopt a favorable attitude toward (*fortune smiled on me*). **5** *intr.* (foll. by *at*) **a** show indifference to (*smiled at my feeble attempts*). **b** favor; smile on. •*n.* **1** the act of smiling. **2** a smiling expression. ◻◻ **smil·er** *n.* **smil·ey** *adj.* **smil·ing·ly** *adv.*

smirch /smərch/ *v.* & *n.* •*v.tr.* mark, soil, or smear (a thing, a person's reputation, etc.). •*n.* **1** a spot or stain. **2** a blot (on one's character, etc.).

smirk /smərk/ *n.* & *v.* •*n.* an affected, conceited, or silly smile. •*v.intr.* put on or wear a smirk. ◻◻ **smirk·er** *n.* **smirk·ing·ly** *adv.* **smirk·y** *adj.*

smit /smit/ *archaic past part.* of SMITE.

smite /smīt/ *v.tr.* (*past* **smote** /smōt/; *past part.* **smitten** /smít'n/) *archaic* or *literary* **1** strike or hit. **2** chastise; defeat. **3** (in *passive*) **a** have a sudden strong effect on (*smitten by his conscience*). **b** infatuate; fascinate (*smitten by her beauty*). ◻◻ **smit·er** *n.*

smith /smith/ *n.* & *v.* •*n.* **1** (esp. in *comb.*) a worker in metal (*goldsmith*). **2** a blacksmith. **3** a craftsman (*wordsmith*). •*v.tr.* make or treat by forging.

smith·er·eens /smíthəréenz/ *n.pl.* (also **smith·ers** /smíthərz/) small fragments.

smith·er·y /smíthəree/ *n.* (*pl.* **-ies**) **1** a smith's work. **2** (esp. in naval dockyards) a smithy.

smith·y /smíthee/ *n.* (*pl.* **-ies**) a blacksmith's workshop; a forge.

smit·ten *past part.* of SMITE.

smock /smok/ *n.* & *v.* •*n.* **1** a loose shirtlike garment with the upper part closely gathered in smocking. **2** a loose overall. •*v.tr.* adorn with smocking.

smock·ing /smóking/ *n.* an ornamental effect on cloth made by gathering the material tightly into pleats, often with stitches in a decorative pattern.

smog /smog, smawg/ *n.* fog intensified by smoke. ◻◻ **smog·gy** *adj.* (**smoggier, smoggiest**).

smoke /smōk/ *n.* & *v.* •*n.* **1** a visible suspension of carbon, etc., in air, emitted from a burning substance. **2** an act or period of smoking tobacco. **3** *colloq.* a cigarette or cigar (*got a smoke?*). •*v.* **1** *intr.* **a** emit smoke or visible vapor. **b** (of a lamp, etc.) burn badly with the emission of smoke. **c** (of a chimney or fire) discharge smoke into the room. **2 a** *intr.* inhale and exhale the smoke of a cigarette. **b** *intr.* do this habitually. **c** *tr.* use (a cigarette, etc.) in this way. **3** *tr.* darken or preserve by the action of smoke (*smoked salmon*). ◻ **go up in smoke** *colloq.* **1** be destroyed by fire. **2** (of a plan, etc.) come to nothing. **smoke out 1** drive out by means of smoke. **2** drive out of hiding or secrecy, etc. ◻◻ **smok·a·ble** *adj.* (also **smoke·a·ble**).

smoke·less /smṓklis/ *adj.* having or producing little or no smoke.

smok·er /smṓkər/ *n.* **1** a person or thing that smokes, esp. a person who habitually smokes tobacco. **2** a compartment on a train, in which smoking is allowed. **3** an informal social gathering of men.

smoke screen *n.* **1** a cloud of smoke diffused to conceal (esp. military) operations. **2** a device or ruse for disguising one's activities.

smoke·stack /smṓkstak/ *n.* **1** a chimney or funnel for discharging the smoke of a locomotive or steamer. **2** a tall chimney.

smok·ing /smṓking/ *n.* & *adj.* •*n.* the act of inhaling and exhaling from a cigarette, cigar, etc. •*adj.* giving off smoke.

smok·y /smṓkee/ *adj.* (also **smokey**) (**smokier, smokiest**) **1** emitting, veiled or filled with, or obscured by, smoke (*smoky fire; smoky room*). **2** stained with or colored like smoke (*smoky glass*). **3** having the taste or flavor of smoked food (*smoky bacon*). ◻◻ **smok·i·ly** *adv.* **smok·i·ness** *n.*

smol·der /smṓldər/ *v.* & *n.* •*v.intr.* **1** burn slowly with smoke but without a flame. **2** (of emotions, etc.) exist in a suppressed or concealed state. **3** (of a person) show silent anger, hatred, etc. •*n.* a smoldering or slow-burning fire.

smooch /smōōch/ *n.* & *v. colloq.* •*n.* a spell of kissing and caressing. •*v.intr.* engage in a smooch. ◻◻ **smooch·er** *n.* **smooch·y** *adj.* (**smoochier, smoochiest**).

smooth /smōōth/ *adj., v., n.,* & *adv.* •*adj.* **1** having a relatively even and regular surface; free from perceptible projections, lumps, indentations, and roughness. **2** not wrinkled, pitted, scored, or hairy. **3** that can be traversed without check. **4** (of liquids) of even consistency; without lumps. **5** (of the sea, etc.) without waves or undulations. **6** (of a journey, progress, etc.) untroubled by difficulties or adverse conditions. **7** having an easy flow or correct rhythm (*smooth breathing*). **8 a** not harsh in sound or taste. **b** (of wine, etc.) not astringent. **9** (of a person, his or her manner, etc.) suave, conciliatory, flattering (*a smooth talker*). **10** (of movement, etc.) not suddenly varying; not jerky. •*v.* **1** *tr.* & *intr.* (often foll. by *out, down*) make or become smooth. **2** (often foll. by *out, over*) **a** *tr.* reduce or get rid of (differences, faults, difficulties, etc.) in fact or appearance. **b** *intr.* (of difficulties, etc.) diminish. **3** *tr.* modify (a graph, curve, etc.) so as to lessen irregularities. **4** *tr.* free from impediments or discomfort (*smooth the way*). •*n.* **1** a smoothing touch or stroke. **2** the easy part of life (*take the rough with the smooth*). •*adv.* smoothly (*true love never did run smooth*). ◻◻ **smooth·a·ble** *adj.* **smooth·er** *n.* **smooth·ish** *adj.* **smooth·ly** *adv.* **smooth·ness** *n.*

smooth·ie /smōōthee/ *n. colloq.* a person who is smooth (see SMOOTH *adj.* 9).

smooth talk *n. colloq.* bland specious language. ◻◻ **smooth-talk** *v.tr.*

smooth-tongued *adj.* insincerely flattering.

smor·gas·bord /smáwrgəsbawrd/ *n.* a buffet offering a variety of hot and cold meats, salads, hors d'oeuvres, etc.

smor·zan·do /smawrtsaándō/ *adj., adv.,* & *n. Mus.* •*adj.* & *adv.* dying away. •*n.* (*pl.* **-dos** or **smorzandi** /–dee/) a smorzando passage.

smote *past* of SMITE.

smoth·er /smúthər/ *v.* & *n.* •*v.* **1** *tr.* suffocate; stifle. **2** *tr.* (foll. by *with*) overwhelm with (kisses, kindness, etc.). **3** *tr.* (foll. by *in, with*) cover entirely in or with (*smothered in mayonnaise*). **4** *tr.* extinguish or deaden (a fire or flame) by covering it. **5** *intr.* **a** die of suffocation. **b** have difficulty breathing. **6** *tr.* (often foll. by *up*) keep from notice or publicity. **7** *tr.* defeat rapidly or utterly. •*n.* **1** a cloud of dust or smoke. **2** obscurity caused by this.

smudge[1] /smuj/ *n.* & *v.* •*n.* **1** a blurred or smeared line or mark. **2** a stain or blot on a person's character, etc. •*v.* **1** *tr.* make a smudge on. **2** *intr.* become smeared or blurred (*smudges easily*). **3** *tr.* smear or blur the lines of (writing, etc.) (*smudge the outline*). **4** *tr.* defile, sully, stain, or disgrace (a person's name, etc.).

smudge[2] /smuj/ *n.* an outdoor fire with dense smoke made to keep off insects, protect plants against frost, etc.

smudg·y /smújee/ *adj.* (**smudgier, smudgiest**) **1** smudged. **2** likely to produce smudges. ▫▫ **smudg·i·ly** *adv.* **smudg·i·ness** *n.*

smug /smug/ *adj.* (**smugger, smuggest**) self-satisfied. ▫▫ **smug·ly** *adv.* **smug·ness** *n.*

smug·gle /smúgəl/ *v.tr.* **1** (also *absol.*) import or export (goods) illegally, esp. without payment of customs duties. **2** (foll. by *in, out*) convey secretly. **3** (foll. by *away*) put into concealment. ▫▫ **smug·gler** *n.* **smug·gling** *n.*

smut /smut/ *n. & v.* • *n.* **1** a small flake of soot, etc. **2** a spot or smudge made by this. **3** obscene or lascivious talk, pictures, or stories. **4** a fungal disease of cereals. • *v.* (**smutted, smutting**) **1** *tr.* mark with smuts. **2** *tr.* infect (a plant) with smut. **3** *intr.* (of a plant) contract smut. ▫▫ **smut·ty** *adj.* (**smuttier, smuttiest**) (esp. in sense 3 of *n.*). **smut·ti·ly** *adv.* **smut·ti·ness** *n.*

Sn *symb. Chem.* the element tin.

snack /snak/ *n. & v.* • *n.* **1** a light, casual, or hurried meal. **2** a small amount of food eaten between meals. • *v.intr.* eat a snack.

snack bar *n.* a place where snacks are sold.

snaf·fle /snáfəl/ *n. & v.* • *n.* (in full **snaffle bit**) a simple bridle bit without a curb. • *v.tr.* put a snaffle on.

sna·fu /snafóo/ *adj. & n. sl.* • *adj.* in utter confusion or chaos. • *n.* this state.

snag /snag/ *n. & v.* • *n.* **1** an unexpected or hidden obstacle or drawback. **2** a jagged or projecting point or broken stump. **3** a tear in material, etc. • *v.tr.* (**snagged, snagging**) **1** catch or tear on a snag. **2** clear (land, a waterway, a tree trunk, etc.) of snags. ▫▫ **snagged** *adj.* **snag·gy** *adj.*

snail /snayl/ *n.* any slow-moving gastropod mollusk with a spiral shell. ▫▫ **snail·like** *adj.*

snake /snayk/ *n. & v.* • *n.* **1 a** any long, limbless reptile of the suborder Ophidia, including boas, pythons, cobras, and vipers. **b** a limbless lizard or amphibian. **2** (also **snake in the grass**) a treacherous person or secret enemy. • *v.intr.* move or twist like a snake. ▫▫ **snake·like** *adj.*

snake charm·er *n.* a person appearing to make snakes move by music, etc.

snake oil *n.* any of various concoctions sold as medicine but without medicinal value.

snake pit *n.* **1** a pit containing snakes. **2** a scene of vicious behavior. **3** a mental hospital in which inhumane treatment is known or suspect.

snak·y /snáykee/ *adj.* **1** of or like a snake. **2** winding; sinuous. **3** showing coldness, ingratitude, venom, or guile. ▫▫ **snak·i·ly** *adv.* **snak·i·ness** *n.*

snap /snap/ *v., n., adv., & adj.* • *v.* (**snapped, snapping**) **1** *intr. & tr.* break suddenly or with a snap. **2** *intr. & tr.* emit or cause to emit a sudden sharp sound or crack. **3** *intr. & tr.* open or close with a snapping sound (*snapped shut*). **4 a** *intr.* (often foll. by *at*) speak irritably or spitefully (*did not mean to snap at you*). **b** *tr.* say irritably or spitefully. **5** *intr.* (often foll. by *at*) (esp. of a dog, etc.) make a sudden audible bite. **6** *tr. & intr.* move quickly (*snap into action*). **7** *tr.* take a snapshot of. **8** *tr. Football* put (the ball) into play on the ground by a quick backward movement. • *n.* **1** an act or sound of snapping. **2** a crisp cookie (*gingersnap*). **3** a snapshot. **4** (in full **cold snap**) a sudden brief spell of cold weather. **5** crispness of style; zest; dash; spring. **6** *sl.* an easy task (*it was a snap*). **7** (also **snap fas·ten·er**) *n.* a two-piece device that snaps together, used esp. on garments, etc. (e.g., instead of buttons). **8** *Football* the beginning of a play, when the ball is passed quickly back. • *adv.* with the sound of a snap (*heard it go snap*). • *adj.* done or taken on the spur of the moment (*snap decision*). ▫ **snap one's fingers 1** make an audible fillip, esp. in rhythm to music, etc. **2** (often foll. by *at*) defy; show contempt for. **snap off** break off or bite off. **snap out** say irritably. **snap out of** *sl.* get rid of (a mood, habit, etc.) by a sudden effort. **snap up 1** accept (an offer) quickly or eagerly. **2** pick up or catch hastily or smartly.

snap·drag·on /snápdragən/ *n.* a plant of the genus *Antirrhinum*, esp. *Antirrhinum majus*, with a bag-shaped flower like a dragon's mouth.

snap·per /snápər/ *n.* **1** a person or thing that snaps. **2** any of several fish of the family Lutjanidae, used as food.

snap·ping tur·tle *n.* any large American freshwater turtle of the family Chelydridae which seizes prey with a snap of its jaws.

snap·pish /snápish/ *adj.* **1** (of a person's manner) curt; ill-tempered. **2** (of a dog, etc.) inclined to snap. ▫▫ **snap·pish·ly** *adv.* **snap·pish·ness** *n.*

snap·py /snápee/ *adj.* (**snappier, snappiest**) *colloq.* **1** brisk; full of zest. **2** neat and elegant (*a snappy dresser*). **3** snappish. ▫ **make it snappy** be quick about it. ▫▫ **snap·pi·ly** *adv.* **snap·pi·ness** *n.*

snap·shot /snápshot/ *n.* a casual photograph taken with a hand-held camera.

snare /snair/ *n. & v.* • *n.* **1** a trap for catching birds or animals, esp. with a noose of wire or cord. **2** a thing that acts as a temptation. **3** a device for tempting an enemy, etc., to expose himself or herself to danger, failure, loss, capture, defeat, etc. **4** (in *sing.* or *pl.*) *Mus.* twisted strings of gut, hide, or wire stretched across the lower head of a snare drum to produce a rattling sound. **5** (in full **snare drum**) a small, double-headed drum fitted with snares, usu. played in a jazz or military band. • *v.tr.* **1** catch in a snare. **2** trap with a snare. ▫▫ **snar·er** *n.* (also in *comb.*).

snarl[1] /snaarl/ *v. & n.* • *v.* **1** *intr.* (of a dog) make an angry growl with bared teeth. **2** *intr.* (of a person) speak cynically; make bad-tempered complaints. **3** *tr.* (often foll. by *out*) **a** utter in a snarling tone. **b** express (discontent, etc.) by snarling. • *n.* the act or sound of snarling. ▫▫ **snarl·er** *n.* **snarl·ing·ly** *adv.* **snarl·y** *adj.* (**snarlier, snarliest**).

snarl[2] /snaarl/ *v. & n.* • *v.* **1** *tr.* (often foll. by *up*) twist; entangle; confuse and hamper the movement of (traffic, etc.). **2** *intr.* (often foll. by *up*) become entangled, congested, or confused. • *n.* a knot or tangle.

snatch /snach/ *v. & n.* • *v.tr.* **1** seize quickly, eagerly, or unexpectedly. **2** steal (a wallet, etc.). **3** secure with difficulty (*snatched an hour's rest*). **4** (foll. by *away, from*) take away or from, esp. suddenly (*snatched away my hand*). **5** (foll. by *from*) rescue narrowly. **6** (foll. by *at*) **a** try to seize by stretching or grasping suddenly. **b** take (an offer, etc.) eagerly. • *n.* **1** an act of snatching (*made a snatch at it*). **2** a fragment of a song or talk, etc. **3** *sl.* a kidnapping. ▫ **in** (or **by**) **snatches** in fits and starts. ▫▫ **snatch·er** *n.* (esp. in sense 3 of *n.*). **snatch·y** *adj.*

snaz·zy /snázee/ *adj.* (**snazzier, snazziest**) *sl.* smart or attractive, esp. in an ostentatious way. ▫▫ **snaz·zi·ly** *adv.* **snaz·zi·ness** *n.*

sneak /sneek/ *v., n., & adj.* • *v.* (**sneaked** or **snuck, sneak·ing**) **1** *intr. & tr.* (foll. by *in, out, past, away,* etc.) go or convey furtively; slink. **2** *tr. sl.* steal unobserved. **3** *intr.* (as **sneaking** *adj.*) **a** furtive; undisclosed (*a sneaking affection for him*). **b** persistent in one's mind (*a sneaking feeling*). • *n.* a mean-spirited, cowardly, underhanded person. • *adj.* acting or done without warning; secret. ▫▫ **sneak·ing·ly** *adv.*

sneak·er /snéekər/ *n.* each of a pair of rubber-soled canvas, etc., shoes.

sneak·y /snéekee/ *adj.* (**sneakier, sneakiest**) given to or characterized by sneaking; furtive; underhanded. □□ **sneak·i·ly** *adv.* **sneak·i·ness** *n.*

sneer /sneer/ *n. & v.* • *n.* a derisive smile or remark. • *v.* **1** *intr.* (often foll. by *at*) smile derisively. **2** *tr.* say sneeringly. **3** *intr.* (often foll. by *at*) speak derisively. □□ **sneer·er** *n.* **sneer·ing·ly** *adv.*

sneeze /sneez/ *n. & v.* • *n.* **1** a sudden involuntary expulsion of air from the nose and mouth caused by irritation of the nostrils. **2** the sound of this. • *v.intr.* make a sneeze. □ **not to be sneezed at** *colloq.* not contemptible; considerable. □□ **sneez·er** *n.* **sneez·y** *adj.*

snick·er /sníkər/ *v. & n.* • *v.intr.* **1** = SNIGGER *v.* **2** whinny; neigh. • *n.* **1** = SNIGGER *n.* **2** a whinny, a neigh.

snide /snīd/ *adj. & n.* • *adj.* **1** sneering; slyly derogatory. **2** counterfeit. **3** underhanded. • *n.* a snide person or remark. □□ **snide·ly** *adv.* **snide·ness** *n.*

sniff /snif/ *v. & n.* • *v.* **1** *intr.* draw up air audibly through the nose. **2** *tr.* (often foll. by *up*) draw in through the nose. **3** *tr.* draw in the scent of (food, flowers, etc.) through the nose. • *n.* **1** an act or sound of sniffing. **2** the amount of air, etc., sniffed up. □ **sniff at 1** try the smell of. **2** show contempt for. **sniff out** detect; discover by investigation. □□ **sniff·ing·ly** *adv.*

sniff·er /snífər/ *n.* **1** a person who sniffs, esp. one who sniffs a drug or toxic substances (often in *comb.*: *glue-sniffer*). **2** *sl.* the nose. **3** *colloq.* any device for detecting gas, radiation, etc.

snif·fle /snífəl/ *v. & n.* • *v.intr.* sniff slightly or repeatedly. • *n.* **1** the act of sniffling. **2** (in *sing.* or *pl.*) a cold in the head causing a running nose and sniffling. □□ **snif·fler** *n.*

snif·fy /snífee/ *adj. colloq.* (**sniffier, sniffiest**) **1** inclined to sniff. **2** disdainful. □□ **sniff·i·ly** *adv.* **sniff·i·ness** *n.*

snif·ter /sníftər/ *n.* **1** *sl.* a small drink of alcohol. **2** a balloon glass for brandy.

snifter

snig·ger /snígər/ *n. & v.* • *n.* a half-suppressed secretive laugh. • *v.intr.* utter such a laugh. □□ **snig·ger·er** *n.* **snig·ger·ing·ly** *adv.*

snip /snip/ *v. & n.* • *v.tr.* (**snipped, snipping**) (also *absol.*) cut with scissors or shears, esp. in small, quick strokes. • *n.* **1** an act of snipping. **2** a piece of material, etc., snipped off. **3** *sl.* something easily achieved. **4** (in *pl.*) hand shears for metal cutting. □□ **snip·ping** *n.*

snipe /snīp/ *n. & v.* • *n.* (*pl.* same or **snipes**) any of various wading birds frequenting marshes, with a long, straight bill. • *v.* **1** *intr.* fire shots from hiding, usu. at long range. **2** *intr.* (foll. by *at*) make a sly critical attack. □□ **snip·er** *n.*

snip·pet /snípit/ *n.* **1** a small piece cut off. **2** (usu. in *pl.*; often foll. by *of*) **a** a scrap or fragment of information, knowledge, etc. **b** a short extract from a book, etc. □□ **snip·pet·y** *adj.*

snip·py /snípee/ *adj.* (**snippier, snippiest**) *colloq.* faultfinding; snappish; sharp. □□ **snip·pi·ly** *adv.* **snip·pi·ness** *n.*

snit /snit/ *n.* a rage; a sulk (esp. *in a snit*).

snitch /snich/ *v. & n. sl.* • *v.* **1** *tr.* steal. **2** *intr.* (often foll. by *on*) inform on a person. • *n.* an informer.

sniv·el /snívəl/ *v. & n.* • *v.intr.* **1** weep with sniffling. **2** run at the nose. **3** show tearful sentiment. • *n.* **1** running mucus. **2** hypocritical talk. □□ **sniv·el·er** *n.* **sniv·el·ing** *adj.* **sniv·el·ing·ly** *adv.*

snob /snob/ *n.* **1** a person with an exaggerated respect for social position or wealth and who despises socially inferior connections. **2** a person who behaves with servility to social superiors. **3** a person who despises others whose (usu. specified) tastes or attainments are considered inferior (*an intellectual snob*). □□ **snob·ber·y** *n.* (*pl.* **-ies**). **snob·bish** *adj.* **snob·bish·ly** *adv.* **snob·bish·ness** *n.* **snob·by** *adj.* (**snobbier, snobbiest**).

snood /sno͝od/ *n.* **1** an ornamental hairnet usu. worn at the back of the head. **2** a ring of woolen, etc., material worn as a hood. **3** a short line attaching a hook to a main line in sea fishing.

snook /sno͝ok, sno͞ok/ *n. sl.* a contemptuous gesture with the thumb to the nose and the fingers spread out.

snook·er /sno͝okər, sno͞ok-/ *n. & v.* • *n.* **1** a game similar to pool in which the players use a cue ball (white) to pocket the other balls (15 red and 6 balls of other colors) in a set order. **2** a position in this game in which a direct shot at a permitted ball is impossible. • *v.tr.* **1** (also *refl.*) subject (oneself or another player) to a snooker. **2** (esp. as **snookered** *adj.*) *sl.* defeat; thwart.

snoop /sno͞op/ *v. & n. colloq.* • *v.intr.* **1** pry into matters one need not be concerned with. **2** (often foll. by *about, around*) investigate in order to find out about transgressions of the law, etc. • *n.* **1** an act of snooping. **2** a person who snoops; a detective. □□ **snoop·er** *n.* **snoop·y** *adj.*

snoot /sno͞ot/ *n. sl.* the nose.

snoot·y /sno͞otee/ *adj.* (**snootier, snootiest**) *colloq.* supercilious; conceited. □□ **snoot·i·ly** *adv.* **snoot·i·ness** *n.*

snooze /sno͞oz/ *n. & v. colloq.* • *n.* a short sleep, esp. in the daytime. • *v.intr.* take a snooze. □□ **snooz·er** *n.* **snooz·y** *adj.* (**snooz·i·er, snooz·i·est**).

snore /snawr/ *n. & v.* • *n.* a snorting or grunting sound in breathing during sleep. • *v.intr.* make this sound. □□ **snor·er** *n.* **snor·ing·ly** *adv.*

snor·kel /snáwrkəl/ *n. & v.* • *n.* **1** a breathing tube for an underwater swimmer. **2** a device for supplying air to a submerged submarine. • *v.intr.* use a snorkel. □□ **snor·kel·er** *n.*

snort /snawrt/ *n. & v.* • *n.* **1** an explosive sound made by the sudden forcing of breath through the nose, esp. expressing indignation or incredulity. **2** a similar sound made by an engine, etc. **3** *colloq.* a small drink of liquor. **4** *sl.* an inhaled dose of a (usu. illegal) powdered drug. • *v.* **1** *intr.* make a snort. **2** *tr.* (also *absol.*) *sl.* inhale (esp. cocaine or heroin).

snot /snot/ *n. sl.* **1** nasal mucus. **2** a term of contempt for a person.

snot·ty /snótee/ *adj.* (**snottier, snottiest**) *sl.* **1** running or foul with nasal mucus. **2** contemptible. **3** supercilious; conceited. □□ **snot·ti·ly** *adv.* **snot·ti·ness** *n.*

snout /snowt/ *n.* **1** the projecting nose and mouth of an animal. **2** *derog.* a person's nose. **3** the pointed front of a thing; a nozzle. □□ **snout·ed** *adj.* (also in *comb.*). **snout·y** *adj.*

snow /snō/ *n. & v.* • *n.* **1** atmospheric vapor frozen into ice crystals and falling to earth in light white flakes. **2** a fall of this, or a layer of it on the ground. **3** a thing resembling snow in whiteness or texture, etc. **4** a mass of flickering white spots on a television or radar screen, caused by interference or a poor signal. **5** *sl.* cocaine. • *v.* **1** *intr.* (prec. by *it* as subject) snow falls (*it is snowing*). **2** *tr.* (foll. by *in, over, up,* etc.) block with large quantities of snow. **3** *tr. & intr.* sprinkle or scatter or fall as or like snow. **4** *intr.* come in large numbers or quantities. □ **be snowed under** be overwhelmed, esp. with work. □□ **snow·less** *adj.* **snow·like** *adj.*

snow·ball /snṓbawl/ *n. & v.* • *n.* **1** snow pressed together into a ball, esp. for throwing in play. **2** anything that grows or increases rapidly like a snowball rolled on snow. • *v.* **1** *intr. & tr.* throw or pelt with snowballs. **2** *intr.* increase rapidly.

snow·bird /snṓbərd/ *n.* **1** a bird, such as the junco, commonly seen in snowy regions. **2** *colloq.* a person who moves from a cold climate to a warmer climate during the winter.

snow·blink /snṓblingk/ *n.* the reflection in the sky of snow or ice fields.

snow·board /snṓbawrd/ *n.* a flat board similar to a wide ski, ridden over snow in an upright or surfing position. □□ **snow·board·er** *n.*

snow·bound /snṓbownd/ *adj.* prevented by snow from going out or traveling.

snow·cap /snṓkap/ *n.* **1** the tip of a mountain when covered with snow. **2** a white-crowned hummingbird, *Microchera albocoronata*, native to Central America. □□ **snow·capped** *adj.*

snow·drift /snṓdrift/ *n.* a bank of snow heaped up by the action of the wind.

snow·drop /snṓdrop/ *n.* a bulbous plant, *Galanthus nivalis*, with white drooping flowers in the early spring.

snow·fall /snṓfawl/ *n.* **1** a fall of snow. **2** *Meteorol.* the amount of snow that falls on one occasion or on a given area within a given time.

snow·field /snṓfeeld/ *n.* a permanent wide expanse of snow in mountainous or polar regions.

snow·flake /snṓflayk/ *n.* each of the small collections of crystals in which snow falls.

snow job *n. sl.* an attempt at flattery or deception.

snow leop·ard *n.* = OUNCE[2].

snow·man /snṓman/ *n.* (*pl.* **-men**) a figure resembling a man, made of compressed snow.

snow·mo·bile /snṓməbeel, -mō-/ *n.* a motor vehicle, esp. with runners or revolving treads, for traveling over snow.

snow·plow /snṓplow/ *n.* a device, or a vehicle equipped with one, for clearing roads of thick snow.

snow·shoe /snṓshōō/ *n.* a flat device like a racket attached to a boot for walking on snow without sinking in.

snowshoes

snow·storm /snṓstawrm/ *n.* a heavy fall of snow, esp. with a high wind.

snow-white *adj.* pure white.

snow·y /snṓee/ *adj.* (**snowier, snowiest**) **1** of or like snow. **2** (of the weather, etc.) with much snow.

snow·y owl *n.* a large white owl, *Nyctea scandiaca*, native to the Arctic.

snub /snub/ *v., n., & adj.* • *v.tr.* (**snubbed, snubbing**) rebuff or humiliate with sharp words or a marked lack of cordiality. • *n.* an act of snubbing; a rebuff. • *adj.* short and blunt in shape.

snuff[1] /snuf/ *n. & v.* • *n.* the charred part of a candlewick. • *v.tr.* trim the snuff from (a candle). □ **snuff out** **1** extinguish by snuffing. **2** kill; put an end to.

snuff[2] /snuf/ *n. & v.* • *n.* powdered tobacco or medicine taken by sniffing it up the nostrils. • *v.intr.* take snuff. □ **snuff-colored** dark yellowish-brown. **up to snuff** *colloq.* up to standard.

snuff·box /snúfboks/ *n.* a small usu. ornamental box for holding snuff.

snuff·er /snúfər/ *n.* **1** a small hollow cone with a handle used to extinguish a candle. **2** (in *pl.*) an implement like scissors used to extinguish a candle or trim its wick.

snuff·y[1] /snúfee/ *adj.* (**snuffier, snuffiest**) **1** annoyed. **2** irritable. **3** supercilious or contemptuous.

snuff·y[2] /snúfee/ *adj.* like snuff in color or substance.

snug /snug/ *adj.* (**snugger, snuggest**) **1 a** cozy, comfortable; sheltered; well enclosed or placed or arranged. **b** cozily protected from the weather or cold. **c** close-fitting. **2** (of an income, etc.) allowing comfort and comparative ease. □□ **snug·ly** *adv.* **snug·ness** *n.*

snug·gle /snúgəl/ *v.intr. & tr.* (usu. foll. by *down, up, together*) settle or draw into a warm comfortable position.

So. *abbr.* South.

so[1] /sō/ *adv. & conj.* • *adv.* **1** to such an extent, or to the extent implied (*why are you so angry?*; *they were so pleased that they gave us a bonus*). **2** (with *neg.*) to the extent to which ... is or does, etc., or to the extent implied (*was not so late as I expected*; *am not so eager as you*). **3** (foll. by *that* or *as* + clause) to the degree or in the manner implied (*so expensive that few can afford it*; *so small as to be invisible*). **4** (adding emphasis) to that extent (*I want to leave and so does she*). **5** to a great degree (*I am so glad*). **6** (with verbs of state) in the way described (*am not very fond of it but may become so*). **7** (with verb of saying or thinking, etc.) as previously mentioned or described (*I think so*; *so he said*). • *conj.* **1** with the result that (*there was none left, so we had to go without*). **2** in order that (*came home early so that I could see you*). **3** and then; as the next step (*so then the car broke down*). **4 a** (introducing a question) then; after that (*so what did you tell them?*). **b** (*absol.*) = *so what?* □ **and so on** (or **forth**) **1** and others of the same kind. **2** and in other similar ways. **so as** (foll. by *to* + infin.) in order to (*did it so as to get it finished*). **so be it** an expression of acceptance or resignation. **so far** see FAR. **so far as** see FAR. **so far so good** see FAR. **so long!** *colloq.* good-bye until we meet again. **so long as** see LONG[1]. **so much 1** a certain amount (of). **2** a great deal of (*so much nonsense*). **3** (with *neg.*) **a** less than; to a lesser extent (*not so much forgotten as ignored*). **b** not even (*didn't give me so much as a penny*). **so much for** that is all that need be done or said about. **so to say** (or **speak**) an expression of reserve or apology for an exaggeration, etc. **so what?** *colloq.* why should that be considered significant?

so[2] var. of SOL.

soak /sōk/ *v. & n.* • *v.* **1** *tr. & intr.* make or become thoroughly wet through saturation with or in liquid. **2** *tr.* (of rain, etc.) drench. **3** *tr.* (foll. by *in, up*) **a** absorb (liquid). **b** acquire (knowledge, etc.) copiously. **4** *refl.* steep (oneself) in a subject of study, etc. **5** *intr.* (foll. by *into, through*) (of liquid) make its way or penetrate by saturation. **6** *tr. colloq.* extract money from by an extortionate charge, taxation, etc. (*soak the rich*). **7** *intr. colloq.* drink persistently; booze. **8** *tr.* (as **soaked** *adj.*) very drunk. • *n.* **1** the act of soaking or the state of being soaked. **2** a drinking bout. **3** *colloq.* a hard drinker. □□ **soak·age** *n.* **soak·ing** *n. & adj.*

so-and-so /sṓəndsō/ *n.* (*pl.* **so-and-sos**) **1** a particular person or thing not needing to be specified (*told me to do so-and-so*). **2** *colloq.* a person disliked or regarded with disfavor (*the so-and-so left me behind*).

soap /sōp/ *n. & v.* • *n.* **1** a cleansing agent which when rubbed in water yields a lather used in washing. **2** *colloq.* = SOAP OPERA. • *v.tr.* **1** apply soap to. **2** scrub with soap.

soap·box /sṓpboks/ *n.* **1** a box for holding soap. **2** a makeshift stand for a public speaker.

soap op·er·a *n.* a broadcast drama, usu. serialized in many episodes, dealing with sentimental or melodramatic domestic themes (so called because orig. sponsored in the US by soap and detergent manufacturers).

soap·stone /sṓpstōn/ *n.* a soft, easily carved rock consisting largely of talc. Also called **steatite**.

soap·y /sṓpee/ *adj.* (**soapier, soapiest**) **1** of or like soap. **2** containing or smeared with soap. **3** (of a person or manner) unctuous or flattering.

soar /sawr/ *v.intr.* **1** fly or rise high. **2** reach a high level or standard (*prices soared*). **3** maintain height in the air without flapping the wings or using power. ▫▫ **soar·ing·ly** *adv.*

S.O.B. *abbr. sl.* (also **SOB**) = SON OF A BITCH.

sob /sob/ *v. & n.* • *v.* (**sobbed, sobbing**) **1** *intr.* draw breath in convulsive gasps usu. with weeping under mental distress or physical exhaustion. **2** *tr.* (usu. foll. by *out*) utter with sobs. **3** *tr.* bring (oneself) to a specified state by sobbing (*sobbed themselves to sleep*). • *n.* a convulsive drawing of breath, esp. in weeping. ▫▫ **sob·bing·ly** *adv.*

so·ber /sṓbər/ *adj. & v.* • *adj.* (**soberer, soberest**) **1** not affected by alcohol. **2** not given to excessive drinking of alcohol. **3** moderate; well-balanced; tranquil; sedate. **4** not fanciful or exaggerated (*the sober truth*). **5** (of a color, etc.) quiet and inconspicuous. • *v.tr. & intr.* (often foll. by *down, up*) make or become sober or less wild, reckless, enthusiastic, visionary, etc. (*a sobering thought*). ▫ **as sober as a judge** completely sober. ▫▫ **so·ber·ly** *adv.*

so·bri·e·ty /səbrī́-itee/ *n.* the state of being sober.

so·bri·quet /sṓbrikay, -ket/ *n.* (also **sou·bri·quet** /sṓō-/) **1** a nickname. **2** an assumed name.

sob sto·ry *n.* a story or explanation appealing mainly to the emotions.

Soc. *abbr.* **1** Socialist. **2** Society.

so-called *adj.* commonly known as, often incorrectly.

soc·cer /sókər/ *n.* a game played by two teams of eleven players with a round ball that cannot be touched with the hands during play except by the goalkeepers.

so·cia·ble /sṓshəbəl/ *adj.* **1** fitted for or liking the society of other people; ready and willing to talk and act with others. **2** (of a person's manner or behavior, etc.) friendly. **3** (of a meeting, etc.) not stiff or formal. ▫▫ **so·cia·bil·i·ty** /-bílitee/ *n.* **so·cia·bly** *adv.*

so·cial /sṓshəl/ *adj. & n.* • *adj.* **1** of or relating to society or its organization. **2** concerned with the mutual relations of human beings or of classes of human beings. **3** living in organized communities; unfitted for a solitary life (*a human is a social animal*). **4 a** needing companionship; gregarious; interdependent. **b** cooperative; practicing the division of labor. **5 a** (of insects) living together in organized communities. **b** (of birds) nesting near each other in communities. • *n.* a social gathering. ▫▫ **so·ci·al·i·ty** /sṓsheeálitee/ *n.* **so·cial·ly** *adv.*

so·cial climb·er *n. derog.* a person anxious to gain a higher social status.

so·cial con·tract *n.* (also **so·cial com·pact**) an agreement to cooperate for social benefits, e.g., by sacrificing some individual freedom for government protection.

so·cial dis·ease *n.* a venereal disease.

so·cial·ism /sṓshəlizəm/ *n.* **1** a political and economic theory which advocates that the community as a whole should own and control the means of production, distribution, and exchange. **2** policy based on this theory. ▫▫ **so·cial·ist** *n. & adj.* **so·cial·is·tic** *adj.*

so·cial·ite /sṓshəlīt/ *n.* a person prominent in fashionable society.

so·cial·ize /sṓshəlīz/ *v.* **1** *intr.* act in a sociable manner. **2** *tr.* make social. **3** *tr.* organize on socialistic principles. ▫▫ **so·cial·i·za·tion** *n.*

so·cial sci·ence *n.* **1** the scientific study of human society and social relationships. **2** a branch of this (e.g., politics or economics). ▫▫ **so·cial sci·en·tist** *n.*

so·cial se·cu·ri·ty *n.* (usu. **So·cial Se·cu·ri·ty**) a US government program of assistance to the elderly, disabled, etc., funded by mandatory contributions from employers and employees.

so·cial serv·ic·es *n.pl.* services provided by the government for the community, esp. education, health, and housing.

so·cial work *n.* work of benefit to those in need of help or welfare, esp. done by specially trained personnel. ▫▫ **so·cial work·er** *n.*

so·ci·e·ty /səsī́ətee/ *n.* (*pl.* **-ties**) **1** the sum of human conditions and activity regarded as a whole functioning interdependently. **2** a social community (*all societies must have firm laws*). **3 a** a social mode of life. **b** the customs and organization of an ordered community. **4** *Ecol.* a plant community. **5 a** the socially advantaged or prominent members of a community (*society would not approve*). **b** this, or a part of it, qualified in some way (*is not done in polite society*). **6** participation in hospitality; other people's homes or company (*avoids society*). **7** companionship; company (*avoids the society of such people*). **8** an association of persons united by a common aim or interest (*a music society*). ▫▫ **so·ci·e·tal** *adj.* (esp. in sense 1).

So·ci·e·ty of Friends *n.* see QUAKER.

So·ci·e·ty of Je·sus *n.* see JESUIT.

socio- /sṓseeō, sṓsheeō/ *comb.form* **1** of society (and). **2** of or relating to sociology (and).

so·ci·o·cul·tur·al /sṓseeōkúlchərəl, sṓsheeō-/ *adj.* combining social and cultural factors. ▫▫ **so·ci·o·cul·tur·al·ly** *adv.*

so·ci·o·ec·o·nom·ic /sṓseeōékənómik, -éekə-, sṓsheeō-/ *adj.* relating to the interaction of social and economic factors. ▫▫ **so·ci·o·ec·o·nom·i·cal·ly** *adv.*

so·ci·o·lin·guis·tic /sṓseeōlinggwístik, sṓsheeō-/ *adj.* relating to or concerned with language in its social aspects. ▫▫ **so·ci·o·lin·guist** *n.* **so·ci·o·lin·guis·ti·cal·ly** *adv.*

so·ci·o·lin·guis·tics /sṓseeōlinggwístiks, sṓsheeō-/ *n.* the study of language in relation to social factors.

so·ci·ol·o·gy /sṓseeóləjee, sṓshee-/ *n.* **1** the study of the development, structure, and functioning of human society. **2** the study of social problems. ▫▫ **so·ci·o·log·i·cal** /-əlójikəl/ *adj.* **so·ci·o·log·i·cal·ly** *adv.* **so·ci·ol·o·gist** *n.*

so·ci·o·path /sṓseeopáth, sṓshee-/ *n. Psychol.* a person who is asocial or antisocial and who lacks a social conscience, as a psychopath. ▫▫ **so·ci·o·path·ic** *adj.*

sock[1] /sok/ *n.* (*pl.* **socks** or *colloq.* **sox** /soks/) a short knitted covering for the foot. ▫ **put a sock in it** *sl.* be quiet.

sock[2] /sok/ *v. & n. colloq.* • *v.tr.* hit forcefully. • *n.* a hard blow. ▫ **sock it to** attack or address (a person) vigorously.

sock·et /sókit/ *n.* **1** a natural or artificial hollow for something to fit into or stand firm or revolve in. **2** *Electr.* a device receiving a plug, lightbulb, etc., to make a connection.

So·crat·ic /səkrátik, sō-/ *adj.* of or relating to the Greek philosopher Socrates (d. 399 BC) or his philosophy, esp. the method associated with him of seeking the truth by a series of questions and answers.

So·crat·ic i·ro·ny *n.* a pose of ignorance assumed in order to entice others into making statements that can then be challenged.

sod /sod/ *n.* **1** turf or a piece of turf. **2** the surface of the ground. ▫ **under the sod** in the grave.

so·da /sṓdə/ *n.* **1** any of various compounds of sodium in common use, e.g., washing soda, baking soda. **2** (in full **soda water**) water made effervescent by impregnation with carbon dioxide under pressure. **3** (also **so·da pop**) a sweet effervescent soft drink.

so·da foun·tain *n.* **1** a device supplying soda. **2** a store or counter equipped with this. **3** a store or counter for preparing and serving sodas and ice cream.

sod·den /sódən/ *adj.* **1** saturated; soaked through. **2** rendered stupid or dull, etc., with drunkenness. ▫▫ **sod·den·ly** *adv.*

so·di·um /sṓdeeəm/ *n. Chem.* a soft silver-white reactive metallic element, occurring naturally in soda, salt, etc., that is important in industry and is an essential element in living organisms. ▫▫ **so·dic** *adj.*

so·di·um bi·car·bon·ate *n.* a white soluble powder used in the manufacture of fire extinguishers and effervescent drinks.

so·di·um chlo·ride *n.* a colorless crystalline compound occurring naturally in sea water and halite; common salt.

so·di·um hy·drox·ide *n.* a deliquescent compound which is strongly alkaline.

Sod·om /sódəm/ *n.* a wicked or depraved place (from Gen. 18-19).

sod·om·ite /sódəmīt/ *n.* a person who practices sodomy.

sod·om·y /sódəmee/ *n.* sexual intercourse involving anal or oral copulation. ▫▫ **sod·om·ize** *v.tr.*

so·ev·er /sō-évər/ *adv. literary* of any kind; to any extent (*how great soever it may be*).

-soever /sō-évər/ *comb. form* (added to relative pronouns, adverbs, and adjectives) of any kind; to any extent (*whatsoever*; *howsoever*).

so·fa /sṓfə/ *n.* a long upholstered seat with a back and arms.

so·fa bed *n.* a sofa that can be converted into a temporary bed.

sof·fit /sófit/ *n.* the underside of an architrave, arch, balcony, etc.

soft /sawft, soft/ *adj.* & *adv.* • *adj.* **1** (of a substance, material, etc.) lacking hardness or firmness; yielding to pressure; easily cut. **2** (of cloth, etc.) having a smooth surface or texture; not rough or coarse. **3** (of air, etc.) mellow; mild; balmy; not noticeably cold or hot. **4** (of water) free from mineral salts and therefore good for lathering. **5** (of a light or color, etc.) not brilliant or glaring. **6** (of a voice or sounds) gentle and pleasing. **7** *Phonet.* **a** (of a consonant) sibilant or palatal (as *c* in *ice*, *g* in *age*). **b** voiced or unaspirated. **8** (of an outline, etc.) not sharply defined. **9** (of an action or manner, etc.) gentle; conciliatory; complimentary; amorous. **10** (of the heart or feelings, etc.) compassionate; sympathetic. **11** (of a person) **a** feeble; lenient; silly; sentimental. **b** weak; not robust. **12** *colloq.* (of a job, etc.) easy. **13** (of drugs) mild; not likely to cause addiction. **14** (of radiation) having little penetrating power. **15** (also **soft-core**) (of pornography) suggestive or erotic but not explicit. **16** *Stock Exch.* (of currency, prices, etc.) likely to fall in value. **17** *Polit.* moderate; willing to compromise (*the soft left*). • *adv.* softly (*play soft*). ▫ **be soft on** *colloq.* **1** be lenient toward. **2** be infatuated with. **have a soft spot for** be fond of or affectionate toward (a person). ▫▫ **soft·ish** *adj.* **soft·ness** *n.*

soft·ball /sáwftbawl, sóft-/ *n.* **1** a ball like a baseball but larger. **2** a modified form of baseball using this.

soft-boiled *adj.* (of an egg) lightly boiled with the yolk soft or liquid.

soft·cov·er /sáwftcəvər/ *adj.* & *n.* • *adj.* (of a book) bound in flexible covers; paperback. • *n.* a softcover book.

soft drink *n.* a nonalcoholic drink, esp. a carbonated one.

soft·en /sáwfən, sófən/ *v.* **1** *tr.* & *intr.* make or become soft or softer. **2** *tr.* **a** reduce the strength of (defenses) by preliminary attack. **b** reduce the resistance of (a person). ▫▫ **soft·en·er** *n.*

soft-head·ed *adj.* feebleminded. ▫▫ **soft-head·ed·ness** *n.*

soft·heart·ed /sáwft-haartid, sóft-/ *adj.* tender; compassionate. ▫▫ **soft·heart·ed·ness** *n.*

soft·ie var. of SOFTY.

soft·ly /sáwftlee, sóft-/ *adv.* in a soft, gentle, or quiet manner. ▫ **softly softly** (of an approach or strategy) cautious; discreet and cunning.

soft pal·ate *n.* the rear part of the palate.

soft ped·al *n.* & *v.* • *n.* a pedal on a piano that makes the tone softer. • (**soft-ped·al**) *v.tr.* downplay.

soft sell *n.* restrained or subtly persuasive salesmanship. ▫▫ **soft-sell** *v.tr.* (*past* and *past part.* **-sold**)

soft soap *n.* **1** a semifluid soap. **2** *colloq.* persuasive flattery. ▫▫ **soft-soap** *v.tr.*

soft-spo·ken *adj.* speaking with a gentle voice.

soft touch *n. colloq.* a gullible person, esp. over money.

soft·ware /sáwftwair, sóft-/ *n.* the programs and other operating information used by a computer.

soft·y /sáwftee, sóftee/ *n.* (also **soft·ie**; *pl.* **-ies**) *colloq.* a weak or softhearted person.

sog·gy /sógee/ *adj.* (**soggier**, **soggiest**) sodden; saturated; dank. ▫▫ **sog·gi·ly** *adv.* **sog·gi·ness** *n.*

soil[1] /soyl/ *n.* **1** the upper layer of earth in which plants grow. **2** ground belonging to a nation; territory. ▫▫ **soil·less** *adj.*

soil[2] /soyl/ *v.* & *n.* • *v.tr.* **1** make dirty; smear or stain (*soiled linen*). **2** tarnish; defile; bring discredit to (*would not soil my hands with it*). • *n.* **1** a dirty mark. **2** filth; refuse.

soi·rée /swaaráy/ *n.* an evening party for conversation or music.

so·journ /sójərn/ *n.* & *v.* • *n.* a temporary stay. • *v.intr.* stay temporarily. ▫▫ **so·journ·er** *n.*

soke /sōk/ *n. Brit. hist.* **1** a right of local jurisdiction. **2** a district under a particular jurisdiction.

Sol /sol/ *n.* (in Roman mythology) the sun, esp. as a personification.

sol /sōl/ *n.* (also **so** /sō/) *Mus.* **1** (in tonic sol-fa) the fifth note of a major scale. **2** the note G in the fixed do system.

sol·ace /sóləs/ *n.* & *v.* • *n.* comfort in distress, disappointment, or tedium. • *v.tr.* give solace to.

so·lar /sṓlər/ *adj.* of, relating to, or reckoned by the sun (*solar eclipse*; *solar time*).

solar bat·ter·y *n.* a battery composed of solar cells.

so·lar cell *n.* a device converting solar radiation into electricity.

so·lar·i·um /səláireeəm/ *n.* (*pl.* **solaria** /-reeə/) a room equipped with sunlamps or fitted with extensive areas of glass for exposure to the sun.

so·lar·ize /sṓlərīz/ *v.intr.* & *tr. Photog.* undergo or cause to undergo change in the relative darkness of parts of an image by long exposure. ▫▫ **so·lar·i·za·tion** *n.*

so·lar pan·el *n.* a panel designed to absorb the sun's rays as a source of energy for operating electricity or heating.

so·lar plex·us *n.* a complex of nerves at the pit of the stomach.

so·lar sys·tem *n.* the sun and the celestial bodies whose motion it governs.

sold *past* and *past part.* of SELL.

sol·der /sódər/ *n.* & *v.* • *n.* a fusible alloy used to join less fusible metals or wires, etc. • *v.tr.* join with solder. ▫▫ **sol·der·a·ble** *n.*

sol·dier /sṓljər/ *n.* & *v.* • *n.* **1** a person serving in an army. **2** (in full **common soldier**) an enlisted person in an army. **3** a military commander of specified ability (*a great soldier*). •*v.intr.* serve as a soldier (*was off soldiering*). ▫ **soldier on** *colloq.* persevere doggedly. ▫▫ **sol·dier·ly** *adj.*

sol·dier of for·tune *n.* a mercenary.

sole[1] /sōl/ *n.* & *v.* •*n.* **1** the undersurface of the foot. **2** the part of a shoe, sock, etc., corresponding to this (esp. excluding the heel). **3** the lower surface or base of a plow, golf club head, etc. •*v.tr.* provide (a shoe, etc.) with a sole. ▫▫ **-soled** *adj.* (in *comb.*).

sole[2] /sōl/ *n.* any flatfish of the family Soleidae, esp. *Solea solea*, used as food.

sole[3] /sōl/ *adj.* (*attrib.*) one and only; single; exclusive (*the sole reason*; *has the sole right*). ▫▫ **sole·ly** *adv.*

sol·e·cism /sólisizəm/ *n.* **1** a mistake of grammar or idiom. **2** a piece of bad manners or incorrect behavior.

sol·emn /sóləm/ *adj.* **1** serious and dignified (*a solemn occasion*). **2** formal; accompanied by ceremony (*a solemn oath*). **3** mysteriously impressive. **4** serious or cheerless in manner (*looks rather solemn*). **5** full of importance; weighty (*a solemn warning*). **6** grave; sober; deliberate (*a solemn promise*). ▫▫ **sol·emn·ly** *adv.*

so·lem·ni·ty /səlémnitee/ *n.* (*pl.* **-ties**) **1** the state of being solemn; a solemn character or feeling; solemn behavior. **2** a rite or celebration; a piece of ceremony.

sol·em·nize /sóləmnīz/ *v.tr.* **1** duly perform (a ceremony, esp. of marriage). **2** celebrate (a festival, etc.). **3** make solemn. ▫▫ **sol·em·ni·za·tion** *n.*

so·le·noid /sṓlənoyd, sól-/ *n.* a cylindrical coil of wire acting as a magnet when carrying electric current. ▫▫ **so·le·noi·dal** /-nóyd'l/ *adj.*

sol-fa /sṓlfaa/ *n.* = SOLMIZATION (cf. TONIC SOL-FA).

sol·feg·gio /solféjeeō/ *n.* (*pl.* **solfeggi** /–jee/) (also **solfège**) *Mus.* **1** an exercise in singing using sol-fa syllables. **2** solmization.

so·li *pl.* of SOLO.

so·lic·it /səlísit/ *v.* (**solicited, soliciting**) **1** *tr.* & (foll. by *for*) *intr.* ask repeatedly or earnestly for (business, etc.). **2** *tr.* make a request to (a person). **3** *tr.* accost (a person) and offer one's services as a prostitute. ▫▫ **so·lic·i·ta·tion** *n.*

so·lic·i·tor /səlísitər/ *n.* **1** a person who solicits. **2** a canvasser. **3** the chief law officer of a city, county, etc.

so·lic·i·tous /səlísitəs/ *adj.* **1** showing interest or concern. **2** (foll. by *to* + infin.) eager; anxious. ▫▫ **so·lic·i·tous·ly** *adv.*

so·lic·i·tude /səlísitōōd, -tyōōd/ *n.* **1** the state of being solicitous; solicitous behavior. **2** anxiety or concern.

sol·id /sólid/ *adj.* & *n.* •*adj.* (**solider, solidest**) **1** firm and stable in shape; not liquid or fluid (*solid food*; *water becomes solid at 32°F*). **2** of one material throughout, not hollow (*a solid sphere*). **3** of the same substance throughout (*solid silver*). **4** of strong material or construction or build; not flimsy or slender, etc. **5 a** having three dimensions. **b** concerned with solids (*solid geometry*). **6 a** sound and reliable (*solid arguments*). **b** dependable (*a solid Republican*). **7** sound but without any special flair (*a solid piece of work*). **8** financially sound. **9** (of time) uninterrupted (*spend four solid hours on it*). **10 a** unanimous; undivided (*support has been pretty solid so far*). **b** (foll. by *for*) united in favor of. •*n.* **1** a solid substance or body. **2** (in *pl.*) solid food. **3** *Geom.* a body or magnitude having three dimensions. ▫▫ **sol·id·ly** *adv.* **sol·id·ness** *n.*

sol·i·dar·i·ty /sólidáritee/ *n.* **1** unity of feeling or action. **2** mutual dependence.

sol·i·di *pl.* of SOLIDUS.

so·lid·i·fy /səlídifī/ *v.tr.* & *intr.* (**-fies, -fied**) make or become solid. ▫▫ **so·lid·i·fi·ca·tion** /-fikáyshən/ *n.*

so·lid·i·ty /səlíditee/ *n.* the state of being solid; firmness.

sol·id-state *adj.* using the electronic properties of solids (e.g., a semiconductor) to replace those of vacuum tubes, etc.

sol·i·dus /sólidəs/ *n.* (*pl.* **solidi** /-dī/) an oblique stroke (/) used in writing fractions ($^3/_4$), to separate other figures and letters, or to denote alternatives (*and/or*) and ratios (*miles/day*).

so·lil·o·quy /səlíləkwee/ *n.* (*pl.* **-quies**) **1** the act of talking when alone or regardless of any hearers, esp. in drama. **2** part of a play involving this. ▫▫ **so·lil·o·quize** *v.intr.*

sol·ip·sism /sólipsizəm/ *n. Philos.* the view that the self is all that exists or can be known. ▫▫ **sol·ip·sist** *n.* **sol·ip·sis·tic** *adj.*

sol·i·taire /sólitáir/ *n.* **1** a diamond or other gem set by itself. **2** a ring having a single gem. **3** any of several card games for one player.

sol·i·tar·y /sóliteree/ *adj.* & *n.* •*adj.* **1** living alone; not gregarious; lonely (*a solitary existence*). **2** (of a place) secluded. **3** single or sole (*a solitary instance*). **4** (of an insect) not living in communities. **5** *Bot.* growing singly; not in a cluster. •*n.* (*pl.* **-ies**) **1** a recluse or anchorite. **2** *colloq.* = SOLITARY CONFINEMENT. ▫▫ **sol·i·tar·i·ly** *adv.* **sol·i·tar·i·ness** *n.*

sol·i·tude /sólitōōd, -tyōōd/ *n.* **1** the state of being solitary. **2** a lonely place.

sol·mi·za·tion /sólmizáyshən/ *n. Mus.* a system of associating each note of a scale with a particular syllable, now usu. *do re mi fa sol la ti*, with do as C in the fixed-do system and as the keynote in the tonic sol-fa system.

so·lo /sṓlō/ *n.*, *v.*, & *adv.* •*n.* (*pl.* **-los**) **1** (*pl.* **-los** or **soli** /-lee/) **a** a vocal or instrumental piece or passage, or a dance, performed by one person with or without accompaniment. **b** (*attrib.*) performed or performing as a solo (*solo passage*; *solo violin*). **2 a** an unaccompanied flight by a pilot in an aircraft. **b** anything done by one person unaccompanied. **c** (*attrib.*) unaccompanied. **3** (in full **solo whist**) a card game like whist in which one player may oppose the others. •*v.* (**-loes, -loed**) **1** *intr.* perform a solo. **2** *tr.* perform or achieve as a solo. •*adv.* unaccompanied; alone (*flew solo for the first time*).

so·lo·ist /sṓlōist/ *n.* a performer of a solo, esp. in music.

sol·stice /sólstis, sṓl-, sáwl-/ *n.* either of the two times in the year, the summer solstice and the winter solstice, when the sun reaches its highest or lowest point in the sky at noon, marked by the longest and shortest days. ▫▫ **sol·sti·tial** /-stíshəl/ *adj.*

sol·u·ble /sólyəbəl/ *adj.* **1** that can be dissolved, esp. in water. **2** that can be solved. ▫▫ **sol·u·bil·i·ty** /-bílitee/ *n.*

sol·ute /sólyōōt, sṓlōōt/ *n.* a dissolved substance.

so·lu·tion /səlōōshən/ *n.* **1** the act or a means of solving a problem or difficulty. **2 a** the conversion of a solid or gas into a liquid by mixture with a liquid. **b** the state resulting from this (*held in solution*). **3** the act of dissolving or the state of being dissolved. **4** the act of separating or breaking.

solv·ate /sólvayt/ *v.intr.* & *tr.* enter or cause to enter combination with a solvent. ▫▫ **sol·va·tion** /–váyshən/ *n.*

solve /solv/ *v.tr.* find an answer to, or an action or course that removes or effectively deals with (a problem or difficulty). ▫▫ **solv·a·ble** *adj.* **solv·er** *n.*

sol·vent /sólvənt/ *adj.* & *n.* •*adj.* **1** able to dissolve or form a solution with something. **2** having enough money to meet one's liabilities. •*n.* a solvent liquid, etc. ▫▫ **sol·ven·cy** *n.* (in sense 2).

So·ma·li /sōmaálee, sə-/ *n.* & *adj.* •*n.* **1** (*pl.* same or **Somalis**) a member of a Hamitic Muslim people of Somalia in NE Africa. **2** the language of this people. •*adj.* of or relating to this people or language. ▫▫ **So·ma·li·an** *adj.*

so•mat•ic /sōmátik, sə-/ *adj.* of or relating to the body, esp. as distinct from the mind. ▫▫ **so•mat•i•cal•ly** *adv.*

somato- /sōmátō–, sṓmətō–/ *comb. form* the human body.

so•mat•o•gen•ic /sōmátōjénik, sṓmə–/ *adj.* originating in the body.

so•ma•tol•o•gy /sṓmətóləjee/ *n.* the study of the physical characteristics of living bodies.

so•mat•o•tro•phin /sōmátətrṓfin, sṓmə–/ (also **so•mat•o•tro•pin**) *n.* a growth hormone secreted by the pituitary gland.

som•ber /sómbər/ *adj.* (also **som•bre**) **1** dark; gloomy. **2** oppressively solemn or sober. **3** dismal, foreboding (*a somber prospect*). ▫▫ **som•ber•ly** *adv.* **som•ber•ness** *n.*

som•bre•ro /sombráirō/ *n.* (*pl.* **-ros**) a broad-brimmed hat worn esp. in Mexico and the southwest US.

some /sum/ *adj., pron., & adv.* • *adj.* **1** an unspecified amount or number of (*some water; some apples*). **2** that is unknown or unnamed (*will return some day; to some extent*). **3** denoting an approximate number (*waited some twenty minutes*). **4** a considerable amount or number of (*went to some trouble*). **5** (usu. stressed) **a** at least a small amount of (*do have some consideration*). **b** such to a certain extent (*that is some help*). **c** *colloq.* notably such (*I call that some story*). • *pron.* some people or things; some number or amount (*I have some already; would you like some more?*). • *adv. colloq.* to some extent (*we talked some; do it some more*).

-some[1] /səm/ *suffix* forming adjectives meaning: **1** adapted to; productive of (*cuddlesome; fearsome*). **2** characterized by being (*fulsome; lithesome*). **3** apt to (*tiresome; meddlesome*).

-some[2] /səm/ *suffix* forming nouns from numerals, meaning 'a group of (so many)' (*foursome*).

-some[3] /sōm/ *comb. form* denoting a portion of a body, esp. of a cell (*chromosome; ribosome*).

some•bod•y /súmbodee, -budee, -bədee/ *pron. & n.* • *pron.* some person. • *n.* (*pl.* **-ies**) a person of importance (*is really somebody now*).

some•day /súmday/ *adv.* at some time in the future.

some•how /súmhow/ *adv.* **1** for some reason or other (*somehow I never liked them*). **2** in some unspecified or unknown way (*he somehow dropped behind*). **3** no matter how (*must get it finished somehow*).

some•one /súmwun/ *n. & pron.* = SOMEBODY.

some•place /súmplays/ *adv. colloq.* = SOMEWHERE.

som•er•sault /súmərsawlt/ *n. & v.* (also **sum•mer•sault**) • *n.* an acrobatic movement in which a person turns head over heels in the air or on the ground and lands on the feet. • *v.intr.* perform a somersault.

some•thing /súmthing/ *n. & pron.* **1 a** some unspecified or unknown thing (*have something to tell you; something has happened*). **b** (in full **something or other**) as a substitute for an unknown or forgotten description (*a student of something or other*). **2** a known or understood but unexpressed quantity, quality, or extent (*there is something about it I do not like; is something of a fool*). **3** *colloq.* an important or notable person or thing (*the party was quite something*). ▫ **or something** or some unspecified alternative possibility (*must have run away or something*). **see something of** encounter (a person) occasionally. **something else 1** something different. **2** *colloq.* something exceptional. **something like 1** an amount in the region of (*something like a million dollars*). **2** somewhat like (*shaped something like a cigar*). **3** *colloq.* impressive; a fine specimen of. **something of** to some extent; in some sense (*he was something of an expert*).

some•time /súmtīm/ *adv. & adj.* • *adv.* **1** at some unspecified time. **2** formerly. • *attrib.adj.* former (*the sometime mayor*).

some•times /súmtīmz/ *adv.* at some times; occasionally.

some•what /súmhwut, -hwot, -hwət, -wut, -wot, -wət/ *adv.* to some extent (*behavior that was somewhat strange; answered somewhat hastily*).

some•when /súmhwen, -wen/ *adv. colloq.* at some time.

some•where /súmhwair, -wair/ *adv. & pron.* • *adv.* in or to some place. • *pron.* some unspecified place. ▫ **get somewhere** *colloq.* achieve success. **somewhere about** approximately.

som•nam•bu•lism /somnámbyəlizəm/ *n.* **1** sleepwalking. **2** a condition of the brain inducing this. ▫▫ **som•nam•bu•lant** *adj.* **som•nam•bu•list** *n.* **som•nam•bu•lis•tic** *adj.* **som•nam•bu•lis•ti•cal•ly** *adv.*

som•no•lent /sómnələnt/ *adj.* **1** sleepy; drowsy. **2** inducing drowsiness. ▫▫ **som•no•lence** *n.* **som•no•lent•ly** *adv.*

son /sun/ *n.* **1** a boy or man in relation to either or both of his parents. **2 a** a male descendant. **b** (foll. by *of*) a male member of a family, nation, etc. **3** a person regarded as inheriting an occupation, quality, etc., or associated with a particular attribute (*sons of freedom; sons of the soil*). **4** (in full **my son**) a form of address, esp. to a boy. **5** (**the Son**) (in Christian belief) the second person of the Trinity. ▫▫ **son•ship** *n.*

so•nar /sṓnaar/ *n.* **1** a system for the underwater detection of objects by reflected sound. **2** an apparatus for this.

so•na•ta /sənaátə/ *n.* a composition for one instrument or two usu. in several movements.

son•a•ti•na /sónəteénə/ *n.* a simple or short sonata.

song /sawng, song/ *n.* **1** a short poem or other set of words set to music or meant to be sung. **2** singing or vocal music (*burst into song*). **3** a musical composition suggestive of a song. **4** the musical cry of some birds. ▫ **for a song** *colloq.* very cheaply.

song and dance *n. colloq.* a fuss or commotion.

song•bird /sáwngbərd, sóng-/ *n.* a bird with a musical call.

song•smith /sáwngsmith, sóng–/ *n.* a writer of songs.

song•ster /sáwngstər, sóng-/ *n.* (*fem.* **songstress** /-stris/) **1** a singer. **2** a songbird. **3** a poet.

song•writ•er /sáwng-rītər, sóng-/ *n.* a writer of songs or the music for them.

son•ic /sónik/ *adj.* of or relating to or using sound or sound waves. ▫▫ **son•i•cal•ly** *adv.*

son•ic bar•ri•er *n.* = SOUND BARRIER.

son•ic boom *n.* a loud explosive noise caused by the shock wave from an aircraft when it passes the speed of sound.

son-in-law *n.* (*pl.* **sons-in-law**) the husband of one's daughter.

son•net /sónit/ *n.* a poem of 14 lines using any of a number of formal rhyme schemes, in English usu. having ten syllables per line.

son•ny /súnee/ *n. colloq.* a familiar form of address to a young boy.

son of a bitch *n. coarse sl.* a general term of contempt.

son of a gun *n. colloq.* a jocular or affectionate form of address or reference.

son•o•gram /sónəgram/ *n. Med.* an image of internal organs or structures produced by ultrasound waves, used for diagnostic purposes.

so•no•rous /sónərəs, sənáwrəs/ *adj.* **1** having a loud, full, or deep sound. **2** (of a speech, style, etc.) grand. ▫▫ **so•nor•i•ty** /sənáwritee/ *n.* **so•no•rous•ly** *adv.*

sook /sŏŏk/ *n. Austral.* & *NZ sl.* **1** *derog.* a timid bashful person; a coward or sissy. **2** a hand-reared calf.

soon /sōōn/ *adv.* **1** after no long interval of time (*shall* *soon know the result*). **2** relatively early (*must you go so soon?*). **3** (prec. by *how*) early (*how soon will it be ready?*). **4** readily or willingly (in expressing choice or preference: *which would you sooner do?*; *would as soon stay behind*). □ **as** (or **so**) **soon as** at the moment that; not later than; as early as (*came as soon as I heard about it*; *disappears as soon as it's time to pay*). **no sooner . . . than** at the very moment that (*we no sooner arrived than the rain stopped*). **sooner or later** at some future time. □□ **soon·ish** *adv.*

soot /sŏŏt/ *n.* & *v.* • *n.* a black substance rising in fine flakes in smoke and deposited on the sides of a chimney, etc. • *v.tr.* cover with soot.

sooth /sōōth/ *n. archaic* truth; fact. □ **in sooth** really; truly.

soothe /sōōth/ *v.tr.* **1** calm (a person or feelings). **2** soften or mitigate (pain). □□ **sooth·er** *n.* **sooth·ing** *adj.* **sooth·ing·ly** *adv.*

sooth·say·er /sōōthsayər/ *n.* a diviner or seer.

soot·y /sŏŏtee/ *adj.* (**sootier, sootiest**) **1** covered with soot. **2** black or brownish black.

sop /sop/ *n.* & *v.* • *n.* **1** a piece of bread, etc., dipped in gravy, etc. **2** a thing done to pacify or bribe. • *v.* (**sopped, sopping**) **1** *intr.* be drenched (*came home sopping*). **2** *tr.* (foll. by *up*) absorb (liquid) in a towel, etc. **3** *tr.* wet thoroughly.

soph. /sof/ *abbr.* sophomore.

soph·ism /sófizəm/ *n.* a false argument, esp. one intended to deceive.

soph·ist /sófist/ *n.* one who reasons with clever but fallacious arguments. □□ **so·phis·tic** /-fístik/ *adj.* **so·phis·ti·cal** *adj.*

so·phis·ti·cate *v., adj.,* & *n.* • *v.* /səfístikayt/ **1** *tr.* make (a person, etc.) educated, cultured, or refined. **2** *tr.* make (equipment or techniques, etc.) highly developed or complex. **3** *tr.* deprive (a person or thing) of its natural simplicity. • *adj.* /səfístikət/ sophisticated. • *n.* /səfístikət/ a sophisticated person. □□ **so·phis·ti·ca·tion** /-káyshən/ *n.*

so·phis·ti·cat·ed /səfístikaytid/ *adj.* **1** (of a person) educated and refined. **2** (of a thing, idea, etc.) highly developed and complex. □□ **so·phis·ti·cat·ed·ly** *adv.*

soph·ist·ry /sófistree/ *n.* (*pl.* **-ries**) **1** the use of sophisms. **2** a sophism.

soph·o·more /sófəmawr, sófmawr/ *n.* a second-year college or high school student.

soph·o·mor·ic /sofəmáwrik, -mór-/ *adj.* **1** of or relating to a sophomore. **2** overconfident and pretentious but immature and lacking judgment.

sop·o·rif·ic /sópərífik/ *adj.* & *n.* • *adj.* tending to produce sleep. • *n.* a soporific drug or influence. □□ **sop·o·rif·i·cal·ly** *adv.*

sop·ping /sóping/ *adj.* (also **sop·ping wet**) soaked with liquid; wet through.

sop·py /sópee/ *adj.* (**soppier, soppiest**) **1** *colloq.* **a** silly or foolish in a feeble or self-indulgent way. **b** mawkishly sentimental. **2** soaked with water. □□ **sop·pi·ly** *adv.* **sop·pi·ness** *n.*

so·pra·ni·no /sóprənéenō/ *n.* (*pl.* **-nos**) *Mus.* an instrument higher than soprano, esp. a recorder or saxophone.

so·pran·o /səpránō, -praá-/ *n.* & *adj.* • *n.* (*pl.* **-os** or **soprani** /-nee/) **1 a** the highest singing voice. **b** a female or boy singer with this voice. **c** a part written for it. **2** an instrument of a high or the highest pitch in its family. • *adj.* of or relating to such a voice, part, or instrument.

sor·bet /sawrbáy, sáwrbit/ *n.* **1** a frozen confection of water, sugar, and usu. fruit flavoring. **2** = SHERBET 1.

sor·cer·er /sáwrsərər/ *n.* (*fem.* **sorceress** /-ris/) a magician or wizard. □□ **sor·cer·ous** *adj.* **sor·cer·y** *n.* (*pl.* **-ies**).

sor·did /sáwrdid/ *adj.* **1** dirty or squalid. **2** ignoble; mercenary. **3** avaricious or niggardly. □□ **sor·did·ly** *adv.* **sor·did·ness** *n.*

sor·di·no /sawrdéenō/ *n.* (*pl.* **sordini** /-nee/) *Mus.* a mute for a bowed or wind instrument.

sore /sawr/ *adj., n.,* & *adv.* • *adj.* **1** (of a part of the body) painful from injury, disease, etc. (*a sore arm*). **2** suffering pain. **3** angry or vexed. **4** *archaic* grievous or severe (*in sore need*). • *n.* **1** a sore place on the body. **2** a source of distress (*reopen old sores*). • *adv. archaic* grievously; severely. □□ **sore·ness** *n.*

sore·head /sáwrhed/ *n.* a touchy or disgruntled person.

sore·ly /sáwrlee/ *adv.* **1** extremely; badly (*am sorely tempted*; *sorely in need of repair*). **2** severely (*am sorely vexed*).

sore point *n.* a subject causing distress or annoyance.

sor·ghum /sáwrgəm/ *n.* any tropical cereal grass of the genus *Sorghum*.

so·ror·i·ty /səráwritee, -rór-/ *n.* (*pl.* **-ties**) a female students' society in a university or college, usu. for social purposes.

so·ro·sis /sərṓsis/ *n.* (*pl.* **soroses** /-seez/) *Bot.* a fleshy compound fruit, e.g., a pineapple or mulberry.

sor·rel[1] /sáwrəl, sór-/ *n.* any acid leaved herb of the genus *Rumex*, used in salads and for flavoring.

sor·rel[2] /sáwrəl, sór-/ *adj.* & *n.* • *adj.* of a light reddish-brown color. • *n.* **1** this color. **2** a sorrel animal, esp. a horse.

sor·row /sáwrō, sór-/ *n.* & *v.* • *n.* **1** mental distress caused by loss or disappointment, etc. **2** a cause of sorrow. **3** lamentation. • *v.intr.* **1** feel sorrow. **2** mourn. □□ **sor·row·ing** *adj.*

sor·row·ful /sáwrōfŏŏl, sór-/ *adj.* **1** feeling or showing sorrow. **2** distressing; lamentable. □□ **sor·row·ful·ly** *adv.*

sor·ry /sáwree, sór-/ *adj.* (**sorrier, sorriest**) **1** (*predic.*) regretful or penitent (*were sorry for what they had done*; *am sorry that you have to go*). **2** (*predic.*; foll. by *for*) feeling pity or sympathy for. **3** as an expression of apology. **4** wretched (*a sorry sight*). □ **sorry for oneself** dejected. □□ **sor·ri·ness** *n.*

sort /sawrt/ *n.* & *v.* • *n.* **1** a group of things, etc., with common attributes; a class or kind. **2** (foll. by *of*) roughly of the kind specified (*is some sort of doctor*). **3** *colloq.* a person of a specified kind (*a good sort*). **4** *Printing* a letter or piece in a font of type. **5** *Computing* the arrangement of data in a prescribed sequence. • *v.tr.* arrange systematically or according to type, class, etc. □ **after a sort** after a fashion. **in some sort** to a certain extent. **of a sort** (or **of sorts**) *colloq.* not fully deserving the name (*a holiday of sorts*). **out of sorts 1** slightly unwell. **2** irritable. **sort of** *colloq.* to some extent (*I sort of expected it*). **sort out 1** separate into sorts. **2** select from a miscellaneous group. **3** disentangle or put into order. **4** resolve (a problem or difficulty). **5** *colloq.* deal with or reprimand. □□ **sort·er** *n.* **sort·ing** *n.*

▶See note at KIND.

sort·ie /sáwrtee, sawrtée/ *n.* & *v.* • *n.* **1** a sally, esp. from a besieged garrison. **2** an operational flight by a single military aircraft. • *v.intr.* (**sorties, sortied, sortieing**) make a sortie; sally.

SOS /ésō-és/ *n.* (*pl.* **SOSs**) **1** an international code signal of extreme distress. **2** an urgent appeal for help.

so-so /sṓ-sṓ/ *adj.* & *adv.* • *adj.* (usu. *predic.*) indifferent. • *adv.* indifferently.

sos·te·nu·to /sóstənŏŏtō/ *adv., adj.,* & *n. Mus.* • *adv.* & *adj.* in a sustained or prolonged manner. • *n.* (*pl.* **-tos**) a passage to be played in this way.

sot /sot/ *n.* a habitual drunkard. □□ **sot·tish** *adj.*

sot·to vo·ce /sótō vṓchee, sáwt-tō váwche/ *adv.* in an undertone or aside.

sou /soo/ *n.* **1** *hist.* a former French coin of low value. **2** (usu. with *neg.*) *colloq.* a very small amount of money (*hasn't a sou*).

sou·bri·quet var. of SOBRIQUET.

souf·fle /sóofəl/ *n. Med.* a low murmur heard in the auscultation of various organs, etc.

souf·flé /sooflάy/ *n. & adj.* • *n.* a light dish usu. made with flavored egg yolks added to stiffly beaten egg whites and baked (*cheese soufflé*). • *adj.* light and frothy (*omelette soufflé*).

sought *past* and *past part.* of SEEK.

sought-af·ter *adj.* much in demand; generally desired or courted.

soul /sōl/ *n.* **1** the spiritual or immaterial part of a human being, often regarded as immortal. **2** the moral or emotional or intellectual nature of a person. **3** the personification or pattern of something (*the very soul of discretion*). **4** an individual (*not a soul in sight*). **5** a person regarded as the animating or essential part of something (*the life and soul of the party*). **6** emotional or intellectual energy or intensity, esp. as revealed in a work of art (*pictures that lack soul*). **7** African-American culture, music, ethnic pride, etc. □ **upon my soul** an exclamation of surprise. □□ **-souled** *adj.* (in *comb.*).

soul food *n.* traditional African-American foods from the southern US.

soul·ful /sṓlfool/ *adj.* **1** having or expressing or evoking deep feeling. **2** *colloq.* overly emotional. □□ **soul·ful·ly** *adv.* **soul·ful·ness** *n.*

soul·less /sṓl-lis/ *adj.* **1** lacking sensitivity. **2** undistinguished or uninteresting. □□ **soul·less·ly** *adv.* **soul·less·ness** *n.*

soul mate *n.* a person ideally suited to another.

soul mu·sic *n.* a kind of music incorporating elements of rhythm and blues and gospel music, popularized by African Americans.

sound[1] /sownd/ *n. & v.* • *n.* **1** a sensation caused in the ear by the vibration of the surrounding air or other medium. **2** vibrations causing this sensation. **3** what is or may be heard. **4** an idea or impression conveyed by words (*don't like the sound of that*). **5** mere words. **6** (in full **musical sound**) sound produced by continuous and regular vibrations. **7** any of a series of articulate utterances (*vowel and consonant sounds*). **8** music, speech, etc., accompanying a movie or other visual presentation. **9** (often *attrib.*) broadcasting by radio as distinct from television. • *v.* **1** *intr. & tr.* emit or cause to emit sound. **2** *tr.* utter or pronounce (*sound a note of alarm*). **3** *intr.* convey an impression when heard (*you sound worried*). **4** *tr.* give an audible signal for (an alarm, etc.). **5** *tr.* test (the lungs, etc.) by noting the sound produced. **6** *tr.* cause to resound; make known (*sound their praises*). □ **sound off** talk loudly or express one's opinions forcefully. □□ **sound·less** *adj.* **sound·less·ly** *adv.* **sound·less·ness** *n.*

sound[2] /sownd/ *adj. & adv.* • *adj.* **1** healthy; not diseased or injured. **2** (of an opinion or policy, etc.) correct; well-founded; judicious. **3** financially secure (*a sound investment*). **4** undisturbed (*a sound sleep*). • *adv.* soundly (*sound asleep*). □□ **sound·ly** *adv.* **sound·ness** *n.*

sound[3] /sownd/ *v.tr.* **1** test the depth or quality of the bottom of (the sea or a river, etc.). **2** (often foll. by *out*) inquire (esp. cautiously or discreetly) into the opinions or feelings of (a person). □□ **sound·er** *n.*

sound[4] /sownd/ *n.* **1** a narrow passage of water. **2** an arm of the sea.

sound bar·ri·er *n.* the high resistance of air to objects moving at speeds near that of sound.

sound bite *n.* a short extract from a recorded interview, chosen for its pungency or appropriateness.

sound ef·fect *n.* a sound other than speech or music made artificially for use in a play, movie, etc.

sound·ing[1] /sównding/ *n.* **1 a** the action or process of measuring the depth of water, now usu. by means of echo. **b** an instance of this (*took a sounding*). **2** (in *pl.*) cautious investigation (*made soundings as to his suitability*).

sound·ing[2] /sównding/ *adj.* giving forth (esp. loud or resonant) sound (*sounding brass*).

sound·ing board *n.* **1** a canopy over a pulpit, etc., to direct sound toward the congregation. **2** a means of causing opinions, etc., to be more widely known (*used his students as a sounding board*).

sound·proof /sówndproof/ *adj. & v.* • *adj.* impervious to sound. • *v.tr.* make soundproof.

sound·track /sówndtrak/ *n.* **1** the recorded sound element of a movie. **2** this recorded on the edge of a film in optical or magnetic form.

sound wave *n.* a wave of compression and rarefaction, by which sound is propagated in an elastic medium, e.g., air.

soup /soop/ *n. & v.* • *n.* a liquid dish made by boiling meat, fish, or vegetables, etc., in stock or water. • *v.tr.* (usu. foll. by *up*) *colloq.* **1** increase the power and efficiency of (an engine). **2** increase the power or impact of (writing, music, etc.). □ **in the soup** *colloq.* in difficulties.

soup·çon /soopsáwN, soopsón/ *n.* a very small quantity; a dash.

soup kitch·en *n.* a place dispensing soup, etc., to the poor.

soup·spoon /soopspoon/ *n.* a spoon, usu. with a large rounded bowl, for eating soup.

soup·y /soopee/ *adj.* (**soupier, soupiest**) **1** resembling soup. **2** *colloq.* sentimental; mawkish. □□ **soup·i·ly** *adv.* **soup·i·ness** *n.*

sour /sowr/ *adj., n., & v.* • *adj.* **1** having an acid taste like lemon or vinegar, esp. because of unripeness (*sour apples*). **2 a** (of food, esp. milk or bread) bad because of fermentation. **b** smelling or tasting rancid or unpleasant. **3** (of a person, temper, etc.) harsh; bitter. **4** (of a thing) unpleasant; distasteful. • *n.* a drink with lemon or lime juice (*whiskey sour*). • *v.tr. & intr.* make or become sour (*soured the cream; soured by misfortune*). □ **go** (or **turn**) **sour 1** (of food, etc.) become sour. **2** turn out badly (*the job went sour on him*). **3** lose one's enthusiasm. □□ **sour·ish** *adj.* **sour·ly** *adv.* **sour·ness** *n.*

source /sawrs/ *n. & v.* • *n.* **1** a spring or fountainhead from which a stream issues. **2** a place, person, or thing from which something originates (*the source of all our troubles*). **3** a person or document, etc., providing evidence (*reliable sources of information*. **4** a body emitting radiation, etc. • *v.tr.* obtain (esp. components) from a specified source. □ **at source** at the point of origin or issue.

source·book /sáwrsbook/ *n.* a collection of documentary sources for the study of a subject.

sour cream *n.* cream deliberately fermented by adding bacteria.

sour·dough /sówrdō/ *n.* fermenting dough, esp. that left over from a previous baking, used as leaven.

sour·puss /sówrpoos/ *n. colloq.* an ill-tempered person.

sour·sop /sówrsop/ *n.* **1** a W. Indian evergreen tree, *Annona muricata*. **2** the large succulent fruit of this tree.

souse /sows/ *v. & n.* • *v.* **1** *tr.* put (pickles, fish, etc.) in brine. **2** *tr. & intr.* plunge into liquid. **3** *tr.* (as **soused** *adj.*) *colloq.* drunk. • *n.* **1 a** pickling brine made with salt. **b** food, esp. a pig's head, etc., in pickle. **2** a dip, plunge, or drenching in water. **3** *colloq.* **a** a drinking bout. **b** a drunkard.

south /sowth/ *n., adj., & adv.* • *n.* **1** the point of the horizon 90° clockwise from east. **2** the compass point corresponding to this. **3** the direction in which this lies. **4** (usu. **the South**) **a** the part of the world or a country or a town lying to the south. **b** the southern states of the US. • *adj.* **1** toward, at, near, or facing the south (*a south wall; south country*). **2** coming from the south (*south wind*). • *adv.* **1** toward, at, or near the south (*they traveled south*). **2** (foll. by *of*) further south than. □ **to the south** (often foll. by *of*) in a southerly direction.

South Af·ri·can *adj. & n.* • *adj.* of or relating to the republic of South Africa. • *n.* **1** a native or inhabitant of South Africa. **2** a person of South African descent.

South A·mer·i·can *adj. & n.* • *adj.* of or relating to South America. • *n.* a native or inhabitant of South America.

south·bound /sówthbownd/ *adj.* traveling or leading southward.

South·down /sówthdown/ *n.* **1** a sheep of a breed raised esp. for mutton, orig. in England. **2** this breed.

south·east *n., adj., & adv.* • *n.* **1** the point of the horizon midway between south and east. **2** the compass point corresponding to this. **3** the direction in which this lies. • *adj.* of, toward, or coming from the southeast. • *adv.* toward, at, or near the southeast. □□ **south·east·er·ly** *adj., adv.* **south·east·ern** *adj., adv.*

south·east·er /sówtheéstər, sou-eéstər/ *n.* a southeast wind.

south·er /sówthər/ *n.* a south wind.

south·er·ly /sú<u>th</u>ərlee/ *adj., adv., & n.* • *adj. & adv.* **1** in a southern position or direction. **2** (of a wind) blowing from the south. • *n.* (*pl.* **-lies**) a southerly wind.

south·ern /sú<u>th</u>ərn/ *adj.* **1** of or in the south; inhabiting the south. **2** lying or directed toward the south. □□ **south·ern·most** *adj.*

south·ern·er /sú<u>th</u>ərnər/ *n.* a native or inhabitant of the south.

south·ern hem·i·sphere (also **South·ern Hem·i·sphere**) *n.* the half of the earth below the equator.

south·ern lights *n.pl.* the aurora australis.

south·ing /sówthing/ *n.* **1** a southern movement. **2** *Naut.* the distance traveled or measured southward. **3** *Astron.* the angular distance of a star, etc., south of the celestial equator.

south·paw /sówthpaw/ *n. & adj. colloq.* • *n.* a left-handed person, esp. a left-handed pitcher in baseball. • *adj.* left-handed.

south pole see POLE².

South Sea *n.* the southern Pacific Ocean.

south·ward /sówthwərd/ *adj., adv., & n.* • *adj. & adv.* (also **south·wards**) toward the south. • *n.* a southward direction or region.

south·west *n., adj., & adv.* • *n.* **1** the point of the horizon midway between south and west. **2** the compass point corresponding to this. **3** the direction in which this lies. • *adj.* of, toward, or coming from the southwest. • *adv.* toward, at, or near the southwest. □□ **south·west·er·ly** *adj., adv.* **south·west·ern** *adj., adv*

south·west·er /sówthwéstər, sow-wéstər/ *n.* a southwest wind.

sou·ve·nir /sóovəneér/ *n.* (often foll. by *of*) a memento of an occasion, etc.

sou'·west·er /sow-wéstər/ *n.* **1** = SOUTHWESTER. **2** a waterproof hat with a broad flap covering the neck.

sov. /sov/ *abbr. Brit.* sovereign.

sov·er·eign /sóvrin/ *n. & adj.* • *n.* **1** a supreme ruler, esp. a monarch. **2** *Brit. hist.* a gold coin nominally worth £1. • *adj.* **1 a** supreme (*sovereign power*). **b** unmitigated (*sovereign contempt*). **2** excellent; effective (*a sovereign remedy*). **3** possessing independent national power (*a sovereign state*). **4** royal (*our sovereign lord*). □□ **sov·er·eign·ly** *adv.* **sov·er·eign·ty** *n.* (*pl.* **-ties**).

so·vi·et /sóveeət, sóv-/ *n. & adj. hist.* • *n.* **1** an elected local, district, or national council in the former USSR. **2** (**Soviet**) a citizen of the former USSR. **3** a revolutionary council of workers, peasants, etc., before 1917. • *adj.* (usu. **Soviet**) of or concerning the former USSR. □□ **So·vi·et·ize** *v.tr.* **So·vi·et·i·za·tion** *n.*

so·vi·et·ol·o·gist /sóveeətóləjist, sóv–/ *n.* a person who studies the former Soviet Union.

sow¹ /sō/ *v.tr.* (*past* **sowed** /sōd/; *past part.* **sown** /sōn/ or **sowed**) **1** (also *absol.*) **a** scatter or put (seed) on or in the earth. **b** (often foll. by *with*) plant (a field, etc.) with seed. **2** initiate; arouse (*sowed doubt in her mind*). **3** (foll. by *with*) cover thickly with. □ **sow the seeds of** implant (an idea, etc.). □□ **sow·er** *n.* **sow·ing** *n.*

sow² /sow/ *n.* **1** a female adult pig, esp. after farrowing. **2** a female guinea pig. **3** the female of some other species.

sown *past part.* of SOW¹.

sox *colloq. pl.* of SOCK¹.

soy /soy/ *n.* (also **soy·a** /sóyə/) (in full **soy sauce**) a sauce made esp. in Asia from pickled soybeans.

soy·bean /soybeen/ *n.* (also **soy·a bean**) **1** a leguminous plant, *Glycine max*, orig. of SE Asia, cultivated for the edible oil and flour it yields, and used as a replacement for animal protein in certain foods. **2** the seed of this.

spa /spaa/ *n.* **1** a curative mineral spring. **2** a place or resort with this. **3** a hot tub, esp. one with a whirlpool device.

space /spays/ *n. & v.* • *n.* **1 a** a continuous unlimited area or expanse which may or may not contain objects, etc. **b** an interval between one, two, or three dimensional points or objects (*a space of 10 feet*). **c** an empty area; room (*clear a space in the corner; occupies too much space*). **2** a large unoccupied region (*the wide open spaces*). **3** = OUTER SPACE. **4** an interval of time (*in the space of an hour*). **5** the amount of paper used in writing, etc. (*hadn't the space to discuss it*). **6** a blank between printed, typed, or written words, etc. **7** *Mus.* each of the blanks between the lines of a staff. • *v.tr.* **1** set or arrange at intervals. **2** put spaces between (esp. words, lines, etc., in printing, typing, or writing). **3** (as **spaced** *adj.*) (often foll. by *out*) **1** *sl.* in a state of euphoria, esp. from taking drugs. **2** abstracted, forgetful, or dreamily inattentive. □□ **spac·er** *n.* **spac·ing** *n.* (esp. in sense 2 of *v.*).

space age *n.* the era when space travel has become possible.

space ca·det *n. sl.* a person who appears absentminded or removed from reality.

space·craft /spáyskraft/ *n.* a vehicle used for traveling in space.

space heat·er *n.* a heater, usu. electric, that warms a limited space, as a room.

space·man /spáysman/ *n.* (*pl.* **-men**; *fem.* **space·wom·an**, *pl.* **-women**) a traveler in outer space; an astronaut.

space probe *n.* = PROBE n.4.

space·ship /spáys-ship/ *n.* a spacecraft, esp. one controlled by its crew.

space shut·tle *n.* a rocket for repeated use carrying people and cargo between the earth and space.

space sta·tion *n.* an artificial satellite used as a base for operations in space.

space·suit /spáys-sōōt, -syōōt/ *n.* a garment designed to allow an astronaut to survive in space.

spa·cey /spáysee/ *adj.* (also **spacy**) *sl.* **1** seemingly out of touch with reality; disoriented. **2** being in a confused or dazed state because of the influence of mind-altering drugs.

spa·cial var. of SPATIAL.

spa·cious /spáyshəs/ *adj.* having ample space; covering a large area; roomy. ▫▫ **spa·cious·ly** *adv.* **spa·cious·ness** *n.*

spade[1] /spayd/ *n. & v.* • *n.* **1** a tool used for digging or cutting the ground, etc., with a sharp-edged metal blade and a long handle. **2** a tool of a similar shape for various purposes. • *v.tr.* dig over (ground) with a spade. ▫ **call a spade a spade** speak plainly or bluntly. ▫▫ **spade·ful** *n.* (*pl.* **-fuls**).

spade[2] /spayd/ *n.* **1 a** a playing card of a suit denoted by black inverted heart-shaped figures with small stalks. **b** (in *pl.*) this suit. **2** *sl. offens.* an African-American. ▫ **in spades** *sl.* to a high degree; with great force.

spae /spay/ *v.intr. & tr. Sc.* foretell; prophesy.

spa·ghet·ti /spəgétee/ *n.* pasta made in solid strings, between macaroni and vermicelli in thickness.

spa·ghet·ti west·ern *n.* a movie about the American West made cheaply in Italy.

spake /spayk/ *archaic past* of SPEAK.

spall /spawl/ *n. & v.* • *n.* a splinter or chip, esp. of rock. • *v.intr. & tr.* break up or cause (ore) to break up in preparation for sorting.

Spam /spam/ *n. Trademark* a canned meat product made mainly from ham.

span[1] /span/ *n. & v.* • *n.* **1** the full extent from end to end in space or time (*the span of a bridge*; *the whole span of history*). **2** each arch or part of a bridge between piers or supports. **3** the maximum lateral extent of an airplane, its wing, a bird's wing, etc. **4 a** the maximum distance between the tips of the thumb and little finger. **b** this as a measurement, equal to 9 inches. • *v.* (**spanned, spanning**) **1** *tr.* **a** (of a bridge, arch, etc.) stretch from side to side of; extend across (*the bridge spanned the river*). **b** (of a builder, etc.) bridge (a river, etc.). **2** *tr.* extend across (space or a period of time, etc.).

span[2] see SPICK-AND-SPAN.

span[3] /span/ *archaic past* of SPIN.

span·drel /spándril/ *n. Archit.* **1** the almost triangular space between one side of the outer curve of an arch, a wall, and the ceiling or framework. **2** the space between the shoulders of adjoining arches and the ceiling or molding above.

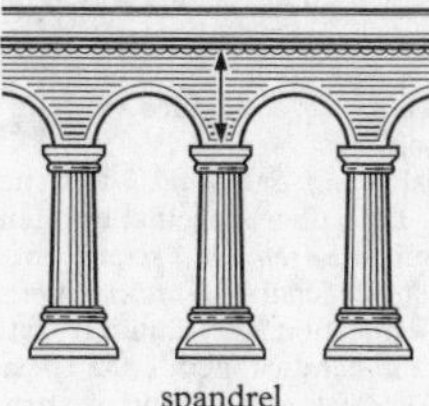

spandrel

spang /spang/ *adv. colloq.* exactly; completely (*spang in the middle*).

span·gle /spánggəl/ *n. & v.* • *n.* a small thin piece of glittering material esp. used in quantity to ornament a dress, etc.; a sequin. • *v.tr.* (esp. as **spangled** *adj.*) cover with or as with spangles (*spangled costume*). ▫▫ **span·gly** /spángglee/ *adj.*

Span·iard /spányərd/ *n.* **a** a native or inhabitant of Spain in southern Europe. **b** a person of Spanish descent.

span·iel /spányəl/ *n.* **1 a** a dog of any of various breeds with a long silky coat and drooping ears. **b** any of these breeds. **2** an obsequious or fawning person.

Span·ish /spánish/ *adj. & n.* • *adj.* of or relating to Spain or its people or language. • *n.* **1** the language of Spain and Spanish America. **2** (prec. by *the*; treated as *pl.*) the people of Spain.

Span·ish A·mer·i·ca *n.* those parts of America orig. settled by Spaniards, including Central and South America and part of the West Indies.

Span·ish Main *n. hist.* the NE coast of South America between the Orinoco River and Panama, and adjoining parts of the Caribbean Sea.

spank /spangk/ *v. & n.* • *v.* **1** *tr.* slap, esp. on the buttocks. **2** *intr.* (of a horse, etc.) move briskly, esp. between a trot and a gallop. • *n.* a slap, esp. on the buttocks.

spank·er /spángkər/ *n.* **1** a person or thing that spanks. **2** *Naut.* a fore-and-aft sail set on the after side of the mizzenmast.

spank·ing /spángking/ *adj., adv., & n.* • *adj.* **1** (esp. of a horse) moving swiftly; lively; brisk. **2** *colloq.* striking; excellent. • *adv. colloq.* very; exceedingly (*spanking clean*). • *n.* the act or an instance of slapping, esp. on the buttocks as a punishment for children.

spar[1] /spaar/ *n.* **1** a stout pole esp. used for the mast, yard, etc., of a ship. **2** the main longitudinal beam of an airplane wing.

spar[2] /spaar/ *v. & n.* • *v.intr.* (**sparred, sparring**) **1** (often foll. by *at*) make the motions of boxing without landing heavy blows. **2** engage in argument. • *n.* **1** a sparring motion. **2** a boxing match.

spar[3] /spaar/ *n.* any crystalline, easily cleavable, and non-lustrous mineral, e.g., calcite. ▫▫ **spar·ry** *adj.*

spare /spair/ *adj., n., & v.* • *adj.* **1 a** not required for ordinary use; extra (*spare cash*; *spare time*). **b** reserved for emergency or occasional use (*the spare room*). **2** lean; thin. **3** scanty; frugal (*a spare diet*; *a spare prose style*). • *n.* **1** a spare part; a duplicate. **2** *Bowling* the knocking down of all the pins with the first two balls. • *v.* **1** *tr.* afford to give or do without; dispense with (*cannot spare him just now*). **2** *tr.* **a** abstain from killing, hurting, wounding, etc. (*spared his feelings*; *spared her life*). **b** abstain from inflicting or causing (*spare me this talk*; *spare my blushes*). **3** *tr.* be frugal or grudging of (*no expense spared*). ▫ **not spare oneself** exert one's utmost efforts. **to spare** left over; additional (*an hour to spare*). ▫▫ **spare·ly** *adv.* **spare·ness** *n.*

spare·ribs /spáir-ríbs/ *n.pl.* closely trimmed ribs of esp. pork.

spare tire *n.* **1** an extra tire carried in a motor vehicle for emergencies. **2** *colloq.* a roll of fat round the waist.

spar·ing /spáiring/ *adj.* **1** economical. **2** restrained; limited. ▫▫ **spar·ing·ly** *adv.*

spark /spaark/ *n. & v.* • *n.* **1** a fiery particle thrown off from a fire, or remaining lit in ashes, or produced by a flint, match, etc. **2** (often foll. by *of*) a particle of a quality, etc. (*not a spark of life*; *a spark of interest*). **3** *Electr.* **a** a light produced by a sudden disruptive discharge through the air, etc. **b** such a discharge serving to ignite the explosive mixture in an internal combustion engine. **4 a** a flash of wit, etc. **b** anything causing interest, excitement, etc. • *v.* **1** *intr.* emit sparks of fire or electricity. **2** *tr.* (often foll. by *off*) stir into activity. **3** *intr. Electr.* produce sparks at the point where a circuit is interrupted. ▫▫ **spark·less** *adj.* **spark·y** *adj.*

spar·kle /spaárkəl/ *v. & n.* • *v.intr.* **1 a** emit or seem to emit sparks; glitter (*her eyes sparkled*). **b** be witty; scintillate (*sparkling repartee*). **2** (of wine, etc.) effervesce (cf. STILL[1] *adj.* 4). • *n.* a gleam or spark. ▫▫ **spar·kly** *adj.*

spar·kler /spaárklər/ *n.* **1** a person or thing that sparkles. **2** a handheld sparkling firework. **3** *colloq.* a diamond or other gem.

spark plug *n.* a device for firing the explosive mixture in an internal combustion engine.

spar·ring part·ner *n.* **1** a boxer employed to engage in sparring with another as training. **2** a person with whom one enjoys arguing.

spar·row /spárō/ *n.* **1** any small brownish gray bird of the genus *Passer*, esp. the house sparrow and tree sparrow. **2** any of various birds of similar appearance such as the hedge sparrow.

spar·row·hawk /spárōhawk/ *n.* a small hawk, *Accipiter nisus*, that preys on small birds.

sparse /spaars/ *adj.* **1** thinly dispersed or scattered; not dense (*sparse population*; *sparse graying hair*). **2** austere; meager. ▫▫ **sparse·ly** *adv.* **sparse·ness** *n.* **spar·si·ty** *n.*

Spar·tan /spaárt'n/ *adj.* & *n.* • *adj.* **1** of or relating to Sparta in ancient Greece. **2 a** possessing courage, endurance, and stern frugality. **b** (of a regime, conditions, etc.) lacking comfort. • *n.* a citizen of Sparta.

spasm /spázəm/ *n.* **1** a sudden involuntary muscular contraction. **2** a sudden convulsive movement or emotion, etc. **3** (usu. foll. by *of*) *colloq.* a brief spell of an activity.

spas·mod·ic /spazmódik/ *adj.* **1** of, caused by, or subject to, a spasm or spasms (*a spasmodic jerk*). **2** occurring or done by fits and starts (*spasmodic efforts*). ▫▫ **spas·mod·i·cal·ly** *adv.*

spas·tic /spástik/ *adj.* & *n.* • *adj.* **1** *Med.* suffering from spasms of the muscles. **2** *sl. offens.* weak; feeble. **3** spasmodic. • *n. offens.* a person suffering from cerebral palsy. ▫▫ **spas·tic·i·ty** /-tísitee/ *n.*

spat[1] *past* and *past part.* of SPIT[1].

spat[2] /spat/ *n.* (usu. in *pl.*) *hist.* a short gaiter protecting the shoe from mud, etc.

spat[3] /spat/ *n.* & *v. colloq.* • *n.* a petty quarrel. • *v.intr.* (**spatted, spatting**) quarrel pettily.

spat[4] /spat/ *n.* & *v.* • *n.* the spawn of shellfish, esp. the oyster. • *v.* (**spatted, spatting**) **1** *intr.* (of an oyster) spawn. **2** *tr.* shed (spawn).

spate /spayt/ *n.* **1** a river flood (*the river is in spate*). **2** a large amount.

spathe /spay<u>th</u>/ *n. Bot.* a large bract or pair of bracts enveloping a spadix.

spa·tial /spáyshəl/ *adj.* (also **spa·cial**) of or concerning space (*spatial extent*). ▫▫ **spa·ti·al·i·ty** /-sheeálitee/ *n.* **spa·tial·ize** *v.tr.* **spa·tial·ly** *adv.*

spa·ti·o·tem·po·ral /spáysheeōtémpərəl/ *adj. Physics* & *Philos.* belonging to both space and time or to space-time. ▫▫ **spa·ti·o·tem·po·ral·ly** *adv.*

spat·ter /spátər/ *v.* & *n.* • *v.* **1** *tr.* **a** (often foll. by *with*) splash (a person, etc.). **b** scatter or splash (liquid, mud, etc.) here and there. **2** *intr.* (of rain, etc.) fall here and there. • *n.* (usu. foll. by *of*) a splash (*a spatter of mud*).

spat·u·la /spáchələ/ *n.* a broad-bladed flat implement used for spreading, lifting, stirring, mixing (food), etc.

spat·u·late /spáchələt/ *adj.* **1** spatula-shaped. **2** (esp. of a leaf) having a broad rounded end.

spawn /spawn/ *v.* & *n.* • *v.* **1 a** *tr.* (also *absol.*) (of a fish, frog, mollusk, or crustacean) produce (eggs). **b** *intr.* be produced as eggs or young. **2** *tr.* produce or generate, esp. in large numbers. • *n.* **1** the eggs of fish, frogs, etc. **2** a white fibrous matter from which fungi are produced. ▫▫ **spawn·er** *n.*

spay /spay/ *v.tr.* sterilize (a female animal) by removing the ovaries.

SPCA *abbr.* Society for the Prevention of Cruelty to Animals.

speak /speek/ *v.* (*past* **spoke** /spōk/; *past part.* **spoken** /spṓkən/) **1** *intr.* make articulate verbal utterances in an ordinary (not singing) voice. **2** *tr.* **a** utter (words). **b** make known or communicate (one's opinion, the truth, etc.) in this way. **3** *intr.* **a** (foll. by *to, with*) hold a conversation. **b** (foll. by *of*) mention in writing, etc. **c** (foll. by *for*) articulate the feelings of (another person, etc.) in speech or writing (*speaks for our generation*). **4** *intr.* (foll. by *to*) **a** address (a person, etc.). **b** speak in confirmation of or with reference to (*spoke to the resolution*). **c** *colloq.* reprove (*spoke to them about their lateness*). **5** *intr.* make a speech before an audience, etc. **6** *tr.* use or be able to use (a specified language) (*cannot speak French*). ▫ **not** (or **nothing**) **to speak of** practically not (or nothing). **speak for itself** need no supporting evidence. **speak for oneself 1** give one's own opinions. **2** not presume to speak for others. **speak one's mind** speak bluntly or frankly. **speak out** speak loudly or freely; give one's opinion. **speak up** = ***speak out***. **speak volumes** (of a fact, etc.) be very significant. **speak volumes for** be abundant evidence of. ▫▫ **speak·a·ble** *adj.*

speak·eas·y /spéekeezee/ *n.* (*pl.* **-ies**) an illicit liquor store or drinking club during Prohibition in the US.

speak·er /spéekər/ *n.* **1** a person who speaks, esp. in public. **2** a person who speaks a specified language (esp. in *comb.*: *a French speaker*). **3** (**Speaker**) the presiding officer in a legislative assembly. **4** = LOUDSPEAKER. ▫▫ **speak·er·ship** *n.*

speak·er·phone /spéekərfōn/ *n.* a telephone equipped with a microphone and loudspeaker, allowing it to be used without picking up the handset.

speak·ing /spéeking/ *n.* & *adj.* • *n.* the act or an instance of uttering words, etc. • *adj.* **1** that speaks; capable of articulate speech. **2** (of a portrait) lifelike (*a speaking likeness*). **3** (in *comb.*) speaking a specified language (*French-speaking*). **4** with a reference or from a point of view specified (*roughly speaking*; *professionally speaking*). ▫ **on speaking terms** (foll. by *with*) **1** slightly acquainted. **2** on friendly terms.

spear /speer/ *n.* & *v.* • *n.* **1** a thrusting or throwing weapon with a pointed usu. steel tip and a long shaft. **2** a similar barbed instrument used for catching fish, etc. **3** a pointed stem of asparagus, etc. • *v.tr.* pierce or strike with or as if with a spear.

spear·head /spéerhed/ *n.* & *v.* • *n.* **1** the point of a spear. **2** an individual or group chosen to lead a thrust or attack. • *v.tr.* act as the spearhead of (an attack, etc.).

spear·mint /spéermint/ *n.* a common garden mint, *Mentha spicata*, used in cooking and to flavor chewing gum.

spec[1] /spek/ *n.* ▫ **on spec** *colloq.* in the hope of success.

spec[2] /spek/ *n. colloq.* a detailed working description; a specification.

spe·cial /spéshəl/ *adj.* & *n.* • *adj.* **1 a** particularly good; exceptional. **b** peculiar; specific; not general. **2** for a particular purpose (*sent on a special assignment*). **3** in which a person specializes (*statistics is his special field*). **4** denoting education for children with particular needs, e.g., the handicapped. • *n.* a special person or thing, e.g., a special train, edition of a newspaper, dish on a menu, etc. ▫▫ **spe·cial·ly** *adv.* **spe·cial·ness** *n.*

spe·cial de·liv·er·y *n.* a delivery of mail in advance of the regular delivery.

spe·cial ef·fects *n.pl.* movie or television illusions created by props, or camera work, or generated by computer.

Spe·cial Forc·es *n.pl.* US Army personnel specially trained in guerrilla warfare.

spe·cial in·ter·est (group) *n.* an organization, corporation, etc., that seeks advantage, usu. by lobbying for favorable legislation.

spe·cial·ist /spéshəlist/ *n.* (usu. foll. by *in*) **1** a person who is trained in a particular branch of a profession, esp. medicine. **2** a person who especially or exclusively studies a subject or a particular branch of a subject. ▫▫ **spe·cial·ism** *n.*

spe·ci·al·i·ty /spésheeálitee/ *n.* (*pl.* **-ties**) *Brit.* = SPECIALTY 1.

spe·cial·ize /spéshəlīz/ *v.* **1** *intr.* (often foll. by *in*) **a** be or become a specialist (*specializes in optics*). **b** make a habit of engaging in a particular activity, interest, etc. (*specializes in insulting people*). **2** *Biol.* **a** *tr.* (esp. in *passive*) adapt or set apart (an organ, etc.) for a particular purpose. **b** *intr.* (of an organ, etc.) become adapted, etc., in this way. **3** *tr.* make specific. ▫▫ **spe·cial·i·za·tion** *n.*

spe·cial·ty /spéshəltee/ *n.* (*pl.* **-ties**) a special pursuit, product, operation, etc., to which a company or a person gives special attention.

spe·ci·a·tion /speésheeáyshən, speés-/ *n. Biol.* the formation of a new species in the course of evolution.

spe·cie /speéshee, -see/ *n.* coin money as opposed to paper money.

spe·cies /speésheez, -seez/ *n.* (*pl.* same) **1** a class of things having some characteristics in common. **2** *Biol.* a category of living organisms consisting of similar individuals capable of exchanging genes or interbreeding. **3** a kind or sort.

spe·cif·ic /spisífik/ *adj. & n.* • *adj.* **1** clearly defined; definite (*has no specific name; told me so in specific terms*). **2** relating to a particular subject; peculiar (*a style specific to that*). • *n.* a specific aspect or factor (*shall we discuss specifics?*). ▫▫ **spe·cif·i·cal·ly** *adv.* **spec·i·fic·i·ty** /spésifisitee/ *n.*

spec·i·fi·ca·tion /spésifikáyshən/ *n.* **1** the act or an instance of specifying. **2** (esp. in *pl.*) a detailed description of the construction, workmanship, materials, etc., of work done or to be done.

spec·i·fy /spésifī/ *v.tr.* (**-fies, -fied**) **1** (also *absol.*) name or mention expressly (*specified the type he needed*). **2** (usu. foll. by *that* + clause) name as a condition (*specified that he must be paid at once*). **3** include in specifications (*a French window was not specified*). ▫▫ **spec·i·fi·a·ble** /-fīəbəl/ *adj.* **spec·i·fi·er** *n.*

spec·i·men /spésimən/ *n.* **1** an individual or part taken as an example of a class or whole, esp. when used for investigation or scientific examination. **2** *Med.* a sample of urine for testing. **3** *colloq.* a person of a specified sort.

spe·cious /speéshəs/ *adj.* **1** superficially plausible but actually wrong (*a specious argument*). **2** misleadingly attractive in appearance. ▫▫ **spe·cious·ly** *adv.* **spe·cious·ness** *n.*

speck /spek/ *n. & v.* • *n.* **1** a small spot or stain. **2** (foll. by *of*) a particle (*speck of dirt*). • *v.tr.* (esp. as **specked** *adj.*) mark with specks. ▫▫ **speck·less** *adj.*

speck·le /spékəl/ *n. & v.* • *n.* a small spot, mark, or stain, esp. in quantity on the skin, a bird's egg, etc. • *v.tr.* (esp. as **speckled** *adj.*) mark with speckles.

specs /speks/ *n.pl. colloq.* a pair of eyeglasses.

spec·ta·cle /spéktəkəl/ *n.* **1** a public show, ceremony, etc. **2** anything attracting public attention (*a charming spectacle; a disgusting spectacle*). ▫ **make a spectacle of oneself** make oneself an object of ridicule.

spec·ta·cles /spéktəkəlz/ *n.pl. old-fashioned* or *joc.* eyeglasses.

spec·tac·u·lar /spektákyələr/ *adj. & n.* • *adj.* **1** of or like a public show; striking. **2** strikingly large or obvious (*a spectacular increase in output*). • *n.* an event intended to be spectacular, esp. a musical. ▫▫ **spec·tac·u·lar·ly** *adv.*

spec·tate /spéktayt/ *v.intr.* be a spectator, esp. at a sporting event.

spec·ta·tor /spéktáytər/ *n.* a person who looks on at a show, game, incident, etc. ▫▫ **spec·ta·to·ri·al** /-tətáwreeəl/ *adj.*

spec·ta·tor sport *n.* a sport attracting spectators rather than participants.

spec·ter /spéktər/ *n.* **1** a ghost. **2** a haunting presentiment or preoccupation (*the specter of war*).

spec·tra *pl.* of SPECTRUM.

spec·tral /spéktrəl/ *adj.* **1 a** of or relating to specters. **b** ghostlike. **2** of or concerning spectra or the spectrum (*spectral colors*). ▫▫ **spec·tral·ly** *adv.*

spectro- /spéktrō/ *comb.form* a spectrum.

spec·trom·e·ter /spektrómitər/ *n.* an instrument used for the measurement of observed spectra. ▫▫ **spec·tro·met·ric** /spéktrəmétrik/ *adj.* **spec·trom·e·try** *n.*

spec·tro·scope /spéktrəskōp/ *n.* an instrument for producing and recording spectra for examination. ▫▫ **spec·tro·scop·ic** /-skópik/ *adj.* **spec·tro·scop·ist** /-tróskəpist/ *n.* **spec·tros·co·py** /-tróskəpee/ *n.*

spec·trum /spéktrəm/ *n.* (*pl.* **spectra** /-trə/) **1** the band of colors, as seen in a rainbow, etc. **2** the entire range of wavelengths of electromagnetic radiation. **3** an image or distribution of parts of electromagnetic radiation arranged in a progressive series according to wavelength. **4** a similar image or distribution of energy, mass, etc., arranged according to frequency, charge, etc. **5** the entire range or a wide range of anything arranged by degree or quality, etc.

spec·u·la *pl.* of SPECULUM.

spec·u·late /spékyəlayt/ *v.* **1** *intr.* (usu. foll. by *on, upon, about*) form a theory or conjecture, esp. without a firm factual basis (*speculated on their prospects*). **2** *tr.* (foll. by *that, how*, etc., + clause) conjecture; consider (*speculated how he might achieve it*). **3** *intr.* invest in stocks, etc., in the hope of gain but with the possibility of loss. ▫▫ **spec·u·la·tor** *n.*

spec·u·la·tion /spékyəláyshən/ *n.* **1** the act of speculating; a conjecture. **2 a** a speculative investment or enterprise. **b** the practice of business speculating.

spec·u·la·tive /spékyələtiv, -lay-/ *adj.* **1** of, based on or inclined to speculation. **2** (of a business investment) involving the risk of loss. ▫▫ **spec·u·la·tive·ly** *adv.*

spec·u·lum /spékyələm/ *n.* (*pl.* **specula** /-lə/) **1** *Surgery* an instrument for dilating the cavities of the human body for inspection. **2** a mirror, usu. of polished metal, esp. in a reflecting telescope.

sped *past* and *past part.* of SPEED.

speech /speech/ *n.* **1** the faculty or act of speaking. **2** a usu. formal address or discourse delivered to an audience or assembly. **3** a manner of speaking (*a man of blunt speech*). **4** the language of a nation, region, group, etc. ▫▫ **speech·ful** *adj.*

speech·i·fy /speéchifī/ *v.intr.* (**-fies, -fied**) *joc.* or *derog.* make boring or long speeches. ▫▫ **speech·i·fi·er** *n.*

speech·less /speéchlis/ *adj.* **1** temporarily unable to speak because of emotion, etc. (*speechless with rage*). **2** mute. ▫▫ **speech·less·ly** *adv.* **speech·less·ness** *n.*

speed /speed/ *n. & v.* • *n.* **1** rapidity of movement (*at full speed*). **2** a rate of progress or motion over a distance in time. **3** an arrangement of gears yielding a specific ratio in a bicycle or automobile transmission. **4** *Photog.* **a** the sensitivity of film to light. **b** the light-gathering power of a lens. **c** the duration of an exposure. **5** *sl.* an amphetamine drug, esp. methamphetamine. • *v.* (*past* and *past part.* **sped** /sped/) **1** *intr.* go fast. **2** (*past* and *past part.* **speeded**) *intr.* (of a motorist, etc.) travel at an illegal or dangerous speed. **3** *tr.* send fast or on its way (*speed an arrow from the bow*). **4** *intr. & tr. archaic* be or make prosperous or successful (*God speed you!*). ▫ **speed up** move or work at greater speed. ▫▫ **speed·er** *n.*

speed·ball /speédbawl/ *n. sl.* a mixture of cocaine with heroin or morphine.

speed·boat /speédbōt/ *n.* a motor boat designed for high speed.

speed bump *n.* a transverse ridge in the road to control the speed of vehicles.

speed·om·e·ter /spidómitər/ *n.* an instrument on a motor vehicle, etc., indicating its speed to the driver.

speed·way /spé̱edway/ *n.* **1 a** a track used for automobile racing. **b** a highway for high-speed travel. **2 a** motorcycle racing. **b** a stadium used for this.

speed·y /spé̱edee/ *adj.* (**speedier, speediest**) **1** moving quickly. **2** done without delay (*a speedy answer*). ▫▫ **speed·i·ly** *adv.* **speed·i·ness** *n.*

spe·le·ol·o·gy /spé̱eleeóləjee/ *n.* **1** the scientific study of caves. **2** the exploration of caves. ▫▫ **spe·le·o·log·i·cal** /-leeəlójikəl/ *adj.* **spe·le·ol·o·gist** *n.*

spell[1] /spel/ *v.tr.* (*past* and *past part.* **spelled**) **1** (also *absol.*) write or name the letters that form (a word) in correct sequence. **2 a** (of letters) make up or form (a word). **b** (of circumstances, a scheme, etc.) result in; involve (*spell ruin*). ▫ **spell out 1** make out (words) letter by letter. **2** explain in detail (*spelled out what the change would mean*).

spell[2] /spel/ *n.* **1** a form of words used as a magical charm or incantation. **2** an attraction or fascination exercised by a person, activity, quality, etc. ▫ **under a spell** mastered by or as if by a spell.

spell[3] /spel/ *n.* **1** a short or fairly short period (*a cold spell in April*). **2** a period of work (*did a spell of woodwork*).

spell·bind /spélbīnd/ *v.tr.* (*past* and *past part.* **spellbound**) **1** bind with or as if with a spell; entrance. **2** (as **spellbound** *adj.*) entranced or fascinated, esp. by a speaker, activity, quality, etc. ▫▫ **spell·bind·er** *n.* **spell·bind·ing·ly** *adv.*

spell·er /spélər/ *n.* a person who spells in a specified way (*a poor speller*).

spell·ing /spéling/ *n.* **1** the process or activity of writing or naming the letters of a word, etc. **2** the way a word is spelled. **3** the ability to spell (*his spelling is weak*).

spell·ing bee *n.* a spelling competition.

spe·lunk·er /spilúngkər, spé̱elung-/ *n.* a person who explores caves, esp. as a hobby. ▫▫ **spe·lunk·ing** *n.*

spend /spend/ *v.tr.* (*past* and *past part.* **spent** /spent/) **1** (usu. foll. by *on*) **a** (also *absol.*) pay out (money) in making a purchase, etc. **b** pay out (money) for a particular person's benefit or for the improvement of a thing (*had to spend $200 on the car*). **2 a** use or consume (time or energy). **b** (also *refl.*) use up; exhaust. **3** *tr.* (as **spent** *adj.*) having lost its original force or strength (*the storm is spent; spent bullets*). ▫▫ **spend·a·ble** *adj.* **spend·er** *n.*

spend·thrift /spéndthrift/ *n.* & *adj.* • *n.* an extravagant person; a prodigal. • *adj.* extravagant; prodigal.

sperm /spərm/ *n.* (*pl.* same or **sperms**) **1** = SPERMATOZOON. **2** the male reproductive fluid containing spermatozoa; semen.

sper·mat·ic /spərmátik/ *adj.* of or relating to a sperm.

sper·mat·ic cord *n.* a bundle of nerves, ducts, and blood vessels passing to the testicles.

sper·ma·tid /spə́rmətid/ *n. Biol.* an immature male sex cell formed from a spermatocyte and which may develop into a spermatozoon. ▫▫ **sper·ma·ti·dal** /–tíd'l/ *adj.*

spermato- /spərmátō, spə́rmətō/ *comb. form Biol.* a sperm or seed.

sper·mat·o·cyte /spərmátəsīt, spə́rmətō–/ *n.* a cell produced from a spermatogonium and which may divide by meiosis into spermatids.

sper·mat·o·gen·e·sis /spərmátəjénisis, spə́rmətə–/ *n.* the production or development of mature spermatozoa. ▫▫ **sper·mat·o·ge·net·ic** /–jinétik/ *adj.*

sper·mat·o·go·ni·um /spərmátəgṓneeəm, spə́rmə–/ *n.* (*pl.* **spermatogonia** /–neeə/) a cell produced at an early stage in the formation of spermatozoa, from which spermatocytes develop.

sper·mat·o·phyte /spərmátəfīt, spə́rmə–/ *n.* any seed-bearing plant.

sper·ma·to·zo·id /spərmátəzṓid, spə́rmə–/ *n.* the mature motile male sex cell of some plants.

sper·ma·to·zo·on /spərmátəzṓ-on, -ən, spə́rmə-/ *n.* (*pl.* **spermatozoa** /-zṓə/) the mature motile sex cell in animals. ▫▫ **sper·ma·to·zo·al** *adj.* **sper·ma·to·zo·an** *adj.*

sper·mi·cide /spə́rmisīd/ *n.* a substance able to kill spermatozoa. ▫▫ **sper·mi·cid·al** /-síd'l/ *adj.*

sperm whale *n.* a large whale, *Physeter macrocephalus*, hunted for spermaceti and ambergris.

spew /spyoo/ *v.* (also **spue**) **1** *tr.* & *intr.* vomit. **2** (often foll. by *out*) **a** *tr.* expel (contents) rapidly and forcibly. **b** *intr.* (of contents) be expelled in this way. ▫▫ **spew·er** *n.*

SPF *abbr.* sun protection factor.

spheno- /sfé̱enō/ *comb. form* wedge-shaped.

sphere /sfeer/ *n.* **1** a solid figure, or its surface, with every point on its surface equidistant from its center. **2** an object having this shape; a ball or globe. **3** *hist.* each of a series of revolving concentrically arranged spherical shells in which celestial bodies were formerly thought to be set in a fixed relationship. **4 a** a field of action, influence, or existence. **b** a (usu. specified) stratum of society or social class. ▫ **music** (or **harmony**) **of the spheres** the natural harmonic tones supposedly produced by the movement of the celestial spheres (see sense 3) or the bodies fixed in them. ▫▫ **spher·al** *adj.*

sphere of in·flu·ence *n.* the claimed or recognized area of a nation's interests, an individual's control, etc.

spher·ic /sfé̱erik, sfér-/ *adj.* = SPHERICAL. ▫▫ **sphe·ric·i·ty** /-rísitee/ *n.*

spher·i·cal /sfé̱erikəl, sfér-/ *adj.* **1** shaped like a sphere. **2** of or relating to the properties of spheres (*spherical geometry*). ▫▫ **spher·i·cal·ly** *adv.*

sphe·roid /sfé̱eroyd/ *n.* a spherelike but not perfectly spherical body. ▫▫ **sphe·roi·dal** /-óyd'l/ *adj.* **sphe·roi·dic·i·ty** /-dísitee/ *n.*

spher·ule /sfé̱erool, –yool, sfér–/ *n.* a small sphere. ▫▫ **sphe·ru·lar** *adj.*

sphinc·ter /sfíngktər/ *n. Anat.* a ring of muscle surrounding and serving to guard or close an opening or tube, esp. the anus. ▫▫ **sphinc·ter·al** *adj.* **sphinc·ter·ic** /-térik/ *adj.*

sphinx /sfingks/ *n.* **1** (**Sphinx**) (in Greek mythology) the winged monster of Thebes, having a woman's head and a lion's body, whose riddle Oedipus guessed. **2** *Antiq.* **a** any of several ancient Egyptian stone figures having a lion's body and a human or animal head. **b** (**the Sphinx**) the huge stone figure of a sphinx near the Pyramids at Giza. **3** an enigmatic or inscrutable person.

sphygmo- /sfígmō/ *comb. form Physiol.* a pulse or pulsation.

sphyg·mo·ma·nom·e·ter /sfígmōmənómitər/ *n.* an instrument for measuring blood pressure. ▫▫ **sphyg·mo·man·o·met·ric** /-nəmétrik/ *adj.*

spice /spīs/ *n.* & *v.* • *n.* **1** an aromatic or pungent vegetable substance used to flavor food, e.g., cloves, pepper, or mace. **2** spices collectively (*a dealer in spice*). **3** an interesting or piquant quality. • *v.tr.* **1** flavor with spice. **2** add an interesting or piquant quality to (*a book spiced with humor*).

spick-and-span /spík ənd spán/ (also **spic-and-span**) *adj.* **1** fresh and new. **2** neat and clean.

spic·y /spísee/ *adj.* (**spicier, spiciest**) **1** of, flavored with, or fragrant with spice. **2** piquant; pungent; sensational (*a spicy story*). ▫▫ **spic·i·ly** *adv.* **spic·i·ness** *n.*

spi·der /spídər/ *n.* & *v.* • *n.* **1 a** any eight-legged arthropod of the order Araneae with a round unsegmented body, many of which spin webs for the capture of insects as food. **b** any of various similar or related arachnids. **2** any object comparable to a spider, esp. as having numerous legs or radiating spokes. •*v.* **1** *intr.* move in a scuttling manner suggestive of a spider. **2** *tr.* cause to move or appear in this way. ▫▫ **spi·der·ish** *adj.*

spi·der crab *n.* any of various crabs of the family Majidae with a pear-shaped body and long thin legs.

spi·der mon·key *n.* any S. American monkey of the genus *Ateles,* with long limbs and a prehensile tail.

spi·der·y /spídəree/ *adj.* elongated and thin (*spidery handwriting*).

spiel /speel, shpeel/ *n. & v. sl.* •*n.* a glib speech or story, esp. a salesman's patter. •*v.* **1** *intr.* speak glibly. **2** *tr.* reel off (patter, etc.). ▫▫ **spiel·er** *n.*

spif·fy /spífee/ *adj.* (**spiffier, spiffiest**) *sl.* stylish; smart. ▫▫ **spif·fi·ly** *adv.*

spig·ot /spígət/ *n.* **1** a small peg or plug, esp. for insertion into the vent of a cask. **2 a** a faucet. **b** a device for controlling the flow of liquid in a faucet.

spike[1] /spīk/ *n. & v.* •*n.* **1 a** a sharp point. **b** a pointed piece of metal, esp. the top of an iron railing, etc. **2 a** any of several metal points set into the sole of a running shoe to prevent slipping. **b** (in *pl.*) running shoes with spikes. **3** = SPINDLE *n.* 4. •*v.tr.* **1 a** fasten or provide with spikes. **b** fix on or pierce with spikes. **2** (of a newspaper editor, etc.) reject (a story), esp. by filing it on a spindle. **3** *colloq.* **a** lace (a drink) with alcohol, a drug, etc. **b** contaminate (a substance) with something added. **4** *hist.* plug up the vent of (a gun) with a spike.

spike[2] /spīk/ *n. Bot.* a flower cluster formed of many flower heads attached closely on a long stem. ▫▫ **spike·let** *n.*

spik·y /spíkee/ *adj.* (**spikier, spikiest**) **1** like a spike; having many spikes. **2** *colloq.* easily offended; prickly. ▫▫ **spik·i·ly** *adv.* **spik·i·ness** *n.*

spile /spīl/ *n. & v.* •*n.* **1** a wooden peg or spigot. **2** a large timber or pile for driving into the ground. **3** a small spout for tapping the sap from a sugar maple, etc. •*v.tr.* tap (a cask, etc.) with a spile in order to draw off liquid.

spill[1] /spil/ *v. & n.* •*v.* (*past* and *past part.* **spilled** or **spilt**) **1** *intr. & tr.* fall or run or cause (a liquid, powder, etc.) to fall or run out of a vessel, esp. unintentionally. **2 a** *tr.* throw from a vehicle, saddle, etc. **b** *intr.* (esp. of a crowd) tumble out quickly from a place, etc. **3** *tr. sl.* disclose (information, etc.). •*n.* **1 a** the act or an instance of spilling or being spilled. **b** a quantity spilled. **2** a tumble or fall, esp. from a horse, etc. (*had a nasty spill*). ▫ **spill the beans** *colloq.* divulge information. **spill blood** be guilty of bloodshed. **spill the blood of** kill or injure (a person). **spill over 1** overflow. **2** (of a surplus population) be forced to move. ▫▫ **spill·age** /spílij/ *n.* **spill·er** *n.*

spill[2] /spil/ *n.* a thin strip of wood, folded or twisted paper, etc., used for lighting a fire, candles, a pipe, etc.

spill·o·ver /spílōvər/ *n.* **1 a** the process or an instance of spilling over. **b** a thing that spills over. **2** a consequence, repercussion, or by-product.

spill·way /spílway/ *n.* a passage for surplus water from a dam.

spin /spin/ *v. & n.* •*v.* (**spinning**; *past* and *past part.* **spun** /spun/) **1** *intr. & tr.* turn or cause (a person or thing) to turn or whirl around quickly. **2** *tr.* (also *absol.*) **a** draw out and twist (wool, cotton, etc.) into threads. **b** make (yarn) in this way. **3** *tr.* (of a spider, silkworm, etc.) make (a web, a cocoon, etc.) by extruding a fine viscous thread. **4** *tr.* tell or write (a story, etc.) (*spins a good tale*). **5** *tr.* impart spin to (a ball). **6** *intr.* (of a person's head, etc.) be dizzy through excitement, astonishment, etc. **7** *tr.* (as **spun** *adj.*) converted into threads (*spun sugar*). **8** *tr.* toss (a coin). •*n.* **1** a spinning motion. **2** an aircraft's diving descent combined with rotation. **3 a** a revolving motion through the air, esp. in a ball struck aslant. **b** *Baseball* a twisting motion given to the ball in pitching. **4** *colloq.* a brief drive in a motor vehicle, etc., esp. for pleasure. **5** emphasis; interpretation. ▫ **spin off** throw off by centrifugal force in spinning. **spin out 1** prolong (a discussion, etc.). **2** make (a story, money, etc.) last as long as possible. **3** consume (time, etc., by discussion or in an occupation, etc.).

spi·na bif·i·da /spínə bífidə/ *n.* a congenital defect of the spine, in which part of the spinal cord and its meninges are exposed through a gap in the backbone.

spin·ach /spínich, -nij/ *n.* **1** a green garden vegetable, *Spinacia oleracea,* with succulent leaves. **2** the leaves of this plant used as food. ▫▫ **spin·ach·y** *adj.*

spi·nal /spín'l/ *adj.* of or relating to the spine (*spinal curvature; spinal disease*). ▫▫ **spi·nal·ly** *adv.*

spi·nal col·umn *n.* the spine.

spi·nal cord *n.* a cylindrical structure of the central nervous system enclosed in the spine.

spin·dle /spínd'l/ *n.* **1 a** a pin in a spinning wheel used for twisting and winding the thread. **b** a small bar with tapered ends used for the same purpose in hand spinning. **c** a pin bearing the bobbin of a spinning machine. **2** a pin or axis that revolves or on which something revolves. **3** a turned piece of wood used as a banister, chair leg, etc. **4 a** a pointed metal rod standing on a base and used for filing news items, etc., esp. when rejected for publication. **b** a similar spike used for bills, etc.

spin·dly /spíndlee/ *adj.* (**spindlier, spindliest**) long or tall and thin.

spin doc·tor *n.* a political pundit employed to promote a favorable interpretation of developments to the media.

spin·drift /spíndrift/ *n.* spray blown along the surface of the sea.

spine /spīn/ *n.* **1** a series of vertebrae extending from the skull to the small of the back; the backbone. **2** *Zool. & Bot.* any hard pointed process or structure. **3** a sharp ridge or projection, esp. of a mountain range or slope. **4** a central feature, main support, or source of strength. **5** the part of a book's jacket or cover that encloses the fastened edges of the pages. ▫▫ **spined** *adj.*

spine chill·er *n.* a frightening story, movie, etc. ▫▫ **spine-chill·ing** *adj.*

spine·less /spínlis/ *adj.* **1 a** having no spine; invertebrate. **b** (of a fish) having no spines. **2** (of a person) weak and purposeless. ▫▫ **spine·less·ly** *adv.* **spine·less·ness** *n.*

spin·et /spínit, spinét/ *n. Mus. hist.* a small harpsichord with oblique strings.

spine-ting·ling *adj.* thrilling; pleasurably exciting.

spin·na·ker /spínəkər/ *n.* a large triangular sail carried opposite the mainsail of a racing yacht running before the wind.

spin·ner /spínər/ *n.* **1** a person or thing that spins. **2** *Cricket* **a** a spin bowler. **b** a spun ball. **3 a** a real or artificial fly for esp. trout fishing. **b** revolving bait. **4** a manufacturer or merchant engaged in (esp. cotton) spinning.

spin·ner·et /spínəret/ *n.* **1** the spinning organ in a spider, etc. **2** a device for forming filaments of synthetic fiber.

spin·ney /spínee/ *n.* (*pl.* **-neys**) *Brit.* a small wood; a thicket.

spin·ning /spíning/ *n.* the act or an instance of spinning.

spin·ning jen·ny *n. hist.* a machine for spinning with more than one spindle at a time.

spin·ning wheel *n.* a household machine for spinning yarn or thread with a spindle driven by a wheel attached to a crank or treadle.
spin-off *n.* an incidental result or results, esp. as a side benefit from industrial technology.
spin·ster /spínstər/ *n.* **1** an unmarried woman. **2** a woman, esp. elderly, thought unlikely to marry. ▫▫ **spin·ster·hood** *n.* **spin·ster·ish** *adj.*
spin·y /spínee/ *adj.* (**spinier, spiniest**) **1** full of spines; prickly. **2** perplexing; troublesome. ▫▫ **spin·i·ness** *n.*
spin·y lob·ster *n.* any of various large edible crustaceans of the family Palinuridae, esp. *Palinuris vulgaris*, with a spiny shell and no large anterior claws.
spi·ral /spírəl/ *adj., n., & v.* •*adj.* **1** winding about a center in an enlarging or decreasing continuous circular motion, either on a flat plane or rising in a cone; coiled. **2** winding continuously along or as if along a cylinder, like the thread of a screw. •*n.* **1** a plane or three-dimensional spiral curve. **2** a spiral spring. **3** a spiral formation in a shell, etc. **4** a spiral galaxy. **5** a progressive rise or fall of prices, wages, etc., each responding to an upward or downward stimulus provided by the other (*a spiral of rising prices and wages*). **6** *Football* a kick or pass in which the ball rotates on its long axis while in the air. •*v.* (**spiraled** or **spiralled, spiraling** or **spiralling**) **1** *intr.* move in a spiral course, esp. upward or downward. **2** *tr.* make spiral. **3** *intr.* esp. *Econ.* (of prices, wages, etc.) rise or fall, esp. rapidly. ▫▫ **spi·ral·ly** *adv.*
spi·ral gal·axy *n.* a galaxy in which the matter is concentrated mainly in one or more spiral arms.
spi·rant /spírənt/ *adj. & n. Phonet.* •*adj.* (of a consonant) uttered with a continuous expulsion of breath, esp. fricative. •*n.* such a consonant.
spire /spīr/ *n. & v.* •*n.* **1** a tapering cone- or pyramid-shaped structure built esp. on a church tower. **2** any tapering thing, e.g., the spike of a flower. •*v.tr.* provide with a spire. ▫▫ **spir·y** /spíree/ *adj.*
spi·ril·lum /spīríləm/ *n.* (*pl.* **spirilla** /–lə/) **1** any bacterium of the genus *Spirillum*, characterized by a rigid spiral structure. **2** any bacterium with a similar shape.
spir·it /spírit/ *n. & v.* •*n.* **1 a** the vital animating essence of a person or animal (*broken in spirit*). **b** the soul. **2 a** a rational or intelligent being without a material body. **b** a supernatural being. **3** a prevailing mental or moral condition or attitude (*took it in the wrong spirit*). **4 a** (in *pl.*) strong distilled liquor, e.g., brandy, whiskey, gin, rum. **b** a distilled volatile liquid (*wood spirits*). **c** purified alcohol (*methylated spirits*). **d** a solution of a volatile principle in alcohol (*spirits of ammonia*). **5 a** a person's mental nature, usu. specified (*an unbending spirit*). **b** a person viewed as possessing these (*is an ardent spirit*). **c** courage; energy; vivacity (*played with spirit*). **6** the real meaning as opposed to lip service or verbal expression (*the spirit of the law*). •*v.tr.* (**spirited, spiriting**) (usu. foll. by *away, off*, etc.) convey rapidly and secretly by or as if by spirits. ▫ **in spirit** inwardly (*will be with you in spirit*).
spir·it·ed /spíritid/ *adj.* **1** full of spirit; animated or courageous (*a spirited attack*). **2** having a spirit or spirits of a specified kind (*a high-spirited person*). ▫▫ **spir·it·ed·ly** *adv.* **spir·it·ed·ness** *n.*
spir·it·less /spíritlis/ *adj.* lacking courage, vigor, or vivacity. ▫▫ **spir·it·less·ly** *adv.* **spir·it·less·ness** *n.*
spir·it lev·el *n.* a bent glass tube nearly filled with alcohol used to test horizontality by the position of an air bubble.
spir·it·u·al /spírichōōəl/ *adj. & n.* •*adj.* **1** of or concerning the spirit as opposed to matter. **2** concerned with sacred or religious things (*spiritual songs*). **3** (of the mind, etc.) refined; sensitive. **4** concerned with the spirit, etc., not with external reality (*his spiritual home*). •*n.* a religious song derived from the musical traditions of African-American people in the southern US. ▫▫ **spir·it·u·al·i·ty** /–chōō-álitee/ *n.* **spir·it·u·al·ly** *adv.* **spir·it·u·al·ness** *n.*
spir·it·u·al·ism /spírichōōəlizəm/ *n.* **1** the belief that the spirits of the dead can communicate with the living, esp. through mediums. **2** the practice of this. ▫▫ **spir·it·u·al·ist** *n.* **spir·it·u·al·is·tic** *adj.*
spir·it·u·al·ize /spírichōōəlīz/ *v.tr.* **1** make (a person or a person's thoughts, etc.) spiritual; elevate. **2** attach a spiritual as opposed to a literal meaning to. ▫▫ **spir·it·u·al·i·za·tion** *n.*
spir·it·u·ous /spírichōōəs/ *adj.* **1** containing much alcohol. **2** distilled, as whiskey, rum, etc. (*spirituous liquor*).
spiro-[1] /spírō/ *comb. form* a coil.
spiro-[2] /spírō/ *comb. form* breath.
spi·ro·chete /spírōkeet/ *n.* (also **spi·ro·chaete**) any of various flexible spiral-shaped bacteria.
spi·ro·gy·ra /spírōjírə/ *n.* any freshwater alga of the genus *Spirogyra*, with cells containing spiral bands of chlorophyll.
spirt var. of SPURT.
spit[1] /spit/ *v. & n.* •*v.* (**spitting**; *past* and *past part.* **spat** /spat/ or **spit**) **1** *intr.* **a** eject saliva from the mouth. **b** do this as a sign of hatred or contempt (*spat at him*). **2** *tr.* (usu. foll. by *out*) **a** eject from the mouth (*spat the meat out*). **b** utter vehemently (*"Damn you!" he spat*). **3** *intr.* (of a fire, pan, etc.) send out sparks, hot fat, etc. **4** *intr.* (of rain) fall lightly (*it's only spitting*). **5** *intr.* (esp. of a cat) make a spitting or hissing noise in anger or hostility. •*n.* **1** spittle. **2** the act or an instance of spitting. ▫ **the spit of** *colloq.* the exact double of. **spit it out** *colloq.* say what is on one's mind. **spit up** regurgitate; vomit. ▫▫ **spit·ter** *n.*
spit[2] /spit/ *n. & v.* •*n.* **1** a slender rod on which meat is skewered before being roasted on a fire, etc. **2 a** a small point of land projecting into the sea. **b** a long narrow underwater bank. •*v.tr.* (**spitted, spitting**) **1** thrust a spit through (meat, etc.). **2** pierce with a sword, etc. ▫▫ **spit·ty** *adj.*
spit and pol·ish *n.* **1** the cleaning and polishing duties of a soldier, etc. **2** exaggerated neatness and smartness.
spit·ball /spítbawl/ *n. & v.* •*n.* **1** a ball of chewed paper, etc., used as a missile. **2** a baseball moistened by the pitcher to affect its flight. •*v.intr.* throw out suggestions for discussion. ▫▫ **spit·ball·er** *n.*
spite /spīt/ *n. & v.* •*n.* **1** ill will; malice toward a person. **2** a grudge. •*v.tr.* thwart; mortify; annoy (*does it to spite me*). ▫ **in spite of** notwithstanding. **in spite of oneself** though one would rather have done otherwise.
spite·ful /spítfōōl/ *adj.* motivated by spite. ▫▫ **spite·ful·ly** *adv.* **spite·ful·ness** *n.*
spit·fire /spítfīr/ *n.* a person with a fiery temper.
spit·ting dis·tance *n.* a very short distance.
spit·ting im·age *n.* (foll. by *of*) *colloq.* the exact double of (another person or thing).
spit·tle /spít'l/ *n.* saliva, esp. as ejected from the mouth.
spit·toon /spitóon/ *n.* a metal or earthenware pot with esp. a funnel-shaped top, used for spitting into.
splash /splash/ *v. & n.* •*v.* **1** *intr. & tr.* spatter or cause (liquid) to spatter in small drops. **2** *tr.* cause (a person) to be spattered with liquid, etc. **3** *intr.* **a** (of a person) cause liquid to spatter (*was splashing about*). **b** (usu. foll. by *across, along*, etc.) move while spattering liquid, etc. **c** step, fall, or plunge, etc., into a liquid, etc., so as to cause a splash. **4** *tr.* display (news) prominently. **5** *tr.* decorate with scattered color. •*n.* **1** the act or an instance of splashing. **2 a** a quantity of liquid splashed. **b** the resulting noise. **3** a spot of dirt, etc., splashed on to a thing. **4** a prominent news feature, etc. **5** a daub or patch of color. **6** *colloq.* a small

quantity of liquid, esp. of soda water, etc., to dilute liquor. □ **make a splash** attract much attention, esp. by extravagance. □□ **splash·y** *adj.* (**splashier, splashiest**).

splash·down /spláshdown/ *n.* the landing of a spacecraft in the sea.

splat[1] /splat/ *n.* a flat piece of thin wood in the center of a chair back.

splat[2] /splat/ *n., adv., & v. colloq.* • *n.* a sharp cracking or slapping sound. • *adv.* with a splat (*fell splat into the puddle*). • *v.intr. & tr.* (**splatted, splatting**) fall or hit with a splat.

splat·ter /splátər/ *v. & n.* • *v.* **1** *tr. & intr.* splash esp. with a continuous noisy action. **2** *tr.* (often foll. by *with*) make wet or dirty by splashing. • *n.* a noisy splashing sound.

splay /splay/ *v., n., & adj.* • *v.* **1** *tr.* (usu. foll. by *out*) spread (the feet, etc.) out. **2** *intr.* (of an aperture or its sides) diverge in shape or position. **3** *tr.* construct (a window, aperture, etc.) so that it diverges or is wider at one side of the wall than the other. • *n.* a surface making an oblique angle with another. • *adj.* **1** wide and flat. **2** turned outward.

spleen /spleen/ *n.* **1** an abdominal organ involved in maintaining the proper condition of blood in most vertebrates. **2** lowness of spirits; ill temper, spite (from the earlier belief that the spleen was the seat of such feelings) (*vented their spleen*). □□ **spleen·y** *adj.*

splen- /spleen/ *comb. form Anat.* the spleen.

splen·dent /spléndənt/ *adj. formal* **1** shining; lustrous. **2** illustrious.

splen·did /spléndid/ *adj.* **1** magnificent; gorgeous; brilliant. **2** dignified; impressive (*splendid isolation*). **3** excellent; fine (*a splendid chance*). □□ **splen·did·ly** *adv.* **splen·did·ness** *n.*

splen·dif·er·ous /splendífərəs/ *adj. colloq.* or *joc.* splendid.

splen·dor /spléndər/ *n.* **1** dazzling brightness. **2** magnificence; grandeur.

sple·nec·to·my /splinéktəmee/ *n.* (*pl.* **-mies**) the surgical excision of the spleen.

sple·net·ic /splinétik/ *adj.* **1** ill-tempered. **2** of or concerning the spleen. □□ **sple·net·i·cal·ly** *adv.*

splen·ic /splénik/ *adj.* of or in the spleen. □□ **splen·oid** /spleénoyd/ *adj.*

sple·ni·tis /spleenítis/ *n.* inflammation of the spleen.

sple·nol·o·gy /spleenóləjee/ *n.* the scientific study of the spleen.

sple·no·meg·a·ly /spleenəmégəlee/ *n.* a pathological enlargement of the spleen.

sple·not·o·my /spleenótəmee/ *n.* (*pl.* **-mies**) a surgical incision into or dissection of the spleen.

splice /splīs/ *v. & n.* • *v.tr.* **1** join the ends of (ropes) by interweaving strands. **2** join (pieces of timber, film, etc.) in an overlapping position. **3** (esp. as **spliced** *adj.*) *colloq.* join in marriage. • *n.* a joint consisting of two ropes, pieces of wood, film, etc., made by splicing. □ **splice the main brace** *Naut. hist.* issue an extra tot of rum. □□ **splic·er** *n.*

spliff /splif/ *n.* (also **splif**) *sl.* a marijuana cigarette.

spline /splīn/ *n. & v.* • *n.* **1** a rectangular key fitting into grooves in the hub and shaft of a wheel and allowing longitudinal play. **2** a slat. • *v.tr.* fit with a spline (sense 1).

splint /splint/ *n. & v.* • *n.* **1 a** a strip of rigid material used for holding a broken bone, etc., when set. **b** a strip of esp. wood used in basketwork, etc. **2** a thin strip of wood, etc., used to light a fire, pipe, etc. • *v.tr.* secure with a splint or splints.

splin·ter /splíntər/ *v. & n.* • *v.tr. & intr.* break into fragments. • *n.* a small thin sharp-edged piece broken off from wood, stone, etc. □□ **splin·ter·y** *adj.*

splin·ter group *n.* (also **splin·ter par·ty**) a group or party that has broken away from a larger one.

split /split/ *v. & n.* • *v.* (**splitting;** *past* and *past part.* **split**) **1 a** *intr. & tr.* break or cause to break forcibly into parts, esp. with the grain or into halves. **b** *intr. & tr.* (often foll. by *up*) divide into parts (*split into groups*). **c** *tr. Stock Exch.* divide into two or more shares for each share owned. **2** *tr. & intr.* (often foll. by *off, away*) remove or be removed by breaking, separating, or dividing (*split away from the group*). **3** *intr. & tr.* **a** (usu. foll. by *up*) separate esp. through discord. **b** (foll. by *with*) quarrel or cease association with (another person, etc.). **4** *tr.* cause the fission of (an atom). **5** *intr. & tr. sl.* leave, esp. suddenly. **6** *intr.* **a** (as **splitting** *adj.*) (esp. of a headache) very painful; acute. **b** (of the head) suffer great pain from a headache, noise, etc. • *n.* **1** the act or an instance of splitting; the state of being split. **2** a fissure, crack, cleft, etc. **3** a separation into parties; a schism. **4** (in *pl.*) the athletic feat of leaping in the air or sitting down with the legs at right angles to the body in front and behind, or at the sides with the trunk facing forward. **5 a** half a bottle of mineral water. **b** half a glass of liquor. **6** *colloq.* a division of money, esp. the proceeds of crime. □ **split the difference** take the average of two proposed amounts. **split hairs** make insignificant distinctions. **split one's sides** be convulsed with laughter. **split the ticket** (or **one's vote**) vote for candidates of more than one party in one election. **split the vote** (of a candidate or minority party) attract votes from another so that both are defeated by a third. □□ **split·ter** *n.*

split in·fin·i·tive *n.* a phrase consisting of an infinitive with an adverb, etc., inserted between *to* and the verb, e.g., *seems to really like it.*

split-lev·el *adj.* (of a building) having a room or rooms a fraction of a story higher than other parts.

split pea *n.* a dried pea split in half for cooking.

split per·son·al·i·ty *n.* the alteration or dissociation of personality occurring in some mental illnesses, esp. schizophrenia and hysteria.

split screen *n.* a screen on which two or more separate images are displayed.

split sec·ond *n.* a very brief moment of time.

splotch /sploch/ *n. & v.tr. colloq.* • *n.* a daub, blot, or smear. • *v.tr.* make a large, esp. irregular, spot or patch on. □□ **splotch·y** *adj.*

splurge /splərj/ *n. & v. colloq.* • *n.* **1** an ostentatious display. **2** an instance of great extravagance. • *v.intr.* (usu. foll. by *on*) spend large sums of money.

splut·ter /splútər/ *v. & n.* • *v.* **1** *intr.* **a** speak in a hurried, vehement, or choking manner. **b** emit spitting sounds. **2** *tr.* **a** speak or utter rapidly or incoherently. **b** emit (food, sparks, etc.) with a spitting sound. • *n.* spluttering speech. □□ **splut·ter·er** *n.* **splut·ter·ing·ly** *adv.*

spoil /spoyl/ *v. & n.* • *v.* (*past* and *past part.* **spoiled**) **1** *tr.* **a** damage; diminish the value of (*spoiled by the rain*). **b** reduce a person's enjoyment, etc., of (*the news spoiled his dinner*). **2** *tr.* injure the character of (a child, pet, etc.) by excessive indulgence. **3** *intr.* **a** (of food) go bad; decay. **b** (usu. in *neg.*) (of a joke, secret, etc.) become stale through long keeping. **4** *tr.* render (a ballot) invalid by improper marking. • *n.* **1** (usu. in *pl.*) **a** plunder taken from an enemy in war, or seized by force. **b** profit or advantage gained by succeeding to public office, high position, etc. **2** earth, etc., thrown up in excavating, dredging, etc. □ **be spoiling for** aggressively seek (a fight, etc.).

spoil·age /spóylij/ *n.* **1** paper spoiled in printing. **2** the spoiling of food, etc., by decay.

spoil·er /spóylər/ *n.* **1** a person or thing that spoils. **2 a** a device on an aircraft to retard its speed by interrupting the air flow. **b** a similar device on a vehicle to improve road-holding at speed.

spoil·sport /spóylspawrt/ *n.* a person who spoils others' pleasure.

spoils sys·tem *n.* the practice of giving public office to the adherents of a successful party.

spoke[1] /spōk/ *n.* & *v.* • *n.* **1** each of the bars running from the hub to the rim of a wheel. **2** a rung of a ladder. • *v.tr.* **1** provide with spokes. **2** obstruct (a wheel, etc.) by thrusting a spoke in. ▫▫ **spoke·wise** *adv.*

spoke[2] *past* of SPEAK.

spo·ken /spṓkən/ *past part.* of SPEAK. *adj.* (in *comb.*) speaking in a specified way (*smooth-spoken*; *well-spoken*). ▫ **spoken for** claimed; requisitioned.

spoke·shave /spṓkshayv/ *n.* a blade set between two handles, used for shaping spokes and other esp. curved work.

spokes·man /spṓksmən/ *n.* (*pl.* **-men**; *fem.* **spokes·wom·an**, *pl.* **-wom·en**) **1** a person who speaks on behalf of others, esp. in the course of public relations. **2** a person deputed to express the views of a group, etc.

spokes·per·son /spṓkspərsən/ *n.* (*pl.* **-persons** or **-people**) a spokesman or spokeswoman.

spo·li·a·tion /spṓleeáyshən/ *n.* **1** plunder or pillage, esp. of neutral vessels in war. **2** extortion.

spon·dee /spóndee/ *n. Prosody* a foot consisting of two long (or stressed) syllables.

sponge /spunj/ *n.* & *v.* • *n.* **1** any aquatic animal of the phylum Porifera, with pores in its body wall and a rigid internal skeleton. **2 a** the skeleton of a sponge, esp. the soft light elastic absorbent kind used in bathing, etc. **b** a piece of porous rubber or plastic, etc., used similarly. **3** a thing of spongelike absorbency or consistency, e.g., a sponge cake, porous metal, etc. **4** = SPONGER. **5** cleaning with or as with a sponge (*gave the stove a quick sponge*). • *v.* **1** *tr.* wipe or clean with a sponge. **2** *tr.* (also *absol.*; often foll. by *down*, *over*) sluice water over (the body, a car, etc.). **3** *tr.* (often foll. by *out*, *away*, etc.) wipe off or efface (writing, etc.) with or as with a sponge. **4** *tr.* (often foll. by *up*) absorb with or as with a sponge. **5** *intr.* (often foll. by *on*, *off*) live as a parasite. **6** *tr.* obtain (drink, etc.) by sponging. **7** *intr.* gather sponges. **8** *tr.* apply paint with a sponge to (walls, furniture, etc.). ▫▫ **sponge·a·ble** *adj.* **sponge·like** *adj.* **spon·gi·form** *adj.* (esp. in senses 1, 2).

sponge cake *n.* a very light cake with a spongelike consistency.

spong·er /spúnjər/ *n.* a person who contrives to live at another's expense.

spon·gy /spúnjee/ *adj.* (**spongier**, **spongiest**) like a sponge, esp. in being porous, compressible, elastic, or absorbent. ▫▫ **spon·gi·ly** *adv.* **spon·gi·ness** *n.*

spon·sion /spónshən/ *n.* **1** being a surety for another. **2** a pledge or promise made on behalf of the government by an agent not authorized to do so.

spon·sor /spónsər/ *n.* & *v.* • *n.* **1** a person who supports an activity done for charity by pledging money in advance. **2 a** a person or organization that promotes or supports an artistic or sporting activity, etc. **b** a business organization that promotes a broadcast program in return for advertising time. **3** an organization lending support to an election candidate. **4** a person who introduces a proposal for legislation. **5** a godparent at baptism or esp. a person who presents a candidate for confirmation. **6** a person who makes himself or herself responsible for another. • *v.tr.* be a sponsor for. ▫▫ **spon·so·ri·al** /sponsáwreeəl/ *adj.* **spon·sor·ship** *n.*

spon·ta·ne·ous /spontáyneeəs/ *adj.* **1** acting or done or occurring without external cause. **2** without external incitement (*made a spontaneous offer of his services*). **3** (of bodily movement, literary style, etc.) gracefully natural and unconstrained. **4** (of sudden movement, etc.) involuntary; not due to conscious volition. **5** growing naturally without cultivation. ▫▫ **spon·ta·ne·i·ty** /spóntənéeitee, –náyitee/ *n.* **spon·ta·ne·ous·ly** *adv.* **spon·ta·ne·ous·ness** *n.*

spon·ta·ne·ous com·bus·tion *n.* the ignition of a substance from heat engendered within itself.

spon·ta·ne·ous gen·er·a·tion *n.* the supposed production of living from nonliving matter as inferred from the appearance of life (due in fact to bacteria, etc.) in some infusions.

spoof /spoof/ *n.* & *v. colloq.* • *n.* **1** a parody. **2** a hoax or swindle. • *v.tr.* **1** parody. **2** hoax; swindle. ▫▫ **spoof·er** *n.* **spoof·er·y** *n.*

spook /spŏŏk/ *n.* & *v.* • *n.* **1** *colloq.* a ghost. **2** *sl.* a spy. • *v. sl.* **1** *tr.* frighten; unnerve; alarm. **2** *intr.* take fright; become alarmed.

spook·y /spŏŏkee/ *adj.* (**spookier**, **spookiest**) **1** *colloq.* ghostly; eerie. **2** *sl.* nervous. ▫▫ **spook·i·ly** *adv.* **spook·i·ness** *n.*

spool /spool/ *n.* & *v.* • *n.* **1 a** a reel for winding magnetic tape, etc., on. **b** a reel for winding thread or wire on. **c** a quantity of tape, etc., wound on a spool. **2** the revolving cylinder of an angler's reel. • *v.tr.* wind on a spool.

spoon /spoon/ *n.* & *v.* • *n.* **1 a** a utensil consisting of an oval or round bowl and a handle for conveying food (esp. liquid) to the mouth, for stirring, etc. **b** a spoonful, esp. of sugar. **2** a spoon-shaped thing, esp.: **a** (in full **spoon-bait**) a bright revolving piece of metal used as a lure in fishing. **b** an oar with a broad curved blade. • *v.* **1** *tr.* (often foll. by *up*, *out*) take (liquid, etc.) with a spoon. **2** *intr. colloq.* behave in an amorous way, esp. foolishly. ▫ **born with a silver spoon in one's mouth** born into affluence. ▫▫ **spoon·er** *n.* **spoon·ful** *n.* (*pl.* **-fuls**).

spoon·bill /spóonbil/ *n.* any large wading bird of the subfamily Plataleidae, having a bill with a very broad flat tip.

spoon·er·ism /spóonərizəm/ *n.* a transposition, usu. accidental, of the initial letters, etc., of two or more words, e.g., *you have hissed the mystery lectures*.

spoon·feed /spóonfeed/ *v.tr.* (*past* and *past part.* **-fed**) **1** feed (a baby, etc.) with a spoon. **2** provide help, information, etc., to (a person) without requiring any effort on the recipient's part.

spo·rad·ic /spərádik, spaw–/ *adj.* occurring only here and there or occasionally; scattered. ▫▫ **spo·rad·i·cal·ly** *adv.*

spo·ran·gi·um /spəránjeeəm/ *n.* (*pl.* **sporangia** /–jeeə/) *Bot.* a receptacle in which spores are found. ▫▫ **spor·an·gi·al** *adj.*

spore /spawr/ *n.* a specialized reproductive cell of many plants and microorganisms.

sporo- /spáwrō/ *comb. form Biol.* a spore.

spo·ro·gen·e·sis /spáwrəjénisis/ *n.* the process of spore formation.

spo·rog·e·nous /spərójinəs/ *adj.* producing spores.

spo·ro·phyte /spáwrəfīt/ *n.* a spore-producing form of plant with alternating sexua and asexual generations. ▫▫ **spor·o·phyt·ic** /–fítik/ *adj.* **spor·o·phyt·i·cal·ly** *adv.*

sport /spawrt/ *n.* & *v.* • *n.* **1 a** a game or competitive activity, esp. an outdoor one involving physical exertion. **b** such activities collectively. **2** amusement; fun. **3** *colloq.* **a** a fair or generous person. **b** a person behaving in a specified way, esp. regarding games, rules, etc. (*a bad sport at tennis*). **c** a form of address, esp. between males. **4** *Biol.* an animal or plant deviating from the normal type. **5** a plaything or laughingstock (*the sport of Fortune*). • *v.* **1** *intr.* divert oneself; take part in a pastime. **2** *tr.* wear, exhibit, or produce, esp. ostentatiously. **3** *intr. Biol.* become or produce a sport. ▫ **in sport**

jestingly. **make sport of** make fun of; ridicule. ▫▫ **sport·er** *n.*

sport·ing /spáwrting/ *adj.* **1** interested in sports (*a sporting man*). **2** sportsmanlike; generous (*a sporting offer*). **3** concerned with sports (*sporting news*). ▫▫ **sport·ing·ly** *adv.*

spor·tive /spáwrtiv/ *adj.* playful. ▫▫ **spor·tive·ly** *adv.* **spor·tive·ness** *n.*

sports car *n.* a usu. open, low-built fast car.

sports·cast /spáwrtskast/ *n.* a broadcast of a sports event or information about sports. ▫▫ **sports·cast·er** *n.*

sports coat *n.* (also **sports jacket**) a man's jacket for informal wear.

sports·man /spáwrtsmən/ *n.* (*pl.* **-men**; *fem.* **sports·wom·an**, *pl.* **-wom·en**) **1** a person who takes part in sports, esp. professionally. **2** a person who behaves fairly and generously. ▫▫ **sports·man·like** *adj.* **sports·man·ly** *adj.* **sports·man·ship** *n.*

sports·wear /spáwrtswair/ *n.* clothes worn for sports or for casual use.

sport u·til·i·ty ve·hi·cle *n.* a high-performance passenger vehicle with a light-truck chassis and four-wheel drive. ¶ Abbr.: **SUV**.

sport·y /spáwrtee/ *adj.* (**sportier**, **sportiest**) *colloq.* **1** fond of sports. **2** rakish; showy. ▫▫ **sport·i·ly** *adv.* **sport·i·ness** *n.*

spot /spot/ *n.* & *v.* • *n.* **1 a** a small part of the surface of a thing distinguished by color, texture, etc., usu. round or less elongated than a streak or stripe. **b** a small mark or stain. **c** a pimple. **d** a small circle or other shape used in various numbers to distinguish playing cards in a suit, etc. **e** a moral blemish or stain. **2 a** a particular place; a definite locality (*on this precise spot*). **b** a place used for a particular activity (often in *comb.*: *nightspot*). **c** (prec. by *the*) *Soccer* the place from which a penalty kick is taken. **3** a particular part of one's body or aspect of one's character. **4 a** *colloq.* one's esp. regular position in an organization, program, etc. **b** a place or position in a show (*did the spot before intermission*). **5** = SPOTLIGHT. **6** (usu. *attrib.*) money paid or goods delivered immediately after a sale (*spot cash*). • *v.* (**spotted, spotting**) **1** *tr.* **a** *colloq.* single out beforehand (the winner of a race, etc.). **b** *colloq.* recognize the identity, nationality, etc., of. **c** watch for and take note of (trains, talent, etc.). **d** *colloq.* catch sight of. **e** *Mil.* locate (an enemy's position), esp. from the air. **2 a** *tr.* & *intr.* mark or become marked with spots. **b** *tr.* stain; soil (a person's character, etc.). **3** *intr.* rain slightly (*it was spotting with rain*). ▫ **on the spot 1** at the scene of an action or event. **2** *colloq.* in a position such that response or action is required. **3** then and there. **put on the spot** *sl.* make to feel uncomfortable, awkward, etc.

spot·less /spótlis/ *adj.* immaculate. ▫▫ **spot·less·ly** *adv.* **spot·less·ness** *n.*

spot·light /spótlīt/ *n.* & *v.* • *n.* **1** a beam of light directed on a small area. **2** a lamp projecting this. **3** full attention or publicity. • *v.tr.* (*past* and *past part.* **-lighted** or **-lit**) **1** direct a spotlight on. **2** draw attention to.

spot·ted /spótid/ *adj.* marked or decorated with spots. ▫▫ **spot·ted·ness** *n.*

spot·ter /spótər/ *n.* **1** (often in *comb.*) a person who spots people or things (*train spotter*). **2** an aviator or aircraft employed in locating enemy positions, etc.

spot·ty /spótee/ *adj.* (**spottier, spottiest**) **1** marked with spots. **2** patchy; irregular. ▫▫ **spot·ti·ly** *adv.* **spot·ti·ness** *n.*

spouse /spows, spowz/ *n.* a husband or wife.

spout /spowt/ *n.* & *v.* • *n.* **1 a** a projecting tube or lip through which a liquid, etc., is poured from a teapot, kettle, etc., or issues from a fountain, pump, etc. **b** a sloping trough down which a thing may be shot into a receptacle. **2** a jet or column of liquid, grain, etc. **3** (in full **spout hole**) a whale's blowhole. • *v.tr.* & *intr.* **1** discharge or issue forcibly in a jet. **2** utter (verses, etc.) or speak in a declamatory manner. ▫▫ **spout·er** *n.*

sprain /sprayn/ *v.* & *n.* • *v.tr.* wrench (an ankle, wrist, etc.) violently so as to cause pain and swelling but not dislocation. • *n.* **1** such a wrench. **2** the resulting inflammation and swelling.

sprang *past* of SPRING.

sprat /sprat/ *n.* **1** a small European herring-like fish, *Sprattus sprattus*, much used as food. **2** a similar fish, e.g., a sand eel or a young herring. ▫▫ **sprat·ting** *n.*

sprawl /sprawl/ *v.* & *n.* • *v.* **1 a** *intr.* sit or lie or fall with limbs flung out or in an ungainly way. **b** *tr.* spread (one's limbs) in this way. **2** *intr.* (of handwriting, a plant, a town, etc.) be of irregular or straggling form. • *n.* **1** a sprawling movement or attitude. **2** a straggling group or mass. **3** the straggling expansion of an urban or industrial area. ▫▫ **sprawl·ing·ly** *adv.*

spray[1] /spray/ *n.* & *v.* • *n.* **1** water or other liquid flying in small drops from the force of the wind or waves, the action of an atomizer, etc. **2** a liquid preparation to be applied in this form with an atomizer, etc., esp. for medical purposes. **3** an instrument for such application. • *v.tr.* (also *absol.*) **1** throw (liquid) in the form of spray. **2** sprinkle (an object) with small drops or particles. **3** (*absol.*) (of a tomcat) mark its environment with the smell of its urine. ▫▫ **spray·a·ble** *adj.* **spray·er** *n.*

spray[2] /spray/ *n.* **1** a sprig of flowers or leaves, or a branch of a tree with branchlets or flowers. **2** an ornament in a similar form (*a spray of diamonds*). ▫▫ **spray·ey** *adj.*

spray gun *n.* a gunlike device for spraying paint, etc.

spray paint *v.tr.* paint (a surface) by means of a spray.

spread /spred/ *v.* & *n.* • *v.* (*past* and *past part.* **spread**) **1** *tr.* (often foll. by *out*) **a** open or extend the surface of. **b** cause to cover a larger surface (*spread butter on bread*). **c** display to the eye or the mind (*the view spread before us*). **2** *intr.* (often foll. by *out*) have a wide or specified or increasing extent (*spreading trees*). **3** *intr.* & *tr.* become or make widely known, felt, etc. (*rumors are spreading*). **4** *tr.* **a** cover the surface of. **b** lay (a table). • 1*n.* **1** the act or an instance of spreading. **2** capability of expanding (*has a large spread*). **3** diffusion (*spread of learning*). **4** breadth; compass (*arches of equal spread*). **5** an aircraft's wingspan. **6** increased bodily girth (*middle-aged spread*). **7** the difference between two rates, prices, etc. **8** *colloq.* an elaborate meal. **9** a food paste for spreading on bread, etc. **10** a bedspread. **11** printed matter spread across more than one column. **12** a ranch with extensive land. ▫ **spread one's wings** see WING. ▫▫ **spread·a·ble** *adj.* **spread·er** *n.*

spread ea·gle *n.* **1** a representation of an eagle with legs and wings extended as an emblem. **2** *Skating* a straight glide made with the feet in a line, with the heels touching, and the arms stretched out to either side. **3** *hist.* a person secured with arms and legs spread out, esp. to be flogged.

spread-ea·gle *v.* & *adj.* • *v.* **1** *tr.* (usu. as **spread-eagled** *adj.*) place (a person) with arms and legs spread out. **2** *tr.* defeat utterly. **3** spread out. **4** *intr.* *Skating* to execute a spread eagle. • *adj.* bombastic, esp. noisily patriotic.

spread·sheet /sprédsheet/ *n.* a computer program allowing manipulation and flexible retrieval of esp. tabulated numerical data.

spree /spree/ *n.* & *v.* *colloq.* • *n.* **1** a lively extravagant outing (*shopping spree*). **2** a bout of fun or drinking, etc. ● *v.intr.* (**sprees, spreed**) have a spree. □ **on a spree** engaged in a spree.

sprig[1] /sprig/ *n.* & *v.* ● *n.* **1** a small branch or shoot. **2** an ornament resembling this, esp. on fabric. ● *v.tr.* (**sprigged, sprigging**) ornament with sprigs (*sprigged muslin*).

sprig[2] /sprig/ *n.* a small tapering headless tack; a brad.

spright·ly /sprítlee/ *adj.* (**sprightlier, sprightliest**) vivacious; lively; brisk. □□ **spright·li·ness** *n.*

spring /spring/ *v.* & *n.* ● *v.* (*past* **sprang** /sprang/also **sprung** /sprung/; *past part.* **sprung**) **1** *intr.* jump; move rapidly or suddenly. **2** *intr.* move rapidly as from a constrained position or by the action of a spring. **3** *intr.* (usu. foll. by *from*) originate or arise. **4** *intr.* (usu. foll. by *up*) appear, esp. suddenly (*a breeze sprang up*). **5** *tr.* cause to act suddenly, esp. by means of a spring (*spring a trap*). **6** *tr.* (often foll. by *on*) produce suddenly or unexpectedly (*loves to spring surprises*). **7** *tr. sl.* contrive the escape or release of. **8** *tr.* rouse (game) from earth or covert. **9** *intr.* become warped or split. **10** *tr.* (usu. as **sprung** *adj.*) provide (a motor vehicle, etc.) with springs. ● *n.* **1** a jump. **2** a backward movement from a constrained position. **3** ability to spring back strongly. **4** a resilient device usu. of bent or coiled metal used esp. to drive clockwork or for cushioning in furniture or vehicles. **5 a** the season in which vegetation begins to appear; the first season of the year. **b** *Astron.* the period from the vernal equinox to the summer solstice. **c** (often foll. by *of*) the early stage of life, etc. **d** = SPRING TIDE. **6** a place where water, oil, etc., wells up from the earth; the basin or flow so formed. **7** the motive for or origin of an action, custom, etc. (*the springs of human action*). □ **spring a leak** develop a leak (orig. *Naut.*, from timbers springing out of position). □□ **spring·less** *adj.* **spring·like** *adj.*

spring bal·ance *n.* a balance that measures weight by the tension of a spring.

spring·board /springbawrd/ *n.* **1** a springy board giving impetus in leaping, diving, etc. **2** a source of impetus in any activity.

spring chick·en *n.* **1** a young fowl for eating (orig. available only in spring). **2** (esp. with *neg.*) a young person (*she's no spring chicken*).

spring·er /springər/ *n.* **1** a person or thing that springs. **2** a small spaniel of a breed used to spring game.

spring fe·ver *n.* a restless or lethargic feeling sometimes associated with spring.

spring-load·ed *adj.* containing a compressed or stretched spring pressing one part against another (*a switchblade with a spring-loaded clip*).

spring roll *n.* an Asian snack consisting of a pancake filled with vegetables, etc., and fried.

spring·tail /springtayl/ *n.* any wingless insect of the order Collembola, leaping by means of a springlike caudal part.

spring·tide /springtīd/ *n. poet.* = SPRINGTIME.

spring tide *n.* a tide just after new and full moon when there is the greatest difference between high and low water.

spring·time /springtīm/ *n.* **1** the season of spring. **2** a time compared to this.

spring wa·ter *n.* water from a spring, as opposed to river or rain water.

spring·y /springee/ *adj.* (**springier, springiest**) **1** springing back quickly when squeezed or stretched. **2** (of movements) as of a springy substance. □□ **spring·i·ly** *adv.* **spring·i·ness** *n.*

sprin·kle /springkəl/ *v.* & *n.* ● *v.tr.* **1** scatter (liquid, ashes, crumbs, etc.) in small drops or particles. **2** (often foll. by *with*) subject (the ground or an object) to sprinkling with liquid, etc. **3** (of liquid, etc.) fall on in this way. **4** distribute in small amounts. ● *n.* (usu. foll. by *of*) **1** a light shower. **2** = SPRINKLING. **3** (in *pl.*) candy particles used as a topping on ice cream.

sprin·kler /springklər/ *n.* a device for sprinkling water on a lawn or to extinguish fires.

sprin·kling /springkling/ *n.* a small thinly distributed number or amount.

sprint /sprint/ *v.* & *n.* ● *v.* **1** *intr.* run a short distance at full speed. **2** *tr.* run (a specified distance) in this way. ● *n.* **1** such a run. **2** a short spell of maximum effort in cycling, swimming, auto racing, etc. □□ **sprint·er** *n.*

sprit /sprit/ *n.* a small spar reaching diagonally from the mast to the upper outer corner of the sail.

sprite /sprīt/ *n.* an elf, fairy, or goblin.

sprit·sail /spritsəl, –sayl/ *n.* **1** a sail extended by a sprit. **2** *hist.* a sail extended by a yard set under the bowsprit.

spritz /sprits/ *v.* & *n.* ● *v.tr.* sprinkle, squirt, or spray. ● *n.* the act or an instance of spritzing.

spritz·er /spritsər/ *n.* a mixture of wine and soda water.

sprock·et /sprókit/ *n.* **1** each of several teeth on a wheel engaging with links of a chain, e.g., on a bicycle, or with holes in film or tape or paper. **2** (also **sprock·et wheel**) a wheel with sprockets.

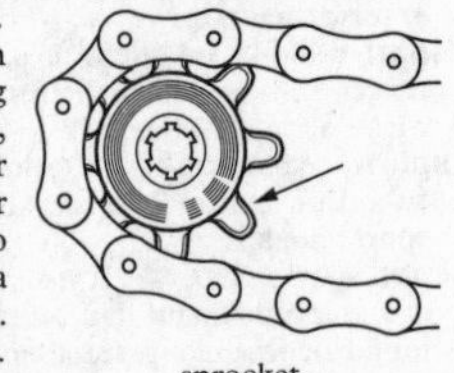

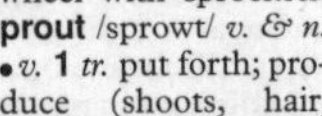

sprocket

sprout /sprowt/ *v.* & *n.* ● *v.* **1** *tr.* put forth; produce (shoots, hair, etc.) (*he had sprouted a mustache*). **2** *intr.* begin to grow; put forth shoots. **3** *intr.* spring up, grow to a height. ● *n.* **1** a shoot of a plant. **2** = BRUSSELS SPROUT.

spruce[1] /sprōōs/ *adj.* & *v.* ● *adj.* neat in dress and appearance; trim; neat and fashionable. ● *v.tr.* & *intr.* (also *refl.*; usu. foll. by *up*) make or become neat and fashionable. □□ **spruce·ly** *adv.* **spruce·ness** *n.*

spruce[2] /sprōōs/ *n.* **1** any coniferous tree of the genus *Picea*, with dense foliage growing in a conical shape. **2** the wood of this tree.

sprung see SPRING.

spry /sprī/ *adj.* (**spryer, spryest**) active; lively. □□ **spry·ly** *adv.* **spry·ness** *n.*

spud /spud/ *n.* & *v.* ● *n.* **1** *sl.* a potato. **2** a small narrow spade for cutting the roots of weeds, etc. ● *v.tr.* (**spudded, spudding**) **1** (foll. by *up*, *out*) remove (weeds) with a spud. **2** (also *absol.*; often foll. by *in*) make the initial drilling for (an oil well).

spue var. of SPEW.

spu·man·te /spōōmaantee, –tay/ *n.* a sweet white Italian sparkling wine.

spume /spyōōm/ *n.* & *v.intr.* froth; foam. □□ **spu·mous** *adj.* **spum·y** *adj.*

spun *past* and *past part.* of SPIN.

spunk /spungk/ *n.* **1** touchwood. **2** *colloq.* courage; spirit.

spunk·y /spúngkee/ *adj.* (**spunkier, spunkiest**) *colloq.* spirited. □□ **spunk·i·ly** *adv.*

spur /spər/ *n.* & *v.* ● *n.* **1** a device with a small spike or a spiked wheel worn on a rider's heel for urging a horse forward. **2** a stimulus or incentive. **3** a spur-shaped thing, esp.: **a** a projection from a mountain. **b** a branch road or railway. **c** a hard projection on a rooster's leg. ● *v.* (**spurred, spurring**) **1** *tr.* prick (a horse) with spurs. **2** *tr.* **a** (often foll. by *on*) incite (a person). **b** stimulate (interest, etc.). **3** *intr.* (often foll. by *on*, *forward*) ride a horse hard. **4** *tr.* (esp. as **spurred** *adj.*) provide with spurs. □ **on the spur of the moment** on a momentary impulse. □□ **spur·less** *adj.*

spurge /spərj/ *n.* any plant of the genus *Euphorbia*, exuding an acrid juice.

spu·ri·ous /spyŏŏreeəs/ *adj.* **1** not genuine; not being what it purports to be (*a spurious excuse*). **2** having an outward similarity of form or function only. **3** (of offspring) illegitimate. ▫▫ **spu·ri·ous·ly** *adv.* **spu·ri·ous·ness** *n.*

spurn /spərn/ *v.tr.* **1** reject with disdain; treat with contempt. **2** repel or thrust back with one's foot.

spur-of-the-mo·ment *adj.* unpremeditated.

spurt /spərt/ *v.* & *n.* • *v.* **1** (also **spirt**) **a** *intr.* gush out in a jet or stream. **b** *tr.* cause (liquid, etc.) to do this. **2** *intr.* make a sudden effort. • *n.* **1** (also **spirt**) a sudden gushing out; a jet. **2** a short sudden effort or increase of pace, esp. in racing.

sput·nik /spŏŏtnik, spút–/ *n.* (sometimes *cap.*) each of a series of Russian artificial satellites that was launched from 1957.

sput·ter /spútər/ *v.* & *n.* • *v.* **1** *intr.* emit spitting sounds, esp. when being heated. **2** *intr.* (often foll. by *at*) speak in a hurried or vehement fashion. **3** *tr.* emit with a spitting sound. **4** *tr.* speak or utter rapidly or incoherently. • *n.* a sputtering sound, esp. sputtering speech. ▫▫ **sput·ter·er** *n.*

spu·tum /spyŏŏtəm/ *n.* (*pl.* **sputa** /–tə/) **1** saliva; spittle. **2** a mixture of saliva and mucus expectorated from the respiratory tract, usu. a sign of disease or illness.

spy /spī/ *n.* & *v.* • *n.* (*pl.* **spies**) **1** a person who secretly collects and reports information on the activities, etc., of an enemy, competitor, etc. **2** a person who keeps watch on others, esp. furtively. • *v.* (**spies, spied**) **1** *tr.* discern or make out, esp. by careful observation. **2** *intr.* (often foll. by *on*) act as a spy; keep a close and secret watch. **3** *intr.* (often foll. by *into*) pry. ▫ **spy out** explore or discover, esp. secretly.

spy·glass /spíglas/ *n.* a small telescope.

sq. *abbr.* square.

squab /skwob/ *n.* & *adj.* • *n.* **1** a short fat person. **2** a young, esp. unfledged, pigeon or other bird. **3** a stuffed cushion. **4** a sofa. • *adj.* squat.

squab·ble /skwóbəl/ *n.* & *v.* • *n.* a petty or noisy quarrel. • *v.intr.* engage in a squabble. ▫▫ **squab·bler** *n.*

squab·by /skwóbee/ *adj.* (**squabbier, squabbiest**) short and fat; squat.

squad /skwod/ *n.* **1** a small group of people sharing a task, etc. **2** *Mil.* a small number of soldiers assembled for drill, etc. **3** *Sports* a group of players forming a team. **4** (often in *comb.*) a specialized unit within a police force (*drug squad*).

squad car *n.* a police car having a radio link with headquarters.

squad·ron /skwódrən/ *n.* **1** an organized body of persons. **2** a principal division of a cavalry regiment or armored formation, consisting of two troops. **3** a detachment of warships employed on a particular duty. **4** a unit of the US Air Force with two or more flights.

squal·id /skwólid/ *adj.* **1** repulsively dirty. **2** degraded or poor in appearance. **3** wretched; sordid. ▫▫ **squa·lid·i·ty** *n.* /–líditee/ **squal·id·ly** *adv.* **squal·id·ness** *n.*

squall /skwawl/ *n.* & *v.* • *n.* **1** a sudden or violent gust or storm of wind, esp. with rain or snow or sleet. **2** a discordant cry; a scream. **3** (esp. in *pl.*) trouble; difficulty. • *v.* **1** *intr.* utter a squall; scream. **2** *tr.* utter in a screaming or discordant voice. ▫▫ **squal·ly** *adj.*

squal·or /skwólər/ *n.* the state of being filthy or squalid.

squan·der /skwóndər/ *v.tr.* spend wastefully. ▫▫ **squan·der·er** *n.*

square /skwair/ *n., adj., adv.,* & *v.* • *n.* **1** an equilateral rectangle. **2 a** an object of this shape or approximately this shape. **b** a small square area on a game board. **c** a square scarf. **3 a** an open (usu. four-sided) area surrounded by buildings. **b** an open area at the meeting of streets. **c** an area within barracks, etc., for drill. **d** a block of buildings bounded by four streets. **4** the product of a number multiplied by itself (*81 is the square of 9*). **5** an L-shaped or T-shaped instrument for obtaining or testing right angles. **6** *sl.* a conventional or old-fashioned person. **7** a square arrangement of letters, figures, etc. **8** a body of infantry drawn up in rectangular form. • *adj.* **1** having the shape of a square. **2** having or in the form of a right angle (*table with square corners*). **3** angular and not round (*a square jaw*). **4** designating a unit of measure equal to the area of a square whose side is one of the unit specified (*square meter*). **5** (often foll. by *with*) **a** level; parallel. **b** on a proper footing; even. **6** (usu. foll. by *to*) at right angles. **7** having the breadth more nearly equal to the height than is usual (*a man of square frame*). **8** properly arranged; settled (*get things square*). **9** (also **all square**) **a** not in debt; with no money owed. **b** having equal scores. **c** (of scores) equal. **10** fair and honest. **11** uncompromising; direct. (*a square refusal*). **12** *sl.* conventional or old-fashioned. • *adv.* **1** squarely (*sat square on her seat*). **2** fairly; honestly (*play square*). • *v.* **1** *tr.* make square or rectangular; give a rectangular cross-section to (timber, etc.). **2** *tr.* multiply (a number) by itself (*3 squared is 9*). **3** *tr.* & *intr.* (usu. foll. by *to, with*) make or be suitable or consistent (*the results do not square with your conclusions*). **4** *tr.* mark out in squares. **5** *tr.* settle or pay (a bill, etc.). **6** *tr.* place (one's shoulders, etc.) squarely facing forward. **7** *tr. colloq.* **a** pay or bribe. **b** secure the acquiescence, etc., of (a person) in this way. **8** *tr.* (also *absol.*) make the scores of (a match, etc.) all square. ▫ **back to square one** *colloq.* back to the starting point with no progress made. **get square with** pay or compound with (a creditor). **on the square** *adj. colloq.* honest; fair. • *adv. colloq.* honestly; fairly. **out of square** not at right angles. **square peg in a round hole** see PEG. **square up** settle an account, etc. **square up to 1** move toward (a person) in a fighting attitude. **2** face and tackle (a difficulty, etc.) resolutely. ▫▫ **square·ly** *adv.* **square·ness** *n.* **squar·ish** *adj.*

square dance *n.* a dance with usu. four couples facing inward from four sides.

square deal *n.* a fair bargain; fair treatment.

square knot *n.* a double knot made symmetrically to hold securely and cast off easily.

square meal *n.* a substantial and satisfying meal.

square meas·ure *n.* measure expressed in square units.

square num·ber *n.* the square of an integer e.g., 1, 4, 9, 16.

square root *n.* the number that multiplied by itself gives a specified number (*3 is the square root of 9*).

square sail *n.* a four-cornered sail extended on a yard slung to the mast by the middle.

square shoot·er *n.* a person who is honest, fair, and straightforward.

square-shoul·dered *adj.* with broad and not sloping shoulders (cf. ROUND-SHOULDERED).

squash[1] /skwosh/ *v.* & *n.* • *v.* **1** *tr.* crush or squeeze flat or into pulp. **2** *intr.* (often foll. by *into*) make one's way by squeezing. **3** *tr.* pack tight; crowd. **4** *tr.* **a** silence (a person) with a crushing retort, etc. **b** dismiss (a proposal, etc.). **c** quash (a rebellion). • *n.* **1** a crowd; a crowded assembly. **2** a sound of or as of something being squashed, or of a soft body falling. **3** a game played with rackets and a small ball against the walls of a closed court. **4** a squashed thing or mass. **5** *Brit.* a drink made of diluted crushed fruit, etc. ▫▫ **squash·y** *adj.* (**squashier, squashiest**). **squash·i·ly** *adv.* **squash·i·ness** *n.*

squash[2] /skwosh/ *n.* (*pl.* same or **squashes**) **1** any of various gourdlike trailing plants of the genus *Cucurbita,* whose fruits may be used as a vegetable. **2** the fruit of these cooked and eaten.

squat /skwot/ *v., adj., & n.* •*v.* (**squatted, squatting**) **1** *intr.* **a** crouch with the buttocks resting on the backs of the heels. **b** sit on the ground, etc., with the knees drawn up and the heels close to or touching the hams. **2** *intr. colloq.* sit down. **3 a** *intr.* act as a squatter. **b** *tr.* occupy (a building) as a squatter. **4** *intr.* (of an animal) crouch close to the ground. •*adj.* (**squatter, squattest**) **1** (of a person, etc.) dumpy. **2** in a squatting posture. •*n.* **1** a squatting posture. **2 a** a place occupied by a squatter or squatters. **b** being a squatter. ▫▫ **squat·ness** *n.*

squat·ter /skwótər/ *n.* **1** a person who takes unauthorized possession of unoccupied premises. **2** a person who settles on new, esp. public, land without title. **3** a person who squats.

squaw /skwaw/ *n.* often *offens.* a Native American woman or wife.

squawk /skwawk/ *n. & v.* •*n.* **1** a loud harsh cry, esp. of a bird. **2** a complaint. •*v.tr. & intr.* utter with or make a squawk. ▫▫ **squawk·er** *n.*

squeak /skweek/ *n. & v.* •*n.* **1 a** a short shrill cry as of a mouse. **b** a slight high-pitched sound as of an unoiled hinge. **2** (also **narrow squeak**) a narrow escape; a success barely attained. •*v.* **1** *intr.* make a squeak. **2** *tr.* utter shrilly. **3** *intr.* (foll. by *by, through*) *colloq.* pass narrowly. **4** *intr. sl.* turn informer.

squeak·er /skwéekər/ *n.* **1** a person or thing that squeaks. **2** a young bird, esp. a pigeon. **3** *colloq.* a close contest.

squeak·y /skwéekee/ *adj.* (**squeakier, squeakiest**) making a squeaking sound. ▫▫ **squeak·i·ly** *adv.* **squeak·i·ness** *n.*

squeal /skweel/ *n. & v.* •*n.* a prolonged shrill sound, esp. a cry of a child or a pig. •*v.* **1** *intr.* make a squeal. **2** *tr.* utter with a squeal. **3** *intr. sl.* turn informer. **4** *intr. sl.* protest loudly or excitedly. ▫▫ **squeal·er** *n.*

squeam·ish /skwéemish/ *adj.* **1** easily nauseated or disgusted. **2** fastidious. ▫▫ **squeam·ish·ly** *adv.* **squeam·ish·ness** *n.*

squee·gee /skwéejee/ *n. & v.* •*n.* a rubber-edged implement often set on a long handle and used for cleaning windows, etc. •*v.tr.* (**squeegees, squeegeed**) treat with a squeegee.

squeeze /skweez/ *v. & n.* •*v.* **1** *tr.* **a** exert pressure on from opposite or all sides, esp. in order to extract moisture or reduce size. **b** compress with one's hand or between two bodies. **c** reduce the size of or alter the shape of by squeezing. **2** *tr.* (often foll. by *out*) extract (moisture) by squeezing. **3 a** *tr.* force into or through a small or narrow space. **b** *intr.* make one's way by squeezing. **c** *tr.* make (one's way) by squeezing. **4** *tr.* **a** harass by exactions; extort money, etc., from. **b** bring pressure to bear on. **c** (usu. foll. by *out of*) obtain (money, etc.) by extortion, entreaty, etc. **5** *tr.* press as a sign of sympathy, etc. **6** *tr.* (often foll. by *out*) produce with effort. •*n.* **1** an instance of squeezing. **2 a** a close embrace. **b** *sl.* a girlfriend or boyfriend. **3** a crush. **4** a small quantity produced by squeezing (*a squeeze of lemon*). **5** *Econ.* a restriction on borrowing, investment, etc., in a financial crisis. **6** *Baseball* bunting a ball to the infield to enable a runner on third base to start for home as soon as the ball is pitched. ▫ **put the squeeze on** *colloq.* coerce or pressure (a person). ▫▫ **squeez·a·ble** *adj.* **squeez·er** *n.*

squeeze box *n. colloq.* an accordion or concertina.

squelch /skwelch/ *v. & n.* •*v.* **1** *intr.* **a** make a sucking sound as of treading in thick mud. **b** move with a squelching sound. **2** *tr.* **a** disconcert; silence. **b** stamp on; put an end to. •*n.* an instance of squelching. ▫▫ **squelch·y** *adj.*

squib /skwib/ *n.* **1** a small firework burning with a hissing sound and usu. with a final explosion. **2** a short satirical composition; a lampoon.

squid /skwid/ *n.* any of various ten-armed cephalopods, esp. of the genus *Loligo* and other related genera, used as bait or food.

squig·gle /skwígəl/ *n. & v.* •*n.* a short curly line, esp. in handwriting or doodling. •*v.* **1** *tr.* write in a squiggly manner. **2** *intr.* wriggle. ▫▫ **squig·gly** *adj.*

squinch /skwinch/ *n.* a straight or arched structure across an interior angle of a square tower to carry a superstructure, e.g., a dome.

squint /skwint/ *v., n., & adj.* •*v.* **1** *intr.* have the eyes turned in different directions; have a squint. **2** *intr.* (often foll. by *at*) look obliquely or with half-closed eyes. **3** *tr.* close (one's eyes) quickly; hold (one's eyes) half shut. •*n.* **1** = STRABISMUS. **2** a stealthy or sidelong glance. **3** *colloq.* a glance or look (*had a squint at it*). **4** an oblique opening through the wall of a church affording a view of the altar. •*adj.* **1** squinting. **2** looking different ways. ▫▫ **squint·y** *adj.*

squire /skwīr/ *n. & v.* •*n.* **1** a country gentleman, esp. the chief landowner in a district. **2** *hist.* a knight's attendant. •*v.tr.* (of a man) attend upon or escort (a woman). ▫▫ **squire·ling** *n.* **squire·ly** *adj.* **squire·ship** *n.*

squirl /skwərl/ *n. colloq.* a flourish or twirl, esp. in handwriting.

squirm /skwərm/ *v. & n.* •*v.intr.* **1** wriggle; writhe. **2** show or feel embarrassment or discomfiture. •*n.* a squirming movement. ▫▫ **squirm·er** *n.* **squirm·y** *adj.* (**squirmier, squirmiest**).

squir·rel /skwə́rəl, skwúr–/ *n. & v.* •*n.* **1** any rodent of the family Sciuridae, often of arboreal habits, with a bushy tail. **2** the fur of this animal. **3** a person who hoards objects, food, etc. •*v.* (**squirreled** or **squirrelled, squirreling** or **squirrelling**) *tr.* (often foll. by *away*) hoard (objects, food, time, etc.)

squir·rel·ly /skwə́rəlee, skwúr–/ *adj.* **1** like a squirrel. **2** nervous. **3** *sl.* eccentric; flighty.

squir·rel-mon·key *n.* a small yellow-haired monkey, *Saimiri sciureus*, native to S. America.

squirt /skwərt/ *v. & n.* •*v.* **1** *tr.* eject (liquid or powder) in a jet as from a syringe. **2** *intr.* (of liquid or powder) be discharged in this way. **3** *tr.* splash with liquid or powder ejected by squirting. •*n.* **1 a** a jet of water, etc. **b** a small quantity produced by squirting. **2** a syringe. **3** *colloq.* an insignificant but presumptuous person. ▫▫ **squirt·er** *n.*

squish /skwish/ *n. & v.* •*n.* a slight squelching sound. •*v.* **1** *intr.* move with a squish. **2** *tr. colloq.* squash; squeeze. ▫▫ **squish·y** *adj.* (**squishier, squishiest**).

Sr *symb. Chem.* the element strontium.

Sr. *abbr.* **1** Senior. **2** Señor. **3** Signor. **4** *Eccl.* Sister.

Sri Lan·kan /shree lángkən, sree/ *n. & adj.* •*n.* **1** a native or inhabitant of Sri Lanka (formerly Ceylon), an island in the Indian Ocean. **2** a person of Sri Lankan descent. •*adj.* of or relating to Sri Lanka or its people.

SRO *abbr.* standing room only.

SS *abbr.* **1** steamship. **2** Saints. **3** *hist.* Nazi special police force.

SSA *abbr.* Social Security Administration.

SSE *abbr.* south-southeast.

SST *abbr.* supersonic transport.

SSW *abbr.* south-southwest.

St. *abbr.* **1** Street. **2** Saint.

st. *abbr.* **1** stanza. **2** state. **3** statute. **4** stone (in weight).

sta. *abbr.* station.

stab /stab/ *v. & n.* •*v.* (**stabbed, stabbing**) **1** *tr.* pierce or wound with a pointed tool or weapon. **2** *intr.* (often foll. by *at*) aim a blow with such a weapon. **3** *intr.*

cause a sensation like being stabbed (*stabbing pain*). **4** *tr.* hurt or distress (a person, feelings, conscience, etc.). •*n.* **1 a** an instance of stabbing. **b** a blow or thrust with a knife, etc. **2** a wound made in this way. **3** a sharply painful physical or mental sensation. **4** *colloq.* an attempt; a try. □ **stab in the back** *n.* a treacherous or slanderous attack. •*v.tr.* slander or betray. □□ **stab·ber** *n.*

sta·bil·i·ty /stəbílitee/ *n.* the quality or state of being stable.

sta·bi·lize /stáybilīz/ *v.tr. & intr.* make or become stable. □□ **sta·bi·li·za·tion** *n.*

sta·bi·liz·er /stáybilīzər/ *n.* a device or substance used to keep something stable, esp.: **1** a gyroscope device to prevent rolling of a ship. **2** the horizontal airfoil in the tail assembly of an aircraft.

sta·ble[1] /stáybəl/ *adj.* (**stabler, stablest**) **1** firmly fixed or established; not easily adjusted, destroyed, or altered (*a stable structure; a stable government*). **2 a** firm; resolute; not wavering or fickle (*a stable and steadfast friend*). **b** sane; sensible. **3** *Chem.* (of a compound) not readily decomposing. **4** *Physics* (of an isotope) not subject to radioactive decay. □□ **sta·bly** *adv.*

sta·ble[2] /stáybəl/ *n. & v.* •*n.* **1** a building for keeping horses. **2** an establishment where racehorses are kept and trained. **3** the racehorses of a particular stable. **4** persons, products, etc., having a common origin or affiliation. **5** such an origin or affiliation. •*v.tr.* put or keep (a horse) in a stable. □□ **sta·ble·ful** *n.* (*pl.* **-fuls**).

sta·ble·man /stáybəlmən/ *n.* (*pl.* **·men**; *fem.* **sta·ble·wom·an,** *pl.* **·wom·en**) a person employed in a stable.

sta·bling /stáybling/ *n.* accommodation for horses.

stac·ca·to /stəkaátō/ *adv., adj., & n.* esp. *Mus.* •*adv. & adj.* with each sound or note sharply detached or separated from the others. •*n.* (*pl.* **-tos**) **1** a staccato passage in music, etc. **2** staccato delivery or presentation.

stack /stak/ *n. & v.* •*n.* **1** a pile or heap, esp. in orderly arrangement. **2** a circular or rectangular pile of hay, straw, etc., or of grain in sheaf, often with a sloping thatched top. **3** *colloq.* a large quantity. **4 a** a number of chimneys in a group. **b** = SMOKESTACK. **c** a tall factory chimney. **5** a stacked group of aircraft. **6** (also **stacks**) a part of a library where books are compactly stored. **7** *Computing* a set of storage locations which store data in such a way that the most recently stored item is the first to be retrieved. •*v.tr.* **1** pile in a stack. **2 a** arrange (cards) secretly for cheating. **b** manipulate (circumstances, etc.) to one's advantage. **3** cause (aircraft) to fly round the same point at different levels while waiting to land at an airport. □ **stack up** *colloq.* present oneself; measure up. □□ **stack·a·ble** *adj.* **stack·er** *n.*

stad·dle /stádəl/ *n.* a platform or framework supporting a rick, etc.

sta·di·um /stáydeeəm/ *n.* (*pl.* **stadiums**) an athletic or sports arena with tiers of seats for spectators.

staff /staf/ *n. & v.* •*n.* **1 a** a stick or pole for use in walking or climbing or as a weapon. **b** a stick or pole as a sign of office or authority. **c** a flagstaff. **2 a** a body of persons employed in a business, etc. (*editorial staff of a newspaper*). **b** those in authority within an organization, esp. the teachers in a school. **c** *Mil.*, etc. a body of officers assisting an officer in high command and concerned with an army, regiment, fleet, or air force as a whole (*general staff*). **3** (*pl.* **staffs** or **staves** /stayvz/) *Mus.* a set of usu. five parallel lines on or between which notes are placed to indicate their pitch. •*v.tr.* provide (an institution, etc.) with staff. □□ **staffed** *adj.* (also in *comb.*).

staff·er /stáfər/ *n.* a member of a staff, esp. of a newspaper.

stag /stag/ *n., adj., & v.* •*n.* **1** an adult male deer, esp. one with a set of antlers. **2** a man who attends a social gathering unaccompanied by a woman. •*adj.* **1** for men only, as a party. **2** intended for men only, esp. pornographic material. **3** unaccompanied by a date. •*v.tr.* (**stagged, stagging**) to attend a gathering unaccompanied.

stage /stayj/ *n. & v.* •*n.* **1** a point or period in a process or development (*a critical stage; in the larval stage*). **2 a** a raised floor or platform, esp. one on which plays, etc., are performed. **b** (prec. by *the*) the theatrical profession, dramatic art or literature. **c** the scene of action (*the stage of politics*). **d** = LANDING STAGE. **3 a** a regular stopping place on a route. **b** the distance between two stopping places. **4** a section of a rocket with a separate engine, jettisoned when its propellant is exhausted. •*v.tr.* **1** present (a play, etc.) on stage. **2** arrange the occurrence of (*staged a demonstration*). □ **go on the stage** become an actor. **hold the stage** dominate a conversation, etc. **set the stage for** prepare the way for; provide the basis for. □□ **stage·a·ble** *adj.* **stage·a·bil·i·ty** /stáyjəbílitee/ *n.* **stag·er** *n.*

stage·coach /stáyjkōch/ *n. hist.* a large enclosed horse-drawn coach running regularly by stages between two places.

stage·craft /stáyjkraft/ *n.* skill or experience in writing or staging plays.

stage door *n.* an actors' and workers' entrance from the street to a theater behind the stage.

stage fright *n.* nervousness on facing an audience, esp. for the first time.

stage·hand /stáyjhand/ *n.* a person handling scenery, etc., during a performance on stage.

stage name *n.* a name assumed for professional purposes by an actor.

stage-struck *adj.* filled with an inordinate desire to go on the stage.

stag·ey var. of STAGY.

stag·fla·tion /stagfláyshən/ *n. Econ.* a state of inflation without a corresponding increase of demand and employment.

stag·ger /stágər/ *v. & n.* •*v.* **1 a** *intr.* walk unsteadily; totter. **b** *tr.* cause to totter (*was staggered by the blow*). **2 a** *tr.* shock; confuse. **b** *intr.* waver in purpose. **3** *tr.* arrange (events, hours of work, etc.) so that they do not coincide. **4** *tr.* arrange (objects) so that they are not in line. •*n.* **1** a tottering movement. **2** (in *pl.*) **a** a disease of the brain and spinal cord, esp. in horses and cattle, causing staggering. **b** giddiness. **3** an overhanging or zigzag arrangement of like parts in a structure, etc. □□ **stag·ger·er** *n.*

stag·ger·ing /stágəring/ *adj.* **1** astonishing; bewildering. **2** that staggers. □□ **stag·ger·ing·ly** *adv.*

stag·ing /stáyjing/ *n.* **1** the presentation of a play, etc. **2** a platform or support or scaffolding, esp. temporary.

stag·ing ar·e·a *n.* an intermediate assembly point for troops, etc., in transit.

stag·nant /stágnənt/ *adj.* **1** (of liquid) motionless, having no current. **2** showing no activity, dull, sluggish. □□ **stag·nan·cy** *n.* **stag·nant·ly** *adv.*

stag·nate /stágnayt/ *v.intr.* be stagnant. □□ **stag·na·tion** /–náyshən/ *n.*

stag·y /stáyjee/ *adj.* (also **stag·ey**) (**stagier, stagiest**) theatrical; artificial; exaggerated. □□ **stag·i·ly** *adv.* **stag·i·ness** *n.*

staid /stayd/ *adj.* of quiet and steady character; sedate. □□ **staid·ly** *adv.* **staid·ness** *n.*

stain /stayn/ *v. & n.* •*v.* **1** *tr. & intr.* discolor or be discolored by the action of liquid sinking in. **2** *tr.* spoil; damage (a reputation, character, etc.). **3** *tr.* color (wood, glass, etc.) by a process other than painting or covering the surface. **4** *tr.* impregnate (a specimen) for microscopic examination with coloring matter that makes the structure visible. •*n.* **1** a discoloration, a spot or mark caused esp. by foreign matter and not easily removed. **2 a** a blot or blemish. **b** damage to a reputation, etc. (*a stain on one's character*). **3** a substance used in staining. ◻◻ **stain·a·ble** *adj.* **stain·er** *n.*

stained glass *n.* dyed or colored glass, esp. in a lead framework in a window (also (with hyphen) *attrib.*: *stained-glass window*).

stain·less /stáynlis/ *adj.* **1** (esp. of a reputation) without stains. **2** not liable to stain.

stain·less steel *n.* chrome steel not liable to rust or tarnish under ordinary conditions.

stair /stair/ *n.* **1** each of a set of fixed steps. **2** (usu. in *pl.*) a set of steps.

stair·case /stáirkays/ *n.* **1** a flight of stairs and the supporting structure. **2** a part of a building containing a staircase.

stair·head /stáirhed/ *n.* a level space at the top of stairs.

stair rod *n.* a rod for securing a carpet against the base of the riser.

stair·way /stáirway/ *n.* **1** a flight of stairs; a staircase. **2** the way up this.

stair·well /stáirwel/ *n.* the shaft in which a staircase is built.

stake[1] /stayk/ *n.* & *v.* •*n.* **1** a stout stick or post sharpened at one end and driven into the ground as a support, boundary mark, etc. **2** *hist.* **a** the post to which a person was tied to be burned alive. **b** (prec. by *the*) death by burning as a punishment (*condemned to the stake*). •*v.tr.* **1** fasten or support with a stake or stakes. **2** (foll. by *off, out*) mark off (an area) with stakes. **3** state or establish (a claim). ◻ **stake out** *colloq.* **1** place under surveillance. **2** place (a person) to maintain surveillance.

stake[2] /stayk/ *n.* & *v.* •*n.* **1** a sum of money, etc., wagered on an event, esp. deposited with a stakeholder. **2** (often foll. by *in*) an interest or concern, esp. financial. **3** (in *pl.*) **a** money offered as a prize, esp. in a horse race. **b** such a race (*maiden stakes*; *trial stakes*). •*v.tr.* wager (*staked $5 on the next race*). ◻ **at stake 1** risked; to be won or lost (*life itself is at stake*). **2** at issue; in question.

stake·out /stáykowt/ *n. colloq.* a period of surveillance.

sta·lac·tite /stəláktīt, stáləktīt/ *n.* a deposit of calcium carbonate having the shape of a large icicle, formed by the trickling of water from the roof of a cave. ◻◻ **sta·lac·tic** /–láktik/ *adj.* **stal·ac·tit·ic** /–títik/ *adj.*

sta·lag·mite /stəlágmīt, stáləg–/ *n.* a deposit of calcium carbonate formed by the dripping of water into the shape of a large inverted icicle rising from the floor of a cave, etc., often uniting with a stalactite. ◻◻ **stal·ag·mit·ic** /–mítik/ *adj.*

stale[1] /stayl/ *adj.* & *v.* •*adj.* (**staler, stalest**) **1 a** not fresh; not quite new (*stale bread*). **b** musty, insipid, or otherwise the worse for age or use. **2** trite or unoriginal (*a stale joke*). **3** (of an athlete or other performer) having ability impaired by excessive exertion or practice. •*v. tr.* & *intr.* make or become stale. ◻◻ **stale·ness** *n.*

stale[2] /stayl/ *n.* & *v.* •*n.* the urine of horses and cattle. •*v.intr.* (esp. of horses and cattle) urinate.

stale·mate /stáylmayt/ *n.* & *v.* •*n.* **1** *Chess* a position counting as a draw, in which a player is not in check but cannot move except into check. **2** a deadlock or drawn contest. •*v.tr.* **1** *Chess* bring (a player) to a stalemate. **2** bring to a standstill.

stalk[1] /stawk/ *n.* **1** the main stem of a herbaceous plant. **2** the slender attachment or support of a leaf, flower, fruit, etc. **3** a similar support for an organ, etc., in an animal. **4** a slender support or linking shaft in a machine, object, etc., e.g., the stem of a wineglass. ◻◻ **stalked** *adj.* (also in *comb.*). **stalk·less** *adj.* **stalk·like** *adj.* **stalk·y** *adj.*

stalk[2] /stawk/ *v.* & *n.* •*v.* **1** *tr.* pursue or approach (game or an enemy) stealthily. **2** *intr.* stride, walk in a stately or haughty manner. •*n.* **1** the stalking of game. **2** an imposing gait. ◻◻ **stalk·er** *n.* (also in *comb.*).

stall[1] /stawl/ *n.* & *v.* •*n.* **1** a trader's stand or booth in a market, etc. **2 a** a stable or cowhouse. **b** a compartment for one animal in this. **3** a fixed seat in the choir or chancel of a church, more or less enclosed at the back and sides and often canopied. **4 a** a compartment for one person in a shower, toilet, etc. **b** a compartment for one horse at the start of a race. **5 a** the stalling of an engine or aircraft. **b** the condition resulting from this. **6** a receptacle for one object. •*v.* **1 a** *intr.* (of a motor vehicle or its engine) stop because of an overload on the engine or an inadequate supply of fuel to it. **b** *intr.* (of an aircraft) reach a condition where the speed is too low to allow effective operation of the controls. **c** *tr.* cause (an engine or vehicle or aircraft) to stall. **2** *tr.* put or keep (cattle, etc.) in a stall or stalls.

stall[2] /stawl/ *v.* **1** *intr.* play for time when being questioned, etc. **2** *tr.* delay; obstruct.

stal·lion /stályən/ *n.* an uncastrated adult male horse, esp. for breeding.

stal·wart /stáwlwərt/ *adj.* & *n.* •*adj.* **1** strongly built. **2** resolute; determined (*stalwart supporters*). •*n.* a stalwart person, esp. a loyal uncompromising partisan. ◻◻ **stal·wart·ly** *adv.*

sta·men /stáymən/ *n.* the male fertilizing organ of a flowering plant, including the anther containing pollen. ◻◻ **stam·i·nif·er·ous** /stáminífərəs/ *adj.*

stam·i·na /stáminə/ *n.* the ability to endure prolonged physical or mental strain.

stam·i·nate /stáminət, –nayt/ *adj.* (of a plant) having stamens, esp. stamens but not pistils.

stam·mer /stámər/ *v.* & *n.* •*v.* **1** *intr.* speak with halting articulation, esp. with pauses or rapid repetitions of the same syllable. **2** *tr.* (often foll. by *out*) utter (words) in this way. •*n.* **1** a tendency to stammer. **2** an instance of stammering. ◻◻ **stam·mer·er** *n.* **stam·mer·ing·ly** *adv.*

stamp /stamp/ *v.* & *n.* •*v.* **1 a** *tr.* bring down (one's foot) heavily on the ground, etc. **b** *tr.* crush, flatten, or bring into a specified state in this way (*stamped down the earth around the plant*). **c** *intr.* walk with heavy steps. **2** *tr.* **a** impress (a pattern, mark, etc.) on metal, paper, etc., with a die or similar instrument of metal, wood, rubber, etc. **b** impress (a surface) with a pattern, etc., in this way. **3** *tr.* affix a postage or other stamp to (an envelope or document). **4** *tr.* assign a specific character to; characterize (*stamps the story an invention*). •*n.* **1** an instrument for stamping a pattern or mark. **2 a** a mark or pattern made by this. **b** the impression of an official mark required to be made on deeds, bills of exchange, etc., as evidence of payment of tax. **3** a small adhesive piece of paper indicating that a price, fee, or tax has been paid, esp. a postage stamp. **4** a mark impressed on or label, etc., affixed to a commodity as evidence of quality, etc. **5 a** a heavy downward blow with the foot. **b** the sound of this. **6** a characteristic mark or impression (*bears the stamp of genius*). ◻ **stamp on 1** impress (an idea, etc.) on (the memory, etc.). **2** suppress. **stamp out 1** produce by cutting out with a die, etc. **2** put an end to; destroy. ◻◻ **stamp·er** *n.*

stam·pede /stampéed/ *n.* & *v.* •*n.* **1** a sudden flight and scattering of a number of horses, cattle, etc. **2** a sudden flight or hurried movement of people due to interest or panic. **3** the spontaneous response of many persons to a common impulse. **4** *W. US & Canada* a festival combining a rodeo and other events and competitions. •*v.* **1** *intr.* take part in a stampede. **2** *tr.* cause to do this. **3** *tr.* cause to act hurriedly. ▫▫ **stam·ped·er** *n.*

stance /stans/ *n.* **1** an attitude or position of the body, esp. when hitting a ball, etc. **2** a standpoint; an attitude of mind.

stanch[1] /stawnch, stanch, staanch/ *v.tr.* (also **staunch**) **1** restrain the flow of (esp. blood). **2** restrain the flow from (esp. a wound).

stanch[2] var. of STAUNCH[1].

stan·chion /stánshən, –chən/ *n.* **1** a post or pillar; an upright support. **2** an upright bar, pair of bars, or frame for confining cattle in a stall.

stand /stand/ *v.* & *n.* • *v.* (*past* and *past part.* **stood** /stŏŏd/) **1** *intr.* have or take or maintain an upright position, esp. on the feet or a base. **2** *intr.* be situated or located. **3** *intr.* be of a specified height (*stands six foot three*). **4** *intr.* be in a specified condition (*stands accused; the thermometer stood at 90°*). **5** *tr.* place or set in an upright or specified position (*stood it against the wall*). **6** *intr.* **a** move to and remain in a specified position (*stand aside*). **b** take a specified attitude (*stand aloof*). **7** *intr.* maintain a position; avoid falling or moving or being moved. **8** *intr.* assume a stationary position; cease to move. **9** *intr.* remain valid or unaltered; hold good. **10** *intr. Naut.* hold a specified course (*stand in for the shore*). **11** *tr.* endure; tolerate (*cannot stand the pain; how can you stand him?*). **12** *tr.* provide for another or others at one's own expense (*stood him a drink*). **13** *intr.* act in a specified capacity (*stood proxy*). **14** *tr.* undergo (trial). • *n.* **1** a cessation from motion or progress. **2 a** a halt made for the purpose of resistance. **b** resistance to attack or compulsion (esp. *make a stand*). **3 a** a position taken up (*took his stand near the door*). **b** an attitude adopted. **4** a rack, set of shelves, table, etc., on or in which things may be placed. **5** a small open-fronted structure for a trader outdoors or in a market, etc. **6** a standing place for vehicles. **7 a** a raised structure for persons to sit or stand on. **b** a witness box. **8** *Theatr.* each halt made on a tour to give one or more performances. **9** a group of growing plants (*stand of trees*). ▫ **as it stands 1** in its present condition; unaltered. **2** in the present circumstances. **it stands to reason** see REASON. **stand alone** be unequaled. **stand and deliver!** *hist.* a highwayman's order to hand over valuables, etc. **stand back 1** take up a position further from the front. **2** withdraw psychologically in order to take an objective view. **stand by 1** stand nearby (*will not stand by and see him ill-treated*). **2** uphold; support. **3** adhere to; abide by (terms or promises). **4** *Naut.* stand ready to take hold of or operate (an anchor, etc.). **stand a chance** see CHANCE. **stand corrected** accept correction. **stand down** withdraw from a team, witness box, or similar position. **stand for 1** represent; signify (*"US" stands for "United States"; democracy stands for a great deal more than that*). **2** (often with *neg.*) *colloq.* endure, tolerate. **stand one's ground** maintain one's position, not yield. **stand in** (usu. foll. by *for*) deputize; act in place of another. **stand in good stead** see STEAD. **stand off** move or keep away; keep one's distance. **stand on** insist on; observe scrupulously (*stand on ceremony; stand on one's dignity*). **stand on one's own (two) feet**) be self-reliant or independent. **stand out 1** be prominent or conspicuous or outstanding. **2** (usu. foll. by *against, for*) persist in opposition or support or endurance. **stand over 1** stand close to (a person) to watch, control, threaten, etc. **2** be postponed, be left for later settlement, etc. **stand pat** see PAT[2]. **stand to 1** *Mil.* stand ready for an attack (esp. before dawn or after dark). **2** be likely or certain to (*stands to lose everything*). **stand up 1 a** rise to one's feet from a sitting or other position. **b** come to or remain in or place in a standing position. **2** (of an argument, etc.) be valid. **3** *colloq.* fail to keep an appointment with. **stand up for** support; side with; maintain (a person or cause). **stand upon** = *stand on.* **stand up to 1** meet or face (an opponent) courageously. **2** be resistant to the harmful effects of (wear, use, etc.). **stand well** (usu. foll. by *with*) be on good terms or in good repute. **take one's stand on** base one's argument, etc., on; rely on.

stand·ard /stándərd/ *n.* & *adj.* • *n.* **1** an object or quality or measure serving as a basis or example or principle to which others conform or should conform or by which others are judged (*by present-day standards*). **2 a** the degree of excellence, etc., required for a particular purpose (*not up to standard*). **b** average quality (*of a low standard*). **3** the ordinary procedure, or quality or design of a product, without added or novel features. **4** a distinctive flag, esp. the flag of a cavalry regiment as distinct from the colors of an infantry regiment. **5 a** an upright support. **b** an upright water or gas pipe. **6 a** a tree or shrub that grows on an erect stem of full height and stands alone without support. **b** a shrub grafted on an upright stem and trained in tree form (*standard rose*). **7** a thing recognized as a model for imitation, etc. **8** a tune or song of established popularity. • *adj.* **1** serving or used as a standard (*a standard size*). **2** of a normal or prescribed quality or size, etc. **3** having recognized and permanent value (*the standard book on the subject*). **4** (of language) conforming to established educated usage (*Standard English*).

stand·ard-bear·er *n.* **1** a soldier who carries a standard. **2** a prominent leader in a cause.

stand·ard·ize /stándərdīz/ *v.tr.* cause to conform to a standard. ▫▫ **stand·ard·iz·a·ble** *adj.* **stand·ard·i·za·tion** *n.* **stand·ard·iz·er** *n.*

stand·ard of liv·ing *n.* the degree of material comfort available to a person or class or community.

stand·ard time *n.* a uniform time for places in approximately the same longitude.

stand·by /stándbī/ *n.* & *adj.* • *n.* (*pl.* **standbys**) **1** a person or thing ready if needed in an emergency, etc. **2** readiness for duty (*on standby*). • *adj.* **1** ready for immediate use. **2** (of air travel) not booked in advance but allocated on the basis of earliest availability.

stand·ee /standée/ *n. colloq.* a person who stands, esp. when all seats are occupied.

stand-in *n.* a deputy or substitute, esp. for an actor when the latter's acting ability is not needed.

stand·ing /stánding/ *n.* & *adj.* • *n.* **1** esteem or repute, esp. high; status; position (*people of high standing; is of no standing*). **2** duration (*a dispute of long standing*). **3** length of service, membership, etc. • *adj.* **1** that stands; upright. **2 a** established; permanent (*a standing rule*). **b** not made, raised, etc., for the occasion (*a standing army*). **3** (of a jump, start, race, etc.) performed from rest or from a standing position. **4** (of water) stagnant. **5** (of grain) unreaped. ▫ **leave a person standing** make far more rapid progress than he or she.

stand·ing joke *n.* an object of permanent ridicule.

stand·off·ish /stándáwfish, –óf–/ *adj.* cold or distant in manner. ▫▫ **stand·off·ish·ly** *adv.* **stand·off·ish·ness** *n.*

stand·out /stándowt/ *n.* a remarkable person or thing.

stand·pipe /stándpīp/ *n.* a vertical pipe extending from a water supply, esp. one connecting a temporary faucet to the main water supply.

stand·point /stándpoynt/ *n.* **1** the position from which a thing is viewed. **2** a mental attitude.

stand·still /stándstil/ *n.* a stoppage; an inability to proceed.

stand-up *attrib.adj.* **1** (of a meal) eaten standing. **2** (of a fight) violent, thorough, or fair and square. **3** (of a collar) upright, not turned down. **4** (of a comedian) performing by standing before an audience and telling jokes.

stank *past* of STINK.

stan·za /stánzə/ *n.* the basic metrical unit in a poem or verse consisting of a recurring group of lines. □□ **stan·za'd** *adj.* (also **stan·zaed**) (also in *comb.*). **stan·za·ic** /–záyik/ *adj.*

sta·pes /stáypeez/ *n.* (*pl.* same) a small stirrup-shaped bone in the ear of a mammal.

staph·y·lo·coc·cus /stáfiləkókəs/ *n.* (*pl.* **staphylococci** /–kóksī, kókī/) any bacterium of the genus *Staphylococcus,* occurring in grapelike clusters, and sometimes causing pus formation usu. in the skin and mucous membranes of animals. □□ **staph·y·lo·coc·cal** *adj.*

sta·ple[1] /stáypəl/ *n. & v.* • *n.* a U-shaped metal bar or piece of wire with pointed ends for driving through and clinching papers, netting, electric wire, etc. • *v.tr.* provide or fasten with a staple. □□ **sta·pler** *n.*

sta·ple[2] /stáypəl/ *n., adj., & v.* • *n.* **1** the principal or an important article of commerce (*the staples of local industry*). **2** the chief element or a main component, e.g., of a diet. **3** a raw material. **4** the fiber of cotton or wool, etc., as determining its quality (*cotton of fine staple*). • *adj.* **1** main or principal (*staple commodities*). **2** important as a product or an export. • *v.tr.* sort or classify (wool, etc.) according to fiber.

sta·ple gun *n.* a handheld device for driving in staples.

star /staar/ *n. & v.* • *n.* **1** a celestial body appearing as a luminous point in the night sky. **2** (in full **fixed star**) such a body so far from the earth as to appear motionless (cf. PLANET, COMET). **3** a large naturally gaseous body such as the sun. **4** a celestial body regarded as influencing a person's fortunes, etc. (*born under a lucky star*). **5** a thing resembling a star in shape or appearance. **6** a star-shaped mark. **7** a figure or object with radiating points esp. as a mark of rank or excellence. **8 a** a famous or brilliant person; the principal or most prominent performer in a play, movie, etc. (*the star of the show*). **b** (*attrib.*) outstanding; particularly brilliant (*star pupil*). • *v.* (**starred, starring**) **1 a** *tr.* (of a movie, etc.) feature as a principal performer. **b** *intr.* (of a performer) be featured in a movie, etc. **2** (esp. as **starred** *adj.*) **a** mark, set, or adorn with a star or stars. **b** put an asterisk or star beside (a name, an item in a list, etc.). □□ **star·dom** *n.* **star·less** *adj.* **star·like** *adj.*

star·board /staárbərd/ *n. & v. Naut. & Aeron.* • *n.* the right-hand side (looking forward) of a ship, boat, or aircraft (cf. PORT[3]). • *v.tr.* (also *absol.*) turn (the helm) to starboard.

star·burst *n.* **1 a** a pattern of radiating lines or rays around a central object, light source, etc. **b** an explosion or a lens attachment producing this effect. **2** *Astron.* a period of intense activity, apparently star formation, in certain galaxies.

starch /staarch/ *n. & v.* • *n.* **1** an odorless tasteless polysaccharide occurring widely in plants and obtained chiefly from cereals and potatoes, forming an important constituent of the human diet. **2** a preparation of this for stiffening fabric. **3** stiffness of manner; formality. • *v.tr.* stiffen (clothing) with starch. □□ **starch·er** *n.*

starch·y /staárchee/ *adj.* (**starchier, starchiest**) **1 a** of or like starch. **b** containing much starch. **2** (of a person) precise. □□ **starch·i·ly** *adv.* **starch·i·ness** *n.*

star-crossed *adj. archaic* ill-fated.

star·dust /staárdust/ *n.* **1** a twinkling mass. **2** a multitude of stars looking like dust.

stare /stair/ *v. & n.* • *v.* **1** *intr.* (usu. foll. by *at*) look fixedly with eyes open, esp. as the result of curiosity, surprise, admiration, etc. **2** *intr.* (of eyes) be wide open and fixed. **3** *tr.* (foll. by *into*) reduce (a person) to a specified condition by staring (*stared me into silence*). • *n.* a staring gaze. □ **stare down** (or **out**) outstare. **stare a person in the face** be evident or imminent. □□ **star·er** *n.*

star·fish /staárfish/ *n.* (*pl.* usu. same) an echinoderm of the class Asteroidea with five or more radiating arms.

star·gaze /staárgayz/ *v.intr.* **1** gaze at or study the stars. **2** gaze intently.

star·gaz·er /staárgayzər/ *n. colloq.* an astronomer or astrologer.

stark /staark/ *adj. & adv.* • *adj.* **1** desolate; bare (*a stark landscape*). **2** brutally simple. (*in stark contrast; the stark reality*). **3** downright; sheer (*stark madness*). • *adv.* completely (*stark naked*). □□ **stark·ly** *adv.* **stark·ness** *n.*

star·let /staárlit/ *n.* **1** a promising young performer, esp. a woman. **2** a little star.

star·light /staárlīt/ *n.* **1** the light of the stars (*walked home by starlight*). **2** (*attrib.*) = STARLIT (*a starlight night*).

star·ling /staárling/ *n.* a small gregarious partly migratory bird, *Sturnus vulgaris,* with blackish-brown speckled iridescent plumage, chiefly inhabiting cultivated areas.

star·lit /staárlit/ *adj.* **1** lighted by stars. **2** with stars visible.

star of Beth·le·hem *n.* any of various plants with starlike flowers, esp. *Ornithogalum umbellatum,* with white star-shaped flowers striped with green on the outside.

Star of Da·vid *n.* a figure consisting of two interlaced equilateral triangles used as a Jewish and Israeli symbol.

star route *n.* a rural mail delivery route served by private contractors.

star·ry /staáree/ *adj.* (**starrier, starriest**) **1** covered with stars. **2** resembling a star. □□ **star·ri·ly** *adv.* **star·ri·ness** *n.*

star·ry-eyed *adj. colloq.* **1** visionary; enthusiastic but impractical. **2** euphoric.

Stars and Bars *n.* the flag of the Confederate States of the US.

Stars and Stripes *n.* the national flag of the US.

star shell *n.* an explosive projectile designed to burst in the air and light up the enemy's position.

star-span·gled *adj.* (esp. of the US national flag) covered or glittering with stars.

star-stud·ded *adj.* **1** (of the night sky) containing many stars. **2** featuring a number of famous people, esp. actors or sports players.

START /staart/ *abbr.* Strategic Arms Reduction Treaty (or Talks).

start /staart/ *v. & n.* • *v.* **1** *tr. & intr.* begin; commence. **2** *tr.* set (proceedings, an event, etc.) in motion (*start the meeting; started a fire*). **3** *intr.* (often foll. by *on*) make a beginning (*started on a new project*). **4** *intr.* (often foll. by *after, for*) set oneself in motion or action (*'wait!' he shouted, and started after her*). **5** *intr.* set out; begin a journey, etc. **6** (often foll. by *up*) **a** *intr.* (of a machine) begin operating. **b** *tr.* cause (a machine, etc.) to begin operating. **7** *tr.* **a** cause or enable (a person) to make a beginning (with something) (*started me in business with $10,000*). **b** (foll. by pres. part.) cause (a person) to begin (doing something) (*the smoke started me coughing*). **8** *tr.* (often foll. by *up*) found or establish; originate. **9** *intr.* (foll. by *at, with*) have as the first of a series of items, e.g., in a meal (*we started with soup*). **10** *tr.* give a signal to (competitors) to start in a race. **11** *intr.* (often foll. by *up, from,* etc.) make a sudden movement from surprise, pain, etc. (*started at the sound of my voice*). **12** *intr.* (foll. by *out, up, from,* etc.) spring out, up, etc. (*started up from the chair*). **13** *tr.* conceive (a baby). **14** *tr.* rouse (game, etc.) from its lair. **15** *intr.* (of boards, etc.) spring from their proper position; give way. • *n.* **1** a beginning of an event, action, journey, etc. (*missed the start; an early start tomorrow*). **2** the place from which a race, etc., begins. **3** an advantage given at the beginning of a race, etc. (*a 15-second start*). **4** an advantageous initial position in life, business, etc. (*a good start in life*). **5** a sudden jerking movement of surprise, pain, alarm, etc. (*you gave me a start*). **6** an intermittent or spasmodic effort or movement (esp. *in* or *by fits and starts*). □ **for a start** *colloq.* as a beginning; in the first place. **start in** *colloq.* **1** begin. **2** (foll. by *on*) make a beginning on. **start off 1** begin; commence (*started off on a lengthy monologue*). **2** begin to move (*it's time we started off*). **start out 1** begin a journey. **2** *colloq.* (foll. by *to* + infin.) proceed as intending (to do something). **start over** begin again. **start up** arise; occur. **to start with 1** in the first place; before anything else is considered. **2** at the beginning.

start·er /staártər/ *n.* **1** a person or thing that starts. **2** an esp. automatic device for starting the engine of a motor vehicle, etc. **3** a person giving the signal for the start of a race. **4** a horse or competitor starting in a race. **5** *Baseball* **a** the pitcher who pitches first in a game. **b** a pitcher who normally starts games. □ **for starters** *sl.* to start with. **under starter's orders** (of racehorses, etc.) in a position to start a race and awaiting the starting signal.

start·ing block /staárting/ *n.* a shaped rigid block for bracing the feet of a runner at the start of a race.

start·ing gate *n.* a movable barrier for securing a fair start in horse races.

start·ing price *n.* the odds ruling at the start of a horse race.

start·ing stall *n.* a compartment for one horse at the start of a race.

star·tle /staárt'l/ *v.tr.* give a shock or surprise to; cause (a person, etc.) to start with surprise or sudden alarm. □□ **star·tler** *n.*

star·tling /staártling/ *adj.* **1** surprising. **2** alarming. □□ **star·tling·ly** *adv.*

starve /staarv/ *v.* **1** *intr.* die of hunger; suffer from malnourishment. **2** *tr.* cause to die of hunger or suffer from lack of food. **3** *intr. colloq.* (esp. as **starved** or **starving** *adj.*) feel very hungry (*I'm starving*). **4** *intr.* **a** suffer from mental or spiritual want. **b** (foll. by *for*) feel a strong craving for (sympathy, amusement, knowledge, etc.). **5** *tr.* **a** (foll. by *for, of*) deprive of; keep scantily supplied with (*starved for affection*). **b** cause to suffer from mental or spiritual want. **6** *tr.* **a** (foll. by *into*) compel by starving (*starved into submission*). **b** (foll. by *out*) compel to surrender, etc., by starving (*starved them out*). **7** *intr. archaic* or *dial.* perish with or suffer from cold. □□ **star·va·tion** /–váyshən/ *n.*

stash /stash/ *v.* & *n. colloq.* • *v.tr.* (often foll. by *away*) **1** conceal; put in a safe or hidden place. **2** hoard; stow. • *n.* **1** a hiding place. **2** a thing hidden.

sta·sis /stáysis, stásis/ *n.* (*pl.* **stases** /–seez/) **1** inactivity; stagnation; a state of equilibrium. **2** a stoppage of circulation of any of the body fluids.

-stasis /stásis, stáysis/ *comb. form* (*pl.* **·stases** /–seez/) *Physiol.* forming nouns denoting a slowing or stopping (*hemostasis*). □□ **–static** *comb. form* forming adjectives.

-stat /stat/ *comb. form* forming nouns with ref. to keeping fixed or stationary (*rheostat*).

stat. *abbr.* **1** at once. **2** statistics. **3** statute.

state /stayt/ *n.* & *v.* • *n.* **1** the existing condition or position of a person or thing (*in a bad state of repair; in a precarious state of health*). **2** *colloq.* **a** an excited, anxious, or agitated mental condition (esp. *in a state*). **b** an untidy condition. **3 a** an organized political community under one government; a commonwealth; a nation. **b** such a community forming part of a federal republic, esp. the United States of America. **c (the States)** the US. **4** (*attrib.*) **a** of, for, or concerned with the state (*state documents*). **b** reserved for or done on occasions of ceremony (*state apartments; state visit*). **5** (also **State**) civil government (*church and state; Secretary of State*). **6 a** pomp; rank; dignity (*as befits their state*). **b** imposing display; ceremony; splendor (*arrived in state*). • *v.tr.* **1** express, esp. fully or clearly, in speech or writing (*have stated my opinion*). **2** fix; specify (*at stated intervals*). □ **in state** with all due ceremony. **of state** concerning politics or government. □□ **stat·a·ble** *adj.* **state·hood** *n.*

state·craft /stáytkraft/ *n.* the art of conducting affairs of state.

State De·part·ment *n.* the federal government department concerned with foreign affairs.

state·hood /stáythŏŏd/ *n.* the condition or status of being a state, esp. a state of the United States.

state house *n.* the building where the legislature of a state meets.

state·less /stáytlis/ *adj.* **1** (of a person) having no nationality or citizenship. **2** without a state. □□ **state·less·ness** *n.*

state·ly /stáytlee/ *adj.* (**statelier, stateliest**) dignified; imposing; grand. □□ **state·li·ness** *n.*

state·ment /stáytmənt/ *n.* **1** the act or an instance of stating or being stated; expression in words. **2** a thing stated; a declaration (*that statement is unfounded*). **3** a formal account of facts, esp. to the police or in a court of law (*make a statement*). **4** a record of transactions in a bank account, etc. **5** a formal notification of an amount due.

state of the art *n.* & *adj.* • *n.* the current stage of development of a practical or technological subject. • *adj.* (usu. **state-of-the-art**) (*attrib.*) using the latest techniques or equipment (*state-of-the-art weaponry*).

state·room /stáytrōōm, –rŏŏm/ *n.* **1** a private compartment in a passenger ship or train. **2** a state apartment in a palace, hotel, etc.

state's ev·i·dence *n. Law* evidence for the prosecution given by a participant in or accomplice to the crime at issue.

state·side /stáytsīd/ *adj. colloq.* of, in, or toward the United States.

states·man /stáytsmən/ *n.* (*pl.* **-men**; *fem.* **states·wom·an**, *pl.* **-wom·en**) **1** a person skilled in affairs of state, esp. one taking an active part in politics. **2** a distinguished and capable politician. □□ **states·man·like** *adj.* **states·man·ly** *adj.* **states·man·ship** *n.*

state so·cial·ism *n.* a system of state control of industries and services.

states' rights *n.pl.* the rights and powers not assumed by the federal government of the United States but reserved to its individual states.

state u·ni·ver·si·ty *n.* a university managed by the public authorities of a state.

stat·ic /státik/ *adj.* & *n.* • *adj.* **1** stationary; not acting or changing. **2** *Physics* **a** concerned with bodies at rest or forces in equilibrium (opp. DYNAMIC). **b** acting as weight but not moving (*static pressure*). **c** of statics. • *n.* **1** static electricity. **2** electrical disturbances in the atmosphere or the interference with telecommunications caused by this.

stat·i·cal /státikəl/ *adj.* = STATIC. □□ **stat·i·cal·ly** *adv.*

stat·ice /státisee, státis/ *n.* **1** sea lavender. **2** sea pink.

stat·ic e·lec·tric·i·ty *n.* electricity not flowing as a current but produced by friction.

stat·ics /státiks/ *n.pl.* (usu. treated as *sing.*) **1** the science of bodies at rest or of forces in equilibrium (cf. DYNAMICS). **2** = STATIC.

sta·tion /stáyshən/ *n.* & *v.* • *n.* **1 a** a regular stopping place on a railroad line. **b** these buildings (see also BUS STATION). **2** a place or building, etc., where a person or thing stands or is placed, esp. habitually or for a definite purpose. **3** a designated point or establishment where a particular service or activity is based or organized (*police station*; *polling station*). **4** an establishment involved in radio or television broadcasting. **5** a military or naval base. **6** position in life; rank or status (*ideas above your station*). • *v.tr.* **1** assign a station to. **2** put in position.

sta·tion·ar·y /stáyshəneree/ *adj.* **1** not moving (*a stationary car*). **2** not meant to be moved; not portable (*stationary engine*). **3** not changing in magnitude, number, quality, efficiency, etc. (*stationary temperature*). **4** (of a planet) having no apparent motion in longitude. □□ **sta·tion·ar·i·ness** *n.*

▶Be careful to distinguish **stationary** 'not moving, fixed' from **stationery** 'writing paper and other supplies.'

sta·tion break *n.* a pause between or within broadcast programs for an announcement of the identity of the station transmitting them.

sta·tion·er /stáyshənər/ *n.* a person who sells writing materials, etc.

sta·tion·er·y /stáyshəneree/ *n.* writing materials such as paper, pens, etc.

sta·tion of the cross *n.pl. RC Ch., Anglican Ch.* each of a series of usu. 14 images or pictures, representing the events in Christ's passion.

sta·tion wag·on *n.* a car with passenger seating and storage or extra seating area in the rear, accessible by a rear door.

stat·ism /stáytizəm/ *n.* centralized government administration and control of social and economic affairs.

stat·ist /státist, stáytist/ *n.* **1** a statistician. **2** a supporter of statism.

sta·tis·tic /stətístik/ *n.* & *adj.* • *n.* a statistical fact. • *adj.* = STATISTICAL.

sta·tis·ti·cal /stətístikəl/ *adj.* of or relating to statistics. □□ **sta·tis·ti·cal·ly** *adv.*

sta·tis·tics /stətístiks/ *n.pl.* **1** (usu. treated as *sing.*) the science of collecting and analyzing numerical data. **2** any systematic collection or presentation of such facts. □□ **stat·is·ti·cian** /státistíshən/ *n.*

stat·u·ar·y /stáchooeree/ *adj.* & *n.* • *adj.* of or for statues (*statuary art*). • *n.* (*pl.* **-ies**) **1** statues collectively. **2** the art of making statues.

stat·ue /stáchoo/ *n.* a sculptured, cast, carved, or molded figure of a person or animal, esp. life-size or larger (cf. STATUETTE). □□ **stat·ued** *adj.*

stat·u·esque /stáchoo-ésk/ *adj.* like, or having the dignity or beauty of, a statue. □□ **stat·u·esque·ly** *adv.*

stat·u·ette /stáchoo-ét/ *n.* a small statue; a statue less than life-size.

stat·ure /stáchər/ *n.* **1** the height of a (human) body. **2** a degree of eminence, social standing, or advancement. □□ **stat·ured** *adj.* (also in *comb.*).

sta·tus /stáytəs, stát–/ *n.* **1** rank; social position; relation to others; relative importance. **2** a superior social, etc., position. **3** the state of affairs (*let me know if the status changes*).

sta·tus quo /stáytəs kwṓ, státəs/ *n.* the existing state of affairs.

stat·ute /stáchoot/ *n.* **1** a written law passed by a legislative body. **2** a rule of a corporation, founder, etc., intended to be permanent.

stat·ute mile *n.* see MILE 1.

stat·ute of lim·i·ta·tions *n.* a statute that sets a time limit during which legal action can be taken.

stat·u·to·ry /stáchətawree/ *adj.* required, permitted, or enacted by statute. □□ **stat·u·to·ri·ly** *adv.*

stat·u·to·ry rape *n.* the offense of sexual intercourse with a minor.

staunch[1] /stawnch, staanch/ *adj.* (also **stanch**) **1** trustworthy; loyal. **2** (of a ship, joint, etc.) strong, watertight, airtight, etc. □□ **staunch·ly** *adv.* **staunch·ness** *n.*

staunch[2] var. of STANCH[1].

stave /stayv/ *n.* & *v.* • *n.* **1** each of the curved pieces of wood forming the sides of a cask, barrel, etc. **2** = STAFF[1] *n.* 3. **3** a stanza or verse. **4** the rung of a ladder. • *v.tr.* (*past* and *past part.* **stove** /stōv/ or **staved**) **1** break a hole in. **2** crush or knock out of shape. **3** fit or furnish (a cask, etc.) with staves. □ **stave in** crush by forcing inward. **stave off** avert or defer (danger or misfortune).

stave, 1

staves *pl.* of STAFF[1] *n.* 3.

stay[1] /stay/ *v.* & *n.* • *v.* **1** *intr.* continue to be in the same place or condition; not depart or change (*stay here until I come back*). **2** *intr.* (often foll. by *at*, *in*, *with*) have temporary residence as a visitor, etc. (*stayed with them for Christmas*). **3** *tr. archaic* or *literary* stop or check (progress, the inroads of a disease, etc.). **4** *tr.* postpone (judgment, decision, execution, etc.). **5 a** *intr.* show endurance. **b** *tr.* show endurance to the end of (a race, etc.). **6** *intr.* (foll. by *for*, *to*) wait long enough to share or join in an activity, etc. (*stay to supper*; *stay for the video*). • *n.* **1 a** the act or an instance of staying or dwelling in one place. **b** the duration of this (*just a ten-minute stay*). **2** a suspension or postponement of a sentence, judgment, etc. (*was granted a stay of execution*). **3** a prop or support. **4** (in *pl.*) *hist.* a corset esp. with whalebone, etc., stiffening, and laced. □ **has come** (or **is here**) **to stay** *colloq.* must be regarded as permanent. **stay the course** pursue a course of action or endure a struggle, etc., to the end. **stay in** remain indoors or at home, esp. in school after hours as a punishment. **stay the night** remain until the next day. **stay put** remain where it is placed or where one is. **stay up** not go to bed (until late at night). □□ **stay·er** *n.*

stay[2] /stay/ *n.* & *v.* • *n.* **1** *Naut.* a rope or guy supporting a mast, spar, flagstaff, etc. **2** a tie-piece in an aircraft, etc. • *v.tr.* **1** support (a mast, etc.) by stays. **2** put (a ship) on another tack.

STD *abbr.* **1** Doctor of Sacred Theology. **2** sexually transmitted disease.

std. *abbr.* standard.

stead /sted/ *n.* □ **in a person's** (or **thing's**) **stead** as a substitute; instead of him or her or it. **stand a person in good stead** be advantageous to him or her.

stead·fast /stédfast/ *adj.* constant; firm. □□ **stead·fast·ly** *adv.* **stead·fast·ness** *n.*

stead·y /stédee/ *adj.*, *v.*, *adv.*, *int.*, & *n.* • *adj.* (**steadier, steadiest**) **1** firmly fixed or supported or standing or balanced; not tottering, rocking, or wavering. **2** done or operating or happening in a uniform and regular manner (*a steady pace*; *a steady increase*). **3 a** constant in mind or conduct; not changeable. **b** persistent. **4** (of a person) serious and dependable in behavior; of industrious and temperate habits; safe; cautious. **5** regular; established (*a steady girlfriend*). **6** accurately directed; not faltering; controlled (*a steady hand*; *a steady eye*; *steady nerves*). **7** (of a ship) on course and upright. • *v.tr.* & *intr.* (**-ies, -ied**) make or become steady (*steady the boat*). • *adv.* steadily (*hold it steady*). • *int.* as a command or warning to take care. • *n.* (*pl.* **-ies**) *colloq.* a regular boyfriend or girlfriend. □ **go steady** (often foll. by *with*) *colloq.* have as a regular boyfriend or girlfriend. **steady down** become steady. **steady-going** staid; sober. □□ **stead·i·er** *n.* **stead·i·ly** *adv.* **stead·i·ness** *n.*

steak /stayk/ *n.* **1** a thick slice of meat (esp. beef) or fish, often cut for grilling, frying, etc. **2** beef cut for stewing or braising.

steak house *n.* a restaurant specializing in serving beefsteaks.

steal /steel/ *v.* & *n.* • *v.* (*past* **stole** /stōl/; *past part.* **stolen** /stṓlən/) **1** *tr.* (also *absol.*) **a** take (another person's property) illegally. **b** take (property, etc.) without right or permission, esp. in secret with the intention of not returning it. **2** *tr.* obtain surreptitiously or by surprise (*stole a kiss*). **3** *tr.* **a** gain insidiously or artfully. **b** (often foll. by *away*) win or get possession of (a person's affections, etc.), esp. insidiously (*stole her heart away*). **4** *intr.* **a** move, esp. silently or stealthily (*stole out of the room*). **b** (of a sound, etc.) become gradually perceptible. **5** *tr.* **a** (in various sports) gain (a run, the ball, etc.) surreptitiously or by luck. **b** *Baseball* run to (a base) while the pitcher is in the act of delivery. • *n.* **1** *colloq.* the act or an instance of stealing or theft. **2** *colloq.* an unexpectedly easy task or good bargain. □ **steal a march on** get an advantage over by surreptitious means; anticipate. **steal the show** outshine other performers, esp. unexpectedly. **steal a person's thunder** use another person's words, ideas, etc., without permission and without giving credit. □□ **steal·er** *n.* (also in *comb.*).

stealth /stelth/ *n.* & *adj.* • *n.* secrecy; a secret procedure. • *adj.* of an aircraft design intended to avoid detection by radar. □ **by stealth** surreptitiously.

stealth·y /stélthee/ *adj.* (**stealthier, stealthiest**) **1** done with stealth; proceeding imperceptibly. **2** acting or moving with stealth. □□ **stealth·i·ly** *adv.* **stealth·i·ness** *n.*

steam /steem/ *n.* & *v.* • *n.* **1 a** the gas into which water is changed by boiling. **b** a mist of liquid particles of water produced by the condensation of this gas. **2** any similar vapor. **3 a** energy or power provided by a steam engine or other machine. **b** *colloq.* power or energy generally. • *v.* **1** *tr.* **a** cook (food) in steam. **b** soften or make pliable (lumber, etc.) or otherwise treat with steam. **2** *intr.* give off steam or other vapor, esp. visibly. **3** *intr.* **a** move under steam power (*the ship steamed down the river*). **b** (foll. by *ahead, away,* etc.) *colloq.* proceed or travel fast or with vigor. **4** *tr.* & *intr.* (usu. foll. by *up*) **a** cover or become covered with condensed steam. **b** (as **steamed up** *adj.*) *colloq.* angry or excited. **5** *tr.* (foll. by *open*, etc.) apply steam to the adhesive of (a sealed envelope) to get it open. □ **get up steam 1** generate enough power to work a steam engine. **2** work oneself into an energetic or angry state. **let off steam** relieve one's pent up feelings or energy. **run out of steam** lose one's impetus or energy. **under one's own steam** without assistance; unaided.

steam age *n.* the era when trains were pulled by steam locomotives.

steam·boat /steémbōt/ *n.* a boat propelled by a steam engine.

steam en·gine *n.* **1** an engine which uses the expansion or rapid condensation of steam to generate power. **2** a locomotive powered by this.

steam·er /steémər/ *n.* **1** a person or thing that steams. **2** a vessel propelled by steam, esp. a ship. **3** a vessel in which things are cooked by steam.

steam·roll·er /steémrōlər/ *n.* & *v.* • *n.* **1** a heavy slow-moving vehicle with a roller, used to flatten new-made roads. **2** a crushing power or force. • *v.tr.* **1** crush forcibly or indiscriminately. **2** (foll. by *through*) force (a measure, etc.) through a legislature by overriding opposition.

steam·ship /steémship/ *n.* a ship propelled by a steam engine.

steam train *n.* a train driven by a steam engine.

steam·y /steémee/ *adj.* (**steamier, steamiest**) **1** like or full of steam. **2** *colloq.* erotic; salacious. □□ **steam·i·ly** *adv.*

ste·ar·ic ac·id *n.* a solid saturated fatty acid obtained from animal or vegetable fats.

ste·a·rin /steérin/ *n.* **1** a glyceryl ester of stearic acid. **2** a mixture of fatty acids used in candle making.

ste·a·tite /steéətīt/ *n.* a soapstone or other impure form of talc.

steed /steed/ *n.* *archaic* or *poet.* a horse, esp. a fast powerful one.

steel /steel/ *n., adj.,* & *v.* • *n.* **1** any of various alloys of iron and carbon with other elements, much used for making tools, weapons, etc. **2** strength; firmness (*nerves of steel*). **3** a rod of steel on which knives are sharpened. **4** (not in *pl.*) *literary* a sword, lance, etc. (*foemen worthy of their steel*). • *adj.* **1** made of steel. **2** like steel. • *v.tr.* & *refl.* harden or make resolute (*steeled myself for a shock*).

steel band *n.* a group of usu. W. Indian musicians with percussion instruments made from oil drums.

steel·head /steélhed/ *n.* a large N. American rainbow trout.

steel wool *n.* an abrasive substance consisting of a mass of fine steel shavings.

steel·works /steélwərks/ *n.pl.* (usu. treated as *sing.*) a place where steel is manufactured. □□ **steel·work·er** *n.*

steel·y /steélee/ *adj.* (**steelier, steeliest**) **1** of, or hard as, steel. **2** severe; ruthless (*steely composure; steely-eyed glance*). □□ **steel·i·ness** *n.*

steel·yard /steélyaard/ *n.* a kind of balance with a short arm to take the item to be weighed and a long graduated arm along which a weight is moved until it balances.

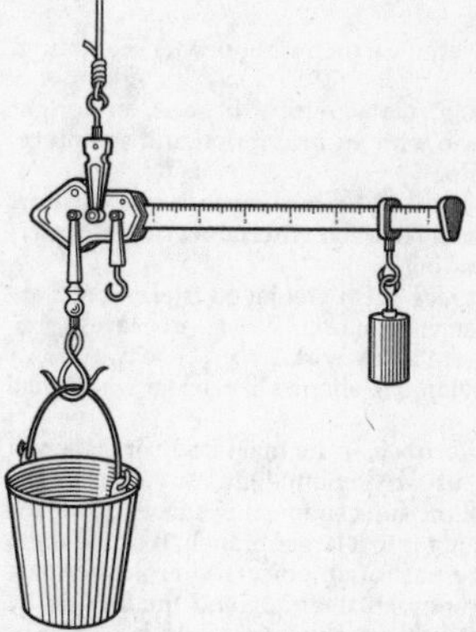

steelyard

steep[1] /steep/ *adj.* & *n.* • *adj.* **1** sloping sharply (*a steep hill; steep stairs*). **2** (of a rise or fall) rapid (*a steep drop in stock prices*). **3** (*predic.*) *colloq.* **a** (of a demand, price, etc.) exorbitant; unreasonable (esp. *a bit steep*). **b** (of a story, etc.) exaggerated; incredible. • *n.* a steep slope. □□ **steep·en** *v.intr.* & *tr.* **steep·ish** *adj.* **steep·ly** *adv.* **steep·ness** *n.*

steep[2] /steep/ *v.* & *n.* • *v.tr.* soak or bathe in liquid. • *n.*

1 the act or process of steeping. 2 the liquid for steeping.

stee·ple /steépəl/ *n.* a tall tower, esp. one surmounted by a spire, above the roof of a church. ▫▫ **stee·pled** *adj.*

stee·ple·chase /steépəlchays/ *n.* **1** a horse race (orig. with a steeple as the goal) across the countryside or on a racetrack with ditches, hedges, etc., to jump. **2** a cross-country foot race. ▫▫ **stee·ple·chas·er** *n.* **stee·ple·chas·ing** *n.*

stee·ple·jack /steépəljak/ *n.* a person who climbs tall chimneys, steeples, etc., to do repairs, etc.

steer[1] /steer/ *v.* **1** *tr.* **a** guide (a vehicle, aircraft, etc.) by a wheel, etc. **b** guide (a vessel) by a rudder or helm. **2** *intr.* guide a vessel or vehicle in a specified direction (*tried to steer left*). **3** *tr.* direct (one's course). **4** *intr.* direct one's course in a specified direction (*steered for the railroad station*). **5** *tr.* guide the movement or trend of (*steered them into the garden; steered the conversation away from that subject*). ▫ **steer clear of** take care to avoid. ▫▫ **steer·a·ble** *adj.* **steer·er** *n.* **steer·ing** *n.* (esp. in senses 1 and 2 of *v.*).

steer[2] /steer/ *n.* a young male bovine animal castrated before sexual maturity, esp. one raised for beef.

steer·age /steérij/ *n.* **1** the act of steering. **2** the effect of the helm on the ship. **3** the part of a ship allotted to passengers traveling at the cheapest rate. **4** *hist.* (in a warship) quarters assigned to midshipmen, etc., just forward of the wardroom.

steer·ing com·mit·tee *n.* a committee deciding the order of business, or priorities and the general course of operations.

steer·ing wheel *n.* a wheel by which a vehicle, etc., is steered.

steers·man /steérzmən/ *n.* (*pl.* **-men**) a helmsman.

steeve /steev/ *n. Naut.* the angle of the bowsprit in relation to the horizontal.

steg·o·sau·rus /stégəsáwrəs/ *n.* any of a group of plant-eating dinosaurs with a double row of large bony plates along the spine.

stein /stīn/ *n.* a large earthenware, pewter, etc., mug, esp. for beer.

ste·la /steélə/ *n.* (*pl.* **stelae** /–lee/) *Archaeol.* an upright slab or pillar usu. with an inscription and sculpture, esp. as a gravestone.

stel·lar /stélər/ *adj.* **1** of or relating to a star or stars. **2** having the quality of a star entertainer or performer; leading; outstanding.

stel·late /stélayt/ *adj.* (also **stel·lat·ed** /stélaytid/) **1** arranged like a star; radiating. **2** *Bot.* (of leaves) surrounding the stem in a whorl.

stel·lu·lar /stélyələr/ *adj.* shaped like, or set with, small stars.

stem[1] /stem/ *n. & v.* • *n.* **1** the main body or stalk of a plant or shrub, usu. rising into light, but occasionally subterranean. **2** the stalk supporting a fruit, flower, or leaf, and attaching it to a larger branch, twig, or stalk. **3** a stem-shaped part of an object: **a** the slender part of a wineglass between the body and the foot. **b** the tube of a tobacco pipe. **c** a vertical stroke in a letter or musical note. **d** the winding shaft of a watch. **4** *Gram.* the root or main part of a noun, verb, etc., to which inflections are added. **5** *Naut.* the main upright timber or metal piece at the bow of a ship (*from stem to stern*). • *v.* (**stemmed, stemming**) **1** *intr.* (foll. by *from*) spring or originate from (*stems from a desire to win*). **2** *tr.* remove the stem or stems from (fruit, tobacco, etc.). **3** *tr.* (of a vessel, etc.) hold its own or make headway against (the tide, etc.). ▫▫ **stem·less** *adj.* **stemmed** *adj.* (also in *comb.*).

stem[2] /stem/ *v.tr.* (**stemmed, stemming**) **1** check or stop. **2** dam up (a stream, etc.).

stem·ware /stémwair/ *n.* glasses with stems.

stench /stench/ *n.* an offensive or foul smell.

stench trap *n.* a trap in a sewer, etc., to prevent the upward passage of gas.

sten·cil /sténsil/ *n. & v.* • *n.* **1** a thin sheet of plastic, metal, card, etc., in which a pattern or lettering is cut, used to produce a corresponding pattern on the surface beneath it by applying ink, paint, etc. **2** the pattern, lettering, etc., produced by a stencil. • *v.tr.* (**stenciled** or **stencilled, stenciling** or **stencilling**) **1** produce (a pattern) with a stencil. **2** decorate or mark (a surface) in this way.

sten·o /sténō/ *n.* (*pl.* **-os**) *colloq.* a stenographer.

ste·nog·ra·phy /stənógrəfee/ *n.* shorthand or the art of writing this. ▫▫ **ste·nog·ra·pher** *n.* **sten·o·graph·ic** /sténəgráfik/ *adj.*

ste·no·sis /stinṓsis/ *n. Med.* the abnormal narrowing of a passage in the body. ▫▫ **ste·not·ic** /–nótik/ *adj.*

sten·o·type /sténətīp/ *n.* **1** a machine like a typewriter for recording speech in syllables or phonemes. **2** a symbol or the symbols used in this process. ▫▫ **ste·no·typ·ist** *n.*

step /step/ *n. & v.* • *n.* **1 a** the complete movement of one leg in walking or running (*step forward*). **b** the distance covered by this. **2** a unit of movement in dancing. **3** a measure taken, esp. one of several in a course of action (*took steps to prevent it; considered it a wise step*). **4 a** a surface on which a foot is placed on ascending or descending a stair. **b** the rung of a ladder. **c** a platform, etc., in a vehicle provided for stepping up or down. **5** a short distance (*only a step from my door*). **6** the sound or mark made by a foot in walking, etc. (*heard a step on the stairs*). **7** the manner of walking, etc., as seen or heard (*know her by her step*). **8 a** a degree in the scale of promotion, advancement, or precedence. **b** one of a series of fixed points on a pay scale, etc. • *v.* (**stepped, stepping**) **1** *intr.* lift and set down one's foot or alternate feet in walking. **2** *intr.* come or go in a specified direction by stepping. **3** *intr.* make progress in a specified way (*stepped into a new job*). **4** *tr.* (foll. by *off, out*) measure (distance) by stepping. **5** *tr.* perform (a dance). ▫ **step down 1** resign. **2** *Electr.* decrease (voltage) using a transformer. **step in 1** enter a room, house, etc. **2 a** intervene. **b** act as a substitute. **step on it** (or **on the gas**) *colloq.* **1** accelerate a motor vehicle. **2** hurry up. **step out 1** leave a room, house, etc. **2** be active socially. **3** take large steps. **step up 1** increase; intensify (*must step up production*). **2** *Electr.* increase (voltage) using a transformer. **turn one's steps** go in a specified direction. ▫▫ **stepped** *adj.* **step·wise** *adv. & adj.*

step- /step/ *comb. form* denoting a relationship resulting from a remarriage.

step ae·ro·bics *n.* an exercise regimen that involves stepping up on and down from a portable block.

step·broth·er /stépbruthər/ *n.* a son of a stepparent by a marriage other than with one's father or mother.

step-by-step *adv.* gradually; cautiously.

step·child /stépchīld/ *n.* (*pl.* **-children**) a child of one's husband or wife by a previous marriage.

step·daugh·ter /stépdawtər/ *n.* a female stepchild.

step·fa·ther /stépfaathər/ *n.* a male stepparent.

step·lad·der /stépladər/ *n.* a short ladder with flat steps and a folding support.

step·moth·er /stépmuthər/ *n.* a female stepparent.

step·par·ent /stép-pairənt/ *n.* a mother's or father's later husband or wife.

steppe /step/ *n.* a level grassy unforested plain, esp. in SE Europe and Siberia.

step·ping-stone *n.* **1** a raised stone in a stream, muddy place, etc., to help in crossing. **2** a means or stage of progress to an end.

step·sis·ter /stépsistər/ *n.* a daughter of a stepparent by a marriage other than with one's father or mother.

step·son /stépsun/ *n.* a male stepchild.

step stool *n.* a stool with usu. folding steps used to reach high shelves, etc.

-ster /stər/ *suffix* denoting a person engaged in or associated with a particular activity or thing (*gangster; youngster*).

stere /steer/ *n.* a unit of volume equal to one cubic meter.

ster·e·o /stéreeō, stéereeō/ *n.* & *adj.* •*n.* (*pl.* **-os**) **1 a** a stereophonic record player, tape recorder, etc. **b** = *stereophony* (see STEREOPHONIC). **2** = STEREOSCOPE. •*adj.* **1** = STEREOPHONIC. **2** = *stereoscopic* (see STEREOSCOPE).

stereo- /stéreeō, stéereeō/ *comb. form* solid; having three dimensions.

ster·e·o·chem·is·try /stéreeōkémistree, stéereeō;n–/ *n.* the branch of chemistry dealing with the three-dimensional arrangement of atoms in molecules.

ster·e·og·ra·phy /stéreeógrəfee, stéeree;n–/ *n.* the art of depicting solid bodies in a plane.

ster·e·o·i·so·mer /stéreeō-ísəmər, stéereeō–/ *n. Chem.* any of two or more compounds differing only in their spatial arrangement of atoms.

ster·e·om·e·try /stéreeómitree, stéeree–/ *n.* the measurement of solid bodies.

ster·e·o·phon·ic /stéreeōfónik, stéereeō–/ *adj.* (of sound reproduction) using two or more channels so that the sound has the effect of being distributed and of coming from more than one source. ▫▫ **ster·e·o·phon·i·cal·ly** *adv.* **ster·e·oph·o·ny** /–reeófənee/ *n.*

ster·e·o·scope /stéreeəskōp, stéereeə–/ *n.* a device by which two photographs of the same object taken at slightly different angles are viewed together, giving an impression of depth and solidity as in ordinary human vision. ▫▫ **ster·e·o·scop·ic** /–skópik/ *adj.* **ster·e·o·scop·i·cal·ly** *adv.* **ster·e·os·co·py** /–reeóskəpee/ *n.*

ster·e·o·type /stéreeətīp, stéeree–/ *n.* & *v.* •*n.* **1 a** a person or thing that conforms to an unjustifiably fixed mental picture. **b** such an impression or attitude. **2** a printing plate cast from a mold of composed type. •*v.tr.* **1** (esp. as **stereotyped** *adj.*) standardize; cause to conform to a type (*the film is weakened by its stereotyped characters*). **2 a** print from a stereotype. **b** make a stereotype of. ▫▫ **ster·e·o·typ·ic** /–típik/ *adj.* **ster·e·o·typ·i·cal** *adj.* **ster·e·o·typ·i·cal·ly** *adv.* **ster·e·o·typ·y** *n.*

ster·ile /stérəl, –īl/ *adj.* **1** not able to produce seeds or fruit or (of an animal) young; barren. **2** unfruitful; unproductive (*sterile discussions*). **3** free from living microorganisms, etc. **4** lacking originality or emotive force; mentally barren. ▫▫ **ste·ril·i·ty** /stərílitee/ *n.*

ster·i·lize /stérilīz/ *v.tr.* **1** make sterile. **2** deprive of the power of reproduction. ▫▫ **ster·i·liz·a·ble** *adj.* **ster·i·li·za·tion** *n.* **ster·i·liz·er** *n.*

ster·ling /stə́rling/ *adj.* & *n.* •*adj.* **1** of or in British money (*pound sterling*). **2** (of a coin or precious metal) genuine; of standard value or purity. **3** (of a person or qualities, etc.) of solid worth; genuine; reliable (*sterling work*). •*n.* British money (*paid in sterling*).

ster·ling sil·ver *n.* silver of 92.5% silver and 7.5% copper.

stern[1] /stərn/ *adj.* severe; enforcing discipline. ▫▫ **stern·ly** *adv.* **stern·ness** *n.*

stern[2] /stərn/ *n.* **1** the rear part of a ship or boat. **2** any rear part. ▫▫ **stern·ward** *adj.* & *adv.* **stern·wards** *adv.*

ster·nal /stə́rnəl/ *adj.* of or relating to the sternum.

ster·num /stə́rnəm/ *n.* (*pl.* **sternums** or **sterna** /–nə/) the breastbone.

ster·nu·ta·tion /stə́rnyətáyshən/ *n. Med.* or *joc.* a sneeze or attack of sneezing.

ster·nu·ta·tor /stə́rnyətaytər/ *n.* a substance, esp. poison gas, that causes nasal irritation, violent coughing, etc. ▫▫ **ster·nu·ta·to·ry** /–nyóotətawree/ *adj.* & *n.* (*pl.* **-ries**).

ste·roid /stéeroyd, stér–/ *n. Biochem.* any of a group of organic compounds with a characteristic structure of four rings of carbon atoms, including many hormones, alkaloids, and vitamins. ▫▫ **ste·roi·dal** /–róyd'l/ *adj.*

ste·rol /stéerawl, –ol, stér–/ *n. Chem.* any of a group of naturally occurring steroid alcohols.

ster·to·rous /stə́rtərəs/ *adj.* (of breathing) labored and noisy. ▫▫ **ster·to·rous·ly** *adv.*

stet /stet/ *v.* (**stetted, stetting**) **1** *intr.* (written on a proof) ignore or cancel the correction or alteration. **2** *tr.* cancel the correction of.

steth·o·scope /stéthəskōp/ *n.* an instrument used in listening to the action of the heart, lungs, etc., usu. consisting of a circular piece placed against the chest, with tubes leading to earpieces.

Stet·son /stétsən/ *n. Trademark* a felt hat with a very wide brim and a high crown.

ste·ve·dore /stéevədawr/ *n.* a person employed in loading and unloading ships.

stew /stoo, styoo/ *v.* & *n.* •*v.* **1** *tr.* & *intr.* cook by long simmering in a closed pot with liquid. **2** *intr. colloq.* be oppressed by heat or humidity. **3** *intr. colloq.* **a** suffer prolonged embarrassment, anxiety, etc. **b** (foll. by *over*) fret or be anxious. **4** *tr.* (as **stewed** *adj.*) *colloq.* drunk. •*n.* **1** a dish of stewed meat, etc. **2** *colloq.* an agitated or angry state (*be in a stew*). ▫ **stew in one's own juices** be left to suffer the consequences of one's own actions.

stew·ard /stóoərd, styóo–/ *n.* & *v.* •*n.* **1** a passengers' attendant on a ship or aircraft or train. **2** an official appointed to keep order or supervise arrangements at a meeting or show or demonstration, etc. **3** = SHOP STEWARD. **4** a person responsible for supplies of food, etc., for a college or club, etc. **5** a person employed to manage another's property. •*v.tr.* act as a steward of (*will steward the meeting*). ▫▫ **stew·ard·ship** *n.*

stew·ard·ess /stóoərdis, styóo–/ *n.* a female steward, esp. on a ship or aircraft.

stick[1] /stik/ *n.* **1 a** a short slender length of wood broken or cut from a tree. **b** this trimmed for use as a support or weapon. **2** a thin rod or spike of wood, etc., for a particular purpose. **3** an implement used to propel the ball in hockey or polo, etc. **4** a gear lever, esp. in a motor vehicle. **5** the lever controlling the ailerons and elevators in an airplane. **6** a conductor's baton. **7 a** a slender piece of celery, dynamite, deodorant, etc. **b** a number of bombs or paratroops released rapidly from aircraft. **8** punishment, esp. by beating. **9** *colloq.* a piece of wood as part of a house or furniture (*a few sticks of furniture*). **10** (in *pl.*; prec. by *the*) *colloq.* remote rural areas; the country (*a dusty town out in the sticks*).

stick[2] /stik/ *v.* (*past* and *past part.* **stuck** /stuk/) **1** *tr.* (foll. by *in, into, through*) insert or thrust (a thing or its point) (*stick a pin through it*). **2** *tr.* insert a pointed thing into; stab. **3** *tr.* & *intr.* (foll. by *in, into, on,* etc.) **a** fix or be fixed on a pointed thing. **b** fix or be fixed by or as by a pointed end. **4** *tr.* & *intr.* fix or become or remain fixed by or as by adhesive, etc. (*the label won't stick*). **5** *intr.* endure; make a continued impression (*the scene stuck in my mind; the name stuck*). **6** *intr.* lose or be deprived of the power of motion or action through adhesion or jamming or other impediment. **7** *colloq.* **a** *tr.* put in a specified position or place, esp. quickly or haphazardly (*stick them down anywhere*). **b** *intr.* remain in a place (*stuck indoors*). **8** *colloq.* **a** *intr.* (of an accusation, etc.) be convincing or regarded as valid (*could not make the charges stick*). **b** *tr.* (foll. by *on*) place the blame for (a thing) on (a person). □ **be stuck for** be at a loss for or in need of. **be stuck on** *colloq.* be infatuated with. **be stuck with** *colloq.* be unable to get rid of or escape from; be permanently involved with. **stick around** *colloq.* linger; remain at the same place. **stick by** (or **with**) stay loyal or close to. **stick fast** adhere or become firmly fixed or trapped in a position or place. **stick in one's throat** be against one's principles. **stick it out** *colloq.* put up with or persevere with a burden, etc., to the end. **stick one's neck** (or **chin**) **out** expose oneself to censure, etc., by acting or speaking boldly. **stick out** protrude or cause to protrude or project (*stuck his tongue out; stick out your chest*). **stick out a mile** (or **like a sore thumb**) *colloq.* be very obvious or incongruous. **stick to 1** remain close to or fixed on or to. **2** remain faithful to. **3** keep to (a subject, etc.) (*stick to the point*). **stick together** *colloq.* remain united or mutually loyal. **stick to one's guns** see GUN. **stick to it** persevere. **stick up 1** be or make erect or protruding upward. **2** fasten to an upright surface. **3** *colloq.* rob or threaten with a gun. **stick up for** support or defend. **stick with** *colloq.* remain in touch with or faithful to; persevere with. □□ **stick·a·bil·i·ty** /stíkəbílitee/ *n.*

stick·ball /stíkbawl/ *n.* a form of baseball played with a stick or broom handle and a rubber ball.

stick·er /stíkər/ *n.* **1** an adhesive label or notice, etc. **2** a person or thing that sticks. **3** a persistent person.

stick·er price *n.* the full price of a new item, esp. the price listed on a sticker attached to a new automobile.

stick·er shock *n. colloq.* surprise at a higher-than-expected retail price.

stick·ing point *n.* the limit of progress, agreement, etc.

stick-in-the-mud *n. colloq.* an unprogressive or old-fashioned person.

stick·le·back /stíkəlbak/ *n.* any small fish of the family Gasterosteidae with sharp spines along the back.

stick·ler /stíklər/ *n.* (foll. by *for*) a person who insists on something.

stick·pin /stíkpin/ *n.* an ornamental tiepin.

stick shift *n.* a manual automotive transmission with a shift lever on the vehicle's floor or steering column.

stick-up *n. colloq.* an armed robbery.

stick·y /stíkee/ *adj.* (**stickier, stickiest**) **1** tending or intended to stick or adhere. **2** glutinous; viscous. **3** humid. **4** *colloq.* awkward or uncooperative; intransigent. **5** *colloq.* difficult; awkward (*a sticky situation*). □□ **stick·i·ly** *adv.* **stick·i·ness** *n.*

stiff /stif/ *adj.* & *n.* • *adj.* **1** rigid; not flexible. **2** hard to bend or move or turn, etc. **3** hard to cope with; needing strength or effort (*a stiff test; a stiff climb*). **4** severe or strong (*a stiff breeze; a stiff penalty*). **5** formal; constrained. **6** (of a muscle or limb, etc., or a person affected by these) aching when used, owing to previous exertion, injury, etc. **7** (of an alcoholic or medicinal drink) strong. **8** (*predic.*) *colloq.* to an extreme degree (*bored stiff; scared stiff*). • *n. sl.* a corpse. □□ **stiff·ish** *adj.* **stiff·ly** *adv.* **stiff·ness** *n.*

stiff·en /stífən/ *v.tr.* & *intr.* make or become stiff. □□ **stiff·en·er** *n.* **stiff·en·ing** *n.*

stiff-necked *adj.* obstinate or haughty.

stiff up·per lip *n.* determination; fortitude.

sti·fle /stífəl/ *v.* **1** *tr.* smother; suppress. **2** *intr.* & *tr.* experience or cause to experience constraint of breathing. **3** *tr.* kill by suffocating. □□ **sti·fling·ly** *adv.*

stig·ma /stígmə/ *n.* (*pl.* **stigmas** or esp. in sense 4 **stigmata** /–mətə, –maátə/) **1** a mark or sign of disgrace or discredit. **2** (foll. by *of*) a distinguishing mark or characteristic. **3** the part of a pistil that receives the pollen in pollination. **4** (in *pl.*) *Eccl.* (in Christian belief) marks corresponding to those left on Christ's body by the Crucifixion, said to have appeared on the bodies of St. Francis of Assisi and others.

stig·mat·ic /stigmátik/ *adj.* & *n.* • *adj.* **1** of or relating to a stigma or stigmas. **2** = ANASTIGMATIC. • *n. Eccl.* a person bearing stigmata. □□ **stig·mat·i·cal·ly** *adv.*

stig·ma·tist /stígmətist/ *n. Eccl.* = STIGMATIC *n.*

stig·ma·tize /stígmətīz/ *v.tr.* describe as unworthy or disgraceful. □□ **stig·ma·ti·za·tion** *n.*

stile /stīl/ *n.* an arrangement of steps allowing people but not animals to climb over a fence or wall.

sti·let·to /stilétō/ *n.* (*pl.* **-tos**) **1** a short dagger. **2** a pointed instrument for making eyelets, etc. **3** (in full **stiletto heel**) **a** a long tapering heel of a shoe. **b** a shoe with such a heel.

still[1] /stil/ *adj., n., adv.,* & *v.* • *adj.* **1** not or hardly moving. **2** with little or no sound; calm and tranquil (*a still evening*). **3** (of sounds) hushed; quieted; subdued. **4** (of a drink) not effervescent. • *n.* **1** deep silence (*in the still of the night*). **2** an ordinary static photograph (as opposed to a motion picture), esp. a single shot from a movie. • *adv.* **1** without moving (*stand still*). **2** even now or at a particular time (*they still did not understand*). **3** nevertheless. **4** (with *compar.*, etc.) even; yet; increasingly (*still greater efforts*). • *v.tr.* & *intr.* make or become still. □□ **still·ness** *n.*

still[2] /stil/ *n.* an apparatus for distilling alcohol, etc.

still·birth /stílbərth/ *n.* the birth of a dead child.

still·born /stílbawrn/ *adj.* **1** born dead. **2** (of an idea, plan, etc.) abortive.

still life *n.* (*pl.* **still lifes**) a painting or drawing of inanimate objects such as fruit or flowers.

stilt /stilt/ *n.* **1** either of a pair of poles with supports for the feet enabling the user to walk at a distance above the ground. **2** each of a set of piles or posts supporting a building, etc.

stilt·ed /stíltid/ *adj.* **1** (of a literary style, etc.) stiff and unnatural; bombastic. **2** standing on stilts. **3** *Archit.* (of an arch) with pieces of upright masonry between the imposts and other stones. □□ **stilt·ed·ness** *n.*

Stil·ton /stílt'n/ *n. Trademark* a kind of strong rich cheese, often with blue veins, orig. sold in Stilton in eastern England.

stim·u·lant /stímyələnt/ *adj.* & *n.* • *adj.* that stimulates, esp. bodily or mental activity. • *n.* **1** a stimulant substance, esp. a drug or a caffeinated beverage. **2** a stimulating influence.

stim·u·late /stímyəlayt/ *v.tr.* **1** apply or act as a stimulus to. **2** animate; excite; arouse. **3** be a stimulant to. □□ **stim·u·lat·ing** *adj.* **stim·u·la·tion** /–láyshən/ *n.*

stim·u·lus /stímyələs/ *n.* (*pl.* **stimuli** /–lī/) **1** a thing that rouses to activity or energy. **2** a stimulating or rousing effect. **3** a thing that evokes a specific functional reaction in an organ or tissue.

sting /sting/ *n.* & *v.* • *n.* **1** a sharp often poisonous wounding organ of an insect, nettle, etc. **2 a** the act of inflicting a wound with this. **b** the wound itself or the pain caused by it. **3** a wounding or painful quality or effect (*stings of remorse*). **4** pungency; sharpness; vigor. **5** *sl.* a swindle or robbery. • *v.* (*past* and *past part.* **stung** /stung/) **1 a** *tr.* wound or pierce with a sting. **b** *intr.* be able to sting. **2** *intr.* & *tr.* feel or cause to feel a tingling physical or sharp mental pain. **3** *tr.* (foll. by *into*) incite by a strong or painful mental effect (*was stung into replying*). **4** *tr. sl.* swindle or charge exorbitantly.

sting·er /stíngər/ *n.* **1** a stinging insect, nettle, etc. **2** the part of an insect or animal that holds a sting. **3** a sharp painful blow. **4** a cocktail containing crème de menthe and brandy.

sting·ray /stíng-ray/ *n.* any of various broad flatfish, esp. of the family Dasyatidae, having a long poisonous serrated spine at the base of its tail.

stin·gy /stínjee/ *adj.* (**stingier, stingiest**) ungenerous; mean. □□ **stin·gi·ly** *adv.* **stin·gi·ness** *n.*

stink /stingk/ *v. & n.* • *v.* (*past* **stank** /stangk/ or **stunk** /stungk/; *past part.* **stunk**) **1** *intr.* emit a strong offensive smell. **2** *tr.* (often foll. by *up*) fill (a place) with a stink. **3** *tr.* (foll. by *out*, etc.) drive (a person) out, etc., by a stink. **4** *intr. colloq.* be or seem very unpleasant, contemptible, or scandalous. **5** *intr.* (foll. by *of*) *colloq.* have plenty of (esp. money). • *n.* **1** a strong or offensive smell; a stench. **2** *colloq.* an outcry or fuss (*the affair caused quite a stink*).

stink·er /stíngkər/ *n.* **1** a person or thing that stinks. **2** *sl.* an objectionable person or thing. **3** *sl.* a difficult task.

stink·ing /stíngking/ *adj. & adv.* • *adj.* **1** that stinks. **2** *sl.* very objectionable. • *adv. sl.* extremely and usu. objectionably (*stinking rich*). ▫▫ **stink·ing·ly** *adv.*

stink·o /stíngkō/ *adj. sl.* drunk.

stink·pot /stíngkpot/ *n. sl.* **1** a term of contempt for a person. **2** a vehicle or boat that emits foul exhaust fumes.

stink·weed /stíngkweed/ *n.* any of several foul-smelling plants.

stint /stint/ *v. & n.* • *v.* **1** *tr.* supply (food or aid, etc.) in an ungenerous amount or grudgingly. **2** (often *refl.*) supply (a person, etc.) in this way. • *n.* **1** a limitation of supply or effort. **2** a fixed or allotted amount of work (*do one's stint*).

sti·pend /stípend/ *n.* a fixed regular allowance or salary.

sti·pen·di·ar·y /stīpéndee-eree/ *adj. & n.* • *adj.* **1** receiving a stipend. **2** working for pay. • *n.* (*pl.* **-ies**) a person receiving a stipend.

stip·ple /stípəl/ *v. & n.* • *v.* **1** *tr. & intr.* draw or paint with dots instead of lines. **2** *tr.* roughen the surface of (paint, cement, etc.). • *n.* **1** the process or technique of stippling. **2** the effect of stippling. ▫▫ **stip·pling** *n.*

stip·u·late /stípyəlayt/ *v.tr.* **1** specify as part of a bargain or agreement. **2** (foll. by *for*) insist upon as an essential condition. **3** (as **stipulated** *adj.*) laid down in the terms of an agreement. ▫▫ **stip·u·la·tion** /–láyshən/ *n.*

stir /stər/ *v. & n.* • *v.* (**stirred, stirring**) **1** *tr.* move a spoon or other implement around and around in (a liquid, etc.) to mix the ingredients. **2 a** *tr.* cause to move, esp. slightly (*a breeze stirred the lake*). **b** *intr.* be or begin to be in motion (*not a creature was stirring*). **c** *refl.* rouse (oneself). **3** *intr.* rise from sleep (*is still not stirring*). **4** *intr.* (foll. by *out of*) leave; go out of. **5** *tr.* arouse strong feeling in (someone); inspire or excite (*was stirred to anger; it stirred the imagination*). • *n.* **1** an act of stirring (*give it a good stir*). **2** commotion or excitement (*caused quite a stir*). **3** the slightest movement (*not a stir*). ▫ **stir in** mix (an added ingredient) with a substance by stirring. **stir up 1** mix thoroughly by stirring. **2** incite (trouble, etc.). **3** excite; arouse (*stirred up their curiosity*).

stir-craz·y *adj.* deranged from long imprisonment.

stir-fry /stə́rfrī/ *v. & n.* • *v.tr.* (**-fries, -fried**) fry rapidly while stirring. • *n.* a dish consisting of stir-fried meat, vegetables, etc.

stirps /stərps/ *n.* (*pl.* **stirpes** /–peez/) **1** *Biol.* a classificatory group. **2** *Law* **a** a branch of a family. **b** its progenitor.

stir·rer /stə́rər/ *n.* a thing or a person that stirs.

stir·ring /stə́ring/ *adj.* **1** stimulating; exciting; arousing. **2** actively occupied.

stir·rup /stə́rəp, stír–/ *n.* **1** each of a pair of devices attached to each side of a horse's saddle, in the form of a loop with a flat base to support the rider's foot. **2** *attrib.* having the shape of a stirrup. **3** (in full **stirrup bone**) = STAPES.

stitch /stich/ *n. & v.* • *n.* **1 a** (in sewing or knitting, etc.) a single pass of a needle or the thread or loop, etc., resulting from this. **b** a particular method of sewing or knitting, etc. (*am learning a new stitch*). **2** (usu. in *pl.*) *Surgery* each of the loops of material used in sewing up a wound. **3** the least bit of clothing (*hadn't a stitch on*). **4** an acute pain in the side of the body induced by running, etc. • *v.tr.* **1** sew; make stitches (in). **2** join or close with stitches. ▫ **in stitches** *colloq.* laughing uncontrollably. ▫▫ **stitch·er** *n.* **stitch·er·y** *n.*

stitch in time *n.* a timely remedy.

stitch·wort /stíchwərt, –wawrt/ *n.* any plant of the genus *Stellaria*, esp. *S. media* with an erect stem and white starry flowers, once thought to cure a stitch in the side.

sto·a /stṓə/ *n.* (*pl.* **stoas**) **1** a portico or roofed colonnade in ancient Greek architecture. **2** (**the Stoa**) the Stoic school of philosophy.

stoat /stōt/ *n.* a carnivorous mammal, *Mustela erminea*, of the weasel family, having brown fur in the summer turning mainly white in the winter.

sto·chas·tic /stōkástik/ *adj.* **1** determined by a random distribution of probabilities. **2** (of a process) characterized by a sequence of random variables. **3** governed by the laws of probability. ▫▫ **sto·chas·ti·cal·ly** *adv.*

stock /stok/ *n., adj., & v.* • *n.* **1** a store of goods, etc., ready for sale or distribution, etc. **2** a supply or quantity of anything for use (*lay in winter stocks of fuel; a great stock of information*). **3** equipment or raw material for manufacture or trade, etc. (*rolling stock; paper stock*). **4** livestock; farm animals or equipment. **5 a** the capital of a business. **b** shares in this. **6** one's reputation or popularity (*his stock is rising*). **7 a** money lent to a government at fixed interest. **b** the right to receive such interest. **8** a line of ancestry (*comes from German stock*). **9** liquid made by stewing bones, vegetables, etc., as a basis for soup, gravy, etc. **10** a plant into which a graft is inserted. **11** the main trunk of a tree. **12** (in *pl.*) *hist.* a wooden frame with holes for the feet in which offenders were locked as a public punishment. • *adj.* **1** kept in stock and so regularly available (*stock sizes*). **2** hackneyed; conventional (*a stock answer*). • *v.tr.* **1** have or keep (goods) in stock. **2 a** provide (a store or a farm, etc.) with goods, equipment, or livestock. **b** fill with items needed (*shelves well-stocked with books*). ▫ **in stock** available immediately for sale, etc. **on the stocks** in construction or preparation. **out of stock** not immediately available for sale. **stock up 1** provide with or get stocks or supplies. **2** (foll. by *with, on*) get in or gather a stock of (food, fuel, etc.). **take stock 1** make an inventory of one's stock. **2** (often foll. by *of*) make a review or estimate of (a situation, etc.).

stock·ade /stokáyd/ *n. & v.* • *n.* **1** a line or enclosure of upright stakes. **2** a military prison. • *v.tr.* fortify with a stockade.

stock·breed·er /stókbreedər/ *n.* a farmer who raises livestock. ▫▫ **stock·breed·ing** *n.*

stock·brok·er /stókbrōkər/ *n.* = BROKER 2. ▫▫ **stock·brok·er·age** *n.* **stock·brok·ing** *n.*

stock car *n.* **1** a specially modified production car for use in racing. **2** a railroad boxcar for transporting livestock.

stock com·pa·ny *n.* a repertory company performing mainly at a particular theater.

stock ex·change *n.* **1** a place where stocks and shares are bought and sold. **2** the dealers working there.

stock·hold·er /stók-hōldər/ *n.* an owner of stocks or shares. ▫▫ **stock·hold·ing** *n.*

stock·i·nette /stókinét/ *n.* (also **stock·i·net**) an elastic knitted material.

stock·ing /stóking/ *n.* **1 a** either of a pair of long separate coverings for the legs and feet, usu. closely woven. **b** = SOCK[1]. **2** any close-fitting garment resembling a stocking (*bodystocking*). **3** a differently colored, usu. white, lower part of the leg of a horse, etc. ▫ **in one's stocking** (or **stockinged**) **feet** wearing stockings or socks but without shoes.

stock·ing cap *n.* a knitted usu. conical cap.

stock·ing stuff·er *n.* a small present suitable for a Christmas stocking.

stock-in-trade *n.* **1** goods kept on sale by a retailer, dealer, etc. **2** all the requisites of a trade or profession. **3** a ready supply of characteristic phrases, attitudes, etc.

stock·man /stókmən/ *n.* (*pl.* **-men**) **1** an owner of livestock. **2** a person in charge of a stock of goods in a warehouse, etc.

stock mar·ket *n.* **1** = STOCK EXCHANGE. **2** transactions on this.

stock·pile /stókpīl/ *n.* & *v.* •*n.* an accumulated stock of goods, materials, weapons, etc., held in reserve. •*v.tr.* accumulate a stockpile of.

stock·pot /stókpot/ *n.* a pot for cooking stock for soup, etc.

stock·room /stókrōōm, –rŏŏm/ *n.* a room for storing goods in stock.

stock-still *adv.* without moving.

stock·tak·ing /stóktayking/ *n.* **1** the process of making an inventory of stock in a store, warehouse, etc. **2** a review of one's position and resources.

stock·y /stókee/ *adj.* (**stockier, stockiest**) short and strongly built. ▫▫ **stock·i·ly** *adv.*

stock·yard /stókyaard/ *n.* an enclosure for the sorting or temporary keeping of cattle.

stodg·y /stójee/ *adj.* (**stodgier, stodgiest**) **1** dull and uninteresting. **2** (of a literary style, etc.) turgid and dull. **3** esp. *Brit.* (of food) heavy and indigestible. ▫▫ **stodg·i·ness** *n.*

sto·gy /stṓgee/ *n.* (also **sto·gie**) (*pl.* **-gies**) a long narrow roughly-made cigar.

Sto·ic /stṓik/ *n.* & *adj.* •*n.* **1** a member of the ancient Greek school of philosophy founded by Zeno *c.*308 BC, which sought virtue as the greatest good and taught control of one's feelings. **2** (**stoic**) a stoical person. •*adj.* **1** of or like the Stoics. **2** (**stoic**) = STOICAL.

sto·i·cal /stṓikəl/ *adj.* showing great self-control in adversity. ▫▫ **sto·i·cal·ly** *adv.*

Sto·i·cism /stṓisizəm/ *n.* **1** the philosophy of the Stoics. **2** (**stoicism**) a stoical attitude.

stoke /stōk/ *v.* (often foll. by *up*) **1 a** *tr.* feed and tend (a fire or furnace, etc.). **b** *intr.* act as a stoker. **2** *intr. colloq.* consume food, esp. steadily and in large quantities.

stoke·hole /stṓk-hōl/ *n.* a space for stokers in front of a furnace.

stok·er /stṓkər/ *n.* a person who tends to the furnace on a steamship.

STOL *abbr. Aeron.* short take-off and landing.

stole[1] /stōl/ *n.* **1** a woman's long garment like a scarf, esp. made of fur, worn around the shoulders. **2** a strip of silk, etc., worn over the shoulders as a vestment by a priest.

stole[2] *past* of STEAL.

sto·len *past part.* of STEAL.

stol·id /stólid/ *adj.* **1** lacking or concealing emotion or animation. **2** not easily excited or moved. ▫▫ **sto·lid·i·ty** /–líditee/ *n.* **stol·id·ly** *adv.* **stol·id·ness** *n.*

sto·ma /stṓmə/ *n.* (*pl.* **stomas** or **stomata** /–mətə/) **1** *Bot.* a minute pore in the epidermis of a leaf. **2** *Surgery* an artificial orifice made in the stomach.

stom·ach /stúmək/ *n.* & *v.* •*n.* **1 a** the internal organ in which the first part of digestion occurs. **b** any of several such organs in animals, esp. ruminants, in which there are four. **2 a** the belly, abdomen, or lower front of the body. **b** a protuberant belly. **3** (usu. foll. by *for*) **a** an appetite. **b** liking, readiness, or inclination (for controversy, conflict, danger, or an undertaking) (*had no stomach for the fight*). •*v.tr.* **1** find sufficiently palatable to swallow or keep down. **2** submit to or endure (an affront, etc.) (usu. with *neg.*: *cannot stomach it*).

stom·ach·ache *n.* a pain in the abdomen or bowels.

stom·ach·er /stúməkər/ *n. hist.* **1** a front piece of a woman's dress covering the breast and pit of the stomach, often jeweled or embroidered. **2** an ornament worn on the front of a bodice.

sto·ma·ta *pl.* of STOMA.

sto·ma·tol·o·gy /stṓmətóləjee/ *n.* the scientific study of the mouth or its diseases. ▫▫ **sto·mat·o·log·i·cal** /–təlójikəl/ *adj.* **sto·mat·ol·o·gist** *n.*

stomp /stomp/ *v.* & *n.* •*v.intr.* tread or stamp heavily. •*n.* a lively jazz dance with heavy stamping. ▫▫ **stomp·er** *n.*

stone /stōn/ *n.* & *v.* •*n.* **1 a** solid nonmetallic mineral matter, of which rock is made. **b** a piece of this, esp. a small piece. **2** *Building* **a** = LIMESTONE (*Portland stone*). **b** = SANDSTONE. **3** *Mineral.* = PRECIOUS STONE. **4** a stony meteorite; an aerolite. **5** (often in *comb.*) a piece of stone of a definite shape or for a particular purpose (*tombstone*; *stepping-stone*). **6 a** a thing resembling stone in hardness or form, e.g., the hard case of the kernel in some fruits. **b** *Med.* (often in *pl.*) a hard concretion in the body, esp. in the kidney or gallbladder (*gallstones*). **7** (*attrib.*) of the color of stone. •*v.tr.* **1** pelt with stones. **2** remove the stones from (fruit). **3** face or pave, etc., with stone. **4** sharpen, polish, etc., by rubbing with or against a stone. ▫ **cast** (or **throw**) **stones** (or **the first stone**) make aspersions on a person's character, etc. **leave no stone unturned** try all possible means. **stone cold** completely cold. **a stone's throw** a short distance. ▫▫ **stoned** *adj.* (also in *comb.*).

Stone Age *n.* a prehistoric period when weapons and tools were made of stone.

stone·crop /stṓnkrop/ *n.* any succulent plant of the genus *Sedum*, usu. having yellow or white flowers and growing among rocks or in walls.

stone·cut·ter /stṓnkutər/ *n.* a person or machine that cuts or carves stone.

stoned /stōnd/ *adj. sl.* under the influence of alcohol or drugs.

stone-deaf *adj.* completely deaf.

stone·fish /stṓnfish/ *n.* (*pl.* same) a venomous tropical fish, *Synanceia verrucosa*, with poison glands underlying its erect dorsal spines. Also called **devilfish**.

stone fruit *n.* a fruit with flesh enclosing a stone.

stone-ground /stṓn-grownd/ *adj.* (of grain) ground with millstones.

stone·ma·son /stṓnmaysən/ *n.* a person who cuts, prepares, and builds with stone. ▫▫ **stone·ma·son·ry** *n.*

stone·wall /stṓnwawl/ *v. tr.* & *intr.* obstruct (discussion or investigation) or be obstructive with evasive answers or denials, etc. ▫▫ **stone·wall·ing** *n.*

stone·ware /stṓnwair/ *n.* ceramic ware that is impermeable and partly vitrified but opaque.

stone·washed /stṓnwawsht, –wosht/ *adj.* (of a garment or fabric, esp. denim) washed with abrasives to produce a worn or faded appearance.

stone·work /stṓnwərk/ *n.* **1** masonry. **2** the parts of a building made of stone.

stone·wort /stṓnwərt, –wawrt/ *n.* any plant of the genus *Chara*, related to green algae, often encrusted with a chalky deposit.

ston·y /stṓnee/ *adj.* (**stonier, stoniest**) **1** full of or covered with stones (*stony soil*; *a stony road*). **2 a** hard; rigid. **b** cold; unfeeling; obdurate; uncompromising.

stood *past* and *past part.* of STAND.

stooge /stōōj/ *n.* & *v. colloq.* •*n.* **1** a butt or foil, esp. for a comedian. **2** an assistant or subordinate, esp. for routine or unpleasant work. **3** a compliant person; a puppet. • *v.intr.* (foll. by *for*) act as a stooge for.

stool /stool/ *n.* & *v.* • *n.* **1** a single seat without a back or arms, typically resting on three or four legs or on a single pedestal. **2** = FOOTSTOOL. **3** = FECES. **4** the root or stump of a tree or plant from which the shoots spring. • *v.intr.* (of a plant) throw up shoots from the root.

stool·ie /stóolee/ *n. sl.* a person acting as a stool pigeon.

stool pi·geon *n.* **1** a person acting as a decoy. **2** a police informer.

stoop[1] /stoop/ *v.* & *n.* • *v.* **1** *tr.* bend (one's head or body) forward and downward. **2** *intr.* carry one's head and shoulders bowed forward. **3** *intr.* (foll. by *to* + infin.) deign or condescend. **4** *intr.* (foll. by *to*) descend or lower oneself to (some conduct) (*has stooped to crime*). • *n.* a stooping posture.

stoop[2] /stoop/ *n.* a porch or small veranda or set of steps in front of a house.

stop /stop/ *v.* & *n.* • *v.* (**stopped, stopping**) **1** *tr.* **a** put an end to (motion, etc.); completely check the progress or motion of. **b** effectively hinder or prevent (*stopped them playing so loudly*). **c** discontinue (an action or sequence of actions) (*stopped playing*). **2** *intr.* come to an end. **3** *intr.* cease from motion or speaking or action. **4** *tr.* cause to cease action; defeat. **5** *tr. sl.* receive (a blow, etc.). **6** *intr.* esp. *Brit.* stay for a short time. **7** *tr.* (often foll. by *up*) block or close up (a hole or leak, etc.). **8** *tr.* not permit or supply as usual (*shall stop their wages*). **9** *tr.* (in full **stop payment of** or **on**) instruct a bank to withhold payment on (a check). **10** *tr.* obtain the required pitch from (the string of a violin, etc.) by pressing at the appropriate point with the finger. • *n.* **1** the act or an instance of stopping; the state of being stopped (*put a stop to*). **2** a place designated for a bus or train, etc., to stop. **3** a device for stopping motion at a particular point. **4** a change of pitch effected by stopping a string. **5 a** (in an organ) a row of pipes of one character. **b** a knob, etc., operating these. **6 a** the effective diameter of a lens. **b** a device for reducing this. **c** a unit of change of relative aperture or exposure. **7** (of sound) = PLOSIVE. □ **put a stop to** cause to end, esp. abruptly. **stop at nothing** be ruthless. **stop by** (also *absol.*) call at (a place). **stop dead** (or **short**) cease abruptly. **stop one's ears 1** put one's fingers in one's ears to avoid hearing. **2** refuse to listen.

stop-and-go *n.* alternate stopping and restarting, esp. in traffic.

stop·cock /stópkok/ *n.* an externally operated valve regulating the flow of a liquid or gas through a pipe, etc.

stop·gap /stópgap/ *n.* (often *attrib.*) a temporary substitute.

stoplight *n.* a red traffic light.

stop·off /stópawf, –of/ *n.* = STOPOVER.

stop·o·ver /stópōvər/ *n.* a break in one's journey.

stop·page /stópij/ *n.* **1** the condition of being blocked or stopped. **2** a stopping (of pay). **3** a stopping or interruption of work in a factory, etc.

stop·per /stópər/ *n.* & *v.* • *n.* **1** a plug for closing a bottle, etc. **2** a person or thing that stops something. • *v.tr.* close with a stopper. □ **put a stopper on 1** put an end to (a thing). **2** keep (a person) quiet.

stop·ple /stópəl/ *n.* & *v.* • *n.* a stopper or plug. • *v.tr.* close with a stopple.

stop·watch /stópwoch/ *n.* a watch with a mechanism for recording elapsed time, used to time races, etc.

stor·age /stáwrij/ *n.* **1 a** the storing of goods, etc. **b** a particular method of storing or the space available for it. **2** the cost of storing. **3** the electronic retention of data in a computer, etc.

stor·age bat·ter·y *n.* (also **storage cell**) a battery (or cell) for storing electricity.

store /stawr/ *n.* & *v.* • *n.* **1** a quantity of something kept available for use. **2** (in *pl.*) **a** articles for a particular purpose accumulated for use (*naval stores*). **b** a supply of these or the place where they are kept. **3 a** = DEPARTMENT STORE. **b** a retail outlet or shop. **c** a shop selling basic necessities (*general store*). • *v.tr.* **1** put (furniture, etc.) in storage. **2** (often foll. by *up, away*) accumulate (provisions, energy, electricity, etc.) for future use. **3** stock or provide with something useful (*a mind stored with facts*). **4** enter or retain (data) for retrieval. □ **in store 1** kept in readiness. **2** coming in the future. **3** (foll. by *for*) destined or intended. **set** (or **lay** or **put**) **store by** (or **on**) consider important or valuable.

store·front /stáwrfrunt/ *n.* **1** the side of a store facing the street. **2** a room at the front of a store.

store·house /stáwrhows/ *n.* a place where things are stored.

store·keep·er /stáwrkeepər/ *n.* the owner or manager of a store.

store·room /stáwr-room, –room/ *n.* a room in which items are stored.

sto·ried /stáwreed/ *adj. literary* celebrated in or associated with stories.

stork /stawrk/ *n.* any long-legged large wading bird of the family Ciconiidae, esp. *Ciconia ciconia* with white plumage, black wingtips, a long reddish beak, and red feet, nesting esp. on tall buildings.

storm /stawrm/ *n.* & *v.* • *n.* **1** a violent disturbance of the atmosphere with strong winds and usu. with thunder and rain or snow, etc. **2** a violent disturbance of the established order in human affairs. **3** (foll. by *of*) **a** a violent shower of missiles or blows. **b** an outbreak of applause, indignation, hisses, etc. (*they were greeted by a storm of abuse*). **4 a** a direct assault by troops on a fortified place. **b** the capture of a place by such an assault. • *v.* **1** *intr.* (often foll. by *at, away*) talk violently; rage; bluster. **2** *intr.* (usu. foll. by *in, out of,* etc.) move violently or angrily (*stormed out of the meeting*). **3** *tr.* attack or capture by storm. **4** *intr.* (of wind, rain, etc.) rage; be violent. □ **take by storm 1** capture by direct assault. **2** rapidly captivate (a person, audience, etc.). □□ **storm·proof** *adj.*

storm door *n.* an additional outer door for protection in bad weather or winter.

storm pet·rel *n.* **1** a small petrel, *Hydrobates pelagicus*, of the North Atlantic, with black and white plumage. **2** a person causing unrest.

storm sail *n.* a sail of smaller size and stouter canvas than the corresponding one used in ordinary weather.

storm sig·nal *n.* a device warning of an approaching storm.

storm troop·er *n.* **1** *hist.* a member of the Nazi political militia. **2** a member of the shock troops.

storm troops *n.pl.* = SHOCK TROOPS.

storm win·dow *n.* an additional outer window used like a storm door.

storm·y /stáwrmee/ *adj.* (**stormier, stormiest**) **1** of or affected by storms. **2** (of a wind, etc.) violent; raging. **3** full of angry feeling or outbursts (*a stormy meeting*). □□ **storm·i·ly** *adv.* **storm·i·ness** *n.*

sto·ry[1] /stáwree/ *n.* (*pl.* **-ries**) **1** an account of imaginary or past events. **2** the past course of the life of a person or institution, etc. **3** (in full **story line**) the plot of a novel or play, etc. **4** facts or experiences that deserve narration. **5** *colloq.* a lie. **6** a narrative or descriptive

See page xii for the *Key to Pronunciation*.

item of news. □ **the old** (or **same old**) **story** the familiar or predictable course of events. **the story goes** it is said. **to cut** (or **make**) **a long story short** a formula excusing the omission of details.

sto·ry[2] /stáwree/ *n.* (*pl.* **-ries**) **1** any of the parts into which a building is divided horizontally; the whole of the rooms having a continuous floor. **2** a thing forming a horizontal division.

sto·ry·board /stáwreebawrd/ *n.* a displayed sequence of pictures, etc., outlining the plan of a movie, television advertisement, etc.

sto·ry·book /stáwreebo͝ok/ *n.* **1** a book of stories for children. **2** (*attrib.*) unreal, romantic (*a storybook ending*).

sto·ry·tell·er /stáwreetelər/ *n.* **1** a person who tells stories. **2** *colloq.* a liar. □□ **sto·ry·tell·ing** *n. & adj.*

stout /stowt/ *adj. & n.* • *adj.* **1** somewhat fat; corpulent. **2** of considerable thickness or strength (*a stout stick*). **3** brave; vigorous (*a stout fellow; stout resistance*). • *n.* a strong dark beer brewed with roasted malt or barley. □□ **stout·ish** *adj.* **stout·ly** *adv.* **stout·ness** *n.*

stout·heart·ed /stówt-hártəd/ *adj.* courageous. □□ **stout·heart·ed·ly** *adv.* **stout·heart·ed·ness** *n.*

stove[1] /stōv/ *n.* a closed apparatus burning fuel or electricity for heating or cooking.

stove[2] *past* and *past part.* of STAVE *v.*

stove·pipe /stṓvpīp/ *n.* a pipe conducting smoke and gases from a stove to a chimney.

stove·pipe hat *n. colloq.* a tall silk hat.

stow /stō/ *v.tr.* **1** pack (goods, etc.) tidily and compactly. **2** *Naut.* place (a cargo or provisions) in its proper place and order. **3** fill (a receptacle) with articles compactly arranged. □ **stow away 1** place (a thing) where it will not cause an obstruction. **2** be a stowaway on a ship, etc.

stow·age /stṓij/ *n.* **1** the act or an instance of stowing. **2** a place for this.

stow·a·way /stṓəway/ *n.* a person who hides on board a ship or aircraft, etc., to get free passage.

STP *abbr.* standard temperature and pressure.

stra·bis·mus /strəbízməs/ *n. Med.* the condition of one or both eyes not correctly aligned in direction; a squint. □□ **stra·bis·mal** *adj.* **stra·bis·mic** *adj.*

strad·dle /strád'l/ *v. & n.* • *v.* **1** *tr.* **a** sit or stand across (a thing) with the legs wide apart. **b** be situated across or on both sides of (*the town straddles the border*). **2** *tr.* part (one's legs) widely. **3** *tr.* drop shots or bombs short of and beyond (a target). • *n.* the act or an instance of straddling. □□ **strad·dler** *n.*

Strad·i·var·i·us /strádiváireeəs/ *n.* a violin or other stringed instrument made by Antonio Stradivari of Cremona (d. 1737) or his followers.

strafe /strayf/ *v. & n.* • *v.tr.* **1** bombard; harass with gunfire. **2** abuse. • *n.* an act of strafing.

strag·gle /strágəl/ *v.intr.* **1** lack compactness or tidiness. **2** be dispersed or sporadic. **3** trail behind others in a march or race, etc. **4** (of a plant, beard, etc.) grow long and loose. □□ **strag·gler** *n.* **strag·gly** *adj.*

straight /strayt/ *adj., n., & adv.* • *adj.* **1** extending uniformly in the same direction; without a curve or bend, etc. **2** successive; uninterrupted (*three straight wins*). **3** in proper order or place or condition; duly arranged (*put things straight*). **4** honest; candid; not evasive. **5** (of thinking, etc.) logical; unemotional. **6** (of drama, etc.) serious as opposed to popular or comic; employing conventional techniques. **7 a** unmodified. **b** (of a drink) undiluted. **8** *colloq.* **a** (of a person, etc.) conventional or respectable. **b** heterosexual. **9** (of a person's back) not bowed. **10** (of the hair) not curly or wavy. **11** (of a knee) not bent. **12** (of a garment) not flared. **13** coming direct from its source. **14** (of an aim, blow, or course) going direct to the mark. • *n.* **1** the straight part of something, esp. a racetrack. **2** a straight condition. **3** a sequence of five cards in poker. **4** *colloq.* **a** a conventional person. **b** a heterosexual. • *adv.* **1** in a straight line; direct (*came straight from Paris*). **2** in the right direction; with a good aim. **3** correctly (*can't see straight*). □ **go straight** live an honest life after being a criminal. **the straight and narrow** morally correct behavior. **straight away** at once; immediately. **straight off** *colloq.* without hesitation. **straight up** *colloq.* **1** truthfully; honestly. **2** without admixture or dilution. □□ **straight·ness** *n.*

straight·a·way /stráytəway/ *adj. & n.* • *adj.* **1** (of a course, etc.) straight. **2** straightforward. • *n.* a straight course, track, road, etc.

straight·edge /stráytej/ *n.* a bar with one edge accurately straight, used for testing.

straight·en /stráyt'n/ *v.tr. & intr.* **1** (often foll. by *out*) make or become straight. **2** (foll. by *up*) stand erect after bending. □□ **straight·en·er** *n.*

straight face *n.* an intentionally expressionless face, esp. avoiding a show of amusement. □□ **straight-faced** *adj.*

straight·for·ward /stráytfáwrwərd/ *adj.* **1** honest or frank. **2** (of a task, etc.) uncomplicated. □□ **straight·for·ward·ly** *adv.* **straight·for·ward·ness** *n.*

straight·jack·et var. of STRAITJACKET.

straight·laced var. of STRAITLACED.

straight man *n.* the person in a comedy duo who speaks lines that give a comedian the opportunity to make jokes.

straight-out *adj.* **1** uncompromising. **2** straightforward; genuine.

straight ra·zor *n.* a razor with a straight blade that is hinged to a handle into which it can be folded.

strain[1] /strayn/ *v. & n.* • *v.* **1** *tr. & intr.* make or become taut or tense. **2** *tr.* exercise (oneself, one's senses, a thing, etc.) intensely or excessively. **3 a** *intr.* make an intensive effort. **b** (foll. by *after*) strive intensely for. **4** *intr.* (foll. by *at*) tug; pull. **5** *intr.* hold out with difficulty under pressure (*straining under the load*). **6** *tr.* distort from the true intention or meaning. **7** *tr.* overtask or injure by overuse or excessive demands (*strain a muscle; strained their loyalty*). **8 a** *tr.* clear (a liquid) of solid matter by passing it through a sieve, etc. **b** *tr.* (foll. by *out*) filter (solids) out from a liquid. **9** *tr.* use (one's ears, eyes, voice, etc.) to the best of one's power. • *n.* **1 a** the act or an instance of straining. **b** the force exerted in this. **2** an injury caused by straining a muscle, etc. **3 a** a severe demand on physical strength or resources. **b** the exertion needed to meet this. **4** (in *sing.* or *pl.*) a snatch or spell of music or poetry. **5** a tone or tendency in speech or writing (*more in the same strain*). □ **strain oneself 1** injure oneself by effort. **2** make undue efforts.

strain[2] /strayn/ *n.* **1** a breed or stock of animals, plants, etc. **2** a moral tendency as part of a person's character (*a strain of aggression*).

strained /straynd/ *adj.* **1** constrained; forced; artificial. **2** (of a relationship) mutually distrustful or tense. **3** (of an interpretation) involving an unreasonable assumption; far-fetched; labored.

strain·er /stráynər/ *n.* a device for straining liquids, vegetables, etc.

strait /strayt/ *n.* **1** (in *sing.* or *pl.*) a narrow passage of water connecting two large bodies of water. **2** (usu. in *pl.*) difficulty, trouble, or distress (usu. *in dire* or *desperate straits*).

strait·en /stráyt'n/ *v.tr.* **1** restrict in range or scope. **2** (as **straitened** *adj.*) (esp. of circumstances) characterized by poverty.

strait·jack·et /stráytjakit/ *n. & v.* (also **straightjacket**) • *n.* **1** a strong garment with long arms for confining the arms of a violent prisoner, mental patient, etc. **2** restrictive measures. •*v.tr.* (**-jacketed, -jacketing**) **1** restrain with a straitjacket. **2** severely restrict.

strait·laced /stráytláyst/ *adj.* (also **straight·laced**) severely virtuous.

strand[1] /strand/ *v. & n.* •*v.tr.* **1** run aground. **2** (as **stranded** *adj.*) left in a helpless position, esp. without money or means of transport. **3** *Baseball* leave (a runner) on base at the end of an inning. •*n. poet.* the margin of a sea, lake, or river.

strand[2] /strand/ *n.* **1** each of the threads or wires twisted around each other to make a rope or cable. **2 a** a single thread or strip of fiber. **b** a constituent filament. **3** an element or strain in any composite whole.

strange /straynj/ *adj.* **1** unusual; peculiar; eccentric. **2** (often foll. by *to*) unfamiliar; alien (*lost in a strange land*). **3** (foll. by *to*) unaccustomed. **4** not at ease; out of one's element. □ **feel strange** be unwell. □□ **strange·ly** *adv.* **strange·ness** *n.*

stran·ger /stráynjər/ *n.* **1** a person who does not know or is not known in a particular place or company. **2** (often foll. by *to*) a person one does not know (*was a complete stranger to me*). **3** (foll. by *to*) a person entirely unaccustomed to (a feeling, experience, etc.) (*no stranger to controversy*).

stran·gle /stránggəl/ *v.tr.* **1** squeeze the windpipe or neck of, esp. so as to kill. **2** hamper or suppress (a movement, impulse, cry, etc.). □□ **stran·gler** *n.*

stran·gle·hold /strángg əlhōld/ *n.* **1** a wrestling hold that throttles an opponent. **2** a deadly grip. **3** complete and exclusive control.

stran·gu·late /stránggyəlayt/ *v.tr. Surgery* **1** prevent circulation through (a vein, intestine, etc.) by compression. **2** remove (a tumor, etc.) by binding with a cord.

stran·gu·la·tion /strángyəláyshən/ *n.* **1** the act of strangling or the state of being strangled. **2** the act of strangulating.

strap /strap/ *n. & v.* •*n.* **1** a strip of leather or other flexible material, often with a buckle or other fastening for holding things together, etc. **2** a thing like this for keeping a garment in place. **3** a loop for grasping to steady oneself in a moving vehicle. •*v.tr.* (**strapped, strapping**) **1** (often foll. by *down, up,* etc.) secure or bind with a strap. **2** beat with a strap. **3** (esp. as **strapped** *adj.*) *colloq.* subject to a shortage. □□ **strap·py** *adj.*

strap·hang·er /stráp-hangər/ *n. sl.* a standing passenger in a bus or subway, esp. a regular commuter.

strap·less /stráplis/ *adj.* (of a garment) without straps, esp. shoulder straps.

strap·ping /stráping/ *adj.* (esp. of a person) large and sturdy.

stra·ta *pl.* of STRATUM.

▶See note at STRATUM.

strat·a·gem /strátəjəm/ *n.* **1** a cunning plan or scheme, esp. for deceiving an enemy. **2** trickery.

stra·tal see STRATUM.

stra·te·gic /strəteéjik/ *adj.* **1** of or serving strategy (*strategic considerations; strategic move*). **2** (of materials) essential in fighting a war. **3** (of bombing or weapons) done or for use against an enemy's home territory as a longer-term military objective (opp. TACTICAL). □□ **stra·te·gi·cal·ly** *adv.*

stra·te·gic de·fense in·i·ti·a·tive *n.* a proposed US system of defense against nuclear weapons using satellites armed with lasers to intercept intercontinental ballistic missiles. Also called **Star Wars.** ¶ Abbr.: **SDI.**

strat·e·gy /strátijee/ *n.* (*pl.* **-gies**) **1** the art of war. **2 a** the art of moving troops, ships, aircraft, etc., into favorable positions (cf. TACTICS). **b** an instance of this or a plan formed according to it. **3** a plan of action or policy in business or politics, etc. □□ **strat·e·gist** *n.*

strat·i *pl.* of STRATUS.

strat·i·fy /strátifī/ *v.tr.* (**-fies, -fied**) **1** (esp. as **stratified** *adj.*) arrange in strata. **2** construct in layers, social grades, etc. □□ **strat·i·fi·ca·tion** /–fikáyshən/ *n.*

strato- /strátō/ *comb. form* stratus.

stra·to·cir·rus /strátōsírəs/ *n.* clouds combining stratus and cirrus features.

stra·to·cu·mu·lus /strátōkyóomyələs/ *n.* clouds combining cumulus and stratus features.

strat·o·sphere /strátəsfeer/ *n.* a layer of atmospheric air above the troposphere extending to about 30 miles above the Earth's surface. □□ **strat·o·spher·ic** /–feérik, –férik/ *adj.*

stra·tum /stráytəm, strát–/ *n.* (*pl.* **strata** /–tə/) **1** esp. *Geol.* or *Archaeol.* a layer or set of successive layers of any deposited substance. **2** an atmospheric layer. **3** a layer of tissue, etc. **4** a social grade, class, etc. (*the various strata of society*). □□ **stra·tal** *adj.*

▶The singular is *stratum,* 'a layer.' The plural, **strata,** is sometimes mistaken for singular.

stra·tus /stráytəs, strát–/ *n.* a continuous horizontal sheet of cloud.

straw /straw/ *n.* **1** dry cut stalks of grain for use as fodder or for thatching, packing, etc. **2** a single stalk of straw. **3** a thin tube for sucking a drink from a glass, etc. **4** the pale yellow color of straw. **5** a straw hat. □ **catch** (or **grasp**) **at straws** resort to an utterly inadequate expedient in desperation. □□ **straw·y** *adj.*

straw·ber·ry /stráwberee/ *n.* (*pl.* **-ries**) **1 a** any plant of the genus *Fragaria,* esp. any of various cultivated varieties, with white flowers and runners. **b** the pulpy red edible fruit of this, having a seed-studded surface. **2** a deep pinkish-red color.

straw·ber·ry blond *n.* **1** reddish blond hair. **2** a person with such hair.

straw·ber·ry mark *n.* a soft reddish birthmark.

straw vote *n.* (also **straw poll**) an unofficial ballot as a test of opinion.

stray /stray/ *v., n., & adj.* •*v.intr.* **1** wander from the right place; become separated from one's companions. **2** deviate morally. **3** (as **strayed** *adj.*) that has gone astray. •*n.* a person or thing that has strayed, esp. a domestic animal. •*adj.* **1** strayed or lost. **2** found or occurring occasionally (*hit by a stray bullet*).

streak /streek/ *n. & v.* •*n.* **1** a long thin usu. irregular line or band, esp. distinguished by color. **2** a strain or element in a person's character (*streak of mischief*). **3** a spell or series (*a winning streak*). •*v.* **1** *tr.* mark with streaks. **2** *intr.* move very rapidly. **3** *intr. colloq.* run naked in a public place as a stunt. □□ **streak·er** *n.*

streak·y /streékee/ *adj.* (**streakier, streakiest**) full of streaks. □□ **streak·i·ly** *adv.* **streak·i·ness** *n.*

stream /streem/ *n. & v.* •*n.* **1** a flowing body of water, esp. a small river. **2 a** the flow of a fluid or of a mass of people (*a stream of lava*). **b** (in *sing.* or *pl.*) a large quantity of something that flows or moves along. **3** a current or direction in which things are moving or tending (*against the stream*). •*v.* **1** *intr.* flow or move as a stream. **2** *intr.* run with liquid (*my eyes were streaming*). **3** *intr.* (of a banner or hair, etc.) float or wave in the wind. **4** *tr.* emit a stream of (blood, etc.).

stream·er /streémər/ *n.* **1** a long narrow flag. **2** a long narrow strip of ribbon or paper, esp. in a coil that unrolls when thrown. **3** a banner headline.

stream·line /streémlīn/ *v.tr.* **1** give (a vehicle, etc.) the form which presents the least resistance. **2** make (an organization, process, etc.) simple or more efficient or better organized. **3** (as **streamlined** *adj.*) **a** having a smooth, slender, or elongated form. **b** having a simplified and more efficient structure or organization.

stream of con·scious·ness *n.* **1** *Psychol.* a person's thoughts and conscious reactions to events perceived as a continuous flow. **2** a literary style depicting events in such a flow in the mind of a character.

street /street/ *n.* **1** a public road in a city, town, or village. **2** this with the houses or other buildings on each side. □ **on the streets 1** living by prostitution. **2** homeless. □□ **street·ed** *adj.* (also in *comb.*).

street·car /stréetkaar/ *n.* a commuter vehicle that operates on rails in city streets.

street smarts *n. colloq.* social awareness gained from hard experience.

street val·ue *n.* the value of drugs sold illicitly.

street·walk·er /stréetwawkər/ *n.* a prostitute seeking customers in the street. □□ **street·walk·ing** *n. & adj.*

street·wise /stréetwīz/ *adj.* familiar with the ways of modern urban life.

strength /strengkth, strength, strenth/ *n.* **1** the state of being strong; the degree or respect in which a person or thing is strong. **2 a** a person or thing affording support. **b** an attribute making for strength of character (*patience is your great strength*). **3** the number of persons present. **4** a full complement (*below strength*). □ **on the strength of** on the basis of.

strength·en /stréngkthən, strén–/ *v.tr. & intr.* make or become stronger. □ **strengthen a person's hand** (or **hands**) encourage a person to vigorous action.

stren·u·ous /strényōōəs/ *adj.* **1** requiring or using great effort. **2** energetic or unrelaxing. □□ **stren·u·ous·ly** *adv.* **stren·u·ous·ness** *n.*

strep /strep/ *n. colloq.* = STREPTOCOCCUS.

strep throat *n. colloq.* an acute sore throat caused by hemolytic streptococci and characterized by fever and inflammation.

strep·to·coc·cus /stréptəkókəs/ *n.* (*pl.* **streptococci** /–kóksī, –kókī/) any bacterium of the genus *Streptococcus*, usu. occurring in chains, some of which cause infectious diseases. □□ **strep·to·coc·cal** *adj.*

strep·to·my·cin /stréptəmísin/ *n.* an antibiotic produced by the bacterium *Streptomyces griseus*, effective against many disease-producing bacteria.

stress /stres/ *n. & v.* • *n.* **1 a** pressure or tension exerted on a material object. **b** a quantity measuring this. **2 a** demand on physical or mental energy. **b** distress caused by this (*suffering from stress*). **3 a** emphasis (*the stress was on the need for success*). **b** accentuation; emphasis laid on a syllable or word. **c** an accent, esp. the principal one in a word (*the stress is on the first syllable*). • *v.tr.* **1** lay stress on; emphasize. **2** subject to mechanical or physical or mental stress.

stress·ful /strésfōōl/ *adj.* causing stress; mentally tiring (*had a stressful day*).

stretch /strech/ *v. & n.* • *v.* **1** *tr. & intr.* draw or be drawn or admit of being drawn out into greater length or size. **2** *tr. & intr.* make or become taut. **3** *tr. & intr.* place or lie at full length or spread out (*with a canopy stretched over them*). **4** *tr.* **a** extend (an arm, leg, etc.). **b** (often *refl.*) thrust out (one's limbs) and tighten (one's muscles) after being relaxed. **5** *intr.* have a specified length or extension; extend (*farmland stretches for many miles*). **6** *tr.* strain or exert extremely or excessively; exaggerate (*stretch the truth*). **7** *tr.* (as **stretched** *adj.*) elongated or extended. • *n.* **1** a continuous extent or expanse or period (*a stretch of open road*). **2** the act of stretching. **3** (*attrib.*) able to stretch; elastic (*stretch fabric*). **4 a** *colloq.* a period of imprisonment. **b** a period of service. □ **at a stretch 1** in one continuous period. **2** with much effort. **stretch one's legs** exercise oneself by walking. **stretch out 1** *tr.* extend (a hand or foot, etc.). **2** *intr. & tr.* last for a longer period; prolong. **3** *tr.* make (money, etc.) last for a sufficient time. □□ **stretch·y** *adj.* **stretch·i·ness** *n.*

stretch·er /stréchər/ *n. & v.* • *n.* **1** a framework of two poles with canvas, etc., between, for carrying sick, injured, or dead persons in a lying position. **2** a brick or stone laid with its long side along the face of a wall. **3** a rod or bar as a tie between chair legs, etc. **4** a board in a boat against which a rower presses the feet. **5** a wooden frame over which a canvas is stretched ready for painting. • *v.tr.* (often foll. by *off*) convey (a sick or injured person) on a stretcher.

stretch marks *n.pl.* marks on the skin resulting from a gain of weight, or on the abdomen after pregnancy.

strew /strōō/ *v.tr.* (*past part.* **strewn** or **strewed**) **1** scatter or spread about over a surface. **2** (usu. foll. by *with*) spread (a surface) with scattered things. □□ **strew·er** *n.*

stri·a /stríə/ *n.* (*pl.* **-ae** /stríee/) *Anat., Zool., Bot., & Geol.* a linear mark on a surface. **2** a slight ridge, furrow, or score.

stri·ate *adj. & v. Anat., Zool., Bot., & Geol.* • *adj.* /stríət/ (also **stri·at·ed** /stríaytid/) marked with striae. • *v.tr.* /stríayt/ mark with striae. □□ **stri·a·tion** /strīáyshən/ *n.*

strick·en /stríkən/ *past part. of* STRIKE • *adj.* **1** affected or overcome with illness or misfortune, etc. (*stricken with measles*; *grief-stricken*). **2** (often foll. by *from*, etc.) *Law* deleted.

strict /strikt/ *adj.* **1** precisely limited or defined (*lives in strict seclusion*). **2** requiring complete compliance or exact performance (*gave strict orders*). □□ **strict·ness** *n.*

strict·ly /stríktlee/ *adv.* **1** in a strict manner. **2** (also **strict·ly speak·ing**) applying words in their strict sense (*he is, strictly, an absconder*). **3** *colloq.* definitely.

stric·ture /stríkchər/ *n.* (usu. in *pl.*; often foll. by *on*, *upon*) a critical or censorious remark. □□ **stric·tured** *adj.*

stride /strīd/ *v. & n.* • *v.* (*past* **strode** /strōd/; *past part.* **stridden** /stríd'n/) **1** *intr. & tr.* walk with long firm steps. **2** *tr.* cross with one step. **3** *tr.* bestride; straddle. • *n.* **1 a** a single long step. **b** the length of this. **2** a person's gait as determined by the length of stride. **3** (usu. in *pl.*) progress (*has made great strides*). **4** a settled rate of progress (*get into one's stride*). □ **take in one's stride 1** clear (an obstacle) without changing one's gait to jump. **2** manage without difficulty. □□ **strid·er** *n.*

stri·dent /stríd'nt/ *adj.* loud and harsh. □□ **stri·den·cy** *n.* **stri·dent·ly** *adv.*

strid·u·late /stríjəlayt/ *v.intr.* (of the cicada and grasshopper) make a shrill sound by rubbing the legs or wing cases together. □□ **strid·u·la·tion** /–láyshən/ *n.*

strife /strīf/ *n.* conflict; struggle between opposed persons or things.

strike /strīk/ *v. & n.* • *v.* (*past* **struck** /struk/; *past part.* **struck** or *archaic* **stricken** /stríkən/) **1 a** *tr.* subject to an impact. **b** *tr.* deliver (a blow) or inflict a blow on. **2** *tr.* come or bring sharply into contact with. **3** *tr.* propel with a blow. **4** *intr.* (foll. by *at*) try to hit. **5** *tr.* cause to penetrate (*struck terror into him*). **6** *tr.* ignite (a match) or produce (sparks, etc.) by rubbing. **7** *tr.* make (a coin) by stamping. **8** *tr.* produce (a musical note) by striking. **9 a** *tr.* (also *absol.*) (of a clock) indicate (the time) by the sounding of a chime, etc. **b** *intr.* (of time) be indicated in this way. **10** *tr.* **a** attack or affect suddenly (*was struck with sudden terror*). **b** (of a disease) afflict. **11** *tr.* cause to become suddenly (*was struck dumb*). **12** *tr.* reach or achieve (*strike a balance*). **13** *tr.* agree on (a bargain). **14** *tr.* assume (an attitude) suddenly and dramatically. **15** *tr.* find (oil, etc.) by drilling. **16** come to the attention of or appear to (*it strikes me as silly*). **17** *intr.* (of employees) cease work as a protest. **18** *tr.* lower or take down (a flag, tent, stage, etc.). • *n.* **1** the act of striking. **2 a** the organized refusal by employees to work until some grievance is remedied. **b** a similar refusal to participate. **3** a sudden find or success. **4** an attack, esp. from the air. **5** *Baseball* a pitched ball counted against a batter, either for failure to hit it into fair territory or because it passes through the strike zone. **6** the act of knocking down all the pins with the first ball in bowling. □ **strike back** strike or attack in return. **strike down 1** knock down. **2** afflict (*struck down by a virus*). **strike home 1** deal an effective blow. **2** have an intended effect (*my words struck home*). **strike it rich** *colloq.* find a source of abundance or success. **strike out 1** hit out. **2** act vigorously. **3** delete (an item or name, etc.). **4** set off or begin (*struck out eastward*). **5** *Baseball* **a** dismiss (a batter) by means of three strikes. **b** be dismissed in this way. **strike through** delete (a word, etc.) with a stroke of one's pen. **strike up 1** start (an acquaintance, conversation, etc.) esp. casually. **2** (also *absol.*) begin playing (a tune, etc.). **strike upon 1** have (an idea, etc.) luckily occur to one. **2** (of light) illuminate. **strike while the iron is hot** act promptly at a good opportunity.

strike•bound /stríkbownd/ *adj.* immobilized or closed by a strike.

strike•break•er /stríkbraykər/ *n.* a person working in place of others who are on strike. □□ **strike•break** *v.intr.*

strike•out /stríkowt/ *n. Baseball* an out charged against a batter who has three strikes and credited to the pitcher.

strik•er /stríkər/ *n.* **1** a person or thing that strikes. **2** an employee on strike. **3** *Sports* the player who is to strike, or who is to be the next to strike, the ball.

strike zone *n. Baseball* an area between a batter's knees and armpits and over home plate through which a pitch must pass in order to be called a strike.

strik•ing /stríking/ *adj.* impressive; attracting attention. □ **within striking distance** near enough to hit or achieve.

string /string/ *n.* & *v.* • *n.* **1** twine or narrow cord. **2** a piece of this or of similar material used for tying or holding together, pulling, etc. **3** a length of catgut or wire, etc., on a musical instrument, producing a note by vibration. **4 a** (in *pl.*) the stringed instruments in an orchestra, etc. **b** (*attrib.*) relating to or consisting of stringed instruments (*string quartet*). **5** (in *pl.*) an awkward condition or complication (*the offer has no strings attached*). **6** a set of things strung together; a series or line of persons or things (*a string of beads*). **7** a tough piece connecting the two halves of a peapod, etc. **8** a piece of catgut, etc., interwoven with others to form the head of a tennis, etc., racket. • *v.tr.* (*past* and *past part.* **strung** /strung/) **1** supply with a string or strings. **2** tie with string. **3** thread (beads, etc.) on a string. **4** arrange in or as a string. **5** remove the strings from (a bean, etc.). □ **on a string** under one's control. **string along** *colloq.* **1** deceive, esp. by appearing to comply with (a person). **2** (often foll. by *with*) keep company (with). **string out** extend; prolong (esp. unduly). **string up 1** hang up on strings, etc. **2** kill by hanging.

string bass *n. Mus.* a double bass.

string bean *n.* any of various beans eaten in their fibrous pods, esp. runner beans or snap beans.

string•board /stringbawrd/ *n.* a supporting timber or skirting in which the ends of a staircase steps are set.

stringed /stringd/ *adj.* (of musical instruments) having strings (also in *comb.*: *twelve-stringed guitar*).

strin•gent /strínjənt/ *adj.* (of rules, etc.) strict; precise; requiring exact performance. □□ **strin•gen•cy** *n.* **strin•gent•ly** *adv.*

string•er /stringər/ *n.* **1** a longitudinal structural member in a framework, esp. of a ship or aircraft. **2** *colloq.* a newspaper correspondent not on the regular staff.

string•y /stringee/ *adj.* (**stringier, stringiest**) **1** (of food, etc.) fibrous; tough. **2** of or like string. **3** (of a person) tall and thin. □□ **string•i•ly** *adv.* **string•i•ness** *n.*

strip[1] /strip/ *v.* & *n.* • *v.* (**stripped, stripping**) **1** *tr.* (often foll. by *of*) remove the clothes or covering from (a person or thing). **2** *intr.* (often foll. by *off*) undress oneself. **3** *tr.* (often foll. by *of*) deprive (a person) of property or titles. **4** *tr.* leave bare of accessories or fittings. **5** *tr.* remove bark and branches from (a tree). **6** *tr.* (often foll. by *down*) remove the accessory fittings of or take apart (a machine, etc.) to inspect or adjust it. **7** *tr.* tear the thread from (a screw). **8** *tr.* tear the teeth from (a gearwheel). **9** *tr.* remove paint from (a surface) with solvent. **10** *tr.* (often foll. by *from*) pull or tear (a covering or property, etc.) off (*stripped the masks from their faces*). **11** *intr.* (of a screw) lose its thread. • *n.* an act of stripping, esp. of undressing in striptease.

strip[2] /strip/ *n.* **1** a long narrow piece (*a strip of land*). **2** (in full **strip cartoon**) = COMIC STRIP.

strip club *n.* a club at which striptease performances are given.

stripe /strīp/ *n.* **1** a long narrow band or strip differing in color or texture from the surface on either side of it (*black with a red stripe*). **2** *Mil.* a chevron, etc., denoting military rank. **3** a category of character, opinion, etc. (*a man of that stripe*). **4** (usu. in *pl.*) *archaic* a blow with a scourge or lash.

striped /strīpt/ *adj.* marked with stripes (also in *comb.*: *red-striped*).

striped bass *n.* a fish, *Morone saxatilis*, with dark stripes along its sides, used for food and game along the N. American coasts.

strip•ling /strípling/ *n.* a youth not yet fully grown.

strip mine *n.* a mine worked by removing the material that overlies the ore, etc. □□ **strip-mine** *v.tr.* & *intr.*

strip•per /strípər/ *n.* **1** a person or thing that strips something. **2** a device or solvent for removing paint, etc. **3** a striptease performer.

strip search *n.* a search of a person involving the removal of all clothes. □□ **strip-search** *v.tr.*

strip•tease /stríptēez/ *n.* & *v.* • *n.* an entertainment in which the performer gradually undresses before the audience. • *v.intr.* perform a striptease.

strip•y /strípee/ *adj.* (**stripier, stripiest**) striped; having many stripes.

strive /strīv/ *v.intr.* (*past* **strove** /strōv/; *past part.* **striv•en** /strívən/) **1** (often foll. by *for*, or *to* + infin.) try hard. **2** (often foll. by *with, against*) struggle. □□ **striv•er** *n.*

strobe /strōb/ *n. colloq.* **1** a stroboscope. **2** a stroboscopic lamp. Also called **strobe light**.

stro•bo•scope /strṓbəskōp/ *n.* **1** *Physics* an instrument for determining speeds of rotation, etc., by shining a bright light at intervals so that a rotating object appears stationary. **2** a lamp made to flash intermittently, esp. for this purpose. Also called **strobe light**. □□ **stro•bo•scop•ic** /–skópik/ *adj.*

strode *past* of STRIDE.

stro•ga•noff /stráwgənawf, strṓ–/ *adj.* (of meat) cut into strips and cooked in a sour cream sauce (*beef stroganoff*).

stroke /strōk/ *n.* & *v.* • *n.* **1** the act of striking; a blow or hit (*with a single stroke*; *a stroke of lightning*). **2** a sudden disabling attack or loss of consciousness caused by an interruption in the flow of blood to the brain, esp. through thrombosis. **3 a** an action or movement esp. as one of a series. **b** the slightest such action (*has not done a stroke of work*). **4** the whole of the motion (of a wing, oar, etc.) until the starting position is regained. **5** (in rowing) the mode or action of moving the oar (*row a fast stroke*). **6** the whole motion (of a piston) in either direction. **7** *Golf* the action of hitting (or hitting at) a ball with a club, as a unit of scoring. **8** a mode of moving the arms and legs in swimming. **9** a specially successful or skillful effort (*a stroke of diplomacy*). **10 a** a mark made by the movement in one direction of a pen or pencil or paintbrush. **b** a similar mark printed. **11** a detail contributing to the general effect in a description. **12** the sound made by a striking clock. **13** (in full **stroke oar**) the oar or oarsman nearest the stern, setting the time of the stroke. **14** the act or a spell of stroking. • *v.tr.* **1** pass one's hand gently along the surface of (hair or fur, etc.). **2** act as the stroke of (a boat or crew). □ **at a stroke** by a single action. **on the stroke** punctually.

stroke of luck *n.* (also **stroke of good luck**) an unforeseen opportune occurrence.

stroll /strōl/ *v. & n.* • *v.intr.* saunter or walk in a leisurely way. • *n.* a short leisurely walk (*go for a stroll*).

stroll·er /strṓlər/ *n.* **1** a person who strolls. **2** a folding chair on wheels, for pushing a child in.

stro·ma /strṓmə/ *n.* (*pl.* **stromata** /–mətə/) *Biol.* **1** the framework of an organ or cell. **2** a fungous tissue containing spore-producing bodies. □□ **stro·mat·ic** /–mátik/ *adj.*

strong /strawng, strong/ *adj. & adv.* • *adj.* (**stronger** /stráwnggər, stróng–/; **strongest** /stráwnggist, stróng–/) **1** having the power of resistance; not easily damaged or overcome (*strong material*; *strong faith*). **2** (of a patient) restored to health. **3** (of a market) having steadily high or rising prices. **4** capable of exerting great force or of doing much. **5** forceful or powerful in effect (*a strong wind*; *a strong protest*). **6** decided or firmly held (*a strong suspicion*; *strong views*). **7** (of an argument, etc.) convincing or striking. **8** powerfully affecting the senses or emotions (*a strong light*; *strong acting*). **9** powerful in terms of size or numbers or quality (*a strong army*). **10** capable of doing much when united (*a strong combination*). **11** formidable; likely to succeed (*a strong candidate*). **12** (of a solution or drink, etc.) containing a large proportion of a substance in water or another solvent (*strong tea*). **13** (of a group) having a specified number (*200 strong*). **14** (of a voice) loud or penetrating. **15** (of food or its flavor) pungent. **16** (of a measure) drastic. **17** *Gram.* in Germanic languages: **a** (of a verb) forming inflections by a change of vowel within the stem rather than by the addition of a suffix (e.g., *swim, swam*). **b** (of a noun or adjective) belonging to a declension in which the stem originally ended otherwise than in *-n*. • *adv.* strongly (*the tide is running strong*). □ **come on strong** act aggressively, flamboyantly, etc. **going strong** *colloq.* continuing action vigorously; in good health. □□ **strong·ish** *adj.* **strong·ly** *adv.*

strong-arm *adj.* using force (*strong-arm tactics*).

strong·box /stráwngboks, stróng–/ *n.* a strongly made small chest for valuables.

strong·hold /stráwnghōld, stróng–/ *n.* **1** a fortified place. **2** a secure refuge. **3** a center of support for a cause, etc.

strong lan·guage *n.* forceful language; swearing.

strong·room /stráwngrōōm, –rŏŏm, stróng–/ *n.* a room designed to protect valuables against fire and theft.

strong suit *n.* **1** a suit at cards in which one can take tricks. **2** a thing at which one excels.

stron·ti·um /strónteeəm/ *n. Chem.* a soft silver white metallic element occurring naturally in various minerals.

stron·ti·um 90 *n.* a radioactive isotope of strontium concentrated selectively in bones and teeth when taken into the body.

strop /strop/ *n. & v.* • *n.* a device, esp. a strip of leather, for sharpening razors. • *v.tr.* (**stropped, stropping**) sharpen on or with a strop.

stro·phe /strṓfee/ *n.* **1 a** a turn in dancing made by an ancient Greek chorus. **b** lines recited during this. **c** the first section of an ancient Greek choral ode or of one division of it. **2** a group of lines forming a section of a lyric poem. □□ **stro·phic** *adj.*

strove *past* of STRIVE.

strow /strō/ *v.tr.* (*past part.* **strown** /strōn/ or **strowed**) *archaic* = STREW.

struck *past* and *past part.* of STRIKE.

struc·tur·al /strúkchərəl/ *adj.* of, concerning, or having a structure. □□ **struc·tur·al·ly** *adv.*

struc·tur·al·ism /strúkchərəlizəm/ *n.* **1** the doctrine that structure rather than function is important. **2** structural linguistics. **3** structural psychology. □□ **struc·tur·al·ist** *n. & adj.*

struc·ture /strúkchər/ *n. & v.* • *n.* **1 a** a whole constructed unit, esp. a building. **b** the way in which a building, etc., is constructed (*has a flimsy structure*). **2** a set of interconnecting parts of any complex thing (*the structure of a sentence*; *a new wages structure*). • *v.tr.* give structure to; organize. □□ **struc·tured** *adj.*

stru·del /strṓōd'l/ *n.* a confection of thin pastry rolled up around a filling and baked (*apple strudel*).

strug·gle /strúgəl/ *v. & n.* • *v.intr.* **1** make forceful or violent efforts to get free of restraint or constriction. **2** (often foll. by *for*, or *to* + infin.) make violent or determined efforts under difficulties (*struggled to get the words out*). **3** (foll. by *with, against*) contend; fight strenuously. **4** make one's way with difficulty. **5** (esp. as **struggling** *adj.*) have difficulty in gaining recognition or a living (*a struggling artist*). • *n.* **1** the act or a spell of struggling. **2** a hard or confused contest. **3** a determined effort under difficulties. □□ **strug·gler** *n.*

strum /strum/ *v. & n.* • *v.tr.* (**strummed, strumming**) **1** play on (a stringed or keyboard instrument), esp. carelessly or unskillfully. **2** play (a tune, etc.) in this way. • *n.* the sound made by strumming. □□ **strum·mer** *n.*

strum·pet /strúmpit/ *n. archaic* or *rhet.* a prostitute.

strung *past* and *past part.* of STRING. □ **strung out** *sl.* **1 a** debilitated from long drug use. **b** agitated or incoherent from using drugs. **2** exhausted physically or emotionally.

strut /strut/ *n. & v.* • *n.* **1** a bar forming part of a framework and designed to resist compression. **2** a strutting gait. • *v.* (**strutted, strutting**) **1** *intr.* walk with a pompous or affected stiff erect gait. **2** *tr.* brace with a strut or struts. □□ **strut·ter** *n.* **strut·ting·ly** *adv.*

stru·thi·ous /strṓōtheeəs/ *adj.* of or like an ostrich.

strych·nine /stríknīn, –nin, –neen/ *n.* a vegetable alkaloid obtained from plants of the genus *Strychnos* (esp. nux vomica), bitter and highly poisonous. □□ **strych·nic** *adj.*

Sts. *abbr.* Saints.

Stu·art /stṓōərt, styṓō–/ *adj. & n.* • *adj.* of or relating to the royal family ruling Scotland 1371–1714 and England 1603–1649 and 1660–1714. • *n.* a member of this family.

stub /stub/ *n. & v.* • *n.* **1** the remnant of a pencil, cigarette, etc., after use. **2** part of a check, receipt, etc., retained as a record. **3** a stunted tail, etc. • *v.tr.* (**stubbed, stubbing**) **1** strike (one's toe) against something. **2** (usu. foll. by *out*) extinguish (a lighted cigarette) by pressing the lighted end against something.

stub·ble /stúbəl/ *n.* **1** the cut stalks of cereal plants left sticking up after the harvest. **2 a** cropped hair or a cropped beard. **b** a short growth of unshaven hair. □□ **stub·bled** *adj.* **stub·bly** *adj.*

stub·born /stúbərn/ *adj.* **1** unreasonably obstinate. **2** unyielding; obdurate; inflexible. **3** refractory; intractable. □□ **stub·born·ly** *adv.* **stub·born·ness** *n.*

stub·by /stúbee/ *adj.* (**stubbier, stubbiest**) short and thick. □□ **stub·bi·ness** *n.*

stuc·co /stúkō/ *n. & v.* • *n.* (*pl.* **-coes**) plaster or cement used for coating wall surfaces or molding into architectural decorations. • *v.tr.* (**-coes, -coed**) coat with stucco.

stuck *past* and *past part.* of STICK[2].

stuck-up *adj. colloq.* affectedly superior and aloof; snobbish.

stud[1] /stud/ *n. & v.* • *n.* **1** a large-headed nail or knob, projecting from a surface esp. for ornament. **2** a double button esp. for use with two buttonholes in a shirt front. **3** a small object projecting slightly from a road surface as a marker, etc. **4** a piece of jewelry consisting of a buttonlike disk with a post attached that slips through a pierced ear or nostril, with a metal backing to hold it in. • *v.tr.* (**studded, studding**) **1** set with or as with studs. **2** (as **studded** *adj.*) (foll. by *with*) thickly set or strewn (*studded with diamonds*). **3** be scattered over or about (a surface).

stud[2] /stud/ *n.* **1 a** a number of horses kept for breeding, etc. **b** a place where these are kept. **2** (in full **stud horse**) a stallion. **3** *colloq.* a young man (esp. one noted for sexual prowess). **4** (in full **stud poker**) a form of poker with betting after the dealing of successive rounds of cards face up.

stud·ding /stúding/ *n.* the woodwork of a lath-and-plaster or plasterboard wall.

stu·dent /stóód'nt, styóód–/ *n.* **1** a person who is studying, esp. at university or another place of higher education. **2** (*attrib.*) studying in order to become (*a student nurse*). **3** a person of studious habits.

stu·dent driv·er *n.* a person who is learning to drive a motor vehicle and has not yet passed a driving test.

stud farm *n.* a place where horses are bred.

stu·di·o /stóódeeō, styóó–/ *n.* (*pl.* **-os**) **1** the workroom of a painter or photographer, etc. **2** a place where movies or recordings are made or where television or radio programs are made or produced.

stu·di·o a·part·ment *n.* an apartment having only one main room, a kitchenette, and bath.

stu·di·o couch *n.* a couch that can be converted into a bed.

stu·di·ous /stóódeeəs, styóó–/ *adj.* **1** devoted to or assiduous in study or reading. **2** deliberate; painstaking (*with studious care*). **3** (foll. by *to* + infin. or *in* + verbal noun) showing care or attention. □□ **stu·di·ous·ly** *adv.* **stu·di·ous·ness** *n.*

stud·y /stúdee/ *n. & v.* • *n.* (*pl.* **-ies**) **1** the devotion of time and attention to acquiring information or knowledge, esp. from books. **2** (in *pl.*) the pursuit of academic knowledge (*continued their studies abroad*). **3** a room used for reading, writing, etc. **4** a piece of work, esp. a drawing, done for practice or as an experiment (*a study of a head*). **5** the portrayal in literature or another art form of an aspect of behavior or character, etc. **6** a musical composition designed to develop a player's skill. • *v.* (**-ies, -ied**) **1** *tr.* make a study of; investigate or examine (a subject) (*study law*). **2** *intr.* (often foll. by *for*) apply oneself to study. **3** (as **studied** *adj.*) deliberate; intentional; affected (*with studied politeness*). □ **make a study of** investigate carefully.

stuff /stuf/ *n. & v.* • *n.* **1** the material that a thing is made of; material that may be used for some purpose. **2** a substance or things or belongings of an indeterminate kind (*there's a lot of stuff about it in the newspapers*). **3** a particular knowledge or activity (*know one's stuff*). **4** valueless matter; trash (*take that stuff away*). **5** (prec. by *the*) **a** *colloq.* an available supply of something, esp. alcohol or drugs. **b** *sl.* money. • *v.* **1** *tr.* pack (a receptacle) tightly. **2** *tr.* (foll. by *in, into*) force or cram (a thing). **3** *tr.* fill out the skin of (an animal or bird, etc.) with material to restore the original shape. **4** *tr.* fill (poultry, etc.) with a mixture, as of rice or seasoned bread crumbs, esp. before cooking. **5 a** *tr. & refl.* fill (a person or oneself) with food. **b** *tr. & intr.* eat greedily. **6** *tr.* push, esp. hastily or clumsily (*stuffed the note behind the cushion*). **7** *tr.* (usu. in *passive*; foll. by *up*) block up (a person's nose, etc.). □ **do one's stuff** *colloq.* do what one has to. **that's the stuff** *colloq.* that is what is wanted. □□ **stuff·er** *n.* (also in *comb.*).

stuffed shirt *n. colloq.* a pompous person.

stuff·ing /stúfing/ *n.* **1** padding used to stuff cushions, etc. **2** a mixture used to stuff poultry, etc., esp. before cooking. □ **knock** (or **take**) **the stuffing out of** *colloq.* beat soundly; defeat.

stuff·y /stúfee/ *adj.* (**stuffier, stuffiest**) **1** (of a room or the atmosphere in it) lacking fresh air or ventilation. **2** dull or uninteresting. **3** (of a person) dull and conventional. □□ **stuff·i·ly** *adv.* **stuff·i·ness** *n.*

stul·ti·fy /stúltifī/ *v.tr.* (**-fies, -fied**) make ineffective, useless, or futile, esp. as a result of tedious routine (*stultifying boredom*). □□ **stul·ti·fi·ca·tion** /–fikáyshən/ *n.*

stum·ble /stúmbəl/ *v. & n.* • *v.intr.* **1** lurch forward or have a partial fall from catching or striking or misplacing one's foot. **2** (often foll. by *along*) walk with repeated stumbles. **3** make a mistake or repeated mistakes in speaking, etc. **4** (foll. by *on, upon, across*) find or encounter by chance. • *n.* an act of stumbling.

stum·ble·bum /stúmbəlbum/ *n. colloq.* a clumsy or inept person.

stum·bling block *n.* an obstacle or circumstance causing difficulty or hesitation.

stump /stump/ *n. & v.* • *n.* **1** the projecting remnant of a cut or fallen tree. **2** the similar remnant of anything else (e.g., a branch or limb) cut off or worn down. **3** (in *pl.*) *joc.* the legs. • *v.* **1** *tr.* (of a question, etc.) be too hard for; puzzle. **2** *tr.* (as **stumped** *adj.*) at a loss; baffled. **3** *intr.* walk stiffly or noisily. **4** *tr.* (also *absol.*) traverse (a district) making political speeches.

stump·er /stúmpər/ *n. colloq.* a puzzling question.

stump·y /stúmpee/ *adj.* (**stumpier, stumpiest**) short and thick.

stun /stun/ *v.tr.* (**stunned, stunning**) **1** knock senseless. **2** bewilder or shock.

stung *past* and *past part.* of STING.

stunk *past* and *past part.* of STINK.

stun·ner /stúnər/ *n. colloq.* a stunning person or thing.

stun·ning /stúning/ *adj. colloq.* extremely impressive or attractive. □□ **stun·ning·ly** *adv.*

stunt[1] /stunt/ *v.tr.* retard the growth or development of. □□ **stunt·ed·ness** *n.*

stunt[2] /stunt/ *n.* **1** something unusual done to attract attention. **2** a trick or daring maneuver.

stunt man *n.* (also **stunt wom·an**) a man (or woman) employed to take an actor's place in performing dangerous stunts.

stu·pa /stóópə/ *n.* a round usu. domed building erected as a Buddhist shrine.

stu·pe·fy /stóópifī, styóó–/ *v.tr.* (**-fies, -fied**) **1** make stupid or insensible. **2** stun with astonishment. □□ **stu·pe·fa·cient** /–fáyshənt/ *adj. & n.* **stu·pe·fac·tion** /–fákshən/ *n.* **stu·pe·fy·ing** *adj.* **stu·pe·fy·ing·ly** *adv.*

stu·pen·dous /stoopéndəs, styóó–/ *adj.* amazing or prodigious, esp. in size or degree (*a stupendous achievement*). □□ **stu·pen·dous·ly** *adv.* **stu·pen·dous·ness** *n.*

stu·pid /stóópid, styóó–/ *adj.* (**stupider, stupidest**) • *adj.* **1** unintelligent; foolish (*a stupid fellow*). **2** typical of stupid persons (*put it in a stupid place*). **3** uninteresting or boring. **4** in a state of stupor or lethargy. **5** obtuse; lacking in sensibility. □□ **stu·pid·i·ty** /–píditee/ *n.* (*pl.* **-ties**). **stu·pid·ly** *adv.*

stu·por /stóópər, styóó–/ *n.* a dazed or amazed state. □□ **stu·por·ous** *adj.*

See page xii for the *Key to Pronunciation.*

stur·dy /stɘ́rdee/ *adj.* (**sturdier, sturdiest**) **1** robust; strongly built. **2** vigorous and determined (*sturdy resistance*). ▫▫ **stur·di·ly** *adv.* **stur·di·ness** *n.*

stur·geon /stɘ́rjən/ *n.* any large sharklike fish of the family Acipenseridae, etc., used as food and a source of caviar and isinglass.

Sturm und Drang /shtŏŏrm ŏŏnt dráng/ *n.* a literary and artistic movement in Germany in the late 18th c., characterized by the expression of emotional unrest and strong feeling.

stut·ter /stútər/ *v. & n.* • *v.* **1** *intr.* stammer, esp. by involuntarily repeating the first consonants of words. **2** *tr.* utter (words) in this way. • *n.* **1** the act or habit of stuttering. **2** an instance of stuttering. ▫▫ **stut·ter·er** *n.*

sty[1] /stī/ *n.* (*pl.* **sties**) **1** a pen or enclosure for pigs. **2** a filthy room or dwelling. **3** a place of debauchery.

sty[2] /stī/ *n.* (also **stye**) (*pl.* **sties** or **styes**) an inflamed swelling on the edge of an eyelid.

Styg·i·an /stíjeeən/ *adj.* **1** (in Greek mythology) of or relating to the Styx, a river in Hades. **2** *literary* dark; gloomy; indistinct.

style /stīl/ *n. & v.* • *n.* **1** a kind or sort, esp. in regard to appearance and form (*an elegant style of house*). **2** a manner of writing or speaking or performing (*written in a florid style*; *started off in fine style*). **3** the distinctive manner of a person or school or period. **4** the correct way of designating a person or thing. **5** a superior quality or manner (*do it in style*). **6** a particular make, shape, or pattern (*in all sizes and styles*). **7** *Bot.* the narrow extension of the ovary supporting the stigma. • *v.tr.* **1** design or make, etc., in a particular style. **2** designate in a specified way. ▫▫ **style·less** *adj.* **styl·er** *n.*

sty·li *pl.* of STYLUS.

styl·ish /stílish/ *adj.* **1** fashionable; elegant. **2** having a superior quality, manner, etc. ▫▫ **styl·ish·ly** *adv.* **styl·ish·ness** *n.*

styl·ist /stílist/ *n.* **1 a** a designer of fashionable styles, etc. **b** a hairdresser. **2 a** a writer noted for or aspiring to good literary style. **b** (in sports or music) a person who performs with style.

sty·lis·tic /stīlístik/ *adj.* of or concerning esp. literary style. ▫▫ **sty·lis·ti·cal·ly** *adv.*

sty·lis·tics /stīlístiks/ *n.* the study of literary style.

styl·ize /stílīz/ *v.tr.* (esp. as **stylized** *adj.*) paint, draw, etc., (a subject) in a conventional nonrealistic style. ▫▫ **styl·i·za·tion** *n.*

sty·lo·bate /stíləbayt/ *n. Archit.* a continuous base supporting a row of columns.

sty·loid /stíloyd/ *adj. & n.* • *adj.* resembling a stylus or pen. • *n.* (in full **styloid process**) a spine of bone, esp. that projecting from the base of the temporal bone.

sty·lus /stíləs/ *n.* (*pl.* **-li** /–lī/ or **-luses**) **1** a hard point following a groove in a phonograph record and transmitting the recorded sound for reproduction. **2** a similar point producing such a groove when recording sound.

sty·mie /stímee/ *n. & v.* (also **sti·my**) • *n.* (*pl.* **-mies**) **1** *Golf* a situation where an opponent's ball lies between the player and the hole (*lay a stymie*). **2** a difficult situation. • *v.tr.* (**stymies, stymied, stymying** or **stymieing**) **1** obstruct; thwart. **2** *Golf* block with a stymie.

styp·tic /stíptik/ *adj. & n.* • *adj.* that checks bleeding. • *n.* a styptic substance.

styp·tic pen·cil *n.* a pencil-shaped wand containing a styptic substance used to check bleeding from minor cuts.

sty·rene /stíreen/ *n. Chem.* a liquid hydrocarbon easily polymerized and used in making plastics, etc.

Sty·ro·foam /stírəfōm/ *n. Trademark* a brand of expanded polystyrene.

sua·sion /swáyzhən/ *n. formal* persuasion as opposed to force (*moral suasion*).

suave /swaav/ *adj.* smooth; polite; sophisticated. ▫▫ **suave·ly** *adv.* **suave·ness** *n.* **suav·i·ty** /–vitee/ *n.* (*pl.* **-ties**).

sub /sub/ *n. & v. colloq.* • *n.* **1** a submarine. **2** a subscription. **3** a substitute. **4** a submarine sandwich. • *v.intr.* (**subbed, subbing**) (usu. foll. by *for*) act as a substitute.

sub- /sub, səb/ *prefix* (also **suc-** before *c*, **suf-** before *f*, **sug-** before *g*, **sup-** before *p*, **sur-** before *r*, **sus-** before *c*, *p*, *t*) **1** at or to or from a lower position (*subordinate*; *submerge*; *subtract*; *subsoil*). **2** secondary or inferior in rank or position (*subclass*; *subcommittee*; *subtotal*). **3** somewhat; nearly; more or less (*subacid*; *subarctic*). **4** (forming verbs) denoting secondary action (*subdivide*; *sublet*).

sub·a·cute /súbəkyŏŏt/ *adj. Med.* (of a condition) between acute and chronic.

sub·al·pine /súbálpīn/ *adj.* of or situated in the higher slopes of mountains just below the timberline.

sub·al·tern /subáwltərn/ *n. & adj.* • *n. Brit. Mil.* an officer below the rank of captain, esp. a second lieutenant. • *adj.* **1** of inferior rank. **2** /súbəltərn/ *Logic* (of a proposition) particular; not universal.

sub·a·quat·ic /súbəkwátik, –əkwótik/ *adj.* **1** of more or less aquatic habits or kind. **2** underwater.

sub·a·que·ous /súbáykweeəs, –ák–/ *adj.* existing or taking place under water.

sub·arc·tic /súbaárktik, –aártik/ *adj.* of or like regions immediately south of the Arctic Circle.

sub·a·tom·ic /súbətómik/ *adj.* occurring in or smaller than an atom.

sub·au·di·tion /súbawdíshən/ *n.* **1** the act of mentally supplying an omitted word or words in speech. **2** the act or process of understanding the unexpressed; reading between the lines.

sub·ax·il·la·ry /súbáksileree/ *adj.* **1** *Bot.* in or growing beneath the axil. **2** beneath the armpit.

sub·cat·e·go·ry /súbkátigawree/ *n.* (*pl.* **-ries**) a secondary or subordinate category. ▫▫ **sub·cat·e·gor·ize** *v.tr.* **sub·cat·e·gor·i·za·tion** *n.*

sub·cau·dal /súbkáwdəl/ *adj.* of or concerning the region under the tail or the back part of the body.

sub·cla·vi·an /súbkláyveeən/ *adj. & n.* • *adj.* (of an artery, etc.) lying or extending under the collar bone. • *n.* such an artery.

sub·clin·i·cal /súbklínikəl/ *adj. Med.* (of a disease) not yet presenting definite symptoms.

sub·com·mit·tee /súbkəmitee/ *n.* a committee composed of some members of a larger committee, board, or other body and reporting to it.

sub·com·pact /səbkómpakt/ *n. & adj.* a car that is smaller than a compact.

sub·con·scious /súbkónshəs/ *adj. & n.* • *adj.* of or concerning the part of the mind which is not fully conscious but influences actions, etc. • *n.* this part of the mind. ▫▫ **sub·con·scious·ly** *adv.* **sub·con·scious·ness** *n.*

sub·con·ti·nent /súbkóntinənt/ *n.* **1** a large land mass, smaller than a continent. **2** a large geographically or politically independent part of a continent. ▫▫ **sub·con·ti·nen·tal** /–nént'l/ *adj.*

sub·con·tract *v. & n.* • *v.* /súbkəntrákt/ **1** *tr.* employ a firm, etc., to do (work) as part of a larger project. **2** *intr.* make or carry out a subcontract. • *n.* /subkóntrakt/ a secondary contract. ▫▫ **sub·con·trac·tor** /–kóntraktər/ *n.*

sub·con·tra·ry /súbkóntreree/ *adj. & n. Logic* • *adj.* (of a proposition) incapable of being false at the same time as another. • *n.* (*pl.* **-ries**) such a proposition.

sub·cul·ture /súbkulchər/ *n.* a cultural group within a larger culture. ▫▫ **sub·cul·tur·al** /–kúlchərəl/ *adj.*

sub·cu·ta·ne·ous /súbkyōōtáyneeəs/ *adj.* under the skin.

sub·di·vide /súbdivíd/ *v.tr. & intr.* divide again after a first division.

sub·di·vi·sion /súbdivízhən/ *n.* **1** the act of subdividing. **2** a secondary or subordinate division. **3** an area of land divided into plots for sale.

sub·dom·i·nant /súbdóminənt/ *n. Mus.* the fourth note of the diatonic scale of any key.

sub·due /səbdóō, –dyóō/ *v.tr.* (**subdues, subdued, subduing**) **1** conquer, subjugate, or tame. **2** (as **subdued** *adj.*) softened; lacking in intensity; toned down (*subdued light; in a subdued mood*).

sub·fam·i·ly /súbfamilee/ *n.* (*pl.* **-lies**) **1** *Biol.* a taxonomic category below a family. **2** any subdivision of a group.

sub·floor /súbflawr/ (also **sub·floor·ing**) *n.* a foundation for a floor in a building.

sub·fusc /súbfusk/ *adj. formal* dull; dusky; gloomy.

sub·gla·cial /súbgláyshəl/ *adj.* next to or at the bottom of a glacier.

sub·group /súbgrōōp/ *n. Math.*, etc., a subset of a group.

sub·head /súbhed/ *n.* (also **sub·head·ing**) **1** a subordinate heading or title. **2** a subordinate division in a classification.

sub·hu·man /súbhyóōmən/ *adj.* **1** (of an animal) closely related to humans. **2** (of behavior, intelligence, etc.) less than human.

subj. *abbr.* **1** subject. **2** subjective. **3** subjunctive.

sub·ject *n., adj., adv., & v.* • *n.* /súbjikt/ **1 a** a matter, theme, etc., to be discussed, described, represented, etc. **b** (foll. by *for*) a person, circumstance, etc., giving rise to specified feeling, action, etc. (*a subject for congratulation*). **2** a field of study (*his best subject is geography*). **3** *Gram.* a noun or its equivalent about which a sentence is predicated and with which the verb agrees. **4 a** any person except a monarch living under a government (*the ruler and his subjects*). **b** any person owing obedience to another. **5** *Mus.* a theme of a fugue or sonata; a leading phrase or motif. **6** a person of specified tendencies (*a hysterical subject*). • *adj.* /súbjikt/ **1** owing obedience to a government, colonizing power, force, etc.; in subjection. **2** (foll. by *to*) liable, exposed, or prone to (*is subject to infection*). **3** (foll. by *to*) conditional upon (*subject to your approval*). • *adv.* /súbjikt/ (foll. by *to*) conditionally upon (*subject to your consent, I propose to try again*). • *v.tr.* /səbjékt/ **1** (foll. by *to*) make liable; expose (*subjected us to hours of waiting*). **2** (usu. foll. by *to*) subdue (a nation, person, etc.) to one's control, etc. ▫▫ **sub·jec·tion** /səbjékshən/ *n.*

sub·jec·tive /səbjéktiv/ *adj. & n.* • *adj.* **1** (of art, literature, written history, a person's views, etc.) proceeding from personal idiosyncrasy or individuality; not impartial or literal. **2** *Gram.* of or concerning the subject. • *n. Gram.* nominative. ▫▫ **sub·jec·tive·ly** *adv.* **sub·jec·tiv·i·ty** /subjektívitee/ *n.*

sub·jec·tiv·ism /səbjéktivizəm/ *n. Philos.* the doctrine that knowledge is merely subjective and that there is no external or objective truth. ▫▫ **sub·jec·tiv·ist** *n.*

sub·join /súbjóyn/ *v.tr.* add (an illustration, anecdote, etc.) at the end.

sub·ju·gate /súbjəgayt/ *v.tr.* bring into subjection; vanquish. ▫▫ **sub·ju·ga·tion** /–gáyshən/ *n.*

sub·junc·tive /səbjúngktiv/ *adj. & n. Gram.* • *adj.* (of a mood) denoting what is imagined or wished or possible (e.g., *if I were you; God help you; be that as it may*). • *n.* **1** the subjunctive mood. **2** a verb in this mood.

sub·lease *n. & v.* • *n.* /súblees/ a lease of a property by a tenant to a subtenant. • *v.tr.* /súblées/ lease (a property) to a subtenant.

sub·les·see /súblesée/ *n.* a person who holds a sublease.

sub·les·sor /súblesáwr/ *n.* a person who grants a sublease.

sub·let *n. & v.* • *n.* /súblet/ = SUBLEASE *n.* • *v.tr.* /súblét/ (**-letting;** *past* and *past part.* **-let**) = SUBLEASE *v.*

sub·li·mate *v., adj., & n.* • *v.* /súblimayt/ **1** *tr. & intr.* divert (the energy of a primitive impulse, esp. sexual) into a culturally more acceptable activity. **2** *tr. & intr. Chem.* convert (a substance) from the solid state directly to its vapor by heat, and usu. allow it to solidify again. **3** *tr.* refine; purify; idealize. • *adj.* /súblimət, –mayt/ **1** *Chem.* (of a substance) sublimated. **2** purified; refined. • *n.* /súblimət/ *Chem.* a sublimated substance. ▫▫ **sub·li·ma·tion** /–máyshən/ *n.*

sub·lime /səblím/ *adj. & v.* • *adj.* (**sublimer, sublimest**) **1** of the most exalted or noble kind; awe inspiring (*sublime genius*). **2** (of indifference, impudence, etc.) arrogantly unruffled; extreme. • *v.* **1** *tr. & intr. Chem.* = SUBLIMATE *v.* 2. **2** *tr.* purify or elevate by or as if by sublimation; make sublime. **3** *intr.* become pure by or as if by sublimation. ▫▫ **sub·lime·ly** *adv.* **sub·lim·i·ty** /–límitee/ *n.*

sub·lim·i·nal /səbliminəl/ *adj. Psychol.* (of a stimulus, etc.) below the threshold of sensation or consciousness. ▫▫ **sub·lim·i·nal·ly** *adv.*

sub·lim·i·nal ad·ver·tis·ing *n.* the use of subliminal images in advertising on television, etc., to influence the viewer at an unconscious level.

sub·lu·nar·y /súblōōnéree, sublóōnəree/ *adj.* **1** beneath the moon. **2** *Astron.* **a** within the moon's orbit. **b** subject to the moon's influence. **3** of this world.

sub·ma·chine gun /súbməshéen/ *n.* a hand-held lightweight machine gun.

sub·mar·gin·al /súbmaárjinəl/ *adj.* **1** esp. *Econ.* not reaching minimum requirements. **2** (of land) that cannot be farmed profitably.

sub·ma·rine /súbməréen/ *n. & adj.* • *n.* **1** a vessel, esp. a warship, capable of operating under water. **2** = SUBMARINE SANDWICH. • *adj.* existing, occurring, done, or used under the surface of the sea (*submarine cable*). ▫▫ **sub·ma·rin·er** /–maréenər, səbmárinər/ *n.*

sub·ma·rine sand·wich *n.* a large sandwich usu. consisting of a halved roll, meat, cheese, lettuce, tomato, etc.

sub·merge /səbmérj/ *v.* **1** *tr.* **a** place under water; flood. **b** inundate with work, problems, etc. **2** *intr.* dive below the surface of water. ▫▫ **sub·mer·gence** *n.* **sub·mer·sion** /–mə́rzhən, –shən/ *n.*

sub·mers·i·ble /səbmə́rsibəl/ *n. & adj.* • *n.* a submarine operating under water for short periods. • *adj.* capable of being submerged.

sub·mi·cro·scop·ic /súbmíkrəskópik/ *adj.* too small to be seen by an ordinary microscope.

sub·mis·sion /səbmíshən/ *n.* **1 a** the act of submitting. **b** anything that is submitted. **2** humility; meekness; obedience (*showed great submission of spirit*). **3** *Law* a theory, etc., submitted by a lawyer to a judge or jury. **4** (in wrestling) the surrender of a participant yielding to the pain of a hold.

sub·mis·sive /səbmísiv/ *adj.* **1** humble; obedient. **2** yielding to power or authority; willing to submit. ▫▫ **sub·mis·sive·ly** *adv.* **sub·mis·sive·ness** *n.*

sub·mit /səbmít/ *v.* (**submitted, submitting**) **1** (usu. foll. by *to*) **a** *intr.* cease resistance; yield (*had to submit to defeat; will never submit*). **b** *refl.* surrender (oneself) to the control of another, etc. **2** *tr.* present for consideration or decision. **3** *tr.* (usu. foll. by *to*) subject (a person or thing) to a process, treatment, etc. (*submitted it* *to the flames*). **4** *tr.* esp. *Law* urge or represent esp. deferentially (*that, I submit, is a misrepresentation*). ▫▫ **sub·mit·ter** *n.*

sub·mul·ti·ple /súbmúltipəl/ *n. & adj.* • *n.* a number that can be divided exactly into a specified number. • *adj.* being such a number.

sub·nor·mal /súbnáwrməl/ *adj.* **1** (esp. as regards intelligence) below normal. **2** less than normal. ▫▫ **sub·nor·mal·i·ty** /–málitee/ *n.*

sub·nu·cle·ar /súbnóökleeər, –nyóö–/ *adj. Physics* occurring in or smaller than an atomic nucleus.

sub·or·bit·al /súbáwrbit'l/ *adj.* **1** situated below the orbit of the eye. **2** (of a spaceship, etc.) not completing a full orbit of the earth.

sub·or·der /súbawrdər/ *n.* a taxonomic category below an order.

sub·or·di·nate *adj., n., & v.* • *adj.* /səbáwrd'nət/ (usu. foll. by *to*) of inferior importance or rank; secondary; subservient. • *n.* /səbáwrd'nət/ a person working under another. • *v.tr.* /səbáwrd'nayt/ (usu. foll. by *to*) **1** make subordinate; treat or regard as of minor importance. **2** make subservient. ▫▫ **sub·or·di·na·tion** /–náyshən/ *n.*

sub·ord·i·nate clause *n.* a clause serving as an adjective, adverb, or noun in a main sentence because of its position or a preceding conjunction.

sub·orn /səbáwrn/ *v.tr.* induce by bribery, etc., to commit perjury or any other unlawful act.

sub·phy·lum /súbfīləm/ *n.* (*pl.* **subphyla** /–lə/) *Biol.* a taxonomic category below a phylum.

sub·plot /súbplot/ *n.* a subordinate plot in a play, etc.

sub·poe·na /səpéenə/ *n. & v.* • *n.* a writ ordering a person to appear in court. • *v.tr.* (*past* and *past part.* **subpoenaed** or **subpoena'd**) serve a subpoena on.

sub·ro·ga·tion /súbrəgáyshən/ *n. Law* the substitution of one party for another as creditor, with the transfer of rights and duties. ▫▫ **sub·ro·gate** /súbrəgayt/ *v.tr.*

sub ro·sa /sub rṓzə/ *adj. & adv.* in secrecy or confidence.

sub·rou·tine /súbrōōteen/ *n. Computing* a routine designed to perform a frequently used operation within a program.

sub·scribe /səbskrīb/ *v.* **1** *tr. & intr.* (usu. foll. by *to,for*) contribute (a specified sum) or make or promise a contribution to a fund, project, charity, etc., esp. regularly. **2** *intr.* (usu. foll. by *to*) express one's agreement with an opinion, resolution, etc. (*cannot subscribe to that*).

sub·scrib·er /səbskrībər/ *n.* **1** a person who subscribes. **2** a person paying for the renting of a telephone line, television cable connection, etc.

sub·script /súbskript/ *adj. & n.* • *adj.* written or printed below the line. • *n.* a subscript number or symbol.

sub·scrip·tion /səbskrípshən/ *n.* **1 a** the act or an instance of subscribing. **b** money subscribed. **2 a** an agreement to take and pay for usu. a specified number of issues of a newspaper, magazine, etc. **b** the money paid by this.

sub·sec·tion /súbsekshən/ *n.* a division of a section.

sub·se·quent /súbsikwənt/ *adj.* (usu. foll. by *to*) following a specified event, etc., in time, esp. as a consequence. ▫▫ **sub·se·quent·ly** *adv.*

sub·ser·vi·ent /səbsə́rveeənt/ *adj.* **1** cringing; obsequious. **2** (usu. foll. by *to*) instrumental. **3** (usu. foll. by *to*) subordinate. ▫▫ **sub·ser·vi·ence** *n.*

sub·set /súbset/ *n.* **1** a secondary part of a set. **2** *Math.* a set all the elements of which are contained in another set.

sub·side /səbsīd/ *v.intr.* **1** become tranquil; abate (*excitement subsided*). **2** (of water, suspended matter, etc.) sink. **3** (of the ground) cave in; sink. **4** (of a building, ship, etc.) sink lower in the ground or water. **5** (of a swelling, etc.) become less. **6** usu. *joc.* (of a person) sink into a sitting, kneeling, or lying posture.

sub·sid·i·ar·i·ty /səbsídeeáritee/ *n.* (*pl.* **-ties**) **1** the quality of being subsidiary. **2** the principle that a central authority should perform only tasks which cannot be performed effectively at a local level.

sub·sid·i·ar·y /səbsídee-airee/ *adj. & n.* • *adj.* **1** serving to assist or supplement. **2** (of a company) controlled by another. • *n.* (*pl.* **-ies**) **1** a subsidiary thing or person. **2** a subsidiary company.

sub·si·dize /súbsidīz/ *v.tr.* **1** pay a subsidy to. **2** reduce the cost of by subsidy (*subsidized lunches*). ▫▫ **sub·si·di·za·tion** *n.*

sub·si·dy /súbsidee/ *n.* (*pl.* **-dies**) **1** money granted by the government or a public body, etc., to keep down the price of commodities, etc. (*housing subsidy*). **2** money granted to a charity or other undertaking held to be in the public interest. **3** any grant of money.

sub·sist /səbsíst/ *v.intr.* **1** (often foll. by *on*) keep oneself alive (*subsists on vegetables*). **2** remain in being; exist. **3** (foll. by *in*) be attributable to (*its excellence subsists in its freshness*). ▫▫ **sub·sist·ent** *adj.*

sub·sist·ence /səbsístəns/ *n.* **1** the state or an instance of subsisting. **2 a** the means of supporting life; a livelihood. **b** a minimal level of existence or the income providing this (*a bare subsistence*).

sub·sist·ence farm·ing *n.* farming which directly supports the farmer's household without producing a significant surplus for trade.

sub·soil /súbsoyl/ *n.* soil lying immediately under the surface soil.

sub·son·ic /súbsónik/ *adj.* relating to speeds less than that of sound.

sub·spe·cies /súbspeesheez, –seez/ *n.* (*pl.* same) *Biol.* a taxonomic category below a species, usu. a fairly permanent geographically isolated variety. ▫▫ **sub·spe·cif·ic** /–spəsífik/ *adj.*

subst. *abbr.* **1** substantive. **2** substitute.

sub·stance /súbstəns/ *n.* **1 a** the essential material forming a thing (*the substance was transparent*). **b** a particular kind of material having uniform properties (*this substance is salt*). **2 a** reality; solidity (*ghosts have no substance*). **b** seriousness or steadiness of character (*there is no substance in him*). **3** addictive drugs or alcohol, etc. (*problems of substance abuse*). **4** the theme or subject of a work of art, argument, etc. (*prefer the substance to the style*). **5** the real meaning or essence of a thing. **6** wealth and possessions (*a woman of substance*).

sub·stand·ard /súbstándərd/ *adj.* **1** of less than the required or normal quality or size; inferior. **2** (of language) not conforming to standard usage.

sub·stan·tial /səbstánshəl/ *adj.* **1 a** of real importance or validity (*made a substantial contribution*). **b** of large size or amount (*awarded substantial damages*). **2** of solid material or structure (*a substantial house*). **3** commercially successful. **4** true in large part (*substantial truth*). **5** having substance. ▫▫ **sub·stan·ti·al·i·ty** /–sheeálitee/ *n.* **sub·stan·tial·ly** *adv.*

sub·stan·ti·ate /səbstánsheeayt/ *v.tr.* prove the truth of (a charge, statement, claim, etc.); give good grounds for. ▫▫ **sub·stan·ti·a·tion** /–áyshən/ *n.*

sub·stan·tive /súbstəntiv/ *adj. & n.* • *adj.* (also /səbstántiv/) **1** having separate and independent existence. **2** *Gram.* expressing existence. **3** *Mil.* (of a rank, etc.) permanent, not acting or temporary. • *n. Gram.* = NOUN.

sub·stan·tive verb *n.* the verb 'to be'.

sub·sta·tion /súbstayshən/ *n.* a subordinate station, esp. one reducing the high voltage of electric power transmission to that suitable for supply to consumers.

sub·stit·u·ent /səbstíchōōənt/ *adj. & n. Chem.* • *adj.* (of a group of atoms) replacing another atom or group in a compound. • *n.* such a group.

sub·sti·tute /súbstitōōt, –tyōōt/ *n.* & *v.* • *n.* **1** (also *attrib.*) a person or thing acting or serving in place of another. **2** an artificial alternative to a natural substance (*butter substitute*). • *v.* **1** *intr.* & *tr.* act or cause to act as a substitute; put or serve in exchange (*substituted for her mother; substituted it for the broken one*). **2** *tr.* (usu. foll. by *by, with*) *colloq.* replace (a person or thing) with another. ▫▫ **sub·sti·tut·a·ble** *adj.* **sub·sti·tu·tion** /–tóōshən, –tyóō–/ *n.* **sub·sti·tu·tive** *adj.*

sub·strate /súbstrayt/ *n.* **1** = SUBSTRATUM. **2** a surface to be painted, printed, etc., on. **3** *Biol.* **a** the substance upon which an enzyme acts. **b** the surface or material on which any particular organism grows.

sub·stra·tum /súbstraytəm, –strát–/ *n.* (*pl.* **substrata** /–tə/) **1** an underlying layer or substance. **2** a layer of rock or soil beneath the surface. **3** a basis.

sub·struc·ture /súbstrukchər/ *n.* an underlying or supporting structure.

sub·sume /səbsóōm, –syóōm/ *v.tr.* (usu. foll. by *under*) include (an instance, idea, category, etc.) in a rule, class, category, etc. ▫▫ **sub·sump·tion** /–súmpshən/ *n.*

sub·ter·fuge /súbtərfyōōj/ *n.* **1 a** an attempt to avoid blame or defeat, esp. by lying or deceit. **b** a statement, etc., resorted to for such a purpose. **2** this as a practice or policy.

sub·ter·ra·ne·an /súbtəráyneeən/ *adj.* **1** existing, occurring, or done under the earth's surface. **2** secret; underground; concealed.

sub·text /súbtekst/ *n.* an underlying theme.

sub·ti·tle /súbtīt'l/ *n.* & *v.* • *n.* **1** a secondary or additional title of a book, etc. **2** a caption at the bottom of a movie, etc., esp. translating dialogue. • *v.tr.* provide with subtitles.

sub·tle /sút'l/ *adj.* (**subtler, subtlest**) **1** evasive or mysterious; hard to grasp (*subtle charm; a subtle distinction*). **2** (of scent, color, etc.) faint; delicate (*subtle perfume*). **3 a** capable of making fine distinctions; perceptive (*subtle intellect; subtle senses*). **b** ingenious (*a subtle device*). ▫▫ **sub·tle·ness** *n.* **sub·tly** *adv.*

sub·tle·ty /sút'ltee/ *n.* (*pl.* **-ties**) **1** the quality of being subtle. **2** a fine distinction, feature, or argument.

sub·ton·ic /súbtónik/ *n. Mus.* the note below the tonic, the seventh note of the diatonic scale of any key.

sub·to·tal /súbtōt'l/ *n.* the total of one part of a group of figures to be added.

sub·tract /səbtrákt/ *v.tr.* deduct (a part, quantity, or number) from another. ▫▫ **sub·trac·tion** /–trákshən/ *n.* **sub·trac·tive** *adj.*

sub·trop·ics /súbtrópiks/ *n.pl.* the regions adjacent to the tropics. ▫▫ **sub·trop·i·cal** *adj.*

sub·urb /súbərb/ *n.* an outlying district of a city, esp. residential.

sub·ur·ban /səbə́rbən/ *adj.* **1** of or characteristic of suburbs. **2** *derog.* provincial, or naïve. ▫▫ **sub·ur·ban·ite** *n.* **sub·ur·ban·ize** *v.tr.* **sub·ur·ban·i·za·tion** *n.*

sub·ur·bi·a /səbə́rbeeə/ *n.* often *derog.* the suburbs, their inhabitants, and their way of life.

sub·ven·tion /səbvénshən/ *n.* a grant of money from a government, etc.

sub·ver·sive /səbvə́rsiv/ *adj.* & *n.* • *adj.* seeking to subvert (esp. a government). • *n.* a subversive person. ▫▫ **sub·ver·sion** /–və́rzhən, –shən/ *n.* **sub·ver·sive·ly** *adv.* **sub·ver·sive·ness** *n.*

sub·vert /səbvə́rt/ *v.tr.* esp. *Polit.* overturn, overthrow, or upset (religion, government, morality, etc.). ▫▫ **sub·vert·er** *n.*

sub·way /súbway/ *n.* **1** an underground railroad. **2 a** a tunnel beneath a road, etc., for pedestrians. **b** an underground passage for pipes, cables, etc.

sub·ze·ro /súbzéerō/ *adj.* (esp. of temperature) lower than zero.

suc- /suk, sək/ *prefix* assim. form of SUB- before *c.*

suc·ceed /səkséed/ *v.* **1** *intr.* **a** have success (*succeeded in his ambition*). **b** (of a plan, etc.) be successful. **2 a** *tr.* follow in order; come immediately after (*night succeeded day*). **b** *intr.* (foll. by *to*) come next; be subsequent. **3** *intr.* (often foll. by *to*) come by an inheritance, office, title, or property (*succeeded to the throne*). **4** *tr.* take over an office, property, inheritance, etc., from (*succeeded his father; succeeded the manager*).

suc·cess /səksés/ *n.* **1** the accomplishment of an aim; a favorable outcome (*their efforts met with success*). **2** the attainment of wealth, fame, or position (*spoiled by success*). **3** a thing or person that turns out well.

suc·cess·ful /səksésfōōl/ *adj.* having success; prosperous. ▫▫ **suc·cess·ful·ly** *adv.* **suc·cess·ful·ness** *n.*

suc·ces·sion /səkséshən/ *n.* **1 a** the process of following in order; succeeding. **b** a series of things or people in succession. **2 a** the right of succeeding to a throne, an office, inheritance, etc. **b** the act or process of so succeeding. **c** those having such a right. ▫ **in succession** one after another. **in succession to** as the successor of. ▫▫ **suc·ces·sion·al** *adj.*

suc·ces·sive /səksésiv/ *adj.* following one after another; consecutive. ▫▫ **suc·ces·sive·ly** *adv.*

suc·ces·sor /səksésər/ *n.* a person or thing that succeeds another.

suc·cinct /səksíngkt/ *adj.* briefly expressed; terse; concise. ▫▫ **suc·cinct·ly** *adv.* **suc·cinct·ness** *n.*

suc·cor /súkər/ *n.* & *v.* • *n.* aid; assistance, esp. in time of need. • *v.tr.* assist or aid (esp. a person in danger or distress).

suc·co·tash /súkətash/ *n.* a dish of corn and lima beans boiled together.

Suc·coth /sóōkəs, sōōkṓt/ *n.* (also **Suk·koth**) the Jewish autumn thanksgiving festival commemorating the sheltering in the wilderness.

suc·cu·bus /súkyəbəs/ *n.* (*pl.* **succubi** /–bī/) a female demon believed to have sexual intercourse with sleeping men.

suc·cu·lent /súkyələnt/ *adj.* & *n.* • *adj.* **1** juicy; palatable. **2** *colloq.* desirable. **3** *Bot.* (of a plant, its leaves, or stems) thick and fleshy. • *n. Bot.* a succulent plant. ▫▫ **suc·cu·lence** *n.* **suc·cu·lent·ly** *adv.*

suc·cumb /səkúm/ *v.intr.* (usu. foll. by *to*) **1** be forced to give way; be overcome (*succumbed to temptation*). **2** be overcome by death (*succumbed to his injuries*).

such /such/ *adj.* & *pron.* • *adj.* **1** (often foll. by *as*) of the kind or degree in question or under consideration (*such a person; such people*). **2** (usu. foll. by *as to* + infin. or *that* + clause) so great; in such high degree (*had such a fright that he fainted*). **3** of a more than normal kind or degree (*we had such an enjoyable evening*). **4** of the kind or degree already indicated, or implied by the context (*there are no such things*). • *pron.* **1** the thing or action in question or referred to (*such was not my intention*). **2 a** *Commerce* or *colloq.* the aforesaid thing or things (*those without tickets should purchase such*). **b** similar things; suchlike (*brought sandwiches and such*). ▫ **as such** as being what has been indicated or named (*there is no theater as such*). **such and such** *adj.* of a particular kind but not needing to be specified. *n.* a person or thing of this kind. **such and such a person** someone; so-and-so. **such as 1** of a kind that (*a person such as we all admire*). **2** for example (*insects, such as moths and bees*). **3** those who (*such as don't need help*). **such as it is** despite its shortcomings (*you are welcome to it, such as it is*).

such·like /súchlīk/ *adj.* & *n. colloq.* • *adj.* of such a kind. • *n.* things, people, etc., of such a kind.

suck /suk/ *v.* & *n.* • *v.* **1** *tr.* draw (a fluid) into the mouth by making a partial vacuum. **2** *tr.* (also *absol.*) **a** draw milk or other fluid from or through (the breast, etc., or a container). **b** extract juice from (a fruit) by sucking. **3** *tr.* **a** draw sustenance, knowledge, or advantage from (a book, etc.). **b** imbibe or gain (knowledge, advantage, etc.) as if by sucking. **4** *tr.* roll the tongue around (a candy, teeth, one's thumb, etc.). **5** *intr.* make a sucking action or sound (*sucking at his pipe*). **6** *intr. sl.* be very unpleasant, contemptible, or unfair. • *n.* the act or an instance of sucking. □ **suck dry 1** exhaust the contents of by sucking. **2** exhaust (a person's sympathy, resources, etc.) as if by sucking. **suck in 1** absorb. **2** involve (a person) in an activity, etc., esp. against his or her will. **suck up to** *colloq.* behave obsequiously, esp. for one's own advantage.

suck•er /súkər/ *n.* & *v.* • *n.* **1 a** a person or thing that sucks. **b** a sucking pig, newborn whale, etc. **2** *sl.* **a** a gullible person. **b** (foll. by *for*) a person especially susceptible to. **3 a** a rubber cup, etc., that adheres by suction. **b** an organ enabling an organism to cling by suction. **4** *Bot.* a shoot springing from the rooted part of a stem, from the root at a distance from the main stem, from an axil, or from a branch. **5** *colloq.* a lollipop. • *v. Bot.* **1** *tr.* remove suckers from. **2** *intr.* produce suckers. **3** *tr. sl.* cheat; fool.

suck•ing /súking/ *adj.* not yet weaned.

suck•le /súkəl/ *v.* **1** *tr.* **a** feed (young) from the breast or udder. **b** nourish (*suckled his talent*). **2** *intr.* feed by sucking the breast, etc. □□ **suck•ler** *n.*

suck•ling /súkling/ *n.* an unweaned child or animal.

su•crose /sóōkrōs/ *n. Chem.* sugar; a disaccharide obtained from sugar cane, sugar beet, etc.

suc•tion /súkshən/ *n.* **1** the act of sucking. **2 a** the production of a partial vacuum by the removal of air, etc., in order to force in liquid, etc., or procure adhesion. **b** the force produced by this process (*suction keeps the lid on*).

Su•da•nese /sóōdənéez/ *adj.* & *n.* • *adj.* of or relating to Sudan, a republic in NE Africa, or the Sudan region south of the Sahara. • *n.* (*pl.* same) **1** a native, national, or inhabitant of Sudan. **2** a person of Sudanese descent.

sud•den /súd'n/ *adj.* & *n.* • *adj.* occurring or done unexpectedly or without warning; abrupt; hurried (*a sudden storm; a sudden departure*). □ **all of a sudden** suddenly. □□ **sud•den•ly** *adv.* **sud•den•ness** *n.*

sud•den death *n. colloq.* a decision in a tied game, etc., dependent on one move, card, toss of a coin, etc.

sud•den in•fant death syn•drome *n. Med.* the death of a seemingly healthy infant from an unknown cause; crib death. ¶ Abbr.: **SIDS**.

suds /sudz/ *n.* & *v.* • *n.pl.* **1** froth of soap and water. **2** *colloq.* beer. • *v.* **1** *intr.* form suds. **2** *tr.* lather, cover, or wash in soapy water. □□ **suds•y** *adj.*

sue /sōō/ *v.* (**sues, sued, suing**) **1** *tr.* (also *absol.*) *Law* institute legal proceedings against (a person). **2** *intr. Law* make application to a court of law for redress. **3** *intr.* make entreaty to a person for a favor.

suede /swayd/ *n.* (often *attrib.*) **1** leather with the flesh side rubbed to make a velvety nap. **2** (also **suede cloth**) a woven fabric resembling suede.

su•et /sóō-it/ *n.* the hard white fat on the kidneys or loins of beef, etc., used in cooking, etc. □□ **su•et•y** *adj.*

su•et pud•ding *n.* a pudding of suet and flour, usu. boiled or steamed.

suf- /suf, səf/ *prefix* assim. form of SUB- before *f.*

suf•fer /súfər/ *v.* **1** *intr.* undergo pain, grief, etc. (*suffers acutely; suffers from neglect*). **2** *tr.* undergo, experience, or be subjected to (pain, loss, defeat, etc.) (*suffered banishment*). **3** *tr.* tolerate (*does not suffer fools gladly*). **4** *intr.* undergo martyrdom. □□ **suf•fer•er** *n.* **suf•fer•ing** *n.*

suf•fer•ance /súfərəns, súfrəns/ *n.* tacit consent. □ **on sufferance** with toleration implied by lack of consent or objection.

suf•fice /səfís/ *v.* **1** *intr.* be enough or adequate (*that will suffice for our purpose*). **2** *tr.* satisfy (*six sufficed him*). □ **suffice it to say** I shall content myself with saying.

suf•fi•cien•cy /səfíshənsee/ *n.* (*pl.* **-cies**) an adequate amount or adequate resources.

suf•fi•cient /səfíshənt/ *adj.* sufficing; adequate; enough (*is sufficient for a family; didn't have sufficient funds*). □□ **suf•fi•cient•ly** *adv.*

suf•fix /súfiks/ *n.* & *v.* • *n.* **1** a verbal element added at the end of a word to form a derivative (e.g., *-ation, -fy, -ing, -itis*). **2** *Math.* = SUBSCRIPT. • *v.tr.* (also /səfíks/) append, esp. as a suffix. □□ **suf•fix•a•tion** *n.*

suf•fo•cate /súfəkayt/ *v.* **1** *tr.* choke or kill by stopping breathing. **2** *tr.* (often foll. by *by, with*) produce a choking or breathless sensation in. **3** *intr.* be or feel suffocated or breathless. □□ **suf•fo•cat•ing** *adj.* **suf•fo•cat•ing•ly** *adv.* **suf•fo•ca•tion** /–káyshən/ *n.*

suf•frage /súfrij/ *n.* the right to vote in political elections (*full adult suffrage*).

suf•fra•gette /súfrəjét/ *n. hist.* a woman seeking the right to vote through organized protest.

suf•fra•gist /súfrəjist/ *n.* esp. *hist.* a person who advocates the extension of suffrage, esp. to women. □□ **suf•fra•gism** *n.*

suf•fuse /səfyóōz/ *v.tr.* **1** (of color, moisture, etc.) spread from within to color or moisten (*a blush suffused her cheeks*). **2** cover with color, etc. □□ **suf•fu•sion** /–fyóōzhən/ *n.*

Su•fi /sóōfee/ *n.* (*pl.* **Sufis**) a Muslim mystic. □□ **Su•fic** *adj.* **Su•fism** *n.*

sug- /sug, səg/ *prefix* assim. form of SUB- before *g.*

sug•ar /shóōgər/ *n.* & *v.* • *n.* **1** a sweet crystalline substance obtained from various plants, esp. the sugar cane and sugar beet, used in cooking, confectionery, brewing, etc. **2** *Chem.* any of a group of soluble usu. sweet-tasting crystalline carbohydrates, e.g., glucose. **3** *colloq.* darling; dear (used as a term of address). **4** sweet words; flattery. **5** anything comparable to sugar encasing a pill in reconciling a person to what is unpalatable. • *v.tr.* **1** sweeten with sugar. **2** make (one's words, meaning, etc.) more pleasant or welcome. **3** coat with sugar.

sug•ar beet *n.* a beet, *Beta vulgaris*, from which sugar is extracted.

sug•ar cane *n.* any perennial tropical grass of the genus *Saccharum*, esp. *S. officinarum*, with tall stout jointed stems from which sugar is made.

sug•ar-coat *v.tr.* **1** enclose (food) in sugar. **2** make superficially attractive. □□ **sug•ar-coat•ed** *adj.*

sug•ar dad•dy *n.* (*pl.* **-dies**) *sl.* an older man who lavishes gifts on a younger partner.

sug•ar ma•ple *n.* any of various trees, esp. *Acer saccharum*, from the sap of which sugar is made.

sug•ar•plum /shóōgərplum/ *n. archaic* a small round candy of flavored boiled sugar.

sug•ar•y /shóōgəree/ *adj.* **1** containing or resembling sugar. **2** excessively sweet or sentimental. **3** falsely sweet (*sugary compliments*). □□ **sug•ar•i•ness** *n.*

sug•gest /səgjést, səjést/ *v.tr.* **1** propose (a theory, plan, or hypothesis) (*suggested to them that they should wait*). **2 a** cause (an idea, memory, association, etc.) to present itself. **b** hint at (*his behavior suggests guilt*). □ **suggest itself** (of an idea, etc.) come into the mind.

sug•gest•i•ble /səgjéstəbəl, səjés–/ *adj.* **1** capable of being suggested. **2** open to suggestion; easily swayed. □□ **sug•gest•i•bil•i•ty** *n.*

sug•ges•tion /səgjéschən, səjés–/ *n.* **1** the act of suggesting. **2** a theory, plan, etc., suggested (*made a helpful suggestion*). **3** a slight trace (*a suggestion of garlic*). **4** *Psychol.* **a** the insinuation of a belief, etc., into the mind. **b** such a belief, etc.

sug·ges·tive /səgjéstiv, səjés–/ *adj.* **1** (usu. foll. by *of*) conveying a suggestion. **2** (esp. of a remark, etc.) indecent; improper; risqué. ▫▫ **sug·ges·tive·ly** *adv.* **sug·ges·tive·ness** *n.*

su·i·cid·al /sōōisíd'l/ *adj.* **1** inclined to commit suicide. **2** of or concerning suicide. **3** self-destructive; fatally or disastrously rash. ▫▫ **su·i·cid·al·ly** *adv.*

su·i·cide /sōōisīd/ *n. & v.* • *n.* **1 a** the intentional killing of oneself. **b** a person who commits suicide. **2** a self-destructive action or course (*political suicide*). • *v.intr.* commit suicide.

su·i ge·ne·ris /sōō-ī jénəris, sōō-ee, sōō-ee gén–/ *adj.* of its own kind; unique.

suit /sōōt/ *n. & v.* • *n.* **1 a** a set of outer clothes of matching material for men, consisting of a jacket, trousers, and sometimes a vest. **b** a similar set of clothes for women, usu. having a skirt instead of trousers. **c** (esp. in *comb.*) a set of clothes for a special occasion, occupation, etc. (*playsuit*; *swimsuit*). **2** any of the four sets (spades, hearts, diamonds, clubs) into which a pack of cards is divided. **3** (in full **suit at law**) a lawsuit (*criminal suit*). **4 a** a petition, esp. to a person in authority. **b** the process of courting a woman (*paid suit to her*). **5** (usu. foll. by *of*) a set of sails, armor, etc. • *v.tr.* **1** go well with (a person's figure, features, etc.). **2** (also *absol.*) meet the demands or requirements of (*does not suit all tastes*). **3** make fitting or appropriate (*suited his style to his audience*). **4** (as **suited** *adj.*) appropriate; well-fitted (*not suited to be an engineer*). ▫ **suit oneself 1** do as one chooses. **2** find something that satisfies one.

suit Middle English: from *sieute*, from a feminine past participle of an alteration of Latin *sequi* 'follow.' Early senses included 'attendance at a court' and 'legal process.' The notion of 'make agreeable or appropriate' dates from the late 16th century.

suit·a·ble /sōōtəbəl/ *adj.* (usu. foll. by *to*, *for*) well fitted for the purpose; appropriate. ▫▫ **suit·a·bil·i·ty** *n.* **suit·a·ble·ness** *n.* **suit·a·bly** *adv.*

suit·case /sōōtkays/ *n.* a usu. oblong case for carrying clothes, etc., having a handle and often a flat hinged lid. ▫▫ **suit·case·ful** *n.* (*pl.* **-fuls**).

suite /sweet/ *n.* **1** a set of things belonging together, esp.: **a** a set of rooms in a hotel, etc. **b** furniture intended for the same room and of the same design. **2** *Mus.* **a** a set of instrumental compositions to be played in succession. **b** a set of selected pieces from an opera, etc., to be played as one instrumental work. **3** a set of people in attendance.

suit·or /sōōtər/ *n.* **1** a man seeking to marry a specified woman; a wooer. **2** a plaintiff or petitioner in a lawsuit.

su·ki·ya·ki /sōōkeeyaákee, skeeyaá–/ *n.* a Japanese dish of sliced meat simmered with vegetables and sauce.

Suk·koth var. of SUCCOTH.

sul·fa /súlfə/ *n.* any drug derived from sulfanilamide (often *attrib.*: *sulfa drug*).

sul·fate /súlfayt/ *n.* a salt or ester of sulfuric acid.

sul·fide /súlfīd/ *n. Chem.* a binary compound of sulfur.

sul·fite /súlfīt/ *n. Chem.* a salt or ester of sulfurous acid.

sul·fon·a·mide /sulfónəmīd/ *n.* a substance derived from an amide of a sulfonic acid, able to prevent the multiplication of some pathogenic bacteria.

sul·fur /súlfər/ *n.* **1 a** a pale yellow nonmetallic element having crystalline and amorphous forms, burning with a blue flame and a suffocating smell. **b** (*attrib.*) like or containing sulfur. **2** the material of which hellfire and lightning were believed to consist. **3** a pale greenish yellow color. ▫▫ **sul·fur·y** *adj.*

sul·fur di·ox·ide *n.* a colorless pungent gas formed by burning sulfur in air and used as a food preservative.

sul·fu·re·ous /sulfyōōreeəs/ *adj.* **1** of, like, or suggesting sulfur. **2** sulfur-colored; yellow.

sul·fu·ric /sulfyōōrik/ *adj. Chem.* containing sexivalent sulfur.

sul·fu·ric ac·id *n.* a dense, oily, colorless, highly acid and corrosive fluid.

sul·fur·ous /súlfərəs, –fyōōr–/ *adj.* **1** relating to or suggestive of sulfur, esp. in color. **2** *Chem.* containing quadrivalent sulfur.

sulk /sulk/ *v. & n.* • *v.intr.* be sulky. • *n.* (also in *pl.*, prec. by *the*) a period of sullen, esp. resentful, silence (*having a sulk*; *got the sulks*). ▫▫ **sulk·er** *n.*

sulk·y /súlkee/ *n. & adj.* • *n.* (*pl.* **-ies**) a light two-wheeled horse-drawn vehicle for one, esp. in harness racing. • *adj.* (**sulkier, sulkiest**) sullen, morose, or silent, esp. from resentment or ill temper. ▫▫ **sulk·i·ly** *adv.* **sulk·i·ness** *n.*

sul·len /súlən/ *adj.* **1** morose; resentful; sulky. **2 a** (of a thing) slow moving. **b** dismal (*a sullen sky*). ▫▫ **sul·len·ly** *adv.* **sul·len·ness** *n.*

sul·ly /súlee/ *v.tr.* (**-lies, -lied**) **1** disgrace or tarnish (a person's reputation or character, a victory, etc.). **2** *poet.* dirty; soil.

sul·tan /súlt'n/ *n.* a Muslim sovereign. ▫▫ **sul·tan·ate** /–nayt/ *n.*

sul·tan·a /sultánə, –taánə/ *n.* **1 a** a seedless raisin used in cakes, etc. **b** the small, pale yellow grape producing this. **2** the mother, wife, concubine, or daughter of a sultan.

sul·try /súltree/ *adj.* (**sultrier, sultriest**) **1** (of the atmosphere or the weather) hot or oppressive. **2** (of a person, character, etc.) passionate; sensual. ▫▫ **sul·tri·ly** *adv.* **sul·tri·ness** *n.*

sum /sum/ *n. & v.* • *n.* **1** the total amount resulting from the addition of two or more items, etc. **2** a particular amount of money. • *v.tr.* (**summed, summing**) find the sum of. ▫ **in sum** in brief. **sum up 1** (esp. of a judge) recapitulate or review the evidence in a case, etc. **2** form or express an idea of the character of (a person, etc.). **3** collect into or express as a total.

su·mac /sōōmak, shōō–/ *n.* (also **su·mach**) **1** any shrub or tree of the genus *Rhus*, having reddish cone-shaped fruits used as a spice in cooking. **2** the dried and ground leaves of this used in tanning and dyeing.

Su·me·ri·an /sōōméereeən, –mér;n–/ *adj. & n.* • *adj.* of or relating to the early and non-Semitic element in the civilization of ancient Babylonia. • *n.* **1** a member of the early non-Semitic people of ancient Babylonia. **2** the Sumerian language.

sum·ma cum lau·de /sōōmə kōōm lówday, –də, –dee/ *adv. & adj.* (of a degree, diploma, etc.) of the highest standard; with the highest distinction.

sum·ma·rize /súmərīz/ *v.tr.* make or be a summary of; sum up. ▫▫ **sum·mar·ist** *n.* **sum·ma·riz·a·ble** *adj.* **sum·ma·ri·za·tion** *n.* **sum·ma·riz·er** *n.*

sum·ma·ry /súmaree/ *n. & adj.* • *n.* (*pl.* **-ries**) a brief statement or account of the main points of something. • *adj.* **1** dispensing with needless details or formalities; brief (*a summary account*). **2** *Law* without the customary legal formalities (*summary justice*). ▫▫ **sum·mar·i·ly** /səmáirilee/ *adv.* **sum·mar·i·ness** *n.*

sum·ma·tion /səmáyshən/ *n.* **1** the finding of a total or sum; an addition. **2** a summing-up.

sum·mer /súmər/ *n. & v.* • *n.* **1** the warmest season of the year. **2** *Astron.* the period from the summer solstice to the autumnal equinox. **3** the hot weather typical of summer. **4** (often foll. by *of*) the mature stage of life; the height of achievement, etc. **5** (*attrib.*) characteristic of or suitable for summer. • *v.intr.*

(usu. foll. by *at, in*) pass the summer. ▫▫ **sum·mer·y** *adj.*

sum·mer·sault var. of SOMERSAULT.

sum·mer sol·stice *n.* the time at which the sun is farthest north from the equator, about June 21 in the northern hemisphere.

sum·mer squash *n.* any of various cultivated squashes whose fruit is used as a vegetable.

sum·mer·time /súmərtīm/ *n.* the season or period of summer.

sum·ming-up *n.* **1** a review of evidence and a direction given by a judge to a jury. **2** a recapitulation of the main points of an argument, case, etc.

sum·mit /súmit/ *n.* **1** the highest point, esp. of a mountain. **2** the highest degree of power, ambition, etc. **3** (in full **summit meeting, talks**, etc.) a discussion, esp. on disarmament, etc., between heads of government.

sum·mon /súmən/ *v.tr.* **1** call upon to appear, esp. as a defendant or witness in a court of law. **2** (usu. foll. by *to* + infin.) call upon (*summoned her to assist*). **3** call together for a meeting or other purpose. ▫▫ **sum·mon·er** *n.*

sum·mons /súmənz/ *n. & v.* • *n.* (*pl.* **summonses**) **1** an authoritative or urgent call to attend on some occasion or do something. **2 a** a call to appear before a judge or magistrate. **b** the writ containing such a summons. • *v.tr.* esp. *Law* serve with a summons.

su·mo /sŏŏmō/ *n.* (*pl.* **-mos**) **1** a style of Japanese wrestling in which a participant is defeated by touching the ground with any part of the body except the soles of the feet or by moving outside the marked area. **2** a sumo wrestler.

sump /sump/ *n.* **1** a pit, well, hole, etc., in which superfluous liquid collects in mines, machines, etc. **2** a cesspool.

sump·tu·ous /súmpchōōəs/ *adj.* rich; lavish; costly (*a sumptuous setting*). ▫▫ **sump·tu·os·i·ty** /–ósitee/ *n.* **sump·tu·ous·ly** *adv.* **sump·tu·ous·ness** *n.*

sum to·tal *n.* = SUM *n.* 1.

Sun. *abbr.* Sunday.

sun /sun/ *n. & v.* • *n.* **1 a** the star around which the earth orbits and from which it receives light and warmth. **b** any similar star in the universe with or without planets. **2** the light or warmth received from the sun (*keep out the sun*). • *v.* (**sunned, sunning**) **1** *refl.* bask in the sun. **2** *tr.* expose to the sun. ▫ **under the sun** anywhere in the world. ▫▫ **sun·less** *adj.*

sun·bathe /súnbayth/ *v.intr.* bask in the sun. ▫▫ **sun·bath·er** *n.*

sun·beam /súnbeem/ *n.* a ray of sunlight.

sun·belt /súnbelt/ *n.* a strip of territory receiving a high amount of sunshine.

sun·block /súnblok/ *n.* a cream or lotion for protecting the skin from the sun.

sun·burn /súnbərn/ *n. & v.* • *n.* reddening and inflammation of the skin caused by overexposure to the sun. • *v.intr.* **1** suffer from sunburn. **2** (as **sunburned** or **sunburnt** *adj.*) suffering from sunburn.

sun·burst /súnbərst/ *n.* **1** something resembling the sun and its rays, esp.: **a** a brooch, etc. **b** a firework. **2** the sun shining suddenly from behind clouds.

sun·dae /súnday, –dee/ *n.* a dish of ice cream with fruit, nuts, syrup, etc.

Sun·day /súnday, –dee/ *n. & adv.* • *n.* **1** the first day of the week, a Christian holiday and day of worship. **2** a newspaper published on a Sunday. • *adv. colloq.* **1** on Sunday. **2** (**Sundays**) on Sundays; each Sunday.

Sun·day best *n.* a person's best clothes, kept for Sunday use.

Sun·day school *n.* a school, usu. affiliated with a Christian church, for the religious instruction of children on Sundays.

sun·der /súndər/ *v.tr. & intr. archaic* separate; sever.

sun·di·al /súndīəl/ *n.* an instrument showing the time by the shadow of a pointer cast by the sun onto a graduated disk.

sundial

sun·down /súndown/ *n.* sunset.

sun·dress /súndres/ *n.* a dress without sleeves and with a low neck.

sun·dry /súndree/ *adj. & n.* • *adj.* various; several (*sundry items*). • *n.* (*pl.* **-dries**) (in *pl.*) various items not important enough to be mentioned individually.

sun·fish /súnfish/ *n.* any of various almost spherical fish, esp. a large ocean fish, *Mola mola*.

sun·flow·er /súnflowr/ *n.* any tall plant of the genus *Helianthus*, esp. *H. annuus*, with very large, showy, golden-rayed flowers, grown also for its seeds which yield an edible oil.

sung *past part.* of SING.

sun·glass·es /súnglasiz/ *n.pl.* glasses tinted to protect the eyes from sunlight or glare.

sunk *past* and *past part.* of SINK.

sunk·en /súngkən/ *adj.* **1** that has been sunk. **2** beneath the surface; submerged. **3** (of the eyes, cheeks, etc.) hollow; depressed.

sun lamp *n.* **1** a lamp giving ultraviolet rays for an artificial suntan, therapy, etc. **2** *Cinematog.* a large lamp with a parabolic reflector used in filmmaking.

sun·light /súnlīt/ *n.* light from the sun. ▫▫ **sun·lit** *adj.*

sun·lit /súnlit/ *adj.* illuminated by sunlight.

Sun·ni /sŏŏnee/ *n. & adj.* • *n.* (*pl.* same or **Sunnis**) **1** one of the two main branches of Islam, regarding the Sunna as equal in authority to the Koran (cf. SHIA). **2** an adherent of this branch of Islam. • *adj.* of or relating to Sunni.

sun·ny /súnee/ *adj.* (**sunnier, sunniest**) **1 a** bright with sunlight. **b** exposed to or warmed by the sun. **2** cheery in temperament. ▫▫ **sun·ni·ly** *adv.* **sun·ni·ness** *n.*

sun·ny-side up /súneesīd/ *adj.* (of an egg) fried on one side and served.

sun·rise /súnrīz/ *n.* **1** the sun's rising at dawn. **2** the colored sky associated with this. **3** the time at which sunrise occurs.

sun·rise in·dus·try *n.* any newly established industry regarded as signaling prosperity.

sun·roof /súnrōōf/ *n.* a section of an automobile roof that can be slid open.

sun·screen *n.* a cream or lotion rubbed into the skin that contains an ingredient that blocks ultraviolet rays.

sun·set /súnset/ *n.* **1** the sun's setting in the evening. **2** the colored sky associated with this. **3** the time at which sunset occurs.

sun·shade /súnshayd/ *n.* **1** a parasol. **2** an awning.

sun·shine /súnshīn/ *n.* **1 a** the light of the sun. **b** an area lit by the sun. **2** good weather. **3** cheerfulness. ▫▫ **sun·shin·y** *adj.*

sun·spot /súnspot/ *n.* one of the dark patches observed on the sun's surface.

sun·stroke /súnstrōk/ *n.* acute prostration or collapse from the excessive heat of the sun.

sun·tan /súntan/ *n. & v.* • *n.* the brownish coloring of skin caused by exposure to the sun. • *v.intr.* (**-tanned, -tanning**) color the skin with a suntan.

sun·up /súnup/ *n.* sunrise.

sup- /sup, səp/ *prefix* assim. form of SUB- before *p*.

su·per /sŏŏpər/ *adj. & n.* • *adj.* (also **su·per-du·per** /–dŏŏpər/) *colloq.* (also as *int.*) exceptional; splendid. • *n. colloq.* **1** *Theatr.* a supernumerary actor. **2** a superintendent. **3** superphosphate. **4** an extra, unwanted, or unimportant person.

super- /sóōpər/ *prefix* forming nouns, adjectives, and verbs, meaning: **1** above, beyond, or over (*superstructure*; *superimpose*). **2** to a great or extreme degree (*superabundant*). **3** extra good or large of its kind (*supertanker*). **4** of a higher kind (*superclass*).

su·per·a·ble /sóōpərəbəl/ *adj.* able to be overcome.

su·per·a·bound /sóōpərəbównd/ *v.intr.* be very or too abundant.

su·per·a·bun·dant /sóōpərəbúndənt/ *adj.* abounding beyond what is normal or right. ▫▫ **su·per·a·bun·dance** *n.* **su·per·a·bun·dant·ly** *adv.*

su·per·add /sóōpərád/ *v.tr.* add over and above. ▫▫ **su·per·ad·di·tion** /–ədíshən/ *n.*

su·per·an·nu·ate /sóōpərányōōayt/ *v.tr.* **1** retire (a person) with a pension. **2** dismiss or discard as too old. **3** (as **superannuated** *adj.*) too old.

su·per·an·nu·a·tion /sóōpərányōō-áyshən/ *n.* **1** a pension paid to a retired person. **2** the process of superannuating.

su·perb /sōōpárb/ *adj.* **1** of the most impressive, splendid, or majestic kind. **2** *colloq.* excellent; fine. ▫▫ **su·perb·ly** *adv.* **su·perb·ness** *n.*

su·per·cal·en·der /sóōpərkálindər/ *v.tr.* give a highly glazed finish to (paper) by extra calendering.

su·per·car·go /sóōpərkaargō/ *n.* (*pl.* **-goes**) an officer in a merchant ship managing sales, etc., of cargo.

su·per·charge /sóōpərchaarj/ *v.tr.* **1** (usu. foll. by *with*) charge (the atmosphere, etc.) with energy, emotion, etc. **2** use a supercharger on.

su·per·charg·er /sóōpərchaarjər/ *n.* a device supplying air or fuel to an internal combustion engine at above normal pressure to increase efficiency.

su·per·cil·i·ous /sóōpərsíleeəs/ *adj.* assuming an air of contemptuous indifference or superiority. ▫▫ **su·per·cil·i·ous·ly** *adv.* **su·per·cil·i·ous·ness** *n.*

su·per·com·put·er /sóōpərkəmpyóōtər/ *n.* a powerful computer capable of dealing with complex problems. ▫▫ **su·per·com·put·ing** *n.*

su·per·con·duc·tiv·i·ty /sóōpərkónduktívitee/ *n. Physics* the property of zero electrical resistance in some substances at very low absolute temperatures. ▫▫ **su·per·con·duct·ing** /–kəndúkting/ *adj.* **su·per·con·duc·tive** *adj.*

su·per·con·duc·tor /sóōpərkəndúktər/ *n. Physics* a substance having superconductivity.

su·per·con·scious /sóōpərkónshəs/ *adj.* transcending human consciousness. ▫▫ **su·per·con·scious·ly** *adv.* **su·per·con·scious·ness** *n.*

su·per·cool /sóōpərkóōl/ *v.* & *adj.* • *v. Chem.* **1** *tr.* cool (a liquid) below its freezing point without solidification or crystallization. **2** *intr.* (of a liquid) be cooled in this way. • *adj. sl.* very cool, relaxed, etc.

su·per·crit·i·cal /sóōpərkrítikəl/ *adj. Physics* of more than critical mass, etc.

su·per-du·per var. of SUPER *adj.*

su·per·e·go /sóōpəreégō, –égō/ *n.* (*pl.* **-gos**) *Psychol.* the part of the mind that acts as a conscience and responds to social rules.

su·per·er·o·ga·tion /sóōpərérəgáyshən/ *n.* the performance of more than duty requires. ▫▫ **su·per·er·og·a·to·ry** /–irógətawree/ *adj.*

su·per·fat·ted /sóōpərfátid/ *adj.* (of soap) containing extra fat.

su·per·fi·cial /sóōpərfíshəl/ *adj.* **1** of or on the surface; lacking depth. **2** swift or cursory. **3** apparent but not real (*a superficial resemblance*). **4** (esp. of a person) having no depth of character or knowledge. ▫▫ **su·per·fi·ci·al·i·ty** /–sheeálitee/ *n.* (*pl.* **-ties**). **su·per·fi·cial·ly** *adv.*

su·per·fine /sóōpərfīn/ *adj.* **1** *Commerce* of high quality. **2** pretending great refinement.

su·per·flu·i·ty /sóōpərflóōitee/ *n.* (*pl.* **-ties**) **1** the state of being superfluous. **2** a superfluous amount or thing.

su·per·flu·ous /sōōpárflōōəs/ *adj.* more than enough; redundant; needless. ▫▫ **su·per·flu·ous·ly** *adv.* **su·per·flu·ous·ness** *n.*

su·per·heat /sóōpərheét/ *v.tr. Physics* **1** heat (a liquid) above its boiling point without vaporization. **2** heat (a vapor) above its boiling point. ▫▫ **su·per·heat·er** *n.*

su·per·high·way /sóōpərhīway/ *n.* a multilane main road for fast traffic.

su·per·hu·man /sóōpərhyóōmən/ *adj.* **1** beyond normal human capability. **2** higher than man. ▫▫ **su·per·hu·man·ly** *adv.*

su·per·im·pose /sóōpərimpóz/ *v.tr.* (usu. foll. by *on*) lay (a thing) on something else. ▫▫ **su·per·im·po·si·tion** /–pəzíshən/ *n.*

su·per·in·cum·bent /sóōpərinkúmbənt/ *adj.* lying on something else.

su·per·in·tend /sóōpərinténd/ *v.tr.* & *intr.* supervise and inspect. ▫▫ **su·per·in·tend·ence** *n.* **su·per·in·tend·en·cy** *n.*

su·per·in·tend·ent /sóōpərinténdənt/ *n.* & *adj.* • *n.* **1 a** a person who superintends. **b** a director of an institution, etc. **2** a high-ranking official, often the chief of a police department. **3** the caretaker of a building. • *adj.* superintending.

su·pe·ri·or /sōōpeéreeər/ *adj.* & *n.* • *adj.* **1** in a higher position; of higher rank. **2 a** above average in quality, etc. (*superior leather*). **b** supercilious (*a superior air*). **3** (often foll. by *to*) **a** better or greater in some respect. **b** above yielding, making concessions, etc. (*superior to bribery*). **4** *Printing* (of figures or letters) placed above the line. • *n.* **1** a person superior to another in rank, character, etc. **2** (*fem.* **superioress** /–ris/) *Eccl.* the head of a monastery or other religious institution (*Mother Superior*). **3** *Printing* a superior letter or figure. ▫▫ **su·pe·ri·or·ly** *adv.*

su·pe·ri·or·i·ty /sōōpeéree-áwritee, –ór–/ *n.* the state of being superior.

su·pe·ri·or·i·ty com·plex *n. Psychol.* an undue conviction of one's own superiority to others.

su·per·la·tive /sōōpárlətiv/ *adj.* & *n.* • *adj.* **1** of the highest quality or degree (*superlative wisdom*). **2** *Gram.* (of an adjective or adverb) expressing the highest or a very high degree of a quality (e.g., *bravest, most fiercely*). • *n.* **1** *Gram.* **a** the superlative expression or form of an adjective or adverb. **b** a word in the superlative. **2** something embodying excellence. **3** an exaggerated or excessive statement, comment, etc. ▫▫ **su·per·la·tive·ly** *adv.* **su·per·la·tive·ness** *n.*

su·per·lu·na·ry /sóōpərlóōnəree/ *adj.* **1** situated beyond the moon. **2** celestial.

su·per·man /sóōpərman/ *n.* (*pl.* **-men**) **1** esp. *Philos.* the ideal superior man of the future. **2** *colloq.* a man of exceptional strength or ability.

su·per·mar·ket /sóōpərmaarkit/ *n.* a large self-service store selling foods, household goods, etc.

su·per·nal /sōōpárnəl/ *adj.* esp. *poet.* **1** heavenly; divine. **2** of or concerning the sky. **3** lofty. ▫▫ **su·per·nal·ly** *adv.*

su·per·nat·u·ral /sóōpərnáchərəl/ *adj.* & *n.* • *adj.* attributed to or thought to reveal some force above the laws of nature; magical; mystical. • *n.* (prec. by *the*) supernatural, occult, or magical forces, effects, etc. ▫▫ **su·per·nat·u·ral·ism** *n.* **su·per·nat·u·ral·ly** *adv.* **su·per·nat·u·ral·ness** *n.*

su·per·nor·mal /sóōpərnáwrməl/ *adj.* beyond what is normal or natural. ▫▫ **su·per·nor·mal·i·ty** /–málitee/ *n.*

su·per·no·va /sóōpərnṓvə/ *n.* (*pl.* **-novae** /–vee/ or **-novas**) *Astron.* a star that suddenly increases very greatly in brightness because of an explosion ejecting most of its mass.

su·per·nu·mer·ar·y /sóopərnóomərerée, –nyóo–/ *adj.* & *n.* • *adj.* **1** in excess of the normal number. **2** engaged for extra work. **3** (of an actor) appearing on stage but not speaking. • *n.* (*pl.* **-ies**) **1** an extra or unwanted person or thing. **2** a person engaged for extra work.

su·per·phys·i·cal /sóopərfízikəl/ *adj.* **1** unexplainable by physical causes; supernatural. **2** beyond what is physical.

su·per·pose /sóopərpóz/ *v.tr.* (usu. foll. by *on*) esp. *Geom.* place (a thing or a geometric figure) on or above something else, esp. so as to coincide. ▫▫ **su·per·po·si·tion** /–pəzíshən/ *n.*

su·per·pow·er /sóopərpowr/ *n.* a nation of supreme power and influence, esp. the US and the former USSR.

su·per·sat·u·rate /sóopəsáchərayt/ *v.tr.* add to (esp. a solution) beyond saturation point. ▫▫ **su·per·sat·u·ra·tion** /–ráyshən/ *n.*

su·per·scribe /sóopərskríb/ *v.tr.* **1** write (an inscription) at the top of or on the outside of a document, etc. **2** write an inscription over or on (a thing). ▫▫ **su·per·scrip·tion** /–skrípshən/ *n.*

su·per·script /sóopərskript/ *adj.* & *n.* • *adj.* written or printed above. • *n.* a superscript number or symbol.

su·per·sede /sóopərséed/ *v.tr.* **1 a** adopt or appoint another person or thing in place of. **b** set aside; cease to employ. **2** (of a person or thing) take the place of. ▫▫ **su·per·ses·sion** /–séshən/ *n.*

su·per·son·ic /sóopərsónik/ *adj.* designating or having a speed greater than that of sound. ▫▫ **su·per·son·i·cal·ly** *adv.*

su·per·son·ics /sóopərsóniks/ *n.pl.* (treated as *sing.*) = ULTRASONICS.

su·per·star /sóopərstaar/ *n.* an extremely famous movie star, athlete, etc. ▫▫ **su·per·star·dom** *n.*

su·per·sti·tion /sóopərstíshən/ *n.* **1** credulity regarding the supernatural. **2** an irrational fear of the unknown. **3** misdirected reverence. **4** a practice, opinion, or religion based on these tendencies. **5** a widely held but unjustified idea. ▫▫ **su·per·sti·tious** *adj.* **su·per·sti·tious·ly** *adv.* **su·per·sti·tious·ness** *n.*

su·per·store /sóopərstawr/ *n.* a very large store selling a wide range of goods.

su·per·struc·ture /sóopərstrukchər/ *n.* **1** the part of a building above its foundations. **2** a structure built on top of something else. **3** a concept or idea based on others. ▫▫ **su·per·struc·tur·al** *adj.*

su·per·tank·er /sóopərtangkər/ *n.* a very large tanker ship.

su·per·ter·res·tri·al /sóopərtəréstreeəl/ *adj.* **1** in or belonging to a region above the Earth. **2** celestial.

su·per·ton·ic /sóopərtónik/ *n. Mus.* the note above the tonic; the second note of the diatonic scale of any key.

su·per·vene /sóopərvéen/ *v.intr.* occur as an interruption in or a change. ▫▫ **su·per·ven·ient** *adj.* **su·per·ven·tion** /–vénshən/ *n.*

su·per·vise /sóopərvīz/ *v.tr.* superintend; oversee. ▫▫ **su·per·vi·sion** /–ví<u>zh</u>ən/ *n.* **su·per·vi·sor** *n.* **su·per·vi·so·ry** *adj.*

su·per·wom·an /sóopərwoomən/ *n.* (*pl.* **-women**) *colloq.* a woman of exceptional strength or ability.

su·pi·nate /sóopinayt/ *v.tr.* put (a hand or foreleg, etc.) into a supine position. ▫▫ **su·pi·na·tion** /–náyshən/ *n.*

su·pine *adj.* /sóopín/ **1** lying face upwards (cf. PRONE). **2** inert; indolent. ▫▫ **su·pine·ly** /–pínlee/ *adv.* **su·pine·ness** *n.*

sup·per /súpər/ *n.* an informal evening meal. ▫ **sing for one's supper** do something in return for a benefit.

sup·plant /səplánt/ *v.tr.* dispossess and take the place of, esp. by underhand means. ▫▫ **sup·plant·er** *n.*

sup·ple /súpəl/ *adj.* (**suppler, supplest**) flexible; pliant. ▫▫ **sup·ple·ness** *n.*

sup·ple·ly var. of SUPPLY[2].

sup·ple·ment *n.* & *v.* • *n.* /súplimənt/ **1** a thing or part added to remedy deficiencies (*dietary supplement*). **2** a part added to a book, etc., to provide further information. **3** a separate section, esp. a color magazine, added to a newspaper or periodical. • *v.tr.* (also /súpliment/) provide a supplement for. ▫▫ **sup·ple·men·tal** /–mént'l/ *adj.* **sup·ple·men·tal·ly** *adv.* **sup·ple·men·ta·tion** /–mentáyshən/ *n.*

sup·ple·men·ta·ry /súpliméntəree/ *adj.* forming or serving as a supplement; additional. ▫▫ **sup·ple·men·tar·i·ly** *adv.*

sup·pli·ant /súpleeənt/ *adj.* & *n.* • *adj.* **1** supplicating. **2** expressing supplication. • *n.* a supplicating person. ▫▫ **sup·pli·ant·ly** *adv.*

sup·pli·cate /súplikayt/ *v.* **1** *tr.* petition humbly to (a person) or for (a thing). **2** *intr.* (foll. by *to, for*) make a petition. ▫▫ **sup·pli·cant** *adj.* & *n.* **sup·pli·ca·tion** /–áyshən/ *n.* **sup·pli·ca·to·ry** *adj.*

sup·ply[1] /səplí/ *v.* & *n.* • *v.tr.* (**-plies, -plied**) **1** provide or furnish (a thing needed). **2** (often foll. by *with*) provide (a person, etc., with a thing needed). **3** meet or make up for (a deficiency or need, etc.). **4** fill (a vacancy, etc.) as a substitute. • *n.* (*pl.* **-plies**) **1** the act or an instance of providing what is needed. **2** a stock, amount, etc., of something provided or obtainable. **3** (in *pl.*) the provisions and equipment for an army, expedition, etc. ▫ **in short supply** available in limited quantity. ▫▫ **sup·pli·er** *n.*

sup·ply[2] /súplee/ *adv.* (also **sup·ple·ly** /súpəlee/) in a supple manner.

sup·ply and de·mand *n. Econ.* quantities available and required as factors regulating the price of commodities.

sup·ply-side *adj. Econ.* denoting a policy of low taxation and other incentives to produce goods and invest.

sup·port /səpáwrt/ *v.* & *n.* • *v.tr.* **1** carry all or part of the weight of. **2** keep from falling or sinking or failing. **3** provide with a home and the necessities of life. **4** enable to last out; give strength to. **5** tend to substantiate or corroborate (a statement, theory, etc.). **6** back up; second. **7** speak in favor of (a resolution, etc.). **8** be actively interested in (a particular team or sport). **9** take a part that is secondary to (a principal actor, etc.). **10** endure; tolerate (*can no longer support the noise*). • *n.* **1** the act of supporting. **2** a person or thing that supports. ▫ **in support of** in order to support. ▫▫ **sup·port·a·ble** *adj.*

sup·port·er /səpáwrtər/ *n.* a person or thing that supports, esp. a person supporting a team, sport, political candidate, etc.

sup·port·ive /səpáwrtiv/ *adj.* providing support or encouragement. ▫▫ **sup·port·ive·ly** *adv.* **sup·port·ive·ness** *n.*

sup·pose /səpóz/ *v.tr.* (often foll. by *that* + clause) **1** assume, esp. in default of knowledge; be inclined to think. **2** take as a possibility or hypothesis (*let us suppose you are right*). **3** (in *imper.*) as a formula of proposal (*suppose we go to the party*). **4** (of a theory or result, etc.) require as a condition; imply (*design supposes a creator*). **5** in the circumstances that; if (*supposing we stay*). **6** (as **supposed** (/səpózid/) *adj.*) generally accepted as being so (*his supposed brother*). **7** (in *passive*; foll. by *to* + infin.) **a** be expected or required (*was supposed to write to you*). **b** (with *neg.*) not have to; not be allowed to (*you are not supposed to go there*). ▫ **I suppose so** an expression of hesitant agreement. ▫▫ **sup·pos·a·ble** *adj.*

sup·pos·ed·ly /səpṓzidlee/ *adv.* as is generally supposed.

sup·po·si·tion /súpəzíshən/ *n.* **1** a fact or idea, etc., supposed. **2** the act or an instance of supposing. ▫▫ **sup·po·si·tion·al** *adj.*

sup·pos·i·to·ry /səpózitawree/ *n.* (*pl.* **-ries**) a medical preparation in the form of a cone, cylinder, etc., to be inserted into the rectum or vagina to melt.

sup·press /səprés/ *v.tr.* **1** end the activity or existence of, esp. forcibly. **2** prevent (information, feelings, etc.) from being seen, heard, or known. **3 a** partly or wholly eliminate (electrical interference, etc.). **b** equip (a device) to reduce such interference due to it. ▫▫ **sup·press·i·ble** *adj.* **sup·pres·sion** *n.* **sup·pres·sor** *n.*

sup·pres·sant /səprésənt/ *n.* a suppressing or restraining agent, esp. a drug that suppresses the appetite.

sup·pu·rate /súpyərayt/ *v.intr.* **1** form pus. **2** fester. ▫▫ **sup·pu·ra·tion** /–ráyshən/ *n.* **sup·pu·ra·tive** /–rətiv/ *adj.*

su·pra /sṓoprə/ *adv.* above or earlier on (in a book, etc.).

supra- /sṓoprə/ *prefix* **1** above. **2** beyond; transcending (*supranational*).

su·prem·a·cist /sōoprémәsist/ *n. & adj.* ● *n.* an advocate of the supremacy of a particular group. ● *adj.* advocating such supremacy. ▫▫ **su·prem·a·cism** *n.*

su·prem·a·cy /sōopréməsee/ *n.* (*pl.* **-cies**) the state of being supreme.

su·preme /sōopreém/ *adj.* **1** highest in authority or rank. **2** greatest; most important. **3** (of a penalty or sacrifice, etc.) involving death. ▫▫ **su·preme·ly** *adv.*

Su·preme Be·ing *n.* a name for God.

Su·preme Court *n.* the highest judicial court in a nation, etc.

su·pre·mo /sōopreémō/ *n. Brit.* (*pl.* **-mos**) **1** a supreme leader or ruler. **2** a person in overall charge.

Supt. *abbr.* Superintendent.

su·rah /sṓorə/ *n.* a soft twilled silk for scarves, etc.

sur·cease /sə́rsees, sərseés/ *n. & v. literary* ● *n.* a cessation. ● *v.intr. & tr.* cease.

sur·charge *n. & v.* ● *n.* /sə́rchaarj/ **1** an additional charge or payment. **2** a mark printed on a postage stamp changing its value. **3** an additional or excessive load. ● *v.tr.* /sə́rchaarj, –cháarj/ **1** exact a surcharge from. **2** exact (a sum) as a surcharge. **3** mark (a postage stamp) with a surcharge. **4** overload. **5** fill to excess.

sur·cin·gle /sə́rsinggəl/ *n.* a strap around a horse's body, used to keep a pack or other equipment in place.

sur·coat /sə́rkōt/ *n.* **1** *hist.* a loose robe worn over armor. **2** a similar sleeveless garment worn as part of the insignia of an order of knighthood. **3** *hist.* an outer coat of rich material.

surd /sərd/ *adj. & n.* ● *adj.* **1** *Math.* (of a number) irrational. **2** *Phonet.* (of a sound) uttered with the breath and not the voice (e.g., *f, k, p, s, t*). ● *n.* **1** *Math.* a surd number, esp. the root of an integer. **2** *Phonet.* a surd sound.

sure /shoor/ *adj. & adv.* ● *adj.* **1** having or seeming to have adequate reason for a belief or assertion. **2** (often foll. by *of*, or *that* + clause) convinced. **3** (foll. by *of*) having confident anticipation or satisfactory knowledge of. **4** reliable or unfailing (*one sure way to find out*). **5** (foll. by *to* + infin.) certain. **6** undoubtedly true or truthful. ● *adv. colloq.* certainly. ▫ **be sure** (in *imper.* or *infin.*; foll. by *that* + clause or *to* + infin.) take care to; not fail to. **for sure** *colloq.* without doubt. **make sure 1** make or become certain. **2** (foll. by *of*) establish the truth or ensure the existence or happening of. **sure enough** *colloq.* **1** in fact; certainly. **2** with near certainty. **sure thing** *n.* a certainty. *int. colloq.* certainly. **to be sure 1** it is undeniable or admitted. **2** it must be admitted. ▫▫ **sure·ness** *n.*

▶Unless intending an informal effect, do not use **sure** when the adverb **surely** is meant: *It surely was foolhardy to take on all these problems yourself. I surely was happy to see them again.*

sure-fire *adj. colloq.* certain to succeed.

sure-foot·ed *adj.* never stumbling or making a mistake. ▫▫ **sure-foot·ed·ly** *adv.* **sure-foot·ed·ness** *n.*

sure·ly /shoorlee/ *adv.* **1** with certainty (*slowly but surely*). **2** as an appeal to reason (*surely that can't be right*). **3** securely (*the goat plants its feet surely*).

sur·e·ty /shooritee/ *n.* (*pl.* **-ties**) **1** a person who takes responsibility for another's performance of an undertaking, e.g., to appear in court, or payment of a debt. **2** a certainty. ▫ **stand surety** become a surety; stand bail. ▫▫ **sur·e·ty·ship** *n.*

surf /sərf/ *n. & v.* ● *n.* **1** the swell of the sea breaking on the shore or reefs. **2** the foam produced by this. ● *v.intr.* ride the surf, with or as with a surfboard. ▫▫ **surf·er** *n.* **surf·y** *adj.*

sur·face /sə́rfis/ *n. & v.* ● *n.* **1 a** the outside of a material body. **b** the area of this. **2** any of the limits terminating a solid. **3** the upper boundary of a liquid or of the ground, etc. **4** the outward aspect of anything (*quiet on the surface*). **5** *Geom.* a set of points that has length and breadth but no thickness. **6** (*attrib.*) **a** of or on the surface. **b** superficial (*surface politeness*). ● *v.* **1** *tr.* give the required surface to (a road, paper, etc.). **2** *intr. & tr.* rise or bring to the surface. **3** *intr.* become visible or known. **4** *intr. colloq.* wake up. ▫ **come to the surface** become perceptible after being hidden. ▫▫ **sur·faced** *adj.* (usu. in *comb.*). **sur·fac·er** *n.*

sur·face ten·sion *n.* the tension of the surface film of a liquid, tending to minimize its surface area.

sur·fac·tant /surfáktənt/ *n.* a substance which reduces surface tension.

surf·board /súrfbawrd/ *n.* a long narrow board used in surfing.

surf cast·ing *n.* fishing by casting a line into the sea from the shore.

sur·feit /súrfit/ *n. & v.* ● *n.* **1** an excess, esp. in eating or drinking. **2** a feeling of disgust resulting from this. ● *v.* (**surfeited, surfeiting**) **1** *tr.* overfeed. **2** *intr.* overeat. **3** *intr. & tr.* (foll. by *with*) be or cause to be wearied through excess.

surg. *abbr.* **1** surgeon. **2** surgery. **3** surgical.

surge /surj/ *n. & v.* ● *n.* **1** a sudden or impetuous onset (*a surge of anger*). **2** the swell of the waves at sea. **3** a heavy forward or upward motion. **4** a rapid increase in price, activity, etc. **5** a sudden marked increase in voltage of an electric current. ● *v.intr.* **1** (of waves, etc.) rise and fall or move heavily forward. **2** (of a crowd, etc.) move suddenly and powerfully forward. **3** (of an electric current, etc.) increase suddenly.

sur·geon /súrjən/ *n.* **1** a medical practitioner qualified to practice surgery. **2** a medical officer in a navy or army or military hospital.

sur·geon gen·er·al *n.* (*pl.* **surgeons general**) the head of a public health service or of an army, etc., medical service.

sur·ger·y /súrjəree/ *n.* (*pl.* **-ies**) the branch of medicine concerned with treatment of injuries or disorders of the body by incision, manipulation or alteration of organs, etc., with the hands or with instruments.

sur·gi·cal /sə́rjikəl/ *adj.* **1** of or relating to or done by surgeons or surgery. **2** resulting from surgery. **3 a** used in surgery. **b** worn to correct a deformity, etc. **4** extremely precise. ▫▫ **sur·gi·cal·ly** *adv.*

sur·ly /sə́rlee/ *adj.* (**surlier, surliest**) bad-tempered and unfriendly; churlish. ▫▫ **sur·li·ly** *adv.* **sur·li·ness** *n.*

sur·mise /sərmíz/ *n. & v.* •*n.* a conjecture. •*v.* **1** *tr.* (often foll. by *that* + clause) infer doubtfully; make a surmise about. **2** *tr.* suspect the existence of. **3** *intr.* make a guess.

---

surmise late Middle English (denoting a formal legal allegation): from Anglo-Norman French and Old French *surmise*, feminine past participle of *surmettre* 'accuse,' from late Latin *supermittere* 'throw upon, put in afterwards, ' from *super-* 'over' + *mittere* 'send.'

---

sur·mount /sərmównt/ *v.tr.* overcome or get over (a difficulty or obstacle). **2** (usu. in *passive*) cap or crown. ◻◻ **sur·mount·a·ble** *adj.*

sur·name /sə́rnaym/ *n. & v.* •*n.* a hereditary name common to members of a family (*her surname is "Johnson"*). •*v.tr.* **1** give a surname to. **2** give (a person a surname). **3** (as **surnamed** *adj.*) having as a family name.

sur·pass /sərpás/ *v.tr.* **1** be greater or better than. **2** (as **surpassing** *adj.*) preeminent. ◻◻ **sur·pass·ing·ly** *adv.*

sur·plice /sə́rplis/ *n.* a loose white linen vestment worn over a cassock by clergy and choristers. ◻◻ **sur·pliced** *adj.*

sur·plus /sə́rpləs, –plus/ *n. & adj.* •*n.* **1** an amount left over. **2 a** an excess of revenue over expenditure. **b** the excess value of a company's assets over the face value of its stock. •*adj.* exceeding what is needed or used.

sur·prise /sərpríz/ *n. & v.* •*n.* **1** an unexpected or astonishing event or circumstance. **2** the emotion caused by this. **3** the act of catching a person, etc., unawares, or the process of being caught unawares. **4** (*attrib.*) unexpected (*a surprise visit*). •*v.tr.* **1** affect with surprise; turn out contrary to the expectations of (*your answer surprised me*). **2** (usu. in *passive*; foll. by *at*) shock (*I am surprised at you*). **3** capture or attack by surprise. **4** come upon (a person) unawares. **5** (foll. by *into*) startle (a person) by surprise into an action, etc. ◻ **take by surprise** affect with surprise, esp. by an unexpected encounter or statement. ◻◻ **sur·pris·ing** *adj.* **sur·pris·ing·ly** *adv.*

sur·ra /sŏŏrə/ *n.* a febrile disease transmitted by bites of flies and affecting horses and cattle in the tropics.

sur·re·al /sərēēəl/ *adj.* **1** having the qualities of surrealism. **2** strange; bizarre. ◻◻ **sur·re·al·i·ty** /–ree-álitee/ *n.* **sur·re·al·ly** *adv.*

sur·re·al·ism /sərēēəlizəm/ *n.* a 20th-c. movement in art and literature aiming at expressing the subconscious mind, e.g., by the irrational juxtaposition of images. ◻◻ **sur·re·al·ist** *n. & adj.* **sur·re·al·is·tic** *adj.* **sur·re·al·is·ti·cal·ly** *adv.*

sur·ren·der /səréndər/ *v. & n.* •*v.* **1** *tr.* hand over; relinquish possession of, give into another's power or control. **2** *intr.* **a** accept an enemy's demand for submission. **b** give oneself up; submit. **3** *intr. & refl.* (foll. by *to*) give oneself over to a habit, emotion, influence, etc. **4** *tr.* give up rights under (a life-insurance policy) in return for a smaller sum received immediately. •*n.* the act or an instance of surrendering.

sur·rep·ti·tious /sə́rəptíshəs/ *adj.* **1** covert; kept secret. **2** done by stealth; clandestine. ◻◻ **sur·rep·ti·tious·ly** *adv.* **sur·rep·ti·tious·ness** *n.*

sur·rey /sə́ree, súree/ *n.* (*pl.* **surreys**) a light four-wheeled carriage with two seats facing forward.

sur·ro·gate /sə́rəgət, –gayt, súr–/ *n.* a substitute, esp. for a person in a specific role or office. ◻◻ **sur·ro·ga·cy** *n.* **sur·ro·gate·ship** *n.*

sur·ro·gate moth·er *n.* **1** a person acting the role of mother. **2** a woman who bears a child on behalf of another woman, usu. from her own egg fertilized by the other woman's partner.

sur·round /sərównd/ *v. & n.* •*v.tr.* **1** come or be all around; encircle; enclose. **2** (in *passive*; foll. by *by, with*) have on all sides. •*n.* an area or substance surrounding something. ◻◻ **sur·round·ing** *adj.*

sur·round·ings /sərówndingz/ *n.pl.* the things in the neighborhood of, or the conditions affecting, a person or thing.

sur·tax /sə́rtaks/ *n. & v.* •*n.* an additional tax, esp. levied on incomes above a certain level. •*v.tr.* impose a surtax on.

sur·veil·lance /sərváyləns/ *n.* close observation, esp. of a suspected person.

sur·vey *v. & n.* •*v.tr.* /sərváy/ **1** take or present a general view of. **2** examine the condition of (a building, etc.). **3** determine the boundaries, ownership, etc., of (a district, etc.). •*n.* /sə́rvay/ **1** a general view or consideration of something. **2 a** the act of surveying opinions, etc. **b** the result or findings of this. **3** an inspection or investigation. **4** a map or plan made by surveying an area.

sur·vey·or /sərváyər/ *n.* **1** a person who surveys land and buildings, esp. professionally. **2** a person who carries out surveys.

sur·viv·al /sərvívəl/ *n.* **1** the process or an instance of surviving. **2** a person, thing, or practice that has remained from a former time. ◻ **survival of the fittest** the process or result of natural selection.

sur·viv·al·ism /sərvívəlizəm/ *n.* the practicing of outdoor survival skills as a sport or hobby. ◻◻ **sur·viv·al·ist** *adj. & n.*

sur·vi·val kit *n.* emergency rations, etc., esp. carried by military personnel, etc.

sur·vive /sərvív/ *v.* **1** *intr.* continue to live or exist. **2** *tr.* live or exist longer than. **3** *tr.* remain alive after or continue to exist in spite of (a danger, accident, etc.).

sur·vi·vor /sərvívər/ *n.* a person who survives or has survived.

sus·cep·ti·bil·i·ty /səséptibílitee/ *n.* (*pl.* **-ties**) **1** the state of being susceptible. **2** (in *pl.*) a person's sensitive feelings.

sus·cep·ti·ble /səséptibəl/ *adj.* **1** impressionable; sensitive; easily moved by emotion. **2** (*predic.*) **a** (foll. by *to*) liable or vulnerable to (*susceptible to pain*). **b** (foll. by *of*) admitting of (*facts not susceptible of proof*). ◻◻ **sus·cep·ti·bly** *adv.*

su·shi /sŏŏshee/ *n.* a Japanese dish of balls of cold rice flavored and garnished, esp. with raw fish or shellfish.

sus·pect *v., n., & adj.* •*v.tr.* /səspékt/ **1** have an impression of the existence or presence of. **2** (foll. by *to be*) believe tentatively, without clear ground. **3** (foll. by *that* + clause) be inclined to think. **4** (often foll. by *of*) be inclined to mentally accuse (*suspect him of complicity*). **5** doubt the genuineness or truth of. •*n.* /súspekt/ a suspected person. •*adj.* /súspekt/ subject to or deserving suspicion or distrust.

sus·pend /səspénd/ *v.tr.* **1** hang up. **2** keep inoperative or undecided for a time. **3** bar temporarily from a school, function, office, etc. **4** (as **suspended** *adj.*) (of solid particles or a body in a fluid medium) sustained somewhere between top and bottom.

sus·pend·ed an·i·ma·tion *n.* a temporary cessation of the vital functions without death.

sus·pend·er /səspéndər/ *n.* (in *pl.*) straps worn across the shoulders and supporting trousers.

sus·pense /səspéns/ *n.* a state of anxious uncertainty or expectation. ◻ **keep in suspense** delay informing (a person) of urgent information. ◻◻ **sus·pense·ful** *adj.*

sus·pen·sion /səspénshən/ *n.* **1** the act of suspending. **2** the means by which a vehicle is supported on its axles. **3** a substance consisting of particles suspended in a medium.

sus·pen·sion bridge *n.* a bridge with a roadway suspended from cables supported by structures at each end.

suspension bridge

sus·pi·cion /səspíshən/ *n.* **1** the feeling or thought of a person who suspects. **2** the act of suspecting. **3** (foll. by *of*) a slight trace of. □ **above suspicion** too obviously good, etc., to be suspected. **under suspicion** suspected.

sus·pi·cious /səspíshəs/ *adj.* **1** prone to or feeling suspicion. **2** indicating suspicion. **3** inviting suspicion. □□ **sus·pi·cious·ly** *adv.* **sus·pi·cious·ness** *n.*

suss /sus/ *v.* & *n.* (also **sus**) esp. *Brit. sl.* • *v.tr.* (**sussed, sussing**) **1** suspect of a crime. **2** (usu. foll. by *out*) **a** investigate; inspect. **b** work out; grasp (*he had the market sussed*). • *n.* **1** a suspect. **2** a suspicion; suspicious behavior. □ **on suss** on suspicion (of having committed a crime).

sus·tain /səstáyn/ *v.tr.* **1** support, bear the weight of, esp. for a long period. **2** encourage; support. **3** (of food) give nourishment to. **4** endure; stand. **5** undergo or suffer (defeat etc.). **6** (of a court, etc.) uphold (an objection, etc.). **7** substantiate (a statement or charge). **8** maintain or keep (a sound, effort, etc.) going continuously. **9** continue to represent (a part, character, etc.) adequately. □□ **sus·tain·a·ble** *adj.* **sus·tain·ed·ly** /–stáynidlee/ *adv.* **sus·tain·er** *n.* **sus·tain·ment** *n.*

sus·te·nance /sústinəns/ *n.* **1 a** nourishment; food. **b** the process of nourishing. **2** a means of support; a livelihood.

su·sur·ra·tion /so͞osəráyshən/ *n.* (also **su·sur·rus** /so͞osə́rəs/) *literary* a sound of whispering or rustling.

Su·tra /so͞otrə/ *n.* **1** an aphorism or set of aphorisms in Hindu literature. **2** a narrative part of Buddhist literature.

sut·tee /sutée, sútee/ *n.* (also **sa·ti**) (*pl.* **suttees** or **satis**) esp. *hist.* **1** the Hindu practice of a widow immolating herself on her husband's funeral pyre. **2** a widow who undergoes or has undergone this.

su·ture /so͞ochər/ *n.* & *v.* • *n.* **1** *Surgery* **a** the joining of the edges of a wound or incision by stitching. **b** the thread or wire used for this. **2** the seamlike junction of two bones, esp. in the skull. • *v.tr. Surgery* stitch up with a suture. □□ **su·tur·al** *adj.* **su·tured** *adj.*

SUV *abbr.* sport utility vehicle.

su·ze·rain /so͞ozərən, –rayn/ *n.* **1** a feudal overlord. **2** a sovereign state having some control over another state that is internally autonomous. □□ **su·ze·rain·ty** *n.*

s.v. *abbr.* (in a textual reference) under the word or heading given (from Latin *sub voce* or *sub verbo*).

svelte /svelt/ *adj.* slender; graceful.

SW *abbr.* (also **SW**) **1** southwest. **2** southwestern. **3** switch. **4** short wave.

swab /swob/ *n.* & *v.* (also **swob**) • *n.* **1** a mop or other absorbent device for cleaning or mopping up. **2 a** an absorbent pad used in surgery. **b** a specimen of a possibly morbid secretion taken with a swab for examination. • *v.tr.* (**swabbed, swabbing**) **1** clean with a swab. **2** (foll. by *up*) absorb (moisture) with a swab.

swad·dle /swód'l/ *v.tr.* swathe (esp. an infant) in garments or bandages, etc.

swag /swag/ *n.* & *v.* • *n.* **1** *sl.* **a** the booty carried off by burglars, etc. **b** illicit gains. **2 a** an ornamental festoon of flowers, etc. **b** a carved, etc., representation of this. **c** drapery of similar appearance. • *v.* (**swagged, swagging**) **1** *tr.* arrange (a curtain, etc.) in swags. **2** *intr.* **a** hang heavily. **b** sway from side to side. **3** *tr.* cause to sway or sag.

swag·ger /swágər/ *v.* & *n.* • *v.intr.* **1** walk arrogantly or self-importantly. **2** behave arrogantly; be domineering. • *n.* **1** a swaggering gait or manner. **2** swaggering behavior. **3** a dashing or confident air or way of doing something. □□ **swag·ger·er** *n.* **swag·ger·ing·ly** *adv.*

swag·ger stick *n.* a short cane carried by a military officer.

Swa·hi·li /swaahéelee/ *n.* (*pl.* same) **1** a member of a Bantu people of Zanzibar and adjacent coasts. **2** their language widely spoken in E. Africa.

swain /swayn/ *n.* **1** *archaic* a country youth. **2** *poet.* a young male lover or suitor.

swal·low[1] /swólō/ *v.* & *n.* • *v.* **1** *tr.* cause or allow (food, etc.) to pass down the throat. **2** *intr.* perform the muscular movement of the esophagus required to do this. **3** *tr.* **a** accept meekly. **b** accept credulously. **4** *tr.* resist the expression of (*swallow one's pride*). **5** *tr.* articulate (words, etc.) indistinctly. **6** *tr.* (often foll. by *up*) engulf or absorb; exhaust. • *n.* **1** the act of swallowing. **2** an amount swallowed in one action.

swal·low[2] /swólō/ *n.* any of various migratory swift-flying insect-eating birds of the family Hirundinidae, with a forked tail and long pointed wings.

swal·low·tail /swólōtayl/ *n.* **1** a deeply forked tail. **2** anything resembling this shape. **3** any butterfly of the family Papilionidae with wings extended at the back to this shape. □□ **swal·low-tailed** *adj.*

swam *past* of SWIM.

swa·mi /swáamee/ *n.* (*pl.* **swamis**) a Hindu male religious teacher.

swamp /swaamp/ *n.* & *v.* • *n.* a piece of waterlogged ground. • *v.* **1 a** *tr.* overwhelm or soak with water. **b** *intr.* become swamped. **2** *tr.* overwhelm with an excess or large amount of something. □□ **swamp·y** *adj.* (**swampier, swampiest**).

swan /swon/ *n.* a large water bird of the genus *Cygnus*, etc., having a long flexible neck, webbed feet, and in most species white plumage.

swan dive *n.* a dive with the arms outspread until close to the water.

swank /swangk/ *n.*, *v.*, & *adj. colloq.* • *n.* ostentation; swagger; bluff. • *v.intr.* behave with swank; show off. • *adj.* = SWANKY.

swank·y /swángkee/ *adj.* (**swankier, swankiest**) **1** ostentatiously smart or showy. **2** (of a person) boastful. □□ **swank·i·ly** *adv.*

swan·ner·y /swónəree/ *n.* (*pl.* **-ies**) a place where swans are bred.

swans·down /swónzdown/ *n.* **1** the fine down of a swan, used in trimming clothing, etc. **2** a kind of thick cotton cloth with a soft nap on one side.

swan song *n.* a person's last work or act before death or retirement, etc.

swap /swop/ *v.* & *n.* (also **swop**) • *v.tr.* & *intr.* (**swapped, swapping**) exchange (one thing for another). • *n.* **1** an act of swapping. **2** a thing suitable for swapping. □□ **swap·per** *n.*

swap meet *n.* **1** a gathering at which enthusiasts or collectors trade or exchange items of common interest (*a computer swap meet*). **2** a flea market.

sward /swawrd/ *n. literary* **1** an expanse of short grass. **2** turf. □□ **sward·ed** *adj.*

swarm[1] /swawrm/ *n.* & *v.* • *n.* **1** a cluster of bees leaving the hive with the queen to establish a new colony. **2** a large number of insects or birds moving in a cluster. **3** a large group of people, esp. moving over or filling a large area. **4** (in *pl.*; foll. by *of*) great numbers. •*v.intr.* **1** move in or form a swarm. **2** (foll. by *with*) (of a place) be overrun, crowded, or infested.

swarm[2] /swawrm/ *v.intr.* (foll. by *up*) & *tr.* climb (a rope or tree, etc.), esp. in a rush, by clasping or clinging with the hands and knees, etc.

swarth·y /swáwrthee/ *adj.* (**swarthier, swarthiest**) dark; dark-complexioned. ▫▫ **swarth·i·ly** *adv.* **swarth·i·ness** *n.*

swash·buck·ler /swóshbuklər/ *n.* **1** a swaggering bully or ruffian. **2** a dashing or daring adventurer, esp. in a novel, movie, etc. ▫▫ **swash·buck·ling** *adj. & n.*

swas·ti·ka /swóstikə/ *n.* **1** an ancient symbol formed by an equal-armed cross with each arm continued at a right angle. **2** this with clockwise continuations as the symbol of Nazi Germany.

swat /swot/ *v. & n.* •*v.tr.* (**swatted, swatting**) **1** crush (a fly, etc.) with a sharp blow. **2** hit hard. •*n.* **1** a swatting blow. **2** a homerun in baseball.

swatch /swoch/ *n.* **1** a sample, esp. of cloth. **2** a collection of samples.

swath /swoth, swawth/ *n.* (also **swathe** /swoth, swayth/) (*pl.* **swaths** /swoths, swawths/ or **swathes** /swothz, swaythz/) **1** a ridge of grass or grain lying after being cut. **2** a space left clear after the passage of a mower. **3** a broad strip.

swathe /swoth, swayth/ *v. & n.* •*v.tr.* bind or enclose in bandages or garments, etc. •*n.* a bandage or wrapping.

swat·ter /swótər/ *n.* an implement for swatting flies.

sway /sway/ *v. & n.* •*v.* **1** *intr. & tr.* lean or cause to lean unsteadily in different directions alternately. **2** *intr.* oscillate irregularly; waver. **3** *tr.* **a** control the motion or direction of. **b** have influence or rule over. •*n.* **1** rule, influence, or government (*hold sway*). **2** a swaying motion or position.

swear /swair/ *v.* (*past* **swore** /swor/; *past part.* **sworn** /sworn/) **1** *tr.* **a** (often foll. by *to* + infin. or *that* + clause) state or promise solemnly or on oath. **b** take (an oath). **2** *tr. colloq.* say emphatically. **3** *tr.* cause to take an oath (*swore them to secrecy*). **4** *intr.* (often foll. by *at*) use profane or indecent language. **5** *tr.* (often foll. by *against*) make a sworn affirmation of (*swear treason against*). **6** *intr.* (foll. by *by*) **a** appeal to as a witness in taking an oath (*swear by Almighty God*). **b** *colloq.* have or express great confidence in (*swears by yoga*). **7** *intr.* (foll. by *to*; usu. in *neg.*) admit the certainty of (*could not swear to it*). ▫ **swear in** induct into office, etc., by administering an oath. **swear off** *colloq.* promise to abstain from (drink, etc.). ▫▫ **swear·er** *n.*

sweat /swet/ *n. & v.* •*n.* **1** moisture exuded through the pores of the skin, esp. from heat or nervousness. **2** a state or period of sweating. **3** *colloq.* a state of anxiety (*in a sweat about it*). **4** *colloq.* **a** drudgery; effort. **b** a laborious task or undertaking. **5** condensed moisture on a surface. •*v.* (*past* and *past part.* **sweat** or **sweated**) **1** *intr.* exude sweat. **2** *intr.* be terrified, suffering, etc. **3** *intr.* (of a wall, etc.) exhibit surface moisture. **4** *intr.* drudge; toil. **5** *tr.* heat (meat or vegetables) slowly in fat or water to extract the juices. **6** *tr.* emit (blood, gum, etc.) like sweat. **7** *tr.* make (a horse, athlete, etc.) sweat by exercise. **8** *tr.* (as **sweat** *adj.*) (of goods, workers, or labor) produced by or subjected to long hours under poor conditions. ▫ **by the sweat of one's brow** by one's own hard work. **no sweat** *colloq.* there is no need to worry. **sweat blood** *colloq.* **1** work strenuously. **2** be extremely anxious. **sweat it out** *colloq.* endure a difficult experience to the end.

sweat·band /swétband/ *n.* a band of absorbent material inside a hat or around a wrist, etc., to soak up sweat.

sweat·er /swétər/ *n.* a knitted jersey, pullover, or cardigan.

sweat gland *n. Anat.* a spiral tubular gland below the skin that secretes sweat.

sweat·pants /swétpants/ *n.pl.* loose pants of absorbent cotton material worn for exercise, etc.

sweat·shirt /swétshərt/ *n.* a sleeved cotton pullover of absorbent material, as worn by athletes before and after exercise.

sweat·shop /swétshop/ *n.* a shop where employees work under poor conditions and for low wages.

sweat·y /swétee/ *adj.* (**sweatier, sweatiest**) **1** sweating; covered with sweat. **2** causing sweat. ▫▫ **sweat·i·ly** *adv.* **sweat·i·ness** *n.*

Swede /sweed/ *n.* **1** a native or national of Sweden. **2** a person of Swedish descent.

Swed·ish /sweédish/ *adj. & n.* •*adj.* of or relating to Sweden or its people or language. •*n.* the language of Sweden.

sweep /sweep/ *v. & n.* •*v.* (*past* and *past part.* **swept** /swept/) **1** *tr.* clean or clear (a room or area, etc.) with or as with a broom. **2** *intr.* (often foll. by *up*) clean a room, etc., in this way. **3** *tr.* (often foll. by *up*) collect or remove (dirt or litter, etc.) by sweeping. **4** *tr.* (foll. by *aside*, *away*, etc.) **a** push with or as with a broom. **b** dismiss or reject abruptly. **5** *tr.* (foll. by *along*, *down*, etc.) carry or drive along with force. **6** *tr.* (foll. by *off*, *away*, etc.) remove or clear forcefully. **7** *tr.* traverse swiftly or lightly. **8** *tr.* impart a sweeping motion to. **9** *tr.* swiftly cover or affect (*a new fashion swept the country*). **10** *intr.* **a** glide swiftly; speed along. **b** go majestically. •*n.* **1** the act or motion of sweeping. **2** a curve in the road, a sweeping line of a hill, etc. **3** range or scope (*beyond the sweep of the human mind*). **4** = CHIMNEY SWEEP. **5** a sortie by aircraft. **6** *colloq.* = SWEEPSTAKE. ▫ **make a clean sweep of 1** completely abolish or expel. **2** win all the prizes, etc., in (a competition, etc.). **sweep away 1** abolish swiftly. **2** (usu. in *passive*) powerfully affect, esp. emotionally. **sweep under the carpet** see CARPET.

sweep·er /sweépər/ *n.* **1** a person who cleans by sweeping. **2** a device for sweeping carpets, etc. **3** *Soccer* a defensive player positioned close to the goalkeeper.

sweep·ing /sweéping/ *adj. & n.* •*adj.* **1** wide in range or effect (*sweeping changes*). **2** taking no account of particular cases or exceptions (*a sweeping statement*). •*n.* (in *pl.*) dirt, etc., collected by sweeping.

sweep·stakes /sweépstayks/ *n.* **1** a form of gambling on horse races or other contests in which all competitors' stakes are divided among the winners. **2** a race or contest with betting of this kind. **3** a prize or prizes won in a sweepstakes.

sweet /sweet/ *adj.* **1** having the pleasant taste characteristic of sugar. **2** smelling pleasant like roses or perfume, etc. **3** (of sound, etc.) melodious or harmonious. **4 a** not salt, sour, or bitter. **b** fresh, with flavor unimpaired by rottenness. **c** (of water) fresh and readily drinkable. **5** highly gratifying or attractive. **6** amiable; pleasant (*has a sweet nature*). **7** *colloq.* (of a person or thing) pretty; charming; endearing. **8** (foll. by *on*) *colloq.* fond of; in love with. ▫▫ **sweet·ish** *adj.* **sweet·ly** *adv.* **sweet·ness** /sweétnis/ *n.*

sweet·bread /sweétbred/ *n.* the pancreas or thymus of an animal, esp. as food.

sweet·bri·er /sweétbrīər/ *n.* (also **sweet·bri·ar**) a wild rose, *Rosa eglanteria* of Europe and central Asia, with hooked thorns and small fragrant pink flowers.

sweet clo·ver *n.* a leguminous plant of the genus *Melilotus*, with trifoliate leaves, small flowers, and a scent of hay when dried.

sweet corn *n.* **1** a kind of corn with kernels having a high sugar content. **2** these kernels, eaten as a vegetable when young.

sweet·en /swe͞et'n/ *v.tr. & intr.* **1** make or become sweet or sweeter. **2** make agreeable or less painful. □ **sweeten the pill** see PILL. □□ **sweet·en·ing** *n.*

sweet·en·er /swe͞et'nər/ *n.* **1** a substance used to sweeten food or drink. **2** *colloq.* a bribe or inducement.

sweet·heart /swe͞et-haart/ *n.* **1** a lover or darling. **2** a term of endearment.

sweet·heart a·gree·ment *n.* (also **sweet·heart contract** or **deal**) *colloq.* an industrial agreement reached privately by employers and labor union representatives.

sweet·ie /swe͞etee/ *n. colloq.* **1** a sweetheart. **2** (also **sweet·ie-pie**) a term of endearment.

sweet·ness /swe͞etnis/ *n.* the quality of being sweet; fragrance, melodiousness, etc. □ **sweetness and light** a display of (esp. uncharacteristic) mildness and reason.

sweet pea *n.* any climbing plant of the genus *Lathyrus*, esp. *L. odoratus* with fragrant flowers in many colors.

sweet pep·per *n.* a small *Capsicum* pepper with a relatively mild taste.

sweet po·ta·to *n.* **1** a tropical climbing plant, *Ipomoea batatas*, with sweet tuberous roots used for food. **2** the root of this.

sweet talk *n. colloq.* flattery; blandishment. □□ **sweet-talk** *v.tr.*

sweet tooth *n.* a liking for sweet-tasting foods.

sweet wil·liam *n.* a plant, *Dianthus barbatus*, with clusters of vivid fragrant flowers.

swell /swel/ *v., n., & adj.* • *v.* (*past part.* **swollen** /swṓlən/ or **swelled**) **1** *intr. & tr.* grow or cause to grow bigger or louder or more intense. **2** *intr.* (often foll. by *up*) & *tr.* rise or raise up from the surrounding surface. **3** *intr.* (foll. by *out*) bulge. **4** *intr.* (of the heart) feel full of joy, pride, relief, etc. **5** *intr.* (foll. by *with*) be hardly able to restrain (pride, etc.). • *n.* **1** an act or the state of swelling. **2** the heaving of the sea with waves that do not break. **3 a** a crescendo. **b** a mechanism in an organ, etc., for obtaining a crescendo or diminuendo. **4** *colloq.* a person of dashing or fashionable appearance. • *adj. colloq.* **1** fine; splendid; excellent. **2** smart, fashionable. □□ **swell·ish** *adj.*

swelled (or **swol·len**) **head** *n. colloq.* conceit.

swell·ing /swéling/ *n.* an abnormal protuberance on or in the body.

swel·ter /swéltər/ *v. & n.* • *v.intr.* be uncomfortably hot. • *n.* a sweltering atmosphere or condition. □□ **swel·ter·ing·ly** *adv.*

swept *past* and *past part.* of SWEEP.

swerve /swərv/ *v. & n.* • *v.intr. & tr.* change or cause to change direction, esp. abruptly. • *n.* **1** a swerving movement. **2** divergence from a course.

swift /swift/ *adj., adv., & n.* • *adj.* **1** quick; rapid. **2** speedy; prompt (*was swift to act*). • *adv.* (*archaic* except in *comb.*) swiftly (*swift-moving*). • *n.* any swift-flying insect-eating bird of the family Apodidae, with long wings and a superficial resemblance to a swallow. □□ **swift·ly** *adv.* **swift·ness** *n.*

swig /swig/ *v. & n. colloq.* • *v.tr. & intr.* (**swigged, swigging**) drink in large swallows. • *n.* a swallow of drink, esp. a large amount. □□ **swig·ger** *n.*

swill /swil/ *v. & n.* • *v. tr. & intr.* drink greedily. • *n.* **1** mainly liquid refuse as pig food. **2** inferior liquor. □□ **swill·er** *n.*

swim /swim/ *v. & n.* • *v.* (**swimming**; *past* **swam** /swam/; *past part.* **swum** /swum/) **1** *intr.* propel the body through water by working the arms and legs, or (of a fish) the fins and tail. **2** *tr.* **a** traverse by swimming. **b** compete in (a race) by swimming. **c** use (a particular stroke) in swimming. **3** *intr.* float on or at the surface of a liquid. **4** *intr.* appear to undulate or reel or whirl. **5** *intr.* have a dizzy effect or sensation. **6** *intr.* (foll. by *in, with*) be flooded. • *n.* **1** a spell or the act of swimming. **2** a deep pool frequented by fish in a river. □ **in the swim** involved in or acquainted with what is going on. □□ **swim·ma·ble** *adj.* **swim·mer** *n.*

swim blad·der *n.* a gas-filled sac in fishes used to maintain buoyancy.

swim·ming·ly /swíminglee/ *adv.* with easy and unobstructed progress.

swim·ming pool *n.* an indoor or outdoor pool for swimming.

swim·suit /swímso͞ot/ *n.* garment worn for swimming. □□ **swim·suit·ed** *adj.*

swim·wear /swímwair/ *n.* clothing worn for swimming.

swin·dle /swínd'l/ *v. & n.* • *v.tr.* (often foll. by *out of*) **1** cheat (a person) of money, possessions, etc. **2** cheat a person of (money, etc.) (*swindled all his savings out of him*). • *n.* **1** an act of swindling. **2** a person or thing represented as what it is not. **3** a fraudulent scheme. □□ **swin·dler** *n.*

swine /swīn/ *n.* (*pl.* same) **1** a pig. **2** *colloq.* (*pl.* **swine** or **swines**) **a** a term of contempt or disgust for a person. **b** a very unpleasant or difficult thing. □□ **swin·ish** *adj.* (esp. in sense 2). **swin·ish·ly** *adv.* **swin·ish·ness** *n.*

swine·herd /swínhərd/ *n.* a person who tends pigs.

swing /swing/ *v. & n.* • *v.* (*past* and *past part.* **swung** /swung/) **1** *intr. & tr.* move or cause to move with a to-and-fro or curving motion, as of an object attached at one end and hanging free at the other. **2** *intr. & tr.* **a** sway. **b** hang so as to be free to sway. **c** oscillate or cause to oscillate. **3** *intr. & tr.* revolve or cause to revolve. **4** *intr.* move by gripping something and leaping, etc. **5** *intr.* go with a swinging gait. **6** *intr.* (foll. by *around*) move around to the opposite direction. **7** *intr.* change from one opinion or mood to another. **8** *intr.* (foll. by *at*) attempt to hit or punch. **9 a** *intr.* (also **swing it**) play music with a swing. **b** *tr.* play (a tune) with swing. **10** *intr. colloq.* **a** be lively or up to date; enjoy oneself. **b** be promiscuous. **11** *intr. colloq.* (of a party, etc.) be lively, etc. **12** *tr.* have a decisive influence on (esp. voting, etc.). **13** *tr. colloq.* deal with or achieve. **14** *intr. colloq.* be executed by hanging. • *n.* **1** the act or an instance of swinging. **2** the motion of swinging. **3** the extent of swinging. **4** a swinging or smooth gait or rhythm or action. **5 a** a seat slung by ropes or chains, etc., for swinging on or in. **b** a spell of swinging on this. **6** an easy but vigorous continued action. **7 a** jazz or dance music with an easy flowing rhythm. **b** the rhythmic feeling or drive of this music. **8** a discernible change in opinion, esp. the amount by which votes change from one side to another. □□ **swing·er** *n.* (esp. in sense 10 of *v.*).

swing bridge *n.* a bridge that can be swung to one side to allow the passage of ships.

swinge /swinj/ *v.tr.* (**swingeing**) *archaic* strike hard; beat.

swing·ing /swínging/ *adj.* **1** (of gait, melody, etc.) vigorously rhythmical. **2** *colloq.* **a** lively; up to date. **b** promiscuous. □□ **swing·ing·ly** *adv.*

swing shift *n.* a work shift from afternoon to late evening.

swing wing *n.* an aircraft wing that can move from a right-angled to a swept-back position.

swing·y /swíngee/ *adj.* (**swingier, swingiest**) **1** (of music) characterized by swing (see SWING *n.* 7). **2** (of a skirt or dress) designed to swing with body movement.

swipe /swīp/ *v. & n. colloq.* • *v.* **1** *tr. &* (often foll. by *at*) *intr.* hit hard and recklessly. **2** *tr.* steal. **3** *tr.* run (a credit card, etc.) through an electronic card reader. • *n.* a reckless hard hit or attempted hit. □□ **swip·er** *n.*

swirl /swərl/ *v. & n.* • *v.intr. & tr.* move or flow or carry along with a whirling motion. • *n.* **1** a swirling motion of or in water, air, etc. **2** the act of swirling. **3** a twist or curl, esp. as part of a pattern or design. ▫▫ **swirl·y** *adj.*

swish /swish/ *v., n., & adj.* •*v.* **1** *tr.* swing (a scythe or stick, etc.) audibly through the air, grass, etc. **2** *intr.* move with or make a swishing sound. **3** *tr.* (foll. by *off*) cut (a flower, etc.) in this way. •*n.* a swishing action or sound. •*adj. colloq.* smart, fashionable. ▫▫ **swish·y** *adj.*

Swiss /swis/ *adj. & n.* •*adj.* of or relating to Switzerland in Western Europe or its people. •*n.* (*pl.* same) **1** a native or inhabitant of Switzerland. **2** a person of Swiss descent.

Swiss cheese *n.* a type of hard cheese with large holes that form during ripening.

switch /swich/ *n. & v.* •*n.* **1** a device for making and breaking the connection in an electric circuit. **2 a** a transfer, change-over, or deviation. **b** an exchange. **3** a slender flexible shoot cut from a tree. **4** a light tapering rod. **5** a device at the junction of railroad tracks for transferring a train from one track to another. **6** a tress of false or detached hair tied at one end used in hairdressing. •*v.* **1** *tr.* (foll. by *on, off*) turn (an electrical device) on or off. **2** *intr.* change or transfer position, subject, etc. **3** *tr.* change or transfer. **4** *tr.* reverse the positions of; exchange. **5** *tr.* beat or flick with a switch. ▫ **switch off** *colloq.* cease to pay attention. **switch over** change or exchange. ▫▫ **switch·er** *n.*

switch·back /swíchbak/ *n.* (often *attrib.*) a railroad or road with alternate sharp ascents and descents.

switch·blade /swíchblayd/ *n.* a pocket knife with the blade released by a spring.

switch·board /swíchbawrd/ *n.* an apparatus for varying connections between electric circuits, esp. for completing telephone calls.

switch hit·ter *n. Baseball* a batter able to hit right-handed or left-handed.

swiv·el /swívəl/ *n. & v.* •*n.* a coupling between two parts enabling one to revolve without turning the other. •*v.tr. & intr.* (**swiveled, swiveling** or **swivelled, swivelling**) turn on or as on a swivel.

swiz·zle stick *n.* a stick used for stirring drinks.

swob var. of SWAB.

swol·len *past part.* of SWELL.

swoon /swo͞on/ *v. & n. literary* •*v.intr.* faint. •*n.* an occurrence of fainting.

swoop /swo͞op/ *v. & n.* •*v.* **1** *intr.* (often foll. by *down*) descend rapidly like a bird of prey. **2** *intr.* (often foll. by *on*) make a sudden attack. **3** *tr.* (often foll. by *up*) *colloq.* snatch the whole of at one swoop. •*n.* a swooping or snatching movement or action. ▫ **at** (or **in**) **one fell swoop** see FELL[4].

swoosh /swo͞osh/ *n.* the noise of a sudden rush of liquid, air, etc.

swop var. of SWAP.

sword /sawrd/ *n.* **1** a weapon usu. of metal with a long blade and hilt with a handguard. **2** (prec. by *the*) **a** war. **b** military power. ▫ **put to the sword** kill, esp. in war.

sword·fish /sáwrdfish/ *n.* a large marine fish, *Xiphias gladius*, with an extended swordlike upper jaw.

sword of Dam·o·cles /dáməkleez/ *n.* an imminent danger.

sword·play /sáwrdplay/ *n.* **1** fencing. **2** repartee; cut-and-thrust argument.

swords·man /sáwrdzmən/ *n.* (*pl.* **-men**) a person of (usu. specified) skill with a sword. ▫▫ **swords·man·ship** *n.*

sword·stick /sáwrdstik/ *n.* a hollow walking stick containing a blade that can be used as a sword.

sword·tail /sáwrdtayl/ *n.* **1** a tropical fish, *Xiphophorus helleri*, with a long tail. **2** = HORSESHOE CRAB.

swore *past* of SWEAR.

sworn /swawrn/ *past part.* of SWEAR. *adj.* bound by or as by an oath (*sworn enemies*).

swum *past part.* of SWIM.

swung *past* and *past part.* of SWING.

syb·a·rite /síbərīt/ *n. & adj.* •*n.* a person who is self-indulgent or devoted to sensuous luxury. •*adj.* fond of luxury or sensuousness. ▫▫ **syb·a·rit·ic** /–rítik/ *adj.* **syb·a·rit·i·cal** *adj.* **syb·a·rit·i·cal·ly** *adv.* **syb·a·rit·ism** *n.*

syc·a·more /síkəmawr/ *n.* **1** any of several plane trees, esp. *Platanus occidentalis* of N. America, or its wood. **2** (in full **sycamore maple**) **a** a large maple, *Acer pseudoplatanus*, with winged seeds. **b** its wood.

syc·o·phant /síkəfant, síkə–/ *n.* a servile flatterer; a toady. ▫▫ **syc·o·phan·cy** *n.* **syc·o·phan·tic** /–fántik/ *adj.* **syc·o·phan·ti·cal·ly** *adv.*

syl- /sil/ *prefix* assim. form of SYN- before *l.*

syl·la·bar·y /síləberee/ *n.* (*pl.* **-ies**) a list of written characters representing syllables.

syl·la·bi *pl.* of SYLLABUS.

syl·lab·ic /silábik/ *adj.* of, relating to, or based on syllables. ▫▫ **syl·lab·i·cal·ly** *adv.*

syl·lab·i·ca·tion /silabikáyshən/ *n.* (also **syl·lab·i·fi·ca·tion** /–bifikáyshən/) division into or articulation by syllables. ▫▫ **syl·lab·i·fy** *v.tr.* (**-fies, -fied**).

syl·la·bize /síləbīz/ *v.tr.* divide into or articulate by syllables.

syl·la·ble /síləbəl/ *n.* **1** a unit of pronunciation uttered without interruption, forming the whole or a part of a word and usu. having one vowel sound often with a consonant or consonants before or after. **2** a character or characters representing a syllable. **3** (usu. with *neg.*) the least amount of speech or writing (*did not utter a syllable*). ▫▫ **syl·la·bled** *adj.* (also in *comb.*).

syl·la·bub /síləbub/ *n.* (also **sil·la·bub**) a dessert made of cream or milk, flavored, sweetened, and whipped to thicken it.

syl·la·bus /síləbəs/ *n.* (*pl.* **syllabuses** or **syllabi** /–bī/) **1** the program or outline of a course of study, teaching, etc. **2** a statement of the requirements for a particular examination.

syl·lep·sis /silépsis/ *n.* (*pl.* **syllepses** /–seez/) a figure of speech in which a word is applied to two others in different senses (e.g., *caught the train and a bad cold*) or to two others of which it grammatically suits one only (e.g., *neither they nor it is working*). ▫▫ **syl·lep·tic** *adj.* **syl·lep·ti·cal·ly** *adv.*

syl·lo·gism /síləjizəm/ *n.* a form of reasoning in which a conclusion is drawn from two given or assumed propositions (premises). ▫▫ **syl·lo·gis·tic** *adj.*

syl·lo·gize /síləjīz/ *v.* **1** *intr.* use syllogisms. **2** *tr.* put (facts or an argument) in the form of syllogism.

sylph /silf/ *n.* **1** an elemental spirit of the air. **2** a slender graceful woman or girl. ▫▫ **sylph·like** *adj.*

syl·van /sílvən/ *adj.* (also **sil·van**) **1 a** of the woods. **b** having woods. **2** rural.

syl·vi·cul·ture var. of SILVICULTURE.

sym. *abbr.* **1** symbol. **2** symphony.

sym- /sim/ *prefix* assim. form of SYN- before *b, m, p.*

sym·bi·ont /símbeeont, –ənt/ *n.* an organism living in symbiosis.

sym·bi·o·sis /símbee-ósis, –bī–/ *n.* (*pl.* **symbioses** /–seez/) **1 a** an interaction between two different organisms living in close physical association, usu. to the advantage of both. **b** an instance of this. **2 a** a mutually advantageous association or relationship between persons. **b** an instance of this. ▫▫ **sym·bi·ot·ic** /–bīótik/ *adj.* **sym·bi·ot·i·cal·ly** /–bīótikəlee/ *adv.*

sym·bol /símbəl/ *n.* **1** a thing conventionally regarded as typifying, representing, or recalling something, esp. an idea or quality. **2** a mark or character taken as the conventional sign of some object, idea, function, or process. ▫▫ **sym·bol·o·gy** /–bóləjee/ *n.*

sym·bol·ic /simbólik/ *adj.* (also **sym·bol·i·cal** /–bólikəl/) **1** of or serving as a symbol. **2** involving the use of symbols or symbolism. ▫▫ **sym·bol·i·cal·ly** *adv.*

sym·bol·ism /símbəlizəm/ *n.* **1 a** the use of symbols to represent ideas. **b** symbols collectively. **2** an artistic and poetic movement or style using symbols and indirect suggestion to express ideas, emotions, etc. ▫▫ **sym·bol·ist** *n.*

sym·bol·ize /símbəlīz/ *v.tr.* **1** be a symbol of. **2** represent by means of symbols. ▫▫ **sym·bol·i·za·tion** *n.*

sym·me·try /símitree/ *n.* (*pl.* **-tries**) **1 a** correct proportion of the parts of a thing. **b** beauty resulting from this. **2 a** a structure that allows an object to be divided into parts of an equal shape and size. **b** the possession of such a structure. **c** approximation to such a structure. **3** the repetition of exactly similar parts facing each other or a center. ▫▫ **sym·met·ric** /simétrik/ *adj.* **sym·met·ri·cal** *adj.* **sym·met·ri·cal·ly** *adv.*

sym·pa·thet·ic /símpəthétik/ *adj.* **1** of, showing, or expressing sympathy. **2** due to sympathy. **3** likable or capable of evoking sympathy. **4** (of a person) friendly and cooperative. **5** (foll. by *to*) inclined to favor (*sympathetic to the idea*). **6 a** designating the part of the nervous system consisting of nerves leaving the thoracic and lumbar regions of the spinal cord and connecting with the nerve cells in or near the viscera. **b** (of a nerve or ganglion) belonging to this system. ▫▫ **sym·pa·thet·i·cal·ly** *adv.*

sym·pa·thize /símpəthīz/ *v.intr.* (often foll. by *with*) **1** feel or express sympathy. **2** agree with a sentiment or opinion. ▫▫ **sym·pa·thiz·er** *n.*

sym·pa·thy /símpəthee/ *n.* (*pl.* **-thies**) **1 a** the state of being simultaneously affected with the same feeling as another. **b** the capacity for this. **2** (often foll. by *with*) **a** the act of sharing or tendency to share in an emotion or sensation or condition of another person or thing. **b** (in *sing.* or *pl.*) compassion or commiseration; condolences. **3** (often foll. by *for*) approval. **4** (in *sing.* or *pl.*; often foll. by *with*) agreement (with a person, etc.) in opinion or desire. **5** (*attrib.*) in support of another cause (*sympathy strike*). ▫ **in sympathy** (often foll. by *with*) having or showing or resulting from sympathy (with another).

sym·phon·ic /simfónik/ *adj.* (of music) relating to or having the form or character of a symphony. ▫▫ **sym·phon·i·cal·ly** *adv.*

sym·phon·ic po·em *n.* an extended orchestral piece, usu. in one movement, on a descriptive or rhapsodic theme.

sym·pho·ny /símfənee/ *n.* (*pl.* **-nies**) **1** an elaborate composition usu. for full orchestra, and in several movements. **2** = SYMPHONY ORCHESTRA.

sym·pho·ny or·ches·tra *n.* a large orchestra suitable for playing symphonies, etc.

sym·po·si·um /simpṓzeeəm/ *n.* (*pl.* **symposia** /–zeeə/) **1 a** a conference or meeting to discuss a particular subject. **b** a collection of essays or papers for this purpose. **2** a philosophical or other friendly discussion.

symp·tom /símptəm/ *n.* **1** *Med.* a change in the physical or mental condition of a person, regarded as evidence of a disorder. **2** a sign of the existence of something.

symp·to·mat·ic /símptəmátik/ *adj.* serving as a symptom. ▫▫ **symp·to·mat·i·cal·ly** *adv.*

symp·tom·a·tol·o·gy /símptəmətóləjee/ *n.* the branch of medicine concerned with the study and interpretation of symptoms.

syn. *abbr.* **1** synonym. **2** synonymous. **3** synonymy.

syn- /sin/ *prefix* with, together, alike.

syn·a·gogue /sínəgog/ *n.* **1** the house of worship where a Jewish congregation meets for religious observance and instruction. **2** the assembly itself. ▫▫ **syn·a·gog·al** /–gógəl/ *adj.* **syn·a·gog·i·cal** /–gójikəl/ *adj.*

syn·apse /sínaps, sináps/ *n. Anat.* a junction of two nerve cells.

syn·ap·sis /sinápsis/ *n.* (*pl.* **synapses** /–seez/) **1** *Anat.* = SYNAPSE. **2** *Biol.* the fusion of chromosome pairs at the start of meiosis. ▫▫ **syn·ap·tic** /–náptik/ *adj.* **syn·ap·ti·cal·ly** *adv.*

sync /singk/ *n. & v.* (also **synch**) *colloq.* • *n.* synchronization. • *v.tr. & intr.* synchronize. ▫ **in** (or **out of**) **sync** (often foll. by *with*) harmonizing or agreeing well (or badly).

syn·car·pous /sinkaárpəs/ *adj.* (of a flower or fruit) having the carpels united.

synch var. of SYNC.

synchro- /síngkrō/ *comb. form* synchronized; synchronous.

syn·chro·mesh /síngkrōmesh/ *n. & adj.* • *n.* a system of changing gears, esp. in motor vehicles, in which the driving and driven gearwheels are made to revolve at the same speed during engagement. • *adj.* relating to or using this system.

syn·chron·ic /singkrónik/ *adj.* describing a subject (esp. a language) as it exists at one point in time. ▫▫ **syn·chron·i·cal·ly** *adv.*

syn·chro·nism /síngkrənizəm/ *n.* **1** = SYNCHRONY. **2** the process of synchronizing sound and picture in cinematography, television, etc. ▫▫ **syn·chro·nis·tic** *adj.* **syn·chro·nis·ti·cal·ly** *adv.*

syn·chro·nize /síngkrənīz/ *v.* **1** *intr.* (often foll. by *with*) occur at the same time. **2** *tr.* cause to occur at the same time. **3** *tr.* carry out the synchronism of (a movie). **4** *tr.* ascertain or set forth the correspondence in the date of (events). **5 a** *tr.* cause (clocks, etc.) to show a standard or uniform time. **b** *intr.* (of clocks, etc.) be synchronized. ▫▫ **syn·chro·ni·za·tion** *n.* **syn·chro·niz·er** *n.*

syn·chro·nized swim·ming *n.* a form of swimming in which participants make coordinated leg and arm movements in time to music.

syn·chro·nous /síngkrənəs/ *adj.* (often foll. by *with*) existing or occurring at the same time. ▫▫ **syn·chro·nous·ly** *adv.*

syn·chro·tron /síngkrətron/ *n. Physics* a cyclotron in which the magnetic field strength increases with the energy of the particles to keep their orbital radius constant.

syn·cline /síngklīn/ *n.* a rock bed forming a trough. ▫▫ **syn·cli·nal** *adj.*

syn·co·pate /síngkəpayt/ *v.tr.* **1** *Mus.* displace the beats or accents in (a passage) so that strong beats become weak and vice versa. **2** shorten (a word) by dropping interior sounds or letters. ▫▫ **syn·co·pa·tion** /–páyshən/ *n.* **syn·co·pa·tor** *n.*

syn·co·pe /síngkəpee/ *n.* **1** *Gram.* the omission of interior sounds or letters in a word. **2** *Med.* a temporary loss of consciousness caused by a fall in blood pressure. ▫▫ **syn·co·pal** *adj.*

syn·cre·tism /síngkrətizəm/ *n.* **1** *Philos.* & *Theol.* the process or an instance of syncretizing (see SYNCRETIZE). **2** *Philol.* the merging of different inflectional varieties in the development of a language. ▫▫ **syn·cret·ic** /; n-krétik/ *adj.* **syn·cre·tist** *n.* **syn·cre·tis·tic** /–krətístik/ *adj.*

syn·cre·tize /síngkrətīz/ *v.tr. Philos. & Theol.* attempt, esp. inconsistently, to unify or reconcile differing schools of thought. ▫▫ **syn·cret·ic** /–krétik/ *adj.* **syn·cre·tism** /síngkrətizəm/ *n.* **syn·cre·tist** *n.*

syn·di·cal·ism /síndikəlizəm/ *n. hist.* a movement for transferring the ownership and control of the means of production and distribution to workers' unions. ▫▫ **syn·di·cal·ist** *n.*

1 make a synthesis of. **2** combine into a coherent whole.

syn·di·cate *n. & v.* •*n.* /síndikət/ **1** a combination of individuals or commercial firms united to promote some common interest. **2** an agency supplying material simultaneously to a number of newspapers or periodicals. **3** a group of people who combine to buy or rent property, gamble, etc. **4** a committee of syndics. •*v.tr.* /síndikayt/ **1** form into a syndicate. **2** publish or broadcast (material) simultaneously in a number of newspapers, television stations, etc. (*her cartoon strip is syndicated in 1,400 newspapers*). ▫▫ **syn·di·ca·tion** /–káyshən/ *n.*

syn·drome /síndrōm/ *n.* **1** a group of concurrent symptoms of a disease. **2** a characteristic combination of opinions, behavior, etc.

syne /sīn/ *adv., conj., & prep. Sc.* since.

syn·ec·do·che /sinékdəkee/ *n.* a figure of speech in which a part is made to represent the whole or vice versa, as in *England lost by six wickets* (meaning "the English cricket team.") ▫▫ **syn·ec·doch·ic** /–dókik/ *adj.*

syn·e·col·o·gy /sinikóləjee/ *n.* the ecological study of plant or animal communities. ▫▫ **syn·ec·o·log·i·cal** /–kəlójikəl/ *adj.* **syn·e·col·o·gist** *n.*

syn·er·gism /sínərjizəm/ *n.* (also **syn·er·gy** /sínərjee/) the combined effect of drugs, organs, etc., that exceeds the sum of their individual effects. ▫▫ **syn·er·get·ic** /–jétik/ *adj.* **syn·er·gis·tic** *adj.* **syn·er·gis·ti·cal·ly** *adv.*

syn·er·gist /sínərjist/ *n.* a medicine or a bodily organ (e.g., a muscle) that cooperates with another or others.

syn·od /sínəd/ *n.* **1** an Episcopal council attended by delegated clergy and sometimes laity. **2** a Presbyterian ecclesiastical court above the presbyteries and subject to the General Assembly.

syn·od·ic /sinódik/ *adj. Astron.* relating to or involving the conjunction of stars, planets, etc.

syn·o·nym /sínənim/ *n.* a word or phrase that means exactly or nearly the same as another in the same language (e.g., *shut* and *close*). ▫▫ **syn·o·nym·i·ty** /–nímitee/ *n.*

syn·on·y·mous /sinónimәs/ *adj.* (often foll. by *with*) **1** having the same meaning; being a synonym (of). **2** suggestive of or associated with another (*excessive drinking regarded as synonymous with violence*). ▫▫ **syn·on·y·mous·ly** *adv.*

syn·on·y·my /sinónimee/ *n.* (*pl.* **-mies**) **1** the state of being synonymous. **2** the collocation of synonyms for emphasis (e.g., *in any shape or form*).

syn·op·sis /sinópsis/ *n.* (*pl.* **synopses** /–seez/) **1** a summary or outline. **2** a brief general survey. ▫▫ **syn·op·size** *v.tr.*

syn·op·tic /sinóptik/ *adj. & n.* •*adj.* **1** of, forming, or giving a synopsis. **2** of the Synoptic Gospels. •*n.* **1** a Synoptic Gospel. **2** the writer of a Synoptic Gospel. ▫▫ **syn·op·ti·cal** *adj.* **syn·op·ti·cal·ly** *adv.*

syn·o·vi·a /sinṓveeə, sī–/ *n. Physiol.* a viscous fluid lubricating joints and tendon sheaths. ▫▫ **syn·o·vi·al** *adj.*

syn·tac·tic /sintáktik/ *adj.* of or according to syntax. ▫▫ **syn·tac·ti·cal** *adj.* **syn·tac·ti·cal·ly** *adv.*

syn·tax /síntaks/ *n.* **1** the grammatical arrangement of words, showing their connection and relation. **2** a set of rules for or an analysis of this.

syn·the·sis /sínthisis/ *n.* (*pl.* **syntheses** /–seez/) **1** the process or result of building up separate elements, esp. ideas, into a connected whole, esp. into a theory or system. **2** a combination or composition. **3** *Chem.* the artificial production of compounds from their constituents, as distinct from extraction from plants, etc. **4** the surgical joining of divided parts. ▫▫ **syn·the·sist** *n.*

syn·the·size /sínthisīz/ *v.tr.* (also **syn·the·tize** /–tīz/) **1** make a synthesis of. **2** combine into a coherent whole.

syn·the·siz·er /sínthisīzər/ *n.* an electronic musical instrument, esp. operated by a keyboard, producing a wide variety of sounds by generating and combining signals of different frequencies.

syn·thet·ic /sinthétik/ *adj. & n.* •*adj.* **1** made by chemical synthesis, esp. to imitate a natural product (*synthetic rubber*). **2** (of emotions, etc.) insincere. •*n. Chem.* a synthetic substance. ▫▫ **syn·thet·i·cal** *adj.* **syn·thet·i·cal·ly** *adv.*

syph·i·lis /sífilis/ *n.* a contagious venereal disease progressing from infection of the genitals to the bones, muscles, and brain. ▫▫ **syph·i·lit·ic** /–lítik/ *adj.*

sy·phon var. of SIPHON.

Syr·i·an /séereeən/ *n. & adj.* •*n.* **1** a native or inhabitant of the modern nation of Syria in the Middle East; a person of Syrian descent. **2** a native or inhabitant of the region of Syria in antiquity or later. •*adj.* of or relating to the region or state of Syria.

sy·rin·ga /siríngɡə/ *n.* **1** = MOCK ORANGE. **2** any plant of the genus *Syringa*, esp. the lilac.

sy·ringe /sirínj/ *n. & v.* •*n.* **1** *Med.* **a** a tube with a nozzle and piston or bulb for sucking in and ejecting liquid in a fine stream. **b** (in full **hypodermic syringe**) a similar device with a hollow needle for insertion under the skin. **2** any similar device used in cooking, etc. •*v.tr.* sluice or spray (the ear, a plant, etc.) with a syringe.

syr·up /sírəp, sə́r–/ *n.* (also **sir·up**) **1 a** a sweet sauce made by dissolving sugar in boiling water, often used for preserving fruit, etc. **b** a similar sauce of a specified flavor as a drink, medicine, etc. **2** the condensed juice of sugar cane or the sugar maple; molasses. **3** excessive sweetness of style or manner. ▫▫ **syr·up·y** *adj.*

sys·tal·tic /sistáltik, sistáwl–/ *adj.* (esp. of the heart) contracting and dilating rhythmically.

sys·tem /sístəm/ *n.* **1** a complex whole; a set of connected things or parts; an organized body of things. **2** a set of devices (e.g., pulleys) functioning together. **3** *Physiol.* **a** a set of organs in the body with a common structure or function. **b** the human or animal body as a whole. **4 a** method; considered principles of procedure. **b** classification. **5** orderliness. **6 a** a body of theory or practice relating to or prescribing a particular form of government, religion, etc. **b** (prec. by *the*) the prevailing political or social order. **7** a method of choosing one's procedure in gambling, etc. **8** *Computing* a group of related hardware units or programs or both. **9** a major group of geological strata (*the Devonian system*). ▫ **get a thing out of one's system** *colloq.* be rid of a preoccupation or anxiety.

sys·tem·at·ic /sístəmátik/ *adj.* **1** done or conceived according to a plan or system. **2** regular; deliberate (*a systematic liar*). ▫▫ **sys·tem·at·i·cal·ly** *adv.* **sys·tem·a·tist** /sístəmətist/ *n.*

sys·tem·at·ics /sístəmátiks/ *n.pl.* (usu. treated as *sing.*) the study or a system of classification; taxonomy.

sys·tem·a·tize /sístəmətīz/ *v.tr.* **1** make systematic. **2** devise a system for. ▫▫ **sys·tem·a·ti·za·tion** *n.* **sys·tem·a·tiz·er** *n.*

sys·tem·ic /sistémik/ *adj.* **1** *Physiol.* of or concerning the whole body (*systemic infection*). **2** (of an insecticide, etc.) entering the plant via the roots or shoots and passing through the tissues. ▫▫ **sys·tem·i·cal·ly** *adv.*

sys·tem·ize /sístəmīz/ *v.tr.* = SYSTEMATIZE. ▫▫ **sys·tem·i·za·tion** *n.* **sys·tem·iz·er** *n.*

sys·tems a·nal·y·sis *n.* the analysis of a complex process or operation in order to improve its efficiency, esp. by applying a computer system.

sys·to·le /sístəlee/ *n. Physiol.* the contraction of the heart, when blood is pumped into the arteries (cf. DIASTOLE). ▫▫ **sys·tol·ic** /sistólik/ *adj.*

T

T /tee/ *n.* (also **t**) (*pl.* **Ts** or **T's**) **1** the twentieth letter of the alphabet. **2** a T-shaped thing (esp. *attrib.*: *T-joint*). □ **to a T** exactly; to perfection.

't *pron. contr.* of IT[1] (*'tis*).

Ta *symb. Chem.* the element tantalum.

tab[1] /tab/ *n.* & *v.* • *n.* **1** a small flap or strip of material attached for grasping, fastening, or hanging up, or for identification. **2** *colloq.* a bill or check (*picked up the tab*). **3** a small or drawn-aside stage curtain. • *v.tr.* (**tabbed, tabbing**) provide with a tab or tabs. □ **keep tabs** (or **a tab**) **on** *colloq.* **1** keep account of. **2** have under observation.

tab[2] /tab/ *n.* **1 a** a device on a typewriter for advancing to a sequence of set positions in tabular work. **b** a programmable key on a computer keyboard that moves the cursor forward a designated number of spaces. **2** = TABULATOR 3.

Ta·bas·co /təbáskō/ *n. Trademark* a pungent pepper sauce made from the fruit of *Capsicum frutescens.*

tab·bou·leh /təbóōlə, –lee/ *n.* an Arabic vegetable salad made with cracked wheat.

tab·by /tábee/ *n.* (*pl.* **-bies**) **1** (in full **tabby cat**) **a** a gray, orange, or brownish cat mottled or streaked with dark stripes. **b** any domestic cat, esp. female. **2** a kind of watered silk. **3** a plain weave.

tab·er·nac·le /tábərnakəl/ *n.* **1** *hist.* a tent used as a sanctuary for the Ark of the Covenant by the Israelites during the Exodus. **2** *Eccl.* a canopied niche or receptacle esp. for the Eucharistic elements. **3** a place of worship, esp. in some Christian denominations. □□ **tab·er·nac·led** *adj.*

ta·bla /taáblə, túb–/ *n. Ind. Mus.* a pair of small drums played with the hands.

tab·la·ture /táblachər/ *n. Mus.* an early form of notation indicating fingering (esp. in playing the lute), rhythm, and features other than notes.

ta·ble /táybəl/ *n.* & *v.* • *n.* **1** a piece of furniture with a flat top and one or more legs, providing a level surface for eating, writing, or working at, playing games on, etc. **2** a flat surface serving a specified purpose (*altar table*; *bird table*). **3 a** food provided in a household (*keeps a good table*). **b** a group seated at a table for dinner, etc. **4 a** a set of facts or figures systematically displayed, esp. in columns (*a table of contents*). **b** matter contained in this. **c** = MULTIPLICATION TABLE. **5** a flat surface for working on or for machinery to operate on. **6 a** a slab of wood or stone, etc., for bearing an inscription. **b** matter inscribed on this. **7** = TABLELAND. • *v.tr.* **1** postpone consideration of (a matter). **2** *Brit.* bring forward for discussion or consideration at a meeting. □ **on the table** offered for discussion. **turn the tables** (often foll. by *on*) reverse one's relations (with), esp. by turning an inferior into a superior position (orig. in backgammon). **under the table** *colloq.* **1** drunk. **2** (esp. of a payment) covertly; secretly.

tab·leau /tabló, táblō/ *n.* (*pl.* **tableaux** /–lōz/) a picturesque presentation.

ta·ble·cloth /táybəlklawth, –kloth/ *n.* a cloth spread over the top of a table, esp. for meals.

ta·ble·land /táybəl-land/ *n.* an extensive elevated region with a level surface; a plateau.

ta·ble man·ners *n.pl.* decorum or correct behavior while eating.

ta·ble·spoon /táybəlspōōn/ *n.* **1** a large spoon for serving food. **2** an amount held by this. **3** a unit of measure equal to $^1/_2$ fl. oz. or 15 ml. □□ **ta·ble·spoon·ful** *n.* (*pl.* **-fuls**).

tab·let /táblit/ *n.* **1** a small measured and compressed amount of a substance, esp. of a medicine or drug. **2** a small flat piece of soap, etc. **3** a flat slab of stone or wood, esp. for display or an inscription. **4** a writing pad.

ta·ble ten·nis *n.* an indoor game based on tennis, played with paddles and a ball bounced on a table divided by a net.

ta·ble·top /táybəltop/ *n.* **1** the top or surface of a table. **2** (*attrib.*) that can be placed or used on a tabletop.

ta·ble·ware /táybəlwair/ *n.* dishes, plates, utensils, glasses, napkins, etc., for use at mealtimes.

tab·loid /tábloyd/ *n.* & *adj.* • *n.* **1** a newspaper, usu. popular in style with bold headlines and large photographs, having pages of half size. **2** anything in a compressed or concentrated form. • *adj.* printed on newsprint and folded once lengthwise so as to be read like a magazine.

ta·boo /təbóō, ta–/ *n., adj.,* & *v.* (also **ta·bu**) • *n.* (*pl.* **taboos** or **tabus**) **1** a system or the act of setting a person or thing apart as sacred or accursed. **2** a prohibition or restriction imposed by social custom. • *adj.* **1** avoided or prohibited, esp. by social custom (*taboo words*). **2** designated as sacred and prohibited. • *v.tr.* (**taboos, tabooed** or **tabus, tabued**) **1** put (a thing, practice, etc.) under taboo. **2** exclude or prohibit by authority or social influence.

ta·bor /táybər/ *n. hist.* a small drum, esp. one used to accompany a pipe.

ta·bu var. of TABOO.

tab·u·lar /tábyələr/ *adj.* **1** of or arranged in tables or lists. **2** broad and flat like a table. **3** (of a crystal) having two broad flat faces. **4** formed in thin plates. □□ **tab·u·lar·ly** *adv.*

tab·u·late /tábyəlayt/ *v.tr.* arrange (figures or facts) in tabular form. □□ **tab·u·la·tion** /–láyshən/ *n.*

tab·u·la·tor /tábyəlaytər/ *n.* **1** a person or thing that tabulates. **2** = TAB[2] 1. **3** *Computing* a machine that produces lists or tables from a data storage medium such as punched cards.

tach *n. colloq.* = TACHOMETER.

tach·ism /táshizəm/ *n.* (also **ta·chisme**) a form of action painting with dabs of color arranged randomly to evoke a subconscious feeling.

tacho- /tákō/ *comb. form* speed.

tach·o·graph /tákəgraf/ *n.* a device used esp. in heavy trucks and buses, etc., for automatically recording speed and travel time.

ta·chom·e·ter /təkómitər, ta–/ *n.* an instrument for measuring the rate of rotation of a shaft and hence the speed of an engine or the speed or velocity of a vehicle.

tachy- /tákee/ *comb. form* swift.

tach·y·car·di·a /tákikaárdeeə/ *n. Med.* an abnormally rapid heart rate.

ta·chym·e·ter /təkímitər, ta;n–/ *n.* **1** *Surveying* an instrument used to locate points rapidly. **2** a speed indicator.

tac·it /tásit/ *adj.* understood or implied without being stated (*tacit consent*). ▫▫ **tac·it·ly** *adv.*

tac·i·turn /tásitərn/ *adj.* reserved in speech; saying little; uncommunicative. ▫▫ **tac·i·tur·ni·ty** /–tə́rnitee/ *n.* **tac·i·turn·ly** *adv.*

tack[1] /tak/ *n. & v.* •*n.* **1** a small sharp broad-headed nail. **2** a pin used to attach papers, etc., to a bulletin board or other surface. **3** a long stitch used in fastening fabrics, etc., lightly or temporarily together. **4 a** the direction in which a ship moves as determined by the position of its sails and regarded in terms of the direction of the wind (*starboard tack*). **b** a temporary change of direction in sailing to take advantage of a side wind, etc. **5** a course of action or policy (*try another tack*). **6** a sticky condition of varnish, etc. •*v.* **1** *tr.* (often foll. by *down*, etc.) fasten with tacks. **2** *tr.* stitch (pieces of cloth, etc.) lightly together. **3** *tr.* (foll. by *to, on*) annex (a thing). **4** *intr.* **a** change a ship's course by turning its head to the wind (cf. WEAR[2]). **b** make a series of tacks. **5** *intr.* change one's conduct or policy, etc. ▫▫ **tack·er** *n.*

tack[2] /tak/ *n.* the saddle, bridle, etc., of a horse.

tack·le /tákəl/ *n. & v.* •*n.* **1** equipment for a task or sport (*fishing tackle*). **2** a mechanism, esp. of ropes, pulley blocks, hooks, etc., for lifting weights, managing sails, etc. (*block and tackle*). **3** a windlass with its ropes and hooks. **4** an act of tackling in football, etc. **5** *Football* **a** the position next to the end of the forward line. **b** the player in this position. •*v.tr.* **1** try to deal with (a problem or difficulty). **2** grapple with or try to overcome (an opponent). **3** enter into discussion with. **4** *Football* obstruct or seize and stop (a player running with the ball). **5** secure by means of tackle. ▫▫ **tack·ler** *n.* **tack·ling** *n.*

tack·le block *n.* a pulley over which a rope runs.

tack·y[1] /tákee/ *adj.* (**tackier, tackiest**) (of glue or paint, etc.) still slightly sticky after application. ▫▫ **tack·i·ness** *n.*

tack·y[2] /tákee/ *adj.* (**tackier, tackiest**) *colloq.* **1** showing poor taste or style. **2** shoddy or seedy. ▫▫ **tack·i·ly** *adv.* **tack·i·ness** *n.*

ta·co /taákō/ *n.* (*pl.* **-cos**) a tortilla filled with meat, cheese, lettuce, tomatoes, etc.

tact /takt/ *n.* **1** adroitness in dealing with others or with difficulties arising from personal feeling. **2** intuitive perception of the right thing to do or say.

tact·ful /táktfŏŏl/ *adj.* having or showing tact. ▫▫ **tact·ful·ly** *adv.* **tact·ful·ness** *n.*

tac·tic /táktik/ *n.* **1** a tactical maneuver. **2** = TACTICS.

tac·ti·cal /táktikəl/ *adj.* **1** of, relating to, or constituting tactics (*a tactical retreat*). **2** (of bombing or weapons) done or for use in immediate support of military or naval operations (opp. STRATEGIC). **3** adroitly planning or planned. ▫▫ **tac·ti·cal·ly** *adv.*

tac·tics /táktiks/ *n.pl.* **1** (also treated as *sing.*) the art of disposing armed forces esp. in contact with an enemy (cf. STRATEGY). **2 a** the plans and means adopted in carrying out a scheme or achieving some end. **b** a skillful device or devices. ▫▫ **tac·ti·cian** /taktíshən/ *n.*

tac·tile /táktəl, –tīl/ *adj.* **1** of or connected with the sense of touch. **2** perceived by touch. **3** tangible. ▫▫ **tac·tu·al** /tákchōōəl/ *adj.* (in senses 1, 2). **tac·til·i·ty** /–tílitee/ *n.*

tact·less /táktlis/ *adj.* having or showing no tact. ▫▫ **tact·less·ly** *adv.* **tact·less·ness** *n.*

tad /tad/ *n. colloq.* a small amount (often used adverbially: *a tad salty*).

tad·pole /tádpōl/ *n.* a larva of an amphibian, esp. a frog, toad, or newt, in its aquatic stage and breathing through gills.

tae kwon do /tī kwón dṓ/ *n.* a Korean martial art similar to karate.

taf·fe·ta /táfitə/ *n.* a fine lustrous silk or silklike fabric.

taf·fy /táfee/ *n.* (*pl.* **-fies**) **1** a chewy boiled sugar or molasses candy. **2** insincere flattery.

tag[1] /tag/ *n. & v.* •*n.* **1 a** a label, esp. one for tying on an object to show its address, price, etc. **b** *colloq.* an epithet or popular name serving to identify a person or thing. **2** a metal or plastic point at the end of a lace, etc., to assist insertion. **3** a loop at the back of a boot used in pulling it on. **4** a license plate of a motor vehicle. **5** a loose or ragged end of anything. **6** a ragged lock of wool on a sheep. **7** *Theatr.* a closing speech addressed to the audience. **8** a trite quotation or stock phrase. •*v.tr.* (**tagged, tagging**) **1** provide with a tag or tags. **2** (often foll. by *on, onto*) join or attach. **3** esp. *Brit. colloq.* follow closely or trail behind. **4** *Computing* identify (an item of data) by its type for later retrieval. **5** label radioactively (see LABEL *v.* 3). **6 a** find rhymes for (verses). **b** string (rhymes) together. **7** shear away tags from (sheep). **8** give a ticket to, as for a traffic or parking violation. ▫ **tag along** (often foll. by *with*) go along or accompany passively.

tag[2] /tag/ *n. & v.* •*n.* **1** a children's game in which one chases the rest, and anyone who is caught then becomes the pursuer. **2** *Baseball* the act of tagging a runner. •*v.tr.* (**tagged, tagging**) **1** touch in a game of tag. **2** (often foll. by *out*) put (a runner) out by touching with the ball or with the hand holding the ball.

Ta·ga·log /təgaáləg, -lawg/ *n. & adj.* •*n.* **1** a member of the principal people of the Philippine Islands. **2** the language of this people. •*adj.* of or relating to this people or language.

Ta·hi·tian /təheéshən/ *n. & adj.* •*n.* **1** a native or inhabitant of Tahiti in the S. Pacific. **2** the language of Tahiti. •*adj.* of or relating to Tahiti or its people or language.

t'ai chi ch'uan /tī chee chwaán/ *n.* (also **t'ai chi**) a Chinese martial art and system of calisthenics consisting of sequences of very slow controlled movements.

t'ai chi ch'uan Chinese, literally 'great ultimate boxing', from *tài* 'extreme' + *ji* 'limit' + *quán* 'fist, boxing.' In Taoism *t'ai chi* denoted the ultimate point, both source and limit, of the life force; t'ai chi ch'uan, believed to have been developed by a Taoist priest, is intended as a spiritual as well as physical exercise.

tai·ga /tígə/ *n.* coniferous forest lying between tundra and steppe, esp. in Siberia.

tail /tayl/ *n. & v.* •*n.* **1** the hindmost part of an animal, esp. when prolonged beyond the rest of the body. **2 a** a thing like a tail in form or position, esp. something extending downward or outward at an extremity. **b** the rear end of anything, e.g., of a procession. **c** a long train or line of people, vehicles, etc. **3 a** the rear part of an airplane, with the horizontal stabilizer and rudder, or of a rocket. **b** the rear part of a motor vehicle. **4** the luminous trail of particles following a comet. **5** the inferior or weaker part of anything, esp. in a sequence. **6 a** the part of a shirt below the waist. **b** the hanging part of the back of a coat. **7** (in *pl.*) *colloq.* **a** a tailcoat. **b** evening dress including this. **8** (in *pl.*) the reverse of a coin as a choice when tossing. **9** *colloq.* a person following or shadowing another. **10** an extra strip attached to the lower end of a kite. **11** the stem of a note in music. **12** the lower part of a letter (e.g., *y, q,* or *g*. **13 a** the exposed end of a slate or tile in a roof. **b** the unexposed end of a brick or stone in a wall. **14 a** the buttocks. **b** *sl. offens.* a (usu. female) sexual partner. •*v.* **1** *tr.* remove the stalks of (fruit). **2** *tr. &* (foll. by *after*) *intr. colloq.* shadow or follow closely. **3** *tr.* provide with a tail. **4** *tr.* dock the tail of (a lamb, etc.). **5** *tr.* (often foll. by *onto*) join (one thing to another).

□ **on a person's tail** closely following a person. **tail off** (or **away**) **1** become fewer, smaller, or fainter. **2** fall behind or away in a scattered line. **with one's tail between one's legs** in a state of dejection or humiliation. **with one's tail up** in good spirits; cheerful. □□ **tailed** *adj.* (also in *comb.*). **tail·less** *adj.*

tail·back /táylbak/ *n. Football* on offense, a player positioned behind the quarterback.

tail·coat /táylkōt/ *n.* a man's morning or evening coat with a long skirt divided at the back into tails and cut away in front, worn as part of formal dress.

tail cov·ert *n.* any of the feathers covering the base of a bird's tail feathers.

tail·gate /táylgayt/ *n. & v.* • *n.* **1 a** a hinged or removable flap at the rear of a station wagon, truck, etc. **b** the tail door of a station wagon or hatchback. **2** the lower end of a canal lock. • *v. colloq.* **1** *intr.* drive too closely behind another vehicle. **2** *tr.* follow (a vehicle) too closely. □□ **tail·gat·er** *n.*

tail·light /táyllīt/ *n.* a usu. red light at the rear of a train, motor vehicle, or bicycle.

tai·lor /táylər/ *n. & v.* • *n.* a maker of clothes, esp. one who makes men's outer garments to measure. • *v.* **1** *tr.* make (clothes) as a tailor. **2** *tr.* make or adapt for a special purpose. **3** *intr.* work as or be a tailor. **4** *tr.* (esp. as **tailored** *adj.*) make clothes for. **5** *tr.* (as **tailored** *adj.*) = TAILOR-MADE. □□ **tai·lor·ing** *n.*

tai·lored /táylərd/ *adj.* (of clothing) well or closely fitted.

tai·lor-made *adj. & n.* • *adj.* **1** (of clothing) made to order by a tailor. **2** made or suited for a particular purpose (*a job tailor-made for me*). • *n.* a tailor-made garment.

tail·piece /táylpees/ *n.* **1** an appendage at the rear of anything. **2** the final part of a thing. **3** a decoration in a blank space at the end of a chapter, etc., in a book.

tail·pipe /táylpīp/ *n.* the rear section of the exhaust pipe of a motor vehicle.

tail·spin /táylspin/ *n. & v.* • *n.* **1** a spin (see SPIN *n.* 2) by an aircraft with the tail spiraling. **2** a state of chaos or panic. • *v.intr.* (**-spinning**; *past* and *past part.* **-spun**) perform a tailspin.

tail wind *n.* a wind blowing in the direction of travel of a vehicle or aircraft, etc.

taint /taynt/ *n. & v.* • *n.* **1** a spot or trace of decay, infection, or some bad quality. **2** a corrupt condition or infection. • *v.* **1** *tr.* affect with a taint. **2** *tr.* (foll. by *with*) affect slightly. **3** *intr.* become tainted. □□ **taint·less** *adj.*

tai·pan /tīpán/ *n.* the head of a foreign business in China.

take /tayk/ *v. & n.* • *v.* (**took** /tŏŏk/; **taken** /táykən/) **1** *tr.* lay hold of; get into one's hands. **2** *tr.* acquire; get possession of; capture, earn, or win. **3** *tr.* get the use of by purchase or formal agreement (*take an apartment*). **4** *tr.* (in a recipe) avail oneself of; use. **5** *tr.* use as a means of transport (*took a taxi*). **6** *tr.* regularly buy or subscribe to (a particular newspaper or periodical, etc.). **7** *tr.* obtain after fulfilling the required conditions (*take a degree*). **8** *tr.* occupy (*take a chair*). **9** *tr.* make use of (*take precautions*). **10** *tr.* consume as food or medicine (*took the pills*). **11** *intr.* **a** be successful or effective (*the inoculation did not take*). **b** (of a plant, seed, etc.) begin to grow. **12** *tr.* **a** require or use up (*will only take a minute*; *these things take time*). **b** accommodate; have room for (*the elevator takes three people*). **13** *tr.* cause to come or go with one; convey (*take the book home*; *the bus will take you all the way*). **14** *tr.* **a** remove; dispossess a person of (*someone has taken my pen*). **b** destroy; annihilate (*took her own life*). **c** (often foll. by *for*) *sl.* defraud; swindle. **15** *tr.* catch or be infected with (fire or fever, etc.). **16** *tr.* **a** experience or be affected by (*take fright*; *take pleasure*). **b** give play to (*take comfort*). **c** exert (*take courage*; *take no notice*). **d** exact; get (*take revenge*). **17** *tr.* find out and note (a name and address; a person's temperature, etc.) by inquiry or measurement. **18** *tr.* grasp mentally; understand (*I take your point*). **19** *tr.* treat or regard in a specified way (*took the news calmly*). **20** *tr.* (foll. by *for* or *to be*) regard as being (*do you take me for an idiot?*). **21** *tr.* **a** accept (*take the offer*). **b** submit to (*take a joke*; *take no nonsense*). **22** *tr.* choose or assume (*took a job*; *took responsibility*). **23** *tr.* derive (*takes its name from the inventor*). **24** *tr.* (foll. by *from*) subtract (*take 3 from 9*). **25** *tr.* execute, make, or undertake; perform or effect (*take notes*; *take an oath*; *take a decision*). **26** *tr.* occupy or engage oneself in; indulge in; enjoy (*take a rest*; *take exercise*; *take a vacation*). **27** *tr.* conduct (*took the early class*). **28** *tr.* deal with in a certain way (*took the corner too fast*). **29** *tr.* **a** teach or be taught (a subject). **b** be examined in (a subject). **30** *tr.* make (a photograph) with a camera; photograph (a person or thing). **31** *tr.* use as an instance (*let us take Napoleon*). **32** *tr. Gram.* have or require as part of the appropriate construction (*this verb takes an object*). **33** *tr.* have sexual intercourse with (a woman). **34** *tr.* (in *passive*; foll. by *by*, *with*) be attracted or charmed by. **35** *tr. Baseball* to refrain from swinging at (a pitch). • *n.* **1** an amount taken or caught in one session or attempt, etc. **2** a scene or sequence of film or videotape photographed continuously at one time. **3** money received by a business, esp. money received at a theater for seats. □ **be taken ill** become ill, esp. suddenly. **have what it takes** *colloq.* have the necessary qualities, etc., for success. **on the take** *sl.* accepting bribes. **take after** resemble (esp. a parent or ancestor). **take apart 1** dismantle. **2** *colloq.* beat or defeat. **take away 1** remove or carry elsewhere. **2** subtract. **take back 1** retract (a statement). **2** convey (a person or thing) to his or her or its original position. **3** carry (a person) in thought to a past time. **4** *Printing* transfer to the previous line. **take a bath** *sl.* lose money. **take the cake** *colloq.* be the most remarkable. **take down 1** write down (spoken words). **2** remove (a structure) by separating it into pieces. **3** humiliate. **take five (or ten)** take a break, esp. from work. **take heart** be encouraged. **take the heat** endure criticism, punishment, etc. **take home** earn. **take in 1** accept as a boarder, etc. **2** undertake (work) at home. **3** make (a garment, etc.) smaller. **4** understand (*did you take that in?*). **5** cheat (*managed to take them all in*). **6** include or comprise. **7** *colloq.* visit (a place) on the way to another (*shall we take in the White House*). **8** furl (a sail). **9** regularly buy (a newspaper, etc.). **10** attend; watch (*take in a show*). **11** arrest. **take in hand 1** undertake; start doing or dealing with. **2** undertake the control or reform of (a person). **take it 1** (often foll. by *that* + clause) assume (*I take it that you have finished*). **2** see TAKE *v.* 19. **take it from me** (or **take my word for it**) I can assure you. **take it on one** (or **oneself**) (foll. by *to* + infin.) venture or presume. **take it or leave it** (esp. in *imper.*) an expression of indifference or impatience about another's decision after making an offer. **take it out on** relieve one's frustration by attacking or treating harshly. **take off 1 a** remove (clothing) from one's or another's body. **b** remove or lead away. **2** deduct (part of an amount). **3** depart, esp. hastily (*took off in a fast car*). **4** *colloq.* mimic humorously. **5** jump from the ground. **6** become airborne. **7** (of a scheme, enterprise, etc.) become successful or popular. **8** have (a period) away from work. **take on 1** undertake (work, a responsibility, etc.). **2** engage (an employee). **3** be willing or ready to meet (an adversary in a sport, an argument, etc., esp. a stronger one). **4** acquire (a new meaning, etc.). **take out 1** remove from within a place; extract. **2** escort on an outing. **3** get (a license or summons, etc.) issued. **4** buy (food) at a store, restaurant, etc., for eating elsewhere. **5** *Bridge* remove (a partner or a partner's call) from a suit by bidding a different one or no trump. **6** murder or destroy. **take over 1** succeed to the management or ownership of. **2** take control. **3** *Printing* transfer to the next line. **take shape** assume a distinct form; develop into something definite. **take sick** *colloq.* be taken ill. **take that!** an exclamation accompanying a blow, etc. **take one's time** not hurry. **take to 1** begin or fall into the habit of (*took to drink*). **2** have recourse to. **3** adapt oneself to. **4** form a liking for. **5** make for (*took to the hills*). **take up 1** become interested or engaged in (a pursuit, a cause, etc.). **2** adopt as a protégé. **3** occupy (time or space). **4** begin (residence, etc.). **5** resume after an interruption. **6** interrupt or question (a speaker). **7** accept (an offer, etc.). **8** shorten (a garment). **9** lift up. **10** absorb (*sponges take up water*). **11** take (a person) into a vehicle. **12** pursue (a matter, etc.) further. **take a person up on** accept (a person's offer, etc.). **take up with** begin to associate with. ▫▫ **tak·a·ble** *adj.* (also **take·a·ble**).

take-home pay *n.* the pay received by an employee after the deduction of taxes, etc.

take·off /táykawf/ *n.* **1** the act of becoming airborne. **2** *colloq.* an act of mimicking. **3** a place from which one jumps.

take-out *adj. & n.* • *adj.* (of food) bought at a shop or restaurant for eating elsewhere. • *n.* food sold for consumption elsewhere.

take·o·ver /táykōvər/ *n.* the assumption of control (esp. of a business); the buying out of one company by another.

tak·er /táykər/ *n.* **1** a person who takes a bet. **2** a person who accepts an offer.

tak·ing /táyking/ *adj.* attractive or captivating.

talc /talk/ *n.* **1** talcum powder. **2** any crystalline form of magnesium silicate that occurs in soft flat plates, usu. white or pale green and used as a lubricant, etc. ▫▫ **talc·ose** *adj.* **talc·ous** *adj.* **talc·y** *adj.* (in sense 1).

tal·cum /tálkəm/ *n.* **1** = TALC. **2** (in full **talcum powder**) powdered talc for toilet and cosmetic use, usu. perfumed.

tale /tayl/ *n.* **1** a narrative or story, esp. fictitious and imaginatively treated. **2** a report of an alleged fact, often malicious or in breach of confidence (*all sorts of tales will get about*). **3** a lie; a falsehood.

tal·ent /tálənt/ *n.* **1** a special aptitude or faculty. **2** high mental ability. **3** a person or persons of talent (*is a real talent*; *plenty of local talent*). **4** an ancient weight and unit of currency, esp. among the Greeks. ▫▫ **tal·ent·ed** *adj.* **tal·ent·less** *adj.*

tal·ent scout *n.* a person looking for talented performers, esp. in sports and entertainment.

ta·li *pl.* of TALUS.

tal·i·pes /tálipeez/ *n. Med.* = CLUBFOOT.

tal·is·man /tálizmən/ *n.* (*pl.* **talismans**) **1** an object, esp. an inscribed ring or stone, supposed to be endowed with magic powers esp. of averting evil from or bringing good luck to its holder. **2** a charm or amulet; a thing supposed to be capable of working wonders. ▫▫ **tal·is·man·ic** /–mánik/ *adj.*

talk /tawk/ *v. & n.* • *v.* **1** *intr.* (often foll. by *to*, *with*) converse or communicate ideas by spoken words. **2** *intr.* have the power of speech. **3** *intr.* (foll. by *about*) **a** have as the subject of discussion. **b** (in *imper.*) *colloq.* as an emphatic statement (*talk about expense! It cost me $50*). **4** *tr.* express or utter in words; discuss (*you are talking nonsense*; *talked football all day*). **5** *tr.* use (a language) in speech (*is talking Spanish*). **6** *intr.* (foll. by *at*) address pompously. **7** *tr.* (usu. foll. by *into*, *out of*) bring into a specified condition, etc., by talking (*talked himself hoarse*; *how did you talk them into it?*; *talked them out of the difficulty*). **8** *intr.* reveal (esp. secret) information; betray secrets. **9** *intr.* gossip (*people are beginning to talk*). **10** *intr.* have influence (*money talks*). **11** *intr.* communicate by radio. • *n.* **1** conversation or talking. **2** a particular mode of speech (*baby talk*). **3** an informal address or lecture. **4 a** rumor or gossip (*there is talk of a merger*). **b** its theme (*their success was the talk of the town*). **c** empty words; verbiage (*mere talk*). **5** (often in *pl.*) extended discussions or negotiations. ▫ **know what one is talking about** be expert or authoritative. **now you're talking** *colloq.* I like what you say, suggest, etc. **talk back 1** reply defiantly. **2** respond on a two-way radio system. **talk big** *colloq.* talk boastfully. **talk down** denigrate; belittle. **talk down to** speak patronizingly or condescendingly to. **talk a person down 1** silence a person by greater loudness or persistence. **2** bring (a pilot or aircraft) to landing by radio instructions from the ground. **talk of 1** discuss or mention. **2** (often foll. by verbal noun) express some intention of (*talked of moving to Dallas*). **talk of the town** what is being talked about generally. **talk over** discuss at length. **talk shop** talk, esp. tediously or inopportunely, about one's occupation, business, etc. **talk tall** boast. **talk to** reprove or scold (a person). **talk up** discuss (a subject) in order to arouse interest in it. ▫▫ **talk·er** *n.*

talk·a·tive /táwkətiv/ *adj.* fond of or given to talking. ▫▫ **talk·a·tive·ly** *adv.* **talk·a·tive·ness** *n.*

talk·ie /táwkee/ *n.* esp. *hist.* a movie with a soundtrack, as distinct from a silent movie.

talk·ing /táwking/ *adj. & n.* • *adj.* **1** that talks. **2** having the power of speech (*a talking parrot*). **3** expressive (*talking eyes*). • *n.* in senses of TALK *v.*

talk·ing book *n.* a recorded reading of a book, esp. for the blind.

talk·ing head *n. colloq.* a commentator, etc., on television, speaking to the camera and viewed in close-up.

talk·ing-to *n. colloq.* a reproof or reprimand (*gave them a good talking-to*).

talk show *n.* a television or radio program featuring discussion of topical issues.

tall /tawl/ *adj. & adv.* • *adj.* **1** of more than average height. **2** of a specified height (*looks about six feet tall*). **3** higher than the surrounding objects (*a tall building*). **4** *colloq.* extravagant or excessive (*a tall story*; *tall talk*). • *adv.* as if tall; proudly; in a tall or extravagant way (*sit tall*). ▫▫ **tall·ish** *adj.* **tall·ness** *n.*

tall·boy /táwlboy/ *n.* a tall chest of drawers sometimes in lower and upper sections or mounted on legs.

tal·lith /taális, taaleét/ *n.* a scarf worn by Jewish men esp. at prayer.

tall or·der *n.* an exorbitant or unreasonable demand.

tal·low /tálō/ *n. & v.* • *n.* the harder kinds of (esp. animal) fat melted down for use in making candles, soap, etc. • *v.tr.* grease with tallow. ▫▫ **tal·low·ish** *adj.* **tal·low·y** *adj.*

tall ship *n.* a sailing ship with more than one high mast.

tal·ly /tálee/ *n. & v.* • *n.* (*pl.* **-lies**) **1** the reckoning of a debt or score. **2** a total score or amount. **3 a** a mark registering a fixed number of objects delivered or received. **b** such a number as a unit. **4** *hist.* **a** a piece of wood scored across with notches for the items of an account and then split into halves, each party keeping one. **b** an account kept in this way. **5** a ticket or label for identification. **6** a corresponding thing, counterpart, or duplicate. • *v.* (**-lies, -lied**) (often foll. by *with*) **1** *intr.* agree or correspond. **2** *tr.* record or reckon by tally. ▫▫ **tal·li·er** *n.*

tal·ly·ho /táleehṓ/ *int.*, *n.*, *& v.* • *int.* a huntsman's cry to the hounds on sighting a fox. • *n.* (*pl.* **-hos**) an utterance of this. • *v.* (**-hoes, -hoed**) **1** *intr.* utter a cry of "tallyho." **2** *tr.* indicate (a fox) or urge (hounds) with this cry.

Tal·mud /taálmŏŏd, –məd, tál–/ *n.* the body of Jewish civil and ceremonial law and legend comprising the Mishnah and the Gemara. □□ **Tal·mud·ic** /–mŏŏdik, myŏŏ–/ *adj.* **Tal·mud·i·cal** *adj.* **Tal·mud·ist** *n.*

tal·on /tálən/ *n.* **1** a claw, esp. of a bird of prey. **2** the cards left after the deal in a card game. □□ **tal·oned** *adj.* (also in *comb.*).

ta·lus /táyləs, tál–/ *n.* (*pl.* **tali** /–lī/) *Anat.* the ankle bone supporting the tibia. Also called **astragalus.**

ta·ma·le /təmaálee/ *n.* a Mexican food of seasoned meat and corn flour steamed or baked in corn husks.

tam·a·rack /támərak/ *n.* **1** an American larch, *Larix laricina.* **2** the wood from this.

tam·a·rind /támərind/ *n.* **1** a tropical evergreen tree, *Tamarindus indica.* **2** the fruit of this, containing an acid pulp used as food and in making drinks.

tam·a·risk /támərisk/ *n.* any shrub of the genus *Tamarix,* usu. with long slender branches and small pink or white flowers, that thrives by the sea.

tam·bour /támbŏŏr/ *n.* & *v.* • *n.* **1** a drum. **2 a** a circular frame for holding fabric taut while it is being embroidered. **b** material embroidered in this way. • *v.tr.* (also *absol.*) decorate or embroider on a tambour.

tam·bou·ra /tambŏŏrə/ *n. Mus.* an E. Indian stringed instrument used as a drone.

tam·bou·rine /támbəreén/ *n.* a percussion instrument consisting of a hoop with a parchment stretched over one side and jingling disks in slots around the hoop. □□ **tam·bou·rin·ist** *n.*

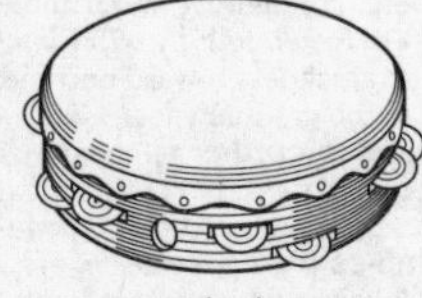
tamborine

tame /taym/ *adj.* & *v.* • *adj.* **1** (of an animal) domesticated; not wild or shy. **2** insipid; lacking spirit or interest; dull (*tame acquiescence*). **3** (of a person) amenable and available. **4 a** (of land) cultivated. **b** (of a plant) produced by cultivation. • *v.tr.* **1** make tame; domesticate; break in. **2** subdue; curb; humble; break the spirit of. □□ **tame·ly** *adv.* **tame·ness** *n.* **tam·er** *n.* (also in *comb.*).

Tam·il /támil, túm–, taá–/ *n.* & *adj.* • *n.* **1** a member of a Dravidian people inhabiting South India and Sri Lanka. **2** the language of this people. • *adj.* of this people or their language. □□ **Ta·mil·ian** /–míleeən/ *adj.*

tam-o'-shan·ter /táməshántər/ *n.* a round woolen or cloth cap of Scottish origin fitting closely around the brows but large and full above.

tamp /tamp/ *v.tr.* ram down (concrete, pipe tobacco, etc.). □□ **tam·per** *n.* **tamp·ing** *n.*

tam·per /támpər/ *v.intr.* (foll. by *with*) **1** meddle with or make unauthorized changes in. **2** exert a secret or corrupt influence upon; bribe. □□ **tam·per·er** *n.* **tam·per·proof** *adj.*

tam·pon /támpon/ *n.* & *v.* • *n.* a plug of soft material used to absorb fluid, esp. one inserted into the vagina during menstruation. • *v.tr.* (**tamponed, tamponing**) plug with a tampon.

tam-tam /támtam/ *n.* a large metal gong.

tan[1] /tan/ *n., adj.,* & *v.* • *n.* **1** a brown skin color resulting from exposure to ultraviolet light. **2** a yellowish-brown color. **3** = TANBARK. • *adj.* yellowish-brown. • *v.* (**tanned, tanning**) **1** *tr.* & *intr.* make or become brown by exposure to ultraviolet light. **2** *tr.* convert (rawhide) into leather by soaking in a liquid containing tannic acid or by the use of mineral salts, etc. **3** *tr. sl.* beat; whip. □□ **tan·na·ble** *adj.* **tan·ning** *n.* **tan·nish** *adj.*

tan[2] /tan/ *abbr.* tangent.

tan·a·ger /tánəjər/ *n.* any small American bird of the subfamily Thraupidae, the male usu. having brightly-colored plumage.

tan·bark /tánbaark/ *n.* **1** the bark of oak and other trees, used to obtain tannin. **2** bark, esp. of oak, bruised and used to tan hides.

tan·dem /tándəm/ *n.* **1** a bicycle or tricycle with two or more seats one behind another. **2 a** a group of two persons or machines, etc., with one behind or following the other. **b** (in full **tandem trailer**) a truck hauling two or more trailers. □ **in tandem** one behind another.

tan·door·i /tandŏŏree/ *n.* food cooked over charcoal in a tandoor (often *attrib.*: *tandoori chicken*).

Tang /tang/ *n.* **1** a dynasty ruling China 618–*c.*906. **2** (*attrib.*) designating art and artifacts of this period.

tang /tang/ *n.* **1** a strong taste or flavor or smell. **2 a** a characteristic quality. **b** a trace; a slight hint of some quality, ingredient, etc.

tan·ge·lo /tánjəlō/ *n.* (*pl.* **-los**) a hybrid of the tangerine and grapefruit.

tan·gent /tánjənt/ *n.* & *adj.* • *n.* **1** a straight line, curve, or surface that meets another curve or curved surface at a point, but if extended does not intersect it at that point. **2** the ratio of the sides opposite and adjacent to an angle in a right-angled triangle. • *adj.* **1** (of a line or surface) that is a tangent. **2** touching. □ **on a tangent** diverging from a previous course of action or thought, etc. (*go off on a tangent*). □□ **tan·gen·cy** *n.*

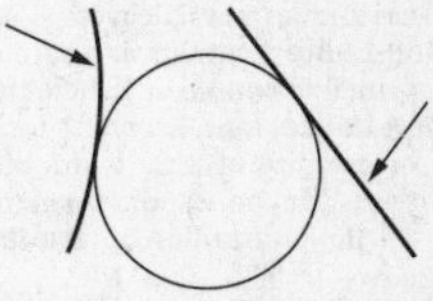

tangent, 1

tan·gen·tial /tanjénshəl/ *adj.* **1** of or along a tangent. **2** divergent. **3** peripheral. □□ **tan·gen·tial·ly** *adv.*

tan·ge·rine /tánjəreén/ *n.* **1** a small sweet orange-colored citrus fruit with a thin skin; a mandarin. **2** a deep orange-yellow color.

tan·gi·ble /tánjəbəl/ *adj.* **1** perceptible by touch. **2** definite; clearly intelligible; not elusive or visionary (*tangible proof*). □□ **tan·gi·bil·i·ty** *n.* **tan·gi·ble·ness** *n.* **tan·gi·bly** *adv.*

tan·gle /tánggəl/ *v.* & *n.* • *v.* **1 a** *tr.* intertwine (threads or hairs, etc.) in a confused mass; entangle. **b** *intr.* become tangled. **2** *intr.* (foll. by *with*) *colloq.* become involved (esp. in conflict or argument) with (*don't tangle with me*). **3** *tr.* complicate (*a tangled affair*). • *n.* **1** a confused mass of intertwined threads, etc. **2** a confused or complicated state (*be in a tangle*; *a love tangle*).

tan·go /tánggō/ *n.* & *v.* • *n.* (*pl.* **-gos**) **1** a slow S. American ballroom dance. **2** the music for this. • *v.intr.* (**-goes, -goed**) dance the tango.

tan·gram /tánggram/ *n.* a Chinese puzzle square cut into seven pieces to be combined into various figures.

tang·y /tángee/ *adj.* (**tangier, tangiest**) having a strong usu. spicy tang. □□ **tang·i·ness** *n.*

tanh /tansh, tanáych/ *abbr.* hyperbolic tangent.

tank /tangk/ *n.* & *v.* • *n.* **1** a large receptacle or storage chamber usu. for liquid or gas. **2** a heavy armored fighting vehicle carrying guns and moving on a tracked carriage. **3** a container for the fuel supply in a motor vehicle. **4** the part of a locomotive tender containing water for the boiler. **5** a reservoir. **6** *colloq.* a prison cell or holding cell. **7** = TANK TOP. • *v.* (usu. foll. by *up*) **1** *tr.* store or place in a tank. **2** *tr.* fill the tank of (a vehicle, etc.) with fuel. **3** *intr.* & *colloq. tr.* (in *passive*) drink heavily; become drunk. □□ **tank·ful** *n.* (*pl.* **-fuls**). **tank·less** *adj.*

tan•kard /tángkərd/ *n.* **1** a tall mug with a handle and sometimes a hinged lid, esp. of silver or pewter for beer. **2** the contents of or an amount held by a tankard.

tank•er /tángkər/ *n.* a ship, aircraft, or truck for carrying liquids or gases in bulk.

tank top *n.* a sleeveless, close-fitting, collarless upper garment.

tan•ner /tánər/ *n.* a person who tans hides.

tan•ner•y /tánəree/ *n.* (*pl.* **-ies**) a place where hides are tanned.

tan•nic /tánik/ *adj.* **1** of or produced from tanbark. **2** (of wine) astringent; tasting of tannin. □□ **tan•nate** /–nayt/ *n.*

tan•nic ac•id *n.* a complex natural organic compound of a yellowish color used as a mordant and astringent.

tan•nin /tánin/ *n.* any of a group of complex organic compounds found in certain tree barks and oak galls, used in leather production and ink manufacture.

tan•sy /tánzee/ *n.* (*pl.* **-sies**) any plant of the genus *Tanacetum*, esp. *T. vulgare* with yellow buttonlike flowers and aromatic leaves.

tan•ta•lite /tántəlīt/ *n.* a rare dense black mineral, the principal source of the element tantalum.

tan•ta•lize /tántəlīz/ *v.tr.* **1** torment or tease by the sight or promise of what is unobtainable. **2** raise and then dash the hopes of; torment with disappointment. □□ **tan•ta•li•za•tion** *n.* **tan•ta•liz•er** *n.* **tan•ta•liz•ing•ly** *adv.*

tan•ta•lum /tántələm/ *n. Chem.* a rare hard white metallic element occurring naturally in tantalite, resistant to heat and the action of acids, and used in surgery and for electronic components. ¶ Symb.: **Ta.** □□ **tan•tal•ic** /–tálik/ *adj.*

tan•ta•lus /tántələs/ *n.* **1** *Brit.* a stand in which liquor decanters may be locked up but visible. **2** a wood ibis, *Mycteria americana*.

tan•ta•mount /tántəmownt/ *predic.adj.* (foll. by *to*) equivalent to (*was tantamount to a denial*).

tan•tra /tántrə, tún–/ *n.* any of a class of Hindu or Buddhist mystical and magical writings. □□ **tan•tric** *adj.* **tan•trism** *n.* **tan•trist** *n.*

tan•trum /tántrəm/ *n.* an outburst of bad temper or petulance (*threw a tantrum*).

Tao•ism /tówizəm, dów–/ *n.* a Chinese philosophy based on the writings of Lao-tzu (*c.*500 BC), advocating humility and religious piety. □□ **Tao•ist** /–ist/ *n.* **Tao•is•tic** /–ístik/ *adj.*

Taos /tows/ *n.* **1 a** a N. American people native to New Mexico. **b** a member of this people. **2** the language of this people.

tap[1] /tap/ *n. & v.* •*n.* **1** = FAUCET. **2** an act of tapping a telephone, etc.; also, the device used for this. **3** *Brit.* a taproom. **4** an instrument for cutting the thread of a female screw. •*v.tr.* (**tapped, tapping**) **1 a** provide (a cask) with a tap. **b** let out (a liquid) by means of, or as if by means of, a tap. **2** draw sap from (a tree) by cutting into it. **3 a** obtain information or supplies or resources from. **b** establish communication or trade with. **4** connect a listening device to (a telephone or telegraph line, etc.) to listen to a call or transmission. **5** cut a female screw thread in. □ **on tap 1** ready to be drawn off by tap. **2** *colloq.* ready for immediate use; freely available. □□ **tap•less** *adj.* **tap•pa•ble** *adj.*

tap[2] /tap/ *v. & n.* •*v.* (**tapped, tapping**) **1** *intr.* (foll. by *at, on*) strike a gentle but audible blow. **2** *tr.* strike lightly (*tapped me on the shoulder*). **3** *tr.* (foll. by *against*, etc.) cause (a thing) to strike lightly (*tapped a stick against the window*). **4** select as if by tapping (*tapped for membership*). **5** *intr.* = TAP-DANCE. •*n.* **1 a** a light blow; a rap. **b** the sound of this (*heard a tap at the door*). **2 a** = TAP DANCE (*goes to tap classes*). **b** a piece of metal attached to the toe and heel of a tap dancer's shoe to make the tapping sound. **3** (in *pl.*, usu. treated as *sing.*) **a** a bugle call for lights to be put out in army quarters. **b** a similar call played at a military funeral. □□ **tap danc•er** *n.* **tap danc•ing** *n.* **tap•per** *n.*

tap dance *n.* a form of display dance performed wearing shoes fitted with metal taps, with rhythmical tapping of the toes and heels. □□ **tap-dance** *v.intr.*

tape /tayp/ *n. & v.* •*n.* **1** a narrow strip of woven material for tying up, fastening, etc. **2 a** a strip of material stretched across the finishing line of a race. **b** a similar strip for marking off an area or forming a notional barrier. **3** (in full **adhesive tape**) a strip of opaque or transparent paper or plastic, etc., esp. coated with adhesive for fastening, sticking, masking, insulating, etc. **4 a** = MAGNETIC TAPE. **b** a tape recording or tape cassette. **5** = TAPE MEASURE. •*v.tr.* **1 a** tie up or join, etc., with tape. **b** apply tape to. **2** (foll. by *off*) seal or mark off an area or thing with tape. **3** record on magnetic tape. **4** measure with tape. □ **break the tape** win a race. **on tape** recorded on magnetic tape. □□ **tape•a•ble** *adj.* (esp. in sense 3 of *v.*). **tape•less** *adj.* **tape•like** *adj.*

tape deck *n.* an audio device for playing and usu. recording magnetic tape.

tape meas•ure *n.* a strip of tape or thin flexible metal marked for measuring lengths.

tap•er /táypər/ *n. & v.* •*n.* **1** a wick coated with wax, etc., for lighting fires, candles, etc. **2** a slender candle. •*v.* (often foll. by *off*) **1** *intr. & tr.* diminish or reduce in thickness toward one end. **2** *tr. & intr.* make or become gradually less.

tape re•cord•er *n.* apparatus for recording sounds on magnetic tape and afterwards reproducing them. □□ **tape-re•cord** *v.tr.* **tape re•cord•ing** *n.*

tap•es•try /tápistree/ *n.* (*pl.* **-tries**) **1 a** a thick textile fabric in which colored weft threads are woven to form pictures or designs. **b** embroidery imitating this, usu. in wools on canvas. **c** a piece of such embroidery. **2** events or circumstances, etc., compared with a tapestry in being intricate, interwoven, etc. (*life's rich tapestry*). □□ **tap•es•tried** *adj.*

tape•worm /táypwərm/ *n.* any flatworm of the class Cestoda, with a body like segmented tape, living as a parasite in the intestines.

tap•i•o•ca /tápeeṓkə/ *n.* a starchy substance in hard white grains obtained from cassava and used for puddings, etc.

ta•pir /táypər, təpéer/ *n.* any nocturnal hoofed mammal of the genus *Tapirus*, native to Central and S. America and Malaysia, having a short flexible protruding snout.

tap•pet /tápit/ *n.* a lever or projecting part used in machinery to give intermittent motion, often in conjunction with a cam.

tap•room /tápro͞om, –ro͝om/ *n.* a room in which alcoholic drinks are available on tap; a barroom.

tap•root *n.* a tapering root growing vertically downwards.

tap wa•ter *n.* water from a piped supply.

tar[1] /taar/ *n. & v.* •*n.* **1** a dark, thick, flammable liquid distilled from wood or coal, etc., and used as a preservative of wood and iron, in making roads, as an antiseptic, etc. **2** a similar substance formed in the combustion of tobacco, etc. •*v.tr.* (**tarred, tarring**) cover with tar. □ **tar and feather** smear with tar and then cover with feathers as a punishment. **tarred with the same brush** having the same faults.

tar[2] /taar/ *n. colloq.* a sailor.

tar•an•tel•la /tárəntélə/ *n.* (also **tar•an•telle** /–tél/) **1** a rapid whirling S. Italian dance. **2** the music for this.

ta•ran•tu•la /təránchələ/ *n.* **1** any large, hairy, tropical spider of the family Theraphosidae. **2** a large black spider, *Lycosa tarentula*, whose bite was formerly held to cause dancing mania.

tar·dy /taárdee/ *adj.* (**tardier, tardiest**) **1** slow to act or come or happen. **2** delaying or delayed beyond the right or expected time. □□ **tar·di·ly** *adv.* **tar·di·ness** *n.*

tare[1] /tair/ *n.* **1** vetch, esp. as a weed or fodder. **2** (in *pl.*) *Bibl.* an injurious grain weed (Matt. 13:24-30).

tare[2] /tair/ *n.* **1** an allowance made for the weight of the packing or wrapping around goods. **2** the weight of a motor vehicle without its fuel or load.

tar·get /taárgit/ *n. & v.* •*n.* **1** a mark or point fired or aimed at, esp. a round or rectangular object marked with concentric circles. **2** a person or thing aimed at, or exposed to gunfire, etc. (*they were an easy target*). **3** (also *attrib.*) an objective or result aimed at (*our export targets; target date*). **4** a person or thing against whom criticism, abuse, etc., is or may be directed. **5** *archaic* a shield or buckler, esp. a small round one. •*v.tr.* (**targeted, targeting**) **1** identify or single out (a person or thing) as an object of attention or attack. **2** aim or direct (*missiles targeted on major cities*. □□ **tar·get·a·ble** *adj.*

tar·iff /tárif/ *n.* **1** a table of fixed charges. **2 a** a duty on a particular class of imports or exports. **b** a list of duties or customs to be paid.

Tar·mac /taármak/ *n. & v.* •*n. Trademark* **1** = TARMACADAM. **2** a surface made of this, e.g., a runway. •*v.tr.* (**tarmac**) (**tarmacked, tarmacking**) apply tarmacadam to.

tar·mac·ad·am /taármәkádәm/ *n.* a material of stone or slag bound with tar, used in paving roads, etc.

tarn /taarn/ *n.* a small mountain lake.

tar·na·tion /taarnáyshәn/ *int.* esp. *dial. sl.* damn; blast.

tar·nish /taárnish/ *v. & n.* •*v.* **1** *tr.* lessen or destroy the luster of (metal, etc.). **2** *tr.* impair (one's reputation, etc.). **3** *intr.* (of metal, etc.) lose luster. •*n.* **1 a** a loss of luster. **b** a film of color formed on an exposed surface of a mineral or metal. **2** a blemish; a stain. □□ **tar·nish·a·ble** *adj.*

ta·ro /taárō, tárō/ *n.* (*pl.* **-ros**) a tropical plant of the arum family, *Colocasia esculenta*, with tuberous roots used as food. Also called **eddo**.

ta·rot /tárō, tәrṓ/ *n.* **1** (in *sing.* or *pl.*) **a** any of several games played with a pack of cards having five suits, the last of which is a set of permanent trump. **b** a similar pack used in fortune-telling. **2 a** any of the trump cards. **b** any of the cards from a fortune-telling pack.

tarp /taarp/ *n. colloq.* tarpaulin.

tar·pau·lin /taarpáwlin, taárpә–/ *n.* **1** heavy-duty waterproof cloth, esp. of tarred canvas or heavy plastic. **2** a sheet or covering of this.

tar·pon /taárpon/ *n.* **1** a large silvery fish, *Tarpon atlanticus*, common in the tropical Atlantic. **2** a similar fish, *Megalops cyprinoides*, of the Pacific ocean.

tar·ra·gon /tárәgәn/ *n.* a bushy herb, *Artemisia dracunculus*, with leaves used to flavor salads, stuffings, vinegar, etc.

tar·ry[1] /taáree/ *adj.* (**tarrier, tarriest**) of or like or smeared with tar. □□ **tar·ri·ness** *n.*

tar·ry[2] /táree/ *v.intr.* (**-ries, -ried**) *archaic* or *literary* linger; stay; wait.

tar·sal /taársәl/ *adj. & n.* •*adj.* of or relating to the bones in the ankle. •*n.* a tarsal bone.

tar·si·er /taárseeәr/ *n.* any small, large-eyed, arboreal, nocturnal primate of the genus *Tarsius*, native to Borneo, the Philippines, etc., with a long tail and long hind legs.

tar·sus /taársәs/ *n.* (*pl.* **tarsi** /–sī, –see/) *Anat.* the group of bones forming the ankle and upper foot.

tart[1] /taart/ *n.* **1** a small pie containing jam, fruit, etc., having no upper crust. **2** a pie with a fruit or sweet filling. □□ **tart·let** *n.*

tart[2] /taart/ *n. & v.* •*n. sl.* **1** a prostitute; a promiscuous woman. **2** *sl. offens.* a girl or woman. •*v.* (foll. by *up*) *colloq.* **1** *tr.* (usu. *refl.*) dress (oneself or a thing) up, esp. flashily or gaudily. **2** *intr.* dress up gaudily. □□ **tart·y** *adj.*

tart[3] /taart/ *adj.* **1** sharp or acid in taste. **2** (of a remark, etc.) cutting; bitter. □□ **tart·ly** *adv.* **tart·ness** *n.*

tar·tan /taárt'n/ *n.* **1** a pattern of colored stripes crossing at right angles, esp. the distinctive plaid worn by the Scottish Highlanders to denote their clan. **2** woolen fabric woven in this pattern (often *attrib.*: *a tartan scarf*).

Tar·tar /taártәr/ *n. & adj.* (also **Ta·tar** /taátәr/except in sense 2 of *n.*) •*n.* **1 a** a member of a group of Central Asian peoples including Mongols and Turks. **b** the Turkic language of these peoples. **2** (**tartar**) a violent-tempered or intractable person. •*adj.* **1** of or relating to the Tartars. **2** of or relating to Central Asia east of the Caspian Sea. □□ **Tar·tar·i·an** /–táireeәn/ *adj.*

tar·tar /taártәr/ *n.* **1** a hard deposit of saliva, calcium phosphate, etc., that forms on the teeth. **2** a deposit of acid potassium tartrate that forms a hard crust on the inside of a cask during the fermentation of wine. □□ **tar·tar·ize** *v.tr.*

tar·tar·ic ac·id /taartárik/ *n.* a natural carboxylic acid found esp. in unripe grapes, used in baking powders and as a food additive.

tar·tar sauce *n.* (also **tar·tare sauce** or **sauce tar·tare**) a sauce of mayonnaise and chopped pickles, capers, etc.

task /task/ *n. & v.* •*n.* a piece of work to be done or undertaken. •*v.tr.* **1** make great demands on (a person's powers, etc.). **2** assign a task to. □ **take to task** rebuke; scold.

task force *n.* (also **task group**) **1** *Mil.* an armed force organized for a special operation. **2** a unit specially organized for a task.

task·mas·ter /táskmastәr/ *n.* (*fem.* **task·mis·tress** /–mistris/) a person who imposes a task or burden, esp. regularly or severely.

Tas·ma·ni·an /tazmáyneeәn/ *n. & adj.* •*n.* **1** a native of Tasmania, an island state of Australia. **2** a person of Tasmanian descent. •*adj.* of or relating to Tasmania.

Tas·ma·ni·an dev·il *n.* a nocturnal carnivorous marsupial similar to a badger, *Sarcophilus harrisii*, now found only in Tasmania.

Tass /tas, taas/ *n. hist.* the official news agency of the former Soviet Union.

tas·sel /tásәl/ *n.* **1** a tuft of loosely hanging threads or cords, etc., attached for decoration to a cushion, scarf, cap, etc. **2** a tassellike head of some plants, esp. a flowerhead with prominent stamens at the top of a corn stalk.

taste /tayst/ *n. & v.* •*n.* **1 a** the sensation characteristic of a soluble substance caused in the mouth and throat by contact with that substance (*disliked the taste of garlic*). **b** the faculty of perceiving this sensation (*was bitter to the taste*). **2 a** a small portion of food or drink taken as a sample. **b** a hint or touch of some ingredient or quality. **3** a slight experience (*a taste of success*). **4** (often foll. by *for*) a liking or predilection (*has expensive tastes; is not to my taste*). **5 a** aesthetic discernment in art, literature, conduct, etc., esp. of a specified kind (*a person of taste; dresses in poor taste*). **b** a style or manner based on this (*a novel of Victorian taste*). •*v.* **1** *tr.* sample or test the flavor of (food, etc.) by taking it into the mouth. **2** *tr.* (also *absol.*) perceive the flavor of (*could taste the lemon; cannot taste with a cold*). **3** *tr.* (esp. with *neg.*) eat or drink a small portion of (*had not tasted food for days*). **4** *tr.* have experience of (*had never tasted failure*). **5** *intr.* (often foll. by *of*) have a specified flavor (*tastes bitter; tastes of onions*). □ **a bad** (or **bitter**, etc.)

taste *colloq.* a strong feeling of regret or unease. **to taste** in the amount needed for a pleasing result (*add salt and pepper to taste*). ▫▫ **taste·a·ble** *adj.*

taste bud *n.* any of the cells or nerve endings on the surface of the tongue by which things are tasted.

taste·ful /táystfool/ *adj.* having, or done in, good taste. ▫▫ **taste·ful·ly** *adv.* **taste·ful·ness** *n.*

taste·less /táystlis/ *adj.* **1** lacking flavor. **2** having, or done in, bad taste. ▫▫ **taste·less·ly** *adv.* **taste·less·ness** *n.*

tast·er /táystər/ *n.* **1** a person employed to test food or drink by tasting it, esp. for quality or *hist.* to detect poisoning. **2** a small cup used by a wine taster. **3** an instrument for extracting a small sample from within a cheese. **4** a sample of food, etc.

tast·ing /táysting/ *n.* a gathering at which food or drink (esp. wine) is tasted and evaluated.

tast·y /táystee/ *adj.* (**tastier, tastiest**) (of food) pleasing in flavor; appetizing. ▫▫ **tast·i·ly** *adv.* **tast·i·ness** *n.*

tat[1] /tat/ *v.* (**tatted, tatting**) **1** *intr.* do tatting. **2** *tr.* make by tatting.

tat[2] see TIT[2].

ta-ta /taatáa/ *int. joc.* good-bye.

Ta·tar var. of TARTAR.

ta·ter /táytər/ *n. sl.* = POTATO.

tat·ter /tátər/ *n.* (usu. in *pl.*) a rag; an irregularly torn piece of cloth or paper, etc. ▫ **in tatters 1** ragged and torn. **2** *colloq.* (of a negotiation, argument, etc.) ruined; demolished.

tat·tered /tátərd/ *adj.* in tatters; ragged.

tat·ting /táting/ *n.* **1** a kind of knotted lace made by hand with a small shuttle and used as trim, etc. **2** the process of making this.

tat·tle /tát'l/ *v.* & *n.* •*v.* **1** *intr.* prattle; chatter; gossip idly; speak indiscreetly. **2** *tr.* utter (words) idly; reveal (secrets). •*n.* gossip; idle or trivial talk. ▫▫ **tat·tler** *n.*

tat·tle·tale /tát'ltayl/ *n.* one who tells tales or informs, esp. a child.

tat·too[1] /tatóo/ *n.* (*pl.* **tattoos**) **1** an evening drum or bugle signal recalling soldiers to their quarters. **2** an elaboration of this with music and marching, presented as an entertainment. **3** a rhythmic tapping or drumming.

tat·too[2] /tatóo/ *v.* & *n.* •*v.tr.* (**tattoos, tattooed**) **1** mark (the skin) with an indelible design by puncturing it and inserting pigment. **2** make (a design) in this way. •*n.* (*pl.* **tattoos**) a design made by tattooing. ▫▫ **tat·too·er** *n.* **tat·too·ist** *n.*

tau /tow, taw/ *n.* the nineteenth letter of the Greek alphabet (Τ, τ).

taught *past* and *past part.* of TEACH.

taunt /tawnt/ *n.* & *v.* •*n.* a thing said in order to anger or wound a person. •*v.tr.* **1** assail with taunts. **2** reproach (a person) contemptuously. ▫▫ **taunt·er** *n.* **taunt·ing·ly** *adv.*

taupe /tōp/ *n.* a gray with a tinge of another color, usu. brown.

Tau·rus /táwrəs/ *n.* **1** a constellation. **2 a** the second sign of the zodiac (the Bull). **b** a person born under this sign. ▫▫ **Tau·re·an** *adj.* & *n.*

taut /tawt/ *adj.* **1** (of a rope, muscles, etc.) tight; not slack. **2** (of nerves) tense. **3** (of a ship, etc.) in good order or condition. ▫▫ **taut·en** *v.tr.* & *intr.* **taut·ly** *adv.* **taut·ness** *n.*

tauto- /táwtō/ *comb. form* the same.

tau·tog /tawtóg/ *n.* a fish, *Tautoga onitis*, found off the Atlantic coast of N. America, used as food.

tau·tol·o·gy /tawtóləjee/ *n.* (*pl.* **-gies**) the saying of the same thing twice in different words, esp. as a fault of style (e.g., *arrived one after the other in succession*). ▫▫ **tau·to·log·ic** /–t'lójik/ *adj.* **tau·to·log·i·cal** *adj.* **tau·to·log·i·cal·ly** *adv.* **tau·tol·o·gist** *n.* **tau·tol·o·gize** *v.intr.* **tau·tol·o·gous** /–ləgəs/ *adj.*

tau·to·mer /táwtəmər/ *n. Chem.* a substance that exists as two mutually convertible isomers in equilibrium. ▫▫ **tau·to·mer·ic** /–mérik/ *adj.* **tau·tom·er·ism** /–tómərizəm/ *n.*

tav·ern /távərn/ *n.* an inn or bar.

taw·dry /táwdree/ *adj.* & *n.* •*adj.* (**tawdrier, tawdriest**) **1** showy but worthless. **2** overly ornamented; gaudy; vulgar. •*n.* cheap or gaudy finery. ▫▫ **taw·dri·ly** *adv.* **taw·dri·ness** *n.*

---

tawdry early 17th century: short for *tawdry lace*, a fine silk lace or ribbon worn as a necklace in the 16th–17th centuries, a contraction of *St. Audrey's lace*: *Audrey* was a later form of *Etheldrida* (died 679), patron saint of the English city of Ely, where tawdry laces, along with cheap imitations and other cheap finery, were traditionally sold at a fair.

---

taw·ny /táwnee/ *adj.* (**tawnier, tawniest**) of an orangish or yellowish brown color. ▫▫ **taw·ni·ness** *n.*

tax /taks/ *n.* & *v.* •*n.* **1** a contribution to government revenue compulsorily levied on individuals, property, or businesses (often foll. by *on*: *a tax on luxury goods*). **2** (usu. foll. by *on, upon*) a strain or heavy demand; an oppressive or burdensome obligation. •*v.tr.* **1** impose a tax on (persons or goods, etc.). **2** deduct tax from (income, etc.). **3** make heavy demands on (a person's powers or resources, etc.) (*you really tax my patience*). **4** (foll. by *with*) confront (a person) with a wrongdoing, etc. **5** call to account. **6** *Law* examine and assess (costs, etc.). ▫▫ **tax·a·ble** *adj.* **tax·er** *n.* **tax·less** *adj.*

tax·a·tion /taksáyshən/ *n.* the imposition or payment of tax.

tax-de·duct·i·ble *adj.* (of expenditure) that may be paid out of income before the deduction of income tax.

tax e·va·sion *n.* the illegal nonpayment or underpayment of income tax.

tax-ex·empt *adj.* **1** exempt from taxes. **2** bearing tax-exempt interest.

tax ha·ven *n.* a country, etc., where income tax is low.

tax·i /táksee/ *n.* & *v.* •*n.* (*pl.* **taxis**) **1** (in full **taxicab**) an automobile licensed to carry passengers for a fee and usu. fitted with a taximeter. **2** a boat, airplane, etc., similarly used. •*v.* (**taxis, taxied, taxiing** or **taxying**) **1 a** *intr.* (of an aircraft or pilot) move along the ground under the machine's own power before takeoff or after landing. **b** *tr.* cause (an aircraft) to taxi. **2** *intr.* & *tr.* go or convey in a taxi.

tax·i·der·my /táksidərmee/ *n.* the art of preparing, stuffing, and mounting the skins of animals with lifelike effect. ▫▫ **tax·i·der·mal** /–dórməl/ *adj.* **tax·i·der·mic** /–dórmik/ *adj.* **tax·i·der·mist** *n.*

tax·i·me·ter /tákseemeetər/ *n.* an automatic device fitted to a taxi, recording the distance traveled and the fare payable.

tax·i stand *n.* (*Brit.* **taxi rank**) a place where taxis wait to be hired.

tax·man /táksman/ *n. colloq.* (*pl.* **-men**) an inspector or collector of taxes.

tax·on /táksən/ *n.* (*pl.* **taxa** /táksə/) any taxonomic group.

tax·on·o·my /taksónəmee/ *n.* **1** the science of the classification of living and extinct organisms. **2** the practice of this. ▫▫ **tax·o·nom·ic** /–sənómik/ *adj.* **tax·o·nom·i·cal** /–sənómikəl/ *adj.* **tax·o·nom·i·cal·ly** /–sənómiklee/ *adv.* **tax·on·o·mist** *n.*

tax·pay·er /tákspayər/ *n.* a person who pays taxes.

tax re·turn *n.* a declaration of income for taxation purposes.

tax shel·ter *n.* a means of organizing business affairs, etc., to minimize payment of tax.

tay·ber·ry *n.* (*pl.* **-ries**) a dark red soft fruit produced by crossing a blackberry and a raspberry.

TB *abbr.* **1** tubercle bacillus. **2** tuberculosis.

Tb *symb. Chem.* the element terbium.

T-bar /téebaar/ *n.* **1** (in full **T-bar lift**) a type of ski lift in the form of a series of inverted T-shaped bars for towing skiers uphill. **2** (often *attrib.*) a T-shaped fastening on a shoe or sandal.

T-bone /téebōn/ *n.* a T-shaped bone, esp. in steak from the thin end of a loin.

tbs. *abbr.* (also **tbsp.**) tablespoon.

Tc *symb. Chem.* the element technetium.

T-cell *n.* a lymphocyte of a type produced or processed by the thymus gland and active in the immune response.

TD *abbr.* **1** touchdown. **2** Treasury Department.

Te *symb. Chem.* the element tellurium.

tea /tee/ *n.* **1 a** (in full **tea plant**) an evergreen shrub or small tree, *Camellia sinensis*, of India, China, etc. **b** its dried leaves. **2** a drink made by infusing tea leaves in boiling water. **3** a similar drink made from the leaves of other plants or from another substance (*chamomile tea; beef tea*). **4 a** *Brit.* a light afternoon meal consisting of tea, bread, cakes, etc. **b** a cooked evening meal. **5** an afternoon party or reception at which tea is served.

tea bag *n.* a small porous bag of tea leaves for infusion.

tea ball *n.* a ball of perforated metal to hold tea leaves, over which boiling water is poured to make a drink of tea.

tea cad·dy *n.* a container for tea leaves.

tea cer·e·mo·ny *n.* an elaborate Japanese ritual of serving and drinking tea, as an expression of Zen Buddhist philosophy.

teach /teech/ *v.tr.* (*past* and *past part.* **taught** /tawt/) **1 a** give systematic information to (a person) or about (a subject or skill). **b** (*absol.*) practice this professionally. **c** enable (a person) to do something by instruction and training (*taught me how to dance*). **2** advocate as a moral, etc., principle (*my parents taught me tolerance*). **3** (foll. by *to* + infin.) **a** induce (a person) by example or punishment to do or not to do a thing (*that will teach you to sit still*). **b** *colloq.* make (a person) disinclined to do a thing (*I will teach you to interfere*). □ **teach a person a lesson** see LESSON. **teach school** be a teacher in a school.

teach·a·ble /téechəbəl/ *adj.* **1** apt at learning. **2** (of a subject) that can be taught. □□ **teach·a·bil·i·ty** /–bílitee/ *n.* **teach·a·ble·ness** *n.*

teach·er /téechər/ *n.* a person who teaches, esp. in a school. □□ **teach·er·ly** *adj.*

teach·ing /téeching/ *n.* **1** the profession of a teacher. **2** (often in *pl.*) what is taught; a doctrine.

tea co·zy *n.* a cover to keep a teapot warm.

tea·cup /téekup/ *n.* **1** a cup from which tea or other hot beverages are drunk. **2** an amount held by this, about 4 fluid ounces. □□ **tea·cup·ful** *n.* (*pl.* **-fuls**).

teak /teek/ *n.* **1** a large deciduous tree, *Tectona grandis*, native to India and SE Asia. **2** its hard durable wood, used in shipbuilding and for furniture.

teal /teel/ *n.* (*pl.* same) **1** any of various small freshwater ducks of the genus *Anas*, esp. *A. crecca*. **2** a dark greenish blue color.

team /teem/ *n.* & *v.* • *n.* **1** a set of players forming one side in a game, debate, etc. (*a hockey team*). **2** two or more persons working together. **3 a** a set of draft animals. **b** one animal or more in harness with a vehicle. • *v.* **1** *intr.* & *tr.* (usu. foll. by *up*) join in a team or in common action (*decided to team up with them*). **2** *tr.* harness (horses, etc.) in a team. **3** *tr.* (foll. by *with*) match or coordinate (clothes).

team·mate /téemmayt/ *n.* a member of the same team or group.

team·ster /téemstər/ *n.* **1 a** a truck driver. **b** a member of the Teamsters Union. **2** a driver of a team of animals.

team·work /téemwərk/ *n.* the combined action of a team, group, etc., esp. when effective and efficient.

tea·pot /téepot/ *n.* a pot with a handle, spout, and lid, in which tea is brewed and from which it is poured.

tear[1] /tair/ *v.* & *n.* • *v.* (*past* **tore** /tor/; *past part.* **torn** /torn/) **1** *tr.* (often foll. by *up*) pull apart or to pieces with some force (*tear it in half; tore up the letter*). **2** *tr.* **a** make a hole or rent in by tearing (*have torn my coat*). **b** make (a hole or rent). **3** *tr.* (foll. by *away, off,* etc.) pull violently or with some force (*tore the book away from me; tore off the cover; tore a page out; tore down the notice*). **4** *tr.* violently disrupt or divide (*torn by conflicting emotions*). **5** *intr. colloq.* go or travel hurriedly or impetuously (*tore across the road*). **6** *intr.* undergo tearing (*the curtain tore down the middle*). **7** *intr.* (foll. by *at,* etc.) pull violently or with some force. • *n.* **1** a hole or other damage caused by tearing. **2** the torn part of a piece of cloth, etc. **3** *sl.* a spree; a drinking bout. □ **be torn between** have difficulty in choosing between. **tear apart 1** search (a place) exhaustively. **2** criticize forcefully. **tear into 1** attack verbally; reprimand. **2** make a vigorous start on (an activity). **tear oneself away** leave despite a strong desire to stay. **tear one's hair out** behave with extreme desperation or anger. **tear to shreds** *colloq.* refute or criticize thoroughly. □□ **tear·a·ble** *adj.* **tear·er** *n.*

tear[2] /teer/ *n.* **1** a drop of clear salty liquid secreted by glands that serves to moisten and wash the eye and is shed from it in grief or other strong emotions. **2** a tearlike thing; a drop. □ **in tears** crying; shedding tears. □□ **tear·like** *adj.*

tear duct *n.* a drain for carrying tears to the eye or from the eye to the nose.

tear·ful /téerfŏŏl/ *adj.* **1** crying or inclined to cry. **2** causing or accompanied with tears; sad (*a tearful event*). □□ **tear·ful·ly** *adv.* **tear·ful·ness** *n.*

tear gas *n.* gas that disables by causing severe irritation to the eyes.

tear·jerk·er /téerjərkər/ *n. colloq.* a story, film, etc., calculated to evoke sadness or sympathy.

tea·room /téeroŏm, –rōōm/ *n.* a small restaurant or café where tea is served.

tease /teez/ *v.* & *n.* • *v.tr.* (also *absol.*) **1 a** make fun of (a person or animal) playfully or unkindly or annoyingly. **b** tempt or allure, esp. sexually, while refusing to satisfy the desire aroused. **2** pick (wool, hair, etc.) into separate fibers. **3** dress (cloth) esp. with teasels. • *n.* **1** *colloq.* a person fond of teasing. **2** an instance of teasing (*it was only a tease*). **3** = TEASER 3. □ **tease out 1** separate (strands, etc.) by disentangling. **2** search out; elicit (information, etc.). □□ **teas·ing·ly** *adv.*

tea·sel /téezəl/ (also **tea·zel, tea·zle**) *n.* **1** any plant of the genus *Dipsacus*, with large prickly heads that are dried and used to raise the nap on woven cloth. **2** a device used as a substitute for teasels.

teas·er /téezər/ *n.* **1** *colloq.* a hard question or task. **2** a teasing person. **3** (also **tease**) a short introductory advertisement, etc.

tea set *n.* a set of china or silver, etc., for serving tea.

tea·spoon /téespōōn/ *n.* **1** a small spoon for stirring tea. **2** an amount held by this. **3** a unit of measure equal to $^1/_3$ tablespoon, approx. $^1/_6$ fl. oz. or 5 ml. □□ **tea·spoon·ful** *n.* (*pl.* **-fuls**).

teat /teet/ *n.* **1** a mammary nipple, esp. of an animal. **2** *Brit.* a thing resembling this, esp. a device of rubber, etc., for sucking milk from a bottle; a nipple.

tech /tek/ *n. colloq.* **1** a technician. **2** a technical college.

tech·ne·ti·um /teknéeshəm, –sheeəm/ *n. Chem.* an artificially produced radioactive metallic element. ¶ Symb.: **Tc**.

tech·ni·cal /téknikəl/ *adj.* **1** of or involving or concerned with the mechanical arts and applied sciences (*technical college*; *a technical education*). **2** of or relating to a particular subject or craft, etc., or its techniques (*technical terms*; *technical merit*). **3** (of a book or discourse, etc.) using technical language; requiring special knowledge to be understood. **4** due to mechanical failure (*a technical hitch*). **5** legally such; such in strict interpretation (*lost on a technical point*). □□ **tech·ni·cal·ly** *adv.* **tech·ni·cal·ness** *n.*

tech·ni·cal foul *n. Basketball* a foul called for a technical rule violation not involving actual play.

tech·ni·cal·i·ty /téknikálitee/ *n.* (*pl.* **-ties**) **1** the state of being technical. **2** a technical expression. **3** a technical point or detail, as in a legal matter (*was acquitted on a technicality*).

tech·ni·cal knock·out *n. Boxing* a termination of a fight by the referee on the grounds of a contestant's inability to continue, the opponent being declared the winner.

tech·ni·cian /teknishən/ *n.* **1** an expert in technology or in the practical application of a science. **2** a person skilled in the technique of an art or craft. **3** a person employed to look after technical equipment and do practical work in a laboratory, clinic, etc.

Tech·ni·col·or /téknikulər/ *n.* (often *attrib.*) **1** *Trademark* a process of color cinematography using synchronized monochrome films, each of a different color, to produce a color print. **2** (usu. **technicolor**) *colloq.* **a** vivid color. **b** artificial brilliance. □□ **tech·ni·col·ored** *adj.*

tech·nique /teknéek/ *n.* **1** mechanical skill in an art. **2** a means of achieving one's purpose, esp. skillfully. **3** a manner of artistic execution in music, painting, etc.

tech·no·bab·ble /téknōbábəl/ *n. colloq.* incomprehensible technical jargon.

tech·noc·ra·cy /teknókrəsee/ *n.* (*pl.* **-cies**) **1** the government or control of society or industry by technology or technical experts. **2** an instance or application of this. □□ **tech·no·crat** *n.* **tech·no·crat·ic** *adj.* **tech·no·crat·i·cal·ly** *adv.*

tech·no·crat /téknəkrat/ *n.* an exponent or advocate of technocracy. □□ **tech·no·crat·ic** /–krátik/ *adj.* **tech·no·crat·i·cal·ly** *adv.*

tech·no·log·i·cal /téknəlójikəl/ *adj.* of, using, or ascribable to technology or technicians. □□ **tech·no·log·i·cal·ly** *adv.*

tech·nol·o·gy /teknóləjee/ *n.* (*pl.* **-gies**) **1** the study, application, or use of the mechanical arts and applied sciences. **2** these subjects collectively. □□ **tech·nol·o·gist** *n.*

tec·ton·ic /tektónik/ *adj.* **1** *Geol.* relating to the deformation of the earth's crust or to the structural changes caused by this (see PLATE TECTONICS). **2** of or relating to building or construction. □□ **tec·ton·i·cal·ly** *adv.*

tec·ton·ics /tektóniks/ *n.pl.* (usu. treated as *sing.*) *Geol.* the study of large-scale structural features (cf. PLATE TECTONICS).

ted·dy /tédee/ *n.* (also **Ted·dy**) (*pl.* **-dies**) (in full **teddy bear**) **1** a stuffed toy bear. **2** a woman's undergarment.

Te De·um /tee déeəm, tay dáyəm/ **1 a** a hymn beginning *Te Deum laudamus*, 'We praise Thee, O God.' **b** the music for this. **2** an expression of thanksgiving or exultation.

te·di·ous /téedeeəs/ *adj.* tiresomely long; wearisome. □□ **te·di·ous·ly** *adv.* **te·di·ous·ness** *n.*

te·di·um /téedeeəm/ *n.* the state of being tedious; boredom.

tee[1] /tee/ *n.* = T[1].

tee[2] /tee/ *n. & v.* • *n.* **1** *Golf* **a** a cleared space from which a golf ball is struck at the beginning of play for each hole. **b** a small support of wood or plastic from which a ball is struck at a tee. **2** a mark aimed at in lawn bowling, quoits, curling, etc. • *v.tr.* (**tees, teed**) (often foll. by *up*) *Golf* place (a ball) on a tee ready to strike it. □ **tee off 1** *Golf* play a ball from a tee. **2** *colloq.* start; begin.

tee-hee /teehée/ *n. & v.* (also **te-hee**) • *n.* **1** a titter. **2** a restrained or contemptuous laugh. • *v.intr.* (**tee-hees, tee-heed**) titter or laugh in this way.

teem[1] /teem/ *v.intr.* **1** be abundant (*fish teem in these waters*). **2** (foll. by *with*) be full of or swarming with (*teeming with fish*; *teeming with ideas*).

teem[2] /teem/ *v.intr.* (often foll. by *down*) (of water, etc.) flow copiously; pour (*it was teeming with rain*).

teen /teen/ *adj. & n.* • *adj.* = TEENAGE. • *n.* = TEENAGER.

teen·age /téenayj/ *adj.* relating to or characteristic of teenagers. □□ **teen·aged** *adj.*

teen·ag·er /téenayjər/ *n.* a person from 13 to 19 years of age.

teens /teenz/ *n.pl.* the years of one's age from 13 to 19 (*in one's teens*).

teen·sy /téensee/ *adj.* (**teensier, teensiest**) *colloq.* = TEENY.

tee·ny /téenee/ *adj.* (**teenier, teeniest**) *colloq.* tiny.

tee·ny·bop·per /téeneebopər/ *n. colloq.* a young teenager, usu. a girl, who follows the latest fashions in clothes, pop music, etc.

tee·pee var. of TEPEE.

tee·shirt var. of T-SHIRT.

tee·ter /téetər/ *v.intr.* **1** totter; stand or move unsteadily. **2** hesitate; be indecisive. □ **teeter on the brink** (or **edge**) be in imminent danger (of disaster, etc.).

teeth *pl.* of TOOTH.

teethe /teeth/ *v.intr.* grow or cut teeth, esp. baby teeth. □□ **teeth·ing** *n.*

tee·to·tal /téetṓt'l/ *adj.* advocating or characterized by total abstinence from alcohol. □□ **tee·to·tal·ism** *n.*

tee·to·tal·er /téetṓt'lər/ *n.* (also **tee·to·tal·ler**) a person advocating or practicing abstinence from alcoholic beverages.

Tef·lon /téflon/ *n. Trademark* polytetrafluoroethylene, esp. used as a nonstick coating for kitchen utensils, etc.

teg·u·ment /tégyəmənt/ *n.* the natural covering of an animal's body or part of its body. □□ **teg·u·men·tal** /–mént'l/ *adj.* **teg·u·men·ta·ry** /–méntəree/ *adj.*

tele- /télee/ *comb. form* **1** at or to a distance (*telekinesis*). **2** forming names of instruments for operating over long distances (*telescope*). **3** television (*telecast*). **4** done by means of the telephone (*teleconference*).

tel·e·cast /télikast/ *n. & v.* • *n.* a television broadcast. • *v.tr.* transmit by television. □□ **tel·e·cast·er** *n.*

tel·e·com·mu·ni·ca·tion /télikəmyóonikáyshən/ *n.* **1** communication over a distance by cable, telegraph, telephone, or broadcasting. **2** (usu. in *pl.*) the branch of technology concerned with this.

tel·e·com·mute /télikəmyóot/ *v.intr.* (**telecommuted, telecommuting**) work, esp. at home, communicating electronically with one's employer, etc., by computer, fax, and telephone.

tel·e·con·fer·ence /télikónfərəns, –frəns/ *n.* a conference with participants in different locations linked by telecommunication devices. □□ **tel·e·con·fer·enc·ing** *n.*

tel·e·gen·ic /télijénik/ *adj.* having an appearance or manner that looks attractive on television.

tel·e·gram /téligram/ *n.* a message sent by telegraph.

tel·e·graph /téligraf/ *n. & v.* • *n.* **1** a system of or device for transmitting messages or signals over a distance esp. by making and breaking an electrical connection. **2** (*attrib.*) used in this system (*telegraph pole; telegraph wire*). •*v.* **1** *tr.* send a message to by telegraph. **2** *tr.* send by telegraph. **3** *tr.* give an advance indication of. **4** *intr.* make signals (*telegraphed to me to come up*). ▫▫ **te·leg·ra·pher** /tilégrəfər, téligrafər/ *n.*

tel·e·graph·ic /téligráfik/ *adj.* **1** of or by telegraphs or telegrams. **2** economically worded. ▫▫ **tel·e·graph·i·cal·ly** *adv.*

te·leg·ra·phy /təlégrəfee/ *n.* the science or practice of using or constructing communication systems for the reproduction of information.

tel·e·ki·ne·sis /télikinéesis, –kī/ *n. Psychol.* movement of objects at a distance supposedly by paranormal means. ▫▫ **tel·e·ki·net·ic** /–nétik/ *adj.*

tel·e·mark /télimaark/ *n.* & *v. Skiing* •*n.* a swing turn with one ski advanced and the knee bent, used to change direction or stop short. •*v.intr.* perform this turn.

tel·e·mar·ket·ing /télimaárkiting/ *n.* the marketing of goods, etc., by means of usu. unsolicited telephone calls. ▫▫ **tel·e·mar·ket·er** *n.*

te·lem·e·ter /tilémitər, télimeetər/ *n.* & *v.* •*n.* an apparatus for recording the readings of an instrument and transmitting them by radio. •*v.* **1** *intr.* record readings in this way. **2** *tr.* transmit (readings, etc.) to a distant receiving set or station. ▫▫ **tel·e·met·ric** /teləmétrik/ *adj.* **te·lem·e·try** /tilémitree/ *n.*

tel·e·ol·o·gy /téleeóləjee, tée–/ *n.* (*pl.* **-gies**) *Philos.* **1** the explanation of phenomena by the purpose they serve rather than by postulated causes. **2** *Theol.* the doctrine of design and purpose in the material world. ▫▫ **tel·e·o·log·ic** /–leeəlójik/ *adj.* **tel·e·o·log·i·cal** *adj.* **tel·e·o·log·i·cal·ly** *adv.* **tel·e·ol·o·gism** *n.* **tel·e·ol·o·gist** *n.*

tel·e·path /télipath/ *n.* a telepathic person.

te·lep·a·thy /təlépəthee/ *n.* the supposed communication of thoughts or ideas otherwise than by the known senses. ▫▫ **tel·e·path·ic** /télipáthik/ *adj.* **tel·e·path·i·cal·ly** *adv.* **te·lep·a·thist** *n.* **te·lep·a·thize** *v.tr.* & *intr.*

tel·e·phone /télifōn/ *n.* & *v.* •*n.* **1** an apparatus for transmitting sound (esp. speech) over a distance by wire or cord or radio, esp. by converting acoustic vibrations to electrical signals. **2** a transmitting and receiving instrument used in this. **3** a system of communication using a network of telephones. •*v.* **1** *tr.* speak to (a person) by telephone. **2** *tr.* send (a message) by telephone (*telephoned my congratulations*). **3** *intr.* make a telephone call. ▫ **on the telephone** by use of or using the telephone. **over the telephone** by use of or using the telephone. ▫▫ **tel·e·phon·er** *n.* **tel·e·phon·ic** /–fónik/ *adj.* **tel·e·phon·i·cal·ly** /–fóniklee/ *adv.*

tel·e·phone booth *n.* a public booth or enclosure from which telephone calls can be made.

te·leph·o·ny /təléfənee/ *n.* the use or a system of telephones.

tel·e·pho·to·graph·ic /télifṓtəgráfik/ *adj.* of or for or using telephotography. ▫▫ **tel·e·pho·to·graph·i·cal·ly** *adv.*

tel·e·pho·tog·ra·phy /télifətógrəfee/ *n.* the photographing of distant objects with a system of lenses giving a large image.

tel·e·pho·to lens /télifṓtō/ *n.* a lens used in telephotography.

tel·e·port[1] /télipawrt/ *v.tr. Psychol.* move by telekinesis. ▫▫ **tel·e·por·ta·tion** *n.*

tel·e·port[2] /télipawrt/ *n.* a center providing interconnections between different forms of telecommunications, esp. one that links satellites to ground-based communications.

Tel·e·Promp·Ter /télipromptər/ *n. Trademark* a device used in television and film-making to project a speaker's script out of sight of the audience (cf. AUTOCUE).

tel·e·scope /téliskōp/ *n.* & *v.* •*n.* **1** an optical instrument using lenses or mirrors or both to make distant objects appear nearer and larger. **2** = RADIO TELESCOPE. •*v.* **1** *tr.* press or drive (sections of a tube, colliding vehicles, etc.) together so that one slides into another like the sections of a folding telescope. **2** *intr.* close or be driven or be capable of closing in this way. **3** *tr.* compress so as to occupy less space or time.

tel·e·scop·ic /téliskópik/ *adj.* **1 a** of, relating to, or made with a telescope (*telescopic observations*). **b** visible only through a telescope (*telescopic stars*). **2** (esp. of a lens) able to focus on and magnify distant objects. **3** consisting of sections that telescope. ▫▫ **tel·e·scop·i·cal·ly** *adv.*

tel·e·scop·ic sight *n.* a telescope used for sighting on a rifle, etc.

tel·e·soft·ware /télisawftwair, –sóft–/ *n.* software transmitted or broadcast to receiving terminals.

tel·e·text /télitekst/ *n.* a news and information service, in the form of text and graphics, from a computer source transmitted to televisions with appropriate receivers.

tel·e·thon /télithon/ *n.* an exceptionally long television program, esp. to raise money for a charity.

Tel·e·type /télitīp/ *n. Trademark* telegraphic apparatus for direct exchange of printed messages.

tel·e·type·writ·er /télitīprītər/ *n.* a device for transmitting telegraph messages as they are keyed, and for printing messages received.

tel·e·van·ge·list /télivánjəlist/ *n.* an evangelical preacher who appears regularly on television to promote beliefs and appeal for funds.

tel·e·view·er /télivyōōər/ *v.tr.* a person who watches television. ▫▫ **tel·e·view·ing** *adj.*

tel·e·vise /télivīz/ *v.tr.* transmit by television. ▫▫ **tel·e·vis·a·ble** *adj.*

tel·e·vi·sion /télivízhən/ *n.* **1** a system for reproducing on a screen visual images transmitted (usu. with sound) by radio waves. **2** (in full **television set**) a device with a screen for receiving these signals. **3** the medium, art form, or occupation of broadcasting on television; the content of television programs.

tel·ex /téleks/ *n.* & *v.* (also **Telex**) •*n.* an international system of telegraphy with printed messages transmitted and received by teletypewriters using the public telecommunications network. •*v.tr.* send or communicate with by telex.

tell /tel/ *v.* (*past* and *past part.* **told** /tōld/) **1** *tr.* relate or narrate in speech or writing; give an account of (*tell me a story*). **2** *tr.* make known; express in words; divulge (*tell me what you want*). **3** *tr.* reveal or signify to (a person) (*your face tells me everything*). **4** *tr.* **a** utter (*don't tell lies*). **b** warn (*I told you so*). **5** *intr.* **a** (often foll. by *of, about*) divulge information or a description; reveal a secret. **b** (foll. by *on*) *colloq.* inform against (a person). **6** *tr.* (foll. by *to* + infin.) give (a person) a direction or order. **7** *tr.* assure (*it's true, I tell you*). **8** *tr.* explain in writing; instruct (*this book tells you how to cook*). **9** *tr.* decide determine; distinguish (*how do you tell one from the other?*). **10** *intr.* **a** (often foll. by *on*) produce a noticeable effect (*the strain was beginning to tell on me*). **b** reveal the truth (*time will tell*). **c** have an influence (*the evidence tells against you*). **11** *tr.* (often *absol.*) count (votes) at a meeting, election, etc. ▫ **tell apart** distinguish between (usu. with *neg.* or *interrog.*: *could not tell them apart*). **tell me another** *colloq.* an expression of incredulity. **tell off 1** *colloq.* reprimand; scold. **2** count off or detach for duty. **tell tales** report a discreditable fact about another. **tell (the) time** determine the time from the face of a clock or watch.

there is no telling it is impossible to know (*there's no telling what may happen*). **you're telling me** *colloq.* I agree wholeheartedly. ▫▫ **tell·a·ble** *adj.*
tell·er /télər/ *n.* **1** a person employed to receive and pay out money in a bank, etc. **2** a person who counts (votes). **3** a person who tells esp. stories (*a teller of tales*). ▫▫ **tell·er·ship** *n.*
tell·ing /téling/ *adj.* **1** having a marked effect; striking. **2** significant. ▫▫ **tell·ing·ly** *adv.*
tell·tale /téltayl/ *n.* **1** a person who reveals (esp. discreditable) information about another's private affairs or behavior. **2** (*attrib.*) that reveals or betrays (*a telltale smile*). **3** a device for automatic indicating, monitoring, or registering of a process, etc.
tel·lu·ri·an /telŏŏreeən/ *adj. & n.* • *adj.* of or inhabiting the earth. • *n.* an inhabitant of the earth.
tel·lu·ri·um /telŏŏreeəm/ *n. Chem.* a rare brittle lustrous silver-white element occurring naturally in ores of gold and silver, used in semiconductors. ¶ Symb.: **Te.** ▫▫ **tel·lu·ride** /télyərīd/ *n.* **tel·lu·rite** /télyərīt/ *n.* **tel·lu·rous** *adj.*
te·mer·i·ty /timéritee/ *n.* **1** rashness. **2** audacity; impudence.
temp /temp/ *n. & v. colloq.* • *n.* a temporary employee. • *v.intr.* work as a temp.
temp. /temp/ *abbr.* temperature.
tem·per /témpər/ *n. & v.* • *n.* **1** habitual or temporary disposition of mind esp. as regards composure (*a person of calm temper*). **2 a** irritation or anger (*in a fit of temper*). **b** an instance of this (*flew into a temper*). **3** a tendency to have fits of anger (*have a temper*). **4** composure or calmness (*keep one's temper; lose one's temper*). **5** the condition of metal as regards hardness and elasticity. • *v.tr.* **1** bring (metal or clay) to a proper hardness or consistency. **2** (often foll. by *with*) moderate or mitigate (*temper justice with mercy*). ▫▫ **tem·per·a·ble** *adj.* **tem·pered** *adj.*

---

temper Old English *temprian* 'bring something into the required condition by mixing it with something else,' from Latin *temperare* 'mingle, restrain oneself.' Sense development was probably influenced by Old French *temprer* 'to temper, moderate.' The noun originally denoted a correct or proportionate mixture of elements or qualities, also the combination of the four bodily humors, believed in medieval times to be the basis of temperament, hence sense 1 (late Middle English).

---

tem·per·a /témpərə/ *n.* a method of painting using an emulsion, e.g., of pigment with egg, esp. on canvas.
tem·per·a·ment /témprəmənt/ *n.* **1** a person's distinct nature and character, esp. as determined by physical constitution and permanently affecting behavior (*a nervous temperament; the artistic temperament*). **2** a creative or spirited personality (*was full of temperament*).
tem·per·a·men·tal /témprəmént'l/ *adj.* **1** of temperament. **2 a** (of a person) prone to erratic or moody behavior. **b** (of a thing, e.g., a machine) working unpredictably; unreliable. ▫▫ **tem·per·a·men·tal·ly** *adv.*
tem·per·ance /témpərəns, témprəns/ *n.* **1** moderation or self-restraint esp. in eating and drinking. **2 a** total or partial abstinence from alcohol. **b** (*attrib.*) advocating or concerned with abstinence.
tem·per·ate /témpərət, témprət/ *adj.* **1** avoiding excess; self-restrained. **2** moderate. **3** (of a region or climate) characterized by mild temperatures. **4** abstemious. ▫▫ **tem·per·ate·ly** *adv.* **tem·per·ate·ness** *n.*
tem·per·a·ture /témprichər/ *n.* **1** the degree or intensity of heat of a body, air mass, etc., in relation to others, esp. as shown by a thermometer or perceived by touch, etc. **2** *Med.* the degree of internal heat of the body. **3** *colloq.* a body temperature above the normal (*have a temperature*). **4** the degree of excitement in a discussion, etc.
-tempered /témpərd/ *comb. form* having a specified temper or disposition (*bad-tempered; hot-tempered*). ▫▫ **-temperedly** *adv.* **-temperedness** *n.*
tem·pest /témpist/ *n.* **1** a violent windy storm. **2** violent agitation or tumult.
tem·pes·tu·ous /tempéschŏŏəs/ *adj.* **1** stormy. **2** (of a person, emotion, etc.) turbulent; violent; passionate. ▫▫ **tem·pes·tu·ous·ly** *adv.* **tem·pes·tu·ous·ness** *n.*
tem·plate /témplit, –playt/ *n.* (also **tem·plet**) **1** a pattern or gauge, usu. a piece of thin board or metal plate, used as a guide in cutting or drilling metal, stone, wood, etc. **2** a flat card or plastic pattern esp. for cutting cloth for patchwork, etc.
tem·ple[1] /témpəl/ *n.* **1** a building devoted to the worship, or regarded as the dwelling place, of a god or gods or other objects of religious reverence. **2** *hist.* any of three successive religious buildings of the Jews in Jerusalem. **3** a Reform or Conservative synagogue. **4** a place of Christian public worship, esp. a Protestant church in France. **5** any place in which God is regarded as residing, as the body of a Christian (I Cor. 6:19).
tem·ple[2] /témpəl/ *n.* the flat part of either side of the head between the forehead and the ear.
tem·po /témpō/ *n.* (*pl.* **-pos** or **tempi** /–pee/) **1** *Mus.* the speed at which music is or should be played, esp. as characteristic (*waltz tempo*). **2** the rate of motion or activity (*the tempo of the war is quickening*).
tem·po·ral /témpərəl, témprəl/ *adj.* **1** of worldly as opposed to spiritual affairs; of this life; secular. **2** of or relating to time. **3** *Gram.* relating to or denoting time or tense (*temporal conjunction*). ▫▫ **tem·po·ral·ly** *adv.*
tem·po·ral lobe *n.* each of the paired lobes of the brain lying beneath the temples, including areas concerned with the understanding of speech.
tem·po·rar·y /témpəréree/ *adj. & n.* • *adj.* lasting or meant to last only for a limited time (*temporary buildings; temporary relief*). • *n.* (*pl.* **-ies**) a person employed temporarily (cf. TEMP). ▫▫ **tem·po·rar·i·ly** /–pəráirilee/ *adv.* **tem·po·rar·i·ness** *n.*
tem·po·rize /témpərīz/ *v.intr.* **1** avoid committing oneself so as to gain time; employ delaying tactics. **2** comply temporarily with the requirements of the occasion; adopt a time-serving policy. ▫▫ **tem·po·ri·za·tion** *n.* **tem·po·riz·er** *n.*
tempt /tempt/ *v.tr.* **1** entice or incite (a person) to do a wrong or forbidden thing (*tempted him to steal it*). **2** allure; attract. **3** risk provoking (esp. an abstract force or power) (*would be tempting fate to try it*). **4** *archaic* make trial of; try the resolution of (*God did tempt Abraham*). ▫ **be tempted to** be strongly disposed to (*I am tempted to question this*). ▫▫ **tempt·a·ble** *adj.* **tempt·a·bil·i·ty** /témptəbílitee/ *n.*
temp·ta·tion /temptáyshən/ *n.* **1** the act or an instance of tempting; the state of being tempted; incitement esp. to wrongdoing. **2** an attractive thing or course of action.
tempt·er /témptər/ *n.* (*fem.* **tempt·ress** /–tris/) a person who tempts.
tempt·ing /témpting/ *adj.* **1** attractive; inviting. **2** enticing to evil. ▫▫ **tempt·ing·ly** *adv.*
tem·pu·ra /tempŏŏrə/ *n.* a Japanese dish of fish, shellfish, or vegetables, dipped in batter and deep-fried.
ten /ten/ *n. & adj.* • *n.* **1** one more than nine. **2** a symbol for this (10, x, X). **3** a size, etc., denoted by ten. **4** the time of ten o'clock (*is it ten yet?*). **5** a playing card with ten pips. **6** a ten-dollar bill. **7** a set of ten. • *adj.* **1** that amount to ten. **2** (as a round number) several (*ten times as easy*).

---

ten Old English *tēn, tīen,* of Germanic origin; related to Dutch *tien* and German *zehn,* from an Indo-European root shared by Sanskrit *daśa*, Greek *deka*, and Latin *decem*.

ten·a·ble /ténəbəl/ *adj.* **1** that can be maintained or defended against attack or objection (*a tenable position; a tenable theory*). **2** (foll. by *for, by*) (of an office, etc.) that can be held for (a specified period) or by (a specified class of person). □□ **ten·a·bil·i·ty** *n.* **ten·a·ble·ness** *n.*

te·na·cious /tináyshəs/ *adj.* **1** (often foll. by *of*) keeping a firm hold of property, principles, life, etc.; not readily relinquishing. **2** (of memory) retentive. **3** holding fast. **4** strongly cohesive. **5** persistent; resolute. **6** adhesive; sticky. □□ **te·na·cious·ly** *adv.* **te·na·cious·ness** *n.* **te·nac·i·ty** /tinásitee/ *n.*

ten·an·cy /ténənsee/ *n.* (*pl.* **-cies**) **1** the status of a tenant; possession as a tenant. **2** the duration or period of this.

ten·ant /ténənt/ *n.* & *v.* • *n.* **1** a person who rents land or property from a landlord. **2** (often foll. by *of*) the occupant of a place. **3** *Law* a person holding real property by private ownership. • *v.tr.* occupy as a tenant. □□ **ten·ant·a·ble** *adj.* **ten·ant·less** *adj.*

tend[1] /tend/ *v.intr.* **1** be apt or inclined (to) (*tends to lose his temper*). **2** be moving; be directed; hold a course (*tends to the same conclusion*).

tend[2] /tend/ *v.* **1** *tr.* take care of; look after (a person, esp. an invalid; animals, esp. sheep; a machine). **2** *intr.* (foll. by *on, upon*) wait on. **3** *intr.* (foll. by *to*) give attention to.

ten·den·cy /téndənsee/ *n.* (*pl.* **-cies**) **1** (often foll. by *to, toward*) a leaning or inclination; a way of tending. **2** a group within a larger political party or movement.

ten·den·tious /tendénshəs/ *adj. derog.* (of writing, etc.) calculated to promote a particular cause or viewpoint; having an underlying purpose. □□ **ten·den·tious·ly** *adv.* **ten·den·tious·ness** *n.*

ten·der[1] /téndər/ *adj.* (**tenderer, tenderest**) **1** easily cut or chewed; not tough (*tender steak*). **2** easily touched or wounded; susceptible to pain or grief (*a tender heart*). **3** easily hurt; sensitive (*tender skin*). **4 a** delicate; fragile (*a tender plant*). **b** gentle; soft (*a tender touch*). **5** loving; affectionate; fond (*tender parents; wrote tender verses*). **6** requiring tact or careful handling; ticklish (*a tender subject*). **7** (of age) early; immature (*of tender years*). □□ **ten·der·ly** *adv.* **ten·der·ness** *n.*

ten·der[2] /téndər/ *v.* & *n.* • *v.* **1** *tr.* **a** offer; present (one's services, apologies, resignation, etc.). **b** offer (money, etc.) as payment. **2** *intr.* (often foll. by *for*) make a tender for the supply of a thing or the execution of work. • *n.* an offer, esp. an offer in writing to execute work or supply goods at a fixed price. □ **put out to tender** seek tenders or bids for (work, etc.). □□ **ten·der·er** *n.*

tend·er[3] /téndər/ *n.* **1** a person who looks after people or things. **2** a vessel attending a larger one to supply stores, convey passengers or orders, etc. **3** a special car closely coupled to a steam locomotive to carry fuel, water, etc.

ten·der·foot /téndərfŏŏt/ *n.* a newcomer or novice, esp. to the outdoor life or to the Scouts.

ten·der·ize /téndərīz/ *v.tr.* make tender, esp. make (meat) tender by pounding, etc. □□ **ten·der·iz·er** *n.*

ten·der·loin /téndərloyn/ *n.* **1** a long tender cut of beef or pork from the loin, along the vertebrae. **2** *sl.* a district of a city where vice and corruption are prominent.

ten·don /téndən/ *n.* **1** a cord or strand of strong tissue attaching a muscle to a bone, etc. **2** (in a quadruped) = HAMSTRING. □□ **ten·di·ni·tis** /téndinítis/ *n.* **ten·di·nous** /–dinəs/ *adj.*

ten·dril /téndril/ *n.* **1** each of the slender leafless shoots by which some climbing plants cling for support. **2** a slender curl of hair, etc.

ten·e·ment /ténimənt/ *n.* **1** a room or a set of rooms forming a separate residence within a house or apartment building. **2** a house divided into and rented in tenements, esp. one that is overcrowded, in poor condition, etc. **3** a dwelling place. **4 a** a piece of land held by an owner. **b** *Law* any kind of permanent property, e.g., lands or rents held from another.

ten·et /ténit/ *n.* a doctrine, dogma, or principle held by a group or person.

ten·fold /ténfōld/ *adj.* & *adv.* **1** ten times as much or as many. **2** consisting of ten parts.

Tenn. *abbr.* Tennessee.

ten·nis /ténis/ *n.* a game in which two or four players strike a ball with rackets over a net stretched across a court.

ten·nis el·bow *n.* chronic inflammation caused by or as by playing tennis.

ten·nis shoe *n.* a light canvas or leather rubbersoled shoe suitable for tennis or general casual wear.

ten·on /ténən/ *n.* & *v.* • *n.* a projecting piece of wood made for insertion into a corresponding cavity (esp. a mortise) in another piece. • *v.tr.* **1** cut as a tenon. **2** join by means of a tenon. □□ **ten·on·er** *n.*

ten·or /ténər/ *n.* **1 a** a singing voice between baritone and alto or countertenor, the highest of the ordinary adult male range. **b** a singer with this voice. **c** a part written for it. **2** an instrument, esp. a viola, recorder, or saxophone, of which the range is roughly that of a tenor voice. **3** (usu. foll. by *of*) the general purport or drift of a document or speech. **4** (usu. foll. by *of*) a settled or prevailing course or direction, esp. the course of a person's life or habits.

ten·pin bowl·ing *n.* a game in which ten pins are set up at the end of an alley and bowled at to be knocked down.

tense[1] /tens/ *adj.* & *v.* • *adj.* **1** stretched tight; strained (*tense cord; tense nerves*). **2** causing tenseness (*a tense moment*). • *v.tr.* & *intr.* make or become tense. □ **tense up** become tense. □□ **tense·ly** *adv.* **tense·ness** *n.* **ten·si·ty** *n.*

tense[2] /tens/ *n. Gram.* **1** a form taken by a verb to indicate the time (also the continuance or completeness) of the action, etc. (*present tense; imperfect tense*). **2** a set of such forms for the various persons and numbers. □□ **tense·less** *adj.*

ten·sile /ténsəl, –sīl/ *adj.* **1** of or relating to tension. **2** capable of being drawn out or stretched. □□ **ten·sil·i·ty** /tensílitee/ *n.*

ten·sile strength *n.* resistance to breaking under tension.

ten·sion /ténshən/ *n.* & *v.* • *n.* **1** the act or an instance of stretching; the state of being stretched; tenseness. **2** mental strain or excitement. **3** a strained (political, social, etc.) state or relationship. **4** *Mech.* the stress by which a bar, cord, etc., is pulled when it is part of a system in equilibrium or motion. **5** electromagnetic force (*high tension; low tension*). • *v.tr.* subject to tension. □□ **ten·sion·al** *adj.* **ten·sion·al·ly** *adv.* **ten·sion·less** *adj.*

tent /tent/ *n.* **1** a portable shelter or dwelling of canvas, cloth, etc., supported by a pole or poles and stretched by cords attached to pegs driven into the ground. **2** *Med.* a tentlike enclosure for control of the air supply to a patient.

ten·ta·cle /téntəkəl/ *n.* **1** a long slender flexible appendage of an (esp. invertebrate) animal, used for feeling, grasping, or moving. **2** a thing used like a tentacle as a feeler, etc. **3** *Bot.* a sensitive hair or filament. □□ **ten·ta·cled** *adj.* (also in *comb.*). **ten·tac·u·lar** /–tákyələr/ *adj.* **ten·tac·u·late** /–tákyələt, –layt/ *adj.*

ten·ta·tive /téntətiv/ *adj.* **1** done by way of trial; experimental. **2** hesitant; not definite (*tentative suggestion; tentative acceptance*). ▫▫ **ten·ta·tive·ly** *adv.* **ten·ta·tive·ness** *n.*

tent cat·er·pil·lar *n.* any of several caterpillars of the genus *Malacosoma*, including *M. americanum* and *M. disstria* (forest tent caterpillar), that construct and live in large tentlike webs in trees.

ten·ter·hook /téntərho͝ok/ *n.* any of the hooks to which cloth is fastened on a tenter. ▫ **on tenterhooks** in a state of suspense or mental agitation due to uncertainty.

tenth /tenth/ *n.* & *adj.* • *n.* **1** the position in a sequence corresponding to the number 10 in the sequence 1-10. **2** something occupying this position. **3** one of ten equal parts of a thing. **4** *Mus.* **a** an interval or chord spanning an octave and a third in the diatonic scale. **b** a note separated from another by this interval. • *adj.* that is the tenth. ▫▫ **tenth·ly** *adv.*

ten·u·ous /tényo͞oəs/ *adj.* **1** slight; of little substance (*tenuous connection*). **2** (of a distinction, etc.) oversubtle. **3** thin; slender; small. **4** rarefied. ▫▫ **ten·u·ous·ly** *adv.* **ten·u·ous·ness** *n.*

ten·ure /tényər/ *n.* **1** a condition, or form of right or title, under which (esp. real) property is held. **2** (often foll. by *of*) **a** the holding or possession of an office or property. **b** the period of this (*during his tenure of office*). **3** guaranteed permanent employment, esp. as a teacher or professor after a probationary period.

ten·ured /tényərd/ *adj.* **1** (of an official position) carrying a guarantee of permanent employment. **2** (of a teacher, professor, etc.) having guaranteed tenure of office.

te·pee /téepee/ *n.* (also **tee·pee**) a conical tent, made of skins, cloth, or canvas on a frame of poles, orig. used by Native Americans.

tepee

tep·id /tépid/ *adj.* **1** slightly warm. **2** unenthusiastic. ▫▫ **tep·id·i·ty** /tipíditee/ *n.* **tep·id·ly** *adv.* **tep·id·ness** *n.*

te·qui·la /tekéelə/ *n.* a Mexican liquor made from an agave.

ter- /ter/ *comb. form* three; threefold (*tercentenary; tervalent*).

tera- /térə/ *comb. form* denoting a factor of 10^{12}.

ter·bi·um /tárbeeəm/ *n. Chem.* a silvery metallic element of the lanthanide series. ¶ Symb.: **Tb**.

terce /tərs/ *n. Eccl.* **1** the office of the canonical hour of prayer appointed for the third daytime hour (i.e., 9 a.m.). **2** this hour.

ter·cen·ten·ar·y /tə́rsenténəree, tərséntineree/ *n.* & *adj.* • *n.* (*pl.* **-ies**) **1** a three-hundredth anniversary. **2** a celebration of this. • *adj.* of this anniversary.

ter·cen·ten·ni·al /tə́rsenténeeəl/ *adj.* & *n.* • *adj.* **1** occurring every three hundred years. **2** lasting three hundred years. • *n.* a tercentenary.

ter·e·binth /téribinth/ *n.* a small Southern European tree, *Pistacia terebinthus*, yielding turpentine.

ter·gi·ver·sate /tə́rjiversáyt/ *v.intr.* **1** be apostate; change one's party or principles. **2** equivocate; make conflicting or evasive statements. **3** turn one's back on something. ▫▫ **ter·gi·ver·sa·tion** /–sáyshən/ *n.* **ter·gi·ver·sa·tor** *n.*

ter·i·ya·ki /tereeyókee/ *n.* a dish consisting of meat, poultry, or fish that is marinated in seasoned soy sauce and grilled, sautéed, or broiled.

term /tərm/ *n.* & *v.* • *n.* **1** a word used to express a definite concept, esp. in a particular branch of study, etc. (*a technical term*). **2** (in *pl.*) language used; mode of expression (*answered in no uncertain terms*). **3** (in *pl.*) a relation or footing (*we are on familiar terms*). **4** (in *pl.*) **a** conditions or stipulations (*cannot accept your terms; do it on your own terms*). **b** charge or price (*his terms are $20 a lesson*). **5 a** a limited period of some state or activity (*for a term of five years*). **b** a period over which operations are conducted or results contemplated (*in the short term*). **c** a period of some weeks, alternating with holidays or vacation, during which instruction is given in a school, college, or university, or during which a court of law holds sessions. **d** a period of imprisonment. **e** a period of tenure. **6** *Logic* a word or words that may be the subject or predicate of a proposition. **7** *Math.* **a** each of the two quantities in a ratio. **b** each quantity in a series. **c** a part of an expression joined to the rest by + or – (e.g., *a*, *b*, *c* in $a + b - c$). **8** the completion of a normal length of pregnancy. **9** an appointed day, time, etc. **10** (in full *US* **term for years** or *Brit.* **term of years**) *Law* an interest in land for a fixed period. • *v.tr.* denominate; call; assign a term to (*the music termed classical*). ▫ **bring to terms** cause to accept conditions. **come to terms** yield; give way. **come to terms with 1** reconcile oneself to (a difficulty, etc.). **2** conclude an agreement with. **in terms of 1** in the language peculiar to; using as a basis of expression or thought. **2** by way of. **make terms** conclude an agreement. **on terms** on terms of friendship or equality. ▫▫ **term·less** *adj.* **term·ly** *adj.* & *adv.*

ter·ma·gant /tə́rməgənt/ *n.* an overbearing or brawling woman; a virago or shrew.

ter·mi·na·ble /tə́rminəbəl/ *adj.* **1** that may be terminated. **2** coming to an end after a certain time (*terminable annuity*). ▫▫ **ter·mi·na·ble·ness** *n.*

ter·min·al /tə́rminəl/ *adj.* & *n.* • *adj.* **1 a** (of a disease) ending in death; fatal. **b** (of a patient) in the last stage of a fatal disease. **c** (of a morbid condition) forming the last stage of a fatal disease. **d** *colloq.* ruinous; disastrous; very great (*terminal laziness*). **2** of or forming a limit or terminus (*terminal station*). **3 a** *Zool.*, etc., ending a series (*terminal joints*). **b** *Bot.* growing at the end of a stem, etc. **4** of or done, etc., each term (*terminal accounts; terminal examinations*). • *n.* **1** a terminating thing; an extremity. **2** a terminus for trains or long-distance buses. **3** a departure and arrival building for air passengers. **4** a point of connection for closing an electric circuit. **5** an apparatus for transmission of messages between a user and a computer, communications system, etc. **6** an installation where oil is stored at the end of a pipeline or at a port. ▫▫ **ter·mi·nal·ly** *adv.*

ter·mi·nal ve·loc·i·ty *n.* a velocity of a falling body such that the resistance of the air, etc., prevents further increase of speed under gravity.

ter·mi·nate /tə́rminayt/ *v.* **1** *tr.* & *intr.* bring or come to an end. **2** *intr.* (foll. by *in*) (of a word) end in (a specified letter or syllable, etc.). **3** *tr.* end (a pregnancy) before term by artificial means. **4** *tr.* bound; limit. ▫▫ **ter·mi·na·tion** /tə́rmináyshən/ *n.* **ter·mi·na·tor** /tə́rminaytər/ *n.*

ter·mi·nol·o·gy /tə́rminóləjee/ *n.* (*pl.* **-gies**) **1** the system of terms used in a particular subject. **2** the science of the proper use of terms. ▫▫ **ter·mi·no·log·i·cal** *adj.* **ter·mi·no·log·i·cal·ly** *adv.* **ter·mi·nol·o·gist** *n.*

ter·mi·nus /tə́rminəs/ *n.* (*pl.* **termini** /–nī/ or **terminuses**) **1** a station or destination at the end of a railroad or bus route. **2** a point at the end of a pipeline, etc. **3** a final point; a goal. **4** a starting point. **5** *Math.* the end point of a vector, etc.

ter·mite /tə́rmīt/ *n.* a small antlike social insect of the order *Isoptera*, chiefly tropical and destructive to wood.

term pa·per *n.* an essay or dissertation representative of the work done during a term.

tern /tərn/ *n.* any marine bird of the subfamily *Sterninae*, like a gull but usu. smaller and with a long forked tail.

ter·na·ry /tə́rnəree/ *adj.* **1** composed of three parts. **2** *Math.* using three as a base (*ternary scale*).

terp·si·cho·re·an /tə́rpsikəréeən, –káwreeən / *adj.* of or relating to dancing.

terr. *abbr.* **1** terrace. **2** territory.

ter·race /térəs/ *n.* & *v.* • *n.* **1** each of a series of flat areas formed on a slope and used for cultivation. **2** a level paved area next to a house. **3 a** a row of houses on a raised level or along the top or face of a slope. **b** *Brit.* a row of houses built in one block of uniform style; a set of row houses. **4** *Geol.* a raised beach, or a similar formation beside a river, etc. • *v.tr.* form into or provide with a terrace or terraces.

ter·ra-cot·ta /térəkótə/ *n.* & *adj.* • *n.* **1 a** unglazed usu. brownish red earthenware used chiefly as an ornamental building material and in modeling. **b** a statuette of this. **2** the color terra-cotta. • *adj.* made of or resembling terra-cotta.

ter·ra fir·ma /térə fə́rmə/ *n.* dry land; firm ground.

ter·rain /teráyn/ *n.* a tract of land as regarded by the physical geographer or the military tactician.

ter·ra·pin /térəpin/ *n.* any of various N. American edible freshwater turtles of the family *Emydidae*, found in fresh or brackish water.

ter·rar·i·um /teráireeəm/ *n.* (*pl.* **terrariums** or **terraria** /–reeə/) **1** a vivarium for small land animals. **2** a sealed transparent globe, etc., containing growing plants.

ter·res·tri·al /təréstreeəl/ *adj.* & *n.* • *adj.* **1** of or on or relating to the earth; earthly. **2 a** of or on dry land. **b** *Zool.* living on or in the ground (opp. AQUATIC, ARBOREAL, AERIAL). **c** *Bot.* growing in the soil (opp. AQUATIC, EPIPHYTIC). **3** *Astron.* (of a planet) similar in size or composition to the earth. **4** of this world; worldly (*terrestrial interests*). • *n.* an inhabitant of the earth. □□ **ter·res·tri·al·ly** *adv.*

ter·ri·ble /téribəl/ *adj.* **1** *colloq.* very great or bad (*a terrible bore*). **2** *colloq.* very incompetent (*terrible at tennis*). **3** causing terror; fit to cause terror; awful; dreadful; formidable. **4** (*predic.*; usu. foll. by *about*) *colloq.* full of remorse; sorry (*I felt terrible about it*). □□ **ter·ri·ble·ness** *n.*

ter·ri·bly /tériblee/ *adv.* **1** *colloq.* very; extremely (*he was terribly nice about it*). **2** in a terrible manner.

ter·ri·er /téreeər/ *n.* **1 a** a small dog of various breeds originally used for driving out foxes, etc., from their holes. **b** any of these breeds. **2** an eager or tenacious person or animal.

ter·rif·ic /tərífik/ *adj.* **1** *colloq.* **a** of great size or intensity. **b** excellent (*did a terrific job*). **c** excessive (*making a terrific noise*). **2** causing terror. □□ **ter·rif·i·cal·ly** *adv.*

ter·ri·fy /térifī/ *v.tr.* (**-fies, -fied**) fill with terror; frighten severely (*terrified them into submission*; *is terrified of dogs*). □□ **ter·ri·fi·er** *n.* **ter·ri·fy·ing** *adj.* **ter·ri·fy·ing·ly** *adv.*

ter·ri·to·ri·al /téritáwreeəl/ *adj.* **1** of territory (*territorial possessions*). **2** limited to a district (*the right was strictly territorial*). **3** (of a person or animal, etc.) tending to defend an area of territory. **4** of any of the territories of the US or Canada. □□ **ter·ri·to·ri·al·i·ty** /–reeálitee/ *n.* **ter·ri·to·ri·al·ize** *v.tr.* **ter·ri·to·ri·al·i·za·tion** *n.* **ter·ri·to·ri·al·ly** *adv.*

ter·ri·to·ri·al wa·ters *n.pl.* the waters under the jurisdiction of a nation, esp. the part of the sea within a stated distance of the shore (traditionally three miles from the low water mark).

ter·ri·to·ry /téritawree/ *n.* (*pl.* **-ries**) **1** the extent of the land under the jurisdiction of a ruler, nation, city, etc. **2** (**Territory**) an organized division of a country, esp. one not yet admitted to the full rights of a state. **3 a** sphere of action or thought; a province of something. **4** the area over which a sales representative or distributor operates. **5** *Zool.* an area defended by an animal or animals against others of the same species. **6** an area defended by a team or player in a game. **7** a large tract of land.

ter·ror /térər/ *n.* **1** extreme fear. **2 a** a person or thing that causes terror. **b** (also **holy terror**) *colloq.* a formidable person; a troublesome person or thing (*the twins are little terrors*). **3** the use of organized intimidation; terrorism.

ter·ror·ist /térərist/ *n.* (also *attrib.*) a person who uses or favors violent and intimidating methods of coercing a government or community. □□ **ter·ror·ism** *n.* **ter·ror·is·tic** *adj.* **ter·ror·is·ti·cal·ly** *adv.*

---

terrorist late 18th century: from French *terroriste*, from Latin *terror* (source of *terror*). The word was originally applied to supporters of the Jacobins in the French Revolution, who advocated repression and violence in pursuit of the principles of democracy and equality.

---

ter·ror·ize /térərīz/ *v.tr.* **1** fill with terror. **2** use terrorism against. □□ **ter·ror·i·za·tion** *n.* **ter·ror·iz·er** *n.*

ter·ror-strick·en *adj.* (also **ter·ror-struck**) affected with terror.

ter·ry /téree/ *n.* & *adj.* • *n.* (*pl.* **-ries**) a pile fabric with the loops uncut, used esp. for towels. • *adj.* of this fabric.

terse /ters/ *adj.* (**terser, tersest**) **1** (of language) brief; concise; to the point. **2** curt; abrupt. □□ **terse·ly** *adv.* **terse·ness** *n.*

ter·ti·ar·y /tə́rshee-eree, –shəri/ *adj.* & *n.* • *adj.* **1** third in order or rank, etc. **2** (**Tertiary**) *Geol.* of or relating to the first period in the Cenozoic era with evidence of the development of mammals and flowering plants (cf. PALEOCENE, EOCENE, OLIGOCENE, MIOCENE, PLIOCENE). • *n.* *Geol.* this period or system.

tes·la /téslə/ *n.* a unit of magnetic flux density.

tes·sel·late /tésəlayt/ *v.tr.* **1** make from tesserae. **2** *Math.* cover (a plane surface) by repeated use of a single shape.

tes·sel·lat·ed /tésəlaytid/ *adj.* **1** of or resembling mosaic. **2** *Bot.* & *Zool.* regularly checkered.

tes·ser·a /tésərə/ *n.* (*pl.* **tesserae** /–ree/) **1** a small square block used in mosaic. **2** *Gk* & *Rom. Antiq.* a small square of bone, etc., used as a token, ticket, etc. □□ **tes·ser·al** *adj.*

tes·si·tu·ra /tésitŏŏrə/ *n.* *Mus.* the range within which most tones of a voice part fall.

test /test/ *n.* & *v.* • *n.* **1** a critical examination or trial of a person's or thing's qualities. **2** the means of so examining; a standard for comparison or trial; circumstances suitable for this (*success is not a fair test*). **3** a minor examination, esp. in school (*spelling test*). **4** *Brit. colloq.* a test match in cricket or rugby. **5** a ground for admission or rejection (*is excluded by our test*). **6** *Chem.* a reagent or a procedure employed to reveal the presence of another in a compound. **7** (*attrib.*) done or performed in order to test (*a test run*). • *v.tr.* **1** put to the test; make trial of (a person or thing or quality). **2** try severely; tax a person's powers of endurance, etc. **3** *Chem.* examine by means of a reagent. □ **put to the test** cause to undergo a test. **test out** put (a theory, etc.) to a practical test. □□ **test·a·ble** *adj.* **test·a·bil·i·ty** /téstəbílitee/ *n.* **test·ee** /testée/ *n.*

Test. *abbr.* Testament.

tes·ta /téstə/ *n.* (*pl.* **testae** /–tee/) *Bot.* a seed coat.

tes·ta·ment /téstəmənt/ *n.* **1** a will (esp. *last will and tes-*

tament). **2** (usu. foll. by *to*) evidence; proof (*is testament to his loyalty*). **3** *Bibl.* **a** a covenant or dispensation. **b** (**Testament**) a division of the Christian Bible (see OLD TESTAMENT, NEW TESTAMENT). **c** (**Testament**) a copy of the New Testament.

tes·ta·men·ta·ry /téstəméntəree/ *adj.* of or by or in a will.

tes·tate /téstayt/ *adj.* & *n.* • *adj.* having left a valid will at death. • *n.* a testate person. ▫▫ **tes·ta·cy** *n.* (*pl.* **-cies**).

tes·ta·tor /téstaytər, testáytər/ *n.* (*fem.* **tes·ta·trix** /testáytriks/) a person who has made a will, esp. one who dies testate.

test case *n. Law* a case setting a precedent for other cases involving the same question of law.

test drive *n.* & *v.* • *n.* a drive taken to determine the qualities of a motor vehicle with a view to its regular use. • *v.tr.* (**test-drive**) (*past* **-drove**; *past part.* **-driven**) drive a vehicle for this purpose.

test·er[1] /téstər/ *n.* **1** a person or thing that tests. **2** a sample of a cosmetic, etc., allowing customers to try it before purchase.

tes·ter[2] /téstər/ *n.* a canopy, esp. over a four-poster bed.

tes·tes *pl.* of TESTIS.

test flight *n.* a flight during which the performance of an aircraft is tested. ▫▫ **test-fly** *v.tr.* (**-flies**; *past* **-flew**; *past part.* **-flown**)

tes·ti·cle /téstikəl/ *n.* a male organ that produces spermatozoa, etc., esp. one of a pair enclosed in the scrotum behind the penis of a man and most mammals. ▫▫ **tes·tic·u·lar** /–stíkyələr/ *adj.*

tes·tic·u·late /testíkyələt/ *adj.* **1** having or shaped like testicles. **2** *Bot.* (esp. of an orchid) having pairs of tubers so shaped.

tes·ti·fy /téstifī/ *v.* (**-fies**, **-fied**) **1** *intr.* (of a person or thing) bear witness (*testified to the facts*). **2** *intr. Law* give evidence. **3** *tr.* affirm or declare (*testified his regret*; *testified that she had been present*). **4** *tr.* (of a thing) be evidence of; evince. ▫▫ **tes·ti·fi·er** *n.*

tes·ti·mo·ni·al /téstimṓneeəl/ *n.* **1** a certificate of character, conduct, or qualifications. **2** a gift presented to a person (esp. in public) as a mark of esteem, in acknowledgment of services, etc.

tes·ti·mo·ny /téstimōnee/ *n.* (*pl.* **-nies**) **1** *Law* an oral or written statement under oath or affirmation. **2** declaration or statement of fact. **3** evidence; demonstration (*called him in testimony*; *produce testimony*).

tes·tis /téstis/ *n.* (*pl.* **testes** /–teez/) *Anat.* & *Zool.* a testicle.

tes·tos·ter·one /testóstərōn/ *n.* a steroid androgen formed in the testicles.

test pat·tern *n.* a still television picture transmitted outside normal program hours and designed for use in judging the quality and position of the image.

test pi·lot *n.* a pilot who test-flies aircraft.

test tube *n.* a thin glass tube closed at one end used for chemical tests, etc.

tes·tu·di·nal /testṓṓd'nəl, –tyṓṓd–/ *adj.* of or shaped like a tortoise.

tes·ty /téstee/ *adj.* (**testier**, **testiest**) irritable; touchy. ▫▫ **tes·ti·ly** *adv.* **tes·ti·ness** *n.*

tet·a·nus /tét'nəs/ *n.* a bacterial disease affecting the nervous system and marked by tonic spasm of the voluntary muscles.

tetch·y /téchee/ *adj.* (also **tech·y**) (**-ier**, **-iest**) peevish; irritable. ▫▫ **tetch·i·ly** *adv.* **tetch·i·ness** *n.*

tête-à-tête /táytaatáyt, tétaatét/ *n.*, *adv.*, & *adj.* • *n.* a private conversation or interview usu. between two persons. • *adv.* together in private (*dined tête-à-tête*). • *adj.* **1** private; confidential. **2** concerning only two persons.

teth·er /té<u>th</u>ər/ *n.* & *v.* • *n.* a rope, etc., by which an animal is tied to confine it to the spot. • *v.tr.* tie (an animal) with a tether. ▫ **at the end of one's tether** having reached the limit of one's patience, resources, abilities, etc.

tetra- /tétrə/ *comb. form* (also **tetr-** before a vowel) **1** four (*tetrapod*). **2** *Chem.* (forming names of compounds) containing four atoms or groups of a specified kind (*tetroxide*).

tet·ra·chord /tétrəkawrd/ *n. Mus.* **1** a scale pattern of four notes, the interval between the first and last being a perfect fourth. **2** a musical instrument with four strings.

tet·ra·cy·cline /tétrəsíkleen, –klin/ *n.* an antibiotic with a molecule of four rings.

tet·rad /tétrad/ *n.* **1** a group of four. **2** the number four.

tet·ra·dac·tyl /tétrədáktil/ *n. Zool.* an animal with four toes on each foot. ▫▫ **tet·ra·dac·tyl·ous** *adj.*

tet·ra·gon /tétrəgon/ *n.* a plane figure with four angles and four sides.

te·trag·o·nal /tetrágənəl/ *adj.* of or like a tetragon. ▫▫ **te·trag·o·nal·ly** *adv.*

tet·ra·gram /tétrəgram/ *n.* a word of four letters.

tet·ra·he·dron /tétrəhéedrən/ *n.* (*pl.* **tetrahedra** /–drə/ or **tetrahedrons**) a four-faced regular solid; a triangular pyramid. ▫▫ **tet·ra·he·dral** *adj.*

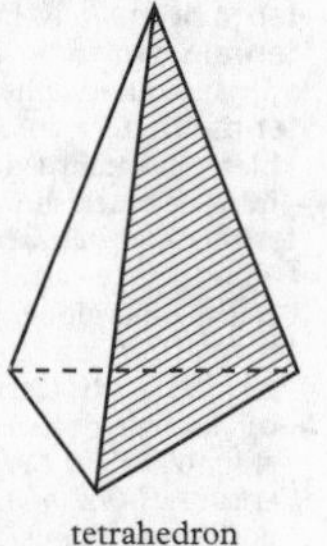
tetrahedron

te·tral·o·gy /tetráləjee, –tról–/ *n.* (*pl.* **-gies**) **1** a group of four related literary or operatic works. **2** *Gk Antiq.* a trilogy of tragedies with a satyric drama.

te·tram·e·ter /tetrámitər/ *n. Prosody* a verse of four measures.

tet·ra·ple·gi·a /tétrəpléejeeə, –jə/ *n. Med.* = QUADRIPLEGIA. ▫▫ **tet·ra·ple·gic** *adj.* & *n.*

tet·ra·ploid /tétrəployd/ *adj.* & *n. Biol.* • *adj.* (of an organism or cell) having four times the haploid set of chromosomes. • *n.* a tetraploid organism or cell.

tet·ra·pod /tétrəpod/ *n.* **1** *Zool.* an animal with four feet. **2** a structure supported by four feet radiating from a center. ▫▫ **te·trap·o·dous** /titrápədəs/ *adj.*

te·trarch /tétraark/ *n.* **1** *Rom.Hist.* **a** the governor of a fourth part of a country or province. **b** a subordinate ruler. **2** one of four joint rulers. ▫▫ **te·trarch·ate** /–kayt/ *n.* **te·trar·chi·cal** /–raárkikəl/ *adj.* **te·trar·chy** *n.* (*pl.* **-chies**).

te·trath·lon /tetráthlən/ *n.* a contest comprising four events, esp. riding, shooting, swimming, and running.

tet·ra·va·lent /tétrəváylənt/ *adj. Chem.* having a valence of four; quadrivalent.

Teu·ton /tṓṓt'n, tyṓṓtən/ *n.* a member of a Teutonic nation, esp. a German.

Teu·ton·ic /tōōtónik, tyōō–/ *adj.* **1** relating to or characteristic of the Germanic peoples or their languages. **2** German.

Tex. *abbr.* Texas.

Tex·an /téksən/ *n.* & *adj.* • *n.* a native or inhabitant of Texas. • *adj.* of or relating to Texas.

Tex-Mex /téksméks/ *adj.* combining cultural elements from Texas and Mexico, as in cooking, music, etc.

text /tekst/ *n.* **1** the main body of a book as distinct from notes, appendices, pictures, etc. **2** the original words of an author or document, esp. as distinct from a paraphrase of or commentary on them. **3** a passage quoted from Scripture, esp. as the subject of a sermon. **4** a subject or theme. **5** (in *pl.*) books prescribed for study. **6** a textbook. **7** data in textual form, esp. as stored, processed or displayed in a word processor etc. ▫▫ **textless** *adj.*

text·book /tékstbŏŏk/ *n.* & *adj.* • *n.* a book for use in studying, esp. a standard account of a subject. • *attrib.adj.* **1** exemplary; accurate (cf. COPYBOOK). **2** instructively typical. ▫▫ **text·book·ish** *adj.*

text ed·i·tor *n. Computing* a system or program allowing the user to enter and edit text.

tex·tile /tékstīl/ *n. & adj.* • *n.* **1** any woven material. **2** any cloth. • *adj.* **1** of weaving or cloth (*textile industry*). **2** woven (*textile fabrics*). **3** suitable for weaving (*textile materials*).

tex·tu·al /tékschōōəl/ *adj.* of, in, or concerning a text (*textual errors*). ▫▫ **tex·tu·al·ly** *adv.*

tex·tu·al·ist /tékschōōəlist/ *n.* a person who adheres strictly to the letter of the text. ▫▫ **tex·tu·al·ism** *n.*

tex·ture /tékschər/ *n. & v.* • *n.* **1** the feel or appearance of a surface or substance. **2** the arrangement of threads, etc., in textile fabric. **3** the arrangement of small constituent parts. **4** the quality of a piece of writing, esp. with reference to imagery, alliteration, etc. **5** quality or style resulting from composition (*the texture of her life*). • *v.tr.* (usu. as **textured** *adj.*) provide with a texture. ▫▫ **tex·tur·al** *adj.* **tex·tur·al·ly** *adv.* **tex·ture·less** *adj.*

tex·tur·ize /tékschərīz/ *v.tr.* (usu. as **texturized** *adj.*) impart a particular texture to (fabrics or food).

Th *symb. Chem.* the element thorium.

Th. *abbr.* Thursday.

Thai /tī/ *n. & adj.* • *n.* (*pl.* same or **Thais**) **1 a** a native or inhabitant of Thailand in SE Asia; a member of the largest ethnic group in Thailand. **b** a person of Thai descent. **2** the language of Thailand. • *adj.* of or relating to Thailand or its people or language.

thal·a·mus /tháləməs/ *n.* (*pl.* **thalami** /–mī/) *Anat.* either of two masses of gray matter in the forebrain, serving as relay stations for sensory tracts. ▫▫ **tha·lam·ic** /thəlámik, tháləmik/ *adj.*

tha·lid·o·mide /thəlídəmīd/ *n.* a drug formerly used as a sedative but found in 1961 to cause fetal malformation when taken by a mother early in pregnancy.

thal·li·um /tháleeəm/ *n. Chem.* a rare soft white metallic element, occurring naturally in zinc blende and some iron ores. ¶ Symb.: **Tl**.

thal·lus /tháləs/ *n.* (*pl.* **thalli** /–lī/) a plant body without vascular tissue and not differentiated into root, stem, and leaves. ▫▫ **thal·loid** *adj.*

than /t͟han, t͟hən/ *conj.* **1** introducing the second element in a comparison (*you are older than he is*; *you are older than he*). ▶It is also possible to say *you are older than him*, with *than* treated as a preposition, esp. in less formal contexts. **2** introducing the second element in a statement of difference (*anyone other than me*).

thank /thangk/ *v. & n.* • *v.tr.* **1** express gratitude to (*thanked him for the present*). **2** hold responsible (*you can thank yourself for that*). • *n.* (in *pl.*) **1** gratitude (*expressed his heartfelt thanks*). **2** an expression of gratitude (*give thanks to all who helped*). **3** (as a formula) thank you (*thanks for your help*; *thanks very much*). ▫ **give thanks** say grace at a meal. **no** (or **small**) **thanks to** despite. **thank goodness** (or **God** or **heavens**, etc.) **1** *colloq.* an expression of relief or pleasure. **2** an expression of pious gratitude. **thanks to** as the (good or bad) result of (*thanks to my foresight*; *thanks to your obstinacy*). **thank you** a polite formula acknowledging a gift or service or an offer accepted or refused.

thank·ful /thángkfōōl/ *adj.* **1** grateful; pleased. **2** (of words or acts) expressive of thanks. ▫▫ **thank·ful·ness** *n.*

thank·ful·ly /thángkfōōlee/ *adv.* **1** in a thankful manner. **2** *disp.* let us be thankful; fortunately (*thankfully, nobody was hurt*).

thank·less /thángklis/ *adj.* **1** not expressing or feeling gratitude. **2** (of a task, etc.) giving no pleasure or profit. **3** not deserving thanks. ▫▫ **thank·less·ly** *adv.* **thank·less·ness** *n.*

thanks·giv·ing /thángksgíving/ *n.* **1 a** the expression of gratitude, esp. as a prayer. **b** a form of words for this. **2** (**Thanksgiving** or **Thanksgiving Day**) a national holiday for giving thanks, the fourth Thursday in November in the US, usu. the second Monday in October in Canada.

thank-you *n. colloq.* an instance of expressing thanks.

that /t͟hat/ *pron., adj., adv., & conj.* • *demons.pron.* (*pl.* **those** /t͟hōz/) **1** the person or thing indicated, named, or understood, esp. when observed by the speaker or when familiar to the person addressed (*I heard that*; *who is that in the yard?*; *I knew all that before*; *that is not fair*). **2** (contrasted with *this*) the further or less immediate or obvious, etc., of two (*this bag is much heavier than that*). **3** the action, behavior, or circumstances just observed or mentioned (*don't do that again*). **4** *Brit.* (on the telephone, etc.) the person spoken to (*who is that?*). **5** esp. *Brit. colloq.* referring to a strong feeling just mentioned (*'Are you glad?' 'I am that'*). **6** (esp. in relative constructions) the one, the person, etc., described or specified in some way (*those who have cars can take the luggage*; *those unfit for use*; *a table like that described above*). **7** /t͟hət/ (*pl.* **that**) used instead of *which* or *whom* to introduce a defining clause, esp. one essential to identification (*the book that you sent me*; *there is nothing here that matters*). ▶As a relative *that* usually specifies, whereas *who* or *which* need not: compare *the book that you sent me is lost* with *the book, which I gave you, is lost*. • *demons.adj.* (*pl.* **those** /t͟hōz/) **1** designating the person or thing indicated, named, understood, etc. (cf. sense 1 of *pron.*) (*look at that dog*; *what was that noise?*; *things were easier in those days*). **2** contrasted with *this* (cf. sense 2 of *pron.*) (*this bag is heavier than that one*). **3** expressing strong feeling (*shall not easily forget that day*). • *adv.* **1** to such a degree; so (*have done that much*; *will go that far*). **2** *colloq.* very (*not that good*). **3** /t͟hət/ at which, on which, etc. (*at the speed that he was going he could not stop*; *the day that I first met her*). ▶Often omitted in this sense: *the day I first met her*. • *conj.* /t͟hət/ except when stressed introducing a subordinate clause indicating: **1** a statement or hypothesis (*they say that he is better*; *there is no doubt that he meant it*; *the result was that the handle fell off*). **2** a purpose (*we live that we may eat*). **3** a result (*am so sleepy that I cannot keep my eyes open*). **4** a reason or cause (it is rather that he lacks the time). **5** a wish (*Oh, that summer were here!*).

▶Often omitted in senses 1 and 3: *they say he is better*. ▫ **all that** very (*not all that good*). **and all that** (or **and that** *colloq.*) and all or various things associated with or similar to what has been mentioned; and so forth. **like that 1** of that kind (*is fond of books like that*). **2** in that manner, as you are doing, as he has been doing, etc. (*wish they would not talk like that*). **3** *colloq.* without effort (*did the job like that*). **4** of that character (*he would not accept any payment — he is like that*). **that is** (or **that is to say**) a formula introducing or following an explanation of a preceding word or words. **that's** *colloq.* you are (by virtue of present or future obedience, etc.) (*that's a good boy*). **that's more like it** an acknowledgment of improvement. **that's right** an expression of approval or *colloq.* assent. **that's that** a formula concluding a narrative or discussion or indicating completion of a task. **that there** *sl.* = sense 1 of *adj.* **that will do** no more is needed or desirable.

▶See note at WHICH.

thatch /thach/ *n. & v.* • *n.* **1** a roofing material of straw, reeds, palm leaves, or similar material. **2** *colloq.* the hair of the head esp. when extremely thick. • *v.tr.* (also *absol.*) cover (a roof or a building) with thatch. ▫▫ **thatch·er** *n.*

thaw /thaw/ *v. & n.* • *v.* **1** *intr.* (often foll. by *out*) (of ice or snow or a frozen thing) pass into a liquid or unfrozen state. **2** *intr.* (usu. prec. by *it* as subject) (of the weather) become warm enough to melt ice, etc. (*it began to thaw*). **3** *intr.* become warm enough to lose numbness, etc. **4** *intr.* become less cold or stiff in manner; become genial. **5** *tr.* (often foll. by *out*) cause to thaw. **6** *tr.* make cordial or animated. • *n.* **1** the act or an instance of thawing. **2** the warmth of weather that thaws (*a thaw has set in*). **3** *Polit.* a relaxation of control or restriction. ▫▫ **thaw·less** *adj.*

the /before a vowel thee, before a consonant thə, when stressed thee/ *adj. & adv.* • *adj.* (called the definite article) **1** denoting one or more persons or things already mentioned, under discussion, implied, or familiar (*gave the man a wave*; *shall let the matter drop*; *hurt myself in the arm*; *went to the theater*). **2** serving to describe as unique (*the President*; *the Mississippi*). **3 a** (foll. by defining adj.) which is, who are, etc. (*ignored the embarrassed Mr. Smith*; *Edward the Seventh*). **b** (foll. by adj. used *absol.*) denoting a class described (*from the sublime to the ridiculous*). **4** best known or best entitled to the name (with *the* stressed: *no relation to the Hemingway*; *this is the book on this subject*). **5** used to indicate a following defining clause or phrase (*the book that you borrowed*; *the best I can do for you*; *the bottom of a well*). **6 a** used to indicate that a singular noun represents a species, class, etc. (*the cat loves comfort*; *has the novel a future?*; *plays the harp well*). **b** used with a noun which figuratively represents an occupation, pursuit, etc. (*went on the stage*; *too fond of the bottle*). **c** (foll. by the name of a unit) a; per (*$5 the square yard*; *allow 8 minutes to the mile*). **d** *colloq.* designating a disease, affliction, etc. (*the measles*; *the toothache*; *the blues*). **7** (foll. by a unit of time) the present; the current (*man of the moment*; *questions of the day*; *book of the month*). **8** *colloq.* my; our (*the dog*; *the car*). **9** used before the surname of the chief of a Scottish or Irish clan (*the Macnab*). • *adv.* (preceding comparatives in expressions of proportional variation) in or by that (or such a) degree; on that account (*the more the merrier*; *the more he gets the more he wants*).

the·a·ter /théeətər/ *n.* (*Brit.* **theatre**) **1 a** a building or outdoor area for dramatic performances. **b** (in full **mov·ie the·a·ter**) a building used for showing movies. **2 a** the writing and production of plays. **b** effective material for the stage (*makes good theater*). **c** action with a dramatic quality; dramatic character or effect. **3** a room or hall for lectures, etc., with seats in tiers. **4** (in full **operating theater**) **a** a room or lecture hall with rising tiers of seats to accommodate students' viewing of surgical procedures **b** *Brit.* = OPERATING ROOM. **5 a** a scene or field of action (*the theater of war*). **b** (*attrib.*) designating weapons intermediate between tactical and strategic (*theater nuclear missiles*). **6** a natural land formation in a gradually rising part-circle like ancient Greek and Roman theaters.

the·a·ter-in-the-round *n.* a dramatic performance on a stage surrounded by spectators.

the·at·ric /theeátrik/ *adj. & n.* • *adj.* = THEATRICAL. • *n.* (in *pl.*) theatrical actions.

the·at·ri·cal /theeátrikəl/ *adj. & n.* • *adj.* **1** of or for the theater; of acting or actors. **2** (of a manner, speech, gesture, or person) calculated for effect; showy; artificial; affected. • *n.* (in *pl.*) **1** dramatic performances (*amateur theatricals*). **2** theatrical actions. ▫▫ **the·at·ri·cal·ism** *n.* **the·at·ri·cal·i·ty** /–kálitee/ *n.* **the·at·ri·cal·ize** *v.tr.* **the·at·ri·cal·i·za·tion** *n.* **the·at·ri·cal·ly** *adv.*

thee /thee/ *pron.* *objective case* of THOU[1].

theft /theft/ *n.* **1** the act or an instance of stealing. **2** *Law* dishonest appropriation of another's property with intent to deprive him or her of it permanently.

their /thair/ *poss.pron.* (*attrib.*) **1** of or belonging to them or themselves (*their house*; *their own business*). **2** *disp.* as a third person sing. indefinite meaning 'his or her' (*has anyone lost their purse?*).

▶**Their** is a possessive pronoun; **there** is an adverb meaning 'at that place'; and **they're** is a contraction of 'they are': *They're having a party at their camp next week; why don't we drive there?*

theirs /thairz/ *poss.pron.* the one or ones belonging to or associated with them (*it is theirs*; *theirs are over here*). ▫ **of theirs** of or belonging to them (*a friend of theirs*).

the·ism /théeizəm/ *n.* belief in the existence of gods or a god, esp. a god sustaining a personal relationship to his creatures. ▫▫ **the·ist** *n.* **the·is·tic** *adj.* **the·is·ti·cal** *adj.* **the·is·ti·cal·ly** *adv.*

them /them, thəm/ *pron. & adj.* • *pron.* **1** *objective case* of THEY (*I saw them*). **2** *colloq.* they (*it's them again*; *is older than them*). **3** *archaic* themselves (*they fell and hurt them*). • *adj. sl.* or *dial.* those (*them bones*).

the·mat·ic /theemátik/ *adj.* **1** of or relating to subjects or topics (*thematic philately*; *the arrangement of the anthology is thematic*). **2** *Mus.* of melodic subjects (*thematic treatment*). ▫▫ **the·mat·i·cal·ly** *adv.*

theme /theem/ *n. & v.* • *n.* **1** a subject or topic on which a person speaks, writes, or thinks. **2** *Mus.* a prominent or frequently recurring melody or group of notes in a composition. **3** a school exercise, esp. an essay, on a given subject. • *v.* (as **themed** *adj.*) **1** (of a leisure park, restaurant, event, etc.) designed around a theme to unify ambience, decor, etc. **2** (often in *comb.*) having a particular theme (*war-themed computer game.*).

theme park *n.* an amusement park organized around a unifying idea.

theme song *n.* **1** a recurrent melody in a musical play or movie. **2** a signature tune.

them·selves /themsélvz, –thəm;n–/ *pron.* **1 a** *emphat. form* of THEY or THEM. **b** *refl. form* of THEM; (cf. HERSELF). **2** in their normal state of body or mind (*are quite themselves again*). ▫ **be themselves** act in their normal, unconstrained manner.

then /then/ *adv., adj., & n.* • *adv.* **1** at that time; at the time in question (*was then too busy*; *then comes the trouble*; *the then existing laws*). **2 a** next; afterwards; after that (*then he told me to come in*). **b** and also (*then, there are the children to consider*). **c** after all (*it is a problem, but then that is what we are here for*). **3 a** in that case; therefore; it follows that (*then you should have said so*). **b** if what you say is true (*but then why did you take it?*). **c** (implying grudging or impatient concession) if you must have it so (*all right then, have it your own way*). **d** used parenthetically to resume a narrative, etc. (*the policeman, then, knocked on the door*). • *adj.* that or who was such at the time in question (*the then Senator*). • *n.* that time (*until then*). ▫ **then and there** immediately and on the spot.

thence /thens/ *adv.* (also **from thence**) *archaic* or *literary* **1** from that place or source. **2** for that reason.

thence·forth /thénsfáwrth/ *adv.* (also **from thence·forth**) *formal* from that time onward.

thence·for·ward /thénsfáwrwərd/ *adv. formal* thenceforth.

theo- /théeō/ *comb. form* God or gods.

the·o·cen·tric /théeəséntrik/ *adj.* having God or a god as its center.

the·oc·ra·cy /theeókrəsee/ *n.* (*pl.* **-cies**) a form of government by God or a god directly or through a priestly order, etc. ▫▫ **the·o·crat** /théeəkrat/ *n.* **the·o·crat·ic** /theeəkrátik/ *adj.* **the·o·crat·i·cal·ly** *adv.*

the·od·o·lite /theeód'līt/ *n.* a surveying instrument for measuring horizontal and vertical angles with a rotating telescope. ▫▫ **the·od·o·lit·ic** /–lítik/ *adj.*

theol. *abbr.* **1** theological. **2** theology.

the·o·lo·gian /theeəlṓjən/ *n.* a person trained in theology.

the·o·log·i·cal /theeəlójikəl/ *adj.* of theology. ▫▫ **the·o·log·i·cal·ly** *adv.*

the·ol·o·gy /theeóləjee/ *n.* (*pl.* **-gies**) **1** the study of theistic (esp. Christian) religion. **2** a system of theistic (esp. Christian) religion. **3** the rational analysis of a religious faith. ▫▫ **the·o·log·i·cal** *adj.* **the·o·log·i·cal·ly** *adv.* **the·ol·o·gist** *n.* **the·ol·o·gize** *v.tr. & intr.*

the·o·rem /theeərəm, theerəm/ *n.* esp. *Math.* **1** a general proposition not self-evident but proved by a chain of reasoning; a truth established by means of accepted truths (cf. PROBLEM). **2** a rule in algebra, etc., esp. one expressed by symbols or formulae (*binomial theorem*). ▫▫ **the·o·re·mat·ic** /–mátik/ *adj.*

the·o·ret·i·cal /theeərétikəl/ *adj.* **1** concerned with knowledge but not with its practical application. **2** based on theory rather than experience or practice. ▫▫ **the·o·ret·i·cal·ly** *adv.*

the·o·rist /theeərist, theerist/ *n.* a holder or inventor of a theory or theories.

the·o·rize /theeərīz, theerīz/ *v.intr.* evolve or indulge in theories. ▫▫ **the·o·riz·er** *n.*

the·o·ry /theeəree, theeree/ *n.* (*pl.* **-ries**) **1** a supposition or system of ideas explaining something, esp. one based on general principles independent of the particular things to be explained (cf. HYPOTHESIS) (*atomic theory; theory of evolution*). **2** a speculative (esp. fanciful) view (*one of my pet theories*). **3** the sphere of abstract knowledge or speculative thought (*this is all very well in theory, but how will it work in practice?*). **4** the exposition of the principles of a science, etc. (*the theory of music*). **5** *Math.* a collection of propositions to illustrate the principles of a subject (*probability theory; theory of equations*).

the·os·o·phy /theeósəfee/ *n.* (*pl.* **-phies**) any of various philosophies professing to achieve a knowledge of God by spiritual ecstasy, direct intuition, or special individual relations, esp. a modern movement following Hindu and Buddhist teachings and seeking universal brotherhood. ▫▫ **the·os·o·pher** *n.* **the·o·soph·ic** /theeəsófik/ *adj.* **the·o·soph·i·cal** *adj.* **the·o·soph·i·cal·ly** *adv.* **the·os·o·phist** *n.*

ther·a·peu·tic /thérəpyṓōtik/ *adj.* **1** of, for, or contributing to the cure of disease. **2** contributing to general, esp. mental, well-being (*finds walking therapeutic*). ▫▫ **ther·a·peu·ti·cal** *adj.* **ther·a·peu·ti·cal·ly** *adv.*

ther·a·peu·tics /thérəpyṓōtiks/ *n.pl.* (usu. treated as *sing.*) the branch of medicine concerned with the treatment of disease and the action of remedial agents.

ther·a·py /thérəpee/ *n.* (*pl.* **-pies**) **1** the treatment of physical or mental disorders, other than by surgery. **2 a** a particular type of such treatment. **b** psychotherapy. ▫▫ **ther·a·pist** *n.*

there /thair/ *adv., n., & int.* • *adv.* **1** in, at, or to that place or position (*lived there for some years; goes there every day*). **2** at that point (in speech, performance, writing, etc.) (*there he stopped*). **3** in that respect (*I agree with you there*). **4** used for emphasis in calling attention (*you there!; there goes the bell*). **5** used to indicate the fact or existence of something (*there is a house on the corner*). • *n.* that place (*lives somewhere near there*). • *int.* **1** expressing confirmation, triumph, dismay, etc. (*there! what did I tell you?*). **2** used to soothe a child, etc. (*there, there, never mind*). ▫ **so there** *colloq.* that is my final decision (whether you like it or not). **there and then** immediately and on the spot. **there it is 1** that is the trouble. **2** nothing can be done about it. **there you are** (or **go**) *colloq.* **1** this is what you wanted, etc. **2** expressing confirmation, triumph, resignation, etc. ▶See note at THEIR.

there·a·bouts /tháirəbówts/ *adv.* (also **there·a·bout**) **1** near that place (*somewhere thereabouts*). **2** near that number, quantity, etc. (*two acres or thereabouts*).

there·af·ter /tháiráftər/ *adv.* after that.

there·by /tháirbī/ *adv.* by that means; as a result of that.

there·fore /tháirfawr/ *adv.* for that reason; accordingly; consequently.

there·from /tháirfrúm, –fróm/ *adv. formal* from that or it.

there·in /tháirín/ *adv. formal* **1** in that place, etc. **2** in that respect.

there·of /tháirúv, –óv/ *adv. formal* of that or it.

there·on /tháirón, –áwn/ *adv. archaic* on that or it (of motion or position).

there·to /tháirtṓō/ *adv. formal* **1** to that or it. **2** in addition; to boot.

there·up·on /tháirəpón, –páwn/ *adv.* **1** in consequence of that. **2** soon or immediately after that. **3** *archaic* upon that (of motion or position).

there·with /tháirwíth, –wíth/ *adv. archaic* **1** with that. **2** soon or immediately after that.

therm /thərm/ *n.* a unit of heat, equivalent to 100,000 British thermal units or 1.055 x 10^8 joules.

ther·mal /thə́rməl/ *adj. & n.* • *adj.* **1** of, for, or producing heat. **2** promoting the retention of heat (*thermal underwear*). • *n.* a rising current of heated air (used by gliders, balloons, and birds to gain height). ▫▫ **ther·mal·ly** *adv.*

ther·mal print·er *n. Comp.* a printer that makes a text image by application of heat to thermally sensitive paper.

therm·i·on·ic /thə́rmīónik/ *adj.* of or relating to electrons emitted from a substance at very high temperature.

thermo- /thə́rmō/ *comb. form* denoting heat.

ther·mo·chem·is·try /thə́rmōkémistree/ *n.* the branch of chemistry dealing with the quantities of heat evolved or absorbed during chemical reactions. ▫▫ **ther·mo·chem·i·cal** *adj.*

ther·mo·cou·ple /thə́rmōkupəl/ *n.* a pair of different metals in contact at a point, generating a thermoelectric voltage that can serve as a measure of temperature at this point relative to their other parts.

ther·mo·dy·nam·ics /thə́rmōdīnámiks/ *n.pl.* (usu. treated as *sing.*) the science of the relations between heat and other (mechanical, electrical, etc.) forms of energy. ▫▫ **ther·mo·dy·nam·ic** *adj.* **ther·mo·dy·nam·i·cal** *adj.* **ther·mo·dy·nam·i·cal·ly** *adv.* **ther·mo·dy·nam·i·cist** /–misist/ *n.*

ther·mo·e·lec·tric /thə́rmōiléktrik/ *adj.* producing electricity by a difference of temperatures. ▫▫ **ther·mo·e·lec·tri·cal·ly** *adv.* **ther·mo·e·lec·tric·i·ty** /–ilektrísitee/ *n.*

ther·mo·gram /thə́rməgram/ *n.* a record made by a thermograph.

ther·mo·graph /thə́rməgraf/ *n.* **1** an instrument that gives a continuous record of temperature. **2** an apparatus used to obtain an image produced by infrared radiation from a human or animal body. ▫▫ **ther·mo·graph·ic** /–gráfik/ *adj.*

ther·mog·ra·phy /thərmógrəfee/ *n. Med.* the taking or use of infrared thermograms, esp. to detect tumors.

ther·mo·la·bile /thə́rmōláybīl, –bil/ *adj.* (of a substance) unstable when heated.

ther·mo·lu·mi·nes·cence /thə́rmōlṓōminésəns/ *n.* the property of becoming luminescent when pretreated and subjected to high temperatures, used as a means of dating ancient artifacts. ▫▫ **ther·mo·lu·mi·nes·cent** *adj.*

ther·mom·e·ter /thərmómitər/ *n.* an instrument for

measuring temperature, esp. a graduated glass tube with a small bore containing mercury or alcohol which expands when heated. ▫▫ **ther·mo·met·ric** /thərməmétrik/ *adj.* **ther·mo·met·ri·cal** *adj.* **ther·mom·e·try** *n.*

ther·mo·nu·cle·ar /thérmōnóokleeər, –nyóo–/ *adj.* **1** relating to or using nuclear reactions that occur only at very high temperatures. **2** relating to or characterized by weapons using thermonuclear reactions.

ther·mo·phile /thérmōfīl/ *n.* & *adj.* (also **ther·mo·phil** /–fil/) • *n.* a bacterium, etc., growing optimally at high temperatures. • *adj.* of or being a thermophile. ▫▫ **ther·mo·phil·ic** /–fílik/ *adj.*

ther·mo·plas·tic /thérmōplástik/ *adj.* & *n.* • *adj.* (of a substance) that becomes plastic on heating and hardens on cooling, and is able to repeat these processes. • *n.* a thermoplastic substance.

ther·mos /thérməs/ *n.* (in full **thermos bottle** or **flask**) *Trademark* a bottle, etc., with a double wall enclosing a vacuum so that the liquid in the inner receptacle retains its temperature.

ther·mo·sphere /thérməsfeer/ *n.* the region of the atmosphere beyond the stratosphere and the mesosphere.

ther·mo·stat /thérməstat/ *n.* a device that automatically regulates temperature, as in a heating or cooling unit, or that activates a device when the temperature reaches a certain point, as in a fire alarm system. ▫▫ **ther·mo·stat·ic** *adj.* **ther·mo·stat·i·cal·ly** *adv.*

the·sau·rus /thisáwrəs/ *n.* (*pl.* **thesauri** /–rī/ or **thesauruses**) **1 a** a collection of concepts or words arranged according to sense. **b** a book of synonyms and antonyms. **2** a dictionary or encyclopedia.

these *pl.* of THIS.

the·sis /théesis/ *n.* (*pl.* **theses** /–seez/) **1** a proposition to be maintained or proved. **2** a dissertation, esp. by a candidate for a degree.

thes·pi·an /théspeeən/ *adj.* & *n.* • *adj.* of or relating to tragedy or drama. • *n.* an actor or actress.

the·ta /tháytə, thée–/ *n.* the eighth letter of the Greek alphabet (Θ, ϑ).

they /thay/ *pron.* (*obj.* **them**; *poss.* **their, theirs**) **1** the people, animals, or things previously named or in question (*pl.* of HE, SHE, IT[1]). **2** people in general (*they say we are wrong*). **3** those in authority (*they have raised the fees*). **4** *disp.* as a third person sing. indefinite pronoun meaning 'he or she' (*anyone can come if they want to*). ▶See note at EVERYBODY.

they'd /thayd/ *contr.* **1** they had. **2** they would.

they'll /thayl/ *contr.* **1** they will. **2** they shall.

they're /thair/ *contr.* they are.
▶See note at THEIR.

they've /thayv/ *contr.* they have.

thi·a·mine /thíəmin, –meen/ *n.* (also **thi·a·min**) a vitamin of the B complex, found in unrefined cereals, beans, and liver, a deficiency of which causes beriberi. Also called **vitamin B$_1$**, or **aneurin**.

thick /thik/ *adj.*, *n.*, & *adv.* • *adj.* **1 a** of great or specified extent between opposite surfaces (*a thick wall*; *a wall two feet thick*). **b** of large diameter (*a thick rope*). **2 a** (of a line, etc.) broad; not fine. **b** (of script or type, etc.) consisting of thick lines. **3 a** arranged closely; crowded together; dense. **b** numerous (*fell thick as peas*). **c** bushy; luxuriant (*thick hair*; *thick growth*). **4** (usu. foll. by *with*) densely covered or filled (*air thick with snow*). **5 a** firm in consistency; containing much solid matter; viscous (*a thick paste*; *thick soup*). **b** made of thick material (*a thick coat*). **6** muddy; cloudy; impenetrable by sight (*thick darkness*). **7** *colloq.* (of a person) stupid; dull. **8 a** (of a voice) indistinct. **b** (of an accent) pronounced; exaggerated. **9** *colloq.* intimate or very friendly (esp. *thick as thieves*). • *n.* a thick part of anything. • *adv.* thickly (*snow was falling thick*; *blows rained down thick and fast*). ▫ **a bit thick** *colloq.* unreasonable or intolerable. **in the thick of 1** at the busiest part of. **2** heavily occupied with. **through thick and thin** under all conditions; in spite of all difficulties. ▫▫ **thickish** *adj.* **thick·ly** *adv.*

thick·en /thíkən/ *v.* **1** *tr.* & *intr.* make or become thick or thicker. **2** *intr.* become more complicated (*the plot thickens*). ▫▫ **thick·en·er** *n.*

thick·et /thíkit/ *n.* a tangle of shrubs or trees.

thick·head /thík-hed/ *n. colloq.* a stupid person; a blockhead. ▫▫ **thick·head·ed** *adj.* **thick·head·ed·ness** *n.*

thick·ness /thíknis/ *n.* **1** the state of being thick. **2** the extent to which a thing is thick. **3** a layer of material of a certain thickness (*three thicknesses of cardboard*). **4** a part that is thick or lies between opposite surfaces (*steps cut in the thickness of the wall*).

thick·set /thíksét/ *adj.* & *n.* • *adj.* **1** heavily or solidly built. **2** set or growing close together. • *n.* a thicket.

thick-skinned *adj.* not sensitive to reproach or criticism.

thief /theef/ *n.* (*pl.* **thieves** /theevz/) a person who steals, esp. secretly and without violence.

thieve /theev/ *v.* **1** *intr.* be a thief. **2** *tr.* steal (a thing).

thiev·er·y /théevəree/ *n.* the act or practice of stealing.

thieves *pl.* of THIEF.

thigh /thī/ *n.* **1** the part of the human leg between the hip and the knee. **2** a corresponding part in other animals. ▫▫ **-thighed** *adj.* (in *comb.*).

thim·ble /thímbəl/ *n.* a metal or plastic cap, usu. with a closed end, worn to protect the finger and push the needle in sewing.

thim·ble·ful /thímbəlfool/ *n.* (*pl.* **-fuls**) a small quantity, esp. of liquid to drink.

thin /thin/ *adj.*, *adv.*, & *v.* • *adj.* (**thinner, thinnest**) **1** having the opposite surfaces close together; of small thickness or diameter. **2 a** (of a line) narrow or fine. **b** (of a script or type, etc.) consisting of thin lines. **3** made of thin material (*a thin dress*). **4** lean; not plump. **5 a** not dense or copious (*thin hair*; *a thin haze*). **b** not full or closely packed (*a thin audience*). **6** of slight consistency (*a thin paste*). **7** weak; lacking an important ingredient (*thin blood*; *a thin voice*). **8** (of an excuse, argument, disguise, etc.) flimsy or transparent. • *adv.* thinly (*cut the bread very thin*). • *v.* (**thinned, thinning**) **1** *tr.* & *intr.* make or become thin or thinner. **2** *tr.* & *intr.* (often foll. by *out*) reduce; make or become less dense or crowded or numerous. **3** *tr.* (often foll. by *out*) remove some of a crop of (seedlings, saplings, etc.) or some young fruit from (a vine or tree) to improve the growth of the rest. ▫ **thin on top** balding. ▫▫ **thin·ly** *adv.* **thin·ness** *n.* **thin·nish** *adj.*

thin air *n.* a state of invisibility or nonexistence (*vanished into thin air*).

thine /thīn/ *poss.pron. archaic* or *dial.* **1** (*predic.* or *absol.*) of or belonging to thee. **2** (*attrib.* before a vowel) = THY.

thing /thing/ *n.* **1** a material or nonmaterial entity, idea, action, etc., that is or may be thought about or perceived. **2** an inanimate material object (*take that thing away*). **3** an unspecified object or item (*have a few things to buy*). **4** an act, idea, or utterance (*a silly thing to do*). **5** an event (*an unfortunate thing to happen*). **6** a quality (*patience is a useful thing*). **7** (with ref. to a person) expressing pity, contempt, or affection (*poor thing!*; *a dear old thing*). **8** a specimen or type of something (*quarks are an important thing in physics*). **9** *colloq.* **a** one's special interest or concern (*not my thing at all*). **b** an obsession, fear, or prejudice (*spiders are a thing of mine*). **10** esp. *Brit. colloq.* something remarkable (*now there's a thing!*). **11** (prec. by *the*) *colloq.* **a** what is conventionally proper or fashionable. **b** what is needed or required (*your suggestion was just the thing*). **c** what is to be considered (*the thing is, shall we go or not?*). **d** what is important (*the thing about them is their reliability*). **12** (in *pl.*) personal belongings or clothing (*where have I left my things?*). **13** (in *pl.*) equipment (*painting things*). **14** (in *pl.*) affairs in general (*not in the nature of things*). **15** (in *pl.*) circumstances or conditions (*things look good*). **16** (in *pl.* with a following adjective) all that is so describable (*all things Greek*). □ **do one's own thing** *colloq.* pursue one's own interests or inclinations. **do things to** *colloq.* affect remarkably. **have a thing about** *colloq.* be obsessed, fearful, or prejudiced about. **make a thing of** *colloq.* **1** regard as essential. **2** cause a fuss about. **one** (or **just one**) **of those things** *colloq.* something unavoidable or to be accepted.

thing·a·ma·jig /thíngəməjig/ (also **thing·a·ma·bob** /thíngəməbob/ *n. colloq.* a thing whose name one has forgotten or does not know or does not wish to mention (*one of those thingamajigs for keeping all the fireplace tools together*).

thing·y /thíngee/ *n.* (*pl.* **-ies**) = THINGAMAJIG.

think /thingk/ *v.* & *n.* • *v.* (*past* and *past part.* **thought** /thawt/) **1** *tr.* (foll. by *that* + clause) be of the opinion (*we think that they will come*). **2** *tr.* (foll. by *that* + clause or *to* + infin.) judge or consider (*is thought to be a fraud*). **3** *intr.* exercise the mind positively with one's ideas, etc. (*let me think for a moment*). **4** *tr.* (foll. by *of* or *about*) **a** consider; be or become mentally aware of (*think of you constantly*). **b** form or entertain the idea of; imagine to oneself (*couldn't think of such a thing*). **c** choose mentally; hit upon (*think of a number*). **d** form or have an opinion of (*what do you think of them?*). **5** *tr.* have a half-formed intention (*I think I'll stay*). **6** *tr.* form a conception of (*cannot think how you do it*). **7** *tr.* reduce to a specified condition by thinking (*cannot think away a toothache*). **8** *tr.* recognize the presence or existence of (*the child thought no harm*). **9** *tr.* (foll. by *to* + infin.) intend or expect (*thinks to deceive us*). **10** *tr.* (foll. by *to* + infin.) remember (*did not think to lock the door*). • *n. colloq.* an act of thinking (*must have a think about that*). □ **think again** revise one's plans or opinions. **think out loud** utter one's thoughts as soon as they occur. **think back to** recall (a past event or time). **think better of** change one's mind about (an intention) after reconsideration. **think fit** see FIT[1]. **think for oneself** have an independent mind or attitude. **think little** (or **nothing**) **of** consider to be insignificant or unremarkable. **think much** (or **highly**) **of** have a high opinion of. **think out** **1** consider carefully. **2** produce (an idea, etc.) by thinking. **think over** reflect upon in order to reach a decision. **think through** reflect fully upon (a problem, etc.). **think twice** use careful consideration, avoid hasty action, etc. **think up** *colloq.* devise; produce by thought. □□ **think·a·ble** *adj.*

think·er /thíngkər/ *n.* **1** a person who thinks, esp. in a specified way (*an original thinker*). **2** a person with a skilled or powerful mind.

think·ing /thíngking/ *adj.* & *n.* • *adj.* using thought or rational judgment. • *n.* **1** opinion or judgment. **2** thought; train of thought. □ **put on one's thinking cap** *colloq.* meditate on a problem.

think tank *n.* a body of experts providing advice and ideas on specific national or commercial problems.

thin·ner /thínər/ *n.* a volatile liquid used to dilute paint, etc.

thin-skinned *adj.* sensitive to reproach or criticism; easily upset.

third /thərd/ *n.* & *adj.* • *n.* **1** the position in a sequence corresponding to that of the number 3 in the sequence 1– 3. **2** something occupying this position. **3** each of three equal parts of a thing. **4** *Mus.* **a** an interval or chord spanning three consecutive notes in the diatonic scale (e.g., C to E). **b** a note separated from another by this interval. • *adj.* that is the third. □□ **third·ly** *adv.*

▶See note at FIRST.

third class *n.* the third-best group or category, esp. of hotel and train accommodation. □□ **third-class** *adj.*

third de·gree *n.* long and severe questioning, esp. by police to obtain information or a confession.

third-de·gree *adj. Med.* denoting burns of the most severe kind, affecting lower layers of tissue.

third par·ty *n.* **1** another party besides the two principals. **2** a bystander, etc.

third-rate *adj.* inferior; very poor in quality.

Third Reich *n.* the Nazi regime, 1933–45.

Third World *n.* (usu. prec. by *the*) the developing countries of Asia, Africa, and Latin America.

thirst /thərst/ *n.* & *v.* • *n.* **1** a physical need to drink liquid, or the feeling of discomfort caused by this. **2** a strong desire or craving (*a thirst for power*). • *v.intr.* (often foll. by *for* or *after*) **1** feel thirst. **2** have a strong desire.

thirst·y /thə́rstee/ *adj.* (**thirstier, thirstiest**) **1** feeling thirst. **2** (of land, a season, etc.) dry or parched. **3** (often foll. by *for* or *after*) eager. **4** *colloq.* causing thirst (*thirsty work*). □□ **thirst·i·ly** *adv.* **thirst·i·ness** *n.*

thir·teen /thə́rtéen/ *n.* & *adj.* • *n.* **1** one more than twelve, or three more than ten. **2** a symbol for this (13, xiii, XIII). **3** a size, etc., denoted by thirteen. • *adj.* that amount to thirteen. □□ **thir·teenth** *adj.* & *n.*

thir·ty /thə́rtee/ *n.* & *adj.* • *n.* (*pl.* **-ties**) **1** the product of three and ten. **2** a symbol for this (30, xxx, XXX). **3** (in *pl.*) the numbers from 30 to 39, esp. the years of a century or of a person's life. • *adj.* that amount to thirty. □□ **thir·ti·eth** *adj.* & *n.* **thir·ty·fold** *adj.* & *adv.*

this /t͟his/ *pron., adj.,* & *adv.* • *demons.pron.* (*pl.* **these** /t͟heez/) **1** the person or thing close at hand or indicated or already named or understood (*can you see this?; this is my cousin*). **2** (contrasted with *that*) the person or thing nearer to hand or more immediately in mind. **3** the action, behavior, or circumstances under consideration (*this won't do at all; what do you think of this?*). **4** (on the telephone): **a** the person spoken to. **b** the person speaking. • *demons.adj.* (*pl.* **these** /t͟heez/) **1** designating the person or thing close at hand, etc. (cf. senses 1, 2 of *pron.*). **2** (of time): **a** the present or current (*am busy all this week*). **b** relating to today (*this morning*). **c** just past or to come (*have been asking for it these three weeks*). **3** *colloq.* (in narrative) designating a person or thing previously unspecified (*then up came this policeman*). • *adv.* to this degree or extent (*knew him when he was this high; did not reach this far*). □ **this and that** *colloq.* various unspecified examples of things (esp. trivial). **this here** *sl.* this particular (person or thing). **this much** the amount or extent about to be stated (*I know this much, that he was not there*).

this·tle /thísəl/ *n.* **1** any of various prickly composite herbaceous plants of the genus *Cirsium*, *Carlina*, or *Carduus*, etc., usu. with globular heads of purple flowers. **2** this as the Scottish national emblem.

thistle

this·tle·down /thísəldown/ *n.* a light fluffy stuff attached to thistle seeds and blown about in the wind.

thith·er /thít͟hər, t͟hi–/ *adv. archaic* or *formal* to or toward that place.

thix·ot·ro·py /thiksótrəpee/ *n.* the property of becoming temporarily liquid when shaken or stirred, etc., and returning to a gel on standing. ▫▫ **thix·o·trop·ic** /thíksətrópik/ *adj.*

tho' var. of THOUGH.

thong /thong/ *n.* **1** a narrow strip of hide or leather used as the lash of a whip, as a halter or rein, etc. **2** = FLIP-FLOP 1.

tho·rax /tháwraks, thṓr–/ *n.* (*pl.* **thoraxes** or **thoraces** /tháwrəseez/) *Anat. & Zool.* the part of the trunk between the neck and the abdomen. ▫▫ **tho·ra·cal** /thórəkəl/ *adj.* **tho·rac·ic** /thawrásik/ *adj.*

tho·ri·um /tháwreeəm, thṓr–/ *n. Chem.* a radioactive metallic element, used in alloys and for nuclear power. ¶ Symb.: **Th.**

thorn /thawrn/ *n.* **1** a stiff sharp-pointed projection on a plant. **2** a thorn-bearing shrub or tree. ▫ **a thorn in one's side** (or **flesh**) a constant annoyance. ▫▫ **thorn·less** *adj.* **thorn·proof** *adj.*

thorn ap·ple *n.* **1** a poisonous plant of the nightshade family, *Datura stramonium*; jimsonweed. **2** the prickly fruit of this.

thorn·y /tháwrnee/ *adj.* (**thornier, thorniest**) **1** having many thorns. **2** (of a subject) hard to handle without offense; problematic. ▫▫ **thorn·i·ly** *adv.* **thorn·i·ness** *n.*

thor·ough /thúrō/ *adj.* **1** complete and unqualified; not superficial (*needs a thorough change*). **2** acting or done with great care and completeness (*the report is most thorough*). **3** absolute (*a thorough nuisance*). ▫▫ **thor·ough·ly** *adv.* **thor·ough·ness** *n.*

thor·ough·bass /thúrəbays/ *n.* = CONTINUO.

thor·ough·bred /thə́rōbred, thə́rə–, thúr–/ *adj. & n.* • *adj.* **1** of pure breeding. **2** high-spirited. • *n.* **1** a thoroughbred animal, esp. a horse. **2** (**Thoroughbred**) **a** a breed of racehorses originating from English mares and Arab stallions. **b** a horse of this breed.

thor·ough·fare /thə́rōfair, thə́rə–, thúr–/ *n.* a road or path open at both ends, esp. for traffic.

thor·ough·go·ing /thə́rōgōing, thə́rə–, thúr–/ *adj.* **1** uncompromising; not superficial. **2** (usu. *attrib.*) extreme; out-and-out.

those *pl.* of THAT.

thou[1] /thow/ *pron.* (*obj.* **thee** /thee/; *poss.* **thy** or **thine**; *pl.* **ye** or **you**) second person singular pronoun, now replaced by *you* except in some formal, liturgical, dialect, and poetic uses.

thou[2] /thow/ *n.* (*pl.* same or **thous**) *colloq.* **1** a thousand. **2** one thousandth.

though /thō/ *conj. & adv.* • *conj.* **1** despite the fact that (*though it was early we went to bed*; *though annoyed, I agreed*). **2** (introducing a possibility) even if (*ask him though he may refuse*). **3** and yet; nevertheless (*she read on, though not to the very end*). **4** in spite of being (*ready though unwilling*). • *adv. colloq.* however; all the same (*I wish you had told me, though*).

thought[1] /thawt/ *n.* **1** the process or power of thinking; the faculty of reason. **2** a way of thinking characteristic of or associated with a particular time, people, group, etc. (*medieval European thought*). **3 a** sober reflection or consideration (*gave it much thought*). **b** care; regard; concern (*had no thought for others*). **4** an idea or piece of reasoning produced by thinking (*many good thoughts came out of the discussion*). **5** (foll. by *of* + verbal noun or *to* + infin.) a partly formed intention or hope (*gave up all thoughts of winning*; *had no thought to go*). **6** (usu. in *pl.*) what one is thinking; one's opinion (*have you any thoughts on this?*). **7** the subject of one's thinking (*my one thought was to get away*).

thought[2] *past* and *past part.* of THINK.

thought·ful /tháwtfōōl/ *adj.* **1** engaged in or given to meditation. **2** (of a book, writer, remark, etc.) giving signs of serious thought. **3** (often foll. by *of*) (of a person or conduct) considerate; not haphazard or unfeeling. ▫▫ **thought·ful·ly** *adv.* **thought·ful·ness** *n.*

thought·less /tháwtlis/ *adj.* **1** careless of consequences or of others' feelings. **2** due to lack of thought. ▫▫ **thought·less·ly** *adv.* **thought·less·ness** *n.*

thought-pro·vok·ing *adj.* stimulating serious thought.

thou·sand /thówzənd/ *n. & adj.* • *n.* (*pl.* **thousands** or (in sense 1) **thousand**) (in *sing.* prec. by *a* or *one*) **1** the product of a hundred and ten. **2** a symbol for this (1,000, m, M). **3** a set of a thousand things. **4** (in *sing.* or *pl.*) *colloq.* a large number. • *adj.* that amount to a thousand. ▫▫ **thou·sand·fold** *adj. & adv.* **thou·sandth** *adj. & n.*

thrall /thrawl/ *n. literary* **1** (often foll. by *of, to*) a slave (of a person, power, or influence). **2** bondage; a state of slavery or servitude (*in thrall*). ▫▫ **thrall·dom** *n.* (also **thral·dom**) .

thrash /thrash/ *v. & n.* • *v.* **1** *tr.* beat severely, esp. with a stick or whip. **2** *tr.* defeat thoroughly in a contest. **3** *intr.* (of a paddle wheel, branch, etc.) act like a flail; deliver repeated blows. **4** *intr.* (foll. by *about, around*) move or fling the limbs about violently or in panic. **5** *intr.* (of a ship) keep striking the waves; make way against the wind or tide (*thrash to windward*). **6** *tr.* = THRESH 1. • *n.* **1** an act of thrashing. **2** *Brit. colloq.* a party, esp. a lavish one. ▫ **thrash out** discuss to a conclusion. ▫▫ **thrash·ing** *n.*

thrash·er[1] /thráshər/ *n.* **1** a person or thing that thrashes. **2** = THRESHER.

thrash·er[2] /thráshər/ *n.* any of various long-tailed N. American thrushlike birds of the family *Mimidae*.

thread /thred/ *n. & v.* • *n.* **1 a** a spun filament of cotton, silk, or glass, etc.; yarn. **b** a length of this. **2** a thin cord of twisted yarns used esp. in sewing and weaving. **3** anything regarded as threadlike with reference to its continuity or connectedness (*lost the thread of his argument*). **4** the spiral ridge of a screw. **5** (in *pl.*) clothes. **6** a thin seam or vein of ore. • *v.tr.* **1** pass a thread through the eye of (a needle). **2** put (beads) on a thread. **3** arrange (material in a strip form, e.g., film or magnetic tape) in the proper position on equipment. **4** make (one's way) carefully through a crowded place, over a difficult route, etc. ▫ **hang by a thread** be in a precarious state, position, etc. ▫▫ **thread·er** *n.* **thread·like** *adj.*

thread·bare /thrédbair/ *adj.* **1** (of cloth) so worn that the nap is lost and the thread visible. **2** (of a person) wearing such clothes. **3 a** hackneyed. **b** feeble or insubstantial (*a threadbare excuse*).

thread·worm /thrédwərm/ *n.* any of various, esp. parasitic, threadlike nematode worms, e.g., the pinworm.

threat /thret/ *n.* **1 a** a declaration of an intention to punish or hurt. **b** *Law* a menace of bodily hurt or injury, such as may restrain a person's freedom of action. **2** an indication of something undesirable coming (*the threat of war*). **3** a person or thing as a likely cause of harm, etc.

threat·en /thrét'n/ *v.tr.* **1 a** make a threat or threats against. **b** constitute a threat to; be likely to harm; put into danger. **2** be a sign or indication of (something undesirable). **3** (foll. by *to* + infin.) announce one's intention to do an undesirable or unexpected thing (*threatened to resign*). **4** (also *absol.*) give warning of the infliction of (harm, etc.) (*the clouds were threatening rain*). ▫▫ **threat·en·er** *n.* **threat·en·ing** *adj.* **threat·en·ing·ly** *adv.*

three /three/ *n. & adj.* • *n.* **1 a** one more than two, or seven less than ten. **b** a symbol for this (3, iii, III). **2** a size, etc., denoted by three. **3** the time of three o'clock. **4** a set of three. **5** a card with three pips. • *adj.* that amount to three.

three-di·men·sion·al *adj.* having or appearing to have length, breadth, and depth.

three·fold /thréefōld/ *adj. & adv.* **1** three times as much or as many. **2** consisting of three parts.
three-leg·ged race *n.* a running race between pairs, one member of each pair having the left leg tied to the right leg of the other.
three parts *n. & adj.* three quarters.
three-piece *adj.* consisting of three items.
three-ply *adj. & n.* • *adj.* of three strands, webs, or thicknesses. • *n.* **1** three-ply wool. **2** three-ply wood made by gluing together three layers with the grain in different directions.
three-point land·ing *n. Aeron.* the landing of an aircraft on the two main wheels and the tail wheel or skid or front wheel simultaneously.
three-ring cir·cus *n.* **1** a circus with three rings for simultaneous performances. **2** an extravagant display.
three Rs *n.pl.* (with *the*) reading, writing (*joc.* 'riting), and arithmetic (*joc.* 'rithmetic), regarded as the fundamentals of learning.
three·score /thréeskáwr/ *n. archaic* sixty.
three·some /thréesəm/ *n.* **1** a group of three persons. **2** a game, etc., for three.
three-wheel·er *n.* a vehicle with three wheels.
thren·o·dy /thrénədee/ *n.* (also **thre·node** /thrénōd/) (*pl.* **-dies** or **threnodes**) **1** a lamentation, esp. on a person's death. **2** a song of lamentation. ▫▫ **thre·no·di·al** /–nṓdeeəl/ *adj.* **thre·nod·ic** /–nódik/ *adj.* **thren·o·dist** /–nədist/ *n.*
thresh /thresh/ *v.* **1** *tr.* beat out or separate grain from (wheat, etc.). **2** *intr.* = THRASH *v.* 4. **3** *tr.* (foll. by *over*) analyze (a problem, etc.) in search of a solution.
thresh·er /thréshər/ *n.* **1** a person or machine that threshes. **2** a shark, *Alopias vulpinus*, with a long upper lobe to its tail, that it can lash about.
thresh·old /thréshōld, thrésh-hōld/ *n.* **1** a strip of wood or stone forming the bottom of a doorway and crossed in entering a house or room, etc. **2** a point of entry or beginning (*on the threshold of a new century*). **3** *Physiol. & Psychol.* a limit below which a stimulus causes no reaction (*pain threshold*).
threw *past* of THROW.
thrice /thrīs/ *adv. archaic* or *literary* **1** three times. **2** (esp. in *comb.*) highly (*thrice-blessed*).
thrift /thrift/ *n.* **1** frugality; economical management. **2** a plant of the genus *Armeria*, esp. the sea pink (*A. maritima*). **3** a savings and loan association or savings bank.
thrift shop *n.* (also **thrift store**) a store selling secondhand items.
thrift·y /thríftee/ *adj.* (**thriftier, thriftiest**) **1** economical; frugal. **2** thriving; prosperous. ▫▫ **thrift·i·ly** *adv.* **thrift·i·ness** *n.*
thrill /thril/ *n. & v.* • *n.* **1 a** a wave or nervous tremor of emotion or sensation. **b** a thrilling experience. **2** a throb or pulsation. **3** *Med.* a vibratory movement or resonance heard in auscultation. • *v.* **1** *intr. & tr.* feel or cause to feel a thrill. **2** *intr.* quiver or throb with or as with emotion. **3** *intr.* (foll. by *through, over, along*) (of an emotion, etc.) pass with a thrill through, etc. (*fear thrilled through my veins*). ▫▫ **thrill·ing** *adj.* **thrill·ing·ly** *adv.*
thrill·er /thrílər/ *n.* an exciting or sensational story or play, etc., esp. one involving crime or espionage.
thrips /thrips/ *n.* (*pl.* same) any insect of the order *Thysanoptera*, esp. a pest injurious to plants.
thrive /thrīv/ *v.intr.* (*past* **throve** /thrōv/ or **thrived**; *past part.* **thriven** /thrívən/ or **thrived**) **1** prosper or flourish. **2** grow rich. **3** (of a child, animal, or plant) grow vigorously.
throat /thrōt/ *n.* **1 a** the windpipe or gullet. **b** the front part of the neck containing this. **2** *literary* **a** a voice, esp. of a songbird. **b** a thing compared to a throat, esp. a narrow passage, entrance, or exit. ▫ **cut one's own throat** bring about one's own downfall. **ram** (or **shove**) **down a person's throat** force (a thing) on a person's attention. ▫▫ **-throated** *adj.* (in *comb.*).
throat·y /thrṓtee/ *adj.* (**throatier, throatiest**) **1** (of a voice) deficient in clarity; hoarsely resonant. **2** guttural; uttered in the throat. **3** having a prominent or capacious throat. ▫▫ **throat·i·ly** *adv.* **throat·i·ness** *n.*
throb /throb/ *v. & n.* • *v.intr.* (**throbbed, throbbing**) **1** palpitate or pulsate, esp. with more than the usual force or rapidity. **2** vibrate or quiver with a persistent rhythm or with emotion. • *n.* **1** a throbbing. **2** a palpitation or (esp. violent) pulsation.
throe /thrō/ *n.* (usu. in *pl.*) **1** a violent pang, esp. of childbirth or death. **2** anguish. ▫ **in the throes of** struggling with the task of.
throm·bo·sis /thrombṓsis/ *n.* (*pl.* **thromboses** /–seez/) the coagulation of the blood in a blood vessel or organ. ▫▫ **throm·bot·ic** /–bótik/ *adj.*
throm·bus /thrómbəs/ *n.* (*pl.* **thrombi** /–bī/) a blood clot formed in the vascular system and impeding blood flow.
throne /thrōn/ *n. & v.* • *n.* **1** a chair of state for a sovereign or bishop, etc. **2** sovereign power (*came to the throne*). **3** (in *pl.*) the third order of the ninefold celestial hierarchy. • *v.tr.* place on a throne. ▫▫ **throne·less** *adj.*
throng /thrawng, throng/ *n. & v.* • *n.* **1** a crowd of people. **2** (often foll. by *of*) a multitude, esp. in a small space. • *v.* **1** *intr.* come in great numbers (*crowds thronged to the stadium*). **2** *tr.* flock into or crowd around; fill with or as with a crowd (*crowds thronged the streets*).
throt·tle /thrót'l/ *n. & v.* • *n.* **1 a** (in full **throttle valve**) a valve controlling the flow of fuel or steam, etc., in an engine. **b** (in full **throttle lever**) a lever or pedal operating this valve. **2** the throat, gullet, or windpipe. • *v.tr.* **1** choke or strangle. **2** prevent the utterance, etc., of. **3** control (an engine or steam, etc.) with a throttle. ▫ **throttle back** (or **down**) reduce the speed of (an engine or vehicle) by throttling. ▫▫ **throt·tler** *n.*
through /thrōō/ *prep., adv., & adj.* (also **thru**) • *prep.* **1 a** from end to end or from side to side of. **b** going in one side or end and out the other of. **2** between or among (*swam through the waves*). **3** from beginning to end of (*read through the letter; went through many difficulties; through the years*). **4** because of; by the agency, means, or fault of (*lost it through carelessness*). **5** up to and including (*Monday through Friday*). • *adv.* **1** through a thing; from side to side, end to end, or beginning to end; completely; thoroughly (*went through to the garden; would not let us through*). **2** having completed (esp. successfully) (*are through their exams*). **3** so as to be connected by telephone (*will put you through*). • *attrib.adj.* **1** (of a journey, route, etc.) done without a change of line or vehicle, etc., or with one ticket. **2** (of traffic) going through a place to its destination. ▫ **be through** *colloq.* **1** (often foll. by *with*) have finished. **2** (often foll. by *with*) cease to have dealings. **3** have no further prospects (*is through as a politician*). **through and through** **1** thoroughly; completely. **2** through again and again.
through·out /thrōō-ówt/ *prep. & adv.* • *prep.* right through; from end to end of (*throughout the town; throughout the 18th century*). • *adv.* in every part or respect (*the timber was rotten throughout*).
through·put /thrṓōpōōt/ *n.* the amount of material put through a process, esp. in manufacturing or computing.

through·way /thrṓō-way/ *n.* (also **thru·way**) a thoroughfare, esp. a highway.

throve *past* of THRIVE.

throw /thrō/ *v. & n.* • *v.tr.* (*past* **threw** /thrōō/; *past part.* **thrown** /thrōn/) **1** propel with some force through the air or in a particular direction. **2** force violently into a specified position or state. **3** compel suddenly to be in a specified condition (*was thrown out of work*). **4** turn or move (part of the body) quickly or suddenly (*threw an arm out*). **5** project or cast (light, a shadow, a spell, etc.). **6 a** bring to the ground in wrestling. **b** (of a horse) unseat (its rider). **7** *colloq.* disconcert (*the question threw me for a moment*). **8** (foll. by *on, off*, etc.) put (clothes, etc.) hastily on or off, etc. **9 a** cause (dice) to fall on a table. **b** obtain (a specified number) by throwing dice. **10** cause to pass or extend suddenly to another state or position (*threw in the army; threw a bridge across the river*). **11** move (a switch or lever) so as to operate it. **12 a** form (pottery) on a potter's wheel. **b** turn (wood, etc.) on a lathe. **13** have (a fit or tantrum, etc.). **14** give (a party). **15** *colloq.* lose (a contest or race, etc.) intentionally. • *n.* **1** an act of throwing. **2** the distance a thing is or may be thrown. **3** the act of being thrown in wrestling. **4** *Geol. & Mining* **a** a fault in strata. **b** the amount of vertical displacement caused by this. **5** a machine or device giving rapid rotary motion. **6 a** the movement of a crank or cam, etc. **b** the extent of this. **7** the distance moved by the pointer of an instrument, etc. **8 a** a light cover for furniture. **b** (in full **throw rug**) a light rug. **c** a shawl or scarf. **9** (prec. by *a*) *sl.* each; per item (*sold at $10 a throw*). □ **throw around** (or **about**) **1** throw in various directions. **2** spend (one's money) ostentatiously. **throw away 1** discard as useless or unwanted. **2** waste or fail to make use of (an opportunity, etc.). **3** discard (a card). **4** *Theatr.* speak (lines) with deliberate underemphasis. **5** (in *passive*; often foll. by *on*) be wasted (*the advice was thrown away on him*). **throw back** revert to ancestral character. **throw cold water on** see COLD. **throw down** cause to fall. **throw down the gauntlet** (or **glove**) issue a challenge. **throw good money after bad** incur further loss in a hopeless attempt to recoup a previous loss. **throw one's hand in 1** abandon one's chances in a card game, esp. poker. **2** give up; withdraw from a contest. **throw in 1** interpose (a word or remark). **2** include at no extra cost. **3** throw (a soccer ball) from the edge of the field where it has gone out of play. **4** *Baseball & Cricket* return (the ball) from the outfield. **5** *Cards* give (a player) the lead, to the player's disadvantage. **throw in one's lot with** see LOT. **throw in the towel** admit defeat. **throw light on** see LIGHT[1]. **throw off 1** discard; contrive to get rid of. **2** write or utter in an offhand manner. **3** confuse or distract (a person speaking, thinking, or acting) from the matter in hand. **4** (of hounds or a hunt) begin hunting; make a start. **throw oneself at** seek blatantly as a spouse or sexual partner. **throw oneself into** engage vigorously in. **throw oneself on** (or **upon**) **1** rely completely on. **2** attack. **throw open** (often foll. by *to*) **1** cause to be suddenly or widely open. **2** make accessible. **throw out 1** put out forcibly or suddenly. **2** discard as unwanted. **3** expel (a troublemaker, etc.). **4** put forward tentatively. **5** reject (a proposal, etc.) **throw over** desert or abandon. **throw stones** cast aspersions. **throw together 1** assemble hastily. **2** bring into casual contact. **throw up 1** abandon. **2** *colloq.* vomit. **3** erect hastily. **throw one's weight around** *colloq.* act with unpleasant self-assertiveness. □□ **throw·a·ble** *adj.* **throw·er** *n.* (also in *comb.*).

throw·a·way /thrṓəway/ *adj. & n.* • *adj.* **1** meant to be thrown away after (one) use. **2** (of lines, etc.) deliberately underemphasized. • *n.* a thing to be thrown away after (one) use.

throw·back /thrṓbak/ *n.* **1** reversion to ancestral character. **2** an instance of this.

thru var. of THROUGH.

thrum /thrum/ *v.* (**thrummed, thrumming**) **1** *tr.* play (a stringed instrument) monotonously or unskillfully. **2** *intr.* (often foll. by *on*) beat or drum idly or monotonously.

thrush[1] /thrush/ *n.* any small or medium-sized songbird of the family *Turdidae*, esp. a song thrush or mistle thrush (see SONG THRUSH).

thrush[2] /thrush/ *n.* **1** a fungal disease, esp. of children, marked by whitish vesicles in the mouth and throat. **2** a similar disease of the vagina.

thrust /thrust/ *v. & n.* • *v.* (*past* and *past part.* **thrust**) **1** *tr.* push with a sudden impulse or with force (*thrust the letter into my pocket*). **2** *tr.* (foll. by *on*) impose (a thing) forcibly; enforce acceptance of (a thing) (*had it thrust on me*). **3** *intr.* (foll. by *at, through*) pierce or stab; make a sudden lunge. **4** *tr.* make (one's way) forcibly. **5** *intr.* (foll. by *through, past*, etc.) force oneself (*thrust past me abruptly*). • *n.* **1** a sudden or forcible push or lunge. **2** the propulsive force developed by a jet or rocket engine. **3** a strong attempt to penetrate an enemy's line or territory. **4** a remark aimed at a person. **5** the stress between the parts of an arch, etc. **6** (often foll. by *of*) the chief theme or gist of remarks, etc. **7** an attack with the point of a weapon. **8** (in full **thrust fault**) *Geol.* a low-angle reverse fault, with older strata displaced horizontally over newer.

thru·way var. of THROUGHWAY.

thud /thud/ *n. & v.* • *n.* a low dull sound as of a blow on a nonresonant surface. • *v.intr.* (**thudded, thudding**) make or fall with a thud. □□ **thud·ding·ly** *adv.*

thud late Middle English (originally Scots): probably from Old English *thyddan* 'to thrust, push'; related to *thoden* 'violent wind.' The noun is recorded earlier, denoting a sudden blast or gust of wind, later the sound of a thunderclap, whence a dull heavy sound. The verb dates from the early 16th century.

thug /thug/ *n.* **1** a vicious or brutal gangster or ruffian. **2** (**Thug**) *hist.* a member of a religious organization of robbers and assassins in India. □□ **thug·ger·y** *n.* **thug·gish** *adj.* **thug·gish·ly** *adv.* **thug·gish·ness** *n.*

thumb /thum/ *n. & v.* • *n.* **1 a** a short thick terminal projection on the human hand, set lower and apart from the other four and opposable to them. **b** a digit of other animals corresponding to this. **2** part of a glove, etc., for a thumb. • *v.* **1** *tr.* wear or soil (pages, etc.) with a thumb (*a well-thumbed book*). **2** *intr.* turn over pages with or as with a thumb (*thumbed through the directory*). **3** *tr.* request or obtain (a lift in a passing vehicle) by signaling with a raised thumb. **4** *tr.* gesture at (a person) with the thumb. □ **be all thumbs** be clumsy with one's hands. **thumb one's nose 1** put one's thumb up to one's nose with fingers extended up, a gesture of contempt. **2** display contempt or disdain. **under a person's thumb** completely dominated by a person. □□ **thumbed** *adj.* (also in *comb.*). **thumb·less** *adj.*

thumb·nail /thúmnayl/ *n.* **1** the nail of a thumb. **2** (*attrib.*) denoting conciseness (*a thumbnail sketch*).

thumb·print /thúmprint/ *n.* an impression of a thumb, esp. as used for identification.

thumb·screw /thúmskrōō/ *n.* an instrument of torture for crushing the thumbs.

thumbs-down *n.* an indication of rejection or failure.

thumbs-up *n.* an indication of satisfaction or approval.

thumb·tack /thúmtak/ *n.* a tack with a flat head pressing in with the thumb.

thump /thump/ *v. & n.* • *v.* **1** *tr.* beat or strike heavily, esp. with the fist (*thumped the table for attention*). **2** *intr.* throb or pulsate strongly (*my heart was thumping*). **3** *intr.* (foll. by *at*, *on*, etc.) deliver blows, esp. to attract attention (*thumped on the door*). **4** *tr.* (often foll. by *out*) play (a tune on a piano, etc.) with a heavy touch. **5** *intr.* tread heavily. • *n.* **1** a heavy blow. **2** the sound of this. □□ **thump·er** *n.*

thun·der /thúndər/ *n. & v.* • *n.* **1** a loud rumbling or crashing noise heard after a lightning flash and due to the expansion of rapidly heated air. **2** a resounding loud deep noise (*the thunder of an explosion*). **3** strong censure or denunciation. • *v.* **1** *intr.* (prec. by *it* as subject) thunder sounds (*if it thunders*). **2** *intr.* make or proceed with a noise suggestive of thunder. **3** *tr.* utter or communicate (approval, disapproval, etc.) loudly or impressively. **4** *intr.* (foll. by *against*, etc.) **a** make violent threats, etc., against. **b** criticize violently. □ **steal a person's thunder** spoil the effect of another's idea, action, etc., by expressing or doing it first. □□ **thun·der·er** *n.* **thun·der·less** *adj.* **thun·der·y** *adj.*

thun·der·bolt /thúndərbōlt/ *n.* **1 a** a flash of lightning with a simultaneous crash of thunder. **b** a stone, etc., imagined to be a destructive bolt. **2** a sudden or unexpected occurrence or item of news. **3** a supposed bolt or shaft as a destructive agent.

thun·der·clap /thúndərklap/ *n.* **1** a crash of thunder. **2** something startling or unexpected.

thun·der·cloud /thúndərklowd/ *n.* a cumulus cloud with a tall diffuse top, charged with electricity and producing thunder and lightning.

thun·der·head /thúndərhed/ *n.* a rounded cumulus cloud projecting upwards and heralding a thunderstorm.

thun·der·ous /thúndərəs/ *adj.* **1** like thunder. **2** very loud. □□ **thun·der·ous·ly** *adv.* **thun·der·ous·ness** *n.*

thun·der·show·er /thə́ndərshowər/ *n.* a brief rain shower accompanied by thunder and sometimes lightning.

thun·der·storm /thúndərstawrm/ *n.* a storm with thunder and lightning and usu. heavy rain or hail.

thun·der·struck /thúndərstruk/ *adj.* amazed; overwhelmingly surprised or startled.

Thur. *abbr.* Thursday.

Thurs. *abbr.* Thursday.

Thurs·day /thə́rzday, –dee/ *n. & adv.* • *n.* the fifth day of the week, following Wednesday. • *adv. colloq.* **1** on Thursday. **2** (**Thursdays**) on Thursdays; each Thursday.

thus /thus/ *adv. formal* **1 a** in this way. **b** as indicated. **2 a** accordingly. **b** as a result or inference. **3** to this extent; so (*thus far*; *thus much*).

▶There is never a need to expand the adverb **thus** to "thusly."

thwart /thwawrt/ *v., n., prep., & adv.* • *v.tr.* frustrate or foil (a person or purpose, etc.). • *n.* a rower's seat placed across a boat.

thy /thī/ *poss. pron.* (*attrib.*) (also **thine** /thīn/before a vowel) of or belonging to thee: now replaced by *your* except in some formal, liturgical, dialect, and poetic uses (*love thy neighbor*).

thyme /tīm/ *n.* any herb or shrub of the genus *Thymus* with aromatic leaves, esp. *T. vulgaris* grown for culinary use. □□ **thym·y** *adj.*

thy·mine /thímeen/ *n. Biochem.* a compound found in all living tissue as a component base of DNA.

thy·mus /thíməs/ *n.* (*pl.* **-muses** or **-mi** /–mī/) (in full **thymus gland**) *Anat.* a lymphoid organ situated in the neck of vertebrates producing lymphocytes for the immune response.

thy·roid /thíroyd/ *n.* (in full **thyroid gland**) a large ductless gland in the neck of vertebrates secreting a hormone which regulates growth and development through the rate of metabolism.

thy·rox·ine /thīróksin, –seen/ *n.* the main hormone produced by the thyroid gland, involved in controlling the rate of metabolic processes.

thy·self /thīsélf/ *pron. archaic* emphat. & refl. form of THOU[1], THEE.

Ti *symb. Chem.* the element titanium.

ti /tee/ *n.* (also **te**) **1** (in tonic sol-fa) the seventh note of a major scale. **2** the note B in the fixed-do system.

ti·ar·a /teeárə, –aárə, –áirə/ *n.* **1** a jeweled ornamental band worn on the front of a woman's hair. **2** a three-crowned diadem worn by a pope.

Ti·bet·an /tibét'n/ *n. & adj.* • *n.* **1 a** a native of Tibet. **b** a person of Tibetan descent. **2** the language of Tibet. • *adj.* of or relating to Tibet or its language.

tib·i·a /tíbeeə/ *n.* (*pl.* **tibiae** /–bee-ee/) *Anat.* the inner and usu. larger of two bones extending from the knee to the ankle. □□ **tib·i·al** *adj.*

tic /tik/ *n.* **1** a habitual spasmodic contraction of the muscles, esp. of the face. **2** a personality or behavioral quirk.

tick[1] /tik/ *n. & v.* • *n.* **1** a slight recurring click, esp. that of a watch or clock. **2** esp. *Brit. colloq.* a moment; an instant. **3** *Brit.* a mark (') to denote correctness, check items in a list, etc. • *v.* **1** *intr.* **a** (of a clock, etc.) make ticks. **b** (foll. by *away*) (of time, etc.) pass. **2** *intr.* (of a mechanism) work; function (*take it apart to see how it ticks*). **3** *tr. Brit.* **a** mark (a written answer, etc.) with a tick. **b** (often foll. by *off*) mark (an item in a list, etc.) with a tick in checking. □ **tick off** *sl.* annoy, anger; dispirit. **what makes a person tick** *colloq.* a person's motivation. □□ **tick·less** *adj.*

tick[2] /tik/ *n.* **1** any of various arachnids of the order *Acarina*, parasitic on the skin of warm-blooded vertebrates. **2** any of various insects of the family *Hippoboscidae*, parasitic on sheep and birds, etc. **3** *colloq.* an unpleasant or despicable person.

tick[3] /tik/ *n.* **1** the cover of a mattress or pillow. **2** = TICKING.

tick·er /tíkər/ *n. colloq.* **1** the heart. **2** a watch. **3** a machine that receives and prints telegraphed messages onto paper tape.

tick·er tape *n.* **1** a paper strip from a ticker. **2** this or similar material thrown from windows, etc., along the route of a parade honoring a hero, etc.

tick·et /tíkit/ *n. & v.* • *n.* **1** a written or printed piece of paper or card entitling the holder to enter a place, participate in an event, travel by public transport, use a public amenity, etc. **2** an official notification of a traffic offense, etc. (*parking ticket*). **3** *Brit.* a certificate of discharge from the army. **4** a certificate of qualification as a ship's master, ship or airplane pilot, etc. **5** a label attached to a thing and giving its price or other details. **6** a list of candidates put forward by one group, esp. a political party. **7** (prec. by *the*) *colloq.* what is correct or needed. • *v.tr.* (**ticketed**, **ticketing**) attach or serve a ticket to. □□ **tick·et·ed** *adj.* **tick·et·less** *adj.*

tick·ing /tíking/ *n.* a stout usu. striped material used to cover mattresses, etc.

tick·le /tíkəl/ *v. & n.* • *v.* **1 a** *tr.* apply light touches or strokes to (a person or part of a person's body) so as to excite the nerves and usu. produce laughter and spasmodic movement. **b** *intr.* feel this sensation (*my foot tickles*). **2** *tr.* excite agreeably; amuse or divert (a person, a sense of humor, vanity, etc.) (*was tickled at the idea*; *this will tickle your fancy*). • *n.* **1** an act of tickling. **2** a tickling sensation. □ **tickled pink** (or **to death**) *colloq.* extremely amused or pleased. □□ **tick·ler** *n.* **tick·ly** *adj.*

tickle Middle English (in the sense 'be delighted or thrilled,' surviving in *tickled pink*): perhaps a frequentative of TICK[1], or an alteration of Scots and dialect *kittle* 'to tickle,' of Germanic origin and related to Dutch *kittelen* and German *kizzeln.*

tick·lish /tíklish/ *adj.* **1** sensitive to tickling. **2** (of a matter or person to be dealt with) difficult; requiring careful handling. □□ **tick·lish·ly** *adv.* **tick·lish·ness** *n.*

tick-tack-toe *n.* (also **tic-tac-toe**) a game in which players alternate turns, seeking to complete a series of three Xs or Os marked in a nine-square grid.

tick·y-tack·y /tíkeetákee/ *n. & adj. colloq.* •*n.* inferior or cheap material, esp. used in suburban buildings. •*adj.* (esp. of a building or housing development) made of inferior material; cheap or in poor taste.

tid·al /tíd'l/ *adj.* relating to, like, or affected by tides (*tidal basin; tidal river*). □□ **tid·al·ly** *adv.*

tid·al bore *n.* a large wave or bore caused by constriction of the spring tide as it enters a long narrow shallow inlet.

tid·al wave *n.* **1** = TSUNAMI. **2** a widespread manifestation of feeling, etc.

tid·bit /tídbit/ *n.* (*Brit.* **tit·bit** /tít–/) **1** a small morsel. **2** a choice item of news, etc.

tid·dly-winks /tídleewingks/ *n.* (also **tid·dle·dy-** /tíd'ldee–/) a game played by flicking counters into a cup, etc.

tide /tīd/ *n.* **1 a** the periodic rise and fall of the sea due to the attraction of the moon and sun (see EBB *n.* 1, FLOOD *n.* 3). **b** the water as affected by this. **2** a time or season (usu. in *comb.*: *Whitsuntide*). **3** a marked trend of opinion, fortune, or events. □ **tide over** enable or help (a person) to deal with an awkward situation, difficult period, etc. (*the money will tide me over until Friday*). □□ **tide·less** *adj.*

tide·land /tīdland/ *n.* **1** land that is submerged at high tide. **2** land below the low-water mark but within a nation's territorial waters.

tide·wa·ter *n.* **1** water brought by or affected by tides. **2** (*attrib.*) affected by tides (*tidewater region*).

ti·dings /tīdingz/ *n.* (as *sing.* or *pl.*) news; information.

ti·dy /tīdee/ *adj., n., & v.* •*adj.* (**tidier, tidiest**) **1** neat; orderly; methodically arranged. **2** (of a person) methodically inclined. **3** *colloq.* considerable (*it cost a tidy sum*). •*n.* (*pl.* **-dies**) **1** a receptacle for holding small objects. **2** esp. *Brit.* an act or spell of tidying. **3** a detachable ornamental cover for a chair back, arms, etc. •*v.tr.* (**-dies, -died**) (also *absol.*; often foll. by *up*) put in good order; make (oneself, a room, etc.) tidy. □□ **ti·di·ly** *adv.* **ti·di·ness** *n.*

tie /tī/ *v. & n.* •*v.* (**tying**) **1** *tr.* **a** attach or fasten with string or cord, etc. (*tie the dog to the gate; tie his hands together; tied on a label*). **b** link conceptually. **2** *tr.* **a** form (a string, ribbon, shoelace, necktie, etc.) into a knot or bow. **b** form (a knot or bow) in this way. **3** *tr.* restrict or limit (a person) as to conditions, occupation, place, etc. (*is tied to his family*). **4** *intr.* (often foll. by *with*) achieve the same score or place as another competitor (*they tied at ten games each*). **5** *tr.* hold (rafters, etc.) together by a crosspiece, etc. **6** *tr. Mus.* **a** unite (written notes) by a tie. **b** perform (two notes) as one unbroken note. •*n.* **1** a cord, line, or chain, etc., used for fastening. **2** a strip of material worn round the collar and tied in a knot at the front with the ends hanging down. **3** a thing that unites or restricts persons; a bond or obligation (*family ties; ties of friendship*). **4** a draw, dead heat, or equality of score among competitors. **5** *Brit.* a match between any pair from a group of competing players or teams. **6** (also **tie beam**, etc.) a rod or beam holding parts of a structure together. **7** *Mus.* a curved line above or below two notes of the same pitch indicating that they are to be played for the combined duration of their time values. **8** a beam laid horizontally as a support for railroad rails. **9** a shoe tied with a lace. □ **fit to be tied** *colloq.* very angry. **tie down** = TIE *v.* 3 above. **tie in** (foll. by *with*) bring into or have a close association or agreement. **tie the knot** *colloq.* get married. **tie up 1** bind or fasten securely with cord, etc. **2** invest or reserve (capital, etc.) so that it is not immediately available for use. **3** moor (a boat). **4** secure (an animal). **5** obstruct; prevent from acting freely. **6** secure or complete (an undertaking, etc.). **7** (often foll. by *with*) = *tie in.* **8** (usu. in *passive*) fully occupy (a person). □□ **tie·less** *adj.*

tie·back *n.* a decorative strip of fabric or cord for holding a curtain back from the window.

tie-dye *n.* a method of producing dyed patterns by tying string, etc., to protect parts of the fabric from the dye.

tie-in *n.* **1** a connection or association. **2** (often *attrib.*) a form of sale or advertising that offers or requires more than a single purchase. **3** the joint promotion of related commodities, etc. (e.g., a book and a movie).

tie·pin /tīpin/ *n.* an ornamental pin or clip for holding a tie in place.

tier /teer/ *n.* **1** a row or rank or unit of a structure, as one of several placed one above another (*tiers of seats*). **2** a layer or rank. □□ **tiered** *adj.* (also in *comb.*).

tiff /tif/ *n. & v.* •*n.* **1** a slight or petty quarrel. **2** a fit of peevishness. •*v.intr.* have a petty quarrel; bicker.

ti·ger /tīgər/ *n.* **1 a** a large Asian feline, *Panthera tigris*, having a yellowish brown coat with black stripes. **b** a similar feline, as the jaguar or ocelot. **2** a domestic cat with similar stripping. **3** a fierce, energetic, or formidable person. □□ **ti·ger·ish** *adj.* **ti·ger·ish·ly** *adv.*

ti·ger cat *n.* **1** any moderate-sized feline resembling the tiger, .e.g, the ocelot, serval, or margay. **2** *Austral.* any of various carnivorous marsupials of the genus *Dasyurus*, including the Tasmanian devil.

ti·ger-eye *n.* (also **ti·ger's-eye**) **1** a yellowish brown striped gem of brilliant luster. **2** a pottery glaze of similar appearance.

ti·ger lil·y *n.* a tall garden lily, *Lilium tigrinum*, with flowers of dull orange spotted with black or purple.

tight /tīt/ *adj., n., & adv.* •*adj.* **1** closely held, drawn, fastened, fitting, etc. (*a tight hold; a tight skirt*). **2 a** closely and firmly put together (*a tight joint*). **b** close; evenly matched (*a tight finish*). **3** (of clothes, etc.) too closely fitting (*my shoes are rather tight*). **4** impermeable, impervious, esp. (in *comb.*) to a specified thing (*watertight*). **5** tense; stretched so as to leave no slack. **6** *colloq.* drunk. **7** *colloq.* (of a person) mean; stingy. **8 a** (of money or materials) not easily obtainable. **b** (of a money market) in which money is tight. **9 a** (of precautions, a program, a schedule, etc.) stringent; demanding. **b** presenting difficulties (*a tight situation*). **c** (of an organization, group, or member) strict; disciplined. **10** produced by or requiring great exertion or pressure (*a tight squeeze*). **11** (of control, etc.) strictly imposed. **12** *colloq.* friendly; close (*the two girls quickly became tight*) •*adv.* tightly (*hold tight!*). □□ **tight·ly** *adv.* **tight·ness** *n.*

tight·en /tīt'n/ *v.tr. & intr.* (also foll. by *up*) make or become tight or tighter. □ **tighten one's belt** see BELT.

tight-fist·ed *adj.* stingy.

tight-fit·ting *adj.* (of a garment) fitting (often too) close to the body.

tight-lipped *adj.* with or as with the lips compressed to restrain emotion or speech.

tight·rope /tītrōp/ *n.* a rope stretched tightly high above the ground, on which acrobats perform.

tights /tīts/ *n.pl.* **1** a thin but not sheer close-fitting wool or nylon, etc., garment covering the legs and the lower part of the torso. **2** a similar garment worn by a dancer, acrobat, etc.

tight·wad /tītwod/ *n. colloq.* a person who is miserly or stingy.

ti·gress /tīgris/ *n.* **1** a female tiger. **2** a fierce or passionate woman.

tike var. of TYKE.

ti·la·pi·a /ti-lay-pia/ *n.* a freshwater fish of the African genus *Tilapia* or a related genus, widely introduced for food.

til·de /tíldə/ *n.* a mark (~), put over a letter, e.g., over a Spanish *n* when pronounced *ny* (as in *señor*) or a Portuguese *a* or *o* when nasalized (as in *Sãao Paulo*).

tile /tīl/ *n. & v.* •*n.* **1** a thin slab of concrete or baked clay, etc., used in series for covering a roof or pavement, etc. **2** a similar slab of glazed pottery, cork, linoleum, etc., for covering a floor, wall, etc. **3** a thin flat piece used in a game (esp. mah-jongg). •*v.tr.* cover with tiles.

til·ing /tīling/ *n.* **1** the process of fixing tiles. **2** an area of tiles.

till[1] /til/ *prep. & conj.* •*prep.* **1** up to or as late as (*wait till six o'clock; did not return till night*). **2** up to the time of (*faithful till death; waited till the end*). •*conj.* **1** up to the time when (*wait till I return*). **2** so long that (*laughed till I cried*). ▶*Until* is more usual when beginning a sentence.

▶See note at UNTIL.

till[2] /til/ *n.* **1** a drawer for money in a store or bank, etc., esp. with a device recording the amount of each purchase. **2** a supply of money.

till[3] /til/ *v.tr.* prepare and cultivate (land) for crops. □□ **till·a·ble** *adj.* **till·er** *n.*

till·age /tílij/ *n.* **1** the preparation of land for bearing crops. **2** tilled land.

till·er /tílər/ *n.* a horizontal bar fitted to the head of a boat's rudder to turn it in steering.

tilt /tilt/ *v. & n.* •*v.* **1 a** *intr. & tr.* assume or cause to assume a sloping position; heel over. **b** incline or lean or cause to lean toward one side of an opinion, action, controversy, etc. **2** *intr.* (foll. by *at*) strike, thrust, or run at with a weapon, esp. in jousting. **3** *intr.* (foll. by *with*) engage in a contest. •*n.* **1** the act or an instance of tilting. **2** a sloping position. **3** an inclination or bias. **4** (of medieval knights, etc.) the act of charging with a lance against an opponent or at a mark, done for exercise or as a sport. **5** an encounter between opponents; an attack, esp. with argument or satire (*have a tilt at*). □ **full** (or **at full**) **tilt 1** at full speed. **2** with full force. □□ **tilt·er** *n.*

tim·bale /tímbəl, taNbaal/ *n.* a drum-shaped dish of ground meat or fish baked in a mold or pastry shell.

tim·ber /tímbər/ *n.* **1** large standing trees suitable for lumber; woods or forest. **2** (esp. as *int.*) a warning cry that a tree is about to fall. **3** a prepaid piece of wood or beam, esp. as the rib of a vessel. **4** *Brit.* wood prepared for building, carpentry, etc. □□ **tim·ber·ing** *n.*

tim·bered /tímbərd/ *adj.* **1** (esp. of a building) made wholly or partly of lumber, esp. with partly exposed beams. **2** (of country) wooded.

tim·ber·land /tímbərland/ *n.* land covered with forest yielding timber.

tim·ber·line /tímbərlīn/ *n.* (on a mountain) the line or level above which no trees grow.

tim·ber wolf *n.* a type of large N. American gray wolf.

tim·bre /támbər, táNbrə/ (also **tim·ber**) *n.* the distinctive character of a musical sound or voice apart from its pitch and intensity.

time /tīm/ *n. & v.* •*n.* **1** the indefinite continued progress of existence, events, etc., in past, present, and future regarded as a whole. **2** the progress of this as affecting persons or things (*stood the test of time*). **3** a more or less definite portion of time belonging to particular events or circumstances (*the time of the Plague; prehistoric times; the scientists of the time*). **4** an allotted, available, or measurable portion of time; the period of time at one's disposal (*am wasting my time; had no time to visit; how much time do you need?*). **5** a point of time, esp. in hours and minutes (*the time is 7:30; what time is it?*). **6** (prec. by *a*) an indefinite period (*waited for a time*). **7** time or an amount of time as reckoned by a conventional standard (*the time allowed is one hour; ran the mile in record time; eight o'clock Eastern Standard time*). **8 a** an occasion (*last time I saw you*). **b** an event or occasion qualified in some way (*had a good time*). **9** a moment or definite portion of time destined or suitable for a purpose, etc. (*now is the time to act; shall we set a time?*). **10** (in *pl.*) expressing multiplication (*is four times as old; five times six is thirty*). **11** a lifetime (*will last my time*). **12** (in *sing.* or *pl.*) **a** the conditions of life or of a period (*hard times; times have changed*). **b** (prec. by *the*) the present age, or that being considered. **13** *colloq.* a prison sentence (*is doing time*). **14 a** an apprenticeship (*served his time*). **b** a period of military service. **15** a period of gestation. **16** the date or expected date of childbirth (*is near her time*) or of death (*my time is drawing near*). **17** measured time spent in work (*put them on short time*). **18 a** any of several rhythmic patterns of music (*in waltz time*). **b** the duration of a note as indicated by a quarter note, whole note, etc. **19** *Brit.* the moment at which a bar closes. **20** = TIME OUT. •*v.tr.* **1** choose the time or occasion for (*time your remarks carefully*). **2** do at a chosen or correct time. **3** arrange the time of arrival of. **4** ascertain the time taken by (a process or activity, or a person doing it). **5** regulate the duration or interval of; set times for (*trains are timed to arrive every hour*). □ **against time** with utmost speed; so as to finish by a specified time (*working against time*). **ahead of time** earlier than expected. **ahead of one's time** having ideas too enlightened or advanced to be accepted by one's contemporaries. **all the time 1** during the whole of the time referred to (often despite some contrary expectation, etc.) (*we never noticed, but he was there all the time*). **2** constantly (*cries all the time*). **3** at all times (*leaves a light on all the time*). **at one time 1** in or during a known but unspecified past period. **2** simultaneously (*ran three businesses at one time*). **at the same time 1** simultaneously; at a time that is the same for all. **2** nevertheless (*at the same time, I do not want to offend you*). **at a time** separately in the specified groups or numbers (*came three at a time*). **at times** occasionally; intermittently. **before one's time** prematurely (*old before his time*). **for the time being** for the present; until some other arrangement is made. **half the time** *colloq.* as often as not. **have no time for 1** be unable or unwilling to spend time on. **2** dislike. **have the time 1** be able to spend the time needed. **2** know from a watch, etc., what time it is. **have a time of it** undergo trouble or difficulty. **in no** (or **less than no**) **time 1** very soon. **2** very quickly. **in one's own good time** at a time and a rate decided by oneself. **in time 1** not late; punctual (*was in time to catch the bus*). **2** eventually (*in time you may agree*). **3** in accordance with a given rhythm or tempo, esp. of music. **in one's time** at or during some previous period of one's life (*in his time he was a great hurdler*). **keep good** (or **bad**) **time 1** (of a clock, etc.) record time accurately (or inaccurately). **2** be habitually punctual (or not punctual). **keep time** move or sing, etc., in time. **know the time of day** be well informed. **lose no time** (often foll. by *in* + verbal noun) act immediately. **no time** *colloq.* a very short interval (*it was no time before they came*). **on one's own time** outside working hours. **on time** see ON. **out of time 1** unseasonable; unseasonably. **2** not in rhythm. **pass the time of day** *colloq.* exchange a greeting or casual remarks. **time after time 1** repeatedly; on many occasions. **2** in many instances. **time and** (or **time and time**) **again** on many occasions. **the time of day** the hour by the clock. **the time of one's life** a period or occasion of exceptional enjoyment. **time out of mind** see TIME IMMEMORIAL. **time was** there was a time (*time was when I could do that*).

time and a half *n.* a rate of payment for work at one and a half times the normal rate.

time bomb *n.* a bomb designed to explode at a preset time.

time cap•sule *n.* a box, etc., containing objects typical of the present time, buried for discovery in the future.

time clock *n.* **1** a clock with a device for recording workers' hours of work. **2** a switch mechanism activated at preset times by a built-in clock.

time ex•po•sure *n.* the exposure of photographic film for longer than the maximum normal shutter setting.

time frame *n.* period of time during which an action occurs or will occur.

time-hon•ored *adj.* esteemed by tradition or through custom.

time im•me•mo•ri•al *n.* a longer time than anyone can remember or trace.

time•keep•er /tímkeepər/ *n.* **1** a person who records time, esp. of workers or in a game. **2 a** a watch or clock as regards accuracy (*a good timekeeper*). **b** a person as regards punctuality. □□ **time•keep•ing** *n.*

time-lapse *n.* (of photography) using frames taken at long intervals to photograph a slow process, and shown continuously as if at normal speed.

time•less /tímlis/ *adj.* not affected by the passage of time; eternal. □□ **time•less•ly** *adv.* **time•less•ness** *n.*

time•ly /tímlee/ *adj.* (**timelier, timeliest**) opportune; coming at the right time. □□ **time•li•ness** *n.*

time off *n.* time for rest or recreation, etc.

time out *n.* **1** a brief intermission in a game, etc. **2** time for rest or recreation away from one's usual work or studies.

time•piece /tímpees/ *n.* an instrument, such as a clock or watch, for measuring time.

tim•er /tímər/ *n.* **1** a person or device that measures or records time taken. **2** an automatic mechanism for activating a device, etc., at a preset time.

time-share *n.* a share in a property under a time-sharing arrangement.

time-shar•ing *n.* **1** the operation of a computer system by several users for different operations at one time. **2** the use of a vacation home at agreed different times by several joint owners.

time sheet *n.* a sheet of paper for recording hours of work, etc.

time sig•na•ture *n.* *Mus.* an indication of tempo following a clef, expressed as a fraction with the numerator giving the number of beats in each bar and the denominator giving the kind of note getting one beat.

time•ta•ble /tímtaybəl/ *n.* & *v.* • *n.* a list of times at which events are scheduled to take place, esp. the arrival and departure of buses or trains, etc., or *Brit.* a lesson plan in a school or college. • *v.tr.* include in or arrange to a timetable; schedule.

time warp *n.* an imaginary distortion of space in relation to time, whereby persons or objects of one age can be moved to another.

time•worn /tímwawrn/ *n.* impaired by age.

time zone *n.* a range of longitudes where a common standard time is used.

tim•id /tímid/ *adj.* (**timider, timidest**) easily frightened; apprehensive; shy. □□ **ti•mid•i•ty** /–míditee/ *n.* **tim•id•ly** *adv.* **tim•id•ness** *n.*

tim•ing /tíming/ *n.* **1** the way an action or process is timed, esp. in relation to others. **2** the regulation of the opening and closing of valves in an internal combustion engine.

tim•or•ous /tímərəs/ *adj.* **1** timid; easily alarmed. **2** frightened. □□ **tim•or•ous•ly** *adv.* **tim•or•ous•ness** *n.*

tim•pa•ni /tímpənee/ *n.pl.* (also **tym•pa•ni**) kettledrums. □□ **tim•pa•nist** *n.*

tin /tin/ *n.* & *v.* • *n.* **1** *Chem.* a silvery white malleable metallic element resisting corrosion, occurring naturally in cassiterite and other ores, and used esp. in alloys and for plating thin iron or steel sheets to form tin plate. ¶ Symb.: **Sn. 2** a vessel or container made of tin or tin-plated iron. **3** = TIN PLATE. • *v.tr.* (**tinned, tinning**) **1** esp. *Brit.* seal (food) in an airtight can for preservation. **2** cover or coat with tin.

tinc•ture /tíngkchər/ *n.* & *v.* • *n.* (often foll. by *of*) **1** a slight flavor or trace. **2** a tinge (of a color). **3** a medicinal solution (of a drug) in alcohol (*tincture of quinine*). **4** *Heraldry* an inclusive term for the metals, colors, and furs used in coats of arms. • *v.tr.* **1** color slightly; tinge, flavor. **2** (often foll. by *with*) affect slightly (with a quality).

tin•der /tíndər/ *n.* a dry substance such as wood that readily catches fire from a spark. □□ **tin•der•y** *adj.*

tin•der•box /tíndərboks/ *n.* **1** *hist.* a box containing tinder, flint, and steel, formerly used for kindling fires. **2** a potentially explosive or violent person, place, situation, etc.

tine /tīn/ *n.* a prong or tooth or point of a fork, comb, antler, etc. □□ **tined** *adj.* (also in *comb.*).

ting /ting/ *n.* & *v.* • *n.* a tinkling sound as of a bell. • *v.intr.* & *tr.* emit or cause to emit this sound.

tinge /tinj/ *v.* & *n.* • *v.tr.* (also **tinge•ing**) (often foll. by *with*; often in *passive*) **1** color slightly (*is tinged with red*). **2** affect slightly (*regret tinged with satisfaction*). • *n.* **1** a tendency toward or trace of some color. **2** a slight admixture of a feeling or quality.

tin•gle /tínggəl/ *v.* & *n.* • *v.* **1** *intr.* **a** feel a slight prickling, stinging, or throbbing sensation. **b** cause this (*the reply tingled in my ears*). **2** *tr.* make (the ear, etc.) tingle. • *n.* a tingling sensation.

tin•gly /tíngglee/ *adj.* (**tinglier, tingliest**) causing or characterized by tingling.

tin•horn /tínhawrn/ *n.* & *adj. sl.* • *n.* a pretentious but unimpressive person. • *adj.* cheap; pretentious.

tin•ker /tíngkər/ *n.* & *v.* • *n.* **1** an itinerant mender of kettles and pans, etc. **2** *Sc.* & *Ir.* a gypsy. **3** a spell of tinkering. • *v.* **1** *intr.* (foll. by *at*, *with*) work in an amateurish or desultory way, esp. to adjust or mend machinery, etc. **2 a** *intr.* work as a tinker. **b** *tr.* repair (pots and pans). □□ **tin•ker•er** *n.*

tin•kle /tíngkəl/ *v.* & *n.* • *v.* **1** *intr.* & *tr.* make or cause to make a succession of short light ringing sounds. **2** *intr. colloq.* urinate. • *n.* **1** a tinkling sound. **2** *Brit. colloq.* a telephone call (*will give you a tinkle on Monday*). **3** *colloq.* an act of urinating.

tin•ni•tus /tinítəs, tíni–/ *n.* *Med.* a ringing in the ears.

tin•ny /tínee/ *adj.* (**tinnier, tinniest**) **1** of or like tin. **2** (of a metal object) flimsy; insubstantial; of poor quality. **3 a** sounding like struck tin. **b** (of reproduced sound) thin and metallic, lacking low frequencies. □□ **tin•ni•ly** *adv.* **tin•ni•ness** *n.*

Tin Pan Al•ley *n.* the name given to a district in New York where many songwriters, arrangers and music publishers were formerly based.

tin plate *n.* sheet iron or sheet steel coated with tin. □□ **tin-plate** *v.tr.*

tin·pot /tínpot/ *adj.* cheap; inferior.

tin·sel /tínsəl/ *n.* & *v.* • *n.* **1** glittering metallic strips, threads, etc., used as decoration to give a sparkling effect. **2** a fabric adorned with tinsel. **3** superficial brilliance or splendor. **4** (*attrib.*) showy; gaudy; flashy. • *v.tr.* (**tinseled, tinseling** or **tinselled, tinselling**) adorn with or as with tinsel. ▫▫ **tin·seled** *adj.* **tin·sel·ly** *adj.*

tint /tint/ *n.* & *v.* • *n.* **1** a variety of a color, esp. one made lighter by adding white. **2** a tendency toward or admixture of a different color (*red with a blue tint*). **3** a faint color spread over a surface, esp. as a background for printing on. **4** a dye for the hair. • *v.tr.* apply a tint to; color. ▫▫ **tint·er** *n.*

tin·tin·nab·u·la·tion /tíntinábyəláyshən/ *n.* a ringing or tinkling of bells.

ti·ny /tínee/ *adj.* (**tinier, tiniest**) very small or slight. ▫▫ **ti·ni·ly** *adv.* **ti·ni·ness** *n.*

tip[1] /tip/ *n.* & *v.* • *n.* **1** an extremity or end, esp. of a small or tapering thing (*tips of the fingers*). **2** a small piece or part attached to the end of a thing, e.g., a ferrule on a stick. **3** a leaf bud of tea. • *v.tr.* (**tipped, tipping**) **1** provide with a tip. **2** (foll. by *in*) attach (a loose sheet) to a page at the inside edge. ▫ **on the tip of one's tongue** about to be said, esp. after difficulty in recalling to mind. **the tip of the iceberg** a small evident part of something much larger or more significant. ▫▫ **tip·less** *adj.* **tip·py** *adj.* (in sense 3).

tip[2] /tip/ *v.* & *n.* • *v.* (**tipped, tipping**) **1 a** *intr.* lean or slant. **b** *tr.* cause to do this. **2** *tr.* (foll. by *into*, etc.) **a** overturn or cause to overbalance (*was tipped into the pond*). **b** discharge the contents of (a container, etc.) in this way. • *n.* **1 a** a slight push or tilt. **b** a glancing stroke, esp. in baseball. **2** *Brit.* a place where material (esp. trash) is dumped. ▫ **tip the balance** make the critical difference. **tip the scales** see SCALE[2].

tip[3] /tip/ *v.* & *n.* • *v.* (**tipped, tipping**) **1** *tr.* make a small present of money to, esp. for a service given (*have you tipped the waiter?*). **2** *tr.* name as the likely winner of a race or contest, etc. • *n.* **1** a small gift of money, esp. for a service given. **2** a piece of private or special information, esp. regarding betting or investment. **3** a small or casual piece of advice. ▫ **tip off 1** give (a person) a hint or piece of special information or warning, esp. discreetly or confidentially. **2** *Basketball* start play by throwing the ball up between two opponents. ▫▫ **tip·per** *n.*

tip-off *n.* **1** a hint or warning, etc., given discreetly or confidentially. **2** *Basketball* the act of starting play with a tip off.

tip·ple /típəl/ *v.* & *n.* • *v.* **1** *intr.* drink intoxicating liquor habitually. **2** *tr.* drink (liquor) repeatedly in small amounts. • *n. colloq.* a drink, esp. a strong one. ▫▫ **tip·pler** *n.*

tip·sy /típsee/ *adj.* (**tipsier, tipsiest**) **1** slightly intoxicated. **2** caused by or showing intoxication (*a tipsy leer*). ▫▫ **tip·si·ly** *adv.* **tip·si·ness** *n.*

tip·toe /típtō/ *n., v.,* & *adv.* • *n.* the tips of the toes. • *v.intr.* (**tiptoes, tiptoed, tiptoeing**) walk on tiptoe, or very stealthily. • *adv.* (also **on tip·toe**) with the heels off the ground and the weight on the balls of the feet.

tip-top /típtóp/ *adj., adv.,* & *n. colloq.* • *adj.* & *adv.* highest in excellence; very best. • *n.* the highest point of excellence.

ti·rade /tírayd, tīráyd/ *n.* a long vehement denunciation or declamation.

tire[1] /tīr/ *v.* **1** *tr.* & *intr.* make or grow weary. **2** *tr.* exhaust the patience or interest of; bore. **3** *tr.* (in *passive*; foll. by *of*) have had enough of; be fed up with (*was tired of arguing*).

tire[2] /tīr/ *n.* **1** a rubber covering, usu. inflatable, that fits around a wheel rim. **2** a band of metal placed around the rim of a wheel to strengthen it.

tired /tīrd/ *adj.* **1** weary; exhausted; ready for sleep. **2** (of an idea, etc.) hackneyed. ▫▫ **tired·ly** *adv.* **tired·ness** *n.*

tire·less /tírlis/ *adj.* having inexhaustible energy. ▫▫ **tire·less·ly** *adv.* **tire·less·ness** *n.*

tire·some /tírsəm/ *adj.* **1** wearisome; tedious. **2** *Brit. colloq.* annoying (*how tiresome of you!*). ▫▫ **tire·some·ly** *adv.* **tire·some·ness** *n.*

'tis /tiz/ *archaic* it is.

tis·sue /tíshoo/ *n.* **1** any of the coherent collections of specialized cells of which animals or plants are made (*muscular tissue*; *nervous tissue*). **2** = TISSUE PAPER. **3** a disposable piece of thin soft absorbent paper for wiping, drying, etc. **4** fine woven esp. gauzy fabric. **5** (foll. by *of*) a connected series; a web (*a tissue of lies*).

tis·sue pa·per *n.* thin soft paper for wrapping or protecting fragile or delicate articles.

tit[1] /tit/ *n.* any of various small birds, esp. of the family Paridae.

tit[2] /tit/ *n.* ▫ **tit for tat** /tat/ blow for blow; retaliation.

tit[3] /tit/ *n.* **1** *colloq.* a nipple. **2** *coarse sl.* a woman's breast. ▶Usually considered a taboo word in sense 2.

Ti·tan /tít'n/ *n.* **1** (often **titan**) a person of very great strength, intellect, or importance. **2** (in Greek mythology) a member of a family of early gigantic gods, the offspring of Heaven and Earth.

ti·tan·ic /tītánik/ *adj.* **1** of or like the Titans. **2** gigantic; colossal. ▫▫ **ti·tan·i·cal·ly** *adv.*

ti·ta·ni·um /tītáyneeəm, tee–/ *n. Chem.* a gray metallic element occurring naturally in many clays, etc., and used to make strong light alloys that are resistant to corrosion. ¶ Symb.: **Ti**.

tithe /tīth/ *n.* & *v.* • *n.* **1** one tenth of the annual product of land or labor, formerly taken as a tax for the support of the church and clergy. **2** a tenth part. • *v.* **1** *tr.* subject to tithes. **2** *intr.* pay tithes. ▫▫ **tith·a·ble** *adj.*

tit·il·late /tít'layt/ *v.tr.* **1** excite pleasantly. **2** tickle. ▫▫ **tit·il·lat·ing·ly** *adv.* **tit·il·la·tion** /–láyshən/ *n.*

ti·tle /tít'l/ *n.* & *v.* • *n.* **1** the name of a book, work of art, piece of music, etc. **2** the heading of a chapter, poem, document, etc. **3 a** the contents of the title page of a book. **b** a book regarded in terms of its title (*published 20 new titles*). **4** a caption or credit in a movie, broadcast, etc. **5** a form of nomenclature indicating a person's status (e.g., *professor, queen*) or used as a form of address or reference (e.g., *Lord, Mr.*). **6** a sports championship. **7** *Law* **a** the right to ownership of property with or without possession. **b** the facts constituting this. **c** (foll. by *to*) a just or recognized claim. **8** *Eccl.* **a** a fixed sphere of work and source of income as a condition for ordination. **b** a parish church in Rome under a cardinal. • *v.tr.* **1** give a title to. **2** call by a title; term.

ti·tled /tít'ld/ *adj.* having a title of nobility or rank.

ti·tle role *n.* the part in a play, etc., that gives it its name (e.g., Othello).

tit·mouse /títmows/ *n.* (*pl.* **titmice** /–mīs/) any of various small tits, esp. of the genus *Parus*.

ti·trate /títrayt/ *v.tr. Chem.* ascertain the amount of a constituent in (a solution) by measuring the volume of a known concentration of reagent required to complete the reaction. ▫▫ **ti·trat·a·ble** *adj.* **ti·tra·tion** /–tráyshən/ *n.*

tit·ter /títər/ *v.* & *n.* • *v.intr.* laugh in a furtive or restrained way; giggle. • *n.* a furtive or restrained laugh. ▫▫ **tit·ter·er** *n.* **tit·ter·ing·ly** *adv.*

tit·tle /tít'l/ *n.* **1** a small written or printed stroke or dot. **2** a particle; a whit (esp. in *not one jot or tittle*).

tit·tle-tat·tle /tít'ltat'l/ *n.* & *v.* • *n.* petty gossip; foolish chatter. • *v.intr.* gossip; chatter. ▫▫ **tit·tle-tat·tler** *n.*

tit·ty /títee/ *n.* (*pl.* **-ties**) *sl.* = TIT[3].

tit·u·lar /tíchələr/ *adj.* & *n.* ●*adj.* **1** of or relating to a title (*the book's titular hero*). **2** existing, or being what is specified, in name or title only (*titular ruler; titular sovereignty*). ●*n.* **1** the holder of an office, etc., esp. a benefice without the corresponding functions or obligations. **2** a titular saint. □□ **tit·u·lar·ly** *adv.*

tiz·zy /tízee/ *n.* (*pl.* **-zies**) (also **tizz, tiz**) *colloq.* a state of nervous agitation (*in a tizzy*).

TKO *abbr. Boxing* technical knockout.

Tl *symb. Chem.* the element thallium.

TLC *abbr. colloq.* tender loving care.

Tlin·git /tlíngkət, –gət, klíng–/ *n.* & *adj.* ●*n.* **1 a** a N. American people native to southern Alaska. **b** a member of this people. **2** the language of this people. ●*adj.* of or relating to this people or their language.

TM *abbr.* **1** Transcendental Meditation. **2** trademark

Tm *symb. Chem.* the element thulium.

TN *abbr.* Tennessee (in official postal use).

TNT *abbr.* trinitrotoluene, a high explosive formed from toluene.

to /too; tə (when unstressed)/ *prep.* & *adv.* ●*prep.* **1** introducing a noun: **a** expressing what is reached, approached, or touched (*fell to the ground; went to Paris; put her face to the window; five minutes to six*). **b** expressing what is aimed at: often introducing the indirect object of a verb (*throw it to me; explained the problem to them*). **c** as far as; up to (*went on to the end; have to stay from Tuesday to Friday*). **d** to the extent of (*were all drunk to a man; was starved to death*). **e** expressing what is followed (*according to instructions; made to order*). **f** expressing what is considered or affected (*am used to that; that is nothing to me*). **g** expressing what is caused or produced (*turn to stone; tear to shreds*). **h** expressing what is compared (*nothing to what it once was; equal to the occasion; won by three to two*). **i** expressing what is increased (*add it to mine*). **j** expressing what is involved or composed as specified (*there is nothing to it; more to him than meets the eye*). **k** *archaic* for; by way of (*took her to wife*). **2** introducing the infinitive: **a** as a verbal noun (*to get there is the priority*). **b** expressing purpose, consequence, or cause (*we eat to live; left him to starve; am sorry to hear that*). **c** as a substitute for *to* + infinitive (*wanted to come but was unable to*). ●*adv.* **1** in the normal or required position or condition (*come to; heave to*). **2** (of a door) in a nearly closed position. □ **to and fro 1** backward and forward. **2** repeatedly between the same points.

toad /tōd/ *n.* **1** any froglike amphibian of the family *Bufonidae*, esp. of the genus *Bufo*, breeding in water but living chiefly on land. **2** any of various similar amphibians, including the Surinam toad. **3** a repulsive or detestable person. □□ **toad·ish** *adj.*

toad·flax /tṓdflaks/ *n.* **1** any plant of the genus *Linaria* or *Chaenorrhinum*, with flaxlike leaves and spurred yellow or purple flowers. **2** a related plant, *Cymbalaria muralis*, with lilac flowers and ivy-shaped leaves.

toad·stool /tṓdstool/ *n.* the spore-bearing structure of various fungi, usu. poisonous, with a round top and slender stalk.

toad·y /tṓdee/ *n.* & *v.* ●*n.* (*pl.* **-ies**) a sycophant; an obsequious hanger-on. ●*v.tr.* & (foll. by *to*) *intr.* (**-ies, -ied**) behave servilely to; fawn upon. □□ **toad·y·ish** *adj.* **toad·y·ism** *n.*

toast /tōst/ *n.* & *v.* ●*n.* **1** bread in slices browned on both sides by radiant heat. **2 a** a person (orig. esp. a woman) or thing in whose honor a company is requested to drink. **b** a call to drink or an instance of drinking in this way. **3** a person or thing that is very popular or held in high regard (*the toast of the town*). ●*v.* **1** *tr.* cook or brown (bread, etc.) by radiant heat. **2** *intr.* (of bread, etc.) become brown in this way. **3** *tr.* warm (one's feet, oneself, etc.) at a fire, etc. **4** *tr.* drink to the health or in honor of (a person or thing).

toast late Middle English (as a verb in the sense 'burn as the sun does, parch'): from Old French *toster* 'roast,' from Latin *torrere* 'parch.' Sense 2 derives from the practice of placing a small piece of toasted bread, flavored with spices, into a drink such as wine, later associated with the practice of toasting a woman in whose honor a company was requested to drink.

toast·er /tṓstər/ *n.* an electrical device for making toast.

toast·mas·ter /tṓstmastər/ *n.* an official responsible for announcing toasts at a public occasion.

toast·y /tṓstee/ *adj.* (**toastier, toastiest**) comfortably warm, cozy and warm. □□ **toast·i·ness** *n.*

to·bac·co /təbákō/ *n.* (*pl.* **-cos**) **1** any plant of the genus *Nicotiana*, of American origin, with narcotic leaves used for smoking, chewing, or snuff. **2** its leaves, esp. as prepared for smoking.

to·bac·co·nist /təbákənist/ *n.* a retail dealer in tobacco and cigarettes, etc.

to·bog·gan /təbógən/ *n.* & *v.* ●*n.* a long light narrow sled curled up at the front for sliding downhill, esp. over compacted snow or ice. ●*v.intr.* ride on a toboggan. □□ **to·bog·gan·er** *n.* **to·bog·gan·ing** *n.* **to·bog·gan·ist** *n.*

toc·ca·ta /təkaátə/ *n.* a musical composition for a keyboard instrument designed to exhibit the performer's touch and technique.

to·coph·er·ol /tōkófərawl, –rol/ *n.* any of several closely related vitamins found in wheat germ oil, egg yolk, and leafy vegetables, and important in the stabilization of cell membranes, etc. Also called **vitamin E**.

to·day /tədáy/ *adv.* & *n.* ●*adv.* **1** on or in the course of this present day (*shall we go today?*). **2** nowadays; in modern times. ●*n.* **1** this present day (*today is my birthday*). **2** modern times.

tod·dle /tód'l/ *v.* & *n.* ●*v.intr.* **1** walk with short unsteady steps like those of a small child. **2** *colloq.* **a** (often foll. by *around, to*, etc.) take a casual or leisurely walk. **b** (usu. foll. by *off*) depart. ●*n.* **1** a toddling walk. **2** *colloq.* a stroll or short walk.

tod·dler /tódlər/ *n.* a child who is just beginning to walk. □□ **tod·dler·hood** *n.*

tod·dy /tódee/ *n.* (*pl.* **-dies**) **1** a drink of liquor with hot water and sugar or spices. **2** the sap of some kinds of palm, fermented to produce arrack.

to-do /tədoo/ *n.* a commotion or fuss.

toe /tō/ *n.* & *v.* ●*n.* **1** any of the five terminal projections of the foot. **2** the corresponding part of an animal. **3** the part of an item of footwear that covers the toes. **4** the lower end or tip of an implement, etc. ●*v.* (**toes, toed, toeing**) **1** *tr.* touch (a starting line, etc.) with the toes before starting a race. **2** *tr.* **a** mend the toe of (a sock, etc.). **b** provide with a toe. □ **on one's toes** alert; eager. **toe the line** conform to a general policy or principle, esp. unwillingly or under pressure. **turn up one's toes** *colloq.* die. □□ **toed** *adj.* (also in *comb.*). **toe·less** *adj.*

toe·cap /tṓkap/ *n.* the (usu. strengthened) outer covering of the toe of a boot or shoe.

toe clip *n.* a clip on a bicycle pedal to prevent the foot from slipping.

toe·nail /tṓnayl/ *n.* the nail at the tip of each toe.

tof·fee /táwfee, tóf–/ *n.* (also **tof·fy**) (*pl.* **toffees** or **toffies**) **1** a kind of firm or hard candy softening when sucked or chewed, made by boiling sugar, butter, etc. **2** a small piece of this.

to·fu /tṓfoo/ *n.* a curd made from mashed soy beans.

tog /tog/ *n.* & *v. colloq.* ●*n.* (usu. in *pl.*) an item of clothing. ●*v.tr.* & *intr.* (**togged, togging**) (foll. by *out, up*) dress, esp. elaborately.

to·ga /tṓgə/ *n. hist.* an ancient Roman citizen's loose flowing outer garment. ▫▫ **to·gaed** *adj.*

to·geth·er /təgéthər/ *adv. & adj.* • *adv.* **1** in company or conjunction (*walking together; built it together; were at school together*). **2** simultaneously; at the same time (*both shouted together*). **3** one with another (*were talking together*). **4** into conjunction; so as to unite (*tied them together; put two and two together*). **5** into company or companionship (*came together in friendship*). **6** uninterruptedly (*could talk for hours together*). • *adj. colloq.* well organized or controlled. ▫ **together with** as well as; and also.

to·geth·er·ness /təgéthərnis/ *n.* **1** the condition of being together. **2** a feeling of comfort from being together.

tog·gle /tógəl/ *n. & v.* • *n.* **1** a device for fastening (esp. a garment), consisting of a crosspiece which can pass through a hole or loop in one position but not in another. **2** a pin or other crosspiece put through the eye of a rope, a link of a chain, etc., to keep it in place. **3** a pivoted barb on a harpoon. **4** *Computing* a switch action that is operated the same way but with opposite effect on successive occasions. • *v.tr.* provide or fasten with a toggle.

tog·gle switch *n.* an electric switch with a projecting lever to be moved usu. up and down.

toil /toyl/ *v. & n.* • *v.intr.* **1** work laboriously or incessantly. **2** make slow painful progress (*toiled along the path*). • *n.* prolonged or intensive labor; drudgery. ▫▫ **toil·er** *n.*

toil Middle English (in the senses 'strife' and 'contend verbally'): from Old French *tooillier* (verb), *tooil* (noun) 'confusion,' from Latin *tudiculare* 'stir about,' from *tudicula* 'machine for crushing olives,' related to *tundere* 'crush.'

toile /twaal/ *n.* **1** a type of sheer fabric. **2** a garment reproduced in muslin or other cheap material for fitting or for making copies.

toi·let /tóylit/ *n.* **1 a** a fixture, as in a bathroom, etc., for defecating and urinating. **b** a bathroom or lavatory. **2** the process of washing oneself, dressing, etc. (*make one's toilet*).

toilet mid-16th century: from French *toilette* 'cloth, wrapper,' diminutive of *toile*. The word originally denoted a cloth used as a wrapper for clothes, or occasionally a cloth placed around the shoulders during hairdressing; hence, the articles needed for washing and dressing or the process involved (sense 2). In the US the word came to denote a dressing-room, especially one with washing facilities, hence, a bathroom (early 20th century).

toi·let pa·per *n.* (also **toi·let tis·sue**) paper for cleaning oneself after excreting.

toi·let·ry /tóylitree/ *n.* (*pl.* **-ries**) (usu. in *pl.*) any of various articles or cosmetics used in washing, dressing, etc.

toi·lette /twaalét/ *n.* = TOILET 2.

toi·let wa·ter *n.* a diluted form of perfume used esp. after washing.

toil·some /tóylsəm/ *adj.* involving toil; laborious. ▫▫ **toil·some·ly** *adv.* **toil·some·ness** *n.*

to·ken /tṓkən/ *n.* **1** a thing serving as a symbol, reminder, or distinctive mark of something (*as a token of affection; in token of my esteem*). **2** a thing serving as evidence of authenticity or as a guarantee. **3** a voucher exchangeable for goods (often of a specified kind), given as a gift. **4** anything used to represent something else, esp. a metal disk, etc., used instead of money in coin-operated machines, as subway fare, etc. **5** (*attrib.*) **a** nominal or perfunctory (*token effort*). **b** conducted briefly to demonstrate strength of feeling (*token resistance; token strike*). **c** serving to acknowledge a principle only (*token payment*). **d** chosen by way of tokenism to represent a particular group (*the token woman on the committee*). ▫ **by the same token 1** similarly. **2** moreover.

to·ken·ism /tṓkənizəm/ *n.* **1** esp. *Polit.* the principle or practice of granting minimum concessions, esp. to appease radical demands, etc. (cf. TOKEN 5d). **2** making only a token effort.

told *past* and *past part.* of TELL.

tol·er·a·ble /tólərəbəl/ *adj.* **1** able to be endured; bearable; supportable; allowable. **2** fairly good; mediocre. ▫▫ **tol·er·a·bil·i·ty** /–bílitee/ *n.* **tol·er·a·ble·ness** *n.* **tol·er·a·bly** *adv.*

tol·er·ance /tólərəns/ *n.* **1** a willingness or ability to tolerate; forbearance. **2** the capacity to tolerate. **3** an allowable variation in any measurable property. **4** the ability to tolerate the effects of a drug, etc., after continued use.

tol·er·ant /tólərənt/ *adj.* **1** disposed or accustomed to tolerate others or their acts or opinions. **2** (foll. by *of*) enduring or patient. **3** exhibiting tolerance of a drug, etc. ▫▫ **tol·er·ant·ly** *adv.*

tol·er·ate /tólərayt/ *v.tr.* **1** allow the existence or occurrence of without authoritative interference. **2** leave unmolested. **3** endure or permit, esp. with forbearance. **4** sustain or endure (suffering, etc.). **5** be capable of continued subjection to (a drug, radiation, etc.) without harm. **6** find or treat as endurable. ▫▫ **tol·er·a·tor** *n.*

tol·er·a·tion /tóləráyshən/ *n.* the process or practice of tolerating, esp. the allowing of differences in religious opinion without discrimination.

toll[1] /tōl/ *n.* **1** a charge payable for permission to pass a barrier or use a bridge or road, etc. **2** the cost or damage caused by a disaster, battle, etc., or incurred in an achievement (*death toll*). **3** a charge for a long distance telephone call. ▫ **take its toll** be accompanied by loss or injury, etc.

toll[2] /tōl/ *v. & n.* • *v.* **1 a** *intr.* (of a bell) sound with a slow uniform succession of strokes. **b** *tr.* ring (a bell) in this way. **c** *tr.* (of a bell) announce or mark (a death, etc.) in this way. **2** *tr.* strike (the hour). • *n.* **1** the act of tolling. **2** a stroke of a bell.

toll·booth /tṓlbōōth/ *n.* a booth on a toll road or toll bridge, etc., from which tolls are collected.

toll·house /tṓlhows/ *n.* a house at a tollgate or toll bridge, used by a toll collector.

Tol·tec /tṓltek, tól–/ *n.* **1** a member of a Native American people that flourished in Mexico before the Aztecs. **2** the language of this people. ▫▫ **Tol·tec·an** *adj.*

tol·u·ene /tólyōō-een/ *n.* a colorless aromatic liquid hydrocarbon derivative of benzene, orig. obtained from tolu, used in the manufacture of explosives, etc. Also called **methyl benzene**. ▫▫ **to·lu·ic** *adj.* **tol·u·ol** *n.*

tom /tom/ *n.* a male of various animals, esp. (in full **tomcat**) a male cat.

tom·a·hawk /tóməhawk/ *n. & v.* • *n.* **1** a Native American war ax with a stone or iron head. **2** *Austral.* a hatchet. • *v.tr.* strike, cut, or kill with a tomahawk.

to·ma·to /təmáytō, –maá–/ *n.* (*pl.* **-toes**) **1** a glossy red or yellow pulpy edible fruit. **2** a plant, *Lycopersicon esculentum*, bearing this. ▫▫ **to·ma·to·ey** *adj.*

tomb /tōōm/ *n.* **1** a large, esp. underground, vault for the burial of the dead. **2** an enclosure cut in the earth or in rock to receive a dead body. **3** a sepulchral monument. **4** (prec. by *the*) the state of death.

tom·boy /tómboy/ *n.* a girl who behaves in a boisterous boyish way. ◻◻ **tom·boy·ish** *adj.* **tom·boy·ish·ness** *n.*

tomb·stone /to͞omstōn/ *n.* a stone standing or laid over a grave, usu. with an epitaph.

tome /tōm/ *n.* a large heavy book or volume.

tom·fool /tómfo͞ol/ *n.* **1** a foolish person. **2** (*attrib.*) silly; foolish (*a tomfool idea*).

tom·fool·er·y /tómfo͞oləree/ *n.* (*pl.* **-ies**) **1** foolish behavior; nonsense. **2** an instance of this.

tom·my gun /tómee/ *n.* a type of submachine gun.

tom·my·rot /tómeerot/ *n. sl.* nonsense.

to·mog·ra·phy /təmógrəfee/ *n.* a method of radiography displaying details in a selected plane within the body.

to·mor·row /təmáwrō, –mór–/ *adv. & n.* • *adv.* **1** on the day after today. **2** at some future time. • *n.* **1** the day after today. **2** the near future. ◻ **tomorrow morning** (or **afternoon**, etc.) in the morning (or afternoon, etc.) of tomorrow.

tom·tit /tómtit/ *n.* any of various tit birds, esp. a blue tit.

tom-tom /tómtom/ *n.* **1** an early drum beaten with the hands. **2** a tall drum beaten with the hands and used in jazz bands, etc.

ton /tun/ *n.* **1** (in full **short ton**) a unit of weight equal to 2,000 lb. (907.19 kg). **2** (in full **long ton**) a unit of weight equal to 2,240 lb. (1,016.05 kg). **3** = METRIC TON. **4 a** (in full **displacement ton**) a unit of measurement of a ship's weight or volume in terms of its displacement of water with the loadline just immersed, equal to 2,240 lb. or 35 cu. ft. (0.99 cubic meters). **b** (in full **freight ton**) a unit of weight or volume of cargo, equal to a metric ton (1,000 kg) or 40 cu. ft. **5 a** (in full **gross ton**) a unit of gross internal capacity, equal to 100 cu. ft. (2.83 cubic meters). **b** (in full **net** or **register ton**) an equivalent unit of net internal capacity. **6** a measure of capacity for various materials, esp. 40 cu. ft. of lumber. **7** (usu. in *pl.*) *colloq.* a large number or amount (*tons of money*). **8** esp. *Brit. sl.* **a** a speed of 100 m.p.h. **b** a sum of £100. **c** a score of 100. ◻ **weigh a ton** *colloq.* be very heavy.

ton·al /tṓnəl/ *adj.* **1** of or relating to tone or tonality. **2** (of a fugue, etc.) having repetitions of the subject at different pitches in the same key. ◻◻ **ton·al·ly** *adv.*

to·nal·i·ty /tōnálitee/ *n.* (*pl.* **-ties**) **1** *Mus.* **a** the relationship between the tones of a musical scale. **b** the observance of a single tonic key as the basis of a composition. **2** the tone or color scheme of a picture.

tone /tōn/ *n. & v.* • *n.* **1** a musical or vocal sound, esp. with reference to its pitch, quality, and strength. **2** (often in *pl.*) modulation of the voice expressing a particular feeling or mood (*a cheerful tone*; *suspicious tones*). **3** a manner of expression in writing. **4** *Mus.* **a** a musical sound, esp. of a definite pitch and character. **b** an interval of a major second, e.g., C–D. **5 a** the general effect of color or of light and shade in a picture. **b** the tint or shade of a color. **6 a** the prevailing character of the morals and sentiments, etc., in a group. **b** an attitude or sentiment expressed, esp. in a letter, etc. **7** the proper firmness of bodily organs. **8** a state of good or specified health or quality. • *v.* **1** *tr.* give the desired tone to. **2** *tr.* modify the tone of. **3** *intr.* (often foll. by *to*) attune. **4** *intr.* (foll. by *with*) be in harmony (esp. of color) (*does not tone with the wallpaper*). ◻ **tone down 1** make or become softer in tone of sound or color. **2** make (a statement, etc.) less harsh or emphatic. **tone up 1** make or become stronger in tone of sound or color. **2** make (a statement, etc.) more emphatic. **3** make (muscles) firm by exercise, etc.; make or become fitter. ◻◻ **tone·less** *adj.* **tone·less·ly** *adv.* **ton·er** *n.*

tone arm *n.* the movable arm supporting the pickup of a record player.

tone-deaf *adj.* unable to perceive differences of musical pitch accurately. ◻◻ **tone deaf·ness** *n.*

tone row *n. Mus.* a series of varying tones that recur in sequence throughout a composition.

tongs /tawngz, tongz/ *n.pl.* (also **pair of tongs** *sing.*) an instrument with two hinged or sprung arms for grasping and holding.

tongue /tung/ *n. & v.* • *n.* **1** the fleshy muscular organ in the mouth used in tasting, licking, and swallowing, and (in humans) for speech. **2** the tongue of an ox, etc., as food. **3** the faculty of or a tendency in speech (*a sharp tongue*). **4** a particular language (*the German tongue*). **5** a thing like a tongue in shape or position, esp.: **a** a long low promontory. **b** a strip of leather, etc., attached at one end only, under the laces in a shoe. **c** the clapper of a bell. **d** the pin of a buckle. **e** the projecting strip on a wooden, etc., board fitting into the groove of another. **f** a vibrating slip in the reed of some musical instruments. **g** a jet of flame. • *v.* (**tongues, tongued, tonguing**) **1** *tr.* produce staccato, etc., effects with (a flute, etc.) by means of tonguing. **2** *intr.* use the tongue in this way. ◻ **find** (or **lose**) **one's tongue** be able (or unable) to express oneself after a shock, etc. **speaking in tongues** vocal sounds uttered during religious ecstasy. **keep a civil tongue in one's head** avoid rudeness. **with one's tongue hanging out** eagerly or expectantly. ◻◻ **tongued** *adj.* (also in *comb.*). **tongue·less** *adj.*

tongue-and-groove *adj.* applied to boards in which a tongue along one edge fits into a groove along the edge of the next, each board having a tongue on one edge and a groove on the other.

tongue de·pres·sor *n.* a doctor's implement for holding the tongue in place while examining the throat or mouth.

tongue-in-cheek *adj. & adv.* • *adj.* ironic; slyly humorous. • *adv.* insincerely or ironically.

tongue-lash·ing *n.* a severe scolding or reprimand.

tongue-tied *adj.* too shy or embarrassed to speak.

tongue twist·er *n.* a sequence of words difficult to pronounce quickly and correctly.

tongu·ing /túnging/ *n. Mus.* the technique of playing a wind instrument using the tongue to articulate certain notes.

ton·ic /tónik/ *n. & adj.* • *n.* **1** an invigorating medicine. **2** anything serving to invigorate. **3** = TONIC WATER. **4** *Mus.* the first degree of a scale, forming the keynote of a piece (see KEYNOTE 3). • *adj.* **1** serving as a tonic; invigorating. **2** *Mus.* denoting the first degree of a scale. ◻◻ **ton·i·cal·ly** *adv.*

ton·ic sol-fa *n. Mus.* a system of notation used esp. in teaching singing, with do as the keynote of all major keys and la as the keynote of all minor keys.

ton·ic wa·ter *n.* a carbonated mineral water containing quinine.

to·night /tənít/ *adv. & n.* • *adv.* on the present or approaching evening or night. • *n.* the evening or night of the present day.

ton·nage /túnij/ *n.* **1** a ship's internal cubic capacity or freight-carrying capacity, measured in tons. **2** the total carrying capacity, esp. of a country's merchant marine. **3** a charge per ton on freight or cargo.

tonne /tun/ *n.* = METRIC TON.

ton·sil /tónsəl/ *n.* either of two small masses of lymphoid tissue on each side of the root of the tongue. ◻◻ **ton·sil·lar** *adj.*

ton·sil·lec·to·my /tónsiléktəmee/ *n.* (*pl.* **-mies**) the surgical removal of the tonsils.

ton·sil·li·tis /tónsilítis/ *n.* inflammation of the tonsils.

ton·so·ri·al /tonsáwreeəl/ *adj.* usu. *joc.* of or relating to a hairdresser or barber or hairdressing.

ton·sure /tónshər/ *n. & v.* • *n.* **1** the shaving of the crown of the head or the entire head, esp. of a person entering a priesthood or monastic order. **2** a bare patch made in this way. • *v.tr.* give a tonsure to.

ton·y /tṓnee/ *adj.* (**tonier, toniest**) *colloq.* stylish; fashionable; trendy.

too /to͞o/ *adv.* **1** to a greater extent than is desirable, permissible, or possible for a specified or understood purpose (*too colorful for my taste; too large to fit*). **2** *colloq.* extremely (*you're too kind*). **3** in addition (*are they coming too?*). **4** moreover (*we must consider, too, the time of year*). □ **none too 1** somewhat less than (*feeling none too good*). **2** barely. **too bad** see BAD.

took *past* of TAKE.

tool /to͞ol/ *n. & v.* • *n.* **1** any device or implement used to carry out mechanical functions whether manually or by a machine. **2** a thing used in an occupation or pursuit (*the tools of one's trade; literary tools*). **3** a person used as a mere instrument by another. **4** *coarse sl.* the penis. ▶Usually considered a taboo use. • *v.tr.* **1** dress (stone) with a chisel. **2** impress a design on (a leather book cover). **3** (foll. by *along, around,* etc.) *sl.* drive or ride, esp. in a casual or leisurely manner. **4** (often foll. by *up*) equip with tools. □ **tool up 1** *sl.* arm oneself. **2** equip oneself. □□ **tool·er** *n.*

tool·bar /to͞olbar/ *n. Computing* a strip of icons used to select from a set of software applications.

tool·mak·er /to͞olmaykər/ *n.* a person who makes precision tools, esp. tools used in a press. □□ **tool·mak·ing** *n.*

toot /to͞ot/ *n. & v.* • *n.* **1** a short sharp sound as made by a horn, trumpet, or whistle. **2** *sl.* cocaine or a snort (see SNORT *n.* 4) of cocaine. **3** *sl.* a drinking session; a binge; a spree. • *v.* **1** *tr.* sound (a horn, etc.) with a short sharp sound. **2** *intr.* give out such a sound. □□ **toot·er** *n.*

tooth /to͞oth/ *n. & v.* • *n.* (*pl.* **teeth** /teeth/) **1** each of a set of hard bony enamel-coated structures in the jaws of most vertebrates, used for biting and chewing. **2** a toothlike part or projection, especially one of a series that function or engage together, e.g., the cog of a gearwheel, the point of a saw or comb, etc. **3** (often foll. by *for*) one's sense of taste; an appetite or liking. **4** (in *pl.*) force or effectiveness (*the penalties give the contract teeth*). • *v.* **1** *tr.* provide with teeth. **2** *intr.* (of cogwheels) engage, interlock. □ **armed to the teeth** completely and elaborately armed or equipped. **fight tooth and nail** fight very fiercely. **get** (or **sink**) **one's teeth into** devote oneself seriously to. **in the teeth of 1** in spite of (opposition or difficulty, etc.). **2** contrary to (instructions, etc.). **3** directly against (the wind, etc.). **set a person's teeth on edge** see EDGE. □□ **toothed** *adj.* (also in *comb.*). **tooth·less** *adj.* **tooth·like** *adj.*

tooth·ache /to͞othayk/ *n.* a (usu. prolonged) pain in a tooth or teeth.

tooth·brush /to͞othbrush/ *n.* a brush for cleaning the teeth.

tooth·paste /to͞othpayst/ *n.* a paste for cleaning the teeth.

tooth·pick /to͞othpik/ *n.* a small sharp instrument for removing small pieces of food lodged between the teeth.

tooth·some /to͞othsəm/ *adj.* **1** (of food) delicious; appetizing. **2** attractive, esp. sexually. □□ **tooth·some·ly** *adv.* **tooth·some·ness** *n.*

tooth·y /to͞othee/ *adj.* (**toothier, toothiest**) having or showing large, numerous, or prominent teeth (*a toothy grin*). □□ **tooth·i·ly** *adv.*

too·tle /to͞ot'l/ *v.intr.* **1** toot gently or repeatedly. **2** (usu. foll. by *along, around,* etc.) *colloq.* move casually or aimlessly. □□ **too·tler** *n.*

top[1] /top/ *n., adj., & v.* • *n.* **1** the highest point or part (*the top of the house*). **2 a** the highest rank or place (*at the top of the school*). **b** a person occupying this (*was top in spelling*). **c** esp. *Brit.* the upper end or head (*the top of the table*). **3** the upper surface of a thing, esp. of the ground, a table, etc. **4** the upper part of a thing, esp.: **a** a blouse, sweater, etc., for wearing with a skirt or pants. **b** the upper part of a shoe or boot. **c** the stopper of a bottle. **d** the lid of a jar, saucepan, etc. **e** the creamy part of unhomogenized milk. **f** the folding roof of a car, carriage, etc. **g** the upper edge or edges of a page or pages in a book (*gilt top*). **5** the utmost degree; height (*called at the top of his voice*). **6** (in *pl.*) *colloq.* a person or thing of the best quality (*he's tops at swimming*). **7** (esp. in *pl.*) the leaves, etc., of a plant grown esp. for its root (*turnip tops*). **8** (usu. in *pl.*) a bundle of long wool fibers prepared for spinning. **9** *Naut.* a platform around the head of the lower mast. **10** *Baseball* the first half of an inning. **11** = TOPSPIN. • *adj.* **1** highest in position (*the top shelf*). **2** highest in degree or importance (*at top speed; the top job*). • *v.tr.* (**topped, topping**) **1** provide with a top, cap, etc. (*cake topped with icing*). **2** remove the top of (a plant, fruit, etc.), esp. to improve growth, prepare for cooking, etc. **3** be higher or better than; surpass; be at the top of (*topped the list*). **4** *Brit. sl.* **a** execute, esp. by hanging; kill. **b** (*refl.*) commit suicide. **5** reach the top of (a hill, etc.). **6 a** hit (a ball) above the center. **b** make (a hit or stroke) in this way. □ **from top to toe** from head to foot; completely. **off the top of one's head** see HEAD. **on top 1** in a superior position; above. **2** on the upper part of the head (*bald on top*). **on top of 1** fully in command of. **2** in close proximity to. **3** in addition to. **4** above; over. **on top of the world** *colloq.* exuberant. **over the top 1** over the parapet of a trench (and into battle). **2** into a final or decisive state. **3** to excess; beyond reasonable limits (*that joke was over the top*). **top off 1** put an end or the finishing touch to (a thing). **2** fill up, esp. a container already partly full. **top out** put the highest stone on (a building). **top one's part** esp. *Theatr.* act or discharge one's part to perfection. □□ **top·most** *adj.*

top[2] /top/ *n.* a wooden or metal toy, usu. conical, spherical, or pear-shaped, spinning on a point when set in motion by hand, string, etc.

to·paz /tṓpaz/ *n.* a transparent or translucent aluminum silicate mineral, usu. yellow, used as a gem.

top brass *n.* esp. *Mil. colloq.* the highest ranking officers, heads of industries, etc.

top·coat /tópkōt/ *n.* **1** an overcoat. **2** an outer coat of paint, etc.

top dog *n. colloq.* a person who is successful or dominant in their field.

top draw·er *n.* **1** the uppermost drawer in a chest, etc. **2** *colloq.* high quality, social position or class. □□ **top-drawer** *adj. colloq.*

tope /tōp/ *v.intr.* drink alcohol to excess, esp. habitually. □□ **top·er** *n.*

top hat *n.* a man's tall silk hat.

top-heav·y /tóphévee/ *adj.* **1** disproportionately heavy at the top so as to be in danger of toppling. **2 a** (of an organization, business, etc.) having a disproportionately large number of people in senior administrative positions. **b** overcapitalized. **3** *colloq.* (of a woman) having a disproportionately large bust. □□ **top-heav·i·ly** *adv.* **top-heav·i·ness** *n.*

to·pi·ar·y /tópee-eree/ *adj. & n.* • *adj.* concerned with or formed by clipping shrubs, trees, etc., into ornamental shapes. • *n.* (*pl.* **-ies**) **1** topiary art. **2** an example of this. □□ **to·pi·ar·i·an** /–peeáireeən/ *adj.* **to·pi·a·rist** *n.*

top·ic /tópik/ *n.* **1** a theme for a book, discourse, essay, sermon, etc. **2** the subject of a conversation or argument.

top·i·cal /tópikəl/ *adj.* **1** dealing with the news, current affairs, etc. (*a topical song*). **2** dealing with a place; local. **3** *Med.* (of an ailment, medicine, etc.) affecting a part of the body. **4** of or concerning topics. ▫▫ **top·i·cal·i·ty** /–kálitee/ *n.* **top·i·cal·ly** *adv.*

top·knot /tópnot/ *n.* a knot, tuft, crest, or bow worn on the head or growing on the head.

top·less /tóplis/ *adj.* **1** without or seeming to be without a top. **2 a** (of clothes) having no upper part. **b** (of a person) wearing such clothes; barebreasted. **c** (of a place, esp. a beach, bar, etc.) where women go topless. ▫▫ **top·less·ness** *n.*

top-lev·el *adj.* of the highest level of importance or prestige (*top-level talks*).

top·loft·y /tópláwftee, –lóf–/ *adj. colloq.* haughty.

top·mast /tópmast/ *n. Naut.* the mast next above the lower mast.

top-notch *adj. colloq.* first rate.

to·pog·ra·phy /təpógrəfee/ *n.* **1 a** a detailed description, representation on a map, etc., of the natural and artificial features of a town, district, etc. **b** such features. **2** *Anat.* the mapping of the surface of the body with reference to the parts beneath. ▫▫ **to·pog·ra·pher** *n.* **top·o·graph·ic** /tópəgráfik/ *adj.* **top·o·graph·i·cal** *adj.* **top·o·graph·i·cal·ly** *adv.*

to·poi *pl.* of TOPOS.

to·pol·o·gy /təpóləjee/ *n. Math.* the study of geometrical properties and spatial relations unaffected by the continuous change of shape or size of figures. ▫▫ **top·o·log·i·cal** /tópəlójikəl/ *adj.* **top·o·log·i·cal·ly** *adv.* **to·pol·o·gist** *n.*

top·o·nym /tópənim/ *n.* **1** a place-name. **2** a descriptive place-name, usu. derived from a topographical feature of the place.

to·pon·y·my /təpónimee/ *n.* the study of the place-names of a region. ▫▫ **top·o·nym·ic** /tópənímik/ *adj.*

to·pos /tṓpōs, –pos/ *n.* (*pl.* **topoi** /–poy/) a stock theme in literature, etc.

top·ping /tóping/ *adj.* & *n.* • *adj.* **1** preeminent in position, rank, etc. **2** *Brit. archaic sl.* excellent. • *n.* anything that tops something else, esp. icing, etc., on a cake.

top·ple /tópəl/ *v.intr.* & *tr.* (usu. foll. by *over*, *down*) **1 a** fall or cause to fall as if top-heavy. **b** fall or cause to fall from power. **2** totter or cause to totter and fall.

top·sail /tópsayl, –səl/ *n.* a square sail next above the lowest fore-and-aft sail on a gaff.

top se·cret *adj.* of the highest secrecy.

top·side /tópsīd/ *n.* **1** the side of a ship above the waterline. **2** *Brit.* the outer side of a round of beef.

top·soil /tópsoyl/ *n.* the top layer of soil.

top·spin /tópspin/ *n.* a fast forward spinning motion imparted to a ball in tennis, etc., by hitting it forward and upward.

top·sy-tur·vy /tópseetə́rvee/ *adv., adj.,* & *n.* • *adv.* & *adj.* **1** upside down. **2** in utter confusion. • *n.* utter confusion. ▫▫ **top·sy-tur·vi·ly** *adv.* **top·sy-tur·vi·ness** *n.*

toque /tōk/ *n.* **1** a woman's small brimless hat. **2** *hist.* a small cap or bonnet for a man or woman.

tor /tor/ *n.* a hill or rocky peak.

To·rah /tṓrə, táwrə, tōráa/ *n.* **1** (usu. prec. by *the*) **a** the first five books of the Hebrew scriptures (the Pentateuch). **b** a scroll containing this. **2** the will of God as revealed in Mosaic law.

torch /tawrch/ *n.* & *v.* • *n.* **1 a** a piece of wood, cloth, etc., soaked in tallow and lighted for illumination. **b** any similar lamp, e.g., an oil lamp on a pole. **2** a source of heat, illumination, or enlightenment (*bore aloft the torch of freedom*). **3** = BLOWTORCH. **4** *sl.* an arsonist. **5** (also **electric torch**) *Brit.* = FLASHLIGHT 1. • *v.tr. sl.* set alight with or as with a torch. ▫ **carry a torch for** suffer from unrequited love for. **put to the torch** destroy by burning.

torch·light /táwrchlīt/ *n.* the light of a torch or torches.

torch song *n.* a popular song of unrequited love. ▫▫ **torch sing·er** *n.*

tore[1] *past* of TEAR[1].

tore[2] /tawr/ *n.* = TORUS 1, 4.

tor·e·a·dor /táwreeədor/ *n.* a bullfighter, esp. on horseback.

tor·e·a·dor pants *n.pl.* close-fitting calf-length women's slacks.

to·ri *pl.* of TORUS.

tor·ment *n.* & *v.* • *n.* /táwrment/ **1** severe physical or mental suffering (*was in torment*). **2** a cause of this. **3** *archaic* **a** torture. **b** an instrument of torture. • *v.tr.* /tawrmént/ **1** subject to torment (*tormented with worry*). **2** tease or worry excessively (*enjoyed tormenting the teacher*). ▫▫ **tor·ment·ed·ly** *adv.* **tor·ment·ing·ly** *adv.* **tor·men·tor** *n.*

torn *past part.* of TEAR[1].

tor·na·do /tawrnáydō/ *n.* (*pl.* **-does**) a violent storm of small extent with whirling winds, esp. over a narrow path, often accompanied by a funnel-shaped cloud. ▫▫ **tor·na·dic** /–nádik/ *adj.*

to·roi·dal /tawróyd'l/ *adj. Geom.* of or resembling a torus. ▫▫ **to·roi·dal·ly** *adv.*

tor·pe·do /tawrpéedō/ *n.* & *v.* • *n.* (*pl.* **-does**) **1** a cigar-shaped self-propelled underwater missile that explodes on impact with a ship. **2** a similar device dropped from an aircraft. • *v.tr.* (**-does, -doed**) **1** destroy or attack with a torpedo. **2** make (a policy, institution, plan, etc.) ineffective or inoperative; destroy. ▫▫ **tor·pe·do·like** *adj.*

tor·pid /táwrpid/ *adj.* **1** sluggish; inactive; dull; apathetic. **2** numb. **3** (of a hibernating animal) dormant. ▫▫ **tor·pid·i·ty** /–píditee/ *n.* **tor·pid·ly** *adv.* **tor·pid·ness** *n.*

tor·por /táwrpər/ *n.* torpidity. ▫▫ **tor·por·if·ic** /–pərífik/ *adj.*

torque /tawrk/ *n.* **1** *Mech.* the moment of a system of forces tending to cause rotation.

torque con·vert·er *n.* a device to transmit the correct torque from the engine to the axle in a motor vehicle.

tor·rent /táwrənt, tór–/ *n.* **1** a rushing stream of water, lava, etc. **2** (usu. in *pl.*) a great downpour of rain (*came down in torrents*). **3** (usu. foll. by *of*) a violent or copious flow (*uttered a torrent of abuse*). ▫▫ **tor·ren·tial** /tərénshəl/ *adj.* **tor·ren·tial·ly** /tərénshəlee/ *adv.*

tor·rid /táwrid, tór–/ *adj.* **1 a** (of the weather) very hot and dry. **b** (of land, etc.) parched by such weather. **2** (of language or actions) emotionally charged; passionate; intense. ▫▫ **tor·rid·i·ty** /–ríditee/ *n.* **tor·rid·ly** *adv.* **tor·rid·ness** *n.*

tor·rid zone *n.* the central belt of the earth between the Tropics of Cancer and Capricorn.

tor·sion /táwrshən/ *n.* **1** twisting, esp. of one end of a body while the other is held fixed. **2** *Math.* the extent to which a curve departs from being planar. ▫▫ **tor·sion·al** *adj.* **tor·sion·al·ly** *adv.* **tor·sion·less** *adj.*

tor·sion bar *n.* a bar forming part of a vehicle suspension, twisting in response to the motion of the wheels, and absorbing their vertical movement.

tor·so /táwrsō/ *n.* (*pl.* **-sos** or **-si**) **1** the trunk of the human body. **2** a statue of a human consisting of the trunk alone, without head or limbs.

tort /tawrt/ *n. Law* a breach of duty (other than under contract) leading to liability for damages.

torte /táwrt/ *n.* (*pl.* **torten** /táwrt'n/ or **tortes**) an elaborate sweet cake.

tort·fea·sor /táwrtfeezər/ *n. Law* a person guilty of tort.

tor·til·la /tawrtéeyə/ *n.* a thin flat orig. Mexican corn or wheat bread eaten hot or cold with or without a filling.

tor·toise /táwrtəs/ *n.* **1** any slow-moving, esp. land reptile of the family *Testudinidae*, encased in a scaly or leathery domed shell, and having a retractile head and elephantine legs. **2** *Rom.Antiq.* = TESTUDO. ◻◻ **tor·toise·like** *adj. & adv.*

tor·toise·shell /táwrtəs-shel/ *n. & adj.* •*n.* **1** the yellowish brown mottled or clouded outer shell of some turtles, used for decorative combs, jewelry, brushes, etc. **2 a** = TORTOISESHELL BUTTERFLY. **b** = TORTOISESHELL CAT. •*adj.* having the coloring or appearance of tortoiseshell.

tor·toise·shell but·ter·fly *n.* any of various butterflies of the genus *Aglais* or *Nymphalis* with wings mottled like tortoiseshell.

tor·toise·shell cat *n.* a domestic cat with markings resembling tortoiseshell.

tor·tu·ous /táwrchōōəs/ *adj.* **1** full of twists and turns (*followed a tortuous route*). **2** devious; circuitous; crooked (*has a tortuous mind*). ◻◻ **tor·tu·os·i·ty** /–ósitee/ *n.* (*pl.* **-ties**). **tor·tu·ous·ly** *adv.* **tor·tu·ous·ness** *n.* ▶**Tortuous** means 'full of twists and turns' or 'devious; circuitous,' e.g., *Both paths were tortuous and are strewn with boulders.* **Torturous** is derived from *torture* and means 'involving torture; excruciating,' e.g., *I found the concert torturous because of the music's volume.*

tor·ture /táwrchər/ *n. & v.* •*n.* **1** the infliction of severe bodily pain, esp. as a punishment or a means of persuasion. **2** severe physical or mental suffering (*the torture of defeat*). •*v.tr.* **1** subject to torture (*tortured by guilt*). **2** force out of a natural position or state; deform; pervert. ◻◻ **tor·tur·a·ble** *adj.* **tor·tur·er** *n.* **tor·tur·ous** *adj.* **tor·tur·ous·ly** *adv.*

to·rus /táwrəs/ *n.* (*pl.* **tori** /–rī/) **1** *Archit.* a large convex molding, esp. as the lowest part of the base of a column. **2** *Bot.* the receptacle of a flower. **3** *Anat.* a smooth ridge of bone or muscle. **4** *Geom.* a surface or solid formed by rotating a closed curve, esp. a circle, about a line in its plane but not intersecting it.

To·ry /táwree/ *n. & adj.* •*n.* (*pl.* **-ries**) **1** esp. *Brit. colloq.* = CONSERVATIVE *n.* 2. **2** *Brit. hist.* a member of the party that gave rise to the Conservative party (opp. WHIG). **3** a colonist loyal to the English during the American Revolution. •*adj. colloq.* = CONSERVATIVE *adj.* 3. ◻◻ **To·ry·ism** *n.*

toss /taws, tos/ *v. & n.* •*v.* **1** *tr.* throw up (a ball, etc.) esp. with the hand. **2** *tr. & intr.* roll about, throw, or be thrown, restlessly or from side to side (*the ship tossed on the ocean*; *was tossing and turning all night*; *tossed her head angrily*). **3** *tr.* (usu. foll. by *to*, *away*, *aside*, *out*, etc.) throw (a thing) lightly or carelessly (*tossed the letter away*). **4** *tr.* **a** throw (a coin) into the air to decide a choice, etc., by the side on which it lands. **b** (also *absol.*; often foll. by *for*) settle a question or dispute with (a person) in this way (*tossed him for the armchair*; *tossed for it*). **5** *tr.* **a** (of a bull, etc.) throw (a person, etc.) up with the horns. **b** (of a horse, etc.) throw (a rider) off its back. **6** *tr.* coat (food) with dressing, etc., by mixing or shaking. **7** *tr.* bandy about in debate; discuss (*tossed the question back and forth*). •*n.* **1** the act or an instance of tossing (a coin, the head, etc.). **2** a fall, esp. from a horse. ◻◻ **toss·er** *n.*

toss-up *n.* **1** a situation in which any of two or more outcomes or options is equally possible. **2** the tossing of a coin to make a decision between two alternatives.

tos·ta·da /tōstaádə/ *n.* a crisp fried tortilla, often topped with meat, cheese, etc.

tot /tot/ *n.* **1** a small child (*a tiny tot*). **2** esp. *Brit.* a dram of liquor.

to·tal /tṓt'l/ *adj., n., & v.* •*adj.* **1** complete; comprising the whole (*the total number of people*). **2** absolute; unqualified (*in total ignorance*; *total abstinence*). •*n.* a total number or amount. •*v.* (**totaled, totaling** or **totalled, totalling**) **1** *tr.* **a** amount in number to (*they totaled 131*). **b** find the total of (things, a set of numbers, etc.). **2** *intr.* (foll. by *to*, *up to*) amount to; mount up to. **3** *tr. sl.* wreck completely; demolish. ◻◻ **to·tal·ly** *adv.*

to·tal e·clipse *n.* an eclipse in which the whole disk (of the sun, moon, etc.) is obscured.

to·tal·i·tar·i·an /tōtálitáireeən/ *adj. & n.* •*adj.* of or relating to a centralized dictatorial form of government requiring complete subservience to the state. •*n.* a person advocating such a system. ◻◻ **to·tal·i·tar·i·an·ism** *n.*

to·tal·i·ty /tōtálitee/ *n.* **1** the complete amount or sum. **2** *Astron.* the time during which an eclipse is total.

to·tal re·call *n.* the ability to remember every detail of one's experience clearly.

to·tal war *n.* a war in which all available weapons and resources are employed.

tote /tōt/ *v.tr. colloq.* carry or convey, esp. a heavy load (*toting a gun*). ◻◻ **tot·er** *n.* (also in *comb.*).

tote bag *n.* a large open-topped bag for shopping, etc.

to·tem /tṓtəm/ *n.* **1** a natural object, esp. an animal, adopted by Native American people as an emblem of a clan or an individual. **2** an image of this. ◻◻ **to·tem·ic** /–témik/ *adj.* **to·tem·ism** *n.* **to·tem·ist** *n.* **to·tem·is·tic** /–təmístik/ *adj.*

to·tem pole *n.* **1** a pole on which totems are carved or hung. **2** a hierarchy.

totem pole

tot·ter /tótər/ *v. & n.* •*v.intr.* **1** stand or walk unsteadily or feebly (*tottered out of the bar*). **2 a** (of a building, etc.) shake or rock as if about to collapse. **b** (of a system of government, etc.) be about to fall. •*n.* an unsteady or shaky movement or gait. ◻◻ **tot·ter·er** *n.* **tot·ter·y** *adj.*

tou·can /tóōkan/ *n.* any tropical American fruit-eating bird of the family *Ramphastidae*, with an immense beak and brightly colored plumage.

touch /tuch/ *v. & n.* •*v.* **1** *tr.* come into or be in physical contact with (another thing). **2** *tr.* (often foll. by *with*) bring the hand, etc., into contact with. **3 a** *intr.* (of two things, etc.) be in or come into contact with one another (*the cars were touching*). **b** *tr.* bring (two things) into mutual contact (*they touched hands*). **4** *tr.* produce feelings of affection, gratitude, or sympathy in (*was touched by his loyalty*). **5** *tr.* strike lightly. **6** *tr.* (usu. with *neg.*) **a** disturb or harm (*don't touch my things*). **b** have any dealings with (*won't touch bricklaying*). **c** consume; use up; make use of (*has not touched her breakfast*; *need not touch your savings*). **d** cope with; affect; manage (*soap won't touch this dirt*). **7** *tr.* **a** deal with (a subject) lightly or in passing (*touched the matter of their expenses*). **b** concern (*it touches you closely*). **8** *tr.* **a** reach or rise as far as, esp. momentarily (*the thermometer touched 90°*). **b** (usu. with *neg.*) approach in excellence, etc. (*can't touch him for style*). **9** *tr.* affect slightly; modify (*pity touched with fear*). **10** *tr.* (as **touched** *adj.*) slightly mad. **11** *tr.* esp. *Art* mark lightly; put in (features, etc.) with a brush, pencil, etc. **12** *tr.* **a** strike (the keys, strings, etc., of a musical instrument). **b** strike the keys or strings of (a piano, etc.). **13** *tr.* (usu. foll. by *for*) *sl.* ask for and get money, etc., from (a person) as a loan or gift (*touched him for $5*). **14** *tr.* injure slightly (*blossom touched by frost*). **15** *tr. Geom.* be tangent to (a curve). • *n.* **1** the act or an instance of touching, esp. with the body or hand (*felt a touch on my arm*). **2 a** the faculty of perception through physical contact, esp. with the fingers (*has no sense of touch in her right hand*). **b** the qualities of an object, etc., as perceived in this way (*the soft touch of silk*). **3** a small amount; a slight trace (*a touch of salt*; *a touch of irony*). **4 a** a musician's manner of playing keys or strings. **b** the manner in which the keys or strings respond to touch. **c** an artist's or writer's style of workmanship, writing, etc. (*has a delicate touch*). **5** a distinguishing quality or trait (*a professional touch*). **6** (esp. in *pl.*) **a** a light stroke with a pen, pencil, etc. **b** a slight alteration or improvement (*speech needs a few touches*). **7** = TAG[2]. **8** (prec. by *a*) slightly (*is a touch too arrogant*). **9** *sl.* **a** the act of asking for and getting money, etc., from a person. **b** a person from whom money, etc., is so obtained. **10** *Soccer & Rugby* the part of the field outside the side limits. □ **at a touch** if touched, however lightly (*opened at a touch*). **get** (or **put**) **in** (or **into**) **touch with** come or cause to come into communication with; contact. **in touch** (often foll. by *with*) **1** in communication. **2** up to date, esp. regarding news, etc. **3** aware; conscious; empathetic (*not in touch with her own feelings*). **keep in touch** (often foll. by *with*) **1** remain informed. **2** continue correspondence, a friendship, etc. **lose touch** (often foll. by *with*) **1** cease to be informed. **2** cease to correspond with or be in contact with another person. **lose one's touch** not show one's customary skill. **out of touch** (often foll. by *with*) **1** not in correspondence. **2** not up to date or modern. **3** lacking in awareness or sympathy (*out of touch with his son's beliefs*). **to the touch** when touched (*was cold to the touch*). **touch and go** uncertain regarding a result; risky (*it was touch and go whether we'd catch the train*). **touch at** (of a ship) call at (a port, etc.). **touch base (with)** make contact with; briefly communicate with. **touch bottom 1** reach the bottom of water with one's feet. **2** be at the lowest or worst point. **3** be in possession of the full facts. **touch down** (of an aircraft or spacecraft) make contact with the ground in landing. **touch off 1** represent exactly (in a portrait, etc.). **2** explode by touching with a match, etc. **3** initiate (a process) suddenly (*touched off a run on the peso*). **touch on** (or **upon**) **1** treat (a subject) briefly; refer to or mention casually. **2** verge on (*that touches on impudence*). **touch up** make small improvements to something. □□ **touch·a·ble** *adj.* **touch·er** *n.*

touch-and-go *adj. & n.* • *adj.* (of an outcome) possible but very uncertain (*it was touch-and-go whether we'd make it home that day*). • *n.* an airplane landing and immediate takeoff done esp. as practice.

touch·back /túchbak/ *n. Football* a play in which the ball is downed behind the goal line after it has been caught there; the ball is put back in play at the 20-yard line of the team making the catch, who then take over on offense.

touch·down /túchdown/ *n.* **1** the act or an instance of an aircraft or spacecraft making contact with the ground during landing. **2** *Football* the act or an instance of scoring by crossing the goal line.

tou·ché /tōōsháy/ *int.* **1** the acknowledgment of a hit by a fencing opponent. **2** the acknowledgment of a justified accusation, a witticism, or a point made in reply to one's own.

touch foot·ball *n.* football with touching in place of tackling.

touch·ing /túching/ *adj. & prep.* • *adj.* moving; pathetic (*a touching incident*; *touching confidence*). • *prep.* concerning; about. □□ **touch·ing·ly** *adv.* **touch·ing·ness** *n.*

touch-me-not *n.* any of various plants of the genus *Impatiens*, with ripe seed capsules bursting open when touched.

touch screen *n.* a touch-sensitive video screen for display of data, as information to customers in a store, etc.

touch·stone /túchstōn/ *n.* **1** a fine-grained dark schist or jasper used for testing alloys of gold, etc., by marking it with them and observing the color of the mark. **2** a standard or criterion.

touch-tone *adj.* **1** of or relating to a tone dialing telephone system. **2** (**Touch-tone**) *Trademark* a telephone that produces tones when buttons are pushed.

touch-type *v.intr.* type without looking at the keys. □□ **touch typ·ing** *n.* **touch-typ·ist** *n.*

touch·y /túchee/ *adj.* (**touchier, touchiest**) **1** apt to take offense; overly sensitive. **2** not to be touched without danger; ticklish; risky; awkward. □□ **touch·i·ly** *adv.* **touch·i·ness** *n.*

tough /tuf/ *adj. & n.* • *adj.* **1** hard to break, cut, tear, or chew; durable; strong. **2** (of a person) able to endure hardship; hardy. **3** unyielding; stubborn; difficult (*it was a tough job*; *a tough customer*). **4** *colloq.* **a** acting sternly; hard (*get tough with*). **b** (of circumstances, luck, etc.) severe; unpleasant; hard; unjust. **5** *colloq.* criminal or violent (*tough guys*). • *n.* a tough person, esp. a gangster or criminal. □ **tough it out** *colloq.* endure or withstand difficult conditions. □□ **tough·en** *v.tr. & intr.* **tough·en·er** *n.* **tough·ish** *adj.* **tough·ness** *n.*

tou·pee /tōōpáy/ *n.* a wig or artificial hairpiece to cover a bald spot.

tour /tŏŏr/ *n. & v.* • *n.* **1 a** a journey from place to place as a vacation. **b** an excursion, ramble, or walk (*made a tour of the yard*). **2 a** a period of duty on military or diplomatic service. **b** the time to be spent at a particular post. **3** a series of performances, games, etc., at different places on a route through a country, etc. • *v.* **1** *intr.* (usu. foll. by *through*) make a tour (*toured through Italy*). **2** *tr.* make a tour of (a country, etc.). □ **on tour** (esp. of a sports team, theater company, etc.) touring.

tour de force /tŏŏr də fáwrs/ *n.* a feat of strength or skill.

tour·ism /tŏŏrizəm/ *n.* the organization and operation of tours, esp. as a commercial enterprise.

tour·ist /tŏŏrist/ *n.* a person making a visit or tour as a vacation; a traveler. (often *attrib.*: *tourist accommodations*). □□ **tour·is·tic** *adj.* **tour·is·ti·cal·ly** *adv.*

tour·ma·line /tŏŏrməlin, –leen/ *n.* a boron aluminum silicate mineral of various colors, possessing unusual electrical properties, and used in electrical and optical instruments and as a gemstone.

tour·na·ment /tŏŏrnəmənt, tə́r–/ *n.* **1** any contest of skill between a number of competitors, esp. played in heats or a series of games (*chess tournament*; *tennis tournament*). **2** (in the UK) a display of military exercises, etc. **3** *hist.* **a** a pageant with jousting. **b** a meeting for jousting.

tour·ne·dos /tŏŏrnədō/ *n.* (*pl.* same /–dōz/) a small round thick cut from a tenderloin of beef.

tour·ney /tŏŏrnee, tə́r–/ *n. & v.* • *n.* (*pl.* **-neys**) a tournament. • *v.intr.* (**-neys, -neyed**) take part in a tournament.

tour·ni·quet /tərnikit, tŏŏr–/ *n.* a device for stopping the flow of blood through an artery by constriction.

tou·sle /tówzəl/ *v.tr.* **1** make (esp. the hair) untidy; rumple. **2** handle roughly or rudely.

tout /towt/ *v. & n.* • *v.* **1** *intr.* (usu. foll. by *for*) solicit patronage persistently; pester customers (*touting for business*). **2** *tr.* solicit the patronage of (a person) or for (a thing). **3** *intr.* **a** *Brit.* spy out the movements and condition of racehorses in training. **b** offer racing tips for a share of the resulting profit. •*n.* a person employed in touting. ▫▫ **tout·er** *n.*

tout Old English *tȳtan* 'look out,' of Germanic origin; related to Dutch *tuit* 'spout, nozzle.' The Old English meaning gave rise to the sense 'be on the lookout,' hence 'be on the lookout for customers, solicit' (mid-18th century), also 'watch, spy on' (early 19th century).

tow /tō/ *v. & n.* •*v.tr.* **1** (of a motor vehicle, horse, or person controlling it) pull (a boat, another motor vehicle, a trailer, etc.) along by a rope, tow bar, etc. **2** pull (a person or thing) along behind one. •*n.* the act or an instance of towing; the state of being towed. ▫ **have in tow 1** be towing. **2** be accompanied by and often in charge of (a person). ▫▫ **tow·a·ble** *adj.* **tow·age** /tṓij/ *n.*

to·ward /tawrd, təwáwrd, twawrd/ *prep. & adj.* (also **to·wards** /tawrdz, təwáwrdz, twawrdz/) **1** in the direction of (*set out toward town*). **2** as regards; in relation to (*his attitude toward death*). **3** as a contribution to; for (*put this toward your expenses*). **4** near (*toward the end of our journey*).

tow·el /tówəl/ *n. & v.* •*n.* **1 a** a piece of absorbent cloth used for drying oneself or a thing after washing. **b** absorbent paper used for this. **c** a cloth used for drying plates, dishes, etc.; a dish towel. •*v.* (**toweled, toweling** or **towelled, towelling**) **1** *tr.* (often *refl.*) wipe or dry with a towel. **2** *intr.* wipe or dry oneself with a towel. ▫▫ **tow·el·ing** or **tow·el·ling** *n.*

tow·er /tówər/ *n. & v.* •*n.* **1 a** a tall esp. square or circular structure, often part of a church, castle, etc. **b** a fortress, etc., comprising or including a tower. **c** a tall structure housing machinery, apparatus, operators, etc. (*cooling tower; control tower*). **2** a place of defense; a protection. •*v.intr.* **1** (usu. foll. by *above, high*) reach or be high or above; be superior. **2** (of a bird) soar or hover. **3** (as **towering** *adj.*) **a** high, lofty (*towering intellect*). **b** violent (*towering rage*).

tow·head /tṓhed/ *n.* **1** tow-colored or blond hair. **2** a person with such hair. ▫▫ **tow·head·ed** *adj.*

town /town/ *n.* **1 a** an urban area with a name, defined boundaries, and local government, being larger than a village and usu. not incorporated as a city. **b** any densely populated area, esp. as opposed to the country or suburbs. **c** the people of a town (*the whole town knows of it*). **2 a** *Brit.* London or the chief city or town in an area (*went up to town*). **b** the central business or shopping area in a neighborhood (*just going into town*). ▫ **go to town** *colloq.* act or work with energy or enthusiasm. **on the town** *colloq.* enjoying the entertainments, esp. the nightlife, of a town; celebrating. ▫▫ **town·ish** *adj.* **town·let** *n.* **town·ward** *adj. & adv.* **town·wards** *adv.*

town clerk *n.* the officer of a town in charge of records, etc.

town cri·er *n. hist.* an officer employed by a town council, etc., to make public announcements in the streets or marketplace.

town hall *n.* a building for the administration of local government, having public meeting rooms, etc.

town·ie /tównee/ *n. colloq.* a person living in a town, esp. as opposed to a student, tourist, etc.

town·scape /tównskayp/ *n.* **1** the visual appearance of a town or towns. **2** a picture of a town.

towns·folk /tównzfōk/ *n.* the inhabitants of a particular town or towns.

town·ship /tównship/ *n.* a division of a county in some states with some corporate powers.

towns·man /tównzmən/ *n.* (*pl.* **-men**; *fem.* **towns·wom·an**, *pl.* **-women**) an inhabitant of a town; a fellow citizen.

towns·peo·ple /tównzpeepəl/ *n.pl.* the people of a town.

tox·e·mi·a /tokséemeeə/ *n.* (*Brit.* **tox·ae·mi·a**) **1** blood poisoning. **2** a condition in pregnancy characterized by increased blood pressure. ▫▫ **tox·e·mic** *adj.*

tox·ic /tóksik/ *adj.* **1** of or relating to poison (*toxic symptoms*). **2** poisonous (*toxic gas*). **3** caused by poison (*toxic anemia*). ▫▫ **tox·i·cal·ly** *adv.* **tox·ic·i·ty** /–sísitee/ *n.*

tox·i·col·o·gy /tóksikóləjee/ *n.* the scientific study of poisons. ▫▫ **tox·i·co·log·i·cal** /–kəlójikəl/ *adj.* **tox·i·col·o·gist** *n.*

tox·in /tóksin/ *n.* a poison produced by a living organism, esp. one formed in the body and stimulating the production of antibodies.

toy /toy/ *n. & v.* •*n.* **1 a** a plaything, esp. for a child. **b** (often *attrib.*) a model or miniature replica of a thing, esp. as a plaything (*toy airplane*). **2 a** a thing, esp. a gadget or instrument, regarded as providing amusement or pleasure. **b** a task or undertaking regarded in an unserious way. **3** (usu. *attrib.*) a diminutive breed or variety of dog, etc. (*toy poodle*). •*v.intr.* (usu. foll. by *with*) **1** trifle; amuse oneself, esp. with a person's affections; flirt (*toyed with the idea of going to Africa*). **2 a** move a material object idly (*toyed with her necklace*). **b** nibble at food, etc., unenthusiastically (*toyed with her dinner*).

tp. *abbr.* **1** (also **t.p.**) title page. **2** township. **3** troop.

tra·bec·u·la /trəbékyələ/ *n.* (*pl.* **trabeculae** /–lee/) **1** *Anat.* a supporting band or bar of connective or bony tissue, esp. dividing an organ into chambers. **2** *Bot.* a beamlike projection or process within a hollow structure. ▫▫ **tra·bec·u·lar** *adj.* **tra·bec·u·late** /–lət, –layt/ *adj.*

trace[1] /trays/ *v. & n.* •*v.tr.* **1 a** observe, discover, or find vestiges or signs of by investigation. **b** (often foll. by *along, through, to*, etc.) follow or mark the track or position of (*traced their footprints in the mud; traced the outlines of a wall*). **c** (often foll. by *back*) follow to its origins (*can trace my family to the 12th century; the report has been traced back to you*). **2** (often foll. by *over*) copy (a drawing, etc.) by drawing over its lines on a superimposed piece of translucent paper, or by using carbon paper. **3** (often foll. by *out*) mark out, delineate, sketch, or write, often laboriously (*traced out a plan of the district; traced out his vision of the future*). **4** pursue one's way along (a path, etc.). •*n.* **1 a** a sign or mark or other indication of something having existed; a vestige (*no trace remains of the castle*). **b** a very small quantity. **c** an amount of rainfall, etc., too small to be measured. **2** a track or footprint left by a person or animal. **3** a track left by the moving pen of an instrument, etc. **4** a line on the screen of a cathode-ray tube showing the path of a moving spot. ▫▫ **trace·a·ble** *adj.* **trace·a·bil·i·ty** /tráysəbílitee/ *n.* **trace·less** *adj.*

trace[2] /trays/ *n.* each of the two straps, chains, or ropes by which a horse draws a vehicle. ▫ **kick over the traces** become insubordinate or reckless.

trace el·e·ment *n.* **1** a chemical element occurring in minute amounts. **2** a chemical element required only in minute amounts by living organisms for normal growth.

trac·er /tráysər/ *n.* **1** a person or thing that traces. **2** *Mil.* a bullet, etc., that is visible in flight because of flames, etc., emitted. **3** an artificially produced radioactive isotope capable of being followed through the body by the radiation it produces.

trac·er·y /tráysəree/ *n.* (*pl.* **-ies**) **1** ornamental stone openwork, esp. in the upper part of a Gothic window. **2** a fine decorative pattern. ▫▫ **trac·er·ied** *adj.*

tra·che·a /tráykeeə/ *n.* (*pl.* **tracheae** /–kée-ee/ or **tracheas**) the passage, reinforced by rings of cartilage, through which air reaches the bronchial tubes from the larynx; the windpipe. □□ **tra·che·al** /tráykeeəl/ *adj.* **tra·che·ate** /tráykeeayt/ *adj.*

tra·che·ot·o·my /traykeeótəmee/ *n.* (also **tra·che·os·to·my** /–óstəmee/) (*pl.* **-mies**) an incision made in the trachea to relieve an obstruction to breathing.

trac·ing /tráysing/ *n.* **1** a copy of a drawing, etc., made by tracing. **2** = TRACE[1] *n.* 3. **3** the act or an instance of tracing.

track /trak/ *n.* & *v.* • *n.* **1 a** a mark or marks left by a person, animal, or thing in passing. **b** (in *pl.*) such marks, esp. footprints. **2** a rough path, esp. one beaten by use. **3** a continuous railway line (*laid three miles of track*). **4 a** a course for racing horses, dogs, etc. **b** a prepared course for runners, etc. **c** various sports performed on a track, as running or hurdles. **5 a** a groove on a phonograph record. **b** a section of a phonograph record, compact disk, etc., containing one song, etc. (*this side has six tracks*). **c** a lengthwise strip of magnetic tape containing one sequence of signals. **6 a** a line of travel, passage, or motion (*followed the track of the hurricane*). **b** the path traveled by a ship, aircraft, etc. (cf. COURSE *n.* 2c). **7** a continuous band around the wheels of a tank, tractor, etc. **8** the transverse distance between a vehicle's wheels. **9** = SOUNDTRACK. **10** a line of reasoning or thought (*this track proved fruitless*). **11** any of several levels of instruction to which students are assigned based on their abilities, interests, etc. **12** a course of action or planned future (*management track*) • *v.* **1** *tr.* follow the track of (an animal, person, spacecraft, etc.). **2** *tr.* make out (a course, development, etc.); trace by vestiges. **3** *intr.* (often foll. by *back, in,* etc.) (of a movie or television camera) move in relation to the subject being filmed. **4** *intr.* (of wheels) run so that the back ones are exactly in the track of the front ones. **5** *intr.* (of a record stylus) follow a groove. **6** *tr.* **a** make a track with (dirt, etc.) from the feet. **b** leave such a track on (a floor, etc.). □ **in one's tracks** *colloq.* where one stands; then and there (*stopped him in his tracks*). **keep** (or **lose**) **track of** follow (or fail to follow) the course or development of. **make tracks** *colloq.* go or run away. **make tracks for** *colloq.* go in pursuit of or toward. **off the track** away from the subject. **on a person's track 1** in pursuit of him or her. **2** in possession of a clue to a person's conduct, plans, etc. **on the wrong side of the tracks** *colloq.* in an inferior or dubious part of town. **on the wrong** (or **right**) **track** following the wrong (or right) line of inquiry. **track down** reach or capture by tracking. □□ **track·age** *n.* **track·less** *adj.*

track·ing /tráking/ *n.* **1** assignment of students in a track system. **2** *Electr.* the formation of a conducting path over the surface of an insulating material.

track·ing sta·tion *n.* an establishment set up to track objects in the sky.

track·lay·er /tráklayər/ *n.* **1** a person employed in laying or repairing railroad tracks. **2** a tractor or other vehicle equipped with continuous tracks (see TRACK[1] *n.* 7).

track·less /tráklis/ *adj.* **1** without a track or tracks; untrodden. **2** leaving no track or trace. **3** not running on a track.

track rec·ord *n.* a person's past performance or achievements.

track shoe *n.* a spiked shoe worn by a runner.

tract[1] /trakt/ *n.* **1** a region or area of indefinite, esp. large, extent (*pathless desert tracts*). **2** *Anat.* an area of an organ or system (*respiratory tract*). **3** *Brit. archaic* a period of time, etc.

tract[2] /trakt/ *n.* a short treatise in pamphlet form, esp. on a religious subject.

trac·ta·ble /tráktəbəl/ *adj.* **1** (of a person) easily handled; manageable; docile. **2** (of material, etc.) pliant; malleable. □□ **trac·ta·bil·i·ty** /–bílitee/ *n.* **trac·ta·ble·ness** *n.* **trac·ta·bly** *adv.*

trac·tion /trákshən/ *n.* **1** the act of drawing or pulling a thing over a surface, esp. a road or track (*steam traction*). **2 a** a sustained pulling on a limb, muscle, etc., by means of pulleys, weights, etc. **b** contraction, e.g., of a muscle. **3** the grip of a tire on a road, a wheel on a rail, etc. □□ **trac·tion·al** *adj.* **trac·tive** /tráktiv/ *adj.*

trac·tor /tráktər/ *n.* **1** a motor vehicle used for hauling, esp. farm machinery, heavy loads, etc. **2** a traction engine.

trac·tor-trail·er *n.* a truck consisting of a tractor or cab unit attached to a trailer.

trade /trayd/ *n.* & *v.* • *n.* **1 a** buying and selling. **b** buying and selling conducted between nations, etc. **c** business conducted for profit (esp. as distinct from a profession) (*a butcher by trade*). **d** business of a specified nature or time (*Christmas trade; tourist trade*). **2** a skilled craft, esp. requiring an apprenticeship (*learned a trade; his trade is plumbing*). **3** (usu. prec. by *the*) the people engaged in a specific trade (*trade inquiries only*). **4** a transaction, esp. a swap. **5** (usu. in *pl.*) a trade wind. • *v.* **1** *intr.* (often foll. by *in, with*) engage in trade; buy and sell (*trades in plastic novelties; we trade with Japan*). **2** *tr.* **a** exchange in commerce; barter (goods). **b** exchange (insults, blows, etc.). **c** (foll. by *for*) swap, exchange. **3** *intr.* (usu. foll. by *with, for*) have a transaction with a person for a thing. □ **trade in** (often foll. by *for*) exchange (esp. a used car, etc.) in esp. part payment for another. **trade off** exchange, esp. as a compromise. **trade on** take advantage of (a person's credulity, one's reputation, etc.). □□ **trad·a·ble, trade·a·ble** *adj.*

trade def·i·cit *n.* (also **trade gap**) the extent by which a country's imports exceed its exports.

trade-in *n.* a thing, esp. a car, exchanged in part payment for another.

trade jour·nal *n.* a periodical containing news, etc., concerning a particular trade.

trade·mark /tráydmaark/ *n.* **1** a device, word, or words, secured by legal registration or established by use as representing a company, product, etc. **2** a distinctive characteristic, etc.

trade name *n.* **1** a name by which a thing is called in a trade. **2** a name given to a product. **3** a name under which a business trades.

trade-off *n.* an exchange; a swap.

trad·er /tráydər/ *n.* **1** a person engaged in trade. **2** a merchant ship.

trade se·cret *n.* **1** a secret device or technique used esp. in a trade. **2** *joc.* any secret.

trades·man /tráydzmən/ *n.* (*pl.* **-men**; *fem.* **trades·wom·an**, *pl.* **-women**) a person engaged in trading or a trade, as a skilled craftsman or Brit. a shopkeeper.

trade un·ion *n.* esp. *Brit.* = LABOR UNION.

trade wind *n.* a wind blowing continually toward the equator and deflected westward.

trad·ing /tráyding/ *n.* the act of engaging in trade.

trad·ing post *n.* a store, etc., established in a remote or unsettled region.

trad·ing stamp *n.* a stamp given to customers by some stores that is exchangeable in large numbers for various articles.

tra·di·tion /trədíshən/ *n.* **1 a** a custom, opinion, or belief handed down to posterity, esp. orally or by practice. **b** this process of handing down. **2** esp. *joc.* an established practice or custom. **3** artistic, literary, etc., principles based on experience and practice; any one of these (*stage tradition; traditions of the Dutch School*).

□□ **tra·di·tion·ar·y** *adj.* **tra·di·tion·ist** *n.* **tra·di·tion·less** *adj.*

tra·di·tion·al /trədíshənəl/ *adj.* **1** of, based on, or obtained by tradition. **2** (of jazz) in the style of the early 20th c. □□ **tra·di·tion·al·ly** *adv.*

tra·di·tion·al·ism /trədíshənəlizəm/ *n.* respect, esp. excessive, for tradition, esp. in religion. □□ **tra·di·tion·al·ist** *n.* **tra·di·tion·al·is·tic** *adj.*

tra·duce /trədóos, –dyóos/ *v.tr.* speak ill of; misrepresent. □□ **tra·duce·ment** *n.* **tra·duc·er** *n.*

traf·fic /tráfik/ *n.* & *v.* • *n.* **1** (often *attrib.*) **a** vehicles moving on a public highway, esp. of a specified kind, density, etc. (*heavy traffic on the interstate*; *traffic cop*). **b** such movement in the air or at sea. **2** (usu. foll. by *in*) trade, esp. illegal (*the traffic in drugs*). **3 a** the transportation of goods; the coming and going of people or goods by road, rail, air, sea, etc. **b** the persons or goods so transported. **4** dealings or communication between people, etc. (*had no traffic with them*). **5** the messages, signals, etc., transmitted through a communications system; the flow or volume of such business. • *v.* (**trafficked, trafficking**) **1** *intr.* (usu. foll. by *in*) deal in something, esp. illegally (*trafficked in narcotics*; *traffics in innuendo*). **2** *tr.* deal in; barter. □□ **traf·fick·er** *n.* **traf·fic·less** *adj.*

traf·fic cir·cle *n.* a road junction at which traffic moves in one direction around a central island.

traf·fic jam *n.* traffic at a standstill because of construction, an accident, etc.

traf·fic light *n.* (also **traf·fic sig·nal**) a usu. automatic signal with colored lights to control road traffic, esp. at intersections.

tra·ge·di·an /trəjéedeeən/ *n.* **1** a writer of tragedies. **2** an actor in tragedy.

tra·ge·di·enne /trəjéedee-én/ *n.* an actress in tragedy.

trag·e·dy /trájidee/ *n.* (*pl.* **-dies**) **1** a serious accident, crime, or natural catastrophe. **2** a sad event; a calamity (*the team's defeat is a tragedy*). **3 a** a play in verse or prose dealing with tragic events and with an unhappy ending, esp. concerning the downfall of the protagonist. **b** tragic plays as a genre (cf. COMEDY).

trag·ic /trájik/ *adj.* **1** (also **trag·i·cal** /–kəl/) sad; calamitous; greatly distressing (*a tragic tale*). **2** of, or in the style of, tragedy (*tragic drama*; *a tragic actor*). □□ **trag·i·cal·ly** *adv.*

trag·ic i·ro·ny *n.* a device, orig. in Greek tragedy, by which words carry a tragic, esp. prophetic, meaning to the audience, unknown to the character speaking.

trag·i·com·e·dy /trájikómidee/ *n.* (*pl.* **-dies**) **1 a** a play having a mixture of comedy and tragedy. **b** plays of this kind as a genre. **2** an event, etc., having tragic and comic elements. □□ **trag·i·com·ic** /–kómik/ *adj.* **trag·i·com·i·cal·ly** *adv.*

trail /trayl/ *n.* & *v.* • *n.* **1 a** a track left by a thing, person, etc., moving over a surface (*left a trail of wreckage*; *a slug's slimy trail*). **b** a track or scent followed in hunting, seeking, etc. (*he's on the trail*). **2** a beaten path or track, esp. through a wild region. **3** a part dragging behind a thing or person; an appendage (*a trail of smoke*; *a condensation trail*). • *v.* **1** *tr.* & *intr.* draw or be drawn along behind, esp. on the ground. **2** *intr.* (often foll. by *behind*) walk wearily; lag; straggle. **3** *tr.* follow the trail of; pursue (*trailed him to his home*). **4** *intr.* be losing in a game or other contest (*trailing by three points*). **5** *intr.* (usu. foll. by *away*, *off*) peter out; tail off. **6** *intr.* **a** (of a plant, etc.) grow or hang over a wall, along the ground, etc. **b** (of a garment, etc.) hang loosely. **7** *tr.* (often *refl.*) drag (oneself, one's limbs, etc.) along wearily, etc. **8** *tr.* advertise (a movie, a radio or television program, etc.) in advance by showing extracts, etc.

trail·blaz·er /tráylblayzər/ *n.* **1** a person who marks a new track through wild country. **2** a pioneer; an innovator.

trail·blaz·ing /tráylblayzing/ *n.* & *adj.* • *n.* the act or process of blazing a trail. • *attrib.adj.* blazing a trail; pioneering.

trail·er /tráylər/ *n.* **1** a person or thing that trails. **2** a series of brief extracts from a movie, etc., used to advertise it in advance. **3** a vehicle towed by another, esp.: **a** the rear section of a tractor-trailer. **b** an open cart. **c** a platform for transporting a boat, etc. **d** a camper. **4** a mobile home. **5** a trailing plant.

trail·er park *n.* a place where trailers are parked as dwellings, often with special amenities.

train /trayn/ *v.* & *n.* • *v.* **1 a** *tr.* (often foll. by *to* + infin.) teach (a person, animal, oneself, etc.) a specified skill, esp. by practice (*trained the dog to beg*; *was trained in midwifery*). **b** *intr.* undergo this process (*trained as a teacher*). **2** *tr.* & *intr.* bring or come into a state of physical fitness by exercise, diet, etc.; undergo physical exercise, esp. for a specific purpose. **3** *tr.* cause (a plant) to grow in a required shape. **4** (usu. as **trained** *adj.*) make (the mind, eye, etc.) sharp or discerning as a result of instruction, practice, etc. **5** *tr.* (often foll. by *on*) point or aim (a gun, camera, etc.) at an object, etc. **6** *intr. colloq.* go by train. • *n.* **1** a series of railroad cars drawn by an engine. **2** something dragged along behind or forming the back part of a dress, robe, etc. **3** a succession or series of people, things, events, etc. (*a long train of camels*; *interrupted my train of thought*). **4** a body of followers; a retinue (*a train of admirers*). **5** a succession of military vehicles, etc., including artillery, supplies, etc. (*baggage train*). **6** a line of gunpowder, etc., to fire an explosive charge. **7** a series of connected wheels or parts in machinery. □□ **train·a·ble** *adj.* **train·a·bil·i·ty** /tráynəbílitee/ *n.* **train·ee** /–née/ *n.* **train·less** *adj.*

train·er /tráynər/ *n.* **1** a person who trains. **2** a person who trains or provides medical assistance, etc., to horses, athletes, etc., as a profession. **3** an aircraft or device simulating it used to train pilots. **4** *Brit.* a soft running shoe of leather, canvas, etc.

train·ing /tráyning/ *n.* the act or process of teaching or learning a skill, discipline, etc. (*physical training*). □ **go into training** begin physical training. **in training 1** undergoing physical training. **2** physically fit as a result of this. **out of training 1** no longer training. **2** physically unfit.

train·man /tráynmən/ *n.* (*pl.* **-men**) a railroad employee working on trains.

traipse /trayps/ *v.intr. colloq.* tramp or trudge wearily.

trait /trayt/ *n.* a distinguishing feature or characteristic, esp. of a person.

---

trait late 15th century (as a rare usage denoting arrows or other missiles): from French, from Latin *tractus* 'drawing, draft.' An early sense was 'stroke of the pen or pencil,' giving rise to the notion of 'a trace,' hence the current sense 'a characteristic' (mid-18th century).

---

trai·tor /tráytər/ *n.* (*fem.* **trai·tress** /–tris/) (often foll. by *to*) a person who is treacherous or disloyal, esp. to his or her country. □□ **trai·tor·ous** *adj.* **trai·tor·ous·ly** *adv.*

tra·jec·to·ry /trəjéktəree/ *n.* (*pl.* **-ries**) **1** the path described by a projectile flying or an object moving under the action of given forces. **2** *Geom.* a curve or surface cutting a system of curves or surfaces at a constant angle.

tram /tram/ *n.* = STREETCAR.

tram·mel /tráməl/ *n.* & *v.* • *n.* **1** (usu. in *pl.*) an impediment to free movement; a hindrance (*the trammels of domesticity*). **2** a triple dragnet for fish. **3** an instrument for drawing ellipses, etc., with a bar sliding in upright grooves. **4** a beam compass. **5** a hook in a fireplace for a kettle, etc. •*v.tr.* (**trammeled, trammeling** or **trammelled, trammelling**) confine or hamper with or as if with trammels.

tramp /tramp/ *v. & n.* •*v.* **1** *intr.* **a** walk heavily and firmly (*tramping about upstairs*). **b** go on foot, esp. a distance. **2** *tr.* **a** cross on foot, esp. wearily or reluctantly. **b** cover (a distance) in this way (*tramped forty miles*). **3** *tr.* (often foll. by *down*) tread on; trample; stamp on. **4** *intr.* live as a tramp. •*n.* **1** an itinerant vagrant or beggar. **2** the sound of a person, or esp. people, walking, marching, etc., or of horses' hooves. **3** a journey on foot, esp. protracted. **4 a** an iron plate protecting the sole of a boot used for digging. **b** the part of a spade that it strikes. **5** *sl. derog.* a promiscuous woman. **6** (also **tramp steam•er**) a merchant ship that takes on any cargo available. ▫▫ **tramp•er** *n.* **tramp•ish** *adj.*

tram•ple /trámpəl/ *v. & n.* •*v.tr.* **1** tread underfoot. **2** press down or crush in this way. •*n.* the sound or act of trampling. ▫ **trample on** (or **underfoot**) **1** tread heavily on. **2** treat roughly or with contempt; disregard (a person's feelings, etc.). ▫▫ **tram•pler** *n.*

tram•po•line /trámpəleen/ *n.* a strong fabric sheet connected by springs to a horizontal frame, used by gymnasts, etc., for somersaults, as a springboard, etc. ▫▫ **tram•po•lin•ist** *n.*

trance /trans/ *n.* **1 a** a sleeplike or half-conscious state without response to stimuli. **b** a hypnotic or cataleptic state. **2** such a state as entered into by a medium. ▫▫ **trance•like** *adj.*

tran•quil /trángkwil/ *adj.* calm; serene; unruffled. ▫▫ **tran•quil•li•ty** /–kwílitee/ *n.* **tran•quil•ly** *adv.*

tran•quil•ize /trángkwilīz/ *v.tr.* make tranquil, esp. by a drug, etc.

tran•quil•iz•er /trángkwilīzər/ *n.* a drug used to diminish anxiety.

trans- /trans, tranz/ *prefix* **1** across; beyond (*transcontinental*; *transgress*). **2** on or to the other side of (*transatlantic*). **3** through (*transpierce*). **4** into another state or place (*transform*; *transcribe*). **5** surpassing; transcending (*transfinite*). **6** *Chem.* **a** (of an isomer) having the same atom or group on opposite sides of a given plane in the molecule. **b** having a higher atomic number than (*transuranic*).

trans. *abbr.* **1** transaction. **2** transfer. **3** transitive. **4** (also **transl.**) translated. **5** (also **transl.**) translation. **6** (also **transl.**) translator. **7** transmission. **8** transportation. **9** transpose. **10** transposition. **11** transverse.

trans•act /tranzákt, –sákt/ *v.tr.* perform or carry through (business). ▫▫ **trans•ac•tor** *n.*

trans•ac•tion /tranzákshən, –sák–/ *n.* **1 a** a piece of esp. commercial business done; a deal (*a profitable transaction*). **b** the management of business, etc. **2** (in *pl.*) published reports of discussions, papers read, etc., at the meetings of a learned society. ▫▫ **trans•ac•tion•al** *adj.* **trans•ac•tion•al•ly** *adv.*

trans•al•pine /tránzálpīn, trans–/ *adj.* beyond the Alps, esp. from the Italian point of view.

trans•at•lan•tic /tránzətlántik, trans–/ *adj.* **1** beyond the Atlantic, esp.: **a** European. **b** *Brit.* American. **2** crossing the Atlantic (*a transatlantic flight*).

trans•ax•le /tranzáksəl/ *n.* a unit in front-wheel-drive vehicles that combines the functions of the transmission and differential.

tran•scend /transénd/ *v.tr.* **1** be beyond the range or grasp of (human experience, reason, belief, etc.). **2** excel; surpass.

tran•scend•ent /transéndənt/ *adj. & n.* •*adj.* **1** excelling; surpassing (*transcendent merit*). **2** transcending human experience. **3** (esp. of the supreme being) existing apart from the material universe (opp. IMMANENT). •*n. Philos.* a transcendent thing. ▫▫ **tran•scend•ence** *n.* **tran•scend•en•cy** *n.* **tran•scend•ent•ly** *adv.*

tran•scen•den•tal /tránsendént'l/ *adj.* **1** = TRANSCENDENT. **2 a** presupposed in and necessary to experience; a priori. **b** explaining matter and objective things as products of the subjective mind. **c** regarding the divine as the guiding principle in man. **3 a** visionary; abstract. **b** vague; obscure. ▫▫ **tran•scen•den•tal•ly** *adv.*

tran•scen•den•tal•ism /tránsendént'lizəm/ *n.* **1** transcendental philosophy. **2** exalted or visionary language. ▫▫ **tran•scen•den•tal•ist** *n.* **tran•scen•den•tal•ize** *v.tr.*

tran•scen•den•tal med•i•ta•tion *n.* a method of detaching oneself from problems, anxiety, etc., by silent meditation and repetition of a mantra.

trans•con•ti•nen•tal /tránzkontinént'l, trans–/ *adj. & n.* •*adj.* (of a railroad, etc.) extending across a continent. •*n.* a transcontinental railroad or train. ▫▫ **trans•con•ti•nen•tal•ly** *adv.*

tran•scribe /transkríb/ *v.tr.* **1** make a copy of, esp. in writing. **2** transliterate. **3** write out (shorthand, notes, etc.) in ordinary characters or continuous prose. **4 a** record for subsequent reproduction. **b** broadcast in this form. **5** arrange (music) for a different instrument, etc. ▫▫ **tran•scrib•er** *n.* **tran•scrip•tion** /–skrípshən/ *n.* **tran•scrip•tion•al** *adj.* **tran•scrip•tive** /–skríptiv/ *adj.*

tran•script /tránskript/ *n.* **1** a written or recorded copy. **2** any copy.

trans•duc•er /tranzdóōsər, –dyóō–, trans–/ *n.* any device for converting a nonelectrical signal into an electrical one, e.g., pressure into voltage.

tran•sect /transékt/ *v.tr.* cut across or transversely. ▫▫ **tran•sec•tion** *n.*

tran•sept /tránsept/ *n.* **1** either arm of the part of a cross-shaped church at right angles to the nave (*north transept*; *south transept*). **2** this part as a whole. ▫▫ **tran•sep•tal** *adj.*

trans•fer *v. & n.* •*v.* /transfə́r/ (**transferred, transferring**) **1** *tr.* (often foll. by *to*) **a** convey, remove, or hand over (a thing, etc.). **b** make over the possession of (property, a ticket, rights, etc.) to a person. **2** *tr. & intr.* change or move to another group, club, department, school, etc. **3** *intr.* change from one station, route, etc., to another on a journey. **4** *tr.* **a** convey (a drawing, etc.) from one surface to another, esp. to a lithographic stone by means of transfer paper. **b** remove (a picture) from one surface to another, esp. from wood or a wall to canvas. **5** *tr.* change (the sense of a word, etc.) by extension or metaphor. •*n.* /tránsfər/ **1** the act or an instance of transferring or being transferred. **2 a** a design, etc., conveyed or to be conveyed from one surface to another. **b** a small usu. colored picture or design on paper, which is transferable to another surface; a decal. **3** a student, etc., who is or is to be transferred. **4 a** the conveyance of property, a right, etc. **b** a document effecting this. **5** a ticket allowing a journey to be continued on another route, etc. ▫▫ **trans•fer•ee** /–rée/ *n.* **trans•fer•or** /–fə́rər/ esp. *Law n.* **trans•fer•rer** /–fə́rər/ *n.*

trans•fer•a•ble /transfə́rəbəl/ *adj.* capable of being transferred. ▫▫ **trans•fer•a•bil•i•ty** /–bilitee/ *n.*

trans•fer•ence /transfə́rəns, tránsfər–/ *n.* **1** the act or an instance of transferring; the state of being transferred. **2** *Psychol.* the redirection of childhood emotions to a new object, esp. to a psychoanalyst.

trans•fer RNA *n.* RNA conveying an amino acid molecule from the cytoplasm to a ribosome for use in protein synthesis, etc.

trans·fig·u·ra·tion /transfigyəráyshən/ *n.* **1** a change of form or appearance. **2 a** Christ's appearance in radiant glory to three of his disciples (Matt. 17:2, Mark 9:2–3). **b** (**Transfiguration**) the festival of Christ's transfiguration, Aug. 6.

trans·fig·ure /transfigyər/ *v.tr.* change in form or appearance, esp. so as to elevate or idealize.

trans·fix /transfiks/ *v.tr.* **1** pierce with a sharp implement or weapon. **2** root (a person) to the spot with horror or astonishment; paralyze the faculties of. ▫▫ **trans·fix·ion** /–fikshən/ *n.*

trans·form *v.* /transfáwrm/ **1 a** *tr.* make a thorough or dramatic change in the form, outward appearance, character, etc., of. **b** *intr.* (often foll. by *into, to*) undergo such a change. **2** *tr. Electr.* change the voltage, etc., of (a current). ▫▫ **trans·form·a·ble** *adj.* **trans·form·a·tive** *adj.*

trans·for·ma·tion /tránsfərmáyshən/ *n.* **1** the act or an instance of transforming; the state of being transformed. **2** *Zool.* a change of form at metamorphosis, esp. of insects, amphibians, etc. **3** the induced or spontaneous change of one element into another. **4** *Math.* a change from one geometrical figure, expression, or function to another of the same value, magnitude, etc. ▫▫ **trans·for·ma·tion·al** *adj.* **trans·for·ma·tion·al·ly** *adv.*

trans·form·er /transfáwrmər/ *n.* **1** an apparatus for reducing or increasing the voltage of an alternating current. **2** a person or thing that transforms.

trans·fuse /transfyóoz/ *v.tr.* **1 a** permeate (*purple dye transfused the water*). **b** instill (an influence, quality, etc.) into (*transfused enthusiasm into everyone*). **2 a** transfer (blood) from one person or animal to another. **b** inject (liquid) into a blood vessel to replace lost fluid. **3** cause (fluid, etc.) to pass from one vessel, etc., to another. ▫▫ **trans·fu·sion** /–fyóozhən/ *n.*

trans·gress /tranzgrés/ *v.tr.* (also *absol.*) go beyond the bounds or limits set by (a commandment, law, etc.); violate; infringe. ▫▫ **trans·gres·sion** /–gréshən/ *n.* **trans·gres·sive** *adj.* **trans·gres·sor** *n.*

tran·sient /tránzhənt, –shənt, –zeeənt/ *adj.* & *n.* • *adj.* of short duration; momentary; passing; impermanent. • *n.* a temporary visitor, worker, etc. ▫▫ **tran·sience** *n.* **tran·sien·cy** *n.* **tran·sient·ly** *adv.*

tran·sis·tor /tranzístər/ *n.* **1** a semiconductor device with three connections, capable of amplification in addition to rectification. **2** (in full **transistor radio**) a portable radio with transistors.

tran·sit /tránzit, –sit/ *n.* & *v.* • *n.* **1** the act or process of going, conveying, or being conveyed, esp. over a distance (*transit by rail; made a transit of the lake*). **2** a passage or route (*the overland transit*). **3 a** the apparent passage of a celestial body across the meridian of a place. **b** such an apparent passage across the sun or a planet. **4** the local conveyance of passengers on public transportation. • *v.* (**transited, transiting**) **1** *tr.* make a transit across. **2** *intr.* make a transit. ▫ **in transit** while going or being conveyed.

tran·si·tion /tranzíshən, –síshən/ *n.* **1** a passing or change from one place, state, condition, etc., to another (*an age of transition; a transition from plains to hills*). **2** *Mus.* a momentary modulation. **3** *Art* a change from one style to another, esp. *Archit.* from Norman to Early English. **4** *Physics* a change in an atomic nucleus or orbital electron with emission or absorption of radiation. ▫▫ **tran·si·tion·al** *adj.* **tran·si·tion·al·ly** *adv.* **tran·si·tion·ar·y** *adj.*

tran·si·tive /tránzitiv, –si–/ *adj. Gram.* (of a verb or sense of a verb) that takes a direct object (whether expressed or implied), e.g., *saw* in *saw the donkey, saw that she was ill* (opp. INTRANSITIVE). ▫▫ **tran·si·tive·ly** *adv.* **tran·si·tive·ness** *n.* **tran·si·tiv·i·ty** /–tívitee/ *n.*

tran·si·to·ry /tránzitawree/ *adj.* not permanent; brief; transient. ▫▫ **tran·si·to·ri·ly** /–táwrilee/ *adv.* **tran·si·to·ri·ness** /–táwreenis/ *n.*

tran·sit vi·sa *n.* a visa allowing only passage through a country.

trans·late /tránzláyt, tráns–/ *v.* **1** *tr.* (also *absol.*) **a** (often foll. by *into*) express the sense of (a word, sentence, speech, book, etc.) in another language. **b** do this as a profession, etc. (*translates for the UN*). **2** *intr.* (of a literary work, etc.) be translatable; bear translation (*does not translate well*). **3** *tr.* express (an idea, book, etc.) in another, esp. simpler, form. **4** *tr.* interpret the significance of; infer as (*translated his silence as dissent*). **5** *tr.* move or change, esp. from one person, place, or condition, to another (*was translated by joy*). **6** *intr.* (foll. by *into*) result in; be converted into; manifest itself as. ▫▫ **trans·lat·a·ble** *adj.* **trans·lat·a·bil·i·ty** /–laytəbílitee/ *n.*

trans·la·tion /tranzláyshən, trans–/ *n.* **1** the act or an instance of translating. **2** a written or spoken expression of the meaning of a word, speech, book, etc., in another language. ▫▫ **trans·la·tion·al** *adj.* **trans·la·tion·al·ly** *adv.*

trans·la·tor /tránzláytər, trans–/ *n.* **1** a person who translates from one language into another. **2** a television relay transmitter. **3** a program that translates from one (esp. programming) language into another.

trans·lit·er·ate /tranzlítərayt, trans–/ *v.tr.* represent (a word, etc.) in the closest corresponding letters or characters of a different alphabet or language. ▫▫ **trans·lit·er·a·tion** /–ráyshən/ *n.* **trans·lit·er·a·tor** *n.*

trans·lu·cent /tranzlóosənt, tráns–/ *adj.* **1** allowing light to pass through diffusely; semitransparent. **2** transparent. ▫▫ **trans·lu·cence** *n.* **trans·lu·cen·cy** *n.* **trans·lu·cent·ly** *adv.*

trans·mi·grate /tranzmígrayt, tráns–/ *v.intr.* **1** (of the soul) pass into a different body. **2** migrate. ▫▫ **trans·mi·gra·tion** /–gráyshən/ *n.* **trans·mi·gra·tor** *n.* **trans·mi·gra·to·ry** /–mígrətawree/ *adj.*

trans·mis·sion /tranzmíshən, trans–/ *n.* **1** the act or an instance of transmitting; the state of being transmitted. **2** a broadcast radio or television program. **3** the mechanism by which power is transmitted from an engine to the axle in a motor vehicle.

trans·mit /tranzmít, trans–/ *v.tr.* (**transmitted, transmitting**) **1 a** pass or hand on; transfer (*transmitted the message; how diseases are transmitted*). **b** communicate (ideas, emotions, etc.). **2 a** allow (heat, light, sound, electricity, etc.) to pass through; be a medium for. **b** be a medium for (ideas, emotions, etc.) (*his message transmits hope*). **3** broadcast (a radio or television program). ▫▫ **trans·mis·si·ble** /–mísəbəl/ *adj.* **trans·mis·sive** /–mísiv/ *adj.* **trans·mit·ta·ble** *adj.* **trans·mit·tal** *n.*

trans·mit·ter /tránzmítər, trans–/ *n.* **1** a person or thing that transmits. **2** a set of equipment used to generate and transmit electromagnetic waves carrying messages, signals, etc., esp. those of radio or television. **3** = NEUROTRANSMITTER.

trans·mog·ri·fy /tranzmógrifī, trans–/ *v.tr.* (**-fies, -fied**) *joc.* transform, esp. in a magical or surprising manner. ▫▫ **trans·mog·ri·fi·ca·tion** /–fikáyshən/ *n.*

trans·mute /tranzmyóot, trans–/ *v.tr.* **1** change the form, nature, or substance of. **2** *Alchemy hist.* subject (base metals) to the supposed process of changing base metals into gold. ▫▫ **trans·mut·a·ble** *adj.* **trans·mut·a·bil·i·ty** /–təbílitee/ *n.* **trans·mu·ta·tion** *n.* **trans·mu·ta·tive** /–myóotətiv/ *adj.* **trans·mut·er** *n.*

trans·na·tion·al /tránznáshənəl, tráns–/ *adj.* extending beyond national boundaries.

trans·o·ce·an·ic /tránzṓshiánik, tráns–/ *adj.* **1** situated beyond the ocean. **2** concerned with crossing the ocean (*transoceanic flight*).

tran·som /tránsəm/ *n.* **1** a horizontal bar of wood or stone across a window or the top of a door (cf. MULLION). **2** each of several beams fixed across the sternpost of a ship. **3** a beam across a saw pit to support a log. **4** a strengthening crossbar. **5** = TRANSOM WINDOW. ▫▫ **tran·somed** *adj.*

tran·som win·dow *n.* **1** a window divided by a transom. **2** a window placed above the transom of a door or larger window.

trans·par·en·cy /tranzpárənsee, –páirənsee, trans–/ *n.* (*pl.* **-cies**) **1** the condition of being transparent. **2** *Photog.* a positive transparent photograph on glass or in a frame to be viewed using a slide projector, etc. **3** a picture, inscription, etc., made visible by a light behind it.

trans·par·ent /tranzpáirənt, –párənt, trans–/ *adj.* **1** allowing light to pass through so that bodies can be distinctly seen (cf. TRANSLUCENT). **2 a** (of a disguise, pretext, etc.) easily seen through. **b** (of a motive, quality, etc.) easily discerned; evident; obvious. **3** (of a person, etc.) easily understood; frank; open. ▫▫ **trans·par·ent·ly** *adv.* **trans·par·ent·ness** *n.*

tran·spire /transpír/ *v.* **1** *intr.* (of a secret or something unknown) leak out; come to be known. **2** *intr. disp.* **a** (prec. by *it* as subject) turn out; prove to be the case (*it transpired he knew nothing about it*). **b** occur; happen. **3** *tr. & intr.* emit (vapor, sweat, etc.), or be emitted, through the skin or lungs; perspire. **4** *intr.* (of a plant or leaf) release water vapor. ▫▫ **tran·spir·a·ble** *adj.* **tran·spi·ra·tion** /–spiráyshən/ *n.* **tran·spir·a·to·ry** /–spírətawree/ *adj.*

trans·plant *v. & n.* ● *v.tr.* /tranzplánt, trans–/ **1 a** plant in another place (*transplanted the daffodils*). **b** move to another place (*whole nations were transplanted*). **2** *Surgery* transfer (living tissue or an organ) and implant in another part of the body or in another body. ● *n.* /tránzplant, tráns–/ **1** *Surgery* **a** the transplanting of an organ or tissue. **b** such an organ, etc. **2** a thing, esp. a plant, transplanted. ▫▫ **trans·plant·a·ble** *adj.* **trans·plan·ta·tion** /–táyshən/ *n.* **trans·plant·er** *n.*

tran·spon·der /tranzpóndər, trans–/ *n.* a device for receiving a radio signal and automatically transmitting a different signal.

trans·port *v. & n.* ● *v.tr.* /tranzpáwrt, trans–/ **1** take or carry (a person, goods, troops, baggage, etc.) from one place to another. **2** *hist.* take (a criminal) to a penal colony; deport. **3** (as **transported** *adj.*) (usu. foll. by *with*) affected with strong emotion. ● *n.* /tránzpawrt, tráns–/ **1 a** a system of conveying people, goods, etc., from place to place. **b** esp. *Brit.* the means of this (*our transport has arrived*). **2** a ship, aircraft, etc., used to carry soldiers, stores, etc. **3** (esp. in *pl.*) vehement emotion (*transports of joy*). ▫▫ **trans·port·a·ble** /tranzpáwrtəbəl, trans–/ *adj.*

trans·por·ta·tion /tránzpərtáyshən, tráns–/ *n.* **1** the act of conveying or the process of being conveyed. **2 a** a system of conveying. **b** the means of this. **3** *hist.* removal to a penal colony.

trans·port·er /tránzpáwrtər, tráns–/ *n.* **1** a person or device that transports. **2** a vehicle used to transport other vehicles or large pieces of machinery, etc., by road.

trans·pose /tranzpṓz, trans–/ *v.tr.* **1 a** cause (two or more things) to change places. **b** change the position of (a thing) in a series. **2** change the order or position of (words or a word) in a sentence. **3** *Mus.* write or play in a different key. **4** *Algebra* transfer (a term) with a changed sign to the other side of an equation. ▫▫ **trans·pos·a·ble** *adj.* **trans·pos·al** *n.* **trans·pos·er** *n.*

trans·po·si·tion /tránzpəzíshən, tráns–/ *n.* the act or an instance of transposing; the state of being transposed. ▫▫ **trans·po·si·tion·al** *adj.* **trans·pos·i·tive** /–pózitiv/ *adj.*

trans·sex·u·al /tránsékshōōəl/ *adj. & n.* ● *adj.* having the physical characteristics of one sex and the supposed psychological characteristics of the other. ● *n.* **1** a transsexual person. **2** a person whose sex has been changed by surgery. ▫▫ **trans·sex·u·al·ism** *n.*

trans·ship /tranz-shíp, trans–/ *v.tr.* (also **tran·ship**) *intr.* (**-shipped, -shipping**) transfer from one ship or form of transport to another. ▫▫ **trans·ship·ment** *n.*

tran·sub·stan·ti·a·tion /tránsəbstánsheeáyshən/ *n.* *Theol. & RC Ch.* the conversion of the Eucharistic elements wholly into the body and blood of Christ, only the appearance of bread and wine still remaining.

trans·verse /tránzvə́rs, tráns–/ *adj.* situated, arranged, or acting in a crosswise direction. ▫▫ **trans·verse·ly** *adv.*

trans·ves·tism /tranzvéstizəm, trans–/ *n.* (also **trans·ves·ti·tism** /–véstitizəm/) the practice of wearing the clothes of the opposite sex, esp. as a sexual stimulus. ▫▫ **trans·ves·tist** *n.*

trans·ves·tite /tranzvéstīt, trans–/ *n.* a person given to transvestism.

trap /trap/ *n. & v.* ● *n.* **1 a** an enclosure or device, often baited, for catching animals, usu. by affording a way in but not a way out. **b** a device with bait for killing vermin, esp. = MOUSETRAP. **2** a trick betraying a person into speech or an act (*is this question a trap?*). **3** an arrangement to catch an unsuspecting person, e.g., a speeding motorist. **4** a device for hurling an object such as a clay pigeon into the air to be shot at. **5** a compartment from which a greyhound is released at the start of a race. **6** a shoe-shaped wooden device with a pivoted bar that sends a ball from its heel into the air on being struck at the other end with a bat. **7 a** a curve in a downpipe, etc., that fills with liquid and forms a seal against the upward passage of gases. **b** a device for preventing the passage of steam, etc. **8** *Golf* a bunker. **9** a device allowing pigeons to enter but not leave a loft. **10** a two-wheeled carriage (*a pony and trap*). **11** = TRAPDOOR. **12** *sl.* the mouth (esp. *shut one's trap*). **13** (esp. in *pl.*) *colloq.* a percussion instrument, esp. in a jazz band. ● *v.tr.* (**trapped, trapping**) **1** catch (an animal) in a trap. **2** catch (a person) by means of a trick, plan, etc. **3** stop and retain in or as in a trap. **4** provide (a place) with traps. ▫▫ **trap·like** *adj.*

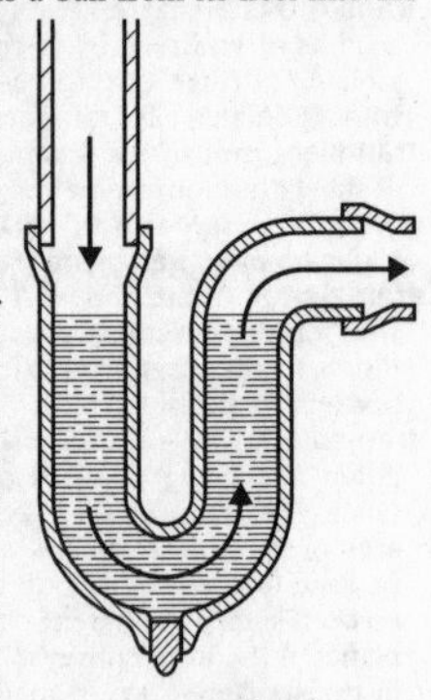

trap, 7a

trap·door /trápdawr/ *n.* a door or hatch in a floor, ceiling, or roof, usu. made flush with the surface.

tra·peze /trapéez/ *n.* a crossbar or set of crossbars suspended by ropes used as a swing for acrobatics, etc.

tra·pe·zi·um /trəpéezeeəm/ *n.* (*pl.* **trapezia** /–zeeə/ or **trapeziums**) **1** a quadrilateral with no two sides parallel. **2** *Brit.* = TRAPEZOID 1.

trap·e·zoid /trápizoyd/ *n.* **1** a quadrilateral with only one pair of sides parallel. **2** *Brit.* = TRAPEZIUM 1. ▫▫ **trap·e·zoi·dal** *adj.*

trap·per /trápər/ *n.* a person who traps wild animals, esp. to obtain furs.

trap·pings /trápingz/ *n.pl.* **1** ornamental accessories, esp. as an indication of status (*the trappings of office*). **2** the harness of a horse, esp. when ornamental.

trash /trash/ *n. & v.* •*n.* **1 a** worthless or poor quality stuff, esp. literature. **b** rubbish; refuse. **c** absurd talk or ideas; nonsense. **2** a worthless person or persons. **3** a thing of poor workmanship or material. •*v.tr.* **1** *colloq.* wreck. **2** *colloq.* expose the worthless nature of; disparage. **3** *colloq.* throw away; discard.

trash·y /tráshee/ *adj.* (**trashier, trashiest**) (esp. of items of popular culture) of poor quality (*trashy novels*). ▫▫ **trash·i·ly** *adv.* **trash·i·ness** *n.*

trat·to·ri·a /trátəreéə/ *n.* an Italian restaurant.

trau·ma /trówmə, tráw–/ *n.* (*pl.* **traumata** /–mətə/ or **traumas**) **1** any physical wound or injury. **2** physical shock following this, characterized by a drop in body temperature, mental confusion, etc. **3** *Psychol.* emotional shock following a stressful event, sometimes leading to long-term neurosis. ▫▫ **trau·ma·tize** *v.tr.*

trau·mat·ic /trəmátik, trow–, traw–/ *adj.* **1** of or causing trauma. **2** *colloq.* (in general use) distressing; emotionally disturbing (*a traumatic experience*). **3** of or for wounds. ▫▫ **trau·mat·i·cal·ly** *adv.*

tra·vail /trəváyl, trávayl/ *n. & v.* •*n.* **1** painful or laborious effort. **2** the pangs of childbirth. •*v.intr.* undergo a painful effort, esp. in childbirth.

trav·el /trávəl/ *v. & n.* •*v.intr. & tr.* (**traveled, traveling** or **travelled, travelling**) **1** *intr.* go from one place to another; make a journey, esp. of some length or abroad. **2** *tr.* **a** journey along or through (a country). **b** cover (a distance) in traveling. **3** *intr. colloq.* withstand a long journey (*wines that do not travel*). **4** *intr.* go from place to place as a salesman. **5** *intr.* move or proceed in a specified manner or at a specified rate (*light travels faster than sound*). **6** *intr. colloq.* move quickly. **7** *intr.* pass esp. in a deliberate or systematic manner from point to point (*the photographer's eye traveled over the scene*). **8** *intr.* (of a machine or part) move or operate in a specified way. •*n.* **1 a** the act of traveling, esp. in foreign countries. **b** (often in *pl.*) a time or occurrence of this (*have returned from their travels*). **2** the range, rate, or mode of motion of a part in machinery. ▫▫ **trav·el·er** /trávələr, trávlər/ *n.* **trav·el·ing** *adj.*

trav·el a·gen·cy *n.* (also **trav·el bu·reau**) an agency that makes the necessary arrangements for travelers. ▫▫ **trav·el a·gent** *n.*

trav·eled /trávəld/ *adj.* experienced in traveling (also in *comb.*: *much traveled*).

trav·el·er's check *n.* a check for a fixed amount that may be cashed on signature, usu. internationally.

trav·el·ing sales·man *n.* a person who travels to solicit orders as a representative of a company, etc.

trav·e·logue /trávəlog/ *n.* (also **trav·e·log**) a movie or illustrated lecture about travel.

trav·erse /trávərs, trəvə́rs/ *v. & n.* •*v.* **1** *tr.* travel or lie across (*traversed the country*; *a pit traversed by a beam*). **2** *tr.* consider or discuss the whole extent of (a subject). **3** *tr.* turn (a large gun) horizontally. **4** *tr.* thwart, frustrate, or oppose (a plan or opinion). **5** *intr.* (of the needle of a compass, etc.) turn on or as on a pivot. **6** *intr.* (of a horse) walk obliquely. **7** *intr.* make a traverse in climbing. •*n.* **1** a sideways movement. **2** an act of traversing. **3** a thing, esp. part of a structure, that crosses another. **4** a gallery extending from side to side of a church or other building. **5 a** a single line of survey, usu. plotted from compass bearings and with chained or paced distances between angular points. **b** a tract surveyed in this way. **6** *Naut.* a zigzag line taken by a ship because of contrary winds or currents. **7** a skier's similar movement on a slope. **8** the sideways movement of a part in a machine. **9 a** a sideways motion across a rock face from one practicable line of ascent or descent to another. **b** a place where this is necessary. ▫▫ **tra·vers·a·ble** *adj.* **tra·vers·al** *n.* **tra·vers·er** *n.*

trav·es·ty /trávistee/ *n. & v.* •*n.* (*pl.* **-ties**) a grotesque misrepresentation or imitation (*a travesty of justice*). •*v.tr.* (**-ties, -tied**) make or be a travesty of.

tra·vois /trəvóy/ *n.* (*pl.* same /–vóyz/) a vehicle of two joined poles pulled by a horse, etc., for carrying a burden, orig. used by Native American people of the Plains.

trawl /trawl/ *v. & n.* •*v.* **1** *intr.* **a** fish with a trawl or seine. **b** seek a suitable candidate, etc., by sifting through a large number. **2** *tr.* **a** catch by trawling. **b** seek a suitable candidate, etc., from (a certain area or group, etc.). •*n.* **1** an act of trawling. **2** (in full **trawl net**) a large wide-mouthed fishing net dragged by a boat along the bottom. **3** (in full **trawl line**) a long sea fishing line buoyed and supporting short lines with baited hooks.

trawl·er /tráwlər/ *n.* **1** a boat used for trawling. **2** a person who trawls.

tray /tray/ *n.* **1** a flat shallow vessel usu. with a raised rim for carrying dishes, etc., or containing small articles, papers, etc. **2** a shallow lidless box forming a compartment of a trunk. ▫▫ **tray·ful** *n.* (*pl.* **-fuls**).

treach·er·ous /tréchərəs/ *adj.* **1** guilty of or involving treachery. **2** (of the weather, ice, the memory, etc.) not to be relied on; likely to fail or give way. ▫▫ **treach·er·ous·ly** *adv.* **treach·er·ous·ness** *n.*

treach·er·y /tréchəree/ *n.* (*pl.* **-ies**) **1** violation of faith or trust; betrayal. **2** an instance of this.

trea·cle /treékəl/ *n.* **1** esp. *Brit.* **a** a syrup produced in refining sugar. **b** molasses. **2** cloying sentimentality or flattery. ▫▫ **trea·cly** *adj.*

tread /tred/ *v. & n.* •*v.* (**trod** /trod/; **trodden** /tród'n/ or **trod**) **1** *intr.* (often foll. by *on*) **a** set down one's foot; walk or step (*do not tread on the grass*; *trod on a snail*). **b** (of the foot) be set down. **2** *tr.* **a** walk on. **b** (often foll. by *down*) press or crush with the feet. **3** *tr.* perform (steps, etc.) by walking (*trod a few paces*). **4** *tr.* make (a hole, etc.) by treading. **5** *intr.* (foll. by *on*) suppress; subdue mercilessly. **6** *tr.* make a track with (dirt, etc.) from the feet. **7** *tr.* (often foll. by *in, into*) press down into the ground with the feet (*trod dirt into the carpet*). **8** *tr.* (also *absol.*) (of a male bird) copulate with (a hen). •*n.* **1** a manner or sound of walking. **2** the top surface of a step or stair. **3** the thick molded part of a vehicle tire for gripping the road. **4 a** the part of a wheel that touches the ground or rail. **b** the part of a rail that the wheels touch. **5** the part of the sole of a shoe that rests on the ground. **6** (of a male bird) copulation. ▫ **tread the boards** (or **stage**) be or become an actor; appear on the stage. **tread on a person's toes** offend a person or encroach on a person's privileges, etc. **tread water** maintain an upright position in the water by moving the feet with a walking movement and the hands with a downward circular motion. ▫▫ **tread·er** *n.*

trea·dle /trédəl/ *n. & v.* •*n.* a lever worked by the foot and imparting motion to a machine. •*v.intr.* work a treadle.

tread·mill /trédmil/ *n.* **1** a device for producing motion by the weight of persons or animals stepping on movable steps on the inner surface of a revolving upright wheel. **2** monotonous routine work.

trea·son /treézən/ *n.* violation by a subject of allegiance to the sovereign or to the nation, esp. by attempting to kill or overthrow the sovereign or to overthrow the government. ▫▫ **trea·son·ous** *adj.*

treas·ure /trézhər/ *n. & v.* •*n.* **1 a** precious metals or gems. **b** a hoard of these. **c** accumulated wealth. **2** a thing valued for its rarity, workmanship, associations, etc. (*art treasures*). **3** *colloq.* a much loved or highly valued person. • *v.tr.* **1** (often foll. by *up*) store up as valuable. **2** value (esp. a long-kept possession) highly.

treas·ure hunt *n.* **1** a search for treasure. **2** a game in which players seek a hidden object from a series of clues.

treas·ur·er /trézhərər/ *n.* **1** a person appointed to administer the funds of a society or municipality, etc. **2** an officer authorized to receive and disburse public revenues. ▫▫ **treas·ur·er·ship** *n.*

treas·ure trove *n.* **1** *Law* treasure of unknown ownership found hidden. **2** a hidden store of valuables.

treas·ur·y /trézhəree/ *n.* (*pl.* **-ies**) **1** a place or building where treasure is stored. **2** the funds or revenue of a nation, institution, or society. **3** (**Treasury**) **a** the department managing the public revenue of a country. **b** the offices and officers of this. **c** the place where the public revenues are kept.

treas·ur·y bill *n.* a bill of exchange issued by the government to raise money for temporary needs. ¶ Abbr.: **T-bill.**

treat /treet/ *v. & n.* • *v.* **1** *tr.* act or behave toward or deal with (a person or thing) in a certain way. **2** *tr.* deal with or apply a process to; act upon to obtain a particular result (*treat it with acid*). **3** *tr.* apply medical care or attention to. **4** *tr.* present or deal with (a subject) in literature or art. **5** *tr.* (often foll. by *to*) provide with food or drink or entertainment, esp. at one's own expense (*treated us to dinner*). **6** *intr.* (often foll. by *with*) negotiate terms (with a person). • *n.* **1** an event or circumstance (esp. when unexpected or unusual) that gives great pleasure. **2** a meal, entertainment, etc., provided by one person for the enjoyment of another or others. **3** *Brit.* (prec. by *a*) extremely good or well (*they looked a treat; has come on a treat*). ▫▫ **treat·a·ble** *adj.* **treat·er** *n.* **treat·ing** *n.*

trea·tise /tréetis/ *n.* a written work dealing formally and systematically with a subject.

treat·ment /tréetmənt/ *n.* **1** a process or manner of behaving toward or dealing with a person or thing (*received rough treatment*). **2** the application of medical care or attention to a patient. **3** a manner of treating a subject in literature or art. **4** (prec. by *the*) *colloq.* the customary way of dealing with a person, situation, etc. (*got the full treatment*).

trea·ty /tréetee/ *n.* (*pl.* **-ties**) **1** a formally concluded and ratified agreement between nations. **2** an agreement between individuals or parties, esp. for the purchase of property.

tre·ble /trébəl/ *adj., n., & v.* • *adj.* **1 a** threefold. **b** triple. **c** three times as much or many (*treble the amount*). **2** (of a voice) high-pitched. **3** *Mus.* = SOPRANO (esp. of an instrument or with ref. to a boy's voice). • *n.* **1** a treble quantity or thing. **2** *Darts* a hit on the narrow ring enclosed by the two middle circles of a dartboard, scoring treble. **3 a** *Mus.* = SOPRANO (esp. a boy's voice or part, or an instrument). **b** a high-pitched voice. **4** the high-frequency output of a radio, record player, etc., corresponding to the treble in music. • *v.* **1** *tr. & intr.* make or become three times as much or many; increase threefold; multiply by three. **2** *tr.* amount to three times as much as. ▫▫ **tre·bly** *adv.* (in sense 1 of *adj.*).

tre·ble clef *n.* a clef placing G above middle C on the second lowest line of the staff.

tre·cen·to /traychéntō/ *n.* the style of Italian art and literature of the 14th c. ▫▫ **tre·cen·tist** *n.*

tree /tree/ *n.* **1 a** a perennial plant with a woody self-supporting main stem or trunk when mature and usu. unbranched for some distance above the ground (cf. SHRUB[1]). **b** any similar plant having a tall erect usu. single stem, e.g., palm tree. **2** a piece or frame of wood, etc., for various purposes (*shoe tree*). ▫▫ **tree·less** *adj.* **tree·less·ness** *n.* **tree·like** *adj.*

tree·creep·er /tréekreepər/ *n.* any small creeping bird, esp. of the family *Certhiidae*, feeding on insects in the bark of trees.

tree frog *n.* any arboreal tailless amphibian, esp. of the family *Hylidae*, climbing by means of adhesive pads on its toes.

tree house *n.* a structure in a tree for children to play in.

tree ring *n.* a ring in a cross section of a tree, from one year's growth.

tree sur·geon *n.* a person who treats decayed trees in order to preserve them. ▫▫ **tree sur·ger·y** *n.*

tree toad *n.* = TREE FROG.

tree to·ma·to *n.* = TAMARILLO.

tree·top /tréetop/ *n.* the topmost part of a tree.

tref /tráyf/ *adj.* (also **trefa** /tráyfə/and other variants) not kosher.

tre·foil /tréefoyl, tréf–/ *n. & adj.* • *n.* **1** any leguminous plant of the genus *Trifolium*, with leaves of three leaflets and flowers of various colors, esp. clover. **2** any plant with similar leaves. **3** a three-lobed ornamentation, esp. in tracery windows. **4** a thing arranged in or with three lobes. • *adj.* of or concerning a three-lobed plant, window tracery, etc. ▫▫ **tre·foiled** *adj.* (also in *comb.*).

trek /trek/ *v. & n.* • *v.intr.* (**trekked, trekking**) **1** travel or make one's way arduously (*trekking through the forest*). **2** esp. *S. Afr. hist.* migrate or journey with one's belongings by ox wagon. • *n.* **1 a** a journey or walk made by trekking. **b** each stage of such a journey. **2** an organized migration of a body of persons. ▫▫ **trek·ker** *n.*

trel·lis /trélis/ *n. & v.* • *n.* (in full **trelliswork**) a lattice or grating of light wooden or metal bars used esp. as a support for fruit trees or creepers and often fastened against a wall. • *v.tr.* (**trellised, trellising**) **1** provide with a trellis. **2** support (a vine, etc.) with a trellis.

trem·a·tode /trémətōd, trée–/ *n.* any parasitic flatworm of the class *Trematoda*, esp. a fluke, equipped with hooks or suckers, e.g., a liver fluke.

trem·ble /trémbəl/ *v. & n.* • *v.intr.* **1** shake involuntarily from fear, excitement, weakness, etc. **2** be in a state of extreme apprehension (*trembled at the very thought of it*). **3** move in a quivering manner (*leaves trembled in the breeze*). • *n.* a trembling state or movement; a quiver (*couldn't speak without a tremble*). ▫▫ **trem·bling·ly** *adv.*

tre·men·dous /triméndəs/ *adj.* **1** awe inspiring; fearful; overpowering. **2** *colloq.* remarkable; considerable; excellent (*a tremendous explosion; gave a tremendous performance*). ▫▫ **tre·men·dous·ly** *adv.* **tre·men·dous·ness** *n.*

trem·o·lo /tréməlō/ *n. Mus.* **1** a tremulous effect in playing stringed and keyboard instruments or singing, esp. by rapid reiteration of a note; in other instruments, by rapid alternation between two notes (cf. VIBRATO). **2** a device in an organ producing a tremulous effect.

trem·or /trémər/ *n. & v.* • *n.* **1** a shaking or quivering. **2** a thrill (of fear or exultation, etc.). **3** a slight earthquake. • *v.intr.* undergo a tremor or tremors.

trem·u·lous /trémyələs/ *adj.* **1** trembling or quivering (*in a tremulous voice*). **2** (of a line, etc.) drawn by a tremulous hand. **3** timid or vacillating. ▫▫ **trem·u·lous·ly** *adv.* **trem·u·lous·ness** *n.*

trench /trench/ *n. & v.* • *n.* **1** a long narrow usu. deep depression or ditch. **2** *Mil.* **a** this dug by troops to stand in and be sheltered from enemy fire. **b** (in *pl.*) a defensive system of these. **3** a long narrow deep depression in the ocean bed. • *v.* **1** *tr.* dig a trench or trenches in (the ground). **2** *tr.* turn over the earth of (a field, garden, etc.) by digging a succession of adjoining ditches.

trench·ant /trénchənt/ *adj.* **1** (of a style or language, etc.) incisive; terse; vigorous. **2** *archaic* or *poet.* sharp; keen. ▫▫ **trench·an·cy** *n.* **trench·ant·ly** *adv.*

trench coat *n.* **1** a soldier's lined or padded waterproof coat. **2** a loose belted raincoat.

trench·er /trénchər/ *n. hist.* a wooden or earthenware platter for serving food.

trench·er·man /trénchərmən/ *n.* (*pl.* **-men**) a person who eats well, or in a specified manner (*a good trencherman*).

trench war·fare *n.* hostilities carried on from more or less permanent trenches.

trend /trend/ *n. & v.* • *n.* a general direction and tendency (esp. of events, fashion, or opinion, etc.). • *v.intr.* **1** bend or turn away in a specified direction. **2** be chiefly directed; have a general and continued tendency.

trend·set·ter /tréndsetər/ *n.* a person who leads the way in fashion, etc. ▫▫ **trend·set·ting** *adj.*

trend·y /tréndee/ *adj. & n. colloq.* • *adj.* (**trendier, trendiest**) often *derog.* fashionable; following fashionable trends. • *n.* (*pl.* **-ies**) a fashionable person. ▫▫ **trend·i·ly** *adv.* **trend·i·ness** *n.*

trep·i·da·tion /trépidáyshən/ *n.* **1** a feeling of fear or alarm; perturbation of the mind. **2** tremulous agitation.

tres·pass /tréspəs, –pas/ *v. & n.* • *v.intr.* **1** (usu. foll. by *on, upon*) make an unlawful or unwarrantable intrusion (esp. on land or property). **2** (foll. by *on*) make unwarrantable claims (*shall not trespass on your hospitality*). **3** (foll. by *against*) *literary* or *archaic* offend. • *n.* **1** *Law* a voluntary wrongful act against the person or property of another, esp. unlawful entry to a person's land or property. **2** *archaic* a sin or offense. ▫▫ **tres·pass·er** *n.*

tress /tres/ *n.* **1** a long lock of human (esp. female) hair. **2** (in *pl.*) a woman's or girl's head of hair. ▫▫ **tressed** *adj.* (also in *comb.*).

tres·tle /trésəl/ *n.* **1** a supporting structure for a table, etc., consisting of two frames fixed at an angle or hinged or of a bar supported by two divergent pairs of legs. **2** (in full **trestle table**) a table consisting of a board or boards laid on trestles or other supports. **3** (also **trestlework**) an open braced framework to support a bridge, etc.

tri·ad /tríad/ *n.* a group of three (esp. notes in a chord).

tri·age /tree-aázh, trée-aazh/ *n.* **1** the act of sorting according to quality. **2** the assignment of degrees of urgency to decide the order of treatment of wounds, illnesses, etc.

tri·al /tríəl/ *n.* **1** a judicial examination and determination of issues between parties by a judge with or without a jury (*stood trial for murder*). **2 a** a process or mode of testing qualities. **b** experimental treatment. **c** a test (*will give you a trial*). **d** an attempt. **e** (*attrib.*) experimental. **3** a trying thing or experience or person, esp. hardship or trouble (*the trials of old age*). **4** a preliminary contest to test the ability of players eligible for selection to a team, etc. **5** *Brit.* a test of individual ability on a motorcycle over rough ground or on a road. **6** any of various contests involving performance by horses, dogs, or other animals. ▫ **on trial 1** being tried in a court of law. **2** being tested; to be chosen or retained only if suitable.

tri·al and er·ror *n.* repeated (usu. varied and unsystematic) attempts or experiments continued until successful.

tri·al run *n.* a preliminary test of a vehicle, vessel, machine, etc.

tri·an·gle /tríanggəl/ *n.* **1** a plane figure with three sides and angles. **2** any three things not in a straight line, with imaginary lines joining them. **3** an implement of this shape. **4** a musical instrument consisting of a steel rod bent into a triangle and sounded by striking it with a smaller steel rod. **5** a situation, esp. an emotional relationship, involving three people. **6** a right-angled triangle of wood, etc., as a drawing implement.

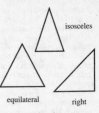

isosceles

equilateral

right

triangles

tri·an·gu·lar /triánggyələr/ *adj.* **1** triangle-shaped; three-cornered. **2** (of a contest or treaty, etc.) between three persons or parties. **3** (of a pyramid) having a three-sided base. ▫▫ **tri·an·gu·lar·i·ty** /–láiritee/ *n.* **tri·an·gu·lar·ly** *adv.*

tri·an·gu·late *v.tr.* /triánggyəlayt/ **1** divide (an area) into triangles for surveying purposes. **2 a** measure and map (an area) by the use of triangles with a known base length and base angles. **b** determine (a height, distance, etc.) in this way. ▫▫ **tri·an·gu·la·tion** /–láyshən/ *n.*

Tri·as·sic /triásik/ *adj. & n. Geol.* • *adj.* of or relating to the earliest period of the Mesozoic era with evidence of an abundance of reptiles (including the earliest dinosaurs) and the emergence of mammals. • *n.* this period or system.

tri·ath·lon /triáthlən, –lon/ *n.* an athletic contest consisting of three different events, esp. running, swimming, and bicycling. ▫▫ **tri·ath·lete** /–leet/ *n.*

tri·a·tom·ic /triətómik/ *adj. Chem.* **1** having three atoms (of a specified kind) in the molecule. **2** having three replacement atoms or radicals.

tri·ax·i·al /triákseeəl/ *adj.* having three axes.

trib. *abbr.* **1** tribunal. **2** tribune. **3** tributary.

trib·al /tríbəl/ *adj.* of, relating to, or characteristic of a tribe or tribes. ▫▫ **trib·al·ly** *adv.*

trib·al·ism /tríbəlizəm/ *n.* **1** tribal organization. **2** strong loyalty to one's tribe, group, etc. ▫▫ **trib·al·ist** *n.* **trib·al·is·tic** *adj.*

tribe /trīb/ *n.* **1** a group of (esp. primitive) families or communities, linked by social, economic, religious, or blood ties, and usu. having a common culture and dialect, and a recognized leader. **2** any similar natural or political division. **3** each of the 12 divisions of the Israelites. **4** a set or number of persons, esp. of one profession, etc., or family (*the whole tribe of actors*).

tribes·man /tríbzmən/ *n.* (*pl.* **-men**) a member of a tribe or of one's own tribe.

tri·bol·o·gy /trībóləjee/ *n.* the study of friction, wear, lubrication, and the design of bearings; the science of interacting surfaces in relative motion. ▫▫ **tri·bol·o·gist** *n.*

trib·u·la·tion /tríbyəláyshən/ *n.* **1** great affliction or oppression. **2** a cause of this (*was a real tribulation to me*).

tri·bu·nal /trībyóonəl, tri–/ *n.* **1** a board appointed to adjudicate in some matter, esp. one appointed by the government to investigate a matter of public concern. **2** a court of justice. **3** a seat or bench for a judge or judges. **4 a** a place of judgment. **b** judicial authority (*the tribunal of public opinion*).

trib·une[1] /tríbyoon, tribyóon/ *n.* **1** a popular leader or demagogue. **2** (in full **tribune of the people**) an official in ancient Rome chosen by the people to protect their interests. **3** (in full **military tribune**) a Roman legionary officer. ▫▫ **trib·u·nate** /–nət, –nayt/ *n.* **trib·une·ship** *n.*

trib·une[2] /tríbyoon, tribyóon/ *n.* **1** *Eccl.* **a** a bishop's throne in a basilica. **b** an apse containing this. **2** a dais or rostrum. **3** a raised area with seats.

trib·u·tar·y /tríbyəteree/ *n. & adj.* • *n.* (*pl.* **-ies**) **1** a river or stream flowing into a larger river or lake. **2** *hist.* a person or nation paying or subject to tribute. • *adj.* **1** (of a river, etc.) that is a tributary. **2** *hist.* **a** paying tribute. **b** serving as tribute. ▫▫ **trib·u·tar·i·ly** /–táirilee/ *adv.* **trib·u·tar·i·ness** /–táireenis/ *n.*

trib·ute /tríbyoot/ *n.* **1** a thing said or done or given as a mark of respect or affection, etc. (*paid tribute to their achievements*; *floral tributes*). **2** *hist.* **a** a payment made periodically by one nation or ruler to another, esp. as a sign of dependence. **b** an obligation to pay this (*was paid under tribute*). **3** (foll. by *to*) an indication of (some praiseworthy quality) (*their success is a tribute to their perseverance*).

trice /trīs/ *n.* ▫ **in a trice** in a moment; instantly.

tri·cen·ten·ar·y /trísenténəree/ *n.* (*pl.* **-ies**) = TERCENTENARY.

tri·ceps /tríseps/ *adj. & n.* • *adj.* (of a muscle) having three heads or points of attachment. • *n.* any triceps muscle, esp. the large muscle at the back of the upper arm.

tri·cer·a·tops /trísérətops/ *n.* an herbivorous dinosaur with three sharp horns on the forehead and a wavy-edged collar around the neck.

tri·chi·na /trikínə/ *n.* (*pl.* **trichinae** /–nee/) any hairlike parasitic nematode worm of the genus *Trichinella.* ▫▫ **trich·i·nous** *adj.*

trich·in·o·sis /tríkinósis/ *n.* a disease caused by trichinae, usu. ingested in meat, and characterized by digestive disturbance, fever, and muscular rigidity.

tri·chot·o·my /trīkótəmee/ *n.* (*pl.* **-mies**) a division (esp. sharply defined) into three categories, esp. of human nature into body, soul, and spirit. ▫▫ **trich·o·tom·ic** /–kətómik/ *adj.*

trick /trik/ *n. & v.* • *n.* **1** an action or scheme undertaken to fool, outwit, or deceive. **2** an optical or other illusion (*a trick of the light*). **3** a special technique; a knack or special way of doing something. **4 a** a feat of skill or dexterity. **b** an unusual action (e.g., begging) learned by an animal. **5** a mischievous, foolish, or discreditable act; a practical joke (*a mean trick to play*). **6** a peculiar or characteristic habit or mannerism (*has a trick of repeating himself*). **7 a** the cards played in a single round of a card game, usu. one from each player. **b** such a round. **c** a point gained as a result of this. **8** (*attrib.*) done to deceive or mystify or to create an illusion (*trick photography*; *trick question*). **9** *Naut.* a sailor's turn at the helm, usu. two hours. **10 a** a prostitute's client. **b** a sexual act performed by a prostitute and a client. • *v.tr.* **1** deceive by a trick; outwit. **2** (often foll. by *out of*, or *into* + verbal noun) cheat; treat deceitfully so as to deprive (*were tricked into agreeing*; *were tricked out of their savings*). **3** (of a thing) foil or baffle; take by surprise; disappoint the calculations of. ▫ **do the trick** *colloq.* accomplish one's purpose; achieve the required result. **not miss a trick** see MISS[1]. **trick out** (or **up**) dress, decorate, or deck out, esp. showily. **turn tricks** engage in prostitution. **up to one's tricks** *colloq.* misbehaving. ▫▫ **trick·er** *n.* **trick·ish** *adj.* **trick·less** *adj.*

trick·er·y /tríkəree/ *n.* (*pl.* **-ies**) **1** the practice or an instance of deception. **2** the use of tricks.

trick·le /tríkəl/ *v. & n.* • *v.* **1** *intr. & tr.* flow or cause to flow in drops or a small stream (*water trickled through the crack*). **2** *intr.* come or go slowly or gradually (*information trickles out*). • *n.* a trickling flow.

trick or treat *n.* a children's custom of calling at houses at Halloween with the threat of pranks if they are not given candy.

trick·ster /tríkstər/ *n.* a person who cheats or deceives people.

trick·y /tríkee/ *adj.* (**trickier, trickiest**) **1** difficult or intricate; requiring care and adroitness (*a tricky job*). **2** crafty or deceitful. **3** resourceful or adroit. ▫▫ **trick·i·ly** *adv.* **trick·i·ness** *n.*

tri·clin·ic /trīklínik/ *adj.* **1** (of a mineral) having three unequal oblique axes. **2** denoting the system classifying triclinic crystalline substances.

tri·col·or /tríkulər/ *n. & adj.* • *n.* a flag of three colors, esp. the French national flag of blue, white, and red. • *adj.* (also **tri·col·ored**) having three colors.

tri·corn /tríkawrn/ *adj.* (also **tri·corne**) **1** having three horns. **2** (of a hat) having a brim turned up on three sides.

tri·cot /treékō/ *n.* **1 a** a hand-knitted woolen fabric. **b** an imitation of this. **2** a ribbed woolen cloth.

tri·cy·cle /trísikəl/ *n.* **1** a vehicle having three wheels, two on an axle at the back and one at the front, driven by pedals in the same way as a bicycle. **2** a three-wheeled motor vehicle for a disabled driver. ▫▫ **tri·cy·clist** *n.*

tri·dac·tyl /trīdáktil/ *adj.* (also **tri·dac·tyl·ous** /–dáktiləs/) having three fingers or toes.

tri·dent /tríd'nt/ *n.* **1** a three-pronged spear, esp. as an attribute of Poseidon (Neptune) or Britannia. **2** (**Trident**) a type of submarine-launched ballistic missile.

tried *past* and *past part.* of TRY.

tri·en·ni·al /trī-éneeəl/ *adj.* **1** lasting three years. **2** recurring every three years. ▫▫ **tri·en·ni·al·ly** *adv.*

tri·fid /trífid/ *adj.* esp. *Biol.* partly or wholly split into three divisions or lobes.

tri·fle /trífəl/ *n. & v.* • *n.* **1** a thing of slight value or importance. **2 a** a small amount, esp. of money (*was sold for a trifle*). **b** (prec. by *a*) somewhat (*seems a trifle annoyed*). **3** *Brit.* a confection of sponge cake with custard, jelly, fruit, cream, etc. • *v.* **1** *intr.* talk or act frivolously. **2** *intr.* (foll. by *with*) **a** treat or deal with frivolously or derisively; flirt heartlessly with. **b** refuse to take seriously. **3** *tr.* (foll. by *away*) waste (time, energies, money, etc.) frivolously. ▫▫ **tri·fler** *n.*

tri·fling /trífling/ *adj.* **1** unimportant; petty. **2** frivolous. ▫▫ **tri·fling·ly** *adv.*

tri·fo·cal /trīfókəl/ *adj. & n.* • *adj.* having three focuses, esp. of a lens with different focal lengths. • *n.* (in *pl.*) trifocal eyeglasses.

tri·fo·li·ate /trīfóleeət/ *adj.* **1** (of a compound leaf) having three leaflets. **2** (of a plant) having such leaves.

tri·fo·ri·um /trīfáwreeəm/ *n.* (*pl.* **triforia** /–reeə/) a gallery or arcade above the arches of the nave, choir, and transepts of a church.

trig /trig/ *n. colloq.* trigonometry.

trig·ger /trígər/ *n. & v.* • *n.* **1** a movable device for releasing a spring or catch and so setting off a mechanism (esp. that of a gun). **2** an event, occurrence, etc., that sets off a chain reaction. • *v.tr.* **1** (often foll. by *off*) set (an action or process) in motion; initiate; precipitate. **2** fire (a gun) by the use of a trigger. ▫ **quick on the trigger** quick to respond. ▫▫ **trig·gered** *adj.*

trig·ger·fish *n.* any usu. tropical marine fish of the family *Balistidae* with a first dorsal fin spine that can be depressed by pressing on the second.

trig·ger-hap·py *adj.* apt to shoot without or with slight provocation.

trig·o·nom·e·try /trígənómitree/ *n.* the branch of mathematics dealing with the relations of the sides and angles of triangles and with the relevant functions of any angles. ▫▫ **trig·o·no·met·ric** /–nəmétrik/ *adj.* **trig·o·no·met·ri·cal** *adj.*

tri·graph /trígraf/ *n.* (also **tri·gram** /–gram/) **1** a group of three letters representing one sound. **2** a figure of three lines.

tri·he·dron /trīhéedrən/ *n.* a figure of three intersecting planes.

trike /trīk/ *n. & v.intr. colloq.* tricycle.

tri·lat·er·al /trīlátərəl/ *adj.* **1** of, on, or with three sides. **2** shared by or involving three parties, countries, etc. (*trilateral negotiations*).

tril·by /trílbee/ *n.* (*pl.* **-bies**) *Brit.* a soft felt hat with a narrow brim and indented crown. ▫▫ **tril·bied** *adj.*

tri·lin·gual /trīlínggwəl/ *adj.* **1** able to speak three languages, esp. fluently. **2** spoken or written in three languages. ▫▫ **tri·lin·gual·ism** *n.*

trill /tril/ *n. & v.* •*n.* **1** a quavering or vibratory sound, esp. a rapid alternation of sung or played notes. **2** a bird's warbling sound. **3** the pronunciation of *r* with a vibration of the tongue. •*v.* **1** *intr.* produce a trill. **2** *tr.* warble (a song) or pronounce (*r*, etc.) with a trill.

tril·lion /trílyən/ *n.* (*pl.* same or (in sense 3) **trillions**) **1** a million million (1,000,000,000,000 or 10^{12}). **2** esp. *Brit.* a million million million (1,000,000,000,000,000,000 or 10^{18}). **3** (in *pl.*) *colloq.* a very large number (*trillions of times*). ▫▫ **tril·lionth** *adj. & n.*

tri·lo·bite /trílәbīt/ *n.* any fossil marine arthropod of the class *Trilobita* of Palaeozoic times, characterized by a three-lobed body.

tril·o·gy /trílәjee/ *n.* (*pl.* **-gies**) a group of three related literary or operatic works.

trim /trim/ *v., n., & adj.* •*v.* (**trimmed, trimming**) **1** *tr.* **a** set in good order. **b** make neat or of the required size or form, esp. by cutting away irregular or unwanted parts. **2** *tr.* (foll. by *off, away*) remove by cutting off (such parts). **3** *tr.* **a** (often foll. by *up*) make (a person) neat in dress and appearance. **b** ornament or decorate (esp. clothing, a hat, etc., by adding ribbons, lace, etc.). **4** *tr.* adjust the balance of (a ship or aircraft) by the arrangement of its cargo, etc. **5** *tr.* arrange (sails) to suit the wind. **6** *intr.* **a** associate oneself with currently prevailing views, esp. to advance oneself. **b** hold a middle course in politics or opinion. **7** *tr. colloq.* **a** rebuke sharply. **b** thrash. **c** get the better of in a bargain, etc. •*n.* **1** the state or degree of readiness or fitness (*found everything in perfect trim*). **2** ornament or decorative material. **3** dress or equipment. **4** the act of trimming a person's hair. **5** the inclination of an aircraft to the horizontal. •*adj.* **1** neat, slim, or tidy. **2** in good condition or order; well arranged or equipped. ▫ **in trim 1** looking smart, healthy, etc. **2** *Naut.* in good order. ▫▫ **trim·ly** *adv.* **trim·ness** *n.*

tri·ma·ran /trímәran/ *n.* a vessel like a catamaran, with three hulls side by side.

tri·mes·ter /trīméstər/ *n.* a period of three months, esp. of human gestation or as a college or university term. ▫▫ **tri·mes·tral** *adj.* **tri·mes·tri·al** *adj.*

trim·e·ter /trímitər/ *n. Prosody* a verse of three measures. ▫▫ **tri·met·ric** /trīmétrik/ *adj.* **tri·met·ri·cal** *adj.*

trim·ming /tríming/ *n.* **1** ornamentation or decoration, esp. for clothing. **2** (in *pl.*) *colloq.* the usual accompaniments, esp. of the main course of a meal. **3** (in *pl.*) pieces cut off in trimming.

tri·ni·tro·tol·u·ene /trīnítrōtólyōōeen/ *n.* (also **tri·ni·tro·tol·u·ol** /–tólyōō-awl, –ōl/) = TNT.

trin·i·ty /trínitee/ *n.* (*pl.* **-ties**) **1** the state of being three. **2** a group of three. **3** (**the Trinity** or **Holy Trinity**) *Theol.* the three persons of the Christian Godhead (Father, Son, and Holy Spirit).

trin·ket /tríngkit/ *n.* a trifling ornament, jewel, etc., esp. one worn on the person. ▫▫ **trin·ket·ry** *n.*

tri·no·mi·al /trīnṓmeeəl/ *adj. & n.* •*adj.* consisting of three terms. •*n.* a scientific name or algebraic expression of three terms.

tri·o /trée-ō/ *n.* (*pl.* **-os**) **1** a set or group of three. **2** *Mus.* **a** a composition for three performers. **b** a group of three performers. **c** the central, usu. contrastive, section of a minuet, scherzo, or march. **3** (in piquet) three aces, kings, queens, or jacks in one hand.

trip /trip/ *v. & n.* •*v.intr. & tr.* (**tripped, tripping**) **1** *intr.* **a** walk or dance with quick light steps. **b** (of a rhythm, etc.) run lightly. **2 a** *intr. & tr.* (often foll. by *up*) stumble or cause to stumble, esp. by catching or entangling the feet. **b** *intr. & tr.* (foll. by *up*) make or cause to make a slip or blunder. **3** *tr.* detect (a person) in a blunder. **4** *intr.* make an excursion to a place. **5** *tr.* release (part of a machine) suddenly by knocking aside a catch, etc. **6 a** release and raise (an anchor) from the bottom by means of a cable. **b** turn (a yard, etc.) from a horizontal to a vertical position for lowering. **7** *intr. colloq.* have a hallucinatory experience caused by a drug. •*n.* **1** a journey or excursion, esp. for pleasure. **2 a** a stumble or blunder. **b** the act of tripping or the state of being tripped up. **3** a nimble step. **4** *colloq.* a hallucinatory experience caused by a drug. **5** a contrivance for a tripping mechanism, etc.

tri·par·tite /trīpáartīt/ *adj.* **1** consisting of three parts. **2** shared by or involving three parties. **3** *Bot.* (of a leaf) divided into three segments almost to the base. ▫▫ **tri·par·tite·ly** *adv.* **tri·par·ti·tion** /–tíshən/ *n.*

tripe /trīp/ *n.* **1** the first or second stomach of a ruminant, esp. an ox, as food. **2** *colloq.* nonsense; rubbish (*don't talk such tripe*).

tri·plane /tríplayn/ *n.* an early type of airplane having three sets of wings, one above the other.

tri·ple /trípəl/ *adj., n., & v.* •*adj.* **1** consisting of three usu. equal parts or things; threefold. **2** involving three parties. **3** three times as much or many (*triple the amount; triple thickness*). •*n.* **1** a threefold number or amount. **2** a set of three. **3** a base hit allowing a batter to safely reach third base. **4** (in *pl.*) a peal of changes on seven bells. •*v.intr. & tr.* **1** multiply or increase by three. **2** to hit a triple.

tri·ple crown *n.* the act of winning all three of a group of important events in horse racing, etc.

tri·ple jump *n.* an athletic exercise or contest comprising a hop, a step, and a jump.

tri·ple play *n. Baseball* the act of making all three outs in a single play.

tri·plet /tríplit/ *n.* **1** each of three children or animals born at one birth. **2** a set of three things, esp. of equal notes played in the time of two or of verses rhyming together.

trip·li·cate *adj., n., & v.* •*adj.* /tríplikət/ **1** existing in three examples or copies. **2** having three corresponding parts. **3** tripled. •*n.* /tríplikət/ each of a set of three copies or corresponding parts. •*v.tr.* /tríplikayt/ **1** make in three copies. **2** multiply by three. ▫ **in triplicate** consisting of three exact copies. ▫▫ **trip·li·ca·tion** /–káyshən/ *n.*

trip·loid /tríployd/ *n. & adj. Biol.* •*n.* an organism or cell having three times the haploid set of chromosomes. •*adj.* of or being a triploid.

trip·me·ter /trípmeetər/ *n.* a vehicle instrument that can be set to record the distance of individual journeys.

tri·pod /trípod/ *n.* **1** a three-legged stand for supporting a camera, etc. **2** a stool, table, or utensil resting on three feet or legs. ▫▫ **trip·o·dal** /trípəd'l/ *adj.*

trip·tych /tríptik/ *n.* **1 a** a picture or relief carving on three panels, usu. hinged vertically together and often used as an altarpiece. **b** a set of three associated pictures placed in this way. **2** a set of three writing tablets hinged or tied together. **3** a set of three artistic works.

trip wire *n.* a wire stretched close to the ground, operating an alarm, etc., when disturbed.

---

tri•reme /tríreem/ *n.* an ancient Greek warship, with three banks of oarsmen on each side.

tri•sac•cha•ride /trīsákərīd/ *n. Chem.* a sugar consisting of three linked monosaccharides.

tri•sect /trīsékt/ *v.tr.* cut or divide into three (usu. equal) parts. □□ **tri•sec•tion** /–sékshən/ *n.* **tri•sec•tor** *n.*

tris•mus /trízməs/ *n. Med.* a variety of tetanus with tonic spasm of the jaw muscles causing the mouth to remain tightly closed.

trite /trīt/ *adj.* (of a phrase, opinion, etc.) hackneyed; worn out by constant repetition. □□ **trite•ly** *adv.* **trite•ness** *n.*

trit•i•um /tríteeəm/ *n. Chem.* a radioactive isotope of hydrogen with a mass about three times that of ordinary hydrogen. ¶ symb.: **T.**

trit•u•rate /tríchərayt/ *v.tr.* **1** grind to a fine powder. **2** masticate thoroughly. □□ **trit•u•ra•ble** *adj.* **trit•u•ra•tion** /–ráyshən/ *n.* **trit•u•ra•tor** *n.*

tri•umph /tríəmf, –umf/ *n.* & *v.* •*n.* **1 a** the state of victory or success (*returned home in triumph*). **b** a great success or achievement. **2** a supreme example (*a triumph of engineering*). **3** joy at success; exultation (*could see triumph in her face*). **4** the processional entry of a victorious general into ancient Rome. •*v.intr.* **1** (often foll. by *over*) gain a victory; be successful; prevail. **2** ride in triumph. **3** (often foll. by *over*) exult.

tri•um•phal /trīúmfəl/ *adj.* of or used in or celebrating a triumph.

▶**Triumphant**, the more common of these words, means 'victorious' or 'exultant,' e.g., *She led an arduous campaign to its triumphant conclusion*, or *He returned triumphant with a patent for his device.* **Triumphal** means 'used in or celebrating a triumph,' e.g., *a triumphal arch, a triumphal parade.*

tri•um•phant /trīúmfənt/ *adj.* **1** victorious or successful. **2** exultant. □□ **tri•um•phant•ly** *adv.*

tri•um•vir /tríəmveer, –úmvər/ *n.* (*pl.* **triumvirs** or **triumviri** /–rī/) **1** each of three men holding a joint office. **2** a member of a triumvirate. □□ **tri•um•vi•ral** *adj.*

tri•um•vi•rate /trīúmvirət/ *n.* **1** a board or ruling group of three men, esp. in ancient Rome. **2** the office of triumvir.

tri•va•lent /trīváylənt/ *adj. Chem.* having a valence of three. □□ **tri•va•lence** *n.* **tri•va•len•cy** *n.*

triv•et /trívit/ *n.* **1** an iron tripod or bracket for a hot pot, kettle, or dish to stand on. **2** an iron bracket designed to hook on to bars of a grate for a similar purpose.

triv•i•a /tríveeə/ *n.pl.* **1** insignificant factual details. **2** trifles or trivialities.

triv•i•al /tríveeəl/ *adj.* **1** of small value or importance; trifling (*raised trivial objections*). **2** (of a person) concerned only with trivial things. **3** *archaic* commonplace or humdrum (*the trivial round of daily life*). □□ **triv•i•al•i•ty** /–veeálitee/ *n.* (*pl.* **-ties**). **triv•i•al•ly** *adv.* **triv•i•al•ness** *n.*

triv•i•al•ize /tríveeəlīz/ *v.tr.* make trivial or apparently trivial; minimize. □□ **triv•i•al•i•za•tion** *n.*

tRNA *abbr.* transfer RNA.

tro•chee /trṓkee/ *n. Prosody* a foot consisting of one long or stressed syllable followed by one short or unstressed syllable.

troch•le•a /trókleeə/ *n.* (*pl.* **trochleae** /–lee-ee/) *Anat.* a pulleylike structure or arrangement of parts, e.g., the groove at the lower end of the humerus.

tro•choid /trṓkoyd/ *adj.* & *n.* •*adj.* **1** *Anat.* rotating on its own axis. **2** *Geom.* (of a curve) traced by a point on a radius of a circle rotating along a straight line or another circle. •*n.* a trochoid joint or curve. □□ **tro•choi•dal** *adj.*

trod *past* and *past part.* of TREAD.

trod•den *past part.* of TREAD.

trog•lo•dyte /trógləd īt/ *n.* **1** a cave dweller, esp. of prehistoric times. **2** a hermit. **3** *derog.* a willfully obscurantist or old-fashioned person. □□ **trog•lo•dyt•ic** /–dítik/ *adj.* **trog•lo•dyt•i•cal** /–dítikəl/ *adj.* **trog•lo•dyt•ism** *n.*

troi•ka /tróykə/ *n.* **1 a** a Russian vehicle with a team of three horses abreast. **b** this team. **2** a group of three people, esp. as an administrative council.

troil•ism /tróylizəm/ *n.* sexual activity involving three participants.

Tro•jan /trṓjən/ *adj.* & *n.* •*adj.* of or relating to ancient Troy in Asia Minor. •*n.* **1** a native or inhabitant of Troy. **2** a person who works, fights, etc., courageously (*works like a Trojan*).

Tro•jan Horse *n.* **1** a hollow wooden horse said to have been used by the Greeks to enter Troy. **2** a person or device secreted, intended to bring about ruin at a later time. **3** *Computing* a set of instructions hidden in a program that cause damage or mischief.

troll[1] /trōl/ *n.* (in Scandinavian folklore) a fabled being, esp. a giant or dwarf dwelling in a cave.

troll[2] /trōl/ *v.* & *n.* •*v.* **1** *intr.* sing out in a carefree jovial manner. **2** *tr.* & *intr.* fish by drawing bait along in the water. **3** *intr.* esp. *Brit.* walk; stroll. •*n.* **1** the act of trolling for fish. **2** a line or bait used in this. □□ **troll•er** *n.*

trol•ley /trólee/ *n.* (*pl.* **-leys**) **1** esp. *Brit.* a table, stand, or basket on wheels or castors for serving food, transporting luggage or shopping, gathering purchases in a supermarket, etc. **2** esp. *Brit.* a low truck running on rails. **3** (in full **trolley wheel**) a wheel attached to a pole, etc., used to carry current from an overhead electric wire to drive a vehicle. **4** (in full **trolley car**) a streetcar powered by electricity obtained from an overhead cable by means of a trolley wheel.

trol•lop /tróləp/ *n.* **1** a disreputable girl or woman. **2** a prostitute. □□ **trol•lop•ish** *adj.* **trol•lop•y** *adj.*

trom•bone /trombṓn/ *n.* **1 a** a large brass wind instrument with a sliding tube. **b** its player. **2** an organ stop with the quality of a trombone. □□ **trom•bon•ist** *n.*

trompe-l'œil /troNplṓyə, trámpláy, –loi/ *n.* a still life painting, etc., designed to give an illusion of reality.

troop /trōōp/ *n.* & *v.* •*n.* **1** an assembled company; an assemblage of people or animals. **2** (in *pl.*) soldiers or armed forces. **3** a cavalry unit commanded by a captain. **4** a unit of artillery and armored formation. **5** a unit of Girl Scouts, Boy Scouts, etc. •*v. intr.* (foll. by *in, out, off*, etc.) come together or move in large numbers.

troop•er /trṓōpər/ *n.* **1** a soldier in a cavalry or armored unit. **2 a** a mounted police officer. **b** a state police officer. □ **swear like a trooper** swear extensively or forcefully.

tro•phy /trṓfee/ *n.* (*pl.* **-phies**) **1** a cup or other decorative object awarded as a prize or memento of victory or success in a contest, etc. **2** a memento or souvenir, e.g., a deer's antlers, taken in hunting. **3** *Gk & Rom. Antiq.* the weapons, etc., of a defeated army set up as a memorial of victory. **4** an ornamental group of symbolic or typical objects arranged for display. □□ **tro•phied** *adj.* (also in *comb.*).

trop•ic /trópik/ *n.* & *adj.* •*n.* **1** the parallel of latitude 23°27′ north (**trop•ic of Can•cer**) or south (**trop•ic of Cap•ri•corn**) of the Equator. **2** each of two corresponding circles on the celestial sphere where the sun appears to turn after reaching its greatest declination. **3** (**the Tropics**) the region between the tropics of Cancer and Capricorn. •*adj.* **1** = TROPICAL 1. **2** of tropism.

trop•i•cal /trópikəl/ *adj.* **1** of, peculiar to, or suggesting the Tropics (*tropical fish*; *tropical diseases*). **2** very hot; passionate; luxuriant. **3** of or by way of a trope. ▫▫ **trop·i·cal·ly** *adv.*

tro·pism /trṓpizəm/ *n. Biol.* the turning of all or part of an organism in a particular direction in response to an external stimulus.

trop·o·sphere /trópəsfeer, trṓ–/ *n.* a layer of atmospheric air extending upward from the earth's surface, in which the temperature falls with increasing height (cf. STRATOSPHERE, IONOSPHERE). ▫▫ **trop·o·spher·ic** /–sférik, –sféer–/ *adj.*

trot /trot/ *v. & n.* •*v.* (**trotted, trotting**) **1** *intr.* (of a person) run at a moderate pace, esp. with short strides. **2** *intr.* (of a horse) proceed at a steady pace faster than a walk lifting each diagonal pair of legs alternately. **3** *intr. colloq.* walk or go. **4** *tr.* cause (a horse or person) to trot. **5** *tr.* traverse (a distance) at a trot. •*n.* **1** the action or exercise of trotting (*proceed at a trot*; *went for a trot*). **2** (**the trots**) *sl.* an attack of diarrhea. **3** a brisk steady movement or occupation. ▫ **trot out 1** cause (a horse) to trot to show his paces. **2** produce or introduce (as if) for inspection and approval, esp. tediously or repeatedly.

troth /trawth, trōth/ *n. archaic* **1** faith; loyalty. **2** truth. ▫ **pledge** (or **plight**) **one's troth** pledge one's word esp. in marriage or betrothal.

trou·ba·dour /tróobədawr/ *n.* **1** any of a number of French medieval lyric poets composing and singing in Provençal in the 11th–13th c. on the theme of courtly love. **2** a singer or poet.

trou·ble /trúbəl/ *n. & v.* •*n.* **1** difficulty or distress; vexation; affliction (*am having trouble with my car*). **2 a** inconvenience; unpleasant exertion; bother (*went to a lot of trouble for nothing*). **b** a cause of this (*the child was no trouble at all*). **3** a cause of annoyance or concern (*the trouble with you is that you can't say no*). **4** a faulty condition or operation (*kidney trouble*; *engine trouble*). **5 a** fighting; disturbance (*crowd trouble*; *don't want any trouble*). **b** (in *pl.*) political or social unrest; public disturbances. **6** disagreement; strife (*is having trouble at home*). •*v.* **1** *tr.* cause distress or anxiety to; disturb (*were much troubled by their debts*). **2** *intr.* be disturbed or worried (*don't trouble about it*). **3** *tr.* afflict; cause pain, etc., to (*am troubled with arthritis*). **4** *tr. & intr.* (often *refl.*) subject or be subjected to inconvenience or unpleasant exertion (*sorry to trouble you*; *don't trouble yourself*). ▫ **ask** (or **look**) **for trouble** *colloq.* invite trouble or difficulty by one's actions, behavior, etc.; behave rashly or indiscreetly. **be no trouble** cause no inconvenience, etc. **go to the trouble** (or **some trouble**, etc.) exert oneself to do something. **in trouble** involved in a matter likely to bring censure or punishment. **take trouble** (or **the trouble**) exert oneself to do something. ▫▫ **trou·bler** *n.*

trou·bled /trúbəld/ *adj.* showing, experiencing, or reflecting trouble, anxiety, etc. (*a troubled mind*; *a troubled childhood*).

trou·ble·mak·er /trúbəlmaykər/ *n.* a person who habitually causes trouble. ▫▫ **trou·ble·mak·ing** *n.*

trou·ble·shoot·er /trúbəlshootər/ *n.* **1** a mediator in industrial or diplomatic, etc., disputes. **2** a person who traces and corrects faults in machinery, etc. ▫▫ **trou·ble·shoot·ing** *n.*

trou·ble·some /trúbəlsəm/ *adj.* **1** causing trouble. **2** vexing; annoying. ▫▫ **trou·ble·some·ly** *adv.* **trou·ble·some·ness** *n.*

trou·ble spot *n.* a place where difficulties regularly occur.

trough /trawf, trof/ *n.* **1** a long narrow open receptacle for water, animal feed, etc. **2** a channel for conveying a liquid. **3** an elongated region of low barometric pressure. **4** a hollow between two wave crests. **5** the time of lowest economic performance, etc. **6** a region around the minimum on a curve of variation of a quantity. **7** a low point or depression.

trounce /trowns/ *v.tr.* **1** defeat heavily. **2** beat; thrash. **3** punish severely. ▫▫ **trounc·er** *n.* **trounc·ing** *n.*

troupe /troop/ *n.* a company of actors or acrobats, etc.

troup·er /tróopər/ *n.* **1** a member of a theatrical troupe. **2** a staunch reliable person, esp. during difficult times.

trou·sers /trówzərz/ *n.pl.* **1** = PANTS. **2** (**trouser**) (*attrib.*) designating parts of this (*trouser leg*). ▫▫ **trou·sered** *adj.* **trou·ser·less** *adj.*

trous·seau /tróosō, troosṓ/ *n.* (*pl.* **trousseaus** or **trousseaux** /–sōz/) the clothes and other possessions collected by a bride for her marriage.

trout /trowt/ *n.* (*pl.* same or **trouts**) **1** any of various freshwater fish of the genus *Salmo* of the northern hemisphere, valued as food. **2** a similar fish of the family Salmonidae. ▫▫ **trout·let** *n.* **trout·ling** *n.* **trout·y** *adj.*

trove /trōv/ *n.* = TREASURE TROVE.

trow·el /trówəl/ *n. & v.* •*n.* **1** a small hand tool with a flat pointed blade, used to apply and spread mortar, etc. **2** a similar tool with a curved scoop for lifting plants or earth. •*v.tr.* (**troweled, troweling** *or* **trowelled, trowelling**) **1** apply (plaster, etc.). **2** plaster (a wall, etc.) with a trowel.

troy /troy/ *n.* (in full **troy weight**) a system of weights used for precious metals and gems, with a pound of 12 ounces or 5,760 grains.

tru·ant /tróoənt/ *n., adj., & v.* •*n.* **1** a child who stays away from school without leave or explanation. **2** a person missing from work, etc. •*adj.* (of a person, conduct, thoughts, etc.) shirking; idle; wandering. •*v.intr.* (also **play truant**) stay away as a truant. ▫▫ **tru·an·cy** *n.*

truce /troos/ *n.* **1** a temporary agreement to cease hostilities. **2** a suspension of private feuding or bickering. ▫▫ **truce·less** *adj.*

truck[1] /truk/ *n. & v.* •*n.* **1** a vehicle for carrying heavy or bulky cargo, etc. **2** *Brit.* a railroad freight car. **3** a vehicle for transporting troops, supplies, etc. **4** a swiveling wheel frame of a railroad car. **5** a wheeled stand for transporting goods; a handcart. •*v.* **1** *tr.* convey on or in a truck. **2** *intr.* drive a truck. **3** *intr. sl.* proceed; go. ▫▫ **truck·age** *n.*

truck[2] /truk/ *n.* **1** dealings; exchange; barter. **2** small wares. **3** small farm or garden produce (*truck farm*). **4** *colloq.* odds and ends. **5** *hist.* the payment of workers in kind. ▫ **have no truck with** avoid dealing with.

truck·er /trúkər/ *n.* **1** a long-distance truck driver. **2** a firm dealing in long-distance transportation of goods.

truck·ing /trúking/ *n.* transportation of goods by truck.

truck·le /trúkəl/ *n. & v.* •*n.* **1** (in full **truckle bed**) = TRUNDLE BED. **2** orig. *dial.* a small barrel-shaped cheese. •*v.intr.* (foll. by *to*) submit obsequiously. ▫▫ **truck·ler** *n.*

truck stop *n.* a facility, esp. for truck drivers, usu. by a major highway and including a gas station, restaurant, etc.

truc·u·lent /trúkyələnt/ *adj.* **1** aggressively defiant. **2** aggressive; pugnacious. **3** fierce; savage. ▫▫ **truc·u·lence** *n.* **truc·u·len·cy** *n.* **truc·u·lent·ly** *adv.*

trudge /truj/ *v. & n.* •*v.* **1** *intr.* go on foot, esp. laboriously. **2** *tr.* traverse (a distance) in this way. •*n.* a trudging walk. ▫▫ **trudg·er** *n.*

true /troo/ *adj., adv., & v.* •*adj.* **1** in accordance with fact or reality (*a true story*). **2** genuine; rightly or strictly so called; not spurious or counterfeit (*a true friend*; *the true heir to the throne*). **3** (often foll. by *to*) loyal or faithful (*true to one's word*). **4** (foll. by *to*) accurately conforming (to a standard or expectation, etc.) (*true to form*). **5** correctly positioned or balanced; upright; level. **6** exact; accurate (*a true aim*; *a true copy*). **7** (*absol.*) (also **it is true**) certainly; admittedly (*true, it would cost more*). **8** (of a note) exactly in tune. **9** *archaic* honest; upright (*twelve good men and true*). • *adv.* **1** truly (*tell me true*). **2** accurately (*aim true*). **3** without variation (*breed true*). • *v.tr.* (**trues, trued, trueing** or **truing**) bring (a tool, wheel, frame, etc.) into the exact position or form required. □ **come true** actually happen or be the case. **out of true** (or **the true**) not in the correct or exact position. **true to form** (or **type**) being or behaving, etc., as expected. **true to life** accurately representing life. □□ **true·ish** *adj.* **true·ness** *n.*

true-blue *adj.* extremely loyal or orthodox.

true north *n.* north according to the earth's axis, not magnetic north.

truf·fle /trúfəl/ *n.* **1** any strong-smelling underground fungus of the order Tuberales, used as a culinary delicacy and found esp. in France by trained dogs or pigs. **2** a usu. round candy made of chocolate mixture covered with cocoa, etc.

tru·ism /tróoizəm/ *n.* **1** an obviously true or hackneyed statement. **2** a proposition that states nothing beyond what is implied in any of its terms. □□ **tru·is·tic** /–ístik/ *adj.*

tru·ly /tróolee/ *adv.* **1** sincerely; genuinely (*am truly grateful*). **2** really; indeed (*truly, I do not know*). **3** faithfully; loyally (*served them truly*). **4** accurately; truthfully (*is not truly depicted*; *has been truly stated*). **5** rightly; properly (*well and truly*).

trump /trump/ *n.* & *v.* • *n.* **1** a playing card of a suit ranking above the others. **2** an advantage, esp. involving surprise. • *v.* **1 a** *tr.* defeat (a card or its player) with a trump. **b** *intr.* play a trump card when another suit has been led. **2** *tr. colloq.* gain a surprising advantage over (a person, proposal, etc.). □ **trump up** fabricate or invent (an accusation, excuse, etc.) (*on a trumped-up charge*).

trump card *n.* **1** a card belonging to, or turned up to determine, a trump suit. **2** *colloq.* **a** a valuable resource. **b** a surprise move to gain an advantage.

trump·er·y /trúmpəree/ *n.* & *adj.* • *n.* (*pl.* **-ies**) **1 a** worthless finery. **b** a worthless article. **2** junk. • *adj.* **1** showy but worthless (*trumpery jewels*). **2** delusive; shallow (*trumpery arguments*).

trum·pet /trúmpit/ *n.* & *v.* • *n.* **1 a** a tubular or conical brass instrument with a flared bell and a bright penetrating tone. **b** its player. **c** an organ stop with a quality resembling a trumpet. **2 a** the tubular corona of a daffodil, etc. **b** a trumpet-shaped thing (*ear trumpet*). **3** a sound of or like a trumpet. • *v.* (**trumpeted, trumpeting**) **1** *intr.* **a** blow a trumpet. **b** (of an enraged elephant, etc.) make a loud sound as of a trumpet. **2** *tr.* proclaim loudly (a person's or thing's merit). □□ **trum·pet·less** *adj.*

trum·pet·er /trúmpitər/ *n.* **1** a person who plays or sounds a trumpet, esp. a cavalry soldier giving signals. **2** a bird making a trumpetlike sound, esp.: **a** a variety of domestic pigeon. **b** a large black S. American cranelike bird of the genus *Psophia*.

trum·pet·er swan *n.* a large N. American wild swan, *Cygnus buccinator*.

trun·cate /trúngkayt/ *v.tr.* cut the top or the end from (a tree, a body, a piece of writing, etc.). □□ **trun·cate·ly** *adv.* **trun·ca·tion** /–káyshən/ *n.*

trun·cheon /trúnchən/ *n.* **1** a short club or cudgel, esp. carried by a policeman; a billy club. **2** a staff or baton as a symbol of authority.

trun·dle /trúnd'l/ *v.tr.* & *intr.* roll or move heavily or noisily, esp. on or as on wheels.

trun·dle bed *n.* a low bed on wheels that can be stored under a larger bed.

trunk /trungk/ *n.* **1** the main stem of a tree as distinct from its branches and roots. **2** a person's or animal's body apart from the limbs and head. **3** the main part of any structure. **4** a large box with a hinged lid for transporting luggage, clothes, etc. **5** the luggage compartment of an automobile. **6** an elephant's elongated prehensile nose. **7** (in *pl.*) men's often close-fitting shorts worn for swimming, boxing, etc. **8** the main body of an artery, nerve, communications network, etc. **9** an enclosed shaft or conduit for cables, ventilation, etc. □□ **trunk·ful** *n.* (*pl.* **-fuls**). **trunk·less** *adj.*

truss /trus/ *n.* & *v.* • *n.* **1** a framework, e.g., of rafters and struts, supporting a roof or bridge, etc. **2** a surgical appliance worn to support a hernia. • *v.tr.* **1** tie up (a fowl) compactly for cooking. **2** (often foll. by *up*) tie (a person) up with the arms to the sides. **3** support (a roof or bridge, etc.) with a truss or trusses. □□ **truss·er** *n.*

trust /trust/ *n.* & *v.* • *n.* **1 a** a firm belief in the reliability or truth or strength, etc., of a person or thing. **b** the state of being relied on. **2** a confident expectation. **3 a** a thing or person committed to one's care. **b** the resulting obligation or responsibility (*am in a position of trust*; *have fulfilled my trust*). **4** a person or thing confided in (*is our sole trust*). **5** reliance on the truth of a statement, etc., without examination. **6** commercial credit (*obtained merchandise on trust*). **7** *Law* **a** confidence placed in a person by making that person the nominal owner of property to be used for another's benefit. **b** the right of the latter to benefit by such property. **c** the property so held. **d** the legal relation between the holder and the property so held. **8 a** a body of trustees. **b** an organization managed by trustees. **c** an organized association of several companies for the purpose of reducing or defeating competition, etc., esp. one in which all or most of the stock is transferred to a central committee and shareholders lose their voting power although remaining entitled to profits. • *v.* **1** *tr.* place trust in; believe in; rely on the character or behavior of. **2** *tr.* (foll. by *with*) allow (a person) to have or use (a thing) from confidence in its proper use (*was reluctant to trust them with my books*). **3** *tr.* (often foll. by *that* + clause) have faith or confidence or hope that a thing will take place (*I trust you will not be late*; *I trust that she is recovering*). **4** *tr.* (foll. by *to*) consign (a thing) to (a person) with trust. **5** *tr.* (foll. by *for*) allow credit to (a customer) for (merchandise). **6** *intr.* (foll. by *in*) place reliance in (*we trust in you*). **7** *intr.* (foll. by *to*) place (esp. undue) reliance on (*shall have to trust to luck*). □ **in trust** *Law* held on the basis of trust (see sense 7 of *n.*). **on trust 1** on credit. **2** on the basis of trust or confidence. **take on trust** accept (an assertion, claim, etc.) without evidence or investigation. □□ **trust·a·ble** *adj.* **trust·er** *n.*

trust·ee /trustée/ *n.* **1** *Law* a person or member of a board given control or powers of administration of property in trust with a legal obligation to administer it solely for the purposes specified. **2** a nation made responsible for the government of an area. □□ **trust·ee·ship** *n.*

trust·ful /trústfool/ *adj.* **1** full of trust or confidence. **2** not feeling or showing suspicion. □□ **trust·ful·ly** *adv.* **trust·ful·ness** *n.*

trust fund *n.* a fund of money, etc., held in trust.

trust·ing /trústing/ *adj.* having trust (esp. characteristically); trustful. □□ **trust·ing·ly** *adv.* **trust·ing·ness** *n.*

trust·wor·thy /trústwurthee/ *adj.* deserving of trust; reliable. □□ **trust·wor·thi·ly** *adv.* **trust·wor·thi·ness** *n.*

trust·y /trústee/ *adj.* & *n.* • *adj.* (**trustier, trustiest**) **1** *archaic* or *joc.* trustworthy (*a trusty steed*). **2** *archaic* loyal (to a sovereign) (*my trusty subjects*). • *n.* (*pl.* **-ies**) a prisoner who is given special privileges for good behavior. ▫▫ **trust·i·ly** *adv.* **trust·i·ness** *n.*

truth /trooth/ *n.* (*pl.* **truths** /troothz, trooths/) **1** the quality or a state of being true or truthful. **2 a** what is true (*tell us the whole truth; the truth is that I forgot*). **b** what is accepted as true (*one of the fundamental truths*). ▫ **in truth** truly; really. **to tell the truth** (or **truth to tell**) to be frank. ▫▫ **truth·less** *adj.*

truth·ful /tróothfool/ *adj.* **1** habitually speaking the truth. **2** (of a story, etc.) true. **3** (of a likeness, etc.) corresponding to reality. ▫▫ **truth·ful·ly** *adv.* **truth·ful·ness** *n.*

try /trī/ *v.* & *n.* •*v.* (**-tries, -tried**) **1** *intr.* make an effort with a view to success (often foll. by *to* + infin.; *colloq.* foll. by *and* + infin.: *tried to be on time; try and be early; I shall try hard*). ▶Use with *and* is uncommon in the past tense and in negative contexts (except in *imper.*). **2** *tr.* make an effort to achieve (*tried my best; had better try something easier*). **3** *tr.* **a** test (the quality of a thing) by use or experiment. **b** test the qualities of (a person or thing) (*try it before you buy*). **4** *tr.* make severe demands on (a person, quality, etc.) (*my patience has been sorely tried*). **5** *tr.* examine the effectiveness or usefulness of for a purpose (*try cold water; have you tried kicking it?*). **6** *tr.* ascertain the state of fastening of (a door, window, etc.). **7** *tr.* **a** investigate and decide (a case or issue) judicially. **b** subject (a person) to trial (*will be tried for murder*). **8** *tr.* make an experiment in order to find out (*let us try which takes longest*). **9** *intr.* (foll. by *for*) **a** apply or compete for. **b** seek to reach or attain (*am going to try for a gold medal*). **10** *tr.* (often foll. by *out*) **a** extract (oil) from fat by heating. **b** treat (fat) in this way. **11** *tr.* (often foll. by *up*) smooth (roughly planed wood) with a plane to give an accurately flat surface. •*n.* (*pl.* **-ies**) **1** an effort to accomplish something; an attempt (*give it a try*). **2** *Rugby* the act of touching the ball down behind the opposing goal line, scoring points and entitling the scoring side to a kick at the goal. **3** *Football* an attempt to score one or two extra points after a touchdown. ▫ **tried and true** (or **tested**) proved reliable by experience; dependable. **try on for size** try out or test for suitability. **try one's hand** see how skillful one is, esp. at the first attempt. **try on** put on (clothes, etc.) to see if they fit or suit the wearer. **try out 1** put to the test. **2** test thoroughly.

try·ing /trī́-ing/ *adj.* annoying; vexatious; hard to endure. ▫▫ **try·ing·ly** *adv.*

tryst /trist/ *n.* **1** a time and place for a meeting, esp. of lovers. **2** such a meeting (*keep a tryst; break one's tryst*). ▫▫ **tryst·er** *n.*

tsar var. of CZAR.

tsa·ri·na var. of CZARINA.

tset·se /tsétsee, tét–, tseétsee, teé–/ *n.* any fly of the genus *Glossina* native to Africa that feeds on human and animal blood with a needlelike proboscis and transmits trypanosomiasis.

T-shirt /teéshərt/ *n.* (also **tee-shirt**) a short-sleeved collarless casual top, usu. of knitted cotton and having the form of a T when spread out.

tsp. *abbr.* (*pl.* **tsps.**) teaspoon; teaspoonful.

T square /teé skwair/ *n.* a T-shaped instrument for drawing or testing right angles.

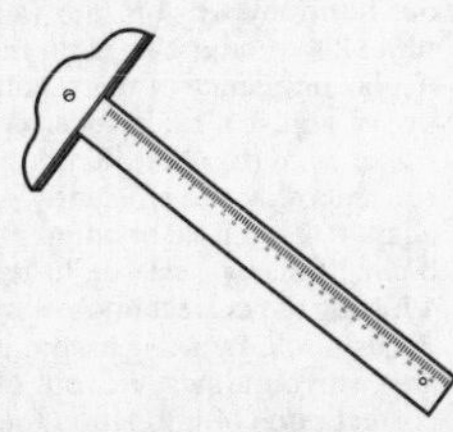
T square

tsu·na·mi /tsoonaámee/ *n.* (*pl.* **tsunamis**) a long high sea wave caused by underwater earthquakes or other disturbances; tidal wave.

tub /tub/ *n.* & *v.* •*n.* **1** an open flat-bottomed usu. round container for various purposes. **2** a tub-shaped (usu. plastic) carton. **3** the amount a tub will hold. **4** *Brit. colloq.* a bath. **5 a** *colloq.* a clumsy slow boat. **b** a stout roomy boat for rowing practice. •*v.* (**tubbed, tubbing**) **1** *tr.* & *intr.* esp. *Brit.* plant, bathe, or wash in a tub. **2** *tr.* enclose in a tub. ▫▫ **tub·ba·ble** *adj.* **tub·bish** *adj.* **tub·ful** *n.* (*pl.* **-fuls**).

tu·ba /tóobə, tyóo–/ *n.* (*pl.* **tubas**) **1 a** a low-pitched brass wind instrument. **b** its player. **2** an organ stop with the quality of a tuba.

tub·al /tóobəl, tyóo–/ *adj. Anat.* of or relating to a tube, esp. the bronchial or Fallopian tubes.

tub·by /túbee/ *adj.* (**tubbier, tubbiest**) **1** (of a person) short and fat; tub-shaped. **2** (of a violin) dull-sounding; lacking resonance. ▫▫ **tub·bi·ness** *n.*

tube /toob, tyoob/ *n.* & *v.* •*n.* **1** a long hollow rigid or flexible cylinder, esp. for holding or carrying air, liquids, etc. **2** a soft metal or plastic cylinder sealed at one end and having a screw cap at the other, for holding a semiliquid substance ready for use (*a tube of toothpaste*). **3** *Anat.* & *Zool.* a hollow cylindrical organ in the body (*bronchial tubes; Fallopian tubes*). **4** (often prec. by *the*) *colloq.* the London subway system. **5 a** a cathode-ray tube, esp. in a television set. **b** (prec. by *the*) *colloq.* television. **6** = VACUUM TUBE. **7** = INNER TUBE. **8** the cylindrical body of a wind instrument. **9** (in full **tube top**) an elasticized upper garment shaped like a tube. **10** *Austral. sl.* a can of beer. •*v.tr.* **1** equip with tubes. **2** enclose in a tube. ▫▫ **tube·less** *adj.* (esp. in sense 7 of *n.*). **tube·like** *adj.*

tu·ber /tóobər, tyóo–/ *n.* **1** the short thick rounded part of a stem or rhizome, usu. found underground and covered with modified buds, e.g., a potato. **2** the similar root of a dahlia, etc.

tu·ber·cle /tóobərkəl, tyóo–/ *n.* **1** a small rounded protuberance, esp. on a bone. **2** a small rounded swelling on the body or in an organ, esp. a nodular lesion characteristic of tuberculosis in the lungs, etc. ▫▫ **tu·ber·cu·late** /–bə́rkyələt, –layt/ *adj.* **tu·ber·cu·lous** /–bə́rkyələs/ *adj.*

tu·ber·cu·lar /toobə́rkyələr, tyoo–/ *adj.* & *n.* •*adj.* of or having tubercles or tuberculosis. •*n.* a person with tuberculosis.

tu·ber·cu·lin /toobə́rkyəlin, tyoo–/ *n.* a sterile liquid from cultures of tubercle bacillus, used in the diagnosis and treatment of tuberculosis.

tu·ber·cu·lo·sis /toobə́rkyəlósis, tyoo–/ *n.* an infectious disease caused by the bacillus *Mycobacterium tuberculosis*, characterized by tubercles, esp. in the lungs.

tu·ber·ose /tóobərōs, tyóo–/ *adj.* **1** covered with tubers; knobby. **2** of or resembling a tuber. **3** bearing tubers. ▫▫ **tu·ber·os·i·ty** /–rósitee/ *n.*

tu·ber·ous /tóobərəs, tyóo–/ *adj.* = TUBEROSE.

tub·ing /tóobing, tyóo–/ *n.* **1** a length of tube. **2** a quantity of tubes.

tu·bu·lar /tóobyələr, tyóo–/ *adj.* **1** tube-shaped. **2** having or consisting of tubes. **3** (of furniture, etc.) made of tubular pieces.

tu·bu·lar bells *n.pl.* an orchestral instrument consisting of a row of vertically suspended brass tubes that are struck with a hammer.

tu·bule /tóobyool, tyóo–/ *n.* a small tube in a plant or an animal body.

tuck /tuk/ *v.* & *n.* •*v.* **1** *tr.* (often foll. by *in, up*) **a** draw, fold, or turn the outer or end parts of (cloth or clothes, etc.) close together so as to be held; thrust in the edge of (a thing) so as to confine it (*tucked his shirt into his trousers*). **b** thrust in the edges of bedclothes around (a person) (*came to tuck me in*). **2** *tr.* draw together into a small space (*the bird tucked its head under its wing*). **3** *tr.* stow (a thing) away in a specified place or way (*tucked it out of sight*). **4** *tr.* **a** make a stitched fold in (material, a garment, etc.). **b** shorten, tighten, or ornament with stitched folds. • *n.* **1** a flattened usu. stitched fold in material, a garment, etc., often one of several parallel folds for shortening, tightening, or ornament. **2** *Brit. colloq.* food, esp. cake and candy eaten by children (also *attrib.*: *tuck box*). **3** (in full **tuck position**) (in diving, gymnastics, etc.) a position with the knees bent upward into the chest and the hands clasped around the shins. □ **tuck away** (or **into**) *colloq.* eat (food) heartily (*tucked into their dinner*; *could really tuck it away*).

tuck·er /túkər/ *n.* & *v.* • *n.* **1** a person or thing that tucks. **2** *hist.* a piece of lace or linen, etc., in or on a woman's bodice. **3** *Austral. colloq.* food. • *v.tr.* (esp. in *passive*; often foll. by *out*) *colloq.* tire; exhaust.

Tu·dor /tóōdər, tyóō–/ *adj. hist.* **1** of, characteristic of, or associated with the royal family of England ruling 1485–1603 or this period. **2** of or relating to the architectural style of this period, esp. with half-timbering and elaborately decorated houses.

Tues. *abbr.* (also **Tue.**) Tuesday.

Tues·day /tóōzday, –dee, tyóōz–/ *n.* & *adv.* • *n.* the third day of the week, following Monday. • *adv.* **1** *colloq.* on Tuesday. **2** (**Tuesdays**) on Tuesdays; each Tuesday.

tu·fa /tóōfə, tyóō–/ *n.* **1** a porous rock composed of calcium carbonate and formed around mineral springs. **2** = TUFF. □□ **tu·fa·ceous** /–fáyshəs/ *adj.*

tuff /tuf/ *n.* rock formed by the consolidation of volcanic ash. □□ **tuff·a·ceous** /tufáyshəs/ *adj.*

tuft /tuft/ *n.* & *v.* • *n.* a bunch or collection of threads, grass, feathers, hair, etc., held or growing together at the base. • *v.* **1** *tr.* provide with a tuft or tufts. **2** *tr.* make depressions at regular intervals in (a mattress, etc.) by passing a thread through. **3** *intr.* grow in tufts. □□ **tuft·y** *adj.*

tuft·ed /túftid/ *adj.* **1** having or growing in a tuft or tufts. **2** (of a bird) having a tuft of feathers on the head.

tug /tug/ *v.* & *n.* • *v.* (**tugged, tugging**) **1** *tr.* & (foll. by *at*) *intr.* pull hard or violently; jerk (*tugged it from my grasp*; *tugged at my sleeve*). **2** *tr.* tow (a ship, etc.) by means of a tugboat. • *n.* **1** a hard, violent, or jerky pull (*gave a tug on the rope*). **2** a sudden strong emotional feeling (*felt a tug as I watched them go*). **3** a small powerful boat for towing larger boats and ships. □□ **tug·ger** *n.*

tug·boat /túgbōt/ *n.* = TUG *n.* 3.

tug-of-war *n.* **1** a trial of strength between two sides pulling against each other on a rope. **2** a decisive or severe contest.

tu·i·tion /tōō-íshən, tyōō–/ *n.* **1** teaching or instruction, esp. if paid for (*driving tuition*; *music tuition*). **2** a fee for this. □□ **tu·i·tion·al** *adj.*

tu·lip /tóōlip, tyóō–/ *n.* **1** any bulbous spring-flowering plant of the genus *Tulipa*, esp. one of the many cultivated forms with showy cup-shaped flowers of various colors and markings. **2** a flower of this plant.

tu·lip tree *n.* any of various trees, esp. of the genus *Liriodendron*, producing tuliplike flowers.

tulle /tōōl/ *n.* a soft fine silk, etc., net for veils and dresses.

tum·ble /túmbəl/ *v.* & *n.* • *v.* **1** *intr.* & *tr.* fall or cause to fall suddenly, clumsily, or headlong. **2** *intr.* fall rapidly in amount, etc. (*prices tumbled*). **3** *intr.* (often foll. by *about*, *around*) roll or toss erratically or helplessly back and forth. **4** *intr.* move or rush in a headlong or blundering manner (*the children tumbled out of the car*). **5** *intr.* (often foll. by *to*) *colloq.* grasp the meaning or hidden implication of an idea, circumstance, etc. (*they quickly tumbled to our intentions*). **6** *tr.* overturn; fling or push roughly or carelessly. **7** *intr.* perform acrobatic feats, esp. somersaults. **8** *tr.* rumple or disarrange; disorder. **9** *tr.* dry (laundry) in a tumble dryer. **10** *tr.* clean (castings, gemstones, etc.) in a tumbling barrel. **11** *intr.* (of a pigeon) turn over backward in flight. • *n.* **1** a sudden or headlong fall. **2** a somersault or other acrobatic feat. **3** an untidy or confused state.

---

tumble Middle English (also in the sense 'dance with contortions'): of Germanic origin; related to German *taumeln* 'be giddy, stagger,' Swedish *tumla* 'tumble down'; related to Old English *tumbian* 'to dance.' The sense was probably influenced by Old French *tomber* 'to fall.' The noun dates from the mid-17th century.

---

tum·ble·down /túmbəldown/ *adj.* falling or fallen into ruin; dilapidated.

tum·ble-dry *v.tr.* dry laundry in a machine that has a heated rotating drum.

tum·bler /túmblər/ *n.* **1** a drinking glass with no handle or foot (formerly with a rounded bottom so as not to stand upright). **2** an acrobat, esp. one performing somersaults. **3** a pivoted piece in a lock that holds the bolt until lifted by a key. □□ **tum·bler·ful** *n.* (*pl.* **-fuls**).

tum·ble·weed /túmbəlweed/ *n.* a plant, *Amaranthus albus*, that forms a globular bush that breaks off in late summer and is tumbled about by the wind.

tum·brel /túmbrəl/ *n.* (also **tum·bril** /–ril/) *hist.* an open cart in which condemned persons were conveyed to their execution, esp. to the guillotine during the French Revolution.

tu·mes·cent /tōōmésənt, tyōō–/ *adj.* **1** becoming tumid; swelling. **2** swelling as a response to sexual stimulation. □□ **tu·mes·cence** *n.* **tu·mes·cent·ly** *adv.*

tum·my /túmee/ *n.* (*pl.* **-mies**) *colloq.* the stomach.

tu·mor /tóōmər, tyóō–/ *n.* a swelling, esp. from an abnormal growth of tissue. □□ **tu·mor·ous** *adj.*

tu·mult /tóōmult, tyóō–/ *n.* **1** an uproar or din, esp. of a disorderly crowd. **2** an angry demonstration by a mob; a riot; a public disturbance. **3** a conflict of emotions in the mind.

tu·mul·tu·ous /tōōmúlchōōəs, tyōō–/ *adj.* **1** noisily vehement; uproarious; making a tumult (*a tumultuous welcome*). **2** disorderly. **3** agitated. □□ **tu·mul·tu·ous·ly** *adv.* **tu·mul·tu·ous·ness** *n.*

tun /tun/ *n.* & *v.* • *n.* **1** a large beer or wine cask. **2** a brewer's fermenting vat. **3** a measure of capacity, equal to 252 gallons. • *v.tr.* (**tunned, tunning**) store (wine, etc.) in a tun.

tu·na /tóōnə, tyóō–/ *n.* (*pl.* same or **tunas**) **1** any marine fish of the family *Scombridae* native to tropical and warm waters, having a round body and pointed snout, and used for food. Also called esp. *Brit.* TUNNY. **2** (in full **tuna fish**) the flesh of the tuna, usu. preserved in oil or brine.

tun·dra /túndrə/ *n.* a vast level treeless region of the Arctic usu. with a marshy surface and underlying permafrost.

tune /tōōn, tyōōn/ *n.* & *v.* • *n.* a melody with or without harmony. • *v.* **1** *tr.* put (a musical instrument) in tune. **2 a** *tr.* adjust (a radio receiver, etc.) to the particular frequency of the required signals. **b** *intr.* (foll. by *in*) adjust a radio receiver to the required signal (*tuned in to the news*). **3** *tr.* adjust (an engine, etc.) to run smoothly and efficiently. **4** *tr.* (foll. by *to*) adjust or adapt to a required or different purpose, situation, etc. **5** *intr.* (foll. by *with*) be in harmony with. □ **in tune 1** having the correct pitch or intonation (*sings in tune*). **2** (usu. foll. by *with*) harmonizing with one's associates, surroundings, etc. **out of tune 1** not having the correct pitch or intonation (*always plays out of tune*). **2** (usu. foll. by *with*) clashing with one's associates, etc.

to the tune of *colloq.* to the considerable sum or amount of. **tuned in 1** (of a radio, etc.) adjusted to a particular frequency, station, etc. **2** (foll. by *on, to*) *sl.* in rapport or harmony with. **3** *colloq.* up to date; aware of what is going on. **tune up 1** (of an orchestra) bring the instruments to the proper or uniform pitch. **2** begin to play or sing. **3** bring to the most efficient condition. □□ **tun•a•ble** *adj.* (also **tune•a•ble**).

tune•ful /tóonfool, tyóon–/ *adj.* melodious; musical. □□ **tune•ful•ly** *adv.* **tune•ful•ness** *n.*

tune•less /tóonlis, tyóon–/ *adj.* **1** unmelodious; unmusical. **2** out of tune. □□ **tune•less•ly** *adv.* **tune•less•ness** *n.*

tun•er /tóonər, tyóo–/ *n.* **1** a person who tunes musical instruments, esp. pianos. **2** a device for tuning a radio receiver.

tung•sten /túngstən/ *n. Chem.* a steel-gray dense metallic element with a very high melting point, used for the filaments of electric lamps and for alloying steel, etc. ¶ Symb.: **W.** □□ **tung•state** /–stayt/ *n.* **tung•stic** /–stik/ *adj.* **tung•stous** /–stəs/ *adj.*

tung•sten car•bide *n.* a very hard black substance used in making dies and cutting tools.

tu•nic /tóonik, tyóo–/ *n.* **1** a close-fitting short coat as part of a police or military, etc., uniform. **2** a loose, often sleeveless garment usu. reaching to about the knees, as worn in ancient Greece and Rome. **3** any of various loose, pleated dresses gathered at the waist with a belt or cord. **4** a tunicle.

tun•ing /tóoning, tyóo–/ *n.* the process or a system of putting a musical instrument in tune.

tun•ing fork *n.* a two-pronged steel fork that gives a particular note when struck, used in tuning.

tuning fork

tun•nel /túnəl/ *n. & v.* • *n.* **1** an artificial underground passage through a hill or under a road or river, etc., esp. for a railroad or road to pass through, or in a mine. **2** an underground passage dug by a burrowing animal. **3** a prolonged period of difficulty or suffering (esp. in metaphors, e.g., *the end of the tunnel*). • *v.* (**tunneled, tunneling** or **tunnelled, tunnelling**) **1** *intr.* (foll. by *through, into,* etc.) make a tunnel through (a hill, etc.). **2** *tr.* make (one's way) by tunneling. □□ **tun•nel•er** *n.*

tun•nel vi•sion *n.* **1** vision that is defective in not adequately including objects away from the center of the field of view. **2** *colloq.* inability to grasp the wider implications of a situation.

tu•pe•lo /tóopilō, tyóo–/ *n.* (*pl.* **-los**) **1** any of various Asian and N. American deciduous trees of the genus *Nyssa,* with colorful foliage and growing in swampy conditions. **2** the wood of this tree.

Tu•pi /tóopee/ *n. & adj.* • *n.* (*pl.* same or **Tupis**) **1** a member of a Native American people native to the Amazon valley. **2** the language of this people. • *adj.* of or relating to this people or language.

tup•pence /túpəns/ *n. Brit.* = TWOPENCE.

tup•pen•ny /túpənee/ *adj. Brit.* = TWOPENNY.

tuque /took/ *n.* a Canadian stocking cap.

tur•ban /tárbən/ *n.* **1** a man's headdress of cotton or silk wound around a cap or the head, worn esp. by Muslims and Sikhs. **2** a woman's headdress or hat resembling this. □□ **tur•baned** *adj.*

tur•bid /tárbid/ *adj.* **1** (of a liquid or color) muddy; thick; not clear. **2** (of a style, etc.) confused; disordered. □□ **tur•bid•i•ty** /–bíditee/ *n.* **tur•bid•ly** *adv.* **tur•bid•ness** *n.*

▶**Turbid** is used of a liquid or color to mean 'muddy, not clear,' or of literary style, etc., to mean 'confused,' e.g., *the turbid utterances and twisted language of Carlyle.* **Turgid** means 'swollen, inflated, enlarged.' When used of literary style it means 'pompous, bombastic': *Communications from headquarters were largely turgid exercises in self-congratulation.*

tur•bine /tárbin, –bīn/ *n.* a rotary motor or engine driven by a flow of water, steam, gas, wind, etc., esp. to produce electrical power.

tur•bo /tárbō/ *n.* (*pl.* **-bos**) = TURBOCHARGER.

tur•bo•charg•er /tárbōchaarjər/ *n.* a supercharger driven by a turbine powered by the engine's exhaust gases.

tur•bo•fan /tárbōfan/ *n.* **1** a jet engine in which a turbine-driven fan provides additional thrust. **2** an aircraft powered by this.

tur•bo•jet /tárbōjet/ *n. Aeron.* **1** a jet engine in which the jet also operates a turbine-driven compressor for the air drawn into the engine. **2** an aircraft powered by this.

tur•bo•prop /tárbōprop/ *n. Aeron.* **1** a jet engine in which a turbine is used as in a turbojet and also to drive a propeller. **2** an aircraft powered by this.

tur•bo•shaft /tárbōshaft/ *n.* a gas turbine that powers a shaft for driving heavy vehicles, generators, pumps, etc.

tur•bot /tárbət/ *n.* **1** a flatfish, *Psetta maxima,* having large bony tubercles on the body and head and prized as food. **2** any of various similar fishes including halibut.

tur•bu•lence /tárbyələns/ *n.* **1** an irregularly fluctuating flow of air or fluid. **2** *Meteorol.* stormy conditions as a result of atmospheric disturbance. **3** a disturbance, commotion, or tumult.

tur•bu•lent /tárbyələnt/ *adj.* **1** disturbed; in commotion. **2** (of a flow of air, etc.) varying irregularly; causing disturbance. **3** tumultuous. **4** insubordinate; riotous. □□ **tur•bu•lent•ly** *adv.*

turd /tərd/ *n. coarse sl.* **1** a lump of excrement. **2** a term of contempt for a person. ▶Often considered a taboo word, esp. in sense 2.

tu•reen /tooréen, tyoo–/ *n.* a deep covered dish for serving soup, etc.

turf /tərf/ *n. & v.* • *n.* (*pl.* **turfs** or **turves**) **1 a** a layer of grass, etc., with earth and matted roots as the surface of grassland. **b** a piece of this cut from the ground. **c** an artificial ground covering, as on a playing field, etc. **2** a slab of peat for fuel. **3** (prec. by *the*) **a** horse racing generally. **b** a general term for racetracks. **4** *sl.* a person's territory or sphere of influence. • *v.tr.* **1** cover (ground) with turf. **2** (foll. by *out*) esp. *Brit. colloq.* expel or eject (a person or thing).

tur•gid /tárjid/ *adj.* **1** swollen; inflated; enlarged. **2** (of language) pompous; bombastic. □□ **tur•gid•i•ty** /–jíditee/ *n.* **tur•gid•ly** *adv.* **tur•gid•ness** *n.*

Turk /tərk/ *n.* **1 a** a native or inhabitant of Turkey in SE Europe and Asia Minor. **b** a person of Turkish descent. **2** a member of a central Asian people from whom the Ottomans derived, speaking Turkic languages. **3** *offens.* a ferocious, wild, or unmanageable person.

tur•key /tárkee/ *n.* (*pl.* **-keys**) **1** a large mainly domesticated game bird, *Meleagris gallopavo,* orig. of N. America, having dark plumage with a green or bronze sheen, prized as food, esp. on festive occasions including Christmas and Thanksgiving. **2** the flesh of the turkey as food. **3** *sl.* **a** a theatrical failure; a flop. **b** a stupid or inept person. □ **talk turkey** *colloq.* talk frankly and straightforwardly; get down to business.

tur·key vul·ture *n.* (also **tur·key buz·zard**) an American vulture, *Cathartes aura.*

Turk·ish /tə́rkish/ *adj. & n.* • *adj.* of or relating to Turkey in SE Europe and Asia Minor, or to the Turks or their language. • *n.* this language.

Turk·ish bath *n.* **1** a hot air or steam bath followed by washing, massage, etc. **2** (in *sing.* or *pl.*) a building for this.

Turk·ish tow·el *n.* a towel made of cotton terry cloth.

tur·mer·ic /tə́rmərik/ *n.* **1** an E. Indian plant, *Curcuma longa*, of the ginger family, yielding aromatic rhizomes used as a spice and for yellow dye. **2** this powdered rhizome used as a spice, esp. in curry powder.

tur·moil /tə́rmoyl/ *n.* **1** violent confusion; agitation. **2** din and bustle.

turn /tərn/ *v. & n.* • *v.* **1** *tr. & intr.* move around a point or axis so that the point or axis remains in a central position; give a rotary motion to or receive a rotary motion (*turned the wheel*; *the wheel turns*; *the key turns in the lock*). **2** *tr. & intr.* change in position so that a different side, end, or part becomes outermost or uppermost, etc.; invert or reverse or cause to be inverted or reversed (*turned inside out*; *turned it upside down*). **3 a** *tr.* give a new direction to (*turn your face this way*). **b** *intr.* take a new direction (*turn left here*; *my thoughts have often turned to you*). **4** *tr.* aim in a certain way (*turned the hose on them*). **5** *intr. & tr.* (foll. by *into*) change in nature, form, or condition to (*turned into a dragon*; *then turned him into a frog*; *turned the book into a play*). **6** *intr.* (foll. by *to*) **a** apply oneself to; set about (*turned to doing the ironing*). **b** have recourse to; begin to indulge in habitually (*turned to drink*; *turned to me for help*). **c** go on to consider next (*let us now turn to your report*). **7** *intr. & tr.* become or cause to become (*turned hostile*; *has turned informer*). **8 a** *tr. & intr.* (foll. by *against*) make or become hostile to (*has turned them against us*). **b** *intr.* (foll. by *on, upon*) become hostile to; attack (*suddenly turned on them*). **9** *intr.* (of hair or leaves) change color. **10** *intr.* (of milk) become sour. **11** *intr.* (of the stomach) be nauseated. **12** *intr.* (of the head) become giddy. **13** *tr.* cause (milk) to become sour, (the stomach) to be nauseated, or (the head) to become giddy. **14** *tr.* translate (*turn it into French*). **15** *tr.* move to the other side of; go around (*turned the corner*). **16** *tr.* pass the age or time of (*he has turned 40*; *it has now turned 4 o'clock*). **17** *intr.* (foll. by *on*) depend on; be determined by; concern (*it all turns on the weather tomorrow*; *the conversation turned on my motives*). **18** *tr.* send or put into a specified place or condition; cause to go (*was turned loose*; *turned the water out into a basin*). **19** *tr.* **a** perform (a somersault, etc.) with rotary motion. **b** twist (an ankle) out of position; sprain. **20** *tr.* remake (a garment or a sheet) putting the worn outer side on the inside. **21** *tr.* make (a profit). **22** *tr.* (also foll. by *aside*) divert; deflect (something material or immaterial). **23** *tr.* blunt (the edge of a knife, slot of a screw, etc.). **24** *tr.* shape (an object) on a lathe. **25** *tr.* give an (esp. elegant) form to (*turn a compliment*). **26** *intr.* (of the tide) change from flood to ebb or vice versa. • *n.* **1** the act or process or an instance of turning; rotary motion (*a single turn of the handle*). **2 a** a changed or a change of direction or tendency (*took a sudden turn to the left*). **b** a deflection or deflected part (*full of twists and turns*). **3** a point at which a turning or change occurs. **4** a turning of a road. **5** a change of the tide from ebb to flow or from flow to ebb. **6** a change in the course of events. **7** a tendency or disposition (*is of a mechanical turn of mind*). **8** an opportunity or obligation, etc., that comes successively to each of several persons, etc. (*your turn will come*; *my turn to read*). **9** a short walk or ride (*shall take a turn around the block*). **10** a short performance on stage or in a circus, etc. **11** service of a specified kind (*did me a good turn*). **12** purpose (*served my turn*). **13** *colloq.* a momentary nervous shock or ill feeling (*gave me quite a turn*). □ **at every turn** continually; at each new stage, etc. **by turns** in rotation of individuals or groups; alternately. **in turn** in succession; one by one. **in one's turn** when one's turn or opportunity comes. **not know which way** (or **where**) **to turn** be completely at a loss, unsure how to act, etc. **out of turn 1** at a time when it is not one's turn. **2** inappropriately; inadvisedly or tactlessly (*did I speak out of turn?*). **take turns** act or work alternately or in succession. **turn around 1** move so as to face in a new direction. **2 a** *Commerce* unload and reload (a ship, vehicle, etc.). **b** receive, process, and send out again; cause to progress through a system. **3** adopt new opinions or policy. **turn aside** see TURN *v.* 22 above. **turn away 1** turn to face in another direction. **2** refuse to accept; reject. **3** send away. **turn back 1** begin or cause to retrace one's steps. **2** fold back. **turn the corner 1** pass around it into another street. **2** pass the critical point in an illness, difficulty, etc. **turn down 1** reject (a proposal, application, etc.). **2** reduce the volume or strength of (sound, heat, etc.) by turning a knob, etc. **3** fold down. **4** place downward. **turn in 1** hand in or over; deliver. **2** achieve or register (a performance, score, etc.). **3** *colloq.* go to bed in the evening. **4** fold inward. **5** incline inward (*his toes turn in*). **6** *colloq.* abandon (a plan, etc.). **turn in one's grave** see GRAVE[1]. **turn off 1 a** stop the flow or operation of (water, electricity, etc.) by means of a faucet, switch, etc. **b** operate (a faucet, switch, etc.) to achieve this. **2 a** enter a side road. **b** (of a side road) lead off from another road. **3** *colloq.* repel; cause to lose interest (*turned me right off with their complaining*). **turn on 1 a** start the flow or operation of (water, electricity, etc.) by means of a faucet, switch, etc. **b** operate (a faucet, switch, etc.) to achieve this. **2** *colloq.* excite; stimulate the interest of, esp. sexually. **3** *tr. & intr. colloq.* intoxicate or become intoxicated with drugs. **turn one's stomach** make one nauseous or disgusted. **turn out 1** expel. **2** extinguish (an electric light, etc.). **3** dress or equip (*well turned out*). **4** produce (manufactured goods, etc.). **5** esp. *Brit.* empty or clean out (a room, etc.). **6** empty (a pocket) to see the contents. **7** *colloq.* **a** get out of bed. **b** go out of doors. **8** *colloq.* assemble; attend a meeting, etc. **9** (often foll. by *to* + infin. or *that* + clause) prove to be the case; result (*turned out to be true*; *we shall see how things turn out*). **10** *Mil.* call (a guard) from the guardroom. **turn over 1** reverse or cause to reverse vertical position; bring the underside or reverse into view (*turn over the page*). **2** upset; fall or cause to fall over. **3 a** cause (an engine) to run. **b** (of an engine) start running. **4** consider thoroughly. **5** (foll. by *to*) transfer the care or conduct of (a person or thing) to (a person) (*shall turn it all over to my deputy*; *turned him over to the authorities*). **6** do business to the amount of (*turns over $5,000 a week*). **turn over a new leaf** improve one's conduct or performance. **turn the other cheek** respond meekly to insult or abuse. **turn tail** turn one's back; run away. **turn the tide** reverse the trend of events. **turn to** set about one's work (*came home and immediately turned to*). **turn up 1** increase the volume or strength of (sound, heat, etc.) by turning a knob, etc. **2** place upward. **3** discover or reveal. **4** be found, esp. by chance. **5** happen or present itself; (of a person) put in an appearance. **6** shorten (a garment) by increasing the size of the hem. **turn up one's nose** (or **turn one's nose up**) react with disdain.

turn·a·bout /tə́rnəbowt/ *n.* **1** an act of turning about. **2** an abrupt change of policy, etc.

turn·a·round *n.* (also *Brit.* **turn·a·round**) **1 a** the process of loading and unloading. **b** the process of receiving, processing, and sending out again; progress through a system. **2** the reversal of an opinion or tendency.

turn·coat /tə́rnkōt/ *n.* a person who changes sides in a conflict, dispute, etc.

turn·down /tə́rndown/ *n. & adj.* • *n.* a rejection, a refusal. • *adj.* (of a collar) turned down.

turn·ing /tə́rning/ *n.* **1 a** a road that branches off another; a turn. **b** a place where this occurs. **2 a** use of the lathe. **b** (in *pl.*) chips or shavings from a lathe.

turn·ing point *n.* a point at which a decisive change occurs.

tur·nip /tə́rnip/ *n.* **1** a cruciferous plant, *Brassica rapa*, with a large white globular root and sprouting leaves. **2** this root used as a vegetable. ▫▫ **tur·nip·y** *adj.*

turn·key /tə́rnkee/ *n. & adj.* • *n.* (*pl.* **-keys**) *archaic* a jailer. • *adj.* (of a contract, etc.) providing for a supply of equipment in a state ready for operation.

turn·off /tə́rnof/ *n.* **1** a turning off a main road. **2** *colloq.* something that repels or causes a loss of interest.

turn-on *n. colloq.* a person or thing that causes (esp. sexual) arousal.

turn·out /tə́rnowt/ *n.* **1** the number of people attending a meeting, voting in an election, etc. (*rain reduced the turnout*). **2** the quantity of goods produced in a given time. **3** a set or display of equipment, clothes, etc. **4 a** a railroad siding. **b** a place where a highway widens so cars may park, pass, etc.

turn·o·ver /tə́rnōvər/ *n.* **1** the act or an instance of turning over. **2** the amount of money taken in a business. **3** the number of people entering and leaving employment, etc. **4** a small pastry made by folding a piece of pastry crust over a filling. **5** a change in a business' goods as items are sold, new merchandise arrives, etc.

turn·pike /tə́rnpīk/ *n.* **1** a highway, esp. one on which a toll is charged. **2** *hist.* **a** a tollgate. **b** a road on which a toll was collected at a tollgate. **3** *hist.* a defensive frame of spikes.

turn sig·nal *n.* any of the flashing lights on the front or back of an automobile that are activated by a driver to indicate that the vehicle is about to turn or change lanes.

turn·stile /tə́rnstīl/ *n.* a gate for admission or exit, with revolving arms allowing people through singly.

turn·stone /tə́rnstōn/ *n.* any wading bird of the genus *Arenaria*, related to the plover, that looks under stones for small animals to eat.

turn·ta·ble /tə́rntaybəl/ *n.* **1** a circular revolving plate supporting a phonograph record that is being played. **2** a circular revolving platform for turning a railroad locomotive or other vehicle.

tur·pen·tine /tə́rpəntīn/ *n.* an oleoresin secreted by several trees, esp. of the genus *Pinus*, *Pistacia*, *Syncarpia*, or *Copaifera*, and used in various commercial preparations.

tur·pi·tude /tə́rpitōōd, –tyōōd/ *n. formal* baseness; depravity; wickedness.

turps /tərps/ *n. colloq.* oil of turpentine.

tur·quoise /tə́rkwoyz, –koyz/ *n. & adj.* • *n.* **1** a semiprecious stone, usu. opaque and greenish blue or blue, consisting of hydrated copper aluminum phosphate. **2** a greenish blue color. • *adj.* of this color.

tur·ret /tə́rit, túr–/ *n.* **1** a small tower, usu. projecting from the wall of a building as a decorative addition. **2** a low flat usu. revolving armored tower for a gun and gunners in a ship, aircraft, fort, or tank. ▫▫ **tur·ret·ed** *adj.*

tur·tle /tə́rt'l/ *n.* **1** any of various terrestrial, marine, or freshwater reptiles of the order *Chelonia*, encased in a shell of bony plates, and having flippers or webbed toes used in swimming. **2** the flesh of the turtle, esp. used for soup. **3** *Computing* a directional cursor in a computer graphics system for children that can be instructed to move around a screen. ▫ **turn turtle** capsize.

tur·tle·dove /tə́rt'lduv/ *n.* any wild dove of the genus *Streptopelia*, esp. *S. turtur*, noted for its soft cooing and its affection for its mate and young.

tur·tle·neck /tərt'lnek/ *n.* **1** a high close-fitting turned over collar on a garment. **2** an upper garment with such a collar.

Tus·can /túskən/ *n. & adj.* • *n.* **1** an inhabitant of Tuscany in central Italy. **2** the classical Italian language of Tuscany. • *adj.* **1** of or relating to Tuscany or the Tuscans. **2** *Archit.* denoting the least ornamented of the classical orders.

Tus·ca·ro·ra /təskərṓrə, –ráwr–/ *n.* **1 a** a N. American people native to N. Carolina and later to New York. **b** a member of this people. **2** the language of this people.

tush /tŏŏsh/ *n. sl.* the buttocks.

tusk /tusk/ *n. & v.* • *n.* **1** a long pointed tooth, esp. protruding from a closed mouth, as in the elephant, walrus, etc. **2** a tusklike tooth or other object. • *v.tr.* gore, thrust at, or tear up with a tusk or tusks. ▫▫ **tusked** *adj.* (also in *comb.*). **tusk·y** *adj.*

tus·sle /túsəl/ *n. & v.* • *n.* a struggle or scuffle. • *v.intr.* engage in a tussle.

tus·sock /túsək/ *n.* a clump of grass, etc.

tu·te·lage /tṓōt'lij, tyṓō–/ *n.* **1** guardianship. **2** the state or duration of being under this. **3** instruction.

tu·te·lar·y /tṓōt'lairee, tyṓō–/ *adj.* (also **tu·te·lar** /–t'lər/) **1 a** serving as guardian. **b** relating to a guardian (*tutelary authority*). **2** giving protection (*tutelary saint*).

tu·tor /tṓōtər, tyṓō–/ *n. & v.* • *n.* **1** a private teacher, esp. in general charge of a person's education. **2** esp. *Brit.* a university teacher supervising the studies or welfare of assigned undergraduates. **3** *Brit.* a book of instruction in a subject. • *v.* **1** *tr.* act as a tutor to. **2** *intr.* work as a tutor. **3** *tr.* restrain; discipline. **4** *intr.* receive instruction. ▫▫ **tu·tor·age** /–rij/ *n.* **tu·tor·ship** *n.*

tu·to·ri·al /tōōtáwreeəl, tyōō–/ *adj. & n.* • *adj.* of or relating to a tutor or tuition. • *n.* **1** a period of individual instruction given by a tutor. **2** *Computing* a routine that allows one to instruct oneself in using a software program. ▫▫ **tu·to·ri·al·ly** *adv.*

tut·ti /tṓōtee/ *adv. & n. Mus.* • *adv.* with all voices or instruments together. • *n.* (*pl.* **tuttis**) a passage to be performed in this way.

tut·ti-frut·ti /tṓōteefrṓōtee/ *n.* (*pl.* **-fruttis**) a confection, esp. ice cream, of or flavored with mixed fruits.

tu·tu /tṓōtōō/ *n.* a ballet dancer's short skirt of stiffened projecting frills.

tux /tuks/ *n. colloq.* = TUXEDO.

tux·e·do /tukseédō/ *n.* (*pl.* **-dos** or **-does**) **1** a man's short black formal jacket. **2** a suit of clothes including this.

TV *abbr.* **1** television. **2** transvestite

TVA *abbr.* Tennessee Valley Authority.

TVP *abbr. Trademark* textured vegetable protein (in foods made from vegetable but given a meatlike texture).

twad·dle /twód'l/ *n. & v.* • *n.* useless, senseless, or dull writing or talk. • *v.intr.* indulge in this. ▫▫ **twad·dler** *n.*

twain /twayn/ *adj. & n. archaic* two (usu. *in twain*).

twang /twang/ *n. & v.* • *n.* **1** a strong ringing sound made by the plucked string of a musical instrument or bow. **2** the nasal quality of a voice compared to this.

See page xii for the *Key to Pronunciation*.

•*v.* **1** *intr.* & *tr.* emit or cause to emit this sound. **2** *tr.* usu. *derog.* play (a tune or instrument) in this way. □□ **twang·y** *adj.*

'twas /twuz, twoz/ *archaic* it was.

tweak /tweek/ *v.* & *n.* •*v.tr.* **1** pinch and twist sharply; pull with a sharp jerk; twitch. **2** make small adjustments to (a mechanism). •*n.* an instance of tweaking.

tweed /tweed/ *n.* **1** a rough-surfaced woolen cloth, usu. of mixed colors, orig. produced in Scotland. **2** (in *pl.*) clothes made of tweed.

tweed·y /twéedee/ *adj.* (**tweedier, tweediest**) **1** of or relating to tweed cloth. **2** characteristic of the country gentry; heartily informal. □□ **tweed·i·ly** *adv.* **tweed·i·ness** *n.*

'tween /tween/ *prep. archaic* = BETWEEN.

tweet /tweet/ *n.* & *v.* •*n.* the chirp of a small bird. •*v.intr.* make a chirping noise.

tweet·er /twéetər/ *n.* a loudspeaker designed to reproduce high frequencies.

tweeze /tweez/ *v.tr.* pluck out with tweezers (*tweeze eyebrow hair*).

tweez·ers /twéezərz/ *n.pl.* a small pair of pincers for picking up small objects, plucking out hairs, etc.

twelfth /twelfth/ *n.* & *adj.* •*n.* **1** the position in a sequence corresponding to the number 12 in the sequence 1–12. **2** something occupying this position. **3** each of twelve equal parts of a thing. **4** *Mus.* **a** an interval or chord spanning an octave and a fifth in the diatonic scale. **b** a note separated from another by this interval. •*adj.* that is the twelfth. □□ **twelfth·ly** *adv.*

twelve /twelv/ *n.* & *adj.* •*n.* **1** one more than eleven; the product of two units and six units. **2** a symbol for this (12, xii, XII). **3** a size, etc., denoted by twelve. **4** the time denoted by twelve o'clock (*is it twelve yet?*). **5** (**the Twelve**) the twelve apostles. •*adj.* that amount to twelve.

twelve·fold /twélvfōld/ *adj.* & *adv.* **1** twelve times as much or as many. **2** consisting of twelve parts.

twen·ty /twéntee/ *n.* & *adj.* •*n.* (*pl.* **-ties**) **1** the product of two and ten. **2** a symbol for this (20, xx, XX). **3** (in *pl.*) the numbers from 20 to 29, esp. the years of a century or of a person's life. **4** *colloq.* a large indefinite number (*have told you twenty times*). •*adj.* that amount to twenty. □□ **twen·ti·eth** *adj.* & *n.* **twen·ty·fold** *adj.* & *adv.*

twen·ty-one *n.* the card game BLACKJACK in which players try to acquire cards with a face value totaling 21 points and no more.

twen·ty-twen·ty *adj.* (or **20/20**) **1** denoting vision of normal acuity. **2** *colloq.* denoting clear perception or hindsight.

'twere /twər/ *archaic* it were.

twerp /twərp/ *n. sl.* a stupid or objectionable person.

twice /twīs/ *adv.* **1** two times (esp. of multiplication); on two occasions. **2** in double degree or quantity (*twice as good*).

twid·dle /twíd'l/ *v.* & *n.* •*v.* **1** *tr.* & (foll. by *with*, etc.) *intr.* twirl, adjust, or play randomly or idly. **2** *intr.* move twirlingly. •*n.* **1** an act of twiddling. **2** a twirled mark or sign. □ **twiddle one's thumbs 1** make them rotate around each other. **2** have nothing to do. □□ **twid·dler** *n.* **twid·dly** *adj.*

twig[1] /twig/ *n.* a small branch or shoot of a tree or shrub. □□ **twigged** *adj.* (also in *comb.*). **twig·gy** *adj.*

twig[2] /twig/ *v.tr.* (**twigged, twigging**) *Brit. colloq.* **1** (also *absol.*) understand; grasp the meaning or nature of. **2** perceive; observe.

twi·light /twílīt/ *n.* **1** the soft glowing light from the sky when the sun is below the horizon, esp. in the evening. **2** the period of this. **3** a faint light. **4** a state of imperfect knowledge or understanding. **5** a period of decline or destruction. **6** *attrib.* of, resembling, or occurring at twilight.

twi·light zone *n.* any physical or conceptual area that is undefined or intermediate, esp. one that is eerie or unreal.

twi·lit /twílit/ *adj.* (also **twi·light·ed** /–lītid/) dimly illuminated by or as by twilight.

twill /twil/ *n.* & *v.* •*n.* a fabric so woven as to have a surface of diagonal parallel ridges. •*v.tr.* (esp. as **twilled** *adj.*) weave (fabric) in this way. □□ **twilled** *adj.*

'twill /twil/ *archaic* it will.

twin /twin/ *n., adj.,* & *v.* •*n.* **1** each of a closely related or associated pair, esp. of children or animals born at one birth. **2** the exact counterpart of a person or thing. **3** a compound crystal one part of which is in a reversed position with reference to the other. **4** (**the Twins**) the zodiacal sign or constellation Gemini. •*adj.* **1** forming, or being one of, such a pair (*twin brothers*). **2** *Bot.* growing in pairs. **3** consisting of two closely connected and similar parts. •*v.* (**twinned, twinning**) **1** *tr.* & *intr.* **a** join intimately together. **b** (foll. by *with*) pair. **2** *intr.* bear twins. **3** *intr.* grow as a twin crystal. □□ **twin·ning** *n.*

twin bed *n.* each of a pair of single beds.

twine /twīn/ *n.* & *v.* •*n.* **1** a strong thread or string of two or more strands of hemp or cotton, etc., twisted together. **2** a coil or twist. **3** a tangle; an interlacing. •*v.* **1** *tr.* form (a string or thread, etc.) by twisting strands together. **2** *tr.* form (a garland, etc.) of interwoven material. **3** *tr.* (often foll. by *with*) garland (a brow, etc.). **4** *intr.* (often foll. by *around, about*) coil or wind. **5** *intr.* & *refl.* (of a plant) grow in this way. □□ **twin·er** *n.*

twinge /twinj/ *n.* & *v.* •*n.* a sharp momentary local pain or pang (*a twinge of toothache; a twinge of conscience*). •*v.intr.* & *tr.* experience or cause to experience a twinge.

twin·kle /twíngkəl/ *v.* & *n.* •*v.* **1** *intr.* (of a star or light, etc.) shine with rapidly intermittent gleams. **2** *intr.* (of the eyes) sparkle. **3** *intr.* (of the feet in dancing) move lightly and rapidly. **4** *tr.* emit (a light or signal) in quick gleams. **5** *tr.* blink or wink (one's eyes). •*n.* **1 a** a sparkle or gleam of the eyes. **b** a blink or wink. **2** a slight flash of light; a glimmer. **3** a short rapid movement. □ **in a twinkle** (or **a twinkling** or **the twinkling of an eye**) in an instant. □□ **twin·kler** *n.* **twin·kly** *adj.*

twirl /twərl/ *v.* & *n.* •*v.tr.* & *intr.* spin or swing or twist quickly and lightly around. •*n.* **1** a twirling motion. **2** a form made by twirling, esp. a flourish made with a pen. □□ **twirl·er** *n.* **twirl·y** *adj.*

twist /twist/ *v.* & *n.* •*v.* **1 a** *tr.* change the form of by rotating one end and not the other or the two ends in opposite directions. **b** *intr.* undergo such a change; take a twisted position (*twisted around in his seat*). **c** *tr.* wrench or pull out of shape with a twisting action (*twisted my ankle*). **2** *tr.* **a** wind (strands, etc.) around each other. **b** form (a rope, etc.) by winding the strands. **c** (foll. by *with, in with*) interweave. **d** form by interweaving or twining. **3 a** *tr.* give a spiral form to (a rod, column, cord, etc.) as by rotating the ends in opposite directions. **b** *intr.* take a spiral form. **4** *tr.* (foll. by *off*) break off or separate by twisting. **5** *tr.* distort or misrepresent the meaning of (words). **6 a** *intr.* take a winding course. **b** *tr.* make (one's way) in a winding manner. **7** *tr. Brit. colloq.* cheat (*twisted me out of my allowance*). **8** *tr.* cause (the ball, esp. in billiards) to rotate while following a curved path. **9** *tr.* (as **twisted** *adj.*) (of a person or mind) emotionally unbalanced. **10** *intr.* dance the twist. •*n.* **1** the act or an instance of twisting. **2 a** a twisted state. **b** the manner or degree in which a thing is twisted. **3** a thing formed by or as by twisting, esp. a thread or rope, etc., made by winding strands together. **4** the point at which a thing twists or bends. **5** usu. *derog.* a peculiar tendency of mind or character, etc. **6 a** an unexpected development of events, esp. in a story, etc. **b** an unusual interpretation or variation. **c** a distortion or bias. **7** a fine strong silk thread used by tailors, etc. **8** a roll of bread, tobacco, etc., in the form of a twist. **9** *Brit.* a paper package with the ends twisted shut. **10** a curled piece of lemon, etc., peel to flavor a drink. **11** a spinning motion given to a ball in throwing, etc., to make it curve. **12 a** a twisting strain. **b** the amount of twisting of a rod, etc., or the angle showing this. **c** forward motion combined with rotation about an axis. **13** *Brit.* a drink made of two ingredients mixed together. **14** (prec. by *the*) a dance with a twisting movement of the body, popular in the 1960s. □ **twist a person's arm** *colloq.* persuade someone to do something that they might be reluctant to do. **twist around one's finger** see FINGER. □□ **twist·a·ble** *adj.* **twist·y** *adj.* (**twistier, twistiest**).

twist·er /twístər/ *n. colloq.* a tornado, waterspout, etc.

twit[1] /twit/ *n. sl.* a silly or foolish person.

twit[2] /twit/ *v.tr.* (**twitted, twitting**) reproach or taunt, usu. good-humoredly.

twitch /twich/ *v. & n.* • *v.* **1** *intr.* (of the features, muscles, limbs, etc.) move or contract spasmodically. **2** *tr.* give a short sharp pull at. • *n.* **1** a sudden involuntary contraction or movement. **2** a sudden pull or jerk. **3** *colloq.* a state of nervousness. **4** a noose and stick for controlling a horse during a veterinary operation. □□ **twitch·y** *adj.* (**twitchier, twitchiest**) (in sense 3 of *n.*).

twit·ter /twítər/ *v. & n.* • *v.* **1** *intr.* (of or like a bird) emit a succession of light tremulous sounds. **2** *tr.* utter or express in this way. • *n.* **1** the act or an instance of twittering. **2** *colloq.* a tremulously excited state. □□ **twit·ter·er** *n.* **twit·ter·y** *adj.*

'twixt /twikst/ *prep. archaic* = BETWIXT.

two /to͞o/ *n. & adj.* • *n.* **1** one more than one; the sum of one unit and another unit. **2** a symbol for this (2, ii, II). **3** a size, etc., denoted by two. **4** the time of two o'clock (*is it two yet?*). **5** a set of two. **6** a card with two pips. **7** a two-dollar bill. • *adj.* that amount to two. □ **in two** in or into two pieces. **in two shakes** see SHAKE. **or two** denoting several (*a thing or two* = several things). **put two and two together** make (esp. an obvious) inference from what is known or evident. **that makes two of us** *colloq.* that is true of me also. **two by two** (or **two and two**) in pairs. **two can play at that game** *colloq.* another person's behavior can be copied to that person's disadvantage.

two-bit *adj. colloq.* cheap; petty.

two-by-four *n.* a length of lumber with a rectangular cross section nominally 2 in. by 4 in.

two-di·men·sion·al *adj.* **1** having or appearing to have length and breadth but no depth. **2** lacking depth or substance; superficial.

two-faced *adj.* **1** having two faces. **2** insincere; deceitful.

two·fold /to͞ofōld/ *adj. & adv.* **1** twice as much or as many. **2** consisting of two parts.

two-hand·ed *adj.* **1** having, using, or requiring the use of two hands. **2** (of a card game) for two players.

two·pence /túpəns/ *n. Brit.* **1** the sum of two pence, esp. before decimalization. **2** *colloq.* (esp. with *neg.*) a thing of little value (*don't care twopence*).

two·pen·ny /túpənee/ *adj. Brit.* **1** costing two pence, esp. before decimalization. **2** *colloq.* cheap; worthless.

two-ply *adj. & n.* • *adj.* of two strands, webs, or thicknesses. • *n.* **1** two-ply wool. **2** two-ply wood made by gluing together two layers with the grain in different directions.

two·some /to͞osəm/ *n.* **1** two persons together. **2** a game, dance, etc., for two persons.

two-step *n.* a dance with a sliding step in march or polka time.

two-stroke *adj.* (also **two-cy·cle**) (of an internal combustion engine) having its power cycle completed in one up-and-down movement of the piston.

two-time *v.tr. colloq.* **1** deceive or be unfaithful to (esp. a partner or lover). **2** swindle; double-cross. □□ **two-tim·er** *adj.*

two-tone *n.* having two colors or sounds.

'twould /two͝od/ *archaic* it would.

two-way *adj.* **1** involving two ways or participants. **2** (of a switch) permitting a current to be switched on or off from either of two points. **3** (of a radio) capable of transmitting and receiving signals. **4** (of a faucet, etc.) permitting fluid, etc., to flow in either of two channels or directions. **5** (of traffic, etc.) moving in two esp. opposite directions.

two-way mir·ror *n.* a panel of glass that can be seen through from one side and is a mirror on the other.

TX *abbr.* Texas (in official postal use).

ty·coon /tīko͞on/ *n.* **1** a business magnate. **2** *hist.* a title applied by foreigners to the shogun of Japan 1854–68.

ty·ing *pres. part.* of TIE.

tyke /tīk/ *n.* (also **tike**) a small child.

tym·pa·na *pl.* of TYMPANUM.

tym·pa·ni var. of TIMPANI.

tym·pan·ic /timpánik/ *adj.* **1** *Anat.* of, relating to, or having a tympanum. **2** resembling or acting like a drumhead.

tym·pan·ic mem·brane *n. Anat.* the membrane separating the outer ear and middle ear and transmitting vibrations resulting from sound waves to the inner ear.

tym·pa·num /tímpənəm/ *n.* (*pl.* **tympanums** or **tympana** /–nə/) **1** *Anat.* **a** the middle ear. **b** the tympanic membrane. **2** *Zool.* the membrane covering the hearing organ on the leg of an insect. **3** *Archit.* **a** a vertical triangular space forming the center of a pediment. **b** a similar space over a door between the lintel and the arch; a carving on this space.

type /tīp/ *n. & v.* • *n.* **1 a** a class of things or persons having common characteristics. **b** a kind or sort (*would like a different type of car*). **2** a person, thing, or event serving as an illustration, symbol, or characteristic specimen of another, or of a class. **3** (in *comb.*) made of, resembling, or functioning as (*ceramic-type material; Cheddar-type cheese*). **4** *colloq.* a person, esp. of a specified character (*is rather a quiet type; is not really my type*). **5** an object, conception, or work of art serving as a model for subsequent artists. **6** *Printing* **a** printed characters or letters. **b** a piece of metal, etc., with a raised letter or character on its upper surface, for use in letterpress printing. **c** such pieces collectively. **d** a kind or size of such pieces (*printed in large type*). **e** printed characters produced by type. **7** a device on either side of a medal or coin. **8** *Biol.* an organism having or chosen as having the essential characteristics of its group and giving its name to the next highest group. • *v.* **1** *tr.* be a type or example of. **2** *tr. & intr.* write with a typewriter or keyboard. **3** *tr.* esp. *Biol.* & Med. assign to a type; classify. **4** *tr.* = TYPECAST. □□ **typ·al** *adj.*

a	**a**	*a*
roman	boldface	italic

type

type·cast /típkast/ *v.tr.* (*past* and *past part.* **-cast**) assign (an actor or actress) repeatedly to the same type of role.

See page xii for the *Key to Pronunciation*.

type•face /típfays/ *n. Printing* **1** a set of type or characters in a particular design. **2** the inked part of type, or the impression made by this.

type•set•ter /típsetər/ *n. Printing* **1** a person who composes type. **2** a composing machine. ▫▫ **type•set•ting** *n.*

type•write /típrīt/ *v.tr. & intr.* (*past* **-wrote**; *past part.* **-written**) = TYPE *v.* 2.

type•writ•er /típrītər/ *n.* a machine with keys for producing printlike characters one at a time on paper inserted around a roller.

type•writ•ten /típrit'n/ *adj.* produced with a typewriter.

ty•phoid /tífoyd/ *n.* **1** (in full **typhoid fever**) an infectious bacterial fever with an eruption of red spots on the chest and abdomen and severe intestinal irritation. **2** a similar disease of animals. ▫▫ **ty•phoi•dal** *adj.*

ty•phoon /tīfo͞on/ *n.* a violent hurricane in E. Asia. ▫▫ **ty•phon•ic** /–fónik/ *adj.*

ty•phus /tífəs/ *n.* an infectious fever caused by rickettsiae, characterized by a purple rash, headaches, fever, and usu. delirium. ▫▫ **ty•phous** *adj.*

typ•i•cal /típikəl/ *adj.* **1** serving as a characteristic example; representative. **2** characteristic of or serving to distinguish a type. **3** (often foll. by *of*) conforming to expected behavior, attitudes, etc. (*is typical of them to forget*). **4** symbolic. ▫▫ **typ•i•cal•i•ty** /–kálitee/ *n.* **typ•i•cal•ly** *adv.*

typ•i•fy /típifī/ *v.tr.* (**-fies, -fied**) **1** be a representative example of; embody the characteristics of. **2** represent by a type or symbol; serve as a type, figure, or emblem of; symbolize. ▫▫ **typ•i•fi•ca•tion** /–fikáyshən/ *n.* **typ•i•fi•er** *n.*

typ•ist /típist/ *n.* a person who types at a typewriter or keyboard.

ty•po /típō/ *n.* (*pl.* **-pos**) *colloq.* **1** a typographical error. **2** a typographer.

ty•pog•ra•pher /tīpógrəfər/ *n.* a person skilled in typography.

ty•pog•ra•phy /tīpógrəfee/ *n.* **1** printing as an art. **2** the style and appearance of printed matter. ▫▫ **ty•po•graph•ic** /–pəgráfik/ *adj.* **ty•po•graph•i•cal** *adj.* **ty•po•graph•i•cal•ly** *adv.*

ty•ran•ni•cal /tiránikəl/ *adj.* **1** acting like a tyrant; imperious; arbitrary. **2** given to or characteristic of tyranny. ▫▫ **ty•ran•ni•cal•ly** *adv.*

tyr•an•nize /tírənīz/ *v.tr. &* (foll. by *over*) *intr.* behave like a tyrant toward; rule or treat despotically or cruelly.

ty•ran•no•sau•rus /tiránəsáwrəs/ *n.* (also **ty•ran•no•saur**) any bipedal carnivorous dinosaur of the genus *Tyrannosaurus*, esp. *T. rex* having powerful hind legs, small clawlike front legs, and a long well-developed tail.

tyr•an•ny /tíranee/ *n.* (*pl.* **-nies**) **1** the cruel and arbitrary use of authority. **2** a tyrannical act; tyrannical behavior. **3 a** rule by a tyrant. **b** a period of this. **c** a nation ruled by a tyrant. ▫▫ **tyr•an•nous** /–rənəs/ *adj.* **tyr•an•nous•ly** *adv.*

ty•rant /tírənt/ *n.* **1** an oppressive or cruel ruler. **2** a person exercising power arbitrarily or cruelly.

ty•ro /tírō/ *n.* (*pl.* **-ros**) a beginner or novice.

Ty•ro•le•an /tirṓleeən, tī–/ *adj.* of or characteristic of the Tyrol, an Alpine province of Austria. ▫▫ **Ty•ro•lese** *adj.* & *n.*

U

U[1] /yoō/ *n.* (also **u**) (*pl.* **Us** or **U's**) **1** the twenty-first letter of the alphabet. **2** a U-shaped object or curve (esp. in *comb.*: *U-bolt*).

U[2] *symb. Chem.* the element uranium.

U[3] *abbr.* (also **U.**) university.

u·bi·e·ty /yoōbíətee/ *n.* the fact or condition of being in a definite place; local relation.

u·biq·ui·tous /yoōbíkwitəs/ *adj.* **1** present everywhere or in several places simultaneously. **2** often encountered. ▫▫ **u·biq·ui·tous·ly** *adv.* **u·biq·ui·tous·ness** *n.* **u·biq·ui·ty** *n.*

U-boat /yoōbōt/ *n. hist.* a German submarine.

ud·der /údər/ *n.* the mammary gland of cattle, sheep, etc., hanging as a baglike organ with several teats. ▫▫ **ud·dered** *adj.* (also in *comb.*).

UFO /yoō-ef-ó, yoōfō/ *n.* (also **ufo**) (*pl.* **UFOs** or **ufos**) unidentified flying object.

u·fol·o·gy /yoōfóləjee/ *n.* the study of UFOs. ▫▫ **u·fol·o·gist** *n.*

ugh /əkh, ug, ukh/ *int.* **1** expressing disgust or horror. **2** the sound of a cough or grunt.

Ug·li /úglee/ *n.* (*pl.* **Uglis** or **Uglies**) *Trademark* a mottled green and yellow citrus fruit, a hybrid of a grapefruit and tangerine.

ug·ly /úglee/ *adj.* (**uglier, ugliest**) **1** unpleasing or repulsive to see or hear (*an ugly scar*; *spoke with an ugly snarl*). **2** unpleasantly suggestive; discreditable (*ugly rumors are about*). **3** threatening; dangerous (*the sky has an ugly look*; *an ugly mood*). **4** morally repulsive; vile (*ugly vices*). ▫▫ **ug·li·ly** *adv.* **ug·li·ness** *n.*

ug·ly duck·ling *n.* a person who turns out to be beautiful or talented, etc., against all expectations (with ref. to a cygnet in a brood of ducks in a tale by Andersen).

UHF *abbr.* ultrahigh frequency.

uh-huh /uhú/ *int. colloq.* expressing assent.

UHT *abbr.* **1** ultrahigh temperature. **2** ultra-heat-treated (esp. of milk, for long keeping).

UK *abbr.* United Kingdom.

u·kase /yoōkáys, –káyz/ *n.* **1** an arbitrary command. **2** *hist.* an edict of the czarist Russian government.

U·krain·i·an /yoōkráyneeən/ *n. & adj.* •*n.* **1** a native of Ukraine. **2** the language of Ukraine. •*adj.* of or relating to Ukraine or its people or language.

u·ku·le·le /yoōkəláylee/ *n.* a small, four-stringed Hawaiian (orig. Portuguese) guitar.

ul·cer /úlsər/ *n.* **1** an open sore on an external or internal surface of the body, often forming pus. **2 a** a moral blemish. **b** a corroding or corrupting influence, etc. ▫▫ **ul·cered** *adj.* **ul·cer·ous** *adj.*

ul·cer·ate /úlsərayt/ *v.tr. & intr.* form into or affect with an ulcer. ▫▫ **ul·cer·a·ble** *adj.* **ul·cer·a·tion** /–ráyshən/ *n.* **ul·cer·a·tive** *adj.*

ul·na /úlnə/ *n.* (*pl.* **ulnae** /–nee/) **1** the thinner and longer bone in the forearm, on the side opposite to the thumb (cf. RADIUS 3). **2** *Zool.* a corresponding bone in an animal's foreleg or a bird's wing. ▫▫ **ul·nar** *adj.*

ul·ster /úlstər/ *n.* a man's long, loose overcoat of rough cloth.

ult. *abbr.* **1** ultimo. **2** ultimate.

ul·te·ri·or /ultéereeər/ *adj.* **1** existing in the background, or beyond what is evident or admitted; hidden; secret (esp. *ulterior motive*). **2** situated beyond. **3** more remote; not immediate; in the future. ▫▫ **ul·te·ri·or·ly** *adv.*

ul·ti·ma·ta *pl.* of ULTIMATUM.

ul·ti·mate /últimət/ *adj. & n.* •*adj.* **1** last; final. **2** beyond which no other exists or is possible (*the ultimate analysis*). **3** fundamental; primary; unanalyzable (*ultimate truths*). **4** maximum (*ultimate tensile strength*). •*n.* **1** (prec. by *the*) the best achievable or imaginable. **2** a final or fundamental fact or principle. ▫▫ **ul·ti·mate·ly** *adj.* **ul·ti·mate·ness** *n.*

ul·ti·ma·tum /últimáytəm/ *n.* (*pl.* **ultimatums** or **ultimata** /–tə/) a final demand or statement of terms by one party, the rejection of which by another could cause a breakdown in relations, war, or an end of cooperation, etc.

ul·ti·mo /últimō/ *adj. Commerce* of last month (*the 28th ultimo*).

ul·tra /últrə/ *adj. & n.* •*adj.* favoring extreme views or measures, esp. in religion or politics. •*n.* an extremist.

ultra- /últrə/ *comb. form* **1** beyond; on the other side of. **2** extreme(ly), excessive(ly) (*ultraconservative*; *ultramodern*).

ul·tra·high /últrəhí/ *adj.* **1** (of a frequency) in the range 300 to 3,000 megahertz. **2** extremely high (*ultrahigh prices*; *ultrahigh suspension bridge*).

ul·tra·ist /últrəist/ *n.* the holder of extreme positions in politics, religion, etc. ▫▫ **ul·tra·ism** *n.*

ul·tra·light /últrəlīt/ *n.* a kind of motorized hang glider.

ul·tra·ma·rine /últrəmərēen/ *n. & adj.* •*n.* **1 a** a brilliant blue pigment orig. obtained from lapis lazuli. **b** an imitation of this from powdered fired clay, sodium carbonate, sulfur, and resin. **2** the color of this. •*adj.* of this color.

ul·tra·mon·tane /últrəmontáyn/ *adj. & n.* •*adj.* **1** situated on the other side of the mountains (esp. the Alps) from the point of view of the speaker. **2** advocating supreme papal authority in matters of faith and discipline. •*n.* **1** a person living on the other side of the mountains (esp. the Alps). **2** a person advocating supreme papal authority.

ul·tra·son·ic /últrəsónik/ *adj.* of or involving sound waves with a frequency above the upper limit of human hearing. ▫▫ **ul·tra·son·i·cal·ly** *adv.*

ul·tra·son·ics /últrəsóniks/ *n.pl.* (usu. treated as *sing.*) the science and application of ultrasonic waves.

ul·tra·sound /últrəsownd/ *n.* **1** sound having an ultrasonic frequency. **2** ultrasonic waves.

ul·tra·struc·ture /últrəstrukchər/ *n. Biol.* fine structure not visible with an optical microscope.

ul·tra·vi·o·let /últrəvíələt/ *adj. Physics* **1** having a wavelength (just) beyond the violet end of the visible spectrum. **2** of or using such radiation.

u·lu /óōloō/ *n.* a short-handled knife with a broad crescent-shaped blade, usu. used by Eskimo women.

ul·u·late /úlyəlayt, yóōl–/ *v.intr.* howl; wail. ▫▫ **ul·u·lant** *adj.* **ul·u·la·tion** /–láyshən/ *n.*

um /um, əm/ *int.* expressing hesitation or a pause in speech.

um·bel /úmbəl/ *n. Bot.* a flower cluster in which stalks nearly equal in length spring from a common center and form a flat or curved surface, as in parsley. ◻◻ **um·bel·lar** *adj.* **um·bel·late** /–bəlit, –layt, umbélit/ *adj.* **um·bel·lule** /úmbəlyo͞ol, –bélyo͞ol/ *adj.*

um·bel·lif·er /umbélifər/ *n.* any plant of the family Umbelliferae bearing umbels, including parsley and parsnip. ◻◻ **um·bel·lif·er·ous** /–bəlífərəs/ *adj.*

um·ber /úmbər/ *n. & adj.* • *n.* **1** a natural pigment like ocher but darker and browner. **2** the color of this. • *adj.* **1** of this color. **2** dark; dusky.

um·bil·i·cal /umbílikəl/ *adj.* **1** of, situated near, or affecting the navel. **2** centrally placed.

um·bil·i·cal cord *n.* **1** a flexible, cordlike structure attaching a fetus to the placenta. **2** *Astronaut.* a supply cable linking a missile to its launcher, or an astronaut in space to a spacecraft.

um·bil·i·cus /umbílikəs/ *n.* (*pl.* **umbilici** /–bílisī/ or **umbilicuses**) **1** *Anat.* the navel. **2** *Bot. & Zool.* a navel-like formation.

um·bra /úmbrə/ *n.* (*pl.* **umbras** or **umbrae** /–bree/) *Astron.* **1** a total shadow usu. cast on the earth by the moon during a solar eclipse. **2** the dark central part of a sunspot (cf. PENUMBRA). ◻◻ **um·bral** *adj.*

um·brage /úmbrij/ *n.* **1** offense; a sense of slight or injury (esp. give or take umbrage at). **2** *archaic* **a** shade. **b** what gives shade.

um·brel·la /umbrélə/ *n.* **1** a light, portable device for protection against rain, strong sun, etc., consisting of a usu. circular canopy of cloth mounted by means of a collapsible metal frame on a central stick. **2** protection or patronage. **3** (often *attrib.*) a coordinating or unifying agency (*umbrella organization*). **4** a screen of fighter aircraft or a curtain of fire put up as a protection against enemy aircraft. **5** *Zool.* the gelatinous disk of a jellyfish, etc., which it contracts and expands to move through the water. ◻◻ **um·brel·laed** /–ləd/ *adj.* **um·brel·la·like** *adj.*

u·mi·ak /o͞omeeak/ *n.* an Inuit skin-and-wood open boat propelled with paddles.

um·laut /o͝omlowt/ *n.* **1** a mark (¨) used over a vowel, esp. in Germanic languages, to indicate a vowel change. **2** such a vowel change, e.g., German *Mann, Männer*, English *man, men*, due to *i, j*, etc. (now usu. lost or altered) in the following syllable.

ump /ump/ *n. colloq.* an umpire.

um·pire /úmpīr/ *n. & v.* • *n.* **1** a person chosen to enforce the rules and settle disputes in various sports. **2** a person chosen to arbitrate between disputants, or to see fair play. • *v.* **1** *intr.* (usu. foll. by *for, in*, etc.) act as umpire. **2** *tr.* act as umpire in (a game, etc.). ◻◻ **um·pir·age** /–pīrij, –pərij/ *n.* **um·pire·ship** *n.*

ump·teen /úmptéen/ *adj. & pron. sl.* • *adj.* indefinitely many; a lot of. • *pron.* indefinitely many. ◻◻ **ump·teenth** *adj.*

UN *abbr.* United Nations.

un-[1] /un/ *prefix* **1** added to adjectives and participles and their derivative nouns and adverbs, meaning: **a** not: denoting the absence of a quality or state (*unusable; unhappiness*). **b** reverse of, usu. with an implication of approval or disapproval (*unselfish; unscientific*). **2** (less often) added to nouns, meaning 'a lack of' (*unrest; untruth*).

un-[2] /un/ *prefix* added to verbs and (less often) nouns, forming verbs denoting: **1** reversal or cancellation of an action or state (*undress; unsettle*). **2** deprivation or separation (*unmask*). **3** release from (*unburden*). **4** causing to be no longer (*unman*).

'un /ən/ *pron. colloq.* one (*that's a good 'un*).

un·a·bat·ed /únəbáytid/ *adj.* not abated; undiminished. ◻◻ **un·a·bat·ed·ly** *adv.*

un·a·bridged /únəbríjd/ *adj.* (of a text, etc.) complete; not abridged.

un·ac·com·pa·nied /únəkúmpəneed/ *adj.* **1** not accompanied. **2** *Mus.* without accompaniment.

un·ac·com·plished /únəkómplisht/ *adj.* **1** not accomplished; uncompleted. **2** lacking accomplishments.

un·ac·count·a·ble /únəkówntəbəl/ *adj.* **1** unable to be explained. **2** unpredictable or strange in behavior. **3** not responsible. ◻◻ **un·ac·count·a·bil·i·ty** /–bílitee/ *n.* **un·ac·count·a·ble·ness** *n.* **un·ac·count·a·bly** *adv.*

un·ac·count·ed /únəkówntid/ *adj.* of which no account is given. ◻ **unaccounted for** unexplained; not included in an account.

un·ac·cus·tomed /únəkústəmd/ *adj.* **1** (usu. foll. by *to*) not accustomed. **2** not customary; unusual (*his unaccustomed silence*). ◻◻ **un·ac·cus·tomed·ly** *adv.*

un·a·dul·ter·at·ed /únədúltəraytid/ *adj.* **1** not adulterated; pure; concentrated. **2** sheer; complete; utter (*unadulterated nonsense*).

un·ad·vised /únədvízd/ *adj.* **1** indiscreet; rash. **2** not having had advice. ◻◻ **un·ad·vis·ed·ly** /–zidlee/ *adv.* **un·ad·vis·ed·ness** *n.*

un·af·fect·ed /únəféktid/ *adj.* **1** (usu. foll. by *by*) not affected. **2** free from affectation; genuine; sincere. **3** unaffected by; impervious to; immune to. ◻◻ **un·af·fect·ed·ly** *adv.* **un·af·fect·ed·ness** *n.*

un·al·ien·a·ble /únáyleeənəbəl/ *adj. Law* = INALIENABLE.

un·al·loyed /únəlóyd, únál–/ *adj.* **1** not alloyed; pure. **2** complete; utter (*unalloyed joy*).

un-A·mer·i·can /únəmérikən/ *adj.* **1** not in accordance with American characteristics, etc. **2** contrary to the interests of the US; (in the US) treasonable. ◻◻ **un-A·mer·i·can·ism** *n.*

u·nan·i·mous /yo͞onánimәs/ *adj.* **1** all in agreement (*the committee was unanimous*). **2** (of an opinion, vote, etc.) held or given by general consent (*the unanimous choice*). ◻◻ **u·na·nim·i·ty** /–nənímitee/ *n.* **u·nan·i·mous·ly** *adv.* **u·nan·i·mous·ness** *n.*

un·an·swer·a·ble /únánsərəbəl/ *adj.* **1** unable to be refuted (*has an unanswerable case*). **2** unable to be answered (*an unanswerable question*). ◻◻ **un·an·swer·a·ble·ness** *n.* **un·an·swer·a·bly** *adv.*

un·ap·proach·a·ble /únəpróchəbəl/ *adj.* **1** not approachable; remote; inaccessible. **2** (of a person) unfriendly. ◻◻ **un·ap·proach·a·bil·i·ty** *n.* **un·ap·proach·a·ble·ness** *n.* **un·ap·proach·a·bly** *adv.*

un·apt /únápt/ *adj.* **1** (usu. foll. by *for*) not suitable. **2** (usu. foll. by *to* + infin.) not apt. ◻◻ **un·apt·ly** *adv.* **un·apt·ness** *n.*

un·ar·gu·a·ble /únaárgyo͞oəbəl/ *adj.* not arguable; certain.

un·armed /únaármd/ *adj.* not armed; without weapons.

un·ar·rest·ing /únəréstinq/ *adj.* uninteresting; dull. ◻◻ **un·ar·rest·ing·ly** *adv.*

un·ar·tis·tic /únaartístik/ *adj.* not artistic, esp. not concerned with art. ◻◻ **un·ar·tis·ti·cal·ly** *adv.*

un·a·shamed /únəsháymd/ *adj.* **1** feeling no guilt, shameless. **2** blatant; bold. ◻◻ **un·a·sham·ed·ly** /–midlee/ *adv.* **un·a·sham·ed·ness** /–midnis/ *n.*

un·as·sail·a·ble /únəsáyləbəl/ *adj.* unable to be attacked or questioned; impregnable. ◻◻ **un·as·sail·a·bil·i·ty** /–bílitee/ *n.* **un·as·sail·a·ble·ness** *n.* **un·as·sail·a·bly** *adv.*

un·as·sum·ing /únəso͞oming/ *adj.* not pretentious or arrogant; modest. ◻◻ **un·as·sum·ing·ly** *adv.* **un·as·sum·ing·ness** *n.*

un·at·tached /únətácht/ *adj.* **1** (often foll. by *to*) not attached, esp. to a particular body, organization, etc. **2** not engaged or married.

un·at·tend·ed /únəténdid/ *adj.* **1** (usu. foll. by *to*) not attended. **2** (of a person, vehicle, etc.) not accompanied; alone; uncared for.

un·at·trib·ut·a·ble /únətríbyətəbəl/ *adj.* (esp. of information) that cannot or may not be attributed to a source, etc. ◻◻ **un·at·trib·ut·a·bly** *adv.*

un·at·trib·ut·ed /únətríbyətəd/ *adj.* (of a painting, quotation, etc.) not attributed to a source, etc.

un·a·void·a·ble /únəvóydəbəl/ *adj.* not avoidable; inevitable. ▫▫ **un·a·void·a·bil·i·ty** *n.* **un·a·void·a·ble·ness** *n.* **un·a·void·a·bly** *adv.*

un·a·ware /únəwáir/ *adj. & adv.* •*adj.* **1** (usu. foll. by *of*, or *that* + clause) not aware; ignorant (*unaware of her presence*). **2** (of a person) insensitive; unperceptive. •*adv.* = UNAWARES. ▫▫ **un·a·ware·ness** *n.*

un·a·wares /únəwáirz/ *adv.* **1** unexpectedly (*met them unawares*). **2** inadvertently (*dropped it unawares*).

un·bal·ance /únbáləns/ *v. & n.* •*v.tr.* **1** upset the physical or mental balance of (*unbalanced by the blow*; *the shock unbalanced him*). **2** (as **unbalanced** *adj.*) **a** not balanced. **b** (of a mind or a person) unstable or deranged. •*n.* lack of balance; instability, esp. mental.

un·bear·a·ble /únbáirəbəl/ *adj.* not bearable. ▫▫ **un·bear·a·ble·ness** *n.* **un·bear·a·bly** *adv.*

un·beat·a·ble /únbeétəbəl/ *adj.* not beatable; excelling.

un·beat·en /únbeét'n/ *adj.* **1** not beaten. **2** (of a record, etc.) not surpassed.

un·be·com·ing /únbikúming/ *adj.* **1** (esp. of clothing) not flattering or suiting a person. **2** (usu. foll. by *to*, *for*) not fitting; indecorous or unsuitable. ▫▫ **un·be·com·ing·ly** *adv.* **un·be·com·ing·ness** *n.*

un·be·known /únbinṓn/ *adj.* (also **un·be·knownst** /–nṓnst/) (foll. by *to*) without the knowledge of (*was there all the time unbeknown to us*).

un·be·lief /únbileéf/ *n.* the state of not believing, esp. in religious matters. ▫▫ **un·be·liev·er** *n.* **un·be·liev·ing** *adj.* **un·be·liev·ing·ly** *adv.* **un·be·liev·ing·ness** *n.*

un·be·liev·a·ble /únbileévəbəl/ *adj.* not believable; incredible. ▫▫ **un·be·liev·a·bil·i·ty** *n.* **un·be·liev·a·ble·ness** *n.* **un·be·liev·a·bly** *adv.*

un·bend /únbénd/ *v.* (*past* and *past part.* **unbent**) **1** *tr. & intr.* change from a bent position; straighten. **2** *intr.* relax from strain or severity; become affable.

un·bend·ing /únbénding/ *adj.* **1** not bending; inflexible. **2** firm; austere (*unbending rectitude*). **3** relaxing from strain, activity, or formality. ▫▫ **un·bend·ing·ly** *adv.* **un·bend·ing·ness** *n.*

un·bi·ased /únbíəst/ *adj.* not biased; impartial.

un·blink·ing /únblíngking/ *adj.* **1** not blinking. **2** steadfast; not hesitating. **3** stolid; cool. ▫▫ **un·blink·ing·ly** *adv.*

un·block /únblók/ *v.tr.* **1** remove an obstruction from (esp. a pipe, drain, etc.). **2** (also *absol.*) *Cards* allow the later unobstructed play of (a suit) by playing a high card.

un·bolt /únbṓlt/ *v.tr.* release (a door, etc.) by drawing back the bolt.

un·born /únbáwrn/ *adj.* **1** not yet born (*an unborn child*). **2** never to be brought into being (*unborn hopes*).

un·bos·om /únbŏŏzəm/ *v.tr.* **1** disclose (thoughts, secrets, etc.). **2** (*refl.*) unburden (oneself) of one's thoughts, secrets, etc.

un·bound /únbównd/ *adj.* **1** not bound or tied up. **2** unconstrained. **3 a** (of a book) not having a binding. **b** having paper covers. **4** (of a substance or particle) in a loose or free state.

un·bound·ed /únbówndid/ *adj.* not bounded; infinite (*unbounded optimism*). ▫▫ **un·bound·ed·ly** *adv.* **un·bound·ed·ness** *n.*

un·bri·dle /únbríd'l/ *v.tr.* **1** remove a bridle from (a horse). **2** remove constraints from (one's tongue, a person, etc.). **3** (as **unbridled** *adj.*) unconstrained (*unbridled insolence*).

un·bro·ken /únbrṓkən/ *adj.* **1** not broken. **2** not tamed (*an unbroken horse*). **3** not interrupted (*unbroken sleep*). **4** not surpassed (*an unbroken record*). ▫▫ **un·bro·ken·ly** *adv.* **un·bro·ken·ness** /–ən-nis/ *n.*

un·buck·le /únbúkəl/ *v.tr.* release the buckle of (a strap, shoe, etc.).

un·bur·den /únbúrd'n/ *v.tr.* **1** relieve of a burden. **2** (esp. *refl.*; often foll. by *to*) relieve (oneself, one's conscience, etc.) by confession, etc. ▫▫ **un·bur·dened** *adj.*

un·but·ton /únbút'n/ *v.tr.* **1 a** unfasten (a coat, etc.) by taking the buttons out of the buttonholes. **b** unbutton the clothes of (a person). **2** (*absol.*) *colloq.* relax from tension or formality, become communicative. **3** (as **unbuttoned** *adj.*) **a** not buttoned. **b** *colloq.* communicative; informal.

un·called-for *adj.* (of an opinion, action, etc.) impertinent or unnecessary (*an uncalled-for remark*).

un·can·ny /únkánee/ *adj.* (**uncannier, uncanniest**) seemingly supernatural; mysterious. ▫▫ **un·can·ni·ly** *adv.* **un·can·ni·ness** *n.*

un·cap /únkáp/ *v.tr.* (**uncapped, uncapping**) remove the cap from (a jar, bottle, etc.).

un·cared-for /únkáirdfawr/ *adj.* disregarded; neglected.

un·car·ing /unkáiring/ *adj.* lacking compassion or concern for others.

un·ceas·ing /únseésing/ *adj.* not ceasing; continuous (*unceasing effort*). ▫▫ **un·ceas·ing·ly** *adv.*

un·cer·e·mo·ni·ous /únserimṓneeəs/ *adj.* **1** lacking ceremony or formality. **2** abrupt; discourteous. ▫▫ **un·cer·e·mo·ni·ous·ly** *adv.* **un·cer·e·mo·ni·ous·ness** *n.*

un·cer·tain /únsə́rt'n/ *adj.* **1** not certainly knowing or known (*uncertain what it means*; *the result is uncertain*). **2** unreliable (*his aim is uncertain*). **3** changeable; erratic (*uncertain weather*). ▫ **in no uncertain terms** clearly and forcefully. ▫▫ **un·cer·tain·ly** *adv.*

un·cer·tain·ty /únsə́rt'ntee/ *n.* (*pl.* **-ties**) **1** the fact or condition of being uncertain. **2** an uncertain matter or circumstance.

un·cer·ti·fied /únsə́rtifīd/ *adj.* **1** not attested as certain. **2** not guaranteed by a certificate of competence, etc. **3** not certified as insane.

un·chain /úncháyn/ *v.tr.* **1** remove the chains from. **2** release; liberate.

un·char·i·ta·ble /úncháritəbəl/ *adj.* censorious; severe in judgment. ▫▫ **un·char·i·ta·ble·ness** *n.* **un·char·i·ta·bly** *adv.*

un·chart·ed /únchaártid/ *adj.* not charted, mapped, or surveyed.

un·chart·ered /únchaártərd/ *adj.* **1** not furnished with a charter; not formally privileged or constituted. **2** unauthorized; illegal.

un·checked /únchékt/ *adj.* **1** not checked. **2** freely allowed; unrestrained (*unchecked violence*).

un·chris·tian /únkríschən/ *adj.* **1 a** not professing Christianity or its teachings. **b** not Christian. **2** *colloq.* outrageous. ▫▫ **un·chris·tian·ly** *adv.*

un·church /únchərch/ *v.tr.* excommunicate.

un·ci·al /únsheeəl, únshəl/ *adj. & n.* •*adj.* **1** of or written in large writing with rounded, unjoined letters found in manuscripts of the 4th–8th c., from which modern capitals are derived. **2** of or relating to an inch or an ounce. •*n.* **1** an uncial letter. **2** an uncial style or manuscript.

uncial

uncial

un·cir·cum·cised /únsə́rkəmsīzd/ *adj.* **1** not circumcised. **2** spiritually impure; heathen. ▫▫ **un·cir·cum·ci·sion** /–sízhən/ *n.*

un·civ·il /únsívil/ *adj.* **1** ill-mannered; impolite. **2** not public-spirited. ▫▫ **un·civ·il·ly** *adv.*

un·civ·i·lized /únsívilīzd/ *adj.* **1** not civilized. **2** rough; uncultured.

See page xii for the *Key to Pronunciation*.

un·clasp /únklásp/ *v.tr.* **1** loosen the clasp or clasps of. **2** release the grip of (a hand, etc.).
un·clas·si·fied /únklásifīd/ *adj.* **1** not classified. **2** (of government information) not secret.
un·cle /úngkəl/ *n.* **1 a** the brother of one's father or mother. **b** an aunt's husband. **2** *colloq.* a name given by children to a male family friend. **3** *sl.* esp. *hist.* a pawnbroker.
un·clean /únkléen/ *adj.* **1** not clean. **2** unchaste. **3** unfit to be eaten; ceremonially impure. ▫▫ **un·clean·ly** *adv.* **un·clean·ly** /–klénlee/ *adj.* **un·clean·li·ness** /–klénleenis/ *n.* **un·clean·ness** *n.*
un·clear /únkléer/ *adj.* **1** not clear or easy to understand; obscure; uncertain. **2** (of a person) doubtful; uncertain (*I'm unclear as to what you mean*). ▫▫ **un·clear·ly** *adv.* **un·clear·ness** *n.*
Un·cle Sam *n. colloq.* the federal government or citizens of the US (*will fight for Uncle Sam*).
Un·cle Tom *n. derog.* a black man considered to be servile, cringing, etc. (from the hero of H. B. Stowe's *Uncle Tom's Cabin*, 1852).
un·clog /únklóg/ *v.tr.* (**unclogged, unclogging**) unblock (a drain, pipe, etc.).
un·clothe /únklṓth/ *v.tr.* **1** remove the clothes from. **2** strip of leaves or vegetation (*trees unclothed by the wind*). **3** expose; reveal. ▫▫ **un·clothed** *adj.*
un·cloud·ed /únklówdid/ *adj.* **1** not clouded; clear; bright. **2** untroubled (*unclouded serenity*).
un·clut·tered /únklútərd/ *adj.* not cluttered; austere; simple.
un·col·ored /únkúlərd/ *adj.* **1** having no color. **2** not influenced; impartial. **3** not exaggerated.
un·com·fort·a·ble /únkúmftəbəl, –kúmfərtə–/ *adj.* **1** not comfortable. **2** uneasy; causing or feeling disquiet (*an uncomfortable silence*). ▫▫ **un·com·fort·a·ble·ness** *n.* **un·com·fort·a·bly** *adv.*
un·com·mit·ted /únkəmítid/ *adj.* **1** not committed. **2** unattached to any specific political cause or group.
un·com·mon /únkómən/ *adj. & adv.* • *adj.* **1** not common; unusual; remarkable. **2** remarkably great, etc. (*an uncommon fear of spiders*). • *adv. archaic* uncommonly (*he was uncommon fat*). ▫▫ **un·com·mon·ly** *adv.* **un·com·mon·ness** /–mən-nis/ *n.*
un·com·mu·ni·ca·tive /únkəmyóonikətiv/ *adj.* not wanting to communicate; taciturn. ▫▫ **un·com·mu·ni·ca·tive·ly** *adv.* **un·com·mu·ni·ca·tive·ness** *n.*
un·com·pro·mis·ing /únkómprəmīzing/ *adj.* unwilling to compromise; stubborn; unyielding. ▫▫ **un·com·pro·mis·ing·ly** *adv.* **un·com·pro·mis·ing·ness** *n.*
un·con·cern /únkənsə́rn/ *n.* lack of concern; indifference; apathy. ▫▫ **un·con·cerned** *adj.* **un·con·cern·ed·ly** /–nidlee/ *adv.*
un·con·di·tion·al /únkəndíshənəl/ *adj.* not subject to conditions; complete (*unconditional surrender*). ▫▫ **un·con·di·tion·al·i·ty** /–nálitee/ *n.* **un·con·di·tion·al·ly** *adv.*
un·con·di·tioned /únkəndíshənd/ *adj.* **1** not subject to conditions or to an antecedent condition. **2** (of behavior, etc.) not determined by conditioning; natural.
un·con·di·tioned re·flex *n.* an instinctive response to a stimulus.
un·con·nect·ed /únkənéktid/ *adj.* **1** not physically joined. **2** not connected or associated. **3** (of speech, etc.) disconnected; not joined in order or sequence (*unconnected ideas*). **4** not related by family ties. ▫▫ **un·con·nect·ed·ly** *adv.* **un·con·nect·ed·ness** *n.*
un·con·scion·a·ble /únkónshənəbəl/ *adj.* **1 a** having no conscience. **b** contrary to conscience. **2 a** unreasonably excessive (*an unconscionable length of time*). **b** not right or reasonable. ▫▫ **un·con·scion·a·ble·ness** *n.* **un·con·scion·a·bly** *adv.*
un·con·scious /únkónshəs/ *adj. & n.* • *adj.* not conscious (*unconscious of any change; fell unconscious on the floor; an unconscious prejudice*). • *n.* that part of the mind which is inaccessible to the conscious mind but which affects behavior, emotions, etc. ▫▫ **un·con·scious·ly** *adv.* **un·con·scious·ness** *n.*
un·con·sti·tu·tion·al /únkonstitóoshənəl, –tyóo–/ *adj.* not in accordance with the political constitution or with procedural rules. ▫▫ **un·con·sti·tu·tion·al·i·ty** /–nálitee/ *n.* **un·con·sti·tu·tion·al·ly** *adv.*
un·con·ven·tion·al /únkənvénshənəl/ *adj.* not bound by convention or custom; unusual; unorthodox. ▫▫ **un·con·ven·tion·al·ism** *n.* **un·con·ven·tion·al·i·ty** /–nálitee/ *n.* **un·con·ven·tion·al·ly** *adv.*
un·cool /únkóol/ *adj. sl.* **1** unrelaxed; unpleasant. **2** (of jazz) not cool.
un·co·or·di·nat·ed /únkō-áwrd'naytid/ *adj.* **1** not coordinated. **2** (of a person's movements, etc.) clumsy.
un·cork /únkáwrk/ *v.tr.* **1** draw the cork from (a bottle). **2** allow (feelings, etc.) to be vented.
un·cor·rob·o·rat·ed /únkəróbəraytid/ *adj.* (esp. of evidence, etc.) not corroborated.
un·count·ed /únkówntid/ *adj.* **1** not counted. **2** very many; innumerable.
un·couth /únkóoth/ *adj.* (of a person, manners, appearance, etc.) lacking in ease and polish; uncultured; rough (*uncouth voices; behavior was uncouth*). ▫▫ **un·couth·ly** *adv.* **un·couth·ness** *n.*
un·cov·er /únkúvər/ *v.* **1** *tr.* **a** remove a cover or covering from. **b** make known; disclose (*uncovered the truth at last*). **2** *intr. archaic* remove one's hat, cap, etc. **3** *tr.* (as **uncovered** *adj.*) **a** not covered by a roof, clothing, etc. **b** not wearing a hat.
un·cross /únkráws, –krós/ *v.tr.* **1** remove from a crossed position. **2** (as **uncrossed** *adj.*) **a** (of a letter or symbol, etc.) not crossed (*I recognize his writing by the uncrossed t's*). **b** not thwarted or challenged. **c** not wearing a cross.
un·crown /únkrówn/ *v.tr.* **1** deprive (a monarch, etc.) of a crown. **2** deprive (a person) of a position. **3** (as **uncrowned** *adj.*) **a** not crowned. **b** having the status but not the name of (*the uncrowned king of boxing*).
unc·tion /úngkshən/ *n.* **1 a** the act of anointing with oil, etc., as a religious rite. **b** the oil, etc., so used. **2 a** soothing words or thought. **b** excessive or insincere flattery. **3 a** the act of anointing for medical purposes. **b** an ointment so used. **4 a** a fervent or sympathetic quality in words or tone caused by or causing deep emotion. **b** a pretense of this.
unc·tu·ous /úngkchooəs/ *adj.* **1** (of behavior, speech, etc.) unpleasantly flattering; oily. **2** (esp. of minerals) having a greasy or soapy feel; oily. ▫▫ **unc·tu·ous·ly** *adv.* **unc·tu·ous·ness** *n.*
un·cul·tured /únkúlchərd/ *adj.* **1** not cultured; unrefined. **2** (of soil or plants) not cultivated.
un·cured /únkyóord/ *adj.* **1** not cured. **2** (of pork, etc.) not salted or smoked.
un·cut /únkút/ *adj.* **1** not cut. **2** (of a book) with the pages not cut open or with untrimmed margins. **3** (of a book, film, etc.) complete; uncensored. **4** (of a stone, esp. a diamond) not shaped by cutting. **5** (of fabric) having its pile loops intact.
un·de·cid·ed /úndisídid/ *adj.* **1** not settled or certain (*the question is undecided*). **2** hesitating; irresolute (*undecided about their relative merits*). ▫▫ **un·de·cid·ed·ly** *adv.*
un·de·mon·stra·tive /úndimónstrətiv/ *adj.* not expressing feelings, etc., outwardly; reserved. ▫▫ **un·de·mon·stra·tive·ly** *adv.* **un·de·mon·stra·tive·ness** *n.*
un·de·ni·a·ble /úndiníəbəl/ *adj.* **1** unable to be denied or disputed; certain. **2** excellent (*was of undeniable character*). ▫▫ **un·de·ni·a·ble·ness** *n.* **un·de·ni·a·bly** *adv.*
un·der /úndər/ *prep., adv., & adj.* • *prep.* **1 a** in or to a

position lower than; below; beneath (*fell under the table; under the left eye*). **b** within; on the inside of (a surface, etc.) (*wore a vest under his jacket*). **2 a** inferior to; less than (*a captain is under a major; is under 18*). **b** at or for a lower cost than (*was under $20*). **3 a** subject or liable to; controlled or bound by (*lives under oppression; under pain of death; born under Saturn; the country prospered under him*). **b** undergoing (*is under repair*). **c** classified or subsumed in (*that book goes under biology; goes under many names*). **4** at the foot of or sheltered by (*hid under the wall; under the cliff*). **5** planted with (a crop). **6** powered by (sail, steam, etc.). • *adv.* **1** in or to a lower position or condition (*kept him under*). **2** *colloq.* in or into a state of unconsciousness (*put her under for the operation*). • *adj.* lower (*the under jaw*). □ **under separate cover** in another envelope. **under the sun** anywhere in the world. **under way** in motion; in progress. □□ **un·der·most** *adj.*

under- /úndər/ *prefix* in senses of UNDER: **1** below; beneath (*underground*). **2** lower in status; subordinate (*undersecretary*). **3** insufficiently; incompletely (*undercook; underdeveloped*).

un·der·a·chieve /úndərəchéev/ *v.intr.* do less well than might be expected (esp. scholastically). □□ **un·der·a·chieve·ment** *n.* **un·der·a·chiev·er** *n.*

un·der·age /undəráyj/ *adj.* **1** not old enough, esp. not yet of adult status. **2** involving underage persons (*underage smoking and drinking*).

un·der·arm /úndəraarm/ *adj., adv., & n.* • *adj. & adv.* **1** *Sports* with the arm below shoulder level. **2** under the arm. **3** in the armpit. • *n.* the armpit.

un·der·bel·ly /úndərbélee/ *n.* (*pl.* **-lies**) the underside of an animal, vehicle, etc., esp. as an area vulnerable to attack.

un·der·bid *v. & n.* • *v.tr.* /úndərbíd/ (**-bidding**; *past* and *past part.* **-bid**) **1** make a lower bid than (a person). **2** (also *absol.*) *Bridge*, etc., bid less on (one's hand) than its strength warrants. • *n.* /úndərbid/ **1** such a bid. **2** the act or an instance of underbidding.

un·der·brush /úndərbrúsh/ *n.* undergrowth in a forest.

un·der·car·riage /úndərkárij/ *n.* **1** a wheeled structure beneath an aircraft, usu. retracted when not in use, to receive the impact on landing and support the aircraft on the ground, etc. **2** the supporting frame of a vehicle.

un·der·charge /úndərcháarj/ *v.tr.* **1** charge too little for (a thing) or to (a person). **2** give less than the proper charge to (a gun, an electric battery, etc.).

un·der·class /úndərklas/ *n.* a subordinate social class.

un·der·clothes /úndərklōz, –klōthz/ *n.pl.* clothes worn under others, esp. next to the skin.

un·der·cloth·ing /úndərklṓthing/ *n.* underclothes collectively.

un·der·coat /úndərkōt/ *n. & v.* • *n.* **1 a** a preliminary layer of paint under the finishing coat. **b** the paint used for this. **2** an animal's under layer of hair or down. **3** a coat worn under another. • *v.tr.* seal the underpart of (esp. a motor vehicle) against rust, etc., with an undercoat. □□ **un·der·coat·ing** *n.*

un·der·cov·er /úndərkúvər/ *adj.* (usu. *attrib.*) **1** surreptitious. **2** engaged in spying, esp. by working with or among those to be observed (*undercover agent*).

un·der·cur·rent /úndərkərənt, –kur–/ *n.* **1** a current below the surface. **2** an underlying, often contrary, feeling, activity, or influence (*an undercurrent of protest*).

un·der·cut *v. & n.* • *v.tr.* /úndərkút/ (**-cutting**; *past* and *past part.* **-cut**) **1** sell or work at a lower price or lower wages than. **2** *Golf* strike (a ball) so as to make it rise high. **3 a** cut away the part below or under (a thing). **b** cut away material to show (a carved design, etc.) in relief. **4** render unstable or less firm; undermine. • *n.* /úndərkut/ **1** a notch cut in a tree trunk to guide its fall when felled. **2** any space formed by the removal or absence of material from the lower part of something.

un·der·de·vel·oped /úndərdivéləpt/ *adj.* **1** not fully developed; immature. **2** (of a country, etc.) below its potential economic level. **3** *Photog.* not developed sufficiently to give a normal image. □□ **un·der·de·vel·op·ment** *n.*

un·der·dog /úndərdawg, –dog/ *n.* **1** a dog, or usu. a person, losing a fight. **2** a person whose loss in a contest, etc., is expected. **3** a person who is in a state of inferiority or subjection.

un·der·done /úndərdún/ *adj.* **1** not thoroughly done. **2** (of food) lightly or insufficiently cooked.

un·der·dress /úndərdrés/ *v.tr. & intr.* dress with too little formality or too lightly.

un·der·em·ployed /úndərimplóyd/ *adj.* **1** not fully employed. **2** having employment inadequate to one's abilities, education, etc. □□ **un·der·em·ploy·ment** *n.*

un·der·es·ti·mate *v. & n.* • *v.tr.* /úndəréstimayt/ form too low an estimate of. • *n.* /úndəréstimət/ an estimate that is too low. □□ **un·der·es·ti·ma·tion** /–máyshən/ *n.*

un·der·ex·pose /úndərikspṓz/ *v.tr. Photog.* expose (film) for too short a time or with insufficient light. □□ **un·der·ex·po·sure** /–pṓzhər/ *n.*

un·der·foot /úndərfŏŏt/ *adv.* **1** under one's feet. **2** on the ground. **3** in a state of subjection. **4** so as to obstruct or inconvenience.

un·der·gar·ment /úndərgaarmənt/ *n.* a piece of underclothing.

un·der·glaze /úndərglayz/ *adj. & n.* • *adj.* **1** (of painting on ceramics and pottery, etc.) done before the glaze is applied. **2** (of colors) used in such painting. • *n.* underglaze painting.

un·der·go /úndərgṓ/ *v.tr.* (*3rd sing. present* **-goes**; *past* **-went**; *past part.* **-gone**) be subjected to; suffer; endure.

un·der·grad·u·ate /úndərgrájŏŏət/ *n.* a student at a college or university who has not yet taken a degree.

un·der·ground *adv., adj., n., & v.* • *adv.* /úndərgrównd/ **1** beneath the surface of the ground. **2** in or into secrecy or hiding. • *adj.* /úndərgrownd/ **1** situated underground. **2** secret, hidden, esp. working secretly to subvert a ruling power. **3** unconventional; experimental (*underground press*). • *n.* /úndərgrownd/ **1** a secret group or activity, esp. aiming to subvert the established order. **2** *Brit.* a subway system. • *v.tr.* /úndərgrownd/ lay (cables) below ground level.

Un·der·ground Rail·road *n. US Hist.* a covert system of escape through which abolitionists helped fugitive slaves reach safe destinations, before 1863.

un·der·growth /úndərgrōth/ *n.* a dense growth of shrubs, etc., esp. under large trees.

un·der·hand *adj. & adv.* • *adj.* /úndərhand/ **1** secret; clandestine; not aboveboard. **2** deceptive; crafty. **3** *Sports* underarm. • *adv.* /úndərhánd/ in an underhand manner.

un·der·hand·ed /úndərhándid/ *adj. & adv.* = UNDERHAND.

un·der·lay[1] *v. & n.* • *v.tr.* /úndərláy/ (*past* and *past part.* **-laid**) lay something under (a thing) to support or raise it. • *n.* /úndərlay/ a thing laid under another, esp. material laid under a carpet or mattress as protection or support.

un·der·lay[2] *past* of UNDERLIE.

un·der·lie /úndərlí/ *v.tr.* (**-lying**; *past* **-lay**; *past part.* **-lain**) **1** (also *absol.*) lie or be situated under (a stratum, etc.). **2** (also *absol.*) (esp. as **underlying** *adj.*) (of a principle, reason, etc.) be the basis of (a doctrine, law, conduct, etc.). **3** exist beneath the superficial aspect of.

un·der·line *v. & n.* • *v.tr.* /úndərlín/ **1** draw a line under (a word, etc.) to give emphasis or draw attention or indicate italic or other special type. **2** emphasize; stress. • *n.* **1** a line drawn under a word, etc. **2** a caption below an illustration.

un•der•ling /úndərling/ *n.* usu. *derog.* a subordinate.

un•der•ly•ing *pres. part.* of UNDERLIE.

un•der•manned /úndərmánd/ *adj.* having too few people as crew or staff.

un•der•mine /úndərmín/ *v.tr.* **1** injure (a person, reputation, influence, etc.) by secret or insidious means. **2** weaken, injure, or wear out (health, etc.) imperceptibly or insidiously. **3** wear away the base or foundation of (*rivers undermine their banks*). □□ **un•der•min•er** *n.* **un•der•min•ing•ly** *adv.*

un•der•neath /úndərneéth/ *prep., adv., n., & adj.* • *prep.* **1** at or to a lower place than, below. **2** on the inside of, within. • *adv.* **1** at or to a lower place. **2** inside. • *n.* the lower surface or part. *adj.* lower.

un•der•nour•ished /úndərnórisht, –núr–/ *adj.* insufficiently nourished. □□ **un•der•nour•ish•ment** *n.*

un•der•paid *past* and *past part.* of UNDERPAY.

un•der•pants /úndərpants/ *n.pl.* an undergarment covering the lower part of the torso and sometimes part of the legs.

un•der•part /úndərpaart/ *n.* **1** a lower part, esp. of an animal. **2** a subordinate part in a play, etc.

un•der•pass /úndərpas/ *n.* **1** a road, etc., passing under another. **2** a crossing of this form.

un•der•pay /úndərpáy/ *v.tr.* (*past* and *past part.* **-paid**) pay too little to (a person) or for (a thing). □□ **un•der•pay•ment** *n.*

un•der•pin /úndərpín/ *v.tr.* (**-pinned, -pinning**) **1** support from below with masonry, etc. **2** support; strengthen.

un•der•pin•ning /úndərpíning/ *n.* **1** a physical or metaphorical foundation. **2** the action or process of supporting from below.

un•der•plant /úndərplánt/ *v.tr.* (usu. foll. by *with*) plant or cultivate the ground about (a tall plant) with smaller ones.

un•der•play /úndərpláy/ *v.* **1** *tr.* play down the importance of. **2** *intr. & tr. Theatr.* perform with deliberate restraint.

un•der•priv•i•leged /úndərprívilijd, –prívlijd/ *adj.* **1** less privileged than others. **2** not enjoying the normal standard of living or rights in a society.

un•der•rate /úndəráyt/ *v.tr.* have too low an opinion of.

un•der•score *v.tr.* /úndərskáwr/ = UNDERLINE *v.*

un•der•sea /úndərsee/ *adj.* below the sea or the surface of the sea; submarine.

un•der•sec•re•tar•y /úndərsékrəteree/ *n.* (*pl.* **-ies**) a subordinate official, esp. one subordinate to a cabinet secretary.

un•der•sell /úndərsél/ *v.tr.* (*past* and *past part.* **-sold**) **1** sell at a lower price than (another seller). **2** sell at less than the true value.

un•der•sexed /úndərsékst/ *adj.* having unusually weak sexual desires.

un•der•shirt /úndərshərt/ *n.* an undergarment worn under a shirt.

un•der•shoot *v. & n.* • *v.tr.* /úndərshóót/ (*past* and *past part.* **-shot**) **1** (of an aircraft) land short of (a runway, etc.). **2** shoot short of or below. • *n.* /úndərshōōt/ the act or an instance of undershooting.

un•der•shorts /úndərsháwrts/ *n.* short underpants; trunks.

un•der•side /úndərsīd/ *n.* the lower or under side or surface.

un•der•signed /úndərsínd/ *adj.* whose signature is appended (*we, the undersigned, wish to state…*).

un•der•sized /úndərsízd/ *adj.* of less than the usual size.

un•der•staffed /úndərstáft/ *adj.* having too few staff.

un•der•stand /úndərstánd/ *v.* (*past* and *past part.* **-stood** /–stóód/) **1** *tr.* perceive the meaning of (words, a person, a language, etc.) (*understood you perfectly; cannot understand French*). **2** *tr.* perceive the significance or explanation or cause of (*do not understand why he came*). **3** *tr.* be sympathetically aware of the character or nature of, know how to deal with (*cannot understand him at all; could never understand algebra*). **4** *tr.* **a** (often foll. by *that* + clause) infer esp. from information received; take as implied; take for granted (*I understand that it begins at noon; am I to understand that you refuse?*). **b** (*absol.*) believe or assume from knowledge or inference (*he is coming tomorrow, I understand*). **5** *tr.* supply (a word) mentally (*the verb may be either expressed or understood*). **6** *tr.* accept (terms, conditions, etc.) as part of an agreement. **7** *intr.* have understanding (in general or in particular). □ **understand each other 1** know each other's views or feelings. **2** be in agreement or collusion. □□ **un•der•stand•a•ble** *adj.* **un•der•stand•a•bly** *adv.* **un•der•stand•er** *n.*

un•der•stand•ing /úndərstánding/ *n. & adj.* • *n.* **1 a** the ability to understand or think; intelligence. **b** the power of apprehension; the power of abstract thought. **2** an individual's perception or judgment of a situation, etc. **3** an agreement; a thing agreed upon, esp. informally (*had an understanding with the rival company*). **4** harmony in opinion or feeling (*disturbed the good understanding between them*). **5** sympathetic awareness or tolerance. • *adj.* **1** having understanding or insight or good judgment. **2** sympathetic to others' feelings. □□ **un•der•stand•ing•ly** *adv.*

un•der•state /úndərstáyt/ *v.tr.* (often as **understated** *adj.*) **1** express in greatly or unduly restrained terms. **2** represent as being less than it actually is. □□ **un•der•state•ment** /úndərstáytmənt/ *n.* **un•der•stat•er** *n.*

un•der•stood *past* and *past part.* of UNDERSTAND.

un•der•stud•y /úndərstúdee/ *n. & v.* esp. *Theatr.* • *n.* (*pl.* **-ies**) a person who studies another's role or duties in order to act at short notice in the absence of the other. • *v.tr.* (**-ies, -ied**) **1** study (a role, etc.) as an understudy. **2** act as an understudy to (a person).

un•der•take /úndərtáyk/ *v.tr.* (*past* **-took**; *past part.* **-taken**) **1** bind oneself to perform; make oneself responsible for; engage in; enter upon (work, an enterprise, a responsibility). **2** (usu. foll. by *to* + infin.) accept an obligation; promise.

un•der•tak•er /úndərtaykər/ *n.* **1** a person whose business is to make arrangements for funerals. **2** (also /–táykər/) a person who undertakes to do something.

un•der•tak•ing /úndərtáyking/ *n.* **1** work, etc., undertaken; an enterprise (*a serious undertaking*). **2** a pledge or promise. **3** /úndərtayking/ the management of funerals as a profession.

un•der•things /úndərthingz/ *n.pl. colloq.* underclothes.

un•der•tone /úndərtōn/ *n.* **1** a subdued tone of sound or color. **2** an underlying quality. **3** an undercurrent of feeling.

un•der•took *past* of UNDERTAKE.

un•der•tow /úndərtō/ *n.* a current below the surface of the sea moving in the opposite direction to the surface current.

un•der•wa•ter /úndərwáwtər, –wótər/ *adj. & adv.* • *adj.* situated or done under water. • *adv.* in and covered by water.

un•der•way /úndərwáy/ *adj.* occurring while in progress or in motion (*the ship's underway food service was excellent*).

un•der•wear /úndərwair/ *n.* underclothes.

un•der•weight *adj. & n.* • *adj.* /úndərwáyt/ weighing less than is normal or desirable. • *n.* /úndərwayt/ insufficient weight.

un•der•went *past* of UNDERGO.

un·der·whelm /úndərhwelm, –wélm/ *v.tr. joc.* fail to impress.
un·der·work /úndərwə́rk/ *v.* **1** *tr.* impose too little work on. **2** *intr.* do too little work.
un·der·world /úndərwərld/ *n.* **1** the part of society comprising those who live by organized crime and immorality. **2** the mythical abode of the dead under the earth.
un·der·write /úndər-rít/ *v.* (*past* **-wrote;** *past part.* **-written**) **1 a** *tr.* sign, and accept liability under (an insurance policy). **b** *tr.* accept (liability) in this way. **c** *intr.* practice insurance. **2** *tr.* undertake to finance or support. **3** *tr.* engage to buy all the stock in (a company, etc.) not bought by the public. **4** *tr.* write below (*the underwritten names*). ▫▫ **un·der·writ·er** /úndər-rītər/ *n.*
un·de·sir·a·ble /úndizírəbəl/ *adj. & n.* • *adj.* not desirable; objectionable; unpleasant. • *n.* an undesirable person. ▫▫ **un·de·sir·a·bil·i·ty** /–bílitee/ *n.* **un·de·sir·a·ble·ness** *n.* **un·de·sir·a·bly** *adv.*
un·de·ter·mined /únditə́rmind/ *adj.* = UNDECIDED.
un·did *past* of UNDO.
un·dies /úndeez/ *n.pl. colloq.* (esp. women's) underclothes.
un·di·gest·ed /úndijéstid, úndī–/ *adj.* **1** not digested. **2** (esp. of information, facts, etc.) not properly arranged or considered.
un·dig·ni·fied /úndígnifīd/ *adj.* lacking dignity.
un·dis·crim·i·nat·ing /úndiskríminayting/ *adj.* not showing good judgment.
un·dis·put·ed /úndispyóótid/ *adj.* not disputed or called in question.
un·di·vid·ed /úndivídid/ *adj.* not divided or shared; whole, entire (*gave him my undivided attention*).
un·do /úndóó/ *v.tr.* (*3rd sing. present* **-does;** *past* **-did;** *past part.* **-done**) **1 a** unfasten or untie (a coat, button, package, etc.). **b** unfasten the clothing of (a person). **2** annul; cancel (*cannot undo the past*). **3** ruin the prospects, reputation, or morals of.
un·doc·u·ment·ed /úndókyəmentid/ *adj.* **1** not having the appropriate document. **2** not proved by or recorded in documents.
un·do·ing /úndóóing/ *n.* **1** ruin or a cause of ruin. **2** the process of reversing what has been done. **3** the action of opening or unfastening.
un·done /úndún/ *adj.* **1** not done; incomplete (*left the job undone*). **2** not fastened (*left the buttons undone*). **3** *archaic* ruined.
un·doubt·ed /úndówtid/ *adj.* certain; not questioned; not regarded as doubtful. ▫▫ **un·doubt·ed·ly** *adv.*
un·dreamed /úndreémd/ *adj.* (also **un·dreamt** /úndrémt/) (often foll. by *of*) not dreamed or thought of or imagined.
un·dress /úndrés/ *v.* **1** *intr.* take off one's clothes. **2** *tr.* take the clothes off (a person).
un·dressed /úndrést/ *adj.* **1** not or no longer dressed; partly or wholly naked. **2** (of leather, etc.) not treated. **3** (of food) **a** not having a dressing (*undressed salad*). **b** prepared simply, with no sauce, stuffing, etc. (*undressed turkey*).
un·drink·a·ble /úndríngkəbəl/ *adj.* unfit for drinking.
un·due /úndóó, –dyóó/ *adj.* **1** excessive; disproportionate. **2** not suitable. **3** not owed. ▫▫ **un·du·ly** *adv.*
un·du·lant /únjələnt, –dyə–, –də–/ *adj.* moving like waves; fluctuating.
un·du·late *v.* /únjəlayt, –dyə–, –də–/ *intr. & tr.* have or cause to have a wavy motion or look.
un·du·la·tion /únjəláyshən, –dyə–, –də–/ *n.* **1** a wavy motion or form; a gentle rise and fall. **2** each wave of this. **3** a set of wavy lines.
un·dy·ing /úndī́-ing/ *adj.* **1** immortal. **2** never-ending (*undying love*). ▫▫ **un·dy·ing·ly** *adv.*
un·earned in·come *n.* income from interest payments, etc., as opposed to salary, wages, or fees.
un·earth /únə́rth/ *v.tr.* **1** discover by searching or in the course of digging or rummaging. **2** dig out of the earth.
un·earth·ly /únə́rthlee/ *adj.* **1** supernatural; mysterious. **2** *colloq.* absurdly early or inconvenient (*an unearthly hour*). **3** not earthly. ▫▫ **un·earth·li·ness** *n.*
un·ease /úneéz/ *n.* lack of ease; discomfort; distress.
un·eas·y /úneézee/ *adj.* (**uneasier, uneasiest**) **1** disturbed or uncomfortable in mind or body (*passed an uneasy night*). **2** disturbing (*had an uneasy suspicion*). ▫▫ **un·eas·i·ly** *adv.* **un·eas·i·ness** *n.*
un·ec·o·nom·i·cal /únekənómikəl, –eekə–/ *adj.* not economical; wasteful.
un·em·ployed /únimplóyd/ *adj.* **1** not having paid employment; out of work. **2** not in use.
un·em·ploy·ment /únimplóymənt/ *n.* **1** the state of being unemployed. **2** the condition or extent of this in a country or region, etc. (*the Northeast has higher unemployment*).
un·en·cum·bered /úninkúmbərd/ *adj.* **1** (of an estate) not having any liabilities (e.g., a mortgage) on it. **2** having no encumbrance; free.
un·e·qual /úneékwəl/ *adj.* **1** (often foll. by *to*) not equal. **2** of varying quality. **3** lacking equal advantage to both sides (*an unequal bargain*). ▫▫ **un·e·qual·ly** *adv.*
un·e·qualed /úneékwəld/ *adj.* (also esp. *Brit.* **unequalled**) superior to all others.
un·e·quiv·o·cal /únikwívəkəl/ *adj.* not ambiguous; plain; unmistakable. ▫▫ **un·e·quiv·o·cal·ly** *adv.* **un·e·quiv·o·cal·ness** *n.*
un·err·ing /únéring/ *adj.* not erring, failing, or missing the mark; true; certain. ▫▫ **un·err·ing·ly** *adv.* **un·err·ing·ness** *n.*
UNESCO /yóónéskō/ *abbr.* United Nations Educational, Scientific, and Cultural Organization.
un·eth·i·cal /únéthikəl/ *adj.* not ethical, esp. unscrupulous in business or professional conduct. ▫▫ **un·eth·i·cal·ly** *adv.*
un·e·ven /úneévən/ *adj.* **1** not level or smooth. **2** not uniform or equable. **3** (of a contest) unequal. ▫▫ **un·e·ven·ly** *adv.* **un·e·ven·ness** *n.*
un·ex·am·pled /únigzámpəld/ *adj.* having no precedent or parallel.
un·ex·cep·tion·a·ble /úniksépshənəbəl/ *adj.* with which no fault can be found; entirely satisfactory. ▫▫ **un·ex·cep·tion·a·ble·ness** *n.* **un·ex·cep·tion·a·bly** *adv.*
▶ See note at EXCEPTIONABLE. [NB: unexceptionable not actually handled in that note]
un·ex·cep·tion·al /úniksépshənəl/ *adj.* not out of the ordinary; usual; normal. ▫▫ **un·ex·cep·tion·al·ly** *adv.*
un·ex·pect·ed /únikspéktid/ *adj.* not expected; surprising. ▫▫ **un·ex·pect·ed·ly** *adv.* **un·ex·pect·ed·ness** *n.*
un·ex·pur·gat·ed /únékspərgaytid/ *adj.* (esp. of a text, etc.) not expurgated; complete.
un·fail·ing /únfáyling/ *adj.* **1** not failing. **2** not running short. **3** constant. **4** reliable. ▫▫ **un·fail·ing·ly** *adv.* **un·fail·ing·ness** *n.*
un·fair /unfáir/ *adj.* **1** not equitable or honest (*obtained by unfair means*). **2** not impartial or according to the rules (*unfair play*). ▫▫ **un·fair·ly** *adv.* **un·fair·ness** *n.*
un·faith·ful /únfáythfóól/ *adj.* **1** not faithful, esp. adulterous. **2** not loyal. **3** treacherous. ▫▫ **un·faith·ful·ly** *adv.* **un·faith·ful·ness** *n.*
un·fal·ter·ing /únfáwltəring/ *adj.* not faltering; steady; resolute. ▫▫ **un·fal·ter·ing·ly** *adv.*
un·fas·ten /únfásən/ *v.* **1** *tr. & intr.* make or become loose. **2** *tr.* open the fastening(s) of. **3** *tr.* detach.
un·fa·vor·a·ble /únfáyvərəbəl/ *adj.* not favorable;

adverse; hostile. □□ **un·fa·vor·a·ble·ness** *n.* **un·fa·vor·a·bly** *adv.*

un·fazed /únfáyzd/ *adj. colloq.* untroubled; not disconcerted.

un·feel·ing /únféeling/ *adj.* **1** unsympathetic; harsh; not caring about others' feelings. **2** lacking sensation or sensitivity. □□ **un·feel·ing·ly** *adv.* **un·feel·ing·ness** *n.*

un·feigned /únfáynd/ *adj.* genuine; sincere. □□ **un·feign·ed·ly** /–fáynidlee/ *adv.*

un·fem·i·nine /únféminin/ *adj.* not in accordance with, or appropriate to, female character. □□ **un·fem·i·nin·i·ty** /–nínitee/ *n.*

un·fet·tered /únfétərd/ *adj.* unrestrained; unrestricted.

un·fit /únfít/ *adj. & v.* • *adj.* (often foll. by *for*, or *to* + infin.) not fit. • *v.tr.* (**unfitted, unfitting**) (usu. foll. by *for*) make unsuitable. □□ **un·fit·ly** *adv.* **un·fit·ness** *n.*

un·fit·ting /únfíting/ *adj.* not fitting or suitable; unbecoming. □□ **un·fit·ting·ly** *adv.*

un·flag·ging /únfláging/ *adj.* tireless; persistent. □□ **un·flag·ging·ly** *adv.*

un·flap·pa·ble /únflápəbəl/ *adj. colloq.* imperturbable; remaining calm in a crisis. □□ **un·flap·pa·bil·i·ty** /–bílitee/ *n.* **un·flap·pa·bly** *adv.*

un·fold /únfṓld/ *v.* **1** *tr.* open the fold or folds of; spread out. **2** *tr.* reveal (thoughts, etc.). **3** *intr.* become opened out. **4** *intr.* develop. □□ **un·fold·ment** *n.*

un·forced /únfáwrst/ *adj.* **1** not produced by effort; easy; natural. **2** not compelled or constrained. □□ **un·forc·ed·ly** /–fáwrsidlee/ *adv.*

un·for·get·ta·ble /únfərgétəbəl/ *adj.* that cannot be forgotten; memorable; wonderful (*an unforgettable experience*). □□ **un·for·get·ta·bly** *adv.*

un·formed /únfáwrmd/ *adj.* **1** not formed. **2** shapeless. **3** not developed.

un·for·tu·nate /únfáwrchənət/ *adj. & n.* • *adj.* **1** having bad fortune; unlucky. **2** unhappy. **3** regrettable. **4** disastrous. • *n.* an unfortunate person.

un·for·tu·nate·ly /únfáwrchənətlee/ *adv.* **1** (qualifying a whole sentence) it is unfortunate that. **2** in an unfortunate manner.

un·found·ed /únfówndid/ *adj.* having no foundation (*unfounded hopes; unfounded rumor*). □□ **un·found·ed·ly** *adv.* **un·found·ed·ness** *n.*

un·friend·ly /únfréndlee/ *adj.* (**unfriendlier, unfriendliest**) not friendly. □□ **un·friend·li·ness** *n.*

un·fruit·ful /únfróotfool/ *adj.* **1** not producing good results; unprofitable. **2** not producing fruit or crops. □□ **un·fruit·ful·ly** *adv.* **un·fruit·ful·ness** *n.*

un·fun·ny /únfúnee/ *adj.* (**unfunnier, unfunniest**) not amusing (though meant to be). □□ **un·fun·ni·ly** *adv.* **un·fun·ni·ness** *n.*

un·furl /únfərl/ *v.* **1** *tr.* spread out (a sail, umbrella, etc.). **2** *intr.* become spread out.

un·gain·ly /úngáynlee/ *adj.* (of a person, animal, or movement) awkward; clumsy. □□ **un·gain·li·ness** *n.*

un·god·ly /úngódlee/ *adj.* **1** impious; irreligious. **2** *colloq.* unreasonably inconvenient (*an ungodly hour to arrive*). □□ **un·god·li·ness** *n.*

un·gov·ern·a·ble /úngúvərnəbəl/ *adj.* uncontrollable; violent. □□ **un·gov·ern·a·bil·i·ty** /–bílitee/ *n.* **un·gov·ern·a·bly** *adv.*

un·gra·cious /úngráyshəs/ *adj.* **1** not kindly or courteous; unkind. **2** unattractive. □□ **un·gra·cious·ly** *adv.* **un·gra·cious·ness** *n.*

un·gram·mat·i·cal /úngrəmátikəl/ *adj.* contrary to the rules of grammar. □□ **un·gram·mat·i·cal·i·ty** /–kálitee/ *n.* **un·gram·mat·i·cal·ly** *adv.* **un·gram·mat·i·cal·ness** *n.*

un·guard·ed /úngaárdid/ *adj.* **1** incautious; thoughtless (*an unguarded remark*). **2** not guarded; without a guard. □ **in an unguarded moment** unawares. □□ **un·guard·ed·ly** *adv.* **un·guard·ed·ness** *n.*

un·guent /únggwənt/ *n.* a soft substance used as ointment or for lubrication.

un·guid·ed /úngídid/ *adj.* not guided in a particular path or direction; left to take its own course.

un·gu·la /úngyələ/ *n.* (*pl.* **un·gu·lae** /–lee/) a hoof or claw.

un·gu·late /úngyələt, –layt/ *adj. & n.* • *adj.* hoofed. • *n.* a hoofed mammal.

un·hand /únhánd/ *v.tr. rhet.* or *joc.* **1** take one's hands off (a person). **2** release from one's grasp.

un·hand·y /únhándee/ *adj.* **1** not easy to handle or manage; awkward. **2** not skillful in using the hands. □□ **un·hand·i·ly** *adv.* **un·hand·i·ness** *n.*

un·hap·py /únhápee/ *adj.* (**unhappier, unhappiest**) **1** not happy; miserable. **2** unsuccessful; unfortunate. **3** causing misfortune. **4** disastrous. **5** inauspicious. □□ **un·hap·pi·ly** *adv.* **un·hap·pi·ness** *n.*

un·health·y /únhélthee/ *adj.* (**unhealthier, unhealthiest**) **1** not in good health. **2 a** (of a place, etc.) harmful to health. **b** unwholesome. **c** *sl.* dangerous to life. □□ **un·health·i·ly** *adv.* **un·health·i·ness** *n.*

un·heard /únhə́rd/ *adj.* **1** not heard. **2** (usu. **unheard-of**) unprecedented; unknown.

un·hinge /únhínj/ *v.tr.* **1** take (a door, etc.) off its hinges. **2** (esp. as **unhinged** *adj.*) unsettle or disorder (a person's mind, etc.); make (a person) crazy.

un·ho·ly /únhṓlee/ *adj.* (**unholier, unholiest**) **1** impious; profane; wicked. **2** *colloq.* dreadful; outrageous (*made an unholy ordeal out of nothing*). **3** not holy. □□ **un·ho·li·ness** *n.*

un·hook /únhóok/ *v.tr.* **1** remove from a hook or hooks. **2** unfasten by releasing a hook or hooks.

un·horse /únháwrs/ *v.tr.* **1** throw or drag from a horse. **2** (of a horse) throw (a rider). **3** dislodge; overthrow.

un·hu·man /únhyóomən/ *adj.* **1** not human. **2** superhuman. **3** inhuman; brutal.

uni- /yóonee/ *comb. form* one; having or consisting of one.

u·ni·cam·er·al /yóonikámərəl/ *adj.* with a single legislative chamber.

UNICEF /yóonisef/ *abbr.* United Nations Children's (orig. International Children's Emergency) Fund.

u·ni·cel·lu·lar /yóonisélyələr/ *adj.* (of an organism, organ, tissue, etc.) consisting of a single cell.

u·ni·corn /yóonikawrn/ *n.* a mythical animal with a horse's body and a single straight horn.

u·ni·cy·cle /yóonisīkəl/ *n.* a single-wheeled cycle, esp. as used by acrobats. □□ **u·ni·cy·clist** *n.*

u·ni·fi·ca·tion /yóonifikáyshən/ *n.* the act or an instance of unifying; the state of being unified. □□ **u·ni·fi·ca·tor·y** *adj.*

u·ni·form /yóonifawrm/ *adj., n., & v.* • *adj.* **1** not changing in form or character; the same; unvarying (*present a uniform appearance; all of uniform size and shape*). **2** conforming to the same standard, rules, or pattern. **3** constant in the course of time (*uniform acceleration*). **4** (of a tax, law, etc.) not varying with time or place. • *n.* distinctive uniform clothing worn by members of the same body, e.g., by soldiers, police, and schoolchildren. • *v.tr.* clothe in uniform (*a uniformed officer*). □□ **u·ni·form·ly** *adv.*

u·ni·form·i·ty /yóonifáwrmitee/ *n.* (*pl.* **-ties**) **1** being uniform; sameness; consistency. **2** an instance of this.

u·ni·fy /yóonifī/ *v.tr.* (also *absol.*) (**-fies, -fied**) reduce to unity or uniformity. □□ **u·ni·fi·er** *n.*

u·ni·lat·er·al /yóonilátərəl/ *adj.* **1** performed by or affecting only one person or party (*unilateral disarmament; unilateral declaration of independence*). **2** one-sided. □□ **u·ni·lat·er·al·ly** *adv.*

u·ni·lat·er·al·ism /yóonilátərəlizəm/ *n.* **1** unilateral disarmament. **2** the pursuit of a foreign policy without allies. □□ **u·ni·lat·er·al·ist** *n. & adj.*

u·ni·lin·gual /yóonilínggwəl/ *adj.* of or in only one language. ▫▫ **u·ni·lin·gual·ly** *adv.*

un·im·peach·a·ble /únimpéechəbəl/ *adj.* giving no opportunity for censure; beyond reproach or question. ▫▫ **un·im·peach·a·bly** *adv.*

un·im·proved /únimpróovd/ *adj.* **1** not made better. **2** not made use of. **3** (of land) not used for agriculture or building; not developed.

un·in·cor·po·rat·ed /úninkáwrpəraytid/ *adj.* **1** not incorporated or united. **2** not formed into a corporation.

un·in·flam·ma·ble /úninflámәbəl/ *adj.* not flammable.

un·in·i·ti·at·ed /úninísheeaytid/ *adj.* not initiated; not admitted or instructed.

un·in·ter·est·ed /únintrəstid, –təristid, –təres–/ *adj.* **1** not interested. **2** unconcerned; indifferent. ▫▫ **un·in·ter·est·ed·ly** *adv.* **un·in·ter·est·ed·ness** *n.*

▶See note at DISINTERESTED.

un·ion /yóonyən/ *n.* **1** the act or an instance of uniting; the state of being united. **2 a** a whole resulting from the combination of parts or members. **b** a political unit formed in this way, esp. (**Union**) the US (esp. as distinct from the Confederacy during the Civil War), the UK, or South Africa. **3** = LABOR UNION. **4** marriage; matrimony. **5** concord; agreement (*lived together in perfect union*). **6** (**Union**) (in the UK) **a** a general social club and debating society at some universities and colleges. **b** the buildings or accommodations of such a society. **7** *Math.* the totality of the members of two or more sets. **8** a part of a flag with a device emblematic of union, normally occupying the upper corner next to the staff. **9** a joint or coupling for pipes, etc.

un·ion·ist /yóonyənist/ *n.* **1 a** a member of a labor union. **b** an advocate of labor unions. **2** (usu. **Unionist**) an advocate of union, esp.: **a** a person opposed to the rupture of the parliamentary union between Great Britain and Northern Ireland (formerly between Great Britain and Ireland). **b** *hist.* a person who opposed secession during the US Civil War. ▫▫ **un·ion·ism** *n.* **un·ion·is·tic** /–nístik/ *adj.*

un·ion·ize /yóonyənīz/ *v.tr.* & *intr.* bring or come under labor-union organization or rules. ▫▫ **un·ion·i·za·tion** *n.*

Un·ion Jack *n.* (also **Un·ion flag**) the national ensign of the United Kingdom formed by the union of the crosses of St. George, St. Andrew, and St. Patrick.

un·ion shop *n.* a shop, factory, trade, etc., in which employees must belong to a labor union or join one within an agreed time.

un·ion suit *n.* a single undergarment for the body and legs; combinations.

u·nip·ar·ous /yoonípərəs/ *adj.* producing one offspring at a birth.

u·ni·ped /yóoniped/ *n.* & *adj.* • *n.* a person having only one foot or leg. • *adj.* one-footed; one-legged.

u·nique /yoonéek/ *adj.* & *n.* • *adj.* **1** of which there is only one; unequaled; having no like, equal, or parallel (*his position was unique; this vase is considered unique*). **2** *disp.* unusual; remarkable (*the most unique man I ever met*). • *n.* a unique thing or person. ▫▫ **u·nique·ly** *adv.* **u·nique·ness** *n.*

▶See note at PERFECT.

u·ni·sex /yóoniseks/ *adj.* (of clothing, hairstyles, etc.) designed to be suitable for both sexes.

u·ni·sex·u·al /yóonisékshóoəl/ *adj.* **1 a** of one sex. **b** *Bot.* having stamens or pistils but not both. **2** unisex. ▫▫ **u·ni·sex·u·al·i·ty** /–shóoálitee/ *n.* **u·ni·sex·u·al·ly** *adv.*

u·ni·son /yóonisən/ *n.* **1** *Mus.* **a** coincidence in pitch of sounds or notes. **b** this regarded as an interval. **2** *Mus.* a combination of voices or instruments at the same pitch or at pitches differing by one or more octaves (*sang in unison*). **3** agreement; concord (*acted in perfect unison*).

u·nit /yóonit/ *n.* **1 a** an individual thing, person, or group regarded as single and complete, esp. for purposes of calculation. **b** each of the (smallest) separate individuals or groups into which a complex whole may be analyzed (*the family as the unit of society*). **2** a quantity chosen as a standard in terms of which other quantities may be expressed (*unit of heat; SI unit; mass per unit volume*). **3** the smallest share in a unit trust. **4** a device with a specified function forming part of a complex mechanism. **5** a piece of furniture for fitting with others like it or made of complementary parts. **6** a group with a special function in an organization. **7** a group of buildings, wards, etc., in a hospital. **8** the number 'one.'

u·ni·tard /yóonətaard/ *n.* a one-piece leotard that covers the legs as well as the torso.

U·ni·tar·i·an /yóonitáireeən/ *n.* & *adj.* • *n.* **1** a person who believes that God is not a Trinity but one being. **2** a member of a religious body maintaining this and advocating freedom from formal dogma or doctrine. • *adj.* of or relating to the Unitarians. ▫▫ **U·ni·tar·i·an·ism** *n.*

u·ni·tar·y /yóoniteree/ *adj.* **1** of a unit or units. **2** marked by unity or uniformity. ▫▫ **u·ni·tar·i·ly** *adv.* **u·ni·tar·i·ty** /–téritee/ *n.*

u·nit cell *n.* *Crystallog.* the smallest repeating group of atoms, ions, or molecules in a crystal.

u·nit cost *n.* the cost of producing one item of manufacture.

u·nite /yoonít/ *v.* **1** *tr.* & *intr.* join together; make or become one; combine. **2** *tr.* & *intr.* join together for a common purpose or action (*united in their struggle against injustice*). **3** *tr.* & *intr.* join in marriage. **4** *tr.* possess (qualities, features, etc.) in combination (*united anger with mercy*). **5** *intr.* & *tr.* form or cause to form a physical or chemical whole (*oil will not unite with water*). ▫▫ **u·ni·tive** /yóonitiv/ *adj.* **u·ni·tive·ly** *adv.*

u·nit·ed /yoonítid/ *adj.* **1** that has united or been united. **2 a** of or produced by two or more persons or things in union; joint. **b** resulting from the union of two or more parts (esp. in the names of churches, societies, and athletic clubs). **3** in agreement; of like mind. ▫▫ **u·nit·ed·ly** *adv.*

U·nit·ed Na·tions *n.pl.* (orig., in 1942) those united against the Axis powers in the war of 1939–45, (later) a supranational peace-seeking organization of these and many other nations.

u·nit price *n.* the price charged for each unit of goods supplied.

u·ni·ty /yóonitee/ *n.* (*pl.* **-ties**) **1** oneness; being one, single, or individual; being formed of parts that constitute a whole; due interconnection and coherence of parts (*the pictures lack unity; national unity*). **2** harmony or concord between persons, etc. (*lived together in unity*). **3** a thing forming a complex whole (*a person regarded as a unity*). **4** *Math.* the number 'one,' the factor that leaves unchanged the quantity on which it operates.

Univ. *abbr.* University.

u·ni·va·lent *adj.* & *n.* • *adj.* **1** /yóoniváylənt/ *Chem.* having a valence of one. **2** /yóonívələnt/ *Biol.* (of a chromosome) remaining unpaired during meiosis. • *n.* /yoonívələnt/ *Biol.* a univalent chromosome.

u·ni·valve /yóonivalv/ *adj.* & *n.* *Zool.* • *adj.* having one valve. • *n.* a univalve mollusk.

u·ni·ver·sal /yóonivə́rsəl/ *adj.* & *n.* • *adj.* **1** of, belonging to, or done, etc., by all persons or things in the world or in the class concerned; applicable to all cases (*the feeling was universal; met with universal approval*). **2** *Log-*

ic (of a proposition) in which something is asserted of all of a class (opp. PARTICULAR 5). • *n.* **1** *Logic* a universal proposition. **2** *Philos.* **a** a term or concept of general application. **b** a nature or essence signified by a general term. □□ **u·ni·ver·sal·i·ty** /–sálitee/ *n.* **u·ni·ver·sal·ize** *v.tr.* **u·ni·ver·sal·i·za·tion** /–lizáyshən/ *n.* **u·ni·ver·sal·ly** *adv.*

u·ni·ver·sal·ist /yóonivə́rsəlist/ *n. Theol.* **1** a person who holds that all mankind will eventually be saved. **2** a member of an organized body of Christians who hold this. □□ **u·ni·ver·sal·ism** *n.* **u·ni·ver·sal·is·tic** /–lístik/ *adj.*

u·ni·ver·sal joint *n.* (also **u·ni·ver·sal cou·pling**) a joint or coupling that can transmit rotary power by a shaft at any selected angle.

U·ni·ver·sal Prod·uct Code *n.* a bar code on products that can be read by an electronic scanner, usu. providing price and product identification.

u·ni·verse /yóonivərs/ *n.* **1 a** all existing things; the whole creation; the cosmos. **b** a sphere of existence, influence, activity, etc. **2** all mankind.

u·ni·ver·si·ty /yóonivə́rsitee/ *n.* (*pl.* **-ties**) **1** an educational institution designed for instruction, examination, or both, of students in many branches of advanced learning, conferring degrees in various faculties, and often embodying colleges and similar institutions. **2** the members of this collectively.

u·niv·o·cal /yoonívəkəl, yóonivṓkəl/ *adj. & n.* • *adj.* (of a word, etc.) having only one proper meaning. • *n.* a univocal word. □□ **u·niv·o·cal·i·ty** /yóonivōkálitee/ *n.* **u·niv·o·cal·ly** *adv.*

un·just /únjúst/ *adj.* not just; contrary to justice or fairness. □□ **un·just·ly** *adv.* **un·just·ness** *n.*

un·kempt /únkémpt/ *adj.* **1** untidy; of neglected appearance. **2** uncombed; disheveled. □□ **un·kempt·ly** *adv.* **un·kempt·ness** *n.*

un·kept /únképt/ *adj.* **1** (of a promise, law, etc.) not observed; disregarded. **2** not tended; neglected.

un·kind /únkínd/ *adj.* **1** not kind. **2** harsh; cruel. **3** unpleasant. □□ **un·kind·ly** *adv.* **un·kind·ness** *n.*

un·know·a·ble /ún-nṓəbəl/ *adj. & n.* • *adj.* that cannot be known. • *n.* **1** an unknowable thing. **2** (**the Unknowable**) the postulated absolute or ultimate reality.

un·know·ing /ún-nṓing/ *adj. & n.* • *adj.* (often foll. by *of*) not knowing; ignorant; unconscious. • *n.* ignorance (*cloud of unknowing*). □□ **un·know·ing·ly** *adv.* **un·know·ing·ness** *n.*

un·known /ún-nṓn/ *adj. & n.* • *adj.* (often foll. by *to*) not known; unfamiliar (*his purpose was unknown to me*). • *n.* **1** an unknown thing or person. **2** an unknown quantity (*equation in two unknowns*). □ **unknown to** without the knowledge of (*did it unknown to me*). □□ **un·known·ness** *n.*

Un·known Sol·dier *n.* an unidentified representative member of a country's armed forces killed in war, given burial with special honors in a national memorial.

un·lace /únláys/ *v.tr.* **1** undo the lace or laces of. **2** unfasten or loosen in this way.

un·lade /únláyd/ *v.tr.* **1** take the cargo out of (a ship). **2** discharge (a cargo, etc.) from a ship.

un·law·ful /únláwfool/ *adj.* not lawful; illegal; not permissible. □□ **un·law·ful·ly** *adv.* **un·law·ful·ness** *n.*

un·lead·ed /únlédid/ *adj.* **1** (of gasoline, etc.) without added lead. **2** not covered, weighted, or framed with lead.

un·learn /únlə́rn/ *v.tr.* (*past* and *past part.* **unlearned** or **unlearnt**) **1** discard from one's memory. **2** rid oneself of (a habit, false information, etc.).

un·learn·ed[1] /únlə́rnid/ *adj.* not well educated; untaught; ignorant. □□ **un·learn·ed·ly** *adv.*

un·learned[2] /únlə́rnd/ *adj.* (also **un·learnt** /–lérnt/) that has not been learned.

un·leash /únleésh/ *v.tr.* **1** release from a leash or restraint. **2** set free to engage in pursuit or attack.

un·leav·ened /únlévənd/ *adj.* not leavened; made without yeast or other raising agent.

un·less /unlés, ən–/ *conj.* if not; except when (*shall go unless I hear from you; always walked unless I had a bicycle*).

un·let·tered /únlétərd/ *adj.* **1** illiterate. **2** not well educated.

un·like /únlík/ *adj. & prep.* • *adj.* **1** not like; different from (*is unlike both his parents*). **2** uncharacteristic of (*such behavior is unlike him*). **3** dissimilar; different. • *prep.* differently from (*acts quite unlike anyone else*). □□ **un·like·ness** *n.*

un·like·ly /únlíklee/ *adj.* (**unlikelier, unlikeliest**) **1** improbable (*unlikely tale*). **2** (foll. by *to* + infin.) not to be expected to do something (*he's unlikely to be available*). **3** unpromising (*an unlikely candidate*). □□ **un·like·li·hood** *n.* **un·like·li·ness** *n.*

un·like signs *n. Math.* plus and minus.

un·lim·it·ed /únlímitid/ *adj.* without limit; unrestricted; very great in number or quantity (*has unlimited possibilities; an unlimited expanse of sea*). □□ **un·lim·it·ed·ly** *adv.* **un·lim·it·ed·ness** *n.*

un·lined[1] /únlínd/ *adj.* **1** (of paper, etc.) without lines. **2** (of a face, etc.) without wrinkles.

un·lined[2] /únlínd/ *adj.* (of a garment, etc.) without lining.

un·link /únlíngk/ *v.tr.* **1** undo the links (of a chain, etc.). **2** detach or set free.

un·list·ed /únlístid/ *adj.* not included in a published list, esp. of stock exchange prices or of telephone numbers.

un·lived-in /únlívdin/ *adj.* **1** appearing to be uninhabited. **2** unused by the inhabitants.

un·load /únlṓd/ *v.tr.* **1** (also *absol.*) remove a load from (a vehicle, etc.). **2** remove (a load) from a vehicle, etc. **3** remove the charge from (a firearm, etc.). **4** *colloq.* get rid of. **5** (often foll. by *on*) *colloq.* **a** divulge (information). **b** (also *absol.*) give vent to (feelings). □□ **un·load·er** *n.*

un·lock /únlók/ *v.tr.* **1 a** release the lock of (a door, box, etc.). **b** release or disclose by unlocking. **2** release thoughts, feelings, etc., from (one's mind, etc.).

un·looked-for /únlóoktfawr/ *adj.* unexpected; unforeseen.

un·loose /únlóos/ *v.tr.* (also **un·loos·en**) loose; set free.

un·luck·y /únlúkee/ *adj.* (**unluckier, unluckiest**) **1** not fortunate or successful. **2** wretched. **3** bringing bad luck. **4** ill-judged. □□ **un·luck·i·ly** *adv.* **un·luck·i·ness** *n.*

un·made /únmáyd/ *adj.* **1** not made. **2** destroyed; annulled.

un·make /únmáyk/ *v.tr.* (*past* and *past part.* **unmade**) undo the making of; destroy; depose; annul.

un·man /únmán/ *v.tr.* (**unmanned, unmanning**) **1** deprive of supposed manly qualities (e.g., self-control, courage); cause to weep, etc.; discourage. **2** deprive (a ship, etc.) of men.

un·man·age·a·ble /únmánijəbəl/ *adj.* not (easily) managed, manipulated, or controlled. □□ **un·man·age·a·ble·ness** *n.* **un·man·age·a·bly** *adv.*

un·man·ner·ly /únmánərlee/ *adj.* **1** without good manners. **2** (of actions, speech, etc.) showing a lack of good manners. □□ **un·man·ner·li·ness** *n.*

un·marked /únmaárkt/ *adj.* **1** not marked. **2** not noticed.

un·mask /únmásk/ *v.* **1** *tr.* **a** remove the mask from. **b** expose the true character of. **2** *intr.* remove one's mask. □□ **un·mask·er** *n.*

un·matched /únmácht/ *adj.* not matched or equaled.

un·men·tion·a·ble /únménshənəbəl/ *adj. & n.* • *adj.* that cannot (properly) be mentioned. • *n.* **1** (in *pl.*) *joc.* **a** undergarments. **b** *archaic* trousers. **2** a person or thing not to be mentioned. ▫▫ **un·men·tion·a·bil·i·ty** /–bílitee/ *n.* **un·men·tion·a·ble·ness** *n.* **un·men·tion·a·bly** *adv.*

un·mer·ci·ful /únmərsifoo͝l/ *adj.* merciless. ▫▫ **un·mer·ci·ful·ly** *adv.* **un·mer·ci·ful·ness** *n.*

un·met /únmét/ *adj.* (of a quota, demand, goal, etc.) not achieved or fulfilled.

un·mis·tak·a·ble /únmistáykəbəl/ *adj.* that cannot be mistaken or doubted; clear. ▫▫ **un·mis·tak·a·bil·i·ty** /–bílitee/ *n.* **un·mis·tak·a·ble·ness** *n.* **un·mis·tak·a·bly** *adv.*

un·mit·i·gat·ed /únmítigaytid/ *adj.* **1** not mitigated or modified. **2** absolute; unqualified (*an unmitigated disaster*). ▫▫ **un·mit·i·gat·ed·ly** *adv.*

un·mor·al /únmáwrəl, –mór–/ *adj.* not concerned with morality (cf. IMMORAL). ▫▫ **un·mor·al·i·ty** /–rálitee/ *n.* **un·mor·al·ly** *adv.*

un·moved /únmoo͞vd/ *adj.* **1** not moved. **2** not changed in one's purpose. **3** not affected by emotion. ▫▫ **un·mov·a·ble** *adj.* (also **un·move·a·ble**).

un·mu·si·cal /únmyoo͞zikəl/ *adj.* **1** not pleasing to the ear. **2** unskilled in or indifferent to music. ▫▫ **un·mu·si·cal·i·ty** /–kálitee/ *n.* **un·mu·si·cal·ly** *adv.* **un·mu·si·cal·ness** *n.*

un·name·a·ble /ún-náyməbəl/ *adj.* that cannot be named, esp. too bad to be named.

un·named /ún-náymd/ *adj.* not named.

un·nat·u·ral /ún-náchərəl/ *adj.* **1** contrary to nature or the usual course of nature; not normal. **2 a** lacking natural feelings. **b** extremely cruel or wicked. **3** artificial. **4** affected. ▫▫ **un·nat·u·ral·ly** *adv.* **un·nat·u·ral·ness** *n.*

un·nec·es·sar·y /ún-nésəseree/ *adj. & n.* • *adj.* **1** not necessary. **2** more than is necessary (*with unnecessary care*). • *n.* (*pl.* **-ies**) (usu. in *pl.*) an unnecessary thing. ▫▫ **un·nec·es·sar·i·ly** *adv.* **un·nec·es·sar·i·ness** *n.*

un·nerve /ún-nərv/ *v.tr.* deprive of strength or resolution. ▫▫ **un·nerv·ing·ly** *adv.*

un·num·bered /ún-númbərd/ *adj.* **1** not marked with a number. **2** not counted. **3** countless.

un·ob·jec·tion·a·ble /únəbjékshənəbəl/ *adj.* not objectionable; acceptable. ▫▫ **un·ob·jec·tion·a·ble·ness** *n.* **un·ob·jec·tion·a·bly** *adv.*

un·ob·tru·sive /únəbtroo͞siv/ *adj.* not making oneself or itself noticed. ▫▫ **un·ob·tru·sive·ly** *adv.* **un·ob·tru·sive·ness** *n.*

un·of·fend·ing /únəfénding/ *adj.* not offending; harmless; innocent. ▫▫ **un·of·fend·ed** *adj.*

un·of·fi·cial /únəfishəl/ *adj.* **1** not officially authorized or confirmed. **2** not characteristic of officials. ▫▫ **un·of·fi·cial·ly** *adv.*

un·op·posed /únəpṓzd/ *adj.* not opposed, esp. in an election.

un·or·gan·ized /únáwrgənīzd/ *adj.* not organized (cf. DISORGANIZE).

un·o·rig·i·nal /únəríjinəl/ *adj.* lacking originality; derivative. ▫▫ **un·o·rig·i·nal·i·ty** /–nálitee/ *n.* **un·o·rig·i·nal·ly** *adv.*

un·owned /únṓnd/ *adj.* **1** unacknowledged. **2** having no owner.

un·pack /únpák/ *v.tr.* **1** (also *absol.*) open and remove the contents of (a package, luggage, etc.). **2** take (a thing) out from a package, etc. ▫▫ **un·pack·er** *n.*

un·paired /únpáird/ *adj.* **1** not arranged in pairs. **2** not forming one of a pair.

un·pal·at·a·ble /únpálətəbəl/ *adj.* **1** not pleasant to taste. **2** (of an idea, suggestion, etc.) disagreeable; distasteful. ▫▫ **un·pal·at·a·bil·i·ty** *n.* **un·pal·at·a·ble·ness** *n.*

un·par·al·leled /únpárəleld/ *adj.* having no parallel or equal.

un·peo·ple *v. & n.* • *v.tr.* /únpeépəl/ depopulate. • *n.pl.* /únpeepəl/ unpersons.

un·per·son /únpərsən/ *n.* a person whose name or existence is denied or ignored.

un·pin /únpín/ *v.tr.* (**unpinned, unpinning**) **1** unfasten or detach by removing a pin or pins. **2** *Chess* release (a piece that has been pinned).

un·place·a·ble /únpláysəbəl/ *adj.* that cannot be placed or classified (*his accent was unplaceable*).

un·placed /únpláyst/ *adj.* not placed, esp. not placed as one of the first three finishing in a race, etc.

un·play·a·ble /únpláyəbəl/ *adj.* **1** *Sports* (of a ball) that cannot be struck or returned. **2** that cannot be played. ▫▫ **un·play·a·bly** *adv.*

un·plug /únplúg/ *v.tr.* (**unplugged, unplugging**) **1** disconnect (an electrical device) by removing its plug from the socket. **2** unstop.

un·pol·ished /únpólisht/ *adj.* **1** not polished; rough. **2** without refinement; crude.

un·pop·u·lar /únpópyələr/ *adj.* not popular; not liked by the public or by people in general. ▫▫ **un·pop·u·lar·i·ty** /–láritee/ *n.* **un·pop·u·lar·ly** *adv.*

un·prac·ti·cal /únpráktikəl/ *adj.* **1** not practical. **2** (of a person) not having practical skill. ▫▫ **un·prac·ti·cal·i·ty** /–kálitee/ *n.* **un·prac·ti·cal·ly** *adv.*

un·prac·ticed /únpráktist/ *adj.* **1** not experienced or skilled. **2** not put into practice.

un·prec·e·dent·ed /únprésidentid/ *adj.* **1** having no precedent; unparalleled. **2** novel. ▫▫ **un·prec·e·dent·ed·ly** *adv.*

un·pre·ten·tious /únpriténshəs/ *adj.* not making a great display; simple; modest. ▫▫ **un·pre·ten·tious·ly** *adv.* **un·pre·ten·tious·ness** *n.*

un·prin·ci·pled /únprínsipəld/ *adj.* lacking or not based on good moral principles. ▫▫ **un·prin·ci·pled·ness** *n.*

un·print·a·ble /únpríntəbəl/ *adj.* that cannot be printed, esp. because too indecent or libelous or blasphemous. ▫▫ **un·print·a·bly** *adv.*

un·pro·fes·sion·al /únprəféshənəl/ *adj.* **1** contrary to professional standards of behavior, etc. **2** not belonging to a profession; amateur. ▫▫ **un·pro·fes·sion·al·ly** *adv.*

un·prom·is·ing /únprómising/ *adj.* not likely to turn out well. ▫▫ **un·prom·is·ing·ly** *adv.*

un·prompt·ed /únprómptid/ *adj.* spontaneous.

un·proved /únproo͞vd/ *adj.* (also **un·prov·en** /–vən/) not proved.

un·pro·vid·ed /únprəvídid/ *adj.* (usu. foll. by *with*) not furnished, supplied, or equipped.

un·pro·voked /únprəvṓkt/ *adj.* (of a person or act) without provocation.

un·qual·i·fied /únkwólifīd/ *adj.* **1** not competent (*unqualified to give an answer*). **2** not legally or officially qualified (*an unqualified practitioner*). **3** not modified or restricted; complete (*unqualified assent*; *unqualified success*).

un·ques·tion·a·ble /únkwéschənəbəl/ *adj.* that cannot be disputed or doubted. ▫▫ **un·ques·tion·a·bil·i·ty** *n.* **un·ques·tion·a·ble·ness** *n.* **un·ques·tion·a·bly** *adv.*

un·ques·tioned /únkwéschənd/ *adj.* not disputed or doubted; definite; certain.

un·ques·tion·ing /únkwéschəning/ *adj.* **1** asking no questions. **2** done, etc., without asking questions. ▫▫ **un·ques·tion·ing·ly** *adv.*

un·qui·et /únkwíət/ *adj.* **1** restless; agitated; stirring. **2** perturbed, anxious. ▫▫ **un·qui·et·ly** *adv.* **un·qui·et·ness** *n.*

un·quote /únkwṓt/ *v.tr.* (as *int.*) (in dictation, reading aloud, etc.) indicate the presence of closing quotation marks (cf. QUOTE *v.* 5 b).

un·quot·ed /únkwṓtid/ *adj.* not quoted, esp. on a stock exchange.

un·rav·el /únrávəl/ *v.* **1** *tr.* cause to be no longer raveled, tangled, or intertwined. **2** *tr.* probe and solve (a mystery, etc.). **3** *tr.* undo (a fabric, esp. a knitted one). **4** *intr.* become disentangled or unknitted.

un·read /únréd/ *adj.* **1** (of a book, etc.) not read. **2** (of a person) not well-read.

un·read·a·ble /únréedəbəl/ *adj.* **1** too dull or too difficult to be worth reading. **2** illegible. □□ **un·read·a·bil·i·ty** /–bílitee/ *n.* **un·read·a·bly** *adv.*

un·re·al /únréeəl/ *adj.* **1** not real. **2** imaginary; illusory. **3** *sl.* incredible, amazing. □□ **un·re·al·i·ty** /–reeálitee/ *n.* **un·re·al·ly** *adv.*

un·rea·son /únréezən/ *n.* lack of reasonable thought or action.

un·rea·son·a·ble /únréezənəbəl/ *adj.* **1** going beyond the limits of what is reasonable or equitable (*unreasonable demands*). **2** not guided by or listening to reason. □□ **un·rea·son·a·ble·ness** *n.* **un·rea·son·a·bly** *adv.*

un·re·lent·ing /únrilénting/ *adj.* **1** not relenting or yielding. **2** unmerciful. **3** not abating or relaxing. □□ **un·re·lent·ing·ly** *adv.* **un·re·lent·ing·ness** *n.*

un·re·li·a·ble /únrilíəbəl/ *adj.* not reliable; erratic. □□ **un·re·li·a·bil·i·ty** *n.* **un·re·li·a·ble·ness** *n.* **un·re·li·a·bly** *adv.*

un·re·mark·a·ble /únrimaárkəbəl/ *adj.* not remarkable; uninteresting. □□ **un·re·mark·a·bly** *adv.*

un·re·mit·ting /únrimíting/ *adj.* never relaxing or slackening; incessant. □□ **un·re·mit·ting·ly** *adv.* **un·re·mit·ting·ness** *n.*

un·re·morse·ful /únrimáwrsfŏŏl/ *adj.* lacking remorse. □□ **un·re·morse·ful·ly** *adv.*

un·re·mu·ner·a·tive /únrimyŏŏnərətiv, –raytiv/ *adj.* bringing no, or not enough, profit or income. □□ **un·re·mu·ner·a·tive·ly** *adv.* **un·re·mu·ner·a·tive·ness** *n.*

un·re·peat·a·ble /únripéetəbəl/ *adj.* **1** that cannot be done, made, or said again. **2** too indecent to be said again. □□ **un·re·peat·a·bil·i·ty** *n.*

un·re·quit·ed /únrikwítid/ *adj.* (of love, etc.) not returned. □□ **un·re·quit·ed·ly** *adv.* **un·re·quit·ed·ness** *n.*

un·re·served /únrizə́rvd/ *adj.* **1** not reserved (*unreserved seats*). **2** without reservations; absolute (*unreserved confidence*). **3** free from reserve (*an unreserved nature*). □□ **un·re·serv·ed·ly** /–vidlee/ *adv.* **un·re·serv·ed·ness** *n.*

un·re·solved /únrizólvd/ *adj.* **1 a** uncertain how to act; irresolute. **b** uncertain in opinion; undecided. **2** (of questions, etc.) undetermined; undecided; unsolved. **3** not broken up or dissolved. □□ **un·re·sol·ved·ly** /–vidlee/ *adv.* **un·re·sol·ved·ness** *n.*

un·re·turned /únritə́rnd/ *adj.* **1** not reciprocated or responded to. **2** not having returned or been returned.

un·right·eous /únríchəs/ *adj.* not righteous; unjust; wicked; dishonest. □□ **un·right·eous·ly** *adv.* **un·right·eous·ness** *n.*

un·ri·valed /únrívəld/ *adj.* having no equal; peerless.

un·robe /únrṓb/ *v.tr.* & *intr.* **1** disrobe. **2** undress.

un·roll /únrṓl/ *v.tr.* & *intr.* **1** open out from a rolled-up state. **2** display or be displayed in this form.

un·ruf·fled /únrúfəld/ *adj.* **1** not agitated or disturbed; calm. **2** not physically ruffled.

un·ruled /únrŏŏld/ *adj.* **1** not ruled or governed. **2** not having ruled lines.

un·ru·ly /únrŏŏlee/ *adj.* (**unrulier, unruliest**) not easily controlled or disciplined; disorderly. □□ **un·ru·li·ness** *n.*

un·said[1] /únséd/ *adj.* not said or uttered.

un·said[2] *past* and *past part.* of UNSAY.

un·sat·is·fac·to·ry /únsatisfáktəree/ *adj.* not satisfactory; poor; unacceptable. □□ **un·sat·is·fac·to·ri·ly** *adv.* **un·sat·is·fac·to·ri·ness** *n.*

un·sat·u·rat·ed /únsáchəraytid/ *adj.* **1** *Chem.* (of a compound, esp. a fat or oil) having double or triple bonds in its molecule and therefore capable of further reaction. **2** not saturated. □□ **un·sat·u·ra·tion** /–ráyshən/ *n.*

un·sa·vor·y /únsáyvəree/ *adj.* **1** disagreeable to the taste, smell, or feelings; disgusting. **2** disagreeable; unpleasant (*an unsavory character*). **3** morally offensive. □□ **un·sa·vor·i·ly** *adv.* **un·sa·vor·i·ness** *n.*

un·say /únsáy/ *v.tr.* (*past* and *past part.* **unsaid**) retract (a statement).

un·scathed /únskáyt͟hd/ *adj.* without suffering any injury.

un·schooled /únskŏŏld/ *adj.* **1** uneducated; untaught. **2** not sent to school. **3** untrained; undisciplined. **4** not made artificial by education.

un·sci·en·tif·ic /únsīəntífik/ *adj.* **1** not in accordance with scientific principles. **2** not familiar with science. □□ **un·sci·en·tif·i·cal·ly** *adv.*

un·scram·ble /únskrámbəl/ *v.tr.* restore from a scrambled state, esp. interpret (a scrambled transmission, etc.). □□ **un·scram·bler** *n.*

un·screw /únskrŏŏ/ *v.* **1** *tr.* & *intr.* unfasten or be unfastened by turning or removing a screw or screws or by twisting like a screw. **2** *tr.* loosen (a screw).

un·script·ed /únskríptid/ *adj.* (of a speech, etc.) delivered without a prepared script.

un·scru·pu·lous /únskrŏŏpyələs/ *adj.* having no scruples; unprincipled. □□ **un·scru·pu·lous·ly** *adv.* **un·scru·pu·lous·ness** *n.*

un·seal /únséel/ *v.tr.* break the seal of; open (a letter, receptacle, etc.).

un·sea·son·a·ble /únséezənəbəl/ *adj.* **1** not appropriate to the season. **2** untimely; inopportune. □□ **un·sea·son·a·ble·ness** *n.* **un·sea·son·a·bly** *adv.*

un·sea·soned /únséezənd/ *adj.* **1** not flavored with salt, herbs, etc. **2** (esp. of timber) not matured. **3** not habituated.

un·seat /únséet/ *v.tr.* **1** remove from a seat, esp. in an election. **2** dislodge from a seat, esp. on horseback.

un·see·ing /únséeing/ *adj.* **1** unobservant. **2** blind. □□ **un·see·ing·ly** *adv.*

un·seem·ly /únséemlee/ *adj.* (**unseemlier, unseemliest**) **1** indecent. **2** unbecoming. □□ **un·seem·li·ness** *n.*

un·sel·fish /únsélfish/ *adj.* mindful of others' interests. □□ **un·sel·fish·ly** *adv.* **un·sel·fish·ness** *n.*

un·ser·vice·a·ble /únsə́rvisəbəl/ *adj.* not serviceable; unfit for use. □□ **un·ser·vice·a·bil·i·ty** *n.*

un·set·tle /únsét'l/ *v.* **1** *tr.* disturb the settled state or arrangement of; discompose. **2** *tr.* derange. **3** *intr.* become unsettled. □□ **un·set·tle·ment** *n.* **un·set·tling** *adj.*

un·set·tled /únsét'ld/ *adj.* **1** not (yet) settled. **2** liable or open to change or further discussion. **3** (of a bill, etc.) unpaid. □□ **un·set·tled·ness** *n.*

un·sex /únséks/ *v.tr.* deprive (a person, esp. a woman) of the qualities of her or his sex.

un·sexed /únsékst/ *adj.* having no sexual characteristics.

un·shack·le /únshákəl/ *v.tr.* **1** release from shackles. **2** set free.

un·shak·a·ble /únsháykəbəl/ *adj.* (also **un·shake·a·ble**) that cannot be shaken; firm; obstinate. □□ **un·shak·a·bil·i·ty** *n.* **un·shak·a·bly** *adv.*

un·sheathe /únshéet͟h/ *v.tr.* remove (a knife, etc.) from a sheath.

un·shod /únshód/ *adj.* not wearing shoes.

un·shrink·a·ble /únshríngkəbəl/ *adj.* (of fabric, etc.) not liable to shrink. □□ **un·shrink·a·bil·i·ty** /–bílitee/ *n.*

un·shrink·ing /únshríngking/ *adj.* unhesitating; fearless. □□ **un·shrink·ing·ly** *adv.*

un·sight·ly /únsítlee/ *adj.* unpleasant to look at; ugly. □□ **un·sight·li·ness** *n.*
un·skilled /únskíld/ *adj.* lacking or not needing special skill or training.
un·so·cia·ble /únsṓshəbəl/ *adj.* not sociable; disliking the company of others. □□ **un·so·cia·bil·i·ty** /–bílitee/ *n.* **un·so·cia·ble·ness** *n.* **un·so·cia·bly** *adv.*
un·so·lic·it·ed /únsəlísitid/ *adj.* not asked for; given or done voluntarily. □□ **un·so·lic·it·ed·ly** *adv.*
un·so·phis·ti·cat·ed /únsəfístikaytid/ *adj.* **1** artless; simple; natural; ingenuous. **2** not adulterated or artificial. □□ **un·so·phis·ti·cat·ed·ly** *adv.* **un·so·phis·ti·cat·ed·ness** *n.* **un·so·phis·ti·ca·tion** /–káyshən/ *n.*
un·sound /únsównd/ *adj.* **1** unhealthy; diseased. **2** rotten; weak. **3 a** ill-founded; fallacious. **b** unorthodox; heretical. **4** unreliable. **5** wicked. □ **of unsound mind** insane. □□ **un·sound·ly** *adv.* **un·sound·ness** *n.*
un·spar·ing /únspáiring/ *adj.* **1** lavish; profuse. **2** merciless. □□ **un·spar·ing·ly** *adv.* **un·spar·ing·ness** *n.*
un·speak·a·ble /únspeékəbəl/ *adj.* **1** that cannot be expressed in words. **2** indescribably bad or objectionable. □□ **un·speak·a·ble·ness** *n.* **un·speak·a·bly** *adv.*
un·spent /únspént/ *adj.* **1** not expended or used. **2** not exhausted or used up.
un·spoiled /únspóyld/ *adj.* **1** not spoiled. **2** not plundered.
un·spoilt /únspóylt/ *adj.* not spoiled.
un·sport·ing /únspáwrting/ *adj.* not sportsmanlike; not fair or generous. □□ **un·sport·ing·ly** *adv.* **un·sport·ing·ness** *n.*
un·sports·man·like /únspáwrtsmənlīk/ *adj.* unsporting.
un·sta·ble /únstáybəl/ *adj.* (**unstabler, unstablest**) **1** not stable. **2** changeable. **3** showing a tendency to sudden mental or emotional changes. □□ **un·sta·ble·ness** *n.* **un·sta·bly** *adv.*
un·stead·y /únstédee/ *adj.* (**unsteadier, unsteadiest**) **1** not steady or firm. **2** changeable; fluctuating. **3** not uniform or regular. □□ **un·stead·i·ly** *adv.* **un·stead·i·ness** *n.*
un·stick *v.* /únstík/ (*past* and *past part.* **unstuck** /–stúk/) *tr.* separate (a thing stuck to another). □ **come unstuck** *colloq.* come to grief; fail.
un·stint·ing /únstínting/ *adj.* ungrudging; lavish. □□ **un·stint·ing·ly** *adv.*
un·stop·pa·ble /únstópəbəl/ *adj.* that cannot be stopped or prevented. □□ **un·stop·pa·bil·i·ty** /–bílitee/ *n.* **un·stop·pa·bly** *adv.*
un·strained /únstráynd/ *adj.* **1** not subjected to straining or stretching. **2** not injured by overuse or excessive demands. **3** not forced or produced by effort. **4** not passed through a strainer.
un·strap /únstráp/ *v.tr.* (**unstrapped, unstrapping**) undo the strap or straps of.
un·stressed /únstrést/ *adj.* **1** (of a word, syllable, etc.) not pronounced with stress. **2** not subjected to stress.
un·string /únstríng/ *v.tr.* (*past* and *past part.* **unstrung**) **1** remove or relax the string or strings of (a bow, harp, etc.). **2** remove from a string. **3** (esp. as **unstrung** *adj.*) unnerve.
un·struc·tured /únstrúkchərd/ *adj.* **1** not structured. **2** informal.
un·stuck *past* and *past part.* of UNSTICK.
un·stud·ied /únstúdeed/ *adj.* easy; natural; spontaneous. □□ **un·stud·ied·ly** *adv.*
un·sub·stan·tial /únsəbstánshəl/ *adj.* having little or no solidity, reality, or factual basis. □□ **un·sub·stan·ti·al·i·ty** /–sheeálitee/ *n.* **un·sub·stan·tial·ly** *adv.*
un·sung /únsúng/ *adj.* **1** not celebrated in song; unknown. **2** not sung.
un·sup·port·a·ble /únsəpáwrtəbəl/ *adj.* **1** that cannot be endured. **2** indefensible. □□ **un·sup·port·a·bly** *adv.*
un·sure /únshŏor/ *adj.* not sure; doubtful. □□ **un·sure·ly** *adv.* **un·sure·ness** *n.*
un·swerv·ing /únswə́rving/ *adj.* **1** steady; constant. **2** not turning aside. □□ **un·swerv·ing·ly** *adv.*
un·tan·gle /úntánggəl/ *v.tr.* **1** free from a tangled state. **2** free from entanglement.
un·tapped /úntápt/ *adj.* not (yet) tapped or wired (*untapped resources*).
un·taught /úntáwt/ *adj.* **1** not instructed by teaching; ignorant. **2** not acquired by teaching; natural; spontaneous.
un·teach /únteéch/ *v.tr.* (*past* and *past part.* **untaught**) **1** cause (a person) to forget or discard previous knowledge. **2** remove from the mind (something known or taught) by different teaching.
un·tem·pered /úntémpərd/ *adj.* (of metal, etc.) not brought to the proper hardness or consistency.
un·ten·a·ble /únténəbəl/ *adj.* not tenable; that cannot be defended. □□ **un·ten·a·bil·i·ty** *n.* **un·ten·a·ble·ness** *n.* **un·ten·a·bly** *adv.*
un·think·a·ble /únthíngkəbəl/ *adj.* **1** that cannot be imagined or grasped by the mind. **2** *colloq.* highly unlikely or undesirable. □□ **un·think·a·bil·i·ty** /–bílitee/ *n.* **un·think·a·ble·ness** *n.* **un·think·a·bly** *adv.*
un·think·ing /únthíngking/ *adj.* **1** thoughtless. **2** unintentional; inadvertent. □□ **un·think·ing·ly** *adv.* **un·think·ing·ness** *n.*
un·thought·ful /únthháwtfŏol/ *adj.* unthinking; unmindful; thoughtless. □□ **un·thought·ful·ly** *adv.* **un·thought·ful·ness** *n.*
un·tie /úntí/ *v.tr.* (*pres. part.* **untying**) **1** undo (a knot, etc.). **2** unfasten the cords, etc., of (a package, etc.). **3** release from bonds or attachment.
un·tied /úntíd/ *adj.* not tied.
un·til /əntíl, un–/ *prep. & conj.* = TILL[1].
▶**Until** is more formal than **till**, and is more usual at the beginning of a sentence, e.g., *Until the 1920s it was quite unusual for women to wear short hair.* **'Til** is considered incorrect in standard English and should be avoided.
un·time·ly /úntímlee/ *adj. & adv.* • *adj.* **1** inopportune. **2** (of death) premature. • *adv. archaic* **1** inopportunely. **2** prematurely. □□ **un·time·li·ness** *n.*
un·tir·ing /úntíring/ *adj.* tireless. □□ **un·tir·ing·ly** *adv.*
un·ti·tled /úntít'ld/ *adj.* having no title.
un·to /úntōō, úntə/ *prep. archaic* = TO (in all uses except as the sign of the infinitive) (*do unto others*; *faithful unto death*; *take unto oneself*).
un·told /úntṓld/ *adj.* **1** not told. **2** not (able to be) counted or measured (*untold misery*).
un·touch·a·ble /úntúchəbəl/ *adj. & n.* • *adj.* that may not or cannot be touched. • *n.* a member of a hereditary Hindu group held to defile members of higher castes on contact.
▶Use of the term, and social restrictions accompanying it, were declared illegal under the Indian constitution in 1949. □□ **un·touch·a·bil·i·ty** *n.* **un·touch·a·ble·ness** *n.*
un·touched /úntúcht/ *adj.* **1** not touched. **2** not affected physically; not harmed, modified, used, or tasted. **3** not affected by emotion. **4** not discussed.
un·to·ward /úntáwrd, –təwáwrd/ *adj.* **1** inconvenient; unlucky. **2** awkward. **3** perverse, refractory. **4** unseemly. □□ **un·to·ward·ly** *adv.* **un·to·ward·ness** *n.*
un·trav·eled /úntrávəld/ *adj.* **1** that has not traveled. **2** that has not been traveled over or through.
un·treat·a·ble /úntreétəbəl/ *adj.* (of a disease, etc.) that cannot be treated.
un·tried /úntríd/ *adj.* **1** not tried or tested. **2** inexperienced. **3** not yet tried by a judge.

un·trou·bled /úntrúbəld/ *adj.* not troubled; calm; tranquil.
un·true /úntróó/ *adj.* **1** not true; contrary to what is the fact. **2** (often foll. by *to*) not faithful or loyal. **3** deviating from an accepted standard. □□ **un·tru·ly** *adv.*
un·truth /úntróóth/ *n.* (*pl.* **untruths** /–tróóthz, –tróóths/) **1** the state of being untrue; falsehood. **2** a false statement (*told me an untruth*). □□ **un·truth·ful** *adj.*
un·ty·ing *pres. part.* of UNTIE.
un·used *adj.* **1** /únyóózd/ **a** not in use. **b** never having been used. **2** /únyóóst/ (foll. by *to*) not accustomed.
un·u·su·al /únyóózhooəl/ *adj.* **1** not usual. **2** exceptional; remarkable. □□ **un·u·su·al·ly** *adv.* **un·u·su·al·ness** *n.*
un·ut·ter·a·ble /únútərəbəl/ *adj.* inexpressible; beyond description (*unutterable torment*; *an unutterable fool*). □□ **un·ut·ter·a·ble·ness** *n.* **un·ut·ter·a·bly** *adv.*
un·val·ued /únvályood/ *adj.* **1** not regarded as valuable. **2** not having been valued.
un·var·nished /únvaárnisht/ *adj.* **1** not varnished. **2** (of a statement or person) plain and straightforward (*the unvarnished truth*).
un·veil /únváyl/ *v.* **1** *tr.* remove a veil from. **2** *tr.* remove a covering from (a statue, plaque, etc.) as part of the ceremony of the first public display. **3** *tr.* disclose; reveal; make publicly known. **4** *intr.* remove one's veil.
un·ven·ti·lat·ed /únvént'laytid/ *adj.* **1** not provided with a means of ventilation. **2** not discussed.
un·versed /únvə́rst/ *adj.* (usu. foll. by *in*) not experienced or skilled.
un·war·rant·ed /únwáwrəntid, –wór–/ *adj.* **1** unauthorized. **2** unjustified.
un·war·y /únwáiree/ *adj.* **1** not cautious. **2** (often foll. by *of*) not aware of possible danger, etc. □□ **un·war·i·ly** *adv.* **un·war·i·ness** *n.*
un·washed /únwósht, –wáwsht/ *adj.* **1** not washed. **2** not usually washed or clean. □ **the great unwashed** *colloq.* the rabble.
un·wea·ried /únwéereed/ *adj.* **1** not wearied or tired. **2** never becoming weary; indefatigable. **3** unremitting. □□ **un·wea·ried·ly** *adv.* **un·wea·ried·ness** *n.*
un·wea·ry·ing /únwéereeing/ *adj.* **1** persistent. **2** not causing or producing weariness. □□ **un·wea·ry·ing·ly** *adv.*
un·wed /únwéd/ *adj.* not married.
un·weighed /únwáyd/ *adj.* **1** not considered; hasty. **2** (of goods) not weighed.
un·wel·come /únwélkəm/ *adj.* not welcome or acceptable. □□ **un·wel·come·ly** *adv.* **un·wel·come·ness** *n.*
un·well /únwél/ *adj.* **1** not in good health; (somewhat) ill. **2** indisposed.
un·whole·some /únhṓlsəm/ *adj.* **1** not promoting, or detrimental to, physical or moral health. **2** unhealthy; insalubrious. **3** unhealthy-looking. □□ **un·whole·some·ly** *adv.* **un·whole·some·ness** *n.*
un·wield·y /únwéeldee/ *adj.* (**unwieldier, unwieldiest**) cumbersome, clumsy, or hard to manage, owing to size, shape, or weight. □□ **un·wield·i·ly** *adv.* **un·wield·i·ness** *n.*
un·will·ing /únwíling/ *adj.* not willing or inclined; reluctant. □□ **un·will·ing·ly** *adv.* **un·will·ing·ness** *n.*
un·wind /únwínd/ *v.* (*past* and *past part.* **unwound** /–wównd/) **1 a** *tr.* draw out (a thing that has been wound). **b** *intr.* become drawn out after having been wound. **2** *intr.* & *tr.* *colloq.* relax.
un·wink·ing /únwíngking/ *adj.* **1** not winking. **2** watchful; vigilant. □□ **un·wink·ing·ly** *adv.*
un·wise /únwíz/ *adj.* **1** foolish; imprudent. **2** injudicious. □□ **un·wise·ly** *adv.*
un·wit·ting /únwíting/ *adj.* **1** unaware of the state of the case (*an unwitting offender*). **2** unintentional. □□ **un·wit·ting·ly** *adv.* **un·wit·ting·ness** *n.*
un·wont·ed /únwáwntid, –wṓn–, –wún–/ *adj.* not customary or usual. □□ **un·wont·ed·ly** *adv.* **un·wont·ed·ness** *n.*
un·work·a·ble /únwə́rkəbəl/ *adj.* not workable; impracticable. □□ **un·work·a·bil·i·ty** *n.* **un·work·a·ble·ness** *n.* **un·work·a·bly** *adv.*
un·worked /únwə́rkt/ *adj.* not cultivated, mined, carved, or wrought into shape.
un·world·ly /únwə́rldlee/ *adj.* **1** spiritually minded. **2** spiritual. □□ **un·world·li·ness** *n.*
un·worn /únwáwrn/ *adj.* not worn or impaired by wear.
un·wor·thy /únwúrthee/ *adj.* (**unworthier, unworthiest**) **1** (often foll. by *of*) not worthy or befitting the character of a person, etc. **2** discreditable; unseemly. **3** contemptible; base. □□ **un·wor·thi·ly** *adv.* **un·wor·thi·ness** *n.*
un·wound[1] /únwównd/ *adj.* not wound or wound up.
un·wound[2] *past* and *past part.* of UNWIND.
un·wrap /únráp/ *v.* (**unwrapped, unwrapping**) **1** *tr.* remove the wrapping from. **2** *tr.* open or unfold. **3** *intr.* become unwrapped.
un·writ·ten /únrít'n/ *adj.* **1** not written. **2** (of a law, etc.) resting originally on custom or judicial decision, not on statute.
un·yield·ing /únyéelding/ *adj.* **1** not yielding to pressure, etc. **2** firm; obstinate. □□ **un·yield·ing·ly** *adv.* **un·yield·ing·ness** *n.*
un·zip /únzíp/ *v.tr.* (**unzipped, unzipping**) unfasten the zipper of.
up /up/ *adv., prep., adj., n., & v.* • *adv.* **1** at, in, or toward a higher place or position (*jumped up in the air*). **2** to or in a place regarded as higher, esp.: **a** northward (*up in New England*). **b** *Brit.* toward a major city or a university (*went up to London*). **3** *colloq.* ahead, etc., as indicated (*went up front*). **4 a** to or in an erect position or condition (*stood it up*). **b** to or in a prepared or required position (*wound up the watch*). **c** in or into a condition of efficiency, activity, or progress (*stirred up trouble*; *the house is up for sale*). **5** in a stronger or winning position or condition (*our team was three goals up*; *am $10 up on the transaction*). **6** (of a computer) running and available for use. **7** to the place or time in question or where the speaker, etc., is (*a child came up to me*; *went straight up to the door*; *has been fine up till now*). **8** at or to a higher price or value (*our costs are up*; *shares are up*). **9 a** completely or effectually (*burn up*; *eat up*; *tear up*; *use up*). **b** more loudly or clearly (*speak up*). **10** in a state of completion; denoting the end of availability, supply, etc. (*time is up*). **11** into a compact, accumulated, or secure state (*pack up*; *save up*; *tie up*). **12 a** awake. **b** out of bed (*are you up yet?*). **13** (of the sun, etc.) having risen. **14** happening, esp. unusually or unexpectedly (*something is up*). **15** esp. *Brit.* (usu. foll. by *on* or *in*) taught or informed (*is well up in French*). **16** (usu. foll. by *before*) appearing for trial, etc. (*was up before the judge*). **17** *Brit.* (of a road, etc.) being repaired. **18** (of a jockey) in the saddle. **19** toward the source of a river. **20** inland. **21** (of the points, etc., in a game): **a** registered on the scoreboard. **b** forming the total score for the time being. **22** upstairs, esp. to bed (*are you going up yet?*). **23** (of a theater curtain) raised, etc., to reveal the stage. **24** (as *int.*) get up. **25** *Baseball* at bat (*he struck out his last time up*). • *prep.* **1** upward along, through, or into (*climbed up the ladder*). **2** from the bottom to the top of. **3** along (*walked up the road*). **4 a** at or in a higher part of (*is situated up the street*). **b** toward the source of (a river). • *adj.* (often in *comb.*) directed upward (*upstroke*). • *n.* a spell of good fortune. • *v.* (**upped, upping**) **1** *intr. colloq.* start up; begin abruptly to say or do something (*upped and hit him*). **2** *intr.* (foll. by *with*) raise; pick up

(*upped with his stick*). **3** *tr.* increase or raise, esp. abruptly (*upped all their prices*). □ **on the up and up** *colloq.* **1** honest(ly); on the level. **2** *Brit.* steadily improving. **something is up** *colloq.* something unusual or undesirable is afoot or happening. **up against 1** close to. **2** in or into contact with. **3** *colloq.* confronted with (*up against a problem*). **up against it** *colloq.* in great difficulties. **up and about** having risen from bed; active. **up and down 1** moving upward and downward. **2** *colloq.* in varying health or spirits. **up for** available for or being considered for (office, etc.). **up to 1** until (*up to the present*). **2** not more than (*you can have up to five*). **3** less than or equal to (*adds up to $10*). **4** incumbent on (*it is up to you to say*). **5** capable of or fit for (*am not up to a long walk*). **6** occupied or busy with (*what have you been up to?*). **up with** *int.* expressing support for a stated person or thing. **what's up?** *colloq.* **1** what is going on? **2** what is the matter?

up-and-com·ing *adj.* (of a person) making good progress and likely to succeed.

u·pas /yóōpəs/ *n.* **1** (in full **upas tree**) **a** a Javanese tree, *Antiaris toxicaria*, yielding a milky sap used as arrow poison. **b** *Mythol.* a Javanese tree thought to be fatal to whatever came near it. **c** a pernicious influence, practice, etc. **2** the poisonous sap of upas and other trees.

up·beat /úpbeet/ *n. & adj.* • *n.* an unaccented beat in music. • *adj. colloq.* optimistic or cheerful.

up·braid /upbráyd/ *v.tr.* (often foll. by *with, for*) chide or reproach (a person). □□ **up·braid·ing** *n.*

up·bring·ing /úpbringing/ *n.* the bringing up of a child; education.

UPC *abbr.* = Universal Product Code.

up·cast *n. & v.* • *n.* /úpkast/ **1** the act of casting up; an upward throw. **2** *Mining* a shaft through which air leaves a mine. • *v.tr.* /úpkást/ (*past* and *past part.* **upcast**) cast up.

up·chuck /úpchuk/ *v.tr. & intr. sl.* vomit.

up·com·ing /úpkúming/ *adj.* forthcoming; about to happen.

up-coun·try /úpkúntree/ *adv. & adj.* inland; toward the interior of a country.

up·date *v. & n.* • *v.tr.* /úpdáyt/ bring up to date. • *n.* /úpdayt/ **1** the act or an instance of updating. **2** an updated version; a set of updated information. □□ **up·dat·er** *n.*

up·draft /úpdraft/ *n.* an upward draft of gas, esp. smoke in a chimney.

up·end /úpénd/ *v.tr. & intr.* set or rise up on end.

up·field /úpfeeld/ *adv.* in or to a position nearer to the opponents' end of a football, etc., field.

up·front /úpfrúnt/ *adv. & adj.* • *adv.* **1** at the front; in front. **2** (of payments) in advance. • *adj.* **1** honest; frank. **2** (of payments) made in advance.

up·grade *v. & n.* • *v.tr.* /úpgráyd/ **1** raise in rank, etc. **2** improve (equipment, machinery, etc.) esp. by replacing components. • *n.* /úpgrayd/ **1** the act or an instance of upgrading. **2** an upgraded piece of equipment, etc. **3** an upward slope. □ **on the upgrade 1** improving in health, etc. **2** advancing; progressing. □□ **up·grad·er** *n.*

up·growth /úpgrōth/ *n.* the process or result of growing upward.

up·heav·al /upheévəl/ *n.* **1** a violent or sudden change or disruption. **2** *Geol.* an upward displacement of part of the earth's crust. **3** the act or an instance of heaving up.

up·heave /upheév/ *v.* **1** *tr.* heave or lift up, esp. forcibly. **2** *intr.* rise up.

up·hill *adv., adj., & n.* • *adv.* /úphíl/ in an ascending direction up a hill, slope, etc. • *adj.* /úphíl/ **1** sloping up; ascending. **2** arduous; difficult (*an uphill task*). • *n.* /úphil/ an upward slope.

up·hold /úphṓld/ *v.tr.* (*past* and *past part.* **upheld** /–held/) **1** confirm or maintain (a decision, etc., esp. of another). **2** give support or countenance to (a person, practice, etc.). □□ **up·hold·er** *n.*

up·hol·ster /uphṓlstər, əpṓl–/ *v.tr.* **1** provide (furniture) with upholstery. **2** furnish (a room, etc.) with furniture, carpets, etc. □□ **up·hol·ster·er** *n.*

up·hol·ster·er /uphṓlstərər, əpṓl–/ *n.* a person who upholsters furniture, esp. professionally.

up·hol·ster·y /uphṓlstəree, əpṓl–/ *n.* **1** textile covering, padding, springs, etc., for furniture. **2** an upholsterer's work.

up·keep /úpkeep/ *n.* **1** maintenance in good condition. **2** the cost or means of this.

up·land /úplənd/ *n. & adj.* • *n.* the higher or inland parts of a country. • *adj.* of or relating to these parts.

up·lift *v. & n.* • *v.tr.* /úplíft/ **1** esp. *Brit.* raise; lift up. **2** elevate or stimulate morally or spiritually. • *n.* /úplift/ **1** the act or an instance of being raised. **2** *Geol.* the raising of part of the earth's surface. **3** *colloq.* a morally or spiritually elevating influence. **4** support for the bust, etc., from a garment. □□ **up·lift·er** *n.* **up·lift·ing** *adj.* (esp. in sense 2 of *v.*).

up·mar·ket /úpmaárkit/ *adj. & adv.* = UPSCALE.

up·most var. of UPPERMOST.

up·on /əpón, əpáwn/ *prep.* = ON.

▶**Upon** is sometimes more formal, and is preferred to **on** in *once upon a time* and *upon my word*, and in uses such as *row upon row of seats* and *Christmas is almost upon us*.

up·per[1] /úpər/ *adj. & n.* • *adj.* **1 a** higher in place; situated above another part (*the upper atmosphere*; *the upper lip*). **b** *Geol.* designating a younger (and usually shallower) part of a stratigraphic division, or the period of its formation (*the Upper Jurassic*). **2** higher in rank or dignity, etc. (*the upper class*). **3** situated on higher ground, further to the north, or further inland (*Upper Egypt*). • *n.* the part of a boot or shoe above the sole. □ **on one's uppers** *colloq.* extremely short of money.

up·per[2] /úpər/ *n. sl.* a stimulant drug, esp. an amphetamine.

up·per·case /úpərkáys/ *adj., n., & v.* • *adj.* (of letters) capital. • *n.* capital letters. • *v.tr.* set or print in uppercase.

up·per class *n.* the highest class of society, esp. (in the UK) the aristocracy. □□ **up·per-class** *adj.*

up·per crust *n. colloq.* (in the UK) the aristocracy. □□ **up·per-crust** *adj.*

up·per·cut /úpərkut/ *n. & v.* • *n.* an upward blow delivered with the arm bent. • *v.tr.* hit with an uppercut.

up·per hand *n.* dominance or control.

up·per house *n.* the higher house in a legislature, e.g., the U.S. Senate.

up·per·most /úpərmōst/ *adj. & adv.* • *adj.* (also **up·most** /úpmōst/) **1** highest in place or rank. **2** predominant. • *adv.* at or to the highest or most prominent position.

up·pi·ty /úpitee/ *adj. colloq.* arrogant; snobbish.

up·right /úprīt/ *adj., adv., & n.* • *adj.* **1** erect; vertical (*an upright posture*; *stood upright*). **2** (of a piano) with vertical strings. **3** (of a person or behavior) righteous; strictly honorable or honest. **4** (of a picture, book, etc.) greater in height than breadth. • *adv.* in a vertical direction; vertically upward; into an upright position. • *n.* **1** a post or rod fixed upright, esp. as a structural support. **2** an upright piano. □□ **up·right·ly** *adv.* **up·right·ness** *n.*

up·ris·ing /úprīzing/ *n.* a rebellion or revolt.

up·roar /úprawr/ *n.* a tumult; a violent disturbance.

up·roar·i·ous /upráwreeəs/ *adj.* **1** very noisy; tumultuous. **2** provoking loud laughter. ▫▫ **up·roar·i·ous·ly** *adv.* **up·roar·i·ous·ness** *n.*

up·root /úpróot, róot/ *v.tr.* **1** pull (a plant, etc.) up from the ground. **2** displace (a person) from an accustomed location. **3** eradicate; destroy. ▫▫ **up·root·er** *n.*

up·sa·dai·sy var. of UPSY-DAISY.

ups and downs *n.pl.* **1** rises and falls. **2** alternate good and bad fortune.

up·scale /úpskáyl/ *adj., v., & n.* • *adj.* toward or relating to the more affluent or upper sector of society or the market. • *v.tr.* improve the quality or value of. • *n.* (as *pl.*) upscale persons collectively (*apartments built for the upscale*).

up·set *v., n., & adj.* • *v.* /úpsét/ (**upsetting**; *past* and *past part.* **upset**) **1 a** *tr. & intr.* overturn or be overturned. **b** *tr.* overcome; defeat. **2** *tr.* disturb the composure or digestion of (*was very upset by the news*; *ate something that upset me*). **3** *tr.* disrupt. **4** *tr.* shorten and thicken (metal, esp. a tire) by hammering or pressure. • *n.* /úpset/ **1** a condition of upsetting or being upset (*a stomach upset*). **2** a surprising result in a game, etc. • *adj.* /úpsét/ disturbed (*an upset stomach*). ▫▫ **up·set·ter** *n.* **up·set·ting·ly** *adv.*

up·shot /úpshot/ *n.* the final or eventual outcome or conclusion.

up·side down /úpsīd dówn/ *adv. & adj.* • *adv.* **1** with the upper part where the lower part should be; in an inverted position. **2** in or into total disorder (*everything was turned upside down*). • *adj.* (also **up·side-down** *attrib.*) that is positioned upside down; inverted.

up·side-down cake *n.* a cake baked with fruit in a syrup at the bottom, and inverted for serving.

up·si·lon /úpsilon, yóop–/ *n.* the twentieth letter of the Greek alphabet (Υ, υ).

up·stage /úpstáyj/ *adj., adv., v., & n.* • *adj. & adv.* **1** nearer the back of a theater stage. **2** snobbish(ly). • *v.tr.* **1** (of an actor) move upstage to make (another actor) face away from the audience. **2** divert attention from (a person) to oneself; outshine. • *n.* the part of the stage farthest from the audience.

up·stairs /úpstáirz/ *adv., adj., & n.* • *adv.* to or on an upper floor. • *adj.* (also **up·stair**) situated upstairs. • *n.* an upper floor.

up·stand·ing /úpstánding/ *adj.* **1** standing up. **2** strong and healthy. **3** honest or straightforward.

up·start /úpstaart/ *n. & adj.* • *n.* a person who has risen suddenly to prominence, esp. one who behaves arrogantly. • *adj.* **1** that is an upstart. **2** of or characteristic of an upstart.

up·state /úpstáyt/ *n., adj., & adv.* • *n.* part of a state remote from its large cities, esp. the northern part (*upstate New York*). • *adj.* of or relating to this part. • *adv.* in or to this part. ▫▫ **up·stat·er** *n.*

up·stream /úpstréem/ *adv. & adj.* • *adv.* against the flow of a stream, etc. • *adj.* moving upstream.

up·surge /úpsərj/ *n.* an upward surge; a rise (esp. in feelings, etc.).

up·swept /úpswept/ *adj.* **1** (of the hair) combed to the top of the head. **2** curved or sloped upward.

up·swing /úpswing/ *n.* an upward movement or trend.

up·sy-dai·sy /úpseedáyzee/ *int.* (also **up·sa-dai·sy**) expressing encouragement to a child who is being lifted or has fallen.

up·take /úptayk/ *n.* **1** *colloq.* understanding; comprehension (esp. *quick* or *slow on the uptake*). **2** the act or an instance of taking up.

up·throw /úpthrō/ *n.* **1** the act or an instance of throwing upward. **2** *Geol.* an upward dislocation of strata.

up·thrust /úpthrust/ *n.* **1** upward thrust, e.g., of a fluid on an immersed body. **2** *Geol.* = UPHEAVAL.

up·tight /úptīt/ *adj. colloq.* **1** nervously tense or angry. **2** rigidly conventional.

up-to-date *adj.* meeting or according to the latest requirements, knowledge, or fashion; modern.

up-to-the-minute *adj.* (usu. *attrib.*) completely up to date.

up·town /úptówn/ *adj., adv., & n.* • *adj.* **1** of or in the residential part of a town or city. **2** characteristic of or suitable to affluent or sophisticated people. • *adv.* in or into this part. • *n.* this part. ▫▫ **up·town·er** *n.*

up·turn *n. & v.* • *n.* /úptərn/ **1** an upward trend; an improvement. **2** an upheaval. • *v.tr.* /úptúrn/ turn up or upside down.

up·ward /úpwərd/ *adv. & adj.* • *adv.* (also **up·wards**) toward what is higher, superior, larger in amount, more important, or earlier. • *adj.* moving, extending, pointing, or leading upward. ▫ **upwards of** more than (*found upwards of forty specimens*).

up·ward·ly /úpwərdlee/ *adv.* in an upward direction.

up·ward·ly mo·bile *adj.* able or aspiring to advance socially or professionally.

up·wind /úpwínd/ *adj. & adv.* against the direction of the wind.

u·ra·ni·um /yŏoráyneeəm/ *n. Chem.* a radioactive, gray, dense metallic element occurring naturally in pitchblende, and capable of nuclear fission and therefore used as a source of nuclear energy. ¶ Symb.: **U.** ▫▫ **u·ran·ic** /–ránik/ *adj.*

U·ran·us /yŏorənəs, yŏoráynəs/ *n.* a planet discovered by Herschel in 1781, seventh in order from the sun.

ur·ban /ərbən/ *adj.* of, living in, or situated in a town or city (*an urban population*) (opp. RURAL).

ur·bane /ərbáyn/ *adj.* courteous; suave; elegant and refined in manner. ▫▫ **ur·bane·ly** *adv.* **ur·bane·ness** *n.*

ur·ban·ite /ərbənīt/ *n.* a dweller in a city or town.

ur·ban·i·ty /ərbánitee/ *n.* **1** an urbane quality; refinement of manner. **2** urban life.

ur·ban·ize /ərbənīz/ *v.tr.* **1** make urban. **2** destroy the rural quality of (a district). ▫▫ **ur·ban·i·za·tion** /–záyshən/ *n.*

ur·ban re·new·al *n.* slum clearance and redevelopment in a city or town.

ur·ban sprawl *n.* the uncontrolled expansion of urban areas.

ur·chin /ərchin/ *n.* **1** a mischievous child, esp. young and raggedly dressed. **2** = SEA URCHIN.

Ur·du /ŏordōo, ər–/ *n.* a language related to Hindi but with many Persian words, an official language of Pakistan and also used in India.

u·re·a /yŏoréeə/ *n. Biochem.* a soluble, colorless, crystalline, nitrogenous compound contained esp. in the urine of mammals. ▫▫ **u·re·al** *adj.*

u·re·mi·a /yŏoréemeeə/ *n. Med.* a morbid condition due to the presence in the blood of urinary matter normally eliminated by the kidneys. ▫▫ **u·re·mic** /–mik/ *adj.*

u·re·ter /yŏoréetər/ *n.* the duct by which urine passes from the kidney to the bladder or cloaca. ▫▫ **u·re·ter·al** *adj.* **u·re·ter·ic** /yóoritérik/ *adj.* **u·re·ter·i·tis** /–rītis/ *n.*

u·re·thane /yŏorithayn/ *n. Chem.* a crystalline amide, ethyl carbamate, used in plastics and paints.

u·re·thra /yŏoréethrə/ *n.* (*pl.* **urethras** or **urethrae** /–ree/) the duct by which urine is discharged from the bladder. ▫▫ **u·re·thral** *adj.* **u·re·thri·tis** /–rithrītis/ *n.*

urge /ərj/ *v. & n.* • *v.tr.* **1** (often foll. by *on*) drive forcibly; impel; hasten (*urged them on*; *urged the horses forward*). **2** (often foll. by *to* + infin. or *that* + clause) encourage or entreat earnestly or persistently (*urged them to go*; *urged them to action*; *urged that they should go*). **3** (often foll. by *on, upon*) advocate (an action or argument, etc.) pressingly or emphatically (to a person). **4** adduce forcefully as a reason or justification (*urged the seriousness of the problem*). **5** ply (a person, etc.) hard with argument or entreaty. • *n.* **1** an urging impulse or tendency. **2** a strong desire.

ur·gent /ə́rjənt/ *adj.* **1** requiring immediate action or attention (*an urgent need for help*). **2** importunate; earnest and persistent in demand. □□ **ur·gen·cy** *n.* **ur·gent·ly** *adv.*

u·ric /yŏŏrik/ *adj.* of or relating to urine.

u·ric ac·id *n.* a crystalline acid forming a constituent of urine.

u·ri·nal /yŏŏrinəl/ *n.* **1** a sanitary fitting, usu. against a wall, for men to urinate into. **2** a place or receptacle for urination.

u·ri·nar·y /yŏŏrineree/ *adj.* **1** of or relating to urine. **2** affecting or occurring in the urinary system (*urinary diseases*).

u·ri·nate /yŏŏrinayt/ *v.intr.* discharge urine. □□ **u·ri·na·tion** /–náyshən/ *n.*

u·rine /yŏŏrin/ *n.* a pale-yellow fluid secreted as waste from the blood by the kidneys, stored in the bladder, and discharged through the urethra. □□ **u·ri·nous** *adj.*

urn /ərn/ *n.* **1** a vase with a foot and usu. a rounded body, esp. for storing the ashes of the cremated dead or as a vessel or measure. **2** a large vessel with a tap, in which tea or coffee, etc., is made or kept hot. □□ **urn·ful** *n.* (*pl.* **-fuls**).

u·ro·gen·i·tal /yŏŏrəjénit'l/ *adj.* of or relating to urinary and genital products or organs.

u·rol·o·gy /yŏŏróləjee/ *n.* the scientific study of the urinary system. □□ **u·ro·log·ic** /–rəlójik/ *adj.* **u·rol·o·gist** *n.*

Ur·sa Ma·jor /ə́rsə máyjər/ *n.* a prominent constellation in the northern sky, including the stars of the Big Dipper.

Ur·sa Mi·nor /ə́rsə mínər/ *n.* a small constellation containing the north celestial pole and the polestar, Polaris.

ur·sine /ə́rsīn/ *adj.* of or like a bear.

ur·ti·car·i·a /ə́rtikáireeə/ *n. Med.* skin rash, usu. from an allergic reaction; hives.

US *abbr.* United States (of America).

us /us, əs/ *pron.* **1** *objective case of* WE (*they saw us*). **2** *colloq.* = WE (*it's us again*). **3** *colloq.* = ME[1] (*give us a kiss*).

USA *abbr.* **1** United States of America. **2** United States Army.

us·a·ble /yŏŏzəbəl/ *adj.* (also **use·a·ble**) that can be used. □□ **us·a·bil·i·ty** /–bílitee/ *n.* **us·a·ble·ness** *n.*

USAF *abbr.* United States Air Force.

us·age /yŏŏsij/ *n.* **1** a manner of using or treating; treatment (*damaged by rough usage*). **2** habitual or customary practice, esp. as creating a right, obligation, or standard.

▶**Usage** means 'manner of use; practice,' while **use** means the 'act of employing.' In discussions of writing, **usage** is the term for normal or prescribed practice: *Standard usage calls for a plural.* In describing particular examples, however, employ **use:** *The use of the plural with this noun is incorrect.*

USCG *abbr.* United States Coast Guard.

use *v. & n.* • *v.tr.* /yōōz/ **1 a** cause to act or serve for a purpose; bring into service; avail oneself of (*rarely uses the car; use your discretion*). **b** consume by eating or drinking; take (alcohol, a drug, etc.), esp. habitually. **2** treat (a person) in a specified manner (*they used him shamefully*). **3** exploit for one's own ends (*they are just using you; used his position*). **4** (in *past* /yōōst/; foll. by *to* + infin.) did or had in the past (but no longer) as a customary practice or state (*I used to be an archaeologist; it used not (or did not use) to rain so often*). **5** (as **used** *adj.*) secondhand. **6** (as **used** /yōōst / *predic. adj.*) (foll. by *to*) familiar by habit; accustomed (*not used to hard work*). **7** apply (a name or title, etc.) to oneself. • *n.* /yōōs/ **1** the act of using or the state of being used; application to a purpose (*put it to good use; is in daily use; worn and polished with use*). **2** the right or power of using (*lost the use of my right arm*). **3 a** the ability to be used (*a flashlight would be of use*). **b** the purpose for which a thing can be used (*it's no use talking*). **4** custom or usage (*long use has reconciled me to it*). **5** the characteristic ritual and liturgy of a church or diocese, etc. **6** *Law hist.* the benefit or profit of lands, esp. in the possession of another who holds them solely for the beneficiary. □ **could use** *colloq.* would be glad to have; would be improved by having. **have no use for 1** be unable to find a use for. **2** dislike or be impatient with. **make use of 1** employ; apply. **2** benefit from. **use a person's name** quote a person as an authority or reference, etc. **use up 1** consume completely; use the whole of. **2** find a use for (something remaining). **3** exhaust or wear out, e.g., with overwork.

▶See note at USAGE.

use·ful /yōōsfŏŏl/ *adj.* **1 a** of use; serviceable. **b** producing or able to produce good results (*gave me some useful hints*). **2** *colloq.* highly creditable or efficient (*a useful performance*). □ **make oneself useful** perform useful services. □□ **use·ful·ly** *adv.* **use·ful·ness** *n.*

use·less /yōōslis/ *adj.* **1** serving no purpose; unavailing (*the contents were made useless by moisture; protest is useless*). **2** *colloq.* feeble or ineffectual (*am useless at swimming; a useless gadget*). □□ **use·less·ly** *adv.* **use·less·ness** *n.*

us·er /yōōzər/ *n.* **1** a person who uses (esp. a particular commodity or service, or a computer). **2** *colloq.* a drug addict. **3** *Law* the continued use or enjoyment of a right, etc.

us·er-friend·ly *adj.* esp. *Computing* (of a machine or system) designed to be easy to use.

ush·er /úshər/ *n. & v.* • *n.* **1** a person who shows people to their seats in an auditorium or theater, etc. **2** a doorkeeper at a court, etc. • *v.tr.* **1** act as usher to. **2** (usu. foll. by *in*) announce or show in, etc. (*ushered us into the room; ushered in a new era*).

USMC *abbr.* United States Marine Corps.

USN *abbr.* United States Navy.

USO *abbr.* (also **U.S.O.**) United Service Organizations.

USPS *abbr.* (also **U.S.P.S.**) United States Postal Service.

USS *abbr.* United States Ship.

USSR *abbr. hist.* Union of Soviet Socialist Republics.

usu. *abbr.* **1** usual. **2** usually.

u·su·al /yōōzhōōəl/ *adj. & n.* • *adj.* such as commonly occurs, or is observed or done; customary; habitual (*the usual formalities; it is usual to tip them; forgot my keys as usual*). • *n.* (prec. by *the, my,* etc.) *colloq.* a person's usual drink, etc. □□ **u·su·al·ly** *adv.*

u·surp /yōōzə́rp, –sə́rp/ *v.* **1** *tr.* seize or assume (a throne or power, etc.) wrongfully. **2** *intr.* (foll. by *on, upon*) encroach. □□ **u·sur·pa·tion** /yōōzərpáyshən, –sər–/ *n.* **u·surp·er** *n.*

u·su·ry /yōōzhəree/ *n.* **1** the act or practice of lending money at interest, esp. at an exorbitant rate. **2** interest at this rate. □□ **u·su·rer** *n.* **u·su·ri·ous** /–zhŏŏreeəs/ *adj.*

UT *abbr.* **1** Utah (in official postal use). **2** universal time.

Ute /yōōt/ *n.* (*pl.* **Ute** or **Utes**) **1** a member of a N. American people native to the area that is now Colorado, New Mexico, Utah, and Arizona. **2** the language of these people.

u·ten·sil /yōōténsəl/ *n.* an implement or vessel, esp. for domestic use (*cooking utensils*).

u·ter·ine /yōōtərin, –rīn/ *adj.* **1** of or relating to the uterus. **2** born of the same mother but not the same father (*sister uterine*).

u·ter·us /yóotərəs/ *n.* (*pl.* **uteri** /–rī/) the womb. ▫▫ **u·ter·i·tis** /–rítis/ *n.*

u·tile /yóotil, –tīl/ *adj.* useful; having utility.

u·til·i·tar·i·an /yootílitáireeən/ *adj.* & *n.* •*adj.* **1** designed to be useful for a purpose rather than attractive; severely practical. **2** of utilitarianism. •*n.* an adherent of utilitarianism.

u·til·i·tar·i·an·ism /yootílitáireeənizəm/ *n.* the doctrine that actions are right if they are useful or for the benefit of a majority.

u·til·i·ty /yootílitee/ *n.* (*pl.* **-ties**) **1** the condition of being useful or profitable. **2** a useful thing. **3** = PUBLIC UTILITY. **4** (*attrib.*) **a** severely practical and standardized (*utility furniture*). **b** made or serving for utility.

u·til·i·ty room *n.* a room equipped with appliances for washing, ironing, and other domestic work.

u·til·i·ty ve·hi·cle *n.* (also **utility truck**, etc.) a vehicle capable of serving various functions.

u·ti·lize /yóot'līz/ *v.tr.* make practical use of; turn to account; use effectively. ▫▫ **u·ti·liz·a·ble** *adj.* **u·ti·li·za·tion** *n.* **u·ti·liz·er** *n.*

ut·most /útmōst/ *adj.* & *n.* •*adj.* furthest, extreme, or greatest (*the utmost limits; showed the utmost reluctance*). •*n.* (prec. by *the*) the utmost point or degree, etc. ▫ **do one's utmost** do all that one can.

U·to·pi·a /yootópeeə/ *n.* an imagined perfect place or state of things.

U·to·pi·an /yootópeeən/ *adj.* & *n.* (also **utopian**) •*adj.* characteristic of Utopia; idealistic. •*n.* an idealistic reformer. ▫▫ **U·to·pi·an·ism** *n.*

ut·ter[1] /útər/ *attrib.adj.* complete; total; absolute (*utter misery; saw the utter absurdity of it*). ▫▫ **ut·ter·ly** *adv.* **ut·ter·ness** *n.*

ut·ter[2] /útər/ *v.tr.* **1** emit audibly (*uttered a startled cry*). **2** express in spoken or written words. **3** *Law* put (esp. forged money) into circulation. ▫▫ **ut·ter·a·ble** *adj.* **ut·ter·er** *n.*

ut·ter·ance /útərəns/ *n.* **1** the act or an instance of uttering. **2** a thing spoken. **3 a** the power of speaking. **b** a manner of speaking.

ut·ter·most /útərmōst/ *adj.* furthest; extreme.

U-turn /yóotərn/ *n.* **1** the turning of a vehicle in a U-shaped course so as to face in the opposite direction. **2** a reversal of policy.

UV *abbr.* ultraviolet.

u·ve·a /yoveeə/ *n.* the pigmented layer of the eye, lying beneath the outer layer.

u·vu·la /yóovyələ/ *n.* (*pl.* **uvulas** *or* **uvulae** /–lee/) **1** a fleshy extension of the soft palate hanging above the throat. **2** a similar process in the bladder or cerebellum. ▫▫ **u·vu·lar** *adj.*

u·vu·lar /yóovyələr/ *adj.* & *n.* •*adj.* **1** of or relating to the uvula. **2** articulated with the back of the tongue and the uvula, as in *r* in French. •*n.* a uvular consonant.

ux·o·ri·al /uksáwreeəl, ugzáwr–/ *adj.* of or relating to a wife.

ux·o·ri·ous /uksáwreeəs, ugzáwr–/ *adj.* **1** greatly or excessively fond of one's wife. **2** (of behavior, etc.) showing such fondness. ▫▫ **ux·o·ri·ous·ly** *adv.* **ux·o·ri·ous·ness** *n.*

V

V[1] /vee/ *n.* (also **v**) (*pl.* **Vs** or **V's**) **1** the twenty-second letter of the alphabet. **2** a V-shaped thing. **3** (as a Roman numeral) five.

V[2] *abbr.* (also **V.**) volt(s).

V[3] *symb. Chem.* the element vanadium.

v. *abbr.* **1** verse. **2** verso. **3** versus. **4** very. **5** *vide.*

VA *abbr.* **1** Veterans Administration. **2** Virginia (in official postal use). **3** vice admiral.

Va. *abbr.* Virginia.

va·can·cy /váykənsee/ *n.* (*pl.* **-cies**) **1 a** the state of being vacant. **b** an instance of this; empty space. **2** an unoccupied job (*there are three vacancies for computer specialists*). **3** an available room in a hotel, etc. **4** emptiness of mind; idleness; listlessness.

va·cant /váykənt/ *adj.* **1** not filled nor occupied. **2** not mentally active; showing no interest (*had a vacant stare*). ▫▫ **va·cant·ly** *adv.*

va·cate /váykayt, vaykáyt/ *v.tr.* **1** leave vacant or cease to occupy (a house, room, etc.). **2** give up tenure of (a post, etc.).

va·ca·tion /vaykáyshən, və–/ *n. & v.* • *n.* **1** a time of rest, recreation, etc., esp. spent away from home or in traveling, during which regular activities (esp. work or schooling) are suspended. **2** a fixed period of cessation from work, esp. in legislatures and courts of law. **3** the act of vacating. • *v.intr.* take a vacation, esp. away from home for pleasure and recreation. ▫▫ **va·ca·tion·er** *n.*

vac·ci·nate /váksinayt/ *v.tr.* inoculate with a vaccine to procure immunity from a disease. ▫▫ **vac·ci·na·tion** /–náyshən/ *n.* **vac·ci·na·tor** *n.*

vac·cine /vákséen/ *n.* a preparation used to stimulate the production of antibodies and procure immunity from one or several diseases.

vac·il·late /vásilayt/ *v.intr.* **1** fluctuate in opinion or resolution. **2** move from side to side; oscillate; waver. ▫▫ **vac·il·la·tion** /–láyshən/ *n.*

vac·u·a *pl.* of VACUUM.

vac·u·ole /vákyoo-ól/ *n. Biol.* a space within the cytoplasm of a cell containing air, fluid, etc. ▫▫ **vac·u·o·lar** /vakyoo-ólər, vákyooələr/ *adj.*

vac·u·ous /vákyooəs/ *adj.* **1** lacking expression (*a vacuous stare*). **2** unintelligent (*a vacuous remark*). **3** empty. ▫▫ **va·cu·i·ty** /vəkyóo-itee/ *n.* **vac·u·ous·ly** *adv.*

vac·u·um /vákyooəm, –yoom, –yəm/ *n. & v.* • *n.* (*pl.* **vacuums** or **vacua** /–yooə/) **1** a space entirely devoid of matter. **2** a space or vessel from which the air has been completely or partly removed by a pump, etc. **3 a** the absence of the normal or previous content of a place, environment, etc. **b** the absence of former circumstances, activities, etc. **4** (*pl.* **vacuums**) *colloq.* a vacuum cleaner. **5** a decrease of pressure below the normal atmospheric value. • *v. colloq.* **1** *tr.* clean with a vacuum cleaner. **2** *intr.* use a vacuum cleaner.

vac·uum clean·er *n.* an apparatus for removing dust, etc., by suction.

vac·uum-packed *adj.* sealed after the partial removal of air.

vac·uum tube *n. Electronics* an evacuated glass tube that regulates the flow of thermionic electrons in one direction, used esp. in the rectification of a current and in radio reception.

vag·a·bond /vágəbond/ *n. & adj.* • *n.* **1** a wanderer, esp. an idle one. **2** *colloq.* a scamp or rascal. • *adj.* having no fixed habitation; wandering. ▫▫ **vag·a·bond·age** *n.*

va·gar·y /váygəree/ *n.* (*pl.* **-ies**) a caprice; an eccentric idea or act (*the vagaries of Fortune*).

va·gi·na /vəjínə/ *n.* (*pl.* **vaginas** or **vaginae** /–nee/) the canal between the uterus and vulva of a woman or other female mammal. ▫▫ **vag·i·nal** /vájin'l/ *adj.* **vag·i·ni·tis** /vájinítis/ *n.*

va·grant /váygrənt/ *n. & adj.* • *n.* **1** a person without a settled home or regular work. **2** a wanderer. • *adj.* **1** wandering or roving (*a vagrant musician*). **2** characteristic of a vagrant. ▫▫ **va·gran·cy** /–grənsee/ *n.*

vague /vayg/ *adj.* **1** of uncertain or ill-defined meaning or character (*gave a vague answer; has some vague idea of emigrating*). **2** inexact in thought, expression, or understanding. ▫▫ **vague·ly** *adv.* **vague·ness** *n.*

vain /vayn/ *adj.* **1** excessively proud or conceited. **2** empty; trivial (*vain boasts; vain triumphs*). **3** useless; followed by no good result (*in the vain hope of dissuading them*). ▫ **in vain** without result or success (*it was in vain that we protested*). **take a person's name in vain** use it lightly or profanely. ▫▫ **vain·ly** *adv.*

vain·glo·ry /vaynglawree/ *n. literary* boastfulness; extreme vanity. ▫▫ **vain·glo·ri·ous** *adj.* **vain·glo·ri·ous·ly** *adv.*

val·ance /váləns, váyl–/ *n.* (also **val·ence**) a short curtain around the frame or canopy of a bed, above a window, or under a shelf. ▫▫ **val·anced** *adj.*

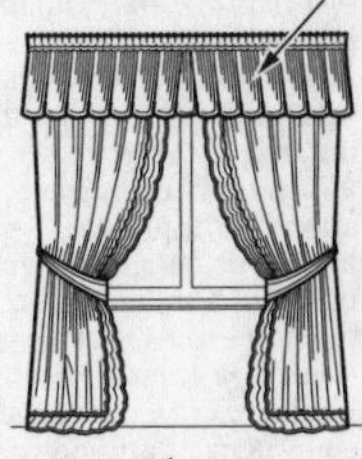
valance

vale /vayl/ *n. archaic* or *poet.* (except in place-names) a valley (*Vale of the White Horse*).

val·e·dic·tion /válidíkshən/ *n.* **1** the act or an instance of bidding farewell. **2** the words used in this.

val·e·dic·to·ri·an /válidiktáwreeən/ *n.* a person who gives a valedictory, esp. the highest-ranking member of a graduating class.

val·e·dic·to·ry /válidíktəree/ *adj. & n.* • *adj.* serving as a farewell. • *n.* (*pl.* **-ries**) a farewell address.

va·lence[1] /váyləns/ *n. Chem.* the combining power of an atom measured by the number of hydrogen atoms it can displace or combine with.

val·ence[2] var. of VALANCE.

val·en·tine /váləntīn/ *n.* **1** a card or gift sent, often anonymously, as a mark of love or affection on St. Valentine's Day (Feb. 14). **2** a sweetheart chosen on this day.

va·le·ri·an /vəléereeən/ *n.* **1** any of various flowering plants of the family Valerianaceae. **2** the root of any of these used as a medicinal sedative.

val·et /valáy, válit, –lay/ *n. & v.* • *n.* **1** a man's personal attendant who looks after his clothes, etc. **2** a hotel, etc., employee with similar duties. **3** a standing rack for holding one's suit, coat, etc. • *v.* (**valeted, valeting**) **1** *intr.* work as a valet. **2** *tr.* act as a valet to.

val·e·tu·di·nar·i·an /válitood'náireeən, –tyood–/ *n. &*

adj. • *n.* a person of poor health or unduly anxious about health. • *adj.* **1** of or being a valetudinarian. **2** of poor health. **3** seeking to recover one's health.

val•e•tu•di•nar•y /válitōōd'neree/ *adj. & n.* (*pl.* **•ies**) = VALETUDINARIAN.

Val•hal•la /valhálə, vaalhaálə/ *n.* **1** (in Norse mythology) a palace in which the souls of slain heroes feasted for eternity. **2** a building used for honoring the illustrious.

val•iant /vályənt/ *adj.* brave. ◻◻ **val•iant•ly** *adv.*

val•id /válid/ *adj.* **1** (of a reason, objection, etc.) sound or defensible. **2 a** executed with the proper formalities (*a valid contract*). **b** legally acceptable (*a valid passport*). **c** not having reached its expiration date. ◻◻ **va•lid•i•ty** /–líditee/ *n.* **val•id•ly** *adv.*

val•i•date /válidayt/ *v.tr.* make valid; ratify. ◻◻ **val•i•da•tion** /–dáyshən/ *n.*

va•lise /vəleés/ *n.* **1** a small suitcase; traveling bag. **2** a knapsack.

Val•i•um /váleeəm/ *n. Trademark* the drug diazepam used as a tranquilizer.

Val•kyr•ie /valkeéree, válkiree/ *n.* (in Norse mythology) each of Odin's twelve handmaidens who selected heroes destined to be slain in battle.

val•ley /válee/ *n.* (*pl.* **-leys**) **1** a low area more or less enclosed by hills and usu. with a stream flowing through it. **2** any depression compared to this. **3** *Archit.* an internal angle formed by the intersecting planes of a roof.

val•or /válər/ *n.* courage, esp. in battle. ◻◻ **val•or•ous** *adj.*

val•or•ize /váləríz/ *v.tr.* raise or fix the price of (a commodity, etc.) by artificial means, esp. by government action. ◻◻ **val•or•i•za•tion** *n.*

val•u•a•ble /vályōōəbəl, vályə–/ *adj. & n.* • *adj.* of great value, price, or worth (*a valuable property*; *valuable information*). • *n.* (usu. in *pl.*) a valuable thing. ◻◻ **val•u•a•bly** *adv.*

val•u•a•tion /vályōō-áyshən/ *n.* **1 a** an estimation (esp. by a professional) of a thing's worth. **b** the worth estimated. **2** the price set on a thing. ◻◻ **val•u•ate** *v.tr.*

val•u•a•tor /vályoo-aytər/ *n.* a person who makes valuations; an appraiser.

val•ue /vályōō/ *n. & v.* • *n.* **1** the worth, desirability, or utility of a thing, or the qualities on which these depend (*the value of regular exercise*). **2** worth as estimated (*set a high value on my time*). **3** the amount for which a thing can be exchanged in the open market. **4** the equivalent of a thing (*paid them the value of their lost property*). **5** (in full **value for money**) something well worth the money spent. **6** the ability of a thing to serve a purpose or cause an effect (*news value*; *nuisance value*). **7** (in *pl.*) one's principles or standards; one's judgment of what is valuable or important in life. **8** *Mus.* the duration of the sound signified by a note. **9** *Math.* the amount denoted by an algebraic term or expression. **10** (foll. by *of*) **a** the meaning (of a word, etc.). **b** the quality (of a spoken sound). **11** the relative rank or importance of a playing card, chess piece, etc. **12** the relation of one part of a picture to others in respect of light and shade; the part being characterized by a particular tone. **13** *Physics & Chem.* the numerical measure of a quantity or a number denoting magnitude on some conventional scale (*the value of gravity at the equator*). • *v.tr.* (**values, valued, valuing**) **1** estimate the value of; appraise (esp. professionally) (*valued the property at $200,000*). **2** have a high or specified opinion of (*a valued friend*).

val•ue-add•ed tax *n.* a tax on the amount by which the value of an article has been increased at each stage of its production.

val•ue judg•ment *n.* an assessment of something as good or bad in terms of one's own standards or priorities.

va•lu•ta /vəlóōtə/ *n.* **1** the value of one currency with respect to another. **2** a currency considered in this way.

valve /valv/ *n.* **1** a device for controlling the passage of fluid through a pipe, etc., esp. an automatic device allowing movement in one direction only. **2** *Anat. & Zool.* a membranous part of an organ, etc., allowing a flow of blood, etc., in one direction only. **3** a device to vary the effective length of the tube in a brass musical instrument. **4** each of the two shells of an oyster, mussel, etc. ◻◻ **valved** *adj.* (also in *comb.*).

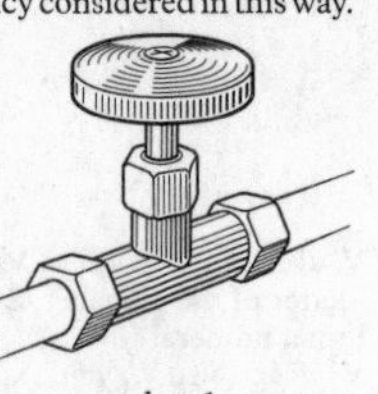
valve, 1

val•vu•lar /válvyələr/ *adj.* **1** having a valve or valves. **2** having the form or function of a valve.

va•moose /vamóōs, və–/ *v.intr.* (esp. as *int.*) *sl.* depart hurriedly.

vamp[1] /vamp/ *n. & v.* • *n.* **1** the upper front part of a boot or shoe. **2** a patched-up article. **3** an improvised musical accompaniment. • *v.* **1** *tr.* (often foll. by *up*) repair or furbish. **2** *tr.* (foll. by *up*) make by patching or from odds and ends. **3 a** *tr. & intr.* improvise a musical accompaniment (to). **b** *tr.* improvise (a musical accompaniment). **4** *tr.* put a new vamp to (a boot or shoe).

vamp[2] /vamp/ *n. & v. colloq.* • *n.* a woman who uses sexual attraction to exploit men. • *v.* **1** *tr.* allure or exploit (a man). **2** *intr.* act as a vamp.

vam•pire /vámpīr/ *n.* **1** a ghost or reanimated corpse supposed to leave its grave at night to suck the blood of persons sleeping. **2** a person who preys ruthlessly on others. **3** (in full **vampire bat**) any tropical (esp. South American) bat of the family *Desmodontidae*, with incisors for piercing flesh and feeding on blood. ◻◻ **vam•pir•ic** /–pírik/ *adj.*

vam•pir•ism /vámpīrizəm/ *n.* **1** belief in the existence of vampires. **2** the practices of a vampire.

van[1] /van/ *n.* **1** a covered vehicle for conveying goods, etc., esp. a large truck or trailer (*moving van*). **2** a smaller such vehicle, similar to a panel truck and used esp. for carrying passengers, traveling gear, etc.

van[2] /van/ *n.* **1** a vanguard. **2** the forefront (*in the van of progress*).

va•na•di•um /vənáydeeəm/ *n. Chem.* a hard, gray, metallic transition element occurring naturally in several ores and used in small quantities for strengthening some steels. ¶ Symb.: **V.** ◻◻ **van•a•date** /vánədayt/ *n.*

Van Al•len belt /van álən/ *n.* (also **Van Al•len lay•er**) each of two regions of intense radiation partly surrounding the earth at heights of several thousand miles.

van•dal /vánd'l/ *n. & adj.* • *n.* **1** a person who willfully or maliciously destroys or damages property. **2** (**Vandal**) a member of a Germanic people that ravaged Gaul, Spain, N. Africa, and Rome in the 4th–5th c., destroying many books and works of art. • *adj.* of or relating to the Vandals.

van•dal•ism /vánd'lizəm/ *n.* willful or malicious destruction or damage to works of art or other property. ◻◻ **van•dal•is•tic** *adj.*

van•dal•ize /vánd'līz/ *v.tr.* destroy or damage willfully or maliciously.

Van•dyke beard *n.* a neat, pointed beard.

Van•dyke brown *n.* a deep rich brown.

vane /vayn/ *n.* **1** (in full **weather vane**) a revolving pointer mounted on a high place to show the direction of the wind (cf. WEATHERCOCK). **2** a blade of a screw propeller or a windmill, etc. **3** the sight of surveying instruments, a quadrant, etc. **4** the flat part of a bird's feather formed by the barbs. ▫▫ **vaned** *adj.*

van•guard /vángaard/ *n.* **1** the foremost part of an army or fleet advancing or ready to advance. **2** the leaders of a movement or of opinion, etc.

va•nil•la /vənílə/ *n.* **1 a** any tropical climbing orchid of the genus *Vanilla*, esp. *V. planifolia*, with fragrant flowers. **b** (in full **vanilla bean**) the fruit of these. **2** a substance obtained from the vanilla bean or synthesized and used to flavor ice cream, chocolate, etc.

va•nil•lin /vənílin/ *n.* **1** the fragrant principle of vanilla. **2** a synthetic preparation used as a vanillalike fragrance or flavoring.

van•ish /vánish/ *v.intr.* **1 a** disappear suddenly. **b** disappear gradually; fade away. **2** cease to exist.

van•ish•ing point *n.* the point at which receding parallel lines viewed in perspective appear to meet.

van•i•ty /vánitee/ *n.* (*pl.* **-ties**) **1** conceit and desire for admiration of one's personal attainments or attractions. **2 a** futility or unsubstantiality (*the vanity of human achievement*). **b** an unreal thing. **3** ostentatious display. **4** a dressing table. **5** a unit consisting of a washbowl set into a flat top with cupboards beneath.

van•quish /vángkwish/ *v.tr. literary* conquer or overcome. ▫▫ **van•quish•er** *n.*

van•tage /vántij/ *n.* **1** (also **van•tage point** or **ground**) a place affording a good view or prospect. **2** *Tennis* = ADVANTAGE.

vap•id /vápid/ *adj.* insipid; flat; dull (*vapid moralizing*). ▫▫ **va•pid•i•ty** /–píditee/ *n.* **vap•id•ly** *adv.*

va•por /váypər/ *n.* **1** moisture or another substance diffused or suspended in air, e.g., mist or smoke. **2** *Physics* a gaseous form of a normally liquid or solid substance (cf. GAS). **3** a medicinal agent for inhaling. **4** (in *pl.*) *archaic* a state of depression or melancholy thought to be caused by exhalations of vapor from the stomach. ▫▫ **va•por•ous** *adj.* **va•por•ing** *n.* **va•por•y** *adj.*

va•por•ize /váypərīz/ *v.tr. & intr.* convert or be converted into vapor. ▫▫ **va•por•i•za•tion** *n.*

va•por•iz•er /váypərīzər/ *n.* a device that vaporizes substances, esp. for medicinal inhalation.

va•por trail *n.* a trail of condensed water from an aircraft or rocket at high altitude, seen as a white streak against the sky.

var. *abbr.* **1** variant. **2** variety.

var•i•a•ble /váireeəbəl/ *adj. & n.* • *adj.* **1 a** that can be varied or adapted. **b** (of a gear) designed to give varying speeds. **2** apt to vary; not constant. **3** *Math.* (of a quantity) indeterminate; able to assume different numerical values. **4** (of wind or currents) tending to change direction. **5** *Astron.* (of a star) periodically varying in brightness. **6** *Bot. & Zool.* (of a species) including individuals or groups that depart from the type. **7** *Biol.* (of an organism or part of it) tending to change in structure or function. • *n.* **1** a variable thing or quantity. **2** *Math.* a variable quantity. ▫▫ **var•i•a•bil•i•ty** /–bílitee/ *n.* **var•i•a•bly** *adv.*

var•i•ance /váireeəns/ *n.* **1** difference of opinion; dispute; disagreement; lack of harmony (*at variance among ourselves*; *a theory at variance with all known facts*). **2** *Law* a discrepancy between statements or documents. **3** *Statistics* a quantity equal to the square of the standard deviation.

var•i•ant /váireeənt/ *adj. & n.* • *adj.* **1** differing in form or details from the main one (*a variant spelling*). **2** having different forms (*forty variant types of pigeon*). **3** variable or changing. • *n.* a variant form, spelling, type, reading, etc.

var•i•a•tion /váireeáyshən/ *n.* **1** the act or an instance of varying. **2** departure from a former or normal condition, action, or amount, or from a standard or type (*prices are subject to variation*). **3** the extent of this. **4** a thing that varies from a type. **5** *Mus.* a repetition of a theme in a changed or elaborated form. ▫▫ **var•i•a•tion•al** *adj.*

var•i•cel•la /váriséla/ *n. Med.* = CHICKEN POX.

var•i•col•ored /váirikúlərd, vári–/ *adj.* **1** variegated in color. **2** of various or different colors.

var•i•cose /várikōs/ *adj.* (esp. of the veins of the legs) affected by a condition causing them to become dilated and swollen. ▫▫ **var•i•cos•i•ty** /–kósitee/ *n.*

var•ied /váireed/ *adj.* showing variety; diverse.

var•i•e•gate /váirigayt, váireeə–, vár–/ *v.tr.* **1** (often as **variegated** *adj.*) mark with irregular patches of different colors. **2** diversify in appearance, esp. in color. **3** (as **variegated** *adj.*) *Bot.* (of plants) having leaves containing two or more colors. ▫▫ **var•i•e•ga•tion** /–gáyshən/ *n.*

va•ri•e•tal /vərīət'l/ *adj.* **1** esp. *Bot. & Zool.* of, forming, or designating a variety. **2** (of wine) made from a single designated variety of grape. ▫▫ **va•ri•e•tal•ly** *adv.*

va•ri•e•ty /vərīətee/ *n.* (*pl.* **-ties**) **1** diversity; absence of uniformity; many-sidedness (*not enough variety in our lives*). **2** a quantity or collection of different things (*for a variety of reasons*). **3 a** a class of things different in some common qualities from the rest of a larger class to which they belong. **b** a specimen or member of such a class. **4** (foll. by *of*) a different form of a thing, quality, etc. **5** *Biol.* **a** a subspecies. **b** a cultivar. **c** an individual or group usually fertile within the species to which it belongs but differing from the species type in some qualities capable of perpetuation. **6** a mixed sequence of dances, songs, comedy acts, etc. (usu. *attrib.*: *a variety show*).

var•i•fo•cal /váirifṓkəl/ *adj. & n.* • *adj.* having a focal length that can be varied, esp. of a lens that allows an infinite number of focusing distances for near, intermediate, and far vision. • *n.* (in *pl.*) varifocal spectacles.

var•i•form /váirifawrm/ *adj.* having various forms.

va•ri•o•la /vərīələ/ *n. Med.* smallpox.

var•i•o•rum /váireeáwrəm/ *adj. & n.* • *adj.* **1** (of an edition of a text) having notes by various editors or commentators. **2** (of an edition of an author's works) including variant readings. • *n.* a variorum edition.

var•i•ous /váireeəs/ *adj.* **1** different; diverse (*too various to form a group*). **2** more than one; several (*for various reasons*). ▫▫ **var•i•ous•ly** *adv.* **var•i•ous•ness** *n.*

var•let /vaárlit/ *n.* **1** *archaic* or *joc.* a menial or rascal. **2** *hist.* a knight's attendant.

var•mint /vaármint/ *n. dial.* a mischievous or discreditable person or animal.

var•nish /vaárnish/ *n. & v.* • *n.* **1** a resinous solution used to give a hard shiny transparent coating to wood, metal, paintings, etc. **2** any other preparation for a similar purpose (*nail varnish*). **3** external appearance or display without an underlying reality. **4** artificial or natural glossiness. • *v.tr.* **1** apply varnish to. **2** gloss over (a fact). ▫▫ **var•nish•er** *n.*

var•si•ty /vaársitee/ *n.* (*pl.* **-ties**) a high school, college, etc., first team in a sport.

var•y /váiree/ *v.* (**-ies**, **-ied**) **1** *tr.* make different; modify; diversify (*seldom varies the routine*; *the style is not sufficiently varied*). **2** *intr.* **a** undergo change; become or be different (*the temperature varies from 30° to 70°*). **b** be of different kinds (*his mood varies*). **3** *intr.* (foll. by *as*) be in proportion to. ▫▫ **var•y•ing•ly** *adv.*

vas /vas/ *n.* (*pl.* **vasa** /váysə/) *Anat.* a vessel or duct.

vas•cu•lar /váskyələr/ *adj.* of, made up of, or containing vessels for conveying blood or sap, etc. (*vascular functions*; *vascular tissue*). ▫▫ **vas·cu·lar·i·ty** /–láritee/ *n.*

vas·cu·lum /váskyələm/ *n.* (*pl.* **vascula** /–lə/) a botanist's (usu. metal) collecting case with a lengthwise opening.

vas de·fe·rens /défərenz/ *n.* (*pl.* **vasa deferentia** /défərénsheeə/) *Anat.* the spermatic duct from the testicle to the urethra.

vase /vays, vayz, vaaz/ *n.* a vessel, usu. tall and circular, used as an ornament or container, esp. for flowers.

vas·ec·to·my /vəséktəmee/ *n.* (*pl.* **-mies**) the surgical removal of part of each vas deferens, esp. as a means of sterilization. ▫▫ **vas·ec·to·mize** *v.tr.*

Vas·e·line /vásileen/ *n. Trademark* a type of petroleum jelly used as an ointment, lubricant, etc.

va·si·form /váyzifawrm, vásə;n–/ *adj.* **1** duct-shaped. **2** vase-shaped.

vaso- /váyzō/ *comb. form* a vessel, esp. a blood vessel (*vasoconstrictive*).

vas·o·ac·tive /vázō-áktiv/ *adj.* = VASOMOTOR.

vas·o·con·stric·tion /vázōkənstríkshən/ *adj.* the constriction of blood vessels. ▫▫ **vas·o·con·stric·tive** /–stríktiv/ *adj.*

vas·o·di·la·tion /vázōdīláyshən/ (also **vas·o·dil·a·ta·tion**) *n.* the dilatation of blood vessels.

vas·o·mo·tor /vázōmṓtər/ *adj.* causing constriction or dilatation of blood vessels.

vas·o·pres·sin /vázōprésin/ *n.* a pituitary hormone acting to reduce diuresis and increase blood pressure. Also called ANTIDIURETIC HORMONE.

vas·sal /vásəl/ *n. hist.* a holder of land by feudal tenure on conditions of homage and allegiance. ▫▫ **vas·sal·age** *n.*

vast /vast/ *adj.* **1** immense; huge (*a vast expanse of water*; *a vast crowd*). **2** *colloq.* great; considerable (*makes a vast difference*). ▫▫ **vast·ly** *adv.* **vast·ness** *n.*

VAT /vat, vée-aytée/ *abbr.* value-added tax.

vat /vat/ *n.* a large tank or other vessel, esp. for holding liquids or something in liquid in the process of brewing, tanning, dyeing, etc.

vat·ic /vátik/ *adj. formal* prophetic or inspired.

Vat·i·can /vátikən/ *n.* **1** the palace and official residence of the Pope in Rome. **2** papal government.

Vat·i·can Cit·y *n.* an independent Papal State in Rome, instituted in 1929.

vaude·ville /váwdvil, váwdə–/ *n.* **1** variety entertainment. **2** a stage play on a trivial theme with interspersed songs. **3** a satirical or topical song with a refrain. ▫▫ **vaude·vil·lian** /–vílyən/ *adj.* & *n.*

vault /vawlt/ *n.* & *v.* •*n.* **1 a** an arched roof. **b** a continuous arch. **c** a set or series of arches whose joints radiate from a central point or line. **2** a vaultlike covering (*the vault of heaven*). **3** an esp. underground chamber: **a** as a place of storage (*bank vaults*). **b** as a place of interment beneath a church or in a cemetery, etc. (*family vault*). **4** an act of vaulting. **5** *Anat.* the arched roof of a cavity. •*v.* **1** *intr.* leap or spring, esp. while resting on one or both hands or with the help of a pole. **2** *tr.* spring over in this way. **3** *tr.* (esp. as **vaulted**) **a** make in the form of a vault. **b** provide with a vault or vaults. ▫▫ **vault·er** *n.*

vault·ing /váwlting/ *n.* **1** arched work in a vaulted roof or ceiling. **2** a gymnastic or athletic exercise in which participants vault over obstacles.

vault·ing horse *n.* a wooden block to be vaulted over by gymnasts.

vaunt /vawnt/ *v.* & *n. literary* •*v.* **1** *intr.* boast. **2** *tr.* boast of; extol boastfully. •*n.* a boast.

VC *abbr.* **1** vice-chairman. **2** vice-chancellor. **3** vice-consul. **4** Victoria Cross. **5** Vietcong.

V-chip /vée chip/ *n.* a computer chip installed in a television receiver that can be programmed to block offensive, esp. violent material.

VCR *abbr.* videocassette recorder.

VD *abbr.* venereal disease.

VDT *abbr.* video display terminal.

V-E *abbr.* Victory in Europe (in 1945).

've *abbr.* (chiefly after pronouns) = HAVE (*I've*; *they've*).

veal /veel/ *n.* calf's flesh as food.

vec·tor /véktər/ *n.* & *v.* •*n.* **1** *Math.* & *Physics* a quantity having direction as well as magnitude. (cf. SCALAR. **2** a carrier of disease. **3** a course to be taken by an aircraft. •*v.tr.* direct (an aircraft in flight) to a desired point. ▫▫ **vec·to·ri·al** /–táwreeəl/ *adj.* **vec·tor·ize** *v.tr.* (in sense 1 of *n.*). **vec·tor·i·za·tion** /–tərīzáyshən/ *n.*

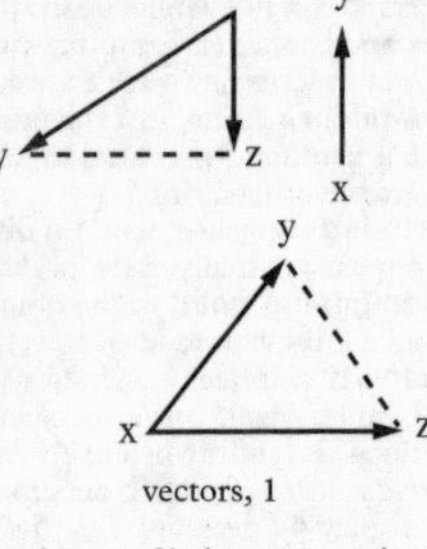

vectors, 1

Ve·da /váydə, vée–/ *n.* (in *sing.* or *pl.*) the most ancient Hindu scriptures.

Ve·dan·ta /vidaántə, vedán–/ *n.* **1** the Upanishads. **2** the Hindu philosophy based on these, esp. in its monistic form. ▫▫ **Ve·dan·tic** *adj.* **Ve·dan·tist** *n.*

V-E Day *n.* May 8, the day marking Victory in Europe in 1945.

Ve·dic /váydik, vée–/ *adj.* & *n.* •*adj.* of or relating to the Veda or Vedas. •*n.* the language of the Vedas, an older form of Sanskrit.

vee /vee/ *n.* **1** the letter V. **2** a thing shaped like a V.

vee·jay /véejay/ *n.* VIDEO JOCKEY.

veer /veer/ *v.* & *n.* •*v.intr.* **1** change direction, esp. (of the wind) clockwise (cf. BACK *v.* 5). **2** change in course, opinion, conduct, emotions, etc. **3** *Naut.* = WEAR[2]. •*n.* a change of course or direction.

veg·an /véjən, véegən/ *n.* & *adj.* •*n.* a person who does not eat or use animal products. •*adj.* using or containing no animal products.

veg·e·ta·ble /véjtəbəl, véjitəbəl/ *n.* & *adj.* •*n.* **1** *Bot.* any of various plants, esp. a herbaceous plant used for food, e.g., a cabbage, potato, or bean. **2** *colloq.* **a** a person who is incapable of normal intellectual activity, esp. through brain injury, etc. **b** a person lacking in animation or living a monotonous life. •*adj.* **1** of, derived from, relating to, or comprising plants or plant life. **2** of or relating to vegetables as food. **3 a** unresponsive to stimulus (*vegetable behavior*). **b** uneventful; monotonous (*a vegetable existence*).

veg·e·tal /véjit'l/ *adj.* **1** of or having the nature of plants (*vegetal growth*). **2** vegetative.

veg·e·tar·i·an /véjitáireeən/ *n.* & *adj.* •*n.* a person who abstains from animal food, esp. that from slaughtered animals, though often not eggs and dairy products. •*adj.* excluding animal food, esp. meat (*a vegetarian diet*). ▫▫ **veg·e·tar·i·an·ism** *n.*

veg·e·tate /véjitayt/ *v.intr.* **1 a** live an uneventful or monotonous life. **b** spend time lazily or passively, exerting oneself neither mentally nor physically. **2** grow as plants do.

veg·e·ta·tion /véjitáyshən/ *n.* **1** plants collectively; plant life. **2** the process of vegetating. ▫▫ **veg·e·ta·tion·al** *adj.*

veg·e·ta·tive /véjitaytiv/ *adj.* **1** concerned with growth and development as distinct from sexual reproduction. **2** of or relating to vegetation or plant life. ▫▫ **veg·e·ta·tive·ly** *adv.*

veg·gie /véjee/ *n.* (also **veg·ie**) *colloq.* **1** a vegetable. **2** a vegetarian.

ve·he·ment /véeəmənt/ *adj.* showing or caused by strong feeling; forceful; ardent. ◻◻ **ve·he·mence** /–məns/ *n.* **ve·he·ment·ly** *adv.*

ve·hi·cle /véeikəl/ *n.* **1** any conveyance for transporting people, goods, etc., esp. on land. **2** a medium for thought, feeling, or action (*the stage is the best vehicle for their talents*). **3** a liquid, etc., as a medium for suspending pigments, drugs, etc. ◻◻ **ve·hic·u·lar** /veehíkyələr/ *adj.*

veil /vayl/ *n. & v.* • *n.* **1** a piece of usu. more or less transparent fabric attached to a woman's hat, etc., esp. to conceal the face or protect against the sun, dust, etc. **2** a piece of linen, etc., as part of a nun's headdress. **3** a curtain, esp. that separating the sanctuary in the Jewish temple. **4** a disguise; a pretext; a thing that conceals (*under the veil of friendship; a veil of mist*). • *v.tr.* **1** cover with a veil. **2** (esp. as **veiled** *adj.*) partly conceal (*veiled threats*). ◻ **draw a veil over** avoid discussing or calling attention to. **take the veil** become a nun.

vein /vayn/ *n. & v.* • *n.* **1 a** any of the tubes by which blood is conveyed to the heart (cf. ARTERY). **b** (in general use) any blood vessel (*has royal blood in his veins*). **2** a veinlike structure in an insect's wing. **3** a rib in the framework of a leaf. **4** a streak of a different color in wood, marble, cheese, etc. **5** a fissure in rock filled with ore or other deposited material. **6** a source of a particular characteristic (*a rich vein of humor*). **7** a distinctive character or tendency; a cast of mind or disposition; a mood (*spoke in a sarcastic vein*). • *v.tr.* fill or cover with or as with veins. ◻◻ **vein·let** *n.* **vein·y** *adj.* (**veinier, veiniest**).

ve·la *pl.* of VELUM.

ve·lar /véelər/ *adj.* **1** of a veil or velum. **2** *Phonet.* (of a sound) pronounced with the back of the tongue near the soft palate.

Vel·cro /vélkrō/ *n. Trademark* a fastener consisting of two strips of fabric which adhere when pressed together. ◻◻ **Vel·croed** *adj.*

veld /velt, felt/ *n.* (also **veldt**) *S.Afr.* open country; grassland.

vel·lum /véləm/ *n.* **1 a** fine parchment orig. from the skin of a calf. **b** a manuscript written on this. **2** smooth writing paper imitating vellum.

ve·loc·i·pede /vilósipeed/ *n.* **1** *hist.* an early form of bicycle propelled by pressure from the rider's feet on the ground. **2** a child's tricycle.

ve·loc·i·rap·tor /vilósiráptər/ *n.* a small bipedal carnivorous dinosaur with an enlarged curved claw on each hind foot.

ve·loc·i·ty /vilósitee/ *n.* (*pl.* **-ties**) **1** the measure of the rate of movement of a usu. inanimate object in a given direction. **2** speed in a given direction. **3** (in general use) speed.

ve·lo·drome /vélədrōm/ *n.* a special place or building with a track for cycling.

ve·lour /vəlŏŏr/ *n.* (also **ve·lours**) a plushlike woven fabric or felt.

ve·lum /véeləm/ *n.* (*pl.* **vela** /–lə/) a membrane, membranous covering, or flap.

vel·vet /vélvit/ *n. & adj.* • *n.* **1** a closely woven fabric of silk, cotton, etc., with a thick short pile on one side. **2** the furry skin on a deer's growing antler. **3** anything smooth and soft like velvet. • *adj.* of, like, or soft as velvet. ◻ **on** (or **in**) **velvet** in an advantageous or prosperous position. ◻◻ **vel·vet·y** *adj.*

vel·vet·een /vélvitéen/ *n.* **1** a cotton fabric with a pile like velvet. **2** (in *pl.*) garments made of this.

vel·vet glove *n.* outward gentleness, esp. cloaking firmness or strength (cf. IRON HAND).

ve·na ca·va /véenə káyvə/ *n.* (*pl.* **venae cavae** /–nee -vee/) each of usu. two veins carrying blood into the heart.

ve·nal /véenəl/ *adj.* **1** able to be bribed or corrupted. **2** characteristic of a venal person. ◻◻ **ve·nal·i·ty** /–nálitee/ *n.*

▶**Venal** and **venial** are sometimes confused. **Venal** means 'corrupt, able to be bribed, or involving bribery,' e.g., *Local customs officials are notoriously venal, and smuggling thrives.* **Venial** is used among Christians to describe a certain type of sin and means 'pardonable, excusable, not mortal,' e.g., *Purgatory, to Catholics, was an intermediate stage in which those who had committed venial sins might earn their way into heaven.*

ve·na·tion /vináyshən/ *n.* the arrangement of veins in a leaf or an insect's wing, etc., or the system of venous blood vessels in an organism. ◻◻ **ve·na·tion·al** *adj.*

vend /vend/ *v.tr.* **1** offer (small wares) for sale. **2** *Law* sell.

ven·det·ta /vendétə/ *n.* **1** a blood feud in which the family of a murdered person seeks vengeance on the murderer or the murderer's family. **2** a prolonged bitter quarrel.

vend·ing ma·chine *n.* a machine that dispenses small articles for sale when a coin or token is inserted.

ven·dor /véndər/ *n.* **1** *Law* the seller in a sale. **2** = VENDING MACHINE.

ve·neer /vinéer/ *n. & v.* • *n.* **1 a** a thin covering of fine wood or other surface material applied to a coarser wood. **b** a layer in plywood. **2** (often foll. by *of*) a deceptive outward appearance of a good quality, etc. • *v.tr.* **1** apply a veneer to. **2** disguise (an unattractive character, etc.) with a more attractive manner, etc.

ven·er·a·ble /vénərəbəl/ *adj.* **1** entitled to veneration on account of character, age, associations, etc. (*a venerable priest; venerable relics*). **2** as the title of an archdeacon in the Church of England. **3** *RC Ch.* as the title of a deceased person who has attained a certain degree of sanctity but has not been fully beatified or canonized. ◻◻ **ven·er·a·bil·i·ty** *n.* **ven·er·a·bly** *adv.*

ven·er·ate /vénərayt/ *v.tr.* **1** regard with deep respect. **2** revere on account of sanctity, etc. ◻◻ **ven·er·a·tion** /–ráyshən/ *n.*

ve·ne·re·al /vinéereeəl/ *adj.* **1** of or relating to sexual desire or intercourse. **2** relating to venereal disease.

ve·ne·re·al dis·ease *n.* any of various diseases contracted chiefly by sexual intercourse with a person already infected.

Ve·ne·tian /vinéeshən/ *n. & adj.* • *n.* **1** a native or citizen of Venice in NE Italy. **2** the Italian dialect of Venice. **3** (**venetian**) = VENETIAN BLIND. • *adj.* of Venice.

ve·ne·tian blind *n.* a window blind of adjustable horizontal slats.

venge·ance /vénjəns/ *n.* punishment inflicted or retribution exacted for wrong to oneself or to a person, etc., whose cause one supports. ◻ **with a vengeance** in a higher degree than was expected or desired; in the fullest sense (*punctuality with a vengeance*).

venge·ful /vénjfŏŏl/ *adj.* vindictive; seeking vengeance. ◻◻ **venge·ful·ly** *adv.* **venge·ful·ness** *n.*

ve·ni·al /véeneeəl/ *adj.* (of a sin or fault) pardonable; not mortal. ◻◻ **ve·ni·al·ly** *adv.*

▶See note at VENAL.

ven·i·son /vénisən, –zən/ *n.* a deer's flesh as food.

Venn di·a·gram /ven/ *n.* a diagram of usu. circular areas representing mathematical sets, the areas intersecting where they have elements in common.

ven·om /vénəm/ *n.* **1** a poisonous fluid secreted by snakes, scorpions, etc. **2** malignity; virulence of feeling, language, or conduct.

ven·om·ous /vénəməs/ *adj.* **1 a** containing, secreting, or injecting venom. **b** (of a snake, etc.) inflicting poisonous wounds by this means. **2** (of a person, etc.) virulent; spiteful; malignant. ▫▫ **ven·om·ous·ly** *adv.*

ve·nous /veénəs/ *adj.* of, full of, or contained in veins.

vent[1] /vent/ *n. & v.* • *n.* **1** an opening allowing motion of air, etc., out of or into a confined space. **2** an outlet; free passage or play (*gave vent to their indignation*). **3** the anus esp. of a lower animal, serving for both excretion and reproduction. **4** (of an otter, beaver, etc.) a means of breathing. **5** an aperture or outlet through which volcanic products are discharged at the earth's surface. **6** a touchhole of a gun. **7** a finger hole in a musical instrument. **8** a flue of a chimney. • *v.* **1** *tr.* **a** make a vent in (a cask, etc.). **b** provide (a machine) with a vent. **2** *tr.* give free expression to (emotions, etc.) (*vented my anger on my drum set*). **3** *intr.* (of an otter or beaver) come to the surface for breath. **4** *tr. & intr.* discharge. ▫ **vent one's spleen on** scold or ill-treat without cause.

vent[2] /vent/ *n.* a slit in a garment, esp. in the lower edge of the back of a coat.

ven·ti·late /vént'layt/ *v.tr.* **1** cause air to circulate freely in (a room, etc.). **2** submit (a question, grievance, etc.) to public consideration and discussion. **3** *Med.* **a** oxygenate (the blood). **b** admit or force air into (the lungs). ▫▫ **ven·ti·la·tion** /–láyshən/ *n.*

ven·ti·la·tor /véntilaytər/ *n.* **1** an appliance or aperture for ventilating a room, etc. **2** *Med.* = RESPIRATOR 2.

ven·tral /véntrəl/ *adj.* **1** *Anat. & Zool.* of or on the abdomen (cf. DORSAL). **2** *Bot.* of the front or lower surface. ▫▫ **ven·tral·ly** *adv.*

ven·tri·cle /véntrikəl/ *n. Anat.* **1** a cavity in the body. **2** a hollow part of an organ, esp. in the brain or heart. ▫▫ **ven·tric·u·lar** /–tríkyələr/ *adj.*

ven·tril·o·quism /ventríləkwizəm/ *n.* the skill of speaking or uttering sounds so that they seem to come from the speaker's dummy or a source other than the speaker. ▫▫ **ven·tril·o·quist** *n.* **ven·tril·o·quize** *v.intr.*

ven·tril·o·quy /ventríləkwee/ *n.* = VENTRILOQUISM.

ven·ture /vénchər/ *n. & v.* • *n.* **1 a** an undertaking of a risk. **b** a risky undertaking. **2** a commercial speculation. • *v.* **1** *intr.* dare; not be afraid (*did not venture to stop them*). **2** *intr.* (usu. foll. by *out*, etc.) dare to go. **3** *tr.* dare to put forward (an opinion, suggestion, etc.). **4 a** *tr.* expose to risk; stake (a bet, etc.). **b** *intr.* take risks. **5** *intr.* (foll. by *on*, *upon*) dare to engage in, etc. (*ventured on a longer journey*). ▫ **at a venture** at random; without previous consideration.

ven·ture cap·i·tal *n.* money put up for speculative business investment.

ven·tur·er /vénchərər/ *n. hist.* a person who undertakes or shares in a trading venture.

ven·ture·some /vénchərsəm/ *adj.* **1** disposed to take risks. **2** risky.

ven·ue /vényōō/ *n.* **1** an appointed meeting place, esp. for a sports event, meeting, concert, etc. **2** a rendezvous.

ven·ule /vényōōl/ *n. Anat.* a small vein adjoining the capillaries.

Ve·nus /veénəs/ *n.* (*pl.* **Venuses**) **1** the planet second from the sun in the solar system. **2** *poet.* **a** a beautiful woman. **b** sexual love; amorous influences or desires. ▫▫ **Ve·nu·si·an** /vinóōshən, –sheeən, –zeeən, –nyóō;n–/ *adj. & n.*

Ve·nus's fly·trap *n.* (also **Ve·nus fly·trap**) a carnivorous plant, *Dionaea muscipula*, with leaves that close on insects, etc.

ve·ra·cious /vəráyshəs/ *adj. formal* **1** speaking or disposed to speak the truth. **2** (of a statement, etc.) true or meant to be true.

ve·rac·i·ty /vərásitee/ *n.* **1** truthfulness; honesty. **2** accuracy (of a statement, etc.).

ve·ran·da /vərándə/ *n.* (also **ve·ran·dah**) an open, roofed porch.

verb /vərb/ *n. Gram.* a word used to indicate an action, state, or occurrence (e.g., *hear*, *become*, *happen*).

ver·bal /vórbəl/ *adj. & n.* • *adj.* **1** of or concerned with words (*made a verbal distinction*). **2** oral; not written (*gave a verbal statement*). **3** *Gram.* of or in the nature of a verb (*verbal inflections*). **4** literal (*a verbal translation*). **5** talkative; articulate. • *n. Gram.* **1** a verbal noun. **2** a word or words functioning as a verb. ▫▫ **ver·bal·ly** *adv.*

ver·bal·ism /vórbəlizəm/ *n.* **1** minute attention to words. **2** merely verbal expression. ▫▫ **ver·bal·ist** *n.* **ver·bal·is·tic** /–lístik/ *adj.*

ver·bal·ize /vórbəlīz/ *v.* **1** *tr.* express in words. **2** *intr.* be verbose. **3** *tr.* make (a noun, etc.) into a verb. ▫▫ **ver·bal·i·za·tion** *n.* **ver·bal·iz·er** *n.*

ver·bal noun *n. Gram.* a noun formed as an inflection of a verb and partly sharing its constructions (e.g., *smoking* in *smoking is forbidden*).

ver·ba·tim /vərbáytim/ *adv. & adj.* in exactly the same words (*copied it verbatim*; *a verbatim report*).

ver·be·na /vərbeénə/ *n.* any plant of the genus *Verbena*, bearing clusters of fragrant flowers.

ver·bi·age /vórbeeij/ *n.* needless accumulation of words.

ver·bose /vərbṓs/ *adj.* using or expressed in more words than are needed. ▫▫ **ver·bose·ly** *adv.* **ver·bos·i·ty** /–bósitee/ *n.*

ver·bo·ten /ferbṓt'n/ *adj.* forbidden, esp. by an authority.

ver·dant /vórd'nt/ *adj.* **1** (of grass, etc.) green, fresh-colored. **2** (of a field, etc.) covered with green grass, etc. **3** (of a person) unsophisticated; raw; green. ▫▫ **ver·dan·cy** /–d'nsee/ *n.*

ver·dict /vórdikt/ *n.* **1** a decision on an issue of fact in a civil or criminal cause or an inquest. **2** a decision; a judgment.

ver·di·gris /vórdigrees, –gris, –gree/ *n.* **1 a** a green crystallized substance formed on copper by the action of acetic acid. **b** this used as a medicine or pigment. **2** green rust on copper or brass.

ver·dure /vórjər/ *n.* **1** green vegetation. **2** the greenness of this.

verge[1] /vərj/ *n.* **1** an edge or border. **2** an extreme limit beyond which something happens (*on the verge of tears*).

verge[2] /vərj/ *v.intr.* **1** incline downward or in a specified direction (*the now verging sun*; *verge to a close*). **2** (foll. by *on*) border on; approach closely (*verging on the ridiculous*).

ver·i·fi·ca·tion /vérifikáyshən/ *n.* **1** the process or an instance of establishing the truth or validity of something. **2** *Philos.* the establishment of the validity of a proposition empirically.

ver·i·fy /vérifī/ *v.tr.* (**-fies, -fied**) **1** establish the truth or correctness of by examination or demonstration (*must verify the statement*; *verified my figures*). **2** (of an event, etc.) bear out or fulfill (a prediction or promise). ▫▫ **ver·i·fi·a·ble** *adj.* **ver·i·fi·er** *n.*

ver·i·ly /vérilee/ *adv. archaic* really; truly.

ver·i·sim·il·i·tude /vérisimílitōōd, –tyōōd/ *n.* **1** the appearance of being true or real. **2** a statement, etc., that seems true. ▫▫ **ver·i·sim·i·lar** /–símilər/ *adj.*

ve·ris·mo /verízmō/ *n.* (esp. of opera) realism.

ver·i·ta·ble /véritəbəl/ *adj.* real; rightly so called (*a veritable feast*). ▫▫ **ver·i·ta·bly** *adv.*

ver·i·ty /véritee/ *n.* (*pl.* **-ties**) **1** a true statement, esp. one of fundamental import. **2** truth. **3** a really existent thing.

ver·meil /vórmil, vərmáyl/ *n.* **1** (/vərmáy/) silver gilt. **2** an orange-red garnet. **3** *poet.* vermilion.

vermi- /vórmee/ *comb. form* worm.

ver·mi·cel·li /vérmichélee/ *n.* pasta made in long slender threads.
ver·mi·cide /vérmisīd/ *n.* a substance that kills worms.
ver·mic·u·lar /vərmíkyələr/ *adj.* **1** like a worm in form or movement. **2** *Med.* of or caused by intestinal worms. **3** marked with close wavy lines.
ver·mic·u·lite /vərmíkyəlīt/ *n.* a hydrous silicate mineral usu. resulting from alteration of mica, and expandable into sponge by heating, used as an insulation material.
ver·mi·form /vérmifawrm/ *adj.* worm-shaped.
ver·mi·form ap·pen·dix *n.* see APPENDIX 1.
ver·mil·ion /vərmílyən/ *n. & adj.* • *n.* **1** cinnabar. **2 a** a brilliant red pigment made by grinding this or artificially. **b** the color of this. • *adj.* of this color.
ver·min /vármin/ *n.* (usu. treated as *pl.*) **1** mammals and birds injurious to game, crops, etc. **2** parasitic worms or insects. **3** vile persons. ▫▫ **ver·min·ous** *adj.*
ver·miv·o·rous /vərmívərəs/ *adj.* feeding on worms.
ver·mouth /vərmóoth/ *n.* a wine flavored with aromatic herbs.
ver·nac·u·lar /vərnákyələr/ *n. & adj.* • *n.* **1** the language or dialect of a particular country (*Latin gave place to the vernacular*). **2** the language of a particular clan or group. **3** plain, direct speech. • *adj.* (of language) of one's native country; not of foreign origin or of learned formation. ▫▫ **ver·nac·u·lar·ize** *v.tr.* **ver·nac·u·lar·ly** *adv.*
ver·nal /vérnəl/ *adj.* of, in, or appropriate to spring (*vernal equinox; vernal breezes*).
ver·nal e·qui·nox *n.* the time in spring (about March 20) when the sun crosses the celestial equator, and day and night are of equal length.
ver·nal·i·za·tion /vérnəlīzáyshən/ *n.* the cooling of seed before planting, in order to accelerate flowering.
ver·nier /vérneeər/ *n.* a small, movable graduated scale for obtaining fractional parts of subdivisions on a fixed main scale of a barometer, sextant, etc.
Ve·ro·nal /vérənəl/ *n. Trademark* a sedative drug, a derivative of barbituric acid.
ve·ron·i·ca /vərónikə/ *n.* **1** any plant of the genus *Veronica* or *Hebe*. **2 a** a cloth supposedly impressed with an image of Christ's face. **b** any similar picture of Christ's face. **3** *Bullfighting* the movement of a matador's cape away from a charging bull.
ver·sa·tile /vérsət'l, –tīl/ *adj.* **1** turning easily or readily from one subject or occupation to another; capable of dealing with many subjects (*a versatile mind*). **2** having many uses. ▫▫ **ver·sa·til·i·ty** /–tílitee/ *n.*
verse /vərs/ *n. & v.* • *n.* **1 a** a metrical composition in general (*wrote pages of verse*). **b** a particular type of this (*English verse*). **2 a** a metrical line in accordance with the rules of prosody. **b** a group of a definite number of such lines. **c** a stanza of a poem or song. **3** each of the short numbered divisions of a chapter in the Bible or other scripture. **4 a** a versicle. **b** a passage (of an anthem, etc.) for solo voice. • *v.tr.* **1** express in verse. **2** (usu. *refl.*; foll. by *in*) instruct; make knowledgeable.
versed /vərst/ *predic.adj.* (foll. by *in*) experienced or skilled in; knowledgeable about.
ver·si·cle /vérsikəl/ *n.* each of the short sentences in a liturgy said or sung by a priest, etc., and alternating with responses.
ver·si·fy /vérsifī/ *v.* (**-fies, -fied**) **1** *tr.* turn into or express in verse. **2** *intr.* compose verses. ▫▫ **ver·si·fi·ca·tion** /–fikáyshən/ *n.* **ver·si·fi·er** *n.*
ver·sion /vérzhən, –shən/ *n.* **1** an account of a matter from a particular person's point of view (*told them my version of the incident*). **2** a book, etc., in a particular edition or translation (*Authorized Version*). **3** a form or variant of a thing as performed, adapted, etc.
vers li·bre /vair léebrə/ = FREE VERSE.
ver·so /vérsō/ *n.* (*pl.* **-sos**) **1 a** the left-hand page of an open book. **b** the back of a printed leaf of paper or manuscript (opp. RECTO). **2** the reverse of a coin.
ver·sus /vérsəs, –səz/ *prep.* against (esp. in legal and sports use). ¶ Abbr.: **v., vs.**
ver·te·bra /vértibrə/ *n.* (*pl.* **vertebrae** /–bray, –bree/) **1** each segment of the backbone. **2** (in *pl.*) the backbone. ▫▫ **ver·te·bral** *adj.*
ver·te·brate /vértibrət, –brayt/ *n. & adj.* • *n.* any animal of the subphylum Vertebrata, having a spinal column. • *adj.* of or relating to the vertebrates.
ver·tex /vérteks/ *n.* (*pl.* **vertices** /–tiseez/or **vertexes**) **1** the highest point; the top or apex. **2** *Geom.* **a** each angular point of a polygon, polyhedron, etc. **b** a meeting point of two lines that form an angle. **c** the point at which an axis meets a curve or surface. **d** the point opposite the base of a figure. **3** *Anat.* the crown of the head.
ver·ti·cal /vértikəl/ *adj. & n.* • *adj.* **1** at right angles to a horizontal plane; perpendicular. **2** in a direction from top to bottom of a picture, etc. **3** of or at the vertex or highest point. **4** at, or passing through, the zenith. **5** *Anat.* of or relating to the crown of the head. **6** involving all the levels in an organizational hierarchy or stages in the production of a class of goods (*vertical integration*). • *n.* a vertical line or plane. ▫▫ **ver·ti·cal·i·ty** /–kálitee/ *n.* **ver·ti·cal·ly** *adv.*
ver·tig·i·nous /vərtíjinəs/ *adj.* of or causing vertigo. ▫▫ **ver·tig·i·nous·ly** *adv.*
ver·ti·go /vértigō/ *n.* a condition with a sensation of whirling and a tendency to lose balance; dizziness; giddiness.
ver·tu var. of VIRTU.
verve /vərv/ *n.* enthusiasm; vigor; spirit.
ver·y /véree/ *adv. & adj.* • *adv.* **1** in a high degree (*did it very easily; had a very bad cough; am very much better*). **2** in the fullest sense (foll. by *own* or superl. adj.: *at the very latest; do your very best; my very own room*). • *adj.* **1** (usu. prec. by *the, this, his,* etc.) **a** actual; truly such (emphasizing identity, significance, or extreme degree: *the very thing we need; those were his very words*). **b** mere; sheer (*the very idea of it was horrible*). **2** *archaic* real; genuine (*very God*). ▫ **not very 1** in a low degree. **2** far from being.
ver·y high fre·quen·cy *n.* (of radio frequency) in the range 30–300 megahertz. *Abbrev.* VHF.
ve·si·ca /vesíkə, vésikə/ *n.* **1** *Anat. & Zool.* a bladder. **2** (in full **vesica piscis** /písis/ or **piscium** /píseeəm/) *Art* a pointed oval used as an aureole in medieval sculpture and painting. ▫▫ **ve·si·cal** *adj.*
ves·i·cate /vésikayt/ *v.tr.* raise blisters on. ▫▫ **ves·i·cant** /–kənt/ *adj. & n.* **ves·i·ca·tion** /–káyshən/ *n.* **ves·i·ca·to·ry** /–kətáwree/ *adj. & n.*
ve·si·cle /vésikəl/ *n.* **1** *Anat., Zool., & Bot.* a small bladder, bubble, or hollow structure. **2** *Geol.* a small cavity in volcanic rock produced by gas bubbles. **3** *Med.* a blister. ▫▫ **ve·sic·u·lar** /–síkyələr/ *adj.* **ve·sic·u·la·tion** /–láyshən/ *n.*
ves·per /véspər/ *n.* **1** Venus as the evening star. **2** *poet.* evening. **3** (in *pl.*) **a** the sixth of the canonical hours of prayer. **b** evensong.
ves·per·tine /véspərtīn, –tin/ *adj.* of or occurring in the evening.
ves·sel /vésəl/ *n.* **1** a hollow receptacle esp. for liquid. **2** a ship or boat, esp. a large one. **3 a** *Anat.* a duct or canal, etc., holding or conveying blood or other fluid, esp. = BLOOD VESSEL. **b** *Bot.* a woody duct carrying or containing sap, etc. **4** *Bibl.* or *joc.* a person regarded as the recipient or exponent of a quality (*a weak vessel*).

---

vest /vest/ *n.* & *v.* • *n.* **1** a waist-length close-fitting, sleeveless garment, often worn under a suit jacket, etc. **2** *Brit.* an undershirt. **3** a usu. V-shaped piece of material to fill the opening at the neck of a woman's dress. • *v.* **1** *tr.* (esp. in *passive*; foll. by *with*) bestow (powers, authority, etc.) on. **2** *tr.* (foll. by *in*) confer (property or power) on with an immediate fixed right of immediate or future possession. **3** *intr.* (foll. by *in*) (of property, a right, etc.) come into the possession of (a person).

ves•tal /vést'l/ *adj.* & *n.* • *adj.* **1** chaste; pure. **2** of or relating to the Roman goddess Vesta. • *n.* **1** a chaste woman. **2** *Rom. Antiq.* a vestal virgin.

ves•tal vir•gin *n. Rom. Antiq.* a virgin consecrated to the goddess Vesta and vowed to chastity.

vest•ed in•ter•est *n.* **1** *Law* an interest (usu. in land or money held in trust) recognized as belonging to a person. **2** a personal interest in a state of affairs, usu. with an expectation of gain.

ves•ti•bule /véstibyōōl/ *n.* **1 a** an antechamber, hall, or lobby next to the outer door of a building. **b** a porch of a church, etc. **2** an enclosed entrance to a railroad car. **3** *Anat.* **a** a chamber or channel communicating with others. **b** part of the mouth outside the teeth. **c** the central cavity of the labyrinth of the inner ear. ▫▫ **ves•tib•u•lar** /–stíbyoolər/ *adj.*

ves•tige /véstij/ *n.* **1** a trace or piece of evidence; a sign (*vestiges of an earlier civilization*; *found no vestige of their presence*). **2** a slight amount; a particle (*without a vestige of clothing*; *showed not a vestige of decency*). **3** *Biol.* a part or organ of an organism that is reduced or functionless but was well developed in its ancestors.

ves•tig•i•al /vestíjeeəl, –jəl/ *adj.* **1** being a vestige or trace. **2** *Biol.* (of an organ) atrophied or functionless from the process of evolution (*a vestigial wing*). ▫▫ **ves•tig•i•al•ly** *adv.*

vest•ment /véstmənt/ *n.* **1** any of the official robes of clergy, choristers, etc., worn during divine service, esp. a chasuble. **2** a garment, esp. an official or state robe.

ves•try /véstree/ *n.* (*pl.* **-tries**) a room or building attached to a church for keeping vestments in.

vet[1] /vet/ *n.* & *v.* • *n. colloq.* a veterinary surgeon. • *v.tr.* (**vetted, vetting**) make a careful and critical examination of (a scheme, work, candidate, etc.).

vet[2] /vet/ *n. colloq.* a veteran.

vetch /vech/ *n.* any plant of the genus *Vicia*, esp. *V. sativa*, largely used for silage or fodder.

vet•er•an /vétərən, vétrən/ *n.* **1** a person who has had long experience of an occupation (*a war veteran*; *a veteran of the theater*; *a veteran marksman*). **2** an ex-serviceman or servicewoman. **3** (*attrib.*) of or for veterans.

Vet•er•an's Day *n.* November 11, a legal holiday in the US, commemorating the end of World War I and of World War II, and honoring all veterans.

vet•er•i•nar•i•an /vétərináireeən, vétrə–/ *n.* a doctor who practices veterinary medicine or surgery.

vet•er•i•nar•y /vétərineree, vétrə–/ *adj.* & *n.* • *adj.* of or for diseases and injuries of animals, or their treatment. • *n.* (*pl.* **-ies**) = VETERINARIAN.

ve•to /véetō/ *n.* & *v.* • *n.* (*pl.* **-toes**) **1 a** a constitutional right to reject a legislative enactment. **b** the right of a permanent member of the UN Security Council to reject a resolution. **c** such a rejection. **d** an official message conveying this. **2** a prohibition (*put one's veto on a proposal*). • *v.tr.* (**-toes, -toed**) **1** exercise a veto against (a measure, etc.). **2** forbid authoritatively.

vex /veks/ *v.tr.* anger by a slight or a petty annoyance; irritate. ▫▫ **vex•ing** *adj.*

vex•a•tion /veksáyshən/ *n.* **1** the act or an instance of vexing; the state of being vexed. **2** an annoying or distressing thing.

vex•a•tious /veksáyshəs/ *adj.* **1** such as to cause vexation. **2** *Law* not having sufficient grounds for action and seeking only to annoy the defendant. ▫▫ **vex•a•tious•ly** *adv.*

vexed /vekst/ *adj.* **1** irritated; angered. **2** (of a problem, issue, etc.) much discussed; problematic. ▫▫ **vex•ed•ly** /véksidlee/ *adv.*

VHF *abbr.* very high frequency.

VI *abbr.* Virgin Islands.

vi•a /véeə, víə/ *prep.* by way of; through (*New York to Los Angeles via Chicago*; *send it via your secretary*).

vi•a•ble /víəbəl/ *adj.* **1** (of a plan, etc.) feasible; practicable, esp. from an economic standpoint. **2 a** (of a plant, animal, etc.) capable of living or existing in a particular climate, etc. **b** (of a fetus or newborn child) capable of maintaining life. **3** (of a seed or spore) able to germinate. ▫▫ **vi•a•bil•i•ty** /–bílitee/ *n.* **vi•a•bly** *adv.*

vi•a•duct /víədukt/ *n.* **1** a long, bridge, esp. a series of arches, carrying a road or railroad across a valley or dip in the ground. **2** such a road or railroad.

vi•al /víəl/ *n.* a small (usu. cylindrical glass) vessel, esp. for holding medicines.

vi•and /víənd/ *n. formal* **1** an article of food. **2** (in *pl.*) provisions; victuals.

vibes /vībz/ *n.pl. colloq.* **1** vibrations, esp. in the sense of feelings or atmosphere communicated (*the house had bad vibes*). **2** = VIBRAPHONE.

vi•brant /víbrənt/ *adj.* **1** vibrating. **2** (often foll. by *with*) thrilling; quivering (*vibrant with emotion*). **3** (of sound) resonant. **4** (of color) bright and vivid. ▫▫ **vi•bran•cy** /–rənsee/ *n.* **vi•brant•ly** *adv.*

vi•bra•phone /víbrəfōn/ *n.* a percussion instrument of tuned metal bars with motor-driven resonators and metal tubes giving a vibrato effect. ▫▫ **vi•bra•phon•ist** *n.*

vi•brate /víbráyt/ *v.* **1** *intr.* & *tr.* move or cause to move continuously and rapidly back and forth. **2** *intr. Physics* move unceasingly back and forth. **3** *intr.* (of a sound) throb; continue to be heard. **4** *intr.* (foll. by *with*) quiver; thrill (*vibrating with passion*). **5** *intr.* (of a pendulum) swing back and forth.

vi•bra•tion /vībráyshən/ *n.* **1** the act or an instance of vibrating. **2** *Physics* an oscillation of the parts of a fluid or an elastic solid whose equilibrium has been disturbed or of an electromagnetic wave. **3** (in *pl.*) **a** a mental (esp. occult) influence. **b** a characteristic atmosphere or feeling in a place, regarded as communicable to people present in it. ▫▫ **vi•bra•tion•al** *adj.*

vi•bra•to /vibraátō/ *n. Mus.* a rapid slight variation in pitch in singing or playing a stringed or wind instrument, producing a tremulous effect (cf. TREMOLO).

vi•bra•tor /víbraytər/ *n.* **1** a device that vibrates or causes vibration, esp. an instrument used in massage or for sexual stimulation. **2** *Mus.* a reed in a reed organ.

vi•bra•to•ry /víbrətawree/ *adj.* causing vibration.

vi•bur•num /vībərnəm, vee–/ *n. Bot.* any shrub of the genus *Viburnum*, usu. with white flowers.

vic•ar /víkər/ *n.* **1 a** (in the Church of England) an incumbent of a parish where tithes formerly passed to a chapter or religious house or layman (cf. RECTOR). **b** (in an Episcopal Church) a member of the clergy deputizing for another. **2** *RC Ch.* a representative or deputy of a bishop. ▫▫ **vic•ar•i•ate** /–káireeət/ *n.*

vic•ar•age /víkərij/ *n.* the residence or benefice of a vicar.

vi•car•i•ous /vikáireeəs/ *adj.* **1** experienced in the imagination through another person (*vicarious pleasure*). **2** acting or done for another (*vicarious suffering*). **3** deputed; delegated (*vicarious authority*). ▫▫ **vi•car•i•ous•ly** *adv.* **vi•car•i•ous•ness** *n.*

vice[1] /vīs/ *n.* **1 a** evil or grossly immoral conduct. **b** a particular form of this, esp. involving prostitution, drugs, etc. **2 a** depravity; evil. **b** an evil habit; a particular form of depravity (*has the vice of gluttony*). **3** a defect of character or behavior (*drunkenness was not among his vices*). **4** a fault or bad habit in a horse, etc.

vice[2] *n. colloq.* = VICE PRESIDENT, VICE ADMIRAL, etc.

vice- *comb. form* forming nouns meaning: **1** acting as a substitute or deputy for (*vice-chancellor*). **2** next in rank to (*vice admiral*).

vice ad·mi·ral /vīs/ *n.* a naval officer ranking below admiral and above rear admiral.

vice-chan·cel·lor /vís-chánsələr/ *n.* a deputy chancellor, esp. of a university, discharging most of the administrative duties.

vice pres·i·dent /vís-prézidənt, –dent/ *n.* an official ranking below and deputizing for a president. ▫▫ **vice pres·i·den·cy** *n.* (*pl.* **-cies**). **vice pres·i·den·tial** /–dénshəl/ *adj.*

vice·re·gal /vísreégəl/ *adj.* of or relating to a viceroy.

vice·roy /vísroy/ *n.* a ruler exercising authority on behalf of a sovereign in a colony, province, etc. ▫▫ **vice·roy·al·ty** *n.*

vice squad *n.* a police department enforcing laws against prostitution, drug abuse, etc.

vice ver·sa /vísə vérsə, vīs/ *adv.* with the order of the terms or conditions changed; the other way around (*could go from left to right or vice versa*).

vi·chys·soise /vísheeswaáz, veé–/ *n.* a creamy soup of leeks and potatoes.

Vi·chy wa·ter /víshee, –veé/ *n.* an effervescent mineral water from Vichy in France.

vi·cin·i·ty /visínitee/ *n.* (*pl.* **-ties**) **1** a surrounding district. **2** (foll. by *to*) nearness. ▫ **in the vicinity** (often foll. by *of*) near (to).

vi·cious /víshəs/ *adj.* **1** bad-tempered; spiteful (*a vicious dog; vicious remarks*). **2** violent (*a vicious attack*). **3** of the nature of or addicted to vice. **4** (of language or reasoning, etc.) faulty or unsound. ▫▫ **vi·cious·ly** *adv.* **vi·cious·ness** *n.*

vi·cis·si·tude /visísitōōd, –tyōōd/ *n.* a change of circumstances.

vic·tim /víktim/ *n.* **1** a person injured or killed (*a road victim; the victims of war*). **2** a person or thing injured or destroyed in pursuit of an object or in gratification of a passion, etc. (*the victim of their ruthless ambition*). **3** a prey; a dupe (*fell victim to a confidence scam*). **4** a living creature sacrificed to a deity or in a religious rite.

vic·tim·ize /víktimīz/ *v.tr.* **1** single out for punishment or unfair treatment. **2** make (a person, etc.) a victim. ▫▫ **vic·tim·i·za·tion** /–izáyshən/ *n.* **vic·tim·iz·er** *n.*

vic·tor /víktər/ *n.* a winner in battle or in a contest.

Vic·to·ri·a Cross /viktáwreeə/ *n.* a UK decoration awarded for bravery in the armed services, instituted by Queen Victoria in 1856.

Vic·to·ri·an /viktáwreeən/ *adj. & n.* • *adj.* **1** of or characteristic of the time of Queen Victoria. **2** associated with attitudes attributed to this time, esp. of prudery and moral strictness. • *n.* a person of this time. ▫▫ **Vic·to·ri·an·ism** *n.*

Vic·to·ri·an·a /viktáwreeánə, –aánə/ *n.pl.* **1** articles, esp. collectors' items, of the Victorian period. **2** attitudes characteristic of this period.

vic·to·ri·ous /viktáwreeəs/ *adj.* **1** conquering; triumphant. **2** marked by victory (*victorious day*). ▫▫ **vic·to·ri·ous·ly** *adv.*

vic·to·ry /víktəree/ *n.* (*pl.* **-ries**) **1** the process of defeating an enemy in battle or war or an opponent in a contest. **2** an instance of this; a triumph.

vict·ual /vít'l/ *n.* (usu. in *pl.*) food; provisions.

vict·ual·ler /vítlər/ *n.* (also **vict·ual·er**) **1** a person, etc., who supplies victuals. **2** a ship carrying stores for other ships.

vi·cu·ña /vīkōōnə, –nyə, –kyōō–, vi–/ *n.* (also **vi·cu·na**) **1** a S. American mammal, *Vicugna vicugna*, related to the llama, with fine silky wool. **2 a** cloth made from its wool. **b** an imitation of this.

vi·de /vídee, veéday/ *v.tr.* (as an instruction in a reference to a passage in a book, etc.) see; consult.

vi·de·li·cet /vidéliset, vī–/ *adv.* = VIZ.

vid·e·o /vídeeō/ *adj., n., & v.* • *adj.* **1** relating to the recording, reproducing, or broadcasting of visual images on magnetic tape or disk. **2** relating to the broadcasting of television pictures. • *n.* (*pl.* **-os**) **1** the process of recording, reproducing, or broadcasting visual images on magnetic tape or disk. **2** the visual element of television broadcasts. **3** *colloq.* = VIDEOCASSETTE RECORDER. **4** a movie, etc., recorded on a videotape. • *v.tr.* (**-oes, -oed**) make a video recording of.

vid·e·o·cam /vídeeōkam/ *n.* (also **vid·e·o·cam·er·a**) a camera for recording images on videotape.

vid·e·o·cas·sette /vídeeōkasét, –kəsét/ *n.* a cassette of videotape.

vid·e·o·cas·sette re·cord·er *n.* an apparatus for recording and playing videotapes ¶ Abbr.: **VCR**.

vid·e·o·disc /vídeeōdisk/ *n.* (also **vid·e·o·disk**) a metal-coated disk on which visual material is recorded for reproduction on a television screen.

vid·e·o dis·play ter·mi·nal *n. Computing* a device displaying data as characters on a screen and usu. incorporating a keyboard.

vid·e·o game *n.* a game played by manipulating images produced by a computer program on a television screen.

vid·e·o jock·ey *n.* a person who introduces music videos, as on television.

vid·e·o·phone /vídeeōfōn/ *n.* a telephone device transmitting a visual image as well as sound.

vid·e·o·tape /vídeeōtayp/ *n. & v.* • *n.* magnetic tape for recording television pictures and sound. • *v.tr.* make a recording of (broadcast material, etc.) with this.

vie /vī/ *v.intr.* (**vying**) (often foll. by *with*) compete; strive for superiority (*vied with each other for recognition*).

Vi·en·nese /veéəneéz/ *adj. & n.* • *adj.* of, relating to, or associated with Vienna in Austria. • *n.* (*pl.* same) a native or citizen of Vienna.

Vi·et·nam·ese /vee-étnəmeéz/ *adj. & n.* • *adj.* of or relating to Vietnam in SE Asia. • *n.* (*pl.* same) **1** a native or national of Vietnam. **2** the language of Vietnam.

view /vyōō/ *n. & v.* • *n.* **1** range of vision (*came into view; in full view of the crowd*). **2 a** what is seen from a particular point; a scene or prospect (*a fine view of the mountains; a room with a view*). **b** a picture, etc., representing this. **3** a visual or mental survey. **4** an opportunity for visual inspection; a viewing (*a private view of the exhibition*). **5 a** an opinion (*holds strong views on morality*). **b** a mental attitude (*took a favorable view of the matter*). **c** a manner of considering a thing (*took a long-term view of it*). • *v.* **1** *tr.* survey visually; inspect (*we are going to view the house*). **2** *tr.* survey mentally (*different ways of viewing a subject*). **3** *tr.* form a mental impression or opinion of; consider (*does not view the matter in the same light*). **4** *intr.* watch television. ▫ **have in view 1** have as one's object. **2** bear (a circumstance) in mind in forming a judgment, etc. **in view of** considering. **on view** being shown; being exhibited. **with a view to 1** with the hope or intention of. **2** with the aim of attaining (*with a view to marriage*). ▫▫ **view·a·ble** *adj.*

view·er /vyōōər/ *n.* **1** a person who views. **2** a person watching television. **3** a device for looking at film transparencies, etc.

view·find·er /vyōōfīndər/ *n.* a device on a camera showing the area covered by the lens in taking a photograph.

view·ing /vyóoing/ *n.* **1** an opportunity or occasion to view; an exhibition. **2** the act or practice of watching television.
view·point /vyóopoynt/ *n.* a point of view; a standpoint.
vig·il /víjil/ *n.* **1 a** keeping awake during the time usually given to sleep, esp. to keep watch or pray (*keep vigil*). **b** a period of this. **2** *Eccl.* the eve of a festival or holy day. **3** (in *pl.*) nocturnal devotions.
vig·i·lance /víjiləns/ *n.* watchfulness; caution.
vig·i·lant /víjilənt/ *adj.* watchful against danger, difficulty, etc. □□ **vig·i·lant·ly** *adv.*
vig·i·lan·te /víjilántee/ *n.* a member of a self-appointed body for the maintenance of order, etc.
vi·gnette /vinyét/ *n. & v.* • *n.* **1** a short descriptive essay or character sketch. **2** an illustration or decorative design. **3** a photograph or portrait showing only the head and shoulders with the background gradually shaded off. **4** a brief scene in a movie, etc. • *v.tr.* make a portrait of (a person) in vignette style.
vig·or /vígər/ *n.* **1** physical strength or energy. **2** a flourishing physical condition. **3** healthy growth. **4 a** mental strength or activity. **b** forcefulness; trenchancy; animation.
vig·or·ous /vígərəs/ *adj.* **1** strong and active; robust. **2** (of a plant) growing strongly. **3** forceful; acting or done with physical or mental vigor; energetic. **4** showing or requiring physical strength or activity. □□ **vig·or·ous·ly** *adv.* **vig·or·ous·ness** *n.*
Vi·king /víking/ *n. & adj.* • *n.* any of the Scandinavian seafaring pirates and traders who raided and settled in parts of NW Europe in the 8th–11th c. • *adj.* of or relating to the Vikings or their time.
vile /vīl/ *adj.* **1** disgusting. **2** depraved. **3** *colloq.* abominably bad (*vile weather*). □□ **vile·ly** *adv.* **vile·ness** *n.*
vil·i·fy /vílifī/ *v.tr.* (**-fies, -fied**) defame; speak evil of. □□ **vil·i·fi·ca·tion** /–fikáyshən/ *n.* **vil·i·fi·er** *n.*
vil·la /vílə/ *n.* **1** *Rom. Antiq.* a large country house with an estate. **2** a country residence. **3** a rented holiday home, esp. abroad.
vil·lage /vílij/ *n.* **1 a** a group of houses and associated buildings, larger than a hamlet and smaller than a town, esp. in a rural area. **b** the inhabitants of a village regarded as a community. **2** a small municipality with limited corporate powers. □□ **vil·lag·er** *n.* **vil·lage·y** *adj.*
vil·lain /vílən/ *n.* **1** a person guilty or capable of great wickedness. **2** *colloq.* usu. *joc.* a rascal or rogue. **3** (also **vil·lain of the piece**) (in a play, etc.) a character whose evil actions or motives are important in the plot.
vil·lain·ous /vílənəs/ *adj.* **1** wicked. **2** *colloq.* abominably bad; vile (*villainous weather*). □□ **vil·lain·ous·ly** *adv.*
vil·lain·y /vílənee/ *n.* (*pl.* **-ies**) **1** villainous behavior. **2** a wicked act.
-ville /vil/ *comb. form colloq.* forming the names of fictitious places with ref. to a particular quality, etc. (*dragsville; squaresville*).
vil·lein /vílin, –ayn, viláyn/ *n. hist.* a feudal tenant entirely subject to a lord or attached to a manor.
vil·lus /víləs/ *n.* (*pl.* **villi** /–lī/) **1** *Anat.* each of the short, fingerlike processes on some membranes, esp. on the mucous membrane of the small intestine. **2** *Bot.* (in *pl.*) long, soft hairs covering fruit, flowers, etc. □□ **vil·li·form** /víləfawrm/ *adj.* **vil·lose** /vílōs/ *adj.* **vil·los·i·ty** /–lósitee/ *n.* **vil·lous** /–əs/ *adj.*
vim /vim/ *n. colloq.* vigor.
VIN *abbr.* = vehicle identification number.
vin·ai·grette /vínigrét/ *n.* **1** (in full **vinaigrette sauce**) a salad dressing of oil, vinegar, and seasoning. **2** a small ornamental bottle for holding smelling salts.
vin·di·cate /víndikayt/ *v.tr.* **1** clear of blame or suspicion. **2** establish the existence, merits, or justice of. **3** justify by evidence or argument. □□ **vin·di·ca·tion** /–káyshən/ *n.* **vin·di·ca·tor** *n.*
vin·di·ca·to·ry /víndikətawree/ *adj.* **1** tending to vindicate. **2** (of laws) punitive.
vin·dic·tive /vindíktiv/ *adj.* **1** tending to seek revenge. **2** spiteful. □□ **vin·dic·tive·ly** *adv.* **vin·dic·tive·ness** *n.*
vine /vīn/ *n.* **1** any climbing or trailing woody-stemmed plant, esp. of the genus *Vitis*, bearing grapes. **2** a slender trailing or climbing stem. □□ **vin·y** *adj.*
vin·e·gar /vínigər/ *n.* **1** a sour liquid obtained from wine, cider, etc., by fermentation and used as a condiment or for pickling. **2** sour behavior or character. □□ **vin·e·gar·y** *adj.*
vin·er·y /vínəree/ *n.* (*pl.* **-ies**) **1** a greenhouse for grapevines. **2** a vineyard.
vine·yard /vínyərd/ *n.* a plantation of grapevines, esp. for wine-making.
vini- /vínee/ *comb. form* wine.
vin·i·cul·ture /vínikulchər/ *n.* the cultivation of grapevines.
vin·i·fi·ca·tion /vínifikáyshən/ *n.* the conversion of grape juice, etc., into wine.
vi·no /véenō/ *n. sl.* wine, esp. a red Italian wine.
vin ordinaire /ván awrdináir/ *n.* inexpensive (usu. red) table wine.
vin·tage /víntij/ *n. & adj.* • *n.* **1 a** a season's produce of grapes. **b** the wine made from this. **2 a** the gathering of grapes for winemaking. **b** the season of this. **3** a wine of high quality from a single identified year and district. **4 a** the year, etc., when a thing was made, etc. **b** a thing made, etc., in a particular year, etc. • *adj.* **1** of high quality, esp. from the past or characteristic of the best period of a person's work. **2** of a past season.
vint·ner /víntnər/ *n.* a wine merchant.
vin·y see VINE.
vi·nyl /vínəl/ *n.* any plastic made by polymerizing a compound containing the vinyl group, esp. polyvinyl chloride.
vi·ol /víəl/ *n.* a stringed musical instrument of the Renaissance, played with a bow and held vertically on the knees or between the legs.
vi·o·la[1] /vee-ólə/ *n.* **1 a** an instrument of the violin family, larger than the violin and of lower pitch. **b** a viola player. **2** a viol.
vi·o·la[2] /vī-ólə, vee–, víələ/ *n.* **1** any plant of the genus *Viola*, including the pansy and violet. **2** a cultivated hybrid of this genus.
vi·o·late /víəlayt/ *v.tr.* **1** disregard; fail to comply with (an oath, treaty, law, etc.). **2** treat (a sanctuary, etc.) profanely or with disrespect. **3** disturb (a person's privacy, etc.). **4** rape. □□ **vi·o·la·tion** /–láyshən/ *n.* **vi·o·la·tor** *n.*
vi·o·lence /víələns/ *n.* **1** the quality of being violent. **2** violent conduct or treatment. **3** *Law* **a** the unlawful exercise of physical force. **b** intimidation by the exhibition of this. □ **do violence to 1** act contrary to; outrage. **2** distort.
vi·o·lent /víələnt/ *adj.* **1** involving or using great physical force (*a violent person; a violent storm*). **2 a** intense; vehement; passionate; furious (*a violent contrast; violent dislike*). **b** vivid (*violent colors*). **3** (of death) resulting from external force or from poison (cf. NATURAL *adj.* 2). **4** involving an unlawful exercise of force (*laid violent hands on him*). □□ **vi·o·lent·ly** *adv.*
vi·o·let /víələt/ *n. & adj.* • *n.* **1 a** any plant of the genus *Viola*, esp. the sweet violet, with usu. purple, blue, or white flowers. **b** any of various plants resembling the sweet violet. **2** the bluish-purple color seen at the end of the spectrum opposite red. **3 a** pigment of this color. **b** clothes or material of this color. • *adj.* of this color.

vi·o·lin /víəlín/ *n.* **1** a musical instrument with four strings of treble pitch played with a bow. **2** a violin player. ▫▫ **vi·o·lin·ist** *n.*

vi·o·list /vee-ṓlist/ *n.* a viola player.

vi·o·lon·cel·lo /vééələnchélō, ví–/ *n.* (*pl.* **-los**) *formal* = CELLO. ▫▫ **vi·o·lon·cel·list** *n.*

VIP *abbr.* very important person.

violin

vi·per /vípər/ *n.* **1** any venomous snake of the family Viperidae, esp. the common viper (see ADDER). **2** a malignant or treacherous person. ▫▫ **vi·per·ish** *adj.* **vi·per·ous** *adj.*

vi·ra·go /viraágō, –ráygō/ *n.* (*pl.* **-gos**) a fierce or abusive woman.

vi·ral /vírəl/ *adj.* of or caused by a virus. ▫▫ **vi·ral·ly** *adv.*

vir·e·o /víreeō/ *n.* (*pl.* **-os**) any small American songbird of the family *Vireonidae*.

Vir·gil·i·an /vərjíleeən/ *adj.* of, or in the style of, the Roman poet Virgil (d. 19 BC).

vir·gin /vərjin/ *n.* & *adj.* • *n.* **1** a person (esp. a woman) who has never had sexual intercourse. **2 a** (**the Virgin**) Christ's mother the Blessed Virgin Mary. **b** a picture or statue of the Virgin. **3** (**the Virgin**) the zodiacal sign or constellation Virgo. **4** *colloq.* a naïve, innocent, or inexperienced person (*a political virgin*). **5** a member of any order of women under a vow to remain virgins. **6** a female insect producing eggs without impregnation. • *adj.* **1** that is a virgin. **2** of or befitting a virgin (*virgin modesty*). **3** not yet used, penetrated, or tried (*virgin soil*). **4** undefiled; spotless. **5** (of clay) not fired. **6** (of metal) made from ore by smelting. **7** (of wool) not yet, or only once, spun or woven. **8** (of olive oil, etc.) obtained from the first pressing of olives, etc.

vir·gin·al /vərjinəl/ *adj.* & *n.* • *adj.* that is or befits or belongs to a virgin. • *n.* (usu. in *pl.*) (in full **pair of virginals**) an early form of spinet in a box. ▫▫ **vir·gin·al·ly** *adv.*

Vir·gin·ia creep·er *n.* a N. American vine, *Parthenocissus quinquefolia*, cultivated for ornament.

Vir·gin·ia reel *n.* a country dance.

vir·gin·i·ty /vərjínitee/ *n.* the state of being a virgin.

Vir·go /vərgō/ *n.* (*pl.* **-gos**) **1** a constellation, traditionally regarded as contained in the figure of a woman. **2 a** the sixth sign of the zodiac (the Virgin). **b** a person born when the sun is in this sign. ▫▫ **Vir·go·an** *n.* & *adj.*

vir·gule /vərgyool/ *n.* **1** a slanting line used to mark division of words or lines. **2** = SOLIDUS 1.

vi·rid·i·an /virídeeən/ *n.* & *adj.* • *n.* **1** a bluish-green chromium oxide pigment. **2** the color of this. • *adj.* bluish-green.

vir·ile /virəl, –il/ *adj.* **1** of or characteristic of a man; having masculine (esp. sexual) vigor or strength. **2** of or having procreative power. **3** of a man as distinct from a woman or child. ▫▫ **vi·ril·i·ty** /virílitee/ *n.*

vi·rol·o·gy /vīróləjee/ *n.* the scientific study of viruses. ▫▫ **vi·ro·log·i·cal** /–rəlójikəl/ *adj.* **vi·rol·o·gist** *n.*

vir·tu /vərtóó/ *n.* (also **vertu**) **1** a knowledge of or expertise in the fine arts. **2** virtuosity. ▫ **article** (or **object**) **of virtu** an article interesting because of its workmanship, antiquity, rarity, etc.

vir·tu·al /vərchooəl/ *adj.* **1** that is such for practical purposes though not in name or according to strict definition (*is the virtual manager of the business*). **2** *Optics* relating to the points at which rays would meet if produced backward (*virtual focus*; *virtual image*). **3** *Mech.* relating to an infinitesimal displacement of a point in a system. **4** *Computing* not physically existing as such but made by software to appear to do so (*virtual memory*). ▫▫ **vir·tu·al·i·ty** /–álitee/ *n.* **vir·tu·al·ly** *adv.*

vir·tu·al re·al·i·ty *n.* the generation by computer software of an image or environment that appears real to the senses.

vir·tue /vərchoo/ *n.* **1** moral excellence; goodness. **2** a particular form of this (*patience is a virtue*). **3** chastity, esp. of a woman. **4** a good quality (*has the virtue of being adjustable*). **5** efficacy (*no virtue in such drugs*). ▫ **by virtue of** on the strength or ground of (*got the job by virtue of his experience*). **make a virtue of necessity** derive some credit or benefit from an unwelcome obligation.

vir·tu·o·so /vərchoo-ṓsō, –zō/ *n.* (*pl.* **virtuosi** /–see, –zee/or **-os**) **1 a** a person highly skilled in the technique of a fine art, esp. music. **b** (*attrib.*) displaying the skills of a virtuoso. **2** a person with a special knowledge of or taste for works of art. ▫▫ **vir·tu·os·i·ty** /–ósitee/ *n.*

vir·tu·ous /vərchooəs/ *adj.* **1** possessing or showing moral rectitude. **2** chaste. ▫▫ **vir·tu·ous·ly** *adv.* **vir·tu·ous·ness** *n.*

vir·u·lent /víyələnt, virə–/ *adj.* **1** strongly poisonous. **2** (of a disease) violent. **3** bitterly hostile. ▫▫ **vir·u·lence** /–ləns/ *n.* **vir·u·lent·ly** *adv.*

vi·rus /vírəs/ *n.* **1** a microscopic organism consisting mainly of nucleic acid in a protein coat, multiplying only in living cells and often causing diseases. **2** *Computing* = COMPUTER VIRUS. **3** a harmful or corrupting influence.

vi·sa /véézə/ *n.* an endorsement on a passport, etc., showing that it has been found correct, esp. as allowing the holder to enter or leave a country.

vis·age /vízij/ *n.* *literary* a face. ▫▫ **vis·aged** *adj.* (also in *comb.*).

vis-à-vis /véézaavéé/ *prep., adv.,* & *n.* • *prep.* **1** in relation to. **2** opposite to. • *adv.* facing one another. • *n.* (*pl.* same) **1** a person or thing facing another, esp. in some dances. **2** a person occupying a corresponding position in another group. **3** a social partner.

▶This expression means 'face to face.' Avoid using it to mean 'about, concerning,' e.g., "He wanted to talk to me vis-à-vis next weekend." In the sense 'in contrast, comparison, or relation to,' however, **vis-à-vis** is generally acceptable: *Let us consider government regulations vis-à-vis employment rates.*

vis·cer·a /vísərə/ *n.pl.* the interior organs in the great cavities of the body (e.g., brain, heart, liver), esp. in the abdomen (e.g., the intestines).

vis·cer·al /vísərəl/ *adj.* **1** of the viscera. **2** relating to inward feelings rather than conscious reasoning. ▫▫ **vis·cer·al·ly** *adv.*

vis·cid /vísid/ *adj.* **1** glutinous; sticky. **2** semifluid.

vis·cose /vískōs/ *n.* **1** a form of cellulose in a highly viscous state suitable for drawing into yarn. **2** rayon made from this.

vis·cos·i·ty /viskósitee/ *n.* (*pl.* **-ties**) **1** the quality or degree of being viscous. **2** *Physics* **a** (of a fluid) internal friction; the resistance to flow. **b** a quantity expressing this.

vis·count /víkownt/ *n.* a British nobleman ranking between an earl and a baron. ▫▫ **vis·count·cy** /–kówntsee/ *n.* (*pl.* **-cies**).

vis·count·ess /víkowntis/ *n.* **1** a viscount's wife or widow. **2** a woman holding the rank of viscount in her own right.

vis·cous /vískəs/ *adj.* **1** glutinous; sticky. **2** semifluid.

3 *Physics* having a high viscosity; not flowing freely. □□ **vis•cous•ly** *adv.*

vis•cus /vískəs/ *n.* (*pl.* **viscera** /vísərə/) (usu. in *pl.*) any of the soft internal organs of the body.

vise /vīs/ *n. & v.* •*n.* an instrument, esp. attached to a workbench, with two movable jaws between which an object may be clamped so as to leave the hands free to work on it. •*v.tr.* secure in a vise. □□ **vise•like** *adj.*

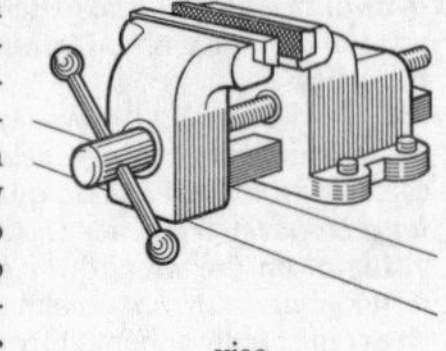
vise

Vish•nu /víshnōō/ *n.* a Hindu god regarded by his worshipers as the supreme deity and savior, by others as the second member of a triad with Brahma and Siva. □□ **Vish•nu•ism** *n.*

vis•i•bil•i•ty /vízibílitee/ *n.* **1** the state of being visible. **2** the range or possibility of vision as determined by the conditions of light and atmosphere.

vis•i•ble /vízibəl/ *adj.* **1 a** that can be seen. **b** (of light) within the range of wavelengths to which the eye is sensitive. **2** that can be perceived or ascertained (*has no visible means of support; spoke with visible impatience*). □□ **vis•i•ble•ness** *n.* **vis•i•bly** *adv.*

Vis•i•goth /vízigoth/ *n.* a West Goth, a member of the branch of the Goths who settled in France and Spain in the 5th c. and ruled much of Spain until 711.

vi•sion /ví<u>zh</u>ən/ *n.* **1** the act or faculty of seeing; sight. **2 a** a thing or person seen in a dream or trance. **b** a supernatural or prophetic apparition. **3** a thing or idea perceived vividly in the imagination (*visions of sandy beaches*). **4** imaginative insight. **5** statesmanlike foresight. **6** a person, etc., of unusual beauty. **7** what is seen on a television screen; television images collectively. □□ **vi•sion•less** *adj.*

vi•sion•ar•y /ví<u>zh</u>əneree/ *adj. & n.* •*adj.* **1** informed or inspired by visions; indulging in fanciful theories. **2** existing in or characteristic of a vision or the imagination. **3** not practicable. •*n.* (*pl.* **-ies**) a visionary person.

vis•it /vízit/ *v. & n.* •*v.* (**visited, visiting**) **1** *tr.* (also *absol.*) go or come to see (a person, place, etc.). **2** *tr.* reside temporarily with (a person) or at (a place). **3** *intr.* be a visitor. **4** *tr.* (of a disease, calamity, etc.) come upon; attack. **5** *tr. Bibl.* **a** (foll. by *with*) punish (a person). **b** (often foll. by *upon*) inflict punishment for (a sin). **6** *intr.* **a** (foll. by *with*) go to see (a person) esp. socially. **b** (usu. foll. by *with*) converse; chat. •*n.* **1 a** an act of visiting (*was on a visit to some friends; paid him a long visit*). **b** temporary residence. **2** (foll. by *to*) an occasion of going to a doctor, dentist, etc. **3** a formal or official call for the purpose of inspection, etc. **4** a chat.

vis•it•ant /vízit'nt/ *n.* a visitor, esp. a supposedly supernatural one.

vis•it•a•tion /vízitáyshən/ *n.* **1** an official visit of inspection. **2** trouble or difficulty regarded as a divine punishment. **3** (**Visitation**) **a** the visit of the Virgin Mary to Elizabeth related in Luke 1:39–56. **b** the festival commemorating this on July 2. **4** the instance of a parent using his or her visitation rights.

vis•it•a•tion rights *n.pl.* legal right of a noncustodial parent to visit or have temporary custody of his or her child.

vis•it•ing /víziting/ *n. & adj.* •*n.* paying a visit or visits. •*attrib.adj.* (of an academic)spending some time at another institution (*a visiting professor*).

vis•it•ing nurse *n.* a nurse, often employed by a public health agency, who visits the sick at home.

vis•i•tor /vízitər/ *n.* a person who visits.

vi•sor /vízər/ *n.* **1 a** a movable part of a helmet covering the face. **b** the projecting front part of a cap. **2** a shield to protect the eyes from unwanted light, esp. one at the top of a vehicle windshield. □□ **vi•sored** *adj.*

vis•ta /vístə/ *n.* **1** a long, narrow view as between rows of trees. **2** a mental view of a long succession of events (*opened up new vistas to his ambition*).

vis•u•al /ví<u>zh</u>ōōəl/ *adj. & n.* •*adj.* of, concerned with, or used in seeing. •*n.* (usu. in *pl.*) a visual image or display; a picture. □□ **vis•u•al•ly** *adv.*

vis•u•al aid *n.* a movie, model, etc., as an aid to learning.

vis•u•al•ize /ví<u>zh</u>ōōəlīz/ *v.tr.* **1** make visible, esp. to one's mind (a thing not visible to the eye). **2** make visible to the eye. □□ **vis•u•al•i•za•tion** /–izáyshən/ *n.*

vi•tal /vít'l/ *adj. & n.* •*adj.* **1** of, concerned with, or essential to organic life (*vital functions*). **2** essential to the existence of a thing or to the matter in hand (*a vital question; secrecy is vital*). **3** full of life or activity. **4** affecting life. **5** fatal to life or to success, etc. (*a vital error*). **6** *disp.* important. •*n.* (in *pl.*) the body's vital organs, e.g., the heart and brain.

vi•tal•ism /vít'lizəm/ *n. Biol.* the doctrine that life originates in a vital principle distinct from chemical and other physical forces. □□ **vi•tal•ist** *n.* **vi•tal•is•tic** *adj.*

vi•tal•i•ty /vītálitee/ *n.* **1** liveliness; animation. **2** the ability to sustain life. **3** (of an institution, language, etc.) the ability to endure and to perform its functions.

vi•tal•ize /vít'līz/ *v.tr.* **1** endow with life. **2** infuse with vigor.

vi•tal•ly /vít'lee/ *adv.* essentially; indispensably.

vi•tal signs *n.pl.* pulse rate, rate of respiration, and body temperature considered as signs of life.

vi•tal sta•tis•tics *n.pl.* data concerning the population, such as the number of births, marriages, and deaths.

vi•ta•min /vítəmin/ *n.* any of a group of organic compounds essential in small amounts for many living organisms to maintain normal health and development.

vi•ta•min A *n.* = RETINOL.

vi•ta•min B com•plex *n.* any of a group of vitamins which, although not chemically related, are often found together in the same foods.

vi•ta•min $\mathbf{B_1}$ *n.* = THIAMINE.

vi•ta•min $\mathbf{B_2}$ *n.* = RIBOFLAVIN.

vi•ta•min $\mathbf{B_6}$ *n.* = PYRIDOXINE.

vi•ta•min $\mathbf{B_{12}}$ *n.* = CYANOCOBALAMIN.

vi•ta•min C *n.* = ASCORBIC ACID.

vi•ta•min D *n.* any of a group of vitamins found in liver and fish oils, essential for the absorption of calcium and the prevention of rickets in children and osteomalacia in adults.

vi•ta•min E *n.* = TOCOPHEROL.

vi•ta•min K *n.* any of a group of vitamins found mainly in green leaves and essential for the blood-clotting process.

vi•ti•ate /vísheeayt/ *v.tr.* **1** impair the quality or efficiency of; debase. **2** make invalid or ineffectual. □□ **vi•ti•a•tion** /–sheeáyshən/ *n.*

vit•i•cul•ture /vítikulchər/ *n.* the cultivation of grapevines; the science or study of this. □□ **vit•i•cul•tur•al** *adj.* **vit•i•cul•tur•ist** *n.*

vit•re•ous /vítreeəs/ *adj.* **1** of, or of the nature of, glass. **2** like glass in hardness, brittleness, transparency, structure, etc. (*vitreous enamel*).

vit•re•ous hu•mor *n.* (also **vit•re•ous bod•y**) *Anat.* a transparent jellylike tissue filling the eyeball.

vit•ri•form /vítrifawrm/ *adj.* having the form or appearance of glass.

vit•ri•fy /vítrifī/ *v.tr. & intr.* (**-fies, -fied**) convert or be converted into glass or a glasslike substance, esp. by heat. ▫▫ **vit·ri·fi·ca·tion** /–fikáyshən/ *n.*

vit·ri·ol /vítreeōl, –əl/ *n.* **1** sulfuric acid or a sulfate. **2** caustic or hostile speech, criticism, or feeling.

vit·ri·ol·ic /vítreeólik/ *adj.* caustic or hostile.

vi·tu·per·ate /vītóōpərayt, –tyóō–, vi–/ *v.tr. & intr.* revile; abuse. ▫▫ **vi·tu·per·a·tion** /–ráyshən/ *n.* **vi·tu·per·a·tive** /–rətiv, –ráytiv/ *adj.*

vi·va /véevə/ *int. & n.* • *int.* long live. • *n.* a cry of this as a salute, etc.

vi·va·ce /viváachay/ *adv. Mus.* in a lively manner.

vi·va·cious /viváyshəs/ *adj.* lively; animated. ▫▫ **vi·va·cious·ly** *adv.* **vi·va·cious·ness** *n.* **vi·vac·i·ty** /vivásitee/ *n.*

vi·va vo·ce /vívə vṓsee, vṓchee, véevə/ *adj. & adv.* • *adj.* oral. • *adv.* orally.

viv·id /vívid/ *adj.* **1** (of light or color) strong; intense (*a vivid flash of lightning; of a vivid green*). **2** (of a mental faculty, impression, or description) clear; lively; graphic. **3** (of a person) lively; vigorous. ▫▫ **viv·id·ly** *adv.* **viv·id·ness** *n.*

viv·i·fy /vívifī/ *v.tr.* (**-fies, -fied**) enliven; animate; make lively or living. ▫▫ **viv·i·fi·ca·tion** /–fikáyshən/ *n.*

vi·vip·a·rous /vīvípərəs, vi–/ *adj.* **1** *Zool.* bringing forth young alive, not hatching them by means of eggs (cf. OVIPAROUS). **2** *Bot.* producing bulbs or seeds that germinate while still attached to the parent plant. ▫▫ **viv·i·par·i·ty** /vívipáritee/ *n.*

viv·i·sect /vívisekt/ *v.tr.* perform vivisection on.

viv·i·sec·tion /vívisékshən/ *n.* **1** dissection or other painful treatment of living animals for purposes of scientific research. **2** unduly detailed or ruthless criticism. ▫▫ **viv·i·sec·tion·ist** *n.* **viv·i·sec·tor** /–sektər/ *n.*

vix·en /víksən/ *n.* **1** a female fox. **2** a spiteful woman. ▫▫ **vix·en·ish** *adj.*

viz. /viz/ *adv.* namely; that is to say; in other words (*came to a firm conclusion, viz. that we were right*).

vi·zier /vizéer, víziər/ *n. hist.* a high official in some Muslim countries.

vi·zor var. of VISOR.

VJ *abbr.* = VIDEO JOCKEY.

V neck /véenék/ *n.* (often *attrib.*) **1** a neck of a sweater, etc., with straight sides meeting at an angle in the front to form a V. **2** a garment with this.

vocab. *abbr.* vocabulary.

vo·cab·u·lar·y /vōkábyəleree/ *n.* (*pl.* **-ies**) **1** the words used in a language or a particular book or branch of science, etc., or by a particular author (*scientific vocabulary; the vocabulary of Shakespeare*). **2** a list of these, arranged alphabetically with definitions or translations. **3** the range of words known to an individual (*his vocabulary is limited*). **4** a set of artistic or stylistic forms or techniques, esp. a range of set movements in ballet, etc.

vo·cal /vṓkəl/ *adj. & n.* • *adj.* **1** of or concerned with or uttered by the voice (*a vocal communication*). **2** expressing one's feelings freely in speech (*was very vocal about her rights*). **3** *Phonet.* voiced. **4** (of music) written for or produced by the voice with or without accompaniment (cf. INSTRUMENTAL). • *n.* **1** (in *sing.* or *pl.*) the sung part of a musical composition. **2** a musical performance with singing. ▫▫ **vo·cal·ly** *adv.*

vo·cal cords *n.pl.* folds of the lining membrane of the larynx, with edges vibrating in the air stream to produce the voice.

vo·cal·ism /vṓkəlizəm/ *n.* **1** the use of the voice in speaking or singing. **2** a vowel sound or system.

vo·cal·ist /vṓkəlist/ *n.* a singer, esp. of jazz or popular songs.

vo·cal·ize /vṓkəlīz/ *v.* **1** *tr.* form (a sound) or utter (a word) with the voice. **2** *intr.* utter a vocal sound. **3** *tr.* write (Hebrew, etc.) with vowel points. **4** *intr. Mus.* sing with several notes to one vowel. ▫▫ **vo·cal·i·za·tion** *n.*

vo·ca·tion /vōkáyshən/ *n.* **1** a strong feeling of fitness for a particular career (in religious contexts regarded as a divine call). **2 a** a person's employment, esp. regarded as requiring dedication. **b** a trade or profession.

vo·ca·tion·al /vōkáyshənəl/ *adj.* **1** of or relating to an occupation or employment. **2** (of education or training) directed at a particular occupation and its skills. ▫▫ **vo·ca·tion·al·ism** *n.* **vo·ca·tion·al·ly** *adv.*

voc·a·tive /vókətiv/ *n. & adj. Gram.* • *n.* the case of nouns, pronouns, and adjectives used in addressing a person or thing. • *adj.* of or in this case.

vo·cif·er·ate /vōsífərayt/ *v.* **1** *tr.* utter (words, etc.) noisily. **2** *intr.* shout; bawl. ▫▫ **vo·cif·er·a·tion** /–ráyshən/ *n.*

vo·cif·er·ous /vōsífərəs/ *adj.* **1** (of a person, speech, etc.) noisy; clamorous. **2** insistently and forcibly expressing one's views. ▫▫ **vo·cif·er·ous·ly** *adv.*

vod·ka /vódkə/ *n.* an alcoholic spirit made orig. in Russia by distillation of rye, etc.

vogue /vōg/ *n.* **1** (prec. by *the*) the prevailing fashion. **2** popular use or currency (*has had a great vogue*). ▫ **in vogue** in fashion. ▫▫ **vogu·ish** *adj.*

voice /voys/ *n. & v.* • *n.* **1 a** sound formed in the larynx, etc., and uttered by the mouth, esp. human utterance in speaking, shouting, singing, etc. (*heard a voice; spoke in a low voice*). **b** the ability to produce this (*has lost her voice*). **2 a** the use of the voice; utterance, esp. in spoken or written words (esp. *give voice*). **b** an opinion so expressed. **c** the right to express an opinion (*I have no voice in the matter*). **d** an agency by which an opinion is expressed. **3** *Gram.* a form or set of forms of a verb showing the relation of the subject to the action (*active voice; passive voice*). **4** *Mus.* **a** a vocal part in a composition. **b** a constituent part in a fugue. **5** *Phonet.* sound uttered with resonance of the vocal cords, not with mere breath. **6** (usu. in *pl.*) the supposed utterance of an invisible guiding or directing spirit. • *v.tr.* **1** express (*the letter voices our opinion*). **2** (esp. as **voiced** *adj.*) *Phonet.* utter with vibration of the vocal cords (e.g., *b, d, g, v, z*). **3** *Mus.* regulate the tone quality of (organ pipes). ▫ **in voice** (or **good voice**) in proper vocal condition for singing or speaking. **with one voice** unanimously. ▫▫ **-voiced** *adj.* (in *comb.*).

voice box *n.* the larynx.

voice·less /vóyslis/ *adj.* **1** dumb; speechless. **2** *Phonet.* uttered without vibration of the vocal cords (e.g., *f, k, p, s, t*). ▫▫ **voice·less·ness** *n.*

voice mail *n.* an automatic telephone answering system that records messages from callers.

voice-o·ver *n.* narration in a movie, etc., not accompanied by a picture of the speaker.

void /voyd/ *adj., n., & v.* • *adj.* **1 a** empty, vacant. **b** (foll. by *of*) free from (*a style void of affectation*). **2** esp. *Law* (of a contract, deed, promise, etc.) invalid; not binding (*null and void*). **3** useless; ineffectual. • *n.* **1** an empty space; a vacuum (*vanished into the void; cannot fill the void made by death*). **2** an unfilled space in a wall or building. • *v.tr.* **1** render invalid. **2** (also *absol.*) excrete. ▫▫ **void·a·ble** *adj.* **void·ness** *n.*

void·ance /vóyd'ns/ *n.* **1** *Eccl.* a vacancy in a benefice. **2** the act or an instance of voiding; the state of being voided.

void·ed /vóydid/ *adj. Heraldry* (of a bearing) having the central area cut away so as to show the field.

voile /voyl, vwaal/ *n.* a thin, semitransparent dress material of cotton, wool, or silk.

vol. *abbr.* volume.

vo·lant /vṓlənt/ *adj.* **1** *Zool.* flying; able to fly. **2** *Heraldry* represented as flying. **3** *literary* nimble; rapid.

vol·a·tile /vólət'l, –tīl/ *adj. & n.* • *adj.* **1** evaporating rapidly (*volatile salts*). **2** changeable; fickle. **3** lively; lighthearted. **4** apt to break out into violence. **5** transient. • *n.* a volatile substance. ▫▫ **vol·a·til·i·ty** /–tílitee/ *n.*

vol·a·til·ize /vólət'līz/ *v.* **1** *tr.* cause to evaporate. **2** *intr.* evaporate. ▫▫ **vol·a·til·iz·a·ble** *adj.* **vol·a·til·i·za·tion** *n.*

vol-au-vent /váwlōvoɴ/ *n.* a round case of puff pastry filled with meat, fish, etc., and sauce.

vol·can·ic /volkánik/ *adj.* (also **vul·can·ic** /vul–/) of, like, or produced by a volcano. ▫▫ **vol·can·i·cal·ly** *adv.* **vol·can·ic·i·ty** /vólkənísitee/ *n.*

vol·ca·no /volkáynō/ *n.* (*pl.* **-noes**) **1** a mountain or hill having an opening or openings in the earth's crust through which lava, cinders, steam, gases, etc., are or have been expelled continuously or at intervals. **2 a** a state of things likely to cause a violent outburst. **b** a violent esp. suppressed feeling.

vol·can·ol·o·gy /vólkənóləjee/ *n.* (also **vul·can·ol·o·gy** /vúl–/) the scientific study of volcanoes. ▫▫ **vol·can·ol·o·gist** *n.*

vole /vōl/ *n.* any small ratlike or mouselike plant-eating rodent of the family *Cricetidae.*

vo·li·tion /vəlíshən/ *n.* **1** the exercise of the will. **2** the power of willing. ▫ **of** (or **by**) **one's own volition** voluntarily. ▫▫ **vo·li·tion·al** *adj.*

vol·ley /vólee/ *n. & v.* • *n.* (*pl.* **-leys**) **1 a** the simultaneous discharge of a number of weapons. **b** the bullets, etc., discharged in a volley. **2** (usu. foll. by *of*) a noisy emission of oaths, etc., in quick succession. **3** *Tennis* the return of a ball in play before it touches the ground. **4** *Soccer* the kicking of a ball in play before it touches the ground. • *v.* (**-leys, -leyed**) **1** *tr.* (also *absol.*) *Tennis & Soccer* return or send (a ball) by a volley. **2** *tr. & absol.* discharge (bullets, abuse, etc.) in a volley. **3** *intr.* (of bullets, etc.) fly in a volley. **4** *intr.* (of guns, etc.) sound together. **5** *intr.* make a sound like a volley of artillery.

vol·ley·ball /vóleebawl/ *n.* a game for two teams of six hitting a large ball by hand over a net.

volt /vōlt/ *n.* the SI unit of electromotive force, the difference of potential that would carry one ampere of current against one ohm resistance. ¶ Abbr.: **V.**

volt·age /vṓltij/ *n.* electromotive force expressed in volts.

volt·ai·c /voltáyik/ *adj.* of electricity from a primary battery; galvanic (*voltaic battery*).

volt·me·ter /vṓltmeetər/ *n.* an instrument for measuring electric potential in volts.

vol·u·ble /vólyəbəl/ *adj.* speaking or spoken vehemently, incessantly, or fluently (*voluble spokesman*; *voluble excuses*). ▫▫ **vol·u·bil·i·ty** *n.* **vol·u·bly** *adv.*

vol·ume /vólyoom/ *n.* **1** a set of sheets of paper, usu. printed, bound together and forming part or the whole of a work or comprising several works (*issued in three volumes*; *a library of 12,000 volumes*). **2 a** solid content; bulk. **b** the space occupied by a gas or liquid. **c** (foll. by *of*) an amount or quantity (*large volume of business*). **3 a** quantity or power of sound. **b** fullness of tone. **4** (foll. by *of*) **a** a moving mass of water, etc. **b** (usu. in *pl.*) a wreath or coil or rounded mass of smoke, etc.

vo·lu·mi·nous /vəloominəs/ *adj.* **1** large in volume; bulky. **2** (of drapery, etc.) loose and ample. **3** consisting of many volumes. **4** (of a writer) producing many books. ▫▫ **vo·lu·mi·nous·ly** *adv.* **vo·lu·mi·nous·ness** *n.*

vol·un·ta·rism /vóləntərizəm/ *n.* **1** the principle of relying on voluntary action rather than compulsion. **2** *Philos.* the doctrine that the will is a fundamental or dominant factor in the individual or the universe. ▫▫ **vol·un·ta·rist** *n.*

vol·un·tar·y /vólənteree/ *adj. & n.* • *adj.* **1** done, acting, or able to act of one's own free will; not compulsory; intentional (*a voluntary gift*). **2** unpaid (*voluntary work*). **3** (of an institution) supported by voluntary contributions. **4** brought about, produced, etc., by voluntary action. **5** (of a movement, muscle, or limb) controlled by the will. **6** (of a confession by a criminal) not prompted by a promise or threat. • *n.* (*pl.* **-ies**) **1 a** an organ solo played before, during, or after a church service. **b** the music for this. **2** (in competitions) a special performance left to the performer's choice. ▫▫ **vol·un·tar·i·ly** *adv.*

vol·un·teer /vóləntéer/ *n. & v.* • *n.* **1** a person who voluntarily undertakes a task or enters military or other service. **2** (usu. *attrib.*) a self-sown plant. • *v.* **1** *tr.* (often foll. by *to* + infin.) undertake or offer (one's services, a remark or explanation, etc.) voluntarily. **2** *intr.* (often foll. by *for*) make a voluntary offer of one's services; be a volunteer.

vo·lup·tu·ar·y /vəlúpchooeree/ *n. & adj.* • *n.* (*pl.* **-ies**) a person given up to luxury and sensual pleasure. • *adj.* concerned with luxury and sensual pleasure.

vo·lup·tu·ous /vəlúpchooəs/ *adj.* **1** of, tending to, occupied with, or derived from, sensuous or sensual pleasure. **2** (of a woman) curvaceous and sexually attractive. ▫▫ **vo·lup·tu·ous·ly** *adv.* **vo·lup·tu·ous·ness** *n.*

vo·lute /vəloot/ *n. & adj.* • *n.* **1** *Archit.* a spiral scroll characteristic of Ionic capitals and also used in Corinthian and composite capitals. **2 a** any marine gastropod mollusk of the genus *Voluta.* **b** the spiral shell of this. • *adj.* esp. *Bot.* rolled up. ▫▫ **vo·lut·ed** *adj.*

vom·it /vómit/ *v. & n.* • *v.tr.* **1** (also *absol.*) eject (matter) from the stomach through the mouth. **2** (of a volcano, chimney, etc.) eject violently; belch (forth). • *n.* matter vomited from the stomach.

voo·doo /voodoo/ *n. & v.* • *n.* **1** use of or belief in religious witchcraft, esp. as practiced in the W. Indies. **2** a person skilled in this. **3** a voodoo spell. • *v.tr.* (**voodoos, voodooed**) affect by voodoo; bewitch.

vo·ra·cious /vawráyshəs, və–/ *adj.* **1** greedy in eating; ravenous. **2** very eager in some activity (*a voracious reader*). ▫▫ **vo·ra·cious·ly** *adv.* **vo·ra·cious·ness** *n.* **vo·rac·i·ty** /vərásitee/ *n.*

-vorous /vərəs/ *comb. form* forming adjectives meaning 'feeding on' (*carnivorous*). ▫▫ **-vora** /vərə/ *comb. form* forming names of groups. **-vore** /vawr/ *comb. form* forming names of individuals.

vor·tex /váwrteks/ *n.* (*pl.* **vortices** /–tiseez/ or **vortexes**) **1** a mass of whirling fluid, esp. a whirlpool or whirlwind. **2** any whirling motion or mass. **3** a system, occupation, pursuit, etc., viewed as swallowing up or engrossing those who approach it (*the vortex of society*). **4** *Physics* a portion of fluid whose particles have rotatory motion. ▫▫ **vor·ti·cal** /–tikəl/ *adj.* **vor·tic·i·ty** /vortísitee/ *n.*

vor·ti·cel·la /váwrtisélə/ *n.* any sedentary protozoan of the family *Vorticellidae*, consisting of a tubular stalk with a bell-shaped opening.

vor·ti·cist /váwrtisist/ *n. Art* a painter, writer, etc., of a school influenced by futurism and using the 'vortices' of modern civilization as a basis. ▫▫ **vor·ti·cism** *n.*

vo·ta·ry /vṓtəree/ *n.* (*pl.* **-ries**; *fem.* **vo·ta·ress**) (usu. foll. by *of*) **1** a person vowed to the service of God or a god or cult. **2** a devoted follower, adherent, or advocate of a person, system, occupation, etc.

vote /vōt/ *n. & v.* • *n.* **1** a formal expression of choice or opinion by means of a ballot, show of hands, etc., concerning a choice of candidate, approval of a motion or resolution, etc. (*let us take a vote on it*; *gave my vote to the independent candidate*) **2** (usu. prec. by *the*) the right to vote, esp. in a government election. **3** an opinion expressed by a majority of votes. **4** the collective votes that are or may be given by or for a particular group (*will lose the Southern vote*; *the Conservative* *vote increased*). **5** a ticket, etc., used for recording a vote. • *v.* **1** *intr.* (often foll. by *for*, *against*, or *to* + infin.) give a vote. **2** *tr.* **a** (often foll. by *that* + clause) enact or resolve by a majority of votes. **b** grant (a sum of money) by a majority of votes. **c** cause to be in a specified position by a majority of votes (*was voted off the committee*). **3** *tr. colloq.* pronounce or declare by general consent (*was voted a failure*). **4** *tr.* (often foll. by *that* + clause) *colloq.* announce one's proposal (*I vote that we all go home*). **5** *tr.* cast a ballot in accordance with (*vote your conscience*). □ **put to a** (or **the**) **vote** submit to a decision by voting. **vote down** defeat (a proposal, etc.) in a vote. **vote in** elect by votes. **vote with one's feet** *colloq.* indicate an opinion by one's presence or absence.

vote of con·fi·dence *n.* a vote showing that the majority support the policy of the governing body, etc.

vote of no con·fi·dence *n.* a vote showing that the majority do not support the policy of the governing body, etc.

vot·er /vṓtər/ *n.* **1** a person with the right to vote at an election. **2** a person voting.

vo·tive /vṓtiv/ *adj.* offered or consecrated in fulfillment of a vow (*votive offering*; *votive picture*; *votive candle*).

vouch /vowch/ *v.intr.* (foll. by *for*) answer for; be surety for (*will vouch for the truth of this*; *can vouch for him*).

vouch·er /vówchər/ *n.* **1** a document which can be exchanged for goods or services. **2** a document establishing the payment of money or the truth of accounts. **3** a person who vouches for a person, statement, etc.

vouch·safe /vówchsáyf/ *v.tr. formal* give or grant something to someone in a condescending manner.

vow /vow/ *n.* & *v.* • *n.* **1** *Relig.* a solemn promise, esp. in the form of an oath to God or another deity or to a saint. **2** (in *pl.*) the promises by which a monk or nun is bound to poverty, chastity, and obedience. **3** a promise of fidelity (*lovers' vows*; *marriage vows*). • *v.tr.* **1** promise solemnly (*vowed obedience*). **2** dedicate to a deity. □ **under a vow** having made a vow.

vow·el /vówəl/ *n.* **1** a speech sound made with vibration of the vocal cords but without audible friction. **2** a letter or letters representing this, as *a, e, i, o, u, aw, ah*. □□ **vow·eled** *adj.* (also in *comb.*).

vox po·pu·li /vóks pópyəlee, –lī/ *n.* public opinion; the general verdict.

voy·age /vóyij/ *n.* & *v.* • *n.* **1** a journey, esp. a long one by water, air, or in space. **2** an account of this. • *v.* **1** *intr.* make a voyage. **2** *tr.* traverse, esp. by water or air. □□ **voy·ag·er** *n.*

vo·yeur /vwaayṓr/ *n.* a person who obtains sexual gratification from observing others' sexual actions or organs. □□ **vo·yeur·ism** *n.* **vo·yeur·is·tic** /–rístik/ *adj.* **vo·yeur·is·ti·cal·ly** /–rístikəlee/ *adv.*

VP *abbr.* vice president.

VS. *abbr.* versus.

V sign /veé sīn/ *n.* **1** a sign of the letter V made with the first two fingers pointing up and the palm of the hand facing outward, as a symbol of victory. **2** *Brit.* a similar sign made with the back of the hand facing outward as a gesture of abuse, contempt, etc.

VSOP *abbr.* very special old pale (brandy).

VT *abbr.* Vermont (in official postal use).

Vt. *abbr.* Vermont.

VTOL /veétol/ *abbr.* vertical takeoff and landing.

vul·can·ic var. of VOLCANIC.

vul·can·ize /vúlkənīz/ *v.tr.* treat (rubber or rubberlike material) with sulfur, etc., esp. at a high temperature to increase its strength. □□ **vul·can·i·za·tion** *n.*

vul·can·ol·o·gy var. of VOLCANOLOGY.

vul·gar /vúlgər/ *adj.* **1 a** of or characteristic of the common people. **b** coarse in manners; low (*vulgar expressions*; *vulgar tastes*). **2** in common use; generally prevalent (*vulgar errors*). □□ **vul·gar·ly** *adv.*

vul·gar·i·an /vulgáireeən/ *n.* a vulgar (esp. rich) person.

vul·gar·ism /vúlgərizəm/ *n.* **1** a word or expression in coarse or uneducated use. **2** an instance of coarse or uneducated behavior.

vul·gar·i·ty /vulgáritee/ *n.* (*pl.* **-ties**) **1** the quality of being vulgar. **2** an instance of this.

vul·gar·ize /vúlgərīz/ *v.tr.* **1** make vulgar. **2** spoil (a scene, sentiment, etc.) by making it too common, frequented, or well known. **3** popularize. □□ **vul·gar·i·za·tion** *n.*

Vul·gate /vúlgayt, –gət/ *n.* **1 a** the Latin version of the Bible prepared mainly by St. Jerome in the late fourth century. **b** the official Roman Catholic Latin text as revised in 1592. **2** (**vulgate**) the traditionally accepted text of any author. **3** (**vulgate**) common or colloquial speech.

vul·ner·a·ble /vúlnərəbəl/ *adj.* **1** that may be wounded or harmed. **2** (foll. by *to*) exposed to damage by a weapon, criticism, etc. □□ **vul·ner·a·bil·i·ty** *n.* **vul·ner·a·bly** *adv.*

vul·ner·ar·y /vúlnəreree/ *adj.* & *n.* • *adj.* useful or used for the healing of wounds. • *n.* (*pl.* **·ies**) a vulnerary drug, plant, etc.

vul·pine /vúlpīn/ *adj.* **1** of or like a fox. **2** crafty; cunning.

vul·ture /vúlchər/ *n.* **1** any of various large birds of prey of the family *Cathartidae* or *Accipitridae*, with the head and neck more or less bare of feathers, feeding chiefly on carrion. **2** a rapacious person.

vul·va /vúlvə/ *n.* (*pl.* **vulvas**) *Anat.* the external female genitals. □□ **vul·var** *adj.* **vul·vi·tis** /–vítis/ *n.*

vv. *abbr.* **1** verses. **2** volumes.

vy·ing *pres. part.* of VIE.

W

W[1] /dúbəlyoo/ *n.* (also **w**) (*pl.* **Ws** or **W's**) the twenty-third letter of the alphabet.
W[2] *abbr.* (also **W.**) **1** watt(s). **2** West; Western. **3** women's (size).
W[3] *symb. Chem.* the element tungsten.
w. *abbr.* **1** warden. **2** wide(s). **3** with. **4** wife. **5** watt(s).
WA *abbr.* Washington (state) (in official postal use).
Wac /wak/ *n.* a member of the US Army's Women's Army Corps.
wack·o /wákō/ *adj. & n.* (also **whack·o**) *sl.* • *adj.* crazy. • *n.* (*pl.* **-os** or **-oes**) a crazy person.
wack·y /wákee/ *adj. & n.* (also **whack·y**) *sl.* • *adj.* (**-ier, -iest**) crazy. • *n.* (*pl.* **-ies**) a crazy person. ◻◻ **wack·i·ly** *adv.* **wack·i·ness** *n.*
wad /wod/ *n. & v.* • *n.* **1** a lump or bundle of soft material used esp. to keep things apart or in place or to stuff up an opening. **2** a disk of felt, etc., keeping powder or shot in place in a gun. **3** a number of bills of currency or documents placed together. **4** (in *sing.* or *pl.*) a large quantity, esp. of money. • *v.tr.* (**wadded, wadding**) **1** stop up (an aperture or a gun barrel) with a wad. **2** keep (powder, etc.) in place with a wad. **3** line or stuff with wadding. **4** protect with wadding. **5** press (cotton, etc.) into a wad or wadding.
wad·ding /wóding/ *n.* **1** soft, pliable material used to line or stuff, or to pack fragile articles. **2** any material from which gun wads are made.
wad·dle /wód'l/ *v. & n.* • *v.intr.* walk with short steps and a swaying motion. • *n.* a waddling gait. ◻◻ **wad·dler** *n.*
wade /wayd/ *v. & n.* • *v.* **1** *intr.* walk through water or some impeding medium. **2** *intr.* make one's way with difficulty or by force. **3** *intr.* (foll. by *through*) read (a book, etc.) in spite of its dullness, etc. **4** *intr.* (foll. by *into*) *colloq.* attack vigorously. **5** *tr.* ford on foot. • *n.* a spell of wading. ◻ **wade in** *colloq.* make a vigorous attack or intervention. ◻◻ **wad·a·ble** *adj.* (also **wade·a·ble**).
wad·er /wáydər/ *n.* **1 a** a person who wades. **b** a wading bird. **2** (in *pl.*) high waterproof boots, or a waterproof garment for the legs and body.
wa·di /wáadee/ *n.* (also **wa·dy**) (*pl.* **wadis** or **wadies**) a rocky watercourse in N. Africa, etc., dry except in the rainy season.
wa·fer /wáyfər/ *n.* **1** a very thin, light, crisp sweet cake, cookie, or biscuit. **2** *RC Ch.* a thin disk of unleavened bread used in the Eucharist. **3** *Electronics* a very thin slice of a semiconductor crystal. ◻◻ **wa·fer·y** *adj.*
wa·fer-thin *adj.* very thin.
waf·fle[1] /wófəl/ *n. & v. colloq.* • *n.* verbose but aimless or ignorant talk or writing. • *v.intr.* indulge in waffle. ◻◻ **waf·fler** *n.* **waf·fly** *adj.*
waf·fle[2] /wófəl/ *n.* a small, crisp batter cake with an indented lattice pattern, baked in a waffle iron and eaten hot with butter or syrup.
waf·fle i·ron *n.* a utensil, usu. of two shallow metal pans hinged together, for cooking waffles.
waft /woft, waft/ *v. & n.* • *v.tr. & intr.* convey or travel easily as through air or over water; sweep smoothly along. • *n.* **1** (usu. foll. by *of*) a whiff or scent. **2** a transient sensation.
wag[1] /wag/ *v. & n.* • *v. tr. & intr.* (**wagged, wagging**) shake or wave energetically back and forth. • *n.* a single wagging motion (*with a wag of his tail*). ◻ **the tail wags the dog** the less or least important member of a society, section of a party, or part of a structure has control. **tongues** (or **chins** or **jaws**) **wag** there is talk.
wag[2] /wag/ *n.* a facetious person; a joker.
wage /wayj/ *n. & v.* • *n.* **1** (in *sing.* or *pl.*) a fixed regular payment, made by an employer to an employee, esp. to a manual or unskilled worker (cf. SALARY). **2** (in *sing.* or *pl.*) requital. **3** (in *pl.*) *Econ.* the part of total production that rewards labor rather than remunerating capital. • *v.tr.* carry on (a war or contest).
wa·ger /wáyjər/ *n. & v.* = BET.
wag·gish /wágish/ *adj.* playful; facetious. ◻◻ **wag·gish·ly** *adv.* **wag·gish·ness** *n.*
wag·gle /wágəl/ *v. & n. colloq.* • *v.* **1** *intr. & tr.* wag. **2** *intr. Golf* swing the club head back and forth over the ball before playing a shot. • *n.* a waggling motion.
wag·gly /wáglee/ *adj.* unsteady.
wag·on /wágən/ *n.* **1 a** a four-wheeled vehicle for heavy loads. **b** a truck. **2** (in full **water wagon**) a vehicle for carrying water. **3** a light horse-drawn vehicle. **4** *colloq.* an automobile, esp. a station wagon. ◻ **on the wagon** *sl.* abstaining from alcohol.
wag·on·er /wágənər/ *n.* the driver of a wagon.
wag·on·ette /wágənét/ *n.* a four-wheeled, horse-drawn vehicle, usu. open, with facing side seats.
wag·tail /wágtayl/ *n.* any small bird of the genus *Motacilla* with a long tail in frequent motion.
waif /wayf/ *n.* **1** a homeless and helpless person, esp. a child. **2** an abandoned pet animal. **3** an object found and unclaimed. ◻◻ **wai·fish** *adj.*
wail /wayl/ *n. & v.* • *n.* **1** a prolonged and plaintive loud, high-pitched cry of pain, grief, etc. **2** a sound like this. • *v.intr.* **1** utter a wail. **2** lament or complain persistently or bitterly. **3** make a sound like a person wailing. ◻◻ **wail·er** *n.* **wail·ing·ly** *adv.*
wain·scot /wáynskət, –skot, –skōt/ *n. & v.* • *n.* boarding or wooden paneling on the lower part of an interior wall. • *v.tr.* line with wainscot.
wain·scot·ing /wáynskōting, –skot–, –skə–/ *n.* **1** a wainscot. **2** material for this.
waist /wayst/ *n.* **1 a** the part of the human body below the ribs and above the hips. **b** the circumference of this. **2** a similar narrow part in the middle of a violin, etc. **3 a** the part of a garment encircling or covering the waist. **b** the narrow middle part of a woman's dress, etc. **c** a blouse or bodice. **4** the middle part of a ship, between the forecastle and the quarterdeck. ◻◻ **waist·ed** *adj.* (also in *comb.*). **waist·less** *adj.*
waist·band /wáystband/ *n.* a strip of cloth forming the waist of a garment.
waist·coat /wéskət, wáystkōt/ *n. Brit.* a close-fitting waist-length garment, without sleeves or collar but usu. buttoned; a vest.
waist·line /wáystlīn/ *n.* the outline or the size of a person's waist.
wait /wayt/ *v. & n.* • *v.* **1** *intr.* **a** defer action or departure for a specified time or until some expected event occurs (*wait a minute*; *wait for a fine day*). **b** be expectant or on the watch (*waited to see what would happen*). **c** (foll. by *for*) refrain from going so fast that (a per-

son) is left behind (*wait for me!*). **2** *tr.* await (an opportunity, one's turn, etc.). **3** *tr.* defer (an activity) until a person's arrival or until some expected event occurs. **4** *intr.* **a** (in full **wait at** or **on table**) act as a waiter. **b** act as an attendant. **5** *intr.* (foll. by *on, upon*) **a** await the convenience of. **b** serve as an attendant to. **c** pay a respectful visit to. • *n.* **1** a period of waiting (*had a long wait*). **2** (usu. foll. by *for*) watching for an enemy; ambush (*lie in wait*). □ **wait and see** await the progress of events. **wait on 1** act as a waiter, etc. **2** be patient; wait. **wait up** (often foll. by *for*) **1** not go to bed until a person arrives or an event happens. **2** slow down until a person catches up, etc. (*wait up, I'm coming with you*). **you wait!** used to imply a threat, warning, or promise.

wait·er /wáytər/ *n.* **1** a person who serves at table in a hotel or restaurant, etc. **2** a person who waits for a time, event, or opportunity. **3** a tray or salver.

wait·ing /wáyting/ *n.* **1** in senses of WAIT *v.* **2 a** official attendance at court. **b** one's period of this.

wait·ing game *n.* a tactic in which one refrains from action for a time in order to act more effectively at a later date.

wait·per·son /wáytpərsən/ *n.* a waiter or waitress.

wait·ress /wáytris/ *n.* a woman who serves at table in a hotel or restaurant, etc.

waive /wayv/ *v.tr.* refrain from insisting on or using (a right, claim, etc.).

▶**Waive,** meaning 'surrender,' and the related noun, *waiver*, should not be confused with **wave,** 'a back-and-forth or up-and-down motion,' or with **waver** 'to go back and forth, vacillate': *He waived potential rights in the case by by signing the waiver. She waved the papers at her friends across the room. Just as we were all ready to go, he wavered and said he wasn't sure whether he should go.*

waiv·er /wáyvər/ *n. Law* the act or an instance of waiving.

wake[1] /wayk/ *v. & n.* • *v.* (*past* **woke** /wōk/or **waked**; *past part.* **woken** /wōkən/or **waked**) **1** *intr. & tr.* (often foll. by *up*) cease or cause to cease to sleep. **2** *intr. & tr.* (often foll. by *up*) become or cause to become alert or active (*needs something to wake him up*). • *n.* a watch beside a corpse before burial.

wake[2] /wayk/ *n.* **1** the track left on the water's surface by a moving ship. **2** turbulent air left behind a moving aircraft, etc. □ **in the wake of** behind; following; as a result of.

wake·ful /wáykfōōl/ *adj.* **1** unable to sleep. **2** (of a night, etc.) passed with little or no sleep. **3** vigilant. □□ **wake·ful·ly** *adv.* **wake·ful·ness** *n.*

wak·en /wáykən/ *v.tr. & intr.* make or become awake.

wale /wayl/ *n. & v.* • *n.* **1** = WEAL. **2** a ridge on a woven fabric, e.g., corduroy. **3** *Naut.* a broad, thick timber along a ship's side. **4** a specially woven strong band around a woven basket. • *v.tr.* provide or mark with wales.

walk /wawk/ *v. & n.* • *v.* **1** *intr.* **a** (of a person or other biped) progress by lifting and setting down each foot in turn, never having both feet off the ground at once. **b** progress with similar movements (*walked on his hands*). **c** go with one's usual gait except when speed is desired. **d** (of a quadruped) go with the slowest gait, always having at least two feet on the ground at once. **2** *intr.* **a** travel or go on foot. **b** take exercise in this way (*walks for two hours each day*). **3** *tr.* **a** perambulate; traverse on foot at walking speed; tread the floor or surface of. **b** traverse or cover (a specified distance) on foot (*walks five miles a day*). **4** *tr.* **a** cause to walk with one. **b** accompany in walking. **c** ride or lead (a horse, dog, etc.) at walking pace. **5** *intr.* (of a ghost) appear. **6** *intr. Cricket* leave the wicket on being out. **7** *Baseball* **a** *intr.* reach first base on balls. **b** *tr.* allow to do this. **8** *intr. sl.* be released from suspicion or from a charge. • *n.* **1 a** an act of walking, the ordinary human gait (*go at a walk*). **b** the slowest gait of an animal. **c** a person's manner of walking. **2 a** taking a (usu. specified) time to walk a distance (*is only ten minutes' walk from here*). **b** an excursion on foot (*go for a walk*). **c** a journey on foot completed to earn money promised for a charity, etc. **3 a** a place, track, or route intended or suitable for walking. **b** a person's favorite place or route for walking. □ **walk all over** *colloq.* **1** defeat easily. **2** take advantage of. **walk away from 1** easily outdistance. **2** refuse to become involved with. **3** survive (an accident, etc.) without serious injury. **walk away with** *colloq.* = *walk off with*. **walk the boards** = *tread the boards* (see TREAD). **walk in** (often foll. by *on*) enter or arrive, esp. unexpectedly or easily. **walk into** *colloq.* encounter through unwariness (*walked into the trap*). **walk off 1** depart (esp. abruptly). **2** get rid of the effects of by walking (*walked off his anger*). **walk off with** *colloq.* **1** steal. **2** win easily. **walk out 1** depart suddenly or angrily. **2** cease work, esp. to go on strike. **walk out on** desert; abandon. **walk over 1** *colloq.* = *walk all over*. **2** (often *absol.*) traverse (a racecourse) without needing to hurry, because one has no opponents or only inferior ones. **walk the plank** see PLANK. **walk the streets 1** be a prostitute. **2** traverse the streets, esp. in search of work, etc. **walk tall** *colloq.* feel justifiable pride. **walk up to** approach (a person) for a talk, etc. □□ **walk·a·ble** *adj.*

walk·a·thon /wáwkəthon/ *n.* an organized fund-raising walk.

walk·er /wáwkər/ *n.* **1** a person or animal that walks. **2 a** a framework in which a baby can learn to walk. **b** a usu. tubular metal frame used by disabled or elderly people to help them walk.

walk·ie-talk·ie /wáwkeetáwkee/ *n.* a two-way radio carried on the person.

walk·ing pa·pers *n.pl. colloq.* dismissal (*gave him his walking papers*).

walk·ing wound·ed *n.* (*pl.* same) (usu. in *pl.*) **1** a casualty able to walk despite injuries. **2** *colloq.* a person or people having esp. mental difficulties.

Walk·man /wáwkmən/ *n.* (*pl.* **-mans**) *Trademark* a type of portable stereo equipment with headphones.

walk-on *n.* **1** (in full **walk-on part**) a nonspeaking dramatic role. **2** the player of this.

walk·out /wáwkowt/ *n.* a sudden angry departure, esp. as a protest or strike.

walk·o·ver /wáwkōvər/ *n.* an easy victory or achievement.

walk-up *adj. & n.* • *adj.* (of a building) allowing access to the upper floors only by stairs. • *n.* a walk-up building.

walk·way /wáwkway/ *n.* a passage or path for walking along.

wall /wawl/ *n. & v.* • *n.* **1 a** a continuous and usu. vertical structure of usu. brick or stone, esp. enclosing, protecting, or dividing a space or supporting a roof. **b** the surface of a wall (*hung the picture on the wall*). **2** anything like a wall in appearance or effect (*a wall of steel bayonets*; *a wall of indifference*). **3** *Anat.* the outermost layer or enclosing membrane, etc., of an organ, structure, etc. **4** the outermost part of a hollow structure (*stomach wall*). • *v.tr.* **1** (esp. as **walled** *adj.*) surround or protect with a wall (*walled garden*). **2 a** (usu. foll. by *up, off*) block or seal with a wall. **b** (foll. by *up*) enclose (a person) within a sealed space (*walled them up in the dungeon*). □ **drive a person up the wall** *colloq.* **1** make a person angry; infuriate. **2** drive a person mad. **go to the wall** be defeated or ruined. **off the wall** *sl.* **1** unconventional. **2** angry. **walls have ears** it is unsafe to speak openly, as there may be eavesdroppers. ◻◻ **wall·ing** *n.* **wall-less** *adj.*

wal·la·by /wóllәbee/ *n.* (*pl.* **-bies**) any of various marsupials of the family *Macropodidae*, smaller than kangaroos, and having large hind feet and long tails.

wall·board /wáwlbawrd/ *n.* a type of wall covering made from wood pulp, plaster, etc.

wal·let /wólit/ *n.* a small flat esp. leather case for holding paper money, etc.

wall·eye /wáwlī/ *n.* **1 a** an eye with a streaked or opaque white iris. **b** an eye squinting outwards. **2** (also **wall·eyed pike**) an American perch, *Stizostedion vitreum*, with large prominent eyes. ◻◻ **wall·eyed** *adj.*

wall·flow·er /wáwlflowr/ *n.* **1 a** a fragrant spring garden plant, *Cheiranthus cheiri*, with brown, yellow, or dark-red clustered flowers. **b** any of various flowering plants of the genus *Cheiranthus* or *Erysimum*, growing wild on old walls. **2** *colloq.* a neglected or socially awkward person, esp. a woman sitting out at a dance for lack of partners.

Wal·loon /wolo͝on/ *n.* & *adj.* •*n.* **1** a member of a French-speaking people inhabiting S. and E. Belgium and neighboring France (see also FLEMING). **2** the French dialect spoken by this people. •*adj.* of or concerning the Walloons or their language.

wal·lop /wólәp/ *v.* & *n. sl.* •*v.tr.* **1 a** thrash; beat. **b** hit hard. **2** (as **walloping** *adj.*) big; thumping (*a walloping profit*). •*n.* a heavy blow; a thump. ◻◻ **wal·lop·ing** *n.*

wal·low /wólō/ *v.* & *n.* •*v.intr.* **1** (esp. of an animal) roll about in mud, water, etc. **2** (usu. foll. by *in*) indulge in unrestrained pleasure, misery, etc. (*wallows in nostalgia*). •*n.* **1** the act or an instance of wallowing. **2 a** a place used by buffalo, etc., for wallowing. **b** the depression in the ground caused by this. ◻◻ **wal·low·er** *n.*

wall·pa·per /wáwlpaypәr/ *n.* & *v.* •*n.* paper sold in rolls for pasting on to interior walls as decoration. •*v.tr.* (often *absol.*) decorate with wallpaper.

Wall Street *n.* a street at the south end of Manhattan where the New York Stock Exchange and other leading American financial institutions are located.

wal·nut /wáwlnut/ *n.* **1** any tree of the genus *Juglans*, having aromatic leaves and drooping catkins. **2** the nut of this tree. **3** the timber of this tree used in cabinetmaking.

wal·rus /wáwlrәs, wól–/ *n.* a large, amphibious, long-tusked arctic mammal, *Odobenus rosmarus*, related to the seal.

waltz /wawlts, wawls/ *n.* & *v.* •*n.* **1** a dance in triple time. **2** the usu. flowing music for this. •*v.* **1** *intr.* dance a waltz. **2** *intr.* (often foll. by *in, out, round*, etc.) *colloq.* move lightly, casually, with deceptive ease, etc. (*waltzed in and took first prize*). **3** *tr.* move (a person) in or as if in a waltz, casually or with ease (*was waltzed off to Paris*). ◻ **waltz·er** *n.*

wam·pum /wómpәm/ *n.* beads made from shells and strung together for use as money, decoration, or as aids to memory by N. American Indians.

wan /won/ *adj.* (**wanner, wannest**) **1** (of a person's complexion or appearance) pale; exhausted; worn. **2** faint. ◻◻ **wan·ly** *adv.* **wan·ness** *n.*

wand /wond/ *n.* **1** a supposedly magic stick used in casting spells or for effect by a fairy, magician, etc. **2** a slender rod carried or used as a marker in the ground. **3** a staff symbolizing authority. **4** *colloq.* a conductor's baton. **5** a handheld electronic device which can be passed over a bar code to read the data this represents.

wan·der /wóndәr/ *v.* & *n.* •*v.* **1** *intr.* (often foll. by *in, off*, etc.) go about from place to place aimlessly. **2** *intr.* **a** (of a person, river, etc.) diverge; meander. **b** get lost; leave home; stray from a path, etc. **3** *intr.* talk or think incoherently. **4** *tr.* cover while wandering (*wanders the world*). •*n.* the act or an instance of wandering (*went for a wander around the garden*). ◻◻ **wan·der·er** *n.* **wan·der·ing** *n.* (esp. in *pl.*).

wan·der·lust /wóndәrlust/ *n.* an eagerness for traveling.

wane /wayn/ *v.* & *n.* •*v.intr.* **1** (of the moon) decrease in apparent size after the full moon (cf. WAX[2]). **2** decrease in importance, brilliance, size, etc.; decline. •*n.* the process of waning. ◻ **on the wane** waning; declining.

wan·gle /wánggәl/ *v.* & *n. colloq.* •*v.tr.* **1** (often *refl.*) obtain (a favor, etc.) by scheming, etc. (*wangled himself a free trip*). **2** alter or fake (a report, etc.) to appear more favorable. •*n.* the act or an instance of wangling. ◻◻ **wan·gler** *n.*

wan·na·be /wónәbee/ *n. sl.* **1** an avid fan who tries to emulate the person he or she admires. **2** anyone who would like to be someone or something else.

want /wont, wawnt/ *v.* & *n.* •*v.* **1** *tr.* **a** (often foll. by *to* + infin.) desire; wish for possession of; need (*wants a toy train; wanted to leave; wanted him to leave*). **b** need or desire (a person, esp. sexually). **c** (foll. by *to* + infin.) *colloq.* ought; should; need (*you want to pull yourself together*). **2** *intr.* (usu. foll. by *for*) lack (*wants for nothing*). **3** *tr.* be without or fall short by (esp. a specified amount or thing) (*the drawer wants a handle*). **4** *intr.* (foll. by *in, out*) *colloq.* desire to be in, out, etc. (*wants in on the deal*). **5** *tr.* (as **wanted** *adj.*) (of a suspected criminal, etc.) sought by the police. •*n.* **1** (often foll. by *of*) **a** a lack (*shows great want of judgment*). **b** poverty; need (*living in great want; in want of necessities*). **2 a** a desire (*meets a long-felt want*). **b** a thing so desired (*can supply your wants*).

want Middle English: the noun from Old Norse *vant*, neuter of *vanr* 'lacking'; the verb from Old Norse *vanta* 'be wanting.' The notions of 'lack' and 'need' became complemented by the notion of 'desire' (i.e., to satisfy the need).

want ad *n.* a classified newspaper advertisement, esp. for something sought.

want·ing /wónting, wáwn–/ *adj.* **1** lacking; deficient (*wanting in judgment*). **2** absent; not provided. ◻ **be found wanting** fail to meet requirements.

wan·ton /wóntәn/ *adj.* **1** licentious; lewd; sexually promiscuous. **2** capricious; random (*wanton destruction*). **3** luxuriant (*wanton extravagance*). ◻◻ **wan·ton·ly** *adv.* **wan·ton·ness** *n.*

wap·i·ti /wópitee/ *n.* (*pl.* **wapitis**) a N. American deer, *Cervus canadensis*.

war /wawr/ *n.* & *v.* •*n.* **1 a** armed hostilities, esp. between nations; conflict (*war broke out*). **b** a specific conflict or the time during which such conflict exists (*was before the war*). **c** the suspension of international law, etc., during such a conflict. **2** (as **the war**) a war in progress; the most recent major war. **3 a** hostility or contention (*war of words*). **b** (often foll. by *on*) a sustained campaign against crime, poverty, etc. •*v.intr.* (**warred, warring**) **1** (as **warring** *adj.*) **a** rival; fighting (*warring factions*). **b** conflicting (*warring principles*). **2** make war. ◻ **at war** (often foll. by *with*) engaged in a war. **go to war** declare or begin a war. **have been in the wars** *colloq.* appear injured, bruised, unkempt, etc.

war Middle English (also in the sense 'dance with contortions'): of Germanic origin; related to German *taumeln* 'be giddy, stagger,' Swedish *tumla* 'tumble down'; related to Old English *tumbian* 'to dance.' The sense was probably influenced by Old French *tomber* 'to fall.' The noun dates from the mid-17th century.

war·ble /wáwrbəl/ *v.* & *n.* •*v.* **1** *intr.* & *tr.* sing in a gentle, trilling manner. **2** *tr.* **a** utter in a warbling manner. **b** express in a song or verse (*warbled his love*). •*n.* a warbled song or utterance.

war·bler /wáwrblər/ *n.* **1** any small, insect-eating songbird of the family *Sylviidae*, including the black cap, or, in N. America, *Parulidae*, including the wood warbler, whitethroat, and chiffchaff. **2** a person, bird, etc., that warbles.

war cry *n.* **1** a phrase or name shouted to rally one's troops. **2** a party slogan, etc.

ward /wawrd/ *n.* **1** a separate room or division of a hospital, etc. **2** an administrative division of a city or town. **3 a** a minor under the care of a guardian appointed by the parents or a court. **b** (in full **ward of the court**) a minor or mentally deficient person placed under the protection of a court. **4** (in *pl.*) the corresponding notches and projections in a key and a lock. □ **ward off 1** parry (a blow). **2** avert (danger, etc.).

-ward /wərd/ *suffix* (also **-wards**) added to nouns of place or destination and to adverbs of direction and forming: **1** adverbs meaning 'toward the place, etc.' (*set off homeward*). **2** adjectives meaning 'turned or tending toward' (*an onward rush*). **3** (less commonly) nouns meaning 'the region toward or about' (*look to the eastward*).

war·den /wáwrd'n/ *n.* **1** (usu. in *comb.*) a supervising official (*churchwarden*; *game warden*). **2** chief administrator of a prison. □□ **war·den·ship** *n.*

ward·er /wáwrdər/ *n.* a guard.

ward heel·er *n.* a party worker in elections, etc.

ward·robe /wáwrdrōb/ *n.* **1** a large movable or built-in case with rails, etc., for storing clothes. **2** a person's stock of clothes. **3** the costume department or costumes of a theater, a movie company, etc.

ward·room /wáwrdrōōm, –rōōm/ *n.* a room in a warship for the use of commissioned officers.

-wards var. of -WARD.

ware[1] /wair/ *n.* **1** (esp. in *comb.*) things of the same kind, esp. ceramics, made usu. for sale (*chinaware*; *hardware*). **2** (usu. in *pl.*) **a** articles for sale (*displayed his wares*). **b** a person's skills, talents, etc. **3** ceramics, etc., of a specified material, factory, or kind (*Wedgwood ware*; *delftware*).

ware[2] /wair/ *v.tr.* (esp. in hunting) look out for; avoid (usu. in *imper.*: *ware hounds!*).

ware·house /wáirhows/ *n.* & *v.* •*n.* **1** a building in which esp. retail goods are stored. **2** a wholesale or large retail store. •*v.tr.* (also /–howz/) store temporarily in a repository. □□ **ware·house·man** *n.* (*pl.* **-men**).

war·fare /wáwrfair/ *n.* a state of war; campaigning, engaging in war (*chemical warfare*).

war game *n.* **1** a military exercise testing or improving tactical knowledge, etc. **2** a battle, etc., conducted with toy soldiers.

war·head /wáwrhed/ *n.* the explosive head of a missile, torpedo, or similar weapon.

war·horse /wáwrhawrs/ *n.* **1** *hist.* a knight's or soldier's powerful horse. **2** *colloq.* a veteran soldier, politician, etc. **3** a song, play, etc., that has been performed to the point of triteness.

war·like /wáwrlīk/ *adj.* **1** hostile. **2** soldierly. **3** of or for war (*warlike preparations*).

war·lock /wáwrlok/ *n.* *archaic* a sorcerer or wizard.

war·lord /wáwrlawrd/ *n.* a military commander or commander in chief.

warm /wawrm/ *adj.*, *v.*, & *n.* •*adj.* **1** of or at a fairly or comfortably high temperature. **2** (of clothes, etc.) affording warmth. **3 a** sympathetic; cordial; loving (*a warm welcome*; *has a warm heart*). **b** enthusiastic; hearty (*was warm in her praise*). **4** animated; heated (*the dispute grew warm*). **5** *colloq. iron.* difficult or hostile (*met a warm reception*). **6** *colloq.* **a** close to the object, etc., sought. **b** near to guessing or finding out a secret. **7** (of a color, light, etc.) reddish, pink, or yellowish, etc., suggestive of warmth. **8** *Hunting* (of a scent) fresh and strong. **9 a** (of a person's temperament) amorous; sexually demanding. **b** erotic; arousing. •*v.* **1** *tr.* **a** make warm (*fire warms the room*). **b** make cheerful (*warms the heart*). **2** *intr.* **a** (often foll. by *up*) warm oneself at a fire, etc. (*warmed himself up*). **b** (often foll. by *to*) become enthusiastic or sympathetic (*warmed to his subject*). •*n.* **1** the act of warming; the state of being warmed (*had a nice warm by the fire*). **2** the warmth of the atmosphere, etc. □ **warm up 1** (of an athlete, performer, etc.) prepare by practicing. **2** (of a room, etc.) become warmer. **3** become enthusiastic, etc. **4** (of an engine, etc.) reach a temperature for efficient working. **5** reheat (food). □□ **warm·er** *n.* (also in *comb.*). **warm·ish** *adj.* **warm·ly** *adv.* **warm·ness** *n.* **warmth** *n.*

warmed-o·ver *adj.* (also **warmed-up**) **1** (of food, etc.) reheated. **2** stale; secondhand.

warm·heart·ed /wáwrmhaártid/ *adj.* kind; friendly. □□ **warm·heart·ed·ly** *adv.* **warm·heart·ed·ness** *n.*

war·mon·ger /wáwrmunggər, –mong–/ *n.* a person who seeks to bring about or promote war. □□ **war·mon·ger·ing** *n.* & *adj.*

warm-up *n.* a period of preparatory exercise for a contest or performance.

warn /wawrn/ *v.tr.* **1** (also *absol.*) **a** (often foll. by *of*, or *that* + clause, or *to* + infin.) inform of danger, unknown circumstances, etc. (*warned them of the danger*). **b** (often foll. by *against*) inform (a person, etc.) about a specific danger, hostile person, etc. (*warned her against trusting him*). **2** (usu. with *neg.*) tell forcefully (*has been warned not to go*). **3** give (a person) cautionary notice (*shall not warn you again*). □□ **warn·er** *n.*

warn·ing /wáwrning/ *n.* **1** in senses of WARN *v.* **2** anything that serves to warn. □□ **warn·ing·ly** *adv.*

warn·ing track *n.* (also **warn·ing path**) *Baseball* dirt strip that borders the outfield just inside the fence.

warp /wawrp/ *v.* & *n.* •*v.* **1** *tr.* & *intr.* **a** make or become bent or twisted out of shape. **b** make or become perverted or strange (*a warped sense of humor*). **2 a** *tr.* haul (a ship) by a rope attached to a fixed point. **b** *intr.* progress in this way. •*n.* **1 a** a state of being warped, esp. of lumber. **b** perversion of the mind or character. **2** the threads stretched lengthwise in a loom. **3** a rope used in towing or warping, or attached to a trawl net. □□ **warp·age** *n.* (esp. in sense 1a of *v.*).

war·path /wáwrpath/ *n.* **1** a warlike expedition of N. American Indians. **2** *colloq.* any hostile course (*on the warpath*).

war·rant /wáwrənt, wór–/ *n.* & *v.* •*n.* **1 a** anything that authorizes a person or an action. **b** a person so authorizing. **2 a** a written authorization, money voucher, etc. (*a dividend warrant*). **b** a written authorization allowing police to search premises, etc. **3** a document authorizing counsel to represent the principal in a lawsuit (*warrant of attorney*). **4** a certificate of service rank held by a warrant officer. •*v.tr.* **1** justify (*nothing can warrant his behavior*). **2** guarantee or attest to. □ **I** (or **I'll**) **warrant** I am certain (*he'll be sorry, I'll warrant*). □□ **war·rant·a·ble** *adj.* **war·rant·er** *n.* **war·ran·tor** *n.*

war·ran·ty /wáwrəntee, wór–/ *n.* (*pl.* **-ties**) **1** an undertaking as to the ownership or quality of a thing sold, leased, etc., often accepting responsibility or liability over a specified period. **2** (usu. foll. by *for* + verbal noun) an authority or justification. **3** an undertaking by an insured person of the truth of a statement or fulfillment of a condition.

▶See note at GUARANTEE.

war·ren /wáwrən, wór–/ *n.* **1 a** a network of interconnecting rabbit burrows. **b** a piece of ground occupied by this. **2** a labyrinthine building or district.

war·ri·or /wáwreeər, wór–/ *n.* **1** a person experienced or distinguished in fighting. **2** a fighting person, esp. a man, esp. of primitive peoples. **3** (*attrib.*) martial (*a warrior nation*).

wart /wawrt/ *n.* **1** a small, hardish, roundish growth on the skin caused by a virus-induced abnormal growth of papillae and thickening of the epidermis. **2** a protuberance on the skin of an animal, surface of a plant, etc. **3** *colloq.* an objectionable person. □ **warts and all** *colloq.* with no attempt to conceal blemishes or inadequacies. □□ **wart·y** *adj.*

wart·hog /wáwrt-hog/ *n.* an African wild pig of the genus *Phacochoerus*, with a large head and warty lumps on its face, and large curved tusks.

war·y /wáiree/ *adj.* (**warier, wariest**) **1** on one's guard; circumspect. **2** (foll. by *of*) cautious; suspicious (*am wary of using elevators*). **3** showing or done with caution or suspicion (*a wary expression*). □□ **war·i·ly** *adv.* **war·i·ness** *n.*

was *1st & 3rd sing. past* of BE.

Wash. *abbr.* Washington.

wash /wosh, wawsh/ *v. & n.* • *v.* **1** *tr.* cleanse with liquid, esp. water. **2** *tr.* (foll. by *out, off, away*, etc.) remove (a stain or dirt, a surface, or some physical feature of the surface) in this way. **3** *intr.* wash oneself or esp. one's hands and face. **4** *intr.* wash clothes, etc. **5** *intr.* (of fabric or dye) bear washing without damage. **6** *intr.* (foll. by *off, out*) (of a stain, etc.) be removed by washing. **7** *tr.* (of a river, sea, etc.) touch (a country, coast, etc.) with its waters. **8** *tr.* (of moving liquid) carry along in a specified direction (*a wave washed him overboard*). **9** *tr.* (also foll. by *away, out*) **a** scoop out (*the water had washed a channel*). **b** erode; denude (*sea-washed cliffs*). **10** *intr.* (foll. by *over, along*, etc.) sweep, move, or splash. **11** *tr.* sift (ore) by the action of water. **12** *tr.* **a** brush a thin coat of watery paint or ink over (paper in watercolor painting, etc., or a wall). **b** (foll. by *with*) coat (inferior metal) with gold, etc. • *n.* **1 a** the act or an instance of washing; the process of being washed (*only needed one wash*). **b** (prec. by *the*) treatment at a laundry, etc. (*sent them to the wash*). **2** a quantity of clothes for washing or just washed. **3** the visible or audible motion of agitated water or air, esp. due to the passage of a ship, etc., or aircraft. **4 a** soil swept off by water. **b** a sandbank exposed only at low tide. **5** kitchen slops given to pigs. **6 a** thin, weak, or inferior liquid food. **b** liquid food for animals. **7** a liquid to spread over a surface to cleanse, heal, or color. **8** a thin coating of watercolor, wall paint, or metal. **9** malt, etc., fermenting before distillation. **10** a lotion or cosmetic. □ **come out in the wash** *colloq.* be clarified, or (of contingent difficulties) be resolved or removed, in the course of time. **wash one's dirty linen in public** see LINEN. **wash down 1** wash completely (esp. a large surface). **2** (usu. foll. by *with*) accompany or follow (food) with a drink. **wash one's hands** *euphem.* go to the lavatory. **wash one's hands of** renounce responsibility for. **wash out 1** clean the inside of (a thing) by washing. **2** clean (a garment, etc.) by brief washing. **3 a** rain out (an event, etc.). **b** *colloq.* cancel. **4** (of a downpour, etc.) make a breach in (a road, etc.). **wash up 1** (also *absol.*) esp. *Brit.* wash (dishes, etc.) after use. **2** wash one's face and hands. **won't** (or **doesn't**) **wash** *colloq.* will not be believed or accepted.

wash·a·ble /wóshəbəl, wáwsh–/ *adj.* that can be washed, esp. without damage. □□ **wash·a·bil·i·ty** /–bílitee/ *n.*

wash·board /wóshbawrd, wáwsh–/ *n.* **1** a board of ribbed wood or a sheet of corrugated zinc on which clothes are scrubbed in washing. **2** this used as a percussion instrument.

wash·cloth /wóshkloth, wáwsh–/ *n.* a cloth for washing the face or body.

washed out *adj.* (hyphenated when *attrib.*) **1** faded by washing. **2** pale. **3** *colloq.* limp; enfeebled.

washed up *adj. sl.* (hyphenated when *attrib.*) defeated, having failed.

wash·er /wóshər, wáwsh–/ *n.* **1 a** a person or thing that washes. **b** a washing machine. **2** a flat ring of rubber, metal, etc., inserted at a joint to prevent leakage. **3** a similar ring placed under a nut, etc. to disperse pressure.

wash·er·wom·an /wóshərwŏŏmən, wáwsh–/ *n.* (*pl.* **-women**) (also **wash·wom·an**) a woman whose occupation is washing clothes; a laundress.

wash·ing /wóshing, wáwsh–/ *n.* a quantity of clothes for washing or just washed.

wash·ing ma·chine *n.* a machine for washing clothes and linen, etc.

wash-out *n.* **1** *colloq.* a fiasco; a complete failure. **2** a breach in a road, etc., caused by flooding.

wash·room /wóshrŏŏm, –rŏŏm, wáwsh–/ *n.* a room with washing and toilet facilities.

wash·stand /wóshstand, wáwsh–/ *n.* a piece of furniture to hold a washbowl, pitcher, soap, etc.

wash·y /wóshee, wáwsh–/ *adj.* (**washier, washiest**) **1** (of liquid food) too watery or weak; insipid. **2** (of color) faded-looking; thin; faint. **3** (of a style, sentiment, etc.) lacking vigor or intensity. □□ **wash·i·ness** *n.*

wasn't /wúzənt, wóz–/ *contr.* was not.

WASP /wosp/ *n.* (also **Wasp**) usu. *derog.* **1** a white Anglo-Saxon Protestant **2** an upper- or middle-class American white Protestant descended from early English settlers. □□ **Wasp·y** *adj.*

wasp /wosp/ *n.* **1** a stinging, often flesh-eating insect of the order *Hymenoptera*, esp. the common social wasp *Vespa vulgaris*, with black and yellow stripes and a very thin waist. **2** (in *comb.*) any of various insects resembling a wasp in some way (*wasp beetle*). □□ **wasp·like** *adj.*

wasp·ish /wóspish/ *adj.* irritable; petulant. □□ **wasp·ish·ly** *adv.* **wasp·ish·ness** *n.*

was·sail /wósəl, wósayl, wosáyl/ *n. & v. archaic* • *n.* **1** a festive occasion; a drinking bout. **2** a kind of liquor drunk on such an occasion. • *v.intr.* make merry; celebrate with drinking, etc. □□ **was·sail·er** *n.*

---

wassail Middle English (as a salutation): from Old Norse *ves heill*, corresponding to the Old English greeting *wæs hǣil* 'be in (good) health!' (source of HAIL[2]). No trace has been found of the use of drinking formulas in Old English, Old Norse or other Teutonic languages; *wassail* (and the reply *drinkhail* 'drink good health') were probably introduced by Danish-speaking inhabitants of England, the use then spreading to the native population. By the 12th century, the usage was considered, by the Normans, characteristic of Englishmen.

---

wast·age /wáystij/ *n.* **1** an amount wasted. **2** loss by use, wear, or leakage. **3** *Commerce* loss of employees other than by layoffs.

waste /wayst/ *v., adj., & n.* • *v.* **1** *tr.* use to no purpose or for inadequate result (*waste time*). **2** *tr.* fail to use (esp. an opportunity). **3** *tr.* (often foll. by *on*) utter (words, etc.), without effect. **4** *tr. & intr.* wear gradually away; wither. **5** *tr.* **a** ravage. **b** *sl.* murder; kill. **6** *tr.* treat as wasted or valueless. **7** *intr.* be expended without useful effect. • *adj.* **1** superfluous. **2** (of a district, etc.) not inhabited nor cultivated. **3** presenting no features of interest. • *n.* **1** the act or an instance of wasting; extravagant or ineffectual use of an asset, of time, etc. **2** waste material or food; refuse; useless remains or by-products. **3** a waste region; a desert, etc. **4** the state of being used up; diminution by wear and tear. **5** = WASTE PIPE. □ **go** (or **run**) **to waste** be wasted. **lay waste** ravage; devastate. **waste not, want not** extravagance leads to poverty. **waste words** see WORD.

waste·bas·ket /wáystbaskit/ *n.* a receptacle for wastepaper, etc.

waste·ful /wáystfo͝ol/ *adj.* **1** extravagant. **2** causing or showing waste. □□ **waste·ful·ly** *adv.* **waste·ful·ness** *n.*

waste·land /wáystland/ *n.* **1** an unproductive or useless area of land. **2** a place or time considered spiritually or intellectually barren.

waste·pa·per /wáystpaypər/ *n.* spoiled, valueless, or discarded paper.

wast·er /wáystər/ *n.* **1** a wasteful person. **2** *colloq.* a wastrel.

wast·rel /wáystrəl/ *n.* **1** a wasteful or good-for-nothing person. **2** a waif; a neglected child.

watch /woch/ *v. & n.* •*v.* **1** *tr.* keep the eyes fixed on; look at attentively. **2** *tr.* **a** keep under observation; follow observantly. **b** monitor or consider carefully (*have to watch my weight*). **3** *intr.* (often foll. by *for*) be in an alert state; be vigilant (*watch for the holes in the road*). **4** *intr.* (foll. by *over*) take care of. •*n.* **1** a small portable timepiece for carrying on one's person. **2** a state of alert observation or attention. **3** *Naut.* **a** a four-hour period of duty. **b** (in full **starboard** or **port watch**) each of the halves, divided according to the position of the bunks, into which a ship's crew is divided to take alternate watches. □ **on the watch** waiting for an expected or feared occurrence. **set the watch** *Naut.* station sentinels, etc. **watch it** (or **oneself**) *colloq.* be careful. **watch one's step** proceed cautiously. **watch out 1** (often foll. by *for*) be on one's guard. **2** as a warning of immediate danger. □□ **watch·a·ble** *adj.* **watch·er** *n.* (also in *comb.*).

watch chain *n.* a metal chain for securing a pocket watch.

watch·dog /wóchdawg, dog/ *n. & v.* •*n.* **1** a dog kept to guard property, etc. **2** a person or body monitoring others' rights, behavior, etc. •*v.tr.* (**-dogged, -dogging**) maintain surveillance over.

watch·ful /wóchfo͝ol/ *adj.* **1** accustomed to watching. **2** on the watch. **3** showing vigilance. **4** *archaic* wakeful. □□ **watch·ful·ly** *adv.* **watch·ful·ness** *n.*

watch·man /wóchmən/ *n.* (*pl.* **-men**) **1** a person employed to look after an empty building, etc., at night. **2** *archaic* or *hist.* a person employed to patrol the streets, etc. at night.

watch·tow·er /wóchtower/ *n.* a tower from which observation can be kept.

watch·word /wóchwərd/ *n.* **1** a phrase summarizing a guiding principle; a slogan. **2** *hist.* a military password.

wa·ter /wáwtər, wót–/ *n. & v.* •*n.* **1** a colorless, transparent, odorless, tasteless liquid compound of oxygen and hydrogen. ¶ Chem. formula: H_2O. **2** a liquid consisting chiefly of this and found in seas, lakes, and rivers, in rain, and in secretions of organisms. **3** an expanse of water; a sea, lake, river, etc. **4** (in *pl.*) part of a sea or river (*in Icelandic waters*). **5** (often as **the waters**) mineral water at a spa, etc. **6** the state of a tide (*high water*). **7** a solution of a specified substance in water (*lavender water*). **8** the quality of the transparency and brilliance of a gem, esp. a diamond. **9** (*attrib.*) **a** found in or near water. **b** of, for, or worked by water. **c** involving, using, or yielding water. •*v.* **1** *tr.* sprinkle or soak with water. **2** *tr.* supply (a plant) with water. **3** *tr.* give water to (an animal) to drink. **4** *intr.* (of the mouth or eyes) secrete water as saliva or tears. **5** *tr.* (as **watered** *adj.*) (of silk, etc.) having irregular wavy glossy markings. **6** *tr.* adulterate (beer, etc.) with water. **7** *tr.* (of a river, etc.) supply (a place) with water. **8** *intr.* (of an animal) go to a pool, etc., to drink. □ **by water** using a ship, etc., for travel or transport. **like water** lavishly; profusely. **like water off a duck's back** see DUCK[1]. **make one's mouth water** cause one's saliva to flow; stimulate one's appetite or anticipation. **of the first water 1** (of a diamond) of the greatest brilliance and transparency. **2** of the finest quality or extreme degree. **on the water** on a ship, etc. **water down 1** dilute with water. **2** make less vivid, forceful, or horrifying. **water under the bridge** past events accepted as past and irrevocable. □□ **wa·ter·er** *n.* **wa·ter·less** *adj.*

wa·ter bed *n.* a mattress of rubber or plastic, etc., filled with water.

wa·ter buf·fa·lo *n.* the common domestic E. Indian buffalo, *Bubalus arnee*.

wa·ter chest·nut *n.* **1** an aquatic plant, *Trapa natans*, bearing an edible seed. **2 a** (in full **Chinese water chestnut**) a sedge, *Eleocharis tuberosa*, with rushlike leaves arising from a corm. **b** this corm used as food.

wa·ter·col·or /wáwtərkúlər, wótər–/ *n.* **1** artists' paint made of pigment to be diluted with water and not oil. **2** a picture painted with this. **3** the art of painting with watercolors. □□ **wa·ter·col·or·ist** *n.*

wa·ter-cooled *adj.* cooled by the circulation of water.

wa·ter·course /wáwtərkawrs, wótər–/ *n.* **1** a brook, stream, or artificial water channel. **2** the bed along which this flows.

wa·ter·cress /wáwtərkres, wótər–/ *n.* a hardy perennial cress, *Nasturtium officinale*, growing in running water, with pungent leaves used in salad.

wa·ter·fall /wáwtərfawl, wótər–/ *n.* a stream or river flowing over a precipice or down a steep hillside.

wa·ter·fowl /wáwtərfowl, wótər–/ *n.* (usu. collect. as *pl.*) birds frequenting water, esp. swimming game birds.

wa·ter·front /wáwtərfrunt, wótər–/ *n.* the part of a town or city adjoining a river, lake, harbor, etc.

wa·ter hole *n.* a shallow depression in which water collects (esp. in the bed of a river otherwise dry).

wa·ter·ing hole *n.* **1** a pool of water from which animals regularly drink; a water hole. **2** *sl.* a bar.

wa·ter lil·y *n.* any aquatic plant of the family *Nymphaeaceae*, with broad flat floating leaves and large usu. cup-shaped floating flowers.

wa·ter·line /wáwtərlīn, wótər–/ *n.* **1** the line along which the surface of water touches a ship's side (marked on a ship for use in loading). **2** a linear watermark.

wa·ter·logged /wáwtərlawgd, –logd, wótər–/ *adj.* **1** saturated with water. **2** (of a boat, etc.) hardly able to float from being filled with water.

Wa·ter·loo /wáwtərlo͞o, wótər–/ *n.* a decisive defeat or contest (*meet one's Waterloo*).

wa·ter main *n.* the main pipe in a water-supply system.

wa·ter·man /wáwtərmən, wótər–/ *n.* (*pl.* **-men**) **1** a boatman plying for hire. **2** an oarsman as regards skill in keeping the boat balanced.

wa·ter·mark /wáwtərmaark, wótər–/ *n. & v.* •*n.* a faint design made in some paper during manufacture, visible when held against the light, identifying the maker, etc. •*v.tr.* mark with this.

wa·ter·mel·on /wáwtərmelən, wótər–/ *n.* a large, smooth, green melon, *Citrullus lanatus*, with red pulp and watery juice.

wa·ter pipe *n.* **1** a pipe for conveying water. **2** a hookah.

wa·ter pis·tol *n.* a toy pistol shooting a jet of water.

wa·ter plan·tain *n.* a plant of the genus *Alisma*, with plantainlike leaves, found esp. in ditches.

wa·ter po·lo *n.* a game played by swimmers, with a ball like a soccer ball.
wa·ter·proof /wáwtərproof, wótər–/ *adj. & v.* • *adj.* impervious to water. • *v.tr.* make waterproof.
wa·ter rat *n.* **1** any rodent of aquatic habits. **2** a muskrat. **3** *sl.* a waterfront vagrant or thug.
wa·ter-re·pel·lent *adj.* not easily penetrated by water.
wa·ter·shed /wáwtərshed, wótər–/ *n.* **1** a line of separation between waters flowing to different rivers, basins, or seas. **2** a turning point in affairs.
wa·ter ski *n. & v.* • *n.* (*pl.* **skis**) each of a pair of skis for skimming the surface of the water when towed by a motorboat. • *v.intr.* (**water-ski**) (**-skis, -skied, -skiing**) travel on water skis. ▫▫ **wa·ter-ski·er** *n.*
wa·ter·spout /wáwtərspowt, wótər–/ *n.* a gyrating column of water and spray formed by a whirlwind between sea and cloud.
wa·ter ta·ble *n.* a level below which the ground is saturated with water.
wa·ter·tight /wáwtərtīt, wótər–/ *adj.* **1** closely fastened or fitted or made so as to prevent the passage of water. **2** (of an argument, etc.) unassailable.
wa·ter·way /wáwtərway, wótər–/ *n.* **1** a navigable channel. **2** a route for travel by water. **3** a thick plank at the outer edge of a deck along which a channel is hollowed for water to run off by.
wa·ter·wheel /wáwtərhweel, wótər–, –weel/ *n.* a wheel driven by water to work machinery, or to raise water.
wa·ter wings *n.pl.* inflated floats fixed on the arms of a person learning to swim.
wa·ter·works /wáwtərwərks, wótər–/ *n.* **1** an establishment for managing a water supply. **2** *colloq.* the shedding of tears.
wa·ter·y /wáwtəree, wótər–/ *adj.* **1** containing too much water. **2** too thin in consistency. **3** of or consisting of water. **4** (of the eyes) suffused with water. **5** (of conversation, style, etc.) vapid; uninteresting. **6** (of color) pale. **7** (of the sun, moon, or sky) rainy-looking. ▫▫ **wa·ter·i·ness** *n.*
watt /wot/ *n.* the SI unit of power, equivalent to one joule per second. ¶ Symb.: **W**.
watt·age /wótij/ *n.* an amount of electrical power expressed in watts.
watt-hour *n.* the energy used when one watt is applied for one hour.
wat·tle[1] /wót'l/ *n. & v.* • *n.* **1 a** interlaced rods as a material for making fences, walls, etc. **b** (in *sing.* or *pl.*) rods and twigs for this use. **2** an Australian acacia with long pliant branches and golden flowers used as the national emblem. • *v.tr.* **1** make of wattle. **2** enclose or fill up with wattles.
wat·tle[2] /wót'l/ *n.* **1** a loose fleshy appendage on the head or throat of a turkey or other birds. **2** = BARB *n.* 3. ▫▫ **wat·tled** *adj.*

wattle[2]

wave /wayv/ *v. & n.* • *v.* **1 a** *intr.* (often foll. by *to*) move a hand, etc., back and forth in greeting or as a signal (*waved to me across the street*). **b** *tr.* move (a hand, etc.) in this way. **2 a** *intr.* show a sinuous motion as of a flag, tree, or a wheat field in the wind. **b** *tr.* impart a waving motion to. **3** *tr.* brandish (a sword, etc.) as an encouragement to followers, etc. **4** *tr.* tell or direct (a person) by waving (*waved them away*). **5** *tr.* express (a greeting, etc.) by waving (*waved good-bye to them*). **6** *tr.* give an undulating form to; make wavy. **7** *intr.* (of hair, etc.) have such a form; be wavy. • *n.* **1** a ridge of water between two depressions. **2** a long body of water curling into an arched form and breaking on the shore. **3** a body of persons in one of successive advancing groups. **4** a gesture of waving. **5 a** the process of waving the hair. **b** an undulating form produced in the hair by waving. **6 a** a temporary occurrence of a condition, emotion, or influence (*a wave of enthusiasm*). **b** a specified period of widespread weather (*heat wave*). **7** *Physics* **a** the disturbance of the particles of a fluid medium to form ridges and troughs for the propagation or direction of motion, heat, sound, etc. **b** a single curve in the course of this motion. **8** *Electr.* a similar variation of an electromagnetic field in the propagation of radiation through a medium or vacuum. ▫ **make waves** *colloq.* cause trouble. **wave aside** dismiss as intrusive or irrelevant. ▫▫ **wave·less** *adj.* **wave·like** *adj. & adv.*
▶See note at WAIVE.
wave·form /wáyvfawrm/ *n. Physics* a curve showing the shape of a wave at a given time.
wave·length /wáyvlengkth, –length, –lenth/ *n.* **1** the distance between successive crests of a wave, esp. points in a sound wave or electromagnetic wave. ¶ Symb.: λ. **2** this as a distinctive feature of radio waves from a transmitter. **3** *colloq.* a particular mode or range of thinking and communicating (*we don't seem to be on the same wavelength*).
wave·let /wáyvlit/ *n.* a small wave on water.
wa·ver /wáyvər/ *v.intr.* **1** be or become unsteady; falter; begin to give way. **2** be undecided between different opinions; be shaken in resolution or belief. **3** (of a light) flicker. ▫▫ **wa·ver·er** *n.* **wa·ver·ing·ly** *adv.*
▶See note at WAIVE.
wav·y /wáyvee/ *adj.* (**wavier, waviest**) (of a line or surface) having waves or alternate contrary curves (*wavy hair*). ▫▫ **wav·i·ness** *n.*
wa-wa /wa̋awaa/ *n.* (also **wah-wah**) *Mus.* an effect achieved on brass instruments by alternately applying and removing a mute, and on an electric guitar by controlling the output from the amplifier with a pedal.
wax[1] /waks/ *n. & v.* • *n.* **1** a sticky, plastic, yellowish substance secreted by bees as the material of honeycomb cells. **2** a white translucent material obtained from this by bleaching and purifying and used for candles, in modeling, as a basis of polishes, and for other purposes. **3** any similar substance, e.g., earwax. **4** *colloq.* **a** a phonograph record. **b** material for the manufacture of this. **5** (*attrib.*) made of wax. • *v.tr.* **1** cover or treat with wax. **2** *colloq.* record for the phonograph. ▫▫ **wax·er** *n.*
wax[2] /waks/ *v.intr.* **1** (of the moon between new and full) have a progressively larger part of its visible surface illuminated, increasing in apparent size (cf. WANE). **2** become larger or stronger. **3** pass into a specified state or mood (*wax lyrical*). ▫ **wax and wane** undergo alternate increases and decreases.
wax·en /wáksən/ *adj.* **1** having a smooth pale translucent surface as of wax. **2** able to receive impressions like wax. **3** *archaic* made of wax.
wax pa·per *n.* (also **waxed pa·per**) paper waterproofed with a layer of wax.
wax·work /wákswərk/ *n.* **1 a** an object, esp. a lifelike dummy, modeled in wax. **b** the making of waxworks. **2** (in *pl.*) an exhibition of wax dummies.
way /way/ *n. & adv.* • *n.* **1** a road, path, etc., for passing along. **2** a route for reaching a place, esp. the best one (*asked the way to Rockefeller Center*). **3** a place of passage into a building, etc. (*could not find the way out*). **4 a** a method for attaining an object (*that is not the way to do it*). **b** the ability to obtain one's object (*has a way with him*). **5 a** a person's chosen course of action. **b** a manner of behaving; a personal peculiarity (*has a way

of forgetting things). **6** a specific manner of procedure (*soon got into the way of it*). **7** the normal course of events (*that is always the way*). **8** a traveling distance; a length traversed or to be traversed (*is a long way away*). **9 a** an unimpeded opportunity of advance. **b** a space free of obstacles. **10** a region or ground over which advance is desired or natural. **11** impetus; progress (*pushed my way through*). **12** movement of a ship, etc. (*gather way; lose way*). **13** the state of being engaged in movement from place to place; time spent in this (*met them on the way home*). **14** a specified direction (*step this way; which way are you going?*). **15** (in *pl.*) parts into which a thing is divided (*split it three ways*). **16** a person's line of occupation or business. **17** a specified condition or state (*in a bad way*). **18** a respect (*useful in some ways*). **19 a** (in *pl.*) a structure of lumber, etc., down which a new ship is launched. **b** parallel rails, etc., as a track for the movement of a machine. • *adv. colloq.* to a considerable extent; far (*you're way off the mark*). □ **across** (or **over**) **the way** opposite. **be on one's way** set off; depart. **by the way 1** incidentally. **2** during a journey. **by way of 1** through; by means of. **2** as a substitute for or as a form of (*did it by way of apology*). **3** with the intention of (*asked by way of discovering the truth*). **come one's way** become available to one; become one's lot. **find a way** discover a means of accomplishing one's plans. **get** (or **have**) **one's way** (or **have it one's own way**, etc.) get what one wants; ensure one's wishes are met. **give way 1 a** make concessions. **b** yield. **2** (often foll. by *to*) concede precedence (to). **3** (of a structure, etc.) be dislodged or broken under a load; collapse. **4** (foll. by *to*) be superseded by. **5** (foll. by *to*) be overcome by (an emotion, etc.). **6** (of rowers) row hard. **go out of one's way** (often foll. by *to* + infin.) make a special effort; act gratuitously or without compulsion (*went out of their way to help*). **go one's own way** act independently, esp. against contrary advice. **go one's way 1** leave; depart. **2** (of events, circumstances, etc.) be favorable to one. **go a person's way** accompany a person (*are you going my way?*). **in its way** if regarded from a particular standpoint appropriate to it. **in no way** not at all; by no means. **in a way** in a certain respect but not altogether or completely. **in the** (or **one's**) **way** forming an obstacle or hindrance. **lead the way 1** act as guide or leader. **2** show how to do something. **look the other way 1** ignore what one should notice. **2** disregard an acquaintance, etc., whom one sees. **one way or another** by some means. **on the** (or **one's**) **way 1** in the course of a journey, etc. **2** having progressed (*is well on the way to completion*). **3** *colloq.* (of a child) conceived but not yet born. **on the way out** *colloq.* going down in status, estimation, or favor; going out of fashion. **the other way around** in an inverted or reversed position. **out of the way 1** no longer an obstacle. **2** disposed of; settled. **3** (of a person) imprisoned or killed. **4** uncommon; remarkable (*nothing out of the way*). **5** (of a place) remote; inaccessible. **out of one's way** not on one's intended route. **put a person in the way of** give a person the opportunity of. **way back** *colloq.* long ago.

way·far·er /wáyfairər/ *n.* a traveler, esp. on foot.

way·lay /wayláy/ *v.tr.* (*past* and *past part.* **waylaid**) **1** lie in wait for. **2** stop to rob or interview.

way·leave /wáyleev/ *n.* a right of way granted over another's property.

-ways /wayz/ *suffix* forming adjectives and adverbs of direction or manner (*sideways*) (cf. -WISE).

ways and means *n.pl.* **1** methods of achieving something. **2** methods of raising government revenue.

way·side /wáysīd/ *n.* **1** the side of a road. **2** the land at the side of a road. □ **fall by the wayside** fail to continue in an endeavor or undertaking (after Luke 8:5).

way·ward /wáywərd/ *adj.* **1** childishly self-willed or perverse; capricious. **2** unaccountable or freakish. □□ **way·ward·ly** *adv.* **way·ward·ness** *n.*

we /wee/ *pron.* (*obj.* **us**; *poss.* **our, ours**) **1** (*pl.* of I²) used by and with reference to more than one person speaking or writing, or one such person and one or more associated persons. **2** used for or by a royal person in a proclamation, etc., and by a writer or editor in a formal context. **3** people in general (cf. ONE *pron.* 2). **4** *colloq.* = I² (*give us a chance*). **5** *colloq.* (often implying condescension) you (*how are we feeling today?*).

weak /week/ *adj.* **1** deficient in strength, power, or number; easily broken or bent or defeated. **2** deficient in vigor (*weak health; a weak imagination*). **3 a** deficient in resolution; easily led (*a weak character*). **b** indicating a lack of resolution (*a weak surrender; a weak chin*). **4** unconvincing or logically deficient (*a weak argument*). **5** (of a mixed liquid or solution) watery; thin; dilute (*weak tea*). **6** (of a style, etc.) not vigorous nor well-knit; diffuse; slipshod. **7** (of a crew) short-handed. **8** (of a syllable, etc.) unstressed. **9** *Gram.* in Germanic languages: **a** (of a verb) forming inflections by the addition of a suffix to the stem. **b** (of a noun or adjective) belonging to a declension in which the stem originally ended in *-n*.

weak·en /wéekən/ *v.* **1** *tr.* & *intr.* make or become weak or weaker. **2** *intr.* relent; give way; succumb to temptation, etc.

weak-kneed *adj. colloq.* lacking resolution.

weak·ling /wéekling/ *n.* a feeble person or animal.

weak·ly /wéeklee/ *adv.* & *adj.* • *adv.* in a weak manner. • *adj.* (**weaklier, weakliest**) sickly; not robust.

weak-mind·ed *adj.* **1** mentally deficient. **2** lacking resolution. □□ **weak-mind·ed·ness** *n.*

weak·ness /wéeknis/ *n.* **1** the state or condition of being weak. **2** a weak point; a defect. **3** the inability to resist a particular temptation. **4** (foll. by *for*) a self-indulgent liking (*have a weakness for chocolate*).

weal /weel/ *n.* & *v.* • *n.* a ridge raised on the flesh by a stroke of a rod or whip. • *v.tr.* mark with a weal.

wealth /welth/ *n.* **1** riches; abundant possessions. **2** the state of being rich. **3** (foll. by *of*) an abundance (*a wealth of new material*).

wealth·y /wélthee/ *adj.* (**wealthier, wealthiest**) having an abundance, esp. of money.

wean /ween/ *v.tr.* **1** accustom (an infant or other young mammal) to food other than milk. **2** (often foll. by *from, away from*) disengage (from a habit, etc.) by enforced discontinuance.

weap·on /wépən/ *n.* **1** a thing designed or used for inflicting bodily harm. **2** a means employed for trying to gain the advantage in a conflict (*irony is a double-edged weapon*). □□ **weap·on·less** *adj.*

weap·on·ry /wépənree/ *n.* weapons collectively.

wear¹ /wair/ *v.* & *n.* • *v.* (*past* **wore** /wawr/; *past part.* **worn** /wawrn/) **1** *tr.* have on one's person as clothing or an ornament, etc. **2** *tr.* be dressed habitually in (*wears green*). **3** *tr.* exhibit or present (a facial expression or appearance) (*wore a frown; the day wore a different aspect*). **4** *tr.* (often foll. by *away, down*) **a** *tr.* injure the surface of, or partly obliterate or alter, by rubbing, stress, or use. **b** *intr.* undergo such injury or change. **5** *tr.* & *intr.* (foll. by *off, away*) rub or be rubbed off. **6** *tr.* make (a hole, etc.) by constant rubbing or dripping, etc. **7** *tr.* & *intr.* (often foll. by *out*) exhaust; tire or be tired. **8** *tr.* (foll. by *down*) overcome by persistence. **9** *intr.* **a** remain for a specified time in working order or a presentable state; last long. **b** (foll. by *well, badly*, etc.) endure continued use or life. **10 a** *intr.* (of time) pass, esp. tediously. **b** *tr.* pass (time) gradually away. •*n.* **1** the act of wearing or the state of being worn (*suitable for informal wear*). **2** things worn; fashionable or suitable clothing (*sportswear; footwear*). **3** (in full **wear and tear**) damage sustained from continuous use. **4** the capacity for resisting wear and tear (*still a great deal of wear left in it*). ▫ **in wear** being regularly worn. **wear off** lose effectiveness or intensity. **wear out 1** use or be used until no longer usable. **2** tire or be tired out. **wear the pants** see PANTS. **wear thin** (of patience, excuses, etc.) begin to fail. **wear** (or **wear one's years**) **well** *colloq.* remain young-looking. ▫▫ **wear·a·ble** *adj.* **wear·a·bil·i·ty** /wáirəbílitee/ *n.* **wear·er** *n.*

wear[2] /wair/ *v.* (*past* and *past part.* **wore** /wawr/) **1** *tr.* bring (a ship) about by turning its head away from the wind. **2** *intr.* (of a ship) come about in this way (cf. TACK[1] *v.* 4a).

wear·i·some /wéereesəm/ *adj.* tedious; tiring by monotony or length.

wear·y /wéeree/ *adj.* & *v.* •*adj.* (**wearier, weariest**) **1** disinclined for further exertion or endurance. **2** (foll. by *of*) dismayed at the continuing of; impatient of. **3** tiring or tedious. •*v.tr.* & intr. (**-ies, -ied**) make or grow weary. ▫▫ **wear·i·ly** *adv.* **wear·i·ness** *n.*

wea·sel /wéezəl/ *n.* & *v.* •*n.* **1** a small, reddish-brown, carnivorous mammal, *Mustela nivalis*, with a slender body. **2** a stoat. **3** *colloq.* a deceitful or treacherous person. •*v.intr.* **1** equivocate or quibble. **2** (foll. by *on, out*) default on an obligation. ▫▫ **wea·sel·ly** *adj.*

weath·er /wéthər/ *n.* & *v.* •*n.* **1** the state of the atmosphere at a place and time as regards heat, cloudiness, dryness, sunshine, wind, and rain, etc. **2** (*attrib.*) *Naut.* windward (*on the weather side*). •*v.* **1** *tr.* expose to atmospheric changes (*weathered shingles*). **2 a** *tr.* (usu. in *passive*) discolor or partly disintegrate (rock or stones) by exposure to air. **b** *intr.* be discolored or worn in this way. **3** *tr.* make (boards or tiles) overlap downward to keep out rain, etc. **4** *tr.* **a** come safely through (a storm). **b** survive (a difficult period, etc.). **5** *tr.* (of a ship or its crew) get to the windward of (a cape, etc.). ▫ **keep a** (or **one's**) **weather eye open** be watchful. **make good** (or **bad**) **weather of it** *Naut.* (of a ship) behave well (or badly) in a storm. **make heavy weather of** *colloq.* exaggerate the difficulty presented by. **under the weather** *colloq.* **1** indisposed or out of sorts. **2** drunk.

weath·er·cock /wéthərkok/ *n.* **1** a weather vane (see VANE 1) in the form of a cock. **2** an inconstant person.

weath·er·ing /wéthəring/ *n.* **1** the action of the weather on materials, etc., exposed to it. **2** exposure to adverse weather conditions (see WEATHER *v.* 1).

weath·er·man /wéthərman/ *n.* (*pl.* **-men**) a meteorologist, esp. one who broadcasts a weather forecast.

weath·er·proof /wéthərproof/ *adj.* & *v.* •*adj.* resistant to the effects of bad weather. •*v.tr.* make weatherproof. ▫▫ **weath·er·proofed** *adj.*

weath·er strip *n.* & *v.* •*n.* a piece of material used to make a door or window proof against rain or wind. •*v.tr.* (**weather-strip**) (**-stripped, -stripping**) install a weather strip on.

weath·er vane see VANE 1.

weave[1] /weev/ *v.* & *n.* •*v.* (*past* **wove** /wōv/; *past part.* **woven** /wṓvən/or **wove**) **1** *tr.* **a** form (fabric) by interlacing long threads in two directions. **b** form (thread) into fabric in this way. **2** *intr.* **a** make fabric in this way. **b** work at a loom. **3** *tr.* make by interlacing rushes or flowers, etc. **4** *tr.* **a** (foll. by *into*) make (facts, etc.) into a story or connected whole. **b** make (a story) in this way. •*n.* a style of weaving.

weave[2] /weev/ *v.intr.* **1** move repeatedly from side to side; take an intricate course to avoid obstructions. **2** *colloq.* maneuver an aircraft in this way; take evasive action. ▫ **get weaving** *sl.* begin action; hurry.

weav·er /wéevər/ *n.* **1** a person whose occupation is weaving. **2** = WEAVERBIRD.

web /web/ *n.* & *v.* •*n.* **1 a** a woven fabric. **b** an amount woven in one piece. **2** a complete structure or connected series (*a web of lies*). **3** a cobweb, gossamer, or a similar product of a spinning creature. **4 a** a membrane between the toes of a swimming animal or bird. **b** the vane of a bird's feather. **5 a** a large roll of paper used in a continuous printing process. **b** an endless wire mesh on rollers, on which this is made. **6** (**the Web**) = WORLD WIDE WEB. •*v.* (**webbed, webbing**) **1** *tr.* weave a web on. **2** *intr.* weave a web. ▫▫ **webbed** *adj.*

web·bing /wébing/ *n.* strong, closely woven fabric used for supporting upholstery, for belts, etc.

we·ber /wébər, váybər/ *n.* the SI unit of magnetic flux, causing the electromotive force of one volt in a circuit of one turn when generated or removed in one second. ¶ Abbr.: **Wb.**

web-foot·ed *adj.* having the toes connected by webs.

Web site *n. Computing* a location on the Internet that maintains one or more pages on the World Wide Web.

wed /wed/ *v.* (**wedding**; *past* and *past part.* **wedded** or **wed**) **1** usu. *formal* or *literary* **a** *tr.* & *intr.* marry. **b** *tr.* join in marriage. **2** *tr.* unite (*wed efficiency to economy*). **3** *tr.* (as **wedded** *adj.*) of or in marriage (*wedded bliss*). **4** *tr.* (as **wedded** *adj.*) (foll. by *to*) obstinately attached or devoted (to a pursuit, etc.).

we'd /weed/ *contr.* **1** we had. **2** we should; we would.

wed·ding /wéding/ *n.* a marriage ceremony (considered by itself or with the associated celebrations).

wed·ding march *n.* a march played at the entrance of the bride or the exit of the couple at a wedding.

wedge[1] /wej/ *n.* & *v.* •*n.* **1** a piece of wood or metal, etc., tapering to a sharp edge, that is driven between two objects or parts of an object to secure or separate them. **2** anything resembling a wedge (*a wedge of cheese; troops formed a wedge*). **3** a golf club with a wedge-shaped head. **4 a** a wedge-shaped heel. **b** a shoe with this. •*v.tr.* **1** tighten, secure, or fasten by means of a wedge (*wedged the door open*). **2** force open or apart with a wedge. **3** (foll. by *in, into*) pack or thrust (a thing or oneself) tightly in or into.

wedge[2] /wej/ *v.tr. Pottery* prepare (clay) for use by cutting, kneading, and throwing down.

wedg·ie /wéjee/ *n. colloq.* **1** a shoe with an extended wedge-shaped heel. **2** the condition of having one's underwear, etc., wedged between one's buttocks.

wed·lock /wédlok/ *n.* the married state. ▫ **born in** (or **out of**) **wedlock** born of married (or unmarried) parents.

Wednes·day /wénzday, –dee/ *n.* & *adv.* •*n.* the fourth day of the week, following Tuesday. •*adv. colloq.* **1** on Wednesday. **2** (**Wednesdays**) on Wednesdays; each Wednesday.

wee /wee/ *adj.* (**weer** /wéeər/; **weest** /wéeist/) **1** esp. *Sc.* little; very small. **2** *colloq.* tiny; extremely small (*a wee bit*).

weed /weed/ *n.* & *v.* •*n.* **1** a wild plant growing where it is not wanted. **2** a thin, weak-looking person or horse. **3** (prec. by *the*) *sl.* **a** marijuana. **b** tobacco. •*v.* **1** *tr.* **a** clear (an area) of weeds. **b** remove unwanted parts from. **2** *tr.* (foll. by *out*) **a** sort out (inferior or unwanted parts, etc.) for removal. **b** rid (a quantity or company) of inferior or unwanted members, etc. **3** *intr.* cut off or uproot weeds. ▫▫ **weed·er** *n.* **weed·less** *adj.*

weed·y /wéedee/ *adj.* (**weedier, weediest**) **1** having many weeds. **2** (esp. of a person) **a** weak; feeble; of poor stature. **b** very thin; lanky. ▫▫ **weed·i·ness** *n.*

week /week/ *n.* **1** a period of seven days reckoned usu. from and to midnight on Saturday–Sunday. **2** a period of seven days reckoned from any point (*would like to* *stay for a week*). **3** the six days between Sundays. **4 a** the five days Monday to Friday. **b** a normal amount of work done in this period (*a 35-hour week*). **5** (in *pl.*) a long time; several weeks (*have not seen you for weeks; did it weeks ago*).

week·day /wéekday/ *n.* a day other than Sunday or other than at a weekend (often *attrib.*: *a weekday afternoon*).

week·end /wéekénd/ *n.* & *v.* • *n.* **1** the end of a week, esp. Saturday and Sunday. **2** this period extended slightly esp. for a vacation or visit, etc. • *v.intr.* spend a weekend (*decided to weekend in the country*).

week·long /wéeklawng, lóng/ *adj.* lasting for a week.

week·ly /wéeklee/ *adj., adv.,* & *n.* • *adj.* done, produced, or occurring once a week. • *adv.* once a week; from week to week. • *n.* (*pl.* **-lies**) a weekly newspaper or periodical.

weep /weep/ *v.* & *n.* • *v.* (*past* and *past part.* **wept** /wept/) **1** *intr.* shed tears. **2 a** *tr.* & (foll. by *for*) *intr.* shed tears for; bewail. **b** *tr.* utter or express with tears (*wept her thanks*). **3 a** *intr.* be covered with or send forth drops. **b** *intr.* & *tr.* come or send forth in drops; exude liquid (*weeping sore*). **4** *intr.* (as **weeping** *adj.*) (of a tree) having drooping branches (*weeping willow*). • *n.* a fit or spell of weeping. ▫▫ **weep·er** /wéepər/ *n.*

weep·y /wéepee/ *adj.* (**weepier, weepiest**) *colloq.* inclined to weep; tearful.

wee·vil /wéevil/ *n.* **1** any beetle of the family Curculionidae, with its head extended into a beak or rostrum and feeding esp. on grain. **2** any insect damaging stored grain. ▫▫ **wee·vi·ly** *adj.*

wee-wee /wéewee/ *n.* & *v. sl.* • *n.* **1** a child's word for the act or instance of urinating. **2** a child's word for urine. • *v.intr.* (**-wees, -weed, -weeing**) urinate.

weft /weft/ *n.* **1** the threads woven across a warp to make fabric. **2** yarn for these. **3** a thing woven.

weigh /way/ *v.* **1** *tr.* find the weight of. **2** *tr.* balance in the hands to guess or as if to guess the weight of. **3** *tr.* (often foll. by *out*) **a** take a definite weight of; take a specified weight from a larger quantity. **b** distribute in exact amounts by weight. **4** *tr.* **a** estimate the relative importance or desirability of (*weighed the consequences; weighed the merits of the candidates*). **b** (foll. by *with, against*) compare (one consideration with another). **5** *tr.* be equal to (a specified weight) (*weighs three pounds*). **6** *intr.* **a** have importance; exert an influence. **b** (foll. by *with*) be regarded as important by (*the point that weighs with me*). **7** *intr.* (often foll. by *on*) be heavy or burdensome (to); be depressing (to). ▫ **weigh anchor** see ANCHOR. **weigh down 1** bring or keep down by exerting weight. **2** be oppressive or burdensome to (*weighed down with worries*). **weigh in** (of a boxer before a contest, or a jockey after a race) be weighed. **weigh into** *colloq.* attack (physically or verbally). **weigh in with** *colloq.* advance (an argument, etc.) assertively or boldly. **weigh up** *colloq.* form an estimate of; consider carefully. **weigh one's words** carefully choose the way one expresses something. ▫▫ **weigh·er** *n.*

---

weigh Old English *wegan*, of Germanic origin; related to Dutch *wegen* 'weigh,' German *bewegen* 'move,' from an Indo-European root shared by Latin *vehere* 'convey.' Early senses included 'transport from one place to another' and 'raise up' (as in *weigh anchor*).

---

weight /wayt/ *n.* & *v.* • *n.* **1** *Physics* **a** the force experienced by a body as a result of the earth's gravitation (cf. MASS[1] *n.* 8). **b** any similar force with which a body tends to a center of attraction. **2** the heaviness of a body regarded as a property of it; its relative mass or the quantity of matter contained by it giving rise to a downward force (*is twice your weight; kept in position by its weight*). **3 a** the quantitative expression of a body's weight (*has a weight of three pounds*). **b** a scale of such weights (*troy weight*). **4** a body of a known weight for use in weighing. **5** a heavy body (*a clock worked by weights*). **6** a load or burden (*a weight off my mind*). **7 a** influence; importance (*carried weight with the public*). **b** preponderance (*the weight of evidence was against them*). **8** a heavy object thrown as an athletic exercise; = SHOT[1] 7. **9** the surface density of cloth, etc., as a measure of its suitability. • *v.tr.* **1 a** attach a weight to. **b** hold down with a weight or weights. **2** (foll. by *with*) impede or burden. **3** *Statistics* multiply the components of (an average) by factors to take account of their importance. **4** assign a handicap weight to (a horse). ▫ **put on weight 1** increase one's weight. **2** get fat. **throw one's weight around** *colloq.* be unpleasantly self-assertive. **worth one's weight in gold** (of a person) exceedingly useful or helpful.

weight·less /wáytlis/ *adj.* not apparently acted on by gravity. ▫▫ **weight·less·ly** *adv.* **weight·less·ness** *n.*

weight·lift·ing /wáytlifting/ *n.* the sport of lifting a heavy weight. ▫▫ **weight·lift·er** *n.*

weight·y /wáytee/ *adj.* (**weightier, weightiest**) **1** weighing much; heavy. **2** momentous; important. **3** (of utterances, etc.) deserving consideration; careful and serious. **4** influential; authoritative. ▫▫ **weight·i·ly** *adv.* **weight·i·ness** *n.*

weir /weer/ *n.* **1** a dam built across a river to raise the level of water upstream or regulate its flow. **2** an enclosure of stakes, etc., set in a stream as a trap for fish.

weird /weerd/ *adj.* **1** uncanny; supernatural. **2** *colloq.* strange; incomprehensible. **3** *archaic* connected with fate. ▫▫ **weird·ly** *adv.* **weird·ness** *n.*

weird·o /wéerdō/ *n.* (*pl.* **-os**) *colloq.* an odd or eccentric person.

welch var. of WELSH.

wel·come /wélkəm/ *n., int., v.,* & *adj.* • *n.* the act or an instance of greeting or receiving gladly; a kind or glad reception (*gave them a warm welcome*). • *int.* expressing such a greeting. • *v.tr.* receive with a welcome. *adj.* **1** that one receives with pleasure. **2** (foll. by *to*, or *to* + infin.) **a** cordially allowed or invited (*you are welcome to use my car*). **b** *iron.* gladly given (an unwelcome task, thing, etc.) (*here's my work and you are welcome to it*). ▫ **make welcome** receive hospitably. **you're** (or **you are**) **welcome** a polite response to thanks. ▫▫ **wel·com·er** *n.* **wel·com·ing·ly** *adv.*

weld /weld/ *v.* & *n.* • *v.tr.* **1 a** hammer or press (pieces of metal) into one piece. **b** join by fusion with an electric arc, etc. **c** form by welding into some article. **2** fashion into an effectual or homogeneous whole. • *n.* a welded joint. ▫▫ **weld·a·ble** *adj.* **weld·a·bil·i·ty** /wéldəbílitee/ *n.* **weld·er** *n.*

wel·fare /wélfair/ *n.* **1** well-being; happiness; health and prosperity. **2 a** the maintenance of persons in such a condition esp. by statutory procedure or social effort. **b** financial support given for this purpose.

wel·far·ism /wélfairizəm/ *n.* principles characteristic of a welfare state. ▫▫ **wel·far·ist** *n.*

wel·kin /wélkin/ *n. poet.* sky; the upper air.

well[1] /wel/ *adv., adj.,* & *int.* • *adv.* (**better, best**) **1** in a satisfactory way. **2** in the right way (*well said; you did well to tell me*). **3** with some talent or distinction. **4** in a kind way. **5 a** thoroughly; carefully (*polish it well*). **b** intimately; closely (*knew them well*). **6** with heartiness or approval. **7** probably; reasonably; advisably (*you may well be right; we might well take the risk*). **8** to a considerable extent (*is well over forty*). **9** successfully; fortunately (*it turned out well*). **10** luckily; opportunely (*well met!*). **11** with a fortunate outcome; without disaster (*were well rid of them*). **12** profitably (*did*

well for themselves). **13** comfortably; abundantly; liberally (*we live well here*; *the job pays well*). • *adj.* (**better, best**) **1** (usu. *predic.*) in good health (*are you well?*; *was not a well person*). **2** (*predic.*) **a** in a satisfactory state or position (*all is well*). **b** advisable (*it would be well to inquire*). • *int.* expressing surprise, resignation, insistence, etc., or resumption or continuation of talk, used esp. after a pause in speaking (*well, I never!*; *well, I suppose so*; *well, who was it?*). □ **as well 1** in addition; to an equal extent. **2** (also **just as well**) with equal reason; with no loss of advantage or need for regret (*may as well give up*; *it would be just as well to stop now*). **as well as** in addition to. **leave** (or **let**) **well enough alone** avoid needless change or disturbance. **take well** react calmly to (a thing, esp. bad news). **well and good** expressing dispassionate acceptance of a decision, etc. **well aware** certainly aware (*well aware of the danger*). **well away** having made considerable progress. **well worth** certainly worth (*well worth a visit*; *well worth visiting*). ▶A hyphen is normally used in combinations of *well-* when used attributively, but not when used predicatively, e.g., *a well-made coat* but *the coat is well made.* □□ **well•ness** /wélnəs/ *n.*
▶See note at GOOD.

well[2] /wel/ *n.* & *v.* • *n.* **1** a shaft sunk into the ground to obtain water, oil, etc. **2** an enclosed space like a well shaft, e.g., in the middle of a building for stairs or an elevator, or for light or ventilation. **3** (foll. by *of*) a source, esp. a copious one (*a well of information*). **4 a** a mineral spring. **b** (in *pl.*) a spa. **5** = INKWELL. **6** a depression for gravy, etc., in a dish or tray, or for a mat in the floor. • *v.intr.* (foll. by *out*, *up*) spring as from a fountain; flow copiously.

we'll /weel, wil/ *contr.* we shall; we will.

well-ad•vised *predic.adj.* (usu. foll. by *to* + infin.) (of a person) prudent (*would be well-advised to wait*).

well-ap•point•ed *adj.* (**well appointed** when *predic.*) having all the necessary equipment.

well-bal•anced *adj.* (**well balanced** when *predic.*) **1** sane; sensible. **2** equally matched. **3** having a symmetrical or orderly arrangement of parts.

well-be•ing *n.* a state of being well, healthy, contented, etc.

well•born /wélbáwrn/ *adj.* of wealthy or noble lineage.

well-dis•posed *adj.* (**well disposed** when *predic.*) (often foll. by *toward*) having a good disposition or friendly feeling (for).

well-done *adj.* (**well done** when *predic.*) **1** (of meat, etc.) thoroughly cooked. **2** (of a task, etc.) performed well (also as *int.*).

well-found•ed *adj.* (**well founded** when *predic.*) (of suspicions, etc.) based on good evidence; having a foundation in fact or reason.

well-groomed *adj.* (**well groomed** when *predic.*) (of a person) with carefully tended hair, clothes, etc.

well-ground•ed *adj.* (**well grounded** when *predic.*) **1** = WELL-FOUNDED. **2** having a good training in or knowledge of the groundwork of a subject.

well•head /wélhed/ *n.* a source esp. of a spring or stream.

well-in•formed *adj.* (**well informed** when *predic.*) having much knowledge or information about a subject.

well-in•ten•tioned *adj.* (**well intentioned** when *predic.*) having or showing good intentions.

well-known *adj.* (**well known** when *predic.*) **1** known to many. **2** known thoroughly.

well-mean•ing *adj.* (also **well-meant**) (**well meaning, well meant** when *predic.*) well-intentioned (but ineffective or unwise).

well-off *adj.* (**well off** when *predic.*) **1** having plenty of money. **2** in a fortunate situation or circumstances.

well-oiled *adj.* (**well oiled** when *predic.*) *colloq.* **1** drunk. **2** operating efficiently (*a well-oiled committee*).

well-pre•served *adj.* (**well preserved** when *predic.*) showing little sign of aging.

well-read *adj.* (**well read** when *predic.*) knowledgeable through much reading.

well-round•ed *adj.* (**well rounded** when *predic.*) **1** complete and symmetrical. **2** (of a phrase, etc.) complete and well expressed. **3** (of a person) having or showing a fully developed personality, ability, etc. **4** fleshy; plump.

well-spo•ken *adj.* articulate or refined in speech.

well-thought-of *adj.* (**well thought of** when *predic.*) having a good reputation; esteemed; respected.

well-thought-out *adj.* (**well thought out** when *predic.*) carefully devised.

well-to-do *adj.* prosperous.

well-worn *adj.* (**well worn** when *predic.*) **1** much worn by use. **2** (of a phrase, joke, etc.) stale; often heard.

Welsh /welsh/ *adj.* & *n.* • *adj.* of or relating to Wales or its people or language. • *n.* **1** the Celtic language of Wales. **2** (prec. by *the*; treated as *pl.*) the people of Wales.

welsh /welsh/ *v.intr.* (also **welch** /welch/) **1** fail to honor a debt or obligation incurred through a promise or agreement. **2** fail to carry out a promise to (a person). □□ **welsh•er** *n.*

Welsh•man /wélshmən/ *n.* (*pl.* **-men**) a person who is Welsh by birth or descent.

Welsh rab•bit *n.* (also **Welsh rare•bit**) a dish of melted cheese, etc., on toast.

Welsh•wom•an /wélshwŏŏmən/ *n.* (*pl.* **-women**) a woman who is Welsh by birth or descent.

welt /welt/ *n.* & *v.* • *n.* **1** a leather rim sewn around the edge of a shoe upper for the sole to be attached to. **2** = WEAL. **3** a ribbed or reinforced border of a garment; a trimming.

wel•ter /wéltər/ *v.* & *n.* • *v.intr.* roll; wallow; be washed about. • *n.* **1** a state of general confusion. **2** a disorderly mixture (*a welter of half-written letters and crude maps*).

wel•ter•weight /wéltərwayt/ *n.* **1** a weight in certain sports intermediate between lightweight and middleweight. **2** an athlete of this weight.

wen /wen/ *n.* a benign tumor on the skin, esp. of the scalp.

wench /wench/ *n.* & *v.* • *n. joc.* a girl or young woman. • *v.intr. archaic* (of a man) consort with prostitutes. □□ **wench•er** *n.*

wend /wend/ *v.tr.* & *intr. literary* or *archaic* go. □ **wend one's way** make one's way.

went *past* of GO[1].

wept *past* of WEEP.

were *2nd sing. past, pl. past, and past subj.* of BE.

we're /weer/ *contr.* we are.

weren't /wərnt, wərənt/ *contr.* were not.

were•wolf /wéerwŏŏlf, wáir–/ *n.* (also **wer•wolf** /wə́r–/) (*pl.* **-wolves**) a mythical being who at times changes from a person to a wolf.

west /west/ *n., adj.,* & *adv.* • *n.* **1 a** the point of the horizon where the sun sets at the equinoxes (cardinal point 90° to the left of north). **b** the compass point corresponding to this. **c** the direction in which this lies. **2** (usu. **the West**) **a** European in contrast to Oriental civilization. **b** *hist.* the non-Communist nations of Europe and N. America. **c** the western part of the late Roman Empire. **d** the western part of a country, town, etc., esp. the American West. **3** *Bridge* a player occupying the position designated 'west'. • *adj.* **1** toward, at, near, or facing west. **2** coming from the west (*west wind*). • *adv.* **1** toward, at, or near the west. **2** (foll. by *of*) further west than. □ **go west** *sl.* be killed or destroyed, etc.

west·er·ly /wéstərlee/ *adj., adv., & n.* • *adj. & adv.* **1** in a western position or direction. **2** (of a wind) blowing from the west. • *n.* (*pl.* **-lies**) a wind blowing from the west.
west·ern /wéstərn/ *adj. & n.* • *adj.* **1** of or in the west; inhabiting the west. **2** lying or directed toward the west. **3** (**Western**) of or relating to the West (see WEST *n.* 2). • *n.* a motion picture or novel about cowboys in western North America. ▫▫ **West·ern·er** *n.*
west·ern hem·i·sphere *n.* the half of the earth containing the Americas.
west·ern·ize /wéstərnīz/ *v.tr.* (also **West·ern·ize**) influence with or convert to the ideas and customs, etc., of the West. ▫▫ **west·ern·i·za·tion** *n.* **west·ern·iz·er** *n.*
West In·dies *n.pl.* the islands of Central America, including Cuba and the Bahamas.
west-north·west *n.* the direction or compass point midway between west and northwest.
west-south·west *n.* the direction or compass point midway between west and southwest.
west·ward /wéstwərd/ *adj., adv., & n.* • *adj. & adv.* toward the west. • *n.* a westward direction or region.
wet /wet/ *adj., v., & n.* • *adj.* (**wetter, wettest**) **1** soaked, covered, or dampened with water or other liquid (*a wet sponge; got my feet wet*). **2** (of the weather, etc.) rainy (*a wet day*). **3** (of paint, ink, etc.) not yet dried. **4** used with water (*wet shampoo*). **5** *sl.* (of a country, of legislation, etc.) allowing the free sale of alcoholic drink. **6** (of a baby or young child) incontinent (*is still wet at night*). • *v.tr.* (**wetting**; *past* and *past part.* **wet** or **wetted**) **1** make wet. **2 a** urinate in or on (*wet the bed*). **b** *refl.* urinate involuntarily. • *n.* **1** moisture. **2** rainy weather; a time of rain. ▫ **wet behind the ears** immature; inexperienced. **wet through** (or **to the skin**) with one's clothes soaked. **wet one's whistle** *colloq.* drink. ▫▫ **wet·ly** *adv.* **wet·ness** *n.* **wet·ta·ble** *adj.* **wet·ting** *n.* **wet·tish** *adj.*
wet·back /wétbak/ *n. offens.* an illegal immigrant from Mexico to the US.
wet dream *n.* an erotic dream with involuntary ejaculation of semen.
wet·lands /wétləndz/ *n.pl.* swamps and other damp areas of land.
wet nurse *n. & v.* • *n.* a woman employed to suckle another's child. • *v.tr.* (**wet-nurse**) **1** act as a wet nurse to. **2** *colloq.* treat as if helpless.
wet suit *n.* a close-fitting rubber garment worn by skin divers, etc., to keep warm.
we've /weev/ *contr.* we have.
whack /hwak, wak/ *v. & n. colloq.* • *v.tr.* strike or beat forcefully with a sharp blow. • *n.* a sharp or resounding blow. ▫ **have a whack at** *sl.* attempt. **out of whack** *sl.* out of order; malfunctioning. ▫▫ **whack·ing** *n.*
whack·o /hwákō, wák–/ *adj. & n.* var. of WACKO.
whack·y var. of WACKY.
whale[1] /hwayl, wayl/ *n.* (*pl.* same or **whales**) any of the larger marine mammals of the order Cetacea, having a streamlined body and horizontal tail, and breathing through a blowhole on the head. ▫ **a whale of a** *colloq.* exceedingly good or fine, etc.
whale[2] /hwayl, wayl/ *v.tr. colloq.* beat; thrash.
whale·bone /hwáylbōn, wáyl–/ *n.* an elastic horny substance growing in thin parallel plates in the upper jaw of some whales, used as stiffening, etc.
whal·er /hwáylər, wáyl–/ *n.* **1** a whaling ship or a seaman engaged in whaling. **2** an Australian shark of the genus *Carcharhinus.*
whal·ing /hwáyling, wáyl–/ *n.* the practice or industry of hunting and killing whales.
wham /hwam, wam/ *int., n., & v. colloq.* • *int.* expressing the sound of a forcible impact. • *n.* such a sound. • *v.* (**whammed, whamming**) **1** *intr.* make such a sound or impact. **2** *tr.* strike forcibly.
wham·my /hwámee, wám–/ *n.* (*pl.* **-mies**) *colloq.* an evil or unlucky influence.
wharf /hwawrf, wawrf/ *n. & v.* • *n.* (*pl.* **wharves** /hwawrvz, wawrvz/or **wharfs**) a level quayside area to which a ship may be moved to load and unload. • *v.tr.* **1** moor (a ship) at a wharf. **2** store (goods) on a wharf.
wharves *pl.* of WHARF.
what /hwot, wot, hwut, wut/ *adj., pron., & adv.* • *interrog.adj.* **1** asking for a choice from an indefinite number or for a statement of amount, number, or kind (*what books have you read?; what news have you?*). **2** *colloq.* = WHICH *interrog.adj.* (*what book have you chosen?*). • *adj.* (usu. in exclam.) how great or remarkable (*what luck!*). • *rel.adj. the or any ... that (*will give you what help I can). *pron.* (corresp. to the functions of the *adj.*) **1** what thing or things? (*what is your name?; I don't know what you mean*). **2** (asking for a remark to be repeated) = what did you say? **3** asking for confirmation or agreement of something not completely understood (*what, you really mean it?*). **4** how much (*what you must have suffered!*). **5** (as *rel.pron.*) that or those which; a or the or any thing which (*what followed was worse; tell me what you think*). • *adv.* to what extent (*what does it matter?*). ▫ **what about** what is the news or position or your opinion of (*what about me?; what about a game of tennis?*). **what-d'you-call-it** (or **whatchamacallit** or **what's-its-name**) *colloq.* a substitute for a name not recalled. **what for** *colloq.* **1** for what reason? **2** a severe reprimand (esp. *give a person what for*). **what have you** *colloq.* (prec. by *or*) anything else similar. **what if? 1** what would result, etc., if? **2** what would it matter if. **what is more** and as an additional point; moreover. **what next?** *colloq.* what more absurd, shocking, or surprising thing is possible? **what not** (prec. by *and*) other similar things. **what of?** what is the news concerning? **what of it?** why should that be considered significant? **what's-his** (or **-its**) **-name** = *what-d'you-call-it.* **what's what** *colloq.* what is useful or important, etc. **what with** *colloq.* because of (usu. several things).
what·e'er /hwotáir, wot–, hwut–, wut–/ *poet.* var. of WHATEVER.
what·ev·er /hwotévər, wot–, hwut, wut–/ *adj. & pron.* **1** = WHAT (in relative uses) with the emphasis on indefiniteness (*lend me whatever you can; whatever money you have*). **2** though anything (*we are safe whatever happens*). **3** (with *neg.* or *interrog.*) at all; of any kind (*there is no doubt whatever*). **4** *colloq.* what at all or in any way (*whatever do you mean?*) ▫ **or whatever** *colloq.* or anything similar.
what·not /hwótnot, wót–, hwút–, wút–/ *n.* **1** an indefinite or trivial thing. **2** a stand with shelves for small objects.
what·so·ev·er /hwótsō-évər, wót–, hwút–, wút–/ *adj. & pron.* = WHATEVER 1–3.
wheat /hweet, weet/ *n.* **1** any cereal plant of the genus *Triticum.* **2** its grain, used in making flour, etc. ▫ **separate the wheat from the chaff** see CHAFF.
wheat·en /hwéetən, wéet–/ *adj.* made of wheat.
wheat germ *n.* the embryo of the wheat grain, extracted as a source of vitamins.
whee /hwee, wee/ *int.* expressing delight or excitement.
whee·dle /hwéedəl, wéedəl/ *v.tr.* **1** coax by flattery or endearments. **2** (foll. by *out*) **a** get (a thing) out of a person by wheedling. **b** cheat (a person) out of a thing by wheedling. ▫▫ **whee·dler** *n.* **whee·dling** *adj.* **whee·dling·ly** *adv.*
wheel /hweel, weel/ *n. & v.* • *n.* **1** a circular frame or disk arranged to revolve on an axle and used to facilitate the motion of a vehicle or for various mechanical

purposes. **2** a wheellike thing (*potter's wheel*; *steering wheel*). **3** motion as of a wheel, esp. the movement of a line of people with one end as a pivot. **4** a machine, etc., of which a wheel is an essential part. **5** (in *pl.*) *sl.* a car. **6** *sl.* = BIGWIG 2. **7** a set of short lines concluding a stanza. • *v.* **1** *intr. & tr.* **a** turn on an axis or pivot. **b** swing around in line with one end as a pivot. **2 a** *intr.* (often foll. by *about*, *around*, *round*) change direction or face another way. **b** *tr.* cause to do this. **3** *tr.* push or pull (a wheeled thing, esp. a wheelbarrow, bicycle, wheelchair, or stroller, or its load or occupant). **4** *intr.* go in circles or curves (*seagulls wheeling overhead*). □ **at the wheel 1** driving a vehicle. **2** directing a ship. **3** in control of affairs. **wheel and deal** engage in political or commercial scheming. □□ **wheeled** *adj.* (also in *comb.*). **wheel·less** *adj.*

wheel·bar·row /hwe̅e̅lbarō, we̅e̅l–/ *n.* a small cart with one wheel and two shafts for carrying garden loads, etc.

wheel·base /hwe̅e̅lbays, we̅e̅l–/ *n.* the distance between the front and rear axles of a vehicle.

wheel·chair /hwe̅e̅lchair, we̅e̅l–/ *n.* a chair on wheels for an invalid or disabled person.

wheel·er-deal·er *n. colloq.* a person who wheels and deals (see WHEEL).

wheel·house /hwe̅e̅lhows, weel–/ *n.* = PILOTHOUSE.

wheel·ie /hwe̅e̅lee, we̅e̅–/ *n. sl.* the stunt of riding a bicycle or motorcycle for a short distance with the front wheel off the ground.

wheel·wright /hwe̅e̅lrīt, we̅e̅l–/ *n.* a person who makes or repairs esp. wooden wheels.

wheeze /hweez, weez/ *v. & n.* • *v.* **1** *intr.* breathe with an audible chesty whistling sound. **2** *tr.* (often foll. by *out*) utter in this way. • *n.* **1** a sound of wheezing. **2** *colloq.* **a** an actor's interpolated joke, etc. **b** a catchphrase. □□ **wheez·er** *n.* **wheez·y** *adj.* (**wheezier, wheeziest**). **wheez·i·ly** *adv.* **wheez·i·ness** *n.*

whelk /hwelk, welk/ *n.* any predatory marine gastropod mollusk of the family *Buccinidae*, esp. the edible kind of the genus *Buccinum*, having a spiral shell.

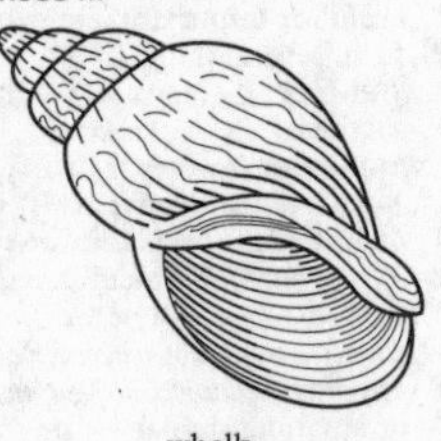
whelk

whelm /hwelm, welm/ *v.tr. poet.* **1** engulf; submerge. **2** crush with weight; overwhelm.

whelp /hwelp, welp/ *n. & v.* • *n.* **1** a young dog; a puppy. **2** *archaic* a cub. **3** an ill-mannered child or youth. **4** (esp. in *pl.*) a projection on the barrel of a capstan or windlass. • *v.tr.* (also *absol.*) **1** bring forth (a whelp or whelps). **2** *derog.* (of a human mother) give birth to. **3** originate (an evil scheme, etc.).

when /hwen, wen/ *adv., conj., pron., & n.* • *interrog.adv.* **1** at what time? **2** on what occasion? **3** how soon? **4** how long ago? • *rel.adv.* (prec. by *time*, etc.) at or on which (*there are times when I could cry*). • *conj.* **1** at the or any time that; as soon as (*come when you like*; *when I was your age*). **2** although; considering that (*why stand up when you could sit down?*). **3** after which; and then; but just then (*was nearly asleep when the bell rang*). • *pron.* what time? (*till when can you stay?*; *since when it has been better*). • *n.* time, occasion, date (*have finally decided on the where and when*).

whence /hwens, wens/ *adv. & conj. formal* • *adv.* from what place? (*whence did they come?*). • *conj.* **1** to the place from which (*return whence you came*). **2** (often prec. by *place*, etc.) from which (*the source whence these errors arise*). **3** and thence (*whence it follows that*). ▶Use of *from whence* as in *the place from whence they came*, though common, is generally considered incorrect.

when·ev·er /hwenévər, wen–/ *conj. & adv.* **1** at whatever time; on whatever occasion. **2** every time that. □ **or whenever** *colloq.* or at any similar time.

where /hwair, wair/ *adv., conj., pron., & n.* • *interrog.adv.* **1** in or to what place or position? (*where is the milk?*; *where are you going?*). **2** in what direction or respect? (*where does the argument lead?*; *where does it concern us?*). **3** in what book, etc.?; from whom? (*where did you read that?*; *where did you hear that?*). **4** in what situation or condition? (*where does that leave us?*). • *rel.adv.* (prec. by *place*, etc.) in or to which (*places where they meet*). • *conj.* **1** in or to the or any place, direction, or respect in which (*go where you like*; *that is where you are wrong*). **2** and there (*reached Albuquerque, where the car broke down*). • *pron.* what place? (*where do you come from?*). • *n.* place; scene of something (see WHEN *n.*).

where·a·bouts *adv. & n.* • *adv.* /hwáirəbówts, wáir–/ where or approximately where? (*whereabouts are they?*; *show me whereabouts to look*). • *n.* /hwáirəbowts, wáir–/ (as *sing.* or *pl.*) a person's or thing's location roughly defined.

where·as /hwairáz, wair–/ *conj.* **1** in contrast or comparison with the fact that. **2** (esp. in legal preambles) taking into consideration the fact that.

where·by /hwairbí, wair–/ *conj.* by what or which means.

where·fore /hwáirfawr, wáir–/ *adv. & n.* • *adv. archaic* **1** for what reason? **2** for which reason. • *n.* a reason (*the whys and wherefores*).

where·in /hwairín, wair–/ *conj. & adv. formal* • *conj.* in what or which place or respect. • *adv.* in what place or respect?

where·of /hwairúv, –óv, wair–/ *conj. & adv. formal* • *conj.* of what or which (*the means whereof*). • *adv.* of what?

where·up·on /hwáirəpón, –páwn, wáir–/ *conj.* immediately after which.

wher·ev·er /hwairévər, wair–/ *adv. & conj.* • *adv.* in or to whatever place. • *conj.* in every place that. □ **or wherever** *colloq.* or in any similar place.

where·with·al /hwáirwithawl, –with–, wáir–/ *n. colloq.* money, etc., needed for a purpose (*has not the wherewithal to do it*).

whet /hwet, wet/ *v. & n.* • *v.tr.* (**whetted, whetting**) **1** sharpen (a scythe or other tool) by grinding. **2** stimulate (the appetite or a desire, interest, etc.). • *n.* the act or an instance of whetting.

wheth·er /hwéthər, wéth–/ *conj.* introducing the first or both of alternative possibilities (*I doubt whether it matters*; *I do not know whether they have arrived or not*).

whet·stone /hwétstōn, wét–/ *n.* **1** a tapered stone used with water to sharpen curved tools (cf. OILSTONE). **2** a thing that sharpens the senses, etc.

whew /hwyo͞o/ *int.* expressing surprise, consternation, or relief.

whey /hway, way/ *n.* the watery liquid left when milk forms curds.

which /hwich, wich/ *adj. & pron.* • *interrog.adj.* asking for choice from a definite set of alternatives (*say which book you prefer*; *which way shall we go?*). • *rel.adj.* being the one just referred to; and this or these (*ten years, during which time they admitted nothing*; *a word of advice, which action is within your power, will set things straight*). • *interrog.pron.* **1** which person or persons (*which of you is responsible?*). **2** which thing or things (*say which you prefer*). • *rel.pron.* (*poss.* **of which, whose** /ho͞oz/) **1** which thing or things, usu. introducing a clause not essential for identification (cf. THAT *pron.* 7) (*the house, which is empty, has been damaged*). **2** used in place of *that* after *in* or *that* (*there is the house in which I was born*; *that which you have just seen*).

▶**Which** should be employed only for nonrestrictive (or nonessential) clauses: The horse, which is in the paddock, is six years old (the *which-* clause contains a nonessential fact, noted in passing; the horse would be six years old wherever it was). A *that*-clause is restrictive (or essential), as it identifies a particular thing: *The horse that is in the paddock is six years old* (not any horse, but the one in the paddock).

which·ev·er /hwichévər, wich–/ *adj. & pron.* **1** any which (*take whichever you like; whichever one you like*). **2** no matter which (*whichever one wins, they both get a prize*).

whiff /hwif, wif/ *n. & v.* •*n.* **1** a puff or breath of air, smoke, etc. (*went outside for a whiff of fresh air*). **2** a smell (*caught the whiff of a cigar*). **3** (foll. by *of*) a trace or suggestion of scandal, etc. •*v.* **1** *tr. & intr.* blow or puff lightly. **2** *tr.* get a slight smell of. **3** *intr. Baseball* strike out by swinging and missing on the third strike. **4** *tr. Baseball* strike out a batter in this way.

Whig /hwig, wig/ *n. hist.* **1** *Polit.* a member of the British reforming and constitutional party that was succeeded in the 19th c. by the Liberal Party (opp. TORY *n.* 2). **2 a** a supporter of the American Revolution. **b** a member of an American political party in the 19th c., succeeded by the Republicans. ▫▫ **Whig·ger·y** *n.* **Whig·gish** *adj.* **Whig·gism** *n.*

while /hwīl, wīl/ *n., conj., v., & adv.* •*n.* **1** a space of time, time spent in some action (*a long while ago; waited a while; all this while*). **2** (prec. by *the*) **a** during some other process. **b** *poet.* during the time that. **3** (prec. by *a*) for some time (*have not seen you a while*). •*conj.* **1** during the time that; at the same time as (*while I was away, the house was burgled; fell asleep while reading*). **2** although; whereas (*while I want to believe it, I cannot*). •*v.tr.* (foll. by *away*) pass (time, etc.) in a leisurely or interesting manner. *rel.adv.* (prec. by *time*, etc.) during which (*the summer while I was abroad*). ▫ **all the while** during the whole time (that). **for a long while** for a long time past. **for a while** for some time. **a good** (or **great**) **while** a considerable time. **in a while** (or **little while**) soon; shortly. **worth while** (or **one's while**) worth the time or effort spent.

whim /hwim, wim/ *n.* **1** a sudden fancy; a caprice. **2** capriciousness.

whim·per /hwímpər, wím–/ *v. & n.* •*v.* **1** *intr.* make feeble, querulous, or frightened sounds; cry and whine softly. **2** *tr.* utter whimperingly. •*n.* **1** a whimpering sound. **2** a feeble note or tone (*the conference ended on a whimper*). ▫▫ **whim·per·er** *n.* **whim·per·ing·ly** *adv.*

whim·si·cal /hwímzikəl, wím–/ *adj.* **1** capricious. **2** fantastic. **3** odd or quaint; fanciful; humorous. ▫▫ **whim·si·cal·i·ty** /–kálitee/ *n.* **whim·si·cal·ly** *adv.*

whim·sy /hwímzee, wím–/ *n.* (also **whim·sey**) (*pl.* **-sies** or **-seys**) **1** a whim; a capricious notion or fancy. **2** capricious or quaint humor.

whine /hwīn, wīn/ *n. & v.* •*n.* **1** a complaining, long-drawn wail as of a dog. **2** a similar shrill, prolonged sound. **3 a** a querulous tone. **b** an instance of feeble or undignified complaining. •*v.* **1** *intr.* emit or utter a whine. **2** *intr.* complain in a querulous tone or undignified way. **3** *tr.* utter in a whining tone. ▫▫ **whin·er** *n.* **whin·ing·ly** *adv.* **whin·y** *adj.* (**whinier, whiniest**).

whin·ny /hwínee, wín–/ *n. & v.* •*n.* (*pl.* **-nies**) a gentle or joyful neigh. •*v.intr.* (**-nies, -nied**) give a whinny.

whip /hwip, wip/ *n. & v.* •*n.* **1** a lash attached to a stick for urging on animals or punishing, etc. **2** a member of a political party in a legislative body appointed to control its party discipline and tactics, esp. ensuring voting in debates. **3** a dessert made with whipped cream, etc. **4** the action of beating cream, eggs, etc., into a froth. **5** = WHIPPER-IN. **6** a rope-and-pulley hoisting apparatus. •*v.* (**whipped, whipping**) **1** *tr.* beat or urge on with a whip. **2** *tr.* beat (cream or eggs, etc.) into a froth. **3** *tr. & intr.* take or move suddenly, unexpectedly, or rapidly (*whipped out a knife; whipped behind the door*). **4** *tr. sl.* **a** excel. **b** defeat. **5** *tr.* bind with spirally wound twine. **6** *tr.* sew with overcast stitches. ▫ **whip in** bring (hounds) together. **whip on** urge into action. **whip up 1** excite or stir up (feeling, etc.). **2** summon up. **3** prepare (a meal, etc.) hurriedly. ▫▫ **whip·less** *adj.* **whip·like** *adj.* **whip·per** *n.*

whip·cord /hwípkawrd, wíp–/ *n.* **1** a tightly twisted cord such as is used for making whiplashes. **2** a close-woven worsted fabric.

whip hand *n.* **1** a hand that holds the whip (in riding, etc.). **2** (usu. prec. by *the*) the advantage or control in any situation.

whip·lash /hwíplash, wíp–/ *n.* **1** the flexible end of a whip. **2** a blow with a whip. **3** an injury to the neck caused by a jerk of the head, esp. as in a motor vehicle accident.

whip·per·snap·per /hwípərsnapər, wíp–/ *n.* **1** a small child. **2** an insignificant but presumptuous or intrusive (esp. young) person.

whip·pet /hwípit, wíp–/ *n.* a crossbred dog of the greyhound type used for racing.

whip·ping /hwíping, wíp–/ *n.* **1** a beating, esp. with a whip. **2** cord wound around in binding.

whip·ping boy *n.* **1** a scapegoat. **2** *hist.* a boy educated with a young prince and punished instead of him.

whip·poor·will /hwípərwil, wíp–/ *n.* an American nightjar, *Caprimulgus vociferus*.

whir /hwər, wər/ *n. & v.* (also **whirr**) •*n.* a continuous rapid buzzing or softly clicking sound as of a bird's wings or of cogwheels in constant motion. •*v.intr.* (**whirred, whirring**) make this sound.

whirl /hwərl, wərl/ *v. & n.* •*v.* **1** *tr. & intr.* swing around and around; revolve rapidly. **2** *tr. & intr.* (foll. by *away*) convey or go rapidly in a vehicle, etc. **3** *tr. & intr.* send or travel swiftly in an orbit or a curve. **4** *intr.* **a** (of the brain, senses, etc.) seem to spin around. **b** (of thoughts, etc.) be confused; follow each other in bewildering succession. •*n.* **1** a whirling movement (*vanished in a whirl of dust*). **2** a state of intense activity (*the social whirl*). **3** a state of confusion (*my mind is in a whirl*). **4** *colloq.* an attempt (*give it a whirl*). ▫▫ **whirl·er** *n.*

whirl·i·gig /hwə́rligig, wə́rl–/ *n.* **1** a spinning or whirling toy. **2** a merry-go-round. **3** a revolving motion. **4** anything regarded as hectic or constantly changing (*the whirligig of time*). **5** any freshwater beetle of the family Gyrinidae that circles about on the surface.

whirl·ing der·vish *n.* (also **howl·ing der·vish**) a dervish performing a wild dance, or howling, as a religious observance.

whirl·pool /hwə́rlpool, wə́rl–/ *n.* a powerful circular eddy in the sea, etc., often causing suction to its center.

whirl·wind /hwə́rlwind, wə́rl–/ *n.* **1** a mass or column of air whirling rapidly around and around in a cylindrical or funnel shape over land or water. **2** a confused tumultuous process. **3** (*attrib.*) very rapid (*a whirlwind romance*). ▫ **reap the whirlwind** suffer worse results of a bad action.

whirr var. of WHIR.

whisk /hwisk, wisk/ *v. & n.* •*v.* **1** *tr.* (foll. by *away, off*) **a** brush with a sweeping movement. **b** take with a sudden motion (*whisked the plate away*). **2** *tr.* whip (cream, eggs, etc.). **3** *tr. & intr.* convey or go (esp. out of sight) lightly or quickly (*whisked me off to the doctor; the mouse whisked into its hole*). **4** *tr.* wave or lightly brandish. •*n.* **1** a whisking action or motion. **2** a utensil for whisking eggs or cream, etc. **3** a bunch of grass, twigs, bristles, etc., for removing dust or flies.

whisk·er /hwískər, wís–/ *n.* **1** (usu. in *pl.*) the hair growing on a man's face, esp. on the cheek. **2** each of the bristles on the face of a cat, etc. **3** *colloq.* a small distance (*within a whisker of; won by a whisker*). **4** a strong, hairlike crystal of metal, etc. ▫ **have** (or **have grown**) **whiskers** *colloq.* (esp. of a story, etc.) be very old. ▫▫ **whisk·ered** *adj.* **whisk·er·y** *adj.*

whis·key /hwískee, wís–/ *n.* (also **whis·ky**) (*pl.* **-keys** or **-kies**) **1** an alcoholic liquor distilled esp. from grain, such as corn or malted barley. **2** a drink of this.
▶Note that the British and Canadian spelling is without the *e*, so that properly one would write of *Scotch whisky* or *Canadian whisky*, but *Kentucky bourbon whiskey*.

whis·per /hwíspər, wís–/ *v.* & *n.* • *v.* **1 a** *intr.* speak very softly without vibration of the vocal cords. **b** *intr.* & *tr.* talk or say in a barely audible tone or in a secret or confidential way. **2** *intr.* speak privately or conspiratorially. **3** *intr.* (of leaves, wind, or water) rustle or murmur. • *n.* **1** whispering speech (*talking in whispers*). **2** a whispering sound. **3** a thing whispered. **4** a rumor or piece of gossip. **5** a brief mention; a hint or suggestion. ▫ **it is whispered** there is a rumor. ▫▫ **whis·per·er** *n.* **whis·per·ing** *n.*

whist /hwist, wist/ *n.* a card game usu. for four players, with the winning of tricks.

whis·tle /hwisəl, wís–/ *n.* & *v.* • *n.* **1** a clear shrill sound made by forcing breath through a small hole between nearly closed lips. **2** a similar sound made by a bird, the wind, a missile, etc. **3** an instrument used to produce such a sound. • *v.* **1** *intr.* emit a whistle. **2 a** *intr.* give a signal or express surprise or derision by whistling. **b** *tr.* (often foll. by *up*) summon or give a signal to (a dog, etc.) by whistling. **3** *tr.* (also *absol.*) produce (a tune) by whistling. **4** *intr.* (foll. by *for*) vainly seek or desire. ▫ **as clean** (or **clear** or **dry**) **as a whistle** very clean or clear or dry. **blow the whistle on** *colloq.* bring (an activity) to an end; inform on (those responsible). **whistle in the dark** pretend to be unafraid. ▫▫ **whis·tler** *n.*

whis·tle·blow·er /hwísəlblōər, wí–/ *n. colloq.* one who reports wrongdoing in a workplace or organization to authorities, the news media, etc.

whit /hwit, wit/ *n.* a particle; a least possible amount (*not a whit better*). ▫ **every whit** the whole; wholly. **no** (or **never a** or **not a**) **whit** not at all.

white /hwīt, wīt/ *adj.*, *n.*, & *v.* • *adj.* **1** resembling a surface reflecting sunlight without absorbing any of the visible rays; of the color of milk or fresh snow. **2** approaching such a color; pale esp. in the face (*turned as white as a sheet*). **3** less dark than other things of the same kind. **4 a** of the human group having light-colored skin. **b** of or relating to white people. **5** albino (*white mouse*). **6 a** (of hair) having lost its color, esp. in old age. **b** (of a person) white-haired. **7** *colloq.* innocent; untainted. **8** (in *comb.*) (of esp. animals) having some white on the body (*white-throated*). **9 a** (of a plant) having white flowers or pale-colored fruit, etc. (*white hyacinth*). **b** (of a tree) having light-colored bark, etc. (*white ash*). **10** (of wine) made from white grapes or dark grapes with the skins removed. **11** *Brit.* (of coffee) with milk or cream added. **12** transparent; colorless (*white glass*). **13** *hist.* counterrevolutionary or reactionary (*white guard; white army*). • *n.* **1** a white color or pigment. **2 a** white clothes or material (*dressed in white*). **b** (in *pl.*) white garments as worn in tennis, etc. **3 a** (in a game or sport) a white piece, ball, etc. **b** the player using such pieces. **4** the white part or albumen around the yolk of an egg. **5** the visible part of the eyeball around the iris. **6** a member of a light-skinned race. ▫ **bleed white** drain (a person, country, etc.) of wealth, etc. ▫▫ **white·ly** *adv.* **white·ness** *n.* **whitish** *adj.*

white ant *n.* a termite.

white·cap /hwītkap, wīt–/ *n.* a white-crested wave at sea.

white cell *n.* (also **white blood cell, white cor·pus·cle**) a leukocyte.

white-col·lar *attrib.adj.* (of a worker) engaged in clerical or administrative rather than manual work.

white el·e·phant *n.* a useless and troublesome possession or thing.

white·fish /hwītfish, wīt–/ *n.* (*pl.* same or **-fishes**) **1** any freshwater fish of the genus *Coregonus*, etc., of the trout family, and used esp. for food. **2** a marine fish, *Caulolatilus princeps*, of California used esp. for food.

white flag *n.* a symbol of surrender or a period of truce.

white·fly /hwītflī, wīt–/ *n.* (*pl.* **-flies**) any small insect of the family Aleyrodidae, having wings covered with white powder and feeding on sap.

white goods *n.pl.* **1** domestic linen. **2** large domestic electrical appliances.

white·head /hwīt-hed, wīt–/ *n. colloq.* a white or white-topped skin pustule.

white heat *n.* **1** the temperature at which metal emits white light. **2** a state of intense passion or activity.

white-hot *adj.* at white heat.

White House *n.* the official residence of the US president and offices of the executive branch of government in Washington.

white lie *n.* a harmless or trivial untruth.

white light *n.* colorless light, e.g., ordinary daylight.

white meat *n.* poultry, veal, rabbit, and pork.

whit·en /hwītən, wīt–/ *v.tr.* & *intr.* make or become white. ▫▫ **whit·en·er** *n.* **whit·en·ing** *n.*

white noise *n.* noise containing many frequencies with equal intensities.

white-out *n.* **1** a dense blizzard in which the features and horizon of snow-covered country are indistinguishable. **2** white correction fluid for covering typing or writing mistakes.

white sale *n.* a sale of household linen.

white sauce *n.* a sauce of flour, melted butter, and milk or cream.

white slave *n.* a woman tricked or forced into prostitution, usu. one taken to a foreign country for this purpose. ▫▫ **white slav·er·y** *n.*

white·smith /hwītsmith, wīt;n–/ *n.* **1** a worker in tin. **2** a polisher or finisher of metal goods.

white tie *n.* a man's white bow tie as part of full evening dress.

white·wall /hwītwawl, wīt–/ *n.* a tire having a white band encircling the outer sidewall.

white·wash /hwītwosh, –wawsh, wīt–/ *n.* & *v.* • *n.* **1** a solution of lime or of whiting and size for whitening walls, etc. **2** a means employed to conceal mistakes or faults in order to clear a person or institution of imputations. • *v.tr.* **1** cover with whitewash. **2** attempt by concealment to clear the reputation of. **3** defeat (an opponent) without allowing any opposing score.

white wa·ter *n.* a shallow or foamy stretch of water.

whit·ey /hwītee, wī–/ *n.* (also **White·y**) (*pl.* **-eys**) *sl. offens.* **1** a white person. **2** white people collectively.

whith·er /hwíthər, wíth–/ *adv.* & *conj. archaic* • *adv.* **1** to what place, position, or state? **2** (prec. by *place*, etc.) to which (*the house whither we were walking*). • *conj.* **1** to the or any place to which (*go whither you will*). **2** and thither (*we saw a house, whither we walked*).

whit·ing[1] /hwīting, wī–/ *n.* (*pl.* same or **whitings**) a small, white-fleshed fish of several species, used as food.

whit·ing[2] /hwíting, wí;n–/ *n.* ground chalk used in whitewashing, etc.

Whit·sun·day /hwítsúnday, wít–/ *n.* the seventh Sunday after Easter, commemorating the descent of the Holy Spirit at Pentecost (Acts 2).

whit·tle /hwítəl, wítəl/ *v.* **1** *tr.* & (foll. by *at*) *intr.* pare (wood, etc.) with repeated slicing with a knife. **2** *tr.* (often foll. by *away, down*) reduce by repeated subtractions.

whiz /hwiz, wiz/ *n.* & *v.* (also **whizz**) *colloq.* •*n.* (*pl.* **whizzes**) **1** the sound made by the friction of a body moving through the air at great speed. **2** (also **wiz**) *colloq.* a person who is remarkable or skillful in some respect (*is a whiz at chess*). •*v.intr.* (**whizzed, whizzing**) move with or make a whiz.

whiz kid *n.* (also **whizz kid**) *colloq.* a brilliant or highly successful young person.

WHO *abbr.* World Health Organization.

who /hoo/ *pron.* (*obj.* **whom** /hoom/or *colloq.* **who**; *poss.* **whose** /hooz/) **1 a** what or which person or persons (*who called?*; *you know who it was*; *whom* or *who did you see?*). ▶In the last example *whom* is correct but *who* is common in less formal contexts. **b** what sort of person or persons? (*who am I to object?*). **2** (a person) that (*anyone who wishes can come*; *the woman whom you met*; *the man who you saw*).
▶In the last two examples *whom* is correct but *who* is common in less formal contexts. **3** and or but he, she, they, etc. (*gave it to Tom, who sold it to Jim*). ☐ **as who should say** like a person who said; as though one said. **who goes there?** see GO[1].
▶**Whom**, the objective case of **who**, is properly used where the word functions as an object: *Our mayor is the one whom you mean. To whom is the package addressed?* In informal usage, **who** often serves in all cases ("Who did you see?"), but in formal writing it is best to maintain the distinction.

whoa /wō/ *int.* used as a command to stop or slow a horse, etc.

who'd /hood/ *contr.* **1** who had. **2** who would.

who·dun·it /hoodúnit/ *n.* (also **who·dun·nit**) *colloq.* a story or play about the detection of a crime, etc., esp. murder.

who·ev·er /hoo-évər/ *pron.* (*obj.* **whomever** /hoom–/or *colloq.* **whoever**; *poss.* **whosever** /hooz–/) **1** the or any person or persons who (*whoever comes is welcome*). **2** though anyone (*whoever else objects, I do not*; *whosever it is, I want it*). **3** *colloq.* (as an intensive) whoever; who at all (*whoever heard of such a thing?*).

whole /hōl/ *adj.* & *n.* •*adj.* **1** in an uninjured, unbroken, intact, or undiminished state (*swallowed it whole*; *there is not a plate left whole*). **2** not less than; all there is of; entire; complete (*waited a whole year*; *the whole school knows*). **3** (of blood or milk, etc.) with no part removed. **4** (of a person) healthy; recovered from illness or injury. •*n.* **1** a thing complete in itself. **2** all there is of a thing (*the whole of the summer*). **3** (foll. by *of*) all members, inhabitants, etc., of (*the whole of Congress knows it*). ☐ **as a whole** as a unity; not as separate parts. **go (the) whole hog** see HOG. **on the whole** taking everything relevant into account; in general. **out of whole cloth** without fact; entirely fictitious. ☐☐ **whole·ness** *n.*

whole·heart·ed /hólhaártid/ *adj.* **1** (of a person) completely devoted or committed. **2** (of an action, etc.) done with all possible effort or sincerity; thorough. ☐☐ **whole·heart·ed·ly** *adv.* **whole·heart·ed·ness** *n.*

whole note *n.* esp. *Mus.* a note having the time value of four quarter notes, and represented by a ring with no stem.

whole num·ber *n.* a number without fractions; an integer.

whole·sale /hólsayl/ *n., adj., adv.,* & *v.* •*n.* the selling of things in large quantities to be retailed by others (cf. RETAIL). •*adj.* & *adv.* **1** by wholesale; at a wholesale price. **2** on a large scale (*wholesale destruction occurred*). •*v.tr.* sell wholesale. ☐☐ **whole·sal·er** *n.*

whole·some /hólsəm/ *adj.* **1** promoting or indicating physical, mental, or moral health. **2** prudent (*wholesome respect*). ☐☐ **whole·some·ly** *adv.* **whole·some·ness** *n.*

whole step *n. Mus.* = TONE 4.

whole-tone scale *n. Mus.* a scale consisting entirely of tones, with no semitones.

whole-wheat *adj.* made of wheat with none of the bran or germ removed.

who·lism var. of HOLISM.

whol·ly /hólee/ *adv.* **1** entirely; without limitation or diminution (*I am wholly at a loss*). **2** purely; exclusively (*a wholly bad example*).

whom *objective case* of WHO.
▶See note at WHO.

whom·ev·er *objective case* of WHOEVER.

whom·so·ev·er *objective case* of WHOSOEVER.

whoop /hoop, hwoop, woop/ *n.* & *v.* (also **hoop**) •*n.* **1** a loud cry of or as of excitement, etc. **2** a long, rasping, indrawn breath in whooping cough. •*v.intr.* utter a whoop. ☐ **whoop it up** *colloq.* **1** engage in revelry. **2** make a stir.

whoop·ee /hwóopeé, wóop–, hwóo–, wóo–/ *int.* & *n. colloq.* •*int.* expressing exuberant joy. •*n.* exuberant enjoyment or revelry. ☐ **make whoopee** *colloq.* **1** rejoice noisily. **2** engage in sexual play.

whoo·pee cush·ion *n.* a rubber cushion that when sat on makes a sound like the breaking of wind.

whoop·er /hóopər, hwóo–, wóo–/ *n.* **1** one that whoops. **2** a whooping crane. **3** (in full **whooper swan**) a swan, *Cygnus cygnus*, with a characteristic whooping sound in flight.

whoop·ing cough *n.* an infectious bacterial disease, esp. of children, with a series of short, violent coughs followed by a whoop.

whoop·ing crane *n.* a white N. American crane with a loud, whooping cry.

whoops /hwoops, woops/ *int. colloq.* expressing surprise or apology, esp. on making an obvious mistake.

whoosh /hwoosh, woosh/ *v., n.,* & *int.* (also **woosh**) •*v.intr.* & *tr.* move or cause to move with a rushing sound. •*n.* a sudden movement accompanied by a rushing sound. •*int.* an exclamation imitating this.

whop·per /hwópər, wóp–/ *n. sl.* **1** something big of its kind. **2** a great lie.

whop·ping /hwóping, wóp–/ *adj. sl.* very big.

whore /hawr/ *n.* & *v.* •*n.* **1** a prostitute. **2** *derog.* a promiscuous woman. •*v.intr.* (of a man) seek or chase after whores.

whore·house /hawrhows/ *n.* a brothel.

whorl /hwawrl, wawrl, hwərl, wərl/ *n.* **1** a ring of leaves or other organs around a stem of a plant. **2** one turn of a spiral, esp. on a shell. **3** a complete circle in a fingerprint. ☐☐ **whorled** *adj.*

whose /hooz/ *pron.* & *adj.* •*pron.* of or belonging to which person (*whose is this book?*). •*adj.* of whom or which (*whose book is this?*; *the man, whose name was Tim*; *the house whose roof was damaged*).
▶It is not necessary to avoid using **whose** in referring to things rather than people. *I admired the houses, whose windows glowed in the sunset* is perfectly acceptable. To say *I admired the houses, the windows of which glowed in the sunset* is more awkward.

whos·ev·er /hoozévər/ *poss.* of WHOEVER.

who·so·ev·er /hóosō-évər/ *pron.* (*obj.* **whomsoever**

/hōōm–/; *poss.* **whosesoever** /hōōz–/) *archaic* = WHOEVER.

why /hwī, wī/ *adv., int., & n.* • *adv.* **1 a** for what reason or purpose (*why did you do it?*). **b** on what grounds (*why do you say that?*). **2** (prec. by *reason*, etc.) for which (*the reasons why I did it*). • *int.* expressing: **1** surprised discovery or recognition (*why, it's you!*). **2** impatience (*why, of course I do!*). **3** reflection (*why, yes, I think so*). **4** objection (*why, what is wrong with it?*). • *n.* (*pl.* **whys**) a reason or explanation (esp. *whys and wherefores*). □ **why so?** on what grounds?; for what reason or purpose?

WI *abbr.* **1** West Indies. **2** West Indian. **3** Wisconsin (in official postal use).

Wich•i•ta /wíchitaw/ *n.* **1 a** a N. American people native to Kansas. **b** a member of this people. **2** the language of this people.

wick /wik/ *n. & v.* • *n.* **1** a strip or thread of fibrous or spongy material feeding a flame with fuel in a candle, lamp, etc. **2** *Surgery* a gauze strip inserted in a wound to drain it. • *v.tr.* draw (moisture) away by capillary action. □ **dip one's wick** *coarse sl.* (of a man) have sexual intercourse.

wick•ed /wíkid/ *adj.* (**wickeder, wickedest**) **1** sinful. **2** spiteful; ill-tempered; intending or intended to give pain. **3** playfully malicious. **4** *colloq.* very bad (*a wicked cough*). **5** *sl.* excellent. □□ **wick•ed•ly** *adv.* **wick•ed•ness** *n.*

wick•er /wíkər/ *n.* plaited twigs or osiers, etc., as material for baskets, etc.

wick•er•work /wíkərwərk/ *n.* **1** wicker. **2** things made of wicker.

wick•et /wíkit/ *n.* **1** (in full **wicket door** or **gate**) a small door or gate, esp. beside or in a larger one or closing the lower part only of a doorway. **2** an aperture in a door or wall, usu. closed with a sliding panel. **3** a croquet hoop. **4** *Cricket* **a** a set of three stumps with the bails in position defended by a batsman. **b** the ground between two wickets. **c** the state of this (*a slow wicket*). **d** an instance of a batsman being got out (*bowler has taken four wickets*). **e** a pair of batsmen batting at the same time (*a third-wicket partnership*).

wide /wīd/ *adj., adv., & n.* • *adj.* **1 a** measuring much or more than other things of the same kind across or from side to side. **b** considerable; more than is needed (*a wide margin*). **2** (following a measurement) in width (*a foot wide*). **3** extending far; embracing much. **4** not tight nor close nor restricted; loose. **5 a** free; liberal; unprejudiced (*takes wide views*). **b** not specialized; general. **6** open to the full extent (*staring with wide eyes*). **7 a** (foll. by *of*) not within a reasonable distance of. **b** at a considerable distance from a point or mark. **8** (in *comb.*) extending over the whole of (*nationwide*). • *adv.* **1** widely. **2** to the full extent (*wide awake*). **3** far from the target, etc. (*is shooting wide*). • *n.* **1** *Cricket* a ball judged beyond the batsman's reach and so scoring a run. **2** (prec. by *the*) the wide world. □ **give a wide berth to** see BERTH. □□ **wide•ness** *n.* **wid•ish** *adj.*

wide-an•gle *attrib.adj.* (of a lens) having a short focal length and hence a field covering a wide angle.

wide•a•wake /wídəwáyk/ *n.* a soft felt hat with a low crown and wide brim.

wide-eyed *adj.* surprised or naïve.

wide•ly /wídlee/ *adv.* **1** far apart. **2** extensively (*widely read*). **3** by many people (*it is widely thought that*). **4** to a large degree (*a widely different view*).

wid•en /wíd'n/ *v.tr. & intr.* make or become wider. □□ **wid•en•er** *n.*

wide o•pen *adj.* (often foll. by *to*) vulnerable (to attack, etc.).

wide•spread /wídspréd/ *adj.* widely distributed or disseminated.

widg•et /wíjit/ *n. colloq.* any gadget or device.

wid•ow /wídō/ *n. & v.* • *n.* **1** a woman who has lost her husband by death and has not married again. **2** a woman whose husband is often away on a specified activity (*golf widow*). **3** extra cards dealt separately and taken by the highest bidder. **4** *Printing* the short last line of a paragraph, esp. at the top of a page or column. • *v.tr.* **1** make into a widow or widower. **2** (as **widowed** *adj.*) bereft by the death of a spouse (*my widowed mother*). **3** (foll. by *of*) deprive of. □□ **wid•ow•hood** *n.*

---

widow Old English *widewe, widuwe*, from an Indo-European root meaning 'be empty, be separated'; related to Sanskrit *vidh* 'be destitute,' Latin *viduus* 'bereft, widowed,' and Greek *ēitheos* 'unmarried man.'

---

wid•ow•er /wídōər/ *n.* a man who has lost his wife by death and has not married again.

wid•ow's peak *n.* a V-shaped growth of hair toward the center of the forehead.

width /width, witth, with/ *n.* **1** measurement or distance from side to side. **2** a large extent. **3** breadth or liberality of views, etc. **4** a strip of material of full width as woven. □□ **width•ways** *adv.* **width•wise** *adv.*

wield /weeld/ *v.tr.* **1** hold and use (a weapon or tool). **2** exert or command (power or authority, etc.). □□ **wield•er** *n.*

wie•ner /wéenər/ *n.* a frankfurter.

wife /wīf/ *n.* (*pl.* **wives** /wīvz/) **1** a married woman, esp. in relation to her husband. **2** *archaic* a woman, esp. an old or uneducated one. **3** (in *comb.*) a woman engaged in a specified activity (*fishwife*; *housewife*; *midwife*). □ **have** (or **take**) **to wife** *archaic* marry (a woman). □□ **wife•ly** *adj.*

wig /wig/ *n.* an artificial head of hair, esp. to conceal baldness or as a disguise, or worn by a judge or barrister or as period dress. □□ **wigged** *adj.* (also in *comb.*). **wig•less** *adj.*

wig•gle /wígəl/ *v. & n. colloq.* • *v.intr. & tr.* move or cause to move quickly from side to side, etc. • *n.* an act of wiggling. □□ **wig•gler** *n.* **wig•gly** *adj.* (**wigglier, wiggliest**)

wig•wam /wígwom/ *n.* **1** a Native American hut or tent of skins, mats, or bark on poles. **2** a similar structure for children, etc.

wild /wīld/ *adj., adv., & n.* • *adj.* **1** (of an animal or plant) in its original natural state; not domesticated nor cultivated. **2** not civilized; barbarous. **3** (of scenery, etc.) having a conspicuously desolate appearance. **4** unrestrained; disorderly (*a wild youth*; *wild hair*). **5** tempestuous (*a wild night*). **6 a** excited; frantic (*wild with excitement*). **b** (of looks, etc.) indicating distraction. **c** (foll. by *about*) *colloq.* enthusiastically devoted to. **7** *colloq.* infuriated (*makes me wild*). **8** haphazard; ill-aimed; rash (*a wild guess*; *a wild shot*). **9** (of a horse, game bird, etc.) easily startled. **10** *colloq.* exciting; delightful. **11** (of a card) having any rank chosen (*the joker is wild*). • *adv.* in a wild manner (*shooting wild*). • *n.* **1** a wild tract. **2** a desert. □ **in the wild** in an uncultivated, etc., state. **in** (or **out in**) **the wilds** *colloq.* far from normal habitation. **run wild** grow or stray unchecked or undisciplined. □□ **wild•ish** *adj.* **wild•ly** *adv.* **wild•ness** *n.*

wild card *n.* **1** see sense 11 of WILD *adj.* **2** *Computing* a character that will match any character or sequence of characters in a file name, etc. **3** *Sports* an extra player or team chosen to enter a competition at the selectors' discretion.

wild•cat /wíldkat/ *n. & adj.* • *n.* **1** a hot-tempered or violent person. **2** any of various smallish cats, esp. the European *Felis sylvestris* or the N. American bobcat. **3** an exploratory oil well. • *adj.* (*attrib.*) **1** reckless; financially unsound. **2** (of a strike) sudden and unauthorized.

wil·de·beest /wíldəbeest, víl–/ *n.* (*pl.* same or **wildebeests**) = GNU.

wil·der·ness /wíldərnis/ *n.* **1** a desert; an uncultivated and uninhabited region. **2** part of a garden left with an uncultivated appearance. **3** (foll. by *of*) a confused assemblage of things.

wild·fire /wíldfīr/ *n. hist.* **1** a combustible liquid formerly used in warfare. **2** = WILL-O'-THE-WISP. □ **spread like wildfire** spread with great speed.

wild·fowl /wíldfowl/ *n.* (*pl.* same) a game bird, esp. an aquatic one.

wild-goose chase *n.* a foolish or hopeless and unproductive quest.

wild·life /wíldlīf/ *n.* wild animals collectively.

wild rice *n.* any tall grass of the genus *Zizania*, yielding edible grains.

Wild West *n.* the western US in a time of lawlessness in its early history.

wile /wīl/ *n. & v.* •*n.* (usu. in *pl.*) a trick or cunning procedure. •*v.tr.* (foll. by *away*, *into*, etc.) lure or entice.

wil·i·ness see WILY.

will[1] /wil/ *v.aux. & tr.* (*3rd sing. present* **will**; *past* **would** /wŏŏd/) (foll. by infin. without *to*, or *absol.*; present and past only in use) **1** (in the 2nd and 3rd persons, and often in the 1st: see SHALL) expressing the future tense in statements, commands, or questions (*you will regret this*; *they will leave at once*; *will you go to the party?*). **2** (in the 1st person) expressing a wish or intention (*I will return soon*). ▶For the other persons in senses 1 and 2, see SHALL. **3** expressing desire, consent, or inclination (*will you have a sandwich?*; *come when you will*; *the door will not open*). **4** expressing ability or capacity (*the jar will hold a quart*). **5** expressing habitual or inevitable tendency (*accidents will happen*; *will sit there for hours*). **6** expressing probability or expectation (*that will be my wife*). □ **will do** *colloq.* expressing willingness to carry out a request.

▶See note at SHALL.

will[2] /wil/ *n. & v.* •*n.* **1** the faculty by which a person decides or is regarded as deciding on and initiating action (*the mind consists of the understanding and the will*). **2** control exercised by deliberate purpose over impulse; self-control; willpower (*has a strong will*). **3** a deliberate or fixed desire or intention (*a will to live*). **4** the power of effecting one's intentions or dominating others. **5** directions in legal form for the disposition of one's property after death (*make one's will*). **6** disposition toward others (*good will*). **7** *archaic* what one desires or ordains (*thy will be done*). •*v.tr.* **1** have as the object of one's will (*what God wills*; *willed that we should succeed*). **2** (*absol.*) exercise willpower. **3** instigate or impel or compel by the exercise of willpower (*you can will yourself into contentment*). **4** bequeath by the terms of a will (*shall will my money to charity*). □ **at will 1** whenever one pleases. **2** *Law* able to be evicted without notice (*tenant at will*). **have one's will** obtain what one wants. **what is your will?** what do you wish done? **where there's a will there's a way** determination will overcome any obstacle. **a will of one's own** obstinacy; willfulness of character. **with a will** energetically or resolutely. □□ **willed** *adj.* (also in *comb.*).

will·ful /wílfŏŏl/ *adj.* **1** (of an action or state) intentional, deliberate (*willful murder*; *willful neglect*; *willful disobedience*). **2** (of a person) obstinate, headstrong. □□ **will·ful·ly** *adv.* **will·ful·ness** *n.*

wil·lies /wíleez/ *n.pl. colloq.* nervous discomfort (esp. *give* or *get the willies*).

will·ing /wíling/ *adj. & n.* •*adj.* **1** ready to consent or undertake (*a willing ally*; *am willing to do it*). **2** given or done, etc., by a willing person (*willing hands*). •*n.* cheerful intention (*show willing*). □□ **will·ing·ly** *adv.* **will·ing·ness** *n.*

will-o'-the-wisp /wíləthəwisp/ *n.* **1** a phosphorescent light seen on marshy ground, perhaps resulting from the combustion of gases. **2** an elusive person. **3** a delusive hope or plan.

wil·low /wílō/ *n.* **1** a tree or shrub of the genus *Salix*, growing usu. near water in temperate climates, with small flowers borne on catkins, and pliant branches. **2** an item made of willow wood, esp. a cricket bat.

wil·low·y /wílō-ee/ *adj.* **1** having or bordered by willows. **2** lithe and slender.

will·pow·er /wílpowr/ *n.* control exercised by deliberate purpose over impulse; self-control (*overcame his shyness by willpower*).

wil·ly-nil·ly /wileenílee/ *adv. & adj.* •*adv.* whether one likes it or not. •*adj.* existing or occurring willy-nilly.

wilt /wilt/ *v. & n.* •*v.* **1** *intr.* (of a plant) wither; droop. **2** *intr.* (of a person) lose one's energy. **3** *tr.* cause to wilt. •*n.* a plant disease causing wilting.

wil·y /wílee/ *adj.* (**wilier, wiliest**) crafty; cunning. □□ **wil·i·ly** *adv.* **wil·i·ness** *n.*

wimp /wimp/ *n. colloq.* a feeble or ineffectual person. □□ **wimp·ish** *adj.* **wimp·ish·ly** *adv.* **wimp·ish·ness** *n.* **wimp·y** *adj.*

wim·ple /wímpəl/ *n.* a linen or silk headdress covering the neck and the sides of the face, formerly worn by women and still worn by some nuns.

win /win/ *v. & n.* •*v.* (**winning**; *past* and *past part.* **won** /wun/) **1** *tr.* acquire or secure as a result of a contest, bet, litigation, or some other effort (*won some money*; *won my admiration*). **2** *tr.* be victorious in (a fight, etc.). **3** *intr.* **a** be the victor (*who won?*). **b** (foll. by *through*, *free*, etc.) make one's way or become by successful effort. **4** *tr.* reach by effort (*win the summit*). **5** *tr.* obtain (ore) from a mine. **6** *tr.* dry (hay, etc.) by exposure to the air. •*n.* victory in a game or bet, etc. □ **win the day** be victorious in battle, argument, etc. **win over** persuade; gain the support of. **win one's spurs** *colloq.* gain distinction or fame. **win out** overcome obstacles. **you can't win** *colloq.* there is no way to succeed. **you can't win them all** *colloq.* a resigned expression of consolation on failure. □□ **win·na·ble** *adj.*

wince /wins/ *n. & v.* •*n.* a start or involuntary shrinking movement showing pain or distress. •*v.intr.* give a wince. □□ **winc·ing·ly** *adv.*

winch /winch/ *n. & v.* •*n.* **1** the crank of a wheel or axle. **2** a windlass. **3** a roller for moving textile fabric through a dyeing vat. •*v.tr.* lift with a winch. □□ **winch·er** *n.*

wind[1] /wind/ *n. & v.* •*n.* **1 a** air in more or less rapid natural motion, esp. from an area of high pressure to one of low pressure. **b** a current of wind blowing from a specified direction or otherwise defined (*north wind*; *opposing wind*). **2 a** breath as needed in physical exertion or in speech. **b** the power of breathing without difficulty while running or making a similar continuous effort (*let me recover my wind*). **c** a spot below the center of the chest where a blow temporarily paralyzes breathing. **3** mere empty words; meaningless rhetoric. **4** flatulence. **5 a** an artificially produced current of air, esp. for sounding an organ or other wind instrument. **b** air stored for use or used as a current. **c** the wind instruments of an orchestra collectively. **6** a scent carried by the wind, indicating the presence or proximity of an animal, etc. •*v.tr.* **1** exhaust the wind of by exertion or a blow. **2** renew the wind of by rest (*stopped to wind the horses*). **3** make breathe quickly and deeply by exercise. **4** detect the presence of by a scent. **5** /wīnd/ (*past* and *past part.* **winded** or **wound** /wownd/) *poet.* sound (a bugle or call) by blowing. □ **before the wind** helped by the wind's force. **between wind and water** at a vulnerable point. **close to** (or **near**) **the wind 1** sailing as nearly against the wind as is consistent with using its force. **2** *colloq.* verging on indecency or dishonesty. **get wind of** begin to suspect that something is happening; hear a rumor of. **how** (or **which way**) **the wind blows 1** what is the state of opinion. **2** what developments are likely. **in the wind** happening or about to happen. **like the wind** swiftly. **off the wind** *Naut.* with the wind on the quarter. **on a wind** *Naut.* against a wind on either bow. **on the wind** (of a sound or scent) carried by the wind. **take the wind out of a person's sails** frustrate a person by anticipating an action or remark, etc. **throw caution to the wind** (or **winds**) not worry about taking risks; be reckless. **to the winds** (or **four winds**) **1** in all directions. **2** into a state of abandonment or neglect. **wind and weather** exposure to the effects of the elements. □□ **wind·less** *adj.*

wind[2] /wīnd/ *v.* & *n.* • *v.* (*past* and *past part.* **wound** /wownd/) **1** *intr.* go in a circular, spiral, curved, or crooked course (*a winding staircase*). **2** *tr.* make (one's way) by such a course (*wind your way up to bed*). **3** *tr.* wrap closely (*wound the blanket around me*). **4 a** *tr.* coil; provide with a coiled thread, etc. (*wound cotton on a reel*). **b** *intr.* coil (*the vine winds around the pole*). **5** *tr.* wind up (a clock, etc.). **6** *tr.* draw with a windlass, etc. (*wound the cable car up the mountain*). • *n.* **1** a bend or turn in a course. **2** a single turn when winding. □ **wind down 1** lower by winding. **2** (of a mechanism) unwind. **3** (of a person) relax. **4** draw gradually to a close. **wind off** unwind (string, wool, etc.). **wind around one's finger** see FINGER. **wind up 1** coil the whole of (a piece of string, etc.). **2 a** *colloq.* increase the tension (*wound myself up to fever pitch*). **b** irritate or provoke to the point of anger. **3** end (*wound up his speech*). **4** *Commerce* **a** arrange the affairs of and dissolve (a company). **b** (of a company) cease business and go into liquidation. **5** *colloq.* end in a specified state or circumstance (*you'll wind up in prison*). **6** *Baseball* (of a pitcher) carry out a windup. **wound up** *adj.* (of a person) excited or tense or angry. □□ **wind·er** *n.*

wind·bag /wíndbag/ *n. colloq.* a person who talks a lot but says little of any value.

wind·blown /wíndblōn/ *adj.* exposed to or blown about by the wind.

wind·break /wíndbrayk/ *n.* a row of trees or a fence or wall, etc., serving to break the force of the winds.

wind·break·er /wíndbraykər/ *n.* a kind of wind-resistant outer jacket with close-fitting neck, cuffs, and lower edge.

wind·burn /wíndbərn/ *n.* inflammation of the skin caused by exposure to the wind.

wind·chill /wíndchil/ *n.* the cooling effect of wind blowing on a surface.

wind·fall /wíndfawl/ *n.* **1** an apple or other fruit blown to the ground by the wind. **2** a piece of unexpected good fortune.

wind·ing-sheet *n.* a sheet in which a corpse is wrapped for burial.

wind in·stru·ment *n.* a musical instrument in which sound is produced by a current of air, esp. the breath.

wind·lass /wíndləs/ *n.* & *v.* • *n.* a machine with a horizontal axle for hauling or hoisting. • *v.tr.* hoist or haul with a windlass.

wind·mill /wíndmil/ *n.* a mill worked by the action of the wind on its sails. □ **throw one's cap** (or **bonnet**) **over the windmill** esp. *Brit.* act recklessly or unconventionally. **tilt at** (or **fight**) **windmills** attack an imaginary enemy or grievance.

win·dow /wíndō/ *n.* **1 a** an opening in a wall, roof, or vehicle, etc., usu. with glass in fixed, sliding, or hinged frames, to admit light or air, etc., and allow the occupants to see out. **b** the glass filling this opening (*have broken the window*). **2** a space for display behind the front window of a shop. **3** an aperture in a wall, etc., through which customers are served in a bank, ticket office, etc. **4** an opportunity to observe or learn. **5** an opening or transparent part in an envelope to show an address. **6** a part of a computer monitor display selected to show a particular category or part of the data. **7 a** an interval during which atmospheric and astronomical circumstances are suitable for the launch of a spacecraft. **b** any interval or opportunity for action. **8** strips of metal foil dispersed in the air to obstruct radar detection. **9** a range of electromagnetic wavelengths for which a medium is transparent. □□ **win·dowed** *adj.* (also in *comb.*). **win·dow·less** *adj.*

win·dow box *n.* a box placed on an outside windowsill for growing flowers.

win·dow dress·ing *n.* **1** the art of arranging a display in a store window, etc. **2** an adroit presentation of facts, etc., to give a deceptively favorable impression.

win·dow·ing /wíndōing/ *n. Computing* the selection of part of a stored image for display or enlargement.

win·dow·pane /wíndōpayn/ *n.* a pane of glass in a window.

win·dow-shop *v.intr.* (**-shopped, -shopping**) look at goods displayed in store windows, usu. without buying anything. □□ **win·dow-shop·per** *n.*

win·dow·sill /wíndōsil/ *n.* a sill below a window.

wind·pipe /wíndpīp/ *n.* the air passage from the throat to the lungs; the trachea.

wind·shield /wíndsheeld/ *n.* a shield of glass at the front of a motor vehicle.

wind·shield wip·er *n.* a device consisting of a rubber blade on an arm, moving in an arc, for keeping a windshield clear of rain, etc.

wind sock *n.* a canvas cylinder or cone on a mast to show the direction of the wind at an airfield, etc.

wind·surf·ing /wíndsərfing/ *n.* the sport of riding on water on a sailboard. □□ **wind·surf** *v.intr.* **wind·surf·er** *n.*

wind·swept /wíndswept/ *adj.* exposed to or swept back by the wind.

wind tun·nel *n.* a tunnellike device to produce an air stream past models of aircraft, etc., for the study of wind effects on them.

wind·up /wíndup/ *n.* **1** a conclusion; a finish. **2** *Baseball* the motions made by a pitcher, esp. arm swinging, in preparation for releasing a pitch.

wind·ward /wíndwərd/ *adj.*, *adv.*, & *n.* • *adj.* & *adv.* on the side from which the wind is blowing (opp. LEEWARD). • *n.* the windward region, side, or direction (*to windward*). □ **get to windward of 1** place oneself there to avoid the smell of. **2** gain an advantage over.

wind·y /wíndee/ *adj.* (**windier, windiest**) **1** stormy with wind (*a windy night*). **2** exposed to the wind; windswept (*a windy plain*). **3** generating or characterized by flatulence. **4** *colloq.* wordy; verbose; empty (*a windy speech*). □□ **wind·i·ness** *n.*

wine /wīn/ *n.* & *v.* • *n.* **1** fermented grape juice as an alcoholic drink. **2** a fermented drink resembling this made from other fruits, etc., as specified (*elderberry wine*; *ginger wine*). **3** the dark-red color of red wine. • *v.* **1** *intr.* drink wine. **2** *tr.* entertain with wine. □ **wine and dine** entertain to or have a meal with wine.

wine cel·lar *n.* **1** a cellar for storing wine. **2** the contents of this.

wine·glass /wínglas/ *n.* **1** a glass for wine, usu. with a stem and foot. **2** the contents of this, a wineglassful.

wine·grow·er /wíngrōər/ *n.* a cultivator of grapes for wine.

wine·press /wínpres/ *n.* a press in which grapes are squeezed in making wine.

win·er·y /wínəree/ *n.* (*pl.* **-ies**) an establishment where wine is made.

wine·tast·ing /wíntaysting/ *n.* **1** judging the quality of wine by tasting it. **2** an occasion for this.

wing /wing/ *n. & v.* •*n.* **1** each of the limbs or organs by which a bird, bat, or insect is able to fly. **2** a rigid horizontal winglike structure forming a supporting part of an aircraft. **3** part of a building, etc., which projects or is extended in a certain direction (*lived in the north wing*). **4 a** a forward player at either end of a line in soccer, hockey, etc. **b** the side part of a playing area. **5** (in *pl.*) the sides of a theater stage out of view of the audience. **6** a section of a political party in terms of the extremity of its views. **7** a flank of a battle array. **8 a** an air-force unit of several squadrons or groups. **b** (in *pl.*) a pilot's badge in the air force, etc. (*get one's wings*). •*v.* **1** *intr. & tr.* travel or traverse on wings or in an aircraft (*winging through the air*; *am winging my way home*). **2** *tr.* wound in a wing or an arm. **3** *tr.* equip with wings. **4** *tr.* enable to fly; send in flight (*fear winged my steps*; *winged an arrow toward them*). □ **give** (or **lend**) **wings to** speed up (a person or a thing). **on the wing** flying or in flight. **on a wing and a prayer** with only the slightest chance of success. **spread one's wings** develop one's powers fully. **take under one's wing** treat as a protégé. **take wing** fly away; soar. **waiting in the wings** holding oneself in readiness. □□ **winged** *adj.* (also in *comb.*). **wing·less** *adj.* **wing·let** *n.* **wing·like** *adj.*

wing chair *n.* a chair with side pieces projecting forward at the top of a high back.

wing·er /wíngər/ *n.* **1** a player on a wing in soccer, hockey, etc. **2** (in *comb.*) a member of a specified political wing (*left-winger*).

wing nut *n.* a nut with projections for the fingers to turn it on a screw.

wing·span /wíngspan/ *n.* (also **wing·spread**) measurement right across the wings of a bird or aircraft.

wing tip *n.* **1** the outer end of an aircraft's or a bird's wing. **2** a style of shoe with a pattern of perforations on the toe resembling extended bird wings.

wink /wingk/ *v. & n.* •*v.* **1 a** *tr.* close and open (one eye or both eyes) quickly. **b** *intr.* close and open an eye. **2** *intr.* (often foll. by *at*) wink one eye as a signal of friendship or greeting or to convey a message to a person. **3** *intr.* (of a light, etc.) shine or flash intermittently. •*n.* **1** the act or an instance of winking. **2** *colloq.* a brief moment of sleep (*didn't sleep a wink*). □ **in a wink** very quickly. **wink at 1** purposely avoid seeing; pretend not to notice. **2** connive at (a wrongdoing, etc.).

win·ner /wínər/ *n.* **1** a person, racehorse, etc., that wins. **2** *colloq.* a successful or highly promising idea, enterprise, etc.

win·ning /wíning/ *adj. & n.* •*adj.* **1** having or bringing victory or an advantage. **2** attractive; persuasive (*a winning smile*; *winning ways*). •*n.* (in *pl.*) money won esp. in betting, etc. □□ **win·ning·ly** *adv.*

win·ning post *n.*> a post marking the end of a race.

win·now /wínō/ *v.tr.* **1** blow (grain) free of chaff, etc., by an air current. **2** (foll. by *out*, *away*, *from*, etc.) get rid of (chaff, etc.) from grain. **3 a** sift; separate. **b** sift or examine (evidence for falsehood, etc.). **c** clear, sort, or weed out (rubbish, etc.). □□ **win·now·er** *n.* (in senses 1, 2).

win·o /wínō/ *n.* (*pl.* **-os**) *sl.* a habitual excessive drinker of cheap wine.

win·some /wínsəm/ *adj.* (of a person, looks, or manner) winning; attractive; engaging. □□ **win·some·ly** *adv.* **win·some·ness** *n.*

win·ter /wíntər/ *n. & v.* •*n.* **1** the coldest season of the year. **2** *Astron.* the period from the winter solstice to the vernal equinox. **3** a bleak or lifeless period or region, etc. (*nuclear winter*). **4** (*attrib.*) **a** characteristic of or suitable for winter (*winter light*; *winter clothes*). **b** (of fruit) ripening late or keeping until or during winter. **c** (of wheat or other crops) sown in autumn for harvesting the following year. •*v.* **1** *intr.* (usu. foll. by *at*, *in*) pass the winter (*likes to winter in Florida*). **2** *tr.* keep or feed (plants, cattle) during winter. □□ **win·ter·er** *n.*

win·ter·green /wíntərgreen/ *n.* any of several plants esp. of the genus *Pyrola* or *Gaultheria* remaining green through the winter.

win·ter·ize /wíntərīz/ *v.tr.* adapt for operation or use in cold weather. □□ **win·ter·i·za·tion** *n.*

win·ter sol·stice *n.* the time at which the sun is farthest south from the equator, about Dec. 22 in the northern hemisphere.

win·try /wíntree/ *adj.* (also **win·ter·y** /–təree/) (**wintrier, wintriest**) **1** characteristic of winter (*a wintry landscape*). **2** (of a smile, greeting, etc.) lacking warmth or enthusiasm. □□ **win·tri·ly** *adv.* **win·tri·ness** *n.*

win·y /wínee/ *adj.* (**winier, winiest**) resembling wine in taste or appearance.

wipe /wīp/ *v. & n.* •*v.tr.* **1** clean or dry the surface of by rubbing with the hands or a cloth, etc. **2** rub (a cloth) over a surface. **3** spread (a liquid, etc.) over a surface by rubbing. **4** (often foll. by *away*, *off*, etc.) **a** clear or remove by wiping. **b** remove or eliminate completely (*the village was wiped off the map*). **5 a** erase (data, a recording, etc., from a magnetic medium). **b** erase data from (the medium). •*n.* **1** an act of wiping (*give the floor a wipe*). **2** a piece of disposable absorbent cloth, usu. treated with a cleansing agent, for wiping something clean (*antiseptic wipes*). □ **wipe down** clean (esp. a vertical surface) by wiping. **wipe the floor with** *colloq.* inflict a humiliating defeat on. **wipe out 1 a** destroy; annihilate. **b** obliterate (*wiped it out of my memory*). **2** *sl.* murder. **3** clean the inside of. **wipe the slate clean** see SLATE.

wiped out *adj. sl.* tired out, exhausted.

wipe·out /wípowt/ *n.* **1** the obliteration of one radio signal by another. **2** an instance of destruction or annihilation. **3** *sl.* a fall from a surfboard.

wire /wīr/ *n. & v.* •*n.* **1 a** metal drawn out a thread or thin flexible rod. **b** a piece of this. **c** (*attrib.*) made of wire. **2** a length or quantity of wire used for fencing or to carry an electric current, etc. **3** a telegram or cablegram. •*v.tr.* **1** provide, fasten, strengthen, etc., with wire. **2** (often foll. by *up*) *Electr.* install electrical circuits in (a building, piece of equipment, etc.). **3** *colloq.* telegraph (*wired me that they were coming*). **4** snare (an animal, etc.) with wire. □ **by wire** by telegraph. **get one's wires crossed** become confused and misunderstood.

wire·draw /wírdraw/ *v.tr.* (*past* **·drew** /–drōō/; *past part.* **·drawn** /–drawn/) **1** draw (metal) out into wire. **2** elongate; protract unduly. **3** (esp. as **wiredrawn** *adj.*) refine or apply or press (an argument, etc.) with idle or excessive subtlety.

wire·haired /wírhaird/ *adj.* (esp. of a dog) having stiff or wiry hair.

wire serv·ice *n.* a business that gathers news and distributes it to subscribers, usu. newspapers.

wire·tap /wírtap/ *v.* (**-tapped, -tapping**) **1** *intr.* connect a listening device to (a telephone or telegraph line, etc.) to listen to a call or transmission. **2** *tr.* obtain (information, etc.) by wiretapping. □□ **wire·tap·per** *n.* **wire·tap·ping** *n.*

wir·ing /wíring/ *n.* **1** a system of wires providing electrical circuits. **2** the installation of this (*came to do the wiring*).

wir·y /wíree/ *adj.* (**wirier, wiriest**) **1** tough and flexible as wire. **2** (of a person) thin and sinewy; untiring. **3** made of wire. □□ **wir·i·ly** *adv.*

Wis. *abbr.* Wisconsin.

wis·dom /wízdəm/ *n.* **1** the state of being wise. **2** experience and knowledge together with the power of applying them. **3** prudence; common sense. **4** wise sayings, thoughts, etc. □ **in his** (or **her**, etc.) **wisdom** usu. *iron.* thinking it would be best (*the committee in its wisdom decided to abandon the project*).

wis·dom tooth *n.* each of four hindmost molars not usu. cut before 20 years of age.

wise[1] /wīz/ *adj.* & *v.* • *adj.* **1** having, determined by, or showing wisdom. **2** prudent; sensible. **3** having knowledge. **4** suggestive of wisdom (*with a wise nod of the head*). **5** *colloq.* **a** alert; crafty. **b** (often foll. by *to*) having (usu. confidential) information (about). • *v.tr.* & *intr.* (foll. by *up*) *colloq.* put or get wise. □ **be** (or **get**) **wise to** *colloq.* become aware of. **no** (or **none the** or **not much**) **wiser** knowing no more than before. **put a person wise** (often foll. by *to*) *colloq.* inform a person (about). **without anyone's being the wiser** undetected. □□ **wise·ly** *adv.*

wise[2] /wīz/ *n. archaic* way, manner, or degree (*on this wise*). □ **in no wise** not at all.

-wise /wīz/ *suffix* forming adjectives and adverbs of manner (*crosswise*; *clockwise*; *lengthwise*) or respect (*moneywise*) (cf. -WAYS).

▶More fanciful phrase-based combinations, such as *employment-wise* (= as regards employment) are *colloq.*, and restricted to informal contexts.

wise·a·cre /wízaykər/ *n.* a person who affects a wise manner; a wise guy.

wise·crack /wízkrak/ *n.* & *v. colloq.* • *n.* a smart pithy remark. • *v.intr.* make a wisecrack. □□ **wise·crack·er** *n.*

wise guy *n.* **1** *colloq.* a know-it-all. **2** *sl.* a member of organized crime.

wish /wish/ *v.* & *n.* • *v.* **1** *intr.* (often foll. by *for*) have or express a desire or aspiration for. **2** *tr.* (often foll. by *that* + clause, usu. with *that* omitted) have as a desire or aspiration (*I wish I could sing*). **3** *tr.* want or demand, usu. so as to bring about what is wanted (*I wish to go*; *I wish you to do it*). **4** *tr.* express one's hopes for (*wished us a pleasant journey*). **5** *tr.* (foll. by *on, upon*) *colloq.* foist on a person. • *n.* **1 a** a desire, request, or aspiration. **b** an expression of this. **2** a thing desired. □ **best** (or **good**) **wishes** hopes felt or expressed for another's happiness, etc. □□ **wish·er** *n.* (in sense 4 of *v.*); (also in *comb.*).

wish·bone /wíshbōn/ *n.* **1** a forked bone between the neck and breast of a cooked bird: when broken between two people the longer portion entitles the holder to make a wish. **2** an object of similar shape.

wish·ful /wíshfŏŏl/ *adj.* **1** (often foll. by *to* + infin.) desiring; wishing. **2** having or expressing a wish. □□ **wish·ful·ly** *adv.* **wish·ful·ness** *n.*

wish·y-wash·y /wísheewóshee, –wáwshee/ *adj.* **1** feeble, insipid, or indecisive in quality or character. **2** (of tea, soup, etc.) weak; watery.

wisp /wisp/ *n.* **1** a small bundle or twist of straw, etc. **2** a small separate quantity of smoke, hair, etc. **3** a small, thin person, etc. □□ **wisp·y** *adj.* (**wispier, wispiest**). **wisp·i·ly** *adv.* **wisp·i·ness** *n.*

wis·te·ri·a /wisteéreeə/ *n.* (also **wis·tar·i·a** /–stáiriə/) any climbing plant of the genus *Wisteria*, with hanging racemes of blue, purple, or white flowers.

wist·ful /wístfŏŏl/ *adj.* (of a person, looks, etc.) yearningly or mournfully expectant, thoughtful, or wishful. □□ **wist·ful·ly** *adv.* **wist·ful·ness** *n.*

wit[1] /wit/ *n.* **1** (in *sing.* or *pl.*) intelligence; quick understanding. **2 a** the unexpected, quick, and humorous combining or contrasting of ideas or expressions (*conversation sparkling with wit*). **b** the power of giving intellectual pleasure by this. **3** a person possessing such a power. □ **at one's wit's** (or **wits'**) **end** utterly at a loss or in despair. **have** (or **keep**) **one's wits about one** be alert or vigilant or of lively intelligence. **live by one's wits** live by ingenious or crafty expedients, without a settled occupation. **out of one's wits** mad; distracted.

wit[2] /wit/ *v.* □ **to wit** that is to say; namely.

witch /wich/ *n.* & *v.* • *n.* **1** a sorceress, esp. a woman supposed to have dealings with the devil or evil spirits. **2** an ugly old woman; a hag. **3** a fascinating girl or woman. • *v.tr. archaic* **1** bewitch. **2** fascinate; charm; lure. □□ **witch·ing** *adj.* **witch·like** *adj.*

witch·craft /wíchkraft/ *n.* the use of magic; sorcery.

witch doc·tor *n.* a tribal magician of primitive people.

witch·er·y /wíchəree/ *n.* **1** witchcraft. **2** power exercised by beauty or eloquence or the like.

witch ha·zel *n.* **1** any American shrub of the genus *Hamamelis*, with bark yielding an astringent lotion. **2** this lotion, esp. from the leaves of *H. virginiana*.

witch-hunt *n.* **1** *hist.* a search for and persecution of supposed witches. **2** a campaign directed against a particular group of those holding unpopular or unorthodox views.

with /wi<u>th</u>, with/ *prep.* expressing: **1** an instrument or means used (*cut with a knife*). **2** association or company (*lives with his mother*; *lamb with mint sauce*). **3** cause or origin (*shiver with fear*). **4** possession; attribution (*the woman with dark hair*). **5** circumstances; accompanying conditions (*sleep with the window open*). **6** manner adopted or displayed (*behaved with dignity*; *won with ease*). **7** agreement or harmony (*sympathize with*). **8** disagreement; antagonism; competition (*stop arguing with me*). **9** responsibility for (*the decision rests with you*). **10** material (*made with gold*). **11** addition or supply; possession of as a material, attribute, circumstance, etc. (*fill it with water*; *threaten with dismissal*; *decorate with flowers*). **12** reference or regard (*be patient with them*; *how are things with you?*). **13** relation or causative association (*changes with the weather*). **14** an accepted circumstance or consideration (*with all your faults, we like you*). □ **away** (or **in** or **out**, etc.) **with** (as *int.*) take, send, or put (a person or thing) away, in, out, etc. **be with a person 1** agree with and support a person. **2** *colloq.* follow a person's meaning (*are you with me?*). **one with** part of the same whole as. **with child** (or **young**) *literary* pregnant. **with that** thereupon.

with·draw /wi<u>th</u>dráw, with–/ *v.* (*past* **withdrew** /–drŏŏ/; *past part.* **withdrawn** /–dráwn/) **1** *tr.* pull or take aside or back. **2** *tr.* discontinue; cancel; retract (*withdrew my support*). **3** *tr.* remove; take away (*withdrew the child from school*). **4** *tr.* take (money) out of an account. **5** *intr.* retire or go away; move away or back. **6** *intr.* (as **withdrawn** *adj.*) abnormally shy and unsociable.

with·draw·al /wi<u>th</u>dráwəl, with–/ *n.* **1** the act or an instance of withdrawing or being withdrawn. **2** a process of ceasing to take addictive drugs. **3** = COITUS INTERRUPTUS.

with·er /wí<u>th</u>ər/ *v.* **1** *tr.* & *intr.* (often foll. by *up*) make or become dry and shriveled. **2** *tr.* & *intr.* (often foll. by *away*) deprive of or lose vigor, freshness, or importance. **3** *intr.* decay; decline. **4** *tr.* **a** blight with scorn, etc. **b** (as **withering** *adj.*) scornful (*a withering look*). □□ **with·er·ing·ly** *adv.*

with·ers /wí<u>th</u>ərz/ *n.pl.* the ridge between a horse's shoulder blades.

with·hold /wi<u>th</u>-hṓld, with–/ *v.tr.* (*past* and *past part.* **-held** /–héld/) **1** (often foll. by *from*) hold back; restrain. **2** refuse to give, grant, or allow (*withhold one's consent*).

with•in /wit͟hín, with–/ *adv., prep. & n.* •*adv. archaic* or *literary* **1** inside. **2** indoors. **3** in spirit (*make me pure within*). •*prep.* **1** inside; enclosed or contained by. **2 a** not beyond or exceeding (*within one's means*). **b** not transgressing (*within the law*). **3** not further off than (*within three miles of a station; within ten days*). •*n.* the inside part of a place, building, etc. □ **within reach** (or **sight**) **of** near enough to be reached or seen.

with•out /wit͟hówt, with–/ *prep. & adv.* •*prep.* **1** not having, feeling, or showing (*without any money; without hesitation*). **2** with freedom from (*without fear*). **3** in the absence of (*cannot live without you*). **4** with neglect or avoidance of (*do not leave without telling me*). •*adv. archaic* or *literary* outside (*seen from without*). □ **without end** infinite; eternal.

with•stand /wit͟hstánd, with–/ *v.* (*past* and *past part.* **-stood** /–stŏŏd/) **1** *tr.* resist; hold out against (a person, force, etc.). **2** *intr.* make opposition; offer resistance.

wit•less /wítlis/ *adj.* **1** lacking wits; foolish; stupid. **2** crazy. □□ **wit•less•ly** *adv.* **wit•less•ness** *n.*

wit•ness /wítnis/ *n. & v.* •*n.* **1** a person present at some event and able to give information about it (cf. EYEWITNESS). **2 a** a person giving sworn testimony. **b** a person attesting another's signature to a document. **3** (foll. by *to, of*) a person or thing whose existence, condition, etc., attests or proves something (*is a living witness to their generosity*). **4** testimony; evidence; confirmation. •*v.* **1** *tr.* be a witness of (an event, etc.). **2** *tr.* be witness to the authenticity of (a document or signature). **3** *tr.* serve as evidence or an indication of. **4** *intr.* (foll. by *against, for, to*) give or serve as evidence. □ **bear witness to** (or **of**) **1** attest the truth of. **2** state one's belief in. **call to witness** appeal to for confirmation, etc.

wit•ti•cism /wítisizəm/ *n.* a witty remark.

wit•ting /wíting/ *adj.* **1** aware. **2** intentional. □□ **wit•ting•ly** *adv.*

wit•ty /wítee/ *adj.* (**wittier, wittiest**) **1** showing verbal wit. **2** characterized by wit or humor. □□ **wit•ti•ly** *adv.* **wit•ti•ness** *n.*

wives *pl.* of WIFE.

wiz var. of WHIZ *n.* 2.

wiz•ard /wízərd/ *n.* **1** a sorcerer; a magician. **2** a genius. **3** a conjuror. □□ **wiz•ard•ly** *adj.* **wiz•ard•ry** *n.*

wiz•ened /wízənd/ *adj.* (also **wiz•en**) (of a person or face, etc.) shriveled-looking.

wk. *abbr.* **1** week. **2** work.

wks. *abbr.* weeks.

WNW *abbr.* west-northwest.

WO *abbr.* warrant officer.

wob•be•gong /wóbigong/ *n.* an Australian brown shark, *Orectolobus maculatus*, with buff patterned markings.

wob•ble /wóbəl/ *v. & n.* •*v.* **1 a** *intr.* sway or vibrate unsteadily from side to side. **b** *tr.* cause to do this. **2** *intr.* stand or go unsteadily. **3** *intr.* waver; vacillate. **4** *intr.* (of the voice or sound) quaver; pulsate. •*n.* **1** a wobbling movement. **2** an instance of wobbling. □□ **wob•bler** *n.*

wob•bly /wóblee/ *adj.* (**wobblier, wobbliest**) **1** wobbling or tending to wobble. **2** wavy (*a wobbly line*). **3** weak after illness (*feeling wobbly*). **4** wavering; insecure (*the economy was wobbly*). □□ **wob•bli•ness** *n.*

woe /wō/ *n. archaic* or *literary* **1** affliction; bitter grief; distress. **2** (in *pl.*) calamities; troubles. **3** *joc.* problems (*told me a tale of woe*). □ **woe is me** an exclamation of distress.

woe•be•gone /wṓbigon, –gawn/ *adj.* dismal-looking.

woe•ful /wṓfŏŏl/ *adj.* **1** sorrowful. **2** causing sorrow or affliction. **3** very bad (*woeful ignorance*). □□ **woe•ful•ly** *adv.* **woe•ful•ness** *n.*

wok /wok/ *n.* a bowl-shaped metal pan used in esp. Chinese cooking.

woke *past* of WAKE[1].

wok•en *past part.* of WAKE[1].

wolf /wŏŏlf/ *n. & v.* •*n.* (*pl.* **wolves** /wŏŏlvz/) **1** a wild, flesh-eating, tawny-gray mammal related to the dog, esp. *Canis lupus*. **2** *sl.* a man given to seducing women. **3** a rapacious or greedy person. •*v.tr.* (often foll. by *down*) devour (food) greedily. □ **cry wolf** raise repeated false alarms (so that a genuine one is disregarded). **keep the wolf from the door** avert hunger or starvation. **throw to the wolves** sacrifice without compunction. **wolf in sheep's clothing** a hostile person who pretends friendship. □□ **wolf•ish** *adj.* **wolf•ish•ly** *adv.* **wolf•like** *adj. & adv.*

wolf•hound /wŏŏlfhownd/ *n.* a borzoi or other dog of a kind used orig. to hunt wolves.

wolf•ram /wŏŏlfrəm/ *n.* **1** tungsten. **2** tungsten ore.

wol•ver•ine /wŏŏlvəreen/ *n.* a voracious carnivorous mammal, *Gulo gulo*, of the weasel family.

wolves *pl.* of WOLF.

wom•an /wŏŏmən/ *n.* (*pl.* **women** /wímin/) **1** an adult human female. **2** the female sex; any or an average woman (*how does woman differ from man?*). **3** a wife or female sexual partner. **4** (prec. by *the*) emotions or characteristics traditionally associated with women (*brought out the woman in him*). **5** a man with characteristics traditionally associated with women. **6** (*attrib.*) female (*woman driver*). **7** (as second element in *comb.*) a woman of a specified nationality, profession, skill, etc. (*Englishwoman; horsewoman*). **8** *colloq.* a female domestic servant.

wom•an•hood /wŏŏmənhŏŏd/ *n.* **1** female maturity. **2** womanly instinct. **3** womankind.

wom•an•ish /wŏŏmənish/ *adj.* usu. *derog.* **1** (of a man) effeminate; unmanly. **2** suitable to or characteristic of a woman.

wom•an•ize /wŏŏmənīz/ *v. intr.* chase after women; philander. □□ **wom•an•iz•er** *n.*

wom•an•kind /wŏŏmənkīnd/ *n.* (also **wom•en•kind** /wímin–/) women in general.

wom•an•ly /wŏŏmənlee/ *adj.* (of a woman) having or showing qualities traditionally associated with women. □□ **wom•an•li•ness** *n.*

womb /wōōm/ *n.* **1** the organ of conception and gestation in a woman and other female mammals; the uterus. **2** a place of origination and development. □□ **womb•like** *adj.*

wom•bat /wómbat/ *n.* any burrowing, plant-eating Australian marsupial of the family *Vombatidae*.

wom•en *pl.* of WOMAN.

wom•en•folk /wíminfōk/ *n.* **1** women in general. **2** the women in a family.

wom•en•kind var. of WOMANKIND.

wom•en's lib•er•a•tion *n.* the liberation of women from inequalities and subservient status in relation to men.

won *past* and *past part.* of WIN.

won•der /wúndər/ *n. & v.* •*n.* **1** surprise mingled with admiration or curiosity. **2** a strange or remarkable person or thing, event, etc. **3** (*attrib.*) having marvelous properties, etc. (*a wonder drug*). **4** a surprising thing (*it is a wonder you were not hurt*). •*v.* **1** *intr.* (often foll. by *at*, or *to* + infin.) be filled with wonder or great surprise. **2** *tr.* (foll. by *that* + clause) be surprised to find. **3** *tr.* desire or be curious to know (*I wonder what the time is*). **4** *tr.* expressing a tentative inquiry (*I wonder whether you would mind?*). **5** *intr.* (foll. by *about*) ask oneself with puzzlement or doubt about; question (*wondered about the sense of the decision*). □ **I shouldn't**

wonder *colloq.* I think it likely. **I wonder** I very much doubt it. **no** (or **small**) **wonder** (often foll. by *that* + clause) one cannot be surprised. **wonders will** (or **will wonders**) **never cease** an exclamation of extreme (usu. agreeable) surprise. **work** (or **do**) **wonders 1** do miracles. **2** succeed remarkably. ▫▫ **won·der·er** *n.*

won·der·ful /wúndərfo͝ol/ *adj.* **1** very remarkable or admirable. **2** arousing wonder. ▫▫ **won·der·ful·ly** *adv.* **won·der·ful·ness** *n.*

won·der·ing /wúndəring/ *adj.* filled with wonder; marveling (*their wondering gaze*). ▫▫ **won·der·ing·ly** *adv.*

won·der·land /wúndərland/ *n.* **1** a fairyland. **2** a land of surprises or marvels.

won·der·ment /wúndərmənt/ *n.* surprise; awe.

won·drous /wúndrəs/ *adj. & adv. poet.* • *adj.* wonderful. • *adv. archaic* or *literary* wonderfully (*wondrous kind*). ▫▫ **won·drous·ly** *adv.*

wont /wōnt, wawnt, wunt/ *adj. & n.* • *predic.adj. archaic* or *literary* (foll. by *to* + infin.) accustomed (*as we were wont to say*). • *n. formal* or *joc.* what is customary; one's habit (*as is my wont*).

won't /wōnt/ *contr.* will not.

wont·ed /wṓntid, wáwn–, wún–/ *attrib.adj.* habitual; accustomed; usual.

won·ton /wúntun/ *n.* (in Chinese cookery) a small round dumpling or roll with a savory filling, usu. eaten boiled in soup.

woo /wo͞o/ *v.tr.* (**woos, wooed**) **1** court; seek the hand or love of (a woman). **2** try to win (fame, fortune, etc.). **3** seek the favor or support of. **4** coax or importune. ▫▫ **woo·er** *n.*

wood /wo͝od/ *n.* **1 a** a hard fibrous material from the trunk or branches of a tree or shrub. **b** this cut for lumber or for fuel. **2** (in *sing.* or *pl.*) growing trees densely occupying a tract of land. **3** (prec. by *the*) wooden storage, esp. a cask, for wine, etc. (*poured straight from the wood*). **4** a wooden-headed golf club. **5** = BOWL[2] *n.* 1. ▫ **out of the woods** out of danger or difficulty.

wood·bine /wo͝odbīn/ *n.* **1** wild honeysuckle. **2** Virginia creeper.

wood·carv·ing /wo͝odkaarving/ *n.* **1** (also *attrib.*) the act or process of carving wood. **2** a design in wood produced by this art.

wood·chuck /wo͝odchuk/ *n.* a reddish-brown and gray N. American marmot, *Marmota monax*. Also called GROUNDHOG.

wood·cock /wo͝odkok/ *n.* (*pl.* same) any game bird of the genus *Scolopax*.

wood·craft /wo͝odkraft/ *n.* **1** skill in woodwork. **2** knowledge of woodland, esp. in camping, scouting, etc.

wood·cut /wo͝odkut/ *n.* **1** a relief cut on a block of wood sawn along the grain. **2** a print made from this. **3** the technique of making such reliefs and prints.

wood·cut·ter /wo͝odkutər/ *n.* **1** a person who cuts wood. **2** a maker of woodcuts.

wood·ed /wo͝odid/ *adj.* having woods or many trees.

wood·en /wo͝od'n/ *adj.* **1** made of wood. **2** like wood. **3 a** stiff, clumsy, or stilted; without animation or flexibility. **b** expressionless (*a wooden stare*). ▫▫ **wood·en·ly** *adv.* **wood·en·ness** *n.*

wood·land /wo͝odlənd/ *n.* wooded country; woods (often *attrib.*: *woodland scenery*). ▫▫ **wood·land·er** *n.*

wood·man /wo͝odmən/ *n.* (*pl.* **-men**) **1** a forester. **2** a woodcutter.

wood·peck·er /wo͝odpekər/ *n.* any bird of the family *Picidae* that climbs and taps tree trunks in search of insects.

wood pulp *n.* wood fiber reduced chemically or mechanically to pulp as raw material for paper.

wood·shed /wo͝odshed/ *n.* a shed where wood for fuel is stored.

woods·man /wo͝odzmən/ *n.* (*pl.* **-men**) **1** a person who lives in or is familiar with woodland. **2** a person skilled in woodcraft.

woodsy /wo͝odzee/ *adj.* like or characteristic of woods.

wood·wind /wo͝odwind/ *n.* (often *attrib.*) **1** (*collect.*) wind instruments that were (mostly) orig. made of wood, e.g., the flute and clarinet. **2** (usu. in *pl.*) an individual instrument of this kind or its player.

wood·work /wo͝odwərk/ *n.* **1** the making of things in wood. **2** things made of wood. ▫ **crawl** (or **come**) **out of the woodwork** *colloq.* (of something unwelcome) appear; become known. ▫▫ **wood·work·er** *n.* **wood·work·ing** *n.*

wood·y /wo͝odee/ *adj.* (**woodier, woodiest**) **1** (of a region) wooded; abounding in woods. **2** like or of wood. ▫▫ **wood·i·ness** *n.*

woof[1] /wo͝of/ *n. & v.* • *n.* the gruff bark of a dog. • *v.intr.* give a woof.

woof[2] /wo͝of, wo͞of/ *n.* = WEFT.

woof·er /wo͝ofər/ *n.* a loudspeaker designed to reproduce low frequencies (cf. TWEETER).

wool /wo͝ol/ *n.* **1** fine, soft, wavy hair from the fleece of sheep, goats, etc. **2 a** yarn produced from this hair. **b** cloth or clothing made from it. **3** any of various wool-like substances (*steel wool*). **4** soft, short, underfur or down. **5** *colloq.* a person's hair, esp. when short and curly. ▫ **pull the wool over a person's eyes** deceive a person. ▫▫ **wool·like** *adj.*

wool·en /wo͝olən/ *adj. & n.* (also **wool·len**) • *adj.* made wholly or partly of wool. • *n.* **1** a fabric produced from wool. **2** (in *pl.*) woolen garments.

wool·ly /wo͝olee/ *adj.* (**woollier, woolliest**) **1** bearing or naturally covered with wool. **2** resembling or suggesting wool (*woolly clouds*). **3** (of a sound) indistinct. **4** (of thought) vague or confused. **5** *Bot.* downy. **6** lacking in definition, luminosity, or incisiveness. ▫▫ **wool·li·ness** *n.*

wool·ly bear *n.* a large hairy caterpillar, esp. of the tiger moth.

wool·y *adj.* (**woolier, wooliest**) var. of WOOLLY.

woosh var. of WHOOSH.

wooz·y /wo͞ozee/ *adj.* (**woozier, wooziest**) *colloq.* **1** dizzy or unsteady. **2** dazed or slightly drunk. **3** vague. ▫▫ **wooz·i·ly** *adv.* **wooz·i·ness** *n.*

wop /wop/ *n. sl. offens.* an Italian or other S. European.

word /wərd/ *n. & v.* • *n.* **1** a sound or combination of sounds forming a meaningful element of speech, usu. shown with a space on either side of it when written or printed. **2** speech, esp. as distinct from action (*bold in word only*). **3** one's promise or assurance (*gave us their word*). **4** (in *sing.* or *pl.*) a thing said, a remark or conversation. **5** (in *pl.*) the text of a song or an actor's part. **6** (in *pl.*) angry talk (*they had words*). **7** news; intelligence. **8** a command, password, or motto (*gave the word to begin*). **9** a basic unit of the expression of data in a computer. • *v.tr.* put into words; select words to express (*how shall we word that?*). ▫ **at a word** as soon as requested. **be as good as one's word** fulfill (or exceed) what one has promised. **break one's word** fail to do what one has promised. **have no words for** be unable to express. **have a word** (often foll. by *with*) speak briefly (to). **in other words** expressing the same thing differently. **in so many words** explicitly or bluntly. **in a word** briefly. **keep one's word** do what one has promised. **my** (or **upon my**) **word** an exclamation of surprise or consternation. **not the word for it** not an adequate or appropriate description. **of few words** taciturn. **of one's word** reliable in keeping promises (*a woman of her word*). **put into words** express in speech or writing. **take a person at his** or **her word** interpret a person's words literally or exactly. **take a person's word for it**

believe a person's statement without investigation, etc. **too ... for words** too ... to be adequately described (*was too funny for words*). **waste words** talk in vain. **words fail me** an expression of disbelief, dismay, etc. **a word to the wise** enough said. □□ **word·age** *n.* **word·less** *adj.* **word·less·ly** *adv.* **word·less·ness** *n.*

word·ing /wə́rding/ *n.* **1** a form of words used. **2** the way in which something is expressed.

word of hon·or *n.* an assurance given upon one's honor.

word of mouth *n.* spoken language; informal or unofficial discourse.

word·play /wə́rdplay/ *n.* use of words to witty effect, esp. by punning.

word proc·es·sor *n.* a computer software program for electronically storing text entered from a keyboard, incorporating corrections, and providing a printout.

word·y /wə́rdee/ *adj.* (**wordier, wordiest**) **1** using or expressed in many or too many words; verbose. **2** consisting of words. □□ **word·i·ly** *adv.* **word·i·ness** *n.*

wore[1] *past* of WEAR[1].

wore[2] *past* and *past part.* of WEAR[2].

work /wərk/ *n. & v.* • *n.* **1** the application of mental or physical effort to a purpose; the use of energy. **2 a** a task to be undertaken. **b** the materials for this. **c** (prec. by *the*; foll. by *of*) a task occupying (no more than) a specified time (*the work of a moment*). **3** a thing done or made by work; the result of an action; an achievement. **4** a person's employment or occupation, etc., esp. as a means of earning income (*looked for work; is out of work*). **5 a** a literary or musical composition. **b** (in *pl.*) all such by an author or composer, etc. **6** actions or experiences of a specified kind (*good work!; this is thirsty work*). **7** (in *comb.*) things or parts made of a specified material or with specified tools, etc. (*ironwork; needlework*). **8** (in *pl.*) the operative part of a clock or machine. **9** *Physics* the exertion of force overcoming resistance or producing molecular change (*convert heat into work*). **10** (in *pl.*) *colloq.* all that is available; everything needed. **11** (in *pl.*) operations of building or repair (*road works*). **12** (usu. in *pl.* or in *comb.*) a defensive structure (*earthworks*). **13** (in *comb.*) **a** ornamentation of a specified kind (*scrollwork*). **b** articles having this. • *v.* (*past* and *past part.* **worked** or (esp. as *adj.*) **wrought**) **1** *intr.* (often foll. by *at, on*) do work; be engaged in bodily or mental activity. **2** *intr.* **a** be employed in certain work (*works in industry; works as a secretary*). **b** (foll. by *with*) be the coworker of (a person). **3** *intr.* (often foll. by *for*) make efforts (*works for peace*). **4** *intr.* (foll. by *in*) be a craftsman (in a material). **5** *intr.* operate or function, esp. effectively (*how does this machine work?; your idea will not work*). **6** *intr.* (of a part of a machine) run; revolve; go through regular motions. **7** *tr.* carry on, manage, or control (*cannot work the machine*). **8** *tr.* **a** put or keep in operation or at work (*this mine is no longer worked; works the staff very hard*). **b** cultivate (land). **9** *tr.* bring about; produce as a result (*worked miracles*). **10** *tr.* knead; hammer; bring to a desired shape or consistency. **11** *tr.* do, or make by, needlework, etc. **12** *tr. & intr.* (cause to) progress or penetrate, or make (one's way), gradually or with difficulty in a specified way (*worked our way through the crowd; worked the peg into the hole*). **13** *intr.* (foll. by *loose*, etc.) gradually become (loose, etc.) by constant movement. **14** *tr.* artificially excite (*worked themselves into a rage*). **15** *tr.* solve (an equation, etc.) by mathematics. **16** *tr.* **a** purchase with one's labor instead of money (*work one's passage*). **b** obtain by labor the money for (one's way through college, etc.). **17** *intr.* (foll. by *on, upon*) have influence. **18** *intr.* be in motion or agitated; cause agitation; ferment (*his features worked violently; the yeast began to work*). □ **at work** in action or engaged in work. **give a person the works 1** *colloq.* give or tell a person everything. **2** *colloq.* treat a person harshly. **3** *sl.* kill a person. **have one's work cut out** be faced with a hard task. **in the works** *colloq.* in progress; in the pipeline. **out of work** unemployed. **set to work** begin or cause to begin operations. **work away** (or **on**) continue to work. **work in** find a place for. **work it** *colloq.* bring it about; achieve a desired result. **work off** get rid of by work or activity. **work out 1** solve (an equation, etc.) or find out (an amount) by calculation; resolve (a problem, etc.). **2** (foll. by *at*) be calculated (*the total works out at 230*). **3** give a definite result (*this sum will not work out*). **4** have a specified result (*the plan worked out well*). **5** provide for the details of (*has worked out a plan*). **6** accomplish or attain with difficulty (*work out one's salvation*). **7** exhaust with work (*the mine is worked out*). **8** engage in physical exercise or training. **work over 1** examine thoroughly. **2** *colloq.* treat with violence. **work up 1** bring gradually to an efficient state. **2** (foll. by *to*) advance gradually to a climax. **3** elaborate or excite by degrees. **4** mingle (ingredients) into a whole. **work wonders** see WONDER. □□ **work·less** *adj.*

work·a·ble /wə́rkəbəl/ *adj.* **1** that can be worked or will work. **2** that is worth working; practicable; feasible (*a workable plan*). □□ **work·a·bil·i·ty** (/–bílitee/) *n.* **work·a·bly** *adv.*

work·a·day /wə́rkəday/ *adj.* **1** ordinary; everyday; practical. **2** fit for, used, or seen on workdays.

work·a·hol·ic /wə́rkəhólik/ *n. & adj. colloq.* (a person) addicted to working.

work·bench /wə́rkbench/ *n.* a bench for doing mechanical or practical work, esp. carpentry.

work·day /wə́rkday/ *n.* a day on which work is usually done.

work·er /wə́rkər/ *n.* **1** a person who works, esp. a manual or industrial employee. **2** a neuter or undeveloped female of various social insects, esp. a bee or ant, that does the basic work of its colony.

work·force /wə́rkfawrs/ *n.* **1** the workers engaged or available in an industry, etc. **2** the number of such workers.

work·horse /wə́rk-hawrs/ *n.* a horse, person, or machine that performs hard work.

work·house /wə́rk-hows/ *n.* **1** a house of correction for petty offenders. **2** *Brit. hist.* a public institution in which the destitute of a parish received board and lodging in return for work.

work·ing /wə́rking/ *adj. & n.* • *adj.* **1** engaged in work, esp. in manual or industrial labor. **2** functioning or able to function. • *n.* **1** the activity of work. **2** the act or manner of functioning of a thing. **3 a** a mine or quarry. **b** the part of this in which work is being or has been done (*a disused working*).

work·ing class *n.* the class of people who are employed for wages, esp. in manual or industrial work. □□ **work·ing-class** *adj.*

work·ing or·der *n.* the condition in which a machine works (satisfactorily or as specified).

work·load /wə́rklōd/ *n.* the amount of work to be done by an individual, etc.

work·man /wə́rkmən/ *n.* (*pl.* **-men**) **1** a person employed to do manual labor. **2** a person considered with regard to skill in a job (*a good workman*).

work·man·like /wə́rkmənlīk/ *adj.* characteristic of a good workman; showing practiced skill.

work·man·ship /wə́rkmənship/ *n.* **1** the degree of skill with which a product is made or a job done; craftsmanship. **2** a thing made or created by a specified person, etc.

work of art *n.* a fine picture, poem, or building, etc.

work·out /wə́rkowt/ *n.* a session of physical exercise.

work·piece /wə́rkpees/ *n.* a thing worked on with a tool or machine.

work·place /wə́rkplays/ *n.* a place at which a person works; an office, factory, etc.

work sheet *n.* **1** a paper for recording work done or in progress. **2** a paper listing questions or activities for students, etc., to work through.

work·shop /wə́rkshop/ *n.* **1** a room or building in which goods are manufactured. **2 a** a meeting for concerted discussion or activity (*a dance workshop*). **b** the members of such a meeting.

work·sta·tion /wə́rkstayshən/ *n.* **1** the location of a stage in a manufacturing process. **2** a computer terminal or the desk, etc., where this is located.

work-stud·y pro·gram *n.* a system of combining academic studies with related practical employment.

world /wərld/ *n.* **1 a** the earth, or a planetary body like it. **b** its countries and their inhabitants. **c** all people. **2 a** the universe or all that exists; everything. **b** everything that exists outside oneself (*dead to the world*). **3 a** the time, state, or scene of human existence. **b** (prec. by *the, this*) mortal life. **4** secular interests and affairs. **5** human affairs; active life (*how goes the world with you?*). **6** average, respectable, or fashionable people or their customs or opinions. **7** all that concerns or all who belong to a specified class, time, or sphere of activity (*the medieval world; the world of baseball*). **8** (foll. by *of*) a vast amount (*that makes a world of difference*). **9** (*attrib.*) affecting many nations, of all nations (*world politics; a world champion*). □ **be worlds apart** differ greatly, esp. in nature or opinion. **bring into the world** give birth to. **come into the world** be born. **for all the world** (foll. by *like, as if*) precisely (*looked for all the world as if they were real*). **get the best of both worlds** benefit from two incompatible sets of ideas, circumstances, etc. **in the world** of all; at all (used as an intensifier in questions) (*what in the world is it?*). **man** (or **woman**) **of the world** a person experienced and practical in human affairs. **the next** (or **other**) **world** life after death. **out of this world** *colloq.* extremely good, etc. **see the world** travel widely; gain wide experience. **think the world of** have a very high regard for. **the** (or **all the**) **world over** throughout the world. **the world's end** the farthest attainable point of travel. **the world to come** supposed life after death.

world-class *adj.* of a quality or standard regarded as high throughout the world.

world·ly /wə́rldlee/ *adj.* (**worldlier, worldliest**) **1** temporal or earthly (*worldly goods*). **2** engrossed in temporal affairs, esp. the pursuit of wealth and pleasure. □□ **world·li·ness** *n.*

World Se·ries *n.* the championship for North American major-league baseball teams.

world-wea·ry *adj.* bored with the world and life on it. □□ **world-wea·ri·ness** *n.*

world·wide /wə́rldwíd/ *adj.* & *adv.* • *adj.* affecting, occurring in, or known in all parts of the world. • *adv.* throughout the world.

World Wide Web *n. Computing* a widely used information system on the Internet that provides facilities for electronic documents to be interconnected by hypertext links, enabling the user to search for information by moving from one document to another. ¶ Abbr.: **WWW**.

worm /wərm/ *n.* & *v.* • *n.* **1** any of various types of creeping or burrowing invertebrate animals with long, slender bodies and no limbs. **2** the long, slender larva of an insect. **3** (in *pl.*) internal parasites. **4** a slowworm. **5** a maggot supposed to eat dead bodies in the grave. **6** an insignificant or contemptible person. **7 a** the spiral part of a screw. **b** a short screw working in a worm gear. • *v.* **1** *intr.* & *tr.* (often *refl.*) move with a crawling motion (*wormed through the bushes; wormed our way through the bushes*). **2** *intr.* & *refl.* (foll. by *into*) insinuate oneself into a person's favor, confidence, etc. **3** *tr.* (foll. by *out*) obtain (a secret, etc.) by cunning persistence (*managed to worm the truth out of them*). **4** *tr.* rid (a plant or dog, etc.) of worms. □ **a** (or **even a**) **worm will turn** the meekest will resist or retaliate if pushed too far. □□ **worm·er** *n.* **worm·like** *adj.*

worm gear *n.* an arrangement of a toothed wheel worked by a revolving spiral.

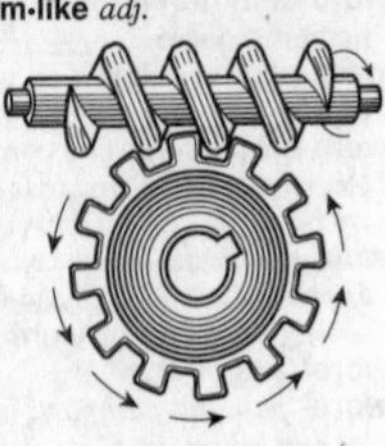
worm gear

worm·wood /wə́rmwood/ *n.* **1** any woody shrub of the genus *Artemisia*, with a bitter aromatic taste. **2** bitter mortification or a source of this.

worm·y /wə́rmee/ *adj.* (**wormier, wormiest**) **1** full of worms. **2** eaten into by worms.

worn /wawrn/ *past part.* of WEAR[1]. • *adj.* **1** damaged by use or wear. **2** looking tired and exhausted. **3** (in full **well-worn**) (of a phrase, joke, etc.) stale; often heard.

wor·ri·some /wə́reesəm, wúr–/ *adj.* causing or apt to cause worry or distress.

wor·ry /wə́ree, wúr–/ *v.* & *n.* • *v.* (**-ries, -ried**) **1** *intr.* allow one's mind to dwell on troubles. **2** *tr.* harass; importune; be a trouble to. **3** *tr.* **a** (of a dog, etc.) shake or pull about with the teeth. **b** attack repeatedly. **4** (as **worried** *adj.*) **a** uneasy; troubled in the mind. **b** suggesting worry (*a worried look*). • *n.* (*pl.* **-ries**) **1** a thing that causes anxiety. **2** a disturbed state of mind. **3** a dog's worrying of its quarry. □ **not to worry** *colloq.* there is no need to worry. **worry along** (or **through**) manage to advance by persistence in spite of obstacles. **worry oneself** (usu. in *neg.*) take needless trouble. **worry out** obtain (the solution to a problem, etc.) by dogged effort. □□ **wor·ried·ly** *adv.* **wor·ri·er** *n.* **wor·ry·ing·ly** *adv.*

wor·ry·wart /wə́reewawrt, wúr–/ *n. colloq.* a person who habitually worries unduly.

worse /wərs/ *adj., adv.,* & *n.* • *adj.* **1** more bad. **2** (*predic.*) in or into worse health or a worse condition. • *adv.* more badly or more ill. • *n.* **1** a worse thing or things (*you might do worse than accept*). **2** (prec. by *the*) a worse condition (*a change for the worse*). □ **none the worse** (often foll. by *for*) not adversely affected (by). **or worse** or as an even worse alternative. **the worse for drink** fairly drunk. **the worse for wear 1** damaged by use. **2** injured. **3** *joc.* drunk. **worse off** in a worse position.

wors·en /wə́rsən/ *v.tr.* & *intr.* make or become worse.

wor·ship /wə́rship/ *n.* & *v.* • *n.* **1 a** homage or reverence paid to a deity. **b** the acts, rites, or ceremonies of worship. **2** adoration or devotion shown toward a person or principle (*the worship of wealth*). • *v.* (**worshiped, worshiping** or **worshipped, worshipping**) **1** *tr.* adore as divine; honor with religious rites. **2** *tr.* regard with adoration (*worships the ground she walks on*). **3** *intr.* attend public worship. **4** *intr.* be full of adoration. □□ **wor·ship·er** or wor·ship·per *n.*

worst /wərst/ *adj., adv., n.,* & *v.* • *adj.* most bad. • *adv.* most badly. • *n.* the worst part, event, circumstance, or possibility (*the worst of the storm is over; prepare for the worst*). *v.tr.* defeat; outdo. □ **at its,** etc., **worst** in the worst state. **at worst** (or **the worst**) in the worst possible case. **do your worst** an expression of defiance. **get** (or **have**) **the worst of it** be defeated. **if worst comes to worst** if the worst happens.

wort /wərt, wawrt/ *n.* **1** *archaic* (except in names) a plant (*St. John's wort*). **2** the infusion of malt which after fermentation becomes beer.

worth /wərth/ *adj. & n.* • *predic.adj.* (governing a noun like a preposition) **1** of a value equivalent to (*is worth $50*). **2** such as to justify or repay (*worth doing; not worth the trouble*). **3** possessing or having property amounting to. • *n.* **1** what a person or thing is worth (*of great worth; persons of worth*). **2** the equivalent of money in a commodity (*ten dollars' worth of gasoline*). □ **for all one is worth** *colloq.* with one's utmost efforts. **for what it is worth** without a guarantee of its truth or value. **worth it** *colloq.* worth the time or effort spent. **worth one's salt** see SALT. **worth while** (or **one's while**) see WHILE.
▶**Worth while** (two words) is used only in the predicate, e.g., *Nobody thought it worth while to call the police,* and means 'worth the time or effort.' **Worthwhile** (one word) also has this meaning, but can be used both predicatively and attributively, e.g., *Would this investment be worthwhile?* (predicative), or *He was a worthwhile candidate for the office* (attributive).

worth•less /wə́rthlis/ *adj.* without value or merit. □□ **worth•less•ness** *n.*

worth•while /wə́rth-hwíl, wíl/ *adj.* that is worth the time or effort spent; of value or importance.

wor•thy /wə́rthee/ *adj. & n.* • *adj.* (**worthier, worthiest**) **1** estimable; having some moral worth (*lived a worthy life*). **2** (of a person) entitled to recognition (*a worthy old couple*). **3 a** (foll. by *of* or *to* + infin.) deserving (*worthy of a mention; worthy to be remembered*). **b** (foll. by *of*) suitable to the dignity, etc., of (*in words worthy of the occasion*). • *n.* (*pl.* **-thies**) **1** a worthy person. **2** a person of some distinction. **3** *joc.* a person. □□ **wor•thi•ly** *adv.* **wor•thi•ness** *n.*

-worthy /wərthee/ *comb. form* forming adjectives meaning: **1** deserving of (*blameworthy; noteworthy*). **2** suitable or fit for (*newsworthy; roadworthy*).

would /wood, when unstressed wəd/ *v.aux.* (*3rd sing.* **would**) *past* of WILL[1], used esp.: **1** (in the 2nd and 3rd persons, and often in the 1st: see SHOULD). **a** in reported speech (*he said he would be home by evening*). **b** to express the conditional mood (*they would have been killed if they had gone*). **2** to express habitual action (*would wait for her every evening*). **3** to express a question or polite request (*would they like it?; would you come in, please?*). **4** to express probability (*I guess she would be over fifty by now*). **5** (foll. by *that* + clause) *literary* to express a wish (*would that you were here*). **6** to express consent (*they would not help*).
▶See note at SHALL.

would-be *attrib.adj.* often *derog.* desiring or aspiring to be (*a would-be politician*).

wouldn't /wood'nt/ *contr.* would not. □ **I wouldn't know** *colloq.* (as is to be expected) I do not know.

wound[1] /woond/ *n. & v.* • *n.* **1** an injury done to living tissue by a cut or blow, etc. **2** an injury to a person's reputation or a pain inflicted on a person's feelings. • *v.tr.* inflict a wound on (*wounded soldiers; wounded feelings*).

wound[2] *past* and *past part.* of WIND[2] (cf. WIND[1] *v.* 5).

wove[1] *past* of WEAVE[1].

wove[2] /wōv/ *adj.* (of paper) made on a wire-gauze mesh and so having a uniform unlined surface.

wo•ven *past part.* of WEAVE[1].

wow[1] /wow/ *int., n., & v.* • *int.* expressing astonishment or admiration. • *n. sl.* a sensational success. • *v.tr. sl.* impress or excite greatly.

wow[2] /wow/ *n.* a slow pitch fluctuation in sound reproduction, perceptible in long notes.

WP *abbr.* word processor; word processing.

w.p.m. *abbr.* words per minute.

wrack /rak/ *n.* **1** seaweed cast up or growing on the shore. **2** destruction. **3** a wreck or wreckage. **5** = RACK[5].

wraith /rayth/ *n.* **1** a ghost or apparition. **2** the spectral appearance of a living person supposed to portend that person's death. □□ **wraith•like** *adj.*

wran•gle /ránggəl/ *n. & v.* • *n.* a noisy argument or dispute. • *v.* **1** *intr.* engage in a wrangle. **2** *tr.* herd (cattle).

wran•gler /rángglər/ *n.* **1** a person who wrangles. **2** a cowboy.

wrap /rap/ *v. & n.* • *v.tr.* (**wrapped, wrapping**) **1** (often foll. by *up*) envelop in folded or soft encircling material (*wrap it up in paper; wrap up a package*). **2** (foll. by *around, about*) arrange or draw (a pliant covering) around (a person) (*wrapped the coat closer around me*). **3** (foll. by *around*) *sl.* crash (a vehicle) into a stationary object. • *n.* **1** a shawl or scarf or other such addition to clothing. **2** material used for wrapping. □ **take the wraps off** disclose. **under wraps** in secrecy. **wrapped up in** engrossed in. **wrap up 1** finish off; bring to completion (*wrapped up the deal in two days*). **2** put on warm clothes (*mind you wrap up well*).

wrap•a•round /rápərownd/ *adj. & n.* • *adj.* **1** (esp. of clothing) designed to wrap around. **2** curving or extending around at the edges. • *n.* anything that wraps around.

wrap•per /rápər/ *n.* **1** a cover for a candy, chocolate, etc. **2** a cover enclosing a newspaper or similar packet for mailing. **3** a paper cover of a book, usu. detachable. **4** a loose enveloping robe or gown. **5** a tobacco leaf of superior quality enclosing a cigar.

wrap•ping pa•per *n.* strong or decorative paper for wrapping packages.

wrath /rath, roth, rawth/ *n. literary* extreme anger.

wrath•ful /ráthfool, róth–, ráwth–/ *adj. literary* extremely angry. □□ **wrath•ful•ly** *adv.*

wreak /reek/ *v.tr.* **1** (usu. foll. by *upon*) put in operation (vengeance or one's anger, etc.). **2** cause (damage, etc.) (*the hurricane wreaked havoc on the crops*).

wreath /reeth/ *n.* (*pl.* **wreaths** /reethz, reeths/) **1** flowers or leaves fastened in a ring. **2** a similar ring of soft twisted material such as silk. **3** a carved representation of a wreath. **4** (foll. by *of*) a curl or ring of smoke or cloud. **5** a light drifting mass of snow, etc.

wreathe /reeth/ *v.* **1** *tr.* encircle as, with, or like a wreath. **2** *tr.* (foll. by *around*) put (one's arms, etc.) around (a person, etc.). **3** *intr.* (of smoke, etc.) move in the shape of wreaths. **4** *tr.* form (flowers, silk, etc.) into a wreath. **5** *tr.* make (a garland).

wreck /rek/ *n. & v.* • *n.* **1** the destruction or disablement, esp. of a ship. **2** a ship that has suffered a wreck (*the shores are strewn with wrecks*). **3** a greatly damaged or disabled thing or person (*had become a physical and mental wreck*). **4** (foll. by *of*) a wretched remnant or disorganized set of remains. **5** *Law* goods, etc., cast up by the sea. • *v.* **1** *tr.* cause the wreck of (a ship, etc.). **2** *tr.* completely ruin (hopes, chances, etc.). **3** *intr.* suffer a wreck. **4** *tr.* (as **wrecked** *adj.*) involved in a shipwreck (*wrecked sailors*). **5** *intr.* deal with wrecked vehicles, etc.

wreck•age /rékij/ *n.* **1** wrecked material. **2** the remnants of a wreck. **3** the action or process of wrecking.

wreck•er /rékər/ *n.* **1** a person or thing that wrecks or destroys. **2** a person employed in demolition, or in recovering a wrecked ship or its contents. **3** a person who breaks up damaged vehicles for spares and scrap. **4** a vehicle or train used in recovering a damaged one.

wren /ren/ *n.* any small, usu. brown, short-winged songbird of the family *Troglodytidae*, esp. *Troglodytes troglodytes* of Europe, having an erect tail.

wrench /rench/ *n. & v.* •*n.* **1** a violent twist or oblique pull or act of tearing off. **2** an adjustable tool for gripping and turning nuts, etc. **3** an instance of painful uprooting or parting (*leaving home was a great wrench*). **4** *Physics* a combination of a couple with the force along its axis. •*v.tr.* **1 a** twist or pull violently around or sideways. **b** injure (a limb, etc.) by undue straining; sprain. **2** (often foll. by *off, away,* etc.) pull off with a wrench. **3** seize or take forcibly. **4** distort (facts) to suit a theory, etc.

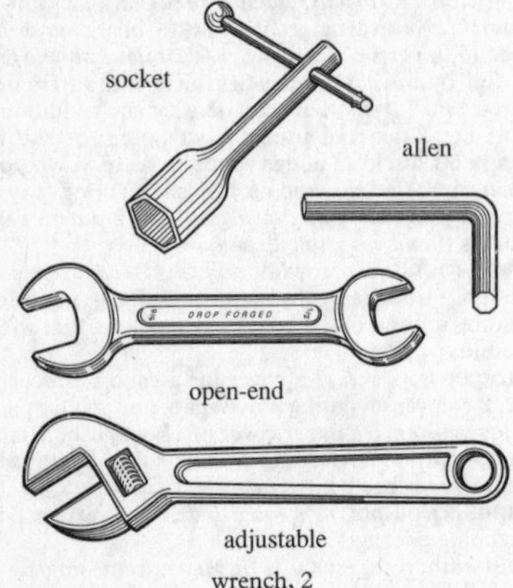

wrench, 2

wrest /rest/ *v.tr.* **1** force or wrench away from a person's grasp. **2** (foll. by *from*) obtain by effort or with difficulty. **3** distort into accordance with one's interests or views (*wrest the law to suit themselves*).

wres·tle /résəl/ *n. & v.* •*n.* **1** a contest in which two opponents grapple and try to throw each other to the ground. **2** a hard struggle. •*v.* **1** *intr.* (often foll. by *with*) take part in a wrestle. **2** *tr.* fight (a person) in a wrestle (*wrestled his opponent to the ground*). **3** *intr.* **a** (foll. by *with, against*) struggle; contend. **b** (foll. by *with*) do one's utmost to deal with (a task, difficulty, etc.). **4** *tr.* move with efforts as if wrestling. □□ **wres·tler** *n.* **wres·tling** *n.*

wretch /rech/ *n.* **1** a pitiable person. **2** (often as a playful term of depreciation) a contemptible person.

wretch·ed /réchid/ *adj.* (**wretcheder, wretchedest**) **1** miserable. **2** of bad quality; contemptible. **3** unsatisfactory or displeasing. □ **feel wretched 1** be unwell. **2** be much embarrassed. □□ **wretch·ed·ly** *adv.* **wretch·ed·ness** *n.*

wrig·gle /rígəl/ *v. & n.* •*v.* **1** *intr.* (of a worm, etc.) twist or turn its body with short, writhing movements. **2** *intr.* (of a person or animal) make wriggling motions. **3** *tr. & intr.* (foll. by *along,* etc.) move or go in this way (*wriggled into the corner; wriggled his hand into the hole*). **4** *tr.* make (one's way) by wriggling. **5** *intr.* practice evasion. •*n.* an act of wriggling. □ **wriggle out of** *colloq.* avoid on a contrived pretext. □□ **wrig·gler** *n.* **wrig·gly** *adj.*

wright /rīt/ *n.* a maker or builder (usu. in *comb.*: *playwright; shipwright*).

wring /ring/ *v. & n.* •*v.tr.* (*past* and *past part.* **wrung** /rung/) **1 a** squeeze tightly. **b** (often foll. by *out*) squeeze and twist. **2** twist forcibly; break by twisting. **3** distress or torture. **4** extract by squeezing. **5** (foll. by *out, from*) obtain by pressure or importunity; extort. •*n.* an act of wringing; a squeeze. □ **wring a person's hand** clasp it forcibly or press it with emotion. **wring one's hands** clasp them as a gesture of great distress.

wring·er /ríngər/ *n.* **1** a device for wringing water from washed clothes, etc. **2** a difficult ordeal (*that exam put me through the wringer*).

wring·ing /ríngìng/ *adj.* (in full **wringing wet**) so wet that water can be wrung out.

wrin·kle /ríngkəl/ *n. & v.* •*n.* **1** a slight crease in the skin such as is produced by age. **2** a similar mark in another flexible surface. **3** *colloq.* a useful tip or clever expedient. •*v.* **1** *tr.* make wrinkles in. **2** *intr.* form wrinkles; become marked with wrinkles.

wrin·kly /ríngklee/ *adj. & n.* •*adj.* (**wrinklier, wrinkliest**) having many wrinkles. •*n.* (also **wrin·klie**) (*pl.* **-klies**) *sl. offens.* an old or middle-aged person.

wrist /rist/ *n.* **1** the part connecting the hand with the forearm. **2** the corresponding part in an animal. **3** the part of a garment covering the wrist.

wrist·band /rístband/ *n.* a band forming or concealing the end of a shirt sleeve; a cuff.

wrist·watch /rístwoch/ *n.* a small watch worn on a strap around the wrist.

writ[1] /rit/ *n.* a form of written command in the name of a sovereign, court, government, etc. □ **serve a writ on** deliver a writ to (a person).

writ[2] /rit/ *archaic past part.* of WRITE. □ **writ large** in magnified or emphasized form.

write /rīt/ *v.* (*past* **wrote** /rōt/; *past part.* **written** /rít'n/) **1** *intr.* mark a surface by means of a pen, pencil, etc., with symbols, letters, or words. **2** *tr.* form (such symbols, etc.). **3** *tr.* form the symbols that represent or constitute (a word or sentence, or a document, etc.). **4** *tr.* fill or complete (a form, check, etc.) with writing. **5** *tr.* put (data) into a computer store. **6** *tr.* (esp. in *passive*) indicate (a quality or condition) by one's or its appearance (*guilt was written on his face*). **7** *tr.* compose (a text, article, novel, etc.) for written or printed reproduction or publication. **8** *intr.* be engaged in composing a text, article, etc. (*writes for the local newspaper*). **9** *intr.* (foll. by *to*) write and send a letter (to a recipient). **10** *tr. colloq.* write and send a letter to (a person) (*wrote him last week*). **11** *tr.* convey (news, information, etc.) by letter (*wrote that they would arrive next Friday*). **12** *tr.* state in written or printed form (*it is written that*). **13** *tr.* cause to be recorded. **14** *tr.* underwrite (an insurance policy). **15** *tr.* (foll. by *into, out of*) include or exclude (a character or episode) in a story by suitable changes of the text. □ **nothing to write home about** *colloq.* of little interest or value. **write in 1** send a suggestion, query, etc., in writing to an organization. **2** add (an extra name) on a list of candidates when voting. **write off 1** write and send a letter. **2** cancel the record of (a bad debt, etc.); acknowledge the loss of or failure to recover (an asset). **3** damage (a vehicle, etc.) so badly that it cannot be repaired. **4** compose with facility. **5** dismiss as insignificant. **write out 1** write in full or in finished form. **2** exhaust (oneself) by writing (*have written myself out*). **write up 1** write a full account of. **2** make a report (of a person) esp. to cite a violation of rules, etc. □□ **writ·a·ble** *adj.* **writ·er** *n.*

writ·er's block *n.* (of a writer) a temporary inability to proceed with the composition of a novel, play, etc.

writ·er's cramp *n.* a muscular spasm due to excessive writing.

write-up *n. colloq.* a written or published account; a review.

writhe /rīth/ *v. & n.* •*v.* **1** *intr.* twist or roll oneself about in or as if in acute pain. **2** *intr.* suffer severe mental discomfort or embarrassment. **3** *tr.* twist (one's body, etc.) about. •*n.* an act of writhing.

writ·ing /ríting/ *n.* **1** a group or sequence of letters or symbols. **2** = HANDWRITING. **3** the art or profession of literary composition. **4** (usu. in *pl.*) a piece of literary work done; a book, article, etc. □ **in writing** in written form. **the writing on the wall** an ominously significant event, etc. (see Dan. 5:5, 25-8).

writ·ten *past part.* of WRITE.

wrong /rawng, rong/ *adj., adv., n., & v.* • *adj.* **1** mistaken; not true; in error (*gave a wrong answer; we were wrong to think that*). **2** less or least desirable (*the wrong road; a wrong decision*). **3** contrary to law or morality (*it is wrong to steal*). **4** out of order; in or into a bad or abnormal condition (*something wrong with my heart*). • *adv.* (usually placed last) in a wrong manner or direction; with an incorrect result (*guessed wrong; told them wrong*). • *n.* **1** what is morally wrong; a wrong action. **2** injustice; unjust action or treatment (*suffer wrong*). • *v.tr.* **1** treat unjustly. **2** mistakenly attribute bad motives to. □ **do wrong** commit sin; transgress; offend. **do wrong to** malign or mistreat (a person). **get in wrong with** incur the dislike or disapproval of (a person). **get on the wrong side of** fall into disfavor with. **get wrong 1** misunderstand (a person, statement, etc.). **2** obtain an incorrect answer to. **get** (or **get hold of**) **the wrong end of the stick** misunderstand completely. **go down the wrong way** (of food) enter the windpipe instead of the esophagus. **go wrong 1** take the wrong path. **2** stop functioning properly. **3** depart from virtuous or suitable behavior. **in the wrong** responsible for a quarrel, mistake, or offense. **on the wrong side of 1** out of favor with (a person). **2** somewhat more than (a stated age). **wrong side out** inside out. **wrong way around** (or **round**) in the reverse of the normal or desirable orientation or sequence, etc. □□ **wrong·ly** *adv.* **wrong·ness** *n.*

wrong·do·er /ráwngdo͞oər, róng–/ *n.* a person who behaves immorally or illegally. □□ **wrong·do·ing** *n.*

wrong·ful /ráwngfo͝ol, róng–/ *adj.* **1** characterized by unfairness or injustice. **2** contrary to law. **3** (of a person) not entitled to the position, etc., occupied. □□ **wrong·ful·ly** *adv.*

wrong·head·ed /ráwnghedid, róng–/ *adj.* perverse and obstinate. □□ **wrong·head·ed·ness** *n.*

wrote *past* of WRITE.

wrought /rawt/ *adj.* (of metals) beaten out or shaped by hammering (from the *archaic past* and *past part.* of WORK.

wrought i·ron *n.* a tough malleable form of iron suitable for forging or rolling.

wrung *past* and *past part.* of WRING.

wry /rī/ *adj.* (**wryer, wryest** or **wrier, wriest**) **1** distorted or turned to one side. **2** (of a smile, etc.) contorted in disgust, disappointment, or mockery. **3** (of humor) dry and mocking. □□ **wry·ly** *adv.* **wry·ness** *n.*

WSW *abbr.* west-southwest.

wt. *abbr.* weight.

WV *abbr.* West Virginia (in official postal use).

W.Va. *abbr.* West Virginia.

WWW *abbr.* = WORLD WIDE WEB.

WY *abbr.* Wyoming (in official postal use).

Wyo. *abbr.* Wyoming.

WYS·I·WYG /wízeewig/ *adj.* (also **wysiwyg**) *Computing* denoting the representation of text onscreen exactly as it will appear on a printout (acronym of *w*hat *y*ou *s*ee *i*s *w*hat *y*ou *g*et).

X¹ /eks/ *n.* (also **x**) (*pl.* **Xs** or **X's**) **1** the twenty-fourth letter of the alphabet. **2** (as a Roman numeral) ten. **3** (usu. **x**) *Algebra* the first unknown quantity. **4** *Geom.* the first coordinate. **5** an unknown or unspecified number or person, etc. **6** a cross-shaped symbol esp. used to indicate position (*X marks the spot*) or incorrectness or to symbolize a kiss or a vote, or as the signature of a person who cannot write.

X² *symb.* = X-RATED.

X chro·mo·some /éks krṓməsōm/ *n.* a sex chromosome of which the number in female cells is twice that in male cells.

Xe *symb. Chem.* the element xenon.

xen·o·lith /zénəlith, zéénə–/ *n. Geol.* an inclusion within an igneous rock mass, usu. derived from the immediately surrounding rock.

xe·non /zénon, zéé–/ *n. Chem.* a heavy, colorless, odorless inert gaseous element occurring in traces in the atmosphere and used in fluorescent lamps. ¶ Symb.: **Xe**.

xen·o·phobe /zénəfōb, zéénə–/ *n.* a person given to xenophobia.

xen·o·pho·bi·a /zénəfṓbeeə, zéénə–/ *n.* a deep dislike of foreigners. ▫▫ **xen·o·pho·bic** *adj.*

xero- /zéérō/ *comb. form* dry.

xe·rog·ra·phy /zeerógrəfee/ *n.* a dry copying process in which powder adheres to parts of a surface remaining electrically charged after exposure of the surface to light from an image of the document to be copied. ▫▫ **xe·ro·graph·ic** /–rəgráfik/ *adj.*

xe·ro·phyte /zéérəfīt/ *n.* (also **xe·ro·phile** /–fīl/) a plant able to grow in very dry conditions.

Xe·rox /zééroks/ *n. & v.* • *n. Trademark* **1** a machine for copying by xerography. **2** a copy made using this machine. • *v.tr.* (**xerox**) reproduce by this process.

Xho·sa /kṓsə, –zə, káw–/ *n. & adj.* • *n.* **1** (*pl.* same or **Xhosas**) a member of a Bantu people of Cape Province, South Africa. **2** the Bantu language of this people. • *adj.* of or relating to this people or language.

xi /zī, sī, ksee/ *n.* the fourteenth letter of the Greek alphabet (Ξ, ξ).

Xmas /krísməs, éksməs/ *n. colloq.* = CHRISTMAS.

X-rat·ed *adj.* (usu. *attrib.*) (of motion pictures, etc.) classified as suitable for adults only.

X ray /éksray/ *n.* (also **X-ray, x-ray**) **1** (in *pl.*) electromagnetic radiation of short wavelength, able to pass through opaque bodies. **2** an image made by the effect of X rays on a photographic plate, esp. showing the position of bones, etc., by their greater absorption of the rays. ▫▫ **X-ray** *adj.* (also **x-ray**).

x-ray /éksray/ *v.tr.* (also **X-ray**) photograph, examine, or treat with X rays.

xy·lem /zílem/ *n. Bot.* woody tissue (cf. PHLOEM).

xy·lene /zíleen/ *n. Chem.* one of three isomeric hydrocarbons formed from benzene by the substitution of two methyl groups, obtained from wood tar or coal tar.

xylo- /zílō/ *comb. form* wood.

xy·lo·phone /zíləfōn/ *n.* a musical instrument of wooden or metal bars graduated in length and struck with a small wooden hammer or hammers. ▫▫ **xy·lo·phon·ist** *n.*

Y

Y[1] /wī/ *n.* (also **y**) (*pl.* **Ys** or **Y's**) **1** the twenty-fifth letter of the alphabet. **2** (usu. **y**) *Algebra* the second unknown quantity. **3** *Geom.* the second coordinate. **4 a** a Y-shaped thing, esp. an arrangement of lines, piping, roads, etc. **b** a forked clamp or support.

Y[2] *symb. Chem.* the element yttrium.

y. *abbr.* year(s).

-y[1] /ee/ *suffix* forming adjectives: **1** from nouns and adjectives, meaning: **a** full of; having the quality of (*messy*; *icy*; *horsy*). **b** addicted to (*boozy*). **2** from verbs, meaning 'inclined to,' 'apt to' (*runny*; *sticky*).

-y[2] /ee/ *suffix* (also **-ey, -ie**) forming diminutive nouns, pet names, etc. (*granny*; *nightie*; *Mickey*).

-y[3] /ee/ *suffix* forming nouns denoting: **1** state, condition, or quality (*courtesy*; *orthodoxy*; *modesty*). **2** an action or its result (*colloquy*; *remedy*; *subsidy*).

yacht /yot/ *n. & v.* • *n.* **1** a light sailing vessel, esp. equipped for racing. **2** a larger usu. power-driven vessel equipped for cruising. • *v.intr.* race or cruise in a yacht. ▫▫ **yacht·ing** *n.*

yachts·man /yótsmən/ *n.* (*pl.* **-men**; *fem.* **yachts·wom·an**, *pl.* **-women**) a person who owns a yacht or sails yachts.

yack /yak/ *n. & v.* (also **yack·e·ty-yack** /yákəteeyák/, **yak**) *sl. derog.* • *n.* trivial or unduly persistent conversation. • *v.intr.* engage in this.

ya·hoo /yaáhōō/ *n.* a coarse, rude, or brutish person.

Yah·weh /yaáway, –we/ *n.* (also **Yah·veh** /–vay, –ve/) the Hebrew name of God in the Old Testament.

yak[1] /yak/ *n.* a long-haired, humped Tibetan ox, *Bos grunniens*.

yak[2] *n. & v.* (**yakked, yakking**) var. of YACK.

yak·e·ty-yack var. of YACK.

y'all *pron.* var. of YOU-ALL.

yam /yam/ *n.* **1 a** any tropical or subtropical climbing plant of the genus *Dioscorea*. **b** the edible starchy tuber of this. **2** a sweet potato.

yam·mer /yámər/ *n. & v. colloq.* or *dial.* • *n.* **1** a lament, wail, or grumble. **2** voluble talk. • *v.intr.* **1** utter a yammer. **2** talk volubly.

yang /yang/ *n.* (in Chinese philosophy) the active male principle of the universe (cf. YIN).

Yank /yangk/ *n.* esp. *Brit. colloq.* often *derog.* an inhabitant of the US; an American.

yank /yangk/ *v. & n. colloq.* • *v.tr.* pull with a jerk. • *n.* a sudden hard pull.

Yan·kee /yángkee/ *n. colloq.* **1** often *derog.* = YANK. **2** an inhabitant of New England or one of the northern states. **3** *hist.* a federal Union soldier in the Civil War. **4** (*attrib.*) of or as of the Yankees.

yap /yap/ *v. & n.* • *v.intr.* (**yapped, yapping**) **1** bark shrilly or fussily. **2** *colloq.* talk noisily, foolishly, or complainingly. • *n.* **1** a sound of yapping. **2** *sl.* the mouth.

yard[1] /yaard/ *n.* **1** a unit of linear measure equal to 3 feet (0.9144 meter). **2** this length of material (*a yard and a half of fabric*). **3** a square or cubic yard, esp. (in building) of sand, etc. **4** a cylindrical spar tapering to each end slung across a mast for a sail to hang from. **5** (in *pl.*; foll. by *of*) *colloq.* a great length (*yards of spare wallpaper*).

yard[2] /yaard/ *n. & v.* • *n.* **1** a piece of ground, esp. attached to a building or used for a particular purpose. **2** the lawn and garden area of a house. **3** a pen or other enclosure for farm animals, livestock, etc. • *v.tr.* put (cattle) into a stockyard.

yard·age /yaárdij/ *n.* **1** a number of yards of material, etc. **2 a** the use of a stockyard, etc. **b** payment for this.

yard·arm /yaárdaarm/ *n.* the outer extremity of a ship's yard.

yard·bird /yaárdbərd/ *n. sl.* **1** a new military recruit. **2** a convict.

yard·man /yaárdmən/ *n.* (*pl.* **-men**) *n.* **1** a person working in a railroad yard or lumberyard. **2** a gardener or a person who does various outdoor jobs.

yard·stick /yaárdstik/ *n.* **1** a standard used for comparison. **2** a measuring rod a yard long, usu. divided into inches, etc.

yar·mul·ke /yaármәlkә, yaámәl–/ *n.* (also **yar·mul·ka**) a skullcap worn by Jewish men.

yarn /yaarn/ *n. & v.* • *n.* **1** any spun thread, esp. for knitting, weaving, rope making, etc. **2** *colloq.* a long or rambling story. • *v.intr. colloq.* tell yarns.

yar·row /yárō/ *n.* any perennial herb of the genus *Achillea*, esp. milfoil.

yash·mak /yaáshmaak, yáshmak/ *n.* a veil concealing the face except the eyes, worn by some Muslim women when in public.

yaw /yaw/ *v. & n.* • *v.intr.* (of a ship or aircraft, etc.) fail to hold a straight course; go unsteadily (esp. turning from side to side). • *n.* the yawing of a ship, etc., from its course.

yawl /yawl/ *n.* **1** a two-masted, fore-and-aft sailing vessel with the mizzenmast stepped far aft. **2** a small kind of fishing boat.

yawn /yawn/ *v. & n.* • *v.* **1** *intr.* (as a reflex) open the mouth wide and inhale, esp. when sleepy or bored. **2** *intr.* (of a chasm, etc.) gape; be wide open. **3** *tr.* utter with a yawn. • *n.* **1** an act of yawning. **2** *colloq.* a boring or tedious idea, activity, etc. ▫▫ **yawn·ing·ly** *adv.*

yaws /yawz/ *n.pl.* (usu. treated as *sing.*) a contagious tropical skin disease with large red swellings.

Yb *symb. Chem.* the element ytterbium.

Y chro·mo·some /wī-krṓməsōm/ *n.* a sex chromosome occurring only in male cells.

yd. *abbr.* yard (measure).

yds. *abbr.* yards (measure).

ye[1] /yee/ *pron. archaic pl.* of THOU[1]. ▫ **ye gods!** *joc.* an exclamation of astonishment.

ye[2] /yee/ *adj. pseudo-archaic* = THE (*ye olde tea shoppe*).

yea /yay/ *adv. & n. formal* • *adv.* **1** yes. **2** indeed (*ready, yea eager*). • *n.* an affirmative vote. ▫ **yea and nay** shilly-shally.

yeah /yeə/ *adv. colloq.* yes. ▫ **oh yeah?** expressing incredulity.

yean /yeen/ *v.tr. & intr. archaic* bring forth (a lamb or kid).

yean·ling /yeénling/ *n. archaic* a young lamb or kid.

year /yeer/ *n.* **1** (also **astronomical year, equinoctial year, natural year, solar year, tropical year**) the time occupied by the earth in one revolution around the sun, 365 days, 5 hours, 48 minutes, and 46 seconds in length. **2** (also **calendar year, civil year**) the period of 365 days (**common year**) or 366 days (see LEAP YEAR) from Jan. 1 to Dec. 31, used for reckoning time in ordinary affairs. **3 a** a period of the same length as this starting at any point (*four years ago*). **b** such a period in terms of a particular activity, etc., occupying its duration (*school year; tax year*). **4** (in *pl.*) age or time of life (*young for his years*). **5** (usu. in *pl.*) *colloq.* a very long time (*it took years to get served*). **6** a group of students entering college, etc., in the same academic year. □ **of the year** chosen as outstanding in a particular year (*sportsman of the year*). **a year and a day** the period specified in some legal matters to ensure the completion of a full year. **year in, year out** continually over a period of years.

year·book /yéerbŏŏk/ *n.* **1** an annual publication dealing with events or aspects of the (usu. preceding) year. **2** such a publication, usu. produced by a school's graduating class and featuring students, activities, sports, etc.

year·ling /yéerling/ *n. & adj.* • *n.* **1** an animal between one and two years old. **2** a racehorse in the calendar year after the year of foaling. • *adj.* a year old; having existed or been such for a year (*a yearling heifer*).

year·long /yéerlóng/ *adj.* lasting a year or the whole year.

year·ly /yéerlee/ *adj. & adv.* • *adj.* **1** done, produced, or occurring once a year. **2** of or lasting a year. • *adv.* once a year; from year to year.

yearn /yərn/ *v.intr.* **1** (usu. foll. by *for*, *after*, or *to* + infin.) have a strong emotional longing. **2** (usu. foll. by *to*, *toward*) be filled with compassion or tenderness. □□ **yearn·ing** *n. & adj.* **yearn·ing·ly** *adv.*

year-round *adj.* existing, etc., throughout the year.

yeast /yeest/ *n.* **1** a grayish-yellow fungous substance obtained esp. from fermenting malt liquors and used as a fermenting agent, to raise bread, etc. **2** any of various unicellular fungi in which vegetative reproduction takes place by budding or fission. □□ **yeast·like** *adj.*

yeast·y /yéestee/ *adj.* (**yeastier, yeastiest**) **1** frothy or tasting like yeast. **2** in a ferment. **3** working like yeast. **4** (of talk, etc.) light and superficial.

yell /yel/ *n. & v.* • *n.* **1** a loud sharp cry of pain, anger, fright, encouragement, delight, etc. **2** a shout. **3** an organized cry, used esp. to support a sports team. • *v.tr. & intr.* utter with or make a yell.

yel·low /yélō/ *adj., n., & v.* • *adj.* **1** of the color between green and orange in the spectrum, of buttercups, lemons, egg yolks, or gold. **2** of the color of faded leaves, ripe wheat, etc. **3** having a yellow skin or complexion. **4** *colloq.* cowardly. **5** (of looks, feelings, etc.) jealous, envious, or suspicious. **6** (of newspapers, etc.) unscrupulously sensational. • *n.* **1** a yellow color or pigment. **2** yellow clothes or material (*dressed in yellow*). **3 a** a yellow ball, piece, etc., in a game or sport. **b** the player using such pieces. **4** (usu. in *comb.*) a yellow moth or butterfly. • *v.tr. & intr.* make or become yellow. □□ **yel·low·ish** *adj.* **yel·low·ness** *n.* **yel·low·y** *adj.*

yel·low-bel·lied *adj.* **1** *colloq.* cowardly. **2** (of a fish, bird, etc.) having yellow underparts.

yel·low·bel·ly /yélōbélee/ *n.* **1** *colloq.* a coward. **2** any of various fish with yellow underparts.

yel·low fe·ver *n.* a tropical virus disease causing fever and jaundice.

yel·low·ham·mer /yélōhamər/ *n.* a bunting, *Emberiza citrinella*, of which the male has a yellow head, neck, and breast.

yel·low jack·et *n.* **1** any of various wasps of the family Vespidae with yellow and black bands. **2** sl. a capsule of phenobarbital.

yel·low jour·nali·sm *n.* journalism that is based on sensationalism.

Yel·low Pag·es *n.pl.* (also **yel·low pag·es**) a telephone directory on yellow paper and listing business subscribers according to the goods or services they offer.

yel·low streak *n. colloq.* a trace of cowardice.

yelp /yelp/ *n. & v.* • *n.* a sharp, shrill cry of or as of a dog in pain or excitement. • *v.intr.* utter a yelp.

yen[1] /yen/ *n.* (*pl.* same) the chief monetary unit of Japan.

yen[2] /yen/ *n. & v. colloq.* • *n.* a longing or yearning. • *v.intr.* (**yenned, yenning**) feel a longing.

yeo·man /yṓmən/ *n.* (*pl.* **-men**) **1** esp. *hist.* a man holding and cultivating a small landed estate. **2** *Brit. hist.* a person qualified by possessing free land of an annual value of 40 shillings to serve on juries. **3** *Brit.* a member of the yeomanry force. **4** *hist.* a servant in a royal or noble household. **5** in the US Navy, a petty officer performing clerical duties on board ship.

yeo·man of the guard *n.* **1** a member of the British sovereign's bodyguard. **2** (in general use) a warder in the Tower of London.

yeo·man ser·vice *n.* (also **yeoman's service**) efficient or useful help in need.

yep /yep/ *adv. & n.* (also **yup** /yup/) *colloq.* = YES.

yes /yes/ *adv. & n.* • *adv.* **1** equivalent to an affirmative sentence: the answer to your question is affirmative; it is as you say or as I have said; the statement, etc., made is correct; the request or command will be complied with; the negative statement, etc., made is not corre **2** (in answer to a summons or address) an acknowledgment of one's presence. • *n.* an utterance of the word *yes*. □ **say yes** grant a request or confirm a statement. **yes? 1** indeed? is that so? **2** what do you want? **yes and no** that is partly true and partly untrue.

yes-man *n.* (*pl.* **-men**) *colloq.* a weakly acquiescent person.

yes·ter·day /yéstərday/ *adv. & n.* • *adv.* **1** on the day before today. **2** in the recent past. • *n.* **1** the day before today. **2** the recent past.

yes·ter·year /yéstəryeer/ *n. literary* **1** last year. **2** the recent past.

yet /yet/ *adv. & conj.* • *adv.* **1** as late as, or until, now or then (*there is yet time; your best work yet*). **2** (with *neg.* or *interrog.*) so soon as, or by, now or then (*it is not time yet; have you finished yet?*). **3** again; in addition (*more and yet more*). **4** in the remaining time available; before all is over (*I will do it yet*). **5** (foll. by *compar.*) even (*a yet more difficult task*). **6** nevertheless; and in spite of that; but for all that (*it is strange, and yet it is true*). • *conj.* but at the same time; but nevertheless (*I won, yet what good has it done?*).

yet·i /yétee/ *n.* = ABOMINABLE SNOWMAN.

yew /yōō/ *n.* **1** any dark-leaved evergreen coniferous tree of the genus *Taxus*, having seeds enclosed in a fleshy red aril, and often planted in landscaped settings. **2** its wood, used formerly as a material for bows and still in cabinetmaking.

Yid·dish /yídish/ *n. & adj.* • *n.* a vernacular used by Jews in or from central and eastern Europe, orig. a German dialect with words from Hebrew and several modern languages. • *adj.* of or relating to this language.

yield /yeeld/ *v. & n.* • *v.* **1** *tr.* (also *absol.*) produce or return as a fruit, profit, or result (*the land yields crops; the land yields poorly; the investment yields 15%*). **2** *tr.* give up; surrender; concede; comply with a demand for (*yielded the fortress; yielded themselves prisoners*). **3** *intr.* (often foll. by *to*) **a** surrender; make submission. **b** give consent or change one's course of action in deference to; respond as required to (*yielded to persuasion*). **4** *intr.* (foll. by *to*) be inferior or confess inferiority to (*I yield to none in understanding the problem*). **5** *intr.* (foll. by *to*) give right of way to other traffic. **6** *intr.* allow another the right to speak in a debate, etc. • *n.* an amount yielded or produced; an output or return. □□ **yield·er** *n.*

yield·ing /yeélding/ *adj.* **1** compliant, submissive. **2** (of a substance) able to bend; not stiff nor rigid.

yin /yin/ *n.* (in Chinese philosophy) the passive female principle of the universe (cf. YANG).

yin and yang

yip·pee /yíppeé/ *int.* expressing delight or excitement.

yip·pie /yípee/ *n.* a hippie associated with political activism, esp. as a member of a radical organization (acronym of *Y*outh *I*nternational *P*arty).

-yl /əl/ *suffix Chem.* forming nouns denoting a radical (*ethyl*; *hydroxyl*; *phenyl*).

YMCA *abbr.* Young Men's Christian Association.

yo /yō/ *int.* used to call attention, express affirmation, or greet informally.

yo·del /yṓd'l/ *v.* & *n.* • *v.tr.* & *intr.* sing with melodious inarticulate sounds and frequent changes between falsetto and the normal voice in the manner of the Swiss mountain-dwellers. • *n.* a yodeling cry. ▫▫ **yo·del·er** *n.*

yo·ga /yṓgə/ *n.* a Hindu system of philosophic meditation and asceticism, a part of which includes the adoption of specific bodily postures.

yo·gi /yṓgee/ *n.* a person proficient in yoga. ▫▫ **yo·gism** *n.*

yo·gurt /yṓgərt/ *n.* (also **yo·ghurt**) a semisolid sourish food prepared from milk fermented by added bacteria.

yoke /yōk/ *n.* & *v.* • *n.* **1** a wooden crosspiece fastened over the necks of two oxen, etc., and attached to the plow or wagon to be drawn. **2** (*pl.* same or **yokes**) a pair (of oxen, etc.). **3** an object like a yoke in form or function, e.g., a wooden shoulder-piece for carrying a pair of pails, the top section of a dress or skirt, etc., from which the rest hangs. **4** sway, dominion, or servitude, esp. when oppressive. **5** a bond of union, esp. that of marriage. **6** a crossbar on which a bell swings. **7** the crossbar of a rudder to whose ends ropes are fastened. • *v.* **1** *tr.* put a yoke on. **2** *tr.* couple or unite (a pair). **3** *tr.* (foll. by *to*) link (one thing) to (another). **4** *intr.* match or work together.

yo·kel /yṓkəl/ *n.* a rustic; a country bumpkin.

yolk /yōk/ *n.* **1** the yellow internal part of an egg that nourishes the young before it hatches. **2** *Biol.* the corresponding part of any animal ovum. ▫▫ **yolked** *adj.* (also in *comb.*). **yolk·less** *adj.* **yolk·y** *adj.*

Yom Kip·pur /yawm kípər, keepṓor, yōm, yom/ *n.* a Jewish high holy day of fasting and atonement.

yon /yon/ *adj., adv.,* & *pron. literary* & *dial.* • *adj.* & *adv.* yonder. • *pron.* yonder person or thing.

yon·der /yóndər/ *adv.* & *adj.* • *adv.* over there; at some distance in that direction; in the place indicated by pointing, etc. • *adj.* situated yonder.

yoo-hoo /yṓohṓo/ *int.* used to attract a person's attention.

yore /yawr/ *n. literary* ▫ **of yore** formerly; in or of old days.

York·shire pud·ding /yáwrksheer/ *n.* a popover made of unsweetened egg batter and often eaten with roast beef.

York·shire ter·ri·er /yáwrksheer/ *n.* a small, long-haired, blue-gray and tan kind of terrier.

Yo·ru·ba /yáwrəbə/ *n.* **1** a member of a black African people inhabiting the west coast, esp. Nigeria. **2** the language of this people.

you /yoo/ *pron.* (*obj.* **you**; *poss.* **your, yours**) **1** used with reference to the person or persons addressed or one such person and one or more associated persons. **2** (as *int.* with a noun) in an exclamatory statement (*you fools!*). **3** (in general statements) one, a person, anyone, or everyone (*it's bad at first, but you get used to it*).

you-all (often **y'all** esp. *Southern US colloq.*) *pron.* you (usu. more than one person).

you and yours *pron.* you together with your family, property, etc.

you'd /yood/ *contr.* **1** you had. **2** you would.

you-know-what *n.* (also **you-know-who**) something or someone unspecified but understood.

you'll /yool, yool/ *contr.* you will; you shall.

young /yung/ *adj.* & *n.* • *adj.* (**younger** /yúnggər/; **youngest** /yúnggist/) **1** not far advanced in life, development, or existence; not yet old. **2** immature or inexperienced. **3** felt in or characteristic of youth (*young love*; *young ambition*). **4** representing young people (*Young Republicans*; *young America*). **5** distinguishing a son from his father (*young Jones*). **6** (**younger**) distinguishing one person from another of the same name (*the younger Davis*). • *n.* (*collect.*) offspring, esp. of animals before or soon after birth. ▫ **with young** (of an animal) pregnant. ▫▫ **young·ish** *adj.*

young·ster /yúngstər/ *n.* a child or young person.

young thing *n. archaic* or *colloq.* an indulgent term for a young person.

Young Turk *n.* **1** a member of a revolutionary party in Turkey in 1908. **2** a young person eager for radical change to the established order.

young 'un *n. colloq.* a youngster.

your /yoor, yawr/ *poss.pron.* (*attrib.*) **1** of or belonging to you (*your house*; *your own business*). **2** *colloq.* usu. *derog.* much talked of; well known (*none so fallible as your self-styled expert*).

you're /yoor, yawr/ *contr.* you are.

yours /yoorz, yawrz/ *poss.pron.* **1** the one or ones belonging to or associated with you (*it is yours*; *yours are over there*). **2** your letter (*yours of the 10th*). **3** introducing a formula ending a letter (*yours ever*; *yours truly*). ▫ **of yours** of or belonging to you (*a friend of yours*).

your·self /yoorsélf, yawr–/ *pron.* (*pl.* **yourselves** /–sélvz/) **1 a** *emphat. form* of YOU. **b** *refl. form* of YOU. **2** in your normal state of body or mind (*are quite yourself again*). ▫ **be yourself** act in your normal, unconstrained manner. **how's yourself?** *sl.* how are you? (esp. after answering a similar inquiry).

youth /yooth/ *n.* (*pl.* **youths** /yoothz/) **1** the state of being young; the period between childhood and adult age. **2** the vigor or enthusiasm, inexperience, or other characteristic of this period. **3** an early stage of development, etc. **4** a young person (esp. male). **5** (*pl.*) young people collectively (*the youth of the country*).

youth·ful /yṓothfool/ *adj.* **1** young, esp. in appearance or manner. **2** having the characteristics of youth (*youthful impatience*). **3** having the freshness or vigor of youth (*a youthful complexion*). ▫▫ **youth·ful·ly** *adv.* **youth·ful·ness** *n.*

youth hos·tel *n.* a place where (esp. young) travelers can put up cheaply for the night. ▫▫ **youth hos·tel·er** *n.*

you've /yoov, yoov/ *contr.* you have.

yowl /yowl/ *n.* & *v.* • *n.* a loud, wailing cry of or as of a cat or dog in pain or distress. • *v.intr.* utter a yowl.

yo-yo /yṓyō/ *n.* & *v.* • *n.* (*pl.* **yo-yos**) **1** *Trademark* a toy consisting of a pair of disks with a deep groove between them in which string is attached and wound, and which can be spun alternately downward and upward by its weight and momentum as the string unwinds and rewinds. **2** a thing that repeatedly falls and rises again. • *v.intr.* (**yo-yoes, yo-yoed, yo-yoing**) **1** play with a yo-yo. **2** move up and down; fluctuate.

yr. *abbr.* **1** year(s). **2** your. **3** younger.

yrs. *abbr.* **1** years. **2** yours.

yt·ter·bi·um /itə́rbeeəm/ *n. Chem.* a silvery metallic element of the lanthanide series occurring naturally as various isotopes. ¶ Symb.: **Yb.**

yt·tri·um /ítreeəm/ *n. Chem.* a grayish metallic element resembling the lanthanides, occurring naturally in uranium ores and used in making superconductors. ¶ Symb.: **Y.**

yu·an /yŏŏ-áan, yö–/ *n.* (*pl.* same) the chief monetary unit of China.

yuc·ca /yúkə/ *n.* any American white-flowered liliaceous plant of the genus *Yucca*, with swordlike leaves.

yuck /yuk/ *int. & n. sl.* • *int.* an expression of strong distaste or disgust. • *n.* something messy or repellent.

yuck·y /yúkee/ *adj.* (**-ier, -iest**) *sl.* **1** messy; repellent. **2** sickly; sentimental.

Yu·go·slav /yṓōgəslaav/ *n. & adj.* (also **Ju·go·slav**) *hist.* • *n.* **1** a native or national of the former republic of Yugoslavia. **2** a person of Yugoslav descent. • *adj.* of or relating to Yugoslavia or its people. ▫▫ **Yu·go·sla·vi·an** *adj. & n.*

yule /yōōl/ *n.* (in full **yuletide**) *archaic* the Christmas festival.

Yule log *n.* **1** a large log burned in the hearth on Christmas Eve. **2** a log-shaped cake eaten at Christmas.

Yu·ma /yṓōmə/ *n.* **1 a** a N. American people native to Arizona. **b** a member of this people. **2** the language of this people.

yum·my /yúmee/ *adj.* (**yummier, yummiest**) *colloq.* tasty; delicious.

yum-yum /yúmyúm/ *int.* expressing pleasure from eating or the prospect of eating.

yup var. of YEP.

yup·pie /yúpee/ *n. & adj.* (also **yup·py**) (*pl.* **-pies**) *colloq.*, usu. *derog.* • *n.* a young, middle-class professional person working in a city. • *adj.* characteristic of a yuppie or yuppies (from *y*oung *u*rban *p*rofessional).

yurt /yərt/ *n.* **1** a circular tent of felt, skins, etc., on a collapsible framework, used by nomads in Mongolia and Siberia. **2** a semisubterranean hut, usu. of timber covered with earth or turf.

YWCA *abbr.* Young Women's Christian Association.

Z

Z /zee/ *n.* (also **z**) (*pl.* **Zs** or **Z's**) **1** the twenty-sixth letter of the alphabet. **2** (usu. **z**) *Algebra* the third unknown quantity. **3** *Geom.* the third coordinate. **4** *Chem.* atomic number.

zag /zag/ *n.* & *v.* •*n.* a sharp change of direction in a zigzag course. •*v.intr.* (**zagged, zagging**) move in one of the two directions in a zigzag course.

za·ny /záynee/ *adj.* & *n.* •*adj.* (**zanier, zaniest**) comically idiotic; crazily ridiculous. •*n.* a buffoon or jester. ◻◻ **za·ni·ly** *adv.* **za·ni·ness** *n.*

zap /zap/ *v., n., & int. sl.* •*v.* (**zapped, zapping**) **1** *tr.* **a** kill or destroy; deal a sudden blow to. **b** hit forcibly (*zapped the ball over the net*). **c** send an electric current, radiation, etc., through (someone or something). **2** *intr.* move quickly and vigorously. **3** *tr.* overwhelm emotionally. **4** *tr. Computing* erase or change (an item in a program). **5** *intr.* (foll. by *through*) fast-forward a videotape to skip a section. **6** *tr.* heat or cook (food) by microwave. **7** *tr.* change (television channels) by remote control. •*n.* **1** energy; vigor. **2** a strong emotional effect. •*int.* expressing the sound or impact of a bullet, ray gun, etc., or any sudden event.

zap·per /zápər/ *n. colloq.* a hand-held remote-control device for changing television channels, adjusting volume, etc.

Zar·a·thus·tri·an var. of ZOROASTRIAN.

zeal /zeel/ *n.* **1** earnestness or fervor in advancing a cause or rendering service. **2** hearty and persistent endeavor.

zeal·ot /zélət/ *n.* **1** an uncompromising or extreme partisan; a fanatic. **2** (**Zealot**) *hist.* a member of an ancient Jewish sect aiming at a world Jewish theocracy and resisting the Romans until AD 70. ◻◻ **zeal·ot·ry** *n.*

zeal·ous /zéləs/ *adj.* full of zeal; enthusiastic. ◻◻ **zeal·ous·ly** *adv.* **zeal·ous·ness** *n.*

ze·bra /zeebrə/ *n.* (*pl.* same or **zebras**) **1** any of various African quadrupeds, esp. *Equus burchelli*, related to the ass and horse, with black and white stripes. **2** (*attrib.*) with alternate dark and pale stripes.

ze·bu /zéeboo/ *n.* a humped ox, *Bos indicus*, of India, E. Asia, and Africa.

zed /zed/ *n. Brit.* the letter Z.

zee /zee/ *n.* the letter Z.

Zen /zen/ *n.* a form of Mahayana Buddhism emphasizing the value of meditation and intuition. ◻◻ **Zen·ist** *n.* (also **Zen·nist**).

ze·nith /zéenith/ *n.* **1** the part of the celestial sphere directly above an observer (opp. NADIR). **2** the highest point in one's fortunes; a time of great prosperity, etc.

ze·o·lite /zéeəlīt/ *n.* each of a number of minerals consisting mainly of hydrous silicates of calcium, sodium, and aluminum, able to act as cation exchangers. ◻◻ **ze·o·lit·ic** /–lítik/ *adj.*

zeph·yr /zéfər/ *n.* **1** *literary* a mild gentle wind or breeze. **2** a fine cotton fabric. **3** an athlete's thin gauzy jersey.

zep·pe·lin /zépəlin/ *n. hist.* a large German dirigible airship of the early 20th c., orig. for military use.

ze·ro /zéerō/ *n.* & *v.* •*n.* (*pl.* **-ros**) **1 a** the figure 0; naught. **b** no quantity or number; nil. **2** a point on the scale of an instrument from which a positive or negative quantity is reckoned. **3** (*attrib.*) having a value of zero; no; not any (*zero population growth*). **4** (in full **zero hour**) **a** the hour at which a planned, esp. military, operation is timed to begin. **b** a crucial moment. **5** the lowest point; a nullity or nonentity. •*v.tr.* (**-roes, -roed**) **1** adjust (an instrument, etc.) to zero point. **2** set the sights of (a gun) for firing. ◻ **zero in on 1** take aim at. **2** focus one's attention on.

ze·ro-sum *adj.* (of a game, political situation, etc.) in which whatever is gained by one side is lost by the other so that the net change is always zero.

zest /zest/ *n.* **1** piquancy; a stimulating flavor or quality. **2 a** keen enjoyment or interest. **b** (often foll. by *for*) relish. **c** gusto (*entered into it with zest*). **3** a scraping of orange or lemon peel as flavoring. ◻◻ **zest·ful** *adj.* **zest·ful·ly** *adv.* **zest·ful·ness** *n.* **zest·y** *adj.* (**zestier, zestiest**).

ze·ta /záytə, zée–/ *n.* the sixth letter of the Greek alphabet (Z, ζ).

zeug·ma /zoogmə/ *n.* a figure of speech using a verb or adjective with two nouns, to one of which it is strictly applicable while the word appropriate to the other is not used (e.g., *with weeping eyes and hearts*) (cf. SYLLEPSIS). ◻◻ **zeug·mat·ic** /–mátik/ *adj.*

zi·do·vu·dine /zīdóvyoodeen/ *n.* = AZT.

zig·gu·rat /zígərat/ *n.* a rectangular stepped tower in ancient Mesopotamia, surmounted by a temple.

zig·zag /zígzag/ *n., adj., adv., & v.* •*n.* **1** a line or course having abrupt alternate right and left turns. **2** (often in *pl.*) each of these turns. •*adj.* having the form of a zigzag; alternating right and left. •*adv.* with a zigzag course. *v.intr.* (**zigzagged, zigzagging**) move in a zigzag course.

zilch /zilch/ *n. sl.* nothing.

zil·lion /zílyən/ *n. colloq.* an indefinite large number. ◻◻ **zil·lionth** *adj.* & *n.*

zinc /zingk/ *n. Chem.* a white metallic element occurring naturally as zinc blende, and used as a component of brass, in galvanizing sheet iron, and in electric batteries. ¶ Symb.: **Zn.** ◻◻ **zinced** *adj.*

zinc ox·ide *n.* a powder used as a white pigment and in medicinal ointments.

zing /zing/ *n.* & *v. colloq.* •*n.* vigor; energy. •*v.intr.* move swiftly or with a shrill sound. ◻◻ **zing·y** *adj.* (**zingier, zingiest**).

zing·er /zíngər/ *n. sl.* **1** a witty retort. **2** an unexpected or startling announcement, etc. **3** an outstanding person or thing.

zin·ni·a /zíneeə/ *n.* a composite plant of the genus *Zinnia*, with showy rayed flowers of deep red and other colors.

Zi·on /zíən/ *n.* (also **Si·on** /síən/) **1** the hill of Jerusalem on which the city of David was built. **2 a** the Jewish people or religion. **b** the Christian church. **3** (in Christian thought) the kingdom of God in heaven.

Zi·on·ism /zíənizəm/ *n.* a movement (orig.) for the reestablishment and (now) the development of a Jewish nation in what is now Israel. ◻◻ **Zi·on·ist** *n.*

zip /zip/ *n.* & *v.* •*n.* **1** a light fast sound, as of a bullet passing through air. **2** energy; vigor. **3** *Brit.* (in full **zip fastener**) = ZIPPER. •*v.* (**zipped, zipping**) **1** *tr.* & *intr.* (often foll. by *up*) fasten with a zipper. **2** *intr.* move with zip or at high speed.

zip code /zip/ *n.* (also **ZIP code**) a US system of postal codes consisting of five-digit or nine-digit numbers.
zip·per /zípər/ *n. & v.* • *n.* a fastening device of two flexible strips with interlocking projections closed or opened by pulling a slide along them. • *v.tr.* (often foll. by *up*) fasten with a zipper. ▫▫ **zip·pered** *adj.*
zip·py /zípee/ *adj.* (**zippier, zippiest**) *colloq.* **1** bright; fresh; lively. **2** fast; speedy. ▫▫ **zip·pi·ly** *adv.* **zip·pi·ness** *n.*
zir·con /zə́rkon/ *n.* a zirconium silicate of which some translucent varieties are cut into gems.
zir·co·ni·um /zərkṓneeəm/ *n. Chem.* a gray metallic element occurring naturally in zircon and used in various industrial applications. ¶ Symb.: **Zr.**
zit /zit/ *n. sl.* a pimple.
zith·er /zíthər/ *n.* a musical instrument consisting of a flat wooden sound box with numerous strings stretched across it, a few of which may be stopped on a fretted fingerboard, placed horizontally and played with the fingers and a plectrum. ▫▫ **zith·er·ist** *n.*
zlo·ty /zláwtee/ *n.* (*pl.* same or **zlotys**) the chief monetary unit of Poland.
Zn *symb. Chem.* the element zinc.
zo·di·ac /zṓdeeak/ *n.* **1 a** a belt of the heavens limited by lines about 8° from the ecliptic on each side, including all apparent positions of the sun, moon, and planets as known to ancient astronomers, and divided into twelve equal parts (**signs of the zodiac**), each formerly containing the similarly named constellation but now by precession of the equinoxes coinciding with the constellation that bears the name of the preceding sign: Aries, Taurus, Gemini, Cancer, Leo, Virgo, Libra, Scorpio, Sagittarius, Capricorn(us), Aquarius, Pisces. **b** a diagram of these signs. **2** a complete cycle, circuit, or compass.
zo·di·a·cal /zədíəkəl/ *adj.* of or in the zodiac.
zo·ic /zṓik/ *adj.* **1** of or relating to animals. **2** *Geol.* (of rock, etc.) containing fossils; with traces of animal or plant life.
zom·bie /zómbee/ *n.* **1** *colloq.* a dull or apathetic person. **2** a corpse said to be revived by witchcraft.
zone /zōn/ *n. & v.* • *n.* **1** an area having particular features, properties, purpose, or use (*danger zone*; *erogenous zone*; *smokeless zone*). **2** any well-defined region of more or less beltlike form. **3 a** an area between two exact or approximate concentric circles. **b** a part of the surface of a sphere enclosed between two parallel planes, or of a cone or cylinder, etc., between such planes cutting it perpendicularly to the axis. **4** (in full **time zone**) a range of longitudes where a common standard time is used. **5** *Geol.*, etc. a range between specified limits of depth, height, etc., esp. a section of strata distinguished by characteristic fossils. **6** *Geog.* any of five divisions of the earth bounded by circles parallel to the equator (see FRIGID, TEMPERATE, TORRID). **7** an encircling band or stripe distinguishable in color, texture, or character from the rest of the object encircled. • *v.tr.* **1** encircle as or with a zone. **2** arrange or distribute by zones. **3** assign as or to a particular area. ▫▫ **zon·al** *adj.* **zon·ing** *n.* (in sense 3 of *v.*).
zonked /zongkt/ *adj. sl.* (often foll. by *out*) exhausted; intoxicated.
zoo /zo͞o/ *n.* a zoological garden.
zoo- /zṓə/ *comb. form* of animals or animal life.
zo·oid /zṓ-oyd/ *n.* **1** a more or less independent invertebrate organism arising by budding or fission. **2** a distinct member of an invertebrate colony. ▫▫ **zo·oi·dal** /–óyd'l/ *adj.*
zool. *abbr.* **1** zoological. **2** zoology.
zo·o·log·i·cal /zṓəlójikəl/ *adj.* of or relating to zoology. ▫▫ **zo·o·log·i·cal·ly** *adv.*
zo·ol·o·gy /zō-óləjee/ *n.* the scientific study of animals, esp. with reference to their structure, physiology, classification, and distribution. ▫▫ **zo·ol·o·gist** *n.*
zoom /zo͞om/ *v. & n.* • *v.* **1** *intr.* move quickly, esp. with a buzzing sound. **2 a** *intr.* cause an airplane to mount at high speed and a steep angle. **b** *tr.* cause (an airplane) to do this. **3 a** *intr.* (of a camera) close up rapidly from a long shot to a close-up. **b** *tr.* cause (a lens or camera) to do this. • *n.* **1** an airplane's steep climb. **2** a zooming camera shot.
zoom lens *n.* a lens allowing a camera to zoom by varying the focal length.
zo·o·mor·phic /zṓəmáwrfik/ *adj.* **1** dealing with or represented in animal forms. **2** having gods of animal form. ▫▫ **zo·o·mor·phism** *n.*
zo·o·phyte /zṓəfīt/ *n.* a plantlike animal, esp. a coral, sea anemone, or sponge. ▫▫ **zo·o·phyt·ic** /–fítik/ *adj.*
zo·o·plank·ton /zṓəplángktən/ *n.* plankton consisting of animals.
Zo·ro·as·tri·an /záwrō-ástreeən/ *adj. & n.* (also **Za·ra·thus·tri·an** /zárəthóostreeən/) • *adj.* of or relating to Zoroaster (or Zarathustra) or the dualistic religious system taught by him or his followers in the Zend-Avesta, sacred writings based on the concept of a conflict between a spirit of light and good and a spirit of darkness and evil. • *n.* a follower of Zoroaster.
ZPG *abbr.* zero population growth.
Zr *symb. Chem.* the element zirconium.
zuc·chi·ni /zo͞okéenee/ *n.* (*pl.* same or **zucchinis**) a green variety of smooth-skinned summer squash.
Zu·lu /zo͞olo͞o/ *n. & adj.* • *n.* **1** a member of a black South African people orig. inhabiting Zululand and Natal. **2** the language of this people. • *adj.* of or relating to this people or language.
Zu·ni /zo͞onee/ *n.* (also **Zuñi** /zo͞onyee/) **1 a** a N. American people native to New Mexico. **b** a member of this people. **2** the language of this people.
zwie·back /zwíbak, –baak, zwée–, swí–, swée–/ *n.* a kind of rusk or biscuit toasted in slices.
zy·go·mat·ic bone *n.* the bone that forms the prominent part of the cheek.
zy·gote /zígōt, zíg–/ *n. Biol.* a cell formed by the union of two gametes. ▫▫ **zy·got·ic** /–gótik/ *adj.* **zy·got·i·cal·ly** /–gótikəlee/ *adv.*

Biographical Entries

Aar·on /áirən/, **Hank (Henry Louis)** 1934– ; U.S. baseball player.
Ab·e·lard /ábəlaard/, **Peter** 1079–1142; French theologian and philosopher.
A·bra·ham /áybrəham/ Hebrew patriarch.
A·che·be /aacháybay/, **Chinua** (born **Albert Chinualumgu**) 1930– ; Nigerian author.
Ach·e·son /áchəsən/, **Dean Gooderham** 1893–1971; U.S. secretary of state (1949–53).
Ad·ams /ádəmz/, **Ansel Easton** 1902–84; U.S. photographer.
Ad·ams family of U.S. politicians, including: **1** John 1735–1826; 2nd president of the U.S. (1797–1801); father of: **2** John Quincy 1767–1848; 6th president of the U.S. (1825–29).
Ad·ams, Samuel 1722–1803; U.S. patriot.
Ad·dams /ádəmz/, **Jane** 1860–1935; U.S. social worker.
Ad·di·son /ádəsən/, **Joseph** 1672–1719; English author.
A·de·nau·er /aád-nowər, ád–/, **Konrad** 1876–1967; chancellor of West Germany (1949–63).
Ad·ler /ádlər/, **Alfred** 1870–1937; Austrian psychiatrist.
Ael·fric /álfrik/ c. 955–c. 1020; English abbot, author, and grammarian.
Aes·chy·lus /éskələs/ c. 525–c. 456 B.C.; Greek playwright.
Ae·sop /éesaap, –səp/ 6th cent. B.C.; Greek writer of fables.
Ag·as·siz /ágəsee/, **(Jean) Louis** 1807–73; U.S. naturalist, born in Switzerland.
Ag·new /ágnoo/, **Spiro Theodore** 1918–96; U.S. vice president (1969–73); resigned.
Ai·ken /áykən/, **Conrad Potter** 1889–1973; U.S. poet.
Ak·bar /ákbər, –baar/, **Jalaludin Muhammad** 1542–1605; Mogul emperor of India (1556–1605).
Akh·na·ton /aaknaátən/ see **Amenhotep IV** (AMENHOTEP).
A·ki·hi·to /aakiheétō/ 1933– ; emperor of Japan (1989–).
Al·a·ric /álərik/ c. 370–410; king of the Visigoths (395–410); captured Rome (410).
Al·bee /áwlbee, ál–/, **Edward** 1928– ; U.S. playwright.
Al·bright /áwlbrīt/, **Madeleine** 1937– ; U.S. secretary of state (1997–), born in Czechoslovakia.
Al·ci·bi·a·des /alsəbíədeez/ c. 450–404 B.C.; Athenian general and statesman.
Al·cott /áwlkət, ál–, –kaat/, **Louisa May** 1832–88; U.S. novelist.
Al·cuin /álkwin/ c. 735–804; English theologian.
Al·ex·an·der /aligzándər/ (called **"the Great"**) 356–323 B.C.; king of Macedonia (336–323 B.C.); conqueror of the Persian Empire.
Al·ex·an·der name of three czars of Russia: **1** Alexander I 1777–1825; reigned 1801–25. **2** Alexander II (called **"the Liberator"**) 1818–81; reigned 1855–81; father of: **3** Alexander III 1845–94; reigned 1881–94.
Al·fred /álfrəd/ (called **"the Great"**) 849–899; Anglo-Saxon king (871–899).
A·li /aaleé, aleé/, **Muhammad** (born **Cassius Marcellus Clay, Jr.**) 1942– ; U.S. boxer.
A·li·ghie·ri /aləgyéree/, **Dante** see DANTE.
Al·len /álən/, **Ethan** 1738–89; American Revolutionary War soldier.
Al·len, Woody (born **Allen Stewart Konigsberg**) 1935– ; U.S. film director, author, and actor.
All·en·de Gos·sens /aayénday gáwsens/, **Salvador** 1908–73; Chilean political leader.
A·ma·ti /əmaátee, aa–/ family of Italian violin-makers, including: **1** Andrea c. 1520–c. 1580; grandfather of: **2** Nicolò 1596–1684.
A·men·ho·tep /aamənhṓtep/ (also **Am·e·no'phis**) name of four kings of Egypt: **1** Amenhotep I reigned 1546–1526 B.C. **2** Amenhotep II reigned 1450–1425 B.C. **3** Amenhotep III reigned 1417–1379 B.C.; built capital city of Thebes. **4** Amenhotep IV (also **Akh·na'ton; Ikh·na'ton**) reigned 1379–1362 B.C.
A·min /aameén/, **Idi** 1925– ; president of Uganda (1971–79); exiled (1979).
An·ax·ag·o·ras /anakságərəs/ c. 500–c. 428 B.C.; Greek philosopher.
An·der·sen /ándərsən, aán–/, **Hans Christian** 1805–75; Danish author.
An·der·son /ándərsən/, **Marian** 1902–93; U.S. contralto.
An·der·son, Maxwell 1888–1959; U.S. playwright.
An·der·son, Sherwood 1876–1941; U.S. author.
An·drew /ándroo/, **St.** died c. 60; apostle of Jesus; patron saint of Scotland.
An·dro·pov /andrṓpawf/, **Yuri** 1914–84; Soviet politician.
An·ge·lou /aánjəloo, –lō/, **Maya** 1928– ; U.S. novelist and poet.
An·nan /aánaan/, **Kofi** 1938– ; Ghanaian secretary-general of the United Nations (1997–).
Anne /an/ 1665–1714; queen of England (1702–14).
Anne Bol·eyn see BOLEYN, ANNE.
Anne of Cleves /kleevz/ 1515–57; 4th wife of Henry VIII.
An·nen·berg /ánənbərg/, **Walter** 1908– ; U.S. publisher and philanthropist.
A·nou·ilh /aanóoee/, **Jean** 1910–87; French playwright.
An·selm /ánselm/, **St.** c. 1033–1109; English theologian.
An·tho·ny /ánthənee/, **Susan B(rownell)** 1820–1906; U.S. suffragist.
An·to·ni·nus Pi·us /antənínəs píəs/ 86–161; Roman emperor (137–161).
An·to·ny /ántənee/, **Mark** (Latin name **Mar'cus An·to'ni·us**) c. 83–30 B.C.; Roman general and political leader.
Ap·ol·lo·ni·us /apəlṓneeəs/ **of Rhodes** /rōdz/ 3rd cent. B.C.; Greek poet.
A·pu·lei·us /apyəláyəs/ 2nd cent.; Roman author.
A·qui·nas /əkwínəs/, **St. Thomas** 1225–74; Italian philosopher and theologian.
Ar·a·fat /árəfat/, **Yasser** 1929– ; Palestinian political leader.
A·ri·os·to /aaree-aástō, –ṓstō/, **Ludovico** 1474–1533; Italian poet.
Ar·is·ti·des /arəstídeez/ (called **"the Just"**) fl. 5th cent. B.C.; Athenian statesman and general.
Ar·is·toph·a·nes /arəstaáfəneez/ c. 450–c. 385 B.C.; Greek comic playwright.
Ar·is·tot·le /árəstaat'l, arəstaát'l/ 384–322 B.C.; Greek philosopher.
Arm·strong /aármstrawng/, **(Daniel) Louis** (called **"Satchmo"**) 1900–71; U.S. jazz trumpeter and bandleader.
Arm·strong, Neil Alden 1930– ; U.S. astronaut; first to walk on the moon (1969).
Ar·nold /aárnəld/, **Benedict** 1741–1801; American Revolutionary War general; turned traitor (1779).
Ar·nold, Matthew 1822–88; English poet and essayist.
Arou·et /áawə/, **François-Marie** see VOLTAIRE.
Ar·ta·xerx·es /aartəzə́rkseez/ name of three kings of Persia: **1** Artaxerxes I reigned 464–424 B.C.; son of Xerxes I. **2** Artaxerxes II reigned 404–358 B.C.; father of: **3** Artaxerxes III reigned 358–338 B.C.
Ar·thur /aárthər/ 5th cent. or 6th cent.; legendary king of Britain. □□ **Ar·thu'ri·an** *adj.*
Ar·thur, Chester Alan 1830–86; 21st president of the U.S. (1881–85).
Ashe /ash/, **Arthur Robert** 1943–93; U.S. tennis player.
As·i·mov /ázəmawf, –mawv/, **Isaac** 1920–92; U.S. scientist and author, born in Russia.
As·sad /aasaád/, **Hafiz al-** 1928– ; president of Syria (1971–).
A·staire /əstáir/, **Fred** (born **Frederick Austerlitz**) 1899–1987; U.S. dancer, singer, and actor.
As·tor /ástər/, **John Jacob** 1763–1848; U.S. capitalist, born in Germany.
As·tu·ri·as /aastóoreeəs, –tyoo–/, **Miguel Angel** 1899–1974; Guatemalan author.
A·ta·türk /átətərk/, **Kemal** (born **Mustafa Kemal**) 1881–1938; president of Turkey (1923–38).
At·ti·la /ətílə, át'lə/ 406–453; king of the Huns (434–453).
Att·lee /átlee/, **Clement Richard** 1883–1967; prime minister of Great Britain (1945–51).
At·tucks /átəks/, **Crispus** c. 1723–70; American patriot; killed in the Boston Massacre.
At·wood /átwood/, **Margaret** 1939– ; Canadian author and critic.
Au·den /áwd'n/, **W(ystan) H(ugh)** 1907–73; U.S. poet, born in England.
Au·du·bon /áwdəbaan, –bən/, **John James** 1785–1851; U.S. naturalist and artist.
Au·gus·tine /áwgusteen, awgústən/ name of two saints: **1** (called **St. Augustine of Hippo**) 354–430; early Christian author. **2** (also known as **Aus'tin**) died c. 604; first archbishop of Canterbury. □□ **Au·gus·tin'i·an** *adj.*
Au·gus·tus /awgústəs/ (also known as **Oc·ta'vi·an**) 63 B.C.–A.D. 14; first Roman emperor.
Aung San Suu Kyi /ówng saán sóo chee/ 1945– ; Burmese political leader.
Au·re·li·us, Marcus see MARCUS AURELIUS.
Aus·ten /áwstən/, **Jane** 1775–1817; English novelist.

Aus·tin /áwstən/, **Stephen Fuller** 1793–1836; Texas pioneer and colonizer.
A·ver·ro·ës /əvérō-eez, avərṓ–/ c. 1126–98; Islamic philosopher, born in Spain.
A·vi·cen·na /avəsénə/ 980–1037; Islamic philosopher and physician, born in Persia.
Ayer /áyər/, **A(lfred) J(ules)** 1910–89; British philosopher.
Ba·ber /baábər/ (also **Ba'bar**; **Ba'bur**) 1483–1530; founder of the Mogul Empire.
Bach /baakh, baak/ family of German composers, including: **1** Johann Sebastian 1685–1750; father of: **2** Wilhelm Friedemann 1710–84; **3** C(arl) P(hilipp) E(manuel) 1714–88; **4** Johann Christoph Friedrich 1732–95; and **5** Johann Christian 1735–82.
Ba·con /báykən/, **Francis** 1561–1626; English statesman and philosopher.
Ba·con, Roger c. 1214–94; English scientist and philosopher.
Ba·den-Pow·ell /bayd'n pṓəl, pówəl/, **(Lord) Robert Stephenson Smyth** 1857–1941; English general; founder of the Boy Scouts (1908).
Bal·an·chine /bálənsheen/, **George** 1904–83; U.S. choreographer and ballet dancer, born in Russia.
Bal·boa /balbṓə/, **Vasco Núñez de** 1475–1517; Spanish explorer of America.
Bald·win /báwldwin/, **James** 1924–87; U.S. author.
Bald·win, Stanley 1867–1947; prime minister of Great Britain (1923–29; 1935–37).
Bal·four /bálfər, –fawr/, **Arthur James** 1848–1930; British statesman.
Ball /bawl/, **Lucille Désirée** 1911–1989; U.S. comedienne.
Bal·ti·more, Lord see CALVERT, GEORGE.
Bal·zac /báwlzak, bál–/, **Honoré de** 1799–1850; French novelist.
Bar·ba·ros·sa /baarbərṓsə/ see FREDERICK I.
Bar·nard /baárnərd/, **Christiaan Neethling** 1922– ; South African physician; performed first human heart transplant (1967).
Bar·num /baárnəm/, **P(hineas) T(aylor)** 1810–91; U.S. showman.
Bar·rett /bárit/, **Elizabeth** see BROWNING, ELIZABETH BARRETT.
Bar·rie /báree/, **(Sir) J(ames) M(atthew)** 1860–1937; Scottish author.
Bar·ry·more /bárimawr/ family of U.S. actors, including three siblings: **1** Lionel 1878–1954; **2** Ethel 1879–1959; and **3** John 1882–1942.
Barth /baarth/, **John** 1930– ; U.S. author.
Barth /baart/, **Karl** 1886–1968; Swiss Protestant theologian.
Barthes /baart/, **Roland** 1915–80; French author and critic.
Bar·tók /baártaak, –tawk/, **Béla** 1881–1945; Hungarian composer.
Bar·ton /baárt'n/, **Clara** 1821–1912; U.S. health worker; founded the American Red Cross (1881).
Ba·rysh·ni·kov /baríshnikawf/, **Mikhail** 1948– dat> U.S. ballet dancer and choreographer, born in Latvia.
Ba·sie /báysee/, **Count (William)** 1904–84; U.S. jazz pianist, bandleader, and composer.
Ba·tis·ta /bəteéstə/, **Fulgencio** 1901–73; president of Cuba (1940–44; 1954–59).
Bau·de·laire /bōd'lair/, **Charles** 1821–67; French poet and critic.
Beards·ley /beérdzlee/, **Aubrey Vincent** 1872–98; English artist.
Be·a·trix /báyətriks/ 1938– ; queen of the Netherlands (1980–).
Beau·mar·chais /bōmaarsháy/, **Pierre Augustin Caron de** 1732–99; French playwright.
Beau·mont /bṓmaant/, **Francis** 1584–1616; English playwright.
Beauvoir, Simone de see DE BEAUVOIR, SIMONE.
Beck·et /békit/, **St. Thomas à** c. 1118–70; archbishop of Canterbury; murdered for opposing King Henry II.
Beck·ett /békit/, **Samuel Barclay** 1906–89; Irish author.
Bede /beed/, **St.** (called **"the Venerable Bede"**) c. 673–735; English theologian and historian.
Bee·cher /beéchər/, **Henry Ward** 1813–87; U.S. abolitionist.
Beer·bohm /beérbōm/, **(Sir) Max (Henry Maximilian)** 1872–1956; English caricaturist and critic.
Bee·tho·ven /báytōvən/, **Ludwig van** 1770–1827; German composer.
Be·gin /bəgeén, báygin/, **Menachem** 1913–92; Israeli political leader.
Be·han /beéən/, **Brendan** 1923–64; Irish playwright and poet.
Bell /bel/, **Alexander Graham** 1847–1922; U.S. inventor of the telephone, born in Scotland.
Bel·li·ni /beleénee/ family of Italian artists, including: **1** Jacopo c. 1400–70; father of: **2** Gentile c. 1429–1507; and **3** Giovanni c. 1430–1516.
Bel·low /bélō/, **Saul** 1915– ; U.S. novelist, born in Canada.
Ben·e·dict /bénədikt/, **St.** c. 480–c. 550; Italian monk; founded Western monasticism.
Be·nét /bənáy/, **Stephen Vincent** 1898–1943; U.S. poet.
Ben-Gu·ri·on /ben gŏŏreeən/, **David** (born **David Gruen** 1886–1973; prime minister of Israel (1948–53; 1955–63), born in Poland.
Ben·ny /bénee/, **Jack** (born **Benjamin Kubelsky**) 1894–1974; U.S. comedian.
Ben·tham /bénthəm/, **Jeremy** 1748–1832; English philosopher and jurist.
Ben·ton /bént'n/ **1** Thomas Hart 1782–1858; U.S. politician; great-uncle of: **2** Thomas Hart 1889–1975; U.S. artist.
Bent·sen /béntsən/, **Lloyd Millard** 1921– ; U.S. politician.
Benz /benz, bents/, **Karl Friedrich** 1844–1929; German automotive engineer.
Berg·son /bérgsən/, **Henri** 1859–1941; French philosopher.
Ber·ing /beéring, bér–/, **Vitus Jonassen** 1681–1741; Danish explorer.
Berke·ley /baárklee, bə́r–/, **George** 1685–1753; Irish philosopher and bishop.
Ber·lin /bərlín/, **Irving** (born **Israel Isidore Baline**) 1888–1989; U.S. composer, born in Russia.
Ber·li·oz /bérlee-ōz/, **Hector Louis** 1803–69; French composer.
Ber·na·dette /bərnədét/, **St.** (born **Marie-Bernarde Soubirous**) 1844–79; French peasant girl who had visions of the Virgin Mary at Lourdes.
Ber·nard /bərnaárd/ **of Clair·vaux** /klairvṓ/ 1090–1153; French theologian.
Bern·hardt /bə́rnhaart/, **Sarah** (born **Henriette Rosine Bernard**) 1844–1923; French actress.
Ber·ni·ni /bərneénee/, **Gianlorenzo** 1598–1680; Italian artist and architect.
Bern·stein /bə́rnstīn, –steen/, **Leonard** 1918–90; U.S. composer and conductor.
Ber·ry /béree/, **Chuck (Charles Edward)** 1931– ; U.S. rock and roll musician.
Bes·se·mer /bésimər/, **(Sir) Henry** 1813–98; English engineer and inventor.
Be·thune /bəthŏŏn, –yŏŏn/, **Mary McLeod** 1875–1955; U.S. educator.
Bet·je·man /béchəmən/, **(Sir) John** 1906–84; English poet.
Beyle /bel/, **Marie Henri** see STENDHAL.
Bhut·to /bŏŏtō/ **1** Zulfikar Ali 1928–79; president (1971–73) and prime minister (1973–77) of Pakistan; father of: **2** Benazir 1953– ; prime minister of Pakistan (1988–91; 1993–96).
Bierce /beers/, **Ambrose Gwinnett** 1842–c. 1914; U.S. author.
Bi·ko /beékō/, **Stephen** 1946–77; South African civil rights activist.
Bis·marck /bízmaark/, **Otto Eduard Leopold von** (called **"the Iron Chancellor"**) 1815–98; chancellor of the German Empire (1871–90).
Bi·zet /beezáy/, **Georges Alexandre César Léopold** 1838–75; French composer.
Black /blak/, **Shirley Temple** 1928– ; U.S. actress and diplomat.
Blair /blair/, **Tony (Anthony Charles Lynton)** 1953– ; prime minister of Great Britain (1997–).
Blake /blayk/, **William** 1757–1827; English artist and poet.
Bligh /blī/, **William** 1754–1817; British naval officer.
Bo·ad·i·ce·a /bōədəseéə/ (also **Bou·dic'ca**) died 62; warrior queen of the ancient Britons.
Boc·cac·ci·o /bəkaácheeō, –chō/, **Giovanni** 1313–75; Italian poet.
Bo·e·thi·us /bō-eétheeəs/, **Anicius Manlius Severinus** c. 480–524; Roman philosopher.
Bo·gart /bṓgaart/, **Humphrey De Forest** 1899–1957; U.S. actor.
Bohr /bawr/, **Niels Henrik David** 1885–1962; Danish nuclear physicist.
Bol·eyn /bŏŏlín, bŏŏlən/, **Anne** 1507–36; 2nd wife of King Henry VIII of England; mother of Queen Elizabeth I; beheaded.
Bol·í·var /bōleévaar, baáləvər/, **Simón** (called **"the Liberator"**) 1783–1830; Venezuelan patriot and liberator of South America.
Bo·na·parte /bṓnəpaart/ see NAPOLEON I; NAPOLEON III.
Boone /bōōn/, **Daniel** c. 1735–1820; American pioneer.
Boor·stin /bŏŏrstin/, **Daniel J(oseph)** 1914– ; U.S. author.
Booth /bōōth/, **John Wilkes** 1838–65; U.S. actor; assassin of President Abraham Lincoln (1865).
Bor·ges /báwrhays/, **Jorge Luis** 1899–1986; Argentine author.
Bor·gi·a /báwrjə, –zhə/ **1** Cesare 1476–1507; Italian cardinal and militarist; brother of: **2** Lucrezia 1480–1519; Italian patron of the arts.
Born /bawrn/, **Max** 1882–1970; German physicist.
Bosch /baash, bawsh/, **Hieronymus** c. 1450–1516; Dutch artist.
Bos·well /baázwel, –wəl/, **James** 1740–95; Scottish author; biographer of Samuel Johnson.
Bot·ti·cel·li /baatəchélee/, **Sandro** 1445–1510; Italian artist.
Bou·dic·ca /bōōdíkə/ see BOADICEA.
Bou·lez /bōōléz/, **Pierre** 1925– ; French conductor and composer.
Bourke-White /bŏŏrk wīt/, **Margaret** 1906–71; U.S. photojournalist.
Bou·tros-Gha·li /bōōtrōs gaalee/, **Boutros** 1922– ; Egyptian statesman; secretary-general of the United Nations (1992–96).
Brad·bur·y /brádberee, –bəree/, **Ray(mond Douglas)** 1920– ; U.S. science-fiction author.
Brad·ford /brádfərd/, **William** 1590–1657; English Puritan governor of Plymouth colony in Massachusetts.
Brad·ley /brádlee/, **Omar Nelson** 1893–1981; U.S. general.
Bra·dy /bráydee/, **Mathew B.** 1823–96; U.S. Civil War photographer.
Brahe /braa, braáhee/, **Tycho** 1546–1601; Danish astronomer.
Brahms /braamz/, **Johannes** 1833–97; German composer.
Bran·deis /brándīs/, **Louis Dembitz** 1856–1941; U.S. Supreme Court justice (1916–39).

Bran·do /brándō/, **Marlon** 1924– ; U.S. actor.
Brandt /braant, brant/, **Willy** (born **Karl Herbert Frahm**) 1913–92; German politician.
Braun /brown/, **Wernher von** 1912–77; U.S. rocket scientist, born in Germany.
Brecht /brekht, brekt/, **Bertolt** 1898–1956; German playwright and poet.
Breu·ghel see BRUEGEL, PIETER.
Brey·er /bríər/, **Stephen Gerald** 1938– ; U.S. Supreme Court justice (1994–).
Brezh·nev /brézhnef, –nyəf/, **Leonid** 1906–83; Soviet political leader.
Bridg·es /brijiz/, **Robert** 1844–1930; English poet and critic.
Brit·ten /brít'n/, **(Edward) Benjamin** 1913–76; English composer.
Brod·sky /braádskee, braát–/, **Joseph** 1940–1996; U.S. poet, born in Russia.
Bron·të /braántee, braántay/ family of English novelists; three sisters: **1** Charlotte 1816–55; **2** Emily Jane 1818–48; and **3** Anne 1820–49.
Brown /brown/, **John** 1800–59; U.S. radical abolitionist.
Brown·ing /brówning/ two English poets: **1** Elizabeth Barrett 1806–61; wife of: **2** Robert 1812–89.
Bruce /broos/, **Robert the** see ROBERT I.
Brue·gel /bróygəl/ (also **Breu'ghel; Brue'ghel**), **Pieter** c. 1525–69; Flemish artist.
Bru·nel·les·chi /broon'léskee/ (also **Bru·nel·les'co**), **Filippo** 1377–1446; Italian architect.
Bru·tus /brootəs/, **Marcus Junius** 85–42 B.C.; Roman senator; an assassin of Julius Caesar.
Bry·an /bríən/, **William Jennings** 1860–1925; U.S. lawyer, politician, and orator.
Bry·ant /bríənt/, **William Cullen** 1794–1878; U.S. poet.
Bryn·ner /brínər/, **Yul** 1915–85; U.S. actor, born in Russia.
Bu·ber /boobər/, **Martin** 1878–1965; Israeli philosopher, born in Austria.
Bu·chan·an /byookánən/, **James** 1791–1868; 15th president of the U.S. (1857–61).
Buck /buk/, **Pearl S(ydenstricker)** 1892–1973; U.S. author.
Buck·ley /búklee/, **William F(rank)** 1925– ; U.S. political commentator and author.
Bud·dha /boodə, boodə/ (born **Siddhartha Gautama**) c. 563–c. 483 B.C.; Indian philosopher; founder of Buddhism.
Bult·mann /booltmaan, –mən/, **Rudolf Karl** 1884–1976; German theologian.
Bunche /bunch/, **Ralph Johnson** 1904–71; U.S. diplomat.
Bu·nin /boonyeen/, **Ivan Alekseyevich** 1870–1953; Russian author and poet.
Bun·yan /búnyən/, **John** 1628–88; English author.
Bur·bank /bərbangk/, **Luther** 1849–1926; U.S. horticulturist.
Bur·ger /bərgər/, **Warren Earl** 1907–95; Chief Justice of the U.S. (1969–86).
Burke /bərk/, **Edmund** 1729–97; British author and politician.
Bur·nett /bərnét, bərnət/, **Frances (Eliza) Hodgson** 1849–1924; U.S. novelist, born in England.
Burns /bərnz/, **George** 1895–1996; U.S. entertainer.
Burns, Robert 1759–96; Scottish poet.
Burn·side /bərnsīd/, **Ambrose Everett** 1824–81; Union general in the American Civil War.
Burr /bər/, **Aaron** 1756–1836; vice president of the U.S. (1801–05).
Bur·roughs /bərōz/, **Edgar Rice** 1875–1950; U.S. author.
Bur·ton /bərt'n/, **Richard** (born **Richard Jenkins**) 1925–84; Welsh actor.
Bur·ton, (Sir) Richard Francis 1821–90; English explorer and anthropologist.
Bush /boosh/, **George Herbert Walker** 1924– ; 41st president of the U.S. (1989–93).
But·ler /bútlər/, **Samuel** 1612–80; English poet.
But·ler, Samuel 1835–1902; English novelist.
Byrd /bərd/, **Richard Evelyn** 1888–1957; U.S. polar explorer.
By·ron /bírən/, **(Lord) George Gordon** 1788–1824; English poet.
Cab·ot /kábət/, **John** (Italian name **Giovanni Caboto**) 1425–c. 1498; Italian explorer.
Ca·bri·ni /kəbreénee/, **St. Frances Xavier** (called **"Mother Cabrini"**) 1850–1917; U.S. nun, born in Italy.
Cad·il·lac /kád'l-ak, kaadeeyaák/, **Antoine de la Mothe** c. 1656–1730; French explorer.
Cae·sar /seézər/, **(Gaius) Julius** 100–44 B.C.; Roman general and statesman; assassinated.
Cag·ney /kágnee/, **James** 1904–86; U.S. actor.
Cal·der /káwldər/, **Alexander Milne** 1898–1976; U.S. sculptor, born in Scotland.
Cal·houn /kalhoon/, **John C(aldwell)** 1782–1850; U.S. politician.
Ca·lig·u·la /kəlígyələ/ (born **Gaius Caesar**) 12–41; Roman emperor (37–41).
Cal·las /káləs, kaál–/, **Maria** (born **Maria Anna Sofia Cecilia Kalogeropoulos**) 1923–77; U.S. operatic soprano.
Cal·vert /kálvərt/ family of English colonial administrators of Maryland, including: **1** (Lord) George (**1st Baron Baltimore**) c. 1580–1632; father of: **2** Cecilius (**2nd Baron Baltimore**) 1605–75; established Maryland colony; **3** Leonard 1606–47; and **4** Charles (**3rd Baron Baltimore**) 1637–1715; son of Cecilius Calvert.
Cal·vin /kálvən/, **John** 1509–64; French Protestant theologian.
Ca·mus /kamóo, kaamý/, **Albert** 1913–60; French author.
Ca·na·let·to /kan'létō/ (born **Giovanni Antonio Canale**) 1697–1768; Italian artist.
Ca·no·va /kənóvə/, **Antonio** 1757–1822; Italian sculptor.
Ca·nute /kənóot, –nyóot/ (also **Cnut; Knut**) died 1035; Danish king of England (1017–35), Denmark (1018–35), and Norway (1028–35).
Ca·pet /kaapáy, káypət/, **Hugh (Hugo)** 938–996; king of France (987–996).
Ca·pone /kəpón/, **Al(phonse)** (called **"Scarface"**) 1899–1947; U.S. gangster, born in Italy.
Ca·po·te /kəpótee/, **Truman** 1924–84; U.S. author.
Ca·ra·vag·gio /kaarəvaájō, –jeeō/, **Michelangelo Merisi da** 1573–1610; Italian artist.
Car·lyle /kaarlíl, kaár–/, **Thomas** 1795–1881; Scottish historian and political philosopher.
Car·mi·chael /kaármīkəl/, **Hoagy (Hoagland Howard)** 1899–1981; U.S. jazz pianist, singer, and composer.
Car·ne·gie /kaárnəgee, kaarnégee/, **Andrew** 1835–1919; U.S. industrialist and philanthropist, born in Scotland.
Car·o·lus Mag·nus /kárələs mágnəs/ see CHARLEMAGNE.
Car·rac·ci /kaaraáchee/ family of Italian artists, including: **1** Ludovico 1555–1619; cousin of two brothers: **2** Agostino 1557–1602; and **3** Annibale 1560–1609.
Car·re·ras /kəréraas/, **José** 1946– ; Spanish operatic tenor.
Car·roll /kárəl/, **Lewis** (pseudonym of **Charles Lutwidge Dodgson**) 1832–98; English author and statesman and logician.
Car·son /kaársən/, **Kit (Christopher)** 1809–68; U.S. frontiersman.
Car·son, Rachel Louise 1907–64; U.S. zoologist and ecologist.
Car·ter /kaártər/, **Jimmy (James Earl)** 1924– ; 39th president of the U.S. (1977–81).
Car·tier /kaartyáy, kaártee-ay/, **Jacques** 1491–1557; French explorer.
Ca·ru·so /kəróosō, –zō/, **Enrico** 1873–1921; Italian operatic tenor.
Car·ver /kaárvər/, **George Washington** 1864–1943; U.S. botanist and educator.
Ca·sals /kəsaálz/, **Pablo** 1876–1973; Spanish cellist and composer.
Cas·a·no·va /kasənóvə, kaz–/, **Giovanni Jacopo** 1725–98; Italian adventurer.
Cash /kash/, **Johnny** 1932– ; U.S. country music singer and songwriter.
Cas·satt /kəsát/, **Mary Stevenson** 1845–1926; U.S. artist.
Cas·sius /káshəs/, **Gaius** died 42 B.C.; Roman general; an assassin of Julius Caesar.
Cas·tro /kástrō/, **Fidel** 1927– ; Cuban revolutionary; president of Cuba (1976–).
Cath·er /káthər/, **Willa Sibert** 1876–1974; U.S. novelist.
Cath·er·ine II /káthərən, káthrən/ (called **"the Great"**) 1729–96; empress of Russia (1762–96), born in Germany.
Ca·the·rine de Méd·i·cis /maydeesées, méd–/ (Italian name **Ca·te·ri·na de' Med·i·ci** /kaatayreénaa də médəchee, mədeéchee/) 1519–89; queen of Henry II of France, born in Florence.
Cath·er·ine of Ar·a·gon /árəgon/ 1485–1536; 1st wife of Henry VIII; mother of Mary I.
Ca·to /káytō/, **Marcus Porcius** (called **"the Elder"** and **"the Censor"**) 234–149 B.C.; Roman statesman, orator, and author.
Catt /kat/, **Carrie Chapman Lane** 1859–1947; U.S. suffragist.
Ca·tul·lus /kətúləs/, **Gaius Valerius** c. 84–c. 54 B.C.; Roman poet.
Ca·vour /kəvóor/, **Camillo Benso** 1810–61; Italian statesman.
Ceau·ses·cu /chowshéshkoo/, **Nicolae** 1918–89; president of Romania (1967–89); executed.
Cel·li·ni /chəleénee/, **Benvenuto** 1500–71; Italian artisan.
Cer·van·tes /sərvánteez, servaántays/ (**Saa·ve'dra**), **Miguel de** 1547–1616; Spanish author.
Cé·zanne /sayzaán/, **Paul** 1839–1906; French artist.
Cha·gall /shəgaál/, **Marc** 1887–1985; French artist, born in Russia.
Chal·lans /chálənz/ **Mary** see RENAULT, MARY.
Cham·ber·lain /cháymbərlən/, **(Arthur) Neville** 1869–1940; prime minister of Great Britain (1937–40).
Cham·plain /shampláyn/, **Samuel de** 1567–1635; French explorer and colonial statesman in Canada.
Chan·dler /chándlər/, **Raymond Thornton** 1888–1959; U.S. novelist.
Cha·nel /shənél/, **Coco (Gabrielle Bonheur)** 1883–1971; French fashion designer.
Chap·lin /cháplən/, **Charlie (Sir Charles Spencer)** 1889–1977; English film actor and director.
Char·le·magne /shaárləmayn/, (called **Carolus Magnus** or **Charles the Great**) 742–814; king of the Franks (768–814); Holy Roman Emperor (800–814).
Charles[1] /chaarlz/ name of two British kings: **1** Charles I 1600–49; reigned 1625–49. **2** Charles II 1630–85; reigned 1660–85.
Charles[2] name of four kings of Spain, including: **1** Charles I 1500–58; reigned 1516–56; (as **Charles V**) Holy Roman Emperor (1519–56). **2** Charles II 1661–1700; reigned 1665–1700.

Charles (Prince of Wales) 1948– ; heir apparent to the throne of the United Kingdom.
Charles Mar·tel /maartél/ c. 688–741; ruler of the Franks (714–741).
Chase /chays/, **Salmon P(ortland)** 1808–73; Chief Justice of the U.S. (1864–73).
Cha·teau·bri·and /shaatōbree-aáN/, **François-René (Vicomte de)** 1768–1848; French author and diplomat.
Chau·cer /cháwsər/, **Geoffrey** c. 1342–1400; English poet.
Chee·ver /cheévər/, **John** 1912–82; U.S. author.
Che·khov /chékawf, –awv/, **Anton Pavlovich** 1860–1904; Russian author.
Che·ops /keéaaps/ (also **Khu'fu**) fl. early 26th cent. B.C.; Egyptian king; built the pyramid at Giza.
Ches·ter·ton /chéstərtən/, **G(ilbert) K(eith)** 1874–1936; English author and critic.
Chiang Kai-shek /cháng kíshék/ 1887–1975; president of China (1928–31; 1943–49) and Taiwan (1950–75).
Chi·rac /shiraák, –rák/, **Jacques** 1932– ; prime minister (1974–76; 1986–88) and president (1995–) of France.
Chi·ri·co /keérikō, kír–/, **Giorgio de** 1888–1978; Italian artist, born in Greece.
Chom·sky /chaámskee/, **(Avram) Noam** 1928– ; U.S. linguist.
Cho·pin /shṓpan, shōpáN/, **Frédéric François** 1810–49; French composer, born in Poland.
Chou En-lai /jṓ énlí/ (also **Zhou En·lai'**) 1898–1976; Chinese political leader.
Chré·tien de Troyes /kraytyáN də trwaá/ 12th cent.; French poet.
Chris·tie /krístee/, **(Dame) Agatha Mary Clarissa Miller** 1890–1976; English author.
Church /chərch/, **Frederick Edwin** 1826–1900; U.S. artist.
Church·ill /chə́rchil/, **John (1st Duke of Marlborough)** 1650–1722; British military commander.
Church·ill, (Sir) Winston Leonard Spencer 1874–1965; British statesman; prime minister of Great Britain (1940–45; 1951–55).
Cic·e·ro /sísərō/, **Marcus Tullius** 106–43 B.C.; Roman statesman and author.
Cid /síd/, **El** (born **Rodrigo Diaz de Vivar**) c. 1043–99; Spanish military hero.
Clap·ton /kláptən/, **Eric** 1945– ; British guitarist and composer.
Clark /klaark/, **1** George Rogers 1752–1818; U.S. frontiersman and soldier; brother of: **2** William 1770–1838; U.S. explorer (with Meriwether Lewis) of the North American continent (1804–06).
Clarke /klaark/, **Arthur C(harles)** 1917– ; English science-fiction author.
Claude Lor·rain /klṓd lawrén/ (born **Claude Gellée**) 1600–82; French landscape artist.
Clau·di·us /kláwdeeəs/ 10 B.C.–A.D. 54; Roman emperor (41–54).
Clau·se·witz /klówzəvits/, **Karl von** 1780–1831; Prussian military theorist.
Cla·vell /kləvél/, **James** 1924–94; U.S. author.
Clay /klay/, **Henry** 1777–1852; U.S. politician.
Clay, Cassius see ALI, MUHAMMAD.
Cle·men·ceau /kleməns̄ṓ/, **Georges Eugène Benjamin** 1841–1929; French political leader.
Clem·ens /klémənz/, **Samuel Langhorne** see TWAIN, MARK.
Cle·o·pat·ra /kleeōpátrə/ **(Cleopatra VII)** 69–30 B.C.; queen of Egypt (47–30 B.C.).
Cleve·land /kleévlənd/, **(Stephen) Grover** 1837–1908; 22nd and 24th president of the U.S. (1885–89; 1893–97).
Clin·ton /klínt'n/, **1** Bill (William Jefferson) 1946– ; 42nd president of the U.S. (1993–); husband of: **2** Hillary Rodham 1947– ; U.S. lawyer.
Clin·ton, DeWitt 1769–1828; governor of New York (1817–23; 1825–28); promoter of the Erie Canal.
Clo·vis /klṓvəs/ 465–511; king of the Franks (481–511).
Cnut /kənṓṓt, –nyṓṓt/ see CANUTE.
Co·chise /kōcheés/ c. 1812–74; Apache Indian chief.
Coc·teau /kaaktṓ/, **Jean** 1889–1963; French playwright and film director.
Co·dy /kṓdee/, **William Frederick** (called **"Buffalo Bill"**) 1846–1917; U.S. army scout and showman.
Co·han /kṓhan/, **George M(ichael)** 1878–1942; U.S. songwriter and theatrical producer.
Cole /cōl/, **Nat King** (born **Nathaniel Adams Coles**) 1919–65; U.S. popular singer and pianist.
Cole, Thomas 1801–48; U.S. artist.
Cole·ridge /kṓlrij, kṓlərij/, **Samuel Taylor** 1772–1834; English poet, critic, and philosopher.
Co·lette /kəlét/ (born **Sidonie Gabrielle Claudine Colette**) 1873–1954; French novelist.
Colt /kōlt/, **Samuel** 1814–62; U.S. inventor; patented the Colt revolver (1836).
Co·lum·ba /kəlúmbə/, **St.** c. 521–597; Irish abbot and missionary.
Co·lum·bus /kəlúmbəs/, **Christopher** 1451–1506; Spanish explorer, born in Italy; initiated colonization of America by Europeans (1492).
Comte /kōNt/, **Auguste** 1798–1857; French philosopher.
Con·fu·cius /kənfyṓṓshəs/ (also **K'ung Fu-tzu**) 551–479 B.C.; Chinese philosopher. ▫▫ **Con·fu'cian** *adj.*
Con·greve /kaán-greev, kaáng–/, **William** 1670–1729; English playwright.
Con·ner·y /kaánəree/, **Sean** (born **Thomas Connery**) 1930– ; Scottish actor.
Con·rad /kaánrad/, **Joseph** 1857–1924; British novelist, born in Poland.
Con·sta·ble /kaánstəbəl/, **John** 1776–1837; English artist.
Con·stan·tine /kaánstənteen, –tīn/ (called **"the Great"**) c. 274–337; Roman emperor (306–337); adopted and sanctioned Christianity.
Cook /kook/, **(Captain) James** 1728–79; English explorer of the Pacific.
Cool·idge /kṓṓlij/, **(John) Calvin** 1872–1933; 30th president of the U.S. (1923–29).
Coop·er /kṓṓpər, kṓṓpər/, **James Fenimore** 1789–1851; U.S. novelist.
Co·per·ni·cus /kəpə́rnikəs/, **Nicolaus** 1473–1543; Polish astronomer; set forth the heliocentric theory of the solar system.
Cop·land /kṓplənd/, **Aaron** 1900–90; U.S. composer.
Cop·ley /kaáplee/, **John Singleton** 1738–1815; U.S. artist.
Cor·day d'Ar·mont /kawrdáy daarmṓN/, **(Marie-Anne) Charlotte** 1768–93; French patriot and political assassin.
Cor·i·o·la·nus /kawreeəláynəs/, **Gaius** (or **Gnaeus**) **Marcius** 6th cent.–5th cent. B.C.; legendary Roman general.
Cor·neille /kawrnáy/, **Pierre** 1606–84; French playwright.
Corn·wal·lis /kawrnwáwləs/, **Charles (1st Marquis)** 1738–1805; British general; surrendered at Yorktown (1781), ending American Revolutionary War.
Co·ro·na·do /kawrənaádō/, **Francisco Vásquez de** 1510–54; Spanish explorer in North America.
Co·rot /kawrṓ/, **(Jean-Baptiste) Camille** 1796–1875; French artist.
Cor·reg·gio /kəréjō, –jeeō/, **Antonio Allegri da** c. 1489–1534; Italian artist.
Cor·tés /kawrtéz, kawrtés/ (also **Cor·tez'**), **Hernando** 1485–1547; Spanish conquistador; conqueror of Mexico.
Cos·by /kózbee/, **Bill (William Henry)** 1937– ; U.S. entertainer.
Cou·pe·rin /kṓṓp(ə)ráN/, **François** 1668–1733; French composer.
Cow·ard /kówərd/, **(Sir) Noel Peirce** 1899–1973; English playwright, actor, and composer.
Cow·per /kṓṓpər, ków–/, **William** 1731–1800; English poet.
Crane /krayn/, **Stephen** 1871–1900; U.S. author.
Cran·mer /kránmər/, **Thomas** 1489–1556; English leader of Protestant Reformation.
Cras·sus /krásəs/, **Marcus Licinius** c. 115–53 B.C.; Roman politician; financier of First Triumvirate.
Cra·zy Horse /kráyzee hawrs/ c. 1849–77; Sioux chief of Oglala tribe; led Sioux uprising (1876–77).
Crick /krik/, **Francis Harry Compton** 1916– ; English biophysicist.
Crock·ett /kraákit/, **Davy (David)** 1786–1836; U.S. frontiersman.
Croe·sus /kreésəs/ died 546 B.C.; Lydian king of legendary wealth.
Crom·well /kraámwel, –wəl/, **Oliver** 1599–1658; English soldier and political leader.
Cro·nin /krṓnən/, **A(rchibald) J(oseph)** 1896–1981; Scottish novelist.
Cron·kite /krónkīt/, **Walter Leland, Jr.** 1916– ; U.S. broadcast journalist.
Cum·mings /kúmingz/, **Edward Estlin** (known as **"e e cummings"**) 1894–1962; U.S. poet.
Cu·rie /kyṓṓree, kyṓṓree/ two French physicists and chemists: **1** Pierre 1859–1906; codiscovered radium and polonium with his wife: **2** Marie (born **Maria Sklowdowska**) 1867–1934; born in Poland.
Cur·tiss /kə́rtəs/, **Glenn Hammond** 1878–1930; U.S. inventor and aviation pioneer.
Cus·ter /kústər/, **George Armstrong** 1839–76; U.S. cavalry commander.
Cym·be·line /símbəleen/ died c. 42; British chieftain of Catuvellauni tribe.
Cyr·a·no de Ber·ge·rac /seérənō də bérzhərak/, **Savinien de** 1619–55; French soldier and author.
Cyr·il /seérəl/, **St.** (called **"the Apostle of the Slavs"**) 826–869; Greek missionary; inventor of the Cyrillic alphabet.
Cy·rus the Great /sírəs/ died 529 B.C.; king of Persia (559–529 B.C.).
Dahl /daal/, **Roald** 1916–90; British author.
Da·lai La·ma /daálī laamə, –lee/ title of the leader of Tibetan Buddhism.
Da·li /daálee/, **Salvador** 1904–89; Spanish surrealist artist.
Da·na /dáynə/, **Richard Henry** 1815–82; U.S. adventurer, author, and lawyer.
d'An·nun·zio /daanṓṓntsee-ō/, **Gabriele** 1863–1938; Italian novelist, playwright, and poet.
Dan·te /daántay, dántee/ (surname **Alighieri**) 1265–1321; Italian poet.
Dan·ton /daaNtṓN/, **Georges-Jacques** 1759–94; French revolutionary leader.
Dare /dar, der/, **Virginia** 1587–?; first child born in W hemisphere of European parents.

Da·ri·us I /dərīəs/ (called **"the Great"**) c. 550–486 B.C.; king of Persia (521–486 B.C.).
Dar·row /dárō/, **Clarence Seward** 1857–1938; U.S. lawyer.
Dar·win /daárwin/, **Charles Robert** 1809–82; English naturalist; promulgated theory of evolution.
Dau·det /dōdáy/, **Alphonse** 1840–97; French author.
Dau·mier /dōmyáy/, **Honoré** 1808–78; French artist.
Da·vid /dáyvid/ died c. 970 B.C.; biblical king of Israel.
Da·vid /daavéed/, **Jacques-Louis** 1748–1825; French artist.
da Vin·ci, Leonardo see LEONARDO DA VINCI.
Da·vis /dáyvəs/, **Jefferson** 1808–89; president of the Confederate States of America (1861–65).
Da·yan /dī-aán, daa-yaán/, **Moshe** 1915–81; Israeli politician and military commander.
de Beau·voir /də bōvwaár/, **Simone** 1908–86; French playwright and novelist.
Debs /debz/, **Eugene Victor** 1855–1926; U.S. labor leader.
De·bus·sy /debyōōsée, dáybyōō–/, **(Achille) Claude** 1862–1918; French composer.
de Fal·la, Manuel see FALLA, MANUEL DE.
De·foe /difṓ/, **Daniel** 1660–1731; English novelist and journalist.
De·gas /daygaá/, **(Hilaire-Germain) Edgar** 1834–1917; French artist.
de Gaulle /də gṓl, gáwl/, **Charles André Joseph Marie** 1890–1970; French general and statesman.
de Klerk /də klérk, klórk/, **F(rederik) W(illem)** 1936– ; president of South Africa (1989–94).
de Koo·ning /də kṓōning/, **Willem** 1904–97; U.S. artist, born in the Netherlands.
De·la·croix /deləkrwaá/, **(Ferdinand Victor) Eugène** 1798–1863; French artist.
de la Mare /del ə már, mér/, **Walter John** 1873–1956; English poet and novelist.
De·li·us /déeleeəs/, **Frederick Theodore Albert** 1862–1934; English composer.
De·moc·ri·tus /dimaákrətəs/ c. 460–c. 370 B.C.; Greek philosopher.
De·mos·the·nes /dimaásthəneez/ 384–322 B.C.; Athenian orator and statesman.
Demp·sey /démpsee/, **Jack (William Harrison)** (called **"the Manassa Mauler"**) 1895–1983; U.S. boxer.
Deng Xiao·ping /dúng shówpíng/ (also **Teng Hsiao-p'ing**) 1904–97; Chinese political leader.
De Quin·cey /də kwínsee/, **Thomas** 1785–1859; English essayist and critic.
de Sade /də saád/, **Marquis** see SADE, DONATIEN.
Des·cartes /daykaárt/, **René** 1596–1650; French philosopher and mathematician.
de So·to /də sṓtō/, **Hernando** 1496–1542; Spanish explorer in Central and North America.
De Va·le·ra /devəlérə, –lírə/, **Eamon** 1882–1975; Irish political leader, born in U.S.
Dew·ey /dṓōee, d(y)ōō–/, **John** 1859–1952; U.S. philosopher and educator.
Dew·ey, Melvil 1851–1931; U.S. librarian; developed decimal system for book classification (1876).
Di·a·ghi·lev /dee-aágəlef/, **Sergei Pavlovich** 1872–1929; Russian ballet impresario.
Di·an·a /dīánə/ **(Princess of Wales)** (born **Diana Frances Spencer**) 1961–97; divorced wife of Charles, Prince of Wales.
Di·as /déeəs, déeaash/ (also **Di'az**), **Bartolomeu** c. 1450–1500; Portuguese explorer.
Dick·ens /díkənz/, **Charles John Huffam** 1812–70; English novelist.
Dick·in·son /díkinsən/, **Emily Elizabeth** 1830–86; U.S. poet.
Di·de·rot /déedərō/, **Denis** 1713–84; French philosopher, encyclopedist, and critic.
Di·Mag·gi·o /dimájeeō/, **Joe (Joseph Paul)** 1914–99; U.S. baseball player.
Di·o·cle·tian /dīəkléeshən/ 245–313; Roman emperor (284–305).
Di·og·e·nes /dī-aájəneez/ c. 400–c. 325 B.C.; Greek philosopher.
Di·o·ny·si·us I /dīənísheeəs, –níseeəs/ (called **"the Elder"**) c. 430–367 B.C.; tyrant of Syracuse.
Dis·ney /díznee/, **Walt (Walter Elias)** 1901–66; U.S. animator, film producer, and theme-park creator.
Dis·rae·li /dizráylee/, **Benjamin (1st Earl of Beaconsfield)** 1804–81; prime minister of Great Britain (1868; 1874–80).
Dodg·son /daájsən/, **Charles Lutwidge** see CARROLL, LEWIS.
Dole /dōl/ **1** Robert Joseph 1923– ; U.S. politician; husband of: **2** Elizabeth Hanford 1936– ; U.S. public official.
Do·min·go /dəmíng-gō/, **Placido** 1941– ; Spanish operatic tenor.
Dom·i·nic /daáminik/, **St.** c. 1170–1221; Spanish cleric; founder of Dominican religious order.
Do·mi·tian /dəmíshən/ 51–96; Roman emperor (81–96).
Don·a·tel·lo /daanətélō/ (born **Donato de Betto di Bardi**) 1386–1466; Italian sculptor.
Don·i·zet·ti /donizétee, dōnə(d)zétee/, **Gaetano** 1797–1848; Italian composer.
Donne /dún/, **John** 1572–1631; English poet and priest.
Dos Pas·sos /dəs pásəs/, **John** 1896–1970; U.S. novelist.
Do·sto·ev·sky /daastəyéfskee, –yév–/ (also **Do·sto·yev·sky**), **Fyodor Mikhailovich** 1821–81; Russian author.
Doug·las /dúgləs/, **Stephen A(rnold)** 1813–61; U.S. political leader and orator.
Doug·lass /dúgləs/, **Frederick** (born **Frederick Augustus Washington Bailey**) c. 1817–95; U.S. abolitionist, author, and orator.
Doyle /doyl/, **(Sir) Arthur Conan** 1859–1930; Scottish author.
Dra·co /dráykō/ 7th cent. B.C.; Athenian lawgiver.
Drake /drayk/, **(Sir) Francis** c. 1540–96; English explorer; circumnavigated the world (1577–80).
Drei·ser /drízər/, **Theodore** 1871–1945; U.S. novelist.
Drey·fus /drífəs/, **Alfred** 1859–1935; French army officer; falsely convicted of treason.
Dry·den /dríd'n/, **John** 1631–1700; English poet.
Dub·ček /dṓōbchek/, **Alexander** 1921–92; Czech political leader.
Du Bois /dōō bóys/, **W(illiam) E(dward) B(urghardt)** 1868–1963; U.S. sociologist and educator.
Du·champ /dY shaáN/, **Marcel** 1887–1968; U.S. artist, born in France.
Du·de·vant /dṓōdəvaaN/, **Amandine-Aurore-Lucile Dupin** see SAND, GEORGE.
Du·fy /dYfée/, **Raoul** 1877–1953; French artist.
Dul·les /dúləs/, **John Foster** 1888–1959; U.S. secretary of state (1953–59).
Dumas /d(y)ōōmaá/ two French playwrights and novelists: **1** Alexandre (called **"Dumas père"**) 1802–70; father of: **2** Alexandre (called **"Dumas fils"**) 1824–95.
Du Mau·ri·er /də máwree-ay, dyōō–/, two English literary figures: **1** George Louis Palmella Busson 1834–96; novelist and illustrator, born in France; grandfather of: **2** (Dame) Daphne 1907-89; novelist.
Dun·can /dúngkən/, **Isadora** 1878–1927; U.S. dancer.
Duns Sco·tus /duns skṓtəs/, **John** c. 1265–1308; Scottish theologian.
du Pont /dōōpónt/, **Eleuthère Irénée** 1771–1834; U.S. industrialist, born in France.
Du·rant /dəránt/ two U.S. historians: **1** Will(iam James) 1885–1981; husband of: **2** Ariel (born **Ida Kaufman**) 1898–1981.
Dü·rer /dṓōrər, dyṓō–/, **Albrecht** 1471–1528; German artist.
Durey /dYré/, **Louis-Edmond** 1888–1979; French composer.
Durk·heim /dYrkém, dórkhīm/, **Émile** 1858–1917; French sociologist.
Du·va·lier /dōōvaalyáy/, **François** (called **"Papa Doc"**) 1907–71; president of Haiti (1957–71).
Dvo·řák /dváwrzhaak/, **Antonin Leopold** 1841–1904; Czech composer.
Dyl·an /dílən/, **Bob** (born **Robert Allen Zimmerman**) 1941– ; U.S. folk-rock singer and songwriter.
Ear·hart /érhaart, éer–/, **Amelia Mary** 1898–1937?; U.S. aviator.
East·man /éestmən/, **George** 1854–1932; U.S. inventor and philanthropist; invented Kodak box camera (1888).
Eco /ékō/, **Umberto** 1932– ; Italian novelist and scholar.
Ed·dy /édee/, **Mary (Morse) Baker** 1821–1910; U.S. founder of the Christian Science Church.
E·den /éed'n/, **(Sir) (Robert) Anthony** 1897–1977; prime minister of Great Britain (1955–57).
Ed·i·son /édisən/, **Thomas Alva** 1847–1931; U.S. inventor.
Ed·ward /édwərd/ name of eight British kings, including: **1** Edward I 1239–1307; reigned 1272–1307. **2** Edward VII 1841–1910; eldest son of Queen Victoria; reigned 1901–10. **3** Edward VIII 1894–1972; reigned 1936; abdicated, became Duke of Windsor.
Ed·wards /édwərdz/, **Jonathan** 1703–58; American theologian and clergyman.
Eich·mann /íkmən, íkhmaan/, **(Karl) Adolf** 1906–62; German Nazi officer; executed as a war criminal.
Eif·fel /ífəl/, **Alexandre Gustave** 1832–1923; French engineer; designer of the Eiffel Tower.
Ein·stein /ínstīn/, **Albert** 1879–1955; U.S. physicist, born in Germany; promulgated theory of relativity.
Ei·sen·how·er /ízənhowər/, **Dwight David** (called **"Ike"**) 1890–1969; U.S. general and 34th president of the U.S. (1953–61).
Ei·sen·staedt /ízənstat/, **Alfred** 1898–1995; U.S. photojournalist, born in Germany.
El Cid see CID, EL.
El·ea·nor /élənər, –nawr/ **of Aq·ui·taine** /ákwitayn/ c. 1122–1204; queen of France (1137–52) and England (1154–89).
El·gar /élgaar, –gər/, **(Sir) Edward William** 1857–1934; English composer.
El Gre·co see GRECO, EL.
E·li·a /éeleeə/ see LAMB, CHARLES.
El·i·ot /éleeət/, **George** (pseudonym of **Mary Ann Evans**) 1819–80; English novelist.
El·i·ot, T(homas) S(tearns) 1888–1965; British poet and critic, born in U.S.
E·liz·a·beth /ilízəbəth/ name of two British monarchs: **1** Elizabeth I 1533–1603; reigned 1558–1603; **2** Elizabeth II 1926– ; reigned 1952– .
El·ling·ton /élingtən/, **Duke (Edward Kennedy)** 1899–1974; U.S. jazz pianist, bandleader, and composer.

El·lis /éləs/, **(Henry) Havelock** 1859–1939; English psychologist.
Em·er·son /émərsən/, **Ralph Waldo** 1803–82; U.S. essayist and poet.
Em·ped·o·cles /empédəkleez/ c. 493–c. 433 B.C.; Greek philosopher.
En·gels /éng-gəlz/, **Friedrich** 1820–95; German political philosopher in England.
En·ni·us /éneeəs/, **Quintus** 239–169 B.C.; Roman poet and playwright.
En·ver Pa·sha /énver paáshə, pəshaá/ 1881–1922; Turkish statesman and military leader.
E·pi·cu·rus /epikyóórəs/ 341–270 B.C.; Greek philosopher.
E·ras·mus /irázməs/, **Desiderius** c. 1469–1536; Dutch theologian and humanist.
Er·ic /érik/ (called **"the Red"**) c. 940–c. 1010; Norse explorer.
Er·ic·son /ériksən/ (also **Er'ics·son**; **Er'iks·son**), **Leif** early 11th cent.; Norse explorer.
Ernst /ernst/, **Max** 1891–1976; German artist.
Eth·el·red II /éthəlred/, (called **"the Unready"**) c. 969–1016; king of England (978–1016).
Eu·clid /yóóklid/ 3rd cent. B.C.; Greek mathematician.
Eu·gé·nie /yóójənee, yóójáynee/ 1826–1920; empress of France (1853–71), born in Spain; wife of Napoleon III.
Eu·rip·i·des /yóóripideez/ 480–c. 406 B.C.; Greek playwright.
Ev·ans /évənz/, **(Sir) Arthur John** 1851–1941; British archaeologist.
Ev·ans, (Dame) Edith 1888–1976; English actress.
Ev·ans, Mary Ann see ELIOT, GEORGE.
Fa·ber·gé /fabərzháy/, **Peter Carl** 1846–1920; Russian goldsmith and jeweler.
Fahd /faad/ 1922– ; king of Saudi Arabia (1982–).
Fair·field /fáirfeeld/, **Cicily Isabel** see WEST, REBECCA.
Fal·la /faáyə/, **Manuel de** 1876–1946; Spanish composer.
Far·a·day /fárədee, –day/, **Michael** 1791–1867; British chemist and physicist.
Fa·rouk /fəróók/ 1920–65; king of Egypt (1936–52).
Far·ra·gut /fárəgət/, **David Glasgow** (born **James Glasgow Farragut**) 1801–70; U.S. naval commander.
Faulk·ner /fáwknər/, **William Cuthbert** 1897–1962; U.S. novelist.
Fau·ré /fawráy/, **Gabriel** 1845–1924; French composer.
Faust /fowst/ (also **Faus·tus**) died c. 1540; German astronomer and necromancer.
Fer·ber /fárbər/, **Edna** 1885–1968; U.S. author.
Fer·di·nand II /fárd'nand/ (called **"the Catholic"**) 1452–1516; W European king who founded the Spanish monarchy; husband of Isabella I.
Fer·mi /férmee/, **Enrico** 1901–54; U.S. nuclear physicist, born in Italy.
Fied·ler /feédlər/, **Arthur** 1894–1979; U.S. conductor.
Field·ing /feélding/, **Henry** 1707–54; English novelist.
Fields /feeldz/, **W. C.** (born **William Claude Dukenfield**) 1880–1946; U.S. vaudevillian and comedic actor.
Fill·more /filmawr, –mōr/, **Millard** 1800–74; 13th president of the U.S. (1850–53).
Fitz·ger·ald /fitsjérəld/, **Ella** 1918–96; U.S. jazz singer.
Fitz·ger·ald, F(rancis) Scott Key 1896–1940; U.S. author.
Flau·bert /flōbér/, **Gustave** 1821–80; French author.
Flem·ing /fléming/, **(Sir) Alexander** 1881–1955; Scottish bacteriologist; discovered and developed penicillin.
Flem·ing, Ian Lancaster 1908–64; English novelist.
Fletch·er /fléchər/, **John** 1579–1625; English playwright.
Foch /fawsh/, **Ferdinand** 1851–1929; French general.
Fon·da /faándə/ family of U.S. actors, including: **1** Henry 1905–82; father of: **2** Jane 1937– .
Fon·teyn /faantáyn/, **(Dame) Margot** (born **Margaret Hookham**) 1919–91; English prima ballerina.
Ford /fawrd/, **Ford Madox** (born **Ford Hermann Hueffer**) 1873–1939; English novelist.
Ford, Gerald Rudolph, Jr. (born **Leslie Lynch King, Jr.**) 1913– ; 38th president of the U.S. (1974–77).
Ford, Henry 1863–1947; U.S. automobile manufacturer.
For·ster /fáwrstər/, **E(dward) M(organ)** 1879–1970; English novelist.
For·syth /fáwrsīth, fawrsíth/, **Frederick** 1938– ; English novelist.
Fos·ter /fáwstər, faástər/, **Stephen Collins** 1826–64; U.S. songwriter.
Fou·cault /fóókó/, **Michel** 1929–84; French philosopher.
Fowles /fowlz/, **John** 1926– ; English novelist.
Fox /faaks/, **George** 1624–91; English founder of the Society of Friends (Quakers).
Fra·go·nard /fragənaár/, **Jean-Honoré** 1732–1806; French artist.
France /frans/, **Anatole** (pseudonym of **Jacques Anatole Thibault**) 1844–1924; French author.
Fran·cis /fránsis/ **of As·si·si** /əsísee, əseézee/, **St.** c. 1181–1226; Italian monk; founder of Franciscan religious order.
Franck /fraangk/, **César** 1822–90; French composer, born in Belgium.
Fran·co /frángkō, fraáng–/, **Francisco** 1892–1975; Spanish general; dictator of Spain (1939–75).
Frank /frangk/, **Anne** 1929–45; Jewish diarist, born in Germany; wrote diary while in hiding from the Nazis.
Frank·furt·er /frángkfərtər/, **Felix** 1882–1965; U.S. Supreme Court justice (1939–62), born in Austria.
Frank·lin /frángklən/, **Aretha** 1943– ; U.S. soul and gospel singer.
Frank·lin, Benjamin 1706–90; U.S. statesman, author, and inventor.
Franz Jo·sef I /fraanz yṓzəf/ 1830–1916; emperor of Austria (1848–1916).
Fra·zer /fráyzər/, **(Sir) James George** 1854–1941; Scottish anthropologist.
Fred·er·ick I /fréd(ə)rik/ (called **"Barbarossa"**) c. 1123–90; Holy Roman emperor (1152–90).
Fred·er·ick II (called **"the Great"**) 1712–86; king of Prussia (1740–86).
Fred·er·ick Wil·liam /wílyəm/ (called **"the Great Elector"**) 1620–88; elector of Brandenburg (1640–88).
Fré·mont /freémaant/, **John Charles** 1813–90; U.S. explorer and politician.
Freud /froyd/, **Lucian** 1922– ; British artist, born in Germany.
Freud, Sigmund 1856–1939; Austrian neurologist; founder of psychoanalysis.
Frie·dan /freedán/, **Betty** (born **Naomi Goldstein**) 1921– ; U.S. feminist and author.
Fried·man /freédmən/, **Milton** 1912– ; U.S. economist.
Frost /frawst/, **Robert Lee** 1874–1963; U.S. poet.
Frye /frī/, **(Herman) Northrop** 1912–91; Canadian literary critic.
Fu·ad /fóó-aád/ two kings of Egypt: **1** Fuad I 1868–1936; reigned 1922–36. **2** Fuad II 1952– ; reigned 1952–53.
Fuen·tes /fwéntays/, **Carlos** 1928– ; Mexican author.
Ful·bright /fóólbrīt/, **(James) William** 1905–95; U.S. senator.
Ful·ler /fóólər/, **R(ichard) Buckminster** 1895–1983; U.S. engineer and architect.
Ful·ler, (Sarah) Margaret 1810–50; U.S. critic and social reformer.
Ful·ton /fóólt'n/, **Robert** 1765–1815; U.S. engineer; developed first commercially successful steamboat.
Ga·ble /gáybəl/, **(William) Clark** 1901–60; U.S. actor.
Gad·da·fi /gədaáfee/ see QADHAFI, MUAMMAR.
Ga·ga·rin /gəgaárən/, **Yuri** 1934–68; Soviet cosmonaut; first human in space.
Gage /gayj/, **Thomas** 1721–87; British general.
Gains·bor·ough /gáynzbrō, –bərə/, **Thomas** 1727–88; English artist.
Gal·braith /gálbrayth/, **John Kenneth** 1908– ; U.S. economist, born in Canada.
Ga·len /gáylən/ c. 130–c. 201; Greek physician.
Gal·i·le·o /galəláyō, –leéō/ 1564–1642; Italian astronomer.
Gals·wor·thy /gáwlzwərthee/, **John** 1867–1933; English novelist and playwright.
Ga·ma /gaámə/, **Vasco da** c. 1469–1524; Portuguese navigator.
Gan·dhi /gaándee/ two Indian prime ministers: **1** Indira Priyadarshini Nehru 1917–84; in office 1966–77; 1980–84; assassinated; mother of: **2** Rajiv 1944–91; in office 1984–89; assassinated.
Gan·dhi, Mahatma (born **Mohandes Karamchand**) 1869–1948; Indian nationalist and spiritual leader.
Gar·bo /gaárbō/, **Greta** (born **Greta Louisa Gustafsson**) 1905–90; U.S. actress, born in Sweden.
Gar·cí·a Lor·ca /gaarseéə láwrkə/, **Federico** 1899–1936; Spanish poet and playwright.
Gar·cí·a Már·quez /gaarseéə maárkays/, **Gabriel** 1928– ; Colombian author.
Gard·ner /gaárdnər/, **Erle Stanley** 1899–1970; U.S. author.
Gar·field /gaárfeeld/, **James Abram** 1831–81; 20th president of the U.S. (1881); assassinated.
Gar·i·bal·di /garəbáwldee/, **Giuseppe** 1807–82; Italian nationalist.
Gar·land /gárlənd/, **Judy** (born **Frances Gumm**) 1922–69; U.S. singer and actress.
Gar·ri·son /gárəsən/, **William Lloyd** 1805–79; U.S. editor and abolitionist.
Gar·vey /gaárvee/, **Marcus Mosiah** 1887–1940; Jamaican black nationalist.
Gates /gayts/, **Bill (William Henry)** 1955– ; U.S. computer executive.
Gates, Horatio c. 1728–1806; American Revolutionary War general, born in England.
Gau·guin /gōgáN/, **(Eugène) Paul** 1848–1903; French artist.
Gaulle see DE GAULLE.
Gau·ta·ma /gówtəmə, gáw–/ see BUDDHA.
Geh·rig /gérig/, **Lou (Henry Louis)** (called **"the Iron Horse"**) 1903–41; U.S. baseball player.
Gei·sel /gízəl/, **Theodor Seuss** see SEUSS, DR.
Gen·ghis Khan /géng-gəs, jeng-gəs kaán/ c. 1162–1227; ruler of the Mongols; conquered most of Asia.
George III /jawrj/ 1738–1820; king of England (1760–1820); reigned during American Revolution.
George, St. died c. 337; patron saint of England.
Ge·ron·i·mo /jəraánəmō/ c. 1829–1909; Apache Indian leader.
Gersh·win /gə́rshwən/ **1** Ira 1896–1983; U.S. lyricist; brother of: **2** George 1898–1937; U.S. composer.
Get·ty /gétee/, **J(ean) Paul** 1892–1976; U.S. industrialist.

Gib·bon /gíbən/, **Edward** 1737–94; English historian.
Gib·ran /jibraán/, **Kahlil** 1883–1931; Lebanese author and artist.
Gide /zheed/, **André** 1869–1951; French author.
Giel·gud /géelgood/, **(Sir) (Arthur) John** 1904– ; English actor and director.
Gil·bert /gílbərt/, **(Sir) W(illiam) S(chwenck)** 1836–1911; English playwright and librettist; collaborated with composer (Sir) Arthur Sullivan.
Gil·les·pie /gəléspee/, **Dizzy (John Birks)** 1917–93; U.S. jazz musician.
Ging·rich /gíngrich/, **Newt(on Leroy)** 1943– ; U.S. politician.
Gins·berg /gínzbərg/, **Allen** 1926–97; U.S. poet.
Gins·berg, Ruth Bader 1933– ; U.S. Supreme Court justice (1993–).
Gior·gio·ne /jawrjṓnay/ c. 1478–1511; Italian artist.
Giot·to /jaátō, jee-aátō/ c. 1267–1337; Florentine artist.
Gis·card d'Es·taing /zheeskaár destáN/, **Valéry** 1926– ; president of France (1974–81).
Gish /gish/, **Lillian** 1896–1993; U.S. actress.
Glad·stone /gládstōn, –stən/, **William Ewart** 1809–98; prime minister of Great Britain (1868–74; 1880–85; 1886; 1892–94).
Glea·son /gléesən/, **Jackie** 1916–87; U.S. entertainer.
Glen·dow·er /glendówər/ (also **Glyn·dwr'**) /glindóor/, **Owen** c. 1355–c. 1417; legendary Welsh rebel.
Glenn /glen/, **John Herschel, Jr.** 1921– ; U.S. astronaut and politician; first American to orbit the earth (1962).
God·dard /gaádərd/, **Robert Hutchings** 1882–1945; U.S. rocket scientist.
Go·di·va /gədívə/, **Lady** died 1080; legendary English noblewoman.
Go·du·nov /gṓd'n-awf, gáwd–/, **Boris** 1550–1605; czar of Russia (1598–1605).
Goeb·bels /gṓbəlz, gə́r–/, **(Paul) Joseph** 1897–1945; German director of Nazi propaganda.
Goe·ring /gṓring, gə́r–/, **Hermann Wilhelm** 1893–1946; German Nazi leader; directed the air force.
Goe·the /gṓtə, gə́r–/, **Johann Wolfgang von** 1749–1832; German poet and statesman.
Go·gol /gṓgawl, gáwgəl/, **Nikolai Vasilievich** 1809–52; Russian novelist and playwright.
Gol·ding /gṓlding/, **(Sir) William** 1911–93; English author.
Gold·smith /gṓldsmith/, **Oliver** 1728–74; Irish author.
Go·li·ath /gəlíəth/ biblical giant killed by David.
Gom·pers /gaámpərz/, **Samuel** 1850–1924; U.S. labor leader, born in England.
Good·man /góodmən/, **Benny (Benjamin David)** (called **"the King of Swing"**) 1909–86; U.S. jazz clarinetist and bandleader.
Good·year /góodyeer/, **Charles** 1800–60; U.S. inventor; developed vulcanized rubber.
Gor·ba·chev /gáwrbəchawf, –chawv/, **Mikhail Sergeyevich** 1931– ; president of the Soviet Union (1988–91).
Gordimer /gáwrdimər/, **Nadine** 1923– ; South African novelist.
Gor·don /gáwrd'n/, **Charles George** 1833–85; British general and colonial administrator.
Gore /gawr/, **Albert, Jr.** 1948– ; U.S. vice president (1993–).
Gor·ky /gáwrkee/, **Maxim** (pseudonym of **Aleksei Maksimovich Peshkov**) 1868–1936; Russian author and revolutionary.
Gou·nod /goonṓ/, **Charles François** 1818–93; French composer.
Go·ya /góyə/, **Francisco** 1746–1828; Spanish artist.
Gra·ham /gráyəm, gram/, **Billy (William Franklin)** 1918– ; U.S. evangelical preacher.
Gra·ham, Katherine 1917– ; U.S. newspaper executive.
Gra·ham, Martha 1893–1991; U.S. dancer and choreographer.
Gra·hame /gráyəm/, **Kenneth** 1859–1932; Scottish author.
Grant /grant/, **Cary** (born **Archibald Alexander Leach**) 1904–86; U.S. actor, born in England.
Grant, Ulysses S(impson) (born **Hiram Ulysses Grant**) 1822–85; Union general in the American Civil War; 18th president of the U.S. (1869–77).
Grass /graas/, **Günter** 1927– ; German novelist and playwright.
Graves /grayvz/, **Robert** 1895–1985; English poet, novelist, and critic.
Gray /gray/, **Thomas** 1716–71; English poet.
Gre·co /grékō/, **El** (born **Domenikos Theotokopoulos**) 1541–1614; Spanish artist, born in Crete.
Gree·ley /gréelee/, **Horace** 1811–72; U.S. journalist and politician.
Greene /green/, **(Henry) Graham** 1904–91; English novelist.
Greene, Nathanael 1742–86; American Revolutionary War general.
Green·span /géenspan/, **Alan** 1926– ; U.S. economist.
Greer /greer/, **Germaine** 1939– ; Australian feminist and author.
Greg·o·ry /grégəree/ name of sixteen popes, including: **1** Gregory I, St. (called **"the Great"**) c. 540–604; pope (590–604); developed the Gregorian chant. **2** Gregory XIII 1502–85; pope (1572–85); introduced the modern calendar.
Gren·ville /grénvil/, **George** 1712–70; prime minister of Great Britain (1763–65).
Grey /gray/, **(Lady) Jane** 1537–54; queen of England (1553); executed by Mary I.
Grey, Zane 1875–1939; U.S. author.
Grieg /greeg/, **Edvard** 1843–1907; Norwegian composer.
Grif·fith /gríﬁth/, **D(avid Lewelyn) W(ark)** 1875–1948; U.S. film director.
Grimm /grim/ two German philologists and folklorists: **1** Jacob Ludwig Karl 1785–1863; brother of: **2** Wilhelm Karl 1786–1859.
Gro·my·ko /grəméekō/, **Andrei** 1909–89; Russian diplomat.
Gro·pi·us /grṓpeeəs/, **Walter** 1883–1969; U.S. architect, born in Germany.
Gue·va·ra /g(w)əvaárə, gay–/, **Che (Ernesto)** 1928–67; Cuban revolutionary, born in Argentina.
Guin·ness /gínəs/, **(Sir) Alec** 1914– ; British actor.
Gus·tav·us A·dol·phus /gustaávəs ədáwlfəs/ 1594–1632; king of Sweden (1611–32).
Gut·en·berg /góot'n-bərg/, **Johannes** c. 1400–68; German inventor of printing with movable type.
Guth·rie /gúthree/, **Woody (Woodrow Wilson)** 1912–67; U.S. folk musician, singer, and songwriter.
Hai·le Se·las·sie /hílee səlaásee, –lás–/ (born **Tafari Makonnen**) 1892–1975; emperor of Ethiopia (1930–74).
Hak·luyt /háklōōt, háklit/, **Richard** c. 1552–1616; English geographer.
Hale /hayl/, **Nathan** 1755–76; American Revolutionary hero; hanged as a spy by British.
Ha·ley /háylee/, **Alex Palmer** 1921–92; U.S. author.
Hal·ley /hálee, háylee/, **Edmund** 1656–1742; English astronomer.
Hals /haals/, **Frans** c. 1580–1666; Dutch artist.
Hal·sey /háwlzee/, **William Frederick** (called **"Bull"**) 1882–1959; U.S. admiral.
Ham·il·ton /hámiltən/, **Alexander** 1755–1804; first U.S. secretary of the treasury (1789–95).
Ham·mar·skjold /haáməshəld, hám–/, **Dag** 1905–61; Swedish statesman; secretary-general of the United Nations (1953–61).
Ham·mer·stein /hámərstīn/, **Oscar, II** 1895–1960; U.S. lyricist and librettist.
Ham·mett /hámit/, **(Samuel) Dashiell** 1894–1961; U.S. author.
Ham·mu·ra·bi /hamərаábee, haam–/ fl. 18th cent. B.C.; king of Babylon (1792–1750 B.C.); instituted early code of laws.
Ham·sun /haámsən/, **Knut** (pseudonym of **Knut Pedersen**) 1859–1952; Norwegian novelist.
Han·cock /hánkaak/, **John** 1737–93; American politician; first signer of the U.S. Declaration of Independence.
Han·del /hánd'l/, **George Frederick** 1685–1759; British composer, born in Germany.
Han·dy /hándee/, **W(illiam) C(hristopher)** 1873–1958; U.S. blues musician and composer.
Hanks /hangks/, **Tom (Thomas J.)** 1956– ; U.S. actor.
Han·ni·bal /hánibəl/ 247–182 B.C.; Carthaginian general.
Har·ding /haárding/, **Warren Gamaliel** 1865–1923; 29th president of the U.S. (1921–23).
Har·dy /haárdee/, **Thomas** 1840–1928; English author.
Harms·worth /haármzwərth/, **Alfred (Viscount Northcliffe)** 1865–1922; English publisher and politician.
Har·ris /háris/, **Joel Chandler** 1848–1908; U.S. author.
Har·ri·son /hárisən/, **George** 1943– ; British pop and rock guitarist, singer, and songwriter.
Har·ri·son, (Sir) Rex 1908–90; English actor.
Har·ri·son, family of U.S. politicians, including: **1** William Henry 1773–1841; 9th president of the U.S. (1841); grandfather of: **2** Benjamin 1833–1901; 23rd president of the U.S. (1889–93).
Hart /haart/, **Lorenz** 1895–1943; U.S. lyricist.
Harte /haart/, **(Francis) Bret** 1836–1902; U.S. author.
Har·vey /haárvee/, **William** 1578–1657; English physician and anatomist.
Hath·a·way /háthəway/, **Anne** c. 1557–1623; wife of William Shakespeare.
Haupt·mann /hówptmaan/, **Gerhart** 1862–1946; German playwright.
Ha·vel /haávəl/, **Václav** 1936– ; Czech author and politician.
Hawke /hawk/, **Bob (Robert James Lee)** 1929– ; prime minister of Australia (1983–91).
Hawk·ing /háwking/, **Stephen William** 1942– ; British scientist.
Haw·thorne /háwthawrn/, **Nathaniel** 1804–64; U.S. author.
Hay /hay/, **John Milton** 1838–1905; U.S. statesman.
Hay·dn /híd'n/, **Franz Joseph** 1732–1809; Austrian composer.
Hayes /hayz/, **Helen** (born **Helen Hayes Brown**) 1900–93; U.S. actress.
Hayes, Rutherford B(irchard) 1822–93; 19th president of the U.S. (1877–81).
Hearst /hərst/, **William Randolph** 1863–1951; U.S. newspaper publisher.
Heath /heeth/, **(Sir) Edward** 1916– ; prime minister of Great Britain (1970–74).
He·gel /háygəl/, **Georg Wilhelm Friedrich** 1770–1831; German philosopher.
Hei·deg·ger /hídigər/, **Martin** 1889–1976; German philosopher.
Hei·fetz /hífəts/, **Jascha** 1901–87; U.S. violinist, born in Lithuania.

Hei·ne /hínə/, **(Christian) Heinrich** 1797–1856; German poet.
Heinz /hīnz/, **Henry John** 1844–1919; U.S. manufacturer of processed foods.
Hel·ler /hélər/, **Joseph** 1923– ; U.S. author.
Hell·man /hélmən/, **Lillian Florence** 1905–84; U.S. playwright.
Hem·ing·way /hémingway/, **Ernest Miller** 1899–1961; U.S. author.
Hen·drix /héndriks/, **Jimi** 1942–70; U.S. rock guitarist, singer, and songwriter.
Hen·ry /hénree/ (called **"the Navigator"**) 1394–1460; prince of Portugal; sponsor of geographic expeditions.
Hen·ry VIII 1491–1547; king of England (1509–47).
Hen·ry, O. (pseudonym of **William Sydney Porter**) 1862–1910; U.S. author.
Hen·ry, Patrick 1736–99; American patriot and orator.
Hen·son /hénsən/, **Jim (James Maury)** 1936–90; U.S. puppeteer; creator of the Muppets.
Hep·burn /hépbərn/, **Audrey** 1929–93; U.S. actress, born in Belgium.
Hep·burn, Katharine 1909– ; U.S. actress.
Her·a·cli·tus /herəklítəs/ c. 500 B.C.; Greek philosopher.
Her·od /hérəd/ several rulers of ancient Palestine, including: **1** Herod I (called **"the Great"**) c. 74–4 B.C.; king of Judea (37–4 B.C.); father of: **2** Herod Antipas 22 B.C.–A.D. c. 40; ruler of Galilee (4 B.C.–A.D. 40). **3** Herod Agrippa I 10 B.C.–A.D. 44; king of Judea (41–44); grandson of Herod I.
He·rod·o·tus /hərádətəs/ (called **"the Father of History"**) fl. 5th cent. B.C.; Greek historian.
Her·rick /hérik/, **Robert** 1591–1674; English poet.
Her·zl /hértsəl/, **Theodor** 1860–1904; Austrian founder of the Zionist movement, born in Hungary.
He·si·od /héeseeəd, hésee–/ fl. 8th cent. B.C.; Greek poet.
Hess /hes/, **(Walter Richard) Rudolf** 1894–1987; German Nazi official, born in Egypt.
Hes·se /hésə/, **Hermann** 1877–1962; Swiss author, born in Germany.
Hey·er·dahl /híərdaal/, **Thor** 1914– ; Norwegian explorer and ethnologist.
Hick·ok /híkaak/, **James Butler** (called **"Wild Bill Hickock"**) 1837–76; U.S. frontiersman.
Hil·la·ry /híləree/, **(Sir) Edmund Percival** 1919– ; New Zealand mountaineer; climbed Mt. Everest (1953).
Hil·ton /hílt'n/, **James** 1900–54; English novelist.
Himm·ler /hímlər/, **Heinrich** 1900–45; German head of the Nazi secret police.
Hin·de·mith /híndəmit/, **Paul** 1895–1963; German composer.
Hin·den·burg /híndinbərg/, **Paul von** 1847–1934; German field marshal; 2nd president of Germany (1925–32).
Hip·poc·ra·tes /hipaákrəteez/ (called **"the Father of Medicine"**) c. 460–c. 377 B.C.; Greek physician.
Hi·ro·hi·to /heeróheétō/ (also known as **Sho'wa**) 1901–89; emperor of Japan (1926–89).
Hitch·cock /híchkaak/, **(Sir) Alfred Joseph** 1899–1980; British film director.
Hit·ler /hítlər/, **Adolf** (born **Adolf Schicklgruber**) (called **"Der Führer"**) 1889–1945; dictator of Nazi Germany (1934–45), born in Austria.
Ho Chi Minh /hō cheé min/ (born **Nguyen That Thanh**) 1890–1969; Vietnamese revolutionary; president of North Vietnam (1954–1969).
Hobbes /haabz/, **Thomas** 1588–1679; English philosopher.
Ho·garth /hógaarth/, **William** 1697–1764; English artist and engraver.
Hol·bein /hólbīn, háwl–/ name of two German artists: **1** Hans (called **"the Elder"**) c. 1465–1524; father of: **2** Hans (called **"the Younger"**) c. 1497–1543; worked in England.
Hol·ins·hed /haálins-hed, –inshed/, **Raphael** died c. 1580; English chronicler.
Holmes /hōlmz, hōmz/ **1** Oliver Wendell 1809–94; U.S. author and physician; father of: **2** Oliver Wendell 1841–1935; U.S. Supreme Court justice (1902–32).
Holst /hōlst/, **Gustav** 1874–1934; English composer.
Ho·mer /hómər/ 8th cent. B.C.; Greek epic poet.
Ho·mer, Winslow 1836–1910; U.S. artist.
Ho·neck·er /hónəkər/, **Erich** 1912–94; head of state of East Germany (1976–89).
Hoo·ver /hóovər/, **Herbert Clark** 1874–1964; 31st president of the U.S. (1929–33).
Hoo·ver, J(ohn) Edgar 1895–1972; director of the Federal Bureau of Investigation (1924–72).
Hope /hōp/, **Bob** (born **Leslie Townes Hope**) 1903– ; U.S. comedian and actor, born in England.
Hop·kins /haápkinz/, **Gerard Manley** 1844–89; English poet.
Hop·per /haápər/, **Edward** 1882–1967; U.S. artist.
Hor·ace /háwrəs/ **(Quintus Horatius Flaccus)** 65–8 B.C.; Roman poet.
Hor·o·witz /háwrəwits, haár–/, **Vladimir** 1904–89; U.S. pianist, born in Russia.
Hou·di·ni /hoodéenee/, **Harry** (born **Ehrich Weiss**) 1874–1926; U.S. magician and escape artist, born in Hungary.
Hous·man /hówsmən/, **A(lfred) E(dward)** 1859–1936; English poet.
Hous·ton /hyóostən/, **Samuel** 1793–1863; U.S. general and president of the Republic of Texas (1836–38).
Howe /how/, **Elias** 1819–67; U.S. inventor of the sewing machine.
Howe, Julia Ward 1819–1910; U.S. social reformer and author.
How·ells /hówəlz/, **William Dean** 1837–1920; U.S. author and editor.
Hox·ha /háwjə/, **Enver** 1908–85; Albanian Communist political leader.
Hud·son /húdsən/, **Henry** died 1611?; English explorer.
Hughes /hyooz, yooz/, **Howard Robard** 1905–76; U.S. aviator and industrialist.
Hughes, (James) Langston 1902–67; U.S. author.
Hughes, Ted 1930–98; English poet.
Hu·go /hyóogō/, **Victor** 1802–85; French author.
Hume /hyoom, yoom/, **David** 1711–76; Scottish philosopher and historian.
Hum·per·dinck /húmpərdingk/, **Engelbert** 1854–1921; German composer.
Hus·sein I /hoosayn/ (also **Hu'sain**) 1935–99; king of Jordan (1953–99).
Hus·sein, Saddam 1937– ; political leader of Iraq.
Hus·serl /húsərl/, **Edmund** 1859–1938; German philosopher.
Hutch·in·son /húchinsən/, **Anne** 1591–1643; American religious leader, born in England.
Hux·ley /húkslee/, **Aldous Leonard** 1894–1963; English novelist.
Ibn Sa·ud /íbən saa-óod/, **Abdul-Aziz** c. 1880–1953; king of Saudi Arabia (1932–53).
Ib·sen /íbsən/, **Henrik** 1828–1906; Norwegian playwright.
Ig·na·tius /ignáyshəs/ **of Loy·o·la** /loyólə/, **St.** 1491–1556; Spanish founder of the Jesuit religious order.
Ikh·na·ton /iknaátən/ see *Amenhotep IV* (AMENHOTEP).
Inge /inj/, **William Motter** 1913–73; U.S. playwright.
In·gres /aNgr/, **Jean** 1780–1867; French artist.
Io·nes·co /yənéskō, eeə–/, **Eugène** 1912–94; French playwright, born in Romania.
Ir·ving /ərving/, **Washington** 1783–1859; U.S. author.
I·sa·bel·la I /izəbélə/ 1474–1504; queen of Castile and Aragon; sponsor of Christopher Columbus.
Ish·er·wood /ishərwood/, **Christopher William Bradshaw** 1904–86; U.S. novelist, born in England.
I·van IV /ívən/ (called **"Ivan the Terrible"**) 1530–84; first czar of Russia (1547–84).
Ives /ivz/, **Charles Edward** 1874–1954; U.S. composer.
Jack·son /jáksən/, **Andrew** (called **"Old Hickory"**) 1767–1845; U.S. general; 7th president of the U.S. (1828–37).
Jack·son, Jesse Louis 1941– ; U.S. clergyman and civil-rights activist.
Jack·son, Michael 1958– ; U.S. pop singer and songwriter.
Jack·son, Shirley 1919–65; U.S. author.
Jack·son, Thomas Jonathan (called **"Stonewall Jackson"**) 1824–63; Confederate general in the American Civil War.
Jag·ger /jágər/, **Mick (Michael Philip)** 1944– ; English rock singer.
James I /jaymz/, 1566–1625; king of England and Ireland (1603–25). ▫▫ **Ja·co·be'an** *adj. & n.*
James, Henry 1843–1916; British novelist and critic, born in the U.S.
James, Jesse Woodson 1847–82; U.S. outlaw.
James, P(hyliss) D(orothy) 1920– ; British author.
James, William 1842–1910; U.S. philosopher and psychologist.
Jef·fer·son /jéfərsən/, **Thomas** 1743–1826; U.S. patriot and statesman; 3rd president of the U.S. (1801–09). ▫▫ **Jef·fer·so'ni·an** /–sóneeən/ *adj.*
Je·rome /jərṓm/, **St.** c. 342–420; early Christian scholar; published the Vulgate Bible.
Je·sus /jéezəs, –zəz/ (also known as **Je'sus Christ'** or **Je'sus of Naz'a·reth**) c. 4 B.C.–c. A.D. 30; source of the Christian religion.
Joan /jōn/ **of Arc, St.** (called **"the Maid of Orleans"**) c. 1412–31; French national heroine and Christian martyr.
John /jaan/ (called **"John Lackland"**) 1165–1216; king of England (1199–1216); signed the Magna Carta (1215).
John Paul II /jaan páwl/ (born **Karol Jozef Wojtyla**) 1920– ; pope (1978–), born in Poland.
Johns /jaanz/, **Jasper** 1930– ; U.S. artist.
John·son /jaánsən/, **Andrew** 1808–75; 17th president of the U.S. (1865–69).
John·son, Lyndon Baines (called **"L.B.J."**) 1908–73; 36th president of the U.S. (1963–69).
John·son, Samuel 1709–84; English lexicographer and author.
Jo·li·et /zhawlyáy/, **Louis** 1645–1700; French-Canadian explorer.
Jones /jōnz/, **Inigo** 1573–1652; English architect.
Jones, John Paul (born **John Paul**) 1747–92; American naval hero, born in Scotland.
Jong /jong/, **Erica** 1942– ; U.S. author.
Jon·son /jaánsən/, **Ben(jamin)** 1572–1637; English playwright and poet.
Jordan /jáwrd'n/, **Michael Jeffrey** 1963– ; U.S. basketball player.
Jo·se·phus /jōséefəs/, **Flavius** c. 37–c. 100; Jewish historian and general.

Joyce /joys/, **James** 1882–1941; Irish author.
Juan Car·los /waan kaárlōs, hwaan/ 1938– ; king of Spain (1975–).
Ju·das Is·car·i·ot /jóódəs iskáireeət/ died c. 30; apostle who betrayed Jesus.
Jul·ius /jóólyəs/, **Caesar** see CAESAR, (GAIUS) JULIUS.
Jung /yoong/, **Carl Gustav** 1875–1961; Swiss psychologist. □□ **Jung'i·an** /–eeən/ *adj.*
Jus·tin·i·an /justíneeən/ 483–565; Byzantine emperor (527–565); codified Roman law.
Ju·ve·nal /jóóvən'l/ c. 60–c. 140; Roman satirist.
Kaf·ka /kaáfkə/, **Franz** 1883–1924; Czech author.
Ka·me·ha·me·ha I /kəmayəmáyhə/ c. 1758–1819; king of Hawaii (1810–19).
Kan·din·sky /kandínskee/, **Wassily** 1866–1944; Russian artist.
Kant /kaant, kant/, **Immanuel** 1724–1804; German philosopher.
Ka·wa·ba·ta /kaawəbaátə, kawaábətə/, **Yasunari** 1899–1972; Japanese author.
Keats /keets/, **John** 1795–1821; English poet.
Kel·ler /kélər/, **Helen Adams** 1880–1968; U.S. author, educator, and social reformer; deaf and blind from infancy.
Kel·ly /kélee/, **Grace** 1928–82; U.S. actress; princess of Monaco (1956–82).
Kem·pis /kémpis/, **Thomas à** (born **Thomas Hemerken**) c. 1379–1471; German monk and author.
Ken·ne·dy U.S. political family, including three brothers: **1** John Fitzgerald (called **"J.F.K."**) 1917–63; 35th president of the U.S. (1961–63); assassinated; **2** Robert Francis 1925–68; U.S. politician; assassinated; and **3** Ted (Edward Moore) 1932– ; U.S. politician.
Ken·ne·dy /kénədee/, **Anthony Mcleod** 1936– ; U.S. Supreme Court justice (1988–).
Ken·yat·ta /kenyaátə/, **Jomo** c. 1891–1978; Kenyan political leader.
Kep·ler /képlər/, **Johannes** 1571–1630; German astronomer.
Kern /kərn/, **Jerome** 1885–1945; U.S. composer.
Ker·ou·ac /kéroo-ak/, **Jack** 1922–69; U.S. author.
Key /kee/, **Francis Scott** 1779–1843; U.S. lawyer; wrote lyrics to "The Star-Spangled Banner."
Keynes /kaynz/, **John Maynard** 1883–1946; English economist. □□ **Keynes·i·an** /káynzeeən/ *adj. & n.*
Kho·mei·ni /khōmáynee, kō–/, **(Ayatollah) Ruhollah** c. 1900–89; Islamic head of state of Iran (1979–89).
Khrush·chev /kroóshchef, –chawf/, **Nikita Sergeyevich** 1894–1971; Russian politician; premier of the Soviet Union (1958–64).
Kidd /kid/, **William** (called **"Captain Kidd"**) 1645–1701; Scottish pirate.
Kier·ke·gaard /keérkəgaard, –gawr/, **Sören** 1813–55; Danish philosopher.
Kil·mer /kílmər/, **(Alfred) Joyce** 1886–1918; U.S. poet.
Kim Il Sung /kim il soong/ 1912–94; premier (1948–72) and president (1972–94) of North Korea.
King /king/, **Martin Luther, Jr.** 1929–68; U.S. civil-rights leader; assassinated.
King, Stephen 1947– ; U.S. author.
Kip·ling /kípling/, **(Joseph) Rudyard** 1865–1936; English author, born in India.
Kis·sin·ger /kísinjər/, **Henry Alfred** 1923– ; U.S. statesman, born in Germany.
Kitch·e·ner /kíchənər/, **(Horatio) Herbert (1st Earl Kitchener of Khartoum)** 1850–1916; British soldier and statesman.
Klee /klay/, **Paul** 1879–1940; Swiss artist.
Knox /naaks/, **Henry** 1750–1806; first U.S. secretary of war (1785–94).
Knox, John 1505–72; Scottish religious leader.
Knut, /kanóót, –nyóót/, see CANUTE.
Kohl /kōl/, **Helmut** 1930– ; German political leader.
Kos·ci·us·ko /kawshchóóshkō, kaasee-óóskō, kaaz–/, **Thaddeus** 1746–1817; Polish patriot; American Revolutionary War general in the Continental army.
Kos·suth /kaásooth, kaasóóth/, **Lajos** 1802–94; Hungarian patriot and statesman.
Kroc /kraak/, **Ray(mond Albert)** 1902–1984; U.S. entrepreneur; founder of McDonald's restaurant chain.
Ku·blai Khan /kóóblə kaán, kóóblī/ c. 1215–94; founder of the Mongol dynasty in China.
K'ung Fu-tzu /kóóngfóódzə/ see CONFUCIUS.
La·fa·yette (also **La Fa·yette**) /laafee-ét, laf–/, **Marie Joseph (Marquis de)** 1757–1834; French statesman; American Revolutionary War general in the Continental army.
La·Fol·lette /ləfaálit/, **Robert Marion** 1855–1925; U.S. politician.
La Fon·taine /laa fawNtén/, **Jean de** 1621–95; French author.
Lamb /lam/, **Charles** (pseudonym **"Elia"**) 1775–1834; English critic and essayist.
Lang·land /lánglənd/, **William** c. 1330–c. 1400; English poet.
Lao-tse /lówdzóó/ (also **Lao-tsze, Lao-tsu**) c. 604–c. 531 B.C.; Chinese philosopher.
La Roche·fou·cauld /laa rawshfóókō/, **François (Duc de)** 1613–80; French author.
La·rousse /laaróós, lə–/, **Pierre** 1817–75; French lexicographer and encyclopedist.
La Salle /laa saál, lə sál/, **René Robert Cavalier (Sieur de)** 1643–87; French explorer.
Law·rence /láwrəns, laár–/, **D(avid) H(erbert)** 1885–1930; English author.
Law·rence, T(homas) E(dward) (called **"Lawrence of Arabia"**) 1888–1935; British soldier and author.
Lay·a·mon /líəmən, láy–/ late 12th cent.; English poet.
Lea·key /leékee/ **1** Louis Seymour Bazett 1903–72; British archaeologist and anthropologist; husband of: **2** Mary Douglas 1913–96; British archaeologist; their son: **3** Richard Erskine Frere Kenyan paleontologist.
Lear /leer/, **Edward** 1812–88; English artist and writer of humorous verse.
Lee /lee/, **Henry** (called **"Light-horse Harry"**) 1756–1818; American Revolutionary War cavalry commander.
Lee, Robert E(dward) 1807–70; Confederate commander in the American Civil War.
Leib·niz /lípnits, líbnəts/, **Gottfried Wilhelm** 1646–1716; German philosopher and mathematician.
L'En·fant /laaNfaáN/, **Pierre Charles** 1754–1825; American soldier and engineer, born in France; designed Washington, D.C.
Le·nin /lénin/ (born **Vladimir Ilich Ulyanov**) 1870–1924; Russian Communist leader.
Len·non /lénən/, **John Winston** 1940–80; English pop and rock musician, singer, and songwriter.
Le·o·nar·do da Vin·ci /leeənaárdō də vínchee/ 1452–1519; Italian artist, inventor, and engineer.
Ler·ner /lórnər/, **Alan Jay** 1918–86; U.S. lyricist and librettist.
Les·seps /léseps, leséps/, **Ferdinand (Vicomte de)** 1805–94; French diplomat; promoter of the Suez Canal.
Lew·is /lóóis/, **C(ecil) Day** 1904–72; English poet and critic.
Lew·is, C(live) S(taples) 1898–1963; English author.
Lew·is, (Harry) Sinclair 1885–1951; U.S. author.
Lew·is, Meriwether 1774–1809; U.S. explorer (with William Clark) of the North American continent (1804–06).
Lin·coln /língkən/, **Abraham** 1809–65; 16th president of the U.S. (1861–65); assassinated.
Lind·bergh /líndbərg, lín–/, **Charles Augustus** 1902–74; U.S. aviator; made first solo transatlantic flight (1927).
Lind·say /líndzee, lín–/, **(Nicholas) Vachel** 1879–1931; U.S. poet.
Lin·nae·us /ləneéəs, –náy–/, **Carolus** 1707–78; Swedish botanist.
Lis·ter /lístər/, **Joseph** 1827–1912; English surgeon; developed antiseptic surgery.
Liszt /list/, **Franz** 1811–86; Hungarian composer.
Liv·ing·stone /lívingstən/, **David** 1813–73; Scottish missionary and explorer.
Liv·y /lívee/ (Latin name **Titus Livius**) 59 B.C.–A.D. 17; Roman historian.
Lloyd George /loyd jáwrj/, **David** 1863–1945; prime minister of Great Britain (1916–22).
Lloyd Web·ber /loyd wébər/, **(Sir) Andrew** 1948– ; English composer.
Locke /laak/, **John** 1632–1704; English philosopher.
Loewe /lō/, **Frederick** 1904–88; U.S. composer, born in Austria.
Lon·don /lúndən/, **Jack (John Griffith)** 1876–1916; U.S. author.
Long /lawng/, **Huey Pierce** (called **"the Kingfish"**) 1893–1935; U.S. politician; assassinated.
Long·fel·low /láwngfelō/, **Henry Wadsworth** 1807–82; U.S. poet.
Lor·rain, Claude see CLAUDE LORRAIN.
Lou·is /lóóee, lwee/ name of eighteen kings of France, including: **1** Louis XIV (called **"the Sun King"**) 1638–1715; reigned 1643–1715. **2** Louis XVI 1754–93; reigned 1774–92.
Lou·is /lóóəs/, **Joe** (born **Joseph Louis Barrow**) (called **"the Brown Bomber"**) 1914–81; U.S. boxer.
Lou·is Phi·lippe /weé fileép, lóóee/ 1773–1850; king of France (1830–48).
Low·ell /lóəl/, **Amy** 1874–1925; U.S. poet.
Low·ell, James Russell 1819–91; U.S. poet and critic.
Low·ell, Robert 1917–77; U.S. poet.
Lu·cre·tius /lookreéshəs/ **(Titus Lucretius Carus)** c. 94–c. 55 B.C.; Roman poet and philosopher.
Lu·ther /lóóthər/, **Martin** 1483–1546; German theologian; key figure of the Protestant Reformation.
Ly·cur·gus /līkórgəs/ fl. 9th cent. B.C.; Spartan lawgiver.
Lyl·y /lílee/, **John** c. 1554–1606; English author.
Ly·on /líən/, **Mary** 1797–1849; U.S. educator.
Mac·Ar·thur /məkaárthər/, **Douglas** 1880–1964; U.S. general.
Ma·cau·lay /məkáwlee/, **Thomas Babington** 1800–59; English author and historian.
Mac·beth /məkbéth, mak–/ c. 1005–57; king of Scotland (1040–57); Shakespearean tragic hero.
Mac·ca·be·us /makəbeéəs/, **Judas** died 160 B.C.; Jewish patriot.
Mac·Don·ald /məkdaánld/, **(James) Ramsay** 1866–1937; prime minister of Great Britain (1924; 1929–35).
Mach /maakh, maak/, **Ernst** 1836–1916; Austrian physicist.
Mach·i·a·vel·li /makeeəvélee/, **Niccolò di Bernardo** 1469–1527; Italian political theorist.

Mac·ken·zie /məkénzee/, **Alexander** 1822–92; prime minister of Canada (1873–78).
Mac·ken·zie, (Sir) Alexander 1764–1820; Scottish explorer of Canada.
Mac·Leish /makleésh/, **Archibald** 1892–1982; U.S. poet and playwright.
Mac·mil·lan /məkmílən/, **(Maurice) Harold** 1895–1987; prime minister of Great Britain (1957–63).
Mad·i·son /mádisən/, **James** 1751–1836; 4th president of the U.S. (1809–17).
Mae·ter·linck /máytərlingk, met–/, **(Count) Maurice** 1862–1947; Belgian poet and playwright.
Ma·gel·lan /məjélən/, **Ferdinand** c. 1480–1521; Portuguese navigator.
Ma·gritte /maagreét/, **René** 1898–1967; Belgian artist.
Mahfouz /maáfoōz/, **Naguib** 1911– ; Egyptian author.
Mah·ler /maálər/, **Gustav** 1860–1911; Austrian composer.
Mail·er /máylər/, **Norman** 1923– ; U.S. author.
Mai·mon·i·des /mīmaánideez/, **Moses** (born **Moses ben Maimon**) 1135–1204; Jewish theologian and scholastic philosopher, born in Spain.
Ma·jor /máyjər/, **John** 1943– ; prime minister of Great Britain (1990–97).
Mal·a·mud /máləməd/, **Bernard** 1914–86; U.S. author.
Mal·colm X /málkəm éks/ (born **Malcolm Little**) 1925–65; U.S. civil-rights activist; assassinated.
Ma·li·now·ski /malináwfskee/, **Bronislaw** 1884–1942; U.S. anthropologist, born in Poland.
Mal·lar·mé /maalaarmáy/, **Stéphane** 1842–98; French poet.
Mal·o·ry /máləree/, **(Sir) Thomas** died 1471; English author.
Mal·raux /malrṓ/, **André** 1901–76; French statesman and author.
Mal·thus /málthəs, máwl–/, **Thomas Robert** 1766–1834; English economist.
Man·de·la /mandélə/, **Nelson** 1918– ; president of South Africa (1994–).
Man·et /manáy, maa–/, **Édouard** 1832–83; French artist.
Mann /man/, **Horace** 1796–1859; U.S. educator.
Mann /maan/, **Thomas** 1875–1955; German author.
Man Ray see RAY, MAN.
Mans·field /mánsfeeld/, **Katherine** (born **Kathleen Beauchamp**) 1888–1923; British author, born in New Zealand.
Man·son /mánsən/, **Charles** 1934– ; U.S. cult leader and criminal.
Mao Ze·dong /mów dzədóóng/ (also **Mao Tse-tung**) 1893–1976; Chinese Communist leader.
Ma·rat /maraá/, **Jean Paul** 1743–93; French revolutionary leader, born in Switzerland; assassinated.
Mar·ci·a·no /maarsee-ánō, –shee–, –aánō/, **Rocky** (born **Rocco Francis Marchegiano**) 1923–69; U.S. boxer.
Mar·co Po·lo see POLO, MARCO.
Mar·co·ni /maarkṓnee/, **Guglielmo** 1874–1937; Italian inventor; pioneered wireless telegraphy.
Mar·cos /maárkōs/, **Ferdinand** 1917–89; president of the Philippines (1965–86).
Mar·cus Au·re·li·us /maárkəs awreéleeəs/ 121–180; Roman emperor and Stoic philosopher.
Mar·cuse /maarkóózə/, **Herbert** 1898–1979; U.S. philosopher, born in Germany.
Mare, Walter de la see DE LA MARE, WALTER.
Mar·gre·the II /maargrétə/ 1940– ; queen of Denmark (1972–).
Ma·rie An·toi·nette /məreé antwənét/ 1755–93; queen of France (1774–92), wife of Louis XVI.
Ma·rie de Mé·di·cis /məreé də maydeeseés/ (Italian name **Ma·ri·a de' Med·i·ci** /máydəchee/) 1573–1642; queen of France (1610–17).
Mark An·to·ny see ANTONY, MARK.
Mark·ham /maárkəm/, **(Charles) Edwin** 1852–1940; U.S. poet.
Marl·bor·ough /márlbərō, máwlbrə/, **1st Duke of** see CHURCHILL, JOHN.
Mar·lowe /maárlō/, **Christopher** 1564–93; English playwright and poet.
Mar·quand /maarkwaánd/, **J(ohn) P(hillips)** 1893–1960; U.S. author.
Mar·quette /maarkét/, **Jacques** 1637–75; Jesuit missionary and explorer of North America, born in France.
Már·quez, Gabriel García see GARCÍA MÁRQUEZ, GABRIEL.
Mar·shall /maárshəl/, **George C(atlett)** 1880–1959; U.S. general and statesman.
Mar·shall, John 1755–1835; Chief Justice of the U.S. (1801–35).
Mar·shall, Thurgood 1908–93; U.S. Supreme Court justice (1967–91).
Mar·tel, Charles see CHARLES MARTEL.
Mar·tial /maárshəl/ 1st cent. A.D.; Roman writer of epigrams, born in Spain.
Marx /maarks/, **Karl Heinrich** 1818–83; German political philosopher.
Mar·y /máiree/ (called **"the Virgin Mary"** or **"Blessed Virgin Mary"**) 1st cent. B.C.–A.D. 1st cent.; mother of Jesus.
Mar·y I (also known as **Mary Tu·dor**) (called **"Bloody Mary"**) 1516–58; queen of England (1553–58).
Mar·y, Queen of Scots (also known as **Mary Stu·art**) 1542–87; queen of Scotland (1542–67).
Ma·sa·ryk /maásaarik/, **Tomáš** 1850–1937; president of Czechoslovakia (1918–35).
Mase·field /máysfeeld/, **John Edward** 1878–1967; English poet, playwright, and novelist.
Mas·ters /mástərz/, **Edgar Lee** 1869–1950; U.S. poet.
Ma·tisse /maateés/, **Henri** 1869–1954; French artist.
Maugham /mawm/, **(William) Somerset** 1874–1965; English author.
Mau·pas·sant /mōpaasaáN/, **(Henri) Guy de** 1850–93; French author.
Mau·riac /mawr-yaák/, **François** 1885–1970; French author.
Max·i·mil·ian /maksimílyən/ 1832–67; emperor of Mexico (1864–67).
Maz·a·rin /maazaaráN/, **Jules** 1602–61; French cardinal and statesman, born in Italy.
Mboy·a /embóyə/, **Tom (Thomas Joseph)** 1930–69; Kenyan political leader; assassinated.
Mc·Car·thy /məkaárthee/, **Joseph Raymond** 1908–57; U.S. politician.
Mc·Car·thy, Mary 1912–89; U.S. author.
Mc·Cart·ney /məkaártnee/, **(James) Paul** 1942– ; English pop and rock musician, singer, and songwriter.
Mc·Clel·lan /məklélən/, **George Brinton** 1826–85; Union general in the American Civil War.
Mc·Cor·mick /məkáwrmik/, **Cyrus Hall** 1809–84; U.S. developer of the mechanical reaper.
Mc·Kin·ley /məkínlee/, **William** 1843–1901; 25th president of the U.S. (1897–1901); assassinated.
Mc·Lu·han /məklóóən/, **(Herbert) Marshall** 1911–80; Canadian communications theorist.
Mead /meed/, **Margaret** 1901–78; U.S. anthropologist.
Meade /meed/, **George Gordon** 1815–72; Union general in the American Civil War.
Med·i·ci /médichee, médeechee/ powerful Italian family, including: **1** Cosimo de' (called **"the Elder"**) 1389–1464; Florentine ruler, banker, and art patron. **2** Lorenzo de' (called **"the Magnificent"**) 1449–92; Florentine ruler and art patron. **3** see CATHERINE DE MÉDICIS. **4** Cosimo de' (called **"the Great"**) 1519–74; duke of Florence (1537–74). **5** Maria de' **see** MARIE DE MÉDICIS.
Mei·ji Ten·no /máyjee ténnō/ (born **Mutsuhito**) 1852–1912; emperor of Japan (1867–1912).
Me·ir /me-eér/, **Golda** (born **Goldie Mabovitch**) 1898–1978; prime minister of Israel (1969–74), born in Russia.
Mel·ba /mélbə/, **(Dame) Nellie** (born **Helen Porter Mitchell**) 1861–1931; Australian operatic soprano.
Mel·lon /mélən/, **Andrew William** 1855–1937; U.S. financier and art patron; U.S. secretary of the treasury (1921–32).
Mel·ville /mélvil/, **Herman** 1819–91; U.S. author.
Me·nan·der /mənándər/ c. 342–292 B.C.; Greek playwright.
Men·ci·us /méncheeəs/ (Latinized name of **Meng-tzu'** or **Meng·zi'**) c. 371–c. 289 B.C.; Chinese philosopher.
Menck·en /méngkən/, **H(enry) L(ouis)** 1880–1956; U.S. journalist and critic.
Men·del /méndəl/, **Gregor Johann** 1822–84; Austrian monk and botanist.
Men·dels·sohn /méndəlsən/, **Felix** 1809–47; German composer.
Me·nes /meéneez/ king of Egypt (c. 3100 B.C.).
Meng-tzu /múng dzóó/ (also **Meng·zi'**) see MENCIUS.
Me·not·ti /mənáwtee/, **Gian Carlo** 1911– ; U.S. composer, born in Italy.
Men·u·hin /ményōōhin/, **Yehudi** 1916–99; U.S. violinist.
Mer·ca·tor /mərkáytər/, **Gerardus** 1512–94; Flemish cartographer.
Mer·e·dith /mérədith/, **George** 1828–1909; English novelist and poet.
Met·ter·nich /métərnik, –nikh/, **(Prince) Klemens** 1773–1859; Austrian statesman.
Mi·chel·an·ge·lo /mikəlánjəlō, mikəl–/ (surname **Buonarroti**) 1475–1564; Italian artist and architect.
Mich·en·er /míchənər, míchnər/, **James A(lbert)** 1907–97; U.S. author.
Mies van der Rohe /mees vaan də rṓə/, **Ludwig** 1886–1969; U.S. architect and designer, born in Germany.
Mill /mil/, **J(ohn) S(tuart)** 1806–73; English philosopher and economist.
Mil·lay /məláy/, **Edna St. Vincent** 1892–1950; U.S. poet.
Mil·ler /mílər/, **Arthur** 1915– ; U.S. playwright.
Mil·ler, (Alton) Glenn 1904–44; U.S. jazz trombonist and bandleader.
Mil·ler, Henry 1891–1980; U.S. author.
Mil·let /meeláy/, **Jean François** 1814–75; French artist.
Milne /miln/, **A(lan) A(lexander)** 1882–1956; English author.
Mil·ton /mílt'n/, **John** 1608–74; English poet.
Min·u·it /mínyōōit/, **Peter** 1580–1638; Dutch colonial administrator in America.
Mi·ró /mee-rṓ/, **Joan** 1893–1983; Spanish artist.
Mitch·ell /míchəl/, **Margaret** 1900–49; U.S. author.
Mit·ford /mítfərd/ **1** Nancy 1904–73; English author; sister of: **2** Jessica 1917–96; U.S. author, born in England.
Mith·ri·da·tes VI /mithrədáyteez/ (called **"the Great"**) c. 132–63 B.C.; king of Pontus (120–63 B.C.).

Mit·ter·rand /meeteraáɴ/, **François** 1916–96; president of France (1981–95).

Mo·bu·tu Se·se Se·ko /məbóōtōō sésay sékō/ 1930–97; president of (the former) Zaire (1965–97).

Mo·di·glia·ni /mōdeel-yaánee/, **Amedeo** 1884–1920; Italian artist.

Mo·ham·med /mōhaámid/ see MUHAMMAD.

Mo·lière /mōlyér/ (pseudonym of **Jean-Baptiste Poquelin**) 1622–73; French playwright.

Mol·nár /mōlnaár/, **Ferenc** 1878–1952; Hungarian author.

Momm·sen /mómsən/, **Theodor** 1817–1903; German historian.

Mon·dale /móndayl/, **Walter Frederick** 1928– ; vice president of the U.S. (1977–81).

Mon·dri·an /máwndree-aan/, **Piet** 1872–1944; Dutch artist.

Mo·net /mawnáy/, **Claude** 1840–1926; French artist.

Mon·roe /mənró/, **James** 1758–1831; 5th president of the U.S. (1817–25).

Mon·roe, Marilyn 1926–62; U.S. actress.

Mon·taigne /mawɴtén, –ténya/, **Michel de** 1533–92; French essayist.

Mont·calm /mōɴkaálm/, **Louis Joseph** 1712–59; French general.

Mon·tes·quieu /maantəskyóō/ 1689–1755; French political philosopher.

Mon·tes·so·ri /maantəsáwree/, **Maria** 1870–1952; Italian educator.

Mon·te·ver·di /maantəvérdee/, **Claudio** 1567–1643; Italian composer.

Mon·te·zu·ma II /maantəzóōmə/ 1466–1520; Aztec emperor (1502–20).

Moon /mōōn/, **Sun Myung** 1920– ; Korean religious leader.

Moore /mawr, mōōr/, **G(eorge) E(dward)** 1873–1958; English philosopher.

Moore, Henry 1898–1986; English sculptor.

Moore, Marianne 1887–1972; U.S. poet.

More /mawr/, **(Sir) Thomas** 1478–1535; English scholar and statesman.

Mor·gan /máwrgən/, **J(ohn) P(ierpont)** 1837–1913; U.S. financier and philanthropist.

Mor·i·son /máwrisən/, **Samuel Eliot** 1887–1976; U.S. historian.

Mo·ri·sot /mawrisó/, **Berthe** 1841–95; French artist.

Mor·ris /máwrəs, maár–/, **Gouverneur** 1752–1816; U.S. statesman.

Mor·ris /máwrəs, maár–/, **Robert** 1734–1806; U.S. statesman and financier, born in England.

Mor·ri·son /máwrisən, maár–/, **Jim** 1943–1971; U.S. singer and songwriter.

Mor·ri·son, Toni 1931– ; U.S. novelist.

Morse /mawrs/, **Samuel F(inley) B(reese)** 1791–1872; U.S. artist and inventor; devised telegraphic code.

Mo·ses /mózíz/ c. 14th cent. B.C.; Hebrew prophet and lawgiver.

Mo·ses /mózíz/, **Anna Mary** (called **"Grandma Moses"**) 1860–1961; U.S. artist.

Mo·ses ben Mai·mon see MAIMONIDES.

Mo·ther Te·re·sa see TERESA, MOTHER.

Mott /maat/, **Lucretia Coffin** 1793–1880; U.S. social reformer.

Mount·bat·ten /mowntbát'n/, **Louis (1st Earl Mountbatten of Burma)** 1900–79; British admiral and statesman.

Mous·sorg·sky /mōōsáwrgskee/ (also **Mus·sorg'sky**), **Modest** 1839–81; Russian composer.

Mo·zart /mótsaart/, **Wolfgang Amadeus** 1756–91; Austrian composer.

Mu·ga·be /mōōgaábee/, **Robert** 1924– ; prime minister (1980–87) and president (1987–) of Zimbabwe.

Mu·ham·mad A·li see ALI, MUHAMMAD.

Mu·ham·mad /mōōhaáməd, mō–/ (also **Mo·ham'med; Ma·hom'et**) c. 570–632; Arab prophet, founder of Islam.

Muir /myōōr/, **John** 1838–1914; U.S. naturalist and explorer, born in Scotland.

Mun·ro /mənró/, **H(ector) H(ugh)** (pseudonym **"Saki"**) 1870–1916; Scottish author, born in Burma.

Mu·rat /myōōraá/, **Joachim** c. 1767–1815; French general and king of Naples (1808–15).

Mur·doch /mə́rdaak/, **Rupert** 1931– ; Australian media executive.

Mur·ray /mə́ree/, **(Sir) James Augustus Henry** 1837–1915; British philologist and lexicographer.

Mus·so·li·ni /mōōsəleénee, mōōsə–/, **Benito** (called **"Il Duce"**) 1883–1945; Fascist dictator of Italy (1922–43).

Mus·sorg·sky see MOUSSORGSKY.

My·ron /mírən/ fl. c. 480–440 B.C.; Greek sculptor.

Na·bo·kov /nábəkawf, nəbáwkəf/, **Vladimir** 1899–1977; U.S. novelist, born in Russia.

Na·der /náydər/, **Ralph** 1934– ; U.S. consumer advocate.

Na·po·le·on I /nəpóleeən/ (surname **Bonaparte**) 1769–1821; French general, born in Corsica; emperor of France (1804–15). ▫▫ **Na·po·le·on'ic** /–leeaánək/ *adj.*

Na·po·le·on III (Louis Napoleon Bonaparte) 1808–73; president (1848–52) and emperor (1852–70) of France.

Nash /nash/, **Ogden** 1902–71; U.S. writer of humorous verse.

Nas·ser /násər/, **Gamal Abdel** 1918–70; president of Egypt (1956–58).

Na·tion /náyshən/, **Carry Amelia Moore** 1846–1911; U.S. temperance activist.

Neb·u·chad·nez·zar /nebəkədnézər/ king of Babylon (605–562 B.C.).

Neh·ru /nérōō, náyrōō/, **Jawaharlal** 1889–1964; prime minister of India (1947–64).

Nel·son /nélsən/, **Horatio** 1758–1805; British admiral.

Ne·ro /neérō/ 37–68; Roman emperor (54–68).

Net·an·ya·hu /netaanyaáhōō/, **Benjamin** 1949–99; prime minister of Israel (1996–).

Neu·mann /nóymaan/, **John von** 1903–57; U.S. mathematician, born in Hungary.

New·man /nóōmən, nyóō–/, **John Henry** 1801–91; English theologian.

New·ton /nóōt'n, nyóō–/, **(Sir) Isaac** 1642–1727; English mathematician and physicist.

Ngo Dinh Di·em /nó dín dee-ém/ 1901–63; president of South Vietnam (1956–63).

Nich·o·las II /níkələs, nikləs/ 1868–1918; last Russian czar (1894–1917); assassinated.

Nich·o·las, St. fl. 4th cent.; Christian bishop in Asia Minor.

Nick·laus /níkləs/, **Jack (William)** (called **"the Golden Bear"**) 1940– ; U.S. golfer.

Nie·buhr /neébōōr/, **Reinhold** 1892–1971; U.S. theologian.

Nie·tzsche /neéchə, –chee/, **Friedrich Wilhelm** 1844–1900; German philosopher.

Night·in·gale /nít'n-gayl/, **Florence** 1820–1910; English nurse.

Ni·jin·sky /nəzhínskee, –jín–/, **Vaslav** 1890–1950; Russian ballet dancer and choreographer.

Nim·itz /nímits/, **Chester William** 1885–1966; U.S. admiral.

Nix·on /níksən/, **Richard Milhous** 1913–94; 37th president of the U.S. (1969–74); resigned.

Nkru·mah /enkróōmə/, **Kwame** 1909–72; Ghanaian political leader.

No·bel /nōbél/, **Alfred Bernhard** 1833–96; Swedish inventor; endowed Nobel Prizes.

North /nawrth/, **Frederick** (called **"Lord North"**) 1732–92; prime minister of Great Britain (1770–82).

Nos·tra·da·mus /naastrədáyməs, naws–, –daáməs/ 1503–66; French astrologer and prophet.

Noyes /noyz/, **Alfred** 1880–1958; English poet and critic.

Nu·re·yev /nōōráyəf, nóōree-ef/, **Rudolf Hametovich** 1939–93; Russian ballet dancer.

O'Ca·sey /ōkáysee/, **Sean** 1880–1964; Irish playwright.

O'Con·nell /ōkaánl/, **Daniel** 1775–1847; Irish nationalist leader.

O'Con·nor /ōkaánər/, **(Mary) Flannery** 1925–1964; U.S. author.

O'Con·nor, Sandra Day 1930– ; U.S. Supreme Court justice (1981–); first woman appointed to Court.

Oc·ta·vi·an /oktávee-ən/ see AUGUSTUS.

O·dets /ōdéts/, **Clifford** 1906–63; U.S. playwright.

Of·fen·bach /áwfənbaakh, –baak/, **Jacques** 1819–80; French composer, born in Germany.

O·gle·thorpe /ógəlthawrp/, **James Edward** 1696–1785; English colonizer of Georgia.

O'Hig·gins /ōhíginz/, **Bernardo** (called **"the Liberator of Chile"**) c. 1778–1842; Chilean revolutionary; dictator of Chile (1817–23).

O'Keeffe /ōkeéf/, **Georgia** 1887–1986; U.S. artist.

O·liv·i·er /əlívee-ay, ō–/, **(Sir) Laurence Kerr** 1907–89; English actor.

Olm·sted /ómstid/, **Frederick Law** 1822–1903; U.S. landscape architect.

O·mar Khay·yám /ōmaar kī-aám, kī-ám/ died 1123; Persian poet and astronomer.

O·nas·sis /ōnásis/ **1** Aristotle (Socrates) c. 1900–75; Greek shipping tycoon, born in Turkey; husband of: **2** Jacqueline Lee Bouvier Kennedy 1929–94; wife of John F. Kennedy (1953–63) and Aristotle Onassis (1968–75).

O'Neill /ōneél/, **Eugene Gladstone** 1888–1953; U.S. playwright.

Op·pen·heim·er /aápənhīmər/, **J(ulius) Robert** 1904–67; U.S. nuclear physicist.

Or·well /áwrwel, –wəl/, **George** (pseudonym of **Eric Arthur Blair**) 1903–50; English author, born in India.

Os·man I /aázmən, aás–/ (also **Oth'man**) 1259–1326; Turkish ruler; founder of the Ottoman Empire.

Os·wald /aázwawld, –wəld/, **Lee Harvey** 1939–63; accused assassin of U.S. president John F. Kennedy.

O·tis /ótis/, **James** 1725–83; American Revolutionary War patriot.

Ov·id /aávid/ (born **Publius Ovidius Naso**) 43 B.C.–c. A.D. 17; Roman poet.

Ow·en /óən/, **David** 1938– ; British politician.

Ow·en, Wilfred 1893–1918; English poet.

Ow·ens /óənz/, **Jesse** (born **James Cleveland Owens**) 1913–80; U.S. Olympic athlete.

Pa·de·rew·ski /padəréfskee, –rév–/, **Ignace** 1860–1941; Polish pianist, composer, and statesman.

Pa·ga·ni·ni /pagəneénee/, **Nicolò** 1782–1840; Italian violinist and composer.

Pah·la·vi /paáləvee/, **Mohammed Reza** 1919–80; shah of Iran (1941–79); exiled.

Paine /payn/, **Thomas** 1737–1809; American patriot and political philosopher, born in England.

Pal·la·dio /pəlaádee-ō/, **Andrea** 1508–80; Italian architect.

Pal·mer /paámər, paálmər/, **Arnold** 1929– ; U.S. golfer.
Pank·hurst /pángkhərst/, **Emmeline Goulden** 1858–1928; English suffragist.
Pa·pan·dre·ou /paapaandráyōō/, **George** 1888–1968; premier of Greece (1963; 1964–65).
Par·ker /paárkər/, **Dorothy Rothschild** 1893–1967; U.S. author and critic.
Park·man /paárkmən/, **Francis** 1823–93; U.S. historian.
Par·men·i·des /paarménideez/ early 5th cent. B.C.; Greek philosopher.
Par·nell /paarnél, paárn'l/, **Charles Stewart** 1846–91; Irish nationalist.
Pas·cal /paskál/, **Blaise** 1623–62; French mathematician and philosopher.
Pas·ter·nak /pástərnak/, **Boris** 1890–1960; Russian poet and novelist.
Pas·teur /pastóor/, **Louis** 1822–95; French chemist and microbiologist.
Pat·rick /pátrik/, **St.** 5th cent.; patron saint of Ireland.
Pat·ton /pát'n/, **George S(mith)** 1885–1945; U.S. general.
Paul /pawl/, **St.** died c. 67; early Christian missionary.
Paul·ing /páwling/, **Linus Carl** 1901–94; U.S. chemist.
Pa·va·rot·ti /paavəraátee, pav–/, **Luciano** 1935– ; Italian operatic tenor.
Pav·lov /paávlawf, páv–, –lawv/, **Ivan** 1849–1936; Russian physiologist.
Pav·lo·va /pávləvə, pavlóvə/, **Anna** 1881–1931; Russian prima ballerina.
Peale /peel/, **Charles Willson** 1741–1827; U.S. artist.
Peale, Norman Vincent 1898–1994; U.S. religious leader.
Pea·ry /péeree/, **Robert Edwin** 1856–1920; U.S. Arctic explorer.
Pe·der·sen /páydərsən/, **Knut** see HAMSUN, KNUT.
Peel /peel/, **(Sir) Robert** 1788–1850; prime minister of Great Britain (1834–35; 1841–46).
Pei /pay/, **I(eoh) M(ing)** 1917– ; U.S. architect, born in China.
Penn /pen/, **William** 1644–1718; English Quaker and founder of Pennsylvania (1682).
Pep·in III /pépin/ (called **"the Short"**) c. 714–768; king of the Franks (751–768); father of Charlemagne.
Pepys /peeps/, **Samuel** 1633–1703; English diarist.
Pé·rez de Cué·llar /pérez de kwáyyaar/, **Javier** 1920– ; Peruvian diplomat; secretary-general of the United Nations (1982–92).
Per·i·cles /périkleez/ c. 495–429 B.C.; Athenian statesman and general.
Per·kins /pérkinz/, **Frances** 1882–1965; U.S. secretary of labor (1933–45); first woman cabinet member.
Pe·rón /pərón, pay–/ **1** Juan Domingo 1895–1974; president of Argentina (1946–55; 1973–74); husband of: **2** (Maria) Evita Duarte Ibarguren (called **"Evita"**) 1919–52; Argentine political figure.
Pe·rot /pəró/, **H(enry) Ross** 1930– ; U.S. business executive and politician.
Per·ry /péree/ **1** Oliver Hazard 1785–1819; U.S. naval officer; brother of: **2** Matthew Calbraith 1794–1858; U.S. commodore.
Per·shing /pérshing, –zhing/, **John J(oseph)** (called **"Black Jack"**) 1860–1948; U.S. commander of American forces during World War I.
Pesh·kov /pyáyshkəf/, **Aleksei Maksimovich** see GORKY, MAXIM.
Pé·tain /paytán/, **Henri Philippe** 1856–1951; premier of Fascist Vichy France (1940–44).
Pe·ter I /péetər/ (called **"the Great"**) 1672–1725; emperor of Russia (1682–1725).
Pe·ter, St. (also known as **Si'mon Pe'ter**) died c. 67; apostle of Jesus.
Pe·ter·son /péetərsən/, **Roger Tory** 1908–1996; U.S. ornithologist, artist, and author.
Pe·trarch /péetraark, pé–/ 1304–74; Italian poet. ▫▫ **Pe·trarch·an** /pətraárkən/ *adj.*
Phid·i·as /fídeeəs/ fl. 5th cent. B.C.; Athenian sculptor.
Phil·ip II /fíləp/ c. 382–336 B.C.; king of Macedonia; father of Alexander the Great.
Pi·af /pee-aáf/, **Edith** (born **Edith Giovanna Gassion**) 1915–63; French singer.
Pia·get /pyaazháy/, **Jean** 1897–1980; Swiss psychologist.
Pi·cas·so /pikaásō, –kás–/, **Pablo** 1881–1973; Spanish artist.
Pick·ett /píkət/, **George Edward** 1825–75; Confederate general in the American Civil War.
Pierce /peers/, **Franklin** 1804–69; 14th president of the U.S. (1853–57).
Pi·late /pílət/, **Pontius** 1st cent. A.D.; Roman procurator of Judea (26–c. 36).
Pin·dar /píndər, –daar/ 518–438 B.C.; Greek lyric poet.
Pink·er·ton /píngkərtən/, **Allan** 1819–84; U.S. detective, born in Scotland.
Pi·no·chet U·gar·te /peenōchét ōōgaártay/, **Augusto** 1915– ; president of Chile (1973–89).
Pin·ter /píntər/, **Harold** 1930– ; English playwright.
Pi·ran·del·lo /peerəndélō/, **Luigi** 1867–1936; Italian author.
Pi·sis·tra·tus /pisístrətəs/ died c. 527 B.C.; Athenian ruler.
Pis·sar·ro /pisaárō/, **Camille** 1830–1903; French artist.
Pitt /pit/ **1** William (**1st Earl of Chatham**) (called **"the Elder Pitt"** and **"the Great Commoner"**) 1708–78; British political leader; father of: **2** William (called **"the Younger Pitt"**) 1759–1806; prime minister of Great Britain (1783–1801; 1804–06).
Pi·zar·ro /pizaárō/, **Francisco** c. 1478–1541; Spanish conquistador; conqueror of Peru.
Planck /plaangk, plangk/, **Max** 1858–1947; German physicist.
Plan·tag·e·net /plantájinit/ British ruling dynasty (1154–1485).
Plath /plath/, **Sylvia** 1932–63; U.S. poet and novelist.
Pla·to /pláytō/ 429–347 B.C.; Greek philosopher.
Plau·tus /pláwtəs/, **Titus Maccius** c. 250–184 B.C.; Roman comic playwright.
Plin·y /plínee/ **1** (called **"the Elder"**) c. 23–79; Roman scholar; uncle of: **2** (called **"the Younger"**) c. 61–c. 112; Roman author.
Plu·tarch /plóotaark/ c. 46–c. 120; Greek biographer.
Po·ca·hon·tas /pōkəhaántəs/ (English name **Rebecca Rolfe**) c. 1595–1617; Native American princess; daughter of Powhatan.
Poe /pō/, **Edgar Allan** 1809–49; U.S. short-story author and poet.
Pol Pot /paal paát, pōl/ c. 1925– ; prime minister of Cambodia (1976–79).
Polk /pōk/, **James Knox** 1795–1849; 11th president of the U.S. (1845–49).
Pol·lock /paálək/, **(Paul) Jackson** 1912–56; U.S. artist.
Po·lo /pólō/, **Marco** 1254–1324; Venetian traveler in E Asia.
Pom·pey /paámpee/ (called **"the Great"**) 106–48 B.C.; Roman general and politician.
Pom·pi·dou /pōNpeedóo/, **Georges** 1911–74; president of France (1969–74).
Ponce de Le·ón /paans də léeən, pónsə day lee-ón, paants, póntsə/, **Juan** c. 1460–1521; Spanish explorer; discovered Florida (1513).
Pon·ti·ac /paántee-ak/ c. 1720–69; Ottawa Indian chief.
Pope /pōp/, **Alexander** 1688–1744; English poet.
Po·que·lin /pōklán/, **Jean-Baptiste** see MOLIÈRE.
Porsche /páwrshə/, **Ferdinand** 1875–1952; Austrian car designer.
Por·ter /páwrtər, pór–/, **Cole Albert** 1891–1964; U.S. composer.
Por·ter, Katherine Anne Maria Veronica Callista Russell 1890–1980; U.S. author.
Por·ter, William Sydney see HENRY, O.
Pot·ter /paátər/, **(Helen) Beatrix** 1866–1943; English author.
Pound /pownd/, **Ezra (Loomis)** 1885–1972; U.S. poet and critic.
Pow·ell /pów'l/, **Colin** 1937– ; U.S. general.
Pow·ha·tan /powətán, pow-hát'n/ c. 1550–1618; Native American chief in early colonial Virginia.
Prax·it·e·les /praksít'l-eez/ fl. 370–330 B.C.; Athenian sculptor.
Pres·ley /prézlee, prés–/, **Elvis Aron** (called **"the King of Rock and Roll"**) 1935–77; U.S. pop and rock singer.
Pre·vin /prévin/, **André** (born **Andreas Priwin**) 1929– ; U.S. composer and conductor, born in Germany.
Price /prīs/, **(Mary) Leontyne** 1927– ; U.S. operatic soprano.
Priest·ley /préestlee/, **J(ohn) B(oynton)** 1894–1984; English author.
Priest·ley, Joseph 1733–1804; English scientist and theologian.
Pro·ko·fiev /prəkáwfyev, –yef, –yəf/, **Sergei** 1891–1953; Russian composer.
Prou·dhon /prōōdóN/, **Pierre Joseph** 1809–65; French author.
Proust /prōōst/, **Marcel** 1871–1922; French author and critic.
Ptol·e·my /taálimee/ fl. 127–151; ancient astronomer and geographer in Alexandria.
Puc·ci·ni /pōōchéenee/, **Giacomo** 1858–1924; Italian opera composer.
Pu·las·ki /pəláskee, pyōō–/, **(Count) Casimir** c. 1748–79; Polish patriot; American Revolutionary War general in Continental army.
Pu·litz·er /póolitsər, pyóo–/, **Joseph** 1847–1911; U.S. newspaper publisher, born in Hungary.
Push·kin /póoshkin/, **Alexander** 1799–1837; Russian author.
Py·thag·o·ras /pəthág(ə)rəs, pī–/ fl. late 6th cent. B.C.; Greek philosopher.
Qa·dha·fi /kədaáfee, –dáf–/ (also **Gad·da'fi**), **Muammar (Muhammad) al-** 1942– ; chief of state of Libya (1969–).
Rab·e·lais /rabəláy/, **François** c. 1494–1553; French satirical author.
Ra·bin /raabéen/, **Yitzhak** 1922–95; prime minister of Israel (1974–77; 1992–95); assassinated.
Rach·ma·ni·noff /raakmaáninawf/, **Sergei** 1873–1943; Russian composer.
Ra·leigh /ráwlee, raálee/ (also **Ra'legh**), **(Sir) Walter** c. 1552–1618; English courtier, explorer, and poet.
Ram·ses /rámseez/ (also **Ram'e·ses**) name of eleven pharaohs of Egypt, including: **1** Ramses I reigned 1320–1318 B.C.; grandfather of: **2** Ramses II reigned 1304–1237 B.C. **3** Ramses III reigned 1198–1166 B.C.
Rand /rand/, **Ayn** 1905–82; U.S. author, born in Russia.
Raph·a·el /ráfeeəl, ráyfee–, raáfee–/ (surname **Sanzio**) 1483–1520; Italian artist.
Ra·spu·tin /raspyóot'n/, **Grigori** 1871–1916; Russian mystic; influential in the court of Czar Nicholas II.
Ra·vel /rəvél/, **Maurice** 1875–1937; French composer.
Ray /ray/, **Man** (born **Emmanuel Rudnitsky**) 1890–1976; U.S. artist and photographer.
Rea·gan /ráygən/, **Ronald Wilson** 1911– ; 40th president of the U.S. (1981–89).

Reed /reed/, **Walter C.** 1851–1902; U.S. army physician.

Rehn·quist /rénkwist/, **William H(ubbs)** 1924– ; Chief Justice of the U.S. (1986–).

Re·marque /rəmaárk/, **Erich Maria** 1898–1970; U.S. author, born in Germany.

Rem·brandt /rémbrant/ (surname **Harmensz van Rijn**) 1606–69; Dutch artist.

Re·nault /rənáwlt/, **Mary** (pseudonym of **Mary Challans**) 1905–83; British novelist.

Re·no /reénō/, **Janet** 1938– ; U.S. attorney general (1993–).

Re·noir /rənwaár/, **Pierre Auguste** 1841–1919; French artist.

Re·vere /rəveér/, **Paul** 1735–1818; American patriot and silversmith.

Reyn·olds /rén'ldz/, **(Sir) Joshua** 1723–92; English artist.

Rhee /ree/, **Syngman** 1875–1965; president of South Korea (1948–60).

Rhodes /rōdz/, **Cecil John** 1853–1902; British colonial administrator in S Africa.

Ri·chard /ríchərd/ name of three kings of England: **1** Richard I (called **"the Lionheart"**) 1157–99; reigned 1189–99. **2** Richard II 1367–1400; reigned 1377–99. **3** Richard III 1452–85; reigned 1483–85.

Rich·ard·son /ríchərdsən/, **Samuel** 1689–1761; English author.

Rich·e·lieu /ríshəloo, –lyoo/, **Armand Jean du Plessis (Duc de)** 1585–1642; French cardinal and statesman.

Rick·o·ver /ríkōvər/, **Hyman George** 1900–86; U.S. admiral.

Ride /rīd/, **Sally Kristen** 1951– ; U.S. astronaut.

Rim·sky-Kor·sa·kov /rimskee káwrsəkawf/, **Nikolai** 1844–1908; Russian composer.

Ri·ve·ra /rivérə/, **Diego** 1886–1957; Mexican artist.

Rob·bins /raábinz/, **Jerome** 1918– ; U.S. ballet dancer and choreographer.

Robert I /róbərt/ (called **"Robert the Bruce"**) 1274–1329; king of Scotland (1306–29).

Robe·son /rṓbsən/, **Paul** 1898–1976; U.S. actor and singer.

Robes·pierre /rṓbzpeer, –pyer/, **Maximilien** 1758–94; French revolutionary leader.

Rob·in·son /raábinsən/, **Edwin Arlington** 1869–1935; U.S. poet.

Rob·in·son, Jackie (John Roosevelt) 1919–72; U.S. baseball player.

Rock·e·fel·ler /rókəfelər/ U.S. family prominent in industry, philanthropy, and politics, including: **1** John D(avison) 1839–1937; oil magnate; father of: **2** John D(avison), Jr. 1874–1960; philanthropist; father of: **3** Nelson 1908–79; politician.

Rock·well /rókwel/, **Norman** 1894–1978; U.S. artist.

Rodg·ers /rójərz/, **Richard** 1902–79; U.S. composer.

Ro·din /rōdáɴ/, **(François) Auguste** 1840–1917; French sculptor.

Roent·gen see Röntgen, Wilhelm Conrad.

Rog·ers /rójərz/, **Will(iam Penn Adair)** 1879–1935; U.S. humorist.

Röl·vaag /rṓlvaag/, **Ole Edvart** 1876–1931; U.S. author, born in Norway.

Rom·berg /rómbərg/, **Sigmund** 1887–1951; U.S. composer, born in Hungary.

Rom·mel /róməl/, **Erwin Johannes Eugen** (called **"the Desert Fox"**) 1891–1944; German general.

Rönt·gen /réntgən, rénchən/ (also **Roent'gen**), **Wilhelm Conrad** 1845–1923; German physicist; discovered X rays.

Roo·se·velt /rṓzəvelt, –vəlt, roo–/ **1** Franklin Delano 1882–1945; 32nd president of the U.S. (1933–45); husband of: **2** (Anna) Eleanor 1884–1962; U.S. diplomat and author.

Roo·se·velt, Theodore 1858–1919; 26th president of the U.S. (1901–08).

Ross /raws/, **Betsy (Elizabeth Griscom)** 1752–1836; reported maker of the first American flag (1776).

Ros·set·ti /rōzétee, –sét–/ **1** Dante Gabriel 1828–82; English poet and artist; brother of: **2** Christina Georgina 1830–94; English poet.

Ros·si·ni /rəseénee, raw–/, **Gioachino** 1792–1868; Italian composer.

Ros·tand /rawstaáɴ, rostánd/, **Edmond** 1868–1918; French playwright.

Roth /rawth/, **Philip** 1933– ; U.S. novelist.

Roth·schild /ráwth-chīld, ráwths–/ European-based family prominent in banking and finance, including: **1** Mayer Amschel 1743–1812; German financier. **2** Lionel Nathan, Baron de 1809–79; British financier.

Rous·seau /roosṓ/, **Jean-Jacques** 1712–78; French philosopher and author, born in Switzerland.

Ru·bens /róobənz/, **Peter Paul** 1577–1640; Flemish artist.

Ru·bin·stein /róobinstīn/, **Arthur** (also **Artur**) 1886–1982; U.S. concert pianist, born in Poland.

Rush·die /róoshdee, rúsh–/, **(Ahmed) Salman** 1947– ; British novelist, born in India.

Rus·kin /rúskin/, **John** 1819–1900; English art and social critic.

Rus·sell /rúsəl/, **Bertrand** 1873–1970; British philosopher, mathematician, and social reformer.

Ruth /rooth/, **Babe (George Herman)** 1895–1948; U.S. baseball player.

Ruth·er·ford /rú<u>th</u>ərfərd, –əfərd/, **(Sir) Ernest** 1871–1937; British nuclear physicist, born in New Zealand.

Ryle /rīl/, **Gilbert** 1900–76; English philosopher.

Saa·ri·nen /saárənən/ two U.S. architects, born in Finland: **1** (Gottlieb) Eliel 1873–1950; father of: **2** Eero 1910–61.

Sa·bin /sáybin/, **Albert Bruce** 1906–93; U.S. microbiologist, born in Russia; developed oral vaccine for polio.

Sac·a·ja·we·a /sakəjəweéə, –wáyə/ (also **Sa·ca·ga·we'a**) c. 1788–1812; Shoshone Indian guide for the Lewis and Clark expedition.

Sa·dat /sədaát, –dát/, **Anwar el-** 1918–81; president of Egypt (1970–81); assassinated.

Sade /saad/, **Donatien (Comte de)** (called **"Marquis de Sade"**) 1740–1814; French novelist and notorious sexual deviant.

Sa·gan /sáygən/, **Carl Edward** 1934–96; U.S. astronomer and author.

Saint-Gau·dens /saynt gáwdnz/, **Augustus** 1848–1907; U.S. sculptor, born in Ireland.

Saint-Saëns /saɴ saáɴs/, **(Charles) Camille** 1835–1921; French composer.

Sa·kha·rov /saá<u>kh</u>ərawf, sák–/, **Andrei Dmitrievich** 1921–89; Russian nuclear physicist.

Sa·ki /saákee/ see Munro, H(ector) H(ugh).

Sal·a·din /sálədeen, –ədin/ 1137–93; sultan of Egypt and Syria (1175–93).

Sa·la·zar /sáləzaar/, **António de Oliveira** 1899–1970; premier of Portugal (1932–68).

Sal·in·ger /sálinjər/, **J(erome) D(avid)** 1919– ; U.S. author.

Salk /saw(l)k/, **Jonas** 1914–95; U.S. physician and microbiologist; developed first polio vaccine (1955).

Sal·lust /sáləst/, (Latin name **Gaius Sallustius Crispus**) 86–34 B.C.; Roman historian and politician.

Sand /sand, saaɴd/, **George** (pseudonym of **Amandine-Aurore-Lucile Dupin Dudevant**) 1804–76; French novelist.

Sand·burg /sánbərg, sánd–/, **Carl** 1878–1967; U.S. poet and biographer.

Sang·er /sángər/, **Margaret Louise Higgins** 1883–1966; U.S. reformer; proponent of birth control.

San·ta An·na /sántə ánə/ (also **San'ta An'a**), **Antonio López de** c. 1795–1876; Mexican military and political leader.

San·ta·ya·na /santəyaánə/, **George** 1863–1952; U.S. philosopher and poet, born in Spain.

Sap·pho /sáfō/ fl. 7th cent.–6th cent. B.C.; Greek lyric poet.

Sar·gent /saárjənt/, **John Singer** 1856–1925; U.S. portrait artist.

Sa·roy·an /səróyən/, **William** 1908–81; U.S. author.

Sar·tre /saártrə, saart/, **Jean-Paul** 1905–80; French philosopher and author.

Saus·sure /sōsóor/, **Ferdinand de** 1857–1913; Swiss linguist.

Sav·o·na·ro·la /savənərṓlə/, **Girolamo** 1452–98; Italian religious reformer.

Sca·li·a /skəleéə/, **Antonin** 1936– ; U.S. Supreme Court justice (1986–).

Scar·lat·ti /skaarlaátee/ two Italian composers: **1** Alessandro 1659–1725; father of: **2** (Giuseppe) Domenico 1685–1757.

Schles·in·ger /shlésinjər/ two U.S. historians: **1** Arthur Meier 1888–1965; father of: **2** Arthur Meier, Jr. 1917– .

Schil·ler /shílər/, **Johann Christoph Friedrich von** 1759–1805; German playwright and poet.

Schlie·mann /shleémaan/, **Heinrich** 1822–90; German archaeologist.

Schön·berg /shṓrnbərg/, **Arnold Franz Walter** 1874–1951; U.S. composer, born in Austria.

Scho·pen·hau·er /shṓpənhowər/, **Arthur** 1788–1860; German philosopher.

Schrö·ding·er /shráydingər, shrṓd–/, **Erwin** 1887–1961; German theoretical physicist.

Schu·bert /shóobərt/, **Franz** 1797–1828; Austrian composer.

Schulz /shoolts/, **Charles M(onroe)** 1922– ; U.S. cartoonist.

Schu·mann /shóomaan, –mən/, **Robert** 1810–56; German composer.

Schwarz·kopf /shwáwrtskawf/, **H. Norman** 1934– ; U.S. general.

Schweit·zer /shwítsər/, **Albert** 1875–1965; French theologian, organist, and medical missionary in Africa.

Scip·i·o /sípee-ō, skíp–/ name of two Roman generals: **1** Publius Cornelius Scipio Africanus Major 236–c. 184 B.C.; defeated Hannibal; adoptive grandfather of: **2** Publius Cornelius Scipio Aemilianus Africanus 185–129 B.C.; destroyed Carthage.

Scott /skot/, **Dred** c. 1795–1858; U.S. slave; subject of a controversial U.S. Supreme Court proslavery decision (1857).

Scott, (Sir) Walter 1771–1832; Scottish novelist and poet.

Scott, Winfield (called **"Old Fuss and Feathers"**) 1786–1866; U.S. general.

Sea·borg /seébawrg/, **Glenn Theodor** 1912–99; U.S. chemist.

Se·go·vi·a /səgṓveeə/, **Andrés** 1893–1987; Spanish classical guitarist.

Se·leu·cus I /səlóokəs/ c. 358–280 B.C.; Macedonian general; founded Seleucid Empire of Syria and Asia Minor.

Sen·e·ca /sénikə/, **Lucius Annaeus** c. 4 B.C.–A.D. 65; Roman philosopher and author.

See page xii for the *Key to Pronunciation*.

Sen·nach·er·ib /sənakərib/ died 681 B.C.; king of Assyria (704–681 B.C.).
Se·quoy·a /sikwóyə/ c. 1770–1843; Cherokee Indian scholar.
Se·ton /seét'n/, **St. Elizabeth Ann Bayley** (called **"Mother Seton"**) 1774–1821; U.S. religious leader and educator.
Seu·rat /səraá/, **Georges** 1859–91; French artist.
Seuss /so͞os/, **Dr.** (pseudonym of **Theodor Seuss Geisel**) 1904–91; U.S. children's author and illustrator.
Sew·ard /so͞oərd/, **William Henry** 1801–72; U.S. politician; advocated U.S. purchase of Alaska.
Shake·speare /sháykspeer/, **William** 1564–1616; English poet and playwright. ▫▫ **Shake·spear'e·an** *adj.* **Shake·spear'i·an** *adj.*
Sha·li·kash·vi·li /shaaleekaashveélee/, **John Malchase** 1936– ; U.S. general, born in Poland; chairman of the Joint Chiefs of Staff (1993–).
Shan·kar /shaángkaar/, **Ravi** 1920– ; Indian sitar player.
Shaw /shaw/, **George Bernard** 1856–1950; Irish playwright, novelist, and critic.
Shel·ley /shélee/ **1** Percy Bysshe 1792–1822; English poet; husband of: **2** Mary Wollstonecraft 1797–1851; English novelist.
Sher·i·dan /shérid'n/, **Phillip Henry** 1831–88; Union general in the American Civil War.
Sher·i·dan, Richard Brinsley 1751–1816; Irish playwright.
Sher·man /shórmən/, **Roger** 1721–93; American statesman and patriot.
Sher·man, William Tecumseh 1820–91; Union general in the American Civil War.
Shev·ard·na·dze /shevərdnaádzə/, **Eduard** 1928– ; president of the Georgian Republic (1992–).
Sho·sta·ko·vich /shostəkṓvich/, **Dmitri** 1906–75; Russian composer.
Sho·wa /shṓwə/ see HIROHITO.
Si·be·li·us /sibáyleeəs/, **Jean** 1865–1957; Finnish composer.
Sid·dhart·ha Gau·ta·ma /sidaártə, –thə; gówtəmə/ see BUDDHA.
Sie·mens /seémənz, zeé–/, **(Ernst) Werner von** 1816–92; German electrical engineer and inventor.
Si·kor·sky /sikáwrskee/, **Igor** 1889–1972; U.S. aircraft designer, born in Russia.
Sills /silz/, **Beverly** (born **Belle Silverman**) 1929– ; U.S. operatic soprano.
Si·mon Pe·ter see PETER, ST.
Si·mon /símən/, **(Marvin) Neil** 1927– ; U.S. playwright.
Simp·son /símpsən/, **O(renthal) J(ames)** 1947– ; U.S. football player and actor.
Si·na·tra /sinaátrə/, **Frank (Francis Albert)** 1915–98; U.S. singer and actor.
Sin·clair /sinklair, –kláir/, **Upton** 1878–1968; U.S. novelist.
Sing·er /síng-ər/, **Isaac Bashevis** 1904–91; U.S. author, born in Poland.
Sing·er, Isaac Merritt 1811–75; U.S. inventor.
Sit·ting Bull /síting bo͝ol/ c. 1831–90; Sioux Indian leader.
Skin·ner /skínər/, **B(urrhus) F(rederic)** 1904–90; U.S. psychologist.
Sme·ta·na /smét'nə/, **Bedřich** 1824–84; Czech composer.
Smith /smith/, **Adam** 1723–90; Scottish philosopher and economist.
Smith, John 1580–1631; English colonist of Virginia.
Smith, Joseph 1805–44; founder of the Mormon Church (1830).
Smol·lett /smólit/, **Tobias George** 1721–71; English novelist.
Smuts /smʏts, smuts/, **Jan Christiaan** 1870–1950; prime minister of South Africa (1919–24; 1939–48).
Soc·ra·tes /sókrəteez/ 469–399 B.C.; Greek philosopher. ▫▫ **So·crat·ic** /səkrátik/ *adj.*
So·lon /sṓlən/ c. 638–559 B.C.; Athenian lawgiver.
Sol·zhe·ni·tsyn /sōlzhəneétsin, sawl–/, **Alexander** 1918– ; Russian novelist.
Sond·heim /sóndhīm/, **Stephen Joshua** 1930– ; U.S. songwriter.
Son·tag /sóntag/, **Susan** 1933– ; U.S. author and critic.
Soph·o·cles /sófəkleez/ c. 496–406 B.C.; Greek tragedian.
Sou·sa /so͞ozə/, **John Philip** 1854–1932; U.S. bandmaster and composer.
Sou·ter /so͞otər/, **David Hackett** 1939– ; U.S. Supreme Court justice (1990–).
Sou·they /súthee, sówthee/, **Robert** 1774–1843; English author.
So·yin·ka /shaw-yíngkə/, **Wole** 1934– ; Nigerian author.
Spar·ta·cus /spaártəkəs/ died 71 B.C.; Thracian gladiator; leader of a slave revolt against Rome.
Spen·ser /spénsər/, **Edmund** c. 1552–99; English poet.
Spiel·berg /speélbərg/, **Steven** 1947– ; U.S. film director, writer, and producer.
Spi·no·za /spinṓzə/, **Baruch (Benedict de)** 1632–77; Dutch philosopher.
Spock /spok/, **Benjamin** 1903–98; U.S. pediatrician and author.
Squan·to /skwaántō/ died 1622; Pawtuxet Indian who befriended Pilgrims at Plymouth Colony in Massachusetts.
Sta·lin /staálən, stál–/, **Joseph** (born **Iosif Vissarionovich Dzhugashvili**) 1879–1953; Soviet political leader.
Stan·dish /stándish/, **Myles** (or **Miles**) c. 1584–1656; English colonist in New England.
Stan·i·slav·sky /stanislaávskee/, **Konstantin** 1863–1938; Russian director and teacher of acting.
Stan·ley /stánlee/, **(Sir) Henry Morton** (born **John Rowlands**) 1841–1904; U.S. explorer and author, born in Wales.
Stan·ton /stánt'n/, **Elizabeth Cady** 1815–1902; U.S. social reformer.
Starr /staar/, **Ringo** (born **Richard Starkey**) 1940– ; British pop and rock drummer and singer.
Stein /stīn/, **Gertrude** 1874–1946; U.S. author.
Stein·beck /stínbek/, **John Ernst** 1902–68; U.S. author.
Stein·em /stínəm/, **Gloria** 1934– ; U.S. journalist, editor, and women's rights activist.
Sten·dhal /stendaál, stanNdaál/ (pseudonym of **Henri Beyle**) 1783–1842; French novelist.
Sterne /stərn/, **Laurence** 1713–68; British novelist.
Steu·ben /styo͞obən, sto͞o–, shtóy–/, **(Baron) Friedrich von** 1730–94; Prussian military leader; American Revolutionary War general in the Continental army.
Ste·vens /steévənz/, **John Paul** 1920– ; U.S. Supreme Court justice (1975–).
Ste·vens, Wallace 1878–1955; U.S. poet.
Ste·ven·son /steévənsən/, **Adlai Ewing** 1900–65; U.S. politician and statesman.
Ste·ven·son, Robert Louis Balfour 1850–94; British novelist.
Stone /stōn/, **Lucy** 1818–93; U.S. suffragist.
Stop·pard /stópaard, –ərd/, **Tom** (born **Thomas Straussler**) 1937– ; English playwright, born in Czechoslovakia.
Stowe /stō/, **Harriet Beecher** 1811–96; U.S. author.
Stra·di·va·ri /stradəvaáree, –vár–/, **Antonio** c. 1644–1737; Italian violin-maker.
Strauss /strows, shtrows/, **Johann** (called **"the Waltz King"**) 1825–99; Austrian composer.
Strauss, Richard Georg 1864–1949; German composer.
Stra·vin·sky /strəvínskee/, **Igor** 1882–1971; U.S. composer, born in Russia.
Strind·berg /strín(d)bərg/, **(Johan) August** 1849–1912; Swedish author.
Stu·art /sto͞oərt/, **Gilbert Charles** 1755–1828; U.S. portrait artist.
Stu·art, Jeb (James Ewell Brown) 1833–64; Confederate general in the American Civil War.
Stuy·ve·sant /stívəsənt/, **Peter** 1592–1672; Dutch colonial administrator in America.
Sue·to·ni·us /sweetṓneeəs/ 75–150; Roman historian.
Su·kar·no /so͞okaárnō/, **Achmed** 1901–70; president of Indonesia (1949–67).
Su·har·to /so͞ohaártō/, **Raden** 1921– ; president of Indonesia (1968–).
Su·lei·man I /so͞olaymaan, –li–/ (called **"the Magnificent"**) c. 1495–1566; sultan of the Ottoman Empire.
Sul·la /súlə/, **Lucius Cornelius** c. 138–78 B.C.; Roman general and political leader.
Sun Yat-sen /so͝on yaátsén/ (also **Sun Yi-xian**) 1866–1925; Chinese political leader.
Suth·er·land /súthərlənd/, **Joan** 1926– ; Australian operatic soprano.
Swift /swift/, **Jonathan** 1667–1745; English clergyman and satirist, born in Ireland.
Swin·burne /swínbərn/, **Algernon Charles** 1837–1909; English poet and critic.
Synge /sing/, **(Edmund) John Millington** 1871–1909; Irish playwright.
Tac·i·tus /tásitəs/, **Cornelius** c. 55–c. 120; Roman historian.
Taft /taft/ **1** William Howard 1857–1930; 27th president of the U.S. (1909–13); Chief Justice of the U.S. (1921–30); father of: **2** Robert A(lphonse) 1889–1953; U.S. politician.
Ta·gore /təgáwr, –gṓr/, **(Sir) Rabindranath** 1861–1941; Indian poet.
Tal·ley·rand-Pé·ri·gord /táleerand perəgáwr/, **Charles Maurice de (Prince de Bénévent)** 1754–1838; French diplomat.
Tam·er·lane /támərlayn/ c. 1336–1405; Mongol ruler.
Tar·king·ton /taárkingtən/, **(Newton) Booth** 1869–1946; U.S. author.
Tay·lor /táylər/, **Elizabeth** 1932– ; U.S. actress, born in England.
Tay·lor, Zachary 1784–1850; 12th president of the U.S. (1849–50).
Tchai·kov·sky /chīkáwfskee, –káwv–/, **Peter Ilyich** 1840–93; Russian composer.
Te Ka·na·wa /tay kaánəwə/, **Kiri** 1944– ; New Zealand operatic soprano.
Te·cum·seh /təkúmsə/ c. 1768–1813; Shawnee Indian leader.
Teil·hard de Char·din /tay-yaár də shaardáN/, **Pierre** 1881–1955; French Jesuit philosopher.
Tel·ler /télər/, **Edward** 1908– ; U.S. nuclear physicist, born in Hungary.
Tem·ple /témpəl/, **Shirley** see BLACK, SHIRLEY TEMPLE.
Teng Hsiao-p'ing /dúng shyówping/ see DENG XIAOPING.
Ten·ny·son /ténəsən/, **Alfred, Lord** 1809–92; English poet.
Te·re·sa /təreésə, –ráyzə/, **Mother** (born **Agnes Gonxha Bojaxhiu**) 1910–97; Roman Catholic missionary nun, born in Albania.
Tes·la /téslə/, **Nikola** 1856–1943; U.S. engineer and inventor.
Thack·er·ay /thákəree/, **William Makepeace** 1811–63; English author.

Tha·les /tháyleez/ fl. early 6th cent. B.C.; Greek philosopher.
Thant /t(h)aant, t(h)ánt/, **U** 1909–74; Burmese diplomat; secretary-general of the United Nations (1962–71).
Thatch·er /tháchər/, **(Lady) Margaret Hilda Roberts** (called **"the Iron Lady"**) 1925– ; prime minister of Great Britain (1979–90).
Thi·bault /teebṓ/, **Jacques Anatole** see FRANCE, ANATOLE.
Thom·as à Kem·pis see KEMPIS, THOMAS À.
Thom·as /taáməs/, **Clarence** 1948– ; U.S. Supreme Court justice (1991–).
Thom·as, Dylan 1914–53; Welsh poet.
Tho·reau /thərṓ, tháwrō/, **Henry David** (born **David Henry Thoreau**) 1817–62; U.S. author.
Thu·cyd·i·des /thoosídədeez, thyoo–/ c. 455–c. 400 B.C.; Greek historian.
Thur·ber /thórbər/, **James Grover** 1894–1961; U.S. cartoonist and author.
Ti·be·ri·us /tībeéreeəs/ 42 B.C.–A.D. 37; Roman emperor (A.D. 14–37).
Til·lich /tílik/, **Paul Johannes** 1886–1965; U.S. theologian, born in Germany.
Tin·to·ret·to /tintərétō/ 1518–94; Italian artist.
Ti·tian /tíshən/ c. 1488–1576; Italian artist.
Ti·to /teétō/, (born **Josip Broz**) 1892–1980; president of Yugoslavia (1953–80).
Tocque·ville /tṓkvil/, **Alexis de** 1805–59; French statesman and author.
Tof·fler /táwflər/, **Alvin** 1928– ; U.S. author.
To·jo /tṓjō/, **Hideki** 1885–1948; war minister (1940–41) and prime minister (1941–44) of Japan; executed.
Tol·kien /taálkeen, tṓl–/, **J(ohn) R(onald) R(euel)** 1892–1973; English author.
Tol·stoy /táwlstoy, tṓl–, taál–/, **(Count) Leo** (or **Lev**) **Nikolaevich** 1828–1910; Russian author.
Tor·que·ma·da /tawrkəmaádə/, **Tomás de** c. 1420–98; Spanish cleric; led Spanish Inquisition.
Tos·ca·ni·ni /toskəneénee/, **Arturo** 1867–1975; Italian conductor.
Tou·louse-Lau·trec /toolóos lōtrék/, **Henri de** 1864–1901; French artist.
Toyn·bee /tóynbee/, **Arnold Joseph** 1889–1975; English historian.
Tra·cy /tráysee/, **Spencer** 1900–67; U.S. actor.
Trev·i·thick /trévəthik/, **Richard** 1771–1833; British engineer.
Trol·lope /trólәp/, **Anthony** 1815–82; English novelist.
Trot·sky /trótskee/, **Leon** (born **Lev Davidovich Bronstein**) 1879–1940; Russian revolutionary.
Tru·deau /troodṓ/, **Pierre Elliott** 1919– ; prime minister of Canada (1968–79; 1980–84).
Tru·man /troomən/ **1** Harry S 1884–1972; 33rd president of the U.S. (1945–53); father of: **2** Margaret 1924– ; U.S. author.
Trump /trump/, **Donald** 1946– ; U.S. business executive.
Tub·man /túbmən/, **Harriet** 1820–1913; U.S. abolitionist.
Tuch·man /túkmən/, **Barbara** 1912–89; U.S. historian.
Tur·ge·nev /toorgáynyəf, –gén–/, **Ivan** 1818–83; Russian novelist.
Tur·ner /tórnər/, **Joseph Mallord William** 1775–1851; English landscape artist.
Tur·ner, Nat 1800–31; U.S. slave insurrectionist.
Tur·ner, Ted (**Robert Edward**) 1938– ; U.S. media executive.
Tut·ankh·a·men /tootaangkaámən, –tang–/ 14th cent. B.C.; Egyptian king.
Tu·tu /tootoo/, **Desmond** (born **Mpilo**) 1931– ; South African archbishop and civil-rights leader.
Twain /twayn/, **Mark** (pseudonym of **Samuel Langhorne Clemens**) 1835–1910; U.S. author.
Tweed /tweed/, **Boss (William Marcy)** 1823–78; U.S. politician.
Ty·ler /tílər/, **John** 1790–1862; 10th president of the U.S. (1841–45).
Tyn·dale /tíndəl, –dayl/, **William** c. 1494–1536; English translator of the Bible.
Up·dike /úpdīk/, **John Hoyer** 1932– ; U.S. novelist.
Va·lé·ry /valəreé/, **Paul Ambroise** 1871–1945; French poet and philosopher.
Van Bu·ren /van byoorən/, **Martin** (called **"Old Kinderhook"**) 1782–1862; 8th president of the U.S. (1837–41).
Van·der·bilt /vándərbilt/, **Cornelius** 1794–1877; U.S. industrialist.
Van Dyck /van dík/, **(Sir) Anthony** 1599–1641; Flemish artist.
Van Eyck /van ík/, **Jan** died 1441; Flemish artist.
Van Gogh /van gṓ, gaákh/, **Vincent** 1853–90; Dutch artist.
Vaughan /vawn/, **Sarah** 1924–90; U.S. jazz singer.
Vaughan Wil·liams /vawn wílyəmz/, **Ralph** 1872–1958; English composer.
Ve·láz·quez /vəláskəs, –kwez/, **Diego** 1599–1660; Spanish artist.
Ver·di /vérdee/, **Giuseppe** 1813–1901; Italian opera composer.
Ver·gil /vórjəl/ see VIRGIL.
Ver·meer /vərmeér/, **Jan** 1632–75; Dutch artist.
Verne /vərn/, **Jules** 1828–1905; French author.
Ves·puc·ci /vespoochee/, **Amerigo** 1451–1512; Italian explorer.
Vic·to·ri·a /viktáwreeə/ 1819–1901; queen of Great Britain (1837–1901).
Vi·dal /vidaál, –dáwl/, **Gore** (born **Eugene Luther Vidal**) 1925– ; U.S. author.
Vil·la /veé-ə/, **Pancho (Francisco)** 1877–1923; Mexican revolutionary.
Vil·lon /vee-yṓN/, **François** 1431–c. 1463; French poet.
Vir·gil /vórjəl/ (also **Ver'gil**) 70–19 B.C.; Roman poet.
Vir·gin Mar·y see MARY.
Vi·val·di /vivaáldee/, **Antonio** 1678–1741; Italian composer.
Vol·ta /vṓwltə/, **(Count) Alessandro** 1745–1827; Italian physicist.
Vol·taire /vōltáir, vawl–, –tér/, (pseudonym of **François-Marie Arouet**) 1694–1778; French author.
Von·ne·gut /vónigət/, **Kurt** 1922– ; U.S. author.
Wag·ner /vaágnər/, **Richard** 1813–83; German composer.
Wald·heim /vaáldhīm/, **Kurt** 1918– ; Austrian political leader and diplomat; secretary-general of the United Nations (1972–82).
Wa·le·sa /vəlénsə, vəwénsə/, **Lech** 1943– ; Polish labor and political leader.
Wal·lace /waáləs/, **Alfred Russel** 1823–1913; British naturalist.
Wal·lace, George Corley 1919–98; U.S. politician.
Wal·pole /wáwlpōl/, **Horace (4th Earl of Orford)** 1717–97; English author.
Wal·ton /wáwlt'n/, **Izaak** 1593–1683; English author.
Wan·kel /vaángkəl/, **Felix** 1902–88; German engineer.
War·hol /wáwrhawl, –hōl/, **Andy** (born **Andrew Warhola**) c. 1930–87; U.S. artist and filmmaker.
War·ren /wáwrən, waár–/, **Earl** 1891–1974; Chief Justice of the U.S. (1953–69).
Wash·ing·ton /waáshingtən, wáwsh–/, **Booker T(aliaferro)** 1856–1915; U.S. educator and reformer.
Wash·ing·ton, George 1732–99; American patriot and Revolutionary War general; 1st president of the U.S. (1789–97).
Wat·son /waátsən/, **James Dewey** 1928– ; U.S. biologist.
Watt /waat/, **James** 1736–1819; Scottish inventor.
Wat·teau /vaatṓ, waa–/, **Jean Antoine** 1684–1721; French artist.
Waugh /waw/, **Evelyn** 1903–66; English novelist.
Wayne /wayn/, **Anthony** (called **"Mad Anthony"**) 1745–96; American Revolutionary War general.
Wayne, John (born **Marion Michael Morrison**) 1907–79; U.S. actor.
We·ber /váybər/, **Max** 1864–1920; German sociologist.
We·ber /wébər/, **Max** 1881–1961; U.S. artist, born in Russia.
Web·ster /wébstər/, **Daniel** 1782–1852; U.S. politician and orator.
Web·ster, Noah 1758–1843; U.S. lexicographer.
Wedg·wood /wéjwood/, **Josiah** 1730–95; English potter.
Weill /vīl/, **Kurt** 1900–50; German composer.
Weiz·mann /vítsmən/, **Chaim** 1874–1952; president of Israel (1949–52).
Wel·ling·ton /wélingtən/, **1st Duke of (Arthur Wellesley)** (called **"the Iron Duke"**) 1769–1852; British general and statesman; prime minister of Great Britain (1828–30).
Wells /welz/, **H(erbert) G(eorge)** 1866–1946; English author.
Wel·ty /wéltee/, **Eudora** 1909– ; U.S. author.
Wes·ley /wéslee, wéz–/, **John** 1703–91; English evangelical leader; founder of Methodism.
West /west/, **Benjamin** 1738–1820; U.S. artist.
West, Rebecca (pseudonym of **Cicily Isabel Fairfield**) 1892–1983; English author.
Whar·ton /(h)wáwrt'n/, **Edith Newbold Jones** 1862–1937; U.S. novelist.
Wheat·ley /(h)weétlee/, **Phillis** c. 1753–84; American poet, probably born in Senegal.
Wheat·stone /(h)weétstōn/, **(Sir) Charles** 1802–75; English physicist and inventor.
Whis·tler /(h)wíslər/, **James Abbott McNeill** 1834–1903; U.S. artist.
White·head /(h)wít-hed/, **Alfred North** 1861–1947; English mathematician and philosopher.
Whit·man /(h)wítmən/, **Walt(er)** 1819–92; U.S. poet.
Whit·ney /(h)wítnee/, **Eli** 1765–1825; U.S. inventor and manufacturer.
Whit·tier /(h)wíteeər/, **John Greenleaf** 1807–92; U.S. poet.
Wie·sel /veezél, wizél/, **Elie** 1928– ; U.S. author and educator, born in Romania.
Wilde /wīld/, **Oscar** 1854–1900; Irish poet and playwright.
Wil·der /wíldər/, **Thornton Niven** 1897–1975; U.S. author.
Wil·lard /wílərd/, **Emma Hart** 1787–1870; U.S. educational reformer.
Wil·liam /wílyəm/ name of four kings of England, including: **1** William I (called **"the Conqueror"**) c. 1027–87; reigned 1066–87. **2** William III 1650–1702; reigned 1689–1702 with his wife, Mary II.
Wil·liams /wílyəmz/, **Roger** c. 1603–83; English clergyman; established Rhode Island colony (1636).
Wil·liams, Tennessee (born **Thomas Lanier Williams**) 1911–83; U.S. playwright.
Wil·liams, William Carlos 1883–1963; U.S. poet.
Wil·son /wílsən/, **Edmund** 1895–1972; U.S. critic and author.
Wil·son, (Lord) (James) Harold 1916–95; prime minister of Great Britain (1964–70; 1974–76).
Wil·son, (Thomas) Woodrow 1856–1924; 28th president of the U.S. (1913–21).

See page xii for the *Key to Pronunciation*.

Win·frey /wínfree/, **Oprah** 1954– ; U.S. television personality and actress.
Witt·gen·stein /vítgənshtīn, –stīn/, **Ludwig** 1889–1951; British philosopher, born in Austria.
Wode·house /wŏŏdhows/, **(Sir) P(elham) G(renville)** 1881–1975; English author.
Wolfe /wŏŏlf/, **Thomas** 1900–38; U.S. author.
Wol·las·ton /wŏŏləstən/, **William Hyde** 1766–1828; English scientist.
Wol·sey /wŏŏlzee/, **Thomas** c. 1474–1530; English cleric and statesman.
Won·der /wúndər/, **Stevie** (born **Stephen Judkins**) 1950– ; U.S. pop singer and songwriter.
Wood /wŏŏd/, **Grant** 1892–1942; U.S. artist.
Woods /wŏŏdz/, **Tiger (Eldrick)** 1975– ; U.S. golfer.
Woolf /wŏŏlf/, **(Adeline) Virginia** 1882–1941; English author.
Words·worth /wə́rdzwərth/, **William** 1770–1850; English poet.
Wouk /wōk/, **Herman** 1915– ; U.S. author.
Wren /ren/, **(Sir) Christopher** 1632–1723; English architect.
Wright /rīt/, **Frank Lloyd** 1869–1959; U.S. architect.
Wright, Richard 1908–60; U.S. author.
Wright two U.S. aviation pioneers: **1** Wilbur 1867–1912; brother of: **2** Orville 1871–1948.
Wy·eth /wíəth/ family of U.S. artists, including: **1** N(ewell) C(onvers) 1882–1945; father of: **2** Andrew Newell 1917– ; father of: **3** Jamie (James Browning) 1946– .
Xa·vi·er /záyvyər, igzáy–/, **St. Francis (Francisco Javier)** 1506–52; Spanish Jesuit missionary of the Far East.
Xen·o·phon /zénəfən, –fon/ c. 428–c. 354 B.C.; Greek author.
Xerx·es I /zórkseez/ c. 519–465 B.C.; king of Persia (486–465 B.C.).
Yeats /yayts/, **William Butler** 1865–1939; Irish poet and playwright.
Yelt·sin /yéltsin/, **Boris** 1931– ; president of the Russian federation (1991–).
Young /yung/, **Brigham** 1801–77; U.S. Mormon leader.
Za·pa·ta /zəpaátə/, **Emiliano** c. 1877–1919; Mexican revolutionary.
Zar·a·thus·tra /zaarəthŏŏstrə/ see ZOROASTER.
Zep·pe·lin /zépəlin/, **(Count) Ferdinand von** 1838–1917; German airship developer.
Zhou En·lai /jō enlí/ see CHOU EN-LAI.
Zhu·kov /zhŏŏkawf, –kawv/, **Georgi Konstantinovich** 1896–1974; Soviet military leader in World War II.
Zieg·feld /zígfeld, zeég–/, **Flo(renz)** 1867–1932; U.S. theater producer.
Zo·la /zṓlə, zōlaá/, **Émile** 1840–1902; French author.
Zo·ro·as·ter /záwrō-astər, zṓr–/ (also **Zar·at·hus'tra**) c. 628–551 B.C.; Persian prophet; founder of Zoroastrianism.

Geographical Entries

Aa·chen /aákhən/ *n.* city in W Germany. Pop. 241,900.
Ab·er·deen /abərdeén/ *n.* port city in E Scotland, United Kingdom. Pop. 218,200.
Ab·i·djan /abijaán/ *n.* port city and commercial capital of Ivory Coast. Pop. 2,797,000.
Ab·i·lene /ábəleen/ *n.* city in central Texas. Pop. 106,654.
A·bu Dha·bi /aábōō daábee/ *n.* capital of the United Arab Emirates. Pop. 363,400.
A·bu·ja /aabóōjaa/ *n.* capital of Nigeria, in the central part. Pop. 339,100.
A·ca·di·a /akáydeeə/ **Na·tion·al Park** *n.* scenic area on the coast of Maine; includes parts of Mount Desert Island, Schoodic Peninsula, and Isle au Haut.
A·ca·pul·co /akəpóōlkō, aak–, –pōōl–/ *n.* port city in S Mexico. Pop. 515,400.
Ac·cra /aákraá/ *n.* port city and capital of Ghana. Pop. 1,781,100.
A·con·ca·gua /aakənkaágwə/ *n.* mountain in the Andes range, in W Argentina; highest in W hemisphere: 22,831 ft.
Ad·dis A·ba·ba /ádis ábəbə/ *n.* capital of Ethiopia, in the central part. Pop. 2,200,200.
Ad·e·laide /ád'layd/ *n.* capital of South Australia, Australia, in the SE part. Pop. 1,023,600.
A·den /aád'n, áyd'n/ *n.* port city and economic capital of Yemen. Pop. 318,000.
A·den, Gulf of *n.* arm of the Arabian Sea, S of Yemen.
Ad·i·ron·dack /adəraándak/ **Moun·tains** *n.* mountain range in NE New York; part of the Appalachian range.
A·dri·at·ic /aydree-átik/ **Sea** *n.* arm of the Mediterranean Sea, between Italy and the Balkan Peninsula.
Ae·ge·an /ijeéən, ee–/ **Sea** *n.* arm of the Mediterranean Sea, between Greece and Turkey.
Af·ghan·i·stan /afgánistan/ *n.* republic in central Asia. Pop. 22,664,000. Capital: Kabul.
Af·ri·ca /áfrikə/ *n.* continent between the Atlantic and Indian oceans, S of Europe. ▫▫ **Af'ri·can** *n. & adj.*
A·gra /aágrə/ *n.* city in N central India; site of the Taj Mahal. Pop. 899,200.
A·guas·ca·lien·tes /aagwaaskaalyéntays/ *n.* state in central Mexico. Pop. 719,700. Capital: Aguascalientes.
Ah·mad·a·bad /aámədəbaad/ *n.* city in W India. Pop. 2,872,900.
Aix-en-Pro·vence /ayks aan prōvaáns, eks/*n.* city in SE France. Pop. 126,900.
Ak·ron /ákrən/ *n.* city in N Ohio. Pop. 223,019.
Al·a·bam·a /aləbámə/ *n.* state in SE U.S. Pop. 4,040,587. Capital: Montgomery. Abbr. **AL**; **Ala.** ▫▫ **Al·a·bam'i·an, Al·a·bam'an** *n. & adj.*
A·las·ka /əláskə/ *n.* state in NW U.S. Pop. 550,043. Capital: Juneau. Abbr. **AK** ▫▫ **A·las'kan** *n. & adj.*
A·las·ka, Gulf of *n.* arm of the N Pacific, on the S coast of Alaska.
Al·ba·ni·a /albáyneeə, awl–/ *n.* republic in S Europe, on the Balkan Peninsula. Pop. 3,249,000. Capital: Tiranë. ▫▫ **Al·ba'ni·an** *n. & adj.*
Al·ba·ny /áwlbənee/ *n.* capital of New York, in the E part. Pop. 101,082.
Al·ber·ta /albúrtə/ *n.* province in W Canada. Pop. 2,662,000. Capital: Edmonton. ▫▫ **Al·ber'tan** *n. & adj.*
Al·bu·quer·que /álbəkərkee/ *n.* city in central New Mexico. Pop. 384,736.
Al·ca·traz /álkətraz/ *n.* island in in San Francisco Bay; site of a former federal penitentiary.
A·lep·po /əlépō/ *n.* city in N Syria. Pop. 1,591,400.
A·leu·tian /əlóōshən/ **Is·lands** *n.* (also called **the A·leu'tians**) island chain in Alaska, between the Bering Sea and the Pacific.
Al·ex·an·dri·a /aligzándreeə/ *n.* **1** port city in N Egypt. Pop. 3,382,000. **2** city in NE Virginia; Pop. 111,183.
Al·ge·ri·a /aljeéreeə/ *n.* republic in NW Africa. Pop. 29,183,000. Capital: Algiers. ▫▫ **Al·ge'ri·an** *n. & adj.*
Al·giers /aljeérz/ *n.* port city and capital of Algeria. Pop. 1,507,200.
Al·lah·a·bad /áləhəbad, –baad/ *n.* city in N India. Pop. 806,400.
Al·le·ghe·ny /aləgáynee/ **Moun·tains** *n.* mountain range in E U.S., extending from Pennsylvania to Virginia; part of the Appalachian range.
Al·len·town /áləntown/ *n.* city in E Pennsylvania. Pop. 105,090.
al-Ma·nam·ah /al mənámə/ *n.* see MANAMA.
Al·ma·ty /aalmaateé/ *n.* (formerly **Alma-Ata** /aalmaá aataá/) former capital of Kazakhstan, in the SE part. Pop. 1,164,000.
Alps /alps/ *n.* mountain range in S Europe, extending from France through Switzerland and to the Balkan Peninsula.
Am·a·ril·lo /aməríló/ *n.* city in NW Texas. Pop. 157,615.
Am·a·zon /áməzaan, –zən/ **Riv·er** *n.* river in N South America, flowing 3,900 mi. from the Andes to the Atlantic; largest river in the world.
A·mer·i·ca /əmérikə, –már–/ *n.* **1** popular term for the United States of America. **2** (also called **the A·mer'i·cas**) the continents of North and South America, considered together. ▫▫ **A·mer'i·can** *n. & adj.*
A·mer·i·can Sa·mo·a /səmṓə/ *n.* (also **East'ern Sa·mo'a**) island group in the S Pacific, comprising the E islands of Samoa; a U.S. territory. Pop. 60,000. Capital: Pago Pago. See also WESTERN SAMOA. ▫▫ **Sa·mo'an** *n. & adj.*
Am·i·ens /aámyan, aamyán/ *n.* city in N France. Pop. 136,200.
Am·man /aamaán/ *n.* capital of Jordan. Pop. 963,500.
Am·rit·sar /əmrítsər/ *n.* city in NW India. Pop. 709,500.
Am·ster·dam /ámstərdam/ *n.* port city and capital of the Netherlands. Pop. 724,100.
An·a·heim /ánəhīm/ *n.* city in SW California. Pop. 266,406.
An·chor·age /ángkərij/ *n.* port city in S Alaska. Pop. 226,338.
An·da·man /ándəmən, –man/ **Is·lands** *n.* island group in the Bay of Bengal, W of the Malay Peninsula.
An·des /ándeez/ *n.* mountain range in W South America, extending from Colombia to Cape Horn. ▫▫ **An'de·an** *n. & adj.*
An·dor·ra /andáwrə/ *n.* republic in W Europe, on the border between France and Spain. Pop. 73,000. Capital: Andorra la Vella.
An·gel /áynjəl/ **Falls** *n.* waterfall in SE Venezuela; highest in the world: 3,212 ft.
An·go·la /ang-gṓlə, an–/ *n.* republic in SW Africa. Pop. 10,343,000. Capital: Luanda. ▫▫ **An·go'lan** *n. & adj.*
An·guil·la /anggwílə/ *n.* island in the E West Indies; dependent territory of the United Kingdom. Pop. 8,700.
An·ka·ra /aángkərə, áng–/ *n.* capital of Turkey, in the central part. Pop. 2,720,000.
An·nap·o·lis /ənápələs/ *n.* capital of Maryland, in the central part; site of U.S. Naval Academy. Pop. 33,187.
Ann Ar·bor /an aárbər/ *n.* city in SE Michigan. Pop. 109,592.
An·ta·na·na·ri·vo /antənanəreévō/ *n.* capital of Madagascar, in the E central part. Pop. 1,052,800.
Ant·arc·ti·ca /antaárktikə, –aártikə/ *n.* **1** largely ice-covered continent surrounding the South Pole. **2 (the Antarctic)** region of Antarctica and surrounding oceans. ▫▫ **ant·arc'tic** *adj.*
An·ti·gua /anteégwə/ **and Bar·bu·da** /baarbóōdə/ *n.* island state in the E West Indies. Pop. 66,000. Capital: St. John's.
An·til·les /antíleez/ *n.* island chain in the West Indies, comprising the Greater Antilles and the Lesser Antilles.
An·tip·o·des /antípədeez/ *n.* **1** collective term for Australia and New Zealand. **2** island group in the S Pacific, SE of New Zealand.
Ant·werp /ántwərp/ *n.* port city in N Belgium. Pop. 462,900.
Ap·en·nines /ápənīnz/ *n.* mountain range extending the length of the Italian peninsula.
A·pi·a /əpeéə/ *n.* port city and capital of Western Samoa. Pop. 32,900.
Ap·pa·la·chi·an /apəláychən, –lách–, –cheeən/ **Moun·tains** *n.* mountain range in E North America, extending from Quebec to Alabama.
Ap·po·mat·tox /apəmátəks/ **Court·house** *n. hist.* former town in central Virginia, at present-day Appomattox; site of Lee's surrender to Grant ending the American Civil War (1865).
A·ra·bi·an /əráybeeən/ **Pen·in·su·la** *n.* (also called **A·ra'bi·a**) peninsula in SW Asia, bounded by the Red Sea and the Persian Gulf, and comprising Kuwait, Oman, Qatar, Saudi Arabia, United Arab Emirates, and Yemen.
A·ra·bi·an Sea *n.* part of the Indian Ocean, between the Arabian Peninsula and India.
Ar·al /árəl/ **Sea** *n.* inland sea in W Asia.
Ar·a·rat /árərat/, **Mount** *n.* mountain in E Turkey; traditional landing site of Noah's Ark.
Arch·an·gel *n.* see ARKHANGELSK.
Arc·tic /aárktik, aártik/ *n.* region delimited by the Arctic Circle.
Arc·tic Cir·cle *n.* imaginary line at latitude 66° 32′ **N, delimiting the Arctic region.**
Arc·tic O·cean *n.* ocean N of North America, Asia, and Europe. Area 5,540,000 sq. mi.
Ar·gen·ti·na /aarjənteénə/ *n.* republic in SE South America. Pop. 34,673,000. Capital: Buenos Aires. ▫▫ **Ar·gen·tine** /aárjənteen, –tīn/ *n. & adj.* **Ar·gen·tin·e·an** /aarjəntíneeən/ *n. & adj.*
Ar·i·zo·na /arəzṓnə/ *n.* state in SW U.S. Pop. 3,665,118. Capital: Phoenix. Abbr. **Ariz.**; **AZ** ▫▫ **Ar·i·zo'nan, Ar·i·zo'ni·an** *n. & adj.*
Ar·kan·sas /aárkənsaw/ *n.* state in S central U.S. Pop. 2,350,725.

Capital: Little Rock. Abbr. **AR**; **Ark.** ▫▫ **Ar·kan·san** /aarkánsən/ *n. & adj.*

Ar·khan·gelsk /aarkangélsk/ *n.* (also **Arch·an′gel**) port city in NW Russia. Pop. 407,100.

Ar·ling·ton /aárlingtən/ *n.* **1** city in N Texas. Pop. 261,721. **2** city in NE Virginia. Pop. 170,936.

Ar·me·ni·a /aarmeéneeə/ *n.* republic in W Asia. Pop. 3,464,000. Capital: Yerevan. ▫▫ **Ar·me′ni·an** *n. & adj.*

A·ru·ba /aaróóbaa/ *n.* self-governing Caribbean island, NW of Venezuela. Pop. 68,000.

Ash·ga·bat /áshkəbat/ *n.* (also **Ashkh′a·bad**) capital of Turkmenistan, in the S part. Pop. 518,000.

A·sia /áyzhə/ *n.* continent bounded by Europe, the Mediterranean and Red seas, and the Indian, Pacific, and Arctic oceans. ▫▫ **A′sian** *n. & adj.*

A·sia Mi·nor *n. hist.* peninsula in W Asia, bounded by the Black and Mediterranean seas; roughly equivalent to present-day Turkey.

As·ma·ra /aasmaárə/ *n.* (also **As·me′ra**) capital of Eritrea, in the central part. Pop. 367,300.

As·ta·na /aastaánaa/ *n.* (formerly **Aqmola**) capital (since 1998) of Kazakhstan, in the central part. Pop. 130,000.

A·sun·ción /aasóónsee-ón/ *n.* capital of Paraguay, in the SW part. Pop. 502,400.

As·wan /áswaan, –waán/ *n.* city in SE Egypt. Pop. 220,000.

A·syut /aasyóót/ *n.* city in E central Egypt. Pop. 321,000.

A·ta·ca·ma /aatəkaámə, at–/ **Des·ert** *n.* arid region in N Chile.

Ath·a·bas·ka /athəbáskə/, **Lake** *n.* lake in W Canada.

Ath·ens /áthənz/ *n.* capital of Greece, in the E part. Pop. 748,100. ▫▫ **A·the·ni·an** /əthéeneeən/ *n. & adj.*

At·lan·ta /ətlántə, at–/ *n.* capital of Georgia, in the NW central part. Pop. 394,017.

At·lan·tic /ətlántik, at–/ **In·tra·coast·al Wa·ter·way** *n.* system of sheltered waterways along the E seaboard of the U.S.

At·lan·tic O·cean *n.* ocean separating the Americas from Europe and Africa. Area 31,530,000 sq. mi.

At·las /átləs/ **Moun·tains** *n.* mountain range in NW Africa, extending from SW Morocco to NE Tunisia.

Auck·land /áwklənd/ *n.* port city in N New Zealand. Pop. 336,500.

Augs·burg /ówksbóórk, áwgzbərg/ *n.* city in S Germany. Pop. 264,800.

Au·gus·ta /əgústə/ *n.* capital of Maine, in the SW part. Pop. 21,325.

Au·ro·ra /əráwrə, –rórə/ *n.* **1** city in NE central Colorado. Pop. 222,103. **2** city in NE Illinois. Pop. 99,581.

Aus·tin /áwstən/ *n.* capital of Texas, in the E central part. Pop. 465,622.

Aus·tral·a·sia /awstrəláyzhə, aas–, –shə/ *n.* region including Australia, New Zealand, and neighboring islands in the S Pacific.

Aus·tral·ia /awstráylyə, aas–/ *n.* **1** continent SE of Asia, bounded by the Indian and Pacific oceans. **2** commonwealth of the states and territories of Australia and Tasmania. Pop. 18,261,000. Capital: Canberra. ▫▫ **Aus·tral′i·an** *n. & adj.*

Aus·tri·a /áwstreeə, áas–/ *n.* republic in central Europe. Pop. 8,023,000. Capital: Vienna. ▫▫ **Aus′tri·an** *n. & adj.*

Az·er·bai·jan /azərbīzhaán, –jaán/ *n.* republic in SW Asia; formerly part of the USSR. Pop. 7,677,000. Capital: Baku. ▫▫ **Az·er·bai·ja′ni** *n. & adj.*

A·zores /áyzawrz/ *n.* island group in the Atlantic, W of Portugal; autonomous region of Portugal.

A·zov /ázawf, áyzawf/, **Sea of** *n.* N arm of the Black Sea.

Bad·lands /bádlanz, –landz/ *n.* barren region in SW South Dakota and NW Nebraska.

Baf·fin /báfin/ **Bay** *n.* inlet of the Arctic Ocean, between Baffin Island and Greenland.

Baf·fin Is·land *n.* island in NE Canada, W of Greenland.

Bagh·dad /bágdad, bagdád/ *n.* (also **Bag′dad**) capital of Iraq, in the E central part. Pop. 4,044,000.

Ba·ha·mas /bəhaáməz/ *n.* island nation in the N West Indies, SE of Florida. Pop. 259,000. Capital: Nassau. ▫▫ **Ba·ha·mi·an** /bəháymeeən/ *n. & adj.*

Bah·rain /baaráyn, baakhráyn/ *n.* sheikdom consisting of islands in the Persian Gulf. Pop. 590,000. Capital: Manama.

Bai·kal /bīkaál, ; n-káwl/, **Lake** *n.* lake in S Russia; deepest in the world: 5,700 ft.

Ba·ja Ca·li·for·nia /baáhaa kalifáwrnyə/ *n.* **1** peninsula in NW Mexico, bounded by the Pacific and the Gulf of California. **2** (formerly **Ba′ja Ca·li·for′nia Nor·te** /náwrtay/) state in NW Mexico; N part of Baja California peninsula. Pop. 1,886,000. Capital: Mexicali.

Ba·ja Ca·li·for·nia Sur /sóór/ *n.* state in NW Mexico; S part of Baja California peninsula. Pop. 317,800. Capital: La Paz.

Ba·kers·field /báykərzfeeld/ *n.* city in S California. Pop. 174,820.

Ba·ku /baakóó/ *n.* port city and capital of Azerbaijan. Pop. 1,080,500.

Bal·e·ar·ic /balee-árik/ **Is·lands** *n.* island group in the W Mediterranean Sea; province of Spain.

Ba·li /baálee, bálee/ *n.* island in Indonesia, E of Java.

Bal·kan /báwlkən/ **Pen·in·su·la** *n.* peninsula in S Europe, bounded by the Adriatic and Black seas, and comprising the Balkan States.

Bal·kan States *n.* (also called **the Bal′kans**) countries of the Balkan Peninsula: Albania, Bulgaria, Greece, Romania, Croatia, Bosnia and Herzegovina, Yugoslavia (including Serbia), Macedonia, and European Turkey.

Bal·tic /báwltik/ **Sea** *n.* sea in N Europe, S of Scandinavian Peninsula.

Bal·ti·more /báwltəmawr/ *n.* port city in N central Maryland. Pop. 736,014.

Ba·ma·ko /báməkō/ *n.* capital of Mali, in the SW part. Pop. 745,800.

Ban·dung /baándŏŏng/ *n.* city in Indonesia, on Java. Pop. 2,026,900.

Ban·ga·lore /baánggəlawr/ *n.* city in SW India. Pop. 2,650,700.

Bang·kok /bángkaak/ *n.* port city and capital of Thailand. Pop. 5,572,700.

Ban·gla·desh /banggləàdésh, baang–/ *n.* republic in S Asia. Pop. 123,063,000. Capital: Dhaka. ▫▫ **Ban·gla·desh′i** *n. & adj.*

Ban·gui /baang-gée/ *n.* capital of Central African Republic, in the SW part. Pop. 524,000.

Ban·jul /baánjŏŏl/ *n.* port city and capital of Gambia. Pop. 44,200.

Bar·ba·dos /baarbáydōs, –ōz/ *n.* island nation in the E West Indies. Pop. 257,000. Capital: Bridgetown. ▫▫ **Bar·ba′di·an** *n. & adj.*

Bar·ba·ry /baárbəree/ **Coast** *n.* Mediterranean coast of the former Barbary States, in N Africa.

Bar·ba·ry States *n. hist.* Morocco, Algiers, Tunis, and Tripoli; refuge for pirates between 1520 and 1830.

Bar·ce·lo·na /baarsəlṓnə/ *n.* port city in NE Spain. Pop. 1,630,900.

Ba·ri /baáree/ *n.* (also called **Ba′ri del·le Pu·glie** /delə póólyee/) port city in SE Italy. Pop. 339,000.

Ba·ro·da /bərṓdə/ *n.* city in W India. Pop. 1,021,100.

Bar·ran·qui·lla /baaraankéeyə, –kéelyə/ *n.* port city in N Colombia. Pop. 1,064,300.

Ba·sel /baázəl/ *n.* city in W Switzerland. Pop. 176,200.

Bas·ra /baásrə, baáz–/ *n.* city in SE Iraq. Pop. 616,700.

Basse·terre /baastér/ *n.* port city and capital of St. Kitts and Nevis. Pop. 15,000.

Basse-Terre /baas tér/ *n.* port city and capital of Guadeloupe. Pop. 14,100.

Ba·su·to·land /bəsóótōōland, –tōland/ *n.* see Lesotho.

Bat·on Rouge /bat′n róózh/ *n.* capital of Louisiana, in the SE central part. Pop. 219,531.

Bat·tle /bát′l/ **Creek** *n.* city in S Michigan. Pop. 53,540.

Ba·ya·món /bīəmṓn/ *n.* city in N Puerto Rico. Pop. 202,100.

Beau·fort /bṓfərt/ **Sea** *n.* part of the Arctic Ocean, NE of Alaska.

Beau·mont /bṓmaant/ *n.* city in SE Texas. Pop. 114,323.

Bea·ver·ton /béevərtən/ *n.* city in NW Oregon. Pop. 53,310.

Beer·she·ba /beershéebə/ *n.* city in S Israel. Pop. 141,400.

Bei·jing /bayjíng, –zhíng/ *n.* (formerly **Peking**) capital of China, in the NE part. Pop. 5,769,600.

Bei·rut /bayróót/ *n.* capital of Lebanon, in the W part. Pop. 1,100,000.

Bel·a·rus /beləróós/ *n.* republic in E Europe; formerly, as Byelorussia, part of the USSR. Pop. 10,416,000. Capital: Minsk.

Bel·fast /bélfast, belfást/ *n.* port city and capital of Northern Ireland, United Kingdom. Pop. 296,700.

Bel·gium /béljəm/ *n.* kingdom in W Europe. Pop. 10,170,000. Capital: Brussels. ▫▫ **Bel′gian** *n. & adj.*

Bel·go·rod /bélgəraad, byél–/ *n.* city in W Russia. Pop. 317,900.

Bel·grade /bélgrayd, –graad/ *n.* capital of Serbia, in the N part; capital of former Yugoslavia. Pop. 1,168,500.

Be·lize /bəléez/ *n.* country in N Central America. Pop. 219,000. Capital: Belmopan.

Belle·vue /bélvyoo/ *n.* city in W central Washington. Pop. 86,874.

Bel·mo·pan /belmōpán/ *n.* capital of Belize, in the central part. Pop. 3,900.

Be·lo Ho·ri·zon·te /báylō hawrizaántee/ *n.* city in SE Brazil. Pop. 1,529,600.

Be·na·res /bənaáris, –eez/ *n.* see Varanasi.

Ben·e·lux /bén′ləks/ *n.* collective term for Belgium, the Netherlands, and Luxembourg.

Ben·gal /ben-gáwl, beng; n–/, **Bay of** *n.* inlet of the Indian Ocean, between India and Burma.

Ben·gha·zi /ben-gaázee/ *n.* port city in N Libya. Pop. 446,300.

Be·nin /bənéen, –nín/ *n.* republic in W Africa. Pop. 5,710,000. Capital: Porto-Novo.

Ber·gen /bérgən/ *n.* port city in SW Norway. Pop. 221,700.

Ber·ing /béering, bér–/ **Sea** *n.* extension of the N Pacific, between Russia and Alaska.

Ber·ing Strait *n.* body of water separating Asia (Russia) from North America (Alaska).

Berke·ley /búrklee/ *n.* city in W California. Pop. 102,724.

Ber·lin /bərlín/ *n.* capital of Germany, in the NE part. Pop. 3,475,400. ▫▫ **Ber·lin′er** *n.*

Ber·mu·da /bərmyóódə/ *n.* (also called **the Ber·mu′das**) island group in the Atlantic, E of North Carolina; British colony. Pop. 62,000. Capital: Hamilton. ▫▫ **Ber·mu′dan, Ber·mu′di·an** *n. & adj.*

Ber·mu·da Tri·an·gle *n.* area in the Atlantic bounded by Puerto Rico, Bermuda, and Florida, where many ships and planes are said to have disappeared mysteriously.

Bern /bərn, bern/ *n.* (also **Berne**) capital of Switzerland, in the W central part. Pop. 134,600. ▫▫ **Ber·nese** /bərnéez, –nées/ *n. & adj.*

Be·thes·da /bəthézdə/ *n.* city in central Maryland. Pop. 62,936.

Bho·pal /bōpaál/ *n.* city in central India. Pop. 1,063,700.

Bhu·tan /bootán, –taán/ *n.* monarchy in the Himalayas, NE of India. Pop. 1,823,000. Capital: Thimphu.

Bia·ly·stok /bee-aáleestawk/ *n.* city in E Poland. Pop. 276,100.

Bie·le·feld /beéləfelt/ *n.* city in W central Germany. Pop. 324,700.

Big Sur /big sər/ *n.* Pacific coastal region of California, from Carmel to San Simeon.

Bil·ba·o /bilbów, –báyō/ *n.* port city in N Spain. Pop. 371,800.

Bil·lings /bílingz/ *n.* city in S central Montana. Pop. 81,151.

Bir·ming·ham *n.* **1** /búrmingham/ city in N central Alabama. Pop. 265,968. **2** /búrmingəm/ city in central England. Pop. 1,024,100.

Bis·cay /biskáy/, **Bay of** *n.* inlet of the Atlantic, between France and Spain.

Bish·kek /bishkék/ *n.* capital of Kyrgyzstan, in the N part. Pop. 597,000.

Bis·marck /bízmaark/ *n.* capital of North Dakota, in the S central part. Pop. 49,256.

Bis·sau /bisów/ *n.* port city and capital of Guinea-Bissau. Pop. 200,000.

Black /blak/ **Hills** *n.* mountains in NE Wyoming and W South Dakota.

Black·pool /blákpool/ *n.* city in NW England. Pop. 146,100.

Black /blak/ **Sea** *n.* sea enclosed by Turkey, the Balkan Peninsula, Ukraine, SW Russia, and Georgia.

Blanc /blaaN/, **Mont** /mawn/ *n.* mountain on the France-Italy-Switzerland border; highest in the Alps: 15,771 ft.

Bloem·fon·tein /bloofaanten/ *n.* judicial capital of South Africa, in the central part. Pop. 126,900.

Bloo·ming·ton /bloomingtən/ *n.* **1** city in SE central Minnesota. Pop. 86,335. **2** city in S central Indiana. Pop. 60,633.

Blue·grass /bloograS/ **Re·gion** *n.* area of central Kentucky noted for thoroughbred horse breeding.

Blue Ridge /bloo rij/ **Moun·tains** *n.* mountain range in E U.S., extending from West Virginia to N Georgia; part of the Appalachian range.

Bo·go·tá /bōgətaá/ *n.* capital of Colombia, in the central part. Pop. 5,237,600.

Boi·se /bóysee, –zee/ *n.* capital of Idaho, in the SW part. Pop. 125,738.

Bo·liv·i·a /bəlíveeə/ *n.* republic in W South America. Pop. 7,165,000. Capitals: La Paz; Sucre. ☐☐ **Bo·liv'i·an** *n. & adj.*

Bo·lo·gna /bəlṓnyə/ *n.* city in N Italy. Pop. 395,000. ☐☐ **Bo·lo·gnese** /bōləneéz/ *n. & adj.*

Bom·bay /baambáy/ *n.* port city in W India. Pop. 14,496,000.

Bonn /baan, bawn/ *n.* city in W Germany; seat of government. Pop. 296,900.

Bon·ne·ville /baánivil/ **Salt Flats** *n.* barren salt flatland in NW Utah.

Bor·deaux /bawrdṓ/ *n.* port city in SW France. Pop. 213,300.

Bor·ne·o /báwrnee-ō/ *n.* island in the Malay Archipelago.

Bos·ni·a /baázneeə/ **and Her·ze·go·vi·na** /hərtsəgōveénə, –gṓvinə/ *n.* (also called **Bos'ni·a-Her·ze·go·vi'na**) republic in S Europe, on the Balkan Peninsula; formerly part of Yugoslavia. Pop. 2,656,000. Capital: Sarajevo.

Bos·po·rus /baáspərəs/ *n.* strait connecting the Sea of Marmara and the Black Sea.

Bos·ton /báwstən/ *n.* capital of Massachusetts, in the E part. Pop. 574,283. ☐☐ **Bos·ton'i·an** /bawstṓneeən/ *n. & adj.*

Both·ni·a /baáthneeə/, **Gulf of** *n.* arm of the Baltic Sea, between Finland and Sweden.

Bot·swa·na /baatswaánə/ *n.* republic in S Africa. Pop. 1,478,000. Capital: Gaborone.

Boul·der /bṓldər/ *n.* city in N central Colorado. Pop. 83,312.

Bourne·mouth /báwrnməth/ *n.* city in S England. Pop. 151,300.

Bramp·ton /brámtən, brámp–/ *n.* city in SE Ontario, Canada. Pop. 234,400.

Bra·sil·ia /brəzílyə/ *n.* capital of Brazil, in the S central part. Pop. 411,300.

Bra·ti·sla·va /braatislaávə/ *n.* capital of Slovakia, in the W part. Pop. 446,700.

Bra·zil /brəzil/ *n.* republic in E South America. Pop. 162,661,000. Capital: Brasilia. ☐☐ **Bra·zil'ian** *n. & adj.*

Braz·za·ville /brázəvil/ *n.* capital of the Republic of the Congo, in the SE part. Pop. 937,600.

Brem·en /brémən/ *n.* port city in NW Germany. Pop. 551,600.

Brem·er·ha·ven /brémərhaavən/ *n.* port city in NW Germany. Pop. 131,500.

Bre·scia /bráyshə/ *n.* city in N Italy. Pop. 191,900.

Brest /brest/ *n.* **1** port city in W France. Pop. 153,100. **2** city in SW Belarus. Pop. 284,000.

Brid·al·veil /bríd'lvayl/ *n.* waterfall in Yosemite National Park, California: 620 ft. high.

Bridge·port /bríjpawrt, –pōrt/ *n.* city in SW Connecticut. Pop. 141,686.

Bridge·town /bríjtown/ *n.* port city and capital of Barbados. Pop. 6,100.

Brigh·ton /brít'n/ *n.* city in SE England. Pop. 143,600.

Bris·bane /brízbən, –bayn/ *n.* port city and capital of Queensland, Australia. Pop. 786,400.

Bris·tol /brístəl/ *n.* port city in SW England. Pop. 399,200.

Brit·ain /brít'n/ *n.* see GREAT BRITAIN.

Brit·ish Co·lum·bi·a /british kəlúmbeeə/ *n.* province in W Canada. Pop. 3,535,000. Capital: Victoria. ☐☐ **Brit'ish Co·lum'bi·an** *n. & adj.*

Brit·ish Em·pire *n. hist.* countries under the control or leadership of the British Crown.

Brit·ish Vir·gin /vərjin/ **Is·lands** *n.* island group in the E West Indies; British possession.

Br·no /búrnō/ *n.* city in E Czech Republic. Pop. 388,000.

Brock·ton /braáktən/ *n.* city in SE Massachusetts. Pop. 92,788.

Bronx /braangks/ *n.* (also **the Bronx**) one of the five boroughs of New York City. Pop. 1,203,789.

Brook·lyn /brooklən/ *n.* one of the five boroughs of New York City. Pop. 2,300,664.

Browns·ville /brównzvil/ *n.* city in S Texas. Pop. 98,962.

Bruges /broozh, bryzh/ *n.* (also called **Brug·ge** /brúgə/) city in NW Belgium. Pop. 116,800.

Bru·nei /brooní/ *n.* sultanate on the NW coast of Borneo. Pop. 300,000. Capital: Bandar Seri Begawan.

Brus·sels /brúsəlz/ *n.* capital of Belgium, in the central part; site of European parliament. Pop. 949,100.

Bry·ansk /bree-aánsk/ *n.* city in W Russia. Pop. 460,900.

Bryce /brīs/ **Can·yon Na·tion·al Park** *n.* area in S Utah noted for its extensive natural rock formations.

Bu·cha·rest /bookərest/ *n.* capital of Romania, in the S part. Pop. 2,064,500.

Bu·da·pest /boodəpest/ *n.* capital of Hungary, in the N central part. Pop. 1,996,000.

Bue·nos Ai·res /bwaynəs éreez/ *n.* port city and capital of Argentina. Pop. 2,961,000.

Buf·fa·lo /búfəlō/ *n.* port city in W New York. Pop. 328,123.

Bu·jum·bu·ra /boojəmboorə/ *n.* capital of Burundi, in the E part. Pop. 300,000.

Bul·gar·i·a /bəlgáreeə, bul–/ *n.* republic in SE Europe. Pop. 8,613,000. Capital: Sofia. ☐☐ **Bul·gar'i·an** *n. & adj.*

Bur·bank /búrbangk/ *n.* city in SW California. Pop. 93,643.

Bur·gos /boorgōs/ *n.* city in N Spain. Pop. 166,300.

Bur·ki·na Fa·so /boorkeénə faásō/ *n.* republic in W Africa. Pop. 10,623,000. Capital: Ouagadougou.

Bur·ma /búrmə/ *n.* (also called **My·an'mar**) republic in SE Asia. Pop. 45,976,000. Capital: Rangoon. ☐☐ **Bur·mese** /bərmeéz/ *n. & adj.*

Bur·sa /boorsaá/ *n.* city in NW Turkey. Pop. 996,600.

Bu·run·di /bəroondee/ *n.* republic in central Africa. Pop. 5,943,000. Capital: Bujumbura.

Bye·lo·rus·sia /byelōrúshə/ *n.* see BELARUS.

Byz·an·tine /bízanteen, ; n-tīn/ **Em·pire** *n. hist.* term for the Eastern Roman Empire from the fall of the Western Empire (476) to the fall of Constantinople (1453).

By·zan·ti·um /bizánshee-əm, –tee-əm/ *n.* see ISTANBUL.

Cá·diz /kədíz/ *n.* port city in SW Spain. Pop. 155,400.

Caen /kaaN/ *n.* city in NW France. Pop. 115,600.

Ca·guas /kaáwaas, –gwaas/ *n.* city in E central Puerto Rico. Pop. 139,800.

Cai·ro /kírō/ *n.* capital of Egypt, in the N part. Pop. 6,849,000.

Cal·cut·ta /kalkútə/ *n.* port city in E India. Pop. 4,399,800.

Cal·ga·ry /kálgəree/ *n.* city in S Alberta, Canada. Pop. 710,700.

Ca·li /kaálee/ *n.* city in SW Colombia. Pop. 1,718,900.

Cal·i·for·nia /kalifáwrnyə/ *n.* state in W U.S. Pop. 29,760,021. Capital: Sacramento. Abbr. **CA**; **Cal.**; **Calif.** ☐☐ **Cal·i·for'ni·an** *n. & adj.*

Cal·i·for·nia, Gulf of *n.* arm of the Pacific, enclosed by Baja California.

Ca·ma·güey /kaaməgwáy/ *n.* city in central Cuba. Pop. 279,000.

Cam·bo·di·a /cambṓdeeə/ *n.* (also called **Kam·pu·che'a**) republic in SE Asia. Pop. 10,861,000. Capital: Phnom Penh. ☐☐ **Cam·bo'di·an** *n. & adj.*

Cam·bridge /káymbrij/ *n.* **1** city in NE Massachusetts. Pop. 95,802. **2** city in SE England. Pop. 113,800.

Cam·den /kámdən/ *n.* city in SW New Jersey. Pop. 87,492.

Cam·e·roon /kamərōon/ *n.* republic in W Africa. Pop. 14,262,000. Capital: Yaoundé.

Camp Da·vid /dáyvid/ *n.* U.S. presidential retreat in Catoctin Mountains of Maryland, NW of Washington, D.C.

Cam·pe·che /kampáychay, –peéchee/ *n.* state in SE Mexico. Pop. 535,200. Capital: Campeche.

Cam·pi·nas /kampeénəs/ *n.* city in SE Brazil. Pop. 748,100.

Can·a·da /kánədə/ *n.* country in N North America. Pop. 28,821,900. Capital: Ottawa. ☐☐ **Ca·na·di·an** /kənáydee-ən/ *n. & adj.*

Ca·nar·y /kənáiree/ **Is·lands** *n.* island group in the Atlantic, off the NW coast of Africa.

Can·ber·ra /kánbərə, –brə/ *n.* capital of Australia, in the SE part. Pop. 303,700.

Can·ter·bur·y /kántərberee, –bree/ *n.* city in SE England; seat of the archbishop who heads the Anglican Church. Pop. 132,400.

Can·ton /kánt'n/ *n.* city in NE Ohio. Pop. 84,161.

Cape Ca·nav·er·al /kənávrəl, –návər–/ *n.* cape on the E central coast of Florida; site of Kennedy Space Center.

Cape Cod /kaad/ *n.* peninsula in SE Massachusetts, bounded by Cape Cod Bay, the Atlantic, and Nantucket Sound.
Cape Hat·ter·as /hátərəs/ *n.* cape on the North Carolina coast.
Cape Horn /hawrn/ *n.* headland of a S Chilean island; the southernmost tip of South America.
Cape of Good Hope /go͝od hōp/ *n.* cape at the SW tip of South Africa.
Cape Town *n.* port city and legislative capital of South Africa, in the SW part. Pop. 854,600.
Cape Verde /vərd/ *n.* republic in NW Africa, comprising an island group W of Senegal. Pop. 449,000. Capital: Praia.
Ca·ra·cas /kərákəs, –raák–/ *n.* capital of Venezuela, in the N part. Pop. 1,822,500.
Car·diff /kaárdif/ *n.* port city and capital of Wales, United Kingdom. Pop. 300,000.
Car·ib·be·an /karəbeéən, kəríbeeən/ **Sea** *n.* arm of the Atlantic, enclosed by the West Indies, N South America, and Central America.
Carls·bad /kaárlzbad/ **Cav·erns** *n.* network of subterranean limestone caves in SE New Mexico.
Car·o·li·na /karəlínə/ *n.* **1** (also called **the Car·o·li·nas**) North and South Carolina. **2** /kaarəleénə/ city in NE Puerto Rico. Pop. 187,100.
Car·o·line /kárəlīn, kér–, –lin/ **Is·lands** *n.* island group in the Pacific, E of the Philippines; U.S. trusteeship.
Car·pa·thi·an /kaarpáytheeən/ **Moun·tains** *n.* mountain range in central Europe.
Car·son /kaársən/ **Cit·y** *n.* capital of Nevada, in the W part. Pop. 40,443.
Car·ta·ge·na /kaartəjeénə, –háynə/ *n.* port city in N Colombia. Pop. 745,700.
Car·thage /kaárthij/ *n. hist.* ancient city-state near present-day Tunis, in N Africa. □□ **Car·tha·gin'i·an** *n. & adj.*□□
Cas·a·blan·ca /kasəblángkə, kaz–/ *n.* port city in NW Morocco. Pop. 2,943,000.
Cas·cade /kaskáyd/ **Range** *n.* mountain range in W U.S., extending from N California into Canada.
Cas·pi·an /káspeeən/ **Sea** *n.* inland salt lake between Europe and Asia, N of Iran.
Cas·tries /kastreé, kaástrees/ *n.* port city and capital of St. Lucia. Pop. 11,100.
Cat·a·li·na /kat'l-eénə/ **Is·land** *n.* see SANTA CATALINA ISLAND.
Ca·ta·nia /kətaányə, –táyn–/ *n.* port city in E Sicily, Italy. Pop. 327,200.
Cats·kill /kátskil/ **Moun·tains** *n.* mountain range in SE New York; part of the Appalachian range.
Cau·ca·sus /káwkəsəs/ **Moun·tains** *n.* mountain range dividing Russia from Georgia and Azerbaijan; traditional division between Europe and Asia.
Cay·enne /kī-én, kay–/ *n.* port city and capital of French Guiana. Pop. 41,700.
Cay·man /káymən/ **Is·lands** *n.* island group in the NW Caribbean; dependent territory of the United Kingdom. Pop. 35,000.
Ce·dar /seédər/ **Rap·ids** *n.* city in E Iowa. Pop. 108,751.
Cel·e·bes /séləbeez/ *n.* see SULAWESI.
Cen·tral Af·ri·can Re·pub·lic *n.* republic in central Africa. Pop. 3,274,000. Capital: Bangui.
Cen·tral A·mer·i·ca *n.* portion of continental North America between Mexico and South America.
Cen·tral Val·ley *n.* valley in W central California, between the San Joaquin and Sacramento rivers.
Cey·lon /silón, say–/ *n.* see SRI LANKA.
Chad /chad/ *n.* republic in N central Africa. Pop. 6,977,000. Capital: N'Djamena. **Chad'i·an** *n. & adj.*
Cham·paign /shampáyn/ *n.* city in E central Illinois. Pop. 63,502.
Cham·plain /shampláyn/, **Lake** *n.* lake in NE U.S., between New York and Vermont.
Chang /chang/ **Riv·er** *n.* (formerly **Yangtze River**) river in central China, flowing 3,400 mi. from Tibet to the East China Sea; longest river in China.
Chan·nel /chánəl/ **Is·lands** *n.* group of British islands in the English Channel, near the coast of France; includes Guernsey and Jersey.
Charles·ton /chaárlstən/ *n.* **1** capital of West Virginia, in the W central part. Pop. 57,287. **2** port city in SE South Carolina. Pop. 80,414.
Char·lotte /shaárlət/ *n.* city in S North Carolina. Pop. 395,934.
Char·lotte·town /shaárlət-town/ *n.* capital of Prince Edward Island, Canada, in the central part. Pop. 15,400.
Chat·ta·hoo·chee /chatəho͞ochee/ **Riv·er** *n.* river in SE U.S., flowing 440 mi. from NE Georgia to the Gulf of Mexico.
Chat·ta·noo·ga /chatəno͞ogə/ *n.* city in S Tennessee. Pop. 152,466.
Chel·ya·binsk /chelyaábinsk/ *n.* city in S Russia. Pop. 1,086,000.
Chem·nitz /k͟hémnits/ *n.* (formerly **Karl-Marx-Stadt**) city in E central Germany. Pop. 274,200.
Ches·a·peake /chésəpeek/ *n.* city in SE Virginia. Pop. 151,976.
Ches·a·peake Bay *n.* inlet of the Atlantic, on the E coast of the U.S.
Che·tu·mal /chaytoōmaál/ *n.* capital of Quintana Roo, Mexico, in the S part. Pop. 111,400.
Chey·enne /shīán, –én/ *n.* capital of Wyoming, in the SE part. Pop. 50,008.
Chi·a·pas /chee-aápəs, chaápəs/ *n.* state in S Mexico. Pop. 3,210,500. Capital: Tuxtla.
Chi·ba /cheébə/ *n.* city in Japan, on Honshu. Pop. 856,900.
Chi·ca·go /shikaágō, –káwgō/ *n.* city in NE Illinois. Pop. 2,783,726. □□ **Chi·ca'go·an** *n.*
Chi·hua·hua /chəwaáwaa, –wə/ *n.* state in N central Mexico. Pop. 2,441,900. Capital: Chihuahua.
Chil·e /chílee, cheélay/ *n.* republic in W South America. Pop. 14,333,000. Capital: Santiago. □□ **Chil'e·an** *n. & adj.*
Chil·pan·cin·go /chilpənsínggō/ *n.* capital of Guerrero, Mexico, in the E central part. Pop. 136,200.
Chi·lung /jeélo͝ong/ *n.* (formerly **Keelung**) port city in N Taiwan. Pop. 352,900.
Chi·na /chínə/ *n.* (official name **People's Republic of China**; abbr. **PRC**) republic in E and central Asia. Pop. 1,210,005,000. Capital: Beijing.
Chi·nan /jěnán/ *n.* see JINAN.
Chis·holm /chízəm/ **Trail** *n. hist.* cattle trail from San Antonio, Texas, to Abilene, Kansas, used after the Civil War.
Chi·şi·nă·u /keesheenúo͞o/ *n.* see KISHINEV.
Chit·ta·gong /chítəgaang, –gawng/ *n.* port city in SE Bangladesh. Pop. 1,599,000.
Chong·qing /chúngchíng, –kíng/ *n.* (formerly **Chungking**) city in S central China. Pop. 2,980,000.
Chon·ju /júnjo͞o/ *n.* city in SW South Korea. Pop. 563,400.
Christ·church /krīschərch, kríst–/ *n.* city in E central New Zealand. Pop. 314,000.
Chuk·chi /chúkchee, cho͝ok–/ **Sea** *n.* arm of the Arctic Ocean, N of the Bering Strait.
Chu·la Vis·ta /cho͞olə vístə/ *n.* city in SW California. Pop. 135,163.
Chung·king /chúngkíng, chŏ́n–/ *n.* see CHONGQING.
Cin·cin·nat·i /sinsinátee/ *n.* port city in SW Ohio. Pop. 364,040.
Cit·rus /sítrəs/ **Heights** *n.* city in central California. Pop. 107,439.
Ciu·dad Gua·ya·na /seeo͞odaád gwaayaánaa, seeyo͞o–/ *n.* see SANTO TOMÉ DE GUAYANA.
Ciu·dad Juá·rez /waáres, hwaáres/ *n.* city in N Mexico. Pop. 544,500.
Ciu·dad Vic·to·ria /veektáwree-ə/ *n.* capital of Tamaulipas, Mexico, in the W central part. Pop. 195,000.
Clear·wa·ter /kleérwawtər, –waatər/ *n.* city in W Florida. Pop. 98,784.
Cleve·land /kleévlənd/ *n.* city in N Ohio. Pop. 505,616.
Co·a·hui·la /kōəweélə, kwaaweélə/ *n.* state in N Mexico. Pop. 1,972,300. Capital: Saltillo.
Co·blenz /kṓblens/ *n.* (also **Ko'blenz**) city in W Germany. Pop. 109,600.
Co·li·ma /kəleémə/ *n.* state in W Mexico. Pop. 428,500. Capital: Colima.
Co·logne /kəlṓn/ *n.* (German name **Köln**) city in W Germany. Pop. 963,800.
Co·lom·bi·a /kəlúmbeeə/ *n.* republic in NW South America. Pop. 36,813,000. Capital: Bogotá. □□ **Co·lom'bi·an** *n. & adj.*
Co·lom·bo /kəlúmbō/ *n.* port city and capital of Sri Lanka. Pop. 615,000.
Col·o·ra·do /kaalərádō, –raádō/ *n.* state in W U.S. Pop. 3,294,394. Capital: Denver. Abbr. **Colo.**; **CO** □□ **Col·o·ra'dan, Col·o·ra'do·an** *n. & adj.*
Col·o·rad·o Riv·er *n.* river in W U.S., flowing 1,450 mi. from Colorado through the Grand Canyon and into the Gulf of California.
Col·o·rad·o Springs *n.* city in E central Colorado. Pop. 281,140.
Co·lum·bi·a /kəlúmbeeə/ *n.* **1** capital of South Carolina, in the central part. Pop. 98,052. **2** city in central Missouri. Pop. 69,101.
Co·lum·bi·a Riv·er *n.* river in W North America, flowing 1,200 mi. from W Canada through Washington and Oregon and into the Pacific.
Co·lum·bus /kəlúmbəs/ *n.* capital of Ohio, in the central part. Pop. 632,910.
Com·o·ros /kaámərōz, kəmáwrōz/ *n.* island republic in the Indian Ocean, between Africa and Madagascar. Pop. 569,000. Capital: Moroni. □□ **Com'o·ran, Co·mo'ri·an** *n. & adj.*
Co·na·kry /kaánəkree/ *n.* port city and capital of Guinea. Pop. 1,508,000.
Con·cep·ción /kənsepsee-ṓn/ *n.* city in S central Chile. Pop. 350,300.
Con·cord /kaángkərd, –kawrd/ *n.* **1** capital of New Hampshire, in the S part. Pop. 36,006. **2** city in W California. Pop. 111,348.
Con·go /kaánggō/ *n.* **1** (formerly **Zaire**) republic in central Africa. Pop. 41,151,000. Capital: Kinshasa. **2** (official name **Re·pub'lic of the Con'go**) republic in central Africa. Pop. 2,528,000. Capital: Brazzaville. □□ **Con·go·lese** /kaanggəleéz, –leés/ *n. & adj.*
Con·go Riv·er *n.* river in central Africa, flowing 3,000 mi. from SE Congo (formerly Zaire) to the Atlantic.
Con·nect·i·cut /kənétikət/ *n.* state in NE U.S. Pop. 3,287,116. Capital: Hartford. Abbr. **Conn.**; **CT**; **Ct.** □□ **Con·nect'i·cut·ter** *n.*
Con·nect·i·cut Riv·er *n.* river in New England, flowing 400 mi. from N New Hampshire to Long Island Sound.
Con·stan·tine /kaánstənteen, KAWNSTAANTEÉN/ *n.* city in NE Algeria. Pop. 440,900.

Con·stan·ti·no·ple /kaanstantənṓpəl/ *n.* see ISTANBUL.

Con·ti·nen·tal Di·vide *n.* (also called **Great Di·vide**) High ridge of the Rocky Mountains; watershed of the North American continent, separating the river systems flowing either W or E and S.

Cook /kŏŏk/ **Is·lands** *n.* island group in the S Pacific, belonging to New Zealand. Pop. 20,000.

Co·pen·ha·gen /kṓpənhaygən, –haagən/ *n.* port city and capital of Denmark. Pop. 1,353,300.

Cor·al /káwrəl/ **Sea** *n.* arm of the S Pacific, NE of Australia.

Cór·do·ba /káwrdəbə, –əvə/ *n.* **1** (also **Cor'do·va**) city in S Spain. Pop. 315,900. **2** city in central Argentina. Pop. 1,208,700.

Cor·fu /kawrfṓō/ *n.* island in Greece, SW of Albania.

Cork /kawrk/ *n.* port city in S Ireland. Pop. 127,000.

Cor·pus Chris·ti /káwrpəs kristee/ *n.* port city in S Texas. Pop. 257,453.

Cor·si·ca /káwrsikə/ *n.* island in the Mediterranean Sea, W of Italy; a department of France. Capital: Ajaccio ▫▫ **Cor'si·can** *n. & adj.*

Cos·ta Bra·va /kṓstə braávə/ *n.* region on the NE coast of Spain.

Cos·ta del Sol /del sṓl/ *n.* region on the S coast of Spain.

Cos·ta Me·sa /kṓstə máysə, káwstə/ *n.* city in SW California. Pop. 96,357.

Cos·ta Ri·ca /kṓstə reékə, káws–/ *n.* republic in S Central America. Pop. 3,463,000. Capital: San José. ▫▫ **Cos'ta Ric'an** *n. & adj.*

Côte d'A·zur /kōt dəzṓŏr/ *n.* region on the SE coast of France.

Côte d'I·voire /kōt deevwaár/ *n.* see IVORY COAST.

Co·to·nou /kōt'n-ṓō/ *n.* port city and government center of Benin. Pop. 533,200.

Cov·en·try /kaávəntree, kúv–/ *n.* city in central England. Pop. 302,500.

Crac·ow /krákow, kraákōof/ *n.* (also **Kra'ków**) city in S central Poland. Pop. 746,000.

Cra·ter /kráytər/ **Lake** *n.* lake in S Oregon formed by an ancient volcanic crater.

Crete /kreet/ *n.* (also called **Can'di·a**) Greek island in the Mediterranean Sea, SE of the mainland.

Cri·me·a /krīmeéə/ *n.* peninsula in S Ukraine, bounded by the Black Sea and the Sea of Azov. ▫▫ **Cri·me'an** *adj.*

Cro·a·tia /krōáyshə/ *n.* republic in S Europe, on the Balkan Peninsula; formerly part of Yugoslavia. Pop. 5,004,000. Capital: Zagreb.

Cu·ba /kyṓōbə, kṓōbə/ *n.* island republic in the W West Indies. Pop. 10,951,000. Capital: Havana. ▫▫ **Cu'ban** *n. & adj.*

Cuer·na·va·ca /kwernəvaákə/ *n.* capital of Morelos, Mexico, in the N part. Pop. 279,200.

Cu·lia·cán /kōōlyəkaán/ *n.* capital of Sinaloa, Mexico, in the central part. Pop. 415,000.

Cum·ber·land /kúmbərlənd/ **Gap** *n.* natural pass through the Appalachian Mountains in Kentucky and Virginia.

Cum·ber·land Road *n.* see NATIONAL ROAD.

Cu·ra·çao /kŏŏrəsów, –sṓw, kyŏŏrə–/ *n.* largest island of the Netherlands Antilles, NW of Venezuela. Capital: Willemstad.

Cy·prus /síprəs/ *n.* island republic in the E Mediterranean Sea. Pop. 745,000. Capital: Nicosia.

Czech·o·slo·va·ki·a /chekəsləvaákeeə/ *n.* former republic of central Europe (1918–93); divided into Czech Republic and Slovakia.

Czech /chek/ **Re·pub·lic** *n.* republic in central Europe; formerly the W part of Czechoslovakia. Pop. 10,321,000. Capital: Prague.

Cze·sto·cho·wa /chenstəkṓvə/ *n.* city in S Poland. Pop. 259,800.

Da·kar /dəkaár, dákaar/ *n.* port city and capital of Senegal. Pop. 785,100.

Da·lian /daályén/ *n.* (formerly **Talien; Lüda**) port city in NE China. Pop. 2,400,300.

Dal·las /dáləs/ *n.* city in NE Texas. Pop. 1,006,877. ▫▫ **Dal'las·ite** *n.*

Da·mas·cus /dəmáskəs/ *n.* capital of Syria, in the SW part. Pop. 1,550,000.

Da·nang /daanaáng, dənáng/ *n.* port city in central Vietnam. Pop. 382,700.

Dan·ube /dányōōb/ **Riv·er** *n.* river in central Europe, flowing 1,720 mi. from SW Germany to the Black Sea.

Dar·da·nelles /daard'nélz/ *n.* strait in Turkey, connecting the Aegean Sea with the Sea of Marmara.

Dar es Sa·laam /daar es səlaám/ *n.* port city and capital of Tanzania. Pop. 1,360,900.

Dav·en·port /dávənpawrt/ *n.* city in E Iowa. Pop. 95,333.

Day·ton /dáyt'n/ *n.* city in SW Ohio. Pop. 182,044.

D.C. *abbr.* (also **DC**) District of Columbia. See also WASHINGTON, D.C.

Dead /ded/ **Sea** *n.* inland salt lake, between Israel and Jordan.

Dear·born /deérbawrn, –bərn/ *n.* city in SE Michigan. Pop. 89,286.

Death /deth/ **Val·ley** *n.* desert basin in E California; lowest point is 282 ft. below sea level.

De·ca·tur /dikáytər/ *n.* city in central Illinois. Pop. 83,885.

Del·a·ware /déləwair, –wer/ *n.* state in E U.S. Pop. 666,168. Capital: Dover. Abbr. **DE; Del.** ▫▫ **Del·a·war'e·an** *n. & adj.*

Del·a·ware Bay *n.* inlet of the Atlantic, between Delaware and New Jersey.

Del·a·ware Riv·er *n.* river in E U.S., flowing 280 mi. from S New York to Delaware Bay.

Del·hi /délee/ *n.* city in N India. Pop. 7,206,700.

Del·mar·va /delmaárvə/ **Pen·in·su·la** *n.* peninsula in E U.S., bounded by the Atlantic and Chesapeake Bay, and comprising parts of Delaware, Maryland, and Virginia.

De·na·li /denaálee/ **Na·tion·al Park** U.S. national park in S central Alaska; contains North America's highest peak, Mount McKinley.

Den·mark /dénmaark/ *n.* kingdom in N Europe. Pop. 5,250,000. Capital: Copenhagen.

Den·ver /dénvər/ *n.* capital of Colorado, in the central part. Pop. 467,610.

Der·by /daárbee/ *n.* city in central England. Pop. 230,500.

Des Moines /di móin/ *n.* capital of Iowa, in the central part. Pop. 193,187.

De·troit /ditróyt, deétroyt/ *n.* city in SE Michigan. Pop. 1,027,974.

Dha·ka /daákə/ *n.* capital of Bangladesh, in the central part. Pop. 3,839,000.

Di·a·mond /dímənd, díə–/ **Head** *n.* extinct volcano on SE coast of Oahu, Hawaii.

Di·jon /dee-zháwn, –zhaán/ *n.* city in E France. Pop. 151,600.

Dis·trict of Co·lum·bi·a /kəlúmbeeə/ *n.* federal district in E U.S., on the Potomac River; coextensive with the national capital, Washington. Abbr. **DC; D.C.**

Dji·bou·ti /jibṓōtee/ *n.* **1** republic in E Africa. Pop. 428,000. Capital: Djibouti. **2** capital of Djibouti, in the E part. Pop. 290,000.

Dni·pro·pe·trovsk /neprōpətráwfsk, dənyeprō–/ *n.* city in E central Ukraine. Pop. 1,147,000.

Do·ha /dṓhə/ *n.* port city and capital of Qatar. Pop. 313,600.

Dom·i·ni·ca /daamineékə, dəmínikə/ *n.* island republic in the E West Indies. Pop. 83,000. Capital: Roseau.

Dom·i·ni·can /dəmínikən/ **Re·pub·lic** *n.* republic in the central West Indies, comprising the E part of Hispaniola. Pop. 8,089,000. Capital: Santo Domingo.

Do·netsk /dənétsk, –nyétsk/ *n.* city in E Ukraine. Pop. 1,088,000.

Don /daan/ **Riv·er** *n.* river in SW Russia, flowing 1,200 mi. from Tula to the Sea of Azov.

Dort·mund /dáwrtmōōnt, –mənd/ *n.* city in W Germany. Pop. 600,900.

Do·ver /dṓvər/ *n.* **1** capital of Delaware, in the central part. Pop. 27,630. **2** port city in SE England. Pop. 32,800.

Dres·den /drézdən/ *n.* city in SE Germany. Pop. 474,400.

Du·bai /dōōbí/ *n.* port city in N United Arab Emirates. Pop. 585,200.

Dub·lin /dúblin/ *n.* capital of the Republic of Ireland, in the E part. Pop. 478,400. ▫▫ **Dub'lin·er** *n. & adj.*

Du·buque /dəbyṓōk/ *n.* city in E Iowa. Pop. 57,546.

Duis·burg /dṓōsbŏŏrk, dyṓōs–, –bərg/ *n.* port city in W Germany. Pop. 536,100.

Du·luth /dəlṓōth/ *n.* city in NE Minnesota. Pop. 85,493.

Dun·dee /dəndeé/ *n.* port city in E Scotland, United Kingdom. Pop. 167,600.

Du·ran·go /dŏŏrránggō, dyŏŏráng–/ *n.* state in N central Mexico. Pop. 1,349,400. Capital: Durango.

Dur·ban /dúrbən/ *n.* port city in SE South Africa. Pop. 715,700.

Dur·ham /dúrəm, dŏŏr–/ *n.* city in NE central North Carolina. Pop. 136,600.

Du·shan·be /dōōshaánbay, dyōō–, –sham–/ *n.* capital of Tadzhikistan, in the W part. Pop. 524,000.

Düs·sel·dorf /dṓōsəldawrf, dyṓōs–/ *n.* port city in W Germany. Pop. 572,600.

Dust Bowl agricultural region of about 50 million acres in central U.S.; site of great dust storms 1935–38.

East Chi·na Sea *n.* arm of the N Pacific, E of mainland China and N of Taiwan.

East Ger·ma·ny *n.* (also called **German Democratic Republic**) German state created in 1949, under Communist government; unified with West Germany in 1990.

East Los An·ge·les /laws ánjələs, –leez/ *n.* city in SW California. Pop. 126,379.

Ec·ua·dor /ékwədawr/ *n.* republic in NW South America. Pop. 11,466,000. Capital: Quito. ▫▫ **Ec·ua·dor'an, Ec·ua·do'ri·an** /–reeən/ *n. & adj.*

Ed·in·burgh /éd'nbərə, –brə/ *n.* capital of Scotland, in the United Kingdom. Pop. 447,600.

Ed·mon·ton /édməntən/ *n.* capital of Alberta, Canada, in the central part. Pop. 616,700.

E·gypt /eéjipt/ *n.* republic in NE Africa. Pop. 63,575,000. Capital: Cairo.

Eir·e /érə, írə/ *n.* see IRELAND 2.

El·ba /élbə/ *n.* Italian island in the Mediterranean Sea, E of Corsica.

El·brus /elbrṓōz/, **Mount** *n.* mountain in the Caucasus range, on the border between Russia and Georgia; highest peak in Europe: 18,481 ft.

El Gi·za *n.* see GIZA.

E·liz·a·beth /ilízəbəth/ *n.* city in NE New Jersey. Pop. 110,002.

El·lis /éləs/ **Is·land** *n.* island in New York Harbor; former arrival point for European immigrants.

El Mon·te /el maántee/ *n.* city in SW California. Pop. 106,209.

El Ni·ño /neényō/ *n.* periodic occasional warm Pacific current that alters climate patterns.
El Pas·o /pásō/ *n.* city in W Texas. Pop. 515,342.
El Sal·va·dor /sálvədawr/ *n.* republic in NW Central America. Pop. 5,829,000. Capital: San Salvador. ▫▫ **Sal·va·do'ran, Sal·va·do'ri·an** /-reeən/ *n. & adj.*
Eng·land /ínggIənd/ *n.* largest division of the United Kingdom. Pop. 44,876,000. Capital: London. ¶ See note at GREAT BRITAIN.
Eng·lish /ínglish/ **Chan·nel** *n.* strait between S England and N France, connecting the Atlantic and the North Sea.
En·sche·de /énskədə/ *n.* city in the E Netherlands. Pop. 147,900.
E·qua·to·ri·al Guin·ea /ekwətóree-əl ginee/ *n.* mainland and island republic in W Africa. Pop. 431,000. Capital: Malabo.
Er·furt /érfoort/ *n.* city in central Germany. Pop. 213,500.
E·rie /eeree/ *n.* city in NW Pennsylvania. Pop. 108,718.
E·rie, Lake *n.* one of the Great Lakes, N of Ohio.
E·rie Ca·nal *n.* canal in New York between Albany and Buffalo, connecting the Hudson River with Lake Erie.
Er·i·tre·a /eritreeə, –tráyə/ *n.* republic in E Africa; formerly a province of Ethiopia. Pop. 3,428,000. Capital: Asmara.
Es·con·di·do /eskəndeedō/ *n.* city in SW California. Pop. 108,635.
Es·fa·han /ésfəhaan/ *n.* see ISFAHAN.
Es·sen /ésən/ *n.* city in W Germany. Pop. 618,000.
Es·to·ni·a /estóneeə/ *n.* republic in N Europe; formerly part of the USSR. Pop. 1,459,000. Capital: Tallinn.
E·thi·o·pi·a /eethee-ópeeə/ *n.* republic in E Africa. Pop. 57,172,000. Capital: Addis Ababa. ▫▫ **E·thi·o'pi·an** *n. & adj.*
Et·na /étnə/, **Mount** *n.* active volcano in Sicily: 11,122 ft. high.
Eu·gene /yoojeen/ *n.* city in W Oregon. Pop. 112,669.
Eu·phra·tes /yoofráyteez/ **Riv·er** *n.* river in SW Asia, flowing 1,700 mi. from central Turkey to the Persian Gulf.
Eu·rope /yóorəp/ *n.* continent bounded by the Arctic and Atlantic oceans, Asia, the Caucasus Mountains, and the Black, Mediterranean, Baltic, and North seas.
Eu·ro·pe·an /yoorəpeeən/ **Un·ion** *n.* (formerly **Eu·ro·pe'an Com·mu'ni·ty**) official name of a confederation of independent European countries.
Ev·ans·ton /évənstən/ *n.* city in NE Illinois. Pop. 73,233.
Ev·ans·ville /évənzvil/ *n.* city in SW Indiana. Pop. 126,272.
Ev·er·est /évrəst, évərəst/, **Mount** *n.* mountain in the Himalayas, on the Tibet-Nepal border; highest in the world: 29,028 ft.
Ev·er·glades /évərglaydz/ *n.* large area of swampland in S Florida.
Faer·oe /fárō, férō/ **Is·lands** *n.* cluster of Danish islands in the N Atlantic, between Iceland and Great Britain.
Fair·banks /fáirbangks, fér–/ *n.* city in central Alaska. Pop. 30,843.
Fai·sa·la·bad /fisaaləbaad/ *n.* (formerly **Lyallpur**) city in E Pakistan. Pop. 1,104,200.
Falk·land /fáwklənd, fáwlk–/ **Is·lands** *n.* (Spanish name **Is·las Mal·vin·as** /eesləs maalveenəs/) island group in the Atlantic, E of Argentina; British possession.
Far East *n.* term for E Asia, including China, Japan, Korea, Mongolia, and adjacent areas.
Far·go /faargō/ *n.* city in E North Dakota. Pop. 74,111.
Fay·ette·ville /fáyətvəl, –vil/ *n.* city in S central North Carolina. Pop. 75,695.
Fed·er·al Dis·trict of Mex·i·co *n.* national government district in Mexico, in the central part.
Fer·ra·ra /fəraarə/ *n.* city in NE Italy. Pop. 137,400.
Fez /fez, fes/ *n.* (also **Fès**) city in N central Morocco. Pop. 564,800.
Fi·ji /feejee/ *n.* independent archipelago in the S Pacific, N of New Zealand. Pop. 782,000. Capital: Suva. ▫▫ **Fi'ji·an** *n. & adj.*
Fin·ger /finggər/ **Lakes** *n.* chain of long, thin lakes in central New York.
Fin·land /finlənd/ *n.* republic in N Europe. Pop. 5,105,000. Capital: Helsinki.
Flan·ders /flándərz/ Atlantic coastal region of Europe in Belgium, France, and the Netherlands.
Flint /flint/ *n.* city in SE central Michigan. Pop. 140,761.
Flor·ence /fláwrəns, flaar–/ *n.* (Italian name **Fi·ren·ze** /feeréntsay, fərénzə/) city in central Italy. Pop. 392,900. ▫▫ **Flor·en·tine** /fláwrənteen, -tīn/ *n. & adj.*
Flor·i·da /fláwrədə, flaar–/ *n.* peninsular state in SE U.S. Pop. 12,937,926. Capital: Tallahassee. Abbr. **FL**; **Fla.** ▫▫ **Flo·rid·i·an** /fləriđeeən/ *n. & adj.*
Flor·i·da Keys *n.* island chain in Florida, extending from the S tip of Florida into the Gulf of Mexico.
Flor·i·da, Straits of *n.* channel separating Florida from Cuba.
For·mo·sa /fawrmósə/ *n.* see TAIWAN.
Fort Col·lins /kaalinz/ *n.* city in N Colorado. Pop. 87,758.
Fort Lau·der·dale /láwdərdayl/ *n.* city in SE Florida. Pop. 149,377.
Fort Wayne /wayn/ *n.* city in NE Indiana. Pop. 173,072.
Fort Worth /wúrth/ *n.* city in N Texas. Pop. 447,619.
France /frans/ *n.* republic in W Europe. Pop. 58,041,000. Capital: Paris.
Frank·fort /frángkfərt/ *n.* capital of Kentucky, in the N central part. Pop. 25,968.
Frank·furt /frángkfərt/ *n.* **1** (also called **Frank'furt am Main** /aam mín/) city in W Germany. Pop. 652,400. **2** (also called **Frank'furt an der O·der** /aan dər ódər/) city in E Germany. Pop. 70,000.
Fred·er·ic·ton /frédriktən/ *n.* capital of New Brunswick, Canada, in the S part. Pop. 46,500.
Free·town /freetown/ *n.* port city and capital of Sierra Leone. Pop. 469,800.
Fre·mont /freemaant/ *n.* city in W California. Pop. 173,339.
French Gui·an·a /geeaanə/ *n.* overseas department of France, on the NE coast of South America. Pop. 151,180. Capital: Cayenne.
French Pol·y·ne·sia /paaləneezhə, –shə/ *n.* island group in the S Pacific; territory of France. Pop. 225,000. Capital: Papeete.
Fres·no /fréznō/ *n.* city in central California. Pop. 354,202.
Fu·ji /foojee/, **Mount** *n.* dormant volcano in central Japan: 12,388 ft. high.
Fu·ku·o·ka /fookoo-ókə/ *n.* city in Japan, on Kyushu. Pop. 1,284,700.
Ful·ler·ton /foolərtən/ *n.* city in SW California. Pop. 114,144.
Fu·na·fu·ti /foonəfootee, fyoonəfyootee/ *n.* capital of Tuvalu, in the central part. Pop. 3,800.
Fun·dy /fúndee/, **Bay of** *n.* inlet of the Atlantic, between New Brunswick and Nova Scotia.
Fu·shun /fooshoon/ *n.* city in NE China. Pop. 1,350,000.
Ga·bon /gabáwn/ *n.* republic in W Africa. Pop. 1,253,000. Capital: Libreville. ▫▫ **Gab·o·nese** /gabəneez, –nees/ *n. & adj.*
Ga·bo·ro·ne /gaabərónee/ *n.* capital of Botswana, in the SE part. Pop. 156,800.
Gaines·ville /gáynzvəl, –vil/ *n.* city in N Florida. Pop. 84,770.
Ga·lá·pa·gos /gəlaapəgəs/ **Is·lands** *n.* archipelago in the Pacific, W of Ecuador; province of Ecuador.
Gal·i·lee /gálilee/, **Sea of** *n.* lake in NE Israel.
Gal·ves·ton /gálvəstən/ **Bay** *n.* inlet of the Gulf of Mexico, SE of Houston, Texas.
Gam·bi·a /gámbeeə, gaam-/ *n.* (also **the Gambia**) republic in W Africa. Pop. 1,205,000. Capital: Banjul.
Gan·ges /gánjeez/ **Riv·er** *n.* river in India, flowing 1,560 mi. from the Himalayas to the Bay of Bengal at Calcutta.
Gar·den Grove /gaardən grōv/ *n.* city in SW California. Pop. 143,050.
Gar·land *n.* city in SW Texas. Pop. 180,650.
Gar·y /géree/ *n.* city in NW Indiana. Pop. 116,646.
Ga·tun /gətóon/ **Lake** *n.* artificial lake forming part of the Panama Canal.
Gaul /gawl/ *n. hist.* province of the ancient Roman Empire, in W Europe.
Ga·za Strip /gaazə/ area of land along the Mediterranean Sea, between Egypt and Israel.
Gdansk /gədaansk, –dánsk/ *n.* port city in N Poland. Pop. 463,100.
Gdy·nia /gədíneeə/ *n.* port city in N Poland. Pop. 251,500.
Ge·ne·va /jəneevə/ *n.* city in SW Switzerland. Pop. 172,700.
Ge·ne·va, Lake *n.* (also called **Lake Le'man**) lake between Switzerland and France.
Gen·o·a /jénəwə/ *n.* port city in N Italy. Pop. 659,800.
George·town /jáwrjtown/ *n.* port city and capital of Guyana. Pop. 248,500.
Geor·gia /jáwrjə/ *n.* **1** state in SE U.S. Pop. 6,478,216. Capital: Atlanta. Abbr. **GA**; **Ga. 2** republic in E Europe; formerly part of the USSR. Pop. 5,220,000. Capital: Tbilisi. ▫▫ **Geor'gian** *n. & adj.*
Ger·ma·ny /júrmənee/ *n.* republic in W Europe. Pop. 83,536,000. Capital: Berlin.
Get·tys·burg /géteezbərg/ *n.* borough in S central Pennsylvania; site of a Civil War battle. Pop. 7,025.
Gha·na /gaanə/ *n.* republic in W Africa. Pop. 17,698,000. Capital: Accra. ▫▫ **Gha'na·ian, Ghan'i·an** *n. & adj.*
Ghent /gent/ *n.* port city in NW central Belgium. Pop. 227,500.
Gi·bral·tar /jibráwltər/ *n.* British crown colony near the S tip of Spain. Pop. 29,000.
Gi·bral·tar, Strait of strait between Europe and Africa, at the Atlantic entrance to the Mediterranean Sea.
Gi·jón /heehón/ *n.* port city in N Spain, on the Bay of Biscay. Pop. 269,600.
Gi·za /geezə/ *n.* (also called **El Gi'za**) city in N Egypt. Pop. 2,144,000.
Glas·gow /gláskō, glázgō/ *n.* port city in SW Scotland, United Kingdom. Pop. 674,800. ▫▫ **Glas·we·gian** /glasweejən, -jeeən/ *n. & adj.*
Glen·dale /gléndayl/ *n.* **1** city in SW California. Pop. 180,038. **2** city in SW central Arizona. Pop. 148,134.
Glouces·ter /glaastər, gláws–/ *n.* port city in SW central England. Pop. 104,800.
Go·bi /góbee/ *n.* desert in E Asia, mostly in Mongolia.
Gö·te·borg /yótəbawr, –bawryə/ *n.* (also **Go·then·burg** /gaathənberg/) port city in SW Sweden. Pop. 449,200.
Got·land /gaatlənd/ *n.* island province in SE Sweden, in the Baltic Sea.
Gra·na·da /grənaadə/ *n.* city in S Spain. Pop. 271,200.
Grand Banks *n.* extensive shoal and fishing grounds SE of Newfoundland.
Grand Can·yon *n.* extensive gorge of the Colorado River, in NW Arizona.
Grand Cou·lee /koolee/ **Dam** *n.* dam on the Columbia River, in NE central Washington; largest concrete dam in U.S.
Grand Rap·ids *n.* city in W Michigan. Pop. 189,126.
Grand Te·ton /teeton/ highest peak in the Teton range: 13,770 ft.
Graz /graats/ *n.* city in SE Austria. Pop. 237,800.

Great Ba·sin *n.* extensive desert region in W U.S.
Great Brit·ain /brít'n/ *n.* **1** island of NW Europe, comprising England, Scotland, and Wales. **2** popular term for the United Kingdom. ¶ *Great Britain* is the overall name given to the island that comprises *England, Scotland, Wales*; the *United Kingdom* includes the preceding and *Northern Ireland*; the *British Isles* include the *United Kingdom* together with the *Channel Islands* and all the other surrounding islands—the *Isles of Scilly*, the *Isle of Man*, and the *Orkney* and *Shetland* islands. The all-encompassing adjective is *British*, which is unlikely to offend anyone. *Welsh, Scottish,* and *English* should be used with care; it is safest to use *British* if unsure.
Great Di·vide *n.* see CONTINENTAL DIVIDE.
Great·er An·til·les /antíleez/ *n.* term for the larger islands of the West Indies: Cuba, Hispaniola, Jamaica, and Puerto Rico. See also LESSER ANTILLES.
Great·er Sun·da /súndə, sŏŏndə/ **Is·lands** *n.* island chain in the Malay Archipelago; includes Borneo, Java, and Sumatra.
Great Lakes *n.* series of five freshwater lakes between the U.S. and Canada: Superior, Michigan, Huron, Erie, and Ontario.
Great Plains *n.* dry, grassy region E of the Rocky Mountains, in Canada and the U.S.
Great Salt Lake *n.* inland salt sea in NW Utah.
Great Salt Lake Des·ert *n.* arid region in NW Utah.
Great Slave Lake *n.* lake in S central Northwest Territories, Canada.
Great Smo·ky /smókee/ **Moun·tains** *n.* mountain range in E U.S., between Tennessee and North Carolina; part of the Appalachian range.
Greece /grees/ *n.* republic in S Europe, on the Balkan Peninsula. Pop. 10,539,000. Capital: Athens.
Green /green/ **Bay** *n.* city in E Wisconsin. Pop. 96,466.
Green·land /greenlənd, –land/ *n.* island territory of Denmark, NE of Canada; largest island in the world. Pop. 58,000. □□ **Green'land·er** *n.* **Green·land'ic** *adj.*
Green·land Sea *n.* arm of the Arctic Ocean, NE of Greenland.
Green /green/ **Moun·tains** *n.* mountain range in E North America, extending from S Quebec through Vermont into W Massachusetts; part of the Appalachian range.
Greens·bo·ro /greenzbərə/ *n.* city in N central North Carolina. Pop. 183,521.
Gre·na·da /grənáydə/ *n.* island country in the E West Indies. Pop. 95,000. Capital: St. George's.
Gre·no·ble /grənṓbəl/ *n.* city in SE France. Pop. 154,000.
Gro·ning·en /grṓningən/ *n.* city in the N Netherlands. Pop. 170,700.
Groz·ny /gráwznee, graáz–/ *n.* city in S Russia. Pop. 364,000.
Gua·da·la·ja·ra /gwaad'ləhaárə/ *n.* capital of Jalisco, Mexico, in the N central part. Pop. 1,650,042.
Gua·dal·ca·nal /gwaad'lkənál/ *n.* island in the W Pacific; largest of the Solomon Islands; site of a World War II battle.
Gua·da·lu·pe /gwaad'lŏŏpay/ *n.* city in NE Mexico. Pop. 535,300.
Gua·de·loupe /gwaad'lŏŏp/ *n.* island in the E West Indies; dependency of France. Pop. 408,000. Capital: Basse-Terre.
Guam /gwaam/ *n.* island in the W Pacific; largest of the Mariana Islands; territory of the U.S. Pop. 157,000. □□ **Gua·ma'ni·an** /-máyneeən/ *n.* & *adj.*
Gua·na·jua·to /gwaanəwaátō, –nəhwaá–/ *n.* state in central Mexico. Pop. 3,982,600. Capital: Guanajuato.
Guan·tá·na·mo /gwaantaánəmō/ *n.* city in SE Cuba; site of a U.S. naval base. Pop. 207,800.
Gua·te·ma·la /gwaatəmaálə/ *n.* republic in N Central America. Pop. 11,278,000. Capital: Guatemala City. □□ **Gua·te·ma'lan** *n.* & *adj.*
Gua·te·ma·la Cit·y *n.* capital of Guatemala, in the S central part. Pop. 823,300.
Guay·a·quil /gwīəkeel/ *n.* port city in Ecuador. Pop. 1,508,400.
Guern·sey /gúrnzee/ island in the English Channel; British crown dependency. Pop. 63,000. Capital: St. Peter Port.
Guer·re·ro /ger-rérō/ *n.* state in S Mexico. Pop. 2,620,600. Capital: Chilpancingo.
Guin·ea /ginee/ *n.* republic in W Africa. Pop. 7,412,000. Capital: Conakry.
Guin·ea-Bis·sau /bisów/ *n.* republic in W Africa. Pop. 1,151,000. Capital: Bissau.
Guin·ea, Gulf of *n.* arm of the Atlantic, on the W coast of Africa.
Gui·yang /gwáyyaáng/ *n.* (formerly **Kuei-yang**) city in S China. Pop. 1,018,600.
Gulf Stream *n.* warm Atlantic current flowing from Gulf of Mexico along the E coast of North America toward Europe.
Guy·a·na /gī-aánə, -ánə/ *n.* republic in NE South America. Pop. 712,000. Capital: Georgetown.
Gyan·dzha /gyaánjə/ *n.* city in W Azerbaijan. Pop. 282,200.
Haar·lem /haárləm/ *n.* city in the W Netherlands. Pop. 149,000.
Hague /hayg/, **The** *n.* city in the SW Netherlands; seat of government. Pop. 444,200.
Hai·fa /hífə/ *n.* port city in NW Israel. Pop. 252,300.
Hai·phong /hífáwng/ *n.* port city in N Vietnam. Pop. 456,000.
Hai·ti /háytee/ *n.* republic in the central West Indies, comprising the W part of Hispaniola. Pop. 6,732,000. Capital: Port-au-Prince. □□ **Hai·tian** /háyshən/ *n.* & *adj.*
Hal·i·fax /hálifaks/ *n.* capital of Nova Scotia, Canada, in the E part. Pop. 320,500.
Hal·le /haálə/ *n.* city in E central Germany. Pop. 290,100.
Ham·a·dan /hamədaán, -dán/ *n.* city in W Iran. Pop. 349,700.
Ham·burg /haámbərg/ *n.* port city in N Germany. Pop. 1,705,900.
Hamp·ton /hámptən/ *n.* city in SE Virginia. Pop. 133,793.
Ha·noi /hanóy/ *n.* capital of Vietnam, in the N part. Pop. 2,154,900.
Han·o·ver /hánōvər/ *n.* city in N central Germany. Pop. 525,800.
Ha·ra·re /həraárray/ *n.* capital of Zimbabwe, in the N part. Pop. 1,184,200.
Har·bin /haarbín/ *n.* city in NE China. Pop. 2,830,000.
Har·ris·burg /hárəsbərg/ *n.* capital of Pennsylvania, in the SE central part. Pop. 52,376.
Hart·ford /haártfərd/ *n.* capital of Connecticut, in the N central part. Pop. 139,739.
Ha·van·a /həvánə/ *n.* port city and capital of Cuba. Pop. 2,241,000.
Ha·wai·i /həwaáee, –wíee, –wáwee/ *n.* **1** state in the U.S. comprising eight Pacific islands. Pop. 1,108,229. Capital: Honolulu. Abbr. **HI 2** largest island of the state of Hawaii. □□ **Ha·wai'ian** /-waáyən, -wíən/ *n.* & *adj.*
Hay·ward /háywərd/ *n.* city in W California. Pop. 111,498.
Heb·ri·des /hébrədeez/ *n.* island group in the Atlantic, off the W coast of Scotland.
Hei·del·berg /híd'lbərg/ *n.* city in SW Germany. Pop. 139,000.
Hel·e·na /hélənə/ *n.* capital of Montana, in the W central part. Pop. 24,569.
Hel·sin·ki /hélsingkee/ *n.* port city and capital of Finland. Pop. 525,000.
He·rá·klei·on /herákleeaan/ *n.* see IRÁKLION.
Her·mo·si·llo /ermōseeyō/ *n.* capital of Sonora, Mexico, in the central part. Pop. 406,417.
Hi·a·le·ah /hīəleeə/ *n.* city in SE Florida. Pop. 188,004.
Hi·dal·go /hidálgō/ *n.* state in E central Mexico. Pop. 1,888,400. Capital: Pachuca.
Him·a·la·yas /himəláyəz, himaályəz, –ləyəz/ *n.* mountain range in S Asia, along the border between India and Tibet.
Hin·du Kush /híndōō kŏŏsh/ *n.* mountain range in central Asia, extending W from the Himalayas.
Hi·ro·shi·ma /heerəsheemə, heerṓshimə/ *n.* port city in Japan, on Honshu; target of first atomic bomb. Pop. 1,108,900.
His·pan·io·la /hispənyṓlə/ *n.* island in the central West Indies, comprising the republic of Haiti and the Dominican Republic.
Ho·bart /hṓbaart/ *n.* capital of Tasmania, Australia, in the SE part. Pop. 129,000.
Ho Chi Minh /hō chee mín/ **Cit·y** *n.* (formerly **Saigon**) city in S Vietnam. Pop. 4,322,300.
Hok·kai·do /haakídō/ *n.* (formerly **Yezo**) island in N Japan.
Hol·land /haálənd/ *n.* see NETHERLANDS, THE.
Hol·ly·wood /haáleewŏŏd/ *n.* **1** city in SE Florida. Pop. 121,697. **2** section of Los Angeles, California; center of U.S. motion-picture industry.
Ho·ly /hṓlee/ **Land** *n.* see PALESTINE.
Ho·ly Ro·man Em·pire *n. hist.* empire of W central Europe from 800 to 1806.
Hon·du·ras /haandŏŏrəs, –dyŏŏ–/ *n.* republic in N Central America. Pop. 5,605,000. Capital: Tegucigalpa. □□ **Hon·du'ran** *n.* & *adj.*
Hong Kong /haáng kaáng, háwng káwng/ *n.* city and commercial center of SE China; formerly (to 1997) a British crown colony. Pop. 6,305,000. Capital: Victoria.
Ho·ni·a·ra /hōnee-aárə/ *n.* capital of the Solomon Islands, on Guadalcanal. Pop. 43,600.
Hon·o·lu·lu /haanəlŏŏlōō, hōn-/ *n.* capital of Hawaii, on the S coast of Oahu. Pop. 365,272.
Hon·shu /haánshōō/ *n.* largest island in Japan, in the central part.
Hood /hŏŏd/, **Mount** *n.* inactive volcanic peak in NW Oregon, in the Cascade range.
Hoo·ver /hṓōvər/ **Dam** dam on the Colorado River, along the Arizona-Nevada border.
Hous·ton /hyṓōstən, yṓōs–/ *n.* city in SE Texas. Pop. 1,630,553.
Huang /hwaang/ **Riv·er** *n.* (also called **Yel'low Riv'er**) river in China, flowing 2,800 mi. from Qinghai to the Yellow Sea.
Hud·son /hədsən/ **Bay** *n.* inland sea in NE Canada; an arm of the Atlantic.
Hud·son Riv·er *n.* river in E New York, flowing 300 mi. from the Adirondacks to New York Bay.
Hull /həl/ *n.* (official name **Kings'ton up·on' Hull**) port city on the Humber River in England. Pop. 269,100.
Hun·ga·ry /húnggəree/ *n.* republic in central Europe. Pop. 10,003,000. Capital: Budapest.
Hun·ting·ton /húntingtən/ *n.* city in SE New York. Pop. 191,474.
Hun·ting·ton Beach *n.* city in SW California. Pop. 181,519.
Hunts·ville /húntsvəl, –vil/ *n.* city in N Alabama. Pop. 159,789.
Hu·ron /hyṓōraan, yṓōraan, –ən/, **Lake** *n.* one of the Great Lakes, W of Michigan.
Hy·der·a·bad /hídərəbaad/ *n.* **1** city in W India. Pop. 3,145,900. **2** city in S Pakistan. Pop. 751,500.
I·ba·dan /ibaád'n/ *n.* city in SW Nigeria. Pop. 1,365,000.
I·be·ri·an /ībeereeən/ **Pen·in·su·la** *n.* (also called **I·be'ri·a**) peninsula in SW Europe, bounded by the Bay of Biscay, the Atlantic, and the Mediterranean Sea, and comprising Portugal and Spain.

Ice·land /íslənd/ *n.* island republic in the N Atlantic, between Scandinavia and Greenland. Pop. 270,000. Capital: Reykjavik.

I·da·ho /ídəhō/ *n.* state in NW U.S. Pop. 1,006,749. Capital: Boise. Abbr. **ID**; **Ida.** □□ **I'da·ho·an** *n. & adj.*

I·guas·sú /eegwaasóó/ **Falls** *n.* waterfall on the Argentina-Brazil border: 210 ft. high.

Il·li·nois /ilənóy, –nóyz/ *n.* state in central U.S. Pop. 11,430,602. Capital: Springfield. Abbr. **IL**; **Ill.** □□ **Il·li·nois'an, Il·li·noi'an** /–nóyən/ *n. & adj.*

Im·pe·ri·al /impéereeəl/ **Val·ley** *n.* valley in S central California.

In·chon /inchaan/ *n.* port city in NW South Korea. Pop. 2,307,600.

In·de·pend·ence /indipéndəns/ *n.* city in W Missouri. Pop. 112,301.

In·di·a /índeeə/ *n.* republic in S Asia. Pop. 952,108,000. Capital: New Delhi.

In·di·an·a /indee-ánə/ *n.* state in central U.S. Pop. 5,544,159. Capital: Indianapolis. Abbr. **IN**; **Ind.** □□ **In·di·an'an** *n. & adj.*

In·di·an·ap·o·lis /indeeənápələs/ *n.* capital of Indiana, in the central part. Pop. 731,327.

In·di·an /indeeən/ **O·cean** *n.* ocean between Africa and Australia, S of Asia. Area 28,350,500 sq. mi.

In·do·chi·na /indōchínə/ *n.* peninsula in SE Asia, bounded by the Bay of Bengal and the S China Sea, and comprising Burma, W Malaysia, Thailand, Cambodia, Laos, and Vietnam.

In·do·ne·sia /indəneézhə/ republic of the Malay Archipelago in SE Asia. Pop. 206,612,000. Capital: Jakarta. □□ **In·do·ne'sian** *n. & adj.*

In·dus /índəs/ **Riv·er** *n.* river in Asia, flowing 1,900 mi. from Tibet through Pakistan and into the Arabian Sea.

Inglewood /ínggəlwŏŏd/ *n.* city in SW California. Pop. 109,602.

Inns·bruck /ínzbrŏŏk/ *n.* city in W Austria. Pop. 118,100.

I·o·ni·an /ī-ṓneeən/ **Sea** *n.* arm of the Mediterranean Sea, between Greece and Italy.

I·o·wa /íəwə/ *n.* state in central U.S. Pop. 2,776,755. Capital: Des Moines. Abbr. **IA**; **Ia.** □□ **I'o·wan** *n. & adj.*

I·o·wa Cit·y *n.* city in E Iowa. Pop. 59,738.

Ips·wich /ípswich/ *n.* city in E England. Pop. 114,800.

I·rá·kli·on /irákleeon/ (also **He·rá'klei·on**) port city and capital of Crete. Pop. 117,200.

I·ran /irán, iraán, īrán/ *n.* (formerly **Persia**) republic in SW Asia. Pop. 66,094,000. Capital: Teheran. □□ **I·ra·ni·an** /iráyneeən/ *n. & adj.*

I·raq /irák, iraák, īrák/ *n.* republic in SW Asia. Pop. 21,422,000. Capital: Baghdad. □□ **I·ra·qi** /irákee/ *n. & adj.*

Ir·bid /eérbid/ *n.* city in N Jordan. Pop. 314,700.

Ire·land /írlənd/ *n.* **1** island in the N Atlantic, W of England. **2** (official name **Re·pub'lic of Ire'land;** also called **Eir'e**) republic in NW Europe; occupies most of the island of Ireland. Pop. 3,567,000. Capital: Dublin. See also NORTHERN IRELAND.

I·rish /írish/ **Sea** *n.* arm of the Atlantic, between England and Ireland.

Ir·kutsk /eerkóótsk/ *n.* city in S Russia. Pop. 654,000.

Ir·vine /úrvīn/ *n.* city in SW California. Pop. 110,330.

Ir·ving /úrving/ *n.* city in NE Texas. Pop. 155,037.

Is·fa·han /isfəhaán/ *n.* (also **Esfahan** or **Ispahan**) city in central Iran; former capital of Persia. Pop. 1,127,000.

Is·lam·a·bad /islaáməbaad/ *n.* capital of Pakistan, in the NE part. Pop. 204,400.

Is·ra·el /ízreeəl, –rayel/ *n.* **1** republic in SW Asia; formed in 1948 as a Jewish state. Pop. 5,422,000 (excluding territory occupied after 1967). Capital: Jerusalem. **2** *hist.* ancient biblical country of the Hebrews. □□ **Is·rae·li** /izráylee/ *n. & adj.*

Is·tan·bul /istaanbóól/ *n.* (formerly **Constantinople**; ancient name **Byzantium**) port city in NW Turkey. Pop. 7,615,500.

It·a·ly /ít'lee/ *n.* republic in S Europe. Pop. 57,460,000. Capital: Rome.

I·vo·ry /ívəree, ; n-vree/ **Coast** *n.* (official name **Côte d'I·voire'**) republic in W Africa. Pop. 14,762,000. Capital: Abidjan. □□ **I·vo·ri·an** /iváwreeən/ *n. & adj.*

I·wo Ji·ma /eewə jeémə, eewō/ *n.* island S of Japan; site of World War II battle.

Iz·mir /izmeér/ *n.* (formerly **Smyrna**) port city in E Turkey. Pop. 1,985,300.

Jack·son /jáksən/ *n.* capital of Mississippi, in the central part. Pop. 196,637.

Ja·kar·ta /jəkaártə/ *n.* capital of Indonesia, on NW coast of Java. Pop. 6,503,400.

Ja·la·pa /həlaápə/ *n.* capital of Veracruz, Mexico, in the central part. Pop. 111,800.

Ja·lis·co /həlískō/ *n.* state in W Mexico. Pop. 5,302,700. Capital: Guadalajara.

Ja·mai·ca /jəmáykə/ *n.* island republic in the W West Indies, S of Cuba. Pop. 2,595,000. Capital: Kingston.

Ja·pan /jəpán/ *n.* island nation E of mainland Asia. Pop. 125,450,000. Capital: Tokyo.

Ja·pan, Sea of *n.* arm of the Pacific, between Japan and mainland Asia.

Ja·va /jaávə, jávə/ *n.* main island of Indonesia, SE of Sumatra.

Jef·fer·son /jéfərsən/ **Cit·y** *n.* capital of Missouri, in the central part. Pop. 35,481.

Je·na /yáynə/ *n.* city in E central Germany. Pop. 102,200.

Jer·sey /júrzee/ island in the English Channel; British crown dependency. Pop. 88,000. Capital: St. Helier.

Jer·sey Cit·y *n.* city in NE New Jersey. Pop. 228,537.

Je·ru·sa·lem /jəróósələm, –sləm/ *n.* capital of Israel, in the E central part. Pop. 504,100.

Jid·da /jídə/ *n.* port city in W Saudi Arabia. Pop. 1,800,000.

Ji·nan /jeenaan/ (also **Chi·nan**) city in NE China. Pop. 1,100,000.

Jodh·pur /jaádpŏŏr/ *n.* city in NW India. Pop. 666,300.

Jo·han·nes·burg /jōhánəsbərg/ *n.* city in NE South Africa. Pop. 712,500.

Jo·li·et /jōlee-ét/ *n.* city in NE Illinois. Pop. 76,836.

Jor·dan /jáwrd'n/ *n.* kingdom in SW Asia, E of Israel. Pop. 4,212,000. Capital: Amman. □□ **Jor·da·ni·an** /jawrdáyneeən/ *n. & adj.*

Jor·dan Riv·er river in SW Asia, flowing 200 mi. from S Lebanon to the Dead Sea.

Juan de Fu·ca /waan də fóókə, fyóó–/, **Strait of** *n.* channel separating Vancouver Island, Canada, from U.S.

Ju·neau /jóónō/ *n.* capital of Alaska, in the SE part. Pop. 26,751.

Jung·frau /yóóngfrow/ *n.* mountain in the Alps, in S Switzerland: 13,642 ft. high.

Ka·bul /kaabóól, kaábəl/ *n.* capital of Afghanistan, in the E part. Pop. 700,000.

Ka·go·shi·ma /kaagōsheémə, kaagṓsheemə/ *n.* port city in S Japan, on Kyushu. Pop. 546,300.

Ka·la·ha·ri /kaləhaaree, kaal–/ *n.* desert in SW Africa, mainly in Botswana.

Kal·a·ma·zoo /kaləməzóó/ *n.* city in SW Michigan. Pop. 80,277.

Ka·li·nin /kəleénin, –nyin/ *n.* (formerly **Tver**) city in W Russia. Pop. 455,000.

Ka·li·nin·grad /kəleéningrad, –nyingrad/ *n.* port city in W Russia. Pop. 419,000.

Kam·chat·ka /kamchaátkə/ *n.* peninsula in E Russia, bounded by the Sea of Okhotsk and the Bering Sea.

Kam·pa·la /kaampaálə/ *n.* capital of Uganda, in the SE part. Pop. 773,500.

Kam·pu·che·a /kampŏŏcheéə/ *n.* see CAMBODIA.

Ka·no /kaánō/ *n.* city in N central Nigeria. Pop. 657,300.

Kan·pur /kaánpŏŏr/ *n.* city in N India. Pop. 1,874,400.

Kan·sas /kánzəs/ *n.* state in central U.S. Pop. 2,477,574. Capital: Topeka. Abbr. **KS**; **Kan.**; **Kans.** □□ **Kan'san** *n. & adj.*

Kan·sas Cit·y *n.* **1** city in W Missouri. Pop. 435,146. **2** city in E Kansas. Pop. 149,767.

Kao·hsiung /gówshee-óóng/ *n.* port city in SW Taiwan. Pop. 1,426,518.

Ka·ra·chi /kəraáchee/ *n.* port city in S Pakistan. Pop. 5,208,100.

Karl-Marx-Stadt /kaarl maárks shtaat/ *n.* see CHEMNITZ.

Karls·ruh·e /kaárlzrōōə/ *n.* city in SW Germany. Pop. 277,000.

Kath·man·du /katmandóó/ *n.* (also **Kat·man·du'**) capital of Nepal, in the central part. Pop. 235,200.

Ka·to·wi·ce /kaatəveétsə/ *n.* city in S Poland. Pop. 355,100.

Kau·nas /kównəs/ *n.* city in S central Lithuania. Pop. 429,000.

Ka·wa·sa·ki /kaawəsaákee/ *n.* port city in Japan, on Honshu. Pop. 1,202,800.

Kay·se·ri /kīzəreé/ *n.* city in central Turkey. Pop. 454,000.

Ka·zakh·stan /kəzaakstaán/ *n.* republic in central Asia; formerly part of the USSR. Pop. 16,916,000. Capital: Astana. □□ **Ka·zakh'** *n.*

Kee·lung /keélóóng/ *n.* see CHILUNG.

Ken·tuck·y /kəntúkee/ *n.* state in E central U.S. Pop. 3,685,296. Capital: Frankfort. Abbr. **KY**; **Ky.** □□ **Ken·tuck'i·an** *n. & adj.*

Ken·ya /kényə, keén–/ *n.* republic in E Africa. Pop. 28,177,000. Capital: Nairobi.

Khar·kiv /kaárkif/ *n.* (formerly **Khar'kov**) city in NE Ukraine. Pop. 1,555,000.

Khar·toum /kaartóóm/ *n.* capital of Sudan, in the E central part. Pop. 476,200.

Ki·ev /keé-ef, –ev/ *n.* capital of Ukraine, in the N central part. Pop. 2,630,000.

Ki·ga·li /kigaálee/ *n.* capital of Rwanda, in the central part. Pop. 232,700.

Ki·lau·e·a /kiləwáyə/ *n.* active volcano on the island of Hawaii.

Kil·i·man·ja·ro /kilimənjaárō/, **Mount** *n.* volcanic mountain in N Tanzania; highest peak in Africa: 19,340 ft.

Kings·ton /kíngstən/ *n.* port city and capital of Jamaica. Pop. 103,800.

Kings·ton up·on Hull *n.* see HULL.

Kings·town /kíngztown/ *n.* port city and capital of St. Vincent and the Grenadines. Pop. 15,500.

Kin·sha·sa /kinshaásə/ *n.* capital of the Congo (formerly Zaire), in the W part. Pop. 4,655,300.

Ki·ri·ba·ti /keereebaátee, kíribas/ *n.* island republic in the W Pacific, along the equator, comprising thirty-three islands. Pop. 81,000. Capital: Tarawa.

Kir·kuk /keerkóók/ *n.* city in N Iraq. Pop. 570,000.

Ki·shi·nev /kíshinef/ *n.* (also called **Chi·şi·nă'u**) capital of Moldova, in the central part. Pop. 662,000.

Ki·ta·kyu·shu /keetaakee-óóshóó/ *n.* port city in Japan, on Kyushu. Pop. 1,019,600.

Kitch·e·ner /kíchənər, kíchnər/ *n.* city in SE Ontario, Canada. Pop. 168,300.

Knox·ville /naákswil/ *n.* city in E Tennessee. Pop. 165,121.

Ko·be /kóbay, –bee/ *n.* port city in Japan, on Honshu. Pop. 1,488,600.

Ko·blenz /kóblents/ *n.* see COBLENZ.

Ko·di·ak /kódee-ak/ **Is·land** *n.* island in Alaska, in the NW Gulf of Alaska.

Köln /köln/ *n.* see COLOGNE.

Kol·we·zi /kōlwáyzee/ *n.* city in S Congo (formerly Zaire). Pop. 417,800.

Kon·ya /kawnyaá/ *n.* city in SW central Turkey. Pop. 576,000.

Ko·re·a /kəreéə/ *n.* peninsula in E Asia, bounded by the Yellow Sea and the Sea of Japan; divided into two countries: **1 North Korea** Pop. 23,904,000. Capital: Pyongyang. **2 South Korea** Pop. 45,482,000. Capital: Seoul. ▫▫ **Ko·re'an** *n. & adj.*

Ko·so·vo /kaásəvō/ *n.* region of S Serbia. Pop. 2,000,000. ▫▫ **Ko'so·var** *n. & adj.*

Kra·ka·to·a /krakətóə/ *n.* (also **Kra·ka·tau** /krákətow/) island volcano in Indonesia; noted for its violent eruption in 1883.

Kra·ków /krákow, kraákoof/ *n.* see CRACOW.

Kras·no·yarsk /kraasnəyaársk/ *n.* city in central Russia. Pop. 869,400.

K2 *n.* (also called **God·win Aus·ten** /gaádwin áwstən/) mountain in N Kashmir; second highest in the world: 28,250 ft.

Kua·la Lum·pur /kwaálə ləmpóor/ *n.* capital of Malaysia, on the SW Malay Peninsula. Pop. 1,100,000.

Kuei-yang /gwáy-yáng/ (also **Kwei·yang**) see GUIYANG.

Kui·by·shev /kweébəshef, –shev/ see SAMARA.

Ku·ma·mo·to /koomәmótō/ *n.* city in Japan, on Kyushu. Pop. 650,300.

Ku·ma·si /koomaásee/ *n.* city in S central Ghana. Pop. 385,200.

Ku·wait /kəwáyt/ *n.* **1** monarchy in W Asia, on the Persian Gulf. Pop. 1,950,000. **2** (also called **Ku·wait' Cit'y**) port city and capital of Kuwait. Pop. 44,200. ▫▫ **Ku·wai'ti** /–tee/ *n. & adj.*

Kwang·ju /gwaángjoó/ *n.* city in SW South Korea. Pop. 1,257,500.

Kyo·to /kee-ótō/ *n.* city in Japan, on Honshu. Pop. 1,463,600.

Kyr·gyz·stan /kirgistaán, –stán/ *n.* republic in W central Asia; formerly part of the USSR. Pop. 4,530,000. Capital: Bishkek.

Kyu·shu /kyóoshoo/ *n.* island in SW Japan.

La·do·ga /laádəgə, lád–/, **Lake** *n.* lake N of St. Petersburg, Russia; largest lake in Europe.

La·hore /ləháwr, –hór/ *n.* city in E Pakistan. Pop. 2,952,700.

Lake Dis·trict *n.* noted scenic region in NW England.

Lake·wood /láykwood/ *n.* city in central Colorado. Pop. 126,481.

La Ma·tan·za /laa mətaánsə/ *n.* city in E Argentina. Pop. 1,111,800.

Lan·sing /lánsing/ *n.* capital of Michigan, in the S part. Pop. 127,321.

La·os /laáōs/ *n.* country in SE Asia, between Thailand and Vietnam. Pop. 4,976,000. Capital: Vientiane. ▫▫ **La·o·tian** /lay-óshən/ *n. & adj.*

La Paz /lə paáz, paás/ *n.* **1** administrative capital of Bolivia, in the W part. Pop. 785,000 **2** capital of Baja California Sur, Mexico, in the S part. Pop. 161,000.

La Pla·ta /plaátə/ *n.* port city in E Argentina. Pop. 643,000.

La·re·do /ləráydō/ *n.* city in S Texas. Pop. 122,899.

Las Cru·ces /laas kroósəs/ *n.* city in S New Mexico. Pop. 62,126.

Las Pal·mas /paálməs/ *n.* port city of the Canary Islands, off the coast of Morocco. Pop. 342,000.

Las Ve·gas /váygəs/ *n.* city in SE Nevada. Pop. 258,295.

Lat·a·ki·a /latəkeéə/ *n.* port city in W Syria. Pop. 306,500.

Lat·vi·a /látveeə/ *n.* republic in N Europe; formerly part of the USSR. Pop. 2,469,000. Capital: Riga. ▫▫ **Lat'vi·an** *n. & adj.*

Lau·sanne /lōzaán, –zán/ *n.* city in W Switzerland. Pop. 116,800.

La·val /laavaál, ləvál/ *n.* city in S Quebec, Canada. Pop. 314,400.

Law·rence /láwrəns, laár–/ *n.* city in NE Massachusetts. Pop. 70,207.

Leb·a·non /lébənaan, –nən/ *n.* republic in SW Asia. Pop. 3,776,000. Capital: Beirut. ▫▫ **Leb·a·nese** /–neéz/ *n. & adj.*

Leeds /leedz/ *n.* city in N England. Pop. 724,400.

Lee·ward /leéwərd, loóərd/ **Is·lands** *n.* island group in the E West Indies, extending from Dominica NW to the U.S. Virgin Islands.

Leg·horn /léghawrn/ *n.* (Italian name **Li·vor'no**) port city in W Italy. Pop. 165,500.

Le Ha·vre /lə haáv, haávrə/ *n.* port city in N France. Pop. 197,200.

Leices·ter /léstər/ *n.* city in central England. Pop. 293,400.

Lei·den /líd'n/ city in the SW Netherlands. Pop. 115,500.

Leip·zig /lípsig, –sik/ *n.* city in E Germany. Pop. 481,100.

Le·man /leémən/, **Lake** *n.* see GENEVA, LAKE.

Le Mans /lə maan/ *n.* city in NW France. Pop. 148,500.

Le·nin·grad /léningrad/ *n.* see SAINT PETERSBURG 1.

Le·ón /lay-áwn/ *n.* **1** city in NW Spain. Pop. 147,300. **2** city in central Mexico. Pop. 758,300.

Le·so·tho /ləsótō, –sóotoo/ *n.* (formerly **Basutoland**) monarchy in S Africa. Pop. 1,971,000. Capital: Maseru.

Less·er An·til·les /antíleez/ *n.* term for the smaller islands of the West Indies, comprising the Leeward and Windward islands, SE of Puerto Rico. See also GREATER ANTILLES.

Le·vant /ləvánt/ *n.* term for the countries on the E coast of the Mediterranean Sea; includes Israel, Syria, and Lebanon.

Lev·it·town /lévit-town/ *n.* city in SE New York, on Long Island. Pop. 53,286.

Lex·ing·ton /léksingtən/ *n.* **1** city in NE central Kentucky. Pop. 225,366. **2** town in NE Massachusetts; site of the first battle of the American Revolution (1775). Pop. 29,000.

Li·be·ri·a /lībeéreeə/ *n.* republic in W Africa. Pop. 2,110,000. Capital: Monrovia. ▫▫ **Li·ber'i·an** *n. & adj.*

Li·bre·ville /leébrəvil/ *n.* port city and capital of Gabon. Pop. 362,400.

Lib·y·a /líbeeə/ *n.* republic in N Africa. Pop. 5,445,000. Capital: Tripoli. ▫▫ **Lib'y·an** *n. & adj.*

Liech·ten·stein /líkhtənshtīn, líktənstīn/ *n.* principality in central Europe. Pop. 31,000. Capital: Vaduz. ▫▫ **Liech'ten·stein·er** *n. & adj.*

Li·ège /lee-ézh/ *n.* city in E Belgium. Pop. 192,400.

Lille /leel/ *n.* city in N France. Pop. 178,300.

Li·long·we /liláwngway/ *n.* administrative capital of Malawi, in the central part. Pop. 395,500.

Li·ma /leémə/ capital of Peru, in the W part. Pop. 421,600.

Li·moges /leemózh/ *n.* city in central France. Pop. 136,400.

Lin·coln /língkən/ *n.* capital of Nebraska, in the E part. Pop. 191,972.

Linz /lins/ *n.* port city in NW Austria. Pop. 203,000.

Lis·bon /lízbən/ *n.* port city and capital of Portugal. Pop. 677,800.

Lith·u·a·ni·a /lithəwáyneeə/ *n.* republic in N Europe; formerly part of the USSR. Pop. 3,646,000. Capital: Vilnius.

Lit·tle Rock /lítəl raak/ *n.* capital of Arkansas, in the central part. Pop. 175,795.

Liv·er·pool /lívərpool/ *n.* port city in W England. Pop. 474,000. ▫▫ **Liv·er·pud·li·an** /livərpúdleeən/ *n. & adj.*

Li·vo·ni·a /livóneeə/ *n.* city in SE Michigan. Pop. 100,850.

Li·vor·no /leeváwrnaw/ *n.* see LEGHORN.

Lju·blja·na /loóblee-aánə, lyoo–/ *n.* capital of Slovenia. Pop. 276,100.

Lla·no Es·ta·ca·do /laanō estəkaádō/ *n.* (also called **Staked Plain**) extensive plateau in Texas and New Mexico.

Loch Ness /laak nes/ *n.* lake in NW Scotland.

Lódz /looj/ city in central Poland. Pop. 828,500.

Lo·mas de Za·mo·ra /lómaas də zəmáwrə/ *n.* city in E Argentina. Pop. 572,800.

Lo·mé /lōmáy/ *n.* port city and capital of Togo. Pop. 366,500.

Lon·don /lúndən/ *n.* **1** capital of England and of the United Kingdom, in the S part of England. Pop. 6,967,500. **2** city in SE Ontario, Canada. Pop. 303,200.

Long /lawng/ **Beach** *n.* city in SW California. Pop. 429,433.

Long Is·land *n.* island in SE New York; includes portions of New York City.

Long Is·land Sound *n.* arm of the Atlantic, separating Connecticut from Long Island, New York.

Look·out /lóokowt/ **Moun·tain** *n.* ridge near Chattanooga in SE Tennessee; site of Civil War battle.

Los An·ge·les /laws ánjələs, –leez/ *n.* city in S California. Pop. 3,485,398. ▫▫ **An·ge·le·no** /anjəleénō/, **Los An·ge·le·no, Los An·ge·le·an** /anjəleéən/ *n.*

Lou·ise /loo-eez, loo–/, **Lake** *n.* glacial lake in SW Alberta, Canada, in the Canadian Rocky Mountains.

Lou·i·si·an·a /loo-eezee-ánə/ *n.* state in S U.S. Pop. 4,219,973. Capital: Baton Rouge. Abbr. **LA; La.** ▫▫ **Lou·i·si·an'an, Lou·i·si·an'i·an** /–áneeən/ *n. & adj.*

Lou·is·ville /lóoeevil, –əvəl/ *n.* city in N central Kentucky. Pop. 269,063. ▫▫ **Lou·is·vill·ian** /looivílyən/ *n.*

Lourdes /loordz, loord/ *n.* town in SW France; site of a Roman Catholic shrine noted for miraculous cures. Pop. 18,100.

Lou·ren·ço Mar·ques /lərénsō maarkés, maárkəs/ *n.* see MAPUTO.

Low Coun·tries *n.* term for low-lying countries along the North Sea; includes Belgium, Luxembourg, and the Netherlands.

Low·ell /lóəl/ *n.* city in NE Massachusetts. Pop. 103,439.

Lu·an·da /loo-aándə/ *n.* port city and capital of Angola. Pop. 2,000,000.

Lub·bock /lúbək/ *n.* city in NW Texas. Pop. 186,206.

Lü·beck /lýbek/ port city in N Germany. Pop. 216,900.

Lu·blin /lóoblin/ *n.* city in E Poland. Pop. 352,500.

Lu·bum·ba·shi /loobоombaáshee/ *n.* city in S Congo (formerly Zaire). Pop. 851,400.

Luck·now /lúknow/ *n.* city in N India. Pop. 1,619,100.

Lü·da /loódaá/ see DALIAN.

Lu·gansk /loogaánsk/ *n.* (formerly **Voroshilovgrad**) city in E Ukraine. Pop. 487,000.

Lu·sa·ka /loosaákə/ *n.* capital of Zambia, in the SE part. Pop. 982,400.

Lux·em·bourg /lúksəmbərg/ *n.* **1** country and grand duchy in W Europe. Pop. 416,000. **2** capital of Luxembourg, in the S part. Pop. 76,400. **3** province in SE Belgium. ▫▫ **Lux'em·bourg·er** *n.* **Lux'em·bourg·i·an** /–bərgeeən/ *n. & adj.*

Lviv /ləveéf/ *n.* (also **Lvov**) city in W Ukraine. Pop. 802,000.

Ly·all·pur /líəlpoor/ *n.* see FAISALABAD.

Lyd·i·a /lídeeə/ *n. hist.* ancient kingdom of W Asia Minor. ▫▫ **Lyd'i·an** *n. & adj.*

Lynn /lin/ *n.* city in NE Massachusetts. Pop. 81,245.

Ly·ons /lee-áwn/ *n.* (also **Lyon**) city in E France. Pop. 422,400.

Maas·tricht /maástrikht/ *n.* city in the SE Netherlands. Pop. 118,300.
Ma·cau /məkṓw/ *n.* overseas territory of Portugal (to 1999), consisting of a peninsula and two islands off the S coast of China. Pop. 497,000. Capital: Macau City.
Mac·e·do·ni·a /masədṓneeə/ *n.* **1** *hist.* ancient country on the Balkan Peninsula, N of Greece. **2** independent state N of Greece; formerly part of Yugoslavia. Pop. 2,104,000. Capital: Skopje. ▫▫ **Mace·do'ni·an** /–neeən/ *n. & adj.*
Mac·ken·zie /məkénzee/ **Riv·er** *n.* river in NW Canada, flowing 1,120 mi. from Great Slave Lake to the Beaufort Sea.
Ma·con /máykən/ *n.* city in central Georgia. Pop. 106,612.
Mad·a·gas·car /madəgáskər/ *n.* (formerly **Malagasy Republic**) island country in the Indian Ocean, E of Mozambique. Pop. 13,671,000. Capital: Antananarivo. ▫▫ **Ma·da·gas'can** *n. & adj.*
Ma·dei·ra /mədeérə, –dérə/ *n.* **1** island group off the NW coast of Africa; part of Portugal. **2** the major island of this group.
Mad·i·son /mádisən/ *n.* capital of Wisconsin, in the S part. Pop. 191,262.
Ma·dras /mədrás, –draás/ *n.* port city in SE India. Pop. 3,841,400.
Ma·drid /mədríd/ *n.* capital of Spain, in the central part. Pop. 3,041,100. ▫▫ **Mad·ri·le·ni·an** /madrileéneeən/ *n. & adj.*
Mag·de·burg /mágdəbərg/ *n.* city in E central Germany. Pop. 265,400.
Ma·hal·la al-Ku·bra /məhálə al kŏŏbrə/ *n.* city in N Egypt. Pop. 408,000.
Maine /mayn/ *n.* state in NE U.S. Pop. 1,227,928. Capital: Augusta. Abbr. **ME; Me.** ▫▫ **Main'er** *n.*
Mainz /mīnts/ *n.* port city in W Germany. Pop. 184,600.
Ma·ju·ro /məjŏŏrō/ *n.* capital of the Marshall Islands, in the SE part. Pop. 20,000.
Ma·la·bo /məlaábō/ *n.* capital of Equatorial Guinea, on the island of Bioko. Pop. 58,000.
Má·la·ga /máləgə/ *n.* port city in S Spain. Pop. 531,400.
Mal·a·gas·y /máləgásee/ **Re·pub·lic** *n.* see MADAGASCAR.
Ma·lang /məlaáng/ *n.* city in Indonesia, on Java. Pop. 650,300.
Ma·la·wi /məlaáwee/ *n.* republic in SE Africa. Pop. 9,453,000. Capitals: Lilongwe; Zomba.
Ma·la·wi, Lake *n.* see NYASA, LAKE.
Ma·lay·a /məláyə/ *n.* **1** see MALAY PENINSULA. **2** former federation of eleven states on the Malay Peninsula; now part of Malaysia.
Ma·lay /máylay/ **Ar·chi·pel·a·go** *n.* (formerly **Malaysia**) extensive group of islands between Australia and mainland Asia; includes the Philippines and Indonesia.
Ma·lay Pen·in·su·la *n.* (also called **Ma·lay'a**) peninsula in SE Asia, bounded by the South China Sea and the Strait of Malacca, and comprising parts of Burma, Malaysia, and Thailand.
Ma·lay·sia /məláyzhə/ **1** constitutional monarchy in SE Asia. Pop. 19,963,000 Capital: Kuala Lumpur. **2** see MALAY ARCHIPELAGO. ▫▫ **Ma·lay'sian** *n. & adj.*
Mal·dives /máwldeevz, –dīvz/ *n.* republic comprising about 2,000 islands in the Indian Ocean, SW of India. Pop. 271,000. Capital: Male. ▫▫ **Mal·div'i·an** /–díveeən/ *n. & adj.*
Ma·le /maálee/ *n.* capital of the Maldives, in the central part. Pop. 63,000.
Ma·li /maálee/ *n.* republic in W Africa. Pop. 9,653,000. Capital: Bamako. ▫▫ **Ma'li·an** *n. & adj.*
Mal·mö /maálmō, –mər/ *n.* port city in S Sweden. Pop. 245,700.
Mal·ta /máwltə/ *n.* island state in the Mediterranean Sea, S of Sicily. Pop. 376,000. Capital: Valletta.
Mal·vi·nas, Is·las *n.* see FALKLAND ISLANDS.
Mam·moth /máməth/ **Cave** *n.* series of limestone caverns in central Kentucky; longest cave system in the world: more than 300 mi. of passages.
Man /man/, **Isle of** *n.* British island in the Irish Sea, between Britain and Ireland. Pop. 74,000. Capital: Douglas. ▫▫ **Manx** /mangks/ *n. & adj.*
Ma·na·gua /mənaágwə/ *n.* capital of Nicaragua, in the W part. Pop. 682,100.
Ma·na·ma /mənámə/ *n.* (also called **al-Ma·nam'ah**) capital of Bahrain. Pop. 140,400.
Ma·náos /maanóws/ *n.* (also **Ma·naus'**) port city in W Brazil. Pop. 613,000.
Man·ches·ter /mánchestər/ *n.* **1** city in S New Hampshire. Pop. 99,600. **2** city in NW England. Pop. 431,100.
Man·da·lay /mandəláy/ *n.* city in N Burma. Pop. 532,900.
Man·hat·tan /manhát'n/ *n.* one of the five boroughs of New York City. Pop. 1,487,536.
Ma·nil·a /məníla/ *n.* port city and capital of the Philippines. Pop. 1,894,700.
Man·i·to·ba /manitṓbə/ *n.* province in central Canada. Pop. 1,116,000. Capital: Winnipeg. ▫▫ **Man·i·to'ban** *n. & adj.*
Mann·heim /maánhīm/ *n.* city in SW Germany. Pop. 316,200.
Ma·pu·to /maapŏŏtō/ *n.* (formerly **Lourenço Marques**) port city and capital of Mozambique. Pop. 931,600.
Mar·a·cai·bo /marəkībō/ *n.* port city in NW Venezuela. Pop. 1,249,700.
Ma·ra·cay /maarəkī/ *n.* city in NE Venezuela. Pop. 354,200.
Mar·i·an·a /maree-ánə, mer–/ **Trench** *n.* Pacific depression SW of the Mariana Islands and E of the Philippines; greatest known ocean depth: 36,201 ft.
Mar·i·time /máritīm/ **Prov·in·ces** *n.* Canadian provinces of New Brunswick, Nova Scotia, and Prince Edward Island.
Ma·ri·u·pol /maaree-ŏŏpawl/ *n.* (formerly **Zhdanov**) city in S Ukraine. Pop. 510,000.
Mar·ma·ra /maármərə/, **Sea of** *n.* sea in W Turkey, between the Black and Mediterranean seas.
Mar·ra·kesh /márəkesh/ *n.* city in W central Morocco. Pop. 602,000.
Mar·seilles /maarsáy/ *n.* port city in SE France. Pop. 807,700.
Mar·shall /maárshəl/ **Is·lands** *n.* republic comprising a group of islands in the Pacific, NE of New Guinea. Pop. 58,000. Capital: Majuro.
Mar·tha's /maárthəz/ **Vine·yard** island in Massachusetts, S of Cape Cod.
Mar·ti·nique /maart'n-eék/ *n.* island in the E West Indies; department of France. Pop. 399,000. Capital: Fort-de-France.
Mar·y·land /mérələnd/ *n.* state in E central U.S. Pop. 4,781,468. Capital: Annapolis. Abbr. **MD; Md.** ▫▫ **Mar'y·land·er** *n.*
Ma·se·ru /maázərōō/ *n.* capital of Lesotho, in the W part. Pop. 109,400.
Ma·son-Dix·on /máysən díksən/ **Line** *n.* boundary between Pennsylvania and Maryland; traditional division between the North and the South.
Mas·sa·chu·setts /masəchŏŏsits/ *n.* state in NE U.S. Pop. 6,016,425. Capital: Boston. Abbr. **MA; Mass.**
Mat·a·mo·ros /matəmáwrəs/ *n.* city in NE Mexico. Pop. 266,100.
Mat·ter·horn /mátərhawrn/ *n.* mountain in the Alps, on the border of Switzerland and Italy: 14,692 ft. high.
Mau·i /mówee/ *n.* island of central Hawaii.
Mau·na Lo·a /mownə lṓə/ *n.* mountain on the island of Hawaii; includes Kilauea volcano.
Mau·ri·ta·ni·a /mawritáyneeə/ *n.* republic in W Africa. Pop. 2,336,000. Capital: Nouakchott.
Mau·ri·tius /mawríshəs/ *n.* island republic in the Indian Ocean, E of Madagascar. Pop. 1,140,000. Capital: Port Louis.
Ma·ya·güez /mīəgwáys/ *n.* port city in W Puerto Rico. Pop. 100,400.
Ma·za·tlán /maazətlaán/ port city in W Mexico. Pop. 262,700.
Mba·bane /m-bəbaán, em–/ *n.* capital of Swaziland, in the W central part. Pop. 47,000.
Mc·Al·len /məkálən/ *n.* city in S Texas. Pop. 84,000.
Mc·Kin·ley /məkínlee/, **Mount** *n.* mountain in central Alaska; highest in North America: 20,320 ft.
Mead /meed/, **Lake** *n.* largest artificial lake in U.S.; formed by Hoover Dam.
Mec·ca /mékə/ *n.* city in W Saudi Arabia; holy site in Islam. Pop. 550,000.
Me·dan /maydaán/ *n.* city in Indonesia, on Sumatra. Pop. 1,686,000.
Me·del·lín /medəyeén/ *n.* city in NW Colombia. Pop. 1,621,400.
Me·di·na /mədeénə/ *n.* city in W Saudi Arabia. Pop. 290,000.
Med·i·ter·ra·ne·an /meditəráyneeən/ **Sea** *adj.* sea with coastlines along Europe, Asia, and Africa.
Mek·nès /meknés/ *n.* city in NE Morocco. Pop. 401,000.
Me·kong /máykáwng/ **Riv·er** *n.* river in SE Asia, flowing 2,600 mi. from S China to the South China Sea.
Mel·a·ne·sia /melənéezhə, –shə/ *n.* island region in the Pacific, NE of Australia.
Mel·bourne /mélbərn, –bawrn/ *n.* port city and capital of Victoria, Australia. Pop. 3,218,100.
Mem·phis /mémfis/ *n.* city in SW Tennessee. Pop. 610,337.
Mé·ri·da /méridə/ *n.* capital of Yucatán, Mexico, in the NW part. Pop. 523,400.
Mer·sin /merseén/ *n.* port city in S Turkey. Pop. 523,000.
Me·sa /máysə/ *n.* city in central Arizona. Pop. 288,091.
Me·shed /məshéd/ *n.* city in NE Iran. Pop. 1,759,200.
Mes·o·po·ta·mi·a /mesəpətáymeeə/ *n.* region in SW Asia, between the Tigris and Euphrates rivers; part of present-day Iraq.
Mes·quite /məskeét/ *n.* city in NE Texas. Pop. 101,484.
Mes·si·na /məseénə/ *n.* port city in NE Sicily. Pop. 233,800.
Met·air·ie /métəree/ *n.* city in SE Louisiana. Pop. 149,428.
Metz /mets/ *n.* city in NE France. Pop. 123,900.
Mex·i·cal·i /meksikálee/ *n.* capital of Baja California, Mexico, in the NE part. Pop. 438,400.
Mex·i·co /méksikō/ *n.* country in S North America. Pop. 95,772,000. Capital: Mexico City. ▫▫ **Mex'i·can** *n. & adj.*
Mex·i·co, Gulf of *n.* arm of the Atlantic, S of the U.S. and E of Mexico.
Mex·i·co Cit·y *n.* capital of Mexico, in the central part. Pop. 9,815,800.
Mi·am·i /mī-ámee/ *n.* city in SE Florida. Pop. 358,548.
Mi·am·i Beach *n.* city in SE Florida. Pop. 92,639.
Mich·i·gan /míshigən/ *n.* peninsular state in N central U.S. Pop. 9,295,297. Capital: Lansing. Abbr. **MI; Mich.** ▫▫ **Mich·i·gan·der** /mishigándər/, **Mich'i·gan·ite** /–gənīt/ *n.*
Mich·i·gan, Lake *n.* one of the Great Lakes, between Wisconsin and the lower peninsula of Michigan.
Mi·cho·a·cán /meéchō-aakaán/ *n.* state in SW Mexico. Pop. 3,548,200. Capital: Morelia.
Mi·cro·ne·sia /mīkrənéezhə, –shə/ *n.* **1** region of Pacific islands E of the Philippines and N of the equator. **2** (official name **Federated States of Micronesia**) federation of islands in the S Pacific. Pop. 125,000. Capital: Palikir.

Mid·dle East *n.* (also **Near East**) region of SW Asia and N Africa, roughly from Afghanistan to Libya.
Mid·land /mídlənd/ *n.* city in W Texas. Pop. 89,443.
Mid·west /mídwést/ *n.* (also called **Mid'dle West**) region of N central U.S., from the Great Plains to the Allegheny Mountains.
Mi·lan /milán, –laán/ *n.* city in N Italy. Pop. 1,334,200. ▫▫ **Mil·an·ese** /miləneéz/ *n. & adj.*
Mil·wau·kee /milwáwkee/ *n.* city in SE Wisconsin. Pop. 628,088.
Min·ne·ap·o·lis /minee-ápələs/ *n.* city in E Minnesota. Pop. 368,383.
Min·ne·so·ta /minəsṓtə/ *n.* state in N central U.S. Pop. 4,375,099. Capital: St. Paul. Abbr. **Minn.**; **MN** ▫▫ **Min·ne·so'tan** *n. & adj.*
Minsk /minsk/ *n.* capital of Belarus. Pop. 1,700,600.
Mis·sis·sau·ga /misisáwgə/ *n.* city in Ontario, Canada. Pop. 463,400.
Mis·sis·sip·pi /misisípee/ *n.* state in S U.S. Pop. 2,573,216. Capital: Jackson. Abbr. **Miss.**; **MS** ▫▫ **Mis·sis·sip'pi·an** *n. & adj.*
Mis·sis·sip·pi Riv·er *n.* river in central U.S., flowing 2,470 mi. from Minnesota to the Gulf of Mexico; largest river in U.S.
Mis·sour·i /mizŏŏree, –ə/ *n.* state in central U.S. Pop. 5,117,073. Capital: Jefferson City. Abbr. **MO**; **Mo.** ▫▫ **Mis·sour'i·an** *n. & adj.*
Mis·sour·i Riv·er *n.* river in central U.S., flowing 2,700 mi. from Montana to the Mississippi River near St. Louis, Missouri.
Mo·bile /mōbeél, mṓbeel/ *n.* port city in SW Alabama. Pop. 196,278.
Mo·bile /mōbeél/ **Bay** *n.* arm of the Gulf of Mexico, S of Alabama.
Mo·de·na /máwd'nə/ *n.* city in N Italy. Pop. 176,600.
Mo·des·to /mədéstō/ *n.* city in central California. Pop. 164,730.
Mo·ga·di·shu /mōgədíshōō, –deéshōō/ *n.* port city and capital of Somalia. Pop. 900,000.
Mo·ja·ve /məhaávee, mō–/ **Des·ert** *n.* arid basin in SE California.
Mol·do·va /məldṓvə/ *n.* (formerly **Mol·da'vi·an** /mawldáyvee-ən/ **Soviet Socialist Republic**) republic in SE Europe; formerly part of the USSR. Pop. 4,464,000. Capital: Kishinev.
Mo·lo·kai /maaləkí, mō–/ *n.* island in central Hawaii.
Mo·luc·cas /məlúkəz/ *n.* (also called **Spice Is'lands**) island group in the S Pacific, in the Malay Archipelago, between New Guinea and Sulawesi.
Mom·ba·sa /maambaásə/ *n.* port city in SE Kenya. Pop. 600,000.
Mon·a·co /maánəkō/ *n.* principality on the Mediterranean Sea, near Nice, France. Pop. 32,300. Capital: Monaco. ▫▫ **Mon'a·can, Mon·e·gasque'** *n. & adj.*
Mön·chen·glad·bach /mönkhən-glaátbaakh/ *n.* city in W Germany. Pop. 266,100.
Mon·go·li·a /maan-gṓleeə, maang–/ *n.* republic in E central Asia. Pop. 2,497,000. Capital: Ulan Bator. ▫▫ **Mon·go'li·an** *n.*
Mon·ro·vi·a /mənrṓveeə/ *n.* port city and capital of Liberia. Pop. 421,100.
Mon·tan·a /maantánə/ *n.* state in NW U.S. Pop. 799,065. Capital: Helena. Abbr. **Mont.**; **MT.** ▫▫ **Mon·tan'an** *n. & adj.*
Mon·te·ne·gro /mäntəneégrō, –negrō/ *n.* republic in SE Europe; formerly part of Yugoslavia. Pop. 635,000. Capital: Podgorica. ▫▫ **Mon·te·ne'gran** *n. & adj.*
Mon·ter·rey /maantəráy/ *n.* capital of Nuevo León, Mexico, in the W part. Pop. 1,069,000.
Mon·te·vi·de·o /maantəvidáyō/ *n.* port city and capital of Uruguay. Pop. 1,378,700.
Mont·gom·er·y /məntgúməree, maant–, –gúmree/ capital of Alabama, in the E central part. Pop. 187,106.
Mont·pel·ier 1 (/maantpeélyər/) *n.* capital of Vermont, in the N central part. Pop. 8,247. **2** (/mawNpelyáy/) *n.* city in S France. Pop. 210,900.
Mont·re·al /maantree-áwl/ *n.* city in S Quebec, Canada. Pop. 1,017,700.
Mont·ser·rat /montsəraát/ *n.* island in the E West Indies; dependent territory of the United Kingdom. Pop. 13,000. Capital: Plymouth.
Mo·re·lia /məráylyə/ *n.* capital of Michoacán, Mexico, in the N part. Pop. 428,500.
Mo·re·los /məráyləs/ *n.* state in S central Mexico. Pop. 1,195,100. Capital: Cuernavaca.
Mo·re·no /məreénō/ **Val·ley** *n.* city in SW California. Pop. 118,779.
Mo·roc·co /məraákō/ *n.* kingdom in NW Africa. Pop. 29,779,000. Capital: Rabat. ▫▫ **Mo·roc'can** /–kən/ *n. & adj.*
Mo·rón /mawrṓn/ *n.* city in E Argentina. Pop. 641,500.
Mo·ro·ni /mawrṓnee/ *n.* capital of Comoros, on Grande Comore Island. Pop. 30,000.
Mos·cow /maáskow, –kō/ *n.* capital of Russia, in the W part; former capital of the USSR. Pop. 8,717,000.
Mo·sul /mōsŏŏl/ *n.* city in W Iraq. Pop. 664,200.
Mo·zam·bique /mōzambeék/ *n.* republic in SE Africa. Pop. 17,878,000. Capital: Maputo. ▫▫ **Mo·zam·bi'can** *n. & adj.*
Mul·tan /mŏŏltaán/ *n.* city in central Pakistan. Pop. 730,100.
Mu·nich /myŏŏnik, –nikh/ *n.* city in SW Germany. Pop. 1,244,700.
Mün·ster /mýnstər, mún–/ *n.* city in NW Germany. Pop. 264,900.
Mur·cia /múrshə, –sheeə/ *n.* city in SE Spain. Pop. 341,500.
Mur·mansk /mŏŏrmánsk/ *n.* port city in NW Russia. Pop. 407,000.
Mus·cat /múskaat, –kət/ *n.* port city and capital of Oman. Pop. 52,000.
My·an·mar /myaánmaar/ *n.* see BURMA.
My·sore /mīsáwr/ *n.* city in S India. Pop. 480,700.
Myu·ko·la·yiv /myōōkəlíf/ *n.* (formerly **Nikolayev**) city in Ukraine. Pop. 508,000.
Na·ga·sa·ki /naagəsaákee/ *n.* port city in Japan, on Kyushu. Pop. 438,700.
Na·go·ya /nəgóyə, naágəyaa/ *n.* city in Japan, on Honshu. Pop. 2,152,300.
Nag·pur /naágpŏŏr/ *n.* city in central India. Pop. 1,624,800.
Nai·ro·bi /nīrṓbee/ *n.* capital of Kenya, in the S central part. Pop. 2,000,000.
Na·mib·i·a /nəmíbeeə/ *n.* republic in SW Africa. Pop. 1,677,000. Capital: Windhoek. ▫▫ **Na·mib'i·an** *n. & adj.*
Nam·p'o /námpṓ/ *n.* city in SW North Korea. Pop. 370,000.
Nam·pu·la /nampŏŏlə/ *n.* city in E Mozambique. Pop. 250,500.
Nan·chang /naánchaáng/ *n.* city in SE China. Pop. 1,350,000.
Nan·cy /naaNseé, nánsee/ *n.* city in NE France. Pop. 102,400.
Nan·jing /naánjíng/ *n.* (formerly **Nan·king**) port city in E China. Pop. 2,500,000.
Nantes /naaNt/ *n.* port city in W France. Pop. 252,000.
Nan·tuck·et /nantúkit/ *n.* island in Massachusetts, S of Cape Cod.
Na·ples /náypəlz/ *n.* (Italian name **Na'po·li**) port city in SW Italy. Pop. 1,061,600.
Nash·u·a /náshōōə/ *n.* city in S New Hampshire. Pop. 79,662.
Nash·ville /náshvil, –vəl/ *n.* capital of Tennessee, in the N central part. Pop. 487,969.
Nas·sau /násaw/ *n.* capital of the Bahamas, on New Providence Island. Pop. 172,200.
Na·tion·al /náshənəl/ **Road** *n.* (also called **National Old Trail Road; Cumberland Road**) first federal road in U.S., extending from Cumberland, Maryland, W to St. Louis, Missouri.
Na·u·ru /naa-ŏŏrōō/ *n.* island republic in the Pacific, W of Kiribati. Pop. 10,000.
Na·ya·rit /nīəreét/ *n.* state in W Mexico. Pop. 824,600. Capital: Tepic.
N'Dja·me·na /enjəmáynə, –meénə/ *n.* capital of Chad, in the W part. Pop. 531,000.
Ndo·la /en-dṓlə/ *n.* city in N Zambia. Pop. 376,300.
Near East *n.* see MIDDLE EAST.
Ne·bras·ka /nəbráskə/ *n.* state in central U.S. Pop. 1,578,385. Capital: Lincoln. Abbr. **NE**; **Nebr.** ▫▫ **Ne·bras'kan** *n. & adj.*
Neg·ev /négev/ **Des·ert** *n.* arid region in S Israel.
Ne·pal /nipáwl, –pál/ *n.* constitutional monarchy in S Asia. Pop. 22,094,000. Capital: Kathmandu. ▫▫ **Ne·pa·lese** /nepəleéz, –leés/ *n. & adj.*
Neth·er·lands /néthərləndz/ *n.* (also called **Hol'land**) kingdom in W Europe. Capital: Amsterdam. Seat of government: The Hague. Pop. 15,568,000. ▫▫ **Neth'er·land·er** *n.*
Neth·er·lands An·til·les /antíleez/ *n.* island group in the West Indies, comprised of islands off the NW coast of Venezuela and islands among the NW Leeward Islands; territory of the Netherlands. Pop. 209,000. Capital: Willemstad.
Ne·tza·hual·có·yotl /netsaawaalkṓyōt'l/ *n.* city in central Mexico. Pop. 1,255,500.
Ne·vad·a /nəvádə, –vaádə/ *n.* state in W U.S. Pop. 1,201,833. Capital: Carson City. Abbr. **Nev.**; **NV** ▫▫ **Ne·vad'an, Ne·vad'i·an** /–deeən/ *n. & adj.*
New·ark /nōōərk, nyōō–/ *n.* city in N New Jersey. Pop. 275,221.
New Bed·ford /nōō bédfərd, nyōō/ *n.* city in SE Massachusetts. Pop. 99,922.
New Bruns·wick /brúnzwik/ *n.* province in SE Canada. Pop. 751,000. Capital: Fredericton.
New Cal·e·do·ni·a /kalidṓneea, –dṓnyə/ *n.* island group in the S Pacific; territory of France. Pop. 188,000. Capital: Nouméa.
New·cas·tle /nōōkasəl, nōōkás–, nyōō–, nyōō–/ *n.* port city in SE Australia. Pop. 427,700.
New·cas·tle up·on Tyne /tīn/ *n.* port city in N England. Pop. 283,600.
New Del·hi /délee/ *n.* capital of India, in the N central part. Pop. 301,300.
New Eng·land /ínggland/ *n.* region of the NE U.S.; includes Connecticut, Maine, Massachusetts, New Hampshire, Rhode Island, and Vermont.
New·found·land /nōōfənlánd, nōōfənlənd, nyōō–, nyōō–, –fənd–/ *n.* **1** island off the Atlantic coast of Canada. **2** province in E Canada, comprising Labrador and the island of Newfoundland. Pop. 581,000. Capital: St. John's. ▫▫ **New'found·land·er** *n.*
New Guin·ea /ginee/ *n.* island in the East Indies, N of Australia; comprises parts of Papua New Guinea and Indonesia.
New Hamp·shire /hámpshər/ *n.* state in NE U.S. Pop. 1,109,252. Capital: Concord. Abbr. **NH**; **N.H.**; **N. Hamp.** ▫▫ **New Hamp'shir·ite, New Hamp'shire·man** /–mən/ *n.*
New Ha·ven /háyvən/ *n.* city in S Connecticut. Pop. 130,474.
New Jer·sey /júrzee/ *n.* state in E U.S. Pop. 7,730,188. Capital: Trenton. Abbr. **NJ**; **N.J.** ▫▫ **New Jer'sey·ite, New Jer'sey·an** *n.*
New Mex·i·co /méksikō/ *n.* state in SW U.S. Pop. 1,515,069. Capital: Santa Fe. Abbr. **NM**; **N. Mex.** ▫▫ **New Mex'i·can** *n. & adj.*
New Or·le·ans /áwrleeənz, áwrlənz, awrleénz/ *n.* port city in SE Louisiana. Pop. 496,938. ▫▫ **New Or·lea'ni·an** /awrlíneeən/ *n.*

New·port News /nóopawrt nóoz, –pərt, nyóo–/ *n.* city in SE Virginia. Pop. 170,045.
New South Wales /waylz/ *n.* state in SE Australia. Pop. 5,426,200. Capital: Sydney.
New York /yáwrk/ *n.* **1** state in NE U.S. Pop. 17,990,455. Capital: Albany. Abbr. **NY; N.Y. 2** (also **New York Cit'y**) city in SE New York. Pop. 7,322,564. Abbr. **NYC.** ▫▫ **New York'er** *n.*
New Zea·land /zéeland/ *n.* island country in the S Pacific, SE of Australia. Pop. 3,548,000. Capital: Wellington. ▫▫ **New Zea'land·er** *n.*
Ni·ag·a·ra /nī-ágrə, ; n-ágərə/ **Falls** *n.* falls of the Niagara River, along the U.S.-Canada border.
Nia·mey /nee-áamay/ *n.* capital of Niger, in the SW part. Pop. 391,900.
Nic·a·ra·gua /nikəráagwə/ *n.* republic in central Central America. Pop. 4,272,000. Capital: Managua. ▫▫ **Nic·a·ra'guan** *n. & adj.*
Nice /nees/ *n.* port city in SE France. Pop. 345,700.
Nic·o·si·a /nikəsée ə/ *n.* capital of Cyprus, in the central part. Pop. 186,400.
Ni·ger /nījər, neezhér/ *n.* republic in NW Africa. Pop. 9,113,000. Capital: Niamey. ▫▫ **Ni·ge·ri·en** /nījéereeən/ *n. & adj.*
Ni·ge·ri·a /nījéereeə/ *n.* republic in W Africa. Pop. 103,912,000. Capital: Abuja. ▫▫ **Ni·ge'ri·an** *n. & adj.*
Ni·ger /nījər/ **Riv·er** *n.* river in W Africa, flowing 2,600 mi. from S Guinea to the Gulf of Guinea.
Ni·ko·la·yev /nikəláayəf/ *n.* see MYUKOLAYIV.
Nile /nīl/ **Riv·er** *n.* river in E Africa, flowing 3,470 mi. from Lake Victoria to the Mediterranean Sea; longest river in the world.
Nîmes /neem/ *n.* city in S France. Pop. 133,600.
Nome /nōm/ *n.* city in W Alaska. Pop. 3,500.
Nor·folk /náwrfək, –fawk/ *n.* city in SE Virginia. Pop. 261,229.
Nor·man /náwrmən/ *n.* city in central Oklahoma. Pop. 80,071.
North Af·ri·ca *n.* term for region of Africa N of the Sahara Desert.
North A·mer·i·ca *n.* continent in the W hemisphere, comprising Canada, the United States, Mexico, and Central America. ▫▫ **North A·mer'i·can** *n. & adj.*
North·amp·ton /nawrthámtən, –hámptən/ *n.* city in central England. Pop. 187,200.
North Car·o·li·na /karəlīnə/ *n.* state in SE U.S. Pop. 6,628,637. Capital: Raleigh. Abbr. **NC; N.C.; N. Car.** ▫▫ **North Car·o·lin'i·an** /–lineeən/ *n.*
North Da·ko·ta /dəkṓtə/ *n.* state in N central U.S. Pop. 638,800. Capital: Bismarck. Abbr. **ND; N.D.; N. Dak.** ▫▫ **North Da·ko'tan** /–kṓt'n/ *n.*
North·ern Ire·land /īrlənd/ *n.* the NE part of the island of Ireland; part of the United Kingdom. Pop. 1,583,000. Capital: Belfast. ¶ See note at GREAT BRITAIN.
North·ern Mar·i·an·a /maree-ánə, mer–/ **Is·lands** *n.* island group in the Pacific, N of Guam; U.S. possession. Pop. 52,000.
North Ko·re·a *n.* see KOREA.
North Pole N end of the earth's axis, in the Arctic Ocean.
North Sea *n.* arm of the Atlantic, between Britain and N Europe.
North·west Ter·ri·to·ries *n.* territory of Canada, in the NW part. Pop. 63,000. Capital: Yellowknife.
Nor·way /náwrway/ *n.* kingdom of N Europe. Pop. 4,384,000. Capital: Oslo.
Nor·we·gian /nawrwéejən/ **Sea** *n.* arm of the Arctic Ocean, between Greenland and Norway.
Nor·wich /náwrij, –ich/ *n.* city in E England. Pop. 128,100.
Not·ting·ham /náatingəm/ *n.* city in central England. Pop. 282,400.
Nou·ak·chott /nóo-áakshaat/ *n.* capital of Mauritania, in the SW part. Pop. 393,300.
No·va Sco·tia /nṓvə skṓshə/ *n.* province in E Canada. Pop. 923,000. Capital: Halifax. ▫▫ **No'va Sco'tian** *n. & adj.*
Nov·go·rod /náavgəraad/ *n.* city in W Russia. Pop. 233,000.
No·vo·si·birsk /nōvōsibéersk/ *n.* city in SW Russia. Pop. 1,369,000.
Nu·bi·an /nóobeeən, nyóo–/ Des·ert *n.* arid region in NE Sudan.
Nue·vo La·re·do /nóo-áyvō ləráydō/ *n.* city in E Mexico, across the Rio Grande from Laredo, Texas. Pop. 218,400.
Nue·vo Le·ón /lay-ṓn/ *n.* state in NE Mexico. Pop. 3,098,700. Capital: Monterrey.
Nu·ku·a·lo·fa /nóokooəláwfə, –lṓfə/ *n.* port city and capital of Tonga. Pop. 34,000.
Nu·rem·berg /nóorəmbərg/ *n.* (German name **Nürnberg** /nýrnbərk/) city in S Germany. Pop. 495,800.
Nya·sa /nī-ásə/, **Lake** *n.* (also called **Lake Malawi**) freshwater lake in SE Africa, E of Malawi.
O·a·hu /ō-áahoo/ *n.* Hawaiian island; includes Honolulu.
Oak·land /ṓklənd/ *n.* city in W California. Pop. 372,242.
Oa·xa·ca /waaháakə/ *n.* state in S Mexico. Pop. 3,019,600. Capital: Oaxaca.
O·ce·an·i·a /ōshee-áneeə/ *n.* collective term for Australia and the Pacific islands.
O·cean·side /ṓshənsīd/ *n.* city in SW California. Pop. 128,398.
O·den·se /ṓd'n-sə/ *n.* port city in S Denmark. Pop. 182,600.
O·der /ṓdər/ Riv·er *n.* river in central Europe, flowing 570 mi. from E Czech Republic to the Baltic Sea.
O·des·sa /ōdésə/ *n.* port city in S Ukraine. Pop. 1,046,000.
Og·bo·mo·sho /aagbəmṓshō/ *n.* city in SW Nigeria. Pop. 711,900.
O·hi·o /ōhī́ō/ *n.* state in E central U.S. Pop. 10,847,115. Capital: Columbus. Abbr. **O.; OH** ▫▫ **O·hi'o·an** *n. & adj.*
O·hi·o Riv·er *n.* river in E central U.S., flowing 980 mi. from W Pennsylvania into the Mississippi River at Cairo, Illinois.
O·ka·ya·ma /ōkəyáamə/ *n.* city in Japan, on Honshu. Pop. 616,100.
O·kee·cho·bee /ōkəchṓbee/, **Lake** *n.* lake in S Florida, in the N part of the Everglades.
O·ke·fe·no·kee /ōkeefənṓkee/ **Swamp** *n.* extensive wooded swamp area in S Georgia.
O·khotsk /əkháwtsk, ōkáatsk/, **Sea of** *n.* arm of the N Pacific, enclosed by the Kamchatka Peninsula and the Kuril Islands.
O·ki·na·wa /ōkináawə/ *n.* Japanese island between the East China Sea and the Pacific; largest of the Ryukyu Islands.
O·kla·ho·ma /ōkləhṓmə/ *n.* state in S central U.S. Pop. 3,145,585. Capital: Oklahoma City. Abbr. **OK; Okla.** ▫▫ **O·kla·ho'man** *n. & adj.*
O·kla·ho·ma Cit·y *n.* capital of Oklahoma, in the central part. Pop. 444,719.
Old Faith·ful /fáythfool/ *n.* regularly erupting geyser in Yellowstone National Park, Wyoming.
O·lym·pi·a /ōlímpeeə/ *n.* **1** capital of Washington, in the W part. Pop. 33,840. **2** *hist.* ancient Greek city; site of the ancient Olympic games.
O·lym·pus /ōlímpəs/ *n.* mountain in N Greece; home of the gods in Greek mythology.
O·ma·ha /ṓməhaa, –haw/ *n.* city in E Nebraska. Pop. 335,795.
O·man /ōmáan, ōmán/ *n.* independent sultanate on the SE Arabian Peninsula. Pop. 2,187,000. Capital: Muscat.
O·man, Gulf of *n.* arm of the Arabian Sea, at the entrance to the Persian Gulf.
Om·dur·man /aamdərmán/ *n.* city in NE central Sudan. Pop. 526,300.
Omsk /awmsk, aamsk/ *n.* city in SW Russia. Pop. 1,163,000.
On·tar·i·o /aantéreeō, –tár–/ *n.* province in S Canada. Pop. 10,746,000. Capital: Toronto. ▫▫ **On·tar'i·an** *n. & adj.*
On·tar·i·o, Lake *n.* easternmost and smallest of the Great Lakes, N of W New York.
O·por·to /ōpáwrtō/ *n.* (also **Pôr'to**) port city in NW Portugal. Pop. 310,600.
O·ran /ōráan/ *n.* port city in NW Algeria. Pop. 609,800.
Or·ange /áwrinj, ór–/ *n.* city in SW California. Pop. 110,658.
O·ran·je·stad /awráanyəstaad, –jəstad/ *n.* city in W Aruba. Pop. 20,000.
Or·e·gon /áwrigən, áar–, –gaan/ *n.* state in NW U.S. Pop. 2,842,321. Capital: Salem. Abbr. **OR; Ore.** ▫▫ **Or·e·go·ni·an** /awrigṓneeən, aar–/ *n. & adj.*
Or·e·gon Trail *n.* 19th-century pioneer route extending W 2,000 mi. from Independence, Missouri, to Oregon.
Ork·ney /áwrknee/ **Is·lands** *n.* island group in the N Atlantic, off the NE tip of Scotland.
Or·lan·do /awrlándō/ *n.* city in central Florida. Pop. 164,693.
Or·lé·ans /awrlayáan/ *n.* city in central France. Pop. 108,000.
O·sa·ka /ōsáakə/ *n.* city in Japan, on Honshu. Pop. 2,602,400.
Osh·kosh /áashkaash/ *n.* city in E Wisconsin. Pop. 55,006.
Os·lo /áazlō, áas–/ *n.* capital of Norway, in the SE part. Pop. 487,900.
O·stra·va /áwstrəvə/ *n.* city in E Czech Republic. Pop. 325,800.
Ot·ta·wa /áatəwə, –waa, –waw/ *n.* capital of Canada, in the SE part of Ontario. Pop. 314,000.
Oua·ga·dou·gou /waagədóogoo/ *n.* capital of Burkina Faso, in the central part. Pop. 690,000.
O·ver·land /ṓvərland, –lənd/ **Park** *n.* city in NE Kansas. Pop. 111,790.
O·vi·e·do /ōvee-áydō/ *n.* city in N Spain. Pop. 201,700.
Ox·ford /áaksfərd/ *n.* city in S England. Pop. 132,000.
Ox·nard /áaksnaard/ *n.* city in SW California. Pop. 142,216.
O·zark /ṓzaark/ **Moun·tains** *n.* mountain range in S central U.S.
Pa·chu·ca /pəchóokə/ *n.* capital of Hidalgo, Mexico, in the central part. Pop. 174,000.
Pa·cif·ic /pəsífik/ **O·cean** *n.* ocean separating Asia and Australia from the Americas. Area 70,000,000 sq. mi.
Pa·cif·ic Rim *n.* the Pacific coastal regions of Asia, Australia, North America, and South America.
Pa·dang /páadaang/ *n.* port city in Indonesia, on Sumatra. Pop. 477,300.
Pad·u·a /pájəwə/ *n.* city in NE Italy. Pop. 212,600.
Pa·go Pa·go /paanggō páanggō/ *n.* capital of American Samoa, on Tutuila Island. Pop. 3,500.
Paint·ed /páyntəd/ **Des·ert** *n.* arid region in N central Arizona featuring multicolored rock surfaces.
Pa·ki·stan /pákistan, paakistáan/ *n.* republic in central Asia. Pop. 129,276,000. Capital: Islamabad. ▫▫ **Pa·ki·stan'i** *n. & adj.*
Pa·lat·i·nate /pəlát'nayt/ *n.* district in Germany, W of the Rhine.
Pa·lem·bang /paaləmbáang/ *n.* port city in Indonesia, on Sumatra. Pop. 1,084,500.
Pa·ler·mo /pəlérmō/ *n.* port city in W Sicily. Pop. 694,700.
Pal·es·tine /páləstīn, –steen/ *n.* **1** *hist.* ancient country on the E coast of the Mediterranean Sea. **2** (also called **Ho'ly Land**) area controlled by British 1923–48; now divided among Egypt, Israel, and Jordan. ▫▫ **Pal·es·tin'i·an** /–stíneeən/ *n. & adj.*
Pal·ma /páalmə/ *n.* (also **Pal'ma de Ma·llor·ca** /day maayáwrkə, maalyáwrkə/) port city on island of Majorca, Spain. Pop. 296,754.

Pal·o Al·to /palō áltō/ *n.* city in W California. Pop. 55,900.
Pam·plo·na /pamplṓnə/ *n.* city in N Spain. Pop. 182,500.
Pan·a·ma /pánəmaa, –maw/ *n.* **1** republic in S Central America. Pop. 2,655,000. **2** (also **Pan'a·ma Cit'y**) port city and capital of Panama. Pop. 411,500. ▫▫ **Pa·na·ma·ni·an** /panəmáyneeən/ *n. & adj.*
Pan·a·ma Ca·nal *n.* canal through the Isthmus of Panama, connecting the Pacific and Atlantic oceans.
Pan·chi·ao /paánchee-ów/ *n.* city in N Taiwan. Pop. 539,100.
Pa·pe·e·te /paapayáytay, paapétee/ port city and capital of French Polynesia, on Tahiti. Pop. 23,600.
Pap·u·a New Guin·ea /paápōōə nōō gínee, nyōō/ *n.* republic in the W Pacific, comprising the E part of New Guinea and nearby islands. Pop. 4,395,000. Capital: Port Moresby.
Par·a·dise /párədīs/ *n.* city in N California. Pop. 124,682.
Par·a·guay /párəgwī, –gway/ *n.* republic in central South America. Pop. 5,504,000. Capital: Asunción. ▫▫ **Par·a·guay'an** *n. & adj.*
Par·a·mar·i·bo /parəmáribō/ *n.* port city and capital of Suriname. Pop. 77,600.
Par·is /páris, paaree/ *n.* port city and capital of France. Pop. 2,175,200. ▫▫ **Pa·ri·sian** /pəreezhən/ *n. & adj.*
Par·ma /paármə/ *n.* city in N Italy. Pop. 169,300.
Pas·a·de·na /pásədeenə/ *n.* city in S California. Pop. 131,591.
Pat·er·son /pátərsən/ *n.* city in N New Jersey. Pop. 140,891.
Pat·na /pútnə/ *n.* city in NE India. Pop. 917,200.
Pearl /pərl/ **Har·bor** *n.* inlet on the S coast of Oahu, Hawaii.
Pe·king /payking, pee–/ *n.* see BEIJING.
Penn·syl·va·nia /pensəlváynyə/ *n.* state in NE U.S. Pop. 11,881,643. Capital: Harrisburg. Abbr. **PA**; **Pa.**; **Penn.**; **Penna.** ▫▫ **Penn·syl·va'nian** *n. & adj.*
Pen·sa·co·la /pensəkṓlə/ *n.* city in NW Florida. Pop. 58,165.
Pe·o·ri·a /pee-áwreeə, –ṓr–/ *n.* city in NW central Illinois. Pop. 113,504.
Perm /perm/ *n.* city in W Russia. Pop. 1,032,000.
Per·nam·bu·co /pərnambóōkō/ see RECIFE.
Per·sia /púrzha/ *n.* **1** *hist.* ancient empire in W Asia. **2** official name (until 1935) of Iran.
Per·sian Gulf *n.* arm of the Arabian Sea, between the Arabian Peninsula and Iran.
Perth /pərth/ *n.* port city and capital of Western Australia, Australia. Pop. 809,000.
Pe·ru /pərōō/ *n.* republic in W South America. Pop. 24,523,000. Capital: Lima. ▫▫ **Pe·ru'vi·an** /–veeən/ *n. & adj.*
Pe·sha·war /pəshaáwər/ *n.* city in N Pakistan. Pop. 566,300.
Pet·ri·fied /pétrifid/ **For·est** *n.* part of the Painted Desert in E Arizona; contains prehistoric fossilized tree trunks.
Phil·a·del·phi·a /filədélfeeə/ *n.* city in SE Pennsylvania. Pop. 1,585,577.
Phil·ip·pines /filipeenz, filipeenz/ *n.* republic consisting of about 7,100 islands in the Pacific, SE of China. Pop. 63,609,000. Capital: Manila.
Phnom Penh /pənaam pén/ *n.* port city and capital of Cambodia. Pop. 920,000.
Phoe·nix /feeniks/ *n.* capital of Arizona, in the central part. Pop. 983,403.
Pierre /peer/ *n.* capital of South Dakota, in the central part. Pop. 12,906.
Pikes /pīks/ **Peak** *n.* mountain in the Rocky Mountains, in E central Colorado.
Pi·rae·us /pīreeəs, piráy–/ *n.* port city in E Greece. Pop. 169,600.
Pi·sa /peezə/ *n.* city in W Italy. Pop. 101,500.
Pitts·burgh /pítsbərg/ *n.* city in W Pennsylvania. Pop. 369,879.
Piu·ra /pyóōraa/ *n.* city in N Peru. Pop. 278,000.
Pla·no /pláynō/ *n.* city in NE Texas. Pop. 128,713.
Plo·es·ti /plaw-yéshtee, –yésht/ *n.* (also **Plo·ies'ti**) city in SE central Romania. Pop. 254,300.
Plym·outh /plíməth/ *n.* **1** port city in SW England. Pop. 255,800. **2** city in SE Massachusetts. Pop. 45,608.
Pod·go·ri·ca /páwdgawreetsaa/ *n.* capital of Montenegro, in the SE part. Pop. 54,500.
Point Bar·row /bárō/ *n.* the N tip of Alaska; the northernmost point of the U.S.
Pointe-Noire /pwaant nwaár, nəwaár/ *n.* port city in the SW Republic of the Congo. Pop. 576,200.
Po·land /pṓlənd/ *n.* republic in central Europe. Pop. 38,643,000. Capital: Warsaw.
Pol·y·ne·sia /paaləneezhə, –shə/ *n.* islands in the central Pacific, from New Zealand N to the Hawaiian Islands; a subdivision of Oceania. ▫▫ **Pol·y·ne'sian** *n. & adj.*
Po·mo·na /pəmṓnə/ *n.* city in S California. Pop. 131,723.
Pom·pa·no /paámpənō/ **Beach** *n.* city in SE Florida. Pop. 72,411.
Pon·ce /páwnsay/ *n.* port city in S Puerto Rico. Pop. 190,500.
Pont·char·train /paánchərtrayn, paanchərtráyn/, **Lake** *n.* shallow inlet of the Gulf of Mexico, N of New Orleans, Louisiana.
Poo·na /póōnə/ *n.* city in W India. Pop. 1,559,600.
Po·po·cat·e·petl /pōpəkaatépit'l/ *n.* volcanic peak in SW Mexico: 17,887 ft. high.
Port-au-Prince /pawrt ō prins, práNs/ *n.* port city and capital of Haiti. Pop. 846,200.
Port E·liz·a·beth /ilízəbəth/ *n.* port city in S South Africa. Pop. 303,400.
Port·land /páwrtlənd/ *n.* **1** city in NW Oregon. Pop. 437,319. **2** city in SW Maine. Pop. 64,358.
Port Lou·is /lóōis, lōō-ee/ *n.* port city and capital of Mauritius. Pop. 144,800.
Port Mores·by /máwrzbee/ *n.* port city and capital of Papua New Guinea. Pop. 193,200.
Pôr·to /páwrtōō/ *n.* see OPORTO.
Pôr·to A·le·gre /əlégrə/ *n.* port city in S Brazil. Pop. 1,237,200.
Port-of-Spain /spayn/ *n.* port city and capital of Trinidad and Tobago. Pop. 52,500.
Por·to-No·vo /pawrtō nṓvō/ *n.* port city and capital of Benin. Pop. 177,700.
Port Sa·id /saa-eed/ *n.* port city in NE Egypt. Pop. 460,000.
Ports·mouth /páwrtsməth/ *n.* **1** port city in SE Virginia. Pop. 103,907. **2** port city in S England. Pop. 189,100.
Por·tu·gal /páwrchəgəl/ *n.* republic in SW Europe, on the Iberian Peninsula. Pop. 9,865,000. Capital: Lisbon.
Port-Vi·la /pawrt veelə/ (also **Vi'la**) port city and capital of Vanuatu.
Po·to·mac /pətṓmik/ **Riv·er** *n.* river in E U.S., flowing 290 mi. from West Virginia to Chesapeake Bay.
Pots·dam /paátsdam/ *n.* city in NE Germany. Pop. 138,300.
Poz·nan /pṓznan, –nanyə/ *n.* city in W central Poland. Pop. 582,300.
Prague /praag/ *n.* capital of the Czech Republic, in the W central part. Pop. 1,213,300.
Prai·a /prīə/ *n.* capital of Cape Verde, on São Tiago Island. Pop. 61,600.
Prai·rie /práiree/ **Prov·in·ces** *n.* term for the Canadian provinces of Alberta, Manitoba, and Saskatchewan.
Pres·i·den·tial Range *n.* mountain range in N New Hampshire; part of the White Mountain range.
Pre·to·ri·a /pritáwreeə/ *n.* administrative capital of South Africa, in the N part. Pop. 525,600.
Prince Ed·ward /prins édwərd/ **Is·land** *n.* island province in E Canada, in the Gulf of St. Lawrence. Pop. 132,000. Capital: Charlottetown.
Prince Wil·liam /wílyəm/ **Sound** *n.* arm of the Gulf of Alaska, off the S coast of Alaska.
Prov·i·dence /praávədəns/ *n.* capital of Rhode Island, in the NE part. Pop. 160,728.
Pro·vo /prṓvō/ *n.* city in N central Utah. Pop. 86,835.
Pue·bla /pwéblaa/ *n.* state in E central Mexico. Pop. 4,126,100. Capital: Puebla.
Pueb·lo /pwéblō, pōō-éblō/ *n.* city in SE central Colorado. Pop. 98,640.
Puer·to Ri·co /páwrtə reekō, pwértō/ *n.* island in the E central West Indies; self-governing commonwealth of the U.S. Pop. 3,819,000. Capital: San Juan. ▫▫ **Puer'to Ri'can** /–kən/ *n. & adj.*
Puer·to Ri·co Trench *n.* Atlantic depression N of Puerto Rico; deepest part of the Atlantic: 28,374 ft.
Pu·get /pyóōjit/ **Sound** *n.* arm of the Pacific, in NW Washington.
Pu·san /póōsaán/ *n.* port city in SE South Korea. Pop. 3,813,800.
Pyong·yang /pyáwng-yaáng/ *n.* capital of North Korea, in the W part. Pop. 2,355,000.
Pyr·e·nees /peerəneez/ *n.* mountain range in SW Europe, between France and Spain.
Qa·tar /kaátər, gútər/ *n.* peninsular emirate on the Persian Gulf. Pop. 548,000. Capital: Doha. ▫▫ **Qa·tar'i** *n. & adj.*
Qing·dao /chingdów/ *n.* (also **Tsing'tao'**) port city in E China. Pop. 1,459,200.
Qom /kōm/ *n.* city in NW Iran; Islamic holy site. Pop. 681,300.
Que·bec /kwibék, kibék/ *n.* **1** principally French-speaking province in E Canada. Pop. 7,209,000. **2** (also **Que·bec' Cit'y**) capital of Quebec, in the S part. Pop. 645,600. ▫▫ **Que·beck'er, Que·bec·ois** /kaybekwaá/ *n.*
Queens /kweenz/ *n.* one of the five boroughs of New York City. Pop. 1,951,598.
Queens·land /kweenzlənd, –land/ *n.* state in NE Australia. Pop. 2,395,100. Capital: Brisbane.
Que·ré·ta·ro /kəráytərō/ *n.* state in central Mexico. Pop. 1,051,200. Capital: Querétaro.
Que·zon /kaysṓn/ **Cit·y** *n.* city in the Philippines, on Luzon. Pop. 1,676,600.
Quil·mes /keelmays/ *n.* city in E Argentina. Pop. 509,400.
Quin·ta·na Ro·o /keentaánə rṓ-ō/ *n.* state in E Mexico. Pop. 493,300. Capital: Chetumal.
Qui·to /keetō/ *n.* capital of Ecuador, in the N central part. Pop. 1,444,400.
Ra·bat /rəbaát/ *n.* port city and capital of Morocco. Pop. 518,600.
Ra·cine /rəseen, ray–/ *n.* city in SE Wisconsin. Pop. 84,298.
Rai·nier /rəneer, ray; n-/, **Mount** *n.* inactive volcano in W central Washington.
Ra·leigh /ráwlee, raálee/ *n.* capital of North Carolina, in the central part. Pop. 207,951.
Ran·cho Cu·ca·mon·ga /ránchō kóōkəmaánggə/ *n.* city in SW California. Pop. 101,409.
Ran·goon /ranggóōn/ *n.* (also **Yan'gon**) port city and capital of Burma. Pop. 3,851,000.

Rap·id /rápid/ **Cit·y** *n.* city in SW South Dakota. Pop. 54,523.
Ra·ven·na /rəvénə/ *n.* city in NE Italy. Pop. 133,600.
Ra·wal·pin·di /raawəlpíndee/ *n.* city in N Pakistan. Pop. 794,800.
Read·ing /réding/ *n.* **1** city in SE Pennsylvania. Pop. 78,380. **2** city in S England. Pop. 137,700.
Re·ci·fe /rəséefə/ *n.* (formerly **Pernambuco**) port city in NE Brazil. Pop. 1,297,000.
Red /red/ **Riv·er** *n.* **1** river in S central U.S., flowing 1,300 mi. from E New Mexico through Texas and into the Mississippi River in Louisiana. **2** (also called **Red Riv'er of the North**) river in N central U.S., flowing 530 mi. along the Minnesota–North Dakota border into Lake Winnipeg in Canada.
Red Sea *n.* arm of the Indian Ocean, between the Arabian Peninsula and Africa.
Re·gi·na /rijínə/ *n.* capital of Saskatchewan, Canada, in the S part. Pop. 179,200.
Reims /rens, reemz/ *n.* city in NE France. Pop. 185,200.
Rennes /ren/ *n.* city in NW France. Pop. 203,500.
Re·no /réenō/ *n.* city in W Nevada. Pop. 133,850.
Ré·u·nion /ree-yóonyən/ *n.* island in the Indian Ocean; overseas department of France. Pop. 679,000. Capital: Saint-Denis.
Rey·kja·vik /ráykyəvik/ *n.* port city and capital of Iceland. Pop. 104,300.
Rhine /rīn/ **Riv·er** *n.* river in W Europe, flowing 820 mi. from Switzerland to the North Sea.
Rhode /rōd/ **Is·land** *n.* (official name **Rhode Island and Providence Plantations**) state in NE U.S. Pop. 1,003,464. Capital: Providence. Abbr. **RI**; **R.I.** □□ **Rhode Is'land·er** *n.*
Rhodes /rōdz/ Greek island in the Aegean Sea, off the SW coast of Turkey.
Rho·de·sia /rōdéezhə, –shə/ *n.* former region of S Africa under British control; in 1965 became independent countries of Southern Rhodesia (now Zimbabwe) and Northern Rhodesia (now Zambia).
Rhone /rōn/ **Riv·er** *n.* river in W Europe, flowing 500 mi. from Switzerland to the Mediterranean Sea.
Rich·mond /ríchmənd/ *n.* capital of Virginia, in the E part. Pop. 203,056.
Ri·ga /réegə/ *n.* port city and capital of Latvia. Pop. 839,700.
Rim·i·ni /ríminee/ *n.* port city in N Italy. Pop. 130,000.
Ri·o de Ja·nei·ro /réeō day zhənérō/ port city in SE Brazil. Pop. 5,473,900.
Ri·o Gran·de /gránd, grándee/ *n.* river in North America, flowing 1,800 mi. from Colorado to the Gulf of Mexico; forms the border between Texas and Mexico.
Riv·er·side /rívərsīd/ *n.* city in SW California. Pop. 226,505.
Ri·yadh /reeaád, reeyaád/ *n.* capital of Saudi Arabia, in the E central part. Pop. 1,800,000.
Ro·a·noke /róənōk/ *n.* city in W Virginia. Pop. 96,397.
Roch·es·ter /raáchestər, –əstər/ *n.* city in W New York. Pop. 231,636.
Rock·ford /raákfərd/ *n.* city in N Illinois. Pop. 173,645.
Rock·y /raákee/ **Moun·tains** *n.* (also called **the Rock'ies**) mountain range in W North America, extending from New Mexico to Alaska.
Ro·ma·ni·a /rōmáyneeə, roo–/ *n.* (also **Ru·ma'ni·a**) republic in SE Europe. Pop. 21,657,000. Capital: Bucharest.
Rome /rōm/ *n.* capital of Italy, in the W central part. Pop. 2,687,900.
Ro·sa·ri·o /rōsaáreeō, –zaár–/ *n.* port city in E central Argentina. Pop. 875,700.
Ro·seau /rōzó/ *n.* port city and capital of Dominica. Pop. 15,900.
Ross /raws, raas/ **Sea** *n.* arm of the S Pacific, extending into Antarctica, S of New Zealand.
Ros·tock /raástaak, –tawk/ *n.* city in N Germany. Pop. 232,600.
Ro·stov /rəstáwf/ *n.* port city in SW Russia. Pop. 1,026,000.
Rot·ter·dam /raátərdam/ *n.* port city in the W Netherlands. Pop. 599,400.
Rou·en /roo–aán/ *n.* city in NW France. Pop. 105,500.
Ru·ma·ni·a /roomáyneeə/ *n.* var. of ROMANIA.
Rush·more /rúshmawr/, **Mount** *n.* peak in the Black Hills of South Dakota, with carving of the faces of four U.S. presidents: Washington, Jefferson, T. Roosevelt, and Lincoln.
Rus·sia /rúshə/ *n.* republic in E Europe and Asia; chief republic of the former USSR. Pop. 148,178,000. Capital: Moscow.
Rwan·da /roo–aándə/ *n.* republic in central Africa. Pop. 6,853,000. Capital: Kigali. □□ **Rwan'dan** *n. & adj.*
Sac·ra·men·to /sakrəméntō/ *n.* capital of California, in the N central part. Pop. 369,365.
Sa·har·a /səhárə, –haárə/ **Des·ert** *n.* extensive arid region in N Africa.
Sa·hel /səháyl, –héel/ *n.* arid region extending S from Senegal to Chad, S of the Sahara Desert.
Sai·gon /sīgaán, sígaan/ *n.* see HO CHI MINH CITY.
Saint Cath·a·rines /káthərinz, káthrinz/ *n.* city in S Ontario, Canada. Pop. 129,300.
St. Chris·to·pher /krístəfər/ **and Nevis** /néevis/ *n.* see ST. KITTS AND NEVIS.
Saint Geor·ge's /jórjəz/ *n.* capital of Grenada, on Grenada Island. Pop. 4,600.
St. Hel·ens, /hélənz/, **Mount** *n.* active volcano in the Cascade Mountains of Washington.
St. John's /jaánz/ *n.* **1** capital of Antigua and Barbuda, on NW Antigua. Pop. 21,500. **2** capital of Newfoundland, Canada, in the NE part. Pop. 171,900.
St. Jo·seph /jṓsəf, –zəf/ *n.* city in NW Missouri. Pop. 71,852.
St. Kitts /kits/ **and Ne·vis** /néevis/ *n.* (formerly **St. Christopher and Nevis**) two-island state in the E West Indies. Pop. 41,000. Capital: Basseterre.
St. Law·rence /láwrəns, laár–/ **Riv·er** *n.* river in SE Canada, flowing 760 mi. from Lake Ontario to the Atlantic.
St. Law·rence Sea·way *n.* international waterway for oceangoing ships, connecting the Great Lakes to the Atlantic.
St. Lou·is /lóois/ *n.* city in E Missouri. Pop. 396,685.
St. Lu·cia /lóoshə/ *n.* island country in the E West Indies. Pop. 158,000. Capital: Castries.
St. Paul /pawl/ *n.* capital of Minnesota, in the E part. Pop. 272,235.
St. Pe·ters·burg /péetərzbərg/ *n.* **1** (formerly **Leningrad** 1924–91) port city in NW Russia. Pop. 4,838,000. **2** city in W central Florida. Pop. 238,629.
St. Vin·cent /vínsənt/ **and the Gren·a·dines** /grénədeenz/ *n.* island state in the SE West Indies. Pop. 118,000. Capital: Kingstown.
Sa·kai /saákī/ *n.* port city in Japan, on Honshu. Pop. 808,100.
Sa·kha·lin /sakəléen/ **Is·land** *n.* island in SE Russia, N of Japan.
Sal·a·man·ca /saaləmaángkə/ *n.* city in W Spain. Pop. 167,400.
Sa·lem /sáyləm/ *n.* capital of Oregon, in the NW part. Pop. 107,786.
Sa·ler·no /səlérnō/ *n.* port city in W Italy. Pop. 146,500.
Sa·li·nas /səléenəs/ *n.* city in W California. Pop. 108,777.
Sa·lon·i·ka /səlaánikə/ *n.* see THESSALONIKE.
Sal·ti·llo /saaltéeō, –téeyō/ *n.* capital of Coahuila, Mexico, in the SW part. Pop. 420,900.
Salt Lake Cit·y *n.* capital of Utah, in the N central part. Pop. 159,936.
Sal·ton /sáwlt'n/ **Sea** *n.* shallow salt lake in S California; 240 ft. below sea level.
Sal·va·dor /sálvədawr, salvədáwr/ *n.* port city in E Brazil. Pop. 2,070,300.
Salz·burg /sáwlzbərg, saálz–, zaálts–/ *n.* city in central Austria. Pop. 144,000.
Sa·ma·ra /səmaárə/ *n.* (formerly **Kuibyshev** 1935–91) port city in E Russia. Pop. 1,239,000.
Sam·ar·kand /sámərkand/ *n.* city in E Uzbekistan. Pop. 368,000.
Sa·mo·a /səmṓə/ *n.* (also **Sa·mo'a Is'lands**) see AMERICAN SAMOA; WESTERN SAMOA.
Sa·naa /sanaá/ *n.* political capital of Yemen, in the W part. Pop. 503,600.
San An·dre·as /san andráyəs/ **Fault** *n.* earthquake zone extending S to N along the California coast.
San An·to·ni·o /san antṓneeō, əntṓ–/ *n.* city in S central Texas. Pop. 935,933.
San Ber·nar·di·no /san bərnədéenō, –nər–/ *n.* city in SE California. Pop. 164,164.
San Bue·na·ven·tu·ra /san bwenəventóorə, –ventyóo–/ *n.* (also **Ventura**) port city in SW California. Pop. 92,575.
San Di·e·go /san dee-áygō/ *n.* city in S California. Pop. 1,110,549.
San Fran·cis·co /san frənsískō, fran–/ *n.* port city in W California. Pop. 723,959. □□ **San Fran·cis'can** *n.*
San Fran·cis·co Bay *n.* inlet of the Pacific, in W central California.
San Joa·quin /san waakéen/ **Val·ley** *n.* rich agricultural area in the S part of California's Central Valley.
San Jo·sé /saan hōzáy/ *n.* capital of Costa Rica, in the central part. Pop. 299,500.
San Jo·se /san hōzáy, əzáy/ *n.* city in W California. Pop. 782,248.
San Juan /san waán, hwaán/ *n.* port city and capital of Puerto Rico. Pop. 438,100.
San Jus·to /saan hóostō/ *n.* city in E Argentina. Pop. 946,700.
San Lu·is Po·to·sí /saan looees pōtəsée/ *n.* state in central Mexico. Pop. 2,003,200. Capital: San Luis Potosí.
San Ma·ri·no /san məréenō/ *n.* republic in S Europe, surrounded by Italy; oldest independent country in Europe. Pop. 25,000. □□ **San Mar·i·nese'** /marənéez, –nées/ *n. & adj.*
San Ni·co·lás de los Gar·zas /saan neekōlaás de laws gaársaas/ *n.* city in NE Mexico. Pop. 436,600.
San Pe·dro Su·la /saan páydrō sóolaa/ *n.* city in NW Honduras. Pop. 368,500.
San Sal·va·dor /san sálvədawr/ *n.* capital of El Salvador, in the S central part. Pop. 422,600.
San·ta An·a /santə ánə/ *n.* city in SW California. Pop. 293,742.
San·ta Bar·ba·ra /baárbərə, –brə/ *n.* city in SW California. Pop. 85,571.
San·ta Cat·a·li·na /kat'léenə/ **Is·land** *n.* (also **Cat·a·li'na Island**) island in SW California.
San·ta Cla·ra /klárə, klérə/ *n.* city in W California. Pop. 93,613.
San·ta Cla·ri·ta /kləréetə/ *n.* city in S California. Pop. 110,642.
San·ta Cruz /saántaa króoz/ *n.* city in central Bolivia. Pop. 767,300.
San·ta Cruz de Te·ne·rife /day tenəréef, –rif, –réefay/ *n.* port city on Tenerife Island, Spain. Pop. 203,900.
San·ta Fe /santə fáy/ *n.* capital of New Mexico, in the N central part. Pop. 55,859.
San·ta Mon·i·ca /maánikə/ *n.* city in SW California. Pop. 86,905.
San·ta Ro·sa /rṓzə/ *n.* city in W California. Pop. 113,313.
San·ti·a·go /saantee–aágō, sant–/ *n.* capital of Chile, in the central part. Pop. 5,076,800.

San·ti·a·go de Cu·ba /saantyaágō day kóobaa, kyóo–/ *n.* port city in SE Cuba. Pop. 440,100.
San·to Do·min·go /sáantō dəmínggō/ *n.* port city and capital of the Dominican Republic. Pop. 1,600,000.
San·to To·mé de Gua·ya·na /tōmáy day gwaayaánə/ *n.* (also **Ciu·dad' Gua·ya'na** /seeōōdaad, seeyōō–/) city in NE Venezuela. Pop. 453,000.
São Pau·lo /sow pówlō/ *n.* city in SE Brazil. Pop. 9,393,800.
São To·mé /təmáy/ capital of São Tomé and Principe, on NE São Tomé Island. Pop. 35,000.
São To·mé and Prin·ci·pe /prínsəpə/ *n.* island republic in W Africa, in the Gulf of Guinea. Pop. 144,000. Capital: São Tomé.
Sap·po·ro /saapórō, –páwrō/ *n.* city in Japan, on Hokkaido. Pop. 1,757,000.
Sar·a·gos·sa /sarəgósə/ *n.* (also **Za·ra·go'za**) city in NE Spain. Pop. 606,600.
Sa·ra·je·vo /sarəyáyvō, saar–/ *n.* capital of Bosnia and Herzegovina, in the E central part. Pop. 526,000.
Sar·a·so·ta /sarəsótə/ *n.* city in W central Florida. Pop. 50,961.
Sar·din·i·a /saardíneeə/ *n.* Italian island in the Mediterranean Sea, W of Italy. Pop. 1,645,192. Capital: Cagliari.
Sas·katch·e·wan /səskáchəwən, sas–, –waan/ *n.* province in central Canada. Pop. 1,003,000. Capital: Regina.
Sas·ka·toon /saskətóon/ *n.* city in S central Saskatchewan, Canada. Pop. 186,100.
Sau·di A·ra·bi·a /sówdee əráybeeə, sáwdee/ *n.* kingdom in SW Asia, on the Arabian Peninsula. Pop. 19,409,000. Capital: Riyadh. ▫▫ **Sau'di, Sau·di A·ra'bi·an** *n. & adj.*
Sa·van·nah /səvánə/ *n.* city in E Georgia. Pop. 137,560.
Sa·van·nah Riv·er *n.* river in S U.S., flowing 300 mi. from NW South Carolina to the Atlantic; forms the boundary between South Carolina and Georgia.
Say·da /sídə/ see SIDON.
Scan·di·na·vi·a /skandináyveeə/ *n.* **1** region of N Europe; includes Denmark, Norway, Sweden, and sometimes Finland, Iceland, and the Faeroe Islands. **2** (also called **Scan·di·na'vi·an Pen·in'su·la**) peninsula in N Europe, bounded by the Norwegian, North, and Baltic seas and the Gulf of Bothnia, and comprising Norway and Sweden. ▫▫ **Scan·di·na'vi·an** *n. & adj.*
Scar·bor·ough /skaárbərō, –brə/ *n.* city in SE Ontario, Canada. Pop. 524,600.
Sche·nec·ta·dy /skənéktədee/ *n.* city in E New York. Pop. 65,566.
Schuyl·kill /skóolkil, skóokəl, skóolkəl/ **Riv·er** *n.* river in Pennsylvania, flowing 130 mi. from E central Pennsylvania into the Delaware River at Philadelphia.
Scil·ly /sílee/, **Isles of** *n.* island group in the Atlantic, off the SW coast of England.
Scot·land /skaátlənd/ *n.* division of the United Kingdom, N of England. Pop. 4,770,600. Capital: Edinburgh.
Scotts·dale /skaátsdayl/ *n.* city in SW central Arizona. Pop. 130,069.
Scran·ton /skránt'n/ *n.* city in NE Pennsylvania. Pop. 81,805.
Se·at·tle /seeát'l/ *n.* port city in W central Washington. Pop. 516,259.
Seine /sayn, sen/ **Riv·er** *n.* river in France, flowing 480 mi. from E France through Paris and into the English Channel.
Se·ma·rang /səmaáraang/ *n.* port city in Indonesia, on Java. Pop. 1,005,300.
Sen·dai /séndī/ *n.* city in Japan, on Honshu. Pop. 971,300.
Sen·e·gal /senəgáwl/ *n.* republic in W Africa. Pop. 9,093,000. Capital: Dakar. ▫▫ **Sen·e·gal·ese** /–eéz/ *n. & adj.*
Seoul /sōl/ *n.* capital of South Korea, in the NW part. Pop. 10,229,300.
Ser·bi·a /súrbeeə/ *n.* republic in SE Europe; formerly part of Yugoslavia. Pop. 9,979,000. Capital: Belgrade. ▫▫ **Serb** *n. & adj.*
Se·vas·to·pol /səvástəpōl, –pawl/ *n.* port city in S Ukraine. Pop. 365,000.
Se·ville /səvíl/ *n.* port city in SW Spain. Pop. 714,100.
Sey·chelles /sayshél, –shélz/ *n.* island republic in the Indian Ocean, NE of Madagascar. Pop. 78,000. Capital: Victoria.
Shang·hai /shanghí, shánghī/ *n.* port city in E China. Pop. 7,830,000.
Shef·field /shéfeeld/ *n.* city in N England. Pop. 530,100.
Shen·yang /shúnyaáng/ *n.* city in NE China. Pop. 4,540,000.
Shet·land /shétlənd/ **Is·lands** *n.* island group in the N Atlantic, off the NE coast of Scotland.
Shi·ko·ku /shikókoo/ *n.* island in Japan, S of Honshu.
Shi·raz /shiraáz/ *n.* city in SW Iran. Pop. 965,100.
Shreve·port /shreévpawrt, –pōrt/ *n.* city in NW Louisiana. Pop. 198,525.
Shub·ra al-Khay·mah /shóobraá al kīmaá, –maákh/ *n.* city in N Egypt. Pop. 834,000.
Si·am /sī-ám/ *n.* see THAILAND.
Si·an /sheéaán/ *n.* see XIAN.
Sic·i·ly /sísəlee/ *n.* Italian island in the Mediterranean Sea, off the SW tip of Italy. Pop. 4,910,000. Capital: Palermo.
Si·don /síd'n/ *n.* (also **Say'da**) port city in SW Lebanon. Pop. 100,000.
Si·er·ra Le·one /see-érə lee-ón/ *n.* republic in W Africa. Pop. 4,793,000. Capital: Freetown. ▫▫ **Si·er'ra Le·o'ne·an** /–neeən/ *n. & adj.*
Si·er·ra Ne·va·da /nəvádə, –vaádə/ **1** mountain range in E California. **2** mountain range in S Spain.
Sil·i·con Val·ley *n.* area in W California, from San Jose to Palo Alto.
Si·mi /simeé, seémee/ **Val·ley** *n.* city in SW California. Pop. 100,217.
Si·nai /sínī/ **Pen·in·su·la** peninsula in NE Egypt, bounded by the gulfs of Suez and Aqaba and the Red Sea.
Si·na·lo·a /seenəlóə/ *n.* state in NW Mexico. Pop. 2,204,100. Capital: Culiacán.
Sin·ga·pore /síngəpawr, sínggə–/ *n.* republic in SE Asia, at the S tip of the Malay Peninsula. Pop. 3,397,000. Capital: Singapore. ▫▫ **Sin·ga·po're·an** /–reeən/ *n.*
Sioux /soo/ **Cit·y** *n.* city in W Iowa. Pop. 80,505.
Sioux Falls *n.* city in SE South Dakota. Pop. 100,814.
Skop·je /skáwpye, –yay/ *n.* capital of Macedonia, in the N part. Pop. 541,300.
Skye /skī/ *n.* island in the Hebrides, off the NW coast of Scotland.
Slo·va·ki·a /sləvaákeeə, slō–/ *n.* (also called **Slo'vak Re·pub'lic**) republic in central Europe; formerly part of Czechoslovakia. Pop. 5,374,000. Capital: Bratislava.
Slo·ve·ni·a /sləveéneeə, slō–/ *n.* republic in S Europe; formerly part of Yugoslavia. Pop. 1,951,000. Capital: Ljubljana. ▫▫ **Slo·ve'ni·an** *n. & adj.*
Smo·lensk /sməlénsk/ *n.* city in W Russia. Pop. 355,000.
Smyr·na /smúrnə/ *n.* see IZMIR.
Snake /snayk/ **Riv·er** *n.* river in NW U.S., flowing 1,040 mi. from Yellowstone National Park, Wyoming, to the Columbia River in Washington.
So·ci·e·ty /səsíətee/ **Is·lands** *n.* island group in the S Pacific, forming part of French Polynesia.
So·fi·a /səfeéə, sō–/ *n.* capital of Bulgaria, in the W part. Pop. 1,116,800.
Sol·o·mon /saáləmən/ **Is·lands** *n.* island country, in the Pacific, E of New Guinea. Pop. 413,000. Capital: Honiara.
So·ma·li·a /səmaályə, –eeə/ *n.* republic in E Africa. Pop. 9,639,000. Capital: Mogadishu. ▫▫ **So·ma'li** *n.* **So·ma'li·an** *adj.*
So·no·ra /sənáwrə/ *n.* state in NW Mexico. Pop. 1,823,600. Capital: Hermosillo.
So·no·ran /sənáwrən/ **Des·ert** *n.* arid region in SW Arizona, SE California, and NW Mexico.
South Af·ri·ca *n.* republic in S Africa. Capitals: Bloemfontein; Cape Town; Pretoria. Pop. 41,743,000. ▫▫ **South' Af'ri·can** *n. & adj.*
South A·mer·i·ca *n.* continent in the W hemisphere, S of Panama. ▫▫ **South' A·mer'i·can** *n. & adj.*
South·amp·ton /sowthámtən, sowth-hámp–/ *n.* port city in S England. Pop. 211,700.
South Aus·tral·ia *n.* state in S central Australia. Pop. 1,285,000. Capital: Adelaide.
South Bend /bend/ *n.* city in N Indiana. Pop. 105,511.
South Car·o·li·na /karəlínə/ *n.* state in SE U.S. Pop. 3,486,703. Capital: Columbia. Abbr. **SC; S.C.; S. Car.** ▫▫ **South Car·o·lin·i·an** /–líneeən/ *n. & adj.*
South Chi·na Sea *n.* arm of the W Pacific, enclosed by Borneo and the Philippines.
South Da·ko·ta /dəkótə/ *n.* state in N central U.S. Pop. 696,004. Capital: Pierre. Abbr. **SD; S.D.; S. Dak.** ▫▫ **South' Da·ko'tan** *n. & adj.*
South Ko·re·a *n.* see KOREA.
South Pole *n.* S end of the earth's axis, on Antarctica.
So·vi·et /sóvee-ət/ **Un·ion** see UNION OF SOVIET SOCIALIST REPUBLICS.
So·we·to /səwétō, –wáytō/ *n.* group of townships in N South Africa. Pop. 596,600.
Spain /spayn/ *n.* monarchy in SW Europe, on the Iberian Peninsula. Pop. 39,181,000. Capital: Madrid.
Spice /spīs/ **Is·lands** *n.* see MOLUCCAS.
Spo·kane /spōkán/ *n.* city in E Washington. Pop. 177,196.
Spring·field /springfeeld/ *n.* **1** capital of Illinois, in the central part. Pop. 105,227. **2** city in SW Massachusetts. Pop. 156,983. **3** city in SW Missouri. Pop. 140,494.
Sri Lan·ka /sree laángkə, shree/ *n.* (formerly **Ceylon**) island republic in the Indian Ocean, off the S tip of India. Pop. 18,553,000. Capital: Colombo. ▫▫ **Sri Lank'an** *n. & adj.*
Staked /staykt/ **Plain** *n.* see LLANO ESTACADO.
Sta·lin·grad /staálingrad/ *n.* see VOLGOGRAD.
Stam·ford /stámfərd/ *n.* city in SW Connecticut. Pop. 108,056.
Stat·en /stát'n/ **Is·land** *n.* island in New York Bay; one of the five boroughs of New York City. Pop. 378,977.
Stav·ro·pol /staavráwpəl, –ró–/ *n.* city in S Russia. Pop. 342,000.
Stock·holm /staákhōlm, –hōm/ *n.* port city and capital of Sweden. Pop. 711,100.
Stock·ton /staáktən/ *n.* city in central California. Pop. 210,943.
Stoke-on-Trent /stōk aan trént/ *n.* city in W central England. Pop. 254,200.
Stras·bourg /straasbóorg, straásbərg/ *n.* city in NE France. Pop. 255,900.
Stutt·gart /shtóotgaart/ *n.* city in SW Germany. Pop. 588,500.
Su·cre /sóokray/ *n.* legislative capital of Bolivia, in the S part. Pop. 145,000.

Su·dan /soodán, –daán/ *n.* republic in NE Africa. Pop. 31,548,000. Capital: Khartoum.

Su·ez /soo-éz, sóoez/ *n.* port city in NE Egypt. Pop. 388,000.

Su·ez Ca·nal *n.* canal in NE Egypt, connecting the Mediterranean and Red seas.

Su·la·we·si /soolaawáysee/ *n.* (formerly **Celebes**) island in central Indonesia, in the Malay Archipelago.

Su·ma·tra /soomaátrə/ *n.* island in W Indonesia.

Sum·ga·it /soomgaa-éet/ *n.* city in E Azerbaijan. Pop. 236,200.

Sun·chon /sóoncháwn/ *n.* city in S South Korea. Pop. 136,000.

Sun·da /sə́ndə, sóondaa/ **Is·lands** *n.* island chain in the Malay Archipelago; includes Borneo, Java, Sumatra, and smaller islands.

Sun·ny·vale /sə́neevayl/ *n.* city in W California. Pop. 117,229.

Su·pe·ri·or /soopéereeər/, **Lake** *n.* northernmost and largest of the Great Lakes, N of Michigan.

Su·ra·ba·ya /soorəbíə/ *n.* port city in Indonesia, on Java. Pop. 2,421,000.

Su·rat /sóorət, sooraát/ *n.* port city in W India. Pop. 1,498,800.

Su·ri·na·me /soorinaám, –nám/ *n.* republic in N South America. Pop. 436,000. Capital: Paramaribo. □□ **Su·ri·na·mese** /soorənəméez, –mées/ *n. & adj.*

Su·va /sóovə/ *n.* port city and capital of Fiji. Pop. 69,700.

Su·won /sóowə́n/ *n.* city in NW South Korea. Pop. 755,500.

Sverd·lovsk /sferdláwfsk/ *n.* (also called **Ye·ka'te·rin·burg**) city in W Russia. Pop. 1,280,000.

Swan·sea /swaánzee/ *n.* port city in S Wales, United Kingdom. Pop. 189,300.

Swa·zi·land /swaázeeland/ *n.* kingdom in S Africa. Pop. 999,000. Capital: Mbabane.

Swe·den /swéed'n/ *n.* kingdom in N Europe. Pop. 8,901,000. Capital: Stockholm. □□ **Swede** /sweed/ *n.* **Swed'ish** *adj.*

Switz·er·land /swítsərlənd/ *n.* republic in central Europe. Pop. 6,779,000. Capital: Bern.

Syd·ney /sídnee/ *n.* port city and capital of New South Wales, Australia. Pop. 3,772,700.

Syr·a·cuse /séerəkyoos, sér–, –kyooz/ *n.* city in central New York. Pop. 163,860.

Syr·i·a /séereeə/ *n.* republic in SW Asia. Pop. 15,609,000. Capital: Damascus. □□ **Syr'i·an** *n. & adj.*

Szcze·cin /shchétseen/ *n.* port city in NW Poland. Pop. 419,600.

Ta·bas·co /təbáskō/ *n.* state in SE Mexico. Capital: Villahermosa. Pop. 1,501,700.

Ta·briz /təbréez/ *n.* city in NW Iran. Pop. 1,089,000.

Ta·co·ma /təkṓmə/ *n.* port city in W central Washington. Pop. 176,664.

Ta·dzhik·i·stan /taajéekistán, –staán/ *n.* republic in central Asia; formerly part of the USSR. Pop. 5,916,000. Capital: Dushanbe. □□ **Ta·dzhik'** *n.*

Tae·gu /tágóo/ *n.* city in SE South Korea. Pop. 2,449,100.

Tae·jon /tájáwn/ *n.* city in central South Korea. Pop. 1,272,100.

Ta·gus /táygəs/ **Riv·er** *n.* river on the Iberian Peninsula, flowing 570 mi. from E central Spain through Portugal and into the Atlantic.

Ta·hi·ti /təhéetee/ *n.* island in the S Pacific; one of the Society Islands. □□ **Ta·hi'tian** /–shən/ *n. & adj.*

Ta·hoe /taáhō/, **Lake** *n.* glacial lake in the Sierra Nevada range, on the California-Nevada border: 6,228 ft. above sea level.

Tai·chung /tíchə́ng/ *n.* city in W central Taiwan. Pop. 761,800.

Ta·if /taáif/ *n.* city in W Saudi Arabia. Pop. 300,000.

Tai·nan /tínaán/ *n.* city in SW Taiwan. Pop. 683,300.

Tai·pei /típáy, –báy/ *n.* capital of Taiwan, in the N part. Pop. 2,626,100.

Tai·wan /tíwaán/ *n.* (also called **For·mo'sa**) island nation in SE China. Pop. 21,466,000. Capital: Taipei. □□ **Tai·wan·ese** /tíwənéez/ *n. & adj.*

Tai·yuan /tíyoo-aán/ *n.* city in N China. Pop. 1,533,900.

Ta·lien /daálee-én/ see DALIAN.

Tal·la·has·see /taləhásee/ *n.* capital of Florida, in the NW part. Pop. 124,773.

Tal·linn /taályin, tál–, –lin/ *n.* port city and capital of Estonia. Pop. 434,800.

Ta·mau·li·pas /taamowléepaas/ *n.* state in NE Mexico. Pop. 2,249,600. Capital: Ciudad Victoria.

Tam·pa /támpə/ *n.* city in W central Florida. Pop. 280,015.

Tam·pi·co /tampéekō/ *n.* port city in E Mexico. Pop. 272,700.

Tan·gan·yi·ka /tangənyéekə, tanggən–/, **Lake** *n.* freshwater lake in central Africa, between Tanzania and Congo (formerly Zaire).

Tan·gier /tanjéer/ *n.* (also **Tan·giers** /–jéerz/) port city in N Morocco. Pop. 307,000.

Tang·shan /taángshaán/ *n.* city in NE China. Pop. 1,500,000.

Tan·za·ni·a /tanzənéeə/ *n.* republic in E Africa, formed by the merger of Tanganyika and Zanzibar. Pop. 29,058,000. Capital: Dar es Salaam. □□ **Tan·za·ni'an** *n. & adj.*

Tash·kent /tashként/ *n.* capital of Uzbekistan, in the E part. Pop. 2,106,000.

Tas·ma·ni·a /tazmáyneeə/ *n.* island state in SE Australia, S of Victoria. Pop. 452,800. Capital: Hobart.

Tbi·li·si /təbəléesee/ *n.* capital of the republic of Georgia, in the SE part. Pop. 1,279,000.

Te·gu·ci·gal·pa /təgoosigálpə, –gaál–/ *n.* capital of Honduras, in the S part. Pop. 608,100.

Teh·ran /tayrán, –raán, tayə–/ *n.* (also **Te·he·ran**) capital of Iran, in the NW central part. Pop. 6,042,600.

Tel A·viv-Jaf·fa /tel əveev jaáfə/ *n.* (also called **Tel A·viv'**) city in W central Israel. Pop. 321,700.

Tem·pe /témpee/ *n.* city in central Arizona. Pop. 141,865.

Ten·nes·see /tenəsée/ *n.* state in S central U.S. Pop. 4,877,185. Capital: Nashville. Abbr. **Tenn.**; **TN** □□ **Ten·nes·see'an** *n. & adj.*

Ten·nes·see Riv·er *n.* river in E central U.S., flowing 650 mi. from E Tennessee through Alabama and W Tennessee and Kentucky and into the Ohio River.

Te·pic /taypéek/ *n.* capital of Nayarit, Mexico, in the W part. Pop. 207,000.

Ter·re Haute /terə hṓt, hə́t/ *n.* city in W Indiana. Pop. 57,483.

Te·ton /téeton/ **Range** *n.* mountain range in W Wyoming, part of the Rocky Mountain range.

Tex·as /téksəs/ *n.* state in S U.S. Pop. 16,986,510. Capital: Austin. Abbr. **Tex.**; **TX.** □□ **Tex'an** *n. & adj.*

Thai·land /tílənd, –land/ *n.* (formerly **Siam**) kingdom in SE Asia. Pop. 58,851,000. Capital: Bangkok.

Thai·land, Gulf of arm of the South China Sea, S and W of Thailand.

Thames /temz/ **Riv·er** *n.* river in S England, flowing 210 mi. from Gloucestershire through London and into the North Sea.

Tha·na /taánə/ *n.* city in W India. Pop. 803,400.

Thes·sa·lo·ni·ke /thesəlawnéekee/ *n.* (also called **Salon'ika**) port city in NE Greece. Pop. 378,000.

Thim·phu /thimpóo/ *n.* official capital of Bhutan. Pop. 30,300.

Thou·sand /thówzənd/ **Is·lands** *n.* group of about 1,700 islands in the St. Lawrence River, between Ontario, Canada, and New York.

Thou·sand Oaks /ōks/ *n.* city in SW California. Pop. 104,352.

Tian·jin /tee-aánjín, tee-én–/ *n.* (formerly **Tientsin**) port city in NE China. Pop. 5,770,000.

Ti·bet /tibét/ *n.* autonomous region of W China. Capital: Lhasa.

Tien·tsin /tíntsín/ *n.* see TIANJIN.

Ti·er·ra del Fue·go /tee-érə del fwáygō/ *n.* island group at the S tip of South America; divided between Chile and Argentina.

Ti·gris /tígris/ **Riv·er** *n.* river in SW Asia, flowing 1,150 mi. from Turkey to the Euphrates River in Iraq.

Ti·jua·na /tihwaánə, teeəwaánə/ *n.* city in NW Mexico. Pop. 698,800.

Til·burg /tílbərg/ *n.* city in the S Netherlands. Pop. 164,100.

Ti·mi·soa·ra /teemishwaárə/ *n.* city in W Romania. Pop. 325,400.

Ti·ra·në /tiraánə/ *n.* capital of Albania, in the central part. Pop. 300,000.

Ti·ti·ca·ca /titeekaákə/, **Lake** *n.* lake on the Bolivia-Peru border: 12,508 ft. above sea level.

Tlax·ca·la /tlaaskaálə, təlaa–/ *n.* state in central Mexico. Pop. 761,300. Capital: Tlaxcala.

To·go /tṓgō/ *n.* country in W Africa. Pop. 4,571,000. Capital: Lomé.

To·ky·o /tṓkeeō/ *n.* capital of Japan, on Honshu. Pop. 7,966,200.

To·le·do /təléedō/ *n.* city in NW Ohio. Pop. 332,943.

To·lu·ca /təlóokə/ *n.* capital of Mexico, Mexico, in the S part. Pop. 827,300.

Ton·ga /taánggə, táwng–/ *n.* island kingdom in the S Pacific, NE of New Zealand. Pop. 106,000. Capital: Nukualofa. □□ **Ton'gan** *n. & adj.*

To·pe·ka /təpéekə/ *n.* capital of Kansas, in the NE part. Pop. 119,883.

To·ri·no /təréenō/ *n.* see TURIN.

To·ron·to /təraántō/ *n.* capital of Ontario, Canada, in the SE part. Pop. 3,893,000.

Tor·rance /táwrəns, taár–/ *n.* city in SW California. Pop. 133,107.

Tor·re·ón /tawray-ṓn/ *n.* city in N Mexico. Pop. 328,100.

Tou·lon /tooláwɴ/ *n.* port city in SE France. Pop. 170,200.

Tou·louse /toolóoz/ *n.* city in S France. Pop. 365,900.

Tours /toor/ *n.* city in NW central France. Pop. 133,400.

Trans·vaal /tranzvaál/ *n.* province in NE South Africa.

Tran·syl·va·nia /transilváyneeə/ *n.* a region and former province of central Romania.

Tren·ton /trént'n/ *n.* capital of New Jersey, in the W central part. Pop. 88,675.

Tri·este /tree-ést/ *n.* port city in NE Italy. Pop. 226,700.

Trin·i·dad /trínidad/ **and To·ba·go** /təbáygō/ *n.* island republic in the SE West Indies. Pop. 1,272,000. Capital: Port-of-Spain.

Trip·o·li /trípəlee/ *n.* **1** capital of Libya, in the NW part. Pop. 591,100. **2** port city in NW Lebanon. Pop. 240,000.

Trond·heim /traánhaym/ *n.* port city in central Norway. Pop. 143,700.

Troy /troy/ *n.* **1** *hist.* ancient city in NW Asia Minor (present-day Turkey). **2** city in E New York. Pop. 72,884. □□ **Tro·jan** /trṓjən/ *adj.*

Tru·ji·llo /troohéeyō/ *n.* port city in NW Peru. Pop. 509,300.

Tsing·tao /tsingtów/ *n.* see QINGDAO.

Tuc·son /tóosaan/ *n.* city in S central Arizona. Pop. 405,390.

Tul·sa /túlsə/ *n.* city in NE Oklahoma. Pop. 367,302.

Tu·nis /tóonis, tyóo–/ *n.* port city and capital of Tunisia. Pop. 674,100.

Tu·ni·sia /tooneézhə, tyoo–, –nízhə/ *n.* republic in N Africa. Pop. 9,020,000. Capital: Tunis. □□ **Tu·ni'sian** *n. & adj.*

Tu·rin /tŏŏrin, tŏŏrín, tyŏŏ–, tyŏŏ–/ *n.* (Italian name **To·ri'no**) city in NW Italy. Pop. 945,600.
Tur·key /tə́rkee/ *n.* republic in W Asia and SE Europe. Pop. 62,484,000. Capital: Ankara.
Turk·me·ni·stan /tərkménistan/ *n.* republic in S Asia; formerly part of the USSR. Pop. 4,149,000. Capital: Ashgabat. ◻◻ **Turk·men** *n.*
Turks /túrks/ **and Cai·cos** /kíkōs, káykōs/ **Is·lands** *n.* two island groups in the N Atlantic, SE of the Bahamas; dependent territory of the United Kingdom. Pop. 14,000. Capital: Grand Turk.
Tus·ca·loo·sa /təskəlóosə/ *n.* city in W Alabama. Pop. 77,759.
Tu·va·lu /tŏŏvaálŏŏ, tyŏŏ–, –vaár–/ *n.* island nation in the S Pacific, N of Fiji. Pop. 10,000. Capital: Funafuti.
Tux·tla /tŏŏstlaa/ *n.* (official name **Tux'tla Gu·ti·ér·rez** /gŏŏtyérays/) capital of Chiapas, Mexico, in the W central part. Pop. 289,600.
Tver /tver/ *n.* see KALININ.
U·fa /ŏŏfaá/ *n.* city in W Russia. Pop. 1,094,000.
U·gan·da /ŏŏgándə, yŏŏ–/ *n.* republic in E Africa. Pop. 20,158,000. Capital: Kampala. ◻◻ **U·gan'dan** *n. & adj.*
U·jung Pan·dang /ŏŏjŏŏng paadaáng/ *n.* port city in Indonesia, on Sulawesi. Pop. 913,200.
U·kraine /yŏŏkráyn/ *n.* republic in E Europe; formerly part of the USSR. Pop. 50,864,000. Capital: Kiev.
U·lan Ba·tor /ŏŏlaan baátawr/ *n.* (also **U·laan·baa'tar**) capital of Mongolia, in the N central part. Pop. 619,000.
Ulm /ŏŏlm/ *n.* city in S Germany. Pop. 115,100.
Ul·san /ŏŏlsaán/ *n.* city in SE South Korea. Pop. 967,400.
Un·ion of So·vi·et So·cial·ist Re·pub·lics *n.* (also called **So'vi·et Un'ion**) former union of fifteen constituent republics under Soviet direction, in E Europe and Asia; dissolved in 1991. Abbr. **USSR** ◻◻ **So'vi·et** *n. & adj.*
U·nit·ed Ar·ab E·mir·ates /árəb émərəts, –rayts/ *n.* independent federation of seven emirates on the Persian Gulf. Pop. 3,057,000. Capital: Abu Dhabi.
U·nit·ed King·dom *n.* monarchy in NW Europe; includes England, Northern Ireland, Scotland, and Wales. Pop. 58,490,000. Capital: London. Abbr. **UK; U.K.**
U·nit·ed States of A·mer·i·ca *n.* federal republic of 50 states: 49 states in North America and the island state of Hawaii in the N Pacific. Pop. 265,563,000. Capital: Washington, D.C. Abbr. **US; U.S.; USA; U.S.A.**
Upp·sa·la /ə́psəlaa, –saalə/ *n.* city in E Sweden. Pop. 183,500.
U·ral /yŏŏrəl/ **Moun·tains** *n.* mountain range in W Russia; considered part of the boundary between Europe and Asia.
Ur·fa /ŏŏrfaá/ *n.* city in SE Turkey. Pop. 357,900.
U·ru·guay /ŏŏrəgwī, yŏŏ–, –gway/ *n.* republic in SE South America. Pop. 3,239,000. Capital: Montevideo. ◻◻ **U·ru·guay'an** *n. & adj.*
Ü·rüm·qi /ŏŏrŏŏm-chee/ *n.* city in W China. Pop. 1,160,000.
USSR *abbr.* see UNION OF SOVIET SOCIALIST REPUBLICS.
U·tah /yŏŏtaa, –taw/ *n.* state in W U.S. Pop. 1,722,850. Capital: Salt Lake City. Abbr. **UT; Ut.** ◻◻ **U·tah·an** /yŏŏtaáən, –táwən, yŏŏtaan, –tawn/ *n. & adj.*
U·trecht /ŏŏtrekt, yŏŏ–/ *n.* city in the central Netherlands. Pop. 235,400.
Uz·bek·i·stan /ŏŏzbékistaan, –stan/ *n.* republic in S central Asia; formerly part of the USSR. Pop. 23,418,000. Capital:Tashkent. ◻◻ **Uz'bek** *n.*
Va·duz /faadŏŏts/ *n.* capital of Liechtenstein, in the W part. Pop. 5,100.
Va·len·ci·a /vaalénseeə, –thyaa/ *n.* **1** port city in E Spain. Pop. 752,900. **2** city in N Venezuela. Pop. 903,100.
Va·lla·do·lid /valədəlíd, –léed/ *n.* city in NW central Spain. Pop. 336,900.
Val·le·jo /vəláyō/ *n.* city in central California. Pop. 109,199.
Val·let·ta /vəlétə/ *n.* port city and capital of Malta. Pop. 9,100.
Val·pa·raí·so /valpərízō/ *n.* port city in central Chile. Pop. 282,200.
Van·cou·ver /vankŏŏvər/ *n.* **1** island in SW Canada, off the SW coast of British Columbia. **2** port city in S British Columbia. Pop. 471,800.
Va·nu·a·tu /vaánəwaátŏŏ, vaányə–/ *n.* island republic in the Pacific, NE of Australia. Pop. 178,000. Capital: Port-Vila.
Va·ra·na·si /vəraánəsee/ *n.* (formerly **Benares**) city in NE India. Pop. 929,300.
Var·na /vaárnə/ *n.* port city in E Bulgaria. Pop. 301,400.
Vat·i·can Cit·y /vátikən/ *n.* independent seat of the Roman Catholic Church, within the city of Rome, Italy.
Ve·ne·zia /vənétseeə/ *n.* see VENICE.
Ven·e·zue·la /venəzwáylə, –zwáylə/ *n.* republic in N South America. Pop. 21,983,000. Capital: Caracas. ◻◻ **Ven·e·zue'lan** *n. & adj.*
Ven·ice /vénis/ *n.* (Italian name **Ve·ne·zia** /vənétseeə/) port city in NE Italy. Pop. 306,400. ◻◻ **Ve·ne·tian** /néeshən/ *n. & adj.*
Ven·tu·ra /ventyŏŏrə, –chŏŏr–/ *n.* See SAN BUENAVENTURA.
Ve·ra·cruz /verəkróos, –króoz/ *n.* **1** state in E central Mexico. Pop. 6,228,200. Capital: Jalapa. **2** port city in E Veracruz, Mexico. Pop. 438,800.
Ver·mont /vərmaánt/ *n.* state in NE U.S. Pop. 562,758. Capital: Montpelier. Abbr. **VT; Vt.** ◻◻ **Ver·mont'er** *n.*
Ve·ro·na /vərṓnə/ *n.* city in N Italy. Pop. 256,800.
Ve·su·vi·us /vəsŏŏveeəs/ *n.* active volcano near Naples, Italy.
Vic·to·ri·a /viktáwreeə/ *n.* **1** capital of British Columbia, Canada, on Vancouver Island. Pop. 71,200. **2** state in SE Australia. Pop. 3,832,400. Capital: Melbourne. **3** port city and capital of Seychelles. Pop. 25,000.
Vic·to·ri·a, Lake *n.* freshwater lake in E central Africa; main source of the Nile River.
Vic·to·ri·a Falls *n.* waterfall in S Africa, on the Zambezi River: 420 ft. high.
Vi·en·na /vee-énə/ *n.* capital of Austria, in the NE part. Pop. 1,533,200. ◻◻ **Vi·en·nese** /veeənéez/ *n. & adj.*
Vien·tiane /vyentyaán/ *n.* capital of Laos, in the NW part. Pop. 178,200.
Vi·et·nam /vee-étnaám, veeət–, –nám/ *n.* republic in SE Asia, on the S China Sea. Pop. 73,977,000. Capital: Hanoi.
Vi·go /véegō/ *n.* port city in NW Spain. Pop. 288,600.
Vi·la /véelə/ *n.* see PORT-VILA.
Vi·lla·her·mo·sa /veeyə-ermṓsə, veelyə–/ *n.* capital of Tabasco, Mexico, in the S central part. Pop. 261,200.
Vil·ni·us /vílneeəs/ *n.* capital of Lithuania, in the SE part. Pop. 590,100.
Vir·gin·ia /vərjínyə/ *n.* state in E U.S. Pop. 6,187,358. Capital: Richmond. Abbr. **VA; Va.** ◻◻ **Vir·gin'ian** *n. & adj.*
Vir·gin·ia Beach *n.* city in SE Virginia. Pop. 393,069.
Vir·gin /vərjin/ **Is·lands of the U·nit·ed States** *n.* island group in the E West Indies; U.S. possession. Pop. 101,800. Capital: Charlotte Amalie.
Vi·sa·kha·pat·nam /visaakəpátnəm/ *n.* port city in E India. Pop. 752,000.
Vla·di·kav·kaz /vlaadəkaáfkaaz/ *n.* city in S Russia. Pop. 325,000.
Vla·di·vos·tok /vladivaástaak, –vəstaák/ *n.* port city in SE Russia. Pop. 632,000.
Vol·ga /vaálgə, váwl–, vṓl–/ **Riv·er** *n.* river in E Europe, flowing 2,320 mi. from W Russia to the Caspian Sea; longest river in Europe.
Vol·go·grad /vaálgəgrad, vṓl–/ *n.* (formerly **Stalingrad**) city in SW Russia. Pop. 1,003,000.
Vo·ro·shi·lov·grad /vərawshéeləfgraad/ *n.* see LUGANSK.
Wa·bash /wáwbash/ **Riv·er** *n.* river in central U.S., flowing 475 mi. from W Ohio through Indiana and into the Ohio River; forms S Indiana-Illinois border.
Wa·co /wáykō/ *n.* city in central Texas. Pop. 103,590.
Wales /waylz/ *n.* division of the United Kingdom, W of England. Capital: Cardiff. Pop. 2,719,200. ¶ See note at GREAT BRITAIN.
War·ren /wáwrən, waár–/ *n.* city in SE Michigan. Pop. 144,864.
War·saw /wáwrsaw/ *n.* capital of Poland, in the E central part. Pop. 1,640,700.
Wash·ing·ton /waáshingtən, wáwsh–/ *n.* state in NW U.S. Pop. 4,866,692. Capital: Olympia. Abbr. **WA; Wash.** ◻◻ **Wash·ing·ton·i·an** /–tṓneeən/ *n. & adj.*
Wash·ing·ton, D.C. *n.* capital of the U.S.; coextensive with the District of Columbia, between Virginia and Maryland. Pop. 606,900.
Wash·ing·ton, Mount *n.* mountain in the White Mountains in N New Hampshire; highest peak in NE U.S.: 6,288 ft.
Wa·ter·bur·y /wáwtərberee, waát–/ *n.* city in W Connecticut. Pop. 108,961.
Wed·dell /wədél, wéd'l/ **Sea** *n.* arm of the Atlantic, E of the Antarctic Peninsula.
Wel·ling·ton *n.* /wélingtən/ *n.* capital of New Zealand, on S North Island. Pop. 158,600.
West Bank *n.* disputed area in the Middle East, W of the Jordan River and the Dead Sea. Pop. 1,428,000.
West·ern Aus·tral·ia *n.* state in W Australia. Pop. 1,273,600. Capital: Perth.
West·ern Sa·mo·a /səmṓə/ *n.* island country in the S Pacific, comprising the W islands of Samoa. Pop. 214,000. Capital: Apia. See also AMERICAN SAMOA. ◻◻ **Sa·mo'an** *n. & adj.*
West Ger·man·y /júrmənee/ *n.* (also called **Federal Republic of Germany**) German state created in 1949, under parliamentary government; unified with East Germany in 1990.
West In·dies /índeez/ *n.* island group off the E coast of North and South America, between the Atlantic and the Caribbean Sea; includes the Greater Antilles, the Lesser Antilles, and the Bahamas.
West Palm /paam, paw(l)m/ **Beach** *n.* city in SE Florida. Pop. 67,643.
West Vir·gin·ia /vərjínyə/ *n.* state in E central U.S. Pop. 1,793,477. Capital: Charleston. Abbr. **WV; W. Va.** ◻◻ **West Vir·gin'ian** *n. & adj.*
Whee·ling /wéeling, hwée–/ *n.* city in N West Virginia. Pop. 148,641.
White·horse /wít-hawrs, hwít–/ *n.* capital of Yukon Territory, Canada, in the S part. Pop. 17,900.
White /wīt/ **Moun·tains** *n.* mountain range in N New Hampshire; part of the Appalachian range. Highest peak: Mount Washington.
Whit·ney /wítnee, hwit–/, **Mount** *n.* mountain in the Sierra Nevada range, in central California; highest peak in conterminous U.S.: 14,495 ft.
Whit·ti·er /wíteeər, hwítee–/ *n.* city in SW California. Pop. 77,671.
Wich·i·ta /wíchətaw, –taa/ *n.* city in S central Kansas. Pop. 304,011.
Wies·ba·den /véesbaad'n/ *n.* city in W Germany. Pop. 266,100.
Wight /wīt/, **Isle of** *n.* island in S England, in the English Channel.

Wil·ming·ton /wílmingtən/ *n.* city in N Delaware. Pop. 71,529.
Wind·hoek /vínthoŏk/ *n.* capital of Namibia, in the central part. Pop. 161,000.
Wind·sor /wínzər/ *n.* city in S Ontario, Canada. Pop. 191,400.
Wind·ward /wíndwərd/ **Is·lands** island group in the E West Indies, extending from Grenada N to Martinique.
Win·ni·peg /wínipeg/ *n.* capital of Manitoba, Canada, in the S part. Pop. 616,800.
Win·ston-Sa·lem /wínstən sáyləm/ *n.* city in N central North Carolina. Pop. 143,485.
Wis·con·sin /wiskaánsən/ *n.* state in N central U.S. Pop. 4,891,769. Capital: Madison. Abbr. **WI; Wis.** □□ **Wis·con'sin·ite** *n.*
Wol·ver·hamp·ton /woŏlvərhamptən, –vəramptən, –amtən/ *n.* city in W England. Pop. 245,100.
Worces·ter /woŏstər/ *n.* city in central Massachusetts. Pop. 169,759.
Wroc·law /vráwtslaaf/ *n.* city in SW Poland. Pop. 642,900.
Wu·han /woŏhaán/ *n.* city in E China. Pop. 3,750,000.
Wup·per·tal /voŏpərtaal/ *n.* city in W Germany. Pop. 383,800.
Wy·o·ming /wīṓming/ *n.* state in W U.S. Pop. 453,588. Capital: Cheyenne. Abbr. **WY; Wyo.** □□ **Wy·o'ming·ite** *n.*
Xi·an /sheéaán/ *n.* (also **Si·an**) city in central China. Pop. 2,760,000.
Ya·mous·sou·kro /yaamoŏsoŏkrō/ *n.* capital of Ivory Coast, in the S central part. Pop. 106,800.
Yan·gon /yaángoŏn/ *n.* see RANGOON.
Yang·tze /yangtseé, –seé/ **Riv·er** *n.* see CHANG.
Ya·oun·dé /yowndáy/ *n.* capital of Cameroon, in the S part. Pop. 800,000.
Ya·ren /yaárən/ *n.* district in SW Nauru; seat of government. Pop. 600.
Ye·ka·te·rin·burg /yikaátərinboŏrg/ *n.* see SVERDLOVSK.
Yel·low·knife /yélōnīf/ *n.* capital of Northwest Territories, Canada, in the S part. Pop. 15,200.
Yel·low /yélō/ **Riv·er** *n.* see HUANG RIVER.
Yel·low Sea *n.* arm of the N Pacific, between Korea and China.
Yel·low·stone /yéləstōn/ **Falls** *n.* waterfall of the Yellowstone River, in NW Wyoming.
Yem·en /yémən, yáymən/ *n.* republic on the SW Arabian Peninsula. Capitals: Aden; Sanaa. Pop. 13,483,000. □□ **Yem'en·ite, Yem'en·i** *n. & adj.*
Ye·re·van /yerəvaán/ *n.* capital of Armenia, in the W part. Pop. 1,226,000.
Ye·zo /yeézaw/ *n.* see HOKKAIDO.
Yo·ko·ha·ma /yōkəhaámə/ *n.* port city in Japan, on Honshu. Pop. 3,307,400.
Yo·ko·su·ka /yōkəsoŏkə/ *n.* port city in Japan, on Honshu. Pop. 432,200.
Yon·kers /yaángkərz/ *n.* city in SE New York. Pop. 188,082.
York /yawrk/ *n.* **1** city in NE England. Pop. 104,000. **2** city in SE Ontario, Canada. Pop. 140,500.
York·town /yáwrktown/ *n.* village in E Virginia; site of British surrender to Washington (1781).
Yo·sem·i·te /yōsémitee/ **Na·tion·al Park** *n.* scenic mountain region in E California.
Youngs·town /yúngstown/ *n.* city in NE Ohio. Pop. 95,732.
Yu·ca·tán /yoōkətán, –taán/ *n.* state in SE Mexico. Pop. 1,362,900. Capital: Mérida.
Yu·go·sla·vi·a /yoōgōslaáveeə/ *n.* federation (1918–92) in SE Europe that included Serbia, Croatia, Bosnia and Herzegovina, Montenegro, Macedonia, and Slovenia.
Yu·kon /yoŏkaan/ **Riv·er** *n.* river in NW North America, flowing 2,000 mi. from Yukon Territory, Canada, through Alaska and into the Bering Sea.
Yu·kon Ter·ri·to·ry *n.* territory in NW Canada, bordering Alaska. Pop. 32,000. Capital: Whitehorse.
Za·ca·te·cas /zaakətáykəs/ *n.* state in N central Mexico. Pop. 1,276,300. Capital: Zacatecas.
Za·greb /zaágreb/ *n.* capital of Croatia, in the N part. Pop. 867,700.
Za·ire /zaa-eér/ *n.* see CONGO 1.
Zam·be·zi /zambeézee/ **Riv·er** *n.* river in S Africa, flowing 1,650 mi. from NW Zambia to the Indian Ocean.
Zam·bi·a /zámbeeə/ *n.* republic in S central Africa. Pop. 9,159,000. Capital: Lusaka. □□ **Zam'bi·an** *n. & adj.*
Zan·zi·bar /zánzibaar/ *n.* island in the Indian Ocean, off the E coast of Tanzania; part of Tanzania.
Za·ra·go·za /saaraagáwsaa/ *n.* see SARAGOSSA.
Zhdan·ov /zhdaánəf/ *n.* see MARIUPOL.
Zim·bab·we /zimbaábway/ *n.* republic in S central Africa. Pop. 11,271,000. Capital: Harare.
Zom·ba /zaámbə/ *n.* legislative capital of Malawi, in the S part. Pop. 62,700.
Zu·rich /zoŏrik/ *n.* city in N Switzerland. Pop. 342,900.

Special Reference Appendices

PRESIDENTS OF THE UNITED STATES OF AMERICA

Name and life dates	Party (term in office)
1. George Washington 1732-99	Federalist (1789-97)
2. John Adams 1735-1826	Federalist (1797-1801)
3. Thomas Jefferson 1743-1826	Democratic-Republican (1801-09)
4. James Madison 1751-1836	Democratic-Republican (1809-17)
5. James Monroe 1758-1831	Democratic-Republican (1817-25)
6. John Quincy Adams 1767-1848	Independent (1825-29)
7 Andrew Jackson 1767-1845	Democrat (1829-37)
8. Martin Van Buren 1782-1862	Democrat (1837-41)
9. William H. Harrison 1773-1841	Whig (1841)
10. John Tyler 1790-1862	Whig, then Democrat (1841-45)
11. James K. Polk 1795-1849	Democrat (1845-49)
12. Zachary Taylor 1784-1850	Whig (1849-50)
13. Millard Fillmore 1800-74	Whig (1850-53)
14. Franklin Pierce 1804-69	Democrat (1853-57)
15. James Buchanan 1791-1868	Democrat (1857-61)
16. Abraham Lincoln 1809-65	Republican (1861-65)
17. Andrew Johnson 1808-75	Democrat (1865-69)
18. Ulysses S. Grant 1822-85	Republican (1869-77)
19. Rutherford B. Hayes 1822-93	Republican (1877-81)
20. James A. Garfield 1831-81	Republican (1881)
21. Chester A. Arthur 1830-86	Republican (1881-85)
22. Grover Cleveland 1837-1908	Democrat (1885-89)
23. Benjamin Harrison 1833-1901	Republican (1889-93)
24. Grover Cleveland (see above)	Democrat (1893-97)
25. William McKinley 1843-1901	Republican (1897-1901)
26. Theodore Roosevelt 1858-1919	Republican (1901-09)
27. William H. Taft 1857-1930	Republican (1909-13)
28. Woodrow Wilson 1856-1924	Democrat (1913-21)
29. Warren G. Harding 1865-1923	Republican (1921-23)
30. Calvin Coolidge 1872-1933	Republican (1923-29)
31. Herbert Hoover 1874-1964	Republican (1929-33)
32. Franklin D. Roosevelt 1882-1945	Democrat (1933-45)
33. Harry S Truman 1884-1972	Democrat (1945-53)
34. Dwight D. Eisenhower 1890-1969	Republican (1953-61)
35. John F. Kennedy 1917-63	Democrat (1961-63)
36. Lyndon B. Johnson 1908-73	Democrat (1963-69)
37. Richard M. Nixon 1913-94	Republican (1969-74)
38. Gerald R. Ford 1913-	Republican (1974-77)
39. James Earl Carter 1924-	Democrat (1977-81)
40. Ronald W. Reagan 1911-	Republican (1981-89)
41. George H.W. Bush 1924-	Republican (1989-93)
42. William J. Clinton 1946-	Democrat (1993-)

STATES OF THE UNITED STATES OF AMERICA

State	Traditional & Postal Abbreviations	Capital
Alabama	Ala.; AL	Montgomery
Alaska	Alas.; AK	Juneau
Arizona	Ariz.; AZ	Phoenix
Arkansas	Ark.; AR	Little Rock
California	Calif.; CA	Sacramento
Colorado	Col.; CO	Denver
Connecticut	Conn.; CT	Hartford
Delaware	Del.; DE	Dover
Florida	Fla.; FL	Tallahassee
Georgia	Ga.; GA	Atlanta
Hawaii	Haw.; HI	Honolulu
Idaho	Id.; ID	Boise
Illinois	Ill.; IL	Springfield
Indiana	Ind.; IN	Indianapolis
Iowa	Ia.; IA	Des Moines
Kansas	Kan.; KS	Topeka
Kentucky	Ky.; KY	Frankfort
Louisiana	La.; LA	Baton Rouge
Maine	Me.; ME	Augusta
Maryland	Md.; MD	Annapolis
Massachusetts	Mass.; MA	Boston
Michigan	Mich.; MI	Lansing
Minnesota	Minn.; MN	St. Paul
Mississippi	Miss.; MS	Jackson
Missouri	Mo.; MO	Jefferson City
Montana	Mont.; MT	Helena
Nebraska	Nebr.; NE	Lincoln
Nevada	Nev.; NV	Carson City
New Hampshire	N.H.; NH	Concord
New Jersey	N.J.; NJ	Trenton
New Mexico	N. Mex.; NM	Santa Fe
New York	N.Y.; NY	Albany
North Carolina	N.C.; NC	Raleigh
North Dakota	N. Dak.; ND	Bismarck
Ohio	O.; OH	Columbus
Oklahoma	Okla.; OK	Oklahoma City
Oregon	Ore.; OR	Salem
Pennsylvania	Pa.; PA	Harrisburg
Rhode Island	R.I.; RI	Providence
South Carolina	S.C.; SC	Columbia
South Dakota	S. Dak.; SD	Pierre
Tennessee	Tenn.; TN	Nashville
Texas	Tex.; TX	Austin
Utah	Ut.; UT	Salt Lake City
Vermont	Vt.; VT	Montpelier
Virginia	Va.; VA	Richmond
Washington	Wash.; WA	Olympia
West Virginia	W. Va.; WV	Charleston
Wisconsin	Wis.; WI	Madison
Wyoming	Wyo.; WY	Cheyenne

STANDARD WEIGHTS AND MEASURES WITH METRIC EQUIVALENTS

Linear Measure

1 inch	= 2.54 centimeters
1 foot = 12 inches	= 0.3048 meter
1 yard = 3 feet	= 0.9144 meter
= 36 inches	
1 (statute) mile = 1,760 yards	= 1.609 kilometers
= 5,280 feet	

Square Measure

1 sq. inch	= 6.45 sq. centimeters
1 sq. foot = 144 sq. inches	= 9.29 sq. decimeters
1 sq. yard = 9 sq. feet	= 0.836 sq. meter
1 acre = 4,840 sq. yards	= 0.405 hectare
1 sq. mile = 640 acres	= 259 hectares

Cubic Measure

1 cu. inch	= 16.4 cu. centimeters
1 cu. foot = 1,728 cu. inches	= 0.0283 cu. meter
1 cu. yard = 27 cu. feet	= 0.765 cu. meter

Capacity Measure

DRY MEASURE

1 pint = 33.60 cu. inches	= 0.550 liter
1 quart = 2 pints	= 1.101 liters
1 peck = 8 quarts	= 8.81 liters
1 bushel = 4 pecks	= 35.3 liters

LIQUID MEASURE

1 fluid ounce	= 29.573 milliliters
1 gill = 4 fluid ounces	= 118.294 milliliters
1 pint = 16 fluid ounces	= 0.473 liter
= 28.88 cu. inches	
1 quart = 2 pints	= 0.946 liter
1 gallon = 4 quarts	= 3.785 liters

Avoirdupois Weight

1 grain	= 0.065 gram
1 dram	= 1.772 grams
1 ounce = 16 drams	= 28.35 grams
1 pound = 16 ounces	= 0.4536 kilograms (0.45359237 exactly)
= 7,000 grains	
1 stone (British) = 14 pounds	= 6.35 kilograms
1 ton = 2,000 pounds	
1 hundredweight (US) = 100 pounds	
20 hundredweight (US) = 2,000 pounds	

CONVERSION FROM STANDARD TO METRIC MEASUREMENTS

Standard	Multiply By	To Get Metric
Length:		
inches	2.5	centimeters
feet	30	centimeters
yards	0.9	meters
miles	1.6	kilometers
Area:		
square inches	6.5	square centimeters
square feet	0.09	square meters
square yards	0.8	square meters
square miles	2.6	square kilometers
acres	0.4	hectares
Weight:		
ounces	28	grams
pounds	0.45	kilograms
short tons	0.9	metric tons
Volume:		
teaspoons	5	milliliters
tablespoons	15	milliliters
cubic inches	16	milliliters
fluid ounces	30	milliliters
cups	0.24	liters
pints	0.47	liters
quarts	0.95	liters
gallons	3.8	liters
cubic feet	0.03	cubic meters
cubic yards	0.76	cubic meters
Temperature:		
degrees Fahrenheit	subtract 32, then multiply by 5/9	degrees Celsius

METRIC WEIGHTS AND MEASURES WITH STANDARD EQUIVALENTS

Linear Measure	
1 millimeter (mm)	= 0.039 inch
1 centimeter (cm) = 10 millimeters	= 0.394 inch
1 decimeter (dm) = 10 centimeters	= 3.94 inches
1 meter (m) = 10 decimeters	= 1.094 yards
1 decameter = 10 meters	= 10.94 yards
1 hectometer = 100 meters	= 109.4 yards
1 kilometer (km) = 1,000 meters	= 0.6214 mile
Square Measure	
1 sq. centimeter	= 0.155 sq. inch
1 sq. meter = 10,000 sq. centimeters	= 1.196 sq. yards
1 are = 100 sq. meters	= 119.6 sq. yards
1 hectare = 100 ares	= 2.471 acres
1 sq. kilometer = 100 hectares	= 0.386 sq. mile
Cubic Measure	
1 cu. centimeter	= 0.061 cu. inch
1 cu. meter = 1,000,000 cu. centimeters	= 1.308 cu. yards
Capacity Measure	
1 milliliter (ml)	= 0.034 fluid ounce
1 centiliter (cl) = 10 milliliters	= 0.34 fluid ounce
1 deciliter (dl) = 10 centiliters	= 3.38 fluid ounces
1 liter (l) = 10 deciliters	= 1.06 quarts
1 decaliter = 10 liters	= 2.64 gallons
1 hectoliter = 100 liters	= 2.75 bushels
Weight	
1 milligram (mg)	= 0.015 grain
1 centigram = 10 milligrams	= 0.154 grain
1 decigram (dg) = 10 centigrams	= 1.543 grains
1 gram (g) = 10 decigrams	= 15.43 grains
1 decagram = 10 grams	= 5.64 drams
1 hectogram = 100 grams	= 3.527 ounces
1 kilogram (kg) = 1,000 grams	= 2.205 pounds
1 ton (metric ton) = 1,000 kilograms	= 0.984 (long) ton

CONVERSION FROM METRIC TO STANDARD MEASUREMENTS

Metric	Multiply By	To Get Standard
Length:		
inches	2.5	centimeters
feet	30	centimeters
yards	0.9	meters
miles	1.6	kilometers
Area:		
square inches	6.5	square centimeters
square feet	0.09	square meters
square yards	0.8	square meters
square miles	2.6	square kilometers
acres	0.4	hectares
Weight:		
ounces	28	grams
pounds	0.45	kilograms
short tons	0.9	metric tons
Volume:		
teaspoons	5	milliliters
tablespoons	15	milliliters
cubic inches	16	milliliters
fluid ounces	30	milliliters
cups	0.24	liters
pints	0.47	liters
quarts	0.95	liters
gallons	3.8	liters
cubic feet	0.03	cubic meters
cubic yards	0.76	cubic meters
Temperature:		
degrees Fahrenheit	subtract 32, then multiply by 5/9	degrees Celsius

CHEMICAL ELEMENTS

Element	Symbol	Atomic Number
actinium	Ac	89
aluminum	Al	13
americium	Am	95
antimony	Sb	51
argon	Ar	18
arsenic	As	33
astatine	At	85
barium	Ba	56
berkelium	Bk	97
beryllium	Be	4
bismuth	Bi	83
bohrium*	Ns	107
boron	B	5
bromine	Br	35
cadmium	Cd	48
calcium	Ca	20
californium	Cf	98
carbon	C	6
cerium	Ce	58
cesium	Cs	55
chlorine	Cl	17
chromium	Cr	24
cobalt	Co	27
copper	Cu	29
curium	Cm	96
dubnium*	Db	105
dysprosium	Dy	66
einsteinium	Es	99
erbium	Er	68
europium	Eu	63
fermium	Fm	100
fluorine	F	9
francium	Fr	87
gadolinium	Gd	64
gallium	Ga	31
germanium	Ge	32
gold	Au	79
hafnium	Hf	72
hassium*	Hs	108
helium	He	2
holmium	Ho	67
hydrogen	H	1
indium	In	49
iodine	I	53
iridium	Ir	77
iron	Fe	26
krypton	Kr	36
lanthanum	La	57
lawrencium	Lr	103
lead	Pb	82
lithium	Li	3
lutetium	Lu	71
magnesium	Mg	12
manganese	Mn	25
meitnerium*	Mt	109
mendelevium	Md	101
mercury	Hg	80
molybdenum	Mo	42
neodymium	Nd	60
neon	Ne	10
neptunium	Np	93
nickel	Ni	28
niobium	Nb	41
nitrogen	N	7
nobelium	No	102
osmium	Os	76
oxygen	O	8
palladium	Pd	46
phosphorus	P	15
platinum	Pt	78
plutonium	Pu	94
polonium	Po	84
potassium	K	19
praseodymium	Pr	59
promethium	Pm	61
protactinium	Pa	91
radium	Ra	88
radon	Rn	86
rhenium	Re	75
rhodium	Rh	45
rubidium	Rb	37
ruthenium	Ru	44
rutherfordium*	Rf	104
samarium	Sm	62
scandium	Sc	21
seaborgium*	Sg	106
selenium	Se	34
silicon	Si	14
silver	Ag	47
sodium	Na	11
strontium	Sr	38
sulfur	S	16
tantalum	Ta	73
technetium	Tc	43
tellurium	Te	52
terbium	Tb	65
thallium	Tl	81
thorium	Th	90
thulium	Tm	69
tin	Sn	50
titanium	Ti	22
tungsten (wolfram)	W	74
uranium	U	92
vanadium	V	23
xenon	Xe	54
ytterbium	Yb	70
yttrium	Y	39
zinc	Zn	30
zirconium	Zr	40

* Names formed systematically based on atomic numbers are preferred by the International Union of Pure and Applied Chemistry (IUPAC) for numbers from 104 onward. These names are formed on the numerical roots *nil* (= 0), *un* (= 1), *bi* (= 2), etc. (e.g., *unnilquadium* = 104, *unnilpentium* = 105, *unnilhexium* = 106, *unnilseptium* = 107, *unniloctium* = 108, *unnilnovium* = 109, etc.).

COUNTRIES OF THE WORLD

Country	Capital	Continent/Area	Nationality
Afghanistan	Kabul	Asia	Afghan
Albania	Tirane	Europe	Albanian
Algeria	Algiers	Africa	Algerian
Andorra	Andorra la Vella	Europe	Andorran
Angola	Luanda	Africa	Angolan
Antigua and Barbuda	Saint John's	North America	Antiguan, Barbudan
Argentina	Buenos Aires	South America	Argentinian
Armenia	Yerevan	Asia	Armenian
Australia	Canberra	Australia	Australian
Austria	Vienna	Europe	Austrian
Azerbaijan	Baku	Asia	Azerbaijani
Bahamas, The	Nassau	North America	Bahamian
Bahrain	Manama	Asia	Bahraini
Bangladesh	Dhaka	Asia	Bangaldeshi
Barbados	Bridgetown	North America	Barbadian
Belarus	Minsk	Europe	Belorussian, Belarussian, or Belarusian
Belgium	Brussels	Europe	Belgian
Belize	Belmopan	North America	Belizean
Benin	Porto-Novo	Africa	Beninese
Bhutan	Thimphu	Asia	Bhutanese
Bolivia	La Paz; Sucre	South America	Bolivian
Bosnia and Herzegovina	Sarajevo	Europe	Bosnian, Herzegovinian
Botswana	Gaborone	Africa	Motswana, sing., Batswana, pl.
Brazil	Brasilia	South America	Brazilian
Brunei	Bandar Seri Begawan	Asia	Bruneian
Bulgaria	Sofia	Europe	Bulgarian
Burkina	Ouagadougou	Africa	Burkinese
Burma (Myanmar)	Rangoon	Asia	Burmese
Burundi	Bujumbura	Africa	Burundian, n.; Burundi, adj.
Cambodia	Phnom Penh	Asia	Cambodian
Cameroon	Yaoundé	Africa	Cameroonian
Canada	Ottawa	North America	Canadian
Cape Verde	Praia	Africa	Cape Verdean
Central African Republic	Bangui	Africa	Central African
Chad	N'Djamena	Africa	Chadian
Chile	Santiago	South America	Chilean
China	Beijing	Asia	Chinese
Colombia	Bogotá	South America	Colombian
Comoros	Moroni	Africa	Comoran
Congo, Republic of the	Brazzaville	Africa	Congolese, n.; Congolese or Congo, adj.
Congo (formerly Zaire)	Kinshasa	Africa	Congolese
Costa Rica	San José	North America	Costa Rican
Côte d'Ivoire (Ivory Coast)	Yamoussoukro	Africa	Ivorian
Croatia	Zagreb	Europe	Croat, n.; Croatian, adj.
Cuba	Havana	North America	Cuban
Cyprus	Nicosia	Europe	Cypriot
Czech Republic	Prague	Europe	Czech
Denmark	Copenhagen	Europe	Dane, n.; Danish, adj.
Djibouti	Djibouti	Africa	Djiboutian
Dominica	Roseau	North America	Dominican
Dominican Republic	Santo Domingo	North America	Dominican
Ecuador	Quito	South America	Ecuadorian
Egypt	Cairo	Africa	Egyptian
El Salvador	San Salvador	North America	Salvadoran
Equatorial Guinea	Malabo	Africa	Equatorial Guinean or Equatoguinean
Eritrea	Asmara	Africa	Eritrean
Estonia	Tallinn	Europe	Estonian
Ethiopia	Addis Ababa	Africa	Ethiopian
Fiji	Suva	Oceania	Fijian

Country	Capital	Continent/Area	Nationality
Finland	Helsinki	Europe	Finn, n.; Finnish, adj.
France	Paris	Europe	French
Gabon	Libreville	Africa	Gabonese
Gambia, The	Banjul	Africa	Gambian
Georgia	T'bilisi	Asia	Georgian
Germany	Berlin	Europe	German
Ghana	Accra	Africa	Ghanaian
Greece	Athens	Europe	Greek
Grenada	Saint George's	North America	Grenadian
Guatemala	Guatemala City	North America	Guatemalan
Guinea	Conakry	Africa	Guinean
Guinea-Bissau	Bissau	Africa	Guinea-Bissauan
Guyana	Georgetown	South America	Guyanese
Haiti	Port-au-Prince	North America	Haitian
Holy See	Vatican City	Europe	
Honduras	Tegucigalpa	North America	Honduran
Hungary	Budapest	Europe	Hungarian
Iceland	Reykjavik	Europe	Icelander, n.; Icelandic, adj.
India	New Delhi	Asia	Indian
Indonesia	Jakarta	Asia	Indonesian
Iran	Tehran	Asia	Iranian
Iraq	Baghdad	Asia	Iraqi
Ireland	Dublin	Europe	Irish
Israel	Jerusalem	Asia	Israeli
Italy	Rome	Europe	Italian
Ivory Coast (see Côte d'Ivoire)			
Jamaica	Kingston	North America	Jamaican
Japan	Tokyo	Asia	Japanese
Jordan	Amman	Asia	Jordanian
Kazakhstan	Astana	Asia	Kazakhstani
Kenya	Nairobi	Africa	Kenyan
Kiribati	Tarawa	Oceania	I-Kiribati
Korea, North	P'yongyang	Asia	North Korean
Korea, South	Seoul	Asia	South Korean
Kuwait	Kuwait	Asia	Kuwaiti
Kyrgyzstan	Bishkek	Asia	Kyrgyz
Laos	Vientiane	Asia	Lao or Laotian
Latvia	Riga	Europe	Latvian
Lebanon	Beirut	Asia	Lebanese
Lesotho	Maseru	Africa	Mosotho, sing.; Basotho, pl.; Basotho, adj.
Liberia	Monrovia	Africa	Liberian
Libya	Tripoli	Africa	Libyan
Liechtenstein	Vaduz	Europe	Liechtensteiner, n.; Liechtenstein, adj.
Lithuania	Vilnius	Europe	Lithuanian
Luxembourg	Luxembourg	Europe	Luxembourger, n.; Luxembourg, adj.
Macedonia, The Former Yugoslav Republic of	Skopje	Europe	Macedonian
Madagascar	Antananarivo	Africa	Malagasy
Malawi	Lilongwe	Africa	Malawian
Malaysia	Kuala Lumpur	Asia	Malaysian
Maldives	Male	Asia	Maldivian
Mali	Bamako	Africa	Malian
Malta	Valletta	Europe	Maltese
Marshall Islands	Majuro	Oceania	Marshallese
Mauritania	Nouakchott	Africa	Mauritanian
Mauritius	Port Louis	Africa	Mauritian
Mexico	Mexico City	North America	Mexican
Micronesia, Federated States of	Kolonia	Oceania	Micronesian
Moldova	Chisinau	Europe	Moldovan
Monaco	Monaco	Europe	Monacan or Monegasque
Mongolia	Ulaanbaatar	Asia	Mongolian

Country	Capital	Continent/Area	Nationality
Morocco	Rabat	Africa	Moroccan
Mozambique	Maputo	Africa	Mozambican
Myanmar (see Burma)			
Namibia	Windhoek	Africa	Namibian
Nauru	Yaren District	Oceania	Nauruan
Nepal	Kathmandu	Asia	Nepalese
Netherlands	Amsterdam; The Hague	Europe	Dutchman or Dutchwoman, n.; Dutch, adj.
New Zealand	Wellington	Oceania	New Zealander, n.; New Zealand, adj.
Nicaragua	Managua	North America	Nicaraguan
Niger	Niamey	Africa	Nigerien
Nigeria	Abuja	Africa	Nigerian
Norway	Oslo	Europe	Norwegian
Oman	Muscat	Asia	Omani
Pakistan	Islamabad	Asia	Pakistani
Palau	Koror	Oceania	Palauan
Panama	Panama	North America	Panamanian
Papua New Guinea	Port Moresby	Oceania	Papua New Guinean
Paraguay	Asunción	South America	Paraguayan
Peru	Lima	South America	Peruvian
Philippines	Manila	Asia	Filipino, n.; Philippine, adj.
Poland	Warsaw	Europe	Pole, n.; Polish, adj.
Portugal	Lisbon	Europe	Portuguese
Qatar	Doha	Asia	Quatari
Romania	Bucharest	Europe	Romanian
Russia	Moscow	Europe & Asia	Russian
Rwanda	Kigali	Africa	Rwandan
Saint Kitts and Nevis	Basseterre	North America	Kittsian; Nevisian
Saint Lucia	Castries	North America	St. Lucian
Saint Vincent and the Grenadines	Kingstown	North America	St. Vincentian or Vincentian
San Marino	San Marino	Europe	Sammarinese
Sao Tome and Principe	Sao Tome	Africa	Sao Tomean
Saudi Arabia	Riyadh	Asia	Saudi or Saudi Arabian
Senegal	Dakar	Africa	Senegalese
Seychelles	Victoria	Indian Ocean	Seychellois, n.; Seychelles, adj.
Sierra Leone	Freetown	Africa	Sierra Leonean
Singapore	Singapore	Asia	Singaporean, n.; Singapore, adj.
Slovakia	Bratislava	Europe	Slovak
Slovenia	Ljubljana	Europe	Slovene, n.; Slovenian, adj.
Solomon Islands	Honiara	Oceania	Solomon Islander
Somalia	Mogadishu	Africa	Somali
South Africa	Pretoria; Cape Town; Bloemfontein	Africa	South African
Spain	Madrid	Europe	Spanish
Sri Lanka	Colombo	Asia	Sri Lankan
Sudan	Khartoum	Africa	Sudanese
Suriname	Paramaribo	South America	Surinamer, n.; Surinamese, adj.
Swaziland	Mbabane	Africa	Swazi
Sweden	Stockholm	Europe	Swede, n.; Swedish, adj.
Switzerland	Bern	Europe	Swiss
Syria	Damascus	Asia	Syrian
Tajikistan	Dushanbe	Asia	Tajik
Tanzania	Dar es Salaam	Africa	Tanzanian
Thailand	Bangkok	Asia	Thai
Togo	Lomé	Africa	Togolese
Tonga	Nuku'alofa	Oceania	Tongan
Trinidad and Tobago	Port-of-Spain	South America	Trinidadian; Tobagonian
Tunisia	Tunis	Africa	Tunisian
Turkey	Ankara	Asia & Europe	Turk, n.; Turkish, adj.
Turkmenistan	Ashgabat	Asia	Turkmen
Tuvalu	Funafuti	Oceania	Tuvaluan
Uganda	Kampala	Africa	Ugandan

Country	Capital	Continent/Area	Nationality
Ukraine	Kiev	Europe	Ukrainian
United Arab Emirates	Abu Dhabi	Africa	Emirian
United Kingdom	London	Europe	Briton, n.; British, collective pl. & adj.
United States of America	Washington, DC	North America	American
Uruguay	Montevideo	South America	Uruguayan
Uzbekistan	Tashkent	Asia	Uzbek
Vanuatu	Port-Vila	Oceania	Ni-Vanuatu
Venezuela	Caracas	South America	Venezuelan
Vietnam	Hanoi	Asia	Vietnamese
Western Samoa	Apia	Oceania	Western Samoan
Yemen	Sanaa	Asia	Yemeni
Yugoslavia	Belgrade	Europe	Yugoslav
(Serbia and Montenegro)			Serb, n.; Serbian, adj; Montenegran
Zaire (see Congo)			
Zambia	Lusaka	Africa	Zambian
Zimbabwe	Harare	Africa	Zimbabwean